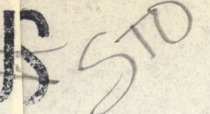

1998

DIRECTORY OF

CORPORATE

AFFILIATIONS

This edition of *Directory of Corporate Affiliations: Master Index* was prepared by National Register Publishing's Database Publishing Group in collaboration with the Publications Systems Department.

Editorial:
    Managing Editor: Christine Kerwin
    Senior Editors: Brittany Hartman, Barbara J. Morse, John R. Platt
    Associate Editors: Matthew Hanagan, Heather M. Lordi
    Assistant Editors: Elizabeth Higgins, Kerri Nelen, Jason Rimmer

Research:
    Director: Judy Redel
    Senior Managing Editor: Lisa Weissbard
    Senior Editor: Beverly A. Heath
    Associate Editors: Barrett Barnes, Laura Naphor

Production:
    Production & Training Director: Mark Van Orman
    Senior Production Editor: Matthew O'Connell

Editorial Systems:
    Vice President, Information Technology: John Roney
    Director, Biographical & Reference Systems: Carter McWilliams
    Manager, Reference & Biographic Systems: Helene Davis
    Senior Programmers: Victoria Maurer, Sophia Pikulin

Vice President, Database Production: Dean Hollister
Senior Editorial Director: Thomas Bachmann
Senior Managing Editor: Patricia Flinsch-Rodriguez

1998

Directory of

Corporate

Affiliations

VOLUME
1

MASTER INDEX

U.S. Public • U.S. Private • International

"WHO OWNS WHOM"

National Register Publishing

A Division of Reed Elsevier Inc.

New Providence, New Jersey

Published by National Register Publishing, a division of Reed Elsevier Inc.

Darryl Fisher - Chief Operating Officer
Andrew W. Meyer - Publisher

Printed and bound in the United States of America.
International Standard Book Number:

    Vol 1: 0-87217-215-5
    Directory of Corporate Affiliations 5-Vol Library: 0-87217-217-1

Library of Congress Catalog Card Number: 67-22770

ISBN 0-87217-215-5

9 780872 172159

CONTENTS

VOLUME I

Preface vii

How to Use the *Directory of Corporate Affiliations* ix

Mergers, Acquisitions and Name Changes 1976 – 1996 xvii

Master Index to Company Names 1

Brand Name Index 543

Master Geographic Index to U.S. Located Companies 1107

Master Geographic Index to Non-U.S. Located Companies 1489

CONTENTS

PREFACE

THE DIRECTORY OF CORPORATE AFFILIATIONS

The *Directory of Corporate Affiliations* (DCA) is a logically organized business reference tool that covers major public and private businesses in the United States and throughout the world. The principle of organization for the set is geographical (by parent company) and hierarchical (by company reportage). Subsidiaries of a parent company, no matter where they are located, will be found in the same volume as the ultimate parent.

Entry criteria for the set are flexible. Generally speaking, domestic companies must demonstrate revenue in excess of $10 million, substantial assets/net worth, or a work force in excess of 300 persons. Non-U.S. based companies must demonstrate revenues in excess of $50 million.

SET ORGANIZATION AND CONTENT

A brief outline of the volumes and their components follows. Please note that every volume in the set, including this one, has a customized 'How-to-Use' guide for the benefit of the researcher. These include extensive listing and referencing examples that go into great detail.

Master Index, Volume I
— Master Company Name Index
— Master Brand Name Index
— Master Geographic Index, U.S.
— Master Geographic Index, Non-U.S.

Master Index, Volume II
— Master S.I.C. Index
— Master Corporate Responsibilities Index

U.S. Public Companies, Volume III
— Public Company Name Index
— Public Company Listings
— Public S.I.C. Index

U.S. Private Companies, Volume IV
— Private Company Name Index
— Private Company Listings
— Private S.I.C. Index

International Public and Private Companies, Volume V
— International Company Name Index
— International Company Listings
— International S.I.C. Index

CUMULATIVE ENTRY STATISTICS FOR THIS EDITION

These statistics show the sum of entry listings across all three volumes. Individual statistics are provided in each volume.

—   14,778 Ultimate parent companies.
—   47,366 U.S. located sub companies.
—   <u>54,432</u> Non-U.S. located sub companies.
— 116,576 Total entry units listed.

—   27,617 Outside service firms.

COMPILATION

The *Directory of Corporate Affiliations* is compiled and updated from information supplied by the companies themselves, business publications, and annual reports. Each company is sent at least one listing mailer for updating prior to publication.

RELATED SERVICES

For information on the CD-ROM version of the directory, *Corporate Affiliations PLUS*, please call (800) 521-8110. Mailing lists compiled from information contained in the directory may be ordered from Rich Lukowski, Reed Elsevier Business Lists, 1350 East Touhy Avenue, Des Plaines, IL 60018; telephone (800) 323-4958, ext. 2340. Electronic database tapes of the directory in raw data format are available for lease. Please contact John Sonta, NRP Electronic Sales, 121 Chanlon Road, New Providence, NJ 07974; telephone (800) 521-8110, ext. 4698. The *Directory of Corporate Affiliations* is also available online through LEXIS-NEXIS and The Dialog Corporation. For LEXIS-NEXIS information please call (800) 227-4908. For more information on DIALOG please call (800) 334-2564.

Companies who wish to add or correct their listings can contact the editors by mailing to: National Register Publishing, DCA Editorial, 121 Chanlon Road, New Providence, NJ 07974, or calling (908) 464-6800.

In addition to keeping the information in our directories as up to date as possible, we are constantly trying to improve their design or add useful new features. Any comments or suggestions in this regard can be directed to the editors at the above address.

HOW TO USE THE DIRECTORY OF CORPORATE AFFILIATIONS

The *Directory of Corporate Affiliations* (DCA) presents extensive information on U.S. and foreign companies, both public and private. Entries include information on financials, personnel, outside service firms, and subsidiaries with an emphasis on hierarchy and reportage. Entry criteria for the set are flexible. Domestic companies generally show revenues in excess of $10 million, employee totals in excess of 300 persons, or substantial assets/net worth. Non-U.S. companies generally show revenue in excess of $50 million.

This user guide is divided into four parts.

— **Part A,** 'How to Locate a Company' gives referencing instructions and samples of indexes. It demonstrates many useful methods for getting the information you need from the DCA set at large.

— **Part B,** 'How to Locate an Executive' shows how to locate names of personnel listed throughout the DCA set.

— **Part C,** 'Sample Entries' shows the various data elements and listing style of a typical DCA company listing.

— **Part D,** 'Understanding Levels of Reportage' demonstrates how company reportage structures are simply and clearly presented throughout DCA.

PART A: HOW TO LOCATE A COMPANY

1. **If you know the name of the company, but do not know its nationality or ownership status:**

   Look in the 'Master Index to Company Names' in volume one of the *Master Index*. This index will direct you to the correct volume of the set (i.e. International, Public, or Private) and the correct page listing therein.

   > AEMTLERHALLE AG—See Hurliman Holding AG; *Int'l*,
   >   pg. 643
   > **AEON GROUP**; *Int'l*, pg. 30
   > **AEQUINTRON MEDICAL, INC.**; *U.S. Public*, pg. 28
   > **AER LINGUS**; *Int'l*, pg. 31
   > AERACOM TECHNOLOGIES, PTE. LTD.—See Ssangyong
   >   Business Group; *Int'l*, pg. 1294
   > **AERCO INTERNATIONAL INC.**; *U.S. Private*, pg. 23

2. **If you do know a parent company's nationality and ownership status:**

   You can turn directly to the company listings in the appropriate volume, all of which are alphabetized by the name of the parent company.

3. **If you know the name of a subsidiary or division:**

You can turn to the 'Master Index of Company Names' in the *Master Index* Volume I or the 'Index of Company Names' in the appropriate volume. In either place, the subsidiary entry will also show you the name of its ultimate parent and the volume and page of its listing.

> JHK & ASSOCIATES, INC.—See Science Applications
>   International Corp.; *U.S. Private*, pg. 986
> JIB GROUP PLC—See Jardine Matheson Holdings Limited;
>   *Int'l*, pg. 711
> JII/SALES PROMOTION ASSOCIATES, INC.—See Jordan
>   Industries, Inc.; *U.S. Private*, pg. 604
> JIT-STAL AB—See Rautaruukki Oy; *Int'l*, pg. 1036
> JJC SPECIALIST CORP.—See The Quick & Reilly Group
>   Inc.; *U.S. Public*, pg. 1397

4. **If you cannot find the company's name in the indexes:**

It may mean that the company has been acquired or changed its name. To confirm this, try looking in the 'Mergers, Acquisitions and Name Changes' section at the front of the appropriate volume. If not successful, you can try the cumulative 'Mergers and Acquisitions' section in the *Master Index* Volume I. This shows such activity from as early as 1976.

Sample of 'Mergers, Acquisitions and Name Changes'

> Friendly Ice Cream Corp.—acquired by Hershey Foods
>   Corp.
> Frigitronics, Inc.—acquired by Revlon, Inc.
> Frontier Oil Corporation—acquired by Wainoco Oil Corpo-
>   ration
> Furr Cafeterias, Inc.—acquired by K Mart Corp.
> GAC Corp.—name changed to Avatar Holdings, Inc.

5. **To locate companies in a given line of business:**

Use the S.I.C. (Standard Industrial Classification) Index. There is one in each volume as well as in the *Master Index* Volume II. This index arranges companies by particular products and services, and is a useful prospecting tool. The index is preceded by two helpful compendia: one sorts the codes alphabetically by the name of the product or service, the other numerically by the code itself.

Sample of Alpha Compendium of S.I.C.s

Description	SIC Code
M	
Machinery, Electrical Equipment & Supplies, NEC	3699
Machinery, Special Industry	3559
Machines & Equipment, General Industry, NEC	3569
Magazine Publishing & Printing	2721
Magazines, Wholesale	5192
Magnesium & Alloys Bars, Rods, Shapes	3356
Magnesium Compounds	2819

Sample of Numeric Compendium of S.I.C.s

Code	Title
62	**SECURITY & COMMODITY BROKERS**
6211	Security Brokers, Dealers & Flotation Companies
6221	Commodity Contracts, Brokers & Dealers
6231	Security & Commodity Exchanges
6282	Investment Advice
6289	Services Allied With Exchange of Securities or Commodities, NEC

Both parent and sub companies are covered in this index; parent companies are printed in bold type, sub companies in regular typeface. The term "NEC" stands for "Not Elsewhere Classified". A sample of the S.I.C. index is shown here:

3552—TEXTILE MACHINERY

APV GAULIN—APV PLC; *Int'l*, Pg. 19

AMERICAN BARMAG CO.; *U.S. Private*, pg. 51

THE AMERICAN GROUP; *U.S. Private*, pg. 56

AMERICAN SAHM CORPORATION—Georg Sahm GmbH & Co. KG Masschinenfabrik; *Int'l*, pg. 1177

AMERICAN SUESSEN—Spindelfabrik Suessen; *Int'l*, pg. 1292

6.   **To locate a company via a particular brand or trade name:**

Look to the 'Brand Name Index' in the *Master Index* Volume I. Brand and trade names of products and services are indexed here showing the name of the company, its listing volume and page number.

JIFFY-GRO—Garden Products—Jiffy Products of America, Inc.; *Int'l*, pg. 714

JIFFY KIT—Automotive Products—Standard Motor Products, Inc.; *U.S. Public*, pg. 1556

JIFFY LUBE—Oil Change Facilities—Jiffy Lube International, Inc.; *U.S. Public*, pg. 1317

JIFFY MIRACLE PEAT—Garden Products—Jiffy Products of America, Inc.; *Int'l*, pg. 714

JIFFY-MIX—Garden Products—Jiffy Products of America, Inc.; *Int'l*, pg. 714

JIFFY POP—Popcorn—American Home Food Products; *U.S. Private*, pg. 530

JIFFY-POTS—Garden Products—Jiffy Products of America, Inc.; *Int'l*, pg. 714

JIFFY PREP—Paint Condition—Jones Blair Company; *U.S. Private*, pg. 602

7. **To locate a company in a given geographical area:**

Look to the 'Geographic Index' in the *Master Index* Volume I. Arranged in two parts — U.S. locations and non-U.S. locations — this index interfiles data from all three volumes of DCA, and shows the company's listing volume and page number.

CALIFORNIA
Los Angeles

A A CATER TRUCK MANUFACTURING COMPANY, INC.,
750 E. Slauson Ave., 90011, pg. 1   **PV**
ABC Entertainment, 2040 Ave. of the Stars, 90067,
pg. 528   **PB**
ABC/Watermark, Inc., 3575 Cahuenga Blvd. W, 90068
pg. 528   **PB**
ABN AMRO Bank, N.V. (Los Angeles), 300 S. Grand Ave.,
Ste. 1115, 90071-7519, pg. 10   **IT**
AAMES FINANCIAL CORPORATION, 3731 Wilshire Blvd.,
10th Fl., 90010, pg. 16   **PB**

PB - *U.S. Public Companies Volume*
PV - *U.S. Private Companies Volume*
IT - *International Public & Private Companies Volume*

PART B: HOW TO LOCATE EXECUTIVES

Personnel are indexed in DCA by their title or area of activity. To find people in a given area or title such as Marketing, Sales, CEO, or Treasurer, use the 'Corporate Responsibilities Index' in the *Master Index* Volume II. This index lists personnel from every parent and subsidiary entry in the set by key areas of responsibility. Also included are their company name, listing volume, and page number.

Hancock, Edward R., Mktg. Dir.—Farnam Sealing Systems
Division, Troy, MI; *U.S. Public*, pg. 411
Hancock, Jayne, V.P.-Sports Mktg.—DirecTV Inc., El
Segundo, CA; *U.S. Public*, pg. 736
Hancock, John, V.P.-Sls. & Mktg.—Coburn Optical Industries
Inc., Tulsa, OK; *U.S. Private*, pg. 249
Hancock, Larry, Mgr.-Mktg. & Opers.—Hayes Microcomputer
Products, Inc., Norcross, GA; *U.S. Private*, pg. 517

PART C: BASIC COMPONENTS OF A DCA COMPANY LISTING

Following is an example of a typical parent company listing with tags to some of its basic components.

STANDARD MEDICAL GROUP——————————— Company Name
560 River Rd.——————————————————— Company Address
Richmond, VA 23219
Tel.: 804-223-3289————————— DE ——— Telecommunications Data & State of
Telex: 95421   Incorporation
Fax: 804-223-3290
E-Mail: info@standardmed.com ———————— Electronic Addresses
Web Site: www.standardmed.com
Year Founded: 1967
SMG—(ASE)————————————————————— Ticker Symbol and Stock Exchanges
Approx Sls.: $16,000,000 ————————————— Financial Information
Assets: $24,000,000
Liabilities: $16,000,000

Net Worth: $8,000,000
Earnings: ($1,500,000)
Emp: 580 ——————————————————— **No. of Employees, Including Sub-entries**
Fiscal Year End: 12/31/97
Business Description: ——————————————— **Business Description**
Research Technology Company that
Develops and Manufactures Medical
Products
Import Export
S.I.C.: 2833, 2834, 3841, 3844 ———————— **Standard Industrial Classification codes**
Personnel:
John R. Callahan (Chm. Bd.) ———————————— **Key Personnel**
Cynthia I. Jenkins (Pres. & Chief Exec. Officer)
William E. Kirkpatrick (Exec. V.P.)
Alvert N. Hackett (V.P.-Res. & Devel.)
Lawrence Woods (V.P.-Sls.)
Board of Directors:
John R. Callahan ————————————————— **Members of the Board**
David C. Abel
William A. Scott
Carolyn H. Trunbull
Paul Underdahl

Legal Firm:
Scott, Morris & Tyler ———————————————— **Name, Address & Phone of**
315 Fifth St.   **Outside Service Firm**
Richmond, VA 23260
Tel.: 804-292-6521

Auditor:
DeCorva & Abbott
19 39th St.
Norfolk, VA 23502
Tel.: 804-466-2121

Following each parent company listing are the entries for each of that company's divisions, subsidiaries, affiliates, joint ventures, units etc. Though companies vary widely in their usage of these terms, some of the more common company designations can be defined as follows:

Affiliate   A chartered business owned by the company at less than 50%.

Division   An internal unit of a company, not incorporated.

Joint Venture   A business in which two or more companies share responsibility and ownership.

Subsidiary   A chartered business owned by the company at 50% or more.

PART D: UNDERSTANDING LEVELS OF REPORTAGE

Each sub-unit of the company will have a number in parentheses to the right of the company name. This number represents the level of reportage for that particular company. Any company with a level (1) reports directly to the parent company. Level (2) companies report to the level (1) company immediately above them. Level (3) companies report to the level (2) company immediately above them, etc.

Subsidiaries:

Brock Corporation
6060 Wall St.
Hartford, CT 06103
Tel: 203-251-6526
Approx. Sls: 2,000,000
Emp.: 98
Mfr. of Pharmaceuticals
S.I.C.: 2834
J.M. McAleer (Pres.)
Michael F. Hamilton (Sr. V.P.-Res. & Devel.)

(1) ——————— **Reports to parent company (Standard Medical Group)**

(100%) ——————— **Percent of Ownership**

Subsidiary:

Clark Technology
601 Pulaski St.
Jackson, MS 39215
Tel: 601-848-4626
Emp.: 850
Mfr. of Sutures and Other Surgical Products
S.I.C.: 3842
Steven Colaccino (Pres.)

(2) ——————— **Reports to level 1 company above (Brock Corporation)**

(100%)

Branch:

Clark Technology
52 Main St.
Wayne, NJ 07435
Tel: 201-662-7654
Mfr. of Sutures
S.I.C. 3842

(3) ——————— **Reports to level 2 company above (Clark Technology)**

Cedar Laboratories
51 16th St.
Wilmington, MA 01887
Tel: 508-223-1000
Emp.: 124
Research & Develop Antibiotics
S.I.C.: 2834
Melissa A. Newman (Chief Oper. Officer)

(1) ——————— **Reports to parent company (Standard Medical Group)**

(40%)

Non-U.S. Subsidiary:

Merieux Pharmaceuticals
1421 rue Gourbet, 75755
Paris, Cedex 15, France
Tel: 42 73 10 08
Approx Sls: $1,500,000
Emp.: 118
Mfr. of Pharmaceuticals
S.I.C.: 2834
G. Bidaud (Pres.)

(1) ——————— **Subsidiary not located in the U.S. Reports to the parent company (Standard Medical Group)**

(100%)

In addition to keeping the information in our directories as up to date as possible, we are constantly trying to improve their design and organization, or to add useful new features. Any comments or suggestions in this regard can be directed to: National Register Publishing, DCA Editorial, 121 Chanlon Road, New Providence, NJ 07974.

Request For Additional Companies Not Now Listed

Directory of Corporate Affiliations
National Register Publishing
121 Chanlon Road, New Providence, NJ 07974
908-464-6800

AS A CURRENT SUBSCRIBER to the *Directory of Corporate Affiliations*, are there companies not currently listed in the directory that you would like to see included? If so, please fill out the following and return to the above address.

Please type or print all information and return completed form.

_____
Company or Institution Name

_____
Address

_____   _____   _____
City   State / Country   Zip / Postal Code

_____   _____
Phone   Fax

_____
Company or Institution Name

_____
Address

_____   _____   _____
City   State / Country   Zip / Postal Code

_____   _____
Phone   Fax

Mergers, Acquisitions and Name Changes
1976-1996

A

A&M Food Services, Inc.—absorbed by Pepsico, Inc.

A & W Brands, Inc.—absorbed by Cadbury Schweppes p.l.c.

A.A. Importing Company—out of business

AAF Investment Corporation Plc—name changed to AAF Industries Plc

AAH plc—acquired by GEHE AG, a subsidiary of Franz Haniel & Cie, GmbH

The AAV Companies—name changed to The Tranzonic Companies

ABA Industries, Inc.—acquired by Clabir Corp.

ABS Industries, Inc.—out of business

ABS Specialty Genetics—company closed

ACA Joe, Inc.—out of business

ACCO International, Inc.—holding co. formed, ACCO World Corporation

ACL Filco Corp.—name changed to ACL Technologies

ACR Mechanical Corporation—out of business

ADT Group PLC—name changed to ADT Limited

AEA, Inc.—acquired by Republic Automotive Parts, Inc. & name changed to Republic Automotive-AEA Division

AEL Industries, Inc.—acquired by Tracor, Inc. & name changed to Tracor-AEL Industries, Inc.

AES Technology Systems Inc.—out of business

AGA Burdox, Inc.—name changed to AGA Gas, Inc.

AGS Computers, Inc.—acquired by Nynex

AIOC—liquidated

A.L. Laboratories, Inc.—name changed to A.L. Pharma Inc.

ALC Communications Corporation—acquired by Frontier Corporation & name changed to Frontier Communications

AM Cable TV Industries, Inc.—name changed to AM Communications

A M Diagnostics Inc—out of business

AMCA International Corporation—name changed to United Dominion Industries Limited

AMEV Holdings, Inc.—name changed to Fortis, Inc.

AMF Inc.—acquired by Minstar, Inc.

AMIC Corp.—acquired by Merrill Lynch & Co. Inc.

A.R.A. Manufacturing Co. of Delaware Inc.—acquired by Schick, Incorporated

ATE Enterprises, Inc.—now ATE Management Service Co., wholly-owned sub. of Ryder Systems

ATO, Inc.—name changed to Figgie International, Inc.

AVC Corp.—acquired by Raybestos-Manhattan, Inc. & merged with Milford Rivet & Machine Co.

AVM Corporation—name changed to American Locker Group, Incorporated

AVX Corporation—acquired by Kyocera Corporation

AXA—merged with Union des Assurances de Paris (UAP) to form AXA-UAP

AZL Resources, Inc.—acquired by & merged into Tosco Corp.

AZP Group, Inc.—name changed to Pinnacle West Capital Corporation

Aaron Brothers, Inc.—acquired by Michaels Stores, Inc.

Abbott Glass Co., Inc.—out of business

A.S. Abell Co.—acquired by The Times Mirror Company

Aberdeen Mfg. Corp.—acquired by CHF Industries, Inc.

Abex Inc.—merged with another company to form Mafco Consolidated Group, Inc.

Abitibi Paper Company Ltd.—name changed to Abitibi-Price, Inc.

Acacia Mutual Life Insurance Co.—name changed to Acacia Group of Companies

Acco World Corp.—acquired by American Brands, Inc.

Accuray Corp.—acquired by Combustion Engineering, Inc.

Acme-Cleveland Corporation—acquired & absorbed by Danaher Corporation

Acme General Corp.—wholly-owned sub. of The Stanley Works, Inc.

Action Auto Rental, Inc.—out of business

Action Auto Sales—out of business

Action Corporation—name changed to Beltran Corp.

Action Dictograph Telecommunications, Inc.—name changed to Connecticut Consolidated Industries, Inc.

Action Staffing Inc.—out of business

Activision, Inc.—name changed to Mediagenic

Actmedia, Inc.—now wholly-owned sub. of Heritage Media

Acton Corporation—name changed to Sunstates Corporation

Actrix Systems, Inc.—out of business

Acushnet Co.—acquired by American Brands, Inc.

Ada Resources, Inc.—name changed to Adams Resources & Energy, Inc.

Adacorp, Inc.—out of business

Adam Meldrum & Anderson Co. Inc.—acquired by Bon-Ton Stores Inc.

Adams Rite Industries, Inc.—name changed to Adams Rite Manufacturing Co.

Adams-Russell Co., Inc.—now wholly-owned sub. of Cablevisions Systems Corporation

Adams-Russell, Inc.—now M/A Com-Adams Russell, wholly-owned sub. of M/A Com

Addison-Wesley Publishing Company—acquired by Pearson, Inc.

Addressograph Multigraph Corp. — name changed to AM International, Inc.

Addsco Industries, Inc. — out of business

Adience Inc. — acquired by The Alpine Group, Inc.

Adler & Shaykin — name changed to Shaykin & Company

Advance Circuits, Inc. — acquired by Johnson Matthey Public Limited Company

Advance Ross Corporation — acquired by CUC International

Advanced Marine Enterprises Inc. — acquired by Nichols Research Corporation

Advanced Systems, Inc. — acquired by URS Corp.

Aegis Corporation — acquired by Minstar, Inc.

Aeicor, Inc. — name changed to Doskocil Cos., Inc.

Aero-Flow Dynamics, Inc. — acquired by United Telecommunications, Inc. & merged into Argo Intl. Corp.

Aeroflex Laboratories, Inc. — name changed to ARX, Inc.

Aerolineas Argentinas — acquired by Grupo Iberia

Aeronautical Radio, Inc. — holding co. formed ARINC, Inc.

Aeronica, Inc. — acquired by Fleet Aerospace

AeroSystems Engineering — acquired by FFVAB

Affholder Inc. — holding co. formed, Institutiform Mid-America, Inc.

Affiliated Bank Corporation of Wyoming — name changed to Wyoming National Bancorporation

Affiliated Business Center, Inc. — out of business

Affiliated Publications, Inc. — acquired & absorbed by The New York Times Company

Ag Equipment Group LP — acquired by AGCO Corporation

Ag-Met, Inc. — name changed to Refinement Intl. Co.

Agnew Group Inc. — acquired by 3226727 Canada Inc.

Agricultural Minerals Company, L.P. — name changed to Terra Nitrogen Company L.P.

Aileen, Inc. — acquired & absorbed by Names for Dames, Inc.

The Ailing & Cory Company — acquired by Union Camp Corporation

Ain Plastics, Inc. — acquired by Thyssen AG

Air Midwest, Inc. — now sub. of Mesa Airlines, Inc.

AIR WIS Services, Inc. — acquired by UAL Corporation

Air Wisconsin, Inc. — holding co. formed, Air Wis Services, Inc.

Aircal, Inc. — acquired by & merged with AMR Corporation

Airco, Inc. — holding co. formed, The BOC Group, Inc.

Airpax Electronics, Inc. — merged into North American Phillips Control Div.

Aker A/S — name changed to Aker Raj Asa

Akzona, Inc. — name changed to Akzo America, Inc.

Akzo N.V. — name changed to Akzo Nobel N.V.

Alabama Bancorporation — name changed to AmSouth Bancorp

Alabama By-Products Corp. — acquired by & merged into Drummond Company, Inc.

Alabama Dry Docking & Shipbuilding Co. — name changed to Addsco Industries

Alabama Gas Corp. — name changed to Alagasco, Inc.

Aladdin Mills, Inc. — acquired by Mohawk Industries, Inc.

Alagasco, Inc. — name changed to Energen Corporation

Alamand Corp. — acquired by & merged into Moraga Corp.

Alamo Rent-A-Car Inc. — acquired by Republic Industries, Inc.

Alaska Bancorporation — out of business

Alaska Interstate Co. — name changed to Enstar Corp.

Alaska National Bank of the North — out of business

Alaska Pacific Bancorporation — acquired by Key Banks, Inc.

Alaska Pulp Corporation — out of business

Alcan Australia Limited — name changed to Capral Aluminum Limited

Alco Gravure Industries, Inc. — absorbed into Maxwell Communications, PLC

Alco Standard Corporation — name changed to Ikon Office Solutions, Inc.

Alcott & Andrews — out of business

The Alderman Company — now Alderman Studios

Aldix International Corporation — absorbed into Automatic Equipment Corporation

Aldrich Chemical Co. & Sigma. Chemical Co. — merged to form Sigma-Aldrich Corporation

Aldus Corporation — acquired by & name changed to Adobe Systems, Incorporated

Alexander & Alexander Services Inc. — acquired by AON Corporation

Alexander Energy Corporation — merged into National Energy Group, Inc.

Alexander Proudfoot plc — name changed to Proudfoot Plc

Alias Research, Inc. — acquired by Silicon Graphics, Inc. & name changed to Alias Wavefront

All Tech Industries, Inc. — name changed to Clabir Corp.

Allbritton Communications Co. — name changed to Perpetual Corp.

Allegheny & Western Energy Corporation — acquired by Eastern American Energy Corporation

Allegheny Airlines, Inc. — name changed to USAir, Inc.

Allegheny Beverage Corporation — name changed to Alleco, Inc.

Allegheny International, Inc. — name changed to Sunbeam-Oster Company, Inc.

Allegheny Ludlum Industries, Inc. — name changed to Allegheny International, Inc.

Allegis Corporation — name changed back to UAL Corp.

Allen-Bradley Co. — acquired by Rockwell Intl., Inc.

Alliance Telecommunications, Inc. — acquired by The Allen Group, Inc.

Alliant Computer Systems Corp. — out of business

Allied Artists Picture Corp. — merged into Allied Artists Industries

Allied Bancshares, Inc.—now First Interstate Bank of Texas, sub. of First Interstate Bancorp

Allied Chemical Corp.—name changed to Allied Corp.

Allied Clinical Laboratories, Inc.—acquired by National Health Laboratories Holdings Inc.

Allied Corporation—new holding company formed, Allied-Signal, Inc.

Allied Equities Corporation—name changed to Precision Technologies

Allied Film Video—merged with HMG Digital Technologies to form Allied Digital Technologies

Allied Maintenance Corp.—acquired by Allied Supermarkets, Inc.

Allied Telephone Co.—merged with Mid Continent Telephone Co. to form Alltel Corp.

Allied Thermal Corp.—acquired by Interpace Corp.

Allied U.S. Holdings, Inc.—name changed to Allied-Lyons North America Corp.

Allis-Chalmers Corporation—liquidated

Allison Engine Company—acquired by Rolls-Royce plc

Allison Mortgage Investment Trust—name changed to First Newport Realty Investors

Allergan Pharmaceuticals, Inc.—acquired by SmithKline Corp.

Allomatic Products Company—now sub. of Raytech Corporation

Alloway Manufacturing—name changed to Alloway Industries

Almy Stores, Inc.—acquired by Stop & Shop, Inc.

Aloha Airlines, Inc.—holding co. formed, Aloha, Inc.

Alpha Metals, Inc.—acquired by Thomas Tilling, Inc.

Alp/Freddy's—liquidated

Alpine Press, Inc.—division of Courier Corporation

Alta Energy Corp.—acquired & absorbed by Devon Energy Corporation

Altai, Inc.—acquired & absorbed by Platinum Technology, Inc.

Altamil Corporation—acquired by & merged into The Marmon Group

Altec Corporation—acquired by Mark IV Industries & name changed to Altec Lansing Corporation

Alterman Foods, Inc.—name changed to Food Giant, Inc.

Altex Oil Corp.—holding co. formed, Altex Industries, Inc.

Altier & Sons Shoes Inc.—name changed to The Shoe Show of Rocky Mt.

Alton Box Board Co.—name changed to Alton Packing Corp.

Alton Packaging Corp.—name changed to Jefferson Smurfit Corporation

Altus Federal Savings Bank—liquidated

Alumax, Inc.—acquired by Amax, Inc.

Alusuisse of America, Inc.—now Alusuisse-Lonza America Inc.

Alza Corporation—acquired by Ciba Geigy Corp.

The Amalgamated Sugar Co.—wholly-owned sub. of Valhi, Inc., formerly LLC Corporation

Amalloy—out of business

Amarlite Architectural Products—name changed to Arch Amarlite Architectural Products

Amax Inc.—merged with Cyprus Minerals Company & name changed to Cyprus Amax Minerals Company

Ambac Industries, Inc.—acquired by United Technologies Corp.

Ambar, Inc.—acquired by The Beacon Group

Amcon Group, Inc.—name changed to Gold Fields American Corp.

Amcord, Inc.—acquired by Gilford-Hill & Company, Inc.

Amdura Corporation—out of business

Amedco Inc.—acquired by Service Corp. International

Amerco, Inc.—name changed to Amerco, A Nevada Corp.

Amerex, Inc.—out of business

Ameribanc, Inc.--acquired by Mercantile Bancorporation Inc.

American Aggregates Corp.—acquired by ARC America Corp.

American Air Filter Co.—acquired by Allis Chalmers Corp.

American Airlines—holding co. formed, AMR Corp.

American Bakeries Company—merged into Interstate Bakeries Corp.

American Bancorp, Inc.—name changed to Meridian Bancorp

American Bank & Trust Co. of Pennsylvania—name changed to American Bancorp, Inc.

American Bankers Life Assurance Co. of Florida—name changed to American Bankers Insurance Group

American Barrick Resources Corporation—name changed to Barrick Gold Corporation

American Bread Company-Sunbeam Company—acquired by Lewis Brothers Bakeries, Inc. & name changed to Lewis Brothers Bakeries

American Broadcasting Companies, Inc.—acquired by Capital Cities/ABC, Inc.

American Buildings Co.—acquired by Cronus Industries, Inc.

American Can Co.—name changed to Primerica Corp.

American Capital Convertible Securities, Inc.--acquired by Primerica Corporation & name changed to American Capital Management & Research Inc.

American Capital Management & Research—name changed to Van Kampen American Capital

American Century Mortgage Investors—name changed to American Century Trust

American Century Trust—out of business

American Chain & Cable Co.—acquired by Babcock International, Inc.

American City Business Journals, Inc.—acquired by Advance Publications, Inc.

American Consumer Industries, Inc. — acquired by Trans Canada Freezers, Ltd.

American Credit Corp. — name changed to Barclays American Corp.

American Distilling Co. — acquired by Amdisco Corp.

American District Telegraph Co. — name changed to ADT, Inc.

American Electronics, Inc. — holding co. formed, AEI Holding Co. Inc.

American Electronics Labs, Inc. — name changed to AEL Industries, Inc.

American Export Industries, Inc. — name changed to Aeicor, Inc.

American Family Corporation — name changed to AFLAC Incorporated

American Finance Group — name changed to Equis Finance Group

American Finance System, Inc. — acquired by Security Pacific Corp.

American Fletcher Corporation — acquired by Banc One Corporation & name changed to Banc One Indiana Corporation

American Forest Products Company — out of business

American Furniture Co., Inc. — acquired by Ladd Furniture, Inc. & name changed to American of Martinsville

American Garden Products, Inc. — acquired by Amfac, Inc.

American General Bond Fund, Inc. — holding co. formed, American Capital Asset Management, Inc.

American General Convertible Securities, Inc. — name changed to American Capital Convertible Securities, Inc.

American Health Companies, Inc. — acquired by Physicians Weight Loss Centers, Inc.

American Hoechst Corp. — acquired by Celanese Corp. & name changed to Hoechst Celanese Corporation

American Hoist & Derrick Co. — name changed to Amdura Corporation

American Hospital Supply Corp. — acquired by & merged into Baxter Travenol Laboratories, Inc.

American Industries Inc. — acquired by Reliance Steel & Aluminum Co. & name changed to American Steel LLC

American International Pictures, Inc. — acquired by Filmways, Inc.

American Investment Co. — acquired by Leucadia National Corp.

American Journal of Nursing Company — acquired by Wolters Kluwer N.V.

American Liberty Financial Corp. — out of business

American Lock & Supply Inc. — name changed to American Security Distribution

American Maize-Products Company — acquired by Eridania Beghin-Say Group

American Manufacturing Company, Inc. (LA) — name changed to The American Group

American Marketing Works & International Corporation — acquired by & absorbed into Signal Apparel

American Medical Affiliates, Inc. — acquired by Unicare Services, Inc.

American Medical International, Inc. — now American Medical Holdings

American Medical Security Holdings, Inc. — acquired by United Wisconsin Services, Inc.

American Medical Services, Inc. — wholly-owned sub. of TW Services, Inc.

American Medicorp, Inc. — acquired by Humana, Inc.

American Microsystems, Inc. — acquired by Gould, Inc.

American Motor Inns, Inc. — acquired by Prime Motor Inns, Inc.

American Motors Corp. — acquired by Chrysler Corp.

American National Bank & Trust Co. of Chicago — acquired by First Chicago NBD Corporation

American National Financial Corp. — name changed to American National Insurance Co.

American Natural Gas Co. — name changed to American National Resources, Inc.

American Plan Corporation — in liquidation

American Pre-Package Company — name changed to River Ranch Southwest, Inc.

American Premier Underwriters, Inc. — acquired by American Financial Corporation & name changed to American Financial Group

American President Companies, Ltd. — name changed to APL Ltd.

American Public Energy Co. — name changed to AmQuest Corp.

American Recreation Products, Inc. — now sub. of Kellwood Company

American Restaurants Corporation — name changed to Hudson's Grill of America, Inc.

American Safety Equipment Corp. — acquired by The Marmon Group, Inc.

American Savings of Florida, FSB — acquired & absorbed by First Union National Bank

American Seating Co. — acquired by Fuqua Industries, Inc.

The American Ship Building Company — name changed to Tampa Ship Building Co.

American Signature — acquired by & merged into Quebecor, Inc.

American Solar King Corporation — now ASK Corporation

American Specialty Corp. — out of business

American Stabilis, Inc. — out of business

American Technical Industries, Inc. — acquired by Papercraft Corp.

American Technical Services Group, Inc. — acquired by Strategic Distribution Inc.

American Travellers Corporation — acquired by Conseco Inc.

American United Global Inc. — name changed to

Hutchenson Seal Corporation

American Vision Centers, Inc. — name changed to AVC/Nu-Vision, Inc.

American Welding & Mfg. Co. — acquired by Papercraft Corp.

American Wilhelmsburger, Inc. — holding co. dissolved, see Michigan Precision Industries, Inc.

America's Favorite Chicken Company — name changed to AFC Enterprises

Americopy Mitchell Acquisition Co., Inc. — name changed to AMI Group, Inc.

AmeriData Technologies, Inc. — acquired by General Electric Company

Ameritrust Corporation — merged into Society Corporation

Amfac, Inc. — acquired by JMB Realty Corporation

Amfesco Industries, Inc. — name changed to New American Shoe Co.

Amfood Industries, Inc. — out of business

Amherst Associates, Inc. — acquired by HBO & Co.

Amicon Corp. — acquired by Hoover Universal, Inc.

Amicor Inc. — name changed to Keystone Camera Products Corporation

Aminco, Inc. — out of business

Amity Leather Products Company — name changed to AR Accessories Group, Inc.

Amoco Petroleum Additives Co. — acquired by Ethyl Petroleum Additives, a division of Ethyl Corp.

Amoskeag Bank Shares, Inc. — now a subsidiary of Bank of Ireland

Ampad Corp. — wholly-owned sub. of The Mead Corp.

Amper S.A. — acquired by Telefonica de Espana, S.A.

Amperif Corporation — acquired by Storage Technology Corp.

Ampex Corp. — acquired by The Signal Companies, Inc.

Amre, Inc. — out of business

Amrecorp Realty Inc. — name changed to Univesco Inc.

Amsco, American Sterilizer Company — now Amsco International Inc.

Amserve Healthcare, Inc. — acquired & absorbed by Star Multi Care Services Inc.

Amstar Corporation — merged with Essex Industries to form Esstar Incorporated; American Sugar Div. sold to Tate & Lyle PLC

Amtel, Inc. — acquired by Dominion Bridge Co., Ltd.

AmTran Corporation — acquired by Navistar International Corporation

The Anaconda Co. — acquired by Atlantic Richfield Co.

Anadite, Inc. — sub. of Industrial Equity Pacific, Ltd.

Analytical Technology Inc. — acquired by Thermo Electron Corporation & name changed to Orion Research Inc.

Anchor Coupling, Inc. — acquired by Amerace Corp.

Anchor Glass Container Corp. — acquired by Vitro S.A.

Anchor Hocking Corp. — wholly-owned sub. of Newell Co.

Anderson Brothers Book Stores, Inc. — merged with Follett Corp.

Anderson Clayton & Co. — acquired by Quaker Oats Co.

Anderson Greenwood & Co. — acquired by Keystone International, Inc.

Anderson Industries Inc. — acquired by Excel Industries, Inc. & name changed to Anderson Enterprises LLC

Anderson Jacobson, Inc. — now CXR Telcom Mergers, Corporation

Andrea Radio Corporation — name changed to Andrea Electronics Corp.

Andros Analyzers Incorporated — name changed to Androw, Inc.

Anglo Co. Ltd. — name changed to Anglo Energy Ltd.

Anglo Energy Inc. — name changed to Nabors Industries, Inc.

Anitec Image Technology Corp. — acquired by International Paper Co. & name changed to Anitec Image Corp.

Anixter Bros., Inc. — wholly-owned sub. of Itel Corporation

Anken Industries — acquired by & merged into Rhone-Poulenc Systems Co.

Ansul Co. — acquired by Wormald Americas, Inc.

Anta Corp. — liquidated

Anthony Industries, Inc. — name changed to K2 Inc.

Anton Smith & Co. Inc. — acquired by Diamond Productions, Inc.

Apeco Corp. — name changed to The Lori Corporation

Apex Express — out of business

Apollo Computer Inc. — now sub. of Hewlett-Packard Co.

Apple Lines, Inc. — name changed to New Apple Lines, Inc.

Applebaums Food Markets, Inc. — acquired by National Tea Co., U.S. sub. of George Weston Ltd.

Application Engineering Corp. — name changed to AEC, Inc.

Applied Communications, Inc. — wholly-owned sub. of US West, Inc.

Applied Data Reseach, Inc. — acquired by Ameritech

Applied Digital Data Systems, Inc. — acquired by NCR Corp.

Applied Machining Technology, Inc. — out of business

Applied Solar Energy Corporation — name changed to Tecstar Inc.

Aqua Fab Industries, Inc. — out of business

Aquatec Quima S/A — acquired & absorbed into Grace Quimicia Cia Ltda.

Arandell Schmidt — name changed to Arandell Corporation

Arbor Acre Farms, Inc. — acquired by Booker PLC

Arcadia Fryers — acquired by Golden Plump Poultry & name changed to Golden Plump Poultry

Arcadian Power Corp. — acquired by The New World Power Corp. & name changed to The New World Grid Power Corp.

Arcata-National Corp. — name changed to Arcata Corp.

Arctic Enterprises, Inc. — name changed to Minstar, Inc.

Arden-Mayfair, Inc. — name changed to Arden Group, Inc.

Argo Petroleum Corp. — 75% sold to Seneca Resources Corp. of National Fuel Gas Co. & 25% sold to Fortune Petroleum

ARGO Systems, Inc. — now wholly-owned sub. of The Boeing Company

Argus Press Limited — name changed to Argus Business Media, Limited

Aries Enterprise — liquidated

Aristar, Inc. — acquired by Gamble-Skogmo, Inc.

Aristek Communities, Inc. — name changed to Homefree Village Resorts, Inc.

Aritech Corp (Delaware) — acquired by Berwind Corporation & name changed to Sentrol Controls Group

Aritmos AB — acquired by Proventus AB

Arizona Bancwest Corporation — acquired by Security Pacific Corp.

Arizona Colorado Land & Cattle Co. — name changed to AZL Resources, Inc.

Arizona Public Service Co. — holding co. formed, AZP Group, Inc.

Arkansas Best Corporation — merged into Carolina Freight Corporation

Arkansas Louisiana Gas Co. — name changed to Arkla, Inc.

Arkansas Oak Flooring — out of business

Arlen Realty & Development Corp. — name changed to Arlen Corporation

Armco Steel Corp. — name changed to Armco, Inc.

Armel, Inc. — acquired by F.W. Woolworth Company

Armstrong Cork Co. — name changed to Armstrong World Industries, Inc.

The Armstrong Rubber Co. — name changed to Armtek Corporation

Armtek Corporation — acquired by Mark IV Industries, Inc.

Arnold Industries, Inc. — name changed to Arnold Transportation Services

Arnolds Interiors, Inc. — acquired by Huffman Koos

The Aro Corporation — acquired by Todd Shipyards Corp.

Artec Distributing, Inc. — out of business

The Arundel Corp. — wholly-owned sub. of Florida Rock Industries, Inc.

Arwood Corp. — acquired by Interlake, Inc.

Asamera Oil Corp. — name changed to Asamera, Inc.

Ashton-Tate — acquired by Borland International Inc.

Asko Deutsche Kaufhaus AG — merged with Kaufop Group to form Metro AG

Aspen Imaging International, Inc. — acquired by Pubco Corporation

Aspen Ribbons Inc. — name changed to Aspen Imaging International, Inc.

Aspro, Inc. — name changed to Dyneer Corp.

Associated Coca-Cola Bottling, Inc. — acquired by Coca-Cola Co.

Associated Dry Goods Corp. — acquired by The May Department Stores Company

The Associated Group Insurance Companies — name changed to Anthem

Associated Hosts, Inc. — acquired by Industrial Equity Pacific Ltd.

Associated Madison Companies, Inc. — acquired by American Can Co.

Associated Natural Gas Corp. — name changed to Pan Energy Natural Gas Corp.

Associated Spring Corp. — name changed to Barnes Group, Inc.

Aston Martin Lagonda of North America — acquired by Ford Motor Company

Astrodata, Inc. — name changed to Adacorp, Inc.

Astrosystems, Inc. — Liquidated

Astrum International Corp. — out of business

Atari Corporation — name changed to JTS Corporation

Atari Games Corporation — acquired by Time Warner Inc. & name changed to Time Warner Interactive

Atari Games Corporation — acquired by WMS Industries Inc.

Atco Industries, Inc. — acquired by FSC Corporation

Atlan-Tol Industries — name changed to Astromed, Inc.

Atlanta Wire Works, Inc. — acquired by JWI Group of Canada

Atlantic Bancorporation — acquired by First Union Corp. & name changed to First Union Bancorporation of Florida

Atlantic City Electric Co. — holding co. formed, Atlantic Energy, Inc.

Atlantic Metropolitan Corp. — name changed to The Halwood Group, Incorporated

Atlantic Research Corp. — wholly-owned sub. of Sequa Corp.

Atlantic Steel Co. — acquired by Ivaco, Inc.

Atlantic to Pacific Bedding Corp. — out of business

Atlas Construction Co. — acquired by Starrett Corporation & name changed to HRH/Atlas Constuction Inc.

Atlas Power Equipment Company — out of business

Atlas Van Lines — acquired by Atlas World Group, Inc.

Attwoods Plc — acquired & absorbed into Browning-Ferris Industries, Inc.

Atwood Industries, Inc. — acquired by Excel Industries, Inc. & name changed to Excel of Rockford

Auburn Faith Community Hospital — acquired by Sutter Health & name changed to Sutter Auburn Faith Community Hospital

Augat, Inc. — acquired by Thomas & Betts Corporation

Audio Specialist, Inc. — out of business

The Austad Company — acquired by Hanover Direct, Inc.

The Austin Co. — acquired by National Gypsum Co.

Austrian Industries AG — name changed to Osterreichische

Industrieholding AG

Auto Crane Company—acquired by Ramsey Industries

Autoclave Engineers, Inc.—acquired by Snap-Tite, Inc.

Autofinance Group, Inc.—acquired by Keycorp & name changed to AFG, Inc.

Automanage—name changed to Performance Automotive Network

Automated Building Components, Inc.—acquired by Redland Brass Corp.

Automatic Radio Manufacturing Co., Inc.—name changed to Armatron International, Inc.

Automatic Switch Co.—acquired by Emerson Electric Co.

Automation Industries, Inc.—acquired by General Cable Corp.

Automation Intelligence, Inc.—out of business

Automotive Industries, Inc.—name changed to Lear Seating Corporation

Automotive Marketing Association—name changed to All Pro Bumper to Bumper Inc.

Automotive Moulding Company—acquired by Guardian Industries Corp.

Automotive Plastic Technologies, Inc.—out of business

Avacare, Inc.—name changed to Carrington Laboratories

Avail, Inc.—acquired by Ryder System, Inc.

Avalon Corporation—acquired by Corona Corporation

Avco Corporation—acquired by Textron, Inc.

Avery International Corporation—merged with Dennison Manufacturing Company to form Avery-Dennison Corporation

Avery Products Corp.—name changed to Avery International, Inc.

The Aviation Group, Inc.—acquired by Primark Corp.

Axia Inc.—name changed to New Axia Holding Corp.

Aztec Oil & Gas Co.—merged into Southland Royal Co.

B

B & B International Holdings, Inc.—now BTU International, Inc.

BBDO International—merged with Doyle Dane Bernbach and Needham Harper Worldwide to form Omnicom Group, Inc.

BCM Engineers Inc.—acquired by Canonie Environmental Services Corp & name changed to Smith Environmental Technologies Corp.

BD Holdings, Inc.—out of business

BDM International, Inc.—wholly-owned sub. of Ford Aerospace & Communications Corp., sub. of Ford Motor Company

B-E Holdings Inc.—name changed to Bucyrus-Erie Company

BET Public Limited Company—acquired & absorbed by Sophus Berendsen A/S

BIW Cable Systems—acquired by Draka Kabel B.V.

BLH Electronics—acquired by Spectra-Physics AB

BLT Manufacturing—name changed to Millennium Technology Services, Inc.

BM Group plc—name changed to Brunel Holding plc

BMA Corp.—name changed to Business Men's Assurance Co. of America

B.M.J. Financial Corp.—acquired by Summit Bancorp

B-O-P Corp.—name changed to Bancorp of Pennsylvania

BTK Industries, Inc.—acquired by McGregor Corp., sub. of Rapid American Corp.

BTU Engineering Corp.—name changed to Holec U.S.A., Inc.

BTU (USA) Inc.—name changed to B & B International Holdings, Inc.

The Babcock & Wilcox Co.—acquired by J. Ray McDermott & Co., Inc.

Babcock International, Inc.—now sub. of FKI Babcock PLC

Bache Group, Inc.—acquired by Prudential Insurance Co. of America

Bacon Henry Building Materials, Inc.—acquired by GAF Corporation & name changed to BMC West

Badger Northland Inc.—acquired by Miller-St. Nazianz, Inc.

Baird-Atomic, Inc.—name changed to Baird Corp.

Baker Industries, Inc.—acquired by Borg-Warner Corp.

Baker International Corp.—wholly-owned sub. of Baker Hughes International

Baker Material Handling Corp.—acquired by Linde AG

Baker Oil Tools, Inc.—name changed to Baker International, Inc.

Baldwin Construction, Inc.—name changed to Alliance Construction Solutions

D.H. Baldwin Co.—merged with United Corp. to form Baldwin United Corp.

Baldwin United Corp.—name changed to Philcorp, Inc.

Ballenger Paving Company, Inc.—acquired by Ashland, Inc. & name changed to APAC/Ballenger Pavings Company Inc.

Y.C. Ballenger Electrical Contractors—out of business

Bally Entertainment Corporation—acquired by Hilton Hotels Corporation

Balsam Sportstattenbau G.m.b.H.—out of business

BancOhio Corp.—acquired by National City Corporation

Banco Espanol de Credito SA—acquired by Banco Santander

Bancorp New Jersey Inc.—acquired & aborbed by UJB Financial Corp.

Bancorp of Pennsylvania—acquired by Dauphin Deposit Corp.

Bancshares of New Jersey—name changed to Northern National Corp.

Bangor Punta Corp.—acquired by Lear Siegler, Inc.

Bank Building & Equipment Corporation of America—out of business

Bank of Commonwealth—acquired by & merged into Comerica Incorporated

Bank of Delaware Corporation—acquired by PNC Financial Corporation

Bank of New England Corporation—now Fleet Bank of New England Corporation, a sub of Fleet/Norstar Financial Group, Inc.

Bank of Virginia Company—now Signet Bank, Virginia, wholly-owned sub. of Signet Banking Corp.

Bankers First Corporation—acquired by & absorbed into SouthTrust Corporation

Bankers Life Co.—name changed to Principal Mutual Life Insurance Co.

Banks of Iowa, Inc.—now Firstar Corp. of Iowa, a wholly-owned sub. of Firstar Corporation

Banks of Mid America, Inc.—name changed to Liberty Bancorp

Banner Industries—acquired Fairchild Industries Inc. and name changed to The Fairchild Industries Inc.

Barbara Lynn Stores, Inc.—merged into Belscot Retailers, Inc.

Barber-Colman Co.—acquired by Siebe PLC

Barber-Greene Co.—acquired by Astec Industries, Inc.

The Barcolene Company—acquired & absorbed by Benjamin Ansehl Company

The Barden Corporation—acquired by FAG Bearings Corporation, a sub of FAG Kugelfischer George Schaefer KGAA

Barefoot, Inc.—acquired by The ServiceMaster Company

Barge Wagener Construction Co.—acquired by Clark Enterprises Inc.

Barnes Engineering Co.—acquired by Edo Corporation

Barnes-Hind, Inc.—acquired by Pilkington Visionary & name changed to Sola Barnes-Hind. Inc.

Barnes-Hind Pharmaceuticals, Inc.—acquired by Revlon, Inc.

Barnett Mortgage Trust—name changed to Treco, Inc.

Baron-Abramson—out of business

Barondata Systems—acquired by Convergent Business Systems, Inc., sub. of Convergent, Inc.

Barrett Haentjens & Co.—acquired by Warman Intl. Inc. & name changed to Hazleton Pumps, Inc.

Barris Industries, Inc.—name changed to The Guber Peters Entertainment Company

Barry Wright Corporation—now wholly-owned sub. of Applied Power Inc.

Barth Spencer Corp.—acquired by Darby Drug Co.

Barton Brands Ltd.—acquired by Canadaigua Wine Company, Inc. & name changed to Barton Incorporated

Barton's Candy Corp.—acquired by American Safety Razor Co.

Bartlett Agri Enterprises Inc.—name changed to Bartlett & Co.

Baruch-Foster Corp.—acquired by and merged with Hadson Energy Resources Corp.

Basco, Inc.—acquired by Best Products Co., Inc.

Basic American Medical, Inc.—acquired by Columbia Hospital Corp.

Basic, Inc.—acquired by Combustion Engineering, Inc.

Basic Resources Corp.—name changed to BASIX Corp.

Basil Blackwell Ltd.—acquired by B.H. Blackwell Ltd. & name changed to Blackwell Publishers Ltd.

Basin Petroleum Corp.—name changed to Reserve Oil, Inc.

Basix Corporation—in process of liquidation

G.H. Bass & Co.—acquired by Chesebrough-Pond's Inc.

Bastian Industries, Inc.—out of business

Bates Fabrics, Inc.—out of business

Bath Iron Works—acquired by General Dynamics Corporation

Batlen, Barton, Durstine & Osborn—name changed to BBDO Worldwide, Inc.

Batus Inc.—disbanded after sale of retail group; remaining companies, Brown & Williamson Tobacco Group and Farmers Group, Inc., now separate companies

Baukol-Noonan, Inc.—name changed to BNI Coal, now sub. of Minnesota Power & Light Company

Baxter Laboratories, Inc.—name changed to Baxter Travenol Laboratories

Baxter Travenol Laboratories—name changed to Baxter International, Inc.

Bay Colony Property Co.—name changed to Bay Financial Corp.

Bay Financial Corporation—out of business

BayBanks, Inc.—acquired by Bank of Boston Corporation & merged to form BankBoston Corporation

Bayly Corporation—liquidated

Beacon Manufacturing Co.—acquired by Pillowtex Corporation

Beacon Photo Service, Inc.—name changed to Imprint Products, Inc.

The Beard Company—name changed to Beard Oil Co.

Beatrice Companies, Inc.—holding co. formed, BCI Holdings, Inc.

Beatrice Company—acquired by ConAgra, Inc.

Beazer USA—acquired by Hanson Industries

Beckman Instruments, Inc.—merged with SmithKline Corp. to form SmithKline Beckman Corp.

Becor Western, Inc.—name changed back to Bucyrus-Erie Company

Bee Chemical Co.—acquired by Morton-Thiokol, Inc.

Beeba's Creations, Inc.—name changed to Niches, Inc.

Beech Aircraft Corp.—acquired by Raytheon Co.

Beech Holdings Corp.—holding company dissolved

Beech-Nut Corp.—sub. of Nestle Enterprises, Inc.

Beehive International—out of business

Beeline Fashions, Inc.—name changed to Beeline, Inc.

Beeline, Inc.—liquidated

Beers Construction Company—acquired by Skanska A.B.

Begley Company—acquired by Rite Aid Corporation

Begley Drug Co.—name changed to Begley Company

Behr Stores Inc.—out of business

The Bekins Co.—acquired by Minstar, Inc.

Belco Petroleum Corp.—acquired by Allied Corporation

Belden Corp.—acquired by Crouse-Hinds Co.

Belden Wire & Cable Company—name changed to Belden Inc.

Belding Heminway Company, Inc.—acquired by Noel Group, Inc.

Beldoch Industries Corporation—acquired by Donnkenny, Inc.

Belgrave Industries—out of business

Belknap, Inc.—out of business

Bell Chemical Company—out of business

Bell Gardens Bycicle Club—name changed to Bicycle Club Casino

Bell Petroleum Services, Inc.—acquired by Regal International Inc.

W. Bell & Co.—out of business

Bellacicco & Sons—out of business

Belliss & Morcom—acquired by Powell Duffryn PLC

Bellofram Corp.—name changed to Marsh Bellofram Corp.

Beloit Corp.—acquired by Harnischfeger Corporation

Belscot Retailers, Inc.—name changed to Albert Lechter, Inc.

Bench Craft, Inc.—now sub. of Universal Furniture Ltd.

Beneficial Standard Corp.—liquidated

Beneficial Standard Mortgage Investors—name changed to Alamand Corp.

Bennett Ringrose Wolsfeld, Inc.—name changed to BRW, Inc.

Benrus Corp.—name changed to Wells-Benrus Corp.

Benson Inc.—acquired by Oce-van der Grinton N.V. & name changed to Oce Graphics

Benson Eyecare Corporation—merged into Essilor International Compagnie Generale d Optique

Tom Benson Glass Co.—name changed to Tom Benson Industries, Inc.

Bentley Laboratories, Inc.—acquired by American Hospital Supply Corp.

Benton & Bowles, Inc.—acquired by D'Arcy Masius Benton & Bowles, Inc.

Benton Harbor Engineering—assets sold

Berg Enterprises, Inc.—acquired by American Can Co.

Bergerat, Monnoyeur S.A.—name changed to Monnoyeur SCA

Bergstrom Paper Co.—acquired by P.H. Glatfelter Co.

Berkey Photo Inc.—name changed to Berkey, Inc.

Berliner Bank AG—acquired by Bankgesellschaft Berlin

Bernzomatic Corp.—acquired by Newell Cos., Inc.

Berol Corporation—now Empire Berol, sub. of Empire Pencil Corporation

Bertea Corp.—acquired by Parker-Hannifin Corp.

Besnier SA—name changed to Compagnie Laitiere BESNIER

Best Brands—acquired by Hero AG

Best Western, Inc.—name changed to Best Western International, Inc.

Besteel Industries, LLC—acquired by American Modular Technologies, L.L.C. & name changed to American Modular Technologies, LLC

Bestop, Inc.—acquired by Douglas & Lomason Company

The Betham Corporation—acquired by Tyco International Ltd.

Bettcher Manufacturing Corp.—acquired by Brittany Corporation

Bettis Corporation—acquired by Daniel Industries, Inc.

Beverage Canners International Corp.—acquired by BCI Holding Corporation

Beverage Management, Inc.—acquired by BMI Acquisition Corp.

Beverage Management, Inc.—now sub. of J.W. Brooks

Bevis Industries, Inc.—liquidated

Bic Pen Corp.—name changed to Bic Corp.

Bickford Corp.—name changed to Bickford's Family Fare, Inc.

Bickford's Family Fare, Inc.—acquired by The Dorsey Corporation

Bicoastal Corporation—liquidated

Big Bear, Inc.—now sub. of Penn Traffic Company

Big Daddy's Lounges, Inc.—name changed to Flanigan's Enterprises, Inc.

Big Drum, Inc.—acquired by Alco Standard Corp.

Big O Tires Incorporated—acquired by TCB Corporation

Big Three Industries, Inc.—sub. of American Air Liquide, Inc.

Big V Pharmacies Co. Limited—acquired by Imasco Limited & name changed to Shoppers Drug Mart, Ltd.

Bigg's Hyper Shoppe—acquired by Super Value Inc.

Billy the Kid, Inc.—name changed to BTK Industries, Inc.

Binney & Smith, Inc.—acquired by Hallmark, Inc.

Bio Medic Corporatin—name changed to Lab Products, Inc.

Bio-Medicus Inc.—now Medtronic Bio-Medicus, Inc., sub. of Medtronic Inc.

Biochem International Inc.—name changed to BCI International

Biocraft Laboratories, Inc.—acquired by Teva Pharmaceutical Industries Ltd. & name changed to Teva USA-Biocraft

Biodor Holding AG—out of business

Biosys, Inc.—out of business

Biotech Research Laboratories, Inc.—merged with Cam-

bridge BioScience Corporation to form Cambridge Biotech Corporation

Biotechnica International, Inc.—acquired by Groupe Limagrain

Bird & Son, Inc.—name changed to Bird, Inc.

Bird Medical Technologies—acquired by Therma Electron Corporation

Birtcher Medical Systems, Incorporated—out of business

Bitco Corp.—acquired by Old Republic International Corp.

Black & Decker Mfg. Co.—name changed to The Black & Decker Corporation

Black & Edgington—name changed to SkyePharma PLC

Black Hills Power & Light Co.—name changed to Black Hills Corp.

Blackstone Corp.—acquired by Armstrong Rubber Corp.

Blackstone Partnership (NYC)—name changed to The Blackstone Group

Blackwood Stocko Corporation—now Stocko Corporation

John Blair & Co.—now two separate companies, Telemundo Group, Inc. & John Blair Communications, Inc.

Blaw Knox Corp.—out of business

Blessings Corp.—acquired by Williamson-Dickey Co.

Blevins Concession Supply Co.—out of business

Bliss & Laughlin Industries—name changed to AXIA Inc.

BLOC Development Corporation—name changed to Tiger Direct, Inc.

Blocker Energy Corp.—name changed to Energy Service Company, Inc.

Blue Bell Holding Co., Inc.—acquired by VF Corporation

Blue Chip Stamps—acquired by Berkshire Hathaway Inc.

Blue Circle Holdings Inc.—now Blue Circle America Inc.

Blue Cross Assn. & Blue Shield Corp.—name changed to Blue Cross & Blue Shield Association

Blue Ridge Transfer Co.—acquired by Lily Transportation Corp.

Boatmen's Bankshares, Inc.—acquired by NationsBank Corporation & name changed to NationsBank West

Bobbie Brooks, Inc.—acquired by Pubco Corporation

Boddington—acquired & absorbed into The Greenalls Group Plc

The Bodine Corp.—name changed to Bodine Assembly and Test Systems

Boewe Passat—name changed to Passat Laundry Systems

Bohemia, Inc.—acquired by Willamette Industries, Inc.

Bon Ton Foods, Inc.—acquired by Amerifoods Companies Inc.

Bonanza International Inc.—name changed to USA Cafes

Bond Industries, Inc.—name changed to The Trump Group

Bonhomme Shirtmakers, Ltd.—acquired by Randa Corp.

Book-of-the-Month, Inc.—acquired by Time, Inc.

Boothe Computer Corp.—name changed to Boothe Courier Corp.

Boothe Courier Corp.—name changed to Boothe Financial Corp.

Boothe Financial Corp.—name changed to Robert Half International

Borchers Bros.—out of business

Borman's Inc.—now sub. of The Great Atlantic & Pacific Tea Company, Inc.

The Boston Co., Inc.—acquired by American Express

Boston Distributors, Inc.—out of business

Boston Trading Ltd. Inc.—out of business; assets acquired by Designs, Inc.

Boury Incorporated—name changed to Boury Enterprises

Bovay—acquired by Rosser International Inc. & name changed to Rosser Bovay

Bow Valley Industries Ltd.—absorbed by Nova Corporation

Bozell & Jacobs, Inc.—acquired by Lorimar, Inc. & name changed to Bozell, Jacobs, Kenyon & Eckhardt, Inc.

Bradford Computer & Systems, Inc.—name changed to Bradford National Corp.

Bradford National Corp.—name changed to Fidata Corp.

Bramlea Limited—liquidated

Branch Banking & Trust—name changed to Southern National

Branch Corp.—name changed to BB&T Financial Corp.

Branch Industries, Inc.—liquidated

Brandon Systems Corporation—acquired by Interim Services Inc.

Brandt, Inc.—acquired by De La Rue plc

Braniff International Corp.—acquired by Hyatt, Inc.

Braniff International Corp.—name changed to Braniff Inc., now separate company

Brass-Craft Mfg. Co.—name changed to Masco Corp.

C.F. Braun & Co.—acquired by Santa Fe International Corp.

Braun Engineering Company—acquired by Masco Industries, Inc.

Brazier Forest Industries, Inc.—out of business

Breeze Corporations, Inc.—acquired by Trans Technology Corp.

Brenco, Inc.—acquired by Varlen Corporation

Brendle's Inc.—liquidated

The Brenlin Group—name changed to The Cypress Companies

Brennand-Paige Industries, Inc.—acquired by & merged into Thackeray Corp.

Brenner Industries—acquired by & merged into Browning-Ferris Industries, Inc.

Bressler's Industries, Inc.—acquired by Yogen Fruz

Worldwide Inc.

Brian Center Management Corporation—acquired by & name changed to Living Centers of America

Brillion Ironworks—acquired by Johnstown America Industries

Brigadier Industries Corp.—acquired by U.S. Homes Corporation

Brinkmann Industries—now sub. of Beijer Industries AB

Bristol Corporation—acquired by Heywood Williams Group plc

Bristol-Myers Company—merged with Squibb Corporation to form Bristol-Myers Squibb Company

Bristol Products, Inc.—name changed to Bristol Corp.

Bristol Steel & Iron Works—liquidated

British Coal Corporation—out of business

British Mohair Spinners Limited—reorganized under British Mohair Holdings Plc

British Syphon Industries Ltd.—name changed to Graystone PLC

British Technology Group International Plc—name changed to BTG Plc

Brix Maritime Co.—acquired by Foss Maritime Co.

Broadway Hale Stores—now Carter Hawley Hale Stores, Inc.

Broadway Stores, Inc.—acquired & absorbed by Camdev Corporation

Brock Hotel Corporation—name changed to Intergra-A Hotel & Restaurant Co.

J.C. Brock Corp.—name changed to Brock's Fresh Foods

Brockhouse Corporation—acquired by Evered Holdings PLC & name changed to Brockhouse Holding USA

Brockton Public Markets, Inc.—name changed to Shaw's Supermarkets, Inc.

Brockway Glass Co., Inc.—name changed to Brockway, Inc. (NY)

Brockway, Inc.—acquired by & merged into Owens-Illinois, Inc.

Brodhead-Garrett Co.—acquired by FSC Educational Inc.

British Syphon Industries Ltd.—name changed to Graystone PLC

Brooke Tool Engineering (Holdings) Ltd.—name changed to Brooke Industrial Holdings Plc

Brooklyn Bancorp, Inc.—absorbed into Republic National Bank of New York

Brooks & Perkins, Inc.—acquired by AAR Corp.

Brooks Beverage Management, Inc.—name changed to Beverage America, Inc.

Brooks-Scanlon, Inc.—acquired by Diamond Intl. Corp. & merged into Diamond Lumber Div.

Brooktree Corporation—acquired by Rockwell International & name changed to Brooktree Rockwell Semiconductor Systems Div.

Brown & Williamson Tobacco Corp.—name changed to Brown & Williamson Industries, Inc.

Brown-Forman Distillers Co.—name changed to Brown-Forman Co.

H.H. Brown Shoe Company, Inc.—acquired by Berkshire Hathaway Inc.

Brown-Minneapolis Tank & Fabricating Co.—acquired by Astrotech International Corp.

Browning—acquired by FN America, Inc.

Browns Lumber & Supply Company—acquired by & name changed to O.C. Cluss Lumber Co.

Brubaker Tool Corp.—acquired by Cincinnati Milacron Inc.

Bruce Rossmeyer's Qeality Toyotaland—name changed to Quality Toyota

Brudi, Inc.—now Swingshift Brudi Inc., a subsidiary of Tredegar Industries Inc.

Bruner Corporation—acquired by Astrum International Corp.

Bryant Universal Roofing, Inc.—out of business

Bucilla Corporation—acquired by Dyson-Kissner-Moran Corporation

Buckbee-Mears Co.—name changed to BMC Industries

Buckeye Federal Savings & Loan Assn.—name changed to Buckeye Financial Corp.

Buckeye Financial Corporation—acquired by National City Corporation

Buckeye International, Inc.—acquired by Worthington Industries, Inc.

Buckhorn, Inc.—acquired by Myers Industries, Inc.

Bucyrus Erie Co.—name changed to Becor Western, Inc.

Buddy L Inc.—acquired by & absorbed into Empire of Carolina, Inc.

Budget Industries, Inc.—name changed to Financial Corp. of America

Bugatti Automobili—out of business

Buehler Corp.—merged with Maul Bros. Inc. to form Maul Technology Corp.

Builders Investment Group—name changed to Winn Industries

Buffalo Forge Co.—acquired by Ampco-Pittsburgh Corp.

Bulova Watch Co., Inc.—acquired by Loews Corp.

Bundy Corp.—sub. of TI Group PLC

Bunker Hill Income Securities, Inc.—out of business

The Bunker Ramo Corp.—acquired by Allied Corp.

Bunton Company—acquired by Textron Inc.

Burdox, Inc.—name changed to AGA Burdox, Inc.

Burgess, Anderson & Tate Inc.—acquired by U.S. Office Products Company

Burgess Industries, Inc.—acquired by Valley Industries, Inc.

Burgess Vibrocrafters, Inc.—acquired by Acme General Corp.

Burlington Holdings—holding co. dissolved & name changed to Burlington Industries Inc.

Burlington Northern, Inc.—merged with St. Louis San Francisco Railway Co.

Burlington Northern, Inc. — merged with Santa Fe Pacific Corporation to form Burlington Northern Santa Fe Corporation

Burlington Northern Inc. — spun-off Burlington Resources, Inc.

Burndy Corporation — acquired by Framatome et Cie

Burnham Broadcasting Company — out of business

Burns Aerospace Corporation — acquired by B/E Aerospace, Inc. & name changed to B/E Aerospace Seating Products

Burns International Security Services, Inc. — acquired by Borg-Warner Corp.

Burris Industries, Inc. — acquired by La-Z-Boy Chair Co.

Burroughs Corporation — merged with Sperry Corp. to form Unisys Corporation

Bushwacker Associates, Inc. — acquired by Bethrum Research & Development, Inc.

Business Men's Assurance Co. of America — holding co. formed, BMA Corp.

BusinessLand Inc. — acquired by JWP Inc.

Business Records Corporation Holding Company — name changed to BRC Holdings

M. Buten & Sons, Inc. — acquired by Duron, Inc. & name changed to Buten, Division of Duron

Butler Aviation Corporation — name changed to Signature Flight Support

Butler International, Inc. — acquired by North American Ventures, Inc.

John O. Butler Co. — acquired by Sunstar Inc.

Bycom Systems Inc. — name changed to Superior Holding Corporation

Byers Communications Systems — name changed to Bycom Systems, Inc.

C

C & K Petroleum, Inc. — acquired by Alaska Interstate Co.

C & S/Sovran Corporation — merged with NCNB & name changed to Nations Bank

CAP Gemini Sogeti (USA) — name changed to CAP Gemini America

CB&T Bancshares, Inc. — name changed to Synovus Financial Corp.

CBI Holdings — out of business

CBI Industries — acquired by Praxair Inc.

CBM Industries, Inc. — name changed to RisComp Industries, Inc.

CBR Cement Corporation — acquired by Heidelberger Zemet A.G.

CBS Inc. — acquired by Westinghouse Electric Corporation

CCH Incorporated — acquired by Wolters Kluwer N.V.

CCP Insurance, Inc. — acquired by Conseco Inc.

CCS Continental Copper & Steel Industries, Inc. — name changed to CCX, Inc.

CDI Corporation — holding co. formed, CDI Corp.

C.E.C. Industries Corp. — out of business

CFI Industries, Inc. — executive office closed; subsidiary acquired by IVEX

CFS Continental Inc. — acquired by A. E. Staley Mfg. Co. & new holding co. formed, Staley Continental Inc.

CGW Southeast Partners — name changed to Cravey, Green & Wahlen Incorporated

CHB Foods, Inc. — name changed to California Home Brands, Inc.

CHF Industries, Inc. — acquired by CC Industries

CI Mortgage Group — name changed to Enterprise Development Corp.

C.I.T. Financial Corp. — acquired by RCA Corp.

CJC Holdings, Inc. — name changed to Commemorative Brands, Inc.

CLC of America, Inc. — absorbed into American River Transportation, Archer Daniels

CMI Investment Corp. — acquired by Greyhound Corp. & name changed to Verex Corp.

CMT Industries, Inc. — name changed to Matrix Corp.

CMX Corporation — acquired by Chyron Corporation

CP National Corporation — acquired by Alltel Corporation

CPI Plastics Inc. — acquired by U.S. Can Company & name changed to U.S. Can Company-Newnan

CR/PL Limited Partnership — name changed to CR LLC

CRA Limited — merged with The RTZ Corporation PLC to form The RTZ-CRA Group

CRS Design Associates, Inc. — name changed to CRS Group, Inc.

The CRS Group, Inc. — name changed to CRS Sirrine

CRSS Inc. — acquired by Tractebel

CS First Boston Group Inc. — acquired by CS Holding

CS Vidar Inc. — name changed to Vidar, Inc.

CSF Holdings, Inc. — acquired by NationsBank Corporation & name changed to NationsBank/Miami

CW Transport, Inc. — acquired by Gerber Products Co.

CWT Specialty Stores, Inc. — name changed to Cherry & Webb

CXR Telcom Corporation — holding co. formed, CXR Corporation

Cabana Foods, Inc. — acquired by Amerifoods Companies Inc.

Cablevision Industries Corp. — acquired by Time Warner, Inc. & name changed to Time Warner Cable Liberty Division

Cabot, Cabot & Forbes Land Trust — name changed to Bay Colony Property Co.

Cabot Medical Corporation — acquired by Circon Corporation

Cabot Safety Corporation — name changed to Aeoro Company

Cadbury Schweppes U.S.A. Inc. — name changed to Cadbury Schweppes Holdings, Inc.

Cadnetix Corporation—merged with Daisy Systems to form Daisy/Cadnetix, Inc.

Cafeterias, Inc.—name changed to Luby's Cafeterias, Inc.

Calberrson— acquired by SNCF

Calbiochem—acquired by American Hoescht Corp.

Caldor, Inc.—acquired by Associated Dry Goods Corp.

California Apricot Advisory Board—out of business

California Artichoke & Vegetable Growers Corp.—name changed to Ocean Mist Farms Corp.

California Biotechnology Inc.—name changed to Scios Inc.

California Computer Products, Inc.—acquired by Sanders Associates, Inc.

California Electric Service—name changed to GDJK, Incorporated

California Federal Bank FSB—merged with First Nationwide Bank to form California Federal Bank

California First Bank—name changed to Union Bank

California Home Brands, Inc.—out of business

California Labels, Inc.—name changed to Cal Emblem Labels, Inc.

California Pacific Utilities Co.—name changed to C.P. National Corp.

California Portland Cement—merged with Conrock Co. to form CalMat Co.

Callahan Mining Corporation—acquired by Coeur d'Alene Mines Corporation

Calumet Industries, Inc.—out of business

Cambridge BioScience Corporation—merged with Biotech Research Laboratories to form Cambridge Biotech Corporation

Cambridge Biotech Corporation—name changed to Aquila Biopharmaceuticals, Inc.

Cambridge Memories, Inc.—name changed to Cambes, Inc.

Cambridge Nuclear Corp.—name changed to Cambridge Medical Technology Corporation

Camco, Inc.—acquired by Midhurst Corp.

Cameron Iron Works, Inc.—acquired by Cooper Industries, Inc.

Campanelli Industries, Inc.—now Realmark Corporation

Campbell Industries—acquired by Marine Construction & Design Co.

Campbell Taggart, Inc.—acquired by Anheuser-Busch Cos., Inc.

Campus Casuals of California—acquired by Chromalloy American Corp.

Canada Malting Co. Limited—acquired by ConAgra, Inc.

Canadian Export Gas & Oil Ltd.—acquired by Placer Development Ltd. & name changed to Placer Cego Petroleum Ltd.

Canadian Homestead Oils Ltd.—acquired by & merged into Inter-City Gas Corp.

Canadian Hydrocarbons Ltd.—acquired by Inter-City Gas Ltd.

Canadian Insurance Group Ltd.—name changed to GIGL Holding Ltd.

Canadians Corp.—out of business

Canal Randolph Corp.—name changed to United Stockyards Corp.

Candle Corporation of America—acquired by Blyth Corporation

Candy Elettrodomestici Srl—name changed to Candy S.p.A.

A.J. Canfield Co.—acquired by Select Bevereges, Inc. & name changed to Select Canfield

The Cannon Group, Inc.—name changed to Pathe Communications Corporation

Cannon Mills Co.—acquired by Pacific Holding Corp.

Canoga Industries—acquired by Zero Mfg. Co.

Canstar Sports Inc.—acquired by Nike Inc.

CAPCO Automotive Products Corporation—acquired & absorbed by Eaton Corporation

Capin Management Corp.—acquired by Family Bargain Corporation & name changed to Factory 2-U

Capital Cities/ABC, Inc.—acquired by The Walt Disney Company

Capital Energy Corp.—name changed to Life Chemistry

Capital Reserve Corp.—name changed to Capital Energy Corp.

Capital Food Industries, Inc.—name changed to Vincent Food Industries

Capital Pacific Homes—name changed to Capital Pacific Holdings

Capitol Intl. Airways, Inc.—name changed to Capitol Air, Inc.

Capitol Products—out of business

Capt. Crab, Inc.—name changed to Bayport Restaurant Group, Inc.

Captech, Inc.—acquired by & merged into A-T-O, Inc.

Carboline Co.—acquired by Sun Company

Carbon Industries—acquired by International Telephone & Telegraph Corp.

The Carborundum Co.—acquired by Kennecott Copper Co.

Card Establishment Services—acquired by First Data Corporation & name changed to CES/Card Establishment Services

Cardinal Communications Group, Inc.—acquired by Unidigital Inc. & name changed to Unidigital/Carolina Corp.

Care Corporation—acquired by Owens-Illinois

CareerTrack Inc.—acquired by Tele-Communications Inc.

Caremark International Inc.—acquired by Medpartners Inc.

Carena Developments Ltd.—name changed to Brookfield Properties Corporation

Carey Machinery & Supply Company—acquired by J. Fegely Inc. & name changed to Carey Division

Carlisle Corp.—name changed to Carlisle Companies, Inc.

Carlisle Plastics, Inc.—acquired & absorbed by Tyco International Ltd.

Carlisle Retailers, Inc.—acquired & absorbed by Peebles, Inc.

Carlsberg Corp.—acquired by Southmark Corp. & name changed to Carlsberg Financial Corporation

Carnation Company—acquired by Nestle Holdings, Inc. & name changed to Nestle Carnation Food Company

Carolina Clinchfield & Ohio Railway—acquired by CSX Corp.

Carolina Energies, Inc.—acquired by South Carolina Electric & Gas Co.

Carolina Freight Carriers Corp.—name changed to Carolina Freight Corp.

Carolina Pipeline Co.—name changed to Carolina Energies, Inc.

Carom Capital Corporation—name changed to Jillians Entertainment Corp.

Carpenter Paper Co. of Nebraska—acquired by Alco Standard Corp.

Carpenter Rigging—name changed to The Carpenter Group

Carrera Eyewear Corporation—name changed to Optimaxx International

Carrier Corp.—acquired by & merged into United Technologies Corp.

Carson Pirie Scott & Company—acquired by P.A. Bergner & Co. sub. of Maus Feres S.A.

Carstensen Freight Line, Inc.—acquired by Wintz Companies

Carter Controls Inc.—now Lin-Act Carter, a division of Figgie International

Carter Holt Harvey Limited—acquired by International Paper Company

Jerry C. Carter Inc.—acquired by Jones Petroleum Co. Inc.

Carter-Jones Lumber Company—name changed to Carter-Jones Companies, Inc.

Carter, Oncor Intl.—name changed to Carter & Associates

Cartwright Communications Co.—acquired by Tessco Technologies, Inc.

CasChem Inc.—acquired by Cambrex Corporation

Casco-Northern Corp.—acquired by Bank of Boston Corp.

Cash America Investments, Inc.—name changed to Cash America International Inc.

Casino-Guichard Perrachon & CIE—acquired by Groupe Casino

Castex Industries Inc.—acquired by Tennant Company & name changed to Castex Incorporated

Casting Material Company—acquired by Hickman, Williams & Co. Inc.

Castle & Cooke Inc.—name changed to Dole Food Company

Castleberry's Food Company—name changed to Castleberry/Snow's Brands Inc.

Castlewood International Corp.—name changed to Big Daddy's Lounges, Inc.

The Casual Male Corporation—acquired by J. Baker Inc.

Caterair International—acquired by Onex Corporation

Caterpillar Tractor Co.—name changed to Caterpillar, Inc.

Carena Developments Ltd.—name changed to Brookfield Properties Corporation

Cavanagh Communities Corp.—name changed to The Royal Group, Ltd.

Cavexsa—acquired by Magellan International Trading

Cavitron Corp.—acquired by & merged into Cooper Laboratories, Inc.

Cawsl Corporation—name changed to Superior Group, Inc.

The Ceco Corporation—merged with H.H. Robertson Co. to form Robertson-Ceco Corporation

Cedar Point, Inc.—name changed to Cedar Fair Limited Partnership

Celanese Corp.—acquired by American Hoescht Corp., now Hoescht-Celanese Corporation

Celeron Corp.—acquired by Goodyear Tire & Rubber Co.

Cellu-Craft Inc.—now sub. of Alusuisse of America, Inc.

Cenco, Inc.—acquired by Manor Care, Inc. & merged into Manor Health Care Corp.

Centech Corporation—out of business

Centennial Corp.—name changed to Foremost Corp. of America

Centerbank—acquired by Center Financial Corporation

Center Financial Corporation—acquired & absorbed by First Union Corporation

Centermark Properties, Inc.—out of business

The Central Bancorporation, Inc.—merged with PNC Financial Corp.

Central Illinois Light Co.—holding co. formed, CILCORP Inc.

Central Illinois Public Service Company—holding co. formed, CIPSCO Incorporated

Central Louisiana Energy Corp.—name changed to Celeron Corp.

Central Pharmaceuticals, Inc.—acquired by Schwarz Pharma AG & name changed to Schwarz Pharma Manufacturing, Inc.

Central Point Software Inc.—acquired by Symantec Corporation

Central Soya Co., Inc.—acquired by Ferruzzi Finanziaria SpA

Central Telephone & Utilities Corp.—name changed to Centel Corporation

Centronics Data Computer Corp.—name changed to Genicom Corp.

Century Acceptance Corp. — acquired by Bank of Boston Corporation & name changed to Fidelity Century Acceptance Corp.

Century Autoline — acquired by Fuchs Petrolub AG

Century Boat Company Inc. — acquired by Yamaha Corporation

Century Computer Marketing — acquired by Aurora Electronics Inc.

Century Factors, Inc. — name changed to Century Business Credit Corp.

Century 21 Real Estate Corp. — acquired by Trans World Corp.

Cenvill Communities, Inc. — name changed to Cenvill Investors, Inc.

Cenvill Development Corp. — acquired by First American Bank & Trust

Cenvill Development Corp. — now CV Reit Inc.

Cenvill Development Corp. — out of business

Cerebronics, Inc. — holding co. formed, Cerbco, Inc.

Cerro Corp. — name changed to Cerro Marmon Corp.

Cerro-Marmon Corp. — name changed to The Marmon Group, Inc.

Certified Corp. — acquired by MEDIQ Incorporated & name changed to Powers Pharmaceutical

Cessna Aircraft Co. — acquired by General Dynamics Corporation

Cetec Corporation — dissolved

Cetus Corporation — merged with Chiron Corporation

Chamberlain Mfg. Corp. — acquired by Duchossois/Thrall Group

Chambers Development Company, Inc. — acquired by USA Waste Services, Inc. & name changed to Chambers USA Waste, Inc.

Champion Home Builders Co. — holding co. formed, Champion Enterprises, Inc.

Champion Motors (1975) Pte. Ltd. — acquired by Inchcape PLC

Champion Parts Rebuilders, Inc. — name changed to Champion Parts, Inc.

Champion Products Inc. — acquired by Sara Lee Corporation

Champion Spark Plug Company — now Champion Spark Plug Division of Cooper Industries, Inc.

Channel Companies, Inc. — acquired by W.R. Grace & Co.

Channel Home Centers, Inc. — acquired by EOS Partners LP & merged into Rickel Home Centers Inc.

Charing Cross Group — out of business

Charlotte Charles, Inc. — acquired by Portland Food Products Co.

Chart House, Inc. — merged with Godfather's Pizza to form Diversifoods Incorporated

Charted New York Corp. — name changed to Irving Bank Corp.

Charter Bancshares, Inc. — acquired by NationsBank Corporation

The Charter Company — sub. of American Financial Corporation

Charter Federal Savings Bank — acquired by First American Corporation & name changed to First American Federal Savings Bank

Charter Press — out of business

Chase Bag Co. — name changed to Chase Packaging Corp.

Chase Convertible Fund of Boston, Inc. — name changed to Phoenix-Chase Convertible Fund Series

Chattem Drug & Chemical Co. — name changed to Chattem, Inc.

Checker Holding Corp. — now Checker Motor Corp.

Chelsea Moore Company — acquired by Western and Southern Life Insurance Company

Chemical Banking Corporation — merged with the Chase Manhattan Corporation

Chemical Express Co. — acquired by TIC Industries, Inc.

Chemical Fabrics Corporation — name changed to Chemfab Corporation

Chemical Leaman Tank Line, Inc. — name changed to Chemical Leaman Corp.

Chemical New York Corp. — name changed to Chemical Banking Corp.

Chemie Linz GmbH — acquired by DSM N.V. & now a joint venture of DSM N.V. & DSM Chemie Linz GmbH

Chemineer, Inc. — acquired by Interpace Corp., sub. of Clevepak Corp.

Chemlawn Corp. — acquired by Ecolab, Inc.

Chemplast, Inc. — acquired by Norton Co. & name changed to Fluoropolymers Div.

Chemtex International — now sub. of Mitsubishi Corporation

Chemtron Corp. — acquired by Allegheny Ludlum Industries, Inc.

Cherne Enterprises, Inc. — out of business

Cherne Industries, Inc. — name changed to Cherne Enterprises, Inc.

The Cherry Corporation — name changed to Cherry Electrical Products Corporation

The Chesapeake Corp. of Virginia — name changed to Chesapeake Corporation

Chesapeake Holding Corp. —- acquired by DWG Corp. & name changed to CFC Holding Corp.

The Chesapeake Life Insurance Co. — acquired by United Insurance Companies, Inc.

Chesebrough-Pond's Inc. — acquired by Unilever United States, Inc.

Chessie Systems, Inc. — merged with Seaboard Coast Line Industries, to form CSX Corp.

Chevy Electrical Products Corp. — now The Chevy Corp.

Chi-Chi's, Inc. — wholly-owned sub. of Foodmaster Corp.

Chicago & North Western Transportation Co. — holding co. formed, CNW Corporation

Chicago and North Western Transportation Company — acquired & absorbed by Union Pacific Corporation

Chicago Bridge & Iron Co.—name changed to CBI Industries

Chicago Mechanical, Inc.—acquired by Scott Companies, Inc.

Chicago Metropolitan Assurance Co.—acquired by Atlanta Life Insurance Company

Chicago Milwaukee Corporation—out of business

Chicago Pacific Corporation—acquired by & merged into Maytag Corporation

Chicago Pneumatic Tool Co.—acquired by Danaher Corp. & Atlas Copco North America, Inc.

Chicken Unlimited Enterprises, Inc.—name changed to Cue Enterprises, Inc.

Child World, Inc.—acquired by Cole National Corp.

Chilewich Group—out of business

Chili's, Inc.—name changed to Brinker International, Inc.

Chilten Capital plc—acquired by Alpha Omikron Limited & name changed to Chilten Group Sam

Chilton Co.—acquired by American Broadcasting Cos.

Chilton Corp.—acquired by Borg-Warner Corporation

ChipCom Corporation—acquired by 3Com Corp. & name changed to 3Com Corporation

Chloride Inc.—name changed to Pacific Chloride, Inc.

Christensen Boyles Corp.—acquired by Layne, Inc.

Chromalloy American Corp.—acquired by Sun Chemical Corp., now Sequa Corporation

Church's Fried Chicken, Inc.—acquired by Popeye's Famous Fried Chicken Inc.

Ciba Geigy Limited Group—merged with Sandoz Ltd. to form Novartis AG

CIMCO—acquired by Hanna M.A. Company

Cincinnati Gas & Electric Company—acquired by CINergy Corp.

Cinderella Clothing Industries, Inc.—liquidated

Cinerama, Inc.—name changed to Forkel Enterprises, Inc.

CINergy—acquired by PSI Resources

Circa Pharmaceuticals, Inc.—acquired by Watson Pharmaceuticals, Inc.

Circle A.W. Products, Company—acquired by Signa-Aldrich Corp.

Circle F Industries, Inc.—acquired by General Telephone & Electronics Corp.

Citadel Life Insurance Co.—acquired by Barclays America

Citadel Life Insurance Co.—acquired by & merged into American Health & Life Insurance Co. of America

The Citation Companies—acquired by Dayton-Walther Corp. & name changed to Citation-Walther Corp.

Cities Service Co.—acquired by Occidental Petroleum Corp.

Citified Financial Corp.—surviving corporation after takeover by RTC is City Savings Bank, F.S.B.

City Meats & Provisions Co.—acquired by Clayton, Dubilier & Rice, Inc.

Citizens & Southern Bank—holding co. formed, Citizens First Bancorp, Inc.

The Citizens & Southern Corporation—merged with Sovran Financial to form holding co., C&S/Sovran Corporation

Citizens & Southern Realty Investors—name changed to Southmark Properties

Citizens Bancorp—acquired & absorbed by Crestar Financial Corporation

Citizens Fidelity Corp.—acquired by & merged with PNC Corp.

Citizens Financial Corporation—out of business

Citizens First Bank of New Jersey—name changed to Citizens First Natl. Bank of New Jersey

Citizens First Natl. Bank of New Jersey—holding co. formed, Citizens First Bancorp, Inc

Citizen's National Bancshares Inc.—out of business

Citizens Savings Financial Corporation—now CSF Holdings Inc.

Citizens Trust Bank—acquired by & merged into Bank of Virginia Company

City Federal Savings & Loan Association—holding co. formed, CityFed Financial Corp.

City Investing Co.—liquidated

Clabir Corporation—now CLR Corporation, sub. of Empire of California

Claremont Capital Corporation—name changed to Bergstrom Capital Corporation

A.D. Clark Inc.—acquired by & absorbed into American Drug Stores Inc.

Clark Consolidated Industries, Inc.—acquired by Wilcox & Gibbs Inc.

Clark Equipment Company—acquired by Ingersoll-Rand Company

J.L. Clark Manufacturing Co.—name changed to Clarcor

Clark Refining & Marketing Inc.—acquired by Horsham Corporation

Clarkson Industries, Inc.—acquired by Thomas Tilling, Inc.

Clarkson Industries, Inc.—now wholly-owned sub. of BTR plc

Clausing Corp.—acquired by Rexnord, Inc.

Clay-Park Labs, Inc.—acquired by Agis Industries Ltd.

Clearing International Inc.—acquired by Verson International Inc.

Clemco Industries—name changed to Aerolyte Systems

Cleveland Machine Controls—acquired by International Motion Control, Inc. & name changed to Cleveland Motion Controls

Clevepak Corp.—acquired by Great American Management & Investment, Inc.

Clevetrust Corp.—name changed to Ameritrust Corp.

Clevite Industries, Inc.—acquired by The Pullman Co.

Clopay Corp.—acquired by Instrument Systems Corp.

Clow Corp.—acquired by McWane, Inc.

Cluette, Peabody & Co., Inc.—acquired by West Point-

Pepperell, Inc.

Coast America Corporation — acquired by American Hoist & Derrick Co., now Amdura Corporation

Coast Holdings Corp. — name changed to Coast America Corporation

Coastal Dairy Products, Inc. — name changed to Mell Buttercup Ice Co.

Coastal States Corp. — acquired by Kaufman & Broad, Inc.

Coastal States Gas Corp. — name changed to The Coastal Corp.

Coated Sales, Inc. — acquired by & absorbed into Brookwood Co.

Cobbledick-Kibbe Inc. — out of business

Cobe Laboratories, Inc. — now wholly-owned sub. of Gambro A.B.

Coble Dairy Products Co-op — out of business

Coca Mines Inc. — acquired by Hecla Mining Corporation

George W. Cochran Co., Inc. — acquired & absorbed by Century Distributors

Cochrane Furniture Co., Inc. — acquired by Chromcraft Revington, Inc.

Coda Energy, Inc. — acquired by Enron Corp.

Code-A-Phone Corp. — out of business

Codex Corp. — acquired by Motorola, Inc.

Coggin O'Steen Investment Corp. — name changed to Coggin Automotive Group

Cogifer Inc. — acquired by ABC Rail Products Corp. & name changed to ABC Rail Cogifer Industries

Cohen Hatfield Industries, Inc. — merged with MacAndrews & Forbes Group, Inc.

Cointreau S.A. — merged with E. Remy Martin et Compagnie SA to form Remy Cointreau

Coldwell, Banker & Co. — acquired by Sears Roebuck & Co.

Coldwell Banker Corp. — acquired by Bechtel Group Inc.

Coldwell Banker/Schlott Realtors — acquired by HFS, Incorporated

Cole National Corporation — holding company formed, CNC Holding Corporation

Coleco Industries, Inc. — operating assets sold to Hasbro, Inc.

Coleman Cable Systems, Inc. — acquired by Kuhlman Corporation

The Coleman Company, Inc. — acquired by MacAndrews & Forbes Group, Inc.

Coleman Dairy Inc. — acquired by Associated Milk Producers, Inc.

Coleman Toyota — name changed to Coleman Oldsmobile, Inc.

College/University Corp. — acquired by Baldwin-United Corp.

Collegiate Concepts Inc. — out of business

Collins & Aikman Corp. — acquired by Wickes Cos., Inc.

Collins Chevrolet, Geo — name changed to Broadway Chevrolet

Collins Foods International, Inc. — now Sizzler International, Inc.

Collum Companies — out of business

Colonial Bancorp, Inc. — acquired by Bank of Boston Corporation

Colonial Gas Energy Systems — acquired by Bank of Boston Corporation

Colonial Life & Accident Insurance Co. — holding co. formed, Colonial Companies, Inc.

Colonial Penn Group, Inc. — acquired by FPL Goup, Inc.

Colonial Petroleum Co. — acquired by Cleveland Capital Holdings & name changed to Petroleum World

Colonial Stores, Inc. — acquired by Grand Union Co.

Color Tile, Inc. — acquired by General Felt Industries

Color Your World, Corp. — name changed to St. Clair Paint and Wallpaper Corporation

Colotone Riverside Inc. — name changed to Charter Press Inc.

Colt Holdings, Inc. — now Coltec Industries, Inc.

Columbia Chase Corp. — name changed to Chase Corp.

Columbia First Bank, FSB — acquired & absorbed by First Union Corporation

Columbia General Corporation — out of business

Columbia Pictures Industries, Inc. — acquired by The Coca-Cola Co.

Columbia Prescolite Moldcast, Inc. — name changed to Prescolite Moldcast Lighting Company

Columbia Technical Corp. — name changed to Columbia Chase Corp.

Columbus & Southern Ohio Electric Co. — acquired by American Electric Power Co., Inc.

The Colwell Company — acquired by Baldwin-United Corp.

Combined Communications Corp. — acquired by Gannett Co, Inc.

Combined Insurance Co. of America — name changed to Combined International, Inc.

Combined International Corp. — name changed to Aon Corporation

Combustion Engineering, Inc. — acquired by ABB Asea Brown-Boveri Inc.

Combustion Equipment Associates, Inc. — name changed to Carter Day Industries

Comdata Holdings Corporation — acquired by Ceridian Corporation & name changed to Comdata Network, Inc.

Comgen Technology, Inc. — acquired by Fox Technology, Inc.

Comlinear Corporation — acquired by National Semiconductor Corp.

Commerce Union Corp. — now Sovran Financial Corp./ Central South

Commercial Alliance Corporation — acquired by First Interstate Bancorp

Commercial Bancorp — acquired by & name changed to

West Coast Bancorp

Commercial Credit Corporation—merged with Primerica Corporation

Commercial Shearing, Inc.—name changed to Commercial Intertech Corporation

Commodore Business Machines, Inc.—name changed to Commodore International, Inc.

Commodore International, Inc.—out of business

Commodore International Limited—out of business

Commonwealth Natural Resources, Inc.—acquired by & merged into Columbia Gas Systems, Inc.

Commonwealth Telephone Enterprises, Inc.—name changed to C-TEX Corporation

Communications & Cable Inc.—now IMNET

Communications Cable, Inc.—acquired by Kuhlman Corporation

Communications Corporation of America—acquired by Contel Corporation & d/b/a Contel Customer Support, Inc.

Communications Industries, Inc.—acquired by Pacific Telesis Group

Communications International—liquidated

Community Health Systems, Inc.—acquired by Forstman Little & Co.

Community Psychiatric Centers—name changed to Traditional Hospitals

Community Public Service Co.—name changed to Texas-New Mexico Power Co.

Community Shares, Ltd.—out of business

Comp-U-Card International—name changed to CUC International, Inc.

Compac Corp.—acquired by Masco Corp.

Complex Industry Corporation—out of business

Compo Industries, Inc.—acquired by Montedison SpA & name changed to Ausimont Compo, N.V.

Component Technology Corp.—liquidated

Compuadd Corporation—acquired by Dimeling, Schreiber & Park & name changed to Compuadd Computer Corporation

Compuserve, Inc.—acquired by H & R Block, Inc.

Compushop Incorporated—acquired by Bell Atlantic Corp.

Computer & Communication Technology Corporation—name changed to Sunward Technologies, Inc.

Computer Assembly Systems Ltd.—name changed to Compas Electronics, Inc.

Computer Consoles, Inc.—acquired by STC, PLC

Computer Dynamics, Inc.—out of business

Computer Entry Systems Corporation—acquired by Banctec, Inc.

Computer Investors Group, Inc.—acquired by TTS, Inc.

Computer Network Corp.—name changed to Comnet Corporation

Computer Resources, Inc.—name changed to OPUS Computer Products, Inc.

Computercraft, Inc.—acquired by Businessland, Inc.

Computervision Corp.—acquired by Prime Computer, Inc.

Comten, Inc.—acquired by NCR Corporation

Con-Way Eastern Express, Inc.—out of business

Concept, Inc.—acquired by Bristol-Myers Squibb

Condec Corporation—acquired by Farley Industries

Confer Tech International—acquired by Frontier Corporation

Conference Management Company—name changed to Ullo International, Inc.

Conna Corporation—acquired by Dairy Mart Convenience Stores, Inc.

Connecticut General Corp.—merged with INA Corp. to form Cigna Corporation

Connecticut General Mortgage & Realty Investments—acquired by Prudential Insurance Insurance Co. & name changed to 745 Property Investments

Connecticut Mutual Life Insurance Company—acquired & absorbed by Massachusetts Mutual Life Insurance Co.

Conner Peripherals, Inc.—acquired & absorbed by Seagate Technology, Inc.

Conoco Inc.—acquired by E.I. DuPont de Nemours & Co.

Conquest Carpet Mills—acquired by Beaulieu of America & name changed to Beaulieu United

Conquest Exploration Company—acquired by and merged into American Exploration Company

Conrock Co.—merged with California Portland Cement to form Calmat Co.

Conrac Corp.—acquired by Mark IV Industries, Inc

Consildated Co-op—acquired by & name changed to West Central Co-op

Consolidated Distilled Products of NWS, Inc.—name changed to NWS, Inc.

Consolidated Foods Corp.—name changed to Sara Lee Corporation

Consolidated Freightways—name changed to CNF Transportation

Consolidated Metro Inc.—acquired by Varlen Corporation

Consolidated Oil & Gas Inc.—out of business

Consumers Gas Co.—merged with Hiram Walker Gooderham & Worts Ltd. & name changed to Hiram-Walker Consumers Home Ltd.

Consumers Markets, Inc.—acquired by Fleming Companies

Consumers Power Co.—holding co. formed, CMS Energy Corp.

Consyne Corp.—acquired by American Hospital Supply Co.

Container Products Inc.—name changed to CPI Plastics Inc.

Context Industries, Inc.—acquired by Evans Industries, Inc.

Contel Corporation—acquired by and merged into GTE

Corporation

Continental Air Lines, Inc.—acquired by Texas Air Corp.

Continental Bancorp, Inc.—merged with Midlantic Banks Inc. to form Midlantic Corporation

Continental Bank—name changed to Continental Bancorp, Inc.

Continental Cablevision Inc.—acquired by U S West Inc.

Continental Can Co., Inc.—name changed to Continental Group, Inc.

Continental Can Company—acquired by Crown Cork & Seal Co., Inc.

Continental Care Centers, Inc.—merged with Beacon Hill America

Continental Conveyor & Equipment Co.—acquired by B.F. Goodrich Co.

The Continental Corporation—acquired by Loews Corporation

Continental Distributing Co. Inc.—out of business

Continental Hair Products, Inc.—name changed to Conair Corp.

Continental Illinois Corporation—name changed to Continental Bank Corporation

Continental Investment Corp.—acquired by Torchmark Corp. & name changed to Liberty Financial Service Company, Inc.

Continental Interests Inc.—name changed to Forum Restaurant Inc.

Continental Medical Systems, Inc.—acquired by Horizon/CMS Healthcare Corporation

Continental Oil Co.—name changed to Conoco, Inc.

Continental Ozark, Inc.—acquired by TransMontaigne Oil Company

Continental Steel Corporation—liquidated

Continental Telecom, Inc.—name changed to Contel Corporation

Continental Telephone Corp.—name changed to Continental Telecom, Inc.

Continental 2001 S.A. Utilidades Domesticas—name changed to BS Continental S.A. Utilidades Domesticas

The Continuum Co., Inc.—acquired by Computer Sciences Corporation

Control Laser Corporation—holding co. formed, Control Laser International Corporation

Controller Power (CPC)—acquired by Chempower, Inc.

Convergent Technologies—name changed to Convergent, Inc.

Converse Inc.—acquired by Interco, Inc.

Convest Energy Corporation—acquired by Edisto Resources Corp.

Convex Computer Corporation—acquired by Hewlett-Packard Company

Conwed Corp.—acquired by Cardiff Equities Corp., sub. of Leucadia National Corporation

Conwest Exploration Company Limited—acquired & absorbed by Alberta Energy Company, Ltd.

Conwood Corporation—name changed to Conwood Company, L.P.

B.C. Cook & Son Enterprises—out of business

Cook Data Services, Inc.—name changed to Blockbuster Entertainment Corporation

Cook Electric Co.—acquired by Bell Canada

Cook Industries, Inc.—name changed to Cook International, Inc.

Cook Paint & Varnish Company—name changed to Cook Composites & Polymers

Cook's United, Inc.—out of business

Cooper Lasersonics, Inc.—now Cooper Life Sciences, Inc.

Cooper Life Sciences, Inc.—now Cooper Companies, Inc.

Coopervision, Inc.—now The Cooper Companies, Inc.

Coordinated Apparel, Inc.—out of business

Copeland Corp.—acquired by Emerson Electric Co.

Copper Range Co.—acquired by Louisiana Land & Exploration Co.

Copperweld Steel Company—out of business

Coradian Corporation—now Mitel Integrated Systems, Inc., a sub of Mitel Corporation

Coral Petroleum Co.—name changed to Coral Petroleum, Inc.

Corber Corporation—acquired by & merged into Masco Corporation

Corco, Inc.—merged to form Liqui-Box Corp.

Corcoran Mfg. Co., Inc.—name changed to Foam Pro Manufacturing

Cordis Corporation—acquired by Johnson & Johnson

Corenco Corp.—acquired by Canadian Pacific Ltd.

Corhan, Inc.—name changed to Petals

The Cornelius Co.—name changed to IMI Cornelius Inc.

Cornerstone Natural Gas, Inc.—acquired by El Paso Energy Corporation

Corporate Software Incorporated—name changed to Stream International

Corroon & Black Corporation—now Willis Corroon Corporation, wholly-owned sub of Willis Corroon plc

Cosco, Inc.—acquired by Walter Kidde & Co.

Cosmair, Inc.—acquired by L'Oreal S.A.

Cosmetic & Fragrance Concepts Inc.—name changed to The Cosmetic Center Inc.

Courtlauds North America, Inc.—now Courtaulds Fibers, Inc.

Cousins Mortgage & Equity Investments—name changed to Newcorp, Inc.

Cowles Broadcasting, Inc.—acquired by Florida Progress Corp.

Cox Broadcasting Corp.—name changed to Cox Communications, Inc.

Craddock-Terry Shoe Corp.—now Craddock-Terry, Inc.

Craft House Corp.—acquired by RPM, Inc.

Cramer Company—acquired by Owasso Corporation

Cramer Electronics, Inc. — acquired by & merged into Arrow Electronics, Inc.

Cray Research, Inc. — acquired by Silicon Graphics, Inc.

Crazy Eddie, Inc. — out of business

Credithrift Financial, Inc. — acquired by American General Corp.

The Crest-Foam Corp. — acquired by Leggett & Platt, Inc.

Crestmont Oil & Gas Co. — acquired by Occidental Petroleum Corp.

Crime Control, Inc. — now ADT Security Systems, Inc., sub. of ADT, Inc.

Crisa Corporation — name changed to World Crisa Corporation

Criton Corp. — acquired by Dyson-Kissner-Moran Corp.

Crocker National Corp. — acquired by & merged into Wells Fargo & Company

The Croker Fels Company — acquired by Physicians Sales and Services Inc.

Crompton Company, Inc. — liquidated

Cronus Industries Inc. — now Business Records Corporation Holding Company

Cross & Trecker Corporation — acquired by Giddings & Lewis, Inc.

Cross Co. — merged with Kearney & Trecker Corp. & formed Cross & Trecker Corp.

Crouse-Hinds Co. — acquired by Cooper Industries, Inc.

Crownx Inc. — name changed to Extendicare, Inc.

Crown Zellerbach Corp. — acquired by James River Corp.

Crum & Forster — name changed to Crum & Forster Insurance Cos.

E.H. Crump Cos., Inc. — name changed to The Crump Cos., Inc.

The Crump Cos., Inc. — sub. of Fred S. James & Co. Inc., sub. of Sedgwick Group, Inc.

Crutcher Resources Corporation — liquidated

Cucina Classica Italiana, Inc. — acquired by Saratoga Brands, Inc.

Cue Enterprises, Inc. — holding co. formed, Cue Industries, Inc.

Cue Industries, Inc. — acquired by Guardian Industries

Culligan International Co. — acquired by Beatrice Foods Co.

Cullinane Corp. — name changed to Cullinane Database Systems, Inc.

Cullinet Software, Inc. — now Computer Associates Cullinet, sub. of Computer Asssociates, Inc.

Culver Textile Corporation — acquired by Noel Group, Inc.

Cumberland-Swan Inc. — acquired by L. Perrigo Company & name changed to Perrigo of Tennessee

Cunningham Drug Stores, Inc. — name changed to Quael Corp.

Curragh Inc. — out of business

Curtis Mathes Corp. — name changed to The Mathes Co.

Curtis Noll Corp. — acquired by Congoleum Corp.

Custom Alloy Corp. — name changed to Custom Energy Services, Inc.

Custom Energy Services, Inc. — name changed to Customedix, Inc.

H.H. Cutler Company — acquired by V.F. Corporation

Cutler-Hammer, Inc. — acquired by Eaton Corp.

Cutlery Corp. of America — now Cutlery World of America, Inc., sub. of James F. Parker Co., Inc.

Cutter Laboratories, Inc. — acquired by Miles Laboratories Inc. & name changed to Cutter Group

Cutting International Limited — out of business

Cyberex, Inc. — acquired by Joslyn Corporation

Cycare Systems, Inc. — acquired by HBO & Company & name changed to HBO & Company/Cycare Business Group

Cycles Peugot — name changed to Cycles Europe

Cyclops Corporation — name changed to Cyclops Industries, Inc.

Cyclops Industries, Inc. — acquired by and merged into ARMCO Inc.

Cypress Mines Corp. — acquired by Standard Oil Co. (Indiana)

Cyprus Corporation — name changed to Astrotech International Corporation

D

D & K Optical Corporation — out of business

D&L Venture Corp. — name changed to The Weathervane Retail Corp.

D.A.B. Industries, Inc. — acquired by J.P. Industries, Inc.

DAF Trucks N.V. — acquired by Paccar Inc.

DCA Food Industries, Inc. — acquired by Allied U.S.

DCNY Corporation — holding co. dissolved, now Discount Corporation of New York

DHJ Industries, Inc. — acquired by Dominion Textile, Ltd.

DM International, Inc. — acquired by Davy McKee Corp. & name changed to Dresser Division

DMR Group — acquired by Amdahl Corporation

DNA Plant Technology Corp. — name changed to DNAP Holding Corp.

Dacobas, Inc. — now Knurr USA, Inc.

Dagens Naeringsliv — out of business

Dahl Invest International A/S — acquired by Forvaltnings AB Ratos & name changed to Dahl International AB

Dahlstrom Manufacturing Company, Inc. — out of business

Daisy Systems Corporation — now Daisy/Cadnetix Inc.

Daka, Inc. — holding co. formed, Daka International, Inc.

Dakin, Inc. — acquired by & absorbed into Applause Enterprises Inc.

Dallas Corp. — name changed to Overhead Door Corp.

Damon Creations, Inc. — now The Apparel Group, Ltd.

Danbury Printing & Lithograph, Inc. — acquired by Banta Corporation

Danfoss Fluid Power Inc.—acquired by Danfoss A/S

Danley Machine Corp.—acquired by Ogden Corp.

Danners, Inc.—acquired by Maxway Corp.

Dart & Kraft, Inc.—separated into two companies, Kraft, Inc. and Premark International

Data Architects, Inc.—acquired by Logica plc

Data Design Laboratories, Inc.—name changed to DDL Electronics, Inc.

Data Documents, Inc.—acquired by Dictaphone Corp.

Data 100 Corp.—acquired by Bell Canada Ltd.

Data Switch Corporation—acquired by General Signal Corporation & name changed to General Signal Networks

Data Terminal Systems, Inc.—acquired by National Semiconductor Co. & name changed to Datachecker/DTS Corp.

Data Translation Inc.—name changed to Media 100

Datamedia Corporation—acquired by Axent Technologies & name changed to Axent Technologies

Dataproducts Corporation—acquired by HND Corporation, a joint venture of Hitachi Koki Co. and Nissei Sangyo Co., Ltd.

Davidson & Associates, Inc.—acquired by CUC International, Inc.

Charles Davis Limited—name changed to Harris Scarfe Holdings Limited

Davis Water & Waste Industries —acquired by U.S. Filter & name changed to U.S. Filter/Davis Water & Waste Industries

Davy McKee Corporation—acquired by Trafalgar House Group Services Ltd.

William Dawson Holdings Plc—name changed to Dawson Holdings Plc

Cecil B. Day Companies, Inc.—name changed to Days Inn of America, Inc.

Day International—now Dayton Polymer Group of M.A. Hanna Co.

Day Mines—acquired & absorbed by Hecla Mining Co.

Dayco Corporation—name changed to Dayco Products, Inc.

Daylin, Inc.—acquired by W. R. Grace & Co.

Days Inns of America—acquired by Reliance Capital

Dayton Malleable Inc.—name changed to AmCast Industrial Corp.

Dayton Power & Light Co.—holding co. formed, DPL, Inc.

Dayton Superior Corp.—now Danis Industries Corporation

Dayton Sure Grip & Shore Co.—name changed to Dayton Superior Corp.

Dayton-Walther Corp.—acquired by Varity Corp.

Dazey Corporation—out of business

De Tomaso Industries, Inc.—name changed to Trident Rowand Group, Inc.

Deans Photo Service, Inc.—name changed to Fuji Trucolor Foto

Debron Corp.—acquired by Bristol Steel & Iron Works, Inc.

De Bussy B.V., Advertising & Jobmarketing—name changed to De Bussy Harms N.V.

Decision Industries Corporation—now Decision Data, Inc.

DeKalb Ag Research, Inc.—name changed to DeKalb Corporation, then split into three separate companies: DeKalb Genetics, DeKalb Energy Company & Pride Petroleum Services, Inc.

DeKalb Energy Company—acquired by Apache Corporation & name changed to Apache Canada Ltd.

Del Monte Corp.—acquired by R.J. Reynolds Industries, Inc.

Del Monte Properties Co.—name changed to Pebble Beach Corp.

Del Webb's Coventry—acquired by Del Webb Corp.

Delcorp—acquired by Harbour Group Ltd. & name changed to Sterling Products Inc.

Della Construction Co. Inc.—out of business

Dellwood Foods, Inc.—now sub. of Investcorp Intl.

The Delmark Co. Inc.—acquired by Sandoz United States, Inc.

Delta Bravo, Inc.—name changed to Magnetics Data Inc.

Delta Consolidated Industries—acquired by Danaher Corporation

Delta Education—acquired by Torstar Corporation

Delta Sugar Corporation—out of business

Delta Surprenant Wire & Cable, Inc.—name changed to Surprenant Cable Corp.

Deltown Foods, Inc.—name changed to Dellwood Foods, Inc.

Deluxe Check Printers, Inc.—now Deluxe Corporation

The DeMars Corp.—name changed to Geupel DeMars, Inc.

Demeter, Inc—acquired by Archer Daniels Midland Company (ADM)

Demoulas Super Markets—name changed to Demoulas Market Basket

Dempster, Inc.—acquired by Toccoa Metal Technology & name changed to Dempster Equipment

Den-Tal-Ez, Inc.—acquired by Syntex Corp.

Dennison Manufacturing Company—merged with Avery International Corporation to form Avery Dennison Corporation

Denny's Inc.—acquired by TW Services, Inc.

Depositors Corp.—name changed to Key Bancshares of Maines, Inc.

Desco Shoe Corp.—name changed to Revelations Shoe Company

Deseret Pharmaceutical Co., Inc.—acquired by Warner-Lambert Co.

Design 1 Interiors—name changed to Sue Firestone & Assoc.

Designer Jewel Industries, Inc.—name changed to De-

signer Industries, Inc.

Destiny Industry, Inc.—acquired by Oakwood Homes Corporation

Detecto Scales, Inc.—div. of United Syndicate, Inc.

Detrex Chemical Industries, Inc.—name changed to Detrex Corporation

Detroitbank Corp.—name changed to Comerica Inc.

Deutsche Spezialgas AG—acquired by Carl-Zeiss-Stiftung

Development Corporation of America—acquired by Lennar Corporation

Devoe Paint Corporation—acquired by Imperial Chemical Industries PLC & name changed to Devoe & Reynolds

Deweese Inc.—name changed to Beach Patrol Inc.

Dexter Shoe Company—acquired by Berkshire Hathaway Inc.

Diagnostek, Inc.—acquired by Value Health Inc. & name changed to Value Behavioral Health

Dial Corp.—acquired by Northwest Bancorporation

Dial Page, Inc.—acquired & absorbed by Nextel

Diamond Electronics, Inc.—acquired by Ultrak Inc.

Diamond M. Co.—acquired by Kaneb Services, Inc.

Diamond Shamrock Corp.—name changed to Maxus Energy Corporation

Diamondhead Corp.—name changed to Purcell Co., Inc.

Dibrell Brothers, Incorporated—name changed to DIMON

Diceon Electronics, Inc.—name changed to Elexsys International, Inc.

Dickenson Mines Ltd.—name changed to Goldcorp Inc.

Dicomed Corp.—acquired by Crosfield Dicomed, Inc., wholly-owned sub. of DeLaRue PLC, Ltd.

Dictaphone Corp.—acquired by Pitney-Bowes, Inc.

Diebold Venture Capital Corp.—name changed to Claremont Capital Corp.

Diet Center, Inc.—acquired by American Health Cos., Inc.

Digicon, Inc.—merged with Veritas Energy Services Inc. to form Veritas DGC Inc.

Digital Electronic Automation—acquired by & absorbed into Brown & Sharpe Manufacturing Company

Digital Research Inc.—acquired by Novell, Inc. of Safeguard Scientifics, Inc.

Digital Switch Corp.—name changed to DCS Communications Corp.

Dillingham Corp.—liquidated June 16, 1987; surviving corp. Dillingham Construction Corporation

Dillon Companies, Inc.—acquired by The Kroger Co.

DIMAC Corporation—acquired by Heritage Media Corporation

Glen Dimplex Limited—name changed to The Glen Dimplex Group

Dinner Bell Foods, Inc.—now division of John Morrell & Co.

Dinwiddie Construction Co—acquired by Fletcher Challenge Limited

Discount Fabrics, Inc.—acquired by & merged into Fabri-

Centers of America, Inc.

Walt Disney Productions—name changed to Walt Disney Company

The Disston Co.—acquired by Greenfield Industries Inc.

Disston, Inc.—acquired by Sandvik, Inc.

Distribuco, Inc.—liquidated Oct. 27, 1987

The Diversey Corp.—acquired by The Molson Cos., Ltd.

Diversified Energies, Inc.—acquired by and merged into Arkla, Inc.

Diversified Mortgage Investors, Inc.—name changed to DMG, Inc.

Diversifoods Incorporated—acquired by The Pillsbury Company

Dixico Inc.—acquired by Bell Fibre Products Corp.

Dixilyn Corp.—acquired by Panhandle Eastern Pipe Line Co.

The Joseph Dixon Crucible Co.—name changed to Dixon Ticonderoga Co.

Dobson Park Industries Plc—acquired by Harnischfeger Industries, Inc.

Docks de France S.A.—acquired by Auchan S.A.

Documentation, Inc.—acquired by Storage Technology Corp.

Docutel Corp.—merged with Olivetti Corp. & name changed to Docutel/Olivetti Corp.

Doehler-Jarvis, Inc.—acquired by Harvard Industries, Inc.

Domain Industries, Inc.—acquired by & merged into Nordson Corp.

Domecq Importers Inc.—acquired by Allied Domecq

Dometic Inc.—merged with White Consolidated Industries, sub. of Electrolux AB

Dominick's Finer Foods—acquired by The Yucaipa Companies

Dominion Bridge Co., Ltd.—acquired by Canadian Pacific Ltd.

Donovan Cos., Inc.—acquired by Midwest Energy Co.

Dorchester Gas Corp.—acquired by & merged into Damson Oil Corp.

Donaldson, Lufkin & Jenrette—acquired by Equitable Life Assurance Society of the United States

Donrey Media Group—acquired by Stephens, Inc.

Doremus & Co.—acquired by BBDO International, Inc.

Dorman-Roth Foods Inc.—acquired by ConAgra, Inc.

Dorr-Oliver Incorporated—acquired by Mannesman A.G.

The Dorsey Corp.—name changed to Constar International, Inc.

Doubleday & Co., Inc.—acquired by Bertelsmann Publishing Group, Inc.

Douglas & Lomason Company—acquired by Magna International Inc. & name changed to Magna Lomason Corp.

Downe Communications, Inc.—acquired by The Charter Co. & name changed to ChartCom, Inc.

Doyle Dane Bernback—merged with Needham Harper Worldwide and BBDO International to form Omnicom Group, Inc.

Dr Pepper Co.—acquired by Hicks & Haas

Dranetz Technologies Inc.—now sub. of Hawken Siddeley Group, Public Limited Company

Draper Corporation—name changed to Draper Texmaco, Inc.

Dreisbach & Sons Cadillac Company—acquired & absorbed by Don Massey Cadillac Inc.

Drexel Bond Debenture Trading Fund—now 1938 Bond Debenture Trading Fund

Drexel Utility Shares, Inc.—name changed to Energy & Utility Shares

Drug Fair, Inc.—acquired by Gray Drug Stores, Inc.

Drum Financial—acquired by St. Regis Paper Co.

Druther's Systems, Inc.—acquired by International Dairy Queen, Inc.

The Duchossois/Thrall Group—name changed to Duchossois Industries

Duckwell-Alco Stores, Inc.—acquired by The E.F. Hutton Group, Inc.

Duckwell Stores, Inc.—name changed to Duckwell-Alco Stores Inc.

Dumez S.A.—name changed to Dumez-GTM

Dundee Mills, Inc.—absorbed into Bath Fashions, a subsidiary of Springs Industries, Inc.

Dunkin' Donuts Incorporated—acquired by Allied-Lyons plc

Dunlop Tire & Rubber Corp.—name changed to Dunlop Tire Corp.

Duplex Products, Inc.—acquired & absorbed by The Reynolds & Reynolds Company

G.B. DuPont Co., Inc.—name changed to Kamax-G.B. DuPont L.P.

Duquesne Light Company—holding co. formed, DQE Inc.

Duracell International Inc.—acquired by The Gillette Company

Durametallic Corp.—acquired by The Duriron Company, Inc.

Durex Industries Inc.—out of business

Durham Corporation—acquired by Capital Holding Corp.

Durham Life Insurance Co.—name changed to Durham Corp.

Duro-Test Corporation—acquired by Duro-Lite International

Durr Beteiligungs-AG—name changed to Durr AG

Dutch Boy, Inc.—name changed to Artra Group, Inc.

Dyko Petroleum Corp.—acquired by Diversified Energies, Inc.

Dymo Industries, Inc.—merged with Esselte Pendaflex Corp.

Dynalectron Corporation—now DynCorp

Dynamic Controls Corp.—acquired & absorbed by United Technologies Corporation

Dynatrend Incorporated—acquired by EG&G, Inc.

Dyneer Corporation—holding co. formed, Westar Industries, Inc.

Dynell Electronics Corp.—acquired by United Technologies Corp. & merged into Norden Systems

Dyson-Kissner Corp.—name changed to The Dyson-Kissner-Moran Corp.

E

E for M Corp.—acquired by Marquette Electronics, Inc.

E Systems, Inc.—acquired by Raytheon, Inc.

E-II Holdings, Inc.—acquired by American Brands

EBP Health Plans, Inc.—acquired by First Data Corporation

ELT, Inc.—name changed to Dutch Boy, Inc.

ERC Corporation—acquired by Getty Oil Co.

ERC Industries, Inc.—name changed to Wood Group Pressure Control

ERC International Inc.—now Odgen-ERC Government Systems Company, a sub. of Ogden Corporation

EZ Communications, Inc.—out of business

Eagle Clothes Inc.—out of business

R.W. Eakin, Inc.—absorbed by Textile Chemical Co., Inc.

Earth Resources co.—acquired by Mapco, Inc.

Earth Technology Corp. USA—acquired by Tyco International Ltd.

The Earthraker Corp.—name changed to Barancorp

Easco Hand Tools, Inc.—acquired by Danaher Corporation

Easel Corporation—acquired by VMark Software, Inc.

Eason Oil Co.—acquired by International Telephone & Telegraph Corp.

Eastern Air Lines, Inc.—acquired by Texas Air Corp.

Eastern Flat Bed Systems—out of business

Eastern Milk—merged with Milk Marketing Inc.

Eastern Technologies Ltd.—name changed to Craig Systems Corp.

Eastex Energy Inc.—acquired by El Paso Natural Gas Co.

Eastmet Corporation—out of business

Eastport International, Inc.—-acquired by Oceaneering International, Inc. & name changed to Oceaneering Technologies

Eastway Delivery Service of Houston, Inc.—acquired by U.S. Delivery Systems & name changed to U.S. Delivery Systems Southwest, Inc.

Eaton & Howard Vance Sanders, Inc.—name changed to Eaton Vance Corp.

Eaton Equipment Corp.—merged into Grassland Equipment & Irrigation Corp.

Eazor Express, Inc.—name changed to Eazor Special Services

Eberhard Faber, Inc.—acquired by Faber-Castell

Eberline Instrument Co.—acquired by Thermo Electron

Corp.

Echevarria Angel Co., Inc.—out of business

Echlin Manufacturing Co.—name changed to Echlin, Inc.

Eck-Adams Corporation—now EAC Corporation, d/b/a Eck-Adams

Eckerd Corporation—acquired by JC Penney Company, Inc.

Eckerd Drugs, Inc.—acquired by Jack Eckerd Corp.

Eclipse Combustion Inc.—name changed to Eclipse Inc.

Economics laboratory, Inc.—name changed to Ecolab Inc.

E. Edelman & Co.—acquired by Parker-Hannifin Corp.

Edgar B. Furniture Co.—out of business

Edgewood Tool & Manufacturing Company—acquired by Tower Automotive & name changed to Tower Automotive Romulus

Edgington Oil Co.—acquired by Penn Central Co.

Educum Corp.—name changed to CareerCom Corp.

Egan Machinery Co.—acquired by Leesona Corp.

Ekco Housewares, Inc.—acquired by Centronics Data Computer Corporation

El Chico Corp.—unit of Gulf & Western Industries, Inc.

El Dorado Tire Co.—acquired by Sumitomo Corporation

The El Paso Co.—acquired by Burlington Northern, Inc.

Elastomeric Technologies, Inc.—acquired by Augat, Inc.

Elco Corp.—unit of Gulf & Western Industries, Inc.

Elco Industries, Inc.—acquired by Textron Inc.

Elcor Chemical Corp.—name changed to Elcor Corp.

Elders International Inc.—now Fosters Brewing Group Limited

Eldon Industries, Inc.—acquired by Rubbermaid Incorporated

Electric Hose & Rubber Co.—acquired by Dayco Corp

Electric Specialty & Supply Corp.—name changed to Branch Electric Supply Co., Inc.

Electro-Biology, Inc.—acquired by Biomet, Inc.

Electro-Nite Co.—acquired by Midland Ross Co.

Electro Wire Products, Inc.—acquired by Aluminum Company of America & name changed to Alcoa Fujikura

ElectroCom Automation L.P.—acquired by Daimler-Benz Aktiengesellschaft

Electrographic Corp.—acquired by Encyclopaedia Britannica, Inc.

Electron House Plc—acquired by CS Holding & name changed to Eurodis Electron Plc

Electronic Arrays, Inc.—name changed to NEC Electronics U.S.A., Inc.

Electronic Assistance Corp.—name changed to EAC Industries, Inc.

Electronic Associates, Inc.—name changed to EA Industries

Electronic Data Systems Corp.—acquired by General Motors Corp.

Electronic Engineering of California—name changed to EECO Inc.

Electronic Memories & Magnetics Corp.—name changed to The Titan Group

Electronic Research Assoc., Inc.—acquired by Refac Technology Development Corp.

Electronics Corp. of America—acquired by Allen-Bradley Co., sub. of Rockwell International Corp.

Electrosound Group, Inc.—out of business

Electrospace Systems, Inc.—acquired by The Chrysler Corp.

Electrovert—acquired by Cookson Group PLC

Elgin National Industries, Inc.—now sub. of The Jupiter Corporation

Eli's Chicago's Finest, Inc.—name changed to Eli's Cheesecake Company

Eljer Industries, Inc.—acquired by Zurn Industries, Inc.

Ellman's Inc.—acquired by & merged into Service Merchandise, Inc.

Elosua S.A.—out of business

Eltra Corp.—acquired by Allied Chemical Corp.

The Elwell-Parker Electric Co.—name changed to Elwell-Parker Limited

Emerald Corporation—company closed

Emery Air Freight Corporation—acquired by Consolidated Freightways, Inc.

Emery Industries, Inc.—acquired by National Distillers & Chemical Corp.

Emhart Corporation—acquired by The Black & Decker Corporation

Empire Airlines, Inc.—acquired by Piedmont Aviation, Inc.

Empire Gas Corporation—name changed to All Star Gas Corporation

Empire, Inc.—name changed to Empire Gas Corporation

Empire Petroleum, Inc.—out of business

Empire West Companies, Inc.—out of business

Employee Leasing of NY—out of business

Employers Casualty Company—liquidated

Employers Insurance of Wausau—holding co. formed, Wausau Insurance Companies

Endata, Inc.—wholly-owned sub. of First Financial Management Corporation

Energas Company—holding co. formed, Atmos Energy Corp.

Energy & Utility Shares, Inc.—name changed to Stratton Monthly Dividend Shares, Inc.

Energy Exchange Corp.—out of business

Energy Resources Corp.—name changed to Enertec Corp.

Energy Service Company, Inc. (ENSCO)—name changed to Ensco International Incorporated

Enertac Corporation—out of business

Enex Resources Corp.—sub. of BTU Operating Co.,

wholly-owned sub. of Pyro Energy Corporation

Engelhard Minerals & Chemicals Corp. — name changed to Philbro Corp.

The Enro Shirt Company Inc. — merged into The Apparel Group Inc.

Enso-Gutzeit Oy — name changed to Enso Oy

Ensource Inc. — out of business

Enstar Corp. — acquired by joint venture of Ultramar America Ltd. & Union Texas Petroleum of Alllied-Signal, Inc.

Enterra Corporation — merged with Weatherford to form Weatherford Enterra, Inc.

Entertainment Marketing Incorporated — name changed to KLH Computers, Inc.

Entex, Inc. — now div. of Arkla, Inc.

Environetics — out of business

Environmental Services of America, Inc. — acquired by ERD Waste Corp.

Environmental Treatment and Technologies Corp. — name changed to OHM Corporation

Envirotech Corp. — acquired by Baker International Corp.

Epsco Incorporated — acquired by Lucas Aerospace Inc.

Equipment Company of America — out of business

Equitable Gas Co., Inc. — name changed to Equitable Resources, Inc.

Equitable General Corp. — acquired by Gulf United Corp. & name changed to Equitable Life Insurance Corp.

Equitable Life Mortgage & Realty Investors — acquired by & merged into Equitable Life Assurance Society of the United States

Equity Enterprises, Inc. — company dissolved

Equity Funding Corp. of America — name changed to Orion Capital Corp.

Erie Press Systems — acquired by EFCO Inc.

Erie Technological Products, Inc. — name changed to Murata Erie North America, Inc.

N. Erlanger, Blumgart & Company, Inc. — name changed to Balsom, Hercules Ltd.

E.C. Ernst — now division of The Philadelphia Bourse, Inc.

Ernst & Winney — merged with Arthur Young to form Ernst & Young

Ernst Home Center, Inc. — liquidated

Ershigs, Inc. — acquired by CBI Industries, Inc.

Esab AB — acquired by Charter PLC

Esmark, Inc. — now The Vigoro Corporation

Esmark Inc. — name changed to Danskin Inc.

Esmor Correctional Services — name changed to Correctional Services Corporation

Esquire Inc. — acquired by Gulf & Western Industries Inc.

Essef Industries, Inc. — name changed to Essef Corp.

Essex Chemical Corporation — acquired by The Dow Chemical Company

Essex Industries — acquired by Assa Abloy AB

Esteben Foods, Inc. — name changed to Ardin International Kitchens, Inc.

Estech Branded Fertilizers, Inc. — acquired by Esmark,

Inc.

Estee Corporation — acquired by The Hain Food Group Inc.

Euroc AB — name changed to Scancem AB

Evaluation Research Corp. — holding co. formed, ERC International, Inc.

Evans-Aristocrat Industries, Inc. — acquired by Masco Corp.

Evans Brothers Company, Inc. — acquired by & name changed to AmeriServe

Evans Products Co. — out of business

EVCON Holdings — acquired by York International Corporation & name changed to EVCON Industries

Evered Bardon Plc — name changed to Bardon Group Plc

Everest & Jennings International Ltd. — acquired by Graham-Field Health Products, Inc.

Evergreen Healthcare Ltd. — acquired by Grancare

Ewing Brothers, Inc. — now Oneida Distribution Services

Ex-Cello Corporation — sub. of Textron, Inc.

Exchange Bancorp Inc. — now wholly-owned sub. of LaSalle National Corporation, sub. of ABN/LaSalle North America, Inc.

Exchange Bancorporation, Inc. — acquired by & merged into NCNB Corp.

Exchange International Corp. — now Exchange Bancorp, Inc.

Executive Industries, Inc. — out of business

Executone, Inc. — acquired by Continental Telephone Co.

Exel Limited — name changed to Exel Insurance Co. Ltd.

The Exolon Co. — name changed to Exolon-Esk Co.

Exploration Surveys, Inc. — name changed to ESI Industries, Inc.

F

F & C Bancshares, Inc. — acquired by First of America Bank & name changed to First of America Bank Florida

F&F Laboratories — name changed to F&F Foods

F & M Distributors Inc. — liquidated

FHP International Corporation — acquired by PacifiCare Health Systems

FL Industries Inc. — acquired by Thomas & Belts Corporation

FLS Holdings Inc. — name changed to AmeriSteel

FN America, Inc. — now Browning America, Inc.

FN Fabrique National Herstal S.A. — name changed to Herstal S.A.

FSC Corporation — name changed to Trilos Corporation

FSC Educational Group — acquired by Bulter Capital Group & name changed to Beckley-Cardy Group

FSF Industries, Inc. — name changed to Trafalgar, Inc.

Faber/Castell Corporation — merged into Newell Company

Fabrics National, Inc.—name changed to Three D Departments, Inc.

Facet Enterprises, Inc.—now wholly-owned sub. of Pennzoil Corporation

Fadal Engineering Company, Inc.—acquired by Giddings & Lewis, Inc.

Fair Lanes Inc.—acquired by & absorbed into AMF Bowling Inc.

Fairbanks Morse Pump Corporation—acquired by General Signal Corp.

Fairchild Camera and Instrument Corp.—acquired by Schlumberger Ltd.

Fairchild Industries, Inc.—sub. of Banner Industries, Inc., now The Fairchild Corporation

The Fairfield Lumber & Supply Company—out of business

Fairmont Foods Co.—acquired by American Financial Corp.

Falcon Seaboard Inc.—acquired by Diamond Shamrock Corp. & name changed to Falco Coal Co., Inc.

Falconbridge Nickel Mines, Ltd.—affil. of Superior Oil Co.

Fall Pete Ford Inc.—name changed to Harold Ziegler Ford-Exeter

Falls Financial Inc.—acquired by Fifth Third Bancorp & name changed to The Fifth Third Bank

Familian Corp.—now wholly-owned sub. of Wolseley PLC

FamTec International, Inc.—name changed to SpeedFam International, Inc.

Fanny Farmer Candy Shops, Inc.—acquired by Amoskeag Co.

Fansteel, Inc.—acquired by H.K. Porter Co., Inc.

Faraday, Inc.—acquired by Cerebus Pyrotronics Inc.

Fargo Clinic Ltd.—name changed to Merit Care Medical Group

Farinon Corp.—acquired by Harris Corp.

Farm & Home Savings Assoc.—acquired by Farm & Home Financial Corp.

Farmers Group, Inc.—now wholly-owned sub. of Batus, Inc.

Farmers Marine Copper Works—acquired by Four Winds Investment Corp.

Farrar, Strauss & Giroux, Inc.—acquired by Verlagsgruppe Gerog von Holtzbrinck GmbH

Fay's Incorporated—acquired by JC Penney Company, Inc.

Federal Paper Board Company, Inc.—acquired by International Paper Company

Federated Bank, S.S.B.—acquired by Firstar Corporation; name changed to Firstar Bank Milwaukee

Federated Capital Corp.—member banks merged into Mercantile Texas Corp.

Federated Dept. Stores, Inc.—acquired by Campeau Corp.

Federated Guaranty Corp.—name changed to Alfa Corp.

Felmont Oil Corp.—wholly-owned sub. of Homestake Mining Co.

The Felsway Corp.—acquired by Heck's, Inc.

Fermec Holdings—acquired by Tenneco Inc.

Ferranti International Plc—out of business

Ferrara Foods & Confections, Inc.—name changed to Colivita USA, Inc.

Ferruzzi Finanziaria SPA—name changed to Compart SpA

Feuer Leather Corporation—out of business

Fibreboard Corp.—acquired by Louisiana-Pacific Corp.

Fidata Corporation—acquired by & merged into Advanced Medical Technologies, Inc.

Fidelco Growth Investors—name changed to FGI Investors

Fidelcor, Inc.—acquired by First Fidelity Bancorporation

Fidelity American Bankshares, Inc.—name changed to Central Fidelity Banks, Inc.

Fidelity Corp.—name changed to Drum Financial Corp.

Fidelity Financial Corp. Fidelity Savings & Loan Assn.—acquired by Citicorp

Fidelity Union Life Insurance Co.—acquired by Allianz of America, Inc.

Field Enterprises—liquidated

Fields Plastics & Chemicals, Inc.—name changed to Cleveland Calendering & Coating Corp.

Filmways, Inc.—name changed to Orion Pictures Corp.

Filtrol Corp.—acquired by U.S. Filter Corp.

Financial Benefit Group, Inc.—acquired by Amvestors Financial Corporation

Financial Corporation of America—out of business

Financial Corporation of Santa Barbara—out of business

Financial Federation, Inc.—acquired by & merged into Great Western Financial Corp.

Financial General Bankshares, Inc.—name changed to First American Bankshares, Inc.

Findley Adhesives, Inc.—acquired by Elf Aquitane & name changed to Ato-Findley, Inc.

Fine Art Acquisitions Ltd.—name changed to Dyansen Corporation

Fine Homes International, L.P.—now Prudential Residential Services

Fingerhut Corp.—acquired by American Can Co.

Firefox Communications, Inc.—absorbed by FTP Software Inc.

Firemans Fund Corporation—now The Fund American Companies, Inc.

The Firestone Tire & Rubber Co.—sub. of Bridgestone Tire Company

Fireman's Fund Insurance Company—acquired by Allianz AG Holdings

First & Merchants Corp.—merged with Virginia National Bankshares, Inc. to form Sovran Financial Corporation

First Advantage Mortgage Corporation—acquired by

Long Island Bancorp & name changed to Entrust Home Financing

1st American Bancorp, Inc. — out of business

First American Bank and Trust — acquired by Barnett Banks

First Amtenn Corp. — name changed to First American Corp.

First Arkansas Bankstock Corp. — name changed to Worthern Banking Corporation

First Bancgroup Alabama, Inc. — name changed to First Gulf Bancorp

First Boston, Inc. — Sub of Credit Suisse, name changed to CS First Boston

First Charter Financial Corp. — acquired by & merged into Financial Corp. of America

First Chicago Corporation — merged with NBD Bancorp, Inc. to form First Chicago NBD Corporation

First Colonial Bankshares Corporation — acquired & absorbed by Firstar Corporation Illinois

First Colony Life Insurance Co. — acquired by Ethyl Corp.

First Colony Life Insurance Co. — acquired by General Electric Company

First Commercial Banks, Inc. — name changed to Key Banks, Inc.

First Farwest Corporation — company in liquidation

First Fidelity Bancorporation — acquired & absorbed by First Union Corporation

First Financial Management — acquired & absorbed by First Data Corporation

1st Franklin Corporation — merged with 1st Franklin Financial Corporation

First Gulf Bancorp — merged with AmSouth Bancorporation

First Illinois Corporation — merged with Banc One Corp.; name changed to Illinois Banc One Corporation

First International Bancshares, Inc. — name changed to Interfirst Corp.

First Interstate Bancorp — acquired by Wells Fargo & Company & name changed to Wells Fargo & Company

First Interstate Corporation of Alaska — taken over by FSLIC

First Interstate Corporation of Wisconsin — now Norwest Bank of Wisconsin

First Jersey Corp. — now National Westminster Bancorp N.J., sub. of National Westminster Bank PLC

First Lincoln Financial Corp. — acquired by American Continental Corp.

First Maryland Bancorp — now wholly-owned sub. of Allied Irish Banks plc

First National Bancorp — acquired by Regions Financial Corporation & name changed to Regions Bank

First National Bank of Commerce — name changed to First Commerce Corp.

First National Bankshares, Inc. — acquired by Merchants National Corporation

First National Boston Corp. — name changed to Bank of Boston Corp.

First National Cincinnati Corp. — now Star Banc Corp.

First National Holding Corp. — name changed to First Atlanta Corp.

First National State Bancorp — name changed to First Fidelity Bancorporation

First National Stores, Inc. — merged with Pick-n-Pay Supermarkets, Inc. & name changed to First National Supermarkets, Inc.

First National Supermarkets, Inc. — 80% acquired by Ahold U.S.A., Inc.

First Nationwide Financial Corp. — acquired by Ford Motor Company

First NH Banks Inc. — acquired by Bank of Ireland

First Northern Savings Bank, S.A. — name changed to First Northern Capitol Corp.

First Ohio Bancshares, Inc. — acquired by Fifth Third Bancorp

First Oklahoma Bancorporation — acquired by FN Bancorporation, sub. of Landmark Land Development Corp.

First Pennsylvania Corporation — acquired by CoreStates Financial Corp.

First Pennsylvania Mortgage Trust — name changed to Atlantic Metropolitan Corp.

First Realty Investment Corp. — name changed to Thor Corp.

First S & L Shares, Inc. — acquired by Golden West Financial Corp. & merged into World Savings & Loan Association

First Savings and Loan Association of Fort Stockton — name changed to Stockton Savings Assn.

First Texas Financial Corp. — acquired by Beneficial Corp.

First Union Bancorporation, Inc. — name changed to Centerre Bancorporation

First United Bancorporation, Inc. — acquired by Interfirst Corp.

First Variable Life Insurance Co. — acquired by Kredietbank N.V.

First Wachovia Corporation — name changed to Wachovia Corporation

First Wisconsin Corporation — now Firstar Corporation

First World Cheese Inc. — name changed to Alpine Lace Brands Inc.

FirstFed Michigan Corporation — merged with Charter One Financial, Inc.

Fischbach & Moore Inc. — name changed to Fischbach Corp.

Fischbach Corporation — acquired by American International Group, Inc.

Fish Engineering & Construction, Partners Ltd. — name changed to KTI Fish

Fisher Foods, Inc. — acquired by Riser Foods, Inc.

Fisher Scientific Co. — acquired by & merged into Allied

Health & Scientific Products Co.

Fishers Big Wheel Inc. — liquidated

Fisons Plc — acquired by Rhone-Poulenc S.A.

Fitchburg Gas and Electric Light Co. — acquired by Unitil Corporation

Flagg Industries, Inc. — acquired by Hillhaven, Inc. of National Medical Enterprises, Inc.

Flagstaff Corp. — name changed to FSF Industries, Inc.

Flambeau Products Corp. — name changed to Flambeau Corp.

Fleck Manufacturing Inc. — acquired by Noma Industries Limited

Fleet Aerospace Corporation — name changed to Magellan Aerospace Corporation

Fleet Financial Group, Inc. — merged with Norstar Bancorp Inc. to form Fleet/Norstar Financial Group, Inc.

Fleet/Norstar Financial Group, Inc. — name changed to Fleet Financial Group, Inc.

Flexonics Inc. — name changed to Senior Flexonics Inc.

S.M. Flickinger — acquired by Scrivner Inc.

FlightSafety International Inc. — acquired by Berkshire Hathaway Inc.

Floating Point Systems, Inc. — out of business

Flock Industries, Inc. — out of business

Florasynth Inc. — acquired by Bayer Group

Florida Capital Corp. — acquired by Alfa-Laval, Inc.

The Florida Companies — acquired by Fairfield Communities, Inc.

Florida East Coast Industries Inc. — now sub. of St. Joe Paper Company

Florida First Bancorp, Inc. — acquired by Regions Financial Corporation

Florida First Federal Savings Bank — name changed to Florida First Bancorp, Inc.

Florida Gas Co. — acquired by Continental Group, Inc. & name changed to Continental Resources Co.

Florida Mining & Materials Corp. — acquired by & merged into Moore McCormack Resources, Inc.

Florida Power & Light Co. — holding co. formed, FPL Group

Florida Power Corp. — name changed to Florida Progress Corp.

Florida Steel Corporation — holding co. formed, FLS Holdings Inc.

Flow General Inc. — became GRC International, Inc.

Flow Systems, Inc. — now Flow International Corp.

Flowmole Corporation — name changed to UTILX Corporation

The Flurocarbon Company — name changed to The Furon Company

Flying Diamond Oil Corp. — acquired by Bow Balley Industries Ltd. & name changed to Bow Valley Exploration (U.S.), Inc.

Foamex International Inc. — acquired by Trace International Holdings, Inc.

Folger Adam Company — name changed to Folger Adam Security Inc.

Food Fair, Inc. — name changed to Pantry Pride, Inc.

Food Giant, Inc. — acquired by Super Value Stores, Inc.

Food Town Stores, Inc. — name changed to Food Lion Inc.

Foodmaker, Inc. d/b/a Jack in the Box — acquired by Gibbon, Green van Ameringen

Foodways National, Inc. — acquired by H.J. Heinz & merged into Ore-Ida Foods Div.

Foote & Davies Inc. — name changed to American Signature

The Foothill Group, Inc. — acquired by Norwest Corporation

Foremost-McKesson Inc. — name changed to McKesson Corp.

Formica Corporation — holding co. formed, FM Holdings Inc.

Fortune Systems Corporation — out of business

Forum Group, Inc. — acquired by Marriott International, Inc.

Forum Re Group Inc. — name changed to The Group, Inc.

Forum Restaurants, Inc. — holding co. formed, Continental Interests, Inc.

Forum Restaurants — out of business

Forum Retirement Partners, L.P. — acquired by Marriott International, Inc.

Foseco Minisep Inc. — now Foseco Holding Inc.

Foster Medical Supply, Inc. — acquired by General Medical Corp.

Foto Interamerica de Peru — acquired by Eastman Kodak

Fotomat Corp. — acquired by Konischiroku Photo Industry Co., Ltd.

Four Phase Systems, Inc. — acquired by Motorola, Inc.

Four Seasons Sunrooms — name changed to Four Seasons Solar Products Corp.

Fourth Financial Corp. — acquired by Boatmen's Bancshares, Inc.

G. Fox — merged with & name changed to Filene's

Fox-Knapp, Inc. — acquired by David Peyser Sportswear, Inc.

Fox Photo, Inc. — wholly-owned sub. of Eastman Kodak Company

The Foxboro Company — acquired by Siebe plc

Franchise Enterprises Inc. — merged into Heartland Food Systems

Franklin Computer Corporation — name changed to Franklin Electronic Publishers, Inc.

Franklin Federal Savings Association — out of business

Franklin Life Insurance Co. — acquired by American Brands, Inc.

Franklin Mint Corp. — acquired by & merged into Warner Communications, Inc.

Franklin Realty & Mortgage Trust—name changed to Franklin Realty Group

Franklin Steel Company—out of business

Frank's Nursery Sales, Inc.—name changed to Frank's Nursery & Crafts, Inc.

Frank's Nursery & Crafts, Inc.—acquired by General Host Co.

Fraser Paper, Ltd.—acquired by Brascan Limited

Frederic Printing Company—acquired by Consolidated Graphics, Inc.

Fredirick & Herrud, Inc.—name changed to Thorn Apple Valley, Inc.

Freeman Shoes Company—out of business

Freeport Minerals Co.—merged with McMoran Oil & Gas Co. to form Freeport-McRan, Inc.

R.T. French Co.—acquired by Reckit & Colman

Fresnillo Co.—acquired by Rosairo Resources Corp.

Fretter, Inc.—liquidated

Freymiller Trucking Inc.—acquired by Ameritruck Distribution Corp.

Friendly Frost, Inc.—acquired by Swanton Corp.

Friendly Ice Cream Corp.—acquired by Hershey Foods Corp.

Friesz Manufacturing Company—acquired by Oshkosh Truck Corporation & name changed to Summit Performance Dist. Inc.

Frigitronics, Inc.—acquired by Revlon, Inc.

Bob Frink Chevrolet Geo Management—name changed to Performance Chevrolet & Geo

Frontier Oil Corporation—acquired by Wainoco Oil Corporation

Frozen Desserts Inc.—name changed to Downfast Frozen Desserts LLC

Fruehauf Corporation—now Fruehauf Trailers, a div. of Terex Trailers

Full Circle Media Corp.—name changed to Conference Management Company

The Fuller Brush Company—acquired by CPAC Inc.

Fuller Company—now sub. of F.L. Smidth & Co. A/S

Fuller-O'Brien Paints—acquired by Imperial Chemical Industries PLC

Furnas Electric Company—acquired by Siemens AG

Furr Cafeterias, Inc.—acquired by K Mart Corp.

G

GAC Corp.—name changed to Avatar Holdings, Inc.

GCA Corp.—now wholly-owned sub. of General Signal Corporation

GEO International Corporation—out of business

GI Export Corporation—name changed to Johnston Industries, Inc.

GIT Industries, Inc.—name changed to United States Banknote Corp.

GK Technologies, Inc.—acquired by Penn Central Corp.

GMR Properties—acquired by Grubb & Ellis Co.

GND Holdings Corp.—out of business

GPD Limited—acquired by Whirlpool Corporation & name changed to GPD/Embraco North America, Inc.

GR Foods, Inc.—name changed to Ground Round Restaurants

GS Technologies—merged with Georgetown Industries to form GS Industries

Gable Industries, Inc.—name changed to Hajoca Corp.

Gabriel Industries, Inc.—acquired by CBS, Inc. & merged into Toy Div.

Galactic Resources Ltd.—out of business

Galaxy Carpet Mills, Inc.—acquired by Peerless Carpet Corp.

Galaxy Cheese Co.—name changed to Galaxy Food Company

Galena Enterprises, Inc.—name changed to Foster & Gallagher Enterprises, Inc.

Gamble-Skogmo, Inc.—merged with Wickes Corp. & name changed to Wickes Companies

The Garber Company—acquired by Carustar Industries, Inc.

The Garcia Corp.—name changed to TGC, Inc.

Gardiner Metal Company—out of business

Gardner-Denver Co.—acquired by Cooper Industries & new companies formed

Garfinckel, Brooks Brothers, Miller & Rhoads, Inc.—acquired by Allied Stores Corp.

Garlock, Inc.—acquired by Colt Industries, Inc.

Garvey Elevators Inc.—out of business

The Gas Service Co.—acquired by Kansas Power & Light Co.

The Gates Corporation—acquired by Tomkins PLC

Gates Learjet Corp.—name changed to Learjet Corp.

Gateway Transportation Co.—acquired by Maislin Transport of Delaware

Gault, Inc.—name changed to Gault Distributors Inc.

Gaylords National Corp.—acquired by Zayre Corporation

Gaynor-Stafford Industries, Inc.—out of business

Gearhart Industries, Inc.—acquired by and absorbed into Halliburton Company

Gearhart-Owen Industries, Inc.—name changed to Gearhart Industries, Inc.

Geico Corporation—acquired by Berkshire Hathaway Inc.

Gelco Corp.—acquired by General Electric Capital Corp., sub. of General Electric Company

Gelman Sciences, Inc.—acquired by Pall Corporation

Gem Industries, Inc.—holding co. formed, Gem Industries Finance Corporation

Gemtec Corp.—out of business

General Aerospace Materials Corporation—company closed

General American Oil Co. of Texas—acquired by Phillips Petrolem Corp. & merged into Phillips Oil Co.

General Automotive Parts Corp. — acquired by Genuine Parts Co.

General Bancshares Corp. — merged with Boatmen's Bancshares, Inc.

General Cable Corp. — name changed to GK Technologies, Inc.

General Care Corp. — acquired by & merged into Hospital Corp. of America

General Ceramics, Inc. — acquired by Tokuyama Soda Co., Ltd.

General Cigar Co., Inc. — name changed to Culbro Corp.

General Computer Corporation — acquired by MedE America Inc. & name changed to MedE America Inc.-Ohio

General Defense Corp. — acquired by Clabir Corporation

General Educational Services Group — name changed to Deon Group, Inc.

General Energy Corp. — acquired by Kirby Exploration Co.

General Felt Industries, Inc. — sub. of Knoll International Holding Inc.

General Foods Corp. — acquired by Philip Morris Inc.

General Growth Properties — in liquidation

General Health Services, Inc. — acquired by Hospital Corp. of America

General Hobbies Corp. — liquidated

General Marine Industries, Inc. — name changed to Century Boat Company

General Medical Corp. — acquired by Whittaker Corp. & name changed to Whittaker General Medical

General Medical Corp. — acquired by McKesson Corporation

General Physics Corp. — 83% owned by National Patent Corporation

General Public Utilities Corporation — name changed to GPU, Inc.

General Re Corp. — name changed to General Reinsurance Corporation

General Refractories Company — acquired by Belmont Industries, Inc.

General Reinsurance Corp. — name changed to General Re Corp.

General Research Corp. — name changed to Flow General, Inc.

General Safety Corporation — acquired by Allied Signal & name changed to Allied Signal Safety Restraints, Inc.

General Ship Corporation — out of business

General Steel Industries, Inc. — acquired by Lukens, Inc. & name changed to Lukens General Industries, Inc.

General Telephone & Electronics Corp. — name changed to GTE Corp.

The General Tire & Rubber Co. — name changed to GenCorp

General Tire, Inc. — now sub. of Continental AG

Genetic Laboratories, Inc. — now Bio Plasty, Inc.

Genetic Systems Corp. — acquired by Bristol-Myers Co.

Genevar Enterprises — out of business

Genex Corporation — acquired by Enzon, Inc.

Genge, Inc. — name changed to Systems Planning Corp.

The Genie Company — acquired by Overhead Door Corporation

Genova, Inc. — name changed to Genova Products, Inc.

Genstar Corp. — acquired by Imasco Limited

Genstar Corp. — dissolved Dec. 1986

Gentex Optics, Inc. — acquired by Essilor International Compagnie Generale d'Optique

Gentry Associates Inc. — acquired by Peak Technologies Group, Inc. & name changed to Peak Technologies Group (S.E. Region)

Geodynamics Corp. — acquired by Logicon, Inc. & name changed to Logicon Geodynamic

Geon Industries, Inc. — name changed to GI Export Corp.

Georgie Boy Manufacturing — acquired by Coachman Industries, Inc.

Geosource, Inc. — acquired by Aetna Life & Csasualty

J. Gerber & Co. Inc. — acquired by Gerber International Inc.

The Gerber Scientific Instrument Co. — name changed to Gerber Scientific, Inc.

Geriatric & Medical Companies, Inc. — acquired by Genesis Health Ventures, Inc. & name changed to Genesis ElderCare

Gerrity Co. Enterprise, Inc. — acquired by Wickes Lumber Co. & name changed to Gerrity Lumber

Gestetner Holdings Plc — acquired by Ricoh Company, Ltd.

Getty Oil Co. — acquired by Texaco, Inc.

Gettys Corp. — acquired by Gould, Inc. & name changed to Gould, Inc. Motion Control Operations

Giant Cement Co. — holding co. formed, Giant Group Ltd.

Giant Industries, Inc. — acquired by Mobex Corporation

Giant Portland Cement Co. — name changed to Giant Portland & Masonry Cement Co.

Gibraltar Financial Corporation — merged into Security Pacific Corporation

C.R. Gibson Co. — acquired by Thomas Nelson, Inc.

Giant Portland & Masonry Cement Co. — holding co. formed, Giant Group Limited

The Gibson-Homans Co. — acquired by Foseco-Minsip, Inc.

Giddings & Lewis, Inc. — acquired by AMCA Intl. Corp.

Giffen Industries, Inc. — name changed to LDB Corp.

Gifford-Hill — acquired by Beazer PLC & name changed to Beazer West, Inc.

Gifford Instrument Laboratories, Inc. — acquired by Corning Glass Works

Gillett Group, Inc. — name changed to Gillett Holdings, Inc.

Gillett Holdings, Inc. — name changed to Vail Resorts, Inc.

Roger Gimbel Accessories, Inc.—name changed to RGA and East End Accessories

M.S. Ginn & Co.—acquired by The Hillman Corp.

Gino's, Inc.—acquired by Marriott Corp. & merged into Restaurant Operation

The Girard Co.—acquired by Mellon National Corp.

The Gitano Group, Inc—acquired by Farley Industries & name changed to Gitano Fashions Ltd.

Gladding Cordage Corp.—reorganized under Chapter 11 & renamed Gladding Braided Products, Inc.

Gladdings Corp.—acquired by Gladding Cordage Corp.

Glasrock Products, Inc.—name changed to Glasrock Medical Services Corp.

Glaxo Holdings P.L.C.—merged with The Wellcome Foundation Limited to form Glaxco Wellcome plc

Glaztile—acquired by The Siam Cement Company Limited

Glico Harmony Foods Corporation—name changed to Harmony Foods Corporation

Global Compression Services Inc.—acquired by General Electric Company

Global Homes, Inc.—out of business

Globe Glass & Mirror Co.—name changed to Vistar, Inc.

Globe Industries, Inc.—acquired by Rieter Holdings & name changed to Rieter Automotive Globe

Globe Life & Accident Insurance Co.—acquired by Liberty National Life Insurance Co.

Globe-Union, Inc.—acquired by Johnson Controls, Inc.

Gloria Jean's Coffee Bean Corp.—acquired by Brothers Gourmet Coffees, Inc.

Glory Mill Papers Ltd.—name changed to Selix F. Schoeller Ltd.

Glynwed Incorporated—now Glynwed Group Services, Inc.

Goal Systems International Inc.—acquired by Legent Corporation

Godfrey Co.—now sub. of Fleming Cos., Inc.

Goetze AG—acquired by T & N Plc

Gold Fields American Corporation—now wholly-owned sub. of Hanson Industries

Goldcorp Inc.—acquired by CSA Management Ltd.

Golden Grain Macaroni Co.—acquired by The Quaker Oats Co.

Golden Nugget, Inc.—name changed to Mirage Resorts, Inc.

Golden West Homes—acquired by Oakwood Homes Corporation

Golden West Mobile Homes, Inc.—name changed to Golden West Homes

Golden Valley Microwave Foods, Inc.—now wholly-owned sub. of ConAgra Corporation

Goldenbanks of Colorado, Inc.—acquired & absorbed by Norwest Corporation

Goldome National Corp.—dissolved

Golodetz Corporation—out of business

W.B. Goode Company, Inc.—acquired by Omega Environmental Inc. & name changed to International Specialty Products

J.E. Goold & Company—acquired by Bindley Western Industries, Inc.

Goolsby Foods, Inc.—out of business

Gordon Jewelry Corporation—acquired by Zale Corporation

Kenneth Gordon New Orleans, Ltd.—name changed to Kenneth Gordon/IAG, Inc.

Gorin Stores, Inc.—name changed to Almy Stores, Inc.

Gott Corp.—acquired by Rubbermaid Inc.

Gould Inc.—now sub. of Nippon Mining Company, Ltd.

Government Employees Insurance Co.—name changed to Geico Corp.

Graham Company—acquired by Danfoss A/S

Gram Industries, Inc.—name changed to Transact Intl. Co.

Grand Central Inc.—acquired by & merged into Fred Meyer, Inc.

Grandy's, Inc.—acquired by American Restaurant Group, Inc.

Granges Inc.—name changed to Vista Gold Corp.

Graniteville Co.—acquired & absorbed by Avondale Incorporated

Grant Industries, Inc.—acquired by Mobex Corporation & name changed to Grant Hardware Company

Grantree Corporation—acquired by & name changed to Globe Furniture Rentals

Graphic Arts Center—acquired by Mail-Well Inc.

Graphic Controls Corp.—acquired by The Times Mirror Co.

Graphic Scanning Corp.—acquired by Bellsouth Corporation

Graphisphere Holding Company—acquired & absorbed by World Color Press, Inc.

Gray Drug Stores, Inc.—acquired by Sherwin-Williams Co.

Gray-Pro, Inc.—name changed to Staffing Solutions

Grazer/Howard Productions, Inc.—acquired by Imagine Entertainment Inc.

Great American First Savings Bank—name changed to Great American SSB Bank

Great American Victory Markets—out of business

Great Dane Holdings, Inc.—acquired by Stamford Capital & name changed to C.R.A. Holdings Inc.

Great Lakes Carbon Corp.—acquired by Horsehead Industries

Great Lakes Dredge & Dock Co.—name changed to Great Lakes International, Inc.

Great Lakes International, Inc.—acquired by Itel Corp.

Great Lakes Terminal & Transport Corp.—name changed to GLS Corporation

Great Northern Nekoosa Corporation—acquired by Georgia-Pacific Corporation

Great Scott Supermarkets, Inc.—acquired by Allied

Supermarkets, Inc.

Great Southwest Industries Corp.—liquidated

Great Western United Corp.—name changed to Hunt International Resources Corp.

Greater Orlando Auto Auction—acquired by Cox Enterprises, Inc. & name changed to Manheim's Greater Orlando Auto Auction

Greatwest Hospitals, Inc.—name changed to Health-Care USA

Greeley Gas Co.—acquired by Atmos Energy Corporation

Green Construction of Indiana, Inc.—out of business

Green Giant Co.—acquired by Pillsbury Company

Green Isle Environmental Services, Inc.—name changed to Reuter Manufacturing Inc.

Green Tree Acceptance, Inc.—name changed to Green Tree Financial Corp.

GreenForest Lumber Corporation—acquired by MacMillan Bloedel Limited

Greenwood Resources, Ltd.—name changed to Greenwood Holdings, Inc.

Greiner Engineering, Inc.—acquired by URS Corporation

Greit Realty Trust—merged with Unicorp American Corp.

The Greyhound Corporation—now Greyhound Dial Corporation

Greyhound Dial Corporation—name changed to Dial Corporation

Greyhound Lines, Inc.—holding co. formed, G.L.I. Holdings Company

Greyvest Financial Services, Inc.—name changed to Greyvest Capitol, Inc.

Grolier Inc.—acquired by Hachette S.A.

Groman Corp.—acquired by & merged into Talley Industries, Inc.

Gross Telecasting, Inc.—liquidated

Groundwater Technology, Inc.—acquired by Fluor Corporation & name changed to Fluor Daniel/GTI, Inc.

Grow Group, Inc.—acquired by Imperial Chemical Industries PLC

Gruen Industries, Inc.—acquired by Jewelcor, Inc.

Gruntal Financial Corp.—acquired by The Home Group, Inc.

Guarantee Financial Corp.—now Guarantee Savings, a div. of Glendale Federal, a sub. of Glenfed, Inc.

Guaranteed Products, Inc.—out of business

Guaranty Commerce Corp.—acquired by Hibernia Corp.

Guaranty National Corporation—now wholly-owned sub. of Orion Capital Corporation

Guardian Mortgage Investors—name changed to The Florida Companies

Guardsman Chemicals, Inc.—name changed to Guardsman Products, Inc.

The Guber Peters Entertainment Company—now wholly-owned sub. of Sony Corporation of America

Gulf + Western Inc.—name changed to Paramount Communications, Inc.

Gulf Applied Technologies, Inc.—now Gulfmark International, Inc.

Gulf Broadcast Co.—liquidated

Gulf Life Holding Co.—name changed to Gulf United Corp.

Gulf Mortgage & Realty Investments—name changed to GMR Properties

Gulf Oil Corp.—name changed to Gulf Corporation

Gulf Resources & Chemical Corporation—name changed to Gulf USA Corporation

Gulf States Utilities Company—acquired by Entergy Corporation

Gulfstream Aerospace Corp.—acquired by Chrysler Corp.

Gulfstream Aerospace Corp.—acquired by Forstmann Little

Gulton Industries, Inc.—wholly-owned sub. of Mark IV Industries, Inc.

Gump's Inc.—acquired by Hanover Direct, Inc.

Gunite Corporation—acquired by Johnstown America Industries

Guy Schoenecker, Inc.—name changed to Schoeneckers Inc.

H

H & H Advertising—out of business

HAI, Inc.—name changed to Hawaiian Airlines, Inc.

HBT, Inc.—acquired by Dewberry & Davis & name changed to Dewberry Design Group

HDM—now Dentsu Young & Rubicam Partnership

HNG/Internorth, Inc.—name changed to Enron Corp.

H.P.H. Industries Ltd.—name changed to Packaging Resources, Incorporated

HUB Inc.—acquired by Wolseley Plc & name changed to Energy & Process Corp.

Haag Drug Co., Inc.—acquired by Peoples Drug Stores

Hackensack Water Co.—name changed to United Water Resources

Hackney & Sons, Inc.—acquired by Transportation Technologies, Inc.

Haddon Craftsmen, Inc.—acquired by RR Donnelley & Sons

Ernest W. Hahn, Inc.—acquired by Trizec Western, Inc.

Hain Pure Food Co., Inc.—acquired by Ogden Corp.

Haines Lundberg Waehter—name changed to HLW International LLP

Hal Richardson, Inc.—now Howe Richardson, Inc.

Halco Products Corp.—acquired by Tobin Packing Co., Inc.

Hale Bros. Associates—name changed to Hale Technology Corp.

W.F. Hall Printing Co.—acquired by Mobil Corp.

Hallcraft Homes, Inc.—name changed to Nu-West Development Corp. of Arizona

Hallmark Healthcare Corporation — acquired & absorbed by Community Health Systems

Hall's Motor Transit Co. — acquired by Tiger International, Inc.

Hamilton Beach, Inc. — now Hamilton/Proctor Silex, Inc. a sub of NACCO Industries

Hamilton International Corp. — merged into Household Finance Corp.

The Hammond Company — acquired by Westcorp

Hammond Corp. — div. of Marmon Group, Inc.

Hancock Peanut Company LP — acquired by Morven Partners, LP

Hanes Companies, Inc. — acquired by Leggett & Platt Inc.

Hanes Corp. — acquired by Consolidated Foods Co.

Hanjin Group — name changed to Hanjin Shipping Company Ltd.

The Hanna Mining Co. — name changed to M.A. Hanna Co.

The Hanover Insurance Company — holding co. formed, All America Financial

Hanover Petroleum Corp. — acquired by Total Petroleum (North America) Ltd.

Hanover Shoe, Inc. — name changed to C & J Clark, Inc.

Hanover Square Realty Investors — merged with Pearce, Mayer & Greer, Inc. to form Pearce, Urstadt, Mayer & Greer, Inc.

Harbour Industries, Inc. — acquired by Marmon Group, Inc.

Harco Technologies Corporation — name changed to Corppro Companies, Inc.

Harcourt Brace Jovanovich, Inc. — acquired by General Cinema Corporation

Hardee's Food Systems, Inc. — name changed to Hardee's Holdings, Inc., sub. of Imasco U.S.A.

Harken Oil & Gas, Incorporated — now Harken Energy Corporation

Harlan Electric Co. — acquired by The L.E. Myers Co. Group

Harley Corp. — acquired by Union Camp Corp.

Harleysville Group — name changed to The Harleysville Insurance Companies

Harman International Industries, Inc. — acquired by Beatrice Foods Co.

Harmeson Manufacturing Company, Inc. — name changed to The Kay Company, Inc.

Harnischfeger Corp. — name changed to Harnischfeger Industries

Harper & Row Publishers, Inc. — acquired by a joint venture of The News Corp., Ltd. & William Collins PLC; name changed to HarperCollins Publishers Inc.

Harrah's — acquired by Holiday Inns, Inc.

Harris & Paulson, Inc. — out of business

Harris Computer Systems Corporation — name changed to Cyberguard Corporation

Harris Graphics Corp. — acquired by AM International Inc.

Hart Schaffner & Marx — name changed to Hartmarx Corp.

Harte Hanks Newspapers, Inc. — name changed to Harte Hanks Communications, Inc.

The Harter Group — acquired by Jami, Inc.

Hartfield Zody's, Inc. — name changed to HRT Industries, Inc.

Hartford National Corp. — merged with Shawmut Corp. to form Shawmut National Corporation

Hartog Food International, Inc. — name changed to Hartog Rahil Foods Inc.

Harvest Foods — out of business

Harvey Construction Company, Inc. — out of business

Harvey Hotels Management Corporation — name changed to Bristol Hotels Management Corporation

Harvey Plant Ltd. — name changed to Lex Harvey Ltd.

Hasbro Bradley Inc. — name changed to Hasbro, Inc.

Hasbro Industries, Inc. — merged with Milton Bradley, Inc. to form Hasbro Bradley, Inc.

Hauserman, Inc. — now Clestra Hauserman, Inc. sub. of Clestra S.A.

Havatampa Corp. — name changed to The Eli Witt Co.

Havens & Emerson, Inc. — acquired by Montgomery Watson & name changed to Montgomery Watson

Hawaii Bancorporation — name changed to Bancorp Hawaii, Inc.

Hawkeye Bancorporation — acquired by Mercantile Bancorporation & name changed to Mercantile of Iowa

Hayes-Albion Corp. — acquired by & merged with Harvard Industries, Inc.

Hayward Mfg Co., Inc. — name changed to Hayward Industries, Inc.

Hazeltine Corp. — acquired by Emerson Electric Co.

Hazelton Laboratories Corp. — wholly-owned sub. of Corning Glass Works, Inc.

Head Sports, Inc. — name changed to Head USA, Inc.

The Heaf Group — out of business

Health Extension Service, Inc. — name changed to Professional Care, Inc.

Health Tecna Corp. — name changed to Criton Corp.

Healthdyne, Inc. — acquired by Matria Healthcare Corporation & name changed to Matria Healthdyne, Inc.

Healthtrust, Inc. — acquired by Columbia/HCA Healthcare Corporation

Healthwise of America — acquired by United Healthcare Corporation

Heck Enterprises, Inc. — name changed to Heck Industries

Heckler Mfg. & Investment Group Inc. — absorbed into Her Majesty Industries Corp.

Heico Inc. — acquired by Pettitance Corp.

G. Heileman Brewing Co., Inc. — sub. of Bond Corp. Holding Ltd.

G. Heilman Brewing Co. — acquired by Heilman Holdings

Heizer Corp. — liquidated

Heldor Industries, Inc. — out of business

Helene Curtis Industries, Inc. — acquired by Unilever Plc

Helian Health Group, Inc. — acquired by TheraTx, Incorporated

Walter E. Heller International Corp. — acquired by The Fuji Bank, Ltd.

Helly-Hensen A/S — acquired by Orkla A.S.

Help Management Corporation — name changed to Hawk Management Corporation

Helzberg's Diamond Shops — acquired by Berkshire Hathaway Inc.

Hemar Group — name changed to HEAF Group

Hemdale Enterprises — name changed to Redlaw Enterprises, Inc.

Hemisphere Fund, Inc. — now Manhattan Fund, Inc.

Hemodynamics, Inc. — name changed to The Thundergroup Industries, Inc.

Henderson Auctioneers — acquired by JAH Enterprises, Inc. & name changed to Mini Henderson Auctions

The Henley Group, Inc. — split into two companies; Henley Properties Inc. and Henley Group Inc.

Henredon Furniture Industries, Inc. — acquired by Masco Corp.

Henri's Food Products Co. Inc. — acquired by CPC International

Her Majesty Industries, Inc. — acquired by Gulf & Western Industries

Herbal Enterprises Inc. — name changed to Right Ideas Inc.

G.R. Herberger's, Inc. — acquired by Proffitt's, Inc.

Heritage Bancorporation — acquired by Midlantic Banks, Inc.

Heritage Financial Corporation — acquired by Crestar Bank

Heritage Wisconsin Corp. — acquired by Marshall & Isley Corp.

Herley Microwave Systems Inc. — now Herley Industries, Inc.

Herman's Sporting Goods, Inc. — out of business

Hershey Oil Corporation — now wholly-owned sub. of American Exploration Company

Hertie Waren und Kaufhaus GmbH — acquired by Karstadt Aktiengesellschaft

The Hertz Corporation — acquired by Ford Motor Co.

Hess's, Inc. — acquired by Crown American Corp.

Hesston Corporation — now AGCO, Inc.

Heublin, Inc. — acquired by R.J. Reynolds Industries, Inc.

Hewitt-Robins Corp. — acquired by W.S. Tyler

Hi-G, Inc. — name changed to Tridex Corporation

Hickinbotham Bros., Ltd. — acquired by Ferro Union Inc. & name changed to Ferro Union

Hicks & Hass Incorporated — now Hass & Partners Incorporated

The Higbee Co. — acquired by Dillard Dept. Stores, Inc.

Highland Capital Corp. — liquidated

The Hillhaven Corporation — acquired & absorbed by Vencor, Inc.

Hills Bros. Coffee, Inc. — acquired by Nestle Holdings, Inc.

Hobart Brothers Co. — acquired by Illinois Tool Works Inc.

Hobart Corp. — acquired by Dart & Kraft, Inc.

Hoerner Waldorf Corp. — acquired by Champion International Corp.

Hoffman Brothers Packing Co. — out of business

Hoffman Electronics Corp. — acquired by Gould, Inc. & name changed to Audio Pulse Div.

Hogan Systems, Inc. — acquired by The Continuum Co.

Hogg Group plc — acquired by Inchcape PLC & name changed to Bain Hogg Group plc

Hok Yhtyma Helsinki — out of business

Holec U.S.A., Inc. — name changed to BTU, Inc.

Holiday Corporation — name changed to Promus Companies Inc.

Holiday Inns Inc. — name changed to Holiday Corporation

Hollinger Mines Ltd. — name changed to Hollinger Argus Ltd.

Holly Farms Corporation — acquired by Tyson Foods, Inc.

Hollywood Alloy Casting Company — name changed to Consolidated Foundries

Home Fashions Inc. — acquired by Newell Company & name changed to Levelor Home Fashions

Home Federal Savings & Loan Association — acquired by Great American First Savings

Home Life Insurance Company — merged with Phoenix Life Insurance Company & name changed to Phoenix Home Life Insurance Company

Home Oil Co. Ltd. — acquired by Consumers Gas Co.

Home Shopping Network, Inc. — merged with Silver King Communications, Inc. to form HSN, Inc.

Homedco Group Inc. — merged into Apria Healthcare Group

Homefed Bank — out of business

Homemaker Shops, Inc. — acquired by The Linen Super Market Inc.

Honorbuilt Industries Inc. — acquired by Sommer Metalcraft Corporation & name changed to SMC Midwest

H.P. Hood, Inc. — acquired by Agway, Inc.

Hoof Products Company — acquired by Dynagear Inc.

Hook Drugs, Inc. — acquired by The Kroger Co.

Hoover Ball & Bearing Co. — name changed to Hoover Universal, Inc.

The Hoover Co. — acquired by Chicago Pacific Corp.

Hope Design Group — out of business

Hopkinson Holdings PLC — acquired & absorbed into Weir Group PLC

Hopson Building Materials—acquired by Wolseley Plc. & name changed to Carolina Builders Corporation

Horizon Industries—acquired by Mohawk Industries

Hornbeck Offshore Services, Inc. — acquired & merged into Tidewater

Horrigan American Inc.—acquired by ABN-AMRO Holding N.V.

Horsham Corporation — merged with Trizec Corporation Ltd. to form TrizecHahn Corporation

Hospital Affiliates International, Inc. — acquired by INA Corp.

Hospital Trust Corp. — name changed to RIHT Financial

Hospitality Motor Inns, Inc. — acquired by Helmsley Enterprises, Inc.

Host International, Inc. — acquired by Marriott Corp.

The House of Vision, Inc. — acquired by Frigitronics, Inc. & merged into Benson Optical Co.

Household Finance Corp. — holding co. formed, Household International, Inc.

Housing Industries of America, Inc. — name changed to HIA, Inc.

Houston Natural Gas Corp. — acquired by & merged into HNG/Internorth, Inc.

Houston Oil & Minerals Corp. — acquired by Tenneco, Inc.

Howaldtswerke-Deutsche Werft AG — acquired by Preussag AG

Howard Hughes Corporation — acquired by The Rouse Company

Howard Johnson Co. — acquired by Prine Motor Inns, Inc.

Howard Manufacturing—acquired by Greenbull Inc.

Howe Richardson, Inc. — now sub. of Staveley Industries, Plc

Howell Instruments Corp. — name changed to Howell Management, Inc.

Howell Petroleum Corp. — acquired by Howell Corp.

Howmet Corp. — name changed to Pechiney Ugine Kuhlann Corp.

The Hoyt Group—out of business

Hubbard Real Estate Investments — name changed to HRE Properties

Harvey Hubbel, Inc. — name changed to Hubbel Inc.

Huck Mfg. Co. — acquired by Federal Mogul Corp.

Hudson & Affiliated Co.—liquidated

Hudson Place Investments Ltd. — out of business

Hudson Pulp & Paper Corp. — acquired by Georgia-Corp.

The Huffman Mfg. Co. — name changed to Huffy Corp.

Hughes Aircraft Co. — acquired by General Motors Corp.

Hughes & Hatcher, Inc. — acquired by The Outlet Co.

Hughes Tool Co. — wholly-owned sub. of Baker-Hughes Incorporated

Humiston-Keeling Inc. — acquired by Cardinal Health, Inc.

Hungry Tiger, Inc. — out of business

Philip A. Hunt Chemical Corp. — acquired by Olin Corp.

Huntington Health Services, Inc. — acquired by & merged into American Health Care Management

Husky Oil Co. — acquired by Marathon Oil Co. of United States Steel Corp.

The E.F. Hutton Group, Inc. — acquired by Shearson Lehman Brothers Holdings, Inc.

Huyck Corp. — acquired by BTR, Inc.

Hybritech Incorporated — acquired by Eli Lilly & Company

Hycel, Inc. — acquired by Boehinger Mannheim Corp.

The Hydraulic Company — name changed to Aquarion Company

Hydrometals, Inc. — acquired by Wallace-Murray Corp.

Hygrade Food Prods. Corp. — acquired by Hanson Industries, Inc.

Hypertronics Corporation — acquired by Smiths Industries PLC

Hyplains Beef, L.C. — acquired by National Beef Packing Company & name changed to National Beef Packing Company, L.P.

Hypro Corporation — acquired by WICOR, Inc.

I

I-T-E Imperial Corp. — merged into Gould, Inc.

IBC Holdings Corp. — name changed to Interstate Bakeries Corporation

IBM Foods — acquired by Polyphase Corporation & name changed to Overhill Farms, Inc.

IC Industries, Inc. — name changed to Whitman Corp.

ICI Incorporated — now ICI America Inc.

ICI United States, Inc. — name changed to ICI Americas, Inc.

ICI Soplant — acquired by Zeneca Group & name changed to Soplant

ICM Industries, Inc.—out of business

ICOT Corporation — name changed to AMATI Communications Corp.

IFS Industries, Inc. — acquired by Service Corp. International

IGC Energy, Inc. — name changed to Indiana Gasco, Inc.

INA Corp. — merged with Connecticut General Corp. to form Cigna Corp.

INI - Instituto Nacional de Indsutria — name changed to TENEO

IRT Realty Services, Inc. — name changed to IRT Property Co.

ISI Manufacturing, Inc.—acquired by IMI Plc & name changed to ISI Norgen, Inc.

ITI Corporation—out of business

ITT Corporation — split into 3 independent publicly traded companies: ITT Corporation, ITT Hartford Group, Inc. & ITT Industries, Inc.

IU International Corp. — acquired by Neoax, Inc.

IVB Financial Corp. — merged with Fidelcor, Inc.

IVHS Technologies Inc.—acquired by Eaton Corporation

IWC Resources Corporation—acquired by NIPSCO Industries, Inc.

Ibstock Johnsen Plc—name changed to Ibstock Plc

Idaho First National Bank—acquired by Moore Financial Group, Inc.

Ideal Pool Corp.—out of business

Ideal Toy Corp.—acquired by CBS, Inc.

Ideon Group, Inc.—acquired by CUC International, Inc.

Idle Wild Foods—acquired by Union Holdings, Inc.

Idun Gimsoy A/S—acquired by Orkla A.S. & name changed to Stabburet A/S

IFINT S.A.—name changed to Exor Group

Igloo Products Corporation—acquired by Brunswick Corporation

Illinois Cereal Mills, Inc.—acquired by Cargill

Illinois Consolidated Telephone Co.—name changed to Consolidated Communications

Illochroma International, S.A.—out of business

Imark Industries Incorporated—liquidated

Imasco USA, Inc.—now Hardee's Food Systems, Inc.

Immuno Nuclear Corp.—name changed to Incstar Corp.

Immuno Science Corp.—acquired by Johnson & Johnson

Imo Delaval Inc.—name changed to IMO Industries Inc.

Imodo, Inc.—acquired by Amtel, Inc.

Imperial Corporation of America—out of business

Imperial Litho/Graphics, Inc.—name changed to Imperial Litho & Dryography

Imperial Pearl Company, Inc.—out of business

Imperial World, Inc.—name changed to IWI Holding Limited

Inacomp Computer Centers—name changed to Inacom Corp.

Inarco Corp.—name changed to International Artware Corp.

Incom International, Inc.—out of business

Income & Capital Shares, Inc.—name changed to P-C Capital Fund, Inc.

Incoterm Corp.—acquired by Honeywell, Inc.

Incstar Corporation—merged with Clinical Sciences, Inc., a sub. of Fiat SpA

Independence Bancorp, Inc.—out of business

Independence Bank Group—acquired by The Marine Corporation

Independent Insurance Group—name changed to Life & Accident Corp.

Independent Life & Accident Insurance Co.—name changed to Independent Insurance Group, Inc.

Indian Head, Inc.—name changed to Thyssen-Bornemisza, Inc.

Indiana Gas Co., Inc.—holding co. formed, Indiana Energy, Inc.

Indiana Group, Inc.—acquired by National Distillors & Chemical Corp.

Indiana National Corporation—name changed to INB Financial Corporation

Indianapolis Power & Light Co.—holding co. formed, IPALCO Enterprises, Inc.

Indresco Inc.—name changed to Life & Accident Corp.

Inductotherm Corp.—name changed to Inductotherm Industries, Inc.

Industra Service Corporation—acquired by American Ecology Corporation

Industrial General Corporation—name changed to G.I. Plastek

Industrial National Corp.—name changed to Fleet Financial Group, Inc.

Industrial Nucleonics Corp.—name changed to AccuRay Corp.

Industrial Valley Bank & Trust Co.—holding co. formed, IVB Financial Corporation

Inexco Oil Co.—acquired by The Louisiana Land & Exploration Co.

Infinity Broadcasting Corporation—acquired by Westinghouse Electric Corporation & name changed to CBS Radio

Inforex, Inc.—acquired by Datapoint Corp.

Informatics General Corp.—acquired by & merged into Sterling Software, Inc.

Information International, Inc.—merged with Autologic Information International

Information Magnetics Corp.—name changed to Computer & Communication Technology Corp.

Infotron Systems Corp.—now Gandalf Systems Group, sub. of Gandalf Technologies Inc.

The Ingersoll Milling Machine Co.—holding co. formed, Ingersoll International, Inc.

Ingersoll Publications Company—name changed to Journal Register Company

Ingredient Technology Corp.—div. of Crompton & Knowles Corp.

Ingrid-Sevko, Inc.—acquired by Lawnware Products & name changed to Ingrid, Div. of Lawncare

Inland Container Corp.—acquired by Time Inc.

Inland Steel Co.—holding co. formed, Inland Steel Industries, Inc.

Inlander-Steindler Paper—acquired & absorbed by Unisource Worldwide, Inc.

Inmac Corp.—acquired by Micro Warehouse, Inc.

Inmar Corp.—out of business

Inmont Corp.—acquired by Carrier Corp.

Insituform Mid-America, Inc.—name changed to Insituform Technologies, Inc.

Inspiration Consolidated Copper Co.—acquired by Hudson Bay Mining & Smelting Co., Ltd.

Inspiration Resources Corporation—name changed to Terra Industries Inc.

Institutional Financing Services—acquired by Tyler Corp.

Instrumentation Laboratory, Inc.—acquired by Allied Corporation

Intech Inc.—acquired by Unitech plc

Intecom, Inc.—acquired by Wang Laboratories, Inc.

Integon Corp.—acquired by Ashland Oil, Inc.

Integra Financial Corporation—acquired by National City Corporation

Integrated Healthcare Facilities, L.P.—out of business

Integrity Entertainment Corp.—name changed to Wherehouse Entertainment, Inc.

Intelogic Trace Inc.—out of business

Inter-Regional Financial Group—name changed to Interra Financial

Interchem Inc.—now Rhone-Poulenc Performance Resins & Coatings Division of Rhone-Poulenc

Interco Incorporated—name changed to Furniture Brands International Inc.

Intercole Automation, Inc.—name changed to Intercole, Inc.

Intercontinental Bank—acquired by NationsBank Corporation

Intercraft Holdings—acquired by Newell Co.

Intercraft Industries Corporation—now Intercraft Holdings, L.P.

Interfinancial, Inc.—acquired by AMEV Holdings, Inc.

Interfirst Corp.—merged with Republic Bank to form First RepublicBank Corporation

Interform Corporation—acquired by Champion Industries

Interim Systems Corporation—now sub. of H&R Block, Inc.

Interlake, Inc.—name changed to The Interlake Corp.

Intermec Corporation—now wholly-owned sub. of Litton Industries Inc.

Intermedco, Inc.—name changed to Intermedco Holdings, Inc.

Intermedics Inc.—sub. of Sulzer Brothers Ltd.

International Bank—holding co. formed, USLICO

International Basic Economy Corp.—name changed to IBEC, Inc.

International Boiler Works Corporation—acquired by Universal Energy Corporation

International Business Interiors, Inc.—name changed to Environetx

International Cheese Company Limited—acquired by Stella Cheese Co., Inc.

International Clinical Laboratories, Inc.—acquired by & absorbed into Smith-Kline Bio-Science Corporation

International Controls Corp.—acquired by Checker Motors Company

International Couriers Corp.—acquired by Gelco Corp. & merged into Gelco Courier Services, Inc.

International Designer Accessories, Inc.—out of business

International Foodservice Corp.—acquired by Acton Corp. & name changed to Acton Foodservice Corp., IFC Div.

International Funeral Services, Inc.—name changed to

IFS Industries, Inc.

International Harvester Co.—name changed to Navistar International

International Income Property Inc.—liquidated June, 1990

International Industries, Inc.—name changed to Ihop Corp.

International Innopac Inc.—name changed to Great Pacific Enterprises

International Jensen Inc.—acquired by Recotron Corporation & name changed to Recotron Auto Corporation

International Kings Table—acquired by Horn & Hardart Corporation

International Lease Finance Corporation—now wholly-owned sub. of American International Group, Inc.

International Marine Holdings, Inc.—acquired by Vector Industries, Inc. & dissolved

International Minerals & Chemicals Corporation—name changed to Imcera Group, Inc.

International Mining Corp.—acquired by Pacific Holding Corp.

International Nickel Co. of Canada Ltd.—name changed to Inco Ltd.

International Paint (USA) Inc.—acquired by Courtaulds plc

International Power Machines Corp.—acquired by Exide Electronics, Inc.

International Protein Corporation—now GR Foods Inc.

International Research & Development Corporation—name changed to MPI Research LLC

International Semi-Tech Micro Electronics Inc.—name changed to Semi-Tech Corporation

International Stretch Products, Inc.—liquidated

International Tapetronics Corporation—out of business

International Telephone & Telegraph Corp.—name changed to ITT Corporation

InterNorth, Inc.—name changed to HNG/Internorth, Inc.

Interpace Corp.—acquired by Clevepak Corp.

Interplastic Corp.—acquired by Phillips Petroleum Corp.

Interpoint Corporation—acquired by Crane Co.

Interprovincial Pipe Line Inc.—acquired by IPL Energy Inc.

Intersil, Inc.—acquired by General Electric Co.

Interstate Electric Supply Company, Inc.—acquired by Branch Group Inc. & name changed to Branch Electric Supply Company

Interstate Stores, Inc.—name changed to Toys "R" Us, Inc.

Interstate United Corp.—acquired by Hanson Industries, Inc.

Interstate United Corp.—merged with Canteen Co., a sub. of TW Services, Inc.

Intertec Data Systems Corp.—out of business

Intertherm, Inc.—acquired by Nortek, Inc.

Intertrans Corporation—acquired by Fritz Companies,

Inc. & name changed to Fritz Air Freight

Interway Corp.—acquired by Transamerica Corp.

Interwest Corporation—now Collum Companies

Intext, Inc.—acquired by National Education Corp.

Intrepid Corp.—name changed to Trek Corporation

Invesco Group Limited—name changed to Invesco Group Asset Management Ltd.

Investment AB Cardo—name changed to Cardo AB

Investment Corp. of Florida—acquired by Ashland Oil Inc.

Investors Bank Corp.—acquired & absorbed by Firstar Corporation

Investors Realty Trust—name changed to IR Property Company

Investors Royalto Co., Inc.—merged into Sabine Royalty Corp.

Invitron Corporation—now Centrocor St. Louis, division of Centocor, Inc.

Iowa Beef Processors, Inc.—acquired by Occidental Petroleum Corp.

Iowa Electric Light & Power Co.—holding co. formed, IE Industries, Inc.

Iowa-Illinois Gas & Electric Company—merged with Midwest Resources Inc. to form MidAmerican Energy Company

Iowa Power & Light Co.—name changed to Iowa Resources, Inc.

Iowa Southern Utilities Co.—holding co. formed, Iowa Southern, Inc.

Ipco Hospital Supply Corp.—name changed to Ipco Corp.

Ireland Coffee Tea, Inc.—acquired by Chock Full O' Nuts Corporation

Irish Cement Ltd.—acquired by CRH, plc

Isoscoles plc—out of business

IVAC Corporation—acquired by Advanced Medical, Inc.

Irvin Industries, Inc.—acquired by Halle & Stieglitz, Inc.

Irving Bank Corporation—acquired by The Bank of New York Company, Inc.

Italgel S.P.A.—acquired & absorbed into Nestle Italiana S.p.A.

Italia Di Navigazione S.p.A.—acquired by IRI Istituto Ricostruzione Industriale

ITEL Corporation—name changed to Anixter International

Itran Corporation—out of business

J.B. Ivey & Co.—acquired by Marshall Field & Co.

Ivy Corp.—acquired by Koppers Corp.

J

J H Collectibles—out of business

J.P. Industries, Inc.—wholly-owned sub. of T&N Plc

JMP Newcor Holdings Inc.—acquired by Patra Ceramics Co., Ltd.

JWT Group, Inc.—acquired by WPP Group, Inc.

Jack Winter, Inc.—name changed to Winjak

Jackson Machine Sales—name changed to Jackson MSC

Jackson National Life Insurance Co.—acquired by Prudential Corp. PLC

Jackson Vibrators, Inc.—name changed to Jackson Jordan, Inc.

Jacobs Suchard Inc.—now E.J. Brach, Inc.

Jacques Jugeat Inc.—acquired by Lalique S.A.

Jaeger Energy Corporation—out of business

The Jaeger Machine Co.—holding co. formed, Jaeger Energy Corp.

Jamaica Water Properties, Inc.—holding co. formed, JWP, Inc.

Jamecon Industries, Inc.—acquired by Watts Industries, Inc.

Fred S. James Co., Inc.—acquired by Transamerica Corp. & name changed to Sedgwick James Inc.

Jamesway Corporation—out of business

Jarnia AB—acquired by Bergman & Beving AB

Jandy Industries—acquired by Allegheny Teledyne Incorporated & name changed to Teledyne Laars Jandy Products

Jantzen, Inc.—acquired by Blue Bell, Inc.

Japan Radion Corporation International, Inc.—name changed to JRC Canida, Inc.

Jardine Emett & Chandler Inc.—now Jardine Insurance Brokers

Jazz Holding Corporation—name changed to Chorus Line Corporation

Jeanette Corp.—acquired by Coca-Cola Bottling Co. of New York, Inc.

Jefferson Corp.—name changed to The Somerset Group, Inc.

Jefferson National Life Insurance Co.—now wholly-owned sub. of Lomas Financial Corporation

Jenn-Air Corp.—acquired by Carrier Corp., sub. of United Technologies Corp.

A/S Jens Villadsens Fabriker—name changed to Icopal a/s

Jerrico, Inc.—now sub. of Castle-Harlan Inc.

Jet America Airlines, Inc.—wholly-owned sub. of Alaska Air Group, Inc.

Jetero Corporation—name changed to Beeler-Sanders, Inc.

Jewel Companies, Inc.—acquired by American Stores Company

Jewelcor Inc.—out of business

Jhirmack Enterprises, Inc.—acquired by Esmark, Inc.

Jill Phoenix—acquired by Dover Corporation

John R. Hollingsworth Co.—out of business

Johns-Manville Corp.—name changed to Manville Corp.

Johnson & Firth Brown Plc—name changed to Firth-Rixson Plc

E.F. Johnson Co.—acquired by Western Union Corp.

Johnson Hill's Inc.—now sub. of Kline Bros., a sub. of

Pubco Corporation

The Johnson Industries Corp—acquired by Q3 Stamped Metal & name changed to Q3 JMC Inc.

Johnstown American Companies—out of business

Jon Douglas Company—acquired by Prudential Insurance Company of America to form The Prudential-Jon Douglas Company

Jonathan Logan, Inc.—acquired by United Merchants & Manufacturers, Inc.

David Jones Ltd.—name changed to DJL Limited

Earle M. Jorgensen Company—now Jorgensen Steel & Aluminum, sub. of Kelso Company

Jos. Schlitz Brewing Co.—acquired by Stroh Brewery Co.

Joslyn Corporation—acquired by Danaher Corporation

Joslyn Mfg. & Supply Co.—name changed to Joslyn Corp.

The Journal Co.—name changed to Journal Communications, Inc.

Joy Manufacturing Co.—name changed to Joy Technologies, Inc.

Judy Bond, Inc.—out of business

Juniper Petroleum Corp.—acquired by & merged into Damson Oil Corp.

Jupiter Industries, Inc.—holding co. formed, The Jupiter Corporation

Jupiter National—acquired by Johnston Industries

Justrite Manufacturing Company—acquired by Federal Signal Corp.

K

K & F Industries Inc.—acquired by Loral Space & Communications

KB Marketing Systems, Inc.—name changed to Kobacker Stores

KDI Corporation—out of business

K-H Corp.—acquired by Andrew Corporation

K-J Distributors, Inc.—acquired by Philip Morris Companies Inc. & name changed to Miller Brands of Phoenix

KKS Holdings A/S—out of business

KMW Systems Corporation—acquired by Andrew Corporation

KSG Inc.—name changed to Kappler Safety Group, Inc.

Kaiser Aluminum & Chemical Corp.—holding co. formed, KaiserTech Limited

Kaiser Aluminum Chemcials Inc.—acquired by Esmark, Inc. now The Vigoro Corporation

Kaiser Cement Corp.—acquired by Hanson Industries, Inc.

Kaiser Steel Corporation—now Kaiser Steel Resources, Inc.

KaiserTech Limited—now unit of Maxxam Group, Inc.

Kal Grafx—acquired by The Excellence Group

Kaldnes Heavy Lift Trucks—acquired by Norskvekst ASA

Kallestad Laboratories, Inc.—acquired by Erbamont, Inc.

Kalvar Corp.—acquired by & merged into Xidex Corp.

Kalvar Corporation—acquired by Electronic Data Systems Corporation, sub. of General Motors Corporation

Kalvex, Inc.—merged into Allied Artists Industries

Kampgrounds of America, Inc.—holding co. formed, KOA Holdings Inc.

Kanawha Steel & Equipment Co.—name changed to Logan Corp.

Kanex America Inc.—name changed to Lake Business Products, Inc.

Kansallis-Osake-Pankki—merged with Unitas to form Merita Ltd.

Kansas-Nebraska Natural Gas Co.—name changed to K N Energy, Inc.

Kansas Power & Light Co.—name changed to Western Resources, Inc.

Kapok Corporation—out of business

Kapok Tree Inns Corp.—name changed to Kapok Corp.

Karl Kassbohrer Fahrzeugwerke GmbH—name changed to Gelandefahrzeug GmbH

Kaufhop Group—merged with Asko Deutsche Kaufhaus AG to form Metro AG

Kaufman & Broad, Inc.—split into Broad, Inc. and Kaufman & Broad Home Corporation

Kawecki Berylco Industries, Inc.—acquired by Cabot Corp.

Kay Corp.—name changed to Balfour Maclaine Corp.

Kay Jewelers, Inc.—acquired by Sterling Inc., sub. of Ratners Group Plc

Kaye Instruments, Inc.—acquired by Bowthorpe Plc

Kearney & Trecker Corp.—merged with Cross Co. to form Cross & Trecker Corp.

Keene Corp.—holding co. formed, Bairnco Corp.

Keene Corporation—out of business

Keller Building Products of Cincinnati—name changed to American Building Products

Keller Ladders Inc.—acquired by U.S. Industries, Inc.

Kelsey Hayes Company—acquired by Varity Corporation

Kemmerer Bottling Group Inc.—name changed to Select Beverages, Inc.

Kemper Corporation—acquired & absorbed by Zurich Insurance Company

Kemper National Insurance Companies—name changed to Kemper Insurance Companies

Ken-Mac Metals, Inc.—acquired by Thyssen A.G.

Kendavis Holding Co.—out of business

Kennecott Copper Corp.—name changed to Kennecott Corp.

Kennecott Corp.—acquired by Standard Oil Co. (Ohio)

Kenner Parker Toys, Inc.—now Parker Brothers, div. of Tonka Corporation

Kent-Moore Corp.—acquired by Sealed Power Corp.

Kentile Floors Inc.—acquired by United Capital Corp. & name changed to Kentile

Kenton Corp.—merged into Rapid American Corp.

Kentron International, Inc.—acquired by Planning Research Corporation

Kentucky Medical Insurance Company (KMIC)—acquired by Michigan Physicians Mutual Liability Inc

Kentucky Utilities Co.—acquired by KU Energy

Kern's Bakeries, Incorporated—acquired by Cooper Smith, Inc.

Kerr Glass Manufacturing Corporation—name changed to Kerr Group, Inc.

Kettenburg Marine Corporation—out of business

Keuffel & Esser Co.—acquired by Kratos, Inc.

Kevex Corporation—now Kevex Instruments Inc., sub. of VG Instruments Group PLC

Kevex Corporation—acquired by Fisons Plc

Kevlin Microwave Corporation—name changed to Kevlin Corporation

Kewanee Industries, Inc.—acquired by Gulf Oil Corp.

Kewanee Oil Co.—name changed to Kewanee Industries, Inc.

The Key Company—acquired by Concord Camera Corp.

Key Manufacturing Group Limited Partnership—acquired by JPE, Inc. & name changed to Industrial & Automotive Fasteners, Inc.

Keyes Fibre Co.—acquired by Arcata Corp.

Keyport Life—acquired by Liberty Mutual Insurance Co.

Keystone Camera Products Corporation—liquidated

Keystone Coffee—name changed to Mr. Wright's Amazing Coffee Factory

Keystone Custodian Funds, Inc.—acquired by Travelers Corp.

Keystone Industries, Inc.—acquired by Varlen Corp.

Keystone Portland Cement Co.—acquired by Giant Group Limited

Keystone Precious Metals Holdings, Inc.—out of business

Kidde, Inc.—acquired by & merged into Hanson Industries, Inc.

Kimbell, Inc.—acquired by & merged into Winn-Dixie Inc.

Kincaid furniture Co., Inc.—acquired by La-Z-Boy Chair Company

Kinder-Care, Inc.—now two separate companies, The Enstar Group, Inc. and Kinder-Care Learning Centers, Inc.

King Bear Enterprises, Inc.—out of business

King O'Lawn, Inc.—name changed to Faas Enterprises, Inc.

King Optical Corp.—name changed to Lee Optical, Inc.

King Radio Corp.—acquired by Allied-Signal Inc.

E.B. Kingman Company—out of business

Kings Department Stores, Inc.—name changed to KDT Industries, Inc.

Kingsbury Machine Tool Corporation—now Kingsbury International

Kingsley Machine Co.—acquired by Illinois Tool Works Inc.

Kingstip, Inc.—acquired by & merged into Justin Industries, Inc.

Kirk-Mayer, Inc.—acquired by Tad Resources

Kirsch Co.—acquired by Cooper Industries, Inc.

Klafs-Saunabau GmbH—name changed to Klafs Saunabau GmbH & Co. KG Medizinische Technik

Kleinwort Benson Ltd.—acquired by Dresden Bank AG

Klockner-Humboldt-Deutz AG (KHD)—name changed to Deutz AG

Kluener Packing Company—name changed to Kluener Foods & Distributing Co. Inc.

Knapp King Size Corp.—name changed to Knapp Shoes, Inc.

Knickerbocker Toy Co., Inc.—acquired by Warner Communications, Inc.

Knogo North America Inc.—name changed to Sentry Technology Corp.

Knoll International Holdings, Inc.—name changed to 21 International Holdings Inc.

Knott Hotels Corp.—name changed to Trusthouse Forte, Inc.

Knox Lumber Co.—acquired by Southwest Forest Industries, Inc.

Knudsen Corp.—acquired by Winn Enterprises

Koehler Manufacturing Company—acquired by Charter plc

Koehring Corp.—acquired by AMCA International Corp.

Koenig & Bauo AG—name changed to Koenig & Bauer-Albert AG

Koenig, Inc.—name changed to Rawson-Koenig, Inc.

The Koger Company—merged with Koger Properties, Inc.

H. Kohnstamm & Co., Inc.—acquired by Universal Foods Corporation & name changed to H.K. Color Group

Koninklijke Borsumij Wehry N.V.—acquired & absorbed into Hagemeyer N.V.

Koolvent Group Inc.—name changed to American Home Improvement

Koppers Company, Inc.—now Beazer Materials & Services Inc., a sub. of Beazer PLC

Koracorp Industries, Inc.—acquired by Levi Strauss, Inc.

Korman Co.—name changed to Korman Services, L.P.

Kraft, Inc.—merged with Dart Industries, Inc. to form Dart & Kraft, Inc.

Kraft, Inc.—acquired by Philip Morris Corporation, now Kraft General Foods

Kraftco Corp.—name changed to Kraft, Inc.

Kransco Group Companies—acquired by Mattel, Inc. & name changed to Mattel Power Wheels

S.S. Kresge Co.—name changed to Kmart Corp.

Kroehler Mfg. Co.—reorganized, now The Rymer Co.

Kroh Operating L.P. — liquidated

W.A. Krueger Company — now Krueger-Ringier, sub. of Ringier AG

Kuhn's Big K Stores Corp. — acquired by Wal-Mart Stores, Inc.

Kymmene Corporation — merged with Repola Corporation to form UPM-Kymmene Corporation

Kysor Industrial Corporation — acquired by Scotsman Industries, Inc.

L

LAC Minerals Ltd. — absorbed by Barrick Gold Corporation

LDB Corporation — name changed to LDBrinkman Co.

LDDS Metromedia Communications, Inc. — name changed to WorldCom, Inc.

LDI Corporation — acquired by NationsBank Corporation & name changed to Nations Credit Commercial Corporation

LFE Corporation — acquired by Mark IV Industries

LLC Corporation — name changed to Valhi, Inc.

LMF Corporation — acquired by Diamond International Corp. & merged into Diamond Retail Div.

LWMCK Corporation — out of business

La Belle Industries, Inc. — name changed to Quest Technologies Inc.

La Fabril S.A. — name changed to Consorto de Alimentos Fabril Pacifico S.A.

John Labatt Limited — acquired by Interbrew S.A. & name changed to Labatt Brewing Company Limited

LaBatt Communications, Inc. — acquired & absorbed by Netstar Communications, Inc.

Lacy Diversified Industries, Inc. — name changed to Lacy Diversified Industries, Ltd.

Lafayette Manufacturing, Inc. — acquired by Waltus & Wolf & name changed to Pressed Lafayette Precast

Lafayette Radio Electronics Corp. — acquired & absorbed by Wards Co., Inc.

Lafayette Steel Co. — acquired by Olympic Steel Inc.

Lake Center Industries — acquired by Guy F. Atkinson Co. of CA

Lake Superior District Power Co. — acquired by Northern States Power Co.

Lake to Lake Dairy — acquired by Land O'Lakes, Inc.

Lakeland Savings Bank — acquired by Valley National Bancorp

Tony Lama Co., Inc. — acquired by Justin Industries, Inc.

Lamaur, Inc. — acquired by Dow Consumer Products, Inc., sub. of Dow Chemical Company

Lancaster Host Resort — name changed to The Holiday Inn Lancaster Host Hotel & Conference Center

Lancaster Press, Inc. — acquired by Cadmus Inc.

Lancer Orthodontics Inc. — sub. of Biomerica, Inc.

Lanchart Industries, Inc. — acquired by LDB Corporation

Land & Houses Co., Ltd. — name changed to Benetone

Land & Houses Co., Ltd.

Landis & Gyr AG — name changed to Landis & Staefa AG

Landmark Bancshares Corporation — acquired by Magna Group, Inc.

Landmark Bank — acquired by California State Bank & name changed to California State Bank-La Habra

Landmark Banking Corp. — acquired by Citizens & Southern Georgia Corp.

Landmark Graphics Corporation — acquired by Halliburton Company

Landmark Hotel Corporation — name changed to Hotel Corporation of America

Lane Bryant, Inc. — acquired by Limited Stores, Inc.

The Lane Co. Inc. — wholly-owned sub. of Interco, Inc.

Lanier Business Products, Inc. — acquired by Harris Corp.

LaPointe Industries, Inc. — out of business

Laramie Tire Distributors Inc. — acquired by Sumitomo Corporation

Larizza Industries, Inc. — acquired by Collins & Aikman Corporation & name changed to Manchester Plastics

The Larsen Co. — acquired by Dean Foods Company

Larson Industries, Inc. — acquired by Arctic Enterprises, Inc. & name changed to Arctic Marine Products, Inc.

LaSalle Deitch Co., Inc. — name changed to LaSalle Bristol

Laser Precision Corp. — acquired by GN Great Nordic Ltd.

Lasky Company — out of business

LaTouraine-Bickford's Foods, Inc. — name changed to Bickford Corporation

Laverdiere's Enterprises — acquired by Rite Aid Corporation & name changed to Rite Aid Pharmacy

Lawry's Foods, Inc. — acquired by Thomas J. Lipton, Inc.

Lawson Mordon Group Limited — acquired by Alusuisse-Lonza Holding Ltd.

Lawter Chemicals, Inc. — name changed to Lawter International, Inc.

Lay Packing Company Inc. — name changed to Lay's Fine Foods

Layne, Inc. — name changed to Layne Christenson Co.

Leader Federal Bank for Savings — acquired & absorbed by Union Planters Corporation

Learjet Corporation — now sub. of Bombardier, Inc.

Lear Siegler Inc. — name changed to Lear Siegler Holdings Corp.

Leaseway Transportation — acquired by Penske Corporation

Leath and Co. — acquired by Gamble-Skogmo, Inc.

Lebanon Chemical Corp. — name changed to Lebanon Seaboard Corp.

LeBlond, Inc. — name changed to LeBlond Makino Machine Tool Co.

Lechmere, Inc. — acquired by Montgomery Ward & Co., Inc.

Lee Data Corporation—now Apertus Technologies Incorporated

Lee Way Motor Freight, Inc.—acquired by Pepsico, Inc.

Leeds & Northrup Co.—acquired by General Signal Corp.

Leeds Permanent Building Society—acquired & absorbed into Halifax Building Society

Leesona Corp.—name changed to John Brown, Inc.

Legent Corporation—acquired by Computer Associates International, Inc. & name changed to Computer Associates

Lehndorff Vermoegensverwaltung AG—out of business

Leichtung, Inc.—acquired by Hanover Direct, Inc. & name changed to LWI Holdings Inc.

Leisure & Technology Corp.—name changed to Leisure Technology Inc.

Leisure Dynamics, Inc.—acquired by Coleco Industries, Inc.

Leonard Silver International, Inc.—acquired by Towle Mfg. Co.

Lennox Industries, Inc.—holding co. formed, Lennox International, Inc.

Lenox, Inc.—acquired by Brown-Forman Corp.

Leslie Salt Co.—acquired by Cargill Corp.

Les Magasins M—out of business

Kenneth Leventhal & Company—acquired by Ernst & Young, LLP & name changed to E & Y Kenneth Leventhal Real Estate Group

Charles Letts (Holdings) Ltd.—out of business

Levitt Industries, Inc.—name changed to Optel Corp.

Levy Security Consultants, Limited—name changed to Levy Security Corp.

A.M. Lewis Inc.—acquired by The Price Company

Lewis Business Forms, inc.—name changed to Lewis Business Products, Inc.

Palmer G. Lewis & Co., Inc.—now sub. of Huttig Sash & Door Co. of Crane Company

Lexitron Corp.—acquired by Raytheon Co.

Libby, McNeil & Libby, Inc.—sub. of Nestle Enterprises, Inc.

Libby-Owens-Ford Co.—name changed to Trinova Corp.

W.S. Libbey Company—out of business

Liberty Fabrics of New York, Inc.—now sub. of Courtaulds plc

Liberty Glass Company—acquired by Pechiney S.A. & name changed to Foster Forbes Glass Development, Inc.

Liberty Loan Corp.—name changed to LLC Corp.

Liberty National Insurance Holding Co.—name changed to Torchmark Corp.

Liberty National Insurance Co.—name changed to Liberty National Insurance Holding Co.

Liberty Tool Corporation—name changed to Liberty Precision Industries

Life & Accident Corporation—acquired & absorbed by American General Corporation

Life Investors—name changed to Aegon USA Inc.

Life Line Nutritionals, Inc.—out of business

Life-Rollway Corp.—name changed to Life Corp.—acquired by Echlin, Inc.

Lifeco Travel Services—acquired by American Express Co.

Lifemark Corp.—acquired by & merged into American Medical International, Inc.

Liggett & Myers Inc.—name changed to Liggett Group, Inc.

Liggett Group, Inc.—name changed to GrandMet USA, Inc.

Lightolier, Inc.—acquired by Bairnco Corp.

Lilly Industrial Coatings, Inc.—name changed to Lilly Industries, Inc.

Lily Lynn, Inc.—name changed to Lynnwear Corporation

Lin Broadcasting Corporation—acquired by McCaw Cellular Communication Inc.

Lincoln American Corp.—acquired by American General Corp.

Lincoln First Banks, Inc.—merged with The Chase Manhattan Corp.

Lincoln Telecommunications Company—name changed to Aliant Communications Inc.

Lincoln Telephone & Telegraph Co.—name changed to Lincoln Telecommunications Co.

Linear Corp.—now sub. of Nortek, Inc.

LinRead Public Limited Co.—acquired by McKechnie PLC

Lipe-Rollway Corp.—name changed to Lipe Corporation

J.B. Lippincott Co.—acquired by Harper & Row Publishers, Inc.

Liquid Air Corp. of North America—name changed to Liquid Air Corp.

Liquidonics Industries, Inc.—acquired by & merged into VSI Corp.

Litco Corp. of New York—name changed to Litco Bancorporation of New York, Inc.

Litronix, Inc.—acquired by Siemens Corp.

Little & Company—name changed to First USA Paymentech, Inc.

Lloyd's Electronic Corp.—now Lloyds Electronic Division of Dynascan Corporation

Lloyd's Electronics, Inc.—acquired by Bacardi Corp.

Loblaw, Inc.—sub. of Peter J. Schmitt Co., Inc., a sub. of George Waston, Ltd.

Lockard Construction, Inc.—acquired by Peters Construction Corp & name changed to Lockard Development, Inc.

Locke Group, Inc.—name changed to Locke Mfg., Inc.

Loctite Corporation—acquired by Henkel KGaA

Locus Computing Corp.—acquired by Platinum Technology Inc.

Lodge & Shipley Co. — now div. of Manuflex Corp., a sub. of Belcan Corporation

Lodgistix, Inc. — now sub. of Sulcus Computer Corp.

Loehmann's Inc. — acquired by Associated Dry Goods Corp.

Logetronics, Inc. — acquired by DBA Systems

Logica UK Limited — name changed to Logica Plc

Logistics Industries Corp. — acquired by & merged into Lydall, Inc.

Lomas & Nettleton Financial Corp. — now Lomas Financial Corporation

Londontown Corp. — acquired by Interco, Inc.

Londontown Holdings Corporation — name changed to London Fog Corporation

Lone Star Cadillac Co. — acquired & absorbed by Don Massey Cadillac Inc.

Lorimar, Inc. — name changed to Lorimar Telepictures Corporation

Lorimar Telepictures Corporation — wholly-owned sub. of Warner Communications Inc.

The Lorvic Corporation — acquired by Young Dental Manufacturing Corp. & name changed to Young Dental/Lorvic Division

Los Angeles Smoking & Curing Company — acquired by Ocean Beauty Seafoods, Inc.

Lotus Development Corporation — acquired by International Business Machines Corporation

Louisiana Bancshares, Inc. — name changed to Premier Bancorp, Inc.

Louisiana Gas System, Inc. — acquired & absorbed by DuPont (E.I. du Pont de Nemours & Co.)

Louisiana General Services, Inc. — acquired by Citizens Utilities & name changed to Louisiana Gas Service

Louisville Gas and Electric Company — holding co. formed, LG&E Energy Corp.

M. Lowenstein Corp. — acquired by Springs Industries Inc.

M. Lowenstein & Sons, Inc. — name changed to M. Lowenstein Corp.

Loyola Capital Corporation — merged into Crestar Bank FSB

Lucas Industries plc — merged with the Varity Corporation to form LucasVarity plc

Luchem Corp. — name changed to BASF America Corp.

Ludlow Corp. — acquired by Tyco Labs, Inc.

Lukenheimer Co. — out of business

Lukens Steel Co. — name changed to Lukens, Inc.

Lumex, Inc. — acquired by Fuqua Enterprises & name changed to Lumex Medical Products

Lund Enterprises, Inc. — now Lune International Holdings, Inc.

Lundy Electronics & Systems, Inc. — acquired by TransTechnology Corporation

Lykes Corp. — acquired by & merged into LTV Corp.

Lykes-Youngstown Corp. — name changed to Lykes Corp.

Lynch Communication Systems — acquired by Alcatel Network Systems

Lynden Transport, Inc. — name changed to Lynden, Inc.

Lynnwear Corp. — name changed to Devon Hall, Div. of Alfo

Lyon Conklin & Company — acquired by Wolseley Plc. & name changed to Ferguson Lyon Conklin & Company Inc.

Lyon Holding Company — name changed to L & D Group

M

M & T Incorporated — name changed to M & T Partners

M-Corp — out of business

M/A-Com Inc. — acquired by AMP Incorporated

MBPXL Corp. — acquired by & merged into Cargill Corp.

MBT Associates, Inc. — name changed to MBT Architecture

MCA, Inc. — acquired by Matsushita Electric Industrial Co. Ltd. & name changed to MCA Universal

MCN Corporation — name changed to MCN Energy Group Inc.

MCO Holdings, Inc. — name changed to Maxxam Inc.

MD Papier GmbH — acquired by Metsa-Serla Corporation

MDL Information Systems, Inc. — acquired by Reed Elsevier Plc

MDS Health Group Limited — name changed to MDS Inc.

MEI Corp. — name changed to MEI Diversified, Inc.

MFS Communications Company, Inc. — acquired by WorldCom, Inc. & name changed to MFS WorldCom, Inc.

MGIC Investment Corp. — acquired by Baldwin-United Corp.

MGM Grand Hotels, Inc. — acquired by Bally Manufacturing Corporation

MGM/UA Communications Co. — now MGM Pathe Communications Co., a sub. of Pathe Communications Co.

MGM/UA Entertainment Co. — acquired by Turner Broadcasting Systems, Inc.

MHB Inc. — out of business

MHI Group, Inc. — acquired by The Loewen Group, Inc.

MHP Machines, Inc. — now Applied Machining Technology, Inc.

The MI Designer Group — out of business

MI Fund Incorporated — out of business

MIPs Computer Systems, Inc. — acquired by Silicon Graphics & name changed to MIPs Technologies, Inc.

MPB Corp. — acquired by Wheelabrator-Frye, Inc.

MRFY Corp. — out of business

MSI Data Corporation — acquired by Symbol Technologies Inc.

MTC Electronic Technologies Co., Ltd.—name changed to GrandeTel Technologies Inc.

The MTLG Acquisition Corporation—out of business

MTM Plc—name changed to Meristem Plc

MWA Co.—acquired by Mitchell Corp. of Owosso

Maccabees Mutual Life Insurance—acquired by Royal Insurance Plc

Macco Constructors, Inc.—acquired by ARB Inc.

MacDonald Dettwiler & Associates Ltd.—acquired by Orbital Sciences Corporation

E.F. MacDonald Co.—acquired by Carlson Companies, Inc.

Macfield Inc.—acquired by Unifi, Inc.

Machado & Co. Incorporated—out of business

Mack Trucks, Inc.—now wholly-owned by Regie Nationale des Usines Renault

Macke Co.—acquired by Allegheny Beverage Corp.

MacKinnon-Parker, Inc.—out of business

Macks Stores, Inc.—acquired by Maxway Corporation

MacLean Hunter Ltd.—acquired by Rogers Communications Inc.

Macmillan, Inc.—acquired by Maxwell Communications PLC

Macmillan Publishers Limited—acquired by Verlagsgruppe International Plc

R.H. Macy & Co., Inc.—acquired by Camdev Corporation & name changed to Macy's East & Macy's West

James Madison Limited—out of business

Madison Square Garden Corp.—acquired by Gulf & Western Industries, Inc.

Magic Chef, Inc.—acquired by Maytag Corporation

Magma Copper Co.—acquired by Broken Hill Proprietary Co. & name changed to BHP Copper North America

Magmetco, Inc.—acquired by Inductotherm Industries, Inc.

Magnet Group Plc—acquired by Berisford International Plc & name changed to Magnet Ltd.

Magnetic Controls Co.—name changed to ADC Telecommunications, Inc.

Magnetics International, Inc.—acquired by H. K. Porter Company, Inc.

Maine Printing & Business Forms Co.—name changed to EPX

Mallinckrodt, Inc.—acquired by Avon Products, Inc.

P.R. Mallory & Co., Inc.—acquired by Dart Industries

Mallory Randall Corp.—acquired by Savoy Industries, Inc.

Malone & Hyde, Inc.—wholly-owned sub. of Fleming Companies, Inc.

Maloya AG—acquired by Fredstein Barden & name changed to Maloya Fredstein

Mammoth Mart, Inc.—acquired by Kings Department Stores, Inc.

Management Assistance, Inc.—liquidated

Management Science America, Inc.—acquired by Dun & Bradstreet Corporation

Manhattan Industries, Inc.—now div. of Salent Corporation

Manhattan Life Corp.—name changed to Manhattan National Corp.

Manpower, Inc.—acquired by The Parker Pen Co.

Manpower, Inc.—now wholly-owned sub. of Blue Arrrow PLC

Manufacturers Hanover Corporation—merged into Chemical Banking Corporation

Manville Corporation—name changed to Schuller Corporation

Marantz Co., Inc.—acquired by Dynascan Corporation

Marathon Mfg. Co.—acquired by Penn Central Corp.

Marathon Oil Co.—acquired by U.S. Steel Corp.

Marcor Resorts, Inc.—name changed to Rio Hotel & Casino Inc.

Maremont Corp.—acquired by Arvin Industries, Inc.

Marine Bank—acquired by PNC Financial Corp.

The Marine Corp.—now Banc One Wisconsin Corp., sub. of Banc One Corporation

Marion Corp.—out of business

Marion Laboratories, Inc.—now Marion Merrell Dow Inc.

Marion Merrell Dow, Inc.—acquired by Hoechst Aktiengesellschaft & name changed to Hoechst Marion Rousel, Inc.

Mark Products, Inc.—acquired by Bralorne Resources, Ltd.

Marketing Communications—acquired by Harte-Hanks Communications, Inc.

Marketing Displays International, Inc.—name changed to MDI

Markwood Inc.—acquired by Howard Miller

Marlene Industries Corp.—acquired by Unishops, Inc.

The Marmon Group, Inc.—name changed to Marmon Corporation

Marquette Co.—acquired by & merged into Gulf & Western Industries, Inc. Natural Resources Group

Mars Stores, Inc.—out of business

Marshall Contractors Inc.—acquired by Fluor Corporation

Marshall Field & Co.—acquired by Batus, Inc.

Jeffrey Martin Inc.—acquired by & merged with Dep Corporation

Martin Pet Foods Inc.—acquired & absorbed by H.J. Heinz Company

Martin Processing, Inc.—name changed to Ronile, Inc.

Martrade—out of business

Maryland Cup Corp.—acquired by Fort Howard Paper Corp.

Maryland National Corp.—name changed to MNC Financial, Inc.

Masco Corp.—now Masco Corp. & Masco Industries

C.H. Masland & Sons—acquired by Burlington Industries, Inc.

Mason & Hanger Silas Mason Co., Inc.—name changed

to Mason & Hanger Corporation, Inc.

Mason Oil Company — acquired by Toms Sierra Company

Masonite Corp. — acquired by U.S. Gypsum Company

Mass Merchandisers, Inc. — acquired by McKesson Corp.

Masters Merchandise Mart, Inc. — liquidated

Mateco Electronics Corp. — company closed

Materials Research Corporation — acquired by Sony Corporation of America

Mathematica, Inc. — acquired by Martin Marietta Corp.

Mathematical Applications Group, Inc. — now MAGI Direct Inc.

The Mathes Co. — name changed to Curtis Mathes Corp.

Matthey Bishop, Inc. — merged with Johnson Matthey & Co., Inc. to form Johnson Matthey, Inc.

Mathieu Corporation — out of business

Matra-Hachette — name changed to Lagardere Groupe

Matrix Corporation — acquired by Bayer U.S.A., Inc.

Matrix Essentials, Inc. — acquired by Bristol-Myers Squibb Co.

Matrix Science Corporation — sub. of AMP Incorporated

Maule Industries, Inc. — acquired by Lone Star Industries & merged into Lone Star Florida, Inc.

Maxtor Corporation — acquired by Hyundai Corporation

Maxus Energy Corporation — acquired by Yacmientos Petroliferos Fiscales-YPF

Maxway Corporation — out of business

Maxway Partners, L.P. — now Maxwell Corporation

Maxwell Communication Corporation plc — liquidated

Maybelline, Inc. — acquired by L'Oreal S.A.

Mayfair Industries, Inc. — acquired by Apparel America Inc.

Mayfair Super Markets, Inc. — acquired by Koninklijke Ahold NV

Mayflower Corp. — name changed to Mayflower Group, Inc.

Mayrath Industries, Inc. — acquired by TIC Industries, Inc.

J.W. Mays, Inc. — out of business

Maywood, Inc. — liquidated

McCarty Foods — acquired by & name changed to Tyson Foods, Inc.

McCord Corp. — acquired by Ex-Cell-O Corp.

McCulloch Oil Corp. — name changed to MCO Holdings, Inc.

J. Ray McDermott & Co., Inc. — name changed to McDermott, Inc.

McDougal, Littell & Co. — acquired by Houghton, Mifflin & Co.

McGill Manufacturing Company, Inc. — acquired by Emerson Electric Company

McGraw-Edison Co. — acquired by Cooper Industries, Inc.

McGregor-Doniger, Inc. — acquired by Rapid-American Corp.

McIntosh Corp. — acquired by Norris Industries, Inc.

McIntyre Mines Ltd. — acquired by Superior Oil Co.

Arthur G. McKee & Co. — name changed to The McKee Corp.

The McKee Corp. — name changed to Davy, Inc.

McKeon Construction — acquired by Barratt America, Inc. & name changed to Barratt-San Francisco

McLean Industries, Inc. — out of business

McLean Trucking Co. — acquired by Meridian Trucking Co.

McLouth Steel — acquired & absorbed by DSC Ltd.

McMoran Exploration Co. — name changed to McMoRan Oil & Gas Co.

McMoRan Oil & Gas Co. — merged with Freeport Minerals Co. & new name is Freeport-McMoRan, Inc.

McNally Manufacturing — acquired by Trelleborg AB

McNeil Corp. — acquired by Pentair, Inc.

McQuay, Inc. — acquired by Snyder General Corporation

McQuay-Perfex, Inc. — name changed to McQuay, Inc.

McRae's, Inc. — acquired by Proffitt's, Inc.

F.W. Means & Co. — name changed to Means Services, Inc.

Means Services, Inc. — acquired by ARA Services, Inc.

Mechanical Heat & Cold Inc. — acquired by Compagnie General Des Eaux

Meco International Limited — out of business

Meco Metal Finishing — acquired by Possehl Co. GmbH & name changed to Possehl Electronic Nederland BV

Meco Metal Finishing Engineers — name changed to Possehl Electronic Nederland bv

Medalist Industries — acquired & absorbed by Illinois Tool Works Inc.

Medallion Group, Inc. — name changed to Health-Chem Corp.

Medchem Products Inc. — acquired by C.R. Bard, Inc.

Medco Jewelry Corp. — name changed to Medco Corp.

Medenco, Inc. — name changed to Lifemark Corp.

Medfield Corp. — acquired by National Medical Enterprises, Inc.

Medford Corp. — acquired by The Amalgamated Sugar Co.

Media America Corp. — name changed to MAC America Communications, Inc.

Medical Imaging Centers of America, Inc. — out of business

Medicine Shoppe International, Inc. — acquired by Cardinal Health, Inc.

Medrad, Inc. — acquired by Schering AG

Medusa Corporation — acquired by Crane Company

Meehan Tooker — out of business

Meiji Mutual Life Insurance Company — name changed to Meiji Life Insurance Company

Mellon National Corp. — name changed to Mellon Bank

Corporation

Melville Corporation — out of business

Melville Shoe Corp. — name changed to Melville Corp.

Members Only By Europe Craft — acquired by Aris Industries, Inc.

Memorex Corp. — acquired by Burroughs Corp.

Menasco Mfg. Co. — acquired by Colt Industries, Inc.

The Mennen Company — acquired by Colgate-Palmolive Company

Mental Health Management, Inc. — name changed to MHM Services

Mentholatum Co. — acquired by Rhoto Pharmaceutical Co.

Mercantile National Bank — name changed to Mercantile Texas Corp.

Mercantile Texas Corp. — merged with Southwest Bancshares, Inc. to form MCorp

Merchants, Inc. — acquired by Meridian Express, Inc.

Merchants National Corporation — acquired by and merged into National City Corporation

Merchants Truck Line, Inc. — company closed

Mercury Savings & Loan Associations — now Mercury Savings & Loan RTC

Mercury Stainless Corp. — acquired by Lukins, Inc. & name changed to Washington Specialty Metals

Meridian Bancorp, Inc. — acquired & absorbed by Core States Financial Corp.

Meridian Express Co. — liquidated

Merry-Go-Round Enterprises, Inc. — out of business

Mesa Limited Partenership — name changed to Mesa Inc.

Mesa Petroleum Co. — name changed to Mesa Limited Partnership

Mesta Machine Co. — acquired by Park Corporation

Metal Lubricants Company — now Fuchs Corporation

Metal Resources Corporation — name changed to Orexana Corporation

Metalbanc Corporation — name changed to Carom Capitol Corporation

Metalcenter, Inc. — acquired by Reliance Steel & Aluminum Co.

Metex Corporation — sub. of United Capital Corporation

Metlox Potteries — out of business

Metpath Inc. — acquired by Corning Glass Works

Metrocare, Inc. — acquired by Merit Care, Inc. & name changed to Merit Care California

Metro Mobile CTS, Inc. — acquired by Bell Atlantic Corporation

Metropolitan Circuits, Inc. — out of business

Metropolitan Consolidated Industries, Inc. — name changed to United Capital Corporation

Metropolitan Greetings, Inc. — name changed to Metropolitan Consolidated Industries, Inc.

Meyers & Co. Inc. — now Alco Health Services Corporation Tiffin Division

Michigan Energy Resources Company — acquired by Utilicorp United Inc. & name changed to Michigan

Gas Utilities

Michigan Gas Utilities Co. — name changed to Michigan Energy Resource Co.

Michigan National Corporation — acquired by National Australia Bank Limited

Michigan Seamless Tube Co. — name changed to Quanex Corp.

Michigan Sugar Co. — acquired by Savannah Foods & Industries, Inc.

Microamerica, Inc. — acquired by Merisel, Inc.

Microband Companies, Inc. — name changed to New York Choice

Microdot, Inc. — liquidated

Microdynamics, Inc. — acquired by Gerber Scientific Inc. & name changed to Gerber Garmet Technology, Inc.

Microfleet Company, Inc. — acquired by Valmont Industries, Inc.

Microform Data Systems, Inc. — name changed to Icot Corp.

Micropump Corporation — acquired by IDEX Corporation

Microwave Associates, Inc. — name changed to M/A-Com, Inc.

Micrcwave Networks Incorporated — acquired by California Microwave, Inc.

Microwave Products of America, Inc. — now Menumaster, Inc. — sub. of Litton Industries, Inc.

Mid-America Industries, Inc. — acquired by CKN PLC, unit of Parts Industries Corporation

Mid Continent Telephone Corp. — merged with Allied Telephone Co. to form Alltel Corp.

Mid-States Petroleum Inc. — out of business

Mid-West Automation Systems, Inc. — acquired by DT Industries Inc.

MidAmerican Energy Company — name changed to MidAmerican Energy Holdings

Midcoast Industrial Services Corporation — name changed to D.C. Taylor Co.

Midcon Corp. — acquired by Occidental Petroleum Corp.

Midcon Industries, Inc. — acquired & absorbed by GIT Industries, Inc.

Middle South Utilities, Inc. — now Entergy Corporation

Middlesex/Patriot General Insurance Company — acquired by Sentry Insurance & name changed to Middlesex Insurance

Midland Color Company — sub. of Sakata Inx Corporation

Midland Cooperatives, Inc. — acquired by & merged into Land O'Lakes, Inc.

Midland Glass Co., Inc. — acquired by Anchor Glass Container Corp.

Midland Mortgage Investors — name changed to Centennial Group, Inc.

Midland Resources, Inc. — name changed to American Midland Corp.

Midlantic Banks, Inc. — merged with Continental Bancorp

Inc. to form Midlantic Corporation

Midlantic Corporation—acquired & absorbed by PNC Bank Corp.

Midwesco Inc.—name changed to MFRI Inc.

Midwest Financial Group, Inc.—acquired by First of America Bank Corporation

Midwest Rubber Reclaiming Co.—acquired by Midcon Industries, Inc.

Midwestern Distribution, Inc.—acquired by Leaseway Transportation Corp.

The Mil Group—name changed to Davie Industries Inc.

Miles Laboratories, Inc.—name changed to Miles, Inc.

Milgo Electronic Corp.—name changed to Racal Milgo, Inc.

Milgray Electronics, Inc.—acquired by Bell Industries, Inc.

Miller Bros. Industries—acquired by Hat Brands

H. Miller & Sons, Inc.—merged with Lennar Corporation

Millstone Cofee, Inc.—acquired by The Procter & Gamble Company

Milton Bradley Co.—merged with Hasbro Industries, Inc. to form Hasbro Bradley, Inc.

Milton Roy Company—acquired by Sunstrand Corporation

Mindscape Inc.—acquired by Software Toolworks, Inc.

Mini Mart, Inc.—acquired by The Kroger Company

Miniscribe Corporation—acquired by Maxtor Corporation

Minneapolis Star and Tribune Co.—name changed to Cowles Media Corp.

Minnesota Fabrics, Inc.—acquired by Hancock Textile Co., sub. of Lucky Stores, Inc.

Minnesota Gas Co.—name changed to Diversified Energies, Inc.

Minnetonka Corporation—now FMG Tsumura, sub. of Tsumura Co.

Mintex Don Limited—acquired by BBA Group plc & name changed to BBA Friction Ltd.

Mirro Corp.—acquired by Newell Companies, Inc.

Mirror Group Newspapers plc—name changed to Mirror Group plc

Mission Equities Corp.—name changed to Mission Insurance Group, Inc.

Mission Investment Trust—name changed to Mission West Properties

Mississippi River Corp.—name changed to Missouri Pacific Corp.

Missouri Pacific Corp.—merged with Union Pacific Railroad & part of Union Pacific Systems

Missouri Portland Cement Co.—acquired by H.K. Porter Co., Inc.

Mitchell International—acquired by International Thomson Inc.

Mitchum Jones & Templeton—holding co. formed, Mitchum Management Corp.

Mitchum Management Corp.—liquidated Dec. 15, 1986

Mite Corporation—acquired by Emhart Corporation

Mitek Inc.—acquired by Bowater Plc

The Mitsubishi Bank Limited—merged with The Bank of Tokyo, Ltd. to form The Bank of Tokyo-Mitsubishi, Ltd.

Mitsubishi Mining & Cement Corporation—out of business

Mitsubishi Petrochemical Co. Ltd.—merged with Mitsubishi Kasei Corp. & name changed Mitsubishi Chemical Corporation

Mitsumi Co., Ltd.—name changed to Mitsumi Electric Co., Ltd.

Mobil Oil Corp.—name changed to Mobil Corp.

Mobile Home Industries, Inc.—name changed to MHI Group, Inc.

Mobilemedia Corporation—name changed to Mobilcomm

Modern Diversified Industries, Inc.—merged with Jemison, Inc.

Modern Maid Food Products, Inc.—acquired by Dalgety, Inc.

Modern Merchandising, Inc.—acquired by Best Products Co., Inc.

Modular Ambulance Corp.—acquired by Amtech Group Ltd.

Modular Computer Systems, Inc.—acquired by AEG Aktiengesellschaft

Moen Incorporated—acquired by American Brands Corporation

The Mogul Corp.—acquired by The Dexter Corporation

Mohawk Data Science Corp.—name changed to Qantel Corporation

Molkerei Zentrale Sued GmbH & Co. KG—name changed to Bayernland GmbH & Co. KG

Molycorp, Inc.—acquired by Union Oil Co. of California

Monarch Import Co. Inc.—acquired by Canandaigua Wine Company, Inc.

Monarch Industries, Inc.—now Coppes-Nappanee Co.

Monarch Marking Systems, Inc.—acquired by PAXAR Corporation

Money Management Corp.—merged into Banc One Corporation

Monfort of Colorado, Inc.—acquired by ConAgra, Inc.

A.C. Monk Co., Inc.—merged with DIMON International, Inc.

Monogram Industries, Inc.—acquired by The Nortek, Inc.

B.L. Montague Co.—company closed

Montana Dakota Utilities Co.—holding co. formed, MDU Resources Group, Inc.

Monterey's Tex Mex Cafe—acquired by Monterey's Acquisition Corp.

Montgomery Elevator Company—acquired by Kone Corporation & name changed to Montgomery Kone Inc.

Monumental Corporation—now AUSA Holding Com-

pany, a direct sub. of Aegnon USA

Monroe Auto Equipment Co.—acquired by Tenneco, Inc.

Monte Dei Paschi Di Siena—name changed to Banca Monte Dei Paschi Di Siena

Moorco International Inc.—acquired & absorbed by FMC Corporation

Moore Financial Group, Inc.—now West One Bancorp

Moore McCormack Resources, Inc.—acquired by Southdown, Inc.

Samuel Moore & Co.—acquired by Eaton Corp.

Morgan Industries Inc.—name changed to AAMCO Transmissions Inc.

Morgan Worcester—name changed to Morgan Construction Co.

Morgan's Restaurants, Inc.—name changed to MorTronics, Inc.

Morris County Savings Bank—acquired by First Fidelity Bancorporation & name changed to Morris Savings Bank

T.J. Morris Company, Inc.—acquired by Nash Finch Company

Morse Electro Products Corp.—acquired by Pilot Audio Systems, Inc.

Morse Operations Inc.—name changed to Ed Morse Automotive Agency

Mortgage Trust of America—name changed to Transamerica Realty Investors

Morton Norwich Products, Inc.—merged with Thiokol Corp. to form Morton Thiokol, Inc.

Morton Thiokol Inc.—split into two companies, Morton International Inc. and Thiokol Corporation

Morton's Shoe Stores, Inc.—name changed to Morton Shoe Companies, Inc.

Mortronics, Inc.—name changed to Morgan's Foods, Inc.

The Moseley Holding Corporation—no longer in business

Motch & Merryweather Machinery Co.—name changed to Oerlikon Motch Corp.

Motor Wheel Corporation—acquired & absorbed by Hayes Wheels International, Inc.

Motter Printing Press Co.—now KBA-Motter Corporation

Mountain Fuel Supply Co.—holding co. formed, Questar Corporation

Movie Star, Inc.—acquired by Sandmark Stardust Inc.

Movielab Inc.—out of business

Moxa Energy Corp.—liquidated

Moxie Industries, Inc.—acquired by ICN Pharmaceuticals, Inc.

Moyer Products, Inc.—out of business

Mrs. Paul's Kitchens, Inc.—acquired by Campbell Soup Co.

Mrs. Smith's Pie Co.—acquired by Kellogg Co.

Muelhens Inc.—company closed

Mueller Holdings Corp.—acquired by Tyco Laboratories

Mulach Parking Structures Corp.—name changed to

MPS Corporation

Multi-Amp Corp.—acquired by Indian Head, Inc.

Multibank Financial Corp.—absorbed by Bank of Boston Corporation

Multimedia, Inc.—acquired & absorbed by Gannet Company, Inc.

Munsingwear, Inc.—name changed to PremiumWear, Inc.

G. C. Murphy Co.—acquired by AKD, Inc., sub. of Ames Department Stores, Inc.

Murphy Industries, Inc.—acquired by Electro-Wire Products, Inc.

Muse Air Corp.—acquired by Southwest Airlines Co. & name changed to TranStar Airlines Corp.

Mutual Assurance, Inc.—name changed to MAIC Holdings

The Myers Group—name changed to F.W. Myers & Co. Inc.

N

NBD Bancorp, Inc.—merged with First Chicago Corporation to form First Chicago NBD Corporation

NBO Stores Inc.—absorbed by Gerald Group

NCA Corporation—acquired by & merged into ASK Computer Systems, Inc.

NCD Financial, Inc.—liquidated

NCNB Corporation—merged with C & S/Sovran, name changed to NationsBank Corporation

NCR Corporation—now wholly-owned sub. of American Telephone & Telegraph Co. (AT&T)

NHD Stores, Inc.—acquired by Aco, Inc. & name changed to NHD Hardware

NI Industries—acquired by Masco Corp. & Masco Industries, Inc.

NLT Corp.—acquired by American General Corp. & name changed to National Life & Accident Insurance Co.

NMC of North America, Inc—name changed to Nomeco, Inc.

NN Corp.—acquired by Armco, Inc. & name changed to Armco Tubular Div.

NUS Corp.—acquired by Halliburton Company

NVF Corp.—acquired by DWG Corp.

NWA Inc.—acquired by Wings Holdings Inc.

Nabisco Brands, Inc.—acquired by R.J. Reynolds Industries, Inc.

NACOLAH Holding Corp. Inc.—acquired by Sammons Enterprises, Inc.

Nacoma Consolidated, Inc.—name changed to Nacoma Products, Inc.

Nadel Partnership, Inc.—name changed to Nadel Architects, Inc. Name Sales One, Inc.—name changed to Persingers, Inc.

Napco Industries, Inc.—now Napco International & Mass Merchandisers, Inc.

Napco International, Inc.—holding co. formed, Venturian Corp.

Narco Scientific Inc.—acquired by & merged into Healthdyne, Inc.

The Narda Microwave Corp.—acquired by Loral Corp.

Natco Industries Inc.—now Retail Ventures, Inc.

National Airlines, Inc.—acquired by & merged with Pan American World Airways

National Association of Blue Shield Plans—name changed to Blue Shield Association

National Aviation & Technology Corporation—merged with National Telecommunications Technology Fund to form AFA Funds Inc.

National Aviation Corp.—name changed to National Aviation & Technology Corp.

National Bedding & Furniture Industries—acquired by & name changed to National Bedding Co.

National Brewing Co.—acquired by Carling O'Keefe Ltd.

National By-Products, Inc.—acquired by The Federal Co.

National CSS, Inc.—acquired by Dun & Bradstreet Corp.

National Can Corp.—acquired by Triangle Industries, Inc.

National Car Rental System, Inc.—acquired by Republic Industries, Inc.

National Central Financial Corp.—merged with Philadelphia National Corp. to form CoreStates Financial Corp.

National Chemsearch Corp.—name changed to NCH Corp.

National Convenience Stores Incorporated—acquired by Diamond Shamrock, Inc.

National Detroit Corp.—name changed to NBD Bancorp, Inc.

National Distillers & Chemical Corp.—now Quantum Chemical Corp.

National Emergeny Services, Inc.—name changed to NES Holdings, Inc.

The National Guardian Corporation—now wholly-owned sub. of LEP Group Plc

National Gypsum Co.—acquired by Anacor Holdings, Inc.

National Health Enterprises, Inc.—acquired by National Medical Enterprises Inc. & merged into Hillhaven Corp.

National Health Laboratories Holdings—merged with Roche Biomedical Laboratories, Inc. to form Laboratory Corp. of America

National Home Corp.—name changed to National Enterprises, Inc.

National Industries, Inc.—acquired by Fuqua Industries

National Kenny Corp.—name changed to Aancor Holdings, Inc.

National Liberty Corp.—acquired by Capital Holding Corp.

National Life of Florida Corp.—name changed to Voy-

ager Group, Inc.

National Live Stock & Meat Board—name changed to National Cattlemen's Beef Association

National Marine Service, Inc.—acquired by Nicor, Inc.

National Medical Care, Inc.—acquired by W.R. Grace

National Merchandise Co., Inc.—out of business

National Mortgage Company—acquired by Boatmen's Bancshares, Inc. & name changed to Boatmen's National Mortgage Inc.

National Mutual Life Association of Australia—acquired by National Mutual Holdings Limited

National Property Analysts, Inc.—name changed to EBL & S Management

National Shoes, Inc.—out of business

National Silver Industries, Inc.—acquired by Towle Mfg. Co.

National Steel Corp.—name changed to National Intergroup, Inc.

National Systems Corp.—name changed to National Education Corp.

National Tea Co.—sub. of George Weston Ltd.

National Union Electric Corp.—acquired by Dometic Inc.

National Utilities & Industries Corp.—name changed to NUI Corp.

Nationwide Cellular Service, Inc.—acquired by MCI Communications Corp. & name changed to MCI Wireless Inc.

Nationwide Corp.—acquired by Nationwide Mutual Insurance Co.

Nationwide Homes, Inc.—acquired by Insilco Corp.

Nationwide Mutual Insurance Company—name changed to Nationwide Insurance Enterprise

Nationwise Automotive, Inc.—out of business

Natomas Co.—acquired by Diamond Shamrock Corp.

Navajo Forest Products Industries—out of business

Neeco, Inc.—now Neeco JWP I/S—acquired by & merged with JWP Inc.

Needham Harper Worldwide—merged with Doyle Dane Bernback and BBDO International to form Omnicom Group, Inc.

Neer Manufacturing Company Inc—acquired by General Signal Corp.

Neisner Brothers, Inc.—acquired by & merged into Ames Dept. Stores, Inc.

Neptune International Corp.—acquired by Wheelabrator-Frye Co.

NESLAB Instruments, Inc.—acquired by Life Sciences International Plc

The Nestle Co., Inc.—sub. of Nestle Holdings, Inc.

Nestle-Lemur Co.—acquired by Kleer-Vu Industries, Inc.

Neumon—out of business

Nevada Savings & Loan Association—acquired by Southwest Gas Corporation

New Axia Holding Corp.—name changed to Axia Incorporated

New Century Entertainment Corp.—now New Visions

Entertainment Corporation

New Dartmouth Bank—Acquired by Shawmut National Corporation & name changed to Shawmut National

New Dimensions in Education Inc.—now a division of Abrams Publishing Inc.

The New England—acquired by Metropolitan Life Insurance Co.

New England Corporation—out of business

New England Gas & Electric Assn.—name changed to Commonwealth Energy System

New England Merchants Co., Inc.—name changed to Bank of New England Corp.

New England Nuclear Corp.—acquired by E.I. DuPont de Nemours & Co., Inc.

New Hampshire Oak—name changed to The General Chemical Group, Inc.

New Idria, Inc.—acquired by Buckhorn, Inc.

New Jersey Natural Gas Co.—name changed to New Jersey Resources Corp.

New London plc—name changed to International Tool & Supply, PLC

New Penn Motor Express, Inc.—name changed to Arnold Industries

New Process Company—now Blair Corp.

New Production Machinery—acquired by FKI plc & name changed to FATA Production Machinery

New Texas Tumbleweed—out of business

New York Carpet World—acquired by Shaw Industries, Inc.

Newbery Energy Corp.—name changed to Newbery Corporation

Newbery Corporation—out of business

Newbury Industries—acquired & absorbed by Mannesmann A.G.

Newcorp, Inc.—merged into Pier 1 Imports, Inc.

Newflo Corporation—acquired by Precision Castparts Corp. & name changed to PCC Flow Technologies, Inc.

Newport Pharmaceuticals International, Inc.—name changed to Systemed, Inc.

Next Software Inc.—acquired & absorbed by Apple Computer Inc.

Niagra Envelope Company, Inc.—acquired & absorbed by American Pad and Paper

Niagara Frontier Services, Inc.—name changed to Tops Markets, Inc.

Nibble With Gibble's, Inc.—acquired by Consolidated Bisquit Co.

Nidec Corporation—acquired by Nippon Densan (NIDEC)

A.C. Nielsen Co.—acquired by The Dun & Bradstreet Corporation

The Nikkel Corporation—out of business

Nobel Industries Sweden AB—acquired by Akzo Nobel N.V. & name changed to Akzo Nobel AB

Nobelpharma AB—name changed to Nobel Biocare

Nolan Helmets S.p.A.—name changed to Opticos S.r.l.

Noland Paper Company—acquired by Spicers Paper Limited

Nolex Corp.—acquired by James Hardie Industries, U.S.A.

Norcliff-Thayer—now Beecham Consumer Products

Norcross Footwear, Inc.—out of business

Norfolk & Western Railway Co.—merged into Southern Railway to form Norfolk Southern Corp.

Norin Corp.—acquired by Canadian Pacific Ltd.

Norlin Corp.—name changed to Service Resources Corp.

Norris NI Industries, Inc.—name changed to NI Industries, Inc.

Norsk Data A/S—out of business

Norstar Bancorp—merged with Fleet Financial Group, Inc. to form Fleet/Norstar Financial Group, Inc.

North American Bancorp, Inc.—acquired by The Bank of New York

North American Biologicals, Inc.—name changed to NABI

The North American Coal Corp.—holding co. formed, NACCO Industries, Inc.

North American Development Corp.—name changed to Scotts Seaboard Corp.

North American Mortgage Investors—acquired by Southmark Corp.

North American National Corporation—acquired & absorbed by Pierce National Life Insurance Co.

The North American National Group—acquired & absorbed by Liberty Corporation

North Central Airlines, Inc.—merged into Southern Airways, Inc. & name changed to Republic Airlines, Inc.

North of New England Building Society—acquired & absorbed into Northern Rock Building Society

North-West Telecommunications, Inc.—acquired by PacificCorp

Northeast Federal Corp.—acquired & absorbed by Shawmut National Corporation

Northeast Utilities Service Co.—name changed to Northeast Utilities

Northern Air Freight, Inc.—now Danzas Northern, sub. of Danzas AG

Northern & Central Gas Corp.—acquired by Norcen Energy Resources Ltd.

Northern Drug Company—acquired by D & K Wholesale Drug, Inc.

Northern Illinois Gas Co.—name changed to Nicor, Inc.

Northern Indiana Public Service Co.—holding co, formed, NIPSCO Industries, Inc.

Northern National Corp.—acquired by & merged into Nicor, Inc.

Northern Natural Gas Co.—name changed to InterNorth, Inc.

Northern Processors, Inc.—name changed to AKF Foods

Northgate Computers, Inc.—out of business

Northwest Airlines, Inc.—holding co. formed, NWA, Inc.

Northwest Bancorp—holding co. formed, Norwest Corp.

Northwest Industries, Inc.—acquired by Farley Industries & name changed to Farley/Northwest Industries, Inc.

Northwestern Mutual Life Mortgage & Realty Investors—acquired by & merged into Northwestern Mutual Life Insurance Co.

Northwestern National Life Insurance Co.—holding co. formed, The NWNL Companies, Inc.

Norton Company—acquired by Saint Gobain

Norton Christensen, Inc.—acquired by Baker Hughes Incorporated

Norton Simon, Inc.—acquired by Esmark, Inc.

Norweco, Inc.—name changed to Oxarc, Inc.

Nova Pharmaceutical Corporation—merged with Scios Inc. to form Scios Nova

Novera Group—out of business

Noxell Corporation—acquired by The Procter & Gamble Company

Nu-West Arizona, Inc.—name changed to Nu-West, Inc.

Nu-West Development Corp. of Arizona—name changed to Nu-West Arizona, Inc.

Nuclear Data, Inc.—now Metropolitan Circuits, Inc.

Nuclear Medical Systems, Inc.—name changed to NMS Pharmaceuticals, Inc.

Nuclear Services Corp.—name changed to Quadrex Corp.

Numac Oil & Gas Ltd.—name changed to Numac Energy Inc.

Numerex Corporation—acquired by Carl Zeiss, Inc.

Nuovo Banco Ambrosiano-Veneto—name changed to Banco Ambrosiano-Veneto

Nutri/System Inc.—acquired by Heico Inc.

Nuttall Equipment Co., Inc.—out of business

Nycomed ASA ADS—name changed to Hafslund Nycomed

Nycor, Inc.—acquired by & absorbed into Fedders Corp.

Nytronics, Inc.—acquired by Bastian Industries, Inc.

O

O&K Orenstein & Koppel—acquired by Fried. Krupp GmbH

OBH Co.—name changed to O.B. Holding

ODI—name changed to Organizational Dynamics Inc.

OK Petroleum AB—name changed to Preem Petroleum AB

OPT Industries, Inc.—acquired by Torotel Products, Inc.

Oakbrook Consolidated, Inc.—name changed to Szabo Food Service

Oakite Products, Inc.—acquired by Chemetall, a subsidiary of Metallgesellschaft AG

O'Brien Energy Systems Inc.—acquired & absorbed by Northern States Power Company

O'Brien Machinery Company—out of business

The Observer Ltd.—name changed to Guardian & Observer

Oce-Printing Systems—name changed to Oce-van de Grinten N.V.

Occupational-Urgent Care Health Systems (OUCH)—acquired by Healthcare Compare Corp.

Office Connection, Inc.—acquired by U.S. Office Products Company

Ogden Publishing Corporation—name changed to Standard Examiner

Ogilvy & Mather International, Inc.—holding co. formed, The Ogilvy Group, Inc.

The Ohio Brass Co.—acquired by Harvey Hubbell Inc.

Ohio Ferro-Alloy Corp.—now Simetco, Inc.

The Ohio Mattress Company—name changed to Sealy Corporation

Ohio-Sealy Mattress Mfg. Co.—name changed to The Ohio Mattress Company

Oil & Gas Supply Company—acquired by Global Compressing Services

Oji Paper Company Ltd.—name changed to New Oji Paper Co., Ltd.

Oklahoma Gas & Electric Company—name changed to OGE Energy Corp.

Oklahoma Natural Gas Co.—name changed to Oneok, Inc.

Old Navy Stores—acquired by The Gap, Inc.

Old Quaker Paint Co.—merged into The Sherwin Williams Company

Olga Co.—acquired by Warnaco, Inc.

Olinkraft, Inc.—acquired by Johns-Manville Corp.

Olla Industries, Inc.—out of business

Olympia Brewing Co.—acquired by & merged into Pabst Brewing Co.

Olympia Broadcasting Corp.—out of business

Omark Industries, Inc.—acquired by Blount, Inc.

OMNI Flight Helicopters, Inc.—name changed to Omniflight, Inc.

Omni Spectra, Inc.—acquired by M/A Com, Inc.

Omron Business Systems, Inc.—holding co. formed, Omron E.E.T. Systems Inc.

On-Line Software International—acquired by & merged into Computer Associates International, Inc.

On-Line Systems, Inc.—acquired by United Telecommunications, Inc.

One Stop Supply—out of business

Opelika Manufacturing Corp.—out of business

Optel Corp.—name changed to Moore Medical Corp.

Optiworld—folded into Lenscrafters

Opto Mechanik, Inc.—out of business

Opto Mechanik, Inc.—acquired by Diagnostics/Retrieval Systems, Inc. and name changed to DRS OMI Corp

Orbanco Financial Services Corporation—now Security Pacific Oregon, Inc., sub. of Security Pacific Corp.

Orbanco, Inc.—name changed to Orbanco Financial

Services, Inc.

Orchard Supply Hardware—acquired by Sears, Roebuck and Co.

Oregon Portland Cement Co.—acquired by Ash Grove Cement, Inc.

Orion Pictures Corporation—merged with The Actava Group, Inc. to form Metromedia International Group

The Ormond Shops, Inc.—company closed

ORNDA HealthCorp—acquired by Tenet Healthcare Corporation & name changed to Tenet Healthcare Corporation-Nashville Office

Orrox Corporation—acquired by CMX Corporation

Oscar Mayer & Co., Inc.—acquired by General Foods Corp.

Otis Elevator Co.—acquired by United Technologies Corp.

O'Tooles Group, Inc.—out of business

Ottenheimer & Company—acquired by Dowling Textile Manufacturing Co. & name changed to Whiteswan/Meta

Ouachita Coca-Cola Bottling Company—acquired by Coca-Cola Enterprises Inc.

Ourso Investment Corporation—out of business

Outdoor Sports Industries, Inc.—acquired by Brown Group, Inc.

Outlet Communications, Inc.—acquired by General Electric Company

Overhead Door Corporation—now sub. of DCO Holdings Corp. c/o Bessemer Capital Partners Ltd.

Overnight Transportation Co.—acquired by Union Pacific Corp.

Overseas Partners, Inc.—out of business

Overseas Securities Co., Inc.—name changed to Interwest Corp.

Owen Steel Co., Inc.—acquired by Commercial Metals Company

Owens-Illinois, Inc.—wholly-owned sub. of Kohlberg Kravis Roberts & Co.

Owens, Minor & Bodeker, Inc.—name changed to Owens & Minor, Inc.

Oxford First Corporation—company dissolved

Oxford Pendaflex Corp.—name changed to Esselte Pendaflex Corp.

Oxoco, Inc.—now American National Petroleum Co., 64%-owned by Ironstone Group

Ozark Holdings, Inc.—acquired by & merged with Trans World Airlines, Inc.

Ozite Corporation—out of business

P

P&C Food Markets, Inc.—now sub. of The Penn Traffic Company

PBA, Inc.—name changed to Profit Systems, Inc.

PBM Office Products—acquired by Boise Cascade Corporation & name changed to Boise Cascade Office Products

PC Distributing Inc.—out of business

PLM Companies, Inc.—name changed to Transcisco Industries, Inc.

P M Company—acquired by Bemis Company, Inc. & name changed to Perfecseal Company

PPA Industries, Inc.—name changed to Premier Metal Products Co.

PSA, Inc.—now PS Group, Inc.

PTT Suises—name changed to Swiss Telecom PTT

PVO International, Inc.—acquired by Kay Corp.

Pace Foods—acquired by Campbell Soup Company

Pace Industries, Inc.—acquired by Leggett & Platt, Incorporated

Pacesetter Financial Corp.—acquired by Old Kent Financial Corp.

Pacific Express Holding, Inc.—liquidated

Pacific Gamble Robinson Co.—acquired by Miller-Cascade, Inc., sub. of Stevedoring Services Group, Inc.

Pacific Gamble Robinson Co.—now Food Services of America

Pacific Hawaiian Ltd.—merged into Sure Save Super market Ltd.

Pacific Lighting Corp.—now Pacific Enterprises

The Pacific Lumber Co.—acquired by Maxxam Group Inc.

Pacific Power & Light Co.—name changed to Pacificorp

Pacific Resources—acquired by Broken Hill Proprietary Co.

Pacific Scene, Inc.—name changed to Monticello Management Co.

Pacific Sound Resources—name changed to PSR

Pacific Wood Treating Corporation—out of business

Packaging Products & Design—acquired by Brawney Plastics, Inc. & name changed to Brawney Plastics West

Paco Pharmaceutical Services, Inc.—acquired by The West Company Incorporated

Paco Pharmaceutical Services, Inc.—wholly-owned sub. of R.P. Scherer Corporation

Pacwest Bancorp—now Key Bank of Oregon of Key Corp.

Page Boy Company, Inc.—out of business

Pain Jacquet Biscottes S.A.—name changed to Pain Jacquet S.A.

Pak-Well Corp.—acquired by Great Northern Nekoosa Corp.

Pako Corporation—out of business

Palm Beach Holdings, Inc.—acquired by Crystal Brands, Inc.

Palmetto Spinning Corp.—acquired by Martin Color-Fi

Palomar Financial Corp.—acquired by & merged into T & N Holdings

Pan American Banks Inc.—acquired by & merged into MCMB Corporation

Pan American Trade Development Corp.—liquidated

Pan Ocean Oil Corp. — acquired by Marathon Oil Co.

Panax Trading Co. — out of business

Pandel-Bradford, Inc. — acquired by Compo Industries, Inc.

Pandick Inc. — out of business, most assets sold to R.R. Donnelly Corp.

Pandora Industries, Inc. — out of business

Panhandle Eastern Corporation — name changed to PanEnergy Corporation

Panhandle Eastern Pipe Line Co. — name changed to Panhandle Eastern Corp.

Panorama Press, Inc. — out of business

Pansophic Systems, Incorporated — acquired by and merged into Computer Associates International, Inc.

Pantasote Wallcovering — out of business

Pantry Pride, Inc. — acquired by McAndrews & Forbes, Inc.

Papetti Hygrade Egg Products — acquired by Michael Foods, Inc.

Paradata Computer Networks Inc. — acquired by World Acceptance Corp.

Paradyne Corporation — acquired by American Telephone & Telegraph Company

Paragon Group, Inc. — name changed to Property Services

Paramount Foods LLC — out of business

Paramount Packaging Corp. — assests aquired by Bemis Company, Inc.

Parisi Inc. — merged with Bankcrafters to form Parisi/Royal Inc.

Parisian, Inc. — acquired by Proffitt's, Inc.

Park Chemical Co. — acquired by Whittaker Corp.

Park Communications, Inc. — acquired & absorbed by Media General, Inc.

Parkmount Hospitality Corp. — wholly-owned sub. of Ramada, Inc.

Parodi Cigar Corp. — name changed to Parodi Industries, Inc.

The Ralph M. Parsons Co. — name changed to The Parsons Corp.

Patrick Petroleum Company — acquired by Goodrich Petroleum Corporation & name changed to Patrick Exploration

Patterson Industries, Inc. — liquidated

Patton Oil Co. — acquired by Great Eastern Energy & Development Corp.

Pauley Petroleum, Inc. — now Hondo Oil & Gas Company

Pavey Envelope & Tag Corp. — acquired by Mail-Well Inc.

Pawnee Industries, Inc. — out of business

The Paxall Group, Inc. — acquired by Sasib S.p.A.

Frank Paxton Company — now sub. of Jeld-Wen, Inc.

Pay-Fone Systems, Inc. — acquired by Paychex, Inc.

Pay Less Drug Stores Northwest, Inc. — acquired by Kmart Corporation

Pay 'N Pak Stores, Inc. — out of business

Pay N Save Corp. — acquired by The Trump Group

Payless Cashways, Inc. — leveraged buyout

Paysaver Catalog Showrooms, Inc. — out of business

Peabody Galion Corp. — name changed to Peabody International Corp.

Peabody International Corp. — acquired by & merged into The Pullman-Peabody Co.

Peachtree Doors, Inc. — acquired by Indal Ltd.

Pearce, Urstadt, Mayer & Greer, Inc. — now Pearce, Mayer & Greer Realty

Pearle Health Services, Inc. — acquired by GrandMet USA, Inc.

Peavey Co. — acquired by ConAgra, Inc.

Pebble Beach Corp. — acquired by Twentieth Century-Fox Film Corp.

Pegasus International Corporation — acquired by Asian & American Assets Management Corporation

Pelouze Scale Co. — acquired by Health O Meter, Inc.

Pemcor, Inc. — acquired by Esmark, Inc.

Pen Holdings, Inc. — acquired by Newell Co. & name changed to Sanford Beros Corp.

Pennant Properties PLC — out of business

Penn-Corp. — acquired by Western Publishing Group, Inc.

Penn Dixie Industries, Inc. — name changed to Continental Steel Corp.

Penn Yan Express Inc. — name changed to Con-Way Eastern Express, Inc.

PennCorp Financial, Inc. — acquired by American Can Co.

Pennex Products Co. Inc. — acquired by Rexall Sundown Inc & name changed to Pennex Laboratories Inc.

Pennsylvania Life Co. — name changed to Penncorp Financial, Inc.

Pennsylvania Petroleum Product Company — out of business

Pennsylvania Power & Light Resources, Inc.-name changed to PP&L Resources

Pennwalt Corporation — now Atochem North America, Inc., acquired by Societe Nationale Elf Acquitaine

Pentair Industries, Inc. — name changed to Pentair, Inc.

People Express Airlines, Inc. — acquired by & merged with Continental Airlines Corp., sub. of Texas Air Corp.

Peoples Drug Stores, Inc. — acquired by Imasco USA, Inc.

Peoples Gas Co. — name changed to Peoples Energy Corp.

Pepcom Industries, Inc. — acquired by Suntory International Corp.

Perenchio — name changed to Chartwell Partners

Perfect Fit Industries — acquired by Foamex International Inc.

Perlmutter Printing Company — acquired by St. Ives plc

Pertec Computer Corp.—acquired by Triumph Adler, Inc.

Pet, Inc.—acquired & absorbed by The Pillsbury Company

Peter Paul Cadbury, Inc.—acquired by Cadbury Schweppes U.S.A., Inc.

J.M. Peters Co.—acquired by Capital Pacific Homes

Petersen Howell & Heather, Inc.—name changed to PHH Group, Inc.

Petersville Sleigh Limited—out of business

Petrolane, Inc.—acquired by Texas Eastern Corp.

Petroleum Corp. of America—name changed to Petroleum & Resources Corp.

Pfaudler-U.S., Inc.—acquired by Robbins & Myers, Inc.

Pharmacaps, Inc.—acquired by Sobel USA & name changed to Banner Pharmacaps Inc.

Pharmacy Management Services, Inc.—acquired by Beverly Enterprises, Inc.

Philbro Corp.—name changed to Philbro-Salomon, Inc.

Philadelphia Life Insurance Co.—acquired by Tenneco Inc.

Philadelphia National Corp.—merged with National Central Financial Corp.

Philadelphia Suburban Corp.—name changed to Enterra Corporation

Philips Industries, Inc.—now Tomkins Industries, Inc., sub. of Tomkins PLC

Phillips Screw Co.—acquired by Rule Industries, Inc.

Phoenix Enterprises Inc.—company closed

The Phoenix Resource Companies, Inc.—acquired by Apache Corporation

Phoenix Steel, Inc.—out of business

PhoneMate, Inc.—acquired by Casio Computer Co., Ltd. & name changed to Phone-Mate, Inc.

Photo Maker II, Inc.—name changed to Pinnacle Coating & Converting, Inc.

Photronics Corp.—sub. of Prognostic/Retrieval Systems, Inc.

Physio Technology Inc.—now PTI

Pick Hotels Corp.—name changed to Americana Hotels Corp.

Pickwick International, Inc.—acquired by American Can Co.

Pictou Industries Limited—out of business

Piedmont Aviation, Inc.—sub. of USAir Group, Inc.

S.S. Pierce Co., Inc.—name changed to Seneca Foods Corporation

Pierce Manufacturing, Inc.—acquired by Oshkosh Truck Corporation

Pilkington Australasia Limited—acquired by Pilkington Plc

The Pillsbury Company—acquired by Grand Metropolitan plc

Pilot Audio Systems, Inc.—now div. of Curtis Mathis Corp.

Pine State Creamery Co.—out of business

Pinkerton's, Inc.—acquired by American Brands, Inc.

Pioneer Financial Corporation—acquired & absorbed by Signet Banking Corporation

Pioneer Food Industries, Inc.—acquired by The Pillsbury Co.

Pioneer Industrial Corporation—acquired by Total S.A. & name changed to Mapa Pioneer Corporation

Pioneer Lifeco Inc.—out of business

Pioneer Texas Corp.—acquired by Coit International, Inc.

Piper Industries, Inc.—name changed to P&E, Inc.

Pistol Pete's Pizza—acquired by & absorbed into Peter Piper, Inc.

Pitman Learning, Inc.—name changed to David S. Lake Publishers

Pittsburgh Brewing Company—acquired by Keystone Brewers, Inc.

Pittsburgh-Des Moines Steel Co.—name changed to Pittsburgh-Des Moines Corp.

Pittsburgh Forgings Co.—acquired by Ampco-Pittsburgh Corp.

Pittsburgh National Corp.—merged with Provident National Corp. to form PNC Financial Corp.

Pizza Hut, Inc.—acquired by Pepsico, Inc.

Plains Petroleum Company—acquired & absorbed by Barrett Resources Corporation

Planning Research Corp.—acquired by Emhart Corp.

Plant Industries, Inc.—out of business

Plasticorp, Inc.—now Plastic Suppliers, Inc.

Playtex Inc.—split into two companies, FP Group Incorporated and Playtex Apparel Partners L.P.

Plaza Home Mortgage—out of business

Plessey North America Corp.—acquired by General Electric Corporation plc

Pleuss-Staufer (North American), Inc.—name changed to Pleuss-Staufer Industries, Inc.

Plus Marketing—name changed to Karp's Plus

Plywood Panels, Inc.—company dissolved

Pneumo Abex Holdings Co.—Pneumo Abex Corporation acquired by The Henley Group, Inc.

Pneumo Corp.—acquired by IC Industries, Inc.

Po Folks, Inc.—out of business

Polar Corporation—name changed to Polar Beverages

Polarad Corp.—name changed to Rohde & Schwarz-Polarad, Inc.

Poliet—acquired by Saint-Gobain

Polive/Tricosteril—now a joint venture of Johnson & Johnson & James River Corporation

Poloron Products, Inc.—now sub. of Centuri

Polychrome Corp.—sub. of DaiNippon Ink & Chemicals Americas, Inc.

Polymer Development Laboratories—acquired by Urethane Technologies, Inc.

Ponderosa, Inc.—wholly-owned sub. of Metromedia Co.

Ponderosa Systems, Inc.—name changed to Ponderosa, Inc.

Pony Industries, Inc.—sold to Baker Hughes Inc.

Pony Sports & Leisure Inc.—acquired by Pentland Group Plc & name changed to Pony U.S.A.

Porex Technologies Corp.—now Medco Entertainment Services, Inc.

Portage Industries Corporation—acquired by Spartech Corporation & name changed to Spartech Plastics

Portland General Electric Co.—holding co. formed, Portland General Corporation

Posi-Seal International, Inc.—acquired by Fisher Controls International, sub. of Monsanto Company

Post Corp.—name changed to Gillet Group, Inc.

Postal Instant Press—now PIP Printing, which was acquired by Kane-Miller Corp.

Potato Sales Company, Inc.—out of business

Pott Industries, Inc.—acquired by Houston Natural Gas Corp.

Potter Instrument Co., Inc.—liquidated

Potter Luke Dodge Inc.—name changed to Dodge of Winter Park

Power Engineering Co. Inc.—out of business

Power King Products Co.—name changed to HCC Inc.

Power Test Corp.—name changed to Getty Petroleum Corp.

Powerline Oil Company Holdings—acquired by Castle Energy Corp.

Powers Regulator Co.—acquired by Mark Controls Corp.

Prairie Producing Co.—acquired by Placer Development Limited

H.C. Prange Company—name changed to American Specialty Corp.

Prange Way—out of business

Henry Pratt Co.—acquired by Amsted Industries, Inc.

Praxis International Inc.—name changed to Computer Corporation of America

Precision Aerotech, Inc.—acquired & absorbed by Vernitron Corporation

Precision Echo, Inc.—acquired by Diagnostic/Retreival Systems

Precisionaire, Inc.—acquired by Flanders Corp.

Precious Metal Holdings, Inc.—name changed to Keystone Precious Metals Holding, Inc.

Precision Technologies—out of business

Prel Corp.—name changed to Landall Corporation

Premier Bancorp, Inc.—acquired by Banc One Corporation

Premiere Industrial Corporation—acquired by Premier Farnell plc & name changed to Premiere Farnell

Prentice-Hall, Inc.—acquired by Gulf + Western Industries, Inc.

Preservative Paint Company—acquired by Kelley-Moore Paint Co.

Presidio Oil Company—acquired by Tom Brown, Inc. & name changed to Tom Brown, Inc.

The Presley Companies—acquired by Pacific Lighting Corporation

Presro Lock, Inc.—out of business

Prestige Foods Corp.—out of business

Presto Food Products, Inc.—acquired by The Morning Star Group

Presto Products, Inc.—acquired by The Coca Cola Co.

Prestolite Electric, Inc.—acquired by Genstar Capital Corporation

Preston Energy Inc.—out of business

Preston Mines Ltd.—acquired by & merged into Rio Algom Ltd.

Price Pfister, Inc.—wholly-owned sub. of Emhart Corp.

Price Stern Sloan Inc.—acquired by Matsushita Electric Industrial Co., Ltd.

Pricel, Inc.—name changed to Chargeurs, Inc.

Prime Computer, Inc.—holding company formed, DR Holdings, Inc.

Prince Corporation—acquired by Johnson Controls, Inc.

Princeton Applied Research Corp.—acquired by EG&G, Inc.

Print Northwest—acquired by Quebecor, Inc.

Printco, Inc.—acquired by Big Flower Press & name changed to Printo Group

Private Patients Health Care—name changed to PPP hc

Pro Corporation—name changed to Summit Plastic Solutions, Inc.

Pro-Fac Cooperative Incorporated—name changed to Curtice Burns/Pro Fac Cooperative Incorporated

Prochemco, Inc.—name changed to Procor, Inc.

Prodigy Systems, Inc.—out of business

Products Research & Chemical Corporation—now wholly-owned sub. of Courtaulds, Plc

Professional Geophysics, Inc.—out of business

Professional Travel, Inc.—acquired by First Travelcorp Inc. & name changed to Professional/First Travelcorp

Profit Systems, Inc.—now Profit/LEP, sub. of LEP Group PLC

Progroup, Inc.—name changed to The Arnold Palmer Golf Company

Property Trust of America—acquired by Security Capital Group Inc. & name changed to Security Capital Pacific Trust

Properties of America, Inc.—out of business

Prospect Foundry, Inc.—acquired by Atchison Casting Corporation

The Prospect Group, Inc.—out of business

Providence Gas Co.—name changed to Providence Energy Corp.

Providence Journal-Bulletin—acquired by A.H. Belo Corporation

Provident Life & Accident Insurance Co. of America—name changed to Provident Companies, Inc.

Provident National Corporation—merged with Pittsburgh National Corp. to form PNC Financial Corp.

Provincial House, Inc.—name changed to Provincial Management, Inc.

Prudential Building Maintenance Corp. — name changed to ISS International Service System, Inc.

The Prudential Group, Inc. — out of business

Prudential Reinsurance Holdings — name changed to Everest Reinsurance Holdings

PSICOR, Inc. — acquired by Baxter International Inc.

Public Service Company of Indiana, Inc. — holding co. formed, PSI Holdings, Inc.

Public Service Company of New Hampshire — acquired by Northeast Utilities

Pueblo International, Inc. — name changed to Pueblo Xtra Int'l, Inc.

The Pullman Company — acquired by Tenneco Inc.

Pullman, Inc. — acquired by Wheelabrator-Frye, Inc.

Pulse Engineering, Inc. — acquired by Technitrol, Inc.

Pulte Home Corporation — holding co. formed, PHM Corporation

Puma AG Rudolf Dassler Sport — acquired by Aritmos AB

Punta Gorda Isles, Inc. — now PGI Incorporated

Purex Industries, Inc. — liquidated February, 1986

Puritan Bennett Corporation — merged with Nellcor Incorporated to form Nellcor Puritan Bennett Incorporated

Purity Supreme, Inc. — absorbed into The Stop & Shop Companies

Purolator Courier Corp. — acquired by Emery Air Freight Corporation

Purolator, Inc. — name changed to Purolator Courier Corp.

G.P. Putnam's Sons — acquired by MCA, Inc.

Pyramid Technology — acquired by Siemens AG

Pytronic Industries, Inc. — absorbed by Reptron Electronics, Inc.

Q

Qantel Corporation — absorbed by Decision Data, Inc.

Quad Cities First Company — now First of America Bank, Quad Cities

Quadrex Corporation — liquidated

Quael Corp. — out of business

Quaker State Oil Refining Corp. — name changed to Quaker State Corporation

Quality Care, Inc. — acquired by GrandMet USA, Inc.

Quality Inns International, Inc. — acquired by Manor Care, Inc.

Quantronix Corporation — name changed to Excel Technology, Inc.

Quantum Health Resources, Inc. — acquired by Olsten Corporation

Quantum Restaurant Group, Inc. — name changed to Morton's Restaurant Group

Quart Products Inc. — acquired by Saint-Gobain & name changed to Saint-Gobain/Norton Industrial Ceramics

Quartet Manufacturing Co. — acquired by General Binding Corporation

Quest Welding Supply Co. — acquired & absorbed by Valley National Gasses Inc.

Quik Wok Corporation — out of business

Quintessence Inc. — acquired by Joh. A. Benckiser GmbH

R

R & S Strauss, Inc. — name changed to Strauss Discount Auto

RAI Research Corporation — merged with Pall Corporation to form Pall RAI, Inc.

RB Industries, Inc. — out of business

RB&W Corporation — acquired by Park-Ohio Industries, Inc.

RCA Corp. — acquired by General Electric Company

RDI, Inc. — out of business

R.E.D.M. Corp. — name changed to REDM Industries, Inc.

R.H. Medical Services, Inc. — co. liquidated & subs. acquired by Media, Inc.

RIHT Properties Inc. — acquired by Bank of Boston Corp.

RJR Nabisco, Inc. — acquired by Kohlberg, Kravis, Roberts

RLC Corp. — now Rollins Truck Leasing Corp.

RMS Electronics, Inc. — name changed to RMS International, Inc.

RMT Properties Inc. — name changed to Frontier Oil & Refining Company

ROC Communities, Inc. — merged with Chateau Properties to form Chateau Communities, Inc.

RPS Corporation — name changed to R.P. Scherer Corporation

RPS Products, Inc. — out of business

RSC Industries, Inc. — name changed to Matec Corp.

RSR Holding Corp. — name changed to Quexco Incorporated

RTE Corp. — acquired by Cooper Industries, Inc.

RTW, Rogers Tool Works, Inc. — acquired by Greenfield Industries Inc.

RTZ Corporation PLC — merged with CRA Limited to form The RTZ-CRA Group

Radiation Technology, Inc. — now RTI Inc.

Radionics, Inc. — acquired by Detection Systems, Inc.

Brad Ragan, Inc. — acquired by The Goodyear Tire & Rubber Co.

Ragen Precision Industries, Inc. — name changed to Ragen Corp.

Rahall Communications Corp. — acquired by & merged into Gulf United Corp.

Rail Products International — name changed to National Electric Coil

The Rainier Companies, Inc. — acquired by G. Heileman Brewing Co., Inc.

Rainier Bancorporation — acquired by Security Pacific

Corporation

Ramada Inc. — now Aztar Corporation

Ranchers Exploration & Development Corp. — acquired by Hecla Mining Co.

Ranco Inc. — wholly-owned sub. of Siebe PLC

Randolph Medical Inc. — merged with General Medical Corp. to form Randolph General Medical Inc.

Random Access, Inc. — acquired by EMCOR Group, Inc. & name changed to ENTEX/Random Access, Inc.

Rand's Inc. — out of business

Rangaire & Company — acquired by Nortek, Inc. & name changed to Rangaire Company

Rangaire Corporation — name changed to Scottish Heritable Trust plc

Ransburg Corporation — acquired by Illinois Tool Works Corporation

Rao Wholesale Tire Centers, Inc. — name changed to The Rao Group Inc.

Ann Raskas Gourmet Confectioners — name changed to Square Shooter Candy Co.

RasterOps Corporation — name changed to Truevision, Inc.

The Rath Packing Co. — liquidated

Ratliff Drilling & Exploration Co. — out of business

Ratners Group plc — name changed to Signet Group plc

Rau Fasteners Company, LLC — out of business

Raub Supply Company — acquired & absorbed by Noland Company

Rauch Industries Inc. — acquired by Syratech Corporation

The Rawplug Company — name changed to Powers Fastening, Inc.

Raybestos-Manhattan, Inc. — name changed to Raymark Corp.

Rayco — acquired by Kaufman & Broad Home Corporation

Raymark Corp. — holding co. formed, Raytech Corporation

Raymark Friction Company — name changed to Universal Raymark Friction Composites Company

Raymond Holdings Inc. — name changed to Raymond International Company

Raymond International Company — out of business

Raymond Precision Industries, Inc. — name changed to Raymond Industries, Inc.

Raypak, Inc. — acquired by Rheem Manufacturing Co., a sub. of Paloma Industries Limited

Reading & Bates Offshore Drilling Co. — name changed to Reading & Bates Corp.

Reading Tube Corp. — acquired by Cambridge-Lee Industries

Real Estate Corp. of Florida — name changed to Landstar Development Company

Real Estate Investment Trust of America — merged into REIT of America which merged into Unicorp American Corporation

Realist, Inc. — now David White, Inc.

Realty & Mortgage Investors of the Pacific — name changed to RAMPAC

Reckitt & Colman North American Inc. — name changed to R.T. French Co.

Recognition International Inc. — acquired & absorbed by BanTec

Recording & Statistical Corporation — out of business

Red Ball Corporation — acquired by Atlas World Group, Inc.

Red Calliope & Associates, Inc. — acquired by Crown Crafts, Inc.

Red Wing Products, Inc. — acquired by Ferguson International Holdings

Redco Foods, Inc. — acquired by Teekane GmbH

Redgate Communications Corp. — acquired by America On-Line Incorporated

Redlaw Enterprises, Inc. — sub. of Galtaco, Inc.

Reed Tool Co. — acquired by Baker International Corp.

Reese Finer Foods, Inc. — name changed to World Finer Foods, Inc.

Reeves Brothers, Inc. — acquired by Schick Inc.

Reeves Communications Corp. — owned by Thames Television Plc

Refrigerated Transport Co., Inc. — name changed to RTC Transportation, Inc.

The Regina Company — acquired by Philips Electronics N.V.

Rego Company — name changed to Engineer Control Intl.

Rehability Corporation — acquired by Living Centers of America

Reichold Chemicals, Inc. — wholly-owned sub. of Dainippon Ink & Chemicals, Inc.

Reidbord Bros., Inc. — out of business

Walter Reist Holding AG — name changed to WRH Walter Reist Holding AG

Relational Technology Inc. — now Ingres Corp.

Reinz-Dichtungs, GmbH — acquired by Dana Corporation

Reliance Electric Co. — acquired by Exxon Corp.

Reliance Universal, Inc. — acquired by Tyler Corp.

Remarks, Inc. — out of business

Remco Enterprises, Inc. — acquired by Thorm EMI Plc & name changed to Remco America, Inc.

Remcor Products Co. — acquired by IMI Plc

Renaissance Communications Corp. — acquired & absorbed by Tribune Company

Renaissance International Hotels, Inc. — name changed to Renaissance Hotel Group N.V.

Renaissance Publishing Co., Inc. — acquired by Bemrose Corporation

Renken Boat Manufacturing Co. — acquired by & absorbed into United Marine Corp.

Rent-A-Center, Inc. — acquired by Thorn-EMI plc

Rentokil Group PLC — name changed to Rentokil Initial

plc

Republic Airlines, Inc. — acquired by NWA, Inc.

Republic Corp. — acquired by Titon Group, Ltd.

Republic Housing Corp. — name changed to Republic Gypsum Co.

Republic Industries Inc. — name changed to NT Dormatic

Republic Mortgage Investors — name changed to Thackeray Corp.

Republic National Life Insurance Co. — acquired by Gulf United Corp.

Republic of Texas Corp. — name changed to Republic Bank Corp.

Republic Steel Corp. — acquired by The LTV Corporation

Republic Health Corporation — name changed to Ornda Healthcorp

Republic Waste Industries, Inc. — name changed to Republic Industries, Inc.

RepublicBank Corp. — merged with Interfirst Corp. to form First RepublicBank Corporation

Reserve Oil & Gas Co. — acquired by & merged into Getty Oil Co.

Resistoflex Corp. — acquired by UMC Industries, Inc.

Resonex Holding Co. — out of business

Resort Condominiums International — acquired by HFS, Incorporated

Resorts International, Inc. — sold to The Griffin Company

Resource Inc. — acquired by International Business Machines Corporation

Restaurant Associates Industries, Inc. — 85% owned by Kyotaru Co., Ltd.

The Ret Income Fund Inc. — acquired by & merged into Cyprus Corp.

Retail Ventures, Inc. — name changed to American Eagle Outfitters, Inc.

Retzlaff Peters Incorporated — name changed to Retzlaff Incorporated

Dr. Reutlinger & Soehne GmbH & Co. KG — out of business

Revelstoke Home Centers Ltd. — acquired by West Fraser Timber Co. Ltd.

Revere Copper & Brass, Inc. — out of business

Revlon, Inc. — acquired by Pantry Pride, Inc.

Rex Plastics, Inc. — acquired by Carlisle Plastics, Inc.

Rex Precision Products, Inc. — acquired by Alco Standard Corp.

Rexham Corp. — sub. of Bowater Industries, Inc.

Rexnord, Inc. — acquired by Banner Industries, Inc.

Rexon Incorporated — acquired by Tecmar Technologies International, Inc. & name changed to Tecmar Technologies, Inc.

R.J. Reynolds Industries Inc. — name changed to RJR Nabisco

Reynolds Securities Intl., Inc. — merged with Dean Witter Organization & name changed to Dean Witter

Reynolds Organization, Inc.

Rhenania Schiffahrts-und Speditions-Gesellschaft mbH — acquired by The Peninsula & Oriental Steam Navigation Company

Rhone Poulenc Systems Co. — name changed to Rhone Poulenc, Inc.

Rial Oil Co. — name changed to Sage Energy Co.

George Rice & Sons — acquired by World Color Press

Rich-Melt Corporation — out of business

Richardson Co. — acquired by Witco Chemical Corp.

Richardson-Merrell, Inc. — name changed to Richardson-Vicks, Inc.

Richardson-Vicks, Inc. — acquired by The Procter & Gamble Co.

Richco Plastics Company — name changed to Richco Inc.

Richford Industries, Inc. — acquired by Great American Industries & name changed to Paeco Indus., Inc.

Richmond Corp. — acquired by Continental Group, Inc.

Ridgeview Motors, Inc. — out of business

Ridgewood News, Inc. — name changed to RNI Publications, Inc.

L.L. Ridgway Enterprises — name changed to Ridgway's Inc.

Riegel Textile Corp. — acquired by Mount Vernon Mills, Inc., sub. of R.B. Pamplin Corp.

Rigway's, Inc. — acquired by YRJ Corporation

Riklis Family Corporation — name changed to McCrory Corporation

The Riley Co. — acquired by U.S. Filter Co. & name changed to U.S. Riley Corp.

Ring Around Products, Inc. — acquired by Occidental Petroleum Corp.

Ringling Bros., Barnum & Bailey Combined Shows — acquired by Irvin & Kenneth Feld Productions, Inc.

Rinsoz & Ormand Tabac SA — out of business

Risdon Mfg. Co. — name changed to Risdon Corp.

Ritasa Freight Service Srl — name changed to A.I. Ocean

Rite Way, Inc. — acquired by Hesco Parts Corporation & name changed to Hesco, Inc.

Rival Holdings, Inc. — name changed to The Rivan Company, 60%-Owned by Fulcrum II., L.P.

River Oaks Industries — name changed to ROC Properties Inc.

Riviania Foods — acquired by Colgate-Palmolive

R.C.S. Rizzoli S.p.A. — name changed to R.c.S. Editori S.p.A.

Roadmaster Industries, Inc. — name changed to R.D.M. Sports Group

Roadway Services, Inc. — name changed to Caliber System, Inc.

Robec Inc. — acquired & absorbed by Ameriquest Technologies

Robel Beef Packers, Inc. — out of business

Roberts & Porter, Inc. — name changed to Midland Color Company

Robertshaw Controls Co.—acquired by Siebe PLC

H.H. Robertson Company—merged with Ceco Industries Inc. to form Robertson-Ceco Corporation

Robertson Tritech A/S—name changed to Simrad Norge

The Robino-Ladd Co.—name changed to Inprojet Corp.

A.H. Robins Co.—acquired by American Home Products Corporation

Robintech Inc.—acquired by CompuDyne Corporation

Roblin Industries, Inc.—out of business

Rochester Community Savings Bank—acquired by RCSB Financial, Inc.

Rockaway Corporation—acquired by Ascom Holding AG

Rockefeller Center Properties, Inc.—acquired & absorbed by Goldman, Sachs & Co.

Rocket Industries, Inc./Excel, The Exercise Co.—out of business

Rocket Research Corp.—name changed to Rockor, Inc.

Rockmont Corporation—out of business

Rockor, Inc.—acquired by Olin Corporation

W.B. Roddenberry Co.—acquired by Dean Foods

Rodeway Inns of America—name changed to Lodging Systems, Inc.

Roffe, Inc.—out of business; assets acquired by Gerry Sportswear Company

Rolland Inc.—acquired by The Cascades Group

Rollins Burdick Hunter Co.—acquired by Combined International Corp.

Rolm Corp.—acquired by International Business Machines Corp.

Rome Manufacturing Co.—out of business

Ronco, Inc.—out of business

Ronco Teleproducts, Inc.—name changed to Ronco, Inc.

Roper Corporation—acquired by General Electric Co.

Rorer-Amchem, Inc.—name changed to Rorer Group, Inc.

Rorer Group, Inc.—now Rhone-Poulenc Rorer Inc., sub. of Rhone-Poulenc S.A.

Rosario Resources Corp.—acquired by Amax, Inc.

Rosemont, Inc.—acquired by Emerson Electric Co.

Rosenau Brothers, Inc.—name changed to Cinderella Clothing Industries, Inc.

Rospatch Corporation—name changed to Ameriwood Industries International Inc.

Ross Engineering Co., Inc.—name changed to Ross Technology Corp.

Rostona Corporation—acquired by Reunion Resources Company & name changed to Oneida Rostore Corporation

Rotron, Inc.—acquired by EG&G, Inc.

Roussel Uclaf S.A.—acquired by Hoechst Aktiengesellschaft

Royal Business Group, Inc.—out of business

Royal Corporation—name changed to Del Monte Royal Corporation

Royal Crown Cola Co.—name changed to Royal Crown Industries, Inc.

Royal Crown Industries, Inc.—name changed to Royal Crown Companies, Inc.

Royal Cruise Line Inc.—acquired & absorbed by Norwegian Cruise Line

Royal Industries—acquired by Lear Siegler, Inc.

Royal Insurance PLC—merged with Sun Alliance Insurance Group PLC to form Royal & Sun Alliance Insurance Group plc

Royal Palm Savings—acquired by Barnett Banks, Inc.

Royston Company—acquired by Universal Leaf Tobacco Co., Inc.

The Rucker Company—acquired by NL Industries, Inc.

Rule Industries, Inc.—acquired by Greenfield Industries Inc.

Rusco Industries, Inc.—name changed to Rusco Hilite

Rush County Farm Bureau Co-op—name changed to Heritage Co-op

Russell, Burdsall & Ward Corp.—name changed to RB&W Corp.

Russell Stadelman & Company—acquired by Timber Products Company, LP

Rust Craft Greeting Cards, Inc.—acquired by Ziff Corp.

Rustenburg Platinum holdings Ltd.—name changed to JCI Limited

Ryan Homes, Inc.—name changed to NVRyan L.P. and again to NVR L.P.

Ryan Properties Inc.—name changed to Ryan Construction Company of Minnesota

S.E. Rykoff & Co.—name changed to Rykoff-Sexton, Inc.

The Rymer Company—now The Rymer Food Company

S

SAE Pinkerton & Laws Inc.—name changed to Pinkerton & Laws Inc.

SCA Services, Inc.—acquired by Waste Management Inc. & Genestar Corporation

SCECorp—name changed to Edison International

SCM Corporation—acquired by Hanson Industries, Inc.

SFFed Corp.—merged with First Nationwide Bank to form California Federal Bank

SFN Companies, Inc.—name changed to SFN Holding Company

SFN Companies, Inc.—liquidated

S-G Metals Industries, Inc.—acquired by Galamet, Inc.

SJL of Kansas Corp.—acquired by Lee Enterprises, Incorporated

S-K-I Limited—acquired by American Skiing Company & name changed to Killington Ltd.

SKZ Inc.—name changed to Zilkha Energy Company

SLM, Inc.—name changed to Buddy L. Inc.

SMD Industries, Inc.—acquired by American Greetings Corp.

SOS Consolidated, Inc.—name changed to Core Indus-

tries, Inc.

SPW Corp. — out of business

SQA, Inc. — acquired by Rational Software Corporation

SSP Industries — acquired by Transtechnology Corp.

STK Enterprises, Inc. — now Furman Lumber Company

STS Holdings, Inc. — name changed to STS Consultants, Inc.

STSC, Inc. — acquired by Continental Telecom, Inc.

SW Industries, Inc. — acquired by BTR, Inc. & new name is Stowe Woodward Co.

SW Industries, Inc. — name changed to SW (Delaware), Inc.

S.W. Jr. Enterprises, Inc. — out of business

Saab-Scania of America, Inc. — now Saab Cars USA, Inc.

Sabine Corporation — now sub. of Pacific Enterprises, Inc.

Sabine Royalty Corp. — name changed to Sabine Corp.

Safeguard Industries, Inc. — name changed to Safeguard Scientifics, Inc.

Safety Fund Corporation — acquired by CFX Bank & name changed to Safety Fund National Bank

Safeway Stores Inc. — now Safeway Incorporated

Safran Printing Co. — acquired by Stecher-Traung-Schmidt Corp.

Saga Corporation — acquired by Marriott Corporation

SAGE Technologies, Inc. — name changed to AmeriData Technologies, Inc.

Sahara Coal — acquired by Sahara Enterprises Co.

St. Ives Laboratories, Inc. — acquired by Alberto-Culver Company

St. Joe Minerals Corp. — acquired by Fluor Corp.

St. Louis-San Francisco Railway Co. — merged with Burlington Northern, Inc. & new name is Frisco International Corp.

St. Regis Corp. — acquired by & merged into Champion International Corporation

Salem Corporation — acquired by Salem Group, Inc.

Samna Corporation — now Lotus Word Processing Division of Lotus Development Corp.

San Diego Gas & Electric Company — acquired by Enova Corporation

San Fernando Electric Mfg. Co. — name changed to SFE Technologies

San Francisco Federal S & L — acquired by SFFed Corp.

San Jose Water Co. — holding co. formed, SJW Corp.

Sanborn Manufacturing Company — acquired by MacAndrews & Forbes

Sanders Associates, Inc. — acquired by Lockheed Corp.

Sandoz Ltd. — merged with Ciba Geigy Limited Group to form Novartis AG

Sandy Corporation — acquired by Automatic Data Processing, Inc.

Sanford Corporation — acquired by the Newell Company

Sanifill, Inc. — acquired by USA Waste Services, Inc.

Sanitary-Dash Manufacturing Co., Inc. — acquired by

Zurn Industries, Inc.

Santa Anita Operating Company and Santa Anita Realty Enterprises, Inc. — merged to form Santa Anita Companies

Santa Fe Pacific Corporation — merged with Burlington Northern Inc. to form Burlington Northern Santa Fe Corporation

Santa Fe Southern Pacific Corportion — name changed to Santa Fe Pacific Corporation

Sarah Coventry, Inc. — out of business

Sargent Industries, Inc. — acquired by Dover Corp.

Sargent-Fletcher Co. — acquired by Corham PLC

The Sargent Sowell Company — name changed to SA-SO Company

Sargent-Welch Scientific Co. — acquired by Artra Group, Inc.

D.L. Saslow Co. — acquired by Thomas Tilling, Inc.

Satellite Technology Management Wireless, Inc. — name changed to STM Wireless, Inc.

Saturn Airways, Inc. — merged into Transamerica Corp.

Saunders System, Inc. — acquired by Ryder System, Inc. & merged with Ryder Truck Rental, Inc.

Sav-A-Stop, Inc. — acquired by Consolidated Foods Corp.

Sav-on-Drugs, Inc. — acquired by Jewel Companies, Inc.

Savannah Electric & Power Co. — merged into The Southern Co.

Save More Food Mart, Inc. — name changed to Fresh Food, Inc.

Save Way Industries — name changed to Windmere Corp.

Savin Business Machines Corp. — name changed to Savin Corp.

Savoy Industries, Inc. — out of business

Saxon Industries, Inc. — acquired by Alco Standard Corp.

Scan-Data Corp. — acquired by & merged into Ban Tec Inc.

Scanforms, Inc. — acquired by Big Flower Press Holdings, Inc.

Schaak Electronics, Inc. — out of business

Schad Industries, Inc. — acquired by Wilsey Bennett Co.

F. & M. Schaefer Corp. — acquired by Stroh Brewery Co.

S. Schaffer Grocery Corporation — out of business

Schenuit Industries, Inc. — acquired by Allegheny Ludlum Industries, Inc.

R.P. Scherer Corporation — holding co. formed, RPS Corporation

Schick Incorporated — now Hart Holding Company, Inc.

Schiller Industries, Inc. — acquired by Rexham Corp.

Schlegel Corporation — acquired by BTR Dunlop, a sub. of BRT plc

Schludeberg-Kurdle Co., Inc. — acquired by Smithfield Foods, Inc.

Scholastic Inc. — holding co. formed, SI Holdings Inc.

Scholl, Inc. — acquired by & merged into Schering-Plough

Corp.

School Pictures, Inc. — acquired by Jostens, Inc. & name changed to Jostens Photography

Schumacher & Forelle — out of business

Schwartz Brothers, Inc. — out of business

Friedrich Wilhelm Schwing GmbH — name changed to Schwing GmbH

Schwitzer, Inc. — acquired by Kuhlman Corporation

Scientific Leasing — now the LINC Group, Inc.

SciMed Life Systems, Inc. — acquired by Boston Scientific Corp.

Scitech Corp. — name changed to ACL Filco Corporation

Scoa Industries, Inc. — now Hills Department Stores, Inc.

Scope Incorporated — acquired by Lexicon Corporation

Scotsman Group, Inc. — name changed to Williams Scotsman Group, Inc.

The Scott Fetzer Co. — acquired by Berkshire Hathaway, Inc.

Scott Foresman & Co. — holding co. formed, SFN Cos., Inc.

Scott Foresman & Co. — sold to Time, Inc. & then to Harper Collins, sub. of News America Corporation

Scott Mills, Inc. — acquired by Kleinert s, Inc. & name changed to Scott Mills

Scott Paper Company — acquired & absorbed by Kimberly-Clark Corporation

The Scottish Heritage Trust PLC — company liquidated

Scott's Seaboard Corp. — acquired by General Host Corp.

Scovill, Inc. — acquired by First City Industries

Richard Screw Anchor Company — acquired by Symons Corporation

Scrivner, Inc. — acquired by Hanamerica, Inc.

Scudder Duo-Vest, Inc. — name changed to Scudder Capital Growth Fund, Inc.

Scurry-Rainbow Oil Ltd. — acquired by Home Oil Co., Ltd.

Sea Containers, Inc. — name changed to Seaco Inc.

Sea Galley Stores — out of business

Sea Land Corp. — wholly-owned sub. of CSX Corporation

Seaboard Coast Line Industries, Inc. — merged with Chessie System, Inc.

Seaboard Farms — acquired by Farmland Industries, Inc. & name changed to Farmstead

Seaboard World Airlines, Inc. — acquired by & merged into Tiger International, Inc.

Seaco Inc. — now Orient Express Hotels Inc.

Seafirst Corp. — acquired by Bank America Corp.

Seagrave Corp. — name changed to Vista Resources Corp.

Seagull Pipeline Corp. — name changed to Segull Energy Corp.

Seal Incorporated — acquired by Bunzl plc

Sealed Power Corporation — now SPX Corporation

Sealy Holdings Inc. — now Sealy Corporation

Seaport Corporation — out of business

G.D. Searle & Co. — acquired by Monsanto Company

Season All Industries, Inc. — acquired by Redland Braas Corp.

Seatrain Lines, Inc. — out of business

Sebastian & Cooke — out of business

Securities Lock Group Inc. — name changed to Assa Alboy Lock Group Inc.

Security Capital Bancorp — acquired by CCB Financial Corporation & name changed to Central Carolina Bank & Trust Company

Security Mortgage Investors — name changed to Security Capital Corp.

Security New York State Corp. — name changed to Security Trust Company

Security Pacific Corporation — acquired by Bank America Corporation

Security Real Estate — acquired by Bechtel Group, Inc. & name changed to Coldwell Banker Security Real Estate

Sedco, Inc. — acquired by Schlumberger Ltd.

Seeburg Industries, Inc. — name changed to X-Cor Intl., Inc.

Seis Pros, Inc. — now Seis Pros, div. of Professional Geophysics, Inc.

Seko Air Freight — name changed to Seko Worldwide Inc.

Selectone Corporation — name changed to SmarTruck Systems, Inc.

Selectro Corp. — now ITT Sealectro, sub. of ITT Corp.

Seligman & Latz, Inc. — split into two companies: Seligman & Latz, Inc. and Finlay Enterprises, Inc.

Semco Flo-Tronics Inc. — name changed to MAC Equipment, Inc.

Seneca Foods Corp. — name changed to S.S. Pierce Co., Inc.

The Sentry Corporation — name changed to Sentry Insurance Company

Serono Baker Diagnostics — acquired by BioChem Pharma Inc. & name changed to Serano BioChem Immuno Systems Inc.

Servam Corporation — acquired by General Electric Co.

Service Fracturing Company — acquired by Nowsco Well Service Ltd.

Servicemaster Industries, Inc. — now Servicemaster Limited Partnership

Servomation Corp. — acquired by City Investing Co.

Seco Maschinenbau GmbH & Co. KG — out of business

Security Chimneys Ltd. — name changed to Security Chimneys International Ltd.

The Seven-Up Co. — acquired by Philip Morris, Inc.

Shakespeare Co. — acquired by Anthony Industries, Inc.

Shaklee Corporation — now sub. of Yamanouchi Pharmaceuticals Ltd.

Shaklee Terraces — name changed to Shaklee Corp.

Shamrock Broadcasting, Inc.—acquired by & absorbed into Chancellor Broadcasting

Sharon-Jay Togs, Inc.—out of business

Shaver Corp. of America—name changed to Cutlery Corp. of America

Shaw Barton, Inc.—acquired by Heritage Communications, Inc.

Shawmut National Corporation—merged into Fleet Financial Group, Inc.

Shearson Hayden Store, Inc.—name changed to Shearson Loeb Rhoades, Inc.

Shearson Loeb Rhoades, Inc.—acquired by American Express Co. & name changed to Shearson/American Express

Sheffield Exploration Company, Inc.—merged with TransMontaigne Oil Company

Sheller-Globe Corp.—acquired by General Felt Industries, Inc., which is now Knoll International Holdings, Inc.

Shenandoah Corp.—sub. of Kenton Corp.

Shenango Furnace Company—name changed to Shenango Industries

Sherritt Inc.—name changed to Viridian Inc. & acquired & absorbed by Agrium Inc.

Sherwood Van Lines, Inc.—company closed

Shoe-Town, Inc.—out of business

Shofar Kosher Foods, Inc.—acquired by Sara Lee Corporation

Shop & Go., Inc.—merged into Circle K Corporation

Shoppers World Stores, Inc.—now 50-Off Stores, Inc.

Shopwell, Inc.—acquired by The Great Atlantic & Pacific Tea Co., Inc.

Showell Farms, Inc.—acquired by Perdue Farms Incorporated

Sieg Company—acquired by A.P.S., Ltd.

Sierra On-Line, Inc.—acquired by CUC International, Inc.

Sierra Research Corp.—acquired by The LTV Corp.

Sigma Instruments, Inc.—acquired by Wheelabrator-Frye, Inc.

Sigma-Tau Industrie Farmaceutiche Riunite S.p.A.—name changed to Sigma-Tau Finanziaria S.p.A.

Sigman Meat Co. Inc.—liquidated

Sigmor Corp.—acquired by Diamond Shamrock Corp. & name changed to Diamond Shamrock Refining & Marketing Co.

The Signal Companies—acquired by Allied-Signal, Inc.

Signet Industries—out of business

Signode Industries, Inc.—acquired by Illinois Tool Works, Inc.

Sikes Corporation—acquired by Primark International, Inc.

Silicon Valley Development—out of business

Silk Greenhouses, Inc.—out of business

Silo, Inc.—acquired by Cyclops Corp.

Siltec Corporation—wholly-owned sub. of Mitsubishi Metal Corporation

Silvercrest Industries, Inc.—leveraged buyout

Silver's Inc.—acquired by Office Depot Inc.

Simba Quix Pty. Ltd.—acquired by Foodcorp Limited

Simmons Co.—acquired by Gulf + Western Industries, Inc.

Simmons Precision Products, Inc.—acquired by Hercules, Inc.

Simmons Upholstered Furniture, Inc.—out of business

Melvin Simon & Associates—name changed to Simon Property Group

Simplex Industries, Inc.—acquired by Anthony Industries, Inc.

Simplicity Pattern Co., Inc.—name changed to MAXXAM Group, Inc.

Simpsons, Ltd.—acquired by Hudson's Bay Co.

The Singer Company—now Bicoastal Corporation

Singh Industries—name changed to Ranjit Corporation

Skaggs Companies, Inc.—merged with American Stores Company

Skandia International Holding A.B.—acquired by Skandia Insurance Company Limited & name changed to Skandia Holding AB

Skil Corp.—acquired by Emerson Electric Co.

Skipper's Inc.—acquired by National Pizza Company

Sky City Stores—acquired by Interco, Inc.

SkyBox International Inc.—acquired by MacAndrews & Forbes Holdings Inc.

Sloan's Supermarkets, Inc.—acquired by Red Apple Companies

Small Tube Products Co., Inc.—acquired by Wolverine Tube Inc.

Smartstar Corporation—acquired by Sapiens International Corp. N.V.

Smarty Pants N Tops Too, Inc.—name changed to Susie's Deals

Smith Metal Arts Company, Inc.—name changed to Smith McDonald Corp.

Smith-Shafer Oil Co.—out of business

Smith Valve Corporation—acquired by Tyco International Ltd.

SmithKline Corp.—merged with Beckman Instruments & new name is SmithKline/Beckman Corp.

SmithKline/Beckman Corporation—merged with Beecham plc to form SmithKline Beecham

Smith's Transfer Corp.—acquired by ARA Services, Inc.

John M. Smyth Co.—acquired by Levitz Furniture Inc.

Sobel USA—acquired by Sobel BV & name changed to Banner Pharmacaps Inc.

Societe Commerciale de Reassurance (SCR)—name changed to SCOR

Softool Corporation—acquired by Platinum Technology, Inc. & name changed to Platinum Technology-Santa Barbara

Softsel Computer Products, Inc.—name changed to

Merisel, Inc.

Software Developers Company, Inc.—name changed to NeTegrity, Inc.

Sola Basic Industries, Inc.—acquired by General Signal Corp.

Solar Press, Inc.—name changed to Solar Communications

Solid State Scientific, Inc.—acquired by The Penn Central Corp. & name changed to Sprague Solid State

Sam Solomon Co., Inc.—acquired by & merged into Service Merchandise Corp.

Solon Automated Services, Inc.—acquired by ARA Services, Inc.

Sonderling Broadcasting Corp.—acquired by Viacom International, Inc.

Sonic Carriers of Arizona, Inc.—acquired by United Parcel Service of America, Inc.

Sonics International, Inc.—name changed to Ozite Corp.

Soo Line Railroad Co.—holding co. formed, Soo Line Corporation

Sorg Paper Co.—acquired by Mosinee Paper Corp.

South Carolina Electric & Gas Co.—holding co. formed, SCANA Corporation

South Carolina Insurance Co.—name changed to The Seibels Bruce Group, Inc.

South Carolina National Corp.—acquired by Wachovia Corporation

South East Coal Co.—out of business

South Shore Pet Center—out of business

Southeast Banking Corporation—acquired by First Union Corporation

Southeastern Capital Corporation—name changed to Property Asset Management

Southern Airways, Inc.—merged with North Central Airlines & new name is Republic Airlines, Inc.

Southern California Edison Co.—holding co. formed SCE Corporation

Southern Connecticut Gas Co.—name changed to Connecticut Energy Corporation

Southern Cross Corporation Ltd.—out of business

Southern Industries Corp.—acquired by Dravo Corp.

Southern National Resources, Inc.—name changed to Sonat, Inc.

Southern Radio Corporation—out of business

Southern Railway Co.—merged with Norfolk & Western Railway Co. & new name is Norfolk Southern Corp.

Southern Union Company—acquired by Metra Mobile CTS, Inc.

SouthernNet, Inc.—acquired by & merged into Telecom USA Inc.

Southam Inc.—acquired by Hollinger Inc.

Southend Property Holdings Plc—name changed to Hampton Trust House Plc

Southland Financial Corporation—acquired by Teachers Insurance and Annuity Association of America

Southland Royalty Co.—acquired by Burlington Northern, Inc.

Southwest Bancshares, Inc.—merged with Mercantile Texas Corp. to form MCorp

Southwest Florida Banks, Inc.—acquired by Landmark Banking Corporation

Southwest Forest Industries, Inc.—acquired by Stone Container Corporation

Southwestern Drug Co.—acquired by Gulf United Corp.

Southwestern Group Financial, Inc.—acquired by Kaneb Services

Southwestern Life Corp.—acquired by Tenneco, Inc.

Sovereign Corporation—now wholly-owned sub. of The Chubb Corporation

Sovran Financial Corporation—merged with Citizens & Southern Corporation to form holding company, C&S Sovran Corporation

Spalding & Evenflo Companies, Inc.—acquired by Kohlberg Kravis Roberts & Co.

Sparkman Energy Corp.—name changed to S. Key, Inc.

Sparkomatic Corporation—acquired by Mark IV Industries & name changed to Altec Lansing Technologies, Inc.

Spartan Food Systems, Inc.—acquired by Trans World Corp.

Spearhead Industries, Inc.—acquired by CSS Industries, Inc.

Specialty Retailers, Inc.—name changed to Stage Stores, Inc.

Spector Industries, Inc.—acquired by Telecom Corp. & merged into Spector Red Ball Freight System, Inc.

Spectral Dynamics Corp. of San Diego—acquired by & merged into Scientific-Atlanta

Spectravision Inc.—out of business

Spectro Industries, Inc.—acquired by McKesson Corp.

Spectrum Color Center—name changed to Prep-Stat/Spectrum

Speedfoam Corp.—name changed to FamTec International, Inc.

Spencer Foods, Inc.—acquired by Land O'Lakes, Inc.

Sperry & Hutchinson Co.—acquired by Baldwin United Corp.

Sperry Corp.—merged with Burroughs Corp. to form Unisys Corporation

Sperry Rand Corp.—name changed to Sperry Corp.

Splentex, Inc.—name changed to Splendor Form International

The Spohn Corporation—name changed to ColeJon Spohn Corporation

SportsTown, Inc.—out of business

Sportsystems Corp.—name changed to Delaware North Companies, Inc.

Spotnails Inc.—acquired by Peace Industries Inc.

Sprague Electric Co.—acquired by General Cable Corp.

Sprague Solid State—now sub. of Sprague Technologies Inc.

Sprague Technologies, Inc.—name changed to STI Group, Inc.

Spreckles Industries, Inc.—acquired by Colombus McKinnon Corp. & name changed to Yale International

Spring Engineers, Inc.—acquired by SEI Holding Corp.

Spring Mills, Inc.—name changed to Springs Industries

Square D Company—acquired by Schneider S.A.

Square Industries, Inc.—acquired by Central Parking Corporation

Squibb Corporation—merged with Bristol-Myers to form Bristol-Myers Squibb Company

Ssangyong Group of Companies—name changed to Ssangyong Business Group

Sta-Rite Industries, Inc.—acquired by Wicor, Inc.

Stafford-Lowden Co.—acquired by American Standard, Inc.

Stainless Equipment Co.—name changed to Molitor Industries, Inc.

A.E. Staley Manufacturing Co.—holding co. formed, Staley Continental, Inc.

A.E. Staley Manufacturing Co.—now sub. of Tate & Lyle plc

Stall Campbell—name changed to Stahl GmbH & Co.

Stanadyne, Inc.—name changed to Moen Incorporated

Standard Alliance Industries, Inc.—acquired by Walco National Corp. & merged into parent co.

Standard Brands, Inc.—merged with Nabisco, Inc. & new name is Nabisco Brands, Inc.

Standard Brands Paint Company—out of business

Standard Chlorine Chemical Company—name changed to Standard Chlorine Cloroben Corporation

Standard Commercial Tobacco Co.—holding co. formed, Standard Commercial Corp.

Standard Container Co.—acquired by Brockway Glass Co., Inc.

Standard Education Corporation—name changed to Ferguson Publishing Company

Standard Gravure Corp./Shea Communications—name changed to Shea Communications

Standard Oil Co. (Indiana)—name changed to Amoco Corporation

Standard Oil Co. of California—name changed to Chevron Corporation

The Standard Oil Co. (Ohio)—name changed to The Standard Oil Corporation

Standard Prudential Corp.—name changed to Sterling Bancorp

Standard Shares, Inc.—merged into Pittway Corporation

Standard Tele Services Supply—name changed to Standard Telecommunications

Standard Tool & Manufacturing Company—liquidated

Stang Dewatering, Inc.—out of business

Stange Co.—acquired by McCormick & Co., Inc.

Stanley Consultants Inc.—holding co. formed, S.C. Companies, Inc.

Stanley Home Products, Inc.—name changed to Stanhome, Inc.

Stanray Corp.—acquired by IC Industries, Inc.

Stanwick Corporation—liquidated

Stanwood Corporation—acquired by Delta Woodside Corporation

Starcraft Corporation—name changed to Starcraft Automotive Corporation

Stardust, Inc.—name changed to Sanmark-Stardust, Inc.

Starlite Industries—acquired by Wynn's International, Inc. & name changed to Starlight Automotive Products, Inc.

State Mutual Securities, Inc.—now State Mutual Securities Trust

State National Bank—acquired by Norwest Corporation

State Savings & Loan Assn.—acquired by NLT Corp.

Statex Petroleum, Inc.—acquired by California Portland Cement Co.

Statler Industries—out of business

Stauffer Chemical Co.—acquired by Chesebrough-Pond's Inc.

Stauffer Chemical Co.—acquired by ICI Americas Inc.

Steadly Company—acquired by Leggett & Platt, Incorporated

Steak 'n Shake—holding co. formed, Consolidated Products, Inc.

Stearns & Foster Co.—acquired by The Ohio Mattress Company

Stecher-Traung-Schmidt Corp.—acquired by International Paper Co.

Steego Corporation—90%-owned by Industrial Equity (Pacific) Limited

Steiger Tractor, Inc.—acquired by J.J. Case Co. of Tenneco, Inc.

Steinbach—acquired by Crowley, Milner & Company

Steiner & Company—name changed to Clover Yarns Inc.

Steinway & Sons—acquired by The Selmer Co., Inc.

Stella D'Oro Biscuit Co.—acquired by RJR Nabisco Holdings

Stellar Industries, Inc.—name changed to Locke Group, Inc.

Steltex, Inc.—now Sharp Distributor Inc.

Sterchi Bros. Stores, Inc.—acquired by Heilig-Meyers Co.

Sterling Drug, Inc.—wholly-owned sub. of Eastman Kodak Company

Sterling Extruder Corp.—now APV Chemical Machinery, Inc., sub. of APV Holdings PLC

Sterling Healthcare Group, Inc.—acquired by FPA Medical Management, Inc.

Sterling Optical—now Sterling Vision

Sterling Precision Corp.—name changed to Steego

Corp.

Sterling Stores, Inc.—acquired by & merged into Duckwall-Alco Stores, Inc.

Sterndent Corp.—acquired by Cooper Laboratories, Inc. & merged into existing groups

Stern's Miracle-Gro Products, Inc.—acquired by The Scotts Company

David G. Steven, Inc.—name changed to Baume Mercier Inc.

Stevens Graphics Corporation—name changed to Stevens International, Inc.

J.P. Stevens & Co., Inc.—acquired by West Point-Pepperell, Inc.

Stevokit, Inc.—acquired by J.P. Stevens & Co. & name changed to Knit & Narrow Fabric Div.

Stewart Foods, Inc.—acquired by Apple Tree Company Inc. & name changed to Americas Foods

Stewart-Warner Corp.—sub. of BTR PLC

Stewart Well Service Co.—name changed to Blue Hawk Well Service

Stillman Seal—name changed to American United Global Inc.

Stixi AG—out of business

Stockton Savings Association—out of business

Stokely-Van Camp, Inc.—acquired by Quaker Oats Co.

Stonco—acquired by The Genolyte Group & name changed to Stonco Genolyte

The Stop & Shop Company, Inc.—acquired by Koninklijke Ahold NV

Stop Shop Save—name changed to Baines Management Co.

Storer Broadcasting Co.—name changed to Storer Communications

Storer Communications, Inc.—now joint venture of Comcast Corporation & Tele-Communications, Inc.

Stouffer Corp.—sub. of Nestle Enterprises, Inc.

Stow Davis Architectural Woodwork Incorporated—acquired by Steelcase Inc. & name changed to Wigland Corporation

Strategic Planning Associates, Inc.—now wholly-owned sub. of Marsh & McLennan Companies, Inc.

Stratford of Texas, Inc.—acquired by Ralston-Purina Co. & name changed to Green Thumb Co., Deco-Plants Co.

Stratton Corp.—acquired by Intrawest Corporation

Strawbridge & Clothier—acquired by The May Department Stores Company & name changed to Hecht's Strawbridges

Streech Electric Company—out of business

O.J. Strobel Oil & Tire Co., Inc.—name changed to Horizon Distribution Inc.

Strongheart Products Inc.—out of business

Stuarts Department Store Inc.—out of business

Structural Fibers, Inc.—name changed to ESSEF Industries, Inc.

Structural Measurement Systems, Inc.—now Structural Measurement Division of Genrad, Inc.

C.H. Stuart, Inc.—name changed to Sarah Coventry

Stuart Hall—acquired by Newell Co.

Studebaker-Worthington, Inc.—acquired by McGraw-Edison Co.

Studio 5 Clothing Stores Inc.—out of business

Stusser Electric Company—acquired by Consolidated Electrical Distributors

Style Auto—name changed to Gilrichco

Su Crest Corp.—name changed to Ingredient Technology Corp.

Suburban Propane Gas Corp.—acquired by National Distiller & Chemical Corp.

Sue Ann, Inc.—name changed to CSA Group, Inc.

Sugardale Foods, Inc.—name changed to Morgan's Restaurants

Sullair Corp.—acquired by Sundstrand Corporation

Summagraphics Corporation—acquired & absorbed by Lockheed Martin Corporation

Summers Electric Co.—acquired by Thomas Tilling, Inc.

The Summit Bancorporation—merged with UJB Financial Corp. to form Summit Bancorp

Summit Communications, Inc.—acquired & absorbed by Time Warner, Inc.

Summit Environmental Group—out of business

Summit Family Restaurants, Inc.—acquired by CKE Restaurants Inc.

Summit Heading Corporation—acquired by United Bankshares & name changed to United National Bank

Sun Alliance Insurance Group PLC—merged with Royal Insurance PLC to form Royal & Sun Alliance Insurance Group plc

Sun Banks, Inc.—merged with Trust Co. of Georgia to form Sun Trust Banks

Sun Carriers, Inc.—now St. Johnsbury Trucking Co., Inc.

Sun Chemical Corp.—merged with Chromalloy Corp. & name changed to Sequa Corp.

Sun Oil Co.—name changed to Sun Co., Inc.

Sunbeam Corp.—acquired by Allegheny International

Sunbeam Corp. Ltd.—name changed to Sunbeam Victa Holdings Ltd.

Sundor Brands Inc.—acquired by Procter & Gamble Co.

Sunergy Communities, Inc.—merged with River Oaks Industries

Sunkyong Limited—name changed to Sunkyong Industries Co.

Sunox, Inc.—acquired by Linde AG & absorbed by Holox Inc.

Sunrise Bancorp—acquired & absorbed by First Banks, Inc.

Sunstates Corp.—merged with Treco, Inc.

Super Food Services, Inc.—acquired by Nash Finch Company

Super Music Corp.—acquired by Blockbuster Music

Super Rite Corporation—acquired by Richfood Holdings, Inc.

Supercuts, Inc.—acquired by Regis Corporation

Superior Care, Inc.—merged with Kimberly Home Health Care, Inc. of Lifetime Corp.

Superior Container, Inc.—acquired by & name changed to Willamette Industries, Inc.

Superior Fast Freight—out of business

Superior Holding Corporation—now Superior Teletec Inc.

The Superior Oil Co.—acquired by Mobil Corporation

Superscope, Inc.—name changed to Marantz Co., Inc.

Supradur Companies, Inc.—acquired by International Specialty Products, Inc. & name changed to GAF Premium Products, Inc.

Surgical Care Affiliates, Inc.—acquired & absorbed by Healthsouth Rehabilitation Corporation

Survival Technology, Inc.—name changed to Meridian Medicad Technology, Inc.

Suter plc—acquired & absorbed by Ascot Holdings Plc

Sutro Mortgage Investment Trust—acquired by & merged into PNB Mortgage & Realty Investors

Swallen's, Inc.—out of business

The Swanson Company Manufacturers—acquired by Crestline Plastic Pipe Co. & name changed to Crestline West Inc.

Swanton Corporation—out of business

Swedish Match Holding Inc.—now Stora Holdings Inc.; Swedish Match AB now Swedish Match NV

Sweetlife Foods, Inc.—acquired by Super Value Inc.

Swell-Wear, Inc.—liquidated

Swift Independent Packing Company—now sub. of Montfort, Inc., sub. of ConAgra Corporation

Sybron Corporation—now Sybron Acquisition Company

Sycor, Inc.—acquired by Bell Canada

Symbion, Inc.—out of business

Synercon Corp.—merged into Coroon & Black Corp.

Synergex Corp.—acquired by Bergen Brunswick Corp.

Syntex Technologies, Inc.—acquired by Phoenix Technologies

Synto Corporation—acquired by Mallinckrodt Group, Inc.

Syracuse China Corp.—acquired by Canadian Pacific Ltd.

Syscon Corp.—wholly-owned sub. of Harnischfeger Industries, Inc.

Systems Engineering & Manufacturing Corp.—out of business

Systems Engineering Laboratories, Inc.—acquired by Gould, Inc.

Systems Planning Corp.—name changed to Greiner Engineering, Inc.

Systems Research and Applications Corporation—name changed to SRA International Inc.

Szabo Food Service, Inc.—acquired by ARA Services, Inc., sub. of ARA Holding Company

T

T & N Holding Co., Inc.—acquired by First Savings & Loan Association of Fort Stockton

T-Bar, Inc.—sub. of Data Switch Corporation

TA Triumph-Adler Vertriebs GmbH—acquired by Olivetti S.p.A.

TABS Associates—out of business

TCC—name changed to Carnival Hotels & Casinos

TEC Incorporated—out of business

TFI Companies, Inc.—acquired by Leucadia National Corp.

TGC Inc.—name changed to Equion Corporation

TI Corporation (of California)—name changed to TICOR

TIC Industries, Inc.—name changed to TIC Investment Corp.

TRE Corp.—acquired by Aluminum Company of America

TSB Group Plc—merged with Lloyds Bank PLC to form Lloyds TSB Group Plc

TSI Industries, Inc.—out of business

TW Services, Inc.—holding co. formed, TW Holding Co.

Tacoma Boatbuilding Company—out of business

Tagsons Papers, Inc.—acquired by American Tissue Inc.

Talcott National Corp.—name changed to Leucadia National Corp.

Tallgrass Technologies Corp.—acquired by Exabyte Corp.

Talman Home Federal Savings & Loan Association of Illinois—acquired by La Salle Bank & name changed to La Salle Talman Bank

Tampa Electric Co.—name changed to TECO Energy, Inc.

Tampax Inc.—name changed to Tambrands, Inc.

Tampella Corp.—name changed to Tamrock Corp.

Tano, L.L.C.—name changed to Tano Automation, Inc.

Tapco Products Company—name changed to Tapco International Corporation

The Tappan Co.—acquired by Dometic Inc.

Taren Holdings, Inc.—out of business

Targeted Marketing, Inc.—acquired by Lion Holding Company

Tash, Inc.—out of business

Taunton Cider Company P.L.C.—merged with Matthew Clark & Sons Ltd. to form Matthew Clark Taunton, Ltd.

Taylor Drug Stores, Inc.—acquired & absorbed by Rite Aid Corporation

Taylor Medical Inc.—acquired by & name changed to Physicians Sales and Services Inc.

Taylor Rental Corp.—acquired by The Stanley Works

Taylor Wine Co., Inc.—acquired by The Coca-Cola Co.

TechAmerica Group, Inc.—now Fermenta Animal Health, sub. of Fermenta AB

Technalysis Corporation—acquired & absorbed

byCompuserve Corporation

Technical Operations, Inc.—name changed to Tech/Ops, Inc.

Technical Publishing Co.—acquired by Dun & Bradstreet Cos., Inc.

Technicolor, Inc.—acquired by MacAndrews & Forbes Group, Inc.

Technicron Corp.—acquired by Revlon, Inc.

Technology Applications Inc.—acquired by Dyncorp

Technology Development Corp.—acquired by Computerland

Technology Inc.—name changed to Krug International

Tech/Ops Landover, Inc.—name changed to Landover, Inc.

Teenform, Inc.—name changed to Wacoal America, Inc.

Tele-Com Products, Inc.—acquired by Zack Electronics & name changed to Zack Electronics/Tele-Com Products

Tejas Power Corporation—name changed to TPC Corporation

Tekken Construction Corporation—name changed to Tekken Corporation

Tele-Communications, Inc.—name changed to TCI Communications Inc.

Telecom USA Inc.—acquired by MCI Communications Corp.

Telecommunications Industries, Inc.—name changed to TII Corp.

Telecrafter Corporation—now Wegener Corporation

Telecredit, Inc.—acquired by Equifax Inc.

Teledyne Inc.—merged with Allegheny Ludlum Corporation to form Allegheny Teledyne Incorporated

Telefile Computer Corporation—name changed to Telefile Inc.

Teleprompter Corp.—acquired by Westinghouse Electric Corp.

Telerate Inc.—now wholly-owned sub. of Dow Jones Company, Inc.

Telerent Leasing Corp.—acquired by The Aviation Group, Inc.

Telesciences, Inc.—now Telesciences Co. Systems, Inc.

Telesphere Communications, Inc.--acquired by The Williams Companies

The Telex Corp.—now Memorex Telex Corporation

Templeton Energy, Inc.—now TGX Corporation

Teneo—name changed to SEPI

Tennelec/Nucleus Inc.—acquired by Oxford Instruments Plc & name changed to Oxford Instruments Group

Tennessee Natural Resources, Inc.—liquidated

Tennessee Valley Bancorp, Inc.—name changed to Commerce Group

Teno AB—name changed to Rosenlewemballage AB

Tensor Corp.—acquired by Shetland Corporation

Teradata Corporation—acquired by NCR Corporation of American Telephone & Telegraph Co. (AT&T)

The Terson Co., Inc.—holding co. formed, Terson Holdings, Ltd.

Texas Air Corporation—name changed to Continental Airlines Holdings Inc.

Texas American Bancshares Inc.—now Team Bancshares Inc.

Texas American Energy Corporation—now Kent Financial Services, Inc.

Texas American Oil Corp.—name changed to Texas American Energy Corp.

Texas Commerce Bancshares, Inc.—wholly-owned sub. of Chemical New York Corporation

Texas Eastern Corporation—now sub. of Panhandle Easern Corporation

Texas Energies, Inc.—acquired by Sunshine Mining Co.

Texas Gas Transmission Corp.—acquired by CSX Corp. & name changed to Texas Gas Resources Corp.

Texas International Company—restructured and name changed to The Phoenix Resources Companies, Inc.

Texas Oil & Gas Corp.—acquired by USX Corporation

Texas Olefins Co.—name changed to Texas Petrochemicals

Texas Steel Co.—acquired by Citation Corp.

Texasgulf, Inc.—acquired by Elf Aquitaine, Inc.

Texon, Inc.—acquired by Emhart Corp.

Textiles, Inc.—name changed to Ti-Caro, Inc.

Textilgruppe Hof—name changed to Neuebaum Woll-Spinnerei und Weberei Hof AG

Thames Television Ltd.—acquired by Pearson plc

Thetford Corporation—acquired by The Dyson-Kissner Moran Corporation

Thiokol Corp.—merged with Morton Norwich Products, Inc. & name changed to Morton Thiokol, Inc.

Third National Corp.—merged with SunTrust Banks, Inc.

Thomas Kotzin Company—out of business

Thomas Pipe & Steel, Inc.—acquired by Harvest Partners Inc.

Thomas Tilling, Inc.—acquired by BTR, Inc.

The Thompson-Minwax Company—acquired by The Sherwin-Williams Company

Thriftway, Inc.—acquired by Winn-Dixie Stores, Inc.

Thrifty Corp.—acquired by Pacific Lighting Corporation

Thrifty Corporation—acquired by Leonard Green & Partners

Thrifty Rent-A-Car System Inc.—now wholly-owned sub. of Chrysler Corporation

Throfare Corp.—name changed to Casablanca Industries, Inc.

Thyssen-Bornemisza, Inc.—name changed to TBG, Inc.

Ti-Caro, Inc.—acquired by Dixie Yarns, Inc.

Ticketron—name changed to Automated Wagering

Ticor—acquired by Southern Pacific Co.

Tidemark Bancorp, Inc.—acquired & absorbed by Crestar Financial

Tidewater Marine Service, Inc.—name changed to Tidewater, Inc.

Tiffany & Co.—spun-off from Avon Products, Inc.

Tiger Direct, Inc. — acquired by Global Equipment Company

Tiger International, Inc. — acquired by & absorbed into Federal Express Corporation

Timberland Industries, Inc. — out of business

Time Holdings, Inc. — acquired by & merged into AMEV Holdings, Inc.

Time Inc. — merged with Warner Communications, Inc. to form Time Warner Inc.

Time Industries, Inc. — name changed to Smurfit Industries, Inc.

Timeplex, Inc. — acquired by Unisys Corporation

Tioxide Group PLC — acquired by Imperial Chemical Industries PLC

Titan Group, Inc. — acquired by Hanover Companies, Inc.

Tobacco Supply Co. — acquired by Luckett Tobaccos Inc.

Tokos Medical Corporation — acquired by Matria Healthcare Corporation & name changed to Matria West

Toledo Edison Co. — merged with The Cleveland Electric Illuminating Co. to form the holding co., Centerior Energy Corporation

Topaz, Inc. — acquired by Square D Company

Topeka Capital-Journal — acquired by Shivers Trading Operating Co.

Topp & Trowsers — name changed to Inmar Corporation

Topps Chewing Gum, Inc. — now Topps Company, Inc.

Torin Corp. — acquired by Clevepak Corp.

Torino Fashions, Inc. — name changed to Dani Michaels, Inc.

Total Assets Protection Inc. — out of business

Total Energold Corporation — acquired by Rigel Energy Limited

Total Energy Services, Inc. — acquired by Enterra Corporation & name changed to FM Enterra Petroleum Equipment Group Inc.

Totes Incorporated — acquired by Barn Capital

Touche Remnant & Co. — acquired by Henderson Administration Group PLC & name changed to Touch Remnant Holdings, Ltd.

Towle Manufacturing Company — acquired by Merrimac Corporation

Town & Country Mobile Homes, Inc. — name changed to Brigadier, Inc.

Towner Petroleum Co. — name changed to SKZ, Inc.

Trace Incorporated — now Trace Products

Trafalgar Industries, Inc. — acquired by Triangle Industries, Inc., now wholly-owned sub. of Towe International, Inc.

Trailways, Inc. — name changed to Trailways Corporation Lines, Inc.

Trailways Corporation Lines, Inc. — now Greyhound Lines, Inc.

Trak International, Inc. — acquired by Harbour Group Ltd.

The Trane Co. — acquired by American Standard

Trans Louisiana Gas Co., Inc. — acquired by Energas

Transco Energy Corporation — acquired & absorbed by The Williams Companies Inc.

Transcon Lines, Inc. — name changed to Transco, Inc.

Transcontinental Energy Corp. — liquidated

Transcontinental Oil Corp. — name changed to Transcontinental Energy Corp.

Transohio Financial Corp. — name changed to Transcapital Financial Corporation

Transport Holdings Inc. — acquired by Conseco Inc.

Transway International Corp. — merged into International Controls Corp.

Transworld Corp. — name changed to TW Services, Inc.

Travel Leisure Concepts — out of business

Travelodge Intl., Inc. — acquired by Trusthouse Forte, Inc.

Treadway Cos., Inc. — acquired by Fair Lanes, Inc.

Treasure Chest Advertising Co., Inc. — acquired by Big Flower Press

Treaty Co. — name changed to Hughes Supply Corp.

Treco, Inc. — name changed to Sunstates Corporation

Tri-Continental Corporation — acquired by J.W. Seligman & Company

Tri-Mark Metal Corp. — out of business

Tri-South Investments, Inc. — name changed to Avalon Properties, Inc.

Triangle Home Products, Inc. — out of business

Triangle Industries, Inc. — now Pechiney Packaging Corp., sub. of Pechiney Corp., sub. of Pechiney S.A.

Triangle Publications, Inc. — acquired by News America Publishing, Inc., sub. of News Corporation, Ltd.

Trico Industries, Inc. — acquired by PACCAR Inc.

Trico Products Corporation — acquired by Stunt Corporation

Trident Seafoods Corp. — acquired by ConAgra, Inc.

Trilogy Ltd. — name changed to ELXSI Ltd.

Trimac Limited — name changed to Trimac Corporation

Trinzic Corporation — acquired & absorbed by Platinum Technology

Trio Products Inc. — acquired by Ivex Packaging Corporation

Triton Group, Ltd. — merged with Intermark Inc.

Triton Oil & Gas Corp. — name changed to Triton Energy Corp.

Tropicana Products, Inc. — acquired by Beatrice Foods Co.

Trus Joist Corp. — now TJ International, Inc.

Trustbank Savings — taken over by Resolution Trust Co., January, 1991

Trusthouse Forte, Inc. — now Trusthouse Forte Hotels, Inc.

Tundra Books Inc. — acquired by McClelland & Stewart

Tur-Vel Industries, Inc. — out of business

Turner Broadcasting System, Inc. — acquired by Time

Warner Inc.

Turner Construction Co. — name changed to The Turner Corporation

Twin City Barge & Towing Co. — name changed to Twin City Barge, Inc.

Twin Fair, Inc. — name changed to Twin Fair Properties, Inc.

Tylan Corporation — merged with Vacuum General to form Tylan General, Inc.

Tylan General — acquired by Millipore Corporation & name changed to Millipore Tylan Products

Tymshare, Inc. — acquired by McDonnell Douglas Corp.

Tyrone Hydraulics, Inc. — acquired by Dana Corporation

U

U and I Incorporated — name changed to UI Group, Inc.

UAL, Inc. — name changed to Allegis Corporation

UC Industries, Inc. — acquired by Owens-Corning Fiberglass Corp.

UDC Homes, Inc. — acquired by DMB & Associates

U.I. Group, Inc. — now AgriNorthwest, Inc.

U.I.P. Corp. — acquired by Eastmet Corp. & name changed to Eastmet Industrial Products Group, Inc.

UMC Industries — name changed to UMI Dynamics Corp.

UNC Resources, Inc. — name changed to UNC Incorporated

UPDW, Inc. — name changed to Pricel, Inc.

UTC International Ltd. — name changed to Basel Trading Company Ltd.

Uarco, Inc. — acquired by City Investing Co.

Ullenberg Corp. — acquired by Imperial World, Inc.

Ultramar Corporation — merged with Diamond Shamrock, Inc. to form Ultramar Diamond Shamrock Corporation

Ultrasystems Incorporated — acquired by Hadson Corp.

Unarco Industries, Inc. — name changed to UNR Industries

William Underwood Co. — acquired by IC Industries, Inc.

Ungerman-Bass, Inc. — wholly-owned sub. of Tanden Computer, Inc.

Unibraze Corp. — acquired by Sanitas Service Corp.

Unicapital Corp. — name changed to Production Operators, Inc.

Unicord Co., Ltd. — name changed to Unicord Public Co. LTD.

Unicorp American Corp. — merged with Institutional Investors Corp.

Unidynamics Corp. — acquired by Crane Company

Uniform Software Systems, Inc. — acquired by Locus Computing Corp.

Unigard Insurance Group — name changed to Unigard Mutual Insurance Co.

Union Bancorp, Inc. — acquired by NBD Bancorp, Inc.

Union Bank of Finland — acquired by Unitas Ltd.

Union Commerce Corp. — acquired by & merged into Huntington Bancshares, Inc.

Union des Assurances de Paris (UAP) — merged with AXA to form AXA-UAP

Union Electric Steel Corp. — acquired by Ampco-Pittsburgh Corporation

Union Energy Inc. — acquired by Westcoast Energy Inc.

Union Fidelity Corp. — acquired by Filmways, Inc.

Union Gas Systems, Inc. — holding co. formed, Union Holding, Inc.

The Union Metal Mfg. Co. — name changed to Unimet Corporation

Union Mutual Life Insurance Co. — holding co. formed, UNUM Corporation

Union Oil Co. of California — name changed to UNOCAL Corporation

Union Trust Bancorp — merged with Bank of Virginia Co.

Union Trust Bancorp — dissolved; assets & liabilities assumed by Signet Banking Corporation

Unionamerica, Inc. — name changed to Westmor Corp.

Uniroyal Chemical Corporation — acquired by Crompton & Knowles Corporation

Uniroyal, Inc. — liquidated

Unishops, Inc. — name changed to The Marcade Group

Unistrut Corporation — acquired by Tyco International Ltd.

Unit Drilling & Exploration Co. — name changed to Unit Corporation

Unitas Ltd. — name changed to Merita Ltd.

Unitech Plc — acquired by Siebe plc

United Aircraft Products, Inc. — acquired by Parker-Hannifin Corp.

United Artists Communications, Inc. — now United Artists Entertainment Company, after merger with United Cable Television Corporation

United Artists Theatre Circuit, Inc. — name changed to United Artists Communications, Inc.

United Bank Corp. — name changed to United Bank Corp. of New York

United Banks of Colorado — now wholly-owned sub. of Norwest Corporation

United Biscuits UK Ltd. — name changed to United Biscuits (Holdings) Plc

United Cable Television Corporation — merged with United Artists Entertainment Company to form United Artists Entertainment Company

United Coatings, Inc. — acquired by Pratt & Lambert, Inc.

The United Corp. — merged with D.H. Baldwin Co. & new name is Baldwin-United Corp.

United Dollar Stores, Inc. — name changed to UDS, Inc.

United Energy Resources, Inc. — acquired by MidCon Corp.

United Envelope Company, Inc. — name changed to Westside Envelope Company, Inc.

United Financial Corp. of California — acquired by National Steel Corp.

United Foam Corp. — liquidated

United Foam Plastics Corporation—name changed to UFP Technology

United Gaming, Inc.—name changed to Alliance Gaming Corporation

United Graphics, Inc.—acquired by Banta Corporation

United Guaranty Corp.—acquired by American International Group, Inc. & name changed to United Guaranty Corp. of North Carolina

United Industrial Syndicate, Inc.—name changed to UIS, Inc.

United Inns, Inc.—acquired & absorbed by Harvey Hotels Management

United Marketing, Inc.—name changed to United Receptical, Inc.

United Medical Corporation—name changed to U.M. Holding Limited

United Michigan Corp.—acquired by NBD Bancorp, Inc.

United Nuclear Corp.—name changed to UNC Resources, Inc.

United Piece Dye Works—name changed to UPDW, Inc.

United Refining Co.—acquired by Coral Petroleum Co.

United Refrigeration Services—name changed to URS Logisitics

United Scientific Holdings P.L.C.—name changed to Alvis Plc

U.S. Banknote Corp.—acquired by Midcon Industries, Inc.

U.S. Delivery Systems—acquired by Corporate Express Inc.

U.S. Enertek, Inc.—out of business

U.S. Fidelity & Guaranty Co.—name changed to USF&G Corp.

United States Filter Corp.—acquired by Ashland Oil, Inc.

United States Gypsum Co.—holding co. formed, USG Corporation

U.S. Healthcare, Inc.—acquired by Aetna Life & Casualty & merged to form Aetna Inc.

U.S. Intec, Inc.—acquired by International Specialty Products, Inc.

United States Leasing International, Inc.—sub. of Ford Motor Company

United States Radium Corp.—name changed to USR Industries, Inc.

U.S. Reduction Co.—acquired by American Can Co.

U.S. Rubber Reclaiming Co., Inc.—acquired by Genstar Ltd.

U.S. Shelter Corporation—name changed to Insignia Financial Group, Inc.

The United States Shoe Corporation—out of business

United States Steel Corp.—name changed to USX Corporation

U.S. Telephone, Inc.—acquired by United Telecommunications, Inc.

United States Testing Co., Inc.—holding co. formed, SGS North America, Inc.

United States Tobacco Co.—name changed to UST, Inc.

United Stores—name changed to United Properties

United Telecommunications Inc.—name changed to the Sprint Corporation

United Transnet, Inc.—acquired by Corporate Express Inc.

United Virginia Bankshares Inc.—now Crestar Financial Corporation

United Westburne Inc.—name changed to Westburne Inc.

Unitek Corp.—acquired by Bristol-Myers Co.

Unity Buying Service Co., Inc.—liquidated

Univar Corporation—acquired by Royal Pakhoed NV

Universal Business Machines, Inc.—acquired by Recognition Equipment Inc. & merged into Recognition Business Systems, Inc.

Universal Cigar Corp.—now Faber, Coe & Gregg, Inc.

Universal Dynamics, Inc.—acquired by Filterwerk Mann & Hummel GmbH

Universal Group, Ltd.—acquired by Universal Foods Corporation

Universal Instruments Corp.—acquired by Dover Corp.

Universal Leaf Tobacco Co.—now Universal Corporation

Universal Resources Corp.—wholly-owned sub. of Questar Corp.

Universal Securities Corporation—out of business

Universal Voltronics Corporation—acquired by Thermo Electron Corporation

University Computing Co.—name changed to Wyly, Inc.

University Savings Assn.—acquired by Entex, Inc.

The Upjohn Company—merged with Pharmacia AB to form Pharmacia & Upjohn, Inc.

Utah International, Inc.—acquired by General Electric Co.

Utah Power & Light Company—acquired by PacifiCorp

Utilities & Industries Corp.—now Shephaug Corporation

Uvex Safety, Inc.—acquired by Bacou S.A.

V

V.G.S. Corp.—name changed to Southland Oil Company

VM Software, Inc.—now Systems Center, Inc.

VMC Fiberglass Products Inc.—acquired by Penda Corporation

VP Schickedanz A.G.—acquired by The Procter & Gamble Company

VSI Corp.—acquired by Fairchild Industries, Inc.

VWR Corporation—name changed to VWR Scientific Products

The Vagabond Inns—name changed to Imperial Hotels

Valid Logic Systems Inc.—acquired by and merged into Cadence Design Systems Inc.

Valley Gas Co.—name changed to Valley Resources,

Inc.

Valley Metallurgical Processing Co.—name changed to Gram Industries, Inc.

Valley National Bank of Arizona—holding co. formed, Valley National Corp.

Valleylab, Inc.—acquired by Pfizer, Inc.

Valmac Industries, Inc.—acquired by Tyson Food, Inc.

Value City Department Stores, Inc.—acquired by Schottenstein Stores Corp.

Value Line Development Capital Corp.—name changed to Sterling Capital Corp.

Value Merchants—out of business

Van Dusen Air Inc.—acquired by & merged with Aviall, Inc. of Ryder Systems, Inc.

Van Dyk Research Corporation—out of business

Van Kampen/American Capital Inc.—acquired by Morgan Stanley Group Inc.

Van Ommeren Ceteco N.V.—name changed to Koninklijke Van Ommeren NV

Vance, Sanders & Co., Inc.—name changed to Eaton & Howard, Vance Sanders, Inc.

Vanguard Technologies International, Inc.—wholly-owned sub. of Cincinnati Bell, Inc.

Varity Corporation—merged with LucasVarity plc & name changed to LucasVarity Inc.

The Vaughn Jacklin Corp.—name changed to Vaughan Products, Inc.

Vaughan Products Inc.—now Vaughan's Seed Co., wholly-owned sub. of Sandoz Ltd.

Vector Graphic, Inc.—out of business

Veeco Instruments Inc.—now Lamda Electronics Inc.

Veeder Industries—acquired by Western Pacific Industries, Inc.

Velobind, Inc.—acquired by General Banking Corp.

The Vendo Company—now sub. of Sanden International Corp.

Venice Industries, Inc.—acquired by Jonathan Logan, Inc.

Ventrex Laboratories, Inc.—acquired by Hycor Biomedical Inc.

Ventura Travelware, Inc.—out of business

Verbatim Corp.—acquired by Eastman Kodak Co.

Vermont America Corporation—acquired by Emerson Electric Company & Robert Bosch GmbH

Vermont Marble Co.—acquired by Pleuss-Stauffer (North America)

Verna Corporation—out of business

Vernitron Corporation—name changed to Axsys Technologies, Inc.

Versitron, Inc.—div. of Keene Corp., sub. of Bairnco

Vetco, Inc.—acquired by Combustion Engineering, Inc.

Vetco Offshore Industries, Inc.—name changed to Vetco, Inc.

Vertex Electronics, Inc.—name changed to Vertex Technology

Vertipile, Inc.—now Quaker Fabric Corp.

Vess Beverages, Inc.—acquired by Cott Corporation

Viacom International Inc.—wholly-owned sub. of Viacom, Inc.

Victor Comptometer Corp.—acquired by Walter Kidde & Co., Inc.

Victoria Bankshares Inc.—acquired & absorbed by Norwest Corporation

Victoria Financial Corporation—name changed to USF&G Corporation

Victory Markets, Inc.—wholly-owned sub. of LNC Industries Limited

View-Master International Group, Inc.—name changed to View-Master Ideal Group, Inc.

Viewlex, Inc.—name changed to Electro Sound Group, Inc.

The Vigoro Corporation—acquired by IMC Global Operations Inc.

Viking Electronics, Inc.—acquired by Wire-Pro Inc.

Viking General Corp.—name changed to American Capital Corp.

Viking Industries, Inc.—acquired by Heath Tecna Corp.

Vikoa, Inc.—name changed to Acton Corp.

Vipont Pharmaceutical Inc.—acquired by Colgate-Palmolive Company

Virginia Chemicals, Inc.—acquired by Celanese Corp.

Virginia Electric & Power Co.—name changed to Dominion Resources, Inc.

Virginia Hot Springs, Inc.—acquired by Club Corporation International & name changed to The Homestead L.C.

Vista Resources, Inc.—name changed to Fuqua Enterprises

Visual Electronics Corp.—name changed to Visual Industries, Inc.

Visual Graphics Corporation—now VGC Corp., sub. of VRG Group N.V.

Viuda De Jose Tolra, S.A.—name changed to Tradicion Textil, S.A.

Vivigen Inc.—acquired by Genzyme Corp.

Vogue & Body Shops, Inc.—name changed to Body Shop of America

Volume Shoe Corp.—acquired by May Dept. Stores Co.

Volunteer Capital Corporation—named changed to J. Alexanders Corporation

Voplex Corp.—acquired by & name changed to Cambridge Industries Inc.

Voyager Group—name changed to Virgin Hotel

Voyager Group, Inc.—acquired by American Can Co.

Vulcan, Inc.—acquired by Ampco-Pittsburgh Corp.

Vyquest, Inc.—out of business

W

W & F Products, Inc.—out of business

W S Holding Co.—acquired by U.S. Food Service Inc.

The WBDC Group—company dissolved

WCIX-TV—acquired by Westinghouse Electric Corp.

WDS, Inc.—liquidated

WEI Enterprises Corp.—liquidated

WG, Inc.—name changed to Willcox & Gibbs, Inc.

WLPF Corp.—name changed to Dartford Partnership

WMX Technologies, Inc.—name changed to Waste Management Inc.

WTC(U.S.A.) Inc.—acquired by & merged into Burlington Air Express Inc.

WUI, Inc.—acquired by Xerox Corp.

Wabash, Inc.—acquired by Dyson-Kissner Moran Corp.

Wabash Magnetics, Inc.—name changed to Wabash, Inc.

The Wachovia Corp.—holding co. formed, First Wachovia Corporation

Wadsworth Publishing Co., Inc.—name changed to Wadsworth, Inc.

Waggoner Corp.—out of business

Walbar, Inc.—acquired by Colt Industries, Inc.

Walco National Corp.—now Industrial General Corp.

Waldorf Corporation—acquired by Rock-Tenn Company

Walk, Haydel & Associates, Inc.—acquired by Hochteif AG

Hiram Walker Gooderham & Worts Ltd.—merged with Consumers Gas Co. & name changed to Hiram Walker-Consumers Home Ltd.

Walker-Home Petroleum Inc.—wholly-owned sub. of Gulf Canada Corp., sub. of Olympia & York Enterprises, sub. of Olympia & York Development

Walker Home Petroleum, Inc.—now HPC, Inc.

Wallace Business Forms, Inc.—name changed to Wallace Computer Services

Wallace Co. Inc.—acquired by & absorbed into Wilson Industries

Wallace Moir Co.—name changed to MIG Moir Financial

Wallace Murray Corp.—acquired by Household International, Inc.

Sam P. Wallace Co., Inc.—holding co. formed, SPW Corporation

Walter Industries, Inc.—acquired by Hillsborough Holdings Corporation

Jim Walter Corp.—now Walter Industries, Inc.

Walter Kidde & Co., Inc.—name changed to Kidde, Inc.

Wango, Inc.—acquired by Perkin-Elmer Corp.

Waples-Platter Cos.—acquired by Fleming Cos., Inc.

S.G. Warburg Group plc—acquired by Swiss Bank Corporation & name changed to SBC Warburg

Ward Foods, Inc.—name changed to The Terson Co., Inc.

Wards Co., Inc.—name changed to Circuit City Stores, Inc.

Warehouse Club—out of business

Warner Communications, Inc.—merged with Time Inc. to form Time Warner Inc.

Warner Electric Brake & Clutch Co.—acquired by Dana Corporation

Washers, Inc.—name changed to Alpha Stamping Inc.

Washington Construction Group—acquired by Morrison Knudsen Corporation & name changed to Morrison Knudsen California Regional Office

Washington Natural Gas Co.—name changed to Washington Energy Co.

Washington Star Communications, Inc.—name changed to Albritton Communications

Washington Steel Corp.—acquired by Blount, Inc.

Waters Associates, Inc.—acquired by Millipore Corp.

Waverly Press, Inc.—now Waverly, Inc.

Wayne-Gossard Corp.—name changed to Signal Apparel Co., Inc.

Wean United, Inc.—now Wean, Inc.

Weasler Engineering Inc.—acquired by Hochtief AG

Weatherhead Co.—acquired by Dana Corporation

W.H. Weaver Construction Co.—name changed to Weaver Contractors, LLC

Web Food Products Corp.—name changed to Worldwide Food Products Inc.

Del E. Webb Corp.—name changed to Del Webb Corp.

Webcor Electronics, Inc.—out of business

Webcraft Technologies, Inc.—acquired by Big Flower Press

Wedco Technology, Inc.—acquired by ICO, Inc.

Weeden Holding Corp.—name changed to Moseley, Hallgarten, Estabrook & Weeden Corp.

Weeks Energy Minerals Corp.—name changed to Energy Minerals Corp.

Barry Wehmiller International Plc—name changed to BWI

Wehr Corporation—split into two companies: Carnes Company, Inc. & Venturedyne, Inc.

Weigh-Tronix, Inc.—now sub. of Stavely Industries PLC

Weight Watchers International, Inc.—acquired by H.J. Heinz Co.

Weil Mclain Co., Inc.—name changed to Wylain, Inc.

Weiners Enterprises, Inc.—name changed to Weiners Stores, Inc.

J. Weingarten, Inc.—sub. of Grand Union Co.

Weisfield's Inc.—acquired by The Ratner Group and merged into Sterling Inc.

Weksler Instruments Corp.—acquired by Dresser Industries, Inc.

Welded Tube Co. of America—now wholly-owned sub. of Palmer Tube Mills

The Wellcome Foundation Limited—merged with Glaxo Holdings P.L.C. to form Glaxo Wellcome plc

Wells-Benrus Corporation—out of business

Wellstead Industries, Inc.—liquidated

WellTech, Inc.—jointly acquired by Bechtel Group of Cos. & Hanna Mining Co.

Welsbach Electric Corp.—acquired by M-Corp Group, Inc.

Werner Continental, Inc.—acquired by & merged into Hall's Motor Transit Co.

Wenczel Tile Co.—out of business

Milton J. Wershow Co.—name changed to Wershow-Ash-Lewis

West Chemical Products, Inc.—out of business

West Dairies, Inc.—acquired by Parmalot S.p.A.

West Lumber Co.—name changed to West Building Materials

West One Bancorp—acquired & absorbed by U.S. Bancorp.

West-Point Pepperell, Inc.—acquired by Farley Industries

West Publishing Company—acquired by The Thomson Corporation & name changed to West Information Publishing Group

Western Air Lines, Inc.—absorbed into Delta Air Lines, Inc.

Western Bancorporation—name changed to First Interstate Bancorp

The Western Company of North America—acquired & absorbed by BJ Services Company

Western Controls—acquired by & name changed to Heatcon Inc.

Western Federal Savings & Loan Association—out of business

Western Financial Corp.—name changed to Western Savings & Loan Association

Western Gear Corp.—acquired by Bucyrus-Erie Co.

Western Health Plans, Inc.—co. has ceased operations

Western Kentucky Gas Co.—acquired by Texas American Energy Corp.

Western Pacific Industries, Inc.—acquired by Danaher Company

Western Preferred Corp.—out of business

Western Publishing Co.—acquired by Mattel, Inc.

Western Savings & Loan Association—company placed in receivership, June 14, 1990

Western States Life Insurance Co.—sub. of Mutual Life of Canada

Western Temporary Services, Inc.—name changed to Western Staff Services, Inc.

Western Waste Industries—acquired by USA Waste Services, Inc.

Westmore Corp.—acquired by Genstar Ltd. & name changed to Western Mortgage Co.

Wheaton Inc.—acquired by Alusuisse-Lonza Holding Ltd.

Wheelabrator-Frye, Inc.—acquired by & merged into The Signal Companies

Wheelabrator-Frye, Inc.—acquired by the Henley Group, Inc., name changed to Wheelabrator Technologies, Inc.

Wheelabrator Technologies, Inc.—now 60% owned by Wheelabrator Group, Inc.

Wheeled Coach Industries, Inc.—acquired by Collins Industries, Inc.

Wherehouse Entertainment, Inc.—acquired by Adler & Shaykin

Whillock Manufacturing Co., Inc.—now Sealy Furniture Company

Whitaker Cable Corp.—name changed to Murphy Industries

White Consolidated Industries, Inc.—acquired by A.B. Electrolux

White County Farm Bureau Co-op Association—name changed to Excel Co-op Inc.

White Motor Corp.—wholly-owned sub. of Volvo North American Corp. & name changed to Volvo White Truck Corp.

White Shield Corp.—name changed to Basic Resources Corp.

White Storage & Retrieval Systems, Inc.—acquired by Pinnacle Automation Inc.

Whitestar Graphics, Inc.—name changed to Capital Graphics Inc.

Whiting Corp.—acquired by Wheelabrator-Frye Co.

Whitmire Distribution—acquired by Cardinal Health, Inc.

Wicat Systems——acquired by Jostens Inc.

Wichita Industries, Inc.—now Wichita River Oil Corp.

Wicker Park L.P.—out of business

The Wickes Corp.—merged with Gamble Skogmo, Inc. to form The Wickes Companies

Wieboldt Stores, Inc.—out of business

Wien Air Alaska, Inc.—acquired by Household Finance Corp.

The Wiener Corp.—name changed to Wiener Enterprises

Willcox & Gibbs Inc.—acquired by Rexel, S.A. & name changed to Rexel, Inc.

R.C. Wiley Home Furnishings—acquired by Berkshire Hathaway Inc.

Wilkata Packaging Corporation—name changed to Mebane Packaging Group, Wilkata Operation

Williamhouse-Regency, Inc.—acquired by American Pad & Paper

The A.L. Williams Corporation—wholly-owned by Primerica Corporation

Williams Electronics, Inc.—name changed to WMS Industries, Inc.

Wilson Brothers—acquired by DWG Corp.

H.J. Wilson Co., Inc.—acquired by & merged into Service Merchandise Co., Inc.

Wilson Foods Corporation—acquired by Doskocil Companies Incorporated

Wincorp Industries, Inc.—name changed to Wincorp Realty Investments

Wincorp Realty Investments, Inc.—acquired by & merged into Coyzel Properties

Windelman Stores, Inc.—acquired by Petrie Stores Corp.

Windmill Holdings Corp.—name changed to WLPF Corp.

Windsor Art, Inc.—acquired by Bentley International, Inc.

Windsor Industries, Inc.—name changed to Windsor Holding Corp.

Windsor Service, Inc.—acquired by Haines Kibblehouse

Wings & Wheels Express, Inc.—name changed to Air Express International

Winn Enterprises—out of business

Winona Knitting Mills, Inc.—acquired by Hampshire Group Ltd.

The Winter Park Telephone Co.—acquired by United Telecommunication, Inc.

Wisconsin Centrifugal, Inc.—acquired by Atlantic Richfield & merged into Anaconda Industries

Wisconsin Electric Power Co.—holding co. formed, Wisconsin Energy Corporation

Wisconsin Pharmacal Company, Inc.—name changed to Female Health Co.

Wisconsin Power & Light Co.—new holding co. formed, WPL Holdings, Inc.

Wisdom Import Sales Co. Inc.—acquired by John Labatt Limited

Witco Chemical Corp.—name changed to Witco Corp.

Wix Corp.—acquired by Dana Corporation

Wolverine Technologies—acquired by Saint-Gobain, Paris

Wometco Enterprises—now WEI Enterprises & Wometco Broadcasting Co.

Wood Industries, Inc.—acquired by M.A.N. of North America, Inc.

Daniel Woodhead, Inc.—name changed to Woodhead Industries, Inc.

Woods Corp.—acquired by & merged into WDS, Inc.

Woods Equipment Company—acquired by Code, Hennessey & Simmons, Inc.

Woodstream Corp.—now wholly-owned sub. of EKCO Group, Inc.

Woodward & Lothrop/John Wanamaker—absorbed into The May Department Stores Company

F.W. Woolworth Co.—holding co. formed, Woolworth Corporation

Worcester Controls Corp.—acquired by SW (Delaware) Inc.

Wordperfect Corporation—acquired by Novell, Inc. & name changed to Novell Application Group

Worlco Data Systems Inc.—out of business

World Computer Corp.—acquired by General Motors

World Service Life Insurance Co.—name changed to Western Preferred Corp.

Worldwide Energy Corp.—acquired by Triton Oil & Gas Corp.

Worthen Banking—acquired & absorbed by Boatmen's Bancshares

Wrather Corporation—acquired by & merged into The Walt Disney Company

Wm. E. Wright Co.—now wholly-owned sub. of Newell Company

Wunda Weve Carpets, Inc.—acquired by & absorbed into World Carpets, Inc.

The Wurlitzer Co.—now Wurltech and The Wurlitzer Company, sub. of Baldwin Piano & Organ Co.

Wylain, Inc.—acquired by & merged into The Marley Company

Wyly Corp.—name changed to UCCEL Corporation

Wyndham Foods, Inc.—now Wyndham Holdings, Inc.—acquired by President Enterprises Corp.

Wyoming Bancorporation—name changed to Western Preferred Corp.

Wyomissing Corp.—acquired by Alco Standard

X

XCor International—name changed to Biscayne Holdings Inc.

Xidex Corporation—acquired by Anacomp, Inc.

Xlogics, Inc.—acquired by Bay Networks, Inc.

Xoil Energy Resources, Inc.—out of business

Xomox Corp.—acquired by Emerson Electric Co.

Xonics, Inc.—liquidated September, 1985

Y

Y.R.J. Corp.—name changed to U.S. Reprographics Corp.

Yale Industrial Trucks of Southern California—name changed to Yale/Chase Materials Handling, Inc.

Yankee Oil & Gas Inc.—name changed to The Yankee Corporation

Yates & Auberle, Ltd.—now Harding Lawson Associates of Harding Associates, Inc.

Yates Industries, Inc.—acquired by Square D Co. & name changed to Square D Manufacturing Facility

Yerger Bros., Inc.—name changed to Great Connections, Inc.

Yoo-Hoo Chocolate Beverage Co.—acquired by Iroquois Brands Ltd.

York International Corporation—holding co., formed, York Holding Corporation

Youngstown Steel Door Co.—acquired by Lamson & Sessions Co.

Younker Bros., Inc.—acquired by Equitable of Iowa Cos.

Yugoslav Airlines—out of business

Z

Zale Corporation—now joint venture of Peoples Jewellers Ltd. & Swasovski Intl. Holding A.G.

Zayre Corporation—acquired by Ames Department Stores, Inc.

Zenith Laboratories—acquired by IVAX Corporation

Zenith Products Corp.—acquired by Masco Corporation

Zeos International, Ltd.—merged with Micron Electron-

ics, Inc.

Zenith Radio Corp.—name changed to Zenith Electronics Corporation

Zentec Corporation—out of business

Ziff Corp.—name changed to Ziff Communications Co.

Ziff-Davis Publishing Company—acquired by Softbank

Zilber Ltd.—out of business

Zima Corporation—acquired by Kusters Corporation

Zimmer Corporation—out of business

John Zink Co.—acquired by Koch Engineering of Koch Industries

Ziyad, Inc.—now Gradco Systems Inc., Printed Products Div.

Zoecon Corp.—acquired by Occidental Petroleum Corp.

Zollner Industries—out of business

The Zondervan Corporation—acquired by Harper & Row Publishers, Inc.

MASTER INDEX TO COMPANY NAMES

A

A A CATER TRUCK MANUFACTURING COMPANY, INC.; *U.S. Private,* pg. 1
A & A ASSOCIATES—See Zimmerman Holdings, Inc.; *U.S. Private,* pg. 1206
A & A INTERNATIONAL, INC.—See Tandy Corporation; *U.S. Public,* pg. 1560
A & A INTERNATIONAL-SEOUL BRANCH—See Tandy Corporation; *U.S. Public,* pg. 1561
A & A INTERNATIONAL-TAIPEI BRANCH—See Tandy Corporation; *U.S. Public,* pg. 1561
A & A INTL. (YICHI-HK) LTD.—See Tandy Corporation; *U.S. Public,* pg. 1561
A & A JAPAN LTD.—See Tandy Corporation; *U.S. Public,* pg. 1561
A&A MANUFACTURING CO.; *U.S. Private,* pg. 1
A & B DEVELOPMENT CO. (CALIFORNIA)—See Alexander & Baldwin; *U.S. Public,* pg. 39
A & B-HAWAII, INC.—See Alexander & Baldwin, Inc.; *U.S. Public,* pg. 39
A & B PLASTICS, INC.—See Bunzl PLC; *Int'l,* pg. 232
A & B PLASTICS-SOUTHWEST, INC.—See Bunzl PLC; *Int'l,* pg. 232
A & B PROPERTIES, INC.—See Alexander & Baldwin, Inc.; *U.S. Public,* pg. 39
A&E STORES, INC.; *U.S. Private,* pg. 1
A&E TELEVISION NETWORKS—See The Hearst Corporation; *U.S. Private,* pg. 515
A&M INSTRUMENTS INC—See BTR plc; *Int'l,* pg. 125
A & M PRODUCTS—See First Brands Corporation; *U.S. Public,* pg. 627
A&M RECORDS—See Philips Electronics N.V.; *Int'l,* pg. 1052
A & N LEASING—See Service Motor Company; *U.S. Private,* pg. 986
A & P COAT, APRON & LINEN SUPPLY; *U.S. Private,* pg. 1
A&P / WALDBAUM'S FOOD MART—See Tengelmann Warenhandelsgesellschaft; *Int'l,* pg. 1375
A & R BARRIERE FRERES S.A.—See Suntory Ltd.; *Int'l,* pg. 1322
A & S BUILDING SYSTEMS, INC.—See NCI Building Systems, Inc.; *U.S. Public,* pg. 1146
A & S TRIBAL INDUSTRIES; *U.S. Private,* pg. 1
A&T CORPORATION—See Tokuyama Corporation; *Int'l,* pg. 1393
A&W COMPANY—See Albright & Wilson plc; *Int'l,* pg. 49
A&W FOOD SERVICES OF CANADA INC.; *Int'l,* pg. 1
A&W RESTAURANTS, INC.; *U.S. Private,* pg. 1
A&W RESTAURANTS, INC.-CAROUSEL DIV.—See A&W Restaurants, Inc.; *U.S. Private,* pg. 2
A&Z HAYWARD, INC.; *U.S. Private,* pg. 2
A B C APPLIANCE INC.; *U.S. Private,* pg. 2
A-B EMBLEM DIV. OF CONRAD INDUSTRIES, INC.; *U.S. Private,* pg. 2
A-B EMBLEMS AND CAPS—See A-B Emblem Div. of Conrad Industries, Inc.; *U.S. Private,* pg. 2
A BAR A RANCH—See Cody Company; *U.S. Private,* pg. 249
A/CD-EAST—See ITT Industries, Inc.; *U.S. Public,* pg. 859
A/CD-WEST—See ITT Industries, Inc.; *U.S. Public,* pg. 859
A-DEC, INC.; *U.S. Private,* pg. 2
A E CLEVITE, INC.—See T & N Plc; *Int'l,* pg. 1334
A-E DIVISION—See Central Allied Enterprises; *U.S. Private,* pg. 222
A4 REKLAMCILIK—See TBWA Chiat/Day; *U.S. Private,* pg. 1062
A-G SAFETY SALES, INC.—See Tyco International Ltd.; *U.S. Public,* pg. 1650
A GREENHOUSE INC.—See Koninklijke BolsWessanen nv; *Int'l,* pg. 752
A J M PACKAGING CORPORATION; *U.S. Private,* pg. 2
A K H COMPANY, INC.; *U.S. Private,* pg. 2

A-L PACKAGING SERVICES LTD.—See Alusuisse-Lonza Holding Ltd.; *Int'l,* pg. 67
A-L SERVICES FRANCE S.N.C.—See Alusuisse-Lonza Holding Ltd.; *Int'l,* pg. 68
A-MARK FINANCIAL; *U.S. Private,* pg. 2
A-MOLD CORP.—See UBE Industries Ltd.; *Int'l,* pg. 1427
A/O AHLSTROM—See A. Ahlstrom Corporation; *Int'l,* pg. 34
A-OK DELAWARE INC.—See GIB Group; *Int'l,* pg. 533
A - 1 MEDICAL EQUIPMENT, INC.—See Integrated Health Services, Inc.; *U.S. Public,* pg. 884
A-1 WIRETECH, INC.—See Inco Limited; *Int'l,* pg. 672
A-P-A TRANSPORT CORP.; *U.S. Private,* pg. 2
A-PARTNERS—See Vendex International N.V.; *Int'l,* pg. 1463
A-R TECHNOLOGIES—See Magellan Aerospace Corporation; *Int'l,* pg. 829
A S H, INC.; *U.S. Private,* pg. 2
A/S/M COMMUNICATIONS, INC.—See VNU Verenigde Nederlandse Uitgeversbedrijven B.V.; *Int'l,* pg. 1446
A S RUFFEL (MOZAMBIQUE) LIMITADA—See Pfizer Inc.; *U.S. Public,* pg. 1282
A S RUFFEL (PRIVATE) LTD.—See Pfizer Inc.; *U.S. Public,* pg. 1282
A TABLE MATSUYA CO., LTD.—See Matsuya Company Ltd.; *Int'l,* pg. 848
A-Z TERMINAL CORPORATION—See Sooner Pipe & Supply Corp.; *U.S. Private,* pg. 1014
AA JAPAN CO.—See American Appraisal Associates, Inc.; *U.S. Private,* pg. 50
AA THE MOTORISTS PUBLICATIONS (PTY.) LIMITED—See The Reader's Digest Association, Inc.; *U.S. Public,* pg. 1368
AAA INVESTMENT COMPANY—See American Automobile Association; *U.S. Private,* pg. 50
AAA PLUMBING POTTERY CORP.—See Gerber Plumbing Fixtures Corporation; *U.S. Private,* pg. 449
AAF CONSULTANTS LTD.—See AAF Industries Plc; *Int'l,* pg. 1
AAF INDUSTRIES PLC; *Int'l,* pg. 1
AAF-INTERNATIONAL—See AAF McQuay, Inc.; *U.S. Private,* pg. 3
AAF MCQUAY, INC.; *U.S. Private,* pg. 2
AAH BUILDERS SUPPLIES LIMITED—See Franz Haniel & Cie, GmbH; *Int'l,* pg. 591
AAH CONSUMER PRODUCTS LTD.—See Franz Haniel & Cie, GmbH; *Int'l,* pg. 591
AAH DISTRIBUTION SERVICES LTD.—See Franz Haniel & Cie, GmbH; *Int'l,* pg. 591
AAH MEDICAL—See Franz Haniel & Cie, GmbH; *Int'l,* pg. 591
AAH MEDITEL LIMITED—See Franz Haniel & Cie, GmbH; *Int'l,* pg. 591
AAH PHARMACEUTICALS LIMITED—See Franz Haniel & Cie, GmbH; *Int'l,* pg. 591
AAH PLC—See Franz Haniel & Cie, GmbH; *Int'l,* pg. 591
AAH RETAIL PHARMACY LIMITED—See Franz Haniel & Cie, GmbH; *Int'l,* pg. 591
AAI/ACL TECHNOLOGIES—See United Industrial Corporation; *U.S. Public,* pg. 1679
AAI CORPORATION—See United Industrial Corporation; *U.S. Public,* pg. 1679
AAL CAPITAL MANAGEMENT CORP.—See Aid Association for Lutherans; *U.S. Private,* pg. 28
AAR ADVANCED STRUCTURES DIV.—See AAR Corp.; *U.S. Public,* pg. 1
AAR AIRCRAFT TURBINE CENTER—See AAR Corp.; *U.S. Public,* pg. 1
AAR ALLEN AIRCRAFT—See AAR Corp.; *U.S. Public,* pg. 1
AAR ALLEN AIRMOTIVE, INC.—See AAR Corp.; *U.S. Public,* pg. 1
AAR AVIATION SERVICES U.K.—See AAR Corp.; *U.S. Public,* pg. 1
AAR CADILLAC MANUFACTURING DIV.—See AAR Corp.; *U.S. Public,* pg. 1

AAR CORP.; *U.S. Public,* pg. 1
AAR DEFENSE SYSTEMS—See AAR Corp.; *U.S. Public,* pg. 1
AAR ENGINE COMPONENT SERVICES—See AAR Corp.; *U.S. Public,* pg. 1
AAR EUROPA—See AAR Corp.; *U.S. Public,* pg. 1
AAR LANDING GEAR CENTER—See AAR Corp.; *U.S. Public,* pg. 1
AAR OKLAHOMA—See AAR Corp.; *U.S. Public,* pg. 1
AAR PACIFIC PTE. LTD.—See AAR Corp.; *U.S. Public,* pg. 1
AAR POWER BOSS—See AAR Corp.; *U.S. Public,* pg. 1
AAR TECHNICAL SERVICE CENTER—See AAR Corp.; *U.S. Public,* pg. 1
AAV AUSTRALIA—See John Fairfax Holdings Limited; *Int'l,* pg. 477
AAV BUSINESS COMMUNICATIONS—See John Fairfax Holdings Limited; *Int'l,* pg. 477
AB-SMALL BUSINESS INVESTMENT COMPANY, INC.—See Bozzuto's Inc.; *U.S. Public,* pg. 249
ABB AB—See ABB Asea Brown Boveri (Holding) Ltd.; *Int'l,* pg. 7
ABB-ADTRANZ HENNINGSDORF—See Daimler-Benz Aktiengesellschaft; *Int'l,* pg. 369
ABB AIR PREHEATER INC.—See ABB Asea Brown Boveri (Holding) Ltd.; *Int'l,* pg. 3
ABB AMDATA—See ABB Asea Brown Boveri (Holding) Ltd.; *Int'l,* pg. 3
ABB ASEA—See ABB Asea Brown Boveri (Holding) Ltd.; *Int'l,* pg. 8
ABB ASEA BROWN BOVERI (HOLDING) LTD.; *Int'l,* pg. 1
ABB ASEA BROWN BOVERI PTY. LTD.—See ABB Asea Brown Boveri (Holding) Ltd.; *Int'l,* pg. 2
ABB ASEA SKANDIA AB—See ABB Asea Brown Boveri (Holding) Ltd.; *Int'l,* pg. 7
ABB CABLES AB—See ABB Asea Brown Boveri (Holding) Ltd.; *Int'l,* pg. 7
ABB C-E POWER PRODUCTS MANUFACTURING—See ABB Asea Brown Boveri (Holding) Ltd.; *Int'l,* pg. 3
ABB C-E SERVICES—See ABB Asea Brown Boveri (Holding) Ltd.; *Int'l,* pg. 3
ABB CEAG POWER SUPPLIES INC.—See ABB Asea Brown Boveri (Holding) Ltd.; *Int'l,* pg. 4
ABB COMBUSTION ENGINEERING BRASIL—See ABB Asea Brown Boveri (Holding) Ltd.; *Int'l,* pg. 5
ABB COMBUSTION ENGINEERING NUCLEAR POWER—See ABB Asea Brown Boveri (Holding) Ltd.; *Int'l,* pg. 3
ABB COMBUSTION ENGINEERING SYSTEMS—See ABB Asea Brown Boveri (Holding) Ltd.; *Int'l,* pg. 3
ABB COMMERCIAL ENGINEERING CANADA—See ABB Asea Brown Boveri (Holding) Ltd.; *Int'l,* pg. 5
ABB CONTROL INC.—See ABB Asea Brown Boveri (Holding) Ltd.; *Int'l,* pg. 8
ABB-DAIMLER BENZ TRANSPORTATION (ADTRANZ)—See ABB Asea Brown Boveri (Holding) Ltd.; *Int'l,* pg. 8
ABB-DAIMLER BENZ TRANSPORTATION (ADTRANZ)—See Daimler-Benz Aktiengesellschaft; *Int'l,* pg. 369
ABB DRYING—See ABB Asea Brown Boveri (Holding) Ltd.; *Int'l,* pg. 5
ABB ELECTRO MECHANICS INC.—See ABB Asea Brown Boveri (Holding) Ltd.; *Int'l,* pg. 3
ABB ENERGY VENTURES INC.—See ABB Asea Brown Boveri (Holding) Ltd.; *Int'l,* pg. 4
ABB ENVIRONMENTAL SERVICES INC.—See ABB Asea Brown Boveri (Holding) Ltd.; *Int'l,* pg. 4
ABB ENVIRONMENTAL SYSTEMS (ABBES)—See ABB Asea Brown Boveri (Holding) Ltd.; *Int'l,* pg. 4
ABB ENVIRONMENTAL SYSTEMS (UTILITIES)—See ABB Asea Brown Boveri (Holding) Ltd.; *Int'l,* pg. 4
ABB FINANCIAL SERVICES INC.—See ABB Asea Brown Boveri (Holding) Ltd.; *Int'l,* pg. 4
ABB FLEXIBLE AUTOMATION—See ABB Asea Brown Boveri (Holding) Ltd.; *Int'l,* pg. 4
ABB GARDEN CITY FAN—See ABB Asea Brown Boveri (Holding) Ltd.; *Int'l,* pg. 4

Company Index

ABB GAS TURBINE BUSINESS—See ABB Asea Brown Boveri (Holding) Ltd.; *Int'l*, pg. 4
ABB GENERATION AB—See ABB Asea Brown Boveri (Holding) Ltd.; *Int'l*, pg. 7
ABB HAFO AB—See ABB Asea Brown Boveri (Holding) Ltd.; *Int'l*, pg. 7
ABB HAFO INC.—See ABB Asea Brown Boveri (Holding) Ltd.; *Int'l*, pg. 4
ABB HV SWITCHGEAR AB—See ABB Asea Brown Boveri (Holding) Ltd.; *Int'l*, pg. 7
ABB HYDRO POWER DIV.—See ABB Asea Brown Boveri (Holding) Ltd.; *Int'l*, pg. 4
ABB IN CANADA—See ABB Asea Brown Boveri (Holding) Ltd.; *Int'l*, pg. 7
ABB INC.—See ABB Asea Brown Boveri (Holding) Ltd.; *Int'l*, pg. 3
ABB INDUSTRI A/S—See ABB Asea Brown Boveri (Holding) Ltd.; *Int'l*, pg. 2
ABB INDUSTRIAL SYSTEMS, INC.—See ABB Asea Brown Boveri (Holding) Ltd.; *Int'l*, pg. 4
ABB INDUSTRIAL SYSTEMS, INC.—See ABB Asea Brown Boveri (Holding) Ltd.; *Int'l*, pg. 4
ABB INVESTMENT MANAGEMENT—See ABB Asea Brown Boveri (Holding) Ltd.; *Int'l*, pg. 4
ABB ISOPROFIL GMBH STAHLPROFIL-UND WARMWALZWERK—See ABB Asea Brown Boveri (Holding) Ltd.; *Int'l*, pg. 2
ABB K-FLOW INC.—See ABB Asea Brown Boveri (Holding) Ltd.; *Int'l*, pg. 4
ABB KABEL UND DRAHT GMBH—See ABB Asea Brown Boveri (Holding) Ltd.; *Int'l*, pg. 2
ABB KENT METERS—See ABB Asea Brown Boveri (Holding) Ltd.; *Int'l*, pg. 4
ABB KENT PLC—See ABB Asea Brown Boveri (Holding) Ltd.; *Int'l*, pg. 7
ABB KENT-TAYLOR LTD.—See ABB Asea Brown Boveri (Holding) Ltd.; *Int'l*, pg. 7
ABB LUMMUS GLOBAL INC.—See ABB Asea Brown Boveri (Holding) Ltd.; *Int'l*, pg. 4
ABB LUMMUS HEAT TRANSFER—See ABB Asea Brown Boveri (Holding) Ltd.; *Int'l*, pg. 5
ABB MASCHINENFABRIK MEYER AG—See ABB Asea Brown Boveri (Holding) Ltd.; *Int'l*, pg. 1
ABB METALLURGY AB—See ABB Asea Brown Boveri (Holding) Ltd.; *Int'l*, pg. 7
ABB METERING SYSTEMS—See ABB Asea Brown Boveri (Holding) Ltd.; *Int'l*, pg. 5
ABB MOTORS AB—See ABB Asea Brown Boveri (Holding) Ltd.; *Int'l*, pg. 4
ABB NEWINGTON OPERATIONS—See ABB Asea Brown Boveri (Holding) Ltd.; *Int'l*, pg. 4
ABB OPERATIONS & MAINTENANCE—See ABB Asea Brown Boveri (Holding) Ltd.; *Int'l*, pg. 4
ABB PAINT FINISHING—See ABB Asea Brown Boveri (Holding) Ltd.; *Int'l*, pg. 5
ABB PETERCEM S.A.—See ABB Asea Brown Boveri (Holding) Ltd.; *Int'l*, pg. 2
ABB PHOENIX CONTROLS—See ABB Asea Brown Boveri (Holding) Ltd.; *Int'l*, pg. 4
ABB PLAST AB—See ABB Asea Brown Boveri (Holding) Ltd.; *Int'l*, pg. 7
ABB POWER GENERATION INC.—See ABB Asea Brown Boveri (Holding) Ltd.; *Int'l*, pg. 3
ABB POWER LTD.—See ABB Asea Brown Boveri (Holding) Ltd.; *Int'l*, pg. 2
ABB POWER PLANT CONTROLS—See ABB Asea Brown Boveri (Holding) Ltd.; *Int'l*, pg. 4
ABB POWER PLANT LABORATORIES—See ABB Asea Brown Boveri (Holding) Ltd.; *Int'l*, pg. 4
ABB POWER T & D COMPANY INC.—See ABB Asea Brown Boveri (Holding) Ltd.; *Int'l*, pg. 4
ABB PROCESS ANALYTICS—See ABB Asea Brown Boveri (Holding) Ltd.; *Int'l*, pg. 5
ABB PROCESS ANALYTICS LTD.—See ABB Asea Brown Boveri (Holding) Ltd.; *Int'l*, pg. 7
ABB PROJECT & EXPORT FINANCE (USA) INC.—See ABB Asea Brown Boveri (Holding) Ltd.; *Int'l*, pg. 4
ABB RANDALL CORPORATION—See ABB Asea Brown Boveri (Holding) Ltd.; *Int'l*, pg. 5
ABB REGIONAL PRODUCT CENTRE PTE. LTD.—See ABB Asea Brown Boveri (Holding) Ltd.; *Int'l*, pg. 2
ABB RELAYS AB—See ABB Asea Brown Boveri (Holding) Ltd.; *Int'l*, pg. 7
ABB ROBOTICS AB—See ABB Asea Brown Boveri (Holding) Ltd.; *Int'l*, pg. 7
ABB SACE LIMITADA—See ABB Asea Brown Boveri (Holding) Ltd.; *Int'l*, pg. 2
ABB SACE S.P.A. COSTRUSIONI ELETTROMECCANICHE—See ABB Asea Brown Boveri (Holding) Ltd.; *Int'l*, pg. 2
ABB SECHERON S.A.—See ABB Asea Brown Boveri (Holding) Ltd.; *Int'l*, pg. 1
ABB SELFA AB—See ABB Asea Brown Boveri (Holding) Ltd.; *Int'l*, pg. 7
ABB SERVICE AB—See ABB Asea Brown Boveri (Holding) Ltd.; *Int'l*, pg. 7
ABB SIMCON, INC.—See ABB Asea Brown Boveri (Holding) Ltd.; *Int'l*, pg. 5
ABB STAL AB—See ABB Asea Brown Boveri (Holding) Ltd.; *Int'l*, pg. 7
ABB STAL REFRIGERATION—See ABB Asea Brown Boveri (Holding) Ltd.; *Int'l*, pg. 4
ABB STEAM POWER GENERATION COMPANY—See ABB Asea Brown Boveri (Holding) Ltd.; *Int'l*, pg. 4
ABB STOTZ-KONTAKT HELLAS S.A.—See ABB Asea Brown Boveri (Holding) Ltd.; *Int'l*, pg. 2
ABB STOTZ-KONTAKT (PORTUGAL) LDA.—See ABB Asea Brown Boveri (Holding) Ltd.; *Int'l*, pg. 2
ABB STOTZ-KONTAKT S.A.—See ABB Asea Brown Boveri (Holding) Ltd.; *Int'l*, pg. 2
ABB TECNOMASIO S.P.A.—See ABB Asea Brown Boveri (Holding) Ltd.; *Int'l*, pg. 2
ABB TRACTION AB—See ABB Asea Brown Boveri (Holding) Ltd.; *Int'l*, pg. 7
ABB TRACTION INC.—See ABB Asea Brown Boveri (Holding) Ltd.; *Int'l*, pg. 5

ABB TRALLFA ROBOT A/S—See ABB Asea Brown Boveri (Holding) Ltd.; *Int'l*, pg. 8
ABB TRANSFORMERS AB—See ABB Asea Brown Boveri (Holding) Ltd.; *Int'l*, pg. 7
ABB TRANSFORMERS INC.—See ABB Asea Brown Boveri (Holding) Ltd.; *Int'l*, pg. 7
ABB TREASURY CENTER (USA) INC.—See ABB Asea Brown Boveri (Holding) Ltd.; *Int'l*, pg. 4
ABB TURBINE MANUFACTURING & SERVICE—See ABB Asea Brown Boveri (Holding) Ltd.; *Int'l*, pg. 4
ABB TURBOCHARGER COMPANY—See ABB Asea Brown Boveri (Holding) Ltd.; *Int'l*, pg. 5
ABB VETCO U.K. LTD.—See ABB Asea Brown Boveri (Holding) Ltd.; *Int'l*, pg. 5
ABC-ADEMCO SECURITY PRODUCTS—See Pittway Corporation; *U.S. Public*, pg. 1306
ABC BULL S.A. TELEMATIC—See Compagnie des Machines Bull; *Int'l*, pg. 318
ABC BULL S/A TELEMATIC—See Compagnie des Machines Bull; *Int'l*, pg. 315
ABC CABLE & INTERNATIONAL BROADCAST, INC.—See The Walt Disney Company; *U.S. Public*, pg. 512
ABC DECO, INC.—See ABC Rail Products Corp.; *U.S. Public*, pg. 2
ABC HOLDING COMPANY, INC.—See The Walt Disney Company; *U.S. Public*, pg. 512
ABC INC.—See The Walt Disney Company; *U.S. Public*, pg. 511
ABC INSTRUMENTACION ANALITICA, S.A. DE C.V.—See Hewlett-Packard Company; *U.S. Public*, pg. 816
ABC/KANE PRODUCTIONS INTERNATIONAL, INC.—See The Walt Disney Company; *U.S. Public*, pg. 511
ABC NEWS & SPORTS—See The Walt Disney Company; *U.S. Public*, pg. 511
ABC NEWS HOLDING COMPANY, INC.—See The Walt Disney Company; *U.S. Public*, pg. 511
ABC NEWS, INC.—See The Walt Disney Company; *U.S. Public*, pg. 511
ABC NEWS INTERCONTINENTAL, INC.—See The Walt Disney Company; *U.S. Public*, pg. 511
ABC PACKAGING MACHINE CORP.; *U.S. Private*, pg. 3
ABC PRODUCTIONS—See The Walt Disney Company; *U.S. Public*, pg. 511
ABC RADIO NETWORK, INC.—See The Walt Disney Company; *U.S. Public*, pg. 512
ABC RAIL COGIFER INDUSTRIES—See ABC Rail Products Corp.; *U.S. Public*, pg. 2
ABC RAIL PRODUCTS CORP.; *U.S. Public*, pg. 2
ABC SPORTS HOLDING COMPANY, INC.—See The Walt Disney Company; *U.S. Public*, pg. 511
ABC SPORTS, INC.—See The Walt Disney Company; *U.S. Public*, pg. 511
ABC SUPPLY COMPANY, INC.; *U.S. Private*, pg. 3
ABC TELEVISION NETWORK—See The Walt Disney Company; *U.S. Public*, pg. 511
ABC TRANSPORTATION CO.—See American Buildings Co.; *U.S. Public*, pg. 69
ABC/WATERMARK, INC.—See The Walt Disney Company; *U.S. Public*, pg. 511
ABCO, INC.—See Fortune Brands, Inc.; *U.S. Public*, pg. 674
ABD GROUP INC.—See Devon Group, Inc.; *U.S. Public*, pg. 503
ABF FREIGHT SYSTEM, INC.—See Arkansas Best Corporation; *U.S. Public*, pg. 130
ABG-FRANCE S.A.R.L.—See Ingersoll-Rand Company; *U.S. Public*, pg. 877
ABG-IBERICA—See Ingersoll-Rand Company; *U.S. Public*, pg. 877
ABH LUBRIFANTS—See Fuchs Petrolub AG Oel + Chemie; *Int'l*, pg. 518
ABI IMTECH NV—See Internatio-Muller N.V.; *Int'l*, pg. 681
ABI MANAGEMENT, INC.—See American Financial Group; *U.S. Public*, pg. 74
ABI NATIONAL ACCOUNTS—See American Business Information, Inc.; *U.S. Public*, pg. 70
ABM CHEMICALS LTD.—See Rhone-Poulenc S.A.; *Int'l*, pg. 1113
ABM INDUSTRIES; *U.S. Public*, pg. 2
ABM INVESTMENT LTD.—See Viag AG; *Int'l*, pg. 1465
ABN AMRO BANK, N.V. (SEATTLE)—See ABN-AMRO Holding N.V.; *Int'l*, pg. 10
ABN-AMRO BANK (SVERIGE) AB—See ABN-AMRO Holding N.V.; *Int'l*, pg. 11
ABN AMRO CHICAGO CORP.—See ABN-AMRO Holding N.V.; *Int'l*, pg. 10
ABN AMRO CHICAGO CORP FINANCIAL SERVICES—See ABN-AMRO Holding N.V.; *Int'l*, pg. 10
ABN AMRO CHICAGO CORPORATION—See ABN-AMRO Holding N.V.; *Int'l*, pg. 10
ABN-AMRO HOLDING N.V.; *Int'l*, pg. 8
ABN-AMRO NORTH AMERICA INC., CHICAGO—See ABN-AMRO Holding N.V.; *Int'l*, pg. 10
ABN-AMRO SECURITIES (U.K.) LTD—See ABN-AMRO Holding N.V.; *Int'l*, pg. 12
ABN-AMRO SECURITIES (USA) INC.—See ABN-AMRO Holding N.V.; *Int'l*, pg. 11
ABN-AMRO TRUST COMPANY (VIRGIN ISLANDS)—See ABN-AMRO Holding N.V.; *Int'l*, pg. 11
ABN FINANZIARIA S.P.A.—See ABN-AMRO Holding N.V.; *Int'l*, pg. 11
ABN (HEAD OFFICE)—See ABN-AMRO Holding N.V.; *Int'l*, pg. 11
ABN INTERNATIONAL DIAMOND DIVISION—See ABN-AMRO Holding N.V.; *Int'l*, pg. 11
ABN INTERNATIONAL FINANCIAL SERVICES CO.—See ABN-AMRO Holding N.V.; *Int'l*, pg. 11
ABN/LASALLE NORTH AMERICA INC.—See ABN-AMRO Holding N.V.; *Int'l*, pg. 11
ABN LEASING ESPANA, S.A.—See ABN-AMRO Holding N.V.; *Int'l*, pg. 11
ABN LEASING ITALIA S.P.A.—See ABN-AMRO Holding N.V.; *Int'l*, pg. 11
ABN (LUXEMBOURG) S.A.—See ABN-AMRO Holding N.V.; *Int'l*, pg. 11

ABN MANAGEMENT SERVICES A.G.—See ABN-AMRO Holding N.V.; *Int'l*, pg. 11
ABN, SUCURSAL EN ESPANA (BARCELONA)—See ABN-AMRO Holding N.V.; *Int'l*, pg. 11
ABN, SUCURSAL EN ESPANA (MADRID)—See ABN-AMRO Holding N.V.; *Int'l*, pg. 11
ABN TRUSTCOMPANY (LUXEMBOURG) S.A.—See ABN-AMRO Holding N.V.; *Int'l*, pg. 11
ABN TRUSTCOMPANY (SUISSE) S.A.—See ABN-AMRO Holding N.V.; *Int'l*, pg. 12
ABP INTERACTIVE LLC—See Adler Boschetto Peebles & Partners, Inc.; *U.S. Private*, pg. 17
ABR ABFALLBESEITIGUNG UND RECYCLING GMBH—See Ruetgers A.G.; *Int'l*, pg. 1148
ABR HANDEL GMBH—See Ruetgers A.G.; *Int'l*, pg. 1148
ABR INFORMATION SERVICES, INC.; *U.S. Public*, pg. 2
ABS BELGIUM NV/SA—See Cardo AB; *Int'l*, pg. 270
ABS BOMBAS LTDA—See Cardo AB; *Int'l*, pg. 270
ABS BOMBAS S.A.—See Cardo AB; *Int'l*, pg. 270
ABS GLOBAL INC.; *U.S. Private*, pg. 3
ABS INDUSTRIA DE BOMBAS CENTRIFUGES LTDA—See Cardo AB; *Int'l*, pg. 270
ABS INTEGRATED SERVICES—See American Bureau of Shipping; *U.S. Private*, pg. 51
ABS MARINE SERVICES, INC.—See American Bureau of Shipping; *U.S. Private*, pg. 51
ABS POMPALAEI LTD.—See Cardo AB; *Int'l*, pg. 270
ABS POMPE SRL—See Cardo AB; *Int'l*, pg. 270
ABS POMPEN B.V.—See Cardo AB; *Int'l*, pg. 270
ABS POMPES S.A.—See Cardo AB; *Int'l*, pg. 270
ABS PRODUCTION S.A.R.L.—See Cardo AB; *Int'l*, pg. 270
ABS PUMP AB—See Cardo AB; *Int'l*, pg. 270
ABS PUMP AB, FAR EAST—See Cardo AB; *Int'l*, pg. 270
ABS PUMP CENTER AG—See Cardo AB; *Int'l*, pg. 270
ABS PUMP PRODUCTION AB—See Cardo AB; *Int'l*, pg. 270
ABS PUMPEN GES.M.B.H.—See Cardo AB; *Int'l*, pg. 270
ABS PUMPEN GMBH—See Cardo AB; *Int'l*, pg. 270
ABS PUMPER A/S—See Cardo AB; *Int'l*, pg. 270
ABS PUMPS CORPORATION—See Cardo AB; *Int'l*, pg. 270
ABS PUMPS INC.—See Cardo AB; *Int'l*, pg. 270
ABS PUMPS INTERNATIONAL AB—See Cardo AB; *Int'l*, pg. 270
ABS PUMPS LTD.—See Cardo AB; *Int'l*, pg. 270
ABS PUMPUT OY—See Cardo AB; *Int'l*, pg. 270
ABS QUALITY EVALUATIONS, INC.—See American Bureau of Shipping; *U.S. Private*, pg. 51
ABS SUBMERSIBLE DIVISION—See Cardo AB; *Int'l*, pg. 270
ABT BUILDING PRODUCTS CORPORATION—See Abitibi-Consolidated Inc.; *Int'l*, pg. 20
ABTCO, INC.—See Abitibi-Consolidated Inc.; *Int'l*, pg. 20
ABX AIR, INC.—See Airborne Freight Corporation; *U.S. Public*, pg. 33
ABX S.A.—See Roche Holding Ltd.; *Int'l*, pg. 1120
AC & S INC.—See Irex Corporation; *U.S. Public*, pg. 913
AC BAKONY KFT.—See General Motors Corporation; *U.S. Public*, pg. 724
AC CORPORATION; *U.S. Private*, pg. 3
AC LEASING CORPORATION—See Action Equipment; *U.S. Private*, pg. 15
A.C. MEDICAL, INC.—See Columbia/HCA Healthcare Corporation; *U.S. Public*, pg. 403
AC PRODUCTS, INC.—See Quaker Chemical Corporation; *U.S. Public*, pg. 1346
AC ROCHESTER CORPORATION—See General Motors Corporation; *U.S. Public*, pg. 721
AC ROCHESTER DIVISION (GENNEVILLIERS)—See General Motors Corporation; *U.S. Public*, pg. 721
AC ROCHESTER DIVISION (SAO PAULO)—See General Motors Corporation; *U.S. Public*, pg. 721
AC ROCHESTER LUXEMBOURG S.A.—See General Motors Corporation; *U.S. Public*, pg. 723
AC ROCHESTER OVERSEAS CORPORATION—See General Motors Corporation; *U.S. Public*, pg. 722
AC ROCHESTER PRODUCTS AUSTRIA GES.M.B.H—See General Motors Corporation; *U.S. Public*, pg. 723
A.C. SCANNING, INC.—See Wallace Computer Services, Inc.; *U.S. Public*, pg. 1735
ACAP CHEMICALS PTE. LTD.—See Aluminum Company of America; *U.S. Public*, pg. 61
ACBJ BUSINESS JOURNALS, INC.—See Advance Publications Inc.; *U.S. Private*, pg. 19
ACBJ BUSINESS PUBLICATIONS, INC.—See Advance Publications Inc.; *U.S. Private*, pg. 19
ACC-BABCOCK LTD.—See FKI Plc; *Int'l*, pg. 474
ACC CORP.; *U.S. Public*, pg. 3
ACC LONG DISTANCE, LTD.—See ACC Corp.; *U.S. Public*, pg. 3
ACC LONG DISTANCE U.K. LTD.—See ACC Corp.; *U.S. Public*, pg. 3
ACC SERVICES, INC.—See Caraustar Industries, Inc.; *U.S. Public*, pg. 303
ACC TELECOM—See ACC Corp.; *U.S. Public*, pg. 3
ACD AGRO CONSULT DRESDEN GMBH—See Heidemij N.V.; *Int'l*, pg. 607
A.C.E. DAIKIN (SINGAPORE) PTE., LTD.—See Daikin Industries, Ltd.; *Int'l*, pg. 365
ACEC AUTOMATISME—See Alcatel Alsthom Compagnie Generale D'Electricite; *Int'l*, pg. 54
ACEC-OSI—See Tractebel; *Int'l*, pg. 1415
ACF INDUSTRIES, INC.—See Icahn & Co., Inc.; *U.S. Private*, pg. 556
ACF MINERA LTDA.—See DSM N.V.; *Int'l*, pg. 354
ACG COMPONENTES, S.A.—See General Motors Corporation; *U.S. Public*, pg. 724
ACH, INC.—See Columbia/HCA Healthcare Corporation; *U.S. Public*, pg. 403
ACI AMERICA HOLDINGS INC.—See BTR plc; *Int'l*, pg. 129
ACI AUSTRALIA LIMITED—See BTR plc; *Int'l*, pg. 128
ACI CLOSURES—See BTR plc; *Int'l*, pg. 128
ACI COMPUTER SERVICES—See BTR plc; *Int'l*, pg. 128

ACI ENGINEERING—See BTR plc; *Int'l*, pg. 128
ACI EUROPE LTD.—See BTR plc; *Int'l*, pg. 129
ACI FIBREGLASS—See BTR plc; *Int'l*, pg. 128
ACI GATEWAY—See Morgan Crucible Co. Plc; *Int'l*, pg. 891
ACI HOLDING INC.—See EULER; *Int'l*, pg. 464
ACI HOLDING INC.—See Swiss Reinsurance Company; *Int'l*, pg. 1332
ACI HOMES—See BTR plc; *Int'l*, pg. 128
ACI INDUSTRIES PTY. LTD.—See BTR plc; *Int'l*, pg. 128
ACI INTERNATIONAL LTD.—See BTR plc; *Int'l*, pg. 128
ACI KIMTRUSS CORP.—See BTR plc; *Int'l*, pg. 129
ACI LIQUITAINERS—See BTR plc; *Int'l*, pg. 128
ACI MILLING PTY. LTD.—See BTR plc; *Int'l*, pg. 128
ACI NEW ZEALAND LTD.—See BTR plc; *Int'l*, pg. 129
ACI OPERATIONS PTY. LTD.—See BTR plc; *Int'l*, pg. 128
ACI PLASTICS CLOSURES—See BTR plc; *Int'l*, pg. 128
ACI RESOURCES LTD.—See BTR plc; *Int'l*, pg. 128
ACI STANDARD—See Morgan Crucible Co. Plc; *Int'l*, pg. 891
ACI SYSTEMS, INC.—See CSA Holdings Ltd.; *Int'l*, pg. 242
ACI TELECENTRICS, INC.; *U.S. Public*, pg. 3
ACI TELECENTRICS INC.—See ACI Telecentrics, Inc.; *U.S. Public*, pg. 3
ACL DRAYTON—See Siebe plc; *Int'l*, pg. 1241
ACN PRODUCT GROUP—See DSM N.V.; *Int'l*, pg. 353
ACNA—See Groupe Air France; *Int'l*, pg. 560
ACO INC.; *U.S. Private*, pg. 3
ACOR (ACIERS DE CONSTRUCTIONS RATIONALISES)—See Groupe Usinor; *Int'l*, pg. 570
ACR GROUP; *U.S. Public*, pg. 3
ACR INDUSTRIES INC.; *U.S. Private*, pg. 3
ACS INDUSTRIES, INC.; *U.S. Private*, pg. 3
ACS INTERNACIONAL S.A. DE C.V.—See ACS Industries, Inc.; *U.S. Private*, pg. 4
ACS MISTERMESH PTY LIMITED—See CSA Holdings Ltd.; *Int'l*, pg. 242
ACS MISTERMESH—See ACS Industries, Inc.; *U.S. Private*, pg. 4
ACT MANUFACTURING; *U.S. Public*, pg. 3
ACT NETWORKS, INC.; *U.S. Public*, pg. 3
ACTC TECHNOLOGIES—See Compagnie des Machines Bull; *Int'l*, pg. 317
ACTE NORDIC COMPONENTS A/S—See Bergman & Beving AB; *Int'l*, pg. 188
ACX TECHNOLOGIES INC.; *U.S. Public*, pg. 3
A.D. DATA SYSTEMS—See PSC Inc.; *U.S. Public*, pg. 1246
AD PLASTICS LTD.—See Dentsply International Inc.; *U.S. Public*, pg. 499
ADA CRUDE OIL COMPANY—See Adams Resources & Energy, Inc.; *U.S. Public*, pg. 19
ADAC LABORATORIES INC.; *U.S. Public*, pg. 3
ADAP INC.; *U.S. Private*, pg. 4
ADC DE MEXICO, S.A. DE C.V.—See ADC Telecommunications, Inc.; *U.S. Public*, pg. 4
ADC EUROPE NV—See ADC Telecommunications, Inc.; *U.S. Public*, pg. 4
ADC L.P.; *U.S. Private*, pg. 4
ADC METRICA—See ADC Telecommunications, Inc.; *U.S. Public*, pg. 4
ADC NEWNET, INC.—See ADC Telecommunications, Inc.; *U.S. Public*, pg. 4
ADC SOLITRA OY—See ADC Telecommunications, Inc.; *U.S. Public*, pg. 4
ADC SYSTEMS INTEGRATION GROUP—See ADC Telecommunications, Inc.; *U.S. Public*, pg. 4
ADC TELECOM CANADA INC.—See ADC Telecommunications, Inc.; *U.S. Public*, pg. 4
ADC TELECOMMUNICATIONS AUSTRALIA PTY. LTD.—See ADC Telecommunications, Inc.; *U.S. Public*, pg. 4
ADC TELECOMMUNICATIONS DO BRASIL LTDA—See ADC Telecommunications, Inc.; *U.S. Public*, pg. 4
ADC TELECOMMUNICATIONS GMBH—See ADC Telecommunications, Inc.; *U.S. Public*, pg. 4
ADC TELECOMMUNICATIONS, INC.; *U.S. Public*, pg. 4
ADC TELECOMMUNICATIONS SINGAPORE PTE LIMITED—See ADC Telecommunications, Inc.; *U.S. Public*, pg. 4
ADC TELECOMMUNICATIONS U.K. LIMITED—See ADC Telecommunications, Inc.; *U.S. Public*, pg. 4
ADC TELECOMUNICACIONES VENEZUELA, S.A.—See ADC Telecommunications, Inc.; *U.S. Public*, pg. 4
ADC WIRELESS SYSTEMS, INC.—See ADC Telecommunications, Inc.; *U.S. Public*, pg. 4
ADCS, INC.—See ATMI, Inc.; *U.S. Public*, pg. 12
ADD, INC.—See Journal Communications Inc.; *U.S. Private*, pg. 601
ADHOC—See Vendex International N.V.; *Int'l*, pg. 1463
ADI—See Tennessee Farmers Co-op; *U.S. Private*, pg. 1076
ADI (ADEMCO DISTRIBUTION, INC.)—See Pittway Corporation; *U.S. Public*, pg. 1306
ADI DATA FURNITURE—See Esselte AB; *Int'l*, pg. 460
ADI MEXICO—See Pittway Corporation; *U.S. Public*, pg. 1307
ADIG ALLGEMEINE DEUTSCHE INVESTMENT GESELLSCHAFTMBH—See Bayerische Vereinsbank Group; *Int'l*, pg. 180
ADIG ALLGEMEINE DEUTSCHE INVESTMENT GESELLSCHAFTMBH—See Commerzbank AG; *Int'l*, pg. 309
ADIG INVESTMENT LUXEMBOURG S.A.—See Bayerische Vereinsbank Group; *Int'l*, pg. 181
ADIG INVESTMENT LUXEMBOURG S.A.—See Commerzbank AG; *Int'l*, pg. 312
ADK PRESSURE EQUIPMENT CORPORATION—See Danaher Corporation; *U.S. Public*, pg. 481
ADM ARKADY—See Archer Daniels Midland Company (ADM); *U.S. Public*, pg. 127
ADM COCOA, INC.—See Archer Daniels Midland Company (ADM); *U.S. Public*, pg. 127
ADM CORN PROCESSING DIVISION—See Archer Daniels Midland Company (ADM); *U.S. Public*, pg. 127

ADM ETHANOL SALES—See Archer Daniels Midland Company (ADM); *U.S. Public*, pg. 127
ADM FOOD ADDITIVES DIVISION—See Archer Daniels Midland Company (ADM); *U.S. Public*, pg. 127
ADM FOOD OILS—See Archer Daniels Midland Company (ADM); *U.S. Public*, pg. 128
ADM/GROWMARK—See Archer Daniels Midland Company (ADM); *U.S. Public*, pg. 128
ADM LECITHINS—See Archer Daniels Midland Company (ADM); *U.S. Public*, pg. 128
ADM MILLING CO.—See Archer Daniels Midland Company (ADM); *U.S. Public*, pg. 128
ADM MILLING CO. - RICE DIVISION—See Archer Daniels Midland Company (ADM); *U.S. Public*, pg. 128
ADM MILLING CO. - VALLEY GRAIN—See Archer Daniels Midland Company (ADM); *U.S. Public*, pg. 128
ADM PROCESSING DIV.—See Archer Daniels Midland Company (ADM); *U.S. Public*, pg. 127
ADM PROTEIN SPECIALTIES—See Archer Daniels Midland Company (ADM); *U.S. Public*, pg. 128
ADMC INC.—See Artco-Bell Corporation; *U.S. Private*, pg. 86
ADN/ADD—See Young & Rubicam Inc.; *U.S. Private*, pg. 1200
ADP FLUOR DANIEL—See Fluor Corporation; *U.S. Public*, pg. 660
ADP MARSHALL CONTRACTORS INC.—See Fluor Corporation; *U.S. Public*, pg. 660
ADR, INC.—See Tracor, Inc.; *U.S. Public*, pg. 1427
ADS ENVIRONMENTAL SERVICES INC.—See Axel Johnson AB; *Int'l*, pg. 709
ADT AUTOMOTIVE, INC.—See Tyco International Ltd.; *U.S. Public*, pg. 1648
ADT DIVERSIFIED SERVICES, INC.—See Tyco International Ltd.; *U.S. Public*, pg. 1649
ADT EUROPE—See Tyco International Ltd.; *U.S. Public*, pg. 1649
ADT GREECE, S.A.—See Tyco International Ltd.; *U.S. Public*, pg. 1649
ADT ITALIANA, S.P.A.—See Tyco International Ltd.; *U.S. Public*, pg. 1649
ADT PHONE & MODERN SECURITY—See Tyco International Ltd.; *U.S. Public*, pg. 1649
ADT/PROEGUR, S.A.—See Tyco International Ltd.; *U.S. Public*, pg. 1649
ADT SECURITY SERVICES—See Tyco International Ltd.; *U.S. Public*, pg. 1648
ADT SECURITY SERVICES, INC.—See Tyco International Ltd.; *U.S. Public*, pg. 1649
ADT SECURITY SYSTEMS—See Tyco International Ltd.; *U.S. Public*, pg. 1649
ADT TRUCK & EQUIPMENT AUCTIONS, INC.—See Tyco International Ltd.; *U.S. Public*, pg. 1648
AE FARMS, INC.—See Anderson Erickson Dairy Company; *U.S. Private*, pg. 72
AE GOETZE AUTOMOTIVE—See T & N Plc; *Int'l*, pg. 1334
AE GOETZE-NORTH AMERICA—See T & N Plc; *Int'l*, pg. 1334
AEA DEVELOPMENT CORP.—See CoreStates Financial Corp.; *U.S. Public*, pg. 447
AEA INC./AUTO PARTS—See Republic Automotive Parts, Inc.; *U.S. Public*, pg. 1377
AEA INVESTORS INC.; *U.S. Private*, pg. 4
AEA OF COLUMBIA—See Republic Automotive Parts, Inc.; *U.S. Public*, pg. 1377
AEA OF RALEIGH—See Republic Automotive Parts, Inc.; *U.S. Public*, pg. 1377
AEC/APPLICATION AUTOMATION, INC.—See Sterling, Inc.; *U.S. Private*, pg. 1041
AEC/APPLICATION ENGINEERING CORPORATION—See Sterling, Inc.; *U.S. Private*, pg. 1041
AEC FOREST PRODUCTS—See Alberta Energy Company, Ltd.; *Int'l*, pg. 48
AEC, INC.—See Harbour Group Ltd.; *U.S. Private*, pg. 500
AEC, INC.—See Sterling, Inc.; *U.S. Private*, pg. 1041
AEC OIL & GAS—See Alberta Energy Company, Ltd.; *Int'l*, pg. 48
AEC PIPELINES—See Alberta Energy Company, Ltd.; *Int'l*, pg. 48
AEC/WHITLOCK, INC.—See Sterling, Inc.; *U.S. Private*, pg. 1041
AECL TECHNOLOGIES INC.—See Atomic Energy of Canada Ltd.; *Int'l*, pg. 97
AEG ELECTROCOM GMBH, KONSTANZ—See Siemens AG; *Int'l*, pg. 1244
AEG HAUSGERATE AG—See Electrolux, AB; *Int'l*, pg. 442
AEG MOBILE COMMUNICATIONS GMBH—See Lagardere Groupe; *Int'l*, pg. 795
AEG RADIOCOMUNICACIONES SA—See Lagardere Groupe; *Int'l*, pg. 795
AEG SORTING SYSTEMS INC.—See Siemens AG; *Int'l*, pg. 1244
AEG STARKSTROMANLAGEN—See Daimler-Benz Aktiengesellschaft; *Int'l*, pg. 367
AEG ZAHLER GMBH—See Schlumberger Limited; *U.S. Public*, pg. 1439
AEI AUSTRALIA PTY. LTD.—See Air Express International Corporation; *U.S. Public*, pg. 30
AEI CABLES—See TT Group PLC; *Int'l*, pg. 1344
AEI HOLDING CO., INC.; *U.S. Private*, pg. 4
AEI ITALY—See Air Express International Corporation; *U.S. Public*, pg. 30
AEI OCEAN SERVICES—See Air Express International Corporation; *U.S. Public*, pg. 30
AEL LEASING CO., INC.—See ABN-AMRO Holding N.V.; *Int'l*, pg. 9
AEP/BORDEN B.V.—See AEP Industries, Inc.; *U.S. Public*, pg. 5
AEP/BORDEN GLOBAL PACKAGING (U.K.) LTD.—See AEP Industries, Inc.; *U.S. Public*, pg. 5
AEP/BORDEN MACAPLE S.A.—See AEP Industries, Inc.; *U.S. Public*, pg. 5
AEP/BORDEN S.A.—See AEP Industries, Inc.; *U.S. Public*, pg. 5

AEP CANADA, INC.—See AEP Industries, Inc.; *U.S. Public*, pg. 5
AEP FRANCE S.A.S.—See AEP Industries, Inc.; *U.S. Public*, pg. 5
AEP GENERATING CO.—See American Electric Power Company, Inc.; *U.S. Public*, pg. 72
AEP INDUSTRIES AUSTRALIA PTY. LTD.—See AEP Industries, Inc.; *U.S. Public*, pg. 5
AEP INDUSTRIES, INC.; *U.S. Public*, pg. 4
AEP INDUSTRIES (NZ) LTD.—See AEP Industries, Inc.; *U.S. Public*, pg. 5
AEP INDUSTRIES PACKAGING ESPANA, S.A.—See AEP Industries, Inc.; *U.S. Public*, pg. 5
AEP RESOURCES SERVICE COMPANY—See American Electric Power Company, Inc.; *U.S. Public*, pg. 72
AEP-SPAN—See United Dominion Industries, Ltd.; *U.S. Public*, pg. 1676
AER TURAS TEO—See Aer Lingus; *Int'l*, pg. 28
AES AIRPORT EQUIPMENT & SERVICES GMBH—See Mannesmann A.G.; *Int'l*, pg. 836
AES AMERICAS—See AES Corporation; *U.S. Public*, pg. 5
AES CHINA GENERATING—See AES Corporation; *U.S. Public*, pg. 5
AES CORPORATION; *U.S. Public*, pg. 5
AES ELECTRIC—See AES Corporation; *U.S. Public*, pg. 5
AES ENTERPRISE—See AES Corporation; *U.S. Public*, pg. 5
AES TRANSPOWER—See AES Corporation; *U.S. Public*, pg. 5
AESA ASTILLEROS ESPANOLES, S.A.—See SEPI; *Int'l*, pg. 1223
AET PACKAGING FILMS—See Applied Extrusion Technologies, Inc.; *U.S. Public*, pg. 122
AET SPECIALTY NETS & PROFILES—See Applied Extrusion Technologies, Inc.; *U.S. Public*, pg. 122
AEW CAPITAL MANAGEMENT, L.P.—See Metropolitan Life Insurance Co.; *U.S. Private*, pg. 737
AEW PARTNERS, L.P.; *U.S. Private*, pg. 5
A.F. & D. MACKAY LTD.—See Norske Skogindustrier A.S; *Int'l*, pg. 966
AF INVESTIMENTOS—See Eureko B.V.; *Int'l*, pg. 464
AF SISTEMAS SA—See Groupe Strafor Facom; *Int'l*, pg. 569
AFA PROTECTIVE SYSTEMS, INC.; *U.S. Public*, pg. 5
AFA PROTECTIVE SYSTEMS, INC.—See AFA Protective Systems, Inc.; *U.S. Public*, pg. 5
AFC CABLE SYSTEMS, INC.; *U.S. Public*, pg. 6
AFC ENTERPRISES; *U.S. Private*, pg. 5
AFCO CREDIT CORP.—See Mellon Bank Corporation; *U.S. Public*, pg. 1085
AFD CONTRACT FURNITURE; *U.S. Private*, pg. 5
AFE (HONG KONG) LTD.—See BTR plc; *Int'l*, pg. 129
AFG, INC.—See Keycorp; *U.S. Public*, pg. 955
AFG INDUSTRIES, INC.—See Asahi Glass Co., Ltd.; *Int'l*, pg. 84
AFGD—See Asahi Glass Co., Ltd.; *Int'l*, pg. 84
AFI HOTELS LIMITED—See Granada Group PLC; *Int'l*, pg. 556
AFIA—See Cigna Corp.; *U.S. Public*, pg. 366
AFIA (CIGNA) CORPORATION, LIMITED—See Cigna Corp.; *U.S. Public*, pg. 364
AFIA FINANCE CORPORATION—See Cigna Corp.; *U.S. Public*, pg. 363
AFIA (INA) CORPORATION, LIMITED—See Cigna Corp.; *U.S. Public*, pg. 366
AFIA SOCIEDAD ANONIMA—See Cigna Corp.; *U.S. Public*, pg. 363
AFIA VENEZUELA, C.A.—See Cigna Corp.; *U.S. Public*, pg. 363
AFM—See Raytech Corporation; *U.S. Public*, pg. 1363
A.F.N. LTD.—See Porsche AG; *Int'l*, pg. 1063
AFP IMAGING CORPORATION; *U.S. Public*, pg. 6
AFP TRANSFORMERS, INC.—See United Capital Corp.; *U.S. Public*, pg. 1674
AFS AVIATION FUEL SERVICES GMBH—See Veba AG; *Int'l*, pg. 1460
AFS INSURANCE SERVICES, INC.—See Associated Food Stores Inc.; *U.S. Private*, pg. 90
AFSA DATA CORP.—See Fleet Financial Group, Inc.; *U.S. Public*, pg. 649
AFSC SIGNATURE FLIGHT SUPPORT—See Japan Airlines Company, Ltd.; *Int'l*, pg. 700
AG-CHEM EQUIPMENT CO., INC.; *U.S. Public*, pg. 6
AG INDUSTRIES, INC.—See AG Ajikawa Corporation; *Int'l*, pg. 40
A.G. INDUSTRIES INC.—See American Greetings Corporation; *U.S. Public*, pg. 78
AG SERVICES OF AMERICA, INC.; *U.S. Public*, pg. 6
AG STANLEY LIMITED—See The Boots Company PLC; *Int'l*, pg. 202
AG SUPERMARKETS INC.—See Associated Grocers of New England, Inc.; *U.S. Private*, pg. 91
AGA AB; *Int'l*, pg. 12
OY AGA AB—See AGA AB; *Int'l*, pg. 13
AGA AG—See AGA AB; *Int'l*, pg. 13
AGA ARGENTINA SACIFIMR—See AGA AB; *Int'l*, pg. 13
AGA A/S—See AGA AB; *Int'l*, pg. 13
AGA CATALOG MARKETING & DESIGN; *U.S. Private*, pg. 5
AGA CATALOG MARKETING & DESIGN—See Cullman Ventures, Inc.; *U.S. Private*, pg. 295
AGA CHILE S.A.—See AGA AB; *Int'l*, pg. 13
AGA COOKERS INC.—See Glynwed International PLC; *Int'l*, pg. 555
AGA-CRYO AB—See AGA AB; *Int'l*, pg. 12
AGA-CRYO GMBH—See AGA AB; *Int'l*, pg. 13
AGA DE MEXICO S.A. DE C.V.—See AGA AB; *Int'l*, pg. 13
AGA DEL ECUADOR C.A.—See AGA AB; *Int'l*, pg. 13
CIA. AGA DEL PERU S.A.—See AGA AB; *Int'l*, pg. 13
AGA-FANO S.A.—See AGA AB; *Int'l*, pg. 13
AGA GAS AB—See AGA AB; *Int'l*, pg. 12
AGA GAS B.V.—See AGA AB; *Int'l*, pg. 13
AGA GAS C.A.—See AGA AB; *Int'l*, pg. 13
AGA GAS GMBH—See AGA AB; *Int'l*, pg. 13

Company Index

AGA GAS, INC.—See AGA AB; *Int'l*, pg. 13
AGA GAS LTD.—See AGA AB; *Int'l*, pg. 13
AGA GAS SPOL.S R.O.—See AGA AB; *Int'l*, pg. 13
AGA GAZ KFT.—See AGA AB; *Int'l*, pg. 13
AGA GAZ SP.Z.O.O.—See AGA AB; *Int'l*, pg. 13
AGA GAZ S.R.L.—See AGA AB; *Int'l*, pg. 13
AGA GES.M.B.H.—See AGA AB; *Int'l*, pg. 13
AGA GLOUCESTER HOUSE—See AGA Catalog Marketing
    & Design; *U.S. Private*, pg. 5
AGA INDUSTRIAL GAS ENGINEERING AB—See AGA AB;
    Int'l, pg. 12
AGA NV/SA—See AGA AB; *Int'l*, pg. 13
AGA PROGAS A/S—See AGA AB; *Int'l*, pg. 13
AGA PUERTO RICO CORP.—See AGA AB; *Int'l*, pg. 13
AGA-QUINSA S.A.—See AGA AB; *Int'l*, pg. 13
AGA RE—See AGA AB; *Int'l*, pg. 13
AGA S.A.—See AGA AB; *Int'l*, pg. 13
AGA S.A. DE C.V.—See AGA AB; *Int'l*, pg. 14
AGA SIA—See AGA AB; *Int'l*, pg. 13
AGA SPECIALGAS AB—See AGA AB; *Int'l*, pg. 14
AGA S.R.L.—See AGA AB; *Int'l*, pg. 14
AGA UAB—See AGA AB; *Int'l*, pg. 14
AGA VENEZOLANA C.A.—See AGA AB; *Int'l*, pg. 14
A.G.C. (ADVANCES) LIMITED—See Westpac Banking
    Corporation; *Int'l*, pg. 1496
P.T. AGC ARTA LEASING—See Westpac Banking
    Corporation; *Int'l*, pg. 1497
A.G.C. (FINANCE) LIMITED—See Westpac Banking
    Corporation; *Int'l*, pg. 1496
AGC FINANCIAL (H.K.) LIMITED—See Westpac Banking
    Corporation; *Int'l*, pg. 1497
A.G.C. (GENERAL FINANCE) LIMITED—See Westpac
    Banking Corporation; *Int'l*, pg. 1496
A.G.C. (INDUSTRIAL) LIMITED—See Westpac Banking
    Corporation; *Int'l*, pg. 1496
AGC LIFE INSURANCE CO.—See American General
    Corporation; *U.S. Public*, pg. 76
AGC (THAILAND) FINANCE & SECURITIES CO.,
    LIMITED—See Westpac Banking Corporation; *Int'l*,
    pg. 1497
AGEFI—See LVMH Moet Hennessy Louis Vuitton; *Int'l*,
    pg. 779
AGF ASSURANCES; *Int'l*, pg. 14
AGG - SA ALUSUISSE GUY GEISLER NV—See Alusuisse-
    Lonza Holding Ltd.; *Int'l*, pg. 68
AGI INC.; *U.S. Private*, pg. 5
AGIP (AFRICA) LTD.—See ENI S.p.A.; *Int'l*, pg. 428
AGIP DEUTSCHLAND AG—See ENI S.p.A.; *Int'l*, pg. 428
AGIP DO BRASIL S.A.—See ENI S.p.A.; *Int'l*, pg. 428
AGIP HUNGARIA R.T.—See ENI S.p.A.; *Int'l*, pg. 428
AGIP INTERNATIONAL B.V.—See ENI S.p.A.; *Int'l*, pg. 429
AGIP (NORTH AFRICA & MIDDLE EAST) LTD.—See ENI
    S.p.A.; *Int'l*, pg. 428
AGIP (OVERSEAS) LTD.—See ENI S.p.A.; *Int'l*, pg. 428
AGIP PETROLEUM CO., INC.—See ENI S.p.A.; *Int'l*,
    pg. 428
AGIP PETROLI—See ENI S.p.A.; *Int'l*, pg. 428
AGIP PETROLI INTERNATIONAL B.V.—See ENI S.p.A.;
    Int'l, pg. 429
AGIP PRAHA LTD.—See ENI S.p.A.; *Int'l*, pg. 428
AGIP SPA—See ENI S.p.A.; *Int'l*, pg. 428
AGIP (SUISSE) S.A.—See ENI S.p.A.; *Int'l*, pg. 428
AGIV GROUP; *Int'l*, pg. 14
AGL ENERGY SERVICES, INC.—See AGL Resources; *U.S.
    Public*, pg. 7
AGL RESOURCES; *U.S. Public*, pg. 6
AGP INDUSTRIAL CORPORATION; *Int'l*, pg. 14
AGR INTERNATIONAL, INC.; *U.S. Private*, pg. 5
AGRA (HONG KONG) LIMITED—See Agra Inc.; *Int'l*,
    pg. 31
AGRA INTERNATIONAL LIMITED—See Agra Inc.; *Int'l*,
    pg. 30
AGRA PLASTICS INC.—See Agra Inc.; *Int'l*, pg. 30
AHF-DUCOMMUN INCORPORATED—See Ducommun
    Incorporated; *U.S. Public*, pg. 534
AHF SALONS, INC.—See Opal Concepts, Inc.; *U.S.
    Private*, pg. 818
AHI ROLL-A-DOOR—See International Paper Company;
    U.S. Public, pg. 904
AHM ALTOS HORNOS DEL MEDITERRANEO, S.A.—See
    SEPI; *Int'l*, pg. 1223
AHP DO BRASIL—See American Home Products
    Corporation; *U.S. Public*, pg. 80
A.H.V. ENSIDESA CAPITAL, S.A.—See SEPI; *Int'l*,
    pg. 1223
A.I. CREDIT CORP.—See American International Group,
    Inc.; *U.S. Public*, pg. 85
AI/FOCS, INC.—See Woodhead Industries, Inc.; *U.S.
    Public*, pg. 1776
A.I. OCEAN; *Int'l*, pg. 14
A.I. OCEAN—See A.I. Ocean; *Int'l*, pg. 14
AIAL (ARIMPEX S.R.L. INDUSTRIE ALIMENTARI)—See
    H.J. Heinz Company; *U.S. Public*, pg. 807
AIB CAPITAL MARKETS PLC—See Allied Irish Banks,
    p.l.c.; *Int'l*, pg. 64
AIB CORPORATE FINANCE LTD.—See Allied Irish Banks,
    p.l.c.; *Int'l*, pg. 64
AIB FINANCE & LEASING LTD.—See Allied Irish Banks,
    p.l.c.; *Int'l*, pg. 64
AIB INTERNATIONAL CONSULTANTS LTD.—See Allied
    Irish Banks, p.l.c.; *Int'l*, pg. 64
AIB INTERNATIONAL FINANCIAL SERVICES LTD—See
    Allied Irish Banks, p.l.c.; *Int'l*, pg. 64
AIB INVESTMENT MANAGERS LTD.—See Allied Irish
    Banks, p.l.c.; *Int'l*, pg. 64
AIB SECURITIES SERVICES LTD.—See Allied Irish Banks,
    p.l.c.; *Int'l*, pg. 64
AIB SOFTWARE DEVELOPMENT LABORATORY—See
    Platinum Technology, Inc.; *U.S. Public*, pg. 1309
AIC-FSS ADVERTISING; *U.S. Private*, pg. 6
AIC-FSS ADVERTISING—See AIC-FSS Advertising; *U.S.
    Private*, pg. 6
AIC HOLDINGS, INC.—See Cigna Corp.; *U.S. Public*,
    pg. 362

AIC IBM PROJECT SUPPORT OFFICE—See Analysts
    International Corporation; *U.S. Public*, pg. 110
AIC INTERNATIONAL, INC.; *U.S. Private*, pg. 6
AIC NATIONAL PROJECTS OFFICE—See Analysts
    International Corporation; *U.S. Public*, pg. 110
AIC TECH WEST—See Analysts International Corporation;
    U.S. Public, pg. 110
A.I.F. INVESTMENTS PTE. LTD.—See Ajinomoto Company
    Inc.; *Int'l*, pg. 40
AIG AVIATION, INC.—See American International Group,
    Inc.; *U.S. Public*, pg. 85
AIG CONSULTANTS, INC.—See American International
    Group, Inc.; *U.S. Public*, pg. 85
AIG LIFE INSURANCE COMPANY—See American
    International Group, Inc.; *U.S. Public*, pg. 84
AIG MARKETING, INC.—See American International
    Group, Inc.; *U.S. Public*, pg. 85
AIG RISK MANAGEMENT, INC.—See American
    International Group, Inc.; *U.S. Public*, pg. 85
AII CLUBMAN—See American International Industries; *U.S.
    Private*, pg. 57
AIL SYSTEMS INC.—See Eaton Corporation; *U.S. Public*,
    pg. 556
AIP B.V.—See Royal Begemann Group; *Int'l*, pg. 1133
AIS MEDIA; *Int'l*, pg. 15
AIS MEDIA—See AIS Media; *Int'l*, pg. 15
AIS MEDIA ADELAIDE—See Dentsu Inc.; *Int'l*, pg. 394
AIS MEDIA BRISBANE—See AIS Media; *Int'l*, pg. 15
AIS MEDIA BRISBANE—See Dentsu Inc.; *Int'l*, pg. 393
AIS MEDIA SOUTH—See AIS Media; *Int'l*, pg. 15
AIS MEDIA SOUTH—See Dentsu Inc.; *Int'l*, pg. 393
AIT - ARBED INTERNATIONAL TRADING S.A.—See Arbed
    S.A.; *Int'l*, pg. 79
AIU CANADA LTD.—See American International Group,
    Inc.; *U.S. Public*, pg. 85
AIU INSURANCE COMPANY—See American International
    Group, Inc.; *U.S. Public*, pg. 84
AJC INTERNATIONAL, INC.; *U.S. Private*, pg. 6
AJD—See HATCO, Inc.; *U.S. Private*, pg. 510
AJL PARK—See FCB; *U.S. Private*, pg. 389
AJM PACKAGING CORPORATION—See A J M Packaging
    Corporation; *U.S. Private*, pg. 2
AK STEEL CORPORATION; *U.S. Public*, pg. 7
AKA INDUSTRIPRODUKTER AB—See Incentive AB; *Int'l*,
    pg. 666
AKAY FLAVOURS & AROMATICS LTD.—See Chr. Hansen
    Holding A/S; *Int'l*, pg. 288
AKF KREDITBANK GMBH. & CO.—See Vorwerk & Co.;
    Int'l, pg. 1481
AKF LEASING BETEILIGUNGSGESELLSCHAFT M.B.H.—
    See Vorwerk & Co.; *Int'l*, pg. 1481
AKF LEASING GMBH & CO. KG—See Vorwerk & Co.; *Int'l*,
    pg. 1481
AKG ACOUSTICS—See Harman International Industries,
    Inc.; *U.S. Public*, pg. 787
AKO ARMATUREN - VERTRIEKS GMBH—See Axel
    Johnson AB; *Int'l*, pg. 710
ALA VERMIETUNGS GMBH—See Commerzbank AG; *Int'l*,
    pg. 310
ALC INCORPORATED—See American Grain & Related
    Industries; *U.S. Private*, pg. 55
OY ALGOL AB; *Int'l*, pg. 15
ALIC, INCORPORATED—See Cigna Corp.; *U.S. Public*,
    pg. 364
ALK BENELUX BV—See Chr. Hansen Holding A/S; *Int'l*,
    pg. 288
ALK LABORATORIES, INC.—See Chr. Hansen Holding A/
    S; *Int'l*, pg. 288
ALK SVERGE AB—See Chr. Hansen Holding A/S; *Int'l*,
    pg. 288
ALM & COMPANY—See Saatchi & Saatchi Advertising
    Worldwide; *U.S. Public*, pg. 1422
ALNAB ARMATUR AB—See GESTRA GmbH; *Int'l*, pg. 549
ALNAB/SCANA ARMATUR A/S—See GESTRA GmbH;
    Int'l, pg. 549
ALR INTERNATIONAL (PTE.) LTD.—See Gateway 2000;
    U.S. Public, pg. 704
ALS TONIC—See BDDP Group; *Int'l*, pg. 116
ALZ N.V.—See Arbed S.A.; *Int'l*, pg. 79
AM CAN—See Frozen Food Express Industries, Inc.; *U.S.
    Public*, pg. 685
AM CONCEPTS INC.—See The Western and Southern Life
    Insurance Company; *U.S. Private*, pg. 1164
AM COSMETICS INC.; *U.S. Private*, pg. 6
AM ENTERTAINMENT—See Allied Advertising Agency,
    Public Relations; *U.S. Private*, pg. 38
AM GENERAL CORPORATION—See Renco Group; *U.S.
    Private*, pg. 922
AM MANAGEMENT CORP.—See The Rouse Company;
    U.S. Public, pg. 1409
AM106/CJAY RADIO—See Rogers Communications, Inc.;
    Int'l, pg. 1123
A.M.A. ASSET MANAGEMENT ADVISORS OF DRESDNER
    BANK—See Dresdner Bank AG; *Int'l*, pg. 418
AMA LEO BURNETT—See Leo Burnett Company, Inc.;
    U.S. Private, pg. 184
AMB AACHENER UND MUENCHENER BETEILIGUNGS-
    AG; *Int'l*, pg. 15
AMB DEVELOPMENT GROUP LLC; *U.S. Private*, pg. 6
AMBI INC.; *U.S. Public*, pg. 7
AMC—See Associated Merchandising Corp. (AMC); *U.S.
    Private*, pg. 92
AMC ENTERTAINMENT, INC.; *U.S. Private*, pg. 6
AMC, INC.; *U.S. Private*, pg. 6
AMD CORPORATION—See Advanced Micro Devices, Inc.;
    U.S. Public, pg. 21
AMD FAR EAST, LTD.—See Advanced Micro Devices, Inc.;
    U.S. Public, pg. 21
AMD GMBH—See Advanced Micro Devices, Inc.; *U.S.
    Public*, pg. 21
AMD INDUSTRIES INC.; *U.S. Private*, pg. 6
AMD INTL LTD.—See Advanced Micro Devices, Inc.; *U.S.
    Public*, pg. 21

AMD PROPERTIES—See Advanced Micro Devices, Inc.;
    U.S. Public, pg. 21
AMD (U.K.) LTD.—See Advanced Micro Devices, Inc.; *U.S.
    Public*, pg. 21
AMEC BUILDING LTD.—See AMEC Plc; *Int'l*, pg. 16
AMEC CIVIL ENGINEERING LTD.—See AMEC Plc; *Int'l*,
    pg. 16
AMEC CONSTRUCTION LTD., INDUSTRIAL
    ENGINEERING DIV.—See AMEC Plc; *Int'l*, pg. 16
AMEC CONSTRUCTION SCOTLAND LTD.—See AMEC
    Plc; *Int'l*, pg. 16
AMEC CONSTRUCTION SERVICES LTD.—See AMEC Plc;
    Int'l, pg. 16
AMEC DEVELOPMENT LTD.—See AMEC Plc; *Int'l*, pg. 16
AMEC ENGINEERING LTD.-C.V. BUCHAN (CONCRETE)
    LTD.—See AMEC Plc; *Int'l*, pg. 16
AMEC MINING LTD.—See AMEC Plc; *Int'l*, pg. 16
AMEC PLC; *Int'l*, pg. 16
AMEC PROCESS & ENERGY—See AMEC Plc; *Int'l*, pg. 16
AMEV BELEGGINGSCONSORTIUM N.V.—See Fortis; *Int'l*,
    pg. 499
AMEV FINANCIERINGEN N.V.—See Fortis; *Int'l*, pg. 499
AMEV GENERAL INSURANCE COMPANY LIMITED—See
    Fortis; *Int'l*, pg. 499
AMEV HYPOTHEEKBEDRIJF—See Fortis; *Int'l*, pg. 499
AMEV LEVENSVERZEKERING N.V.—See Fortis; *Int'l*,
    pg. 499
AMEV NEDERLAND N.V.—See Fortis; *Int'l*, pg. 498
AMEV ONTWIKKELING MAATSCHAPPIJ N.V.—See Fortis;
    Int'l, pg. 499
AMEV PRAKTIJKVOORZIENING N.V.—See Fortis; *Int'l*,
    pg. 499
AMEV SCHADEVERZEKERING N.V.—See Fortis; *Int'l*,
    pg. 499
AMEV V-A ARDANTA—See Fortis; *Int'l*, pg. 499
AMF AZALEA BOWL—See AMF Bowling Worldwide; *U.S.
    Private*, pg. 7
AMF BAKERY SYSTEMS; *U.S. Private*, pg. 6
AMF BOWLING CENTERS INC.—See AMF Bowling
    Worldwide; *U.S. Private*, pg. 7
AMF BOWLING WORLDWIDE; *U.S. Private*, pg. 6
AMF LANG'S BOWLARAMA INC.—See AMF Bowling
    Worldwide; *U.S. Private*, pg. 7
AMF REECE INCORPORATED; *U.S. Private*, pg. 7
AMI—See John Menzies plc; *Int'l*, pg. 707
AMI CAPITAL INC.—See ULLICO Inc.; *U.S. Private*,
    pg. 1116
AMI GIBSON, INC.—See Technitrol, Inc.; *U.S. Public*,
    pg. 1564
AMI GROUP, INC.; *U.S. Private*, pg. 7
AMI INDUSTRIES F.S.C., INC.—See Coltec Holdings Inc.;
    U.S. Public, pg. 401
AMI INDUSTRIES, INC.—See Coltec Holdings Inc.; *U.S.
    Public*, pg. 401
AMI LEASING CORPORATION; *U.S. Private*, pg. 7
AMI METALS, INC.—See Reliance Steel & Aluminum Co.;
    U.S. Public, pg. 1375
AMMB HOLDINGS BERHAD—See The Tokai Bank,
    Limited; *Int'l*, pg. 1391
AMP ASSET MANAGEMENT PLC—See Australian Mutual
    Provident; *Int'l*, pg. 100
AMP EXPORT LTD. S.A.R.L.—See AMP Incorporated; *U.S.
    Public*, pg. 8
AMP INC. FLEXIBLE FILM SENSORS—See AMP
    Incorporated; *U.S. Public*, pg. 7
AMP INC. LYTEL DIVISION—See AMP Incorporated; *U.S.
    Public*, pg. 8
AMP INC. LYTEL DIVISION, INDUSTRIAL—See AMP
    Incorporated; *U.S. Public*, pg. 8
AMP INC. LYTEL/NETCOM DIVISION—See AMP
    Incorporated; *U.S. Public*, pg. 8
AMP INCORPORATED; *U.S. Public*, pg. 7
AMP INDIA PRIVATE LIMITED—See AMP Incorporated;
    U.S. Public, pg. 9
AMP PACKAGING SYSTEMS, INC.—See AMP
    Incorporated; *U.S. Public*, pg. 8
PT AMP PANIN LIFE—See Australian Mutual Provident;
    Int'l, pg. 100
AMP RECYCLING—See Commercial Metals Company; *U.S.
    Public*, pg. 413
AMP SHANGHAI CONNECTOR, LTD.—See AMP
    Incorporated; *U.S. Public*, pg. 9
A.M.P. TRANSPORTS—See Lagardere Groupe; *Int'l*,
    pg. 795
AMP TURKEY—See AMP Incorporated; *U.S. Public*, pg. 9
AMPEP P.L.C.—See AB SKF; *Int'l*, pg. 1157
AMR CORPORATION; *U.S. Public*, pg. 9
AMR EAGLE, INC.—See AMR Corporation; *U.S. Public*,
    pg. 9
AMR INVESTMENT SERVICES, INC.—See AMR
    Corporation; *U.S. Public*, pg. 9
AMR SERVICES CORPORATION—See AMR Corporation;
    U.S. Public, pg. 9
AMRAD PHARMACIA & UPJOHN BIOTECH—See
    Pharmacia & Upjohn, Inc.; *Int'l*, pg. 1047
AMRI INC.—See KSB Aktiengesellschaft; *Int'l*, pg. 721
AMRI NEDERLAND B.V.—See KSB Aktiengesellschaft;
    Int'l, pg. 721
AMRI PTE. LTD.—See KSB Aktiengesellschaft; *Int'l*,
    pg. 721
AMS—See American Management Systems, Inc.; *U.S.
    Public*, pg. 86
AMS MANAGEMENT SYSTEMS AUSTRALIA—See
    American Management Systems, Inc.; *U.S. Public*,
    pg. 86
AMS MANAGEMENT SYSTEMS CANADA INC.—See
    American Management Systems, Inc.; *U.S. Public*,
    pg. 86
AMS MANAGEMENT SYSTEMS DEUTSCHLAND GMBH—
    See American Management Systems, Inc.; *U.S. Public*,
    pg. 87
AMS MANAGEMENT SYSTEMS ESPANA, S.A.—See
    American Management Systems, Inc.; *U.S. Public*,
    pg. 87

AMS MANAGEMENT SYSTEMS EUROPE, SA, NV—See American Management Systems, Inc.; *U.S. Public,* pg. 87

AMS MANAGEMENT SYSTEMS MEXICO S.A. DE C.V.— See American Management Systems, Inc.; *U.S. Public,* pg. 87

AMS MANAGEMENT SYSTEMS NETHERLANDS B.V.— See American Management Systems, Inc.; *U.S. Public,* pg. 87

AMS MANAGEMENT SYSTEMS (SWITZERLAND) AG— See American Management Systems, Inc.; *U.S. Public,* pg. 87

AMS MANAGEMENT SYSTEMS UK LTD—See American Management Systems, Inc.; *U.S. Public,* pg. 87

AMS MEDINVENT S.A.—See Pfizer Inc.; *U.S. Public,* pg. 1283

AMS OPERATIONS CORPORATION, INC.—See American Management Systems, Inc.; *U.S. Public,* pg. 86

AMT—See Oy Nokia Ab/Nokia Group; *Int'l,* pg. 954

AMVI S.A.—See KSB Aktiengesellschaft; *Int'l,* pg. 721

AMW INDUSTRIES INC.—See Crane Co.; *U.S. Public,* pg. 457

ANA HOTEL—See All Nippon Airways Co. Ltd.; *Int'l,* pg. 57

ANF PARTNERS 361

ANI AMERICA, INC.—See Australian National Industries Limited; *Int'l,* pg. 101

ANI AURORA PLC—See Australian National Industries Limited; *Int'l,* pg. 101

ANI BRADKEN—See Australian National Industries Limited; *Int'l,* pg. 100

ANI ENGINEERING—See Australian National Industries Limited; *Int'l,* pg. 100

ANI MINERAL PROCESSING—See Australian National Industries Limited; *Int'l,* pg. 100

ANI STRATA PRODUCTS—See Australian National Industries Limited; *Int'l,* pg. 100

ANI WEAR RESISTANT PRODUCTS—See Australian National Industries Limited; *Int'l,* pg. 100

ANIE-ASSOCIAZIONE NAZIONALE INDUSTRIE ELETTROTECNICHE ED ELETTRONICHE; *Int'l,* pg. 16

ANR ATLANTIC PIPELINE CO.—See The Coastal Corporation; *U.S. Public,* pg. 389

ANR BLUE LAKE COMPANY—See The Coastal Corporation; *U.S. Public,* pg. 389

ANR CREDIT CORPORATION—See The Coastal Corporation; *U.S. Public,* pg. 389

ANR DEVELOPMENT CORPORATION—See The Coastal Corporation; *U.S. Public,* pg. 389

ANR EATON COMPANY—See The Coastal Corporation; *U.S. Public,* pg. 389

ANR FINANCE N.V.—See The Coastal Corporation; *U.S. Public,* pg. 391

ANR FREIGHT SYSTEM, INC.—See The Coastal Corporation; *U.S. Public,* pg. 389

ANR GASIFICATION PROPERTIES CO.—See The Coastal Corporation; *U.S. Public,* pg. 389

ANR IROQUOIS, INC.—See The Coastal Corporation; *U.S. Public,* pg. 389

ANR JACKSON COMPANY—See The Coastal Corporation; *U.S. Public,* pg. 389

ANR NORTHEASTERN GAS STORAGE COMPANY—See The Coastal Corporation; *U.S. Public,* pg. 389

ANR PIPELINE CO.—See The Coastal Corporation; *U.S. Public,* pg. 389

ANR PRODUCTION CO.—See The Coastal Corporation; *U.S. Public,* pg. 389

ANR REN-CEN, INC.—See The Coastal Corporation; *U.S. Public,* pg. 389

ANR SOUTHERN PIPELINE COMPANY—See The Coastal Corporation; *U.S. Public,* pg. 389

ANR STORAGE CO.—See The Coastal Corporation; *U.S. Public,* pg. 389

ANR VENTURE EAGLE POINT COMPANY—See The Coastal Corporation; *U.S. Public,* pg. 389

ANR VENTURE FULTON COMPANY—See The Coastal Corporation; *U.S. Public,* pg. 389

ANR VENTURE MANAGEMENT CO.—See The Coastal Corporation; *U.S. Public,* pg. 389

ANR WESTERN STORAGE CO.—See The Coastal Corporation; *U.S. Public,* pg. 389

ANRFS HOLDINGS, INC.—See The Coastal Corporation; *U.S. Public,* pg. 389

ANT NACHRICHTENTECHNIK GMBH—See Robert Bosch GmbH; *Int'l,* pg. 204

ANZ ASIA LIMITED—See Australia & New Zealand Banking Group Limited; *Int'l,* pg. 98

ANZ AUSTRALIAN CAPITAL TERRITORY—See Australia & New Zealand Banking Group Limited; *Int'l,* pg. 98

ANZ BANK (GUERNSEY) LIMITED—See Australia & New Zealand Banking Group Limited; *Int'l,* pg. 98

ANZ BANK (VANUATU) LIMITED—See Australia & New Zealand Banking Group Limited; *Int'l,* pg. 98

ANZ BANKING GROUP (NEW ZEALAND) LTD.—See Australia & New Zealand Banking Group Limited; *Int'l,* pg. 98

ANZ FUNDS MANAGEMENT—See Australia & New Zealand Banking Group Limited; *Int'l,* pg. 98

ANZ GRINDLAYS BANK PLC UNITED KINGDOM—See Australia & New Zealand Banking Group Limited; *Int'l,* pg. 99

ANZ INTERNATIONAL PTE LIMITED—See Australia & New Zealand Banking Group Limited; *Int'l,* pg. 99

ANZ LIFE ASSURANCE COMPANY LIMITED—See Australia & New Zealand Banking Group Limited; *Int'l,* pg. 98

ANZ MANAGED INVESTMENTS LIMITED—See Australia & New Zealand Banking Group Limited; *Int'l,* pg. 98

ANZ MCCAUGHAN (NZ) LIMITED—See Australia & New Zealand Banking Group Limited; *Int'l,* pg. 99

ANZ MCCAUGHAN SECURITIES (ASIA) LIMITED—See Australia & New Zealand Banking Group Limited; *Int'l,* pg. 99

ANZ MCCAUGHAN SECURITIES LIMITED—See Australia & New Zealand Banking Group Limited; *Int'l,* pg. 98

ANZ NORTHERN TERRITORY—See Australia & New Zealand Banking Group Limited; *Int'l,* pg. 98

P.T. ANZ PANIN BANK—See Australia & New Zealand Banking Group Limited; *Int'l,* pg. 99

ANZ QUEENSLAND—See Australia & New Zealand Banking Group Limited; *Int'l,* pg. 98

ANZ SINGAPORE LIMITED—See Australia & New Zealand Banking Group Limited; *Int'l,* pg. 99

AO ENERCON—See Imatran Voima Oy; *Int'l,* pg. 660

AO FINNCOLOR—See Kemira Oy; *Int'l,* pg. 729

A.O. KROKHA—See Nutricia BV; *Int'l,* pg. 991

A/O PFIZER—See Pfizer Inc.; *U.S. Public,* pg. 1283

AO UNOC EQUIPMENT & SUPPLY—See Caterpillar Inc.; *U.S. Public,* pg. 316

AO ZENECA RUSSIA—See Zeneca Group Plc; *Int'l,* pg. 1525

AOC LADIES—See Amerex USA, Inc.; *U.S. Private,* pg. 49

AOFR PTY LIMITED—See ADC Telecommunications, Inc.; *U.S. Public,* pg. 4

AOK-NERVAL COSMETICS & PERFUMES GMBH—See Henkel KGaA; *Int'l,* pg. 609

AOLP ACQUISITION CORP.—See Cigna Corp.; *U.S. Public,* pg. 357

AOLP MEZZANINE ACQUISITION CORP.—See Cigna Corp.; *U.S. Public,* pg. 357

AON ADVISORS, INC.—See AON Corporation; *U.S. Public,* pg. 117

AON, JAUCH & HUEBENER GRUPPE—See AON Corporation; *U.S. Public,* pg. 118

AON REINSURANCE AGENCY, INC.—See AON Corporation; *U.S. Public,* pg. 117

AON RISK SERVICES, INC.—See AON Corporation; *U.S. Public,* pg. 117

AON SPECIALTY GROUP, INC.—See AON Corporation; *U.S. Public,* pg. 117

A.O.O.T. HENKEL ERA TOSNO—See Henkel KGaA; *Int'l,* pg. 611

AOTEC—See American Optical Corporation; *U.S. Private,* pg. 60

AP AMORTIGUADORES, S.A.—See Kayaba Industry Co., Ltd.; *Int'l,* pg. 727

AP & T GMBH—See Ferrofluidics Corporation; *U.S. Public,* pg. 620

AP & T LTD.—See Ferrofluidics Corporation; *U.S. Public,* pg. 620

A.P. DE ASSURANTIEPARTNERS AMSTERDAM B.V.— See Assicurazioni Generali S.p.A.; *Int'l,* pg. 90

AP-DOW JONES NEWS SERVICE—See Dow Jones & Company, Inc.; *U.S. Public,* pg. 524

AP JOURNALS, INC.—See Harcourt General, Inc.; *U.S. Public,* pg. 783

AP NORTH AMERICAN AFTERMARKET DIVISION—See Charterhouse Group International, Inc.; *U.S. Private,* pg. 230

AP TECHNO GLASS COMPANY—See Asahi Glass Co., Ltd.; *Int'l,* pg. 84

AP TECHNOLOGY MANAGEMENT INC.—See Adolfson & Peterson, Inc.; *U.S. Private,* pg. 18

APAC/BALLENGER PAVING COMPANY, INC.—See Ashland, Inc.; *U.S. Public,* pg. 139

APAC HOLDINGS, INC.—See Ashland, Inc.; *U.S. Public,* pg. 139

APC OPERATING PARTNERSHIP, L.P.—See Apache Corporation; *U.S. Public,* pg. 119

APCI (U.K.), INC.—See Air Products and Chemicals, Inc.; *U.S. Public,* pg. 30

APD CRYOGENICS INC.—See Intermagnetics General Corporation; *U.S. Public,* pg. 894

APG LIME CORP.—See A.P. Green Industries, Inc.; *U.S. Public,* pg. 761

APG SECURITY, INC.; *U.S. Private,* pg. 7

API DEVELOPMENT CORP.—See American Precision Industries Inc.; *U.S. Public,* pg. 90

API-FS CORPORATION—See American Precision Industries Inc.; *U.S. Public,* pg. 90

API-GETTYS CORPORATION—See American Precision Industries Inc.; *U.S. Public,* pg. 90

API GROUP INC.; *U.S. Private,* pg. 7

API HAROWE—See American Precision Industries Inc.; *U.S. Public,* pg. 90

API KATEMA INC.—See American Precision Industries Inc.; *U.S. Public,* pg. 90

API OF CANADA INC.—See American Precision Industries Inc.; *U.S. Public,* pg. 90

APL CORPORATION; *U.S. Private,* pg. 7

APL LAND TRANSPORT SERVICE INC.—See Neptune Orient Lines Ltd.; *Int'l,* pg. 912

APL LIMITED—See Neptune Orient Lines Ltd.; *Int'l,* pg. 912

APP CHEMICALS LIMITED—See Burmah Castrol plc; *Int'l,* pg. 234

APP SYSTEMS—See Oracle Corporation; *U.S. Public,* pg. 1228

APPH AVIATION SERVICES LTD.—See BBA Group plc; *Int'l,* pg. 112

APPH (BOLTON) LTD.—See BBA Group plc; *Int'l,* pg. 112

APPH LTD.—See BBA Group plc; *Int'l,* pg. 112

APPX SOFTWARE INC.—See Tredegar Industries Inc.; *U.S. Public,* pg. 1634

A.P.S.—See APS Holding Corporation; *U.S. Public,* pg. 10

APS—See Pinnacle West Capital Corporation; *U.S. Public,* pg. 1297

APS HOLDING CORPORATION; *U.S. Public,* pg. 10

A.P.S., INC.—See APS Holding Corporation; *U.S. Public,* pg. 10

APS RESOURCES—See Kelley Company, Inc.; *U.S. Private,* pg. 613

APSYS (AEROSPATIALE PROTECTION SYSTEMES)—See Aerospatiale; *Int'l,* pg. 29

APT—See Telephone and Data Systems, Inc.; *U.S. Public,* pg. 1570

APT COIN MACHINES, INC.—See Alliance Gaming Corporation; *U.S. Public,* pg. 47

APV BAKER INC.—See Siebe plc; *Int'l,* pg. 1240

APV BAKER INC., FOOD MACHINERY DIV.—See Siebe plc; *Int'l,* pg. 1240

APV BAKER LIMITED—See Siebe plc; *Int'l,* pg. 1240

APV BAKER PLC—See Siebe plc; *Int'l,* pg. 1240

APV CHEMICAL MACHINERY, INC., PROCESS SYSTEMS DIV.—See Siebe plc; *Int'l,* pg. 1240

APV CHEMICAL MACHINERY LIMITED—See Siebe plc; *Int'l,* pg. 1240

APV CREPACO, INC.—See Siebe plc; *Int'l,* pg. 1240

APV CREPACO, INC., DRYER DIV.—See Siebe plc; *Int'l,* pg. 1240

APV DOUGLAS MACHINE CORP.—See Siebe plc; *Int'l,* pg. 1240

APV FRANKLIN INC.—See Siebe plc; *Int'l,* pg. 1240

APV GAULIN—See Siebe plc; *Int'l,* pg. 1241

APV GAULIN GMBH—See Siebe plc; *Int'l,* pg. 1241

APV GAULIN INC.—See Siebe plc; *Int'l,* pg. 1241

APV GLACIER INDUSTRIES—See Siebe plc; *Int'l,* pg. 1240

APV PASILAC—See Siebe plc; *Int'l,* pg. 485

APV PAVAILLER CANADA—See Financiere Equipment S.A.; *Int'l,* pg. 485

APV PAVAILLER MONZIANI—See Financiere Equipment S.A.; *Int'l,* pg. 485

APV REFINERY PRODUCTS CORP.—See Siebe plc; *Int'l,* pg. 1241

APV ROSISTA GMBH—See Siebe plc; *Int'l,* pg. 1241

APV ROSISTA LTD.—See Siebe plc; *Int'l,* pg. 1241

APV U.K. PLC—See Siebe plc; *Int'l,* pg. 1240

APV VENT-AXIA INC.—See Siebe plc; *Int'l,* pg. 1241

APX INTERNATIONAL; *U.S. Private,* pg. 7

AR ACCESSORIES GROUP, INC.; *U.S. Private,* pg. 7

AR DIVISION OF TELENEX—See General Signal Corporation; *U.S. Public,* pg. 727

A-R TECHNOLOGIES—See Hawker Siddeley Canada Inc.; *Int'l,* pg. 604

ARA/BDDP—See BDDP Group; *Int'l,* pg. 117

ARB INC.; *U.S. Private,* pg. 7

ARB, INC.-BUILDING DIVISION—See ARB Inc.; *U.S. Private,* pg. 7

ARC ADVERTISING; *Int'l,* pg. 17

ARC CENTRAL—See Hanson PLC; *Int'l,* pg. 592

ARC CONBLOC LIMITED—See Hanson PLC; *Int'l,* pg. 592

ARC INTERNATIONAL CORPORATION; *Int'l,* pg. 17

ARC LIMITED—See Hanson PLC; *Int'l,* pg. 592

ARC MARINE LIMITED—See Hanson PLC; *Int'l,* pg. 592

ARC NORTHERN—See Hanson PLC; *Int'l,* pg. 592

ARC PIPES LIMITED—See Hanson PLC; *Int'l,* pg. 592

ARC SOUTH WALES—See Hanson PLC; *Int'l,* pg. 592

ARC SOUTH WESTERN—See Hanson PLC; *Int'l,* pg. 592

ARC SOUTHERN—See Hanson PLC; *Int'l,* pg. 592

ARCA MERCHANT-ABK S.P.A.—See Dresdner Bank AG; *Int'l,* pg. 420

ARI GROUP EUROPE—See Tyco International Ltd.; *U.S. Public,* pg. 1650

ARS CHEMICAL (THAILAND) CO., LTD.—See Otsuka Pharmaceutical Co., Ltd.; *Int'l,* pg. 1014

ARS/DMB&B—See DMB&B Communications; *U.S. Private,* pg. 303

ARS INTEGRATED SYSTEMS GMBH—See Integrated Systems, Inc.; *U.S. Public,* pg. 886

AS. CO S.P.A.—See Bastogi-S.p.A.; *Int'l,* pg. 170

AS LATVIJAS KRASAS—See Kemira Oy; *Int'l,* pg. 729

AS LUMIFOREST—See Enso Oyj; *Int'l,* pg. 457

A.S. MANAGEMENT CORPORATION; *U.S. Private,* pg. 7

AS NEOPAC-ELKSON—See Metsa-Serla Corporation; *Int'l,* pg. 863

ASAB SERVICEFORETAGET AB—See Electrolux, AB; *Int'l,* pg. 438

ASAL INGENIEURE GMBH—See Heidemij N.V.; *Int'l,* pg. 608

ASB—See Vendex International N.V.; *Int'l,* pg. 1463

ASB BANK LIMITED—See Commonwealth Bank Group; *Int'l,* pg. 313

ASB INTERIM—See Vendex International N.V.; *Int'l,* pg. 1463

ASC—See Shizuki Electric Corporation; *Int'l,* pg. 1236

ASC INCORPORATED; *U.S. Private,* pg. 8

ASC, LTDA.—See Hewlett-Packard Company; *U.S. Public,* pg. 816

ASC WEINSBERG KAROSSERIEWERKE WEINSBERG GMBH—See ASC Incorporated; *U.S. Private,* pg. 8

ASCG, INC.—See Arctic Slope Regional Corporation; *U.S. Private,* pg. 80

ASCG INSPECTION SERVICES—See Arctic Slope Regional Corporation; *U.S. Private,* pg. 80

ASCO MUSIC—See Cox Enterprises, Inc.; *U.S. Private,* pg. 282

ASDA GROUP PLC; *Int'l,* pg. 17

ASDC (APPLIED SOFTWARE DEVELOPMENT CENTER)— See The Macneal-Schwendler Corp.; *U.S. Public,* pg. 1031

ASF THOMAS—See Thomas Industries Inc.; *U.S. Public,* pg. 1599

ASF TRANSPORT, INC.—See Giant Eagle, Inc.; *U.S. Private,* pg. 451

A.S.I. (COMPUTER TRAINING) NETHERLANDS B.V.—See Harcourt General, Inc.; *U.S. Public,* pg. 784

ASI CORP.; *U.S. Private,* pg. 8

ASI INVESTMENTS HOLDING CO.—See A. Schulman, Inc.; *U.S. Public,* pg. 1441

ASI LANDMARK, INC.—See Analytical Surveys, Inc.; *U.S. Public,* pg. 91

ASI MARKET RESEARCH, INC.—See IDC Services, Inc.; *U.S. Private,* pg. 554

ASI PROPERTIES, INC.—See American Software, Inc.; *U.S. Public,* pg. 91

ASK-CENTRALEN AB—See Axel Johnson AB; *Int'l,* pg. 708

ASLK-CGER; *Int'l,* pg. 17

A.S.M. INDUSTRIES—See Serfilco, Ltd.; *U.S. Private,* pg. 985

ASM INGENIERIE—See Thomson S.A.; *Int'l,* pg. 1381

ASN INCORPORATED; *U.S. Private,* pg. 8

Company Index

A.S.P. S.A.—See Astra AB; Int'l, pg. 93
ASRC CONTACTING COMPANY, INC. (ACCI)—See Arctic Slope Regional Corporation; U.S. Private, pg. 80
ASRC PARSONS ENGINEERING, LLC.—See Arctic Slope Regional Corporation; U.S. Private, pg. 80
ASSA ABLOY AB; Int'l, pg. 17
ASSA LTD.—See Assa Abloy AB; Int'l, pg. 17
AST ASIA—See Samsung Group; Int'l, pg. 1182
AST BEARINGS DIVISION—See Axsys Technologies, Inc.; U.S. Public, pg. 157
AST BENELUX, N.V.—See Samsung Group; Int'l, pg. 1182
AST CANADA, INC.—See Samsung Group; Int'l, pg. 1182
AST CANADA INC.—See Samsung Group; Int'l, pg. 1182
AST COMPUTER—See Samsung Group; Int'l, pg. 1182
AST COMPUTER (CHINA) LTD.—See Samsung Group; Int'l, pg. 1182
AST COMPUTER NETHERLANDS BV—See Samsung Group; Int'l, pg. 1182
AST COMPUTER & SERVICES—See Samsung Group; Int'l, pg. 1182
AST EUROPE LIMITED—See Samsung Group; Int'l, pg. 1182
AST FORT WORTH FINAL ASSEMBLY—See Samsung Group; Int'l, pg. 1182
AST KOREA—See Samsung Group; Int'l, pg. 1182
AST MIDDLE EAST LIMITED—See Samsung Group; Int'l, pg. 1182
AST NEW ZEALAND LIMITED—See Samsung Group; Int'l, pg. 1182
AST RESEARCH—See Samsung Group; Int'l, pg. 1182
AST RESEARCH ANZ PTY. LTD.—See Samsung Group; Int'l, pg. 1182
AST RESEARCH DEUTSCHLAND GMBH—See Samsung Group; Int'l, pg. 1182
AST RESEARCH FAR EAST LIMITED—See Samsung Group; Int'l, pg. 1182
AST RESEARCH FINLAND OY—See Samsung Group; Int'l, pg. 1182
AST RESEARCH FRANCE S.A.R.L.—See Samsung Group; Int'l, pg. 1182
AST RESEARCH INC.—See Samsung Group; Int'l, pg. 1181
AST RESEARCH INC., BEIJING REPRESENTATIVE OFFICE—See Samsung Group; Int'l, pg. 1182
AST RESEARCH INC.-CHENGDU REPRESENTATIVE—See Samsung Group; Int'l, pg. 1182
AST RESEARCH ITALIA S.P.A.—See Samsung Group; Int'l, pg. 1182
AST RESEARCH ITALIA S.R.L.—See Samsung Group; Int'l, pg. 1182
AST RESEARCH (JAPAN) K.K.—See Samsung Group; Int'l, pg. 1182
AST RESEARCH-NORWAY—See Samsung Group; Int'l, pg. 1182
AST RESEARCH SPAIN, S.L.—See Samsung Group; Int'l, pg. 1182
AST RESEARCH SWITZERLAND S.A.—See Samsung Group; Int'l, pg. 1182
AST SINGAPORE PTE. LIMITED—See Samsung Group; Int'l, pg. 1182
AST SPAIN—See Samsung Group; Int'l, pg. 1183
AST SWEDEN, AB—See Samsung Group; Int'l, pg. 1183
AST TAIWAN LTD.—See Samsung Group; Int'l, pg. 1183
ASTANDER - ASTILLEROS DE SANTANDER S.A.—See SEPI; Int'l, pg. 1223
ASTANO - ASTILLEROS Y TALLERES DEL NOROESTE, S.A.—See SEPI; Int'l, pg. 1223
ASTO BETEILIGUNGS-GMBH—See Freudenberg & Company; Int'l, pg. 506
AST TAIWAN LIMITED—See Samsung Group; Int'l, pg. 1183
AT ACCEPTANCE CORPORATION—See Keycorp; U.S. Public, pg. 955
AT&L RAILROAD—See Wheeler Brothers Grain Co.; U.S. Private, pg. 1171
AT&T ALASCOM—See AT&T Corporation; U.S. Public, pg. 10
AT&T AMERICAN TRANSTECH INC.—See AT&T Corporation; U.S. Public, pg. 10
AT&T BUSINESS COMMUNICATION—See AT&T Corporation; U.S. Public, pg. 11
AT&T BUSINESS COMMUNICATIONS SERVICES—See AT&T Corporation; U.S. Public, pg. 10
AT&T CAPITAL CORPORATION—See Newcourt Credit Group Inc.; Int'l, pg. 924
AT&T COMMUNICATIONS—See AT&T Corporation; U.S. Public, pg. 10
AT&T CONSUMER COMMUNICATIONS SERVICES—See AT&T Corporation; U.S. Public, pg. 10
AT&T CORPORATION; U.S. Public, pg. 10
AT&T CUSTOMER INFORMATION—See AT&T Corporation; U.S. Public, pg. 10
AT&T DATATEK INC.—See AT&T Corporation; U.S. Public, pg. 10
AT&T IMAGE SOLUTION—See AT&T Corporation; U.S. Public, pg. 10
AT&T ISTEL GLOBAL MESSAGING SERVICES LTD.—See AT&T Corporation; U.S. Public, pg. 11
AT&T ISTEL LIMITED—See AT&T Corporation; U.S. Public, pg. 11
AT&T LANGUAGE LINE SERVICES—See AT&T Corporation; U.S. Public, pg. 11
AT&T NETWORK SYSTEMS INTERNATIONAL—See AT&T Corporation; U.S. Public, pg. 11
AT&T NETWORKED COMMERCE SERVICES—See AT&T Corporation; U.S. Public, pg. 11
AT&T QINGDAO POWER SYSTEMS COMPANY LTD.—See Lucent Technologies Inc.; U.S. Public, pg. 1018
AT&T QINGDAO TELECOMMUNICATIONS SYSTEMS LTD.—See Lucent Technologies Inc.; U.S. Public, pg. 1018
AT&T QINGDAO TELECOMMUNICATIONS EQUIPMENT LTD.—See Lucent Technologies Inc.; U.S. Public, pg. 1018

AT&T STRATEGY & NEW SERVICE INNOVATIONS—See AT&T Corporation; U.S. Public, pg. 11
AT&T UNIVERSAL CARD SERVICES CORP.—See AT&T Corporation; U.S. Public, pg. 11
AT&T WIRELESS SERVICES—See AT&T Corporation; U.S. Public, pg. 11
AT FINANCIAL CORPORATION—See Keycorp; U.S. Public, pg. 955
AT INFORMATION PRODUCTS; U.S. Private, pg. 8
AT SUPPLY, INC.—See Teltronics Inc.; U.S. Public, pg. 1573
ATA COMBUSTAO TECNICA S.A.—See Mitsubishi Heavy Industries Ltd.; Int'l, pg. 874
ATA S.A.—See Alcatel Alsthom Compagnie Generale D'Electricite; Int'l, pg. 53
ATA S.P.A.—See Bastogi-S.p.A.; Int'l, pg. 170
ATC CABLEVISION OF SAN MARINO, INC.—See Time Warner Inc.; U.S. Public, pg. 1610
ATC CABLEVISION OF SOUTH PASADENA, INC.—See Time Warner Inc.; U.S. Public, pg. 1610
ATC COMMUNICATIONS GROUP, INC.; U.S. Public, pg. 11
ATC HEALTHCARE—See ATC Healthcare Services Inc.; U.S. Private, pg. 8
ATC HEALTHCARE SERVICES INC.; U.S. Private, pg. 8
ATC, INC.—See UBE Industries Ltd.; Int'l, pg. 1427
ATC INTERNATIONAL TECHNICAL CERAMICS.—See American Technical Ceramics Corp.; U.S. Public, pg. 93
ATE INVESTMENT, INC.—See Conectiv; U.S. Public, pg. 430
ATEA—See Framatome SA; Int'l, pg. 503
ATF, INC.; U.S. Private, pg. 8
A.T.I. TOOLS, INC.—See Snap-On Tools Corporation; U.S. Public, pg. 1480
ATIO CORPORATION USA, INC.—See Venturian Corp.; U.S. Public, pg. 1716
ATL ECHO ULTRASOUND—See ATL Ultrasound, Inc.; U.S. Public, pg. 12
ATL PRODUCTS, INC.—See Odetics Inc.; U.S. Public, pg. 1212
ATL ULTRASOUND, INC.; U.S. Public, pg. 11
ATM FINANCE, INC.—See Diebold, Incorporated; U.S. Public, pg. 506
ATMI ECOSYS CORP.—See ATMI, Inc.; U.S. Public, pg. 12
ATMI, INC.; U.S. Public, pg. 12
ATOR CORPORATION—See Lucent Technologies Inc.; U.S. Public, pg. 1018
ATR SUPPORT—See IRI Istituto Ricostruzione Industriale; Int'l, pg. 653
ATR WIRE & CABLE CO., INC.—See Itochu Corporation; Int'l, pg. 694
ATS AUTOMATION TOOLING SYSTEMS, INC.; Int'l, pg. 18
ATS OMEGA DE MEXICO, S.A. DE C.V.—See Omega Environmental Inc.; U.S. Public, pg. 1222
ATS OMEGA, INC.—See Omega Environmental Inc.; U.S. Public, pg. 1222
ATT NETWORK SYSTEMS INTERNATIONAL, B.V.—See Telefonica de Espana, S.A.; Int'l, pg. 1373
ATX INTERNATIONAL, INC.—See A.T. Cross Co.; U.S. Public, pg. 461
ATX MARKETING CO.—See A.T. Cross Co.; U.S. Public, pg. 461
AU MANAGEMENT CORP.—See The Rouse Company; U.S. Public, pg. 1409
A.U.P. ARMBRUSTER BAUUNTERNHMUNG GMBH—See Bilfinger + Berger Bauaktiengesellschaft; Int'l, pg. 195
AUSA HOLDING COMPANY—See AEGON N.V.; Int'l, pg. 27
AUSA LIFE INSURANCE CO.—See AEGON N.V.; Int'l, pg. 27
AV EUROMEDIA GESELLSCHAFT FUR AUDIOVISION MBH—See Georg von Holtzbrinck GmbH; Int'l, pg. 1478
AVA; U.S. Private, pg. 8
AVA LEASING SERVICE COMPANY—See AVA; U.S. Private, pg. 8
AVC CHEMICAL CORPORATION—See Ishihara Sangyo Kaisha, Ltd.; Int'l, pg. 689
AVC/NU-VISION—See AVC/Nu-Vision, Inc.; U.S. Private, pg. 9
AVC/NU-VISION, INC.; U.S. Private, pg. 9
AVE GESELLSCHAFT FUR FERNSEHPRODUKTION MBH—See Georg von Holtzbrinck GmbH; Int'l, pg. 1478
AVE GESELLSCHAFT FUR HORFUNKBETEILIGUNGEN MBH—See Georg von Holtzbrinck GmbH; Int'l, pg. 1478
AVG ABFALL-VERWERTUNGS-GESELLSCHAFT MBH—See Veba AG; Int'l, pg. 1460
AVG ALLGEMEINE VERTRIEBSGESELLSCHAFT FUR INDUSTRIEERZEUGNISSE—See Mannesmann A.G.; Int'l, pg. 835
AVM INC.—See Arvin Industries, Inc.; U.S. Public, pg. 137
AVO INTERNATIONAL; U.S. Private, pg. 9
AVO INTERNATIONAL—See TBG Management S.A.M.; Int'l, pg. 1335
AVO MULTI-AMP INSTITUTE—See TBG Management S.A.M.; Int'l, pg. 1335
AVO MULTI-AMP SERVICES CORP.—See TBG Management S.A.M.; Int'l, pg. 1335
AVR CHEMIE—See Koninklijke Hoogovens N.V.; Int'l, pg. 754
AVT-MCCORMICK INGREDIENTS—See McCormick & Company, Incorporated; U.S. Public, pg. 1067
AVW AUDIOVISUAL, INC.—See Freeman Decorating Co.; U.S. Private, pg. 426
AVX CONWAY PLANT—See Kyocera Corporation; Int'l, pg. 775
AVX CORP.—See Kyocera Corporation; Int'l, pg. 775
AVX CORPORATION—See Kyocera Corporation; Int'l, pg. 775

AVX FILTERS DIV.—See Kyocera Corporation; Int'l, pg. 775
AVX ISRAEL LTD.—See Kyocera Corporation; Int'l, pg. 776
AVX LEADED PRODUCTS DIV.—See Kyocera Corporation; Int'l, pg. 775
AVX LTD.—See Kyocera Corporation; Int'l, pg. 776
AVX RALEIGH PLANT—See Kyocera Corporation; Int'l, pg. 775
AVX TANTALUM DIV.—See Kyocera Corporation; Int'l, pg. 775
A.W. REALTY CO.—See Southwestern Energy Company; U.S. Public, pg. 1494
AWA A/S—See Norske Skogindustrier A.S; Int'l, pg. 965
AWC MANUFACTURING FACILITY—See Nortek, Inc.; U.S. Public, pg. 1193
AWG ABFALLWIRTSCHAFT—See Tractebel; Int'l, pg. 1415
AWI RETAIL—See Alba-Waldensian, Inc.; U.S. Public, pg. 94
AWS REMEDIATION, INC.—See American Waste Services, Inc.; U.S. Public, pg. 94
AWT INTERNATIONAL TRADE & FINANCE AG—See Creditanstalt-Bankverein; Int'l, pg. 347
AXA ASSET MANAGEMENT EUROPE—See AXA-UAP; Int'l, pg. 19
AXA ASSICURAZIONI—See AXA-UAP; Int'l, pg. 19
AXA ASSURANCES—See AXA-UAP; Int'l, pg. 18
AXA ASSURANCES LUXEMBOURG—See AXA-UAP; Int'l, pg. 19
AXA BANQUE—See AXA-UAP; Int'l, pg. 18
AXA BELGIUM—See AXA-UAP; Int'l, pg. 19
AXA CANADA—See AXA-UAP; Int'l, pg. 19
AXA CREDIT—See AXA-UAP; Int'l, pg. 18
AXA EQUITY & LAW LEVENSVERZEKERINGEN NV—See AXA-UAP; Int'l, pg. 19
AXA EQUITY & LAW LIFE ASSURANCE SOCIETY PLC—See AXA-UAP; Int'l, pg. 18
GIE AXA GESTION DES ACTIFS—See AXA-UAP; Int'l, pg. 18
AXA GESTION INTERESSEMENT—See AXA-UAP; Int'l, pg. 18
AXA INSURANCE—See AXA-UAP; Int'l, pg. 19
AXA LEBEN—See AXA-UAP; Int'l, pg. 19
AXA LIFE OFFICE—See AXA-UAP; Int'l, pg. 19
AXA MARINE & AVIATION INSURANCE UK LTD.—See AXA-UAP; Int'l, pg. 19
AXA RE ASIA—See AXA-UAP; Int'l, pg. 18
AXA RE FRANCE—See AXA-UAP; Int'l, pg. 18
AXA RE UNITED KINGDOM—See AXA-UAP; Int'l, pg. 19
AXA RE UNITED STATES—See AXA-UAP; Int'l, pg. 19
AXA SEGUROS Y REASEGUROS—See AXA-UAP; Int'l, pg. 19
AXA-UAP; Int'l, pg. 18
AXIMS ACOS ESPECIAIS LDA—See Axel Johnson AB; Int'l, pg. 710
A.Y.M. INC.—See A.Y. McDonald Industries, Inc.; U.S. Private, pg. 721
AYP CANADA, INC.—See Electrolux, AB; Int'l, pg. 440
AZU AUTOTEILE U. ZUBEHOR VERTRIEBE GMBH—See Volkswagen AG; Int'l, pg. 1474
AACHENER UND MUENCHENER IMMOBILIEN GMBH—See AMB Aachener und Muenchener Beteiligungs-AG; Int'l, pg. 15
AACHENER UND MUENCHENER INFORMATIK SERVICE—See AMB Aachener und Muenchener Beteiligungs-AG; Int'l, pg. 15
AACHENER UND MUENCHENER LEBENSVERSICHERUNG—See AMB Aachener und Muenchener Beteiligungs-AG; Int'l, pg. 15
AACHENER UND MUENCHENER VERSICHERUNG AKTIENGESELLSCHAFT—See AMB Aachener und Muenchener Beteiligungs-AG; Int'l, pg. 15
AACIPHAR NV—See Akzo Nobel N.V.; Int'l, pg. 44
AAKRONITE NEW ZEALAND—See International Paper Company; U.S. Public, pg. 904
AALBORG PORTLAND HOLDING A/S—See FLS Industries A/S; Int'l, pg. 475
AALLIED DIE CASTING MFG., INC.—See RCM Industries; U.S. Private, pg. 903
AAMCO TRANSMISSIONS, INC.; U.S. Private, pg. 9
AAMES FINANCIAL CORPORATION; U.S. Public, pg. 12
AANNEMINGSBEDRIJF VAN OUDBROEKHUIZEN B.V., NIEUWEGLIN—See Internatio-Muller N.V.; Int'l, pg. 681
AAR COOPER AVIATION—See AAR Corp.; U.S. Public, pg. 1
AARNE LAAKSONEN OY—See Groupe Saint Louis; Int'l, pg. 568
AARON BROTHERS, INC.—See Michaels Stores, Inc.; U.S. Public, pg. 1104
AARON INVESTMENT COMPANY—See Aaron Rents, Inc.; U.S. Public, pg. 12
AARON RENTS CONVENTION FURNISHINGS—See Aaron Rents, Inc.; U.S. Public, pg. 12
AARON RENTS, INC.; U.S. Public, pg. 12
AARON SCRAP METALS—See Commercial Metals Company; U.S. Public, pg. 413
AARON'S RENTAL PURCHASE—See Aaron Rents, Inc.; U.S. Public, pg. 12
THE AARQUE COMPANIES; U.S. Private, pg. 9
AARQUE MANAGEMENT CORP.—See The Aarque Companies; U.S. Private, pg. 9
AARQUE STEEL CORPORATION—See The Aarque Companies; U.S. Private, pg. 9
AARTSENFRUIT BREDA BV—See The Albert Fisher Group PLC; Int'l, pg. 491
ABAX INFORMATICA S.R.L.—See Compagnie des Machines Bull; Int'l, pg. 318
ABAX SERVICE S.R.L.—See Compagnie des Machines Bull; Int'l, pg. 318
ABAY ENGINEERING—See Technip; Int'l, pg. 1361
ABELL ASSOCIATES; U.S. Private, pg. 9
ABBEVILLE-GRIMES RAILWAY COMPANY—See Stone Container Corporation; U.S. Public, pg. 1521
ABBEY CHEMICALS, LTD.—See Contran Corporation; U.S. Private, pg. 271

ABBEY ETNA FOREIGN SALES CORPORATION—See Abbey Etna Machine Company; *U.S. Private*, pg. 9
ABBEY ETNA MACHINE COMPANY; *U.S. Private*, pg. 9
ABBEY NATIONAL PLC; *Int'l*, pg. 19
ABBOT POINT BULKCOAL PTY. LTD—See M.I.M. Holdings Ltd.; *Int'l*, pg. 827
ABBOTT AG—See Abbott Laboratories; *U.S. Public*, pg. 13
ABBOTT AMBULATORY INFUSION—See Abbott Laboratories; *U.S. Public*, pg. 13
ABBOTT AUSTRALIA/ASIA PTY. LTD.—See Abbott Laboratories; *U.S. Public*, pg. 13
ABBOTT BALL COMPANY; *U.S. Private*, pg. 9
ABBOTT CRITICAL CARE SYSTEMS—See Abbott Laboratories; *U.S. Public*, pg. 13
ABBOTT ELECTRONICS, INC.; *U.S. Private*, pg. 9
ABBOTT HOSPITALS INC.—See Abbott Laboratories; *U.S. Public*, pg. 13
ABBOTT IRELAND LTD.—See Abbott Laboratories; *U.S. Public*, pg. 13
J.R. ABBOTT CONSTRUCTION, INC.; *U.S. Private*, pg. 9
ABBOTT LABORATORIES; *U.S. Public*, pg. 12
ABBOTT LABORATORIES/ASHLAND—See Abbott Laboratories; *U.S. Public*, pg. 13
ABBOTT LABORATORIES C.A.—See Abbott Laboratories; *U.S. Public*, pg. 13
ABBOTT LABORATORIES DE MEXICO S.A.—See Abbott Laboratories; *U.S. Public*, pg. 13
ABBOTT LABORATORIES LTD.—See Abbott Laboratories; *U.S. Public*, pg. 13
ABBOTT LABORATORIES LTD.-MFG.—See Abbott Laboratories; *U.S. Public*, pg. 14
ABBOTT LABORATORIES-MOSCOW SALES OFFICE—See Abbott Laboratories; *U.S. Public*, pg. 14
ABBOTT LABORATORIES NZ LTD.—See Abbott Laboratories; *U.S. Public*, pg. 14
ABBOTT LABORATORIES S.A.—See Abbott Laboratories; *U.S. Public*, pg. 14
ABBOTT S.A.—See Abbott Laboratories; *U.S. Public*, pg. 14
ABBOTT SCANDINAVIA AB—See Abbott Laboratories; *U.S. Public*, pg. 14
ABBYLAND FOODS, INC.; *U.S. Private*, pg. 10
ABBYLAND ILLINOIS, INC.—See Abbyland Foods, Inc.; *U.S. Private*, pg. 10
ABBYLAND PORK RACK—See Abbyland Foods, Inc.; *U.S. Private*, pg. 10
ABCO—See Jami, Inc.; *U.S. Private*, pg. 581
ABCO MARKETS, INC.; *U.S. Private*, pg. 10
ABDALLA'S LAFAYETTE, INC.; *U.S. Private*, pg. 10
ABDULLA FOUAD CORPORATION—See Abdulla Fouad Co. Ltd.; *Int'l*, pg. 502
ABEL LEMON & BLEAKLEY—See Laporte plc; *Int'l*, pg. 803
ABELL-HOWE COMPANY; *U.S. Private*, pg. 10
ABELLO DEUTSCHLAND PHARMA GMBH—See Chr. Hansen Holding A/S; *Int'l*, pg. 288
ABELLO LINDE, S.A.—See Linde AG; *Int'l*, pg. 811
M. ABELMAN COMPANY, INC.—See GP Strategies Corporation; *U.S. Public*, pg. 694
ABELSON-TAYLOR, INC.; *U.S. Private*, pg. 10
ABELSON-TAYLOR, INC.—See Abelson-Taylor, Inc.; *U.S. Private*, pg. 10
ABERCROMBIE & FITCH—See The Limited, Inc.; *U.S. Public*, pg. 995
ABERDARE CABLES LTD.—See Pirelli S.p.A.; *Int'l*, pg. 1059
ABERDEEN CITIZEN NEWS-RECORD—See Media General, Inc.; *U.S. Public*, pg. 1079
ABERDEEN MFG. CORPORATION—See Trace International Holdings, Inc.; *U.S. Private*, pg. 1094
ABERDEEN NEWS COMPANY—See Knight-Ridder, Inc.; *U.S. Public*, pg. 963
ABERDEEN SCAFFOLDING COMPANY LTD.—See Sophus Berendsen A/S; *Int'l*, pg. 1285
ABERLY—See Lagardere Groupe; *Int'l*, pg. 791
ABERTAY PAPER SACKS LTD.—See BPB Industries PLC; *Int'l*, pg. 122
ABETONG AMERICA INC.—See Scancem AB; *Int'l*, pg. 1199
ABETONG MILJO AB—See Scancem AB; *Int'l*, pg. 1199
ABETONG PREFAB AB—See Scancem AB; *Int'l*, pg. 1199
ABETONG TEKNIK AB—See Scancem AB; *Int'l*, pg. 1199
ABEX FRICTION PRODUCTS—See Cooper Industries, Inc.; *U.S. Public*, pg. 443
ABFALLVERWERTUNGSGESELLSCHAFT WESTFALEN MBH (AVW)—See Veba AG; *Int'l*, pg. 1460
ABFALLWIRTSCHAFT GMBH—See Tractebel; *Int'l*, pg. 1416
ABFALLWIRTSCHAFTSGESELLSCHAFT DES KREISS WARENDORF MBH—See Harpen AG; *Int'l*, pg. 597
ABIANNE—See Lagardere Groupe; *Int'l*, pg. 791
ABIATAR S.A.—See BellSouth Corporation; *U.S. Public*, pg. 208
STE. ABIDJANAISE—See Accor S.A.; *Int'l*, pg. 21
ABIETA CHEMIE GMBH—See Hercules Incorporated; *U.S. Public*, pg. 810
ABILENE REPORTER NEWS—See Harte-Hanks Communications, Inc.; *U.S. Public*, pg. 601
ABINGDON PRESS—See The United Methodist Publishing House; *U.S. Private*, pg. 1123
ABINGTON-ROCKLAND MARINER—See Gannett Company, Inc.; *U.S. Public*, pg. 700
ABISKO MFG., INC.—See Flexible Products Company; *U.S. Private*, pg. 412
ABITEC—See Associated British Foods plc; *Int'l*, pg. 92
ABITIBI-CONSOLIDATED INC.; *Int'l*, pg. 19
ABITIBI-CONSOLIDATED PAPER SALES CORPORATION—See Abitibi-Consolidated Inc.; *Int'l*, pg. 20
ABLE TRANSLATIONS LIMITED—See Berlitz International, Inc.; *U.S. Public*, pg. 221
ABLESTIK LABORATORIES—See Unilever Plc; *Int'l*, pg. 1435
ABLOY AB—See Assa Abloy AB; *Int'l*, pg. 17

ABLOY OY—See Assa Abloy AB; *Int'l*, pg. 18
ABLOY SECURITY INC.—See Assa Abloy AB; *Int'l*, pg. 18
ABLOY SECURITY LTD.—See Assa Abloy AB; *Int'l*, pg. 17
ABOLITE LIGHTING INC.—See LSI Industries, Inc.; *U.S. Public*, pg. 971
ABRAHAM LINCOLN INSURANCE CO.—See First Commonwealth Corporation; *U.S. Private*, pg. 406
ABRAMS & CO. PUBLISHING INC.; *U.S. Private*, pg. 10
ABRAMS CONSTRUCTION, INC.—See Abrams Industries, Inc.; *U.S. Public*, pg. 14
ABRAMS FIXTURE CORPORATION—See Abrams Industries, Inc.; *U.S. Public*, pg. 14
ABRAMS INDUSTRIES, INC.; *U.S. Public*, pg. 14
ABRAMS PROPERTIES, INC.—See Abrams Industries, Inc.; *U.S. Public*, pg. 14
ABRASIVES, INC.—See Prime Technology, Inc.; *U.S. Private*, pg. 884
ABROS, INC.—See Art Iron, Inc.; *U.S. Private*, pg. 86
ABRU ALUMINIUM LIMITED—See Hepworth Plc; *Int'l*, pg. 615
ABS GENERAL CONTRACTORS, INC.—See Shook National Corporation; *U.S. Private*, pg. 996
ABSORBENT MANUFACTURING & TECHNOLOGY, INC.—See ERD Waste Corp.; *U.S. Public*, pg. 546
ABU AB—See Outdoor Technologies Group; *U.S. Private*, pg. 822
ABU ALLGEMEINE BAU-UNION GMBH & CO. KG—See Bilfinger + Berger Bauaktiengesellschaft; *Int'l*, pg. 195
ABU DHABI COMPANY FOR ONSHORE OIL OPERATIONS—See Royal Dutch/Shell Group of Companies; *Int'l*, pg. 1140
ABU DHABI GAS INDUSTRIES—See Royal Dutch/Shell Group of Companies; *Int'l*, pg. 1140
ABU GARCIA INC.—See Outdoor Technologies Group; *U.S. Private*, pg. 822
ABU GARCIA PRODUKTION AB—See Outdoor Technologies Group; *U.S. Private*, pg. 822
ABU GARCIA PTY. LTD.—See Outdoor Technologies Group; *U.S. Private*, pg. 822
ABU GARCIA (UK) LTD.—See Outdoor Technologies Group; *U.S. Private*, pg. 822
ABURAHI LABORATORIES—See Shionogi & Co., Ltd.; *Int'l*, pg. 1235
ABWASSERSYSTEME GMBH—See Harpen AG; *Int'l*, pg. 597
ACACIA FEDERAL MORTGAGE CORP.—See The Acacia Group - Acacia Life Insurance Co.; *U.S. Private*, pg. 11
ACACIA FINANCIAL CORPORATION—See The Acacia Group - Acacia Life Insurance Co.; *U.S. Private*, pg. 11
THE ACACIA GROUP - ACACIA LIFE INSURANCE CO.; *U.S. Private*, pg. 10
ACACIA NATIONAL LIFE INS. CO.—See The Acacia Group - Acacia Life Insurance Co.; *U.S. Private*, pg. 11
ACACIA NETWORKS, INC.; *U.S. Private*, pg. 11
ACACIA TECHNOLOGIES—See Computer Associates International, Inc.; *U.S. Public*, pg. 420
ACACIA TECHNOLOGIES ASIA—See Computer Associates International, Inc.; *U.S. Public*, pg. 420
ACACIA TECHNOLOGIES AUSTRALIA/NEW ZEALAND—See Computer Associates International, Inc.; *U.S. Public*, pg. 420
ACACIA TECHNOLOGIES UK/EUROPE—See Computer Associates International, Inc.; *U.S. Public*, pg. 420
ACADEMIC BOOKSTORE—See OY Stockmann AB; *Int'l*, pg. 1301
ACADEMIC PRESS, INC.—See Harcourt General, Inc.; *U.S. Public*, pg. 783
ACADEMIC PRESS INTERNATIONAL CORP.—See Harcourt General, Inc.; *U.S. Public*, pg. 783
ACADEMIC YEAR IN AMERICA—See American Institute for Foreign Study; *U.S. Private*, pg. 56
ACADEMIE ACCOR—See Accor S.A.; *Int'l*, pg. 20
ACADEMY CORPORATION; *U.S. Private*, pg. 11
ACADEMY INSURANCE GROUP, INC.—See AEGON N.V.; *Int'l*, pg. 27
ACADEMY LIFE INSURANCE CO.—See AEGON N.V.; *Int'l*, pg. 27
ACADIA INSURANCE COMPANY—See W.R. Berkley Corporation; *U.S. Public*, pg. 215
ACADIAN ASSET MANAGEMENT—See United Asset Management Corporation; *U.S. Public*, pg. 1672
ACAPULCO RESTAURANTS—See Restaurant Associates Corporation; *U.S. Private*, pg. 925
ACCECONES RICCI U.S.A., INC.—See Elf Aquitaine; *Int'l*, pg. 445
ACCEL INTERNATIONAL CORPORATION; *U.S. Public*, pg. 14
ACCELERATED CLAIMS PROCESSING, INC.—See Health Management Systems, Inc.; *U.S. Public*, pg. 802
ACCELERATED FREEZE DRYING CO., LTD.—See Nissin Food Products Co., Ltd.; *Int'l*, pg. 950
ACCELERATION INSURANCE AGENCY, INC.—See ACCEL International Corporation; *U.S. Public*, pg. 14
ACCELERATION INSURANCE AGENCY OF INDIANA, INC.—See ACCEL International Corporation; *U.S. Public*, pg. 14
ACCELERATION LIFE INSURANCE AGENCY, INC.—See ACCEL International Corporation; *U.S. Public*, pg. 14
ACCELERATION NATIONAL INSURANCE COMPANY—See ACCEL International Corporation; *U.S. Public*, pg. 14
ACCENDO TECHNOLOGIES SDN. BHD.—See Knurr AG; *Int'l*, pg. 740
ACCENT FURNITURE, INC.—See Royal Waterbeds; *U.S. Private*, pg. 949
ACCEPTANCE INSURANCE CO., INC.; *U.S. Public*, pg. 14
ACCEPTANCE INSURANCE COMPANIES, INC.—See Acceptance Insurance Co., Inc.; *U.S. Public*, pg. 15
ACCES CAPITAL—See Caisse de depot et placement du Quebec; *Int'l*, pg. 249
ACCES CAPITAL ABITIBI-TEMISCAMINQUE—See Caisse de depot et placement du Quebec; *Int'l*, pg. 249
ACCES CAPITAL QUEBEC—See Caisse de depot et placement du Quebec; *Int'l*, pg. 249

ACCESORIOS DE TUBERIA DE COBRE S.A.—See Delta plc; *Int'l*, pg. 391
ACCESS ADVERTISING LIMITED—See DMB&B Communications; *U.S. Public*, pg. 303
ACCESS BUSINESS UNIT—See Telco Systems, Inc.; *U.S. Public*, pg. 1568
ACCESS CORPORATION—See Oce-van der Grinten N.V.; *Int'l*, pg. 994
ACCESS EQUIPMENT LTD.—See Up-Right, Inc.; *U.S. Private*, pg. 1128
ACCESS INDUSTRIES; *U.S. Private*, pg. 11
THE ACCESS WORKS, INC.—See Fleet Engineers, Inc.; *U.S. Private*, pg. 410
ACCESSORY DESIGN GROUP, LTD.—See Tandy Brands Accessories, Inc.; *U.S. Public*, pg. 1560
ACCESSORY SERVICES-TEXAS—See General Electric Company; *U.S. Public*, pg. 710
ACCIAI KRUPP S.R.L.—See Fried. Krupp AG; *Int'l*, pg. 515
ACCIDENT & MISCELLANEOUS ACCEPTANCES (PTY.) LTD.—See Assicurazioni Generali S.p.A.; *Int'l*, pg. 90
ACCIONES Y VALORES DE MEXICO, S.A. DE C.V.—See Grupo Financiero Banamex/Accival, S.A. de C.V.; *Int'l*, pg. 574
ACCLAIM COMICS—See Acclaim Entertainment, Inc.; *U.S. Public*, pg. 15
ACCLAIM DISTRIBUTION, INC.—See Acclaim Entertainment, Inc.; *U.S. Public*, pg. 15
ACCLAIM ENTERTAINMENT GMBH—See Acclaim Entertainment, Inc.; *U.S. Public*, pg. 15
ACCLAIM ENTERTAINMENT, INC.; *U.S. Public*, pg. 15
ACCLAIM ENTERTAINMENT, LTD.—See Acclaim Entertainment, Inc.; *U.S. Public*, pg. 15
ACCLAIM ENTERTAINMENT, SA—See Acclaim Entertainment, Inc.; *U.S. Public*, pg. 15
ACCLAIM JAPAN, LTD.—See Acclaim Entertainment, Inc.; *U.S. Public*, pg. 15
ACCO BRANDS, INC.—See Fortune Brands, Inc.; *U.S. Public*, pg. 674
ACCO CANADA INC.—See Fortune Brands, Inc.; *U.S. Public*, pg. 674
ACCO CHAIN & LIFTING PRODUCTS—See FKI Plc; *Int'l*, pg. 473
ACCO CONTROLS—See FKI Plc; *Int'l*, pg. 472
ACCO CONTROLS INC.—See FKI Plc; *Int'l*, pg. 472
ACCO EASTLIGHT LIMITED—See Fortune Brands, Inc.; *U.S. Public*, pg. 674
ACCO EUROPE PLC—See Fortune Brands, Inc.; *U.S. Public*, pg. 674
ACCO FRANCE S.A.—See Fortune Brands, Inc.; *U.S. Public*, pg. 675
ACCO PLATEN GMBH—See FKI Plc; *Int'l*, pg. 473
ACCO-REXEL GROUP SERVICES PLC—See Fortune Brands, Inc.; *U.S. Public*, pg. 674
ACCO SYSTEMS DIV.—See FKI Plc; *Int'l*, pg. 472
ACCO UK LIMITED—See Fortune Brands, Inc.; *U.S. Public*, pg. 675
ACCO WORLD CORPORATION—See Fortune Brands, Inc.; *U.S. Public*, pg. 674
ACCOR ASIA PTE—See Accor S.A.; *Int'l*, pg. 21
ACCOR DO BRASIL—See Accor S.A.; *Int'l*, pg. 21
ACCOR GASTONOMIE AG—See Accor S.A.; *Int'l*, pg. 21
ACCOR GMBH—See Accor S.A.; *Int'l*, pg. 21
THE ACCOR GROUP, INC.—See Accor S.A.; *Int'l*, pg. 21
ACCOR HONG KONG LTD.—See Accor S.A.; *Int'l*, pg. 21
ACCOR HOTELLERIE GMBH—See Accor S.A.; *Int'l*, pg. 21
ACCOR NORTH AMERICA—See Accor S.A.; *Int'l*, pg. 21
ACCOR S.A.; *Int'l*, pg. 20
ACCOR TRB—See Accor S.A.; *Int'l*, pg. 21
ACCOR UK—See Accor S.A.; *Int'l*, pg. 21
ACCORD CONTRACT SERVICES—See Veba AG; *Int'l*, pg. 1458
ACCORD CONTROLS, INC.—See Flowserve Corporation; *U.S. Public*, pg. 658
ACCORD ENERGY LTD.—See Centrica Plc; *Int'l*, pg. 279
ACCORD INDUSTRIES—See McKechnie PLC; *Int'l*, pg. 851
ACCORDINATION—See Accor S.A.; *Int'l*, pg. 21
ACCORS HOTELS BELGIUM—See Accor S.A.; *Int'l*, pg. 21
ACCOUNT SPECIFIC MARKETING, INC. (ASM)—See Dugan Valva Contess Inc.; *U.S. Private*, pg. 345
ACCOUNTEMPS—See Robert Half International Inc.; *U.S. Public*, pg. 775
ACCPAC INTERNATIONAL—See Computer Associates International, Inc.; *U.S. Public*, pg. 420
ACCRA PAC GROUP; *U.S. Private*, pg. 11
ACCRAPLY, INC.—See Barry-Wehmiller Company; *U.S. Private*, pg. 118
ACCRES UITGEVERS BV—See VNU Verenigde Nederlandse Uitgeversbedrijven B.V.; *Int'l*, pg. 1445
ACCU-CAST—See Crane Co.; *U.S. Public*, pg. 456
ACCU-SORT CANADA—See Accu-Sort Systems, Inc.; *U.S. Private*, pg. 11
ACCU-SORT SYSTEMS, INC.; *U.S. Private*, pg. 11
ACCU-TIME SYSTEM—See Accu-Sort Systems, Inc.; *U.S. Private*, pg. 11
ACCUCARE DIV.—See Medline Industries, Inc.; *U.S. Private*, pg. 728
ACCUDYNE CORPORATION—See Alliant Techsystems; *U.S. Public*, pg. 47
ACCURATE BOX CO., INC.; *U.S. Private*, pg. 11
ACCURATE BUSHING CO., INC.; *U.S. Private*, pg. 11
ACCURATE DOOR & HARDWARE DIVISION—See Acklands Limited; *Int'l*, pg. 23
ACCURATE FORGING CORP.—See Delta plc; *Int'l*, pg. 391
ACCURATE PERFORATING CO.; *U.S. Private*, pg. 12
ACCURIDE CORP.—See Phelps Dodge Corporation; *U.S. Public*, pg. 1286
ACCUSCAN—See Moore Corporation Limited; *Int'l*, pg. 890
ACCUSCAN INTERNATIONAL—See Moore Corporation Limited; *Int'l*, pg. 890
ACCUSTAFF INCORPORATED; *U.S. Public*, pg. 15
ACE COMB COMPANY INC.—See Newell Co.; *U.S. Public*, pg. 1177

Company Index

ACE DORAN BROKERAGE—See Ace Doran Hauling & Rigging Company; *U.S. Private*, pg. 340
ACE FASTENER—See Peace Industries Inc.; *U.S. Private*, pg. 845
ACE GLASS INCORPORATED; *U.S. Private*, pg. 12
ACE HARDWARE CORPORATION; *U.S. Private*, pg. 12
ACE NOVELTY COMPANY, INC.—See Play by Play Toys & Novelties, Inc.; *U.S. Public*, pg. 1309
ACE NOVELTY FUN SERVICE DIVISION—See Play by Play Toys & Novelties, Inc.; *U.S. Public*, pg. 1309
ACE TANK & EQUIPMENT CO.; *U.S. Private*, pg. 12
ACEITES LUBRICANTES Y GRASAS CASTROL S.A.—See Burmah Castrol plc; *Int'l*, pg. 235
ACER AFRICA PTY. LTD.—See Acer Incorporated; *Int'l*, pg. 22
ACER/ALTOS COMPUTER SYSTEMS—See Acer Incorporated; *Int'l*, pg. 22
ACER AMERICA CORPORATION—See Acer Incorporated; *Int'l*, pg. 22
ACER ARGENTINA—See Acer Incorporated; *Int'l*, pg. 22
ACER BELGIUM N.V.—See Acer Incorporated; *Int'l*, pg. 22
ACER CHILE—See Acer Incorporated; *Int'l*, pg. 22
ACER COMPUTEC LATINO AMERICA—See Acer Incorporated; *Int'l*, pg. 22
ACER COMPUTER AUSTRALIA PTY. LTD.—See Acer Incorporated; *Int'l*, pg. 22
ACER COMPUTER B.V.—See Acer Incorporated; *Int'l*, pg. 22
ACER COMPUTER COLOMBIA—See Acer Incorporated; *Int'l*, pg. 22
ACER COMPUTER (FAR EAST) LTD.—See Acer Incorporated; *Int'l*, pg. 22
ACER COMPUTER FRANCE S.A.R.L.—See Acer Incorporated; *Int'l*, pg. 22
ACER COMPUTER GMBH—See Acer Incorporated; *Int'l*, pg. 22
ACER COMPUTER HANDELSGMBH—See Acer Incorporated; *Int'l*, pg. 22
ACER COMPUTER INTERNATIONAL LTD.—See Acer Incorporated; *Int'l*, pg. 22
ACER COMPUTER (M.E.) LTD.—See Acer Incorporated; *Int'l*, pg. 22
ACER COMPUTER NEW ZEALAND—See Acer Incorporated; *Int'l*, pg. 22
ACER COMPUTER NORWAY A/S—See Acer Incorporated; *Int'l*, pg. 22
ACER COMPUTER TURKEY—See Acer Incorporated; *Int'l*, pg. 22
ACER DE VENEZUELA—See Acer Incorporated; *Int'l*, pg. 22
ACER INCORPORATED; *Int'l*, pg. 22
ACER INCORPORATED, INFORMATION PRODUCTS BUSINESS UNIT—See Acer Incorporated; *Int'l*, pg. 22
ACER ITALY S.R.L.—See Acer Incorporated; *Int'l*, pg. 22
ACER JAPAN CORPORATION—See Acer Incorporated; *Int'l*, pg. 22
ACER KOREA—See Acer Incorporated; *Int'l*, pg. 22
ACER LABS—See Acer Incorporated; *Int'l*, pg. 22
ACER LATIN AMERICA—See Acer Incorporated; *Int'l*, pg. 22
ACER MARKET SERVICES, LTD.—See Acer Incorporated; *Int'l*, pg. 22
ACER PERIPHERALS, INC.—See Acer Incorporated; *Int'l*, pg. 22
ACER PROPERTY DEVELOPMENT INC.—See Acer Incorporated; *Int'l*, pg. 22
ACER SALES & SERVICE SDN. BHD.—See Acer Incorporated; *Int'l*, pg. 22
ACER SCANDINAVIA A/S—See Acer Incorporated; *Int'l*, pg. 22
ACER SERTEK INCORPORATED—See Acer Incorporated; *Int'l*, pg. 22
ACER TWP CORPORATION—See Acer Incorporated; *Int'l*, pg. 22
ACER UK LIMITED—See Acer Incorporated; *Int'l*, pg. 22
ACEREX S.A.—See Alfa, S.A. de C.V.; *Int'l*, pg. 56
ACEROMEX ATLAS, S.A. DE C.V.—See Carpenter Technology Corporation; *U.S. Public*, pg. 308
ACEROMEX-ATLAS S.A. DE C.V.—See Rio Algom Limited; *Int'l*, pg. 1118
ACEROS BOEHLER DEL PERU S.A.—See Voest-Alpine Stahl AG; *Int'l*, pg. 1471
ACEROS BOEHLER S.A.—See Voest-Alpine Stahl AG; *Int'l*, pg. 1471
ACEROS CAMESA S.A. DE C.V.—See Grupo Industrial Camesa S.A. de C.V.; *Int'l*, pg. 575
ACEROS FORTUNA S.A.—See Fried. Krupp AG; *Int'l*, pg. 515
ACEROS KRUPP HOESCH S.A.—See Fried. Krupp AG; *Int'l*, pg. 515
ACEROS NACIONALES—See Altos Hornos de Mexico, S.A.; *Int'l*, pg. 66
ACEROS PHOENIX-BOHLER S.A.—See Voest-Alpine Stahl AG; *Int'l*, pg. 1471
ACESITA SANDVIK TUBOS INOX S.A.—See Sandvik AB; *Int'l*, pg. 1187
ACESSORIOS ELECTRONICOS (BEL FUSE MACAO), LIMITADA—See Bel Fuse Inc.; *U.S. Public*, pg. 200
ACETO AGRICULTURAL CHEMICALS CORP.—See Aceto Corporation; *U.S. Public*, pg. 15
ACETO CORPORATION; *U.S. Public*, pg. 15
ACHATZ GMBH BAUUNTERNEHMUNG—See Bilfinger + Berger Bauaktiengesellschaft; *Int'l*, pg. 195
ACHESON A.N.Z. PTY. LTD.—See Acheson Industries, Inc.; *U.S. Private*, pg. 12
ACHESON COLLOIDEN B.V.—See Acheson Industries, Inc.; *U.S. Private*, pg. 12
ACHESON COLLOIDS (CANADA) LTD.—See Acheson Industries, Inc.; *U.S. Private*, pg. 12
ACHESON COLLOIDS COMPANY—See Acheson Industries, Inc.; *U.S. Private*, pg. 12
ACHESON DO BRASIL IND. E COM LTDA.—See Acheson Industries, Inc.; *U.S. Private*, pg. 12

ACHESON FRANCE S.A.—See Acheson Industries, Inc.; *U.S. Private*, pg. 12
ACHESON INDUSTRIES (EUROPE) LTD.—See Acheson Industries, Inc.; *U.S. Private*, pg. 12
ACHESON INDUSTRIES, INC.; *U.S. Private*, pg. 12
ACHESON INTERNATIONAL S.A.-EQUIPMENT DIV.—See Acheson Industries, Inc.; *U.S. Private*, pg. 12
ACHESON ITALIANA S.R.L.—See Acheson Industries, Inc.; *U.S. Private*, pg. 12
ACHESON (JAPAN) LTD.—See Acheson Industries, Inc.; *U.S. Private*, pg. 12
ACHESON KOREA LTD.—See Acheson Industries, Inc.; *U.S. Private*, pg. 12
ACHIEVE GLOBAL—See The Times Mirror Company; *U.S. Public*, pg. 1617
ACHILLES CORPORATION; *Int'l*, pg. 22
ACHMEA—See Eureko B.V.; *Int'l*, pg. 464
ACHOIA PAPERMILL—See Fort James Corporation; *U.S. Public*, pg. 672
ACIERIES DE PLOERMEL—See Varlen Corporation; *U.S. Private*, pg. 1711
ACIERS FRANCOSTEEL CANADA—See Groupe Usinor; *Int'l*, pg. 572
ACIERS KRUPP S.A.R.L.—See Fried. Krupp AG; *Int'l*, pg. 515
ACIOM 1932 S.P.A.—See Fuchs Petrolub AG Oel + Chemie; *Int'l*, pg. 517
ACKERLEY COMMUNICATIONS OF FLORIDA, INC.—See The Ackerley Group; *U.S. Public*, pg. 16
ACKERLEY COMMUNICATIONS OF THE NORTHWEST-PORTLAND—See The Ackerley Group; *U.S. Public*, pg. 15
ACKERLEY COMMUNICATIONS OF THE NORTHWEST-SEATTLE—See The Ackerley Group; *U.S. Public*, pg. 15
THE ACKERLEY GROUP; *U.S. Public*, pg. 15
ACKERMAN MCQUEEN, INC.; *U.S. Private*, pg. 12
ACKLANDS LIMITED; *Int'l*, pg. 23
ACKLIN STAMPING DIV.—See Tecumseh Products Company; *U.S. Public*, pg. 1565
ACMA S.A.—See N.V. Bekaert S.A.; *Int'l*, pg. 184
ACMAT CORPORATION; *U.S. Public*, pg. 16
ACME BOOT CO., INC.—See Farley, Inc.; *U.S. Private*, pg. 394
ACME BRICK CO.—See Justin Industries, Inc.; *U.S. Public*, pg. 936
ACME CANVAS CO., INC.; *U.S. Private*, pg. 13
ACME/CHASTON PUERTO RICO—See GP Strategies Corporation; *U.S. Private*, pg. 694
ACME CHEMICALS & INSULATION CO.—See Insulating Materials, Inc.; *U.S. Private*, pg. 565
ACME DESIGN TECHNOLOGY, CO.; *U.S. Private*, pg. 13
ACME ELECTRIC CORPORATION; *U.S. Public*, pg. 16
ACME FOUNDRY, INC.; *U.S. Private*, pg. 13
ACME FRAME PRODUCTS, INC.—See American Greetings Corporation; *U.S. Public*, pg. 78
ACME INDUSTRIAL COMPANY—See Jergens Inc.; *U.S. Private*, pg. 586
ACME MARKETS—See American Stores Company; *U.S. Public*, pg. 93
ACME METALS INCORPORATED; *U.S. Public*, pg. 16
ACME MILLS CO. INC.; *U.S. Private*, pg. 13
ACME PACKAGING CORPORATION—See Acme Metals Incorporated; *U.S. Public*, pg. 16
ACME POULTRY COMPANY, INC.; *U.S. Private*, pg. 13
ACME PRINTING INK CO., INC.—See Sumitomo Chemical Company, Ltd.; *Int'l*, pg. 1311
ACME REFRIGERATION OF BATON ROUGE INC.; *U.S. Private*, pg. 13
ACME RESIN CORP.—See Borden, Inc.; *U.S. Private*, pg. 157
ACME RULER CO. LTD.—See Acme United Corporation; *U.S. Public*, pg. 17
ACME STEEL CO.—See Acme Metals Incorporated; *U.S. Public*, pg. 16
ACME TRUCK LINE, INC.; *U.S. Private*, pg. 14
ACME TUBE INC.; *U.S. Private*, pg. 14
ACME UNITED CORPORATION; *U.S. Public*, pg. 17
ACME UNITED LTD.-SURMANCO DIVISION—See Acme United Corporation; *U.S. Public*, pg. 17
ACME VISIBLE RECORDS—See Acme Design Technology, Co.; *U.S. Private*, pg. 13
ACMETRACK—See BTR plc; *Int'l*, pg. 129
ACMIL INDUSTRIES PTY. LTD.—See BTR plc; *Int'l*, pg. 129
ACONCAGUA SEGUROS DE RETIRO, S.A.—See Corporacion MAPFRE, Compania Internacional de Reaseguros, S.A.; *Int'l*, pg. 333
ACORDIA, INC.; *U.S. Public*, pg. 14
ACORDIA NORTHEAST—See Inchcape PLC; *Int'l*, pg. 671
ACORGA MINING CHEMICALS BUSINESS—See Zeneca Group Plc; *Int'l*, pg. 1524
THE ACORN—See Gilmore Bros., Inc.; *U.S. Private*, pg. 454
ACORN COMPUTERS LTD.—See Olivetti SpA; *Int'l*, pg. 1002
ACORN CUSTOM MOLDING/CAL TUBE—See Acorn Engineering Company; *U.S. Private*, pg. 14
ACORN ENGINEERING COMPANY; *U.S. Private*, pg. 14
ACORN PRODUCTS, INC.; *U.S. Public*, pg. 17
ACORN STRUCTURES—See Deck House Inc.; *U.S. Private*, pg. 320
ACORN WINDOW SYSTEMS INC.; *U.S. Private*, pg. 14
ACOS PHOENIX-BOEHLER LTDA.—See Voest-Alpine Stahl AG; *Int'l*, pg. 1471
ACOS VILLARES MECHANICAL ENGINEERING UNIT—See Acos Villares S.A.; *Int'l*, pg. 23
ACOS VILLARES PLANT - DIADEMA—See Acos Villares S.A.; *Int'l*, pg. 23
ACOS VILLARES PLANT - MOGI DAS CRUZ—See Acos Villares S.A.; *Int'l*, pg. 23
ACOS VILLARES PLANT - PINDAMONHANGABA—See Acos Villares S.A.; *Int'l*, pg. 23
ACOS VILLARES S.A.; *Int'l*, pg. 23

ACOS VILLARES SAO CAETANO PLANT—See Acos Villares S.A.; *Int'l*, pg. 23
ACOS VILLARES STEEL UNIT—See Acos Villares S.A.; *Int'l*, pg. 23
N.V. ACOTECH S.A.—See N.V. Bekaert S.A.; *Int'l*, pg. 183
ACOUSTI ENGINEERING CO. OF FLORIDA; *U.S. Private*, pg. 14
ACOUSTIC IMAGING TECHNOLOGIES, INC.—See Daimler-Benz Aktiengesellschaft; *Int'l*, pg. 368
ACQUEDOTTO DI DOMODOSSOLA S.P.A.—See ENI S.p.A.; *Int'l*, pg. 428
ACQUEDOTTO DI SAVONA S.R.L.—See ENI S.p.A.; *Int'l*, pg. 428
ACQUEDOTTO MONFERRATO S.P.A.—See ENI S.p.A.; *Int'l*, pg. 428
ACRISON, INC.; *U.S. Private*, pg. 14
ACROMETAL COMPANIES, INC.; *U.S. Private*, pg. 14
ACSIA—See Fortis; *Int'l*, pg. 499
ACSTAR INSURANCE COMPANY—See ACMAT Corporation; *U.S. Public*, pg. 16
ACTEX, INC.—See Acme Mills Co. Inc.; *U.S. Private*, pg. 13
ACTION CLINTON—See Action Technology Company; *U.S. Private*, pg. 15
ACTION COMMODITIES CORPORATION—See Tennessee Dressed Beef Company; *U.S. Private*, pg. 1076
ACTION CONTROLS PTY. LTD.—See Action Instruments, Inc.; *U.S. Private*, pg. 15
ACTION EQUIPMENT; *U.S. Private*, pg. 14
ACTION INDUSTRIES, INC.—See Furniture Brands International Inc.; *U.S. Public*, pg. 688
ACTION INSTRUMENTS (CHINA) LTD.—See Action Instruments, Inc.; *U.S. Private*, pg. 15
ACTION INSTRUMENTS, INC.; *U.S. Private*, pg. 15
ACTION LIFT—See Medico Industries, Inc.; *U.S. Private*, pg. 728
ACTION MANUFACTURING CO.; *U.S. Private*, pg. 15
ACTION MORTGAGE COMPANY—See Sterling Financial Corporation; *U.S. Public*, pg. 1516
ACTION MUNICIPALE—See C.E.P. Communication Group; *Int'l*, pg. 239
ACTION OILFIELD SERVICES, INC.—See Prima Energy Corporation; *U.S. Public*, pg. 1325
ACTION PAY-PER-VIEW—See Black Entertainment Television Holdings Inc.; *U.S. Public*, pg. 235
ACTION PERFORMANCE COMPANIES, INC.; *U.S. Public*, pg. 17
ACTION ROCKAWAY—See Action Technology Company; *U.S. Private*, pg. 15
ACTION SUPPLY—See Action Equipment; *U.S. Private*, pg. 15
ACTION TECHNOLOGY COMPANY; *U.S. Private*, pg. 15
ACTION TIRE—See Action Equipment; *U.S. Private*, pg. 15
ACTIUM LEASOBJEKT GMBH—See Commerzbank AG; *Int'l*, pg. 310
ACTIV TRAINING LTD.—See ITC Learning Corp.; *U.S. Public*, pg. 859
ACTIVE BIOTECH AB; *Int'l*, pg. 23
ACTIVE ELECTRICAL SUPPLY COMPANY; *U.S. Private*, pg. 15
ACTIVE HOMES CORP.—See Active Tool & Manufacturing Co., Inc.; *U.S. Private*, pg. 16
ACTIVE INDUSTRIES, INC.—See Active Tool & Manufacturing Co., Inc.; *U.S. Private*, pg. 16
ACTIVE INTERNATIONAL; *U.S. Private*, pg. 15
ACTIVE QUILTING DIV.—See Rockville Fabrics Corporation; *U.S. Private*, pg. 938
ACTIVE SOFTWARE, INC.; *U.S. Private*, pg. 15
ACTIVE TOOL & MANUFACTURING CO., INC.; *U.S. Private*, pg. 16
ACTIVE VOICE CORPORATION; *U.S. Public*, pg. 17
ACTIVISION; *U.S. Public*, pg. 17
ACTIVISION UK—See Activision; *U.S. Public*, pg. 17
ACTON ENVIRONMENTAL TESTING—See National Technical Systems, Inc.; *U.S. Public*, pg. 1161
ACTRON MANUFACTURING COMPANY; *U.S. Private*, pg. 16
ACTUATE SOFTWARE CORPORATION; *U.S. Private*, pg. 16
ACTUS CORPORATION—See Minebea Co., Ltd.; *Int'l*, pg. 868
ACUICULTURA DE CEUTA, S.A.—See Caja de Madrid Group; *Int'l*, pg. 252
ACUREX ENVIRONMENTAL CORP.—See Heidemij N.V.; *Int'l*, pg. 607
ACUSHNET COMPANY—See Fortune Brands, Inc.; *U.S. Public*, pg. 675
ACUSHNET INTERNATIONAL INC.—See Fortune Brands, Inc.; *U.S. Public*, pg. 675
ACUSON AB—See Acuson Corporation; *U.S. Public*, pg. 18
ACUSON A/S—See Acuson Corporation; *U.S. Public*, pg. 18
ACUSON CANADA, LTD.—See Acuson Corporation; *U.S. Public*, pg. 18
ACUSON CIS—See Acuson Corporation; *U.S. Public*, pg. 18
ACUSON CORPORATION; *U.S. Public*, pg. 18
ACUSON GMBH—See Acuson Corporation; *U.S. Public*, pg. 18
ACUSON HONG KONG LTD.—See Acuson Corporation; *U.S. Public*, pg. 18
ACUSON LTD.—See Acuson Corporation; *U.S. Public*, pg. 18
ACUSON NIPPON, K.K.—See Acuson Corporation; *U.S. Public*, pg. 18
ACUSON OY—See Acuson Corporation; *U.S. Public*, pg. 18
ACUSON PTY. LTD.—See Acuson Corporation; *U.S. Public*, pg. 18
ACUSON S.A.R.L.—See Acuson Corporation; *U.S. Public*, pg. 18
ACUSON S.P.A.—See Acuson Corporation; *U.S. Public*, pg. 18
ACUSTAR, INC.—See Chrysler Corporation; *U.S. Public*, pg. 353

MASTER INDEX TO COMPANY NAMES

ADMORE

Company Index

ACUSTAR, INC., ELECTRONICS GROUP—See Chrysler Corporation; U.S. Public, pg. 353
ACUSTAR, INC., ENGINEERED PRODUCTS GROUP—See Chrysler Corporation; U.S. Public, pg. 353
ACUTEX DIVISION—See SPX Corporation; U.S. Public, pg. 1421
ACXIOM CORPORATION; U.S. Public, pg. 18
ACXIOM CORPORATION - PUBLICITY CENTRE—See Acxiom Corporation; U.S. Public, pg. 18
ACXIOM TRANSPORTATION SERVICES, INC.—See Acxiom Corporation; U.S. Public, pg. 18
AD AMERICAS—See DavisElen Advertising, Inc.; U.S. Private, pg. 316
AD DAIKO GIFU INC.—See Daiko Advertising, Inc.; Int'l, pg. 366
AD DAIKO KYOTO INC.—See Daiko Advertising, Inc.; Int'l, pg. 366
AD DAIKO NAGOYA INC.—See Daiko Advertising, Inc.; Int'l, pg. 366
THE AD TEAM OF FLORIDA INC.; U.S. Private, pg. 16
ADAIR FEED & GRAIN COMPANY; U.S. Private, pg. 16
ADAIR GREENE ADVERTISING; U.S. Private, pg. 16
ADALET DIV.—See Berkshire Hathaway Inc.; U.S. Public, pg. 217
ADAM & COMPANY GROUP PLC—See The Royal Bank of Scotland plc; Int'l, pg. 1132
ADAM OPEL AG—See General Motors Corporation; U.S. Public, pg. 721
ADAM TECHNOLOGY CO.—See Methode Electronics Inc.; U.S. Public, pg. 1101
ADAMATIC—See Premark International, Inc.; U.S. Public, pg. 1322
ADAMS BUSINESS FORMS; U.S. Private, pg. 16
ADAMS BUSINESS MEDIA; U.S. Private, pg. 16
ADAMS BUSINESS MEDIA—See Adams Business Media; U.S. Private, pg. 16
ADAMS ELEVATOR EQUIPMENT COMPANY—See Schindler Holding AG; Int'l, pg. 1205
ADAMS EXPRESS CO.—See Petroleum & Resources Corp.; U.S. Public, pg. 1280
ADAMS EXTRACT CO., INC.; U.S. Private, pg. 16
ADAMS HOUSE HEALTHCARE—See Vencor, Inc.; U.S. Public, pg. 1711
ADAMS INDUSTRIES, INC.—See Banner Aerospace, Inc.; U.S. Public, pg. 187
ADAMS INVESTMENT COMPANY; U.S. Private, pg. 16
ADAM'S MARK HOTELS & RESORTS—See HBE Corporation/Design Build Divisions; U.S. Private, pg. 489
ADAMS PRODUCTS COMPANY—See CRH, plc; Int'l, pg. 242
RALPH & PAUL ADAMS, INC.—See Jones Dairy Farm; U.S. Private, pg. 596
ADAMS RESOURCES & ENERGY, INC.; U.S. Public, pg. 18
ADAMS RESOURCES EXPLORATION CORP.—See Adams Resources & Energy, Inc.; U.S. Public, pg. 19
ADAMS RITE (EUROPE) LTD.—See Adams Rite Manufacturing Co.; U.S. Private, pg. 17
ADAMS RITE MANUFACTURING CO.; U.S. Private, pg. 17
ADAMS RITE SABRE INTERNATIONAL—See ZMP, Inc.; U.S. Private, pg. 1203
R.P. ADAMS COMPANY, INC.; U.S. Public, pg. 19
ADAMS, S.A.—See Warner-Lambert Company; U.S. Public, pg. 1739
STACY ADAMS SHOE CO.—See Weyco Group, Inc.; U.S. Public, pg. 1763
ADAMS U.S.A.—See Warner-Lambert Company; U.S. Public, pg. 1739
W.A. ADAMS, INC.—See Standard Commercial Corporation; U.S. Public, pg. 1502
ADAMS WINE CO.; U.S. Private, pg. 17
ADAMSVILLE TELEPHONE CO.—See Century Telephone Enterprises, Inc.; U.S. Public, pg. 329
ADANET COMMUNICATIONS—See IIS Intelligent Information Systems Ltd.; Int'l, pg. 645
ADAPT ELECTRONIC PUBLISHING—See Bertelsmann AG; Int'l, pg. 191
ADAPTEC - CENTRAL REGION—See Adaptec, Inc.; U.S. Public, pg. 19
ADAPTEC - CORPORATE HEADQUARTERS—See Adaptec, Inc.; U.S. Public, pg. 19
ADAPTEC EUROPE, S.A.—See Adaptec, Inc.; U.S. Public, pg. 19
ADAPTEC GMBH—See Adaptec, Inc.; U.S. Public, pg. 19
ADAPTEC, INC.; U.S. Public, pg. 19
ADAPTEC - JAPAN—See Adaptec, Inc.; U.S. Public, pg. 19
ADAPTEC - LATIN AMERICA—See Adaptec, Inc.; U.S. Public, pg. 19
ADAPTEC MFG. (SINGAPORE) PTE. LTD.—See Adaptec, Inc.; U.S. Public, pg. 19
ADAPTEC - MIDWESTERN REGION—See Adaptec, Inc.; U.S. Public, pg. 19
ADAPTEC - NEW ENGLAND REGION—See Adaptec, Inc.; U.S. Public, pg. 19
ADAPTEC - ROCKY MOUNTAIN REGION—See Adaptec, Inc.; U.S. Public, pg. 19
ADAPTEC - SOUTHERN REGION—See Adaptec, Inc.; U.S. Public, pg. 19
ADAPTEC - SOUTHWESTERN REGION—See Adaptec, Inc.; U.S. Public, pg. 19
ADAPTIVE ELECTRONICS—See Adec International Automation Corp.; U.S. Private, pg. 17
ADAPTIVE INFORMATION SYSTEMS—See Nissei Sangyo Co., Ltd.; Int'l, pg. 946
ADAPTIVE TECHNOLOGIES CORP.—See Kennametal Inc.; U.S. Public, pg. 950
ADASON PROPERTIES LIMITED—See The Canada Life Assurance Company; Int'l, pg. 254
ADCOM LTD., INC., KENYA—See Hewlett-Packard Company; U.S. Public, pg. 816
ADCOM OF IOWA, INC.—See The Vernon Company; U.S. Private, pg. 1137
ADCOM WIRE COMPANY—See Leggett & Platt, Incorporated; U.S. Public, pg. 986
ADD AGENCY—See Young & Rubicam Inc.; U.S. Private, pg. 1200
ADDED DIMENSIONS—See Catherines Stores Corporation; U.S. Public, pg. 318
ADDEY MILNER LIMITED—See Velcro Industries N.V.; Int'l, pg. 1462
ADDINGTON ENVIRONMENTAL, INC.—See Republic Industries, Inc.; U.S. Public, pg. 1379
ADDINGTON HOLDING CO.—See Republic Industries, Inc.; U.S. Public, pg. 1379
ADDINGTON RESOURCES, INC.—See Republic Industries, Inc.; U.S. Public, pg. 1379
ADDISON INSURANCE AGENCY—See United Fire & Casualty Company; U.S. Public, pg. 1677
ADDISON INSURANCE COMPANY—See United Fire & Casualty Company; U.S. Public, pg. 1677
ADDISON PRODUCTS COMPANY—See Heat Controller, Inc.; U.S. Private, pg. 518
ADDISON SAWS LIMITED—See B. Elliott plc.; Int'l, pg. 448
ADDISON STEEL INC.; U.S. Private, pg. 17
ADDISON TUBE FORMING LIMITED—See B. Elliott plc.; Int'l, pg. 448
ADDISON-WESLEY HIGHER EDUCATION—See Pearson plc; Int'l, pg. 1026
ADDISON-WESLEY LONGMAN—See Pearson plc; Int'l, pg. 1026
ADDISON-WESLEY LONGMAN, INC.—See Pearson plc; Int'l, pg. 1026
ADDISON-WESLEY LONGMAN LTD.—See Pearson plc; Int'l, pg. 1027
ADDISON-WESLEY PUBLISHERS B.V.—See Pearson plc; Int'l, pg. 1027
ADDISON-WESLEY PUBLISHERS JAPAN LTD.—See Pearson plc; Int'l, pg. 1027
ADDISON-WESLEY PUBLISHERS LTD.—See Pearson plc; Int'l, pg. 1027
ADDISON-WESLEY PUBLISHERS PTY. LTD.—See Pearson plc; Int'l, pg. 1027
ADDISON-WESLEY (SINGAPORE) PVT. LTD.—See Pearson plc; Int'l, pg. 1027
ADDRESSES UNLIMITED—See Gannett Company, Inc.; U.S. Public, pg. 699
ADDWEST MINERALS, INC.; U.S. Private, pg. 17
ADEC AUTOMATION—See Adec International Automation Corp.; U.S. Private, pg. 17
ADEC INTERNATIONAL AUTOMATION CORP.; U.S. Private, pg. 17
ADECCO ALFRED MARKS (IRELAND) LTD.—See Adecco S.A.; Int'l, pg. 24
ADECCO APS—See Adecco S.A.; Int'l, pg. 24
ADECCO AUSTRALIA PTY LTD.—See Adecco S.A.; Int'l, pg. 24
ADECCO CR SPOL S.R.O.—See Adecco S.A.; Int'l, pg. 24
ADECCO DO BRASIL LTDA.—See Adecco S.A.; Int'l, pg. 24
ADECCO EMPLOYMENT SERVICES—See Adecco S.A.; Int'l, pg. 24
ADECCO ETT, SA—See Adecco S.A.; Int'l, pg. 24
ADECCO GMBH—See Adecco S.A.; Int'l, pg. 24
ADECCO INDUSTRY—See Adecco S.A.; Int'l, pg. 24
ADECCO JAPAN LTD.—See Adecco S.A.; Int'l, pg. 24
ADECCO LUXEMBOURG SA—See Adecco S.A.; Int'l, pg. 24
ADECCO MAGYARORSZAGI SZEMELYZETI KOZVETITO KFT—See Adecco S.A.; Int'l, pg. 24
ADECCO NEW ZEALAND—See Adecco S.A.; Int'l, pg. 24
ADECCO NORGE AS—See Adecco S.A.; Int'l, pg. 24
ADECCO PERSONALDIENSTLEIST UNGEN GMBH—See Adecco S.A.; Int'l, pg. 24
ADECCO PERSONNEL LTD.—See Adecco S.A.; Int'l, pg. 24
ADECCO PERSONNEL SERVICES PTE. LTD.—See Adecco S.A.; Int'l, pg. 24
ADECCO PERSONNELSDIENSTEN B.V.—See Adecco S.A.; Int'l, pg. 24
ADECCO POLAND SP. Z.O.O.—See Adecco S.A.; Int'l, pg. 24
ADECCO RECURSOS HUMANOS—See Adecco S.A.; Int'l, pg. 24
ADECCO RESOURCES HUMAINES SA—See Adecco S.A.; Int'l, pg. 24
ADECCO S.A.; Int'l, pg. 23
ADECCO UK PLC—See Adecco S.A.; Int'l, pg. 24
ADEL MEDICAL LIMITED—See Stryker Corporation; U.S. Public, pg. 1526
ADELAIDE BREWERY—See Foster's Brewing Group Limited; Int'l, pg. 501
ADELANTOS DE TECNOLOGIA S.A. DE C.V.—See SCI Systems, Inc.; U.S. Public, pg. 1417
ADELPHIA LAMP & SHADE INC.; U.S. Private, pg. 17
ADEMCO AUSTRALIA PTY. LTD.—See Pittway Corporation; U.S. Public, pg. 1307
ADEMCO DE JUAREZ—See Pittway Corporation; U.S. Public, pg. 1307
ADEMCO HONG KONG LTD.—See Pittway Corporation; U.S. Public, pg. 1307
ADEMCO-ITALIA S.P.A.—See Pittway Corporation; U.S. Public, pg. 1307
ADEMCO LTD.—See Hunt Corporation; U.S. Public, pg. 849
ADEMCO MICROTECH LIMITED—See Pittway Corporation; U.S. Public, pg. 1307
ADEMCO MICROTECH SECURITY LTD.—See Pittway Corporation; U.S. Public, pg. 1307
ADEMCO SECURITY GROUP—See Pittway Corporation; U.S. Public, pg. 1306
ADEMCO SENSOR COMPANY—See Pittway Corporation; U.S. Public, pg. 1306
ADEMCO-SONTRIX (AUSTRALIA) PTY. LTD.—See Pittway Corporation; U.S. Public, pg. 1307
ADEMCO-SONTRIX ESPANA, S.A.—See Pittway Corporation; U.S. Public, pg. 1307
ADEMCO-SONTRIX (FAR EAST)—See Pittway Corporation; U.S. Public, pg. 1307
ADENAX SPA—See Scapa Group Plc; Int'l, pg. 1202
ADEPT TECHNOLOGY, INC.; U.S. Public, pg. 19
ADERANS CO., LTD.; Int'l, pg. 24
ADESA INC.—See Minnesota Power; U.S. Public, pg. 1116
ADESA PITTSBURGH AUTO AUCTION—See Minnesota Power; U.S. Public, pg. 1116
ADFLEX SOLUTIONS, INC.; U.S. Public, pg. 20
ADHESIVE AND DISPLAY PRODUCTS LIMITED—See N.V. Koninklijke KNP BT; Int'l, pg. 757
ADHESIVE FILMS—See Bairnco Corporation; U.S. Public, pg. 165
ADHESIVE RESEARCH, INC.—See Topflight Corp.; U.S. Private, pg. 1091
ADHESIVE SOLUTIONS LIMITED—See Burmah Castrol plc; Int'l, pg. 234
ADHESIVES (FAR EAST) PTE. LTD.—See BTR plc; Int'l, pg. 129
ADHESIVES (MALAYSIA) SDN. BHD.—See BTR plc; Int'l, pg. 129
ADHESIVES (THAILAND) LTD.—See BTR plc; Int'l, pg. 129
ADHESIVOS SWIFT DE MEXICO S.A. DE C.V.—See Dainippon Ink & Chemicals, Inc.; Int'l, pg. 370
ADI PUERTO RICO—See Pittway Corporation; U.S. Public, pg. 1307
ADIDAS AG; Int'l, pg. 24
ADIDAS AUSTRIA AG—See Adidas AG; Int'l, pg. 24
ADIDAS BUDAPEST KFT.—See Adidas AG; Int'l, pg. 24
ADIDAS (CANADA) LTD.—See Adidas AG; Int'l, pg. 24
ADIDAS CENTRAL DISTRIBUTION—See Adidas AG; Int'l, pg. 24
ADIDAS CSFR SPOL.S.KO.—See Adidas AG; Int'l, pg. 24
ADIDAS DE MEXICO S.A. DE C.V.—See Adidas AG; Int'l, pg. 24
ADIDAS DO BRASIL LTDA.—See Adidas AG; Int'l, pg. 24
ADIDAS ESPANA, S.A.—See Adidas AG; Int'l, pg. 25
ADIDAS-HANDELS AG—See Adidas AG; Int'l, pg. 25
ADIDAS HONG KONG LTD.—See Adidas AG; Int'l, pg. 25
ADIDAS INTERNATIONAL—See Adidas AG; Int'l, pg. 24
ADIDAS (IRELAND) LTD.—See Adidas AG; Int'l, pg. 25
ADIDAS POLEN SP. Z.O.O.—See Adidas AG; Int'l, pg. 25
ADIDAS RUSSIA—See Adidas AG; Int'l, pg. 25
ADIDAS SARRAGAN FRANCE S.A.R.L.—See Adidas AG; Int'l, pg. 25
ADIDAS SARRAGAN NORGE A/S—See Adidas AG; Int'l, pg. 25
ADIDAS-SARRAGAN SVENSKA AB—See Adidas AG; Int'l, pg. 25
ADIDAS SARRAGEN SPORTS E.U.R.L.—See Adidas AG; Int'l, pg. 25
ADIDAS SOUTH AFRICA LTD.—See Adidas AG; Int'l, pg. 25
ADIDAS SPORT GMBH—See Adidas AG; Int'l, pg. 25
ADIDAS SPORTSCHUHFABRIKEN GMBH—See Adidas AG; Int'l, pg. 25
ADIDAS (UK) LTD.—See Adidas AG; Int'l, pg. 25
ADIENCE INC.—See The Alpine Group, Inc.; U.S. Public, pg. 58
ADIG SERVICEGESELLSCHAFT S.A.—See Commerzbank AG; Int'l, pg. 312
ADIRONDACK BEVERAGES—See Polar Beverages; U.S. Private, pg. 873
ADLER BOSCHETTO PEEBLES & PARTNERS, INC.; U.S. Private, pg. 17
ADLER INDUSTRIENAHMASCHINEN VERKAUF GMBH—See FAG Group; Int'l, pg. 468
ADLER MODEMARKTE GMBH—See Metro AG; Int'l, pg. 863
ADLER SHOE SHOPS—See Weyco Group, Inc.; U.S. Public, pg. 1764
ADMAR, INC.—See The Principal Financial Group; U.S. Private, pg. 885
ADMEDIA BV—See VNU Verenigde Nederlandse Uitgeversbedrijven B.V.; Int'l, pg. 1445
ADMINISTRACION Y MANDATOS LA TRANSADINA—See Corporacion MAPFRE, Compania Internacional de Reaseguros, S.A.; Int'l, pg. 333
ADMINISTRADORA DE FONDOS DE PENSIONES QUALITAS S.A.—See Skandia Insurance Company Limited; Int'l, pg. 1258
ADMINISTRADORA PLUMROSE C.A.—See The East Asiatic Company Ltd. A/S; Int'l, pg. 431
ADMINISTRADORA SOAL S.A. DE C.V.—See Leggett & Platt, Incorporated; U.S. Public, pg. 987
ADMINISTRATION CENTER—See Pacific Capital Bancorp; U.S. Public, pg. 1248
ADMINISTRATION D'AFFICHAGE ET DE PUBLICITE—See Lagardere Groupe; Int'l, pg. 791
ADMINISTRATIVE SERVICES, INC.—See National Life Insurance Company; U.S. Private, pg. 785
ADMIRAL/CDT—See Cable Design Technologies Corporation; U.S. Public, pg. 287
ADMIRAL DISTRIBUTION INC.—See G.T.C. Transcontinental Group Ltd.; Int'l, pg. 539
ADMIRAL EQUIPMENT CO.—See The Dow Chemical Company; U.S. Public, pg. 522
ADMIRAL HEINTZ, INC.—See Myers Industries, Inc.; U.S. Public, pg. 1143
ADMIRAL HEINTZ, INC.—See The Standard Products Company; U.S. Public, pg. 1504
ADMIRAL INSURANCE COMPANY—See W.R. Berkley Corporation; U.S. Public, pg. 216
ADMIRAL MAINTENANCE SERVICE L.P.; U.S. Private, pg. 17
ADMIRAL PACKAGING, INC.—See Union Industries, Inc.; U.S. Private, pg. 1119
ADMIRAL REMCO, INC.—See The Standard Products Company; U.S. Public, pg. 1505
ADMIRATION HOSIERY MILLS, INC.—See Highland Mills Inc.; U.S. Private, pg. 528
ADMON ADVERTISING—See BDDP Group; Int'l, pg. 117
ADMORE INC.—See Ennis Business Forms, Inc.; U.S. Public, pg. 583

Company Index

ADOBE SYSTEMS CO. LIMITED—See Adobe Systems Incorporated; U.S. Public, pg. 20
ADOBE SYSTEMS FRANCE—See Adobe Systems Incorporated; U.S. Public, pg. 20
ADOBE SYSTEMS GMBH—See Adobe Systems Incorporated; U.S. Public, pg. 20
ADOBE SYSTEMS INCORPORATED; U.S. Public, pg. 20
ADOBE SYSTEMS JAPAN—See Adobe Systems Incorporated; U.S. Public, pg. 20
ADOBE SYSTEMS LIMITED—See Adobe Systems Incorporated; U.S. Public, pg. 20
ADOBE SYSTEMS NORDIC PB—See Adobe Systems Incorporated; U.S. Public, pg. 20
ADOBE SYSTEMS UK LIMITED—See Adobe Systems Incorporated; U.S. Public, pg. 20
ADOLFSON & PETERSON, INC., U.S. Private, pg. 17
ADOLPH'S LTD.—See Unilever Plc; Int'l, pg. 1435
ADOLPHUS HOTEL—See Noble House Hotels and Resorts; U.S. Private, pg. 800
ADOLPHUS S.A.—See GESTRA GmbH; Int'l, pg. 549
ADPLUS—See The Lowe Group; U.S. Private, pg. 678
ADRA SYSTEMS, INC.; U.S. Private, pg. 18
ADRAY APPLIANCE & PHOTO CENTER, INC.; U.S. Private, pg. 18
ADREMA LEASING CORPORATION—See Pitney Bowes Inc.; U.S. Public, pg. 1304
ADRIA BANK AG—See Creditanstalt-Bankverein; Int'l, pg. 347
ADRIA PLC—See Charnos plc; Int'l, pg. 280
ADRIA PRODUCTOS ALIMENTICOS LTDA—See Borden, Inc.; U.S. Private, pg. 158
ADRIA-WIEN PIPELINE—See Royal Dutch/Shell Group of Companies; Int'l, pg. 1138
ADRIAFRUIT ITALIA S.R.L.—See Coeclerici Group; Int'l, pg. 303
ADRIAFRUIT PRODUTOS ALIMENTARES FLORESTAIS E DERIVADOS LDA—See Coeclerici Group; Int'l, pg. 304
ADRIAPLAST S.P.A.—See Solvay S.A.; Int'l, pg. 1278
ADRIATIC INSURANCE COMPANY OF CANADA—See Allianz Aktiengesellschaft; Int'l, pg. 61
ADRIATIC LIFE LTD.—See Allianz Aktiengesellschaft; Int'l, pg. 61
ADRIATICA DE SEGUROS C.A.—See Allianz Aktiengesellschaft; Int'l, pg. 61
ADRIATICA GESTIONI—See Allianz Aktiengesellschaft; Int'l, pg. 61
ADRIATICA-SOCIEDAD ANONIMA DE SEGUROS Y REASEGUROS—See Allianz Aktiengesellschaft; Int'l, pg. 61
ADRIAVITA S.P.A.—See Assicurazioni Generali S.p.A.; Int'l, pg. 89
ADRONIT GMBH & CO.—See Plettac AG; Int'l, pg. 1061
ADTEC AB—See Celsius AB; Int'l, pg. 276
ADTEC DETENTION SYSTEMS; U.S. Private, pg. 18
ADTEC (UK) LTD—See Celsius AB; Int'l, pg. 278
ADTECH INC.—See Bowthorpe plc; Int'l, pg. 208
ADTECHS CORPORATION—See JGC Corporation; Int'l, pg. 697
ADTRAN, INC.; U.S. Public, pg. 20
ADTRANS PITTSBURGH—See Daimler-Benz Aktiengesellschaft; Int'l, pg. 369
ADULTCARE, INC.—See Fortis; Int'l, pg. 499
ADVANCE AUTOMOTIVE INDUSTRIES, INC.—See Champion Parts, Inc.; U.S. Public, pg. 335
ADVANCE BUSINESS GRAPHICS; U.S. Private, pg. 18
ADVANCE CIRCUITS, INC.—See Johnson Matthey Public Limited Company; Int'l, pg. 713
ADVANCE ENGINEERING—See IAC Industries; U.S. Private, pg. 553
ADVANCE MACHINE COMPANY—See Nilfisk A/S; Int'l, pg. 932
ADVANCE MECHANICAL SYSTEMS, INC.; U.S. Private, pg. 18
ADVANCE PACKAGING CORPORATION; U.S. Private, pg. 18
ADVANCE PACKAGING CORPORATION-JACKSON FACILITY—See Advance Packaging Corporation; U.S. Private, pg. 18
ADVANCE PUBLICATIONS INC.; U.S. Private, pg. 18
ADVANCE ROSS CORPORATION—See Cendant Corporation; U.S. Public, pg. 320
ADVANCE ROSS ELECTRONICS CORP.—See Cendant Corporation; U.S. Public, pg. 320
ADVANCE ROSS STEEL CO.—See Cendant Corporation; U.S. Public, pg. 320
ADVANCE SECURITY—See U.S. Security Associates, Inc.; U.S. Private, pg. 1126
ADVANCE SEED COMPANY—See Groupe Limagrain; Int'l, pg. 566
ADVANCE STEEL CO.; U.S. Private, pg. 21
ADVANCE THERMAL CORP.—See Transco Inc.; U.S. Private, pg. 1096
ADVANCE TRANSFORMER CO.—See Philips Electronics N.V.; Int'l, pg. 1054
ADVANCED ACCESSORIES SYSTEMS, LLC.; U.S. Private, pg. 21
ADVANCED ANIMATIONS, INC.—See VSI Holdings, Inc.; U.S. Public, pg. 1703
ADVANCED AUTOMATION ASSOCIATES, INC.—See Saztec International, Inc.; U.S. Public, pg. 1435
ADVANCED CARE PRODUCTS—See Johnson & Johnson; U.S. Public, pg. 928
ADVANCED CIRCUIT DESIGN DIV.—See Litton Industries, Inc.; U.S. Public, pg. 1003
ADVANCED CIRCUIT TECHNOLOGY; U.S. Private, pg. 21
ADVANCED CIRCUIT TESTING (ACT) GMBH—See Advantest Corporation; Int'l, pg. 25
ADVANCED COIL INDUSTRIES—See American Eco Corporation; U.S. Public, pg. 74
ADVANCED COMPOUNDING—See Amspec Chemical Corporation; U.S. Private, pg. 68
ADVANCED COMPUTER COMMUNICATIONS (ACC)—See Newbridge Networks Corporation; Int'l, pg. 924
ADVANCED CONTROLS, INC.; U.S. Private, pg. 21

ADVANCED CONVERSION PRODUCTS—See Transistor Devices, Inc.; U.S. Private, pg. 1097
ADVANCED DESIGN ELECTRONICS LIMITED—See Chloride Group PLC; Int'l, pg. 287
ADVANCED DETECTION SYSTEMS—See Venturedyne, Ltd.; U.S. Private, pg. 1136
ADVANCED DIGITAL SYSTEMS INC.—See The Titan Corporation; U.S. Public, pg. 1618
ADVANCED DISTRIBUTION SYSTEM, INC.—See Intrenet, Inc.; U.S. Public, pg. 911
ADVANCED ELECTRONIC SYSTEMS—See Litton Industries, Inc.; U.S. Public, pg. 1002
ADVANCED ENERGY INDUSTRY; U.S. Public, pg. 20
ADVANCED ENERGY TECHNOLOGIES—See UniSource Energy Corporation; U.S. Public, pg. 1670
ADVANCED FILTRATION SYSTEMS, INC.—See Caterpillar Inc.; U.S. Public, pg. 316
ADVANCED FILTRATION SYSTEMS, INC.—See Donaldson Company, Inc.; U.S. Public, pg. 517
ADVANCED FORMING TECHNOLOGY, INC.—See Precision Castparts Corp.; U.S. Public, pg. 1320
ADVANCED GENERAL PRINTING INKS LTD.—See Dainippon Ink & Chemicals, Inc.; Int'l, pg. 370
ADVANCED INFORMATION TECHNOLOGY CENTER—See Toshiba Corporation; Int'l, pg. 1405
ADVANCED INPUT DEVICES, INC.; U.S. Private, pg. 21
ADVANCED INSTRUMENTS, INC.; U.S. Private, pg. 22
ADVANCED LIGHTING TECHNOLOGIES, INC.; U.S. Public, pg. 20
ADVANCED LOGIC RESEARCH (DEUTSCHLAND) GMBH—See Gateway 2000; Int'l, pg. 704
ADVANCED LOGIC RESEARCH, INC.—See Gateway 2000; U.S. Public, pg. 703
ADVANCED LOGIC RESEARCH, INC. (U.K.) LIMITED—See Gateway 2000; U.S. Public, pg. 704
ADVANCED MACHINE VISION CORP.; U.S. Public, pg. 20
ADVANCED MAGNETICS, INC.; U.S. Public, pg. 20
ADVANCED MANUFACTURING & DEVELOPMENT; U.S. Private, pg. 22
ADVANCED MARINE ENTERPRISES, INC.—See Nichols Research Corporation; U.S. Public, pg. 1182
ADVANCED MARKETING CONCEPTS, INC.—See Washington Gas Light Co.; U.S. Public, pg. 1741
ADVANCED MATERIALS AND TECHNOLOGIES N.V.—See UMS Swiss Metalworks Holding Ltd; Int'l, pg. 1427
ADVANCED METAL FORMING CV—See Koninklijke Hoogovens N.V.; Int'l, pg. 753
ADVANCED METALLURGY, INC.—See Technitrol, Inc.; U.S. Public, pg. 1564
ADVANCED MICRO COMPUTERS EXPORT CORPORATION, INC.—See Advanced Micro Devices, Inc.; U.S. Public, pg. 21
ADVANCED MICRO DEVICES AB—See Advanced Micro Devices, Inc.; U.S. Public, pg. 21
ADVANCED MICRO DEVICES EXPORT CORPORATION—See Advanced Micro Devices, Inc.; U.S. Public, pg. 21
ADVANCED MICRO DEVICES GMBH—See Advanced Micro Devices, Inc.; U.S. Public, pg. 21
ADVANCED MICRO DEVICES, INC.; U.S. Public, pg. 21
ADVANCED MICRO DEVICES, KK—See Advanced Micro Devices, Inc.; U.S. Public, pg. 21
ADVANCED MICRO DEVICES OVERSEAS CORPORATION—See Advanced Micro Devices, Inc.; U.S. Public, pg. 21
ADVANCED MICRO DEVICES, S.A.—See Advanced Micro Devices, Inc.; U.S. Public, pg. 21
ADVANCED MICRO DEVICES, SDN BHD—See Advanced Micro Devices, Inc.; U.S. Public, pg. 21
ADVANCED MICRO DEVICES S.P.A.—See Advanced Micro Devices, Inc.; U.S. Public, pg. 21
ADVANCED MICRO DEVICES, (UK), LTD.—See Advanced Micro Devices, Inc.; U.S. Public, pg. 21
ADVANCED MICRO, LTD.—See Advanced Micro Devices, Inc.; U.S. Public, pg. 21
ADVANCED MICROCONTROLLER DIVISION—See Motorola, Inc.; U.S. Public, pg. 1137
ADVANCED MONOBLOC—See CCL Industries, Inc.; Int'l, pg. 238
ADVANCED MONOBLOC CORPORATION—See CCL Industries, Inc.; Int'l, pg. 238
ADVANCED MONOBLOC INC.—See CCL Industries, Inc.; Int'l, pg. 238
ADVANCED POLYMER SYSTEMS; U.S. Public, pg. 22
ADVANCED POLYMERS—See Perstorp AB; Int'l, pg. 1036
ADVANCED POLYMERS CORP.—See Furon Company; U.S. Public, pg. 689
ADVANCED POLYMERS DIVISION - KENT FACILITY—See Furon Company; U.S. Public, pg. 689
ADVANCED PRODUCTS DIVISION—See Methode Electronics Inc.; U.S. Public, pg. 1101
ADVANCED PRODUCTS & SYSTEMS CORP.—See Raytheon Company; U.S. Public, pg. 1365
ADVANCED REMEDIATION INC. (ARM); U.S. Public, pg. 22
ADVANCED RISK MANAGEMENT SERVICES—See Willis Corroon Group PLC; Int'l, pg. 1505
ADVANCED SEMICONDUCTOR MANUFACTURING CORPORATION OF SHANGHAI—See Northern Telecom Limited; Int'l, pg. 970
ADVANCED SEPARATION TECHNOLOGIES INCORPORATED—See Florida Progress Corporation; U.S. Public, pg. 655
ADVANCED SOFTWARE CONCEPTS, INC.—See Platinum Technology; U.S. Public, pg. 1309
ADVANCED STRUCTURES, INC.—See Essef Corporation; U.S. Public, pg. 592
ADVANCED TECHNOLOGY AND DESIGN CENTER—See Northrop Grumman Corporation; U.S. Public, pg. 1198
ADVANCED TECHNOLOGY SERVICES INC.—See Caterpillar Inc.; U.S. Public, pg. 315
ADVANCED TEL, INC.—See Eatelcorp Inc.; U.S. Private, pg. 358
ADVANCED TELEMARKETING CORP.—See ATC Communications Group, Inc.; U.S. Private, pg. 11

ADVANCED TELEVISION TECHNOLOGY CENTER—See Toshiba Corporation; Int'l, pg. 1405
ADVANCO CONSTRUCTORS, INC.—See Zurn Industries, Inc.; U.S. Public, pg. 1795
ADVANSTAR COMMUNICATIONS; U.S. Private, pg. 22
ADVANSWERS MEDIA/PROGRAMMING—See BDDP Group; Int'l, pg. 117
ADVANTA BUSINESS SERVICES—See Advanta Corp.; U.S. Public, pg. 22
ADVANTA CORP.; U.S. Public, pg. 22
ADVANTA INSURANCE COMPANIES—See Advanta Corp.; U.S. Public, pg. 22
ADVANTA MORTGAGE CORP. USA—See Advanta Corp.; U.S. Public, pg. 22
ADVANTA NATIONAL BANK USA—See Advanta Corp.; U.S. Public, pg. 22
ADVANTAGE COMPANIES, INC.; U.S. Private, pg. 22
ADVANTAGE LEARNING SYSTEMS, INC.; U.S. Public, pg. 22
ADVANTAGE LIFE PRODUCTS, INC.; U.S. Public, pg. 22
ADVANTEST AMERICA, INC.—See Advantest Corporation; Int'l, pg. 25
ADVANTEST ASIA PTE. LTD.—See Advantest Corporation; Int'l, pg. 25
ADVANTEST CORPORATION; Int'l, pg. 25
ADVANTEST - ENG(M) SDN. BHD.—See Advantest Corporation; Int'l, pg. 25
ADVANTEST KOREA CO., LTD.—See Advantest Corporation; Int'l, pg. 25
ADVANTEST LABORATORIES—See Advantest Corporation; Int'l, pg. 25
ADVANTEST SHANGHAI LTD.—See Advantest Corporation; Int'l, pg. 25
ADVANTEST (SUZHOU) CO., LTD.—See Advantest Corporation; Int'l, pg. 25
ADVANTICA RESTAURANT GROUP, INC.; U.S. Public, pg. 22
ADVENT INTERNATIONAL; U.S. Private, pg. 22
ADVENT LOUDSPEAKERS—See Recoton Corporation; U.S. Public, pg. 1369
ADVENTURE ISLAND—See Anheuser-Busch Companies, Inc.; U.S. Public, pg. 114
ADVENTURE LANDS OF AMERICA, INC.; U.S. Private, pg. 22
ADVENTURE TOURS USA, INC.; U.S. Private, pg. 22
ADVERTA—See Warwick Baker O'Neill; U.S. Private, pg. 1152
ADVERTISER—See The Gazette Company; U.S. Private, pg. 442
THE ADVERTISER—See Journal Register Company; U.S. Public, pg. 934
THE ADVERTISER CO.—See Gannett Company, Inc.; U.S. Public, pg. 699
ADVERTISING AGE—See Crain Communications, Inc.; U.S. Private, pg. 284
ADVERTISING AGE INTERNATIONAL—See Crain Communications, Inc.; U.S. Private, pg. 285
ADVERTISING CHECKING BUREAU INCORPORATED; U.S. Private, pg. 23
ADVERTISING DISPLAY CO.; U.S. Private, pg. 23
ADVERTISING INVESTMENT SERVICES PTY. LTD.—See Dentsu Inc.; Int'l, pg. 394
ADVERTISING PROMOTIONS—See Scott's Liquid Gold-Inc.; U.S. Public, pg. 1447
THE ADVEST GROUP, INC.; U.S. Public, pg. 23
ADVEST, INC.—See The Advest Group, Inc.; U.S. Public, pg. 23
ADVICO YOUNG & RUBICAM AG—See Young & Rubicam Inc.; U.S. Private, pg. 1198
ADVISERS CAPITAL MANAGEMENT INC.; U.S. Private, pg. 23
ADVISOR'S GROUP—See The Acacia Group - Acacia Life Insurance Co.; U.S. Private, pg. 11
ADVO, INC.; U.S. Public, pg. 23
ADVOCARD RECHTSSCHUTZVERSICHERENG AG—See AMB Aachener und Muenchener Beteiligungs-AG; Int'l, pg. 15
ADVOCATE HEALTH CARE; U.S. Private, pg. 23
ADVOCATE SERVICES, INC.—See TruServ Corporation; U.S. Private, pg. 1108
THE ADVOCATE; U.S. Private, pg. 23
THE ADVOCATE—See The Times Mirror Company; U.S. Public, pg. 1616
ADWEEK—See VNU Verenigde Nederlandse Uitgeversbedrijven B.V.; Int'l, pg. 1446
ADWIN EQUIPMENT CO.—See PECO Energy Company; U.S. Public, pg. 1268
ADWIN REALTY CO.—See PECO Energy Company; U.S. Public, pg. 1268
ADWORK! EURO RSCG PARTNERSHIP—See Havas Advertising; Int'l, pg. 602
ADWORKS, INC.; U.S. Private, pg. 23
AEARO COMPANY; U.S. Private, pg. 23
AEGIS CORPORATE TRAINING, INC.—See Career Blazers Inc.; U.S. Private, pg. 209
THE AEGIS GROUP, INC.—See Automobile Protection Corporation-APCO; U.S. Public, pg. 150
AEGIS, INC.—See Olin Corporation; U.S. Public, pg. 1219
AEGIS SAFETY HOLDINGS, INC.—See Hanover Direct, Inc.; U.S. Public, pg. 782
AB-AEGON ALTALANOS BIZTOSITO RT—See AEGON N.V.; Int'l, pg. 28
AEGON FINANCIAL SERVICES GROUP (UK) LTD.—See AEGON N.V.; Int'l, pg. 28
AEGON INSURANCE COMPANY (UK) LIMITED—See AEGON N.V.; Int'l, pg. 28
AEGON INTERNATIONAL B.V.—See AEGON N.V.; Int'l, pg. 25
AEGON LEBENSVERSICHERUNGS-AG—See AEGON N.V.; Int'l, pg. 28
AEGON LEVENSVERZEKERING NV—See AEGON N.V.; Int'l, pg. 25
AEGON LEVENSVERZEKERING N.V. (LIFE)—See AEGON N.V.; Int'l, pg. 26

AEGON NEDERLAND N.V.—See AEGON N.V.; *Int'l*, pg. 26
AEGON NEVAK HOLDING B.V.—See AEGON N.V.; *Int'l*, pg. 26
AEGON N.V.; *Int'l*, pg. 25
AEGON REINSURANCE COMPANY OF AMERICA—See AEGON N.V.; *Int'l*, pg. 26
AEGON REINSURANCE N.V.—See AEGON N.V.; *Int'l*, pg. 26
AEGON SCHADEVERZEKERING N.V.—See AEGON N.V.; *Int'l*, pg. 26
AEGON U.S. HOLDING CORP.—See AEGON N.V.; *Int'l*, pg. 26
AEGON USA, INC.—See AEGON N.V.; *Int'l*, pg. 26
AEKYUNG & SHELL—See Royal Dutch/Shell Group of Companies; *Int'l*, pg. 1140
AEKYUNG CHEMICAL CO., LTD.—See Dainippon Ink & Chemicals, Inc.; *Int'l*, pg. 371
AELTUS INVESTMENT MANAGEMENT, INC.—See Aetna Inc.; *U.S. Public*, pg. 27
AEMTLERHALLE AG—See Feldschlosschen Hurlimann Holding; *Int'l*, pg. 479
AEON GROUP; *Int'l*, pg. 28
AER LINGUS; *Int'l*, pg. 28
AER LINGUS—See Aer Lingus; *Int'l*, pg. 28
AER RIANTA BEWLEY LIMITED—See Campbells/Bewley Group; *Int'l*, pg. 254
AERACOM TECHNOLOGIES PTE. LTD.—See Ssangyong Business Group; *Int'l*, pg. 1293
AERCO INTERNATIONAL INC.; *U.S. Private*, pg. 23
AERIMPIANTI S.P.A.—See IRI Istituto Ricostruzione Industriale; *Int'l*, pg. 653
AERMACCHI S.P.A.—See IRI Istituto Ricostruzione Industriale; *Int'l*, pg. 653
AERO ASAHI CORPORATION—See The Saison Group; *Int'l*, pg. 1178
AERO-BOUTIQUE DE MEXICO S.A. DE C.V.—See Lagardere Groupe; *Int'l*, pg. 796
AERO CORPORATION—See Whitehall Corporation; *U.S. Public*, pg. 1766
AERO DATA METAL CRAFTERS; *U.S. Private*, pg. 23
AERO ELECTRONICS INCORPORATED—See Memphis Group, Inc.; *U.S. Private*, pg. 731
AERO ENGINE EQUIPMENT GROUP—See BTR plc; *Int'l*, pg. 127
AERO MANUFACTURING, INC.—See Thor Industries, Inc.; *U.S. Public*, pg. 1602
AERO-MOTIVE COMPANY—See Woodhead Industries, Inc.; *U.S. Public*, pg. 1776
AERO MOTIVE (U.K.) LTD.—See Woodhead Industries, Inc.; *U.S. Public*, pg. 1776
AERO OIL CORP.—See Getty Petroleum Marketing Inc.; *U.S. Public*, pg. 741
AERO PERU—See Aero Peru Corporation; *U.S. Private*, pg. 24
AERO PERU CORPORATION; *U.S. Private*, pg. 24
AERO PRODUCTS DIV.—See Litton Industries, Inc.; *U.S. Public*, pg. 1002
AERO SERVICE CORP.—See Litton Industries, Inc.; *U.S. Public*, pg. 1003
AERO SERVICE (GREAT BRITAIN) C/O WESTERN GEOPHYSICAL CO.—See Litton Industries, Inc.; *U.S. Public*, pg. 1004
AERO SYSTEMS AVIATION CORP.; *U.S. Private*, pg. 24
AERO SYSTEMS ENGINEERING INC.—See Celsius AB; *Int'l*, pg. 276
AERO TECH MANUFACTURING INC.—See Toromont Industries Ltd.; *Int'l*, pg. 1400
AERO TECNICA SA—See Hesta Tex AG; *Int'l*, pg. 617
AERO TRASPORTI ITALIANI - A.T.I. S.P.A.—See IRI Istituto Ricostruzione Industriale; *Int'l*, pg. 652
AEROASSURANCES—See Aerospatiale; *Int'l*, pg. 29
AEROBOUTIQUES DE MEXICO—See Lagardere Groupe; *Int'l*, pg. 795
AEROBOUTIQUES FRANCE—See Lagardere Groupe; *Int'l*, pg. 791
AEROCHEM, INC.—See Ducommun Incorporated; *U.S. Public*, pg. 534
AEROCHEM, INC./EL MIRAGE—See Ducommun Incorporated; *U.S. Public*, pg. 534
AEROCLO METAL PRODUCTS—See Precision Valve Corporation; *U.S. Private*, pg. 880
AEROFIN CORP.—See Ampco-Pittsburgh Corporation; *U.S. Public*, pg. 103
AEROFLEX INCORPORATED; *U.S. Public*, pg. 23
AEROFLEX INTERNATIONAL, INC.—See Aeroflex Incorporated; *U.S. Public*, pg. 24
AEROFLEX LABORATORIES INC.—See Aeroflex Incorporated; *U.S. Public*, pg. 24
AEROFLEX LINTER CORP.—See Aeroflex Incorporated; *U.S. Public*, pg. 24
AEROFLEX SYSTEMS CORP.—See Aeroflex Incorporated; *U.S. Public*, pg. 24
AEROGLIDE AMERICAS INTERNATIONAL, INC.—See Aeroglide Corporation; *U.S. Private*, pg. 24
AEROGLIDE CORPORATION; *U.S. Private*, pg. 24
AEROJET—See GenCorp Inc.; *U.S. Public*, pg. 706
AEROJET AZUSA OPERATIONS—See GenCorp Inc.; *U.S. Public*, pg. 706
AEROLINEAS ARGENTINAS—See Grupo Iberia; *Int'l*, pg. 575
AEROLITORAL—See Corporacion Internacional de Aviacion (CINTRA); *Int'l*, pg. 332
AEROLYTE SYSTEMS; *U.S. Private*, pg. 24
AEROMET CORPORATION—See MTS Systems Corporation; *U.S. Public*, pg. 1029
AEROMETRICS, INC.—See TSI Incorporated; *U.S. Public*, pg. 1559
AEROMEXICO—See Corporacion Internacional de Aviacion (CINTRA); *Int'l*, pg. 332
AEROMEXPRESS S.A. DE C.V.—See Corporacion Internacional de Aviacion (CINTRA); *Int'l*, pg. 332
AEROMOTIVE SERVICES CO.—See ASC Incorporated; *U.S. Private*, pg. 8
AEROMOTOR PUMP, INC.—See GSW Inc.; *Int'l*, pg. 538

AERONAUTICAL RADIO, INC.—See Arinc Inc. (Consolidated); *U.S. Public*, pg. 81
AERONCA, INC.—See Magellan Aerospace Corporation; *Int'l*, pg. 829
AERONET EUROPE—See Telxon Corporation; *U.S. Public*, pg. 1573
AEROPLEX OF CENTRAL EUROPE LTD.—See Malev Hungarian Airlines, Plc.; *Int'l*, pg. 834
AEROPORTI DI-ROMA-SOCIETA PER LA GESTIONE DEL AEROPORTUALE DELLA CAPITALE—See IRI Istituto Ricostruzione Industriale; *Int'l*, pg. 652
AEROPOSTALE/CHARTER CLUB—See Federated Department Stores, Inc.; *U.S. Public*, pg. 618
AEROQUIP CORPORATION—See Aeroquip-Vickers, Inc.; *U.S. Public*, pg. 24
AEROQUIP DIVISION, VICKERS SYSTEMS PTY. LTD.—See Aeroquip-Vickers, Inc.; *U.S. Public*, pg. 25
AEROQUIP IBERICA S.A. (AUTOMOTIVE GROUP)—See Aeroquip-Vickers, Inc.; *U.S. Public*, pg. 25
AEROQUIP INOAC COMPANY—See Aeroquip-Vickers, Inc.; *U.S. Public*, pg. 24
AEROQUIP MEXICANA S.A. DE C.V.—See Aeroquip-Vickers, Inc.; *U.S. Public*, pg. 25
AEROQUIP SINGAPORE PRIVATE LIMITED—See Aeroquip-Vickers, Inc.; *U.S. Public*, pg. 25
AEROQUIP STERLING GMBH—See Aeroquip-Vickers, Inc.; *U.S. Public*, pg. 25
AEROQUIP-VICKERS, INC.; *U.S. Public*, pg. 24
AEROS INSTRUMENTS, INC.—See Squire-Cogswell Company; *U.S. Private*, pg. 1028
AEROSERVICES J.T. INC.—See Hudson General Corporation; *U.S. Public*, pg. 845
AEROSONIC CORPORATION; *U.S. Public*, pg. 25
AEROSPACE AVIONICS, INC.—See BTR plc; *Int'l*, pg. 126
AEROSPACE BEARING SUPPORT, INC.—See Banner Aerospace, Inc.; *U.S. Public*, pg. 187
AEROSPACE CORPORATION; *U.S. Private*, pg. 24
AEROSPACE OPERATIONS ASIA PACIFIC—See TI Group plc; *Int'l*, pg. 1337
AEROSPACE PRODUCTS, INC.—See AMETEK, Inc.; *U.S. Public*, pg. 100
AEROSPACE SYSTEMS & EQUIPMENT—See Moog Incorporated; *U.S. Public*, pg. 1127
AEROSPACE TECHNOLOGY—See DynCorp; *U.S. Private*, pg. 351
AEROSPATIALE; *Int'l*, pg. 28
AEROSPATIALE INC.—See Aerospatiale; *Int'l*, pg. 29
AEROSTAR INTERNATIONAL—See Raven Industries, Inc.; *U.S. Public*, pg. 1361
AEROTEST OPERATIONS, INC.—See OEA, Inc.; *U.S. Public*, pg. 1207
AEROTHRUST CORP.—See Celsius AB; *Int'l*, pg. 276
AEROVIRONMENT, INC.; *U.S. Private*, pg. 25
AEROVOX INC.; *U.S. Public*, pg. 25
AERY EXPRESS AIRCRAFT LIMITED—See Royal Nedlloyd Group N.V.; *Int'l*, pg. 1144
AES AURORA—See AES Corporation; *U.S. Public*, pg. 5
AES SILK ROAD—See AES Corporation; *U.S. Public*, pg. 5
AESCULAP AKTIENGESELLSCHAFT; *Int'l*, pg. 29
AESCULAP, INC.—See Aesculap Aktiengesellschaft; *Int'l*, pg. 29
AESOP CO., LTD.—See Hallmark Cards, Inc.; *U.S. Private*, pg. 496
AETHYLEN ROHRLEITUNGS GESELLSCHAFT MBH & CO. KG—See DSM N.V.; *Int'l*, pg. 356
AETNA BEARING COMPANY; *U.S. Private*, pg. 25
AETNA CANADA HOLDINGS LTD.—See Aetna Inc.; *U.S. Public*, pg. 27
AETNA CAPITAL MANAGEMENT INVESTMENT LIMITED—See Aetna Inc.; *U.S. Public*, pg. 27
AETNA FINANCIAL SERVICES INC.—See Aetna Inc.; *U.S. Public*, pg. 26
AETNA HANDBAGS—See Jaclyn, Inc.; *U.S. Public*, pg. 920
AETNA HEALTH (NEW ZEALAND) LIMITED—See Aetna Inc.; *U.S. Public*, pg. 27
AETNA INC.; *U.S. Public*, pg. 26
AETNA INDUSTRIES, INC.; *U.S. Private*, pg. 25
AETNA INTERNATIONAL (AUSTRALIA) PTY. LTD.—See Aetna Inc.; *U.S. Public*, pg. 27
AETNA INTERNATIONAL CHILE S.A.—See Aetna Inc.; *U.S. Public*, pg. 27
AETNA INTERNATIONAL, INC.—See Aetna Inc.; *U.S. Public*, pg. 26
AETNA INVESTMENT MANAGEMENT (JAPAN), K.K.—See Aetna Inc.; *U.S. Public*, pg. 27
AETNA INVESTMENT MANAGEMENT LIMITED—See Aetna Inc.; *U.S. Public*, pg. 27
AETNA LIFE INSURANCE AND ANNUITY CO.—See Aetna Inc.; *U.S. Public*, pg. 26
AETNA LIFE INSURANCE COMPANY—See Aetna Inc.; *U.S. Public*, pg. 26
AETNA LIFE INSURANCE COMPANY OF AMERICA—See Aetna Inc.; *U.S. Public*, pg. 26
AETNA LIFE INSURANCE CO. OF AMERICA (ALICA)—See Aetna Inc.; *U.S. Public*, pg. 27
AETNA LIFE INSURANCE COMPANY OF ILLINOIS—See Aetna Inc.; *U.S. Public*, pg. 26
AETNA PLYWOOD, INC.; *U.S. Private*, pg. 25
AETNA REALTY INVESTORS, INC.—See Aetna Inc.; *U.S. Public*, pg. 26
AETNA UNIVERSAL INSURANCE SDN. BHD.—See Aetna Inc.; *U.S. Public*, pg. 27
AETRIUM-FSA—See Aetrium Inc.; *U.S. Public*, pg. 27
AETRIUM INC.; *U.S. Public*, pg. 27
AFCO METALS, INC.—See Inland Steel Industries, Inc.; *U.S. Public*, pg. 879
AFERFRANS S.A.—See LVMH Moet Hennessy Louis Vuitton; *Int'l*, pg. 782
AFFHOLDER, INC.—See Insituform Technologies, Inc.; *U.S. Public*, pg. 881
AFFICHAGE CENTRE VILLE (A.C.V.)—See Lagardere Groupe; *Int'l*, pg. 795
AFFILIATED BANKS BUILDING CO.—See Banc One Corporation; *U.S. Public*, pg. 173

AFFILIATED BANKS SERVICE CO.—See Banc One Corporation; *U.S. Public*, pg. 173
AFFILIATED BUILDING SERVICES, INC.—See Compagnie Generale Des Eaux; *Int'l*, pg. 322
AFFILIATED CARRIERS, INC.—See Affiliated Foods Cooperative; *U.S. Private*, pg. 25
AFFILIATED COMPUTER SERVICES, INC.; *U.S. Public*, pg. 27
AFFILIATED FINANCE INC.—See Affiliated Foods, Inc.; *U.S. Private*, pg. 25
AFFILIATED FIRST COLORADO LEASE COMPANY—See Banc One Corporation; *U.S. Public*, pg. 173
AFFILIATED FM INSURANCE CO.—See Allendale Mutual Insurance Co.; *U.S. Private*, pg. 37
AFFILIATED FOODS COOPERATIVE; *U.S. Private*, pg. 25
AFFILIATED FOODS, INC.; *U.S. Private*, pg. 25
AFFILIATED FOODS SOUTHWEST; *U.S. Private*, pg. 26
AFFILIATED FUND, INC.—See Lord Abbett & Co.; *U.S. Private*, pg. 675
AFFILIATED FUNDING—See Affiliated Foods, Inc.; *U.S. Private*, pg. 25
AFFILIATED INDEPENDENT DEVELOPMENT—See Affiliated Foods Cooperative; *U.S. Private*, pg. 25
AFFILIATED INSURANCE SERVICES, INC.—See Affiliated Foods Cooperative; *U.S. Private*, pg. 25
AFFILIATED LABORATORIES—See SmithKline Beecham plc; *Int'l*, pg. 1264
AFFILIATED METALS COMPANY—See Metals USA, Inc.; *U.S. Public*, pg. 1100
AFFILIATED PUBLICATIONS, INC.—See The New York Times Company; *U.S. Public*, pg. 1174
AFFILIATED PUBLISHERS, INC.; *U.S. Private*, pg. 26
THE AFFILIATES—See Robert Half International Inc.; *U.S. Public*, pg. 775
AFFIMET—See Pechiney S.A.; *Int'l*, pg. 1028
AFFIVAL INC.—See Viag AG; *Int'l*, pg. 1465
AFFIVAL SA—See Viag AG; *Int'l*, pg. 1466
THE AFFORDABLE MEDICAL NETWORKS—See First Health Group Corp.; *U.S. Public*, pg. 635
AFLAC INCORPORATED; *U.S. Public*, pg. 28
AFORA LTD.—See ABB Asea Brown Boveri (Holding) Ltd.; *Int'l*, pg. 5
AFRAM CARRIERS, INC.—See Kirby Corporation; *U.S. Public*, pg. 962
AFRICAINE DE RAFFINAGE—See Royal Dutch/Shell Group of Companies; *Int'l*, pg. 1136
AFRICAN AMINES (PTY) LTD.—See Sasol Limited; *Int'l*, pg. 1196
AFRICAN LIFE ASSURANCE COMPANY LIMITED—See Anglo American Corporation of South Africa Limited; *Int'l*, pg. 77
AFRICAN OXYGEN LTD.—See The BOC Group plc; *Int'l*, pg. 121
AFRIQUE ASSISTANCE—See Corporacion MAPFRE, Compania Internacional de Reaseguros, S.A.; *Int'l*, pg. 334
AFRISPORTS SA—See Adidas AG; *Int'l*, pg. 25
AFTER DARK VIDEO, INC.—See Playboy Enterprises, Inc.; *U.S. Public*, pg. 1310
AFTERMARKET PRODUCTION DIV.—See Dana Corporation; *U.S. Public*, pg. 479
AFTONBLADET AB; *Int'l*, pg. 29
AG PROCESSING INC., A COOPERATIVE; *U.S. Private*, pg. 26
AGAMERICA, FCB—See Federal Farm Credit Banks Funding Corporation; *U.S. Private*, pg. 398
AGANOR S.A.—See AGA AB; *Int'l*, pg. 13
AGBABIAN ASSOCIATES, INC.—See OYO Corporation; *Int'l*, pg. 1019
AGCAST—See Data Broadcasting Corporation; *U.S. Public*, pg. 484
AGCO ARGENTINA S.A.; *Int'l*, pg. 30
AGCO CORPORATION; *U.S. Public*, pg. 28
AGCO INC.; *U.S. Private*, pg. 26
AGEMA DIRECT SALES AB—See Spectra-Physics AB; *Int'l*, pg. 1289
AGEMA INFRARED SYSTEMS AB—See Spectra-Physics AB; *Int'l*, pg. 1289
AGEMA INFRARED SYSTEMS GMBH—See Spectra-Physics AB; *Int'l*, pg. 1289
AGEMA INFRARED SYSTEMS, INC.—See Spectra-Physics AB; *Int'l*, pg. 1289
AGEMA INFRARED SYSTEMS LTD.—See Spectra-Physics AB; *Int'l*, pg. 1289
AGEMA INFRARED SYSTEMS S.A.R.L.—See Spectra-Physics AB; *Int'l*, pg. 1289
AGEMA INFRARED SYSTEMS SRL—See Spectra-Physics AB; *Int'l*, pg. 1289
AGENCE BELGE BULOW BENNET & CIE—See Norske Skogindustrier A.S; *Int'l*, pg. 966
AGENCE ET MESSAGERIES DE LA PRESSE—See Lagardere Groupe; *Int'l*, pg. 795
AGENCE MARITIME ET CONTENEURS—See Internatio-Muller N.V.; *Int'l*, pg. 682
AGENCES MARITIME ASSOCIES—See Internatio-Muller N.V.; *Int'l*, pg. 682
AGENCIA EFE, S.A.—See Telefonica de Espana, S.A.; *Int'l*, pg. 1372
AGENCIAS BANCARIAS COPACHILE LTDA—See Compagnie Financiere de Paribas; *Int'l*, pg. 319
AGENCY AND REP SERVICES DIV.—See Jefferson-Pilot Corporation; *U.S. Public*, pg. 925
AGENCY AT MALMO—See Pechiney S.A.; *Int'l*, pg. 1030
AGENCY AUTO SALES, INC.—See National Auto Credit Inc.; *U.S. Public*, pg. 1153
AGENCY CHRYSLER-PLYMOUTH, INC.—See National Auto Credit Inc.; *U.S. Public*, pg. 1153
AGENCY.COM—See Omnicom Group Inc.; *U.S. Public*, pg. 1223
AGENCY FORD, INC.—See National Auto Credit Inc.; *U.S. Public*, pg. 1153
AGENCY MEDIA SERVICES, INC.—See Norfolk Southern Corporation; *U.S. Public*, pg. 1190

Company Index

AGENCY SPECIALTY INC.—See The Seibels Bruce Group, Inc.; *U.S. Public*, pg. 1454
AGENZIA CARBONI S.R.L.—See Veba AG; *Int'l*, pg. 1461
AGENZIA LOMBARDA DISTRIBUZIONE GIORNALI E RIVISTE S.R.L.—See Arnoldo Mondadori Editore S.p.A.; *Int'l*, pg. 888
AGEO SEIMITSU MFG. CO., LTD.—See Citizen Watch Company, Ltd.; *Int'l*, pg. 293
AGERIS INTERNATIONAL, S.A.—See Comdisco, Inc.; *U.S. Public*, pg. 408
AGFA AG—See Bayer AG; *Int'l*, pg. 172
AGFA COPAL INC.—See Bayer AG; *Int'l*, pg. 173
AGFA EPS DIVISION—See Bayer AG; *Int'l*, pg. 172
AGFA-GEVAERT AB—See Bayer AG; *Int'l*, pg. 174
AGFA-GEVAERT ARGENTINA S.A.—See Bayer AG; *Int'l*, pg. 174
AGFA-GEVAERT B.V.—See Bayer AG; *Int'l*, pg. 174
AGFA-GEVAERT JAPAN, LTD.—See Bayer AG; *Int'l*, pg. 174
AGFA-GEVAERT LIMITED—See Bayer AG; *Int'l*, pg. 174
AGFA-GEVAERT N.V.—See Bayer AG; *Int'l*, pg. 174
AGFA-GEVAERT S.A.—See Bayer AG; *Int'l*, pg. 174
AGFA-GEVAERT S.P.A.—See Bayer AG; *Int'l*, pg. 174
AGGREGATE HAULERS INC.—See Pioneer International Ltd.; *Int'l*, pg. 1058
AGGREGATE SUPPLY CO., LTD.—See The Siam Cement Public Company Limited; *Int'l*, pg. 1237
AGGREGATES (ULSTER) LIMITED—See RMC Group p.l.c.; *Int'l*, pg. 1079
AGIE AG (FUR INDUSTRIELLE ELEKTRONIK)—See Georg Fischer Ltd.; *Int'l*, pg. 488
AGIE CHARMILLES GROUP—See Georg Fischer Ltd.; *Int'l*, pg. 488
AGIE FRANCE SWISS EDM SARL—See Georg Fischer Ltd.; *Int'l*, pg. 488
AGIE GMBH—See Georg Fischer Ltd.; *Int'l*, pg. 488
AGIE ITALIA SPA—See Georg Fischer Ltd.; *Int'l*, pg. 488
AGIE NIPPON LTD.—See Georg Fischer Ltd.; *Int'l*, pg. 488
AGIE SINGAPORE—See Georg Fischer Ltd.; *Int'l*, pg. 488
AGIE UK LTD.—See Georg Fischer Ltd.; *Int'l*, pg. 488
AGIE USA LTD.—See Georg Fischer Ltd.; *Int'l*, pg. 490
AGIE U.S.A. LTD.—See Georg Fischer Ltd.; *Int'l*, pg. 490
AGIE VERKAUF SCHWEIZ AG—See Georg Fischer Ltd.; *Int'l*, pg. 488
AGILE NETWORKS, INC.—See Lucent Technologies Inc.; *U.S. Public*, pg. 1018
AGIS INDUSTRIES LTD.; *Int'l*, pg. 30
AGLUKON SPEZIALDUNGER GMBH—See Schering AG; *Int'l*, pg. 1203
AGMET LTD.—See Electro-Science Laboratories, Inc.; *U.S. Private*, pg. 369
AGNESI SPA—See Danone Group; *Int'l*, pg. 380
AGNEW GROUP—See The Bentley Agnew Group Inc.; *Int'l*, pg. 187
AGORA—See Lafarge S.A.; *Int'l*, pg. 789
AGOURON PHARMACEUTICALS, INC.; *U.S. Public*, pg. 28
AGPRO GRAIN—See Saskatchewan Wheat Pool; *Int'l*, pg. 1195
AGRA CAMBRIAN INC.—See Agra Inc.; *Int'l*, pg. 30
AGRA CI POWER LIMITED—See Agra Inc.; *Int'l*, pg. 30
AGRA CONSTRUCTION (WUHAN CHINA) LIMITED—See Agra Inc.; *Int'l*, pg. 31
AGRA EARTH & ENVIRONMENTAL, INC.—See Agra Inc.; *Int'l*, pg. 31
AGRA EARTH & ENVIRONMENTAL LIMITED—See Agra Inc.; *Int'l*, pg. 30
AGRA FOUNDATIONS INC.—See Agra Inc.; *Int'l*, pg. 31
AGRA FOUNDATIONS LIMITED—See Agra Inc.; *Int'l*, pg. 30
AGRA FOUNDATIONS (PACIFIC) LIMITED—See Agra Inc.; *Int'l*, pg. 30
AGRA INC.; *Int'l*, pg. 30
AGRA INC.—See Agra Inc.; *Int'l*, pg. 30
AGRA LAND SURVEYS LTD.—See Agra Inc.; *Int'l*, pg. 30
AGRA MARINE CONSTRUCTION LIMITED—See Agra Inc.; *Int'l*, pg. 30
AGRA MONENCO—See Agra Inc.; *Int'l*, pg. 30
AGRA MONENCO, INC.—See Agra Inc.; *Int'l*, pg. 31
P.T. AGRA MONENCO—See Agra Inc.; *Int'l*, pg. 31
AGRA MONENCO QUEBEC, INC.—See Agra Inc.; *Int'l*, pg. 30
AGRA S.A.—See Unilever Plc; *Int'l*, pg. 1436
AGRA SHAWMONT LIMITED—See Agra Inc.; *Int'l*, pg. 30
AGRA SPECTROCAN LIMITED—See Agra Inc.; *Int'l*, pg. 30
AGRA VADEKO INC.—See Agra Inc.; *Int'l*, pg. 30
AGRARCHEMIKALIEN MUNCHEN GMBH.—See DSM N.V.; *Int'l*, pg. 356
AGRARISCH DAGBLAD—See Reed Elsevier plc; *Int'l*, pg. 1099
AGRARISCHE UNIE-VULCAAN BV—See DSM N.V.; *Int'l*, pg. 353
AGRATRADE FINANCING, INC.—See Gold Kist, Inc.; *U.S. Private*, pg. 459
AGRETAS AGREGA INSAAT SAN.VE. TIC. A.S.—See Lafarge S.A.; *Int'l*, pg. 791
AGREVO GMBH—See Hoechst Aktiengesellschaft; *Int'l*, pg. 624
AGREVO GMBH—See Schering AG; *Int'l*, pg. 1203
AGREVO USA COMPANY—See Schering AG; *Int'l*, pg. 1203
AGRI-FINANCIAL SERVICES—See Dairylea Cooperative Inc.; *U.S. Private*, pg. 308
AGRI FINANCIAL SERVICES INC.—See American Grain & Related Industries; *U.S. Private*, pg. 55
AGRI-GRAPHICS, INC.—See Altair Corporation; *U.S. Private*, pg. 46
AGRI-MARK, INC.; *U.S. Private*, pg. 26
AGRI-SERVICE AGENCIES, INC.—See Dairylea Cooperative Inc.; *U.S. Private*, pg. 308
AGRI TERMINAL CORPORATION—See American Grain & Related Industries; *U.S. Private*, pg. 55
AGRIBANK, FCB—See Federal Farm Credit Banks Funding Corporation; *U.S. Private*, pg. 398

AGRIBIOTECH, INC.; *U.S. Public*, pg. 28
AGRIBUSINESS DEPARTMENT—See CVB Financial Corp.; *U.S. Public*, pg. 287
AGRICOLA SAN GIORGIO S.P.A.—See Assicurazioni Generali S.p.A.; *Int'l*, pg. 89
AGRICOLTURA ASSICURAZIONI—See Assicurazioni Generali S.p.A.; *Int'l*, pg. 89
AGRICOMMERCE SA—See The Albert Fisher Group PLC; *Int'l*, pg. 491
AGRICULTURA GMBH—See Norsk Hydro a.s; *Int'l*, pg. 961
THE AGRICULTURAL GROUP, MONSANTO COMPANY—See Monsanto Company; *U.S. Public*, pg. 1125
AGRICULTURAL INSURANCE COMPANY—See American Financial Group; *U.S. Public*, pg. 74
AGRICULTURAL PRODUCTS, INC.—See Summa Industries; *U.S. Public*, pg. 1527
AGRICULTURAL PUBLISHING GROUP—See The Walt Disney Company; *U.S. Public*, pg. 512
AGRICULTURAL WAREHOUSING—See Hydro/Kirby Agri Service, Inc.; *U.S. Private*, pg. 552
AGRIFUTURES INCORPORATED—See American Grain & Related Industries; *U.S. Private*, pg. 55
AGRIGEST—See Allianz Aktiengesellschaft; *Int'l*, pg. 61
AGRILAND COMPANY; *U.S. Private*, pg. 26
AGRILINE—See Compagnie des Machines Bull; *Int'l*, pg. 318
AGRILINK FOODS, INC.—See Pro-Fac Cooperative, Inc.; *U.S. Private*, pg. 887
AGRINET FARM RADIO NETWORK—See Ray Communications, Inc.; *U.S. Private*, pg. 911
AGRINORTHWEST, INC.; *U.S. Private*, pg. 26
AGRIPAC INC.; *U.S. Private*, pg. 26
AGRIPPINA LEBENSVERSICHERUNG AKTIENGESELLSCHAFT—See Zurich Insurance Company; *Int'l*, pg. 1531
AGRIPPINA RECHTSSCHUTZVERSICHERUNG AG—See Zurich Insurance Company; *Int'l*, pg. 1531
AGRIPPINA RUCKVERSICHERUNG AKTIENGESELLSCHAFT—See Zurich Insurance Company; *Int'l*, pg. 1531
AGRIPPINA VERSICHERUNG AKTIENGESELLSCHAFT—See Zurich Insurance Company; *Int'l*, pg. 1531
AGRISTOR CREDIT CORP.—See A.O. Smith Corporation; *U.S. Public*, pg. 1477
AGRIUM INC.; *Int'l*, pg. 31
AGRIUM U.S.—See Agrium Inc.; *Int'l*, pg. 31
AGRO BARTER UNITED AB—See Axel Johnson AB; *Int'l*, pg. 708
AGRO DYNAMICS CANADA INC.—See EcoScience Corporation; *U.S. Public*, pg. 563
AGRO DYNAMICS, INC.—See EcoScience Corporation; *U.S. Public*, pg. 563
CIA. AGRO INDUSTRIAL IGARASSU—See S.A. Industrias Votorantim; *Int'l*, pg. 677
AGRO-KEMI A/S—See Bayer AG; *Int'l*, pg. 174
AGROCHEMICALS DIV.—See Nippon Kayaku Co. Ltd.; *Int'l*, pg. 934
AGROFERM HUNGARIAN JAPANESE FERMENTATION INDUSTRY LTD.—See Kyowa Hakko Kogyo Company, Ltd.; *Int'l*, pg. 778
AGROINDUSTRIAL BIOTROPICAL LTDA.—See Chr. Hansen Holding A/S; *Int'l*, pg. 288
AGROINDUSTRIAS LA SIERRA S.A.—See Corn Products International, Inc.; *U.S. Public*, pg. 448
AGROLASER INC.—See Spectra-Physics AB; *Int'l*, pg. 1289
AGROLINZ AGRARCHEMIKALIEN GESELLSCHAFTMBH BERLIN—See DSM N.V.; *Int'l*, pg. 356
AGROLINZ AGRARCHEMIKALIEN MUNCHEN GESMBH—See DSM N.V.; *Int'l*, pg. 356
AGROLINZ INC.—See DSM N.V.; *Int'l*, pg. 356
AGROLINZ MELAMIN GMBH—See DSM N.V.; *Int'l*, pg. 356
AGROLINZ MELAMIN ITALIA S.R.L.—See DSM N.V.; *Int'l*, pg. 356
AGROMAC INTERNATIONAL, INC.; *U.S. Private*, pg. 27
AGRONAUT GREAT CENTRAL INSURANCE CO.—See Argonaut Group, Inc.; *U.S. Public*, pg. 129
AGRONOVA A/S—See Tiedemanns - Joh.H.Andresen ANS; *Int'l*, pg. 1389
AGROPECUARIA DE GUISSONA, S. COOP. LTDA.; *Int'l*, pg. 31
AGROPLANT SES SAATZUCHT GMBH—See Zeneca Group Plc; *Int'l*, pg. 1525
AGROPUR; *Int'l*, pg. 31
AGROSTAR A.G.—See Novartis AG; *Int'l*, pg. 974
AGROTEC, WILLIAMS INC.—See Williams Controls, Inc.; *U.S. Public*, pg. 1769
AGROTECHNIP S.A.—See Technip; *Int'l*, pg. 1360
AGROZOOFARMA S.P.A.—See Assicurazioni Generali S.p.A.; *Int'l*, pg. 89
AGSCO, INC.; *U.S. Private*, pg. 27
AGTEC INC.—See Ag-Chem Equipment Co., Inc.; *U.S. Public*, pg. 6
AGUADILLA SHOE DIV.—See Wolverine World Wide, Inc.; *U.S. Public*, pg. 1775
AGUADOR S.A.—See KSB Aktiengesellschaft; *Int'l*, pg. 721
AGUAS ARGENTINAS—See Lyonnaise des Eaux S.A.; *Int'l*, pg. 824
AGUAS DE LANJARON—See Danone Group; *Int'l*, pg. 381
AGUAS PURIFICADAS LTDA.—See GESTRA GmbH; *Int'l*, pg. 549
AGUSTA AEROSPACE CORPORATION—See Agusta S.P.A.; *Int'l*, pg. 32
AGUSTA AEROSPACE SERVICES A.A.S., S.A.-BELGIO—See Agusta S.P.A.; *Int'l*, pg. 32
AGUSTA S.P.A.; *Int'l*, pg. 32
AGVESTMENTS, INC.—See Gold Kist, Inc.; *U.S. Private*, pg. 459
AGWAY AGRICULTURAL PRODUCTS (AAP)—See Agway, Inc.; *U.S. Private*, pg. 27
AGWAY ENERGY PRODUCTS (AEP)—See Agway, Inc.; *U.S. Private*, pg. 27

AGWAY GENERAL AGENCY—See Agway, Inc.; *U.S. Private*, pg. 27
AGWAY, INC.; *U.S. Private*, pg. 27
AGWAY INSURANCE CO.—See Agway, Inc.; *U.S. Private*, pg. 27
AGWAY RETAIL SERVICES—See Agway, Inc.; *U.S. Private*, pg. 27
AHERN FIRE PROTECTION—See J.F. Ahern Co.; *U.S. Private*, pg. 27
J.F. AHERN CO.; *U.S. Private*, pg. 27
AHLENS AB—See Axel Johnson AB; *Int'l*, pg. 708
AHLSELL AB—See Trelleborg AB; *Int'l*, pg. 1422
AHLSELL EL AB—See Trelleborg AB; *Int'l*, pg. 1422
AHLSELL KYL AB—See Trelleborg AB; *Int'l*, pg. 1422
AHLSELL VVS AB—See Trelleborg AB; *Int'l*, pg. 1422
A. AHLSTROM CORPORATION; *Int'l*, pg. 32
A. AHLSTROM CORPORATION-STROMFORS WORKS—See A. Ahlstrom Corporation; *Int'l*, pg. 32
A. AHLSTROM GES.M.B.H.—See A. Ahlstrom Corporation; *Int'l*, pg. 34
A. AHLSTROM GMBH—See A. Ahlstrom Corporation; *Int'l*, pg. 34
AHLSTROM ALCORE GMBH-DUSSELDORF CORE PLANT—See A. Ahlstrom Corporation; *Int'l*, pg. 33
AHLSTROM ALCORE LTD.—See A. Ahlstrom Corporation; *Int'l*, pg. 32
AHLSTROM ANZ PTY LTD.—See A. Ahlstrom Corporation; *Int'l*, pg. 32
AHLSTROM AQUAFLOW LTD.—See A. Ahlstrom Corporation; *Int'l*, pg. 34
AHLSTROM A/S AHLSTROM MACHINERY—See A. Ahlstrom Corporation; *Int'l*, pg. 34
AHLSTROM AUTOMATION OY—See A. Ahlstrom Corporation; *Int'l*, pg. 34
AHLSTROM CONSUMER PRODUCTS LTD.—See A. Ahlstrom Corporation; *Int'l*, pg. 32
AHLSTROM DAIICHI CO., LTD.—See A. Ahlstrom Corporation; *Int'l*, pg. 34
AHLSTROM EQUIPAMENTOS LTDA.—See A. Ahlstrom Corporation; *Int'l*, pg. 34
AHLSTROM FILTRATION, INC.-CHATTANOOGA MILL—See A. Ahlstrom Corporation; *Int'l*, pg. 35
AHLSTROM FILTRATION, INC.-MADISONVILLE MILL—See A. Ahlstrom Corporation; *Int'l*, pg. 35
AHLSTROM FILTRATION, INC.—See A. Ahlstrom Corporation; *Int'l*, pg. 35
AHLSTROM GLASSFIBRE LTD.-KARHULA PLANT—See A. Ahlstrom Corporation; *Int'l*, pg. 32
AHLSTROM-HANSSEN S.A.—See A. Ahlstrom Corporation; *Int'l*, pg. 34
AHLSTROM INC.—See A. Ahlstrom Corporation; *Int'l*, pg. 35
AHLSTROM KAMYR INC.—See A. Ahlstrom Corporation; *Int'l*, pg. 34
AHLSTROM KAMYR SERVICES INC.—See A. Ahlstrom Corporation; *Int'l*, pg. 34
AHLSTROM KAUTTUA LTD.—See A. Ahlstrom Corporation; *Int'l*, pg. 35
AHLSTROM KOREA CO., LTD.—See A. Ahlstrom Corporation; *Int'l*, pg. 35
AHLSTROM KOREA CO., LTD.-HYUN POON MILL—See A. Ahlstrom Corporation; *Int'l*, pg. 35
AHLSTROM LTD.—See A. Ahlstrom Corporation; *Int'l*, pg. 33
AHLSTROM MACHINERY—See A. Ahlstrom Corporation; *Int'l*, pg. 33
AHLSTROM MACHINERY AB—See A. Ahlstrom Corporation; *Int'l*, pg. 34
AHLSTROM MACHINERY AB-FIBER PROCESSES—See A. Ahlstrom Corporation; *Int'l*, pg. 34
AHLSTROM MACHINERY AB-HAMMARS—See A. Ahlstrom Corporation; *Int'l*, pg. 34
AHLSTROM MACHINERY AB PROCESS EQUIPMENT—See A. Ahlstrom Corporation; *Int'l*, pg. 34
AHLSTROM MACHINERY AB-RECOVERY PROCESSES—See A. Ahlstrom Corporation; *Int'l*, pg. 35
AHLSTROM MACHINERY AB-SAWMILL MACHINERY—See A. Ahlstrom Corporation; *Int'l*, pg. 35
AHLSTROM MACHINERY (ASIA-PACIFIC) PTE LTD.—See A. Ahlstrom Corporation; *Int'l*, pg. 35
AHLSTROM MACHINERY CHEMICAL RECOVERY—See A. Ahlstrom Corporation; *Int'l*, pg. 33
AHLSTROM MACHINERY ECOMACHINERY—See A. Ahlstrom Corporation; *Int'l*, pg. 33
AHLSTROM MACHINERY FIBER LINE—See A. Ahlstrom Corporation; *Int'l*, pg. 33
AHLSTROM MACHINERY GMBH ECOMACHINERY—See A. Ahlstrom Corporation; *Int'l*, pg. 35
AHLSTROM MACHINERY KARHULA STEEL FOUNDRY—See A. Ahlstrom Corporation; *Int'l*, pg. 33
AHLSTROM MACHINERY INC.—See A. Ahlstrom Corporation; *Int'l*, pg. 35
AHLSTROM MACHINERY MANTTA PUMP FACTORY—See A. Ahlstrom Corporation; *Int'l*, pg. 33
AHLSTROM MACHINERY PAIVARINNE WORKS—See A. Ahlstrom Corporation; *Int'l*, pg. 33
AHLSTROM MACHINERY PUMP INDUSTRY—See A. Ahlstrom Corporation; *Int'l*, pg. 34
AHLSTROM MACHINERY PUMP INDUSTRY AFTER SALES—See A. Ahlstrom Corporation; *Int'l*, pg. 34
AHLSTROM MACHINERY PUMPS INC.—See A. Ahlstrom Corporation; *Int'l*, pg. 33
AHLSTROM MACHINERY RECOVERY BOILERS—See A. Ahlstrom Corporation; *Int'l*, pg. 33
AHLSTROM MACHINERY RECOVERY BOILERS & HEAT ENGINEERING—See A. Ahlstrom Corporation; *Int'l*, pg. 33
AHLSTROM MACHINERY SALO WORKS—See A. Ahlstrom Corporation; *Int'l*, pg. 34
AHLSTROM MACHINERY SAVONLINNA ENGINEERING WORKS—See A. Ahlstrom Corporation; *Int'l*, pg. 34
AHLSTROM PAPEIS LTDA.—See A. Ahlstrom Corporation; *Int'l*, pg. 35

AHLSTROM PAPER AG—See A. Ahlstrom Corporation; *Int'l*, pg. 35
AHLSTROM PAPIER B.V.—See A. Ahlstrom Corporation; *Int'l*, pg. 35
AHLSTROM PAPIERVERTRIEB GMBH—See A. Ahlstrom Corporation; *Int'l*, pg. 35
AHLSTROM PROCESS EQUIPMENT INC. PUMP FACTORY—See A. Ahlstrom Corporation; *Int'l*, pg. 34
AHLSTROM PROCESS EQUIPMENT INC.—See A. Ahlstrom Corporation; *Int'l*, pg. 34
AHLSTROM PULP & PAPER ENGINEERING S.A.—See A. Ahlstrom Corporation; *Int'l*, pg. 35
AHLSTROM RECOVERY INC.—See A. Ahlstrom Corporation; *Int'l*, pg. 34
AHLSTROM RECOVERY INC.-WESTERN REGION—See A. Ahlstrom Corporation; *Int'l*, pg. 35
AHLSTROM REPRESENTATION IN MOSCOW—See A. Ahlstrom Corporation; *Int'l*, pg. 35
AHLSTROM SOUTH AFRICA (PTY) LTD.—See A. Ahlstrom Corporation; *Int'l*, pg. 35
AHLSTROM SUMIJU K.K.—See A. Ahlstrom Corporation; *Int'l*, pg. 35
AHLSTROMFORETAGEN SVENSKA AB—See A. Ahlstrom Corporation; *Int'l*, pg. 33
AHLSTROMFORETAGEN SVENSKA AB-ELJO—See A. Ahlstrom Corporation; *Int'l*, pg. 33
AHLSTROMFORETAGEN SVENSKA AB-MARKARYD CORE PLANT—See A. Ahlstrom Corporation; *Int'l*, pg. 33
AHLSTROMFORETAGEN SVENSKA AB-MATFORS CORE PLANT—See A. Ahlstrom Corporation; *Int'l*, pg. 33
AHLSTROMFORETAGEN SVENSKA AB-NORRKOPING CORE PLANT—See A. Ahlstrom Corporation; *Int'l*, pg. 33
AHMANSON COMMERCIAL DEVELOPMENT CO.—See H.F. Ahmanson & Co.; *U.S. Public*, pg. 29
AHMANSON DEVELOPMENTS, INC.—See H.F. Ahmanson & Co.; *U.S. Public*, pg. 29
H.F. AHMANSON & CO.; *U.S. Public*, pg. 29
AHMANSON MORTGAGE COMPANY—See H.F. Ahmanson & Co.; *U.S. Public*, pg. 29
AHOLD FINANCE COMPANY (NEDERLANDSE ANTILLEN) NV—See Koninklijke Ahold NV; *Int'l*, pg. 750
AHOLD VASTGOED B.V.—See Koninklijke Ahold NV; *Int'l*, pg. 749
AICHELIN-STAHL, INC.—See Stahl Specialty Company; *U.S. Private*, pg. 1029
AICHI-EMERSON ELECTRIC CO.—See Emerson Electric Co.; *U.S. Public*, pg. 578
AICHI MACHINE INDUSTRY CO., LTD.—See Nissan Motor Co., Ltd.; *Int'l*, pg. 943
AICHI NAGOYA NISSAN MOTOR CO., LTD.—See Nissan Motor Co., Ltd.; *Int'l*, pg. 943
AICHI NIKON CO., LTD.—See Nikon Corporation; *Int'l*, pg. 931
AICHI NISSAN MOTOR CO., LTD.—See Nissan Motor Co., Ltd.; *Int'l*, pg. 943
AICHI STEEL WORKS, LTD.; *Int'l*, pg. 35
AICHI TOYOTA MOTOR CO., LTD.—See Toyota Motor Corporation; *Int'l*, pg. 1412
AID ASSOCIATION FOR LUTHERANS; *U.S. Private*, pg. 27
AID AUTO STORES, INC.; *U.S. Public*, pg. 29
AID FINANCE—See Allied Mutual Insurance Company; *U.S. Private*, pg. 39
AIDI CENTER S.P.R.L.—See Etablissements Delhaize Freres Et Cie "Le Lion" S.A.; *Int'l*, pg. 463
AIDSUN LIMITED—See Saint-Gobain; *Int'l*, pg. 1172
AIKEN ELECTRIC COOPERATIVE INC.; *U.S. Private*, pg. 28
AIKEN ELECTRIC SATELLITE—See Aiken Electric Cooperative Inc.; *U.S. Private*, pg. 28
ROBERT B. AIKENS & ASSOCIATES LLC.; *U.S. Private*, pg. 28
THE AILING & CORY COMPANY—See Union Camp Corporation; *U.S. Public*, pg. 1666
AIM ELECTRONICS CORPORATION—See Jordan Industries, Inc.; *U.S. Private*, pg. 598
AIM EQUITY FUNDS, INC.—See Invesco Group Asset Management Ltd.; *Int'l*, pg. 685
AIM FAMILY OF FUNDS—See Invesco Group Asset Management Ltd.; *Int'l*, pg. 685
AIM SAFETY COMPANY INC.; *Int'l*, pg. 36
AIM SERVICES CO., LTD.—See Aramark Corp.; *U.S. Private*, pg. 79
AIMANTS UGIMAG—See Pechiney S.A.; *Int'l*, pg. 1028
AIN PLASTICS, INC.—See Thyssen AG; *Int'l*, pg. 1388
AIR ALLIANCE—See Air Canada; *Int'l*, pg. 36
AIR & FUEL DIV.—See Parker Hannifin Corporation; *U.S. Public*, pg. 1262
AIR & WATER TECHNOLOGIES CORPORATION; *U.S. Public*, pg. 29
AIR BC—See Air Canada; *Int'l*, pg. 36
AIR CALL COMMUNICATIONS LTD.—See Vodafone Group PLC; *Int'l*, pg. 1470
AIR CANADA; *Int'l*, pg. 36
AIR CANADA—See Air Canada; *Int'l*, pg. 36
AIR CANADA VACATIONS INC.—See Air Canada; *Int'l*, pg. 36
AIR CARGO EQUIPMENT CORPORATION—See Zero Corporation; *U.S. Public*, pg. 1791
AIR CHARTER—See Groupe Air France; *Int'l*, pg. 560
AIR CHEFS (PTY) LTD.—See Transnet Ltd.; *Int'l*, pg. 1417
AIR COMFORT PRODUCTS DIV.—See Emerson Electric Co.; *U.S. Public*, pg. 572
AIR CONDITIONER DIVISION—See Toshiba Corporation; *Int'l*, pg. 1406
AIR CONDITIONING CO., INC.; *U.S. Private*, pg. 28
AIR CONDITIONING CO., INC.—See Air Conditioning Co., Inc.; *U.S. Private*, pg. 28
AIR CONDITIONING CO. INC.—See Air Conditioning Co., Inc.; *U.S. Private*, pg. 28
AIR COURIER DISPATCH—See Corporate Express, Inc.; *U.S. Public*, pg. 450

AIR CRAFTERS INC.—See Aero Data Metal Crafters; *U.S. Private*, pg. 24
AIR CRUISERS CO.—See Groupe Zodiac; *Int'l*, pg. 572
AIR-DRY CORPORATION OF AMERICA—See Danaher Corporation; *U.S. Public*, pg. 481
AIR ENGINEERING CO., INC.—See Amelco Corporation; *U.S. Public*, pg. 65
AIR EXPRESS INTL. AGENCY, INC.—See Air Express International Corporation; *U.S. Public*, pg. 30
AIR EXPRESS INTERNATIONAL CORPORATION; *U.S. Public*, pg. 30
AIR EXPRESS INTERNATIONAL (PVT) LTD.—See Air Express International Corporation; *U.S. Public*, pg. 30
AIR EXPRESS INTERNATIONAL (S.A.) (PTY), LTD.—See Air Express International Corporation; *U.S. Public*, pg. 30
AIR EXPRESS INTERNATIONAL SINGAPORE (PTE.) LTD.—See Air Express International Corporation; *U.S. Public*, pg. 30
AIR EXPRESS INTL. USA, INC.—See Air Express International Corporation; *U.S. Public*, pg. 30
AIR FRANCE—See Groupe Air France; *Int'l*, pg. 560
AIR FRANCE C.S. PARTICIPATION—See Groupe Air France; *Int'l*, pg. 560
AIR FRANCE FINANCE—See Groupe Air France; *Int'l*, pg. 560
AIR FRANCE FINANCE IRELAND—See Groupe Air France; *Int'l*, pg. 560
AIR FRANCE (MID ATLANTIC REGION)—See Groupe Air France; *Int'l*, pg. 560
AIR FRANCE (NORTH CENTRAL)—See Groupe Air France; *Int'l*, pg. 560
AIR FRANCE (NORTHEAST REGION)—See Groupe Air France; *Int'l*, pg. 560
AIR FRANCE (SOUTHEASTERN REGION)—See Groupe Air France; *Int'l*, pg. 561
AIR FRANCE (U.S. PACIFIC REGION)—See Groupe Air France; *Int'l*, pg. 561
AIR FRANCE (U.S. REGION)—See Groupe Air France; *Int'l*, pg. 561
AIR FRESH TRUCKING—See Wilsey Bennett Co.; *U.S. Private*, pg. 1180
AIR GAGE COMPANY—See United Dominion Industries, Ltd.; *U.S. Public*, pg. 1676
AIR GUADELOUPE—See Groupe Air France; *Int'l*, pg. 561
AIR GUARD—See CCL Industries, Inc.; *Int'l*, pg. 238
AIR HANSON LIMITED—See Hanson PLC; *Int'l*, pg. 592
AIR INDIA; *Int'l*, pg. 37
AIR INDUSTRIES CORPORATION; *U.S. Public*, pg. 28
AIR JAMAICA LTD.; *U.S. Private*, pg. 28
AIR LAND FORWARDERS, INC.—See The Suddath Companies; *U.S. Private*, pg. 1049
AIR LINK COMMUNICATIONS, INC.—See Motorola, Inc.; *U.S. Public*, pg. 1137
AIR LIQUIDE AMERICA CORPORATION—See Air Liquide S.A.; *Int'l*, pg. 37
AIR LIQUIDE CORPORATION BULK GASES DIVISION—See Air Liquide S.A.; *Int'l*, pg. 37
AIR LIQUIDE ITALY/SIO—See Air Liquide S.A.; *Int'l*, pg. 37
AIR LIQUIDE NORTHERN DIV.—See Air Liquide S.A.; *Int'l*, pg. 37
AIR LIQUIDE S.A.; *Int'l*, pg. 37
AIR LIQUIDE SOUTHERN DIV.—See Air Liquide S.A.; *Int'l*, pg. 37
AIR MALTA - CAIRO—See Air Malta Co. Ltd.; *Int'l*, pg. 38
AIR MALTA CO. LTD.; *Int'l*, pg. 37
AIR MIDWEST, INC.—See Mesa Air Group; *U.S. Public*, pg. 1099
AIR MOVEMENT GROUP LTD.—See Smiths Industries plc; *Int'l*, pg. 1267
AIR NELSON—See Air New Zealand Ltd.; *Int'l*, pg. 38
AIR NEW ZEALAND CARGO SERVICES—See Air New Zealand Ltd.; *Int'l*, pg. 38
AIR NEW ZEALAND CATERING SERVICES—See Air New Zealand Ltd.; *Int'l*, pg. 38
AIR NEW ZEALAND ENGINEERING SERVICES—See Air New Zealand Ltd.; *Int'l*, pg. 38
AIR NEW ZEALAND INFORMATION SERVICES—See Air New Zealand Ltd.; *Int'l*, pg. 38
AIR NEW ZEALAND INTERNATIONAL—See Air New Zealand Ltd.; *Int'l*, pg. 38
AIR NEW ZEALAND LTD.; *Int'l*, pg. 38
AIR NEW ZEALAND LTD. (U.S.A.)—See Air New Zealand Ltd.; *Int'l*, pg. 38
AIR NEW ZEALAND NATIONAL—See Air New Zealand Ltd.; *Int'l*, pg. 38
AIR NEW ZEALAND TERMINAL SERVICES—See Air New Zealand Ltd.; *Int'l*, pg. 38
AIR NOVA—See Air Canada; *Int'l*, pg. 36
AIR ONTARIO—See Air Canada; *Int'l*, pg. 36
AIR POLLUTION CONTROL—See Air & Water Technologies Corporation; *U.S. Public*, pg. 29
AIR POWER, INC.; *U.S. Private*, pg. 28
AIR PRO—See Frozen Food Express Industries, Inc.; *U.S. Public*, pg. 685
AIR PRODUCTS—See Air Products and Chemicals, Inc.; *U.S. Public*, pg. 30
AIR PRODUCTS AND CHEMICALS DE MEXICO S.A. DE C.V.—See Air Products and Chemicals, Inc.; *U.S. Public*, pg. 30
AIR PRODUCTS AND CHEMICALS, INC.; *U.S. Public*, pg. 30
AIR PRODUCTS A/S-GARDNER CRYOGENICS DIV.—See Air Products and Chemicals, Inc.; *U.S. Public*, pg. 31
AIR PRODUCTS A/S PERMIA MARITIME DIV.—See Air Products and Chemicals, Inc.; *U.S. Public*, pg. 31
AIR PRODUCTS ASIA ELECTRONICS—See Air Products and Chemicals, Inc.; *U.S. Public*, pg. 31
AIR PRODUCTS ASIA, INC.—See Air Products and Chemicals, Inc.; *U.S. Public*, pg. 31
AIR PRODUCTS CANADA—See Air Products and Chemicals, Inc.; *U.S. Public*, pg. 31
AIR PRODUCTS CANADA LTD.—See Air Products and Chemicals, Inc.; *U.S. Public*, pg. 31

AIR PRODUCTS CHINA—See Air Products and Chemicals, Inc.; *U.S. Public*, pg. 31
AIR PRODUCTS CHINA INC.—See Air Products and Chemicals, Inc.; *U.S. Public*, pg. 31
AIR PRODUCTS EUROPE, INC.—See Air Products and Chemicals, Inc.; *U.S. Public*, pg. 31
AIR PRODUCTS GASES INDUSTRIAIS LTDA.—See Air Products and Chemicals, Inc.; *U.S. Public*, pg. 31
AIR PRODUCTS GMBH.—See Air Products and Chemicals, Inc.; *U.S. Public*, pg. 31
AIR PRODUCTS GMBH, WERK NORDERSTEDT—See Air Products and Chemicals, Inc.; *U.S. Public*, pg. 31
AIR PRODUCTS GROUP—See York International Corporation; *U.S. Public*, pg. 1789
AIR PRODUCTS HYDROGEN CO., INC.—See Air Products and Chemicals, Inc.; *U.S. Public*, pg. 30
AIR PRODUCTS INDUSTRY CO., LTD.—See Nippon Sanso Corporation; *Int'l*, pg. 939
AIR PRODUCTS INTERNATIONAL CORP.—See Air Products and Chemicals, Inc.; *U.S. Public*, pg. 30
AIR PRODUCTS ITALIA—See Air Products and Chemicals, Inc.; *U.S. Public*, pg. 31
AIR PRODUCTS JAPAN, INC.—See Air Products and Chemicals, Inc.; *U.S. Public*, pg. 31
AIR PRODUCTS KOREA INC.—See Air Products and Chemicals, Inc.; *U.S. Public*, pg. 31
AIR PRODUCTS (MIDDLE EAST) INC.—See Air Products and Chemicals, Inc.; *U.S. Public*, pg. 31
AIR PRODUCTS NEDERLAND B.V.—See Air Products and Chemicals, Inc.; *U.S. Public*, pg. 31
AIR PRODUCTS N.V.—See Air Products and Chemicals, Inc.; *U.S. Public*, pg. 31
AIR PRODUCTS N.V./S.A.—See Air Products and Chemicals, Inc.; *U.S. Public*, pg. 31
AIR PRODUCTS OF PUERTO RICO, INC.—See Air Products and Chemicals, Inc.; *U.S. Public*, pg. 31
AIR PRODUCTS PLC—See Air Products and Chemicals, Inc.; *U.S. Public*, pg. 31
AIR PRODUCTS REF-FUEL HOLDING CORP.—See Air Products and Chemicals, Inc.; *U.S. Public*, pg. 31
AIR PRODUCTS REF-FUEL OF CONNECTICUT (S.E.), INC.—See Air Products and Chemicals, Inc.; *U.S. Public*, pg. 31
AIR PRODUCTS REF-FUEL OF HEMPSTEAD, INC.—See Air Products and Chemicals, Inc.; *U.S. Public*, pg. 31
AIR PRODUCTS RESINAS, S.A. DE C.V.—See Air Products and Chemicals, Inc.; *U.S. Public*, pg. 32
AIR PRODUCTS S.A.—See Air Products and Chemicals, Inc.; *U.S. Public*, pg. 31
AIR PRODUCTS SINGAPORE PTE LTD.—See Air Products and Chemicals, Inc.; *U.S. Public*, pg. 32
AIR PRODUCTS SOUTH AFRICA (PROPRIETARY) LIMITED—See Air Products and Chemicals, Inc.; *U.S. Public*, pg. 32
AIR PRODUCTS/SPEC GAS FACILITY—See Air Products and Chemicals, Inc.; *U.S. Public*, pg. 32
AIR PRODUCTS S.R.O.—See Air Products and Chemicals, Inc.; *U.S. Public*, pg. 32
AIR PRODUCTS WORLD TRADE, INC. C/O CHASE TRADE, INC.—See Air Products and Chemicals, Inc.; *U.S. Public*, pg. 31
AIR-SCENT INTERNATIONAL—See Surco Products, Inc.; *U.S. Private*, pg. 1056
AIR SEA BROKER AG—See Panalpina Welttransport (Holding) AG; *Int'l*, pg. 1022
AIR SEA BROKER BELGIUM N.V.—See Panalpina Welttransport (Holding) AG; *Int'l*, pg. 1022
AIR SEA CHARTER TRANSPORT GMBH—See Panalpina Welttransport (Holding) AG; *Int'l*, pg. 1022
AIR SEAL WEST—See Flanders Corp.; *U.S. Public*, pg. 648
AIR-SHIELDS INC.—See Vickers PLC; *Int'l*, pg. 1468
AIR SUPPLIES & CATERING CO. LTD.—See Air Malta Co. Ltd.; *Int'l*, pg. 37
AIR SYSTEMS LTD.—See Tomkins PLC; *Int'l*, pg. 1398
AIR TECHNIQUES, INC.; *U.S. Private*, pg. 28
AIR TRAFFIC CONTROL SYSTEMS DIVISION—See Harris Corporation; *U.S. Public*, pg. 792
AIR TRANSPORT AVIONICS LIMITED—See TT Group PLC; *Int'l*, pg. 1344
AIR UK LTD.; *Int'l*, pg. 38
AIR UK ENGINEERING—See Air UK Ltd.; *Int'l*, pg. 39
AIR UK ENGINEERING LTD.—See Air UK Ltd.; *Int'l*, pg. 39
AIR UK (LEISURE) LTD.—See Air UK Ltd.; *Int'l*, pg. 39
AIR VENT INC.—See Saint-Gobain; *Int'l*, pg. 1170
AIR WIS SERVICES, INC.—See UAL Corporation; *U.S. Public*, pg. 1653
AIR WISCONSIN, INC.—See UAL Corporation; *U.S. Public*, pg. 1653
AIRBORNE—See Groupe Strafor Facom; *Int'l*, pg. 569
AIRBORNE FREIGHT CORPORATION; *U.S. Public*, pg. 32
AIRBORNE LEISURE LTD.—See Pentland Group PLC; *Int'l*, pg. 1035
AIRBORNE SYSTEMS INTEGRATION DIVISION—See California Microwave, Inc.; *U.S. Public*, pg. 293
AIRBUS INDUSTRIE; *Int'l*, pg. 39
AIRBUS INDUSTRIE AIRSPARES—See Airbus Industrie; *Int'l*, pg. 39
AIRBUS INDUSTRIE BEIJING—See Airbus Industrie; *Int'l*, pg. 39
AIRBUS INDUSTRIE OF NORTH AMERICA, INC.—See Airbus Industrie; *Int'l*, pg. 39
AIRBUS INDUSTRIE TOKYO—See Airbus Industrie; *Int'l*, pg. 39
AIRCAP INDUSTRIES CORP.—See MTD Products, Inc.; *U.S. Private*, pg. 688
AIRCO COMMERCIAL SERVICES, INC.—See Airco Mechanical Inc.; *U.S. Private*, pg. 29
AIRCO MECHANICAL INC.; *U.S. Private*, pg. 29
AIRCRAFT BEARING CORP.—See Banner Aerospace, Inc.; *U.S. Public*, pg. 187
AIRCRAFT DIVISION/BEDEK AVIATION GROUP—See Israel Aircraft Industries Ltd.; *Int'l*, pg. 690
AIRCRAFT OF CANADA LTD.—See Raytheon Company; *U.S. Public*, pg. 1365

AIRCRAFT
DIRECTORY OF CORPORATE AFFILIATIONS
Company Index

AIRCRAFT PRODUCTS COMPANY—See B/E Aerospace, Inc.; *U.S. Public*, pg. 159
AIRCRAFT SERVICE INTERNATIONAL GROUP—See Viad Corp; *U.S. Public*, pg. 1719
AIRCRAFT SYSTEMS DIVISION, LOS ANGELES—See Ancra International LLC; *U.S. Private*, pg. 71
AIRCRAFT TECHNOLOGY, INC.—See HEICO Corporation; *U.S. Public*, pg. 804
AIRCRAFT WHEEL & BRAKE DIV.—See Parker Hannifin Corporation; *U.S. Public*, pg. 1262
AIRE SELLADO, S.A. DE C.V.—See Sealed Air Corporation; *U.S. Public*, pg. 1451
AIRE SERVE HEATING & AIR CONDITIONING, INC.—See The Dwyer Group, Inc.; *U.S. Public*, pg. 538
AIREX AG (AIREX)—See Alusuisse-Lonza Holding Ltd.; *Int'l*, pg. 67
AIRFLEX DIV. EATON CORP.—See Eaton Corporation; *U.S. Public*, pg. 556
AIRFOIL TECHNOLOGIES INTERNATIONAL LLC—See Teleflex Incorporated; *U.S. Public*, pg. 1569
AIRFORCE PIPELINE INC.—See Norfolk Southern Corporation; *U.S. Public*, pg. 1191
AIRFORGE S.A.—See Groupe Usinor; *Int'l*, pg. 571
AIRGAS, INC.; *U.S. Public*, pg. 33
AIRGUARD INDUSTRIES INC.—See CLARCOR, Inc.; *U.S. Public*, pg. 382
AIRKAMAN OF JACKSONVILLE, INC.—See Kaman Corporation; *U.S. Public*, pg. 942
AIRLEASE LTD.; *U.S. Public*, pg. 33
AIRLEASE MANAGEMENT SERVICES, INC.—See Airlease Ltd.; *U.S. Public*, pg. 33
AIRLINE HYDRAULICS CORPORATION; *U.S. Private*, pg. 29
AIRLINE MANUFACTURING COMPANY, INC.; *U.S. Private*, pg. 29
AIRLINK—See Qantas Airways Ltd.; *Int'l*, pg. 1075
AIRMASTER FAN CO.; *U.S. Private*, pg. 29
AIRMATE—See Day & Zimmermann, Inc.; *U.S. Private*, pg. 317
THE AIROLITE COMPANY; *U.S. Private*, pg. 29
AIRONET WIRELESS COMMUNICATIONS, INC.—See Telxon Corporation; *U.S. Public*, pg. 1573
AIRPARK ASSOCIATES—See Cigna Corp.; *U.S. Public*, pg. 361
AIRPLAY MONITOR—See VNU Verenigde Nederlandse Uitgeversbedrijven B.V.; *Int'l*, pg. 1446
AIRPORT '82 ASSOCIATES LTD.—See Family Inns of America, Inc.; *U.S. Private*, pg. 392
AIRPORT GROUP INTERNATIONAL, INC.—See Lockheed Martin Corporation; *U.S. Public*, pg. 1009
AIRSENSORS, INC.; *U.S. Public*, pg. 33
AIRSHOW—See Dynatech Corporation; *U.S. Public*, pg. 539
AIRSTREAM FINANCE LIMITED—See Dresdner Bank AG; *Int'l*, pg. 420
AIRSTREAM, INC.—See Thor Industries, Inc.; *U.S. Public*, pg. 1602
AIRSTREAM PRODUCTS LIMITED—See Smiths Industries plc; *Int'l*, pg. 1267
AIRTEC DIVISION—See Atlas Copco AB; *Int'l*, pg. 96
AIRTEX—See UIS, Inc.; *U.S. Private*, pg. 1113
AIRTEX PRODUCTS—See UIS, Inc.; *U.S. Private*, pg. 1113
AIRTITE CONTRACTORS INC.; *U.S. Private*, pg. 29
AIRTOUCH CABLE—See AirTouch Communications, Inc.; *U.S. Public*, pg. 34
AIRTOUCH CELLULAR—See AirTouch Communications, Inc.; *U.S. Public*, pg. 34
AIRTOUCH CELLULAR - WESTERN REGION—See AirTouch Communications, Inc.; *U.S. Public*, pg. 34
AIRTOUCH COMMUNICATIONS, INC.; *U.S. Public*, pg. 34
AIRTOUCH INTERNATIONAL—See AirTouch Communications, Inc.; *U.S. Public*, pg. 34
AIRTOUCH PAGING—See AirTouch Communications, Inc.; *U.S. Public*, pg. 34
AIRTOUCH PROPERTIES—See AirTouch Communications, Inc.; *U.S. Public*, pg. 34
AIRTOURS PLC; *Int'l*, pg. 39
AIRTROL, INC.; *U.S. Private*, pg. 29
AIRTRON—See Litton Industries, Inc.; *U.S. Public*, pg. 1003
AIRTRONICS CO.—See Katy Industries, Inc.; *U.S. Public*, pg. 944
AIRVAC INC.—See Ebara Corporation; *Int'l*, pg. 431
AIRVISION—See Philips Electronics N.V.; *Int'l*, pg. 1053
AIRVO B.V.—See Celsius AB; *Int'l*, pg. 278
AIRWAVE COMMUNICATIONS CORP.—See Motorola, Inc.; *U.S. Public*, pg. 1137
AISCO SYSTEMS INC.—See Outokumpu Oyj; *Int'l*, pg. 1017
AISHIN CO.—See Caterpillar Inc.; *U.S. Public*, pg. 317
AISIN ASIA PTE. LTD.—See Aisin Seiki Co. Ltd.; *Int'l*, pg. 39
AISIN (AUSTRALIA) PTY. LTD.—See Aisin Seiki Co. Ltd.; *Int'l*, pg. 39
AISIN DEUTSCHLAND GMBH—See Aisin Seiki Co. Ltd.; *Int'l*, pg. 39
AISIN DO BRASIL COM. E. IND. LTDA.—See Aisin Seiki Co. Ltd.; *Int'l*, pg. 39
AISIN EUROPE S.A.—See Aisin Seiki Co. Ltd.; *Int'l*, pg. 39
AISIN SEIKI CO. LTD.; *Int'l*, pg. 39
AISIN (UK) LIMITED—See Aisin Seiki Co. Ltd.; *Int'l*, pg. 39
AISIN U.S.A. MFG. INC.—See Aisin Seiki Co. Ltd.; *Int'l*, pg. 39
AISIN WORLD CORP. OF AMERICA—See Aisin Seiki Co. Ltd.; *Int'l*, pg. 39
AISIN WORLD CORP.-DETROIT—See Aisin Seiki Co. Ltd.; *Int'l*, pg. 39
AIWA AMERICA, INC.—See Sony Corporation; *Int'l*, pg. 1280
AIWA CO., LTD.—See Sony Corporation; *Int'l*, pg. 1280
AIYA CO., LTD.—See Skylark Co., Ltd.; *Int'l*, pg. 1262
AJAX MAGNETHERMIC CANADA LTD.—See BBA Group plc; *Int'l*, pg. 113
AJAX MAGNETHERMIC CORP.—See BBA Group plc; *Int'l*, pg. 113
AJAX MAGNETHERMIC U.K. LTD.—See BBA Group plc; *Int'l*, pg. 113
THE AJAX MANUFACTURING COMPANY—See Park-Ohio Industries, Inc.; *U.S. Public*, pg. 1258
AJAX MANUFACTURING COMPANY, INC.—See Standard Automotive Corporation; *U.S. Private*, pg. 1030
AJAX METAL PROCESSING—See Cold Heading Co.; *U.S. Private*, pg. 250
AJAX PAVING INDUSTRIES INC.; *U.S. Private*, pg. 29
AJAX SERVICES INC.—See BBA Group plc; *Int'l*, pg. 113
AJAY LEISURE PRODUCTS, INC.—See Ajay Sports Inc.; *U.S. Public*, pg. 34
AJAY SPORTS INC.; *U.S. Public*, pg. 34
AJI PHARMA U.S.A., INC.—See Ajinomoto Company Inc.; *Int'l*, pg. 40
AG AJIKAWA CORPORATION; *Int'l*, pg. 39
P.T. AJINEX INTERNATIONAL, MOJOKERTO FACTORY—See Ajinomoto Company Inc.; *Int'l*, pg. 40
P.T. AJINEX INTERNATIONAL—See Ajinomoto Company Inc.; *Int'l*, pg. 40
AJINOMOTO COMPANY INC.; *Int'l*, pg. 40
S.A. AJINOMOTO COORDINATION CENTER N.V.—See Ajinomoto Company Inc.; *Int'l*, pg. 40
AJINOMOTO DEL PERU S.A.—See Ajinomoto Company Inc.; *Int'l*, pg. 40
AJINOMOTO DEL PERU S.A., PLANT—See Ajinomoto Company Inc.; *Int'l*, pg. 40
AJINOMOTO EUROPE SALES G.M.B.H—See Ajinomoto Company Inc.; *Int'l*, pg. 40
AJINOMOTO EUROPE SALES G.M.B.H., LONDON REPRESENTATIVE OFFICE—See Ajinomoto Company Inc.; *Int'l*, pg. 40
AJINOMOTO EUROPE SALES G.M.B.H., MILANO REPRESENTAIVE OFFICE—See Ajinomoto Company Inc.; *Int'l*, pg. 40
AJINOMOTO FROZEN FOODS (THAILAND) CO., LTD., PLANT—See Ajinomoto Company Inc.; *Int'l*, pg. 41
P.T. AJINOMOTO INDONESIA, MOJOKERTO FACTORY—See Ajinomoto Company Inc.; *Int'l*, pg. 40
P.T. AJINOMOTO INDONESIA—See Ajinomoto Company Inc.; *Int'l*, pg. 40
P.T. AJINOMOTO INDONESIA, SURABAYA BRANCH—See Ajinomoto Company Inc.; *Int'l*, pg. 40
AJINOMOTO INTERAMERICANA INDUSTRIA E COMERCIO LTDA.—See Ajinomoto Company Inc.; *Int'l*, pg. 40
AJINOMOTO INTERAMERICANA INDUSTRIA E COMERCIO, LTDA., LIMEIRA PLANT—See Ajinomoto Company Inc.; *Int'l*, pg. 40
AJINOMOTO OSTEUROPA HANDELS-G.M.B.H.—See Ajinomoto Company Inc.; *Int'l*, pg. 40
AJINOMOTO (SINGAPORE) PTE. LTD.—See Ajinomoto Company Inc.; *Int'l*, pg. 40
AJINOMOTO TONG HSING FOODS, INC.—See Ajinomoto Company Inc.; *Int'l*, pg. 40
AJINOMOTO TONG HSING FOODS, INC., CHIA-YI PLANT—See Ajinomoto Company Inc.; *Int'l*, pg. 40
AJINOMOTO U.S.A., INC.—See Ajinomoto Company Inc.; *Int'l*, pg. 40
AJINOMOTO VIETNAM CO., LTD.—See Ajinomoto Company Inc.; *Int'l*, pg. 41
AJINOMTO (MALAYSIA) BERHAD—See Ajinomoto Company Inc.; *Int'l*, pg. 40
AJITRADE PTE. LTD.—See Ajinomoto Company Inc.; *Int'l*, pg. 41
AKADEMIBOKHANDELSGRUPPEN—See KF/Konsum Coop Group; *Int'l*, pg. 718
AKAGANE KAUIN SANGYO KABUSHIKI KAISHA—See Benguet Corporation; *Int'l*, pg. 187
AKAPP ELECTRO INDUSTRIES B.V.—See Woodhead Industries, Inc.; *U.S. Public*, pg. 1776
AKASHIC MEMORIES CORPORATION—See Kubota Corp.; *Int'l*, pg. 762
AKCANSA—See Heidelberger Zement A.G.; *Int'l*, pg. 605
AKEMI PLASTICS INC.—See Maxco, Inc.; *U.S. Public*, pg. 1061
AKER BASE A.S.—See Aker Raj Asa; *Int'l*, pg. 41
AKER BETONG A.S.—See Aker Raj Asa; *Int'l*, pg. 42
AKER BUILDING AND CEMENT MATERIALS—See Aker Raj Asa; *Int'l*, pg. 42
AKER CONTRACTING PLC—See Aker Raj Asa; *Int'l*, pg. 42
AKER ELEMENTBYGG A.S.—See Aker Raj Asa; *Int'l*, pg. 41
AKER ENGINEERING PLC (AE)—See Aker Raj Asa; *Int'l*, pg. 42
AKER EXCLAY A.S.—See Aker Raj Asa; *Int'l*, pg. 42
AKER GULF MARINE—See Aker Raj Asa; *Int'l*, pg. 42
AKER OIL & GAS TECHNOLOGY, INC.—See Aker Raj Asa; *Int'l*, pg. 42
AKER OMEGA INC. (AE)—See Aker Raj Asa; *Int'l*, pg. 42
AKER RAJ ASA; *Int'l*, pg. 41
AKER SINGEL & GRUS A.S.—See Aker Raj Asa; *Int'l*, pg. 42
AKER STORD A.S.—See Aker Raj Asa; *Int'l*, pg. 42
AKER SUBSEA A.S.—See Aker Raj Asa; *Int'l*, pg. 42
AKERLUND & RAUSING—See A. Ahlstrom Corporation; *Int'l*, pg. 33
AB AKERLUND & RAUSING—See A. Ahlstrom Corporation; *Int'l*, pg. 33
AKERLUND & RAUSING A/S—See A. Ahlstrom Corporation; *Int'l*, pg. 33
A/S AKERLUND & RAUSING—See A. Ahlstrom Corporation; *Int'l*, pg. 33
AB AKERLUND & RAUSING GROUP—See A. Ahlstrom Corporation; *Int'l*, pg. 33
AKERLUND & RAUSING LTD.—See A. Ahlstrom Corporation; *Int'l*, pg. 33
AKERLUND & RAUSING NA INC.—See A. Ahlstrom Corporation; *Int'l*, pg. 33
AKERLUND & RAUSING OY—See A. Ahlstrom Corporation; *Int'l*, pg. 32
AKERLUND & RAUSING S.A.R.L.—See A. Ahlstrom Corporation; *Int'l*, pg. 33
AKERLUND & RAUSING VERPACKUNG GMBH—See A. Ahlstrom Corporation; *Int'l*, pg. 33
AKERS PACKAGING SERVICE INC.; *U.S. Private*, pg. 29
AKI BRICOLAGE—See GIB Group; *Int'l*, pg. 534
AKIN SEED COMPANY—See Groupe Limagrain; *Int'l*, pg. 566
AKITA ATORION BUILDING CO., LTD.—See Nippon Life Insurance Co.; *Int'l*, pg. 935
AKITA SHIZUKI CO., INC.—See Shizuki Electric Corporation; *Int'l*, pg. 1236
AKKURAT GRUNDSTUCKS GMBH—See Bayerische Vereinsbank Group; *Int'l*, pg. 178
AKKURAT GRUNDSTUCKS GMBH & CO. BETRIEBS KG—See Bayerische Vereinsbank Group; *Int'l*, pg. 178
AKOH PLANT—See Shionogi & Co., Ltd.; *Int'l*, pg. 1235
AKOM LTD.—See Tultex Corporation; *U.S. Public*, pg. 1644
AKORN, INC.; *U.S. Public*, pg. 34
AKORN MANUFACTURING, INC.—See Akorn, Inc.; *U.S. Public*, pg. 34
THE AKRO CORPORATION—See Collins & Aikman Corporation; *U.S. Public*, pg. 399
AKROCHEM CORPORATION; *U.S. Private*, pg. 30
AKRON AB—See Proventus AB; *Int'l*, pg. 1072
AKRON BRASS COMPANY—See Premier Farnell plc; *Int'l*, pg. 1068
AKRON STANDARD DIVISION—See Illinois Tool Works Inc.; *U.S. Public*, pg. 865
AKROSIL—See International Paper Company; *U.S. Public*, pg. 903
AKROSIL DIVISION—See International Paper Company; *U.S. Public*, pg. 901
AKROSIL EUROPE B.V.—See International Paper Company; *U.S. Public*, pg. 904
AKSBONO BRAKE INDUSTRY CO., LTD.—See AlliedSignal Inc.; *U.S. Public*, pg. 53
AKSEL SKAARUP & CO. A/S—See Knurr AG; *Int'l*, pg. 739
AKTIEBOLAGET LM ERICSSON FINANS—See Telefonaktiebolaget LM Ericsson; *Int'l*, pg. 1363
AKTIENBRAUEREI KAUFBEUREN AG—See Bayerische Vereinsbank Group; *Int'l*, pg. 178
AKTIESELIKABET ESAB—See Charter plc; *Int'l*, pg. 281
AKVAMATIK AB—See Trelleborg AB; *Int'l*, pg. 1422
AKZO CHEMICALS B.V.—See Akzo Nobel N.V.; *Int'l*, pg. 42
AKZO CHEMICALS INC.—See Akzo Nobel N.V.; *Int'l*, pg. 47
AKZO CHEMICALS S.P.A.—See Akzo Nobel N.V.; *Int'l*, pg. 46
AKZO CHEMIE—See Akzo Nobel N.V.; *Int'l*, pg. 46
AKZO CHEMIE BRASIL—See Akzo Nobel N.V.; *Int'l*, pg. 46
AKZO CHEMIE DANMARK A/S—See Akzo Nobel N.V.; *Int'l*, pg. 47
AKZO CHEMIE FRANCE S.A.R.L.—See Akzo Nobel N.V.; *Int'l*, pg. 47
AKZO CHEMIE GMBH—See Akzo Nobel N.V.; *Int'l*, pg. 47
AKZO CHEMIE LTD.—See Akzo Nobel N.V.; *Int'l*, pg. 47
AKZO CHEMIE NEDERLAND BV—See Akzo Nobel N.V.; *Int'l*, pg. 46
AKZO CHEMIE NORGE AS—See Akzo Nobel N.V.; *Int'l*, pg. 47
AKZO CHEMIE UK LTD.—See Akzo Nobel N.V.; *Int'l*, pg. 47
AKZO COATINGS BELGIUM, DIV. OF AKZO BELGIE NV—See Akzo Nobel N.V.; *Int'l*, pg. 43
AKZO COATINGS B.V.—See Akzo Nobel N.V.; *Int'l*, pg. 42
AKZO COATINGS GES. M.B.H.—See Akzo Nobel N.V.; *Int'l*, pg. 43
AKZO COATINGS GMBH—See Akzo Nobel N.V.; *Int'l*, pg. 43
AKZO COATINGS INC.—See Akzo Nobel N.V.; *Int'l*, pg. 46
AKZO COATINGS INC. (MI)—See Akzo Nobel N.V.; *Int'l*, pg. 46
AKZO COATINGS NEDERLAND B.V.—See Akzo Nobel N.V.; *Int'l*, pg. 42
AKZO COATINGS PLC—See Akzo Nobel N.V.; *Int'l*, pg. 43
AKZO COATINGS SA—See Akzo Nobel N.V.; *Int'l*, pg. 43
AKZO COATINGS S.P.A.—See Akzo Nobel N.V.; *Int'l*, pg. 43
AKZO COATINGS (THAILAND LTD.)—See Akzo Nobel N.V.; *Int'l*, pg. 43
AKZO COATINGS-TINTAS WANDA—See Akzo Nobel N.V.; *Int'l*, pg. 43
AKZO DREELAND—See Akzo Nobel N.V.; *Int'l*, pg. 48
AKZO ELECTRONICS MATERIALS CO.—See Akzo Nobel N.V.; *Int'l*, pg. 48
AKZO ENGINEERING PLASTICS, INC.—See Akzo Nobel N.V.; *Int'l*, pg. 47
AKZO LANCHEM CORP.—See Akzo Nobel N.V.; *Int'l*, pg. 47
AKZO NOBEL AB—See Akzo Nobel N.V.; *Int'l*, pg. 48
AKZO NOBEL COATINGS INC.—See Akzo Nobel N.V.; *Int'l*, pg. 48
AKZO NOBEL COATINGS INC. (KY)—See Akzo Nobel N.V.; *Int'l*, pg. 47
AKZO NOBEL FIBERS B.V.—See Akzo Nobel N.V.; *Int'l*, pg. 43
AKZO NOBEL FIBERS, INC.—See Akzo Nobel N.V.; *Int'l*, pg. 48
AKZO NOBEL FORTAFIL FIBERS INC.—See Akzo Nobel N.V.; *Int'l*, pg. 48
AKZO NOBEL INC.—See Akzo Nobel N.V.; *Int'l*, pg. 43
AKZO NOBEL N.V.; *Int'l*, pg. 42
AKZO PHARMA B.V.—See Akzo Nobel N.V.; *Int'l*, pg. 44
AKZO PHARMA NEDERLAND B.V.—See Akzo Nobel N.V.; *Int'l*, pg. 44
AKZO PLASTICS B.V.—See Akzo Nobel N.V.; *Int'l*, pg. 45
AKZO PLASTICS DANMARK A/S—See Akzo Nobel N.V.; *Int'l*, pg. 45
AKZO PLASTICS GMBH—See Akzo Nobel N.V.; *Int'l*, pg. 46
AKZO RESINS & VEHICLES—See Akzo Nobel N.V.; *Int'l*, pg. 48
AKZO SALT INC.—See Akzo Nobel N.V.; *Int'l*, pg. 48
AKZO SALT LIMITED—See Akzo Nobel N.V.; *Int'l*, pg. 43

AKZO SALT OF UTAH—See Akzo Nobel N.V.; *Int'l*, pg. 48
AKZO SALT SPA.—See Akzo Nobel N.V.; *Int'l*, pg. 43
AKZO ZOUT CHEMIE B.V.—See Akzo Nobel N.V.; *Int'l*, pg. 43
AKZO ZOUT CHEMIE DEUTSCHLAND GMBH—See Akzo Nobel N.V.; *Int'l*, pg. 43
AKZO ZOUT CHEMIE FRANCE SARL—See Akzo Nobel N.V.; *Int'l*, pg. 44
AKZO ZOUT CHEMIE NEDERLAND B.V.—See Akzo Nobel N.V.; *Int'l*, pg. 43
AKZO ZOUT CHEMIE SVENSKA AB—See Akzo Nobel N.V.; *Int'l*, pg. 44
AL-ABAR AL-THALATH TRADING CO., W.L.L.—See Mitsui & Co., Ltd.; *Int'l*, pg. 880
AL & ED'S AUTO SOUND CENTER; *U.S. Private*, pg. 30
AL-BAB CARE OF DAEWOO—See Daewoo Corporation; *Int'l*, pg. 357
AL-FUTTAIM WILLIS FABER (PRIVATE) LTD.—See Willis Corroon Group PLC; *Int'l*, pg. 1509
AL FUTTAIM-WIMPEY (PTE.) LTD.—See Tarmac plc; *Int'l*, pg. 1355
AL-JUBAIL PETROCHEMICAL COMPANY—See Exxon Corporation; *U.S. Public*, pg. 601
AL-NABOODAH LAING (PRIVATE) LTD.—See John Laing PLC; *Int'l*, pg. 797
AL-OSAMA CO., LTD.—See BASF AG; *Int'l*, pg. 105
AL OTAIBA-COSTAIN COMPANY—See Costain Group PLC; *Int'l*, pg. 337
A.A. AL-QATAMI'S SONS TRADING CO., LTD.—See Nichimen Corporation; *Int'l*, pg. 928
AL RUSHAID EASTMAN ARABIA LIMITED—See Saint-Gobain; *Int'l*, pg. 1174
AL-TECHNIEK BENELUX B.V.—See Axel Johnson AB; *Int'l*, pg. 710
AL WATANIYA—See Groupe GAN; *Int'l*, pg. 564
ALABAMA ELECTRIC COOPERATIVE, INC.; *U.S. Private*, pg. 30
ALABAMA FARMERS CO-OP; *U.S. Private*, pg. 30
ALABAMA FINE WIRE—See Hicks, Muse, Tate & Furst Inc.; *U.S. Private*, pg. 526
ALABAMA GAS CORPORATION—See Energen Corporation; *U.S. Public*, pg. 581
THE ALABAMA GREAT SOUTHERN RAILROAD CO.—See Norfolk Southern Corporation; *U.S. Public*, pg. 1191
ALABAMA METAL INDUSTRIES CORPORATION; *U.S. Private*, pg. 30
ALABAMA OIL COMPANY—See Spencer Companies Inc.; *U.S. Private*, pg. 1025
ALABAMA PINE PULP COMPANY, INC.—See Parsons & Whittemore, Inc.; *U.S. Private*, pg. 841
ALABAMA POWER CO.—See Southern Company; *U.S. Public*, pg. 1489
ALABAMA RENAL STONE INSTITUTE, INC.—See Prime Medical Services, Inc.; *U.S. Public*, pg. 1327
ALABAMA RIVER CHIP MILLS, INC.—See Parsons & Whittemore, Inc.; *U.S. Private*, pg. 841
ALABAMA RIVER CRUDE TALL OIL, INC.—See Parsons & Whittemore, Inc.; *U.S. Private*, pg. 841
ALABAMA RIVER PULP COMPANY, INC.—See Parsons & Whittemore, Inc.; *U.S. Private*, pg. 841
ALABAMA TENNESSEE NATURAL GAS COMPANY—See Midcoast Energy Resources, Inc.; *U.S. Public*, pg. 1109
ALABASTINE HOLLAND BV (MANUFACTURING)—See Williams Holdings Plc; *Int'l*, pg. 1501
ALABASTINE HOLLAND BV (SALES)—See Williams Holdings Plc; *Int'l*, pg. 1499
ALADDIN CANADA, INC.—See Aladdin Industries, Incorporated; *U.S. Private*, pg. 31
ALADDIN HOLDING COMPANY—See Aladdin Industries, Incorporated; *U.S. Private*, pg. 31
ALADDIN HOTEL & CASINO; *U.S. Private*, pg. 30
ALADDIN INDUSTRIES—See Aladdin Industries, Incorporated; *U.S. Private*, pg. 31
ALADDIN INDUSTRIES, INCORPORATED; *U.S. Private*, pg. 30
ALADDIN INDUSTRIES, LTD.—See Aladdin Industries, Incorporated; *U.S. Private*, pg. 31
ALADDIN INDUSTRIES PTY. LTD.—See Aladdin Industries, Incorporated; *U.S. Private*, pg. 31
ALADDIN MILLS—See Mohawk Industries, Inc.; *U.S. Public*, pg. 1121
ALADDIN PAPERBACKS—See National Amusements, Inc.; *U.S. Private*, pg. 777
ALADDIN SYNERGETICS, INC.—See Aladdin Industries, Incorporated; *U.S. Private*, pg. 31
ALAHAMRANI-FUCHS PETROLEUM PRODUCTS CO. LTD.—See Fuchs Petrolub AG Oel + Chemie; *Int'l*, pg. 518
ALAMAG PROCESSING CORPORATION—See Bayer AG; *Int'l*, pg. 174
ALAMBRADOS AUTOMOTRICES, S.A. DE C.V.—See General Motors Corporation; *U.S. Public*, pg. 721
ALAMBRADOS Y CIRCUITOS ELECTRICOS, S.A. DE C.V.—See General Motors Corporation; *U.S. Public*, pg. 721
ALAMCO-DELAWARE, INC.—See Columbia Energy Group; *U.S. Public*, pg. 403
ALAMCO, INC.—See Columbia Energy Group; *U.S. Public*, pg. 403
ALAMO FOREST PRODUCTS, INC.—See Vaughan & Sons, Inc.; *U.S. Private*, pg. 1135
ALAMO GROUP, INC.; *U.S. Public*, pg. 34
ALAMO INDUSTRIAL GROUP; *U.S. Private*, pg. 31
ALAMO IRON WORKS—See Alamo Industrial Group; *U.S. Private*, pg. 31
ALAMO LUMBER COMPANY—See Vaughan & Sons, Inc.; *U.S. Private*, pg. 1135
ALAMO RENT-A-CAR INC.—See Republic Industries, Inc.; *U.S. Public*, pg. 1379
ALAMO STEEL COMPANY—See Commercial Metals Company; *U.S. Public*, pg. 412
ALAN LITHOGRAPH, INC.; *U.S. Private*, pg. 31
ALANDCO INC.—See FPL Group, Inc.; *U.S. Public*, pg. 608

ALANEX CORPORATION—See Agouron Pharmaceuticals, Inc.; *U.S. Public*, pg. 28
ALANTEC CORP.—See FORE Systems, Inc.; *U.S. Public*, pg. 667
ALARIS MEDICAL, INC.; *U.S. Public*, pg. 35
ALARIS MEDICAL SYSTEMS, INC.—See ALARIS Medical, Inc.; *U.S. Public*, pg. 35
ALARM DEVICE MANUFACTURING COMPANY—See Pittway Corporation; *U.S. Public*, pg. 1306
ALARMCOM AB—See Siemens AG; *Int'l*, pg. 1246
ALARMCOM AG—See Siemens AG; *Int'l*, pg. 1246
ALARMCOM AS—See Siemens AG; *Int'l*, pg. 1246
ALARMCOM GMBH—See Siemens AG; *Int'l*, pg. 1246
ALARMCOM LEUTRON GMBH—See Siemens AG; *Int'l*, pg. 1246
ALARMCOM LOUTRON GMBH—See Siemens AG; *Int'l*, pg. 1246
ALARMCOM LTD.—See Siemens AG; *Int'l*, pg. 1246
ALARMCOM N.V.—See Siemens AG; *Int'l*, pg. 1246
ALARMCOM SECURITY PTY. LTD.—See Siemens AG; *Int'l*, pg. 1246
ALARMCOM SEGURIDAD S.L.—See Siemens AG; *Int'l*, pg. 1246
ALARMCOM S.P.A.—See Siemens AG; *Int'l*, pg. 1246
ALARMCOM S.R.O.—See Siemens AG; *Int'l*, pg. 1246
ALARMGUARD HOLDINGS, INC.; *U.S. Public*, pg. 35
ALARMNET/RADSCAN—See Pittway Corporation; *U.S. Public*, pg. 1306
ALARON ASIA LTD.—See Alaron Inc.; *U.S. Private*, pg. 31
ALARON INC.; *U.S. Private*, pg. 31
ALASKA AIR GROUP, INC.; *U.S. Public*, pg. 35
ALASKA AIRLINES, INC.—See Alaska Air Group, Inc.; *U.S. Public*, pg. 35
ALASKA BOAT CO.—See Wards Cove Packing Company; *U.S. Private*, pg. 1150
ALASKA INDUSTRIAL HARDWARE INC.; *U.S. Private*, pg. 31
ALASKA LUBE AND FUEL—See Arctic Slope Regional Corporation; *U.S. Private*, pg. 80
ALASKA MARINE LINES, INC.—See Lynden Incorporated; *U.S. Private*, pg. 683
ALASKA PACIFIC ASSURANCE COMPANY—See Cigna Corp.; *U.S. Public*, pg. 366
ALASKA PETROLEUM CONTRACTORS—See Arctic Slope Regional Corporation; *U.S. Private*, pg. 80
ALASKA PIPELINE CO.—See Seagull Energy Corporation; *U.S. Public*, pg. 1450
ALASKA REFINERY—See Mapco Inc.; *U.S. Public*, pg. 1042
ALASKA TOOL & EQUIPMENT SERVICE—See Alaska Industrial Hardware Inc.; *U.S. Private*, pg. 31
ALASKA-WEST EXPRESS, INC.—See Lynden Incorporated; *U.S. Private*, pg. 683
ALASKAN COPPER COMPANIES; *U.S. Private*, pg. 31
ALASKAN COPPER WORKS—See Alaskan Copper Companies; *U.S. Private*, pg. 31
ALATEC PRODUCTS, INC.; *U.S. Private*, pg. 31
S.A. ALAVESA DE PRODUCTOS QUIMICOS BAYQUISA—See Bayer AG; *Int'l*, pg. 174
ALBA AMAZONIA S.A. INDUSTRIAS QUIMICAS—See Borden, Inc.; *U.S. Private*, pg. 158
ALBA FORWARDING CO., INC.; *U.S. Private*, pg. 32
ALBA MODA GMBH—See Otto Versand (GmbH & Co.); *Int'l*, pg. 1014
ALBA NORDESTE SA INDUSTRIES QUIMICAS—See Borden, Inc.; *U.S. Private*, pg. 158
ALBA QUIMICA S.A. INDUSTRIA E COMMERCIO—See Borden, Inc.; *U.S. Private*, pg. 158
ALBA-WALDENSIAN EXPORT CORP.—See Alba-Waldensian, Inc.; *U.S. Public*, pg. 36
ALBA-WALDENSIAN, INC.; *U.S. Public*, pg. 35
ALBACOM SPA—See British Telecommunications plc; *Int'l*, pg. 223
ALBACORA FIELD DEVELOPMENT—See Petrobras - Petroleo Brasileiro S.A.; *Int'l*, pg. 1041
ALBADORO S.P.A.—See Borden, Inc.; *U.S. Private*, pg. 158
ALBAN TRACTOR CO. INC.; *U.S. Private*, pg. 32
ALBANK B.V.—See ABN-AMRO Holding N.V.; *Int'l*, pg. 9
ALBANK FINANCIAL CORPORATION; *U.S. Public*, pg. 36
ALBANY DEMOCRAT-HERALD—See Lee Enterprises, Incorporated; *U.S. Public*, pg. 983
ALBANY ENGINEERED SYSTEMS-CANADA—See Thermo Electron Corporation; *U.S. Public*, pg. 1593
ALBANY GLASS—See BTR plc; *Int'l*, pg. 129
THE ALBANY HERALD PUBLISHING CO., INC.—See Gray Communications Systems, Inc.; *U.S. Public*, pg. 759
ALBANY INTERNATIONAL CORP.; *U.S. Public*, pg. 36
ALBANY INTERNATIONAL B.V.—See Albany International Corp.; *U.S. Public*, pg. 37
ALBANY INTERNATIONAL CANADA, INC.—See Albany International Corp.; *U.S. Public*, pg. 37
ALBANY INTERNATIONAL CANADA-PERTH—See Albany International Corp.; *U.S. Public*, pg. 37
ALBANY INTERNATIONAL FELTROS E TELAS INDUSTRIAS LTDA.—See Albany International Corp.; *U.S. Public*, pg. 37
ALBANY INTERNATIONAL GMBH—See Albany International Corp.; *U.S. Public*, pg. 37
ALBANY INTERNATIONAL/INDUSTRIAL ENG PROCESS FABRICS DIVISION—See Albany International Corp.; *U.S. Public*, pg. 36
ALBANY INTERNATIONAL LTD.—See Albany International Corp.; *U.S. Public*, pg. 37
ALBANY INTERNATIONAL PTY., LTD.—See Albany International Corp.; *U.S. Public*, pg. 37
ALBANY INTERNATIONAL RESEARCH CO.—See Albany International Corp.; *U.S. Public*, pg. 36
ALBANY INTERNATIONAL S.A.—See Albany International Corp.; *U.S. Public*, pg. 37
ALBANY INTERNATIONAL S.A. DE C.V.—See Albany International Corp.; *U.S. Public*, pg. 37
ALBANY LIFE ASSURANCE COMPANY LIMITED—See The Canada Life Assurance Company; *Int'l*, pg. 255

ALBANY PORT RAILROAD CO.—See Conrail, Inc.; *U.S. Public*, pg. 432
ALBANY SAVINGS BANK—See Albank Financial Corporation; *U.S. Public*, pg. 36
ALBANY TIMES UNION—See The Hearst Corporation; *U.S. Private*, pg. 517
ALBEMARLE CORPORATION; *U.S. Public*, pg. 37
ALBER ENGINEERING, INC.—See BTR plc; *Int'l*, pg. 126
ALBERGHIERA FIESOLANA S.R.L.—See Sea Containers Ltd.; *Int'l*, pg. 1213
J.S. ALBERICI CONSTRUCTION CO., INC.; *U.S. Private*, pg. 32
ALBEROX CORPORATION—See Morgan Crucible Co. Plc; *Int'l*, pg. 893
MIKE ALBERT LEASING, INC.; *U.S. Private*, pg. 32
R.L. ALBERT & SON, INC.; *U.S. Private*, pg. 32
ALBERTA ENERGY COMPANY, LTD.; *Int'l*, pg. 48
ALBERTA ENVIROFUELS INC.—See Neste Oy; *Int'l*, pg. 914
ALBERTA NATURAL GAS COMPANY LTD.—See Transcanada Pipelines Limited; *Int'l*, pg. 1417
ALBERTA OIL SANDS PIPELINE LTD.—See Alberta Energy Company, Ltd.; *Int'l*, pg. 48
ALBERTA OIL TOOL DIV.—See Dover Corporation; *U.S. Public*, pg. 522
ALBERTA POWER LIMITED—See ATCO Group Co.; *Int'l*, pg. 95
ALBERTO-CULVER COMPANY; *U.S. Public*, pg. 37
ALBERTSON'S, INC.; *U.S. Public*, pg. 38
ALBI MANUFACTURING DIVISION—See Stanchem Inc.; *U.S. Private*, pg. 1030
THE ALBIA DIVISION—See Chicago Rivet & Machine Company; *U.S. Public*, pg. 350
ALBIN KOMPONENTER AB—See Svedala Industri AB; *Int'l*, pg. 1323
ALBIN KOMPONENTER AB—See Trelleborg AB; *Int'l*, pg. 1419
ALBION WIRE, INC.—See Hicks, Muse, Tate & Furst Inc.; *U.S. Private*, pg. 526
ALBION WIRE INC., KENDALLVILLE WIRE DIVISION—See Hicks, Muse, Tate & Furst Inc.; *U.S. Private*, pg. 526
ALBRECHT/BUEHLER COMMUNICATIONS DIV.—See Emerson Electric Co.; *U.S. Public*, pg. 574
THE FRED W. ALBRECHT GROCERY CO.; *U.S. Private*, pg. 32
ALBRECHT INC.—See The Fred W. Albrecht Grocery Co.; *U.S. Private*, pg. 32
ALBRECHT KNAUS VERLAG—See Bertelsmann AG; *Int'l*, pg. 190
ALBRIGHT & WILSON AB—See Albright & Wilson plc; *Int'l*, pg. 49
ALBRIGHT & WILSON AMERICAS INC.—See Albright & Wilson plc; *Int'l*, pg. 49
ALBRIGHT & WILSON AMERICAS LIMITED—See Albright & Wilson plc; *Int'l*, pg. 49
ALBRIGHT & WILSON AMERIQUE LIMITEE—See Albright & Wilson plc; *Int'l*, pg. 49
ALBRIGHT & WILSON A/S—See Albright & Wilson plc; *Int'l*, pg. 49
ALBRIGHT & WILSON ASIA (HK) LTD.—See Albright & Wilson plc; *Int'l*, pg. 49
ALBRIGHT & WILSON (AUSTRALIA) LIMITED—See Albright & Wilson plc; *Int'l*, pg. 49
ALBRIGHT & WILSON (AUSTRALIA) LTD.—See Albright & Wilson plc; *Int'l*, pg. 49
ALBRIGHT & WILSON B.V.—See Albright & Wilson plc; *Int'l*, pg. 49
ALBRIGHT & WILSON CASTIGLIONE SRL—See Albright & Wilson plc; *Int'l*, pg. 49
ALBRIGHT & WILSON COMPANY—See Albright & Wilson plc; *Int'l*, pg. 49
ALBRIGHT & WILSON DENMARK AS—See Albright & Wilson plc; *Int'l*, pg. 49
ALBRIGHT & WILSON ESPANA S.A.—See Albright & Wilson plc; *Int'l*, pg. 49
ALBRIGHT & WILSON GMBH (AUSTRIA)—See Albright & Wilson plc; *Int'l*, pg. 49
ALBRIGHT & WILSON GMBH (GERMANY)—See Albright & Wilson plc; *Int'l*, pg. 49
ALBRIGHT & WILSON IBERICA S.A.—See Albright & Wilson plc; *Int'l*, pg. 49
ALBRIGHT & WILSON, INC.—See Albright & Wilson plc; *Int'l*, pg. 49
ALBRIGHT & WILSON INTERTRADE LTD.—See Albright & Wilson plc; *Int'l*, pg. 49
ALBRIGHT & WILSON IRELAND, LTD.—See Albright & Wilson plc; *Int'l*, pg. 49
ALBRIGHT & WILSON LAVERA—See Albright & Wilson plc; *Int'l*, pg. 49
ALBRIGHT & WILSON LIMITED, JAPAN BRANCH—See Albright & Wilson plc; *Int'l*, pg. 49
ALBRIGHT & WILSON (MALAYSIA) SDN. BHD.—See Albright & Wilson plc; *Int'l*, pg. 49
ALBRIGHT & WILSON (MARCHON) PTE. LIMITED—See Albright & Wilson plc; *Int'l*, pg. 49
ALBRIGHT & WILSON NORTHERN IRELAND, LTD.—See Albright & Wilson plc; *Int'l*, pg. 49
ALBRIGHT & WILSON PATRICIA SRL—See Albright & Wilson plc; *Int'l*, pg. 49
ALBRIGHT & WILSON PLC; *Int'l*, pg. 49
ALBRIGHT & WILSON SAINT MIHIEL S.A.—See Albright & Wilson plc; *Int'l*, pg. 50
ALBRIGHT & WILSON SPECIALTIES P/L—See Albright & Wilson plc; *Int'l*, pg. 49
ALBRIGHT & WILSON TROY DE MEXICO, S.A. DE C.V.—See Albright & Wilson plc; *Int'l*, pg. 50
ALBRIGHT & WILSON UK LIMITED—See Albright & Wilson plc; *Int'l*, pg. 49
ALBRIGHT, MORAJI & PANDIT LTD.—See Albright & Wilson plc; *Int'l*, pg. 49
ALBRO BAKKERIJEN ZWANENBURG B.V.—See Goodman Fielder Limited; *Int'l*, pg. 555
ALBULA VERWALTUNGS-UND BETEILIGUNGS-AG—See Assicurazioni Generali S.p.A.; *Int'l*, pg. 90

ALBUM—See LVMH Moet Hennessy Louis Vuitton; *Int'l,* pg. 779
ALBUQUERQUE AUTO AUCTION INC.—See Tyco International Ltd.; *U.S. Public,* pg. 1648
ALBUQUERQUE CAPITAL MANAGEMENT, INC.—See The Chase Manhattan Corporation; *U.S. Public,* pg. 337
THE ALBUQUERQUE TRIBUNE—See The E.W. Scripps Company; *U.S. Public,* pg. 1447
ALBUS LEASOBJEKT GMBH—See Commerzbank AG; *Int'l,* pg. 310
ALCAIDESA COSTAIN DEVELOPMENTS S.A.—See Costain Group PLC; *Int'l,* pg. 337
ALCAMP, S.R.L.—See Eclipse Inc.; *U.S. Private,* pg. 360
ALCAN ALLUMINIO S.P.A.—See Alcan Aluminium Limited; *Int'l,* pg. 50
ALCAN ALUMINIO DEL URUGUAY S.A.—See Alcan Aluminium Limited; *Int'l,* pg. 50
ALCAN ALUMINIO DO BRASIL S.A.—See Alcan Aluminium Limited; *Int'l,* pg. 50
ALCAN ALUMINIUM FOLIENWERK VERWALTUNGS GMBH—See Alcan Aluminium Limited; *Int'l,* pg. 50
ALCAN ALUMINIUM LIMITED; *Int'l,* pg. 50
ALCAN ALUMINIUM S.A.—See Alcan Aluminium Limited; *Int'l,* pg. 50
ALCAN ALUMINIUMFOLIENWERK GMBH & CO.—See Alcan Aluminium Limited; *Int'l,* pg. 50
ALCAN ALUMINUM CORPORATION—See Alcan Aluminium Limited; *Int'l,* pg. 50
ALCAN (BERMUDA) LTD.—See Alcan Aluminium Limited; *Int'l,* pg. 50
ALCAN CABLE DIVISION—See Alcan Aluminium Limited; *Int'l,* pg. 50
ALCAN CANADA PRODUCTS, LTD.—See Alcan Aluminium Limited; *Int'l,* pg. 50
ALCAN CHEMICALS EUROPE—See Alcan Aluminium Limited; *Int'l,* pg. 51
ALCAN CONSUMER PRODUCTS—See Alcan Aluminium Limited; *Int'l,* pg. 51
ALCAN DEUTSCHLAND GMBH—See Alcan Aluminium Limited; *Int'l,* pg. 50
ALCAN EKCO—See Alcan Aluminium Limited; *Int'l,* pg. 51
ALCAN EMPREENDIMENTOS LTDA.—See Alcan Aluminium Limited; *Int'l,* pg. 50
ALCAN ENFIELD ALLOYS LTD.—See Delta plc; *Int'l,* pg. 391
ALCAN FINANCES (BERMUDA) LTD.—See Alcan Aluminium Limited; *Int'l,* pg. 51
ALCAN FINANCES B.V.—See Alcan Aluminium Limited; *Int'l,* pg. 51
ALCAN FRANCE—See Alcan Aluminium Limited; *Int'l,* pg. 51
ALCAN INTERNATIONAL LIMITED—See Alcan Aluminium Limited; *Int'l,* pg. 50
ALCAN IRELAND LTD.—See Alcan Aluminium Limited; *Int'l,* pg. 51
ALCAN JAMAICA CO.—See Alcan Aluminium Limited; *Int'l,* pg. 51
ALCAN METAL CENTRES—See Alcan Aluminium Limited; *Int'l,* pg. 51
ALCAN POWDERS & PIGMENTS DIVISION—See Alcan Aluminium Limited; *Int'l,* pg. 50
ALCAN PRICE EXTRUSIONS LTD.—See Alcan Aluminium Limited; *Int'l,* pg. 50
ALCAN RECYCLING—See Alcan Aluminium Limited; *Int'l,* pg. 50
ALCAN ROLLED PRODUCTS COMPANY—See Alcan Aluminium Limited; *Int'l,* pg. 50
ALCAN ROLLED PRODUCTS DIVISION—See Alcan Aluminium Limited; *Int'l,* pg. 50
ALCAN ROLLED PRODUCTS RECYCLING—See Alcan Aluminium Limited; *Int'l,* pg. 50
ALCAN RORSCHACH AG—See Alcan Aluminium Limited; *Int'l,* pg. 51
ALCAN SIAM LIMITED—See Alcan Aluminium Limited; *Int'l,* pg. 51
ALCAN SMELTERS & CHEMICALS LTD.—See Alcan Aluminium Limited; *Int'l,* pg. 50
ALCAN SOUTH PACIFIC LTD.—See Alcan Aluminium Limited; *Int'l,* pg. 51
ALCAN SPECIALTY AEROSPACE—See Alcan Aluminium Limited; *Int'l,* pg. 51
ALCAN SPECIALTY EXTRUSIONS—See Alcan Aluminium Limited; *Int'l,* pg. 51
ALCAN TRADING (BERMUDA) LIMITED—See Alcan Aluminium Limited; *Int'l,* pg. 51
ALCAN TUBES—See Alcan Aluminium Limited; *Int'l,* pg. 51
ALCAN WIRE—See Alcan Aluminium Limited; *Int'l,* pg. 51
ALCANTARA—See Tate & Lyle PLC; *Int'l,* pg. 1357
ALCATEL—See Alcatel Alsthom Compagnie Generale D'Electricite; *Int'l,* pg. 52
ALCATEL ALSTHOM COMPAGNIE GENERALE D'ELECTRICITE; *Int'l,* pg. 52
ALCATEL ATFH—See Alcatel Alsthom Compagnie Generale D'Electricite; *Int'l,* pg. 55
ALCATEL AUSTRIA A.G.—See Alcatel Alsthom Compagnie Generale D'Electricite; *Int'l,* pg. 55
ALCATEL BELL TELEPHONE—See Alcatel Alsthom Compagnie Generale D'Electricite; *Int'l,* pg. 55
ALCATEL BUSINESS SYSTEMS (FRANCE)—See Alcatel Alsthom Compagnie Generale D'Electricite; *Int'l,* pg. 55
ALCATEL BUSINESS SYSTEMS UK—See Alcatel Alsthom Compagnie Generale D'Electricite; *Int'l,* pg. 55
ALCATEL CABLE SYSTEMS GROUP—See Alcatel Alsthom Compagnie Generale D'Electricite; *Int'l,* pg. 55
ALCATEL CAVI, S.P.A.—See Alcatel Alsthom Compagnie Generale D'Electricite; *Int'l,* pg. 55
ALCATEL CIT—See Alcatel Alsthom Compagnie Generale D'Electricite; *Int'l,* pg. 55
ALCATEL CIT (S.A.); *Int'l,* pg. 56
ALCATEL ESPACE—See Alcatel Cit (S.A.); *Int'l,* pg. 56
ALCATEL FACE—See Alcatel Alsthom Compagnie Generale D'Electricite; *Int'l,* pg. 55
ALCATEL FRANCE—See Alcatel Alsthom Compagnie Generale D'Electricite; *Int'l,* pg. 55

ALCATEL INDETEL—See Alcatel Alsthom Compagnie Generale D'Electricite; *Int'l,* pg. 56
ALCATEL ISR—See Alcatel Alsthom Compagnie Generale D'Electricite; *Int'l,* pg. 56
ALCATEL ITS INC.—See Alcatel Alsthom Compagnie Generale D'Electricite; *Int'l,* pg. 55
ALCATEL KIRK—See Alcatel Alsthom Compagnie Generale D'Electricite; *Int'l,* pg. 56
ALCATEL N.A. INC.—See Alcatel Alsthom Compagnie Generale D'Electricite; *Int'l,* pg. 55
ALCATEL NETHERLAND—See Alcatel Alsthom Compagnie Generale D'Electricite; *Int'l,* pg. 55
ALCATEL NETWORK SYSTEM, INC.—See Alcatel Alsthom Compagnie Generale D'Electricite; *Int'l,* pg. 55
ALCATEL NETWORK SYSTEMS, INC. (TX)—See Alcatel Alsthom Compagnie Generale D'Electricite; *Int'l,* pg. 55
ALCATEL N.V.—See Alcatel Alsthom Compagnie Generale D'Electricite; *Int'l,* pg. 55
ALCATEL PORTUGAL—See Alcatel Alsthom Compagnie Generale D'Electricite; *Int'l,* pg. 56
ALCATEL SEL—See Alcatel Alsthom Compagnie Generale D'Electricite; *Int'l,* pg. 56
ALCATEL SEP—See Alcatel Alsthom Compagnie Generale D'Electricite; *Int'l,* pg. 56
ALCATEL STANDARD ELECTRICA, S.A—See Alcatel Alsthom Compagnie Generale D'Electricite; *Int'l,* pg. 56
ALCATEL STANDARD ELECTRICA, S.A.—See Telefonica de Espana, S.A.; *Int'l,* pg. 1372
ALCATEL STC AUSTRALIA—See Alcatel Alsthom Compagnie Generale D'Electricite; *Int'l,* pg. 56
ALCATEL SUBMARINE NETWORKS S.A.—See Alcatel Alsthom Compagnie Generale D'Electricite; *Int'l,* pg. 52
ALCATEL TELECOM—See Alcatel Alsthom Compagnie Generale D'Electricite; *Int'l,* pg. 56
ALCATEL TELSPACE—See Alcatel Cit (S.A.); *Int'l,* pg. 56
ALCATEL TRANSCOM—See Alcatel Alsthom Compagnie Generale D'Electricite; *Int'l,* pg. 55
ALCATEL USA CORP—See Alcatel Alsthom Compagnie Generale D'Electricite; *Int'l,* pg. 55
ALCELL TECHNOLOGIES INC.—See Repap Enterprises Inc.; *Int'l,* pg. 1104
ALCHEM PLASTICS CORP.-INDIANA—See Spartech Corporation; *U.S. Public,* pg. 1495
ALCHEM PLASTICS CORP.-MICHIGAN—See Spartech Corporation; *U.S. Public,* pg. 1495
ALCHEM PLASTICS INC.-CALIFORNIA—See Spartech Corporation; *U.S. Public,* pg. 1495
ALCO CHEMICAL—See Unilever Plc; *Int'l,* pg. 1435
ALCO CONTROLS DIV.—See Emerson Electric Co.; *U.S. Public,* pg. 572
ALCO GRAVURE INDUSTRIES, INC.—See Quebecor Inc.; *Int'l,* pg. 1076
ALCO INDUSTRIES, INC.; *U.S. Private,* pg. 32
ALCOA ALUMINIO S.A.—See Aluminum Company of America; *U.S. Public,* pg. 61
ALCOA BUILDING PRODUCTS, INC.—See Aluminum Company of America; *U.S. Public,* pg. 61
ALCOA CHEMIE GMBH—See Aluminum Company of America; *U.S. Public,* pg. 61
ALCOA CHEMIE NEDERLAND B.V.—See Aluminum Company of America; *U.S. Public,* pg. 61
ALCOA CLOSURE SYSTEMS, INTERNATIONAL—See Aluminum Company of America; *U.S. Public,* pg. 60
ALCOA COMPOSITES, INC.—See Aluminum Company of America; *U.S. Public,* pg. 60
ALCOA DEUTSCHLAND GMBH—See Aluminum Company of America; *U.S. Public,* pg. 61
ALCOA DEUTSCHLAND GMBH-WORMS—See Aluminum Company of America; *U.S. Public,* pg. 61
ALCOA ELECTRONIC PACKAGING, INC.—See Aluminum Company of America; *U.S. Public,* pg. 60
ALCOA EUROPE LIMITED—See Aluminum Company of America; *U.S. Public,* pg. 62
ALCOA EXTRUDED PRODUCTS (UK) LTD.—See Aluminum Company of America; *U.S. Public,* pg. 62
ALCOA FORGED PRODUCTS—See Aluminum Company of America; *U.S. Public,* pg. 62
ALCOA FUJIKURA—See Aluminum Company of America; *U.S. Public,* pg. 60
ALCOA FUJIKURA GMBH—See Aluminum Company of America; *U.S. Public,* pg. 62
ALCOA FUJIKURA LTD.—See Aluminum Company of America; *U.S. Public,* pg. 60
ALCOA FUJIKURA LTD.—See Fujikura Ltd.; *Int'l,* pg. 525
ALCOA INTER-AMERICA CANADA LTD.—See Aluminum Company of America; *U.S. Public,* pg. 62
ALCOA INTER-AMERICA, INC.—See Aluminum Company of America; *U.S. Public,* pg. 60
ALCOA INTERNATIONAL FINANCE COMPANY—See Aluminum Company of America; *U.S. Public,* pg. 60
ALCOA INTERNATIONAL HOLDINGS CORP.—See Aluminum Company of America; *U.S. Public,* pg. 60
ALCOA ITALIA S.P.A.—See Aluminum Company of America; *U.S. Public,* pg. 62
ALCOA JAPAN LIMITED—See Aluminum Company of America; *U.S. Public,* pg. 62
ALCOA MANUFACTURING (G.B.) LTD.—See Aluminum Company of America; *U.S. Public,* pg. 62
ALCOA MINERACAO S.A.—See Aluminum Company of America; *U.S. Public,* pg. 62
ALCOA MINERALS OF JAMAICA, INC.—See Aluminum Company of America; *U.S. Public,* pg. 62
ALCOA NEDERLAND HOLDING B. V.—See Aluminum Company of America; *U.S. Public,* pg. 62
ALCOA OF AUSTRALIA LIMITED—See Aluminum Company of America; *U.S. Public,* pg. 62
ALCOA PACKAGING MACHINERY, INC.—See Aluminum Company of America; *U.S. Public,* pg. 60
ALCOA PROPERTIES, INC.—See Aluminum Company of America; *U.S. Public,* pg. 61
ALCOA PROPPANTS, INC.—See Aluminum Company of America; *U.S. Public,* pg. 61
ALCOA RECYCLING CO.—See Aluminum Company of America; *U.S. Public,* pg. 61

ALCOA S.A.—See Aluminum Company of America; *U.S. Public,* pg. 62
ALCOA SECURITIES CORPORATION—See Aluminum Company of America; *U.S. Public,* pg. 61
ALCOA SOUTH CAROLINA, INC.—See Aluminum Company of America; *U.S. Public,* pg. 61
ALCOA STEAMSHIP CO., INC.—See Aluminum Company of America; *U.S. Public,* pg. 61
ALCOHOLES Y VINOS, S.A.—See Suntory Ltd.; *Int'l,* pg. 1322
ALCOLAC LTD.—See Rhone-Poulenc S.A.; *Int'l,* pg. 1113
ALCOM PRINTING GROUP, INC.; *U.S. Private,* pg. 33
ALCON CANADA, INC.—See Nestle S.A.; *Int'l,* pg. 918
ALCON-COUVREUR N.V.—See Nestle S.A.; *Int'l,* pg. 918
ALCON EYE CARE, INC.—See Nestle S.A.; *Int'l,* pg. 916
ALCON IBERHIS S.A.—See Nestle S.A.; *Int'l,* pg. 918
ALCON ITALIA S.P.A.—See Nestle S.A.; *Int'l,* pg. 918
ALCON JAPAN LTD.—See Nestle S.A.; *Int'l,* pg. 918
ALCON LABORATORIES ARGENTINA S.A.—See Nestle S.A.; *Int'l,* pg. 918
ALCON LABORATORIES (AUSTRALIA) PTY. LTD.—See Nestle S.A.; *Int'l,* pg. 918
ALCON LABORATORIES HELLAS E.P.E.—See Nestle S.A.; *Int'l,* pg. 918
ALCON LABORATORIES, INC.—See Nestle S.A.; *Int'l,* pg. 916
ALCON LABORATORIES (UK) LTD.—See Nestle S.A.; *Int'l,* pg. 918
ALCON LABORATORIOS DO BRASIL S.A.—See Nestle S.A.; *Int'l,* pg. 918
ALCON LABORATORIOS S.A. DE C.V.—See Nestle S.A.; *Int'l,* pg. 918
ALCON PHARMA GMBH—See Nestle S.A.; *Int'l,* pg. 918
ALCON PHARMA, INC.—See Nestle S.A.; *Int'l,* pg. 916
ALCON PHARMACEUTICALS LTD.—See Nestle S.A.; *Int'l,* pg. 916
ALCON (PUERTO RICO) INC.—See Nestle S.A.; *Int'l,* pg. 916
ALCON SURGICAL—See Nestle S.A.; *Int'l,* pg. 916
ALCON SYSTEMS, INC.—See Nestle S.A.; *Int'l,* pg. 916
ALCONE MARKETING GROUP—See Omnicom Group Inc.; *U.S. Public,* pg. 1223
ALCONOR S.A.—See Aluminum Company of America; *U.S. Public,* pg. 62
ALCOR ENVELOPE CO.—See Union Camp Corporation; *U.S. Public,* pg. 1666
ALCOSA/SUNWISE—See Hanover Foods Corporation; *U.S. Private,* pg. 499
ALDAN INDUSTRIES; *U.S. Private,* pg. 33
ALDEN AUTO PARTS WAREHOUSE, INC.; *U.S. Private,* pg. 33
ALDEN ELECTRONICS, INC.—See Platinum Equity Holdings, LLC; *U.S. Private,* pg. 872
JOHN ALDEN FINANCIAL CORPORATION; *U.S. Public,* pg. 39
JOHN ALDEN LIFE INSURANCE COMPANY—See John Alden Financial Corporation; *U.S. Public,* pg. 39
ALDEN PRESS—See World Color Press, Inc.; *U.S. Public,* pg. 1778
ALDEN SHOE CO., INC.; *U.S. Private,* pg. 33
ALDI FOOD INC.; *U.S. Private,* pg. 33
ALDINE TECHNOLOGIES INDUSTRIES INC.; *U.S. Private,* pg. 33
BV ALDIPRESS—See VNU Verenigde Nederlandse Uitgeversbedrijven B.V.; *Int'l,* pg. 1445
ALDRICH CHEMICAL CO., INC.—See Sigma-Aldrich Corporation; *U.S. Public,* pg. 1471
ALDRICH CHEMICAL CO., LTD.—See Sigma-Aldrich Corporation; *U.S. Public,* pg. 1472
ALDRICH CHEMIE GMBH & CO. K.G.—See Sigma-Aldrich Corporation; *U.S. Public,* pg. 1472
ALEMITE CORPORATION—See BTR plc; *Int'l,* pg. 127
ALEMITE GMBH—See BTR plc; *Int'l,* pg. 127
ALENCO, INC.—See Alberta Energy Company, Ltd.; *Int'l,* pg. 48
ALENIA—See IRI Istituto Ricostruzione Industriale; *Int'l,* pg. 653
ALENIA AERONAUTICA—See IRI Istituto Ricostruzione Industriale; *Int'l,* pg. 653
ALENIA SISTEMI CIVILI—See IRI Istituto Ricostruzione Industriale; *Int'l,* pg. 653
ALENIA S.P.A.—See IRI Istituto Ricostruzione Industriale; *Int'l,* pg. 653
ALENIA SPAZIO—See IRI Istituto Ricostruzione Industriale; *Int'l,* pg. 653
ALENIA SYSTEMI DIFESA—See IRI Istituto Ricostruzione Industriale; *Int'l,* pg. 653
ALENITE L.P.; *U.S. Private,* pg. 33
ALERGIA E INMUNOLOGIA ABELLO S.A.—See Chr. Hansen Holding A/S; *Int'l,* pg. 288
ALESA ALUSUISSE ENGINEERING CANADA LTD.—See Alusuisse-Lonza Holding Ltd.; *Int'l,* pg. 68
ALESA ALUSUISSE ENGINEERING LTD.-(ALESA)—See Alusuisse-Lonza Holding Ltd.; *Int'l,* pg. 67
ALETSCH AG—See Alusuisse-Lonza Holding Ltd.; *Int'l,* pg. 67
ALEWIFE BOSTON LTD.—See W.R. Grace & Co.; *U.S. Public,* pg. 755
ALEX FRIES—See Land O'Lakes, Inc.; *U.S. Private,* pg. 646
ALEXANDER & ALEXANDER AUSTRALIA HOLDINGS LTD.—See AON Corporation; *U.S. Public,* pg. 117
ALEXANDER & ALEXANDER HOLDINGS NZ LIMITED—See AON Corporation; *U.S. Public,* pg. 117
ALEXANDER & ALEXANDER (HONG KONG) HOLDINGS LTD.—See AON Corporation; *U.S. Public,* pg. 117
ALEXANDER & ALEXANDER INC.—See AON Corporation; *U.S. Public,* pg. 117
ALEXANDER & ALEXANDER SERVICES INC.—See AON Corporation; *U.S. Public,* pg. 117
ALEXANDER & ALEXANDER SERVICES (UK) PLC—See AON Corporation; *U.S. Public,* pg. 118
ALEXANDER & BALDWIN, INC.; *U.S. Public,* pg. 39

MASTER INDEX TO COMPANY NAMES ALL-AMERICAN

Company Index

THE ALEXANDER CONSULTING GROUP INC.—See AON Corporation; *U.S. Public*, pg. 117
ALEXANDER DOLL COMPANY, INC.; *U.S. Private*, pg. 33
ALEXANDER SCHNEIDER LTD.—See Knurr AG; *Int'l*, pg. 739
ALEXANDER'S, INC.—See Vornado Realty Trust; *U.S. Public*, pg. 1725
J. ALEXANDERS CORPORATION; *U.S. Public*, pg. 40
ALEXANDRIA AUTOMOTIVE COMPANY SAE—See Ford Motor Company; *U.S. Public*, pg. 665
ALEXANDRIA DAILY TOWN TALK—See Central Newspapers, Inc.; *U.S. Public*, pg. 326
ALEXANDRIA SALES—See Fairfield Communities, Inc.; *U.S. Public*, pg. 611
ALFA-BETA VASSILOPOULOS S.A.—See Etablissements Delhaize Freres Et Cie "Le Lion" S.A.; *Int'l*, pg. 463
ALFA-CERCAST MICROFUSION DE ALUMINIO S.A.—See Pechiney S.A.; *Int'l*, pg. 1030
ALFA CORPORATION; *U.S. Public*, pg. 40
ALFA FINANCIAL CORPORATION—See Alfa Corporation; *U.S. Public*, pg. 40
ALFA GENERAL INSURANCE CORP.—See Alfa Corporation; *U.S. Public*, pg. 40
ALFA INSURANCE CORP.—See Alfa Corporation; *U.S. Public*, pg. 40
ALFA INVESTMENT CORP. & BUILDERS INC.—See Alfa Corporation; *U.S. Public*, pg. 40
ALFA LANCIA INDUSTRIALE S.P.A.—See Fiat Auto SpA; *Int'l*, pg. 481
ALFA LAVAL AB—See Tetra Laval Group; *Int'l*, pg. 1378
ALFA-LAVAL AB ATHENS—See Tetra Laval Group; *Int'l*, pg. 1380
ALFA-LAVAL AG—See Tetra Laval Group; *Int'l*, pg. 1380
ALFA-LAVAL AGRAR G.M.B.H.—See Tetra Laval Group; *Int'l*, pg. 1377
ALFA LAVAL AGRI AB—See Tetra Laval Group; *Int'l*, pg. 1378
ALFA-LAVAL AGRI INTERNATIONAL AB—See Tetra Laval Group; *Int'l*, pg. 1377
ALFA-LAVAL AGRI LTD—See Tetra Laval Group; *Int'l*, pg. 1380
ALFA-LAVAL AGRI N.V.—See Tetra Laval Group; *Int'l*, pg. 1379
ALFA-LAVAL AGRI SCANDINAVIA AB—See Tetra Laval Group; *Int'l*, pg. 1377
ALFA-LAVAL AGRI SCANDINAVIA A/S—See Tetra Laval Group; *Int'l*, pg. 1377
ALFA-LAVAL AGRI-SCANDINAVIA OY—See Tetra Laval Group; *Int'l*, pg. 1379
ALFA LAVAL CELLECO INC.—See Tetra Laval Group; *Int'l*, *pg. 1378*
ALFA-LAVAL CHEDDAR SYSTEMS LTD.—See Tetra Laval Group; *Int'l*, pg. 1380
ALFA-LAVAL CO. LTD.—See Tetra Laval Group; *Int'l*, pg. 1380
ALFA LAVAL CONTHERM INC.—See Tetra Laval Group; *Int'l*, pg. 1378
ALFA-LAVAL ENGINEERING K.K.—See Tetra Laval Group; *Int'l*, pg. 1380
ALFA-LAVAL EQUIPAMENTOS LTDA.—See Tetra Laval Group; *Int'l*, pg. 1379
ALFA-LAVAL FLOW EQUIPMENT—See Tetra Laval Group; *Int'l*, pg. 1379
ALFA-LAVAL FOOD ENGINEERING AB—See Tetra Laval Group; *Int'l*, pg. 1378
ALFA-LAVAL HAMILTON PTY LTD.—See Tetra Laval Group; *Int'l*, pg. 1379
ALFA LAVAL INC.—See Tetra Laval Group; *Int'l*, pg. 1378
ALFA-LAVAL INDIA LTD—See Tetra Laval Group; *Int'l*, pg. 1380
ALFA-LAVAL INDUSTRIEGESELLSCHAFT AB—See Tetra Laval Group; *Int'l*, pg. 1380
ALFA-LAVAL INDUSTRIETECHNIK G.M.B.H.—See Tetra Laval Group; *Int'l*, pg. 1379
ALFA-LAVAL IRAN CO.—See Tetra Laval Group; *Int'l*, pg. 1380
ALFA-LAVAL (IRELAND) LTD.—See Tetra Laval Group; *Int'l*, pg. 1380
ALFA-LAVAL LTD.—See Tetra Laval Group; *Int'l*, pg. 1379
ALFA-LAVAL (MALAYSIA) SDN BHD—See Tetra Laval Group; *Int'l*, pg. 1380
ALFA-LAVAL NIREX ENGINEERING A/S—See Tetra Laval Group; *Int'l*, pg. 1379
ALFA-LAVAL N.V.—See Tetra Laval Group; *Int'l*, pg. 1380
ALFA-LAVAL (N.Z.) LTD.—See Tetra Laval Group; *Int'l*, pg. 1380
ALFA-LAVAL PTY LTD.—See Tetra Laval Group; *Int'l*, pg. 1379
ALFA LAVAL PUMPS INC.—See Tetra Laval Group; *Int'l*, pg. 1378
ALFA-LAVAL S.A.—See Tetra Laval Group; *Int'l*, pg. 1379
ALFA-LAVAL S.A. DE C.V.—See Tetra Laval Group; *Int'l*, pg. 1380
ALFA-LAVAL S.A.C.I.—See Tetra Laval Group; *Int'l*, pg. 1379
ALFA LAVAL SAUNDERS INC.—See Tetra Laval Group; *Int'l*, pg. 1378
ALFA-LAVAL SEPARATION AB—See Tetra Laval Group; *Int'l*, pg. 1378
ALFA-LAVAL SEPARATION A/S—See Tetra Laval Group; *Int'l*, pg. 1378
ALFA LAVAL SEPARATION INC.—See Tetra Laval Group; *Int'l*, pg. 1378
ALFA-LAVAL SERVICE K.K.—See Tetra Laval Group; *Int'l*, pg. 1380
ALFA-LAVAL SHARPLES—See Tetra Laval Group; *Int'l*, pg. 1378
ALFA-LAVAL SOUTH EAST ASIA PTY LTD.—See Tetra Laval Group; *Int'l*, pg. 1380
ALFA-LAVAL STALLTECHNIK G.M.B.H.—See Tetra Laval Group; *Int'l*, pg. 1379
ALFA-LAVAL THERMAL AB—See Tetra Laval Group; *Int'l*, pg. 1378
ALFA-LAVAL VENEZOLANA S.A.—See Tetra Laval Group; *Int'l*, pg. 1380
OY ALFA-LAVAL ZETA AB—See Tetra Laval Group; *Int'l*, pg. 1379
ALFA-LAVAL ZETA A/S—See Tetra Laval Group; *Int'l*, pg. 1379
ALFA LIFE INSURANCE CORP.—See Alfa Corporation; *U.S. Public*, pg. 40
ALFA REALTY, INC.—See Alfa Corporation; *U.S. Public*, pg. 40
ALFA ROMEO AUTO S.P.A.—See Fiat Auto SpA; *Int'l*, pg. 481
ALFA ROMEO AVIO S.P.A.—See Fiat Auto SpA; *Int'l*, pg. 481
ALFA ROMEO DISTRIBUTORS OF NORTH AMERICA—See Fiat Auto SpA; *Int'l*, pg. 481
ALFA ROMEO E NISSAN AUTOVEICOLI S.P.A.—See Fiat Auto SpA; *Int'l*, pg. 481
ALFA ROMEO ESPANA—See Fiat Auto SpA; *Int'l*, pg. 481
ALFA ROMEO INTERNATIONAL S.A.—See Fiat Auto SpA; *Int'l*, pg. 481
ALFA ROMEO VEICOLI COMM. E LAV MECC. S.P.A.—See Fiat Auto SpA; *Int'l*, pg. 481
ALFA ROMEO VERTRIEBSGES M.B.H.—See Fiat Auto SpA; *Int'l*, pg. 481
ALFA, S.A. DE C.V.; *Int'l*, pg. 56
ALFA SOLO MARGARINEFABRIKKEN AS—See Unilever Plc; *Int'l*, pg. 1436
ALFA SYSTEM PARTNER GMBH—See Mannesmann A.G.; *Int'l*, pg. 835
ALFATEC SPA—See Electrolux, AB; *Int'l*, pg. 442
ALFAX PAPER OF UNITED KINGDOM, LIMITED—See Platinum Equity Holdings, LLC; *U.S. Private*, pg. 872
ALFER CONSULTING IMMOBILIARIO, S.A.—See Vallehermoso, S.A.; *Int'l*, pg. 1447
ALFIGEN S.A.—See Otto Versand (GmbH & Co.); *Int'l*, pg. 1015
ALFIN, INC.; *U.S. Public*, pg. 40
ALFLEX—See Commonwealth Industries, Inc.; *U.S. Public*, pg. 415
ALFORD REFRIGERATED WAREHOUSE, INC.; *U.S. Private*, pg. 33
ALGAS MARINAS S.A.—See Hercules Incorporated; *U.S. Public*, pg. 810
ALGEA PRODUKTER A/S—See Norsk Hydro a.s; *Int'l*, pg. 959
ALGEL S.P.A.—See Unilever Plc; *Int'l*, pg. 1436
ALGEMEEN VRACHTKANTOOR B.V.—See Unilever Plc; *Int'l*, pg. 1436
ALGEMENE BANK NEDERLAND N.V.—See ABN-AMRO Holding N.V.; *Int'l*, pg. 9
ALGEMENE FRIESE ONDERLINGE SCHADEVERZEKERINGMAATSCHAPPIJ 'ZEVENWOUDEN' U.A.—See AEGON N.V.; *Int'l*, pg. 26
B.V. ALGEMENE HOLDING EN FINANCIERINGS MIJ.—See Assicurazioni Generali S.p.A.; *Int'l*, pg. 90
ALGEMENE LEASE MAATSCHAPPIJ B.V.—See ABN-AMRO Holding N.V.; *Int'l*, pg. 9
ALGEMENE LEVENSHERVERZEKERING MAATSCHAAPIJ NV—See Swiss Reinsurance Company; *Int'l*, pg. 1333
ALGEMENE PARTICIPATIEMAATSCHAPPIJ B.V.—See ABN-AMRO Holding N.V.; *Int'l*, pg. 9
ALGEMENE SEIN INDUSTRIE B.V.—See SASIB SpA; *Int'l*, pg. 1194
ALGEMENE ZEEUWSE VERZEKERING MAATSCHAPPIJ N.V.—See ING Groep N.V.; *Int'l*, pg. 647
ALGERNON BLAIR INTERNATIONAL; *U.S. Private*, pg. 33
ALGINATE INDUSTRIES—See Merck & Co., Inc.; *U.S. Public*, pg. 1091
ALGOA OIL & PIPELINE (PTY) LTD.—See ABB Asea Brown Boveri (Holding) Ltd.; *Int'l*, pg. 5
ALGOA OIL DE CABINDA, LTD—See ABB Asea Brown Boveri (Holding) Ltd.; *Int'l*, pg. 5
ALGOL CENTRAL STORAGE DEPOT—See Oy Algol AB; *Int'l*, pg. 15
ALGOL-EESTI AS—See Oy Algol AB; *Int'l*, pg. 15
ALGOL-LATVIJA SIA—See Oy Algol AB; *Int'l*, pg. 15
ALGOMA CENTRAL RAILWAY INC.—See Wisconsin Central Transportation Corporation; *U.S. Public*, pg. 1772
ALGOMA ORE DIVISION—See Algoma Steel Inc.; *Int'l*, pg. 57
ALGOMA STEEL INC.; *Int'l*, pg. 56
ALGONA FOOD EQUIPMENT CO.—See Hormel Foods Corp.; *U.S. Public*, pg. 840
ALGONQUIN GAS TRANSMISSION CORPORATION—See Duke Energy Corporation; *U.S. Public*, pg. 534
ALGOOD FOOD COMPANY; *U.S. Private*, pg. 34
ALGYNVEST—See Tractebel; *Int'l*, pg. 1416
ALHAMBRA LONGMAN S.A.—See Pearson plc; *Int'l*, pg. 1025
ALIADA QUIMICA DE PORTUGAL LDA.—See Kemira Oy; *Int'l*, pg. 728
ALIADA QUIMICA S.A.—See Kemira Oy; *Int'l*, pg. 728
ALIAF-PUBLIC JOINT STOCK CO.—See Bayer AG; *Int'l*, pg. 174
ALIANT CELLULAR TELEPHONE COMPANY—See Aliant Communications Inc.; *U.S. Public*, pg. 40
ALIANT COMMUNICATIONS CO.—See Aliant Communications Inc.; *U.S. Public*, pg. 40
ALIANT COMMUNICATIONS INC.; *U.S. Public*, pg. 40
ALIANT SYSTEMS INC.—See Aliant Communications Inc.; *U.S. Public*, pg. 41
ALIAS WAVEFRONT—See Silicon Graphics, Inc.; *U.S. Public*, pg. 1474
ALICE—See The Lowe Group; *U.S. Private*, pg. 678
ALICEVILLE CASTING CO.—See Crane Co.; *U.S. Public*, pg. 456
ALICO, INC.; *U.S. Public*, pg. 41
ALICON BORMAEGLERSELKAB A/S—See ABN-AMRO Holding N.V.; *Int'l*, pg. 12
ALICORP S.A.; *Int'l*, pg. 57
ALIGAME S.P.A.—See IRI Istituto Ricostruzione Industriale; *Int'l*, pg. 652
ALIMA-GERBER SA—See Novartis AG; *Int'l*, pg. 973
ALIMAK ELEVATOR COMPANY; *U.S. Private*, pg. 34
ALIMED, INC.; *U.S. Private*, pg. 34
ALIMENTATION COUCHE TARD INC.; *Int'l*, pg. 57
ALIMENTERICS, INC.—See American Standard Inc.; *U.S. Public*, pg. 92
ALIMENTOS BALANCEADOS PILGRIM'S PRIDE—See Pilgrim's Pride Corporation; *U.S. Public*, pg. 1296
ALIMENTOS DESHIDRATADOS DEL BAJIO, S.A. DE C.V.—See McCormick & Company, Incorporated; *U.S. Public*, pg. 1067
ALIMENTOS FINDAS S.A. DE C.V.—See Nestle S.A.; *Int'l*, pg. 918
ALIMENTOS HEINZ C.A.—See H.J. Heinz Company; *U.S. Public*, pg. 806
ALIMENTOS KELLOGG S.A.—See Kellogg Company; *U.S. Public*, pg. 947
ALIMENTOS KERN DE GUATEMALA, S.A.—See Riviana Foods Inc.; *U.S. Public*, pg. 1392
ALIMENTOS Y PRODUCTOS DE MAIZ S.A.—See Corn Products International, Inc.; *U.S. Public*, pg. 447
ALIMENTS FLAMINGO; *Int'l*, pg. 57
ALINORD S.P.A.—See Bastogi-S.p.A.; *Int'l*, pg. 170
ALISA, S.A.—See Borden, Inc.; *U.S. Private*, pg. 159
ALISERE S.A.—See Alusuisse-Lonza Holding Ltd.; *Int'l*, pg. 68
ALITALIA—See IRI Istituto Ricostruzione Industriale; *Int'l*, pg. 652
ALITALIA AIRLINES—See IRI Istituto Ricostruzione Industriale; *Int'l*, pg. 652
ALITALIA LINEE AEREE ITALIANE S.P.A.—See IRI Istituto Ricostruzione Industriale; *Int'l*, pg. 652
ALIVEN S.A.—See Corn Products International, Inc.; *U.S. Public*, pg. 447
ALK A/S—See Chr. Hansen Holding A/S; *Int'l*, pg. 288
ALKA NURNBERGER WARENHANDELSGESELLSCHAFT MBH—See Karstadt Aktiengesellschaft; *Int'l*, pg. 724
ALKALINE BATTERIES A/S—See GP Batteries International Ltd.; *Int'l*, pg. 537
ALKALINE BATTERIES VOLTA S.R.L.—See GP Batteries International Ltd.; *Int'l*, pg. 537
ALKCO LIGHTING COMPANY—See Luxo A/S; *Int'l*, pg. 821
ALKEN-MAES—See Danone Group; *Int'l*, pg. 381
ALKEREMES; *U.S. Public*, pg. 41
ALKI CORPORATION—See New Valley Corporation; *U.S. Public*, pg. 1173
ALKOR GMBH KUNSTSTOFFE—See Solvay S.A.; *Int'l*, pg. 1278
ALKOR MARKENHANDELS GMBH—See Solvay S.A.; *Int'l*, *pg. 1278*
ALKOR PLASTICS LTD.—See Solvay S.A.; *Int'l*, pg. 1278
ALKOTA CLEANING SYSTEMS, INC.; *U.S. Private*, pg. 34
ALL AMERICA INSURANCE COMPANY—See Central Mutual Insurance Co.; *U.S. Private*, pg. 224
ALL AMERICAN AGENCY FACILITIES, INC.—See W.R. Berkley Corporation; *U.S. Public*, pg. 216
ALL AMERICAN BOTTLING CORP.; *U.S. Private*, pg. 34
ALL-AMERICAN BOTTLING FINANCIAL CORP.—See All American Bottling Corp.; *U.S. Private*, pg. 34
ALL-AMERICAN CO.—See Riddell Sports, Inc.; *U.S. Public*, *pg. 1389*
ALL AMERICAN COMMUNICATIONS, INC.; *U.S. Public*, pg. 41
ALL AMERICAN HOME CENTER; *U.S. Private*, pg. 34
ALL AMERICAN HOMES, INC.—See Coachmen Industries, Inc.; *U.S. Public*, pg. 388
ALL AMERICAN HOMES OF IOWA INC.—See Coachmen Industries, Inc.; *U.S. Public*, pg. 388
ALL AMERICAN HOMES OF NORTH CAROLINA, INC.—See Coachmen Industries, Inc.; *U.S. Public*, pg. 388
ALL AMERICAN HOMES OF TENNESSEE, INC.—See Coachmen Industries, Inc.; *U.S. Public*, pg. 388
ALL AMERICAN LIFE INSURANCE CO.—See American General Corporation; *U.S. Public*, pg. 77
ALL AMERICAN PIPELINE COMPANY—See The Goodyear Tire & Rubber Company; *U.S. Public*, pg. 753
ALL AMERICAN RECYCLING—See Commercial Metals Company; *U.S. Public*, pg. 413
ALL AMERICAN SEMICONDUCTOR, INC.; *U.S. Public*, pg. 41
ALL AMERICAN SEMICONDUCTOR OF CALIFORNIA, INC.—See All American Semiconductor, Inc.; *U.S. Public*, pg. 41
ALL AMERICAN SEMICONDUCTOR OF FLORIDA, INC.—See All American Semiconductor, Inc.; *U.S. Public*, pg. 41
ALL AMERICAN SEMICONDUCTOR OF HUNTSVILLE, INC.—See All American Semiconductor, Inc.; *U.S. Public*, pg. 41
ALL AMERICAN SEMICONDUCTOR OF MASSACHUSETTS, INC.—See All American Semiconductor, Inc.; *U.S. Public*, pg. 41
ALL AMERICAN SEMICONDUCTOR OF MINNESOTA, INC.—See All American Semiconductor, Inc.; *U.S. Public*, pg. 41
ALL AMERICAN SEMICONDUCTOR OF NEW YORK, INC.—See All American Semiconductor, Inc.; *U.S. Public*, pg. 41
ALL AMERICAN SEMICONDUCTOR OF NORTHERN CALIFORNIA, INC.—See All American Semiconductor, Inc.; *U.S. Public*, pg. 41
ALL AMERICAN SEMICONDUCTOR OF ROCKVILLE, INC.—See All American Semiconductor, Inc.; *U.S. Public*, pg. 41
ALL AMERICAN SEMICONDUCTOR OF SALT LAKE, INC.—See All American Semiconductor, Inc.; *U.S. Public*, pg. 41
ALL AMERICAN SEMICONDUCTOR OF TEXAS, INC.—See All American Semiconductor, Inc.; *U.S. Public*, pg. 41
ALL-AMERICAN SYSTEMS—See NCI Building Systems, Inc.; *U.S. Public*, pg. 1146

Company Index

ALL AMERICAN TECHNOLOGIES—See All American Semiconductor, Inc.; *U.S. Public*, pg. 41
ALL AMERICAN TECHNOLOGIES OF CHICAGO, INC.—See All American Semiconductor, Inc.; *U.S. Public*, pg. 41
ALL AMERICAN TECHNOLOGIES OF PHILADELPHIA, INC.—See All American Semiconductor, Inc.; *U.S. Public*, pg. 41
ALL AMERICAN TECHNOLOGIES OF PORTLAND, INC.—See All American Semiconductor, Inc.; *U.S. Public*, pg. 42
ALL AMERICAN TELEVISION, INC.—See All American Communications, Inc.; *U.S. Public*, pg. 41
ALL-CARE PROFESSIONAL SERVICES, INC.—See Hospital Staffing Services, Inc.; *U.S. Public*, pg. 841
ALL COMPUTERS S.A.—See Hewlett-Packard Company; *U.S. Public*, pg. 816
ALL-LUMINUM PRODUCTS, INC.; *U.S. Private*, pg. 34
ALL NATION INSURANCE CO.—See All Nation Insurance Company; *U.S. Private*, pg. 35
ALL NATION INSURANCE COMPANY; *U.S. Private*, pg. 35
ALL NIPPON AIRWAYS CO. LTD.; *Int'l*, pg. 57
ALL NIPPON AIRWAYS WORLD TOURS CO., LTD.—See All Nippon Airways Co. Ltd.; *Int'l*, pg. 57
ALL NIPPON AIRWAYS-NEW YORK—See All Nippon Airways Co. Ltd.; *Int'l*, pg. 57
ALL NIPPON MANAGEMENT SERVICE INC.—See All Nippon Airways Co. Ltd.; *Int'l*, pg. 57
ALL NIPPON TRAVEL SERVICE INC.—See All Nippon Airways Co. Ltd.; *Int'l*, pg. 57
ALL-PHASE ELECTRIC SUPPLY CO.; *U.S. Private*, pg. 35
ALL PLAST A-S—See Esselte AB; *Int'l*, pg. 460
ALL PRO BUMPER TO BUMPER INC.; *U.S. Private*, pg. 35
ALL-PRO IMAGING—See Air Techniques, Inc.; *U.S. Private*, pg. 28
ALL PRO WINDOW SUPPLY, INC.; *U.S. Private*, pg. 35
ALL SEASONS SERVICES, INC.; *U.S. Private*, pg. 35
ALL SIZE CORRUGATED—See Buckeye Corrugated Inc.; *U.S. Private*, pg. 177
ALL STAR GAS CORPORATION; *U.S. Private*, pg. 35
ALL STAR GAS FIELD SERVICES—See All Star Gas Corporation; *U.S. Private*, pg. 35
ALL STAR GAS TRANSPORTS (MO)—See All Star Gas Corporation; *U.S. Private*, pg. 36
ALL-STATE FORD TRUCK SALES—See Hesco Parts Corporation; *U.S. Private*, pg. 524
ALLAINZ VERSICHERUNGS-AG (DUBAI BRANCH)—See Allianz Aktiengesellschaft; *Int'l*, pg. 60
ALLAIRE CORPORATION; *U.S. Private*, pg. 36
THE ALLAN & GRAY CO.—See Union Camp Corporation; *U.S. Public*, pg. 1666
O.B. ALLAN JEWELLERS—See Henry Birks & Sons (1993) Inc.; *Int'l*, pg. 197
ALLARCOM PAY TELEVISION LIMITED—See WIC Western International Communications Ltd.; *Int'l*, pg. 1481
ALLARD INDUSTRIES; *U.S. Private*, pg. 36
ALLBRITTON COMMUNICATIONS COMPANY—See Perpetual Corporation; *U.S. Private*, pg. 854
ALLBRITTON GROUP, INC.—See Perpetual Corporation; *U.S. Private*, pg. 854
ALLBRITTON JACKSONVILLE, INC—See Perpetual Corporation; *U.S. Private*, pg. 854
ALLBRITTON NEWS BUREAU, INC.—See Perpetual Corporation; *U.S. Private*, pg. 854
ALLBRITTON TELEVISION PRODUCTIONS, INC.—See Perpetual Corporation; *U.S. Private*, pg. 854
ALLCAPS WEICHGELATINEKAPSELN GMBH—See R.P. Scherer Corporation; *U.S. Public*, pg. 1438
ALLCITY INSURANCE CO.—See Leucadia National Corporation; *U.S. Public*, pg. 990
ALLCITY INSURANCE CO., MINEOLA—See Leucadia National Corporation; *U.S. Public*, pg. 990
ALLCITY INSURANCE CO., ROCHESTER—See Leucadia National Corporation; *U.S. Public*, pg. 990
ALLCITY INSURANCE CO., ROCKVILLE CENTRE—See Leucadia National Corporation; *U.S. Public*, pg. 990
ALLCITY INSURANCE CO., SCARSDALE—See Leucadia National Corporation; *U.S. Public*, pg. 990
ALLCOM, INC.—See General Electric Company; *U.S. Public*, pg. 711
ALLDERS INTERNATIONAL (CANADA) LIMITED—See Agra Inc.; *Int'l*, pg. 30
ALLDERS NUANCE—See The Swissair Group; *Int'l*, pg. 1334
ALLEANZA ASSICURAZIONI S.P.A.—See Assicurazioni Generali S.p.A.; *Int'l*, pg. 89
ALLEGA LTD.-(ALLEGA)—See Alusuisse-Lonza Holding Ltd.; *Int'l*, pg. 67
ALLEGAN COUNTY CABLEVISION INC.—See Cable Michigan, Inc.; *U.S. Public*, pg. 287
ALLEGHANY CORPORATION; *U.S. Public*, pg. 42
ALLEGHENY AIRLINES, INC.—See US Airways Group, Inc.; *U.S. Public*, pg. 1680
ALLEGHENY DEVELOPMENT CORP.—See DQE Inc.; *U.S. Public*, pg. 474
ALLEGHENY GEAR CORPORATION—See Astronics Corporation; *U.S. Public*, pg. 142
ALLEGHENY GENERATING CO.—See Allegheny Power System, Inc.; *U.S. Public*, pg. 42
ALLEGHENY HEAT TREATING—See Commercial Metals Company; *U.S. Public*, pg. 412
ALLEGHENY LUDLUM-WASHINGTON PLANT—See Allegheny Teledyne Incorporated; *U.S. Public*, pg. 43
ALLEGHENY LUDLUM-WATERBURY—See Allegheny Teledyne Incorporated; *U.S. Public*, pg. 43
ALLEGHENY PEPSI-COLA BOTTLING COMPANY—See PepsiCo, Inc.; *U.S. Public*, pg. 1277
ALLEGHENY PITTSBURGH COAL CO.—See Allegheny Power System, Inc.; *U.S. Public*, pg. 42
ALLEGHENY POWER SYSTEM, INC.; *U.S. Public*, pg. 42
ALLEGHENY RAIL PRODUCTS—See L.B. Foster Company; *U.S. Public*, pg. 676

ALLEGHENY TELEDYNE INCORPORATED; *U.S. Public*, pg. 43
ALLEGIANCE HEALTHCARE CORP.; *U.S. Public*, pg. 44
ALLEGIANCE HEALTHCARE CORP.—See Allegiance Healthcare Corp.; *U.S. Public*, pg. 44
ALLEGIANCE HEALTHCARE INTERNATIONAL—See Allegiance Healthcare Corp.; *U.S. Public*, pg. 45
ALLEGIANCE INSURANCE COMPANY—See Cigna Corp.; *U.S. Public*, pg. 362
ALLEGIANCE LIFE INSURANCE COMPANY—See Horace Mann Educators Corporation; *U.S. Public*, pg. 836
ALLEGIANT PHYSICIAN SERVICES; *U.S. Public*, pg. 45
ALLEGRIA INC.—See Inner Secrets, Inc.; *U.S. Private*, pg. 565
ALLEGRO MICROSYSTEMS EUROPE LIMITED—See Sanken Electric Co., Ltd.; *Int'l*, pg. 1188
ALLEGRO MICROSYSTEMS INC.—See Sanken Electric Co., Ltd.; *Int'l*, pg. 1188
ALLEGRO MICROSYSTEMS JAPAN, INC.—See Sanken Electric Co., Ltd.; *Int'l*, pg. 1188
ALLEGRO MICROSYSTEMS PHILIPPINES, INC.—See Sanken Electric Co., Ltd.; *Int'l*, pg. 1188
ALLEN & COMPANY INCORPORATED; *U.S. Private*, pg. 36
ALLEN & HANBURYS—See Glaxo Wellcome plc; *Int'l*, pg. 552
ALLEN & HANBURYS LIMITED—See Glaxo Wellcome plc; *Int'l*, pg. 552
ALLEN & HOSHALL—See Allen & Hoshall, Inc.; *U.S. Private*, pg. 36
ALLEN & HOSHALL, INC.; *U.S. Private*, pg. 36
ALLEN & OHARA, INC.; *U.S. Private*, pg. 36
ALLEN AUTOMOTIVE INTERNATIONAL (FRANCE) S.A.R.L.—See Rockwell International Corporation; *U.S. Public*, pg. 1
ALLEN-BRADLEY AG—See Rockwell International Corporation; *U.S. Public*, pg. 1398
ALLEN-BRADLEY CANADA LIMITED—See Rockwell International Corporation; *U.S. Public*, pg. 1398
ALLEN-BRADLEY COMPANY—See Rockwell International Corporation; *U.S. Public*, pg. 1398
ALLEN-BRADLEY DO BRASIL LTDA.—See Rockwell International Corporation; *U.S. Public*, pg. 1398
ALLEN-BRADLEY ENTERPRISE XIAMEN LTD.—See Rockwell International Corporation; *U.S. Public*, pg. 1398
ALLEN-BRADLEY GLOBAL SALES & SUPPORT GROUP—See Rockwell International Corporation; *U.S. Public*, pg. 1397
ALLEN-BRADLEY INDIA LIMITED—See Rockwell International Corporation; *U.S. Public*, pg. 1398
ALLEN-BRADLEY JAPAN CO., LTD.—See Rockwell International Corporation; *U.S. Public*, pg. 1398
ALLEN-BRADLEY PACKAGED CONTROL PRODUCTS—See Rockwell International Corporation; *U.S. Public*, pg. 1397
ALLEN-BRADLEY PTY. LIMITED—See Rockwell International Corporation; *U.S. Public*, pg. 1399
ALLEN-BRADLEY S.R.L.—See Rockwell International Corporation; *U.S. Public*, pg. 1399
ALLEN CANNING COMPANY; *U.S. Private*, pg. 36
ALLEN CODIERGERATE GMBH—See Smiths Industries plc; *Int'l*, pg. 1268
ALLEN COMMUNICATION—See The Times Mirror Company; *U.S. Public*, pg. 1616
ALLEN-EDMONDS SHOE CORP.; *U.S. Private*, pg. 36
ALLEN FOODS, INC.; *U.S. Private*, pg. 37
ALLEN FRANCE SA—See Smiths Industries plc; *Int'l*, pg. 1268
J.W. ALLEN & COMPANY; *U.S. Private*, pg. 37
ALLEN-LEWIS MANUFACTURING CO., INC.—See TCC Industries; *U.S. Public*, pg. 1554
ALLEN MILK CO.—See Lancaster Colony Corporation; *U.S. Public*, pg. 977
ALLEN ORGAN COMPANY; *U.S. Public*, pg. 45
ROBERT ALLEN AMETEK—See Furnishings International, Inc.; *U.S. Private*, pg. 432
ALLEN-ROGERS CO.—See Davis Mining & Manufacturing; *U.S. Private*, pg. 315
ALLEN TELECOM, INC.; *U.S. Public*, pg. 45
THOMAS ALLEN LTD.—See The Peninsular and Oriental Steam Navigation Company; *Int'l*, pg. 1032
ALLEN-BRADLEY ENTERPRISE XIAMEN LTD.—See Rockwell International Corporation; *U.S. Public*, pg. 1398
ALLENDALE MUTUAL INSURANCE CO.; *U.S. Private*, pg. 37
ALLENERGY MARKETING COMPANY, L.L.C.—See Eastern Enterprises; *U.S. Public*, pg. 549
ALLENERGY MARKETING COMPANY, L.L.C.—See New England Electric System; *U.S. Public*, pg. 1172
ALLEN'S CONCRETE, INC.—See Ritchie Corporation; *U.S. Private*, pg. 933
ALLENS OF HASTINGS, INC.; *U.S. Private*, pg. 37
ALLENTOWN CEMENT CO. INC.—See Scancem AB; *Int'l*, pg. 1201
ALLERGAN AUSTRALIA (PTY.) LTD.—See Allergan, Inc.; *U.S. Public*, pg. 46
ALLERGAN DIV.—See SmithKline Beecham plc; *Int'l*, pg. 1265
ALLERGAN, INC.; *U.S. Public*, pg. 46
ALLERGAN K.K.—See Allergan, Inc.; *U.S. Public*, pg. 46
ALLERGAN LIMITED—See Allergan, Inc.; *U.S. Public*, pg. 46
ALLERGAN-LOK PRODUTOS, FARMACEUTICOS, LTDA.—See Allergan, Inc.; *U.S. Public*, pg. 46
ALLERGAN PHARMACEUTICALS (IRELAND) LTD., INC.—See Allergan, Inc.; *U.S. Public*, pg. 46
ALLERGAN S.A. DE C.V.—See Allergan, Inc.; *U.S. Public*, pg. 46
ALLERGAN S.A.E.—See Allergan, Inc.; *U.S. Public*, pg. 46
ALLERGAN S.P.A.—See Allergan, Inc.; *U.S. Public*, pg. 46
ALLEY-CASSETTY COAL CO.; *U.S. Private*, pg. 37
ALLFAST FACILITY—See Allfast Fastening Systems, Inc.; *U.S. Private*, pg. 37

ALLFAST FASTENING SYSTEMS, INC.; *U.S. Private*, pg. 37
ALLFINCO, INC.—See Perpetual Corporation; *U.S. Private*, pg. 854
ALLGAUER ALPENMILCH A.G.—See Nestle S.A.; *Int'l*, pg. 918
ALLGAUER BRAUHAUS AG—See Bayerische Vereinsbank Group; *Int'l*, pg. 178
ALLGEMEINE ASSEKURANZ-VERMITTLUNG GMBH—See Mannesmann A.G.; *Int'l*, pg. 837
ALLGEMEINE BAU- UND VERIETUNGS GMBH—See Mannesmann A.G.; *Int'l*, pg. 839
ALLGEMEINE IMMOBILIEN VERWALTUNGS GMBH—See Assicurazioni Generali S.p.A.; *Int'l*, pg. 89
KG ALLGEMEINE LEASING GMBH & CO.—See Dresdner Bank AG; *Int'l*, pg. 418
ALLGEMEINE PRIVATKUNDENBANK AG—See Bankgesellschaft Berlin; *Int'l*, pg. 159
ALLGEMEINER KUGELLAGERVERTRIEB POLZL GMBH—See FAG Group; *Int'l*, pg. 469
ALLIAGES FRITTES METAFRAM—See Pechiney S.A.; *Int'l*, pg. 1028
ALLIANCE AIR LTD.—See Transnet Ltd.; *Int'l*, pg. 1417
ALLIANCE AMERICA; *U.S. Private*, pg. 37
ALLIANCE & LEICESTER BUILDING SOCIETY—See Alliance Leicester Building Society; *Int'l*, pg. 57
ALLIANCE AUTOMATED; *U.S. Private*, pg. 38
ALLIANCE CAPITAL MANAGEMENT CORP.—See The Equitable Companies Incorporated; *U.S. Public*, pg. 589
ALLIANCE COMMUNICATIONS CORPORATION; *Int'l*, pg. 57
ALLIANCE CONSTRUCTION SOLUTIONS, INC.; *U.S. Private*, pg. 38
ALLIANCE DATA SYSTEMS—See The Limited, Inc.; *U.S. Public*, pg. 995
ALLIANCE DISPLAY & PACKAGING—See Rock-Tenn Company; *U.S. Public*, pg. 1397
ALLIANCE ET GESTION COMMERCIALE (ALGECO) S.A.—See Preussag AG; *Int'l*, pg. 1071
ALLIANCE FLIGHT TRAINING ACADEMY—See Berkshire Hathaway Inc.; *U.S. Public*, pg. 218
ALLIANCE FOREST PRODUCTS INC.; *Int'l*, pg. 57
ALLIANCE GAMING CORPORATION; *U.S. Public*, pg. 46
ALLIANCE HEATER COMPANY—See Watlow Electric Manufacturing Company; *U.S. Private*, pg. 1453
ALLIANCE LEICESTER BUILDING SOCIETY; *Int'l*, pg. 57
ALLIANCE MANAGEMENT, INC.; *U.S. Private*, pg. 38
ALLIANCE PAPER GROUP PLC—See Metsa-Serla Corporation; *Int'l*, pg. 863
ALLIANCE SEMICONDUCTOR CORP.; *U.S. Public*, pg. 47
ALLIANCE UNICHEM PLC; *Int'l*, pg. 57
ALLIANCE VENTURES, INC.—See Highmark Inc.; *U.S. Private*, pg. 529
ALLIANCE WALL MIDWEST REGIONAL OFFICE—See Alliance America; *U.S. Private*, pg. 38
ALLIANT FOODSERVICE—See Clayton, Dubilier & Rice, Inc; *U.S. Private*, pg. 244
ALLIANT FOODSERVICE, INC.—See Clayton, Dubilier & Rice, Inc; *U.S. Private*, pg. 244
ALLIANT TECHSYSTEMS; *U.S. Public*, pg. 47
ALLIANT TECHSYSTEMS (AEROSPACE DIVISION)—See Alliant Techsystems; *U.S. Public*, pg. 47
ALLIANT TECHSYSTEMS-MAGNA—See Alliant Techsystems; *U.S. Public*, pg. 47
ALLIANT TECHSYSTEMS-ROCKET CENTER—See Alliant Techsystems; *U.S. Public*, pg. 47
ALLIANZ AG (EU REPRESENTATIVE OFFICE)—See Allianz Aktiengesellschaft; *Int'l*, pg. 59
ALLIANZ AKTIENGESELLSCHAFT; *Int'l*, pg. 58
ALLIANZ ASIA PACIFIC—See Allianz Aktiengesellschaft; *Int'l*, pg. 59
ALLIANZ ASSET MANAGEMENT (HONG KONG) LTD.—See Allianz Aktiengesellschaft; *Int'l*, pg. 59
ALLIANZ BEIJING REPRESENTATIVE OFFICE—See Allianz Aktiengesellschaft; *Int'l*, pg. 59
ALLIANZ BETEILIGUNGSGESELLSCHAFT MBH—See Allianz Aktiengesellschaft; *Int'l*, pg. 58
ALLIANZ BICE COMPANIA DE SEGUROS DE VIDA S.A.—See Allianz Aktiengesellschaft; *Int'l*, pg. 59
ALLIANZ-BRADESCO CIA. BRASILEIRA DE SEGUROS—See Allianz Aktiengesellschaft; *Int'l*, pg. 59
ALLIANZ-BRADESCO (RIO DE JANEIRO OFFICE)—See Allianz Aktiengesellschaft; *Int'l*, pg. 59
ALLIANZ CANADA—See Allianz Aktiengesellschaft; *Int'l*, pg. 59
ALLIANZ COMPANIA DE SEGUROS S.A.—See Allianz Aktiengesellschaft; *Int'l*, pg. 59
ALLIANZ CORNHILL INSURANCE (FAR EAST) LTD.—See Allianz Aktiengesellschaft; *Int'l*, pg. 59
ALLIANZ FINANCE B.V.—See Allianz Aktiengesellschaft; *Int'l*, pg. 59
ALLIANZ FIRE AND MARINE INSURANCE JAPAN LTD.—See Allianz Aktiengesellschaft; *Int'l*, pg. 59
ALLIANZ GENERAL INSURANCE COMPANY S.A.—See Allianz Aktiengesellschaft; *Int'l*, pg. 59
ALLIANZ GRUNDSTUECKS-AG—See Allianz Aktiengesellschaft; *Int'l*, pg. 58
ALLIANZ GUANGZHOU REPRESENTATIVE OFFICE—See Allianz Aktiengesellschaft; *Int'l*, pg. 59
ALLIANZ HANOI REPRESENTATIVE OFFICE—See Allianz Aktiengesellschaft; *Int'l*, pg. 59
ALLIANZ INSURANCE OF NAMIBIA LTD.—See Allianz Aktiengesellschaft; *Int'l*, pg. 59
ALLIANZ INSURANCE (SINGAPORE) PTE. LTD.—See Allianz Aktiengesellschaft; *Int'l*, pg. 59
ALLIANZ LEBENSVERSICHERUNG (SCHWEIZ) AG—See Allianz Aktiengesellschaft; *Int'l*, pg. 59
ALLIANZ LEBENSVERSICHERUNGS-AG—See Allianz Aktiengesellschaft; *Int'l*, pg. 58
ALLIANZ LIFE INSURANCE COMPANY OF NORTH AMERICA—See Allianz Aktiengesellschaft; *Int'l*, pg. 58
ALLIANZ LIFE INSURANCE COMPANY S.A.—See Allianz Aktiengesellschaft; *Int'l*, pg. 59

ALLIANZ MEXICO S.A. COMPANIA DE SEGUROS—See Allianz Aktiengesellschaft; *Int'l*, pg. 59
ALLIANZ NEDERLAND N.V. IN FA. STANISLAS H. HAINE S.A.—See Allianz Aktiengesellschaft; *Int'l*, pg. 60
ALLIANZ NEDERLAND N.V. (ROTTERDAM OFFICE)—See Allianz Aktiengesellschaft; *Int'l*, pg. 60
ALLIANZ NEDERLAND N.V. (STOCK EXCHANGE OFFICE)—See Allianz Aktiengesellschaft; *Int'l*, pg. 60
ALLIANZ OF AMERICA, INC.—See Allianz Aktiengesellschaft; *Int'l*, pg. 58
ALLIANZ POISTOVNA A.S.—See Allianz Aktiengesellschaft; *Int'l*, pg. 60
ALLIANZ POISTOVNA, A.S.—See Allianz Aktiengesellschaft; *Int'l*, pg. 60
ALLIANZ RAS ARGENTINA—See Allianz Aktiengesellschaft; *Int'l*, pg. 60
ALLIANZ-RAS SEGUROS Y REASEGUROS, S.A.—See Allianz Aktiengesellschaft; *Int'l*, pg. 60
ALLIANZ RAS TUTELA GUIDIZIARIA S.P.A.—See Allianz Aktiengesellschaft; *Int'l*, pg. 60
ALLIANZ SHANGHAI REPRESENTATIVE OFFICE—See Allianz Aktiengesellschaft; *Int'l*, pg. 59
ALLIANZ SUBALPINA S.P.A.—See Allianz Aktiengesellschaft; *Int'l*, pg. 60
ALLIANZ UNDERWRITERS INSURANCE CO.—See Allianz Aktiengesellschaft; *Int'l*, pg. 58
ALLIANZ VERSICHERUNG (SCHWEIZ) AG—See Allianz Aktiengesellschaft; *Int'l*, pg. 58
ALLIANZ VERSICHERUNGS-AG—See Allianz Aktiengesellschaft; *Int'l*, pg. 58
ALLIANZ VIA ASSURANCES—See Allianz Aktiengesellschaft; *Int'l*, pg. 60
ALLIANZ VIA VIE-COMPAGNIE D'ASSURANCES SUR LA VIE—See Allianz Aktiengesellschaft; *Int'l*, pg. 60
ALLIED ADVERTISING—See Allied Advertising Agency, Public Relations; *U.S. Private*, pg. 38
ALLIED ADVERTISING AGENCY, PUBLIC RELATIONS; *U.S. Private*, pg. 38
ALLIED ADVERTISING PUBLIC RELATIONS CANADA, INC.—See Allied Advertising Agency, Public Relations; *U.S. Private*, pg. 38
ALLIED AUTOMOTIVE GROUP—See Allied Holdings, Inc.; *U.S. Public*, pg. 48
ALLIED BANK OF GEORGIA—See Regions Financial Corporation; *U.S. Public*, pg. 1373
ALLIED BOND & COLLECTION AGENCY, INC.—See The Union Corporation; *U.S. Public*, pg. 1667
ALLIED BROADCAST EQUIPMENT, CANADA, LTD.—See Harris Corporation; *U.S. Public*, pg. 791
ALLIED BUILDING PRODUCTS CORPORATION; *U.S. Private*, pg. 38
ALLIED CAPITAL ADVISORS, INC.—See Allied Capital Corporation; *U.S. Public*, pg. 47
ALLIED CAPITAL COMMERCIAL CORPORATION—See Allied Capital Corporation; *U.S. Public*, pg. 47
ALLIED CAPITAL CORPORATION; *U.S. Public*, pg. 47
ALLIED CAPITAL CORPORATION II—See Allied Capital Corporation; *U.S. Public*, pg. 47
ALLIED CAPITAL FINANCIAL CORPORATION—See Allied Capital Corporation; *U.S. Public*, pg. 48
ALLIED CAPITAL LENDING CORPORATION—See Allied Capital Corporation; *U.S. Public*, pg. 48
ALLIED CARBI-TECH, INC.; *U.S. Private*, pg. 38
ALLIED CHUCKER & ENGINEERING COMPANY; *U.S. Private*, pg. 38
ALLIED CLINICAL LABORATORIES, INC.—See Laboratory Corp. of America Holdings; *U.S. Public*, pg. 973
ALLIED COLLOIDS (ASIA) LTD.—See Allied Colloids Group Plc.; *Int'l*, pg. 62
ALLIED COLLOIDS (AUSTRALIA) PTY. LTD.—See Allied Colloids Group Plc.; *Int'l*, pg. 62
N.V. ALLIED COLLOIDS BELGIUM S.A.—See Allied Colloids Group Plc.; *Int'l*, pg. 62
ALLIED COLLOIDS CHEMICALS (FAR EAST) PTE. LTD.—See Allied Colloids Group Plc.; *Int'l*, pg. 62
ALLIED COLLOIDS DE MEXICO S.A. DE C.V.—See Allied Colloids Group Plc.; *Int'l*, pg. 62
ALLIED COLLOIDS DO BRASIL LTDA—See Allied Colloids Group Plc.; *Int'l*, pg. 62
ALLIED COLLOIDS GROUP PLC.; *Int'l*, pg. 62
ALLIED COLLOIDS INC.—See Allied Colloids Group Plc.; *Int'l*, pg. 62
ALLIED COLLOIDS INSURANCE LTD.—See Allied Colloids Group Plc.; *Int'l*, pg. 62
ALLIED COLLOIDS LTD.—See Allied Colloids Group Plc.; *Int'l*, pg. 62
ALLIED COLLOIDS MAGYARORSZAG KFT—See Allied Colloids Group Plc.; *Int'l*, pg. 62
ALLIED COLLOIDS MANUFACTURING GMBH—See Allied Colloids Group Plc.; *Int'l*, pg. 62
ALLIED COLLOIDS NEDERLAND B.V.—See Allied Colloids Group Plc.; *Int'l*, pg. 62
ALLIED COLOUR (N.Z.) LTD.—See Dainippon Ink & Chemicals, Inc.; *Int'l*, pg. 371
ALLIED COMMUNICATIONS GROUP—See The Interpublic Group of Companies, Inc.; *U.S. Public*, pg. 908
ALLIED CONCRETE, INC.—See CalMat Co.; *U.S. Public*, pg. 295
ALLIED CONSTRUCTION PRODUCTS, INC.—See Pubco Corporation; *U.S. Public*, pg. 1339
ALLIED CONSTRUCTION SPECIALITIES—See Allied Oil & Supply, Inc.; *U.S. Private*, pg. 39
ALLIED DEVELOPMENT CORP.—See Allied Capital Corporation; *U.S. Public*, pg. 48
ALLIED DIAGNOSTIC IMAGING RESOURCES, INC.—See CPAC, Inc.; *U.S. Public*, pg. 282
ALLIED DIGITAL TECHNOLOGIES; *U.S. Public*, pg. 48
ALLIED DIGITAL TECHNOLOGIES CORPORATION—See Allied Digital Technologies; *U.S. Public*, pg. 48
ALLIED DOMECQ BRASIL INDUSTRIA E COMERCIO LTDA.—See Allied Domecq PLC; *Int'l*, pg. 63
ALLIED DOMECQ LEISURE—See Allied Domecq PLC; *Int'l*, pg. 63
ALLIED DOMECQ PLC; *Int'l*, pg. 62

ALLIED DOMECQ RETAILING LIMITED—See Allied Domecq PLC; *Int'l*, pg. 63
ALLIED DOMECQ SPIRITS & WINE—See Allied Domecq PLC; *Int'l*, pg. 63
ALLIED DOMECQ SPIRITS & WINE (UK) LTD.—See Allied Domecq PLC; *Int'l*, pg. 63
ALLIED DUNBAR ASSURANCE PLC—See B.A.T Industries P.L.C.; *Int'l*, pg. 110
ALLIED EASTERN CO.—See Zeller Corp.; *U.S. Private*, pg. 1204
ALLIED ELECTRONICS INC.—See Avnet, Inc.; *U.S. Public*, pg. 155
ALLIED FOODS, INC.; *U.S. Private*, pg. 39
ALLIED HEALTHCARE PRODUCTS, INC.; *U.S. Public*, pg. 48
ALLIED HOLDINGS, INC.; *U.S. Public*, pg. 48
ALLIED IMPEX CORP.—See AIC International, Inc.; *U.S. Private*, pg. 6
ALLIED INDUSTRIAL GROUP, INC.; *U.S. Private*, pg. 39
ALLIED INDUS., INC.—See Halliburton Company; *U.S. Public*, pg. 775
ALLIED INSURANCE AGENCY—See The Progressive Corporation; *U.S. Public*, pg. 1334
ALLIED INSURANCE COMPANY—See Cigna Corp.; *U.S. Public*, pg. 362
ALLIED INTERNATIONAL-AMERICAN EAGLE TRADING CORP.—See Itochu Corporation; *Int'l*, pg. 694
ALLIED INVESTMENT CORP.—See Allied Capital Corporation; *U.S. Public*, pg. 48
ALLIED IRISH BANKS, P.L.C.; *Int'l*, pg. 64
ALLIED MERCANTILE COMPANY; *U.S. Private*, pg. 39
ALLIED MINERAL PRODUCTS, INC.; *U.S. Private*, pg. 39
ALLIED MUTUAL INSURANCE COMPANY; *U.S. Private*, pg. 39
ALLIED OFFICE SUPPLIES; *U.S. Private*, pg. 39
ALLIED OIL & SUPPLY—See Allied Oil & Supply, Inc.; *U.S. Private*, pg. 39
ALLIED OIL & SUPPLY, INC.; *U.S. Private*, pg. 39
ALLIED OIL & SUPPLY, INC.—See Allied Oil & Supply, Inc.; *U.S. Private*, pg. 39
ALLIED OIL & SUPPLY, INC.—See Allied Oil & Supply, Inc.; *U.S. Private*, pg. 39
ALLIED OLD ENGLISH, INC.; *U.S. Private*, pg. 39
ALLIED PLYWOOD CORP.; *U.S. Private*, pg. 40
ALLIED PLYWOOD CORPORATION—See Nortek, Inc.; *U.S. Public*, pg. 1193
ALLIED PREMIUM FINANCE—See Credit Suisse Group; *Int'l*, pg. 346
ALLIED PRINTING SERVICES, INC.; *U.S. Private*, pg. 40
ALLIED PRODUCTS CORPORATION; *U.S. Public*, pg. 48
ALLIED RESEARCH CORPORATION; *U.S. Public*, pg. 48
ALLIED RESEARCH CORPORATION LIMITED—See Allied Research Corporation; *U.S. Public*, pg. 49
ALLIED SECURITY, INC.; *U.S. Private*, pg. 41
ALLIED SECURITY INC.—See Allied Security, Inc.; *U.S. Private*, pg. 41
ALLIED SECURITY, INTERNATIONAL; *U.S. Private*, pg. 41
ALLIED SPORTING GOODS INC.; *U.S. Private*, pg. 41
ALLIED THREAD CO. INC.—See Coats Viyella plc; *Int'l*, pg. 299
ALLIED TIRE—See Allied Oil & Supply, Inc.; *U.S. Private*, pg. 39
ALLIED TIRE CO.—See Allied Oil & Supply, Inc.; *U.S. Private*, pg. 39
ALLIED TIRE SALES; *U.S. Private*, pg. 41
ALLIED TOOL PRODUCTS INC.—See Federal Signal Corporation; *U.S. Public*, pg. 617
ALLIED TUBE & CONDUIT CORPORATION—See Tyco International Ltd.; *U.S. Public*, pg. 1650
ALLIED VAN LINES, INC.—See NFC plc; *Int'l*, pg. 901
ALLIED WASTE INDUSTRIES; *U.S. Public*, pg. 49
ALLIED YOUR COFFEE PARTNER—See Allied Office Supplies; *U.S. Private*, pg. 39
ALLIEDSIGNAL AEROSPACE—See AlliedSignal Inc.; *U.S. Public*, pg. 50
ALLIEDSIGNAL AEROSPACE CANADA—See AlliedSignal Inc.; *U.S. Public*, pg. 53
ALLIEDSIGNAL AEROSPACE CANADA, AEROMARINE—See AlliedSignal Inc.; *U.S. Public*, pg. 53
ALLIEDSIGNAL AEROSPACE CANADA, ELECTRONIC SYSTEMS—See AlliedSignal Inc.; *U.S. Public*, pg. 54
ALLIEDSIGNAL AEROSPACE CANADA OCEAN DEFENSE SYSTEMS—See AlliedSignal Inc.; *U.S. Public*, pg. 53
ALLIEDSIGNAL AEROSPACE GMBH—See AlliedSignal Inc.; *U.S. Public*, pg. 52
ALLIEDSIGNAL AEROSPACE LIMITED—See AlliedSignal Inc.; *U.S. Public*, pg. 52
ALLIEDSIGNAL AEROSPACE SERVICE CORPORATION—See AlliedSignal Inc.; *U.S. Public*, pg. 52
ALLIEDSIGNAL AEROSPACE SYSTEMS & EQUIPMENT—See AlliedSignal Inc.; *U.S. Public*, pg. 50
ALLIEDSIGNAL AEROSPATIALE CANADA INC.—See AlliedSignal Inc.; *U.S. Public*, pg. 53
ALLIEDSIGNAL AFTERMARKET EUROPE S.A.—See AlliedSignal Inc.; *U.S. Public*, pg. 53
ALLIEDSIGNAL AIR TRANSPORT AVIONICS—See AlliedSignal Inc.; *U.S. Public*, pg. 50
ALLIEDSIGNAL AIRCRAFT LANDING SYSTEMS—See AlliedSignal Inc.; *U.S. Public*, pg. 50
ALLIEDSIGNAL AIRLINE SERVICES, ALLIED SIGNAL AEROSPACE CANADA—See AlliedSignal Inc.; *U.S. Public*, pg. 50
ALLIEDSIGNAL AMORPHOUS METALS—See AlliedSignal Inc.; *U.S. Public*, pg. 51
ALLIEDSIGNAL (AUSTRALIA) SALES LTD. FIBERS & CHEMICALS—See AlliedSignal Inc.; *U.S. Public*, pg. 52
ALLIEDSIGNAL, AUTOMOTIVE AFTERMARKET—See AlliedSignal Inc.; *U.S. Public*, pg. 51
ALLIEDSIGNAL AUTOMOTIVE ITALIA S.P.A.—See AlliedSignal Inc.; *U.S. Public*, pg. 53
ALLIEDSIGNAL AUTOMOTIVE ITALIA S.P.A., TURBOCOMPRESSORI GARRETT—See AlliedSignal Inc.; *U.S. Public*, pg. 53

ALLIEDSIGNAL AUTOMOTIVE LTDA.—See AlliedSignal Inc.; *U.S. Public*, pg. 52
ALLIEDSIGNAL AUTOMOTIVE LTDA-CAMPINAS PLANT—See AlliedSignal Inc.; *U.S. Public*, pg. 53
ALLIEDSIGNAL AUTOMOTIVE PORTUGAL LTDA.—See AlliedSignal Inc.; *U.S. Public*, pg. 53
ALLIEDSIGNAL AUTOMOTIVE PROVING GROUNDS—See AlliedSignal Inc.; *U.S. Public*, pg. 51
ALLIEDSIGNAL BROMSBELAG GMBH—See AlliedSignal Inc.; *U.S. Public*, pg. 52
ALLIEDSIGNAL CANADA INC., AUTOMOTIVE AFTERMARKET—See AlliedSignal Inc.; *U.S. Public*, pg. 52
ALLIEDSIGNAL CANADA INC.-FILTERS & SPARK PLUGS CANADA—See AlliedSignal Inc.; *U.S. Public*, pg. 54
ALLIEDSIGNAL CERAMIC COMPONENTS—See AlliedSignal Inc.; *U.S. Public*, pg. 50
ALLIEDSIGNAL CHEMICALS—See AlliedSignal Inc.; *U.S. Public*, pg. 52
ALLIEDSIGNAL CHEMICALS CANADA INC.—See AlliedSignal Inc.; *U.S. Public*, pg. 52
ALLIEDSIGNAL CHEMICALS DO BRASIL—See AlliedSignal Inc.; *U.S. Public*, pg. 52
ALLIEDSIGNAL CHEMICALS N.Z. LTD.—See AlliedSignal Inc.; *U.S. Public*, pg. 52
ALLIEDSIGNAL CHINA INC., ALLIEDSIGNAL AEROSPACE SERVICES CORPORATION—See AlliedSignal Inc.; *U.S. Public*, pg. 52
ALLIEDSIGNAL COMMERCIAL AVIONIC SYSTEMS—See AlliedSignal Inc.; *U.S. Public*, pg. 50
ALLIEDSIGNAL COMPUTER-AIDED ENGINEERING CENTER—See AlliedSignal Inc.; *U.S. Public*, pg. 50
ALLIEDSIGNAL CONTROLS & ACCESSORIES—See AlliedSignal Inc.; *U.S. Public*, pg. 50
ALLIEDSIGNAL DE MEXICANO, S.A. DE C.V.—See AlliedSignal Inc.; *U.S. Public*, pg. 52
ALLIEDSIGNAL ENGINES—See AlliedSignal Inc.; *U.S. Public*, pg. 50
ALLIEDSIGNAL ENVIRONMENTAL CATALYSTS—See AlliedSignal Inc.; *U.S. Public*, pg. 52
ALLIEDSIGNAL EUROPE N.V.—See AlliedSignal Inc.; *U.S. Public*, pg. 52
ALLIEDSIGNAL EUROPE S.A.—See AlliedSignal Inc.; *U.S. Public*, pg. 52
ALLIEDSIGNAL FILTERS & SPARK PLUGS—See AlliedSignal Inc.; *U.S. Public*, pg. 51
ALLIEDSIGNAL FLUID SYSTEMS—See AlliedSignal Inc.; *U.S. Public*, pg. 50
ALLIEDSIGNAL FLUOROCARBONS—See AlliedSignal Inc.; *U.S. Public*, pg. 51
ALLIEDSIGNAL FRANCE SPA—See AlliedSignal Inc.; *U.S. Public*, pg. 54
ALLIEDSIGNAL GENERAL AVIATION AVIONICS—See AlliedSignal Inc.; *U.S. Public*, pg. 50
ALLIEDSIGNAL GUIDANCE & CONTROL SYSTEMS—See AlliedSignal Inc.; *U.S. Public*, pg. 50
ALLIEDSIGNAL GUIDANCE SYSTEMS DIV.—See AlliedSignal Inc.; *U.S. Public*, pg. 50
ALLIEDSIGNAL INC.; *U.S. Public*, pg. 49
ALLIEDSIGNAL INC., ALLIEDSIGNAL AUTOMOTIVE—See AlliedSignal Inc.; *U.S. Public*, pg. 51
ALLIEDSIGNAL INC., ALLIEDSIGNAL PLASTIC—See AlliedSignal Inc.; *U.S. Public*, pg. 51
ALLIEDSIGNAL INC., ALLIEDSIGNAL SPECIALTY FILMS—See AlliedSignal Inc.; *U.S. Public*, pg. 51
ALLIEDSIGNAL INC. ASIA—See AlliedSignal Inc.; *U.S. Public*, pg. 52
ALLIEDSIGNAL INC., CHEMICAL INTERMEDIATES—See AlliedSignal Inc.; *U.S. Public*, pg. 51
ALLIEDSIGNAL INC., FLUOROCARBONS—See AlliedSignal Inc.; *U.S. Public*, pg. 51
ALLIEDSIGNAL, INDUSTRIAL FIBERS—See AlliedSignal Inc.; *U.S. Public*, pg. 51
ALLIEDSIGNAL INTERNATIONAL, INC.—See AlliedSignal Inc.; *U.S. Public*, pg. 52
ALLIEDSIGNAL IRELAND LTD.—See AlliedSignal Inc.; *U.S. Public*, pg. 51
ALLIEDSIGNAL-JIDOSHA KIKI CORPORATION—See AlliedSignal Inc.; *U.S. Public*, pg. 51
ALLIEDSIGNAL LAMINATE SYSTEMS—See AlliedSignal Inc.; *U.S. Public*, pg. 51
ALLIEDSIGNAL LAMINATE SYSTEMS GMBH—See AlliedSignal Inc.; *U.S. Public*, pg. 53
ALLIEDSIGNAL LAMINATE SYSTEMS S.A.—See AlliedSignal Inc.; *U.S. Public*, pg. 53
ALLIEDSIGNAL LAMINATE SYSTEMS THAILAND CO., LTD.—See AlliedSignal Inc.; *U.S. Public*, pg. 53
ALLIEDSIGNAL (LTD.) SINGAPORE—See AlliedSignal Inc.; *U.S. Public*, pg. 53
ALLIEDSIGNAL LIMITED TRUCK BRAKE SYSTEMS—See AlliedSignal Inc.; *U.S. Public*, pg. 54
ALLIEDSIGNAL LTD. TURBOCHARGERS—See AlliedSignal Inc.; *U.S. Public*, pg. 54
ALLIEDSIGNAL MATERIAUX DE FRICTION S.A.—See AlliedSignal Inc.; *U.S. Public*, pg. 54
ALLIEDSIGNAL MICROELECTRONICS & TECHNOLOGY CENTER—See AlliedSignal Inc.; *U.S. Public*, pg. 50
ALLIEDSIGNAL OCEAN SYSTEMS—See AlliedSignal Inc.; *U.S. Public*, pg. 50
ALLIEDSIGNAL PERFORMANCE ADDITIVES—See AlliedSignal Inc.; *U.S. Public*, pg. 53
ALLIEDSIGNAL TECHNICAL SERVICE—See AlliedSignal Inc.; *U.S. Public*, pg. 53
ALLIEDSIGNAL TRANSPORTATION INC.—See AlliedSignal Inc.; *U.S. Public*, pg. 51
ALLIEDSIGNAL TRUCK BRAKE SYSTEMS—See AlliedSignal Inc.; *U.S. Public*, pg. 54
ALLIEDSIGNAL TRUCK BRAKE SYSTEMS COMPANY—See Knorr-Bremse AG; *Int'l*, pg. 738
ALLIEDSIGNAL TURBO S.A.—See AlliedSignal Inc.; *U.S. Public*, pg. 53
ALLIEDSIGNAL TURBOCHARGERS, INC.—See AlliedSignal Inc.; *U.S. Public*, pg. 53

ALLIEDSIGNAL DIRECTORY OF CORPORATE AFFILIATIONS

ALLIEDSIGNAL TURBOCHARGING & TRUCK BRAKE SYSTEMS—See AlliedSignal Inc.; *U.S. Public*, pg. 51
ALLIEDSIGNAL TURBOS AUTOMATRICES, S.A. DE C.V.—See AlliedSignal Inc.; *U.S. Public*, pg. 54
ALLING-LANDER—See Regal-Beloit Corporation; *U.S. Public*, pg. 1370
ALLINSURE—See GIB Group; *Int'l*, pg. 532
ALLISON CORPORATION; *U.S. Private*, pg. 41
ALLISON CORPORATION—See Allison Corporation; *U.S. Private*, pg. 41
ALLISON ENGINE COMPANY INC.—See Rolls-Royce plc; *Int'l*, pg. 1127
ALLISON-ERWIN CO. INC.; *U.S. Private*, pg. 41
ALLISON TRANSMISSION—See General Motors Corporation; *U.S. Public*, pg. 719
ALLMAC LUMBER LTD.—See E.R. Probyn Ltd.; *Int'l*, pg. 1071
ALLMERICA FINANCIAL CORPORATION; *U.S. Public*, pg. 54
ALLMERICA SECURITIES TRUST; *U.S. Public*, pg. 54
ALLMETAL SCREW PRODUCTS CORP.; *U.S. Private*, pg. 41
ALLMETAL SCREW PRODUCTS CORP—See Allmetal Screw Products Corp.; *U.S. Private*, pg. 41
ALLNEWSCO, INC.—See Perpetual Corporation; *U.S. Private*, pg. 854
ALLO PRO A.G.—See Sulzer Ltd.; *Int'l*, pg. 1307
ALLO PRO FRANCE SARL—See Sulzer Ltd.; *Int'l*, pg. 1307
ALLO PRO GMBH—See Sulzer Ltd.; *Int'l*, pg. 1307
ALLO PRO ITALIA S.R.L.—See Sulzer Ltd.; *Int'l*, pg. 1307
ALLOMATIC INDUSTRIES—See Raytech Corporation; *U.S.* Public, pg. 1363
ALLOMATIC PRODUCTS COMPANY—See Raytech Corporation; *U.S. Public*, pg. 1363
ALLOU DISTRIBUTORS INC.—See Allou Health & Beauty Care, Inc.; *U.S. Public*, pg. 55
ALLOU HEALTH & BEAUTY CARE, INC.; *U.S. Public*, pg. 55
ALLOU PERSONAL CARE CORP.—See Allou Health & Beauty Care, Inc.; *U.S. Public*, pg. 55
ALLOY PRODUCTS CORP; *U.S. Private*, pg. 42
ALLOY RING SERVICE—See Handy & Harman; *U.S. Public*, pg. 780
ALLOY RODS KOREA CORPORATION—See Charter plc; *Int'l*, pg. 281
ALLOY TECHNOLOGY INTERNATIONAL INC.; *U.S. Private*, pg. 42
ALLOY TOOL STEEL INC.—See Nissho Iwai Corporation; *Int'l*, pg. 947
ALLOYS INTERNATIONAL—See Illinois Tool Works Inc.; *U.S. Public*, pg. 865
ALLOYTEC MECHANICAL—See Canadian Erectors Ltd.; *Int'l*, pg. 256
ALLPARTS, INC.—See JPE, Inc.; *U.S. Public*, pg. 919
ALLRIGHT BALTIMORE, INC.—See Allright Corporation; *U.S. Private*, pg. 42
ALLRIGHT BATON ROUGE, INC.—See Allright Corporation; *U.S. Private*, pg. 42
ALLRIGHT BEAUMONT COMPANY—See Allright Corporation; *U.S. Private*, pg. 42
ALLRIGHT BIRMINGHAM INC.—See Allright Corporation; *U.S. Private*, pg. 42
ALLRIGHT BOSTON PARKING, INC.—See Allright Corporation; *U.S. Private*, pg. 42
ALLRIGHT CAL. INC.—See Allright Corporation; *U.S. Private*, pg. 42
ALLRIGHT CARPARK, INC.—See Allright Corporation; *U.S.* Private, pg. 42
ALLRIGHT CINCINNATI, INC.—See Allright Corporation; *U.S. Private*, pg. 42
ALLRIGHT COLORADO, INC.—See Allright Corporation; *U.S. Private*, pg. 42
ALLRIGHT COLUMBUS PARKING, INC.—See Allright Corporation; *U.S. Private*, pg. 42
ALLRIGHT CORPORATION; *U.S. Private*, pg. 42
ALLRIGHT CORPORATION OF DELAWARE—See Allright Corporation; *U.S. Private*, pg. 42
ALLRIGHT CORPUS CHRISTI, INC.—See Allright Corporation; *U.S. Private*, pg. 42
ALLRIGHT DAYTON PARKING, INC.—See Allright Corporation; *U.S. Private*, pg. 42
ALLRIGHT FLORIDA, INC.—See Allright Corporation; *U.S. Private*, pg. 42
ALLRIGHT L.R., INC.—See Allright Corporation; *U.S. Private*, pg. 42
ALLRIGHT LONG BEACH PARKING—See Allright Corporation; *U.S. Private*, pg. 42
ALLRIGHT LOUISVILLE CO., INC.—See Allright Corporation; *U.S. Private*, pg. 42
ALLRIGHT MIAMI, INC.—See Allright Corporation; *U.S. Private*, pg. 42
ALLRIGHT MISSOURI, INC.—See Allright Corporation; *U.S.* Private, pg. 42
ALLRIGHT NASHVILLE PARKING, INC.—See Allright Corporation; *U.S. Private*, pg. 42
ALLRIGHT NEW ORLEANS, INC.—See Allright Corporation; *U.S. Private*, pg. 43
ALLRIGHT NEW YORK PARKING, INC.—See Allright Corporation; *U.S. Private*, pg. 43
ALLRIGHT PARKING CHARLOTTE, INC.—See Allright Corporation; *U.S. Private*, pg. 43
ALLRIGHT PARKING CHICAGO, INC.—See Allright Corporation; *U.S. Private*, pg. 43
ALLRIGHT PARKING CORPORATION—See Allright Corporation; *U.S. Private*, pg. 43
ALLRIGHT PARKING EL PASO, INC.—See Allright Corporation; *U.S. Private*, pg. 43
ALLRIGHT PARKING MINNESOTA, INC.—See Allright Corporation; *U.S. Private*, pg. 43
ALLRIGHT PARKING OF AUSTIN, INC.—See Allright Corporation; *U.S. Private*, pg. 43
ALLRIGHT PARKING OF CLEVELAND, INC.—See Allright Corporation; *U.S. Private*, pg. 43
ALLRIGHT PARKING OF GEORGIA—See Allright Corporation; *U.S. Private*, pg. 43
ALLRIGHT PARKING OF GEORGIA, INC.—See Allright Corporation; *U.S. Private*, pg. 43
ALLRIGHT PARKING OF INDIANAPOLIS, INC.—See Allright Corporation; *U.S. Private*, pg. 43
ALLRIGHT PARKING OF MILWAUKEE, INC.—See Allright Corporation; *U.S. Private*, pg. 43
ALLRIGHT PARKING OF TEXAS, INC.—See Allright Corporation; *U.S. Private*, pg. 43
ALLRIGHT PARKING - OMAHA—See Allright Corporation; *U.S. Private*, pg. 43
ALLRIGHT PARKING SYSTEM, INC.—See Allright Corporation; *U.S. Private*, pg. 43
ALLRIGHT PARKING VIRGINIA, INC.—See Allright Corporation; *U.S. Private*, pg. 43
ALLRIGHT PARKING WASHINGTON, INC.—See Allright Corporation; *U.S. Private*, pg. 43
ALLRIGHT PENSACOLA PARKING—See Allright Corporation; *U.S. Private*, pg. 43
ALLRIGHT ROANOKE PARKING, INC.—See Allright Corporation; *U.S. Private*, pg. 43
ALLRIGHT SACRAMENTO—See Allright Corporation; *U.S. Private*, pg. 43
ALLRIGHT SAN ANTONIO PARKING, INC.—See Allright Corporation; *U.S. Private*, pg. 43
ALLRIGHT SAN DIEGO PARKING, INC.—See Allright Corporation; *U.S. Private*, pg. 43
ALLRIGHT SAN FRANCISCO PARKING, INC.—See Allright Corporation; *U.S. Private*, pg. 43
ALLRIGHT SHREVEPORT, INC.—See Allright Corporation; *U.S. Private*, pg. 43
ALLRIGHT SIERRA PARKING, INC.—See Allright Corporation; *U.S. Private*, pg. 43
ALLRIGHT SIERRA PARKING INC.—See Allright Corporation; *U.S. Private*, pg. 43
ALLRIGHT SYSTEM PARKING, INC.—See Allright Corporation; *U.S. Private*, pg. 43
ALLRIGHT TENN. INC.—See Allright Corporation; *U.S. Private*, pg. 43
ALLRIGHT TOLEDO, INC.—See Allright Corporation; *U.S. Private*, pg. 43
ALLRIGHT WEST PALM BEACH, INC.—See Allright Corporation; *U.S. Private*, pg. 43
ALLSOP, INC.; *U.S. Private*, pg. 44
ALLSPANN, ALLGEMEINE SPANNBETON GMBH—See Dyckerhoff & Widmann AG; *Int'l*, pg. 423
ALLSPANN, ALLGEMEINE SPANNBETONGESELLSCHAFT M.B.H.—See Dyckerhoff & Widmann AG; *Int'l*, pg. 424
ALLSTATE AUTOMOBILE & FIRE INSURANCE CO., LTD.—See The Saison Group; *Int'l*, pg. 1178
ALLSTATE CAN CORPORATION; *U.S. Private*, pg. 44
THE ALLSTATE CORPORATION; *U.S. Public*, pg. 55
ALLSTEEL, INC.—See HON Industries Inc.; *U.S. Public*, pg. 772
ALLSUPS CONVENIENCE STORES INC.; *U.S. Private*, pg. 44
ALLTEL ALABAMA—See ALLTEL Corporation; *U.S. Public*, pg. 55
ALLTEL ANSWERING SERVICE, INC.—See ALLTEL Corporation; *U.S. Public*, pg. 55
ALLTEL ARKANSAS, INC.—See ALLTEL Corporation; *U.S. Public*, pg. 55
ALLTEL CAROLINA, INC.—See ALLTEL Corporation; *U.S. Public*, pg. 55
ALLTEL COMMUNICATIONS CORPORATION—See ALLTEL Corporation; *U.S. Public*, pg. 55
ALLTEL CORPORATION; *U.S. Public*, pg. 55
ALLTEL DISTRIBUTION, INC.—See ALLTEL Corporation; *U.S. Public*, pg. 55
ALLTEL FINANCE CORPORATION—See ALLTEL Corporation; *U.S. Public*, pg. 55
ALLTEL FLORIDA, INC.—See ALLTEL Corporation; *U.S. Public*, pg. 56
ALLTEL GEORGIA, INC.—See ALLTEL Corporation; *U.S. Public*, pg. 56
ALLTEL INFORMATION SERVICES-HEALTHCARE DIV.—See ALLTEL Corporation; *U.S. Public*, pg. 55
ALLTEL INFORMATION SERVICES, INC.—See ALLTEL Corporation; *U.S. Public*, pg. 56
ALLTEL KENTUCKY, INC.—See ALLTEL Corporation; *U.S. Public*, pg. 56
ALLTEL MISSISSIPPI, INC.—See ALLTEL Corporation; *U.S.* Public, pg. 56
ALLTEL MISSOURI, INC.—See ALLTEL Corporation; *U.S. Public*, pg. 56
ALLTEL MOBILE COMMUNICATIONS, INC.—See ALLTEL Corporation; *U.S. Public*, pg. 56
ALLTEL NEW YORK, INC.—See ALLTEL Corporation; *U.S.* Public, pg. 56
ALLTEL OHIO, INC.—See ALLTEL Corporation; *U.S. Public*, pg. 56
ALLTEL OKLAHOMA, INC.—See ALLTEL Corporation; *U.S.* Public, pg. 56
ALLTEL PENNSYLVANIA, INC.—See ALLTEL Corporation; *U.S. Public*, pg. 56
ALLTEL PUBLISHING CORPORATION—See ALLTEL Corporation; *U.S. Public*, pg. 56
ALLTEL SERVICE CORPORATION—See ALLTEL Corporation; *U.S. Public*, pg. 56
ALLTEL SERVICES, INC.—See ALLTEL Corporation; *U.S. Public*, pg. 56
ALLTEL SOUTH CAROLINA, INC.—See ALLTEL Corporation; *U.S. Public*, pg. 56
ALLTEL SUPPLY, INC.—See ALLTEL Corporation; *U.S. Public*, pg. 55
ALLTEL TELEPHONE SERVICES CORPORATION—See ALLTEL Corporation; *U.S. Public*, pg. 56
ALLTEL TENNESSEE, INC.—See Citizens Utilities Company; *U.S. Public*, pg. 380
ALLTEL TEXAS, INC.—See ALLTEL Corporation; *U.S. Public*, pg. 56
ALLTIMATE CATERING—See Marsh Supermarkets, Inc.; *U.S. Public*, pg. 1049
ALLTRISTA CORPORATION; *U.S. Public*, pg. 56
ALLUMINIO ALUSUISSE SPA—See Alusuisse-Lonza Holding Ltd.; *Int'l*, pg. 68
ALLURE—See Advance Publications Inc.; *U.S. Private*, pg. 20
ALLVAC—See Allegheny Teledyne Incorporated; *U.S. Public*, pg. 43
ALLVIA, ING. GES. FUR PLANUNG UND KONSTRUKTION—See Dyckerhoff & Widmann AG; *Int'l*, pg. 423
ALLYN & BACON—See National Amusements, Inc.; *U.S. Private*, pg. 778
ALMACENADORA BANCOMER—See Bancomer, S.A.; *Int'l*, pg. 145
ALMAGON—See Axel Johnson AB; *Int'l*, pg. 710
ALMANIJ N.V.; *Int'l*, pg. 65
ALMAVER NV—See Almanij N.V.; *Int'l*, pg. 65
ALMAY, INC.—See MacAndrews & Forbes Holdings Inc.; *U.S. Private*, pg. 689
ALME VIS A BILLES SA—See Mannesmann A.G.; *Int'l*, pg. 838
ALMEDA MALL, INC.—See The Rouse Company; *U.S. Public*, pg. 1409
ALMEGA CORPORATION—See ERD Waste Corp.; *U.S. Public*, pg. 546
ALMEGA CORPORATION-CA—See ERD Waste Corp.; *U.S. Public*, pg. 546
ALMET FRANCE—See Pechiney S.A.; *Int'l*, pg. 1028
ALMET METALL-HALBSEUG-VERTRIEBE-GMBH—See Pechiney S.A.; *Int'l*, pg. 1030
ALMETAL HOLDING N.V.—See Arbed S.A.; *Int'l*, pg. 79
ALMETEX—See Alcan Aluminium Limited; *Int'l*, pg. 51
ALMHULTS GJUTERI—See Svedala Industri AB; *Int'l*, pg. 1323
ALMO CORP.; *U.S. Private*, pg. 44
ALMOND ROCA INTERNATIONAL—See Brown & Haley; *U.S. Private*, pg. 173
ALNAB ARMATUR AB—See AB Industrivarden; *Int'l*, pg. 678
ALNO AG; *Int'l*, pg. 65
ALNOR INSTRUMENT COMPANY—See TSI Incorporated; *U.S. Public*, pg. 1559
ALO-JIDAC S.A.—See Fuchs Petrolub AG Oel + Chemie; *Int'l*, pg. 518
ALOE-VERA OF AMERICA—See Forever Living Products International, Inc.; *U.S. Private*, pg. 418
ALOETTE COSMETICS (AUSTRALASIA) PTY. LTD.—See Aloette Cosmetics, Inc.; *U.S. Public*, pg. 57
ALOETTE COSMETICS, INC.; *U.S. Public*, pg. 57
ALOETTE COSMETICS OF CANADA—See Aloette Cosmetics, Inc.; *U.S. Public*, pg. 57
ALOETTE COSMETICS (UK) LTD.—See Aloette Cosmetics, Inc.; *U.S. Public*, pg. 57
ALOHA AIRGROUP, INC.; *U.S. Private*, pg. 44
ALOHA AIRLINES, INC.—See Aloha Airgroup, Inc.; *U.S. Private*, pg. 44
ALOHA AUTO AUCTION—See Tyco International Ltd.; *U.S.* Public, pg. 1648
ALOIS DALLMAYR KAFFEE OHG—See Nestle S.A.; *Int'l*, pg. 918
ALOVERZEE HANDELGESELLSCHAFT MBH—See Fried. Krupp AG; *Int'l*, pg. 515
ALOX CORPORATION—See RPM, Inc.; *U.S. Public*, pg. 1357
ALP'VERRE—See Saint-Gobain; *Int'l*, pg. 1172
ALPAC CONSTRUCTION & SURVEYS LIMITED—See BC Gas Inc.; *Int'l*, pg. 114
ALPARGATAS SANTISTA TEXTIL S.A.—See Sao Paulo Alpargatas S.A.; *Int'l*, pg. 1193
ALPEK, S.A. DE C.V.—See Alfa, S.A. de C.V.; *Int'l*, pg. 56
ALPESCA, S.A.—See National Sea Products Limited; *Int'l*, pg. 909
ALPHA AIRPORTS GROUP PLC; *Int'l*, pg. 65
ALPHA AIRPORTS GROUP PLC—See Alpha Airports Group Plc; *Int'l*, pg. 65
ALPHA ASSOCIATES, INC.; *U.S. Private*, pg. 44
ALPHA ASSURANCES—See AXA-UAP; *Int'l*, pg. 18
ALPHA BOLT COMPANY—See Washers, Incorporated; *U.S. Private*, pg. 1152
ALPHA COATINGS—See Washers, Incorporated; *U.S. Private*, pg. 1152
ALPHA CONTACT—See Generale de Banque S.A.; *Int'l*, pg. 546
THE ALPHA CORPORATION OF TENNESSEE; *U.S. Private*, pg. 44
ALPHA CREDIT—See Generale de Banque S.A.; *Int'l*, pg. 546
ALPHA EDITIONS—See Lagardere Groupe; *Int'l*, pg. 791
ALPHA FOREST PRODUCTS INC.—See Repap Enterprises Inc.; *Int'l*, pg. 1104
ALPHA INDUSTRIES; *U.S. Private*, pg. 45
ALPHA INDUSTRIES, INC.; *U.S. Public*, pg. 57
ALPHA INDUSTRIES SDN. BHD.—See The Furukawa Electric Co., Ltd.; *Int'l*, pg. 530
ALPHA INDUSTRIES, USA, LTD.—See Alpha Industries, Inc.; *U.S. Public*, pg. 57
ALPHA LIFE SA—See Generale de Banque S.A.; *Int'l*, pg. 546
ALPHA METALS, INC.—See Cookson Group plc; *Int'l*, pg. 328
ALPHA MICROSYSTEMS; *U.S. Public*, pg. 57
ALPHA MILLS CORP.; *U.S. Private*, pg. 45
ALPHA MUURVERFFABRIEKEN BV—See Akzo Nobel N.V.; *Int'l*, pg. 43
ALPHA OLEFINS NORTH AMERICA INC.—See Sasol Limited; *Int'l*, pg. 1196
ALPHA OMEGA PUBLICATIONS—See Bridgestone Multi-Media Group; *U.S. Private*, pg. 168
ALPHA OMIKRON LIMITED; *Int'l*, pg. 65
ALPHA ONE EXCHANGE; *U.S. Private*, pg. 45
ALPHA/OWENS CORNING LLC—See The Alpha Corporation Of Tennessee; *U.S. Private*, pg. 45
ALPHA PAY PHONES, LTD. III—See Peoples Telephone Company, Inc.; *U.S. Public*, pg. 1275

Company Index

ALPHA PROPERTY & CASUALTY INSURANCE CO.—See Unitrin, Inc.; *U.S. Public*, pg. 1694
ALPHA Q, INC.; *U.S. Private*, pg. 45
ALPHA SHIRT CO., INC.; *U.S. Private*, pg. 45
ALPHA SYSTEMS LTD.—See Oracle Corporation; *U.S. Public*, pg. 1228
ALPHA THERAPEUTIC CORP.—See The Green Cross Corporation; *Int'l*, pg. 558
ALPHA THERAPEUTIC GMBH—See The Green Cross Corporation; *Int'l*, pg. 558
ALPHA THERAPEUTIC ITALIA, S.P.A.—See The Green Cross Corporation; *Int'l*, pg. 558
ALPHA THERAPEUTIC U.K. LTD.—See The Green Cross Corporation; *Int'l*, pg. 558
ALPHA TUBE—See Acme Metals Incorporated; *U.S. Public*, pg. 17
ALPHA WAVE HEALTHCARE COMMUNICATIONS—See Ketchum Communications Inc.; *U.S. Private*, pg. 617
ALPHA WIRE COMPANY—See Belden Inc.; *U.S. Public*, pg. 201
ALPHABET DE MEXICO—See Stoneridge, Inc.; *U.S. Private*, pg. 1045
ALPHABET DESIGN CENTER—See Stoneridge, Inc.; *U.S. Private*, pg. 1044
ALPHABET DIVISION—See Stoneridge, Inc.; *U.S. Private*, pg. 1044
ALPHABET EUROPEAN SALES OFFICE—See Stoneridge, Inc.; *U.S. Private*, pg. 1045
ALPHAGARY CORPORATION—See Laporte plc; *Int'l*, pg. 802
ALPHAGAZ DIVISION—See Air Liquide S.A.; *Int'l*, pg. 37
ALPHAPAGE—See France Telecom; *Int'l*, pg. 503
ALPHARMA INC.; *U.S. Public*, pg. 57
ALPINA INSURANCE COMPANY—See Zurich Insurance Company; *Int'l*, pg. 1529
ALPINE AKTIENGESELLSCHAFT—See Hosokawa Micron Corporation; *Int'l*, pg. 636
ALPINE AMERICAN—See Hosokawa Micron Corporation; *Int'l*, pg. 635
ALPINE CENTER, S.R.L. (BERLITZ)—See Berlitz International, Inc.; *U.S. Public*, pg. 221
ALPINE ELECTRONICS, INC.—See Alps Electric Co., Ltd.; *Int'l*, pg. 65
ALPINE ELECTRONICS OF AMERICA, INC.—See Alps Electric Co., Ltd.; *Int'l*, pg. 65
THE ALPINE GROUP, INC.; *U.S. Public*, pg. 58
ALPINE INDUSTRIES—See CFA Holding Company; *U.S. Private*, pg. 194
ALPINE LACE BRANDS, INC.—See Land O'Lakes, Inc.; *U.S. Private*, pg. 646
ALPINE PACKING COMPANY; *U.S. Private*, pg. 45
ALPINE TECHNOLOGIES DE VENEZUELA, C.A.—See Eclipse Inc.; *U.S. Private*, pg. 360
ALPINE TERRACE—See Paragon Health Network, Inc.; *U.S. Public*, pg. 1256
ALPNET—See Alpnet Inc.; *U.S. Public*, pg. 58
ALPNET INC.; *U.S. Public*, pg. 58
ALPO PET FOODS—See Nestle S.A.; *Int'l*, pg. 917
ALPO PET FOODS—See Nestle S.A.; *Int'l*, pg. 917
ALPS ELECTRIC CO., LTD.; *Int'l*, pg. 65
ALPS INSTITUTE S.R.L. (BERLITZ)—See Berlitz International, Inc.; *U.S. Public*, pg. 221
ALRA LABORATORIES, INC.; *U.S. Private*, pg. 45
ALRASHID-ABETONG CO. LTD.—See Scancem AB; *Int'l*, pg. 1199
ALRO GROUP; *U.S. Private*, pg. 45
ALRO GROUP, ALPENA—See Alro Group; *U.S. Private*, pg. 46
ALRO GROUP, BATTLE CREEK—See Alro Group; *U.S. Private*, pg. 46
ALRO GROUP, BENTON HARBOR—See Alro Group; *U.S. Private*, pg. 46
ALRO GROUP, BOCA RATON—See Alro Group; *U.S. Private*, pg. 46
ALRO GROUP, CLEARWATER—See Alro Group; *U.S. Private*, pg. 46
ALRO GROUP, DAYTON—See Alro Group; *U.S. Private*, pg. 46
ALRO GROUP, DETROIT—See Alro Group; *U.S. Private*, pg. 46
ALRO GROUP, FLINT—See Alro Group; *U.S. Private*, pg. 46
ALRO GROUP, FORT WAYNE—See Alro Group; *U.S. Private*, pg. 46
ALRO GROUP, GRAND RAPIDS—See Alro Group; *U.S. Private*, pg. 46
ALRO GROUP, INDIANAPOLIS—See Alro Group; *U.S. Private*, pg. 46
ALRO GROUP, JACKSON—See Alro Group; *U.S. Private*, pg. 46
ALRO GROUP, JACKSON PLASTICS—See Alro Group; *U.S. Private*, pg. 46
ALRO GROUP, KALAMAZOO—See Alro Group; *U.S. Private*, pg. 46
ALRO GROUP, LOUISVILLE—See Alro Group; *U.S. Private*, pg. 46
ALRO GROUP, MUNCIE—See Alro Group; *U.S. Private*, pg. 46
ALRO GROUP, ORLANDO—See Alro Group; *U.S. Private*, pg. 46
ALRO GROUP, PERRYSBURG—See Alro Group; *U.S. Private*, pg. 46
ALRO GROUP, SOUTH BEND—See Alro Group; *U.S. Private*, pg. 46
ALRO INDUSTRIAL SUPPLY GROUP—See Alro Group; *U.S. Private*, pg. 46
ALRO SPECIALTY METALS, CHARLOTTE—See Alro Group; *U.S. Private*, pg. 46
ALRO SPECIALTY METALS, MENOMONEE FALLS—See Alro Group; *U.S. Private*, pg. 46
ALRO SPECIALTY METALS, REDFORD—See Alro Group; *U.S. Private*, pg. 46
ALRO SPECIALTY METALS, TALLMADGE—See Alro Group; *U.S. Private*, pg. 46

ALRO SPECIALTY METALS, TONAWANDA—See Alro Group; *U.S. Private*, pg. 46
ALRO SPECIALTY METALS, VILLA PARK—See Alro Group; *U.S. Private*, pg. 46
ALRON CHEFARO KK—See Akzo Nobel N.V.; *Int'l*, pg. 44
ALS CONSEIL—See BDDP Group; *Int'l*, pg. 116
ALSEN-BREITENBURG ZEMENT- UN KALWERKE GMBH—See Holderbank Financiere Glaris Ltd.; *Int'l*, pg. 629
ALSI GESTION—See Credit Nationale; *Int'l*, pg. 344
ALSIDE—See Associated Materials Incorporated; *U.S. Private*, pg. 91
ALSO HOLDING AG—See Schindler Holding AG; *Int'l*, pg. 1204
ALSO S.P.A.—See Unilever Plc; *Int'l*, pg. 1436
ALSONS CEMENT CORPORATION—See Holderbank Financiere Glaris Ltd.; *Int'l*, pg. 629
ALSONS CORPORATION—See Masco Corporation; *U.S. Public*, pg. 1053
ALSTADT INSURANCES—See Zurich Insurance Company; *Int'l*, pg. 1529
ALSTHOM-JEUMONT—See Jeumont-Schneider Trenformeteurs; *Int'l*, pg. 706
ALSTRIP EAST—See Allegheny Teledyne Incorporated; *U.S. Public*, pg. 43
ALSTRIP, INC.—See Allegheny Teledyne Incorporated; *U.S. Public*, pg. 43
ALSTRIP SOUTH—See Allegheny Teledyne Incorporated; *U.S. Public*, pg. 43
ALTA-DENA CERTIFIED DAIRY—See Bongrain S.A.; *Int'l*, pg. 201
ALTA DENA INC.—See Bongrain S.A.; *Int'l*, pg. 201
ALTA GOLD CO.; *U.S. Public*, pg. 58
ALTA LOMA PRODUCTIONS, INC.—See Playboy Enterprises, Inc.; *U.S. Public*, pg. 1310
ALTA PACIFIC CONSTRUCTORS—See The Rados Companies; *U.S. Private*, pg. 907
ALTA VISTA HEALTHCARE—See Vencor, Inc.; *U.S. Public*, pg. 1711
ALTAE BANCO S.A.—See Caja de Madrid Group; *Int'l*, pg. 251
ALTAI DEVELOPMENT LABORATORY—See Platinum Technology, Inc.; *U.S. Public*, pg. 1309
ALTAIR CORPORATION; *U.S. Public*, pg. 46
ALTAMA DELTA CORPORATION; *U.S. Private*, pg. 47
ALTANA AG; *Int'l*, pg. 65
ALTANA EXPLORATION COMPANY—See Montana Power Company; *U.S. Public*, pg. 1127
ALTANA, INC.—See Altana AG; *Int'l*, pg. 66
ALTASTEEL LTD.—See Stelco Inc.; *Int'l*, pg. 1299
ALTE HAIDE GMBH—See Mannesmann A.G.; *Int'l*, pg. 836
ALTE LEIPZIGER RUECKVERSICHERUNG AG—See Alte Leipziger Versicherung Aktiengesellschaft; *Int'l*, pg. 66
ALTE LEIPZIGER VERSICHERUNG AKTIENGESELLSCHAFT; *Int'l*, pg. 66
ALTEC ELECTRONICA DE CHIHUAHUA S. A. DE C. V.—See Ford Motor Company; *U.S. Public*, pg. 665
ALTEC INDUSTRIES, INC.; *U.S. Private*, pg. 47
ALTEC LANSING CORP.—See Greenwich Street Capital Partners, L.P.; *U.S. Private*, pg. 479
ALTEC LANSING TECHNOLOGIES, INC.—See Greenwich Street Capital Partners, Inc.; *U.S. Private*, pg. 479
ALTEGRA CREDIT COMPANY—See National City Corporation; *U.S. Public*, pg. 1154
ALTEK—See Fiat Auto SpA; *Int'l*, pg. 483
ALTENBERG ZINK AG—See Union Miniere; *Int'l*, pg. 1442
THE HARRY ALTER COMPANY—See Temperature Equipment Corporation; *U.S. Private*, pg. 1075
ALTERA CORPORATION; *U.S. Public*, pg. 59
ALTERMAN TRANSPORT LINES, INC.; *U.S. Private*, pg. 47
ALTERNATIVE COMPUTER COMPANY—See General Electric Company; *U.S. Public*, pg. 711
ALTERNATIVE REMEDIAL TECHNOLOGIES, INC.—See Heidemij N.V.; *Int'l*, pg. 607
ALTERNATIVE RESOURCES CORPORATION; *U.S. Public*, pg. 59
ALTERNATIVE TRANSPORT SERVICES LTD.—See Royal Nedlloyd Group N.V.; *Int'l*, pg. 1144
ALTINIA S.P.A.—See Assicurazioni Generali S.p.A.; *Int'l*, pg. 89
ALTO DAIRY COOPERATIVE; *U.S. Private*, pg. 47
ALTO PAPERS COMPANY—See Bradner Central Company; *U.S. Private*, pg. 164
THE ALTON & SOUTHERN RAILWAY CO.—See Union Pacific Corporation; *U.S. Public*, pg. 1668
ALTON TELEGRAPH—See Journal Register Company; *U.S. Public*, pg. 934
ALTOS HORNOS DE MEXICO, S.A.; *Int'l*, pg. 46
ALTPAPIER-VERWERTUNG WATTENSCHEID GMBH—See Stora Kopparbergs Bergslags AB; *Int'l*, pg. 1303
ALTRA MARINE PRODUCTS, INC.—See Greenway Partners, L.P.; *U.S. Private*, pg. 479
ALTRON INCORPORATED; *U.S. Public*, pg. 59
ALTRON SYSTEMS CORPORATION—See Altron Incorporated; *U.S. Public*, pg. 59
ALTUS ENGINEERING (CORSHAM) LTD.—See Delta plc; *Int'l*, pg. 390
ALUCAM-SOCTRAL—See Pechiney S.A.; *Int'l*, pg. 1030
ALUCOBOND FAR EAST PTY LTD—See Alusuisse-Lonza Holding Ltd.; *Int'l*, pg. 68
ALUCON KFT.—See Plettac AG; *Int'l*, pg. 1061
ALUFLUOR AKTIEBOLAG—See Alusuisse-Lonza Holding Ltd.; *Int'l*, pg. 69
ALUFLUOR AKTIEBOLAG—See Kemira Oy; *Int'l*, pg. 729
ALUM-A-THERM—See Lindberg Corporation; *U.S. Public*, pg. 999
ALUMA METALLI—See Electrolux, AB; *Int'l*, pg. 441
ALUMA SHIELD INDUSTRIES, INC.; *U.S. Private*, pg. 47
ALUMA SYSTEMS CORP.—See Tridel Enterprises Inc.; *Int'l*, pg. 1423
ALUMACRAFT BOAT CO.—See Timpte Industries, Inc.; *U.S. Private*, pg. 1088

ALUMAR CONSORTIUM—See Aluminum Company of America; *U.S. Public*, pg. 62
ALUMAX ALUMINUM CORP., MILL PRODUCTS—See Alumax Inc.; *U.S. Public*, pg. 59
ALUMAX ENGINEERED METAL PROCESSES, INC.—See Alumax Inc.; *U.S. Public*, pg. 60
ALUMAX EXTRUSIONS, INC.—See Alumax Inc.; *U.S. Public*, pg. 59
ALUMAX FOILS, INC.—See Alumax Inc.; *U.S. Public*, pg. 60
ALUMAX INC.; *U.S. Public*, pg. 59
ALUMAX MILL PRODUCTS, INC.—See Alumax Inc.; *U.S. Public*, pg. 59
ALUMAX OF SOUTH CAROLINA MT. HOLLY—See Alumax Inc.; *U.S. Public*, pg. 60
ALUMAX PRIMARY ALUMINUM CORPORATION—See Alumax Inc.; *U.S. Public*, pg. 60
ALUMINA COMPANY LIMITED—See Alcan Aluminium Limited; *Int'l*, pg. 51
ALUMINA PARTNERS OF JAMAICA (ALPART)—See Maxxam Inc.; *U.S. Public*, pg. 1062
ALUMINERIE DE BECANCOUR INC. (A.B.I.)—See Pechiney S.A.; *Int'l*, pg. 1030
ALUMINIO REYNOLDS, SANTO DOMINGO, S.A.—See Reynolds Metals Company; *U.S. Public*, pg. 1386
ALUMINIUM DELFZIJL—See Koninklijke Hoogovens N.V.; *Int'l*, pg. 755
ALUMINIUM DELFZIJL BV—See Koninklijke Hoogovens N.V.; *Int'l*, pg. 753
ALUMINIUM EUROPE S.A., EN ABREGE: "ALEUROPE S.A."—See Reynolds Metals Company; *U.S. Public*, pg. 1386
ALUMINO REYNOLDS DE VENEZUELA, S.A.—See Reynolds Metals Company; *U.S. Public*, pg. 1386
ALUMINUM & CHEMIE ROTTERDAM B.V. - (ALUCHEMIE)—See Alusuisse-Lonza Holding Ltd.; *Int'l*, pg. 68
ALUMINUM COMPANY OF AMERICA; *U.S. Public*, pg. 60
ALUMINUM CO. OF MALAYSIA BERHAD—See Alcan Aluminium Limited; *Int'l*, pg. 51
ALUMINUM CORPORATION—See Alcan Aluminium Limited; *Int'l*, pg. 51
ALUMINUM DE GRECE—See Pechiney S.A.; *Int'l*, pg. 1030
ALUMINUM DECIN SPOL. S.R.O.—See Alusuisse-Lonza Holding Ltd.; *Int'l*, pg. 68
ALUMINUM DUNKERQUE S.A.—See Pechiney S.A.; *Int'l*, pg. 1028
ALUMINUM INDUSTRIE WOHMBAU GMBH—See Alusuisse-Lonza Holding Ltd.; *Int'l*, pg. 68
ALUMINUM-METALL ALMET AG—See Pechiney S.A.; *Int'l*, pg. 1030
ALUMINUM NORF GMBH—See Alcan Aluminium Limited; *Int'l*, pg. 51
ALUMINUM OF KOREA LTD.—See Hyundai Motor Company; *Int'l*, pg. 641
ALUMINUM OXID STADE GESELLSCHAFT MIT BESCHRANKTER HAFTUNG—See Reynolds Metals Company; *U.S. Public*, pg. 1386
ALUMINUM PECHINEY—See Pechiney S.A.; *Int'l*, pg. 1028
THE ALUMINUM POWDER COMPANY—See Metallurg, Inc.; *U.S. Private*, pg. 735
ALUMINUM PRECISION EXTRUDERS LTD.—See Norsk Hydro a.s; *Int'l*, pg. 961
ALUMINUM SHAPES, LLC; *U.S. Private*, pg. 47
ALUMINUM SMELTING CO. OF NIGERIA—See Reynolds Metals Company; *U.S. Public*, pg. 1386
ALUMINUM UK LIMITED—See Saint-Gobain; *Int'l*, pg. 1172
ALUMINUM-VERWALTUNGS-GESELLSCHAFT MBH—See Viag AG; *Int'l*, pg. 1466
ALUMITECH—See Hayes Wheels International, Inc.; *U.S. Private*, pg. 513
ALUMITECH, INC.—See Zemex Corporation; *Int'l*, pg. 1523
ALUMOB ALUSUISSE REAL ESTATE LTD.—See Alusuisse-Lonza Holding Ltd.; *Int'l*, pg. 67
ALUNORD S.A.—See Norsk Hydro a.s; *Int'l*, pg. 961
ALUPLAST S.A. DE C.V.—See The West Company, Incorporated; *U.S. Public*, pg. 1756
ALUPOWER, INC.—See Ener-Tek International Corporation; *U.S. Private*, pg. 376
ALUSINGEN GMBH—See Alusuisse-Lonza Holding Ltd.; *Int'l*, pg. 68
ALUSTAR, S.A. DE C.V.—See CCL Industries, Inc.; *Int'l*, pg. 239
ALUSUISSE AUSTRIA GMBH—See Alusuisse-Lonza Holding Ltd.; *Int'l*, pg. 68
ALUSUISSE ESPANA S.A.—See Alusuisse-Lonza Holding Ltd.; *Int'l*, pg. 68
ALUSUISSE FRANCE PRODUITS INDUSTRIELS S.A.—See Alusuisse-Lonza Holding Ltd.; *Int'l*, pg. 68
ALUSUISSE HOLDINGS LTD.—See Alusuisse-Lonza Holding Ltd.; *Int'l*, pg. 67
ALUSUISSE JAPAN LTD.—See Alusuisse-Lonza Holding Ltd.; *Int'l*, pg. 68
ALUSUISSE-LONZA A.G. FUR KREISLAUFWIRTSCHAFT—See Alusuisse-Lonza Holding Ltd.; *Int'l*, pg. 67
ALUSUISSE-LONZA AMERICA INC.—See Alusuisse-Lonza Holding Ltd.; *Int'l*, pg. 67
ALUSUISSE-LONZA AUSTRALASIA PACIFIC PTY LTD.—See Alusuisse-Lonza Holding Ltd.; *Int'l*, pg. 68
ALUSUISSE-LONZA CAPITAL LTD—See Alusuisse-Lonza Holding Ltd.; *Int'l*, pg. 68
ALUSUISSE-LONZA ENERGIE AG—See Alusuisse-Lonza Holding Ltd.; *Int'l*, pg. 67
ALUSUISSE-LONZA EUROPE—See Alusuisse-Lonza Holding Ltd.; *Int'l*, pg. 68
ALUSUISSE-LONZA FRANCE S.A.—See Alusuisse-Lonza Holding Ltd.; *Int'l*, pg. 68
ALUSUISSE-LONZA GMBH—See Alusuisse-Lonza Holding Ltd.; *Int'l*, pg. 68
ALUSUISSE-LONZA HOLDING LTD.; *Int'l*, pg. 66
ALUSUISSE-LONZA HUNGARIA KFT.—See Alusuisse-Lonza Holding Ltd.; *Int'l*, pg. 68

Company Index

ALUSUISSE-LONZA NEDERLAND B.V.—See Alusuisse-Lonza Holding Ltd.; *Int'l*, pg. 68
ALUSUISSE-LONZA SERVICES LTD.—See Alusuisse-Lonza Holding Ltd.; *Int'l*, pg. 67
ALUSUISSE-LONZA TRADING LTD.—See Alusuisse-Lonza Holding Ltd.; *Int'l*, pg. 67
ALUSUISSE-LONZA UK LTD.—See Alusuisse-Lonza Holding Ltd.; *Int'l*, pg. 68
ALUSUISSE NEDERLAND B.V.—See Alusuisse-Lonza Holding Ltd.; *Int'l*, pg. 68
ALUSUISSE OF AUSTRALIA LTD—See Alusuisse-Lonza Holding Ltd.; *Int'l*, pg. 68
ALUSUISSE PRODUITS SPECIAUX SARL—See Alusuisse-Lonza Holding Ltd.; *Int'l*, pg. 68
ALUSUISSE ROAD & RAIL LTD.—See Alusuisse-Lonza Holding Ltd.; *Int'l*, pg. 67
ALUSUISSE SWISS ALUMINIUM LTD.—See Alusuisse-Lonza Holding Ltd.; *Int'l*, pg. 67
ALUVETICA LDA.—See Alusuisse-Lonza Holding Ltd.; *Int'l*, pg. 68
ALVA/AMCO PHARMACAL COMPANIES, INC.; *U.S. Private*, pg. 47
ALVARADO CONVALESCENT & REHABILITATION HOSPITAL SAN DIEGO—See Vencor, Inc.; *U.S. Public*, pg. 1711
LANDULPHO ALVES REFINERY—See Petrobras - Petroleo Brasileiro S.A.; *Int'l*, pg. 1042
ALVESTA GJUTERI AB—See Svedala Industri AB; *Int'l*, pg. 1323
ALVESTA GJUTERI AB—See Trelleborg AB; *Int'l*, pg. 1419
ALVEY SYSTEMS, INC; *U.S. Private*, pg. 47
ALVEY OF MICHIGAN—See Alvey Systems, Inc; *U.S. Private*, pg. 47
ALVIS AEROSPACE & TRANSMISSIONS LIMITED—See Alvis plc; *Int'l*, pg. 69
ALVIS INDUSTRIES LIMITED—See Alvis plc; *Int'l*, pg. 69
ALVIS LOGISTICS LIMITED—See Alvis plc; *Int'l*, pg. 69
ALVIS PLC; *Int'l*, pg. 69
ALVIS-UNIPOWER LIMITED—See Alvis plc; *Int'l*, pg. 69
ALVIS VEHICLES LIMITED—See Alvis plc; *Int'l*, pg. 70
ALWIN SCHOCKEMOHLE & WILLENBORG GMBH U. CO. BLECHHANDEL KG—See Fried. Krupp AG; *Int'l*, pg. 512
ALYESKA PIPELINE SERVICE COMPANY; *U.S. Private*, pg. 47
ALYESKA PIPELINE SERVICE COMPANY—See Alyeska Pipeline Service Company; *U.S. Private*, pg. 48
ALYESKA SEAFOODS, INC.—See Maruha Corporation; *Int'l*, pg. 845
ALZA CORPORATION; *U.S. Public*, pg. 62
ALZA DEVELOPMENT CORPORATION—See Alza Corporation; *U.S. Public*, pg. 62
ALZA INTERNATIONAL—See Alza Corporation; *U.S. Public*, pg. 62
ALZA, LTD.—See Alza Corporation; *U.S. Public*, pg. 62
AMACO B.V., AMSTELVEEN—See Internatio-Muller N.V.; *Int'l*, pg. 682
AMADA BUTSURYU CO., LTD.—See Amada Co., Ltd.; *Int'l*, pg. 70
AMADA CANADA LTD.—See Amada Co., Ltd.; *Int'l*, pg. 70
AMADA CO., LTD.; *Int'l*, pg. 70
AMADA CUTTING TECHNOLOGIES, INC.—See Amada Co., Ltd.; *Int'l*, pg. 70
AMADA ENGINEERING CENTER CO., LTD.—See Amada Co., Ltd.; *Int'l*, pg. 70
AMADA FRANCHISE CENTER CO., LTD.—See Amada Co., Ltd.; *Int'l*, pg. 70
AMADA INFORMATION SERVICE CO., LTD.—See Amada Co., Ltd.; *Int'l*, pg. 70
AMADA SCHIAVI S.R.L.—See Amada Co., Ltd.; *Int'l*, pg. 70
AMADA SONOIKE CO., LTD.—See Amada Co., Ltd.; *Int'l*, pg. 70
AMADA WASINO CO. LTD.—See Amada Co., Ltd.; *Int'l*, pg. 70
AMADEUS FINLAND OY—See FinnAir Oy; *Int'l*, pg. 485
GIE AMADEUS FRANCE—See Groupe Air France; *Int'l*, pg. 560
AMADOR CENTRAL RAILROAD COMPANY—See Georgia-Pacific Corporation; *U.S. Public*, pg. 736
AMADOR LEDGER-DISPATCH—See Central Valley Publishing; *U.S. Private*, pg. 225
AMADOR MOTORS—See Prospect Motors, Inc.; *U.S. Private*, pg. 891
AMAFRUTAS S.A.—See Novartis AG; *Int'l*, pg. 974
AMAGASAKI MILL—See Settsu Corporation; *Int'l*, pg. 1225
AMAGASAKI PLANT—See Kansai Paint Co., Ltd.; *Int'l*, pg. 723
AMAL AB—See Baldwin Technology Company, Inc.; *U.S. Public*, pg. 170
AMALGA N.V.—See Schuttersveld Holding N.V.; *Int'l*, pg. 1210
AMALGAMATED AUTOMOTIVE INDUSTRIES, INC.; *U.S. Private*, pg. 48
AMALGAMATED BEVERAGE INDUSTRIES—See South African Breweries, Ltd.; *Int'l*, pg. 1286
AMALGAMATED GLASS LIMITED—See Saint-Gobain; *Int'l*, pg. 1172
AMALGAMATED METAL CORPORATION PLC—See Preussag AG; *Int'l*, pg. 1071
AMALGAMATED METAL TRADING LTD.—See Preussag AG; *Int'l*, pg. 1071
AMALGAMATED PLASTIC INDUSTRIES (PTY) LTD.—See Royal Packaging Industries Van Leer B.V.; *Int'l*, pg. 1146
AMALGAMATED RETAIL LTD.—See South African Breweries, Ltd.; *Int'l*, pg. 1286
AMALGAMATED SHOE CO. LTD.—See Pentland Group PLC; *Int'l*, pg. 1035
THE AMALGAMATED SUGAR COMPANY LLC; *U.S. Private*, pg. 48
AMALGAMET, INC.—See Preussag AG; *Int'l*, pg. 1071
AMANA FARMS, INC.—See Amana Society, Inc.; *U.S. Private*, pg. 48

AMANA-NORDSTROM MOTEL CO.—See Amana Society, Inc.; *U.S. Private*, pg. 48
AMANA SOCIETY, INC.; *U.S. Private*, pg. 48
AMANA SOCIETY SERVICE CO.—See Amana Society, Inc.; *U.S. Private*, pg. 48
AMANDA FIELDING—See JC Penney Company, Inc.; *U.S. Public*, pg. 917
AMANO CINCINNATI, INC.—See Amano Corporation; *Int'l*, pg. 70
AMANO CINCINNATI INC.—See Amano Corporation; *Int'l*, pg. 71
AMANO CLEANTECH MALAYSIA SDN. BHD.—See Amano Corporation; *Int'l*, pg. 71
AMANO CORPORATION; *Int'l*, pg. 70
AMANO DEUTSCHLAND GMBH—See Amano Corporation; *Int'l*, pg. 71
AMANO ELECTRONICS EUROPE, N.V.—See Amano Corporation; *Int'l*, pg. 71
AMANO INTERNATIONAL TRADING (SHANGHAI) CO. LTD.—See Amano Corporation; *Int'l*, pg. 71
AMANO KOREA CORPORATION—See Amano Corporation; *Int'l*, pg. 71
AMANO PARTNERS U.S.A. INC. (A.P.U.)—See Amano Corporation; *Int'l*, pg. 71
AMANO PIONEER CREDIT CORP.—See Amano Corporation; *Int'l*, pg. 71
AMAPOLY INDUSTRIA E COMERCIO LTDA.—See Sao Paulo Alpargatas S.A.; *Int'l*, pg. 1193
AMARI PLASTICS PLC—See Glynwed International PLC; *Int'l*, pg. 554
AMARILLO HARDWARE COMPANY—See Distribution America; *U.S. Private*, pg. 335
AMARILLO PLANT—See Cooper Industries, Inc.; *U.S. Public*, pg. 444
AMATI COMMUNICATIONS CORP.—See Texas Instruments Incorporated; *U.S. Public*, pg. 1585
AMATRON—See NCH Corporation; *U.S. Public*, pg. 1145
AMAX COAL COMPANY—See Cyprus Amax Minerals Company; *U.S. Public*, pg. 470
AMAX ENERGY, INC.—See Cyprus Amax Minerals Company; *U.S. Public*, pg. 470
AMAX EXPLORATION, INC.—See Cyprus Amax Minerals Company; *U.S. Public*, pg. 470
AMAX GOLD INC.—See Cyprus Amax Minerals Company; *U.S. Public*, pg. 470
AMAX RESEARCH & DEVELOPMENT INC.—See Cyprus Amax Minerals Company; *U.S. Public*, pg. 470
THE AMAZING VIDEO NETWORK—See Cinram Ltd.; *Int'l*, pg. 293
AMAZON.COM, INC.; *U.S. Public*, pg. 62
AMBAC B.V.; *Int'l*, pg. 71
AMBAC CAPITAL CORP.—See AMBAC Financial Group, Inc.; *U.S. Public*, pg. 63
AMBAC FINANCIAL GROUP, INC.; *U.S. Public*, pg. 62
AMBAC INTERNATIONAL CORP.; *U.S. Private*, pg. 48
AMBAR, INC.—See The Beacon Group; *U.S. Private*, pg. 126
AMBAR MARINE, INC.—See The Beacon Group; *U.S. Private*, pg. 126
AMBASSADAIR TRAVEL CLUB, INC.—See Amtran, Inc.; *U.S. Public*, pg. 106
AMBASSADOR OFFICE EQUIPMENT, INC.—See Canon Inc.; *Int'l*, pg. 262
AMBER TOURS, INC.—See Amtran, Inc.; *U.S. Public*, pg. 106
AMBER TRAVEL, INC.—See Amtran, Inc.; *U.S. Public*, pg. 106
AMBICO—See Recoton Corporation; *U.S. Public*, pg. 1369
AMBIT MICROSYSTEMS CORP.—See Acer Incorporated; *Int'l*, pg. 22
AMBOY AGGREGATES—See Great Lakes Dredge & Dock Co.; *U.S. Public*, pg. 474
AMBOY SPECIALTY FOODS—See Dean Foods Company; *U.S. Public*, pg. 490
AMBRAKE CORPORATION—See General Motors Corporation; *U.S. Public*, pg. 721
AMBRASOFT INTERNATIONAL—See Olivetti SpA; *Int'l*, pg. 1002
AMBRIA—See Lettuce Entertain You Enterprises, Inc.; *U.S. Private*, pg. 661
AMBRO ITALIA SOCIETA DI INTERMEDIAZIONE MOBILIARE S.P.A.—See Banco Ambrosiano Veneto S.p.A.; *Int'l*, pg. 138
AMBROFID GESTIONI FIDUCIARIE S.P.A.—See Banco Ambrosiano Veneto S.p.A.; *Int'l*, pg. 138
AMBROSE CARR LINTON CARROLL INC.; *Int'l*, pg. 71
AMBROSI & ASSOCIATES, INC.—See Devon Group, Inc.; *U.S. Public*, pg. 503
AMBROVENETO INTERNATIONAL BANK LTD.—See Banco Ambrosiano Veneto S.p.A.; *Int'l*, pg. 138
AMBULATORY RESOURCES, INC.—See Magellan Health Services, Inc.; *U.S. Public*, pg. 1033
AMBULATORY SERVICES, INC.—See Columbia/HCA Healthcare Corporation; *U.S. Public*, pg. 403
AMCAN SPECIALTY STEELS—See Carpenter Technology Corporation; *U.S. Public*, pg. 308
AMCAST AUTOMOTIVE—See Amcast Industrial Corporation; *U.S. Public*, pg. 63
AMCAST AUTOMOTIVE-CEDARBURG PLANT—See Amcast Industrial Corporation; *U.S. Public*, pg. 63
AMCAST AUTOMOTIVE-FREMONT PLANT—See Amcast Industrial Corporation; *U.S. Public*, pg. 63
AMCAST AUTOMOTIVE-GAS CITY PLANT—See Amcast Industrial Corporation; *U.S. Public*, pg. 63
AMCAST AUTOMOTIVE-RICHMOND PLANT—See Amcast Industrial Corporation; *U.S. Public*, pg. 63
AMCAST AUTOMOTIVE-WAPAKONETA PLANT—See Amcast Industrial Corporation; *U.S. Public*, pg. 63
AMCAST INDUSTRIAL CORPORATION; *U.S. Public*, pg. 63
AMCAST INDUSTRIAL LTD.—See Amcast Industrial Corporation; *U.S. Public*, pg. 63
AMCEL CORP.; *U.S. Private*, pg. 48

AMCLYDE ENGINEERED PRODUCTS CO., INC.—See Halter Marine Group, Inc.; *U.S. Public*, pg. 778
AMCLYDE GULF COAST DIVISION—See Halter Marine Group, Inc.; *U.S. Public*, pg. 778
AMCO CORPORATION—See Leggett & Platt, Incorporated; *U.S. Public*, pg. 985
AMCO FOLDING CARTONS, INC.; *U.S. Private*, pg. 48
AMCOL INTERNATIONAL CORP.; *U.S. Public*, pg. 63
AMCOR CAPITAL CORPORATION; *U.S. Public*, pg. 64
AMCOR EUROPE—See Amcor Limited; *Int'l*, pg. 72
AMCOR FIBRE PACKAGING—See Amcor Limited; *Int'l*, pg. 72
AMCOR FIBRE PACKAGING - ASIA—See Amcor Limited; *Int'l*, pg. 72
AMCOR FLEXIBLES EUROPE—See Amcor Limited; *Int'l*, pg. 72
AMCOR, INC.—See CRH, plc; *Int'l*, pg. 242
AMCOR LIMITED; *Int'l*, pg. 71
AMCOR PRINTING PAPERS GROUP—See Amcor Limited; *Int'l*, pg. 64
AMCORE BANK—See Amcore Financial, Inc.; *U.S. Public*, pg. 64
AMCORE BANK N.A., NORTHWEST—See Amcore Financial, Inc.; *U.S. Public*, pg. 64
AMCORE BANK N.A., ROCK RIVER VALLEY—See Amcore Financial, Inc.; *U.S. Public*, pg. 64
AMCORE BANK N.A., ROCKFORD—See Amcore Financial, Inc.; *U.S. Public*, pg. 64
AMCORE BANK, ROCK RIVER VALLEY—See Amcore Financial, Inc.; *U.S. Public*, pg. 64
AMCORE CAPITAL MANAGEMENT, INC.—See Amcore Financial, Inc.; *U.S. Public*, pg. 64
AMCORE CONSUMER FINANCE COMPANY, INC.—See Amcore Financial, Inc.; *U.S. Public*, pg. 64
AMCORE FINANCIAL, INC.; *U.S. Public*, pg. 64
AMCORE FINANCIAL LIFE INSURANCE COMPANY—See Amcore Financial, Inc.; *U.S. Public*, pg. 64
AMCORE INSURANCE GROUP, INC.—See Amcore Financial, Inc.; *U.S. Public*, pg. 64
AMCORE INVESTMENT GROUP, N.A.—See Amcore Financial, Inc.; *U.S. Public*, pg. 64
AMCORE INVESTMENT SERVICES, INC.—See Amcore Financial, Inc.; *U.S. Public*, pg. 64
AMCORE MORTGAGE, INC.—See Amcore Financial, Inc.; *U.S. Public*, pg. 64
AMCORE TRUST COMPANY—See Amcore Financial, Inc.; *U.S. Public*, pg. 65
AMDAHL AUSTRALIA PTY. LTD.—See Fujitsu Limited; *Int'l*, pg. 527
AMDAHL BELGIUM S.A.—See Fujitsu Limited; *Int'l*, pg. 527
AMDAHL CANADA LIMITED—See Fujitsu Limited; *Int'l*, pg. 527
AMDAHL (CHINA) LIMITED—See Fujitsu Limited; *Int'l*, pg. 527
AMDAHL COMPUTER SYSTEME GESELLSCHAFT M.B.H.—See Fujitsu Limited; *Int'l*, pg. 527
AMDAHL COMPUTER SYSTEMS SUCURSAL EN ESPANA—See Fujitsu Limited; *Int'l*, pg. 527
AMDAHL CORPORATION—See Fujitsu Limited; *Int'l*, pg. 527
AMDAHL DANMARK COMPUTER SYSTEMS A/S—See Fujitsu Limited; *Int'l*, pg. 527
AMDAHL DEUTSCHLAND GMBH—See Fujitsu Limited; *Int'l*, pg. 527
AMDAHL FRANCE S.A.—See Fujitsu Limited; *Int'l*, pg. 527
AMDAHL INTERNATIONAL CORPORATION FILIAL, SVERIGE—See Fujitsu Limited; *Int'l*, pg. 527
AMDAHL INTERNATIONAL CORPORATION SUCURSAL EM PORTUGAL—See Fujitsu Limited; *Int'l*, pg. 527
AMDAHL INTL. HONG KONG—See Fujitsu Limited; *Int'l*, pg. 527
AMDAHL INTERNATIONAL MANAGEMENT SERVICES LIMITED (EUROPEAN HEADQUARTERS)—See Fujitsu Limited; *Int'l*, pg. 527
AMDAHL IRELAND LTD.—See Fujitsu Limited; *Int'l*, pg. 527
AMDAHL ITALIA S.P.A.—See Fujitsu Limited; *Int'l*, pg. 527
AMDAHL LUXEMBOURG SUCCURSALE D'AMDAHL BELGIQUE S.A./N.V.—See Fujitsu Limited; *Int'l*, pg. 527
AMDAHL NEDERLAND B.V.—See Fujitsu Limited; *Int'l*, pg. 527
AMDAHL NEW ZEALAND—See Fujitsu Limited; *Int'l*, pg. 527
AMDAHL NORGE A/S—See Fujitsu Limited; *Int'l*, pg. 527
AMDAHL PACIFIC BASIN OPERATIONS (THAILAND)—See Fujitsu Limited; *Int'l*, pg. 527
AMDAHL PACIFIC SERVICES PTY. LTD.—See Fujitsu Limited; *Int'l*, pg. 527
AMDAHL (SCHWEIZ) AG—See Fujitsu Limited; *Int'l*, pg. 527
AMDAHL SINGAPORE—See Fujitsu Limited; *Int'l*, pg. 527
AMDAHL SOUTH AFRICA (PTY) LTD.—See Fujitsu Limited; *Int'l*, pg. 527
AMDAHL SVENSKA AB—See Fujitsu Limited; *Int'l*, pg. 527
AMDAHL (UK) LTD.—See Fujitsu Limited; *Int'l*, pg. 527
AMDENT AB—See Axel Johnson AB; *Int'l*, pg. 708
S.A. AMECO—See Cockerill Sambre; *Int'l*, pg. 301
AMECOM DIV.—See Litton Industries, Inc.; *U.S. Public*, pg. 1002
AMEDA AG—See Hollister Incorporated; *U.S. Private*, pg. 535
AMEDIA, INC.—See American Software, Inc.; *U.S. Public*, pg. 91
AMEFO BV—See Koninklijke Hoogovens N.V.; *Int'l*, pg. 753
AMELCO CORPORATION; *U.S. Public*, pg. 65
AMELCO, INC.—See Amelco Corporation; *U.S. Public*, pg. 65
AMELIA TELEPHONE CO.—See Telephone and Data Systems, Inc.; *U.S. Public*, pg. 1571
AMER AIR FILTERS—See AAF McQuay, Inc.; *U.S. Private*, pg. 3
AMER-ES AS—See Amer Group Ltd.; *Int'l*, pg. 72
AMER GROUP LTD.; *Int'l*, pg. 72

AMER SPORT OY—See Amer Group Ltd.; *Int'l*, pg. 72
AMER TOBACCO LTD.—See Amer Group Ltd.; *Int'l*, pg. 72
AMERAC ENERGY CORP.—See Southern Mineral Corporation; *U.S. Public*, pg. 1490
AMERADA HESS A/S—See Amerada Hess Corporation; *U.S. Public*, pg. 65
AMERADA HESS CORPORATION; *U.S. Public*, pg. 65
AMERADA HESS NORGE A/S—See Amerada Hess Corporation; *U.S. Public*, pg. 65
AMERADA HESS PIPELINE CORP.—See Amerada Hess Corporation; *U.S. Public*, pg. 65
AMERADA HESS (U.K.) LTD.—See Amerada Hess Corporation; *U.S. Public*, pg. 65
AMERBELLE CORPORATION; *U.S. Private*, pg. 48
AMERCABLE—See Associated Materials Incorporated; *U.S. Private*, pg. 91
AMERCARD—See Nycomed Amersham plc; *Int'l*, pg. 993
AMERCHOL CORPORATION—See Union Carbide Corporation; *U.S. Public*, pg. 1667
AMERCO; *U.S. Private*, pg. 48
AMERCO REAL ESTATE COMPANY—See Amerco; *U.S. Private*, pg. 49
AMERCOAT ESPANA, S.A.—See Ameron International Corporation; *U.S. Public*, pg. 99
AMERCOAT MEXICANA S.A. DE C.V.—See Ameron International Corporation; *U.S. Public*, pg. 99
AMERCORD INC.—See The Ivaco Group; *Int'l*, pg. 696
AMEREN CORPORATION; *U.S. Public*, pg. 65
AMERENCIPS—See Ameren Corporation; *U.S. Public*, pg. 65
AMERENUE—See Ameren Corporation; *U.S. Public*, pg. 66
AMEREX CHILDREN—See Amerex USA, Inc.; *U.S. Private*, pg. 49
AMEREX MEN'S—See Amerex USA, Inc.; *U.S. Private*, pg. 49
AMEREX USA, INC.; *U.S. Private*, pg. 49
AMERFORD FRANCE S.A.—See Thyssen AG; *Int'l*, pg. 1388
AMERFORD INTERNATIONAL CORPORATION—See Thyssen AG; *Int'l*, pg. 1388
AMERFORD INTL. LTD.—See Thyssen AG; *Int'l*, pg. 1388
AMERFORD INTL. NEDERLAND B.V.—See Thyssen AG; *Int'l*, pg. 1388
AMERFORD INTL. (PTY) LTD.—See Thyssen AG; *Int'l*, pg. 1388
AMERFORD INTL. (U.K.) LTD.—See Thyssen AG; *Int'l*, pg. 1388
AMERI-CO CARRIERS, INC.—See AMCOL International Corp.; *U.S. Public*, pg. 63
AMERI-FORGE CORPORATION—See Global Industrial Technologies; *U.S. Public*, pg. 748
AMERIAN APPRAISAL PROPERTY TAX SERVICES, INC.—See American Appraisal Associates, Inc.; *U.S. Private*, pg. 50
AMERIANA BANCORP; *U.S. Public*, pg. 66
AMERIANA BANK—See Ameriana Bancorp; *U.S. Public*, pg. 66
AMERIANA INSURANCE AGENCY—See Ameriana Bancorp; *U.S. Public*, pg. 66
AMERIC DISC—See G.T.C. Transcontinental Group Ltd.; *Int'l*, pg. 539
AMERIC DISC INC.—See G.T.C. Transcontinental Group Ltd.; *Int'l*, pg. 539
AMERICA—See Ark Restaurants Corp.; *U.S. Public*, pg. 130
AMERICA CAFE—See Ark Restaurants Corp.; *U.S. Public*, pg. 130
AMERICA DO SUL LEASING S.A. ARRENDAMENTO MERCANTIL—See The Fuji Bank, Limited; *Int'l*, pg. 521
AMERICA LATINA COMPANHIA DE SEGUROS—See The Tokio Marine & Fire Insurance Company, Ltd.; *Int'l*, pg. 1392
AMERICA NORTH INC.—See EMCON; *U.S. Public*, pg. 571
AMERICA ONLINE INCORPORATED; *U.S. Public*, pg. 66
AMERICA WEST AIRLINES, INC.—See America West Holdings Corporation; *U.S. Public*, pg. 67
AMERICA WEST HOLDINGS CORPORATION; *U.S. Public*, pg. 66
AMERICABLE, INC.—See ENStar, Inc.; *U.S. Public*, pg. 585
AMERICAL CORPORATION; *U.S. Private*, pg. 49
AMERICAN ADJUSTMENT COMPANY, INC.—See Cigna Corp.; *U.S. Public*, pg. 365
AMERICAN AGGREGATES CORP.—See CSR Limited; *Int'l*, pg. 245
AMERICAN AIR FILTERS—See AAF McQuay, Inc.; *U.S. Private*, pg. 3
AMERICAN AIRCRAFT PARTS MANUFACTURING CO.; *U.S. Public*, pg. 49
AMERICAN AIRLINES CARGO—See AMR Corporation; *U.S. Public*, pg. 9
AMERICAN AIRLINES, INC.—See AMR Corporation; *U.S. Public*, pg. 9
AMERICAN ALLOY CASTINGS COMPANY—See American Foundry Group, Inc.; *U.S. Private*, pg. 55
AMERICAN ALLOY PLANT NO. II—See American Foundry Group, Inc.; *U.S. Private*, pg. 55
AMERICAN ALLSAFE CO.—See NCH Corporation; *U.S. Public*, pg. 1145
AMERICAN-AMICABLE LIFE INSURANCE COMPANY OF TEXAS—See PennCorp Financial Group, Inc.; *U.S. Public*, pg. 1271
AMERICAN & EFIRD, INC.—See Ruddick Corporation; *U.S. Public*, pg. 1412
AMERICAN AND FOREIGN INSURANCE CO.—See Royal & Sun Alliance Insurance Group plc; *Int'l*, pg. 1130
AMERICAN ANNUITY GROUP—See American Financial Group; *U.S. Public*, pg. 74
AMERICAN ANTENNA CORP.—See Capsonic Group, Inc.; *U.S. Private*, pg. 207
AMERICAN APPRAISAL (AAR), INC.—See American Appraisal Associates, Inc.; *U.S. Private*, pg. 50
AMERICAN APPRAISAL ASIA, INC.—See American Appraisal Associates, Inc.; *U.S. Private*, pg. 50

AMERICAN APPRAISAL ASSOCIATES, INC.; *U.S. Private*, pg. 49
AMERICAN APPRAISAL CANADA, INC.—See American Appraisal Associates, Inc.; *U.S. Private*, pg. 50
AMERICAN APPRAISAL CAPITAL SERVICES, INC.—See American Appraisal Associates, Inc.; *U.S. Private*, pg. 50
AMERICAN APPRAISAL CHINA, INC.—See American Appraisal Associates, Inc.; *U.S. Private*, pg. 50
THE AMERICAN APPRAISAL CO.—See American Appraisal Associates, Inc.; *U.S. Private*, pg. 50
AMERICAN APPRAISAL CONSULTORES DE AVALIACOA LIMITADA—See American Appraisal Associates, Inc.; *U.S. Private*, pg. 50
AMERICAN APPRAISAL HONG KONG LTD.—See American Appraisal Associates, Inc.; *U.S. Private*, pg. 50
AMERICAN APPRAISAL HUNGARY CO. LTD.—See American Appraisal Associates, Inc.; *U.S. Private*, pg. 50
AMERICAN APPRAISAL ITALIA S.R.L.—See American Appraisal Associates, Inc.; *U.S. Private*, pg. 50
AMERICAN APPRAISAL, LTD.—See American Appraisal Associates, Inc.; *U.S. Private*, pg. 50
AMERICAN APPRAISAL MAROC—See Caja de Madrid Group; *Int'l*, pg. 252
AMERICAN APPRAISAL MEXICO—See American Appraisal Associates, Inc.; *U.S. Private*, pg. 50
AMERICAN APPRAISAL POLAND SP. Z.O.O.—See American Appraisal Associates, Inc.; *U.S. Private*, pg. 50
AMERICAN APPRAISAL THAILAND LTD.—See American Appraisal Associates, Inc.; *U.S. Private*, pg. 50
AMERICAN ARBITRATION ASSOCIATION; *U.S. Private*, pg. 50
AMERICAN ARCHITECTURAL PRODUCTS, INC.; *U.S. Public*, pg. 67
AMERICAN ARTIST—See VNU Verenigde Nederlandse Uitgeversbedrijven B.V.; *Int'l*, pg. 1446
AMERICAN AUTO AUCTION, INC.—See Cox Enterprises, Inc.; *U.S. Private*, pg. 282
AMERICAN AUTOMOBILE ASSOCIATION; *U.S. Private*, pg. 50
AMERICAN AUTOMOBILE INSURANCE CO.—See Allianz Aktiengesellschaft; *Int'l*, pg. 59
AMERICAN AXLE & MANUFACTURING; *U.S. Private*, pg. 51
AMERICAN AZIDE CORPORATION—See American Pacific Corporation; *U.S. Public*, pg. 88
AMERICAN BABY MAGAZINE—See Primedia Inc.; *U.S. Public*, pg. 1328
AMERICAN BALER CO.—See Avis Industrial Corporation; *U.S. Private*, pg. 102
AMERICAN BANK NOTE COMPANY—See American Banknote Corp.; *U.S. Public*, pg. 68
AMERICAN BANKER BOND BUYER—See The Thomson Corporation; *U.S. Public*, pg. 1600
THE AMERICAN BANKERS ASSOCIATION INSURANCE ASSOCIATION—See The American Bankers Association; *U.S. Private*, pg. 51
THE AMERICAN BANKERS ASSOCIATION LEARNING & DEVELOPMENT INCORPORATED—See The American Bankers Association; *U.S. Private*, pg. 51
THE AMERICAN BANKERS ASSOCIATION SECURITIES ASSOCIATION—See The American Bankers Association; *U.S. Private*, pg. 51
THE AMERICAN BANKERS ASSOCIATION; *U.S. Private*, pg. 51
AMERICAN BANKERS INSURANCE CO. OF FLORIDA—See American Bankers Insurance Group, Inc.; *U.S. Public*, pg. 67
AMERICAN BANKERS INSURANCE GROUP, INC.; *U.S. Public*, pg. 67
AMERICAN BANKERS LIFE AGENTS SERVICES, INC.—See American Bankers Insurance Group, Inc.; *U.S. Public*, pg. 67
AMERICAN BANKERS LIFE ASSURANCE CO. OF FLORIDA—See American Bankers Insurance Group, Inc.; *U.S. Public*, pg. 67
AMERICAN BANKNOTE COMPANY GRAFICA E SERVICOS LTDA.—See American Banknote Corp.; *U.S. Public*, pg. 68
AMERICAN BANKNOTE CORP.; *U.S. Public*, pg. 68
AMERICAN BANKNOTE HOLOGRAPHICS—See American Banknote Corp.; *U.S. Public*, pg. 68
AMERICAN BARMAG CO.; *U.S. Private*, pg. 51
AMERICAN BEARING DIVISION, INC.—See LSB Industries, Inc.; *U.S. Public*, pg. 970
AMERICAN BEAUTY MACARONI—See Hershey Foods Corporation; *U.S. Public*, pg. 812
AMERICAN BEVERAGE CORPORATION—See Koninklijke BolsWessanen nv; *Int'l*, pg. 752
AMERICAN BEVERAGE CORP. INC.—See Koninklijke BolsWessanen nv; *Int'l*, pg. 752
AMERICAN BIBLE SOCIETY; *U.S. Private*, pg. 51
AMERICAN BILTRITE (CANADA) LTD.—See American Biltrite Inc.; *U.S. Public*, pg. 69
AMERICAN BILTRITE FAR EAST, INC.—See American Biltrite Inc.; *U.S. Public*, pg. 69
AMERICAN BILTRITE INC.; *U.S. Public*, pg. 68
AMERICAN BINDRY-MIDWEST—See The American Companies, Inc.; *U.S. Private*, pg. 52
AMERICAN BINDRY-SOUTH—See The American Companies, Inc.; *U.S. Private*, pg. 52
AMERICAN BIO CORPORATION—See Groupe Limagrain; *Int'l*, pg. 566
AMERICAN BLDG. MAINTENANCE CO.—See ABM Industries; *U.S. Public*, pg. 2
AMERICAN BOBST HOLDINGS, INC.—See Bobst S.A.; *Int'l*, pg. 198
AMERICAN BREAD CO.—See The Earthgrains Company; *U.S. Public*, pg. 547
AMERICAN BROADCASTING COMPANIES—See The Walt Disney Company; *U.S. Public*, pg. 511

AMERICAN BROKERAGE CORPORATION—See Phoenix Home Life Mutual Insurance Company; *U.S. Private*, pg. 863
AMERICAN BUILDINGS CO.; *U.S. Public*, pg. 69
AMERICAN BUREAU OF SHIPPING; *U.S. Private*, pg. 51
AMERICAN BUSINESS ADVERTISING; *U.S. Private*, pg. 51
AMERICAN BUSINESS INFORMATION, INC.; *U.S. Public*, pg. 69
AMERICAN BUSINESS INFORMATION MARKETING—See American Business Information, Inc.; *U.S. Public*, pg. 70
AMERICAN BUSINESS PRODUCTS, INC.; *U.S. Public*, pg. 70
AMERICAN CABLEVISION HOLDINGS, INC.—See Time Warner Inc.; *U.S. Public*, pg. 1610
AMERICAN CABLEVISION OF BROOKLYN, INC.—See Time Warner Inc.; *U.S. Public*, pg. 1610
AMERICAN CABLEVISION OF CAROLINA, INC.—See Time Warner Inc.; *U.S. Public*, pg. 1610
AMERICAN CABLEVISION OF INDIANAPOLIS, INC.—See Time Warner Inc.; *U.S. Public*, pg. 1610
AMERICAN CABLEVISION OF KANSAS CITY, INC.—See Time Warner Inc.; *U.S. Public*, pg. 1610
AMERICAN CABLEVISION OF MONROEVILLE, INC.—See Time Warner Inc.; *U.S. Public*, pg. 1610
AMERICAN CABLEVISION OF ORANGE, INC.—See Time Warner Inc.; *U.S. Public*, pg. 1610
AMERICAN CABLEVISION OF QUEENS, INC.—See Time Warner Inc.; *U.S. Public*, pg. 1610
AMERICAN CABLEVISION OF ST. LOUIS, INC.—See Time Warner Inc.; *U.S. Public*, pg. 1610
AMERICAN CABLEVISION OF WEST MEMPHIS, INC.—See Time Warner Inc.; *U.S. Public*, pg. 1610
AMERICAN CAMPER—See Brunswick Corporation; *U.S. Public*, pg. 265
AMERICAN CARBON INDUSTRIES—See Morgan Crucible Co. Plc; *Int'l*, pg. 891
AMERICAN CAST IRON PIPE CO.; *U.S. Private*, pg. 51
AMERICAN CASTINGS CO.—See American Foundry Group, Inc.; *U.S. Private*, pg. 55
AMERICAN CELLULAR COMMUNICATIONS CORPORATION—See BellSouth Corporation; *U.S. Public*, pg. 208
AMERICAN CENTERED TECHNOLOGIES—See Fansteel, Inc.; *U.S. Public*, pg. 612
AMERICAN CENTRIFUGAL—See American Cast Iron Pipe Co.; *U.S. Private*, pg. 52
AMERICAN CENTURY COMPANIES, INC.; *U.S. Private*, pg. 52
AMERICAN CENTURY INVESTMENTS—See American Century Companies, Inc.; *U.S. Private*, pg. 52
AMERICAN CHROME & CHEMICALS, INC.—See Harrisons & Crosfield plc; *Int'l*, pg. 598
AMERICAN CHURCH—See American Paper Group, Inc.; *U.S. Private*, pg. 60
AMERICAN CITIES BUSINESS JOURNALS, INC.—See Advance Publications Inc.; *U.S. Private*, pg. 19
AMERICAN CITRUS PRODUCTS CORPORATION—See Home Juice Co.; *U.S. Private*, pg. 537
AMERICAN CITY BUSINESS JOURNALS, INC.—See Advance Publications Inc.; *U.S. Private*, pg. 19
AMERICAN CITY BUSINESS JOURNALS OF FLORIDA, INC.—See Advance Publications Inc.; *U.S. Private*, pg. 19
THE AMERICAN CITY CORP.—See The Rouse Company; *U.S. Public*, pg. 1407
AMERICAN CLASSIC VOYAGERS COMPANY—See Equity Group Investments; *U.S. Private*, pg. 380
AMERICAN COLOR—See Morgan Stanley Dean Witter & Co.; *U.S. Public*, pg. 1133
AMERICAN COLOR & CHEMICAL CORPORATION—See Philips Electronics N.V.; *Int'l*, pg. 1054
AMERICAN COLOR GRAPHICS—See Morgan Stanley Dean Witter & Co.; *U.S. Public*, pg. 1132
AMERICAN COMETRA, INC.—See Groupe Bruxelles Lambert S.A.; *Int'l*, pg. 562
AMERICAN COMMERCIAL CREDIT CORP.—See ABN-AMRO Holding N.V.; *Int'l*, pg. 10
AMERICAN COMMERCIAL LINES INC.—See CSX Corporation; *U.S. Public*, pg. 284
AMERICAN COMMERCIAL SECURITY & INVESTIGATIVE SERVICES—See ABM Industries; *U.S. Public*, pg. 2
AMERICAN COMMONWEALTH COMPANY—See American Water Works Company, Inc.; *U.S. Public*, pg. 95
AMERICAN COMMONWEALTH MANAGEMENT SERVICES COMPANY, INC.—See American Water Works Company, Inc.; *U.S. Public*, pg. 95
AMERICAN COMMUNICATIONS CORP.—See New Valley Corporation; *U.S. Public*, pg. 1173
THE AMERICAN COMPANIES, INC.; *U.S. Private*, pg. 52
AMERICAN COMPUTER ASSEMBLY/COMPAS—See AIM Safety Company Inc.; *Int'l*, pg. 36
AMERICAN CONSOLIDATION SERVICES LTD.—See Neptune Orient Lines Ltd.; *Int'l*, pg. 912
AMERICAN CONSUMER PRODUCTS—See Vista 2000, Inc.; *U.S. Public*, pg. 1142
AMERICAN CONSUMER SERVICES INC.—See Torchmark Corporation; *U.S. Public*, pg. 1623
AMERICAN CONSUMERS, INC.; *U.S. Public*, pg. 70
AMERICAN COPPER & NICKEL COMPANY, INC.—See Inco Limited; *Int'l*, pg. 672
AMERICAN COUNCIL FOR INTERNATIONAL STUDIES—See American Institute for Foreign Study; *U.S. Private*, pg. 57
AMERICAN COUNTRY FINANCIAL SERVICES CORP.—See Stamford Capital; *U.S. Private*, pg. 1030
AMERICAN COUNTRY INSURANCE CO.—See Stamford Capital; *U.S. Private*, pg. 1030
AMERICAN CRANE & EQUIPMENT CORP.; *U.S. Private*, pg. 52
AMERICAN CREDIT SERVICES INC.—See Charter One Financial, Inc.; *U.S. Public*, pg. 336

Company Index

AMERICAN — DIRECTORY OF CORPORATE AFFILIATIONS

AMERICAN CRYSTAL SUGAR COMPANY; *U.S. Private*, pg. 52
AMERICAN DAIRY QUEEN CORPORATION—See Berkshire Hathaway Inc.; *U.S. Public*, pg. 220
AMERICAN DECAL & MFG. CO.; *U.S. Private*, pg. 53
AMERICAN DEMOGRAPHICS, INC.—See Cowles Media Company; *U.S. Private*, pg. 281
AMERICAN DENTAL TECHNOLOGIES; *U.S. Public*, pg. 70
AMERICAN DETENTION SERVICES, INC.—See Adtec Detention Systems; *U.S. Private*, pg. 18
AMERICAN DOOR COMPANY OF MICHIGAN, INC.—See Premdor Inc.; *Int'l*, pg. 1067
AMERICAN DOOR COMPANY OF MICHIGAN, INC.-FLUSH DOOR PLANT—See Premdor Inc.; *Int'l*, pg. 1067
AMERICAN DOWN & TEXTILE COMPANY—See Hanover Direct, Inc.; *U.S. Public*, pg. 782
AMERICAN DREW—See Ladd Furniture, Inc.; *U.S. Public*, pg. 974
AMERICAN DRUG CORPORATION—See American Home Products Corporation; *U.S. Public*, pg. 80
AMERICAN DRUG STORES INC.—See American Stores Company; *U.S. Public*, pg. 93
AMERICAN DUCTILE IRON PIPE DIV.—See American Cast Iron Pipe Co.; *U.S. Private*, pg. 52
AMERICAN DYNAMICS—See Sensormatic Electronics Corporation; *U.S. Public*, pg. 1457
AMERICAN EAGLE—See Federal Signal Corporation; *U.S. Public*, pg. 617
AMERICAN EAGLE GROUP, INC.; *U.S. Public*, pg. 71
AMERICAN EAGLE LINES—See Frozen Food Express Industries, Inc.; *U.S. Public*, pg. 685
AMERICAN EAGLES OUTFITTERS INC.; *U.S. Private*, pg. 53
AMERICAN ECO CORPORATION; *Int'l*, pg. 73
AMERICAN ECO CORPORATION—See American Eco Corporation; *Int'l*, pg. 74
AMERICAN ECOLOGY CORPORATION; *U.S. Public*, pg. 71
AMERICAN ECONO-THERM—See Petro Chem Development Company; *U.S. Private*, pg. 858
AMERICAN EDUCATIONAL PRODUCTS; *U.S. Public*, pg. 71
AMERICAN ELECTRIC CO., LTD.—See Amelco Corporation; *U.S. Public*, pg. 65
AMERICAN ELECTRIC POWER COMPANY, INC.; *U.S. Public*, pg. 71
AMERICAN ELECTRIC POWER SERVICE CORP.—See American Electric Power Company, Inc.; *U.S. Public*, pg. 72
AMERICAN ELECTRONICS, INC.—See AEI Holding Co., Inc.; *U.S. Private*, pg. 5
AMERICAN EMPIRE SURPLUS LINES INSURANCE COMPANY—See American Financial Group; *U.S. Public*, pg. 74
AMERICAN EMULSIONS CO., INC.—See RPM, Inc.; *U.S. Public*, pg. 1357
AMERICAN ENERGY MANAGEMENT—See Madison Gas and Electric Company; *U.S. Public*, pg. 1033
AMERICAN ENTERPRISE INSTITUTE FOR PUBLIC POLICY RESEARCH; *U.S. Private*, pg. 53
AMERICAN ENTERPRISE INVESTMENT SERVICES, INC.—See American Express Company; *U.S. Public*, pg. 73
AMERICAN ENVIRONMENTAL NETWORK, INC.—See Texas Utilities Company; *U.S. Public*, pg. 1587
AMERICAN ENVIRONMENTAL PRODUCTS, INC.—See Washington Gas Light Co.; *U.S. Public*, pg. 1741
AMERICAN EQUIPMENT COMPANY, INC.—See Fluor Corporation; *U.S. Public*, pg. 660
AMERICAN EUROCOPTER CORP.—See Aerospatiale; *Int'l*, pg. 29
AMERICAN EXCELSIOR COMPANY; *U.S. Private*, pg. 53
AMERICAN EXPORT REGISTER—See Thomas Publishing Company; *U.S. Private*, pg. 1082
AMERICAN EXPRESS BANK LTD.—See American Express Company; *U.S. Public*, pg. 73
AMERICAN EXPRESS BANK (SWITZERLAND) S.A.—See American Express Company; *U.S. Public*, pg. 74
AMERICAN EXPRESS COMPANY; *U.S. Public*, pg. 73
AMERICAN EXPRESS CREDIT CORPORATION—See American Express Company; *U.S. Public*, pg. 74
AMERICAN EXPRESS EUROPE LIMITED—See American Express Company; *U.S. Public*, pg. 74
AMERICAN EXPRESS FINANCIAL ADVISOR—See American Express Company; *U.S. Public*, pg. 73
AMERICAN EXPRESS PUBLISHING CORPORATION—See American Express Company; *U.S. Public*, pg. 74
AMERICAN EXPRESS SERVICE EUROPE LTD.—See American Express Company; *U.S. Public*, pg. 74
AMERICAN EXPRESS TRAVEL RELATED SERVICES CO., INC.—See American Express Company; *U.S. Public*, pg. 73
AMERICAN FABRICS COMPANY; *U.S. Private*, pg. 53
AMERICAN FAMILY BROKERAGE, INC.—See American Family Mutual Insurance Co.; *U.S. Private*, pg. 53
AMERICAN FAMILY FINANCIAL SERVICES, INC.—See American Family Mutual Insurance Co.; *U.S. Private*, pg. 53
AMERICAN FAMILY HOME INSURANCE CO.—See The Midland Company; *U.S. Public*, pg. 1110
AMERICAN FAMILY INSURANCE COMPANY—See American Family Mutual Insurance Co.; *U.S. Private*, pg. 53
AMERICAN FAMILY LIFE ASSURANCE CO. OF COLUMBUS—See AFLAC Incorporated; *U.S. Public*, pg. 28
AMERICAN FAMILY LIFE ASSURANCE COMPANY OF NEW YORK—See AFLAC Incorporated; *U.S. Public*, pg. 28
AMERICAN FAMILY LIFE INSURANCE CO.—See American Family Mutual Insurance Co.; *U.S. Private*, pg. 53
AMERICAN FAMILY MUTUAL INSURANCE CO.; *U.S. Private*, pg. 53
AMERICAN FAMILY PUBLISHERS—See Time Warner Inc.; *U.S. Public*, pg. 1612
AMERICAN FAST PRINT, LIMITED; *U.S. Private*, pg. 53
AMERICAN FEDERATION INSURANCE CO.—See Foremost Corporation of America; *U.S. Public*, pg. 667
AMERICAN FELT & FILTER; *U.S. Private*, pg. 54
AMERICAN FENCE & SECURITY COMPANY; *U.S. Private*, pg. 54
AMERICAN FENCE COMPANY AZ—See American Fence & Security Company; *U.S. Private*, pg. 54
AMERICAN FENCE CO. LTD.—See American Fence & Security Company; *U.S. Private*, pg. 54
AMERICAN FENCE CO. OF MIDWEST—See American Fence & Security Company; *U.S. Private*, pg. 54
AMERICAN FIDELITY CORP.; *U.S. Private*, pg. 54
AMERICAN FINANCE GROUP, INC.—See PLM International, Inc.; *U.S. Public*, pg. 1241
AMERICAN FINANCIAL ENTERPRISES, INC.—See American Financial Group; *U.S. Public*, pg. 74
AMERICAN FINANCIAL GROUP—See American Financial Group; *U.S. Public*, pg. 75
AMERICAN FINANCIAL GROUP; *U.S. Public*, pg. 74
AMERICAN FINANCIAL GROUP SECURITIES CORP.—See Equis Financial Group; *U.S. Private*, pg. 380
AMERICAN FINANCIAL SKYLINK INC.—See The American Bankers Association; *U.S. Private*, pg. 51
AMERICAN FINE FOODS, INC.—See Chiquita Brands International, Inc.; *U.S. Public*, pg. 349
AMERICAN FINE FOODS, INC. (NYSSA PLANT)—See Chiquita Brands International, Inc.; *U.S. Public*, pg. 349
AMERICAN FINE WIRE CORP.—See Kulicke & Soffa Industries, Inc.; *U.S. Public*, pg. 969
AMERICAN FINE WIRE LTD.—See Kulicke & Soffa Industries, Inc.; *U.S. Public*, pg. 969
AMERICAN FIRE & CASUALTY CO.—See Ohio Casualty Corporation; *U.S. Public*, pg. 1214
AMERICAN FIRE & INDEMNITY CO.—See American Indemnity Financial Corp.; *U.S. Public*, pg. 83
AMERICAN FLANGE & MANUFACTURING CO. INC.—See Royal Packaging Industries Van Leer B.V.; *Int'l*, pg. 1146
AMERICAN FLOW CONTROL—See American Cast Iron Pipe Co.; *U.S. Private*, pg. 52
AMERICAN FLUORESCENT CORPORATION; *U.S. Private*, pg. 54
AMERICAN FOODS GROUP, INC.; *U.S. Private*, pg. 54
AMERICAN FOODSERVICE CORP.; *U.S. Private*, pg. 54
AMERICAN FOUNDATION LIFE INSURANCE COMPANY—See Protective Life Corporation; *U.S. Public*, pg. 1336
AMERICAN FOUNDRY GROUP, INC.; *U.S. Private*, pg. 54
THE AMERICAN FRANKLIN LIFE INSURANCE CO.—See American General Corporation; *U.S. Public*, pg. 76
AMERICAN FREIGHTWAYS CORPORATION; *U.S. Public*, pg. 75
AMERICAN FROZEN FOODS, INC.; *U.S. Private*, pg. 55
AMERICAN FUEL CELL & COATED FABRICS CO. (AMFUEL); *U.S. Private*, pg. 55
AMERICAN FUND ADVISORS, INC.; *U.S. Private*, pg. 55
AMERICAN FURNITURE COMPANY; *U.S. Private*, pg. 55
AMERICAN FURNITURE COMPANY, INCORPORATED—See Ladd Furniture, Inc.; *U.S. Public*, pg. 974
AMERICAN GASKET & RUBBER—See Action Technology Company; *U.S. Private*, pg. 15
AMERICAN GENERAL CORPORATION; *U.S. Public*, pg. 76
AMERICAN GENERAL LIFE & ACCIDENT INSURANCE CO.—See American General Corporation; *U.S. Public*, pg. 76
AMERICAN GENERAL LIFE INSURANCE COMPANY—See American General Corporation; *U.S. Public*, pg. 76
AMERICAN GENERAL LIFE INSURANCE COMPANY OF NEW YORK—See American General Corporation; *U.S. Public*, pg. 76
AMERICAN GENERAL LIFE INSURANCE COMPANY OF OKLAHOMA—See American General Corporation; *U.S. Public*, pg. 76
AMERICAN GENERAL PROPERTY INSURANCE COMPANY—See American General Corporation; *U.S. Public*, pg. 76
AMERICAN GENERAL SECURITIES INCORPORATED—See American General Corporation; *U.S. Public*, pg. 76
AMERICAN GIRL—See Hecla Mining Company; *U.S. Public*, pg. 804
AMERICAN GLACE—See Integrated Brands Inc.; *U.S. Public*, pg. 883
AMERICAN GLASSMITH, INC.—See American Architectural Products, Inc.; *U.S. Public*, pg. 67
AMERICAN GOLF CORPORATION; *U.S. Private*, pg. 55
AMERICAN GRAIN & RELATED INDUSTRIES; *U.S. Private*, pg. 55
AMERICAN GRANBY, INC.; *U.S. Private*, pg. 55
AMERICAN GRAPHITE CO.—See Dixon Ticonderoga Company; *U.S. Public*, pg. 515
AMERICAN GREETINGS CORPORATION; *U.S. Public*, pg. 77
AMERICAN GREETINGS U.S. GREETING CARD DIVISION—See American Greetings Corporation; *U.S. Public*, pg. 78
THE AMERICAN GROUP; *U.S. Private*, pg. 56
AMERICAN GUARANTEE INSURANCE COMPANY—See First Citizens Banc Shares, Inc.; *U.S. Public*, pg. 629
AMERICAN GUARANTEE & LIABILITY INSURANCE COMPANY—See Zurich Insurance Company; *Int'l*, pg. 1530
AMERICAN HARDWARE MUTUAL INSURANCE CO.—See Motorists Mutual Insurance Co.; *U.S. Private*, pg. 764
AMERICAN HEALTH AND LIFE INSURANCE CO.—See Travelers Group; *U.S. Public*, pg. 1633
AMERICAN HEALTH ASSISTANCE FOUNDATION; *U.S. Private*, pg. 56
AMERICAN HEALTH CONSULTANTS—See The Thomson Corporation; *U.S. Public*, pg. 1601
AMERICAN HEALTH PACKAGING—See AmeriSource Health Corp.; *U.S. Public*, pg. 96
AMERICAN HEALTHCORP INC.; *U.S. Public*, pg. 78
AMERICAN HERITAGE LIFE INSURANCE CO.—See American Heritage Life Investment Corp.; *U.S. Public*, pg. 79
AMERICAN HERITAGE LIFE INVESTMENT CORP.; *U.S. Public*, pg. 78
AMERICAN HERITAGE MAGAZINE—See Forbes, Inc.; *U.S. Private*, pg. 417
AMERICAN HOME ASSURANCE CO.—See American International Group, Inc.; *U.S. Public*, pg. 84
AMERICAN HOME ASSURANCE COMPANY NEW YORK, SWISS BRANCH—See American International Group, Inc.; *U.S. Public*, pg. 85
AMERICAN HOME ENTERTAINMENT—See JAKKS Pacific, Inc.; *U.S. Public*, pg. 923
AMERICAN HOME IMPROVEMENT; *U.S. Private*, pg. 56
AMERICAN HOME PRODUCTS CORPORATION; *U.S. Public*, pg. 79
AMERICAN HOME SHIELD CORPORATION—See The ServiceMaster Company; *U.S. Public*, pg. 1461
AMERICAN HOME STYLE—See Bertelsmann AG; *Int'l*, pg. 190
AMERICAN HOMESTAR CORPORATION; *U.S. Public*, pg. 83
AMERICAN HONDA MOTOR CO., INC.—See Honda Motor Co., Ltd.; *Int'l*, pg. 634
AMERICAN HONDA MOTOR CO., INC. AUTOMOBILE SALES DIVISION—See Honda Motor Co., Ltd.; *Int'l*, pg. 634
AMERICAN HONDA MOTOR CO., INC. MOTORCYCLE DIVISION—See Honda Motor Co., Ltd.; *Int'l*, pg. 634
AMERICAN INCOME HOLDING, INC.—See Torchmark Corporation; *U.S. Public*, pg. 1622
AMERICAN INCOME LIFE INSURANCE COMPANY—See Torchmark Corporation; *U.S. Public*, pg. 1622
AMERICAN INDEMNITY COMPANY—See American Indemnity Financial Corp.; *U.S. Public*, pg. 83
AMERICAN INDEMNITY FINANCIAL CORP.; *U.S. Public*, pg. 83
AMERICAN INDUSTRIAL PARTNERS; *U.S. Private*, pg. 56
AMERICAN INKS & COATINGS CORP.; *U.S. Private*, pg. 56
AMERICAN INNOVATIONS, LTD.—See HM International; *U.S. Private*, pg. 491
AMERICAN INSTITUTE FOR FOREIGN STUDY; *U.S. Private*, pg. 56
AMERICAN INSTITUTE OF C.P.A.'S INC.; *U.S. Private*, pg. 57
AMERICAN INSTITUTE OF C.P.A.'S INC.-HARBORSIDE FIN. CTR.—See American Institute of C.P.A.'s Inc.; *U.S. Private*, pg. 57
AMERICAN INSTITUTIONAL FOODS—See AJC International, Inc.; *U.S. Private*, pg. 6
AMERICAN INSULATED WIRE CORP.—See Leviton Mfg. Co., Inc.; *U.S. Private*, pg. 663
AMERICAN INSURANCE AGENCY, INC.—See Servco Pacific Inc.; *U.S. Private*, pg. 986
AMERICAN INTERACTIVE MEDIA, INC.—See Philips Electronics N.V.; *Int'l*, pg. 1052
AMERICAN INTERNATIONAL ADJUSTMENT COMPANY—See American International Group, Inc.; *U.S. Public*, pg. 85
AMERICAN INTERNATIONAL AIRWAYS; *U.S. Private*, pg. 57
AMERICAN INTERNATIONAL ASSURANCE CO. LTD.—See American International Group, Inc.; *U.S. Public*, pg. 85
AMERICAN INTERNATIONAL CO. LTD.—See American International Group, Inc.; *U.S. Public*, pg. 85
AMERICAN INTERNATIONAL CONTAINER, INC.; *U.S. Private*, pg. 57
AMERICAN INTERNATIONAL FOREST PRODUCTS, INC.—See Forest City Enterprises, Inc.; *U.S. Public*, pg. 669
AMERICAN INTERNATIONAL GROUP, INC.; *U.S. Public*, pg. 83
AMERICAN INTERNATIONAL GROUP-MOSCOW REPRESENTATIVE OFFICE—See American International Group, Inc.; *U.S. Public*, pg. 85
AMERICAN INTERNATIONAL INDUSTRIES; *U.S. Private*, pg. 57
AMERICAN INTERNATIONAL LIFE ASSURANCE COMPANY OF NEW YORK—See American International Group, Inc.; *U.S. Public*, pg. 84
AMERICAN INTERNATIONAL MANAGEMENT CO. (BARBADOS) LTD.—See American International Group, Inc.; *U.S. Public*, pg. 85
AMERICAN INTERNATIONAL MANAGERS LTD.—See American International Group, Inc.; *U.S. Public*, pg. 85
AMERICAN INTERNATIONAL RECOVERY, INC.—See American International Group, Inc.; *U.S. Public*, pg. 85
AMERICAN INTERNATIONAL UNDERWRITERS CORP.—See American International Group, Inc.; *U.S. Public*, pg. 85
AMERICAN INTERNATIONAL UNDERWRITERS OVERSEAS LTD.—See American International Group, Inc.; *U.S. Public*, pg. 85
AMERICAN INTERNATIONAL UNDERWRITERS (UK) LTD.—See American International Group, Inc.; *U.S. Public*, pg. 85
AMERICAN INTERNATIONAL WATER SERVICES COMPANY—See American Water Works Company, Inc.; *U.S. Public*, pg. 95
AMERICAN INVESTMENT BANK, NA—See Leucadia National Corporation; *U.S. Public*, pg. 990
AMERICAN INVESTMENT CASTING CO.—See American Foundry Group, Inc.; *U.S. Private*, pg. 55
AMERICAN INVESTORS LIFE INSURANCE COMPANY—See American Mutual Life Holding Co.; *U.S. Private*, pg. 59
AMERICAN INVESTORS SALES GROUP, INC.—See American Mutual Life Holding Co.; *U.S. Private*, pg. 59
AMERICAN ISRAELI PAPER MILLS LTD.; *Int'l*, pg. 74

AMERICAN ISUZU MOTORS INC.—See Isuzu Motors Limited; *Int'l*, pg. 692
AMERICAN ITALIAN PASTA COMPANY; *U.S. Public*, pg. 85
AMERICAN JOURNAL OF NURSING COMPANY—See Wolters Kluwer N.V.; *Int'l*, pg. 1513
AMERICAN KENNEL CLUB, INC.; *U.S. Private*, pg. 58
AMERICAN LAND CRUISERS—See Budget Group, Inc.; *U.S. Private*, pg. 178
AMERICAN LANDFILL, INC.—See American Waste Services, Inc.; *U.S. Public*, pg. 94
AMERICAN LANDMARK SPRINGS—See Nestle S.A.; *Int'l*, pg. 919
AMERICAN LAUBSCHER CORP.; *U.S. Private*, pg. 58
AMERICAN LENDERS FACILITIES, INC.—See Cigna Corp.; *U.S. Public*, pg. 366
AMERICAN LIBRARY ASSOCIATION; *U.S. Private*, pg. 58
AMERICAN LIFE & ACCIDENT INSURANCE COMPANY—See Torchmark Corporation; *U.S. Public*, pg. 1622
AMERICAN LIFE & CASUALTY INSURANCE CO.—See Conseco Inc.; *U.S. Public*, pg. 433
AMERICAN LIFE HOLDING CORP.—See Conseco Inc.; *U.S. Public*, pg. 432
AMERICAN LIFE INSURANCE CO., UK—See American International Group, Inc.; *U.S. Public*, pg. 85
AMERICAN LIFE INSURANCE COMPANY OF NEW YORK—See Mutual of America Life Insurance Company; *U.S. Private*, pg. 769
AMERICAN LIMESTONE CO.—See Asarco Incorporated; *U.S. Public*, pg. 138
AMERICAN LIST CORPORATION—See Snyder Communications, Inc.; *U.S. Public*, pg. 1481
AMERICAN LITERATURE REVIEW—See Thomas Publishing Company; *U.S. Private*, pg. 1082
AMERICAN LOCKER CO., INC.—See American Locker Group, Inc.; *U.S. Public*, pg. 86
AMERICAN LOCKER CO. OF CANADA LTD.—See American Locker Group, Inc.; *U.S. Public*, pg. 86
AMERICAN LOCKER GROUP, INC.; *U.S. Public*, pg. 85
AMERICAN LOCKER SECURITY SYSTEMS, INC.—See American Locker Group, Inc.; *U.S. Public*, pg. 86
AMERICAN LONGWALL REBUILD INC.—See Harnischfeger Industries, Inc.; *U.S. Public*, pg. 789
AMERICAN LOUVER CO.; *U.S. Private*, pg. 58
AMERICAN MACHINE & TOOL COMPANY, INC.; *U.S. Private*, pg. 58
AMERICAN MAIL-WELL ENVELOPE—See Mail-Well Inc.; *U.S. Public*, pg. 1038
AMERICAN MANAGEMENT SYSTEMS, INC.; *U.S. Public*, pg. 86
AMERICAN MANUFACTURERS MUTUAL INSURANCE COMPANY—See Kemper Insurance Companies; *U.S. Private*, pg. 614
AMERICAN MANUFACTURING COMPANY; *U.S. Private*, pg. 58
AMERICAN MAPLAN CORPORATION—See MAN Aktiengesellschaft; *Int'l*, pg. 825
AMERICAN MARINE HOLDINGS INC.; *U.S. Private*, pg. 58
AMERICAN MARINE PTE. LTD.—See GB Holdings; *Int'l*, pg. 531
AMERICAN MARKETING INDUSTRIES, INC.; *U.S. Private*, pg. 58
AMERICAN MARKETING WORK, INC.—See Signal Apparel Company, Inc.; *U.S. Public*, pg. 1472
AMERICAN MARKING SYSTEMS, INC.; *U.S. Private*, pg. 58
AMERICAN MATHEMATICAL SOCIETY, INC.; *U.S. Private*, pg. 59
AMERICAN MATHEMATICAL SOCIETY WASHINGTON OFFICE—See American Mathematical Society, Inc.; *U.S. Private*, pg. 59
THE AMERICAN MEAT PACKING CORP.—See The Iowa Packing Co.; *U.S. Private*, pg. 575
AMERICAN MEDIA, INC.; *U.S. Public*, pg. 87
AMERICAN MEDICAL RENTALS, INC.—See Integrated Health Services, Inc.; *U.S. Public*, pg. 884
AMERICAN MEDICAL SECURITY HOLDINGS, INC.—See United Wisconsin Services, Inc.; *U.S. Public*, pg. 1692
AMERICAN MEDICAL SYSTEMS, INC.—See Pfizer Inc.; *U.S. Public*, pg. 1281
AMERICAN MEDICORP DEVELOPMENT CO.—See Columbia/HCA Healthcare Corporation; *U.S. Public*, pg. 403
AMERICAN MELAMINE INDUSTRIES INC.—See DSM N.V.; *Int'l*, pg. 355
AMERICAN MERCHANTS CASUALTY CO.—See Motorists Mutual Insurance Co.; *U.S. Private*, pg. 764
AMERICAN METAL & PLASTICS INC.; *U.S. Private*, pg. 59
AMERICAN METAL PRODUCTS—See Masco Corporation; *U.S. Public*, pg. 1053
AMERICAN METER COMPANY—See Ruhrgas Aktiengesellschaft; *Int'l*, pg. 1149
AMERICAN MICROSYSTEMS, INC.—See Japan Energy Corporation; *Int'l*, pg. 702
AMERICAN MILLIBAR DIV.—See Okura & Co.; *Int'l*, pg. 1001
AMERICAN MINE TOOL CO.—See Kennametal Inc.; *U.S. Public*, pg. 950
AMERICAN MODERN HOME INSURANCE CO.—See The Midland Company; *U.S. Public*, pg. 1110
AMERICAN MODULAR TECHNOLOGIES—See American Buildings Company; *U.S. Public*, pg. 69
AMERICAN MONEY MANAGEMENT CORPORATION—See American Financial Group; *U.S. Public*, pg. 74
AMERICAN MOTORISTS INSURANCE CO.—See Kemper Insurance Companies; *U.S. Private*, pg. 614
AMERICAN MULTI-CINEMA, INC.—See AMC Entertainment, Inc.; *U.S. Public*, pg. 6
AMERICAN MUTUAL LIFE HOLDING CO.; *U.S. Private*, pg. 59
AMERICAN NATIONAL BANK & TRUST CO. OF CHICAGO—See First Chicago NBD Corporation; *U.S. Public*, pg. 628

AMERICAN NATIONAL BANK & TRUST OF CHICAGO—See First Chicago NBD Corporation; *U.S. Public*, pg. 627
AMERICAN CAN CANADA INC.—See Pechiney S.A.; *Int'l*, pg. 1029
AMERICAN NATL. CAN CO.—See Pechiney S.A.; *Int'l*, pg. 1029
AMERICAN NATIONAL CAN COMPANY—See Pechiney S.A.; *Int'l*, pg. 1029
AMERICAN NATIONAL FIRE INSURANCE COMPANY—See American Financial Group; *U.S. Public*, pg. 74
AMERICAN NATIONAL GENERAL INSURANCE COMPANY—See American National Insurance Company; *U.S. Public*, pg. 88
AMERICAN NATIONAL GROWTH FUND, INC.—See American National Insurance Company; *U.S. Public*, pg. 87
AMERICAN NATIONAL INCOME FUND, INC.—See American National Insurance Company; *U.S. Public*, pg. 87
AMERICAN NATIONAL INSURANCE COMPANY; *U.S. Public*, pg. 87
AMERICAN NATIONAL INSURANCE SERVICE CO.—See American National Insurance Company; *U.S. Public*, pg. 88
AMERICAN NATIONAL INVESTMENT ACCOUNTS—See American National Insurance Company; *U.S. Public*, pg. 87
AMERICAN NATIONAL LIFE INSURANCE CO. OF TEXAS—See American National Insurance Company; *U.S. Public*, pg. 87
AMERICAN NATIONAL PROPERTY & CASUALTY CO.—See American National Insurance Company; *U.S. Public*, pg. 87
AMERICAN NATIONAL TRIFLEX FUND, INC.—See American National Insurance Company; *U.S. Public*, pg. 87
AMERICAN NATL. CAN CO.—See Pechiney S.A.; *Int'l*, pg. 1029
AMERICAN NATL. CAN CO.-FOOD PLASTIC N. AMERICA—See Pechiney S.A.; *Int'l*, pg. 1029
AMERICAN NATL. CAN CO., GRAPHIC ARTS DIV.—See Pechiney S.A.; *Int'l*, pg. 1029
AMERICAN NATL. CAN CO.-TUBE PACKAGING—See Pechiney S.A.; *Int'l*, pg. 1029
AMERICAN NATURAL OFFSHORE CO.—See The Coastal Corporation; *U.S. Public*, pg. 389
AMERICAN NATURAL SNACKS—See Koninklijke BolsWessanen nv; *Int'l*, pg. 752
AMERICAN NORIT CO. INC.—See NORIT N.V.; *Int'l*, pg. 958
AMERICAN NUCLEONICS CORP.—See Eaton Corporation; *U.S. Public*, pg. 556
AMERICAN NURSERY PRODUCTS, LLC; *U.S. Private*, pg. 59
AMERICAN NUT CO.—See Clements Foods Co.; *U.S. Private*, pg. 245
AMERICAN NUTRITION, INC.; *U.S. Private*, pg. 60
AMERICAN OIL & GAS CORPORATION—See K N Energy, Inc.; *U.S. Public*, pg. 937
AMERICAN ONCOLOGY RESOURCES, INC.; *U.S. Public*, pg. 88
AMERICAN OPTICAL CORPORATION; *U.S. Private*, pg. 60
AMERICAN OPTICAL-SAFETY DIVISION—See Cabot Corporation; *U.S. Public*, pg. 289
AMERICAN OVERSEAS MARINE CORP.—See General Dynamics Corporation; *U.S. Public*, pg. 709
AMERICAN PACIFIC CORPORATION; *U.S. Public*, pg. 88
AMERICAN PACKAGING CORPORATION; *U.S. Private*, pg. 60
AMERICAN PAD AND PAPER COMPANY; *U.S. Public*, pg. 88
AMERICAN PAGING, INC.—See Telephone and Data Systems, Inc.; *U.S. Public*, pg. 1570
AMERICAN PAPER GROUP, INC.; *U.S. Private*, pg. 60
AMERICAN PAPER PRODUCTS—See American Paper Group, Inc.; *U.S. Private*, pg. 60
AMERICAN PASSAGE MEDIA CORPORATION; *U.S. Private*, pg. 60
AMERICAN PAYMENT SYSTEMS, INC.—See United Illuminating Company; *U.S. Public*, pg. 1678
AMERICAN PEPTIDE COMPANY, INC.—See Itoham Foods Inc.; *Int'l*, pg. 695
AMERICAN PETROFINA HOLDING CO.—See Petrofina S.A.; *Int'l*, pg. 1044
AMERICAN PFAUTER CORP.—See Hermann Pfauter GmbH & Co.; *Int'l*, pg. 617
AMERICAN PHARMACEUTICAL SERVICES, INC.—See Paragon Health Network, Inc.; *U.S. Public*, pg. 1257
AMERICAN PHONE CENTERS, INC.—See Comdial Corporation; *U.S. Public*, pg. 407
AMERICAN PHOTO—See Lagardere Groupe; *Int'l*, pg. 795
AMERICAN PHOTO GROUP—See Eastman Kodak Company; *U.S. Public*, pg. 551
AMERICAN PIPE AND CONSTRUCTION INTERNATIONAL—See Ameron International Corporation; *U.S. Public*, pg. 99
AN AMERICAN PLACE—See Ark Restaurants Corp.; *U.S. Public*, pg. 130
AMERICAN PLASTIC TOYS INC.; *U.S. Private*, pg. 60
AMERICAN POWER CONVERSION—See American Power Conversion Corporation; *U.S. Public*, pg. 89
AMERICAN POWER CONVERSION CORPORATION; *U.S. Public*, pg. 89
AMERICAN PRECAST CONCRETE, INC.; *U.S. Private*, pg. 60
AMERICAN PRECISION INDUSTRIES INC.; *U.S. Public*, pg. 90
AMERICAN PRECISION INDUSTRIES (U.K.) LTD.—See American Precision Industries Inc.; *U.S. Public*, pg. 90
AMERICAN PRESIDENT LINES. CANADA, LTD.—See Neptune Orient Lines Ltd.; *Int'l*, pg. 912

AMERICAN PRESIDENT LINES, CHINA CO., LTD.—See Neptune Orient Lines Ltd.; *Int'l*, pg. 912
AMERICAN PRESIDENT LINES, DELAWARE, LTD.—See Neptune Orient Lines Ltd.; *Int'l*, pg. 912
AMERICAN PRESIDENT REAL ESTATE CO., LTD.—See Neptune Orient Lines Ltd.; *Int'l*, pg. 912
AMERICAN PRESIDENT TRUCKING COMPANY, LTD.—See Neptune Orient Lines Ltd.; *Int'l*, pg. 912
AMERICAN PROCUREMENT & LOGISTICS COMPANY—See American Stores Company; *U.S. Public*, pg. 93
AMERICAN PRODUCTS, INC.—See Essef Corporation; *U.S. Public*, pg. 593
AMERICAN PROTECTION INSURANCE CO.—See Kemper Insurance Companies; *U.S. Private*, pg. 614
AMERICAN PUBLISHING MANAGEMENT SERVICES INC.—See Hollinger Inc.; *Int'l*, pg. 632
AMERICAN RADIO RELAY LEAGUE; *U.S. Private*, pg. 60
AMERICAN RAILCAR INDUSTRIES—See Icahn & Co., Inc.; *U.S. Private*, pg. 556
AMERICAN RE CORPORATION—See Munchener Ruckversicherungs-Gesellschaft; *Int'l*, pg. 897
AMERICAN RE-INSURANCE COMPANY—See Munchener Ruckversicherungs-Gesellschaft; *Int'l*, pg. 897
AMERICAN REAL ESTATE INVESTMENT & DEVELOPMENT CO.—See ABN-AMRO Holding N.V.; *Int'l*, pg. 9
AMERICAN RECREATION CENTERS, INC.; *U.S. Public*, pg. 90
AMERICAN RECREATION PRODUCTS, INC.—See Kellwood Company; *U.S. Public*, pg. 948
AMERICAN RED BALL INTERNATIONAL, INC.—See Atlas World Group, Inc.; *U.S. Private*, pg. 97
AMERICAN RED BALL TRANSIT CO. INC.—See Atlas World Group, Inc.; *U.S. Private*, pg. 97
AMERICAN REFRACTORIES & CRUCIBLE CORPORATION—See Morgan Crucible Co. Plc; *Int'l*, pg. 893
AMERICAN REFRACTORIES CO.—See RGP Holding, Inc.; *U.S. Private*, pg. 903
AMERICAN REHABILITY SERVICES, INC.—See Paragon Health Network, Inc.; *U.S. Public*, pg. 1257
AMERICAN RELIABLE INSURANCE COMPANY—See American Bankers Insurance Group, Inc.; *U.S. Public*, pg. 67
AMERICAN RENAISSANCE INSURANCE COMPANY—See Ford Motor Company; *U.S. Public*, pg. 664
AMERICAN REPUBLIC INSURANCE CO.; *U.S. Private*, pg. 61
AMERICAN RESTAURANT GROUP, INC.; *U.S. Private*, pg. 61
AMERICAN RETAIL GROUP; *U.S. Private*, pg. 61
AMERICAN RICE INC.—See Erly Industries, Inc.; *U.S. Public*, pg. 591
AMERICAN RICE, INC.-FREEPORT—See Erly Industries, Inc.; *U.S. Public*, pg. 591
AMERICAN RIGGING & SUPPLY—See The Carpenter Group; *U.S. Private*, pg. 215
AMERICAN RISK ASSOCIATES, LTD.—See Day & Zimmermann, Inc.; *U.S. Private*, pg. 317
AMERICAN RIVER TRANSPORTATION CO.—See Archer Daniels Midland Company (ADM); *U.S. Public*, pg. 128
THE AMERICAN ROAD INSURANCE COMPANY—See Ford Motor Company; *U.S. Public*, pg. 664
AMERICAN ROCHE INTL.—See Roche Holding Ltd.; *Int'l*, pg. 1120
AMERICAN RUG CRAFTSMEN—See Mohawk Industries, Inc.; *U.S. Public*, pg. 1121
AMERICAN SAFETY RAZOR COMPANY—See The Jordan Company; *U.S. Private*, pg. 597
AMERICAN SAFETY TECHNOLOGIES, INC.—See Morgan Crucible Co. Plc; *Int'l*, pg. 892
AMERICAN SAHM CORPORATION—See Georg Sahm GmbH & Co. KG Maschinenfabrik; *Int'l*, pg. 1169
AMERICAN SAVANNAH BROADCASTING CO.—See Raycom Media, Inc.; *U.S. Private*, pg. 912
AMERICAN SAVINGS BANK, F.S.B.—See Hawaiian Electric Industries, Inc.; *U.S. Public*, pg. 800
AMERICAN SAW & MFG. COMPANY; *U.S. Private*, pg. 61
AMERICAN SCANDINAVIAN BANKING CORPORATION—See Merita Ltd.; *Int'l*, pg. 859
AMERICAN SCIENCE & ENGINEERING, INC.; *U.S. Public*, pg. 90
AMERICAN SEATING COMPANY; *U.S. Private*, pg. 61
AMERICAN SEAWAY FOODS, INC.—See Giant Eagle, Inc.; *U.S. Private*, pg. 451
AMERICAN SECURITY DISTRIBUTION; *U.S. Private*, pg. 61
AMERICAN SECURITY GROUP—See Fortis; *Int'l*, pg. 499
AMERICAN SECURITY PROPERTIES, INC.—See First Hawaiian, Inc.; *U.S. Public*, pg. 635
AMERICAN SHARED-CURACARE—See American Shared Hospital Services; *U.S. Public*, pg. 91
AMERICAN SHARED HOSPITAL SERVICES; *U.S. Public*, pg. 91
AMERICAN SHARED RADIOSURGERY SERVICES—See American Shared Hospital Services; *U.S. Public*, pg. 91
AMERICAN SHEAR KNIVE CO.—See Asko, Inc; *U.S. Private*, pg. 89
AMERICAN SIGHTSEEING INTERNATIONAL; *U.S. Private*, pg. 61
AMERICAN SIGN & MARKETING SERVICES, INC.—See Plasti-Line, Inc.; *U.S. Public*, pg. 1309
AMERICAN SILICON PRODUCTS, INC.—See Semiconductor Packaging Materials Co., Inc.; *U.S. Public*, pg. 1456
AMERICAN SKANDIA BUSINESS SERVICES CORPORATION—See Skandia Insurance Company Limited; *Int'l*, pg. 1257
AMERICAN SKANDIA INFORMATION SERVICES & TECNOLOGY CORP.—See Skandia Insurance Company Limited; *Int'l*, pg. 1257
AMERICAN SKANDIA INVESTMENT HOLDING CORPORATION—See Skandia Insurance Company Limited; *Int'l*, pg. 1257

AMERICAN SKANDIA INVESTMENT SERVICES, INC.—See Skandia Insurance Company Limited; *Int'l*, pg. 1257

AMERICAN SKANDIA LIFE ASSURANCE CORPORATION—See Skandia Insurance Company Limited; *Int'l*, pg. 1257

AMERICAN SKANDIA MARKETING, INC.—See Skandia Insurance Company Limited; *Int'l*, pg. 1257

AMERICAN SKIING COMPANY; *U.S. Private*, pg. 61

AMERICAN SOFTWARE, INC.; *U.S. Public*, pg. 91

AMERICAN SOFTWARE, INC., MID-AMERICA—See American Software, Inc.; *U.S. Public*, pg. 91

AMERICAN SOFTWARE, INC., NORTHEAST—See American Software, Inc.; *U.S. Public*, pg. 91

AMERICAN SOFTWARE, INC., SOUTHERN—See American Software, Inc.; *U.S. Public*, pg. 91

AMERICAN SOFTWARE, INC., WESTERN—See American Software, Inc.; *U.S. Public*, pg. 91

AMERICAN SOFTWARE (UK) LTD., EUROPE/MIDDLE EAST/AFRICA—See American Software, Inc.; *U.S. Public*, pg. 91

AMERICAN SOUTHERN FINANCIAL GROUP—See The Keyes Company Realtors; *U.S. Private*, pg. 618

AMERICAN SPECIALTIES INC.; *U.S. Private*, pg. 62

AMERICAN SPEEDY PRINTING CENTERS, INC.; *U.S. Private*, pg. 62

AMERICAN SPORTING GOODS CORPORATION; *U.S. Private*, pg. 62

AMERICAN STANDARD INC.; *U.S. Public*, pg. 91

AMERICAN STANDARD INSURANCE COMPANY OF OHIO—See American Family Mutual Insurance Co.; *U.S. Private*, pg. 53

AMERICAN STANDARD INSURANCE COMPANY OF WISCONSIN—See American Family Mutual Insurance Co.; *U.S. Private*, pg. 53

AMERICAN STATES ECONOMY INSURANCE CO.—See Lincoln National Corporation; *U.S. Public*, pg. 997

AMERICAN STATES INSURANCE COMPANIES—See Lincoln National Corporation; *U.S. Public*, pg. 997

AMERICAN STATES INSURANCE CO. OF TEXAS—See Lincoln National Corporation; *U.S. Public*, pg. 997

AMERICAN STATES LIFE INSURANCE CO.—See Lincoln National Corporation; *U.S. Public*, pg. 997

AMERICAN STATIONERY CO., INC.; *U.S. Private*, pg. 62

AMERICAN STEAMSHIP COMPANY—See GATX Corporation; *U.S. Public*, pg. 690

AMERICAN STEEL CORP.—See NKK Corporation; *Int'l*, pg. 903

AMERICAN STEEL FOUNDRIES—See Amsted Industries Incorporated; *U.S. Private*, pg. 68

AMERICAN STEEL LLC—See Reliance Steel & Aluminum Co.; *U.S. Public*, pg. 1375

AMERICAN STEEL PIPE DIV.—See American Cast Iron Pipe Co.; *U.S. Private*, pg. 52

THE AMERICAN STOCK EXCHANGE; *U.S. Private*, pg. 62

AMERICAN STOCK EXCHANGE CLEARING CORP.—See The American Stock Exchange; *U.S. Private*, pg. 62

AMERICAN STOCK EXCHANGE REALTY ASSOCIATES INC.—See The American Stock Exchange; *U.S. Private*, pg. 62

AMERICAN STONE-MIX, INC.; *U.S. Private*, pg. 62

AMERICAN STORES COMPANY; *U.S. Public*, pg. 92

AMERICAN STORES PROPERTIES, INC.—See American Stores Company; *U.S. Public*, pg. 93

AMERICAN STRIP STEEL INC.; *U.S. Private*, pg. 62

AMERICAN SUESSEN—See Spindelfabrik Suessen; *Int'l*, pg. 1290

AMERICAN SUNROOF COMPANY—See ASC Incorporated; *U.S. Private*, pg. 138

AMERICAN SUZUKI MOTOR CORPORATION—See Suzuki Motor Corporation; *Int'l*, pg. 1323

AMERICAN SWEETNERS, INC.; *U.S. Private*, pg. 63

AMERICAN SYSTEMS CORPORATION; *U.S. Private*, pg. 63

AMERICAN SYSTEMS ENGINEERING CORPORATION—See Science Applications International Corp.; *U.S. Private*, pg. 976

AMERICAN SYSTEMS TECHNOLOGIES—See ABC Rail Products Corp.; *U.S. Public*, pg. 2

AMERICAN TANK & FABRICATING CO.; *U.S. Private*, pg. 63

AMERICAN TAPE CO.—See Intertape Polymer Group Inc.; *Int'l*, pg. 685

AMERICAN TECH MANUFACTURING CORPORATION—See Halma p.l.c.; *Int'l*, pg. 590

AMERICAN TECHNICAL CERAMICS CORP.; *U.S. Public*, pg. 93

AMERICAN TECHNICAL PUBLISHERS, INC.; *U.S. Private*, pg. 63

AMERICAN TECHNICAL SERVICES GROUP, INC.—See Strategic Distribution Inc.; *U.S. Public*, pg. 1523

AMERICAN TECHNOLOGY CORPORATION; *U.S. Private*, pg. 63

AMERICAN TELECASTING, INC.; *U.S. Public*, pg. 93

AMERICAN TELECOMMUNICATIONS CORPORATION—See Comdial Corporation; *U.S. Public*, pg. 407

AMERICAN TELEVISION TIME, INC.; *U.S. Private*, pg. 63

AMERICAN TEXTIL, S.A. DE C.V.—See Guilford Mills, Inc.; *U.S. Public*, pg. 769

AMERICAN THERMOPLASTICS CORPORATION—See Phillips Petroleum Company; *U.S. Public*, pg. 1291

AMERICAN TIRE & SERVICE COMPANY—See Bridgestone Corporation; *Int'l*, pg. 213

AMERICAN TISSUE CORPORATION; *U.S. Private*, pg. 63

AMERICAN TISSUE, INC.—See American Tissue Corporation; *U.S. Private*, pg. 63

AMERICAN TISSUE MILLS OF GREENWICH—See American Tissue Corporation; *U.S. Private*, pg. 63

AMERICAN TOOL COMPANIES, INC.; *U.S. Private*, pg. 63

AMERICAN TOOL COMPANIES, INC.—See American Tool Companies, Inc.; *U.S. Private*, pg. 63

AMERICAN TOURISTER, INC.—See Samsonite Corporation; *U.S. Public*, pg. 1430

AMERICAN TRACTEBEL CORPORATION—See Tractebel; *Int'l*, pg. 1415

AMERICAN TRADING AND PRODUCTION CORPORATION; *U.S. Private*, pg. 63

AMERICAN TRADING & PRODUCTION CORPORATION, OIL & GAS DIV.—See American Trading and Production Corporation; *U.S. Private*, pg. 64

AMERICAN TRADING REAL ESTATE PROPERTIES, INC.—See American Trading and Production Corporation; *U.S. Private*, pg. 64

AMERICAN TRANS AIR EXECUJET, INC.—See Amtran, Inc.; *U.S. Public*, pg. 106

AMERICAN TRANS AIR, INC.—See Amtran, Inc.; *U.S. Public*, pg. 106

AMERICAN TRANS AIR TRAINING CORP.—See Amtran, Inc.; *U.S. Public*, pg. 106

AMERICAN TRAVELLERS CORPORATION—See Conseco Inc.; *U.S. Public*, pg. 433

AMERICAN TRAVELLERS INSURANCE SERVICES—See Conseco Inc.; *U.S. Public*, pg. 433

AMERICAN TRAVELLERS LIFE INSURANCE COMPANY—See Conseco Inc.; *U.S. Public*, pg. 433

AMERICAN TROUSER, INC.; *U.S. Private*, pg. 64

AMERICAN TV & APPLIANCE OF MADISON, INC.; *U.S. Private*, pg. 64

AMERICAN UNIFORM CO.—See Steiner Corporation; *U.S. Private*, pg. 1039

AMERICAN UNITED LIFE INSURANCE COMPANY; *U.S. Private*, pg. 64

AMERICAN VALVE & HYDRANT CO.—See American Cast Iron Pipe Co.; *U.S. Private*, pg. 52

AMERICAN VANGUARD CORPORATION; *U.S. Public*, pg. 94

AMERICAN WASTE MANAGEMENT SERVICES, INC.—See American Waste Services, Inc.; *U.S. Public*, pg. 94

AMERICAN WASTE SERVICES, INC.; *U.S. Public*, pg. 94

AMERICAN WATER HEAT GROUP—See Southcorp Holdings Ltd.; *Int'l*, pg. 1287

AMERICAN WATER WORKS ASSOCIATION; pg. 94

AMERICAN WATER WORKS COMPANY, INC.; *U.S. Public*, pg. 95

AMERICAN WATER WORKS SERVICE COMPANY, INC.—See American Water Works Company, Inc.; *U.S. Public*, pg. 95

AMERICAN WELDING & MANUFACTURING CO.—See Freedom Forge Corporation; *U.S. Private*, pg. 425

AMERICAN WEST INSURANCE COMPANY—See W.R. Berkley Corporation; *U.S. Public*, pg. 216

AMERICAN WEST TRADING CO.—See McRae Industries, Inc.; *U.S. Public*, pg. 1073

AMERICAN WHITE CROSS—See GP Strategies Corporation; *U.S. Public*, pg. 694

AMERICAN WOODMARK CORPORATION; *U.S. Public*, pg. 96

AMERICAN WYOTT CORPORATION—See A.P. Wyott; *U.S. Private*, pg. 1193

AMERICAN XYROFIN INC.—See Cultor Ltd.; *Int'l*, pg. 350

AMERICAN YAZAKI CORP., INC.—See Yazaki Corporation; *Int'l*, pg. 1520

AMERICAN ZETTLER INC.—See Alois Zettler Elektrotechnische Fabrik GmbH; *Int'l*, pg. 1528

AMERICAN ZURICH INSURANCE COMPANY—See Zurich Insurance Company; *Int'l*, pg. 1530

AMERICANA FOODS, INC.—See TCBY Enterprises Inc.; *U.S. Public*, pg. 1554

AMERICANANGLIAN ENVIRONMENTAL TECHNOLOGIES, INC.—See American Water Works Company, Inc.; *U.S. Public*, pg. 95

AMERICA'S BEVERAGE CO.—See The Kroger Co.; *U.S. Public*, pg. 967

AMERICA'S STORE—See USA Networks, Inc.; *U.S. Public*, pg. 1685

AMERICO MANUFACTURING CO., INC.; *U.S. Private*, pg. 64

AMERICOAL SERVICES COMPANY—See Zeigler Coal Holding Company; *U.S. Public*, pg. 1790

AMERICOLD COMPRESSOR CO.—See Electrolux, AB; *Int'l*, pg. 439

AMERICREDIT CORP.; *U.S. Public*, pg. 96

AMERIDATA TECHNOLOGIES, INC.—See General Electric Company; *U.S. Public*, pg. 711

AMERIFOODS INC.; *U.S. Private*, pg. 65

AMERIFOODS SNACKS—See Amerifoods Inc.; *U.S. Private*, pg. 65

AMERIGAS, INC.—See UGI Corporation; *U.S. Public*, pg. 1653

AMERIGAS PARTNERS, L.P.—See UGI Corporation; *U.S. Public*, pg. 1653

AMERIGAS PROPANE—See UGI Corporation; *U.S. Public*, pg. 1653

AMERIMARK INC.—See Owens Corning; *U.S. Public*, pg. 1237

AMERINSURANCE, INC.—See Corporacion MAPFRE, Compania Internacional de Reaseguros, S.A.; *Int'l*, pg. 333

AMERIPATH, INC.; *U.S. Public*, pg. 96

AMERIPOL SYNPOL CORP.; *U.S. Private*, pg. 65

AMERIPRIDE SERVICE COMPANY; *U.S. Private*, pg. 65

AMERIQUEST TECHNOLOGIES; *U.S. Public*, pg. 96

AMERISCRIBE CORPORATION—See Pitney Bowes Inc.; *U.S. Public*, pg. 1303

AMERISERVE FOOD DISTRIBUTION, INC.—See Holberg Industries, Inc.; *U.S. Private*, pg. 533

AMERISERVE OF DENVER—See Holberg Industries, Inc.; *U.S. Private*, pg. 533

AMERISERVE OF FORT WORTH—See Holberg Industries, Inc.; *U.S. Private*, pg. 533

AMERISERVE OF GRAND RAPIDS—See Holberg Industries, Inc.; *U.S. Private*, pg. 533

AMERISERVE OF NORCROSS—See Holberg Industries, Inc.; *U.S. Private*, pg. 533

AMERISOURCE-BIRMINGHAM DIV.—See AmeriSource Health Corp.; *U.S. Public*, pg. 96

AMERISOURCE-DALLAS DIV.—See AmeriSource Health Corp.; *U.S. Public*, pg. 97

AMERISOURCE HEALTH CORP.; *U.S. Public*, pg. 96

AMERISOURCE-IDAHO FALLS DIV.—See AmeriSource Health Corp.; *U.S. Public*, pg. 97

AMERISOURCE-PHOENIX DIV.—See AmeriSource Health Corp.; *U.S. Public*, pg. 97

AMERISOURCE-PORTLAND DIV.—See AmeriSource Health Corp.; *U.S. Public*, pg. 97

AMERISOURCE-SACRAMENTO DIV.—See AmeriSource Health Corp.; *U.S. Public*, pg. 97

AMERISOURCE-SPRINGFIELD—See AmeriSource Health Corp.; *U.S. Public*, pg. 97

AMERISTAR CAPITAL MARKETS, INC.—See First American Corporation; *U.S. Public*, pg. 624

AMERISTAR FINANCIAL CORPORATION—See Lennar Corporation; *U.S. Public*, pg. 987

AMERISTEEL; *U.S. Private*, pg. 65

AMERISURE COMPANIES; *U.S. Private*, pg. 65

AMERITAS LIFE INSURANCE CORP.; *U.S. Private*, pg. 65

AMERITAS VARIABLE LIFE INSURANCE COMPANY—See Ameritas Life Insurance Corp.; *U.S. Private*, pg. 65

AMERITCON, INC.—See Shook National Corporation; *U.S. Private*, pg. 996

AMERITECH—See Ameritech Corporation; *U.S. Public*, pg. 97

AMERITECH ADVERTISING SERVICES—See Ameritech Corporation; *U.S. Public*, pg. 97

AMERITECH APPLIED TECHNOLOGIES, INC.—See Ameritech Corporation; *U.S. Public*, pg. 98

AMERITECH AUDIOTEX SERVICES INC.—See Ameritech Corporation; *U.S. Public*, pg. 98

AMERITECH CAPITAL SERVICES—See Ameritech Corporation; *U.S. Public*, pg. 98

AMERITECH CELLULAR AND PAGING SERVICES—See Ameritech Corporation; *U.S. Public*, pg. 98

AMERITECH COMMUNICATIONS, INC.—See Ameritech Corporation; *U.S. Public*, pg. 98

AMERITECH CONSUMER SERVICES—See Ameritech Corporation; *U.S. Public*, pg. 98

AMERITECH CORP.—See Ameritech Corporation; *U.S. Public*, pg. 98

AMERITECH CORPORATION; *U.S. Public*, pg. 97

AMERITECH CREDIT CORPORATION—See Ameritech Corporation; *U.S. Public*, pg. 98

AMERITECH CUSTOM BUSINESS SERVICES—See Ameritech Corporation; *U.S. Public*, pg. 98

AMERITECH DEVELOPMENT CORPORATION—See Ameritech Corporation; *U.S. Public*, pg. 98

AMERITECH ENHANCED BUSINESS SERVICES—See Ameritech Corporation; *U.S. Public*, pg. 98

AMERITECH INFORMATION SYSTEMS INC.—See Ameritech Corporation; *U.S. Public*, pg. 98

AMERITECH INTERNATIONAL INC.—See Ameritech Corporation; *U.S. Public*, pg. 98

AMERITECH NEW MEDIA—See Ameritech Corporation; *U.S. Public*, pg. 98

AMERITECH PHONE COMPANY—See Ameritech Corporation; *U.S. Public*, pg. 98

AMERITECH PUBLISHING, INC.—See Ameritech Corporation; *U.S. Public*, pg. 98

AMERITECH SMALL BUSINESS SERVICES—See Ameritech Corporation; *U.S. Public*, pg. 98

AMERITRUCK DISTRIBUTION CORPORATION; *U.S. Private*, pg. 65

AMERITRUCK REFRIGERATED TRANSPORT, INC.—See Ameritruck Distribution Corporation; *U.S. Private*, pg. 66

AMERIWOOD INDUSTRIES INTERNATIONAL INC.; *U.S. Public*, pg. 98

AMEROCK CORPORATION—See Newell Co.; *U.S. Public*, pg. 1177

AMERON B.V., FIBERGLASS PIPE DIVISION-EUROPE—See Ameron International Corporation; *U.S. Public*, pg. 99

AMERON B.V., PROTECTIVE COATINGS DIVISION-EUROPE—See Ameron International Corporation; *U.S. Public*, pg. 99

AMERON FIBERGLASS PIPE GROUP—See Ameron International Corporation; *U.S. Public*, pg. 99

AMERON (HONG KONG) LTD.—See Ameron International Corporation; *U.S. Public*, pg. 99

AMERON INTERNATIONAL CORPORATION; *U.S. Public*, pg. 98

AMERON POLE PRODUCTS & SYSTEMS—See Ameron International Corporation; *U.S. Public*, pg. 99

AMERON PROTECTIVE COATINGS DIV.—See Ameron International Corporation; *U.S. Public*, pg. 99

AMERON PROTECTIVE COATINGS GROUP—See Ameron International Corporation; *U.S. Public*, pg. 99

AMERON PROTECTIVE LININGS DIVISION—See Ameron International Corporation; *U.S. Public*, pg. 99

AMERON (PTE) LTD.—See Ameron International Corporation; *U.S. Public*, pg. 99

AMERON SAUDI ARABIA, LTD.—See Ameron International Corporation; *U.S. Public*, pg. 99

AMERPAP EAST LTD.—See Metsa-Serla Corporation; *Int'l*, pg. 863

AMERPAP OY—See Metsa-Serla Corporation; *Int'l*, pg. 863

AMERSHAM AUSTRALIA PTY. LTD.—See Nycomed Amersham plc; *Int'l*, pg. 992

AMERSHAM BELGIUM NV/SA—See Nycomed Amersham plc; *Int'l*, pg. 992

AMERSHAM BÜCHLER GMBH & CO. KG—See Nycomed Amersham plc; *Int'l*, pg. 992

AMERSHAM CANADA LIMITED—See Nycomed Amersham plc; *Int'l*, pg. 992

AMERSHAM CORPORATION—See Nycomed Amersham plc; *Int'l*, pg. 992

AMERSHAM CORPORATION (AMERSHAM QSA)—See Nycomed Amersham plc; *Int'l*, pg. 992

AMERSHAM DENMARK APS—See Nycomed Amersham plc; *Int'l*, pg. 993

AMERSHAM FAR EAST TRADING LIMITED—See Nycomed Amersham plc; *Int'l*, pg. 993

AMERSHAM FRANCE SA—See Nycomed Amersham plc; *Int'l*, pg. 993
AMERSHAM HEALTHCARE—See Nycomed Amersham plc; *Int'l*, pg. 992
AMERSHAM IBERICA SA—See Nycomed Amersham plc; *Int'l*, pg. 993
AMERSHAM ITALIA SRL—See Nycomed Amersham plc; *Int'l*, pg. 993
AMERSHAM K.K.—See Nycomed Amersham plc; *Int'l*, pg. 993
AMERSHAM LIFE SCIENCE, INC.—See Nycomed Amersham plc; *Int'l*, pg. 992
AMERSHAM NEDERLAND BV—See Nycomed Amersham plc; *Int'l*, pg. 993
AMERSHAM SWEDEN AB—See Nycomed Amersham plc; *Int'l*, pg. 993
AMERUS LIFE—See American Mutual Life Holding Co.; *U.S. Private*, pg. 59
AMES AUTOMOTIVE WAREHOUSE—See Aid Auto Stores, Inc.; *U.S. Public*, pg. 29
AMES CO., INC.—See Watts Industries, Inc.; *U.S. Public*, pg. 1746
AMES COMPANY—See U.S. Industries, Inc.; *U.S. Public*, pg. 1683
AMES CROSTA BABCOCK LTD.—See FKI Plc; *Int'l*, pg. 471
AMES DEPARTMENT STORES, INC.; *U.S. Public*, pg. 99
AMES EUROPE B.V.—See Gamma Holding N.V.; *Int'l*, pg. 539
AMES EUROPE ENSCHEDE B.V.—See Gamma Holding N.V.; *Int'l*, pg. 539
AMES EUROPE LTD.—See Gamma Holding N.V.; *Int'l*, pg. 540
AMES EUROPE S.A.—See Gamma Holding N.V.; *Int'l*, pg. 540
AMES EUROPE VEENENDAAL B.V.—See Gamma Holding N.V.; *Int'l*, pg. 540
AMES SAFETY ENVELOPE COMPANY, INC.; *U.S. Private*, pg. 66
AMES TAPING TOOL SYSTEMS CO.—See AXIA Incorporated; *U.S. Private*, pg. 103
AMES TAPING TOOLS CO. OF CANADA LIMITED—See AXIA Incorporated; *U.S. Private*, pg. 103
AMETEK DENMARK—See AMETEK, Inc.; *U.S. Public*, pg. 100
AMETEK DIXSON DIVISION—See AMETEK, Inc.; *U.S. Public*, pg. 100
AMETEK G.M.B.H.—See AMETEK, Inc.; *U.S. Public*, pg. 100
AMETEK, INC.; *U.S. Public*, pg. 99
AMETEK ITALIA—See AMETEK, Inc.; *U.S. Public*, pg. 100
AMETEX FABRICS, INC.—See Furnishings International, Inc.; *U.S. Private*, pg. 432
AMEX COMMODITIES CORPORATION—See The American Stock Exchange; *U.S. Private*, pg. 62
AMEX LIFE ASSURANCE CO.—See General Electric Company; *U.S. Public*, pg. 712
AMFAC AGRIBUSINESS, INC.—See JMB Realty Corporation; *U.S. Private*, pg. 578
AMFAC, INC.—See JMB Realty Corporation; *U.S. Private*, pg. 577
AMFAC/JMB HAWAII, INC.—See JMB Realty Corporation; *U.S. Private*, pg. 577
AMFAC PROPERTY INVESTMENT CORP.—See JMB Realty Corporation; *U.S. Private*, pg. 577
AMFAC SUGAR AND AGRIBUSINESS, INC.—See JMB Realty Corporation; *U.S. Private*, pg. 578
AMFELS INC.—See Keppel Corporation Limited; *Int'l*, pg. 731
AMFIDIS—See GIB Group; *Int'l*, pg. 533
AMGEN AUSTRALIA PTY LTD.—See Amgen Inc.; *U.S. Public*, pg. 101
AMGEN-BIOFARMACEUTICA, LDA.—See Amgen Inc.; *U.S. Public*, pg. 101
AMGEN BOULDER, INC.—See Amgen Inc.; *U.S. Public*, pg. 101
AMGEN B.V.—See Amgen Inc.; *U.S. Public*, pg. 101
AMGEN CANADA INC.—See Amgen Inc.; *U.S. Public*, pg. 101
AMGEN DEVELOPMENT CORPORATION—See Amgen Inc.; *U.S. Public*, pg. 101
AMGEN (EUROPE) AG—See Amgen Inc.; *U.S. Public*, pg. 101
THE AMGEN FOUNDATION, INC.—See Amgen Inc.; *U.S. Public*, pg. 101
AMGEN GMBH—See Amgen Inc.; *U.S. Public*, pg. 101
AMGEN GREATER CHINA, LTD.—See Amgen Inc.; *U.S. Public*, pg. 101
AMGEN HOLDING, INC.—See Amgen Inc.; *U.S. Public*, pg. 101
AMGEN INC.; *U.S. Public*, pg. 100
AMGEN INTERNATIONAL INC.—See Amgen Inc.; *U.S. Public*, pg. 101
AMGEN KABUSHIKI KAISHA—See Amgen Inc.; *U.S. Public*, pg. 101
AMGEN LIMITED—See Amgen Inc.; *U.S. Public*, pg. 101
AMGEN MANUFACTURING, INC.—See Amgen Inc.; *U.S. Public*, pg. 101
AMGEN N.V.—See Amgen Inc.; *U.S. Public*, pg. 101
AMGEN S.A.—See Amgen Inc.; *U.S. Public*, pg. 101
AMGEN SALES CORPORATION—See Amgen Inc.; *U.S. Public*, pg. 101
AMGEN S.P.A.—See Amgen Inc.; *U.S. Public*, pg. 101
AMGEN VENTURES—See Amgen Inc.; *U.S. Public*, pg. 101
AMGRO, INC.—See Allmerica Financial Corporation; *U.S. Public*, pg. 169
AMHERST METAL PRODUCTS, INC.—See Brittany Corporation; *U.S. Private*, pg. 169
AMIANTIT FIBREGLASS INDUS., LTD.—See Owens Corning; *U.S. Public*, pg. 1237
AMIC INDUSTRIES LIMITED—See Anglo American Corporation of South Africa Limited; *Int'l*, pg. 76
AMICA MUTUAL INSURANCE CO.; *U.S. Private*, pg. 66

AMICALE INDUSTRIES, INC.; *U.S. Private*, pg. 66
AMICI—See N.V. Koninklijke Bijenkorf Beheer KBB; *Int'l*, pg. 750
AMICK CONSTRUCTION LTD.; *U.S. Private*, pg. 66
AMICO-HOUSTON DISTR. CENTER—See Alabama Metal Industries Corporation; *U.S. Private*, pg. 30
AMICON CANADA LTD.—See Millipore Corporation; *U.S. Public*, pg. 1113
AMICON G.M.B.H.—See Millipore Corporation; *U.S. Public*, pg. 1113
AMICON (H.K.) LTD.—See Millipore Corporation; *U.S. Public*, pg. 1113
AMICON, INC.—See Millipore Corporation; *U.S. Public*, pg. 1113
AMICON IRELAND LIMITED—See Millipore Corporation; *U.S. Public*, pg. 1113
AMICON LTD.—See Millipore Corporation; *U.S. Public*, pg. 1113
AMICON POLYMERS (H.K.) LTD.—See Millipore Corporation; *U.S. Public*, pg. 1113
AMIGA COMPUTING/GAMEPRO GREECE—See International Data Group; *U.S. Private*, pg. 569
AMILAND SA—See Castorama Dubois Investissements S.C.A.; *Int'l*, pg. 275
AMINKEMI AB—See Kemira Oy; *Int'l*, pg. 728
AMINS, INC.—See ACMAT Corporation; *U.S. Public*, pg. 16
AMISTAD GATHERING CO.—See Hanson PLC; *Int'l*, pg. 593
AMITE FOUNDRY AND MACHINE, INC.—See Atchison Casting Corporation; *U.S. Public*, pg. 142
AMITY—See AR Accessories Group, Inc.; *U.S. Private*, pg. 7
AMKO SERVICE COMPANY—See Praxair Inc.; *U.S. Public*, pg. 1320
AMKOR ELECTRONICS, INC.; *U.S. Private*, pg. 66
AMLECO LEASING LIMITED—See Empire Company Limited; *Int'l*, pg. 454
AMLI REALTY, INC.—See Baldwin & Lyons, Inc.; *U.S. Public*, pg. 169
AMLINGS FLOWERLAND; *U.S. Private*, pg. 66
AMLINGS LANDSCAPE CO.—See Amlings Flowerland; *U.S. Private*, pg. 66
AMLOID CORPORATION; *U.S. Private*, pg. 66
AMMCO TOOLS, INC.—See Danaher Corporation; *U.S. Public*, pg. 480
AMMERAAL CONVEYOR BELTING B.V.—See Gamma Holding N.V.; *Int'l*, pg. 540
AMMEX TAX & DUTY FREE SHOPS—See BAA plc; *Int'l*, pg. 103
AMMEX TAX & DUTY FREE SHOPS WEST, INC.—See BAA plc; *Int'l*, pg. 103
AMMEX WAREHOUSE COMPANY, INC.—See BAA plc; *Int'l*, pg. 103
AMMIRATI, PURIS & LINTAS, INC.; *U.S. Private*, pg. 66
AMMIRATI PURIS LINTAS WORLDWIDE—See The Interpublic Group of Companies.; *U.S. Public*, pg. 908
AMMIRATI & PURIS LTD./TORONTO—See Ammirati, Puris & Lintas, Inc.; *U.S. Private*, pg. 67
AMNIR-RECYCLING INDUSTRIES LTD—See American Israeli Paper Mills Ltd.; *Int'l*, pg. 75
AMOCO ABU DHABI EXPLORATION CO.—See Amoco Corporation; *U.S. Public*, pg. 103
AMOCO ARGENTINA OIL CO.—See Amoco Corporation; *U.S. Public*, pg. 102
AMOCO AUSTRALIA PETROLEUM COMPANY—See Amoco Corporation; *U.S. Public*, pg. 102
AMOCO CANADA PETROLEUM COMPANY LTD.—See Amoco Corporation; *U.S. Public*, pg. 103
AMOCO CANADA RESOURCES LTD.—See Amoco Corporation; *U.S. Public*, pg. 103
AMOCO CHEMICAL BELGIUM N.V.—See Amoco Corporation; *U.S. Public*, pg. 103
AMOCO CHEMICAL (EUROPE) S.A.—See Amoco Corporation; *U.S. Public*, pg. 103
AMOCO CHEMICAL HOLDING CO.—See Amoco Corporation; *U.S. Public*, pg. 102
AMOCO CHEMICAL (UK) LTD.—See Amoco Corporation; *U.S. Public*, pg. 103
AMOCO CHEMICALS—See Amoco Corporation; *U.S. Public*, pg. 102
AMOCO CHEMICALS FAR EAST, LTD.—See Amoco Corporation; *U.S. Public*, pg. 103
AMOCO CHEMICALS PTY. LTD.—See Amoco Corporation; *U.S. Public*, pg. 102
AMOCO COLOMBIA PETROLEUM COMPANY—See Amoco Corporation; *U.S. Public*, pg. 102
AMOCO COMPANY—See Amoco Corporation; *U.S. Public*, pg. 102
AMOCO CORPORATION; *U.S. Public*, pg. 101
AMOCO CREDIT CORPORATION—See Amoco Corporation; *U.S. Public*, pg. 102
AMOCO DEUTSCHLAND GMBH—See Amoco Corporation; *U.S. Public*, pg. 103
AMOCO DEVELOPMENT COMPANY—See Amoco Corporation; *U.S. Public*, pg. 103
AMOCO EGYPT OIL COMPANY—See Amoco Corporation; *U.S. Public*, pg. 102
AMOCO ESPANA EXPLORATION CO.—See Amoco Corporation; *U.S. Public*, pg. 102
AMOCO FABRICS & FIBERS COMPANY—See Amoco Corporation; *U.S. Public*, pg. 102
AMOCO FABRICS & FIBERS, LTD.—See Amoco Corporation; *U.S. Public*, pg. 102
AMOCO FABRICS (U.K.) LTD.—See Amoco Corporation; *U.S. Public*, pg. 103
AMOCO FINA N.V.—See Amoco Corporation; *U.S. Public*, pg. 102
AMOCO FOAM PRODUCTS CO.—See Amoco Corporation; *U.S. Public*, pg. 102
AMOCO GAS COMPANY—See Royal Dutch/Shell Group of Companies; *Int'l*, pg. 1136
AMOCO JAPAN LTD.—See Amoco Corporation; *U.S. Public*, pg. 102

AMOCO LEASING CORPORATION—See Amoco Corporation; *U.S. Public*, pg. 102
AMOCO MADAGASCAR PETROLEUM COMPANY—See Amoco Corporation; *U.S. Public*, pg. 102
AMOCO NETHERLANDS PETROLEUM CO.—See Amoco Corporation; *U.S. Public*, pg. 102
AMOCO NISSEKI CLAF INC. (ANCI)—See Amoco Corporation; *U.S. Public*, pg. 102
AMOCO NORWAY OIL CO.—See Amoco Corporation; *U.S. Public*, pg. 102
AMOCO OIL COMPANY—See Amoco Corporation; *U.S. Public*, pg. 103
AMOCO OIL REFINERY—See Amoco Corporation; *U.S. Public*, pg. 103
AMOCO OMAN PETROLEUM COMPANY—See Amoco Corporation; *U.S. Public*, pg. 102
AMOCO PERFORMANCE PRODUCTS, INC.—See Amoco Corporation; *U.S. Public*, pg. 102
AMOCO PIPELINE CO.—See Amoco Corporation; *U.S. Public*, pg. 102
AMOCO PRODUCTION COMPANY—See Amoco Corporation; *U.S. Public*, pg. 102
AMOCO PROPERTIES INCORPORATED—See Amoco Corporation; *U.S. Public*, pg. 103
AMOCO RAS AL KHAIMAH OIL CO.—See Amoco Corporation; *U.S. Public*, pg. 102
AMOCO REALTY COMPANY—See Amoco Corporation; *U.S. Public*, pg. 103
AMOCO RESEARCH CENTER—See Amoco Corporation; *U.S. Public*, pg. 103
AMOCO SERVICES, INC.—See Amoco Corporation; *U.S. Public*, pg. 103
AMOCO SHARJAH LPG CO.—See Amoco Corporation; *U.S. Public*, pg. 102
AMOCO SHARJAH OIL CO.—See Amoco Corporation; *U.S. Public*, pg. 102
AMOCO SUPPLY & TRADING COMPANY—See Amoco Corporation; *U.S. Public*, pg. 103
AMOCO TECHNOLOGY COMPANY—See Amoco Corporation; *U.S. Public*, pg. 103
AMOCO TRINIDAD OIL CO.—See Amoco Corporation; *U.S. Public*, pg. 103
AMOCO (U.K.) EXPLORATION COMPANY—See Amoco Corporation; *U.S. Public*, pg. 102
AMOCO (U.K.) LTD.—See Amoco Corporation; *U.S. Public*, pg. 103
AMOK LTD.—See COGEMA - Compagnie Generale des Matieres Nucleaires; *Int'l*, pg. 305
AMOL DICALITE LTD.—See RGP Holding, Inc.; *U.S. Private*, pg. 903
AMORTEX—See Arvin Industries, Inc.; *U.S. Public*, pg. 137
AMOS-HILL ASSOCIATES, INC.; *U.S. Public*, pg. 67
AMOT CONTROLS CORPORATION—See Roper Industries, Inc.; *U.S. Public*, pg. 1405
AMOY—See Danone Group; *Int'l*, pg. 380
AMP INC. LYTEL DIVISION—See AMP Incorporated; *U.S. Public*, pg. 8
AMPAC DEVELOPMENT COMPANY—See American Pacific Corporation; *U.S. Public*, pg. 88
AMPACET CORPORATION; *U.S. Private*, pg. 67
AMPAL (ISRAEL) LTD.—See Bank Hapoalim; *Int'l*, pg. 149
AMPCO AUTO SYSTEM PARKING—See ABM Industries; *U.S. Public*, pg. 2
AMPCO METAL, INC.—See Ampco Metal Incorporated; *U.S. Private*, pg. 67
AMPCO METAL INCORPORATED; *U.S. Private*, pg. 67
AMPCO METAL LTD.—See Ampco Metal Incorporated; *U.S. Private*, pg. 67
AMPCO METAL NEDERLANDS B.V.—See Ampco Metal Incorporated; *U.S. Private*, pg. 67
AMPCO METAL NORDISKA AB—See Ampco Metal Incorporated; *U.S. Private*, pg. 67
AMPCO METAL PORTUGAL LTDA.—See Ampco Metal Incorporated; *U.S. Private*, pg. 67
AMPCO METAL S.A.—See Ampco Metal Incorporated; *U.S. Private*, pg. 67
AMPCO-PITTSBURGH CORPORATION; *U.S. Public*, pg. 103
AMPCO SAFTEY TOOLS, DALLAS DIV.—See Ampco Metal Incorporated; *U.S. Private*, pg. 67
AMPER, S.A.—See Telefonica de Espana, S.A.; *Int'l*, pg. 1372
AMPERIF CORPORATION—See Storage Technology Corporation; *U.S. Public*, pg. 1523
AMPERSAND—See Recoton Corporation; *U.S. Public*, pg. 1369
AMPEX CORPORATION; *U.S. Public*, pg. 104
AMPEX CORPORATION—See Ampex Corporation; *U.S. Public*, pg. 104
AMPEX DATA SYSTEMS—See Ampex Corporation; *U.S. Public*, pg. 104
AMPEX DATA SYSTEMS CORPORATION—See Ampex Corporation; *U.S. Public*, pg. 104
AMPEX EUROPA GMBH—See Ampex Corporation; *U.S. Public*, pg. 104
AMPEX GREAT BRITAIN LIMITED—See Ampex Corporation; *U.S. Public*, pg. 104
AMPEX JAPAN LIMITED—See Ampex Corporation; *U.S. Public*, pg. 104
AMPHABEL S.A.—See Carl-Zeiss-Stiftung; *Int'l*, pg. 1523
AMPHENOL CORPORATION—See Kohlberg Kravis Roberts & Co.; *U.S. Public*, pg. 629
AMPHION HOLDINGS INC.—See Skandia Insurance Company Limited; *Int'l*, pg. 1257
AMPLEFLOW LTD.—See Whitbread PLC; *Int'l*, pg. 1499
AMPLEX/SGNIC—See Saint-Gobain; *Int'l*, pg. 1173
AMPLICON, INC.; *U.S. Public*, pg. 104
AMPRO HANDELSONDERNEMING B.V.—See Schuttersveld Holding N.V.; *Int'l*, pg. 1210
AMPROBE INSTRUMENT—See United Dominion Industries, Ltd.; *U.S. Public*, pg. 1676
AMPROP FINANCE COMPANY—See Amoco Corporation; *U.S. Public*, pg. 103

Company Index

AMQUEST, INC.—See American Software, Inc.; U.S. Public, pg. 91

AMQUIP (PROPRIETARY) LIMITED—See Anglo American Corporation of South Africa Limited; Int'l, pg. 76

AMRAIL—See Jeumont-Schneider Trenformeteurs; Int'l, pg. 706

AMRAM'S DISTRIBUTING, LTD.—See Russ Berrie and Company, Inc.; U.S. Public, pg. 223

AMRAY, INC.; U.S. Private, pg. 67

AMREP CORPORATION; U.S. Public, pg. 104

AMREP FINANCIAL CORPORATION—See AMREP Corporation; U.S. Public, pg. 105

AMREP SOLUTIONS, INC.—See AMREP Corporation; U.S. Public, pg. 104

AMREP SOUTHWEST, INC.—See AMREP Corporation; U.S. Public, pg. 104

AMRESCO, INC.—See Cravey, Green & Wahlen, Incorporated; U.S. Private, pg. 287

AMRION INC.—See Whole Foods Market, Inc.; U.S. Public, pg. 1767

AMRO AUSTRALIA LTD.—See ABN-AMRO Holding N.V.; Int'l, pg. 9

AMRO BANK & FINANCE—See ABN-AMRO Holding N.V.; Int'l, pg. 9

AMRO BANK OVERSEAS N.V.—See ABN-AMRO Holding N.V.; Int'l, pg. 9

AMRO BEHEERS-MAATSCHAPPIJ N.V.—See ABN-AMRO Holding N.V.; Int'l, pg. 9

AMRO EFFECTENBEWAARBEDRIJF N.V.—See ABN-AMRO Holding N.V.; Int'l, pg. 9

AMRO FINANCE AND SECURITIES (ASIA) LTD.—See ABN-AMRO Holding N.V.; Int'l, pg. 10

AMRO HANDELSBANK A.G.—See ABN-AMRO Holding N.V.; Int'l, pg. 10

AMSCO—See Quanex Corporation; U.S. Public, pg. 1350

AMSCO SCHOOL PUBLICATIONS, INC.; U.S. Private, pg. 67

AMSLER OTTO WOLPERT WERKE GMBH—See Instron Corporation; U.S. Public, pg. 883

AMSOUTH BANCORPORATION; U.S. Public, pg. 105

AMSOUTH BANK—See AmSouth Bancorporation; U.S. Public, pg. 105

AMSOUTH BANK N.A.—See AmSouth Bancorporation; U.S. Public, pg. 105

AMSOUTH BANK OF GEORGIA—See AmSouth Bancorporation; U.S. Public, pg. 105

AMSOUTH BANK OF WALKER COUNTY—See AmSouth Bancorporation; U.S. Public, pg. 105

AMSOUTH INVESTMENT SERVICES, INC.—See AmSouth Bancorporation; U.S. Public, pg. 105

AMSOUTH OF TUSCALOOSA—See AmSouth Bancorporation; U.S. Public, pg. 105

AMSPEC CHEMICAL CORPORATION, U.S. Private, pg. 67

AMSTAR INSURANCE COMPANY—See Corporacion MAPFRE, Compania Internacional de Reaseguros, S.A.; Int'l, pg. 333

AMSTAR MANAGEMENT COMPANY—See Corporacion MAPFRE, Compania Internacional de Reaseguros, S.A.; Int'l, pg. 333

AMSTED INDUSTRIES INCORPORATED; U.S. Private, pg. 68

AMSTED INDUSTRIES INTERNATIONAL—See Amsted Industries Incorporated; U.S. Private, pg. 68

AMSTEL BREWERY HUNGARY INC.—See Heineken N.V.; Int'l, pg. 608

AMSTEL LEASE N.V.—See ABN-AMRO Holding N.V.; Int'l, pg. 9

AMSTERDAM DEPOSITARY CO. N.V.—See ABN-AMRO Holding N.V.; Int'l, pg. 9

AMSTERDAM-ROTTERDAM BANK N.V.—See ABN-AMRO Holding N.V.; Int'l, pg. 9

AMSTERDAM-ROTTERDAM BANK N.V. NEW YORK—See ABN-AMRO Holding N.V.; Int'l, pg. 9

AMSTORE CORPORATION; U.S. Private, pg. 68

AMTEC CO., LTD.—See Amada Co., Ltd.; Int'l, pg. 70

AMTECH—See Esterline Technologies Corporation; U.S. Public, pg. 594

AMTECH CORPORATION; U.S. Public, pg. 105

AMTECH DIVISION—See Inco Limited; Int'l, pg. 672

AMTECH ELEVATOR SERVICES—See ABM Industries; U.S. Public, pg. 2

AMTECH EUROPE LIMITED—See Amtech Corporation; U.S. Public, pg. 106

AMTECH INTERNATIONAL—See Amtech Corporation; U.S. Public, pg. 106

AMTECH LIGHTING SERVICES CO.—See ABM Industries; U.S. Public, pg. 2

AMTECH SYSTEMS CORPORATION—See Amtech Corporation; U.S. Public, pg. 105

AMTRADE INTERNATIONAL BANK; U.S. Private, pg. 68

AMTRAK-NATIONAL RAILROAD PASSENGER CORP.; U.S. Private, pg. 68

AMTRAN CORPORATION—See Navistar International Corporation; U.S. Public, pg. 1167

AMTRAN, INC.; U.S. Public, pg. 106

AMTROL INC.—See The Cypress Group LLC; U.S. Private, pg. 300

AMURCON CORPORATION; U.S. Private, pg. 69

AMURCON EQUITIES—See Amurcon Corporation; U.S. Private, pg. 69

AMUROL CONFECTIONS CO.—See Wm. Wrigley Jr. Company; U.S. Public, pg. 1781

AMUSEMENT BUSINESS—See VNU Verenigde Nederlandse Uitgeversbedrijven B.V.; Int'l, pg. 1446

AMVAC CHEMICAL CORPORATION—See American Vanguard Corporation; U.S. Public, pg. 94

AMVESTORS ACQUISITION SUBSIDIARY, INC.—See American Mutual Life Holding Co.; U.S. Private, pg. 59

AMVESTORS FINANCIAL CORPORATION—See American Mutual Life Holding Co.; U.S. Private, pg. 59

AMVESTORS INVESTMENT GROUP, INC.—See American Mutual Life Holding Co.; U.S. Private, pg. 59

AMWAY ARGENTINA, INC.—See Amway Corporation; U.S. Private, pg. 69

AMWAY ASIA PACIFIC LTD-HONG KONG BRANCH—See Amway Corporation; U.S. Private, pg. 69

AMWAY BELGIUM CO.—See Amway Corporation; U.S. Private, pg. 69

AMWAY CHILE—See Amway Corporation; U.S. Private, pg. 69

AMWAY CHINA—See Amway Corporation; U.S. Private, pg. 69

AMWAY COLOMBIA—See Amway Corporation; U.S. Private, pg. 69

AMWAY CORPORATION; U.S. Private, pg. 69

AMWAY COSTA RICA—See Amway Corporation; U.S. Private, pg. 69

AMWAY CZECH REPUBLIC—See Amway Corporation; U.S. Private, pg. 69

AMWAY DE ESPAÑA, S.A.—See Amway Corporation; U.S. Private, pg. 69

AMWAY DE GUATEMALA, S.A.—See Amway Corporation; U.S. Private, pg. 69

AMWAY DE MEXICO, S.A. DE C.V.—See Amway Corporation; U.S. Private, pg. 69

AMWAY DE PANAMA S.A.—See Amway Corporation; U.S. Private, pg. 69

AMWAY DE PORTUGAL, INC.—See Amway Corporation; U.S. Private, pg. 69

AMWAY DO BRASIL LTDA.—See Amway Corporation; U.S. Private, pg. 69

AMWAY (EUROPE) LTD.—See Amway Corporation; U.S. Private, pg. 69

AMWAY FRANCE—See Amway Corporation; U.S. Private, pg. 69

AMWAY GESELLSCHAFT M.B.H.—See Amway Corporation; U.S. Private, pg. 70

AMWAY GMBH—See Amway Corporation; U.S. Private, pg. 70

AMWAY HELLAS—See Amway Corporation; U.S. Private, pg. 70

AMWAY HOTEL CORPORATION—See Amway Corporation; U.S. Private, pg. 69

AMWAY HUNGARIA MARKETING KFT.—See Amway Corporation; U.S. Private, pg. 70

AMWAY INDONESIA—See Amway Corporation; U.S. Private, pg. 70

AMWAY ITALIA S.R.L.—See Amway Corporation; U.S. Private, pg. 70

AMWAY (JAPAN) LIMITED—See Amway Corporation; U.S. Private, pg. 70

AMWAY KOREA, LTD.—See Amway Corporation; U.S. Private, pg. 70

AMWAY (MALAYSIA) SDN. BHD.—See Amway Corporation; U.S. Private, pg. 70

AMWAY NEDERLAND LTD.—See Amway Corporation; U.S. Private, pg. 70

AMWAY OF AUSTRALIA PTY. LTD.—See Amway Corporation; U.S. Private, pg. 70

AMWAY OF CANADA, LTD.—See Amway Corporation; U.S. Private, pg. 70

AMWAY OF NEW ZEALAND LIMITED—See Amway Corporation; U.S. Private, pg. 70

AMWAY PHILIPPINES—See Amway Corporation; U.S. Private, pg. 70

AMWAY POLAND—See Amway Corporation; U.S. Private, pg. 70

AMWAY (SCHWEIZ) AG—See Amway Corporation; U.S. Private, pg. 70

AMWAY SLOVENIA—See Amway Corporation; U.S. Private, pg. 70

AMWAY SLOVENSKO, S.R.O.—See Amway Corporation; U.S. Private, pg. 70

AMWAY SOUTH AFRICA—See Amway Corporation; U.S. Private, pg. 70

AMWAY TAIWAN, LTD.—See Amway Corporation; U.S. Private, pg. 70

AMWAY (THAILAND) LIMITED—See Amway Corporation; U.S. Private, pg. 70

AMWAY TURKIYE LTD.—See Amway Corporation; U.S. Private, pg. 70

AMWAY (U.K.) LIMITED—See Amway Corporation; U.S. Private, pg. 70

AMWAY URUGUAY—See Amway Corporation; U.S. Private, pg. 70

AMWEST INSURANCE GROUP, INC.; U.S. Public, pg. 106

AMWEST SURETY INSURANCE COMPANY—See Amwest Insurance Group, Inc.; U.S. Public, pg. 106

AMYCEL, INC.—See Monterey Mushrooms, Inc.; U.S. Private, pg. 758

AMYLUM N.V.—See Tate & Lyle PLC; Int'l, pg. 1357

ANA KALTO AB—See Bergman & Beving AB; Int'l, pg. 188

ANA TRADING & TAKASHIMAYA UK LTD.—See Takashimaya Company, Limited; Int'l, pg. 1350

ANACOMP (CANADA) LTD.—See Anacomp, Inc.; U.S. Public, pg. 107

ANACOMP DO BRASIL LTDA.—See Anacomp, Inc.; U.S. Public, pg. 107

ANACOMP, GMBH—See Anacomp, Inc.; U.S. Public, pg. 107

ANACOMP, INC.; U.S. Public, pg. 106

ANACOMP ITALIA—See Anacomp, Inc.; U.S. Public, pg. 107

ANACOMP (JAPAN) LTD.—See Anacomp, Inc.; U.S. Public, pg. 107

ANACOMP, LTD.—See Anacomp, Inc.; U.S. Public, pg. 107

ANACOMP MAGNETICS, INC.—See Anacomp, Inc.; U.S. Public, pg. 107

ANACOMP MAGNETICS WALES LTD.—See Anacomp, Inc.; U.S. Public, pg. 107

ANACOMP (NEDERLAND) B.V.—See Anacomp, Inc.; U.S. Public, pg. 107

ANACOMP, S.A. (BELGIUM)—See Anacomp, Inc.; U.S. Public, pg. 107

ANACOMP S.A. (FRANCE)—See Anacomp, Inc.; U.S. Public, pg. 107

ANADARKO ALGERIA CORPORATION—See Anadarko Petroleum Corporation; U.S. Public, pg. 107

ANADARKO MARKETING COMPANY—See Anadarko Petroleum Corporation; U.S. Public, pg. 107

ANADARKO OIL & GAS COMPANY—See Anadarko Petroleum Corporation; U.S. Public, pg. 107

ANADARKO PETROLEUM CORPORATION; U.S. Public, pg. 107

ANADARKO TRADING COMPANY—See Anadarko Petroleum Corporation; U.S. Public, pg. 107

ANADERM RESEARCH CORP.—See Pfizer Inc.; U.S. Public, pg. 1281

ANADOLU OTOMOTIV SANAYII VE TICARET A.S.—See Isuzu Motors Limited; Int'l, pg. 692

ANADOLU TASFIYEHANESI—See Royal Dutch/Shell Group of Companies; Int'l, pg. 1141

ANADRILL HOLDINGS LIMITED—See Schlumberger Limited; U.S. Public, pg. 1439

ANADVENTURE II CORPORATION—See Analogic Corporation; U.S. Public, pg. 109

ANAHEIM EXTRUSION CO.—See Universal Molding Company; U.S. Private, pg. 1127

ANAHEIM MANUFACTURING COMPANY; U.S. Private, pg. 70

ANALOG DEVICES—See Analog Devices, Inc.; U.S. Public, pg. 108

ANALOG DEVICES AB—See Analog Devices, Inc.; U.S. Public, pg. 108

ANALOG DEVICES APS—See Analog Devices, Inc.; U.S. Public, pg. 108

ANALOG DEVICES BV—See Analog Devices, Inc.; U.S. Public, pg. 108

ANALOG DEVICES GMBH—See Analog Devices, Inc.; U.S. Public, pg. 108

ANALOG DEVICES GMBH - TECHNISCHES BUERO BERLIN—See Analog Devices, Inc.; U.S. Public, pg. 108

ANALOG DEVICES GMBH - TECHNISCHES BUERO NORD—See Analog Devices, Inc.; U.S. Public, pg. 108

ANALOG DEVICES GMBH - TECHNISCHES BUERO SUEDWEST—See Analog Devices, Inc.; U.S. Public, pg. 108

ANALOG DEVICES GMBH - TECHNISCHES BUERO WEST—See Analog Devices, Inc.; U.S. Public, pg. 108

ANALOG DEVICES HDLSGESMBH—See Analog Devices, Inc.; U.S. Public, pg. 108

ANALOG DEVICES, INC.; U.S. Public, pg. 107

ANALOG DEVICES INTERNATIONAL INC.—See Analog Devices, Inc.; U.S. Public, pg. 108

ANALOG DEVICES K.K.—See Analog Devices, Inc.; U.S. Public, pg. 108

ANALOG DEVICES K.K. TECH CENTER—See Analog Devices, Inc.; U.S. Public, pg. 108

ANALOG DEVICES KOREA—See Analog Devices, Inc.; U.S. Public, pg. 108

ANALOG DEVICES LTD. - EASTERN SALES OFFICE—See Analog Devices, Inc.; U.S. Public, pg. 108

ANALOG DEVICES MARKETING LTD.—See Analog Devices, Inc.; U.S. Public, pg. 108

ANALOG DEVICES NEDERLAND B.V.—See Analog Devices, Inc.; U.S. Public, pg. 108

ANALOG DEVICES (PHILS), INC.—See Analog Devices, Inc.; U.S. Public, pg. 108

ANALOG DEVICES S.A.—See Analog Devices, Inc.; U.S. Public, pg. 108

ANALOG DEVICES, SANTA CLARA—See Analog Devices, Inc.; U.S. Public, pg. 108

ANALOG DEVICES SEMICONDUCTOR—See Analog Devices, Inc.; U.S. Public, pg. 108

ANALOG DEVICES SRL—See Analog Devices, Inc.; U.S. Public, pg. 108

ANALOG DIVISION—See Cadence Design Systems, Inc.; U.S. Public, pg. 290

ANALOGIC CORPORATION; U.S. Public, pg. 109

ANALOGIC FOREIGN SALES CORP.—See Analogic Corporation; U.S. Public, pg. 109

ANALOGIC LTD.—See Analogic Corporation; U.S. Public, pg. 109

ANALOGIC SCIENTIFIC—See Analogic Corporation; U.S. Public, pg. 109

ANALYSIS & APPLIED RESEARCH DIV.—See Tracor, Inc.; U.S. Public, pg. 1627

ANALYSIS & TECHNOLOGY AUSTRALIA PTY LIMITED—See Analysis & Technology, Inc.; U.S. Public, pg. 110

ANALYSIS & TECHNOLOGY, INC.; U.S. Public, pg. 109

ANALYSTS INTERNATIONAL, CENTRAL REGION—See Analysts International Corporation; U.S. Public, pg. 110

ANALYSTS INTERNATIONAL CORPORATION; U.S. Public, pg. 110

ANALYSTS INTERNATIONAL, EASTERN REGION—See Analysts International Corporation; U.S. Public, pg. 110

ANALYSTS INTERNATIONAL, MIDWEST REGION—See Analysts International Corporation; U.S. Public, pg. 110

ANALYSTS INTERNATIONAL, SOUTHERN REGION—See Analysts International Corporation; U.S. Public, pg. 110

ANALYSTS INTERNATIONAL, WESTERN REGION—See Analysts International Corporation; U.S. Public, pg. 110

ANALYTIC TSA GLOBAL ASSET MANAGEMENT INC.—See United Asset Management Corporation; U.S. Public, pg. 1672

ANALYTICAL DEVELOPMENT COMPANY LIMITED—See Halma p.l.c.; Int'l, pg. 589

ANALYTICAL SERVICES CORPORATION—See OHM Corporation; U.S. Public, pg. 1207

ANALYTICAL SURVEYS, INC.; U.S. Public, pg. 110

ANALYTICAL SURVEYS, INC. - NORTHEAST DIVISION—See Analytical Surveys, Inc.; U.S. Public, pg. 110

ANALYTICAL TECHNOLOGIES, INC.—See Bacardi Limited; Int'l, pg. 131

ANALYTICAL TECHNOLOGY & RESEARCH CORPORATION—See Hewlett-Packard Company; U.S. Public, pg. 816

ANALYTISCH BIOCHEMISCH LABORATORIUM B.V.—See Nutricia BV; Int'l, pg. 991

ANAMBRA MOTOR MFG. CO. LTD.—See Daimler-Benz Aktiengesellschaft; Int'l, pg. 368

ANAMET CANADA INC—See Anamet Inc.; U.S. Private, pg. 70
ANAMET EUROPE BV-AMSTERDAM—See Anamet Inc.; U.S. Private, pg. 70
ANAMET INC.; U.S. Private, pg. 70
ANAMINT—See Anglo American Corporation of South Africa Limited; Int'l, pg. 76
ANARAD—See Tech-Sym Corporation; U.S. Public, pg. 1563
ANAREN MICROWAVE INC.; U.S. Public, pg. 110
ANAREN MICROWAVE, LTD.—See Anaren Microwave Inc.; U.S. Public, pg. 111
ANASAZI INC.—See Reed Elsevier plc; Int'l, pg. 1098
ANASAZI TRAVEL RESOURCES INC.—See Reed Elsevier plc; Int'l, pg. 1098
ANC.ETS.CYR.CAMBIER N.V.—See Gamma Holding N.V.; Int'l, pg. 540
THE ANCHOR BANK—See Anchor Financial Corporation; U.S. Public, pg. 111
ANCHOR CHEMICAL GROUP PLC—See Air Products and Chemicals, Inc.; U.S. Public, pg. 32
ANCHOR CONTINENTAL INCORPORATED; U.S. Private, pg. 70
ANCHOR COUPLING INC.—See Caterpillar Inc.; U.S. Public, pg. 315
ANCHOR DIE CAST—See MMI Products, Inc.; U.S. Private, pg. 687
ANCHOR FASTENERS—See Illinois Tool Works Inc.; U.S. Public, pg. 865
ANCHOR FINANCIAL CORPORATION; U.S. Public, pg. 111
ANCHOR FOODS LIMITED—See New Zealand Dairy Board; Int'l, pg. 923
ANCHOR GASOLINE CORPORATION; U.S. Private, pg. 70
ANCHOR GLASS CONTAINER CORPORATION—See Consumers Packaging Inc.; Int'l, pg. 327
ANCHOR HOCKING—See Newell Co.; U.S. Public, pg. 1177
ANCHOR HOCKING CANADA DIV.—See Newell Co.; U.S. Public, pg. 1178
ANCHOR HOCKING CORPORATION—See Newell Co.; U.S. Public, pg. 1177
ANCHOR HOCKING PLASTICS—See Newell Co.; U.S. Public, pg. 1177
ANCHOR INC.—See International Paper Company; U.S. Public, pg. 903
ANCHOR INDUSTRIES INC.; U.S. Private, pg. 71
ANCHOR LAMINA INC.; Int'l, pg. 75
ANCHOR METAL PROCESSING—See Anchor Tool & Die Company; U.S. Private, pg. 71
ANCHOR NATIONAL LIFE INSURANCE CO.—See SunAmerica Inc.; U.S. Public, pg. 1533
ANCHOR OPTICAL CO., INC.—See Edmund Scientific Company; U.S. Private, pg. 364
ANCHOR STAMPINGS—See Illinois Tool Works Inc.; U.S. Public, pg. 865
ANCHOR TOOL & DIE COMPANY; U.S. Private, pg. 71
ANCHOR WIRE CORPORATION OF TENNESSEE—See Textron Inc.; U.S. Public, pg. 1590
ANCHOR WIRE ROPE DIVISION—See Okura & Co.; Int'l, pg. 1001
ANCHORAGE COLD STORAGE CO.—See The Odom Corporation; U.S. Private, pg. 812
ANCIENS ESTABLISSEMENTS GOYOT ET CIE—See Standex International Corporation; U.S. Public, pg. 1507
ANCIRA ENTERPRISES INC.; U.S. Private, pg. 71
ANCO HERLEV—See UPM-Kymmene Corporation; Int'l, pg. 1429
ANCO INSULATIONS, INC.; U.S. Private, pg. 71
ANCO INTERNATIONAL—See Philip Morris Companies Inc.; U.S. Public, pg. 1287
ANCO N.V.—See CSM N.V.; Int'l, pg. 244
ANCO PRODUCTS—See Cooper Industries, Inc.; U.S. Public, pg. 442
ANCO TRAE A/S—See UPM-Kymmene Corporation; Int'l, pg. 1429
ANCO TRANSPORTATION SERVICE, INC.—See Stage Stores, Inc.; U.S. Private, pg. 1029
ANCON INSURANCE COMPANY, INC.—See Exxon Corporation; U.S. Public, pg. 601
ANCRA ABT AB—See Ancra International LLC; U.S. Private, pg. 71
ANCRA AUSTRALIA PTY. LTD.—See Ancra International LLC; U.S. Private, pg. 71
ANCRA CANADA—See Ancra International LLC; U.S. Private, pg. 71
ANCRA CHS—See Ancra International LLC; U.S. Private, pg. 71
ANCRA CINCINATTI—See Ancra International LLC; U.S. Private, pg. 71
ANCRA ESPANA—See Ancra International LLC; U.S. Private, pg. 71
ANCRA INTERNATIONAL LLC; U.S. Private, pg. 71
ANCRA INTERNATIONAL SARL—See Ancra International LLC; U.S. Private, pg. 71
ANCRA JAPAN—See Ancra International LLC; U.S. Private, pg. 71
ANCRA JUNGFALK GMBH—See Ancra International LLC; U.S. Private, pg. 71
ANCRA NEW ZEALAND—See Ancra International LLC; U.S. Private, pg. 71
ANDA PRODUCTS LIMITED—See Smiths Industries plc; Int'l, pg. 1267
ANDAL CORP.; U.S. Public, pg. 111
ANDALUSIA & CONECUH RAILROAD, INC.—See Alabama Electric Cooperative, Inc.; U.S. Private, pg. 30
THE ANDEAN FUND, INC.—See The Chase Manhattan Corporation; U.S. Public, pg. 338
ANDELSSMAR A.M.B.A.—See MD Foods; Int'l, pg. 826
ANDENES HELIKOPTERBASE A.S.—See Statoil; Int'l, pg. 1298
STE. ANDERNOISIENNE DE DISTRIBUTION—See Groupe Casino; Int'l, pg. 563

ANDERSEN CONSULTING—See Andersen Worldwide; U.S. Private, pg. 72
ANDERSEN CORPORATION; U.S. Private, pg. 71
ANDERSEN GROUP, INC.; U.S. Public, pg. 111
ANDERSEN 2000 INC.—See Crown Andersen Inc.; U.S. Public, pg. 462
ANDERSEN WINDOWS, INC.—See Andersen Corporation; U.S. Private, pg. 71
ANDERSEN WORLDWIDE; U.S. Private, pg. 72
ANDERSON & LEMBKE INC.; U.S. Private, pg. 72
AB ARV ANDERSON—See Trelleborg AB; Int'l, pg. 1422
ANDERSON BAKERY CO., INC.—See Amerifoods Inc.; U.S. Private, pg. 65
ANDERSON-BARROWS METALS CORP.—See Watts Industries, Inc.; U.S. Public, pg. 1746
ANDERSON BROTHERS CONSTRUCTION BRAINERD; U.S. Private, pg. 72
ANDERSON, CLAYTON & CO. S.A.—See Unilever Plc; Int'l, pg. 1436
ANDERSON, CLAYTON S.A.—See Unilever Plc; Int'l, pg. 1436
D. ANDERSON & SON LTD.—See Icopal a/s; Int'l, pg. 659
ANDERSON ELECTRIC, INC.; U.S. Private, pg. 72
ANDERSON ELECTRICAL SALES—See Klockner-Moeller GmbH; Int'l, pg. 736
ANDERSON ERICKSON DAIRY COMPANY; U.S. Private, pg. 72
GAVIN ANDERSON & COMPANY—See Omnicom Group Inc.; U.S. Public, pg. 1223
ANDERSON, GREENWOOD & CO.—See Tyco International Ltd.; U.S. Public, pg. 1650
ANDERSON HARDWOOD FLOORS—See Standard Plywoods, Inc.; U.S. Private, pg. 1032
ANDERSON HICKEY, INC.—See Haworth, Inc.; U.S. Private, pg. 512
ANDERSON HILL INSURANCE LIMITED—See PepsiCo, Inc.; U.S. Public, pg. 1277
ANDERSON INDUSTRIES, INC.—See Excel Industries, Inc.; U.S. Public, pg. 599
ANDERSON LITHOGRAPH COMPANY; U.S. Private, pg. 72
ANDERSON LUMBER COMPANY; U.S. Private, pg. 72
THE ANDERSON NEWS—See Landmark Communications, Inc.; U.S. Private, pg. 648
ANDERSON PARK, INC.—See Churchill Downs, Inc.; U.S. Public, pg. 356
ANDERSON POWER PRODUCTS DIV.—See High Voltage Engineering Corporation; U.S. Private, pg. 528
ROY ANDERSON CORP.; U.S. Private, pg. 72
ANDERSON SOLID WASTE, INC.—See Republic Industries, Inc.; U.S. Public, pg. 1379
ANDERSON TRUCKING SERVICE INC.; U.S. Private, pg. 72
ANDERSON-TULLY CO.; U.S. Private, pg. 73
W.E. ANDERSON DIV.—See Dwyer Instruments Inc.; U.S. Private, pg. 350
ANDERSON WHOLESALE COMPANY; U.S. Private, pg. 73
THE ANDERSONS INCORPORATED; U.S. Public, pg. 111
THE ANDERSONS INVESTMENT SERVICES CORP.—See The Andersons Incorporated; U.S. Public, pg. 111
STUART ANDERSON'S BLACK ANGUS/CATTLE COMPANY RESTAURANTS—See American Restaurant Group, Inc.; U.S. Private, pg. 61
THE ANDERSONS WHITE PIGEON TERMINAL—See The Andersons Incorporated; U.S. Public, pg. 111
J.W. ANDERSSON MASKIN AB—See Trelleborg AB; Int'l, pg. 1422
ANDES CANDIES INC.—See Brach & Brock Confections, Inc.; U.S. Private, pg. 163
ANDIAMO, INC.; U.S. Private, pg. 73
ANDIN INTERNATIONAL INC.; U.S. Private, pg. 73
ANDINA DIVISION—See CODELCO Chile (Corporacion Nacional Del Cobre De Chile); Int'l, pg. 302
ANDIS COMPANY; U.S. Private, pg. 73
ANDOVER BANCORP, INC.; U.S. Public, pg. 111
ANDOVER BANK—See Andover Bancorp, Inc.; U.S. Public, pg. 112
ANDOVER BANK NH—See Andover Bancorp, Inc.; U.S. Public, pg. 112
ANDOVER CONTROLS; U.S. Private, pg. 73
ANDOVER CONTROLS CORP.—See BICC plc; Int'l, pg. 120
ANDOVER CONTROLS INTERNATIONAL INC.—See Andover Controls; U.S. Private, pg. 73
ANDOVER CONTROLS SECURITIES—See Andover Controls; U.S. Private, pg. 73
ANDOVER TOGS, INC.; U.S. Public, pg. 112
ANDRAE LEONBERG GMBH—See ABB Asea Brown Boveri (Holding) Ltd.; Int'l, pg. 7
ANDREA ELECTRONICS CORPORATION; U.S. Public, pg. 112
ANDREA INTERNATIONAL—See American International Industries; U.S. Private, pg. 57
ANDREAS GALLERIES, INC.—See Lantzsch-Andreas Enterprises, Inc.; U.S. Private, pg. 650
ANDREN & WERNE LEO BURNETT AB—See Leo Burnett Company, Inc.; U.S. Private, pg. 184
ANDRES WINES (ALBERTA) LTD.—See Andres Wines Ltd.; Int'l, pg. 76
ANDRES WINES (ATLANTIC) LTD.—See Andres Wines Ltd.; Int'l, pg. 76
ANDRES WINES (B.C.) LTD.—See Andres Wines Ltd.; Int'l, pg. 76
ANDRES WINES LTD.; Int'l, pg. 75
DR. ANDREU S.A.—See Roche Holding Ltd.; Int'l, pg. 1120
ANDREW AG—See Andrew Corporation; U.S. Public, pg. 113
ANDREW ANTENNA CO. LTD.—See Andrew Corporation; U.S. Public, pg. 113
ANDREW ANTENNAS—See Andrew Corporation; U.S. Public, pg. 113
ANDREW CORPORATION; U.S. Public, pg. 112
ANDREW CORPORATION (MEXICO) S.A. DE C.V.—See Andrew Corporation; U.S. Public, pg. 113

ANDREW HOUSE HEALTHCARE—See Vencor, Inc.; U.S. Public, pg. 1711
ANDREW INTERNATIONAL CORP.—See Andrew Corporation; U.S. Public, pg. 112
ANDREW SPORTS CLUB INC.; U.S. Private, pg. 73
ANDREW S.R.L.—See Andrew Corporation; U.S. Public, pg. 113
ANDREWS & CLARK—See Thermo Electron Corporation; U.S. Public, pg. 1593
DAYTON ANDREWS INC.; U.S. Private, pg. 74
ANDREWS GROUP, INCORPORATED—See MacAndrews & Forbes Holdings Inc.; U.S. Private, pg. 689
W.E. ANDREWS CO., INC.—See Wallace Computer Services, Inc.; U.S. Public, pg. 1735
W.E. ANDREWS CO., INC., OF CONNECTICUT—See Wallace Computer Services, Inc.; U.S. Public, pg. 1735
ANDREX RADIATION PRODUCTS A/S—See Illinois Tool Works Inc.; U.S. Public, pg. 867
ANDROCK PRODUCTS/NEWELL BULLDOG—See Newell Co.; U.S. Public, pg. 1178
ANDROS INCORPORATED; U.S. Private, pg. 74
ANDROS INCORPORATED INTERNATIONAL—See Andros Incorporated; U.S. Private, pg. 74
ANDROS SERVICE INC.—See Andros Incorporated; U.S. Private, pg. 74
ANDROSCOGGIN SAVINGS BANK; U.S. Private, pg. 74
ANDY'S RESTAURANTS INC.; U.S. Private, pg. 74
ANEDCO, INC.—See The Lubrizol Corporation; U.S. Public, pg. 1016
ANEMOSTAT PRODUCTS—See CTS Corporation; U.S. Public, pg. 286
ANEMOSTAT-WEST—See CTS Corporation; U.S. Public, pg. 286
ANES SECURITY, INC.—See Code-Alarm, Inc.; U.S. Public, pg. 394
ANESCO; U.S. Private, pg. 74
ANGAR SCIENTIFIC CO., INC.—See Emerson Electric Co.; U.S. Public, pg. 574
ANGEL STATION, INC.—See Catalina Lighting, Inc.; U.S. Public, pg. 314
ANGELES FUNDING CORPORATION—See Angeles Housing Concepts; U.S. Private, pg. 74
ANGELES HOUSING CONCEPTS; U.S. Private, pg. 74
ANGELICA CORPORATION; U.S. Public, pg. 113
ANGELICA IMAGE APPAREL—See Angelica Corporation; U.S. Public, pg. 113
ANGELICA INTERNATIONAL, LTD.—See Angelica Corporation; U.S. Public, pg. 113
ANGELICA TEXTILE SERVICES, INC.—See Angelica Corporation; U.S. Public, pg. 113
ANGELO BROTHERS CO.; U.S. Private, pg. 74
ANGENIEUX—See Thomson S.A.; Int'l, pg. 1381
ANGIODYNAMICS—See E-Z-Em, Inc.; U.S. Public, pg. 540
ANGIOGRAPHIC DEVICES—See Thermo Electron Corporation; U.S. Public, pg. 1596
ANGLERS ROSLYN GROUP LTD.; U.S. Private, pg. 74
ANGLESEY ALUMINIUM LIMITED—See Maxxam Inc.; U.S. Public, pg. 1063
ANGLESEY ALUMINIUM LIMITED—See Rio Tinto PLC; Int'l, pg. 1119
ANGLESEY ALUMINIUM LTD. (ANGLESEY)—See Maxxam Inc.; U.S. Public, pg. 1062
ANGLICKA BUSINESS CENTER—See Assicurazioni Generali S.p.A.; Int'l, pg. 90
ANGLO-ALPHA LTD.—See Holderbank Financiere Glaris Ltd.; Int'l, pg. 629
ANGLO AMERICAN CORPORATION OF SOUTH AFRICA LIMITED; Int'l, pg. 76
ANGLO AMERICAN CORPORATION OF SOUTH AFRICA LIMITED (LONDON)—See Anglo American Corporation of South Africa Limited; Int'l, pg. 77
ANGLO-AUSTRIAN MAGNESITE, LTD.—See RGP Holding, Inc.; U.S. Private, pg. 88
ANGLO BLACKWELLS LTD.—See Viag AG; Int'l, pg. 1465
ANGLO/CDT—See Cable Design Technologies Corporation; U.S. Public, pg. 287
ANGLO DUTCH DREDGING CO. LTD.—See Ballast Nedam NV; Int'l, pg. 134
ANGLO-ELEMENTAR VERSICHERUNGS-AG—See Allianz Aktiengesellschaft; Int'l, pg. 60
ANGLO ESPANOLA DE DISTRIBUCION, AED SA—See Diageo Plc; Int'l, pg. 409
ANGLO FABRICS COMPANY, INC.; U.S. Private, pg. 74
ANGLO MEXICANA DE SEGUROS S.A.—See Assicurazioni Generali S.p.A.; Int'l, pg. 90
ANGLO-SWISS ALUMINIUM COMPANY LTD.—See Alusuisse-Lonza Holding Ltd.; Int'l, pg. 68
ANGSTROHM PRECISION, INC.—See Vishay Intertechnology, Inc.; U.S. Public, pg. 1722
ANGUS BELGIUM SA—See Williams Holdings Plc; Int'l, pg. 1500
ANGUS CHEMICAL COMPANY; U.S. Private, pg. 75
ANGUS CHEMICAL (SINGAPORE) PTE. LTD.—See ANGUS Chemical Company; U.S. Private, pg. 75
ANGUS CHEMIE GMBH—See ANGUS Chemical Company; U.S. Private, pg. 75
ANGUS FIRE ARMOUR (AUSTRALIA) PTY LTD.—See Williams Holdings Plc; Int'l, pg. 1500
ANGUS FIRE ARMOUR CORP.—See Williams Holdings Plc; Int'l, pg. 1500
ANGUS FIRE ARMOUR LIMITED—See Williams Holdings Plc; Int'l, pg. 1500
ANGUS FIRE ARMOUR (S.A.) LIMITED—See Williams Holdings Plc; Int'l, pg. 1500
ANGUS FIRE LIMITED—See Williams Holdings Plc; Int'l, pg. 1500
GEORGE ANGUS & CO.—See Freudenberg & Company; Int'l, pg. 507
ANGUS KOREA—See ANGUS Chemical Company; U.S. Private, pg. 75
ANHEUSER-BUSCH ASIA, INC.—See Anheuser-Busch Companies, Inc.; U.S. Public, pg. 115
ANHEUSER-BUSCH COMPANIES, INC.; U.S. Public, pg. 113

Company Index

ANHEUSER-BUSCH

DIRECTORY OF CORPORATE AFFILIATIONS

ANHEUSER-BUSCH EUROPE, INC.—See Anheuser-Busch Companies, Inc.; *U.S. Public*, pg. 115
ANHEUSER-BUSCH EUROPEAN TRADE LTD.—See Anheuser-Busch Companies, Inc.; *U.S. Public*, pg. 115
ANHEUSER-BUSCH, INC.—See Anheuser-Busch Companies, Inc.; *U.S. Public*, pg. 114
ANHEUSER-BUSCH INTERNATIONAL, INC.—See Anheuser-Busch Companies, Inc.; *U.S. Public*, pg. 114
ANHEUSER-BUSCH INVESTMENT CAPITAL CORPORATION—See Anheuser-Busch Companies, Inc.; *U.S. Public*, pg. 114
ANHEUSER-BUSCH RECYCLING CORPORATION—See Anheuser-Busch Companies, Inc.; *U.S. Public*, pg. 114
ANICOM—See Anicom, Inc.; *U.S. Public*, pg. 115
ANICOM, INC.; *U.S. Public*, pg. 115
ANICOM—See Anicom, Inc.; *U.S. Public*, pg. 115
ANIKEM (PROPRIETARY) LTD.—See Nalco Chemical Company; *U.S. Public*, pg. 1150
ANIMAL FAIR—See Princess Soft Toys; *U.S. Private*, pg. 885
ANIMAL HEALTH—See Alpharma Inc.; *U.S. Public*, pg. 58
ANIMAL NUTRITION DIV.—See Continental Grain Company; *U.S. Private*, pg. 268
ANIMAL PLANET—See Discovery Communications, Inc.; *U.S. Private*, pg. 334
ANISERCO S.A.—See Etablissements Delhaize Freres Et Cie "Le Lion" S.A.; *Int'l*, pg. 463
ANITEC IMAGE INTERNATIONAL B.V.—See International Paper Company; *U.S. Public*, pg. 904
ANIXTER ABERDEEN—See Anixter International; *U.S. Public*, pg. 116
ANIXTER ANTWERP—See Anixter International; *U.S. Public*, pg. 116
ANIXTER BRISTOL—See Anixter International; *U.S. Public*, pg. 116
ANIXTER CABLE TV—See Anixter International; *U.S. Public*, pg. 115
ANIXTER CALGARY—See Anixter International; *U.S. Public*, pg. 115
ANIXTER CANADA—See Anixter International; *U.S. Public*, pg. 115
ANIXTER DARLINGTON—See Anixter International; *U.S. Public*, pg. 115
ANIXTER EDMONTON—See Anixter International; *U.S. Public*, pg. 115
ANIXTER GLASGOW U.K.—See Anixter International; *U.S. Public*, pg. 116
ANIXTER HALIFAX—See Anixter International; *U.S. Public*, pg. 115
ANIXTER HARLOW—See Anixter International; *U.S. Public*, pg. 115
ANIXTER HESTON—See Anixter International; *U.S. Public*, pg. 116
ANIXTER INC.—See Anixter International; *U.S. Public*, pg. 115
ANIXTER INTERNATIONAL; *U.S. Public*, pg. 115
ANIXTER LEEDS—See Anixter International; *U.S. Public*, pg. 115
ANIXTER LONDON—See Anixter International; *U.S. Public*, pg. 115
ANIXTER LONDON HAYES—See Anixter International; *U.S. Public*, pg. 115
ANIXTER MONTREAL—See Anixter International; *U.S. Public*, pg. 115
ANIXTER OTTAWA—See Anixter International; *U.S. Public*, pg. 115
ANIXTER QUEBEC CITY—See Anixter International; *U.S. Public*, pg. 116
ANIXTER ROUYN—See Anixter International; *U.S. Public*, pg. 116
ANIXTER ST. JOHNS—See Anixter International; *U.S. Public*, pg. 116
ANIXTER SASKATOON—See Anixter International; *U.S. Public*, pg. 116
ANIXTER SUDBURY—See Anixter International; *U.S. Public*, pg. 116
ANIXTER THUNDER BAY—See Anixter International; *U.S. Public*, pg. 116
ANIXTER TORONTO—See Anixter International; *U.S. Public*, pg. 116
ANIXTER UK—See Anixter International; *U.S. Public*, pg. 116
ANIXTER VANCOUVER—See Anixter International; *U.S. Public*, pg. 116
ANIXTER WARRINGTON—See Anixter International; *U.S. Public*, pg. 116
ANIXTER WINNIPEG—See Anixter International; *U.S. Public*, pg. 116
ANJOU INTERNATIONAL COMPANY—See Compagnie Generale Des Eaux; *Int'l*, pg. 321
ANJU JEWELRY LIMITED—See Town & Country Corporation; *U.S. Public*, pg. 1625
ANKARA METRO CONSORTIUM—See SNC-Lavalin Group Inc.; *Int'l*, pg. 1162
ANLAGE-UND KREDITBANK AKB, ZURICH—See Bayerische Hypotheken-und Wechsel-Bank Aktiengesellschaft; *Int'l*, pg. 176
ANN ARBOR COMPUTER—See Jervis B. Webb Company; *U.S. Private*, pg. 1156
ANNABELLE CANDY COMPANY, INC.; *U.S. Private*, pg. 75
THE ANNAPOLIS BANKING & TRUST CO.—See Mercantile Bankshares Corporation; *U.S. Public*, pg. 1088
ANNIN & COMPANY; *U.S. Private*, pg. 75
ANNING-JOHNSON COMPANY—See Anson Industries, Inc.; *U.S. Private*, pg. 76
ANNTAYLOR, INC.—See AnnTaylor Stores Corporation; *U.S. Public*, pg. 116
ANNTAYLOR STORES CORPORATION; *U.S. Public*, pg. 116
ANNTAYLOR TRAVEL, INC.—See AnnTaylor Stores Corporation; *U.S. Public*, pg. 116
ANNUITY NETWORK INC.—See St. Paul Bancorp, Inc.; *U.S. Public*, pg. 1428
ANO-COIL CORPORATION; *U.S. Private*, pg. 75
ANOKA ELECTRIC COOPERATIVE; *U.S. Private*, pg. 75
ANORAD CORPORATION; *U.S. Private*, pg. 75
ANPING DISTRIBUTORS LTD.—See Nestle S.A.; *Int'l*, pg. 918
ANREM CO.—See American National Insurance Company; *U.S. Public*, pg. 88
ANRITSU AMERICA, INC.-CENTRAL REGION—See Anritsu Corporation; *Int'l*, pg. 77
ANRITSU AMERICA, INC.-WESTERN REGION—See Anritsu Corporation; *Int'l*, pg. 77
ANRITSU CORPORATION; *Int'l*, pg. 77
ANRITSU ELECTRONICA S.A.—See Anritsu Corporation; *Int'l*, pg. 77
ANRITSU ELEKTRONIK GMBH—See Anritsu Corporation; *Int'l*, pg. 77
ANRITSU EUROPE LTD.—See Anritsu Corporation; *Int'l*, pg. 77
ANRITSU WILTRON—See Anritsu Corporation; *Int'l*, pg. 77
ANSALDO ARGENTINA S.A.—See IRI Istituto Ricostruzione Industriale; *Int'l*, pg. 654
ANSALDO COMPONENTI SRL—See IRI Istituto Ricostruzione Industriale; *Int'l*, pg. 653
ANSALDO DE COLOMBIA S.A.—See IRI Istituto Ricostruzione Industriale; *Int'l*, pg. 654
ANSALDO DE MEXICO—See IRI Istituto Ricostruzione Industriale; *Int'l*, pg. 654
ANSALDO DEUTSCHLAND—See IRI Istituto Ricostruzione Industriale; *Int'l*, pg. 654
ANSALDO DO BRASIL EQUIP ELECTROMECANICOS S.A.—See IRI Istituto Ricostruzione Industriale; *Int'l*, pg. 654
ANSALDO GIE S.R.L.—See IRI Istituto Ricostruzione Industriale; *Int'l*, pg. 653
ANSALDO INDUSTRIA S.P.A.—See IRI Istituto Ricostruzione Industriale; *Int'l*, pg. 653
ANSALDO INTERNATIONAL SERVICES—See IRI Istituto Ricostruzione Industriale; *Int'l*, pg. 654
ANSALDO NORTH AMERICA—See IRI Istituto Ricostruzione Industriale; *Int'l*, pg. 653
ANSALDO RICERCHE SRL—See IRI Istituto Ricostruzione Industriale; *Int'l*, pg. 653
ANSALDO SAUDIA LTD.—See IRI Istituto Ricostruzione Industriale; *Int'l*, pg. 654
ANSALDO SIGNAL N.V.; *Int'l*, pg. 77
ANSALDO TRANSPORTI-MILAN PLANT—See IRI Istituto Ricostruzione Industriale; *Int'l*, pg. 653
ANSALDO TRANSPORTI SPA—See IRI Istituto Ricostruzione Industriale; *Int'l*, pg. 653
ANSALDO TRANSPORTI S.P.A.—See IRI Istituto Ricostruzione Industriale; *Int'l*, pg. 653
ANSALDO TRASPORTI SIGNALING LTD.—See Ansaldo Signal N.V.; *Int'l*, pg. 78
ANSALDO VOLUND A/S—See IRI Istituto Ricostruzione Industriale; *Int'l*, pg. 654
HENRY ANSBACHER HOLDING PLC—See First National Bank Holdings Limited; *Int'l*, pg. 487
ANSCHUTZ & CO.—See Carl-Zeiss-Stiftung; *Int'l*, pg. 1523
ANSCHUTZ CORPORATION; *U.S. Private*, pg. 75
THE ANSCHUTZ OVERSEAS CORP.—See Anschutz Corporation; *U.S. Private*, pg. 75
ANSCO PHOTO-OPTICAL PRODUCTS CORP.—See Haking Enterprises; *Int'l*, pg. 587
BENJAMIN ANSEHL COMPANY; *U.S. Private*, pg. 75
ANSELL INTERNATIONAL—See Pacific Dunlop Limited; *Int'l*, pg. 1021
ANSER (ANALYTIC SERVICES INC.); *U.S. Private*, pg. 75
ANSETT TRANSPORT INDUSTRIES LTD.—See The News Corporation Limited; *Int'l*, pg. 925
ANSEVEN—See IRI Istituto Ricostruzione Industriale; *Int'l*, pg. 654
ANSON INDUSTRIES, INC.; *U.S. Private*, pg. 76
ANSPACH GROSSMAN ENTERPRISE—See WPP Group plc; *Int'l*, pg. 1483
ANSUL FIRE PROTECTION—See Tyco International Ltd.; *U.S. Public*, pg. 1650
ANSUL INCORPORATED—See Tyco International Ltd.; *U.S. Public*, pg. 1648
ANSUL S.A.—See Tyco International Ltd.; *U.S. Public*, pg. 1651
ANSUTECH, INC.—See Nippon Sanso Corporation; *Int'l*, pg. 938
ANSVAR AMERICA LIFE INSURANCE COMPANY—See Preferred Risk Mutual Insurance; *U.S. Private*, pg. 880
THE ANSWER—See Catherines Stores Corporation; *U.S. Public*, pg. 318
ANSWER PRODUCTS, INC.—See LDI, Ltd.; *U.S. Private*, pg. 639
ANSWER SYSTEMS DEVELOPMENT LABORATORY—See Platinum Technology, Inc.; *U.S. Public*, pg. 1309
ANTAH SEDGWICK CHARTERED INSURANCE BROKERS SDN BERHAD—See Standard Chartered Bank PLC; *Int'l*, pg. 1297
ANTARCTIC SUPPORT ASSOCIATES—See EG & G, Inc.; *U.S. Public*, pg. 544
ANTARES ALLIANCE GROUP—See Fujitsu Limited; *Int'l*, pg. 528
ANTARES GROUP INC.; *U.S. Private*, pg. 76
ANTEA SA—See Heidemij N.V.; *Int'l*, pg. 607
THE ANTEC CORPORATION; *U.S. Public*, pg. 116
ANTEC GROUP—See The Antec Corporation; *U.S. Public*, pg. 116
ANTEC INTERNATIONAL—See The Antec Corporation; *U.S. Public*, pg. 117
ANTEC MANUFACTURING—See The Antec Corporation; *U.S. Public*, pg. 116
ANTECH LTD.—See American Waste Services, Inc.; *U.S. Public*, pg. 94
ANTELOPE VALLEY WATER COMPANY—See Dominguez Services Corporation; *U.S. Public*, pg. 516
ANTENNA PRODUCTS CORP.—See Cabre Corp.; *U.S. Public*, pg. 289
ANTENNA SYSTEMS—See United Capital Corp.; *U.S. Public*, pg. 1674
ANTENNACRAFT CO.—See Tandy Corporation; *U.S. Public*, pg. 1560
ANTENNES ANDREW S.A.R.L.—See Andrew Corporation; *U.S. Public*, pg. 113
ANTHEM BLUE CROSS & BLUE SHIELD—See Anthem, Inc.; *U.S. Private*, pg. 76
ANTHEM ELECTRONICS INC.—See Arrow Electronics, Inc.; *U.S. Public*, pg. 134
ANTHEM HEALTH COMPANIES—See Anthem, Inc.; *U.S. Private*, pg. 76
ANTHEM HEALTH PLANS OF FLORIDA INC.—See Anthem, Inc.; *U.S. Private*, pg. 76
ANTHEM HEALTH PLANS OF TEXAS—See Anthem, Inc.; *U.S. Private*, pg. 76
ANTHEM, INC.; *U.S. Private*, pg. 76
ANTHEM TECHNOLOGY—See Arrow Electronics, Inc.; *U.S. Public*, pg. 134
ANTHONY AND SYLVAN POOLS CORPORATION—See Essef Corporation; *U.S. Public*, pg. 593
C.R. ANTHONY COMPANY—See Stage Stores, Inc.; *U.S. Private*, pg. 1029
ANTHONY FOREST DIV.—See Anthony Forest Products Co., Inc.; *U.S. Private*, pg. 76
ANTHONY FOREST PRODUCTS CO., INC.; *U.S. Private*, pg. 76
ANTHONY MACARONI CO., INC.—See Borden, Inc.; *U.S. Private*, pg. 158
ANTHRACITE INDUSTRIES, INC.—See Asbury Carbons, Inc.; *U.S. Private*, pg. 87
ANTHROPOLOGIE—See Urban Outfitters, Inc.; *U.S. Public*, pg. 1700
ANTIBIOTICOS S.A.—See Compart SpA; *Int'l*, pg. 324
ANTIBIOTICOS S.P.A.—See Compart SpA; *Int'l*, pg. 324
ANTIFERENCE LTD.—See Wolseley Plc.; *Int'l*, pg. 1511
ANTILLEAN TELEMATICS NV—See KPN Koninklyke PTT Nederland NV; *Int'l*, pg. 720
ANTILLES INTERNATIONAL SALT COMPANY NV—See Akzo Nobel N.V.; *Int'l*, pg. 44
ANTIQUE TRADER PUBLICATIONS—See Landmark Communications, Inc.; *U.S. Private*, pg. 649
ANTOFAGASTA MINE—See The Broken Hill Proprietary Company Limited; *Int'l*, pg. 228
ANTOINE PETIT—See Vendex International N.V.; *Int'l*, pg. 1463
N.V. ANTRADEX NUTRICIA AMERICAS—See Nutricia BV; *Int'l*, pg. 991
N.V. ANTRIEBSTECHNIK BAUKNECHT S.A.—See Deutsche Babcock AG; *Int'l*, pg. 400
ANTWERP DIAMOND DISTRIBUTORS INC.; *U.S. Private*, pg. 76
ANTWERP LOCAL HEAD OFFICE—See Bank Brussels Lambert; *Int'l*, pg. 147
ANTWERPE DIAMANTBANK—See Generale de Banque S.A.; *Int'l*, pg. 546
ANTWERPESE DIAMANTBANK N.V.—See Bank Brussels Lambert; *Int'l*, pg. 147
ANVIL CASES, INC.—See Zero Corporation; *U.S. Public*, pg. 1791
THE ANVIL CONSULTANCY—See Omnicom Group Inc.; *U.S. Public*, pg. 1224
ANVIL PRODUCTS—See Tyco International Ltd.; *U.S. Public*, pg. 1651
ANYL-MEX SA DE CV—See Zeneca Group Plc; *Int'l*, pg. 1525
ANZON INC.—See Cookson Group plc; *Int'l*, pg. 328
AOKI CORPORATION; *Int'l*, pg. 78
AOKI CORPORATION-OSAKA—See Aoki Corporation; *Int'l*, pg. 78
AOMORI HAKUHODO INC.—See Hakuhodo Incorporated; *Int'l*, pg. 587
AON CORPORATION; *U.S. Public*, pg. 117
AON RISK SERVICES INC. OF ILLINOIS—See AON Corporation; *U.S. Public*, pg. 117
APACHE CANADA LTD.—See Apache Corporation; *U.S. Public*, pg. 119
APACHE CORPORATION; *U.S. Public*, pg. 119
APACHE HOSE & BELTING COMPANY, INC.; *U.S. Private*, pg. 76
APACHE INTERNATIONAL FINANCE, N.V.—See Apache Corporation; *U.S. Public*, pg. 119
APACHE INTERNATIONAL, INC.—See Apache Corporation; *U.S. Public*, pg. 119
APACHE PLASTICS, L.P.; *U.S. Private*, pg. 77
THE APACHE RAILWAY COMPANY—See Stone Container Corporation; *U.S. Public*, pg. 1521
APALACHICOLA NORTHERN RR—See St. Joe Corp.; *U.S. Public*, pg. 1427
APARTMENT SERVICE CO.; *U.S. Private*, pg. 77
APARTMENT VENTURES, INC.—See Cooper Communities, Inc.; *U.S. Private*, pg. 274
APASCO S.A. DE C.V.—See Holderbank Financiere Glaris Ltd.; *Int'l*, pg. 629
APAX AUTOPARTS INTERNATIONAL LTD.—See Freudenberg & Company; *Int'l*, pg. 507
APCO ARGENTINA INC.; *U.S. Public*, pg. 119
APCOA, INC.—See Holberg Industries, Inc.; *U.S. Private*, pg. 533
APCOM INC.—See State Industries Inc.; *U.S. Private*, pg. 1037
APERTUS TECHNOLOGIES INCORPORATED; *U.S. Public*, pg. 119
APEX—See Pittway Corporation; *U.S. Public*, pg. 1306
APEX BROACH & MACHINE CO.; *U.S. Private*, pg. 77
APEX COMPUTER CO.—See The Cerplex Group, Inc.; *U.S. Public*, pg. 332
APEX DATA—See Smart Modular Technologies; *U.S. Public*, pg. 1476
APEX GALVANIZING CORP.—See Victaulic Company of America; *U.S. Private*, pg. 1138
APEX INTERNATIONAL, INC.—See Video Display Corporation; *U.S. Public*, pg. 1720
APEX MILLS CORPORATION; *U.S. Private*, pg. 77

APEX MOTOR MFG. CORP.—See Nissho Iwai Corporation; *Int'l*, pg. 947
APEX OIL COMPANY, INC.; *U.S. Private*, pg. 77
APEX OPERATION—See Cooper Industries, Inc.; *U.S. Public*, pg. 444
APEX PRECISION TECHNOLOGY INC.; *U.S. Private*, pg. 77
APEX SERVICE STATIONS LIMITED—See Burmah Castrol plc; *Int'l*, pg. 234
APEX SPECIALTY MATERIALS, INC.; *U.S. Private*, pg. 77
APEX SUPPLY CO., INC.; *U.S. Private*, pg. 77
APITECH—See Applied Power Inc.; *U.S. Public*, pg. 124
APLEX INDUSTRIES INC.—See Pentair, Inc.; *U.S. Public*, pg. 1273
APLI COMBUSTION, S.A.—See Eclipse Inc.; *U.S. Private*, pg. 361
APLIVENTIL, LDA.—See Axel Johnson AB; *Int'l*, pg. 710
THE APOGEE COMPANIES, INC.; *U.S. Private*, pg. 77
APOGEE ENTERPRISES, INC.; *U.S. Public*, pg. 120
APOINT S.A.—See Corporacion MAPFRE, Compania Internacional de Reaseguros, S.A.; *Int'l*, pg. 333
APOLLINARIS & SCHWEPPES GMBH & CO.; *Int'l*, pg. 78
APOLLO COLORS INC.; *U.S. Private*, pg. 77
APOLLO ELECTRONICS CO., LTD.—See Rohm Co., Ltd.; *Int'l*, pg. 1125
APOLLO EXPRESS, INC.—See Mark VII, Inc.; *U.S. Public*, pg. 1046
APOLLO FIRE DETECTORS LIMITED—See Halma p.l.c.; *Int'l*, pg. 589
APOLLO GAS CO.—See USX Corporation; *U.S. Public*, pg. 1661
APOLLO GROUP, INC.; *U.S. Public*, pg. 120
APOLLO HOTEL B.V.—See Granada Group PLC; *Int'l*, pg. 556
APOLO PRODUTOS DE ACO S.A.; *Int'l*, pg. 78
APONTI GMBH—See Nestle S.A.; *Int'l*, pg. 918
APPALACHIAN INSURANCE CO.—See Allendale Mutual Insurance Co.; *U.S. Private*, pg. 37
APPALACHIAN POWER COMPANY—See American Electric Power Company, Inc.; *U.S. Public*, pg. 72
APPALACHIAN REALTY CO.—See The H.T. Hackney Co.; *U.S. Private*, pg. 493
APPARAL AMERICA, INC.—See Apparel America, Inc.; *U.S. Private*, pg. 120
APPARECCHI DI CONTROLLO RANCO, S.R.L.—See Siebe plc; *Int'l*, pg. 1243
APPAREL AMERICA, INC.; *U.S. Public*, pg. 120
THE APPAREL GROUP, LTD.; *U.S. Private*, pg. 78
APPAREL VENTURES, INC.; *U.S. Private*, pg. 78
I. APPEL CORPORATION; *U.S. Private*, pg. 78
APPEL UNIFORMS DIV.—See Superior Surgical Mfg. Co., Inc.; *U.S. Public*, pg. 1539
APPERSON BUSINESS FORMS, INC.; *U.S. Private*, pg. 78
APPLAUSE INC.; *U.S. Private*, pg. 78
APPLE AUTO GLASS, LTD.—See TCG International Inc.; *Int'l*, pg. 1336
APPLE CANADA LTD.—See Apple Computer, Inc.; *U.S. Public*, pg. 121
APPLE COMPUTER AB—See Apple Computer, Inc.; *U.S. Public*, pg. 121
APPLE COMPUTER AUSTRALIA PTY. LTD.—See Apple Computer, Inc.; *U.S. Public*, pg. 121
APPLE COMPUTER B.V.—See Apple Computer, Inc.; *U.S. Public*, pg. 121
APPLE COMPUTER ESPANA S.A.—See Apple Computer, Inc.; *U.S. Public*, pg. 121
APPLE COMPUTER FRANCE SARL—See Apple Computer, Inc.; *U.S. Public*, pg. 121
APPLE COMPUTER GES.MBH—See Apple Computer, Inc.; *U.S. Public*, pg. 121
APPLE COMPUTER, INC.; *U.S. Public*, pg. 121
APPLE COMPUTER INTERNATIONAL LTD.—See Apple Computer, Inc.; *U.S. Public*, pg. 121
APPLE COMPUTER JAPAN, INC.—See Apple Computer, Inc.; *U.S. Public*, pg. 121
APPLE COMPUTER LTD.—See Apple Computer, Inc.; *U.S. Public*, pg. 121
APPLE COMPUTER PTY. LTD.—See Apple Computer, Inc.; *U.S. Public*, pg. 121
APPLE COMPUTER SA—See Apple Computer, Inc.; *U.S. Public*, pg. 121
APPLE COMPUTER (SALES) LTD.—See Apple Computer, Inc.; *U.S. Public*, pg. 121
APPLE COMPUTER SPA—See Apple Computer, Inc.; *U.S. Public*, pg. 121
APPLE COMPUTER (UK) LTD.—See Apple Computer, Inc.; *U.S. Public*, pg. 121
APPLE DE MEXICO—See Apple Computer, Inc.; *U.S. Public*, pg. 121
APPLE EXPO-THE MACUSER SHOW—See EMAP Plc; *Int'l*, pg. 452
APPLE SOUTH, INC.; *U.S. Public*, pg. 121
APPLE VACATIONS WEST INC.; *U.S. Private*, pg. 78
APPLEBEE'S INTERNATIONAL, INC.; *U.S. Public*, pg. 122
APPLETISER SOUTH AFRICA (PTY) LTD.—See South African Breweries, Ltd.; *Int'l*, pg. 1286
APPLETON & LANGE—See National Amusements, Inc.; *U.S. Private*, pg. 778
APPLETON ELECTRIC CO.—See Emerson Electric Co.; *U.S. Public*, pg. 572
APPLETON ELECTRIC LTD.—See Emerson Electric Co.; *U.S. Public*, pg. 575
APPLETON PAPERS INC.—See Groupe Saint Louis; *Int'l*, pg. 567
APPLETON POHL GMBH & CO.—See J.M. Voith, GmbH; *Int'l*, pg. 1473
APPLETON WIRE DIV., ALBANY INTERNATIONAL—See Albany International Corp.; *U.S. Public*, pg. 36
APPLETREE MARKETS; *U.S. Private*, pg. 78
APPLIANCE COMPONENTS LIMITED—See Siebe plc; *Int'l*, pg. 1241
APPLIANCE SYSTEMS GROUP—See Sharp Corporation; *Int'l*, pg. 1228

APPLICATION SYSTEMS—See Great Plains Manufacturing, Inc.; *U.S. Private*, pg. 475
APPLICATIONS MANAGEMENT GROUP—See Sterling Software, Inc.; *U.S. Public*, pg. 1516
APPLICON INC.—See Gores Technology Group; *U.S. Private*, pg. 465
APPLIED AUTOMATION INC.—See Mannesmann A.G.; *Int'l*, pg. 835
APPLIED AUTOMATION U.K. LTD.—See Mannesmann A.G.; *Int'l*, pg. 835
APPLIED BIOCHEMIST INC.—See Laporte plc; *Int'l*, pg. 802
APPLIED BIOSYSTEMS—See The Perkin-Elmer Corporation; *U.S. Public*, pg. 1279
APPLIED COATINGS—See Bel-Art Products; *U.S. Private*, pg. 130
APPLIED COMMUNICATIONS, INC.—See Transaction Systems Architects, Inc.; *U.S. Public*, pg. 1629
APPLIED COMPOSITES AB—See Celsius AB; *Int'l*, pg. 276
APPLIED COMPUTER TECHNOLOGY—See Hewlett-Packard Company; *U.S. Public*, pg. 816
APPLIED CURING TECHNOLOGY, INC.—See Nordson Corporation; *U.S. Public*, pg. 1189
APPLIED CURING TECHNOLOGY, LTD.—See Nordson Corporation; *U.S. Public*, pg. 1189
APPLIED DIGITAL ACCESS; *U.S. Public*, pg. 122
APPLIED DRILLING TECHNOLOGY INC.—See Global Marine Inc.; *U.S. Public*, pg. 748
APPLIED EXTRUSION TECHNOLOGIES, INC.; *U.S. Public*, pg. 122
APPLIED FILMS CORP.—See Donnelly Corporation; *U.S. Public*, pg. 519
APPLIED GRAPHICS—See U.S. News & World Report; *U.S. Private*, pg. 1125
APPLIED GRAPHICS TECHNOLOGIES—See U.S. News & World Report; *U.S. Private*, pg. 1125
APPLIED GRAPHICS TECHNOLOGY—See U.S. News & World Report; *U.S. Private*, pg. 1125
APPLIED IMPLANT TECHNOLOGY—See Applied Materials, Inc.; *U.S. Public*, pg. 123
APPLIED INDUSTRIAL TECHNOLOGIES; *U.S. Public*, pg. 122
APPLIED INDUSTRIAL TECHNOLOGIES—See Applied Industrial Technologies; *U.S. Public*, pg. 122
APPLIED INNOVATION INC.; *U.S. Public*, pg. 122
APPLIED INTELLIGENCE SYSTEMS, INC.—See Electro Scientific Industries, Inc.; *U.S. Public*, pg. 569
APPLIED MAGNETICS CORPORATION; *U.S. Public*, pg. 123
APPLIED MAGNETICS IRELAND, LTD.—See Applied Magnetics Corporation; *U.S. Public*, pg. 123
APPLIED MAGNETICS KOREA, LTD.—See Applied Magnetics Corporation; *U.S. Public*, pg. 123
APPLIED MAGNETICS (MALAYSIA) SDN. BHD.—See Applied Magnetics Corporation; *U.S. Public*, pg. 123
APPLIED MATERIALS ASIA PACIFIC, LTD.—See Applied Materials, Inc.; *U.S. Public*, pg. 123
APPLIED MATERIALS EUROPE BV—See Applied Materials, Inc.; *U.S. Public*, pg. 123
APPLIED MATERIALS, INC.; *U.S. Public*, pg. 123
APPLIED MATERIALS JAPAN, INC.—See Applied Materials, Inc.; *U.S. Public*, pg. 123
APPLIED MICROSYSTEMS CORPORATION; *U.S. Public*, pg. 123
APPLIED POWER INC.; *U.S. Public*, pg. 124
APPLIED POWER JAPAN—See Applied Power Inc.; *U.S. Public*, pg. 125
APPLIED RESEARCH LABORATORIES SA—See Rhone-Poulenc S.A.; *Int'l*, pg. 1111
APPLIED RESEARCH LABS—See Rhone-Poulenc S.A.; *Int'l*, pg. 1111
APPLIED SCIENCE ASSOCIATES, INC.—See Analysis & Technology, Inc.; *U.S. Public*, pg. 109
APPLIED SCIENCES DIVISION—See Caddock Electronics, Inc.; *U.S. Private*, pg. 198
APPLIED SUPER CONETICS, INC.—See Toshiba Corporation; *Int'l*, pg. 1405
APPLIED SYSTEMS—See York International Corporation; *U.S. Public*, pg. 1788
APPLIED TECHNOLOGY—See Litton Industries, Inc.; *U.S. Public*, pg. 1002
APPLIED TECHNOLOGY (GERMANY)—See Litton Industries, Inc.; *U.S. Public*, pg. 1004
APPLIED TECHNOLOGY (UK)—See Litton Industries, Inc.; *U.S. Public*, pg. 1004
APPRAISAL SERVICES, INC.—See Associated Banc-Corp; *U.S. Public*, pg. 141
APRIA HEALTHCARE GROUP INC.; *U.S. Public*, pg. 125
APRICOT COMPUTERS—See Mitsubishi Electric Corporation; *Int'l*, pg. 873
APRIL HILL, INC.—See Grocers Baking Co.; *U.S. Private*, pg. 483
APRON SERVICES (PTY) LTD.—See Transnet Ltd.; *Int'l*, pg. 1417
APTARGROUP, INC.; *U.S. Public*, pg. 125
AQUA-AEROBIC SYSTEMS INC.; *U.S. Private*, pg. 78
AQUA CARE SYSTEMS INC.; *U.S. Public*, pg. 126
AQUA CHEM DIVISION—See Imperial Chemical Industries PLC; *Int'l*, pg. 663
AQUA-CHEM INC.—See Lyonnaise des Eaux S.A.; *Int'l*, pg. 824
AQUA GLASS CORP.—See Masco Corporation; *U.S. Public*, pg. 1053
AQUA POWER MARINE PRODUCTS DIV.—See IMO Industries Inc.; *U.S. Public*, pg. 857
AQUACHLOR (PROPRIETARY) LIMITED—See Olin Corporation; *U.S. Public*, pg. 1219
AQUACONSULT S.A. DE C.V.—See FKI Plc; *Int'l*, pg. 474
AQUALISA PRODUCTS LIMITED—See Newmond PLC; *Int'l*, pg. 925
AQUALON—See Hercules Incorporated; *U.S. Public*, pg. 810

AQUALON BELGIUM N.V.—See Hercules Incorporated; *U.S. Public*, pg. 810
AQUALON B.V.—See Hercules Incorporated; *U.S. Public*, pg. 810
AQUALON CANADA INC.—See Hercules Incorporated; *U.S. Public*, pg. 810
AQUALON DO BRAZIL S.A.—See Hercules Incorporated; *U.S. Public*, pg. 810
AQUALON FRANCE B.V.—See Hercules Incorporated; *U.S. Public*, pg. 810
AQUALON GMBH—See Hercules Incorporated; *U.S. Public*, pg. 810
AQUALON-HOPEWELL—See Hercules Incorporated; *U.S. Public*, pg. 810
AQUALON ITALIA S.P.A.—See Hercules Incorporated; *U.S. Public*, pg. 810
AQUALON-LOUISIANA—See Hercules Incorporated; *U.S. Public*, pg. 810
AQUALON (UK) LIMITED—See Hercules Incorporated; *U.S. Public*, pg. 810
AQUAMATIC—See Osmonics, Inc.; *U.S. Public*, pg. 1234
AQUAMINE, LLC—See Victaulic Company of America; *U.S. Private*, pg. 1138
AQUAPORE MOISTURE SYSTEMS, INC.—See Powell Duffryn PLC; *Int'l*, pg. 1066
AQUARION COMPANY; *U.S. Public*, pg. 126
AQUARION MANAGEMENT SERVICES—See Aquarion Company; *U.S. Public*, pg. 126
AQUARION MANAGEMENT SERVICES, INC.—See Aquarion Company; *U.S. Public*, pg. 126
AQUASEAL LTD.—See Tarmac plc; *Int'l*, pg. 1355
AQUATERRA CORPORATION, CRYSTAL SPRINGS DIV.—See Danone Group; *Int'l*, pg. 1355
AQUATERRA ENVIRONMENTAL CONSULTANTS—See GZA GeoEnvironmental Technologies, Inc.; *U.S. Public*, pg. 697
AQUATIC ANIMAL HEALTH—See Alpharma Inc.; *U.S. Public*, pg. 58
AQUATROL CORPORATION—See J.M. Process Systems Inc.; *U.S. Private*, pg. 577
AQUILA BETEILIGUNGSGESELLSCHAFT MBH—See Allianz Aktiengesellschaft; *Int'l*, pg. 58
AQUILA BIOPHARMACEUTICALS, INC.; *U.S. Public*, pg. 126
AQUILA ENERGY CORP.—See UtiliCorp United Inc.; *U.S. Public*, pg. 1701
AQUILA ENERGY MARKETING—See UtiliCorp United Inc.; *U.S. Public*, pg. 1701
AQUILA ENERGY RESOURCES—See UtiliCorp United Inc.; *U.S. Public*, pg. 1701
AQUILA GAS PIPELINE CORPORATION—See UtiliCorp United Inc.; *U.S. Public*, pg. 1701
AQUINTER S.A.—See Tractebel; *Int'l*, pg. 1415
AQUION; *U.S. Private*, pg. 78
AQUIONICS INC.—See Halma p.l.c.; *Int'l*, pg. 590
ARAB DRILLING & WORKOVER COMPANY—See Kuwait Petroleum Corporation; *Int'l*, pg. 765
THE ARAB-EASTERN INSURANCE COMPANY LIMITED E.C.—See The Tokio Marine & Fire Insurance Company, Ltd.; *Int'l*, pg. 1392
ARAB ELEVATORS CO.—See Schindler Holding AG; *Int'l*, pg. 1205
ARAB INTERNATIONAL INSURANCE COMPANY—See Allianz Aktiengesellschaft; *Int'l*, pg. 61
ARAB-MALAYSIAN MERCHANT BANK BERHAD—See The Tokai Bank, Limited; *Int'l*, pg. 1391
ARAB MEDICAL PRODUCTS—See Hewlett-Packard Company; *U.S. Public*, pg. 816
ARABIA CIGNA INSURANCE COMPANY LIMITED E.C.—See Cigna Corp.; *U.S. Public*, pg. 363
ARABIAN COMPUTER SYSTEMS—See Hewlett-Packard Company; *U.S. Public*, pg. 816
ARABIAN ELEVATOR & ESCALATOR CO. LTD. (AREECO)—See Kone Corporation; *Int'l*, pg. 748
ARABIAN ENVIRONMENTAL SERVICES COMPANY LIMITED—See Halliburton Company; *U.S. Public*, pg. 777
ARABIAN FIBERGLASS INSULATION CO.—See Owens Corning; *U.S. Public*, pg. 1237
ARABIAN GULF INVESTMENTS (FAR EAST) LIMITED—See HSBC Holdings plc; *Int'l*, pg. 581
ARABIAN OIL COMPANY, LTD.; *Int'l*, pg. 78
ARABIAN PAPER PRODUCTS COMPANY (APPCO)—See Huhtamaki Oy; *Int'l*, pg. 639
ARABIAN PIPECOATING COMPANY LTD.—See Shaw Industries Ltd.; *Int'l*, pg. 1231
ARABIAN PLASTIC MANUFACTURING COMPANY—See Georg Fischer Ltd.; *Int'l*, pg. 489
ARABIAN SHAW PIPECOATERS (THAILAND) LIMITED—See Shaw Industries Ltd.; *Int'l*, pg. 1231
ARABTEL—See Jeumont-Schneider Trenformeteurs; *Int'l*, pg. 706
ARACRUZ CELULOSE S.A.; *Int'l*, pg. 78
ARACRUZ CELULOSE (USA) INC.—See Aracruz Celulose S.A.; *Int'l*, pg. 78
ARACRUZ EUROPE S.A.—See Aracruz Celulose S.A.; *Int'l*, pg. 78
ARACRUZ TRADING—See Aracruz Celulose S.A.; *Int'l*, pg. 78
ARAL AG—See Veba AG; *Int'l*, pg. 1460
ARALMEX, S.A. DE C.V.—See General Motors Corporation; *U.S. Public*, pg. 724
**ARAMARK BELGIUM, S.A.—See Aramark Corp.; *U.S. Public*, pg. 79
ARAMARK CORP.; *U.S. Private*, pg. 78
ARAMARK CORRECTIONAL SERVICES—See Aramark Corp.; *U.S. Private*, pg. 79
ARAMARK EDUCATIONAL RESOURCES INC. INC.—See Aramark Corp.; *U.S. Private*, pg. 79
ARAMARK FOOD SERVICES—See Aramark Corp.; *U.S. Private*, pg. 79
ARAMARK HEALTHCARE SUPPORT SERVICES, INC.—See Aramark Corp.; *U.S. Private*, pg. 79

Company Index

ARAMARK MAGAZINE & BOOK DIVISION, INC.—See Aramark Corp.; *U.S. Private*, pg. 79
ARAMARK SERVICES, GMBH—See Aramark Corp.; *U.S. Private*, pg. 79
ARAMARK SERVICES OF TEXAS, INC.—See Aramark Corp.; *U.S. Private*, pg. 79
ARAMARK SERVICES, PLC—See Aramark Corp.; *U.S. Private*, pg. 79
ARAMARK SERVICES, ROSEMONT HORIZON—See Aramark Corp.; *U.S. Private*, pg. 79
ARAMARK SPORTS & ENTERTAINMENT SERVICES GROUP INC.—See Aramark Corp.; *U.S. Private*, pg. 79
ARAMARK SPORTS & ENTERTAINMENT SERVICES INC.—See Aramark Corp.; *U.S. Private*, pg. 79
ARAMARK UNIFORM SERVICES OF PUERTO RICO—See Aramark Corp.; *U.S. Private*, pg. 79
ARAMI FASER-VERTRIEB GMBH—See Akzo Nobel N.V.; *Int'l*, pg. 46
ARAMI FRANCE SARL—See Akzo Nobel N.V.; *Int'l*, pg. 45
ARAMI ITALIANA SRL—See Akzo Nobel N.V.; *Int'l*, pg. 45
ARAMI UK LTD.—See Akzo Nobel N.V.; *Int'l*, pg. 45
ARAMIDE MAATSCHAPPIJ VOF—See Akzo Nobel N.V.; *Int'l*, pg. 45
ARANCIA CPC INDUSTRIAL S.A. DE C.V.—See Corn Products International, Inc.; *U.S. Public*, pg. 448
ARANDELL CORPORATION; *U.S. Private*, pg. 79
ARANDELL-SCHMIDT—See Arandell Corporation; *U.S. Private*, pg. 79
ARAPILES, S.A.—See Vallehermoso, S.A.; *Int'l*, pg. 1447
A. ARAUJO S.A.—See JGC Corporation; *Int'l*, pg. 697
ARBCO ELECTRONICS—See Imperial Chemical Industries PLC; *Int'l*, pg. 664
ARBED S.A.; *Int'l*, pg. 78
THE ARBITRON COMPANY—See Ceridian Corporation; *U.S. Public*, pg. 331
JAN ARBMAN EURO RSCG—See Havas Advertising; *Int'l*, pg. 602
ARBOR ACRES FARM, INC.—See Booker PLC; *Int'l*, pg. 202
ARBOR DRUGS, INC.; *U.S. Public*, pg. 126
ARBOR HEALTH CARE COMPANY—See Extendicare Inc.; *Int'l*, pg. 468
ARBOR SOFTWARE CORPORATION; *U.S. Public*, pg. 127
ARBOS TREE SERVICE—See The F.A. Bartlett Tree Expert Co.; *U.S. Private*, pg. 119
THE ARBOUR HOSPITAL—See Universal Health Services, Inc.; *U.S. Public*, pg. 1696
ARBURG, INC.; *U.S. Private*, pg. 79
ARBY'S CANADA INC.—See Triarc Companies, Inc.; *U.S. Public*, pg. 1635
ARC PROPULSION DIVISION—See Sequa Corporation; *U.S. Public*, pg. 1458
ARC SPORTS—See ARC International Corporation; *Int'l*, pg. 17
ARCADE INC.; *U.S. Private*, pg. 79
ARCADIA INTERNACIONAL S.A.—See Otto Versand (GmbH & Co.); *Int'l*, pg. 1015
ARCADIA SHOPS, INC.—See Claire's Stores Inc.; *U.S. Public*, pg. 381
ARCADIA TELEPHONE CO.—See Telephone and Data Systems, Inc.; *U.S. Public*, pg. 1571
ARCATA REDWOOD COMPANY—See Simpson Investment Co.; *U.S. Private*, pg. 1003
ARCELIK A.S.—See Koc Holding A.S.; *Int'l*, pg. 741
ARCH ALUMINIUM & GLASS L.C.; *U.S. Private*, pg. 79
ARCH COAL, INC.—See Ashland, Inc.; *U.S. Public*, pg. 139
ARCH COMMUNICATIONS GROUP, INC.; *U.S. Public*, pg. 127
ARCHCO INC.—See Ceridian Corporation; *U.S. Public*, pg. 331
ARCHER DANIELS MIDLAND COMPANY (ADM); *U.S. Public*, pg. 127
ARCHER GROUP HOLDINGS PLC—See Chartwell Re Corporation; *U.S. Public*, pg. 337
GW ARCHER & CO.—See Diageo Plc; *Int'l*, pg. 409
ARCHER MANAGING AGENTS LIMITED—See Chartwell Re Corporation; *U.S. Public*, pg. 337
ARCHER PIPE & TUBE CO., INC.—See Marubeni Corporation; *Int'l*, pg. 845
ARCHER TECHNICOAT LIMITED—See Morgan Crucible Co. Plc; *Int'l*, pg. 893
ARCHIBALD CANDY COMPANY—See The Jordan Company; *U.S. Private*, pg. 597
ARCHITECTURAL LANDSCAPE LIGHTING—See Luxo A/S; *Int'l*, pg. 821
ARCHITECTURAL RECORD—See The McGraw-Hill Companies; *U.S. Public*, pg. 1070
ARCHITECTURAL WALL SYSTEMS, LLC—See Fidelity Investments (FMR Corp.); *U.S. Private*, pg. 403
ARCHITECTURE—See VNU Verenigde Nederlandse Uitgeversbedrijven B.V.; *Int'l*, pg. 1446
ARCHIVO STORICO ANSALDO—See IRI Istituto Ricostruzione Industriale; *Int'l*, pg. 653
ARCHWAY COOKIES, INC.; *U.S. Private*, pg. 80
ARCO—See Connor Corporation; *U.S. Private*, pg. 264
ARCO ALASKA INC.—See Atlantic Richfield Company; *U.S. Public*, pg. 144
ARCO ALUMINUM CO.—See Atlantic Richfield Company; *U.S. Public*, pg. 144
ARCO BLUEPRINTERS—See Wallace Computer Services, Inc.; *U.S. Public*, pg. 1735
ARCO BRITISH LIMITED—See Atlantic Richfield Company; *U.S. Public*, pg. 144
ARCO CHEMICAL CO.—See Atlantic Richfield Company; *U.S. Public*, pg. 144
ARCO COAL AUSTRALIA, INC.—See Atlantic Richfield Company; *U.S. Public*, pg. 144
ARCO COAL COMPANY—See Atlantic Richfield Company; *U.S. Public*, pg. 144
ARCO DUBAI, INCORPORATED—See Atlantic Richfield Company; *U.S. Public*, pg. 144
ARCO INTL. OIL & GAS CO.—See Atlantic Richfield Company; *U.S. Public*, pg. 144

ARCO MARINE, INCORPORATED—See Atlantic Richfield Company; *U.S. Public*, pg. 144
ARCO PRODUCTS CO.—See Atlantic Richfield Company; *U.S. Public*, pg. 144
ARCO TRANSPORTATION ALASKA, INC.—See Atlantic Richfield Company; *U.S. Public*, pg. 144
ARCON CONSTRUCTION CO., INC.; *U.S. Private*, pg. 80
ARCONIUM SPECIALTY ALLOYS—See Cookson Group plc; *Int'l*, pg. 328
ARCOPLUS ARGENTINA—See Grupo Synkro, S.A. de C.V.; *Int'l*, pg. 576
ARCTIC ALASKA FISHERIES CORPORATION—See Tyson Foods, Inc.; *U.S. Public*, pg. 1652
ARCTIC ALASKA SEAFOODS, INC.—See Tyson Foods, Inc.; *U.S. Public*, pg. 1652
ARCTIC ALASKA TESTING LABORATORIES—See Shannon & Wilson, Inc.; *U.S. Private*, pg. 989
ARCTIC CAT INC.; *U.S. Public*, pg. 128
ARCTIC SLOPE REGIONAL CORPORATION; *U.S. Private*, pg. 80
ARDATH TOBACCO CO. LTD.—See B.A.T Industries P.L.C.; *Int'l*, pg. 111
ARDCO, INC.; *U.S. Private*, pg. 80
ARDCO/TRAVERSE LIFT—See Pettibone Corporation; *U.S. Private*, pg. 859
ARDEE MUSIC PUBLISHING, INC.—See The Reader's Digest Association, Inc.; *U.S. Public*, pg. 1367
ARDELL INDUSTRIES, INC.—See The Jordan Company; *U.S. Private*, pg. 597
ARDELL INTERNATIONAL, INC.—See American International Industries; *U.S. Private*, pg. 57
ARDEM PISIRICILER VE ISITICI SAN. A.S.—See Koc Holding A.S.; *Int'l*, pg. 741
ARDEN FOODS, INC.—See Schreiber Foods, Inc.; *U.S. Private*, pg. 972
ARDEN GROUP, INC.; *U.S. Public*, pg. 128
ARDEN INTERNATIONAL KITCHENS, INC.—See Schreiber Foods, Inc.; *U.S. Private*, pg. 972
ARDEN-MAYFAIR, INC.—See Arden Group, Inc.; *U.S. Public*, pg. 129
ARDEN WATER COMPANY—See Dominguez Services Corporation; *U.S. Public*, pg. 516
ARDENT SOFTWARE, INC.; *U.S. Public*, pg. 129
THE ARDMORE DAILY ARDMOREITE—See Shivers Trading & Operating Co.; *U.S. Private*, pg. 995
ARDMORE FARMS—See The Quaker Oats Company; *U.S. Public*, pg. 1348
AREA HEADQUARTERS-ASIA & OCEANIA—See Dentsu Inc.; *Int'l*, pg. 393
AREA HEADQUARTERS-CHINA—See Dentsu Inc.; *Int'l*, pg. 393
AREA HEADQUARTERS-EUROPE & MIDDLE EAST—See Dentsu Inc.; *Int'l*, pg. 393
AREA HEADQUARTERS-THE AMERICAS—See Dentsu Inc.; *Int'l*, pg. 393
AREA REYCLERS—See Baker Commodities, Inc.; *U.S. Private*, pg. 111
AREA TRAVEL AGENCY LTD.—See FinnAir Oy; *Int'l*, pg. 485
ARENA AUTO AUCTION INC.—See Tyco International Ltd.; *U.S. Public*, pg. 1648
ARENA DE COLOMBIA SA—See Adidas AG; *Int'l*, pg. 25
ARENA LIGHTING LTD.; *U.S. Private*, pg. 80
ARENDAL SMELTEVERCK A.S.—See Saint-Gobain; *Int'l*, pg. 1174
ARENIA—See Groupe Air France; *Int'l*, pg. 560
ARES S.A.—See Arbed S.A.; *Int'l*, pg. 79
ARES-SERONO S.A.; *Int'l*, pg. 80
ARGENT INSURANCE CO. LIMITED—See Johnson Matthey Public Limited Company; *Int'l*, pg. 714
ARGENTARIA CORPORACION BANCARIA DE ESPANA, S.A.; *Int'l*, pg. 80
CIA. ARGENTINA DE TELEFONOS, S.A.—See Telefonaktiebolaget LM Ericsson; *Int'l*, pg. 1365
ARGENTINA DIVISION (DRILLERS INTERNATIONAL S.A.)—See American Financial Group; *U.S. Public*, pg. 75
ARGO AG—See Coop Switzerland; *Int'l*, pg. 329
ARGO INSTRUMENTS INC.—See Mannesmann A.G.; *Int'l*, pg. 839
ARGO INTERNATIONAL CORP.—See Delcal Enterprises, Inc.; *U.S. Private*, pg. 322
ARGO-TECH CORPORATION; *U.S. Public*, pg. 81
ARGO TERMINAL CO.—See GLS Corporation; *U.S. Private*, pg. 435
ARGON MEDICAL—See Maxxim Medical, Inc.; *U.S. Public*, pg. 129
ARGONAUT CO.—See Argonaut Group, Inc.; *U.S. Public*, pg. 129
ARGONAUT GROUP, INC.; *U.S. Public*, pg. 129
ARGOS COMPANHIA DE SEGUROS—See The Chubb Corporation; *U.S. Public*, pg. 355
THE ARGOS GROUP—See Barton Malow Enterprises, Inc.; *U.S. Private*, pg. 120
ARGOSY ELECTRONICS, INC.; *U.S. Private*, pg. 81
ARGOSYSTEMS, INC.—See The Boeing Company; *U.S. Public*, pg. 240
ARGUS-COURIER—See Pulitzer Publishing Company; *U.S. Public*, pg. 1343
ARGUS PUBLISHERS—See Primedia Inc.; *U.S. Public*, pg. 1328
ARI CANADA LIMITED—See Holman Enterprises; *U.S. Private*, pg. 535
ARIAKE WORKS—See Hitachi Zosen Corporation; *Int'l*, pg. 623
ARIANESPACE, INC.—See Arianespace SA; *Int'l*, pg. 81
ARIANESPACE KOUROU—See Arianespace SA; *Int'l*, pg. 81
ARIANESPACE SA; *Int'l*, pg. 81
ARIDO ABDICHTUNGS-GESELLSCHAFT—See Dyckerhoff & Widmann AG; *Int'l*, pg. 423
ARIEL CORPORATION; *U.S. Public*, pg. 81
ARIELY ADVERTISING—See The Lowe Group; *U.S. Private*, pg. 678

ARINC INC. (CONSOLIDATED); *U.S. Private*, pg. 81
ARIOS SA—See Heidemij N.V.; *Int'l*, pg. 607
ARIS INDUSTRIES, INC.; *U.S. Public*, pg. 129
ARISEPT—See Lafarge S.A.; *Int'l*, pg. 789
ARISTA RECORDS INC.—See Bertelsmann AG; *Int'l*, pg. 192
ARISTECH CHEMICAL CORPORATION—See Mitsubishi Corporation; *Int'l*, pg. 872
ARISTO MANUFACTURING CO.—See The Metal Ware Corp.; *U.S. Private*, pg. 735
ARISTOKRAFT, INC.—See Fortune Brands, Inc.; *U.S. Public*, pg. 675
ARISTON—See Sonoco Products Company; *U.S. Public*, pg. 1486
ARITECH EUROPE & CENTRAL LIFE SAFETY EUROPE—See Berwind Corporation; *U.S. Private*, pg. 139
ARITMOS AB—See Proventus AB; *Int'l*, pg. 1072
ARITROIS—See Lafarge S.A.; *Int'l*, pg. 790
ARITRON INSTRUMENT A.G.—See Mine Safety Appliances Co.; *U.S. Public*, pg. 1114
ARIZONA AUCTION SERVICES, INC.—See Cox Enterprises, Inc.; *U.S. Private*, pg. 282
ARIZONA AUTO AUCTION SERVICES—See Cox Enterprises, Inc.; *U.S. Private*, pg. 282
ARIZONA CARDINALS; *U.S. Private*, pg. 81
ARIZONA CHEMICAL DIV.—See International Paper Company; *U.S. Public*, pg. 901
THE ARIZONA DAILY STAR—See Pulitzer Publishing Company; *U.S. Public*, pg. 1343
THE ARIZONA DAILY SUN—See Pulitzer Publishing Company; *U.S. Public*, pg. 1343
ARIZONA DAIRY—See Shamrock Foods Company; *U.S. Private*, pg. 989
ARIZONA ELEVATOR, INC.—See Dover Corporation; *U.S. Public*, pg. 521
ARIZONA GALVANIZING INC.—See Aztec Manufacturing Co.; *U.S. Public*, pg. 159
ARIZONA GRAINS INC.; *U.S. Private*, pg. 81
ARIZONA INSTITUTIONAL FOODS—See Shamrock Foods Company; *U.S. Private*, pg. 989
ARIZONA INSTRUMENT CORPORATION; *U.S. Public*, pg. 129
ARIZONA LIFE INSURANCE CO.—See Metropolitan Mortgage & Securities Co., Inc.; *U.S. Private*, pg. 739
ARIZONA REFRIGERATION SUPPLIES, INC.—See Kitchell Corporation; *U.S. Private*, pg. 624
ARIZONA SERVICE CENTER—See Pace Analytical Services; *U.S. Private*, pg. 829
ARIZONA SPORTS PROGRAMMING NETWORK—See Cox Communications, Inc.; *U.S. Public*, pg. 455
ARIZONA WHOLESALE SUPPLY COMPANY; *U.S. Private*, pg. 82
ARJAY EQUIPMENT CORPORATION—See RJR Nabisco Holdings Corp.; *U.S. Public*, pg. 1355
ARJAY HOLDINGS, INC.—See RJR Nabisco Holdings Corp.; *U.S. Public*, pg. 1355
ARJO WIGGINS APPLETON PLC—See Groupe Saint Louis; *Int'l*, pg. 567
ARJO WIGGINS BELGIUM S.A.—See Groupe Saint Louis; *Int'l*, pg. 568
ARJO WIGGINS CHEMIE GMBH—See Groupe Saint Louis; *Int'l*, pg. 568
ARJO WIGGINS EUROPE HOLDINGS, LTD.—See Groupe Saint Louis; *Int'l*, pg. 567
ARJO WIGGINS FINLAND HOLDINGS—See Groupe Saint Louis; *Int'l*, pg. 567
ARJO WIGGINS INTERSERVICES S.A.—See Groupe Saint Louis; *Int'l*, pg. 567
ARJO WIGGINS OVERSEAS LTD.—See Groupe Saint Louis; *Int'l*, pg. 567
ARJO WIGGINS RESEARCH AND DEVEL. LTD.—See Groupe Saint Louis; *Int'l*, pg. 567
ARJO WIGGINS SA—See Groupe Saint Louis; *Int'l*, pg. 567
ARK LES CORP.—See Ark-Les Corporation; *U.S. Private*, pg. 82
ARK-LES CORPORATION; *U.S. Private*, pg. 82
ARK LIFE ASSURANCE COMPANY LIMITED—See Allied Irish Banks, p.l.c.; *Int'l*, pg. 64
ARK-MART—See Hale-Halsell Company; *U.S. Private*, pg. 494
ARK RESTAURANTS CORP.; *U.S. Public*, pg. 129
ARK VALLEY CONCRETE, INC.—See Ritchie Corporation; *U.S. Private*, pg. 933
ARKANSAS ALUMINUM ALLOYS—See A. Tenenbaum Co. Inc.; *U.S. Private*, pg. 1076
ARKANSAS & MEMPHIS RAILWAY BRIDGE AND TERMINAL CO.—See Union Pacific Corporation; *U.S. Public*, pg. 1668
ARKANSAS BANK & TRUST—See First Commercial Corporation; *U.S. Public*, pg. 630
ARKANSAS BEST CORPORATION; *U.S. Public*, pg. 130
ARKANSAS CASUALTY INVESTMENT—See Arkansas Farm Bureau Federation; *U.S. Private*, pg. 82
ARKANSAS CHEMICALS, INC.—See Great Lakes Chemical Corporation; *U.S. Public*, pg. 760
THE ARKANSAS CITY DAILY TRAVELER—See Shivers Trading & Operating Co.; *U.S. Private*, pg. 995
ARKANSAS EASTMAN CO.—See Eastman Chemical Company; *U.S. Public*, pg. 550
ARKANSAS ELECTRIC COOPERATIVES INC.; *U.S. Private*, pg. 82
ARKANSAS FARM BUREAU FEDERATION; *U.S. Private*, pg. 82
ARKANSAS FARM BUREAU INVESTMENT—See Arkansas Farm Bureau Federation; *U.S. Private*, pg. 82
ARKANSAS GALVANIZING—See Aztec Manufacturing Co.; *U.S. Public*, pg. 159
ARKANSAS LIME CO.—See United States Lime & Minerals; *U.S. Public*, pg. 1685
ARKANSAS STATE BANK—See First Commercial Corporation; *U.S. Public*, pg. 630
ARKANSAS VALLEY DISTRIBUTING—See Hale-Halsell Company; *U.S. Private*, pg. 494

ARKANSAS WESTERN GAS CO.—See Southwestern Energy Company; *U.S. Public*, pg. 1494

ARKANSAS WESTERN PIPELINE COMPANY—See Southwestern Energy Company; *U.S. Public*, pg. 1494

ARKAS A.G.—See Moore Corporation Limited; *Int'l*, pg. 890

ARKAY PACKAGING CORPORATION; *U.S. Private*, pg. 82

ARKEL MANAGEMENT GROUP B.V.—See Royal Begemann Group; *Int'l*, pg. 1133

ARKLA—See Houston Industries Incorporated; *U.S. Public*, pg. 843

S.A. ARKOVET—See Novartis AG; *Int'l*, pg. 974

ARKWRIGHT, INC—See Oce-van der Grinten N.V.; *Int'l*, pg. 994

THE ARLEN CORPORATION; *U.S. Public*, pg. 131

ARLEN MANAGEMENT CORP.—See The Arlen Corporation; *U.S. Public*, pg. 131

ARLEN METALS CORPORATION—See The Arlen Corporation; *U.S. Public*, pg. 131

ARLEY CORPORATION—See VKO, Inc.; *U.S. Private*, pg. 1130

THE ARLINGTON CITIZEN-JOURNAL—See The Walt Disney Company; *U.S. Public*, pg. 512

ARLINGTON, LTD.—See Avon Products, Inc.; *U.S. Public*, pg. 156

ARLINGTON SECURITIES PLC—See British Aerospace p.l.c.; *Int'l*, pg. 217

ARLON, INC.—See Bairnco Corporation; *U.S. Public*, pg. 165

ARM & HAMMER CONSUMER PRODUCTS—See Church & Dwight Co., Inc.; *U.S. Public*, pg. 356

ARMADA CORPORATION; *U.S. Private*, pg. 82

ARMADA TIMES—See The Walt Disney Company; *U.S. Public*, pg. 513

ARMAND PRODUCTS COMPANY—See Church & Dwight Co., Inc.; *U.S. Public*, pg. 356

ARMATRON INTERNATIONAL, INC.; *U.S. Public*, pg. 131

ARMATURTEKNIK I OSBY AB—See Svedala Industri AB; *Int'l*, pg. 1323

ARMATURTEKNIK I OSBY AB—See Trelleborg AB; *Int'l*, pg. 1419

ARMCO; *U.S. Public*, pg. 131

ARMCO INC.-BUTLER OPERS.—See Armco Inc.; *U.S. Public*, pg. 131

ARMCO INC.-COSHOCTON OPERATIONS—See Armco Inc.; *U.S. Public*, pg. 131

ARMCO INC.-MANSFIELD OPERATIONS—See Armco Inc.; *U.S. Public*, pg. 131

ARMCO INC.-ZANESVILLE OPERATIONS—See Armco Inc.; *U.S. Public*, pg. 131

ARMENONIC DEL ECUADOR, S.A.—See Nissho Iwai Corporation; *Int'l*, pg. 949

ARMIN PLASTICS—See Tyco International Ltd.; *U.S. Public*, pg. 1647

ARMIN PLASTICS DIVISION—See Tyco International Ltd.; *U.S. Public*, pg. 1647

ARMIN PLASTICS, NORTHEAST DIVISION—See Tyco International Ltd.; *U.S. Public*, pg. 1647

ARMIN PLASTICS, TYCO LABS—See Tyco International Ltd.; *U.S. Public*, pg. 1647

ARMISSE—See Lagardere Groupe; *Int'l*, pg. 791

ARMITAGE SHANKS LIMITED—See Blue Circle Industries PLC; *Int'l*, pg. 197

ARMOR ALL PRODUCTS GROUP—See The Clorox Company; *U.S. Public*, pg. 387

ARMOR BOND BUILDING PRODUCTS, INC.—See Jannock Limited; *Int'l*, pg. 699

ARMOR SAFE TECHNOLOGIES—See Phelps Tointon Inc.; *U.S. Private*, pg. 861

ARMOUR FOOD COMPANY—See ConAgra, Inc.; *U.S. Public*, pg. 427

ARMOUR SWIFT ECKRICH—See ConAgra, Inc.; *U.S. Public*, pg. 426

TOMMY ARMOUR GOLF—See U.S. Industries, Inc.; *U.S. Public*, pg. 1683

ARMS COMMUNICATIONS P. LTD.—See True North Diversified Companies; *U.S. Public*, pg. 1642

ARMSTRONG AIR CONDITIONING INC.—See Lennox International Inc.; *U.S. Private*, pg. 659

ARMSTRONG AMORTIGUADORES S.A.—See Caparo Group Ltd.; *Int'l*, pg. 265

ARMSTRONG CORK FINANCE CORP.—See Armstrong World Industries, Inc.; *U.S. Public*, pg. 132

ARMSTRONG ELECTRA LTD.—See John Laing PLC; *Int'l*, pg. 796

ARMSTRONG ENGINEERING LIMITED—See Caparo Group Ltd.; *Int'l*, pg. 265

ARMSTRONG EUROPE SERVICES—See Armstrong World Industries, Inc.; *U.S. Public*, pg. 132

ARMSTRONG FASTENINGS LTD.—See Caparo Group Ltd.; *Int'l*, pg. 265

ARMSTRONG FLUID HANDLING—See Armstrong International, Inc.; *U.S. Private*, pg. 83

ARMSTRONG-HUNT, INC.—See Armstrong International, Inc.; *U.S. Private*, pg. 83

ARMSTRONG INTERNATIONAL, INC.; *U.S. Private*, pg. 83

ARMSTRONG INTERNATIONAL, S.A.—See Armstrong International, Inc.; *U.S. Private*, pg. 83

ARMSTRONG (JAPAN) K.K.—See Armstrong World Industries, Inc.; *U.S. Public*, pg. 132

ARMSTRONG LABS.—See Medeva PLC; *Int'l*, pg. 852

ARMSTRONG-NYLEX PTY. LTD.—See Armstrong World Industries, Inc.; *U.S. Public*, pg. 132

ARMSTRONG PATENTS CO., LTD.—See Caparo Group Ltd.; *Int'l*, pg. 265

ARMSTRONG PRODUCE LTD.; *U.S. Private*, pg. 83

ARMSTRONG SCREWS & FIXINGS LTD.—See Caparo Group Ltd.; *Int'l*, pg. 265

ARMSTRONG (SINGAPORE) PTE. LTD.—See Armstrong World Industries, Inc.; *U.S. Public*, pg. 132

ARMSTRONG VENTURES, INC.—See Armstrong World Industries, Inc.; *U.S. Public*, pg. 132

ARMSTRONG WORLD INDUSTRIES-A.C.I. B.V.—See Armstrong World Industries, Inc.; *U.S. Public*, pg. 132

ARMSTRONG WORLD INDUSTRIES CANADA LTD.—See Armstrong World Industries, Inc.; *U.S. Public*, pg. 132

ARMSTRONG WORLD INDUSTRIES-FRANCE S.A.—See Armstrong World Industries, Inc.; *U.S. Public*, pg. 132

ARMSTRONG WORLD INDUSTRIES, G.M.B.H.—See Armstrong World Industries, Inc.; *U.S. Public*, pg. 132

ARMSTRONG WORLD INDUSTRIES HALID S.R.L.—See Armstrong World Industries, Inc.; *U.S. Public*, pg. 132

ARMSTRONG WORLD INDUSTRIES (H.K.) LIMITED—See Armstrong World Industries, Inc.; *U.S. Public*, pg. 132

ARMSTRONG WORLD INDUSTRIES, INC.; *U.S. Public*, pg. 131

ARMSTRONG WORLD INDUSTRIES LTD.—See Armstrong World Industries, Inc.; *U.S. Public*, pg. 132

ARMSTRONG WORLD INDUSTRIES PTY. LTD.—See Armstrong World Industries, Inc.; *U.S. Public*, pg. 132

ARMSTRONG WORLD INDUSTRIES, S.A.—See Armstrong World Industries, Inc.; *U.S. Public*, pg. 132

ARMSTRONG WORLD INDUSTRIES (SCHWEIZ) AG—See Armstrong World Industries, Inc.; *U.S. Public*, pg. 132

ARMSTRONG YORK PTY., LTD.—See Caparo Group Ltd.; *Int'l*, pg. 265

ARMSTRONG-YOSHITAKE, INC.—See Armstrong International, Inc.; *U.S. Private*, pg. 83

ARMTEC—See Jannock Limited; *Int'l*, pg. 698

ARMTEC DEFENSE PRODUCTS CO.—See Esterline Technologies Corporation; *U.S. Public*, pg. 594

ARMY TIMES PUBLISHING CO.—See Gannett Company, Inc.; *U.S. Public*, pg. 699

ARNAV INDUSTRIES, INC.; *U.S. Public*, pg. 83

ARNDALE COMMUNICATIONS LTD.—See The Peninsular and Oriental Steam Navigation Company; *Int'l*, pg. 1034

THE ARNDALE PROPERTY TRUST LTD.—See The Peninsular and Oriental Steam Navigation Company; *Int'l*, pg. 1034

ARNHOLD AND S. BLEICHROEDER, INC.; *U.S. Private*, pg. 83

ARNHOLDT HOLDING GMBH—See Plettac AG; *Int'l*, pg. 1061

ARNI AG—See Coop Switzerland; *Int'l*, pg. 329

ARNO-SKIL FERRAMENTAS ELECTRICAS LTDA.—See Emerson Electric Co.; *U.S. Public*, pg. 575

ARNOLD ADVERTISING—See Arnold Communications, Inc.; *U.S. Private*, pg. 84

THE ARNOLD AGENCY—See Arnold Communications, Inc.; *U.S. Private*, pg. 84

BEN ARNOLD CO., INC.; *U.S. Private*, pg. 83

ARNOLD COMMUNICATIONS, INC.; *U.S. Private*, pg. 83

ARNOLD DIRECT—See Arnold Communications, Inc.; *U.S. Private*, pg. 84

THE ARNOLD ENGINEERING COMPANY—See SPS Technologies, Inc.; *U.S. Public*, pg. 1420

ARNOLD INDUSTRIES, INC.; *U.S. Public*, pg. 132

ARNOLD INFORMATION TECHNOLOGY—See Arnold Communications, Inc.; *U.S. Private*, pg. 84

ARNOLD INTERACTIVE—See Arnold Communications, Inc.; *U.S. Private*, pg. 84

ARNOLD MACHINERY COMPANY; *U.S. Private*, pg. 84

ARNOLD MACHINERY COMPANY OF ARIZONA—See Arnold Machinery Company; *U.S. Private*, pg. 84

ARNOLD OMEGA—See Omega Environmental Inc.; *U.S. Public*, pg. 1222

THE ARNOLD PALMER GOLF COMPANY; *U.S. Public*, pg. 132

ARNOLD PROJECTS SERVICES LIMITED—See Kumagai Gumi Co., Ltd.; *Int'l*, pg. 764

ARNOLD PUBLIC RELATIONS—See Arnold Communications, Inc.; *U.S. Private*, pg. 84

ARNOLD STEEL COMPANY, INC.; *U.S. Private*, pg. 84

ARNOLD TRANSPORTATION SERVICES—See Arnold Industries, Inc.; *U.S. Public*, pg. 132

TRUMAN ARNOLD COMPANIES; *U.S. Private*, pg. 84

ARNOLD WRAGG (BOLTS & NUTS) LTD.—See Haden Maclellan Holdings plc; *Int'l*, pg. 586

ARNOLDS INTERIORS, INC.—See Huffman Koos; *U.S. Private*, pg. 546

ARNOTTS LIMITED—See Campbell Soup Company; *U.S. Public*, pg. 299

ARNOTTS PLC; *Int'l*, pg. 81

THE ARO CORPORATION—See Ingersoll-Rand Company; *U.S. Public*, pg. 877

ARO CORPORATION S.A.R.L.—See Ingersoll-Rand Company; *U.S. Public*, pg. 877

ARO FLUID PRODUCTS DIVISION—See Ingersoll-Rand Company; *U.S. Public*, pg. 877

ARO GMBH—See Ingersoll-Rand Company; *U.S. Public*, pg. 877

N.V. ARO S.A.—See Ingersoll-Rand Company; *U.S. Public*, pg. 877

AROAIMA BAUXITE COMPANY LTD.—See Reynolds Metals Company; *U.S. Public*, pg. 1386

AROAIMA MINING COMPANY LIMITED—See Reynolds Metals Company; *U.S. Public*, pg. 1386

AROCOM MARKETING GROUP, INC.—See Meldrum & Fewsmith Communications, Inc.; *U.S. Private*, pg. 730

AROMAT CANADA INC.—See Matsushita Electric Works, Ltd.; *Int'l*, pg. 848

ARORA-MATTHEY LIMITED—See Johnson Matthey Public Limited Company; *Int'l*, pg. 714

AROS FONDKOMMISSION AB—See ABB Asea Brown Boveri (Holding) Ltd; *Int'l*, pg. 7

ADRIEN ARPEL—See Alfin, Inc.; *U.S. Public*, pg. 40

PAUL ARPIN VANLINES, INC.; *U.S. Private*, pg. 85

ARRENDADORA BANCOMER—See Bancomer, S.A.; *Int'l*, pg. 145

ARRENDADORA COMERMEX S.A. DE C.V.—See BankAmerica Corporation; *U.S. Public*, pg. 182

ARRENDADORA GORVAC S.A. DE C.V.—See Tootsie Roll Industries, Inc.; *U.S. Public*, pg. 1621

ARRHYTHMIA RESEARCH TECHNOLOGY, INC.; *U.S. Public*, pg. 133

ARRINGTON-HILLGATE INTERNATIONAL—See Arrington Travel Center Inc.; *U.S. Private*, pg. 85

ARRINGTON TRAVEL CENTER INC.; *U.S. Private*, pg. 85

ARROSTO COFFEE COMPANY—See Koo Koo Roo, Inc.; *U.S. Public*, pg. 966

ARROW AFRICA (PTY.), LTD.—See Arrow International, Inc.; *U.S. Public*, pg. 135

ARROW AUTOMOTIVE INDUSTRIES, INC.; *U.S. Public*, pg. 133

ARROW BUILDING CENTERS—See Consolidated Lumber Co.; *U.S. Private*, pg. 265

ARROW CHEVROLET, INC.; *U.S. Private*, pg. 85

ARROW COMMERCIAL SYSTEMS DIV.—See Arrow Electronics, Inc.; *U.S. Public*, pg. 133

ARROW COMMERCIAL SYSTEMS GROUP—See Arrow Electronics, Inc.; *U.S. Public*, pg. 133

ARROW CZECH REPUBLIC—See Arrow International, Inc.; *U.S. Public*, pg. 135

ARROW DE CENTRO-AMERICA LTDA.—See Bidermann International S.A.; *Int'l*, pg. 194

ARROW DE MEXICO S.A. DE C.V.—See Bidermann International S.A.; *Int'l*, pg. 194

ARROW DEUTSCHLAND G.M.B.H.—See Arrow International, Inc.; *U.S. Public*, pg. 135

ARROW ELECTRONICS, INC.; *U.S. Public*, pg. 133

ARROW FASTENER CO., INC.; *U.S. Private*, pg. 85

ARROW FINANCIAL CORPORATION; *U.S. Public*, pg. 135

ARROW FRANCE S.A.—See Arrow International, Inc.; *U.S. Public*, pg. 135

ARROW FREIGHT CORPORATION—See Berguet Corporation; *Int'l*, pg. 186

ARROW GEAR COMPANY; *U.S. Private*, pg. 85

ARROW GROUP INDUSTRIES, INC.—See Leonard Green & Partners; *U.S. Private*, pg. 477

ARROW HART WIRING DEVICES—See Cooper Industries, Inc.; *U.S. Public*, pg. 444

ARROW HELLAS AEE—See Arrow International, Inc.; *U.S. Public*, pg. 135

ARROW HOLLAND MEDICAL PRODUCTS B.V.—See Arrow International, Inc.; *U.S. Public*, pg. 135

ARROW IBERIA, S.A.—See Arrow International, Inc.; *U.S. Public*, pg. 135

ARROW INDUSTRIES, INC.—See ConAgra, Inc.; *U.S. Public*, pg. 426

ARROW INTERNACIONAL DE MEXICO S.A.—See Arrow International, Inc.; *U.S. Public*, pg. 135

ARROW INTERNATIONAL; *U.S. Private*, pg. 85

ARROW INTERNATIONAL, INC.; *U.S. Public*, pg. 135

ARROW JAPAN, LTD.-MAIN OFFICE—See Arrow International, Inc.; *U.S. Public*, pg. 135

ARROW JAPAN, LTD.-SALES OFFICE—See Arrow International, Inc.; *U.S. Public*, pg. 135

ARROW MEDICAL PRODUCTS LTD.—See Arrow International, Inc.; *U.S. Public*, pg. 135

ARROW METAL PRODUCTS CORPORATION; *U.S. Private*, pg. 85

ARROW OILFIELD SERVICE COMPANY—See Texas Pacific Group; *U.S. Private*, pg. 1078

ARROW PAPER SUPPLY FOOD CO.—See JP Foodservice, Inc.; *U.S. Public*, pg. 918

ARROW PNEUMATICS CO. INC.; *U.S. Private*, pg. 85

ARROW/SCHWEBER ELECTRONICS—See Arrow Electronics, Inc.; *U.S. Public*, pg. 133

ARROW/SCHWEBER ELECTRONICS GROUP—See Arrow Electronics, Inc.; *U.S. Public*, pg. 133

ARROW SHIRT COMPANY—See Bidermann International S.A.; *Int'l*, pg. 194

THE ARROW SHIRT COMPANY—See Bidermann International S.A.; *Int'l*, pg. 194

ARROW SINTERED PRODUCTS—See Arrow Pneumatics Co. Inc.; *U.S. Private*, pg. 85

ARROW-SYSCO FOOD SERVICES, INC.—See Sysco Corporation; *U.S. Public*, pg. 1551

ARROW TANK & ENGINEERING CO.; *U.S. Private*, pg. 85

ARROW THOMPSON METALS—See Thompson Steel Co., Inc.; *U.S. Private*, pg. 1083

ARROW TRU-LINE, INC.; *U.S. Private*, pg. 85

ARROWHEAD CONTAINERS INC.—See Southern Missouri Containers Inc.; *U.S. Public*, pg. 1017

ARROWHEAD HOLDING CORPORATION; *U.S. Private*, pg. 86

ARROWHEAD MILLS, INC.; *U.S. Public*, pg. 86

ARROWHEAD MOUNTAIN SPRING WATER COMPANY—See Nestle S.A.; *Int'l*, pg. 919

ARROWLIFT SYSTEMS—See Mustang Tractor & Equip. Co.; *U.S. Private*, pg. 769

ARROWOOD-SOUTHERN COMPANY—See Norfolk Southern Corporation; *U.S. Public*, pg. 1190

ART GRAPHIC CONVERTERS, INC.—See Wurzburg, Inc.; *U.S. Private*, pg. 1193

ART IRON, INC.; *U.S. Private*, pg. 86

ART TECHNOLOGY GROUP; *U.S. Private*, pg. 86

ART VAN FURNITURE INC.; *U.S. Private*, pg. 86

ARTCO-BELL CORPORATION; *U.S. Private*, pg. 86

ARTE FILM—See Testa International; *Int'l*, pg. 1377

ARTE Y CEMENTO SA—See Reed Elsevier plc; *Int'l*, pg. 1099

ARTEAGA, SOCIEDAD ANOMIMA, "ARTEAGA, S.A."—See Reynolds Metals Company; *U.S. Public*, pg. 1386

ARTEC MANUFACTURING—See Kimball International, Inc.; *U.S. Public*, pg. 957

ARTECON, INC.—See Flambeau Corporation; *U.S. Private*, pg. 409

ARTEE-WRAP SPUN—See Culp, Inc.; *U.S. Public*, pg. 467

ARTEK OY AB—See Proventus AB; *Int'l*, pg. 1072

ARTEL UTAH SCIENTIFIC, INC.—See Artel Video Systems, Inc.; *U.S. Private*, pg. 86

ARTEL VIDEO SYSTEMS, INC.; *U.S. Private*, pg. 86

ARTEMIS MANAGEMENT SYSTEMS—See Gores Technology Group; *U.S. Private*, pg. 465

ARTESANIAS BAJA, S.A.—See Hanson PLC; *Int'l*, pg. 594

ARTESIAN RESOURCES CORPORATION; *U.S. Public*, pg. 135

ARTESIAN WASTEWATER MANAGEMENT INC.—See Artesian Resources Corporation; *U.S. Public*, pg. 135

ARTESIAN WATER COMPANY, INC.—See Artesian Resources Corporation; *U.S. Public*, pg. 135
ARTEX LTD.—See BPB Industries PLC; *Int'l*, pg. 122
ARTHROTEK, INC.—See Biomet, Inc.; *U.S. Public*, pg. 231
ARTHUR ANDERSEN—See Andersen Worldwide; *U.S. Private*, pg. 72
ARTHUR D. LITTLE INTERNATIONAL, INC.—See Arthur D. Little, Inc.; *U.S. Private*, pg. 671
ARTHUR-JONES LITHOGRAPHING LIMITED—See Jannock Limited; *Int'l*, pg. 698
ARTHUR TREACHER'S, INC.; *U.S. Public*, pg. 136
ARTIC N.V. S.A.—See TLC Beatrice International Holdings Inc.; *U.S. Private*, pg. 1064
ARTICHOKE INDUSTRIES, INC.; *U.S. Private*, pg. 86
ARTISAN ELECTRONICS CORPORATION—See Morgan Crucible Co. Plc; *Int'l*, pg. 892
ARTISOFT, INC.; *U.S. Public*, pg. 136
ARTIST GRAPHICS—See Control Systems Inc.; *U.S. Private*, pg. 271
ARTISTCARE PTY. LTD.—See Esselte AB; *Int'l*, pg. 460
ARTISTIC BRASS DIV.—See Masco Corporation; *U.S. Public*, pg. 1054
ARTISTIC CARTON COMPANY; *U.S. Private*, pg. 87
ARTISTIC GREETINGS; *U.S. Public*, pg. 136
ARTLAND NEDERLAND B.V.—See Nestle S.A.; *Int'l*, pg. 918
ARTRA GROUP INCORPORATED; *U.S. Public*, pg. 136
ARTS & CRAFTS PRESS—See Continental Graphics Holdings, Inc.; *U.S. Private*, pg. 268
ARTS & ENTERTAINMENT NETWORK/ABC/NBC—See The Walt Disney Company; *U.S. Public*, pg. 512
ART'S-WAY MANUFACTURING CO., INC.; *U.S. Public*, pg. 136
ARTUS, INC.—See Forest City Enterprises, Inc.; *U.S. Public*, pg. 668
ARTUS MINERALQUELLEN GMBH & CO. KG—See Solvay S.A.; *Int'l*, pg. 1279
ARTWOOD PRODUCTS—See Semac Industries Inc.; *U.S. Private*, pg. 983
ARUN TECHNOLOGY LTD.—See The Roxboro Group PLC; *Int'l*, pg. 1130
THE ARUNDEL CORPORATION—See Florida Rock Industries, Inc.; *U.S. Public*, pg. 656
ARUS GROUP—See Arbed S.A.; *Int'l*, pg. 79
PT ARUTMIN INDONESIA—See The Broken Hill Proprietary Company Limited; *Int'l*, pg. 224
ARVEY PAPER & OFFICE PRODUCTS—See International Paper Company; *U.S. Public*, pg. 903
ARVID HOGSTROM AB—See Saint-Gobain; *Int'l*, pg. 1172
ARVIDA—See JMB Realty Corporation; *U.S. Private*, pg. 578
ARVIN AUTOMOTIVE OF CANADA, LTD.—See Arvin Industries, Inc.; *U.S. Public*, pg. 137
ARVIN FINANCE CORP.—See Arvin Industries, Inc.; *U.S. Public*, pg. 137
ARVIN INDUSTRIES, INC.; *U.S. Public*, pg. 136
ARYA OFFSHORE SERVICES PVT LTD.—See Keppel Corporation Limited; *Int'l*, pg. 731
ASAHI ADVERTISING INC.; *Int'l*, pg. 81
ASAHI AMERICA INC.—See Asahi Mutual Life Insurance Company; *Int'l*, pg. 85
ASAHI/AMERICA, INC.; *U.S. Public*, pg. 137
ASAHI BANK BOMBAY REPRESENTATIVE OFFICE—See The Asahi Bank, Ltd.; *Int'l*, pg. 83
ASAHI BANK BUILDING CO., LTD.—See The Asahi Bank, Ltd.; *Int'l*, pg. 82
ASAHI BANK BUILDING MAINTENANCE CO., LTD.—See The Asahi Bank, Ltd.; *Int'l*, pg. 82
ASAHI BANK BUSINESS SERVICE CO., LTD.—See The Asahi Bank, Ltd.; *Int'l*, pg. 82
ASAHI BANK CAREER SERVICE CO., LTD.—See The Asahi Bank, Ltd.; *Int'l*, pg. 82
ASAHI BANK (DEUTSCHLAND) GMBH—See The Asahi Bank, Ltd.; *Int'l*, pg. 83
ASAHI BANK FACTORING CO., LTD.—See The Asahi Bank, Ltd.; *Int'l*, pg. 82
ASAHI BANK FINANCE SERVICE CO., LTD.—See The Asahi Bank, Ltd.; *Int'l*, pg. 82
ASAHI BANK INVESTMENT CO., LTD.—See The Asahi Bank, Ltd.; *Int'l*, pg. 82
ASAHI BANK JIMU SERVICE CO., LTD.—See The Asahi Bank, Ltd.; *Int'l*, pg. 82
ASAHI BANK KOSEI SERVICE CO., LTD.—See The Asahi Bank, Ltd.; *Int'l*, pg. 82
THE ASAHI BANK, LTD.; *Int'l*, pg. 81
ASAHI BANK LOAN BUSINESS CO., LTD.—See The Asahi Bank, Ltd.; *Int'l*, pg. 82
ASAHI BANK (NEDERLAND) N.V.—See The Asahi Bank, Ltd.; *Int'l*, pg. 82
ASAHI BANK PROPERTY CO., LTD.—See The Asahi Bank, Ltd.; *Int'l*, pg. 82
ASAHI BANK RESEARCH INSTITUTE CO., LTD.—See The Asahi Bank, Ltd.; *Int'l*, pg. 82
ASAHI BANK (SCHWEIZ) AG—See The Asahi Bank, Ltd.; *Int'l*, pg. 83
ASAHI BANK SOGO SERVICE CO., LTD.—See The Asahi Bank, Ltd.; *Int'l*, pg. 82
ASAHI BANK SUPPLY CO., LTD.—See The Asahi Bank, Ltd.; *Int'l*, pg. 82
ASAHI BANK SYDNEY BRANCH—See The Asahi Bank, Ltd.; *Int'l*, pg. 82
ASAHI BREWERIES LTD.; *Int'l*, pg. 83
ASAHI BREWERIES U.S.A., INC.—See Asahi Breweries Ltd.; *Int'l*, pg. 83
ASAHI CARD CO., LTD.—See The Asahi Bank, Ltd.; *Int'l*, pg. 82
ASAHI CHEMICAL INDUSTRY - BEIJING—See Asahi Chemical Industry Co., Ltd.; *Int'l*, pg. 84
ASAHI CHEMICAL INDUSTRY CO., LTD.; *Int'l*, pg. 83
ASAHI CHEMICAL INDUSTRY - LONDON—See Asahi Chemical Industry Co., Ltd.; *Int'l*, pg. 84
ASAHI CHEMICAL INDUSTRY - MILAN—See Asahi Chemical Industry Co., Ltd.; *Int'l*, pg. 84

ASAHI CHEMICAL INDUSTRY - SHANGHAI OFFICE—See Asahi Chemical Industry Co., Ltd.; *Int'l*, pg. 84
ASAHI-CIBA LIMITED-MIZUSHIMA PLANT—See Novartis AG; *Int'l*, pg. 975
ASAHI-CIBA LIMITED-OSAKA SALES OFFICE—See Novartis AG; *Int'l*, pg. 975
ASAHI-CIBA LIMITED-R&D DEPARTMENT—See Novartis AG; *Int'l*, pg. 975
ASAHI-CIBA LTD.—See Novartis AG; *Int'l*, pg. 974
ASAHI ELECTRIC MACHINERY CO., LTD.—See The Furukawa Electric Co., Ltd.; *Int'l*, pg. 530
ASAHI ELECTRONICS (SINGAPORE) PTE., LTD.—See Casio Computer Co., Ltd.; *Int'l*, pg. 274
ASAHI ELECTRONICS (THAILAND) CO., LTD.—See Casio Computer Co., Ltd.; *Int'l*, pg. 274
ASAHI FACILITY MANAGEMENT INC.—See Takenaka Corporation; *Int'l*, pg. 1351
ASAHI FINANCE (GUAM) INC.—See Asahi Mutual Life Insurance Company; *Int'l*, pg. 82
ASAHI GLASS AMERICA, INC.—See Asahi Glass Co., Ltd.; *Int'l*, pg. 84
ASAHI GLASS CO., LTD.; *Int'l*, pg. 84
ASAHI GLASS EUROPE B.V.—See Asahi Glass Co., Ltd.; *Int'l*, pg. 84
ASAHI INDUSTRIES CO. LTD.—See The Saison Group; *Int'l*, pg. 1178
ASAHI INDUSTRIES (MALAYSIA) SDN. BHD.—See Casio Computer Co., Ltd.; *Int'l*, pg. 274
ASAHI INTERNATIONAL LTD.—See Asahi Mutual Life Insurance Company; *Int'l*, pg. 85
ASAHI INVESTMENT AUSTRALIA LTD.—See Asahi Mutual Life Insurance Company; *Int'l*, pg. 85
ASAHI INVESTMENT MANAGEMENT CO., LTD.—See The Asahi Bank, Ltd.; *Int'l*, pg. 82
ASAHI KOGYO CO., LTD.—See Hitachi, Ltd.; *Int'l*, pg. 621
ASAHI KOMAG COMPANY LIMITED—See Komag, Incorporated; *U.S. Public*, pg. 966
ASAHI LIFE INVESTMENT EUROPE LTD.—See Asahi Mutual Life Insurance Company; *Int'l*, pg. 85
ASAHI LIFE INVESTMENT HONG KONG LIMITED—See Asahi Mutual Life Insurance Company; *Int'l*, pg. 85
ASAHI METALS (HK) LTD.—See Axel Johnson AB; *Int'l*, pg. 710
ASAHI MUTUAL LIFE INSURANCE COMPANY; *Int'l*, pg. 85
ASAHI MUTUAL LIFE INSURANCE CO.-TAMA HOME OFFICE—See Asahi Mutual Life Insurance Company; *Int'l*, pg. 85
ASAHI-OLIN LTD.—See Olin Corporation; *U.S. Public*, pg. 1219
ASAHI OPTICAL CO., LTD.; *Int'l*, pg. 85
ASAHI OPTICAL (INTERNATIONAL) LTD.—See Asahi Optical Co., Ltd.; *Int'l*, pg. 85
ASAHI ORIKOMI CENTER, LTD.—See Daiko Advertising, Inc.; *Int'l*, pg. 366
ASAHI-PENN CHEMICAL COMPANY LIMITED—See PPG Industries, Inc.; *U.S. Public*, pg. 1245
ASAHI PROPERTY AUSTRALIA PTY. LTD.—See Asahi Mutual Life Insurance Company; *Int'l*, pg. 85
ASAHI PROPERTY BELGIUM S.A./N.V.—See Asahi Mutual Life Insurance Company; *Int'l*, pg. 85
ASAHI PROPERTY U.K.—See Asahi Mutual Life Insurance Company; *Int'l*, pg. 85
ASAHI SECURITIES CO., LTD.—See The Asahi Bank, Ltd.; *Int'l*, pg. 82
ASAHI SOGO KANRI CO., LTD.—See The Asahi Bank, Ltd.; *Int'l*, pg. 82
ASAHI TRUST AND BANKING CO., LTD.—See The Asahi Bank, Ltd.; *Int'l*, pg. 82
ASAHI TRUST (NEDERLAND) B.V.—See The Asahi Bank, Ltd.; *Int'l*, pg. 82
ASAHIGIN GUARANTEE CO., LTD.—See The Asahi Bank, Ltd.; *Int'l*, pg. 82
ASAHIGIN LEASING CO., LTD.—See The Asahi Bank, Ltd.; *Int'l*, pg. 82
ASAHIGIN SOFTWARE CO., LTD.—See The Asahi Bank, Ltd.; *Int'l*, pg. 82
ASAHIGIN SYSTEMS CO., LTD.—See The Asahi Bank, Ltd.; *Int'l*, pg. 82
ASAHIKASEI ASIA PTE. LTD.—See Asahi Chemical Industry Co., Ltd.; *Int'l*, pg. 84
ASAHIKAWA MILL—See Nippon Paper Industries Company Limited; *Int'l*, pg. 938
ASAMA PTE. LTD., ASIA—See Straube Regional Center LLC; *U.S. Private*, pg. 1046
ASAMAGIKEN CO., LTD.—See Honda Motor Co., Ltd.; *Int'l*, pg. 634
ASARCO EXPLORATION CO.—See Asarco Incorporated; *U.S. Public*, pg. 138
ASARCO INCORPORATED; *U.S. Public*, pg. 137
ASARCO INTERNATIONAL CORP.—See Asarco Incorporated; *U.S. Public*, pg. 138
ASARCO SANTA CRUZ—See Asarco Incorporated; *U.S. Public*, pg. 138
ASATSU AMERICA INC.—See Asatsu Inc.; *Int'l*, pg. 86
ASATSU (DEUTSCHLAND) GMBH—See Asatsu Inc.; *Int'l*, pg. 86
ASATSU EUROPE B.V.—See Asatsu Inc.; *Int'l*, pg. 86
ASATSU HONG KONG LTD.—See Asatsu Inc.; *Int'l*, pg. 86
ASATSU INC.; *Int'l*, pg. 85
ASATSU INTERNATIONAL INC.—See Asatsu Inc.; *Int'l*, pg. 86
ASBACH GMBH & CO.—See Diageo Plc; *Int'l*, pg. 412
ASBURY AUTOMOTIVE GROUP; *U.S. Private*, pg. 87
ASBURY CARBONS, INC.; *U.S. Private*, pg. 87
ASBURY EQUIPMENT—See Asbury Carbons, Inc.; *U.S. Private*, pg. 87
ASBURY FLUXMASTER—See Asbury Carbons, Inc.; *U.S. Private*, pg. 87
ASBURY GRAPHITE INC. OF CALIFORNIA—See Asbury Carbons, Inc.; *U.S. Private*, pg. 87
ASBURY GRAPHITE MILLS, INC.—See Asbury Carbons, Inc.; *U.S. Private*, pg. 87

ASBURY LOUISIANA, INC.—See Asbury Carbons, Inc.; *U.S. Private*, pg. 87
ASBURY PARK PRESS, INC.—See Gannett Company, Inc.; *U.S. Public*, pg. 699
ASBURY WILKINSON GRAPHITE & FOUNDRY SUPPLY CO.—See Asbury Carbons, Inc.; *U.S. Private*, pg. 87
ASBURY WORLDWIDE—See The Middleby Corporation; *U.S. Public*, pg. 1110
ASBURY WORLDWIDE, EUROPE—See The Middleby Corporation; *U.S. Public*, pg. 1110
ASBURY WORLDWIDE FRANCE—See The Middleby Corporation; *U.S. Public*, pg. 1110
ASBURY WORLDWIDE KOREA CO., LTD.—See The Middleby Corporation; *U.S. Public*, pg. 1110
ASBURY WORLDWIDE, LATIN AMERICA—See The Middleby Corporation; *U.S. Public*, pg. 1110
ASBURY WORLDWIDE MEXICO S.A. DE C.V.—See The Middleby Corporation; *U.S. Public*, pg. 1110
ASBURY WORLDWIDE, NORTH ASIA—See The Middleby Corporation; *U.S. Public*, pg. 1110
ASCAT VIDA, S.A. DE SEGUROS Y REASEGUROS—See Caixa d'Estalvis de Catalunya; *Int'l*, pg. 250
ASCEND COMMUNICATIONS, INC.; *U.S. Public*, pg. 138
ASCEND FINANCIAL SERVICES—See The Minnesota Mutual Life Insurance Company; *U.S. Private*, pg. 750
ASCENSEURS DROLET KONE INC.—See Kone Corporation; *Int'l*, pg. 747
ASCENSION WATER CO.—See Baton Rouge Water Works Company; *U.S. Private*, pg. 123
ASCENSORES SCHINDLER (CHILE) S.A.—See Schindler Holding AG; *Int'l*, pg. 1205
ASCENSORES SCHINDLER DE COLOMBIA S.A.—See Schindler Holding AG; *Int'l*, pg. 1205
ASCENSORES SCHINDLER DE VENEZUELA S.A.—See Schindler Holding AG; *Int'l*, pg. 1205
ASCENSORES SCHINDLER DEL PERU S.A.—See Schindler Holding AG; *Int'l*, pg. 1205
ASCENSORES SCHINDLER S.A.—See Schindler Holding AG; *Int'l*, pg. 1205
ASCENT ENTERTAINMENT GROUP, INC.; *U.S. Public*, pg. 138
ASCHE AG—See Schering AG; *Int'l*, pg. 1203
ASCO CONTROLS B.V.—See Emerson Electric Co.; *U.S. Public*, pg. 575
ASCO GENERAL SUPPLIES (FAR EAST) LTD.—See Pentland Group PLC; *Int'l*, pg. 1036
ASCO G.M.B.H. & CO.—See Emerson Electric Co.; *U.S. Public*, pg. 575
ASCO (JAPAN) CO. LIMITED—See Emerson Electric Co.; *U.S. Public*, pg. 575
ASCO (UK)—See Emerson Electric Co.; *U.S. Public*, pg. 575
ASCOLECTRIC LIMITED—See Emerson Electric Co.; *U.S. Public*, pg. 575
ASCOM AUSTRIA GES.MBH—See Ascom Holding AG; *Int'l*, pg. 86
ASCOM AUTELCA AG—See Ascom Holding AG; *Int'l*, pg. 86
ASCOM AUTOMATION INC.—See Ascom Holding AG; *Int'l*, pg. 86
ASCOM AUTOMATION S.R.L.—See Ascom Holding AG; *Int'l*, pg. 86
ASCOM BUSINESS SYSTEMS AG—See Ascom Holding AG; *Int'l*, pg. 86
ASCOM CANADA LIMITED—See Ascom Holding AG; *Int'l*, pg. 86
ASCOM EBS ELEKTRONISCHE BANK SYSTEME GMBH—See Ascom Holding AG; *Int'l*, pg. 86
ASCOM ELSYDEL SA—See Ascom Holding AG; *Int'l*, pg. 87
ASCOM ENERGY SYSTEMS—See Ascom Holding AG; *Int'l*, pg. 86
ASCOM ENERGY SYSTEMS AB—See Ascom Holding AG; *Int'l*, pg. 87
ASCOM ENERGY SYSTEMS OY—See Ascom Holding AG; *Int'l*, pg. 87
ASCOM ERICSSON TRANSMISSION AG—See Ascom Holding AG; *Int'l*, pg. 86
ASCOM ERICSSON TRANSMISSION AG—See Telefonaktiebolaget LM Ericsson; *Int'l*, pg. 1364
ASCOM ERICSSON TRANSMISSION LTD.—See Telefonaktiebolaget LM Ericsson; *Int'l*, pg. 1365
ASCOM FINANZ AG—See Ascom Holding AG; *Int'l*, pg. 86
ASCOM FINTEL OY—See Ascom Holding AG; *Int'l*, pg. 87
ASCOM FRAKO GMBH—See Ascom Holding AG; *Int'l*, pg. 87
ASCOM GCT GMBH & CO.—See Ascom Holding AG; *Int'l*, pg. 87
ASCOM GMBH—See Ascom Holding AG; *Int'l*, pg. 87
ASCOM HASLER AG—See Ascom Holding AG; *Int'l*, pg. 86
ASCOM HASLER AG—See Telefonaktiebolaget LM Ericsson; *Int'l*, pg. 1365
ASCOM HASLER BV—See Ascom Holding AG; *Int'l*, pg. 87
ASCOM HASLER GMBH—See Ascom Holding AG; *Int'l*, pg. 87
ASCOM HASLER (JAPAN) LTD.—See Ascom Holding AG; *Int'l*, pg. 87
ASCOM HASLER LTD.—See Ascom Holding AG; *Int'l*, pg. 87
ASCOM HASLER MAILING SYSTEMS AG—See Ascom Holding AG; *Int'l*, pg. 86
ASCOM HASLER MAILING SYSTEMS, INC.—See Ascom Holding AG; *Int'l*, pg. 86
ASCOM HASLER SA—See Ascom Holding AG; *Int'l*, pg. 87
ASCOM HASLER SPA—See Ascom Holding AG; *Int'l*, pg. 87
ASCOM HOLDING AG; *Int'l*, pg. 86
ASCOM HONGKONG LTD.—See Ascom Holding AG; *Int'l*, pg. 87
ASCOM HPF SA—See Ascom Holding AG; *Int'l*, pg. 87
ASCOM IMMOBILIEN AG—See Ascom Holding AG; *Int'l*, pg. 86

ASCOM INFRASYS AG—See Ascom Holding AG; *Int'l,* pg. 86
ASCOM INFRASYS GMBH—See Ascom Holding AG; *Int'l,* pg. 87
ASCOM INSTALLATIONEN AG—See Ascom Holding AG; *Int'l,* pg. 87
ASCOM MONETEL SA—See Ascom Holding AG; *Int'l,* pg. 86
ASCOM NEXION INC.—See Ascom Holding AG; *Int'l,* pg. 87
ASCOM NORDIC A/S—See Ascom Holding AG; *Int'l,* pg. 87
ASCOM SA—See Ascom Holding AG; *Int'l,* pg. 87
ASCOM SAFNAT SPA—See Ascom Holding AG; *Int'l,* pg. 87
ASCOM SYSTEC AG—See Ascom Holding AG; *Int'l,* pg. 86
ASCOM TATECO AB—See Ascom Holding AG; *Int'l,* pg. 87
ASCOM TATECO AG—See Ascom Holding AG; *Int'l,* pg. 87
ASCOM TATECO GMBH—See Ascom Holding AG; *Int'l,* pg. 87
ASCOM TCS SPA—See Ascom Holding AG; *Int'l,* pg. 87
ASCOM TECH AG—See Ascom Holding AG; *Int'l,* pg. 86
ASCOM TELE-NOVA LTD.—See Ascom Holding AG; *Int'l,* pg. 87
ASCOM TELECOMMUNICATIONS LTD.—See Ascom Holding AG; *Int'l,* pg. 87
ASCOM TELEMATIC AG—See Ascom Holding AG; *Int'l,* pg. 86
ASCOM TELETRON B.V.—See Ascom Holding AG; *Int'l,* pg. 87
ASCOM TIMEPLEX—See Ascom Holding AG; *Int'l,* pg. 86
ASCOM TIMEPLEX AUSTRALIA PTY. LTD.—See Ascom Holding AG; *Int'l,* pg. 87
ASCOM TIMEPLEX CANADA INC.—See Ascom Holding AG; *Int'l,* pg. 87
ASCOM TIMEPLEX FAR EAST LTD.—See Ascom Holding AG; *Int'l,* pg. 87
ASCOM TIMEPLEX GMBH—See Ascom Holding AG; *Int'l,* pg. 87
ASCOM TIMEPLEX INC.—See Ascom Holding AG; *Int'l,* pg. 87
ASCOM TIMEPLEX LTD.—See Ascom Holding AG; *Int'l,* pg. 87
ASCOM TIMEPLEX LTD. (NEW ZEALAND)—See Ascom Holding AG; *Int'l,* pg. 87
ASCOM TIMEPLEX SA—See Ascom Holding AG; *Int'l,* pg. 87
ASCOM ZARLI BV—See Ascom Holding AG; *Int'l,* pg. 87
ASCOM ZEAG—See Ascom Holding AG; *Int'l,* pg. 86
ASCOM ZELCOM AG—See Ascom Holding AG; *Int'l,* pg. 86
ASCOMATICA S.A. DE C.V.—See Emerson Electric Co.; *U.S. Public,* pg. 576
ASCOMATION PTY. LTD.—See Emerson Electric Co.; *U.S. Public,* pg. 576
ASCOMETAL—See Groupe Usinor; *Int'l,* pg. 570
ASCONA (BELGIE) P.V.B.A.—See Melitta Unternehmensgruppe Bentz KG; *Int'l,* pg. 857
ASCOR, INC.—See Giga-Tronics Incorporated; *U.S. Public,* pg. 743
ASCOT CIGARETTE CO. LTD.—See Dubek Ltd.; *Int'l,* pg. 421
ASCOT HOLDINGS PLC; *Int'l,* pg. 87
ASCOTT INTERNATIONAL MANAGEMENT PTE. LTD.—See Scotts Holdings Limited; *Int'l,* pg. 1212
THE ASCOTT JAKARTA/BENCHMARK SERVICE—See Scotts Holdings Limited; *Int'l,* pg. 1212
THE ASCOTT KUALA LUMPUR—See Scotts Holdings Limited; *Int'l,* pg. 1212
THE ASCOTT MAYFAIR—See Scotts Holdings Limited; *Int'l,* pg. 1212
THE ASCOTT SINGAPORE—See Scotts Holdings Limited; *Int'l,* pg. 1212
ASCOVAL INDUSTRIA E COMMERCIO LTDA.—See Emerson Electric Co.; *U.S. Public,* pg. 576
ASCUR MANNHEIM VERSICHERUNGSVERMITTLUNGSGES. GMBH—See Corange Limited; *Int'l,* pg. 331
ASDOR INC.—See Aluminum Company of America; *U.S. Public,* pg. 61
ASE RENT, S.A. DE C.V.—See Corporacion MAPFRE, Compania Internacional de Reaseguros, S.A.; *Int'l,* pg. 334
ASEA BICC CAPACITORS LTD.—See ABB Asea Brown Boveri (Holding) Ltd.; *Int'l,* pg. 7
ASEA BROWN BOVERI AG—See ABB Asea Brown Boveri (Holding) Ltd.; *Int'l,* pg. 1
ASEA BROWN BOVERI AKTIENGESELLSCHAFT—See ABB Asea Brown Boveri (Holding) Ltd.; *Int'l,* pg. 2
ASEA BROWN BOVERI AKTIENGESELLSCHAFT MBH—See ABB Asea Brown Boveri (Holding) Ltd.; *Int'l,* pg. 8
ASEA BROWN BOVERI DANMARK A/S—See ABB Asea Brown Boveri (Holding) Ltd.; *Int'l,* pg. 8
ASEA BROWN BOVERI INDUSTRIAL S.A.—See ABB Asea Brown Boveri (Holding) Ltd.; *Int'l,* pg. 3
ASEA BROWN BOVERI LTD.—See ABB Asea Brown Boveri (Holding) Ltd.; *Int'l,* pg. 2
ASEA BROWN BOVERI LTDA.—See ABB Asea Brown Boveri (Holding) Ltd.; *Int'l,* pg. 8
ASEA BROWN BOVERI MACHINERY SERVICE DIV.—See ABB Asea Brown Boveri (Holding) Ltd.; *Int'l,* pg. 2
ASEA BROWN BOVERI NEDERLAND B.V.—See ABB Asea Brown Boveri (Holding) Ltd.; *Int'l,* pg. 8
ASEA BROWN BOVERI S.A.—See ABB Asea Brown Boveri (Holding) Ltd.; *Int'l,* pg. 8
ASEA BROWN BOVERI SAKATI—See ABB Asea Brown Boveri (Holding) Ltd.; *Int'l,* pg. 8
ASEA BROWN BOVERI (S.E.A.) PTE. LTD.—See ABB Asea Brown Boveri (Holding) Ltd.; *Int'l,* pg. 3
ASEA HAGGLUNDS (U.K.) LTD.—See ABB Asea Brown Boveri (Holding) Ltd.; *Int'l,* pg. 8
ASEA JUMET S.A.—See ABB Asea Brown Boveri (Holding) Ltd.; *Int'l,* pg. 7

ASEA LIMITED—See ABB Asea Brown Boveri (Holding) Ltd.; *Int'l,* pg. 8
ASEA REGULADORES S.A. DE C.V.—See ABB Asea Brown Boveri (Holding) Ltd.; *Int'l,* pg. 8
ASEA S.A.—See ABB Asea Brown Boveri (Holding) Ltd.; *Int'l,* pg. 8
ASEA SKANDIA A/S—See ABB Asea Brown Boveri (Holding) Ltd.; *Int'l,* pg. 7
ASEA SKANDIA HAVEMANNS EI A/S—See ABB Asea Brown Boveri (Holding) Ltd.; *Int'l,* pg. 7
ASEA SKANDIA OY—See ABB Asea Brown Boveri (Holding) Ltd.; *Int'l,* pg. 7
ASEA TRUCK AB—See ABB Asea Brown Boveri (Holding) Ltd.; *Int'l,* pg. 7
P.T. ASEAM INDONESIA—See The Dai-Ichi Kangyo Bank, Limited; *Int'l,* pg. 362
ASEAMBANKERS MALAYSIA BERHAD—See The Dai-Ichi Kangyo Bank, Limited; *Int'l,* pg. 362
ASEGURADORA CUAUHTEMOC S.A.—See Allianz Aktiengesellschaft; *Int'l,* pg. 61
ASEGURADORA GENERAL S.A.—See Assicurazioni Generali S.p.A.; *Int'l,* pg. 90
ASEMAP, ASESORAMIENTO E INVERSIONES, S.A.—See Corporacion MAPFRE, Compania Internacional de Reaseguros, S.A.; *Int'l,* pg. 332
ASERI TELLIS AS—See Scancem AB; *Int'l,* pg. 1200
ASESORES PUBLICITARIOS, S.A.—See Young & Rubicam Inc.; *U.S. Private,* pg. 1200
ASFALTI BREITNER S.P.A.—See Redland PLC; *Int'l,* pg. 1092
ASFALTOS ESPANOLES, S.A. (ASESA)—See Compania Espanola de Petroleos, S.A. (CEPSA); *Int'l,* pg. 323
ASGARD FINANCIAL SERVICES LTDA—See Arnotts plc; *Int'l,* pg. 81
ASGROW CANADA, LTD.—See Pharmacia & Upjohn, Inc.; *Int'l,* pg. 1049
ASGROW DO BRASIL SEMENTES LTDA.—See Pharmacia & Upjohn, Inc.; *Int'l,* pg. 1049
ASGROW FRANCE S.A.—See Pharmacia & Upjohn, Inc.; *Int'l,* pg. 1049
ASGROW GMBH—See Pharmacia & Upjohn, Inc.; *Int'l,* pg. 1049
ASGROW INTERNATIONAL CORP.—See Pharmacia & Upjohn, Inc.; *Int'l,* pg. 1048
ASGROW MEXICANA S.A. DE C.V.—See Pharmacia & Upjohn, Inc.; *Int'l,* pg. 1049
ASGROW SEED COMPANY—See Pharmacia & Upjohn, Inc.; *Int'l,* pg. 1048
ASH GROVE CEMENT COMPANY; *U.S. Private,* pg. 87
ASH GROVE CEMENT COMPANY SALES OFFICE—See Ash Grove Cement Company; *U.S. Private,* pg. 87
ASH GROVE CEMENT PLANT—See Ash Grove Cement Company; *U.S. Private,* pg. 88
ASH GROVE CEMENT-WESTERN REGION CEMENT PLANT—See Ash Grove Cement Company; *U.S. Private,* pg. 88
ASH GROVE CEMENT-WESTERN REGION LIME PLANT—See Ash Grove Cement Company; *U.S. Private,* pg. 88
ASH GROVE CEMENT-WESTERN REGION QUARRY—See Ash Grove Cement Company; *U.S. Private,* pg. 87
ASH GROVE LIME PLANT—See Ash Grove Cement Company; *U.S. Private,* pg. 88
ASH GROVE MATERIALS CORP.—See Ash Grove Cement Company; *U.S. Private,* pg. 88
ASH INSTRUMENTS DIVISION, DENTSPLY LTD.—See Dentsply International Inc.; *U.S. Public,* pg. 499
SAM ASH MUSIC CORP.; *U.S. Private,* pg. 88
ASHBY & HORNER FURNISHINGS LTD.—See The Peninsular and Oriental Steam Navigation Company; *Int'l,* pg. 1032
ASHBY & HORNER JOINERY LTD.—See The Peninsular and Oriental Steam Navigation Company; *Int'l,* pg. 1032
ASHBY & HORNER LTD.—See The Peninsular and Oriental Steam Navigation Company; *Int'l,* pg. 1032
ASHBY & HORNER MASONRY LTD.—See The Peninsular and Oriental Steam Navigation Company; *Int'l,* pg. 1032
ASHCOTT LTD.—See Hewlett-Packard Company; *U.S. Public,* pg. 816
ASHDOWN PRESS LTD.—See Shandwick International Plc; *Int'l,* pg. 1226
ASHER CANDY COMPANY—See Marvel Entertainment Group; *U.S. Public,* pg. 1052
ASHER/GOULD ADVERTISING, INC.; *U.S. Private,* pg. 88
ASHER/GOULD ADVERTISING, INC. - LAS VEGAS—See Asher/Gould Advertising, Inc.; *U.S. Private,* pg. 88
ASHERMAN—See Great Plains Manufacturing, Inc.; *U.S. Private,* pg. 475
ASHEVILLE CITIZEN TIMES—See Gannett Company, Inc.; *U.S. Public,* pg. 699
ASHEVILLE INDUSTRIES, INC.—See Newport News Shipbuilding, Inc.; *U.S. Public,* pg. 1180
ASHEVILLE LABORATORY—See Pace Analytical Services; *U.S. Private,* pg. 829
ASHFIELD MEDICAL SYSTEMS, LIMITED—See Furon Company; *U.S. Public,* pg. 689
ASHIKAGA BANK; *Int'l,* pg. 88
ASHLAND-AVEBENE—See Ashland, Inc.; *U.S. Public,* pg. 139
ASHLAND CHEMICAL—See Ashland, Inc.; *U.S. Public,* pg. 139
ASHLAND CHEMICAL CANADA, LTD.—See Ashland, Inc.; *U.S. Public,* pg. 139
ASHLAND CHEMICAL ITALIANA S.P.A.—See Ashland, Inc.; *U.S. Public,* pg. 139
ASHLAND CHEMICAL LTD.—See Ashland, Inc.; *U.S. Public,* pg. 139
ASHLAND-DAVIS COMPANY—See Saint-Gobain; *Int'l,* pg. 1171
ASHLAND DE MEXICO S.A. DE C.V.—See Ashland, Inc.; *U.S. Public,* pg. 139
ASHLAND, INC.; *U.S. Public,* pg. 138

ASHLAND OIL INTL. LTD.—See Ashland, Inc.; *U.S. Public,* pg. 139
ASHLAND OIL (NIGERIA) CO., LTD.—See Ashland, Inc.; *U.S. Public,* pg. 140
ASHLAND PARTCIPACOES LTD.—See Ashland, Inc.; *U.S. Public,* pg. 140
ASHLAND SERVICES COMPANY—See Ashland, Inc.; *U.S. Public,* pg. 139
ASHLAND-SUEDCHEMIE-KERNFEST GMBH—See Ashland, Inc.; *U.S. Public,* pg. 140
B.V. ASHLAND-SUEDCHEMIE V.H. NECOF—See Ashland, Inc.; *U.S. Public,* pg. 140
ASHLEY & ROCK LTD.—See Wolseley Plc; *Int'l,* pg. 1511
ASHLEY CARPET—See Shaw Industries, Inc.; *U.S. Public,* pg. 1464
ASHLEY, DREW & NORTHERN RAILWAY CO.—See Georgia-Pacific Corporation; *U.S. Public,* pg. 736
ASHLEY INTERNATIONAL & PASCHEN; *U.S. Private,* pg. 88
ASHLEY SHOPS (IRELAND) LTD.—See Laura Ashley Holdings Plc; *Int'l,* pg. 804
ASHTEAD GROUP PLC; *Int'l,* pg. 88
ASHTON DRAKE DIV.—See Bradford Exchange Ltd.; *U.S. Private,* pg. 163
ASHTON/SCHOLASTIC PTY. LTD.—See Scholastic Corporation; *U.S. Public,* pg. 1440
ASHWORTH BROS., INC.; *U.S. Public,* pg. 89
ASHWORTH YOUNG & CO., LTD.—See Pentland Group PLC; *Int'l,* pg. 1035
ASIA CABLE ENGINEERING CO., PTE. LTD. (ACECO)—See The Furukawa Electric Co., Ltd.; *Int'l,* pg. 530
ASIA CITI ENTERPRISE (H.K.) LTD.—See Citizen Watch Company, Ltd.; *Int'l,* pg. 295
ASIA COMPUTERWORLD—See International Data Group; *U.S. Private,* pg. 569
ASIA COMPUTERWORLD COMMUNICATIONS—See International Data Group; *U.S. Private,* pg. 569
ASIA ELECTRONICS INC.—See Toshiba Corporation; *Int'l,* pg. 1402
ASIA EQUITY HOLDING LIMITED—See Finance One Public Company Limited; *Int'l,* pg. 485
ASIA FINANCIAL HOLDINGS, LTD.—See The Tokai Bank, Limited; *Int'l,* pg. 1391
ASIA FLEXIBLE AUTOMOTIVE TECH. CORP.—See General Automotive Corporation; *U.S. Private,* pg. 444
ASIA INDUSTRIES, LTD.—See Nippon Paint Company Ltd.; *Int'l,* pg. 937
ASIA MINERALS CORP.—See Royal Oak Mines Inc.; *U.S. Public,* pg. 1411
ASIA/PACIFIC AREA—See CNF Transportation Inc.; *U.S. Public,* pg. 281
ASIA PACIFIC BREWERIES LTD.—See Heineken N.V.; *Int'l,* pg. 608
ASIA PACIFIC CAPITAL CORP., LIMITED—See Citicorp; *U.S. Public,* pg. 378
ASIA-PACIFIC OPERATIONS—See Zurn Industries, Inc.; *U.S. Public,* pg. 1795
ASIA PACIFIC RESIN CORPORATION—See Novartis AG; *Int'l,* pg. 975
ASIA-PACIFIC SPACE & COMMUNICATION LIMITED—See British Aerospace p.l.c.; *Int'l,* pg. 218
ASIA-PACIFIC TRAINING & SIMULATION LIMITED—See British Aerospace p.l.c.; *Int'l,* pg. 218
ASIA REPRESENTATIVE OFFICE—See GATX Corporation; *U.S. Public,* pg. 693
ASIA SHINWA ENGINEERING CO., LTD.—See Ebara Corporation; *Int'l,* pg. 432
ASIAN-AMERICAN MERCHANT BANK LTD—See The Dai-Ichi Kangyo Bank, Limited; *Int'l,* pg. 362
ASIAN BLEACHING EARTH CO., LTD.—See Laporte plc; *Int'l,* pg. 803
ASIAN CAPITAL PARTNERS HOLDINGS LIMITED—See Dresdner Bank AG; *Int'l,* pg. 420
ASIAN COMPUTER SERVICES PTE. LTD.—See Haw Par Brothers International Limited; *Int'l,* pg. 603
ASIAN DEVELOPMENT BANK; *Int'l,* pg. 88
P.T. ASIAN DEVELOPMENT SECURITIES—See Yamaichi Securities Co., Ltd.; *Int'l,* pg. 1517
ASIAN FOOD INDUSTRIES (HK) LIMITED—See Jardine Matheson Holdings Limited; *Int'l,* pg. 703
ASIAN FOOD INDUSTRIES (PROPERTIES) LIMITED—See Jardine Matheson Holdings Limited; *Int'l,* pg. 703
ASIAN HONDA MOTOR CO., LTD.—See Honda Motor Co., Ltd.; *Int'l,* pg. 635
ASIAN PVS CHEMICAL CO., LTD.—See PVS Chemicals, Inc.; *U.S. Private,* pg. 828
ASIAN QUALIPRODUCTS SERVICE LIMITED—See The Reader's Digest Association, Inc.; *U.S. Public,* pg. 1368
ASIAN TRANSMISSION CORP.—See Nissho Iwai Corporation; *Int'l,* pg. 947
ASIAN WALL STREET JOURNAL—See Dow Jones & Company, Inc.; *U.S. Public,* pg. 525
ASIANA AIRLINES; *U.S. Private,* pg. 88
ASIAWEEK LTD.—See Time Warner Inc.; *U.S. Public,* pg. 1613
ASICS TIGER CORPORATION; *U.S. Private,* pg. 89
ASIENTOS DE CASTILLA LEON SA—See Bertrand Faure; *Int'l,* pg. 193
ASIENTOS DEL NORTE SA (ANSA)—See Bertrand Faure; *Int'l,* pg. 193
ASISERVICE S.R.L.—See Corporacion MAPFRE, Compania Internacional de Reaseguros, S.A.; *Int'l,* pg. 334
ASISTENCIA PLUS, S.A.—See Corporacion MAPFRE, Compania Internacional de Reaseguros, S.A.; *Int'l,* pg. 333
ASITRADE AG—See Bobst S.A.; *Int'l,* pg. 198
ASKIT LABORATORIES LTD.—See Roche Holding Ltd.; *Int'l,* pg. 1120
ASKO, INC; *U.S. Private,* pg. 89
ASKOV MINI-KIBAEK SPECIALFABRIK APS—See Schindler Holding AG; *Int'l,* pg. 1205
ASLAN CIMENTO AS—See Lafarge S.A.; *Int'l,* pg. 788
ASLAND S.A.—See Lafarge S.A.; *Int'l,* pg. 788

Company Index

ASMUSSEN GMBH—See Bayerische Vereinsbank Group; *Int'l*, pg. 178
ASOCIACION TELEFONICA PARA ASISTENCIA A MINUSVALIDOS (A.T.A.M.)—See Telefonica de Espana, S.A.; *Int'l*, pg. 1371
ASOMA CORPORATION; *U.S. Private*, pg. 89
ASOTIN TELEPHONE CO.—See Telephone and Data Systems, Inc.; *U.S. Public*, pg. 1571
ASPA BRUK—See Trelleborg AB; *Int'l*, pg. 1423
ASPEC TECHNOLOGY, INC.; *U.S. Private*, pg. 89
ASPEN IMAGING INTERNATIONAL, INC.—See Pubco Corporation; *U.S. Public*, pg. 1339
ASPEN LABORATORIES, INC.—See Conmed Corporation; *U.S. Public*, pg. 431
ASPEN PET PRODUCTS, INC.—See Ekco Group, Inc.; *U.S. Public*, pg. 566
ASPEN PUBLISHERS, INC.—See Wolters Kluwer N.V.; *Int'l*, pg. 1513
ASPEN SYSTEMS CORP.—See Wolters Kluwer N.V.; *Int'l*, pg. 1513
ASPERA S.P.A.—See Fiat Auto SpA; *Int'l*, pg. 480
ASPERA S.R.L.—See Whirlpool Corporation; *U.S. Public*, pg. 1765
ASPHALT PLANT—See Petrobras - Petroleo Brasileiro S.A.; *Int'l*, pg. 1042
ASPLUNDH TREE EXPERT CO.; *U.S. Private*, pg. 89
ASSA AB—See Assa Abloy AB; *Int'l*, pg. 17
ASSA INDUSTRIE AB—See Assa Abloy AB; *Int'l*, pg. 17
ASSAM CARBON PRODUCTS LIMITED—See Morgan Crucible Co. Plc; *Int'l*, pg. 891
ASSCO GERUSTSYSTEME GMBH & CO. KG—See Plettac AG; *Int'l*, pg. 1061
ASSECURANZ-COMPAGNIE MERCUR AG—See Allianz Aktiengesellschaft; *Int'l*, pg. 58
ETS ASSELIN—See N. Schlumberger & Cie; *Int'l*, pg. 1206
ASSEMBLY COMPONENT SYSTEMS, INC.—See Lawson Products, Inc.; *U.S. Public*, pg. 980
ASSET BASED FINANCING—See CVB Financial Corp.; *U.S. Public*, pg. 287
ASSET DEFENSA LEGAL MEXICANA, S.A. DE C.V.—See Corporacion MAPFRE, Compania Internacional de Reaseguros, S.A.; *Int'l*, pg. 334
ASSET DEVELOPMENT CO., LTD.—See The Industrial Finance Corporation of Thailand; *Int'l*, pg. 677
ASSET RECOVERY & MANAGEMENT CORP.—See Payco American Corporation; *U.S. Public*, pg. 1267
ASSI FRANCE S.A.R.L.—See Norske Skogindustrier A.S; *Int'l*, pg. 966
ASSI ITALIANA S.R.L.—See Norske Skogindustrier A.S; *Int'l*, pg. 966
ASSI PULP & PAPER SALES (UK) LTD.—See Norske Skogindustrier A.S; *Int'l*, pg. 967
ASSIBA DISTRIBUZIONE S.R.L.—See Assicurazioni Generali S.p.A.; *Int'l*, pg. 89
ASSIBA SOCIETA DI ASSICUTAZIONI—See Assicurazioni Generali S.p.A.; *Int'l*, pg. 89
ASSICURAZIONI GENERALI (INSURANCE MANAGERS) LTD.—See Assicurazioni Generali S.p.A.; *Int'l*, pg. 90
ASSICURAZIONI GENERALI S.P.A.; *Int'l*, pg. 90
ASSIPROGETTI S.P.A.—See Banco Ambrosiano Veneto S.p.A.; *Int'l*, pg. 138
ASSOCIATED ADMINISTRATORS, INC.—See Regence BlueCross BlueShield of Oregon; *U.S. Private*, pg. 918
ASSOCIATED AIRCRAFT SUPPLY COMPANY; *U.S. Private*, pg. 89
ASSOCIATED AVIATION, INC.—See The Chubb Corporation; *U.S. Public*, pg. 355
ASSOCIATED AVIATION UNDERWRITERS—See The Chubb Corporation; *U.S. Public*, pg. 355
ASSOCIATED BANC-CORP; *U.S. Public*, pg. 140
ASSOCIATED BANK GREEN BAY—See Associated Banc-Corp; *U.S. Public*, pg. 141
ASSOCIATED BANK, NATIONAL ASSOCIATION—See Associated Banc-Corp; *U.S. Public*, pg. 140
ASSOCIATED BANK NORTH—See Associated Banc-Corp; *U.S. Public*, pg. 140
ASSOCIATED BRITISH FOODS PLC; *Int'l*, pg. 92
ASSOCIATED BUILDING SYSTEMS—See Jannock Limited; *Int'l*, pg. 699
ASSOCIATED BUSINESS PRODUCTS, INC.—See Ikon Office Solutions, Inc.; *U.S. Public*, pg. 863
ASSOCIATED CLAIMS MANAGEMENT, INC. OF CALIFORNIA—See Foundation Health Systems, Inc.; *U.S. Public*, pg. 678
ASSOCIATED COMMERCIAL MORTGAGE, INC.—See Associated Banc-Corp; *U.S. Public*, pg. 140
ASSOCIATED COMPANY, INC.; *U.S. Private*, pg. 89
ASSOCIATED COMPANY MANAGEMENT OF EBASCO LIMITED—See Texas Utilities Company; *U.S. Public*, pg. 1587
ASSOCIATED CONCRETE PRODUCTS, INC.—See For Better Living, Inc.; *U.S. Private*, pg. 417
ASSOCIATED DIRECTORY SERVICES—See SBC Communications Inc.; *U.S. Public*, pg. 1415
ASSOCIATED ELECTRIC CO-OP INC.; *U.S. Private*, pg. 89
ASSOCIATED ENGINEERS & CONSULTANTS, INC.—See Stone & Webster, Incorporated; *U.S. Public*, pg. 1519
ASSOCIATED ENGINEERS LTD.—See Jardine Matheson Holdings Limited; *Int'l*, pg. 705
ASSOCIATED ENVIRONMENTAL SYSTEMS—See Craig Systems; *U.S. Private*, pg. 284
ASSOCIATED EQUIPMENT CO., INC.; *U.S. Private*, pg. 90
ASSOCIATED EQUIPMENT COMPANY OF DELAWARE; *U.S. Private*, pg. 90
ASSOCIATED FINANCIAL CENTER, LTD.—See Associated Banc-Corp; *U.S. Public*, pg. 140
ASSOCIATED FOOD STORES INC.; *U.S. Private*, pg. 90
ASSOCIATED FOOD STORES, INC.; *U.S. Private*, pg. 90
ASSOCIATED FUEL PUMP SYSTEMS CORP.—See Robert Bosch GmbH; *Int'l*, pg. 205
ASSOCIATED FURNITURE COMPANIES LTD.—See South African Breweries, Ltd.; *Int'l*, pg. 1286
ASSOCIATED GLOBAL SYSTEMS; *U.S. Private*, pg. 90
ASSOCIATED GROCERS, INC.; *U.S. Private*, pg. 90

ASSOCIATED GROCERS OF FLORIDA, INC.; *U.S. Private*, pg. 91
ASSOCIATED GROCERS OF NEW ENGLAND, INC.; *U.S. Private*, pg. 91
ASSOCIATED GROCERS OF THE SOUTH, INC.; *U.S. Private*, pg. 91
ASSOCIATED HOSTS, INC.—See Brierley Investments Limited; *Int'l*, pg. 215
ASSOCIATED HOSTS OF CALIFORNIA—See Brierley Investments Limited; *Int'l*, pg. 215
ASSOCIATED HOSTS OF INDIANA—See Brierley Investments Limited; *Int'l*, pg. 215
ASSOCIATED HOSTS OF TEXAS, INC.—See Brierley Investments Limited; *Int'l*, pg. 215
ASSOCIATED INDEMNITY CORP.—See Allianz Aktiengesellschaft; *Int'l*, pg. 59
ASSOCIATED INDUSTRIAL SUPPLY, INC.; *U.S. Private*, pg. 91
ASSOCIATED INVESTMENT SERVICES, INC.—See Associated Banc-Corp; *U.S. Public*, pg. 140
ASSOCIATED LEASE CORP.—See Associated Grocers of New England, Inc.; *U.S. Private*, pg. 91
ASSOCIATED LEASING, INC.—See Associated Banc-Corp; *U.S. Public*, pg. 140
ASSOCIATED MATERIALS INCORPORATED; *U.S. Private*, pg. 91
ASSOCIATED MERCHANDISING CORP. (AMC); *U.S. Private*, pg. 91
ASSOCIATED MERCHANDISING-SINGAPORE—See Associated Merchandising Corp. (AMC); *U.S. Private*, pg. 92
ASSOCIATED MERCHANT BANK PTE. LTD.—See The Royal Bank of Scotland plc; *Int'l*, pg. 1133
ASSOCIATED MORTGAGE, INC.—See Associated Banc-Corp; *U.S. Public*, pg. 140
ASSOCIATED MUSIC PUBLISHERS—See Music Sales Corporation; *U.S. Private*, pg. 768
ASSOCIATED NEWSPAPER HOLDINGS LTD.—See Daily Mail & General Trust PLC; *Int'l*, pg. 366
ASSOCIATED OF LOS ANGELES; *U.S. Private*, pg. 92
ASSOCIATED PAN MALAYSIA CEMENT SDN. BERHAD—See Blue Circle Industries PLC; *Int'l*, pg. 198
ASSOCIATED PETROLEUM CARRIERS; *U.S. Private*, pg. 92
ASSOCIATED PHARMACEUTICAL PRODUCTS, LIMITED—See Merck & Co., Inc.; *U.S. Public*, pg. 1091
ASSOCIATED PLASTICS, INC.—See For Better Living, Inc.; *U.S. Private*, pg. 417
ASSOCIATED POWER, INC.; *U.S. Private*, pg. 92
THE ASSOCIATED PRESS; *U.S. Private*, pg. 92
ASSOCIATED PRESS—See The Associated Press; *U.S. Private*, pg. 92
THE ASSOCIATED PRESS AB—See The Associated Press; *U.S. Private*, pg. 92
THE ASSOCIATED PRESS A/S—See The Associated Press; *U.S. Private*, pg. 92
THE ASSOCIATED PRESS (BELGIUM) S.A.—See The Associated Press; *U.S. Private*, pg. 92
THE ASSOCIATED PRESS DE VENEZUELA, S.A.—See The Associated Press; *U.S. Private*, pg. 92
THE ASSOCIATED PRESS GMBH—See The Associated Press; *U.S. Private*, pg. 92
THE ASSOCIATED PRESS, LTD.—See The Associated Press; *U.S. Private*, pg. 92
ASSOCIATED PROCESS CONTROLS; *U.S. Private*, pg. 92
ASSOCIATED REALTY, INC.—See Associated Banc-Corp; *U.S. Public*, pg. 140
ASSOCIATED SAND & GRAVEL CO., INC.—See CSR Limited; *Int'l*, pg. 245
ASSOCIATED SPRING—See Barnes Group Inc.; *U.S. Public*, pg. 190
ASSOCIATED SPRING-ASIA—See Barnes Group Inc.; *U.S. Public*, pg. 190
ASSOCIATED SPRING, LTD.—See Barnes Group Inc.; *U.S. Public*, pg. 190
ASSOCIATED SPRING-RAYMOND—See Barnes Group Inc.; *U.S. Public*, pg. 190
ASSOCIATED SPRING SPEC, LTD.—See Barnes Group Inc.; *U.S. Public*, pg. 190
ASSOCIATED TECHNOLOGIES, INC.—See American Ecology Corporation; *U.S. Public*, pg. 71
ASSOCIATED TESTING LABORATORIES, INC.—See Publicker Industries Inc.; *U.S. Public*, pg. 1341
ASSOCIATED TRUST COMPANY, INC.—See Associated Banc-Corp; *U.S. Public*, pg. 140
ASSOCIATED VALVE—See Canadian Erectors Ltd.; *Int'l*, pg. 256
ASSOCIATED WHOLESALE ELECTRIC CO.—See Associated of Los Angeles; *U.S. Private*, pg. 92
ASSOCIATED WHOLESALE GROCERS, INC.; *U.S. Private*, pg. 93
ASSOCIATED WHOLESALERS INC.; *U.S. Private*, pg. 93
ASSOCIATES COMMERCIAL CORPORATION—See Ford Motor Company; *U.S. Public*, pg. 663
ASSOCIATES DIVERSIFIED INVESTMENTS LTD.—See Ford Motor Company; *U.S. Public*, pg. 665
ASSOCIATES FINANCIAL LIFE INSURANCE COMPANY—See Ford Motor Company; *U.S. Public*, pg. 663
ASSOCIATES FINANCIAL SERVICES CORPORATION—See Ford Motor Company; *U.S. Public*, pg. 663
ASSOCIATES FIRST CAPITAL CORPORATION—See Ford Motor Company; *U.S. Public*, pg. 662
ASSOCIATES INSURANCE COMPANY—See Ford Motor Company; *U.S. Public*, pg. 663
ASSOCIATES INSURANCE GROUP, INC.—See Ford Motor Company; *U.S. Public*, pg. 663
ASSOCIATES INTERNATIONAL MANAGEMENT COMPANY—See Ford Motor Company; *U.S. Public*, pg. 663
ASSOCIATES NATIONAL BANK—See Ford Motor Company; *U.S. Public*, pg. 663
ASSOCIATES NATIONAL MORTGAGE CORPORATION—See Ford Motor Company; *U.S. Public*, pg. 663

ASSOCIATES REAL ESTATE FINANCIAL SERVICES COMPANY, INC.—See Ford Motor Company; *U.S. Public*, pg. 663
ASSOCIATES RELOCATION MANAGEMENT COMPANY, INC.—See Ford Motor Company; *U.S. Public*, pg. 663
ASSOCIATION COOPERATIVE ZELANDAISE DE CARBONISATION—See Groupe Usinor; *Int'l*, pg. 572
ASSOCIATION MANAGEMENT CORP.—See Conseco Inc.; *U.S. Public*, pg. 433
ASSOCIATION OF CREDIT UNION LEAGUE EXECUTIVES—See Credit Union National Association; *U.S. Private*, pg. 288
ASSOCIATION SAND & GRAVEL—See CSR Limited; *Int'l*, pg. 246
ASSU-VIE—See Groupe GAN; *Int'l*, pg. 563
ASSURANCE & FINANCIAL SERVICES—See Skandia Insurance Company Limited; *Int'l*, pg. 1256
ASSURANCE COMPANY OF AMERICA—See Zurich Insurance Company; *Int'l*, pg. 1530
ASSURANCE GLASS CO. OF ALABAMA—See Globe-Amerada Glass Company; *U.S. Private*, pg. 458
ASSURANCE VIE DESJARDINS-LAURENTIENNE—See Desjardins-Laurentian Financial Corporation; *Int'l*, pg. 399
ASSURANCES DE LA POSTE—See Groupe Bruxelles Lambert S.A.; *Int'l*, pg. 562
ASSUREX—See Groupe GAN; *Int'l*, pg. 564
ASSUREX DEVELOPMENT CORPORATION—See Cigna Corp.; *U.S. Public*, pg. 366
ASSURITY LIFE INC.—See Woodmen Accident & Life Co.; *U.S. Private*, pg. 1187
ASTAR PRECISION CO., LTD.—See Citizen Watch Company, Ltd.; *Int'l*, pg. 294
ASTEC AMERICA CORP.—See Emerson Electric Co.; *U.S. Public*, pg. 573
ASTEC AMERICA INC.—See Astec International Limited; *Int'l*, pg. 93
ASTEC EUROPE LIMITED—See Astec International Limited; *Int'l*, pg. 93
ASTEC FINANCIAL SERVICES, INC.—See Astec Industries, Inc.; *U.S. Public*, pg. 141
ASTEC, INC.—See Astec Industries, Inc.; *U.S. Public*, pg. 141
ASTEC INDUSTRIES, INC.; *U.S. Public*, pg. 141
ASTEC INTERNATIONAL LIMITED; *Int'l*, pg. 92
ASTER INSURANCE LTD.—See Harrah's Entertainment, Inc.; *U.S. Public*, pg. 790
H.A. ASTLETT & CO. LTD.—See Internatio-Muller N.V.; *Int'l*, pg. 682
ASTON BROOKE DEVELOPMENT LABORATORY—See Platinum Technology, Inc.; *U.S. Public*, pg. 1309
ASTON MARTIN FINANCE LIMITED—See Ford Motor Company; *U.S. Public*, pg. 665
ASTON MARTIN LAGONDA DESIGN LIMITED—See Ford Motor Company; *U.S. Public*, pg. 665
ASTON MARTIN LAGONDA GROUP LIMITED—See Ford Motor Company; *U.S. Public*, pg. 665
ASTON MARTIN LAGONDA LIMITED—See Ford Motor Company; *U.S. Public*, pg. 665
ASTON MARTIN LAGONDA OF NORTH AMERICA, INC.—See Ford Motor Company; *U.S. Public*, pg. 664
ASTON MARTIN (RDP) LIMITED—See Ford Motor Company; *U.S. Public*, pg. 665
ASTON MARTIN SALES LIMITED—See Ford Motor Company; *U.S. Public*, pg. 665
ASTOR FRANCE S.A.R.L.—See Joh. A. Benckiser GmbH; *Int'l*, pg. 185
MARGARET ASTOR COSMETICS AG—See Joh. A. Benckiser GmbH; *Int'l*, pg. 185
MARGARET ASTOR COSMETICS GES.M.B.H.—See Joh. A. Benckiser GmbH; *Int'l*, pg. 185
S.A. MARGARET ASTOR N.V.—See Joh. A. Benckiser GmbH; *Int'l*, pg. 186
MARGARET ASTOR SPOL.S.R.O.—See Joh. A. Benckiser GmbH; *Int'l*, pg. 185
ASTOR PRODUCTS—See Winn-Dixie Stores, Inc.; *U.S. Public*, pg. 1772
ASTORIA FINANCIAL CORPORATION; *U.S. Public*, pg. 141
ASTRA AB; *Int'l*, pg. 93
ASTRA ARCUS AB—See Astra AB; *Int'l*, pg. 93
ASTRA ARCUS USA—See Astra AB; *Int'l*, pg. 93
ASTRA-CALVE S.A.—See Unilever Plc; *Int'l*, pg. 1436
ASTRA CHARNWOOD—See Astra AB; *Int'l*, pg. 93
ASTRA CHEMICALS S.A.—See Astra AB; *Int'l*, pg. 93
P.T. ASTRA DAIHATSU MOTOR—See Daihatsu Motor Corporation, Ltd.; *Int'l*, pg. 365
ASTRA DANMARK A/S—See Astra AB; *Int'l*, pg. 93
ASTRA DRACO AB—See Astra AB; *Int'l*, pg. 93
ASTRA EXPORT & TRADING AB—See Astra AB; *Int'l*, pg. 93
ASTRA FARMACEUTICI S.P.A.—See Astra AB; *Int'l*, pg. 93
ASTRA FETT-UND OELWERKE AG—See Unilever Plc; *Int'l*, pg. 1436
ASTRA GMBH—See Astra AB; *Int'l*, pg. 93
ASTRA GES. M.B.H.—See Astra AB; *Int'l*, pg. 93
ASTRA HASSLE AB—See Astra AB; *Int'l*, pg. 93
ASTRA HELLAS S.A.—See Astra AB; *Int'l*, pg. 93
ASTRA-IDL LTD.—See Astra AB; *Int'l*, pg. 93
ASTRA INDONESIA—See Astra AB; *Int'l*, pg. 94
ASTRA JAPAN—See Astra AB; *Int'l*, pg. 94
ASTRA JAPAN—See Fujisawa Pharmaceutical Co. Ltd.; *Int'l*, pg. 525
ASTRA JAPAN LTD.—See Astra AB; *Int'l*, pg. 94
ASTRA KOREA LTD.—See Astra AB; *Int'l*, pg. 94
ASTRA LAKEMEDAL AB—See Astra AB; *Int'l*, pg. 93
ASTRA LUXEMBOURG S.A.R.L.—See Astra AB; *Int'l*, pg. 94
ASTRA/MERCK GROUP—See Merck & Co., Inc.; *U.S. Public*, pg. 1091
ASTRA MERCK INC.—See Astra AB; *Int'l*, pg. 93
ASTRA NORGE A/S—See Astra AB; *Int'l*, pg. 94
ASTRA PAIN CONTROL AB—See Astra AB; *Int'l*, pg. 93
ASTRA PHARMA INC.—See Astra AB; *Int'l*, pg. 94

ASTRA PHARMACEUTICA AG—See Astra AB; *Int'l*, pg. 94
ASTRA PHARMACEUTICA B.V.—See Astra AB; *Int'l*, pg. 94
ASTRA PHARMACEUTICAL PRODUCTION AB—See Astra AB; *Int'l*, pg. 93
ASTRA PHARMACEUTICALS (HK) LTD.—See Astra AB; *Int'l*, pg. 94
ASTRA PHARMACEUTICALS (IRELAND) LTD.—See Astra AB; *Int'l*, pg. 94
ASTRA PHARMACEUTICALS KFT.—See Astra AB; *Int'l*, pg. 94
ASTRA PHARMACEUTICALS LTD.—See Astra AB; *Int'l*, pg. 94
ASTRA PHARMACEUTICALS (MALAYSIA) SDN BHD.—See Astra AB; *Int'l*, pg. 94
ASTRA PHARMACEUTICALS (NEW ZEALAND) LTD.—See Astra AB; *Int'l*, pg. 94
ASTRA PHARMACEUTICALS (PHILIPPINES) INC.—See Astra AB; *Int'l*, pg. 94
ASTRA PHARMACEUTICALS PTY. LTD.—See Astra AB; *Int'l*, pg. 94
ASTRA PHARMACEUTICALS (PTY.) LTD.—See Astra AB; *Int'l*, pg. 94
N.V. ASTRA PHARMACEUTICALS S.A.—See Astra AB; *Int'l*, pg. 94
ASTRA PHARMACEUTICALS (SINGAPORE) PTE. LTD.—See Astra AB; *Int'l*, pg. 94
ASTRA PHARMACEUTICALS (TAIWAN) LTD.—See Astra AB; *int'l*, pg. 94
ASTRA PORTUGUESA LDA.—See Astra AB; *Int'l*, pg. 94
ASTRA PRODUCTION CHEMICALS AB—See Astra AB; *Int'l*, pg. 93
ASTRA PRODUCTION LIQUID AB—See Astra AB; *Int'l*, pg. 93
ASTRA PRODUCTION TABLETS AB—See Astra AB; *Int'l*, pg. 93
ASTRA QUIMICA E FARMACEUTICA LTDA.—See Astra AB; *Int'l*, pg. 94
ASTRA S.A. PRODUCTOS FARMACEUTICOS Y QUIMICOS—See Astra AB; *Int'l*, pg. 94
ASTRA SOUTHEAST ASIA AREA OFFICE—See Astra AB; *Int'l*, pg. 94
ASTRA TECH AB—See Astra AB; *Int'l*, pg. 93
ASTRA (THAI) LTD.—See Astra AB; *Int'l*, pg. 94
ASTRA USA, INC.—See Astra AB; *Int'l*, pg. 93
ASTRA VEICOLI INDUSTRIALI S.P.A.; *Int'l*, pg. 94
ASTRA (WUXI) PHARMACEUTICAL—See Astra AB; *Int'l*, pg. 94
ASTRALUX DYNAMICS LTD.—See Wolseley Plc.; *Int'l*, pg. 1511
ASTRE CORPORATE GROUP; *U.S. Private*, pg. 93
ASTREX, INC.; *U.S. Public*, pg. 141
ASTRO AEROSPACE CORP.—See Spar Aerospace Limited; *Int'l*, pg. 1288
ASTRO BUSINESS SOLUTIONS, INC.—See Canon Inc.; *Int'l*, pg. 262
ASTRO DAIRY PRODUCTS LTD.; *Int'l*, pg. 95
ASTRO HOMES—See Cavalier Homes, Inc.; *U.S. Public*, pg. 318
ASTRO, INC.—See UES, Inc.; *U.S. Private*, pg. 1112
ASTRO-MED, INC.; *U.S. Public*, pg. 141
ASTRO POLYFOAM LTD.—See N.V. Koninklijke KNP BT; *Int'l*, pg. 756
ASTRO-VALCOUR INC.—See N.V. Koninklijke KNP BT; *Int'l*, pg. 756
ASTRON S.A.R.L.—See Commercial Intertech Corp.; *U.S. Public*, pg. 411
ASTRONAUTICS C.A. LTD.—See Astronautics Corporation of America; *U.S. Private*, pg. 93
ASTRONAUTICS CORPORATION OF AMERICA; *U.S. Private*, pg. 93
ASTRONAUTICS U.K.—See Astronautics Corporation of America; *U.S. Private*, pg. 93
ASTRONICS CORPORATION; *U.S. Public*, pg. 142
ASTROTURF MANUFACTURING—See Southwest Recreational Industries Inc.; *U.S. Private*, pg. 1018
EBBE C ASTRUP AS—See Keppel Corporation Limited; *Int'l*, pg. 731
ASTRUP DRUGS, INC.; *U.S. Private*, pg. 93
ASULAB S.A.—See SMH Swiss Corporation for Micro Electronics & Watchmaking Indus. Ltd.; *Int'l*, pg. 1160
P.T. ASURANSI ALLIANZ AKEN LIFE—See Allianz Aktiengesellschaft; *Int'l*, pg. 60
P.T. ASURANSI ALLIANZ UTAMA INDONESIA—See Allianz Aktiengesellschaft; *Int'l*, pg. 60
P.T. ASURANSI CIGNA INDONESIA—See Cigna Corp.; *U.S. Public*, pg. 363
P.T. ASURANSI JIWA DHARMALA MANULIFE—See Manulife Financial (The Manufacturers Life Insurance Company); *Int'l*, pg. 841
ASURANSI JIWA PRINCIPAL EGALITA INDONESIA—See The Principal Financial Group; *U.S. Private*, pg. 886
P.T. ASURANSI NIAGA CIGNA LIFE—See Cigna Corp.; *U.S. Public*, pg. 363
P.T. ASURANSI TOKIO MARINE INDONESIA—See The Tokio Marine & Fire Insurance Company, Ltd.; *Int'l*, pg. 1392
ASYMETRIX LEARNING SYSTEMS, INC.; *U.S. Private*, pg. 93
ASYMTEK—See Nordson Corporation; *U.S. Public*, pg. 1188
THE AT-A-GLANCE GROUP—See Cullman Ventures, Inc.; *U.S. Private*, pg. 295
ATA TONIC—See Havas Advertising; *Int'l*, pg. 602
ATALANTA CORPORATION; *U.S. Private*, pg. 93
ATALANTA (U.K.) LTD.—See Atalanta Corporation; *U.S. Private*, pg. 94
ATALLA CORPORATION—See COMPAQ Computer Corporation; *U.S. Public*, pg. 417
ATAPCO AZTECA, S.A. DE C.V.—See American Trading and Production Corporation; *U.S. Private*, pg. 64
ATAPCO CANADA, LTD.—See American Trading and Production Corporation; *U.S. Private*, pg. 64

ATAPCO OFFICE PRODUCTS GROUP—See American Trading and Production Corporation; *U.S. Private*, pg. 64
ATARI GAMES CORPORATION—See WMS Industries Inc.; *U.S. Public*, pg. 1727
ATCHISON CASTING CORPORATION; *U.S. Public*, pg. 142
ATCHISON/ST. JOE DIVISION—See Atchison Casting Corporation; *U.S. Public*, pg. 142
ATCO/EAST-WEST RECORDS—See Time Warner Inc.; *U.S. Public*, pg. 1611
ATCO GAS SERVICES LTD.—See ATCO Group Co.; *Int'l*, pg. 95
ATCO GROUP CO.; *Int'l*, pg. 95
ATCO STRUCTURES INC.—See ATCO Group Co.; *Int'l*, pg. 95
ATCO TRAVEL—See ATCO Group Co.; *Int'l*, pg. 95
ATCOM, INC.; *U.S. Private*, pg. 94
ATCOR ENGINEERING SYSTEMS—See GP Strategies Corporation; *U.S. Public*, pg. 694
ATCOT CORP., INC.—See Coats Viyella plc; *Int'l*, pg. 300
ATECSA—See Dyckerhoff & Widmann AG; *Int'l*, pg. 424
ATELIERS SUCRE LIQUIDE ET CONDITIONNEMENT DE LYON—See Generale Sucriere SNC; *Int'l*, pg. 549
ATELIERS SUCRE LIQUIDE ET CONDITIONNEMENT-LABORATOIRE DE RECHERCHE DE NASSANDRES—See Generale Sucriere SNC; *Int'l*, pg. 549
ATELIERS SUCRE LIQUIDE ET DEPOT DE TOULOUSE/COLOMIERS—See Generale Sucriere SNC; *Int'l*, pg. 549
ATENEA COMUNICACION Y MECENAZGO, S.A.—See Caja de Madrid Group; *Int'l*, pg. 251
ATEVI S.A.—See Carl-Zeiss-Stiftung; *Int'l*, pg. 1523
ATEX ASIA—See Eastman Kodak Company; *U.S. Public*, pg. 551
ATH COSTA RICA—See Banco Popular de Puerto Rico; *U.S. Public*, pg. 176
ATHENA AB—See Incentive AB; *Int'l*, pg. 666
ATHENA VENTURE PARTNERS L.P.—See IDB Holding Corporation; *Int'l*, pg. 644
ATHENEUM BOOKS FOR YOUNG READERS—See National Amusements, Inc.; *U.S. Private*, pg. 777
ATHENIAN BREWERY S.A.—See Heineken N.V.; *Int'l*, pg. 608
ATHENS BRICK CO.—See Texas Industries, Inc.; *U.S. Public*, pg. 1585
ATHENS FIRST BANK & TRUST CO.—See Synovus Financial Corp.; *U.S. Public*, pg. 1549
ATHENS MILL—See Fort James Corporation; *U.S. Public*, pg. 672
ATHENS NEWSPAPERS, INC.—See Shivers Trading & Operating Co.; *U.S. Private*, pg. 996
ATHENS PAPER CO. INC.; *U.S. Private*, pg. 94
ATHENS PAPER CO., INC.—See Athens Paper Co. Inc.; *U.S. Private*, pg. 94
ATHEY PRODUCTS CORPORATION; *U.S. Public*, pg. 142
ATHEY PRODUCTS-SWEEPER DIV.—See Athey Products Corporation; *U.S. Public*, pg. 143
ATHEY PRODUCTS-WASTE CONTROL DIV.—See Athey Products Corporation; *U.S. Public*, pg. 143
THE ATHLETE'S FOOT GROUP, INC.; *U.S. Private*, pg. 94
ATHLETIC ATTIC RETAIL COMPANY—See Just For Feet, Inc.; *U.S. Public*, pg. 936
ATHLETIC EXPRESS—See Woolworth Corporation; *U.S. Public*, pg. 1777
ATHLETIC TRAINING EQUIPMENT COMPANY, INC.—See Sport Supply Group, Inc.; *U.S. Public*, pg. 1499
ATHOL CORPORATION; *U.S. Private*, pg. 94
ATICAM—See AXA-UAP; *Int'l*, pg. 18
FREDERICK ATKINS; *U.S. Private*, pg. 94
ATKINS KROLL INC.—See Inchcape PLC; *Int'l*, pg. 671
ATKINS TECHNICAL COMPANY—See Thermo Electric Co., Inc.; *U.S. Private*, pg. 1080
ATKINSON; *U.S. Public*, pg. 143
ATKINSON CONSTRUCTION—See Atkinson; *U.S. Public*, pg. 143
ATKINSON DYNAMICS COMPANY—See Atkinson; *U.S. Public*, pg. 143
ATKINSON INDUSTRIES, INC.—See Aztec Manufacturing Co.; *U.S. Public*, pg. 159
ATKINSON INTERNATIONAL VENEZUELA—See Atkinson; *U.S. Public*, pg. 143
ATKINSON UNDERGROUND GROUP—See Atkinson; *U.S. Public*, pg. 143
ATLANDIA DESIGN & FURNISHINGS, INC.—See Mirage Resorts Incorporated; *U.S. Public*, pg. 1116
THE ATLANTA & CHARLOTTE AIR LINE RAILWAY CO.—See Norfolk Southern Corporation; *U.S. Public*, pg. 1191
ATLANTA AUTO AUCTION, INC.—See Cox Enterprises, Inc.; *U.S. Private*, pg. 282
ATLANTA BEVERAGE CO.; *U.S. Private*, pg. 94
ATLANTA BLUEPRINT COMPANY—See Wallace Computer Services, Inc.; *U.S. Public*, pg. 1735
ATLANTA BRAVES, INC.—See Time Warner Inc.; *U.S. Public*, pg. 1614
ATLANTA CASUALTY COMPANY—See American Financial Group; *U.S. Public*, pg. 75
ATLANTA GAS LIGHT COMPANY—See AGL Resources; *U.S. Public*, pg. 7
ATLANTA HAWKS, INC.—See Time Warner Inc.; *U.S. Public*, pg. 1614
ATLANTA HILL RESTAURANT CORP.—See Specialty Restaurants Corporation; *U.S. Private*, pg. 1023
THE ATLANTA JOURNAL—See Cox Enterprises, Inc.; *U.S. Private*, pg. 281
ATLANTA LEARNING CENTER—See Berkshire Hathaway Inc.; *U.S. Public*, pg. 218
ATLANTA LIFE INSURANCE COMPANY; *U.S. Private*, pg. 94
ATLANTA MFG. FACILITY—See L.M. Scofield Company; *U.S. Private*, pg. 976

ATLANTA MOB, INC.—See Magellan Health Services, Inc.; *U.S. Public*, pg. 1033
ATLANTA MOTOR SPEEDWAY—See Speedway Motorsports, Inc.; *U.S. Public*, pg. 1498
ATLANTA NATIONAL LEAGUE BASEBALL CLUB, INC.—See Time Warner Inc.; *U.S. Public*, pg. 1614
ATLANTA REGIONAL OFFICE—See Vencor, Inc.; *U.S. Public*, pg. 1715
ATLANTA SALES—See Fairfield Communities, Inc.; *U.S. Public*, pg. 611
ATLANTIC AMERICAN CORPORATION; *U.S. Public*, pg. 143
ATLANTIC AMERICAN LIFE INSURANCE COMPANY—See Atlantic American Corporation; *U.S. Public*, pg. 143
ATLANTIC & EAST CAROLINA RAILWAY COMPANY—See Norfolk Southern Corporation; *U.S. Public*, pg. 1191
ATLANTIC ANTIBODIES, INC.—See Fiat Auto SpA; *Int'l*, pg. 483
ATLANTIC AUTO FINANCE CORP.—See Trace International Holdings, Inc.; *U.S. Private*, pg. 1095
ATLANTIC AVIATION CORP.; *U.S. Private*, pg. 94
ATLANTIC BANK—See First Virginia Banks, Inc.; *U.S. Public*, pg. 642
ATLANTIC BANK OF NEW YORK INC.—See National Bank of Greece S.A.; *Int'l*, pg. 907
ATLANTIC BUILDERS GROUP INC.; *U.S. Private*, pg. 95
ATLANTIC CELLULAR TELEPHONE CORP.—See Vanguard Cellular Systems, Inc.; *U.S. Public*, pg. 1708
ATLANTIC CHEMICAL CORPORATION LIMITED—See Rhone-Poulenc S.A.; *Int'l*, pg. 1111
ATLANTIC CITY HILTON—See Hilton Hotels Corporation; *U.S. Public*, pg. 829
ATLANTIC CITY SHOWBOAT—See Showboat, Incorporated; *U.S. Public*, pg. 1469
ATLANTIC COAST ASPHALT—See Hubbard Construction Co.; *U.S. Private*, pg. 544
ATLANTIC COAST CARTON COMPANY—See Caraustar Industries, Inc.; *U.S. Public*, pg. 303
ATLANTIC CONCRETE PRODUCTS, INC.; *U.S. Private*, pg. 95
ATLANTIC EAST COAST TERMINAL—See St. Joe Corp.; *U.S. Public*, pg. 1427
ATLANTIC ELECTRIC CO.—See Conectiv; *U.S. Public*, pg. 430
ATLANTIC EMPLOYERS INSURANCE COMPANY—See Cigna Corp.; *U.S. Public*, pg. 366
ATLANTIC ENERGY TECHNOLOGY, INC.—See Conectiv; *U.S. Public*, pg. 430
ATLANTIC ENVELOPE CO.—See National Service Industries, Inc.; *U.S. Public*, pg. 1160
ATLANTIC EXPLOSIVES—See Imperial Chemical Industries PLC; *Int'l*, pg. 664
ATLANTIC FEDERAL SAVINGS BANK—See Susquehanna Bancshares, Inc.; *U.S. Public*, pg. 1543
ATLANTIC GENERATION, INC.—See Conectiv; *U.S. Public*, pg. 430
ATLANTIC GUEST, INC.—See Valley Forge Corporation; *U.S. Public*, pg. 1705
ATLANTIC GULF COMMUNITIES CORPORATION; *U.S. Public*, pg. 144
ATLANTIC HARDWARE & SUPPLY CO.—See Colonial Commercial Corp.; *U.S. Public*, pg. 400
ATLANTIC HOMES CORP.—See The Great Atlantic Management Company; *U.S. Private*, pg. 473
ATLANTIC HOMES DIV.—See Champion Enterprises, Inc.; *U.S. Public*, pg. 332
ATLANTIC INTERNATIONAL REINSURANCE COMPANY LTD.—See Swiss Reinsurance Company; *Int'l*, pg. 1333
ATLANTIC INVESTMENT COMPANY—See Norfolk Southern Corporation; *U.S. Public*, pg. 1190
ATLANTIC LUMBER COMPANY—See Sabbeth Industries Ltd; *U.S. Private*, pg. 959
ATLANTIC MACHINE TOOLS INC.—See Haco N.V.; *Int'l*, pg. 585
ATLANTIC METALS CORPORATION; *U.S. Public*, pg. 95
THE ATLANTIC MONTHLY MAGAZINE; *U.S. Private*, pg. 95
ATLANTIC MUTUAL COMPANIES; *U.S. Private*, pg. 95
ATLANTIC MUTUAL INSURANCE CO.—See Atlantic Mutual Companies; *U.S. Private*, pg. 95
ATLANTIC NATIONAL CORPORATION—See Hawthorne Corp.; *U.S. Private*, pg. 512
ATLANTIC PAPER GROUP—See Gould Paper Corporation; *U.S. Private*, pg. 467
ATLANTIC PLUMBING SUPPLY COMPANY; *U.S. Private*, pg. 95
ATLANTIC PUMP & EQUIPMENT CO.—See Hughes Supply, Inc.; *U.S. Public*, pg. 846
ATLANTIC PUMP & EQUIPMENT CO. OF PUERTO RICO—See Hughes Supply, Inc.; *U.S. Public*, pg. 846
ATLANTIC PUMP & EQUIPMENT CO. OF WEST PALM BEACH—See Hughes Supply, Inc.; *U.S. Public*, pg. 846
ATLANTIC RECORDING CORPORATION—See Time Warner Inc.; *U.S. Public*, pg. 1611
ATLANTIC REPROGRAPHICS—See Wallace Computer Services, Inc.; *U.S. Public*, pg. 1736
ATLANTIC RESEARCH CORPORATION—See Sequa Corporation; *U.S. Public*, pg. 1458
ATLANTIC RICHFIELD COMPANY; *U.S. Public*, pg. 144
ATLANTIC SAVINGS BANK FSB—See Wachovia Corporation; *U.S. Public*, pg. 1730
ATLANTIC SCIENTIFIC CORPORATION—See Bowthorpe plc; *Int'l*, pg. 208
ATLANTIC SERVICE CO., LTD.—See Bairnco Corporation; *U.S. Public*, pg. 165
ATLANTIC SERVICE CO. (U.K.) LTD.—See Bairnco Corporation; *U.S. Public*, pg. 165
ATLANTIC SHOPPING CENTRES LIMITED—See Empire Company Limited; *Int'l*, pg. 454
ATLANTIC SOUTHEAST AIRLINES INC.; *U.S. Public*, pg. 144
ATLANTIC SOUTHERN PROPERTIES, INC.—See Conectiv; *U.S. Public*, pg. 430

Company Index

ATLANTIC STATES BANK—See First Citizens Banc
Shares, Inc.; *U.S. Public*, pg. 629
ATLANTIC STEEL INDUSTRIES, INC.—See The Ivaco
Group; *Int'l*, pg. 696
ATLANTIC SUGAR ASSOCIATION, INC.; *U.S. Private*,
pg. 95
ATLANTIC THERMAL SYSTEMS, INC.—See Conectiv; *U.S.
Public*, pg. 430
ATLANTIC 252—See Groupe Bruxelles Lambert S.A.; *Int'l*,
pg. 561
ATLANTIC WEST B.V.—See Bell Atlantic Corporation; *U.S.
Public*, pg. 203
ATLANTIC WHOLESALERS LTD.—See George Weston
Limited; *Int'l*, pg. 1495
ATLANTIC WORKS—See Lucent Technologies Inc.; *U.S.
Public*, pg. 1017
ATLANTIS MOLDED PLASTICS, INC.—See Atlantis Plastic,
Inc.; *U.S. Public*, pg. 145
ATLANTIS PLASTIC FILMS, INC.—See Atlantis Plastic,
Inc.; *U.S. Public*, pg. 145
ATLANTIS PLASTIC, INC.; *U.S. Public*, pg. 145
ATLAPAC TRADING COMPANY, INC.; *U.S. Private*, pg. 96
ATLAS AGGREGATES LIMITED—See RMC Group p.l.c.;
Int'l, pg. 1079
ATLAS ALCHEM PLASTICS, INC.—See Spartech
Corporation; *U.S. Public*, pg. 1495
ATLAS-ALCHEM PLASTICS-MINNESOTA—See Spartech
Corporation; *U.S. Public*, pg. 1496
ATLAS ALLOYS—See Rio Algom Limited; *Int'l*, pg. 1118
ATLAS A.S.—See Etablissement Delhaize Freres Et Cie
"Le Lion" S.A.; *Int'l*, pg. 463
ATLAS ASSET MANAGEMENT INC.—See Midland Walwyn
Inc.; *Int'l*, pg. 865
ATLAS AUTOMOTIVE, INC.—See General Automotive
Corporation; *U.S. Private*, pg. 444
ATLAS BUILDING SYSTEMS, INC.—See Scancem AB;
Int'l, pg. 1201
ATLAS CEMENT CORPORATION—See FLS Industries A/
S; *Int'l*, pg. 475
ATLAS CO. OF BOSTON, INC.—See Tom James
Company; *U.S. Private*, pg. 581
**ATLAS CONSOLIDATED MINING & DEVELOPMENT
CORPORATION**; *Int'l*, pg. 95
ATLAS CONSTRUCTION TOOLS—See Atlas Copco AB;
Int'l, pg. 96
ATLAS COPCO AB; *Int'l*, pg. 95
ATLAS COPCO ACT—See Atlas Copco AB; *Int'l*, pg. 96
ATLAS COPCO AFS INC.—See Atlas Copco AB; *Int'l*,
pg. 96
ATLAS COPCO AIRPOWER N.V.—See Atlas Copco AB;
Int'l, pg. 96
ATLAS COPCO BEREMA AB—See Atlas Copco AB; *Int'l*,
pg. 96
ATLAS COPCO BEREMA, INC.—See Atlas Copco AB; *Int'l*,
pg. 96
ATLAS COPCO COMPRESSOR CANADA—See Atlas
Copco AB; *Int'l*, pg. 96
ATLAS COPCO COMPRESSOR INTERNATIONAL—See
Atlas Copco AB; *Int'l*, pg. 96
ATLAS COPCO COMPRESSORS, INC.—See Atlas Copco
AB; *Int'l*, pg. 96
ATLAS COPCO COMPTEC INC.—See Atlas Copco AB;
Int'l, pg. 96
ATLAS COPCO CRAELIUS—See Atlas Copco AB; *Int'l*,
pg. 96
ATLAS COPCO ELECTRIC TOOLS—See Atlas Copco AB;
Int'l, pg. 96
ATLAS COPCO INDUSTRIAL TOOLS & EQUIPMENT—See
Atlas Copco AB; *Int'l*, pg. 96
ATLAS COPCO NORTH AMERICA INC.—See Atlas Copco
AB; *Int'l*, pg. 96
ATLAS COPCO RENTAL INC.—See Atlas Copco AB; *Int'l*,
pg. 96
ATLAS COPCO ROBBINS—See Atlas Copco AB; *Int'l*,
pg. 96
ATLAS COPCO ROCKDRILLING EQUIPMENT—See Atlas
Copco AB; *Int'l*, pg. 96
ATLAS COPCO TOOLS INC.—See Atlas Copco AB; *Int'l*,
pg. 96
ATLAS COPCO WAGNER INC.—See Atlas Copco AB; *Int'l*,
pg. 96
ATLAS CRANKSHAFT CORPORATION—See Cummins
Engine Company, Inc.; *U.S. Public*, pg. 468
ATLAS CYLINDER—See Parker Hannifin Corporation; *U.S.
Public*, pg. 1261
ATLAS DE MEXICO, S.A. DE C.V.—See Imperial Chemical
Industries PLC; *Int'l*, pg. 664
ATLAS EDITIONS; *Int'l*, pg. 96
ATLAS ELECTRIC DEVICES CO.; *U.S. Private*, pg. 96
ATLAS FOUNDRY & MACHINE CO.—See TIC United
Corporation; *U.S. Private*, pg. 1063
ATLAS HOTELS, INC.; *U.S. Public*, pg. 96
ATLAS INDUSTRIES CHILE S.A.—See Eclipse Inc.; *U.S.
Private*, pg. 361
ATLAS LEDERER CO.—See Columbia National Group,
Inc.; *U.S. Private*, pg. 256
ATLAS LIFT TRUCK RENTALS & SALES, INC.; *U.S.
Private*, pg. 96
ATLAS MAMMOET CO. LTD.—See Royal Nedlloyd Group
N.V.; *Int'l*, pg. 1144
ATLAS PARTICIPACOES S/C LTDA.—See Commerzbank
AG; *Int'l*, pg. 312
ATLAS PEN & PENCIL CORPORATION; *U.S. Public*,
pg. 96
ATLAS REFINERY; *U.S. Private*, pg. 96
ATLAS ROLL-LITE DOOR CORPORATION—See Griffon
Corp.; *U.S. Public*, pg. 766
ATLAS ROOFING CORP.; *U.S. Private*, pg. 96
ATLAS/SOUNDOLIER—See American Trading and
Production Corporation; *U.S. Private*, pg. 64
ATLAS SPECIALIZED TRANSPORTATION—See Atlas
World Group, Inc.; *U.S. Private*, pg. 97
ATLAS STEEL & WIRE—See AmeriSteel; *U.S. Private*,
pg. 65

ATLAS STONE PRODUCTS LIMITED—See Hanson PLC;
Int'l, pg. 592
ATLAS SUL AMERICANA DE FOMENTO COMERCIAL
LIMITADA—See Assicurazioni Generali S.p.A.; *Int'l*,
pg. 90
ATLAS SUPPLY COMPANY; *U.S. Private*, pg. 96
ATLAS SYSTEMS—See Havens Steel Co.; *U.S. Private*,
pg. 511
ATLAS TAG & LABEL INC.—See Bissell Inc.; *U.S. Private*,
pg. 145
ATLAS TERMINAL CO.—See Atlas World Group, Inc.; *U.S.
Private*, pg. 97
ATLAS TOOL INC.; *U.S. Private*, pg. 97
ATLAS VAN LINES (CANADA) LTD.—See Atlas World
Group, Inc.; *U.S. Private*, pg. 97
ATLAS VAN LINES, INC.—See Atlas World Group, Inc.;
U.S. Private, pg. 97
ATLAS-VERMOEGENSVERWALTUNGS-GMBH—See
Commerzbank AG; *Int'l*, pg. 309
ATLAS WEATHERING DSET LABORATORIES—See Atlas
Electric Devices Co.; *U.S. Private*, pg. 96
ATLAS WIRE CORPORATION; *U.S. Private*, pg. 97
ATLAS WORLD-CLASS TRAVEL—See Atlas World Group,
Inc.; *U.S. Private*, pg. 97
ATLAS WORLD GROUP, INC.; *U.S. Private*, pg. 97
ATLET AB; *Int'l*, pg. 97
ATLET FLURFORDERZUEGE GMBH—See Atlet AB; *Int'l*,
pg. 97
ATLET FRANCE S.A.—See Atlet AB; *Int'l*, pg. 97
ATLET, INC.—See Atlet AB; *Int'l*, pg. 97
ATLET LTD.—See Atlet AB; *Int'l*, pg. 97
ATLET-MULTICAR BV—See Atlet AB; *Int'l*, pg. 97
ATLITE LIGHTING EQUIP.—See Cooper Industries,
Inc.; *U.S. Public*, pg. 443
ATMEL CORPORATION; *U.S. Public*, pg. 145
P.T. ATMINDO—See Deutsche Babcock AG; *Int'l*, pg. 398
ATMOS ENERGY CORPORATION; *U.S. Public*, pg. 145
ATMOS LEBENSMITTELTECHNIK G.M.B.H.—See Tetra
Laval Group; *Int'l*, pg. 1379
ATO-FINDLEY, INC.—See Elf Aquitaine; *Int'l*, pg. 445
ATOCHEM—See Elf Aquitaine; *Int'l*, pg. 445
ATOCHEM CANADA INC.—See Elf Aquitaine; *Int'l*, pg. 446
ATOCHEM SAIC—See Elf Aquitaine; *Int'l*, pg. 446
ATOCHEM SERVICES INC.—See Elf Aquitaine; *Int'l*,
pg. 445
ATOCHEM UK LTD.—See Elf Aquitaine; *Int'l*, pg. 446
ATOHAAS B.V.—See Rohm and Haas Company; *U.S.
Public*, pg. 1403
ATOHAAS CANADA INC.—See Rohm and Haas Company;
U.S. Public, pg. 1403
ATOHAAS EUROPE S.C.A.—See Rohm and Haas
Company; *U.S. Public*, pg. 1404
ATOHAAS HOLDING C.V.—See Rohm and Haas
Company; *U.S. Public*, pg. 1403
ATOHAAS MEXICO INC.—See Rohm and Haas Company;
U.S. Public, pg. 1403
ATOHAAS NORTH AMERICA INC.—See Rohm and Haas
Company; *U.S. Public*, pg. 1403
ATOHAAS PACIFIC INC.—See Rohm and Haas Company;
U.S. Public, pg. 1403
ATOHAAS TECHNOLOGIES B.V.—See Rohm and Haas
Company; *U.S. Public*, pg. 1403
ATOLS TOOL AND MOLD CORP.; *U.S. Private*, pg. 97
ATOMA INTERNATIONAL, INC.—See Magna International
Inc.; *Int'l*, pg. 829
ATOMI CORP.—See Dugan Production Corp.; *U.S. Private*,
pg. 345
ATOMIC AUSTRIA GMBH—See Amer Group Ltd.; *Int'l*,
pg. 73
ATOMIC DEUTSCHLAND GMBH—See Amer Group Ltd.;
Int'l, pg. 73
ATOMIC ENERGY OF CANADA LTD.; *Int'l*, pg. 73
ATOMIC FRANCE S.A.—See Amer Group Ltd.; *Int'l*, pg. 73
ATOMIC SKI USA INC.—See Amer Group Ltd.; *Int'l*, pg. 73
ATOMIC SPORTS CANADA—See Amer Group Ltd.; *Int'l*,
pg. 73
ATOS MEDICAL AB—See Perstorp AB; *Int'l*, pg. 1036
ATOTECH U.S.A. INC.; *U.S. Private*, pg. 97
ATREX INCORPORATED; *U.S. Private*, pg. 97
ATRIA NORTH-PHASE II—See SNC-Lavalin Group Inc.;
Int'l, pg. 1162
ATRION CORPORATION; *U.S. Public*, pg. 146
ATRIUM COMPANIES, INC.; *U.S. Private*, pg. 98
ATRIUM COMPANIES, INC.—See Atrium Companies, Inc.;
U.S. Private, pg. 98
THE ATRIUM DEVELOPMENT CO.—See Time Warner
Inc.; *U.S. Public*, pg. 1613
ATSUGI MOTOR PARTS CO., LTD.—See Nissan Motor
Co., Ltd.; *Int'l*, pg. 944
ATTACHMATE; *U.S. Private*, pg. 98
ATTENDOR INDUSTRI OCH HANDEL AB—See Axel
Johnson AB; *Int'l*, pg. 708
ATTENDOR RAW MATERIALS LTD.—See Axel Johnson
AB; *Int'l*, pg. 710
ATTIJARI CREDIT—See Caja de Madrid Group; *Int'l*,
pg. 252
ATTITASH BEAR PEAK—See American Skiing Company;
U.S. Private, pg. 61
ATTORNEYS' TITLE INSURANCE FUND; *U.S. Private*,
pg. 98
ATWOOD & MORRILL CO., INC.—See Weir Group PLC;
Int'l, pg. 1489
ATWOOD BETTER PRODUCTS—See Excel Industries,
Inc.; *U.S. Public*, pg. 598
ATWOOD DEEP SEAS, LTD.—See Cigna Corp.; *U.S.
Public*, pg. 358
ATWOOD DISTRIBUTING, INC.; *U.S. Private*, pg. 98
ATWOOD FALCON I, LTD.—See Cigna Corp.; *U.S. Public*,
pg. 358
ATWOOD MOBILE PRODUCTS—See Excel Industries, Inc.;
U.S. Public, pg. 598
ATWOOD OCEANICS AUSTRALIA PTY. LTD.—See
Atwood Oceanics, Inc.; *U.S. Public*, pg. 146

ATWOOD OCEANICS DRILLING CO.—See Atwood
Oceanics, Inc.; *U.S. Public*, pg. 146
ATWOOD OCEANICS, INC.; *U.S. Public*, pg. 146
AU BON MARCHE; *Int'l*, pg. 97
AU BON PAIN CO., INC.; *U.S. Public*, pg. 146
AU PAIR IN AMERICA—See American Institute for Foreign
Study; *U.S. Private*, pg. 56
AU-SYSTEM RADIO AB—See Telefonaktiebolaget LM
Ericsson; *Int'l*, pg. 1363
AUBREY MANUFACTURING COMPANY—See Nortek, Inc.;
U.S. Public, pg. 1193
W.E. AUBUCHON CO., INC.; *U.S. Private*, pg. 98
AUBURN CONSOLIDATED INDUSTRIES, INC.—See
Kubota Corp.; *Int'l*, pg. 762
AUBURN GENERAL HOSPITAL—See Universal Health
Services, Inc.; *U.S. Public*, pg. 1696
AUBURN HILLS—See Newcor, Inc.; *U.S. Public*, pg. 1176
AUBURN HOSIERY MILLS, INC.; *U.S. Private*, pg. 98
AUBURN MANOR—See Horizon/CMS Healthcare
Corporation; *U.S. Public*, pg. 838
THE AUBURN STATE BANK—See Fort Wayne National
Corporation; *U.S. Public*, pg. 674
AUBURN TECHNOLOGY, INC.—See Bombardier Inc.; *Int'l*,
pg. 200
AUBURNDALE COMPANY, INC.—See The Turner
Corporation; *U.S. Public*, pg. 1645
AUBURNDALE STAR—See Shivers Trading & Operating
Co.; *U.S. Private*, pg. 995
GEORGE W. AUCH CO.; *U.S. Private*, pg. 98
AUCHAN S.A.; *Int'l*, pg. 98
THE AUCHTER COMPANY; *U.S. Private*, pg. 98
AUCTION TRANSPORT INC.—See Tyco International Ltd.;
U.S. Public, pg. 1648
AUDA S.A.—See ETEX; *Int'l*, pg. 430
AUDATEX HOLDING AG—See Automatic Data Processing,
Inc.; *U.S. Public*, pg. 150
AUDAX INDUSTRIES, S.A.—See Harman International
Industries, Inc.; *U.S. Public*, pg. 787
AUDET TIJDSCHRIFTEN—See Reed Elsevier plc; *Int'l*,
pg. 1099
AUDI AG—See Volkswagen AG; *Int'l*, pg. 1473
AUDI FINANCE N.V.—See Volkswagen AG; *Int'l*, pg. 1474
AUDI HUNGARIA MOTOR KFT.—See Volkswagen AG;
Int'l, pg. 1473
AUDI OF AMERICA—See Volkswagen AG; *Int'l*, pg. 1474
AUDIBLE/VISIBLE & WATERFLOW DIVISION—See
Pittway Corporation; *U.S. Public*, pg. 1306
THE AUDICHRON COMPANY—See Electronic Tele-
Communications, Inc.; *U.S. Public*, pg. 570
AUDIO CLUB OF NEW ZEALAND LTD.—See Philips
Electronics N.V.; *Int'l*, pg. 1052
AUDIO KING CORPORATION—See Ultimate Electronics;
U.S. Public, pg. 1662
AUDIO KING MIDWEST—See Ultimate Electronics; *U.S.
Public*, pg. 1662
AUDIOFINA S.A.—See Groupe Bruxelles Lambert S.A.;
Int'l, pg. 561
AUDIOSONIC—See Vendex International N.V.; *Int'l*,
pg. 1463
AUDIOTEX SA—See Lagardere Groupe; *Int'l*, pg. 795
AUDIOTONE, INC.—See Bausch & Lomb Incorporated;
U.S. Public, pg. 194
AUDIOVOX CORPORATION; *U.S. Public*, pg. 147
AUDISIO INDUSTRIE ALUMENTARI SRL—See CSM N.V.;
Int'l, pg. 244
AUDITOIRE—See BDDP Group; *Int'l*, pg. 116
AUDITS & SURVEYS WORLDWIDE; *U.S. Public*, pg. 147
AUDOUR, SOUM, LARUE/SMS—See The Lowe Group;
U.S. Private, pg. 678
AUDREY RESOURCES—See Cambior Inc.; *Int'l*, pg. 253
AUERGESELLSCHAFT GMBH—See Mine Safety
Appliances Co.; *U.S. Public*, pg. 1114
AUER-SOG GLASWERKE GMBH—See Carl-Zeiss-Stiftung;
Int'l, pg. 1523
AUFBAUGESELLSCHAFT BAYERN GMBH—See
Bayerische Vereinsbank Group; *Int'l*, pg. 178
AUFZUGE AG SCHAFFHAUSEN—See Schindler Holding
AG; *Int'l*, pg. 1204
AUGAT AG—See Thomas & Betts Corporation; *U.S. Public*,
pg. 1598
AUGAT ELECTRONICS INC.—See Thomas & Betts
Corporation; *U.S. Public*, pg. 1598
AUGAT GMBH—See Thomas & Betts Corporation; *U.S.
Public*, pg. 1598
AUGAT, INC.—See Thomas & Betts Corporation; *U.S.
Public*, pg. 1597
AUGAT, INC., AUTOMOTIVE COMPONENTS DIVISION-
BOYNE CITY—See Thomas & Betts Corporation; *U.S.
Public*, pg. 1598
AUGAT, INC., AUTOMOTIVE DIVISION—See Thomas &
Betts Corporation; *U.S. Public*, pg. 1598
AUGAT, INC., COMMUNICATIONS DIVISION—See
Thomas & Betts Corporation; *U.S. Public*, pg. 1598
AUGAT, INC., INTERCONNECTION PRODUCTS-CAROL
STREAM—See Thomas & Betts Corporation; *U.S.
Public*, pg. 1598
AUGAT, INC., INTERCONNECTION PRODUCTS-
MASHPEE—See Thomas & Betts Corporation; *U.S.
Public*, pg. 1598
AUGAT, INC., WIRING SYSTEMS—See Thomas & Betts
Corporation; *U.S. Public*, pg. 1598
AUGAT, INC., WIRING SYSTEMS & COMPONENTS
GROUP—See Thomas & Betts Corporation; *U.S.
Public*, pg. 1598
AUGAT, LRC, COMMUNICATIONS DIVISION-
HORSEHEADS PLANT—See Thomas & Betts
Corporation; *U.S. Public*, pg. 1598
AUGAT LTD.—See Thomas & Betts Corporation; *U.S.
Public*, pg. 1598
AUGAT PTE. LTD.—See Thomas & Betts Corporation; *U.S.
Public*, pg. 1598
AUGAT PTY LTD.—See Thomas & Betts Corporation; *U.S.
Public*, pg. 1598

AUGAT S.A.—See Thomas & Betts Corporation; *U.S. Public,* pg. 1598
AUGAT SRL—See Thomas & Betts Corporation; *U.S. Public,* pg. 1598
AUGSBURG FORTRESS, PUBLISHERS; *U.S. Private,* pg. 98
AUGUST LINDBERG OY—See Rautaruukki Oy; *Int'l,* pg. 1088
AUGUST MAX WOMAN—See Casual Corner Group, Inc.; *U.S. Private,* pg. 219
AUGUST WEST SYSTEMS; *U.S. Private,* pg. 98
AUGUSTA MALL, INC.—See The Rouse Company; *U.S. Public,* pg. 1408
AUGUSTA MILL SUPPLY—See Associated Industrial Supply, Inc.; *U.S. Private,* pg. 91
AULT INCORPORATED; *U.S. Public,* pg. 147
AUNT FANNY'S BAKERY—See Flowers Industries, Inc.; *U.S. Public,* pg. 657
AUPPERLE AUFZUGE GMBH—See Kone Corporation; *Int'l,* pg. 747
AURA S.R.L.—See General Motors Corporation; *U.S. Public,* pg. 721
AURA SYSTEMS, INC.; *U.S. Public,* pg. 147
OY AURINKOMATKAT-SUNTOURS LTD.—See FinnAir Oy; *Int'l,* pg. 485
AURO TECH, INC.—See International Flavors & Fragrances, Inc.; *U.S. Public,* pg. 899
AURORA ASSICURAZIONI S.P.A.—See Assicurazioni Generali S.p.A.; *Int'l,* pg. 90
AURORA CASKET COMPANY; *U.S. Private,* pg. 99
AURORA ELECTRONICS—See Aurora Electronics, Inc.; *U.S. Public,* pg. 147
AURORA ELECTRONICS, INC.; *U.S. Public,* pg. 147
AURORA METALS DIVISION L.P.C.—See Hiler Industries; *U.S. Private,* pg. 529
AURORA NATIONAL BANK—See GreatBanc, Inc.; *U.S. Public,* pg. 760
AURORA PACKING CO., INC.; *U.S. Private,* pg. 99
AURORA POLAR—See AXA-UAP; *Int'l,* pg. 19
AURORA PUMP—See General Signal Corporation; *U.S. Public,* pg. 726
AURORA REGIONAL MEDICAL CENTER—See Columbia/ HCA Healthcare Corporation; *U.S. Public,* pg. 403
AURUM BETEILIGUNGS- UND VERWALTUNGS GMBH— See Bayerische Vereinsbank Group; *Int'l,* pg. 178
AURUM FINANCE BV—See Pegasus Gold Corporation; *U.S. Public,* pg. 1269
AURUM PRESS LIMITED—See Really Useful Holdings Limited; *Int'l,* pg. 1089
AUSBAU DRESDEN GMBH—See Bilfinger + Berger Bauaktiengesellschaft; *Int'l,* pg. 195
AUSBAU GROSSENHAIN GMBH—See Dyckerhoff & Widmann AG; *Int'l,* pg. 423
AUSCO PRODUCTS, INC.—See The Cypress Companies; *U.S. Private,* pg. 299
AUSECO, S.A.—See Caja de Madrid Group; *Int'l,* pg. 252
AUSEON—See The Geon Company; *U.S. Public,* pg. 734
AUSHERMAN CONSTRUCTION COMPANY; *U.S. Private,* pg. 99
AUSILIARE SPA—See Brambles Industries Limited; *Int'l,* pg. 212
AUSIMONT S.P.A.—See Compart SpA; *Int'l,* pg. 324
AUSSENHANDEL-FOERDERUNGSGESELLSCHAFT MBH—See Commerzbank AG; *Int'l,* pg. 309
AUST-AMEC PTY.—See AMEC Plc; *Int'l,* pg. 16
THE AUSTAD COMPANY—See Hanover Direct, Inc.; *U.S. Public,* pg. 782
AUSTELL BOX BOARD CORPORATION—See Caraustar Industries, Inc.; *U.S. Public,* pg. 303
AUSTEN & BUTTA—See Royal Dutch/Shell Group of Companies; *Int'l,* pg. 1137
AUSTILL PACKAGING—See Jefferson Smurfit Group p.l.c.; *Int'l,* pg. 1269
AUSTIN COMMERCIAL, INC.—See Austin Industries, Inc.; *U.S. Private,* pg. 99
THE AUSTIN COMPANY; *U.S. Private,* pg. 99
AUSTIN GROUP; *U.S. Private,* pg. 99
AUSTIN INDUSTRIAL, INC.—See Austin Industries, Inc.; *U.S. Private,* pg. 99
AUSTIN INDUSTRIES, INC.; *U.S. Private,* pg. 99
JAMES AUSTIN CO.; *U.S. Private,* pg. 99
AUSTIN JET LTD.; *U.S. Private,* pg. 100
AUSTIN KELLEY ADVERTISING, INC.; *U.S. Private,* pg. 100
AUSTIN POWDER CO.; *U.S. Private,* pg. 100
AUSTIN PRODUCTIONS, INC.; *U.S. Private,* pg. 100
AUSTIN QUALITY FOODS; *U.S. Private,* pg. 100
AUSTIN REED LIMITED—See Hartmarx Corporation; *U.S. Public,* pg. 796
AUSTRAL BRONZE CRANE COPPER LIMITED—See Crane Group Limited; *Int'l,* pg. 340
AUSTRALASIAN HMT PTY. LTD.—See ITEQ, Inc.; *U.S. Public,* pg. 914
AUSTRALASIAN ONLINE SYSTEMS PTY. LTD.— See COMPAQ Computer Corporation; *U.S. Public,* pg. 417
AUSTRALIA & NEW ZEALAND BANKING GROUP LIMITED; *Int'l,* pg. 98
AUSTRALIA AND NEW ZEALAND BANKING GROUP LIMITED, INTERNATIONAL BANKING DIVISION—See Australia & New Zealand Banking Group Limited; *Int'l,* pg. 98
AUSTRALIA & NEW ZEALAND BANKING GROUP (PNG) LIMITED—See Australia & New Zealand Banking Group Limited; *Int'l,* pg. 100
AUSTRALIA POWER PTY LTD—See Morgan Crucible Co. Plc; *Int'l,* pg. 894
AUSTRALIAN ABRASIVES PTY. LTD.—See Saint-Gobain; *Int'l,* pg. 1174
AUSTRALIAN ALUMINIUM (AUSTRALUCO) LIMITED— See Alcan Aluminium Limited; *Int'l,* pg. 51
AUSTRALIAN AMP PTY. LIMITED—See AMP Incorporated; *U.S. Public,* pg. 9
AUSTRALIAN CHAR HOLDING PTY., LTD.—See Nissho Iwai Corporation; *Int'l,* pg. 947

AUSTRALIAN CHEMICAL HOLDINGS LTD.—See Hercules Incorporated; *U.S. Public,* pg. 810
AUSTRALIAN COLEMAN, INC.—See MacAndrews & Forbes Holdings Inc.; *U.S. Private,* pg. 691
AUSTRALIAN DIAGNOSTICS CORPORATION PTY. LTD.— See Novartis AG; *Int'l,* pg. 975
AUSTRALIAN FINANCIAL REVIEW—See John Fairfax Holdings Limited; *Int'l,* pg. 477
AUSTRALIAN GEOGRAPHIC—See John Fairfax Holdings Limited; *Int'l,* pg. 477
AUSTRALIAN GLASS MANUFACTURERS CO.—See BTR plc; *Int'l,* pg. 128
AUSTRALIAN GUARANTEE CORPORATION LIMITED— See Westpac Banking Corporation; *Int'l,* pg. 1496
AUSTRALIAN GUARANTEE CORPORATION (NZ) LIMITED—See Westpac Banking Corporation; *Int'l,* pg. 1497
AUSTRALIAN MANGANESE COMPANY PTY LTD.—See The Broken Hill Proprietary Company Limited; *Int'l,* pg. 224
AUSTRALIAN MUTUAL PROVIDENT; *Int'l,* pg. 100
AUSTRALIAN MUTUAL PROVIDENT SOCIETY—See Australian Mutual Provident; *Int'l,* pg. 100
AUSTRALIAN NATIONAL INDUSTRIES LIMITED; *Int'l,* pg. 100
AUSTRALIAN NEWSPRINT MILLS—See Fletcher Challenge Limited; *Int'l,* pg. 495
AUSTRALIAN OIL & GAS CORPORATION LIMITED; *Int'l,* pg. 101
AUSTRALIAN PERLITE—See Laporte plc; *Int'l,* pg. 803
AUSTRALIAN POWER PRODUCTS PTY LTD—See Morgan Crucible Co. Plc; *Int'l,* pg. 893
AUSTRALIAN RADIO NETWORK—See Clear Channel Communications, Inc.; *U.S. Public,* pg. 386
AUSTRALIAN ROAD CREDIT LIMITED—See Ford Motor Company; *U.S. Public,* pg. 665
AUSTRALIAN SUBMARINE CORPORATION—See Celsius AB; *Int'l,* pg. 277
AUSTRALIAN THREAD PTY. LTD.—See Coats Viyella plc; *Int'l,* pg. 299
AUSTRALIAN TIMKEN PROPRIETARY LTD.—See The Timken Company; *U.S. Public,* pg. 1617
AUSTRALIAN WATER HEATER DIVISION—See Southcorp Holdings Ltd.; *Int'l,* pg. 1287
AUSTRALIAN WINDOW FURNISHINGS (NSW) PTY. LTD.—See Hunter Douglas N.V.; *Int'l,* pg. 639
AUSTRALIE—See Havas Advertising; *Int'l,* pg. 600
AUSTRIA OBI-SYSTEMZENTRALE—See OBI Bau-und Heimwerkermaerkte GmbH & Co. KG; *Int'l,* pg. 993
AUSTRIA PUMA DASSLER GES.M.B.H.—See Proventus AB; *Int'l,* pg. 1072
AUSTRIA III—See TBWA Chiat/Day; *U.S. Private,* pg. 1062
AUSTRIAN AIRLINES; *Int'l,* pg. 101
AUSTRIAN AIRLINES—See Austrian Airlines; *Int'l,* pg. 101
AUSTRIAN POSTAL & TELEGRAPH ADMINISTRATION; *Int'l,* pg. 101
AUSTRO-BAVARIA INVESTMENT AG—See Bayerische Vereinsbank Group; *Int'l,* pg. 180
AUSTRON INC.—See Datum Inc.; *U.S. Public,* pg. 488
AUTARKA GMBH, VERMITTLUNG VON VERSICHERUNGEN ALLER ART—See Dyckerhoff & Widmann AG; *Int'l,* pg. 423
AUTECH JAPAN, INC.—See Nissan Motor Co., Ltd.; *Int'l,* pg. 944
AUTHENTIC FITNESS CORP.; *U.S. Public,* pg. 147
AUTHENTIC FITNESS CORP. EAST COAST REGION— See Authentic Fitness Corp.; *U.S. Public,* pg. 148
AUTO-AIR COMPOSITES, INC.—See Cade Industries, Inc.; *U.S. Public,* pg. 290
AUTO BLANKERS—See Kasle Steel Corporation; *U.S. Private,* pg. 608
AUTO-BON OY—See Amer Group Ltd.; *Int'l,* pg. 72
AUTO-BON OY (IMPORTS)—See Amer Group Ltd.; *Int'l,* pg. 72
AUTO DIREKT VERSICHERUNGS AG—See Nationwide Insurance Enterprise; *U.S. Private,* pg. 789
AUTO DRIVEAWAY CO.; *U.S. Private,* pg. 100
AUTO 5—See GIB Group; *Int'l,* pg. 533
AUTO GLASS SPECIALISTS; *U.S. Private,* pg. 100
AUTO-GRAPH COMPUTER DESIGNING SYSTEMS, INC.— See Masco Corporation; *U.S. Public,* pg. 1053
AUTO INSURANCE SOLUTIONS INC.—See The Progressive Corporation; *U.S. Public,* pg. 1334
AUTO JECTORS, INC.—See Group Dekko; *U.S. Private,* pg. 484
AUTO LEASE HOLLAND B.V.—See ABN-AMRO Holding N.V.; *Int'l,* pg. 9
AUTO LENDERS ACCEPTANCE CORP.—See Fortis; *Int'l,* pg. 499
AUTO MARKETING NETWORK, INC.—See Imperial Credit Industries, Inc.; *U.S. Public,* pg. 872
AUTO-OWNERS INSURANCE; *U.S. Private,* pg. 100
AUTO-OWNERS LIFE INSURANCE CO.—See Auto-Owners Insurance; *U.S. Private,* pg. 100
AUTO-PRODUCTS AB—See Axel Johnson AB; *Int'l,* pg. 708
AUTO-SERVICE—See Groupe Casino; *Int'l,* pg. 563
AUTO-SPAN OY—See Kesko Ltd.; *Int'l,* pg. 732
AUTO TREND PRODUCTS—See Punch Press Products, Inc.; *U.S. Private,* pg. 895
AUTO-TROL, LTD.—See Auto-trol Technology Corporation; *U.S. Public,* pg. 148
AUTO-TROL TECHNOLOGY AB—See Auto-trol Technology Corporation; *U.S. Public,* pg. 148
AUTO-TROL TECHNOLOGY AUSTRALIA—See Auto-trol Technology Corporation; *U.S. Public,* pg. 148
AUTO-TROL TECHNOLOGY (CANADA) LTD.—See Auto-trol Technology Corporation; *U.S. Public,* pg. 148
AUTO-TROL TECHNOLOGY CORP.—See Auto-trol Technology Corporation; *U.S. Public,* pg. 148
AUTO-TROL TECHNOLOGY CORP.-VIRGINIA—See Auto-trol Technology Corporation; *U.S. Public,* pg. 148
AUTO-TROL TECHNOLOGY CORPORATION; *U.S. Public,* pg. 148

AUTO-TROL TECHNOLOGY GMBH—See Auto-trol Technology Corporation; *U.S. Public,* pg. 148
AUTO-TROL TECHNOLOGY SALES—See Auto-trol Technology Corporation; *U.S. Public,* pg. 148
AUTOALLIANCE INTERNATIONAL INC.—See Mazda Motor Corporation; *Int'l,* pg. 849
AUTOBATERIE SPOL.S.R.O.—See VARTA AG; *Int'l,* pg. 1452
AUTOCAM ACQUISITION, INC.—See Autocam Corporation; *U.S. Public,* pg. 148
AUTOCAM CORPORATION; *U.S. Public,* pg. 148
AUTOCAM LASER TECHNOLOGIES, INC.—See Autocam Corporation; *U.S. Public,* pg. 148
AUTOCAM-PAX, INC.—See Autocam Corporation; *U.S. Public,* pg. 148
AUTOCAM SOUTH CAROLINA, INC.—See Autocam Corporation; *U.S. Public,* pg. 148
AUTOCIM PLC—See N.V. Koninklijke KNP BT; *Int'l,* pg. 757
AUTOCLAVE ENGINEERS—See Snap-Tite, Inc.; *U.S. Private,* pg. 1010
AUTOCOMP, INC.—See Wallace Computer Services, Inc.; *U.S. Public,* pg. 1735
AUTOCON INDUSTRIES INC.—See Pearson plc; *Int'l,* pg. 1026
AUTOCON TECHNOLOGIES, INC.—See Hurco Companies, Inc.; *U.S. Public,* pg. 850
AUTOCONT A.S.—See Knurr AG; *Int'l,* pg. 739
AUTODELTA S.P.A.—See Fiat Auto SpA; *Int'l,* pg. 481
AUTODESK—See Autodesk, Inc.; *U.S. Public,* pg. 149
AUTODESK AB—See Autodesk, Inc.; *U.S. Public,* pg. 149
AUTODESK AG—See Autodesk, Inc.; *U.S. Public,* pg. 149
AUTODESK ALAMEDA—See Autodesk, Inc.; *U.S. Public,* pg. 149
AUTODESK ASIA PTE. LTD.—See Autodesk, Inc.; *U.S. Public,* pg. 149
AUTODESK AUSTRALIA PTY. LTD.—See Autodesk, Inc.; *U.S. Public,* pg. 149
AUTODESK BENELUX B.V.—See Autodesk, Inc.; *U.S. Public,* pg. 149
AUTODESK BRAZIL—See Autodesk, Inc.; *U.S. Public,* pg. 149
AUTODESK B.V.—See Autodesk, Inc.; *U.S. Public,* pg. 149
AUTODESK CANADA INC./BURNABY—See Autodesk, Inc.; *U.S. Public,* pg. 149
AUTODESK CANADA INC./MARKHAM—See Autodesk, Inc.; *U.S. Public,* pg. 149
AUTODESK CANADA INC./MONTREAL—See Autodesk, Inc.; *U.S. Public,* pg. 149
AUTODESK CHILE—See Autodesk, Inc.; *U.S. Public,* pg. 149
AUTODESK CHINA—See Autodesk, Inc.; *U.S. Public,* pg. 149
AUTODESK DEVELOPEMENT BV (TECHNICAL & OPERATIONS)—See Autodesk, Inc.; *U.S. Public,* pg. 149
AUTODESK (EUROPE) S.A.—See Autodesk, Inc.; *U.S. Public,* pg. 149
AUTODESK FAR EAST LTD.—See Autodesk, Inc.; *U.S. Public,* pg. 149
AUTODESK GESMBH—See Autodesk, Inc.; *U.S. Public,* pg. 149
AUTODESK GMBH—See Autodesk, Inc.; *U.S. Public,* pg. 149
AUTODESK, INC.; *U.S. Public,* pg. 148
AUTODESK, INC.—See Autodesk, Inc.; *U.S. Public,* pg. 149
AUTODESK, INC. TAIWAN—See Autodesk, Inc.; *U.S. Public,* pg. 149
AUTODESK INDIA—See Autodesk, Inc.; *U.S. Public,* pg. 149
AUTODESK ISRAEL GMBH—See Autodesk, Inc.; *U.S. Public,* pg. 149
AUTODESK KOREA LIMITED—See Autodesk, Inc.; *U.S. Public,* pg. 149
AUTODESK LTD.—See Autodesk, Inc.; *U.S. Public,* pg. 149
AUTODESK LTD. (AFRICA)—See Autodesk, Inc.; *U.S. Public,* pg. 149
AUTODESK MECHANICAL DIVISION—See Autodesk, Inc.; *U.S. Public,* pg. 149
AUTODESK MEXICO—See Autodesk, Inc.; *U.S. Public,* pg. 149
AUTODESK PORTLAND—See Autodesk, Inc.; *U.S. Public,* pg. 149
AUTODESK RUSSIA—See Autodesk, Inc.; *U.S. Public,* pg. 149
AUTODESK S.A.—See Autodesk, Inc.; *U.S. Public,* pg. 149
AUTODESK S.A.R.L.—See Autodesk, Inc.; *U.S. Public,* pg. 150
AUTODESK SOFTWARE LDA—See Autodesk, Inc.; *U.S. Public,* pg. 150
AUTODESK S.P.A.—See Autodesk, Inc.; *U.S. Public,* pg. 150
AUTODESK S.R.O.—See Autodesk, Inc.; *U.S. Public,* pg. 150
AUTODESK VENEZUELA—See Autodesk, Inc.; *U.S. Public,* pg. 150
AUTOEUROPA AUTOMOVELS LDA.—See Volkswagen AG; *Int'l,* pg. 1474
AUTOFIELD ENGINEERS PRIVATE LTD.—See Cummins Engine Company, Inc.; *U.S. Public,* pg. 469
AUTOGERMA S.P.A.—See Volkswagen AG; *Int'l,* pg. 1474
AUTOLATINA—See Volkswagen AG; *Int'l,* pg. 1474
AUTOLATINA ARGENTINA S.A.—See Volkswagen AG; *Int'l,* pg. 1475
AUTOLATINA BRASIL S.A.—See Ford Motor Company; *U.S. Public,* pg. 665
AUTOLATINA FINANCIADORA S.A.-CREDITO, FINANCIAMENTO E INVESTIMENTOS—See Ford Motor Company; *U.S. Public,* pg. 665
AUTOLEASE FLEETS LIMITED—See Britax International plc; *Int'l,* pg. 216

AUTOLEASE LIMITED—See Britax International plc; *Int'l*, pg. 216
AUTOLIASONS FRANCE S.A.—See Barnes Group Inc.; *U.S. Public*, pg. 190
AUTOLIFT INDUSTRIAL LIFT TRUCKS—See Plymouth Industries, Inc.; *U.S. Private*, pg. 873
AUTOLIV DEVELOPMENT AB—See Electrolux, AB; *Int'l*, pg. 438
AUTOLIV ET CIE—See Electrolux, AB; *Int'l*, pg. 441
AUTOLIV GMBH—See Electrolux, AB; *Int'l*, pg. 442
AUTOLIV S.A.—See Electrolux, AB; *Int'l*, pg. 441
AUTOLIV STIL AB—See Electrolux, AB; *Int'l*, pg. 438
AUTOLOGIC INFORMATION INTERNATIONAL—See Volt Information Sciences, Inc.; *U.S. Public*, pg. 1724
AUTOLOGIC INFORMATION INTERNATIONAL AB—See Volt Information Sciences, Inc.; *U.S. Public*, pg. 1724
AUTOLOGIC INFORMATION INTERNATIONAL, INC.—See Volt Information Sciences, Inc.; *U.S. Public*, pg. 1724
AUTOLOGIC INFORMATION INTERNATIONAL LTD.—See Volt Information Sciences, Inc.; *Int'l*, pg. 1724
AUTOLOGIC INFORMATION INTERNATIONAL LTD. (AUSTRALIA)—See Volt Information Sciences, Inc.; *U.S. Public*, pg. 1724
AUTOLOGIC INFORMATION INTERNATIONAL, PTY, LTD.—See Volt Information Sciences, Inc.; *U.S. Public*, pg. 1724
AUTOMATED LABEL SYSTEMS, INC.—See Illinois Tool Works Inc.; *U.S. Public*, pg. 865
AUTOMATED PRODUCTS, INC. (LEADER SYSTEMS, INC.)—See USF&G Corporation; *U.S. Public*, pg. 1659
AUTOMATED STUDIO LIGHTING, INC.—See Sony Corporation; *Int'l*, pg. 1283
AUTOMATED SYSTEMS (H.K.) LIMITED—See CSA Holdings Ltd.; *Int'l*, pg. 242
AUTOMATED SYSTEMS LIMITED—See CSA Holdings Ltd.; *Int'l*, pg. 242
AUTOMATED WAGERING—See Power House Technologies, Inc.; *U.S. Public*, pg. 1319
AUTOMATED WAGERING INTERNATIONAL, INC.—See Power House Technologies, Inc.; *U.S. Public*, pg. 1319
AUTOMATIC ASSEMBLY—See Research, Incorporated; *U.S. Public*, pg. 1382
AUTOMATIC CASTINGS DIVISION—See Leggett & Platt, Incorporated; *U.S. Public*, pg. 986
AUTOMATIC DATA PROCESSING, INC.; *U.S. Public*, pg. 150
AUTOMATIC EQUIPMENT MFG. CO.; *U.S. Private*, pg. 101
AUTOMATIC LIQUID PACKAGING, INC.; *U.S. Private*, pg. 101
AUTOMATIC MACHINE PRODUCTS COMPANY; *U.S. Private*, pg. 101
AUTOMATIC METAL BLANKING, INC.—See The Cypress Group LLC; *U.S. Private*, pg. 300
AUTOMATIC MUSIC SERVICE OF BILLINGS, INC.—See Power House Technologies, Inc.; *U.S. Public*, pg. 1319
AUTOMATIC POWER, INC.—See Spectra-Physics AB; *Int'l*, pg. 1289
AUTOMATIC POWER RJ—See Spectra-Physics AB; *Int'l*, pg. 1289
AUTOMATIC RADIO INTERNATIONAL—See Armatron International, Inc.; *U.S. Public*, pg. 131
AUTOMATIC SCREW MACHINES PRODUCTS COMPANY—See Lawson Products, Inc.; *U.S. Public*, pg. 980
AUTOMATIC SERVICE CO.—See AVA; *U.S. Private*, pg. 8
AUTOMATIC SERVICE CO. OF VIRGINIA, LYNCHBURG BRANCH—See AVA; *U.S. Private*, pg. 8
AUTOMATIC SERVICE CO. OF VIRGINIA, N. VIRGINIA BRANCH—See AVA; *U.S. Private*, pg. 8
AUTOMATIC SIGNAL/EAGLE SIGNAL—See Siemens AG; *Int'l*, pg. 1245
AUTOMATIC SWITCH CO.—See Emerson Electric Co.; *U.S. Public*, pg. 573
AUTOMATIC TIMING & CONTROLS—See Desco Corporation; *U.S. Private*, pg. 327
AUTOMATIC TIMING & CONTROLS, INC.—See Desco Corporation; *U.S. Private*, pg. 327
AUTOMATION CONTROL—See Thyssen AG; *Int'l*, pg. 1389
AUTOMATION FINISHING INC.—See Freeway Corporation; *U.S. Private*, pg. 426
AUTOMATION GROUP—See Parker Hannifin Corporation; *U.S. Public*, pg. 1259
AUTOMATION SOFTWARE, INC.—See Analysis & Technology, Inc.; *U.S. Public*, pg. 110
AUTOMATISERINGCENTRUM IDETA B.V.—See N.V. Koninklijke Bijenkorf Beheer KBB; *Int'l*, pg. 750
AUTOMAX CONTROLS, INC.—See Flowserve Corporation; *U.S. Public*, pg. 658
AUTOMAX FINANCE—See Firstbank Puerto Rico; *U.S. Public*, pg. 644
AUTOMAX, INC.—See Flowserve Corporation; *U.S. Public*, pg. 658
AUTOMAX SISTEMAS E INSTRUMENTOS DE CONTROL LTDA./TAYLOR—See ABB Asea Brown Boveri (Holding) Ltd.; *Int'l*, pg. 5
AUTOMOBIELBEDRIJVEN HOOGENBOOM B.V.—See Britax International plc; *Int'l*, pg. 216
AUTOMOBILE CLUB INSURANCE COMPANY—See American Automobile Association; *U.S. Private*, pg. 51
AUTOMOBILE MAGAZINE—See Primedia Inc.; *U.S. Public*, pg. 1328
AUTOMOBILE PROTECTION CORPORATION-APCO; *U.S. Public*, pg. 150
AUTOMOBILE SPECIALTY CO.—See ASC Incorporated; *U.S. Private*, pg. 8
AUTOMOBILES CITROEN—See PSA Peugeot Citroen; *Int'l*, pg. 1020
AUTOMOBILES PEUGEOT S.A.—See PSA Peugeot Citroen; *Int'l*, pg. 1020
AUTOMOTIVE ACCESSORY CO., LTD.—See UIS, Inc.; *U.S. Private*, pg. 1113
AUTOMOTIVE AFTERMARKET, NORTH AMERICA—See Mark IV Industries Inc.; *U.S. Public*, pg. 1045

AUTOMOTIVE & APPLIANCE CONTROLS DIV.—See Eaton Corporation; *U.S. Public*, pg. 556
AUTOMOTIVE CONNECTORS DIV.—See Parker Hannifin Corporation; *U.S. Public*, pg. 1260
AUTOMOTIVE CONTROLS CORP.—See Echlin Inc.; *U.S. Public*, pg. 560
AUTOMOTIVE DISTRIBUTION SALES DIV.—See Dana Corporation; *U.S. Public*, pg. 479
AUTOMOTIVE ELECTRONIC CONTROL SYSTEMS, INC.—See Robert Bosch GmbH; *Int'l*, pg. 205
AB AUTOMOTIVE ELECTRONICS LIMITED—See TT Group PLC; *Int'l*, pg. 1344
AUTOMOTIVE EMISSION SYSTEMS—See Engelhard Corporation; *U.S. Public*, pg. 582
AUTOMOTIVE ENERGY CONTROLS GROUP—See Motorola, Inc.; *U.S. Public*, pg. 1137
AUTOMOTIVE EXPORT SUPPLIES LIMITED—See Alvis plc; *Int'l*, pg. 70
AUTOMOTIVE FINANCE LIMITED—See Ford Motor Company; *U.S. Public*, pg. 665
AUTOMOTIVE FINANCIAL SERVICES, INC.—See Chrysler Corporation; *U.S. Public*, pg. 354
AUTOMOTIVE GROUP—See Aeroquip-Vickers, Inc.; *U.S. Public*, pg. 24
AUTOMOTIVE MANUFACTURERS (MALAYSIA) SDN. BHD.—See Isuzu Motors Limited; *Int'l*, pg. 692
AUTOMOTIVE MOULDING COMPANY—See Guardian Industries Corp.; *U.S. Private*, pg. 485
AUTOMOTIVE NEWS—See Crain Communications, Inc.; *U.S. Private*, pg. 284
AUTOMOTIVE OPERS.—See Morton International Inc.; *U.S. Public*, pg. 1134
AUTOMOTIVE PRODUCTS USA INC.—See BBA Group plc; *Int'l*, pg. 113
AUTOMOTIVE REBUILDERS—See Richmond Motor Company; *U.S. Private*, pg. 929
AUTOMOTIVE RENTALS, INC. (ARI)—See Holman Enterprises; *U.S. Private*, pg. 535
AUTOMOTIVE SUPPLY ASSOCIATES, INC.; *U.S. Private*, pg. 101
AUTOMOTIVE SYSTEMS DIVISION—See ABB Asea Brown Boveri (Holding) Ltd.; *Int'l*, pg. 4
AUTOMOTIVE TAILORED BLANKS BV—See Koninklijke Hoogovens N.V.; *Int'l*, pg. 753
AUTOMOTIVE WELDING CENTER—See ABB Asea Brown Boveri (Holding) Ltd.; *Int'l*, pg. 4
AUTOMOTIVE WIRING SYSTEMS DIVISION - SYLEA—See Labinal SA; *Int'l*, pg. 785
AUTOMOTIVE WORLDWIDE SECTOR—See TRW Inc.; *U.S. Public*, pg. 1558
AUTOMOTORES CAPITAL LTDA.—See Corporacion MAPFRE, Compania Internacional de Reaseguros, S.A.; *Int'l*, pg. 333
AUTOMOULD (PTY) LIMITED—See Morgan Crucible Co. Plc; *Int'l*, pg. 895
AUTOPARTES DE PRECISION DE SANTANA, S.A. DE C.V.—See Miniature Precision Components; *U.S. Private*, pg. 750
AUTOPRESS COMPOSITES—See DSM N.V.; *Int'l*, pg. 354
AUTOROLL MACHINE CO., LLC; *U.S. Private*, pg. 101
AUTOSHRED INC.—See Allied Waste Industries; *U.S. Public*, pg. 49
AUTOSTRADE INTL.-LUXEMBOURG—See IRI Istituto Ricostruzione Industriale; *Int'l*, pg. 655
AUTOSWAGE PRODUCTS, INC.; *U.S. Private*, pg. 101
AUTOSYSTEMS DEVELOPMENT LABORATORY—See Platinum Technology, Inc.; *U.S. Public*, pg. 1309
AUTOTANK AB—See Mannesmann A.G.; *Int'l*, pg. 839
AUTOTOTE CORPORATION; *U.S. Public*, pg. 150
AUTOTRACTOREXPORT; *Int'l*, pg. 101
AUTOTROL CORPORATION—See Osmonics, Inc.; *U.S. Public*, pg. 1234
AUTOTROL FRANCE, S.A.—See Osmonics, Inc.; *U.S. Public*, pg. 1234
AUTO-TROL TECHNOLOGY CORP.—See Auto-trol Technology Corporation; *U.S. Public*, pg. 148
AUTOVIDRIO, S.A. DE C.V.—See Ford Motor Company; *U.S. Public*, pg. 665
AUTOWEEK—See Crain Communications, Inc.; *U.S. Private*, pg. 284
AUTOZONE, INC.; *U.S. Public*, pg. 150
AUTRANET, INC.—See The Equitable Companies Incorporated; *U.S. Public*, pg. 589
AUTRON INCORPORATED—See Marubeni Corporation; *Int'l*, pg. 845
AUTRONICS CORPORATION—See Bowthorpe plc; *Int'l*, pg. 208
AUTUMN ROSE QUARRY, INC.—See Rock of Ages Corporation; *U.S. Public*, pg. 1396
AUVERGNE ISOLATION—See Saint-Gobain; *Int'l*, pg. 1172
AUXFINA—See Groupe Bruxelles Lambert S.A.; *Int'l*, pg. 562
AUXILEC—See Thomson S.A.; *Int'l*, pg. 1381
AUXILEC, INC.—See Thomson S.A.; *Int'l*, pg. 1383
AUXILIA GRAPHICA S.R.L.—See Dainippon Ink & Chemicals, Inc.; *Int'l*, pg. 370
AUXILIARY POWER INTERNATIONAL CORPORATION (APIC)—See Labinal SA; *Int'l*, pg. 787
AUXINVEST S.A.—See Tractebel; *Int'l*, pg. 1415
AUXISOL—See Saint-Gobain; *Int'l*, pg. 1176
AUXITROL CO.—See Esterline Technologies Corporation; *U.S. Public*, pg. 594
AUXITROL IBERICO S.A.—See Esterline Technologies Corporation; *U.S. Public*, pg. 594
AUXITROL S.A.—See Esterline Technologies Corporation; *U.S. Public*, pg. 594
AVABANK AG—See General Electric Company; *U.S. Public*, pg. 712
AVAC SYSTEMS INC.—See Celsius AB; *Int'l*, pg. 278
AVALMADRID, S.G.R., S.A.—See Caja de Madrid Group; *Int'l*, pg. 252
THE AVALON HILL GAME COMPANY—See Monarch Avalon, Inc.; *U.S. Public*, pg. 1123

AVANA BAKERIES LTD.—See Tomkins PLC; *Int'l*, pg. 1396
AVANT GARDE OPTICS INC.—See Luxottica Group S.p.A.; *Int'l*, pg. 822
AVANTEL, S.A.—See Grupo Financiero Banamex/Accival, S.A. de C.V.; *Int'l*, pg. 574
AVANTI; *U.S. Public*, pg. 151
AVANTI PRESS INC.; *U.S. Private*, pg. 101
AVANZARE—See Lettuce Entertain You Enterprises, Inc.; *U.S. Private*, pg. 661
AVATAR DEVELOPMENT CORP.—See Avatar Holdings Inc.; *U.S. Public*, pg. 151
AVATAR HOLDINGS INC.; *U.S. Public*, pg. 151
AVATAR PROPERTIES INC.—See Avatar Holdings Inc.; *U.S. Public*, pg. 151
AVATAR REALTY, INC.—See Avatar Holdings Inc.; *U.S. Public*, pg. 151
AVATAR UTILITIES, INC.—See Avatar Holdings Inc.; *U.S. Public*, pg. 151
AVATAR VACATION RESORTS, INC.—See Avatar Holdings Inc.; *U.S. Public*, pg. 151
AVATEX CORPORATION; *U.S. Public*, pg. 151
AVCO FINANCIAL SERVICES—See Textron Inc.; *U.S. Public*, pg. 1589
AVCO INSURANCE SERVICES/BALBOA LIFE & CASUALTY—See Textron Inc.; *U.S. Public*, pg. 1589
AVCRON INCORPORATED—See ITT Industries, Inc.; *U.S. Public*, pg. 859
AVDEL TEXTRON—See Textron Inc.; *U.S. Public*, pg. 1590
AVDON (GB) LTD.—See Pechiney S.A.; *Int'l*, pg. 1030
AVEMCO CORPORATION; *U.S. Public*, pg. 151
AVEMCO INSURANCE CO.—See Avemco Corporation; *U.S. Public*, pg. 152
AVEN TOOLS LTD.—See The Black & Decker Corporation; *U.S. Public*, pg. 234
THE AVENAL PROGRESS—See Pulitzer Publishing Company; *U.S. Public*, pg. 1343
AVENIR TECHNOLOGIE INTERNATIONAL—See Compagnie des Machines Bull; *Int'l*, pg. 315
AVENOR, INC.; *Int'l*, pg. 101
AVENT AMERICA INC.—See Cannon Rubber Ltd.; *Int'l*, pg. 261
AVENT DE HONDURAS, S.A. DE C.V.—See Kimberly-Clark Corporation; *U.S. Public*, pg. 959
AVENT, INC.—See Kimberly-Clark Corporation; *U.S. Public*, pg. 959
AVENT, S.A. DE C.V.—See Kimberly-Clark Corporation; *U.S. Public*, pg. 959
AVERY CONVERTED PRODUCTS GROUP—See Avery Dennison Corporation; *U.S. Public*, pg. 152
AVERY DENNISON CORPORATION; *U.S. Public*, pg. 152
AVERY DENNISON CORPORATION LABEL GROUP—See Avery Dennison Corporation; *U.S. Public*, pg. 153
AVERY ETICHETTE ITALIA S.P.A.—See Avery Dennison Corporation; *U.S. Public*, pg. 153
AVERY ETIKETTERING A/S—See Avery Dennison Corporation; *U.S. Public*, pg. 153
AVERY FLIGHT INTERNATIONAL LIMITED—See Bridport-Gundry p.l.c.; *Int'l*, pg. 215
AVERY INTERNATIONAL CONVERTING GROUP—See Avery Dennison Corporation; *U.S. Public*, pg. 152
AVERY INTL. ADHESIVE PRODS., LTD.—See Avery Dennison Corporation; *U.S. Public*, pg. 153
AVERY LABEL LTD.—See Avery Dennison Corporation; *U.S. Public*, pg. 153
AVERY LABEL SYSTEMS LTD.—See Avery Dennison Corporation; *U.S. Public*, pg. 153
AVERY MASCHINEN GMBH—See Avery Dennison Corporation; *U.S. Public*, pg. 153
AVEST, INC.—See Astrex, Inc.; *U.S. Public*, pg. 141
AVESTA AB—See Axel Johnson AB; *Int'l*, pg. 708
AVESTA ABE AB—See British Steel Plc; *Int'l*, pg. 221
AVESTA CALAMO AB—See British Steel Plc; *Int'l*, pg. 221
AVESTA INFORMATION SYSTEMS AB—See British Steel Plc; *Int'l*, pg. 221
AVESTA NORDS AB—See British Steel Plc; *Int'l*, pg. 221
AVESTA PREFAB AB—See British Steel Plc; *Int'l*, pg. 221
AVESTA PRESS PLATE AB—See British Steel Plc; *Int'l*, pg. 221
AVESTA SANDVIK TUBE AB—See British Steel Plc; *Int'l*, pg. 221
AVESTA SHEFFIELD AB—See British Steel Plc; *Int'l*, pg. 221
AVESTA SHEFFIELD ASIA PACIFIC LTD.—See British Steel Plc; *Int'l*, pg. 221
AVESTA SHEFFIELD DISTRIBUTION LTD.—See British Steel Plc; *Int'l*, pg. 221
AVESTA SHEFFIELD EAST, INC.—See British Steel Plc; *Int'l*, pg. 221
AVESTA SHEFFIELD GESMBH—See British Steel Plc; *Int'l*, pg. 221
AVESTA SHEFFIELD, INC.—See British Steel Plc; *Int'l*, pg. 221
AVESTA SHEFFIELD LTD.—See British Steel Plc; *Int'l*, pg. 221
AVESTA SHEFFIELD PIPE CO.—See British Steel Plc; *Int'l*, pg. 221
AVESTA SHEFFIELD PLATE INC.—See British Steel Plc; *Int'l*, pg. 221
AVESTA SHEFFIELD PRECISION STRIP LTD.—See British Steel Plc; *Int'l*, pg. 222
AVESTA SHEFFIELD PTY. LTD.—See British Steel Plc; *Int'l*, pg. 222
AVESTA VALBRUNA AB—See British Steel Plc; *Int'l*, pg. 221
AVESTA WELDING AB—See British Steel Plc; *Int'l*, pg. 221
AVEX ELECTRONICS, INC.—See J.M. Huber Corporation; *U.S. Private*, pg. 545
AVEX ELECTRONICS LTD.—See J.M. Huber Corporation; *U.S. Private*, pg. 545
AVEX ELECTRONICS PTE. LTD.—See J.M. Huber Corporation; *U.S. Private*, pg. 545
AVEYRON EXPRESS—See SNCF; *Int'l*, pg. 1163
AVFALLSTEKNIK AB—See Celsius AB; *Int'l*, pg. 276

MASTER INDEX TO COMPANY NAMES

BAC

Company Index

AVIA—See American Sporting Goods Corporation; *U.S. Private*, pg. 62
AVIA EURO RSCG—See Havas Advertising; *Int'l*, pg. 602
AVIA RADIO A/S—See AAR Corp.; *U.S. Public*, pg. 2
AVIACION Y COMERCIO, S.A.—See SEPI; *Int'l*, pg. 1224
AVIACO—See Grupo Iberia; *Int'l*, pg. 574
AVIALL, INC.; *U.S. Public*, pg. 154
AVIALL, INC.—See Aviall, Inc.; *U.S. Public*, pg. 154
AVIATECA; *Int'l*, pg. 102
AVIATION CONSTRUCTORS, INC.—See Cleveland Group, Inc.; *U.S. Private*, pg. 246
AVIATION PRODUCT SUPPORT INC.—See Teleflex Incorporated; *U.S. Public*, pg. 1569
AVIATION SALES COMPANY; *U.S. Public*, pg. 154
AVIATUBE—See Pechiney S.A.; *Int'l*, pg. 1028
AVIBANK MFG., INC.; *U.S. Private*, pg. 101
AVICA—See Meggitt plc; *Int'l*, pg. 853
AVICA INC.—See Meggitt plc; *Int'l*, pg. 853
AVICOLA PILGRIM'S PRIDE DE MEXICO, S.A. DE C.V.—See Pilgrim's Pride Corporation; *U.S. Public*, pg. 1296
AVID TECHNOLOGY, INC.; *U.S. Public*, pg. 154
AVIGLIANO MILL—See Fort James Corporation; *U.S. Public*, pg. 673
AVIMO GROUP LIMITED—See Alvis plc; *Int'l*, pg. 70
AVIOCART S.P.A.—See The Mead Corporation; *U.S. Public*, pg. 1076
AVIONICS—See Lockheed Martin Corporation; *U.S. Public*, pg. 1008
AVIONICS & COMMUNICATIONS—See Rockwell International Corporation; *U.S. Public*, pg. 1397
AVIONICS SPECIALITIES, INC.—See Aerosonic Corporation; *U.S. Public*, pg. 25
AVIONS DE TRANSPORT REGIONAL - ATR—See IRI Istituto Ricostruzione Industriale; *Int'l*, pg. 654
AVIONS DIV.—See Aerospatiale; *Int'l*, pg. 29
AVIS AUTOVERMIETUNG AG—See Cendant Corporation; *U.S. Public*, pg. 321
AVIS CAR LEASING—See Cendant Corporation; *U.S. Public*, pg. 321
AVIS FORD INC.; *U.S. Private*, pg. 101
AVIS INDUSTRIAL CORPORATION; *U.S. Private*, pg. 102
AVIS RENT A CAR SYSTEM, INC.—See Cendant Corporation; *U.S. Public*, pg. 321
AVITAS INC.—See Det Norske Veritas; *Int'l*, pg. 396
AVIVA SPORT, INC.—See Mattel, Inc.; *U.S. Public*, pg. 1058
AVNET ACCESS LTD.—See Avnet, Inc.; *U.S. Public*, pg. 155
AVNET COMPOSANTS AND AVNET TIME—See Avnet, Inc.; *U.S. Public*, pg. 155
AVNET COMPUTER—See Avnet, Inc.; *U.S. Public*, pg. 155
AVNET EMG SRL—See Avnet, Inc.; *U.S. Public*, pg. 155
AVNET E2000 GMBH—See Avnet, Inc.; *U.S. Public*, pg. 155
AVNET, INC.; *U.S. Public*, pg. 155
AVNET NORTEC AB—See Avnet, Inc.; *U.S. Public*, pg. 155
AVNET TIME LTD.—See Avnet, Inc.; *U.S. Public*, pg. 155
AVNET VSI ELECTRONICS (AUSTRALIA) PTY. LTD.—See Avnet, Inc.; *U.S. Public*, pg. 155
AVNET VSI ELECTRONICS (N.Z.) LTD.—See Avnet, Inc.; *U.S. Public*, pg. 155
AVNET WKK COMPONENTS—See Avnet, Inc.; *U.S. Public*, *pg. 155*
AVON BOOKS—See The Hearst Corporation; *U.S. Private*, pg. 515
AVON PRODUCTS, INC.; *U.S. Public*, pg. 155
AVON WORKSHOP FICKS REED; *U.S. Private*, pg. 102
AVONDALE FOREIGN SALES CORPORATION—See Avondale Incorporated; *U.S. Private*, pg. 103
AVONDALE GULFPORT MARINE INC.—See Avondale Industries, Inc.; *U.S. Public*, pg. 157
AVONDALE INCORPORATED; *U.S. Private*, pg. 102
AVONDALE INDUSTRIES, INC.; *U.S. Public*, pg. 156
AVONDALE INDUSTRIES INC. SHIPYARDS DIV.—See Avondale Industries, Inc.; *U.S. Public*, pg. 157
AVONDALE MILLS, INC.—See Avondale Incorporated; *U.S. Private*, pg. 102
AVONMORE WATERFORD GROUP PLC; *Int'l*, pg. 102
AVONMOUTH TERMINAL—See GATX Corporation; *U.S. Public*, pg. 692
AVRETT, FREE & GINSBERG, INC.; *U.S. Private*, pg. 103
AVROY SHLAIN COSMETICS (PTY.) LTD.—See Sara Lee Corporation; *U.S. Public*, pg. 1434
AWABED - SSANGYONG CONTRACTING CO.—See Ssangyong Business Group; *Int'l*, pg. 1292
AWARD FOODS, INC.—See Koninklijke BolsWessanen nv; *Int'l*, pg. 752
AWARD SERVICES SA—See GIB Group; *Int'l*, pg. 532
AWBREY GLEN GOLF CLUB, INC.—See Brooks Resources Corporation; *U.S. Private*, pg. 172
AWE ABFALLWIRTSCHAFT EBERSWALDE GMBH—See Veba AG; *Int'l*, pg. 1460
AWREY BAKERIES, INC.; *U.S. Private*, pg. 103
AXEL SPRINGER VERLAG AG; *Int'l*, pg. 102
AXELROD FOODS, INC.—See Koninklijke BolsWessanen nv; *Int'l*, pg. 752
AXENT TECHNOLOGIES; *U.S. Public*, pg. 157
AXENT TECHNOLOGIES—See Axent Technologies; *U.S. Public*, pg. 157
AXIA INCORPORATED; *U.S. Private*, pg. 103
AXIOM INC.; *U.S. Public*, pg. 157
AXIOS, LTDA.—See Tenneco Inc.; *U.S. Public*, pg. 1577
AXIS GROUP—See Allied Holdings, Inc.; *U.S. Public*, pg. 48
AXIVA—See AXA-UAP; *Int'l*, pg. 18
AXLAMIN LTD.—See Axel Johnson AB; *Int'l*, pg. 710
AXLES INDIA LIMITED—See Eaton Corporation; *U.S. Public*, pg. 558
AXMARINE OY—See Axel Johnson AB; *Int'l*, pg. 712
AXPRO AXEL JOHNSON GESMBH—See Axel Johnson AB; *Int'l*, pg. 710
AXPRO FRANCE S.A.—See Axel Johnson AB; *Int'l*, pg. 710
AXSON ESPANA—See Axson S.A.; *Int'l*, pg. 103
AXSON FRANCE—See Axson S.A.; *Int'l*, pg. 103
AXSON GMBH—See Axson S.A.; *Int'l*, pg. 103
AXSON-ITALIA—See Axson S.A.; *Int'l*, pg. 103
AXSON S.A.; *Int'l*, pg. 102
AXSYS TECHNOLOGIES, INC.; *U.S. Public*, pg. 157
AXTEC AB—See Axel Johnson AB; *Int'l*, pg. 708
AXTRADE AB—See Axel Johnson AB; *Int'l*, pg. 708
AXTRADE (AUSTRALIA) PTY LTD.—See Axel Johnson AB; *Int'l*, pg. 710
AXTRADE CARE AB—See Axel Johnson AB; *Int'l*, pg. 708
AXTRADE CZECHOSLOVAKIA—See Axel Johnson AB; *Int'l*, pg. 710
AXTRADE DENTAL AB—See Axel Johnson AB; *Int'l*, pg. 708
AXTRADE EAST AB—See Axel Johnson AB; *Int'l*, pg. 708
AXTRADE EAST ASIA LTD.—See Axel Johnson AB; *Int'l*, pg. 708
AXTRADE FLOW AB—See Axel Johnson AB; *Int'l*, pg. 708
AXTRADE KOREA LTD.—See Axel Johnson AB; *Int'l*, pg. 710
AXTRADE LIC MEDICA S.A.—See Axel Johnson AB; *Int'l*, pg. 710
AXTRADE SCANDINAVIA AB—See Axel Johnson AB; *Int'l*, *pg. 708*
AXTRADE SCANDINAVIA A/S—See Axel Johnson AB; *Int'l*, pg. 710
AXXIS NV—See DSM N.V.; *Int'l*, pg. 354
AYASE PRECISION CO., LTD.—See NHK Spring Co., Ltd.; *Int'l*, pg. 901
AYCOCK AUTO AUCTION—See Tyco International Ltd.; *U.S. Public*, pg. 1648
AYCOCK, INC.; *U.S. Private*, pg. 103
AYDIN CONTROLS DIV.—See Aydin Corporation; *U.S. Public*, pg. 158
AYDIN CORPORATION; *U.S. Public*, pg. 158
AYDIN CORPORATION WEST—See Aydin Corporation; *U.S. Public*, pg. 158
AYDIN DISPLAYS (EAST)—See Aydin Corporation; *U.S. Public*, pg. 158
AYDIN ELECTRO-FAB DIV.—See Aydin Corporation; *U.S. Public*, pg. 158
AYDIN EUROPE LTD.—See Aydin Corporation; *U.S. Public*, *pg. 158*
AYDIN INTERNATIONAL U.K.—See Aydin Corporation; *U.S. Public*, pg. 158
AYDIN MOLDED DEVICES DIV.—See Aydin Corporation; *U.S. Public*, pg. 158
AYDIN RAYTOR DIV.—See Aydin Corporation; *U.S. Public*, pg. 158
AYDIN TELECOM DIVISION—See Aydin Corporation; *U.S. Public*, pg. 158
AYDIN VECTOR DIV.—See Aydin Corporation; *U.S. Public*, pg. 158
AYDIN YAZILIM VE ELEKTRONIK SANAYII A.S. (AYES AS)—See Aydin Corporation; *U.S. Public*, pg. 158
AYER FRANCE—See N.W. Ayer & Partners; *U.S. Private*, pg. 104
AYER INTERNATIONAL—See N.W. Ayer & Partners; *U.S. Private*, pg. 104
N.W. AYER & PARTNERS; *U.S. Private*, pg. 103
N.W. AYER & PARTNERS CHICAGO—See N.W. Ayer & Partners; *U.S. Private*, pg. 104
AYER PUBLIC RELATIONS—See N.W. Ayer & Partners; *U.S. Private*, pg. 104
AYERDIRECT—See N.W. Ayer & Partners; *U.S. Private*, pg. 104
AYERST, MCKENNA & HARRISON INC.—See American Home Products Corporation; *U.S. Public*, pg. 80
AYERST-WYETH PHARMACEUTICALS, INC.—See American Home Products Corporation; *U.S. Public*, pg. 79
AYLESBURY AUTOMATION LTD.—See Clayhithe P.L.C.; *Int'l*, pg. 297
JOHN AYLING AND ASSOCIATES LIMITED; *Int'l*, pg. 103
AYMORE GROUP—See ABN-AMRO Holding N.V.; *Int'l*, pg. 12
AYRA SERVICIO SA—See GKN plc; *Int'l*, pg. 535
AYRSHIRE LAND COMPANY—See Cyprus Amax Minerals Company; *U.S. Public*, pg. 471
AYRTON SAUNDERS—See Franz Haniel & Cie, GmbH; *Int'l*, pg. 591
AYTON YOUNG & RUBICAM LTD.—See Young & Rubicam Inc.; *U.S. Private*, pg. 1198
AYUDHYA INVESTMENT AND TRUST PUBLIC CO., LTD.—See The Sakura Bank, Limited; *Int'l*, pg. 1180
AZALEA DEVELOPMENT COMPANY—See Shivers Trading & Operating Co.; *U.S. Private*, pg. 994
AZCON CORP.—See Blue Tee Corporation; *U.S. Private*, pg. 153
AZENIDA AGRICOLA PEROLLA S.R.L.—See Allianz Aktiengesellschaft; *Int'l*, pg. 61
AZERTY INCORPORATED—See Abitibi-Consolidated Inc.; *Int'l*, pg. 20
AZON CORPORATION; *U.S. Private*, pg. 104
AZONIX INC.—See Crane Co.; *U.S. Public*, pg. 457
AZTAR CORPORATION; *U.S. Public*, pg. 158
AZTEC ENVIRONMENTAL CONTROL LIMITED—See Severn Trent Plc; *Int'l*, pg. 1225
AZTEC INDUSTRIES, INC.—See Aztec Manufacturing Co.; *U.S. Public*, pg. 159
AZTEC MANUFACTURING CO.; *U.S. Public*, pg. 159
AZTEC TRADING COMPANY, S.A.—See Georgia-Pacific Corporation; *U.S. Public*, pg. 736
AZTECA FOODS, INCORPORATED; *U.S. Private*, pg. 104
AZTEX ENTERPRISES; *U.S. Private*, pg. 104
AZTRONIC—See Vishay Intertechnology, Inc.; *U.S. Public*, pg. 1722
AZUSA ROCK, INC.—See CalMat Co.; *U.S. Public*, pg. 295
AZZURA-INTERNATIONAL MARKETING & PROMOTIONS—See DMB&B Communications; *U.S. Private*, pg. 303

B

B COMMUNICATIONS/GGK—See TBWA GGK Zurick; *Int'l*, *pg. 1335*
B + B ASIA LIMITED—See Bilfinger + Berger Bauaktiengesellschaft; *Int'l*, pg. 196
B&B CORPORATE HOLDINGS, INC.; *U.S. Private*, pg. 104
B + B FAR EAST LTD.—See Bilfinger + Berger Bauaktiengesellschaft; *Int'l*, pg. 196
B + B GAS AND OIL SERVICES (NIGERIA) LIMITED—See Bilfinger + Berger Bauaktiengesellschaft; *Int'l*, pg. 196
B & B HOMES CORPORATION; *U.S. Private*, pg. 105
B&B MOLDERS; *U.S. Private*, pg. 105
B & B MOTOR & CONTROL CORPORATION; *U.S. Private*, pg. 105
B & C BOTTLERS CORP.—See Bacardi Limited; *Int'l*, pg. 131
B&C DANMARK A/S—See Redland PLC; *Int'l*, pg. 1091
B&C DANMARK BETONTAGSTENSVAERKENE A/S—See Redland PLC; *Int'l*, pg. 1092
B&D DE COSTA RICA, S.A.—See The Black & Decker Corporation; *U.S. Public*, pg. 234
B&D INSTRUMENTS AND AVIONICS, INC.—See Bowthorpe plc; *Int'l*, pg. 208
B&G ELECTRONICS—See Vector Industries, Ltd.; *Int'l*, pg. 1462
B&G FOODS, INC.; *U.S. Private*, pg. 105
B&G REALTY, INC.—See The Marcus Corporation; *U.S. Public*, pg. 1044
B & G WHOLESALERS, INC.; *U.S. Private*, pg. 105
B & J OPERATIONS COMPANY, INC.—See Huntington Bancshares Inc.; *U.S. Public*, pg. 850
B & K STEEL & SUPPLY, INC.; *U.S. Private*, pg. 105
B&K ULTRASOUND A/S—See Analogic Corporation; *U.S. Public*, pg. 109
B & L INSURANCE, LTD.—See Baldwin & Lyons, Inc.; *U.S.* Public, pg. 169
B&L JEWELRY STORE—See Reliable Stores, Inc.; *U.S. Private*, pg. 921
B&L PHARMACEUTICALS, INC.—See Bausch & Lomb Incorporated; *U.S. Public*, pg. 194
B & L PLASTICS INC.—See Illinois Tool Works Inc.; *U.S. Public*, pg. 867
B&M EQUIPMENT, INC.—See Beaudry Ford, Inc.; *U.S. Private*, pg. 127
B&M PRINTING CO., INC.—See Master Graphic, Inc.; *U.S. Private*, pg. 713
B & P MANUFACTURING; *U.S. Private*, pg. 105
B & P VERMOEGENSVERWALTUNGS GMBH—See Commerzbank AG; *Int'l*, pg. 309
B & Q PLC—See Kingfisher plc; *Int'l*, pg. 733
B & R FOODS—See Performance Food Group Company; *U.S. Public*, pg. 1278
B & R INDUSTRIAL AUTOMATION; *U.S. Private*, pg. 105
B&W CO-OP, INC.; *U.S. Private*, pg. 105
B & W FARM CENTER—See B&W Co-op, Inc.; *U.S. Private*, pg. 105
B & W STORMARKNADER AB—See Axel Johnson AB; *Int'l*, pg. 708
B&W STORMARKNADER AB—See KF/Konsum Coop Group; *Int'l*, pg. 718
B-BAR-B FLEXIBLE PACKAGING SYSTEMS—See Liqui-Box Corporation; *U.S. Public*, pg. 1000
B C SUGAR REFINERY, LTD.; *Int'l*, pg. 103
B. DALTON BOOKSELLER, INC.—See Barnes & Noble Inc.; *U.S. Public*, pg. 189
B/E AEROSPACE, INC.; *U.S. Public*, pg. 159
B/E AEROSPACE, INC./IN FLIGHT ENTERTAINMENT GROUP—See B/E Aerospace, Inc.; *U.S. Public*, pg. 159
B-H COMPUTERS—See Pace Resources, Inc.; *U.S. Private*, pg. 830
B-H LABORATORIES, INC.—See Pace Resources, Inc.; *U.S. Private*, pg. 830
B-LINE SYSTEMS, INC.—See Sigma-Aldrich Corporation; *U.S. Public*, pg. 1471
THE B-M GROUP (PTY.) LTD.—See Bristol-Myers Squibb Company; *U.S. Public*, pg. 255
B-MAT LTD.—See N.V. Bekaert S.A.; *Int'l*, pg. 184
B OF B (EUROPE) LIMITED—See The Bank of Bermuda Limited; *Int'l*, pg. 151
B.VIA INTERNATIONAL HOUSEWARES, INC.—See Ekco Group, Inc.; *U.S. Public*, pg. 566
BA AGENCY, INC.—See BankAmerica Corporation; *U.S. Public*, pg. 180
BA ATM, INC.—See BankAmerica Corporation; *U.S. Public*, *pg. 181*
B.A. BANK NOTE—See Quebecor Inc.; *Int'l*, pg. 1077
BA BANKNOTE YVON BOULANGAR—See Quebecor Inc.; *Int'l*, pg. 1077
BA FUTURES, INCORPORATED—See BankAmerica Corporation; *U.S. Public*, pg. 180
BA INSURANCE COMPANY, INC.—See BankAmerica Corporation; *U.S. Public*, pg. 180
BA INVESTMENT MANAGERS—See BankAmerica Corporation; *U.S. Public*, pg. 180
BA LEASING & CAPITAL CORPORATION—See BankAmerica Corporation; *U.S. Public*, pg. 181
B.A. RESOURCES CO., LTD.—See Commercial Metals Company; *U.S. Public*, pg. 414
BAII/NZ, INC.—See Bell Atlantic Corporation; *U.S. Public*, pg. 202
BA VENTURES, INC.—See BankAmerica Corporation; *U.S. Public*, pg. 180
BAA MC ARTHUR-GLEN EUROPE—See The Kaempfer Company, Investment Builders; *U.S. Private*, pg. 604
BAA PLC; *Int'l*, pg. 103
BAC FINANCIAL B.V.—See Bell Atlantic Corporation; *U.S. Public*, pg. 203
BAC FINANCIAL ITALIA S.R.L.—See Bell Atlantic Corporation; *U.S. Public*, pg. 203

BAC DIRECTORY OF CORPORATE AFFILIATIONS
Company Index

BAC FINANCIAL SERVICES INTERNATIONAL B.V.—See Bell Atlantic Corporation; *U.S. Public*, pg. 203
BAC INTERNATIONAL-THE NETHERLANDS B.V.—See Bell Atlantic Corporation; *U.S. Public*, pg. 203
BAC INTERNATIONAL-THE NETHERLANDS B.V. SUCURSAL EN ESPANA—See Bell Atlantic Corporation; *U.S. Public*, pg. 203
BACPE, INC.—See Bell Atlantic Corporation; *U.S. Public*, pg. 202
BACSI (UK) LIMITED—See Bell Atlantic Corporation; *U.S. Public*, pg. 203
BAE-SEMA LIMITED—See British Aerospace p.l.c.; *Int'l*, pg. 217
BAI FACTORING S.P.A.—See Deutsche Bank AG; *Int'l*, pg. 403
BAI GEST S.P.A.—See Deutsche Bank AG; *Int'l*, pg. 403
BAI LEASING S.P.A.—See Deutsche Bank AG; *Int'l*, pg. 403
BAIC INTERNATIONAL—See Farmatic Research, Inc.; *Int'l*, *pg. 478*
BAII—See Banque Nationale de Paris; *Int'l*, pg. 163
BAP-DURHAM, INC.—See Bell Atlantic Corporation; *U.S. Public*, pg. 202
BAP-1800 ARCH LAND PARCEL, INC.—See Bell Atlantic Corporation; *U.S. Public*, pg. 202
BAP-1760 MARKET, INC.—See Bell Atlantic Corporation; *U.S. Public*, pg. 202
BAP-1310 NORTH COURT HOUSE—See Bell Atlantic Corporation; *U.S. Public*, pg. 202
BAP-TUSTIN, INC.—See Bell Atlantic Corporation; *U.S. Public*, pg. 202
BAS COMPONENTS LIMITED—See TT Group PLC; *Int'l*, pg. 1344
BASF AFRIQUE DE L'OUEST S.A.R.L.—See BASF AG; *Int'l*, pg. 105
BASF AG; *Int'l*, pg. 103
BASF AKTIENGESELLSCHAFT—See BASF AG; *Int'l*, pg. 104
BASF AKTIENGESELLSCHAFT EG-VERBINDUNGSBUERO—See BASF AG; *Int'l*, pg. 105
BASF AKTIENGESELLSCHAFT LAENDERBEREICH VERTRIEB DEUTSCHLAND—See BASF AG; *Int'l*, pg. 104
BASF AKTIENGESELLSCHAFT PREDSTAVNISTVO U HRVATSKOJ—See BASF AG; *Int'l*, pg. 105
BASF AKTIENGESELLSCHAFT UNTERNEHMENSBEREICH DUENGEMITTEL—See BASF AG; *Int'l*, pg. 104
BASF AKTIENGESELLSCHAFT UNTERNEHMENSBEREICH PFLANZENSCHUTZ—See BASF AG; *Int'l*, pg. 104
BASF ANTWERPEN N.V.—See BASF AG; *Int'l*, pg. 105
BASF ARGENTINA S.A.—See BASF AG; *Int'l*, pg. 105
BASF AUSTRALIA LTD.—See BASF AG; *Int'l*, pg. 105
BASF BANGLADESH LIMITED—See BASF AG; *Int'l*, pg. 105
BASF BEIJING REPRESENTATIVE OFFICE—See BASF AG; *Int'l*, pg. 105
BASF BELGIUM S.A./N.V.—See BASF AG; *Int'l*, pg. 105
BASF CHEMDYES SDN. BHD.—See BASF AG; *Int'l*, pg. 105
BASF CHILE S.A.—See BASF AG; *Int'l*, pg. 105
BASF CHINA LTD.—See BASF AG; *Int'l*, pg. 105
BASF COATINGS AG—See BASF AG; *Int'l*, pg. 104
BASF COATINGS & INKS BELGIUM N.V./S.A.—See BASF AG; *Int'l*, pg. 105
BASF COATINGS & INKS HONG KONG LTD.—See BASF AG; *Int'l*, pg. 105
BASF COATINGS & INKS HONG KONG LTD. MALAYSIA—See BASF AG; *Int'l*, pg. 105
BASF COATINGS & INKS PHILIPPINES, INC.—See BASF AG; *Int'l*, pg. 105
BASF COATINGS & DRUKINKT B.V.—See BASF AG; *Int'l*, pg. 105
BASF COMPUTER SERVICES GMBH—See BASF AG; *Int'l*, pg. 104
BASF CORPORATION—See BASF AG; *Int'l*, pg. 105
BASF CORPORATION DISPERSIONS—See BASF AG; *Int'l*, pg. 105
BASF CORPORATION POLYMERS DIVISION—See BASF AG; *Int'l*, pg. 105
BASF DE COSTA RICA S.A.—See BASF AG; *Int'l*, pg. 105
BASF CURTEX S.A.—See BASF AG; *Int'l*, pg. 105
BASF DANMARK A/S—See BASF AG; *Int'l*, pg. 105
BASF DE EL SALVADOR, S.A. DE C.V.—See BASF AG; *Int'l*, pg. 105
BASF DE GUATEMALA, S.A.—See BASF AG; *Int'l*, pg. 106
BASF DOMINICANA S.A.—See BASF AG; *Int'l*, pg. 106
BASF EAST AFRICA LTD.—See BASF AG; *Int'l*, pg. 106
BASF ECUATORIANA S.A.—See BASF AG; *Int'l*, pg. 106
BASF ENGINEERING PLASTICS CO., LTD.—See BASF AG; *Int'l*, pg. 106
BASF EOOD—See BASF AG; *Int'l*, pg. 106
BASF EOOD KNOLL PHARMA—See BASF AG; *Int'l*, pg. 106
BASF ESPANOLA S.A.—See BASF AG; *Int'l*, pg. 106
BASF (ETHIOPIA) LIMITED P.L.C.—See BASF AG; *Int'l*, pg. 106
BASF FINANCE EUROPE N.V.—See BASF AG; *Int'l*, pg. 106
BASF-FINLAY (PVT.) LTD.—See BASF AG; *Int'l*, pg. 106
BASF FRANCE S.A.—See BASF AG; *Int'l*, pg. 106
BASF (GHANA) LIMITED—See BASF AG; *Int'l*, pg. 106
BASF GUANGZHOU—See BASF AG; *Int'l*, pg. 106
BASF HEALTH AND NUTRITION (BHN)—See BASF AG; *Int'l*, pg. 106
BASF HORTICULTURE ET JARDIN S.A.—See BASF AG; *Int'l*, pg. 106
BASF HUNGARIA KFT.—See BASF AG; *Int'l*, pg. 106
BASF INDIA LTD.—See BASF AG; *Int'l*, pg. 106
P.T. BASF INDONESIA—See BASF AG; *Int'l*, pg. 106
BASF INTERTRADE AG—See BASF AG; *Int'l*, pg. 106
BASF IRAN AG—See BASF AG; *Int'l*, pg. 106
BASF IRELAND LIMITED—See BASF AG; *Int'l*, pg. 106
BASF ITALIA SPA—See BASF AG; *Int'l*, pg. 106
BASF JAPAN LTD.—See BASF AG; *Int'l*, pg. 106
BASF KOREA LTD.—See BASF AG; *Int'l*, pg. 106
BASF LABIANA S.A.—See BASF AG; *Int'l*, pg. 106
BASF LACKE & FARBEN VERTRIEBSGESELLSCHAFT MBH—See BASF AG; *Int'l*, pg. 106
BASF (MALAYSIA) SDN. BHD.—See BASF AG; *Int'l*, pg. 106
BASF MAROC S.A.—See BASF AG; *Int'l*, pg. 106
BASF NEDERLAND B.V.—See BASF AG; *Int'l*, pg. 106
BASF NEW ZEALAND LTD.—See BASF AG; *Int'l*, pg. 106
BASF NICHIYU COATINGS R&D CO., LTD.—See BASF AG; *Int'l*, pg. 106
BASF (NIGERIA) LIMITED—See BASF AG; *Int'l*, pg. 106
BASF NORGE AS—See BASF AG; *Int'l*, pg. 106
BASF NORGE A/S—See BASF AG; *Int'l*, pg. 106
BASF OESTERREICH (AUSTRIA) GES.M.B.H.—See BASF AG; *Int'l*, pg. 106
BASF OY—See BASF AG; *Int'l*, pg. 106
BASF PAKISTAN (PRIVATE) LIMITED—See BASF AG; *Int'l*, pg. 106
BASF PANAMA S.A.—See BASF AG; *Int'l*, pg. 106
BASF PARAGUAYA S.R.L.—See BASF AG; *Int'l*, pg. 107
BASF PEINTURES & ENCRES S.A.—See BASF AG; *Int'l*, pg. 107
BASF PERUANA S.A.—See BASF AG; *Int'l*, pg. 107
BASF PHILIPPINES, INC.—See BASF AG; *Int'l*, pg. 107
BASF PINTURAS S.A. DE C.V.—See BASF AG; *Int'l*, pg. 107
BASF PITTURE SPA—See BASF AG; *Int'l*, pg. 107
BASF POLYURETHANE—See BASF AG; *Int'l*, pg. 107
BASF PORTUGUESA, LDA.—See BASF AG; *Int'l*, pg. 107
BASF QUIMICA COLOMBIANA S.A.—See BASF AG; *Int'l*, pg. 107
BASF S.A.—See BASF AG; *Int'l*, pg. 107
BASF SCHWARZHEIDE GMBH—See BASF AG; *Int'l*, pg. 104
BASF (SCHWEIZ) AG—See BASF AG; *Int'l*, pg. 107
BASF SHANGHAI REP. OFFICE—See BASF AG; *Int'l*, pg. 107
BASF SINGAPORE PTE. LTD.—See BASF AG; *Int'l*, pg. 107
BASF SISTEMEAS DE IMPRESION, S.A.—See BASF AG; *Int'l*, pg. 107
BASF SLOVENSKO SPOL. S R.O.—See BASF AG; *Int'l*, pg. 107
BASF SLOWENIJA D.O.O.—See BASF AG; *Int'l*, pg. 107
BASF SOUTH AFRICA (PTY.) LTD.—See BASF AG; *Int'l*, pg. 107
BASF SOUTH EAST ASIA REGIONAL HEADQUARTERS PTE. LTD.—See BASF AG; *Int'l*, pg. 107
BASF SPOL. S.R.O.—See BASF AG; *Int'l*, pg. 107
BASF SRL—See BASF AG; *Int'l*, pg. 107
BASF SRL ABT. KNOLL PHARMA—See BASF AG; *Int'l*, pg. 107
BASF-SUEMERBANK TUERK KIMYA SANAYII A.S.—See BASF AG; *Int'l*, pg. 107
BASF SVENSKA AB—See BASF AG; *Int'l*, pg. 107
BASF SVENSKA AB AGRO NORDENL BALTIKUM—See BASF AG; *Int'l*, pg. 107
BASF TAIWAN LTD.—See BASF AG; *Int'l*, pg. 107
BASF TEXTILE & LEATHER DYES & CHEMICALS PTE. LTD.—See BASF AG; *Int'l*, pg. 107
BASF (THAI) LTD.—See BASF AG; *Int'l*, pg. 107
BASF TUERK—See BASF AG; *Int'l*, pg. 107
BASF TUNISIA S.A.—See BASF AG; *Int'l*, pg. 107
BASF URUGUAYA S.A.—See BASF AG; *Int'l*, pg. 107
BASF VENEZOLANA, S.A.—See BASF AG; *Int'l*, pg. 107
BASF-VERTRIEBSSTANDORT AGRO—See BASF AG; *Int'l*, pg. 104
BASF VITA LIMITED—See BASF AG; *Int'l*, pg. 107
BASF ZIMBABWE (PRIVATE) LTD.—See BASF AG; *Int'l*, pg. 107
B.A.S.S., INC.; *U.S. Private*, pg. 105
B.A.S.S. TIMES—See B.A.S.S., Inc.; *U.S. Private*, pg. 105
B.A.T BENELUX S.A.—See B.A.T Industries P.L.C.; *Int'l*, pg. 111
B.A.T CIGARETTENFABRIKEN B.A.T.—See B.A.T Industries P.L.C.; *Int'l*, pg. 111
B.A.T (CYPRUS) LTD.—See B.A.T Industries P.L.C.; *Int'l*, pg. 111
B.A.T (DEUTSCHLAND) EXPORT GMBH—See B.A.T Industries P.L.C.; *Int'l*, pg. 112
B.A.T FINLAND—See B.A.T Industries P.L.C.; *Int'l*, pg. 111
B.A.T INDUSTRIES P.L.C.; *Int'l*, pg. 110
B.A.T INTERNATIONAL FINANCE LTD.—See B.A.T Industries P.L.C.; *Int'l*, pg. 111
B.A.T NETHERLANDS B.V.—See B.A.T Industries P.L.C.; *Int'l*, pg. 111
B.A.T (SUISSE) SA—See B.A.T Industries P.L.C.; *Int'l*, pg. 111
B.A.T (UK & EXPORT) LTD.—See B.A.T Industries P.L.C.; *Int'l*, pg. 111
BATCL-1987-I, INC.—See Bell Atlantic Corporation; *U.S. Public*, pg. 202
BATCL-1987-III, INC.—See Bell Atlantic Corporation; *U.S. Public*, pg. 202
BATCL-1987-II, INC.—See Bell Atlantic Corporation; *U.S. Public*, pg. 202
BATCO-1989-II, INC.—See Bell Atlantic Corporation; *U.S. Public*, pg. 202
BAX GLOBAL—See The Pittston Company; *U.S. Public*, pg. 1305
BB ADMINISTRADORA DE CARTOES DE CREDITO S.A.—See Banco do Brasil; *Int'l*, pg. 141
BB&T CORPORATION; *U.S. Public*, pg. 159
BB&T INTERNATIONAL—See BB&T Corporation; *U.S. Public*, pg. 160
BB&T LEASING CORP.—See BB&T Corporation; *U.S. Public*, pg. 160
BB&T OF SOUTH CAROLINA—See BB&T Corporation; *U.S. Public*, pg. 160
BB&T REGIONAL HEADQUARTERS—See BB&T Corporation; *U.S. Public*, pg. 160
BB&T SAVINGS BANK—See BB&T Corporation; *U.S. Public*, pg. 160
BB-ASSET MANAGEMENT VERMOGENSVERWALTUNG GMBH—See Bankgesellschaft Berlin; *Int'l*, pg. 159
BB-AVAL GESELLSCHAFT FUR AUSSENHANDELSFINANZIERUNGEN MBH—See Bankgesellschaft Berlin; *Int'l*, pg. 159
BB-BETRIEBSSERVICE GMBH—See Bankgesellschaft Berlin; *Int'l*, pg. 159
BB CORRETORA DE SEGUROS E ADMINISTRADORA DE BENS S.A.—See Banco do Brasil; *Int'l*, pg. 141
BB-DATA GESELLSCHAFT FUR INFORMATIONS-UND KOMMUNIKATIONSSYSTEME MBH—See Bankgesellschaft Berlin; *Int'l*, pg. 159
BB EUROPE-BANCO DO BRASIL N.V.—See Banco do Brasil; *Int'l*, pg. 141
BB FINANCEIRA S.A. CREDITO FINANCIAMENTO E INVESTIMENTO—See Banco do Brasil; *Int'l*, pg. 141
BB-KAPITALBETEILIGUNGS GESELLSCHAFT GMBH—See Bankgesellschaft Berlin; *Int'l*, pg. 159
BB LEASING-ARRANDEMENTO MERCANTIL—See Banco do Brasil; *Int'l*, pg. 141
BB LEASING COMPANY LTD.—See Banco do Brasil; *Int'l*, pg. 141
BB-LEASING GMBH—See Bankgesellschaft Berlin; *Int'l*, pg. 159
BB-PRIVAT FINANZ-SERVICE GMBH—See Bankgesellschaft Berlin; *Int'l*, pg. 159
BB SECURITIES LTD.—See Banco do Brasil; *Int'l*, pg. 142
BB-TUR-VIAGENS E TURISMO—See Banco do Brasil; *Int'l*, *pg. 141*
BBA FRICTION INC.—See BBA Group plc; *Int'l*, pg. 113
BBA FRICTION LTD.—See BBA Group plc; *Int'l*, pg. 112
BBA GROUP PLC; *Int'l*, pg. 112
BBB BILDEDELHANDLING AB—See Spectra-Physics AB; *Int'l*, pg. 1289
BBBI BANCO DE INVESTIMENTO—See Banco do Brasil; *Int'l*, pg. 141
BBC BROWN BOVERI S.A. DE C.V.—See ABB Asea Brown Boveri (Holding) Ltd.; *Int'l*, pg. 3
BBC BROWN BOVERI SAUDI ARABIA LTD.—See ABB Asea Brown Boveri (Holding) Ltd.; *Int'l*, pg. 3
BBC MAGAZINES; *Int'l*, pg. 114
BBC WARRANT ACQUISITION CORP.—See Cigna Corp.; *U.S. Public*, pg. 357
BBDO CANADA—See N.W. Ayer & Partners; *U.S. Private*, pg. 104
BBDO OSLO—See Omnicom Group Inc.; *U.S. Public*, pg. 1224
BBDO WORLDWIDE INC.—See Omnicom Group Inc.; *U.S. Public*, pg. 1223
BBG BETIELINGGESELLSCHAFT M.B.H.—See Assicurazioni Generali S.p.A.; *Int'l*, pg. 89
BBGR SA—See Essilor International Compagnie Generale d'Optique; *Int'l*, pg. 462
B.B.H. ASIA PACIFIC—See Bartle Bogle Hegarty Limited; *Int'l*, pg. 169
BBL ASSET MANAGEMENT (SINGAPORE) PTE. LTD.—See Bank Brussels Lambert; *Int'l*, pg. 148
BBL AUSTRALIA LIMITED—See Bank Brussels Lambert; *Int'l*, pg. 148
BBL CAPITAL MANAGEMENT CORPORATION—See Bank Brussels Lambert; *Int'l*, pg. 147
BBL CENTRAL REGION—See Bank Brussels Lambert; *Int'l*, pg. 147
BBL FLEMISH REGION—See Bank Brussels Lambert; *Int'l*, *pg. 147*
BBL INSURANCE—See Bank Brussels Lambert; *Int'l*, pg. 147
BBL INSURANCE BROKERAGE—See Bank Brussels Lambert; *Int'l*, pg. 147
BBL IRELAND—See Bank Brussels Lambert; *Int'l*, pg. 148
BBL LIFE—See Bank Brussels Lambert; *Int'l*, pg. 147
BBL SUCURSAL DE BARCELONA—See Bank Brussels Lambert; *Int'l*, pg. 148
BBL WALLOON REGION—See Bank Brussels Lambert; *Int'l*, pg. 147
BBLP DRILL COMPANY LIMITED—See Bilfinger + Berger Bauaktiengesellschaft; *Int'l*, pg. 196
BBME TRUSTEE (JERSEY) LIMITED—See HSBC Holdings plc; *Int'l*, pg. 580
BBS HOLDINGS, INC.—See BellSouth Corporation; *U.S. Public*, pg. 209
BBS ONTARIO INCORPORATED—See Baton Broadcasting Incorporated; *Int'l*, pg. 171
BBS PRODUCTIONS INC.—See Baton Broadcasting Incorporated; *Int'l*, pg. 171
BBS SASKATCHEWAN INCORPORATED—See Baton Broadcasting Incorporated; *Int'l*, pg. 171
BBX S/A—See Compagnie des Machines Bull; *Int'l*, pg. 315
B.C. CHEMICALS LIMITED—See Canfor Corporation; *Int'l*, pg. 260
BC GAS INC.; *Int'l*, pg. 114
BC GAS UTILITY—See BC Gas Inc.; *Int'l*, pg. 114
B.C. HYDRO; *Int'l*, pg. 114
BC HYDROLITE MACHINERY CO.—See International Pipe Machinery Corp.; *U.S. Private*, pg. 571
BC INTERNATIONAL-COSMETICS AND IMAGE SERVICES, INC.—See BeautiControl Cosmetics, Inc.; *U.S. Public*, pg. 198
BC TELECOM INC.—See GTE Corporation; *U.S. Public*, pg. 697
BC-USA—See Bongrain S.A.; *Int'l*, pg. 201
BCA—See Bertelsmann AG; *Int'l*, pg. 192
BCA—See Reed Elsevier plc; *Int'l*, pg. 1094
BCB BEVERAGES LIMITED—See Cott Corporation; *Int'l*, pg. 338
BCC MEXICO, S.A. DE C.V.—See Boise Cascade Corporation; *U.S. Public*, pg. 243
BCE CAPITAL INC.—See BCE Inc.; *Int'l*, pg. 115
BCE INC.; *Int'l*, pg. 114
BCE MOBILE COMMUNICATIONS INC.—See BCE Inc.; *Int'l*, pg. 115

BCI COCA-COLA BOTTLING COMPANY OF LOS ANGELES—See Coca-Cola Enterprises Inc.; *U.S. Public*, pg. 393
BCI HOLDING CORPORATION; *U.S. Private*, pg. 106
BCI INCORPORATED—See BCE Inc.; *Int'l*, pg. 116
BCI MER ROUGE—See Banque Nationale de Paris; *Int'l*, pg. 163
BCIS SERVICES, INC.—See Bancinsurance Corp.; *U.S. Public*, pg. 175
BCL MAGNETICS—See Tempel Steel Company; *U.S. Private*, pg. 1075
BCN-BARCLAYS BANCO DE INVESTIMENTO S.A.—See Barclays Bank PLC; *Int'l*, pg. 165
BCP—See Eureko B.V.; *Int'l*, pg. 464
BCP GROUP LTD.; *Int'l*, pg. 116
BCP INVESTIMENTOS—See Eureko B.V.; *Int'l*, pg. 464
BCP TECHNICAL SERVICE, INC.; *U.S. Private*, pg. 106
BCS INFORMATION SYSTEMS PRIVATE LIMITED—See HSBC Holdings plc; *Int'l*, pg. 581
BCS RICHLAND INC.—See The Boeing Company; *U.S. Public*, pg. 241
BCS WIRELESS—See The Failure Group, Inc.; *U.S. Public*, pg. 609
BCT, INC.—See Boise Cascade Corporation; *U.S. Public*, pg. 243
BCTS—See Marcam Solutions, Inc.; *U.S. Public*, pg. 1043
BD INDUSTRIE BETEILIGUNGSGESELLSCHAFT MBH—See Bayerische Vereinsbank Group; *Int'l*, pg. 178
BD SYSTEMS, INC; *U.S. Private*, pg. 106
BDAG BALCKE-DURR AG—See Deutsche Babcock AG; *Int'l*, pg. 399
BDC, INC.—See Eclipse Inc.; *U.S. Private*, pg. 360
BDDP—See BDDP Group; *Int'l*, pg. 116
BDDP BELGIQUE—See BDDP Group; *Int'l*, pg. 117
BDDP CORPORATE—See BDDP Group; *Int'l*, pg. 116
BDDP FRANKFURT—See BDDP Group; *Int'l*, pg. 117
BDDP GROUP; *Int'l*, pg. 116
BDDP HOLDINGS (UK) LTD.—See BDDP Group; *Int'l*, pg. 117
BDDP MANCEBO KAYE—See BDDP Group; *Int'l*, pg. 117
BDDP MILAN—See BDDP Group; *Int'l*, pg. 117
BDDP NORTH AMERICA, INC.—See BDDP Group; *Int'l*, pg. 117
BDF DE CENTROAMERICA S.A.—See Beiersdorf Group; *Int'l*, pg. 182
BDF DE CHILE S.A.—See Beiersdorf Group; *Int'l*, pg. 182
BDF EAST AFRICA LTD.—See Beiersdorf Group; *Int'l*, pg. 183
BDF MAROC S.A.—See Beiersdorf Group; *Int'l*, pg. 183
BDF MEXICO S.A. DE C.V.—See Beiersdorf Group; *Int'l*, pg. 183
BDF NIVEA LTDA.—See Beiersdorf Group; *Int'l*, pg. 183
BDG/MCCOLL—See WPP Group plc; *Int'l*, pg. 1482
BDH ADVERTISING LIMITED; *Int'l*, pg. 118
BDL BANCO DI LUGANO—See Union Bank of Switzerland; *Int'l*, pg. 1439
BDM INTERNATIONAL, INC.—See TRW Inc.; *U.S. Public*, pg. 1558
BDO SEIDMAN, LLP; *U.S. Private*, pg. 106
BDW - BAYERISCHES DRUCKGUSS-WERK THURNER GMBH & CO KG—See Alusuisse-Lonza Holding Ltd.; *Int'l*, pg. 68
BDW CORP.—See PP&L Resources; *U.S. Public*, pg. 1244
B/E AEROSPACE SEATING PRODUCTS—See B/E Aerospace, Inc.; *U.S. Public*, pg. 159
B/E AEROSPACE SEATING PRODUCTS GROUP—See B/E Aerospace, Inc.; *U.S. Public*, pg. 159
BE & C ENGINEERS, INC.—See The Boeing Company; *U.S. Public*, pg. 241
BE & K, INC.; *U.S. Public*, pg. 106
B.E. INTERNATIONAL FOODS LTD.—See Danone Group; *Int'l*, pg. 380
BEB ERDGAS UND ERDOEL GMBH—See Exxon Corporation; *Int'l*, pg. 601
BEC GROUP, INC.; *U.S. Public*, pg. 160
BEC INC.; *U.S. Private*, pg. 106
BEI DEFENSE SYSTEMS COMPANY—See BEI Technologies, Inc.; *U.S. Public*, pg. 160
BEI GRAPHICS—See The New Yorker Magazine; *U.S. Private*, pg. 796
BEI MEDICAL SYSTEMS COMPANY; *U.S. Private*, pg. 106
BEI SENSORS AND SYSTEMS COMPANY—See BEI Technologies, Inc.; *U.S. Public*, pg. 160
BEI TECHNOLOGIES, INC.; *U.S. Public*, pg. 160
B.E.L. PRODUCTS—See McKechnie PLC; *Int'l*, pg. 851
BET AFFILIATE MARKETING - YSB & EMERGE MAGAZINES—See Black Entertainment Television Holdings Inc.; *U.S. Public*, pg. 235
BET CABLE NETWORK OPERATIONS—See Black Entertainment Television Holdings Inc.; *U.S. Public*, pg. 235
BET DIRECT—See Black Entertainment Television Holdings Inc.; *U.S. Public*, pg. 235
BET MEDIA SALES—See Black Entertainment Television Holdings Inc.; *U.S. Public*, pg. 235
BET MIDWEST MEDIA/AFFILIATE SALES—See Black Entertainment Television Holdings Inc.; *U.S. Public*, pg. 235
BET NEW YORK MEDIA SALES—See Black Entertainment Television Holdings Inc.; *U.S. Public*, pg. 235
BET WEST COAST MEDIA/AFFILIATE SALES & BET ACTION PAY PER VIEW—See Black Entertainment Television Holdings Inc.; *U.S. Public*, pg. 235
BET WEST COAST OPERATIONS—See Black Entertainment Television Holdings Inc.; *U.S. Public*, pg. 235
BF GOODRICH LANDING SYSTEMS DIVISION—See The B.F. Goodrich Company; *U.S. Public*, pg. 751
BFCE BRAZIL—See Banque Francaise du Commerce Exterieur; *Int'l*, pg. 161
BFC BUILDINGS—See BFC Construction Corporation; *Int'l*, pg. 118
BFC CIVIL—See BFC Construction Corporation; *Int'l*, pg. 118

BFC CONSTRUCTION CORPORATION; *Int'l*, pg. 118
BFC FRONTIER—See BFC Construction Corporation; *Int'l*, pg. 118
BFC INDUSTRIAL NICHOLLS-RADTKE—See BFC Construction Corporation; *Int'l*, pg. 118
BFC PIPELINES—See BFC Construction Corporation; *Int'l*, pg. 118
BFC UTILITIES—See BFC Construction Corporation; *Int'l*, pg. 118
BFCE CHINA—See Banque Francaise du Commerce Exterieur; *Int'l*, pg. 161
BFCE HO CHI MINH CITY—See Banque Francaise du Commerce Exterieur; *Int'l*, pg. 161
BFCE HONG KONG—See Banque Francaise du Commerce Exterieur; *Int'l*, pg. 161
BFCE INDONESIA—See Banque Francaise du Commerce Exterieur; *Int'l*, pg. 161
BFCE MYNAMAR—See Banque Francaise du Commerce Exterieur; *Int'l*, pg. 162
BFCE THAILAND—See Banque Francaise du Commerce Exterieur; *Int'l*, pg. 161
BFCE VIETNAM—See Banque Francaise du Commerce Exterieur; *Int'l*, pg. 161
BFD PRODUCTIONS, INC.—See Precision Systems, Inc.; *U.S. Public*, pg. 1321
BFF ITALIA SRL—See Lamont Holdings Plc; *Int'l*, pg. 798
BFI ACQUISITION, INC.—See Browning-Ferris Industries, Inc.; *U.S. Public*, pg. 263
BFI AVIATION SERVICES, INC.—See Browning-Ferris Industries, Inc.; *U.S. Public*, pg. 263
BFI CONSTRUCTORS—See Browning-Ferris Industries, Inc.; *U.S. Public*, pg. 263
BFI ENERGY SYSTEMS, INC.—See Browning-Ferris Industries, Inc.; *U.S. Public*, pg. 263
BFI ENERGY SYSTEMS OF BERGEN COUNTY, INC.—See Browning-Ferris Industries, Inc.; *U.S. Public*, pg. 263
BFI ENERGY SYSTEMS OF PLYMOUTH, INC.—See Browning-Ferris Industries, Inc.; *U.S. Public*, pg. 263
BFI ENERGY SYSTEMS OF TEXAS, INC.—See Browning-Ferris Industries, Inc.; *U.S. Public*, pg. 263
BFI WASTE SYSTEMS, INC.—See Browning-Ferris Industries, Inc.; *U.S. Public*, pg. 263
BFI WASTE SYSTEMS OF INDIANA, INC.—See Browning-Ferris Industries, Inc.; *U.S. Public*, pg. 263
BFL BETEILIGUNGSGESELLSCHAFT FUR FLUGZEUG LEASING MBH—See Bayerische Vereinsbank Group; *Int'l*, pg. 178
BFP WHOLESALE LTD.—See Royal Gist-Brocades N.V.; *Int'l*, pg. 1142
BFR GMBH—See ISS-International Service System A/S; *Int'l*, pg. 657
BFX HOSPITALITY GROUP, INC.; *U.S. Public*, pg. 160
BG CHECO CONSTRUCTION—See Alcatel Alsthom Compagnie Generale D'Electricite; *Int'l*, pg. 53
BG FINANS A/S—See Solvay S.A.; *Int'l*, pg. 1279
B.G. INDUSTRIES; *U.S. Private*, pg. 106
BG PLC; *Int'l*, pg. 118
BG PLC EXPLORATION & PRODUCTION LTD—See BG Plc; *Int'l*, pg. 118
BG SAS—See Bongrain S.A.; *Int'l*, pg. 201
BGD BODENGESUNDHEITSDIENST GMBH—See Sudzucker AG Mannheim/Ochsenfurt; *Int'l*, pg. 1305
BGE-NH 8 PROJECT—See Lyonnaise des Eaux S.A.; *Int'l*, pg. 823
BGF INDUSTRIES INC.; *U.S. Private*, pg. 106
BGL FINANCE (ASIA) LTD.—See Banque Generale du Luxembourg SA; *Int'l*, pg. 162
BGL TRUSTEES LTD.—See Banque Generale du Luxembourg SA; *Int'l*, pg. 162
BGLS INC.—See Brooke Group Ltd.; *U.S. Public*, pg. 259
BGM HEALTH COMMUNICATIONS, INC.—See Omnicom Group Inc.; *U.S. Public*, pg. 1223
BGS/DMB&B TURIN—See DMB&B Communications; *U.S. Private*, pg. 303
BGS SPAIN—See BGS Systems, Inc.; *U.S. Public*, pg. 161
BGS SYSTEMS FRANCE—See BGS Systems, Inc.; *U.S. Public*, pg. 161
BGS SYSTEMS GMBH—See BGS Systems, Inc.; *U.S. Public*, pg. 161
BGS SYSTEMS, INC.; *U.S. Public*, pg. 161
BGS SYSTEMS, LTD.—See BGS Systems, Inc.; *U.S. Public*, pg. 161
BGS SYSTEMS PTY. LTD.—See BGS Systems, Inc.; *U.S. Public*, pg. 161
BGS SYSTEMS S.R.L.—See BGS Systems, Inc.; *U.S. Public*, pg. 161
BGV BETEILIGUNGSGESELLSCHAFT FUR VERSICHERUNGSAGENTUREN M.B.H.—See Assicurazioni Generali S.p.A.; *Int'l*, pg. 89
BGW SYSTEMS, INC.; *U.S. Private*, pg. 107
B.H. AIRCRAFT CO., INC.; *U.S. Private*, pg. 107
BHA COMPANY, INC.—See BHA Group Holdings Inc.; *U.S. Public*, pg. 161
BHA GROUP HOLDINGS INC.; *U.S. Public*, pg. 161
BHA GROUP INTERNATIONAL, INC.—See BHA Group Holdings Inc.; *U.S. Public*, pg. 161
BHA GROUP INTERNATIONAL PVT. LTD.—See BHA Group Holdings Inc.; *U.S. Public*, pg. 161
BHA INTERNATIONAL GMBH—See BHA Group Holdings Inc.; *U.S. Public*, pg. 161
BHC AEROVOX LTD.—See Aerovox Inc.; *U.S. Public*, pg. 26
BHC COMMUNICATIONS, INC.—See Chris-Craft Industries, Inc.; *U.S. Public*, pg. 352
BHC COMPANY—See Aquarion Company; *U.S. Public*, pg. 126
BHC SECURITIES, INC.—See Fiserv, Inc.; *U.S. Public*, pg. 647
BHCM INC.—See Fiserv, Inc.; *U.S. Public*, pg. 647
BHF & CCF LEASING GMBH—See BHF-BANK AG; *Int'l*, pg. 119
BHF & IKB BAUMANAGEMENT GMBH—See IKB Deutsche Industriebank AG; *Int'l*, pg. 645

BHF & IKB IMMOBILIEN-LEASING GMBH—See BHF-BANK AG; *Int'l*, pg. 119
BHF ASSET MANAGEMENT GMBH—See BHF-BANK AG; *Int'l*, pg. 119
BHF-BANK—See BHF-BANK AG; *Int'l*, pg. 119
BHF BANK—See Credit Commercial de France; *Int'l*, pg. 342
BHF-BANK AG; *Int'l*, pg. 119
BHF-BANK INTERNATIONAL S.A.—See BHF-BANK AG; *Int'l*, pg. 119
BHF-BANK (JERSEY) LTD.—See BHF-BANK AG; *Int'l*, pg. 119
BHF-BANK LIASON OFFICE—See BHF-BANK AG; *Int'l*, pg. 120
BHF-BANK REPRESENTATIVE OFFICE—See BHF-BANK AG; *Int'l*, pg. 120
BHF-BANK (SWITZERLAND) LTD.—See BHF-BANK AG; *Int'l*, pg. 119
BHF-BANK—See BHF-BANK AG; *Int'l*, pg. 119
BHF CAPITAL MANAGEMENT GMBH—See BHF-BANK AG; *Int'l*, pg. 119
BHF - CCF LEASING—See Credit Commercial de France; *Int'l*, pg. 342
BHF FINANCE (NETHERLANDS) B.V.—See BHF-BANK AG; *Int'l*, pg. 119
BHF IMMOBILIEN-GMBH—See BHF-BANK AG; *Int'l*, pg. 119
BHF INVESTMENT MANAGEMENT AG—See BHF-BANK AG; *Int'l*, pg. 120
BHF (LOS ANGELES)—See BHF-BANK AG; *Int'l*, pg. 119
BHF SECURITIES CORP.—See BHF-BANK AG; *Int'l*, pg. 119
BHF TRUST MANAGEMENT GESELLSCHAFT FUR VERMOEGENSVERWALTUNG MBH—See BHF-BANK AG; *Int'l*, pg. 119
BHP AUSTRALIA COAL LTD., MACKAY LABORATORY—See The Broken Hill Proprietary Company Limited; *Int'l*, pg. 227
BHP-BANK REPRESENTATIVE OFFICE—See BHF-BANK AG; *Int'l*, pg. 120
BHP BUILDING AND CONSTRUCTION PRODUCTS—See The Broken Hill Proprietary Company Limited; *Int'l*, pg. 226
BHP CIVIL PRODUCTS—See The Broken Hill Proprietary Company Limited; *Int'l*, pg. 226
BHP COAL—See The Broken Hill Proprietary Company Limited; *Int'l*, pg. 223
BHP COATED STEEL CORP.—See The Broken Hill Proprietary Company Limited; *Int'l*, pg. 226
BHP COPPER—See The Broken Hill Proprietary Company Limited; *Int'l*, pg. 227
THE BHP COPPER GROUP—See The Broken Hill Proprietary Company Limited; *Int'l*, pg. 224
BHP COPPER NORTH AMERICA—See The Broken Hill Proprietary Company Limited; *Int'l*, pg. 224
BHP ENGINEERING—See The Broken Hill Proprietary Company Limited; *Int'l*, pg. 225
BHP FASTENER PRODUCTS—See The Broken Hill Proprietary Company Limited; *Int'l*, pg. 226
BHP GROUP RESOURCES PTY LTD.—See The Broken Hill Proprietary Company Limited; *Int'l*, pg. 225
BHP HAWAII, INC.—See The Broken Hill Proprietary Company Limited; *Int'l*, pg. 225
BHP HOUSE FRAMING—See The Broken Hill Proprietary Company Limited; *Int'l*, pg. 226
BHP INFORMATION TECHNOLOGY—See The Broken Hill Proprietary Company Limited; *Int'l*, pg. 225
BHP INSURANCE—See The Broken Hill Proprietary Company Limited; *Int'l*, pg. 225
BHP INTERNATIONAL LTD.—See The Broken Hill Proprietary Company Limited; *Int'l*, pg. 225
BHP IRON ORE—See The Broken Hill Proprietary Company Limited; *Int'l*, pg. 224
BHP JAPAN—See The Broken Hill Proprietary Company Limited; *Int'l*, pg. 225
BHP LIFTING & INDUSTRIAL PRODUCTS—See The Broken Hill Proprietary Company Limited; *Int'l*, pg. 226
BHP MANGANESE—See The Broken Hill Proprietary Company Limited; *Int'l*, pg. 224
BHP MINERALS—See The Broken Hill Proprietary Company Limited; *Int'l*, pg. 223
BHP MINERALS CANADA LTD.—See The Broken Hill Proprietary Company Limited; *Int'l*, pg. 227
BHP MINERALS INTERNATIONAL EXPLORATION INC.—See The Broken Hill Proprietary Company Limited; *Int'l*, pg. 227
BHP MINERALS LABORATORY—See The Broken Hill Proprietary Company Limited; *Int'l*, pg. 227
BHP MINERALS MALI INC.—See The Broken Hill Proprietary Company Limited; *Int'l*, pg. 224
BHP NEW ZEALAND STEEL LTD.—See The Broken Hill Proprietary Company Limited; *Int'l*, pg. 226
BHP PETROLEUM (AMERICAS) INC.—See The Broken Hill Proprietary Company Limited; *Int'l*, pg. 225
BHP PETROLEUM PTY LTD.—See The Broken Hill Proprietary Company Limited; *Int'l*, pg. 225
BHP PETROLEUM (VIETNAM) PTY LTD.—See The Broken Hill Proprietary Company Limited; *Int'l*, pg. 225
BHP RAIL PRODUCTS—See The Broken Hill Proprietary Company Limited; *Int'l*, pg. 226
BHP REFRACTORIES PTY LTD.—See The Broken Hill Proprietary Company Limited; *Int'l*, pg. 227
BHP REFRACTORIES PTY LTD. RESEARCH & DEVELOPMENT—See The Broken Hill Proprietary Company Limited; *Int'l*, pg. 227
BHP REINFORCING PRODUCTS—See The Broken Hill Proprietary Company Limited; *Int'l*, pg. 226
BHP-RMI HOLDINGS PTY LTD.—See The Broken Hill Proprietary Company Limited; *Int'l*, pg. 226
BHP SERVICE COMPANIES—See The Broken Hill Proprietary Company Limited; *Int'l*, pg. 225
BHP SOUTH PACIFIC, INC.—See The Broken Hill Proprietary Company Limited; *Int'l*, pg. 225

BHP STEEL—See The Broken Hill Proprietary Company Limited; *Int'l*, pg. 225
BHP STEEL BUILDING PRODUCTS (NZ) LTD.—See The Broken Hill Proprietary Company Limited; *Int'l*, pg. 226
BHP STEEL CANADA INC.—See The Broken Hill Proprietary Company Limited; *Int'l*, pg. 227
BHP STEEL ENGINEERING SERVICES SINGAPORE PTE LTD.—See The Broken Hill Proprietary Company Limited; *Int'l*, pg. 227
BHP STEEL EUROPE MIDDLE EAST LTD.—See The Broken Hill Proprietary Company Limited; *Int'l*, pg. 227
PT BHP STEEL INDONESIA—See The Broken Hill Proprietary Company Limited; *Int'l*, pg. 227
BHP STEEL (MALAYSIA) SDN BHD—See The Broken Hill Proprietary Company Limited; *Int'l*, pg. 227
BHP STEEL N ASIA LTD.—See The Broken Hill Proprietary Company Limited; *Int'l*, pg. 227
BHP STEEL SANKEY—See The Broken Hill Proprietary Company Limited; *Int'l*, pg. 227
BHP STEEL SE ASIA PTE LTD.—See The Broken Hill Proprietary Company Limited; *Int'l*, pg. 227
BHP TITANIUM MINERALS—See The Broken Hill Proprietary Company Limited; *Int'l*, pg. 224
BHP TRADING INC.—See The Broken Hill Proprietary Company Limited; *Int'l*, pg. 226
BHP TRADING PHILIPPINES INC.—See The Broken Hill Proprietary Company Limited; *Int'l*, pg. 227
BHP TRANSPORT—See The Broken Hill Proprietary Company Limited; *Int'l*, pg. 225
BHP WIRE PRODUCTS—See The Broken Hill Proprietary Company Limited; *Int'l*, pg. 227
BHP WORLD MINERALS—See The Broken Hill Proprietary Company Limited; *Int'l*, pg. 224
BHS-BAYER, BERG-, HUETTEN-, UND SALZWERKE AG—See Viag AG; *Int'l*, pg. 1464
BHS PLC—See Storehouse PLC; *Int'l*, pg. 1304
BHS-VOITH GETRIEBETECHNIK GMBH—See J.M. Voith, GmbH; *Int'l*, pg. 1473
B.H.V. BELLE-EPINE—See Bazar de L'Hotel de Ville; *Int'l*, pg. 181
B.H.V. CAEN—See Bazar de L'Hotel de Ville; *Int'l*, pg. 181
B.H.V. CRETEIL—See Bazar de L'Hotel de Ville; *Int'l*, pg. 181
B.H.V. FLANDRE—See Bazar de L'Hotel de Ville; *Int'l*, pg. 181
B.H.V. GRADIGNAN—See Bazar de L'Hotel de Ville; *Int'l*, pg. 181
B.H.V. LA PART DIEU—See Bazar de L'Hotel de Ville; *Int'l*, pg. 181
B.H.V. LIMONEST—See Bazar de L'Hotel de Ville; *Int'l*, pg. 181
B.H.V. MONTLHERY—See Bazar de L'Hotel de Ville; *Int'l*, pg. 181
B.H.V. PARLY II—See Bazar de L'Hotel de Ville; *Int'l*, pg. 181
B.H.V. RIVOLI—See Bazar de L'Hotel de Ville; *Int'l*, pg. 181
B.H.V. ROSNY II—See Bazar de L'Hotel de Ville; *Int'l*, pg. 181
B.H.V. ST-GENIS-LAVAL—See Bazar de L'Hotel de Ville; *Int'l*, pg. 181
B.H.V. STRASBOURG—See Bazar de L'Hotel de Ville; *Int'l*, pg. 181
B.H.V. VILLENUEVE-LA-GARENNE—See Bazar de L'Hotel de Ville; *Int'l*, pg. 181
BHW BAUSPARKASSE AG; *Int'l*, pg. 120
BI COMMERCIAL FINANCE LIMITED—See Bank of Ireland; *Int'l*, pg. 153
BI HOLDINGS CORP.—See Blount International, Inc.; *U.S. Public*, pg. 238
B.I. TRANSPORTATION, INC.—See Burlington Industries, Inc.; *U.S. Public*, pg. 268
BIAM AUSTRALIA PTY LTD.—See Bank of Ireland; *Int'l*, pg. 153
BIAO NIGER—See Generale de Banque S.A.; *Int'l*, pg. 547
BIAO TOGO—See Generale de Banque S.A.; *Int'l*, pg. 547
BICC BRAND-REX—See BICC plc; *Int'l*, pg. 120
BICC PLC; *Int'l*, pg. 120
BICC PYROTENAX—See BICC plc; *Int'l*, pg. 120
BIEC INTERNATIONAL INC.—See The Broken Hill Proprietary Company Limited; *Int'l*, pg. 226
BIF—See General Signal Corporation; *U.S. Public*, pg. 726
BIFP, INC.—See Forest City Enterprises, Inc.; *U.S. Public*, pg. 668
BIK INTERIMKANTOOR—See Temco Service Industries; *U.S. Public*, pg. 1574
BIL ASIA HOLDINGS LTD.—See Brierley Investments Limited; *Int'l*, pg. 215
BIL BUROGEBAUDE VERWALTUNGS GMBH—See Bayerische Vereinsbank Group; *Int'l*, pg. 179
BIL BUROGEBAUDE VERWALTUNGS GMBH & CO. LEASING KG—See Bayerische Vereinsbank Group; *Int'l*, pg. 179
BIL BUROGEBAUDE VERWALTUNGS GMBH & CO. VERMIETUNGS KG—See Bayerische Vereinsbank Group; *Int'l*, pg. 179
BIL (FAR EAST HOLDINGS) LTD.—See Brierley Investments Limited; *Int'l*, pg. 215
BIL GRUNDBESITZVERWALTUNGS GMBH & CO. LAGERGEBAUDE—See Bayerische Vereinsbank Group; *Int'l*, pg. 179
BIL GRUNDSTUCKSVERWALTUNGS GMBH—See Bayerische Vereinsbank Group; *Int'l*, pg. 179
BIL GRUNDSTUCKSVERWALTUNGS GMBH & CO. WARENHAUS KG—See Bayerische Vereinsbank Group; *Int'l*, pg. 179
BIL GRUNDSTUCKSVERWALTUNGS GMBH & CO. BUROGEBAUDE KG—See Bayerische Vereinsbank Group; *Int'l*, pg. 179
BIL IMMOBILIEN GMBH—See Bayerische Vereinsbank Group; *Int'l*, pg. 179
BIL IMMOBILIEN GMBH & CO. LAGERHAUS KG—See Bayerische Vereinsbank Group; *Int'l*, pg. 179
BIL IMMOBILIEN GMBH & CO. AM STEINACKER KG—See Bayerische Vereinsbank Group; *Int'l*, pg. 179

BIL IMMOBILIEN GMBH & CO. KELLEREI AM SCHATZBOGEN KG—See Bayerische Vereinsbank Group; *Int'l*, pg. 179
BIL IMMOBILIEN GMBH & CO. LAGERHALLENVERMIETUNGS KG—See Bayerische Vereinsbank Group; *Int'l*, pg. 179
BIL IMMOBILIEN GMBH & CO. MONTAGEHALLEN VERMIETUNGS KG—See Bayerische Vereinsbank Group; *Int'l*, pg. 179
BIL IMMOBILIEN GMBH & CO. SPEDITIONSLAGERHALLE KG—See Bayerische Vereinsbank Group; *Int'l*, pg. 179
BIL IMMOBILIEN GMBH & CO. UNI-DRUCK-KG—See Bayerische Vereinsbank Group; *Int'l*, pg. 179
BIL IMMOBILIEN GMBH & CO. VERMIETUNGS KG—See Bayerische Vereinsbank Group; *Int'l*, pg. 179
BIL IMMOBILIEN GMBH & CO. VERTRIEBSLAGER KG—See Bayerische Vereinsbank Group; *Int'l*, pg. 179
BIL IMMOBILIEN GMBH & CO. VERWALTUNGSGEBAUDE KG—See Bayerische Vereinsbank Group; *Int'l*, pg. 179
BIL IMMOBILIEN GMBH & CO. WEBEREI-LAGEHAUS KG—See Bayerische Vereinsbank Group; *Int'l*, pg. 179
BIL IMMOBILIEN GMBH & CO. BAGRUN KG—See Bayerische Vereinsbank Group; *Int'l*, pg. 179
BIL LEASING GMBH—See Bayerische Vereinsbank Group; *Int'l*, pg. 179
BIL LEASING GMBH & CO. ANTUREX KG—See Bayerische Vereinsbank Group; *Int'l*, pg. 179
BIL LEASING GMBH & CO. ARATO KG—See Bayerische Vereinsbank Group; *Int'l*, pg. 179
BIL LEASING GMBH & CO. ASTARI KG—See Bayerische Vereinsbank Group; *Int'l*, pg. 179
BIL LEASING GMBH & CO. BALBEX KG—See Bayerische Vereinsbank Group; *Int'l*, pg. 179
BIL LEASING GMBH & CO. CANTARO KG—See Bayerische Vereinsbank Group; *Int'l*, pg. 179
BIL LEASING GMBH & CO. ENTRO KG—See Bayerische Vereinsbank Group; *Int'l*, pg. 179
BIL LEASING GMBH & CO. GEWERBEGEBAUDE KG—See Bayerische Vereinsbank Group; *Int'l*, pg. 179
BIL LEASING GMBH & CO. GRUNDSTUCKS KG—See Bayerische Vereinsbank Group; *Int'l*, pg. 179
BIL LEASING GMBH & CO. INDUSTRIEGEBAUDE KG—See Bayerische Vereinsbank Group; *Int'l*, pg. 179
BIL LEASING GMBH & CO. INDUSTRIEHALLEN KG—See Bayerische Vereinsbank Group; *Int'l*, pg. 179
BIL LEASING GMBH & CO. KAUFHAUS KG—See Bayerische Vereinsbank Group; *Int'l*, pg. 179
BIL LEASING GMBH & CO. OBJEKT WACKER PENSIONSKASSE KG—See Bayerische Vereinsbank Group; *Int'l*, pg. 179
BIL LEASING GMBH & CO. TEXTILHAUS—See Bayerische Vereinsbank Group; *Int'l*, pg. 179
BIL LEASING GMBH & CO. VERWALTUNGS KG—See Bayerische Vereinsbank Group; *Int'l*, pg. 179
BIL LEASING GMBH & CO. VERWALTUNGSBAUTEN KG—See Bayerische Vereinsbank Group; *Int'l*, pg. 179
BIL PARTICIPATION S.A.—See Banque Internationale a Luxembourg S.A.; *Int'l*, pg. 162
BIM S.A.—See Sun Microsystems, Inc.; *U.S. Public*, pg. 1531
B. I. P.—See Lagardere Groupe; *Int'l*, pg. 791
BIP SUB1, INC.—See Nationwide Health Properties Inc.; *U.S. Public*, pg. 1166
THE BIS GROUP LIMITED—See Bell Atlantic Corporation; *U.S. Public*, pg. 204
BIW CABLE MANUFACTURING PLANT—See Draka Kabel B.V.; *Int'l*, pg. 417
BIW CABLE SYSTEMS-CONNECTOR SYSTEMS DIV.—See Draka Kabel B.V.; *Int'l*, pg. 417
BIW CABLE SYSTEMS, INC.—See Draka Kabel B.V.; *Int'l*, pg. 417
BJ COIL TECH—See BJ Services Company; *U.S. Public*, pg. 161
B.J. (N.Z.) LIMITED—See International Paper Company; *U.S. Public*, pg. 905
BJ PROCESS & PIPELINE SERVICES LTD.—See BJ Services Company; *U.S. Public*, pg. 161
BJ SERVICES COMPANY; *U.S. Public*, pg. 161
BJ SOFTWARE SYSTEMS—See Thermo Electron Corporation; *U.S. Public*, pg. 1593
BJ-TITAN SERVICES COMPANY (PARTNERSHIP)—See Baker Hughes Incorporated; *U.S. Public*, pg. 166
BJK&E MEDIA GROUP—See True North Diversified Companies; *U.S. Public*, pg. 1642
BJN (FIJI) LIMITED—See Imperial Chemical Industries PLC; *Int'l*, pg. 664
BJ'S WHOLESALE CLUB, INC.; *U.S. Public*, pg. 162
BK&S DIRECT MARKETING—See Biederman, Kelly & Shaffer, Inc.; *U.S. Private*, pg. 143
BK BETEILIGUNGSVERWALTUNG GMBH—See Ruetgers A.G.; *Int'l*, pg. 1148
BK INVESTMENTS—See The Bank of New York Company, Inc.; *U.S. Public*, pg. 179
BK LADENBURG GMBH—See Hoechst Aktiengesellschaft; *Int'l*, pg. 626
BKD BANK BUDAPEST—See Dresdner Bank AG; *Int'l*, pg. 418
BKG FINISHING SYSTEMS, INC.—See Illinois Tool Works Inc.; *U.S. Public*, pg. 865
BKI—See Standex International Corporation; *U.S. Public*, pg. 1506
BKM ENTERPRISES, INC.; *U.S. Private*, pg. 107
BKNT, INC.—See VSI Holdings, Inc.; *U.S. Public*, pg. 1703
BL INDUSTRIA OTICA, LTDA.—See Bausch & Lomb Incorporated; *U.S. Public*, pg. 195
BL JERSEY LTD.—See Bank Leumi le-Israel B.M.; *Int'l*, pg. 150
B.L. PHARMACEUTICALS (PTY.) LTD.—See Bristol-Myers Squibb Company; *U.S. Public*, pg. 255
BLC CORP.—See Citicorp; *U.S. Public*, pg. 377
BLC S.A. (FRANCE)—See Maritz Inc.; *U.S. Private*, pg. 704
BLD EUROPE S.A.—See Dentsu Inc.; *Int'l*, pg. 394
BLD PRODUCTS, LTD.—See MascoTech, Inc.; *U.S. Public*, pg. 1055

BLE CAPITAL LIMITED—See Westpac Banking Corporation; *Int'l*, pg. 1496
BLFC SECURITIES CORPORATION—See Citicorp; *U.S. Public*, pg. 377
BLG BETONLIEFERUNGSGESELLSCHAFT GMBH—See Heidelberger Zement A.G.; *Int'l*, pg. 606
BLH ELECTRONICS, CANADA DIVISION—See Spectra-Physics AB; *Int'l*, pg. 1289
BLH ELECTRONICS, INC.—See Spectra-Physics AB; *Int'l*, pg. 1289
BLH SR-4 SENSOREN GMBH—See Spectra-Physics AB; *Int'l*, pg. 1289
BLK-SIO ENERGIE-UND UMWELTTECHNIK AG—See Deutsche Babcock AG; *Int'l*, pg. 398
BLP COMPONENTS LTD.—See The Roxboro Group PLC; *Int'l*, pg. 1130
BLW PRAZISIONSSCHMIEDE GMBH—See Thyssen AG; *Int'l*, pg. 1387
BM BETEILIGUNGS MANAGEMENT GMBH—See Creditanstalt-Bankverein; *Int'l*, pg. 347
BM MANNHEIM BETEILIGUNGEN GMBH—See Corange Limited; *Int'l*, pg. 331
BMA FINANCIAL SERVICES, INC.—See Assicurazioni Generali S.p.A.; *Int'l*, pg. 90
BMA RESOURCES, INC.—See Seafield Capital Corporation; *U.S. Public*, pg. 1449
BMA SELECTCARE, INC.—See Assicurazioni Generali S.p.A.; *Int'l*, pg. 90
B.M.B. BELGO-MINEIRA BEKAERT ARTEFATOS DE ARAME LTDA.—See N.V. Bekaert S.A.; *Int'l*, pg. 184
BMB COMPANY—See Alamo Group, Inc.; *U.S. Public*, pg. 35
BMB MANAGEMENT CONSULTING FOR DEVELOPMENT BV—See Heidemij N.V.; *Int'l*, pg. 606
BMC FORESTRY CORPORATION—See Benguet Corporation; *Int'l*, pg. 186
BMC INDUSTRIES, INC.; *U.S. Public*, pg. 162
BMC REAL ESTATE, INC.—See Butler Manufacturing Company; *U.S. Public*, pg. 271
BMC SOFTWARE A/S—See BMC Software, Inc.; *U.S. Public*, pg. 162
BMC SOFTWARE (AUSTRALIA) PTY. LTD.—See BMC Software, Inc.; *U.S. Public*, pg. 162
BMC SOFTWARE B.V.—See BMC Software, Inc.; *U.S. Public*, pg. 162
BMC SOFTWARE BELGIUM N.V.-S.A.—See BMC Software, Inc.; *U.S. Public*, pg. 162
BMC SOFTWARE CANADA—See BMC Software, Inc.; *U.S. Public*, pg. 162
BMC SOFTWARE FRANCE—See BMC Software, Inc.; *U.S. Public*, pg. 162
BMC SOFTWARE GMBH—See BMC Software, Inc.; *U.S. Public*, pg. 162
BMC SOFTWARE, INC.; *U.S. Public*, pg. 162
BMC SOFTWARE JAPAN LTD.—See BMC Software, Inc.; *U.S. Public*, pg. 163
BMC SOFTWARE KOREA—See BMC Software, Inc.; *U.S. Public*, pg. 163
BMC SOFTWARE, LIMITED—See BMC Software, Inc.; *U.S. Public*, pg. 163
BMC SOFTWARE. S.A.—See BMC Software, Inc.; *U.S. Public*, pg. 163
BMC SOFTWARE SRL—See BMC Software, Inc.; *U.S. Public*, pg. 163
BMC WEST—See GAF Corporation; *U.S. Private*, pg. 433
BMCA INSULATION PRODUCTS, INC.—See GAF Corporation; *U.S. Private*, pg. 433
BMCG (BUSINESS MARKETING COMMUNICATIONS)—See Griffin Bacal Inc.; *U.S. Private*, pg. 480
BMCI MOROCCO—See Banque Nationale de Paris; *Int'l*, pg. 163
BMG ARIOLA BELGIUM NV—See Bertelsmann AG; *Int'l*, pg. 192
BMG ARIOLA MUSIC LTDA.—See Bertelsmann AG; *Int'l*, pg. 192
BMG ARIOLA MUSICA S.P.A.—See Bertelsmann AG; *Int'l*, pg. 192
BMG ARIOLA S.A. DE C.V. (MEXICO)—See Bertelsmann AG; *Int'l*, pg. 192
BMG ARIOLA S.A. (FRANCE)—See Bertelsmann AG; *Int'l*, pg. 192
BMG/MUSIC—See Bertelsmann AG; *Int'l*, pg. 191
B.M.G. MUSIC SERVICE—See Thomson S.A.; *Int'l*, pg. 1383
B.M.G. RECORDS—See Thomson S.A.; *Int'l*, pg. 1383
BMG MUSIC CANADA—See Bertelsmann AG; *Int'l*, pg. 192
BMI—See Thomson S.A.; *Int'l*, pg. 1381
BMI PTE. LTD., SINGAPORE—See F. J. Benjamin Holdings Ltd.; *Int'l*, pg. 187
B.M.J. FINANCIAL CORP.—See Summit Bancorp; *U.S. Public*, pg. 1528
BMK PRINTING, INC—See Bomarko, Inc.; *U.S. Private*, pg. 156
BMMI ENGINEERING SERVICES—See Moore Products Co.; *U.S. Public*, pg. 1128
BMO FINANCIAL, INC.—See Bank of Montreal; *Int'l*, pg. 154
BMOI—See Banque Nationale de Paris; *Int'l*, pg. 163
BMS, INC.—See Cohu, Inc.; *U.S. Public*, pg. 396
BMS ON-LINE SERVICES, INC.—See Fiserv, Inc.; *U.S. Public*, pg. 647
BMW; *U.S. Private*, pg. 107
BMW AUSTRALIA LTD.—See Bayerische Motoren Werke Aktiengesellschaft; *Int'l*, pg. 178
BMW AUSTRIA GESELLSCHAFT M.B.H.—See Bayerische Motoren Werke Aktiengesellschaft; *Int'l*, pg. 178
BMW BANK GMBH—See Bayerische Motoren Werke Aktiengesellschaft; *Int'l*, pg. 177
BMW BELGIUM S.A./N.V.—See Bayerische Motoren Werke Aktiengesellschaft; *Int'l*, pg. 178
BMW CANADA INC.—See Bayerische Motoren Werke Aktiengesellschaft; *Int'l*, pg. 178
BMW COORDINATION CENTER N.V.—See Bayerische Motoren Werke Aktiengesellschaft; *Int'l*, pg. 178

MASTER INDEX TO COMPANY NAMES BT

Company Index

BMW FINANCE N.V.—See Bayerische Motoren Werke Aktiengesellschaft; *Int'l*, pg. 178
BMW FRANCE S.A.—See Bayerische Motoren Werke Aktiengesellschaft; *Int'l*, pg. 178
BMW (GB) LTD.—See Bayerische Motoren Werke Aktiengesellschaft; *Int'l*, pg. 178
BMW HOLDING AG—See Bayerische Motoren Werke Aktiengesellschaft; *Int'l*, pg. 178
BMW HOLDING B.V.—See Bayerische Motoren Werke Aktiengesellschaft; *Int'l*, pg. 178
BMW IBERICA S.A.—See Bayerische Motoren Werke Aktiengesellschaft; *Int'l*, pg. 178
BMW INGENIEUR ZENTRUM VERWALTUNGS GMBH—See Bayerische Motoren Werke Aktiengesellschaft; *Int'l*, pg. 177
BMW ITALIA S.P.A.—See Bayerische Motoren Werke Aktiengesellschaft; *Int'l*, pg. 178
BMW JAPAN CORP.—See Bayerische Motoren Werke Aktiengesellschaft; *Int'l*, pg. 178
BMW LEASING CORP.—See Bayerische Motoren Werke Aktiengesellschaft; *Int'l*, pg. 177
BMW MOTOREN GES.M.B.H.—See Bayerische Motoren Werke Aktiengesellschaft; *Int'l*, pg. 178
BMW MOTORRAD GMBH—See Bayerische Motoren Werke Aktiengesellschaft; *Int'l*, pg. 177
BMW MOTORSPORT GMBH—See Bayerische Motoren Werke Aktiengesellschaft; *Int'l*, pg. 177
BMW NEDERLAND B.V.—See Bayerische Motoren Werke Aktiengesellschaft; *Int'l*, pg. 178
BMW NEW ZEALAND LTD.—See Bayerische Motoren Werke Aktiengesellschaft; *Int'l*, pg. 178
BMW OVERSEAS ENTERPRISES N.V.—See Bayerische Motoren Werke Aktiengesellschaft; *Int'l*, pg. 178
BMW (SCHWEIZ) AG—See Bayerische Motoren Werke Aktiengesellschaft; *Int'l*, pg. 178
BMW (SOUTH AFRICA) (PTY.) LTD.—See Bayerische Motoren Werke Aktiengesellschaft; *Int'l*, pg. 178
BMW SVERIGE AB—See Bayerische Motoren Werke Aktiengesellschaft; *Int'l*, pg. 178
BMW TECHNIK GMBH—See Bayerische Motoren Werke Aktiengesellschaft; *Int'l*, pg. 177
BMW (US) HOLDING CORPORATION—See Bayerische Motoren Werke Aktiengesellschaft; *Int'l*, pg. 177
BMY CO.—See Harsco Corporation; *U.S. Public*, pg. 793
BMY-WHEELED VEHICLES—See Harsco Corporation; *U.S. Public*, pg. 793
BMZ!FCA—See FCA!BMZ; *Int'l*, pg. 470
BN DIVISION—See Bombardier Inc.; *Int'l*, pg. 200
BNA BUSINESS INFORMATION DIVISION—See The Bureau of National Affairs, Inc.; *U.S. Private*, pg. 181
BNA COMMUNICATIONS, INC.—See The Bureau of National Affairs, Inc.; *U.S. Private*, pg. 182
BNA HEALTH CARE INFORMATION DIVISION—See The Bureau of National Affairs, Inc.; *U.S. Private*, pg. 182
BNA INTERNATIONAL INC.—See The Bureau of National Affairs, Inc.; *U.S. Private*, pg. 182
BNB INVESTMENT CORPORATION—See Broad National Bancorporation; *U.S. Public*, pg. 258
BNCI COMERCIAL EXPORTADORA LTDA.—See The Chase Manhattan Corporation; *U.S. Public*, pg. 339
BNE LAND & DEVELOPMENT CO.—See Boddie-Noell Enterprises Inc.; *U.S. Private*, pg. 154
BNFL; *Int'l*, pg. 120
BNI COAL, LTD.—See Minnesota Power; *U.S. Public*, pg. 1116
BNL CONSULTORIA E SERVICIOS LTDA.—See Banca Nazionale del Lavoro Sj.A.; *Int'l*, pg. 136
BNL DE URUGUAY—See Banca Nazionale del Lavoro Sj.A.; *Int'l*, pg. 136
BNL DISTRIBUIDORA DE TITULOS VAL. MOB. S.A.—See Banca Nazionale del Lavoro Sj.A.; *Int'l*, pg. 136
BNL - FONDIARIA INVERSIONES ARGENTINAS S.A.—See Banca Nazionale del Lavoro Sj.A.; *Int'l*, pg. 136
BNL INTERNATIONAL INVESTMENTS—See Banca Nazionale del Lavoro Sj.A.; *Int'l*, pg. 136
BNL SERVICES S.A.M.—See Banca Nazionale del Lavoro Sj.A.; *Int'l*, pg. 137
BNL US CORPORATION—See Banca Nazionale del Lavoro Sj.A.; *Int'l*, pg. 136
BNP-AK DRESDNER BANK A.S.—See Dresdner Bank AG; *Int'l*, pg. 420
BNP-AK DRESDNER BANK A.S.—See Sabanci Holding A.S.; *Int'l*, pg. 1167
BNP-AK DRESDNER FINANSAL KIRALAMA A.S.—See Dresdner Bank AG; *Int'l*, pg. 421
BNP-AK DRESDNER FINANSAL KIRALAMA A.S.—See Sabanci Holding A.S.; *Int'l*, pg. 1167
BNP ARBITRAGE—See Banque Nationale de Paris; *Int'l*, pg. 163
BNP BAIL—See Banque Nationale de Paris; *Int'l*, pg. 163
BNP BANK N.V.—See Banque Nationale de Paris; *Int'l*, pg. 163
BNP CAPITAL FINANCE LIMITED - IRELAND—See Banque Nationale de Paris; *Int'l*, pg. 163
BNP COOPER NEFF—See Banque Nationale de Paris; *Int'l*, pg. 163
BNP-DRESDNER BANK (BULGARIA) A.D.—See Dresdner Bank AG; *Int'l*, pg. 418
BNP ESPANA S.A.—See Banque Nationale de Paris; *Int'l*, pg. 163
BNP FACTOR - PORTUGAL—See Banque Nationale de Paris; *Int'l*, pg. 163
BNP FINANCE—See Banque Nationale de Paris; *Int'l*, pg. 163
BNP FINANS A/S - NORWAY—See Banque Nationale de Paris; *Int'l*, pg. 163
BNP (IRELAND) LTD.—See Banque Nationale de Paris; *Int'l*, pg. 163
BNP - JERSEY TRUST CORP. LIMITED—See Banque Nationale de Paris; *Int'l*, pg. 163
BNP LEASING SPA—See Banque Nationale de Paris; *Int'l*, pg. 164
PT BNP LIPPO UTAMA LEASING—See Banque Nationale de Paris; *Int'l*, pg. 164
BNP LUXEMBOURG SA—See Banque Nationale de Paris; *Int'l*, pg. 164
BNP (MEXICO) SA—See Banque Nationale de Paris; *Int'l*, pg. 164
BNP-NOUVELLE CALEDONIE—See Banque Nationale de Paris; *Int'l*, pg. 164
BNP PRIVATE BANK & TRUST CAYMAN LIMITED—See Banque Nationale de Paris; *Int'l*, pg. 164
BNP PUBLIC LIMITED CO. (LONDON)—See Banque Nationale de Paris; *Int'l*, pg. 164
BNP SECURITIES (JAPAN) LIMITED—See Banque Nationale de Paris; *Int'l*, pg. 164
BNP SIM S.P.A.—See Banque Nationale de Paris; *Int'l*, pg. 164
BNP UK HOLDINGS LTD.—See Banque Nationale de Paris; *Int'l*, pg. 164
BNP (URUGUAY) SA—See Banque Nationale de Paris; *Int'l*, pg. 164
BNPI—See Banque Nationale de Paris; *Int'l*, pg. 163
BNR EUROPE LIMITED—See Northern Telecom Limited; *Int'l*, pg. 969
BNR, INC.—See Northern Telecom Limited; *Int'l*, pg. 969
BNS INTERNATIONAL (BARBADOS) LIMITED—See The Bank of Nova Scotia; *Int'l*, pg. 156
BNS INTERNATIONAL (HONG KONG) LIMITED—See The Bank of Nova Scotia; *Int'l*, pg. 156
BNU—See Caixa Geral de Depositos; *Int'l*, pg. 250
BNU CAPITAL - SOCIEDADE DE CAPITAL DE RISCO, SA—See Caixa Geral de Depositos; *Int'l*, pg. 250
BNY BROKERAGE, INC.—See The Bank of New York Company, Inc.; *U.S. Public*, pg. 178
BNY CAPITAL MARKETS—See The Bank of New York Company, Inc.; *U.S. Public*, pg. 178
BNY FINANCIAL CORPORATION—See The Bank of New York Company, Inc.; *U.S. Public*, pg. 178
BNY FINANCIAL CORPORATION-CANADA—See The Bank of New York Company, Inc.; *U.S. Public*, pg. 179
BNY FUND MANAGEMENT (IRELAND) LIMITED—See The Bank of New York Company, Inc.; *U.S. Public*, pg. 179
BNY HOLDINGS (NEW JERSEY) CORP.—See The Bank of New York Company, Inc.; *U.S. Public*, pg. 178
BNY INTERNATIONAL FINANCING CORPORATION—See The Bank of New York Company, Inc.; *U.S. Public*, pg. 178
BNY MORTGAGE COMPANY, INC.—See The Bank of New York Company, Inc.; *U.S. Public*, pg. 178
BNY WESTERN TRUST COMPANY—See The Bank of New York Company, Inc.; *U.S. Public*, pg. 179
BOC—See The BOC Group plc; *Int'l*, pg. 121
BOC AG—See The BOC Group plc; *Int'l*, pg. 121
BOC BANGLADESH LTD.—See The BOC Group plc; *Int'l*, pg. 121
BOC CANADA LTD.—See The BOC Group plc; *Int'l*, pg. 121
BOC COATING TECHNOLOGIES—See The BOC Group plc; *Int'l*, pg. 121
BOC COATING TECHNOLOGY—See The BOC Group plc; *Int'l*, pg. 121
BOC DISTRIBUTION SERVICES LTD.—See The BOC Group plc; *Int'l*, pg. 121
BOC DO BRASIL LTDA.—See The BOC Group plc; *Int'l*, pg. 121
BOC GASES ANBA NV—See The BOC Group plc; *Int'l*, pg. 121
BOC GASES AUSTRALIA LTD.—See The BOC Group plc; *Int'l*, pg. 121
BOC GASES FIJI LTD.—See The BOC Group plc; *Int'l*, pg. 121
P.T. BOC GASES INDONESIA—See The BOC Group plc; *Int'l*, pg. 121
BOC GASES IRELAND LTD.—See The BOC Group plc; *Int'l*, pg. 121
BOC GASES NEW ZEALAND LTD—See The BOC Group plc; *Int'l*, pg. 121
BOC GASES PAPUA NEW GUINEA PTY LTD.—See The BOC Group plc; *Int'l*, pg. 121
BOC GASES (SAMOA) LTD.—See The BOC Group plc; *Int'l*, pg. 121
THE BOC GROUP INC. (DELAWARE)—See The BOC Group plc; *Int'l*, pg. 121
THE BOC GROUP PLC; *Int'l*, pg. 121
BOC INDIA LTD.—See The BOC Group plc; *Int'l*, pg. 122
BOC KENYA LTD.—See The BOC Group plc; *Int'l*, pg. 122
BOC LIEN HWA INDUSTRIAL GASES CO. LTD.—See The BOC Group plc; *Int'l*, pg. 122
BOC OHMEDA AB—See The BOC Group plc; *Int'l*, pg. 122
BOC OHMEDA OY—See The BOC Group plc; *Int'l*, pg. 122
BOC PAKISTAN LTD.—See The BOC Group plc; *Int'l*, pg. 122
BOC PROCESS PLANTS LTD.—See The BOC Group plc; *Int'l*, pg. 121
BOC ZIMBABWE—See The BOC Group plc; *Int'l*, pg. 122
BOCM PAULS LIMITED—See Harrisons & Crosfield plc; *Int'l*, pg. 598
BOCM SILCOCK LTD.—See Unilever Plc; *Int'l*, pg. 1434
BOCM SILCOCK (N.I.) LTD.—See Electrolux, AB; *Int'l*, pg. 440
BOK FINANCIAL CORP.; *U.S. Public*, pg. 163
BOS (BEAUCHESNE OSTIGUY & SIMARD)—See TBWA Chiat/Day; *U.S. Private*, pg. 1062
BP AMERICA INC.—See The British Petroleum Company P.L.C.; *Int'l*, pg. 220
BP AUSTRALIA LTD.—See The British Petroleum Company P.L.C.; *Int'l*, pg. 220
BP CHEMICALS, INC.—See The British Petroleum Company P.L.C.; *Int'l*, pg. 220
BP CHEMICALS LTD.—See The British Petroleum Company P.L.C.; *Int'l*, pg. 220
BP EXPLORATION (ALASKA) INC.—See The British Petroleum Company P.L.C.; *Int'l*, pg. 220
BP EXPLORATION COMPANY LIMITED—See The British Petroleum Company P.L.C.; *Int'l*, pg. 220
BP-FINA RWANDA S.A.R.L.—See Petrofina S.A.; *Int'l*, pg. 1044
BP FRANCE—See The British Petroleum Company P.L.C.; *Int'l*, pg. 220
BP INTERNATIONAL LTD.—See The British Petroleum Company P.L.C.; *Int'l*, pg. 220
BP JAPAN KK—See The British Petroleum Company P.L.C.; *Int'l*, pg. 220
BP NORTH AMERICA PETROLEUM INC.—See The British Petroleum Company P.L.C.; *Int'l*, pg. 220
BP OIL CO.—See The British Petroleum Company P.L.C.; *Int'l*, pg. 220
BP OIL INTERNATIONAL LIMITED—See The British Petroleum Company P.L.C.; *Int'l*, pg. 220
BP OIL PIPELINE COMPANY—See The British Petroleum Company P.L.C.; *Int'l*, pg. 220
BP PIPELINES (ALASKA) INC.—See The British Petroleum Company P.L.C.; *Int'l*, pg. 220
BPA INTERNATIONAL; *U.S. Private*, pg. 107
BPA INTERNATIONAL - ENGLEWOOD—See BPA International; *U.S. Private*, pg. 107
BPA INTERNATIONAL - LONDON—See BPA International; *U.S. Private*, pg. 107
BPA INTERNATIONAL - MCLEAN—See BPA International; *U.S. Private*, pg. 107
BPA INTERNATIONAL - TAMPA—See BPA International; *U.S. Private*, pg. 107
BPA INTERNATIONAL - TORRANCE—See BPA International; *U.S. Private*, pg. 107
BPB INDUSTRIES PLC; *Int'l*, pg. 122
BPB PAPER & PACKAGING LTD.—See BPB Industries PLC; *Int'l*, pg. 122
BPC DIVISION—See Heywood Williams Group PLC; *Int'l*, pg. 618
BPCO—See Emco Limited; *Int'l*, pg. 453
BPI COMMUNICATIONS INC.—See VNU Verenigde Nederlandse Uitgeversbedrijven B.V.; *Int'l*, pg. 1446
BPI INC.—See HON Industries Inc.; *U.S. Public*, pg. 772
BPI INC., SALISBURY PLANT—See HON Industries Inc.; *U.S. Public*, pg. 772
BPL SANYO LIMITED—See Sanyo Electric Co., Ltd.; *Int'l*, pg. 1191
BPMC, INC.—See Barry-Wehmiller Company; *U.S. Private*, pg. 118
BPO FINANCE CORPORATION—See Baldwin Piano & Organ Company; *U.S. Public*, pg. 169
BR ASSOCIATES, INC.; *U.S. Private*, pg. 107
BR COMMUNICATIONS—See TCI International Inc.; *U.S. Public*, pg. 1555
B.R. GUEST, LTD.—See Rich Products Corp.; *U.S. Private*, pg. 928
BRAC CREDIT CORP.—See Budget Group, Inc.; *U.S. Private*, pg. 178
BRB—See Grey Advertising Inc.; *U.S. Public*, pg. 765
BRC HOLDINGS; *U.S. Public*, pg. 163
BRC WELDMESH (FE) LTD.—See The Broken Hill Proprietary Company Limited; *Int'l*, pg. 227
BRC WELDMESH (SEA) PTE LTD.—See The Broken Hill Proprietary Company Limited; *Int'l*, pg. 227
BRC WELDMESH (VIETNAM) LTD.—See The Broken Hill Proprietary Company Limited; *Int'l*, pg. 227
BRE GROUP—See Alcatel Alsthom Compagnie Generale D'Electricite; *Int'l*, pg. 52
BRE PROPERTIES, INC.; *U.S. Public*, pg. 163
BRI GROUP—See Alcatel Alsthom Compagnie Generale D'Electricite; *Int'l*, pg. 52
BRL LEASING (PTY) LTD.—See Barlow Ltd.; *Int'l*, pg. 167
BRSG/MAPLES PUBLIC RELATIONS—See Black Rogers Sullivan Goodnight, Inc.; *U.S. Private*, pg. 147
BRT CORPORATION—See PSC Inc.; *U.S. Public*, pg. 1246
BRT TRANSFER TERMINAL, INC.—See Vulcan Materials Company; *U.S. Public*, pg. 1726
BRW, INC.; *U.S. Private*, pg. 107
BRW MEDIA—See John Fairfax Holdings Limited; *Int'l*, pg. 477
BRW PAPER CO., INC.—See Gould Paper Corporation; *U.S. Private*, pg. 467
BS & B PROCESS SYSTEMS, INC.—See International Systems & Controls Corp.; *U.S. Private*, pg. 572
BS & B SAFETY SYSTEMS—See International Systems & Controls Corp.; *U.S. Private*, pg. 572
BS BUILDING SEVICES AG—See Landis & Staefa AG; *Int'l*, pg. 800
BS CONTINENTAL S.A. UTILIDADES DOMESTICAS; *Int'l*, *pg. 123*
BS-SERVICE B.V., ZOETERMEER—See Internatio-Muller N.V.; *Int'l*, pg. 682
BSA ADVERTISING, INC.; *U.S. Private*, pg. 107
BSA ADVERTISING, INC.—See BSA Advertising, Inc.; *U.S. Private*, pg. 108
BSA INTERNATIONAL INC.—See BSA Advertising, Inc.; *U.S. Private*, pg. 108
BSB NAHRUNGSMITTEL GMBH—See Danone Group; *Int'l*, *pg. 380*
BSD TEKNIK—See Eclipse Inc.; *U.S. Private*, pg. 361
B.S.G.L.—See Compagnie des Machines Bull; *Int'l*, pg. 315
BSL ENGINEERING LIMITED—See Brammer plc; *Int'l*, pg. 212
BSL INDUSTRIES S.A.—See Royal Begemann Group; *Int'l*, *pg. 1134*
BSL LIMITED—See Brammer plc; *Int'l*, pg. 212
BSMG WORLDWIDE—See True North Diversified Companies; *U.S. Public*, pg. 1642
BSN LONDON—See Banco Santander; *Int'l*, pg. 144
BSN PORTUGAL—See Banco Santander; *Int'l*, pg. 144
BSN S.A. SOCIEDAD DE VALORES Y BOLSA—See Banco Santander; *Int'l*, pg. 143
BSN TOKYO—See Banco Santander; *Int'l*, pg. 144
BSN VIDRIO ESPANA—See Danone Group; *Int'l*, pg. 381
BST-BDDP—See BDDP Group; *Int'l*, pg. 117
BT ALEX. BROWN INC.—See Bankers Trust New York Corporation; *U.S. Public*, pg. 185
BT AUSTRALASIA PTY LIMITED—See British Telecommunications plc; *Int'l*, pg. 223
BT BROKERAGE CORPORATION—See Bankers Trust New York Corporation; *U.S. Public*, pg. 185

BT BROKERAGE (PHILIPPINES) INC.—See Bankers Trust New York Corporation; *U.S. Public*, pg. 185
BT CABLESHIPS LIMITED—See British Telecommunications plc; *Int'l*, pg. 222
BT CAPITAL PARTNERS—See Bankers Trust New York Corporation; *U.S. Public*, pg. 185
BT (CBP) LIMITED—See British Telecommunications plc; *Int'l*, pg. 222
BT COMMERCIAL CORPORATION—See Bankers Trust New York Corporation; *U.S. Public*, pg. 185
BT COMMUNICATIONS MANAGEMENT LIMITED—See British Telecommunications plc; *Int'l*, pg. 222
B.T. EQUIPMENT CO., INC.—See Gilbane Building Company; *U.S. Private*, pg. 453
BT EQUIPMENT LEASING, INC.—See Bankers Trust New York Corporation; *U.S. Public*, pg. 185
BT FINANCIAL CORPORATION; *U.S. Public*, pg. 163
BT FRANCE SNC—See British Telecommunications plc; *Int'l*, pg. 223
BT FUTURES CORP.—See Bankers Trust New York Corporation; *U.S. Public*, pg. 185
BT (HONG KONG) LIMITED—See British Telecommunications plc; *Int'l*, pg. 223
B.T. INC.—See Takashimaya Company, Limited; *Int'l*, pg. 1349
BT INDUSTRIES AB; *Int'l*, pg. 123
BT INTERNATIONAL TRADING CORP.—See Bankers Trust New York Corporation; *U.S. Public*, pg. 185
BT INVESTMENT MANAGERS, INC.—See Bankers Trust New York Corporation; *U.S. Public*, pg. 185
BT LIMITED—See British Telecommunications plc; *Int'l*, pg. 222
BT NORTH AMERICA, INC.—See British Telecommunications plc; *Int'l*, pg. 223
BT OFFICE PRODUCTS INTERNATIONAL, INC—See N.V. Koninklijke KNP BT; *Int'l*, pg. 756
BT PRIVATE CLIENTS GROUP—See Bankers Trust New York Corporation; *U.S. Public*, pg. 185
BT PROPERTY LTD.—See British Telecommunications plc; *Int'l*, pg. 222
BT SECURITIES CORP.—See Bankers Trust New York Corporation; *U.S. Public*, pg. 185
BT SUBSEA CABLES LIMITED—See British Telecommunications plc; *Int'l*, pg. 222
BT TELECOMUNICACIONES S.A.—See British Telecommunications plc; *Int'l*, pg. 223
BT-U.S.A.—See N.V. Koninklijke KNP BT; *Int'l*, pg. 756
BT (WORLDWIDE) LTD.—See British Telecommunications plc; *Int'l*, pg. 222
BTE BRAUEREI-TECHNIK ESSEN GMBH—See Deutsche Babcock AG; *Int'l*, pg. 400
BTG, INC.; *U.S. Public*, pg. 164
BTGRAPHIC SA DE CV—See N.V. Koninklijke KNP BT; *Int'l*, pg. 757
BTI AMERICAS, INC.; *U.S. Private*, pg. 108
BTL AB; *Int'l*, pg. 123
BTL SWEDEN AB—See BTL AB; *Int'l*, pg. 123
BTM FINANCE AND SECURITIES (THAILAND) LTD.—See The Bank of Tokyo-Mitsubishi, Ltd.; *Int'l*, pg. 157
BTM FINANZIARIA (ITALIA) S.P.A.—See The Bank of Tokyo-Mitsubishi, Ltd.; *Int'l*, pg. 158
BTR FARINGTON LTD.—See BTR plc; *Int'l*, pg. 125
BTR, INC.—See BTR plc; *Int'l*, pg. 125
BTR-MEASUREMENT & FLOW CONTROL DIVISION—See BTR plc; *Int'l*, pg. 125
BTR MED/VET—See BTR plc; *Int'l*, pg. 127
BTR PAPER GROUP—See BTR plc; *Int'l*, pg. 127
BTR PERMALI RP LTD.—See BTR plc; *Int'l*, pg. 124
BTR PLC; *Int'l*, pg. 124
BTR PRECISION DIE CASTING, INC.—See BTR plc; *Int'l*, pg. 127
BTR SILVERTOWN LTD.—See BTR plc; *Int'l*, pg. 125
BTR NYLEX LIMITED—See BTR plc; *Int'l*, pg. 128
BTS—See Robert Bosch GmbH; *Int'l*, pg. 205
BTS INC.—See Robert Bosch GmbH; *Int'l*, pg. 204
BTU ENGINEERING CORPORATION—See BTU International, Inc.; *U.S. Public*, pg. 164
BTU EUROPE—See BTU International, Inc.; *U.S. Public*, pg. 164
BTU (FRANCE) SARL—See BTU International, Inc.; *U.S. Public*, pg. 164
BTU (GERMANY) ENGINEERING GMBH—See BTU International, Inc.; *U.S. Public*, pg. 164
BTU INTERNATIONAL, INC.; *U.S. Public*, pg. 164
BTU (NETHERLANDS)—See BTU International, Inc.; *U.S. Public*, pg. 164
BUFA BAEUERLE GMBH & CO.—See Viag AG; *Int'l*, pg. 1464
BUG ALUTECHNIK GMBH—See Koninklijke Hoogovens N.V.; *Int'l*, pg. 755
B.U.S. BERZELIUS UMWELT-SERVICE GMBH—See Metallgesellschaft AG; *Int'l*, pg. 860
B.U.S. ENVIRONMENTAL SERVICES, INC.—See Metallgesellschaft AG; *Int'l*, pg. 860
BV&K DIRECT—See BVK/McDonald; *U.S. Private*, pg. 108
BV BETEILIGUNGS GMBH & CO. VERWALTUNGS KG—See Bayerische Vereinsbank Group; *Int'l*, pg. 178
BV BETEILIGUNSGESELLSCHAFT MBH—See Bayerische Vereinsbank Group; *Int'l*, pg. 178
BV CAPITAL MANAGEMENT, INC.—See Bayerische Vereinsbank Group; *Int'l*, pg. 180
BV CAPITAL MARKETS (ASIA) LTD.—See Bayerische Vereinsbank Group; *Int'l*, pg. 180
BV CAPITAL MARKETS, INC.—See Bayerische Vereinsbank Group; *Int'l*, pg. 180
BV CONSTRUCTION, INC.—See Forest City Enterprises, Inc.; *U.S. Public*, pg. 668
BV-CONSULT—See Bayerische Vereinsbank Group; *Int'l*, pg. 178
BV EASTDIL GMBH—See Bayerische Vereinsbank Group; *Int'l*, pg. 178
BV EASTDIL GMBH & CO. KG—See Bayerische Vereinsbank Group; *Int'l*, pg. 178

BV EXPORTLEASING GMBH—See Bayerische Vereinsbank Group; *Int'l*, pg. 178
BV FINANCE PRAHA S.R.O.—See Bayerische Vereinsbank Group; *Int'l*, pg. 180
BV FINANCIAL (IRELAND) LTD.—See Bayerische Vereinsbank Group; *Int'l*, pg. 180
BV FINANCIAL MANAGEMENT GMBH—See Bayerische Vereinsbank Group; *Int'l*, pg. 178
BV FINANZIARIA S.P.A.—See Bayerische Vereinsbank Group; *Int'l*, pg. 180
BV GRUNDSTUCKSENTWICKLUNGS GMBH—See Bayerische Vereinsbank Group; *Int'l*, pg. 178
BV GRUNDSTUCKSENTWICKLUNGS GMBH & CO.—See Bayerische Vereinsbank Group; *Int'l*, pg. 178
BV GRUNDSTUCKSENTWICKLUNGS GMBH & CO. DELTA KG—See Bayerische Vereinsbank Group; *Int'l*, pg. 178
BV GRUNDSTUCKSENTWICKLUNGS GMBH & CO. ETA KG—See Bayerische Vereinsbank Group; *Int'l*, pg. 178
BV GRUNDSTUCKSENTWICKLUNGS GMBH & CO. GAMMA KG—See Bayerische Vereinsbank Group; *Int'l*, pg. 178
BV GRUNDSTUCKSENTWICKLUNGS GMBH & CO. LAMBDA KG—See Bayerische Vereinsbank Group; *Int'l*, pg. 178
BV GRUNDSTUCKSENTWICKLUNGS GMBH & CO. OMIKRON KG—See Bayerische Vereinsbank Group; *Int'l*, pg. 178
BV GRUNDSTUCKSENTWICKLUNGS GMBH & CO. SIGMA KG—See Bayerische Vereinsbank Group; *Int'l*, pg. 178
BV IMMOBILIEN EXPERTISE GMBH—See Bayerische Vereinsbank Group; *Int'l*, pg. 179
BV IMMOBILIEN GMBH—See Bayerische Vereinsbank Group; *Int'l*, pg. 179
BV INFORMATIONS VERABEITUNGS GMBH—See Bayerische Vereinsbank Group; *Int'l*, pg. 179
BVA COGEN, INC.—See Yankee Energy System, Inc.; *U.S. Public*, pg. 1787
BVBA VERZEKERINGSKANTOOR SOENEN—See Assicurazioni Generali S.p.A.; *Int'l*, pg. 66
BVE CAPITAL MANAGEMENT S.A.—See Bayerische Vereinsbank Group; *Int'l*, pg. 180
BVK/MCDONALD; *U.S. Private*, pg. 108
BVK/MCDONALD—See BVK/McDonald; *U.S. Private*, pg. 108
BVK/MCDONALD - CHICAGO—See BVK/McDonald; *U.S. Private*, pg. 108
BVK/MCDONALD - NEW ORLEANS—See BVK/McDonald; *U.S. Private*, pg. 108
BVK/MCDONALD - TAMPA—See BVK/McDonald; *U.S. Private*, pg. 108
BVZ GMBH—See N.V. Koninklijke KNP BT; *Int'l*, pg. 757
BW INDUSTRIAL PRODUCTS B.V.—See Blydenstein-Willink N.V.; *Int'l*, pg. 198
BW/IP INTERNATIONAL, INC.—See Flowserve Corporation; *U.S. Public*, pg. 658
BW TRANSPORTATION SERVICES, INC.—See Bindley Western Industries, Inc.; *U.S. Public*, pg. 228
B/W WERBEAGENTUR GWA; *Int'l*, pg. 130
BWAY CORP.; *U.S. Public*, pg. 164
BWC FINANCIAL CORP.; *U.S. Private*, pg. 108
BWD AUTOMOTIVE—See Echlin Inc.; *U.S. Public*, pg. 560
BWD AUTOMOTIVE CORP.—See Echlin Inc.; *U.S. Public*, pg. 560
BWD AUTOMOTIVE CORP. (INTERNATIONAL)—See Echlin Inc.; *U.S. Public*, pg. 561
BWE-BABCOCK & WILCOX ESPANOLA, S.A.—See SEPI; *Int'l*, pg. 1224
BWE ENERGIETECHNIK GMBH—See Deutsche Babcock AG; *Int'l*, pg. 398
BWH KOUTSCHUR GMBH—See Veba AG; *Int'l*, pg. 1454
BWI FORDS HOLMATIC—See BWI Plc; *Int'l*, pg. 130
BWI INEX VISION SYSTEMS—See BWI Plc; *Int'l*, pg. 130
BWI KARTRIDG PAK—See BWI Plc; *Int'l*, pg. 130
BWI PLC; *Int'l*, pg. 130
BWK KRIEGLACH BAUWERKSTOFFE GES. M. B. H.—See Viag AG; *Int'l*, pg. 1465
BWP CONTROLS—See FKI Plc; *Int'l*, pg. 472
BWR GMBH—See DSM N.V.; *Int'l*, pg. 355
BWR WERKSTOFFSYSTEME UND WERKZEUGBAU GMBH—See DSM N.V.; *Int'l*, pg. 354
BYK GULDEN-LOMBERG GMBH—See Altana AG; *Int'l*, pg. 66
BYK GULDEN, S.A. DE C.V.—See Altana AG; *Int'l*, pg. 66
BYK LIPRANDI S.A.C.E.L.—See Altana AG; *Int'l*, pg. 66
BYK QUIMICA E FARMACEUTICA LTDA.—See Altana AG; *Int'l*, pg. 66
BZV ZEITSCHRIFTEN VERLAG GMBH & CO. KG—See Burda Holding GmbH & Co., KG; *Int'l*, pg. 233
BAAR & BEARDS—See Paris Accessories; *U.S. Private*, pg. 839
BAARS FRANCE SA—See Koninklijke BolsWessanen nv; *Int'l*, pg. 752
G.C. BAARS (PTY.) LTD.—See GESTRA GmbH; *Int'l*, pg. 549
BAARS KAAS B.V.—See Koninklijke BolsWessanen nv; *Int'l*, pg. 752
BAARS MARKETING GMBH—See Koninklijke BolsWessanen nv; *Int'l*, pg. 752
CARL BAASEL LASERTECHNIK GMBH—See Mannesmann A.G.; *Int'l*, pg. 836
BAASEL LASERTECH BENELUX BV—See Mannesmann A.G.; *Int'l*, pg. 836
BAASEL LASERTECH ESPANA SA—See Mannesmann A.G.; *Int'l*, pg. 836
BAASEL LASERTECH FRANCE SARL—See Mannesmann A.G.; *Int'l*, pg. 836
BAASEL LASERTECH ITALIA SRL—See Mannesmann A.G.; *Int'l*, pg. 836
BAASEL-RABE LASERTECHNIK GMBH—See Mannesmann A.G.; *Int'l*, pg. 836
BAB IKON GMBH SCHLIESSTECHNIK—See Assa Abloy AB; *Int'l*, pg. 18

BABBAGE'S ETC. LLC; *U.S. Private*, pg. 108
BABCOCK AFRICA (PTY) LTD.—See Babcock International Group PLC; *Int'l*, pg. 131
BABCOCK AMES CROSTA DIV.—See FKI Plc; *Int'l*, pg. 474
BABCOCK & BROWN, INC.—See The Nomura Securities Co., Ltd.; *Int'l*, pg. 956
BABCOCK & WILCOX DE MEXICO SA DE CV—See FKI Plc; *Int'l*, pg. 474
BABCOCK & WILCOX INTERNATIONAL—See McDermott International, Inc.; *U.S. Public*, pg. 1068
BABCOCK & WILCOX ST COMPANY—See McDermott International, Inc.; *U.S. Public*, pg. 1068
BABCOCK ARGENTINA S.A.—See FKI Plc; *Int'l*, pg. 473
BABCOCK AUSTRALIA HOLDINGS LTD.—See FKI Plc; *Int'l*, pg. 474
BABCOCK BLK GIESSEREI GMBH—See Deutsche Babcock AG; *Int'l*, pg. 398
BABCOCK-BRISTOL AB—See FKI Plc; *Int'l*, pg. 473
BABCOCK BRISTOL AFRICA DIV.—See FKI Plc; *Int'l*, pg. 474
BABCOCK-BSH AG—See Deutsche Babcock AG; *Int'l*, pg. 399
BABCOCK-BSH INC.—See Deutsche Babcock AG; *Int'l*, pg. 399
BABCOCK CALORIZING LTD.—See Babcock International Group PLC; *Int'l*, pg. 130
BABCOCK CLAUDIUS PETERS DIV.—See FKI Plc; *Int'l*, pg. 474
BABCOCK CONSTRUCTION CONTRACTORS—See Babcock International Group PLC; *Int'l*, pg. 131
BABCOCK CONSTRUCTION LIMITED—See Babcock International Group PLC; *Int'l*, pg. 130
BABCOCK DIENSTLEISTUNGS-GMBH—See Deutsche Babcock AG; *Int'l*, pg. 398
BABCOCK DUIKER B.V.—See FKI Plc; *Int'l*, pg. 472
BABCOCK ELECTRICAL PROJECTS LTD—See FKI Plc; *Int'l*, pg. 471
BABCOCK ENERGY LIMITED—See Babcock International Group PLC; *Int'l*, pg. 130
BABCOCK ENGINEERING CONTRACTORS (PTY) LTD—See Babcock International Group PLC; *Int'l*, pg. 131
BABCOCK ENGINEERING CONTRACTORS (PTY) LTD.—See FKI Plc; *Int'l*, pg. 474
BABCOCK ENGINEERING LTD.—See FKI Plc; *Int'l*, pg. 474
BABCOCK FATA LTD.—See FKI Plc; *Int'l*, pg. 472
BABCOCK FEUERUNGSSYSTEME GMBH—See Deutsche Babcock AG; *Int'l*, pg. 398
BABCOCK-HITACHI K.K.—See Hitachi, Ltd.; *Int'l*, pg. 621
BABCOCK HOLDING (DEUTSCHLAND) GMBH—See Babcock International Group PLC; *Int'l*, pg. 131
BABCOCK HYDRO-PNEUMATICS LTD.—See FKI Plc; *Int'l*, pg. 471
BABCOCK INDUSTRIAL & ELECTRICAL PRODUCTS LTD.—See FKI Plc; *Int'l*, pg. 472
BABCOCK INDUSTRIAL CONTRACTORS (PTY) LTD.—See FKI Plc; *Int'l*, pg. 474
BABCOCK INDUSTRIEROHRLEITUNGSBAU GMBH—See Deutsche Babcock AG; *Int'l*, pg. 399
BABCOCK INTERNATIONAL GROUP PLC; *Int'l*, pg. 130
BABCOCK INTL. INC.—See Babcock International Group PLC; *Int'l*, pg. 131
BABCOCK INTERNATIONAL INVESTMENTS LTD.—See FKI Plc; *Int'l*, pg. 472
BABCOCK INTERNATIONAL (NZ) LTD.—See FKI Plc; *Int'l*, pg. 474
BABCOCK JENKINS LTD.—See FKI Plc; *Int'l*, pg. 472
BABCOCK KING - WILKINSON LIMITED—See Babcock International Group PLC; *Int'l*, pg. 131
BABCOCK LENTJES KRAFTWERKSTECHNIK—See Deutsche Babcock AG; *Int'l*, pg. 398
BABCOCK LUMBER COMPANY; *U.S. Private*, pg. 108
BABCOCK MATERIALS HANDLING LTD.—See Babcock International Group PLC; *Int'l*, pg. 131
BABCOCK METSTEP DIV.—See FKI Plc; *Int'l*, pg. 474
BABCOCK MEXICO SA DE CV—See FKI Plc; *Int'l*, pg. 474
BABCOCK MINERALS ENGINEERING LTD.—See FKI Plc; *Int'l*, pg. 472
BABCOCK MOXEY DIV.—See FKI Plc; *Int'l*, pg. 474
BABCOCK-MOXEY LTD.—See FKI Plc; *Int'l*, pg. 472
BABCOCK PLANT LEASING LTD.—See FKI Plc; *Int'l*, pg. 472
BABCOCK POWER LIMITED-RESEARCH DIV.—See FKI Plc; *Int'l*, pg. 472
BABCOCK POWER-PRODUCTION DIV.—See FKI Plc; *Int'l*, pg. 472
BABCOCK PROZESSAUTOMATION GMBH—See Deutsche Babcock AG; *Int'l*, pg. 398
BABCOCK ROBEY LIMITED—See FKI Plc; *Int'l*, pg. 472
BABCOCK ROHRLEITUNGSBAU GMBH—See Deutsche Babcock AG; *Int'l*, pg. 399
BABCOCK SEMPELL AG—See Deutsche Babcock AG; *Int'l*, pg. 399
BABCOCK SEMPELL ARMATUREN-SERVICE GMBH—See Deutsche Babcock AG; *Int'l*, pg. 400
BABCOCK SERVICES (BELGIUM)—See FKI Plc; *Int'l*, pg. 474
BABCOCK SPRAYMIXER LTD—See FKI Plc; *Int'l*, pg. 472
BABCOCK TEXTILMASCHINEN GMBH—See Deutsche Babcock AG; *Int'l*, pg. 399
BABCOCK TRANSFORMERS LTD.—See FKI Plc; *Int'l*, pg. 472
BABCOCK TRIPPLEJAY—See Babcock International Group PLC; *Int'l*, pg. 131
BABCOCK TURNKEY OPERATIONS LTD.—See FKI Plc; *Int'l*, pg. 472
BABCOCK TVW DIV.—See FKI Plc; *Int'l*, pg. 474
BABCOCK WELDING PRODUCTS LIMITED—See FKI Plc; *Int'l*, pg. 472
BABCOCK WOODALL-DUCKHAM LTD—See FKI Plc; *Int'l*, pg. 472
BABCOCK WORSLEY LIMITED—See FKI Plc; *Int'l*, pg. 472

BABCOCK-OMNICAL-INDUSTRIEKESSEL GMBH—See Deutsche Babcock AG; *Int'l*, pg. 398
BABCOK & WILCOX FUEL CO. (B & WF CO)—See COGEMA - Compagnie Generale des Matieres Nucleaires; *Int'l*, pg. 305
BABIES "R" US—See Toys "R" Us, Inc.; *U.S. Public*, pg. 1626
BABY TOGS, INC.; *U.S. Private*, pg. 108
BABYHALLEN B.V.—See N.V. Koninklijke Bijenkorf Beheer KBB; *Int'l*, pg. 750
BABYLISS. SA—See Conair Corporation; *U.S. Private*, pg. 261
BAC COLOR FRANSEWEG; *Int'l*, pg. 131
BACARDI CORPORATION—See Bacardi Limited; *Int'l*, pg. 131
BACARDI LIMITED; *Int'l*, pg. 131
BACARDI-MARTINI CARIBBEAN CORPORATION—See Bacardi Limited; *Int'l*, pg. 132
BACARDI-MARTINI PRODUCT DEVELOPMENT INC.—See Bacardi Limited; *Int'l*, pg. 131
BACARDI-MARTINI PRODUCT QUALITY AMERICAS INC.—See Bacardi Limited; *Int'l*, pg. 131
BACARDI-MARTINI PROMOTIONS—See Bacardi Limited; *Int'l*, pg. 131
BACARDI-MARTINI, USA, INC.; *U.S. Private*, pg. 109
BACARDI-MARTINI U.S.A., INC.—See Bacardi Limited; *Int'l*, pg. 131
BACARDI SERVICE CORP., (NORTH AMERICA)—See Bacardi Limited; *Int'l*, pg. 131
BACARDI SERVICES (NORTH AMERICA) CORP.—See Bacardi Limited; *Int'l*, pg. 131
BACCARAT (CIE DES CRISTALLERIES); *Int'l*, pg. 132
BACCARAT, INC.—See Baccarat (Cie des Cristalleries); *Int'l*, pg. 132
BACCO CONSTRUCTION CO.; *U.S. Private*, pg. 109
BACH-SIMPSON LTD.—See Katy Industries, Inc.; *U.S. Public*, pg. 944
BACH-SIMPSON (UK) LTD.—See Katy Industries, Inc.; *U.S. Public*, pg. 944
VINCENT BACH CO.—See Steinway Musical Instruments, Inc.; *U.S. Public*, pg. 1514
BACHARACH INC.; *U.S. Private*, pg. 109
BACHMAN COMPANY; *U.S. Private*, pg. 109
BACHMANN GMBH—See Fried. Krupp AG; *Int'l*, pg. 514
BACHMANN INDUSTRIES, INC.; *U.S. Private*, pg. 109
BACHMAN'S, INC.; *U.S. Private*, pg. 109
BACK BAY ADVISORS, INC.—See Metropolitan Life Insurance Co.; *U.S. Private*, pg. 737
BACK STAGE/SHOOT—See VNU Verenigde Nederlandse Uitgeversbedrijven B.V.; *Int'l*, pg. 1446
ERNST BACKHAUS & CO. GMBH—See Schuttersveld Holding N.V.; *Int'l*, pg. 1210
BACKSTAGE—See VNU Verenigde Nederlandse Uitgeversbedrijven B.V.; *Int'l*, pg. 1446
BACO LEISURE PRODUCTS—See Alcan Aluminium Limited; *Int'l*, pg. 51
BACON GROCERY CO., INC.—See Jones Company, Inc.; *U.S. Private*, pg. 596
J. BACON & SONS—See Mercantile Stores Company, Inc.; *U.S. Public*, pg. 1090
BACON'S INFORMATION, INC.—See Primedia Inc.; *U.S. Public*, pg. 1327
BACOT-ALLAIN S.A.—See Swiss Bank Corporation; *Int'l*, pg. 1331
BACOU S.A.; *Int'l*, pg. 132
BACOU U.S.A., INC.—See Bacou S.A.; *Int'l*, pg. 132
BAD DUBEN PROFILWALZMASCHINEN GMBH—See Rothenberger Group GmbH; *Int'l*, pg. 1128
W.S. BADCOCK CORPORATION; *U.S. Private*, pg. 109
BADEN-WURTTEMBERG BRANCH—See IKB Deutsche Industriebank AG; *Int'l*, pg. 645
BADENIA BAUSPARKASSE AG—See AMB Aachener und Muenchener Beteiligungs-AG; *Int'l*, pg. 15
BADER & CO.; *U.S. Private*, pg. 110
BADER RUTTER & ASSOC. INC.—See Bader Rutter & Assoc., Inc.; *U.S. Private*, pg. 110
BADER RUTTER & ASSOC., INC.; *U.S. Private*, pg. 110
BADGER AIR BRUSH COMPANY; *U.S. Private*, pg. 110
BADGER CRANE CO.—See Avis Industrial Corporation; *U.S. Private*, pg. 102
BADGER EQUIPMENT CO.—See Avis Industrial Corporation; *U.S. Private*, pg. 102
BADGER FARM SYSTEMS, INC.—See Miller-St. Nazianz, Inc.; *U.S. Private*, pg. 748
BADGER FIRE PROTECTION INC.—See Williams Holdings Plc; *Int'l*, pg. 1500
BADGER METER DE MEXICO, S.A. DE C.V.—See Badger Meter, Inc.; *U.S. Public*, pg. 165
BADGER METER EUROPE GMBH—See Badger Meter, Inc.; *U.S. Public*, pg. 165
BADGER METER, INC.; *U.S. Public*, pg. 164
BADGER METER INDUSTRIAL DIV.—See Badger Meter, Inc.; *U.S. Public*, pg. 165
BADGER METER, PMI—See Badger Meter, Inc.; *U.S. Public*, pg. 165
BADGER METER UTILITY DIV.—See Badger Meter, Inc.; *U.S. Public*, pg. 165
BADGER PAPER MILLS, INC.; *U.S. Public*, pg. 165
BADGER PIPE LINE CO.—See Texaco Inc.; *U.S. Public*, pg. 1584
BADGER SERVICE CO.—See Wisconsin Energy Corporation; *U.S. Public*, pg. 1773
BADGER TELECAM, INC.—See Telephone and Data Systems, Inc.; *U.S. Public*, pg. 1571
BADGER TRUCK CENTER, INC.; *U.S. Private*, pg. 110
BADISCHE TABAKMANUFAKTUR ROTH-HANDLE GMBH—See Reemtsma Cigarettenfabriken GmbH, Hamburg; *Int'l*, pg. 1101
BADIX SYSTEMS INC.—See Sulcus Computer Corp.; *U.S. Public*, pg. 1527
BAGCRAFT CORPORATION OF AMERICA—See Artra Group Incorporated; *U.S. Public*, pg. 136

BAGCRAFT CORPORATION OF AMERICA, EASTERN DIV.—See Artra Group Incorporated; *U.S. Public*, pg. 136
BAGCRAFT CORPORATION OF AMERICA, GEORGIA DIV.—See Artra Group Incorporated; *U.S. Public*, pg. 136
BAGCRAFT CORPORATION OF AMERICA, MIDWEST DIV.—See Artra Group Incorporated; *U.S. Public*, pg. 136
BAGHEERA & HAGLOFS AB—See Axel Johnson AB; *Int'l*, pg. 708
BAGLEY S.A.—See Danone Group; *Int'l*, pg. 379
BAGNASCO S.R.L.—See Hollingsworth & Vose Co.; *U.S. Private*, pg. 535
BAGPAK DIV.—See International Paper Company; *U.S. Public*, pg. 901
BAHAMA BREEZE—See Darden Restaurants, Inc.; *U.S. Public*, pg. 484
BAHAMAS OIL REFINING CO. (BORCO)—See Petroleos de Venezuela S.A.; *Int'l*, pg. 1046
I. BAHCALL STEEL & PIPE INC.—See Russel Metals Inc.; *Int'l*, pg. 1150
AB BAHCO VENTILATION—See ABB Asea Brown Boveri (Holding) Ltd.; *Int'l*, pg. 7
BAHNTRANS GMBH—See Thyssen AG; *Int'l*, pg. 1388
BAIGENT FOREST INDUSTRIES LIMITED—See International Paper Company; *U.S. Public*, pg. 905
BAIL EQUIPEMENT—See Groupe GAN; *Int'l*, pg. 563
BAILEY AUTOMATISATZIJA—See ELSAG Bailey Process Automation N.V.; *Int'l*, pg. 449
BAILEY BEIJING CONTROLS COMPANY LTD.—See ELSAG Bailey Process Automation N.V.; *Int'l*, pg. 449
BAILEY CONTROLS COMPANY—See ELSAG Bailey Process Automation N.V.; *Int'l*, pg. 449
BAILEY CONTROLS COMPANY—See IRI Istituto Ricostruzione Industriale; *Int'l*, pg. 654
BAILEY CONTROLS JORDAN FOR PROCESS CONTROLS SERVICES, LTD.—See ELSAG Bailey Process Automation N.V.; *Int'l*, pg. 449
C.R. BAILEY (BELFAST) LTD—See Royal Packaging Industries Van Leer B.V.; *Int'l*, pg. 1146
BAILEY DE VENEZUELA S.A.—See ELSAG Bailey Process Automation N.V.; *Int'l*, pg. 449
BAILEY DO BRASIL INSTRUMENTOS INDUSTRIAIS LTDA.—See ELSAG Bailey Process Automation N.V.; *Int'l*, pg. 449
BAILEY FIRE PROTECTION—See N.G. Bailey & Co. Ltd.; *Int'l*, pg. 133
BAILEY-FISCHER & PORTER B.V.—See ELSAG Bailey Process Automation N.V.; *Int'l*, pg. 449
BAILEY, FISCHER & PORTER COMPANY—See ELSAG Bailey Process Automation N.V.; *Int'l*, pg. 449
BAILEY-FISCHER & PORTER ESPANA S.A.—See ELSAG Bailey Process Automation N.V.; *Int'l*, pg. 449
BAILEY FISCHER & PORTER GMBH—See ELSAG Bailey Process Automation N.V.; *Int'l*, pg. 449
BAILEY-FISCHER & PORTER N.V.—See ELSAG Bailey Process Automation N.V.; *Int'l*, pg. 449
BAILEY-FISCHER & PORTER OY—See ELSAG Bailey Process Automation N.V.; *Int'l*, pg. 449
BAILEY GERMANY—See ELSAG Bailey Process Automation N.V.; *Int'l*, pg. 449
BAILEY HATS—See Bollman Hat Co.; *U.S. Private*, pg. 155
BAILEY ICS PLC—See ELSAG Bailey Process Automation N.V.; *Int'l*, pg. 449
BAILEY JAPAN COMPANY LTD.—See ELSAG Bailey Process Automation N.V.; *Int'l*, pg. 449
BAILEY MAINTENANCE SERVICES—See N.G. Bailey & Co. Ltd.; *Int'l*, pg. 133
BAILEY MEXICO S.A. DE C.V.—See ELSAG Bailey Process Automation N.V.; *Int'l*, pg. 449
N.G. BAILEY & CO. LTD.-DUNDEE BRANCH—See N.G. Bailey & Co. Ltd.; *Int'l*, pg. 132
N.G. BAILEY & CO. LTD.-NEWCASTLE BRANCH—See N.G. Bailey & Co. Ltd.; *Int'l*, pg. 132
BAILEY NETWORK MANAGEMENT—See ELSAG Bailey Process Automation N.V.; *Int'l*, pg. 449
N.G. BAILEY & CO. LTD.; *Int'l*, pg. 132
N.G. BAILEY & CO. LTD.-MIDDLESBROUGH—See N.G. Bailey & Co. Ltd.; *Int'l*, pg. 132
BAILEY NORGE AS—See ELSAG Bailey Process Automation N.V.; *Int'l*, pg. 449
R & A BAILEY & CO.—See Diageo Plc; *Int'l*, pg. 409
BAILEY TELECOM LTD—See N.G. Bailey & Co. Ltd.; *Int'l*, pg. 133
JOSHUA L. BAILY CO., INC.; *U.S. Private*, pg. 110
BAIN & COMPANY LIMITED—See Deutsche Bank AG; *Int'l*, pg. 406
BAIN & COMPANY INC. (TOKYO)—See Deutsche Bank AG; *Int'l*, pg. 406
BAIN & COMPANY NEW ZEALAND LTD.—See Deutsche Bank AG; *Int'l*, pg. 406
BAIN & COMPANY PTE. LTD. (SINGAPORE)—See Deutsche Bank AG; *Int'l*, pg. 406
BAIN & COMPANY (SECURITIES) LTD.—See Deutsche Bank AG; *Int'l*, pg. 406
BAIN CAPITAL; *U.S. Private*, pg. 110
BAIN HOGG GROUP PLC—See Inchcape PLC; *Int'l*, pg. 671
BAIN HOGG INSURANCE BROKERS—See Inchcape PLC; *Int'l*, pg. 671
BAIN HOGG INSURANCE MANAGEMENT GUERNSEY LTD.—See Inchcape PLC; *Int'l*, pg. 671
BAIN SECURITIES, INC.—See Deutsche Bank AG; *Int'l*, pg. 406
BAINES MANAGEMENT CO.; *U.S. Private*, pg. 111
BAIRD & WARNER; *U.S. Private*, pg. 111
HUGH BAIRD & SONS LIMITED—See ConAgra, Inc.; *U.S. Public*, pg. 428
BAIRD, PATRICK & CO., INC.; *U.S. Private*, pg. 111
BAIRNCO CORPORATION; *U.S. Public*, pg. 165
BAJAJ TEMPO LTD.—See Daimler-Benz Aktiengesellschaft; *Int'l*, pg. 368

BAKE-LINE PRODUCTS, INC.—See Flowers Industries, Inc.; *U.S. Public*, pg. 657
BAKELITE AG—See Ruetgers A.G.; *Int'l*, pg. 1148
BAKER / ALTECH—See Justiss Oil Co., Inc.; *U.S. Private*, pg. 602
BAKER & MCKENZIE, ATTORNEYS AT LAW; *U.S. Private*, pg. 111
BAKER & TAYLOR, INC.; *U.S. Private*, pg. 111
BAKER CAC—See Thermo Electron Corporation; *U.S. Public*, pg. 1593
BAKER-CAC, INC.—See Baker Hughes Incorporated; *U.S. Public*, pg. 166
BAKER COMMODITIES, INC.; *U.S. Private*, pg. 111
BAKER CONCRETE CONSTRUCTION, INC.; *U.S. Private*, pg. 111
BAKER CUMMINS, INC.—See IVAX Corporation; *U.S. Public*, pg. 915
BAKER DISTRIBUTING COMPANY—See Watsco, Inc.; *U.S. Public*, pg. 1746
EDWARD BAKER LIMITED—See Harrisons & Crosfield plc; *Int'l*, pg. 598
BAKER ENGINEERING, INC.—See Michael Baker Corporation; *U.S. Public*, pg. 168
BAKER ENGINEERING, NY, INC.—See Michael Baker Corporation; *U.S. Public*, pg. 168
BAKER ENVIRONMENTAL, INC.—See Michael Baker Corporation; *U.S. Public*, pg. 168
H.J. BAKER & BRO., INC.; *U.S. Private*, pg. 112
BAKER HUGHES DRILLING TECHNOLOGIES—See Baker Hughes Incorporated; *U.S. Public*, pg. 166
BAKER HUGHES INCORPORATED; *U.S. Public*, pg. 165
BAKER HUGHES INTEQ—See Baker Hughes Incorporated; *U.S. Public*, pg. 166
BAKER HUGHES MINING TOOLS, INC.—See Baker Hughes Incorporated; *U.S. Public*, pg. 166
BAKER HUGHES PROCESS SYSTEMS COMPANY—See Baker Hughes Incorporated; *U.S. Public*, pg. 166
BAKER HUGHES PRODUCTION TOOLS, INC.—See Baker Hughes Incorporated; *U.S. Public*, pg. 166
J. BAKER, INC.; *U.S. Public*, pg. 167
J.E. BAKER CO.; *U.S. Private*, pg. 112
BAKER MATERIAL HANDLING CORP.—See Linde AG; *Int'l*, pg. 810
BAKER MELLON STUART CONSTRUCTION, INC.—See Michael Baker Corporation; *U.S. Public*, pg. 168
MICHAEL BAKER CORPORATION; *U.S. Public*, pg. 168
MICHAEL BAKER, JR., INC.—See Michael Baker Corporation; *U.S. Public*, pg. 168
BAKER/MO SERVICES, INC.—See Michael Baker Corporation; *U.S. Public*, pg. 168
BAKER NORTON PHARMACEUTICALS, INC.—See IVAX Corporation; *U.S. Public*, pg. 914
BAKER OIL TOOLS—See Baker Hughes Incorporated; *U.S. Public*, pg. 167
BAKER OIL TOOLS FAR EAST (PTY) LTD.—See Baker Hughes Incorporated; *U.S. Public*, pg. 167
BAKER OIL TOOLS GMBH—See Baker Hughes Incorporated; *U.S. Public*, pg. 167
BAKER OIL TOOLS OF CANADA, LTD.—See Baker Hughes Incorporated; *U.S. Public*, pg. 167
BAKER/OTS INTERNATIONAL LTD.—See Michael Baker Corporation; *U.S. Public*, pg. 168
BAKER PERKINS (NZ) LIMITED—See Siebe plc; *Int'l*, pg. 1240
BAKER PERKINS PROPRIETARY LIMITED—See Siebe plc; *Int'l*, pg. 1240
BAKER PETROLITE CORPORATION—See Baker Hughes Incorporated; *U.S. Public*, pg. 166
BAKER SUPPORT SERVICES, INC.—See Michael Baker Corporation; *U.S. Public*, pg. 168
BAKER TRADING CO.—See ABB Asea Brown Boveri (Holding) Ltd.; *Int'l*, pg. 5
BAKERMET INC.—See The Ivaco Group; *Int'l*, pg. 695
BAKERS AS—See Orkla A.S.A.; *Int'l*, pg. 1010
BAKERS CHOICE PRODUCTS, INC.—See Reynolds Metals Company; *U.S. Public*, pg. 1386
BAKERS/LEEDS SHOE STORES—See Edison Brothers Stores, Inc.; *U.S. Public*, pg. 563
BAKERS PRIDE OVEN COMPANY—See A.P. Wyott; *U.S. Private*, pg. 1193
BAKERS SQUARE RESTAURANTS—See Vicorp Restaurants, Inc.; *U.S. Public*, pg. 1719
BAKER'S SUPERMARKETS, INC.—See Fleming Companies, Inc.; *U.S. Public*, pg. 652
THE BAKERSFIELD CALIFORNIAN; *U.S. Private*, pg. 112
BAKERY & CONFECTIONARY DIVISION—See Campbell Soup Company; *U.S. Public*, pg. 299
BAKERY INGREDIENTS DIVISION—See Royal Gist-Brocades N.V.; *Int'l*, pg. 1142
BAKKEN RESEARCH CENTER B.V.—See Medtronic, Inc.; *U.S. Public*, pg. 1083
BAKKER CONTINENTAL—See Vendex International N.V.; *Int'l*, pg. 1463
BALACKE-DURR LTD.—See Deutsche Babcock AG; *Int'l*, pg. 400
BALACKE-DURR SIO AG—See Deutsche Babcock AG; *Int'l*, pg. 400
BALAIR/CTA LTD.—See The Swissair Group; *Int'l*, pg. 1333
BALANCE ENGINEERING CORP.—See Illinois Tool Works Inc.; *U.S. Public*, pg. 865
BALANCED FOODS, INC.—See Koninklijke BolsWessanen nv; *Int'l*, pg. 752
BALCKE-DURR KUHLTURMBAU LEIPZIG GMBH—See Deutsche Babcock AG; *Int'l*, pg. 400
BALCO, INC.—See Energy Systems Industries, Inc.; *U.S. Private*, pg. 376
BALCO, INC.—See Snap-On Tools Corporation; *U.S. Public*, pg. 1480
THE BALCOR COMPANY—See American Express Company; *U.S. Public*, pg. 74
BALCRANK PRODUCTS—See The General Chemical Group, Inc.; *U.S. Public*, pg. 707

Company Index

BALCRON OIL DIVISION—See Equitable Resources, Inc.; *U.S. Public*, pg. 589
BALDERSON INC.—See Caterpillar Inc.; *U.S. Public*, pg. 315
BALDI, BLOOM & WHELAN ADVERTISING; *U.S. Private*, pg. 112
BALDINI & CASTOLDI S.R.L.—See Arnoldo Mondadori Editore S.p.A.; *Int'l*, pg. 888
BALDOR ELECTRIC COMPANY; *U.S. Public*, pg. 168
BALDOR ELECTRIC COMPANY—See Baldor Electric Company; *U.S. Public*, pg. 169
BALDT, INC.; *U.S. Private*, pg. 112
BALDWIN & LYONS, INC.; *U.S. Public*, pg. 169
BALDWIN ASIA PACIFIC LTD.—See Baldwin Technology Company, Inc.; *U.S. Public*, pg. 170
BALDWIN DAMPENING SYSTEMS—See Baldwin Technology Company, Inc.; *U.S. Public*, pg. 170
BALDWIN EUROPE CONSOLIDATED, INC.—See Baldwin Technology Company, Inc.; *U.S. Public*, pg. 170
BALDWIN FILTERS—See CLARCOR, Inc.; *U.S. Public*, pg. 381
BALDWIN FRANCE SARL—See Baldwin Technology Company, Inc.; *U.S. Public*, pg. 170
BALDWIN-GRAFOTEC GMBH—See Baldwin Technology Company, Inc.; *U.S. Public*, pg. 170
BALDWIN GRAPHIC EQUIPMENT BV—See Baldwin Technology Company, Inc.; *U.S. Public*, pg. 170
BALDWIN GRAPHIC EQUIPMENT PTY.—See Baldwin Technology Company, Inc.; *U.S. Public*, pg. 170
BALDWIN HARDWARE CORPORATION—See Masco Corporation; *U.S. Public*, pg. 1053
BALDWIN HARDWARE SERVICE CORPORATION—See Masco Corporation; *U.S. Public*, pg. 1053
BALDWIN INLINE FINISHING—See Baldwin Technology Company, Inc.; *U.S. Public*, pg. 170
BALDWIN INTERNATIONAL, INC.—See Russel Metals Inc.; *Int'l*, pg. 1150
BALDWIN JAPAN LTD.—See Baldwin Technology Company, Inc.; *U.S. Public*, pg. 170
BALDWIN PIANO & ORGAN COMPANY; *U.S. Public*, pg. 169
BALDWIN PRINTING CONTROL EQUIPMENT (BEIJING) COMPANY, LTD.—See Baldwin Technology Company, Inc.; *U.S. Public*, pg. 170
BALDWIN PRINTING CONTROLS LTD.—See Baldwin Technology Company, Inc.; *U.S. Public*, pg. 170
BALDWIN STEEL COMPANY—See Duferco Steel Inc.; *U.S. Private*, pg. 345
BALDWIN STEEL COMPANY—See Deutsche Babcock AG; *Int'l*, pg. 401
BALDWIN STOBB SAN BERNARDINO—See Baldwin Technology Company, Inc.; *U.S. Public*, pg. 170
BALDWIN TECHNOLOGY COMPANY, INC.; *U.S. Public*, pg. 169
BALDWIN (UK) LTD.—See Baldwin Technology Company, Inc.; *U.S. Public*, pg. 170
BALDWIN WEB CONTROLS—See Baldwin Technology Company, Inc.; *U.S. Public*, pg. 170
BALDWINS STEEL (PTY) LIMITED—See Dorbyl Limited; *Int'l*, pg. 416
BALE OF KENTUCKY, INC.; *U.S. Private*, pg. 112
BALFOUR BEATTY LIMITED—See BICC plc; *Int'l*, pg. 120
BALFOUR GUTHRIE FOREST PRODUCTS INC.—See Canfor Corporation; *Int'l*, pg. 260
L.G. BALFOUR CO., INC.—See Commemorative Brands, Inc.; *U.S. Private*, pg. 258
BALFOUR TIMBER LTD.—See Canfor Corporation; *Int'l*, pg. 260
BALFOUR, WILLIAMSON & CO. LTD.—See Lonrho plc; *Int'l*, pg. 817
BALI COMPANY—See Sara Lee Corporation; *U.S. Public*, pg. 1433
BALKAMP, INC.—See Genuine Parts Company; *U.S. Public*, pg. 732
BALL AEROSPACE & TECHNOLOGIES CORP.—See Ball Corporation; *U.S. Public*, pg. 171
BALL AEROSPACE SYSTEMS DIVISION—See Ball Corporation; *U.S. Public*, pg. 171
BALL CORPORATION; *U.S. Public*, pg. 170
BALL FLORAPLANT—See Ball Horticultural Company; *U.S. Private*, pg. 112
BALL HORTICULTURAL COMPANY; *U.S. Private*, pg. 112
BALL METAL BEVERAGE CONTAINER CORP.—See Ball Corporation; *U.S. Public*, pg. 171
BALL METAL FOOD CONTAINER CORP.—See Ball Corporation; *U.S. Public*, pg. 171
BALL PACKAGING HOLDINGS CORP.—See Ball Corporation; *U.S. Public*, pg. 171
BALL PACKAGING PRODUCTS CANADA INC.—See Ball Corporation; *U.S. Public*, pg. 171
BALL PRODUCTS, INC.—See The Oilgear Company; *U.S. Public*, pg. 1215
BALL PUBLISHING—See W. Atlee Burpee Co.; *U.S. Private*, pg. 188
BALL SCREWS & ACTUATORS CO., INC.—See Danaher Corporation; *U.S. Public*, pg. 482
BALL SEED CO.—See Ball Horticultural Company; *U.S. Private*, pg. 112
BALL SUPERIOR LTD.—See Ball Horticultural Company; *U.S. Private*, pg. 112
BALL SYSTEMS ENGINEERING OPERATIONS—See Ball Corporation; *U.S. Public*, pg. 171
BALL TELECOMMUNICATION PRODUCTS DIVISION—See Ball Corporation; *U.S. Public*, pg. 171
BALLANTINE BOOKS—See Advance Publications Inc.; *U.S. Private*, pg. 21
THE BALLANTYNE CASHMERE COMPANY LTD—See Dawson International PLC; *Int'l*, pg. 385
BALLANTYNE CASHMERE USA LTD.—See Dawson International PLC; *Int'l*, pg. 386
BALLANTYNE OF OMAHA, INC.—See ARC International Corporation; *Int'l*, pg. 17
BALLARD MEDICAL PRODUCTS; *U.S. Public*, pg. 171

P.T. BALLAST INDONESIA CONSTRUCTION—See Ballast Nedam NV; *Int'l*, pg. 134
BALLAST NEDAM & INDUSTRIE & TOELEVERING B.V.—See Ballast Nedam NV; *Int'l*, pg. 133
BALLAST NEDAM ARUBA N.V.—See Ballast Nedam NV; *Int'l*, pg. 134
BALLAST NEDAM BAU- UND BAGGER GMBH.—See Ballast Nedam NV; *Int'l*, pg. 134
BALLAST NEDAM BETON EN WATERBOUW B.V.—See Ballast Nedam NV; *Int'l*, pg. 133
BALLAST NEDAM BOUWMATERIEEL B.V.—See Ballast Nedam NV; *Int'l*, pg. 133
BALLAST NEDAM CONSTRUCTION INC.—See Ballast Nedam NV; *Int'l*, pg. 134
BALLAST NEDAM DREDGING—See Ballast Nedam NV; *Int'l*, pg. 133
BALLAST NEDAM ENGINEERING B.V.—See Ballast Nedam NV; *Int'l*, pg. 133
BALLAST NEDAM EQUIPMENT SERVICES B.V.—See Ballast Nedam NV; *Int'l*, pg. 133
BALLAST NEDAM EQUIPMENT SERVICES PTE. LTD.—See Ballast Nedam NV; *Int'l*, pg. 134
BALLAST NEDAM FAR EAST PTE. LTD.—See Ballast Nedam NV; *Int'l*, pg. 134
BALLAST NEDAM FUNDERINGSTECHNIEKEN B.V.—See Ballast Nedam NV; *Int'l*, pg. 133
BALLAST NEDAM GROEP N.V.—See Ballast Nedam NV; *Int'l*, pg. 134
BALLAST NEDAM GROEP N.V. (MALAYSIA) SDN. BHD.—See Ballast Nedam NV; *Int'l*, pg. 134
BALLAST NEDAM GROND EN WEGEN B.V.—See Ballast Nedam NV; *Int'l*, pg. 133
BALLAST NEDAM GROND EN WEGEN PROJECTEN B.V.—See Ballast Nedam NV; *Int'l*, pg. 133
BALLAST NEDAM GROND EN WEGEN SPECIALITEITEN B.V.—See Ballast Nedam NV; *Int'l*, pg. 133
BALLAST NEDAM GRONDSTOFFEN B.V.—See Ballast Nedam NV; *Int'l*, pg. 133
BALLAST NEDAM IGB B.V.—See Ballast Nedam NV; *Int'l*, pg. 133
BALLAST NEDAM INDUSTRIEBOUW B.V.—See Ballast Nedam NV; *Int'l*, pg. 133
BALLAST NEDAM INTERNATIONAL B.V.—See Ballast Nedam NV; *Int'l*, pg. 133
BALLAST NEDAM INTERNATIONAL B.V.-PHILIPPINE BRANCH—See Ballast Nedam NV; *Int'l*, pg. 134
BALLAST NEDAM INTERNATIONAL (MALAYSIA) SDN. BHD.—See Ballast Nedam NV; *Int'l*, pg. 134
BALLAST NEDAM MILIEUTECHNIEK B.V.—See Ballast Nedam NV; *Int'l*, pg. 134
BALLAST NEDAM NV; *Int'l*, pg. 133
BALLAST NEDAM PETROL STATIONS—See Ballast Nedam NV; *Int'l*, pg. 133
BALLAST NEDAM PROJECTONTWIKKELING B.V.—See Ballast Nedam NV; *Int'l*, pg. 134
BALLAST NEDAM SERVICES B.V.—See Ballast Nedam NV; *Int'l*, pg. 134
BALLAST NEDAM SURINAME N.V.—See Ballast Nedam NV; *Int'l*, pg. 134
BALLAST NEDAM TELECOM INFRASTRUCTURES—See Ballast Nedam NV; *Int'l*, pg. 134
BALLAST NEDAM WONINGBOUW B.V.—See Ballast Nedam NV; *Int'l*, pg. 134
BALLAST NEDAN CANADA LTD.—See Ballast Nedam NV; *Int'l*, pg. 134
BALLAST NORD AB—See NCC AB; *Int'l*, pg. 899
BALLAST OST AB—See NCC AB; *Int'l*, pg. 899
BALLAST PHOENIX LTD.—See Ballast Nedam NV; *Int'l*, pg. 133
BALLAST STOCKHOLM AB—See NCC AB; *Int'l*, pg. 899
BALLAST SYD AB—See NCC AB; *Int'l*, pg. 899
BALLAST VAST AB—See NCC AB; *Int'l*, pg. 899
BALLAST WILTSHIER PLC—See Ballast Nedam NV; *Int'l*, pg. 134
BALLAST WILTSHIER PLC - NORTH EAST REGION—See Ballast Nedam NV; *Int'l*, pg. 135
BALLAST WILTSHIER PLC - NORTH WEST REGION—See Ballast Nedam NV; *Int'l*, pg. 135
BALLAST WILTSHIER PLC - SCOTLAND—See Ballast Nedam NV; *Int'l*, pg. 135
BALLAST WILTSHIER PLC - SOUTH EAST REGION—See Ballast Nedam NV; *Int'l*, pg. 135
BALLAST WILTSHIER PLC - SOUTH WEST REGION—See Ballast Nedam NV; *Int'l*, pg. 135
BALLAST WILTSHIER PLC - AIRPORT SERVICES DIV.—See Ballast Nedam NV; *Int'l*, pg. 135
BALLATORE CHAMPAGNE CELLARS—See E. & J. Gallo Winery; *U.S. Private*, pg. 438
BALLIEVEY LTD.—See Lamont Holdings Plc; *Int'l*, pg. 797
BALLINGER PUBLISHING CO.—See The News Corporation Limited; *Int'l*, pg. 927
BALLINGER SCHALTTECHNIK G.M.B.H.—See Raytheon Company; *U.S. Public*, pg. 1366
BALLINGSLOVS AB—See Electrolux, AB; *Int'l*, pg. 438
BALLOGRAF BIC AB—See Societe BIC S.A.; *Int'l*, pg. 1273
OY BALLOGRAF BIC AB—See Societe BIC S.A.; *Int'l*, pg. 1273
B.A. BALLOU & CO. INC.; *U.S. Private*, pg. 112
BALLSTON DEVELOPMENT CORPORATION—See Forest City Enterprises, Inc.; *U.S. Public*, pg. 668
BALLY AUSTRALIA PTY. LTD.—See Oerlikon-Buhrle Holding AG; *Int'l*, pg. 997
BALLY-BIVER S.A.R.L.—See Oerlikon-Buhrle Holding AG; *Int'l*, pg. 997
BALLY DEUTSCHLAND GMBH—See Oerlikon-Buhrle Holding AG; *Int'l*, pg. 997
BALLY GAMING INC.—See Alliance Gaming Corporation; *U.S. Public*, pg. 47
BALLY GESELLSCHAFT MBH—See Oerlikon-Buhrle Holding AG; *Int'l*, pg. 997
BALLY GROUP (UK) LIMITED—See Oerlikon-Buhrle Holding AG; *Int'l*, pg. 997
BALLY HONG KONG LTD.—See Oerlikon-Buhrle Holding AG; *Int'l*, pg. 997

BALLY, INC.—See Oerlikon-Buhrle Holding AG; *Int'l*, pg. 997
BALLY (ITALIA) S.R.L.—See Oerlikon-Buhrle Holding AG; *Int'l*, pg. 997
BALLY JAPAN LTD.—See Oerlikon-Buhrle Holding AG; *Int'l*, pg. 997
BALLY MANAGEMENT—See Oerlikon-Buhrle Holding AG; *Int'l*, pg. 998
BALLY MANAGEMENT AG—See Oerlikon-Buhrle Holding AG; *Int'l*, pg. 996
BALLY MODA SA—See Oerlikon-Buhrle Holding AG; *Int'l*, pg. 997
BALLY SCHOENHANDEL B.V.—See Oerlikon-Buhrle Holding AG; *Int'l*, pg. 997
BALLY SCHUHFABRIKEN S.A.—See Oerlikon-Buhrle Holding AG; *Int'l*, pg. 996
BALLY (SCHWEIZ) S.A.—See Oerlikon-Buhrle Holding AG; *Int'l*, pg. 996
BALLY SHOE CO. LTD.—See Oerlikon-Buhrle Holding AG; *Int'l*, pg. 997
BALLY SINGAPORE (PTE) LTD.—See Oerlikon-Buhrle Holding AG; *Int'l*, pg. 997
BALLY SOUTH AFRICA LTD.—See Oerlikon-Buhrle Holding AG; *Int'l*, pg. 997
BALLY TOTAL FITNESS CORPORATION—See Bally Total Fitness Holdings Corporation; *U.S. Public*, pg. 171
BALLY TOTAL FITNESS HOLDINGS CORPORATION; *U.S. Public*, pg. 171
BALLY TRADING AG—See Oerlikon-Buhrle Holding AG; *Int'l*, pg. 996
BALLY UK SALES LTD.—See Oerlikon-Buhrle Holding AG; *Int'l*, pg. 997
BALLY'S GRAND INC. (LAS VEGAS)—See Hilton Hotels Corporation; *U.S. Public*, pg. 829
BALLY'S PARK PLACE, INC.—See Hilton Hotels Corporation; *U.S. Public*, pg. 829
BALLY'S SHOE FACTORIES (NORWICH) LTD.—See Oerlikon-Buhrle Holding AG; *Int'l*, pg. 997
PIERRE BALMAIN—See SMH Swiss Corporation for Micro Electronics & Watchmaking Indus. Ltd.; *Int'l*, pg. 1160
BALMANTA S.A.—See Baltek Corporation; *U.S. Public*, pg. 172
BALMER LAWRIE-FUCHS LIMITED—See Fuchs Petrolub AG Oel + Chemie; *Int'l*, pg. 518
BALMER LAWRIE - VAN LEER LTD.—See Royal Packaging Industries Van Leer B.V.; *Int'l*, pg. 1146
BALSA DEVELOPMENT CORPORATION—See Baltek Corporation; *U.S. Public*, pg. 171
BALSA ECUADOR LUMBER CORPORATION—See Baltek Corporation; *U.S. Public*, pg. 171
BALSON-HERCULES LTD.—See Consoltex Group Inc.; *Int'l*, pg. 326
BALSTER GMBH—See Freudenberg & Company; *Int'l*, pg. 506
BALTEA—See Olivetti SpA; *Int'l*, pg. 1002
BALTEC MASCHINENBAU AG—See Feintool International Holding AG; *Int'l*, pg. 479
BALTEK CORPORATION; *U.S. Public*, pg. 171
BALTEK FOREIGN SALES CORPORATION—See Baltek Corporation; *U.S. Public*, pg. 172
BALTEK LTD.—See Baltek Corporation; *U.S. Public*, pg. 172
BALTEK S.A.—See Baltek Corporation; *U.S. Public*, pg. 172
BALTI PAKEND—See A. Ahlstrom Corporation; *Int'l*, pg. 33
BALTI PAKEND LTD.—See A. Ahlstrom Corporation; *Int'l*, pg. 33
BALTIC CABLE AB—See Veba AG; *Int'l*, pg. 1457
BALTIC COUNTRY MANOR—See Horizon/CMS Healthcare Corporation; *U.S. Public*, pg. 838
BALTIC LINEN COMPANY, INC.; *U.S. Private*, pg. 113
BALTIC POWER (ESTONIA) LTD.—See Vattenfall AB; *Int'l*, pg. 1453
BALTIC POWER (LATVIA) LTD.—See Vattenfall AB; *Int'l*, pg. 1453
BALTIMORE AIRCOIL COMPANY—See Amsted Industries Incorporated; *U.S. Private*, pg. 68
BALTIMORE BUSINESS PUBLICATIONS, INC.—See Advance Publications Inc.; *U.S. Private*, pg. 19
BALTIMORE CENTER, INC.—See The Rouse Company; *U.S. Public*, pg. 1407
BALTIMORE GAS AND ELECTRIC COMPANY; *U.S. Public*, pg. 172
BALTIMORE STATIONERY CO./TOTAL OFFICE; *U.S. Private*, pg. 113
THE BALTIMORE SUN NEWSPAPERS—See The Times Mirror Company; *U.S. Public*, pg. 1616
BALTIMORE TRUST COMPANY—See Mercantile Bankshares Corporation; *U.S. Public*, pg. 1088
BALTIMORE-WASHINGTON AUTO EXCHANGE INC.—See Tyco International Ltd.; *U.S. Public*, pg. 1648
BALZARETTI MODIGLIANI—See Saint-Gobain; *Int'l*, pg. 1176
BALZERS—See Oerlikon-Buhrle Holding AG; *Int'l*, pg. 997
BALZERS DUNNSCHICHT-KOMPONENTEN GMBH—See Oerlikon-Buhrle Holding AG; *Int'l*, pg. 997
BALZERS HOCHVAKUUM AG—See Oerlikon-Buhrle Holding AG; *Int'l*, pg. 997
BALZERS LTD.—See Oerlikon-Buhrle Holding AG; *Int'l*, pg. 997
S.A. BALZERS N.V.—See Oerlikon-Buhrle Holding AG; *Int'l*, pg. 998
BALZERS PROCESS SYSTEMS EURPOE N.V.—See Oerlikon-Buhrle Holding AG; *Int'l*, pg. 997
BALZERS PROCESS SYSTEMS, INC.—See Oerlikon-Buhrle Holding AG; *Int'l*, pg. 997
BALZERS S.A.—See Oerlikon-Buhrle Holding AG; *Int'l*, pg. 997
BALZERS SANDVIK COATING AB—See Oerlikon-Buhrle Holding AG; *Int'l*, pg. 997
BALZERS-SILMAX S.P.A.—See Oerlikon-Buhrle Holding AG; *Int'l*, pg. 997
BALZERS TOOL COATING, INC.—See Oerlikon-Buhrle Holding AG; *Int'l*, pg. 997

BALZERS TRECHNOVAC COMERCIAL LTDA.—See Oerlikon-Buhrle Holding AG; *Int'l*, pg. 997
BALZERS VERSCHLEISSSCHUTZ GMBH—See Oerlikon-Buhrle Holding AG; *Int'l*, pg. 997
BAM MEDIA; *U.S. Private*, pg. 113
BAMBERGER KALIKO GMBH—See Continental AG; *Int'l*, pg. 327
BAMBURI PORTLAND CEMENT CO LTD—See Lafarge S.A.; *Int'l*, pg. 789
BAMBURI TANKERS HOLDING (NAURU) CORP.—See Lafarge S.A.; *Int'l*, pg. 789
BAMIYAN CO., LTD.—See Skylark Co., Ltd.; *Int'l*, pg. 1262
BANACOL MARKETING CORP.; *U.S. Private*, pg. 113
AB BANAN-KOMPANIET—See Axel Johnson AB; *Int'l*, pg. 708
BANANA REPUBLIC—See The Gap, Inc.; *U.S. Public*, pg. 702
BANANZA AIR MANAGEMENT SYSTEMS, INC.—See Rapid Engineering Inc.; *U.S. Private*, pg. 910
BANC LIFE INSURANCE CORPORATION—See Associated Banc-Corp; *U.S. Public*, pg. 140
BANC ONE BUILDING MANAGEMENT CORPORATION—See Banc One Corporation; *U.S. Public*, pg. 173
BANC ONE CAPITAL CORPORATION—See Banc One Corporation; *U.S. Public*, pg. 175
BANC ONE CORPORATION; *U.S. Public*, pg. 172
BANC ONE CREDIT CORPORATION—See Banc One Corporation; *U.S. Public*, pg. 175
BANC ONE FINANCIAL SERVICES, INC.—See Banc One Corporation; *U.S. Public*, pg. 173
BANC ONE INDIANA CORPORATION—See Banc One Corporation; *U.S. Public*, pg. 173
BANC ONE KENTUCKY CORPORATION—See Banc One Corporation; *U.S. Public*, pg. 173
BANC ONE LEASING CORPORATION—See Banc One Corporation; *U.S. Public*, pg. 175
BANC ONE LIFE INSURANCE CO.—See Banc One Corporation; *U.S. Public*, pg. 175
BANC ONE MORTGAGE CORPORATION—See Banc One Corporation; *U.S. Public*, pg. 175
BANC ONE-NEWARK—See Banc One Corporation; *U.S. Public*, pg. 173
BANC ONE OHIO CORPORATION—See Banc One Corporation; *U.S. Public*, pg. 173
BANC ONE REALTY COLUMBUS CORP.—See Banc One Corporation; *U.S. Public*, pg. 175
BANC ONE SECURITIES CORPORATION—See Banc One Corporation; *U.S. Public*, pg. 175
BANC ONE SERVICES CORPORATION—See Banc One Corporation; *U.S. Public*, pg. 174
BANCA AGRICOLA MANTOVANA SARL; *Int'l*, pg. 135
BANCA AGRICOLA MILANESE S.P.A.—See Banca Popolare di Milano; *Int'l*, pg. 137
BANCA BBA-CREDITANSTALT S.A.—See Creditanstalt-Bankverein; *Int'l*, pg. 347
BANCA BRIANTEA SPA—See Banca Popolare di Milano; *int'l*, pg. 137
BANCA C. STEINHAUSLIN & C., S.P.A.—See Creditanstalt-Bankverein; *Int'l*, pg. 347
BANCA CANTRADE LUGANO SA—See Union Bank of Switzerland; *Int'l*, pg. 1439
BANCA COMMERCIALE ITALIANA; *Int'l*, pg. 135
BANCA COMMERCIALE ITALIANA S.P.A.—See IRI Istituto Ricostruzione Industriale; *Int'l*, pg. 652
BANCA D'AMERICA E D'ITALIA S.P.A.—See Deutsche Bank AG; *Int'l*, pg. 403
BANCA DEL GOTTARDO—See The Sumitomo Bank, Limited; *Int'l*, pg. 1310
BANCA DI ROMA; *Int'l*, pg. 135
BANCA DI TRENTO E BOLZANO S.P.A.—See Banca Ambrosiano Veneto S.p.A.; *Int'l*, pg. 138
BANCA FIDEURAN S.P.A.—See Istituto Mobiliare Italiano; *Int'l*, pg. 692
BANCA HIPOTECARIA—See Bancomer, S.A.; *Int'l*, pg. 145
BANCA JOVER—See Credit Lyonnais S.A.; *Int'l*, pg. 344
BANCA MARCH S.A.; *Int'l*, pg. 136
BANCA MEDITERRANEA S.P.A.—See Banca di Roma; *Int'l*, pg. 135
BANCA MERCANTILE S.P.A.—See La Fondiaria Assicurazioni S.p.A.; *Int'l*, pg. 784
BANCA MONTE DEI PASCHI DI SIENA S.P.A.; *Int'l*, pg. 136
BANCA MONTE PASCHI BELGIO—See Bank Brussels Lambert; *Int'l*, pg. 147
BANCA NAZIONALE DEL LAVORO—See Banca Nazionale del Lavoro SjA.; *Int'l*, pg. 137
BANCA NAZIONALE DEL LAVORO SJA.; *Int'l*, pg. 136
BANCA NAZIONALE DELL'AGRICOLTURA S.P.A.—See Banca di Roma; *Int'l*, pg. 135
BANCA PATRIMONIAL—See Bancomer, S.A.; *Int'l*, pg. 145
BANCA POPOLARE DI MILANO; *Int'l*, pg. 137
BANCA PRIVADA D'ANDORRA—See Caixa d'Estalvis de Catalunya; *Int'l*, pg. 250
BANCA SERFIN, S.N.C.; *Int'l*, pg. 137
BANCBOSTON BROKERAGE INC.—See BankBoston Corporation; *U.S. Public*, pg. 184
BANCBOSTON CAPITAL, INC.—See BankBoston Corporation; *U.S. Public*, pg. 184
BANCBOSTON FINANCIAL CO.—See BankBoston Corporation; *U.S. Public*, pg. 184
BANCBOSTON INVESTMENT INC.—See BankBoston Corporation; *U.S. Public*, pg. 184
BANCBOSTON LEASING INC.—See BankBoston Corporation; *U.S. Public*, pg. 184
BANCBOSTON REAL ESTATE CAPITOL CORPORATION—See BankBoston Corporation; *U.S. Public*, pg. 184
BANCBOSTON VENTURES INC.—See BankBoston Corporation; *U.S. Public*, pg. 184
BANCINSURANCE CORP.; *U.S. Public*, pg. 175
BANCIRELAND/FIRST FINANCIAL INC.—See Bank of Ireland; *Int'l*, pg. 152
BANCO AMBROSIANO VENETO S.P.A.; *Int'l*, pg. 138

BANCO AMERICA DO SUL S.A.—See The Fuji Bank, Limited; *Int'l*, pg. 521
BANCO BANIF DE GESTION PRIVADA—See Banco Central Hispanoamericano S.A.; *Int'l*, pg. 139
BANCO BANQUE NATIONALE DE PARIS BRASIL S/A—See Banque Nationale de Paris; *Int'l*, pg. 164
BANCO BILBAO VIZCAYA, S.A.; *Int'l*, pg. 138
BANCO BNL DO BRASIL S.A.—See Banca Nazionale del Lavoro SjA.; *Int'l*, pg. 137
BANCO BOAVISTA INTERATLANTICO SA—See Banco Espirito Santo e Comercial de Lisboa SA; *Int'l*, pg. 142
BANCO BRADESCO S.A.; *Int'l*, pg. 139
BANCO CCF BRAZIL—See Credit Commercial de France; *Int'l*, pg. 342
BANCO CENTRAL CANADA—See Banco Central Hispanoamericano S.A.; *Int'l*, pg. 140
BANCO CENTRAL CORP. (PUERTO RICO)—See Banco Central Hispanoamericano S.A.; *Int'l*, pg. 139
BANCO CENTRAL HISPANOAMERICANO S.A.; *Int'l*, pg. 139
BANCO CHASE MANHATTAN, S.A.—See The Chase Manhattan Corporation; *U.S. Public*, pg. 339
BANCO COMERCIAL TRANSATLANTICO, S.A. (BANCOTRANS) (BARCELONA)—See Deutsche Bank AG; *Int'l*, pg. 403
BANCO COMERCIAL TRANSATLANTICO, S.A. (BANCOTRANS) (MADRID)—See Deutsche Bank AG; *Int'l*, pg. 403
BANCO CREDIBANCO S.A.—See The Bank of New York Company, Inc.; *U.S. Public*, pg. 179
BANCO CREFISUL DE INVESTIMENTO, S.A.—See Citicorp; *U.S. Public*, pg. 378
BANCO DE ASUNCION—See Banco Central Hispanoamericano S.A.; *Int'l*, pg. 140
BANCO DE BOSTON—See BankBoston Corporation; *U.S. Public*, pg. 184
BANCO DE COMERCIO E INDUSTRIA, S.A.—See Banco Santander; *Int'l*, pg. 144
BANCO DE CREDITO LOCAL—See Argentaria Corporacion Bancaria de Espana, S.A.; *Int'l*, pg. 80
BANCO DE EXTREMADURA, S.A.—See Caixa Geral de Depositos; *Int'l*, pg. 251
BANCO DE FORMENTO—See Banco Central Hispanoamericano S.A.; *Int'l*, pg. 139
BANCO DE HONDURAS S.A.—See Citicorp; *U.S. Public*, pg. 378
BANCO DE JEREZ—See Banco Central Hispanoamericano S.A.; *Int'l*, pg. 139
BANCO DE LA NACION ARGENTINA; *Int'l*, pg. 140
BANCO DE LA PROVINCIA DE BUENOS AIRES; *Int'l*, pg. 140
BANCO DE MONTEVIDEO—See Deutsche Bank AG; *Int'l*, pg. 403
BANCO DE MONTREAL S.A.—See Bank of Montreal; *Int'l*, pg. 155
BANCO DE TOKYO-MITSUBISHI BRASIL S/A—See The Bank of Tokyo-Mitsubishi, Ltd.; *Int'l*, pg. 158
BANCO DE VALENCIA—See Banco Central Hispanoamericano S.A.; *Int'l*, pg. 139
BANCO DEL DESARROLLO—See Credit Agricole; *Int'l*, pg. 341
BANCO DI NAPOLI; *Int'l*, pg. 140
BANCO DI ROMA—See IRI Istituto Ricostruzione Industriale; *Int'l*, pg. 652
BANCO DI SICILIA; *Int'l*, pg. 140
BANCO DO BRASIL; *Int'l*, pg. 141
BANCO DO BRASIL S.A.-PARAGUAY—See Banco do Brasil; *Int'l*, pg. 141
BANCO ESPANOL DE CREDITO SA—See Banco Santander; *Int'l*, pg. 143
BANCO ESPIRITO SANTO DO ORIENTE SARL (BESOR)—See Banco Espirito Santo e Comercial de Lisboa SA; *Int'l*, pg. 142
BANCO ESPIRITO SANTO E COMERCIAL DE LISBOA SA; *Int'l*, pg. 142
BANCO ESPIRITO SANTO SA (BESSA)—See Banco Espirito Santo e Comercial de Lisboa SA; *Int'l*, pg. 142
BANCO EXTERIOR, S.A.—See Argentaria Corporacion Bancaria de Espana, S.A.; *Int'l*, pg. 81
BANCO FINANCIAL PORTUGUES-BRAZIL—See Caixa Geral de Depositos; *Int'l*, pg. 251
BANCO GALLEGO; *Int'l*, pg. 145
BANCO HIPOTECARIO DE ESPANA—See Argentaria Corporacion Bancaria de Espana, S.A.; *Int'l*, pg. 80
BANCO HISPANO AMERICANO-BENELUX, S.A./NV—See Banco Central Hispanoamericano S.A.; *Int'l*, pg. 140
BANCO HISPANO DE INVESTIMENTO, S.A.—See Banco Central Hispanoamericano S.A.; *Int'l*, pg. 140
BANCO INTER-ATLANTICO S.A.—See Credit Agricole; *Int'l*, pg. 341
BANCO INTERFINANZAS S.A.—See Creditanstalt-Bankverein; *Int'l*, pg. 347
BANCO INTERNACIONAL DE COLOMBIA, S.A.—See Citicorp; *U.S. Public*, pg. 378
BANCO INTERNACIONAL DE COMERCIO—See Banco Central Hispanoamericano S.A.; *Int'l*, pg. 139
BANCO INTERNACIONAL DE CREDITO S.A.—See Banco Espirito Santo e Comercial de Lisboa SA; *Int'l*, pg. 142
BANCO INTERNATIONAL DE CREDITO SA (PORTUGAL)—See Credit Agricole; *Int'l*, pg. 341
BANCO ITAU S.A.; *Int'l*, pg. 142
BANCO ITAU S.A.—See Banco Itau S.A.; *Int'l*, pg. 142
BANCO J.P. MORGAN S.A.—See J.P. Morgan Co. Incorporated; *U.S. Public*, pg. 1130
BANCO LUSO ESPANOL S.A.—See Caixa Geral de Depositos; *Int'l*, pg. 251
BANCO MAPFRE, S.A.—See Corporacion MAPFRE, Compania Internacional de Reaseguros, S.A.; *Int'l*, pg. 332
BANCO MERCANTIL DE TARRAGONA—See Banco Central Hispanoamericano S.A.; *Int'l*, pg. 139
BANCO MUNDIAL—See The World Bank; *U.S. Private*, pg. 1189

BANCO NACIONAL DE MEXICO, S.A. (BANAMEX)—See Grupo Financiero Banamex/Accival, S.A. de C.V.; *Int'l*, pg. 574
BANCO NATWEST ESPANA SA—See National Westminster Bank PLC; *Int'l*, pg. 911
BANCO NORCHEM, S.A.—See The Chase Manhattan Corporation; *U.S. Public*, pg. 339
BANCO POPULAR—See Banco Popular de Puerto Rico; *U.S. Public*, pg. 176
BANCO POPULAR ARGENTINO—See Banco Central Hispanoamericano S.A.; *Int'l*, pg. 140
BANCO POPULAR DE PUERTO RICO; *U.S. Public*, pg. 175
BANCO POPULAR, FSB—See Banco Popular de Puerto Rico; *U.S. Public*, pg. 176
BANCO POPULAR HIPOTCARIO—See Bayerische Hypotheken-und Wechsel-Bank Aktiengesellschaft; *Int'l*, pg. 176
BANCO POPULAR, ILLINOIS—See Banco Popular de Puerto Rico; *U.S. Public*, pg. 176
BANCO POPULAR, N.A. (CALIFORNIA)—See Banco Popular de Puerto Rico; *U.S. Public*, pg. 176
BANCO POPULAR, N.A. (FLORIDA)—See Banco Popular de Puerto Rico; *U.S. Public*, pg. 176
BANCO PORTUGUES DE INVESTIMENTO, S.A.—See The Sanwa Bank Limited; *Int'l*, pg. 1190
BANCO PROVINCIAL S.A. BANCO UNIVERSAL; *Int'l*, pg. 142
BANCO QUILMES; *Int'l*, pg. 142
BANCO SANTANDER; *Int'l*, pg. 143
BANCO SANTANDER—See Banco Santander; *Int'l*, pg. 143
BANCO SANTANDER ARGENTINA—See Banco Santander; *Int'l*, pg. 143
BANCO SANTANDER-ARGENTINA—See Banco Santander; *Int'l*, pg. 143
BANCO SANTANDER-CHILE—See Banco Santander; *Int'l*, pg. 143
BANCO SANTANDER DE NEGOCIOS—See Banco Santander; *Int'l*, pg. 144
BANCO SANTANDER (GUERNSEY) LTD.—See Banco Santander; *Int'l*, pg. 143
BANCO SANTANDER INTERNATIONAL—See Banco Santander; *Int'l*, pg. 143
BANCO SANTANDER INTERNATIONAL MIAMI—See Banco Santander; *Int'l*, pg. 143
BANCO SANTANDER PERU—See Banco Santander; *Int'l*, pg. 144
BANCO SANTANDER PHILIPPINES LTD.—See Banco Santander; *Int'l*, pg. 144
BANCO SANTANDER PUERTO RICO—See Banco Santander; *Int'l*, pg. 143
BANCO SANTANDER PUERTO RICO, NEW YORK BRANCH—See Banco Santander; *Int'l*, pg. 143
BANCO SANTANDER-SUIZA—See Banco Santander; *Int'l*, pg. 143
BANCO SANTANDER SWITZERLAND—See Banco Santander; *Int'l*, pg. 144
BANCO SANTANDER TRUST & BANKING CORPORATION (BAHAMAS) LTD.—See Banco Santander; *Int'l*, pg. 143
BANCO SANTANDER URUGUAY S.A.—See Banco Santander; *Int'l*, pg. 143
BANCO STANDARD TOTTA DE MOCAMBIQUE, SARL—See Standard Chartered Bank PLC; *Int'l*, pg. 1296
BANCO SUMITOMO BRASILEIRO S.A.—See The Sumitomo Bank, Limited; *Int'l*, pg. 1310
BANCO SURINVEST S.A.—See Rabobank Nederland; *Int'l*, pg. 1082
BANCO TOTTA & ACORES—See Banco Totta & Acores; *Int'l*, pg. 145
BANCO TOTTA & ACORES; *Int'l*, pg. 144
BANCO 21; *Int'l*, pg. 145
BANCO URQUIJO S.A.—See Banca March S.A.; *Int'l*, pg. 136
BANCO VITALICIO DE ESPANA COMPANIA ANONIMA DE SEGUROS—See Assicurazioni Generali S.p.A.; *Int'l*, pg. 90
BANCOMER LONDON BRANCH—See Bancomer, S.A.; *Int'l*, pg. 145
BANCOMER LOS ANGELES INTERNATIONAL BANKING BRANCH—See Bancomer, S.A.; *Int'l*, pg. 145
BANCOMER, S.A.; *Int'l*, pg. 145
BANCOMM—See Datum Inc.; *U.S. Public*, pg. 488
BANCORP INVESTMENT GROUP, LTD.—See Pacific Century Financial Corporation; *U.S. Public*, pg. 1248
BANCORP SOUTH INC.; *U.S. Public*, pg. 176
BANCROFT HOUSE HEALTHCARE—See Vencor, Inc.; *U.S. Public*, pg. 1711
BANCROFT-WHITNEY CO.—See The Thomson Corporation; *U.S. Public*, pg. 1602
BANCTEC (AUSTRALIA) PTY. LIMITED—See BancTec, Inc.; *U.S. Public*, pg. 177
BANCTEC (CANADA), INC.—See BancTec, Inc.; *U.S. Public*, pg. 177
BANCTEC FINANCIAL SYSTEMS—See BancTec, Inc.; *U.S. Public*, pg. 177
BANCTEC, INC.; *U.S. Public*, pg. 176
BANCTEC, INC.-ATLANTA—See BancTec, Inc.; *U.S. Public*, pg. 177
BANCTEC, INC.-CHICAGO—See BancTec, Inc.; *U.S. Public*, pg. 177
BANCTEC, INC.-LOS ANGELES—See BancTec, Inc.; *U.S. Public*, pg. 177
BANCTEC, INC.-NEW YORK—See BancTec, Inc.; *U.S. Public*, pg. 177
BANCTEC LTD.—See BancTec, Inc.; *U.S. Public*, pg. 177
BANCTEC PAYMENT SYSTEMS—See BancTec, Inc.; *U.S. Public*, pg. 177
BANCTEC (PUERTO RICO), INC.—See BancTec, Inc.; *U.S. Public*, pg. 177
BANCTEC SERVICE CORP.—See BancTec, Inc.; *U.S. Public*, pg. 177

BANCTEC TECHNOLOGIES—See BancTec, Inc.; *U.S. Public*, pg. 177
BAND-IT-IDEX, INC.—See IDEX Corporation; *U.S. Public*, pg. 862
BANDAG AG—See Bandag, Incorporated; *U.S. Public*, pg. 178
BANDAG CANADA, LTD.—See Bandag, Incorporated; *U.S. Public*, pg. 178
BANDAG DE MEXICO S.A. DE C.V.—See Bandag, Incorporated; *U.S. Public*, pg. 178
BANDAG DO BRASIL LTDA.—See Bandag, Incorporated; *U.S. Public*, pg. 178
BANDAG EUROPE NV—See Bandag, Incorporated; *U.S. Public*, pg. 178
BANDAG, INCORPORATED; *U.S. Public*, pg. 177
BANDAG INC. OF S.A. (PTY.) LTD.—See Bandag, Incorporated; *U.S. Public*, pg. 178
BANDAG LICENSING CORPORATION—See Bandag, Incorporated; *U.S. Public*, pg. 177
BANDAG NEW ZEALAND LTD.—See Bandag, Incorporated; *U.S. Public*, pg. 178
BANDAI CO., LTD.; *Int'l*, pg. 145
BANDFIX AG—See Beiersdorf Group; *Int'l*, pg. 183
BANDINI FERTILIZER COMPANY; *U.S. Private*, pg. 113
BANDO AMERICA, INC.—See Bando Chemical Industries, Ltd.; *Int'l*, pg. 145
BANDO CHEMICAL INDUSTRIES, LTD.; *Int'l*, pg. 145
BANDO MANUFACTURING OF AMERICA, INC.—See Bando Chemical Industries, Ltd.; *Int'l*, pg. 145
BANDWIDTH OPTIMIZATION BUSINESS UNIT—See Telco Systems, Inc.; *U.S. Public*, pg. 1568
BANEXI (BANQUE POUR L'EXPANSION INDUSTRIELLE)—See Banque Nationale de Paris; *Int'l*, pg. 163
BANEXI INTERNATIONAL FINANCIAL SERVICES (NORTH AMERICA) CORP.—See Banque Nationale de Paris; *Int'l*, pg. 163
BANFI PRODUCT CORP—See Banfi Vintners; *U.S. Private*, pg. 113
BANFI VINTNERS; *U.S. Private*, pg. 113
OY BANG & OLUFSEN AB—See Bang & Olufsen A/S; *Int'l*, pg. 146
S.A. BANG & OLUFSEN BELGIUM N.V.—See Bang & Olufsen A/S; *Int'l*, pg. 146
BANG & OLUFSEN AG—See Bang & Olufsen A/S; *Int'l*, pg. 146
BANG & OLUFSEN A/S; *Int'l*, pg. 145
BANG & OLUFSEN ESPANA S.A.—See Bang & Olufsen A/S; *Int'l*, pg. 146
BANG & OLUFSEN FRANCE S.A.—See Bang & Olufsen A/S; *Int'l*, pg. 146
BANG & OLUFSEN GES. M.B.H.—See Bang & Olufsen A/S; *Int'l*, pg. 146
BANG & OLUFSEN G.M.B.H.—See Bang & Olufsen A/S; *Int'l*, pg. 146
BANG & OLUFSEN OF JAPAN LTD.—See Bang & Olufsen A/S; *Int'l*, pg. 146
BANG & OLUFSEN SVENSKA AB—See Bang & Olufsen A/S; *Int'l*, pg. 146
BANG & OLUFSEN UNITED KINGDOM LTD.—See Bang & Olufsen A/S; *Int'l*, pg. 146
J.C. BANGERTER & SONS, LTD.—See Ameritruck Distribution Corporation; *U.S. Private*, pg. 66
BANGKOK ATHLETIC CO., LTD.—See Bangkok Rubber Public Co., Ltd.; *Int'l*, pg. 146
BANGKOK BANK BERHAD—See Bangkok Bank Public Company Limited; *Int'l*, pg. 146
BANGKOK BANK OF COMMERCE LTD.; *Int'l*, pg. 146
BANGKOK BANK PUBLIC COMPANY LIMITED; *Int'l*, pg. 146
BANGKOK CENTRAL LEASING CO., LTD.—See The Tokai Bank, Limited; *Int'l*, pg. 1391
BANGKOK FIRST TOKAI COMPANY LIMITED—See The Tokai Bank, Limited; *Int'l*, pg. 1391
BANGKOK INDUSTRIAL GAS CO., LTD.—See Air Products and Chemicals, Inc.; *U.S. Public*, pg. 32
BANGKOK INTERNATIONAL BANKING FACILITY—See The Sanwa Bank Limited; *Int'l*, pg. 1190
BANGKOK KOMATSU CO., LTD.—See Komatsu Ltd.; *Int'l*, pg. 745
BANGKOK OA COMS CO., LTD.—See Hewlett-Packard Company; *U.S. Public*, pg. 816
BANGKOK RUBBER PUBLIC CO., LTD.; *Int'l*, pg. 146
BANGKOK SAKURA LEASING CO., LIMITED—See The Sakura Bank, Limited; *Int'l*, pg. 1180
BANGKOK STEEL INDUSTRY CO. LTD.—See Nissho Iwai Corporation; *Int'l*, pg. 947
BANGKOK TELECOM CO., LTD. (BTC)—See The Furukawa Electric Co., Ltd.; *Int'l*, pg. 531
BANGKOK WASTE WATER PROJECT—See Nishimatsu Construction Co., Ltd.; *Int'l*, pg. 942
BANGLADESH TOBACCO CO. LTD.—See B.A.T Industries P.L.C.; *Int'l*, pg. 111
BANGOR & AROOSTOOK RAILROAD CO.—See Iron Road Railways Inc.; *U.S. Private*, pg. 575
BANGOR HYDRO-ELECTRIC COMPANY; *U.S. Public*, pg. 178
BANGOR-PACIFIC HYDRO ASSOCIATES—See Bangor Hydro-Electric Company; *U.S. Public*, pg. 178
BANGOR VAR COMPANY, INC.—See Bangor Hydro-Electric Company; *U.S. Public*, pg. 178
BANISTER MAJESTIC—See BFC Construction Corporation; *Int'l*, pg. 118
BANK AND OFFICE INTERIORS—See BKM Enterprises, Inc.; *U.S. Private*, pg. 107
BANK AUFINA—See Union Bank of Switzerland; *Int'l*, pg. 1439
PT BANK BNP LIPPO INDONESIA—See Banque Nationale de Paris; *Int'l*, pg. 164
BANK BRUSSELS LAMBERT; *Int'l*, pg. 146
BANK BRUSSELS LAMBERT - DUBLIN—See Bank Brussels Lambert; *Int'l*, pg. 148
BANK BRUSSELS LAMBERT, SEDE DI MILANO—See Bank Brussels Lambert; *Int'l*, pg. 147

BANK CARD COMPANY—See Bank Brussels Lambert; *Int'l*, pg. 147
BANK CARD SERVICES DEPARTMENT—See CVB Financial Corp.; *U.S. Public*, pg. 287
BANK CREDITANSTALT S.A.—See Creditanstalt-Bankverein; *Int'l*, pg. 347
PT BANK DBS BUANA—See DBS Bank Ltd.; *Int'l*, pg. 350
P.T. BANK FINCONESIA—See Commerzbank AG; *Int'l*, pg. 312
BANK FOR EUROPE LTD.—See Dresdner Bank AG; *Int'l*, pg. 490
THE BANK FUNDS COMPANY LLC; *U.S. Private*, pg. 113
BANK FUR KARNTEN UND STEIERMARK AG—See Creditanstalt-Bankverein; *Int'l*, pg. 347
BANK FUR OBEROSTERREICH UND SALZBURG—See Creditanstalt-Bankverein; *Int'l*, pg. 347
BANK FUR TIROL UND VORARLBERG AG—See Creditanstalt-Bankverein; *Int'l*, pg. 347
BANK GIROTEL AG—See Bankgesellschaft Berlin; *Int'l*, pg. 159
BANK HAPOALIM; *Int'l*, pg. 149
BANK HAPOALIM (BERLIN)—See Bank Hapoalim; *Int'l*, pg. 149
BANK HAPOALIM B.M.—See Bank Hapoalim; *Int'l*, pg. 149
BANK HAPOALIM (SANTIAGO)—See Bank Hapoalim; *Int'l*, pg. 149
BANK IN LIECHTENSTEIN (FRANKFURT) GMBH AUSTRALIA—See Liechtenstein Global Trust Limited; *Int'l*, pg. 809
BANK LEUMI LE-ISRAEL B.M.; *Int'l*, pg. 150
BANK LEUMI LE-ISRAEL B.M.—See Bank Leumi le-Israel B.M.; *Int'l*, pg. 150
BANK LEUMI LE-ISRAEL (SWITZERLAND)—See Bank Leumi le-Israel B.M.; *Int'l*, pg. 150
BANK LEUMI (UK) P.L.C.—See Bank Leumi le-Israel B.M.; *Int'l*, pg. 150
BANK LEUMI (UK) PLC—See Bank Leumi le-Israel B.M.; *Int'l*, pg. 150
P.T. BANK LTCB CENTRAL ASIA—See The Long-Term Credit Bank of Japan, Limited; *Int'l*, pg. 816
BANK MARKETING ASSOCIATION—See The American Bankers Association; *U.S. Private*, pg. 51
BANK MEES & HOPE NV—See ABN-AMRO Holding N.V.; *Int'l*, pg. 9
BANK MENDES GANS NV—See ING Groep N.V.; *Int'l*, pg. 647
P.T. BANK MERINCORP—See The Sumitomo Bank, Limited; *Int'l*, pg. 1310
M.F. BANK & COMPANY, INC.; *U.S. Private*, pg. 113
BANK OF AGRICULTURE & COMMERCE; *U.S. Private*, pg. 114
BANK OF AMERICA—See BankAmerica Corporation; *U.S. Public*, pg. 180
BANK OF AMERICA ALASKA, N.A.—See BankAmerica Corporation; *U.S. Public*, pg. 180
BANK OF AMERICA AUTO LEASE CENTER—See BankAmerica Corporation; *U.S. Public*, pg. 181
BANK OF AMERICA BUSINESS CREDIT—See BankAmerica Corporation; *U.S. Public*, pg. 180
BANK OF AMERICA CALIFORNIA—See BankAmerica Corporation; *U.S. Public*, pg. 180
BANK OF AMERICA CAPITAL—See BankAmerica Corporation; *U.S. Public*, pg. 180
BANK OF AMERICA IDAHO—See BankAmerica Corporation; *U.S. Public*, pg. 180
BANK OF AMERICA ILLINOIS—See BankAmerica Corporation; *U.S. Public*, pg. 180
BANK OF AMERICA ILLINOIS TRUST COMPANY OF FLORIDA, N.A.—See BankAmerica Corporation; *U.S. Public*, pg. 181
BANK OF AMERICA MALAYSIA BERHAD—See BankAmerica Corporation; *U.S. Public*, pg. 182
BANK OF AMERICA NEVADA—See BankAmerica Corporation; *U.S. Public*, pg. 180
BANK OF AMERICA NEW MEXICO—See BankAmerica Corporation; *U.S. Public*, pg. 180
BANK OF AMERICA NT&SA—See BankAmerica Corporation; *U.S. Public*, pg. 182
BANK OF AMERICA OREGON—See BankAmerica Corporation; *U.S. Public*, pg. 180
BANK OF AMERICA PUBLIC FINANCE—See BankAmerica Corporation; *U.S. Public*, pg. 180
BANK OF AMERICA S.A.—See BankAmerica Corporation; *U.S. Public*, pg. 182
BANK OF AMERICA TEXAS—See BankAmerica Corporation; *U.S. Public*, pg. 180
BANK OF AMERICA-THE SEQUOR GROUP—See BankAmerica Corporation; *U.S. Public*, pg. 181
BANK OF BERMUDA (CAYMAN) LIMITED—See The Bank of Bermuda Limited; *Int'l*, pg. 151
BANK OF BERMUDA (GUERNSEY) LIMITED—See The Bank of Bermuda Limited; *Int'l*, pg. 151
BANK OF BERMUDA (ISLE OF MAN) LIMITED—See The Bank of Bermuda Limited; *Int'l*, pg. 151
THE BANK OF BERMUDA LIMITED; *Int'l*, pg. 150
BANK OF BERMUDA (LUXEMBOURG) S.A—See The Bank of Bermuda Limited; *Int'l*, pg. 151
BANK OF BERMUDA (NEW YORK) LIMITED—See The Bank of Bermuda Limited; *Int'l*, pg. 151
BANK OF BOSTON—See BankBoston Corporation; *U.S. Public*, pg. 184
BANK OF BOSTON CANADA—See BankBoston Corporation; *U.S. Public*, pg. 184
BANK OF BOSTON CONNECTICUT—See BankBoston Corporation; *U.S. Public*, pg. 184
BANK OF BOSTON - FLORIDA, N.A.—See BankBoston Corporation; *U.S. Public*, pg. 184
BANK OF BOSTON INTERNATIONAL—See BankBoston Corporation; *U.S. Public*, pg. 184
BANK OF BOSTON LTD.—See BankBoston Corporation; *U.S. Public*, pg. 184
BANK OF BOSTON OF THE PHILIPPINES—See BankBoston Corporation; *U.S. Public*, pg. 184

BANK OF BOSTON S.A.—See BankBoston Corporation; *U.S. Public*, pg. 185
BANK OF BOSTON TRUST CO. (BAHAMAS) LIMITED—See BankBoston Corporation; *U.S. Public*, pg. 185
BANK OF CARROLL—See MainStreet BankGroup Incorporated; *U.S. Public*, pg. 1038
BANK OF CHINA; *Int'l*, pg. 152
BANK OF COMMERCE—See Union Planters Corporation; *U.S. Public*, pg. 1669
BANK OF COMMERCE (M) BERHAD—See The Sanwa Bank Limited; *Int'l*, pg. 1190
BANK OF COMMERCE TRINIDAD AND TOBAGO LIMITED—See Canadian Imperial Bank of Commerce; *Int'l*, pg. 257
BANK OF COMMERCE TRUST COMPANY BARBADOS LIMITED—See Canadian Imperial Bank of Commerce; *Int'l*, pg. 257
BANK OF COWETA—See Synovus Financial Corp.; *U.S. Public*, pg. 1549
BANK OF DWIGHT—See Pontiac Bancorp, Inc.; *U.S. Public*, pg. 1316
BANK OF EAST TENNESSEE—See Union Planters Corporation; *U.S. Public*, pg. 1669
BANK OF FERRUM—See MainStreet BankGroup Incorporated; *U.S. Public*, pg. 1038
THE BANK OF FUKUOKA, LTD.; *Int'l*, pg. 152
BANK OF GOODLETSVILLE—See Union Planters Corporation; *U.S. Public*, pg. 1669
BANK OF HAWAII—See Pacific Century Financial Corporation; *U.S. Public*, pg. 1248
BANK OF HAWAII INTERNATIONAL CORPORATION, NEW YORK—See Pacific Century Financial Corporation; *U.S. Public*, pg. 1248
BANK OF HAZLEHURST—See Synovus Financial Corp.; *U.S. Public*, pg. 1549
THE BANK OF HIROSHIMA-FOREIGN DEPT.—See The Hiroshima Bank, Ltd.; *Int'l*, pg. 620
BANK OF HOMEWOOD—See Great Lakes Financial Resources, Inc.; *U.S. Private*, pg. 474
BANK OF HUNDRED—See Huntington Bancshares Inc.; *U.S. Public*, pg. 850
BANK OF IRELAND; *Int'l*, pg. 152
BANK OF IRELAND—See Bank of Ireland; *Int'l*, pg. 153
BANK OF IRELAND ASSET MANAGEMENT LIMITED—See Bank of Ireland; *Int'l*, pg. 152
BANK OF IRELAND COMMERCIAL FINANCE LTD.—See Bank of Ireland; *Int'l*, pg. 152
BANK OF IRELAND CORPORATE & INTERNATIONAL BANKING—See Bank of Ireland; *Int'l*, pg. 153
BANK OF IRELAND CORPORATE BANKING—See Bank of Ireland; *Int'l*, pg. 152
BANK OF IRELAND CREDIT CARD CENTRE—See Bank of Ireland; *Int'l*, pg. 152
BANK OF IRELAND DISCOUNTING—See Bank of Ireland; *Int'l*, pg. 153
BANK OF IRELAND FINANCE LTD.—See Bank of Ireland; *Int'l*, pg. 152
BANK OF IRELAND HOME MORGAGES LIMITED—See Bank of Ireland; *Int'l*, pg. 153
BANK OF IRELAND INTERNATIONAL FINANCE LIMITED—See Bank of Ireland; *Int'l*, pg. 152
BANK OF IRELAND INTERNATIONAL SERVICES LIMITED—See Bank of Ireland; *Int'l*, pg. 152
BANK OF IRELAND INVESTMENT MANAGERS LIMITED—See Bank of Ireland; *Int'l*, pg. 153
BANK OF IRELAND (IOM) LIMITED—See Bank of Ireland; *Int'l*, pg. 153
BANK OF IRELAND (JERSEY) LIMITED—See Bank of Ireland; *Int'l*, pg. 153
BANK OF IRELAND SECURITIES SERVICES LIMITED—See Bank of Ireland; *Int'l*, pg. 153
BANK OF IRELAND - TOKYO REPRESENTATIVE OFFICE—See Bank of Ireland; *Int'l*, pg. 153
BANK OF IRELAND TRUST SERVICES—See Bank of Ireland; *Int'l*, pg. 152
BANK OF IRELAND (U.S.A.)—See Bank of Ireland; *Int'l*, pg. 153
BANK OF LAKE COUNTY, N.A.—See Westamerica Bancorporation; *U.S. Public*, pg. 1756
BANK OF LINCOLNWOOD—See GSC Enterprises, Inc.; *U.S. Private*, pg. 436
BANK OF MATTESON—See Great Lakes Financial Resources, Inc.; *U.S. Private*, pg. 474
THE BANK OF MID-JERSEY—See Summit Bancorp; *U.S. Public*, pg. 1528
BANK OF MILLEN—See Regions Financial Corporation; *U.S. Public*, pg. 1371
BANK OF MISSISSIPPI—See Bancorp South Inc.; *U.S. Public*, pg. 176
BANK OF MONTREAL; *Int'l*, pg. 153
BANK OF MONTREAL GLOBAL, INC.—See Bank of Montreal; *Int'l*, pg. 154
BANK OF MONTREAL INVESTOR SERVICES LIMITED—See Bank of Montreal; *Int'l*, pg. 153
BANK OF MONTREAL TRUST COMPANY—See Bank of Montreal; *Int'l*, pg. 154
BANK OF MONTREAL TRUST COMPANY (C.I.) LTD.—See Bank of Montreal; *Int'l*, pg. 155
BANK OF MORGAN COUNTY—See Regions Financial Corporation; *U.S. Public*, pg. 1371
THE BANK OF NEW YORK—See The Bank of New York Company, Inc.; *U.S. Public*, pg. 179
THE BANK OF NEW YORK COMPANY, INC.; *U.S. Public*, pg. 178
THE BANK OF NEW YORK—See The Bank of New York Company, Inc.; *U.S. Public*, pg. 179
BANK OF NEW ZEALAND—See National Australia Bank Limited; *Int'l*, pg. 906
THE BANK OF NORTH ARKANSAS—See First United Bancshares, Inc.; *U.S. Public*, pg. 641
BANK OF NORTH DAKOTA; *U.S. Private*, pg. 114
THE BANK OF NOVA SCOTIA; *Int'l*, pg. 155
THE BANK OF NOVA SCOTIA ASIA LIMITED—See The Bank of Nova Scotia; *Int'l*, pg. 156

THE BANK OF NOVA SCOTIA BERHAD—See The Bank of Nova Scotia; *Int'l*, pg. 156
THE BANK OF NOVA SCOTIA CHANNEL ISLANDS LIMITED—See The Bank of Nova Scotia; *Int'l*, pg. 156
THE BANK OF NOVA SCOTIA INTERNATIONAL LIMITED—See The Bank of Nova Scotia; *Int'l*, pg. 156
THE BANK OF NOVA SCOTIA JAMAICA LIMITED—See The Bank of Nova Scotia; *Int'l*, pg. 156
THE BANK OF NOVA SCOTIA PROPERTIES—See The Bank of Nova Scotia; *Int'l*, pg. 155
THE BANK OF NOVA SCOTIA TRINIDAD AND TOBAGO LIMITED—See The Bank of Nova Scotia; *Int'l*, pg. 157
THE BANK OF NOVA SCOTIA TRUST COMPANY (BAHAMAS) LIMITED—See The Bank of Nova Scotia; *Int'l*, pg. 156
THE BANK OF NOVA SCOTIA TRUST COMPANY (CAYMAN) LIMITED—See The Bank of Nova Scotia; *Int'l*, pg. 156
THE BANK OF NOVA SCOTIA TRUST COMPANY (CARIBBEAN) LIMITED—See The Bank of Nova Scotia; *Int'l*, pg. 157
THE BANK OF NOVA SCOTIA TRUST COMPANY CHANNEL ISLANDS LIMITED—See The Bank of Nova Scotia; *Int'l*, pg. 157
THE BANK OF NOVA SCOTIA TRUST COMPANY OF NEW YORK—See The Bank of Nova Scotia; *Int'l*, pg. 156
THE BANK OF NOVA SCOTIA TRUST COMPANY OF TRINIDAD AND TOBAGO LIMITED—See The Bank of Nova Scotia; *Int'l*, pg. 157
BANK OF OKLAHOMA, N.A.—See BOK Financial Corp.; *U.S. Public*, pg. 163
BANK OF PENNSYLVANIA—See Allied Irish Banks, p.l.c.; *Int'l*, pg. 64
BANK OF PENSACOLA—See Synovus Financial Corp.; *U.S. Public*, pg. 1549
BANK OF PONTIAC—See Pontiac Bancorp, Inc.; *U.S. Public*, pg. 1316
BANK OF PONTIAC-WEST—See Pontiac Bancorp, Inc.; *U.S. Public*, pg. 1316
BANK OF RALEIGH—See Horizon Bancorp, Inc.; *U.S. Public*, pg. 836
BANK OF SAN FRANCISCO—See The San Francisco Co.; *U.S. Public*, pg. 1430
BANK OF SAN FRANCISCO SECURITIES BROKERAGE—See The San Francisco Co.; *U.S. Public*, pg. 1430
BANK OF SMITHTOWN; *U.S. Private*, pg. 114
BANK OF SOUTHERN MARYLAND—See Mercantile Bankshares Corporation; *U.S. Public*, pg. 1088
BANK OF THE HUDSON—See Poughkeepsie Financial Corp.; *U.S. Public*, pg. 1319
BANK OF THE WEST—See Banque Nationale de Paris; *Int'l*, pg. 163
THE BANK OF TOKYO-MITSUBISHI (CANADA)—See The Bank of Tokyo-Mitsubishi, Ltd.; *int'l*, pg. 158
BANK OF TOKYO-MITSUBISHI (DEUTSCHLAND) AG—See The Bank of Tokyo-Mitsubishi, Ltd.; *Int'l*, pg. 158
THE BANK OF TOKYO-MITSUBISHI (HOLLAND) N.V.—See The Bank of Tokyo-Mitsubishi, Ltd.; *Int'l*, pg. 158
THE BANK OF TOKYO-MITSUBISHI, LTD.; *Int'l*, pg. 157
THE BANK OF TOKYO-MITSUBISHI, LTD.—See The Bank of Tokyo-Mitsubishi, Ltd.; *Int'l*, pg. 157
BANK OF TOKYO-MITSUBISHI, LTD.—See The Bank of Tokyo-Mitsubishi, Ltd.; *Int'l*, pg. 157
THE BANK OF TOKYO-MITSUBISHI, LTD. (HOUSTON AGENCY)—See The Bank of Tokyo-Mitsubishi, Ltd.; *int'l*, pg. 157
BANK OF TOKYO-MITSUBISHI LTD. (MIAMI AGENCY)—See The Bank of Tokyo-Mitsubishi, Ltd.; *Int'l*, pg. 157
BANK OF TOKYO-MITSUBISHI LTD., PARIS BRANCH—See The Bank of Tokyo-Mitsubishi, Ltd.; *Int'l*, pg. 158
BANK OF TOKYO-MITSUBISHI, LTD. (RIO DE JANIERO REPRESENTATIVE OFFICE)—See The Bank of Tokyo-Mitsubishi, Ltd.; *Int'l*, pg. 158
BANK OF TOKYO-MITSUBISHI LTD., ZURICH REPRESENTATIVE OFFICE—See The Bank of Tokyo-Mitsubishi, Ltd.; *Int'l*, pg. 158
THE BANK OF TOKYO-MITSUBISHI (LUXEMBOURG) S.A.—See The Bank of Tokyo-Mitsubishi, Ltd.; *Int'l*, pg. 158
THE BANK OF TOKYO-MITSUBISHI (PANAMA BRANCH)—See The Bank of Tokyo-Mitsubishi, Ltd.; *Int'l*, pg. 158
BANK OF TOKYO-MITSUBISHI TRUST COMPANY—See The Bank of Tokyo-Mitsubishi, Ltd.; *Int'l*, pg. 157
THE BANK OF TOKYO-MITSUBISHI (UK) LIMITED—See The Bank of Tokyo-Mitsubishi, Ltd.; *Int'l*, pg. 158
BANK OF TONGA—See Pacific Century Financial Corporation; *U.S. Public*, pg. 1248
BANK OF TUSCALOOSA—See Synovus Financial Corp.; *U.S. Public*, pg. 1549
BANK OF UNION—See First Charter Corporation; *U.S. Public*, pg. 627
BANK OF UTAH; *U.S. Private*, pg. 114
BANK OF WESTERN MASSACHUSETTES—See Chittenden Corporation; *U.S. Public*, pg. 351
BANK OF WESTERN SAMOA—See Australia & New Zealand Banking Group Limited; *Int'l*, pg. 100
BANK OF YOKOHAMA; *Int'l*, pg. 158
BANK OF YOKOHAMA SHANGHAI—See Bank of Yokohama; *Int'l*, pg. 159
BANK ONE, ARIZONA, NA—See Banc One Corporation; *U.S. Public*, pg. 173
BANK ONE, CHICAGO—See Banc One Corporation; *U.S. Public*, pg. 173
BANK ONE, CINCINNATI—See Banc One Corporation; *U.S. Public*, pg. 173
BANK ONE, COLORADO—See Banc One Corporation; *U.S. Public*, pg. 173
BANK ONE, INTERNATIONAL SERVICES CORPORATION—See Banc One Corporation; *U.S. Public*, pg. 173
BANK ONE, KENTUCKY, NA—See Banc One Corporation; *U.S. Public*, pg. 173

BANK ONE, LOUISIANA—See Banc One Corporation; *U.S. Public*, pg. 173
BANK ONE, MORTGAGE COMPANY—See Banc One Corporation; *U.S. Public*, pg. 174
BANK ONE, OHIO TRUST COMPANY, N.A.—See Banc One Corporation; *U.S. Public*, pg. 173
BANK ONE, ROCKFORD, NA—See Banc One Corporation; *U.S. Public*, pg. 173
BANK ONE, TEXAS CORP.—See Banc One Corporation; *U.S. Public*, pg. 173
BANK ONE VENTURE CORPORATION—See Banc One Corporation; *U.S. Public*, pg. 174
BANK ONE, WISCONSIN—See Banc One Corporation; *U.S. Public*, pg. 174
BANK ONE WISCONSIN BANKCARD CORPORATION—See Banc One Corporation; *U.S. Public*, pg. 174
BANK ONE WISCONSIN INVESTMENT SERVICES CORPORATION—See Banc One Corporation; *U.S. Public*, pg. 174
BANK ROHNER LTD.—See Union Bank of Switzerland; *Int'l*, pg. 1439
BANK ROZWOJU EKSPORTU SA—See Commerzbank AG; *Int'l*, pg. 312
P.T. BANK SAKURA SWADHARMA—See The Sakura Bank, Limited; *Int'l*, pg. 1180
BANK SBC WARBURG SODITIC AG—See Swiss Bank Corporation; *Int'l*, pg. 1331
P.T. BANK SUMITOMO NIAGA—See The Sumitomo Bank, Limited; *Int'l*, pg. 1310
P.T. BANK SUMITOMO NIAGA-SURABAYA BRANCH—See The Sumitomo Bank, Limited; *Int'l*, pg. 1309
BANK VON ERNST & CIE AG—See Bayerische Vereinsbank Group; *Int'l*, pg. 180
BANKA CREDITANSTALT D.D.—See Creditanstalt-Bankverein; *Int'l*, pg. 347
BANKAMERICA—See BankAmerica Corporation; *U.S. Public*, pg. 181
BANKAMERICA CAPITAL CORP.—See BankAmerica Corporation; *U.S. Public*, pg. 181
BANKAMERICA CAPITAL INVESTMENTS, INC.—See BankAmerica Corporation; *U.S. Public*, pg. 181
BANKAMERICA CORPORATION; *U.S. Public*, pg. 179
BANKAMERICA FINANCIAL SERVICES SYSTEM, INC.—See BankAmerica Corporation; *U.S. Public*, pg. 181
BANKAMERICA INSURANCE GROUP—See BankAmerica Corporation; *U.S. Public*, pg. 181
BANKAMERICA INTERNATIONAL—See BankAmerica Corporation; *U.S. Public*, pg. 181
BANKAMERICA REALTY SERVICES, INC.—See BankAmerica Corporation; *U.S. Public*, pg. 181
BANKAMERICA SUTTER MORTGAGE CORPORATION—See BankAmerica Corporation; *U.S. Public*, pg. 181
BANKAMERICA TRUST & BANKING CORP. (CAYMAN) LTD.—See BankAmerica Corporation; *U.S. Public*, pg. 183
BANKAMERICA TRUST CO. OF NEW YORK—See BankAmerica Corporation; *U.S. Public*, pg. 181
BANKATLANTIC BANCORP, INC.; *U.S. Public*, pg. 183
BANKBOSTON CORPORATION; *U.S. Public*, pg. 183
BANKENUNION AKTIENGESELLSCHAFT—See Frankfurter Sparkasse; *Int'l*, pg. 504
BANKER'S ACCEPTANCE CORPORATION, INC.—See National Auto Credit Inc.; *U.S. Public*, pg. 1153
BANKERS AMERICAN LIFE ASSURANCE COMPANY—See American Bankers Insurance Group, Inc.; *U.S. Public*, pg. 68
BANKERS BOX/RECORDS STORAGE SYSTEMS—See Fellowes Manufacturing Co.; *U.S. Private*, pg. 400
BANKERS FIDELITY LIFE INSURANCE COMPANY—See Atlantic American Corporation; *U.S. Public*, pg. 143
BANKERS FINANCIAL LIFE INSURANCE COMPANY—See AEGON N.V.; *Int'l*, pg. 27
BANKERS LEASING CORP.—See Citicorp; *U.S. Public*, pg. 377
BANKERS LIFE & CASUALTY COMPANY—See Conseco Inc.; *U.S. Public*, pg. 433
BANKERS LIFE HOLDING CORP.—See Conseco Inc.; *U.S. Public*, pg. 433
BANKERS LIFE INSURANCE CO. OF NEW YORK—See Indianapolis Life Insurance Co.; *U.S. Private*, pg. 560
BANKERS NATIONAL LIFE INSURANCE CO.—See Conseco Inc.; *U.S. Public*, pg. 433
BANKERS SECURITY LIFE INSURANCE SOCIETY—See ReliaStar Financial Corp.; *U.S. Public*, pg. 1375
BANKERS STANDARD FIRE & MARINE COMPANY—See Cigna Corp.; *U.S. Public*, pg. 365
BANKERS STANDARD INSURANCE COMPANY—See Cigna Corp.; *U.S. Public*, pg. 365
BANKERS SYSTEMS INCORPORATED; *U.S. Private*, pg. 114
BANKERS TRUST AG—See Bankers Trust New York Corporation; *U.S. Public*, pg. 185
BANKERS TRUST BANK OF CANADA—See Bankers Trust New York Corporation; *U.S. Public*, pg. 186
BANKERS TRUST COMPANY—See Bankers Trust New York Corporation; *U.S. Public*, pg. 185
BANKERS TRUST COMPANY OF CALIFORNIA, N.A.—See Bankers Trust New York Corporation; *U.S. Public*, pg. 185
BANKERS TRUST CO. OF FLORIDA, N.A.—See Bankers Trust New York Corporation; *U.S. Public*, pg. 185
BANKERS TRUST (DELAWARE)—See Bankers Trust New York Corporation; *U.S. Public*, pg. 185
BANKERS TRUST INTERNATIONAL (ASIA) LTD.—See Bankers Trust New York Corporation; *U.S. Public*, pg. 186
BANKERS TRUST NEW YORK CORPORATION; *U.S. Public*, pg. 185
BANKGESCHAFT HEINRICH ALTEN MBH—See Bayerische Vereinsbank Group; *Int'l*, pg. 179
BANKGESELLSCHAFT BERLIN; *Int'l*, pg. 159
BANKGESELLSCHAFT BERLIN INTERNATIONAL S.A.—See Bankgesellschaft Berlin; *Int'l*, pg. 159

BANKGESELLSCHAFT BERLIN INVESTMENT GMBH—See Bankgesellschaft Berlin; *Int'l*, pg. 159
BANKGESELLSCHAFT BERLIN (IRELAND) PLC—See Bankgesellschaft Berlin; *Int'l*, pg. 160
BANKGESELLSCHAFT BERLIN (UK) PLC—See Bankgesellschaft Berlin; *Int'l*, pg. 160
BANKHAUS BAUER AG—See Commerzbank AG; *Int'l*, pg. 309
BANKHAUS GEBRUDER BETHMANN—See Bayerische Vereinsbank Group; *Int'l*, pg. 179
BANKHAUS LOEBBECKE & CO.—See Cassa di Risparmio delle Provincie Lombarde SpA (CARIPLO); *Int'l*, pg. 275
BANKHAUS NEELMEYER AG—See Bayerische Vereinsbank Group; *Int'l*, pg. 179
BANKHAUS REUSCHEL & CO.—See Dresdner Bank AG; *Int'l*, pg. 418
BANKHAUS SCHLIEP & CO.—See Bayerische Vereinsbank Group; *Int'l*, pg. 179
BANKHEAD ENTERPRISES INC.; *U.S. Private*, pg. 114
BANKING COMPUTER SERVICES PRIVATE LIMITED—See HSBC Holdings plc; *Int'l*, pg. 581
BANKING SYSTEMS DIVISION—See Sterling Commerce, Inc.; *U.S. Public*, pg. 1516
BANKMANAGERS CORP.; *U.S. Private*, pg. 114
BANKMONT FINANCIAL CORP.—See Bank of Montreal; *Int'l*, pg. 154
BANKNORTH GROUP INC.; *U.S. Public*, pg. 186
BANKNORTH MORTGAGE COMPANY—See Banknorth Group Inc.; *U.S. Public*, pg. 187
BANKNOTE & SECURITIES DIVISION—See Stevens International, Inc.; *U.S. Public*, pg. 1517
BANKS-BALDWIN—See The Thomson Corporation; *U.S. Public*, pg. 1602
BANKS ENVIRONMENTAL SERVICE TECHNOLOGIES, INC.—See M.F. Bank & Company, Inc.; *U.S. Private*, pg. 114
BANKSTON FORD OF FRISCO, LTD. CO.—See Republic Industries, Inc.; *U.S. Public*, pg. 1379
BANKSTON NISSAN IN IRVING, INC.—See Republic Industries, Inc.; *U.S. Public*, pg. 1379
W.O. BANKSTON ENTERPRISES INC.—See Republic Industries, Inc.; *U.S. Public*, pg. 1379
W.O. BANKSTON LINCOLN MERCURY—See Republic Industries, Inc.; *U.S. Public*, pg. 1379
W.O. BANKSTON NISSAN INC.—See Republic Industries, Inc.; *U.S. Public*, pg. 1379
BANKSYS—See Bank Brussels Lambert; *Int'l*, pg. 147
BANKVISION SOFTWARE, LTD.—See Jack Henry & Associates, Inc.; *U.S. Public*, pg. 809
BANNER AEROSPACE, INC.; *U.S. Public*, pg. 187
BANNER AIRCRAFT INTERNATIONAL, INC.—See Banner Aerospace, Inc.; *U.S. Public*, pg. 187
BANNER ASSOCIATES INC.; *U.S. Private*, pg. 114
BANNER ENGINEERING CORP.; *U.S. Private*, pg. 114
BANNER LIFE INSURANCE CO.—See Legal & General Group PLC; *Int'l*, pg. 805
BANNER PHARMACAPS INC.—See Sobel NV; *Int'l*, pg. 1272
BANNER WHOLESALE GROCERS, INC.; *U.S. Private*, pg. 114
BANNINGER FRANCE—See Delta plc; *Int'l*, pg. 391
BANNINGER G.M.B.H—See Delta plc; *Int'l*, pg. 391
BANNINGER ITALIA SRL—See Delta plc; *Int'l*, pg. 391
BANPONCE CORPORATION—See Banco Popular de Puerto Rico; *U.S. Public*, pg. 176
BANPONCE FINANCIAL CORP.—See Banco Popular de Puerto Rico; *U.S. Public*, pg. 176
BANQUE ARJIL—See Lagardere Group; *Int'l*, pg. 792
BANQUE ATLANTIQUE COTE D'IVOIRE (BACI)—See Generale de Banque S.A.; *Int'l*, pg. 547
BANQUE BELGE (GUERNSEY) LTD—See Generale de Banque S.A.; *Int'l*, pg. 547
BANQUE BELGE GUERNSEY LUXEMBOURG SA—See Generale de Banque S.A.; *Int'l*, pg. 547
BANQUE BELGE TRUST COMPANY LTD.—See Generale de Banque S.A.; *Int'l*, pg. 547
BANQUE BELGOLAISE—See Generale de Banque S.A.; *Int'l*, pg. 546
BANQUE BONNASSE—See Groupe GAN; *Int'l*, pg. 563
BANQUE DE BOSTON S.A.—See BankBoston Corporation; *U.S. Public*, pg. 185
BANQUE BRUXELLES LAMBERT FRANCE—See Bank Brussels Lambert; *Int'l*, pg. 148
BANQUE BRUXELLES LAMBERT FRANCE SUCCURSALE DE LILLE—See Bank Brussels Lambert; *Int'l*, pg. 148
BANQUE BRUXELLES LAMBERT (JERSEY) LTD.—See Bank Brussels Lambert; *Int'l*, pg. 148
BANQUE BRUXELLES LAMBERT (SUISSE)—See Bank Brussels Lambert; *Int'l*, pg. 148
BANQUE BRUXELLES LAMBERT (SUISSE)-BASEL—See Bank Brussels Lambert; *Int'l*, pg. 148
BANQUE BRUXELLES LAMBERT (SUISSE)-LAUSANNE—See Bank Brussels Lambert; *Int'l*, pg. 148
BANQUE BRUXELLES LAMBERT (SUISSE)-LUGANO—See Bank Brussels Lambert; *Int'l*, pg. 148
BANQUE BRUXELLES LAMBERT TRUST COMPANY LTD.—See Bank Brussels Lambert; *Int'l*, pg. 148
BANQUE CANTONALE VAUDOISE; *Int'l*, pg. 160
BANQUE CANTRADE LAUSANNE S.A.—See Union Bank of Switzerland; *Int'l*, pg. 1439
BANQUE CANTRADE, ORMOND BURRUS SA—See Union Bank of Switzerland; *Int'l*, pg. 1439
BANQUE COGEBA-GONET LUXEMBOURG SA—See Generale de Banque S.A.; *Int'l*, pg. 547
BANQUE COMMERCIALE DU BURUNDI SARL—See Bank Brussels Lambert; *Int'l*, pg. 148
BANQUE COMMERCIALE DU RWANDA S.A.—See Bank Brussels Lambert; *Int'l*, pg. 148
BANQUE COMMERCIALE ZAIROISE—See Generale de Banque S.A.; *Int'l*, pg. 547
BANQUE CONTINENTALE DU LUXEMBOURG—See Compagnie Financiere de Paribas; *Int'l*, pg. 319

BANQUE COVEFI S.A.—See Otto Versand (GmbH & Co.); Int'l, pg. 1015
BANQUE DE CREDIT DE BUJUMBURA—See Generale de Banque S.A.; Int'l, pg. 547
BANQUE DE FRANCE; Int'l, pg. 160
BANQUE DE KIGALI—See Generale de Banque S.A.; pg. 548
BANQUE DE LA POSTE—See Generale de Banque S.A.; Int'l, pg. 547
BANQUE DE L'AQUITAINE—See Generale de Banque S.A.; Int'l, pg. 548
BANQUE DE LUXEMBOURG—See Deutsche Bank AG; Int'l, pg. 406
BANQUE DE NEUFLIZE, SCHLUMBERGER, MALLET—See ABN-AMRO Holding N.V.; Int'l, pg. 12
BANQUE DE NOUVELLE CALEDONIE—See Pacific Century Financial Corporation; U.S. Public, pg. 1248
BANQUE DE TAHITI—See Pacific Century Financial Corporation; U.S. Public, pg. 1248
BANQUE D'HAWAII (VANUATU) LIMITED—See Pacific Century Financial Corporation; U.S. Public, pg. 1248
BANQUE DIAMANTAIRE ANVERSOISE (SUISSE) SA—See Generale de Banque S.A.; Int'l, pg. 548
BANQUE D'ORSAY—See Westdeutsche Landesbank Girozentrale; Int'l, pg. 1493
BANQUE DU CAIRE BARCLAYS INTL. BANK SAE—See Barclays Bank PLC; Int'l, pg. 165
BANQUE DU CREDIT AGRICOLE (SUISSE) S.A.—See Credit Agricole; Int'l, pg. 341
BANQUE DUMENIL-LEBLE—See CERUS - Compagnies Europeennes Reunies; Int'l, pg. 240
BANQUE DUPUY DE PARCEVAL—See Generale de Banque S.A.; Int'l, pg. 548
BANQUE EUROPEENNE POUR L'AMERIQUE LATINE (BEAL)—See Westdeutsche Landesbank Girozentrale; Int'l, pg. 1493
BANQUE FERRIER LULLIN (LUXEMBOURG) SA—See Ferrier Lullin & Cie SA; Int'l, pg. 480
BANQUE FRANCAISE COMMERCIALE—See Compagnie de Suez; Int'l, pg. 313
BANQUE FRANCAISE DE L'ORIENT—See Compagnie de Suez; Int'l, pg. 314
BANQUE FRANCAISE DU COMMERCE EXTERIEUR; Int'l, pg. 160
BANQUE FRANCO PORTUGAISE, SA—See Caixa Geral de Depositos; Int'l, pg. 251
BANQUE GENERALE DE LUXEMBOURG—See Generale de Banque S.A.; Int'l, pg. 548
BANQUE GENERALE DU COMMERCE S.A.—See Banca di Roma; Int'l, pg. 136
BANQUE GENERALE DU LUXEMBOURG SA; Int'l, pg. 161
BANQUE GENERALE DU LUXEMBOURG SA—See Banque Generale du Luxembourg SA; Int'l, pg. 162
BANQUE GENERALE DU LUXEMBOURG SA—See Banque Generale du Luxembourg SA; Int'l, pg. 162
BANQUE GENERALE DU LUXEMBOURG SA—See Generale de Banque S.A.; Int'l, pg. 548
BANQUE GENERALE DU LUXEMBOURG (SUISSE) SA—See Banque Generale du Luxembourg SA; Int'l, pg. 162
BANQUE HIEAUX—See Generale de Banque S.A.; Int'l, pg. 548
BANQUE HYDRO-ENERGIE—See Lyonnaise des Eaux S.A.; Int'l, pg. 822
BANQUE IBJ (FRANCE) S.A.—See The Industrial Bank of Japan, Limited; Int'l, pg. 676
BANQUE INDOSUEZ—See Compagnie de Suez; Int'l, pg. 313
BANQUE INDOSUEZ ESPANA S.A.—See Compagnie de Suez; Int'l, pg. 315
BANQUE INDOSUEZ GENERALE EURO TURK AS—See Generale de Banque S.A.; Int'l, pg. 548
BANQUE INTERNATIONAL A LUXEMBOURG—See Credit Communal De Belgique SA; Int'l, pg. 343
BANQUE INTERNATIONALE A LUXEMBOURG BIL (ASIA) LTD.—See Banque Internationale a Luxembourg S.A.; Int'l, pg. 162
BANQUE INTERNATIONALE A LUXEMBOURG BIL (SUISSE) S.A.—See Banque Internationale a Luxembourg S.A.; Int'l, pg. 162
BANQUE INTERNATIONALE A LUXEMBOURG S.A.; Int'l, pg. 162
BANQUE INTERNATIONALE A LUXEMBOURG S.A., LONDON BRANCH—See Banque Internationale a Luxembourg S.A.; Int'l, pg. 162
BANQUE INTERNATIONALE A LUXEMBOURG S.A.-REPRASENTANT FUR DIE—See Banque Internationale a Luxembourg S.A.; Int'l, pg. 162
BANQUE INTERNATIONALE A LUXEMBOURG S.A.-TOKYO REPRESENTATIVE OFFICE—See Banque Internationale a Luxembourg S.A.; Int'l, pg. 162
BANQUE INTERNATIONALE DE CREDIT ET DE GESTION MONACO—See Bayerische Vereinsbank Group; Int'l, pg. 180
BANQUE INTERNATIONALE DE PLACEMENT S.A.—See Dresdner Bank AG; Int'l, pg. 419
BANQUE INTERNATIONALE DU BURKINA (BIB)—See Generale de Banque S.A.; Int'l, pg. 548
BANQUE INTERNATIONALE POUR L'AFRIQUE EN GUINEE (BIAG)—See Generale de Banque S.A.; Int'l, pg. 548
BANQUE INTERNATIONALE POUR LE COMMERCE ET L'INDUSTRIE DE LA COTE D'IVOIRE (BICICI)—See Bank Brussels Lambert; Int'l, pg. 148
BANQUE INTERNATIONALE POUR LE COMMERCE ET L'INDUSTRIE DE LA GUINEE (BICI-GUI)—See Bank Brussels Lambert; Int'l, pg. 149
BANQUE INTERNATIONALE POUR LE COMMERCE ET L'INDUSTRIE DU GABON (BICIG)—See Bank Brussels Lambert; Int'l, pg. 148
BANQUE INTERNATIONALE POUR LE COMMERCE ET L'INDUSTRIE DU SENEGAL (BICIS)—See Bank Brussels Lambert; Int'l, pg. 149

BANQUE INTERNATIONALE POUR LE COMMERCE, L'INDUSTRIE ET L'AGRICULTURE DU BURKINA (BICIAB)—See Bank Brussels Lambert; Int'l, pg. 148
BANQUE IPPA—See Groupe Bruxelles Lambert S.A.; Int'l, pg. 562
BANQUE IPPA & ASSOCIATES—See Groupe Bruxelles Lambert S.A.; Int'l, pg. 562
BANQUE KLEINWORT BENSON SA—See Dresdner Bank AG; Int'l, pg. 420
BANQUE LAVORO S.A.—See Banca Nazionale del Lavoro SjA.; Int'l, pg. 137
BANQUE LEUMI FRANCE S.A.—See Bank Leumi le-Israel B.M.; Int'l, pg. 150
BANQUE LEUMI FRANCE S.A.-STRASBOURG—See Bank Leumi le-Israel B.M.; Int'l, pg. 150
BANQUE MALGACHE DE L'OCEAN INDIEN S.A. (BMOI)—See Bank Brussels Lambert; Int'l, pg. 149
BANQUE MONDIALE—See The World Bank; U.S. Private, pg. 1189
BANQUE MORGAN GRENFELL EN SUISSE S. A. (SWITZERLAND)—See Deutsche Bank AG; Int'l, pg. 406
BANQUE NAGELMACKERS SA—See CoreStates Financial Corp.; U.S. Public, pg. 447
BANQUE NATIONALE DE BELGIQUE; Int'l, pg. 162
BANQUE NATIONALE DE GRECE—See National Bank of Greece S.A.; Int'l, pg. 907
BANQUE NATIONALE DE PARIS; Int'l, pg. 163
BANQUE NATIONALE DE PARIS (CANADA)—See Banque Nationale de Paris; Int'l, pg. 164
BANQUE NATIONALE DE PARIS-GUYANE—See Banque Nationale de Paris; Int'l, pg. 164
BANQUE NATIONALE DE PARIS (PANAMA) SA—See Banque Nationale de Paris; Int'l, pg. 164
BANQUE NATIONALE DE PARIS (SUISSE) S.A.—See Banque Nationale de Paris; Int'l, pg. 164
BANQUE NOMURA FRANCE—See The Nomura Securities Co., Ltd.; Int'l, pg. 956
BANQUE PARIBAS-CHICAGO—See Compagnie Financiere de Paribas; Int'l, pg. 319
BANQUE PARIBAS-DALLAS—See Compagnie Financiere de Paribas; Int'l, pg. 319
BANQUE PARIBAS-HOUSTON—See Compagnie Financiere de Paribas; Int'l, pg. 319
BANQUE PARIBAS-LOS ANGELES—See Compagnie Financiere de Paribas; Int'l, pg. 319
BANQUE PARIBAS PORTUGAL—See Compagnie Financiere de Paribas; Int'l, pg. 320
BANQUE PARIBAS-SAN FRANCISCO—See Compagnie Financiere de Paribas; Int'l, pg. 319
BANQUE PARISIENNE DE CREDIT—See Generale de Banque S.A.; Int'l, pg. 548
BANQUE PIGUET & CIE S.A.—See Banque Cantonale Vaudoise; Int'l, pg. 160
BANQUE POUR L'EUROPE S.A.-EUROPA BANK AG—See Dresdner Bank AG; Int'l, pg. 419
BANQUE POUR L'INDUSTRIE FRANCAISE—See Groupe GAN; Int'l, pg. 563
BANQUE PSA FINANCE HOLDING—See PSA Peugeot Citroen; Int'l, pg. 1021
BANQUE REGIONALE—See Groupe GAN; Int'l, pg. 563
BANQUE REGIONALE DE L'AIN—See Groupe GAN; Int'l, pg. 563
BANQUE REGIONALE DU NORD—See Generale de Banque S.A.; Int'l, pg. 548
BANQUE RIVAUD—See Northern Trust Corporation; U.S. Public, pg. 1197
BANQUE SAINT DOMINIQUE—See Credit Nationale; Int'l, pg. 344
BANQUE SCALBERT DUPONT—See Groupe GAN; Int'l, pg. 563
BANQUE TONGOLAISE POUR LE COMMERCE ET L'INDUSTRIE (BTCI)—See Bank Brussels Lambert; Int'l, pg. 149
BANQUE TRANSATLANTIQUE—See Groupe GAN; Int'l, pg. 563
BANQUE VERNES ET COMMERCIALE DE PARIS—See Compagnie de Suez; Int'l, pg. 313
BANQUE VEUVE MORIN-PONS—See Dresdner Bank AG; Int'l, pg. 419
BANRENTA COMPANIA DE SEGUROS DE VIDA S.A.—See The Principal Financial Group; U.S. Private, pg. 886
BANSAFINA—See Banco Santander; Int'l, pg. 143
BANSALEASING—See Banco Santander; Int'l, pg. 143
BANTA BOOK GROUP—See Banta Corporation; U.S. Public, pg. 188
BANTA BOOK GROUP-HARRISONBURG—See Banta Corporation; U.S. Public, pg. 188
BANTA CATALOG GROUP—See Banta Corporation; U.S. Public, pg. 188
BANTA CORPORATION; U.S. Public, pg. 187
BANTA DIGITAL GROUP—See Banta Corporation; U.S. Public, pg. 188
BANTA DIRECT MARKETING GROUP—See Banta Corporation; U.S. Public, pg. 188
BANTA GLOBAL TURNKEY—See Banta Corporation; U.S. Public, pg. 188
BANTA HEALTHCARE PRODUCTS—See Banta Corporation; U.S. Public, pg. 188
BANTA INFORMATION SERVICES GROUP—See Banta Corporation; U.S. Public, pg. 188
BANTA INTEGRATED MEDIA—See Banta Corporation; U.S. Public, pg. 188
BANTA MERCHANDISING PRODUCTS—See Banta Corporation; U.S. Public, pg. 188
BANTA PACKAGING & FULFILLMENT—See Banta Corporation; U.S. Public, pg. 188
BANTA PUBLICATIONS GROUP—See Banta Corporation; U.S. Public, pg. 188
BANTAM BOOK CANADA INC.—See Bertelsmann AG; Int'l, pg. 191
BANTAM BOOKS LTD.—See Bertelsmann AG; Int'l, pg. 191

BANTAM DOUBLEDAY DELL PUBLISHING GROUP, INC.—See Bertelsmann AG; Int'l, pg. 191
BANTAM PAPERBACKS UK—See Bertelsmann AG; Int'l, pg. 191
BANTAM PRESS UK—See Bertelsmann AG; Int'l, pg. 191
BANTREL INC.—See BFC Construction Corporation; Int'l, pg. 189
BANYAN SYSTEMS INC.; U.S. Public, pg. 189
BANYU PHARMACEUTICAL CO. LTD.—See Merck & Co., Inc.; U.S. Public, pg. 1091
P.T. BAPINDO LOKA SENTRA LEASING—See The Tokai Bank, Limited; Int'l, pg. 1391
BAR-S FOODS CO.; U.S. Private, pg. 114
BARABOO-SYSCO FOOD SERVICES, INC.—See Sysco Corporation; U.S. Public, pg. 1550
BARANCORP; U.S. Private, pg. 115
BARANSKI & ASSOCIATES—See Barancorp; U.S. Private, pg. 115
D.A. BARANSKI & CO.—See Barancorp; U.S. Private, pg. 115
JOSEPH A. BARANSKI LITERARY AGENCY—See Barancorp; U.S. Private, pg. 115
BARANSKI PUBLISHING COMPANY—See Barancorp; U.S. Private, pg. 115
BARBADOS DAIRY INDUSTRIES LTD.—See New Zealand Dairy Board; Int'l, pg. 923
THE BARBADOS LIGHT & POWER CO. LTD.—See Leucadia National Corporation; U.S. Public, pg. 990
BARBARY COAST STEEL CO.—See Birmingham Steel Corporation; U.S. Public, pg. 232
BARBEQUE KING—See Standex International Corporation; U.S. Public, pg. 1507
BARBER & COLMAN LTD.—See Siebe plc; Int'l, pg. 1243
BARBER BROTHERS CONTRACTING COMPANY; U.S. Private, pg. 115
BARBER-COLMAN COMPANY—See Siebe plc; Int'l, pg. 1242
BARBER-COLMAN INDEV—See Siebe plc; Int'l, pg. 1242
BARBER DAIRIES, INC.; U.S. Private, pg. 115
EDWARD BARBER & CO.—See Tyco International Ltd.; U.S. Public, pg. 1651
BARBER ICE CREAM COMPANY—See Barber Dairies, Inc.; U.S. Private, pg. 115
BARBER INDUSTRIES INC.; Int'l, pg. 164
BARBER INDUSTRIES, INC.—See Barber Industries Inc.; Int'l, pg. 164
BARBER INDUSTRIES LTD.-SERVICE CENTER—See Barber Industries Inc.; Int'l, pg. 164
BARBER PURE MILK CO.—See Barber Dairies, Inc.; U.S. Private, pg. 115
BARBERO 1891 SPA; Int'l, pg. 164
BARBERO S.P.A.—See Allied Domecq PLC; Int'l, pg. 64
THE BARBERS, HAIRSTYLING FOR MEN & WOMEN, INC.; U.S. Private, pg. 115
BARBOT ENTERPRISE—See Groupe Usinor; Int'l, pg. 571
BARBOUR THREAD—See Hicking Pentecost Plc; Int'l, pg. 618
BARBOUR THREAD INC.—See Hicking Pentecost Plc; Int'l, pg. 618
BARBOUR THREAD, INC.—See Hicking Pentecost Plc; Int'l, pg. 618
BARBOUR THREADS, INC.—See Hicking Pentecost Plc; Int'l, pg. 618
BARCALOUNGER COMPANY—See Consolidated Furniture Corporation; U.S. Private, pg. 265
BARCELONA TERMINAL—See GATX Corporation; U.S. Public, pg. 692
BARCLAY & SONS—See Reliable Stores, Inc.; U.S. Private, pg. 921
BARCLAY FURNITURE COMPANY—See Ladd Furniture, Inc.; U.S. Public, pg. 974
JACK BARCLAY LTD.—See Lonrho plc; Int'l, pg. 817
BARCLAY TRAVEL AGENCY—See Day & Zimmermann, Inc.; U.S. Private, pg. 317
BARCLAY WHITE INCORPORATED; U.S. Private, pg. 115
BARCLAYS AMERICAN/MORTGAGE CORP.—See Barclays Bank PLC; Int'l, pg. 165
BARCLAYS BANK COMMERCIAL GROUP—See Barclays Bank PLC; Int'l, pg. 165
BARCLAYS BANK FINANCE CO. (GUERNSEY) LTD.—See Barclays Bank PLC; Int'l, pg. 165
BARCLAYS BANK FINANCE CO. (JERSEY) LTD.—See Barclays Bank PLC; Int'l, pg. 165
BARCLAYS BANK OF BOTSWANA LIMITED—See Barclays Bank PLC; Int'l, pg. 165
BARCLAYS BANK OF CANADA—See Barclays Bank PLC; Int'l, pg. 165
BARCLAYS BANK OF GHANA LTD.—See Barclays Bank PLC; Int'l, pg. 165
BARCLAYS BANK OF KENYA LTD.—See Barclays Bank PLC; Int'l, pg. 165
BARCLAYS BANK OF SIERRA LEONE LTD.—See Barclays Bank PLC; Int'l, pg. 165
BARCLAYS BANK OF SWAZILAND LTD.—See Barclays Bank PLC; Int'l, pg. 165
BARCLAYS BANK OF UGANDA LTD.—See Barclays Bank PLC; Int'l, pg. 165
BARCLAYS BANK OF ZAMBIA LTD.—See Barclays Bank PLC; Int'l, pg. 165
BARCLAYS BANK OF ZIMBABWE LTD.—See Barclays Bank PLC; Int'l, pg. 165
BARCLAYS BANK PLC; Int'l, pg. 164
BARCLAYS BANK PLC—See Barclays Bank PLC; Int'l, pg. 165
BARCLAYS BANK PLC, CARIBBEAN—See Barclays Bank PLC; Int'l, pg. 165
BARCLAYS BANK PLC, USA—See Barclays Bank PLC; Int'l, pg. 165
BARCLAYS BANK SA—See Barclays Bank PLC; Int'l, pg. 166
BARCLAYS BANK SA-MADRID—See Barclays Bank PLC; Int'l, pg. 166
BARCLAYS BANK SZARL—See Barclays Bank PLC; Int'l, pg. 166

BARCLAYS BANK TRUST CO. LTD.—See Barclays Bank PLC; *Int'l*, pg. 164
BARCLAYS DISCOUNT BANK LTD.—See Barclays Bank PLC; *Int'l*, pg. 166
BARCLAYS EUROPEAN INVESTMENT HOLDINGS SA—See Barclays Bank PLC; *Int'l*, pg. 164
BARCLAYS FINANCIAL SERVICES CO. LTD.—See Barclays Bank PLC; *Int'l*, pg. 164
BARCLAYS INSURANCE BROKERS INTERNATIONAL LTD.—See Barclays Bank PLC; *Int'l*, pg. 164
BARCLAYS INSURANCE SERVICES CO. LTD.—See Barclays Bank PLC; *Int'l*, pg. 165
BARCLAYS LIFE ASSURANCE CO. LTD.—See Barclays Bank PLC; *Int'l*, pg. 165
BARCLAYS MERCANTILE BUSINESS FINANCE LIMITED—See Barclays Bank PLC; *Int'l*, pg. 165
BARCLAYS PROPERTY HOLDINGS—See Barclays Bank PLC; *Int'l*, pg. 165
BARCLAYS STOCKBROKERS LTD.—See Barclays Bank PLC; *Int'l*, pg. 165
BARCLAYS TRUST & BANKING COMPANY (JAPAN) LTD.—See Barclays Bank PLC; *Int'l*, pg. 166
BARCLAYS UNICORN LTD.—See Barclays Bank PLC; *Int'l*, pg. 165
BARCLAYTRUST INVESTMENT SERVICES LTD.—See Barclays Bank PLC; *Int'l*, pg. 166
BARCO OF CALIFORNIA; *U.S. Private*, pg. 115
BARCREST LTD.—See Bass PLC; *Int'l*, pg. 170
BARCROFT CO.—See Rhone-Poulenc S.A.; *Int'l*, pg. 1110
BARD ACCESS SYSTEMS—See C.R. Bard, Inc.; *U.S. Public*, pg. 189
C.R. BARD, INC.; *U.S. Public*, pg. 189
BARD DIAGNOSTIC SCIENCES—See C.R. Bard, Inc.; *U.S. Public*, pg. 189
BARD INTERVENTIONAL PRODUCTS—See C.R. Bard, Inc.; *U.S. Public*, pg. 189
BARD MFG. CO.; *U.S. Private*, pg. 116
BARD RADIOLOGY DIV.—See C.R. Bard, Inc.; *U.S. Public*, pg. 189
BARDEN & ROBESON CORPORATION; *U.S. Private*, pg. 116
THE BARDEN CORPORATION—See FAG Group; *Int'l*, pg. 468
BARDEN CORPORATION GMBH—See FAG Group; *Int'l*, pg. 468
THE BARDEN CORP., (U.K.) LTD.—See FAG Group; *Int'l*, pg. 468
BARDEN PRECISION BEARINGS—See FAG Group; *Int'l*, pg. 468
BARDEN SARL—See FAG Group; *Int'l*, pg. 468
BARDES CORP.—See Ilsco; *U.S. Private*, pg. 558
BARDON (ENGLAND) LTD.—See Bardon Group PLC; *Int'l*, pg. 166
BARDON GROUP PLC; *Int'l*, pg. 166
BARDON USA INC.—See Bardon Group PLC; *Int'l*, pg. 166
BARDONS & OLIVER, INC.; *U.S. Private*, pg. 116
BARED JEWELERS—See BAA plc; *Int'l*, pg. 103
BARENBRUG (BELGIUM) MAES NV/SA—See Barenbrug Holland BV; *Int'l*, pg. 167
BARENBRUG FRANCE SA—See Barenbrug Holland BV; *Int'l*, pg. 167
BARENBRUG HOLLAND BV; *Int'l*, pg. 166
BARENBRUG LUXEMBOURG SA—See Barenbrug Holland BV; *Int'l*, pg. 167
BARENBRUG NORTHEAST—See Barenbrug Holland BV; *Int'l*, pg. 167
BARENBRUG POLSKA SP. Z.O.O.—See Barenbrug Holland BV; *Int'l*, pg. 167
BARENBRUG RESEARCH USA—See Barenbrug Holland BV; *Int'l*, pg. 166
BARENBRUG RESEARCH WOLFHEZE—See Barenbrug Holland BV; *Int'l*, pg. 166
BARENBRUG SOUTHEAST—See Barenbrug Holland BV; *Int'l*, pg. 167
BARENBRUG TOURNEUR RECHERCHES SA—See Barenbrug Holland BV; *Int'l*, pg. 167
BARENBRUG U.K. LTD.—See Barenbrug Holland BV; *Int'l*, pg. 167
BARENBRUG USA—See Barenbrug Holland BV; *Int'l*, pg. 166
BARETT S.A.—See Rohto Pharmaceutical Co.; *Int'l*, pg. 1126
BARGAIN SUPPLY COMPANY; *U.S. Private*, pg. 116
BARGER BUILDERS; *U.S. Private*, pg. 116
BARING ASSET MANAGEMENT—See ING Groep N.V.; *Int'l*, pg. 648
BARING ASSET MANAGEMENT (AUSTRALIA) LTD.—See ING Groep N.V.; *Int'l*, pg. 648
BARING ASSET MANAGEMENT (BAHRAIN) LTD.—See ING Groep N.V.; *Int'l*, pg. 648
BARING ASSET MANAGEMENT (FRANCE)—See ING Groep N.V.; *Int'l*, pg. 648
BARING ASSET MANAGEMENT HOLDINGS, INC.—See ING Groep N.V.; *Int'l*, pg. 647
BARING ASSET MANAGEMENT INC.—See ING Groep N.V.; *Int'l*, pg. 647
BARING ASSET MANAGEMENT (INDIA)—See ING Groep N.V.; *Int'l*, pg. 648
BARING BROTHERS—See ING Groep N.V.; *Int'l*, pg. 648
BARING BROTHERS BURROWS & CO. LTD.—See ING Groep N.V.; *Int'l*, pg. 648
BARING BROTHERS (DEUTSCHLAND)—See ING Groep N.V.; *Int'l*, pg. 648
BARING BROTHERS INTERNATIONAL—See ING Groep N.V.; *Int'l*, pg. 648
BARING CAPITAL GMBH—See ING Groep N.V.; *Int'l*, pg. 648
BARING CAPITAL INVESTORS SARL—See ING Groep N.V.; *Int'l*, pg. 648
BARING HELLENIC VENTURES S.A.—See ING Groep N.V.; *Int'l*, pg. 648
BARING, HOUSTON & SAUNDERS—See ING Groep N.V.; *Int'l*, pg. 648

BARING HOUSTON & SAUNDERS INC.—See ING Groep N.V.; *Int'l*, pg. 647
BARING INTERNATIONAL INVESTMENT (CANADA)—See ING Groep N.V.; *Int'l*, pg. 648
BARING (ISLE OF MAN)—See ING Groep N.V.; *Int'l*, pg. 648
BARING PRIVATE EQUITY PARTNERS—See ING Groep N.V.; *Int'l*, pg. 647
BARING SECURITIES INTERNATIONAL—See ING Groep N.V.; *Int'l*, pg. 648
BARING TRUSTEE (GUERNSEY) LTD.—See ING Groep N.V.; *Int'l*, pg. 648
BARING VENTURE PARTNERS—See ING Groep N.V.; *Int'l*, pg. 648
BARING VENTURE PARTNERS LIMITED—See ING Groep N.V.; *Int'l*, pg. 647
BARINGS (FRANCE)—See ING Groep N.V.; *Int'l*, pg. 648
BARIS SHOE COMPANY, INC.; *U.S. Private*, pg. 116
BARIVEN, S.A.—See Petroleos de Venezuela S.A.; *Int'l*, pg. 1045
BARKERS LANDING 365
BARKLEY & EVERGREEN ADVERTISING, INC.; *U.S. Private*, pg. 116
BARKLEY EVERGREEN & PARTNERS PUBLIC RELATIONS—See Barkley & Evergreen Advertising, Inc.; *U.S. Private*, pg. 116
BARKO HYDRAULICS—See Pettibone Corporation; *U.S. Private*, pg. 859
BARKSDALE, INC.—See Crane Co.; *U.S. Public*, pg. 457
BARLETTA MATERIALS & CONSTRUCTION; *U.S. Private*, pg. 116
BARLEY EXPORTS LIMITED—See Avonmore Waterford Group plc; *Int'l*, pg. 102
BARLOW & EATON—See Reliable Stores, Inc.; *U.S. Private*, pg. 921
BARLOW HANDLING (PTY) LTD.—See Barlow Ltd.; *Int'l*, pg. 167
BARLOW INFORMATION SYSTEMS (PTY) LTD.—See Barlow Ltd.; *Int'l*, pg. 167
BARLOW INTERNATIONAL INVESTMENTS PLC—See Barlow Ltd.; *Int'l*, pg. 167
BARLOW LTD.; *Int'l*, pg. 167
BARLOW MOTOR INVESTMENTS LTD.—See Barlow Ltd.; *Int'l*, pg. 167
BARLOW TRACTOR INTERNATIONAL—See Barlow Ltd.; *Int'l*, pg. 167
BARLOWS EQUIPMENT CO.—See Barlow Ltd.; *Int'l*, pg. 167
BARLOWS EQUIPMENT MANUFACTURING CO. SA—See Barlow Ltd.; *Int'l*, pg. 167
BARMAG FAR EAST LTD.—See Akzo Nobel N.V.; *Int'l*, pg. 45
BARMAG MASCHINENFABRIK AG—See Akzo Nobel N.V.; *Int'l*, pg. 46
BARNARDSVILLE TELEPHONE CO.—See Telephone and Data Systems, Inc.; *U.S. Public*, pg. 1571
BARNASUD, S.A.—See Caixa d'Estalvis de Catalunya; *Int'l*, pg. 250
BARNES & NOBLE DIRECT—See Barnes & Noble Inc.; *U.S. Public*, pg. 189
BARNES & NOBLE INC.; *U.S. Public*, pg. 189
BARNES & REINECKE, INC.—See Allied Research Corporation; *U.S. Public*, pg. 49
BARNES ENGINEERING—See EDO Corporation; *U.S. Public*, pg. 542
BARNES GROUP AEROSPACE COMPONENTS—See Barnes Group Inc.; *U.S. Public*, pg. 190
BARNES GROUP INC.; *U.S. Public*, pg. 189
BARNES PUMPS, INC.—See Crane Co.; *U.S. Public*, pg. 457
BARNETT ANNUITIES CORP.—See NationsBank Corporation; *U.S. Public*, pg. 1162
BARNETT BANK N.A.—See NationsBank Corporation; *U.S. Public*, pg. 1162
BARNETT BANK OF SOUTHEAST GEORGIA, N.A.—See NationsBank Corporation; *U.S. Public*, pg. 1162
BARNETT BANK OF SOUTHWEST GEORGIA—See NationsBank Corporation; *U.S. Public*, pg. 1162
BARNETT BANKS, INC.—See NationsBank Corporation; *U.S. Public*, pg. 1162
BARNETT BANKS SERVICES INSURANCE, INC.—See NationsBank Corporation; *U.S. Public*, pg. 1162
BARNETT CAPITAL ADVISORS INC.—See NationsBank Corporation; *U.S. Public*, pg. 1162
BARNETT INC.—See Waxman Industries, Inc.; *U.S. Public*, pg. 1749
BARNETT INTERNATIONAL/PAREXEL—See PAREXEL International Corporation; *U.S. Public*, pg. 1258
BARNETT INVESTMENTS INC.—See NationsBank Corporation; *U.S. Public*, pg. 1162
BARNETT MERCHANT SERVICES CORP.—See NationsBank Corporation; *U.S. Public*, pg. 1162
BARNETT MILLWORKS, INC.; *U.S. Private*, pg. 116
BARNETT MORTGAGE COMPANY—See NationsBank Corporation; *U.S. Public*, pg. 1162
BARNETT RECOVERY CORPORATION—See NationsBank Corporation; *U.S. Public*, pg. 1162
BARNETT TECHNOLOGIES, INC.—See NationsBank Corporation; *U.S. Public*, pg. 1162
BARNEY POINT COAL TERMINAL—See The Broken Hill Proprietary Company Limited; *Int'l*, pg. 223
BARNEYS INC.; *U.S. Private*, pg. 116
BARNHARDT MANUFACTURING CO.; *U.S. Private*, pg. 117
BARNHILL CONTRACTING COMPANY; *U.S. Private*, pg. 117
BARNIER S.A.—See Scapa Group Plc; *Int'l*, pg. 1202
BARNSTEAD/THERMOLYNE CORPORATION—See Sybron International Corporation; *U.S. Public*, pg. 1545
BARNWELL GEOTHERMAL CORPORATION—See Barnwell Industries, Inc.; *U.S. Public*, pg. 191
BARNWELL HAWAIIAN PROPERTIES, INC.—See Barnwell Industries, Inc.; *U.S. Public*, pg. 191
BARNWELL INDUSTRIES, INC.; *U.S. Public*, pg. 190

BARNWELL MANAGEMENT CO., INC.—See Barnwell Industries, Inc.; *U.S. Public*, pg. 191
BARNWELL OF CANADA LTD.—See Barnwell Industries, Inc.; *U.S. Public*, pg. 191
BARNWELL OVERSEAS, INC.—See Barnwell Industries, Inc.; *U.S. Public*, pg. 191
BARNWELL SHALLOW OIL, INC.—See Barnwell Industries, Inc.; *U.S. Public*, pg. 191
BAROID DRILLING FLUIDS DIVISION—See Dresser Industries, Inc.; *U.S. Public*, pg. 528
BARON TECHNICAL SERVICES LTD.—See Knurr AG; *Int'l*, pg. 739
BARONE FOODS—See Clayton, Dubilier & Rice, Inc; *U.S. Private*, pg. 244
BAROUH EATON ALLEN CORPORATION; *U.S. Private*, pg. 117
BARPROP LTD.—See RMP Properties Ltd.; *Int'l*, pg. 1081
BARR & BARR, INC.; *U.S. Private*, pg. 117
BARR BROTHERS & CO., INC.; *U.S. Private*, pg. 117
BARR ELECTRIC CORPORATION; *U.S. Private*, pg. 117
BARR LABORATORIES INC.; *U.S. Public*, pg. 191
W.M. BARR & CO., INC.; *U.S. Private*, pg. 117
BARRA, INC.; *U.S. Public*, pg. 191
BARRACUDA FIELD DEVELOPMENT—See Petrobras - Petroleo Brasileiro S.A.; *Int'l*, pg. 1041
BARRATT AMERICAN INC.—See Barratt Developments Plc; *Int'l*, pg. 168
BARRATT BRISTOL—See Barratt Developments Plc; *Int'l*, pg. 168
BARRATT CENTRAL—See Barratt Developments Plc; *Int'l*, pg. 168
BARRATT CHESTER—See Barratt Developments Plc; *Int'l*, pg. 168
BARRATT COMMERCIAL—See Barratt Developments Plc; *Int'l*, pg. 168
BARRATT CONSTRUCTION—See Barratt Developments Plc; *Int'l*, pg. 168
BARRATT DEVELOPMENTS PLC; *Int'l*, pg. 167
BARRATT EAST MIDLANDS—See Barratt Developments Plc; *Int'l*, pg. 168
BARRATT EAST SCOTLAND—See Barratt Developments Plc; *Int'l*, pg. 168
BARRATT EASTERN COUNTIES—See Barratt Developments; *Int'l*, pg. 168
BARRATT HOMES—See Barratt Developments Plc; *Int'l*, pg. 168
BARRATT LEEDS—See Barratt Developments Plc; *Int'l*, pg. 168
BARRATT LONDON—See Barratt Developments Plc; *Int'l*, pg. 168
BARRATT MANCHESTER—See Barratt Developments Plc; *Int'l*, pg. 168
BARRATT NEWCASTLE—See Barratt Developments Plc; *Int'l*, pg. 168
BARRATT NORTH LONDON—See Barratt Developments Plc; *Int'l*, pg. 168
BARRATT NORTHAMPTON—See Barratt Developments Plc; *Int'l*, pg. 168
BARRATT NORTHERN—See Barratt Developments Plc; *Int'l*, pg. 168
BARRATT SOUTH LONDON—See Barratt Developments Plc; *Int'l*, pg. 168
BARRATT SOUTH WALES—See Barratt Developments Plc; *Int'l*, pg. 168
BARRATT SOUTHAMPTON—See Barratt Developments Plc; *Int'l*, pg. 168
BARRATT SOUTHERN—See Barratt Developments Plc; *Int'l*, pg. 168
BARRATT SOUTHERN COUNTIES—See Barratt Developments Plc; *Int'l*, pg. 168
BARRATT WEST MIDLANDS—See Barratt Developments Plc; *Int'l*, pg. 168
BARRATT WEST SCOTLAND—See Barratt Developments Plc; *Int'l*, pg. 168
BARRATT YORK—See Barratt Developments Plc; *Int'l*, pg. 168
BARREL O'FUN SNACK FOODS CO.; *U.S. Private*, pg. 118
BARRERAS HIJOS DE J. BARRERAS, S.A.—See SEPI; *Int'l*, pg. 1223
BARRETT FUELS CORPORATION—See Barrett Resources Corporation; *U.S. Public*, pg. 191
BARRETT HARDWARE & INDUSTRIAL SUPPLY COMPANY—See Distribution America; *U.S. Private*, pg. 335
BARRETT RESOURCES CORPORATION; *U.S. Public*, pg. 191
BARRICK CHILE LTDA.—See Barrick Gold Corporation; *Int'l*, pg. 169
BARRICK GOLD—See Barrick Gold Corporation; *Int'l*, pg. 169
BARRICK GOLD CORPORATION; *Int'l*, pg. 168
BARRICK GOLD PERU S.A.—See Barrick Gold Corporation; *Int'l*, pg. 169
BARRICK GOLD RESOURCES CORPORATION—See Barrick Gold Corporation; *Int'l*, pg. 169
BARRICK MINERALS (CANADA) INC.—See Barrick Gold Corporation; *Int'l*, pg. 169
BARRICK POWER GOLD CORPORATION OF CHINA LIMITED—See Barrick Gold Corporation; *Int'l*, pg. 169
BARRIE KNITWEAR—See Dawson International PLC; *Int'l*, pg. 385
BARRIER FILMS CORP.—See World Class Film Corporation; *U.S. Private*, pg. 1190
BARRINGER ASIA-PACIFIC—See Barringer Technologies Inc.; *U.S. Public*, pg. 192
BARRINGER EUROPE, SARL—See Barringer Technologies Inc.; *U.S. Public*, pg. 192
BARRINGER INSTRUMENTS, INC.—See Barringer Technologies Inc.; *U.S. Public*, pg. 192
BARRINGER INSTRUMENTS-U.K.-LTD.—See Barringer Technologies Inc.; *U.S. Public*, pg. 192
BARRINGER TECHNOLOGIES INC.; *U.S. Public*, pg. 191

Company Index

BARRIS MUSIC, INC.—See Sony Corporation; Int'l, pg. 1283
BARRIS PRODUCTIONS, INC.—See Sony Corporation; Int'l, pg. 1283
BARRISTER INFORMATION SYSTEMS CORPORATION; U.S. Public, pg. 192
BARRO MARKETING & PUBLICIDADE—See Testa International; Int'l, pg. 1377
BARRON'S THE DOW JONES BUSINESS & FINANCIAL WEEKLY—See Dow Jones & Company, Inc.; U.S. Public, pg. 524
BARROW CABLE TV—See Arctic Slope Regional Corporation; U.S. Private, pg. 80
BARROW, HANLEY, MEWHINNEY & STRAUSS, INC.—See United Asset Management Corporation; U.S. Public, pg. 1672
BARRY BLAU & PARTNERS OF MARYLAND, INC.—See Blau Marketing Technologies, Inc.; U.S. Private, pg. 148
BARRY BLAU & PARTNERS OF NEW YORK—See Blau Marketing Technologies, Inc.; U.S. Private, pg. 148
BARRY CALLEBAUT—See Barry Callebaut N.V.; Int'l, pg. 252
BARRY CONTROLS—See Applied Power Inc.; U.S. Public, pg. 124
BARRY CONTROLS CORP.—See Applied Power Inc.; U.S. Public, pg. 124
BARRY CONTROLS INTERNATIONAL GMBH—See Applied Power Inc.; U.S. Public, pg. 125
BARRY DISTRIBUTION OF SAN ANGELO—See R.G. Barry Corporation; U.S. Public, pg. 192
BARRY OF CIUDAD ACUNA—See R.G. Barry Corporation; U.S. Public, pg. 192
BARRY OF LAREDO—See R.G. Barry Corporation; U.S. Public, pg. 192
BARRY OF NUEVO LAREDO—See R.G. Barry Corporation; U.S. Public, pg. 192
BARRY OF SAN ANGELO—See R.G. Barry Corporation; U.S. Public, pg. 192
R.G. BARRY CORPORATION; U.S. Public, pg. 192
THEODORE BARRY & ASSOCIATES; U.S. Private, pg. 118
THEODORE BARRY & ASSOCIATES—See Theodore Barry & Associates; U.S. Private, pg. 118
BARRY-WEHMILLER COMPANY; U.S. Private, pg. 118
BARRY-WEHMILLER PACKAGING SYSTEMS—See Barry-Wehmiller Company; U.S. Private, pg. 118
BARRY'S JEWELERS, INC.; U.S. Public, pg. 192
THE BARTELL DRUG COMPANY; U.S. Private, pg. 118
E.J. BARTELLS CO.; U.S. Private, pg. 118
E.J. BARTELLS MATERIAL MANAGEMENT CO.—See E.J. Bartells Co.; U.S. Private, pg. 118
BARTLE BOGLE HEGARTY LIMITED; Int'l, pg. 169
BARTLETT & CO.—See Legg Mason, Inc.; U.S. Public, pg. 985
BARTLETT AND COMPANY; U.S. Private, pg. 118
BARTLETT BRAINARD EACOTT, INC.; U.S. Private, pg. 118
THE F.A. BARTLETT TREE EXPERT CO.; U.S. Private, pg. 119
BARTLETT STATE JAIL—See Corrections Corporation of America; U.S. Public, pg. 450
BARTON ALUMINUM FOUNDRIES—See Caparo Group Ltd.; Int'l, pg. 264
BARTON-ASCHMAN ASSOCIATES, INC.—See Parsons Corporation; U.S. Private, pg. 841
BARTON BEERS, LTD.—See Canandaigua Wine Company, Inc.; U.S. Public, pg. 300
BARTON BRANDS, LTD.—See Canandaigua Wine Company, Inc.; U.S. Public, pg. 300
BARTON BRANDS OF CALIFORNIA, INC.—See Canandaigua Wine Company, Inc.; U.S. Public, pg. 300
BARTON BRANDS OF GEORGIA, INC.—See Canandaigua Wine Company, Inc.; U.S. Public, pg. 300
BARTON CONDUITS—See Caparo Group Ltd.; Int'l, pg. 264
BARTON CREEK CAPITAL, INC.—See TCC Industries; U.S. Public, pg. 1554
BARTON DISTILLERS IMPORT CORP.—See Canandaigua Wine Company, Inc.; U.S. Public, pg. 300
E.C. BARTON & COMPANY; U.S. Private, pg. 119
BARTON ENGINEERING LTD.—See Caparo Group Ltd.; Int'l, pg. 264
BARTON HANDLING & STORAGE SYSTEMS LTD.—See Caparo Group Ltd.; Int'l, pg. 264
BARTON INCORPORATED—See Canandaigua Wine Company, Inc.; U.S. Public, pg. 300
BARTON MALOW CO.—See Barton Malow Enterprises, Inc.; U.S. Private, pg. 120
BARTON MALOW ENTERPRISES, INC.; U.S. Private, pg. 120
BARTON-MALOW RIGGING CO.—See Barton Malow Enterprises, Inc.; U.S. Private, pg. 120
BARTON NELSON DE MEXICO—See Barton Nelson Inc.; U.S. Private, pg. 120
BARTON NELSON EUROPE B.V.—See Barton Nelson Inc.; U.S. Private, pg. 120
BARTON NELSON INC.; U.S. Private, pg. 120
BARTON PRESS, INC.; U.S. Private, pg. 120
BARTON'S OF DUMAS—See E.C. Barton & Company; U.S. Private, pg. 119
BARTON'S OF EUDORA—See E.C. Barton & Company; U.S. Private, pg. 119
BARTON'S OF HARRISBURG—See E.C. Barton & Company; U.S. Private, pg. 119
BARTON'S OF JONESBORO—See E.C. Barton & Company; U.S. Private, pg. 119
BARTON'S OF KENNETT—See E.C. Barton & Company; U.S. Private, pg. 119
BARTON'S OF LAKE VILLAGE—See E.C. Barton & Company; U.S. Private, pg. 119
BARTON'S OF LEACHVILLE—See E.C. Barton & Company; U.S. Private, pg. 119

BARTON'S OF LEPANTO—See E.C. Barton & Company; U.S. Private, pg. 119
BARTON'S OF MALDEN—See E.C. Barton & Company; U.S. Private, pg. 119
BARTON'S OF MANILA—See E.C. Barton & Company; U.S. Private, pg. 119
BARTON'S OF MCGEHEE—See E.C. Barton & Company; U.S. Private, pg. 119
BARTON'S OF MONETTE—See E.C. Barton & Company; U.S. Private, pg. 119
BARTON'S OF MONTICELLO—See E.C. Barton & Company; U.S. Private, pg. 119
BARTON'S OF OSCEOLA—See E.C. Barton & Company; U.S. Private, pg. 119
BARTON'S OF PARAGOULD—See E.C. Barton & Company; U.S. Private, pg. 119
BARTON'S OF PINE BLUFF—See E.C. Barton & Company; U.S. Private, pg. 119
BARTON'S OF PORTAGEVILLE—See E.C. Barton & Company; U.S. Private, pg. 119
BARTON'S OF SIKESTON—See E.C. Barton & Company; U.S. Private, pg. 119
BARTON'S OF STUTTGART—See E.C. Barton & Company; U.S. Private, pg. 119
BARTON'S OF TRUMANN—See E.C. Barton & Company; U.S. Private, pg. 119
BARTON'S OF WALNUT RIDGE—See E.C. Barton & Company; U.S. Private, pg. 119
BARTON'S OF WEINER—See E.C. Barton & Company; U.S. Private, pg. 119
BARTON'S OF WEST MEMPHIS—See E.C. Barton & Company; U.S. Private, pg. 119
CARL BARTSCH KG—See Freudenberg & Company; Int'l, pg. 506
BARUM CONTINENTAL SPOL. S.R.O.—See Continental AG; Int'l, pg. 327
BARYTINE DE CHAILLAC S.A.—See Solvay S.A.; Int'l, pg. 1279
BARZON CORPORATION—See Greif Brothers Corporation; U.S. Public, pg. 763
BASALT PRECAST DIVISION—See Dillingham Construction Corporation; U.S. Private, pg. 333
BASBERG PAPIR AS—See Mo och Domsjo AB; Int'l, pg. 886
BASCO DIV.—See American Precision Industries Inc.; U.S. Public, pg. 90
BASCULE-REST—See GIB Group; Int'l, pg. 532
BASE DE CAZAUX—See Dassault Aviation Group; Int'l, pg. 383
BASEL TRADING COMPANY LTD.; Int'l, pg. 169
BASELINE FINANCIAL SERVICES, INC.—See Primark Corporation; U.S. Public, pg. 1325
BASELINE INDUSTRIES—See Mine Safety Appliances Co.; U.S. Public, pg. 1114
BASES INTERNATIONAL—See BASES Worldwide; U.S. Private, pg. 120
BASES INTERNATIONAL RESEARCH DIVISION—See BASES Worldwide; U.S. Private, pg. 120
BASES SERVICES & DURABLES DIVISION—See BASES Worldwide; U.S. Private, pg. 120
BASES WORLDWIDE; U.S. Private, pg. 120
BASES WORLDWIDE—See BASES Worldwide; U.S. Private, pg. 120
BASHAS'; U.S. Private, pg. 120
BASIC AMERICAN FOODS; U.S. Private, pg. 121
BASIC AMERICAN MEDICAL, INC.—See Columbia/HCA Healthcare Corporation; U.S. Public, pg. 403
BASIC AMERICAN MEDICAL PRODUCTS, INC.—See Graham-Field Health Products, Inc.; U.S. Public, pg. 758
BASIC AMERICAN METAL PRODUCTS—See Columbia/HCA Healthcare Corporation; U.S. Public, pg. 404
BASIC AMERICAN WOOD PRODUCTS—See Columbia/HCA Healthcare Corporation; U.S. Public, pg. 404
BASIC BOOKS, INC.—See The News Corporation Limited; Int'l, pg. 927
BASIC CHEMICALS DIV.—See Rhone-Poulenc S.A.; Int'l, pg. 1109
BASIC CONSTRUCTION COMPANY; U.S. Private, pg. 121
BASIC ENGINEERING (SUPEN)—See Petrobras - Petroleo Brasileiro S.A.; Int'l, pg. 1042
BASIC FOOD INTERNATIONAL, INC.; U.S. Private, pg. 121
BASIC RESOURCES, INC.—See Texas Utilities Company; U.S. Public, pg. 1587
BASIC VEGETABLE PRODUCTS—See Basic American Foods; U.S. Private, pg. 121
PETER A. BASILE SONS INC.; U.S. Private, pg. 121
BASIN CO-OPERATIVE SERVICES—See Basin Electric Power Cooperative; U.S. Private, pg. 121
BASIN CREEK MINE—See Pegasus Gold Corporation; U.S. Public, pg. 1269
BASIN ELECTRIC POWER COOPERATIVE; U.S. Private, pg. 121
BASIN PIPELINE CORP.—See Energen Corporation; U.S. Public, pg. 581
BASIN RESOURCES—See Montana Power Company; U.S. Public, pg. 1127
BASIN TELECOMMUNICATION, INC.—See Basin Electric Power Cooperative; U.S. Private, pg. 121
BASINFORM-BASTOGI SERVIZI INFORMATICI S.P.A.—See Bastogi-S.p.A.; Int'l, pg. 170
BASIS PETROLEUM, INC.—See Valero Energy Corporation; U.S. Public, pg. 1704
BASISMARKT—See Vendex International N.V.; Int'l, pg. 1463
BASKIN-ROBBINS CANADA—See Allied Domecq PLC; Int'l, pg. 63
BASKIN-ROBBINS INCORPORATED—See Allied Domecq PLC; Int'l, pg. 63
BASKIN-ROBBINS INTERNATIONAL CO.—See Allied Domecq PLC; Int'l, pg. 63
BASKIN ROBBINS PRODUCTION FACILITY—See Allied Domecq PLC; Int'l, pg. 63

BASKIN-ROBBINS USA CO.—See Allied Domecq PLC; Int'l, pg. 63
BASLER ELECTRIC COMPANY; U.S. Private, pg. 121
BASO PRECISION OPTICS—See Eastman Kodak Company; U.S. Public, pg. 551
BASS—See Novartis AG; Int'l, pg. 975
BASS ANGLER SPORTSMAN SOCIETY—See B.A.S.S., Inc.; U.S. Private, pg. 105
BASS BLOCK & BUILDING SUPPLIES—See Holderbank Financiere Glaris Ltd.; Int'l, pg. 629
BASS BREWERS LTD.—See Bass PLC; Int'l, pg. 170
BASS ENTERPRISES PRODUCTION COMPANY; U.S. Private, pg. 122
G.H. BASS & CO.—See Phillips-Van Heusen Corporation; U.S. Public, pg. 1291
BASS HOLDINGS LTD.—See Bass PLC; Int'l, pg. 170
BASS INTERNATIONAL BREWERS—See Bass PLC; Int'l, pg. 170
BASS INVESTMENTS PLC—See Bass PLC; Int'l, pg. 170
BASS LEISURE—See Bass PLC; Int'l, pg. 170
BASS PLC; Int'l, pg. 169
BASS PRO SHOPS, INC.; U.S. Private, pg. 122
BASS RETAIL DIV.—See Phillips-Van Heusen Corporation; U.S. Public, pg. 1291
BASS TAVERNS LTD.—See Bass PLC; Int'l, pg. 170
BASSANI MANUFACTURING; U.S. Private, pg. 122
BASSETT CHAIR CO.—See Bassett Furniture Industries, Incorporated; U.S. Public, pg. 193
BASSETT FURNITURE CO.—See Bassett Furniture Industries, Incorporated; U.S. Public, pg. 193
BASSETT FURNITURE INDUSTRIES, INCORPORATED; U.S. Public, pg. 193
BASSETT FURNITURE INDUSTRIES OF NORTH CAROLINA INC.—See Bassett Furniture Industries, Incorporated; U.S. Public, pg. 193
J.D. BASSETT MFG. CO.—See Bassett Furniture Industries, Incorporated; U.S. Public, pg. 193
BASSETT MOTION DIVISION—See Bassett Furniture Industries, Incorporated; U.S. Public, pg. 193
BASSETT PRINTERS—See Kervick Enterprises, Inc.; U.S. Private, pg. 616
BASSETT ROTARY TOOL CO.—See Federal Signal Corporation; U.S. Public, pg. 617
BASSETT SUPERIOR LINES—See Bassett Furniture Industries, Incorporated; U.S. Public, pg. 193
BASSETT TABLE CO.—See Bassett Furniture Industries, Incorporated; U.S. Public, pg. 193
BASSETT UPHOLSTERY DIVISION—See Bassett Furniture Industries, Incorporated; U.S. Public, pg. 193
THE W.E. BASSETT COMPANY; U.S. Private, pg. 122
BASSETT-WALKER—See VF Corporation; U.S. Public, pg. 1702
W.M. BASSETT FURNITURE CO.—See Bassett Furniture Industries, Incorporated; U.S. Public, pg. 193
BASSICK BY KASPAR; U.S. Private, pg. 122
BASSMASTER MAGAZINE—See B.A.S.S., Inc.; U.S. Private, pg. 105
THE BASSMASTER TELEVISION SERIES—See B.A.S.S., Inc.; U.S. Private, pg. 105
BASSMASTER TOURNAMENT TRAIL—See B.A.S.S., Inc.; U.S. Private, pg. 105
BAST CHEVROLET INC.; U.S. Private, pg. 122
BASTOGI-S.P.A.; Int'l, pg. 170
BAT OFFICE PRODUCTS—See U.S. Office Products Company; U.S. Public, pg. 1686
BATA SHOE CO., INC.—See CHB Corp.; U.S. Private, pg. 195
BATAAN OPTICAL INC.—See Essilor International Compagnie Generale d'Optique; Int'l, pg. 462
BATANGAS BAY TERMINAL, INC.—See Nissho Iwai Corporation; Int'l, pg. 947
BATAVIA WINE CELLARS—See Canandaigua Wine Company, Inc.; U.S. Public, pg. 300
BATCHELORS FOODS, LTD.—See Unilever Plc; Int'l, pg. 1434
BATCHELORS (IRELAND) LTD.—See Northern Foods plc; Int'l, pg. 968
BATEAUX NANTAIS—See Sodexho S.A.; Int'l, pg. 1274
BATEAUX PARISIENS—See Sodexho S.A.; Int'l, pg. 1274
BATEMAN BROTHERS LUMBER CO., INC.; U.S. Private, pg. 122
BATEMAN FOOD & NUTRITION FOR HEALTHCARE—See Compass Group plc; Int'l, pg. 324
BATES CONTAINER, INC.; U.S. Private, pg. 122
BATES DIV.—See Wolverine World Wide, Inc.; U.S. Public, pg. 1775
BATES EMBALLAGE A/S—See FLS Industries A/S; Int'l, pg. 476
BATESCO QUARRIES DIVISION—See Ash Grove Cement Company; U.S. Private, pg. 88
BATESVILLE AMERICAN MFG.—See Kimball International, Inc.; U.S. Public, pg. 957
BATESVILLE CASKET COMPANY, INC.—See Hillenbrand Industries, Inc.; U.S. Public, pg. 828
BATEY ADS MALAYSIA SDN. BHD.—See BDDP Group; Int'l, pg. 117
BATEY ADS SINGAPORE—See BDDP Group; Int'l, pg. 170
BATEY ADS TAIWAN—See BDDP Group; Int'l, pg. 117
BATEY ADS THAILAND—See BDDP Group; Int'l, pg. 117
BATEY COULDREY JONES ADVERTISING—See BDDP Group; Int'l, pg. 117
BATEY KAZOO—See BDDP Group; Int'l, pg. 117
BATH & BODY WORKS—See The Limited, Inc.; U.S. Public, pg. 995
BATH & PORTLAND STONE LIMITED—See Hanson PLC; Int'l, pg. 592
BATH IRON WORKS CORPORATION—See General Dynamics Corporation; U.S. Public, pg. 709
BATI RECORD—See Groupe Casino; Int'l, pg. 563
BATI-SERVICE—See Kaufman and Broad Home Corporation; Int'l, pg. 945
BATIROC—See ETEX; Int'l, pg. 430
BATON BROADCAST SALES—See Baton Broadcasting Incorporated; Int'l, pg. 171

BATON BROADCASTING INCORPORATED; *Int'l*, pg. 170
BATON ROUGE MACHINE WORKS INC.—See Weir Group PLC; *Int'l*, pg. 1489
BATON ROUGE WATER WORKS COMPANY; *U.S. Private*, pg. 122
BATSON-COOK COMPANY; *U.S. Private*, pg. 123
BATSON MILL LP—See Newpark Resources, Inc.; *U.S. Public*, pg. 1179
BATTAILLE S.A.—See Kemira Oy; *Int'l*, pg. 728
BATTEAST CONSTRUCTION COMPANY, INC.; *U.S. Private*, pg. 123
BATTELLE MEMORIAL INSTITUTE; *U.S. Private*, pg. 123
BATTEN CONVERTER SERVICES—See Jannock Limited; *Int'l*, pg. 698
BATTEN GRAPHICS—See Schawk, Inc.; *U.S. Public*, pg. 1437
BATTENFELD ANLAGENTECHNIK GMBH—See MAN Aktiengesellschaft; *Int'l*, pg. 825
BATTENFELD AUSTRALIA PTY. LTD.—See MAN Aktiengesellschaft; *Int'l*, pg. 825
BATTENFELD AUTOMATISIERUNGSTECHNIK GES.M.B.H.—See MAN Aktiengesellschaft; *Int'l*, pg. 825
BATTENFELD BELGIUM N.V.—See MAN Aktiengesellschaft; *Int'l*, pg. 825
BATTENFELD CANADA LTD.—See MAN Aktiengesellschaft; *Int'l*, pg. 825
BATTENFELD CHEN EXTRUSION SYSTEMS LTD.—See MAN Aktiengesellschaft; *Int'l*, pg. 825
BATTENFELD DANMARK A/S—See MAN Aktiengesellschaft; *Int'l*, pg. 825
BATTENFELD EXTRUSIONSTECHNIK GMBH—See MAN Aktiengesellschaft; *Int'l*, pg. 825
BATTENFELD FRANCE S.A.—See MAN Aktiengesellschaft; *Int'l*, pg. 825
BATTENFELD GLOENCO EXTRUSION SYSTEMS LTD.—See MAN Aktiengesellschaft; *Int'l*, pg. 825
BATTENFELD GLOUCESTER ENGINEERING CO. INC.; *U.S. Private*, pg. 123
BATTENFELD GLOUCESTER ENGINEERING CO., INC.—See MAN Aktiengesellschaft; *Int'l*, pg. 825
BATTENFELD GMBH—See MAN Aktiengesellschaft; *Int'l*, pg. 825
BATTENFELD IBERICA S.A.—See MAN Aktiengesellschaft; *Int'l*, pg. 825
BATTENFELD INDIA LTD.—See MAN Aktiengesellschaft; *Int'l*, pg. 826
BATTENFELD ITALIA S.R.L.—See MAN Aktiengesellschaft; *Int'l*, pg. 826
BATTENFELD KUNSTSTOFFMASCHINEN GES. M.B.H.—See MAN Aktiengesellschaft; *Int'l*, pg. 825
BATTENFELD KUNSTSTOFFMASCHINEN GES. M. B. H.—See MAN Aktiengesellschaft; *Int'l*, pg. 826
BATTENFELD OF AMERICA—See MAN Aktiengesellschaft; *Int'l*, pg. 825
BATTENFELD OF AMERICA, INC.—See MAN Aktiengesellschaft; *Int'l*, pg. 825
BATTENFELD-PUGLIESE EQUIPAMENTOS LTDA.—See MAN Aktiengesellschaft; *Int'l*, pg. 825
BATTENFELD SCHWEIZ AG—See MAN Aktiengesellschaft; *Int'l*, pg. 826
BATTENFELD SERVICE GMBH—See MAN Aktiengesellschaft; *Int'l*, pg. 825
BATTENFELD SVERGIE AB—See MAN Aktiengesellschaft; *Int'l*, pg. 825
BATTENFELD UK LTD.—See MAN Aktiengesellschaft; *Int'l*, pg. 825
BATTERYMARCH FINANCIAL MANAGEMENT—See Legg Mason, Inc.; *U.S. Public*, pg. 985
BATTEY MACHINERY COMPANY; *U.S. Private*, pg. 123
BATTLE CREEK ENQUIRER—See Gannett Company, Inc.; *U.S. Public*, pg. 700
BATTLE CREEK GAS COMPANY—See Southeastern Michigan Gas Enterprises, Inc.; *U.S. Public*, pg. 1489
BATTLE MOUNTAIN (AUSTRALIA) INC.—See Battle Mountain Gold Company; *U.S. Public*, pg. 193
BATTLE MOUNTAIN CANADA LTD.—See Battle Mountain Gold Company; *U.S. Public*, pg. 193
BATTLE MOUNTAIN EXPLORATION COMPANY—See Battle Mountain Gold Company; *U.S. Public*, pg. 193
BATTLE MOUNTAIN GOLD (AFRICA)—See Battle Mountain Gold Company; *U.S. Public*, pg. 193
BATTLE MOUNTAIN GOLD (ARGENTINA)—See Battle Mountain Gold Company; *U.S. Public*, pg. 193
BATTLE MOUNTAIN GOLD (AUSTRALIA)—See Battle Mountain Gold Company; *U.S. Public*, pg. 193
BATTLE MOUNTAIN GOLD (BOLIVIA)—See Battle Mountain Gold Company; *U.S. Public*, pg. 193
BATTLE MOUNTAIN GOLD COMPANY; *U.S. Public*, pg. 193
BATTLE MOUNTAIN GOLD (INDONESIA)—See Battle Mountain Gold Company; *U.S. Public*, pg. 194
BATTLE MOUNTAIN GOLD (MEXICO)—See Battle Mountain Gold Company; *U.S. Public*, pg. 194
BATTLEFIELD EQUIPMENT RENTALS—See Toromont Industries Ltd.; *Int'l*, pg. 1400
RAULF BAU GMBH—See Hollandsche Beton Groep NV; *Int'l*, pg. 630
BAU-UNION POTSDAM GMBH—See Bilfinger + Berger Bauaktiengesellschaft; *Int'l*, pg. 196
BAUCHEMIE LEIPZIG GMBH—See Lafarge S.A.; *Int'l*, pg. 791
BAUDA A/S—See Toyota Motor Corporation; *Int'l*, pg. 1413
BAUER APPAREL INC.—See Nike, Inc.; *U.S. Public*, pg. 1184
BAUER HISS AB—See Kone Corporation; *Int'l*, pg. 747
BAUER MACHINERIES & INDUSTRIAL CORPORATION—See GESTRA GmbH; *Int'l*, pg. 549
BAUER SPORTS INC.—See Nike, Inc.; *U.S. Public*, pg. 1184
BAUER SVERGE AB—See Nike, Inc.; *U.S. Public*, pg. 1184
BAUGH CONSTRUCTION COMPANY; *U.S. Private*, pg. 123

BAUGHER CHEVROLET-BUICK INC.; *U.S. Private*, pg. 123
BAUKJE BEHEER BV—See CSM N.V.; *Int'l*, pg. 243
A.W. BAULDERSTONE HOLDINGS PTY. LTD.—See Bilfinger + Berger Bauaktiengesellschaft; *Int'l*, pg. 196
BAUM PRINTING HOUSE, INC.—See Wallace Computer Services, Inc.; *U.S. Public*, pg. 1735
BAUM USA—See Stahl GmbH & Co.; *Int'l*, pg. 1293
W.A. BAUM COMPANY, INC.; *U.S. Private*, pg. 124
BAUMANN FEDERN AG; *Int'l*, pg. 171
BAUMANN GMBH—See Baumann Federn AG; *Int'l*, pg. 171
BAUMANN, HINDE & CO., LTD.—See Lonrho plc; *Int'l*, pg. 817
BAUMANN MUELLES, S.A.—See Baumann Federn AG; *Int'l*, pg. 171
BAUMANN SPRING CO. (S) PTE. LTD.—See Baumann Federn AG; *Int'l*, pg. 171
BAUMANN SPRINGS & PRESSINGS (UK) LTD.—See Baumann Federn AG; *Int'l*, pg. 171
BAUMANN SPRINGS USA, INC.—See Baumann Federn AG; *Int'l*, pg. 171
BAUMBERGER-GETRANKE AG—See Feldschlosschen Hurlimann Holding; *Int'l*, pg. 479
BAUME MERCIER, INC.; *U.S. Private*, pg. 124
BAUMGARTEN STAMP CO.—See American Marking Systems; *U.S. Private*, pg. 58
KARL BAUMGARTNER & PARTNER CONSULTING GMBH & CO. KG—See Commerzbank AG; *Int'l*, pg. 309
BAUMINERAL GMBH HERTEN—See Veba AG; *Int'l*, pg. 1460
OY BAUSCH & LOMB FINLAND A.B.—See Bausch & Lomb Incorporated; *U.S. Public*, pg. 195
BAUSCH & LOMB INC.—See Bausch & Lomb Incorporated; *U.S. Public*, pg. 194
P.T. BAUSCH & LOMB MANUFACTURING—See Bausch & Lomb Incorporated; *U.S. Public*, pg. 195
BAUSCH & LOMB AG/SA—See Bausch & Lomb Incorporated; *U.S. Public*, pg. 195
BAUSCH & LOMB AUSTRALIA PTY. LTD.—See Bausch & Lomb Incorporated; *U.S. Public*, pg. 195
BAUSCH & LOMB BERMUDA, LIMITED—See Bausch & Lomb Incorporated; *U.S. Public*, pg. 195
BAUSCH & LOMB B.V.—See Bausch & Lomb Incorporated; *U.S. Public*, pg. 195
BAUSCH & LOMB CHINA, INC.—See Bausch & Lomb Incorporated; *U.S. Public*, pg. 195
BAUSCH & LOMB CONTACT LENS DIVISION-FL—See Bausch & Lomb Incorporated; *U.S. Public*, pg. 194
BAUSCH & LOMB DANMARK A/S—See Bausch & Lomb Incorporated; *U.S. Public*, pg. 195
BAUSCH & LOMB DE COLUMBIA S.A.—See Bausch & Lomb Incorporated; *U.S. Public*, pg. 195
BAUSCH & LOMB ESPANA S.A.—See Bausch & Lomb Incorporated; *U.S. Public*, pg. 195
BAUSCH & LOMB EYEWEAR DIVISION-MD—See Bausch & Lomb Incorporated; *U.S. Public*, pg. 194
BAUSCH & LOMB EYEWEAR DIVISION-TX—See Bausch & Lomb Incorporated; *U.S. Public*, pg. 194
BAUSCH & LOMB FRANCE S.A.—See Bausch & Lomb Incorporated; *U.S. Public*, pg. 195
BAUSCH & LOMB FRIBOURG S.A.—See Bausch & Lomb Incorporated; *U.S. Public*, pg. 195
BAUSCH & LOMB G.M.B.H.—See Bausch & Lomb Incorporated; *U.S. Public*, pg. 195
BAUSCH & LOMB HEARING SYSTEMS DIVISION—See Bausch & Lomb Incorporated; *U.S. Public*, pg. 194
BAUSCH & LOMB (HONG KONG) LTD.—See Bausch & Lomb Incorporated; *U.S. Public*, pg. 195
BAUSCH & LOMB INCORPORATED; *U.S. Public*, pg. 194
BAUSCH & LOMB INDIA LTD.—See Bausch & Lomb Incorporated; *U.S. Public*, pg. 195
BAUSCH & LOMB INSTITUTO OFTALMICO MEDIOLANUM—See Bausch & Lomb Incorporated; *U.S. Public*, pg. 195
BAUSCH & LOMB INSURANCE COMPANY—See Bausch & Lomb Incorporated; *U.S. Public*, pg. 194
BAUSCH & LOMB INTERNATIONAL, INC.—See Bausch & Lomb Incorporated; *U.S. Public*, pg. 195
BAUSCH & LOMB IRELAND LIMITED—See Bausch & Lomb Incorporated; *U.S. Public*, pg. 195
BAUSCH & LOMB JAPAN CO., LTD.—See Bausch & Lomb Incorporated; *U.S. Public*, pg. 195
BAUSCH & LOMB KOREA, LTD.—See Bausch & Lomb Incorporated; *U.S. Public*, pg. 195
BAUSCH & LOMB (NEW ZEALAND) LIMITED—See Bausch & Lomb Incorporated; *U.S. Public*, pg. 195
BAUSCH & LOMB NORWAY A/S—See Bausch & Lomb Incorporated; *U.S. Public*, pg. 195
BAUSCH & LOMB OPTICARE, INC.—See Bausch & Lomb Incorporated; *U.S. Public*, pg. 194
BAUSCH & LOMB ORAL CARE DIVISION—See Bausch & Lomb Incorporated; *U.S. Public*, pg. 194
BAUSCH & LOMB PERSONAL PRODUCTS DIVISION-SC—See Bausch & Lomb Incorporated; *U.S. Public*, pg. 194
BAUSCH & LOMB PHARMACEUTICAL DIVISION—See Bausch & Lomb Incorporated; *U.S. Public*, pg. 194
BAUSCH & LOMB PUERTO RICO, INC.—See Bausch & Lomb Incorporated; *U.S. Public*, pg. 194
BAUSCH & LOMB (SINGAPORE) PRIVATE LIMITED—See Bausch & Lomb Incorporated; *U.S. Public*, pg. 195
BAUSCH & LOMB SVENSKA AB—See Bausch & Lomb Incorporated; *U.S. Public*, pg. 195
BAUSCH & LOMB TAIWAN LIMITED—See Bausch & Lomb Incorporated; *U.S. Public*, pg. 195
BAUSCH & LOMB U.K. LTD.—See Bausch & Lomb Incorporated; *U.S. Public*, pg. 195
BAUSPARKASSE GEMEINSCHAFT DER FREUNDE WUESTENROT GEM.GMBH—See Wuestenrot Holding GmbH; *Int'l*, pg. 1514
BAUSTAHL SCHODER GMBH (SSH)—See Veba AG; *Int'l*, pg. 1459

BAUSTOFF UNION GMBH & CO. KG BAUMARKT FRANKEN—See Veba AG; *Int'l*, pg. 1459
BAUSTOFFWERKE DURMERSHEIM GMBH & CO. KG—See Heidelberger Zement A.G.; *Int'l*, pg. 606
BAUVERLAG GMBH—See EMAP Plc; *Int'l*, pg. 451
BAUVERLAG G.M.B.H.—See Rogers Communications, Inc.; *Int'l*, pg. 1124
BAVARIA FILMKUNST GMBH—See Bayerische Vereinsbank Group; *Int'l*, pg. 179
BAVARIA KEYTRONIC TECHNOLOGIE GMBH—See Rogerson Aircraft Corporation; *U.S. Private*, pg. 940
BAVARIA LLOYD REISEBURO GMBH—See Bayerische Motoren Werke Aktiengesellschaft; *Int'l*, pg. 177
BAVARIA SERVICOS DE REPRESENTACAO COMERCIAL LTDA.—See Bayerische Vereinsbank Group; *Int'l*, pg. 180
BAVARIA WIRTSCHAFTSAGENTUR GMBH—See Bayerische Motoren Werke Aktiengesellschaft; *Int'l*, pg. 177
BAVARIAN FINANCE COMPANY B.V.—See Bayerische Vereinsbank Group; *Int'l*, pg. 180
BAVARIAN REINSURANCE COMPANY LTD.—See Swiss Reinsurance Company; *Int'l*, pg. 1333
BAVARIAN REINSURANCE IRELAND LTD.—See Swiss Reinsurance Company; *Int'l*, pg. 1333
BAWDEN CORPORATION; *U.S. Private*, pg. 124
BAWDEN PRINTING, INC.—See Bawden Corporation; *U.S. Private*, pg. 124
BAX BUROSYSTEME VERTRIEBSGESELLSCHAFT MBH—See N.V. Koninklijke KNP BT; *Int'l*, pg. 757
THE BAXENDEN CHEMICAL CO., LTD.—See Witco Corporation; *U.S. Public*, pg. 1774
BAXENDEN SCANDINAVIA APS—See Witco Corporation; *U.S. Public*, pg. 1774
THE BAXTER BULLETIN—See Gannett Company, Inc.; *U.S. Public*, pg. 699
BAXTER COUNTY NEWSPAPERS, INC.—See Gannett Company, Inc.; *U.S. Public*, pg. 699
BAXTER FENWAL DIVISION—See Baxter International Inc.; *U.S. Public*, pg. 196
BAXTER GLOBAL BUSINESS CORPORATION—See Baxter International Inc.; *U.S. Public*, pg. 196
BAXTER HEALTHCARE CORPORATION—See Baxter International Inc.; *U.S. Public*, pg. 196
BAXTER HODELL DONNELLY PRESTON INC.; *U.S. Private*, pg. 124
BAXTER-HYLAND—See Baxter International Inc.; *U.S. Public*, pg. 196
BAXTER INTERNATIONAL INC.; *U.S. Public*, pg. 196
J.H. BAXTER & COMPANY; *U.S. Private*, pg. 124
BAXTER NOVACOR DIVISION—See Baxter International Inc.; *U.S. Public*, pg. 196
BAXTER/PEAS—See Baxter Hodell Donnelly Preston Inc.; *U.S. Private*, pg. 124
BAXTER RESEARCH MEDICAL, INC.—See Baxter International Inc.; *U.S. Public*, pg. 196
BAXTER TUBE COMPANY—See The Tranzonic Companies; *U.S. Public*, pg. 1632
G.G. BAXTERS—See Hillsdown Holdings Plc; *Int'l*, pg. 619
THE BAY—See Hudson's Bay Company; *Int'l*, pg. 637
BAY AREA BANCSHARES; *U.S. Private*, pg. 124
BAY AREA MEDICAL CENTER—See Columbia/HCA Healthcare Corporation; *U.S. Public*, pg. 404
BAY BREEZE CENTER—See Horizon/CMS Healthcare Corporation; *U.S. Public*, pg. 836
BAY CITIES AUTO AUCTION—See Cox Enterprises, Inc.; *U.S. Private*, pg. 282
BAY CITY FORGE OPERATIONS—See Zurn Industries, Inc.; *U.S. Public*, pg. 1794
BAY CORRECTIONAL FACILITY—See Corrections Corporation of America; *U.S. Public*, pg. 450
BAY COUNTY JAIL—See Corrections Corporation of America; *U.S. Public*, pg. 450
BAY INDUSTRIES INC.; *U.S. Private*, pg. 124
BAY INSULATION—See Bay Industries Inc.; *U.S. Private*, pg. 124
BAY MEADOWS RACE TRACK—See Patriot American Hospitality, Inc.; *U.S. Public*, pg. 1265
BAY MILLS (DELAWARE), INC.—See Saint-Gobain; *Int'l*, pg. 1170
BAY MILLS LIMITED—See Saint-Gobain; *Int'l*, pg. 1177
BAY NETWORKS, INC.; *U.S. Public*, pg. 196
BAY PARK, INC.—See Allright Corporation; *U.S. Private*, pg. 43
BAY SHIPBUILDING CO.—See The Manitowoc Company, Inc.; *U.S. Public*, pg. 1041
BAY 6 (BUILDING MATERIALS) LIMITED—See RMC Group p.l.c.; *Int'l*, pg. 1080
BAY STATE CRUISE COMPANY—See Sodexho S.A.; *Int'l*, pg. 1274
BAY STATE ENERGY DEVELOPMENT, INC.—See Bay State Gas Company; *U.S. Public*, pg. 196
BAY STATE GAS COMPANY; *U.S. Public*, pg. 196
BAY STATE GAS COMPANY—See Bay State Gas Company; *U.S. Public*, pg. 197
BAY STATE MILLING CO.; *U.S. Private*, pg. 124
BAY STATE SA—See Saint-Gobain; *Int'l*, pg. 1174
BAY VIEW BANK—See Bay View Capital Corporation; *U.S. Public*, pg. 197
BAY VIEW CAPITAL CORPORATION; *U.S. Public*, pg. 197
BAY WEST PAPER CORPORATION—See Wausau-Mosinee Paper Corporation; *U.S. Public*, pg. 1747
BAY WEST PAPER TOWEL & TISSUE DIV.—See Wausau-Mosinee Paper Corporation; *U.S. Public*, pg. 1747
BAYBANK, N.A.—See BankBoston Corporation; *U.S. Public*, pg. 184
BAYBANKS, INC.—See BankBoston Corporation; *U.S. Public*, pg. 184
BAYCO INDUSTRIES—See Derlan Industries Limited; *Int'l*, pg. 395
BAYCOAT—See DoFasco, Inc.; *Int'l*, pg. 414
BAYCOAT LIMITED—See Stelco Inc.; *Int'l*, pg. 1299
BAYER AG; *Int'l*, pg. 171

BAYER AG—See Bayer AG; *Int'l,* pg. 172
BAYER ANTWERPEN N.V.—See Bayer AG; *Int'l,* pg. 174
BAYER ARGENTINA S.A.—See Bayer AG; *Int'l,* pg. 175
BAYER A/S—See Bayer AG; *Int'l,* pg. 174
BAYER AUSTRALIA LTD.—See Bayer AG; *Int'l,* pg. 175
BAYER AUSTRIA G.M.B.H.—See Bayer AG; *Int'l,* pg. 175
BAYER BELGIUM S.A.-N.V.—See Bayer AG; *Int'l,* pg. 175
BAYER B.V.—See Bayer AG; *Int'l,* pg. 175
BAYER (CANADA) INC.—See Bayer AG; *Int'l,* pg. 174
BAYER CAPITAL CORPORATION N.V.—See Bayer AG; *Int'l,* pg. 172
BAYER CLOTHING GROUP; *U.S. Private,* pg. 124
BAYER CORP. PHARMACEUTICALS—See Bayer AG; *Int'l,* pg. 173
BAYER CORPORATION—See Bayer AG; *Int'l,* pg. 172
BAYER CORPORATION/AGRICULTURE DIVISION—See Bayer AG; *Int'l,* pg. 173
BAYER CORPORATION/CONSUMER CARE DIVISION—See Bayer AG; *Int'l,* pg. 173
BAYER CORPORATION/DIAGNOSTICS DIVISION—See Bayer AG; *Int'l,* pg. 173
BAYER CORPORATION/FIBERS, ORGANICS & RUBBER DIVISION—See Bayer AG; *Int'l,* pg. 172
BAYER CORPORATION/PHARMACEUTICAL DIVISION—See Bayer AG; *Int'l,* pg. 173
BAYER DE CHILE S.A.—See Bayer AG; *Int'l,* pg. 175
BAYER DE MEXICO, S.A. DE C.V.—See Bayer AG; *Int'l,* pg. 175
BAYER DO BRAZIL S.A.—See Bayer AG; *Int'l,* pg. 175
BAYER FASER GMBH—See Bayer AG; *Int'l,* pg. 172
BAYER FINANCE S.A.—See Bayer AG; *Int'l,* pg. 175
BAYER FOREIGN INVESTMENTS LTD. (BAYFORIN)—See Bayer AG; *Int'l,* pg. 175
BAYER FRANCE S.A.—See Bayer AG; *Int'l,* pg. 175
BAYER HISPANIA COMERCIAL S.A.—See Bayer AG; *Int'l,* pg. 175
BAYER HISPANIA INDUSTRIAL, S.A.—See Bayer AG; *Int'l,* pg. 175
BAYER (INDIA) LTD.—See Bayer AG; *Int'l,* pg. 174
P.T. BAYER INDONESIA—See Bayer AG; *Int'l,* pg. 174
BAYER INDUSTRIAL S.A.—See Bayer AG; *Int'l,* pg. 175
BAYER INTERNATIONAL FINANCE N.V.—See Bayer AG; *Int'l,* pg. 174
BAYER (IRELAND) LTD.—See Bayer AG; *Int'l,* pg. 174
BAYER ITALIA S.P.A.—See Bayer AG; *Int'l,* pg. 175
BAYER JAPAN LTD.—See Bayer AG; *Int'l,* pg. 174
BAYER-KAUFHAUS GMBH—See Bayer AG; *Int'l,* pg. 172
BAYER MAROC S.A.—See Bayer AG; *Int'l,* pg. 175
BAYER-MILES (PTY.) LTD.—See Bayer AG; *Int'l,* pg. 175
BAYER OWENS/CORNING GLASSWOOL S.A.—See Bayer AG; *Int'l,* pg. 175
BAYER PHARMA S.A. (BELGIUM)—See Bayer AG; *Int'l,* pg. 175
BAYER PHARMACEUTICALS (NIGERIA) LTD.—See Bayer AG; *Int'l,* pg. 175
BAYER PHILIPPINES, INC.—See Bayer AG; *Int'l,* pg. 175
BAYER PORTUGAL S.A.R.L.—See Bayer AG; *Int'l,* pg. 175
BAYER QUIMICAS UNIDAS S.A.—See Bayer AG; *Int'l,* pg. 175
BAYER-SCHWEIZ AG—See Bayer AG; *Int'l,* pg. 175
BAYER-SHELL ISOCYANATES N.V.—See Royal Dutch/Shell Group of Companies; *Int'l,* pg. 1138
BAYER SOUTH AFRICA (PTY.) LTD.—See Bayer AG; *Int'l,* pg. 175
BAYER SVERIGE AB—See Bayer AG; *Int'l,* pg. 175
BAYER TURK KIMYA SANAYI LTD. STI—See Bayer AG; *Int'l,* pg. 175
BAYER UK LTD.—See Bayer AG; *Int'l,* pg. 175
BAYER-WOHNUNGEN GMBH—See Bayer AG; *Int'l,* pg. 172
BAYER YAKUHIN, LTD.—See Bayer AG; *Int'l,* pg. 174
BAYERISCHE-BULGARISCHE HANDELSBANK GMBH—See Bayerische Vereinsbank Group; *Int'l,* pg. 179
BAYERISCHE HANDELSBANK AG—See Bayerische Vereinsbank Group; *Int'l,* pg. 175
BAYERISCHE HYPOTHEKEN-UND WECHSEL-BANK AKTIENGESELLSCHAFT; *Int'l,* pg. 175
BAYERISCHE HYPOTHEKEN-UND WECHSEL-BANK AKTIENGESELLSCHAFT NEW YORK BRANCH—See Bayerische Hypotheken-und Wechsel-Bank Aktiengesellschaft; *Int'l,* pg. 176
BAYERISCHE HYPOTHEKEN-UND WECHSEL-BANK AG (CAYMAN ISLANDS)—See Bayerische Hypotheken-und Wechsel-Bank Aktiengesellschaft; *Int'l,* pg. 176
BAYERISCHE HYPOTHEKEN-UND WECHSEL-BANK AG (HONG KONG)—See Bayerische Hypotheken-und Wechsel-Bank Aktiengesellschaft; *Int'l,* pg. 176
BAYERISCHE IMMOBILIEN-LEASING GMBH—See Bayerische Vereinsbank Group; *Int'l,* pg. 179
BAYERISCHE KAPITALANLAGEGESELLSCHAFT MBH—See Bayerische Vereinsbank Group; *Int'l,* pg. 179
BAYERISCHE LANDESBANK; *Int'l,* pg. 176
BAYERISCHE LANDESBANK GIROZENTRALE—See Bayerische Landesbank; *Int'l,* pg. 177
BAYERISCHE LANDESBANK - LABUAN BRANCH—See Bayerische Landesbank; *Int'l,* pg. 176
BAYERISCHE MANUFACTUR FUR KLUBER LUBRICATION GMBH—See Freudenberg & Company; *Int'l,* pg. 506
BAYERISCHE MOTOREN WERKE AKTIENGESELLSCHAFT; *Int'l,* pg. 177
BAYERISCHE VEREINSBANK AG—See Bayerische Vereinsbank Group; *Int'l,* pg. 180
BAYERISCHE VEREINSBANK AG-LONDON BRANCH—See Bayerische Vereinsbank Group; *Int'l,* pg. 181
BAYERISCHE VEREINSBANK GROUP; *Int'l,* pg. 178
BAYERISCHE VEREINSBANK INTERNATIONAL S.A.—See Bayerische Vereinsbank Group; *Int'l,* pg. 181
BAYERISCHE VEREINSBANK S.A. (BV FRANCE)—See Bayerische Vereinsbank Group; *Int'l,* pg. 181
BAYERISCHE VERSICHERUNGSBANK-AG—See Allianz Aktiengesellschaft; *Int'l,* pg. 58
BAYERISCHE WOHNUNGSGESELLSCHAFT FUR HANDEL UND INDUSTRIE MBH—See Bayerische Vereinsbank Group; *Int'l,* pg. 179

BAYERN-CHEMIE GMBH—See Daimler-Benz Aktiengesellschaft; *Int'l,* pg. 367
BAYERNHYPO FINANCE N.V.—See Bayerische Hypotheken-und Wechsel-Bank Aktiengesellschaft; *Int'l,* pg. 176
BAYERNLAND GMBH & CO. KG; *Int'l,* pg. 181
BAYERNWERK AG—See Viag AG; *Int'l,* pg. 1464
BAYEX INCORPORATED—See Saint-Gobain; *Int'l,* pg. 1170
BAYEX LTD.—See Saint-Gobain; *Int'l,* pg. 1177
ROBERT E. BAYLEY CONSTRUCTION; *U.S. Private,* pg. 125
WILLIAM BAYLEY/FOLGER ADAM SECURITY, INC.; *U.S. Private,* pg. 125
BAYLEY/FAN GROUP—See Tomkins PLC; *Int'l,* pg. 1398
BAYLOR COMPANY—See Royal Begemann Group; *Int'l,* pg. 1134
BAYMONT MALAYSIA SDN BHD—See Agra Inc.; *Int'l,* pg. 31
BAYMONT TECHNOLOGIES INC.—See Agra Inc.; *Int'l,* pg. 31
BAYMONT TECHNOLOGIES (PTE) LTD.—See Agra Inc.; *Int'l,* pg. 31
BAYOU CITY BARGE LINES—See Adams Resources & Energy, Inc.; *U.S. Public,* pg. 19
BAYOU COGENERATION—See Air Liquide S.A.; *Int'l,* pg. 37
BAYOU STATE OIL CORPORATION; *U.S. Private,* pg. 125
BAYOU STEEL CORPORATION; *U.S. Public,* pg. 197
BAYOU STEEL CORPORATION (TENNESSEE)—See Bayou Steel Corporation; *U.S. Public,* pg. 197
BAYSIDE AUTO AUCTION OF TAMPA INC.—See Tyco International Ltd.; *U.S. Public,* pg. 1648
BAYSIDE FUEL OIL CORP.—See Bayside Fuel Oil Depot Corp.; *U.S. Private,* pg. 125
BAYSIDE FUEL OIL DEPOT CORP.; *U.S. Private,* pg. 125
BAYSIDE MOTION GROUP; *U.S. Private,* pg. 125
BAYSIDE TRAFFIC SERVICES OF MARYLAND—See Giant Food Inc.; *U.S. Public,* pg. 741
BAYSIDE UNDERWRITERS INSURANCE AGENCY, INC.—See The Progressive Corporation; *U.S. Public,* pg. 1334
BAYVIEW HOSPITAL—See Columbia/HCA Healthcare Corporation; *U.S. Public,* pg. 404
THE BAYWATCH PRODUCTION COMPANY—See All American Communications, Inc.; *U.S. Public,* pg. 41
BAZAAR & NOVELTY—See Stuart Entertainment Inc.; *U.S. Public,* pg. 1526
BAZAR DE L'HOTEL DE VILLE; *Int'l,* pg. 181
BAZARS ALENCONNAIS—See Au Bon Marche; *Int'l,* pg. 97
BAZIMO—See GIB Group; *Int'l,* pg. 533
BB KARTENSERVICE GMBH—See Bankgesellschaft Berlin; *Int'l,* pg. 159
BE-DELFT ELECTRONICS LTD.—See Delft Instruments N.V.; *Int'l,* pg. 389
BE-LO MARKETS INC.—See Camellia Food Stores, Inc.; *U.S. Private,* pg. 203
BEACH BELT CHEVROLET CO.; *U.S. Private,* pg. 125
BEACH MOLD & TOOL INC.; *U.S. Private,* pg. 125
BEACH PATROL INC.; *U.S. Private,* pg. 125
BEACHWOOD PLACE, INC.—See The Rouse Company; *U.S. Public,* pg. 1408
BEACON COMMUNICATIONS—See Ascent Entertainment Group, Inc.; *U.S. Public,* pg. 138
BEACON CONTAINER CORPORATION; *U.S. Private,* pg. 125
BEACON CONTAINER OF PA—See Beacon Container Corporation; *U.S. Private,* pg. 125
BEACON EYE CENTRE INC—See Hawker Siddeley Canada Inc.; *Int'l,* pg. 604
BEACON GROUP; *U.S. Private,* pg. 126
BEACON GROUP—See Beacon Group; *U.S. Private,* pg. 126
THE BEACON GROUP; *U.S. Private,* pg. 125
THE BEACON JOURNAL PUBLISHING COMPANY—See Knight-Ridder, Inc.; *U.S. Public,* pg. 963
BEACON MFG. CO.—See Pillowtex Corporation; *U.S. Public,* pg. 1296
THE BEACON-NEWS—See The Copley Press, Inc.; *U.S. Private,* pg. 275
BEACON PRESS, INC.—See Media General, Inc.; *U.S. Public,* pg. 1077
BEACON SALES CORPORATION; *U.S. Private,* pg. 126
BEACON WINCH COMPANY—See Beacon Group; *U.S. Private,* pg. 126
BEAD INDUSTRIES INC.; *U.S. Private,* pg. 126
BEADLES LUMBER COMPANY, INC.; *U.S. Private,* pg. 126
BEAIRD INDUSTRIES, INC.—See Trinity Industries Inc.; *U.S. Public,* pg. 1639
BEAIRD INDUSTRIES, INC. OF ORANGE—See Trinity Industries Inc.; *U.S. Public,* pg. 1639
BEAL - BOGOTA—See Westdeutsche Landesbank Girozentrale; *Int'l,* pg. 1493
BEAL - CARACAS—See Westdeutsche Landesbank Girozentrale; *Int'l,* pg. 1493
BEAL MOUNTAIN MINING INC.—See Pegasus Gold Corporation; *U.S. Public,* pg. 1269
BEAL - SANTIAGO—See Westdeutsche Landesbank Girozentrale; *Int'l,* pg. 1494
BEALL'S DEPT. STORES—See Beall's, Inc.; *U.S. Private,* pg. 126
BEALL'S, INC.; *U.S. Private,* pg. 126
BEALLS OUTLET INC.—See Beall's, Inc.; *U.S. Private,* pg. 126
BEAM INDUSTRIES—See Electrolux, AB; *Int'l,* pg. 440
BEAMISH & CRAWFORD PLC—See Scottish & Newcastle plc; *Int'l,* pg. 1212
BEAMIX HOLDING B.V.—See Heidelberger Zement A.G.; *Int'l,* pg. 605
BEAMIX-BEL S.A.—See Heidelberger Zement A.G.; *Int'l,* pg. 606
D.D. BEAN & SONS (CANADA) LTD.—See D.D. Bean & Sons Co.; *U.S. Private,* pg. 127

D.D. BEAN & SONS CO.; *U.S. Private,* pg. 126
D.D. BEAN & SONS (N.C.) INC.—See D.D. Bean & Sons Co.; *U.S. Private,* pg. 127
BEAR CREEK CORPORATION—See Yamanouchi Pharmaceutical Co. Ltd.; *Int'l,* pg. 1518
BEAR CREEK GARDENS, INC.—See Yamanouchi Pharmaceutical Co. Ltd.; *Int'l,* pg. 1518
BEAR CREEK STORES, INC.—See Yamanouchi Pharmaceutical Co. Ltd.; *Int'l,* pg. 1518
BEAR ISLAND PAPER CO.—See Brant Allen Industries, Inc.; *U.S. Private,* pg. 166
BEAR ISLAND PAPER CO.—See Dow Jones & Company, Inc.; *U.S. Public,* pg. 525
BEAR ISLAND TIMBERLANDS COMPANY, L.P.—See The Washington Post Company; *U.S. Public,* pg. 1743
THE LEWIS BEAR COMPANY; *U.S. Private,* pg. 127
BEAR STEARNS—See The Bear Stearns Companies Inc.; *U.S. Public,* pg. 198
BEAR STEARNS BANK PLC—See The Bear Stearns Companies Inc.; *U.S. Public,* pg. 198
THE BEAR STEARNS COMPANIES INC.; *U.S. Public,* pg. 197
BEAR STEARNS FIDUCIARY SERVICES, INC.—See The Bear Stearns Companies Inc.; *U.S. Public,* pg. 198
BEAR STEARNS MORTGAGE CAPITAL CORPORATION—See The Bear Stearns Companies Inc.; *U.S. Public,* pg. 198
BEAR STEARNS REAL ESTATE GROUP INC.—See The Bear Stearns Companies Inc.; *U.S. Public,* pg. 198
BEAR STEARNS SINGAPORE PTE. LIMITED—See The Bear Stearns Companies Inc.; *U.S. Public,* pg. 198
BEAR VALLEY, INC.—See Forest City Enterprises, Inc.; *U.S. Public,* pg. 668
BEARDEN LUMBER COMPANY, INC.; *U.S. Private,* pg. 127
BEARDSLEY & PIPER, L.L.C.—See Pettibone Corporation; *U.S. Private,* pg. 859
BEARING DISTRIBUTORS, INC.; *U.S. Private,* pg. 127
BEARING HEADQUARTERS CO.; *U.S. Private,* pg. 127
BEARING SERVICE COMPANY; *U.S. Private,* pg. 127
BEATRICE CHEESE—See ConAgra, Inc.; *U.S. Public,* pg. 426
BEATRICE CORPORATION—See Mrs. Alison's Cookie Company; *U.S. Private,* pg. 765
BEATSON CLARK PLC—See TT Group PLC; *Int'l,* pg. 1344
F.B. BEATTIE & COMPANY, INC.—See SAFECO Corporation; *U.S. Public,* pg. 1423
BEAU INTERCONNECT SYSTEMS—See Axsys Technologies, Inc.; *U.S. Public,* pg. 157
BEAU MARAIS S.A. (FRANCE)—See McCain Foods Limited; *Int'l,* pg. 850
BEAUCHAMP DISTRIBUTING COMPANY; *U.S. Private,* pg. 127
BEAUD-CHALLES-SOLAP S.A.—See ETEX; *Int'l,* pg. 430
BEAUDREY MAPLE PRODUCTS, INC.—See Borden, Inc.; *U.S. Private,* pg. 159
BEAUDRY FORD, INC.; *U.S. Private,* pg. 127
BEAULIEU GROUP; *U.S. Private,* pg. 127
BEAULIEU UNITED—See Beaulieu Group; *U.S. Private,* pg. 128
BEAULIEU VINEYARD—See Diageo Plc; *Int'l,* pg. 410
BEAUMONT ENTERPRISE—See The Hearst Corporation; *U.S. Private,* pg. 517
BEAUMONT PETROCHEMICAL PLANT—See Mobil Oil Corporation; *U.S. Public,* pg. 1118
BEAUMONT POLYETHYLENE PLANT—See Mobil Oil Corporation; *U.S. Public,* pg. 1118
BEAUMONT-BENNETT A/S—See Jotun A/S; *Int'l,* pg. 714
BEAUT-EASE CORPORATION—See Hyde Manufacturing Co.; *U.S. Private,* pg. 551
BEAUTE CREAURS S.A.—See Otto Versand (GmbH & Co.); *Int'l,* pg. 1015
BEAUTICONTROL COSMETICS CANADA LTD.—See BeautiControl Cosmetics, Inc.; *U.S. Public,* pg. 199
BEAUTICONTROL COSMETICS, INC.; *U.S. Public,* pg. 198
BEAUTICONTROL INTERNATIONAL, INC.—See BeautiControl Cosmetics, Inc.; *U.S. Public,* pg. 198
S.A. BEAUTOR—See Cockerill Sambre; *Int'l,* pg. 302
BEAUTY ENTERPRISES INC.; *U.S. Private,* pg. 128
BEAUTY INTERNATIONAL LTD.—See Joh. A. Benckiser GmbH; *Int'l,* pg. 185
BEAVER FOODS LIMITED—See Cara Operations Limited; *Int'l,* pg. 266
BEAVER FREE CORP.—See Pacifica Real Estate Group; *U.S. Private,* pg. 832
BEAVER LUMBER COMPANY LIMITED—See The Molson Companies Limited; *Int'l,* pg. 887
BEAVER STREET FISHERIES, INC.; *U.S. Private,* pg. 128
THE BEAVER WOOD FIBER COMPANY LTD.—See Georgia-Pacific Corporation; *U.S. Public,* pg. 739
BEAZER GROUP PLC; *Int'l,* pg. 181
BEAZER HOMES (BEDFORD) LIMITED—See Beazer Group Plc; *Int'l,* pg. 182
BEAZER HOMES (BIRMINGHAM)—See Beazer Group Plc; *Int'l,* pg. 182
BEAZER HOMES (BRIDGWATER) LIMITED—See Beazer Group Plc; *Int'l,* pg. 182
BEAZER HOMES (BRISTOL) LTD.—See Beazer Group Plc; *Int'l,* pg. 182
BEAZER HOMES (COLCHESTER) LIMITED—See Beazer Group Plc; *Int'l,* pg. 182
BEAZER HOMES (DONCASTER) LIMITED—See Beazer Group Plc; *Int'l,* pg. 182
BEAZER HOMES (EDINBURGH) LIMITED—See Beazer Group Plc; *Int'l,* pg. 182
BEAZER HOMES (GLASTON) LIMITED—See Beazer Group Plc; *Int'l,* pg. 182
BEAZER HOMES (REDDITCH) LIMITED—See Beazer Group Plc; *Int'l,* pg. 182
BEAZER HOMES (REIGATE) LTD.—See Beazer Group Plc; *Int'l,* pg. 182
BEAZER HOMES (STOCKPORT) LIMITED—See Beazer Group Plc; *Int'l,* pg. 182

MASTER INDEX TO COMPANY NAMES BEISSIER
Company Index

BEAZER HOMES (YATELY) LIMITED—See Beazer Group Plc; *Int'l*, pg. 182
BEBER & SILVERSTEIN & PARTNERS, INC.; *U.S. Private, pg. 128*
BEBIT INFORMATIONS-TECHNIK GMBH—See Bilfinger + Berger Bauaktiengesellschaft; *Int'l*, pg. 195
BEBO-PLASTIK GMBH—See Schmalbach-Lubeca AG; *Int'l, pg. 1206*
BECEMA—See Royal Begemann Group; *Int'l*, pg. 1134
BECHARA OBEGI—See BASF AG; *Int'l*, pg. 107
BECHTEL CIVIL, INC.—See Bechtel Group, Inc.; *U.S. Private*, pg. 128
BECHTEL ENTERPRISES, INC.—See Bechtel Group, Inc.; *U.S. Private*, pg. 128
BECHTEL FINANCING SERVICES, INC.—See Bechtel Group, Inc.; *U.S. Private*, pg. 128
BECHTEL GROUP, INC.; *U.S. Private*, pg. 128
BECHTEL LTD.—See Bechtel Group, Inc.; *U.S. Private*, pg. 128
BECHTEL MINING & METALS—See Bechtel Group, Inc.; *U.S. Private*, pg. 128
BECHTEL NATIONAL, INC.—See Bechtel Group, Inc.; *U.S. Private*, pg. 128
BECHTEL PETROLEUM & CHEMICAL—See Bechtel Group, Inc.; *U.S. Private*, pg. 128
BECHTEL POWER CORPORATION—See Bechtel Group, Inc.; *U.S. Private*, pg. 128
BECHTEL WATER TECHNOLOGY LTD.—See Bechtel Group, Inc.; *U.S. Private*, pg. 128
BECK/ARNLEY WORLDPARTS CORP.—See Echlin Inc.; *U.S. Public*, pg. 561
BECK ELECTRIC MANUFACTURING COMPANY—See Noma Industries Limited; *Int'l*, pg. 955
BECK MANUFACTURING, INC.—See Bitrek Corporation; *U.S. Private*, pg. 146
R.W. BECK, INC.; *U.S. Private*, pg. 128
BECKER—See Harman International Industries, Inc.; *U.S. Public*, pg. 787
BECKER CPA REVIEW—See DeVry Institutes; *U.S. Public*, pg. 504
BECKER MILK CO. LTD.; *Int'l*, pg. 182
ROBERT A. BECKER—See Havas Advertising; *Int'l*, pg. 601
BECKETT PAPERS—See International Paper Company; *U.S. Public*, pg. 903
BECKLEY CARDY GROUP—See Butler Capital Corp.; *U.S. Private*, pg. 190
BECKMAN COULTER—See Beckman Instruments, Inc.; *U.S. Public*, pg. 199
BECKMAN INDUSTRIAL CORPORATION—See Emerson Electric Co.; *U.S. Public*, pg. 574
BECKMAN INSTRUMENTS—See Beckman Instruments, Inc.; *U.S. Public*, pg. 199
BECKMAN INSTRUMENTS, INC.; *U.S. Public*, pg. 199
BECKMAN-IPD/DORIC—See Emerson Electric Co.; *U.S. Public*, pg. 574
BECKWITH ELEVATOR CO.; *U.S. Private*, pg. 128
BECKWITH MACHINERY COMPANY; *U.S. Private*, pg. 129
BECO ENGINEERING COMPANY; *U.S. Private*, pg. 129
BECON CONSTRUCTION COMPANY, INC.—See Bechtel Group, Inc.; *U.S. Private*, pg. 128
BECQUET S.A.—See Otto Versand (GmbH & Co.); *Int'l*, pg. 1015
BECTON DICKINSON & CO., LTD.—See Becton Dickinson & Company; *U.S. Public*, pg. 200
BECTON DICKINSON & CO., MASSACHUSETTS DIV.—See Becton Dickinson & Company; *U.S. Public*, pg. 199
BECTON DICKINSON & COMPANY; *U.S. Public*, pg. 199
BECTON DICKINSON CANADA INC.—See Becton Dickinson & Company; *U.S. Public*, pg. 200
BECTON DICKINSON CONSUMER PRODS.—See Becton Dickinson & Company; *U.S. Public*, pg. 199
BECTON DICKINSON EUROPE—See Becton Dickinson & Company; *U.S. Public*, pg. 200
BECTON DICKINSON IMMUNOCYTOMETRY SYSTEMS—See Becton Dickinson & Company; *U.S. Public*, pg. 199
BECTON DICKINSON IND. CIRURGICAS, S.A.—See Becton Dickinson & Company; *U.S. Public*, pg. 200
BECTON DICKINSON INFUSION THERAPY, INC.—See Becton Dickinson & Company; *U.S. Public*, pg. 199
BECTON DICKINSON LABORATORY PRODUCTS-EUROPE—See Becton Dickinson & Company; *U.S. Public*, pg. 200
BECTON DICKINSON LABWARE—See Becton Dickinson & Company; *U.S. Public*, pg. 199
BECTON DICKINSON MEDICAL PRODUCTS-EUROPE—See Becton Dickinson & Company; *U.S. Public*, pg. 200
BECTON DICKINSON MEXICO—See Becton Dickinson & Company; *U.S. Public*, pg. 200
BECTON DICKINSON MICROBIOLOGY SYSTEMS—See Becton Dickinson & Company; *U.S. Public*, pg. 199
BECTON DICKINSON PHARMACEUTICAL SYSTEMS—See Becton Dickinson & Company; *U.S. Public*, pg. 199
BECTON DICKINSON PRIMARY CARE DIAGNOSTICS—See Becton Dickinson & Company; *U.S. Public*, pg. 199
BECTON DICKINSON PTY LTD.—See Becton Dickinson & Company; *U.S. Public*, pg. 200
BECTON DICKINSON RESEARCH CENTER—See Becton Dickinson & Company; *U.S. Public*, pg. 199
BECTON DICKINSON SINGAPORE—See Becton Dickinson & Company; *U.S. Public*, pg. 200
BECTON DICKINSON URUGUAY—See Becton Dickinson & Company; *U.S. Public*, pg. 200
BECTON DICKINSON VACUTAINER SYSTEMS—See Becton Dickinson & Company; *U.S. Public*, pg. 199
BECTON DICKINSON VACUTAINER SYSTEMS EUROPE—See Becton Dickinson & Company; *U.S. Public*, pg. 200
BED BATH & BEYOND INC.; *U.S. Public*, pg. 200
BEDARCO NOOTER, INC.—See Nooter Corporation; *U.S. Private*, pg. 801
BEDEK AVIATION GROUP (IAI)—See Israel Aircraft Industries Ltd.; *Int'l*, pg. 690
BEDFORD ASSOCIATES, INC.—See BT Financial Corporation; *U.S. Public*, pg. 164
BEDFORD ASSOCIATES, INC.—See British Airways PLC; *Int'l*, pg. 219
BEDFORD BULLETIN—See Landmark Communications, Inc.; *U.S. Private*, pg. 648
BEDFORD INDUSTRIES, INC.; *U.S. Private*, pg. 129
BEDROOM SUPERSTORES; *U.S. Private*, pg. 129
BEDRUIJENCENTRUM REGIO KORTRIJK N.V.—See Tractebel; *Int'l*, pg. 1415
BEE-GEE SHOE CORP.—See The Elder-Beerman Stores Corp.; *U.S. Private*, pg. 367
BEE LINE COMPANY; *U.S. Private*, pg. 129
BEEBE RUBBER COMPANY—See The Chardon Rubber Co.; *U.S. Private*, pg. 229
BEECH ACCEPTANCE CORP., INC.—See Raytheon Company; *U.S. Public*, pg. 1365
BEECH AEROSPACE SERVICES, INC.—See Raytheon Company; *U.S. Public*, pg. 1365
BEECH COAL COMPANY—See Cyprus Amax Minerals Company; *U.S. Public*, pg. 471
BEECH HOLDINGS, INC.—See Raytheon Company; *U.S. Public*, pg. 1365
BEECH ISUZU—See Beechmont Investments Inc.; *U.S. Private*, pg. 129
BEECH-NUT NUTRITION CORPORATION—See Ralcorp Holdings Inc.; *U.S. Public*, pg. 1359
BEECH TREE BOOKS—See The Hearst Corporation; *U.S. Private*, pg. 515
BEECHAM (AUSTRALIA) PTY. LTD.—See SmithKline Beecham plc; *Int'l*, pg. 1265
BEECHAM RESEARCH LABORATORIES—See SmithKline Beecham plc; *Int'l*, pg. 1265
BEECHAM-WULFING G.M.B.H. & CO. K.G.—See SmithKline Beecham plc; *Int'l*, pg. 1266
BEECHMONT CHEVROLET, INC—See Beechmont Investments Inc.; *U.S. Private*, pg. 129
BEECHMONT HYUNDAI—See Beechmont Investments Inc.; *U.S. Private*, pg. 129
BEECHMONT INVESTMENTS INC.; *U.S. Private*, pg. 129
BEECHMONT PORSCHE AUDI INC.—See Beechmont Investments Inc.; *U.S. Private*, pg. 129
BEECHWOOD INSURANCE AGENCY, INC.—See Summit Bancorp; *U.S. Public*, pg. 1528
BEEF DISTRIBUTORS, INC.—See Keeners, Inc.; *U.S. Private*, pg. 611
BEEFAMERICA OPERATING CO., INC.; *U.S. Private*, pg. 130
BEEHIVE MACHINERY CO.—See Weiler & Company, Inc.; *U.S. Private*, pg. 1160
BEEKMAN 1766 TAVERN—See Ark Restaurants Corp.; *U.S. Public*, pg. 130
BEEMAK PLASTICS—See Jordan Industries, Inc.; *U.S. Private*, pg. 598
GEOFFREY BEENE FRAGRANCES—See French Fragrances Inc.; *U.S. Public*, pg. 681
GEOFFREY BEENE RETAIL—See Phillips-Van Heusen Corporation; *U.S. Public*, pg. 1291
BEENUP MINE—See The Broken Hill Proprietary Company Limited; *Int'l*, pg. 224
BEEPEE MUSIC—See Cox Enterprises, Inc.; *U.S. Private*, pg. 282
BEEPER COMMUNICATIONS ISRAEL LTD.—See Motorola, Inc.; *U.S. Public*, pg. 1139
BEER NUTS, INC.; *U.S. Private*, pg. 130
BEERS CONSTRUCTION COMPANY—See Skanska AB; *Int'l*, pg. 1261
BEETON RUMFORD LTD.—See The Peninsular and Oriental Steam Navigation Company; *Int'l*, pg. 1032
BEFAB-SAFELAND, LTD.—See Datron Incorporated; *U.S. Private*, pg. 313
BEFICO LIMITED—See Novartis AG; *Int'l*, pg. 975
BEGEMANN BELGIUM N.V.—See Royal Begemann Group; *Int'l*, pg. 1134
BEGEMANN INC—See Royal Begemann Group; *Int'l*, pg. 1134
BEGEMANN RUSLAND B.V.—See Royal Begemann Group; *Int'l*, pg. 1134
BEGHIN-MEIJI INDUSTRIES—See Meiji Seika Kaisha, Ltd.; *Int'l*, pg. 856
BEGIMMO N.V.—See Royal Begemann Group; *Int'l*, pg. 1134
BEGINNER BOOKS—See Advance Publications Inc.; *U.S. Private*, pg. 21
BEGINNING READERS' PROGRAM—See Lagardere Groupe; *Int'l*, pg. 794
BEHAVIORAL HEALTH SERVICES—See Central DuPage Health System; *U.S. Private*, pg. 223
BEHAVIORAL HEALTH SYSTEMS OF INDIANA, INC.—See Magellan Health Services, Inc.; *U.S. Public*, pg. 1033
BEHAVIORAL HEALTHCARE OPTIONS, INC.—See Sierra Health Services, Inc.; *U.S. Public*, pg. 1469
BEHLEN MFG. CO.; *U.S. Private*, pg. 130
BEHN, MEYER & CO. (PTE.) LTD.—See BASF AG; *Int'l*, pg. 107
BEHR IBERICA S.A.—See Durr AG; *Int'l*, pg. 422
BEHR INDUSTRIAL EQUIPMENT LTD.—See Durr AG; *Int'l, pg. 422*
JOSEPH BEHR & SONS INC.; *U.S. Private*, pg. 130
BEHR SYSTEMS, INC.—See Durr AG; *Int'l*, pg. 421
BEHRINGWERKE AG—See Hoechst Aktiengesellschaft; *Int'l*, pg. 624
KATHRYN BEICH, INC.—See Nestle S.A.; *Int'l*, pg. 917
BEIERSDORF AB—See Beiersdorf Group; *Int'l*, pg. 183
BEIERSDORF AG—See Beiersdorf Group; *Int'l*, pg. 182
BEIERSDORF (AUSTRALIA) LTD.—See Beiersdorf Group; *Int'l*, pg. 183
BEIERSDORF (DENMARK) A/S—See Beiersdorf Group; *Int'l*, pg. 183
BEIERSDORF ESPANOLA S.A.—See Beiersdorf Group; *Int'l*, pg. 183
BEIERSDORF GES. MBH—See Beiersdorf Group; *Int'l*, pg. 183
BEIERSDORF GROUP; *Int'l*, pg. 182
BEIERSDORF HELLAS AE—See Beiersdorf Group; *Int'l*, pg. 183
BEIERSDORF, INC.—See Beiersdorf Group; *Int'l*, pg. 182
P.T. BEIERSDORF INDONESIA—See Beiersdorf Group; *Int'l*, pg. 183
BEIERSDORF JAPAN K.K.—See Beiersdorf Group; *Int'l*, pg. 183
BEIERSDORF KFT—See Beiersdorf Group; *Int'l*, pg. 183
BEIERSDORF (MALAYSIA) SDN. BHD.—See Beiersdorf Group; *Int'l*, pg. 183
BEIERSDORF NORGE A/S—See Beiersdorf Group; *Int'l*, pg. 183
BEIERSDORF NV—See Beiersdorf Group; *Int'l*, pg. 183
S.A. BEIERSDORF NV—See Beiersdorf Group; *Int'l*, pg. 183
BEIERSDORF OY—See Beiersdorf Group; *Int'l*, pg. 183
BEIERSDORF PORTUGUESA LDA—See Beiersdorf Group; *Int'l*, pg. 183
BEIERSDORF S.A.—See Beiersdorf Group; *Int'l*, pg. 183
BEIERSDORF SPA—See Beiersdorf Group; *Int'l*, pg. 183
BEIERSDORF SPOL. S.R.O.—See Beiersdorf Group; *Int'l*, pg. 183
BEIERSDORF (THAILAND) CO. LTD.—See Beiersdorf Group; *Int'l*, pg. 183
BEIJING AGIE INDUSTRIAL ELECTRONICS LTD.—See Georg Fischer Ltd.; *Int'l*, pg. 488
BEIJING AIRPORT FOODS SERVICE CO., LTD.—See Suntory Ltd.; *Int'l*, pg. 1322
BEIJING AP BEIFEN GASES INDUSTRY COMPANY, LTD.—See Air Products and Chemicals, Inc.; *U.S. Public*, pg. 32
BEIJING AUTOMATED COMPUTER SYSTEMS CO. LTD., WUHAN—See CSA Holdings Ltd.; *Int'l*, pg. 242
BEIJING AUTOMATED COMPUTER SYSTEMS CO. LTD., BEIJING—See CSA Holdings Ltd.; *Int'l*, pg. 242
BEIJING AUTOMATED COMPUTER SYSTEMS CO. LTD.—See CSA Holdings Ltd.; *Int'l*, pg. 242
BEIJING AUTOMATED COMPUTER SYSTEMS CO. LTD., GUANGZHOU—See CSA Holdings Ltd.; *Int'l*, pg. 242
BEIJING AUTOMATED COMPUTER SYSTEMS CO. LTD., SHANGHAI—See CSA Holdings Ltd.; *Int'l*, pg. 242
BEIJING AUTOMATED COMPUTER SYSTEMS CO. LTD., SHENZHEN—See CSA Holdings Ltd.; *Int'l*, pg. 242
BEIJING AUTOMATED COMPUTER SYSTEMS CO. LTD, XIAMEN—See CSA Holdings Ltd.; *Int'l*, pg. 243
BEIJING BEILING SPECIAL AUTOMOBILE CO., LTD.—See Isuzu Motors Limited; *Int'l*, pg. 692
BEIJING CHINATUHSU MAKRO PROPERTY CO. LTD.—See SHV Holdings N.V.; *Int'l*, pg. 1155
BEIJING CHINEFARGE CEMENT LIMITED LIABILITY CO.—See Lafarge S.A.; *Int'l*, pg. 791
BEIJING CIBA-GEIGY PHARMA LTD.—See Novartis AG; *Int'l*, pg. 975
BEIJING CROWN CAN COMPANY LTD.—See Crown Cork & Seal Company, Inc.; *U.S. Public*, pg. 465
BEIJING DENTSU ADVERTISING CO., LTD.—See Dentsu Inc.; *Int'l*, pg. 393
BEIJING DENTSU SHANGHAI BRANCH (DENTSU SHANGHAI)—See Dentsu Inc.; *Int'l*, pg. 393
BEIJING DESCENTE CO., LTD.—See Descente Ltd.; *Int'l*, pg. 396
BEIJING EAST PALACE APARTMENT CO., LTD.—See Daiwa House Industry Co., Ltd.; *Int'l*, pg. 374
BEIJING EASTERN ROHM AND HAAS COMPANY, LIMITED—See Rohm and Haas Company; *U.S. Public*, pg. 1403
BEIJING - FANUC MECHATRONICS CO., LTD.—See Fanuc Ltd.; *Int'l*, pg. 478
BEIJING GOT BUSINESS COMPUTER SYSTEM CO. LTD.—See Omron Corporation; *Int'l*, pg. 1005
BEIJING HUADE LINING MATERIALS INDUSTRY CO. LTD.—See Superior Metal Printing Limited; *Int'l*, pg. 1322
BEIJING HUADE METAL PACKAGING CONTAINER CO. LTD.—See Superior Metal Printing Limited; *Int'l*, pg. 1322
BEIJING JI TONG-BELLSOUTH COMMUNICATION & INFORMATION ENGINEERING CO., LTD.—See BellSouth Corporation; *U.S. Public*, pg. 208
BEIJING JIAI PHARMACEUTICALS LIMITED LIABILITY COMPANY—See IVAX Corporation; *U.S. Public*, pg. 915
BEIJING LUFTHANSA CENTER CO., LTD.—See Daewoo Corporation; *Int'l*, pg. 358
BEIJING MITSUKOSHI RESTAURANT LTD.—See Mitsukoshi, Ltd.; *Int'l*, pg. 884
BEIJING NOKIA HANG XINGTELECOMS SYSTEMS CO. LTD.—See Oy Nokia Ab/Nokia Group; *Int'l*, pg. 953
BEIJING OFFICE—See Mitsubishi Chemical Corporation; *Int'l*, pg. 871
BEIJING PRAXAIR INC.—See Praxair Inc.; *U.S. Public*, pg. 1320
BEIJING SANYO ELECTRONICS (SHEKOU) LTD.—See Sanyo Electric Co., Ltd.; *Int'l*, pg. 1191
BEIJING SHIMADZU MEDICAL EQUIPMENT CO., LTD.—See Shimadzu Corporation; *Int'l*, pg. 1232
BEIJING TOTO CO., LTD.—See Toto Ltd.; *Int'l*, pg. 1410
BEIJING WACOAL CO., LTD.—See Wacoal Corporation; *Int'l*, pg. 1484
BEIJING WIRE COMMUNICATIONS PLANT—See Knurr AG; *Int'l*, pg. 739
BEIJING ZHONG AN FIRE SECURITY ELECTRONICS COMPANY LTD.—See Siemens AG; *Int'l*, pg. 1246
BEIJING ZHULI DIANTONG OPTOELECTRONICS TECHNOLOGY CO., LTD.—See Sumitomo Electric Industries, Ltd.; *Int'l*, pg. 1313
BEISERDORF UK LTD.—See Beiersdorf Group; *Int'l*, pg. 183
BEISSIER S.A.—See Dyckerhoff AG; *Int'l*, pg. 423

BEKAERT A/S—See N.V. Bekaert S.A.; *Int'l*, pg. 184
BEKAERT ASIA—See N.V. Bekaert S.A.; *Int'l*, pg. 184
BEKAERT ASIA SHANGHAI OFFICE—See N.V. Bekaert S.A.; *Int'l*, pg. 184
BEKAERT ASSOCIATES, INC.—See N.V. Bekaert S.A.; *Int'l*, pg. 184
BEKAERT (AUSTRALIA) PTY. LTD.—See Gamma Holding N.V.; *Int'l*, pg. 540
BEKAERT BENELUX N.V.—See N.V. Bekaert S.A.; *Int'l*, pg. 183
BEKAERT-BHP STEEL CORD PTY. LTD.—See N.V. Bekaert S.A.; *Int'l*, pg. 184
BEKAERT BUILDING PRODUCTS LTD.—See N.V. Bekaert S.A.; *Int'l*, pg. 184
BEKAERT COMPOSITES, S.A.—See N.V. Bekaert S.A.; *Int'l*, pg. 183
BEKAERT CONSULTING—See N.V. Bekaert S.A.; *Int'l*, pg. 184
BEKAERT COORDINATIECENTRUM—See N.V. Bekaert S.A.; *Int'l*, pg. 183
BEKAERT CORPORATION—See N.V. Bekaert S.A.; *Int'l*, pg. 184
BEKAERT DEUTSCHLAND GMBH—See N.V. Bekaert S.A.; *Int'l*, pg. 184
BEKAERT ENGINEERING—See N.V. Bekaert S.A.; *Int'l*, pg. 183
BEKAERT ENGINEERING DO BRASIL LTDA.—See N.V. Bekaert S.A.; *Int'l*, pg. 184
BEKAERT ENGINEERING OF NORTH AMERICA—See N.V. Bekaert S.A.; *Int'l*, pg. 184
BEKAERT FIBRE TECHNOLOGIES:—See N.V. Bekaert S.A.; *Int'l*, pg. 184
BEKAERT FRANCE—See N.V. Bekaert S.A.; *Int'l*, pg. 184
BEKAERT GES.M.B.H.—See N.V. Bekaert S.A.; *Int'l*, pg. 184
BEKAERT IBERICA, S.A.—See N.V. Bekaert S.A.; *Int'l*, pg. 184
BEKAERT INTERNATIONAL TRADE—See N.V. Bekaert S.A.; *Int'l*, pg. 183
BEKAERT (IRELAND) LTD.—See N.V. Bekaert S.A.; *Int'l*, pg. 184
BEKAERT KOTLARNIA SP.Z.O.O.—See N.V. Bekaert S.A.; *Int'l*, pg. 184
LEON BEKAERT S.P.A.—See N.V. Bekaert S.A.; *Int'l*, pg. 184
LEON BEKAERT SVENSKA A/B—See N.V. Bekaert S.A.; *Int'l*, pg. 184
BEKAERT NEDERLAND B.V.—See N.V. Bekaert S.A.; *Int'l*, pg. 184
BEKAERT NORGE A/S—See N.V. Bekaert S.A.; *Int'l*, pg. 184
BEKAERT NORTHEAST SALES COMPANY—See N.V. Bekaert S.A.; *Int'l*, pg. 184
BEKAERT PORTUGAL-IMPORTACAO COMERCIALIZACAO DE ARAMES E SEUS DERIVADOS, LTDA.—See N.V. Bekaert S.A.; *Int'l*, pg. 184
N.V. BEKAERT S.A.; *Int'l*, pg. 183
N.V. BEKAERT S.A.—See N.V. Bekaert S.A.; *Int'l*, pg. 183
BEKAERT (SCHWEIZ) AG—See N.V. Bekaert S.A.; *Int'l*, pg. 184
BEKAERT SINGAPORE PTE. LTD.—See N.V. Bekaert S.A.; *Int'l*, pg. 184
BEKAERT-STANWICK CONSULTANTS—See N.V. Bekaert S.A.; *Int'l*, pg. 184
BEKAERT TEXTILES N.V.—See Gamma Holding N.V.; *Int'l*, pg. 540
BEKAERT-TINSLEY—See N.V. Bekaert S.A.; *Int'l*, pg. 183
BEKAERT TRADE LATIN AMERICA N.V.—See N.V. Bekaert S.A.; *Int'l*, pg. 184
BEKAERT-STANWICK N.V.—See N.V. Bekaert S.A.; *Int'l*, pg. 183
BEKINA LEBENSMITTEL GMBH—See Nutricia BV; *Int'l*, pg. 991
BEKINS DISTRIBUTION SERVICES CO.—See Hospitality Worldwide Services, Inc.; *U.S. Public*, pg. 841
BEKINTEX N.V.—See N.V. Bekaert S.A.; *Int'l*, pg. 183
BEKO—See The Macneal-Schwendler Corp.; *U.S. Public*, pg. 1031
BEKO ELEKTRONIK A.S.—See Koc Holding A.S.; *Int'l*, pg. 741
BEKO SPOL. S.R.O.—See The Macneal-Schwendler Corp.; *U.S. Public*, pg. 1031
BEKO U.K. LTD.—See Koc Holding A.S.; *Int'l*, pg. 742
BEKSA CELIK KORD SANAYI VE TICARET A.S.—See N.V. Bekaert S.A.; *Int'l*, pg. 185
BEKSA CELIK KORD SANAYI VE TICARET A.S.—See Sabanci Holding A.S.; *Int'l*, pg. 1167
BEL-AIR FENCE BRANCH—See The Ivaco Group; *Int'l*, pg. 695
BEL-AIR FENCE DIVISION—See The Ivaco Group; *Int'l*, pg. 695
BEL AIR MARKETS—See Raley's & Bel Air; *U.S. Private*, pg. 908
BEL-AIR PATROL—See Borg-Warner Security Corporation; *U.S. Public*, pg. 245
BEL-ART PRODUCTS; *U.S. Private*, pg. 130
BEL (CAYMAN) LIMITED—See Bangkok Bank Public Company Limited; *Int'l*, pg. 146
BEL FUSE INC.; *U.S. Public*, pg. 200
BEL FUSE LTD.—See Bel Fuse Inc.; *U.S. Public*, pg. 200
BEL/KAUKAUNA USA; *U.S. Private*, pg. 130
BEL-RAY COMPANY, INC.; *U.S. Private*, pg. 130
BEL RTL—See Groupe Bruxelles Lambert S.A.; *Int'l*, pg. 561
BELA VISTA LIMITADA—See Jardine Matheson Holdings Limited; *Int'l*, pg. 704
BELAIR INSURANCE COMPANY—See ING Groep N.V.; *Int'l*, pg. 648
BELARUS MACHINERY, INC.—See AutotractorExport; *Int'l*, pg. 101
BELASSI S.A.—See Freudenberg & Company; *Int'l*, pg. 507
BELCAN CORPORATION; *U.S. Private*, pg. 131

BELCOSA DISTRIBUIDORA DE COSMETICOS LTDA.—See Wella Group; *Int'l*, pg. 1489
BELDEN & BLAKE CORPORATION—See Texas Pacific Group; *U.S. Private*, pg. 1078
BELDEN ASSOCIATES—See VNU Verenigde Nederlandse Uitgeversbedrijven B.V.; *Int'l*, pg. 1447
BELDEN INC.; *U.S. Public*, pg. 200
BELDEN WIRE & CABLE COMPANY—See Belden Inc.; *U.S. Public*, pg. 201
BELDOCH INDUSTRIES—See Donnkenny, Inc.; *U.S. Public*, pg. 519
BELDOCH POPPER DIVISION—See Donnkenny, Inc.; *U.S. Public*, pg. 520
BELDRAY LIMITED—See Krug International Corp.; *U.S. Public*, pg. 968
N.V. BELEGGINGS-EN KREDIETKANTOOR VAN POPERINGE—See Assicurazioni Generali S.p.A.; *Int'l*, pg. 90
BELEGGINGSMAATSCHAPPIJ DE GRACHTEN B.V.—See Assicurazioni Generali S.p.A.; *Int'l*, pg. 90
B.V. BELEGGINGSMAATSCHAPPIJ NEDASINVEST—See Assicurazioni Generali S.p.A.; *Int'l*, pg. 90
BELEGGINGSMAATSCHAPPIJ ZAANDIJK B.V.—See Schmalbach-Lubeca AG; *Int'l*, pg. 1207
BELFAST TERMINAL—See GATX Corporation; *U.S. Public*, pg. 692
BELFE S.P.A.; *Int'l*, pg. 185
BELFIN S.A.—See Tractebel; *Int'l*, pg. 1415
BELFOX—See Bank Brussels Lambert; *Int'l*, pg. 147
BELGAMANCHE—See Tractebel; *Int'l*, pg. 1415
BELGATOM S.A.—See Tractebel; *Int'l*, pg. 1415
S.A. BELGE LE CARBONE—See Pechiney; *Int'l*, pg. 1030
BELGELECTRIC FINANCE B.V.—See Tractebel; *Int'l*, pg. 1416
BELGIAN FUELLING AND SERVICES COMPANY—See Sabena; *Int'l*, pg. 1168
BELGIAN PIPE CONTROL S.A.—See Tractebel; *Int'l*, pg. 1415
BELGIAN SHELL, S.A.—See Royal Dutch/Shell Group of Companies; *Int'l*, pg. 1138
BELGICA INSURANCE HOLDING S.A.—See Assicurazioni Generali S.p.A.; *Int'l*, pg. 90
BELGIUM UNION DES ASSUREURS, BELGIQUE—See La Fondiaria Assicurazioni S.p.A.; *Int'l*, pg. 784
BELGO-FACTORS, N.V.—See Generale de Banque S.A.; *Int'l*, pg. 547
BELGOLAISE—See Generale de Banque S.A.; *Int'l*, pg. 548
BELGO-MINEIRA BEKAERT TREFILARIAS LTDA.—See N.V. Bekaert S.A.; *Int'l*, pg. 184
BELGONUCLEAIRE S.A.—See Tractebel; *Int'l*, pg. 1415
BELGOREST S.A.—See Sodexho S.A.; *Int'l*, pg. 1274
BELIN/LU—See Danone Group; *Int'l*, pg. 380
BELIZE FOOD PRODUCTS LTD.—See Nestle S.A.; *Int'l*, pg. 918
BELIZE TELECOMMUNICATIONS LIMITED—See British Telecommunications plc; *Int'l*, pg. 223
BELK STORES SERVICES INC.; *U.S. Private*, pg. 131
BELL—See BCE Inc.; *Int'l*, pg. 115
BELL AG—See Coop Switzerland; *Int'l*, pg. 329
BELL & HOWELL ACCEPTANCE CORPORATION—See Bell & Howell Holdings; *U.S. Public*, pg. 201
BELL & HOWELL DOCUMENT MANAGEMENT PRODUCTS COMPANY—See Bell & Howell Holdings; *U.S. Public*, pg. 201
BELL & HOWELL FRANCE S.A.—See Bell & Howell Holdings; *U.S. Public*, pg. 201
BELL & HOWELL GMBH—See Bell & Howell Holdings; *U.S. Public*, pg. 201
BELL & HOWELL HOLDINGS; *U.S. Public*, pg. 201
BELL & HOWELL JAPAN CO. K.K.—See Bell & Howell Holdings; *U.S. Public*, pg. 201
BELL & HOWELL LTD.—See Bell & Howell Holdings; *U.S. Public*, pg. 201
BELL & HOWELL LTD., (UK) MAILHANDLING DIV.—See Bell & Howell Holdings; *U.S. Public*, pg. 201
BELL & HOWELL MAILMOBILE CO.—See Bell & Howell Holdings; *U.S. Public*, pg. 201
BELL & HOWELL NEDERLAN B.V.—See Bell & Howell Holdings; *U.S. Public*, pg. 201
BELL & HOWELL PUBLICATION SYSTEMS COMPANY—See Bell & Howell Holdings; *U.S. Public*, pg. 201
BELL ATLANTIC—See Bell Atlantic Corporation; *U.S. Public*, pg. 202
BELL ATLANTIC ADMINISTRATIVE SERVICES, INC.—See Bell Atlantic Corporation; *U.S. Public*, pg. 202
BELL ATLANTIC ARGENTINA, INC.—See Bell Atlantic Corporation; *U.S. Public*, pg. 202
BELL ATLANTIC ASIA, INC.—See Bell Atlantic Corporation; *U.S. Public*, pg. 202
BELL ATLANTIC AUSTRALIA PTY LIMITED—See Bell Atlantic Corporation; *U.S. Public*, pg. 204
BELL ATLANTIC CAPITAL ADVISORS, INC.—See Bell Atlantic Corporation; *U.S. Public*, pg. 202
BELL ATLANTIC CAPITAL CORPORATION—See Bell Atlantic Corporation; *U.S. Public*, pg. 202
BELL ATLANTIC CAPITAL FUNDING CORP.—See Bell Atlantic Corporation; *U.S. Public*, pg. 202
BELL ATLANTIC CAPITAL INVESTMENTS, INC.—See Bell Atlantic Corporation; *U.S. Public*, pg. 202
BELL ATLANTIC CELLULAR CONSULTING GROUP, INC.—See Bell Atlantic Corporation; *U.S. Public*, pg. 202
BELL ATLANTIC CORPORATION; *U.S. Public*, pg. 201
BELL ATLANTIC CREDIT COMPANY—See Bell Atlantic Corporation; *U.S. Public*, pg. 202
BELL ATLANTIC CUSTOMER SERVICES INTERNATIONAL, INC.—See Bell Atlantic Corporation; *U.S. Public*, pg. 202
BELL ATLANTIC-DE—See Bell Atlantic Corporation; *U.S. Public*, pg. 202
BELL ATLANTIC DIRECTORY GRAPHICS, INC.—See Bell Atlantic Corporation; *U.S. Public*, pg. 203

BELL ATLANTIC EDUCATION SERVICES, INC.—See Bell Atlantic Corporation; *U.S. Public*, pg. 202
BELL ATLANTIC ENTERPRISES CORPORATION—See Bell Atlantic Corporation; *U.S. Public*, pg. 202
BELL ATLANTIC EUROPE S.A.—See Bell Atlantic Corporation; *U.S. Public*, pg. 204
BELL ATLANTIC FINANCIAL FRANCE S.A.—See Bell Atlantic Corporation; *U.S. Public*, pg. 204
BELL ATLANTIC FINANCIAL OVERSEAS CORPORATION—See Bell Atlantic Corporation; *U.S. Public*, pg. 202
BELL ATLANTIC FINANCIAL S.A.—See Bell Atlantic Corporation; *U.S. Public*, pg. 202
BELL ATLANTIC FINANCIAL SERVICES—See Bell Atlantic Corporation; *U.S. Public*, pg. 202
BELL ATLANTIC FINANCIAL (U.K.) LIMITED—See Bell Atlantic Corporation; *U.S. Public*, pg. 204
BELL ATLANTIC FOREIGN SALES CORPORATION—See Bell Atlantic Corporation; *U.S. Public*, pg. 202
BELL ATLANTIC FOUNDATION—See Bell Atlantic Corporation; *U.S. Public*, pg. 202
BELL ATLANTIC FUNDING COMPANY—See Bell Atlantic Corporation; *U.S. Public*, pg. 202
BELL ATLANTIC GMBH—See Bell Atlantic Corporation; *U.S. Public*, pg. 204
BELL ATLANTIC HOLDINGS LIMITED—See Bell Atlantic Corporation; *U.S. Public*, pg. 204
BELL ATLANTIC INFORMATION SYSTEMS, INC.—See Bell Atlantic Corporation; *U.S. Public*, pg. 202
BELL ATLANTIC INTERNATIONAL—See Bell Atlantic Corporation; *U.S. Public*, pg. 202
BELL ATLANTIC INTERNATIONAL, INC.—See Bell Atlantic Corporation; *U.S. Public*, pg. 202
BELL ATLANTIC INTERNATIONAL-ITALIA S.R.L.—See Bell Atlantic Corporation; *U.S. Public*, pg. 204
BELL ATLANTIC INTERNATIONAL WIRELESS SERVICES, INC.—See Bell Atlantic Corporation; *U.S. Public*, pg. 202
BELL ATLANTIC INVESTMENT DEVELOPMENT CORPORATION—See Bell Atlantic Corporation; *U.S. Public*, pg. 202
BELL ATLANTIC INVESTMENTS, INC.—See Bell Atlantic Corporation; *U.S. Public*, pg. 202
BELL ATLANTIC LAND DEVELOPMENT, INC.—See Bell Atlantic Corporation; *U.S. Public*, pg. 202
BELL ATLANTIC-MD—See Bell Atlantic Corporation; *U.S. Public*, pg. 202
BELL ATLANTIC MM HOLDINGS, INC.—See Bell Atlantic Corporation; *U.S. Public*, pg. 202
BELL ATLANTIC MOBILE—See Bell Atlantic Corporation; *U.S. Public*, pg. 202
BELL ATLANTIC MOBILFUNK GMBH—See Bell Atlantic Corporation; *U.S. Public*, pg. 204
BELL ATLANTIC NETWORK FUNDING CORPORATION—See Bell Atlantic Corporation; *U.S. Public*, pg. 202
BELL ATLANTIC NETWORK SERVICES, INC.—See Bell Atlantic Corporation; *U.S. Public*, pg. 202
BELL ATLANTIC NEW ENGLAND—See Bell Atlantic Corporation; *U.S. Public*, pg. 202
BELL ATLANTIC NEW ZEALAND INVESTMENTS, INC.—See Bell Atlantic Corporation; *U.S. Public*, pg. 203
BELL ATLANTIC NEW ZEALAND LIMITED—See Bell Atlantic Corporation; *U.S. Public*, pg. 204
BELL ATLANTIC-NJ—See Bell Atlantic Corporation; *U.S. Public*, pg. 202
BELL ATLANTIC NORTH—See Bell Atlantic Corporation; *U.S. Public*, pg. 203
BELL ATLANTIC-PA—See Bell Atlantic Corporation; *U.S. Public*, pg. 203
BELL ATLANTIC PAGING—See Bell Atlantic Corporation; *U.S. Public*, pg. 203
BELL ATLANTIC PERSONAL COMMUNICATIONS, INC.—See Bell Atlantic Corporation; *U.S. Public*, pg. 203
BELL ATLANTIC PROPERTIES, INC.—See Bell Atlantic Corporation; *U.S. Public*, pg. 203
BELL ATLANTIC PROPERTIES II, INC.—See Bell Atlantic Corporation; *U.S. Public*, pg. 203
BELL ATLANTIC PROPERTY HOLDINGS, INC.—See Bell Atlantic Corporation; *U.S. Public*, pg. 203
BELL ATLANTIC PUERTO RICO, INC.—See Bell Atlantic Corporation; *U.S. Public*, pg. 203
BELL ATLANTIC SERVICES—See Bell Atlantic Corporation; *U.S. Public*, pg. 203
BELL ATLANTIC SOFTWARE AND SYSTEMS SOLUTIONS, INC.—See Bell Atlantic Corporation; *U.S. Public*, pg. 203
BELL ATLANTIC SPECIALTY GUIDES—See Bell Atlantic Corporation; *U.S. Public*, pg. 203
BELL ATLANTIC SYSTEMS INTEGRATION CORP.—See Bell Atlantic Corporation; *U.S. Public*, pg. 203
BELL ATLANTIC SYSTEMS LEASING INTERNATIONAL, INC.—See Bell Atlantic Corporation; *U.S. Public*, pg. 203
BELL ATLANTIC SYSTEMS MARKETING—See Bell Atlantic Corporation; *U.S. Public*, pg. 203
BELL ATLANTIC TELEPRODUCTS CORP.—See Bell Atlantic Corporation; *U.S. Public*, pg. 203
BELL ATLANTIC-VA—See Bell Atlantic Corporation; *U.S. Public*, pg. 203
BELL ATLANTIC VEHICLE MANAGEMENT, INC.—See Bell Atlantic Corporation; *U.S. Public*, pg. 203
BELL ATLANTIC VENTURES XX, INC.—See Bell Atlantic Corporation; *U.S. Public*, pg. 203
BELL ATLANTIC VENTURES XXI, INC.—See Bell Atlantic Corporation; *U.S. Public*, pg. 203
BELL ATLANTIC VENTURES II, INC.—See Bell Atlantic Corporation; *U.S. Public*, pg. 203
BELL ATLANTIC-WASHINGTON, D.C., INC.—See Bell Atlantic Corporation; *U.S. Public*, pg. 203
BELL ATLANTIC-WV—See Bell Atlantic Corporation; *U.S. Public*, pg. 203
BELL ATLANTIC YELLOW PAGES—See Bell Atlantic Corporation; *U.S. Public*, pg. 203

MASTER INDEX TO COMPANY NAMES BENFORD
Company Index

BELL ATLANTICOM SYSTEMS, INC.—See Bell Atlantic Corporation; U.S. Public, pg. 203
BELL CABLEMEDIA PLC—See BCE Inc.; Int'l, pg. 116
BELL CANADA—See BCE Inc.; Int'l, pg. 115
BELL CANADA INTERNATIONAL, INC.—See BCE Inc.; Int'l, pg. 115
BELL CARTER DISTRIBUTING—See Bell-Carter Foods, Inc.; U.S. Private, pg. 131
BELL-CARTER FOODS, INC.; U.S. Private, pg. 131
BELL DAIRY PRODUCTS, INC.—See Dean Foods Company; U.S. Public, pg. 490
BELL DISTRIBUTING—See A. Levy & J. Zentner Co.; U.S. Private, pg. 664
BELL-ESCHER WYSS LTD.—See Sulzer Ltd.; Int'l, pg. 1305
BELL FASHION, LTD.—See Kanebo, Ltd.; Int'l, pg. 722
BELL FLAVORS & FRAGRANCES; U.S. Private, pg. 131
BELL GAS, INC.; U.S. Private, pg. 131
BELL-GRUPPE—See Coop Switzerland; Int'l, pg. 329
BELL HELICOPTER TEXTRON—See Textron Inc.; U.S. Public, pg. 1588
BELL HORIZON SERVICES—See BCE Inc.; Int'l, pg. 115
BELL INDUSTRIES, INC.; U.S. Public, pg. 204
BELL-IRH INDUSTRIES PTY. LTD.—See Delta plc; Int'l, pg. 391
JAN BELL MARKETING INC.; U.S. Public, pg. 207
BELL LABS—See Lucent Technologies Inc.; U.S. Public, pg. 1018
BELL LOCAL SERVICES—See BCE Inc.; Int'l, pg. 115
BELL MOBILITY CELLULAR INC.—See BCE Inc.; Int'l, pg. 115
BELL MOBILITY PAGING INC.—See BCE Inc.; Int'l, pg. 115
BELL MOBILITY RADIO INC.—See BCE Inc.; Int'l, pg. 115
BELL-NORTHERN RESEARCH LTD.—See BCE Inc.; Int'l, pg. 116
BELL-NORTHERN RESEARCH LTD.—See Northern Telecom Limited; Int'l, pg. 969
BELL PACKAGING CORPORATION-GRAND RAPIDS DIV.—See Pratt Industries; Int'l, pg. 1066
BELL PACKAGING CORPORATION-MARION DIV.—See Pratt Industries; Int'l, pg. 1066
BELL PACKAGING CORPORATION-MENOMINEE DIV.—See Pratt Industries; Int'l, pg. 1066
BELL PACKAGING CORPORATION-SOUTH HOLLAND DIV.—See Pratt Industries; Int'l, pg. 1066
RAY BELL CONSTRUCTION CO. INC.; U.S. Private, pg. 131
BELL SPORTS AUSTRALIA—See Bell Sports Corp.; U.S. Public, pg. 207
BELL SPORTS CANADA—See Bell Sports Corp.; U.S. Public, pg. 207
BELL SPORTS CORP.; U.S. Public, pg. 207
BELL TELEPHONE LABORATORIES INC.—See Lucent Technologies Inc.; U.S. Public, pg. 1018
BELL TEXTILE, LTD.—See Kanebo, Ltd.; Int'l, pg. 722
BELL (U.K.) COMMUNICATIONS LIMITED—See Bell Atlantic Corporation; U.S. Public, pg. 204
BELL (U.K.) SERVICES LIMITED—See Bell Atlantic Corporation; U.S. Public, pg. 204
BELLAIRE CORPORATION—See NACCO Industries, Inc.; U.S. Public, pg. 1149
BELLAMY BROTHERS CONTRACTING COMPANY—See Bellamy Brothers, Inc.; U.S. Private, pg. 132
BELLAMY BROTHERS, INC.; U.S. Private, pg. 132
BELLASERA—See Del Webb Corporation; U.S. Public, pg. 495
BELLAST NEDAM CARIBBEAN N.V.—See Ballast Nedam NV; Int'l, pg. 134
BELLCORE—See Science Applications International Corp.; U.S. Private, pg. 976
BELLCREST HOLDING CO., INC.—See The Suddath Companies; U.S. Private, pg. 1049
BELLE FOURCHE PIPELINE CO.—See True Companies; U.S. Private, pg. 1107
BELLE TIRE DISTRIBUTOR INC.; U.S. Private, pg. 132
BELLEMEAD DEVELOPMENT CORP.—See The Chubb Corporation; U.S. Public, pg. 355
BELLETECH CORP.—See Asahi Glass Co., Ltd.; Int'l, pg. 84
BELLEVILLE CENTER—See The Cascades Group; Int'l, pg. 273
BELLEVILLE NEWS-DEMOCRAT—See Knight-Ridder, Inc.; U.S. Public, pg. 964
THE BELLINGHAM HERALD—See Gannett Company, Inc.; U.S. Public, pg. 700
BELLISS & MORCOM—See Powell Duffryn PLC; Int'l, pg. 1065
BELLISS & MORCOM INDIA—See Powell Duffryn PLC; Int'l, pg. 1065
BELLISS & MORCOM (USA) INC.—See Powell Duffryn PLC; Int'l, pg. 1065
BELLSOUTH ADVERTISING & PUBLISHING CORP.—See BellSouth Corporation; U.S. Public, pg. 208
BELLSOUTH APPLIED TECHNOLOGIES, INC.—See BellSouth Corporation; U.S. Public, pg. 209
BELLSOUTH CELLULAR CORP.—See BellSouth Corporation; U.S. Public, pg. 208
BELLSOUTH CELLULAR NATIONAL MARKETING, INC.—See BellSouth Corporation; U.S. Public, pg. 208
BELLSOUTH CHILE S.A.—See BellSouth Corporation; U.S. Public, pg. 208
BELLSOUTH CHINA, INC.—See BellSouth Corporation; U.S. Public, pg. 208
BELLSOUTH COMMUNICATION SYSTEMS, INC.—See BellSouth Corporation; U.S. Public, pg. 209
BELLSOUTH COMUNICACIONES S.A.—See BellSouth Corporation; U.S. Public, pg. 208
BELLSOUTH CORPORATION; U.S. Public, pg. 207
BELLSOUTH ENTERPRISES, INC.—See BellSouth Corporation; U.S. Public, pg. 208
BELLSOUTH EUROPE—See BellSouth Corporation; U.S. Public, pg. 208
BELLSOUTH FINANCIAL SERVICES CORPORATION—See BellSouth Corporation; U.S. Public, pg. 209
BELLSOUTH INFORMATION SYSTEMS, INC. (BIS)—See BellSouth Corporation; U.S. Public, pg. 208
BELLSOUTH INTERNATIONAL, INC.—See BellSouth Corporation; U.S. Public, pg. 208
BELLSOUTH ISRAEL, INC. (CELLCOM ISRAEL LTD.)—See BellSouth Corporation; U.S. Public, pg. 208
BELLSOUTH MOBILE DATA, INC.—See BellSouth Corporation; U.S. Public, pg. 208
BELLSOUTH MOBILE SYSTEMS GROUP—See BellSouth Corporation; U.S. Public, pg. 208
BELLSOUTH MOBILITY, INC.—See BellSouth Corporation; U.S. Public, pg. 208
BELLSOUTH NETWORK SOLUTIONS, INC.—See BellSouth Corporation; U.S. Public, pg. 209
BELLSOUTH NEW ZEALAND—See BellSouth Corporation; U.S. Public, pg. 208
BELLSOUTH PERSONAL COMMUNICATIONS, INC.—See BellSouth Corporation; U.S. Public, pg. 208
BELLSOUTH PRODUCTS, INC.—See BellSouth Corporation; U.S. Public, pg. 209
BELLSOUTH RESOURCES, INC.—See BellSouth Corporation; U.S. Public, pg. 208
BELLSOUTH SHANGHAI CENTRE, LTD.—See BellSouth Corporation; U.S. Public, pg. 208
BELLSOUTH TELECOMMUNICATIONS, INC.—See BellSouth Corporation; U.S. Public, pg. 209
BELLSOUTH WIRELESS, INC.—See BellSouth Corporation; U.S. Public, pg. 208
BELLWETHER TECHNOLOGY CORPORATION; U.S. Private, pg. 132
BELMEDCO PHARMACY—See Vencor, Inc.; U.S. Public, pg. 1712
BELMONT DYERS COMPANY—See Meridian Industries, Inc.; U.S. Private, pg. 732
BELMONT INDUSTRIES, INC.—See RGP Holding, Inc.; U.S. Private, pg. 903
BELMONT METALS, INC.; U.S. Private, pg. 132
BELMONT PLASTICS CO.—See Foam Pro Manufacturing; U.S. Private, pg. 415
BELMONT TELEPHONE COMPANY—See Lynch Corporation; U.S. Public, pg. 1022
A.H. BELO CORPORATION; U.S. Public, pg. 209
BELOIT CORPORATION—See Harnischfeger Industries, Inc.; U.S. Public, pg. 789
BELOIT LENOX, DIV.—See Harnischfeger Industries, Inc.; U.S. Public, pg. 789
BELOIT MANHATTAN INC.—See Harnischfeger Industries, Inc.; U.S. Public, pg. 789
BELSHAW BROTHERS, INC.—See Berisford plc; Int'l, pg. 188
BELSON PRODUCTS DIV.—See Windmere-Durable Holdings; U.S. Public, pg. 1771
THE BELT RAILWAY CO. OF CHICAGO—See CSX Corporation; U.S. Public, pg. 284
THE BELT RAILWAY CO. OF CHICAGO—See Conrail, Inc.; U.S. Public, pg. 432
THE BELT RAILWAY CO. OF CHICAGO—See Illinois Central Corporation; U.S. Public, pg. 865
THE BELT RAILWAY CO. OF CHICAGO—See Norfolk Southern Corporation; U.S. Public, pg. 1191
BELTONE ELECTRONICS CORPORATION; U.S. Private, pg. 132
BELTSVILLE DISTRIBUTION POINT—See Cloister Pure Spring Water Co., Inc.; U.S. Private, pg. 247
BELTWAY COMMUNITY HOSPITAL, INC.—See Magellan Health Services, Inc.; U.S. Public, pg. 1033
BELVEDERE—See Excel Industries, Inc.; U.S. Public, pg. 598
BELVEDERE COMPANY—See Smith Investment Company; U.S. Private, pg. 1008
BELWITH INTERNATIONAL DIV.—See FKI Plc; Int'l, pg. 473
BELZ ENTERPRISES; U.S. Private, pg. 132
BEMIS COMPANY, INC.; U.S. Public, pg. 210
BEMIS CRAFTIL, S.A.—See Bemis Company, Inc.; U.S. Public, pg. 210
BEMIS MARAL, S.A. DE C.V.—See Bemis Company, Inc.; U.S. Public, pg. 210
BEMIS POLYETHYLENE PACKAGING DIV.—See Bemis Company, Inc.; U.S. Public, pg. 210
BEMROSE CORPORATION; Int'l, pg. 185
BEMROSE USA, INC.—See Bemrose Corporation; Int'l, pg. 185
BEN & JERRY'S HOMEMADE INC.; U.S. Public, pg. 210
BENCARD—See SmithKline Beecham plc; Int'l, pg. 1265
BENCH CRAFT, INC.—See Furnishings International, Inc.; U.S. Private, pg. 432
BENCHMARK APPRAISAL GROUP—See Mercantile Bankshares Corporation; U.S. Public, pg. 1089
BENCHMARK CONTRACTORS, INC.—See Morley Builders; U.S. Private, pg. 761
BENCHMARK ELECTRONICS INC.; U.S. Public, pg. 210
BENCHMARK ELECTRONICS, INC.—See Benchmark Electronics Inc.; U.S. Public, pg. 211
BENCHMARK ELECTRONICS, INC.-WINONA DIVISION—See Benchmark Electronics Inc.; U.S. Public, pg. 211
BENCHMARK, INC.—See Baxter International Inc.; U.S. Public, pg. 196
BENCHMARK INDUSTRIES; U.S. Private, pg. 132
BENCHMARK INSURANCE COMPANY—See Associated Wholesale Grocers, Inc.; U.S. Private, pg. 93
BENCKISER AG—See Joh. A. Benckiser GmbH; Int'l, pg. 185
BENCKISER AUSTRALIA PTY. LTD.—See Joh. A. Benckiser GmbH; Int'l, pg. 185
BENCKISER AUSTRIA GES.M.B.H.—See Joh. A. Benckiser GmbH; Int'l, pg. 185
BENCKISER B.V.—See Joh. A. Benckiser GmbH; Int'l, pg. 185
BENCKISER CONSUMER PRODUCTS INC.—See Joh. A. Benckiser GmbH; Int'l, pg. 185
BENCKISER COSMETICS ARGENTINA S.A.—See Joh. A. Benckiser GmbH; Int'l, pg. 185
BENCKISER COSMETICS SP.Z.O.O.—See Joh. A. Benckiser GmbH; Int'l, pg. 185
BENCKISER DEUTSCHLAND GMBH—See Joh. A. Benckiser GmbH; Int'l, pg. 185
BENCKISER HELLAS AG—See Joh. A. Benckiser GmbH; Int'l, pg. 185
BENCKISER INC.—See Joh. A. Benckiser GmbH; Int'l, pg. 185
BENCKISER (INDIA) PRIVATE LTD.—See Joh. A. Benckiser GmbH; Int'l, pg. 185
BENCKISER (JAPAN) LTD.—See Joh. A. Benckiser GmbH; Int'l, pg. 185
JOH. A. BENCKISER GMBH; Int'l, pg. 185
JOH. A. BENCKISER (PORTUGAL) LDA.—See Joh. A. Benckiser GmbH; Int'l, pg. 185
BENCKISER KFT.—See Joh. A. Benckiser GmbH; Int'l, pg. 185
BENCKISER LTD.—See Joh. A. Benckiser GmbH; Int'l, pg. 185
BENCKISER NEW ZEALAND LTD.—See Joh. A. Benckiser GmbH; Int'l, pg. 185
S.A. BENCKISER N.V.—See Joh. A. Benckiser GmbH; Int'l, pg. 185
BENCKISER POLEN SP.Z.O.O.—See Joh. A. Benckiser GmbH; Int'l, pg. 186
BENCKISER PRODUKTIONS GMBH—See Joh. A. Benckiser GmbH; Int'l, pg. 185
BENCKISER S.A.—See Joh. A. Benckiser GmbH; Int'l, pg. 186
BENCKISER ST. MARC S.A.—See Joh. A. Benckiser GmbH; Int'l, pg. 186
BENCKISER (SCHWEIZ) AG—See Joh. A. Benckiser GmbH; Int'l, pg. 186
BENCKISER SLOVAKIA SPOL.S.R.O.—See Joh. A. Benckiser GmbH; Int'l, pg. 186
BENCKISER SPOL. S.R.O.—See Joh. A. Benckiser GmbH; Int'l, pg. 186
BENCKISER TURKEI A.S.—See Joh. A. Benckiser GmbH; Int'l, pg. 186
BENCO PET FOODS, INC.—See Ralston Purina Company; U.S. Public, pg. 1360
MATTHEW BENDER & COMPANY, INCORPORATED—See The Times Mirror Company; U.S. Public, pg. 1616
BENDER SHIPBUILDING & REPAIR COMPANY, INC.; U.S. Private, pg. 132
BENDERSON DEVELOPMENT CO., INC.; U.S. Private, pg. 132
BENDIX ATLANTIC INFLATER CO.—See AlliedSignal Inc.; U.S. Public, pg. 51
BENDIX CONNECTOR, OPERATIONS—See AlliedSignal Inc.; U.S. Public, pg. 51
BENDIX DEUTSCHLAND G.M.B.H.—See AlliedSignal Inc.; U.S. Public, pg. 54
BENDIX ENVIRONMENTAL RESEARCH—See AlliedSignal Inc.; U.S. Public, pg. 51
BENDIX FLUID POWER DIVISION—See AlliedSignal Inc.; U.S. Public, pg. 51
BENDIX FRICTION MATERIALS DIVISION—See AlliedSignal Inc.; U.S. Public, pg. 51
BENDIX MINTEX PTY., LTD.—See AlliedSignal Inc.; U.S. Public, pg. 54
BENDIX SECURITY SYSTEMS—See AlliedSignal Inc.; U.S. Public, pg. 51
BENDIX TOLEDO STAMPING—See AlliedSignal Inc.; U.S. Public, pg. 51
BENECKE-KALIKO AG—See Continental AG; Int'l, pg. 327
BENEFICIAL CANADA INC.—See Beneficial Corporation; U.S. Public, pg. 211
BENEFICIAL CORPORATION; U.S. Public, pg. 211
BENEFICIAL CREDIT SERVICES, INC.—See Beneficial Corporation; U.S. Public, pg. 211
BENEFICIAL INSURANCE GROUP, INC.—See Beneficial Corporation; U.S. Public, pg. 211
BENEFICIAL LIFE INSURANCE—See Deseret Management Corporation; U.S. Private, pg. 327
BENEFICIAL MANAGEMENT CORPORATION—See Beneficial Corporation; U.S. Public, pg. 211
BENEFICIAL MANAGEMENT CORPORATION OF AMERICA & AFFILIATED CORPS.—See Beneficial Corporation; U.S. Public, pg. 211
BENEFICIAL NATIONAL BANK—See Beneficial Corporation; U.S. Public, pg. 211
BENEFICIAL SAVINGS BANK, FSB—See Beneficial Corporation; U.S. Public, pg. 211
BENEFICIAL STANDARD LIFE INSURANCE COMPANY—See Conseco Inc.; U.S. Public, pg. 433
BENEFICIAL TAX MASTERS INC.—See Beneficial Corporation; U.S. Public, pg. 211
BENEFICIAL TECHNOLOGY CORPORATION—See Beneficial Corporation; U.S. Public, pg. 211
BENEFIT CONSULTANTS, INC. (CT)—See Cendant Corporation; U.S. Public, pg. 320
BENEFIT PLANS ADMINISTRATIVE SERVICES, INC.—See Community Bank System, Inc.; U.S. Public, pg. 416
BENEFITAMERICA—See UNUM Corporation; U.S. Public, pg. 1699
BENEKE—See Sanderson Plumbing Products Inc.; U.S. Private, pg. 964
BENELLI/MOTO GUZZI NORTH AMERICA—See Fiat Auto SpA; Int'l, pg. 482
BENELUX DIVISION—See Computer Sciences Corporation; U.S. Public, pg. 423
BENELUX PERIODIEKEN BV—See VNU Verenigde Nederlandse Uitgeversbedrijven B.V.; Int'l, pg. 1445
BENETONE LAND & HOUSES CO., LTD.; Int'l, pg. 186
BENETTON GROUP S.P.A.; Int'l, pg. 186
BENETTON U.S.A. CORP.—See Benetton Group S.p.A.; Int'l, pg. 186
BENETTON U.S.A. CORPORATION—See Benetton Group S.p.A.; Int'l, pg. 186
BENFORD LIMITED—See Powerscreen International Plc; Int'l, pg. 1066

BENGTSSONS MASKIN AB—See AB Industrivarden; *Int'l*, pg. 678

BENGUET CORPORATION; *Int'l*, pg. 186

BENGUET EBARA REAL ESTATE CORP.—See Benguet Corporation; *Int'l*, pg. 187

BENGUET.EBARA REAL ESTATE CORPORATION—See Ebara Corporation; *Int'l*, pg. 432

BENHAM & COMPANY—See Trinidad/Benham Corp.; *U.S. Private*, pg. 1103

BENIHANA ENCINO CORP.—See Benihana, Inc.; *U.S. Public*, pg. 212

BENIHANA, INC.; *U.S. Public*, pg. 211

BENIHANA INTERNATIONAL, INC.—See Benihana, Inc.; *U.S. Public*, pg. 212

BENIHANA LOMBARD CORP.—See Benihana, Inc.; *U.S. Public*, pg. 212

BENIHANA NATIONAL CORP.—See Benihana, Inc.; *U.S. Public*, pg. 212

BENIHANA NATIONAL OF FLORIDA CORP.—See Benihana, Inc.; *U.S. Public*, pg. 212

BENIHANA OF BETHESDA CORP.—See Benihana, Inc.; *U.S. Public*, pg. 212

BENIHANA OF TEXAS, INC.—See Benihana, Inc.; *U.S. Public*, pg. 212

BENIHANA ORLANDO CORP.—See Benihana, Inc.; *U.S. Public*, pg. 212

BENIHANA PUENTE HILLS CORP.—See Benihana, Inc.; *U.S. Public*, pg. 212

BENIHANA SCHAUMBURG CORP.—See Benihana, Inc.; *U.S. Public*, pg. 212

BENIHANA SUNRISE CORP.—See Benihana, Inc.; *U.S. Public*, pg. 212

BENJAMENS, VAN DOORN EURO RSCG—See Havas Advertising; *Int'l*, pg. 602

BENJAMIN CENTER ASSOCIATES—See Cigna Corp.; *U.S. Public*, pg. 361

THE BENJAMIN/CUMMINGS PUBLISHING COMPANY—See Pearson plc; *Int'l*, pg. 1026

F. J. BENJAMIN HOLDINGS LTD.; *Int'l*, pg. 187

F.J. BENJAMIN MULTIMEDIA PTE LTD.—See F. J. Benjamin Holdings Ltd.; *Int'l*, pg. 187

F.J. BENJAMIN FASHIONS (AUST) PTY. LTD.—See F. J. Benjamin Holdings Ltd.; *Int'l*, pg. 187

F.J. BENJAMIN FASHIONS (HK) LTD.—See F. J. Benjamin Holdings Ltd.; *Int'l*, pg. 187

F.J. BENJAMIN FASHIONS (M) SDN. BHD.—See F. J. Benjamin Holdings Ltd.; *Int'l*, pg. 187

F.J. BENJAMIN FASHIONS (SINGAPORE) PTE. LTD.—See F. J. Benjamin Holdings Ltd.; *Int'l*, pg. 187

BENJAMIN FRANKLIN LITERARY & MEDICAL SOCIETY, INC.; *U.S. Private*, pg. 133

BENJAMIN METALS COMPANY; *U.S. Private*, pg. 133

BENJAMIN MOORE & CO.; *U.S. Private*, pg. 133

BENJAMIN MOORE & CO.—See Benjamin Moore & Co.; *U.S. Private*, pg. 133

BENJAMIN SHERIDAN CO.—See Crosman Corp.; *U.S. Private*, pg. 291

JOHN BENJAMINS BV; *Int'l*, pg. 187

JOHN BENJAMINS NORTH AMERICA INC—See John Benjamins BV; *Int'l*, pg. 187

BENMAR MARINE ELECTRONICS, INC.; *U.S. Private*, pg. 133

BENMARK PTE. LTD.—See F. J. Benjamin Holdings Ltd.; *Int'l*, pg. 187

BENN IRON FOUNDRY, LTD—See Cardo AB; *Int'l*, pg. 271

BENNETT BROTHERS, INC.; *U.S. Private*, pg. 133

BENNETT BROTHERS, INC.—See Bennett Brothers, Inc.; *U.S. Private*, pg. 133

BENNIE LIFTS LTD.—See Kone Corporation; *Int'l*, pg. 747

BENNIGAN'S—See Metromedia Company; *U.S. Private*, pg. 736

BENNINGTON IRON WORKS, INC.; *U.S. Private*, pg. 133

BENOIST GIRARD & CIE S.C.A.—See Pfizer Inc.; *U.S. Public*, pg. 1283

BENSDROP GES. M.B.H.—See Unilever Plc; *Int'l*, pg. 1436

BENSON & HEDGES LIMITED—See Gallaher Limited; *Int'l*, pg. 539

BENSON AUTOMOTIVE WORLD; *U.S. Private*, pg. 133

BENSON CORP.—See Gem Industries Finance Corporation; *U.S. Private*, pg. 443

BENSON INDUSTRIES, INC.; *U.S. Private*, pg. 133

BENSON MOTORS CORPORATION; *U.S. Private*, pg. 134

BENSONS—See Esselte AB; *Int'l*, pg. 460

BENSON'S, INC.; *U.S. Private*, pg. 134

BENSONS INTERNATIONAL SYSTEMS—See Esselte AB; *Int'l*, pg. 460

BENSONS INTERNATIONAL SYSTEMS BV—See Esselte AB; *Int'l*, pg. 460

BENSONS INTERNATIONAL SYSTEMS INC.—See Esselte AB; *Int'l*, pg. 460

BENSONS INTERNATIONAL SYSTEMS PTY. LTD.—See Esselte AB; *Int'l*, pg. 460

BENSONS METAL PRODUCTS PTE. LTD.—See Esselte AB; *Int'l*, pg. 460

BENSONS METAL PRODUCTS SDN BHD—See Esselte AB; *Int'l*, pg. 460

BENSON'S OLD HOME KITCHENS—See Benson's, Inc.; *U.S. Private*, pg. 134

BENT CO. COLORADO CORRECTIONAL FACILITY—See Corrections Corporation of America; *U.S. Public*, pg. 450

S. BENT & BROTHERS, INC.; *U.S. Private*, pg. 134

BENT TUBE, INC.; *U.S. Private*, pg. 134

BENTALLS PLC; *Int'l*, pg. 187

BENTEX KIDDIE CORPORATION; *U.S. Private*, pg. 134

BENTHOS, INC.; *U.S. Public*, pg. 212

THE BENTLEY AGNEW GROUP INC.; *Int'l*, pg. 187

BENTLEY & BENTLEY—See J.R. Wood Inc.; *U.S. Public*, pg. 1186

BENTLEY GROUP—See The Bentley Agnew Group Inc.; *Int'l*, pg. 187

THE BENTLEY-HARRIS MANUFACTURING CO.—See T & N Plc; *Int'l*, pg. 1334

BENTLEY INTERNATIONAL, INC.; *U.S. Public*, pg. 212

BENTLEY LEATHERS INC.—See The Bentley Agnew Group Inc.; *Int'l*, pg. 187

BENTLEY MILLS, INC.—See Interface Inc.; *U.S. Public*, pg. 889

BENTLEY PHARMACEUTICALS, INC.; *U.S. Public*, pg. 212

BENTLEY SYSTEMS, INC.; *U.S. Private*, pg. 134

BENTLY NEVADA, AUSTRALIA—See Bently Nevada Corporation; *U.S. Private*, pg. 134

BENTLY NEVADA CANADA LTD.—See Bently Nevada Corporation; *U.S. Private*, pg. 134

BENTLY NEVADA CORPORATION; *U.S. Private*, pg. 134

BENTLY NEVADA EUROPA B.V.—See Bently Nevada Corporation; *U.S. Private*, pg. 134

BENTLY NEVADA FRANCE S.A.R.L.—See Bently Nevada Corporation; *U.S. Private*, pg. 134

BENTLY NEVADA GMBH—See Bently Nevada Corporation; *U.S. Private*, pg. 134

BENTLY NEVADA SALES & SERVICE SINGAPORE PTE. LTD.—See Bently Nevada Corporation; *U.S. Private*, pg. 134

BENTLY NEVADA (UK) LTD.—See Bently Nevada Corporation; *U.S. Private*, pg. 134

BENTLY ROTOR DYNAMICS RESEARCH CORP.—See Bently Nevada Corporation; *U.S. Private*, pg. 134

BENTON OIL & GAS COMPANY; *U.S. Public*, pg. 212

BENTON PLASTICS, INC.—See Durakon Industries, Inc.; *U.S. Public*, pg. 537

BENTON STATE BANK—See First Commercial Corporation; *U.S. Public*, pg. 630

BENTONE-CHEMIE GMBH—See Contran Corporation; *U.S. Private*, pg. 271

BENTONE-ELECTRO OIL AB—See Trelleborg AB; *Int'l*, pg. 1422

BENTONE-SUD S.A.—See Contran Corporation; *U.S. Private*, pg. 271

BENZING VENTILATOREN GMBH—See Smiths Industries plc; *Int'l*, pg. 1268

BEPAC SC (ROPAC PRODUCTS)—See TI Group plc; *Int'l*, pg. 1339

BEPCO, INC.; *U.S. Private*, pg. 134

BEPEX CORPORATION—See Hosokawa Micron Corporation; *Int'l*, pg. 636

BEQUET PAUL—See Lafarge S.A.; *Int'l*, pg. 789

BERAG GMBH—See Willis Corroon Group PLC; *Int'l*, pg. 1502

BERCEN INC.—See Cranston Print Works Company; *U.S. Private*, pg. 287

HENRY BERCHTOLD AG—See Huber & Suhner AG; *Int'l*, pg. 637

BERCO S.P.A.—See Fried. Krupp AG; *Int'l*, pg. 511

BERCUM BOENDER CARDOZO & WERKENDAM B.V.—See Young & Rubicam Inc.; *U.S. Private*, pg. 1198

BERDEL, INC.—See Pennsylvania Real Estate Investment Trust; *U.S. Public*, pg. 1272

BEREAN CHRISTIAN STORES—See Standex International Corporation; *U.S. Public*, pg. 1506

P.T. BERECA HARDAYAPERKASA—See Hewlett-Packard Company; *U.S. Public*, pg. 816

BEREL INDUSTRIES INC.; *U.S. Private*, pg. 135

BEREMENDI CEMENT-ES MESZIPARI RT.—See Heidelberger Zement A.G.; *Int'l*, pg. 605

JOH. BERENBERG, GOSSLER & CO.—See CoreStates Financial Corp.; *U.S. Public*, pg. 447

BERENDSEN COMPONENTS AB—See Sophus Berendsen A/S; *Int'l*, pg. 1284

BERENDSEN COMPONENTS A/S—See Sophus Berendsen A/S; *Int'l*, pg. 1284

BERENDSEN COMPONENTS OY—See Sophus Berendsen A/S; *Int'l*, pg. 1284

BERENDSEN FLUID POWER, INC.—See Sophus Berendsen A/S; *Int'l*, pg. 1284

BERENDSEN FLUID POWER LTD.—See Sophus Berendsen A/S; *Int'l*, pg. 1284

BERENDSEN FLUID POWER PTY. LTD.—See Sophus Berendsen A/S; *Int'l*, pg. 1285

BERENDSEN PMC AB—See Sophus Berendsen A/S; *Int'l*, pg. 1285

BERENDSEN PMC A/S—See Sophus Berendsen A/S; *Int'l*, pg. 1284

BERENDSEN PMC B.V.—See Sophus Berendsen A/S; *Int'l*, pg. 1285

BERENDSEN PMC GMBH—See Sophus Berendsen A/S; *Int'l*, pg. 1285

BERENDSEN PMC N.V./S.A.—See Sophus Berendsen A/S; *Int'l*, pg. 1285

BERENDSEN PMC OY AB—See Sophus Berendsen A/S; *Int'l*, pg. 1285

BERENDSEN TEXTIL SERVICE A/S—See Sophus Berendsen A/S; *Int'l*, pg. 1284

BERENFIELD CONTAINERS (CLARENDON), INC.—See Berenfield Containers, Inc.; *U.S. Private*, pg. 135

BERENFIELD CONTAINERS, INC.; *U.S. Private*, pg. 135

BERENFIELD CONTAINERS LTD.—See Berenfield Containers, Inc.; *U.S. Private*, pg. 135

BERENFIELD CONTAINERS (MASON), INC.—See Berenfield Containers, Inc.; *U.S. Private*, pg. 135

BERENFIELD CONTAINERS (NORTHEAST), INC.—See Berenfield Containers, Inc.; *U.S. Private*, pg. 135

BERENTER GREENHOUSE & WEBSTER, INC.; *U.S. Private*, pg. 135

P. BERETTA S.P.A.; *Int'l*, pg. 187

BERETTA U.S.A. CORP.—See P. Beretta S.P.A.; *Int'l*, pg. 188

BERFLA, INC.—See Pennsylvania Real Estate Investment Trust; *U.S. Public*, pg. 1272

ALFRED BERG FONDKOMMISSION AB—See ABN-AMRO Holding N.V.; *Int'l*, pg. 12

BERG/CBOS ELECTRONICS AB—See Berg Electronics; *U.S. Public*, pg. 212

BERG CO.—See DEC International, Inc.; *U.S. Private*, pg. 301

BERG ELECTRONICS; *U.S. Public*, pg. 212

BERG ELECTRONICS—See Berg Electronics; *U.S. Public*, pg. 213

BERG ELECTRONICS BEIJING OFFICE—See Berg Electronics; *U.S. Public*, pg. 213

BERG ELECTRONICS BV—See Berg Electronics; *U.S. Public*, pg. 213

BERG ELECTRONICS CANADA, INC.—See Berg Electronics; *U.S. Public*, pg. 213

BERG ELECTRONICS CONNECTOR SYSTEMS LTD.—See Berg Electronics; *U.S. Public*, pg. 213

BERG ELECTRONICS CORP.—See Berg Electronics; *U.S. Public*, pg. 213

BERG ELECTRONICS DK—See Berg Electronics; *U.S. Public*, pg. 213

BERG ELECTRONICS GMBH—See Berg Electronics; *U.S. Public*, pg. 213

BERG ELECTRONICS GROUP, INC.—See Berg Electronics; *U.S. Public*, pg. 213

BERG ELECTRONICS HONG KONG LTD.—See Berg Electronics; *U.S. Public*, pg. 213

BERG ELECTRONICS JAPAN K.K.—See Berg Electronics; *U.S. Public*, pg. 213

BERG ELECTRONICS S.A.—See Berg Electronics; *U.S. Public*, pg. 213

BERG ELECTRONICS SHANGHAI OFFICE—See Berg Electronics; *U.S. Public*, pg. 213

BERG ELECTRONICS SINGAPORE PTE. LTD.—See Berg Electronics; *U.S. Public*, pg. 213

BERG ELECTRONICS SRL—See Berg Electronics; *U.S. Public*, pg. 213

BERG ELECTRONICS TAIWAN LTD.—See Berg Electronics; *U.S. Public*, pg. 213

BERG KOREA ELECTRONICS LTD.—See Berg Electronics; *U.S. Public*, pg. 213

BERGALL CORPORATION—See Staff Builders Inc.; *U.S. Public*, pg. 1501

BERGBAUSTAHL GMBH—See Fried. Krupp AG; *Int'l*, pg. 513

BERGDORF GOODMAN—See Harcourt General, Inc.; *U.S. Public*, pg. 785

BERGELECTRIC CORPORATION; *U.S. Private*, pg. 135

BERGEMANN GMBH MASCHINEN-UND APPARATEBAU—See Deutsche Babcock AG; *Int'l*, pg. 398

BERGEMANN-ILMARINE AG—See Deutsche Babcock AG; *Int'l*, pg. 398

BERGEMANN-SIO—See Deutsche Babcock AG; *Int'l*, pg. 398

BERGEMANN USA, INC.—See Deutsche Babcock AG; *Int'l*, pg. 401

BERGEN BRUNSWIG CORPORATION; *U.S. Public*, pg. 213

BERGEN BRUNSWIG DRUG COMPANY—See Bergen Brunswig Corporation; *U.S. Public*, pg. 213

BERGEN BRUNSWIG MEDICAL CORPORATION—See Bergen Brunswig Corporation; *U.S. Public*, pg. 214

BERGEN BRUNSWIG MEDICAL CORPORATION (DURR DRUG)—See Bergen Brunswig Corporation; *U.S. Public*, pg. 214

BERGEN CABLE TECHNOLOGIES, INC.—See Matec Corporation; *U.S. Public*, pg. 1056

BERGEN RECORD CORP.—See Macromedia Incorporated; *U.S. Private*, pg. 693

A/S BERGEN STAL DIKEMA—See Cockerill Sambre; *Int'l*, pg. 302

F. BERGER & CO. B.V.—See ABN-AMRO Holding N.V.; *Int'l*, pg. 9

BERGER INSTRUMENTS—See Chicago Steel Tape; *U.S. Private*, pg. 235

BERGER LAHR GMBH—See SIG Schweizersiche Industrie-Gesellschaft Holding AG; *Int'l*, pg. 1156

LOUIS BERGER INTERNATIONAL INC.; *U.S. Private*, pg. 135

BERGER TRANSFER & STORAGE, INC.; *U.S. Private*, pg. 135

BERGES ELECTRONIC, GMBH—See TB Wood's Corporation; *U.S. Public*, pg. 1562

BERGES ELECTRONIC, S.R.L.—See TB Wood's Corporation; *U.S. Public*, pg. 1562

BERGESEN D.Y. A.S.; *Int'l*, pg. 188

BERGHUIZER-ENSO FORMAATFABRIEK B.V.—See Enso Oyj; *Int'l*, pg. 458

S.A. BERGIERS N.V.—See Charter plc; *Int'l*, pg. 281

BERGIS PRODUKTION AB—See Electrolux, AB; *Int'l*, pg. 438

BERGIS TEXTIL SERVICE AB—See Sophus Berendsen A/S; *Int'l*, pg. 1285

BERGLEN ASSOCIATES LIMITED—See Masco Corporation; *U.S. Public*, pg. 1054

BERGLEN DISTRIBUTORS LIMITED—See Masco Corporation; *U.S. Public*, pg. 1055

BERGLEN GROUP LIMITED—See Masco Corporation; *U.S. Public*, pg. 1055

BERGMAN & BEVING AB; *Int'l*, pg. 188

BERNHARD M. BERGMAN AB—See Axel Johnson AB; *Int'l*, pg. 708

BERGMAN MANUFACTURING—See Datron Incorporated; *U.S. Private*, pg. 313

THE BERGQUIST COMPANY; *U.S. Private*, pg. 135

BERGQUIST ITC, GMBH—See The Bergquist Company; *U.S. Private*, pg. 135

BERGQUIST UK. LIMITED—See The Bergquist Company; *U.S. Private*, pg. 135

BERGSTROM CAPITAL CORPORATION; *U.S. Public*, pg. 215

BERGSTROM PAPER DIV.—See P.H. Glatfelter Company; *U.S. Public*, pg. 746

BERGTRONICS DY—See Berg Electronics; *U.S. Public*, pg. 213

BERGVIK CHEMIE B.V.—See International Paper Company; *U.S. Public*, pg. 904

BERGVIK CHEMIE GMBH—See International Paper Company; *U.S. Public*, pg. 904

BERGVIK KEMI AB—See International Paper Company; U.S. Public, pg. 906
BERGVIK SALES LIMITED—See International Paper Company; U.S. Public, pg. 904
BERIAC—See Oracle Corporation; U.S. Public, pg. 1228
BERING MARINE CORPORATION—See Lynden Incorporated; U.S. Public, pg. 683
BERINGEN—See TI Group plc; Int'l, pg. 1341
BERINGER DIVISION—See Kvaerner a.s.a.; Int'l, pg. 774
BERINGER HYDRAULIK GMBH—See Akzo Nobel N.V.; Int'l, pg. 46
BERINGER WINE ESTATES HOLDINGS, INC.—See Texas Pacific Group; U.S. Private, pg. 1078
BERISFORD PLC; Int'l, pg. 188
BERJAYA GENERAL INSURANCE SDN. BHD.—See The Tokio Marine & Fire Insurance Company, Ltd.; Int'l, pg. 1392
BERK PHARMACEUTICALS LTD.—See Rhone-Poulenc S.A.; int'l, pg. 1111
BERK SPENCER ACIDS LTD.—See Rhone-Poulenc S.A.; Int'l, pg. 1113
BERKAT-HONEYWELL SDN BHD HONEYWELL ENG SDN BHD—See Honeywell Inc.; U.S. Public, pg. 834
BERKEL INCORPORATED—See The General Electric Company, p.l.c.; Int'l, pg. 545
BERKELEY FINANCIAL GROUP—See John Hancock Mutual Life Insurance Company; U.S. Private, pg. 589
BERKELEY MAGAZINE LTD.—See The Reader's Digest Association, Inc.; U.S. Public, pg. 1368
BERKELEY MARINA RESTAURANT CORP.—See Specialty Restaurants Corporation; U.S. Private, pg. 1022
THE BERKELEY PUBLISHING GROUP—See The Seagram Company Ltd.; Int'l, pg. 1215
BERKLEY ADMINISTRATORS—See W.R. Berkley Corporation; U.S. Public, pg. 216
BERKLEY CARE NETWORK, INC.—See W.R. Berkley Corporation; U.S. Public, pg. 216
BERKLEY DEAN & COMPANY, INC.—See W.R. Berkley Corporation; U.S. Public, pg. 216
BERKLEY, INC.—See Outdoor Technologies Group; U.S. Private, pg. 822
BERKLEY INFORMATION SERVICES—See W.R. Berkley Corporation; U.S. Public, pg. 216
BERKLEY INTERNATIONAL, S.A.—See W.R. Berkley Corporation; U.S. Public, pg. 216
BERKLEY PUBLISHING CORP.—See Pearson plc; Int'l, pg. 1027
BERKLEY RISK MANAGERS—See W.R. Berkley Corporation; U.S. Public, pg. 215
BERKLEY RISK SERVICES, INC.—See W.R. Berkley Corporation; U.S. Public, pg. 215
W.R. BERKLEY CORPORATION; U.S. Public, pg. 215
BERKLIFF CORPORATION; U.S. Public, pg. 135
THE BERKLINE CORPORATION—See Furnishings International, Inc.; U.S. Private, pg. 432
BERKLINE, INC.—See Furnishings International, Inc.; U.S. Private, pg. 432
BERKMANNS ANTRIEBE GMBH—See Groschopp & Co. GmbH EMW Elektromotoren-Feinbauwerk; Int'l, pg. 559
J.E. BERKOWITZ, LP; U.S. Private, pg. 135
BERKS PRODUCTS CORPORATION; U.S. Private, pg. 136
BERKSHIRE BREWERY—See Scottish & Newcastle plc; Int'l, pg. 1212
BERKSHIRE FURNITURE CO.—See Leggett & Platt, Incorporated; U.S. Public, pg. 985
THE BERKSHIRE GAS COMPANY; U.S. Public, pg. 216
BERKSHIRE HATHAWAY INC.; U.S. Public, pg. 217
BERKSHIRE INDUSTRIES, INC.; U.S. Private, pg. 136
BERKSHIRE LIFE INSURANCE COMPANY; U.S. Private, pg. 136
BERKSHIRE REALTY COMPANY, INC.; U.S. Public, pg. 221
BERLACK STRASSENMARKIERUNGSFARBEN—See Lafarge S.A.; Int'l, pg. 791
BERLAMONT—See Castorama Dubois Investissements S.C.A.; Int'l, pg. 275
BERLEX CANADA, INC.—See Schering AG; Int'l, pg. 1204
BERLI JUCKER PUBLIC CO. LTD.—See First Pacific Company Limited; Int'l, pg. 487
BERLIMED—PRODUCTOS QUIMICOS FARMACEULICOS E BIOLOGICOS LTDA.—See Schering AG; Int'l, pg. 1204
BERLIN GLOVE COMPANY LTD.; U.S. Private, pg. 136
BERLIN-GORHAM OPERATIONS—See Crown Vantage Inc.; U.S. Public, pg. 465
BERLIN INDUSTRIES, INC.; U.S. Private, pg. 136
BERLIN INDUSTRIES, INC.—See Berlin Industries, Inc.; U.S. Private, pg. 136
THE BERLIN STEEL CONSTRUCTION COMPANY; U.S. Private, pg. 136
BERLIN WORKS—See Fried. Krupp AG; Int'l, pg. 516
BERLINER BANK AG—See Bankgesellschaft Berlin; Int'l, pg. 159
BERLINER COMMERZ BETEILIGUNGS GMBH—See Commerzbank AG; Int'l, pg. 309
BERLINER HYPOTHEKEN-UND PFANDBRIEFBANK AG—See Bankgesellschaft Berlin; Int'l, pg. 159
BERLINER KRAFT-UND LICHT (BEWAG) AG—See Veba AG; Int'l, pg. 1456
BERLINER SCHMIERSTOFFGESELLSCHAFT MBH—See Fuchs Petrolub AG Oel + Chemie; Int'l, pg. 517
BERLINGER DIV.—See Kvaerner a.s.a.; Int'l, pg. 773
OY BERLITZ AB—See Berlitz International, Inc.; U.S. Public, pg. 221
BERLITZ A/S—See Berlitz International, Inc.; U.S. Public, pg. 221
BERLITZ DE MEXICO, S.A. DE C.V.—See Berlitz International, Inc.; U.S. Public, pg. 221
BERLITZ ESCOLA DE IDIOMAS LTDA.—See Berlitz International, Inc.; U.S. Public, pg. 221
BERLITZ ESCUELAS DE IDIOMAS LTDA.—See Berlitz International, Inc.; U.S. Public, pg. 222
BERLITZ FRANCE S.A.—See Berlitz International, Inc.; U.S. Public, pg. 222

BERLITZ INTERNATIONAL DANMARK A/S—See Berlitz International, Inc.; U.S. Public, pg. 222
BERLITZ INTERNATIONAL, INC.; U.S. Public, pg. 221
BERLITZ KFT—See Berlitz International, Inc.; U.S. Public, pg. 222
BERLITZ LANGUAGE CENTERS OF CANADA LTD.—See Berlitz International, Inc.; U.S. Public, pg. 222
BERLITZ LANGUAGE CENTERS, S.R.L.—See Berlitz International, Inc.; U.S. Public, pg. 222
BERLITZ-POLSKA LIMITED LIABILITY COMPANY—See Berlitz International, Inc.; U.S. Public, pg. 222
BERLITZ PUBLISHING COMPANY INC.—See Berlitz International, Inc.; U.S. Public, pg. 221
BERLITZ SCHOOLS OF LANGUAGES AB—See Berlitz International, Inc.; U.S. Public, pg. 222
BERLITZ SCHOOLS OF LANGUAGES AG—See Berlitz International, Inc.; U.S. Public, pg. 222
BERLITZ SCHOOLS OF LANGUAGES B.V.—See Berlitz International, Inc.; U.S. Public, pg. 222
BERLITZ SCHOOLS OF LANGUAGES CZECHSOLOVAKIA SPOL.SR.O—See Berlitz International, Inc.; U.S. Public, pg. 222
BERLITZ SCHOOLS OF LANGUAGES GMBH—See Berlitz International, Inc.; U.S. Public, pg. 222
THE BERLITZ SCHOOLS OF LANGUAGES (JAPAN) INC.—See Berlitz International, Inc.; U.S. Public, pg. 222
BERLITZ SCHOOLS OF LANGUAGES LTD.—See Berlitz International, Inc.; U.S. Public, pg. 222
BERLITZ SCHOOLS OF LANGUAGES OF ARGENTINA S.A.—See Berlitz International, Inc.; U.S. Public, pg. 222
BERLITZ SCHOOLS OF LANGUAGES OF BENELUX S.A.—See Berlitz International, Inc.; U.S. Public, pg. 222
BERLITZ SOVINCENTER—See Berlitz International, Inc.; U.S. Public, pg. 222
BERLITZ SPRACHSCHULEN GMBH—See Berlitz International, Inc.; U.S. Public, pg. 222
BERLITZ THAILAND LTD.—See Berlitz International, Inc.; U.S. Public, pg. 222
BERLITZ TRANSLATION SERVICES, INC.—See Berlitz International, Inc.; U.S. Public, pg. 221
BERLEX LABORATORIES INC.—See Schering AG; Int'l, pg. 1204
BERLUTI—See LVMH Moet Hennessy Louis Vuitton; Int'l, pg. 779
BERMCO PAPER COMPANY—See Gould Paper Corporation; U.S. Private, pg. 467
BERMEAD INSURANCE COMPANY LTD.—See The Mead Corporation; U.S. Public, pg. 1076
BERMIL INDUSTRIES CORP.; U.S. Private, pg. 136
BERMO, INC.; U.S. Private, pg. 136
BERMO LTDA.—See GESTRA GmbH; Int'l, pg. 550
BERMO SCOTLAND, LTD—See Bermo, Inc.; U.S. Private, pg. 136
BERMUDA INTERNATIONAL (DUBLIN) LIMITED—See The Bank of Bermuda Limited; Int'l, pg. 151
BERMUDA INTERNATIONAL INVESTMENT MANAGEMENT (EUROPE) LIMITED—See The Bank of Bermuda Limited; Int'l, pg. 151
BERMUDA INTERNATIONAL SECURITIES (UK) LIMITED—See The Bank of Bermuda Limited; Int'l, pg. 151
BERMUDA TRUST (CAYMAN) LTD.—See The Bank of Bermuda Limited; Int'l, pg. 151
BERMUDA TRUST (COOK ISLANDS) LIMITED—See The Bank of Bermuda Limited; Int'l, pg. 151
BERMUDA TRUST (DUBLIN) LIMITED—See The Bank of Bermuda Limited; Int'l, pg. 151
BERMUDA TRUST EXECUTORS (JERSEY) LIMITED—See The Bank of Bermuda Limited; Int'l, pg. 151
BERMUDA TRUST (FAR EAST) LIMITED—See The Bank of Bermuda Limited; Int'l, pg. 151
BERMUDA TRUST (GUERNSEY) LIMITED—See The Bank of Bermuda Limited; Int'l, pg. 151
BERMUDA TRUST (HONG KONG) LIMITED—See The Bank of Bermuda Limited; Int'l, pg. 151
BERMUDA TRUST (ISLE OF MAN) LIMITED—See The Bank of Bermuda Limited; Int'l, pg. 151
BERMUDA TRUST (JERSEY) LIMITED—See The Bank of Bermuda Limited; Int'l, pg. 151
BERMUDA TRUST (MAURITIUS) LIMITED—See The Bank of Bermuda Limited; Int'l, pg. 151
BERMUDA TRUST (NEW ZEALAND) LIMITED—See The Bank of Bermuda Limited; Int'l, pg. 151
BERMUDA TRUST (SINGAPORE) LIMITED—See The Bank of Bermuda Limited; Int'l, pg. 151
BERMUDA TRUST (ST. HELIER) LIMITED—See The Bank of Bermuda Limited; Int'l, pg. 151
BERMUDA TRUST (UK) LIMITED—See The Bank of Bermuda Limited; Int'l, pg. 151
BERMUDA TRUST (WESTERN SAMOA) LIMITED—See The Bank of Bermuda Limited; Int'l, pg. 151
BERMUDEZ-BINSWANGER—See Binswanger; U.S. Private, pg. 144
P.T. BERNADI UTAMA SK—See Internatio-Muller N.V.; Int'l, pg. 681
BERNAL DIVISION—See Stevens International, Inc.; U.S. Public, pg. 1517
BERNARD JOHNSON YOUNG INC.; U.S. Private, pg. 136
BERNARD KRIEF MOTIVATION, S.A., CARLSON MARKETING GROUP—See Carlson Companies, Inc.; U.S. Private, pg. 212
BERNARD MATTHEWS PLC; Int'l, pg. 189
BERNARDI ITALIAN FOODS—See Windsor Quality Food Co., Ltd.; U.S. Private, pg. 1182
BERNARDIN OF CANADA, LTD.—See Alltrista Corporation; U.S. Public, pg. 56
BERNARDS BROTHERS, INC.; U.S. Private, pg. 136
HANS BERNEBURG GMBH & CO. KG—See Philipp Holzmann AG; Int'l, pg. 632
BERNER BROS. INC.—See Berner Ltd.; Int'l, pg. 189
BERNER CZ—See Berner Ltd.; Int'l, pg. 189
BERNER EESTI AS—See Berner Ltd.; Int'l, pg. 189

BERNER INTERNATIONAL CO. LTD.—See Incentive AB; Int'l, pg. 669
BERNER LTD.; Int'l, pg. 189
ARNOLD BERNHARD & CO.; U.S. Private, pg. 137
BERNHARDT FURNITURE CO.; U.S. Private, pg. 137
BERNHEIM-COMOFI—See Groupe Bruxelles Lambert S.A.; Int'l, pg. 562
BERNINA HOLDING AG; Int'l, pg. 189
BERNINA NAEHMASCHINENFABRIK AG—See Bernina Holding AG; Int'l, pg. 189
BERNINA OF AMERICA INC.—See Bernina Holding AG; Int'l, pg. 189
BERNIS—See SNCF; Int'l, pg. 1163
BERNISCHE GROSSMOSTEREI—See Coop Switzerland; Int'l, pg. 329
BERNSTEIN-REIN ADVERTISING, INC.; U.S. Private, pg. 137
SANFORD C. BERNSTEIN & CO., INC.; U.S. Private, pg. 137
BERNZOMATIC—See Newell Co.; U.S. Public, pg. 1177
BEROL CORPORATION—See Newell Co.; U.S. Public, pg. 1178
BEROL INC.—See Newell Co.; U.S. Public, pg. 1177
RUSS BERRIE AND COMPANY, INC.; U.S. Public, pg. 222
RUSS BERRIE (U.K.) LIMITED—See Russ Berrie and Company, Inc.; U.S. Public, pg. 223
BERRIEL VITTEL FRANCE—See Nestle S.A.; Int'l, pg. 918
BERRY BEARING COMPANY—See Genuine Parts Company; U.S. Public, pg. 732
BERRY-BROWN ADVERTISING, INC.; U.S. Private, pg. 137
BERRY COMPANIES, INC.; U.S. Private, pg. 137
BERRY CONTRACTING; U.S. Private, pg. 137
BERRY, HARTELL, EVERS & OSBORNE, INC.—See Northern Trust Corporation; U.S. Public, pg. 1196
L.M. BERRY AND COMPANY—See BellSouth Corporation; U.S. Public, pg. 137
BERRY NETWORK, INC.; U.S. Private, pg. 137
BERRY OIL TRADING AND TRANSPORTATION—See Berry Petroleum Company; U.S. Public, pg. 223
BERRY PETROLEUM COMPANY; U.S. Public, pg. 223
BERRY PETROLEUM COMPANY-COASTAL OPERATIONS—See Berry Petroleum Company; U.S. Public, pg. 223
BERRY PLASTICS CORPORATION; U.S. Private, pg. 137
BERRYMAN PRODUCTS, INC.; U.S. Private, pg. 138
BERRYVILLE GRAPHICS INC.—See Bertelsmann AG; Int'l, pg. 191
BERSON MILIEUTECHNIEK B.V.—See Halma p.l.c.; Int'l, pg. 590
BERTAN HIGH VOLTAGE—See Del Global Technologies; U.S. Public, pg. 494
BERTEK, INC.—See Mylan Laboratories, Inc.; U.S. Public, pg. 1143
BERTELLI SPA—See Akzo Nobel N.V.; Int'l, pg. 47
BERTELSMANN AG; Int'l, pg. 189
BERTELSMANN CLUB GMBH—See Bertelsmann AG; Int'l, pg. 189
BERTELSMANN INC.—See Bertelsmann AG; Int'l, pg. 191
BERTELSMANN LEXIOTHEK VERLAG GMBH—See Bertelsmann AG; Int'l, pg. 189
BERTELSMANN MUSIC GROUP—See Bertelsmann AG; Int'l, pg. 191
BERTELSMANN PRINTING & MANUFACTURING CORP.—See Bertelsmann AG; Int'l, pg. 191
BERTOLLI AUSTRALIA PTY LTD.—See IRI Istituto Ricostruzione Industriale; Int'l, pg. 655
BERTOLLI CANADA INC.—See IRI Istituto Ricostruzione Industriale; Int'l, pg. 655
BERTOLLI USA, INC.—See IRI Istituto Ricostruzione Industriale; Int'l, pg. 655
BERTRAM & GRAF GMBH—See Bairnco Corporation; U.S. Public, pg. 165
BERTRAND FAURE; Int'l, pg. 192
BERTRAND FAURE ARGENTINA SA—See Bertrand Faure; Int'l, pg. 193
BERTRAND FAURE COMPONENTES SA—See Bertrand Faure; Int'l, pg. 193
BERTRAND FAURE COMPONENTS LTD.—See Bertrand Faure; Int'l, pg. 193
BERTRAND FAURE COMPONENTS LTD. - NORFINCH PLANT—See Bertrand Faure; Int'l, pg. 193
BERTRAND FAURE EQUIPAMENTOS PARA AUTOMOVEIS SA—See Bertrand Faure; Int'l, pg. 193
BERTRAND FAURE EQUIPEMENTS SA—See Bertrand Faure; Int'l, pg. 192
BERTRAND FAURE JAPON KK—See Bertrand Faure; Int'l, pg. 193
BERTRAND FAURE SEATING LTD.—See Bertrand Faure; Int'l, pg. 193
BERTRAND FAURE SITZTECHNIK GMBH & CO. KG—See Bertrand Faure; Int'l, pg. 193
BERTRAND FAURE TECHNICAL CENTER INC.—See Bertrand Faure; Int'l, pg. 193
BERTSCHINGER TEXTILMASCHINEN AG—See Rieter Holdings; Int'l, pg. 1116
BERWEIN WERTPAPIERHANDELS-UND BORSENMAKLER GMBH—See Swiss Bank Corporation; Int'l, pg. 1331
BERWICK BAY OIL CO. INC.; U.S. Private, pg. 138
BERWICK INDUSTRIES, INC.—See CSS Industries, Inc.; U.S. Public, pg. 284
BERWIND CORPORATION; U.S. Private, pg. 138
BERWIND FINANCIAL GROUP—See Berwind Corporation; U.S. Private, pg. 139
BERWIND INDUSTRIES, INC.—See Berwind Corporation; U.S. Private, pg. 138
BERWIND PHARMACEUTICAL SERVICES, INC.—See Berwind Corporation; U.S. Private, pg. 139
BERWIND PROPERTY GROUP, INC.—See Berwind Corporation; U.S. Private, pg. 138
BES-PAK & CO., INC.—See Chelsea Industries, Inc.; U.S. Private, pg. 231
BESAM AB—See AB Industrivarden; Int'l, pg. 678

BESAN-BESIN SANAYI VE TICARET A.S.—See Bestfoods; U.S. Public, pg. 224
BESCHE OIL COMPANY, INC.; U.S. Private, pg. 139
BESNIER USA—See Compagnie Laitiere BESNIER; Int'l, pg. 323
BESPAK PLC; Int'l, pg. 193
BESS EATON DONUT FLOUR CO., INC.; U.S. Private, pg. 139
BESS HYGIENE AG—See The Procter & Gamble Company; U.S. Public, pg. 1333
BESSEMER GROUP, INC.; U.S. Private, pg. 139
BESSER/APPCO—See Besser Company; U.S. Private, pg. 139
BESSER CANADA, LTD.—See Besser Company; U.S. Private, pg. 139
BESSER COMPANY; U.S. Private, pg. 139
BESSEY JUICE INC.—See Cott Corporation; Int'l, pg. 337
BESSIN CORPORATION—See Sara Lee Corporation; U.S. Public, pg. 1433
BEST ACCESS SYSTEMS; U.S. Public, pg. 223
A.M. BEST COMPANY; U.S. Private, pg. 139
BEST AVIATION—See Fieldale Corporation; U.S. Private, pg. 403
BEST BRANDS—See Hero; Int'l, pg. 617
BEST BUY CO., INC.; U.S. Public, pg. 223
BEST FOODS—See Bestfoods; U.S. Public, pg. 224
BEST FOODS CANADA, INC.—See Bestfoods; U.S. Public, pg. 224
BEST FOODS CARIBBEAN, INC.—See Bestfoods; U.S. Public, pg. 224
BEST FOODS EXPORTS—See Bestfoods; U.S. Public, pg. 224
BEST FOODS GROCERY PRODUCTS GROUP—See Bestfoods; U.S. Public, pg. 224
BEST FOODS JORDAN—See Bestfoods; U.S. Public, pg. 224
BEST FOODS SAUDI ARABIA CO. LTD.—See Bestfoods; U.S. Public, pg. 225
BEST HOSPITAL SUPPLY DIV.—See Best Manufacturing, Inc.; U.S. Private, pg. 140
BEST INSURORS, INC.—See Walter Industries, Inc.; U.S. Public, pg. 1736
BEST MANUFACTURING, INC.; U.S. Private, pg. 139
AB BEST MATIC—See Ingersoll-Rand Company; U.S. Public, pg. 877
BEST MFG. INC.-HOSPITALITY DIV.—See Best Manufacturing, Inc.; U.S. Private, pg. 140
BEST MFG. INC.-SERVICE APPAREL DIV.—See Best Manufacturing, Inc.; U.S. Private, pg. 140
BEST POWER; U.S. Private, pg. 140
BEST PRODUCTS CO., INC.—See Shaykin & Company; U.S. Private, pg. 990
BEST PROVISION CO., INC.; U.S. Private, pg. 140
BEST SOFTWARE, INC.; U.S. Public, pg. 223
BEST S.P.A.—See Nortek, Inc.; U.S. Public, pg. 1194
BEST TEMPORARIES FEDERAL SYSTEMS, INC.—See Western Staff Services; U.S. Public, pg. 1760
BEST TEXTILE CO. DIV.—See Best Manufacturing, Inc.; U.S. Private, pg. 140
BEST UNIVERSAL LOCK LTD.—See Best Access Systems; U.S. Public, pg. 223
BEST'WARE BV—See N.V. Koninklijke KNP BT; Int'l, pg. 756
BEST WESTERN INTERNATIONAL, INC.; U.S. Private, pg. 140
BEST WESTERN OGDEN PARK HOTEL—See Sunstone Hotel Investors, Inc.; U.S. Public, pg. 1537
BEST WESTERN WHEELING INN—See Boury Enterprises; U.S. Private, pg. 162
BEST WHOLESALE CO., INC.—See Old Fashion Foods, Inc.; U.S. Private, pg. 814
BEST-WOOD LIMITED—See International Paper Company; U.S. Public, pg. 905
BESTFOODS; U.S. Public, pg. 223
BESTFORM FOUNDATIONS, INC.; U.S. Private, pg. 140
BESTFRIEND PET FOODS LIMITED—See H.J. Heinz Company; U.S. Public, pg. 807
BESTINFO—See Intergraph Corporation; U.S. Public, pg. 890
BESTMED, INC.—See Saatchi & Saatchi Advertising Worldwide; U.S. Public, pg. 1422
BESTOBELI AVIATION—See Meggitt plc; Int'l, pg. 853
BESTOBELL MOBREY AG—See Meggitt plc; Int'l, pg. 854
BESTOBELL MOBREY GESMBH—See Meggitt plc; Int'l, pg. 854
BESTOBELL MOBREY GMBH—See Meggitt plc; Int'l, pg. 854
BESTOBELL SERVICE CO. LTD.—See Meggitt plc; Int'l, pg. 853
BESTOLIFE CORP.—See Quexco Incorporated; U.S. Private, pg. 900
BESTOP, INC.—See Magna International Inc.; Int'l, pg. 830
BESTROM—See Royal Begemann Group; Int'l, pg. 1134
BESTUURCENTRUM DER VERENIGDE BEDRIJVEN NUTRICIA B.V.—See Nutricia BV; Int'l, pg. 991
BETA MEDICAL EQUIPMENT, INC.—See Integrated Health Services, Inc.; U.S. Public, pg. 884
BETA PLASTICS—See Alpha Industries; U.S. Private, pg. 45
BETA RAVEN INC.—See Raven Industries, Inc.; U.S. Public, pg. 1361
BETA SQUARED, INC.—See Photronics, Inc.; U.S. Public, pg. 1293
BETA TRANSFORMERS—See ILC Industries, Inc.; U.S. Private, pg. 555
BETA TUBE—See Acme Metals Incorporated; U.S. Public, pg. 17
BETAC CORPORATION—See Betac International Corporation; U.S. Private, pg. 140
BETAC INTERNATIONAL CORPORATION; U.S. Private, pg. 140
BETACOM PLC; Int'l, pg. 193
BETANCOURT BARBA EURO RSCG—See Havas Advertising; Int'l, pg. 603

BETAO LIZ S.A.—See Lafarge S.A.; Int'l, pg. 790
CHANNING L. BETE CO., INC.; U.S. Private, pg. 140
BETECH A/S—See Bergman & Beving AB; Int'l, pg. 188
BETECNA—See Lafarge S.A.; Int'l, pg. 789
BETEILIGUNGS- UND HANDELSGESELLSCHAFT IN HAMBURG MBH—See Bayerische Vereinsbank Group; Int'l, pg. 179
BETEILIGUNGSGESELLSCHAFT FUER INDUSTRIE UND HANDEL MBH—See Commerzbank AG; Int'l, pg. 309
BETEILIGUNGSGESELLSCHAFT FUR DIE DEUTSCHE WIRTSCHAFT GMBH—See Dresdner Bank AG; Int'l, pg. 418
BETEILIGUNGSGESELLSCHAFT FUR INDUSTRIE UND HANDEL MBH—See Bayerische Vereinsbank Group; Int'l, pg. 179
BETEILIGUNGS-KG DER DEFAG DEUTSCHE FLUGZEUGV. AG & CO. KG—See Hapag-Lloyd AG; Int'l, pg. 596
BETEN S.A.—See Schmalbach-Lubeca AG; Int'l, pg. 1207
BETHANY LEARNING CENTER—See Berkshire Hathaway Inc.; U.S. Public, pg. 218
BETHEL MILLS, INC.; U.S. Private, pg. 141
BETHEL MILLS KITCHEN & BATH—See Bethel Mills, Inc.; U.S. Private, pg. 141
THE BETHLEHEM CORPORATION; U.S. Public, pg. 225
BETHLEHEM INTL. SALES CORP.—See The Bethlehem Corporation; U.S. Public, pg. 226
BETHLEHEM STEEL CORPORATION; U.S. Public, pg. 226
BETHMANN LIEGENSCHAFTS KG—See Bayerische Vereinsbank Group; Int'l, pg. 179
BETHMANN VERMOGENSBETREUUNG GMBH—See Bayerische Vereinsbank Group; Int'l, pg. 179
BETHURUM RESEARCH & DEVELOPMENT, INC.; U.S. Private, pg. 141
BETMAR HATS, INC.—See M. Grossman & Son, Inc.; U.S. Private, pg. 483
BETOMA AB—See Axel Johnson AB; Int'l, pg. 708
BETOMIX AO—See Scancem AB; Int'l, pg. 1200
CARL LOTZ BETON GMBH & CO.—See Dyckerhoff AG; Int'l, pg. 422
BETON DE PARIS—See Lafarge S.A.; Int'l, pg. 788
BETON MIX BRNO A.S.—See Heidelberger Zement A.G.; Int'l, pg. 605
BETON-UND MONIERBAU GMBH—See Preussag AG; Int'l, pg. 1069
BETON UNION AACHEN GMBH & CO. KG—See Dyckerhoff AG; Int'l, pg. 422
BETON UNION DUSSELFÖRF GMBH & CO. KG—See Dyckerhoff AG; Int'l, pg. 422
BETON UNION ESSEN GMBH & CO.—See Dyckerhoff AG; Int'l, pg. 422
BETON UNION GMBH & CO. KG—See Dyckerhoff AG; Int'l, pg. 422
BETON UNION KOLN-BONN—See Dyckerhoff AG; Int'l, pg. 422
BETON UNION MONCHENGLADBACH GMBH & CO. KG—See Dyckerhoff AG; Int'l, pg. 422
BETON UNION RADEVORMWALD GMBH & CO. KG—See Dyckerhoff AG; Int'l, pg. 422
BETONGINDUSTRI AB—See Scancem AB; Int'l, pg. 1199
BETRA MARKETING—See Berner Ltd.; Int'l, pg. 189
BETRAND FAURE COMPONENTS LTD. - VIPOND PLANT—See Bertrand Faure; Int'l, pg. 193
BETRIEBSMITTELBAU GMBH—See FAG Group; Int'l, pg. 468
BETRIEBSWINTSCHAFT LICHER VERLAG DR. TH. GABLER GMBH—See Bertelsmann AG; Int'l, pg. 189
BETT-TECHNOLOGY IN EDUCATIONS—See EMAP Plc; Int'l, pg. 452
BETTCHER MANUFACTURING CORP.—See Brittany Corporation; U.S. Private, pg. 169
BETTCHER MANUFACTURING CORPORATION—See Brittany Corporation; U.S. Private, pg. 169
BETTER BAKED FOODS, INC.; U.S. Private, pg. 141
BETTER BATH COMPONENTS, INC.—See Kevco, Inc.; U.S. Public, pg. 953
BETTER BRANDS OF ATLANTA, INC.; U.S. Private, pg. 141
BETTER HOMES AND GARDENS BOOKS—See Meredith Corporation; U.S. Public, pg. 1094
BETTER HOMES AND GARDENS MAGAZINE—See Meredith Corporation; U.S. Public, pg. 1094
BETTER HOMES AND GARDENS REAL ESTATE SERVICE—See Meredith Corporation; U.S. Public, pg. 1094
BETTER HOMES AND GARDENS SPECIAL INTEREST PUBLICATIONS—See Meredith Corporation; U.S. Public, pg. 1094
BETTER HOMES AND GARDENS WOOD MAGAZINE—See Meredith Corporation; U.S. Public, pg. 1094
BETTER HOMES INSURANCE ASSOCIATES, INC.—See AEGON N.V.; Int'l, pg. 27
BETTER LIVING INC.; U.S. Private, pg. 141
BETTERBRANDS, LTD.—See Young's Holdings Inc.; U.S. Private, pg. 1202
BETTIGOLE, ANDREWS & CLARK, INC.—See Thermo Electron Corporation; U.S. Public, pg. 1593
BETTIS CANADA LIMITED—See Daniel Industries, Inc.; U.S. Public, pg. 483
BETTIS CORPORATION—See Daniel Industries, Inc.; U.S. Public, pg. 482
BETTIS ELECTRIC ACTUATOR COMPANY—See Daniel Industries, Inc.; U.S. Public, pg. 483
BETTIS FRANCE—See Daniel Industries, Inc.; U.S. Public, pg. 483
BETTIS UK LIMITED—See Daniel Industries, Inc.; U.S. Public, pg. 483
BETTOR S.A.—See Viag AG; Int'l, pg. 1465
BETTY CROCKER PRODUCTS—See General Mills, Inc.; U.S. Public, pg. 718
BETZDEARBORN AB—See BetzDearborn Inc.; U.S. Public, pg. 227
BETZDEARBORN AUSTRALIA PTY LIMITED—See BetzDearborn Inc.; U.S. Public, pg. 227

BETZDEARBORN B.V.—See BetzDearborn Inc.; U.S. Public, pg. 227
BETZDEARBORN CANADA, INC.—See BetzDearborn Inc.; U.S. Public, pg. 227
BETZDEARBORN HYDROCARBON PROCESS GROUP—See BetzDearborn Inc.; U.S. Public, pg. 226
BETZDEARBORN IBERICA, S.A.—See BetzDearborn Inc.; U.S. Public, pg. 227
BETZDEARBORN INC.; U.S. Public, pg. 226
BETZDEARBORN INC.—See BetzDearborn Inc.; U.S. Public, pg. 227
BETZDEARBORN INDIA, PVT., LTD.—See BetzDearborn Inc.; U.S. Public, pg. 227
BETZDEARBORN K.K.—See BetzDearborn Inc.; U.S. Public, pg. 227
BETZDEARBORN KOREA, LTD.—See BetzDearborn Inc.; U.S. Public, pg. 227
BETZDEARBORN LTD.—See BetzDearborn Inc.; U.S. Public, pg. 227
BETZDEARBORN (MALAYSIA) SDN. BHD.—See BetzDearborn Inc.; U.S. Public, pg. 227
BETZDEARBORN METALS PROCESS GROUP—See BetzDearborn Inc.; U.S. Public, pg. 226
BETZDEARBORN OY—See BetzDearborn Inc.; U.S. Public, pg. 227
BETZDEARBORN PAPER PROCESS GROUP—See BetzDearborn Inc.; U.S. Public, pg. 226
BETZDEARBORN PORTUGESA, L.D.A.—See BetzDearborn Inc.; U.S. Public, pg. 227
BETZDEARBORN S.P.A.—See BetzDearborn Inc.; U.S. Public, pg. 227
BETZDEARBORN TAIWAN, LTD.—See BetzDearborn Inc.; U.S. Public, pg. 227
BETZDEARBORN (THAILAND) CO., LTD.—See BetzDearborn Inc.; U.S. Public, pg. 227
BETZDEARBORN VENEZUELA, C.A.—See BetzDearborn Inc.; U.S. Public, pg. 227
BETZDEARBORN WATER MANAGEMENT GROUP—See BetzDearborn Inc.; U.S. Public, pg. 226
BEUTLER HEATING & AIR CONDITIONING INC.; U.S. Private, pg. 141
BEUTLICH, L.P.; U.S. Private, pg. 141
BEVALOID AUSTRALIA (PTY) LTD.—See Rhone-Poulenc S.A.; Int'l, pg. 1113
BEVALOID CHEMICALS LTD.—See Rhone-Poulenc S.A.; Int'l, pg. 1113
BEVALOID LTD.—See Rhone-Poulenc S.A.; Int'l, pg. 1113
BEVALOID SA—See Rhone-Poulenc S.A.; Int'l, pg. 1113
BEVERAGE-AIR CO.—See Specialty Equipment Companies Inc.; U.S. Public, pg. 1496
BEVERAGE AMERICA, INC.; U.S. Private, pg. 141
BEVERAGE CANNERS INTERNATIONAL CORP.—See BCI Holding Corporation; U.S. Public, pg. 59
THE BEVERAGE SOURCE, INC.—See Erly Industries, Inc.; U.S. Public, pg. 591
BEVERIDGE PAPER CO.—See Simkins Industries, Inc.; U.S. Private, pg. 1000
BEVERLY BANCORPORATION INC.; U.S. Public, pg. 227
BEVERLY ENTERPRISES, INC.; U.S. Public, pg. 227
THE BEVERLY HILLS HOTEL; U.S. Private, pg. 142
BEVERLY NATIONAL BANK—See Beverly Bancorporation Inc.; U.S. Public, pg. 227
BEVERLY TRUST COMPANY—See Beverly Bancorporation Inc.; U.S. Public, pg. 227
BEVERWAL BETEILIGUNGS UND VERWALTUNGSGESELLSCHAFT MBH—See Bayerische Vereinsbank Group; Int'l, pg. 188
BEVINGGRUPPEN AB—See Bergman & Beving AB; Int'l, pg. 188
BEVRACHTINGSKANTOOR TWENTHE-RIJN BV—See Akzo Nobel N.V.; Int'l, pg. 43
BEWLEY'S MANUFACTURING LTD.—See Campbells/Bewley Group; Int'l, pg. 254
BEWLEY'S TEA & COFFEE LTD.—See Campbells/Bewley Group; Int'l, pg. 254
BEWLEYS COFFEE USA—See Campbells/Bewley Group; Int'l, pg. 254
BEWLEYS COFFEEMAN LIMITED—See Campbells/Bewley Group; Int'l, pg. 254
BEWLEYS FRANCHISING LIMITED—See Campbells/Bewley Group; Int'l, pg. 254
BEWLEYS HAMPERS LIMITED—See Campbells/Bewley Group; Int'l, pg. 254
BEWLEYS HANOVER STREET LIMITED—See Campbells/Bewley Group; Int'l, pg. 254
BEWLEYS ORIENTAL CAFES LIMITED—See Campbells/Bewley Group; Int'l, pg. 254
BEXLEY COMERCIO E PARTICIPACAO LTDA., BRAZIL DIV.—See Borden, Inc.; U.S. Private, pg. 159
BEXLEY FINANCE S.A.—See Borden, Inc.; U.S. Private, pg. 159
BEYELA S.A.—See Otto Versand (GmbH & Co.); Int'l, pg. 1015
BFA EDUCATIONAL MEDIA—See The Phoenix Learning Group, Inc.; U.S. Private, pg. 863
BFG RAILWAY INVESTORS LP—See Berwind Corporation; U.S. Private, pg. 139
BGB FINANCE (IRELAND) PLC—See Bankgesellschaft Berlin; Int'l, pg. 160
BHARAT BIJLEE LTD.—See Schindler Holding AG; Int'l, pg. 1205
BHARAT COKING COAL LIMITED—See Coal India Limited; Int'l, pg. 298
BHARAT EXPLOSIVES LIMITED—See Mining Services International, Inc.; U.S. Public, pg. 1115
BHARAT PETROLEUM CORPORATION LTD.; Int'l, pg. 194
BHF-REPRESENTATIVE OFFICE—See BHF-BANK AG; Int'l, pg. 120
BI-LO INC.—See Koninklijke Ahold NV; Int'l, pg. 749
BI-TECH ENGINEERING—See The Glen Dimplex Group; Int'l, pg. 554
BI WAVERLY PVT. LTD.—See Waverly, Inc.; U.S. Public, pg. 1748

MASTER INDEX TO COMPANY NAMES BINSWANGER

Company Index

BIAMP SYSTEMS CORP.—See Rauland-Borg Corporation; *U.S. Private*, pg. 911
J. BIBBY & SONS PLC—See Barlow Ltd.; *Int'l*, pg. 167
BIBLER BROTHERS, INC.; *U.S. Private*, pg. 142
BIBLIO DISTRIBUTION CTR.—See University Press of America, Inc.; *U.S. Private*, pg. 1128
BIC ASSEMBLAGE S.A.R.L.—See Societe BIC S.A.; *Int'l*, pg. 1273
BIC BENELUX NEDERLAND BV—See Societe BIC S.A.; *Int'l*, pg. 1273
BIC BENELUX S.A.—See Societe BIC S.A.; *Int'l*, pg. 1273
BIC COMMERCIAL S.A.—See Societe BIC S.A.; *Int'l*, pg. 1273
BIC CORPORATION—See Societe BIC S.A.; *Int'l*, pg. 1273
BIC DE GUATEMALA—See Societe BIC S.A.; *Int'l*, pg. 1273
BIC ERZEUGNISSE GMBH—See Societe BIC S.A.; *Int'l*, pg. 1273
BIC HELLAS A.E.—See Societe BIC S.A.; *Int'l*, pg. 1273
BIC INC.—See Societe BIC S.A.; *Int'l*, pg. 1273
BIC INDUSTR. ESFEROGRAFICA BRASILEIRA—See Societe BIC S.A.; *Int'l*, pg. 1273
BIC ITALIA SPA—See Societe BIC S.A.; *Int'l*, pg. 1273
BIC MARINE S.A.—See Societe BIC S.A.; *Int'l*, pg. 1273
BIC SPECIAL MKTS. DIV.—See Societe BIC S.A.; *Int'l*, pg. 1273
BIC SPORT—See Societe BIC S.A.; *Int'l*, pg. 1273
BIC TECHNIQUE S.A.R.L.—See Societe BIC S.A.; *Int'l*, pg. 1273
BIC URUGUAY S.A.—See Societe BIC S.A.; *Int'l*, pg. 1273
BICAPA-BJOERNKLAEDER AB—See Sophus Berendsen A/S; *Int'l*, pg. 1285
BICKER CAARTEN EN OBREEN N.V.—See ABN-AMRO Holding N.V.; *Int'l*, pg. 9
BICKFORD'S FAMILY RESTAURANTS—See ELXSI Corporation; *U.S. Public*, pg. 545
BICK'S PICKLES & RELISHES—See International Multifoods Corporation; *U.S. Public*, pg. 901
BICOMP, S.A. DE C.V.—See Emerson Electric Co.; *U.S. Public*, pg. 576
BICRON PRODUCTS PRIVATE LIMITED—See Saint-Gobain; *Int'l*, pg. 1174
BICRON VERTRIEBES GMBH—See Saint-Gobain; *Int'l*, pg. 1174
BICYCLE CLUB CASINO; *U.S. Private*, pg. 142
BIDDLE SAWYER CORPORATION; *U.S. Private*, pg. 142
BIDDULPH AUTOMOTIVE GROUP; *U.S. Private*, pg. 142
BIDERMANN CO., LTD.—See Bidermann International S.A.; *Int'l*, pg. 194
BIDERMANN INTERNATIONAL S.A.; *Int'l*, pg. 194
BIDERMANN SHIRT GROUP—See Bidermann International S.A.; *Int'l*, pg. 194
BIDWELL DIV.—See CMI Corporation; *U.S. Public*, pg. 279
BIDWELL INDUSTRIAL GROUP, INC.; *U.S. Private*, pg. 142
ALBERT BIECKER GMBH & CO. KG—See Plettac AG; *Int'l*, pg. 1061
A. BIEDERMAN, INC.—See Triumph Group, Inc.; *U.S. Public*, pg. 1640
BIEDERMAN, KELLY & SHAFFER, INC.; *U.S. Private*, pg. 142
BIENEFELD-PEUKERT GMBH & CO. KG—See Freudenberg & Company; *Int'l*, pg. 505
BIENES RENTABLES MORELOS, S.A. DE C.V.—See Unilever Plc; *Int'l*, pg. 1436
BIENES Y SERVICIOS BISERCA—See Petroleos de Venezuela S.A.; *Int'l*, pg. 1045
BIENFANG PAPER DIV.—See Hunt Corporation; *U.S. Public*, pg. 849
BIERBRAUEREI FOHRENBURG; *Int'l*, pg. 194
BIFFA WASTE SERVICES LIMITED—See Severn Trent Plc; *Int'l*, pg. 1225
BIFFA WASTE SERVICES SA—See Severn Trent Plc; *Int'l*, *pg. 1226*
BIFFI ITALIA S.R.L.—See Tyco International Ltd.; *U.S. Public*, pg. 1650
BIFIN B.V.—See Exor Group; *Int'l*, pg. 467
BIFURCATED ENGINEERING FRANCE S.A.—See Clayhithe P.L.C.; *Int'l*, pg. 297
BIG A AUTO PARTS—See APS Holding Corporation; *U.S. Public*, pg. 10
BIG BALL SPORTS—See Signal Apparel Company, Inc.; *U.S. Public*, pg. 1472
BIG BALLOON BV—See VNU Verenigde Nederlandse Uitgeversbedrijven B.V.; *Int'l*, pg. 1445
BIG BEAR STORES COMPANY—See The Penn Traffic Company; *U.S. Public*, pg. 1270
BIG BOWL CAFE—See Lettuce Entertain You Enterprises, Inc.; *U.S. Private*, pg. 661
BIG DOG HOLDINGS INC.; *U.S. Public*, pg. 227
BIG FLOWER PRESS HOLDINGS, INC.; *U.S. Public*, pg. 228
BIG FOOT CATTLE CO.—See Vienna Sausage Mfg. Co.; *U.S. Private*, pg. 1140
BIG 'G' DIV.—See General Mills, Inc.; *U.S. Public*, pg. 718
BIG HORN CO-OP MARKETING ASSOCIATION; *U.S. Private*, pg. 143
BIG HORN REDI-MIX—See Monroc, Inc.; *U.S. Public*, pg. 1124
BIG J SUPER STORES, INC.—See Jones Company, Inc.; *U.S. Private*, pg. 596
BIG JOE MANUFACTURING CO.; *U.S. Private*, pg. 143
BIG M, INC.; *U.S. Private*, pg. 143
BIG O TIRES INCORPORATED—See TBC Corporation; *U.S. Public*, pg. 1553
BIG RIVER GRILLE & BREWERY WORKS—See Rock Bottom Restaurants; *U.S. Public*, pg. 1396
BIG RIVER INDUSTRIES—See CRH, plc; *Int'l*, pg. 242
BIG SANDY GAS COMPANY—See Cabot Oil & Gas Corporation; *U.S. Public*, pg. 289
BIG SANDY WHOLESALE CO.—See The H.T. Hackney Co.; *U.S. Private*, pg. 493
BIG SPLASH KENDALL CORP.—See Benihana, Inc.; *U.S. Public*, pg. 212
BIG STONE CHEESE FACTORY—See Stella Foods, Inc.; *U.S. Private*, pg. 1040
BIG V SUPERMARKETS, INC.; *U.S. Private*, pg. 143
BIG VALLEY MARKETING CORP.—See J.R. Wood Inc.; *U.S. Private*, pg. 1186
BIG Y FOODS INC.; *U.S. Private*, pg. 143
BIGGS GILMORE COMMUNICATIONS; *U.S. Private*, pg. 143
BIGG'S HYPER SHOPPES, INC.—See SuperValu, Inc.; *U.S. Public*, pg. 1541
BIGG'S SA—See GIB Group; *Int'l*, pg. 533
BIGSBY & KRUTHERS COMPANIES; *U.S. Private*, pg. 143
BIJHUIS ANTWERPEN—See Commerzbank AG; *Int'l*, pg. 312
BIJUR LUBRICATING CORPORATION; *U.S. Private*, pg. 143
BIKE ATHLETIC CO.; *U.S. Private*, pg. 143
BIL-JAX INC.—See Plettac AG; *Int'l*, pg. 1061
BIL LEASING GMBH & CO. BETRIEBSGEBAUDE KG—See Bayerische Vereinsbank Group; *Int'l*, pg. 179
BIL LEASING GMBH & CO. DAKIA KG—See Bayerische Vereinsbank Group; *Int'l*, pg. 179
BIL LEASING GMBH & CO. PRODUKTIONSGEBAUDE KG—See Bayerische Vereinsbank Group; *Int'l*, pg. 179
BIL MAR FOODS, INC.—See Sara Lee Corporation; *U.S. Public*, pg. 1433
BILAR BILGI ARACLARI TICARET A.S.—See Ricoh Company, Ltd.; *Int'l*, pg. 1115
BILBAO COMPANIA ANONIMA DE SEGUROS Y REASEGUROS—See Fortis; *Int'l*, pg. 499
BILBAO TERMINAL—See GATX Corporation; *U.S. Public*, pg. 693
BILBAO/Y&R—See Young & Rubicam Inc.; *U.S. Private*, pg. 1200
BILDUNGSAKADEMIE BERLIN-BRANDENBURG GMBH—See Bankgesellschaft Berlin; *Int'l*, pg. 159
BILFINGER + BERGER AUSTRALIA PTY. LTD.—See Bilfinger + Berger Bauaktiengesellschaft; *Int'l*, pg. 196
BILFINGER + BERGER BAUAKTIENGESELLSCHAFT; *Int'l*, pg. 194
BILFINGER + BERGER BAUAKTIENGESELLSCHAFT—See Bilfinger + Berger Bauaktiengesellschaft; *Int'l*, pg. 196
BILFINGER + BERGER BAUAKTIENGESELLSCHAFT BENGHAZI, S.P.L.A.J.—See Bilfinger + Berger Bauaktiengesellschaft; *Int'l*, pg. 196
BILFINGER + BERGER BAUAKTIENGESELLSCHAFT TRIPOLI, S.P.L.A.J.—See Bilfinger + Berger Bauaktiengesellschaft; *Int'l*, pg. 196
BILFINGER + BERGER BAUAKTIENGESELLSCHAFT—See Bilfinger + Berger Bauaktiengesellschaft; *Int'l*, pg. 196
BILFINGER + BERGER BAUAKTIENGESELLSCHAFT BANGRAK—See Bilfinger + Berger Bauaktiengesellschaft; *Int'l*, pg. 196
BILFINGER + BERGER BAUSTOFFE GMBH—See Bilfinger + Berger Bauaktiengesellschaft; *Int'l*, pg. 195
BILFINGER + BERGER BOUWMAATSCHAPPIJ B.V.—See Bilfinger + Berger Bauaktiengesellschaft; *Int'l*, pg. 196
BILFINGER + BERGER (M) SDN. BHD.—See Bilfinger + Berger Bauaktiengesellschaft; *Int'l*, pg. 196
BILFINGER + BERGER PORTUGAL CONSTRUCOES LDA.—See Bilfinger + Berger Bauaktiengesellschaft; *Int'l*, pg. 196
BILFINGER + BERGER PROJEKTENTWICKLUNG GMBH—See Bilfinger + Berger Bauaktiengesellschaft; *Int'l*, pg. 195
BILFINGER + BERGER S.A.R.L.—See Bilfinger + Berger Bauaktiengesellschaft; *Int'l*, pg. 196
BILFINGER + BERGER STAVEBNI S.R.O.—See Bilfinger + Berger Bauaktiengesellschaft; *Int'l*, pg. 196
BILFINGER + BERGER (THAI) CONSTRUCTION COMPANY LIMITED—See Bilfinger + Berger Bauaktiengesellschaft; *Int'l*, pg. 196
BILFINGER + BERGER U.K. LTD.—See Bilfinger + Berger Bauaktiengesellschaft; *Int'l*, pg. 196
BILFINGER + BERGER UMWELTVERFAHRENSTECHNIK GMBH—See Bilfinger + Berger Bauaktiengesellschaft; *Int'l*, pg. 195
BILFINGER + BERGER VORSPANNTECHNIK GMBH—See Bilfinger + Berger Bauaktiengesellschaft; *Int'l*, pg. 195
N.V. BILFINGER + BERGER BELGIUM S.A.—See Bilfinger + Berger Bauaktiengesellschaft; *Int'l*, pg. 196
BILFINGER Y BERGER ESPANA S.A.—See Bilfinger + Berger Bauaktiengesellschaft; *Int'l*, pg. 196
BILGER GETRANKE AG—See Feldschlosschen Hurlimann Holding; *Int'l*, pg. 479
BILL ACCEPTANCE CORPORATION LIMITED—See Westpac Banking Corporation; *Int'l*, pg. 1496
BILL ACCEPTANCE CORPORATION LIMITED - VICTORIA—See Westpac Banking Corporation; *Int'l*, pg. 1496
BILL BLASS, INC.—See MacAndrews & Forbes Holdings Inc.; *U.S. Private*, pg. 689
BILL COMMUNICATIONS, INC.—See VNU Verenigde Nederlandse Uitgeversbedrijven B.V.; *Int'l*, pg. 1446
BILL GETRANKE AG—See Feldschlosschen Hurlimann Holding; *Int'l*, pg. 479
BILL SWITCHGEAR LTD.—See Delta plc; *Int'l*, pg. 390
BILL WINK CHEVROLET; *U.S. Private*, pg. 144
BILLBOARD MAGAZINE—See VNU Verenigde Nederlandse Uitgeversbedrijven B.V.; *Int'l*, pg. 1446
BILLCOM AKRON—See VNU Verenigde Nederlandse Uitgeversbedrijven B.V.; *Int'l*, pg. 1446
BILLCOM EXPOSITION & CONFERENCE—See VNU Verenigde Nederlandse Uitgeversbedrijven B.V.; *Int'l*, pg. 1446
BILLIARDS DIV. OF BRUNSWICK—See Brunswick Corporation; *U.S. Public*, pg. 265
BILLING METAL TRADING AB—See British Steel Plc; *Int'l*, *pg. 221*
BILLING STAINLESS—See British Steel Plc; *Int'l*, pg. 222
BILLINGS & CO., INC.—See The Advest Group, Inc.; *U.S. Public*, pg. 23
THE BILLINGS GAZETTE—See Lee Enterprises, Incorporated; *U.S. Public*, pg. 983
BILLION SA—See Mannesmann A.G.; *Int'l*, pg. 836
BILLION (UK) LTD.—See Mannesmann A.G.; *Int'l*, pg. 836
BILLITON METALS, INC.—See Royal Dutch/Shell Group of Companies; *Int'l*, pg. 1136
A. BILLITZ S.R.L.—See Coeclerici Group; *Int'l*, pg. 303
BILL'S DOLLAR STORES, INC.; *U.S. Private*, pg. 144
AUGUST BILSTEIN GMBH & CO. KG—See Fried. Krupp AG; *Int'l*, pg. 507
BILSTEIN CORPORATION OF AMERICA—See Fried. Krupp AG; *Int'l*, pg. 507
BILSTON INVESTMENTS—See Delta plc; *Int'l*, pg. 392
BILTBEST WINDOWS—See U.S. Industries, Inc.; *U.S. Public*, pg. 1683
THE BILTRITE CORPORATION; *U.S. Private*, pg. 144
BILTRUST MANAGEMENT AKTIENGESELLSCHAFT—See Liechtenstein Global Trust Limited; *Int'l*, pg. 809
BILTWELL COMPANY, INC.—See Hartmarx Corporation; *U.S. Public*, pg. 795
BIMAR BAKERIES—See Grupo Industrial Bimbo S.A. de C.V.; *Int'l*, pg. 575
BIMBO S.A.—See The Earthgrains Company; *U.S. Public*, pg. 548
BIMCOR INC.—See BCE Inc.; *Int'l*, pg. 115
BIN HAM TRADING AGENCIES—See GESTRA GmbH; *Int'l*, pg. 550
AB BINAB—See NCC AB; *Int'l*, pg. 899
BINDERLINE DEVELOPMENT, INC./DRAFTLINE ENGINEERING CO., INC.—See Defiance, Inc.; *U.S. Public*, pg. 493
BINDICATOR COMPANY—See Berwind Corporation; *U.S. Private*, pg. 138
BINDLEY WESTERN, AUSTELL DIVISION—See Bindley Western Industries, Inc.; *U.S. Public*, pg. 228
BINDLEY WESTERN, CAROLINA DIVISION—See Bindley Western Industries, Inc.; *U.S. Public*, pg. 228
BINDLEY WESTERN, DALLAS DIVISION—See Bindley Western Industries, Inc.; *U.S. Public*, pg. 228
BINDLEY WESTERN DRUG COMPANY—See Bindley Western Industries, Inc.; *U.S. Public*, pg. 228
BINDLEY WESTERN, HOUSTON DIVISION—See Bindley Western Industries, Inc.; *U.S. Public*, pg. 228
BINDLEY WESTERN, INDIANAPOLIS DIVISION—See Bindley Western Industries, Inc.; *U.S. Public*, pg. 228
BINDLEY WESTERN INDUSTRIES, INC.; *U.S. Public*, pg. 228
BINDLEY WESTERN, KENDALL DIVISION—See Bindley Western Industries, Inc.; *U.S. Public*, pg. 228
BINDLEY WESTERN, MIDDLETOWN DIVISION—See Bindley Western Industries, Inc.; *U.S. Public*, pg. 228
BINDLEY WESTERN, MID-SOUTH DIVISION—See Bindley Western Industries, Inc.; *U.S. Public*, pg. 228
BINDLEY WESTERN, ORANGE DIVISION—See Bindley Western Industries, Inc.; *U.S. Public*, pg. 228
BINDLEY WESTERN, ORLANDO DIVISION—See Bindley Western Industries, Inc.; *U.S. Public*, pg. 228
BINDLEY WESTERN, SOUTHEASTERN DIVISION—See Bindley Western Industries, Inc.; *U.S. Public*, pg. 228
BINDLEY WESTERN, SOUTHERN CALIFORNIA DIVISION—See Bindley Western Industries, Inc.; *U.S. Public*, pg. 229
BINDLEY WESTERN, SOUTHWESTERN DIVISION—See Bindley Western Industries, Inc.; *U.S. Public*, pg. 229
BINDLEY WESTERN, TENNESSEE WHOLESALE DIVISION—See Bindley Western Industries, Inc.; *U.S. Public*, pg. 229
BINESA-BIOQUIMICA INDUSTRIAL ESPANOLA, S.A.—See Pfizer Inc.; *U.S. Public*, pg. 1283
BINET FEUTRES—See J.M. Voith, GmbH; *Int'l*, pg. 1473
BING STEEL INC.; *U.S. Private*, pg. 144
SAMUEL BINGHAM CO; *U.S. Private*, pg. 144
BINGHAMS COOKED MEATS LTD.—See Northern Foods plc; *Int'l*, pg. 968
BINGHAMTON CEL TEL CO.—See Vanguard Cellular Systems, Inc.; *U.S. Public*, pg. 1708
BINGO EXPRESS CO., LTD.—See Nippon Express Co., Ltd.; *Int'l*, pg. 934
BINKLEY COMPANY—See The Holland Hitch Company; *U.S. Private*, pg. 534
BINKS-BULLOWS (AUST.) PTY. LTD.—See Binks Sames Corporation; *U.S. Public*, pg. 229
BINKS-BULLOWS, LTD.—See Binks Sames Corporation; *U.S. Public*, pg. 229
BINKS-BULLOWS SWEDEN AB—See Binks Sames Corporation; *U.S. Public*, pg. 229
BINKS DE MEXICO, S.A. DE S.V.—See Binks Sames Corporation; *U.S. Public*, pg. 229
BINKS DEUTSCHLAND GMBH—See Binks Sames Corporation; *U.S. Public*, pg. 229
BINKS INTERNATIONAL, FRANCE—See Binks Sames Corporation; *U.S. Public*, pg. 229
BINKS INTERNATIONAL, S.A.—See Binks Sames Corporation; *U.S. Public*, pg. 229
BINKS JAPAN, LTD.—See Binks Sames Corporation; *U.S. Public*, pg. 229
BINKS MANUFACTURING CO. OF CANADA, LTD.—See Binks Sames Corporation; *U.S. Public*, pg. 229
BINKS MANUFACTURING COMPANY—See Binks Sames Corporation; *U.S. Public*, pg. 229
BINKS MANUFACTURING FACILITY—See Binks Sames Corporation; *U.S. Public*, pg. 229
BINKS RESEARCH & DEVELOPMENT CORP.—See Binks Sames Corporation; *U.S. Public*, pg. 229
BINKS SAMES CORPORATION; *U.S. Public*, pg. 229
BINNEY & SMITH INC.—See Hallmark Cards, Inc.; *U.S. Private*, pg. 496
BINNING'S BUILDING PRODUCTS, INC.—See American Architectural Products, Inc.; *U.S. Public*, pg. 67
BINO (SOCIETE CIVILE IMMOBILIERE)—See Compagnie des Machines Bull; *Int'l*, pg. 317
BINSWANGER; *U.S. Private*, pg. 144

BINSWANGER GLASS COMPANY—See BTR plc; *Int'l*, pg. 129
BINSWANGER MANAGEMENT CORP.—See Binswanger; *U.S. Private*, pg. 144
BINSWANGER REALTY GROUP—See Binswanger; *U.S. Private*, pg. 144
BINTER CANARIAS—See Grupo Iberia; *Int'l*, pg. 574
BINTER CANARIAS, S.A.—See SEPI; *Int'l*, pg. 1224
BINTER FINANCE, B.V.—See SEPI; *Int'l*, pg. 1225
BINTER MEDITERRANEO—See Grupo Iberia; *Int'l*, pg. 574
BINTER MEDITERRANEO, S.A.—See SEPI; *Int'l*, pg. 1224
BIO DERMIS CORPORATION—See Inamod Corporation; *U.S. Public*, pg. 873
BIO-ENERGY PARTNERS—See Caterpillar Inc.; *U.S. Public*, pg. 315
BIO ENTERICS CORPORATION—See Inamed Corporation; *U.S. Public*, pg. 873
BIO-KIL LABORATORIES LIMITED—See Laporte plc; *Int'l*, pg. 802
BIO-LAB, INC.—See Great Lakes Chemical Corporation; *U.S. Public*, pg. 760
BIO-LOGIC FSC INTERNATIONAL CORP.—See Bio-Logic Systems Corp.; *U.S. Public*, pg. 230
BIO-LOGIC SYSTEMS CORP.; *U.S. Public*, pg. 230
BIO MEDIC DATA SYSTEMS—See Lab Products, Inc.; *U.S. Private*, pg. 641
BIO-RAD CLINICAL DIV.—See Bio-Rad Laboratories, Inc.; *U.S. Public*, pg. 230
BIO-RAD DIGILAB DIV.—See Bio-Rad Laboratories, Inc.; *U.S. Public*, pg. 230
BIO-RAD LABORATORIES AG—See Bio-Rad Laboratories, Inc.; *U.S. Public*, pg. 230
BIO-RAD LABORATORIES BV—See Bio-Rad Laboratories, Inc.; *U.S. Public*, pg. 230
BIO-RAD LABORATORIES (CANADA) LTD.—See Bio-Rad Laboratories, Inc.; *U.S. Public*, pg. 230
BIO-RAD LABORATORIES, GES.M.B.H.—See Bio-Rad Laboratories, Inc.; *U.S. Public*, pg. 230
BIO-RAD LABORATORIES, GMBH—See Bio-Rad Laboratories, Inc.; *U.S. Public*, pg. 230
BIO-RAD LABORATORIES, INC.; *U.S. Public*, pg. 230
BIO-RAD LABORATORIES LTD.—See Bio-Rad Laboratories, Inc.; *U.S. Public*, pg. 230
BIO-RAD LABORATORIES PTY. LIMITED—See Bio-Rad Laboratories, Inc.; *U.S. Public*, pg. 230
BIO-RAD LABORATORIES S.R.L.—See Bio-Rad Laboratories, Inc.; *U.S. Public*, pg. 230
BIO-RAD LASERSHARP LTD.—See Bio-Rad Laboratories, Inc.; *U.S. Public*, pg. 230
BIO-RAD PACIFIC—See Bio-Rad Laboratories, Inc.; *U.S. Public*, pg. 230
BIO-RAD S.A.—See Bio-Rad Laboratories, Inc.; *U.S. Public*, pg. 230
BIO-RAD SANZ—See Bio-Rad Laboratories, Inc.; *U.S. Public*, pg. 230
BIO-RAD SEMICONDUCTOR SYSTEMS DIV.—See Bio-Rad Laboratories, Inc.; *U.S. Public*, pg. 230
BIO-RAD S.P.D.—See Bio-Rad Laboratories, Inc.; *U.S. Public*, pg. 230
BIO-TEK INSTRUMENTS, INC.; *U.S. Private*, pg. 144
BIOCARE MEDICAL, INC.—See Integrated Health Services, Inc.; *U.S. Public*, pg. 884
BIOCHEM IMMUNOSYSTEMS, INC.—See BioChem Pharma Inc.; *Int'l*, pg. 196
BIOCHEM IMMUNOSYSTEMS INC.—See BioChem Pharma Inc.; *Int'l*, pg. 196
BIOCHEM PHARMA INC.; *Int'l*, pg. 196
BIOCHEM THERAPEUTIC INC.—See BioChem Pharma Inc.; *Int'l*, pg. 196
BIO-CHEM VALVE INC.—See Halma p.l.c.; *Int'l*, pg. 590
BIOCHEMIE GESELLSCHAFT M.B.H.—See Novartis AG; *Int'l*, pg. 975
BIOCHEMIE S.A.—See Novartis AG; *Int'l*, pg. 975
BIOCINE COMPANY—See Novartis AG; *Int'l*, pg. 973
THE BIOCINE COMPANY—See Chiron Corporation; *U.S. Public*, pg. 350
BIOCINE S.A.R.L.—See Chiron Corporation; *U.S. Public*, pg. 350
BIOCINE S.P.A.—See Chiron Corporation; *U.S. Public*, pg. 350
BIOCRAFT CEPHALOSPORIN DOSAGE PLANT—See Teva Pharmaceutical Industries Ltd.; *Int'l*, pg. 1381
BIOCRAFT NON-PENICILLIN PLANT—See Teva Pharmaceutical Industries Ltd.; *Int'l*, pg. 1381
BIOCRAFT PENICILLIN DOSAGE PLANT—See Teva Pharmaceutical Industries Ltd.; *Int'l*, pg. 1381
BIO-CYPHER LABORATORIES; *U.S. Private*, pg. 145
BIOFIN HOLDING INTERNATIONAL BV—See Fiat Auto SpA; *Int'l*, pg. 483
BIOFIN S.P.A.—See Pfizer Inc.; *U.S. Public*, pg. 1283
BIOGALENICA QUIMICA E FARMACEUTICA LTDA.—See Novartis AG; *Int'l*, pg. 975
BIOGEN FRANCE SA—See Biogen, Inc.; *U.S. Public*, pg. 231
BIOGEN GMBH—See Biogen, Inc.; *U.S. Public*, pg. 231
BIOGEN, INC.; *U.S. Public*, pg. 230
BIOGEN LIMITED—See Biogen, Inc.; *U.S. Public*, pg. 231
BIOGRAM AB—See Norsk Hydro a.s; *Int'l*, pg. 961
BIOIMAGE PRODUCTS—See Millipore Corporation; *U.S. Public*, pg. 1112
BIOINDUSTRIA FARMACEUTICI S.P.A.—See Pfizer Inc.; *U.S. Public*, pg. 1283
BIOINVENT INTERNATIONAL AB—See Norsk Hydro a.s; *Int'l*, pg. 961
BIOITALIA-BIOPRO ITALIA S.P.A.—See Lafarge S.A.; *Int'l*, pg. 790
BIOKAT ATBE—See Mannesmann A.G.; *Int'l*, pg. 836
BIOKAT INTERNATIONAL (BAHRAIN) EC—See Mannesmann A.G.; *Int'l*, pg. 836
BIOKYOWA INC.—See Kyowa Hakko Kogyo Company, Ltd.; *Int'l*, pg. 778
BIOLAC—See Solvay S.A.; *Int'l*, pg. 1278
BIOMAKOR LTD.—See Sigma-Aldrich Corporation; *U.S. Public*, pg. 1472

BIOMAR A.S.—See Norsk Hydro a.s; *Int'l*, pg. 959
BIOMEDICAL SENSORS (HOLDINGS) LTD.—See Pfizer Inc.; *U.S. Public*, pg. 1283
BIOMET AUSTRALIA PTY LTD.—See Biomet, Inc.; *U.S. Public*, pg. 231
BIOMET CANADA, INC.—See Biomet, Inc.; *U.S. Public*, pg. 231
BIOMET DEUTSCHLAND GMBH—See Biomet, Inc.; *U.S. Public*, pg. 232
BIOMET EUROPE LTD.—See Biomet, Inc.; *U.S. Public*, pg. 232
BIOMET, INC.; *U.S. Public*, pg. 231
BIOMET LTD.—See Biomet, Inc.; *U.S. Public*, pg. 232
BIOMET ORTHOPAEDICS LTD.—See Biomet, Inc.; *U.S. Public*, pg. 232
BIOMET POLSKA LTD.—See Biomet, Inc.; *U.S. Public*, pg. 232
BIOMET SA—See Biomet, Inc.; *U.S. Public*, pg. 232
BIOMET SPA—See Biomet, Inc.; *U.S. Public*, pg. 232
THE BIONETICS CORPORATION; *U.S. Private*, pg. 145
BIOPLEX CORP.—See Datascope Corp.; *U.S. Public*, pg. 487
BIOPLEX MEDICAL B.V.—See Datascope Corp.; *U.S. Public*, pg. 487
BIOPLEXUS CORPORATION—See Inamed Corporation; *U.S. Public*, pg. 874
BIOPRODUCTS, INC.; *U.S. Private*, pg. 145
BIOPRODUCTS, INC.-RESEARCH & DEVELOPMENT—See Bioproducts, Inc.; *U.S. Private*, pg. 145
BIORIGINAL FOOD & SCIENCE CORP.—See Saskatchewan Wheat Pool; *Int'l*, pg. 1195
BIOS-COUTELIER SA—See UCB, S.A.; *Int'l*, pg. 1427
BIOSENAL, S.A. DE C.V.—See Hewlett-Packard Company; *U.S. Public*, pg. 816
BIOSOL S.P.A.—See Incentive AB; *Int'l*, pg. 667
BIOSPHERICS INCORPORATED; *U.S. Public*, pg. 232
BIOTEC INTERNATIONAL S.R.L.—See Medtronic, Inc.; *U.S. Public*, pg. 1083
BIOTECHNICA INTERNATIONAL—See Groupe Limagrain; *Int'l*, pg. 566
BIOTER-BIONA S.A.—See ConAgra, Inc.; *U.S. Public*, pg. 429
BIOTON AG INDUSTRIEAKTIENGESELLSCHAFT FUR KOSMETIK UND FRISEURBEDARF—See Wella Group; *Int'l*, pg. 1489
BIOTRACK—See Novartis AG; *Int'l*, pg. 973
BIOWHITTAKER, INC.—See Cambrex Corporation; *U.S. Public*, pg. 297
BIOWHITTAKER UK LTD.—See Cambrex Corporation; *U.S. Public*, pg. 297
BIOZIM B.V.—See Novartis AG; *Int'l*, pg. 975
BIOZYM GESELLSCHAFT M.B.H.—See Novartis AG; *Int'l*, pg. 986
BIPIEMME FIDUCIARIA SPA—See Banca Popolare di Milano; *Int'l*, pg. 137
BIPIEMME-GESTIONE POLIZZE DI ASSICURAZIONE S.P.A.—See Banca Popolare di Milano; *Int'l*, pg. 137
BIRCHWOOD CARE CENTER—See Horizon/CMS Healthcare Corporation; *U.S. Public*, pg. 837
BIRCHWOOD CONCRETE PRODUCTS LTD.—See British Building & Engineering Appliances Plc; *Int'l*, pg. 219
BIRCHWOOD TERRACE HEALTHCARE—See Vencor, Inc.; *U.S. Public*, pg. 1712
WILLIAM M. BIRD & CO., INC.; *U.S. Private*, pg. 145
BIRD INCORPORATED—See Saint-Gobain; *Int'l*, pg. 1170
BIRD-JOHNSON COMPANY—See Axel Johnson AB; *Int'l*, pg. 709
BIRD-JOHNSON COMPANY-GULF COAST OPERATIONS—See Axel Johnson AB; *Int'l*, pg. 709
BIRD-JOHNSON COMPANY-SEATTLE OPERATIONS—See Axel Johnson AB; *Int'l*, pg. 709
BIRD-KATEMA—See Baker Hughes Incorporated; *U.S. Public*, pg. 166
BIRD LIFE DESIGNS—See Thermo Electron Corporation; *U.S. Public*, pg. 1591
BIRD MACHINE COMPANY—See Baker Hughes Incorporated; *U.S. Public*, pg. 166
BIRD PRODUCTS CORPORATION—See Thermo Electron Corporation; *U.S. Public*, pg. 1591
BIRD ROOFING PRODUCTS, INC.—See Saint-Gobain; *Int'l*, pg. 1171
BIRD TREATMENT SERVICES—See Baker Hughes Incorporated; *U.S. Public*, pg. 166
BIRD VINYL—See Jannock Limited; *Int'l*, pg. 699
BIRDAIR, INC.—See Taiyo Kogyo Corporation; *Int'l*, pg. 1348
BIRDS EYE WALLS LTD.—See Unilever Plc; *Int'l*, pg. 1434
BIRDSALL, INC.—See NICOR Inc.; *U.S. Public*, pg. 1182
BIRDSONG CORPORATION; *U.S. Private*, pg. 145
BIRFIELD PLANT OF GKN HARDY SPICER—See GKN plc; *Int'l*, pg. 534
BIRIA ERICSSON OPTICAL LTD.—See Telefonaktiebolaget LM Ericsson; *Int'l*, pg. 1365
BIRKIM FCAI—See FCAIBMZ; *Int'l*, pg. 470
BIRKETT CUTMASTER LIMITED—See Carclo Engineering Group plc; *Int'l*, pg. 268
FRANCIS W. BIRKETT & SONS LIMITED—See Carclo Engineering Group plc; *Int'l*, pg. 268
BIRKHÄUSER + GBC AG—See Coop Switzerland; *Int'l*, pg. 329
HENRY BIRKS & SONS (1993) INC.; *Int'l*, pg. 196
HENRY BIRKS JEWELERS, INC.—See Henry Birks & Sons (1993) Inc.; *Int'l*, pg. 197
BIRLA KENNAMETAL LTD.—See Kennametal Inc.; *U.S. Public*, pg. 951
BIRLA 3M LTD.—See 3M; *U.S. Public*, pg. 1606
BIRLESIK ALMAN ILAC FABRIKALARI TURK A.S.—See Bayer AG; *Int'l*, pg. 175
BIRMID HOLDINGS LTD.—See Thyssen AG; *Int'l*, pg. 1387
BIRMINGHAM—See National Westminster Bank PLC; *Int'l*, pg. 910
BIRMINGHAM AL STEEL DIVISION—See Birmingham Steel Corporation; *U.S. Public*, pg. 232

BIRMINGHAM BASEBALL CLUB, INC.—See Suntory Ltd.; *Int'l*, pg. 1321
BIRMINGHAM CABLE COMMUNICATIONS, INC.—See Time Warner Inc.; *U.S. Public*, pg. 1610
BIRMINGHAM FIELD OFFICE—See Manulife Financial (The Manufacturers Life Insurance Company); *Int'l*, pg. 840
BIRMINGHAM FIRE INSURANCE CO. OF PENNSYLVANIA—See American International Group, Inc.; *U.S. Public*, pg. 84
BIRMINGHAM MIDSHIRES—See Bayerische Hypotheken-und Wechsel-Bank Aktiengesellschaft; *Int'l*, pg. 176
BIRMINGHAM NEWS—See Advance Publications Inc.; *U.S. Private*, pg. 20
BIRMINGHAM POST-HERALD COMPANY—See The E.W. Scripps Company; *U.S. Public*, pg. 1447
BIRMINGHAM SOUTH—See Pinnacle Bank; *U.S. Public*, pg. 1297
BIRMINGHAM SOUTHEAST—See Birmingham Steel Corporation; *U.S. Public*, pg. 232
BIRMINGHAM STEEL CORP., CLEVELAND DIV.—See Birmingham Steel Corporation; *U.S. Public*, pg. 232
BIRMINGHAM STEEL CORPORATION; *U.S. Public*, pg. 232
BIRMINGHAM STEELS OVERSEAS, LTD.—See Birmingham Steel Corporation; *U.S. Public*, pg. 232
BIRMINGHAM VENTURES INC.—See Birmingham Steel Corporation; *U.S. Public*, pg. 232
BIRNBACH COMPANY, INC.—See Bell Industries, Inc.; *U.S. Public*, pg. 207
MAX BIRNGRUBE KG—See Freudenberg & Company; *Int'l*, pg. 506
BIRO BIC LTD.—See Societe BIC S.A.; *Int'l*, pg. 1273
BIRRA MORETTI S.P.A.—See Interbrew S.A.; *Int'l*, pg. 680
BIRRA PERONI INDUSTRIALE—See Danone Group; *Int'l*, pg. 381
BIRTCHER—See Zero Corporation; *U.S. Public*, pg. 1791
BIRTLEY ENGINEERING LTD.—See Royal Dutch/Shell Group of Companies; *Int'l*, pg. 1139
BIRTLEY ENGINEERING LTD.—See Taylor Woodrow plc; *Int'l*, pg. 1359
BISCAYNE APPAREL INC.; *U.S. Public*, pg. 232
BISCEGLIA BROTHERS WINE CO.—See Canandaigua Wine Company, Inc.; *U.S. Public*, pg. 300
BISCHOF & KLEIN (U.K.) LTD.—See BPB Industries PLC; *Int'l*, pg. 122
BISCHOFSZELL CANNING FACTORY AG—See Migros; *Int'l*, pg. 865
BISCO INDUSTRIES, INC; *U.S. Private*, pg. 145
BISCUITERIE BOONE S.A.—See Diageo Plc; *Int'l*, pg. 411
BISCUITERIE MUGUET N.V.—See Borden, Inc.; *U.S. Private*, pg. 159
BISCUITERIE VINCHON-JEANETTE S.A.—See Sara Lee Corporation; *U.S. Public*, pg. 1435
N.V. BISCUITS DELACRE S.A.—See Campbell Soup Company; *U.S. Public*, pg. 300
BISHOP BROTHERS AUTO AUCTION—See Cox Enterprises, Inc.; *U.S. Private*, pg. 282
THE BISMARCK TRIBUNE—See Lee Enterprises, Incorporated; *U.S. Public*, pg. 983
BISON BASEBALL INC.—See Rich Products Corp.; *U.S. Private*, pg. 928
BISON CANNING CO., INC.—See Goya Foods, Inc.; *U.S. Private*, pg. 468
BISS LIMITED—See Wang Laboratories, Inc.; *U.S. Public*, pg. 1737
BISSELL INC.; *U.S. Private*, pg. 145
BISSELL INC.—See Bissell Inc.; *U.S. Private*, pg. 145
BISSETT & ROGERS—See Willis Corroon Group PLC; *Int'l*, pg. 1502
BISSEUIL—See Bouygues; *Int'l*, pg. 206
BISTA (TAIWAN) CO. LTD.—See Clarins; *Int'l*, pg. 295
BISTRO SOUPS, LTD.—See Vienna Sausage Mfg. Co.; *U.S. Private*, pg. 1140
BITBURGER BIER-GMBH KOLN—See Bitburger Brauerei Th. Simon GmbH; *Int'l*, pg. 197
BITBURGER BRAUEREI TH. SIMON GMBH; *Int'l*, pg. 197
BITOPI ADVERTISING LTD.—See Leo Burnett Company, Inc.; *U.S. Private*, pg. 184
BITOR AMERICA CORP.—See Petroleos de Venezuela S.A.; *Int'l*, pg. 1045
BITOR EUROPE—See Petroleos de Venezuela S.A.; *Int'l*, pg. 1046
BITREK CORPORATION; *U.S. Private*, pg. 145
BITUMA CORPORATION—See Gencor Industries, Inc.; *U.S. Public*, pg. 705
BITUMENES ORINOCO, S.A. (BITOR)—See Petroleos de Venezuela S.A.; *Int'l*, pg. 1045
BITUMEN-VERKAUF GMBH—See Veba AG; *Int'l*, pg. 1460
BITUMEX S.A. DE C.V.—See Kao Corporation; *Int'l*, pg. 717
BITUMINOUS CASUALTY CORP.—See Old Republic International Corporation; *U.S. Public*, pg. 1218
BITUMINOUS FIRE AND MARINE INSURANCE CO.—See Old Republic International Corporation; *U.S. Public*, pg. 1218
BITUMINOUS ROADWAYS, INC.; *U.S. Private*, pg. 146
BIVONA INC.—See L'Oreal S.A.; *Int'l*, pg. 818
BIWAG-GETRANKE AG—See Feldschlosschen Hurlimann Holding; *Int'l*, pg. 479
BIXBY INTERNATIONAL CORP.; *U.S. Private*, pg. 146
BIZIMGAZ A.S.—See SHV Holdings N.V.; *Int'l*, pg. 1155
BIZTEL CORPORATION—See WorldCom, Inc.; *U.S. Public*, pg. 1779
BIZZACK INC.; *U.S. Public*, pg. 146
BJOLVEFOSSEN—See Elkem ASA; *Int'l*, pg. 448
BJORNEBORGS JERNVERKS AB—See Axel Johnson AB; *Int'l*, pg. 708
BJORNKLADER AB—See Electrolux, AB; *Int'l*, pg. 438
BLACK & CO.; *U.S. Private*, pg. 146
THE BLACK & DECKER CORPORATION; *U.S. Public*, pg. 233

BLACK & DECKER HOUSEHOLD PRODUCTS GROUP—See The Black & Decker Corporation; *U.S. Public*, pg. 234

BLACK & DECKER INC.—See The Black & Decker Corporation; *U.S. Public*, pg. 234

BLACK & DECKER (NEDERLAND) B.V.—See The Black & Decker Corporation; *U.S. Public*, pg. 234

BLACK & DECKER S.A. DE C.V.—See The Black & Decker Corporation; *U.S. Public*, pg. 234

BLACK & EDGINGTON LTD.; *Int'l*, pg. 197

BLACK & VEATCH; *U.S. Private*, pg. 146

BLACK & VEATCH INTERNATIONAL-ENERGY—See Black & Veatch; *U.S. Private*, pg. 146

BLACK & VEATCH PRITCHARD, INC.—See Black & Veatch; *U.S. Private*, pg. 146

BLACK BAG COMMUNICATIONS, INC.—See Warwick Baker O'Neill; *U.S. Private*, pg. 1152

BLACK BOX CORPORATION OF PA; *U.S. Public*, pg. 235

BLACK CADILLAC OLDS, INC.; *U.S. Private*, pg. 146

THE BLACK CLAWSON COMPANY; *U.S. Private*, pg. 147

BLACK DIAMOND ENERGY, INC.—See Oglethorpe Power Corp.; *U.S. Private*, pg. 812

BLACK DOT GRAPHICS, INC.—See Devon Group, Inc.; *U.S. Public*, pg. 503

BLACK EARTH TELEPHONE CO.—See Telephone and Data Systems, Inc.; *U.S. Public*, pg. 1571

BLACK ENTERTAINMENT TELEVISION HOLDINGS INC.; *U.S. Public*, pg. 235

BLACK FIN YACHT CORPORATION; *U.S. Private*, pg. 147

FRANK B. BLACK RESEARCH CENTER—See Hubbell Incorporated; *U.S. Public*, pg. 844

BLACK HILLS CORPORATION; *U.S. Public*, pg. 235

BLACK HILLS POWER & LIGHT COMPANY—See Black Hills Corporation; *U.S. Public*, pg. 235

BLACK HILLS TRUCKING CO.—See True Companies; *U.S. Private*, pg. 1107

BLACK HORSE AGENCIES LTD.—See Lloyds TSB Group PLC; *Int'l*, pg. 813

BLACK HORSE FINANCIAL SERVICES LTD.—See Lloyds TSB Group PLC; *Int'l*, pg. 813

BLACK HORSE RELOCATION SERVICES LIMITED—See Lloyds TSB Group PLC; *Int'l*, pg. 813

BLACK MILLWORK CO., INC.; *U.S. Private*, pg. 147

BLACK MOUNTAIN PLANT—See Cooper Industries, Inc.; *U.S. Public*, pg. 443

BLACK PINE MINE—See Pegasus Gold Corporation; *U.S. Public*, pg. 1269

BLACK ROGERS SULLIVAN GOODNIGHT, INC.; *U.S. Private*, pg. 147

BLACK WARRIOR METHANE CORP.—See Walter Industries, Inc.; *U.S. Public*, pg. 1737

BLACK WARRIOR TRANSMISSION CORP.—See Sonat Inc.; *U.S. Public*, pg. 1485

BLACK WARRIOR TRANSMISSION CORP.—See Walter Industries, Inc.; *U.S. Public*, pg. 1737

BLACKCOMB SKIING ENTERPRISES LTD.—See Intrawest Corporation; *Int'l*, pg. 685

STANLEY BLACKER, INC.; *U.S. Private*, pg. 147

BLACKEYED PEA RESTAURANTS INC.—See DenAmerica Corp.; *U.S. Public*, pg. 498

BLACKHAWK—See Newcor, Inc.; *U.S. Public*, pg. 1176

BLACKHAWK AUTOMOTIVE LIMITED—See Hein-Werner Corporation; *U.S. Public*, pg. 805

BLACKHAWK COAL CO.—See American Electric Power Company, Inc.; *U.S. Public*, pg. 72

BLACKHAWK COLLISION REPAIR INC.—See Hein-Werner Corporation; *U.S. Public*, pg. 805

BLACKHAWK GMBH—See Hein-Werner Corporation; *U.S. Public*, pg. 805

BLACKHAWK HOLDING COMPANY—See Torchmark Corporation; *U.S. Public*, pg. 1623

BLACKHAWK ITALIA S.R.L.—See Hein-Werner Mendenhall Corporation; *U.S. Public*, pg. 805

BLACKHAWK S.A.—See Hein-Werner Corporation; *U.S. Public*, pg. 805

BLACKMAN UHLER CHEMICAL CO.—See Synalloy Corporation; *U.S. Public*, pg. 1548

BLACKMER PUMP/DOVER RESOURCES CO—See Dover Corporation; *U.S. Public*, pg. 521

BLACKROCK VENTURES INC.—See Rayrock Yellowknife Resources Inc.; *Int'l*, pg. 1089

THE BLACKSTONE GROUP; *U.S. Private*, pg. 147

BLACKSTONE MFG. CO., INC.—See Echlin Inc.; *U.S. Public*, pg. 560

BLACKSTONE VALLEY ELECTRIC CO.—See Eastern Utilities Associates; *U.S. Public*, pg. 549

BLACKVILLE LUMBER INC.—See Repap Enterprises Inc.; *Int'l*, pg. 1104

BLACKWATER MINE—See The Broken Hill Proprietary Company Limited; *Int'l*, pg. 223

B.H. BLACKWELL LTD.; *Int'l*, pg. 197

BLACKWELL LAND CO.—See Pearson plc; *Int'l*, pg. 1027

BLACKWELL PUBLISHERS, INC.—See B.H. Blackwell Ltd.; *Int'l*, pg. 197

BLACKWELL PUBLISHERS LTD.—See B.H. Blackwell Ltd.; *Int'l*, pg. 197

BLACKWELL SCIENCE—See B.H. Blackwell Ltd.; *Int'l*, pg. 197

BLACKWELL SCIENTIFIC PUBLICATIONS (AUSTRALIA) PTY. LTD.—See B.H. Blackwell Ltd.; *Int'l*, pg. 197

BLACKWELL SCIENTIFIC PUBLICATIONS, INC.—See B.H. Blackwell Ltd.; *Int'l*, pg. 197

BLACKWOOD BROTHERS LTD—See Dawson International PLC; *Int'l*, pg. 385

BLACKWOOD HODGE (BELGIE) N.V.—See Brunel Holdings Plc; *Int'l*, pg. 231

BLADE COMMUNICATIONS, INC.; *U.S. Private*, pg. 147

BLAGGE ENTERPRISES; *U.S. Private*, pg. 148

BLAIR ATHOL COAL—See BTR plc; *Int'l*, pg. 128

BLAIR CORPORATION; *U.S. Public*, pg. 236

D.L. BLAIR EUROPE—See D.L. Blair Inc.; *U.S. Private*, pg. 148

D.L. BLAIR INC.; *U.S. Private*, pg. 148

D.L. BLAIR INC.—See D.L. Blair Inc.; *U.S. Private*, pg. 148

BLAIR TELEVISION; *U.S. Private*, pg. 148

BLAIR TOWER LIMITED PARTNERSHIP—See Cooper Communities; *U.S. Private*, pg. 274

WILLIAM BLAIR & COMPANY L.L.C.; *U.S. Private*, pg. 148

WHITNEY BLAKE COMPANY OF VERMONT, INC.; *U.S. Private*, pg. 148

BLAKENHURST H.M. PRISON—See Corrections Corporation of America; *U.S. Public*, pg. 451

BLANCETT—See Racine Federated, Inc.; *U.S. Private*, pg. 906

E.W. BLANCH CAPITAL RISK SOLUTIONS, INC.—See E.W. Blanch Holdings, Inc.; *U.S. Public*, pg. 236

E.W. BLANCH HOLDINGS, INC.; *U.S. Public*, pg. 236

E.W. BLANCH INTERNATIONAL, INC.—See E.W. Blanch Holdings, Inc.; *U.S. Public*, pg. 236

E.W. BLANCH WHOLESALE INSURANCE SERVICES INC.—See E.W. Blanch Holdings, Inc.; *U.S. Public*, pg. 236

WM. BLANCHARD CO.; *U.S. Private*, pg. 148

BLANCPAIN S.A.—See SMH Swiss Corporation for Micro Electronics & Watchmaking Indus. Ltd.; *Int'l*, pg. 1160

BLANDIN PAPER COMPANY—See Fletcher Challenge Limited; *Int'l*, pg. 495

BLANELLA LTD.—See The Glen Dimplex Group; *Int'l*, pg. 554

BLANVALET VERLAG GMBH—See Bertelsmann AG; *Int'l*, pg. 190

D.H. BLATTNER & SONS, INC.; *U.S. Private*, pg. 148

BARRY BLAU & PARTNERS, INC.—See Blau Marketing Technologies, Inc.; *U.S. Private*, pg. 148

BLAU CONSULTING GROUP—See Blau Marketing Technologies, Inc.; *U.S. Private*, pg. 148

BLAU DIRECT EDGE, INC.—See Blau Marketing Technologies, Inc.; *U.S. Private*, pg. 148

BLAU GLOBAL NETWORK—See Blau Marketing Technologies, Inc.; *U.S. Private*, pg. 148

BLAU HEALTHDIRECT—See Blau Marketing Technologies, Inc.; *U.S. Private*, pg. 148

BLAU MARKETING TECHNOLOGIES, INC.; *U.S. Private*, pg. 148

BLAU MEDIA DIRECT—See Blau Marketing Technologies, Inc.; *U.S. Private*, pg. 149

BLAU TECHNOLOGY GROUP—See Blau Marketing Technologies, Inc.; *U.S. Private*, pg. 149

BLAU WILLIAMS TELEVISION TIME—See Blau Marketing Technologies, Inc.; *U.S. Private*, pg. 149

BLAUE QUELLEN MINERAL- UND HEILBRUNNEN AG—See Nestle S.A.; *Int'l*, pg. 919

BLAUER MANUFACTURING CO., INC.; *U.S. Private*, pg. 149

BLAUPUNKT-WERKE GMBH—See Robert Bosch GmbH; *Int'l*, pg. 203

BLAW-KNOX CONSTRUCTION EQUIPMENT CORPORATION—See Ingersoll-Rand Company; *U.S. Public*, pg. 877

BLAZER FINANCIAL SERVICES—See Washington Mutual Inc.; *U.S. Public*, pg. 1741

BLAZER PLC—See Moss Bros Group PLC; *Int'l*, pg. 896

BLEAKLEY FINE CHEMICALS—See Laporte plc; *Int'l*, pg. 803

BLEFA GMBH—See Fried. Krupp AG; *Int'l*, pg. 508

BLEIM STEEL COMPANY—See Marubeni Corporation; *Int'l*, pg. 845

BLENDAX-RICHARDSON AG—See The Procter & Gamble Company; *U.S. Public*, pg. 1331

BLESSINGS CORPORATION—See Williamson-Dickie Mfg. Co.; *U.S. Private*, pg. 1179

BLEU WATER COMPANY—See Central Coca-Cola Bottling Company, Inc.; *U.S. Private*, pg. 223

BLEVINS INC.; *U.S. Private*, pg. 149

BLEYCO PAPER CO. OF MICHIGAN—See A.W. Mendenhall Co., Inc.; *U.S. Private*, pg. 731

BLIKMAN & SARTORIUS B.V.—See Internatio-Muller N.V.; *Int'l*, pg. 682

BLIMPIE INTERNATIONAL, INC.; *U.S. Public*, pg. 236

BLIMPIE INTERNATIONAL, INC.—See Blimpie International, Inc.; *U.S. Public*, pg. 236

BLIMPIE SUBS & SALADS—See Blimpie International, Inc.; *U.S. Public*, pg. 236

BLISH-MIZE CO.—See Distribution America; *U.S. Private*, pg. 335

BLISS—See CNB International, Inc.; *U.S. Private*, pg. 196

JAMES BLISS & CO.—See West Marine, Inc.; *U.S. Public*, pg. 1756

BLISS MANUFACTURING COMPANY—See HMI Industries; *U.S. Public*, pg. 771

BLISS-SALEM, INC.; *U.S. Private*, pg. 149

WILLIAM B. BLISS DIV.—See Falcon Safety Products Inc.; *U.S. Private*, pg. 392

BLISSFIELD MANUFACTURING COMPANY; *U.S. Private*, pg. 149

BLISTEX, INC.; *U.S. Private*, pg. 149

BLISTEX LIMITED—See Blistex, Inc.; *U.S. Private*, pg. 149

BLITZ USA, INC.; *U.S. Private*, pg. 149

BLOCH & BEHRENS APS—See The East Asiatic Company Ltd. A/S; *Int'l*, pg. 430

BLOCH & BEHRENS (ITALIA) S.R.L.—See The East Asiatic Company Ltd. A/S; *Int'l*, pg. 431

BLOCH & BEHRENS (NEW ZEALAND) LIMITED—See The East Asiatic Company Ltd. A/S; *Int'l*, pg. 431

BLOCH & BEHRENS PTY. LTD.—See The East Asiatic Company Ltd. A/S; *Int'l*, pg. 431

BLOCH/NEW ENGLAND, INC.; *U.S. Private*, pg. 149

BLOCK DISTRIBUTING COMPANY; *U.S. Private*, pg. 149

BLOCK DRUG CO. (CANADA) LTD.—See Block Drug Company; *U.S. Public*, pg. 237

BLOCK DRUG CO., INC.; *U.S. Public*, pg. 236

BLOCK DRUG CO. (PHILIPPINES) INC.—See Block Drug Company; *U.S. Public*, pg. 237

BLOCK DRUG CORPORATION DENTAL PRODUCTS CO.—See Block Drug Company; *U.S. Public*, pg. 237

BLOCK INDUSTRIES, INC.; *U.S. Private*, pg. 150

M. BLOCK & SONS, INC.; *U.S. Private*, pg. 150

BLOCKBUSTER ENTERTAINMENT CORPORATION LIMITED (U.K.)—See National Amusements, Inc.; *U.S. Private*, pg. 776

BLOCKBUSTER ENTERTAINMENT GROUP—See National Amusements, Inc.; *U.S. Private*, pg. 775

BLOCKBUSTER HOLDING CORP.—See National Amusements, Inc.; *U.S. Private*, pg. 775

BLOCKBUSTER MUSIC HOLDING CORPORATION—See National Amusements, Inc.; *U.S. Private*, pg. 775

BLOCKBUSTER PICTURES HOLDING CORPORATION—See National Amusements, Inc.; *U.S. Private*, pg. 776

BLOCKBUSTER VIDEO LIMITED PARTNERSHIP—See National Amusements, Inc.; *U.S. Private*, pg. 776

BLOCKBUSTER VIDEOS INC.—See National Amusements, Inc.; *U.S. Private*, pg. 776

BLOCKHOUSE CO., INC.; *U.S. Private*, pg. 150

BLODGETT COMBI—See Maytag Corporation; *U.S. Public*, pg. 1064

G.S. BLODGETT CORPORATION—See Maytag Corporation; *U.S. Public*, pg. 1064

BLODGETT INTERNATIONAL—See Maytag Corporation; *U.S. Public*, pg. 1064

THE BLODGETT OVEN CO., INC.—See Maytag Corporation; *U.S. Public*, pg. 1064

BLOHM + VOSS AG—See Thyssen AG; *Int'l*, pg. 1387

BLOHORN S.A.—See Unilever Plc; *Int'l*, pg. 1436

BLOMMER CHOCOLATE CO.; *U.S. Private*, pg. 150

BLOMSTERCENTRALEN AB—See Axel Johnson AB; *Int'l*, pg. 708

BLONDER-TONGUE LABORATORIES, INC.; *U.S. Private*, pg. 237

BLOOD CELLS, INC.—See IGI, Inc.; *U.S. Public*, pg. 855

BLOODSTOCK & GENERAL INSURANCE SERVICES LIMITED—See Willis Corroon Group PLC; *Int'l*, pg. 1502

BLOOM ELECTRIC SERVICES, INC.; *U.S. Private*, pg. 150

BLOOMBERG L.P.; *U.S. Private*, pg. 150

BLOOMFIELD INDUSTRIES CANADA LTD.—See Specialty Equipment Companies Inc.; *U.S. Public*, pg. 1497

BLOOMINGDALE'S—See Federated Department Stores, Inc.; *U.S. Public*, pg. 617

BLOOMINGDALE'S BY MAIL, LTD.—See Federated Department Stores, Inc.; *U.S. Public*, pg. 618

BLOOMINGTON-NORMAL SEATING COMPANY—See Magna International Inc.; *Int'l*, pg. 830

BLOOMSBURG MILLS INC.; *U.S. Private*, pg. 150

BLOUNT CANADA LTD.—See Blount International, Inc.; *U.S. Public*, pg. 238

BLOUNT DEVELOPMENT CORP.—See Blount International, Inc.; *U.S. Public*, pg. 239

BLOUNT EUROPE, S.A.—See Blount International, Inc.; *U.S. Public*, pg. 238

BLOUNT GMBH—See Blount International, Inc.; *U.S. Public*, pg. 239

BLOUNT HOLDINGS LTD.—See Blount International, Inc.; *U.S. Public*, pg. 239

BLOUNT, INC.—See Blount International, Inc.; *U.S. Public*, pg. 238

BLOUNT, INC. OREGON CUTTING SYSTEMS DIVISION—See Blount International, Inc.; *U.S. Public*, pg. 238

BLOUNT, INC. SPORTING EQUIPMENT GROUP—See Blount International, Inc.; *U.S. Public*, pg. 238

BLOUNT INDUSTRIAL DE CORRENTES LTDA.—See Blount International, Inc.; *U.S. Public*, pg. 239

BLOUNT INTERNATIONAL, INC.; *U.S. Public*, pg. 237

BLOUNT JAPAN INC.—See Blount International, Inc.; *U.S. Public*, pg. 239

BLOUNT U.K. LIMITED—See Blount International, Inc.; *U.S. Public*, pg. 239

BLU-RAY—See Bidwell Industrial Group, Inc.; *U.S. Private*, pg. 142

BLUE ANCHOR, INC.; *U.S. Private*, pg. 150

BLUE & GRAY BROKERAGE—See US 1 Industries Inc.; *U.S. Public*, pg. 1687

BLUE & GRAY TRANSPORTATION—See US 1 Industries Inc.; *U.S. Public*, pg. 1687

BLUE BELL CREAMERIES, L.P.; *U.S. Private*, pg. 150

BLUE BELL/KING KOIL, INC.; *U.S. Private*, pg. 150

BLUE BIRD COACH LINES INC.; *U.S. Private*, pg. 150

BLUE BIRD CORPORATION; *U.S. Private*, pg. 151

BLUE BOAR CAFETERIA CO.; *U.S. Private*, pg. 151

BLUE CHIP STAMPS—See Berkshire Hathaway Inc.; *U.S. Public*, pg. 217

BLUE CIRCLE AGGREGATES, INC.—See Blue Circle Industries PLC; *Int'l*, pg. 198

BLUE CIRCLE AMERICA INC.—See Blue Circle Industries PLC; *Int'l*, pg. 197

BLUE CIRCLE INDUSTRIES PLC; *Int'l*, pg. 197

BLUE CIRCLE MATERIALS, INC.—See Blue Circle Industries PLC; *Int'l*, pg. 198

BLUE CIRCLE SOUTHERN CEMENT LIMITED—See Boral Limited; *Int'l*, pg. 203

BLUE CORAL QUAKER STATE INTERNATIONAL—See Quaker State Corporation; *U.S. Public*, pg. 1348

BLUE CORAL/SLICK 50—See Quaker State Corporation; *U.S. Public*, pg. 1348

BLUE CORAL SYSTEMS—See Quaker State Corporation; *U.S. Public*, pg. 1348

BLUE CRAB LOUNGE—See Lettuce Entertain You Enterprises, Inc.; *U.S. Private*, pg. 661

BLUE CROSS AND BLUE SHIELD ASSOCIATION; *U.S. Private*, pg. 151

BLUE CROSS & BLUE SHIELD OF ILLINOIS; *U.S. Private*, pg. 151

BLUE CROSS AND BLUE SHIELD OF MASSACHUSETTS; *U.S. Private*, pg. 151

BLUE CROSS & BLUE SHIELD OF MICHIGAN; *U.S. Private*, pg. 151

BLUE CROSS AND BLUE SHIELD OF OKLAHOMA; *U.S. Private*, pg. 151

BLUE CROSS & BLUE SHIELD OF TEXAS, INC.; *U.S. Private*, pg. 152

BLUE CROSS LABORATORIES; *U.S. Private*, pg. 152

BLUE CROSS OF CALIFORNIA; *U.S. Private*, pg. 152
BLUE CROSS S.R.L.—See Pfizer Inc.; *U.S. Public*,
  pg. 1283
BLUE DEVIL INDUSTRIES, INC.—See Laporte plc; *Int'l*,
  pg. 802
BLUE DIAMOND GROWERS; *U.S. Private*, pg. 152
BLUE FOX TACKLE CO.—See Normark Corporation; *U.S.
  Private*, pg. 802
BLUE GRASS CHRYSLER-PLYMOUTH INC.; *U.S. Private*,
  pg. 152
BLUE GRASS COOPERAGE CO.—See Brown-Forman
  Corporation; *U.S. Public*, pg. 261
BLUE GRASS PHYSICIAN MANAGEMENT GROUP, INC.—
  See Magellan Health Services, Inc.; *U.S. Public*,
  pg. 1033
BLUE GRASS QUALITY MEATS; *U.S. Private*, pg. 152
BLUE HAWK LTD.—See BPB Industries PLC; *Int'l*, pg. 122
BLUE ISLAND RAILROAD—See Illinois Central
  Corporation; *U.S. Public*, pg. 865
BLUE LINE DISTRIBUTING—See Little Caesar Enterprises,
  Inc.; *U.S. Private*, pg. 671
BLUE M ELECTRIC CO.—See General Signal Corporation;
  U.S. Public, pg. 726
BLUE MARBLE ADVANCED COMMUNICATIONS
  GROUP—See N.W. Ayer & Partners; *U.S. Private*,
  pg. 104
BLUE MOUNTAIN CONSOLIDATED WATER COMPANY—
  See Citizens Utilities Company; *U.S. Public*, pg. 379
BLUE MOUNTAIN PRODUCTION CO.—See Oil-Dri
  Corporation of America; *U.S. Public*, pg. 1215
BLUE PACIFIC TOURS—See Air New Zealand Ltd.; *Int'l*,
  pg. 38
BLUE RIDGE ELECTRIC COOPERATIVE INC.; *U.S.
  Private*, pg. 153
BLUE RIDGE ELECTRIC MEMBERSHIP CORP.; *U.S.
  Private*, pg. 153
BLUE RIDGE FARMS, INC.; *U.S. Private*, pg. 153
BLUE RIDGE FINANCE CO., INC.—See Carolina First
  Corporation; *U.S. Public*, pg. 306
BLUE RIDGE INDEMNITY CO.—See Credit Suisse Group;
  Int'l, pg. 345
BLUE RIDGE INSURANCE CO.—See Credit Suisse Group;
  Int'l, pg. 345
BLUE RIDGE PRESSURE CASTINGS, INC.; *U.S. Private*,
  pg. 153
BLUE RIDGE PRINTING—See Champion Industries; *U.S.
  Public*, pg. 333
THE BLUE SEA COMPANY W.L.L.—See Daewoo
  Corporation; *Int'l*, pg. 357
BLUE SEAL FEEDS, INC.—See Varied Investments, Inc.;
  U.S. Private, pg. 1134
BLUE SHIELD OF CALIFORNIA; *U.S. Private*, pg. 153
BLUE SPRINGS EXAMINER—See Shivers Trading &
  Operating Co.; *U.S. Private*, pg. 995
BLUE STAR LTD.—See Hewlett-Packard Company; *U.S.
  Public*, pg. 816
BLUE TEE CORPORATION; *U.S. Private*, pg. 153
BLUE WATER BROADCASTING LIMITED—See Rogers
  Communications, Inc.; *Int'l*, pg. 1123
BLUEBERRY HILL HEALTHCARE—See Vencor, Inc.; *U.S.
  Public*, pg. 1712
BLUEBIRD FOODS LTD—See Goodman Fielder Limited;
  Int'l, pg. 556
BLUECREST FREEBOOKER LTD.—See Booker PLC; *Int'l*,
  pg. 202
BLUEFIELD GAS COMPANY—See Roanoke Gas
  Company; *U.S. Public*, pg. 1393
BLUEFIELD VALLEY WATER WORKS CO.—See American
  Water Works Company, Inc.; *U.S. Public*, pg. 96
BLUEGRASS COCA-COLA BOTTLING COMPANY—See
  Coca-Cola Enterprises Inc.; *U.S. Public*, pg. 393
BLUELINCS HMO—See Blue Cross and Blue Shield of
  Oklahoma; *U.S. Public*, pg. 152
BLUELINE SOFTWARE INC.—See Apertus Technologies
  Incorporated; *U.S. Public*, pg. 120
BLUEPOINTS CO., INC.—See The First Republic
  Corporation of America; *U.S. Public*, pg. 637
BLUEWATER; *U.S. Private*, pg. 153
BLUEWAVE INN CORPORATION—See Orix Corporation;
  Int'l, pg. 1008
BLUFF CITY DISTRIBUTING CO., INC.; *U.S. Private*, pg.
  153
BLUFFTON AGRI/INDUSTRIAL CORP. D/B/A BAIC—See
  Farmatic Research, Inc.; *Int'l*, pg. 478
BLUMBERG COMMUNICATIONS INC.—See Caribiner
  International, Inc.; *U.S. Public*, pg. 305
BLUMBERG COMMUNICATIONS OF FLORIDA INC.—See
  Caribiner International, Inc.; *U.S. Public*, pg. 305
BLUMENFELD BRENNSTOFFE GMBH—See Fried. Krupp
  AG; *Int'l*, pg. 513
BLUMENTHAL MILLS—See Blumenthal Print Works, Inc.;
  U.S. Private, pg. 153
BLUMENTHAL PRINT WORKS, INC.; *U.S. Private*, pg. 153
BLUMENTHAL/LANSING COMPANY—See Noel Group,
  Inc.; *U.S. Public*, pg. 1187
BLUMHARDT MANUFACTURING COMPANY—See TIC
  United Corporation; *U.S. Private*, pg. 1063
BLYDENSTEIN-WILLINK N.V.; *Int'l*, pg. 198
BLYTH INDUSTRIES; *U.S. Public*, pg. 239
BOAM CHEMICALS CO., INC.—See MacAndrews & Forbes
  Holdings Inc.; *U.S. Private*, pg. 689
BOAM PRODUCE (OVERSEAS) LTD.—See MacAndrews &
  Forbes Holdings Inc.; *U.S. Private*, pg. 689
BOARDMAN COMMUNITY CARE CENTER—See Horizon/
  CMS Healthcare Corporation; *U.S. Public*, pg. 838
BOARDWALK REGENCY CORPORATION—See Starwood
  Hotels & Resorts; *U.S. Public*, pg. 1512
BOART INTERNATIONAL LIMITED—See Anglo American
  Corporation of South Africa Limited; *Int'l*, pg. 76
BOART LONGYEAR B.V.—See Anglo American
  Corporation of South Africa Limited; *Int'l*, pg. 76
BOART LONGYEAR GMBH—See Anglo American
  Corporation of South Africa Limited; *Int'l*, pg. 76

BOART LONGYEAR INC.—See Anglo American
  Corporation of South Africa Limited; *Int'l*, pg. 76
BOART LONGYEAR LIMITED—See Anglo American
  Corporation of South Africa Limited; *Int'l*, pg. 76
BOART LONGYEAR LTD.—See Anglo American
  Corporation of South Africa Limited; *Int'l*, pg. 76
BOART LONGYEAR LTDA.—See Anglo American
  Corporation of South Africa Limited; *Int'l*, pg. 76
BOART LONGYEAR PTY. LTD.—See Anglo American
  Corporation of South Africa Limited; *Int'l*, pg. 76
BOART LONGYEAR S.A.—See Anglo American
  Corporation of South Africa Limited; *Int'l*, pg. 76
BOART LONGYEAR S.A. DE C.V.—See Anglo American
  Corporation of South Africa Limited; *Int'l*, pg. 76
BOART MSA (PTY.) LTD.—See Mine Safety Appliances
  Co.; *U.S. Public*, pg. 1114
BOAT AMERICA CORP.; *U.S. Private*, pg. 153
BOATMEN'S MORTGAGE COMPANY—See NationsBank
  Corporation; *U.S. Public*, pg. 1164
BOATMEN'S NATIONAL MORTGAGE INC.—See
  NationsBank Corporation; *U.S. Public*, pg. 1165
BOATMEN'S TRUST COMPANY, INC.—See NationsBank
  Corporation; *U.S. Public*, pg. 1164
BOATWRIGHT INSULATION COMPANY, INC.—See Irex
  Corporation; *U.S. Public*, pg. 913
BOAZ PLANT—See Cooper Industries, Inc.; *U.S. Public*,
  pg. 443
BOBIT PUBLISHING COMPANY; *U.S. Private*, pg. 154
BOB'S INDUSTRIA E COMERCIA LTDA.—See Nestle S.A.;
  Int'l, pg. 919
BOB'S STORES, INC.—See CVS Corp.; *U.S. Public*,
  pg. 287
BOBST (AFRICA & MIDDLE EAST). LTD—See Bobst S.A.;
  Int'l, pg. 198
BOBST BENELUX N.V.—See Bobst S.A.; *Int'l*, pg. 198
BOBST BRASIL LTDA.—See Bobst S.A.; *Int'l*, pg. 198
BOBST CANADA, INC.—See Bobst S.A.; *Int'l*, pg. 198
BOBST EASTERN EUROPE SPOL. S.R.O.—See Bobst
  S.A.; *Int'l*, pg. 198
BOBST EQUIPMENT FINANCE CO.—See Bobst S.A.; *Int'l*,
  pg. 198
BOBST (FAR EAST) LTD.—See Bobst S.A.; *Int'l*, pg. 198
BOBST GMBH—See Bobst S.A.; *Int'l*, pg. 199
BOBST GROUP INC.—See Bobst S.A.; *Int'l*, pg. 198
BOBST ITALIANA SPA—See Bobst S.A.; *Int'l*, pg. 199
BOBST JAPAN LTD.—See Bobst S.A.; *Int'l*, pg. 199
BOBST KO LTD.—See Bobst S.A.; *Int'l*, pg. 199
BOBST (MALAYSIA) SDN. BHD.—See Bobst S.A.; *Int'l*,
  pg. 199
BOBST PARTICIPATIONS SA—See Bobst S.A.; *Int'l*,
  pg. 198
BOBST S.A.; *Int'l*, pg. 198
BOBST (SEA) PTE LTD—See Bobst S.A.; *Int'l*, pg. 199
BOBST (TAIWAN) LTD.—See Bobst S.A.; *Int'l*, pg. 199
BOCA GREENS INC.—See Lennar Corporation; *U.S.
  Public*, pg. 987
BOCA RATON CONVALESCENT CENTER—See Vencor,
  Inc.; *U.S. Public*, pg. 1712
BOCA RATON NEWS, INC.—See Community Newspaper
  Holdings Inc.; *U.S. Private*, pg. 259
BOCA RESEARCH INC.; *U.S. Public*, pg. 239
BOCK INDUSTRIES INC.—See Caparo Group Ltd.; *Int'l*,
  pg. 265
BOD DATENSYSTEMEM GMBH—See Compagnie des
  Machines Bull; *Int'l*, pg. 317
BODDIE-NOELL ENTERPRISES INC.; *U.S. Private*,
  pg. 154
W.H. BODDINGTON & CO. LTD.—See Wolseley Plc.; *Int'l*,
  pg. 1511
BODE CHEMIE GMBH & CO.—See Beiersdorf Group; *Int'l*,
  pg. 182
BODEGAS CHANDON S.A.—See LVMH Moet Hennessy
  Louis Vuitton; *Int'l*, pg. 782
BODENSEEWERK PERKIN-ELMER & CO. G.M.B.H.—See
  The Perkin-Elmer Corporation; *U.S. Public*, pg. 1279
BODINE ASSEMBLY AND TEST SYSTEMS; *U.S. Private*,
  pg. 154
BODINE ELECTRIC COMPANY; *U.S. Private*, pg. 154
BODOLAY/PRATT DIV.—See Package Machinery Co.; *U.S.
  Private*, pg. 832
BODY DRAMA (FAR EAST) LTD.—See Niches, Inc.; *U.S.
  Public*, pg. 1182
BODY DRAMA, INC.—See Niches, Inc.; *U.S. Public*,
  pg. 1182
THE BODY SHOP—See The Body Shop International; *Int'l*,
  pg. 199
THE BODY SHOP INC.—See The Body Shop International;
  Int'l, pg. 199
THE BODY SHOP INTERNATIONAL; *Int'l*, pg. 199
BODY SHOP OF AMERICA; *U.S. Private*, pg. 154
S. BOEG-THOMSEN A/S—See Taylor Woodrow plc; *Int'l*,
  pg. 1359
BOEHME CHEMIE GESELLSCHAFT MBH—See Henkel
  KGaA; *Int'l*, pg. 609
BOEHME FETTCHEMIE GMBH—See Henkel KGaA; *Int'l*,
  pg. 609
BOEHME FILATEX INC.—See Dr. Th. Boehme KG Chem.
  Fabrik GmbH & Co.; *Int'l*, pg. 199
DR. TH. BOEHME KG CHEM. FABRIK GMBH & CO.; *Int'l*,
  pg. 199
BOEHMERS—See Holderbank Financiere Glaris Ltd.; *Int'l*,
  pg. 629
C.F. BOEHRINGER & SOEHNE GMBH—See Corange
  Limited; *Int'l*, pg. 331
BOEHRINGER INGELHEIM—See Boehringer Ingelheim
  GmbH; *Int'l*, pg. 199
BOEHRINGER INGELHEIM ANIMAL HEALTH INC.—See
  Boehringer Ingelheim GmbH; *Int'l*, pg. 199
BOEHRINGER INGELHEIM CORPORATION—See
  Boehringer Ingelheim GmbH; *Int'l*, pg. 199
BOEHRINGER INGELHEIM GMBH; *Int'l*, pg. 199
BOEHRINGER INGELHEIM ITALIA S.P.A.—See Boehringer
  Ingelheim GmbH; *Int'l*, pg. 199

BOEHRINGER INGELHEIM PHARMACEUTICALS, INC.—
  See Boehringer Ingelheim GmbH; *Int'l*, pg. 199
BOEHRINGER MANNHEIM BIOCHEMICALS DIV.—See
  Corange Limited; *Int'l*, pg. 331
BOEHRINGER MANNHEIM CORPORATION—See Corange
  Limited; *Int'l*, pg. 331
BOEHRINGER MANNHEIM GMBH—See Corange Limited;
  Int'l, pg. 331
BOEHRINGER MANNHEIM JAPAN K.K.—See Corange
  Limited; *Int'l*, pg. 331
BOEHRINGER MANNHEIM PHARM—See Corange Limited;
  Int'l, pg. 331
BOEHRINGER MANNHEIM PHARMACEUTICALS CORP.—
  See Corange Limited; *Int'l*, pg. 331
BOEHRINGER MANNHEIM YAMANOUCHI K.K.—See
  Corange Limited; *Int'l*, pg. 331
BOEING ADVANCED SYSTEMS—See The Boeing
  Company; *U.S. Public*, pg. 240
BOEING AEROSPACE & ELECTRONICS, INC.—See The
  Boeing Company; *U.S. Public*, pg. 240
BOEING AEROSPACE & ELECTRONICS, IRVING—See
  The Boeing Company; *U.S. Public*, pg. 240
BOEING AEROSPACE & ELECTRONICS, OAK RIDGE—
  See The Boeing Company; *U.S. Public*, pg. 240
BOEING AEROSPACE OPERATIONS—See The Boeing
  Company; *U.S. Public*, pg. 241
BOEING AGRI-INDUSTRIAL CO.—See The Boeing
  Company; *U.S. Public*, pg. 242
BOEING BAO—See The Boeing Company; *U.S. Public*,
  pg. 240
BOEING CAPITAL CORP.—See The Boeing Company; *U.S.
  Public*, pg. 240
BOEING CHINA, INC.—See The Boeing Company; *U.S.
  Public*, pg. 242
BOEING COMMERCIAL AIRPLANE GROUP—See The
  Boeing Company; *U.S. Public*, pg. 240
THE BOEING COMPANY; *U.S. Public*, pg. 239
THE BOEING COMPANY—See The Boeing Company; *U.S.
  Public*, pg. 242
THE BOEING COMPANY CANADA LTD.—See The Boeing
  Company; *U.S. Public*, pg. 242
BOEING COMPUTER SERVICES—See The Boeing
  Company; *U.S. Public*, pg. 240
BOEING COMPUTER SUPPORT SERVICES, INC.—See
  The Boeing Company; *U.S. Public*, pg. 240
BOEING DEFENSE & SPACE GROUP—See The Boeing
  Company; *U.S. Public*, pg. 240
BOEING ELECTRONICS, INC.—See The Boeing Company;
  U.S. Public, pg. 240
BOEING FABRICATION DIVISION—See The Boeing
  Company; *U.S. Public*, pg. 240
BOEING GEORGIA INC.—See The Boeing Company; *U.S.
  Public*, pg. 242
BOEING HELICOPTER DIVISION—See The Boeing
  Company; *U.S. Public*, pg. 241
BOEING HELICOPTERS—See The Boeing Company; *U.S.
  Public*, pg. 241
BOEING INFORMATION & SUPPORT SERVICES—See
  The Boeing Company; *U.S. Public*, pg. 241
BOEING INTERNATIONAL CORPORATION—See The
  Boeing Company; *U.S. Public*, pg. 242
BOEING JAPAN—See The Boeing Company; *U.S. Public*,
  pg. 242
BOEING JAPAN, LTD.—See The Boeing Company; *U.S.
  Public*, pg. 242
BOEING LOUISIANA, INC.—See The Boeing Company;
  U.S. Public, pg. 242
BOEING MIDDLE EAST LIMITED—See The Boeing
  Company; *U.S. Public*, pg. 242
BOEING MILITARY AIRPLANES—See The Boeing
  Company; *U.S. Public*, pg. 241
BOEING NORTH AMERICA, AUTONETICS ELECTRONICS
  SYS DIV—See The Boeing Company; *U.S. Public*,
  pg. 241
BOEING NORTH AMERICA, AUTONETICS ELECTRONIC
  SYSTEMS DIVISION—See The Boeing Company; *U.S.
  Public*, pg. 241
BOEING NORTH AMERICA, NORTH AMERICAN
  AIRCRAFT DIVISION—See The Boeing Company; *U.S.
  Public*, pg. 241
BOEING NORTH AMERICA, NORTH AMERICAN
  AIRCRAFT MODIFICATION DIVISION—See The
  Boeing Company; *U.S. Public*, pg. 241
BOEING NORTH AMERICA, ROCKETDYNE DIVISION—
  See The Boeing Company; *U.S. Public*, pg. 241
BOEING NORTH AMERICA, SPACE SYSTEMS
  DIVISION—See The Boeing Company; *U.S. Public*,
  pg. 241
BOEING NORTH AMERICA, SYSTEMS DEVELOPMENT
  CENTER—See The Boeing Company; *U.S. Public*,
  pg. 241
BOEING NORTH AMERICA, TACTICAL SYSTEMS
  DIVISION—See The Boeing Company; *U.S. Public*,
  pg. 241
BOEING NORTH AMERICAN—See The Boeing Company;
  U.S. Public, pg. 241
BOEING OF PORTLAND—See The Boeing Company; *U.S.
  Public*, pg. 242
BOEING PETROLEUM SERVICES, INC.—See The Boeing
  Company; *U.S. Public*, pg. 242
BOEING REALTY CORPORATION—See The Boeing
  Company; *U.S. Public*, pg. 241
BOEING SERVICES, INC.—See The Boeing Company; *U.S.
  Public*, pg. 242
BOEING SPOKANE—See The Boeing Company; *U.S.
  Public*, pg. 241
BOEING TECHNICAL OPERATIONS, INC.—See The
  Boeing Company; *U.S. Public*, pg. 242
THE BOEING TRAVEL COMPANY—See The Boeing
  Company; *U.S. Public*, pg. 241
BOEKELO FOLIEN B.V.—See Solvay S.A.; *Int'l*, pg. 1278
BOERTIEN & PARTNERS—See Reed Elsevier plc; *Int'l*,
  pg. 1094
BOFORS AB—See Celsius AB; *Int'l*, pg. 276

BOFORS CANADA LTD—See Celsius AB; *Int'l*, pg. 278
BOFORS CARL GUSTAF AB—See Celsius AB; *Int'l*, pg. 276
BOFORS DEUTSCHLAND GMBH—See Celsius AB; *Int'l*, pg. 278
BOFORS EXPLOSIVES AB—See Celsius AB; *Int'l*, pg. 276
BOFORS LIAB AB—See Celsius AB; *Int'l*, pg. 276
AS BOFORS NORGE—See Celsius AB; *Int'l*, pg. 278
BOFORS S A MARINE AB—See Celsius AB; *Int'l*, pg. 276
BOFORS UNDERWATER SYSTEMS AB—See Celsius AB; *Int'l*, pg. 276
BOGANYI ES FIA KFT—See GESTRA GmbH; *Int'l*, pg. 550
BOGE CAUCHO METAL SA—See Mannesmann A.G.; *Int'l*, pg. 835
BOGE ESPANA SA—See Mannesmann A.G.; *Int'l*, pg. 835
BOGE FRANCE SARL—See Mannesmann A.G.; *Int'l*, pg. 835
BOGE GMBH & CO.—See Mannesmann A.G.; *Int'l*, pg. 835
BOGE HANDELS GMBH—See Mannesmann A.G.; *Int'l*, pg. 835
BOGE SUSPENSION SYSTEMS, INC.—See Mannesmann A.G.; *Int'l*, pg. 835
BOGE (UK) LTD.—See Mannesmann A.G.; *Int'l*, pg. 835
BOGEN COMMUNICATIONS, INC.—See Geotek Communications; *U.S. Public*, pg. 739
BOH BROS. CONSTRUCTION CO., LLC; *U.S. Private*, pg. 154
BOHAI & MHI PLATFORM ENGINEERING CO., LTD.—See Mitsubishi Heavy Industries Ltd.; *Int'l*, pg. 874
BOHAIN JEUMONT CABLES—See Jeumont-Schneider Trenformeteurs; *Int'l*, pg. 706
BOHLER—See Voest-Alpine Stahl AG; *Int'l*, pg. 1471
BOHLER ACIERS SPECIAUX S.A.R.L.—See Voest-Alpine Stahl AG; *Int'l*, pg. 1471
BOHLER AG—See Voest-Alpine Stahl AG; *Int'l*, pg. 1471
BOHLER BV—See Voest-Alpine Stahl AG; *Int'l*, pg. 1471
BOHLER GES.M.B.H.—See Voest-Alpine Stahl AG; *Int'l*, pg. 1470
BOHLER HELLAS A.E.B.E.—See Voest-Alpine Stahl AG; *Int'l*, pg. 1471
BOHLER KERESKEDALMI KFT—See Voest-Alpine Stahl AG; *Int'l*, pg. 1471
BOHLER S.A.—See Voest-Alpine Stahl AG; *Int'l*, pg. 1471
BOHLER STEEL GOMEI KAISHA—See Voest-Alpine Stahl AG; *Int'l*, pg. 1471
BOHLER STEELS PTY. LTD.—See Voest-Alpine Stahl AG; *Int'l*, pg. 1471
BOHLER UDDEHOLM AG—See Voest-Alpine Stahl AG; *Int'l*, pg. 1471
BOHLER-UDDEHOLM CORP.—See Voest-Alpine Stahl AG; *Int'l*, pg. 1471
BOHLER U.K. LTD.—See Voest-Alpine Stahl AG; *Int'l*, pg. 1471
BOHLER YBBSTALWERKE GES.M.B.H.—See Voest-Alpine Stahl AG; *Int'l*, pg. 1470
BOHLERIT GES.M.B.H.—See Voest-Alpine Stahl AG; *Int'l*, pg. 1470
BOHLIN INSTRUMENTS INC.—See Bowthorpe plc; *Int'l*, pg. 208
BOHLIN INSTRUMENTS LTD.—See Bowthorpe plc; *Int'l*, pg. 207
BOHLIN INSTRUMENTS VETRIEBS GMBH—See Bowthorpe plc; *Int'l*, pg. 208
BOIE-TAKEDA CHEMICALS, INC.—See Takeda Chemical Industries, Ltd.; *Int'l*, pg. 1350
THE BOILER INSPECTION & INSURANCE CO. OF CANADA—See The Hartford Steam Boiler Inspection & Insurance Co.; *U.S. Public*, pg. 795
BOIS ET SCIAGES DE SOUGY S.A.—See UPM-Kymmene Corporation; *Int'l*, pg. 1429
BOIS J.L.P. INC.—See Leggett & Platt, Incorporated; *U.S. Public*, pg. 987
BOISE CASCADE ASIA LTD.—See Boise Cascade Corporation; *U.S. Public*, pg. 243
BOISE CASCADE BUILDING MATERIALS DISTRIBUTION DIV.—See Boise Cascade Corporation; *U.S. Public*, pg. 243
BOISE CASCADE CORPORATION; *U.S. Public*, pg. 242
BOISE CASCADE OFFICE PRODUCTS CORPORATION—See Boise Cascade Corporation; *U.S. Public*, pg. 243
BOISE CASCADE PAPER DIV.—See Boise Cascade Corporation; *U.S. Public*, pg. 243
BOISE CASCADE SALES LTD.—See Boise Cascade Corporation; *U.S. Public*, pg. 243
BOISE CASCADE TIMBER & WOOD PRODUCTS DIVISION—See Boise Cascade Corporation; *U.S. Public*, pg. 243
BOISE PARK SUITES—See Sunstone Hotel Investors, Inc.; *U.S. Public*, pg. 1537
BOJANGLES' RESTARAUNTS, INC.; *U.S. Private*, pg. 154
DAVID BOLAND, INC.; *U.S. Private*, pg. 154
BOLANDS LIMITED—See The Oshawa Group Limited; *Int'l*, pg. 1012
BOLD—See The Lowe Group; *U.S. Private*, pg. 678
BOLDING VERPAKKINGEN B.V.—See Viag AG; *Int'l*, pg. 1466
BOLER COMPANY; *U.S. Private*, pg. 155
BOLETTI F.B. S.R.L.—See Fiat Auto SpA; *Int'l*, pg. 482
BOLEY G.M.B.H.—See Citizen Watch Company, Ltd.; *Int'l*, pg. 294
BOLIDEN AB—See Trelleborg AB; *Int'l*, pg. 1422
BOLIDEN ALLIS AB—See Trelleborg AB; *Int'l*, pg. 1423
BOLIDEN BERGSOE AB—See Trelleborg AB; *Int'l*, pg. 1422
BOLIDEN BERGSOE A/S—See Trelleborg AB; *Int'l*, pg. 1423
BOLIDEN CONTECH AB—See Trelleborg AB; *Int'l*, pg. 1422
BOLIDEN INTERMARKET AB—See Trelleborg AB; *Int'l*, pg. 1422
BOLIDEN INTERNATIONAL MINING AB—See Trelleborg AB; *Int'l*, pg. 1422
BOLIDEN MINERAL AB—See Trelleborg AB; *Int'l*, pg. 1422

BOLIDEN ORE & METALS—See Trelleborg AB; *Int'l*, pg. 1422
BOLIDEN WP-CONTECH AB—See Trelleborg AB; *Int'l*, pg. 1422
BOLIVAR, COMPANIA DE SEGUROS DEL ECUADOR—See The Chubb Corporation; *U.S. Public*, pg. 355
BOLIVAR STAMPING LTD.—See Delta plc; *Int'l*, pg. 390
BOLLIGER, INC.; *U.S. Private*, pg. 155
BOLLINGER ALGIERS INC.—See Bollinger Shipyards, Inc.; *U.S. Private*, pg. 155
BOLLINGER INDUSTRIES INC.; *U.S. Public*, pg. 243
BOLLINGER SHIPYARDS, INC.; *U.S. Private*, pg. 155
BOLLMAN HAT CO.; *U.S. Private*, pg. 155
BOLS BENELUX B.V.—See Koninklijke BolsWessanen nv; *Int'l*, pg. 751
BOLS-CYNAR, AG—See Koninklijke BolsWessanen nv; *Int'l*, pg. 751
BOLS INTERNATIONAL B.V.—See Koninklijke BolsWessanen nv; *Int'l*, pg. 751
BOLS LATIN AMERICA NV—See Koninklijke BolsWessanen nv; *Int'l*, pg. 751
BOLS MILANI LTD.—See Koninklijke BolsWessanen nv; *Int'l*, pg. 751
BOLS ROYAL DISTILLERIES—See Koninklijke BolsWessanen nv; *Int'l*, pg. 751
BOLS STROTHMANN BRENNEREIEN GMBH & CO. KG—See Koninklijke BolsWessanen nv; *Int'l*, pg. 751
BOLSWESSANEN AG—See Koninklijke BolsWessanen nv; *Int'l*, pg. 752
BOLSWESSANEN BETEILIGUNG GMBH—See Koninklijke BolsWessanen nv; *Int'l*, pg. 752
BOLSWESSANEN BETEILIGUNG GMBH OSTERREICH—See Koninklijke BolsWessanen nv; *Int'l*, pg. 752
BOLSWESSANEN COORDINATION CENTER—See Koninklijke BolsWessanen nv; *Int'l*, pg. 752
BOLSWESSANEN INTERNATIONAL BV—See Koninklijke BolsWessanen nv; *Int'l*, pg. 751
BOLSWESSANEN NEDERLAND BV—See Koninklijke BolsWessanen nv; *Int'l*, pg. 751
BOLSWESSANEN TRANSATLANTIC HOLDINGS BV—See Koninklijke BolsWessanen nv; *Int'l*, pg. 751
BOLSWESSANEN UK HOLDING LTD.—See Koninklijke BolsWessanen nv; *Int'l*, pg. 752
BOLSWESSANEN USA, INC.—See Koninklijke BolsWessanen nv; *Int'l*, pg. 752
BOLT GEOPHYSICAL CORPORATION—See Bolt Technology Corporation; *U.S. Public*, pg. 244
BOLT TECHNOLOGY CORPORATION; *U.S. Public*, pg. 244
WM. BOLTHOUSE FARMS, INC.; *U.S. Private*, pg. 155
BOMAG—See United Dominion Industries, Ltd.; *U.S. Public*, pg. 1677
BOMAINE CORPORATION; *U.S. Private*, pg. 155
BOMARKO, INC.; *U.S. Private*, pg. 156
BOMBARDIER CAPITAL GROUP—See Bombardier Inc.; *Int'l*, pg. 200
BOMBARDIER CAPITAL INC.—See Bombardier Inc.; *Int'l*, pg. 200
BOMBARDIER CORPORATION—See Bombardier Inc.; *Int'l*, pg. 200
BOMBARDIER CREDIT LTD.—See Bombardier Inc.; *Int'l*, pg. 200
BOMBARDIER EURORAIL—See Bombardier Inc.; *Int'l*, pg. 200
BOMBARDIER FINANCE INC.—See Bombardier Inc.; *Int'l*, pg. 200
BOMBARDIER INC.; *Int'l*, pg. 199
BOMBARDIER INC. CANADAIR—See Bombardier Inc.; *Int'l*, pg. 200
BOMBARDIER, LEARJET INC.—See Bombardier Inc.; *Int'l*, pg. 200
BOMBARDIER MOTORIZED CONSUMER PRODUCTS GROUP—See Bombardier Inc.; *Int'l*, pg. 200
BOMBARDIER-NORDTRAC OY—See Bombardier Inc.; *Int'l*, pg. 200
BOMBARDIER PRORAIL LTD.—See Bombardier Inc.; *Int'l*, pg. 200
BOMBARDIER REAL ESTATE LTD.—See Bombardier Inc.; *Int'l*, pg. 200
BOMBARDIER RECREATIONAL PRODUCTS—See Bombardier Inc.; *Int'l*, pg. 200
BOMBARDIER REGIONAL AIRCRAFT DIVISION—See The Boeing Company; *U.S. Public*, pg. 242
BOMBARDIER-ROTAX GMBH MOTORENFABRIK—See Bombardier Inc.; *Int'l*, pg. 200
BOMBARDIER-WIEN SCHIENENFAHRZEUGE AG—See Bombardier Inc.; *Int'l*, pg. 200
BOMBARDIER-CONCARRIL, S.A. DE C.V.—See Bombardier Inc.; *Int'l*, pg. 200
BOMBAS GOULDS DE MEXICO, S.A. DE C.V.—See ITT Industries, Inc.; *U.S. Public*, pg. 861
BOMBAS GOULDS DE VENEZUELA C.A.—See ITT Industries, Inc.; *U.S. Public*, pg. 861
THE BOMBAY COMPANY, INC.; *U.S. Public*, pg. 244
THE BOMBAY SPIRITS COMPANY—See Diageo Plc; *Int'l*, pg. 409
BOMEM—See Mannesmann A.G.; *Int'l*, pg. 835
BOMFORD TURNER LIMITED—See Alamo Group, Inc.; *U.S. Public*, pg. 35
BOMMER INDUSTRIES, INC.; *U.S. Private*, pg. 156
BON JOUR INTERNATIONAL LTD.; *U.S. Private*, pg. 156
THE BON MARCHE, INC.—See Federated Department Stores, Inc.; *U.S. Public*, pg. 617
BON PRIX HANDELSGESELLSCHAFT MBH—See Otto Versand (GmbH & Co.); *Int'l*, pg. 1014
BON TON FOODS, INC.—See Amerifoods Inc.; *U.S. Private*, pg. 65
THE BON TON STORES, INC.; *U.S. Public*, pg. 244
BONAIRE PETROLEUM CORP., N.V. (BOPEC)—See Petroleos de Venezuela S.A.; *Int'l*, pg. 1046
BONANZA BOOKS—See Advance Publications, Inc.; *U.S. Private*, pg. 21
BONANZA BUS LINES, INC.; *U.S. Private*, pg. 156

BONANZA RESTAURANTS—See Metromedia Company; *U.S. Private*, pg. 736
BONATO GMBH—See Ruhrgas Aktiengesellschaft; *Int'l*, pg. 1148
BONAVENTURA—See Reed Elsevier plc; *Int'l*, pg. 1099
BONDED FIBRE FABRIC LTD.—See Lamont Holdings Plc; *Int'l*, pg. 798
BONDEX INTL., INC.—See RPM, Inc.; *U.S. Public*, pg. 1357
BONDINA LTD.—See Freudenberg & Company; *Int'l*, pg. 507
BONDIOLI & PAVESI-FRANCE S.A.—See Bondioli & Pavesi S.p.A.; *Int'l*, pg. 201
BONDIOLI & PAVESI GMBH DEUTSCHLAND—See Bondioli & Pavesi S.p.A.; *Int'l*, pg. 201
BONDIOLI & PAVESI GS.M.B.H.—See Bondioli & Pavesi S.p.A.; *Int'l*, pg. 201
BONDIOLI & PAVESI INC.—See Bondioli & Pavesi S.p.A.; *Int'l*, pg. 201
BONDIOLI & PAVESI S.P.A.; *Int'l*, pg. 201
BONDIOLI Y PAVESI IBERICA S.A.—See Bondioli & Pavesi S.p.A.; *Int'l*, pg. 201
BONDO/MAR-HYDE CORPORATION—See RPM, Inc.; *U.S. Public*, pg. 1357
BONDSTRAND, LTD.—See Ameron International Corporation; *U.S. Public*, pg. 99
BONDUEL TELEPHONE CO.—See Telephone and Data Systems, Inc.; *U.S. Public*, pg. 1571
BONDWARE—See Dover Industries Limited; *Int'l*, pg. 417
BONES/LINCOLNWOOD—See Lettuce Entertain You Enterprises, Inc.; *U.S. Private*, pg. 661
BONGARD—See Groupe Strafor Facom; *Int'l*, pg. 570
BONGARD GMBH—See Groupe Strafor Facom; *Int'l*, pg. 570
BONGARDS CREAMERIES INC.; *U.S. Private*, pg. 156
BONGRAIN CHEESE USA—See Bongrain S.A.; *Int'l*, pg. 201
BONGRAIN - GERARD & CIE.—See Bongrain S.A.; *Int'l*, pg. 201
BONGRAIN S.A.; *Int'l*, pg. 201
BONHOMME—See Randa Corp.; *U.S. Private*, pg. 909
BONIFACE THIEM S.A.—See Borden, Inc.; *U.S. Private*, pg. 159
J. BONIFACIO & CIA., LDA.—See Fuchs Petrolub AG Oel + Chemie; *Int'l*, pg. 517
BONIFACIUS KOHLE TRANSPORT UND HANDELSGESELLSCHAFT MBH & CO. KG—See Veba AG; *Int'l*, pg. 1457
BONIFICA-ARGENTINA—See IRI Istituto Ricostruzione Industriale; *Int'l*, pg. 655
BONIFICA-BELGIUM—See IRI Istituto Ricostruzione Industriale; *Int'l*, pg. 655
BONIFICA-COSTA RICA—See IRI Istituto Ricostruzione Industriale; *Int'l*, pg. 655
BONIFICA-CROATIA—See IRI Istituto Ricostruzione Industriale; *Int'l*, pg. 655
BONIFICA-GUATEMALA—See IRI Istituto Ricostruzione Industriale; *Int'l*, pg. 655
BONIFICA-HUNGARY—See IRI Istituto Ricostruzione Industriale; *Int'l*, pg. 655
BONIFICA-MOZAMBIQUE—See IRI Istituto Ricostruzione Industriale; *Int'l*, pg. 655
BONIFICA-PERU—See IRI Istituto Ricostruzione Industriale; *Int'l*, pg. 655
BONIFICA-POLAND—See IRI Istituto Ricostruzione Industriale; *Int'l*, pg. 655
BONIFICA-TUNISIA—See IRI Istituto Ricostruzione Industriale; *Int'l*, pg. 655
BONIG & YAMAOKA INTERNATIONAL PUBLIC RELATIONS—See Scholz & Friends GmbH; *Int'l*, pg. 1210
BONLAND INDUSTRIES, INC.; *U.S. Private*, pg. 156
BONMETS—See Groupe Casino; *Int'l*, pg. 563
F.H. BONN COMPANY; *U.S. Private*, pg. 156
WILLIAM L. BONNELL CO., INC.—See Tredegar Industries Inc.; *U.S. Public*, pg. 1634
BONNET RESOURCES CORP.—See Banc One Corporation; *U.S. Public*, pg. 175
BONNEVILLE INTERNATIONAL CORP.—See Deseret Management Corporation; *U.S. Private*, pg. 327
BONNEVILLE PACIFIC CORPORATION; *U.S. Public*, pg. 244
BONNEY FORGE CORPORATION; *U.S. Private*, pg. 156
BONNIE BAKING CO.—See Lewis Brothers Bakeries, Inc.; *U.S. Private*, pg. 665
BONNIE INTERNATIONAL—See Jaclyn, Inc.; *U.S. Public*, pg. 920
BONOMELLI S.R.L.; *Int'l*, pg. 201
BONS N.V.—See Campbell Soup Company; *U.S. Public*, pg. 299
BONTEX AUSTRALIA—See Georgia-Bonded Fibers, Inc.; *U.S. Public*, pg. 734
BONTEX DE MEXICO, S.A. DE C.V.—See Georgia-Bonded Fibers, Inc.; *U.S. Public*, pg. 734
BONTEX INTERNATIONAL (F.S.C.)—See Georgia-Bonded Fibers, Inc.; *U.S. Public*, pg. 734
BONTEX ITALIA S.R.L.—See Georgia-Bonded Fibers, Inc.; *U.S. Public*, pg. 734
BONTEX KOREA—See Georgia-Bonded Fibers, Inc.; *U.S. Public*, pg. 734
BONTEX S.A.—See Georgia-Bonded Fibers, Inc.; *U.S. Public*, pg. 734
BONTEX TAIWAN—See Georgia-Bonded Fibers, Inc.; *U.S. Public*, pg. 734
BONUM ANLAGE- UND BETEILIGUNGS GMBH—See Bayerische Vereinsbank Group; *U.S. Public*, pg. 179
THE BOOK CLUB FINANCE AND SECURITIES PUBLIC COMPANY LTD.—See The Long-Term Credit Bank of Japan, Limited; *Int'l*, pg. 816
BOOK OF THE MONTH CLUB—See Time Warner Inc.; *U.S. Public*, pg. 1612
BOOKAZINE COMPANY, INC.; *U.S. Private*, pg. 156
BOOKCRAFTERS U.S.A. INC.—See American Business Products, Inc.; *U.S. Public*, pg. 70

BOOKER AGRIBUSINESS LTD.—See Booker PLC; Int'l, pg. 202
BOOKER ENTERTAINMENT—See Booker PLC; Int'l, pg. 202
BOOKER OVERSEAS TRADING—See Booker PLC; Int'l, pg. 202
BOOKER PLC; Int'l, pg. 202
BOOKER TATE—See Booker PLC; Int'l, pg. 202
BOOKER TATE LTD.—See Tate & Lyle PLC; Int'l, pg. 1357
BOOKER WHOLESALE FOODS—See Booker PLC; Int'l, pg. 202
BOOKERS SUGAR CO.—See Booker PLC; Int'l, pg. 202
THE BOOKPOINT (INDIA) PVT. LTD.—See Pearson plc; Int'l, pg. 1026
BOOKS-A-MILLION, INC.; U.S. Public, pg. 244
BOOKS FOR PROFESSIONALS, INC.—See Harcourt General, Inc.; U.S. Public, pg. 783
BOOKS & HOME ENTERTAINMENT DIV.—See The Reader's Digest Association, Inc.; U.S. Public, pg. 1367
BOOKS MANAGEMENT, INC.—See Deb Shops, Inc.; U.S. Public, pg. 491
BOOKSTOP, INC.—See Barnes & Noble Inc.; U.S. Public, pg. 189
BOOLE & BABBAGE EUROPE—See Boole & Babbage, Inc.; U.S. Public, pg. 245
BOOLE & BABBAGE, INC.; U.S. Public, pg. 244
BOOMTOWN-BILOXI—See Hollywood Park, Inc.; U.S. Public, pg. 831
BOOMTOWN-RENO—See Hollywood Park, Inc.; U.S. Public, pg. 831
BOON EDAM B.V.; Int'l, pg. 202
BOON EDAM INC.—See Boon Edam B.V.; Int'l, pg. 202
BOONVILLE MINING SERVICES, INC.—See Bucyrus International; U.S. Private, pg. 177
JOHN BOOS & COMPANY; U.S. Private, pg. 156
WILHELM BOOS JR., GMBH & CO.—See Fiskars Oy AB; Int'l, pg. 492
BOOTH AMERICAN; U.S. Private, pg. 156
BOOTH/CRYSTAL TIPS—See Scotsman Industries, Inc.; U.S. Public, pg. 1445
BOOTH NEWSPAPERS, INC.; U.S. Private, pg. 157
THE BOOTS COMPANY PLC; Int'l, pg. 202
BOOTS CONTRACT MANUFACTURING—See The Boots Company PLC; Int'l, pg. 202
BOOTS HEALTHCARE INTERNATIONAL—See The Boots Company PLC; Int'l, pg. 202
BOOTS OPTICIANS—See The Boots Company PLC; Int'l, pg. 202
BOOTS PROPERTIES—See The Boots Company PLC; Int'l, pg. 203
BOOTS THE CHEMISTS—See The Boots Company PLC; Int'l, pg. 203
BOOZ, ALLEN & HAMILTON INC.; U.S. Private, pg. 157
BORAL ACROW LTD. (NEW ZEALAND)—See Boral Limited; Int'l, pg. 203
BORAL AUSTRALIAN GYPSUM LTD.—See Boral Limited; Int'l, pg. 203
BORAL BRICKS INC.—See Boral Limited; Int'l, pg. 203
BORAL BRICKS PTY. LTD.—See Boral Limited; Int'l, pg. 203
BORAL CONCRETE PRODUCTS INC.—See Boral Limited; Int'l, pg. 203
BORAL CONCRETE PRODUCTS PTY. LTD.—See Boral Limited; Int'l, pg. 203
BORAL GAS LIMITED—See Boral Limited; Int'l, pg. 203
BORAL GYPSUM INC.—See Boral Limited; Int'l, pg. 203
BORAL INDUSTRIES INC.—See Boral Limited; Int'l, pg. 203
BORAL LIMITED; Int'l, pg. 203
BORAL RESOURCES LTD.—See Boral Limited; Int'l, pg. 203
BORAL (UK) LTD.—See Boral Limited; Int'l, pg. 203
BORALEX INC.—See The Cascades Group; Int'l, pg. 273
BORALLON—See Corrections Corporation of America; U.S. Public, pg. 451
BORDELAIS, LEMEUNIER-LEO BURNETT PARIS—See Leo Burnett Company, Inc.; U.S. Private, pg. 184
BORDEN AUSTRALIA (PTY) LTD.—See Borden, Inc.; U.S. Private, pg. 159
BORDEN (BRAY) LTD.—See Borden, Inc.; U.S. Private, pg. 159
THE BORDEN CO., LIMITED—See Borden, Inc.; U.S. Private, pg. 159
BORDEN DECORATIVE PRODUCTS—See Borden, Inc.; U.S. Private, pg. 158
BORDEN, EXPORTS LIMITED—See Borden, Inc.; U.S. Private, pg. 159
BORDEN FOODS CANADA—See Borden, Inc.; U.S. Private, pg. 159
BORDEN FOODS CORPORATION—See Borden, Inc.; U.S. Private, pg. 157
BORDEN FOODS LIMITED—See Borden, Inc.; U.S. Private, pg. 159
BORDEN FRANCE S.A.—See Borden, Inc.; U.S. Private, pg. 159
BORDEN GRAPHICS DIVISION—See Borden, Inc.; U.S. Private, pg. 157
BORDEN, INC.; U.S. Private, pg. 157
BORDEN INTERNATIONAL, INC.—See Borden, Inc.; U.S. Private, pg. 158
BORDEN INTL. PACKAGING, LTD.—See Borden, Inc.; U.S. Private, pg. 159
BORDEN ITALIAN FOODS—See Borden, Inc.; U.S. Private, pg. 158
BORDEN KJEMI NORGE A/S—See Borden, Inc.; U.S. Private, pg. 159
BORDEN (NEDERLAND) B.V.—See Borden, Inc.; U.S. Private, pg. 159
BORDEN OVERSEAS CAPITAL CORPORATION N.V.—See Borden, Inc.; U.S. Private, pg. 159
BORDEN (PROPRIETY) LIMITED—See Borden, Inc.; U.S. Private, pg. 159
BORDEN THERMOFORMING, B.V.—See Borden, Inc.; U.S. Private, pg. 159

BORDEN (U.K.) LTD.—See Borden, Inc.; U.S. Private, pg. 159
BORDER STATES INDUSTRIES, INC.; U.S. Private, pg. 160
BORDER STATES PAVING, INC.—See Border States Industries, Inc.; U.S. Private, pg. 160
BORDERS GROUP, INC.; U.S. Public, pg. 245
BORDERS, INC.—See Borders Group, Inc.; U.S. Public, pg. 245
BORDEX (BELGIUM) N.V.—See Borden, Inc.; U.S. Private, pg. 159
BORDEX B.V.—See Borden, Inc.; U.S. Private, pg. 159
BORDEX (NEDERLAND), B.V.—See Borden, Inc.; U.S. Private, pg. 159
BOREALIS ANTWERPEN N.V.—See Neste Oy; Int'l, pg. 914
BOREALIS A/S—See Neste Oy; Int'l, pg. 914
BOREALIS HOLDING A/S—See Neste Oy; Int'l, pg. 914
BOREALIS N.V.—See Neste Oy; Int'l, pg. 914
BOREALIS PETROKEMI AB—See Neste Oy; Int'l, pg. 914
BOREALIS POLIMEROS S.A.—See Neste Oy; Int'l, pg. 914
BOREALIS POLYETEN AB—See Neste Oy; Int'l, pg. 914
BOREALIS POLYMERS OY—See Neste Oy; Int'l, pg. 913
BOREALIS S.A.—See Neste Oy; Int'l, pg. 914
BOREAS S.A. IARD—See Allianz Aktiengesellschaft; Int'l, pg. 61
BOREL & DUNNER, INC.—See Brown & Sharpe Manufacturing Company; U.S. Public, pg. 260
BOREN CLAY PRODUCTS COMPANY—See Jannock Limited; Int'l, pg. 699
BORENS AB—See Luxo A/S; Int'l, pg. 821
BV BOREON—See Heidemij N.V.; Int'l, pg. 607
BORG & BECK DE VENEZUELA SA—See Mannesmann A.G.; Int'l, pg. 835
BORG WARNER AUTOMOTIVE-ALABAMA DIV.—See Borg Warner Automotive, Inc.; U.S. Public, pg. 245
BORG WARNER AUTOMOTIVE, INC.; U.S. Public, pg. 245
BORG-WARNER PROTECTIVE SERVICES CORPORATION—See Borg-Warner Security Corporation; U.S. Public, pg. 245
BORG-WARNER SECURITY CORPORATION; U.S. Public, pg. 245
BORGHETTO—See TI Group plc; Int'l, pg. 1341
BORLAND CANADA—See Borland International, Inc.; U.S. Public, pg. 246
BORLAND COMPANY LTD.—See Borland International, Inc.; U.S. Public, pg. 246
BORLAND EMM—See Borland International, Inc.; U.S. Public, pg. 246
BORLAND FRANCE—See Borland International, Inc.; U.S. Public, pg. 246
BORLAND (HONG KONG) LTD.—See Borland International, Inc.; U.S. Public, pg. 246
BORLAND HUNGARY ONLINE/DELPHI-SZOFT KFT—See Borland International, Inc.; U.S. Public, pg. 246
BORLAND INTERNATIONAL (AUST) PTY LTD.—See Borland International, Inc.; U.S. Public, pg. 246
BORLAND INTERNATIONAL B.V.—See Borland International, Inc.; U.S. Public, pg. 246
BORLAND INTERNATIONAL, INC.; U.S. Public, pg. 246
BORLAND INTERNATIONAL (NEW ZEALAND) LTD.—See Borland International, Inc.; U.S. Public, pg. 246
BORLAND LATIN AMERICA—See Borland International, Inc.; U.S. Public, pg. 246
BORLAND REPRESENTATIVE OFFICE—See Borland International, Inc.; U.S. Public, pg. 246
BORLAND SRO—See Borland International, Inc.; U.S. Public, pg. 246
BORLAND TAIWAN LTD.—See Borland International, Inc.; U.S. Public, pg. 246
BORLAND UK—See Borland International, Inc.; U.S. Public, pg. 246
BORLETTI CLIMATIZZAZIONE S.R.L.—See Fiat Auto SpA; Int'l, pg. 482
BORON LEPORE GROUP; U.S. Public, pg. 246
BORREGAARD INDUSTRIES LIMITED—See Orkla A.S.A.; Int'l, pg. 1011
BORREGAARD NEA—See Orkla A.S.A.; Int'l, pg. 1011
BORREGAARD SKOGER AS—See Orkla A.S.A.; Int'l, pg. 1011
BORRI S.P.A.—See General Signal Corporation; U.S. Public, pg. 727
BORSCH, STENGEL & PARTNER GMBH; Int'l, pg. 203
BORSIG DE VENEZUELA C.A.—See Deutsche Babcock AG; Int'l, pg. 399
BORSIG KUGELHAHN GMBH—See Deutsche Babcock AG; Int'l, pg. 400
BORSIG SERVICE BOHLEN GMBH—See Deutsche Babcock AG; Int'l, pg. 399
THOMAS BORTHWICK & SONS (AUSTRALIA) PTY. LTD.—See Nippon Meat Packers, Inc.; Int'l, pg. 936
BORVI AS—See Perstorp AB; Int'l, pg. 1040
BOSAM S.A.—See Bobst S.A.; Int'l, pg. 199
HUGO BOSCA CO., INC.; U.S. Private, pg. 160
BOSCARALE/TOM TOGS—See Vista 2000, Inc.; U.S. Private, pg. 1142
BOSCH & BUTZ—See The Lowe Group; U.S. Private, pg. 678
BOSCH BRAKING SYSTEMS-NORTH AMERICA—See Robert Bosch GmbH; Int'l, pg. 204
BOSCH BRAKING SYSTEMS-NORTH AMERICA, ENGINEERING CENTER—See Robert Bosch GmbH; Int'l, pg. 205
BOSCH KOREA LTD.—See Robert Bosch GmbH; Int'l, pg. 205
ROBERT BOSCH BV—See Robert Bosch GmbH; Int'l, pg. 205
ROBERT BOSCH COMPANY LTD.—See Robert Bosch GmbH; Int'l, pg. 205
ROBERT BOSCH CORPORATION—See Robert Bosch GmbH; Int'l, pg. 204
ROBERT BOSCH D.O.O.—See Robert Bosch GmbH; Int'l, pg. 205
ROBERT BOSCH ESPANA SA—See Robert Bosch GmbH; Int'l, pg. 205

ROBERT BOSCH FLUID POWER CORPORATION—See Robert Bosch GmbH; Int'l, pg. 204
ROBERT BOSCH FOOD—See Robert Bosch GmbH; Int'l, pg. 205
ROBERT BOSCH GMBH; Int'l, pg. 203
ROBERT BOSCH GMBH—See Robert Bosch GmbH; Int'l, pg. 204
ROBERT BOSCH GMBH THERMOTECHNIK DIVISION—See Robert Bosch GmbH; Int'l, pg. 204
ROBERT BOSCH HAUSGERATE GMBH—See Robert Bosch GmbH; Int'l, pg. 204
ROBERT BOSCH KFT—See Robert Bosch GmbH; Int'l, pg. 205
ROBERT BOSCH LIMITED—See Robert Bosch GmbH; Int'l, pg. 205
ROBERT BOSCH LTD.—See Robert Bosch GmbH; Int'l, pg. 205
ROBERT BOSCH OY—See Robert Bosch GmbH; Int'l, pg. 205
ROBERT BOSCH SA—See Robert Bosch GmbH; Int'l, pg. 205
ROBERT BOSCH (SOUTH EAST ASIA) PTE. LTD.—See Robert Bosch GmbH; Int'l, pg. 206
ROBERT BOSCH SP. Z.O.O.—See Robert Bosch GmbH; Int'l, pg. 206
ROBERT BOSCH SPOL. S.R.O.—See Robert Bosch GmbH; Int'l, pg. 206
ROBERT BOSCH S.R.L.—See Robert Bosch GmbH; Int'l, pg. 206
ROBERT BOSCH T.A.A.—See Robert Bosch GmbH; Int'l, pg. 206
ROBERT BOSCH T.O.O.—See Robert Bosch GmbH; Int'l, pg. 205
ROBERT BOSCH VERTRIEBSGESELLSCHAFT MBH—See Robert Bosch GmbH; Int'l, pg. 205
BOSCH-SIEMENS HAUSGERAETE GMBH—See Robert Bosch GmbH; Int'l, pg. 204
BOSCH-SIEMENS HAUSGERAETE GMBH—See Siemens AG; Int'l, pg. 1245
BOSCH TELECOM OFFENTLICHE VERMITTLUNGSTECHNIK GMBH—See Robert Bosch GmbH; Int'l, pg. 204
BOSCOV'S DEPARTMENT STORE, INC.; U.S. Private, pg. 160
BOSE A/S—See Bose Corporation; U.S. Private, pg. 160
BOSE CORPORATION; U.S. Private, pg. 160
BOSENBERG BAUCHEMIE GMBH—See Lafarge S.A.; Int'l, pg. 790
L. BOSENDORFER KLAVIERFABRIK GMBH—See Kimball International, Inc.; U.S. Public, pg. 958
BOSENDORFER USA—See Kimball International, Inc.; U.S. Public, pg. 957
BOSMAN BROWAR SZCZECIN S.A.—See Bitburger Brauerei Th. Simon GmbH; Int'l, pg. 197
BOSS CANADA, INC.—See Vista 2000, Inc.; U.S. Private, pg. 1142
BOSS DE MEXICO, S.A.—See Vista 2000, Inc.; U.S. Private, pg. 1142
BOSS MANUFACTURING COMPANY—See Vista 2000, Inc.; U.S. Private, pg. 1142
BOSSO CARTE SPECIALI S.P.A.—See A. Ahlstrom Corporation; Int'l, pg. 35
BOSTA BETON SP.Z.O.O.—See Scancem AB; Int'l, pg. 1200
BOSTIK, INC.—See Total S.A.; Int'l, pg. 1409
BOSTIK INC.—See Total S.A.; Int'l, pg. 1409
BOSTIK LTD.—See Total S.A.; Int'l, pg. 1409
BOSTON ACOUSTICS FOREIGN SALES CORP.—See Boston Acoustics, Inc.; U.S. Public, pg. 246
BOSTON ACOUSTICS, INC.; U.S. Public, pg. 246
BOSTON BEER COMPANY; U.S. Public, pg. 246
BOSTON CELTICS LIMITED PARTNERSHIP; U.S. Public, pg. 246
BOSTON CHICKEN, INC.; U.S. Public, pg. 247
BOSTON COMPANIA ARGENTINA DE SEGUROS S.A.—See Cigna Corp.; U.S. Public, pg. 364
BOSTON COMPANIA ARGENTINA DE SEGUROS S.A.—See UNUM Corporation; U.S. Public, pg. 1700
THE BOSTON COMPANY, INC.—See Mellon Bank Corporation; U.S. Public, pg. 1085
BOSTON DIGITAL CORP.; U.S. Private, pg. 161
BOSTON EDISON COMPANY; U.S. Public, pg. 247
BOSTON ENERGY TECHNOLOGY GROUP, INC.—See Boston Edison Company; U.S. Public, pg. 247
BOSTON FACTORS OF CANADA, INC.—See BankBoston Corporation; U.S. Public, pg. 185
BOSTON FINANCIAL DATA SERVICES, INC.—See Kansas City Southern Industries, Inc.; U.S. Public, pg. 944
BOSTON FINANCIAL DATA SERVICES, INC.—See State Street Corporation; U.S. Public, pg. 1513
BOSTON GAS COMPANY—See Eastern Enterprises; U.S. Public, pg. 549
BOSTON GEAR—See IMO Industries Inc.; U.S. Public, pg. 857
THE BOSTON GLOBE—See The New York Times Company; U.S. Public, pg. 1175
BOSTON GLOBE ELECTRONIC PUBLISHING, INC.—See The New York Times Company; U.S. Public, pg. 1175
BOSTON GLOBE INVESTMENTS—See The New York Times Company; U.S. Public, pg. 1175
THE BOSTON HERALD—See The News Corporation Limited; Int'l, pg. 926
BOSTON INTERNATIONAL DATA SERVICES, INC.—See BankBoston Corporation; U.S. Public, pg. 184
BOSTON INVERSIONES SERVICIOS Y ADMINISTRACION LTDA.—See BankBoston Corporation; U.S. Public, pg. 185
BOSTON INVERSORA DE VALORES S.A.—See BankBoston Corporation; U.S. Public, pg. 185
THE BOSTON INVESTMENT GROUP S.A.—See BankBoston Corporation; U.S. Public, pg. 185
BOSTON MUTUAL LIFE INSURANCE CO.; U.S. Private, pg. 161

BOSTON OLD COLONY INSURANCE CO.—See Loews Corporation; *U.S. Public,* pg. 1010
BOSTON OPERATIONS—See Cooper Industries, Inc.; *U.S. Public,* pg. 443
BOSTON OVERSEAS FINANCIAL CORPORATION S.A.—See BankBoston Corporation; *U.S. Public,* pg. 185
BOSTON OVERSEAS HOLDING CORP.—See BankBoston Corporation; *U.S. Public,* pg. 184
BOSTON PACIFIC, INC.—See CKE Restaurants Inc.; *U.S. Public,* pg. 278
BOSTON PIANO COMPANY—See Steinway Musical Instruments, Inc.; *U.S. Public,* pg. 1514
BOSTON SAFE DEPOSIT & TRUST CO.—See Mellon Bank Corporation; *U.S. Public,* pg. 1085
BOSTON SCIENTIFIC CORP.; *U.S. Public,* pg. 247
BOSTON SCIENTIFIC SYMBIOSIS—See Boston Scientific Corp.; *U.S. Public,* pg. 247
BOSTON SECURITY COUNSELLORS, INC.—See The Advest Group, Inc.; *U.S. Public,* pg. 23
BOSTON STORE—See Carson Pirie Scott & Co.; *U.S. Public,* pg. 309
BOSTON TRADE BANK—See BankBoston Corporation; *U.S. Public,* pg. 184
BOSTON WEATHERHEAD DIV.—See Dana Corporation; *U.S. Public,* pg. 479
BOSTON WHALER, INC.—See MacAndrews & Forbes Holdings Inc.; *U.S. Private,* pg. 689
BOSTON WHARF COMPANY—See The Peninsular and Oriental Steam Navigation Company; *Int'l,* pg. 1035
BOSTONIAN SHOE CO.—See Clarks International; *Int'l,* pg. 297
BOSTONIAN WHOLESALE DIVISION—See Clarks International; *Int'l,* pg. 297
BOSTROM SEATING, INC.—See Johnstown America Industries; *U.S. Public,* pg. 933
THE BOTSFORD GROUP—See Fitzgerald & Co.; *U.S. Private,* pg. 409
JOHN BOUCHARD & SONS COMPANY; *U.S. Private,* pg. 161
N.V. BOUCQUILLON S.A.—See Veba AG; *Int'l,* pg. 1458
BOULDER CITY CARE CENTER—See Horizon/CMS Healthcare Corporation; *U.S. Public,* pg. 837
BOULDER PUBLISHING, INC.—See The E.W. Scripps Company; *U.S. Public,* pg. 1447
BOULEVARD BANCORP, INC.—See U.S. Bancorp; *U.S. Public,* pg. 1680
BOULEVARD DISTILLERS AND IMPORTERS INC.—See Groupe Pernod Ricard; *Int'l,* pg. 567
BOULEVARD MANOR NURSING CENTER—See Paragon Health Network, Inc.; *U.S. Public,* pg. 1256
BOU-MATIC—See DEC International, Inc.; *U.S. Private,* pg. 301
BOUNTY BOOKS—See Reed Elsevier plc; *Int'l,* pg. 1093
BOURAS INDUSTRIES; *U.S. Private,* pg. 161
BOURBON WAREHOUSE RECEIPTS, INC.—See Fortune Brands, Inc.; *U.S. Public,* pg. 675
BOURGEY MONTREUIL—See GEODIS; *Int'l,* pg. 549
BOURNS AG & BOURNS (SCHWEIZ) AG—See Bourns, Inc.; *U.S. Private,* pg. 161
BOURNS BENELUX B.V.—See Bourns, Inc.; *U.S. Private,* pg. 161
BOURNS DE MEXICO—See Bourns, Inc.; *U.S. Private,* pg. 161
BOURNS ELECTRONICS, LTD.—See Bourns, Inc.; *U.S. Private,* pg. 161
BOURNS, GMBH—See Bourns, Inc.; *U.S. Private,* pg. 161
BOURNS, INC.; *U.S. Private,* pg. 161
BOURNS INTEGRATED TECHNOLOGIES DIVISION—See Bourns, Inc.; *U.S. Private,* pg. 161
BOURNS-OHMIC S.A.—See Bourns, Inc.; *U.S. Private,* pg. 161
BOURNS PRESSURE PRODUCTS—See Bourns, Inc.; *U.S. Private,* pg. 161
BOURNS SENSORS & CONTROLS DIVISION—See Bourns, Inc.; *U.S. Private,* pg. 161
BOURQUE PRINTING—See Champion Industries; *U.S. Public,* pg. 333
BOURTON GROUP; *U.S. Private,* pg. 162
BOURTON GROUP—See Bourton Group; *U.S. Private,* pg. 162
BOURY ENTERPRISES; *U.S. Private,* pg. 162
BOUSQUET COMPLEX—See Barrick Gold Corporation; *Int'l,* pg. 169
H.L. BOUTON COMPANY INC.; *U.S. Private,* pg. 162
BOUYGUES; *Int'l,* pg. 206
BOUYGUES NIGERIA LIMITED (B.N.L.)—See Bouygues; *Int'l,* pg. 207
BOUYGUES OFFSHORE—See Bouygues; *Int'l,* pg. 206
BOUYGUES OFFSHORE USA—See Bouygues; *Int'l,* pg. 206
BOVAIRD SUPPLY CO.; *U.S. Private,* pg. 162
BOVAR INC.—See Trimac Corporation; *Int'l,* pg. 1424
BOVIL—See BDDP Group; *Int'l,* pg. 117
BOVIS CONSTRUCTION GROUP—See The Peninsular and Oriental Steam Navigation Company; *Int'l,* pg. 1032
BOVIS CONSTRUCTION LTD.—See The Peninsular and Oriental Steam Navigation Company; *Int'l,* pg. 1032
BOVIS HOME LTD.—See The Peninsular and Oriental Steam Navigation Company; *Int'l,* pg. 1032
BOVIS INC.—See The Peninsular and Oriental Steam Navigation Company; *Int'l,* pg. 1033
BOVIS INTERNATIONAL CALIFORNIA—See The Peninsular and Oriental Steam Navigation Company; *Int'l,* pg. 1035
BOVIS INTERNATIONAL LTD.—See The Peninsular and Oriental Steam Navigation Company; *Int'l,* pg. 1032
BOVIS URBAN RENEWAL LTD.—See The Peninsular and Oriental Steam Navigation Company; *Int'l,* pg. 1032
BOWATER COATED PAPER & PULP DIV.—See Bowater Incorporated; *U.S. Public,* pg. 247
BOWATER INCORPORATED; *U.S. Public,* pg. 247
BOWATER INDUSTRIES AUSTRALIA LTD.—See Rexam PLC; *Int'l,* pg. 1107

BOWATER MERSEY PAPER COMPANY, LTD.—See Bowater Incorporated; *U.S. Public,* pg. 248
BOWATER NEWSPRINT DIVISION—See Bowater Incorporated; *U.S. Public,* pg. 248
BOWATER WINDOWS—See Rexam PLC; *Int'l,* pg. 1106
BOWDEN BROS & CO., LTD.—See Ruhrgas Aktiengesellschaft; *Int'l,* pg. 1149
BOWDEN INDUSTRIES LIMITED—See GP Batteries International Ltd.; *Int'l,* pg. 537
BOWDENS MEDIA MONITORING LIMITED—See Rogers Communications, Inc.; *Int'l,* pg. 1124
BOWEN BROTHERS FRUIT CO., INC.; *U.S. Private,* pg. 162
BOWEN COKE PTY.—See M.I.M. Holdings Ltd.; *Int'l,* pg. 827
BOWEN TOOLS—See IRI International Corporation; *U.S. Public,* pg. 858
BOWEN TOOLS, LTD.—See IRI International Corporation; *U.S. Public,* pg. 858
BOWENS INTERNATIONAL LTD.—See Wolseley Plc; *Int'l,* pg. 1511
BOWES PUBLISHERS LIMITED—See Sun Media Corporation; *Int'l,* pg. 1320
BOWHEAD EQUIPMENT COMPANY—See Lynden Incorporated; *U.S. Private,* pg. 683
R.R. BOWKER—See Reed Elsevier plc; *Int'l,* pg. 1096
BOWKER-SAUR LTD.—See Reed Elsevier plc; *Int'l,* pg. 1094
BOWL AMERICA, INCORPORATED; *U.S. Public,* pg. 248
BOWLERAMA LANES, INC.—See Great Lakes Realty Corp.; *U.S. Private,* pg. 475
BOWLES FLUIDICS CORPORATION; *U.S. Public,* pg. 248
BOWLING GREEN HEALTH CARE CENTER—See Vencor, Inc.; *U.S. Public,* pg. 1712
BOWMAN & KEMP REBAR—See B & K Steel & Supply, Inc.; *U.S. Private,* pg. 105
BOWMAN & KEMP STEEL & SUPPLY COMPANY—See B & K Steel & Supply, Inc.; *U.S. Private,* pg. 105
BOWMAN DISTRIBUTION—See Barnes Group Inc.; *U.S. Public,* pg. 190
BOWMAN DISTRIBUTION (CANADA) LTD.—See Barnes Group Inc.; *U.S. Public,* pg. 190
BOWMAN DISTRIBUTION-EUROPE—See Barnes Group Inc.; *U.S. Public,* pg. 190
BOWMAN DISTRIBUTION FRANCE—See Barnes Group Inc.; *U.S. Public,* pg. 190
BOWMAR INSTRUMENT CORPORATION; *U.S. Public,* pg. 248
BOWMAR TECHNOLOGIES—See Bowmar Instrument Corporation; *U.S. Public,* pg. 248
BOWNE & CO., INC.; *U.S. Public,* pg. 248
BOWNE BUSINESS COMMUNICATIONS, INC.—See Bowne & Co., Inc.; *U.S. Public,* pg. 248
BOWNE INSURANCE DIVISION—See Bowne & Co., Inc.; *U.S. Public,* pg. 248
BOWNE INTERNATIONAL INC.—See Bowne & Co., Inc.; *U.S. Public,* pg. 248
BOWTHORPE AUSTRALIA PTY. LTD.—See Bowthorpe plc; *Int'l,* pg. 208
BOWTHORPE BV—See Bowthorpe plc; *Int'l,* pg. 208
BOWTHORPE EMP LIMITED—See Bowthorpe plc; *Int'l,* pg. 207
BOWTHORPE GMBH—See Bowthorpe plc; *Int'l,* pg. 208
BOWTHORPE-HELLERMANN DISTRIBUTORS—See Bowthorpe plc; *Int'l,* pg. 207
BOWTHORPE-HELLERMANN (PTY.) LTD.—See Bowthorpe plc; *Int'l,* pg. 208
BOWTHORPE (NZ) LIMITED—See Bowthorpe plc; *Int'l,* pg. 208
BOWTHORPE PLC; *Int'l,* pg. 207
BOWTHORPE THERMOMETRICS—See Bowthorpe plc; *Int'l,* pg. 207
BOWTHORPE THERMOMETRICS (INDIA) PVT. LTD.—See Bowthorpe plc; *Int'l,* pg. 208
BOX HILL FEDERAL SYSTEMS—See Box Hill Systems Corporation; *U.S. Public,* pg. 249
BOX HILL SYSTEMS CORPORATION; *U.S. Public,* pg. 249
BOX HILL SYSTEMS EUROPE LTD.—See Box Hill Systems Corporation; *U.S. Public,* pg. 249
BOX USA INC.—See Four M Corporation, Inc.; *U.S. Private,* pg. 421
BOXHOLMS SKOGAR AB/SKANSKA FORESTRY GROUP—See Skanska AB; *Int'l,* pg. 1260
BOXMAG-RAPID LTD.—See Wolseley Plc.; *Int'l,* pg. 1511
BOYD FLOTATION, INC.—See Royal Waterbeds; *U.S. Private,* pg. 949
BOYD GAMING CORPORATION; *U.S. Public,* pg. 249
BOYE NEEDLE—See Wm. E. Wright Limited Partnership; *U.S. Private,* pg. 1192
BOYER CANDY COMPANY INC.; *U.S. Private,* pg. 162
BOYERS & CO. LIMITED—See Arnotts plc; *Int'l,* pg. 81
BOYKIN LODGING CO.; *U.S. Public,* pg. 249
BOYKIN MANAGEMENT CO.; *U.S. Private,* pg. 162
BOYLE ENGINEERING CORP.; *U.S. Private,* pg. 163
BOYLES GALVANIZING CO.—See Kinark Corporation; *U.S. Public,* pg. 960
BOYNE SMELTERS LIMITED—See Comalco Limited; *Int'l,* pg. 307
BOZ-WHITE HILLS INC.—See Bozzuto's Inc.; *U.S. Public,* pg. 249
BOZELL RETAIL; *U.S. Public,* pg. 209
BOZELL WORLDWIDE, INC.—See True North Diversified Companies; *U.S. Public,* pg. 1642
BOZEMAN CARE CENTER—See Vencor, Inc.; *U.S. Public,* pg. 1712
BOZZALLA & LESNA S.P.A.; *Int'l,* pg. 209
BOZZUTO'S INC.; *U.S. Public,* pg. 249
BRAAS BENELUX S.A.—See Redland PLC; *Int'l,* pg. 1092
BRAAS BERLIN GMBH & CO.—See Redland PLC; *Int'l,* pg. 1091
BRAAS DACHSTEINWERKE GMBH—See Redland PLC; *Int'l,* pg. 1091

BRAAS DACHSYSTEME GMBH—See Redland PLC; *Int'l,* pg. 1091
BRAAS FLACHDACHSYSTEME GMBH—See Redland PLC; *Int'l,* pg. 1091
BRAAS FRANCE S.A.R.L.—See Redland PLC; *Int'l,* pg. 1092
BRAAS GMBH—See Redland PLC; *Int'l,* pg. 1091
THE BRAAS GROUP—See Redland PLC; *Int'l,* pg. 1091
BRAAS ITALIA S.P.A.—See Redland PLC; *Int'l,* pg. 1092
BRAAS SCANDINAVIA AB—See Redland PLC; *Int'l,* pg. 1092
BRAAS SCHWEIZ AG—See Redland PLC; *Int'l,* pg. 1092
BRABANT ALUCAST INTERNATIONAL BV—See Koninklijke Hoogovens N.V.; *Int'l,* pg. 753
BRABANT NEWSPAPERS LTD.—See Hollinger Inc.; *Int'l,* pg. 631
BRABANT PERS BV—See VNU Verenigde Nederlandse Uitgeversbedrijven B.V.; *Int'l,* pg. 1445
BRABANTS NIEUWSBLAD BV—See VNU Verenigde Nederlandse Uitgeversbedrijven B.V.; *Int'l,* pg. 1445
BRACCO DIAGNOSTICS, INC.—See Bracco S.p.A.; *Int'l,* pg. 210
BRACCO RESEARCH, INC.—See Bracco S.p.A.; *Int'l,* pg. 210
BRACCO S.P.A.; *Int'l,* pg. 209
BRACH & BROCK CONFECTIONS, INC.; *U.S. Private,* pg. 163
E.J. BRACH, INC.—See Brach & Brock Confections, Inc.; *U.S. Private,* pg. 163
BRACONNOT—See Royal Dutch/Shell Group of Companies; *Int'l,* pg. 1138
BRADBURY COMPANY, INC.; *U.S. Private,* pg. 163
BRADEN MANUFACTURING CO.—See Jason Incorporated; *U.S. Public,* pg. 924
BRADEN-METRIO—See Jason Incorporated; *U.S. Public,* pg. 924
THE BRADENTON HERALD, INC.—See Knight-Ridder, Inc.; *U.S. Public,* pg. 964
BRADESCO LEASING S.A. ARRENDAMENTO MERCANTIL—See Orix Corporation; *Int'l,* pg. 1009
BRADFORD & BINGLEY BUILDING SOCIETY; *Int'l,* pg. 210
BRADFORD COMPANY; *U.S. Private,* pg. 163
BRADFORD ELECTRONIC INC.—See Vishay Intertechnology, Inc.; *U.S. Public,* pg. 1722
BRADFORD EXCHANGE LTD.; *U.S. Private,* pg. 163
BRADFORD INDUSTRIES, INC.; *U.S. Private,* pg. 163
J.C. BRADFORD & CO.; *U.S. Private,* pg. 163
THE BRADFORD NATIONAL BANK OF GREENVILLE; *U.S. Private,* pg. 164
BRADFORD OIL COMPANY, INC.; *U.S. Private,* pg. 164
BRADFORD-WHITE CORPORATION; *U.S. Private,* pg. 164
BRADLEES INC.; *U.S. Public,* pg. 249
A. BRADLEY PRESENCE SENSING—See Rockwell International Corporation; *U.S. Public,* pg. 1397
ALLEN BRADLEY CREONICS—See Rockwell International Corporation; *U.S. Public,* pg. 1397
BRADLEY CORPORATION; *U.S. Private,* pg. 164
BRADLEY MARKETING SERVICES—See W.C. Bradley Co.; *U.S. Private,* pg. 164
BRADLEY PHARMACEUTICALS; *U.S. Public,* pg. 249
BRADLEY PRINTING COMPANY—See World Color Press, Inc.; *U.S. Public,* pg. 1778
BRADLEY REAL ESTATE, INC.; *U.S. Public,* pg. 250
BRADLEY SPECIALTY RETAILING—See W.C. Bradley Co.; *U.S. Private,* pg. 164
W.C. BRADLEY CO.; *U.S. Private,* pg. 164
W.C. BRADLEY FARMS INC.—See W.C. Bradley Co.; *U.S. Private,* pg. 164
BRADNER CENTRAL COMPANY; *U.S. Private,* pg. 164
BRADNER SMITH & CO.—See Bradner Central Company; *U.S. Private,* pg. 164
BRADNER SMITH & CO. OF WISCONSIN—See Bradner Central Company; *U.S. Private,* pg. 165
BRADSHAW-PRAEGER CO.—See RPM, Inc.; *U.S. Public,* pg. 1358
BRADSTOCK BLUNT & CRAWLEY (AVIATION) LTD—See Bradstock Group plc; *Int'l,* pg. 210
BRADSTOCK BLUNT & CRAWLEY LTD.—See Bradstock Group plc; *Int'l,* pg. 210
BRADSTOCK BLUNT & THOMPSON—See Bradstock Group plc; *Int'l,* pg. 210
BRADSTOCK BLUNT (PLASTICS) LTD.—See Bradstock Group plc; *Int'l,* pg. 210
BRADSTOCK FINANCIAL SERVICES LTD.—See Bradstock Group plc; *Int'l,* pg. 210
BRADSTOCK GROUP PLC; *Int'l,* pg. 210
BRADSTOCK GROUP SERVICES LIMITED—See Bradstock Group plc; *Int'l,* pg. 210
BRADSTOCK INSURANCE BROKERS LIMITED—See Bradstock Group plc; *Int'l,* pg. 210
BRADY ENTERPRISES, INC.; *U.S. Private,* pg. 165
BRADY GRAPHICS SOLUTIONS LTD.—See W.H. Brady Co.; *U.S. Public,* pg. 250
BRADY INTERNATIONAL CO.—See W.H. Brady Co.; *U.S. Public,* pg. 250
BRADY MARKETING COMPANY; *U.S. Private,* pg. 165
BRADY PLANT—See Oglebay Norton Company; *U.S. Public,* pg. 1213
BRADY PRECISION TAPE CO.—See W.H. Brady Co.; *U.S. Public,* pg. 250
BRADY SERVICE CO.—See W.H. Brady Co.; *U.S. Public,* pg. 250
BRADY USA, INC.—See W.H. Brady Co.; *U.S. Public,* pg. 250
W.H. BRADY CO.; *U.S. Public,* pg. 250
BRAEBURN ALLOY STEEL—See CCX, Inc.; *U.S. Private,* pg. 193
BRAEMAR APPAREL INC.—See Dylex Limited; *Int'l,* pg. 425
BRAID ELECTRIC COMPANY; *U.S. Private,* pg. 165
THE BRAIDWATER SPINNING COMPANY LTD.—See Lamont Holdings Plc; *Int'l,* pg. 797

BRAIN FORUM CO., LTD.—See Skylark Co., Ltd.; *Int'l*, pg. 1262
BRAIN POWER INC.—See HON Industries Inc.; *U.S. Public*, pg. 772
BRAINCO DEL PERU S.A.—See Pechiney S.A.; *Int'l*, pg. 1030
BRAINERD DAILY DISPATCH—See Shivers Trading & Operating Co.; *U.S. Private*, pg. 995
BRAINTREE FORUM—See Gannett Company, Inc.; *U.S. Public*, pg. 700
BRAKE BROS PLC; *Int'l*, pg. 210
BRAKE CABLES LTD—See FKI Plc; *Int'l*, pg. 472
BRAKE FLUID OPERATIONS—See Cooper Industries, Inc.; *U.S. Public*, pg. 443
BRAKE PARTS, INC.—See Echlin Inc.; *U.S. Public*, pg. 560
BRAKE-PRO SYSTEMS, INC.—See Tenneco Inc.; *U.S. Public*, pg. 1578
BRAKE SUPPLY CO.—See George Koch Sons, Inc.; *U.S. Private*, pg. 628
BRAKES INDIA LTD.—See LucasVarity plc; *Int'l*, pg. 820
BRALEMEX S.A. DE C.V.—See Fried. Krupp AG; *Int'l*, pg. 515
BRAMAC DACHSYSTEME INTERNATIONAL GMBH—See Redland PLC; *Int'l*, pg. 1092
BRAMAC D.O.O.—See Redland PLC; *Int'l*, pg. 1092
BRAMAC KFT—See Redland PLC; *Int'l*, pg. 1092
BRAMAC SPOL. SR.O.—See Redland PLC; *Int'l*, pg. 1092
BRAMAN WORLD CAR CENTER; *U.S. Private*, pg. 165
DAVID A. BRAMBLE, INC.; *U.S. Private*, pg. 165
BRAMBLES BULK HAULAGE—See Brambles Industries Limited; *Int'l*, pg. 211
BRAMBLES CONTAINER SERVICES—See Brambles Industries Limited; *Int'l*, pg. 211
BRAMBLES DIV. OF BRAMBLES EQUIPMENT SERVICES INC.—See Brambles Industries Limited; *Int'l*, pg. 211
BRAMBLES EQUIPMENT & FORKLIFTS—See Brambles Industries Limited; *Int'l*, pg. 211
BRAMBLES EQUIPMENT SERVICES INC.—See Brambles Industries Limited; *Int'l*, pg. 211
BRAMBLES EUROPE S.A.—See Brambles Industries Limited; *Int'l*, pg. 212
BRAMBLES HOLDINGS LIMITED—See Brambles Industries Limited; *Int'l*, pg. 211
BRAMBLES INDUSTRIES LIMITED; *Int'l*, pg. 210
BRAMBLES INDUSTRIES LTD.—See Brambles Industries Limited; *Int'l*, pg. 212
BRAMBLES INDUSTRIES (N.Z.) LTD.—See Brambles Industries Limited; *Int'l*, pg. 212
BRAMBLES INTERNATIONAL FREIGHT PTY. LIMITED—See Brambles Industries Limited; *Int'l*, pg. 211
BRAMBLES MANFORD—See Brambles Industries Limited; *Int'l*, pg. 211
BRAMBLES MARINE SERVICES PTY. LTD.—See Brambles Industries Limited; *Int'l*, pg. 211
BRAMBLES RECORD MANAGEMENT—See Brambles Industries Limited; *Int'l*, pg. 211
BRAMBLES SEACARGO—See Brambles Industries Limited; *Int'l*, pg. 211
BRAMBLES SECURITIES SERVICES LIMITED—See Brambles Industries Limited; *Int'l*, pg. 211
BRAMBLES SECURITY SERVICES INC.—See Brambles Industries Limited; *Int'l*, pg. 211
BRAMBLES SHIPPING—See Brambles Industries Limited; *Int'l*, pg. 211
BRAMBLES TEXTILE RENTAL & LAUNDRY SERVICES—See Brambles Industries Limited; *Int'l*, pg. 211
BRAMBLES TRANSPORT (FREIGHT FORWARDING) DIVISION—See Brambles Industries Limited; *Int'l*, pg. 211
BRAMBLES (U.K.) LTD.—See Brambles Industries Limited; *Int'l*, pg. 212
BRAMBLES USA INC.—See Brambles Industries Limited; *Int'l*, pg. 211
BRAMCO, INC.—See Greenway Partners, L.P.; *U.S. Private*, pg. 478
BRAMMER PLC; *Int'l*, pg. 212
BRAMPTON PLANT—See Fort James Corporation; *U.S. Public*, pg. 672
BRAN & LUEBBE (G.B.) LTD.—See Tetra Laval Group; *Int'l*, pg. 1380
BRAN & LUEBBE G.M.B.H.—See Tetra Laval Group; *Int'l*, pg. 1379
BRAN & LUEBBE INC.—See Tetra Laval Group; *Int'l*, pg. 1378
BRAN & LUEBBE S.A.R.L.—See Tetra Laval Group; *Int'l*, pg. 1380
BRAN & LUEBBE S.R.L.—See Tetra Laval Group; *Int'l*, pg. 1380
BRANCE KRACHY COMPANY, INC.; *U.S. Private*, pg. 165
BRANCH BANKING & TRUST—See BB&T Corporation; *U.S. Public*, pg. 160
BRANCH DATA COMM—See Branch Group Inc.; *U.S. Private*, pg. 165
BRANCH ELECTRIC SUPPLY CO.—See Branch Group Inc.; *U.S. Private*, pg. 165
BRANCH ELECTRIC SUPPLY CO., INC.—See Branch Group Inc.; *U.S. Private*, pg. 165
BRANCH GROUP INC.; *U.S. Private*, pg. 165
THE BRAND COMPANY—See BDDP Group; *Int'l*, pg. 116
BRANDEIS AFRICA-LUTECE DIVISION AGENCY—See Pechiney S.A.; *Int'l*, pg. 1030
BRANDEIS AFRICA (PTY) LTD.—See Pechiney S.A.; *Int'l*, pg. 1030
BRANDEIS BROKERS LTD.—See Pechiney S.A.; *Int'l*, pg. 1030
BRANDEIS CHILE LTDA.—See Pechiney S.A.; *Int'l*, pg. 1030
BRANDEIS DIVISION OF PWT (USA) INC.—See Pechiney S.A.; *Int'l*, pg. 1029
BRANDEIS HAUCK & PARTNERS—See Pechiney S.A.; *Int'l*, pg. 1030
BRANDEIS INTSEL DEUTSCHLAND—See Pechiney S.A.; *Int'l*, pg. 1030
BRANDEIS (ITALIA) S.R.L.—See Pechiney S.A.; *Int'l*, pg. 1030
BRANDEIS LTD.—See Pechiney S.A.; *Int'l*, pg. 1030
BRANDEIS LTD.-REP. OFFICE OF PECHINEY HANDELSGESELLSCHAFT IN ROMANIA—See Pechiney S.A.; *Int'l*, pg. 1030
BRANDEIS SERVICES INC.—See Pechiney S.A.; *Int'l*, pg. 1029
BRANDEIS US DIVISION-REP. OFFICE IN MEXICO—See Pechiney S.A.; *Int'l*, pg. 1030
E. BRANDLE AG—See Freudenberg & Company; *Int'l*, pg. 506
A.J. BRANDON—See Kellwood Company; *U.S. Public*, pg. 948
BRANDSOLUTIONS—See EvansGroup; *U.S. Private*, pg. 385
BRANDT, INC.—See De La Rue plc; *Int'l*, pg. 387
BRANDWEEK—See VNU Verenigde Nederlandse Uitgeversbedrijven B.V.; *Int'l*, pg. 1446
BRANDYWINE FOODS, INC.—See Tyson Foods, Inc.; *U.S. Public*, pg. 1652
BRANDYWINE HALL CARE CENTER—See Genesis Health Ventures, Inc.; *U.S. Public*, pg. 728
BRANDYWINE REALTY & DEVELOPMENT, INC.—See Brandywine Sports, Inc.; *U.S. Private*, pg. 165
BRANDYWINE SPORTS, INC.; *U.S. Private*, pg. 165
BRANDYWINE VALLEY RAILROAD COMPANY—See Lukens Inc.; *U.S. Public*, pg. 1020
BRANDYWOOD ESTATES, INC.—See Washington Gas Light Co.; *U.S. Public*, pg. 1741
BRANFORD REVIEW—See Journal Register Company; *U.S. Public*, pg. 934
BRANFORD SAVINGS BANK; *U.S. Public*, pg. 250
BRANFORD SAVINGS BANK-BRANFORD—See Branford Savings Bank; *U.S. Public*, pg. 250
BRANFORD SAVINGS BANK-EAST HAVEN—See Branford Savings Bank; *U.S. Public*, pg. 250
BRANFORD SAVINGS BANK-FOXON—See Branford Savings Bank; *U.S. Public*, pg. 250
BRANFORD SAVINGS BANK-NORTH BRANFORD—See Branford Savings Bank; *U.S. Public*, pg. 250
BRANFORD VIBRATOR COMPANY—See ABB Asea Brown Boveri (Holding) Ltd.; *Int'l*, pg. 4
BRANI READY MIX PTE. LTD.—See Ssangyong Business Group; *Int'l*, pg. 1293
THE BRANIGAR ORGANIZATION, INC.—See Union Camp Corporation; *U.S. Public*, pg. 1666
BRANN LTD.; *Int'l*, pg. 212
BRANSON (EUROPA) B.V.—See Emerson Electric Co.; *U.S. Public*, pg. 576
BRANSON INTERNATIONAL PLASMA CORP.—See Emerson Electric Co.; *U.S. Public*, pg. 574
BRANSON PLASTIC JOINING—See Emerson Electric Co.; *U.S. Public*, pg. 574
BRANSON SONIC POWER, S.A.—See Emerson Electric Co.; *U.S. Public*, pg. 576
BRANSON ULTRASONICS—See Emerson Electric Co.; *U.S. Public*, pg. 574
BRANSON ULTRASONICS (ASIA PACIFIC) CO. LTD.—See Emerson Electric Co.; *U.S. Public*, pg. 576
BRANSON ULTRASONICS CORP.-PLASTICS JOINING DIV.—See Emerson Electric Co.; *U.S. Public*, pg. 574
BRANSON ULTRASONICS CORP. - PRECISION CLEANING DIV.—See Emerson Electric Co.; *U.S. Public*, pg. 574
BRANSON ULTRASONIDOS, S.A.E.—See Emerson Electric Co.; *U.S. Public*, pg. 576
BRANSON ULTRASUONI S.P.A.—See Emerson Electric Co.; *U.S. Public*, pg. 576
BRANT ALLEN INDUSTRIES, INC.; *U.S. Private*, pg. 165
BRAODBAND COMMUNICATIONS DIVISION—See ADC Telecommunications, Inc.; *U.S. Public*, pg. 4
BRASCADE RESOURCES INC.—See EdperBrascan Corporation; *Int'l*, pg. 433
BRASCAN BRAZIL—See EdperBrascan Corporation; *Int'l*, pg. 435
BRASIL ASISTENCIA—See Corporacion MAPFRE, Compania Internacional de Reaseguros, S.A.; *Int'l*, pg. 334
BRASIL BETON—See Lafarge S.A.; *Int'l*, pg. 790
CIA. BRASILEIRA DE ALUMINIO—See S.A. Industrias Votorantim; *Int'l*, pg. 677
BRASILIAN AMERICAN MERCHANT BANK—See Banco do Brasil; *Int'l*, pg. 142
BRASILIT DA AMAZONIA—See Saint-Gobain; *Int'l*, pg. 1171
BRASILIT DO OESTE—See Saint-Gobain; *Int'l*, pg. 1171
BRASILIT S.A.—See Saint-Gobain; *Int'l*, pg. 1171
BRASILUX S.A.—See Arbed S.A.; *Int'l*, pg. 79
BRASOIL U.K. LTD.—See Petrobras - Petroleo Brasileiro S.A.; *Int'l*, pg. 1042
BRASPETRO ANGOLA—See Petrobras - Petroleo Brasileiro S.A.; *Int'l*, pg. 1042
BRASPETRO COLUMBIA—See Petrobras - Petroleo Brasileiro S.A.; *Int'l*, pg. 1042
BRASPETRO LIBYA—See Petrobras - Petroleo Brasileiro S.A.; *Int'l*, pg. 1042
BRASPETRO OIL SERVICES CO. - BRASOIL—See Petrobras - Petroleo Brasileiro S.A.; *Int'l*, pg. 1042
BRASS-CRAFT CANADA, LTD.—See Masco Corporation; *U.S. Public*, pg. 1054
BRASS-CRAFT HOLDING CO.—See Masco Corporation; *U.S. Public*, pg. 1053
BRASS-CRAFT MANUFACTURING COMPANY—See Masco Corporation; *U.S. Public*, pg. 1053
BRASS-CRAFT WESTERN COMPANY—See Masco Corporation; *U.S. Public*, pg. 1053
BRASS EAGLE INC.; *U.S. Public*, pg. 250
BRASSERIES DE BOURBON S.A.—See Heineken N.V.; *Int'l*, pg. 608
BRASSERIES DU LOGONE S.A.—See Unilever Plc; *Int'l*, pg. 1436
BRASSERIES ET LIMONADERIES DU BURUNDI "BRARUDI" S.A.R.L.—See Heineken N.V.; *Int'l*, pg. 608
BRASSERIES ET LIMONADERIES DU RWANDA "BRALIRWA" S.A.R.L.—See Heineken N.V.; *Int'l*, pg. 608
BRASSERIES, LIMONADERIES ET MALTERIES DU ZAIRE "BRALIMA" S.A.R.L.—See Heineken N.V.; *Int'l*, pg. 608
BRASTEMP S.A.—See Whirlpool Corporation; *U.S. Public*, pg. 1765
BRASWELL CONCRETE PRODUCTS, INC.—See Holderbank Financiere Glaris Ltd.; *Int'l*, pg. 628
BRASWELL INDUSTRIES—See Holderbank Financiere Glaris Ltd.; *Int'l*, pg. 628
BRASWELL SAND & GRAVEL COMPANY, INC.—See Holderbank Financiere Glaris Ltd.; *Int'l*, pg. 628
BRATRI BOHLEROVE A.S.—See Voest-Alpine Stahl AG; *Int'l*, pg. 1472
BRAUEREI AG—See Feldschlosschen Hurlimann Holding; *Int'l*, pg. 479
BRAUEREI EICHHOF; *Int'l*, pg. 213
BRAUM ICE CREAM STORES INC.; *U.S. Private*, pg. 166
BRAUN AG—See The Gillette Company; *U.S. Public*, pg. 744
BRAUN-BRUMFIELD, INC.—See The Sheridan Group; *U.S. Private*, pg. 993
BRAUN CANADA LTD.—See The Gillette Company; *U.S. Public*, pg. 744
BRAUN DE MEXICO Y COMPANIA DE C.V.—See The Gillette Company; *U.S. Public*, pg. 744
B. BRAUN-DEXON SA—See American Home Products Corporation; *U.S. Public*, pg. 80
BRAUN ESPANOLA, S.A.—See The Gillette Company; *U.S. Public*, pg. 744
F. BRAUN & CO. PTY. LTD.—See Wella Group; *Int'l*, pg. 1489
BRAUN FINLAND OY—See The Gillette Company; *U.S. Public*, pg. 744
BRAUN FRANCE S.A.—See The Gillette Company; *U.S. Public*, pg. 744
BRAUN IRELAND LTD.—See The Gillette Company; *U.S. Public*, pg. 744
BRAUN ITALIA, S.R.L.—See The Gillette Company; *U.S. Public*, pg. 744
BRAUN JAPAN K.K.—See The Gillette Company; *U.S. Public*, pg. 744
BRAUN NEDERLAND B.V.—See The Gillette Company; *U.S. Public*, pg. 744
BRAUN, NORTH AMERICA—See The Gillette Company; *U.S. Public*, pg. 743
BRAUN TRANSWORLD CORP.—See Kuwait Petroleum Corporation; *Int'l*, pg. 765
BRAUN (U.K.) LTD.—See The Gillette Company; *U.S. Public*, pg. 744
W. BRAUN COMPANY; *U.S. Private*, pg. 166
W. BRAUN CO.—See W. Braun Company; *U.S. Private*, pg. 166
W. BRAUN INTERNATIONAL—See W. Braun Company; *U.S. Private*, pg. 166
BRAUNS FASHIONS CORPORATION; *U.S. Public*, pg. 251
BRAUNSCHWEIGISCHE KOHLEN-BERGWERKE AG—See Veba AG; *Int'l*, pg. 1456
BRAVIKEN PAPER MILL—See Mo och Domsjo AB; *Int'l*, pg. 885
THE BRAVO GROUP—See Young & Rubicam Inc.; *U.S. Private*, pg. 1197
BRAVO NETWORK—See Cablevision Systems Corporation; *U.S. Public*, pg. 288
BRAWN OF CALIFORNIA, INC.—See Hanover Direct, Inc.; *U.S. Public*, pg. 782
BRAWNEY PLASTICS, INC.; *U.S. Private*, pg. 166
BRAWNY PLASTICS WEST—See Brawney Plastics, Inc.; *U.S. Private*, pg. 166
BRAYTON INTERNATIONAL INC.—See Steelcase Inc.; *U.S. Private*, pg. 1038
BRAZOS ELECTRIC POWER COOPERATIVE, INC.; *U.S. Private*, pg. 166
BRAZOS FUEL COMPANY INC.—See Brazos Electric Power Cooperative, Inc.; *U.S. Private*, pg. 166
BRAZOS POINT, INC.—See Centex Corporation; *U.S. Public*, pg. 322
BRAZOS SPORTSWEAR INC.; *U.S. Public*, pg. 251
BREAD & ROLLS DISTRIBUTION—See Campbell Soup Company; *U.S. Public*, pg. 299
BREATHING AND RELIEF, INC.—See Integrated Health Services, Inc.; *U.S. Public*, pg. 884
BRECK OPERATING CORP.—See States, Inc.; *U.S. Private*, pg. 1037
BRECKENRIDGE MATERIAL COMPANY; *U.S. Private*, pg. 166
BRECKETT PTY. LIMITED—See Brambles Industries Limited; *Int'l*, pg. 211
BRECKLAND FARMS—See J. Sainsbury plc; *Int'l*, pg. 1170
BRECKS—See Foster & Gallagher, Inc.; *U.S. Private*, pg. 420
BREDA SUGAR FACTORY—See CSM N.V.; *Int'l*, pg. 244
BREDERO-SHAW—See Dresser Industries, Inc.; *U.S. Public*, pg. 529
BREED TECHNOLOGIES—See Breed Technologies, Inc.; *U.S. Public*, pg. 251
BREED TECHNOLOGIES, INC.; *U.S. Public*, pg. 251
BREED UK LIMITED—See Breed Technologies, Inc.; *U.S. Public*, pg. 251
BREEDER'S SEEDS LTD.—See Novartis AG; *Int'l*, pg. 975
BREEMARS ASSURANTIEN B.V.—See Royal Begemann Group; *Int'l*, pg. 1133
DANIEL BREEN AND CO.—See Compagnie de Suez; *Int'l*, pg. 313
BREEZE EASTERN—See TransTechnology Corporation; *U.S. Public*, pg. 1632
BREEZE INDUSTRIAL—See TransTechnology Corporation; *U.S. Public*, pg. 1632

BREGAL, BREMER GALVANISLERUNGS GMBH—See Arbed S.A.; *Int'l*, pg. 79

BREHM COMMUNICATIONS INC.; *U.S. Private*, pg. 166

PETER BREITENBACH GMBH—See Mannesmann A.G.; *Int'l*, pg. 838

PETER BREITENBACH SANITAR UND HEIZUNGSFACHHANDEL GMBH—See Mannesmann A.G.; *Int'l*, pg. 838

BREKELMANS BV—See Koninklijke BolsWessanen nv; *Int'l*, pg. 751

BREMANGER POWER PLANT—See Elkem ASA; *Int'l*, pg. 447

BREMEN S.A.—See N.V. Bekaert S.A.; *Int'l*, pg. 185

BREMER & LEGUIL HANDELSGESELLSCHAFT MBH—See Fuchs Petrolub AG Oel + Chemie; *Int'l*, pg. 517

BREMER FINANCIAL CORPORATION; *U.S. Private*, pg. 167

BREMER REISEBURO GMBH—See Hapag-Lloyd AG; *Int'l*, pg. 596

BREMER SCHIFFSVERCHARTERUNGS AG—See Hapag-Lloyd AG; *Int'l*, pg. 596

BREMERTON SUN—See The E.W. Scripps Company; *U.S. Public*, pg. 1447

BREMIN MINERALOEL GMBH & CO.—See Fuchs Petrolub AG Oel + Chemie; *Int'l*, pg. 517

BREMNER, INC.—See Ralcorp Holdings Inc.; *U.S. Public*, pg. 1359

BREMSON DATA SYSTEMS, INC.—See Eastman Kodak Company; *U.S. Public*, pg. 551

BRENCAL CONTRACTORS INC.—See BEC Inc.; *U.S. Private*, pg. 106

BRENCO, INC.—See Varlen Corporation; *U.S. Public*, pg. 1710

BRENDERUP TRAILERS A/S—See Eldon AB; *Int'l*, pg. 436

BRENFORD—See Campbells/Bewley Group; *Int'l*, pg. 254

GEORG A. BRENNER ARZNEIMITTEL-FABRIK GMBH—See American Home Products Corporation; *U.S. Public*, pg. 80

BRENNTAG AG—See Veba AG; *Int'l*, pg. 1458

BRENNTAG EUROCHEM GMBH—See Veba AG; *Int'l*, pg. 1458

BRENNTAG INTERCHEM GMBH—See Veba AG; *Int'l*, pg. 1458

BRENNTAG INTERCHEM, INC.—See Veba AG; *Int'l*, pg. 1458

BRENNTAG INTERPLAST GMBH—See Veba AG; *Int'l*, pg. 1458

BRENT LEISURE LIMITED—See Namco Ltd.; *Int'l*, pg. 905

BRENT TRANSPORTATION CO.—See Kirby Corporation; *U.S. Public*, pg. 961

BRENTON BANK—See Brenton Banks, Inc.; *U.S. Public*, pg. 251

BRENTON BANKS, INC.; *U.S. Public*, pg. 251

BRENTON ENGINEERING COMPANY—See Derlan Industries Limited; *Int'l*, pg. 395

BRENTON SAVINGS BANK, FSB—See Brenton Banks, Inc.; *U.S. Public*, pg. 251

BRENTWOOD BENSON PUBLISHING GROUP—See Zomba Recording Corp.; *Int'l*, pg. 1529

BRENTWOOD LABEL GROUP—See Zomba Recording Corp.; *Int'l*, pg. 1529

BRESLER'S INDUSTRIES, INC.—See Yogen Fruz Worldwide Inc.; *Int'l*, pg. 1520

BRESLUBE DIVISION OF SAFETY-KLEEN CANADA INC.—See Safety-Kleen Corp.; *U.S. Public*, pg. 1426

BRETEC INC.—See Tamrock Corp.; *Int'l*, pg. 1352

BRETEC OY—See Tamrock Corp.; *Int'l*, pg. 1352

BRETLIN, INC.—See The Dixie Group, Inc.; *U.S. Public*, pg. 514

BRETTON WOODS TELEPHONE COMPANY—See Lynch Corporation; *U.S. Public*, pg. 1021

BREUER/TORNADO; *U.S. Private*, pg. 167

BREVARD DIV.—See NUI Corporation; *U.S. Public*, pg. 1148

C. BREWER & COMPANY, LIMITED—See Buyco, Inc.; *U.S. Private*, pg. 190

THE BREWER COMPANY; *U.S. Private*, pg. 167

BREWER ENVIRONMENTAL INDUSTRIES, LLC—See Buyco, Inc.; *U.S. Private*, pg. 190

BREWER OIL CO.; *U.S. Private*, pg. 167

BREWERY INGREDIENTS GROUP—See Cultor Ltd.; *Int'l*, pg. 349

BREWO GRUNDSTUCKSVERWALTUNGS GMBH—See Assicurazioni Generali S.p.A.; *Int'l*, pg. 89

THE BREWSKELLER—See Ark Restaurants Corp.; *U.S. Public*, pg. 130

BREWSTER TRANSPORT CO. LTD.—See Viad Corp; *U.S. Public*, pg. 1719

BREWSTER WHOLESALER COMPANY—See Sonesta International Hotels Corporation; *U.S. Public*, pg. 1485

BREYER CHEMIE B.V.—See Harrisons & Crosfield plc; *Int'l*, pg. 599

BRIAN CONTROLS—See Weir Group PLC; *Int'l*, pg. 1489

BRIAN CONTROLS DIVISION—See Axel Johnson AB; *Int'l*, pg. 711

BRIAN UNLIMITED DISTRIBUTION COMPANY, INC.; *U.S. Private*, pg. 167

BRICE BUILDING CO., INC.; *U.S. Private*, pg. 167

BRICE MANUFACTURING COMPANY, INC.—See Ducommun Incorporated; *U.S. Public*, pg. 534

BRICO BELGIUM SA—See GIB Group; *Int'l*, pg. 533

BRICO INTERNATIONAL GROUP—See GIB Group; *Int'l*, pg. 533

BRICO SRL—See Luxottica Group S.p.A.; *Int'l*, pg. 822

BRICODIS—See GIB Group; *Int'l*, pg. 534

BRICOGAL—See GIB Group; *Int'l*, pg. 534

BRICOREV—See Castorama Dubois Investissements S.C.A.; *Int'l*, pg. 275

ETS, BRICQ & CIE S.A.—See Scapa Group Plc; *Int'l*, pg. 1202

BRIDE'S—See Advance Publications Inc.; *U.S. Private*, pg. 20

BRIDGE—See Welsh Carson Anderson & Stowe; *U.S. Private*, pg. 1162

BRIDGE PACIFIC LTD.—See Compagnie des Machines Bull; *Int'l*, pg. 317

THE BRIDGEFORD GROUP—See The Industrial Bank of Japan, Limited; *Int'l*, pg. 674

BRIDGEMAN'S RESTAURANTS INC.; *U.S. Private*, pg. 167

BRIDGEND PAPER MILL—See Fort James Corporation; *U.S. Public*, pg. 672

BRIDGEPORT BRASS CORPORATION—See Olin Corporation; *U.S. Public*, pg. 1219

BRIDGEPORT CORRECTION FACILITY—See Corrections Corporation of America; *U.S. Public*, pg. 450

BRIDGEPORT FITTINGS, INC.; *U.S. Private*, pg. 168

BRIDGEPORT MACHINES, INC.; *U.S. Public*, pg. 251

BRIDGES & COMPANY, INC.; *U.S. Private*, pg. 168

BRIDGESTONE AUSTRALIA LTD.—See Bridgestone Corporation; *Int'l*, pg. 214

BRIDGESTONE CORPORATION; *Int'l*, pg. 213

BRIDGESTONE CYCLE CO., LTD.—See Bridgestone Corporation; *Int'l*, pg. 213

BRIDGESTONE CYCLE (U.S.A.), INC.—See Bridgestone Corporation; *Int'l*, pg. 213

BRIDGESTONE EARTHMOVER TYRES PTY. LTD.—See Bridgestone Corporation; *Int'l*, pg. 214

BRIDGESTONE/FIRESTONE CANADA INC.—See Bridgestone Corporation; *Int'l*, pg. 214

BRIDGESTONE/FIRESTONE CANADA, INC.—See Bridgestone Corporation; *Int'l*, pg. 214

BRIDGESTONE/FIRESTONE CREDIT SERVICES COMPANY—See Bridgestone Corporation; *Int'l*, pg. 213

BRIDGESTONE/FIRESTONE DE LA ARGENTINA S.A.I.C.—See Bridgestone Corporation; *Int'l*, pg. 214

BRIDGESTONE/FIRESTONE DE MEXICO, S.A. DE C.V.—See Bridgestone Corporation; *Int'l*, pg. 214

BRIDGESTONE/FIRESTONE DO BRASIL INDUSTRIA E COMMERCIO LTDA—See Bridgestone Corporation; *Int'l*, pg. 214

BRIDGESTONE/FIRESTONE EUROPE, S.A.—See Bridgestone Corporation; *Int'l*, pg. 214

BRIDGESTONE/FIRESTONE HISPANIA S.A.—See Bridgestone Corporation; *Int'l*, pg. 214

BRIDGESTONE/FIRESTONE, INC.—See Bridgestone Corporation; *Int'l*, pg. 213

BRIDGESTONE/FIRESTONE INC. RETAIL OPERATIONS—See Bridgestone Corporation; *Int'l*, pg. 213

BRIDGESTONE/FIRESTONE, INC.—See Bridgestone Corporation; *Int'l*, pg. 213

BRIDGESTONE/FIRESTONE INFORMATION SERVICES COMPANY—See Bridgestone Corporation; *Int'l*, pg. 213

BRIDGESTONE/FIRESTONE ITALIA S.P.A.—See Bridgestone Corporation; *Int'l*, pg. 214

BRIDGESTONE/FIRESTONE OFF ROAD TIRE COMPANY—See Bridgestone Corporation; *Int'l*, pg. 213

BRIDGESTONE/FIRESTONE OFF ROAD TIRE COMPANY-BLOOMINGTON—See Bridgestone Corporation; *Int'l*, pg. 213

BRIDGESTONE/FIRESTONE ORIGINAL EQUIPMENT TIRE SALES COMPANY—See Bridgestone Corporation; *Int'l*, pg. 213

BRIDGESTONE/FIRESTONE RESEARCH LABORATORIES—See Bridgestone Corporation; *Int'l*, pg. 213

BRIDGESTONE/FIRESTONE TECHNOLOGY COMPANY—See Bridgestone Corporation; *Int'l*, pg. 213

BRIDGESTONE/FIRESTONE TIRE MANUFACTURING OPERATIONS—See Bridgestone Corporation; *Int'l*, pg. 213

BRIDGESTONE/FIRESTONE TIRE MANUFACTURING OPERATIONS-DECATUR—See Bridgestone Corporation; *Int'l*, pg. 213

BRIDGESTONE/FIRESTONE TIRE MANUFACTURING OPERATIONS-LAVERGNE—See Bridgestone Corporation; *Int'l*, pg. 213

BRIDGESTONE/FIRESTONE TIRE MANUFACTURING OPERATIONS-WARREN COUNTY—See Bridgestone Corporation; *Int'l*, pg. 213

BRIDGESTONE/FIRESTONE TIRE MANUFACTURING OPERATIONS-WILSON—See Bridgestone Corporation; *Int'l*, pg. 213

BRIDGESTON/FIRESTONE TIRE MANUFACTURING OPERATIONS-JOLIETTE—See Bridgestone Corporation; *Int'l*, pg. 213

BRIDGESTONE/FIRESTONE TIRE SALES COMPANY—See Bridgestone Corporation; *Int'l*, pg. 213

BRIDGESTONE/FIRESTONE U.K. LTD.—See Bridgestone Corporation; *Int'l*, pg. 214

BRIDGESTONE/FIRESTONE VENEZOLANA, C.A.—See Bridgestone Corporation; *Int'l*, pg. 214

BRIDGESTONE FRANCE S.A.R.L.—See Bridgestone Corporation; *Int'l*, pg. 214

BRIDGESTONE MULTI-MEDIA GROUP; *U.S. Private*, pg. 168

BRIDGESTONE REIFEN GMBH—See Bridgestone Corporation; *Int'l*, pg. 214

BRIDGESTONE (SCHWEIZ) AG—See Bridgestone Corporation; *Int'l*, pg. 214

BRIDGESTONE TAIWAN CO., LTD.—See Bridgestone Corporation; *Int'l*, pg. 214

BRIDGESTONE TIRE CO. A/S—See Bridgestone Corporation; *Int'l*, pg. 214

P.T. BRIDGESTONE TIRE INDONESIA—See Bridgestone Corporation; *Int'l*, pg. 214

BRIDGESTONE TRADING CO., (PTE.) LTD.—See Bridgestone Corporation; *Int'l*, pg. 214

BRIDGESTONE TRADING CO.—See Bridgestone Corporation; *Int'l*, pg. 214

BRIDGEWATER PAPER LIMITED—See Abitibi-Consolidated Inc.; *Int'l*, pg. 20

BRIDGEWATER RESOURCES CORPORATION; *U.S. Private*, pg. 168

BRIDGEWAY HOSPITAL—See Universal Health Services, Inc.; *U.S. Public*, pg. 1696

BRIDGFORD DISTRIBUTING CO.—See Bridgford Foods Corporation; *U.S. Public*, pg. 252

BRIDGFORD FOODS CORPORATION; *U.S. Public*, pg. 252

BRIDGFORD FOODS OF ILLINOIS—See Bridgford Foods Corporation; *U.S. Public*, pg. 252

BRIDGFORD FROZEN-RITE FOODS—See Bridgford Foods Corporation; *U.S. Public*, pg. 252

BRIDON AMERICAN CORP.—See Bridon PLC; *Int'l*, pg. 215

BRIDON CORDAGE INC.—See Bridon PLC; *Int'l*, pg. 215

BRIDON PLC; *Int'l*, pg. 215

BRIDPORT AVIATION PRODUCTS—See Bridport-Gundry p.l.c.; *Int'l*, pg. 215

BRIDPORT-GRUNDY MARINE—See Bridport-Gundry p.l.c.; *Int'l*, pg. 215

BRIDPORT-GRUNDY NETTING LIMITED—See Bridport-Gundry p.l.c.; *Int'l*, pg. 215

BRIDPORT-GUNDRY LTD. (U.K.)—See Bridport-Gundry p.l.c.; *Int'l*, pg. 215

BRIDPORT-GUNDRY P.L.C.; *Int'l*, pg. 215

BRIERLEY & PARTNERS; *U.S. Private*, pg. 168

BRIERLEY & PARTNERS—See Brierley & Partners; *U.S. Private*, pg. 168

BRIERLEY INVESTMENTS LIMITED; *Int'l*, pg. 215

BRIERLEY INVESTMENTS LTD.—See Brierley Investments Limited; *Int'l*, pg. 215

BRIGADIER HOMES OF NORTH CAROLINA—See Cavalier Homes, Inc.; *U.S. Public*, pg. 318

BRIGGS & STRATTON AUSTRALIA PTY. LIMITED—See Briggs & Stratton Corporation; *U.S. Public*, pg. 252

BRIGGS & STRATTON CANADA INC.—See Briggs & Stratton Corporation; *U.S. Public*, pg. 252

BRIGGS & STRATTON CORPORATION; *U.S. Public*, pg. 252

BRIGGS & STRATTON FRANCE S.A.R.L.—See Briggs & Stratton Corporation; *U.S. Public*, pg. 252

BRIGGS & STRATTON GERMANY—See Briggs & Stratton Corporation; *U.S. Public*, pg. 252

BRIGGS & STRATTON INTERNATIONAL SALES—See Briggs & Stratton Corporation; *U.S. Public*, pg. 252

BRIGGS & STRATTON NEW ZEALAND LIMITED—See Briggs & Stratton Corporation; *U.S. Public*, pg. 252

BRIGGS & STRATTON U.K. LIMITED—See Briggs & Stratton Corporation; *U.S. Public*, pg. 252

BRIGGS INDUSTRIES, INC.; *U.S. Private*, pg. 168

BRIGGS & STRATTON MEXICO S.A. DE C.V.—See Briggs & Stratton Corporation; *U.S. Public*, pg. 252

BRIGGS WEAVER VINSON—See Sammons Enterprises, Inc.; *U.S. Private*, pg. 963

WM. BRIGGS & CO. LIMITED—See Coats Viyella plc; *Int'l*, pg. 299

BRIGHAM'S, INC.—See Grotech Capital Group, Inc.; *U.S. Private*, pg. 483

BRIGHT NATIONAL BANK—See First Financial Bancorp; *U.S. Public*, pg. 633

BRIGHT OF AMERICA, INC.—See Russ Berrie and Company, Inc.; *U.S. Public*, pg. 223

BRIGHT STAR INDUSTRIES, INC.—See Publicker Industries Inc.; *U.S. Public*, pg. 1341

BRIGHT STAR TECHNOLOGY, INC.—See Cendant Corporation; *U.S. Public*, pg. 321

BRIGHTON COMMUNICATION CORP.—See Lynch Corporation; *U.S. Public*, pg. 1021

BRIGHTON CORPORATION—See Haseko Corporation; *Int'l*, pg. 600

BRIGHT'S & MARTIN'S FOODS—See Diageo Plc; *Int'l*, pg. 411

BRIGHTWARE, INC.; *U.S. Private*, pg. 168

BRIKER SA—See Castorama Dubois Investissements S.C.A.; *Int'l*, pg. 275

BRIKO DEPOT SA—See GIB Group; *Int'l*, pg. 533

BRIKO DEPOT AG—See Emess PLC; *Int'l*, pg. 453

BRILLIANT LIGHTING (AUSTRALIA)—See Emess PLC; *Int'l*, pg. 453

BRILLION IRON WORKS, INC.—See Johnstown America Industries; *U.S. Public*, pg. 933

BRIM HEALTH CARE—See Brim, Inc.; *U.S. Private*, pg. 168

BRIM HEALTHCARE—See Brim, Inc.; *U.S. Private*, pg. 168

BRIM, INC.; *U.S. Private*, pg. 168

BRIMA MINERALOL-VERTRIEBS-UNION GMBH—See Veba AG; *Int'l*, pg. 1457

BRIMAX BOOKS LIMITED—See Reed Elsevier plc; *Int'l*, pg. 1093

BRIMMS INC.; *U.S. Private*, pg. 169

BRINER PAINT MANUFACTURING CO., INC.—See RPM, Inc.; *U.S. Public*, pg. 1358

BRINK ELECTRIC CONSTRUCTION COMPANY; *U.S. Private*, pg. 169

BRINKER INTERNATIONAL, INC.; *U.S. Public*, pg. 253

BRINKMANN INSTRUMENTS (CANADA) LTD.—See Brinkmann Instruments, Inc.; *U.S. Private*, pg. 169

BRINKMANN INSTRUMENTS, INC.; *U.S. Private*, pg. 169

BRINKS-ALLIED—See Arnotts plc; *Int'l*, pg. 81

BRINK'S HOME SECURITY, INC.—See The Pittston Company; *U.S. Public*, pg. 1305

BRINK'S, INC.—See The Pittston Company; *U.S. Public*, pg. 1305

BRINKS-NEDLLOYD V.O.F.—See Royal Nedlloyd Group N.V.; *Int'l*, pg. 1144

BRIOLE S.A.—See Velcro Industries N.V.; *Int'l*, pg. 1462

BRISA BRIDGESTONE SABANCI LASTIK SANAYI VE TICARET A.S.—See Bridgestone Corporation; *Int'l*, pg. 213

BRISA BRIDGESTONE SABANCI LASTIK SANAYI VE TICARET A.S.—See Sabanci Holding A.S.; *Int'l*, pg. 1167

BRISBANE BREWERY—See Foster's Brewing Group Limited; *Int'l*, pg. 501

BRISBANE DIRECTORY OF CORPORATE AFFILIATIONS
Company Index

BRISBANE MARKET MILL—See The Broken Hill Proprietary Company Limited; Int'l, pg. 227
FRANK BRISCOE CO. INC.; U.S. Private, pg. 169
R.T. BRISCOE (NIGERIA) PLC—See The East Asiatic Company Ltd. A/S; Int'l, pg. 431
BRISTER PHARMACY, INC.—See Integrated Health Services, Inc.; U.S. Public, pg. 884
BRISTER'S MEDICAL ASSOCIATES, INC.—See Integrated Health Services, Inc.; U.S. Public, pg. 884
BRISTILE CLAY TILES, LTD.; Int'l, pg. 216
BRISTOL—See National Westminster Bank PLC; Int'l, pg. 910
BRISTOL AEROSPACE LIMITED—See Magellan Aerospace Corporation; Int'l, pg. 829
BRISTOL AEROSPACE LTD.—See Rolls-Royce plc; Int'l, pg. 1127
BRISTOL & WARREN GAS COMPANY—See Valley Resources, Inc.; U.S. Public, pg. 1706
BRISTOL & WEST BUILDING SOCIETY; Int'l, pg. 216
BRISTOL BABCOCK CANADA—See FKI Plc; Int'l, pg. 473
BRISTOL BABCOCK, INC.—See FKI Plc; Int'l, pg. 472
BRISTOL-BABCOCK LTD.—See FKI Plc; Int'l, pg. 474
BRISTOL BREWERY—See Scottish & Newcastle plc; Int'l, pg. 1212
BRISTOL COMPRESSORS, INC.—See York International Corporation; U.S. Public, pg. 1788
BRISTOL CONCRETE PRODS. CORP.—See Marley PLC; Int'l, pg. 843
BRISTOL EUROPE S.P.A.—See Bristol-Myers Squibb Company; U.S. Public, pg. 255
BRISTOL FARMACEUTICA, S.A.—See Bristol-Myers Squibb Company; U.S. Public, pg. 255
BRISTOL HELLAS A.E.B.E.—See Bristol-Myers Squibb Company; U.S. Public, pg. 255
BRISTOL HOTELS & RESORTS; U.S. Public, pg. 253
BRISTOL INDUSTRIES; U.S. Private, pg. 169
BRISTOL INSTRUMENTS DIV.—See FKI Plc; Int'l, pg. 472
BRISTOL ITALIANA (SUD), S.P.A.—See Bristol-Myers Squibb Company; U.S. Public, pg. 255
BRISTOL LABORATORIES INTERNATIONAL, S.A.—See Bristol-Myers Squibb Company; U.S. Public, pg. 255
BRISTOL LABORATORIES (PHILIPPINES), INC.—See Bristol-Myers Squibb Company; U.S. Public, pg. 255
BRISTOL LINGERIE—See House of Ronnie, Inc.; U.S. Private, pg. 542
BRISTOL METALS, L.P.—See Synalloy Corporation; U.S. Public, pg. 1548
BRISTOL MOTOR SPEEDWAY—See Speedway Motorsports, Inc.; U.S. Public, pg. 1498
BRISTOL-MYERS AB—See Bristol-Myers Squibb Company; U.S. Public, pg. 255
BRISTOL MYERS BARCELONETA INC.—See Bristol-Myers Squibb Company; U.S. Public, pg. 254
BRISTOL-MYERS BELGIUM S.A, N.V.—See Bristol-Myers Squibb Company; U.S. Public, pg. 255
BRISTOL-MYERS B.V.—See Bristol-Myers Squibb Company; U.S. Public, pg. 255
BRISTOL-MYERS COMPANY LIMITED—See Bristol-Myers Squibb Company; U.S. Public, pg. 255
BRISTOL-MYERS COMPANY PTY. LIMITED—See Bristol-Myers Squibb Company; U.S. Public, pg. 255
BRISTOL-MYERS DE MEXICO, S.A. DE C.V.—See Bristol-Myers Squibb Company; U.S. Public, pg. 255
BRISTOL-MYERS DE VENEZUELA, S.A.—See Bristol-Myers Squibb Company; U.S. Public, pg. 255
BRISTOL-MYERS ECUATORIANA, S.A.—See Bristol-Myers Squibb Company; U.S. Public, pg. 255
BRISTOL-MYERS EQUIBLE CANADA INC.—See Bristol-Myers Squibb Company; U.S. Public, pg. 255
OY BRISTOL-MYERS (FINLAND) AB—See Bristol-Myers Squibb Company; U.S. Public, pg. 255
BRISTOL-MYERS G.M.B.H.—See Bristol-Myers Squibb Company; U.S. Public, pg. 255
BRISTOL-MYERS HEALTH CARE GROUP—See Bristol-Myers Squibb Company; U.S. Public, pg. 253
BRISTOL-MYERS (HONG KONG) LIMITED—See Bristol-Myers Squibb Company; U.S. Public, pg. 255
P.T. BRISTOL-MYERS INDONESIA—See Bristol-Myers Squibb Company; U.S. Public, pg. 255
BRISTOL-MYERS INTERNATIONAL GROUP—See Bristol-Myers Squibb Company; U.S. Public, pg. 254
BRISTOL-MYERS LION LTD.—See Bristol-Myers Squibb Company; U.S. Public, pg. 255
BRISTOL-MYERS (MALAYSIA) SDN. BHD.—See Bristol-Myers Squibb Company; U.S. Public, pg. 255
BRISTOL-MYERS MARKETING SERVICES PTY. LTD.—See Bristol-Myers Squibb Company; U.S. Public, pg. 255
BRISTOL-MYERS (N.Z.) LIMITED—See Bristol-Myers Squibb Company; U.S. Public, pg. 255
BRISTOL-MYERS ONCOLOGY DIVISION—See Bristol-Myers Squibb Company; U.S. Public, pg. 254
BRISTOL-MYERS OVERSEAS FINANCE N.V.—See Bristol-Myers Squibb Company; U.S. Public, pg. 255
BRISTOL-MYERS (PACIFIC) LIMITED—See Bristol-Myers Squibb Company; U.S. Public, pg. 255
BRISTOL-MYERS PERUANA S.A.—See Bristol-Myers Squibb Company; U.S. Public, pg. 255
BRISTOL-MYERS PHARMACEUTICAL RESEARCH & DEVELOPMENT DIVISION—See Bristol-Myers Squibb Company; U.S. Public, pg. 254
BRISTOL-MYERS PRODUCTS—See Bristol-Myers Squibb Company; U.S. Public, pg. 254
BRISTOL-MYERS PRODUCTS S.A.—See Bristol-Myers Squibb Company; U.S. Public, pg. 255
BRISTOL-MYERS RESEARCH—See Bristol-Myers Squibb Company; U.S. Public, pg. 254
BRISTOL-MYERS S.A.—See Bristol-Myers Squibb Company; U.S. Public, pg. 255
BRISTOL-MYERS S.A.E.—See Bristol-Myers Squibb Company; U.S. Public, pg. 255
BRISTOL-MYERS (SINGAPORE) PTE. LTD.—See Bristol-Myers Squibb Company; U.S. Public, pg. 256
BRISTOL-MYERS SQUIBB—See Bristol-Myers Squibb Company; U.S. Public, pg. 256
BRISTOL-MYERS SQUIBB CANADA INC.—See Bristol-Myers Squibb Company; U.S. Public, pg. 256
BRISTOL-MYERS SQUIBB COMPANY; U.S. Public, pg. 253
BRISTOL-MYERS SQUIBB U.S. PHARMACEUTICAL GROUP—See Bristol-Myers Squibb Company; U.S. Public, pg. 255
BRISTOL ORGANICS, LTD.—See Sigma-Aldrich Corporation; U.S. Public, pg. 1472
BRISTOL PHARMACEUTICAL INFORMATION CENTER, S.A.—See Bristol-Myers Squibb Company; U.S. Public, pg. 256
THE BRISTOL PRESS—See Journal Register Company; U.S. Public, pg. 934
BRISTOL STREET MOTORS LIMITED—See Britax International plc; Int'l, pg. 216
BRISTOLIPE DIVISION—See Heywood Williams Group PLC; Int'l, pg. 618
BRITA (USA), INC.—See The Clorox Company; U.S. Public, pg. 387
BRITAINS PETITE INC.—See Harnischfeger Industries, Inc.; U.S. Public, pg. 789
BRITAINS PETITE LTD.—See Harnischfeger Industries, Inc.; U.S. Public, pg. 789
BRITANNIA AIRWAYS LTD.—See The Thomson Corporation; U.S. Public, pg. 1601
BRITANNIA BRANDS (HONG KONG) LTD.—See Danone Group; Int'l, pg. 380
BRITANNIA BRANDS (MALAYSIA) SON BHD—See Danone Group; Int'l, pg. 380
BRITANNIA INDUSTRIES LTD.—See Danone Group; Int'l, pg. 380
BRITANNIA MUSIC CO. LTD.—See Philips Electronics N.V.; Int'l, pg. 1052
BRITANNIA REFINED METALS LTD.—See M.I.M. Holdings Ltd.; Int'l, pg. 827
BRITANNIC AVIATION LIMITED—See Bridport-Gundry p.l.c.; Int'l, pg. 215
BRITAX AUTOLEASE B.V.—See Britax International plc; Int'l, pg. 216
BRITAX AUTOZUBEHOR GMBH—See Britax International plc; Int'l, pg. 216
BRITAX-BRYLITE PTY. LTD.—See Britax International plc; Int'l, pg. 216
BRITAX CHILDCARE PRODUCTS PTY.—See Britax International plc; Int'l, pg. 216
BRITAX-EXCELSIOR LIMITED—See Britax International plc; Int'l, pg. 216
BRITAX (GECO) S.A.—See Britax International plc; Int'l, pg. 216
BRITAX INTERNATIONAL PLC; Int'l, pg. 216
BRITAX (P.M.G.) LIMITED—See Britax International plc; Int'l, pg. 216
BRITAX PUERICULTURE S.A.R.L.—See Britax International plc; Int'l, pg. 216
BRITAX VEGA LIMITED—See Britax International plc; Int'l, pg. 216
BRITAX WINGARD LIMITED—See Britax International plc; Int'l, pg. 216
BRITCAIR, LTD.—See Merck & Co., Inc.; U.S. Public, pg. 1091
BRITE HOLDING AG—See Brite Voice Systems, Inc.; U.S. Public, pg. 257
BRITE VOICE SYSTEMS—See Brite Voice Systems, Inc.; U.S. Public, pg. 257
BRITE VOICE SYSTEMS EUROPE—See Brite Voice Systems, Inc.; U.S. Public, pg. 257
BRITE VOICE SYSTEMS GROUP, LTD.—See Brite Voice Systems, Inc.; U.S. Public, pg. 257
BRITE VOICE SYSTEMS, INC.; U.S. Public, pg. 257
BRITE VOICE SYSTEMS, INC.—See Brite Voice Systems, Inc.; U.S. Public, pg. 257
BRITE VUE GLASS SYSTEMS—See Alumax Inc.; U.S. Public, pg. 60
BRITHOL MICHCOMA MOCAMBIQUE LIMITADA—See BASF AG; Int'l, pg. 107
BRITISH AEROSPACE AIRBUS LIMITED—See British Aerospace p.l.c.; Int'l, pg. 217
BRITISH AEROSPACE AUSTRALIA LIMITED—See British Aerospace p.l.c.; Int'l, pg. 218
BRITISH AEROSPACE BNI B.V. - QATAR—See Ballast Nedam NV; Int'l, pg. 134
BRITISH AEROSPACE (CONSULTANCY SERVICES) LIMITED—See British Aerospace p.l.c.; Int'l, pg. 217
BRITISH AEROSPACE DEFENCE LIMITED—See British Aerospace p.l.c.; Int'l, pg. 217
BRITISH AEROSPACE DEFENCE LIMITED (DYNAMICS)—See British Aerospace p.l.c.; Int'l, pg. 217
BRITISH AEROSPACE DEFENCE LIMITED (MILITARY AIRCRAFT)—See British Aerospace p.l.c.; Int'l, pg. 217
BRITISH AEROSPACE DEFENCE LIMITED (ROYAL ORDNANCE)—See British Aerospace p.l.c.; Int'l, pg. 217
BRITISH AEROSPACE DEFENCE LIMITED (SYSTEMS & SERVICES)—See British Aerospace p.l.c.; Int'l, pg. 217
BRITISH AEROSPACE FLYING COLLEGE LTD.—See British Aerospace p.l.c.; Int'l, pg. 217
BRITISH AEROSPACE HOLDINGS INC.—See British Aerospace p.l.c.; Int'l, pg. 218
BRITISH AEROSPACE (LIVERPOOL AIRPORT) LIMITED—See British Aerospace p.l.c.; Int'l, pg. 217
BRITISH AEROSPACE P.L.C.; Int'l, pg. 217
BRITISH AEROSPACE REGIONAL AIRCRAFT, AVRO INTL. AEROSPACE DIV.—See British Aerospace p.l.c.; Int'l, pg. 218
BRITISH AEROSPACE REGIONAL AIRCRAFT LIMITED—See British Aerospace p.l.c.; Int'l, pg. 218
BRITISH AEROSPACE (SYSTEMS AND EQUIPMENT) LTD.—See British Aerospace p.l.c.; Int'l, pg. 217
BRITISH AIRWAYS—See British Airways PLC; Int'l, pg. 219
BRITISH AIRWAYS CARGO—See British Airways PLC; Int'l, pg. 219
BRITISH AIRWAYS HOLIDAYS LTD.—See British Airways PLC; Int'l, pg. 219
BRITISH AIRWAYS PLC; Int'l, pg. 218
BRITISH ALCAN ALUMINIUM PLC—See Alcan Aluminium Limited; Int'l, pg. 51
BRITISH ALCAN BUILDING PRODUCTS LTD.—See Alcan Aluminium Limited; Int'l, pg. 51
BRITISH ALCAN ROLLED PRODUCTS LIMITED—See Alcan Aluminium Limited; Int'l, pg. 51
BRITISH AMERICAN OFFSHORE LIMITED—See Rowan Companies, Inc.; U.S. Public, pg. 1410
BRITISH-AMERICAN TOBACCO CO. (BARBADOS) LTD.—See B.A.T Industries P.L.C.; Int'l, pg. 111
BRITISH AMERICAN TOBACCO CO. (HONG KONG) LTD.—See B.A.T Industries P.L.C.; Int'l, pg. 111
BRITISH-AMERICAN TOBACCO CO. LTD.—See B.A.T Industries P.L.C.; Int'l, pg. 111
BRITISH-AMERICAN TOBACCO CO. (SINGAPORE) LTD.—See B.A.T Industries P.L.C.; Int'l, pg. 111
BRITISH-AMERICAN TOBACCO (GERMANY) GMBH—See B.A.T Industries P.L.C.; Int'l, pg. 111
BRITISH & SOVIET INTERNATIONAL CARBON LIMITED—See Morgan Crucible Co. Plc; Int'l, pg. 894
BRITISH ARAB COMMERCIAL BANK LTD.—See HSBC Holdings plc; Int'l, pg. 579
BRITISH BAKERIES LIMITED—See Tomkins PLC; Int'l, pg. 1396
BRITISH BAKERIES (MIDLANDS) LIMITED—See Tomkins PLC; Int'l, pg. 1396
BRITISH BAKERIES (SCOTLAND) LIMITED—See Tomkins PLC; Int'l, pg. 1396
THE BRITISH BANK OF THE MIDDLE EAST—See HSBC Holdings plc; Int'l, pg. 579
BRITISH BUILDING & ENGINEERING APPLIANCES PLC; Int'l, pg. 219
BRITISH CAR AUCTION GROUP—See Tyco International Ltd.; U.S. Public, pg. 1649
BRITISH CARIBBEAN INSURANCE COMPANY LIMITED—See The Bank of Nova Scotia; Int'l, pg. 156
BRITISH CHROME & CHEMICALS LTD.—See Harrisons & Crosfield plc; Int'l, pg. 598
BRITISH COLUMBIA PACKERS LIMITED—See George Weston Limited; Int'l, pg. 1495
BRITISH DREDGING AGGREGATES LIMITED—See RMC Group p.l.c.; Int'l, pg. 1081
BRITISH ELECTRICAL REPAIRS LTD.—See Delta plc; Int'l, pg. 390
BRITISH EUROPEAN ASSOCIATED PUBLISHERS LTD.—See VNU Verenigde Nederlandse Uitgeversbedrijven B.V.; Int'l, pg. 1445
BRITISH FERMENTATION PRODUCTS LTD.—See Royal Gist-Brocades N.V.; Int'l, pg. 1143
BRITISH FILM INSTITUTE; Int'l, pg. 219
BRITISH GAS ENERGY CENTRES LTD.—See Centrica Plc; Int'l, pg. 279
BRITISH GAS SERVICES LTD.—See Centrica Plc; Int'l, pg. 279
BRITISH GAS TRADING LTD.—See Centrica Plc; Int'l, pg. 279
BRITISH GYPSUM LTD.—See BPB Industries PLC; Int'l, pg. 122
BRITISH INDUSTRIAL SAND SA—See Hepworth Plc; Int'l, pg. 615
THE BRITISH LAND COMPANY PLC; Int'l, pg. 219
THE BRITISH LAND CORPORATION LIMITED—See The British Land Company PLC; Int'l, pg. 219
BRITISH LAND INVESTMENTS N.V.—See The British Land Company PLC; Int'l, pg. 219
BRITISH MOHAIR HOLDINGS PLC; Int'l, pg. 219
BRITISH MOHAIR SPINNERS LIMITED—See British Mohair Holdings Plc; Int'l, pg. 219
BRITISH PEPPER & SPICE CO. LTD.—See Burns, Philp & Company Limited; Int'l, pg. 236
THE BRITISH PETROLEUM COMPANY P.L.C.; Int'l, pg. 219
BRITISH PHARMACEUTICALS PTY. LTD.—See Akzo Nobel N.V.; Int'l, pg. 44
BRITISH PIPELINE AGENCY—See Royal Dutch/Shell Group of Companies; Int'l, pg. 1139
BRITISH PRINTING COMPANY LTD.; Int'l, pg. 220
BRITISH RAILWAYS BOARD; Int'l, pg. 220
BRITISH RESERVE—See Allianz Aktiengesellschaft; Int'l, pg. 61
BRITISH SALT—See Staveley Industries PLC; Int'l, pg. 1298
BRITISH STEEL CANADA INC.—See British Steel Plc; Int'l, pg. 222
BRITISH STEEL ENGINEERING—See British Steel Plc; Int'l, pg. 220
BRITISH STEEL GENERAL STEELS DIVISION—See British Steel Plc; Int'l, pg. 220
BRITISH STEEL, INC.—See British Steel Plc; Int'l, pg. 221
BRITISH STEEL PLC; Int'l, pg. 220
BRITISH STEEL SEAMLESS TUBES—See British Steel Plc; Int'l, pg. 221
BRITISH STEEL SEAMLESS TUBES-WEDNESFIELD WORKS—See British Steel Plc; Int'l, pg. 220
BRITISH STEEL SERVICE CENTRES LTD.—See British Steel Plc; Int'l, pg. 221
BRITISH STEEL TUBES & PIPES—See British Steel Plc; Int'l, pg. 221
BRITISH STERILIZER LTD.—See Getinge Industrier AB; Int'l, pg. 551
BRITISH SUGAR PLC—See Associated British Foods plc; Int'l, pg. 92
BRITISH TELECOM TYMNET—See British Telecommunications plc; Int'l, pg. 223
BRITISH TELECOMMUNICATIONS PLC; Int'l, pg. 222
BRITISH TIMKEN DIV.—See The Timken Company; U.S. Public, pg. 1617
BRITISH TISSUES LIMITED—See Fort James Corporation; U.S. Public, pg. 672
BRITISH TRIMMINGS LTD.—See Conso Products Company; U.S. Public, pg. 434

BRITISH UNITED TURKEYS LTD.—See Merck & Co., Inc.; U.S. Public, pg. 1091
THE BRITISH VAN HEUSEN COMPANY LIMITED—See Coats Viyella plc; Int'l, pg. 299
BRITOOL LTD.—See Groupe Strafor Facom; Int'l, pg. 570
BRITRAIL TRAVEL INTERNATIONAL INC.—See SNCF; Int'l, pg. 1165
BRITT INDUSTRIES, INC.—See Kurdziel Industries, Inc.; U.S. Private, pg. 637
BRITTANY CORPORATION; U.S. Private, pg. 169
BRITTANY DYEING & PRINTING CORPORATION; U.S. Private, pg. 170
BRITTANY HOLDINGS LTD.—See Petrofina S.A.; Int'l, pg. 1044
BRITTON OPERATION—See Sheldahl, Inc.; U.S. Public, pg. 1465
BRITVIC SOFT DRINKS LTD.—See Whitbread PLC; Int'l, pg. 1499
BROAD NATIONAL BANCORPORATION; U.S. Public, pg. 257
BROAD NATIONAL BANK—See Broad National Bancorporation; U.S. Public, pg. 257
BROAD NATIONAL BANK-BAYWAY—See Broad National Bancorporation; U.S. Public, pg. 257
BROAD NATIONAL BANK-EAST ORANGE—See Broad National Bancorporation; U.S. Public, pg. 257
BROAD NATIONAL BANK-ELIZABETH—See Broad National Bancorporation; U.S. Public, pg. 257
BROAD NATIONAL BANK-IRONBOUND—See Broad National Bancorporation; U.S. Public, pg. 257
BROAD NATIONAL BANK-JACKSON—See Broad National Bancorporation; U.S. Public, pg. 258
BROAD NATIONAL BANK-LIVINGSTON—See Broad National Bancorporation; U.S. Public, pg. 258
BROAD NATIONAL BANK-MILLBURN—See Broad National Bancorporation; U.S. Public, pg. 258
BROAD NATIONAL BANK-NORTH ARLINGTON—See Broad National Bancorporation; U.S. Public, pg. 258
BROAD NATIONAL BANK-NORTH NEWARK—See Broad National Bancorporation; U.S. Public, pg. 258
BROAD NATIONAL BANK-PERTH AMBOY—See Broad National Bancorporation; U.S. Public, pg. 258
BROAD NATIONAL BANK-PRUDENTIAL PLAZA—See Broad National Bancorporation; U.S. Public, pg. 258
BROAD NATIONAL REALTY CORPORATION—See Broad National Bancorporation; U.S. Public, pg. 258
BROAD RACK STRUCTURES—See Broad, Vogt & Conant, Inc.; U.S. Private, pg. 170
BROAD STEEL CONSTRUCTION-MEXICO OPERATIONS OFFICE—See Broad, Vogt & Conant, Inc.; U.S. Private, pg. 170
BROAD, VOGT & CONANT, INC.; U.S. Private, pg. 170
BROAD, VOGT & CONANT S.W., INC.—See Broad, Vogt & Conant, Inc.; U.S. Private, pg. 170
BROADBAND BUSINESS UNIT—See Telco Systems, Inc.; U.S. Public, pg. 1568
BROADBAND CONNECTIVITY GROUP—See ADC Telecommunications, Inc.; U.S. Public, pg. 4
BROADBAND NETWORKS GROUP—See General Instrument Corporation; U.S. Public, pg. 716
BROADCAST AND VIDEO ENTERPRISES INC.—See Landmark Communications, Inc.; U.S. Private, pg. 647
BROADCAST ELECTRONICS, INC.—See Hoak Capital; U.S. Private, pg. 531
BROADCAST OPERATIONS & ENGINEERING—See The Walt Disney Company; U.S. Public, pg. 511
BROADCAST PROGRAMMING—See Hoak Capital; U.S. Private, pg. 531
BROADCAST SUPPLY WORLDWIDE, INC.; U.S. Private, pg. 170
BROADCASTING DATASERVICES LTD.—See BBC Magazines; Int'l, pg. 114
BROADCOM EIREANN RESEARCH LTD.—See Telefonaktiebolaget LM Ericsson; Int'l, pg. 1365
BROADCORT CAPITAL CORP.—See Merrill Lynch & Co., Inc.; U.S. Public, pg. 1097
BROADHURST ENVIRONMENTAL, INC.—See Republic Industries, Inc.; U.S. Public, pg. 1379
BROADMOOR HOTEL, INC.; U.S. Private, pg. 170
BROADTEX LTD.—See Freudenberg & Company; Int'l, pg. 507
BROADVISION, INC.; U.S. Public, pg. 258
BROADWAY & SEYMOUR, INC.; U.S. Public, pg. 258
BROADWAY CHEVROLET; U.S. Private, pg. 170
BROAN LIMITED—See Nortek, Inc.; U.S. Public, pg. 1194
BROAN MFG. CO., INC.—See Nortek, Inc.; U.S. Public, pg. 1193
BROCK COMMUNICATIONS, INC.—See Peoples Telephone Company, Inc.; U.S. Public, pg. 1275
BROCK EXPLORATION CORPORATION—See Key Production Company, Inc.; U.S. Public, pg. 953
BROCK INTERNATIONAL INC.; U.S. Public, pg. 258
M.J. BROCK & SONS, INC.—See The Ryland Group, Inc.; U.S. Public, pg. 1414
BROCK MANUFACTURING—See CTB International Corp.; U.S. Public, pg. 285
BROCK TELECOM LIMITED—See Northern Telecom Limited; Int'l, pg. 969
GEORGE F. BROCKE & SONS, INC.; U.S. Private, pg. 170
BROCKHOUSE C & F MACHINING LIMITED—See EIP Group plc; Int'l, pg. 426
BROCKHOUSE CANADA LIMITED—See EIP Group plc; Int'l, pg. 426
BROCKHOUSE FORGINGS LIMITED—See EIP Group plc; Int'l, pg. 426
BROCKHOUSE MODERNFOLD LIMITED—See EIP Group plc; Int'l, pg. 426
BROCKMORE LIMITED—See Avonmore Waterford Group plc; Int'l, pg. 102
BROCKWAY STANDARD INC.—See BWAY Corp.; U.S. Public, pg. 164
BROCKWAY STANDARD OHIO, INC.—See BWAY Corp.; U.S. Public, pg. 164

BRODARD ET TAUPIN—See Lagardere Groupe; Int'l, pg. 792
BRODARD GRAPHIQUE SNC—See Lagardere Groupe; Int'l, pg. 792
BRODART—See Brodart Company; U.S. Private, pg. 170
BRODART COMPANY; U.S. Private, pg. 170
BRODART SALES CO.—See Brodart Company; U.S. Private, pg. 170
BRODER BROS. CO.; U.S. Private, pg. 170
BRODER BROS. CO. OF ALBANY—See Broder Bros. Co.; U.S. Private, pg. 171
BRODER BROS. CO. OF DALLAS—See Broder Bros. Co.; U.S. Private, pg. 171
BRODER BROS. CO. OF FLORIDA, INC.—See Broder Bros. Co.; U.S. Private, pg. 171
BRODERBUND SOFTWARE, INC.; U.S. Public, pg. 258
BRODERICK & BASCOM ROPE CO.—See Amsted Industries Incorporated; U.S. Private, pg. 68
BRODERNA BERNER HAB—See Berner Ltd.; Int'l, pg. 189
BRODERNA EDSTRAND AB—See Trelleborg AB; Int'l, pg. 1422
BRODRENE BOCKMANN A/S—See Saint-Gobain; Int'l, pg. 1172
BRODRENE DAHL A/S—See Dahl International AB; Int'l, pg. 359
BRODY CO. DIV.—See Lancaster Colony Corporation; U.S. Public, pg. 976
BROE COMPANIES; U.S. Private, pg. 171
BROEX, S.A.—See Borden, Inc.; U.S. Private, pg. 159
BROILMASTER DIVISION—See Martin Industries, Inc. (AL); U.S. Private, pg. 709
WILLIAM BROJACK LUMBER COMPANY; U.S. Private, pg. 171
BROKEN BOW GAS CO.—See Energy West Inc.; U.S. Public, pg. 581
THE BROKEN HILL PROPRIETARY COMPANY LIMITED; Int'l, pg. 223
BROMAR INC.; U.S. Private, pg. 171
BROMLEY, AGUILAR & ASSOCIATES—See The MacManus Group, Inc.; U.S. Private, pg. 692
BRONATOREO—See Broad National Bancorporation; U.S. Public, pg. 258
BRONBORGER & KESSLER HANDELSGESELLSCHAFT GMBH—See ENI S.p.A.; Int'l, pg. 428
BRONNER SLOSBERG HUMPHREY/STRATEGIC INTERACTIVE GROUP; U.S. Private, pg. 1277
BRONSON SPECIALTIES, INC.—See Solvay S.A.; Int'l, pg. 1277
BRONTO SKYLIFT OY AB—See Federal Signal Corporation; U.S. Public, pg. 617
THE BRONX ENGINEERING COMPANY LIMITED—See MetalTech International PLC; Int'l, pg. 862
BRONZE HEADQUARTERS—See Bearing Headquarters Co.; U.S. Private, pg. 127
BROOKDALE RESORTS, INC.—See Starwood Hotels & Resorts; U.S. Public, pg. 1512
BROOKE CUTTING TOOLS LTD.—See Brooke Industrial Holdings Plc; Int'l, pg. 228
BROOKE GROUP LTD.; U.S. Public, pg. 259
BROOKE INDUSTRIAL HOLDINGS PLC; Int'l, pg. 228
BROOKES & GATEHOUSE, LTD.—See Vector Industries, Ltd.; Int'l, pg. 1461
BROOKFIELD ENGINEERING LABORATORIES, INC.; U.S. Private, pg. 171
BROOKFIELD HOMES—See Brookfield Properties Corporation; Int'l, pg. 228
BROOKFIELD HOMES CALIFORNIA INC.—See Brookfield Properties Corporation; Int'l, pg. 228
BROOKFIELD HOMES LTD.—See Brookfield Properties Corporation; Int'l, pg. 228
BROOKFIELD HOMES-ORANGE COUNTY—See Brookfield Properties Corporation; Int'l, pg. 228
BROOKFIELD HOMES PARTNERS—See Brookfield Properties Corporation; Int'l, pg. 228
BROOKFIELD HOMES-SAN FRANCISCO—See Brookfield Properties Corporation; Int'l, pg. 228
BROOKFIELD HOMES-WESTERN REGION—See Brookfield Properties Corporation; Int'l, pg. 228
BROOKFIELD PROPERTIES CORPORATION; Int'l, pg. 228
BROCKHOLLOW CORP.—See Texas Industries, Inc.; U.S. Public, pg. 1585
BROOKHOLLOW OF VIRGINIA, INC.—See Texas Industries, Inc.; U.S. Public, pg. 1585
BROOKHURST, INC.; U.S. Private, pg. 171
BROOKLINE SAVINGS BANK; U.S. Private, pg. 171
BROOKLYN BOTTLING CO. OF MILTON, NY; U.S. Private, pg. 171
BROOKLYN INTERSTATE—See Brooklyn Union; U.S. Public, pg. 259
BROOKLYN UNION; U.S. Public, pg. 259
BROOKLYNS LIMITED—See Tarmac plc; Int'l, pg. 1355
BROOKS BEVERAGE MANAGEMENT, INC.—See Beverage America, Inc.; U.S. Private, pg. 142
BROOKS BROTHERS—See Marks & Spencer PLC; Int'l, pg. 843
BROOKS/COLE PUBLISHING CO.—See The Thomson Corporation; U.S. Public, pg. 1600
BROOKS COUNTY SAUSAGE—See Smithfield Foods, Inc.; U.S. Public, pg. 1479
E.J. BROOKS—See E.J. Brooks Company; U.S. Private, pg. 172
E.J. BROOKS COMPANY; U.S. Private, pg. 172
E.J. BROOKS EUROPE LTD.—See E.J. Brooks Company; U.S. Private, pg. 172
E.J. BROOKS INDUSTRIES, LTD.—See E.J. Brooks Company; U.S. Private, pg. 172
BROOKS FOODS—See Pro-Fac Cooperative, Inc.; U.S. Private, pg. 887
BROOKS INSTRUMENT—See Emerson Electric Co.; U.S. Public, pg. 574
BROOKS INSTRUMENT B.V.—See Emerson Electric Co.; U.S. Public, pg. 576

BROOKS INSTRUMENT (CANADA)—See Emerson Electric Co.; U.S. Public, pg. 576
BROOKS INSTRUMENT (GERMANY)—See Emerson Electric Co.; U.S. Public, pg. 576
BROOKS INSTRUMENT (JAPAN)—See Emerson Electric Co.; U.S. Public, pg. 576
BROOKS, MONTAGUE & ASSOCIATES, INC.—See National Commerce Bancorporation; U.S. Public, pg. 1155
BROOKS PROVISIONS INC.; U.S. Private, pg. 172
BROOKS RESOURCES CORPORATION; U.S. Private, pg. 172
BROOKS RESOURCES SALES CORP.—See Brooks Resources Corporation; U.S. Private, pg. 172
BROOKS-SELLOS DA SEGURANCA DO BRAZIL LTDA—See E.J. Brooks Company; U.S. Private, pg. 172
BROOKS-SHETTLE CO.—See Avemco Corporation; U.S. Public, pg. 152
BROOKS TECHNOLOGY—See Premier Farnell plc; Int'l, pg. 1068
BROOKS-TODO—See E.J. Brooks Company; U.S. Private, pg. 172
BROOKSHIRE BROS., LTD.; U.S. Private, pg. 172
BROOKSHIRE GROCERY; U.S. Private, pg. 172
BROOKSTONE COMPANY, INC.; U.S. Public, pg. 259
BROOKSVILLE PRIMARY CARE CLINIC, INC.—See Integrated Health Services, Inc.; U.S. Public, pg. 884
BROOKTREE ASIA PACIFIC—See Rockwell International Corporation; U.S. Public, pg. 1398
BROOKTREE CENTRAL EUROPE—See Rockwell International Corporation; U.S. Public, pg. 1398
BROOKTREE LTD.—See Rockwell International Corporation; U.S. Public, pg. 1398
BROOKTREE PTE.—See Rockwell International Corporation; U.S. Public, pg. 1398
BROOKTREE ROCKWELL SEMICONDUCTOR SYSTEMS DIV.—See Rockwell International Corporation; U.S. Public, pg. 1398
BROOKVILLE TELEPHONE COMPANY—See ALLTEL Corporation; U.S. Public, pg. 56
BROOKWOOD COMPANIES INC.—See The Hallwood Group Incorporated; U.S. Private, pg. 777
BROSSARD—See Sara Lee Corporation; U.S. Public, pg. 1435
BROSSETTE BTI SA—See Wolseley Plc.; Int'l, pg. 1511
BROTHER CORPORATION (ASIA) LTD.—See Brother Industries, Ltd.; Int'l, pg. 229
BROTHER FINANCE (NETHERLANDS) B.V.—See Brother Industries, Ltd.; Int'l, pg. 229
BROTHER FINANCE (U.K.) PLC—See Brother Industries, Ltd.; Int'l, pg. 229
BROTHER FRANCE S.A.—See Brother Industries, Ltd.; Int'l, pg. 229
BROTHER HOLDING (EUROPE)—See Brother Industries, Ltd.; Int'l, pg. 229
BROTHER INDUSTRIAL ESPANA S.A.—See Brother Industries, Ltd.; Int'l, pg. 229
BROTHER INDUSTRIAL SEWING MACHINES DIV.—See Brother Industries, Ltd.; Int'l, pg. 229
BROTHER INDUSTRIES (AUSTRALIA) PTY. LTD.—See Brother Industries, Ltd.; Int'l, pg. 229
BROTHER INDUSTRIES (IRELAND) LTD.—See Brother Industries, Ltd.; Int'l, pg. 229
BROTHER INDUSTRIES (JOHOR) SDN. BHD.—See Brother Industries, Ltd.; Int'l, pg. 229
BROTHER INDUSTRIES, LTD.; Int'l, pg. 229
BROTHER INDUSTRIES TECHNOLOGY (M) SDN. BHD.—See Brother Industries, Ltd.; Int'l, pg. 229
BROTHER INDUSTRIES (U.K.) LTD.-RUABON FACTORY—See Brother Industries, Ltd.; Int'l, pg. 229
BROTHER INDUSTRIES (USA) INC.—See Brother Industries, Ltd.; Int'l, pg. 229
S.A. BROTHER INTERNATIONAL (BELGIUM) N.V.—See Brother Industries, Ltd.; Int'l, pg. 229
BROTHER INTERNATIONAL CORPORATION—See Brother Industries, Ltd.; Int'l, pg. 229
BROTHER INTERNATIONAL CORPORATION (CANADA) LTD.—See Brother Industries, Ltd.; Int'l, pg. 229
BROTHER INTERNATIONAL CORPORATION DO BRAZIL—See Brother Industries, Ltd.; Int'l, pg. 229
BROTHER INTERNATIONAL DE CHILE, LTDA.—See Brother Industries, Ltd.; Int'l, pg. 229
BROTHER INTERNATIONAL DE MEXICO, S.A. DE C.V.—See Brother Industries, Ltd.; Int'l, pg. 229
BROTHER INTERNATIONAL G.M.B.H.—See Brother Industries, Ltd.; Int'l, pg. 229
BROTHER INTERNATIONAL (GULF) CORPORATION—See Brother Industries, Ltd.; Int'l, pg. 229
BROTHER INTERNATIONAL HUNGARY KFT.—See Brother Industries, Ltd.; Int'l, pg. 229
BROTHER INTERNATIONAL MASKINAKTIESELSKAB A/S—See Brother Industries, Ltd.; Int'l, pg. 229
BROTHER INTERNATIONAL (NEDERLAND) B.V.—See Brother Industries, Ltd.; Int'l, pg. 229
BROTHER INTERNATIONAL (NZ) LIMITED—See Brother Industries, Ltd.; Int'l, pg. 229
BROTHER INTERNATIONAL (PORTUGAL) DISTRIBUIDORES DE EQUIPAMENTOS ELECTRICOS LDA.—See Brother Industries, Ltd.; Int'l, pg. 230
BROTHER INTERNATIONAL (SINGAPORE) PTE. LTD.—See Brother Industries, Ltd.; Int'l, pg. 230
BROTHER INTERNATIONAL, S.R.O.—See Brother Industries, Ltd.; Int'l, pg. 230
BROTHER INTERNATIONAL SWEDEN A.B.—See Brother Industries, Ltd.; Int'l, pg. 230
BROTHER INTERNATIONALE INDUSTRIEMASCHINEN G.M.B.H.—See Brother Industries, Ltd.; Int'l, pg. 230
BROTHER MACCHINE INDUSTRIALI S.R.L.—See Brother Industries, Ltd.; Int'l, pg. 230
BROTHER NORGE A.S.—See Brother Industries, Ltd.; Int'l, pg. 230
BROTHER OFFICE EQUIPMENT S.P.A.—See Brother Industries, Ltd.; Int'l, pg. 230

BROTHER (SCHWEIZ) A.G.—See Brother Industries, Ltd.; *Int'l*, pg. 230
BROTHER U.K., LTD.—See Brother Industries, Ltd.; *Int'l*, pg. 230
BROTHERS GOURMET COFFEES, INC.; *U.S. Public*, pg. 259
BROTHERS SALES, LTD.—See Brother Industries, Ltd.; *Int'l*, pg. 229
BROTHERTON CHEMICALS LTD.—See Church & Dwight Co., Inc.; *U.S. Public*, pg. 356
BROUGHER AGENCY, INC.—See Eureko B.V.; *Int'l*, pg. 464
BROUGHTON FOODS COMPANY; *U.S. Public*, pg. 259
BROUGHTON FOODS COMPANY—See Broughton Foods Company; *U.S. Public*, pg. 259
BROWER COMPANY—See Bay Industries Inc.; *U.S. Private*, pg. 124
BROWER EQUIPMENT—See Hawkeye Steel Products, Inc.; *U.S. Private*, pg. 511
BROWER PRODUCTS; *U.S. Private*, pg. 172
ABBOT BROWN & SONS LTD.—See Wolseley Plc.; *Int'l*, pg. 1511
BROWN & BIGELOW, INC.; *U.S. Private*, pg. 172
BROWN & BROWN VENTURE GROUP, LLC; *U.S. Private*, pg. 172
BROWN AND CALDWELL; *U.S. Private*, pg. 173
BROWN & COMPANY SECURITIES CORPORATION—See The Chase Manhattan Corporation; *U.S. Public*, pg. 337
BROWN & HALEY; *U.S. Private*, pg. 173
BROWN & ROOT CIVIL—See Halliburton Company; *U.S. Public*, pg. 775
BROWN & ROOT DEVELOPMENT, INC.—See Halliburton Company; *U.S. Public*, pg. 775
BROWN & ROOT ENERGY SERVICES—See Halliburton Company; *U.S. Public*, pg. 775
BROWN & ROOT ENVIRONMENTAL—See Halliburton Company; *U.S. Public*, pg. 775
BROWN & ROOT INC.—See Halliburton Company; *U.S. Public*, pg. 775
BROWN & ROOT INDUSTRIAL SERVICES—See Halliburton Company; *U.S. Public*, pg. 775
BROWN & ROOT INTERNATIONAL, INC.—See Halliburton Company; *U.S. Public*, pg. 775
BROWN & ROOT LTD.—See Halliburton Company; *U.S. Public*, pg. 776
BROWN & ROOT NEDERLAND B.V.—See Halliburton Company; *U.S. Public*, pg. 776
BROWN & ROOT PETROLEUM AND CHEMICALS—See Halliburton Company; *U.S. Public*, pg. 775
BROWN & ROOT POWER & MFG.—See Halliburton Company; *U.S. Public*, pg. 775
BROWN & ROOT SERVICES CORPORATION—See Halliburton Company; *U.S. Public*, pg. 775
BROWN & ROOT U.S.A. INC.—See Halliburton Company; *U.S. Public*, pg. 775
BROWN & SHARPE INTL. CAPITAL CORP.—See Brown & Sharpe Manufacturing Company; *U.S. Public*, pg. 260
BROWN & SHARPE LIMITED—See Brown & Sharpe Manufacturing Company; *U.S. Public*, pg. 260
BROWN & SHARPE MANUFACTURING COMPANY; *U.S. Public*, pg. 260
BROWN & WILLIAMSON TOBACCO CORP.—See B.A.T Industries P.L.C.; *Int'l*, pg. 111
BROWN & WILLIAMSON TOBACCO CORP.-MACON PLANT—See B.A.T Industries P.L.C.; *Int'l*, pg. 111
BROWN AUTOMOTIVE GROUP; *U.S. Private*, pg. 173
BILL BROWN FORD INC.; *U.S. Private*, pg. 173
BROWN BOVERI IRAN (PRIVATE JOINT STOCK COMPANY)—See ABB Asea Brown Boveri (Holding) Ltd.; *Int'l*, pg. 3
BROWN BOVERI-YORK SUISSE—See ABB Asea Brown Boveri (Holding) Ltd.; *Int'l*, pg. 1
BROWN-BRIDGE—See Lynch Corporation; *U.S. Public*, pg. 1022
BROWN BROTHERS & COMPANY LTD.—See Vickers PLC; *Int'l*, pg. 1466
BROWN BROTHERS HARRIMAN & CO.; *U.S. Private*, pg. 173
BROWN BROTHERS HARRIMAN LIMITED—See Brown Brothers Harriman & Co.; *U.S. Private*, pg. 173
BROWN BROTHERS HARRIMAN TRUSTEE SERVICES (IRELAND) LIMITED—See Brown Brothers Harriman & Co.; *U.S. Private*, pg. 173
BROWN CITY BANNER—See The Walt Disney Company; *U.S. Public*, pg. 513
DONALD BROWN & CO. LTD.—See Pechiney S.A.; *Int'l*, pg. 1030
DONALD BROWN (BROWNALL) LTD.—See Delta plc; *Int'l*, pg. 390
EARLE PALMER BROWN; *U.S. Private*, pg. 173
EARLE PALMER BROWN/BETHESDA—See Earle Palmer Brown; *U.S. Private*, pg. 174
EARLE PALMER BROWN/NEW YORK—See Earle Palmer Brown; *U.S. Private*, pg. 174
EARLE PALMER BROWN PUBLIC RELATIONS—See Earle Palmer Brown; *U.S. Private*, pg. 174
BROWN EVANS DISTRIBUTING CO.; *U.S. Private*, pg. 174
F.M. BROWN SONS, INC.; *U.S. Private*, pg. 174
BROWN-FORMAN BEVERAGES WORLDWIDE—See Brown-Forman Corporation; *U.S. Public*, pg. 261
BROWN-FORMAN CORPORATION; *U.S. Public*, pg. 261
BROWN GROUP, INC.; *U.S. Public*, pg. 262
H.H. BROWN SHOE COMPANY, INC.—See Berkshire Hathaway Inc.; *U.S. Public*, pg. 217
BROWN, HARRIS, STEVENS, INC.; *U.S. Private*, pg. 174
BROWN INDUSTRIES, INC.; *U.S. Private*, pg. 174
J. BROWN & ASSOCIATES MINNEAPOLIS/ST. PAUL—See Grey Advertising Inc.; *U.S. Public*, pg. 764
J. BROWN/LMC GROUP—See Grey Advertising Inc.; *U.S. Public*, pg. 764
JERED BROWN BROTHERS INC.—See Vickers PLC; *Int'l*, pg. 1468

JOHN BROWN/DAVY INTERNATIONAL—See Kvaerner a.s.a.; *Int'l*, pg. 772
JOHN BROWN E & C CORPORATE OFFICES (U.S.)—See Kvaerner a.s.a.; *Int'l*, pg. 774
JOHN BROWN - ENGINEERING & CONSTRUCTION SECTOR—See Kvaerner a.s.a.; *Int'l*, pg. 772
JOHN BROWN ENGINEERING LIMITED—See Kvaerner a.s.a.; *Int'l*, pg. 772
JOHN BROWN, INC.—See Kvaerner a.s.a.; *Int'l*, pg. 774
JOHN BROWN PLASTICS MACHINERY—See Kvaerner a.s.a.; *Int'l*, pg. 773
BROWN JORDAN COMPANY; *U.S. Private*, pg. 174
BROWN MACHINE—See Kvaerner a.s.a.; *Int'l*, pg. 774
BROWN MACHINE DIV.—See Kvaerner a.s.a.; *Int'l*, pg. 773
BROWN MARKETING COMMUNICATIONS; *U.S. Private*, pg. 174
MATHEW BROWN PLC—See Scottish & Newcastle plc; *Int'l*, pg. 1211
BROWN-MINNEAPOLIS TANK & FABRICATING CO.—See ITEQ, Inc.; *U.S. Public*, pg. 914
BROWN MOTORS; *U.S. Private*, pg. 174
OWEN BROWN B DEVELOPMENT CO.—See The Rouse Company; *U.S. Public*, pg. 1409
BROWN PRINTING CENTRAL—See Bertelsmann AG; *Int'l*, pg. 190
BROWN PRINTING CO., INC.—See Bertelsmann AG; *Int'l*, pg. 190
BROWN PRINTING EAST—See Bertelsmann AG; *Int'l*, pg. 190
BROWN RETAIL DEVELOPMENT CO.—See Brown Group, Inc.; *U.S. Public*, pg. 262
R.J. BROWN AMERICA, INC.—See Kvaerner a.s.a.; *Int'l*, pg. 766
R.J. BROWN AND ASSOCIATES CORPORATION AG—See Kvaerner a.s.a.; *Int'l*, pg. 766
R.J. BROWN & ASSOCIATES (UK) LIMITED—See Kvaerner a.s.a.; *Int'l*, pg. 772
BROWN-SERVICE FUNERAL HOMES CO., INC.—See Torchmark Corporation; *U.S. Public*, pg. 1622
BROWN SHOE COMPANY—See Brown Group, Inc.; *U.S. Public*, pg. 262
BROWN SHOE CO. OF CANADA LTD.—See Brown Group, Inc.; *U.S. Public*, pg. 262
BROWN STEEL DIV.—See Lapham-Hickey Steel Corp.; *U.S. Private*, pg. 651
BROWN-STRAUSS STEEL—See Blue Tee Corporation; *U.S. Private*, pg. 153
TOM BROWN, INC.; *U.S. Public*, pg. 262
BROWN WOOD PRESERVING COMPANY; *U.S. Private*, pg. 174
BROWN WOOTEN/BALLSTON PLANT—See Brown Wooten Mills, Inc.; *U.S. Private*, pg. 175
BROWN WOOTEN MILLS, INC.; *U.S. Private*, pg. 174
E.T. BROWNE DRUG CO., INC.; *U.S. Private*, pg. 175
BROWNFIELD CORRECTION FACILITY—See Corrections Corporation of America; *U.S. Public*, pg. 450
BROWNING CHEMICAL CORPORATION; *U.S. Private*, pg. 175
BROWNING-FERRIS, INC.—See Browning-Ferris Industries, Inc.; *U.S. Public*, pg. 263
BROWNING-FERRIS INDUSTRIES CHEMICAL SERVICES, INC.—See Browning-Ferris Industries, Inc.; *U.S. Public*, pg. 263
BROWNING-FERRIS INDUSTRIES, INC.; *U.S. Public*, pg. 262
BROWNING-FERRIS INDUSTRIES OF FLORIDA, INC.—See Browning-Ferris Industries, Inc.; *U.S. Public*, pg. 263
BROWNING SA—See Herstal S.A.; *Int'l*, pg. 617
BROWNSTONE DEVELOPMENT LABORATORY—See Platinum Technology, Inc.; *U.S. Public*, pg. 1309
THE ANDREW BROWNSWORD COLLECTION—See Hallmark Cards, Inc.; *U.S. Private*, pg. 496
ANDREW BROWNSWORD GIFTS, LTD.—See Hallmark Cards, Inc.; *U.S. Private*, pg. 496
BROWNVILLE POWER COMPANY—See Boise Cascade Corporation; *U.S. Public*, pg. 243
BROYHILL FURNITURE INDUSTRIES, INC.—See Furniture Brands International Inc.; *U.S. Public*, pg. 688
BRUBAKER TOOL CORP.—See Cincinnati Milacron Inc.; *U.S. Public*, pg. 368
BRUCE FOODS CORP.; *U.S. Private*, pg. 175
BRUCE HARDWOOD FLOORS—See Triangle Pacific Corporation; *U.S. Public*, pg. 1634
BRUCE HARDWOOD FLOORS, LTD.—See Triangle Pacific Corporation; *U.S. Public*, pg. 1634
BRUCE INDUSTRIES, INC.; *U.S. Private*, pg. 175
T. BRUCE SALES, INC.; *U.S. Private*, pg. 175
BRUCKEN-, STRASSEN-UND TIEFBAU GESELLSCHAFT MBH—See Bilfinger + Berger Bauaktiengesellschaft; *Int'l*, pg. 190
BRUCKNER GRUNDBAU GMBH—See Hochtief AG; *Int'l*, pg. 623
BRUCKNER MACHINE & TOOL CORP.; *U.S. Private*, pg. 175
BRUDER KUNZ GES.M.B.H.—See Julius Meinl AG; *Int'l*, pg. 856
M.A. BRUDER & SONS, INCORPORATED; *U.S. Private*, pg. 175
BRUDI, INC.—See Long Reach Holdings Inc.; *U.S. Private*, pg. 675
JAMES BRUDNICK COMPANY—See C.D. Smith Drug Company; *U.S. Private*, pg. 1007
BRUEL & KJAER MEASUREMENTS A/S—See AGIV Group; *Int'l*, pg. 14
M. BRUENGER & CO., INC.; *U.S. Private*, pg. 175
BRUENING BEARINGS, INC.—See Applied Industrial Technologies; *U.S. Public*, pg. 122
BRUENINGHAUS HYDRAULIK GMBH—See Mannesmann A.G.; *Int'l*, pg. 838
BRUENINGHAUS HYDRAULIK GMBH & CO.—See Mannesmann A.G.; *Int'l*, pg. 838
BRUGMAN ADMINISTRATIE EN DISTRIBUTIECENTRUM B.V.—See Vorwerk & Co.; *Int'l*, pg. 1481

BRUGMAN BADKAMERS B.V.—See Vorwerk & Co.; *Int'l*, pg. 1481
BRUGMAN BEHEER B.V.—See Vorwerk & Co.; *Int'l*, pg. 1481
BRUGMAN GMBH & CO.—See Vorwerk & Co.; *Int'l*, pg. 1480
BRUGMAN KEUKENS B.V.—See Vorwerk & Co.; *Int'l*, pg. 1481
BRUGMAN VERWALTUNGS GMBH—See Vorwerk & Co.; *Int'l*, pg. 1480
DICK BRUHN INCORPORATED; *U.S. Private*, pg. 175
BRUIL SPECIALISTISCHE BOUWTECHNIEKEN B.V.—See Ballast Nedam NV; *Int'l*, pg. 134
BRUINSMA SEEDS, B.V.—See Pharmacia & Upjohn, Inc.; *U.S. Public*, pg. 1049
BRUKENS HARDVERKSTADER AB—See Voest-Alpine Stahl AG; *Int'l*, pg. 1471
THE BRULIN CORPORATION; *U.S. Private*, pg. 176
BRUMKO MAGNETICS—See Magnetics Data Inc.; *U.S. Private*, pg. 696
BRUNCOR, INC.; *Int'l*, pg. 230
BRUNEI COLDGAS—See Royal Dutch/Shell Group of Companies; *Int'l*, pg. 1139
BRUNEI LNG—See Royal Dutch/Shell Group of Companies; *Int'l*, pg. 1139
BRUNEI SHELL MARKETING—See Royal Dutch/Shell Group of Companies; *Int'l*, pg. 1139
BRUNEI SHELL PETROLEUM CO SDN BHD—See Royal Dutch/Shell Group of Companies; *Int'l*, pg. 1139
BRUNEL HOLDINGS PLC; *Int'l*, pg. 230
BRUNER-IVORY HANDLE COMPANY—See O.P. Link Handle Company; *U.S. Private*, pg. 669
BRUNER WATER TREATMENT SYSTEMS—See Culligan International Company; *U.S. Public*, pg. 467
BRUNING PAINT COMPANY; *U.S. Private*, pg. 176
BRUNINGHAUS SCHMIEDE GMBH—See Fried. Krupp AG; *Int'l*, pg. 508
DR. CHRISTIAN BRUNNENGRABER CHEMISCHE FABRIK GMBH—See Novartis AG; *Int'l*, pg. 975
BRUNNER & LAY, INC.; *U.S. Private*, pg. 176
BRUNNER ENGINEERING & MANUFACTURING, INC.; *U.S. Private*, pg. 176
BRUNO'S BIRMINGHAM—See Bruno's Inc.; *U.S. Public*, pg. 265
BRUNO'S INC.; *U.S. Public*, pg. 265
BRUNO'S INC.-GEORGIA—See Bruno's Inc.; *U.S. Public*, pg. 265
BRUNSCHWIG & FILS, INC.; *U.S. Private*, pg. 176
BRUNSWICK BICYLES DIV.—See Brunswick Corporation; *U.S. Public*, pg. 265
BRUNSWICK BOWLING & BILLIARDS CORP.—See Brunswick Corporation; *U.S. Public*, pg. 265
BRUNSWICK CORPORATION; *U.S. Public*, pg. 265
BRUNSWICK GMBH—See Brunswick Corporation; *U.S. Public*, pg. 266
BRUNSWICK HAW PAR HOLDINGS PTE LTD.—See Haw Par Brothers International Limited; *Int'l*, pg. 604
BRUNSWICK INDOOR RECREATION GROUP—See Brunswick Corporation; *U.S. Public*, pg. 265
BRUNSWICK INTERNATIONAL (CANADA) LIMITED—See Brunswick Corporation; *U.S. Public*, pg. 266
BRUNSWICK MINING & SMELTING CORP. LTD.—See EdperBrascan Corporation; *Int'l*, pg. 434
BRUNSWICK OUTDOOR RECREATION GROUP—See Brunswick Corporation; *U.S. Public*, pg. 265
BRUNSWICK PLANT—See Cooper Industries, Inc.; *U.S. Public*, pg. 444
BRUNSWICK PULP & PAPER COMPANY—See Georgia-Pacific Corporation; *U.S. Public*, pg. 736
BRUNSWICK SQUARE LTD.—See Bruncor, Inc.; *Int'l*, pg. 230
BRUNTEL HOLDINGS LTD.—See Bruncor, Inc.; *Int'l*, pg. 230
BRUNTONS AREO PRODUCT—See Carclo Engineering Group plc; *Int'l*, pg. 268
BRUSH ELECTRICAL MACHINES LTD.—See BTR plc; *Int'l*, pg. 124
BRUSH RESEARCH MANUFACTURING COMPANY; *U.S. Private*, pg. 176
BRUSH TRANSFORMERS LTD.—See BTR plc; *Int'l*, pg. 124
BRUSH WELLMAN GMBH—See Brush Wellman Inc.; *U.S. Public*, pg. 266
BRUSH WELLMAN INC.; *U.S. Public*, pg. 266
BRUSH WELLMAN (JAPAN) LTD.—See Brush Wellman Inc.; *U.S. Public*, pg. 266
BRUSH WELLMAN LTD.—See Brush Wellman Inc.; *U.S. Public*, pg. 266
BRUTGER EQUITIES, INC.; *U.S. Private*, pg. 176
BRUZA GUSUM VIROR AB—See Scapa Group Plc; *Int'l*, pg. 1202
BRYAN FOODS—See Sara Lee Corporation; *U.S. Public*, pg. 1433
BRYAN METALS, INC.—See Olin Corporation; *U.S. Public*, pg. 1219
BRYAN STEAM CORPORATION; *U.S. Private*, pg. 176
BRYANT ELECTRIC COMPANY, INC.; *U.S. Private*, pg. 176
BRYANT ELECTRIC SUPPLY COMPANY, INC.; *U.S. Private*, pg. 177
BRYANT ELECTRICAL, INC.—See Hubbell Incorporated; *U.S. Public*, pg. 844
BRYANT FINANCIAL CORP.—See Washington Mutual Inc.; *U.S. Public*, pg. 1741
BRYANT, FULTON & SHEE—See The Lowe Group; *U.S. Private*, pg. 678
BRYANT GRINDER CORP.—See Goldman Financial Group; *U.S. Private*, pg. 461
BRYANT MANUFACTURING PTY LIMITED—See Britax International plc; *Int'l*, pg. 217
BRYANT MUNGO DIVISION—See Temperature Equipment Corporation; *U.S. Private*, pg. 1075
BRYANT NURSING CENTER—See Horizon/CMS Healthcare Corporation; *U.S. Public*, pg. 839

BRYANT PARK GRILL—See Ark Restaurants Corp.; *U.S. Public*, pg. 130
BRYANT SUGAR HOUSE—See United States Sugar Corporation; *U.S. Public*, pg. 1126
JOHN BRYCE (GLASGOW) LTD.—See Oracle Corporation; *U.S. Public*, pg. 1228
BRYCE LLC CORPORATION; *U.S. Private*, pg. 177
ROBERT BRYCE & CO., LTD.—See Internatio-Muller N.V.; *Int'l*, pg. 682
BRYLANE L.P.—See The Limited, Inc.; *U.S. Public*, pg. 996
BRYLITE PTY LIMITED—See Britax International plc; *Int'l*, pg. 217
BTR AERSPACE GROUP—See BTR plc; *Int'l*, pg. 127
BUB CITY CRABSHACK & BAR-B-Q—See Lettuce Entertain You Enterprises, Inc.; *U.S. Private*, pg. 661
BUBBE S.A.—See Clarins; *Int'l*, pg. 295
BUCCANEER HOMES, INC.—See Cavalier Homes, Inc.; *U.S. Public*, pg. 318
BUCHANAN CONSTRUCTION PRODUCTS, INC.—See Ideal Industries, Inc.; *U.S. Private*, pg. 557
BUCHANAN INDUSTRIES, INC.—See Martin Color-Fi; *U.S. Public*, pg. 1052
BUCHART HORN INC.—See Pace Resources, Inc.; *U.S. Private*, pg. 830
BUCILLA CORPORATION—See The Dyson-Kissner-Moran Corporation; *U.S. Private*, pg. 352
BUCK & HICKMAN LIMITED—See The Peninsular and Oriental Steam Navigation Company; *Int'l*, pg. 1032
BUCK KNIVES, INC.; *U.S. Private*, pg. 177
BUCKA, SPIERO COMERCIO INDUSTRIA E IMPORTACAO LTDA./WALTER KIDDE S.A. INDUSTRIA E COMERCIO—See Hanson PLC; *Int'l*, pg. 594
BUCKAU-WALTHER AG—See Fried. Krupp AG; *Int'l*, pg. 516
BUCKBEE-MEARS EUROPE GMBH—See BMC Industries, Inc.; *U.S. Public*, pg. 162
BUCKEYE BISCUIT COMPANY—See President Enterprises Corp.; *Int'l*, pg. 1069
BUCKEYE CABLEVISION—See Blade Communications, Inc.; *U.S. Private*, pg. 147
BUCKEYE CELLULOSE CORP.—See The Procter & Gamble Company; *U.S. Public*, pg. 1331
BUCKEYE CONTAINER—See Buckeye Corrugated Inc.; *U.S. Private*, pg. 177
BUCKEYE CORRUGATED INC.; *U.S. Private*, pg. 177
THE BUCKEYE OILSEED PRODUCTS CO.—See The Procter & Gamble Company; *U.S. Public*, pg. 1331
BUCKEYE PACIFIC CORP., INC.—See Forest City Enterprises, Inc.; *U.S. Public*, pg. 669
BUCKEYE PARTNERS, L.P.; *U.S. Public*, pg. 266
BUCKEYE PIPE LINE COMPANY, L.P.—See Buckeye Partners, L.P.; *U.S. Public*, pg. 266
BUCKEYE SPECIALTIES DIVISION—See Seaway Food Town, Inc.; *U.S. Public*, pg. 1453
BUCKEYE STEEL CASTINGS COMPANY—See Worthington Industries, Inc.; *U.S. Public*, pg. 1780
BUCKEYE TANK TERMINALS L.P.—See Buckeye Partners, L.P.; *U.S. Public*, pg. 266
BUCKHORN CANADA LTD.—See Myers Industries, Inc.; *U.S. Public*, pg. 1143
BUCKHORN INC.—See Myers Industries, Inc.; *U.S. Public*, pg. 1143
BUCKHORN MATERIAL HANDLING GROUP INC.—See Myers Industries, Inc.; *U.S. Public*, pg. 1143
BUCKHORN RUBBER PRODUCTS INC.—See Myers Industries, Inc.; *U.S. Public*, pg. 1143
THE BUCKLE, INC.; *U.S. Public*, pg. 267
BUCKLEIGH, INC.—See Promus Hotel Corporation; *U.S. Public*, pg. 1335
BUCKMAN LABORATORIES INC.—See Bulab Holdings, Inc.; *U.S. Private*, pg. 180
BUCKSPORT DIVISION—See Consumers Water Company; *U.S. Public*, pg. 438
BUCKSPORT MILL, CHAMPION INTERNATIONAL CORP.—See Champion International Corp.; *U.S. Public*, pg. 334
BUCKYEYE UNION INSURANCE CO.—See Loews Corporation; *U.S. Public*, pg. 1010
BUCON, INC.—See Butler Manufacturing Company; *U.S. Public*, pg. 271
BUCYRUS (AFRICA) PROPRIETARY LTD.—See Bucyrus International; *U.S. Private*, pg. 177
BUCYRUS (AUSTRALIA) PROPRIETARY LTD.—See Bucyrus International; *U.S. Private*, pg. 177
BUCYRUS BLADES DE MEXICO—See Esco Corporation; *U.S. Private*, pg. 383
BUCYRUS BLADES INC.—See Esco Corporation; *U.S. Private*, pg. 383
BUCYRUS BLADES OF CANADA LTD.—See Esco Corporation; *U.S. Private*, pg. 383
BUCYRUS (BRASIL) LTDA.—See Bucyrus International; *U.S. Private*, pg. 177
BUCYRUS CHILE LTDA.—See Bucyrus International; *U.S. Private*, pg. 177
BUCYRUS-ERIE CO. OF CANADA LTD.—See Bucyrus International; *U.S. Private*, pg. 177
BUCYRUS-EUROPE LTD.—See Bucyrus International; *U.S. Private*, pg. 177
BUCYRUS INTERNATIONAL; *U.S. Private*, pg. 177
BUD BAILEY CONSTRUCTION INC.—See Swinerton Inc.; *U.S. Private*, pg. 1059
BUD INDUSTRIES, INC.; *U.S. Private*, pg. 178
BUD WEST, INC.—See Bud Industries, Inc.; *U.S. Private*, pg. 178
BUDAPEST MARRIOTT HOTEL; *Int'l*, pg. 232
BUDCO GROUP INC.; *U.S. Private*, pg. 178
THE BUDD COMPANY—See Thyssen AG; *Int'l*, pg. 1388
BUDD PLASTICS DESIGN CENTER—See Thyssen AG; *Int'l*, pg. 1388
BUDD PLASTICS RESEARCH & DEVELOPMENT CENTER—See Thyssen AG; *Int'l*, pg. 1388
BUDD TECHNICAL CENTER—See Thyssen AG; *Int'l*, pg. 1388

BUDDE & WESTERMANN—See Fleming Packaging Corp.; *U.S. Private*, pg. 411
CARL BUDDIG & COMPANY; *U.S. Private*, pg. 178
BUDERUS AG—See Metallgesellschaft AG; *Int'l*, pg. 861
BUDERUS SCHLEIFTECHNIK GMBH—See Rothenberger Group GmbH; *Int'l*, pg. 1128
BUDGET GROUP, INC.; *U.S. Public*, pg. 178
BUDGET MARKETING, INC.; *U.S. Private*, pg. 178
BUDGET RENT A CAR CORPORATION—See Budget Group, Inc.; *U.S. Public*, pg. 178
BUDGETEL INNS, INC.—See The Marcus Corporation; *U.S. Public*, pg. 1044
BUEHLER, LIMITED—See Emerson Electric Co.; *U.S. Public*, pg. 574
BUEHLER MET GMBH—See Emerson Electric Co.; *U.S. Public*, pg. 575
BUEHLER U.K. LTD.—See Emerson Electric Co.; *U.S. Public*, pg. 575
BUELL MOTORCYCLE COMPANY—See Harley-Davidson, Inc.; *U.S. Public*, pg. 786
BUENA VISTA HOME VIDEO—See The Walt Disney Company; *U.S. Public*, pg. 513
BUENA VISTA INTERNATIONAL, INC.—See The Walt Disney Company; *U.S. Public*, pg. 513
BUENA VISTA PICTURES DISTRIBUTION INC.—See The Walt Disney Company; *U.S. Public*, pg. 513
BUENA VISTA WINERY—See A. Racke GmbH; *Int'l*, pg. 1083
BUENAVENTURA S.A.—See Motorola, Inc.; *U.S. Public*, pg. 1139
BUERKLE BUICK-HONDA CO.; *U.S. Private*, pg. 178
BUFETE DE INGENIERIA CLINICA, S.A.—See Hewlett-Packard Company; *U.S. Public*, pg. 816
BUFETE INDUSTRIAL S.A. DE C.V.; *Int'l*, pg. 232
BUFFALO AIR HANDLING—See Ampco-Pittsburgh Corporation; *U.S. Public*, pg. 103
BUFFALO CHINA, INC.—See Oneida Ltd.; *U.S. Public*, pg. 1226
BUFFALO COLOR CORPORATION; *U.S. Public*, pg. 178
BUFFALO EVENING NEWS, INC.—See Berkshire Hathaway Inc.; *U.S. Public*, pg. 217
BUFFALO HOSPITAL SUPPLY CO., INC.; *U.S. Private*, pg. 179
BUFFALO LAW JOURNAL—See Advance Publications Inc.; *U.S. Private*, pg. 19
BUFFALO PAPERBOARD CORPORATION—See Caraustar Industries, Inc.; *U.S. Public*, pg. 303
BUFFALO PUMPS, INC.—See Ampco-Pittsburgh Corporation; *U.S. Public*, pg. 103
BUFFALO ROCK COMPANY; *U.S. Private*, pg. 179
BUFFALO TRUCK CENTER; *U.S. Private*, pg. 179
BUFFALO WATERFRONT RESTAURANT CORP.—See Specialty Restaurants Corporation; *U.S. Private*, pg. 1023
BUFFELEN WOODWORKING COMPANY; *U.S. Private*, pg. 179
BUFFET MONTPARNASSE SA—See Accor S.A.; *Int'l*, pg. 20
BUFFETS, INC.; *U.S. Public*, pg. 267
BUFKOR, INC.; *U.S. Private*, pg. 179
BUFORD GAZETTE—See McClatchy Newspapers Inc.; *U.S. Public*, pg. 1065
BUGAMOR PHARMA SRL MILAN—See Pharmaceutical Marketing Services Inc.; *U.S. Public*, pg. 1284
BUGLE BOY INDUSTRIES, INC.; *U.S. Private*, pg. 179
BUHLER INC.; *U.S. Private*, pg. 179
BUHRMAN-PHARR HARDWARE COMPANY; *U.S. Private*, pg. 179
BUHRMANN-UBBENS PAPIER BV—See N.V. Koninklijke KNP BT; *Int'l*, pg. 756
BUHRMANN-VROMEN VERPAKKING BV—See N.V. Koninklijke KNP BT; *Int'l*, pg. 756
BUICK MOTOR DIV. GENERAL MOTORS CORP.—See General Motors Corporation; *U.S. Public*, pg. 720
BUILDER MARTS OF AMERICA, INC.; *U.S. Private*, pg. 179
BUILDERS DEVELOPMENT INC.—See Garvey Industries, Inc.; *U.S. Private*, pg. 440
BUILDERS INC.—See Garvey Industries, Inc.; *U.S. Private*, pg. 440
BUILDERS MATERIAL COMPANY—See E.C. Barton & Company; *U.S. Private*, pg. 119
BUILDERS SQUARE, INC.—See Leonard Green & Partners; *U.S. Private*, pg. 477
BUILDERS SUPPLY AND LUMBER CO., INC.—See Pulte Corporation; *U.S. Public*, pg. 1344
BUILDERS TRANSPORT, INCORPORATED; *U.S. Public*, pg. 267
BUILDERS TRANSPORT OF TEXAS, INC.—See Builders Transport, Incorporated; *U.S. Public*, pg. 267
BUILDING & INDUSTRIAL PRODUCTS DIVISION—See The Broken Hill Proprietary Company Limited; *Int'l*, pg. 225
BUILDING & INDUSTRIAL PRODUCTS RESEARCH—See The Broken Hill Proprietary Company Limited; *Int'l*, pg. 227
BUILDING MAINTENANCE PRODUCTS, INC.—See Temco Service Industries; *U.S. Public*, pg. 1574
BUILDING MANAGEMENT DIVISION—See Tokyu Corporation; *Int'l*, pg. 1395
BUILDING MATERIAL INDUSTRY DIVISION—See ABB Asea Brown Boveri (Holding) Ltd.; *Int'l*, pg. 4
BUILDING MATERIALS CORPORATION OF AMERICA—See GAF Corporation; *U.S. Private*, pg. 433
BUILDING PLASTICS, INC.; *U.S. Public*, pg. 180
BUILDING PRODUCTS INC.; *U.S. Private*, pg. 180
BUILDING PRODUCTS INC. OF S.D.—See Building Products Inc.; *U.S. Private*, pg. 180
BUILDING TECHNOLOGIES ENGINEERING—See Energy Systems Industries, Inc.; *U.S. Private*, pg. 376
BUILDINGS DIVISION—See Black & Veatch; *U.S. Private*, pg. 146
BUITONI SPA—See Nestle S.A.; *Int'l*, pg. 919

BUJIAS CHAMPION DE MEXICO, S.A. DE C.V.—See Cooper Industries, Inc.; *U.S. Public*, pg. 444
P.T. BUKAKA FUJI ELECTRIC—See Fuji Electric Co., Ltd.; *Int'l*, pg. 522
BUL A/O—See Compagnie des Machines Bull; *Int'l*, pg. 317
BULAB HOLDINGS, INC.; *U.S. Private*, pg. 180
BULGARI CORPORATION OF AMERICA—See Bulgari SPA; *Int'l*, pg. 232
BULGARI SPA; *Int'l*, pg. 232
BULK MINING EXPLOSIVES—See Mining Services International, Inc.; *U.S. Public*, pg. 1115
BULK SYSTEMS MANAGEMENT LTD.—See Trimac Corporation; *Int'l*, pg. 1424
BULK TERMINAL ANCONA S.P.A.—See Coeclerici Group; *Int'l*, pg. 303
BULK TERMINAL TORRES S.P.A.—See Coeclerici Group; *Int'l*, pg. 303
BULKITALIA INTERNATIONAL N.V.—See Coeclerici Group; *Int'l*, pg. 304
BULKITALIA INVESTMENTS N.V.—See Coeclerici Group; *Int'l*, pg. 304
BULKITALIA OVERSEAS N.V.—See Coeclerici Group; *Int'l*, pg. 304
BULKITALIA S.P.A.—See Coeclerici Group; *Int'l*, pg. 304
BULKITALIA (U.K.) LTD.—See Coeclerici Group; *Int'l*, pg. 304
BULKLIFT A/S—See Norsk Vekst ASA; *Int'l*, pg. 965
BULKNEDLLOYD ANTILLES N.V.—See Coeclerici Group; *Int'l*, pg. 304
BULKNEDLLOYD HOLDING B.V.—See Coeclerici Group; *Int'l*, pg. 304
BULL AB—See Compagnie des Machines Bull; *Int'l*, pg. 317
BULL AE—See Compagnie des Machines Bull; *Int'l*, pg. 317
BULL AFRIQUE—See Compagnie des Machines Bull; *Int'l*, pg. 315
BULL AG—See Compagnie des Machines Bull; *Int'l*, pg. 317
BULL ALPHA—See Compagnie des Machines Bull; *Int'l*, pg. 315
BULL ARGENTINA SACI—See Compagnie des Machines Bull; *Int'l*, pg. 315
BULL A/S—See Compagnie des Machines Bull; *Int'l*, pg. 317
BULL BENELUX N.V.—See Compagnie des Machines Bull; *Int'l*, pg. 317
BULL CALVERT PACE—See The Lowe Group; *U.S. Private*, pg. 678
BULL CAMEROUN—See Compagnie des Machines Bull; *Int'l*, pg. 315
BULL CHILE INFORMATICA LTDA.—See Compagnie des Machines Bull; *Int'l*, pg. 315
BULL COMPUTER & SERVICES D.O.O.—See Compagnie des Machines Bull; *Int'l*, pg. 318
BULL COMPUTERS SOUTH AFRICA PTY. LTD.—See Compagnie des Machines Bull; *Int'l*, pg. 315
BULL CONGO—See Compagnie des Machines Bull; *Int'l*, pg. 315
BULL CORPORATION OF JAPAN—See Compagnie des Machines Bull; *Int'l*, pg. 318
BULL COTE D'IVOIRE—See Compagnie des Machines Bull; *Int'l*, pg. 315
BULL CP8, S.A.—See Compagnie des Machines Bull; *Int'l*, pg. 315
BULL DATA AB—See Compagnie des Machines Bull; *Int'l*, pg. 317
BULL DATA SYSTEMS INC.—See Compagnie des Machines Bull; *Int'l*, pg. 316
BULL DATA SYSTEMS N.V.—See Compagnie des Machines Bull; *Int'l*, pg. 316
BULL DEL URUGUAY S.A.—See Compagnie des Machines Bull; *Int'l*, pg. 315
BULL DO BRASIL SISTEMAS DE INFORMATICAO LTDA.—See Compagnie des Machines Bull; *Int'l*, pg. 315
BULL D.O.O. - CROAZIA—See Compagnie des Machines Bull; *Int'l*, pg. 318
BULL EGYPTE—See Compagnie des Machines Bull; *Int'l*, pg. 316
BULL ELECTRONICS—See Compagnie des Machines Bull; *Int'l*, pg. 316
BULL ELECTRONICS ANGERS—See Compagnie des Machines Bull; *Int'l*, pg. 316
BULL ENGENHARIA DE SISTEMAS LTDA.—See Compagnie des Machines Bull; *Int'l*, pg. 315
BULL (ESPANA) S.A.—See Compagnie des Machines Bull; *Int'l*, pg. 316
BULL EUROCENTER—See Compagnie des Machines Bull; *Int'l*, pg. 318
BULL EUROPE CENTRALE ET ORIENTALE S.A.—See Compagnie des Machines Bull; *Int'l*, pg. 317
BULL FAR EAST PTE. LTD.—See Compagnie des Machines Bull; *Int'l*, pg. 315
BULL FINANCE CORPORATION—See Compagnie des Machines Bull; *Int'l*, pg. 316
BULL FINANSERVICES—See Compagnie des Machines Bull; *Int'l*, pg. 316
BULL GABON—See Compagnie des Machines Bull; *Int'l*, pg. 315
BULL HN INFORMATION SYSTEMS (ASIA) INC.—See Compagnie des Machines Bull; *Int'l*, pg. 316
BULL HN INFORMATION SYSTEMS AUSTRALIA PTY LTD.—See Compagnie des Machines Bull; *Int'l*, pg. 317
BULL HN INFORMATION SYSTEMS INC.—See Compagnie des Machines Bull; *Int'l*, pg. 316
BULL HN INFORMATION SYSTEMS ITALIA S.P.A.—See Compagnie des Machines Bull; *Int'l*, pg. 317
BULL HN INFORMATION SYSTEMS LTD./SYSTEMS INFORMATIQUES BULL NH—See Compagnie des Machines Bull; *Int'l*, pg. 317

BULL HN INFORMATION SYSTEMS NEW ZEALAND LTD.—See Compagnie des Machines Bull; *Int'l*, pg. 317
BULL HN INFORMATION SYSTEMS (THAILAND) LTD.—See Compagnie des Machines Bull; *Int'l*, pg. 316
BULL HN INFORMATION SYSTEMS WHOLESALE PTY. LTD.—See Compagnie des Machines Bull; *Int'l*, pg. 316
BULL HN JUGOSLAVIA D.O.O.—See Compagnie des Machines Bull; *Int'l*, pg. 318
BULL HN SISTEMAS DE INFORMACION S.A. DE C.V.—See Compagnie des Machines Bull; *Int'l*, pg. 317
BULL HN SUD S.P.A.—See Compagnie des Machines Bull; *Int'l*, pg. 317
BULL HOLDING—See Compagnie des Machines Bull; *Int'l*, pg. 317
BULL HUNGARY—See Compagnie des Machines Bull; *Int'l*, pg. 317
BULL, INC.—See Science Applications International Corp.; *U.S. Private*, pg. 976
BULL INFORMATION SYSTEMS (HONG KONG) LTD.—See Compagnie des Machines Bull; *Int'l*, pg. 315
BULL INFORMATION SYSTEMS IRELAND—See Compagnie des Machines Bull; *Int'l*, pg. 318
BULL INFORMATION SYSTEMS (KOREA) LTD.—See Compagnie des Machines Bull; *Int'l*, pg. 318
BULL INFORMATION SYSTEMS LTD.—See Compagnie des Machines Bull; *Int'l*, pg. 318
BULL INFORMATION SYSTEMS (MALAYSIA)—See Compagnie des Machines Bull; *Int'l*, pg. 315
BULL INFORMATION SYSTEMS NIGERIA LTD.—See Compagnie des Machines Bull; *Int'l*, pg. 315
BULL INFORMATION SYSTEMS PTE. LTD.—See Compagnie des Machines Bull; *Int'l*, pg. 315
BULL INFORMATION SYSTEMS TAIWAN LTD.—See Compagnie des Machines Bull; *Int'l*, pg. 315
BULL INFORMATION TECHNOLOGY (SOUTHERN AFRICA) PTY. LTD.—See Compagnie des Machines Bull; *Int'l*, pg. 315
BULL INGENIERIE S.A.—See Compagnie des Machines Bull; *Int'l*, pg. 316
BULL INTERNATIONAL N.V.—See Compagnie des Machines Bull; *Int'l*, pg. 317
BULL INTERNATIONAL S.A.—See Compagnie des Machines Bull; *Int'l*, pg. 315
BULL KABUSHIKI KAISHA—See Compagnie des Machines Bull; *Int'l*, pg. 316
BULL MADAGASCAR S.A.—See Compagnie des Machines Bull; *Int'l*, pg. 315
BULL MAROC—See Compagnie des Machines Bull; *Int'l*, pg. 315
BULL MIDDLE EAST PTE. LTD.—See Compagnie des Machines Bull; *Int'l*, pg. 315
BULL MOOSE TUBE COMPANY—See Caparo Group Ltd.; *Int'l*, pg. 265
BULL MOOSE TUBES LTD.—See Caparo Group Ltd.; *Int'l*, pg. 265
BULL NIGER—See Compagnie des Machines Bull; *Int'l*, pg. 315
S.A. BULL N.V.—See Compagnie des Machines Bull; *Int'l*, pg. 318
BULL OMEGA—See Compagnie des Machines Bull; *Int'l*, pg. 316
BULL ORGANISATIONSSYSTEME GMBH I.L.—See Compagnie des Machines Bull; *Int'l*, pg. 317
BULL PENSION TRUSTEES IRELAND LTD.—See Compagnie des Machines Bull; *Int'l*, pg. 318
BULL PENSION TRUSTEES LTD.—See Compagnie des Machines Bull; *Int'l*, pg. 318
BULL PERIPHERALS GMBH—See Compagnie des Machines Bull; *Int'l*, pg. 316
BULL POLSKA SP. Z.O.O.—See Compagnie des Machines Bull; *Int'l*, pg. 318
BULL PORTUGUESA COMPUTADORES LDA.—See Compagnie des Machines Bull; *Int'l*, pg. 318
BULL RUN CORPORATION; *U.S. Public*, pg. 267
BULL S.A.—See Compagnie des Machines Bull; *Int'l*, pg. 315
BULL S.A. FINANCIERE LTD.—See Compagnie des Machines Bull; *Int'l*, pg. 316
BULL S.A.L.—See Compagnie des Machines Bull; *Int'l*, pg. 315
BULL (SCHWEIZ) AG—See Compagnie des Machines Bull; *Int'l*, pg. 318
BULL SCION SERVICES—See Compagnie des Machines Bull; *Int'l*, pg. 317
BULL SENEGAL—See Compagnie des Machines Bull; *Int'l*, pg. 315
BULL SLOVAKIA S.R.O.—See Compagnie des Machines Bull; *Int'l*, pg. 317
BULL SPOL S.R.O.—See Compagnie des Machines Bull; *Int'l*, pg. 317
BULL SYSTEMHAUS DRESDEN GMBH I.L.—See Compagnie des Machines Bull; *Int'l*, pg. 317
BULL WORLDWIDE INFORMATION SYSTEMS LTD.—See Compagnie des Machines Bull; *Int'l*, pg. 318
BULLAL B.V.—See Compagnie des Machines Bull; *Int'l*, pg. 317
E.D. BULLARD COMPANY; *U.S. Private*, pg. 180
BULLCOL B.V.—See Compagnie des Machines Bull; *Int'l*, pg. 317
BULLDOG CO.—See Newell Co.; *U.S. Public*, pg. 1176
BULLDOG VSI—See Newell Co.; *U.S. Public*, pg. 1176
BULLDOM B.V.—See Compagnie des Machines Bull; *Int'l*, pg. 317
THE BULLETIN COMPANY—See Gannett Company, Inc.; *U.S. Public*, pg. 700
BULLEY & ANDREWS COMPANY; *U.S. Private*, pg. 180
BULLFROG MINE—See Barrick Gold Corporation; *Int'l*, pg. 169
BULLFROG PRODUCTIONS LTD.—See Electronic Arts; *U.S. Public*, pg. 569
BULLINVEST B.V.—See Compagnie des Machines Bull; *Int'l*, pg. 315

CURT BULLOCK BUILDERS, INC.; *U.S. Private*, pg. 180
H.P. BULMER HOLDINGS PLC; *Int'l*, pg. 232
BULOVA CORPORATION—See Loews Corporation; *U.S. Public*, pg. 1010
BULOVA WATCH COMPANY LIMITED—See Loews Corporation; *U.S. Public*, pg. 1011
SARL BULOW BENNET FRANCE—See Norske Skogindustrier A.S.; *Int'l*, pg. 966
BULTHAUP GMBH & CO.—See Toto Ltd.; *Int'l*, pg. 1410
BUM-A PETROLEUM CO., LTD.—See Ssangyong Business Group; *Int'l*, pg. 1292
BUMBLE BEE INTERNATIONAL INC.—See Hicks, Muse, Tate & Furst Inc.; *U.S. Private*, pg. 526
BUMBLE BEE SEAFOODS INC.—See Hicks, Muse, Tate & Furst Inc.; *U.S. Private*, pg. 526
P.T. BUMI DAYA-IBJ LEASING—See The Industrial Bank of Japan, Limited; *Int'l*, pg. 676
BUNDABERG SUGAR COMPANY—See Tate & Lyle PLC; *Int'l*, pg. 1357
BUNDY AB—See TI Group plc; *Int'l*, pg. 1341
BUNDY ARGENTINA SA—See TI Group plc; *Int'l*, pg. 1342
BUNDY A/S—See TI Group plc; *Int'l*, pg. 1341
BUNDY ASIA PACIFIC—See TI Group plc; *Int'l*, pg. 1341
BUNDY BELGIUM SA—See TI Group plc; *Int'l*, pg. 1341
BUNDY COLOMBIA S.A.—See TI Group plc; *Int'l*, pg. 1342
BUNDY CORPORATION, ENGINEERING CENTER—See TI Group plc; *Int'l*, pg. 1340
BUNDY CORPORATION, WASHINGTON COURT HOUSE PLANT—See TI Group plc; *Int'l*, pg. 1341
BUNDY CORPORATION, WINCHESTER TOOL PLANT—See TI Group plc; *Int'l*, pg. 1341
BUNDY G.M.B.H.—See TI Group plc; *Int'l*, pg. 1341
BUNDY GROUP—See TI Group plc; *Int'l*, pg. 1341
BUNDY INDIA LTD.—See TI Group plc; *Int'l*, pg. 1341
BUNDY INTERNATIONAL—See TI Group plc; *Int'l*, pg. 1340
BUNDY JAPAN LTD.—See TI Group plc; *Int'l*, pg. 1341
BUNDY KFT—See TI Group plc; *Int'l*, pg. 1342
BUNDY LATIN AMERICA—See TI Group plc; *Int'l*, pg. 1342
BUNDY MEXICO SA—See TI Group plc; *Int'l*, pg. 1342
BUNDY NORTH AMERICA—See TI Group plc; *Int'l*, pg. 1340
BUNDY OF CANADA LTD.—See TI Group plc; *Int'l*, pg. 1341
BUNDY PROPERTIES—See Roll International Corporation; *U.S. Private*, pg. 941
BUNDY SA—See TI Group plc; *Int'l*, pg. 1341
BUNDY SA - SUCURSAL PORTUGESA—See TI Group plc; *Int'l*, pg. 1341
BUNDY SNC—See TI Group plc; *Int'l*, pg. 1342
BUNDY SOUTH AFRICA—See TI Group plc; *Int'l*, pg. 1341
BUNDY SPA—See TI Group plc; *Int'l*, pg. 1341
BUNDY S.R.O.—See TI Group plc; *Int'l*, pg. 1342
BUNDY SUD SRL—See TI Group plc; *Int'l*, pg. 1342
BUNDY SYSTEMS KOREA—See TI Group plc; *Int'l*, pg. 1341
BUNDY SYSTEMWERK—See TI Group plc; *Int'l*, pg. 1342
BUNDY TUBING CO. (AUSTRALIA) PTY. LTD.—See TI Group plc; *Int'l*, pg. 1341
BUNDY TUBING (NEW ZEALAND) LTD.—See TI Group plc; *Int'l*, pg. 1341
BUNDY U.K. LTD.—See TI Group plc; *Int'l*, pg. 1341
BUNDY VENEZOLANA C.A.—See TI Group plc; *Int'l*, pg. 1342
BUNKER HILL FOODS INC.—See Castleberry/Snow's Brands Inc.; *U.S. Private*, pg. 219
BUNKERBETRIEBE BUCHTING KG—See Harpen AG; *Int'l*, pg. 597
BUNN-O-MATIC CORPORATION; *U.S. Private*, pg. 180
BUNNAHABHAIN DISTILLERY—See The Highland Distilleries Company; *Int'l*, pg. 619
BUNNELL PLASTICS DIVISION—See Furon Company; *U.S. Public*, pg. 689
BUNNY BREAD CO., INC.—See Flowers Industries, Inc.; *U.S. Public*, pg. 657
THE BUNTIN GROUP; *U.S. Private*, pg. 181
BUNTIN OUT OF HOME MEDIA—See The Buntin Group; *U.S. Private*, pg. 181
BUNTING WARBURG INC.—See Swiss Bank Corporation; *Int'l*, pg. 1331
BUNTON DIVISION—See Textron Inc.; *U.S. Public*, pg. 1589
BUNZL EXTRUSION—See Bunzl PLC; *Int'l*, pg. 232
BUNZL PLC; *Int'l*, pg. 232
BUQUET & LE BLANC INC.; *U.S. Private*, pg. 181
BURBANK AIRCRAFT SUPPLY INC.—See Banner Aerospace, Inc.; *U.S. Public*, pg. 187
BURBERRYS SHIRTS—See Bidermann International S.A.; *Int'l*, pg. 194
BURD & FLETCHER COMPANY; *U.S. Private*, pg. 181
BURDA GMBH—See Burda Holding GmbH & Co., KG; *Int'l*, pg. 233
BURDA HOLDING GMBH & CO., KG; *Int'l*, pg. 233
BURDA PUBLICATIONS, INC.—See Burda Holding GmbH & Co., KG; *Int'l*, pg. 233
BURDICK, INC.; *U.S. Private*, pg. 618
BURDINES—See Federated Department Stores, Inc.; *U.S. Public*, pg. 618
BUREAU BASF ALGERIE—See BASF AG; *Int'l*, pg. 107
S.A. BUREAU INTERNATIONAL DE RECHERCHES POUR LA DESTRUCTION DES IMMONDICES B.I.R.D.I.—See Cockerill Sambre; *Int'l*, pg. 301
BUREAU OF ENGRAVING; *U.S. Private*, pg. 181
THE BUREAU OF NATIONAL AFFAIRS, INC.; *U.S. Private*, pg. 181
BUREAU RHONE-POULENC—See Rhone-Poulenc S.A.; *Int'l*, pg. 1112
BUREAU RHONE-POULENC SA—See Rhone-Poulenc S.A.; *Int'l*, pg. 1112
C.F. BURGER CREAMERY COMPANY; *U.S. Private*, pg. 182
BURGER KING CORPORATION—See Diageo Plc; *Int'l*, pg. 411

BURGER KING, EUROPE/MIDDLE EAST/AFRICA—See Diageo Plc; *Int'l*, pg. 411
BURGER KING (UK) LIMITED—See Diageo Plc; *Int'l*, pg. 411
BURGESS & NIPLE, LIMITED; *U.S. Private*, pg. 182
BURGESS ARCHITECTURAL PRODUCTS LIMITED—See TT Group PLC; *Int'l*, pg. 1344
BURGESS GMBH—See Williams Holdings Plc; *Int'l*, pg. 1500
BURGESS-NORTON MFG. CO.—See Amsted Industries Incorporated; *U.S. Private*, pg. 68
BURGESS PIGMENT CO.; *U.S. Private*, pg. 182
BURGESS SAIA CO. INC.—See Williams Holdings Plc; *Int'l*, pg. 1500
BURGESS-SAIA HONG KONG LIMITED—See Williams Holdings Plc; *Int'l*, pg. 1500
BURGESS-SAIA INC.—See Williams Holdings Plc; *Int'l*, pg. 1500
BURGMANN DALIAN—See Feodor Burgmann Dichtungswerke GmbH; *Int'l*, pg. 234
BURGMANN DO BRASIL—See Feodor Burgmann Dichtungswerke GmbH; *Int'l*, pg. 233
BURGMANN ENDUSTRIYEL SIZDIRMALIK SAN VE TIC LTD STI—See Feodor Burgmann Dichtungswerke GmbH; *Int'l*, pg. 233
FEODOR BURGMANN DICHTUNGSWERKE GMBH; *Int'l*, pg. 233
BURGMANN INDIA PVT. LTD—See Feodor Burgmann Dichtungswerke GmbH; *Int'l*, pg. 234
P.T. BURGMANN INDONESIA—See Feodor Burgmann Dichtungswerke GmbH; *Int'l*, pg. 233
BURGMANN KOREA LTD.—See Feodor Burgmann Dichtungswerke GmbH; *Int'l*, pg. 233
BURGMANN MALAYSIA SDN BHD—See Feodor Burgmann Dichtungswerke GmbH; *Int'l*, pg. 233
BURGMANN MEXICO S.A. DE C.V.—See Feodor Burgmann Dichtungswerke GmbH; *Int'l*, pg. 233
BURGMANN MIDDLE EAST—See Feodor Burgmann Dichtungswerke GmbH; *Int'l*, pg. 234
BURGMANN SEALS AMERICA, INC.—See Feodor Burgmann Dichtungswerke GmbH; *Int'l*, pg. 233
BURGMANN SEALS AUSTRALIA PTY. LTD.—See Feodor Burgmann Dichtungswerke GmbH; *Int'l*, pg. 234
BURGMANN SEALS SOUTH AFRICA (PTY) LTD.—See Feodor Burgmann Dichtungswerke GmbH; *Int'l*, pg. 234
BURGMANN SHANGHAI LTD.—See Feodor Burgmann Dichtungswerke GmbH; *Int'l*, pg. 234
BURGMANN THAILAND CO. LTD.—See Feodor Burgmann Dichtungswerke GmbH; *Int'l*, pg. 234
BURGOPACK-STAMPA, TRASFORMAZIONE, IMBALLAGGI S.P.A.—See Viag AG; *Int'l*, pg. 1466
BURGOYNE, INC.; *U.S. Private*, pg. 182
BURHOLME WOODS JOINT VENTURE—See Prime Bancorp, Inc.; *U.S. Public*, pg. 1326
BURK ROYALTY CO.; *U.S. Private*, pg. 182
THE BURKE CO.—See Tridel Enterprises Inc.; *Int'l*, pg. 1423
BURKE ENGINEERING COMPANY; *U.S. Private*, pg. 183
BURKE FLOORING PRODUCTS DIV.—See Burke Industries, Inc.; *U.S. Private*, pg. 183
BURKE FUEL & HEATING CO.—See Meenan Oil Co. L.P.; *U.S. Private*, pg. 1058
BURKE INDUSTRIES, INC.; *U.S. Private*, pg. 183
THE BURKE INSTITUTE—See BASES Worldwide; *U.S. Private*, pg. 120
BURKE LUMBER CO.—See WTD Industries, Inc.; *U.S. Public*, pg. 1729
BURKE MILLS, INC.; *U.S. Public*, pg. 267
BURKE RUBBER CO.—See Burke Industries, Inc.; *U.S. Private*, pg. 183
BURKHALTER HOLDING AG—See Hesta Tex AG; *Int'l*, pg. 618
BURKHARDT GMBH—See Mannesmann A.G.; *Int'l*, pg. 836
BURLINGTON BASKET CO.; *U.S. Private*, pg. 183
BURLINGTON, BRIGHTON & WHEATLAND TELEPHONE CO.—See Telephone and Data Systems, Inc.; *U.S. Public*, pg. 1571
BURLINGTON COAT FACTORY WAREHOUSE CORPORATION; *U.S. Public*, pg. 268
BURLINGTON DENIM—See Burlington Industries, Inc.; *U.S. Public*, pg. 268
BURLINGTON FREE PRESS—See Gannett Company, Inc.; *U.S. Public*, pg. 700
BURLINGTON HOUSE AREA RUGS—See Burlington Industries, Inc.; *U.S. Public*, pg. 268
BURLINGTON INDUSTRIES, INC.; *U.S. Public*, pg. 268
BURLINGTON MADISON YARN—See Burlington Industries, Inc.; *U.S. Public*, pg. 268
BURLINGTON MENSWEAR—See Burlington Industries, Inc.; *U.S. Public*, pg. 268
BURLINGTON MOTOR HOLDINGS INC.; *U.S. Private*, pg. 183
BURLINGTON NORTHERN SANTA FE CORPORATION; *U.S. Public*, pg. 268
BURLINGTON RESOURCES INC.; *U.S. Public*, pg. 269
BURLINGTON TIMBER INC.—See Burlington Basket Co.; *U.S. Private*, pg. 183
BURLINGTON WOODS CONVALESCENT HOME—See Genesis Health Ventures, Inc.; *U.S. Public*, pg. 728
BURMAH ADHESIVES & SEALANTS (PTY) LTD.—See Burmah Castrol plc; *Int'l*, pg. 235
BURMAH CASTROL CHEMICALS DIVISION—See Burmah Castrol plc; *Int'l*, pg. 234
BURMAH CASTROL CHEMICALS LTD.—See Burmah Castrol plc; *Int'l*, pg. 234
BURMAH CASTROL FRANCE HOLDINGS SA—See Burmah Castrol plc; *Int'l*, pg. 235
BURMAH CASTROL IRELAND, LTD.—See Burmah Castrol plc; *Int'l*, pg. 235
BURMAH CASTROL LUBRICANTS DIVISION—See Burmah Castrol plc; *Int'l*, pg. 234
BURMAH CASTROL NZ LTD.—See Burmah Castrol plc; *Int'l*, pg. 235

MASTER INDEX TO COMPANY NAMES BUSS

Company Index

BURMAH CASTROL PLC; *Int'l*, pg. 234
BURMAH CASTROL (SOUTH AFRICA) (PTY.) LTD.—See Burmah Castrol plc; *Int'l*, pg. 235
BURMAH CASTROL TRADING, LTD.—See Burmah Castrol plc; *Int'l*, pg. 234
BURMAH CASTROL USA INC.—See Burmah Castrol plc; *Int'l*, pg. 235
BURMAH GAS TRANSPORT LTD.—See Burmah Castrol plc; *Int'l*, pg. 235
BURMAH LNG SHIPPING, INC.—See Burmah Castrol plc; *Int'l*, pg. 235
BURMAH MOL TRANSPORT LIMITED—See Burmah Castrol plc; *Int'l*, pg. 235
BURMAH OIL AUSTRALIA LTD.—See Burmah Castrol plc; *Int'l*, pg. 235
THE BURMAH OIL COMPANY (PAKISTAN TRADING) LIMITED—See Burmah Castrol plc; *Int'l*, pg. 235
THE BURMAH OIL (DEUTSCHLAND) GMBH—See Burmah Castrol plc; *Int'l*, pg. 235
BURMAH OIL INDONESIA LIMITED—See Burmah Castrol plc; *Int'l*, pg. 235
BURMAH OIL INVESTMENTS HOLDINGS LTD.—See Burmah Castrol plc; *Int'l*, pg. 234
BURMAH OIL TANKERS LTD.—See Burmah Castrol plc; *Int'l*, pg. 235
BURMAH TRANSPORT HOLDINGS LTD.—See Burmah Castrol plc; *Int'l*, pg. 235
BURMEISTER & WAIN ENERGI A/S—See Deutsche Babcock AG; *Int'l*, pg. 398
JAMES BURN BINDERS—See Standex International Corporation; *U.S. Public*, pg. 1507
JAMES BURN INTERNATIONAL AB—See Standex International Corporation; *U.S. Public*, pg. 1507
JAMES BURN INTERNATIONAL GMBH—See Standex International Corporation; *U.S. Public*, pg. 1507
JAMES BURN INTERNATIONAL LIMITED—See Standex International Corporation; *U.S. Public*, pg. 1507
JAMES BURN INTERNATIONAL S.A.—See Standex International Corporation; *U.S. Public*, pg. 1507
JAMES BURN INTL.—See Standex International Corporation; *U.S. Public*, pg. 1506
BURNER SYSTEMS INTERNATIONAL, INC.—See The Dyson-Kissner-Moran Corporation; *U.S. Private*, pg. 351
LEO BURNETT ADVERTISING—See Leo Burnett Company, Inc.; *U.S. Private*, pg. 184
LEO BURNETT ADVERTISING CO., LTD.-BEIJING—See Leo Burnett Company, Inc.; *U.S. Private*, pg. 184
LEO BURNETT ADVERTISING, REPRESENTATIVE OFFICE—See Leo Burnett Company, Inc.; *U.S. Private, pg. 184*
LEO BURNETT ADVERTISING SDN.BHD.—See Leo Burnett Company, Inc.; *U.S. Private*, pg. 184
LEO BURNETT ADVERTISING SPOL.SR.O—See Leo Burnett Company, Inc.; *U.S. Private*, pg. 184
LEO BURNETT & MORADPOUR/MOSCOW—See Leo Burnett Company, Inc.; *U.S. Private*, pg. 184
LEO BURNETT & TARGET—See Leo Burnett Company, Inc.; *U.S. Private*, pg. 184
LEO BURNETT & WIRZ—See Leo Burnett Company, Inc.; *U.S. Private*, pg. 184
LEO BURNETT A/S—See Leo Burnett Company, Inc.; *U.S.* Private, pg. 184
LEO BURNETT ATHENS—See Leo Burnett Company, Inc.; *U.S. Private*, pg. 184
LEO BURNETT BUDAPEST KFT—See Leo Burnett Company, Inc.; *U.S. Private*, pg. 185
LEO BURNETT CHILE—See Leo Burnett Company, Inc.; *U.S. Private*, pg. 185
LEO BURNETT (CHINA) ADVERTISING CO., LTD.-GUANGZHOU—See Leo Burnett Company, Inc.; *U.S. Private*, pg. 184
LEO BURNETT CO. INC.—See Leo Burnett Company, Inc.; *U.S. Private*, pg. 185
LEO BURNETT COLUMBIANA, S.A.—See Leo Burnett Company, Inc.; *U.S. Private*, pg. 185
LEO BURNETT COMPANY, INC.; *U.S. Private*, pg. 183
LEO BURNETT COMPANY LTD.—See Leo Burnett Company, Inc.; *U.S. Private*, pg. 185
LEO BURNETT COMPANY, LTD.-TAIWAN BRANCH—See Leo Burnett Company, Inc.; *U.S. Private*, pg. 185
LEO BURNETT CO., S.R.L.—See Leo Burnett Company, Inc.; *U.S. Private*, pg. 185
LEO BURNETT COMUNICA S.A.—See Leo Burnett Company, Inc.; *U.S. Private*, pg. 185
LEO BURNETT/CONNAGHAN & MAY PTY. LTD.—See Leo Burnett Company, Inc.; *U.S. Private*, pg. 185
LEO BURNETT-COSTA RICA—See Leo Burnett Company, Inc.; *U.S. Private*, pg. 185
LEO BURNETT DENMARK—See Leo Burnett Company, Inc.; *U.S. Private*, pg. 185
LEO BURNETT GREATER CHINA—See Leo Burnett Company, Inc.; *U.S. Private*, pg. 185
LEO BURNETT INC.—See Leo Burnett Company, Inc.; *U.S.* Private, pg. 185
LEO BURNETT KYIV—See Leo Burnett Company, Inc.; *U.S. Private*, pg. 185
LEO BURNETT KYODO CO. LTD.—See Leo Burnett Company, Inc.; *U.S. Private*, pg. 185
LEO BURNETT LIMITED—See Leo Burnett Company, Inc.; *U.S. Private*, pg. 185
LEO BURNETT LTD. THAILAND—See Leo Burnett Company, Inc.; *U.S. Private*, pg. 185
LEO BURNETT PTE. LTD.—See Leo Burnett Company, Inc.; *U.S. Private*, pg. 185
LEO BURNETT PUBLICIDADE, LTDA.—See Leo Burnett Company, Inc.; *U.S. Private*, pg. 185
LEO BURNETT S.A. DE C.V.—See Leo Burnett Company, Inc.; *U.S. Private*, pg. 185
LEO BURNETT (SHANGHAI) ADVERTISING CO., LTD.—See Leo Burnett Company, Inc.; *U.S. Private*, pg. 185
LEO BURNETT SONYON INC.—See Leo Burnett Company, Inc.; *U.S. Private*, pg. 185
LEO BURNETT VENEZUELA, C.A.—See Leo Burnett Company, Inc.; *U.S. Private*, pg. 186
LEO BURNETT WARSAW SP.Z.O.O.—See Leo Burnett Company, Inc.; *U.S. Private*, pg. 186
LEO BURNETT WORLDWIDE ASIA/PACIFIC HDQTRS.—See Leo Burnett Company, Inc.; *U.S. Private*, pg. 186
LEO BURNETT WORLDWIDE, LATIN AMERICAN HDQTRS.—See Leo Burnett Company, Inc.; *U.S. Private*, pg. 184
BURNETT POLYMER ENGINEERING—See McKechnie PLC; *Int'l*, pg. 851
WM. T. BURNETT & CO., INC.; *U.S. Private*, pg. 186
BURNHAM—See Investcorp International; *Int'l*, pg. 686
BURNHAM GENERAL PARTNER, INC.—See Investcorp International; *Int'l*, pg. 686
JOHN BURNHAM & CO.; *U.S. Private*, pg. 186
BURNHAM; *U.S. Public*, pg. 270
BURNHAM WORLD FORWARDING INC.—See Investcorp International; *Int'l*, pg. 686
BURNS & MCDONNELL ENGINEERS-ARCHITECTS-CONSULTANTS; *U.S. Private*, pg. 187
BURNS & MCDONNELL WASTE CONSULTANTS, INC.—See Burns & McDonnell Engineers-Architects-Consultants; *U.S. Private*, pg. 187
BURNS & ROE CONSTRUCTION GROUP INC.—See Burns & Roe Enterprises, Inc.; *U.S. Private*, pg. 187
BURNS & ROE ENTERPRISES, INC.; *U.S. Private*, pg. 187
BURNS & ROE ENVIRONMENTAL SERVICES—See Burns & Roe Enterprises, Inc.; *U.S. Private*, pg. 187
BURNS & ROE INDUSTRIAL SERVICES COMPANY—See Burns & Roe Enterprises, Inc.; *U.S. Private*, pg. 187
BURNS & ROE SERVICES CORP.—See Burns & Roe Enterprises, Inc.; *U.S. Private*, pg. 187
BURNS & ROE WORLEY—See Burns & Roe Enterprises, Inc.; *U.S. Private*, pg. 187
BURNS & WILCOX—See H.W. Kaufman Financial Group, Inc.; *U.S. Private*, pg. 609
BURNS & WILCOX LTD.—See H.W. Kaufman Financial Group, Inc.; *U.S. Private*, pg. 609
BURNS BROS. INC.; *U.S. Private*, pg. 187
BURNS DRILLING COMPANY—See Harken Energy Corporation; *U.S. Public*, pg. 785
BURNS, PHILP & CO.—See Burns, Philp & Company Limited; *Int'l*, pg. 236
BURNS, PHILP & COMPANY LIMITED; *Int'l*, pg. 236
BURNS PHILP COMPANY OF SAN FRANCISCO—See Burns, Philp & Company Limited; *Int'l*, pg. 236
BURNS, PHILP INC.—See Burns, Philp & Company Limited; *Int'l*, pg. 236
BURNS, PHILP PACIFIC DIVISION—See Burns, Philp & Company Limited; *Int'l*, pg. 237
BURNSIDE CONSTRUCTION CO.; *U.S. Private*, pg. 187
BURNSTAD BROTHERS, INC.; *U.S. Private*, pg. 187
BURNSTEAD CONSTRUCTION COMPANY; *U.S. Private*, pg. 187
BURNUP & SIMS COMMUNICATIONS SERVICES—See MasTec, Inc.; *U.S. Public*, pg. 1056
BURNUP & SIMS COMTEC, INC.—See MasTec, Inc.; *U.S. Public*, pg. 1056
BURNUP & SIMS OF CALIFORNIA, INC.—See MasTec, Inc.; *U.S. Public*, pg. 1056
BURNUP & SIMS OF TX—See MasTec, Inc.; *U.S. Public*, pg. 1056
BURNUP & SIMS TELCOM, INC.—See MasTec, Inc.; *U.S. Public*, pg. 1056
BURO BRITAIN—See Stena Line AB; *Int'l*, pg. 1300
BURO NEUSS—See Koninklijke Hoogovens N.V.; *Int'l*, pg. 754
BURO SCANDINAVIA—See Stena Line AB; *Int'l*, pg. 1300
BUROHAUS VERMIETUNGS UND VERWALTUNGS GMBH & CO. KG—See Creditanstalt-Bankverein; *Int'l*, pg. 347
W. ATLEE BURPEE CO.; *U.S. Private*, pg. 187
BURR-BROWN CORPORATION; *U.S. Public*, pg. 270
BURRELL COMMUNICATIONS GROUP INC.; *U.S. Private, pg. 188*
BURRELL/DFA ADVERTISING—See Burrell Communications Group Inc.; *U.S. Private*, pg. 188
BURREN, INC.—See Pennsylvania Real Estate Investment Trust; *U.S. Public*, pg. 1272
BURRIS FOODS, INC.; *U.S. Private*, pg. 188
BURRISS CORP.; *U.S. Private*, pg. 188
BURRO PIPELINE CORP.—See Tipperary Corporation; *U.S.* Public, pg. 1618
BURROUGHS WELLCOME & CO (BANGLADESH) LTD—See Glaxo Wellcome plc; *Int'l*, pg. 553
BURROUGHS WELLCOME & CO. (HONG KONG) LTD.—See Glaxo Wellcome plc; *Int'l*, pg. 553
BURROUGHS WELLCOME (FAR EAST) LTD—See Glaxo Wellcome plc; *Int'l*, pg. 553
P.T. BURROUGHS WELLCOME INDONESIA—See Glaxo Wellcome plc; *Int'l*, pg. 553
BURROUGHS WELLCOME INTL. LTD.—See Glaxo Wellcome plc; *Int'l*, pg. 552
BURROWS PAPER CORPORATION; *U.S. Private*, pg. 188
BURSIL, INC.—See Giant Food Inc.; *U.S. Public*, pg. 741
BURSON-MARSTELLER—See Young & Rubicam Inc.; *U.S.* Private, pg. 1197
F.N. BURT COMPANY, INC.; *U.S. Private*, pg. 188
BURTCO, INC.; *U.S. Private*, pg. 188
BURTCO METAL SYSTEMS—See Burtco, Inc.; *U.S. Private*, pg. 188
BURTMAN IRON WORKS, INC.; *U.S. Private*, pg. 188
THE BURTON COMPANY—See Hilb, Rogal and Hamilton Company; *U.S. Public*, pg. 826
BURTON ELECTRICAL ENGINEERING—See Wyle Laboratories, Inc.; *U.S. Private*, pg. 1193
THE BURTON GROUP PLC; *Int'l*, pg. 237
BURTON MEDICAL PRODUCTS CORPORATION—See Luxo A/S; *Int'l*, pg. 821
BURY COOPER WHITEHEAD LTD.—See Scapa Group Plc; *Int'l*, pg. 1202
BUSCH AGRICULTURAL RESOURCES, INC.—See Anheuser-Busch Companies, Inc.; *U.S. Public*, pg. 114
AUGUST A. BUSCH & CO. OF MASSACHUSETTS, INC.—See Anheuser-Busch Companies, Inc.; *U.S. Public*, pg. 114
BUSCH CREATIVE SERVICES CORPORATION—See Anheuser-Busch Companies, Inc.; *U.S. Public*, pg. 114
BUSCH ENTERTAINMENT CORP.—See Anheuser-Busch Companies, Inc.; *U.S. Public*, pg. 114
BUSCH GARDENS WILLIAMSBURG—See Anheuser-Busch Companies, Inc.; *U.S. Public*, pg. 114
BUSCH GMBH—See The Monarch Machine Tool Company; *U.S. Public*, pg. 1124
BUSCH-JAEGER ELEKTRO GMBH—See ABB Asea Brown Boveri (Holding) Ltd.; *Int'l*, pg. 2
BUSCH PROPERTIES, INC.—See Anheuser-Busch Companies, Inc.; *U.S. Public*, pg. 114
BUSCH U.S.—See The Monarch Machine Tool Company; *U.S. Public*, pg. 1124
BUSCH-JAEGER LUDENSCHEIDER METALLWERK GMBH—See UMS Swiss Metalworks Holding Ltd; *Int'l*, pg. 1427
THE BUSCHMAN CO.; *U.S. Private*, pg. 188
THE BUSCHMAN COMPANY—See Pinnacle Automation Inc.; *U.S. Private*, pg. 866
BUSH BEACH ENGINEERING LTD.—See Mannesmann A.G.; *Int'l*, pg. 835
BUSH BOAKE ALLEN, INC—See Union Camp Corporation; *U.S. Public*, pg. 1666
BUSH BOAKE ALLEN LTD.—See Union Camp Corporation; *U.S. Public*, pg. 1666
BUSH BROTHERS & COMPANY; *U.S. Private*, pg. 189
BUSH BROTHERS & COMPANY PLANT—See Bush Brothers & Company; *U.S. Private*, pg. 189
BUSH HOG DIVISION—See Allied Products Corporation; *U.S. Public*, pg. 48
BUSH INDUSTRIES INC.; *U.S. Public*, pg. 270
BUSHNELL CORPORATION—See Worldwide Sports & Recreation, Inc.; *U.S. Private*, pg. 1191
BUSHWHACKER ASSOCIATES, INC.—See Bethurum Research & Development, Inc.; *U.S. Private*, pg. 141
BUSINESS AIR—See Horizon Enterprises Group LLC; *U.S. Private*, pg. 539
BUSINESS & PROFESSIONAL PRODUCTS GROUP—See Sony Corporation; *Int'l*, pg. 1284
BUSINESS BANKING GROUP—See California State Bank; *U.S. Public*, pg. 294
BUSINESS COMPUTING SHOW (JV WITH MONTBUILD LTD.)—See EMAP Plc; *Int'l*, pg. 452
THE BUSINESS DEPOT, LTD.—See Staples, Inc.; *U.S. Public*, pg. 1510
BUSINESS EQUIPMENT CENTER; *U.S. Private*, pg. 189
BUSINESS FIRST OF COLUMBUS, INC.—See Advance Publications Inc.; *U.S. Private*, pg. 19
BUSINESS FIRST OF NEW YORK, INC.—See Advance Publications Inc.; *U.S. Private*, pg. 19
BUSINESS FIRST OF NEW YORK, LLC—See Advance Publications Inc.; *U.S. Private*, pg. 19
BUSINESS GUIDES INC.—See Lebhar-Friedman, Inc.; *U.S.* Private, pg. 656
BUSINESS INFORMATION GROUP—See Conseco Inc.; *U.S. Public*, pg. 433
BUSINESS INFORMATION TECHNOLOGY—See Ciber, Inc.; *U.S. Public*, pg. 356
BUSINESS INSURANCE—See Crain Communications, Inc.; *U.S. Private*, pg. 285
BUSINESS INSURANCE CORPORATION—See Foundation Health Systems, Inc.; *U.S. Public*, pg. 678
THE BUSINESS JOURNAL OF PORTLAND, INC.—See Advance Publications Inc.; *U.S. Private*, pg. 19
BUSINESS JOURNAL PUBLICATIONS, INC.—See Advance Publications Inc.; *U.S. Private*, pg. 19
BUSINESS JOURNALS OF NORTH CAROLINA, LLC—See Advance Publications Inc.; *U.S. Private*, pg. 19
BUSINESS MACHINE CENTER, INC. (NSL)—See Ikon Office Solutions, Inc.; *U.S. Public*, pg. 863
BUSINESS MACHINES COMPANY W.L.L.—See BASF AG; *Int'l*, pg. 107
BUSINESS MAGAZINE—See Pearson plc; *Int'l*, pg. 1025
BUSINESS MANAGEMENT & FINANCE INTERNATIONAL LTD.—See Swiss Bank Corporation; *Int'l*, pg. 1332
BUSINESS MANAGEMENT PERSONNEL, INC.—See General Employment Enterprises, Inc.; *U.S. Public*, pg. 714
BUSINESS MARKETING—See Crain Communications, Inc.; *U.S. Private*, pg. 285
BUSINESS MARKETS ORGANIZATION—See Sprint Corporation; *U.S. Public*, pg. 1500
BUSINESS MEN'S ASSURANCE COMPANY OF AMERICA—See Assicurazioni Generali S.p.A.; *Int'l*, pg. 90
BUSINESS MENS INSURANCE CORPORATION; *U.S. Private*, pg. 189
THE BUSINESS OUTLET, INC.—See ABN-AMRO Holding N.V.; *Int'l*, pg. 9
BUSINESS TRAVEL MANAGEMENT, INC.—See Mary Kay Corporation; *U.S. Private*, pg. 711
BUSINESS WEEK—See The McGraw-Hill Companies; *U.S. Public*, pg. 1069
BUSINESSHIP INTERNATIONAL INC.; *U.S. Private*, pg. 189
BUSINESSLAND JAPAN COMPANY, LTD.—See AMP Incorporated; *U.S. Public*, pg. 9
BUSLEASE, INC.—See Consorcio G. Grupo Dina, S.A. de C.V.; *Int'l*, pg. 326
BUSS AG—See Georg Fischer Ltd.; *Int'l*, pg. 490
BUSS (AMERICA) INC.—See Georg Fischer Ltd.; *Int'l*, pg. 490
BUSS (BENELUX) B.V.—See Georg Fischer Ltd.; *Int'l*, pg. 490
BUSS HOLDING GMBH—See Georg Fischer Ltd.; *Int'l*, pg. 490
BUSS (JAPAN) LTD.—See Georg Fischer Ltd.; *Int'l*, pg. 490
BUSS-SMS GMBH VERFAHRENSTECHNIK—See Georg Fischer Ltd.; *Int'l*, pg. 490
BUSS S.R.L.—See Georg Fischer Ltd.; *Int'l*, pg. 490
BUSS WAESCHLE HOLDING CORP.—See Georg Fischer Ltd.; *Int'l*, pg. 490

BUSS WAESCHLE LTD.—See Georg Fischer Ltd.; *Int'l*, pg. 490
BUSS WAESCHLE SARL—See Georg Fischer Ltd.; *Int'l*, pg. 490
BUSSE BROTHERS INC.—See Pinnacle Automation Inc.; *U.S. Private*, pg. 866
BUSSMANN DIVISION—See Cooper Industries, Inc.; *U.S. Public*, pg. 443
BUSTELO COFFEE ROASTING CO.—See The Tetley Group Limited; *Int'l*, pg. 1377
BUSTER BROWN APPAREL, INC.; *U.S. Private*, pg. 189
BUTACHIMIE—See Du Pont (E.I. Du Pont De Nemours & Co.); *U.S. Public*, pg. 533
BUTCHER & CO., INC.; *U.S. Private*, pg. 189
THE BUTCHER COMPANY; *U.S. Private*, pg. 189
BUTCHER ENERGY—See Butcher & Co., Inc.; *U.S. Private*, pg. 189
BUTEN, DIVISION OF DURON—See Duron, Inc.; *U.S. Private*, pg. 349
BUTERA FINER FOODS INC.; *U.S. Private*, pg. 189
BUTLER AUTO AUCTION—See Cox Enterprises, Inc.; *U.S. Private*, pg. 282
BUTLER AUTOMATIC, INC.; *U.S. Private*, pg. 189
BUTLER BUILDING SYSTEMS LTD.—See Butler Manufacturing Company; *U.S. Public*, pg. 271
BUTLER BUILDINGS DIVISION—See Butler Manufacturing Company; *U.S. Public*, pg. 271
BUTLER CAPITAL CORP.; *U.S. Private*, pg. 190
BUTLER DESIGN SERVICES, INC.—See Butler International, Inc.; *U.S. Public*, pg. 271
BUTLER FLEET SERVICES, INC.—See Butler International, Inc.; *U.S. Public*, pg. 271
BUTLER FOODS, INC.; *U.S. Private*, pg. 190
BUTLER INTERNATIONAL, INC.; *U.S. Public*, pg. 270
JOHN O. BUTLER CO.—See Sunstar Inc.; *Int'l*, pg. 1320
JOHN O. BUTLER COMPANY (CANADA)—See Sunstar Inc.; *Int'l*, pg. 1320
JOHN O. BUTLER COMPANY (SWEDEN)—See Sunstar Inc.; *Int'l*, pg. 1321
BUTLER LUTOS SUTTON WILKINSON; *Int'l*, pg. 237
BUTLER MANUFACTURING COMPANY; *U.S. Public*, pg. 271
BUTLER METAL PRODUCTS—See BBA Group plc; *Int'l*, pg. 113
BUTLER NEWALL GMBH—See B. Elliott plc.; *Int'l*, pg. 449
BUTLER NEWALL LIMITED-BUTLER MACHINE TOOL DIV.—See B. Elliott plc.; *Int'l*, pg. 448
BUTLER PHARMA PAK, INC.—See Sunstar Inc.; *Int'l*, pg. 1320
BUTLER REAL ESTATE—See Butler Manufacturing Company; *U.S. Public*, pg. 271
BUTLER SERVICE GROUP, INC.—See Butler International, Inc.; *U.S. Public*, pg. 271
BUTLER SERVICE GROUP - U.K. LTD.—See Butler International, Inc.; *U.S. Public*, pg. 271
BUTLER SERVICES, INC.—See Butler International, Inc.; *U.S. Public*, pg. 271
BUTLER (SHANGHAI), INC.—See Butler Manufacturing Company; *U.S. Public*, pg. 271
BUTLER TECHNOLOGY SOLUTIONS, INC.—See Butler International, Inc.; *U.S. Public*, pg. 271
BUTLER TELECOM, INC.—See Butler International, Inc.; *U.S. Public*, pg. 271
BUTLER TELEPHONE COMPANY, INC.—See Telephone and Data Systems, Inc.; *U.S. Public*, pg. 1571
BUTLER UTILITIES SERVICES, INC.—See Butler International, Inc.; *U.S. Public*, pg. 271
BUTLER VENTAMATIC CORP.; *U.S. Public*, pg. 190
BUTLER WHOLESALE PRODUCTS, INC.; *U.S. Private*, pg. 190
BUTLER'S (GRINDERS & OPERATORS) LTD.—See The Peninsular and Oriental Steam Navigation Company; *Int'l*, pg. 1033
BUTLER'S WAREHOUSING & DISTRIBUTION LTD.—See The Peninsular and Oriental Steam Navigation Company; *Int'l*, pg. 1033
BUTLIN'S LIMITED—See The Rank Group PLC; *Int'l*, pg. 1086
GIO. BUTON S.P.A.—See Diageo Plc; *Int'l*, pg. 409
H.E. BUTT GROCERY CO.; *U.S. Private*, pg. 196
BUTTE CONVALESCENT CENTER—See Horizon/CMS Healthcare Corporation; *U.S. Public*, pg. 837
BUTTE PARK ROYAL—See Horizon/CMS Healthcare Corporation; *U.S. Public*, pg. 837
BUTTER KERNEL PRODUCTS—See Faribault Foods Inc.; *U.S. Private*, pg. 393
BUTTERBALL TURKEY COMPANY—See ConAgra, Inc.; *U.S. Public*, pg. 426
BUTTERFIELD DAY DEVITO HOCKNEY LTD.; *Int'l*, pg. 237
BUTTERICK COMPANY, INC.; *U.S. Private*, pg. 190
BUTTERLEY AGGREGATES LIMITED—See RMC Group p.l.c.; *Int'l*, pg. 1079
BUTTERLEY BRICK LTD.—See Hanson PLC; *Int'l*, pg. 592
BUTTERLEY ENGINEERING LTD.—See Haden Maclellan Holdings plc; *Int'l*, pg. 585
BUTTERWORTH & CO. PUBLISHERS LTD.—See Reed Elsevier plc; *Int'l*, pg. 1095
BUTTERWORTH-HEINEMANN LIMITED—See Reed Elsevier plc; *Int'l*, pg. 1094
BUTTERWORTH-HEINEMANN USA—See Reed Elsevier plc; *Int'l*, pg. 1094
BUTTERWORTH OF PUERTO RICO INC.—See Reed Elsevier plc; *Int'l*, pg. 1095
BUTTERWORTHS ASIA—See Reed Elsevier plc; *Int'l*, pg. 1095
BUTTERWORTHS ASIA (HONG KONG)—See Reed Elsevier plc; *Int'l*, pg. 1095
BUTTERWORTHS AUSTRALIA—See Reed Elsevier plc; *Int'l*, pg. 1095
BUTTERWORTHS BRITISH AND IRISH LEGAL—See Reed Elsevier plc; *Int'l*, pg. 1095
BUTTERWORTHS CANADA—See Reed Elsevier plc; *Int'l*, pg. 1095

BUTTERWORTHS INDIA—See Reed Elsevier plc; *Int'l*, pg. 1095
BUTTERWORTHS IRELAND—See Reed Elsevier plc; *Int'l*, pg. 1095
BUTTERWORTHS MALAYSIA—See Reed Elsevier plc; *Int'l*, pg. 1095
BUTTERWORTHS NEW ZEALAND—See Reed Elsevier plc; *Int'l*, pg. 1095
BUTTERWORTHS SOUTH AFRICA—See Reed Elsevier plc; *Int'l*, pg. 1095
BUTTES DRILLING-C COMPANY—See Reunion Industries, Inc.; *U.S. Public*, pg. 1383
BUTTLE WILSON GROUP LTD.—See Swiss Bank Corporation; *Int'l*, pg. 1331
BUTTREY FOOD & DRUG COMPANY; *U.S. Public*, pg. 271
BUXTON MINERAL WATER COMPANY LTD.—See Nestle S.A.; *Int'l*, pg. 919
BUXTON & SKINNER PRINTING COMPANY—See Pubco Corporation; *U.S. Public*, pg. 1339
BUYCO, INC.; *U.S. Private*, pg. 190
BUYPASS CORPORATION—See CoreStates Financial Corp.; *U.S. Public*, pg. 446
BUZEN TOSHIBA ELECTRONICS CORPORATION—See Toshiba Corporation; *Int'l*, pg. 1402
BYARD KENWEST ENGINEERING LIMITED—See Costain Group PLC; *Int'l*, pg. 336
BYER & MCGUGGART, INC.—See BDDP Group; *Int'l*, pg. 117
BYER CALIFORNIA; *U.S. Private*, pg. 191
BYERLY FORD-NISSAN INC.; *U.S. Private*, pg. 191
BYERLY'S INC.—See Lund Food Holdings, Inc.; *U.S. Private*, pg. 680
BYERS INDUSTRIES, INC.; *U.S. Private*, pg. 191
BYERS PORTLAND WILLAMETTE—See Byers Industries, Inc.; *U.S. Private*, pg. 191
BYGGS SPRUTBETONG AB—See NCC AB; *Int'l*, pg. 899
CARL BYOIR & ASSOCIATES, INC.—See WPP Group plc; *Int'l*, pg. 1483
BYPY HYDRAULICS AND TRANSMISSIONS LTD.—See Wolseley Plc.; *Int'l*, pg. 1511
BYPY HYDRAULICS & TRANSMISSIONS LTD.—See Bondioli & Pavesi S.p.A.; *Int'l*, pg. 201
JACK BYRNE FORD & MERCURY, INC.; *U.S. Private*, pg. 191
JACK BYRNE MINUTEMAN LUBE—See Jack Byrne Ford & Mercury, Inc.; *U.S. Private*, pg. 191
BYRNES & KIEFER COMPANY; *U.S. Private*, pg. 191
BYRON MEDIPLASTICS LIMITED—See Harnischfeger Industries, Inc.; *U.S. Public*, pg. 789
BYRON VALVE FACILITY—See Parker Hannifin Corporation; *U.S. Public*, pg. 1260
BYRON'S, INC.—See Rich Products Corp.; *U.S. Private*, pg. 928
BYTE PUBLICATIONS—See The McGraw-Hill Companies, Inc.; *U.S. Public*, pg. 1070
BYTEX CORPORATION—See Storage Technology Corporation; *U.S. Public*, pg. 1522
BYTEX DATACOM LTD.—See Storage Technology Corporation; *U.S. Public*, pg. 1522
BYTEX GMBH—See Storage Technology Corporation; *U.S. Public*, pg. 1522

C

C.A.L.—See Cultor Ltd.; *Int'l*, pg. 349
C&C ASSOCIATES—See Couristan Inc.; *U.S. Private*, pg. 279
C & C BAKERY—See Grupo Industrial Bimbo S.A. de C.V.; *Int'l*, pg. 575
C & C - COLORING & COMPOUNDING SRL—See Mazzucchelli Polimeri Srl; *Int'l*, pg. 850
C & C MANUFACTURING INC.—See IMI Plc; *Int'l*, pg. 646
C & C (WHOLESALE) LTD.—See Allied Domecq PLC; *Int'l*, pg. 64
C&D CHARTER POWER SYSTEMS; *U.S. Public*, pg. 271
C D DISTRIBUTING CO. INC.—See Borden, Inc.; *U.S. Private*, pg. 158
C&D GROVES—See Cigna Corp.; *U.S. Public*, pg. 365
C & D LEASINGSERVICE GMBH—See Commerzbank AG; *Int'l*, pg. 309
C & D TECHNOLOGIES, INC.; *U.S. Public*, pg. 272
C & J CLARK AMERICA, INC.—See Clarks International; *Int'l*, pg. 297
C & J CLARK CANADA, LTD.—See Clarks International; *Int'l*, pg. 297
C & J CLARK DIRECT MARKETING DIVISION—See Clarks International; *Int'l*, pg. 297
C & J CLARK RETAIL, INC.—See Clarks International; *Int'l*, pg. 297
C & K COLOURS (H.K.) LIMITED—See Crompton & Knowles Corporation; *U.S. Public*, pg. 460
C & K COLOURS (UK) LTD.—See Crompton & Knowles Corporation; *U.S. Public*, pg. 460
C & K MARKET, INC.; *U.S. Private*, pg. 191
C & K TRACKING, INC.—See Rock of Ages Corporation; *Int'l*, pg. 1396
C&L COMMUNICATIONS, INC.; *U.S. Private*, pg. 191
C & L MARKETING INC.—See EMI Group plc; *Int'l*, pg. 428
C & L PROCESSORS PARTNERSHIP—See Du Pont (E.I. Du Pont De Nemours & Co.); *U.S. Public*, pg. 531
C & M CORPORATION; *U.S. Private*, pg. 191
C & M EUROPE—See C & M Corporation; *U.S. Private*, pg. 192
C & S WHOLESALE GROCERY INC.; *U.S. Private*, pg. 192
C & W RAILWAY CO.—See Oregon Steel Mills Inc.; *U.S. Public*, pg. 1230
C&W REFRACTORIES, LTD.—See CFB Industries, Inc.; *U.S. Public*, pg. 216
C. CAKEBREAD—See Esselte AB; *Int'l*, pg. 460
C-COR ELECTRONICS CANADA, INC.—See C-COR Electronics, Inc.; *U.S. Public*, pg. 272
C-COR ELECTRONICS, INC.; *U.S. Public*, pg. 272

C-COR ELECTRONICS, INC.—See C-COR Electronics, Inc.; *U.S. Public*, pg. 272
C-COR EUROPE, B.V.—See C-COR Electronics, Inc.; *U.S. Public*, pg. 272
C-CUBE MICROSYSTEMS; *U.S. Public*, pg. 272
C-E BRASIL COMERCIA E INDUSTRIAL LTDA. SUBSIDIARIA DE COMBUSTION ENGINEERING—See ABB Asea Brown Boveri (Holding) Ltd.; *Int'l*, pg. 5
C-E EUROPE—See ABB Asea Brown Boveri (Holding) Ltd.; *Int'l*, pg. 5
C-E INTERNATIONAL—See ABB Asea Brown Boveri (Holding) Ltd.; *Int'l*, pg. 5
C-E INTERNATIONAL (TECHNOLOGICAL BRANCH)—See ABB Asea Brown Boveri (Holding) Ltd.; *Int'l*, pg. 5
C-LINE PRODUCTS, INC.; *U.S. Private*, pg. 192
C P CONVERTERS, INC.; *U.S. Private*, pg. 192
C S CRABLE SPORTSWEAR, INC.—See The Midland Company; *U.S. Public*, pg. 1111
C S K AUTO INC.—See The Trump Group; *U.S. Private*, pg. 1108
C-T ENGINEERING—See Premier Farnell plc; *Int'l*, pg. 1068
CA BAU-FINANZIERUNGSBERATUNG GMBH—See Creditanstalt-Bankverein; *Int'l*, pg. 347
CA CAPITAL MANAGEMENT LIMITED—See Creditanstalt-Bankverein; *Int'l*, pg. 347
CA COMMUNICATIONS—See Creative Alliance, Inc.; *U.S. Private*, pg. 287
CA-CONSULT INTERNATIONAL INVESTITIONSPROJEKTBERSTUNGESELLSCHAFT M.B.H.—See Creditanstalt-Bankverein; *Int'l*, pg. 347
CA-EA INVESTMENT GMBH—See Creditanstalt-Bankverein; *Int'l*, pg. 347
CA FUND ADVISORY FONDS BERATUNGS GMBH—See Creditanstalt-Bankverein; *Int'l*, pg. 347
CA-GENERALI VERSICHERUNGS AG—See Assicurazioni Generali S.p.A.; *Int'l*, pg. 106
CA GLOBAL FUTURES TERMINKONTRAKTE AG—See Creditanstalt-Bankverein; *Int'l*, pg. 347
CA GLOBAL PROPERTY INTERNATIONALE IMMOBILIEN AG—See Creditanstalt-Bankverein; *Int'l*, pg. 347
CA-GVG-HOLDING GMBH—See Creditanstalt-Bankverein; *Int'l*, pg. 347
THE CA HUNGARY INVESTMENT PARTNERS LTD.—See Creditanstalt-Bankverein; *Int'l*, pg. 347
CA IMMOBILIEN INVEST AG—See Creditanstalt-Bankverein; *Int'l*, pg. 347
CA-INFORMATIONS-TECHNOLOGIE BERATUNGS GMBH—See Creditanstalt-Bankverein; *Int'l*, pg. 347
CA-LEASING GMBH—See Creditanstalt-Bankverein; *Int'l*, pg. 347
CA MANAGEMENT-SYSTEMS-CONSULT GMBH—See Creditanstalt-Bankverein; *Int'l*, pg. 347
CA-1 SERVICES—See Delaware North Companies, Inc.; *U.S. Private*, pg. 322
CA PAWN, INC. OF OHIO—See Cash America International, Inc.; *U.S. Public*, pg. 312
CA-3 BANKEN BETEILIGUNGSFONDS AG—See Creditanstalt-Bankverein; *Int'l*, pg. 347
CA-3 BANKEN VENTURE FONDS AG—See Creditanstalt-Bankverein; *Int'l*, pg. 347
CA II PANTBELANING AB—See Cash America International, Inc.; *U.S. Public*, pg. 312
C.A. VENCEMOS PERTIGALETE—See Lafarge S.A.; *Int'l*, pg. 791
CA-VERSICHERUNGSDIENST GMBH—See Creditanstalt-Bankverein; *Int'l*, pg. 347
CA-VERSICHERUNGSHOLDING GMBH—See Creditanstalt-Bankverein; *Int'l*, pg. 347
CAB (CORPORATION FOR AMERICAN BANKING)—See The American Bankers Association; *U.S. Private*, pg. 51
CAC LEASING A.S., PRAGUE—See Creditanstalt-Bankverein; *Int'l*, pg. 348
CAC MEDICAL CENTERS, INC.—See United HealthCare Corporation; *U.S. Public*, pg. 1678
CAC U.K.—See Thermo Electron Corporation; *U.S. Public*, pg. 1593
CACESA - COMPANIA AUXILIAR AL CARGO EXPRES, S.A.—See SEPI; *Int'l*, pg. 1224
CACI INTERNATIONAL INC; *U.S. Public*, pg. 272
CACI N.V.—See CACI International Inc; *U.S. Public*, pg. 272
C.A.C.O. SERVICES, INC.—See Magellan Health Services, Inc.; *U.S. Public*, pg. 1033
CAD SERVICE NV—See N.V. Koninklijke KNP BT; *Int'l*, pg. 757
CAE DIVISION—See Cadence Design Systems, Inc.; *U.S. Public*, pg. 290
CAE ELECTRONICS (AUSTRALIA) PTY. LTD.—See CAE Inc.; *Int'l*, pg. 238
CAE ELECTRONICS INC.-NEW YORK—See CAE Inc.; *Int'l*, pg. 237
CAE ELECTRONICS, LTD.—See CAE Inc.; *Int'l*, pg. 237
CAE ELECTRONICS PLC—See CAE Inc.; *Int'l*, pg. 238
CAE ELEKTRONIK GMBH—See CAE Inc.; *Int'l*, pg. 238
CAE INC.; *Int'l*, pg. 237
CAE MACHINERY LTD.—See CAE Inc.; *Int'l*, pg. 237
CAE RANSOHOFF INC.—See CAE Inc.; *Int'l*, pg. 237
CAE SCREENPLATES AB—See CAE Inc.; *Int'l*, pg. 238
CAE SCREENPLATES-FINLAND—See CAE Inc.; *Int'l*, pg. 238
CAE SCREENPLATES INC.—See CAE Inc.; *Int'l*, pg. 237
CAE TRISLOT N.V.—See CAE Inc.; *Int'l*, pg. 238
CAE VANGUARD, INC.—See CAE Inc.; *Int'l*, pg. 237
CAF HOLDING COMPANY; *U.S. Private*, pg. 192
CAG ANLAGEFONDSLEITUNG—See Coop Switzerland; *Int'l*, pg. 329
CAI—See Recon/Optical, Inc.; *U.S. Private*, pg. 914
CAI HOLDING COMPANY, INC.—See The Western and Southern Life Insurance Company; *U.S. Public*, pg. 1164
CAIB-AUSTRIA OEVA GMBH—See Brambles Industries Limited; *Int'l*, pg. 212

C.A.I.B./EVA NEDERLAND B.V.—See Brambles Industries Limited; *Int'l*, pg. 212

CAIB-GERMANY, EVA GMBH—See Brambles Industries Limited; *Int'l*, pg. 212

CAIB SA - COMPOSANTS ALUMINIUM INDUSTRIALISES POUR LE BATIMENT SA—See Alusuisse-Lonza Holding Ltd.; *Int'l*, pg. 68

CAIB UK LIMITED—See Brambles Industries Limited; *Int'l*, pg. 212

CAM—See Imetal; *Int'l*, pg. 662

CAM INTERNATIONAL HOLDINGS LTD.; *Int'l*, pg. 238

CAMI AUTOMOTIVE, INC.—See General Motors Corporation; *U.S. Public*, pg. 722

CANCOM—See WIC Western International Communications Ltd.; *Int'l*, pg. 1482

CAP GEMINI AMERICA (MANAGEMENT CONSULTING BRANCH)—See CAP Gemini S.A.; *Int'l*, pg. 264

CAP GEMINI AUSTRIA—See CAP Gemini S.A.; *Int'l*, pg. 264

CAP GEMINI ESPANA—See CAP Gemini S.A.; *Int'l*, pg. 264

CAP GEMINI INOVATION—See CAP Gemini S.A.; *Int'l*, pg. 263

CAP GEMINI (ITALIA)—See CAP Gemini S.A.; *Int'l*, pg. 264

CAP GEMINI SUISSE—See CAP Gemini S.A.; *Int'l*, pg. 264

CAP PROGRAMMATOR—See CAP Gemini S.A.; *Int'l*, pg. 264

CAP RECHTSSCHUTZ—See Allianz Aktiengesellschaft; *Int'l*, pg. 60

CAP SESA FINANCE—See CAP Gemini S.A.; *Int'l*, pg. 263

CAP SESA HOSKYNS—See CAP Gemini S.A.; *Int'l*, pg. 263

CAP SESA INDUSTRIE—See CAP Gemini S.A.; *Int'l*, pg. 263

CAP SESA INFORMATIQUE HOSPITALIERE—See CAP Gemini S.A.; *Int'l*, pg. 263

CAP SESA MAINTENENCE TOUR ANJOU—See CAP Gemini S.A.; *Int'l*, pg. 263

CAP SESA TELECOM—See CAP Gemini S.A.; *Int'l*, pg. 263

CAP SESA TERTIAIRE—See CAP Gemini S.A.; *Int'l*, pg. 263

CAP VOLMAC—See CAP Gemini S.A.; *Int'l*, pg. 264

CAPL—See SAS Holdings Limited; *Int'l*, pg. 1152

CAPS—See SAS Holdings Limited; *Int'l*, pg. 1152

CARBOEX - SOCIEDAD ESPANOLA DE CARBON EXTERIOR, S.A.—See SEPI; *Int'l*, pg. 1224

CASA - CONSTRUCCIONES AERONAUTICAS, S.A.—See SEPI; *Int'l*, pg. 1224

CB & T BANK OF MIDDLE GEORGIA—See Synovus Financial Corp.; *U.S. Public*, pg. 1549

CB & T BANK OF RUSSELL COUNTY—See Synovus Financial Corp.; *U.S. Public*, pg. 1549

CB BANCSHARES, INC. (CITY BANK)—See The Sakura Bank, Limited; *Int'l*, pg. 1179

CB BETEILIGUNGS UND VERWALTUNGSGESELLSCHAFT MBH—See The Chase Manhattan Corporation; *U.S. Public*, pg. 339

CB COMMERCIAL REAL ESTATE; *U.S. Public*, pg. 272

CB COMMERCIAL REAL ESTATE GROUP CENTRAL DIVISION—See CB Commercial Real Estate; *U.S. Public*, pg. 272

CB COMMERCIAL REAL ESTATE GROUP EASTERN DIVISION—See CB Commercial Real Estate; *U.S. Public*, pg. 272

CB COMMERCIAL REAL ESTATE GROUP, INC.—See CB Commercial Real Estate; *U.S. Public*, pg. 272

CB COMMERCIAL REAL ESTATE GROUP, NEW YORK—See CB Commercial Real Estate; *U.S. Public*, pg. 273

CB COMPUTER SERVICES GMBH—See The Chase Manhattan Corporation; *U.S. Public*, pg. 339

CB DIRECT—See Eureko B.V.; *Int'l*, pg. 464

CB FINANCE COMPANY B.V.—See Commerzbank AG; *Int'l*, pg. 312

CB GERMAN INDEX FUND MANAGEMENT COMPANY S.A.—See Commerzbank AG; *Int'l*, pg. 311

CB NORTH AMERICA, INC.; *U.S. Private*, pg. 192

CB PARTNERS—See Cigna Corp.; *U.S. Public*, pg. 357

CB SARREGUEMINES—See Castorama Dubois Investissements S.C.A.; *Int'l*, pg. 275

CB SPORTS INC.—See CB North America, Inc.; *U.S. Private*, pg. 192

CBBM BV—See Reed Elsevier plc; *Int'l*, pg. 1100

CBC INDUSTRIAS PESADAS S.A.—See Mitsubishi Heavy Industries Ltd.; *Int'l*, pg. 874

CBC-U.S.A INC.—See The Chase Manhattan Corporation; *U.S. Public*, pg. 337

C.B.E TECHNOLOGIES INC.—See Richton International Corporation; *U.S. Public*, pg. 1389

CBFC LIMITED—See Commonwealth Bank Group; *Int'l*, pg. 313

CBG CHEMIE BETEILIGUNGSGESELLSCHAFT M.B.H.—See Internatio-Muller N.V.; *Int'l*, pg. 682

CBI INSURANCE CO.—See Commerce Bancshares, Inc.; *U.S. Public*, pg. 410

CBL & ASSOCIATES PROPERTIES, INC.; *U.S. Public*, pg. 273

CBM AMERICA CORP.; *U.S. Private*, pg. 192

CBM GUADELOUPE IMMEUBLE EVC—See Hewlett-Packard Company; *U.S. Public*, pg. 816

CBP RESOURCES—See CBP Resources, Inc.; *U.S. Private*, pg. 192

CBP RESOURCES-GASTONIA DIVISION—See CBP Resources, Inc.; *U.S. Private*, pg. 192

CBP RESOURCES, INC.; *U.S. Private*, pg. 192

CBP RESOURCES-NORFOLK DIVISION—See CBP Resources, Inc.; *U.S. Private*, pg. 192

CBR INVESTMENT CORPORATION OF AMERICA—See Heidelberger Zement A.G.; *Int'l*, pg. 605

CBS—See CBS Corporation; *U.S. Public*, pg. 274

CBS AFFILIATE RELATIONS DIVISION—See CBS Corporation; *U.S. Public*, pg. 274

CBS (AUTOMOTIVE & INDUSTRIAL) LTD.—See BBA Group plc; *Int'l*, pg. 113

CBS BROADCAST GROUP—See CBS Corporation; *U.S. Public*, pg. 274

CBS BROADCAST SERVICES LTD.—See CBS Corporation; *U.S. Public*, pg. 275

CBS CORPORATION; *U.S. Public*, pg. 273

CBS ENTERPRISES DIVISION—See CBS Corporation; *U.S. Public*, pg. 274

CBS ENTERTAINMENT—See CBS Corporation; *U.S. Public*, pg. 274

CBS MARKETING DIVISION—See CBS Corporation; *U.S. Public*, pg. 274

CBS/MTM COMPANY—See CBS Corporation; *U.S. Public*, pg. 275

CBS NEWS—See CBS Corporation; *U.S. Public*, pg. 274

CBS OPERATIONS & ADMINISTRATION DIV.—See CBS Corporation; *U.S. Public*, pg. 274

CBS PENSION TRUSTEES U.K. LIMITED—See CBS Corporation; *U.S. Public*, pg. 275

CBS RADIO—See CBS Corporation; *U.S. Public*, pg. 274

CBS RADIO DIV.—See CBS Corporation; *U.S. Public*, pg. 274

CBS SPORTS DIV.—See CBS Corporation; *U.S. Public*, pg. 274

CBS TELEVISION NETWORK—See CBS Corporation; *U.S. Public*, pg. 274

CBS TELEVISION STATIONS DIV.—See CBS Corporation; *U.S. Public*, pg. 274

CBT SYSTEMS USA—See CBT Systems USA Ltd.; *U.S. Public*, pg. 275

CBT SYSTEMS USA LTD.; *U.S. Public*, pg. 275

CC-BANK, A.G.—See Banco Santander; *Int'l*, pg. 144

CC BANQUE BELGIQUE—See Banco Santander; *Int'l*, pg. 144

C C BEVERAGE PACKING INC.—See Coca-Cola Bottling Co. Consolidated; *U.S. Public*, pg. 391

CC INDUSTRIES, INC.; *U.S. Private*, pg. 192

CC PLAZA CO.—See CalMat Co.; *U.S. Public*, pg. 295

CC SERVICES—See Country Life Insurance Company; *U.S. Private*, pg. 279

CCA INDUSTRIES, INC.; *U.S. Public*, pg. 276

CCA INTERNATIONAL, INC.—See Corrections Corporation of America; *U.S. Public*, pg. 451

CCA SYSTEMS, PTY. LTD.—See COMPAQ Computer Corporation; *U.S. Public*, pg. 418

CCAIR, INC.; *U.S. Public*, pg. 276

CCB CO-OP BANK LIMITED—See Coop Switzerland; *Int'l*, pg. 329

CCB FINANCIAL CORPORATION; *U.S. Public*, pg. 276

CCB/NILS, INC.—See The Walt Disney Company; *U.S. Public*, pg. 512

CCB STAL AS—See Rautaruukki Oy; *Int'l*, pg. 1089

CCC CONVEYORS, INC.—See The Dyson-Kissner-Moran Corporation; *U.S. Private*, pg. 351

CCC INFORMATION SERVICES—See InfoVest, Inc.; *U.S. Private*, pg. 562

CCC STEEL, INC.—See Reliance Steel & Aluminum Co.; *U.S. Public*, pg. 1375

CCCE NELSON/BABYLONE—See BDDP Group; *Int'l*, pg. 116

CCF ASIA LTD—See Credit Commercial de France; *Int'l*, pg. 342

CCF FINANCE MOYEN-ORIENT—See Credit Commercial de France; *Int'l*, pg. 342

CCF FOSTER-BRAITHWAITE—See Credit Commercial de France; *Int'l*, pg. 342

CCF HUNGARY—See Credit Commercial de France; *Int'l*, pg. 342

CCF INTERNATIONAL FINANCE CORP.—See Credit Commercial de France; *Int'l*, pg. 342

CCF KAZAKHSTAN—See Credit Commercial de France; *Int'l*, pg. 342

CCF LISBON—See Credit Commercial de France; *Int'l*, pg. 342

CCF (LUXEMBOURG) S.A.—See Credit Commercial de France; *Int'l*, pg. 342

CCF MELLON PARTNERS—See Credit Commercial de France; *Int'l*, pg. 342

CCF (MONACO) S.A.M.—See Credit Commercial de France; *Int'l*, pg. 342

CCF RANDBURG—See Credit Commercial de France; *Int'l*, pg. 342

CCF REPRESENTACAO E ASSESSORIA S/C LTDA.—See Credit Commercial de France; *Int'l*, pg. 342

CCF ROMANIA—See Credit Commercial de France; *Int'l*, pg. 342

CCF UZBEKISTAN—See Credit Commercial de France; *Int'l*, pg. 342

CCG—See Nichols Research Corporation; *U.S. Public*, pg. 1182

CCG CAPITAL LIMITED—See Confederation Life Insurance Company; *Int'l*, pg. 326

CCG CORP.—See Builders Transport, Incorporated; *U.S. Public*, pg. 267

CCG EQUIPMENT LIMITED—See Confederation Life Insurance Company; *Int'l*, pg. 326

CCG IRELAND—See Confederation Life Insurance Company; *Int'l*, pg. 326

CCH ASIA LIMITED—See Wolters Kluwer N.V.; *Int'l*, pg. 1513

CCH AUSTRALIA LIMITED—See Wolters Kluwer N.V.; *Int'l*, pg. 1513

CCH CANADIAN LTD.—See Wolters Kluwer N.V.; *Int'l*, pg. 1513

CCH COMPUTAX INC.—See Wolters Kluwer N.V.; *Int'l*, pg. 1513

CCH EDITIONS LIMITED—See Wolters Kluwer N.V.; *Int'l*, pg. 1514

CCH EUROPE, INC.—See Wolters Kluwer N.V.; *Int'l*, pg. 1513

CCH INCORPORATED—See Wolters Kluwer N.V.; *Int'l*, pg. 1513

CCH JAPAN LIMITED—See Wolters Kluwer N.V.; *Int'l*, pg. 1513

CCH LEGAL INFORMATION SERVICES, INC.—See Wolters Kluwer N.V.; *Int'l*, pg. 1513

CCH NEW ZEALAND LIMITED—See Wolters Kluwer N.V.; *Int'l*, pg. 1513

CCI CORPORATION; *U.S. Private*, pg. 193

CCI CRANE CORPORATION INTERNATIONAL HANDELSGES. MBH—See Fried. Krupp AG; *Int'l*, pg. 510

CCI/TRIAD AUTOMOTIVE—See CCI/Triad Corporation; *U.S. Private*, pg. 193

CCI/TRIAD CORPORATION; *U.S. Private*, pg. 193

CCIC FINANCE LIMITED—See The Industrial Bank of Japan, Limited; *Int'l*, pg. 676

C.C.K., INC.—See Kunzler & Company, Inc.; *U.S. Private*, pg. 637

CCL CUSTOM MANUFACTURING—See CCL Industries, Inc.; *Int'l*, pg. 238

CCL CUSTOM MANUFACTURING CORP.—See CCL Industries, Inc.; *Int'l*, pg. 239

CCL INDUSTRIES, INC.; *Int'l*, pg. 238

CCL INDUSTRIES LIMITED—See CCL Industries, Inc.; *Int'l*, pg. 239

CCL LABEL—See CCL Industries, Inc.; *Int'l*, pg. 238

CCL LABEL DE MEXICO S.A. DE C.V.—See CCL Industries, Inc.; *Int'l*, pg. 238

CCL LABEL PRODUCT DEVELOPMENT—See CCL Industries, Inc.; *Int'l*, pg. 238

CCL LABEL SALES & MARKETING—See CCL Industries, Inc.; *Int'l*, pg. 238

CCL LABELING EQUIPMENT—See CCL Industries, Inc.; *Int'l*, pg. 238

CCL LTD.—See The Peninsular and Oriental Steam Navigation Company; *Int'l*, pg. 1034

CCL PHARMACEUTICALS—See CCL Industries, Inc.; *Int'l*, pg. 239

CCL SECURITY PRODUCTS—See The Eastern Company; *U.S. Public*, pg. 548

CCL TECHNOLOGIES—See CCL Industries, Inc.; *Int'l*, pg. 238

CCM FRAMLINGTON GROUP PLC—See Credit Commercial de France; *Int'l*, pg. 342

CCM, INC.—See Magellan Health Services, Inc.; *U.S. Public*, pg. 1033

CCM LIMITED—See Sketchley Plc; *Int'l*, pg. 1261

CCMCS, INC.—See Clear Channel Communications, Inc.; *U.S. Public*, pg. 383

CCMP N.V.—See AB Industrivarden; *Int'l*, pg. 678

CCP POSITIONING S.R.L.—See Dentsu Inc.; *Int'l*, pg. 394

CCR-TITRISATION—See Commerzbank AG; *Int'l*, pg. 312

CCS—See Blade Communications; *U.S. Private*, pg. 147

CCS DESKPRO COMPUTER AB—See COMPAQ Computer Corporation; *U.S. Public*, pg. 418

CCS MENDOTA—See R.R. Donnelley & Sons Company; *U.S. Public*, pg. 518

CCT HOLDINGS CORP.—See Charter Communications, Inc.; *U.S. Private*, pg. 230

CCTF—See Emco Limited; *Int'l*, pg. 453

CCW STAMP CO.—See American Marking Systems; *U.S. Private*, pg. 58

CCX FIBERGLASS PRODUCTS—See CCX, Inc.; *U.S. Private*, pg. 193

CCX, INC.; *U.S. Private*, pg. 193

C.D. PACKAGING SYSTEMS LTD.—See American Israeli Paper Mills Ltd.; *Int'l*, pg. 75

CD PLUS S.A.—See Ceridian Corporation; *U.S. Public*, pg. 331

CD PRODUCTS, INC.; *U.S. Public*, pg. 276

CD-ROM TECHNOLOGIES—See American Business Information, Inc.; *U.S. Public*, pg. 70

CDA DISTRIBUTORS—See International Paper Company; *U.S. Public*, pg. 903

CDA INVESTMENT TECHNOLOGIES, INC.—See The Thomson Corporation; *U.S. Public*, pg. 1600

CDB INFOTEC INC.; *U.S. Private*, pg. 193

CDF NORTHEAST—See Cameron Ashley Building Products, Inc.; *U.S. Public*, pg. 298

CDI CORP.; *U.S. Public*, pg. 276

CDI ENGINEERING GROUP, INC.—See CDI Corp.; *U.S. Public*, pg. 277

CDI MANAGED SERVICES—See CDI Corp.; *U.S. Public*, pg. 277

CDI MARINE COMPANY—See CDI Corp.; *U.S. Public*, pg. 277

C.D.I. TECHNOLOGIES, LTD.—See Masco Corporation; *U.S. Public*, pg. 1055

CDI TELECOMMUNICATIONS, INC.—See CDI Corp.; *U.S. Public*, pg. 277

CDM ENGINEERS & CONSTRUCTORS INC.—See Camp Dresser & McKee Inc.; *U.S. Private*, pg. 204

CDM FEDERAL PROGRAMS CORPORATION—See Camp Dresser & McKee Inc.; *U.S. Private*, pg. 204

CDM (PROPRIETARY) LIMITED—See Anglo American Corporation of South Africa Limited; *Int'l*, pg. 77

CDP; *Int'l*, pg. 239

CDP & PARTNERS LTD.—See Dentsu Inc.; *Int'l*, pg. 393

THE CDP MEDIA CO. LTD.—See Dentsu Inc.; *Int'l*, pg. 393

CDR INTERNATIONAL NU/SA—See Flint Ink Corp.; *U.S. Private*, pg. 413

CDR PIGMENTS & DISPERSIONS—See Flint Ink Corp.; *U.S. Private*, pg. 413

CDT INTERNATIONAL—See Cable Design Technologies Corporation; *U.S. Public*, pg. 287

CDW COMPUTER CENTERS, INC.; *U.S. Public*, pg. 277

CDZ—See Lafarge S.A.; *Int'l*, pg. 789

C.E. SERVICES—See Fujitsu Limited; *Int'l*, pg. 527

CE SONORA S.A. DE C.V.—See Cummins Engine Company; *U.S. Public*, pg. 468

CEA-INDUSTRIE (COMMISSARIAT A L'ENERGIE ATOMIQUE); *Int'l*, pg. 239

C.E.A.I.S.A.—See Petrofina S.A.; *Int'l*, pg. 1043

CEC, CHUO ELECTRONICS CO., LTD.—See Knurr AG; *Int'l*, pg. 739

CEDIPSA—See Compania Espanola de Petroleos, S.A. (CEPSA); *Int'l,* pg. 323
CEF SAFETY SYSTEMS B.V.—See Halma p.l.c.; *Int'l,* pg. 590
CEGF—See FMC Corporation; *U.S. Public,* pg. 606
CEGF (USA) INC.—See FMC Corporation; *U.S. Public,* pg. 606
CEGP, CONSULTING ENGINEERS GRABOWSKY & POORT)—See Heidemij N.V.; *Int'l,* pg. 607
CEI ENTERPRISES—See Astec Industries, Inc.; *U.S. Public,* pg. 141
CEM COMPUTERS LIMITED—See Siemens AG; *Int'l,* pg. 1247
CEM CORPORATION; *U.S. Public,* pg. 277
CEM GMBH—See CEM Corporation; *U.S. Public,* pg. 277
CEM (MICROWAVE TECHNOLOGIES) LTD.—See CEM Corporation; *U.S. Public,* pg. 277
CEM SOUTH—See T.L. Smith Machine; *U.S. Private,* pg. 1009
CEM S.R.L.—See CEM Corporation; *U.S. Public,* pg. 277
CEM ZEMENTVERKAUF GMBH—See Heidelberger Zement A.G.; *Int'l,* pg. 605
C.E.P. COMMUNICATION GROUP; *Int'l,* pg. 239
CEP GROUP, INC.—See PP&L Resources; *U.S. Public,* pg. 1244
CEPER-CONDUCTORES ELECTRICOS PERUANOS S.A.—See Pirelli S.p.A.; *Int'l,* pg. 1059
CEPSA CIA. PORTUGUESA DE PETROLEOS, LDA.—See Compania Espanola de Petroleos, S.A. (CEPSA); *Int'l,* pg. 323
CEPSA ESTACIONES DE SERVICIO, S.A.—See Compania Espanola de Petroleos, S.A. (CEPSA); *Int'l,* pg. 323
CEPSA GIBRALTAR, LTD.—See Compania Espanola de Petroleos, S.A. (CEPSA); *Int'l,* pg. 323
CEPSA ITALIA, S.P.A.—See Compania Espanola de Petroleos, S.A. (CEPSA); *Int'l,* pg. 323
CEPSA U.K., LTD.—See Compania Espanola de Petroleos, S.A. (CEPSA); *Int'l,* pg. 323
C.E.R.T.—See Lagardere Groupe; *Int'l,* pg. 795
CERUS - COMPAGNIES EUROPEENNES REUNIES; *Int'l,* pg. 240
CES/CARD ESTABLISHMENT SERVICES INC.—See First Data Corporation; *U.S. Public,* pg. 631
CES THERMAL SERVICES LIMITED-ALEXANDER FIREPROOFING—See American Eco Corporation; *Int'l,* pg. 74
CESA - COMPANIA ESPANOLA DE SISTEMAS AERONAUTICOS, S.A.—See SEPI; *Int'l,* pg. 1224
CESAF (COMPAGNIE D'EXPLOITATION DES SERVICES AUXILLIAIRES FERROVIAIRES)—See Groupe Air France; *Int'l,* pg. 560
CESI CENTRO ELABORAZIONI E STUDI INFORMATICI S.P.A.—See Telefonaktiebolaget LM Ericsson; *Int'l,* pg. 1365
CESL ENGINEERING LIMITED—See Cominco, Ltd.; *Int'l,* pg. 307
CET LTD.—See Hewlett-Packard Company; *U.S. Public,* pg. 816
CETT (COMPAGNIE EUROPEENE DE TELETRANSMISSION)—See Alcatel Alsthom Compagnie Generale D'Electricite; *Int'l,* pg. 53
CF & I STEEL, L.P.—See Oregon Steel Mills Inc.; *U.S. Public,* pg. 1230
CF CABLE TV INC.—See CFCF Inc.; *Int'l,* pg. 240
CF GROUP; *U.S. Public,* pg. 193
CF INDUSTRIES, INC.; *U.S. Private,* pg. 193
CF INVESTMENT COMPANY—See Carolina First Corporation; *U.S. Public,* pg. 306
CF2GS; *U.S. Private,* pg. 194
CF2GS—See CF2GS; *U.S. Private,* pg. 194
CFA HOLDING COMPANY; *U.S. Private,* pg. 194
CFAN-AM—See Rogers Communications, Inc.; *Int'l,* pg. 1123
CFB COMMERZ FONDS BETEILIGUNGS GMBH—See Commerzbank AG; *Int'l,* pg. 309
CFB INDUSTRIES, INC.; *U.S. Private,* pg. 194
CFC DATA CORP.—See Chemical Financial Corporation; *U.S. Public,* pg. 345
CFCF INC.; *Int'l,* pg. 240
CFCF 12—See CFCF Inc.; *Int'l,* pg. 241
CFCI S.A.—See Unilever Plc; *Int'l,* pg. 1436
CFC INVESTMENT CORP.—See Cincinnati Financial Corp.; *U.S. Public,* pg. 368
CFCN COMMUNICATIONS LIMITED—See Rogers Communications, Inc.; *Int'l,* pg. 1123
CFCN-TV (CALGARY & LETHBRIDGE)—See Rogers Communications, Inc.; *Int'l,* pg. 1123
CFCO RADIO-AM—See Rogers Communications, Inc.; *Int'l,* pg. 1123
CFCY-AM/CHLQ-FM—See Rogers Communications, Inc.; *Int'l,* pg. 1124
CFE COMPANY—See AlliedSignal Inc.; *U.S. Public,* pg. 51
CFEM—See Groupe Usinor; *Int'l,* pg. 571
CFG SA—See Heidemij N.V.; *Int'l,* pg. 608
CFI INSURERS, LTD.—See Sizzler International, Inc.; *U.S. Public,* pg. 1475
CFI PTY., LTD.—See Sizzler International, Inc.; *U.S. Public,* pg. 1475
C.F.I.T.R. S.A.—See Fuchs Petrolub AG Oel + Chemie; *Int'l,* pg. 517
CFM INTERNATIONAL INC.—See SNECMA - Societe Nationale d'Etude et de Construction de Moteurs d'Aviation; *Int'l,* pg. 1166
CFM INTERNATIONAL SA—See SNECMA - Societe Nationale d'Etude et de Construction de Moteurs d'Aviation; *Int'l,* pg. 1166
CFNY-FM RADIO—See Rogers Communications, Inc.; *Int'l,* pg. 1124
CFP FOODS—See Saskatchewan Wheat Pool; *Int'l,* pg. 1195
CFPL-TV—See Baton Broadcasting Incorporated; *Int'l,* pg. 171
CFQC-TV—See Baton Broadcasting Incorporated; *Int'l,* pg. 171

CFRN-TV—See Electrohome Ltd.; *Int'l,* pg. 438
CFS NEW ZEALAND LTD.—See Circle International Group, Inc.; *U.S. Public,* pg. 372
CFTO-TV—See Baton Broadcasting Incorporated; *Int'l,* pg. 171
CFX BANK; *U.S. Public,* pg. 277
CFX FUNDING, L.L.C.—See CFX Bank; *U.S. Public,* pg. 278
CFX MORTGAGE, INC.—See CFX Bank; *U.S. Public,* pg. 278
CG&E RESOURCE MARKETING, INC.—See Cinergy Corp.; *U.S. Public,* pg. 369
CG EQUITY VENTURES, INC.—See Cigna Corp.; *U.S. Public,* pg. 365
CG INDIVIDUAL TAX BENEFITS PAYMENTS, INC.—See Cigna Corp.; *U.S. Public,* pg. 358
CG LIFE PENSION BENEFITS PAYMENTS, INC.—See Cigna Corp.; *U.S. Public,* pg. 358
CG LINA PENSION BENEFITS PAYMENTS, INC.—See Cigna Corp.; *U.S. Public,* pg. 358
CG PROJECTS, INC.—See Conrail, Inc.; *U.S. Public,* pg. 432
CG TRUST COMPANY—See Cigna Corp.; *U.S. Public,* pg. 358
CGA-HBS—See Alcatel Alsthom Compagnie Generale D'Electricite; *Int'l,* pg. 53
CGA-HBS (COMPAGNIE GENERALE D'AUTOMATISME)—See Alcatel Alsthom Compagnie Generale D'Electricite; *Int'l,* pg. 53
CGAS, INC.—See Enron Corp.; *U.S. Public,* pg. 585
CGC ENERGY, INC.—See Cascade Natural Gas Corporation; *U.S. Public,* pg. 311
CGC INC.—See USG Corporation; *U.S. Public,* pg. 1660
CGC PROPERTIES INC.—See Cascade Natural Gas Corporation; *U.S. Public,* pg. 311
CGC RESOURCES, INC.—See Cascade Natural Gas Corporation; *U.S. Public,* pg. 311
CGE CORPORATION—See Cinergy Corp.; *U.S. Public,* pg. 369
CGE ECK, INC.—See Cinergy Corp.; *U.S. Public,* pg. 369
CGEP (CIE GENERALE D'ELECTROLYSE DU PALAIS)—See Pechiney S.A.; *Int'l,* pg. 1028
CGF INDUSTRIES; *U.S. Private,* pg. 194
CGF SIGN, INC.—See CGF Industries; *U.S. Private,* pg. 194
CGG AMERICAN SERVICES INC.—See CGG Group; *Int'l,* pg. 241
CGG CHEMOGAS GMBH—See Linde AG; *Int'l,* pg. 811
CGG GEOPHYSICS CANADA LTD.—See CGG Group; *Int'l,* pg. 241
CGG GROUP; *Int'l,* pg. 241
CGG NORGE A/S—See CGG Group; *Int'l,* pg. 241
CGG PAN INDIA LTD.—See CGG Group; *Int'l,* pg. 241
CGI PARTNERS LP—See Cigna Corp.; *U.S. Public,* pg. 357
CGR COMMUNICATIONS—See Saatchi & Saatchi Advertising Worldwide; *U.S. Public,* pg. 1422
CGRM—See AXA-UAP; *Int'l,* pg. 19
CGS INDUSTRIES, INC.; *U.S. Private,* pg. 194
CGTM—See Labinal SA; *Int'l,* pg. 787
CGTX CALGARY OFFICE—See GATX Corporation; *U.S. Public,* pg. 693
CGTX INC.—See Hawker Siddeley Canada Inc.; *Int'l,* pg. 604
CGTX, INC.—See GATX Corporation; *U.S. Public,* pg. 693
CGTX TORONTO OFFICE—See GATX Corporation; *U.S. Public,* pg. 693
CH & A CORPORATION—See SGS Societe Generale de Surveillance Holding S.A.; *Int'l,* pg. 1153
CH MORTGAGE COMPANY—See Continental Homes Holding Corp.; *U.S. Public,* pg. 441
C H RESOURCES, INC.—See Central Hudson Gas & Electric Corporation; *U.S. Public,* pg. 325
CHB CORP.; *U.S. Private,* pg. 194
CHBX/CJIC-TV—See Baton Broadcasting Incorporated; *Int'l,* pg. 171
CHCH-TV—See Rogers Communications, Inc.; *Int'l,* pg. 1124
CHF INDUSTRIES, INC.—See Trace International Holdings, Inc.; *U.S. Private,* pg. 1094
CHI FINANCE CORP.—See Continental Homes Holding Corp.; *U.S. Public,* pg. 441
CHNS/CHFX RADIO—See Maritime Broadcasting System Ltd.; *Int'l,* pg. 842
CHR DIVISION—See Furon Company; *U.S. Public,* pg. 689
CHR INDUSTRIES, INC.—See Furon Company; *U.S. Public,* pg. 689
CHRO-TV—See Baton Broadcasting Incorporated; *Int'l,* pg. 171
CHT STEEL COMPANY INC.—See Stelco Inc.; *Int'l,* pg. 1299
CH2M HILL COMPANIES, LTD.; *U.S. Private,* pg. 195
CH2M HILL, INC.—See CH2M Hill Companies, Ltd.; *U.S. Private,* pg. 195
CH2M HILL INDUSTRIAL DESIGN CORP.—See CH2M Hill Companies, Ltd.; *U.S. Private,* pg. 195
CHWI-TV—See Baton Broadcasting Incorporated; *Int'l,* pg. 171
CHYM/CKGL RADIO—See Rogers Communications, Inc.; *Int'l,* pg. 1124
CHYR RADIO-AM—See Rogers Communications, Inc.; *Int'l,* pg. 1124
C.I. HOLDINGS BERHAD—See Redland PLC; *Int'l,* pg. 1092
C.I. PROPERTY & INVESTMENTS LIMITED—See Christies International plc; *Int'l,* pg. 290
CIBC ASIA LIMITED—See Canadian Imperial Bank of Commerce; *Int'l,* pg. 257
CIBC AUSTRALIA HOLDINGS LIMITED—See Canadian Imperial Bank of Commerce; *Int'l,* pg. 257
CIBC AUSTRALIA LIMITED—See Canadian Imperial Bank of Commerce; *Int'l,* pg. 257
CIBC AVIATION, INC.—See Canadian Imperial Bank of Commerce; *Int'l,* pg. 257

CIBC BANK AND TRUST COMPANY (CAYMAN) LIMITED—See Canadian Imperial Bank of Commerce; *Int'l,* pg. 257
CIBC BANK AND TRUST COMPANY (CHANNEL ISLANDS) LIMITED—See Canadian Imperial Bank of Commerce; *Int'l,* pg. 257
CIBC CAPITAL CORPORATION—See Canadian Imperial Bank of Commerce; *Int'l,* pg. 257
CIBC CONTRACTORS UK LIMITED—See Canadian Imperial Bank of Commerce; *Int'l,* pg. 257
CIBC FINANCE B.V.—See Canadian Imperial Bank of Commerce; *Int'l,* pg. 257
CIBC FINANCE PLC—See Canadian Imperial Bank of Commerce; *Int'l,* pg. 257
CIBC FINANZ AG—See Canadian Imperial Bank of Commerce; *Int'l,* pg. 257
CIBC HOLDINGS (CAYMAN) LIMITED—See Canadian Imperial Bank of Commerce; *Int'l,* pg. 257
CIBC HOLDINGS G.M.B.H.—See Canadian Imperial Bank of Commerce; *Int'l,* pg. 257
CIBC (HONG KONG) LIMITED—See Canadian Imperial Bank of Commerce; *Int'l,* pg. 257
CIBC INC.—See Canadian Imperial Bank of Commerce; *Int'l,* pg. 257
CIBC INVESTMENT MANAGEMENT LIMITED—See Canadian Imperial Bank of Commerce; *Int'l,* pg. 257
CIBC JAMAICA LTD.—See Canadian Imperial Bank of Commerce; *Int'l,* pg. 258
CIBC LIMITED—See Canadian Imperial Bank of Commerce; *Int'l,* pg. 257
CIBC MORTGAGE CORPORATION—See Canadian Imperial Bank of Commerce; *Int'l,* pg. 256
CIBC MORTGAGES PLC—See Canadian Imperial Bank of Commerce; *Int'l,* pg. 257
CIBC NEW ZEALAND HOLDINGS LIMITED—See Canadian Imperial Bank of Commerce; *Int'l,* pg. 258
CIBC NEW ZEALAND LIMITED—See Canadian Imperial Bank of Commerce; *Int'l,* pg. 258
CIBC OPPENHEIMER CORP.—See Canadian Imperial Bank of Commerce; *Int'l,* pg. 257
CIBC SECURITIES EUROPE LIMITED—See Canadian Imperial Bank of Commerce; *Int'l,* pg. 257
CIBC SECURITIES, INC.—See Canadian Imperial Bank of Commerce; *Int'l,* pg. 256
CIBC UNIT TRUST MANAGERS PLC—See Canadian Imperial Bank of Commerce; *Int'l,* pg. 257
CIBC (U.K.) HOLDINGS LIMITED—See Canadian Imperial Bank of Commerce; *Int'l,* pg. 257
CIBC VENTURES, INC.—See Canadian Imperial Bank of Commerce; *Int'l,* pg. 256
THE CIBC WOOD GUNDY CORPORATION—See Canadian Imperial Bank of Commerce; *Int'l,* pg. 256
CIBC WOOD GUNDY INC.—See Canadian Imperial Bank of Commerce; *Int'l,* pg. 256
CIC FINANCIAL—See Loews Corporation; *U.S. Public,* pg. 1011
CIC PARIS—See Groupe GAN; *Int'l,* pg. 564
CICA SUPERANNUATION NOMINEES, PTY., LTD.—See AON Corporation; *U.S. Public,* pg. 118
CICI/CKNC-TV—See Baton Broadcasting Incorporated; *Int'l,* pg. 171
CICM FUND MANAGEMENT LTD.—See Commerzbank AG; *Int'l,* pg. 309
CICM (IRELAND) LIMITED—See Commerzbank AG; *Int'l,* pg. 309
CID FCA/BMZ SEVILLA—See FCA/BMZ CID; *Int'l,* pg. 469
CIE AMERICA, INC.—See Itochu Corporation; *Int'l,* pg. 694
C.I.E. COMPUTER AND INDUSTRIAL ENGINEERING—See Hewlett-Packard Company; *U.S. Public,* pg. 817
CIE SYSTEMS—See Itochu Corporation; *Int'l,* pg. 694
CIECO (AMERICA), INC.—See Itochu Corporation; *Int'l,* pg. 694
CIED CENTRO INTERNACIONAL DE EDUCACION Y DESARROLLO—See Petroleos de Venezuela S.A.; *Int'l,* pg. 1045
CIEL CARIBBEAN INTERNATIONAL EQUIPMENT LTD.—See Confederation Life Insurance Company; *Int'l,* pg. 326
CIFRA, S.A. DE C.V.; *Int'l,* pg. 241
CIG EXPLORATION, INC.—See The Coastal Corporation; *U.S. Public,* pg. 390
CIG MEDISHIELD CO.—See Hewlett-Packard Company; *U.S. Public,* pg. 816
CIGL HOLDINGS LTD.; *Int'l,* pg. 241
CII-HONEYWELL BULL CAMEROUN SARL—See Compagnie des Machines Bull; *Int'l,* pg. 316
CII-HONEYWELL BULL CONGO SARL—See Compagnie des Machines Bull; *Int'l,* pg. 318
CII-HONEYWELL BULL COTE-D'IVOIRE S.A.—See Compagnie des Machines Bull; *Int'l,* pg. 316
CII-HONEYWELL BULL FINANCE BV—See Compagnie des Machines Bull; *Int'l,* pg. 318
CII-HONEYWELL BULL GABON SARL—See Compagnie des Machines Bull; *Int'l,* pg. 316
CII-HONEYWELL BULL NIGER SARL—See Compagnie des Machines Bull; *Int'l,* pg. 316
CII-HONEYWELL BULL SENEGAL SARL—See Compagnie des Machines Bull; *Int'l,* pg. 316
CIMAF-COMPANHIA INDUSTRIAL E MERCANTIL DE ARTEFATOS DE FERRO—See N.V. Bekaert S.A.; *Int'l,* pg. 184
CIMCO REFRIGERATION—See Toromont Industries Ltd.; *Int'l,* pg. 1400
CIMS DEVELOPMENT LABORATORY—See Platinum Technology, Inc.; *U.S. Public,* pg. 1309
CINBA SA—See Diageo Plc; *Int'l,* pg. 409
CIO PUBLISHING CORP.—See International Data Group; *U.S. Private,* pg. 569
CIOK-FM RADIO—See Rogers Communications, Inc.; *Int'l,* pg. 1124
CIP—See Banque Nationale de Paris; *Int'l,* pg. 163
CIREX - CIA. DE REPRESENTACIONES, INVERSIONES Y EXPORTAC, S.A.—See SEPI; *Int'l,* pg. 1224
CIS—See IRI Istituto Ricostruzione Industriale; *Int'l,* pg. 654

C.I.S. CO. OF ALABAMA—See Central Illinois Steel Company; *U.S. Private*, pg. 223
CIS TECHNOLOGIES, INC.—See National Data Corporation; *U.S. Public*, pg. 1155
CITA TABACOS DE CANARIAS, S.A.—See Tabacalera, S.A.; *Int'l*, pg. 1346
CITEX—See Technip; *Int'l*, pg. 1360
CITRA—See SNCF; *Int'l*, pg. 1163
CIWLT MERE & SUCCURSALES—See Accor S.A.; *Int'l*, pg. 21
C.J. TOWER INC.—See The McGraw-Hill Companies; *U.S. Public*, pg. 1071
CJCW-AM—See Rogers Communications, Inc.; *Int'l*, pg. 1124
CJOH-TV—See Baton Broadcasting Incorporated; *Int'l*, pg. 171
C.K. TRADING CORP.—See Baltek Corporation; *U.S. Public*, pg. 172
CKBI/CIPA-TV, PRINCE ALBERT—See Baton Broadcasting Incorporated; *Int'l*, pg. 171
CKC—See Asko, Inc; *U.S. Private*, pg. 89
CKCK-TV—See Baton Broadcasting Incorporated; *Int'l*, pg. 171
CKCO-TV—See Electrohome Ltd.; *Int'l*, pg. 438
CKCW-AM/CFQM-FM—See Rogers Communications, Inc.; *Int'l*, pg. 1124
CKDH RADIO AM—See Rogers Communications, Inc.; *Int'l*, pg. 1124
CKE RESTAURANTS INC.; *U.S. Public*, pg. 278
CKNB-AM—See Rogers Communications, Inc.; *Int'l*, pg. 1124
CKNG-FM/CHED-AM RADIO—See Rogers Communications, Inc.; *Int'l*, pg. 1124
CKNX-TV—See Baton Broadcasting Incorporated; *Int'l*, pg. 171
CKNY/CHNB-TV—See Baton Broadcasting Incorporated; *Int'l*, pg. 171
CKOS/CICC TV—See Baton Broadcasting Incorporated; *Int'l*, pg. 171
CKS GROUP; *U.S. Private*, pg. 195
CKS PARTNERS/LONDON—See CKS Group; *U.S. Private*, pg. 195
CKS PARTNERS/PORTLAND—See CKS Group; *U.S. Private*, pg. 195
CKS PARTNERS/SAN FRANCISCO—See CKS Group; *U.S. Private*, pg. 195
CKTY/CFGX—See Rogers Communications, Inc.; *Int'l*, pg. 1123
CKYC-AM RADIO—See Rogers Communications, Inc.; *Int'l*, pg. 1124
CL CAPITAL MANAGEMENT, INC.—See The Canada Life Assurance Company; *Int'l*, pg. 255
CL CAPITAL MANAGEMENT INC.—See Confederation Life Insurance Company; *Int'l*, pg. 326
CLAI LIMITED—See The Canada Life Assurance Company; *Int'l*, pg. 255
CLCL CARIBBEAN INTERNATIONAL CAPITAL LTD.—See Confederation Life Insurance Company; *Int'l*, pg. 326
CLGB PROPERTY COMPANY LIMITED—See The Canada Life Assurance Company; *Int'l*, pg. 255
CLIC COMPANY I—See The Western and Southern Life Insurance Company; *U.S. Private*, pg. 1164
CLMS REALTY LTD.—See The Canada Life Assurance Company; *Int'l*, pg. 254
CLR CORPORATION—See Empire of Carolina, Inc.; *U.S. Public*, pg. 579
CLS LASER SYSTEMS—See Litton Industries, Inc.; *U.S. Public*, pg. 1002
CLT DEUTSCHLAND—See Groupe Bruxelles Lambert S.A.; *Int'l*, pg. 561
CLT-UFA—See Groupe Bruxelles Lambert S.A.; *Int'l*, pg. 561
CLT UK RADIO—See Groupe Bruxelles Lambert S.A.; *Int'l*, pg. 561
CLT USA—See Groupe Bruxelles Lambert S.A.; *Int'l*, pg. 561
CLTV NEWS—See Tribune Company; *U.S. Public*, pg. 1635
CM CHAIN DIVISION—See Columbus McKinnon Corp.; *U.S. Public*, pg. 405
CM CHEMICAL—See Metallgesellschaft AG; *Int'l*, pg. 861
CM GRAPHICS—See PrimeSource Corporation; *U.S. Public*, pg. 1329
CM HOIST DIVISION—See Columbus McKinnon Corp.; *U.S. Public*, pg. 405
CM HUMAN SERVICES CO. LTD.—See Caterpillar Inc.; *U.S. Public*, pg. 317
CM MATERIALS AB—See Celsius AB; *Int'l*, pg. 276
CM MECHANICAL HANDLING SYSTEMS—See Columbus McKinnon Corp.; *U.S. Public*, pg. 405
CM PARTNERS, INC.; *U.S. Private*, pg. 195
CM SHREDDER DIV.—See Columbus McKinnon Corp.; *U.S. Public*, pg. 405
CMAC INVESTMENT CORPORATION; *U.S. Public*, pg. 278
CMB SONOCO COMPOSITES—See Sonoco Products Company; *U.S. Public*, pg. 1486
CMC (AUSTRALIA) PTY. LIMITED—See Commercial Metals Company; *U.S. Public*, pg. 413
CMC-CAYCE—See Commercial Metals Company; *U.S. Public*, pg. 412
CMC FAREAST LIMITED—See Commercial Metals Company; *U.S. Public*, pg. 413
CMC INTERNATIONAL (S.E. ASIA) PTE. LIMITED—See Commercial Metals Company; *U.S. Public*, pg. 413
CMC KALAMAZOO INC.—See Stamford Capital; *U.S. Private*, pg. 1030
CMC-LEXINGTON—See Commercial Metals Company; *U.S. Public*, pg. 412
CMC-NORTH AUGUSTA—See Commercial Metals Company; *U.S. Public*, pg. 412
C.M.C. SA—See Lagardere Groupe; *Int'l*, pg. 792
CMC STEEL FABRICATORS, INC.—See Commercial Metals Company; *U.S. Public*, pg. 412
CMC STEEL HOLDING CO.—See Commercial Metals Company; *U.S. Public*, pg. 412

CMC TRADING AG—See Commercial Metals Company; *U.S. Public*, pg. 414
CMC (UK) LIMITED—See Commercial Metals Company; *U.S. Public*, pg. 414
CMCA, INC.—See Magellan Health Services, Inc.; *U.S. Public*, pg. 1033
CMCI, INC.—See Magellan Health Services, Inc.; *U.S. Public*, pg. 1033
C.M.D. CHATEL MEDICAL DEVICES S.A.—See Nutricia BV; *Int'l*, pg. 991
CME—See California Manufacturing Enterprises; *U.S. Private*, pg. 201
CME KHBB; *Int'l*, pg. 241
CMEC CO., LTD.—See Caterpillar Inc.; *U.S. Public*, pg. 317
CMFC, INC.—See Magellan Health Services, Inc.; *U.S. Public*, pg. 1033
CMF&Z PUBLIC RELATIONS—See Young & Rubicam Inc.; *U.S. Private*, pg. 1197
CMG HEALTH—See Magellan Health Services, Inc.; *U.S. Public*, pg. 1036
CMG MORTGAGE INSURANCE COMPANY—See CUNA Mutual Insurance Society; *U.S. Private*, pg. 296
CMH HOMES, INC.—See Clayton Homes, Inc.; *U.S. Public*, pg. 383
CMH MANUFACTURING, INC.—See Clayton Homes, Inc.; *U.S. Public*, pg. 383
CMH PARKS, INC.—See Clayton Homes, Inc.; *U.S. Public*, pg. 383
CMI-ATLANTA—See Creative Marketing International Corp.; *U.S. Private*, pg. 287
CMI-CALIFORNIA—See Creative Marketing International Corp.; *U.S. Private*, pg. 287
CMI CORPORATION; *U.S. Public*, pg. 278
C.M.I. DEFENCE SYSTEMS LTD.—See Cockerill Sambre; *Int'l*, pg. 302
CMI-DETROIT—See Creative Marketing International Corp.; *U.S. Private*, pg. 287
CMI ENERGY CONVERSION SYSTEMS, INC.—See CMI Corporation; *U.S. Public*, pg. 279
CMI GROUP, INC.—See The ServiceMaster Company; *U.S. Public*, pg. 1462
CMI HOLDING CO.—See Torchmark Corporation; *U.S. Public*, pg. 1623
CMI HOLDING CORP.; *U.S. Private*, pg. 195
CMI INDUSTRIES, INC.; *U.S. Private*, pg. 195
CMI INDUSTRIES, INC.—See CMI Industries, Inc.; *U.S. Private*, pg. 195
CMI INDUSTRIES INC.-FINISHED FABRICS DIVISION—See CMI Industries, Inc.; *U.S. Private*, pg. 195
CMI INTERNATIONAL—See CMI Corporation; *U.S. Public*, pg. 279
CMI INTERNATIONAL, INC.; *U.S. Private*, pg. 195
C.M.I. INTERNATIONAL LTD.—See Cockerill Sambre; *Int'l*, pg. 302
CMI LLOYDS—See Central Mutual Insurance Co.; *U.S. Private*, pg. 224
CMI LOAD KING TRAILER DIVISION—See CMI Corporation; *U.S. Public*, pg. 279
C.M.I. MALAYSIA—See Cockerill Sambre; *Int'l*, pg. 302
CMI METRO PAVE—See CMI Corporation; *U.S. Public*, pg. 279
CMI OIL CORPORATION—See CMI Corporation; *U.S. Public*, pg. 279
CMI-TORONTO—See Creative Marketing International Corp.; *U.S. Private*, pg. 287
CMI WEIGHING EQUIPMENT DIVISION—See CMI Corporation; *U.S. Public*, pg. 279
CMIC SA—See Alusuisse-Lonza Holding Ltd.; *Int'l*, pg. 68
CML GROUP, INC.; *U.S. Public*, pg. 279
CMM TRANSPORTATION INC.—See Abbott Laboratories; *U.S. Public*, pg. 13
CMP MEDIA, INC.; *U.S. Public*, pg. 279
CMS CHILE S.A.—See Inco Limited; *Int'l*, pg. 672
C.M.S. COMPANIA ANONIMA—See Saint-Gobain; *Int'l*, pg. 1174
CMS ENERGY CORPORATION; *U.S. Public*, pg. 279
CMS ENGINEERING CO.—See CMS Energy Corporation; *U.S. Public*, pg. 280
CMS ENHANCEMENTS, PTE. LTD.—See Ameriquest Technologies; *U.S. Public*, pg. 96
CMS ENTERPRISES, INC.—See CMS Energy Corporation; *U.S. Public*, pg. 279
CMS GENERATION CO.—See CMS Energy Corporation; *U.S. Public*, pg. 280
CMS GILBRETH PACKAGING SYSTEMS—See IMPAXX, Inc.; *U.S. Public*, pg. 558
CMS MIDLAND, INC.—See CMS Energy Corporation; *U.S. Public*, pg. 280
CMS NOMECO—See CMS Energy Corporation; *U.S. Public*, pg. 280
CMS THERAPIES, INC.—See Horizon/CMS Healthcare Corporation; *U.S. Public*, pg. 839
CMS TRANSPORTATION & DISTRIBUTION—See Ameritruck Distribution Corporation; *U.S. Private*, pg. 66
CMSF, INC.—See Magellan Health Services, Inc.; *U.S. Public*, pg. 1033
CMT DASCO S.A.—See BASF AG; *Int'l*, pg. 107
CMT DYNAMICS—See Caparo Group Ltd.; *Int'l*, pg. 265
CMT ENGINEERING LTD.—See Caparo Group Ltd.; *Int'l*, pg. 265
CMT ENGINEERING INSULATION—See Caparo Group Ltd.; *Int'l*, pg. 265
CMT STEELS & SUPPLIES—See Caparo Group Ltd.; *Int'l*, pg. 265
CMV CREDIET MAATSCHAPPIJ VENLO N.V. STEEGH ASSURANTIEN B.V.—See ABN-AMRO Holding N.V.; *Int'l*, pg. 9
CNA FINANCIAL CORP.—See Loews Corporation; *U.S. Public*, pg. 1010
CNA INSURANCE COMPANIES—See Loews Corporation; *U.S. Public*, pg. 1010
CNB BANCSHARES, INC.; *U.S. Public*, pg. 280
CNB INTERNATIONAL—See CNB International, Inc.; *U.S. Private*, pg. 196

CNB INTERNATIONAL, INC.; *U.S. Private*, pg. 196
CNB INTERNATIONAL, L.L.C.—See CNB International, Inc.; *U.S. Private*, pg. 196
CNBC—See General Electric Company; *U.S. Public*, pg. 712
CNF CONSTRUCTORS INC.—See Kenetech Corp.; *U.S. Public*, pg. 950
CNF INDUSTRIES INC.—See Kenetech Corp.; *U.S. Public*, pg. 950
CNF S.A.—See Unilever Plc; *Int'l*, pg. 1436
CNF TRANSPORTATION INC.; *U.S. Public*, pg. 281
CNG COAL CO.—See Consolidated Natural Gas Company; *U.S. Public*, pg. 435
CNG ENERGY SERVICES CORPORATION—See Consolidated Natural Gas Company; *U.S. Public*, pg. 435
CNG INTERNATIONAL CORP.—See Consolidated Natural Gas Company; *U.S. Public*, pg. 435
CNG POWER SERVICES CORPORATION—See Consolidated Natural Gas Company; *U.S. Public*, pg. 435
CNG PRODUCING CO.—See Consolidated Natural Gas Company; *U.S. Public*, pg. 435
CNG REALTY CO.—See CTG Resources, Inc.; *U.S. Public*, pg. 285
CNG TRANSMISSION CORPORATION—See Consolidated Natural Gas Company; *U.S. Public*, pg. 435
CNJ DISTRIBUTING; *U.S. Public*, pg. 281
CNL BULL—See Compagnie des Machines Bull; *Int'l*, pg. 318
CNL FINANCIAL CORP.; *U.S. Public*, pg. 281
CNL/RESOURCE MARKETING CORP.—See CNL Financial Corp.; *U.S. Public*, pg. 282
CNN (CABLE NEWS NETWORK)—See Time Warner Inc.; *U.S. Public*, pg. 1614
CNN HEADLINE NEWS—See Time Warner Inc.; *U.S. Public*, pg. 1614
CNN RADIO—See Time Warner Inc.; *U.S. Public*, pg. 1614
CNO N.V.—See BASF AG; *Int'l*, pg. 107
CNP ASSURANCES; *Int'l*, pg. 241
C.N.P. S.A.—See Tractebel; *Int'l*, pg. 1415
CNS-COMMUNITY NEWS SERVICE WEEKLY NEWSPAPERS—See The Dispatch Printing Company; *U.S. Private*, pg. 335
CNT FRANCE S.A.—See Computer Network Technology Corporation; *U.S. Public*, pg. 421
CNT INTERNATIONAL—See Computer Network Technology Corporation; *U.S. Public*, pg. 421
CNTIC FUSHUN IMPORT & EXPORT—See China National Technical Import & Export Corporation (CNTIC); *Int'l*, pg. 285
CNTIC HAINAN INDUSTRIAL CO.—See China National Technical Import & Export Corporation (CNTIC); *Int'l*, pg. 285
CNTIC HUIZHOU IMPORT & EXPORT CO.—See China National Technical Import & Export Corporation (CNTIC); *Int'l*, pg. 285
CNTIC NORTH CHINA IMPORT & EXPORT CO.—See China National Technical Import & Export Corporation (CNTIC); *Int'l*, pg. 285
CNTIC NORTH WEST IMPORT & EXPORT CO.—See China National Technical Import & Export Corporation (CNTIC); *Int'l*, pg. 285
CNTIC REPRESENTATIVE OFFICE IN USA—See China National Technical Import & Export Corporation (CNTIC); *Int'l*, pg. 285
CNTIC SHANGHAI IMPORT & EXPORT CO.—See China National Technical Import & Export Corporation (CNTIC); *Int'l*, pg. 285
CNTIC SHENZHEN IMPORT & EXPORT CO.—See China National Technical Import & Export Corporation (CNTIC); *Int'l*, pg. 285
CNTIC SOUTH CHINA IMPORT & EXPORT CO.—See China National Technical Import & Export Corporation (CNTIC); *Int'l*, pg. 285
CNTIC STRAIT I/E CORP.—See China National Technical Import & Export Corporation (CNTIC); *Int'l*, pg. 285
CNTIC TIANJIN IMPORT & EXPORT CO.—See China National Technical Import & Export Corporation (CNTIC); *Int'l*, pg. 285
CNTIC TIANSHAN IMPORT & EXPORT CO.—See China National Technical Import & Export Corporation (CNTIC); *Int'l*, pg. 285
CNTIC ZHUHAI IMPORT & EXPORT CO.—See China National Technical Import & Export Corporation (CNTIC); *Int'l*, pg. 285
COBE IBERICA S.A.—See Incentive AB; *Int'l*, pg. 667
COBE INTERNATIONAL LTD—See Incentive AB; *Int'l*, pg. 667
COBE LABORATORIES, INC.—See Incentive AB; *Int'l*, pg. 667
COBE LABORATORIES, K.K.—See Incentive AB; *Int'l*, pg. 667
COBE LABORATORIES PTY LTD.-MELBOURNE—See Incentive AB; *Int'l*, pg. 667
COBE LABORATORIES PTY LTD.-SYDNEY—See Incentive AB; *Int'l*, pg. 667
COBE RENAL CARE, INC.—See Incentive AB; *Int'l*, pg. 667
C.O.F.E.C.—See Lagardere Groupe; *Int'l*, pg. 792
COFINEC (COMPAGNIE FINANCIERE POUR L'EUROPE CENTRALE)—See CERUS - Compagnies Europeennes Reunies; *Int'l*, pg. 240
COFIR (CORPORACION FINANCIERA REUNIDA)—See CERUS - Compagnies Europeennes Reunies; *Int'l*, pg. 240
COGECOM—See France Telecom; *Int'l*, pg. 503
COM/ENERGY ACUSHNET REALTY—See Commonwealth Energy System; *U.S. Public*, pg. 414
COM/ENERGY CAMBRIDGE REALTY—See Commonwealth Energy System; *U.S. Public*, pg. 414
COM/ENERGY ENTERPRISES—See Commonwealth Energy System; *U.S. Public*, pg. 414

COM/ENERGY FREETOWN REALTY—See Commonwealth Energy System; *U.S. Public*, pg. 414
COM/ENERGY RESEARCH PARK REALTY—See Commonwealth Energy System; *U.S. Public*, pg. 414
COM/ENERGY RESOURCES INC.—See Commonwealth Energy System; *U.S. Public*, pg. 414
COM/ENERGY SERVICES CO.—See Commonwealth Energy System; *U.S. Public*, pg. 414
COM/ENERGY STEAM CO.—See Commonwealth Energy System; *U.S. Public*, pg. 414
COMSIP AL A'ALI W.L.L.—See Alcatel Alsthom Compagnie Generale D'Electricite; *Int'l*, pg. 53
COMSIP AUTOMATION BENELUX, S.A.—See Alcatel Alsthom Compagnie Generale D'Electricite; *Int'l*, pg. 53
COMSIP CAM—See Alcatel Alsthom Compagnie Generale D'Electricite; *Int'l*, pg. 53
COMSIP LTD.—See Alcatel Alsthom Compagnie Generale D'Electricite; *Int'l*, pg. 53
COMSIP NEDERLAND B.V.—See Alcatel Alsthom Compagnie Generale D'Electricite; *Int'l*, pg. 53
COP COMMUNICATIONS; *U.S. Private*, pg. 196
COPAL SNC—See Alusuisse-Lonza Holding Ltd.; *Int'l*, pg. 68
CORPA REINSURANCE COMPANY—See AEGON N.V.; *Int'l*, pg. 28
CORS; *U.S. Private*, pg. 196
CP8 - MICROELECTRONIQUE—See Compagnie des Machines Bull; *Int'l*, pg. 316
CP8 - OBERTHUR—See Compagnie des Machines Bull; *Int'l*, pg. 316
C.P. REHAB CORP. OF DELAWARE—See Prime Medical Services, Inc.; *U.S. Public*, pg. 414
CPA/AJI (TAIWAN) LTD.—See Ajinomoto Company Inc.; *Int'l*, pg. 41
THE CPAC CONCRETE PRODUCTS CO., LTD.—See The Siam Cement Public Company Limited; *Int'l*, pg. 1237
CPAC EQUIPMENT DIVISION—See CPAC, Inc.; *U.S. Public*, pg. 282
CPAC EUROPE N.V.—See CPAC, Inc.; *U.S. Public*, pg. 282
CPAC, INC.; *U.S. Public*, pg. 282
CPAC ITALIA, S.R.L./CHIMIFOTO ORNANO—See CPAC, Inc.; *U.S. Public*, pg. 282
THE CPAC READY MIXED CONCRETE CO., LTD.—See The Siam Cement Public Company Limited; *Int'l*, pg. 1237
CPAC ROOF TILE CO., LIMITED—See Redland PLC; *Int'l*, pg. 1092
THE CPAC ROOF TILE CO., LTD.—See The Siam Cement Public Company Limited; *Int'l*, pg. 1237
CPB INC.; *U.S. Public*, pg. 282
CPB PROPERTIES, INC.—See CPB Inc.; *U.S. Public*, pg. 283
CPC/AJI (ASIA) LTD.—See Ajinomoto Company Inc.; *Int'l*, pg. 41
CPC/AJI (ASIA) LTD.—See Bestfoods; *U.S. Public*, pg. 225
CPC/AJI (HONG KONG) LTD.—See Ajinomoto Company Inc.; *Int'l*, pg. 41
CPC/AJI (HONG KONG) LTD.—See Bestfoods; *U.S. Public*, pg. 225
CPC/AJI (MALAYSIA) SDN. BERHAD—See Ajinomoto Company Inc.; *Int'l*, pg. 41
CPC/AJI (MALAYSIA) SDN. BERHAD—See Bestfoods; *U.S. Public*, pg. 225
CPC/AJI (SINGAPORE) PTE. LTD.—See Ajinomoto Company Inc.; *Int'l*, pg. 41
CPC/AJI (SINGAPORE) PTE. LTD.—See Bestfoods; *U.S. Public*, pg. 225
CPC/AJI (TAIWAN) LTD.—See Bestfoods; *U.S. Public*, pg. 225
CPC/AJI (TAIWAN) PLANT—See Ajinomoto Company Inc.; *Int'l*, pg. 41
CPC/AJI (THAILAND) LTD.—See Ajinomoto Company Inc.; *Int'l*, pg. 41
CPC/AJI (THAILAND) LTD.—See Bestfoods; *U.S. Public*, pg. 224
CPC/AJI (THAILAND) LTD., BANGPOO PLANT—See Ajinomoto Company Inc.; *Int'l*, pg. 40
CPC/AJI (THAILAND) LTD., GATEWAY PLANT—See Ajinomoto Company Inc.; *Int'l*, pg. 41
CPC AMINO S.P. ZO.O.—See Bestfoods; *U.S. Public*, pg. 225
CPC ASIA CONSUMER FOODS DIVISION—See Bestfoods; *U.S. Public*, pg. 224
CPC ASIA LTD. OPERATIONS—See Bestfoods; *U.S. Public*, pg. 224
CPC BAKING BUSINESS—See Bestfoods; *U.S. Public*, pg. 224
CPC BENELUX B.V.—See Bestfoods; *U.S. Public*, pg. 225
CPC-COMPANHIA PETROQUIMICA CAMACCARI LTDA.—See Nissho Iwai Corporation; *Int'l*, pg. 947
CPC COOPERATIVE MANAGEMENT GROUP—See Corn Products International, Inc.; *U.S. Public*, pg. 447
CPC DEUTSCHLAND GMBH—See Bestfoods; *U.S. Public*, pg. 225
CPC EUROPE CONSUMER FOODS DIVISION—See Bestfoods; *U.S. Public*, pg. 224
CPC EXPORT (AFRICA/MIDDLE EAST) AG—See Bestfoods; *U.S. Public*, pg. 225
CPC FOODS AB—See Bestfoods; *U.S. Public*, pg. 225
CPC FOODS A/S—See Bestfoods; *U.S. Public*, pg. 225
CPC FOODS CO. LTD. BEIJING—See Bestfoods; *U.S. Public*, pg. 224
CPC FOODS COMPANY LTD.—See Bestfoods; *U.S. Public*, pg. 225
CPC FOODS (IRELAND) LTD.—See Bestfoods; *U.S. Public*, pg. 225
CPC FOODS OY—See Bestfoods; *U.S. Public*, pg. 225
CPC FOODSERVICE GROUP—See Bestfoods; *U.S. Public*, pg. 225
CPC FRANCE—See Bestfoods; *U.S. Public*, pg. 225
CPC (GUANGZHOU) FOODS LTD.—See Bestfoods; *U.S. Public*, pg. 224
CPC (HELLAS) A.B.E.E.—See Bestfoods; *U.S. Public*, pg. 225

CPC HUNGARY LTD.—See Bestfoods; *U.S. Public*, pg. 225
CPC INDUSTRIAL PRODUCTS—See Bestfoods; *U.S. Public*, pg. 225
CPC INDUSTRIAL PRODUCTS (KENYA) LTD.—See Corn Products International, Inc.; *U.S. Public*, pg. 447
C.P.C. INSTRUMENTACAO—See Hewlett-Packard Company; *U.S. Public*, pg. 816
CPC ITALIA S.P.A.—See Bestfoods; *U.S. Public*, pg. 225
CPC JAPAN, LTD.—See Corn Products International, Inc.; *U.S. Public*, pg. 447
CPC KENYA LTD.—See Bestfoods; *U.S. Public*, pg. 225
CPC (LANKA) LTD.—See Bestfoods; *U.S. Public*, pg. 225
CPC LATIN AMERICA CORN REFINING DIVISION—See Corn Products International, Inc.; *U.S. Public*, pg. 448
CPC LATIN AMERICAN CONSUMER FOODS DIVISION—See Corn Products International, Inc.; *U.S. Public*, pg. 447
CPC MAGHREB S.A.—See Bestfoods; *U.S. Public*, pg. 225
CPC-MONDA N.V./S.A.—See Bestfoods; *U.S. Public*, pg. 224
CPC OF LOUISIANA, INC.—See Vencor, Inc.; *U.S. Public*, pg. 1712
CPC OF TEXAS, INC.—See Vencor, Inc.; *U.S. Public*, pg. 1712
CPC PHARMACY, INC.—See Vencor, Inc.; *U.S. Public*, pg. 1712
CPC RAFHAN LTD.—See Bestfoods; *U.S. Public*, pg. 224
CPC RAFHAN LTD.—See Corn Products International, Inc.; *U.S. Public*, pg. 447
CPC ROMANIA—See Bestfoods; *U.S. Public*, pg. 225
CPC RUFHAN LIMITED—See Bestfoods; *U.S. Public*, pg. 225
CPC (SHANGHAI) FOODS LTD.—See Bestfoods; *U.S. Public*, pg. 224
CPC SPAIN, S.A.—See Bestfoods; *U.S. Public*, pg. 225
CPC SPECIALTY MARKETS GROUP—See Bestfoods; *U.S. Public*, pg. 224
CPC (UNITED KINGDOM) LTD.—See Bestfoods; *U.S. Public*, pg. 225
C.P.C.S.I.—See Hewlett-Packard Company; *U.S. Public*, pg. 816
CPF DEUTSCHLAND GMBH—See Canon Inc.; *Int'l*, pg. 262
CPI CORP.; *U.S. Public*, pg. 283
CPI ENGINEERING SERVICES, INC.—See The Lubrizol Corporation; *U.S. Public*, pg. 1016
CPI ESPANA, S.A.—See Eli Lilly and Company; *U.S. Public*, pg. 993
CPI GROUP—See Loews Corporation; *U.S. Public*, pg. 1011
CPI PRINTS PLUS, INC.—See CPI Corp.; *U.S. Public*, pg. 283
CPM—See Gencor Industries, Inc.; *U.S. Public*, pg. 705
CPM & COMPAGNIE—See BDDP Group; *Int'l*, pg. 116
CPM EUROPE B.V.—See Gencor Industries, Inc.; *U.S. Public*, pg. 705
CPM/EUROPE LTD.—See Gencor Industries, Inc.; *U.S. Public*, pg. 705
CPM, INC.; *U.S. Private*, pg. 196
CPM INTERNATIONAL—See Omnicom Group Inc.; *U.S. Public*, pg. 1225
CPS ASSOCIATES, INC.—See Magellan Health Services, Inc.; *U.S. Public*, pg. 1033
CPS CHEMICAL COMPANY INC.; *U.S. Private*, pg. 196
CPS CORPORATION—See Fox Valley Corporation; *U.S. Private*, pg. 422
CPS CREDIT CORP.—See Carson Pirie Scott & Co.; *U.S. Public*, pg. 309
CPS DIRECT, INC.; *U.S. Private*, pg. 196
C.P.T.E. S.A.—See Electrabel S.A.; *Int'l*, pg. 437
CPX CONSTRUCTORS, INC.—See Corporex Companies, Inc.; *U.S. Private*, pg. 276
CQCA MINE—See The Broken Hill Proprietary Company Limited; *Int'l*, pg. 223
CR BRIGGS CORPORATION—See Canyon Resources Corporation; *U.S. Public*, pg. 302
CR INDUSTRIES PTY. LTD.—See AB SKF; *Int'l*, pg. 1157
CR INTERNATIONAL CORPORATION—See Canyon Resources Corporation; *U.S. Public*, pg. 302
CR KENDALL CORPORATION—See Canyon Resources Corporation; *U.S. Public*, pg. 302
CR LLC; *U.S. Private*, pg. 196
CR MINERALS CORPORATION—See Canyon Resources Corporation; *U.S. Public*, pg. 302
CR QUALITY SERVICES, INC.—See Conrail, Inc.; *U.S. Public*, pg. 432
CR SERVICES—See AB SKF; *Int'l*, pg. 1157
C.R.A. HOLDINGS INC.—See Stamford Capital; *U.S. Private*, pg. 1029
CRA LIMITED—See Rio Tinto PLC; *Int'l*, pg. 1119
CRB DAEWOO SECURITIES LTD.—See Daewoo Securities Co., Ltd.; *Int'l*, pg. 359
CRC; *Int'l*, pg. 241
CRC INDUSTRIES, INC.—See Berwind Corporation; *U.S. Private*, pg. 138
CRC PROPERTIES, INC.—See Conrail, Inc.; *U.S. Public*, pg. 432
CREA—See Lyonnaise des Eaux S.A.; *Int'l*, pg. 824
C.R.H INTERNATIONAL, INC.—See Hills Stores Co.; *U.S. Public*, pg. 828
CRH, PLC; *Int'l*, pg. 242
CRI LIQUIDATING REIT, INC.—See CRIIMI MAE; *U.S. Public*, pg. 459
CRINC. - WELLMAN LTD.—See Wellman, Inc.; *U.S. Public*, pg. 1753
CRL ASSET MANAGEMENT CORP.—See Central Reserve Life Corporation; *U.S. Public*, pg. 326
C.R.L.F.—See Lagardere Groupe; *Int'l*, pg. 792
CRMA—See Groupe Air France; *Int'l*, pg. 560
CRN INTERNATIONAL, INC.; *U.S. Private*, pg. 197
CRR INDUSTRIES, INC.—See Conrail, Inc.; *U.S. Public*, pg. 432
CRR INVESTMENTS, INC.—See Conrail, Inc.; *U.S. Public*, pg. 432

CRS DATA AB—See Axel Johnson AB; *Int'l*, pg. 708
CRS DATABUILDING AB—See Axel Johnson AB; *Int'l*, pg. 708
CRS DATASYSTEM AB—See Axel Johnson AB; *Int'l*, pg. 708
CRS FINANCIAL SERVICES, INC.—See Reliance Group Holdings, Inc.; *U.S. Public*, pg. 1374
CRSS ARABIA LTD.—See Tractebel; *Int'l*, pg. 1415
CRSS CAPITAL, INC.—See Tractebel; *Int'l*, pg. 1415
CRSS CIVIL ENGINEERS, INC.—See Tractebel; *Int'l*, pg. 1415
CRSS CONSTRUCTORS, INC.—See Jacobs Engineering Group Inc.; *U.S. Public*, pg. 922
CRSS DEUTSCHLAND—See Tractebel; *Int'l*, pg. 1415
CRSS INC.—See Tractebel; *Int'l*, pg. 1415
CRSS INTERNATIONAL, INC.—See Jacobs Engineering Group Inc.; *U.S. Public*, pg. 922
CRSS INTERNATIONAL, INC.—See Tractebel; *Int'l*, pg. 1415
CRSS INTERNATIONAL, INC. (TAIWAN)—See Tractebel; *Int'l*, pg. 1415
CRSS STRATEGIC CONSULTANTS—See Tractebel; *Int'l*, pg. 1415
C.R.T. S.P.A.—See Telefonaktiebolaget LM Ericsson; *Int'l*, pg. 1365
CRX INC.—See Allied Waste Industries; *U.S. Public*, pg. 49
C.S. ALUMINIUM CORPORATION—See China Steel Corporation; *Int'l*, pg. 285
CS BROOKS CANADA INC.; *U.S. Private*, pg. 197
CS CARTIERA DEL NORD S.R.L.—See Groupe Saint Louis; *Int'l*, pg. 567
CS LIFE—See Credit Suisse Group; *Int'l*, pg. 345
C.S. POLYMER, INC.—See Canon Inc.; *Int'l*, pg. 261
CSA (AUSTRALASIA) PTY LIMITED—See CSA Holdings Ltd.; *Int'l*, pg. 243
CSA AUTOMATED (MACAU) LTD.—See CSA Holdings Ltd.; *Int'l*, pg. 243
CSA AUTOMATED PRIVATE LIMITED—See CSA Holdings Ltd.; *Int'l*, pg. 242
CSA DISTRIBUTION (M) SDN. BHD.—See CSA Holdings Ltd.; *Int'l*, pg. 243
CSA DISTRIBUTION PTE. LTD.—See CSA Holdings Ltd.; *Int'l*, pg. 242
CSA HOLDINGS LTD.; *Int'l*, pg. 242
CSA, LTD.—See COMSAT Corporation; *U.S. Public*, pg. 424
CSA MANAGED GOLD MUTUAL FUNDS—See CSA Management Inc.; *Int'l*, pg. 243
CSA MANAGEMENT INC.; *Int'l*, pg. 243
CSA PRIVATE LIMITED—See CSA Holdings Ltd.; *Int'l*, pg. 242
CSA RECHERCHE LTEE—See CSA Holdings Ltd.; *Int'l*, pg. 243
CSA RESEARCH PTE. LTD.—See CSA Holdings Ltd.; *Int'l*, pg. 242
CSAR FRANCE—See CSA Holdings Ltd.; *Int'l*, pg. 243
CSB BUREAUTIQUE—See CAP Gemini S.A.; *Int'l*, pg. 263
CSC AUSTRALIA—See Computer Sciences Corporation; *U.S. Public*, pg. 423
CSC CONSULTING GROUP—See Computer Sciences Corporation; *U.S. Public*, pg. 422
CSC CREDIT SERVICES, INC.—See Computer Sciences Corporation; *U.S. Public*, pg. 423
CSC DISPOSAL AND LANDFILL, INC.—See Republic Industries, Inc.; *U.S. Public*, pg. 1379
CSC FINANCIAL SERVICES GROUP—See Computer Sciences Corporation; *U.S. Public*, pg. 422
CSC, HALIFAX—See WIC Western International Communications Ltd.; *Int'l*, pg. 1482
CSC HEALTHCARE GROUP—See Computer Sciences Corporation; *U.S. Public*, pg. 423
CSC HEALTHCARE SYSTEMS—See Computer Sciences Corporation; *U.S. Public*, pg. 423
CSC INDEX, INC.—See Computer Sciences Corporation; *U.S. Public*, pg. 422
CSC LOGIC, INC.—See Computer Sciences Corporation; *U.S. Public*, pg. 422
CSC, LTD.—See The Reserve Group; *U.S. Private*, pg. 924
CSC, OTTAWA—See WIC Western International Communications Ltd.; *Int'l*, pg. 1482
CSC PINNACLE ALLIANCE—See Computer Sciences Corporation; *U.S. Public*, pg. 423
CSC PLOENZKE—See Computer Sciences Corporation; *U.S. Public*, pg. 423
CSC, SASKATOON—See WIC Western International Communications Ltd.; *Int'l*, pg. 1482
CSC UNITED STATES; *U.S. Private*, pg. 197
CSD DAYTON OFFICE—See United Technologies Corporation; *U.S. Public*, pg. 1689
CSD HATHAWAY LIMITED—See Hathaway Corporation; *U.S. Public*, pg. 799
CSD, INC.—See Philips Electronics N.V.; *Int'l*, pg. 1053
CSD, VANDENBERG AFB—See United Technologies Corporation; *U.S. Public*, pg. 1690
CSE INSURANCE GROUP; *U.S. Private*, pg. 197
CSE MARINE SERVICES INC.—See Canadian Shipbuilding & Engineering Ltd.; *Int'l*, pg. 259
CSELT—See Telecom Italia S.p.A.; *Int'l*, pg. 1362
CSEMEGE-JULIUS MEINL—See Julius Meinl AG; *Int'l*, pg. 856
CSG SYSTEMS INTERNATIONAL, INC.; *U.S. Public*, pg. 283
C.S.I.—See Olivetti SpA; *Int'l*, pg. 1002
C.S.I. CORPORACION SIDERURGIA INTEGRAL, S.A.—See SEPI; *Int'l*, pg. 1224
CSI EUROPEAN HEADQUARTERS—See Emerson Electric Co.; *U.S. Public*, pg. 573
CSI INTERNATIONAL CORPORATION; *U.S. Private*, pg. 197
CSI SERVICES—See Emerson Electric Co.; *U.S. Public*, pg. 573
CSIC MICROCONTROLLER DIVISION—See Motorola, Inc.; *U.S. Public*, pg. 1137
CSM FOOD DIVISION—See CSM N.V.; *Int'l*, pg. 243

MASTER INDEX TO COMPANY NAMES CABVAL

Company Index

CSM INGREDIENTS DIVISION—See CSM N.V.; Int'l, pg. 243
CSM N.V.; Int'l, pg. 243
CSM SUGAR DIVISION—See CSM N.V.; Int'l, pg. 243
CSM SUIKER BV—See CSM N.V.; Int'l, pg. 243
C.S.O. CENTRALE SUPPORTI OPERATIVI S.P.A.—See Banco Ambrosiano Veneto S.p.A.; Int'l, pg. 138
CSO DIVISION/CSK—See Marcam Solutions, Inc.; U.S. Public, pg. 1043
CSO SERVICE CO. INC.—See Compagnie des Machines Bull; Int'l, pg. 316
CSP INC.; U.S. Public, pg. 283
CSP PACIFIC—See Fletcher Challenge Limited; Int'l, pg. 495
CSR—See Raytheon Company; U.S. Public, pg. 1365
CSR AMERICA INC.—See CSR Limited; Int'l, pg. 245
CSR CENTRAL—See CSR Limited; Int'l, pg. 245
CSR FLORIDA—See CSR Limited; Int'l, pg. 245
CSR LIMITED; Int'l, pg. 245
CSR PAMPRYL—See Groupe Pernod Ricard; Int'l, pg. 566
CSR WEST—See CSR Limited; Int'l, pg. 245
CSS INDUSTRIES, INC.; U.S. Public, pg. 283
CSS USA—See True North Diversified Companies; U.S. Public, pg. 1642
CSSI CORPORATION—See Nichols Research Corporation; U.S. Public, pg. 1182
P.T. CSSL INDONESIA—See Marcam Solutions, Inc.; U.S. Public, pg. 1043
CSSL (M) SDN BHD—See Marcam Solutions, Inc.; U.S. Public, pg. 1043
CSW COMMUNICATIONS, INC.—See Central and South West Corporation; U.S. Public, pg. 324
CSW CREDIT, INC.—See Central and South West Corporation; U.S. Public, pg. 324
CSW ENERGY, INC.—See Central and South West Corporation; U.S. Public, pg. 324
CSW FINANCIAL INC.—See Central and South West Corporation; U.S. Public, pg. 324
CSW LEASING, INC.—See Central and South West Corporation; U.S. Public, pg. 324
CSX CORPORATION; U.S. Public, pg. 284
CSX INTERMODAL, INC.—See CSX Corporation; U.S. Public, pg. 284
CSX LIS—See CSX Corporation; U.S. Public, pg. 284
CSX TECHNOLOGY—See CSX Corporation; U.S. Public, pg. 284
CSX TECHNOLOGY, INC.—See CSX Corporation; U.S. Public, pg. 284
CSX TRANSPORTATION, INC.—See CSX Corporation; U.S. Public, pg. 284
CT & E ENVIRONMENTAL SERVICES INC.—See SGS Societe Generale de Surveillance Holding S.A.; Int'l, pg. 1153
CT&I CORP. OF WISCONSIN—See Chicago Tube & Iron Co.; U.S. Private, pg. 235
CT CORPORATION SYSTEM—See Wolters Kluwer N.V.; Int'l, pg. 1513
CT FINANCIAL SERVICES, INC.—See B.A.T Industries P.L.C.; Int'l, pg. 112
CT PAGING SDN. BHD.—See Telefonaktiebolaget LM Ericsson; Int'l, pg. 1365
CT RADIOSET SDN. BHD.—See Telefonaktiebolaget LM Ericsson; Int'l, pg. 1365
CTB, INC.—See CTB International Corp.; U.S. Public, pg. 285
CTB, INC.—See The Dickerson Group, Inc.; U.S. Private, pg. 331
CTB INTERNATIONAL CORP.; U.S. Public, pg. 284
CTB/MCGRAW HILL—See The McGraw-Hill Companies; U.S. Public, pg. 1070
CTC CONSULTING—See U.S. Trust Corporation; U.S. Public, pg. 1688
CTC ILLINOIS TRUST COMPANY—See The Bank of New York Company, Inc.; U.S. Public, pg. 179
CTC PARCA AB—See Trelleborg AB; Int'l, pg. 1422
CTD DE MEXICO, S.A.—See Kennametal Inc.; U.S. Public, pg. 950
CTE - COMPANIA TRASATLANTICA ESPANOLA, S.A.—See SEPI; Int'l, pg. 1224
CTEL CORPORATION (EUROPE)—See IDB Holding Corporation; Int'l, pg. 643
CTEL CORPORATION (NORTH AMERICA)—See IDB Holding Corporation; Int'l, pg. 643
CTG RESOURCES, INC.; U.S. Public, pg. 285
CTI COMPANIA DE TELEFONOS DEL INTERIOR S.A.—See GTE Corporation; U.S. Public, pg. 697
CTI COMPANIA DE TELEFONOS DEL INTERIOR S.A.—See Lucent Technologies Inc.; U.S. Public, pg. 1019
CTI CRYOGENICS DIV.—See Helix Technology Corp.; U.S. Public, pg. 808
CTI NORTE COMPANIA DE TELEFONOS DEL INTERIOR S.A.—See GTE Corporation; U.S. Public, pg. 697
CTI NORTE COMPANIA DE TELEFONOS DEL INTERIOR S.A.—See Lucent Technologies Inc.; U.S. Public, pg. 1019
CTI SINGAPORE, PTE—See M.A. Hanna Company; U.S. Public, pg. 781
CTIP S.P.A.—See Bastogi-S.p.A.; Int'l, pg. 170
CTL STEEL CO.—See Clark Grave Vault Co.; U.S. Private, pg. 243
CTS BROWNSVILLE/ELECTROMECHANICAL—See CTS Corporation; U.S. Public, pg. 285
CTS COMPONENTS TAIWAN, LTD.—See CTS Corporation; U.S. Public, pg. 286
CTS CORPORATION; U.S. Public, pg. 285
CTS CORPORATION-CONNECTOR DIVISION—See CTS Corporation; U.S. Public, pg. 285
CTS DE MEXICO, S.A.—See CTS Corporation; U.S. Public, pg. 286
CTS OF CANADA, LTD.—See CTS Corporation; U.S. Public, pg. 286
CTS SINGAPORE PTE., LTD.—See CTS Corporation; U.S. Public, pg. 286
CTS U.K., LTD.—See CTS Corporation; U.S. Public, pg. 286
CTT MANAGEMENT GMBH—See Sandvik AB; Int'l, pg. 1186
CTT SCETA—See SNCF; Int'l, pg. 1163
CTX INTERNATIONAL—See Motorola, Inc.; U.S. Public, pg. 1137
CTX MORTGAGE CO., INC.—See Centex Corporation; U.S. Public, pg. 323
CU CAPITALCORP—See Citizens Utilities Company; U.S. Public, pg. 380
CU POWER INTERNATIONAL LTD.—See ATCO Group Co.; Int'l, pg. 95
CUC INTERNATIONAL, INC.—See Cendant Corporation; U.S. Public, pg. 320
CUC PUBLISHING—See Cendant Corporation; U.S. Public, pg. 320
CUC TRAVEL SERVICES INC.—See Cendant Corporation; U.S. Public, pg. 320
CUI CORPORATION—See Inamed Corporation; U.S. Public, pg. 873
C.U.P. SNC—See Continental AG; Int'l, pg. 328
CV HOME FURNISHINGS LIMITED—See Coats Viyella plc; Int'l, pg. 299
C.V. REALTY, INC.—See Central Vermont Public Service Corporation; U.S. Public, pg. 328
CV REIT, INC.; U.S. Public, pg. 286
CV WOVEN FABRICS LIMITED—See Coats Viyella plc; Int'l, pg. 299
CVB FINANCIAL CORP.; U.S. Public, pg. 286
C.V.B.G. (CONSORTIUM VINICOLE DE BORDEAUX ET DE LA GIRONDE)—See Koninklijke BolsWessanen nv; Int'l, pg. 751
CVC OF OHIO—See Citizens Utilities Company; U.S. Public, pg. 380
CVC PRODUCTS, INC.; U.S. Private, pg. 197
CVD INCORPORATED—See Morton International Inc.; U.S. Public, pg. 1135
C.V.G. ALUMINIO DEL CARONI, S.A.—See Reynolds Metals Company; U.S. Public, pg. 1386
CVG AVIATION—See Comair Holdings, Inc.; U.S. Public, pg. 406
CVS CORP.; U.S. Public, pg. 287
C.V.T.-R & D COMPANY N.V.—See Royal Begemann Group; Int'l, pg. 1134
CVU-CONSULTING FUR VERSORGUNGSUNTERNEHMEN GMBH—See Ruhrgas Aktiengesellschaft; Int'l, pg. 1148
CVV NELTEG—See Novartis AG; Int'l, pg. 975
CW COMMUNICACIONES S/A—See International Data Group; U.S. Private, pg. 569
CW/COMMUNICATIONS AB—See International Data Group; U.S. Private, pg. 569
CW LEASE BELGIUM—See ING Groep N.V.; Int'l, pg. 648
CW LEASE NEDERLAND—See ING Groep N.V.; Int'l, pg. 647
CW PUBLIKATIONEN AG—See International Data Group; U.S. Private, pg. 569
CW RENT BELGIUM N.V.—See ING Groep N.V.; Int'l, pg. 648
C.W.A. HOLDINGS LTD.—See Unilever Plc; Int'l, pg. 1434
CWC CASTINGS TEXTRON—See Textron Inc.; U.S. Public, pg. 1590
CWC TEXTRON COMPANY—See Textron Inc.; U.S. Public, pg. 1590
CWI INTERNATIONAL CHINA, LTD.—See Waxman Industries, Inc.; U.S. Public, pg. 1749
CWK AG—See Coop Switzerland; Int'l, pg. 329
CWR TRANSPORTATION COMPANY—See Curran Group, Inc.; U.S. Private, pg. 297
CWS INTERNATIONAL A.G.—See Franz Haniel & Cie, GmbH; Int'l, pg. 592
CWT DISTRIBUTION LIMITED; Int'l, pg. 246
CWT FARMS INTERNATIONAL—See Booker PLC; Int'l, pg. 202
CWW-GERKO AKUSTIK GMBH & CO. KG—See Ruetgers A.G.; Int'l, pg. 1148
CX-GRUS—See Scancem AB; Int'l, pg. 1200
CXA LTD.—See Imperial Chemical Industries PLC; Int'l, pg. 664
CXR SA—See Microtel International Inc.; U.S. Public, pg. 1108
CXR TELCOM CORPORATION—See Microtel International Inc.; U.S. Public, pg. 1108
CYDSA S.A.; Int'l, pg. 246
C.Y.E.D.E. CIA, LTDA.—See Hewlett-Packard Company; U.S. Public, pg. 816
CA. TEL S.P.A.—See Telefonaktiebolaget LM Ericsson; Int'l, pg. 1365
CAB-O-SIL DIV. CABOT CORP.—See Cabot Corporation; U.S. Public, pg. 289
CABANO KINGSWAY TRANSPORT—See Russel Metals Inc.; Int'l, pg. 1150
CABELCO APS—See Telefonaktiebolaget LM Ericsson; Int'l, pg. 1365
CABELEC—See Labinal SA; Int'l, pg. 785
CABELL CONSTRUCTION COMPANY—See Elgin National Industries, Inc.; U.S. Private, pg. 370
CABIN CRAFTS CARPETS—See Shaw Industries, Inc.; U.S. Public, pg. 1464
CABINAS TELEFONICAS, S.A. (CABITEL)—See Telefonica de Espana, S.A.; Int'l, pg. 1371
CABLE & WIRELESS COMMUNICATIONS INC.-TEXAS—See Cable and Wireless plc; Int'l, pg. 247
CABLE & WIRELESS COMMUNICATIONS INC.—See Cable and Wireless plc; Int'l, pg. 247
CABLE & WIRELESS COMMUNICATIONS PLC—See Cable and Wireless plc; Int'l, pg. 247
CABLE & WIRELESS MANAGEMENT SERVICES—See Cable and Wireless plc; Int'l, pg. 247
CABLE & WIRELESS (N.Y.) INC.—See Cable and Wireless plc; Int'l, pg. 247
CABLE & WIRELESS OF NORTH AMERICA, INC.—See Cable and Wireless plc; Int'l, pg. 247
CABLE AND WIRELESS PLC; Int'l, pg. 247
CABLE CAR BEVERAGE CORPORATION—See Triarc Companies, Inc.; U.S. Public, pg. 1635
CABLE/CISCO—See The Carpenter Group; U.S. Private, pg. 215
CABLE CONSTRUCTORS, INC.; U.S. Private, pg. 197
CABLE DESIGN TECHNOLOGIES CORPORATION; U.S. Public, pg. 287
CABLE/HOME COMMUNICATIONS CORP.—See General Instrument Corporation; U.S. Public, pg. 716
CABLE MANAGEMENT CORP.—See TCI Communications, Inc.; U.S. Public, pg. 1555
CABLE MICHIGAN, INC.; U.S. Public, pg. 287
CABLE PRODUCTOS DE CHIHUAHUA, S.A. DE C.V.—See Zenith Electronics Corp.; U.S. Public, pg. 1790
CABLE SERVICES GROUP—See CSG Systems International, Inc.; U.S. Public, pg. 283
CABLE SPINNING EQUIPMENT INC.; U.S. Private, pg. 197
CABLE TECH COMPANY LIMITED—See Noma Industries Limited; Int'l, pg. 955
CABLEADOS S.A. DE C.V.—See General Motors Corporation; U.S. Public, pg. 721
CABLECO—See The Carpenter Group; U.S. Private, pg. 215
CABLECRAFT INC.—See Tuthill Corporation; U.S. Private, pg. 1110
CABLEDATA, INC.—See USCS International, Inc.; U.S. Public, pg. 1659
CABLEDATA INTERNATIONAL, LTD.—See USCS International, Inc.; U.S. Public, pg. 1659
CABLEDATA TELECOMMUNICATIONS, INC.—See USCS International, Inc.; U.S. Public, pg. 1659
CABLELEASE, INC.—See USCS International, Inc.; U.S. Public, pg. 1659
CABLELINK-CALIFORNIA—See Robinson Nugent, Inc.; U.S. Public, pg. 1394
CABLELINK, INCORPORATED—See Robinson Nugent, Inc.; U.S. Public, pg. 1394
CABLEREP, INC.—See Cox Communications, Inc.; U.S. Public, pg. 455
CABLES PIRELLI S.A.—See Pirelli S.p.A.; Int'l, pg. 1059
CABLESA-INDUSTRIA DE COMPONENTES ELECTRICOS SOCIEDADE ANONIMA—See General Motors Corporation; U.S. Public, pg. 721
CABLETEL COMMUNICATIONS INC.—See ARC International Corporation; Int'l, pg. 17
CABLETRON SYSTEMS, INC.; U.S. Public, pg. 288
CABLETRON SYSTEMS, INC.-ASIA—See Cabletron Systems, Inc.; U.S. Public, pg. 288
CABLETRON SYSTEMS, INC.-AUSTRALIA—See Cabletron Systems, Inc.; U.S. Public, pg. 288
CABLETRON SYSTEMS, INC.-EUROPE—See Cabletron Systems, Inc.; U.S. Public, pg. 288
CABLEVISION—See Cablevision Systems Corporation; U.S. Public, pg. 288
CABLEVISION OF BOSTON—See Cablevision Systems Corporation; U.S. Public, pg. 288
CABLEVISION OF DURHAM, INC.—See Time Warner Inc.; U.S. Public, pg. 1610
CABLEVISION OF RALEIGH, INC.—See Time Warner Inc.; U.S. Public, pg. 1610
CABLEVISION OF SHREVEPORT—See Time Warner Inc.; U.S. Public, pg. 1610
CABLEVISION VII, INC.—See TCI Communications, Inc.; U.S. Public, pg. 1555
CABLEVISION VI, INC.—See TCI Communications, Inc.; U.S. Public, pg. 1555
CABLEVISION SYSTEMS CORPORATION; U.S. Public, pg. 288
CABLEWARE TECHNOLOGY DIV.—See Loos & Co., Inc.; U.S. Private, pg. 675
CABLEWAVE SYSTEMS; U.S. Private, pg. 197
CABLINAL—See Labinal SA; Int'l, pg. 785
CABLINAL ESPANA—See Labinal SA; Int'l, pg. 785
CABLINAL PORTUGUESA—See Labinal SA; Int'l, pg. 785
CABOT CANADA LTD.—See Cabot Corporation; U.S. Public, pg. 289
CABOT CORPORATION; U.S. Public, pg. 288
CABOT CREAMERY CO-OPERATIVE INC.—See Agri-Mark, Inc.; U.S. Private, pg. 26
CABOT EUROPE LIMITED—See Cabot Corporation; U.S. Public, pg. 289
CABOT HULS GMBH—See Veba AG; Int'l, pg. 1454
CABOT INTERNATIONAL SERVICES CORP.—See Cabot Corporation; U.S. Public, pg. 289
CABOT MEDICAL CORPORATION—See Circon Corporation; U.S. Public, pg. 373
CABOT OIL & GAS CORPORATION; U.S. Public, pg. 289
CABOT OIL & GAS MARKETING CORPORATION—See Cabot Oil & Gas Corporation; U.S. Public, pg. 289
CABOT PETROLEUM NORTH SEA LIMITED—See Cabot Oil & Gas Corporation; U.S. Public, pg. 289
CABOT PLACE LTD.—See Manulife Financial (The Manufacturers Life Insurance Company); Int'l, pg. 840
CABOT PLASTICS BELGIUM S.A.—See Cabot Corporation; U.S. Public, pg. 289
CABOT PLASTICS INTERNATIONAL—See Cabot Corporation; U.S. Public, pg. 289
SAMUEL CABOT, INC.; U.S. Private, pg. 198
CABOTO GESTIONI SIM S.P.A.—See Banco Ambrosiano Veneto S.p.A.; Int'l, pg. 138
CABOTO HOLDING SOCIETA DI INTERMEDIAZIONE MOBILIARE S.P.A.—See Banco Ambrosiano Veneto S.p.A.; Int'l, pg. 138
CABOTO HOLDING S.P.A.—See Banco Ambrosiano Veneto S.p.A.; Int'l, pg. 138
CABOTO INTERNATIONAL S.A.—See Banco Ambrosiano Veneto S.p.A.; Int'l, pg. 138
CABOTO SIM S.P.A.—See Banco Ambrosiano Veneto S.p.A.; Int'l, pg. 138
CABRE CORP.; U.S. Public, pg. 289
CABRE EXPLORATION LTD.; Int'l, pg. 247
CABVAL—See Haynes International, Inc.; U.S. Public, pg. 801

Company Index

CACAO DIRECTORY OF CORPORATE AFFILIATIONS

CACAO DE ZAAN B.V.—See Archer Daniels Midland Company (ADM); *U.S. Public*, pg. 128
CACHE, INC.; *U.S. Public*, pg. 289
CACHE SCIENTIFIC, INC.—See Tektronix, Inc.; *U.S. Public*, pg. 1567
CACIQUE—See The Limited, Inc.; *U.S. Public*, pg. 995
CACIQUE, INC.; *U.S. Private*, pg. 198
CACTUS FEEDERS, INC.; *U.S. Private*, pg. 198
CAD SERVER LTD —See The Macneal-Schwendler Corp.; *U.S. Public*, pg. 1031
CADACO—See Rapid Mounting & Finishing Co.; *U.S. Private*, pg. 910
CADAM INC.—See International Business Machines Corporation; *U.S. Public*, pg. 896
CADARACHE FUEL FABRICATION UTILITY (CFCA)—See COGEMA - Compagnie Generale des Matieres Nucleaires; *Int'l*, pg. 305
CADBURY BEVERAGES—See Cadbury Schweppes p.l.c.; *Int'l*, pg. 248
CADBURY BEVERAGES CANADA INC.—See Cadbury Schweppes p.l.c.; *Int'l*, pg. 248
CADBURY BEVERAGES NORTH AMERICA—See Cadbury Schweppes p.l.c.; *Int'l*, pg. 248
CADBURY BEVERAGES SEVEN UP—See Cadbury Schweppes p.l.c.; *Int'l*, pg. 248
CADBURY CHOCOLATE CANADA, INC.—See Cadbury Schweppes p.l.c.; *Int'l*, pg. 248
CADBURY INTERNATIONAL LIMITED—See Cadbury Schweppes p.l.c.; *Int'l*, pg. 248
CADBURY IRELAND P.L.C.—See Cadbury Schweppes p.l.c.; *Int'l*, pg. 248
CADBURY KENYA LIMITED—See Cadbury Schweppes p.l.c.; *Int'l*, pg. 248
CADBURY LIMITED—See Cadbury Schweppes p.l.c.; *Int'l*, pg. 248
CADBURY NIGERIA PLC—See Cadbury Schweppes p.l.c.; *Int'l*, pg. 248
CADBURY SCHWEPPES AUSTRALIA LTD—See Cadbury Schweppes p.l.c.; *Int'l*, pg. 248
CADBURY SCHWEPPES P.L.C.; *Int'l*, pg. 247
CADBURY SCHWEPPES SOUTH AFRICA LTD.—See Cadbury Schweppes p.l.c.; *Int'l*, pg. 248
CADCO LTD.—See Autodesk, Inc.; *U.S. Public*, pg. 150
CADDOCK ELECTRONICS EUROPE B.V.—See Caddock Electronics, Inc.; *U.S. Private*, pg. 198
CADDOCK ELECTRONICS, INC.; *U.S. Private*, pg. 198
CADDOCK NETWORK DIVISION—See Caddock Electronics, Inc.; *U.S. Private*, pg. 198
CADDY CORP. OF AMERICA; *U.S. Private*, pg. 198
CADE COMPOSITES, INC.—See Cade Industries, Inc.; *U.S. Public*, pg. 290
CADE INDUSTRIES, INC.; *U.S. Public*, pg. 289
CADE INTERNATIONAL, INC.—See Cade Industries, Inc.; *U.S. Public*, pg. 290
CADEC SYSTEMS INC.—See Cummins Engine Company, Inc.; *U.S. Public*, pg. 468
CADEL DIV.—See UAP, Inc.; *Int'l*, pg. 1426
CADENA COMERCIAL OXXO, S.A. DE CV—See Fomento Economico Mexicano, S.A. de CV; *Int'l*, pg. 496
CADENCE DESIGN SYSTEMS, INC.; *U.S. Public*, pg. 290
CADET MANUFACTURING COMPANY; *U.S. Private*, pg. 198
CADEV—See Caisse de depot et placement du Quebec; *Int'l*, pg. 249
CADILLAC ELECTRIC—See Premier Farnell plc; *Int'l*, pg. 1068
CADILLAC MOTOR CAR DIVISION—See General Motors Corporation; *U.S. Public*, pg. 720
CADILLAC PIPE—See Premarc Corporation; *U.S. Private*, pg. 881
CADILLAC PLASTIC—See M.A. Hanna Company; *U.S. Public*, pg. 781
CADILLAC PLASTIC & CHEMICAL CO.—See M.A. Hanna Company; *U.S. Public*, pg. 781
CADILLAC PLASTIC (CANADA) LTD.—See M.A. Hanna Company; *U.S. Public*, pg. 781
CADILLAC PLASTIC FRANCE S.A.—See M.A. Hanna Company; *U.S. Public*, pg. 781
CADILLAC PLASTIC GMBH—See M.A. Hanna Company; *U.S. Public*, pg. 781
CADILLAC PLASTIC (NEW ZEALAND) LTD.—See M.A. Hanna Company; *U.S. Public*, pg. 781
CADILLAC PRODUCTS, INC.; *U.S. Private*, pg. 198
CADIM—See Caisse de depot et placement du Quebec; *Int'l*, pg. 249
CADIZ ELECTRONICS, S.A.—See Ford Motor Company; *U.S. Public*, pg. 655
THE CADMAN COMPANIES—See Heidelberger Zement A.G.; *Int'l*, pg. 605
CADMUS—See Cadmus Communications Corporation; *U.S. Public*, pg. 290
CADMUS-ATLANTA MANUFACTURING—See Cadmus Communications Corporation; *U.S. Public*, pg. 290
CADMUS-BYRD MANUFACTURING—See Cadmus Communications Corporation; *U.S. Public*, pg. 290
CADMUS CATALOGS—See Cadmus Communications Corporation; *U.S. Public*, pg. 290
CADMUS COMMUNICATIONS CORPORATION; *U.S. Public*, pg. 290
CADMUS CREATIVE—See Cadmus Communications Corporation; *U.S. Public*, pg. 290
CADMUS CUSTOM PUBLISHING—See Cadmus Communications Corporation; *U.S. Public*, pg. 290
CADMUS DIRECT MARKETING, INC.—See Cadmus Communications Corporation; *U.S. Public*, pg. 290
CADMUS-EASTON MANUFACTURING—See Cadmus Communications Corporation; *U.S. Public*, pg. 290
CADMUS FINANCIAL—See Cadmus Communications Corporation; *U.S. Public*, pg. 290
CADMUS FINANCIAL COMMUNICATIONS—See Cadmus Communications Corporation; *U.S. Public*, pg. 290
CADMUS/GE PRINT SERVICES—See Cadmus Communications Corporation; *U.S. Public*, pg. 291
CADMUS INTERACTIVE—See Cadmus Communications Corporation; *U.S. Public*, pg. 291
CADMUS JOURNAL SERVICES—See Cadmus Communications Corporation; *U.S. Public*, pg. 290
CADMUS JOURNAL SERVICES, INC.—See Cadmus Communications Corporation; *U.S. Public*, pg. 291
CADMUS JOURNAL SERVICES-TAPSCO—See Cadmus Communications Corporation; *U.S. Public*, pg. 291
CADMUS-LANCASTER MANUFACTURING—See Cadmus Communications Corporation; *U.S. Public*, pg. 291
CADMUS MAGAZINES—See Cadmus Communications Corporation; *U.S. Public*, pg. 291
CADMUS MARKETING SERVICES—See Cadmus Communications Corporation; *U.S. Public*, pg. 291
CADMUS PROMOTIONAL PRINTING—See Cadmus Communications Corporation; *U.S. Public*, pg. 291
CADMUS-RICHMOND MANUFACTURING—See Cadmus Communications Corporation; *U.S. Public*, pg. 291
CADMUS SPECIALTY PACKAGING—See Cadmus Communications Corporation; *U.S. Public*, pg. 291
CADMUS TECHNOLOGY SOLUTIONS—See Cadmus Communications Corporation; *U.S. Public*, pg. 291
CADSAND MEDICA B.V.—See Pfizer Inc.; *U.S. Public*, pg. 1284
CADSAND MEDICA N.V.—See Pfizer Inc.; *U.S. Public*, pg. 1284
CADY LIFTERS—See Columbus McKinnon Corp.; *U.S. Public*, pg. 405
CAERE CORPORATION; *U.S. Public*, pg. 291
CAERE FSC CORPORATION—See Caere Corporation; *U.S. Public*, pg. 291
CAERE GMBH—See Caere Corporation; *U.S. Public*, pg. 291
CAESARS PALACE CORP.—See Starwood Hotels & Resorts; *U.S. Public*, pg. 1512
CAESARS WORLD, INC.—See Starwood Hotels & Resorts; *U.S. Public*, pg. 1512
CAESARS WORLD MERCHANDISING, INC.—See Starwood Hotels & Resorts; *U.S. Public*, pg. 1512
CAF CASINO—See Groupe Casino; *Int'l*, pg. 563
THE CAFARO CO.; *U.S. Private*, pg. 198
CAFCO—See Central Mutual Insurance Co.; *U.S. Private*, pg. 224
CAFE BA-BA-REEBA—See Lettuce Entertain You Enterprises, Inc.; *U.S. Private*, pg. 661
CAFE CONTINENTAL S.A. DE C.V.—See Nestle S.A.; *Int'l*, pg. 919
CAFE GRAND MERE S.A.—See Philip Morris Companies Inc.; *U.S. Public*, pg. 1289
CAFE ST-LOUIS—See GIB Group; *Int'l*, pg. 534
CAFES LA ESTRELLA S.A.—See Nestle S.A.; *Int'l*, pg. 919
CAFFARO S.P.A.; *Int'l*, pg. 248
CAGLE'S INC.; *U.S. Public*, pg. 291
CAHILL MAY ROBERTS GROUP PLC.—See Franz Haniel & Cie, GmbH; *Int'l*, pg. 592
CAILA Y PARES SA—See Akzo Nobel N.V.; *Int'l*, pg. 47
CAIN & BULTMAN; *U.S. Private*, pg. 199
CAIN'S COFFEE CO.—See Chock Full O' Nuts Corporation; *U.S. Public*, pg. 351
CAINS FOODS, L.P.; *U.S. Private*, pg. 199
CAIRE, INC.—See Minnesota Valley Engineering/Cryogenic Association; *U.S. Private*, pg. 751
CAIRNGORM INSURANCE LTD.—See Burmah Castrol plc; *Int'l*, pg. 235
CAIRNS BREWERY—See Foster's Brewing Group Limited; *Int'l*, pg. 501
A.B. CAIRNS LIMITED—See Taylor Woodrow plc; *Int'l*, pg. 1359
CAIRO FOODS INDUSTRIES SAE—See H.J. Heinz Company; *U.S. Public*, pg. 806
CAISSE CENTRAL DE REESCOMPTE-GESTION—See Commerzbank AG; *Int'l*, pg. 312
CAISSE CENTRALE DE REESCOMPTE, S.A.—See Commerzbank AG; *Int'l*, pg. 312
CAISSE DE DEPOT ET PLACEMENT DU QUEBEC; *Int'l*, pg. 249
CAISSE FRATERNELLE D'EPARGNE—See Groupe GAN; *Int'l*, pg. 563
CAISSE FRATERNELLE VIE—See Groupe GAN; *Int'l*, pg. 564
CAISSE HYPOTHECAIRE DU LUXEMBOURG—See Banque Internationale a Luxembourg S.A.; *Int'l*, pg. 162
CAISSE NATIONALE DE CREDIT AGRICOLE INTERNATIONAL DIVISION—See Credit Agricole; *Int'l*, pg. 341
CAIXA CATALUNYA GESTIO—See Caixa d'Estalvis de Catalunya; *Int'l*, pg. 250
CAIXA D'ESTALVIS DE CATALUNYA; *Int'l*, pg. 249
CAIXA GERAL DE DEPOSITOS; *Int'l*, pg. 250
CAIXA GERAL DE DEPOSITOS—See Caixa Geral de Depositos; *Int'l*, pg. 250
CAIXA GERAL DE DEPOSITOS (FRANCE)—See Caixa Geral de Depositos; *Int'l*, pg. 251
CAIXA-IMOBILIARIO-SOCIEDADE DE GESTAO E INVESTIMENTO IMOBILIARIO S.A.—See Caixa Geral de Depositos; *Int'l*, pg. 250
CAIXA PARTICIPACOES, SGPS. S.A.—See Caixa Geral de Depositos; *Int'l*, pg. 250
CAIXA - SISTEMAS DE INFORMACAO, SA—See Caixa Geral de Depositos; *Int'l*, pg. 250
CAIXAGEST—See Caixa Geral de Depositos; *Int'l*, pg. 250
CAJA DE MADRID DE SEGUROS GENERALES, S.A. DE SEGUROS Y REASEGUROS—See Caja de Madrid Group; *Int'l*, pg. 251
CAJA DE MADRID GROUP; *Int'l*, pg. 251
CAJA DE PREVISION Y SOCORRO S.A.—See Assicurazioni Generali S.p.A.; *Int'l*, pg. 90
CAJA MADRID DE PENSIONES, E.G.F.P., S.A.—See Caja de Madrid Group; *Int'l*, pg. 251
CAJA MADRID VIDA, S.A. DE SEGUROS Y REASEGUROS—See Caja de Madrid Group; *Int'l*, pg. 251
CAJA REASEGURADORA DE ARGENTINA, S.A.—See Corporacion MAPFRE, Compania Internacional de Reaseguros, S.A.; *Int'l*, pg. 335
CAJA REASEGURADORA DE CHILE, S.A.—See Corporacion MAPFRE, Compania Internacional de Reaseguros, S.A.; *Int'l*, pg. 335
CAJA SALUD, S.A. DE SEGUROS Y REASEGUROS—See Caja de Madrid Group; *Int'l*, pg. 251
CAJUN BAYOU DISTRIBUTORS & MANAGEMENT, INC.—See Piccadilly Cafeterias, Inc.; *U.S. Public*, pg. 1294
CAJUN ELECTRIC POWER CO-OP; *U.S. Private*, pg. 199
CAL-AG INSURANCE SERVICES, INC.—See Zenith National Insurance Corp.; *U.S. Public*, pg. 1791
CAL-AIR INC.; *U.S. Private*, pg. 199
CAL EMBLEM, INC.—See Cal Emblem Labels, Inc.; *U.S. Private*, pg. 199
CAL EMBLEM LABELS, INC.; *U.S. Private*, pg. 199
CAL LITHO COLOR—See Alan Lithograph, Inc.; *U.S. Private*, pg. 31
CAL-MAINE EGG PRODUCTS INC.—See Cal-Maine Foods, Inc.; *U.S. Public*, pg. 292
CAL-MAINE FARMS—See Cal-Maine Foods, Inc.; *U.S. Public*, pg. 292
CAL-MAINE FOODS, INC.; *U.S. Public*, pg. 292
CALAMERICA LIFE INSURANCE CO.—See SunAmerica Inc.; *U.S. Public*, pg. 1533
CALANDA HALDENGUT AG—See Heineken N.V.; *Int'l*, pg. 608
CALAVERAS CEMENT COMPANY—See Heidelberger Zement A.G.; *Int'l*, pg. 605
CALAVO FOODS DE MEXICO, S.A. DE C.V.—See Calavo Growers of California; *U.S. Private*, pg. 200
CALAVO FOODS, INC.—See Calavo Growers of California; *U.S. Private*, pg. 199
CALAVO GROWERS OF CALIFORNIA; *U.S. Private*, pg. 199
CALBERSON—See GEODIS; *Int'l*, pg. 549
CALBERSON—See SNCF; *Int'l*, pg. 1163
CALBERSON DANZAS—See SNCF; *Int'l*, pg. 1163
CALBERSON FREIGHT NETWORK DIVISION—See SNCF; *Int'l*, pg. 1163
CALBERSON INTERNATIONAL—See SNCF; *Int'l*, pg. 1163
CALBERSON INTERNATIONAL STRASBOURG—See SNCF; *Int'l*, pg. 1163
CALBERSON OVERSEAS—See GEODIS; *Int'l*, pg. 549
CALBERSON PICARDIE—See SNCF; *Int'l*, pg. 1163
CALCASIEU LUMBER COMPANY; *U.S. Private*, pg. 200
CALCIA—See Ciments Francais; *Int'l*, pg. 292
CALCITEK, INC.—See Sulzer Ltd.; *Int'l*, pg. 1307
CALCO INTERNATIONAL, INC.—See Itoham Foods Inc.; *Int'l*, pg. 695
CALCOMP TECHNOLOGY, INC.—See Lockheed Martin Corporation; *U.S. Public*, pg. 1007
CALCOR SPACE FACILITY, INC.; *U.S. Private*, pg. 200
CALCOT, LTD.; *U.S. Private*, pg. 200
CALDOR, INC.; *U.S. Public*, pg. 292
CALDWELL BUTTON COMPANY—See Empire of Carolina, Inc.; *U.S. Public*, pg. 579
CALDWELL MANUFACTURING COMPANY; *U.S. Private*, pg. 200
CALDWELL TANKS, INC.; *U.S. Private*, pg. 200
CALDWELL VANRIPER, INC.; *U.S. Private*, pg. 200
CALDYNE, INC.—See Tenneco Inc.; *U.S. Public*, pg. 1579
CALEB BRETT USA INC.—See Inchcape PLC; *Int'l*, pg. 671
CALEDONIAN AIRWAYS LTD—See British Airways PLC; *Int'l*, pg. 219
CALEDONIAN PAPER PLC—See UPM-Kymmene Corporation; *Int'l*, pg. 1430
CALEFFI S.P.A.; *Int'l*, pg. 252
CALENERGY CO.; *U.S. Public*, pg. 292
CALENZANO PLANT—See Fort James Corporation; *U.S. Public*, pg. 673
CALFARM INSURANCE AGENCY—See Zenith National Insurance Corp.; *U.S. Public*, pg. 1791
CALFARM INSURANCE COMPANY—See Zenith National Insurance Corp.; *U.S. Public*, pg. 1791
CALGARY FLAMES HOCKEY CLUB; *Int'l*, pg. 252
CALGARY HERALD—See Hollinger Inc.; *Int'l*, pg. 631
THE CALGARY SUN—See Sun Media Corporation; *Int'l*, pg. 1320
CALGENE LLC—See Monsanto Company; *U.S. Public*, pg. 1124
CALGON CARBON CANADA, INC.—See Calgon Carbon Corporation; *U.S. Public*, pg. 293
CALGON CARBON CORPORATION; *U.S. Public*, pg. 292
CALGON CARBON CORP., CATLETTSBURG—See Calgon Carbon Corporation; *U.S. Public*, pg. 293
CALGON CARBON CORP., NEVILLE ISLAND—See Calgon Carbon Corporation; *U.S. Public*, pg. 293
CALGON CORPORATION—See English China Clays Plc; *Int'l*, pg. 455
CALGON FAR EAST CO. LTD.—See Calgon Carbon Corporation; *U.S. Public*, pg. 293
CALGON INTERAMERICAN CORP.—See English China Clays Plc; *Int'l*, pg. 455
CALHAC, INC.—See Honda Motor Co., Ltd.; *Int'l*, pg. 634
CALHOUN CITY TELEPHONE COMPANY—See Telephone and Data Systems, Inc.; *U.S. Public*, pg. 1571
CALIBER ONE INDEMNITY COMPANY—See Pennsylvania Manufacturers Corp.; *U.S. Public*, pg. 1272
CALIBER SYSTEM, INC.—See FDX Corporation; *U.S. Public*, pg. 604
CALIBRON, INC.—See Recoton Corporation; *U.S. Public*, pg. 1369
CALICO CORNERS—See Everfast Inc.; *U.S. Private*, pg. 386
CALICO PRINTERS ASSN. (U.S.A. LTD.)—See Coats Viyella plc; *Int'l*, pg. 300
CALIFIA COMPANY—See Enova Corp; *U.S. Public*, pg. 584
CALIFORNIA AGRIWASTE CORPORATION—See Thermo Electron Corporation; *U.S. Public*, pg. 1591
CALIFORNIA-AMERICAN WATER CO.—See American Water Works Company, Inc.; *U.S. Public*, pg. 95

MASTER INDEX TO COMPANY NAMES CAMDEL

Company Index

CALIFORNIA & HAWAIIAN SUGAR COMPANY INC.—See Alexander & Baldwin, Inc.; *U.S. Public*, pg. 39
CALIFORNIA AUTO DEALERS EXCHANGE, INC.—See Cox Enterprises, Inc.; *U.S. Private*, pg. 282
CALIFORNIA B.V.—See CSM N.V.; *Int'l*, pg. 243
CALIFORNIA CAPITAL INSURANCE COMPANY—See Kelly-Moore Paint Company, Inc.; *U.S. Private*, pg. 613
CALIFORNIA CASH MANAGEMENT COMPANY—See Nationwide Insurance Enterprise; *U.S. Private*, pg. 788
CALIFORNIA CEDAR PRODUCTS, INC.; *U.S. Private*, pg. 200
CALIFORNIA CHO HUNG BANK—See Cho Hung Bank; *Int'l*, pg. 287
CALIFORNIA CLOSET COMPANY, INC.—See Williams-Sonoma, Inc.; *U.S. Public*, pg. 1770
CALIFORNIA COMMERCE BANK—See Grupo Financiero Banamex/Accival, S.A. de C.V.; *Int'l*, pg. 574
CALIFORNIA CUSTOM FOODS—See Pacific Coast Producers; *U.S. Private*, pg. 831
CALIFORNIA DROP FORGE—See Fansteel, Inc.; *U.S. Public*, pg. 612
CALIFORNIA ENERGY INTERNATIONAL, LTD.—See CalEnergy Co.; *U.S. Public*, pg. 292
CALIFORNIA ENERGY OPERATING COMPANY—See CalEnergy Co.; *U.S. Public*, pg. 292
CALIFORNIA FARM PRODUCTS—See J.M. Smucker Company; *U.S. Public*, pg. 1480
CALIFORNIA FASHION INDUSTRIES INC.; *U.S. Private*, pg. 200
CALIFORNIA FEDERAL BANK—See MacAndrews & Forbes Holdings Inc.; *U.S. Private*, pg. 690
CALIFORNIA FRESH APRICOT COUNCIL; *U.S. Private*, pg. 200
CALIFORNIA HARDWARE COMPANY—See Distribution America; *U.S. Private*, pg. 335
CALIFORNIA HOSPITAL MEDICAL CENTER—See UniHealth; *U.S. Private*, pg. 1118
CALIFORNIA MANUFACTURING CO., INC.—See Ajinomoto Company Inc.; *Int'l*, pg. 41
CALIFORNIA MANUFACTURING CO., INC., LAS PINAS PLANT—See Ajinomoto Company Inc.; *Int'l*, pg. 41
CALIFORNIA MANUFACTURING CO., INC., PARANAQUE PLANT—See Ajinomoto Company Inc.; *Int'l*, pg. 41
CALIFORNIA MANUFACTURING ENTERPRISES; *U.S. Private*, pg. 201
CALIFORNIA MEC, INC.—See Mitsubishi Estate Co., Ltd.; *Int'l*, pg. 873
CALIFORNIA MFG. CO., INC.—See Bestfoods; *U.S. Public*, pg. 225
CALIFORNIA MICRO DEVICES; *U.S. Public*, pg. 293
CALIFORNIA MICROWAVE FOREIGN SALES CORPORATION—See California Microwave, Inc.; *U.S. Public*, pg. 293
CALIFORNIA MICROWAVE, INC.; *U.S. Public*, pg. 293
CALIFORNIA MICROWAVE, INC.-GOVERNMENT GRP.—See California Microwave, Inc.; *U.S. Public*, pg. 293
CALIFORNIA MICROWAVE, INC.-WIRELESS PRODUCTS GRP.—See California Microwave, Inc.; *U.S. Public*, pg. 293
CALIFORNIA MICROWAVE NAVIGATION SYSTEMS, INC.—See California Microwave, Inc.; *U.S. Public*, pg. 293
CALIFORNIA MICROWAVE-TELECOM TRANSMISSION SYSTEMS, INC.—See California Microwave, Inc.; *U.S. Public*, pg. 293
CALIFORNIA MILK PRODUCERS; *U.S. Private*, pg. 201
CALIFORNIA NEWSPAPERS, INC.—See Gannett Company, Inc.; *U.S. Public*, pg. 700
CALIFORNIA OFFSET PRINTERS, INC.—See COP Communications; *U.S. Private*, pg. 196
CALIFORNIA PANEL & VENEER COMPANY; *U.S. Private*, pg. 201
CALIFORNIA PHYSICIANS INSURANCE CORP.—See Blue Shield of California; *U.S. Private*, pg. 153
CALIFORNIA PIZZA KITCHEN INC.—See PepsiCo, Inc.; *U.S. Public*, pg. 1277
CALIFORNIA PRETZEL COMPANY—See GF Industries, Inc.; *U.S. Private*, pg. 434
CALIFORNIA PRODUCTS CORP.; *U.S. Private*, pg. 201
CALIFORNIA RECONVEYANCE CO.—See Washington Mutual Inc.; *U.S. Public*, pg. 1741
CALIFORNIA SCHOOL BOOK FAIRS, INC.—See Scholastic Corporation; *U.S. Public*, pg. 1440
CALIFORNIA SEVEN ASSOCIATES LIMITED PARTNERSHIP—See Cigna Corp.; *U.S. Public*, pg. 359
CALIFORNIA STATE BANK; *U.S. Public*, pg. 294
CALIFORNIA STATE BANK-ALHAMBRA—See California State Bank; *U.S. Public*, pg. 294
CALIFORNIA STATE BANK-ANAHEIM—See California State Bank; *U.S. Public*, pg. 294
CALIFORNIA STATE BANK-ARCADIA—See California State Bank; *U.S. Public*, pg. 294
CALIFORNIA STATE BANK-BEAUMONT—See California State Bank; *U.S. Public*, pg. 294
CALIFORNIA STATE BANK-BREA—See California State Bank; *U.S. Public*, pg. 294
CALIFORNIA STATE BANK-CITY OF INDUSTRY—See California State Bank; *U.S. Public*, pg. 294
CALIFORNIA STATE BANK-COVINA DOWNTOWN—See California State Bank; *U.S. Public*, pg. 294
CALIFORNIA STATE BANK-COVINA MAIN—See California State Bank; *U.S. Public*, pg. 294
CALIFORNIA STATE BANK-GLENDORA—See California State Bank; *U.S. Public*, pg. 294
CALIFORNIA STATE BANK-IRVINE—See California State Bank; *U.S. Public*, pg. 294
CALIFORNIA STATE BANK-LA HABRA—See California State Bank; *U.S. Public*, pg. 294
CALIFORNIA STATE BANK-LA PALMA—See California State Bank; *U.S. Public*, pg. 294
CALIFORNIA STATE BANK-LAKE FOREST IRVINE—See California State Bank; *U.S. Public*, pg. 294
CALIFORNIA STATE BANK-NEWPORT BEACH—See California State Bank; *U.S. Public*, pg. 294
CALIFORNIA STATE BANK-ONTARIO—See California State Bank; *U.S. Public*, pg. 294
CALIFORNIA STATE BANK-ORANGE—See California State Bank; *U.S. Public*, pg. 294
CALIFORNIA STATE BANK-PLACENTIA—See California State Bank; *U.S. Public*, pg. 294
CALIFORNIA STATE BANK-RANCHO CUCAMONGA—See California State Bank; *U.S. Public*, pg. 294
CALIFORNIA STATE BANK-VICTORVILLE—See California State Bank; *U.S. Public*, pg. 294
CALIFORNIA STATE BANK-WEST COVINA—See California State Bank; *U.S. Public*, pg. 294
CALIFORNIA STRAWBERRY COMMISSION; *U.S. Private*, pg. 201
CALIFORNIA WATER SERVICE CO.; *U.S. Public*, pg. 294
CALIFORNIA WOODFIBER CORP.—See Marubeni Corporation; *Int'l*, pg. 845
CALIQUA AG—See Sulzer Ltd.; *Int'l*, pg. 1306
CALISAR ASSOCIATES—See Cigna Corp.; *U.S. Public*, pg. 361
CALISTOGA WATER CO.—See Nestle S.A.; *Int'l*, pg. 919
CALITEK CORPORATION—See SATEC Systems Inc.; *U.S. Private*, pg. 967
THE CALKINS MANUFACTURING COMPANY; *U.S. Private*, pg. 201
CALL CONNECTIONS LIMITED—See British Telecommunications plc; *Int'l*, pg. 222
CALL INTERACTIVE—See First Data Corporation; *U.S. Public*, pg. 631
CALLAHAN ENTERPRISES—See Groupe Limagrain; *Int'l*, pg. 566
CALLAHAN MINING CORPORATION—See Coeur D'Alene Mines Corporation; *U.S. Public*, pg. 394
CALLANAN INDUSTRIES, INC.—See CRH, plc; *Int'l*, pg. 242
CALLAWAY CHEMICAL COMPANY—See Vulcan Materials Company; *U.S. Public*, pg. 1726
CALLAWAY CHEMICAL LIMITED—See Vulcan Materials Company; *U.S. Public*, pg. 1726
CALLAWAY GOLF COMPANY; *U.S. Public*, pg. 294
CALLAWAY GOLF (U.K.) LIMITED—See Callaway Golf Company; *U.S. Public*, pg. 295
CALLAWAY VINEYARD & WINERY—See Allied Domecq PLC; *Int'l*, pg. 63
BARRY CALLEBAUT N.V.; *Int'l*, pg. 252
CALLERY CHEMICAL CO.—See Mine Safety Appliances Co.; *U.S. Public*, pg. 1114
CALLIDUS TECHNOLOGIES INC.—See ChemFirst Inc.; *U.S. Public*, pg. 344
CALLITHEKE INTERNATIONAL LTD.—See Diageo Plc; *Int'l*, pg. 409
CALLON OFFSHORE PRODUCTION—See Callon Petroleum Company; *U.S. Public*, pg. 295
CALLON PETROLEUM COMPANY; *U.S. Public*, pg. 295
CALMANN-LEVY—See Lagardere Groupe; *Int'l*, pg. 792
CALMAR INC.; *U.S. Private*, pg. 201
CALMAT CO.; *U.S. Public*, pg. 295
CALMAT CO. OF ARIZONA—See CalMat Co.; *U.S. Public*, pg. 295
CALMAT CO. OF NEW MEXICO—See CalMat Co.; *U.S. Public*, pg. 295
CALMAT LAND CO.—See CalMat Co.; *U.S. Public*, pg. 295
CALMAT LEASING CO.—See CalMat Co.; *U.S. Public*, pg. 295
CALMAT OF CENTRAL CALIFORNIA—See CalMat Co.; *U.S. Public*, pg. 295
CALNEV PIPELINE COMPANY—See GATX Corporation; *U.S. Public*, pg. 692
CALOR-EMAG ELEKTRIZITATS-AKTIENGESELLSCHAFT—See ABB Asea Brown Boveri (Holding) Ltd.; *Int'l*, pg. 2
CALOR GAS LTD.—See SHV Holdings N.V.; *Int'l*, pg. 1155
CALOR GAS NORTHERN IRELAND LTD.—See SHV Holdings N.V.; *Int'l*, pg. 1155
CALOR GROUP PLC—See SHV Holdings N.V.; *Int'l*, pg. 1155
CALOR S.A.—See Groupe SEB; *Int'l*, pg. 568
CALOR TEORANTA—See SHV Holdings N.V.; *Int'l*, pg. 1155
CALORSTAT INDUSTRIES SA—See Senior Engineering Group, plc; *Int'l*, pg. 1222
CALPINE CORPORATION; *U.S. Public*, pg. 296
CALPIS AJINMOTO DANONE—See Danone Group; *Int'l*, pg. 379
CALPIS AJINMOTO DANONE CO. LTD.—See Danone Group; *Int'l*, pg. 380
CALPIS FOOD INDUSTRY CO. LTD.; *Int'l*, pg. 252
CALPROP CORPORATION; *U.S. Public*, pg. 296
CALSEG S.A.—See ETEX; *Int'l*, pg. 430
CALSONIC CLIMATE CONTROL, INC.—See Nissan Motor Co., Ltd.; *Int'l*, pg. 944
CALSONIC CORP.—See Nissan Motor Co., Ltd.; *Int'l*, pg. 944
CALSONIC HARRISON CO., LTD.—See General Motors Corporation; *U.S. Public*, pg. 724
CALSONIC INTERNATIONAL, INC.—See Nissan Motor Co., Ltd.; *Int'l*, pg. 944
CALSONIC MFG. CORP.—See Nissan Motor Co., Ltd.; *Int'l*, pg. 944
CALSONIC YOROZU CORPORATION—See Nissan Motor Co., Ltd.; *Int'l*, pg. 944
CALSPAN OPERATIONS—See Veridian; *U.S. Private*, pg. 1136
CALSPAN SRL CORPORATION—See Veridian; *U.S. Private*, pg. 1136
CALTERM—See Applied Power Inc.; *U.S. Public*, pg. 124
P.T. CALTEX PACIFIC INDONESIA—See Chevron Corporation; *U.S. Public*, pg. 348
CALTEX PETROLEUM CORPORATION—See Chevron Corporation; *U.S. Public*, pg. 348
CALTEX SERVICES CORP.—See Chevron Corporation; *U.S. Public*, pg. 348
CALTON HOMES, INC.—See Calton, Inc.; *U.S. Public*, pg. 296
CALTON, INC.; *U.S. Public*, pg. 296
CALTROL, INC.; *U.S. Private*, pg. 201
CALTY DESIGN RESEARCH, INC.—See Toyota Motor Corporation; *Int'l*, pg. 1412
CALUMET CARTON COMPANY; *U.S. Private*, pg. 201
CALUMET CONSTRUCTION CORPORATION; *U.S. Private*, pg. 201
CALUMET CONSTRUCTION CORPORATION-INDIANAPOLIS DIVISION—See Calumet Construction Corporation; *U.S. Private*, pg. 202
CALUMET CONSTRUCTION CORPORATION-SOUTH BEND DIVISION—See Calumet Construction Corporation; *U.S. Private*, pg. 202
CALUMET FLORIDA, INC.—See Plains Resources Inc.; *U.S. Public*, pg. 1308
CALUMET PHOTOGRAPHIC, INC.; *U.S. Private*, pg. 202
CALVE-DE BETUWE B.V.—See Unilever Plc; *Int'l*, pg. 1436
CALVEL—See SNCF; *Int'l*, pg. 1163
CALVERT BANK & TRUST CO.—See Mercantile Bankshares Corporation; *U.S. Public*, pg. 1088
THE CALVERT CO.—See Aztec Manufacturing Co.; *U.S. Public*, pg. 159
CALVERT GROUP, LTD.—See The Acacia Group - Acacia Life Insurance Co.; *U.S. Private*, pg. 11
CALVIN BULLOCK, LTD.—See Sun Life Assurance Company of Canada; *Int'l*, pg. 1319
CALVIN KLEIN COSMETICS COMPANY—See Unilever Plc; *Int'l*, pg. 1435
CALVIN KLEIN, INC.; *U.S. Private*, pg. 202
CALVIN KLEIN SPORT, INC.—See Calvin Klein, Inc.; *U.S. Private*, pg. 202
CALWER DECKEN-UND TUCHFABRIKEN AG; *Int'l*, pg. 253
CALWEST COMPRESS & WAREHOUSE CO., INC.—See Itochu Corporation; *Int'l*, pg. 694
CAM AM CASTERS—See Standex International Corporation; *U.S. Public*, pg. 1507
CAM CARS—See Chrysler Corporation; *U.S. Public*, pg. 354
CAM MANUFACTURING, INC.—See Crown Holdings, Inc.; *U.S. Private*, pg. 293
CAM-STAT, INC.—See Watsco, Inc.; *U.S. Public*, pg. 1746
CAMALLOY, INCORPORATED; *U.S. Private*, pg. 202
CAMARIN LIMITED—See MacMillan Bloedel Limited; *Int'l*, pg. 829
CAMBEX CORPORATION; *U.S. Public*, pg. 296
CAMBIAR INVESTORS, INC.—See United Asset Management Corporation; *U.S. Public*, pg. 1672
CAMBINEX EXPLORATION—See Cambior Inc.; *Int'l*, pg. 253
CAMBIOR DE MEXICO S.A. DE C.V.—See Cambior Inc.; *Int'l*, pg. 253
CAMBIOR INC.; *Int'l*, pg. 253
CAMBIOR USA, INC.—See Cambior Inc.; *Int'l*, pg. 253
CAMBIUM CORPORATION—See Forest City Enterprises, Inc.; *U.S. Public*, pg. 668
CAMBREX CORPORATION; *U.S. Public*, pg. 297
CAMBREX HONG KONG LTD.—See Cambrex Corporation; *U.S. Public*, pg. 297
CAMBREX-INDIA—See Cambrex Corporation; *U.S. Public*, pg. 297
CAMBREX PRC—See Cambrex Corporation; *U.S. Public*, pg. 297
CAMBRIDGE CONSULTANTS LIMITED—See Arthur D. Little, Inc.; *U.S. Private*, pg. 671
CAMBRIDGE ELECTRIC LIGHT CO.—See Commonwealth Energy System; *U.S. Public*, pg. 414
CAMBRIDGE INDUSTRIES INC.; *U.S. Private*, pg. 202
CAMBRIDGE INDUSTRIES, INC.—See Cambridge Industries Inc.; *U.S. Private*, pg. 202
CAMBRIDGE INDUSTRIES - WOODSTOCK—See Cambridge Industries Inc.; *U.S. Private*, pg. 202
CAMBRIDGE LEASEHOLDS LIMITED—See Cambridge Shopping Centres Limited; *Int'l*, pg. 253
CAMBRIDGE-LEE (EUROPE) LTD.—See Cambridge-Lee Industries, Inc.; *U.S. Private*, pg. 202
CAMBRIDGE-LEE INDUSTRIES, INC.; *U.S. Private*, pg. 202
CAMBRIDGE PRODUCTS CORPORATION—See Jordan Industries, Inc.; *U.S. Private*, pg. 598
CAMBRIDGE RESEARCH BIOCHEMICALS LIMITED—See Zeneca Group Plc; *Int'l*, pg. 1524
CAMBRIDGE SHOPPING CENTRES LIMITED; *Int'l*, pg. 253
CAMBRIDGE SOUNDWORKS, INC.; *U.S. Private*, pg. 202
CAMBRIDGE STREET METAL CO.; *U.S. Private*, pg. 203
CAMBRIDGE TECHNOLOGY PARTNERS—See Safeguard Scientifics, Inc.; *U.S. Public*, pg. 1424
CAMBRIDGE VACUUM ENGINEERING LTD.—See TI Group plc; *Int'l*, pg. 1337
CAMBRIDGE WESTERN LEASEHOLDS LIMITED—See Cambridge Shopping Centres Limited; *Int'l*, pg. 253
CAMBRIDGE-LEE CANADA LTD.—See Cambridge-Lee Industries, Inc.; *U.S. Private*, pg. 202
CAMBRO MANUFACTURING COMPANY; *U.S. Private*, pg. 203
CAMBY—See Bouygues; *Int'l*, pg. 207
CAMCAR TEXTRON—See Textron Inc.; *U.S. Public*, pg. 1589
CAMCO CANADA—See Emerson Electric Co.; *U.S. Public*, pg. 576
CAMCO DRILLING GROUP—See Camco International Inc.; *U.S. Public*, pg. 298
CAMCO EUROPE—See Emerson Electric Co.; *U.S. Public*, pg. 576
CAMCO INC.—See General Electric Company; *U.S. Public*, pg. 713
CAMCO INTERNATIONAL INC.; *U.S. Public*, pg. 297
CAMCO INTERNATIONAL INC.—See Camco International Inc.; *U.S. Public*, pg. 298
CAMCO PRODUCTS & SERVICES COMPANY—See Camco International Inc.; *U.S. Public*, pg. 298
CAMDEL METALS DIVISION—See Handy & Harman; *U.S. Public*, pg. 780

THE CAMDEN FIRE INSURANCE ASSN.—See General Accident Fire and Life Assurance Corporation p.l.c.; *Int'l*, pg. 543

CAMDEN MEDICAL SUPPLY, INC.—See Integrated Health Services, Inc.; *U.S. Public*, pg. 884

CAMDEN MILL, WOOD PRODUCTS DIV.—See Champion International Corp.; *U.S. Public*, pg. 334

CAMDEN MOTORS LTD.—See Barclays Bank PLC; *Int'l*, pg. 165

CAMDEN PAPERBOARD CORPORATION—See Caraustar Industries, Inc.; *U.S. Public*, pg. 303

CAMDEN PROPERTY TRUST; *U.S. Public*, pg. 298

CAMDEN/ROCKLAND DIVISION—See Consumers Water Company; *U.S. Public*, pg. 298

CAMDEN WIRE CO., INC.—See Hicks, Muse, Tate & Furst Inc.; *U.S. Private*, pg. 526

CAMDEV PROPERTIES INC.—See O&Y Properties Corporation; *Int'l*, pg. 993

CAMEA S.A.—See Alcan Aluminium Limited; *Int'l*, pg. 51

CAMECANICA, S.A.—See Corporacion MAPFRE, Compania Internacional de Reaseguros, S.A.; *Int'l*, pg. 333

CAMELIA WERK AG—See Kimberly-Clark Corporation; *U.S. Public*, pg. 959

CAMELLIA FOOD STORES, INC.; *U.S. Private*, pg. 203

CAMELOT COMMUNICATIONS, INC.; *U.S. Private*, pg. 203

CAMELOT MUSIC, INC.; *U.S. Private*, pg. 203

CAMEO WINDOW FURNISHINGS—See Trace International Holdings, Inc.; *U.S. Private*, pg. 1094

CAMERA HOUSE LIMITED—See Ricoh Company, Ltd.; *Int'l*, pg. 1115

CAMERA, INC.—See Sensormatic Electronics Corporation; *U.S. Public*, pg. 1457

AMERICAN INTERNATIONAL—See ConAgra, Inc.; *U.S. Public*, pg. 426

CAMERON; *U.S. Public*, pg. 298

CAMERON & BARKLEY COMPANY; *U.S. Private*, pg. 203

CAMERON ASHLEY—See Cameron Ashley Building Products, Inc; *U.S. Public*, pg. 298

CAMERON ASHLEY BUILDING PRODUCTS, INC; *U.S. Public*, pg. 298

N.C. CAMERON & SONS, LTD.—See Stanhome Inc.; *U.S. Public*, pg. 1508

CAMEROON AIRLINES—See Groupe Air France; *Int'l*, pg. 561

CAMERZ PHOTO PRODUCTS—See Photo Control Corporation; *U.S. Public*, pg. 1292

CAMFORD AUTOMOTIVE SYSTEMS LTD.—See Fried. Krupp AG; *Int'l*, pg. 507

CAMFORD DESIGN LTD.—See Fried. Krupp AG; *Int'l*, pg. 507

CAMFORD ENGINEERING PLC—See Fried. Krupp AG; *Int'l*, pg. 507

CAMFORD PRESSINGS LTD.—See Fried. Krupp AG; *Int'l*, pg. 507

CAMILLUS CUTLERY CO.; *U.S. Private*, pg. 203

CAMINO REAL CHEVROLET & GEO; *U.S. Private*, pg. 203

CAMINO REAL FOODS, INC.—See Nissin Food Products Co., Ltd.; *Int'l*, pg. 949

CAMISAS BAHIA KINO S.A. DE C.V.—See Oxford Industries, Inc.; *U.S. Public*, pg. 1239

CAMISUS DE JUAREZ, S.A. DE C.V.—See Jones Apparel Group, Inc.; *U.S. Public*, pg. 933

CAMLOC FASTENER GMBH—See The Fairchild Corporation; *U.S. Public*, pg. 610

CAMLOC INTERNATIONAL—See The Fairchild Corporation; *U.S. Public*, pg. 610

CAMOSY, INC.; *U.S. Private*, pg. 203

CAMP—See Alcatel Alsthom Compagnie Generale D'Electricite; *Int'l*, pg. 53

CAMP AMERICA—See American Institute for Foreign Study; *U.S. Private*, pg. 57

S.A. CAMP AND GROUP—See Joh. A. Benckiser GmbH; *Int'l*, pg. 186

CAMP DRESSER & MCKEE INC.; *U.S. Private*, pg. 203

CAMP DRESSER & MCKEE INTERNATIONAL INC.—See Camp Dresser & McKee Inc.; *U.S. Private*, pg. 204

CAMP HEALTHCARE—See True Life; *Int'l*, pg. 1425

CAMP LEJEUNE RAILROAD COMPANY—See Norfolk Southern Corporation; *U.S. Public*, pg. 1191

CAMPBELL BEWLEY PROPERTIES LTD.—See Campbells/Bewley Group; *Int'l*, pg. 254

CAMPBELL CATERING INTERNATIONAL LTD.—See Campbells/Bewley Group; *Int'l*, pg. 254

CAMPBELL CATERING LIMITED—See Campbells/Bewley Group; *Int'l*, pg. 254

CAMPBELL CATERING NI LIMITED—See Campbells/Bewley Group; *Int'l*, pg. 254

CAMPBELL DISTILLERS LIMITED—See Groupe Pernod Ricard; *Int'l*, pg. 567

CAMPBELL-EWALD ADVERTISING—See The Interpublic Group of Companies, Inc.; *U.S. Public*, pg. 908

CAMPBELL FINANCE CORP.—See Campbell Soup Company; *U.S. Public*, pg. 299

CAMPBELL GROCERY PRODUCTS LTD.—See Campbell Soup Company; *U.S. Public*, pg. 299

THE CAMPBELL GROUP, INC.—See United Asset Management Corporation; *U.S. Public*, pg. 1672

CAMPBELL HAUSFE.D DIVISION OF SCOTT FETZER—See Berkshire Hathaway Inc.; *U.S. Public*, pg. 217

CAMPBELL INDUSTRIES, INC.—See Marine Construction & Design Co.; *U.S. Private*, pg. 703

CAMPBELL INFLIGHT LIMITED—See Campbells/Bewley Group; *Int'l*, pg. 254

CAMPBELL INTERNATIONAL TRADING HOUSE LIMITED—See Campbells/Bewley Group; *Int'l*, pg. 254

CAMPBELL JAPAN, INC.—See Campbell Soup Company; *U.S. Public*, pg. 299

JOHN J. CAMPBELL CO., INC.; *U.S. Private*, pg. 204

JOSEPH CAMPBELL COMPANY—See Campbell Soup Company; *U.S. Public*, pg. 299

CAMPBELL LEE COMPUTER SERVICES LTD.—See Marcam Solutions, Inc.; *U.S. Public*, pg. 1043

CAMPBELL MANAGEMENT SERVICES LIMITED—See Campbells/Bewley Group; *Int'l*, pg. 254

CAMPBELL MEDIA ALLIANCE—See True North Communications Inc.; *U.S. Public*, pg. 1641

CAMPBELL MITHUN ESTY; *U.S. Private*, pg. 204

CAMPBELL-MITHUN-ESTY—See Campbell Mithun Esty; *U.S. Private*, pg. 204

CAMPBELL OIL CO.; *U.S. Private*, pg. 204

CAMPBELL PLASTICS DIV.—See The Standard Products Company; *U.S. Public*, pg. 1504

CAMPBELL SALES—See Campbell Soup Company; *U.S. Public*, pg. 299

CAMPBELL SALES COMPANY—See Campbell Soup Company; *U.S. Public*, pg. 299

CAMPBELL SOUP COMPANY; *U.S. Public*, pg. 298

CAMPBELL SOUP COMPANY LTD.—See Campbell Soup Company; *U.S. Public*, pg. 299

CAMPBELL SOUP (TEXAS) INC.—See Campbell Soup Company; *U.S. Public*, pg. 299

CAMPBELL SOUPS (FAYETTEVILLE PLANT)—See Campbell Soup Company; *U.S. Public*, pg. 299

CAMPBELL USA—See Campbell Soup Company; *U.S. Public*, pg. 299

CAMPBELL WELLS CORPORATION—See USA Waste Services, Inc.; *U.S. Public*, pg. 1686

CAMPBELLS/BEWLEY GROUP; *Int'l*, pg. 253

CAMPBELL'S DE MEXICO, S.A. DE C.V.—See Campbell Soup Company; *U.S. Public*, pg. 299

CAMPBELL'S FRESH, INC.—See Campbell Soup Company; *U.S. Public*, pg. 299

CAMPBELL'S SOUPS (AUST.) PTY. LTD.—See Campbell Soup Company; *U.S. Public*, pg. 299

CAMPBELL'S (U.K.) LIMITED—See Campbell Soup Company; *U.S. Public*, pg. 299

CAMPENON BERNARD—See Compagnie Generale Des Eaux; *Int'l*, pg. 321

CAMPINA AG—See Campina Melkunie BV; *Int'l*, pg. 254

CAMPINA MELKUNIE BV; *Int'l*, pg. 254

CAMPINA MELKUNIE INTERNATIONAL DIVISION—See Campina Melkunie BV; *Int'l*, pg. 254

CAMPINA N.V./S.A.—See Campina Melkunie BV; *Int'l*, pg. 254

CIA. CAMPINEIRA DE ALIMENTOS—See Danone Group; *Int'l*, pg. 380

CAMPING WORLD, INC.; *U.S. Private*, pg. 204

CAMPMOR INC.; *U.S. Private*, pg. 204

CAMPOS VELAZQUEZ, S.A.—See SEPI; *Int'l*, pg. 1224

CAMPUS POINT REALTY CORPORATION—See Science Applications International Corp.; *U.S. Private*, pg. 976

CAMPUS TELEPHONE SERVICES, INC.—See Peoples Telephone Company, Inc.; *U.S. Public*, pg. 1275

CAMPUS THOMSON—See Thomson S.A.; *Int'l*, pg. 1381

CAMROSE PIPE COMPANY—See Oregon Steel Mills Inc.; *U.S. Public*, pg. 1230

CAMTEC ELECTRONIC LTD.—See Telefonaktiebolaget LM Ericsson; *Int'l*, pg. 1365

CAMTRONICS FOREIGN SALES CORP.—See Analogic Corporation; *U.S. Public*, pg. 109

CAMTRONICS LTD.—See Analogic Corporation; *U.S. Public*, pg. 109

CAN CORPORATION OF AMERICA; *U.S. Private*, pg. 204

CANA INC.—See Alcatel Alsthom Compagnie Generale D'Electricite; *Int'l*, pg. 55

CANAC KITCHENS LTD—See Kohler Company; *U.S. Private*, pg. 630

CANADA ALLOY CASTINGS, LTD.—See Atchison Casting Corporation; *U.S. Public*, pg. 142

CANADA BRICK DIV.—See Jannock Limited; *Int'l*, pg. 698

CANADA DRY DIVISION—See Cadbury Schweppes p.l.c.; *Int'l*, pg. 248

CANADA LIFE ASSURANCE COMPANY OF GREAT BRITAIN LIMITED—See The Canada Life Assurance Company; *Int'l*, pg. 255

THE CANADA LIFE ASSURANCE COMPANY OF IRELAND LIMITED—See The Canada Life Assurance Company; *Int'l*, pg. 255

THE CANADA LIFE ASSURANCE COMPANY; *Int'l*, pg. 254

THE CANADA LIFE ASSURANCE COMPANY (U.K.) LIMITED—See The Canada Life Assurance Company; *Int'l*, pg. 255

CANADA LIFE ASSURANCE (IRELAND) LTD.—See The Canada Life Assurance Company; *Int'l*, pg. 255

CANADA LIFE CAPITAL CORPORATION—See The Canada Life Assurance Company; *Int'l*, pg. 254

CANADA LIFE CASUALTY INSURANCE COMPANY—See The Canada Life Assurance Company; *Int'l*, pg. 254

CANADA LIFE FINANCIAL SERVICES COMPANY LIMITED—See The Canada Life Assurance Company; *Int'l*, pg. 255

CANADA LIFE FINANCIAL SERVICES COMPANY OF IRELAND LIMITED—See The Canada Life Assurance Company; *Int'l*, pg. 255

THE CANADA LIFE GROUP (U.K.) LIMITED—See The Canada Life Assurance Company; *Int'l*, pg. 255

CANADA LIFE HOLDINGS (U.K.) LIMITED—See The Canada Life Assurance Company; *Int'l*, pg. 255

CANADA LIFE INSURANCE COMPANY OF AMERICA—See The Canada Life Assurance Company; *Int'l*, pg. 255

CANADA LIFE INSURANCE COMPANY OF NEW YORK—See The Canada Life Assurance Company; *Int'l*, pg. 255

CANADA LIFE INVESTMENT MANAGEMENT LIMITED—See The Canada Life Assurance Company; *Int'l*, pg. 255

CANADA LIFE IRELAND HOLDINGS—See The Canada Life Assurance Company; *Int'l*, pg. 255

CANADA LIFE MANAGEMENT (U.K.) LIMITED—See The Canada Life Assurance Company; *Int'l*, pg. 255

CANADA LIFE MORTGAGE SERVICES LTD.—See The Canada Life Assurance Company; *Int'l*, pg. 255

CANADA LIFE OF AMERICA FINANCIAL SERVICES, INC.—See The Canada Life Assurance Company; *Int'l*, pg. 255

CANADA LIFE PENSION & ANNUITIES (IRELAND) LIMITED—See The Canada Life Assurance Company; *Int'l*, pg. 255

CANADA LIFE SECURING CORPORATION—See The Canada Life Assurance Company; *Int'l*, pg. 255

CANADA LIFE TRUSTEE SERVICES (U.K.) LIMITED—See The Canada Life Assurance Company; *Int'l*, pg. 255

CANADA LIFE (UK) LTD.—See The Canada Life Assurance Company; *Int'l*, pg. 255

CANADA LIFE UNIT TRUST MANAGERS LIMITED—See The Canada Life Assurance Company; *Int'l*, pg. 255

CANADA MALTING CO. LIMITED—See ConAgra, Inc.; *U.S. Public*, pg. 428

CANADA MARITIME LIMITED—See Canadian Pacific Limited; *Int'l*, pg. 259

CANADA PORTS CORPORATION; *Int'l*, pg. 255

CANADA SAFEWAY LIMITED—See Safeway Inc.; *U.S. Public*, pg. 1426

THE CANADA TRUST COMPANY—See B.A.T Industries P.L.C.; *Int'l*, pg. 112

CANADA TRUSTCO MORTGAGE COMPANY—See B.A.T Industries P.L.C.; *Int'l*, pg. 112

CANADA WEST INDIES MOLASSES CO. LTD.—See Tate & Lyle PLC; *Int'l*, pg. 1357

CANADELLE, INC.—See Sara Lee Corporation; *U.S. Public*, pg. 1434

CANADIAN AD-CHECK SERVICES INC.—See Rogers Communications, Inc.; *Int'l*, pg. 1124

CANADIAN ADHESIVES LTD.—See Viag AG; *Int'l*, pg. 1466

CANADIAN AIRLINES CORPORATION; *Int'l*, pg. 255

CANADIAN AIRLINES INTERNATIONAL LTD.—See Canadian Airlines Corporation; *Int'l*, pg. 256

CANADIAN AMERICAN RAILROAD COMPANY—See Iron Road Railways Inc.; *U.S. Private*, pg. 575

CANADIAN ART PRINTS—See Devon Group, Inc.; *U.S. Public*, pg. 503

CANADIAN AUTOPARTS TOYOTA, INC.—See Toyota Motor Corporation; *Int'l*, pg. 1413

CANADIAN BRINE LTD.—See Morton International Inc.; *U.S. Public*, pg. 1135

CANADIAN BROADCAST SALES—See WIC Western International Communications Ltd.; *Int'l*, pg. 1482

CANADIAN BUILDING SYSTEMS INC.—See Jannock Limited; *Int'l*, pg. 698

CANADIAN CEMENT LTD.—See Medusa Corporation; *U.S. Public*, pg. 1084

THE CANADIAN COLEMAN CO., LTD.—See MacAndrews & Forbes Holdings Inc.; *U.S. Private*, pg. 691

CANADIAN COLEMAN SUPPLY CO., INC.—See MacAndrews & Forbes Holdings Inc.; *U.S. Private*, pg. 691

CANADIAN COMETRA, INC.—See Groupe Bruxelles Lambert S.A.; *Int'l*, pg. 562

CANADIAN ENERGY SERVICES—See American Eco Corporation; *Int'l*, pg. 74

CANADIAN EQUIPMENT FINANCE CORPORATION—See Deere & Company; *U.S. Public*, pg. 492

CANADIAN ERECTORS LTD.; *Int'l*, pg. 256

CANADIAN ERECTORS PIPE—See Canadian Erectors Ltd.; *Int'l*, pg. 256

CANADIAN FABRICATED PRODUCTS—See Chrysler Corporation; *U.S. Public*, pg. 354

CANADIAN FERRO HOT METAL SPECIALTIES, LTD.—See Oglebay Norton Company; *U.S. Public*, pg. 1214

CANADIAN FOREST OIL LTD.—See Forest Oil Corporation; *U.S. Public*, pg. 670

CANADIAN FOREST PRODUCTS LTD.—See Canfor Corporation; *Int'l*, pg. 260

CANADIAN FOREST PRODUCTS LTD., PANEL & FIBRE DIVISION—See Canfor Corporation; *Int'l*, pg. 260

CANADIAN FOREST PRODUCTS LTD., PRINCE GEORGE PULP & PAPER MILLS DIV.—See Canfor Corporation; *Int'l*, pg. 260

CANADIAN FOREST PRODUCTS LTD., TAYLOR DIVISION—See Canfor Corporation; *Int'l*, pg. 260

CANADIAN FREIGHTWAYS LTD.—See Consolidated Freightways Corp.; *U.S. Public*, pg. 435

CANADIAN GAS GATHERING SYSTEMS II, INC.—See Morrison Petroleums Ltd.; *Int'l*, pg. 895

CANADIAN HARDINGS MACHINE TOOLS LTD.—See Hardings, Inc.; *U.S. Private*, pg. 502

CANADIAN HUNTER EXPLORATION LTD.—See EdperBrascan Corporation; *Int'l*, pg. 433

CANADIAN IMPERIAL BANK OF COMMERCE; *Int'l*, pg. 256

CANADIAN IMPERIAL FUND MANAGERS (CAYMAN) LIMITED—See Canadian Imperial Bank of Commerce; *Int'l*, pg. 257

CANADIAN IMPERIAL HOLDINGS, INC.—See Canadian Imperial Bank of Commerce; *Int'l*, pg. 257

CANADIAN IMPERIAL SERVICE CO.—See Canadian Imperial Bank of Commerce; *Int'l*, pg. 257

CANADIAN KAWASAKI MOTORS INC.—See Kawasaki Heavy Industries, Ltd.; *Int'l*, pg. 726

CANADIAN KENWORTH CO.—See Paccar Inc.; *U.S. Public*, pg. 1247

CANADIAN LIMITED—See Wolters Kluwer N.V.; *Int'l*, pg. 1513

CANADIAN LIQUID AIR LTD.-AIR LIQUIDE CANADA LTEE—See Air Liquide S.A.; *Int'l*, pg. 37

CANADIAN LIQUIDAIRE PROPERTIES LTD.—See Air Liquide S.A.; *Int'l*, pg. 37

CANADIAN LOCKER CO., LTD.—See American Locker Group, Inc.; *U.S. Public*, pg. 86

CANADIAN MAAS RIVER INVESTMENT N.V.—See MacMillan Bloedel Limited; *Int'l*, pg. 829

CANADIAN MARCONI COMPANY—See The General Electric Company, p.l.c.; *Int'l*, pg. 545

CANADIAN MEDIA DISTRIBUTORS—See G.T.C. Transcontinental Group Ltd.; *Int'l*, pg. 539

CANADIAN METER COMPANY, INC.—See Ruhrgas Aktiengesellschaft; *Int'l*, pg. 1149
CANADIAN MINI-WAREHOUSE PROPERTIES, LTD.—See Public Storage, Inc.; *U.S. Public*, pg. 1341
CANADIAN MIST DISTILLERS LTD.—See Brown-Forman Corporation; *U.S. Public*, pg. 262
CANADIAN-MONTANA GAS CO., LTD.—See Montana Power Company; *U.S. Public*, pg. 1127
CANADIAN-MONTANA PIPELINE CO.—See Montana Power Company; *U.S. Public*, pg. 1127
CANADIAN NATIONAL RAILWAY COMPANY; *Int'l*, pg. 258
CANADIAN NATURAL RESOURCES LIMITED; *Int'l*, pg. 258
CANADIAN OCCIDENTAL PETROLEUM LTD.—See Occidental Petroleum Corporation; *U.S. Public*, pg. 1210
CANADIAN PACIFIC LIMITED; *Int'l*, pg. 258
CANADIAN PACIFIC RAILWAY—See Canadian Pacific Limited; *Int'l*, pg. 258
CANADIAN POOL AGENCIES LTD.—See Saskatchewan Wheat Pool; *Int'l*, pg. 1195
CANADIAN PRESS CLIPPING SERVICES—See Rogers Communications, Inc.; *Int'l*, pg. 1124
CANADIAN PUBLISHING—See Rogers Communications, Inc.; *Int'l*, pg. 1123
CANADIAN PUREGAS EQUIPMENT LTD.—See American Financial Group; *U.S. Public*, pg. 75
CANADIAN REYNOLDS METALS COMPANY, LTD.—See Reynolds Metals Company; *U.S. Public*, pg. 1386
CANADIAN ROAD CREDIT COMPANY, LIMITED—See Ford Motor Company; *U.S. Public*, pg. 665
CANADIAN ROXY PETROLEUM LTD.—See Westcoast Energy Inc.; *Int'l*, pg. 1492
THE CANADIAN SALT CO. LTD.—See Morton International Inc.; *U.S. Public*, pg. 1135
CANADIAN SATELLITE COMMUNICATIONS INC.—See WIC Western International Communications Ltd.; *Int'l*, pg. 1481
CANADIAN SHADE TREE SERVICE, LTD.—See The Davey Tree Expert Company; *U.S. Private*, pg. 314
CANADIAN SHIPBUILDING & ENGINEERING LTD.; *Int'l*, pg. 259
CANADIAN STEBBINS ENGINEERING & MFG. CO. LTD.—See Stebbins Engineering & Mfg. Co.; *U.S. Private*, pg. 1037
CANADIAN STEEL FOUNDRIES, LTD.—See Atchison Casting Corporation; *U.S. Public*, pg. 142
CANADIAN THERMOS PRODUCTS LTD.—See Nippon Sanso Corporation; *Int'l*, pg. 938
CANADIAN TIMKEN LTD.—See The Timken Company; *U.S. Public*, pg. 1617
CANADIAN TIRE ACCEPTANCE LTD.—See Canadian Tire Corporation Limited; *Int'l*, pg. 259
CANADIAN TIRE CORPORATION LIMITED; *Int'l*, pg. 259
CANADIAN TRANSPORT COMPANY—See Northern Navigation International Inc.; *Int'l*, pg. 805
CANADIAN UTILITIES LIMITED—See ATCO Group Co.; *Int'l*, pg. 95
CANADIAN WESTERN BANK; *Int'l*, pg. 259
CANADIAN WESTERN NATURAL GAS COMPANY LIMITED—See ATCO Group Co.; *Int'l*, pg. 95
CANADIAN WESTERN TRUST—See Canadian Western Bank; *Int'l*, pg. 259
CANADIAN WHITE PINE DIVISION—See MacMillan Bloedel Limited; *Int'l*, pg. 828
CANAGEX INVESTMENTS LIMITED—See Desjardins-Laurentian Financial Corporation; *Int'l*, pg. 396
CANAL ELECTRIC CO.—See Commonwealth Energy System; *U.S. Public*, pg. 415
CANAL MARINE—See Canadian Shipbuilding & Engineering Ltd.; *Int'l*, pg. 259
CANAL REFINING CO.—See Anchor Gasoline Corporation; *U.S. Public*, pg. 71
D. CANALE FOOD SERVICES, INC.; *U.S. Private*, pg. 204
CANALL RESOURCES INC.—See Sinochem International Petroleum Co. Ltd.; *Int'l*, pg. 1255
CANAMERA FOODS—See Saskatchewan Wheat Pool; *Int'l*, pg. 1195
CANANDAIGUA PLASTICS DIV.—See Cambridge Industries Inc.; *U.S. Private*, pg. 202
CANANDAIGUA WINE COMPANY, INC.; *U.S. Public*, pg. 300
CANATOM HEAVY WATER LIMITED—See Texas Utilities Company; *U.S. Public*, pg. 1587
CANATOM INC.—See Agra Inc.; *Int'l*, pg. 31
CANBERRA CRUISES LTD.—See The Peninsular and Oriental Steam Navigation Company; *Int'l*, pg. 1033
CANCARB GAS SERVICES LIMITED—See Transcanada Pipelines Limited; *Int'l*, pg. 1417
CANCARB LIMITED—See Transcanada Pipelines Limited; *Int'l*, pg. 1417
CAND INVESTMENTS INC.—See Deposit Guaranty Corp.; *U.S. Public*, pg. 501
CANDELA CORPORATION; *U.S. Public*, pg. 300
CANDELA EUROPE—See Candela Corporation; *U.S. Public*, pg. 300
CANDELA IBERICA, S.A.—See Candela Corporation; *U.S. Public*, pg. 300
CANDELA K.K.—See Candela Corporation; *U.S. Public*, pg. 301
CANDELA SINGAPORE—See Candela Corporation; *U.S. Public*, pg. 301
CANDELA SKIN CARE CENTER—See Candela Corporation; *U.S. Public*, pg. 300
CANDELA SKIN CARE CENTER OF BOSTON—See Candela Corporation; *U.S. Public*, pg. 300
CANDELA SKIN CARE CENTERS, INC.—See Candela Corporation; *U.S. Public*, pg. 300
CANDEV FINANCIAL SERVICES LTD.—See BCE Inc.; *Int'l*, pg. 115
CANDIAN REGIONAL AIRLINES—See Canadian Airlines Corporation; *Int'l*, pg. 256
CANDLE CORPORATION; *U.S. Private*, pg. 204

CANDLE CORPORATION OF AMERICA—See Blyth Industries; *U.S. Public*, pg. 239
CANDLE-LITE, A LANCASTER COLONY CO.—See Lancaster Colony Corporation; *U.S. Public*, pg. 976
CANDLESTICK WATERFRONT REST. CORP.—See Specialty Restaurants Corporation; *U.S. Private*, pg. 1022
CANDLEWICK DIVISION—See Consumers Water Company; *U.S. Public*, pg. 438
CANDLEWICK GROUP—See The Dixie Group, Inc.; *U.S. Public*, pg. 514
P.T. CANDRA SARI—See Novartis AG; *Int'l*, pg. 975
CANDRAFT DETAILING, INC.—See Pitt-Des Moines, Inc.; *U.S. Public*, pg. 1305
CANDY DOMESTIC APPLIANCES LIMITED—See Candy S.p.A.; *Int'l*, pg. 260
CANDY IBERICA S.A.—See Candy S.p.A.; *Int'l*, pg. 260
CANDY S.P.A.; *Int'l*, pg. 259
CANEFCO LIMITED—See Electric Furnace Co.; *U.S. Private*, pg. 368
CANFOR CORPORATION; *Int'l*, pg. 260
CANFOR U.S.A., BELLINGHAM DIVISION—See Canfor Corporation; *Int'l*, pg. 260
CANFOR U.S.A. CORPORATION—See Canfor Corporation; *Int'l*, pg. 260
CANIDA RUBBER COMPANY—See Lancaster Colony Corporation; *U.S. Public*, pg. 976
CANISCO RESOURCES, INC.; *U.S. Public*, pg. 301
CANLIFE-IBI INVESTMENT SERVICES LIMITED—See The Canada Life Assurance Company; *Int'l*, pg. 255
CANLUBANG AUTOMOTIVE RESOURCES CORP.—See Nissho Iwai Corporation; *Int'l*, pg. 947
CANLYTE INCORPORATED—See The Genlyte Group Incorporated; *U.S. Public*, pg. 730
CANMAKERS (NIGERIA) LTD.—See Crown Cork & Seal Company, Inc.; *U.S. Public*, pg. 463
CANNELTON INC.—See Cyprus Amax Minerals Company; *U.S. Public*, pg. 471
CANNELTON INDUSTRIES, INC.—See Cyprus Amax Minerals Company; *U.S. Public*, pg. 471
CANNING-LIPPERT LTD.—See Fuchs Petrolub AG Oel + Chemie; *Int'l*, pg. 518
CANNON; *U.S. Private*, pg. 205
CANNON EQUIPMENT—See IMI Plc; *Int'l*, pg. 646
CANNON EQUIPMENT CO.—See IMI Plc; *Int'l*, pg. 646
CANNON EXPRESS CORP.—See Cannon Express Inc.; *U.S. Public*, pg. 301
CANNON EXPRESS INC.; *U.S. Public*, pg. 301
CANNON INDUSTRIES LTD.—See The General Electric Company, p.l.c.; *Int'l*, pg. 543
CANNON MILITARY/AEROSPACE—See ITT Industries, Inc.; *U.S. Public*, pg. 859
CANNON-MUSKEGON CORP.—See SPS Technologies, Inc.; *U.S. Public*, pg. 1420
CANNON RUBBER LTD.; *Int'l*, pg. 261
CANNONDALE CORPORATION; *U.S. Public*, pg. 301
CANNONGATE TECHNOLOGY LIMITED—See Scottish & Newcastle plc; *Int'l*, pg. 1211
CANON (ANGLIA) OFFICE AUTOMATION LTD.—See Canon Inc.; *Int'l*, pg. 262
CANON APTEX INC.—See Canon Inc.; *Int'l*, pg. 261
CANON A/S—See Canon Inc.; *Int'l*, pg. 262
CANON AUDIO LTD.—See Canon Inc.; *Int'l*, pg. 262
CANON AUSTRALIA PTY. LTD.—See Canon Inc.; *Int'l*, pg. 262
CANON BENELUX N.V.—See Canon Inc.; *Int'l*, pg. 262
CANON BENELUX N.V./S.A.—See Canon Inc.; *Int'l*, pg. 262
CANON BRETAGNE S.A.—See Canon Inc.; *Int'l*, pg. 262
CANON BUSINESS MACHINES DE MEXICO S.A. DE C.V.—See Canon Inc.; *Int'l*, pg. 262
CANON BUSINESS SERVICE (UK) LTD.—See Canon Inc.; *Int'l*, pg. 262
CANON CAMERA (MALAYSIA) SDN. BHD.—See Canon Inc.; *Int'l*, pg. 262
CANON CHEMICALS INC.—See Canon Inc.; *Int'l*, pg. 261
CANON CHILE S.A.—See Canon Inc.; *Int'l*, pg. 262
CANON COMMUNICATIONS—See Canon Inc.; *Int'l*, pg. 261
CANON COMPONENTS, INC.—See Canon Inc.; *Int'l*, pg. 261
CANON COMPUTER SYSTEMS, INC.—See Canon Inc.; *Int'l*, pg. 262
CANON COPYER SALES CO., LTD.—See Canon Inc.; *Int'l*, pg. 261
CANON CZ SPOL S.R.O.—See Canon Inc.; *Int'l*, pg. 262
CANON DALIAN BUSINESS MACHINES, INC.—See Canon Inc.; *Int'l*, pg. 262
CANON DEUTSCHLAND GMBH—See Canon Inc.; *Int'l*, pg. 262
CANON DO BRASIL INDUSTRIA E COMERCIO LIMITADA—See Canon Inc.; *Int'l*, pg. 262
CANON EAST EUROPE VERTRIEBSGESELLSCHAFT MBH—See Canon Inc.; *Int'l*, pg. 262
CANON ELECTRONIC BUSINESS MACHINES (H.K.) CO., LTD.—See Canon Inc.; *Int'l*, pg. 262
CANON ELECTRONICS INC.—See Canon Inc.; *Int'l*, pg. 261
CANON ENGINEERING (THAILAND) LTD.—See Canon Inc.; *Int'l*, pg. 262
CANON ESPANA, S.A.—See Canon Inc.; *Int'l*, pg. 262
CANON EURO-PHOTO HANDELSGESELLSCHAFT MBH—See Canon Inc.; *Int'l*, pg. 262
CANON EUROPA N.V.—See Canon Inc.; *Int'l*, pg. 262
CANON FINANCE AUSTRALIA PTY. LTD.—See Canon Inc.; *Int'l*, pg. 262
CANON FINANCE NEW ZEALAND LTD.—See Canon Inc.; *Int'l*, pg. 262
CANON FINANCIAL SERVICES, INC.—See Canon Inc.; *Int'l*, pg. 262
CANON FRANCE S.A.—See Canon Inc.; *Int'l*, pg. 262
CANON GIESSEN GMBH—See Canon Inc.; *Int'l*, pg. 262
CANON GMBH—See Canon Inc.; *Int'l*, pg. 262

CANON HI-TECH (THAILAND) LTD.—See Canon Inc.; *Int'l*, pg. 262
CANON HONGKONG CO., LTD.—See Canon Inc.; *Int'l*, pg. 262
CANON HUNGRIA KERESKEDELMI KFT.—See Canon Inc.; *Int'l*, pg. 262
CANON INC.; *Int'l*, pg. 261
CANON INC., TAIWAN—See Canon Inc.; *Int'l*, pg. 262
CANON INFORMATION SYSTEMS, INC.—See Canon Inc.; *Int'l*, pg. 261
CANON INFORMATION SYSTEMS RESEARCH AUSTRALIA PTY. LTD.—See Canon Inc.; *Int'l*, pg. 262
CANON INTERNATIONAL (SHANGHAI) CO., LTD.—See Canon Inc.; *Int'l*, pg. 263
CANON (IRL) BUSINESS EQUIPMENT LTD.—See Canon Inc.; *Int'l*, pg. 262
CANON ITALIA S.P.A.—See Canon Inc.; *Int'l*, pg. 263
CANON LATIN AMERICA, INC.—See Canon Inc.; *Int'l*, pg. 262
CANON MANUFACTURING U.K., LTD.—See Canon Inc.; *Int'l*, pg. 262
CANON MARKETING (MALAYSIA) SDN. BHD.—See Canon Inc.; *Int'l*, pg. 263
CANON MARKETING (THAILAND) CO., LTD.—See Canon Inc.; *Int'l*, pg. 263
CANON (MERSEY) BUSINESS MACHINES LTD.—See Canon Inc.; *Int'l*, pg. 262
CANON MEXICANA, S. DE R.L. DE C.V.—See Canon Inc.; *Int'l*, pg. 263
CANON MILANO S.P.A.—See Canon Inc.; *Int'l*, pg. 263
CANON NEW ZEALAND LTD.—See Canon Inc.; *Int'l*, pg. 263
CANON OFFICE MACHINES (AUSTRALIA) PTY. LTD.—See Canon Inc.; *Int'l*, pg. 263
CANON OPTO (MALAYSIA) SDN. BHD.—See Canon Inc.; *Int'l*, pg. 262
CANON OY—See Canon Inc.; *Int'l*, pg. 263
CANON PANAMA, S.A.—See Canon Inc.; *Int'l*, pg. 263
CANON PHOTO VIDEO FRANCE S.A.—See Canon Inc.; *Int'l*, pg. 263
CANON POLSKA SPOL Z.O.O.—See Canon Inc.; *Int'l*, pg. 263
CANON PRECISION INC.—See Canon Inc.; *Int'l*, pg. 261
CANON RESEARCH CENTER AMERICA, LTD.—See Canon Inc.; *Int'l*, pg. 261
CANON RESEARCH CENTRE EUROPE LTD.—See Canon Inc.; *Int'l*, pg. 262
CANON RESEARCH CENTRE FRANCE S.A.—See Canon Inc.; *Int'l*, pg. 262
CANON S.A.—See Canon Inc.; *Int'l*, pg. 263
CANON SALES CO., INC.—See Canon Inc.; *Int'l*, pg. 261
CANON (SCHWEIZ) AG—See Canon Inc.; *Int'l*, pg. 263
CANON (SCOTLAND) BUSINESS MACHINES LTD.—See Canon Inc.; *Int'l*, pg. 263
CANON SEMICONDUCTOR ENGINEERING KOREA INC.—See Canon Inc.; *Int'l*, pg. 263
CANON SINGAPORE PTE. LTD.—See Canon Inc.; *Int'l*, pg. 263
CANON SOFTWARE INC.—See Canon Inc.; *Int'l*, pg. 261
CANON SVENSKA AB—See Canon Inc.; *Int'l*, pg. 263
CANON (SW) BUSINESS SYSTEMS LTD.—See Canon Inc.; *Int'l*, pg. 263
CANON ZHUHAI, INC.—See Canon Inc.; *Int'l*, pg. 262
CANPLAS INDUSTRIES LTD.—See ETEX; *Int'l*, pg. 430
CANRAD INC.—See ARC International Corporation; *Int'l*, pg. 17
CANROCK PIPELINE COMPANY, LTD.—See Groupe Bruxelles Lambert S.A.; *Int'l*, pg. 562
CANRON FABRICATION CORPORATION - EASTERN DIVISION—See The Ivaco Group; *Int'l*, pg. 695
CANRON FABRICATION CORPORATION - WESTERN DIVISION—See The Ivaco Group; *Int'l*, pg. 695
CANRON INC.—See The Ivaco Group; *Int'l*, pg. 695
CANSTAR APPAREL INC.—See Nike, Inc.; *U.S. Public*, pg. 1184
CANTAY HOLDINGS INC.—See Manulife Financial (The Manufacturers Life Insurance Company); *Int'l*, pg. 840
CANTEEN CORPORATION—See Compass Group plc; *Int'l*, pg. 324
CANTEL INDUSTRIES, INC.; *U.S. Public*, pg. 301
CANTERBURY CORPORATE SERVICES, INC.; *U.S. Public*, pg. 301
CANTERBURY HOTEL—See Taj International Hotels; *U.S. Private*, pg. 1067
CANTERBURY TIMBER PRODUCTS LIMITED—See International Paper Company; *U.S. Public*, pg. 905
CANTERBURY VILLA OF ALLIANCE—See Horizon/CMS Healthcare Corporation; *U.S. Public*, pg. 838
CANTEX CORP.—See BBA Group plc; *Int'l*, pg. 113
CANTEX INC.—See Sumitomo Corporation; *Int'l*, pg. 1312
CANTIERI ITALIANI NAVALI (FINCANTIERI)—See IRI Istituto Ricostruzione Industriale; *Int'l*, pg. 652
CANTIERI RIVA S.P.A.—See Vickers PLC; *Int'l*, pg. 1468
CANTON AGGREGATE DIVISION—See Central Allied Enterprises; *U.S. Private*, pg. 222
CANTON DROP FORGE; *U.S. Private*, pg. 205
CANTON L.D. CORPORATION—See Forest City Enterprises, Inc.; *U.S. Public*, pg. 668
CANTON MILL, CHAMPION INTERNATIONAL CORPORATION—See Champion International Corp.; *U.S. Public*, pg. 334
CANTON NEWS—See Gannett Company, Inc.; *U.S. Public*, pg. 700
CANTON SALES & STORAGE CO.—See National Presto Industries, Inc.; *U.S. Public*, pg. 1159
CANTRADE BANCA PRIVATA LUGANO SA—See Union Bank of Switzerland; *Int'l*, pg. 1439
CANTRADE PRIVATE BANK LTD.—See Union Bank of Switzerland; *Int'l*, pg. 1439
CANTRADE PRIVATE LTD.—See Union Bank of Switzerland; *Int'l*, pg. 1439
CANTRELL & COCHRANE GROUP—See Allied Domecq PLC; *Int'l*, pg. 63

Company Index

CANTROCK REALTY CORP.—See John Hassall, Inc.; *U.S. Private,* pg. 509
CANUCK ENGINEERING INC.—See Agra Inc.; *Int'l,* pg. 31
CANUSA—See Shaw Industries Ltd.; *Int'l,* pg. 1231
CANUSA - CPS—See Shaw Industries Ltd.; *Int'l,* pg. 1231
CANUSA-EMI—See Shaw Industries Ltd.; *Int'l,* pg. 1231
CANUSA SYSTEMS LIMITED—See Shaw Industries Ltd.; *Int'l,* pg. 1231
CANUSA SYSTEMS LIMITED - EMI—See Shaw Industries Ltd.; *Int'l,* pg. 1231
CANUSA WOOD PRODUCTS LTD.—See Meyer International PLC; *Int'l,* pg. 864
CANWEL DISTRIBUTION LTD.—See Canfor Corporation; *Int'l,* pg. 260
CANYON RESOURCES CORPORATION; *U.S. Public,* pg. 301
CANYON ROADS—See Ark Restaurants Corp.; *U.S. Public,* pg. 130
CANYON VENEZUELA CA—See Canyon Resources Corporation; *U.S. Public,* pg. 302
CAP GEMINI AMERICA—See CAP Gemini S.A.; *Int'l,* pg. 263
CAP GEMINI S.A.; *Int'l,* pg. 263
CAP NATIONWIDE MOTOR RESEARCH—See EMAP Plc; *Int'l,* pg. 451
CAP TOYS, INC.—See Hasbro, Inc.; *U.S. Public,* pg. 797
CAPACITY OF TEXAS, INC.—See Collins Industries, Inc.; *U.S. Public,* pg. 151
CAPARO GROUP LTD.; *Int'l,* pg. 264
CAPARO INDUSTRIES PLC—See Caparo Group Ltd.; *Int'l,* pg. 264
CAPARO INDUSTRIES PLC—See Caparo Group Ltd.; *Int'l,* pg. 265
CAPARO INSURANCE LTD.—See Caparo Group Ltd.; *Int'l,* pg. 265
CAPARO MERCHANT BAR PLC—See Caparo Group Ltd.; *Int'l,* pg. 265
CAPARO STEEL STOCKHOLDERS LTD.—See Caparo Group Ltd.; *Int'l,* pg. 265
CAPARO WIRE COMPANY LTD.—See Caparo Group Ltd.; *Int'l,* pg. 265
CAPAX ELECTRISCHE APPARATENFABRIEK B.V.—See Emerson Electric Co.; *U.S. Public,* pg. 576
CAPCO U.S.A., INC. (DETROIT)—See Central Automotive Products, Ltd.; *Int'l,* pg. 279
CAPE BRETON DEVELOPMENT CORPORATION; *Int'l,* pg. 265
CAPE BRETON POST—See Hollinger Inc.; *Int'l,* pg. 631
CAPE COD POTATO CHIP COMPANY; *U.S. Private,* pg. 205
CAPE CORAL NATIONAL BANK—See F.N.B. Corporation; *U.S. Public,* pg. 607
CAPE CORAL REALTY, INC.—See Avatar Holdings Inc.; *U.S. Public,* pg. 151
CAPE MENTELLE VINEYARDS LIMITED—See LVMH Moet Hennessy Louis Vuitton; *Int'l,* pg. 782
CAPE PLC.—See Charter plc; *Int'l,* pg. 280
CAPE PUBLICATIONS, INC.—See Gannett Company, Inc.; *U.S. Public,* pg. 700
CAPE TOWN IRON AND STEEL WORKS (PTY) LTD.—See Iscor; *Int'l,* pg. 689
CAPEZIO BALLET MAKERS INC.; *U.S. Private,* pg. 205
CAPINTEC INC.; *U.S. Private,* pg. 205
CAPINTEC INSTRUMENTS INC.—See Capintec Inc.; *U.S. Private,* pg. 205
CAPITAL AGRICULTURAL PROPERTY SERVICES, INC.—See The Prudential Insurance Company of America; *U.S. Private,* pg. 892
CAPITAL ALLIANCE INSURANCE COMPANY, INC.—See Skandia Insurance Company Limited; *Int'l,* pg. 1258
CAPITAL AMERICAN FINANCE—See Conseco Inc.; *U.S. Public,* pg. 433
CAPITAL ANALYSTS, INCORPORATED—See The Western and Southern Life Insurance Company; *U.S. Private,* pg. 1164
CAPITAL ASSOCIATES, INC.; *U.S. Public,* pg. 302
CAPITAL ASSURANCE COMPANY, INC.—See Skandia Insurance Company Limited; *Int'l,* pg. 1257
CAPITAL AUTO AUCTION INC.—See Tyco International Ltd.; *U.S. Public,* pg. 1648
CAPITAL BANK, N.A.; *U.S. Private,* pg. 205
CAPITAL CITIES/ABC BROADCAST GROUP—See The Walt Disney Company; *U.S. Public,* pg. 511
CAPITAL CITIES/ABC NATIONAL TELEVISION SALES, INC.—See The Walt Disney Company; *U.S. Public,* pg. 511
CAPITAL CITIES/ABC OWNED RADIO STATIONS—See The Walt Disney Company; *U.S. Public,* pg. 512
CAPITAL CITIES/ABC OWNED TELEVISION STATIONS—See The Walt Disney Company; *U.S. Public,* pg. 512
CAPITAL CITIES/ABC PUBLISHING GROUP—See The Walt Disney Company; *U.S. Public,* pg. 512
CAPITAL CITIES/ABC RADIO—See The Walt Disney Company; *U.S. Public,* pg. 512
CAPITAL CITIES MEDIA, INC.—See The Walt Disney Company; *U.S. Public,* pg. 511
CAPITAL CITY MANUFACTURING COMPANY—See House of Perfection, Inc.; *U.S. Private,* pg. 542
CAPITAL CITY PRESS, INC.; *U.S. Private,* pg. 205
CAPITAL CITY COMMUNICATIONS CDPQ—See Caisse de depot et placement du Quebec; *Int'l,* pg. 249
CAPITAL CONCEPT & ENGINEERING—See Synergis Technologies Group; *U.S. Private,* pg. 1060
CAPITAL CONTROLS COMPANY INC.—See Severn Trent Plc; *Int'l,* pg. 1226
CAPITAL CONTROLS LTD.—See Severn Trent Plc; *Int'l,* pg. 1225
CAPITAL CREDIT CORPORATION—See The Union Corporation; *U.S. Public,* pg. 1667
CAPITAL D'AMERIQUE CDPQ—See Caisse de depot et placement du Quebec; *Int'l,* pg. 249
CAPITAL DATA SYSTEMS, INC.—See Chesapeake Utilities Corporation; *U.S. Public,* pg. 347
CAPITAL DEVELOPMENT CO.; *U.S. Private,* pg. 205

CAPITAL EQUIPMENT DIV.—See Athey Products Corporation; *U.S. Public,* pg. 143
CAPITAL FACTORS, INC.—See Union Planters Corporation; *U.S. Public,* pg. 1669
CAPITAL FOR BUSINESS, INC.—See Commerce Bancshares, Inc.; *U.S. Public,* pg. 410
CAPITAL-GAZETTE COMMUNICATIONS, INC.—See Landmark Communications, Inc.; *U.S. Private,* pg. 649
CAPITAL GOODS & MANUFACTURED PRODUCTS BUSINESS GROUP—See Thyssen AG; *Int'l,* pg. 1387
CAPITAL GRAPHICS INC.; *U.S. Private,* pg. 206
THE CAPITAL GROUP COMPANIES INC.; *U.S. Private,* pg. 206
THE CAPITAL GROUP INTERNATIONAL—See The Capital Group Companies Inc.; *U.S. Private,* pg. 206
CAPITAL HOUSE INVESTMENT MANAGEMENT LIMITED—See The Royal Bank of Scotland plc; *Int'l,* pg. 1132
CAPITAL IMAGING; *U.S. Private,* pg. 206
CAPITAL INDUSTRIES, INC.; *U.S. Private,* pg. 206
CAPITAL INTERNATIONAL CDPQ—See Caisse de depot et placement du Quebec; *Int'l,* pg. 249
CAPITAL INTERNATIONAL CDPQ INC.—See Caisse de depot et placement du Quebec; *Int'l,* pg. 249
CAPITAL INTERNATIONAL CDPQ - MANILA—See Caisse de depot et placement du Quebec; *Int'l,* pg. 249
CAPITAL INTERNATIONAL CDPQ - POLAND—See Caisse de depot et placement du Quebec; *Int'l,* pg. 249
CAPITAL INVESTMENT TRUST CORPORATION—See Commerzbank AG; *Int'l,* pg. 312
CAPITAL LENDING SERVICES, INC.; *U.S. Private,* pg. 206
CAPITAL LIBERTY, L.P.—See AEGON N.V.; *Int'l,* pg. 26
CAPITAL MANAGEMENT SCIENCES—See Data Broadcasting Corporation; *U.S. Public,* pg. 484
CAPITAL MARKETS ASSURANCE CORPORATION—See MBIA Inc.; *U.S. Public,* pg. 1023
CAPITAL MERCURY SHIRT; *U.S. Private,* pg. 206
CAPITAL NATIONAL INSURANCE COMPANY—See OHM Corporation; *U.S. Public,* pg. 1207
CAPITAL NOMURA SECURITIES PUBLIC COMPANY LIMITED—See The Nomura Securities Co., Ltd.; *Int'l,* pg. 957
CAPITAL ONE FINANCIAL CORPORATION; *U.S. Public,* pg. 302
CAPITAL PACIFIC HOLDINGS; *U.S. Public,* pg. 302
CAPITAL PAVING CO., INC.—See Killearn Properties, Inc.; *U.S. Public,* pg. 956
CAPITAL PLUMBING & HEATING SUPPLY CO.—See Granite Group Wholesale LLC; *U.S. Private,* pg. 469
CAPITAL PLUMBING & HEATING SUPPLY CO. INC.—See Granite Group Wholesale LLC; *U.S. Private,* pg. 469
CAPITAL RE CORPORATION—See Minnesota Power; *U.S. Public,* pg. 1116
THE CAPITAL RESEARCH & MANAGEMENT CO.—See The Capital Group Companies Inc.; *U.S. Private,* pg. 206
CAPITAL RESOURCES GROUP, LTD.—See The Weitz Company, Inc.; *U.S. Private,* pg. 1161
CAPITAL RESOURCES, INC.—See Alex Lee, Inc.; *U.S. Private,* pg. 657
CAPITAL SENIOR LIVING, INC.; *U.S. Public,* pg. 302
CAPITAL TIRE, INC.; *U.S. Private,* pg. 206
CAPITOL BROADCASTING CO., INC.; *U.S. Private,* pg. 206
CAPITOL CADILLAC, CORP.—See Don Massey Cadillac Inc.; *U.S. Private,* pg. 712
CAPITOL CHEVROLET CADILLAC GEO SUBARU INC.; *U.S. Private,* pg. 206
CAPITOL CITY PUBLISHING CO., INC.-THE TRENTONIAN—See Journal Register Company; *U.S. Public,* pg. 934
CAPITOL CITY STEEL CO.—See Commercial Metals Company; *U.S. Public,* pg. 413
CAPITOL CONSOLIDATED—See Bunzl PLC; *Int'l,* pg. 233
CAPITOL CONSTRUCTION GROUP, INC.; *U.S. Private,* pg. 206
CAPITOL COUNTY MUTUAL FIRE INSURANCE CO.—See The Reliable Life Insurance Company; *U.S. Public,* pg. 1374
CAPITOL DATA SYSTEMS—See EMI Group plc; *Int'l,* pg. 428
CAPITOL ENGINEERING—See Dewberry & Davis; *U.S. Private,* pg. 329
CAPITOL EQUIPMENT—See Canadian Erectors Ltd.; *Int'l,* pg. 256
CAPITOL FACILITIES CORP.—See Capitol Indemnity Corporation; *U.S. Public,* pg. 302
CAPITOL FINANCE GROUP, INC.—See First Union Corporation; *U.S. Public,* pg. 640
CAPITOL GROUP; *U.S. Private,* pg. 206
CAPITOL HARDWARE, INC.—See RHC/Spacemaster Corporation; *U.S. Private,* pg. 904
CAPITOL INDEMNITY CORPORATION; *U.S. Public,* pg. 302
CAPITOL INDEMNITY CORPORATION—See Capitol Indemnity Corporation; *U.S. Public,* pg. 302
CAPITOL INDUSTRIES-EMI INC.—See EMI Group plc; *Int'l,* pg. 427
CAPITOL MANUFACTURING CO.—See Harsco Corporation; *U.S. Public,* pg. 793
CAPITOL METALS COMPANY; *U.S. Private,* pg. 206
CAPITOL OUTDOOR ACQUISITION CO., INC.—See Cigna Corp.; *U.S. Public,* pg. 361
CAPITOL OUTDOOR ADVERTISING, INC.—See Cigna Corp.; *U.S. Public,* pg. 361
CAPITOL OUTDOOR LEASING CO., INC.—See Cigna Corp.; *U.S. Public,* pg. 361
CAPITOL PIPE & STEEL—See Canadian Erectors Ltd.; *Int'l,* pg. 256
CAPITOL PIPE SUPPORTS—See Canadian Erectors Ltd.; *Int'l,* pg. 256
CAPITOL RECORDS, INC.—See EMI Group plc; *Int'l,* pg. 428

CAPITOL RECORDS-EMI OF CANADA LTD.—See EMI Group plc; *Int'l,* pg. 427
CAPITOL SPECIALTY INSURANCE CORPORATION—See Capitol Indemnity Corporation; *U.S. Public,* pg. 302
CAPITOL STEEL, INC.—See Commercial Metals Company; *U.S. Public,* pg. 412
CAPITOL STEEL-SLIDELL—See Commercial Metals Company; *U.S. Public,* pg. 412
CAPITOL STREET CORP.; *U.S. Private,* pg. 207
CAPITOLINE INVESTMENT SERVICES, INC.—See Crestar Financial Corporation; *U.S. Public,* pg. 458
CAPP, INC.; *U.S. Private,* pg. 207
CARL FR. CAPPEL—See BASF AG; *Int'l,* pg. 104
CAPRAL ALUMINIUM-ALUMINIUM CENTERS—See Capral Aluminium Limited; *Int'l,* pg. 266
CAPRAL ALUMINIUM-EXTRUSION—See Capral Aluminium Limited; *Int'l,* pg. 266
CAPRAL ALUMINIUM-FOIL—See Capral Aluminium Limited; *Int'l,* pg. 266
CAPRAL ALUMINIUM LIMITED; *Int'l,* pg. 266
CAPRAL ALUMINIUM-SHEETS—See Capral Aluminium Limited; *Int'l,* pg. 266
CAPRAL ALUMINIUM-SMELTER—See Capral Aluminium Limited; *Int'l,* pg. 266
CAPRAL ALUMINIUM-TRADING—See Capral Aluminium Limited; *Int'l,* pg. 266
CAPRAL NZ LIMITED—See Capral Aluminium Limited; *Int'l,* pg. 266
CAPRI SUN INC.—See Philip Morris Companies Inc.; *U.S. Public,* pg. 1288
CAPRICORN TRANSPORTATION, INC.—See Mark VII, Inc.; *U.S. Public,* pg. 1046
CAPRIUS, INC.; *U.S. Public,* pg. 303
CAPRO, INC.—See Teleflex Incorporated; *U.S. Public,* pg. 1569
CAPROFEM S.A.—See Kingfisher plc; *Int'l,* pg. 734
CAPSEALS, LIMITED—See Sonoco Products Company; *U.S. Public,* pg. 1486
CAPSONIC GROUP, INC.; *U.S. Private,* pg. 207
CAPSTAR PARTNERS, INC.—See The Long-Term Credit Bank of Japan, Limited; *Int'l,* pg. 816
CAPSTEAD MORTGAGE CORPORATION; *U.S. Public,* pg. 303
CAPSTONE ELECTRONICS CORP.—See Arrow Electronics, Inc.; *U.S. Public,* pg. 134
CAPSUGEL—See Warner-Lambert Company; *U.S. Public,* pg. 1739
S.A. CAPSUGEL N.V.—See Warner-Lambert Company; *Int'l,* pg. 1739
CAPSULAS METALICAS S.A.—See Aluminum Company of America; *U.S. Public,* pg. 62
CAPSURE HOLDINGS CORP.; *U.S. Public,* pg. 303
CAPTAIN D'S RESTAURANT—See Shoney's, Inc.; *U.S. Public,* pg. 1467
CAPTIVE-AIRE SYSTEMS, INC.; *U.S. Private,* pg. 207
CAPTIVE MANAGEMENT COMPANY SA (CAPTIMA)—See Generale de Banque S.A.; *Int'l,* pg. 548
CAPTIVE PLASTICS; *U.S. Private,* pg. 207
CAPUAVA REFINERY—See Petrobras - Petroleo Brasileiro S.A.; *Int'l,* pg. 1042
CAPUCCI CREATIONS INTERNATIONAL, INC.; *U.S. Private,* pg. 207
CAPY U.S.A. INC.—See Calpis Food Industry Co. Ltd.; *Int'l,* pg. 253
CAR AND DRIVER—See Lagardere Groupe; *Int'l,* pg. 795
CAR BRITE, INC.—See E & A Industries, Inc.; *U.S. Private,* pg. 352
CAR FINANCE BELGIUM N.V.—See Royal Begemann Group; *Int'l,* pg. 1134
CAR-FRESHNER CORPORATION; *U.S. Private,* pg. 207
CAR-LAC ELECTRONICS—See Premier Farnell plc; *Int'l,* pg. 1068
CAR MAX—See Circuit City Stores, Inc.; *U.S. Public,* pg. 374
CAR PRODUCT DEVELOPMENT—See Ford Motor Company; *U.S. Public,* pg. 662
CAR PROGRAMS MANAGEMENT—See Ford Motor Company; *U.S. Public,* pg. 662
CAR-X MUFFLER & BRAKE—See Tenneco Inc.; *U.S. Public,* pg. 1578
CARA CORPORATION—See William Blair & Company L.L.C.; *U.S. Private,* pg. 148
CARA OPERATIONS LIMITED; *Int'l,* pg. 266
CARACCIOLOSSIGENO S.R.L.—See Linde AG; *Int'l,* pg. 811
CARADCO—See Aluminum Company of America; *U.S. Public,* pg. 61
CARADON PLC; *Int'l,* pg. 266
CARADON (USA) INC.—See Caradon Plc; *Int'l,* pg. 267
CARAIBE ASSURANCES S.A.—See Assicurazioni Generali S.p.A.; *Int'l,* pg. 90
CARALOE, INC.—See Carrington Laboratories, Inc.; *U.S. Public,* pg. 309
CARAMELOS ROYAL C.A.—See Nestle S.A.; *Int'l,* pg. 919
CARAT ICG; *U.S. Private,* pg. 207
CARAT ICG—See Carat ICG; *U.S. Private,* pg. 207
CARAT ICG (PORTLAND, OR)—See Carat ICG; *U.S. Private,* pg. 207
CARAT ICG RETAIL/CO-OP DIV. OF CARAT ICG—See Carat ICG; *U.S. Private,* pg. 207
CARAT ICG (SAN FRANCISCO)—See Carat ICG; *U.S. Private,* pg. 208
CARAT MBS; *U.S. Private,* pg. 208
CARAUSTAR INDUSTRIES, INC.; *U.S. Public,* pg. 303
CARAUSTAR PAPER SALES, INC.—See Caraustar Industries, Inc.; *U.S. Public,* pg. 303
CARAVAN BROKAY—See Caravan Products Company, Inc.; *U.S. Private,* pg. 208
CARAVAN PRODUCTS COMPANY, INC.; *U.S. Private,* pg. 208
CARAVELLE TECHNOLOGY AS—See Keppel Corporation Limited; *Int'l,* pg. 731
CARBIDE & GRAPHITE TECHNOLOGIES S.R.L.—See Morgan Crucible Co. Plc; *Int'l,* pg. 891

CARBIDE CONDO, S.A. DE C.V.—See The Reader's Digest Association, Inc.; *U.S. Public*, pg. 1368
THE CARBIDE/GRAPHITE GROUP, INC.; *U.S. Public*, pg. 304
CARBO PLC; *Int'l*, pg. 268
CARBODERIVADOS S.A.—See Elkem ASA; *Int'l*, pg. 447
CARBOGAL-CARBONOS DE PORTUGAL, S.A.—See Petrogal, s.a.; *Int'l*, pg. 1045
CARBOGHISE S.P.A.—See Coeclerici Group; *Int'l*, pg. 303
CARBOINDUSTRIAL—See Elkem ASA; *Int'l*, pg. 447
CARBOLINE CO.—See RPM, Inc.; *U.S. Public*, pg. 1357
CARBOLON DIVISION—See High Voltage Engineering Corporation; *U.S. Private*, pg. 528
CARBOMEDICS, INC.—See Sulzer Ltd.; *Int'l*, pg. 1307
CARBON BLACK DIV.—See Cabot Corporation; *U.S. Public*, pg. 289
CARBON BRUSH MFG. CO., PTY LIMITED—See Morgan Crucible Co. Plc; *Int'l*, pg. 894
CARBON MECHANICAL PRODUCTS PTY LIMITED—See Morgan Crucible Co. Plc; *Int'l*, pg. 891
CARBON MECHANICAL PRODUCTS (S) PTE.—See Morgan Crucible Co. Plc; *Int'l*, pg. 891
CARBON PRODUCTS OPERATION INC.—See Morgan Crucible Co. Plc; *Int'l*, pg. 891
CARBON TECHNOLOGY INC.—See Morgan Crucible Co. Plc; *Int'l*, pg. 891
CARBONE DANMARK A/S—See Pechiney S.A.; *Int'l*, pg. 1030
CARBONE-LORRAINE DE COLOMBIA S.A.—See Pechiney S.A.; *Int'l*, pg. 1030
CARBONE-LORRAINE GMBH—See Pechiney S.A.; *Int'l*, pg. 1030
CARBONE-LORRAINE KOREA CO. LTD.—See Pechiney S.A.; *Int'l*, pg. 1030
CARBONE-LORRAINE NORTH AMERICA—See Pechiney S.A.; *Int'l*, pg. 1028
CARBONE OF AMERICA—See Pechiney S.A.; *Int'l*, pg. 1028
CARBONE OF AMERICA, CARBON BRUSH DIV.—See Pechiney S.A.; *Int'l*, pg. 1028
CARBONE OF AMERICA, CHEMICAL EQUIPMENT DIV.—See Pechiney S.A.; *Int'l*, pg. 1028
CARBONE OF AMERICA, COMMUTATION COMPONENTS DIV.—See Pechiney S.A.; *Int'l*, pg. 1028
CARBONE OF AMERICA, GRAPHITE MATERIALS DIV.—See Pechiney S.A.; *Int'l*, pg. 1028
CARBONE OF AMERICA (LCL) LTD.—See Pechiney S.A.; *Int'l*, pg. 1028
CARBONE OF AMERICA, ULTRA CARBON DIV.—See Pechiney S.A.; *Int'l*, pg. 1028
CARBONO-LORENA DE MEXICO S.A.—See Pechiney S.A.; *Int'l*, pg. 1030
CARBONO-LORENA S.A.—See Pechiney S.A.; *Int'l*, pg. 1030
CARBORUNDUM ABRASIVES INC./CARBORUNDUM ABRASIFS INC.—See Saint-Gobain; *Int'l*, pg. 1174
CARBORUNDUM ABRASIVES NORTH AMERICA—See Saint-Gobain; *Int'l*, pg. 1174
THE CARBORUNDUM CORPORATION—See Saint-Gobain; *Int'l*, pg. 1173
CARBOSIL INDUSTRIAL LIMITADA—See Morgan Crucible Co. Plc; *Int'l*, pg. 894
CARBOSULF CHEMISCHE WERKE GMBH—See Akzo Nobel N.V.; *Int'l*, pg. 47
CARBOTRADE INTERNATIONAL AB—See Scancem AB; *Int'l*, pg. 1201
CARBOZULIA, S.A.—See Petroleos de Venezuela S.A.; *Int'l*, pg. 1045
S.E. CARBUROS METALICOS S.A.—See Air Products and Chemicals, Inc.; *U.S. Public*, pg. 32
CARCLIN S.A.—See Henkel KGaA; *Int'l*, pg. 612
CARCLO ENGINEERING GROUP PLC; *Int'l*, pg. 268
CARCO ELECTRONICS; *U.S. Private*, pg. 208
CARCO INTERNATIONAL, INC.; *U.S. Private*, pg. 208
CARD PAK, INC.; *U.S. Private*, pg. 208
CARD TECHNOLOGY CORP.—See NBS Technologies, Inc.; *Int'l*, pg. 898
CARDEM INSURANCE CO., LTD.—See Walter Industries, Inc.; *U.S. Public*, pg. 1736
CARDER CONCRETE PRODUCTS CO.; *U.S. Private*, pg. 208
CARDER, INC.; *U.S. Private*, pg. 208
CARDIAC SERVICES COMPANY—See Hewlett-Packard Company; *U.S. Public*, pg. 816
CARDINAL ALUMINUM CO.; *U.S. Private*, pg. 208
CARDINAL BUSINESS MEDIA, VISION CARE GRP.—See Ullo International, Inc.; *U.S. Private*, pg. 1116
CARDINAL CONCRETE CO.—See Florida Rock Industries, Inc.; *U.S. Public*, pg. 656
CARDINAL DISTRIBUTION—See Cardinal Health Inc.; *U.S. Public*, pg. 304
CARDINAL EG SAWS CORP.—See Brooke Industrial Holdings Plc; *Int'l*, pg. 228
CARDINAL HEALTH INC.; *U.S. Public*, pg. 304
CARDINAL INC.; *U.S. Private*, pg. 208
CARDINAL OPERATING CO.—See American Electric Power Company, Inc.; *U.S. Public*, pg. 72
CARDINAL REDEVELOPMENT CORPORATION—See Ford Motor Company; *U.S. Public*, pg. 663
CARDINAL SCALE MANUFACTURING COMPANY; *U.S. Private*, pg. 209
CARDINAL SYSTEMS—See Tetra Laval Group; *Int'l*, pg. 1379
CARDIO DATA SERVICES—See U.M. Holding Limited; *U.S. Private*, pg. 1114
CARDIO-FITNESS CORPORATION—See H.J. Heinz Company; *U.S. Public*, pg. 806
CARDIORHYTHM—See Medtronic, Inc.; *U.S. Public*, pg. 1083
CARDIOTRON MEDIZINTECHNIK GMBH—See Medtronic, Inc.; *U.S. Public*, pg. 1083
CARDIOVASCULAR INNOVATIONS CANADA, INC.—See Pfizer Inc.; *U.S. Public*, pg. 1282

CARDIVAN CO.—See Jackpot Enterprises, Inc.; *U.S. Public*, pg. 920
CARDKEY SYSTEMS, INC.—See Amtech Corporation; *U.S. Public*, pg. 105
CARDO AB; *Int'l*, pg. 268
CARDO DOOR AB—See Cardo AB; *Int'l*, pg. 269
CARDO DOOR (ASIA)—See Cardo AB; *Int'l*, pg. 269
CARDO DOOR EXPORT AB—See Cardo AB; *Int'l*, pg. 269
CARDO DOOR INTERNATIONAL AG—See Cardo AB; *Int'l*, pg. 269
CARDO DOOR LOGISTICS B.V.—See Cardo AB; *Int'l*, pg. 269
CARDO DOOR PRODUCTION A/S—See Cardo AB; *Int'l*, pg. 269
CARDO DOOR PRODUCTION FRANCE S.A.S.—See Cardo AB; *Int'l*, pg. 269
CARDO PUMP AB—See Cardo AB; *Int'l*, pg. 270
CARDO RAILWAY AB—See Cardo AB; *Int'l*, pg. 271
S.A. CARDONER—See Novartis AG; *Int'l*, pg. 984
CARDOX DIVISION—See Air Liquide S.A.; *Int'l*, pg. 37
THE CARDWELL MACHINE COMPANY; *U.S. Private*, pg. 209
CARDWELL-FREIGHT COMPONENTS—See Cardo AB; *Int'l*, pg. 271
CARE AMERICA-SOUTHERN CA—See Blue Shield of California; *U.S. Private*, pg. 153
CARE CENTER OF LOPATCONG—See Genesis Health Ventures, Inc.; *U.S. Public*, pg. 729
CARE CENTER OF PHILLIPSBURG—See Genesis Health Ventures, Inc.; *U.S. Public*, pg. 729
CARE FREE ALUMINUM PRODUCTS, INC.—See CFA Holding Company; *U.S. Private*, pg. 194
THE CARE GROUP, INC.; *U.S. Public*, pg. 305
THE CARE GROUP OF TEXAS, INC.—See The Care Group, Inc.; *U.S. Public*, pg. 305
CARE LINE, INC.—See The Care Group, Inc.; *U.S. Public*, pg. 305
CARE MATRIX CORP.; *U.S. Public*, pg. 305
CARE MEDICAL SUPPLIES, INC.—See Integrated Health Services, Inc.; *U.S. Public*, pg. 884
THE CARE PAVILION OF WALNUT PARK PLAZA—See Genesis Health Ventures, Inc.; *U.S. Public*, pg. 729
CAREAL HOLDING AG; *Int'l*, pg. 271
CARECO, INC.—See Staff Builders Inc.; *U.S. Public*, pg. 1501
CAREER BLAZERS AGENCY, INC.—See Career Blazers Inc.; *U.S. Private*, pg. 209
CAREER BLAZERS INC.; *U.S. Private*, pg. 209
CAREER BLAZERS LEARNING CENTER—See Career Blazers Inc.; *U.S. Private*, pg. 209
CAREER BLAZERS LEARNING CENTER OF MELVILLE—See Career Blazers Inc.; *U.S. Private*, pg. 209
CAREER BLAZERS LEARNING CENTER OF STAMFORD—See Career Blazers Inc.; *U.S. Private*, pg. 209
CAREER BLAZERS OF WASHINGTON, DC—See Career Blazers Inc.; *U.S. Private*, pg. 209
CAREER BLAZERS OF WHITE PLAINS, INC.—See Career Blazers Inc.; *U.S. Private*, pg. 209
CAREER BLAZERS SERVICE COMPANY, INC.—See Career Blazers Inc.; *U.S. Private*, pg. 209
CAREER BLAZERS TEMPORARY PERSONNEL—See Career Blazers Inc.; *U.S. Private*, pg. 209
CAREER EDUCATION CORPORATION; *U.S. Private*, pg. 209
CAREERS USA INC.; *U.S. Private*, pg. 209
CAREERSTAFF UNLIMITED, INC.—See Sun Healthcare Group Inc.; *U.S. Public*, pg. 1531
CAREERTRACK INC.—See TCI Communications, Inc.; *U.S. Public*, pg. 1555
CAREERWEB—See Landmark Communications, Inc.; *U.S. Private*, pg. 647
CAREFREE CAMPING LIMITED—See Eurocamp Plc; *Int'l*, pg. 465
CAREFREE OF COLORADO—See Berkshire Hathaway Inc.; *U.S. Public*, pg. 217
CAREL FOUCHE INDUSTRIES (CFI)—See Jeumont-Schneider Trenformeteurs; *Int'l*, pg. 706
CARELLO S.P.A.—See Fiat Auto SpA; *Int'l*, pg. 482
CAREMARK INTERNATIONAL INC—See Medpartners Inc.; *U.S. Public*, pg. 1082
CAREWOOD TRANSPORT LTD.—See SNCF; *Int'l*, pg. 1165
CAREY DIVISION—See J. Fegely Inc.; *U.S. Private*, pg. 399
W.P. CAREY & CO., INC.; *U.S. Private*, pg. 209
CARFEL, INC.; *U.S. Private*, pg. 210
CARFTIQUE, INC.—See Pulaski Furniture Corporation; *U.S. Public*, pg. 1342
CARGILL; *U.S. Private*, pg. 210
CARGILL ANIMAL NUTRITION DIV.—See Cargill; *U.S. Private*, pg. 210
CARGILL CITRO-AMERICA, INC.—See Cargill; *U.S. Private*, pg. 210
CARGILL DETROIT CORP.; *U.S. Private*, pg. 210
CARGILL FLOUR DIV.—See Cargill; *U.S. Private*, pg. 210
CARGILL LTD.—See Cargill; *U.S. Private*, pg. 210
CARGILL SALT—See Cargill; *U.S. Private*, pg. 210
CARGILL SALT INC.—See Akzo Nobel N.V.; *Int'l*, pg. 48
CARGILL SEED DIV.—See Cargill; *U.S. Private*, pg. 210
CARGO FURNITURE & ACCENTS—See Tandycrafts, Inc.; *U.S. Public*, pg. 1561
CARGOSUR, S.A.—See SEPI; *Int'l*, pg. 1225
CARGOTRANS UMSCHLAGS- UND SPEDITIONSGESELLSCHAFT MBH—See Harpen AG; *Int'l*, pg. 597
CARHARTT, INC.; *U.S. Private*, pg. 210
CARIANE—See SNCF; *Int'l*, pg. 1165
CARIB TELECONSULT NV—See KPN Koninklyke PTT Nederland NV; *Int'l*, pg. 720
CARIBBEAN AIR SERVICE DOMINICANA—See Caribe Express; *U.S. Private*, pg. 211

CARIBBEAN AMERICAN LIFE ASSURANCE COMPANY—See American Bankers Insurance Group, Inc.; *U.S. Public*, pg. 67
CARIBBEAN ANTILLES MOLASSES CO. LTD.—See Tate & Lyle PLC; *Int'l*, pg. 1357
CARIBBEAN CEMENT CARRIERS CORPORATION—See Puerto Rican Cement Co., Inc.; *U.S. Public*, pg. 1342
CARIBBEAN CEMENT CO., LTD.—See Scancem AB; *Int'l*, pg. 1201
CARIBBEAN FOREIGN TRADE CORPORATION—See Ceteco N.V.; *Int'l*, pg. 279
CARIBBEAN MOLASSES CO. LTD.—See Tate & Lyle PLC; *Int'l*, pg. 1357
CARIBBEAN MOVING & STORAGE, INC.—See The Suddath Companies; *U.S. Private*, pg. 1049
CARIBBEAN OUTERWEAR CORP.—See Standard Manufacturing Co., Inc.; *U.S. Private*, pg. 1032
CARIBE BIOCHEMICALS, INC.—See Du Pont (E.I. Du Pont De Nemours & Co.); *U.S. Public*, pg. 531
CARIBE EXPRESS; *U.S. Private*, pg. 211
CARIBE EXPRESS LATIN AMERICAN DIV.—See Caribe Express; *U.S. Private*, pg. 211
CARIBE FREIGHT—See Caribe Express; *U.S. Private*, pg. 211
CARIBE GROLIER, INC.—See Lagardere Groupe; *Int'l*, pg. 794
CARIBINER INTERNATIONAL, INC.; *U.S. Public*, pg. 305
CARIFONE—See Peoples Telephone Company, Inc.; *U.S. Public*, pg. 1275
CARILLO, PASTORE EURO RSCG—See Havas Advertising; *Int'l*, pg. 603
CARILLON IMPORTERS, LTD.—See Diageo Plc; *Int'l*, pg. 409
CARIPLO (BEIJING)—See Cassa di Risparmio delle Provincie Lombarde SpA (CARIPLO); *Int'l*, pg. 275
CARIPLO FINANCE INC.—See Cassa di Risparmio delle Provincie Lombarde SpA (CARIPLO); *Int'l*, pg. 275
CARIPLO GRAND CAYMAN—See Cassa di Risparmio delle Provincie Lombarde SpA (CARIPLO); *Int'l*, pg. 275
CARIPLO HONG KONG—See Cassa di Risparmio delle Provincie Lombarde SpA (CARIPLO); *Int'l*, pg. 275
CARIPLO LONDON—See Cassa di Risparmio delle Provincie Lombarde SpA (CARIPLO); *Int'l*, pg. 275
CARIPLO MADRID—See Cassa di Risparmio delle Provincie Lombarde SpA (CARIPLO); *Int'l*, pg. 275
CARIPLO NEW YORK—See Cassa di Risparmio delle Provincie Lombarde SpA (CARIPLO); *Int'l*, pg. 275
CARIPLO (TAIPEI)—See Cassa di Risparmio delle Provincie Lombarde SpA (CARIPLO); *Int'l*, pg. 275
CARISTRAP DE MEXICO S.A. DE C.V.—See Caristrap International Inc.; *Int'l*, pg. 272
CARISTRAP INDIA—See Caristrap International Inc.; *Int'l*, pg. 272
CARISTRAP INTERNATIONAL INC.; *Int'l*, pg. 271
CARITAS CENTRALE D'ARTICLES DE MARQUES S.A.—See Reemtsma Cigarettenfabriken GmbH, Hamburg; *Int'l*, pg. 1101
CARL M. FREEMAN MGMT CO—See Carl M. Freeman Associates, Inc.; *U.S. Private*, pg. 426
CARLAND, INC.—See Kansas City Southern Industries, Inc.; *U.S. Public*, pg. 944
CARLANDER-DIALYSEN AB—See Incentive AB; *Int'l*, pg. 667
CARLESS REFINING & MARKETING B.V.—See Repsol S.A.; *Int'l*, pg. 1104
THE P.J. CARLIN CONSTRUCTION COMPANY; *U.S. Private*, pg. 211
CARLINGFORD SWIRE ASSURANCE LTD.—See HSBC Holdings plc; *Int'l*, pg. 581
CARLISLE COATED STONE—See RMC Group p.l.c.; *Int'l*, pg. 1079
CARLISLE COATING & WATERPROOFING—See Carlisle Companies Incorporated; *U.S. Public*, pg. 305
CARLISLE COMPANIES INCORPORATED; *U.S. Public*, pg. 305
CARLISLE CONTAINER MANUFACTURING COMPANY—See Carlisle Companies Incorporated; *U.S. Public*, pg. 305
CARLISLE CRANE CO—See Carlisle Equipment Company; *U.S. Private*, pg. 211
CARLISLE ENGINEERED PRODUCTS—See Carlisle Companies Incorporated; *U.S. Public*, pg. 305
CARLISLE EQUIPMENT CO—See Carlisle Equipment Company; *U.S. Private*, pg. 211
CARLISLE EQUIPMENT COMPANY; *U.S. Private*, pg. 211
CARLISLE FOOD SERVICE PRODUCTS—See Carlisle Companies Incorporated; *U.S. Public*, pg. 305
CARLISLE FOOD SERVICE PRODUCTS COMPANY—See Carlisle Companies Incorporated; *U.S. Public*, pg. 305
CARLISLE INSURANCE COMPANY—See Markel Corporation; *U.S. Public*, pg. 1046
CARLISLE POULTRY & EGG ASSOCIATES—See Sun City Industries, Inc.; *U.S. Public*, pg. 1529
CARLISLE SYNTEC INC.—See Carlisle Companies Incorporated; *U.S. Public*, pg. 305
CARLISLE TIRE & WHEEL COMPANY—See Carlisle Companies Incorporated; *U.S. Public*, pg. 305
JOHN CARLO INC.; *U.S. Private*, pg. 211
CARLON CHIMES CO.—See The Lamson & Sessions Co.; *U.S. Public*, pg. 976
CARLOR FINLAND OY—See Pechiney S.A.; *Int'l*, pg. 1030
CARLOR MAROC—See Pechiney S.A.; *Int'l*, pg. 1030
P.T. CARLORINDO UTAMA—See Pechiney S.A.; *Int'l*, pg. 1030
CARL'S JR.—See CKE Restaurants Inc.; *U.S. Public*, pg. 278
CARLSBERG FINANCIAL CORP.; *U.S. Private*, pg. 211
CARLSON ACQUISITION GROUP—See Carlson Companies, Inc.; *U.S. Private*, pg. 212
CARLSON & PARTNERS, INC.; *U.S. Private*, pg. 211
CARLSON COMPANIES, INC.; *U.S. Private*, pg. 212
CARLSON INTERNATIONAL DIVISION—See Carlson Companies, Inc.; *U.S. Private*, pg. 212

CARLSON LEARNING COMPANY—See Carlson Companies, Inc.; *U.S. Private,* pg. 212
CARLSON LEASING, INC.—See Carlson Companies, Inc., Inc.; *U.S. Private,* pg. 212
CARLSON MARKETING GROUP (AUST.) PTY. LIMITED—See Carlson Companies, Inc.; *U.S. Private,* pg. 212
CARLSON MARKETING GROUP, INC.—See Carlson Companies, Inc.; *U.S. Private,* pg. 212
CARLSON MARKETING GROUP JAPAN CO. LTD.—See Carlson Companies, Inc.; *U.S. Private,* pg. 212
CARLSON MARKETING GROUP JAPAN KK—See Carlson Companies, Inc.; *U.S. Private,* pg. 212
CARLSON MARKETING GROUP LTD.—See Carlson Companies, Inc.; *U.S. Private,* pg. 212
CARLSON MARKETING GROUP SCANDINAVIA MOTIVATION SERVICE AB—See Carlson Companies, Inc.; *U.S. Private,* pg. 212
CARLSON MARKETING GROUP (U.K.) LIMITED—See Carlson Companies, Inc.; *U.S. Private,* pg. 212
CARLSON PROMOTION DIVISION—See Carlson Companies, Inc.; *U.S. Private,* pg. 212
CARLSON REAL ESTATE COMPANY—See Carlson Companies, Inc.; *U.S. Private,* pg. 212
CARLSON RETAIL MARKETING—See Carlson Companies, Inc.; *U.S. Private,* pg. 212
CARLSON SYSTEMS; *U.S. Private,* pg. 212
CARLSON TRAVEL GROUP, INC.—See Carlson Companies, Inc.; *U.S. Private,* pg. 212
CARLSON TRAVEL NETWORK INTERNATIONAL—See Carlson Companies, Inc.; *U.S. Private,* pg. 212
CARLSON WAGONLIT TRAVEL—See Carlson Companies, Inc.; *U.S. Private,* pg. 212
AB CARLSSON & MOLLER—See AB Industrivarden; *Int'l,* pg. 678
CARLTON & UNITED BREWERIES INTERNATIONAL—See Foster's Brewing Group Limited; *Int'l,* pg. 501
CARLTON & UNITED BREWERIES LTD.—See Foster's Brewing Group Limited; *Int'l,* pg. 500
CARLTON BREWERY (FIJI) LIMITED—See Foster's Brewing Group Limited; *Int'l,* pg. 501
CARLTON BREWERY NEW ZEALAND—See Foster's Brewing Group Limited; *Int'l,* pg. 501
CARLTON CARDS DIVISION—See American Greetings Corporation; *U.S. Public,* pg. 78
CARLTON CARDS FRANCE—See American Greetings Corporation; *U.S. Public,* pg. 78
CARLTON CARDS LTD.—See American Greetings Corporation; *U.S. Public,* pg. 78
CARLTON COMMUNICATIONS PLC; *Int'l,* pg. 272
CARLTON FILM DISTRIBUTORS—See Carlton Communications Plc; *Int'l,* pg. 272
CARLTON, INC.—See Maescher Industries, Inc.; *U.S. Private,* pg. 694
CARLTON MANUFACTURING, INC.; *U.S. Private,* pg. 212
CARLTON PAPER CORP. LTD.—See Kimberly-Clark Corporation; *U.S. Public,* pg. 959
CARLTON SPECIAL BEVERAGES—See Foster's Brewing Group Limited; *Int'l,* pg. 501
CARLYLE & CO. JEWELERS; *U.S. Private,* pg. 213
CARLYLE COMPRESSOR CO., INC.—See United Technologies Corporation; *U.S. Public,* pg. 1690
THE CARLYLE GROUP—See Carlyle Holding Corporation; *U.S. Private,* pg. 213
CARLYLE HOLDING CORPORATION; *U.S. Private,* pg. 213
CARLYLE INDUSTRIES, INC.—See Noel Group, Inc.; *U.S. Public,* pg. 1187
CARMAG—See Groupe Casino; *Int'l,* pg. 563
CARME' COSMECEUTICAL SCIENCES, INC.; *U.S. Private,* pg. 213
CARMEDA AB—See Norsk Hydro a.s; *Int'l,* pg. 961
CARMEDA A/S—See Norsk Hydro a.s; *Int'l,* pg. 959
CARMEL CONTAINER SYSTEMS LTD.—See American Israeli Paper Mills Ltd.; *Int'l,* pg. 75
A/S CARMEN CLAIROL—See Bristol-Myers Squibb Company; *U.S. Public,* pg. 256
CARMICHAEL LYNCH, INC.; *U.S. Private,* pg. 213
CARMIKE CINEMAS, INC.; *U.S. Public,* pg. 305
CARMOR HELLAS LTD.—See Pechiney S.A.; *Int'l,* pg. 1030
CARMUN INTERNATIONAL—See IMI Plc; *Int'l,* pg. 646
CARNATION DE MEXICO S.A. DE C.V.—See Nestle S.A.; *Int'l,* pg. 919
CARNATION FOODS LTD.—See Nestle S.A.; *Int'l,* pg. 919
CARNATION GROCERY PRODUCTS DIV.—See Nestle S.A.; *Int'l,* pg. 916
CARNATION HELLAS S.A.I.—See Nestle S.A.; *Int'l,* pg. 919
CARNATION ITALIA S.P.A.—See Nestle S.A.; *Int'l,* pg. 919
CARNATION MANUFACTURING CO. (THAILAND) LTD.—See Nestle S.A.; *Int'l,* pg. 919
CARNATION NEDERLAND B.V.—See Nestle S.A.; *Int'l,* pg. 919
S.A. CARNATION N.V.—See Nestle S.A.; *Int'l,* pg. 919
CARNATION PRODUCTS DIV.—See Nestle S.A.; *Int'l,* pg. 916
CARNAUDMETALBOX—See Crown Cork & Seal Company, Ltd.; *U.S. Public,* pg. 463
D. CARNEGIE AB—See Carnegie Holding AB; *Int'l,* pg. 272
CARNEGIE HOLDING AB; *Int'l,* pg. 272
CARNEGIE INC.—See Carnegie Holding AB; *Int'l,* pg. 272
CARNEGIE INTERNATIONAL LIMITED—See Carnegie Holding AB; *Int'l,* pg. 272
CARNEGIE NATURAL GAS CO.—See USX Corporation; *U.S. Public,* pg. 1661
CARNIVAL CORPORATION; *U.S. Public,* pg. 306
CARNIVAL CREATIONS; *U.S. Private,* pg. 213
CARNIVAL HOTELS & CASINOS—See Patriot American Hospitality, Inc.; *U.S. Public,* pg. 1265
CARNRICK LABORATORIES, INC.—See GWC Health, Inc.; *U.S. Private,* pg. 436
CARO KNIT (JEFFERSON PLANT)—See The Dixie Group, Inc.; *U.S. Public,* pg. 514

CARO PRODUCE & INSTITUTIONAL FOODS—See Performance Food Group Company; *U.S. Public,* pg. 1278
CARO TRANS INTL—See Arkansas Best Corporation; *U.S. Public,* pg. 130
CAROHOME LLC—See Carolina Power & Light Company; *U.S. Public,* pg. 307
CAROL CABLE COMPANY—See Wassall Plc; *Int'l,* pg. 1487
T.J. CAROLAN & SON LTD.—See Allied Domecq PLC; *Int'l,* pg. 63
CAROLE FABRICS CORP.—See Hunter Douglas N.V.; *Int'l,* pg. 639
CAROLINA ABSORBENT COTTON CO.—See Barnhardt Manufacturing Co.; *U.S. Private,* pg. 117
CAROLINA BIOLOGICAL SUPPLY CO.; *U.S. Private,* pg. 213
CAROLINA BUILDERS CORPORATION—See Wolseley Plc.; *Int'l,* pg. 1512
CAROLINA BY-PRODUCTS CO. GREENSBORO DIVISION—See CBP Resources, Inc.; *U.S. Private,* pg. 192
CAROLINA CASUALTY INSURANCE COMPANY—See W.R. Berkley Corporation; *U.S. Public,* pg. 216
CAROLINA COMMERCIAL HEAT TREATING, INC.—See Gibraltar Steel Corp.; *U.S. Public,* pg. 742
CAROLINA CUT SHEETS—See Champion Industries; *U.S. Public,* pg. 333
CAROLINA EASTMAN CO.—See Eastman Chemical Company; *U.S. Public,* pg. 550
CAROLINA FIRST BANK—See Carolina First Corporation; *U.S. Public,* pg. 306
CAROLINA FIRST CORPORATION; *U.S. Public,* pg. 306
CAROLINA FIRST MORTGAGE COMPANY—See Carolina First Corporation; *U.S. Public,* pg. 306
CAROLINA GLOVE CO.; *U.S. Private,* pg. 214
CAROLINA HOLDINGS, INC.—See Wolseley Plc.; *Int'l,* pg. 1512
CAROLINA LOGISTICS—See US 1 Industries Inc.; *U.S. Public,* pg. 1687
CAROLINA MAIDEN CORP.—See Carolina Mills, Inc.; *U.S. Private,* pg. 214
CAROLINA MAILING SERVICE—See Wallace Computer Services, Inc.; *U.S. Public,* pg. 1735
CAROLINA METALS, INC.—See Starmet Corporation; *U.S. Public,* pg. 1511
CAROLINA MILLS, INC.; *U.S. Private,* pg. 214
CAROLINA MIRROR COMPANY; *U.S. Private,* pg. 214
CAROLINA NATIONAL TRANSPORTATION—See US 1 Industries Inc.; *U.S. Public,* pg. 1687
CAROLINA PAPER BOARD COMPANY, INC.—See Caraustar Industries, Inc.; *U.S. Public,* pg. 303
CAROLINA PAPER BOX COMPANY, INC.—See Caraustar Industries, Inc.; *U.S. Public,* pg. 303
CAROLINA POWER & LIGHT COMPANY; *U.S. Public,* pg. 306
CAROLINA PUMP & SUPPLY CORP.—See Hughes Supply, Inc.; *U.S. Public,* pg. 846
CAROLINA QUARRIES, INC.—See Rock of Ages Corporation; *U.S. Public,* pg. 1396
CAROLINA RECYCLING, INC.—See Caraustar Industries, Inc.; *U.S. Public,* pg. 303
CAROLINA REPROGRAPHICS—See Wallace Computer Services, Inc.; *U.S. Public,* pg. 1736
CAROLINA SHOE COMPANY—See Berkshire Hathaway Inc.; *U.S. Public,* pg. 217
CAROLINA STEEL CORPORATION; *U.S. Private,* pg. 214
CAROLINA STEEL-FAB SHOP—See Carolina Steel Corporation; *U.S. Private,* pg. 214
CAROLINA STEEL-GREENVILLE PLANT—See Carolina Steel Corporation; *U.S. Private,* pg. 214
CAROLINA STEEL-HICKORY PLANT—See Carolina Steel Corporation; *U.S. Private,* pg. 214
CAROLINA STEEL-SALEM PLANT—See Carolina Steel Corporation; *U.S. Private,* pg. 214
CAROLINA STEEL-MONTGOMERY PLANT—See Carolina Steel Corporation; *U.S. Private,* pg. 214
CAROLINA STEEL-NASH COUNTY PLANT—See Carolina Steel Corporation; *U.S. Private,* pg. 214
CAROLINA TANK CORP.—See Kuhlman Corporation; *U.S. Public,* pg. 968
CAROLINA TRACTOR & EQUIPMENT CO.; *U.S. Private,* pg. 214
CAROLMET DIVISION—See Union Miniere; *Int'l,* pg. 1442
CAROLINE INTERNATIONAL—See National Spinning Co., Inc.; *U.S. Private,* pg. 786
CARONET LLC—See Carolina Power & Light Company; *U.S. Public,* pg. 307
CAROT INSIGHT—See TMD Carat Advertising Limited; *Int'l,* pg. 1342
CAROTELL PAPER BOARD CORPORATION—See Caraustar Industries, Inc.; *U.S. Public,* pg. 303
CAROTHERS ROAD, INC.—See Forest City Enterprises, Inc.; *U.S. Public,* pg. 668
CARPAP LIBERT SA—See N.V. Koninklijke KNP BT; *Int'l,* pg. 757
CARPENTARIA GOLD PTY. LTD.—See M.I.M. Holdings Ltd.; *Int'l,* pg. 786
CARPENTER CO.; *U.S. Private,* pg. 214
THE CARPENTER GROUP; *U.S. Private,* pg. 215
GUY CARPENTER & CO., INC—See Marsh & McLennan Companies, Inc.; *U.S. Public,* pg. 1048
CARPENTER INDUSTRIES, INC.; *U.S. Private,* pg. 215
CARPENTER INVESTMENTS, INC.—See Carpenter Technology Corporation; *U.S. Public,* pg. 307
CARPENTER RESERVE PRINTING COMPANY—See Wallace Computer Services, Inc.; *U.S. Public,* pg. 1735
CARPENTER RIGGING—See The Carpenter Group; *U.S. Private,* pg. 215
CARPENTER STEEL DIV.—See Carpenter Technology Corporation; *U.S. Public,* pg. 307
CARPENTER TECHNOLOGY (CANADA) LTD.—See Carpenter Technology Corporation; *U.S. Public,* pg. 308

CARPENTER TECHNOLOGY CORP. (TAIWAN) LTD.—See Carpenter Technology Corporation; *U.S. Public,* pg. 308
CARPENTER TECHNOLOGY CORPORATION; *U.S. Public,* pg. 307
CARPENTER TECHNOLOGY (DEUTSCHLAND) GMBH—See Carpenter Technology Corporation; *U.S. Public,* pg. 308
CARPENTER TECHNOLOGY (EUROPE) S.A.—See Carpenter Technology Corporation; *U.S. Public,* pg. 308
CARPENTER TECHNOLOGY (FRANCE) SARL—See Carpenter Technology Corporation; *U.S. Public,* pg. 308
CARPENTER TECHNOLOGY (ITALY) S.R.L.—See Carpenter Technology Corporation; *U.S. Public,* pg. 308
CARPENTER TECHNOLOGY (U.K.) LIMITED—See Carpenter Technology Corporation; *U.S. Public,* pg. 308
CARPENTRY & HARDWARE SERVICES—See Harkins Builders, Inc.; *U.S. Private,* pg. 503
CARPETERIA, INC.; *U.S. Private,* pg. 215
CARPLASTIC S.A. DE C.V.—See Ford Motor Company; *U.S. Public,* pg. 665
CARQUEST CANADA LTD.—See General Parts, Inc.; *U.S. Private,* pg. 445
CARQUEST CORP.—See General Parts, Inc.; *U.S. Private,* pg. 445
CARQUEST CORPORATION; *U.S. Private,* pg. 215
CARR ASSET MANAGEMENT INC.—See Compagnie de Suez; *Int'l,* pg. 313
CARR GOTTSTEIN FOODS; *U.S. Public,* pg. 308
CARR REAL ESTATE SERVICES—See CarrAmerica Realty; *U.S. Public,* pg. 309
W.I. CARR—See Compagnie de Suez; *Int'l,* pg. 314
W.I. CARR (AMERICA) LTD.—See Compagnie de Suez; *Int'l,* pg. 314
W.I. CARR INDOSUEZ CAPITAL ASIA LTD.—See Compagnie de Suez; *Int'l,* pg. 314
W.I. CARR LTD.—See Compagnie de Suez; *Int'l,* pg. 314
CARRABBA'S ITALIAN GRILL, INC.—See Outback Steakhouse Inc.; *U.S. Public,* pg. 1235
CARRAFIELLO, DIEHL & ASSOCIATES, INC.; *U.S. Private,* pg. 215
CARRAMERICA REALTY; *U.S. Public,* pg. 308
CARREFOUR; *Int'l,* pg. 272
CARREFOUR ARGENTINE S.A.—See Carrefour; *Int'l,* pg. 272
CARREFOUR CHINA—See Carrefour; *Int'l,* pg. 272
CARREFOUR COMMERCIO E INDUSTRIA—See Carrefour; *Int'l,* pg. 272
CARREFOUR - ERTECO—See Carrefour; *Int'l,* pg. 272
CARREFOUR - FRANCE—See Carrefour; *Int'l,* pg. 272
CARREFOUR - ITALY—See Carrefour; *Int'l,* pg. 272
CARREFOUR KOREA LTD.—See Carrefour; *Int'l,* pg. 272
CARREFOUR - MALAYSIA—See Carrefour; *Int'l,* pg. 272
CARREFOUR MEXICO—See Carrefour; *Int'l,* pg. 272
CARREFOUR NEDERLAND B.V.—See Carrefour; *Int'l,* pg. 273
CARREFOUR - PICARD SURGELES—See Carrefour; *Int'l,* pg. 272
CARREFOUR - PORTUGAL—See Carrefour; *Int'l,* pg. 273
CARREFOUR-TAIWAN—See Carrefour; *Int'l,* pg. 273
CARREFOUR TICARET MERKEZI A.S.—See Carrefour; *Int'l,* pg. 273
CARREIRO HOLDINGS S.A. DE C.V.—See Leggett & Platt, Incorporated; *U.S. Public,* pg. 987
CARRIAGE DESIGNS, INC.—See The Dixie Group, Inc.; *U.S. Public,* pg. 514
CARRIAGE HILL FOODS—See Fresh Mark, Inc.; *U.S. Private,* pg. 427
CARRIAGE HOUSE INNS—See Atlas Hotels, Inc.; *U.S. Private,* pg. 96
CARRIAGE INDUSTRIES, INC.—See The Dixie Group, Inc.; *U.S. Public,* pg. 514
CARRIAGE TRANSPORT, INC.—See The Dixie Group, Inc.; *U.S. Public,* pg. 514
CARRIER AIR TERMINAL FACILITY—See United Technologies Corporation; *U.S. Public,* pg. 1689
CARRIER BUILDING SERVICES—See United Technologies Corporation; *U.S. Public,* pg. 1689
CARRIER BUILDING SYSTEMS & SERVICES—See United Technologies Corporation; *U.S. Public,* pg. 1689
CARRIER CANADA LTD.—See United Technologies Corporation; *U.S. Public,* pg. 1691
CARRIER CORP.—See United Technologies Corporation; *U.S. Public,* pg. 1690
CARRIER CORP. LATIN AMER OPERS—See United Technologies Corporation; *U.S. Public,* pg. 1689
CARRIER CORP. RCD—See United Technologies Corporation; *U.S. Public,* pg. 1689
CARRIER CORP. TRANSICOLD DIVISION—See United Technologies Corporation; *U.S. Public,* pg. 1689
CARRIER CORPORATION—See United Technologies Corporation; *U.S. Public,* pg. 1689
CARRIER GUAM—See United Technologies Corporation; *U.S. Public,* pg. 1691
CARRIER MARKETS—See Sprint Corporation; *U.S. Public,* pg. 1500
CARRIER NORTH AMERICA—See United Technologies Corporation; *U.S. Public,* pg. 1689
CARRIER ONTARIO—See United Technologies Corporation; *U.S. Public,* pg. 1691
CARRIER PIDGIN—See United Technologies Corporation; *U.S. Public,* pg. 1689
CARRIER PUERTO RICO—See United Technologies Corporation; *U.S. Public,* pg. 1691
CARRIER SALES—See MCI Communications Corp.; *U.S. Public,* pg. 1024
CARRIER SINGAPORE (PTE.) LTD.—See United Technologies Corporation; *U.S. Public,* pg. 1691
CARRIER VIBRATING EQUIPMENT, INC.; *U.S. Private,* pg. 215
CARRILLON—See Pechiney S.A.; *Int'l,* pg. 1028
CARRINGTON LABORATORIES, INC.; *U.S. Public,* pg. 309
CARRINGTON PARFUMS LTD.—See MacAndrews & Forbes Holdings Inc.; *U.S. Private,* pg. 689

CARRINGTON VIYELLA GARMENTS LTD.—See Coats Viyella plc; *Int'l*, pg. 299
CARRIS FINANCIAL GROUP; *U.S. Private*, pg. 215
CARRIS OF CALIFORNIA, INC.—See Carris Financial Group; *U.S. Private*, pg. 215
CARRIS OF CONNECTICUT, INC.—See Carris Financial Group; *U.S. Private*, pg. 215
CARRIS REELS, INC.—See Carris Financial Group; *U.S. Private*, pg. 215
CARRIS REELS, INC.-INDIANA DIV.—See Carris Financial Group; *U.S. Private*, pg. 215
CARRIS REELS, INC.-MICHIGAN DIV.—See Carris Financial Group; *U.S. Private*, pg. 215
CARRIS REELS, INC.-NORTH CAROLINA PLASTICS DIV.—See Carris Financial Group; *U.S. Private*, pg. 215
CARRIS REELS, INC.-NORTH CAROLINA WOOD DIV.—See Carris Financial Group; *U.S. Private*, pg. 215
CARROLL COUNTY TIMES—See Landmark Communications, Inc.; *U.S. Private*, pg. 648
P.J. CARROLL HOLDINGS P.L.C.—See Rothmans UK Holdings Limited; *Int'l*, pg. 1130
CARROLL TOUCH, INC.—See AMP Incorporated; *U.S. Public*, pg. 8
CARROLL TOUCH INTERNATIONAL, LTD.—See AMP Incorporated; *U.S. Public*, pg. 9
W.G. CARROLL, INC.—See The McGraw-Hill Companies; *U.S. Public*, pg. 1071
CARROLL'S FOODS, INC.; *U.S. Private*, pg. 215
CARROLS CORPORATION; *U.S. Private*, pg. 216
CARSE OIL CO. INC.; *U.S. Private*, pg. 216
CARSEN GROUP INC.—See Cantel Industries, Inc.; *U.S. Public*, pg. 301
CARSEY-WERNER COMPANY, LLC; *U.S. Private*, pg. 216
CARSON CONVALESCENT CENTER—See Horizon/CMS Healthcare Corporation; *U.S. Public*, pg. 837
CARSON INDUSTRIES—See Millhouse Group; *U.S. Private*, pg. 748
CARSON PIRIE SCOTT & CO.; *U.S. Public*, pg. 309
CARSON PIRIE SCOTT & COMPANY-DEPT. STORES DIV.—See Carson Pirie Scott & Co.; *U.S. Public*, pg. 309
CARSON PRODUCTS COMPANY; *U.S. Public*, pg. 309
CARSON WATER CO.—See Southwest Gas Corporation; *U.S. Public*, pg. 1493
CARSTENS INC.; *U.S. Private*, pg. 216
CARTALL DIV.—See Peco Mfg. Co., Inc.; *U.S. Private*, pg. 846
CARTELLAS S.A.—See Fort James Corporation; *U.S. Public*, pg. 672
CARTER & ASSOCIATES; *U.S. Private*, pg. 216
CARTER CHAMBERS SUPPLY, INC.; *U.S. Private*, pg. 216
CARTER COMPANIES; *U.S. Private*, pg. 216
CARTER DAY INDUSTRIES (CANADA) LTD.—See Carter Day International; *U.S. Private*, pg. 217
CARTER DAY INTERNATIONAL; *U.S. Private*, pg. 216
CARTER HOLT BUILDING SUPPLIES—See International Paper Company; *U.S. Public*, pg. 905
CARTER HOLT HARVEY BUILDING PRODUCTS GROUP LIMITED—See International Paper Company; *U.S. Public*, pg. 904
CARTER HOLT HARVEY FORESTS LIMITED—See International Paper Company; *U.S. Public*, pg. 905
CARTER HOLT HARVEY GARAGE DOORS—See International Paper Company; *U.S. Public*, pg. 904
CARTER HOLT HARVEY LIMITED—See International Paper Company; *U.S. Public*, pg. 904
CARTER HOLT HARVEY PLASTIC PRODUCTS—See International Paper Company; *U.S. Public*, pg. 904
CARTER HOLT HARVEY PLASTIC PRODUCTS (AUSTRALIA) PTY. LIMITED—See International Paper Company; *U.S. Public*, pg. 905
CARTER HOLT HARVEY PLASTIC PRODUCTS-BEVERAGE DIVISION—See International Paper Company; *U.S. Public*, pg. 904
CARTER HOLT HARVEY PLASTIC PRODUCTS GROUP LIMITED—See International Paper Company; *U.S. Public*, pg. 904
CARTER HOLT HARVEY ROOFING INTERNATIONAL—See International Paper Company; *U.S. Public*, pg. 904
CARTER HOLT HARVEY ROOFING USA, INC.—See International Paper Company; *U.S. Public*, pg. 905
CARTER HOLT HARVEY TIMBER LIMITED—See International Paper Company; *U.S. Public*, pg. 904
CARTER HOLT HARVEY WOOD PRODUCTS LIMITED—See International Paper Company; *U.S. Public*, pg. 904
J.C. CARTER COMPANY, INC.—See Argo-Tech Corporation; *U.S. Private*, pg. 81
CARTER-JONES COMPANIES, INC.; *U.S. Private*, pg. 217
CARTER-JONES LUMBER CO.—See Carter-Jones Companies, Inc.; *U.S. Private*, pg. 217
CARTER MACHINERY COMPANY, INC.—See Caterpillar Inc.; *U.S. Public*, pg. 315
CARTER PRODUCTS, CANADA—See Carter-Wallace, Inc.; *U.S. Public*, pg. 310
CARTER PRODUCTS DIV.—See Carter-Wallace, Inc.; *U.S. Public*, pg. 310
CARTER RICE—See International Paper Company; *U.S. Public*, pg. 903
THE ROBERT CARTER CORP.—See United Dominion Industries, Ltd.; *U.S. Public*, pg. 1676
CARTER RYLEY THOMAS-EPB—See Earle Palmer Brown; *U.S. Private*, pg. 174
CARTER-WALLACE (AUSTRALIA) PTY. LIMITED—See Carter-Wallace, Inc.; *U.S. Public*, pg. 310
CARTER-WALLACE DRUGS, INC.—See Carter-Wallace, Inc.; *U.S. Public*, pg. 310
CARTER-WALLACE, INC.; *U.S. Public*, pg. 309
CARTER-WALLACE INTERNATIONAL DIV.—See Carter-Wallace, Inc.; *U.S. Public*, pg. 310
CARTER-WALLACE LIMITED (UNITED KINGDOM)—See Carter-Wallace, Inc.; *U.S. Public*, pg. 310
CARTER-WALLACE MANUFACTURING DIV.—See Carter-Wallace, Inc.; *U.S. Public*, pg. 310

CARTER-WALLACE, S.A.—See Carter-Wallace, Inc.; *U.S. Public*, pg. 310
THE WILLIAM CARTER COMPANY; *U.S. Private*, pg. 217
CARTERS (J&A) LTD.—See Invacare Corporation; *U.S. Public*, pg. 911
CARTIBERIA, S.A.—See Enso Oyj; *Int'l*, pg. 458
CARTIERA DEL TIRRENO MILL—See Fort James Corporation; *U.S. Public*, pg. 673
CARTIERA DI SUBIACO S.P.A.—See Groupe Saint Louis; *Int'l*, pg. 567
CARTMILLS, S.A.—See Abitibi-Consolidated Inc.; *Int'l*, pg. 20
CARTON-CRAFT CORPORATION; *U.S. Private*, pg. 217
CARTON DE COLUMBIA, S.A.—See Jefferson Smurfit Group p.l.c.; *Int'l*, pg. 1271
CARTONAJES INTERNATIONAL, S.A.—See International Paper Company; *U.S. Public*, pg. 905
CARTONPACK S.A.—See Metsa-Serla Corporation; *Int'l*, pg. 864
THE CARTOON NETWORK—See Time Warner Inc.; *U.S. Public*, pg. 1614
CARTWRIGHT COMMUNICATIONS CO.—See Tessco Technologies, Inc.; *U.S. Public*, pg. 1582
CARUS CHEMICAL COMPANY, CHEMICAL DIV.—See Carus Corporation; *U.S. Private*, pg. 217
CARUS CORPORATION; *U.S. Private*, pg. 217
CARVAJAL, S.A.—See Hewlett-Packard Company; *U.S. Public*, pg. 816
CARVEL HALL—See Syratech Corporation; *U.S. Private*, pg. 1061
CARVEL PRINT GRUPO SERIGRAPH—See Serigraph, Inc.; *U.S. Private*, pg. 985
CARVER CORPORATION; *U.S. Public*, pg. 310
CARVER FEDERAL SAVINGS BANK; *U.S. Public*, pg. 310
CARVER, INC.; *U.S. Private*, pg. 217
CASA AIRCRAFT USA INCORPORATED—See SEPI; *Int'l*, pg. 1224
CASA ARENA BLANCA—See Horizon/CMS Healthcare Corporation; *U.S. Public*, pg. 838
CASA BONITA, INC.—See CKE Restaurants Inc.; *U.S. Public*, pg. 278
CASA CIENTIFICA—See Hewlett-Packard Company; *U.S. Public*, pg. 816
CASA DE BOLSA BANCOMER—See Bancomer, S.A.; *Int'l*, pg. 145
CASA DE CAMBIO BANCOMER—See Bancomer, S.A.; *Int'l*, pg. 145
CASA DEL SOL—See Horizon/CMS Healthcare Corporation; *U.S. Public*, pg. 838
CASA DI BERTACCHI—See Rich Products Corp.; *U.S. Private*, pg. 928
CASA EXPORT, LTD.—See Universal Corporation; *U.S. Public*, pg. 1695
CASA EXPORT LIMITED—See Universal Corporation; *U.S. Public*, pg. 1695
CASA GRANDE MFG. DIVISION—See R.R. Donnelley & Sons Company; *U.S. Public*, pg. 518
CASA LEY S.A.—See Safeway Inc.; *U.S. Public*, pg. 1426
CASA MADRID DEVELOPPEMENT—See Caja de Madrid Group; *Int'l*, pg. 252
CASA MARIA HEALTH CARE CENTER—See Horizon/CMS Healthcare Corporation; *U.S. Public*, pg. 838
CASA REAL HEALTH CARE CENTER—See Horizon/CMS Healthcare Corporation; *U.S. Public*, pg. 838
CASABLANCA FAN COMPANY—See Hunter Fan Company; *U.S. Private*, pg. 549
CASALETTO S.R.L.—See Assicurazioni Generali S.p.A.; *Int'l*, pg. 90
CASCADE (AFRICA) PTY. LTD.—See Cascade Corporation; *U.S. Public*, pg. 311
CASCADE AUTOVON CO.—See PacifiCorp; *U.S. Public*, pg. 1252
CASCADE (CANADA) INC.—See Cascade Corporation; *U.S. Public*, pg. 311
CASCADE CONTROLS, INC.—See Synergism, Inc.; *U.S. Private*, pg. 1060
CASCADE CORPORATION; *U.S. Public*, pg. 310
CASCADE DESIGN AUTOMATION—See Oki Electric Industry Company, Ltd.; *Int'l*, pg. 1000
CASCADE DESIGN AUTOMATION JAPAN CO., LTD.—See Oki Electric Industry Company, Ltd.; *Int'l*, pg. 999
CASCADE DIAMOND—See The Cascades Group; *Int'l*, pg. 274
CASCADE DJUPAGOW AB—See The Cascades Group; *Int'l*, pg. 274
CASCADE DUFFEL NV—See The Cascades Group; *Int'l*, pg. 274
CASCADE EMPIRE CORPORATION—See Forest City Enterprises, Inc.; *U.S. Public*, pg. 669
CASCADE EUROPE—See Cascade Corporation; *U.S. Public*, pg. 311
CASCADE (JAPAN) LTD.—See Cascade Corporation; *U.S. Public*, pg. 311
CASCADE (KOREA) LTD.—See Cascade Corporation; *U.S. Public*, pg. 311
CASCADE LAND LEASING CO.—See Cascade Natural Gas Corporation; *U.S. Public*, pg. 311
CASCADE NATURAL GAS CORPORATION; *U.S. Public*, pg. 311
CASCADE PACIFIC ENGINEERING, INC.—See Republic Industries, Inc.; *U.S. Public*, pg. 1379
CASCADE STEEL ROLLING MILLS, INC.—See Schnitzer Steel Industries, Inc.; *U.S. Public*, pg. 1440
CASCADE (U.K.) INC.—See Cascade Corporation; *U.S. Public*, pg. 311
CASCADES CARTECH INC.—See The Cascades Group; *Int'l*, pg. 273
CASCADES COMMERCIALISATION S.A.—See The Cascades Group; *Int'l*, pg. 274
CASCADES CONVERSION INC.—See The Cascades Group; *Int'l*, pg. 273
CASCADES DISMED INC.—See The Cascades Group; *Int'l*, pg. 273

CASCADES DOMINION INC.—See The Cascades Group; *Int'l*, pg. 273
CASCADES EAST ANGUS INC.—See The Cascades Group; *Int'l*, pg. 273
CASCADES ENERGIE INC.—See The Cascades Group; *Int'l*, pg. 273
CASCADES FORMA-PAK INC.—See The Cascades Group; *Int'l*, pg. 273
THE CASCADES GROUP; *Int'l*, pg. 273
CASCADES, INC.—See The Cascades Group; *Int'l*, pg. 273
CASCADES INDUSTRIES INC.—See The Cascades Group; *Int'l*, pg. 273
CASCADES JONQUIERE INC.—See The Cascades Group; *Int'l*, pg. 273
CASCADES LUPEL INC.—See The Cascades Group; *Int'l*, pg. 273
CASCADES MOULDED PULP, INC.—See The Cascades Group; *Int'l*, pg. 274
CASCADES MULTI-PRO INC.—See The Cascades Group; *Int'l*, pg. 273
CASCADES NIAGARA FALLS—See The Cascades Group; *Int'l*, pg. 274
CASCADES PAPERBOARD INTERNATIONAL INC.—See The Cascades Group; *Int'l*, pg. 273
CASCADES P.S.H. INC.—See The Cascades Group; *Int'l*, pg. 273
CASCADES S.A.—See The Cascades Group; *Int'l*, pg. 274
CASCADES SEALED AIR INC.—See The Cascades Group; *Int'l*, pg. 273
CASCADIA TECHNOLOGY CORPORATION—See Novametrix Medical Systems Inc.; *U.S. Public*, pg. 1203
CASCADIA TRANSPORT—See Lynden Incorporated; *U.S. Private*, pg. 683
CASCHEM INC.—See Cambrex Corporation; *U.S. Public*, pg. 297
CASCO CABLE TELEVISION INC.—See The Pfaltzgraff Co.; *U.S. Private*, pg. 860
CASCO INC.—See Corn Products International, Inc.; *U.S. Public*, pg. 448
CASCO NOBEL AB—See Akzo Nobel N.V.; *Int'l*, pg. 48
CASCO-NORTHERN CORPORATION—See BankBoston Corporation; *U.S. Public*, pg. 184
CASCO PRODUCTS CORPORATION—See Sequa Corporation; *U.S. Public*, pg. 1458
CASCO SIGNAL LTD.—See SASIB SpA; *Int'l*, pg. 1195
CASE ADVERTISING, INC.—See Coca-Cola Bottling Co. Consolidated; *U.S. Public*, pg. 391
CASE CORPORATION; *U.S. Public*, pg. 311
CASE ENGINE HOLDING COMPANY, INC.—See Case Corporation; *U.S. Public*, pg. 311
CASE FARMS, INC.—See Case Foods, Inc.; *U.S. Private*, pg. 218
CASE FARMS OF OHIO—See Case Foods, Inc.; *U.S. Private*, pg. 218
CASE FOODS, INC.; *U.S. Private*, pg. 217
CASE FRANCE, S.A.—See Tenneco Inc.; *U.S. Public*, pg. 1579
THE CASE-HOYT CORPORATION—See Avanti Press Inc.; *U.S. Private*, pg. 101
CASE INTERNATIONAL—See Tenneco Inc.; *U.S. Public*, pg. 1579
CASE INTERNATIONAL, AGR ENGINEERING—See Tenneco Inc.; *U.S. Public*, pg. 1579
J.I. CASE (AUSTRALIA) PTY., LTD.—See Tenneco Inc.; *U.S. Public*, pg. 1579
J.I. CASE CREDIT CORP.—See Case Corporation; *U.S. Public*, pg. 312
J.I. CASE CREDIT CORPORATION OF AUSTRALIA PTY. LIMITED—See Tenneco Inc.; *U.S. Public*, pg. 1579
J.I. CASE DO BRASIL & CIA (A PARTNERSHIP)—See Tenneco Inc.; *U.S. Public*, pg. 1579
J.I. CASE INTERNATIONAL SALES—See Case Corporation; *U.S. Public*, pg. 312
J.I. CASE NORGE A/S—See Tenneco Inc.; *U.S. Public*, pg. 1579
J.I. CASE SOUTH AFRICA (PTY.) LTD.—See Tenneco Inc.; *U.S. Public*, pg. 1580
J.I. CASE SWEDEN AB—See Tenneco Inc.; *U.S. Public*, pg. 1580
J.I. CASE LEASING CORPORATION—See Case Corporation; *U.S. Public*, pg. 312
J.I. CASE THRESHING MACHINE COMPANY—See Case Corporation; *U.S. Public*, pg. 312
CASE MANAGEMENT—See Maxxim Medical, Inc.; *U.S. Public*, pg. 1063
CASE PAPER CO., INC.; *U.S. Private*, pg. 218
CASE PAPER CO.—See Case Paper Co., Inc.; *U.S. Private*, pg. 218
CASE PAPER CO. OF COLORADO—See Case Paper Co., Inc.; *U.S. Private*, pg. 218
CASE PAPER CO. OF FLORIDA, INC.—See Case Paper Co., Inc.; *U.S. Private*, pg. 218
CASE POCLAIN GMBH & CO.—See Tenneco Inc.; *U.S. Public*, pg. 1579
CASE-SWAYNE CO. INC.; *U.S. Private*, pg. 218
CASE TRACTEURS, S.A.—See Tenneco Inc.; *U.S. Public*, pg. 1579
CASE TRAKTOREN GMBH—See Tenneco Inc.; *U.S. Public*, pg. 1579
CASE TRAKTORI OY—See Tenneco Inc.; *U.S. Public*, pg. 1579
CASE UNITED KINGDOM LIMITED—See Tenneco Inc.; *U.S. Public*, pg. 1579
CASE VENTURES CORPORATION—See Case Corporation; *U.S. Public*, pg. 312
W.R. CASE & SONS CUTLERY COMPANY—See Zippo Manufacturing Company; *U.S. Private*, pg. 1207
CASELLA WASTE SYSTEMS, INC.; *U.S. Public*, pg. 312
NV CASEMA—See KPN Koninklyke PTT Nederland NV; *Int'l*, pg. 720
CASEY CO.; *U.S. Private*, pg. 218
THE CASEY COUNTY NEWS—See Landmark Communications, Inc.; *U.S. Private*, pg. 648
CASEY'S GENERAL STORES, INC.; *U.S. Public*, pg. 312

CASH AMERICA, INC. OF KENTUCKY—See Cash America International, Inc.; *U.S. Public,* pg. 312
CASH AMERICA, INC. OF LOUISIANA—See Cash America International, Inc.; *U.S. Public,* pg. 312
CASH AMERICA, INC. OF NORTH CAROLINA—See Cash America International, Inc.; *U.S. Public,* pg. 312
CASH AMERICA, INC. OF OKLAHOMA—See Cash America International, Inc.; *U.S. Public,* pg. 312
CASH AMERICA, INC. OF SOUTH CAROLINA—See Cash America International, Inc.; *U.S. Public,* pg. 312
CASH AMERICA, INC. OF TENNESSEE—See Cash America International, Inc.; *U.S. Public,* pg. 312
CASH AMERICA INTERNATIONAL, INC.; *U.S. Public,* pg. 312
CASH & CARRY GROCER INC.; *U.S. Private,* pg. 218
CASH BASES INCORPORATED—See Tridex Corporation; *U.S. Public,* pg. 1637
CASH FLOW, INC.—See NationsBank Corporation; *U.S. Public,* pg. 1163
CASH INVEST MANAGEMENT S.A.—See Tractebel; *Int'l,* pg. 1416
CASH PLUS, INC., *U.S. Private,* pg. 218
CASH WERBEAGENTUR AG/DMB&B ZURICH—See DMB&B Communications; *U.S. Private,* pg. 303
CASHCO, INC., *U.S. Private,* pg. 218
CASHIN SYSTEMS CORP.—See Tetra Laval Group; *Int'l,* pg. 1378
CASHWAY BUILDING CENTRES LTD.; *Int'l,* pg. 274
CASI-RUSCO EUROPE—See CASI-RUSCO Inc.; *U.S. Private,* pg. 218
CASI-RUSCO INC.; *U.S. Private,* pg. 218
CASIA GRUNDSTUECKS - VERMIETUNGS- UND VERWALTUNGS GMBH—See Commerzbank AG; *Int'l,* pg. 310
CASINO AZTAR—See Aztar Corporation; *U.S. Public,* pg. 158
CASINO ELECTRONICS, INC.—See Alliance Gaming Corporation; *U.S. Public,* pg. 47
CASINO FRANCE—See Groupe Casino; *Int'l,* pg. 563
CASINO-GUICHARD PERRACHON & CIE—See Groupe Casino; *Int'l,* pg. 562
CASINO MODERNE MENU SYSTEME GMBH—See Nestle S.A.; *Int'l,* pg. 919
CASINO PROPERTIES, INC.—See Santa Fe Gaming Corporation; *U.S. Public,* pg. 1432
CASINO REALTY INC.—See Groupe Casino; *Int'l,* pg. 563
CASINO RHONE-ALPES—See Groupe Casino; *Int'l,* pg. 563
CASINO U.S.A.—See Groupe Casino; *Int'l,* pg. 563
CASIO ASIA PTE. LTD.—See Casio Computer Co., Ltd.; *Int'l,* pg. 274
CASIO CANADA, LTD.—See Casio Computer Co., Ltd.; *Int'l,* pg. 274
CASIO COMPUTER CO. G.M.B.H. DEUTSCHLAND—See Casio Computer Co., Ltd.; *Int'l,* pg. 274
CASIO COMPUTER CO., LTD.; *Int'l,* pg. 274
CASIO COMPUTER (HONG KONG) LTD.—See Casio Computer Co., Ltd.; *Int'l,* pg. 274
CASIO ELECTROMEX S.A. DE C.V.—See Casio Computer Co., Ltd.; *Int'l,* pg. 274
CASIO ELECTRONICS CO., LTD.—See Casio Computer Co., Ltd.; *Int'l,* pg. 274
CASIO, INC.—See Casio Computer Co., Ltd.; *Int'l,* pg. 274
CASIO KOREA CO., LTD. (SOUTH)—See Casio Computer Co., Ltd.; *Int'l,* pg. 274
CASIO (MALAYSIA) SDN. BHD.—See Casio Computer Co., Ltd.; *Int'l,* pg. 274
CASIO MANUFACTURING CORPORATION—See Casio Computer Co., Ltd.; *Int'l,* pg. 274
CASIO PHONE-MATE, INC.—See Casio Computer Co., Ltd.; *Int'l,* pg. 274
CASIO TAIWAN LTD.—See Casio Computer Co., Ltd.; *Int'l,* pg. 274
CASIOPEA REASEGURADORA, S.A.—See Telefonica de Espana, S.A.; *Int'l,* pg. 1371
CASKET SHELLS, INC., *U.S. Private,* pg. 218
S.A. CASMITJANA MENSA—See Henkel KGaA; *Int'l,* pg. 612
CASPAR & CO. HANDEL GMBH & CO.—See Mannesmann A.G.; *Int'l,* pg. 838
CASPAR VERWALTUNGS GMBH—See Mannesmann A.G.; *Int'l,* pg. 838
CASPER WYOMING PRODUCTION DISTRICT OFFICE—See Hunt Oil Company; *U.S. Private,* pg. 548
CASPIAN SHIPYARD COMPANY LIMITED—See Keppel Corporation Limited; *Int'l,* pg. 731
CASS-CLAY CREAMERY, *U.S. Private,* pg. 218
CASSA DI RISPARMIO DELLE PROVINCIE LOMBARDE SPA (CARIPLO); *Int'l,* pg. 274
CASSANO'S INC.; *U.S. Private,* pg. 218
CASSCO ICE & COLD STORAGE, INC.—See WLR Foods, Inc.; *U.S. Public,* pg. 1727
CASSENS TRANSPORT COMPANY; *U.S. Private,* pg. 219
CASSIDY'S LTD.; *Int'l,* pg. 275
CASSINA—See Groupe Strafor Facom; *Int'l,* pg. 570
CAST-MATIC CORPORATION—See Intermet Corporation; *U.S. Public,* pg. 894
CAST METALS OPERATIONS—See Zurn Industries, Inc.; *U.S. Public,* pg. 1794
CASTAGNETTI—See Fiat Auto SpA; *Int'l,* pg. 481
CASTCRAFT INDUSTRIES, INC.; *U.S. Private,* pg. 219
CASTCRAFT SOFTWARE OPTIFONT—See Castcraft Industries, Inc.; *U.S. Private,* pg. 219
CASTELAZO & ASSOCIATES—See The McGraw-Hill Companies; *U.S. Public,* pg. 1071
CASTELL INTERLOCKS INC.—See Halma p.l.c.; *Int'l,* pg. 590
CASTELL SAFETY INTERNATIONAL LIMITED—See Halma p.l.c.; *Int'l,* pg. 589
CASTELLI S.P.A.—See Haworth, Inc.; *U.S. Private,* pg. 512
CASTELLO BANFI SRL—See Banfi Vintners; *U.S. Private,* pg. 113
CASTELMAC, S.P.A.—See Scotsman Industries, Inc.; *U.S. Public,* pg. 1445

CASTEX INCORPORATED—See Tennant Company; *U.S. Public,* pg. 1577
CASTING MATERIALS DIVISION—See Hickman, Williams & Co. Inc.; *U.S. Private,* pg. 525
A.M. CASTLE & CO.; *U.S. Public,* pg. 312
A.M. CASTLE & CO. (CANADA), INC.—See A.M. Castle & Co.; *U.S. Public,* pg. 313
CASTLE & COOKE INC.; *U.S. Public,* pg. 313
CASTLE & OVERTON—See Haindl Papier GmbH; *Int'l,* pg. 586
CASTLE CEMENT LIMITED—See Scancem AB; *Int'l,* pg. 1201
CASTLE CEMENT LTD. (CLITHEROE)—See Scancem AB; *Int'l,* pg. 1201
CASTLE CEMENT LTD. (GRAYS)—See Scancem AB; *Int'l,* pg. 1201
CASTLE CEMENT LTD. (MOLD)—See Scancem AB; *Int'l,* pg. 1201
CASTLE CEMENT LTD. (PORT OF BRISTOL)—See Scancem AB; *Int'l,* pg. 1201
CASTLE CEMENT LTD. (STAMFORD)—See Scancem AB; *Int'l,* pg. 1201
CASTLE CEMENT LTD. (STRATHCLYDE)—See Scancem AB; *Int'l,* pg. 1201
CASTLE CONCRETE CO.—See Continental Materials Corporation; *U.S. Public,* pg. 441
CASTLE CONVERTIBLE FUND, INC.; *U.S. Public,* pg. 313
CASTLE ENERGY CORPORATION; *U.S. Public,* pg. 313
CASTLE-HARLAN, INC.; *U.S. Private,* pg. 219
CASTLE HARLAN PARTNERS III, L.P.—See Castle-Harlan, Inc.; *U.S. Private,* pg. 219
CASTLE HARLAN PARTNERS II, L.P.—See Castle-Harlan, Inc.; *U.S. Private,* pg. 219
CASTLE OIL CORPORATION; *U.S. Private,* pg. 219
CASTLE ROCK CONTAINER CO.—See Consolidated Papers, Inc.; *U.S. Public,* pg. 436
CASTLE RUBBER CO.—See Park-Ohio Industries, Inc.; *U.S. Public,* pg. 1258
CASTLEBERG'S—See Reliable Stores, Inc.; *U.S. Private,* pg. 219
CASTLEBERRY KNITS, LTD.—See The Leslie Fay Companies, Inc.; *U.S. Public,* pg. 989
CASTLEBERRY/SNOW'S BRANDS INC.; *U.S. Private,* pg. 219
CASTLEGATE INC.—See Premdor Inc.; *Int'l,* pg. 1067
CASTLEREAGH PHARMACEUTICALS—See Franz Haniel & Cie, GmbH; *Int'l,* pg. 591
CASTLETON BEVERAGE CORP.—See Bacardi Limited; *Int'l,* pg. 132
CASTLETON NETWORK SYSTEMS—See Newbridge Networks Corporation; *Int'l,* pg. 924
CASTNER KNOTT CO.—See Mercantile Stores Company, Inc.; *U.S. Public,* pg. 1090
CASTORAMA BOURGES—See Castorama Dubois Investissements S.C.A.; *Int'l,* pg. 275
CASTORAMA DIFFUSION—See Castorama Dubois Investissements S.C.A.; *Int'l,* pg. 275
CASTORAMA DUBOIS INVESTISSEMENTS S.C.A.; *Int'l,* pg. 275
CASTORAMA ITALIA—See Castorama Dubois Investissements S.C.A.; *Int'l,* pg. 276
GIE CASTORAMA TRANSPORTS—See Castorama Dubois Investissements S.C.A.; *Int'l,* pg. 276
CASTOWEST—See Castorama Dubois Investissements S.C.A.; *Int'l,* pg. 275
CASTROL AB—See Burmah Castrol plc; *Int'l,* pg. 235
CASTROL A/S—See Burmah Castrol plc; *Int'l,* pg. 235
CASTROL AUSTRALIA PTY LTD.—See Burmah Castrol plc; *Int'l,* pg. 235
CASTROL AUSTRIA GMBH—See Burmah Castrol plc; *Int'l,* pg. 235
CASTROL BRASIL LIMITADA—See Burmah Castrol plc; *Int'l,* pg. 235
CASTROL CANADA INC.—See Burmah Castrol plc; *Int'l,* pg. 235
CASTROL CHILE SA—See Burmah Castrol plc; *Int'l,* pg. 235
CASTROL CHINA LTD.—See Burmah Castrol plc; *Int'l,* pg. 235
CASTROL DEL PERU SA—See Burmah Castrol plc; *Int'l,* pg. 235
CASTROL ESPANA SA—See Burmah Castrol plc; *Int'l,* pg. 235
CASTROL FRANCE SA—See Burmah Castrol plc; *Int'l,* pg. 235
CASTROL HELLAS S.A.—See Burmah Castrol plc; *Int'l,* pg. 235
CASTROL INC., SPECIALTY PRODUCTS DIV.—See Burmah Castrol plc; *Int'l,* pg. 235
CASTROL INDUSTRIAL—See Burmah Castrol plc; *Int'l,* pg. 235
CASTROL ITALIANA SPA—See Burmah Castrol plc; *Int'l,* pg. 236
CASTROL K.K.—See Burmah Castrol plc; *Int'l,* pg. 236
CASTROL KOREA LIMITED—See Burmah Castrol plc; *Int'l,* pg. 236
CASTROL LTD.—See Burmah Castrol plc; *Int'l,* pg. 234
CASTROL (MALAYSIA) SB—See Burmah Castrol plc; *Int'l,* pg. 236
CASTROL MARINE OIL GMBH—See Burmah Castrol plc; *Int'l,* pg. 236
CASTROL NEDERLAND B.V.—See Burmah Castrol plc; *Int'l,* pg. 236
CASTROL NORGE A/S—See Burmah Castrol plc; *Int'l,* pg. 236
CASTROL NORTH AMERICA—See Burmah Castrol plc; *Int'l,* pg. 235
CASTROL NV—See Burmah Castrol plc; *Int'l,* pg. 236
CASTROL NZ LTD.—See Burmah Castrol plc; *Int'l,* pg. 236
CASTROL OVERSEAS—See Burmah Castrol plc; *Int'l,* pg. 234
CASTROL SINGAPORE PTE. LTD.—See Burmah Castrol plc; *Int'l,* pg. 236

CASTROL SOUTH AFRICA (PTY.) LTD.—See Burmah Castrol plc; *Int'l,* pg. 236
CASTROL (SWITZERLAND) AG—See Burmah Castrol plc; *Int'l,* pg. 236
CASTROL (TAIWAN) LIMITED—See Burmah Castrol plc; *Int'l,* pg. 236
CASTROL (U.K.) LIMITED—See Burmah Castrol plc; *Int'l,* pg. 234
CASTROL ZIMBABWE (PVT.) LTD.—See Burmah Castrol plc; *Int'l,* pg. 236
MIKE CASTRUCCI CHEVROLET; *U.S. Private,* pg. 219
CASU TRANSPORT LIMITED—See The East Asiatic Company Ltd. A/S; *Int'l,* pg. 431
CASUAL CORNER GROUP, INC.; *U.S. Private,* pg. 219
CASUAL CORNER GROUP, INC.—See Casual Corner Group, Inc.; *U.S. Private,* pg. 219
CASUAL CORNER OUTLET—See Casual Corner Group, Inc.; *U.S. Private,* pg. 219
CASUAL CORNER WOMAN—See Casual Corner Group, Inc.; *U.S. Private,* pg. 219
CASUALTY INSURANCE CO.—See Fremont General Corporation; *U.S. Public,* pg. 681
CASUDA CANYON RESTAURANT CORP.—See Specialty Restaurants Corporation; *U.S. Public,* pg. 1022
CASWELL-MASSEY CO. LTD.; *U.S. Private,* pg. 219
CAT PUMPS AG—See Diversified Dynamics Corporation; *U.S. Private,* pg. 336
CAT PUMPS CORPORATION—See Diversified Dynamics Corporation; *U.S. Private,* pg. 336
CAT PUMPS DEUTSCHLAND GMBH—See Diversified Dynamics Corporation; *U.S. Private,* pg. 336
CAT PUMPS INTERNATIONAL N.V.—See Diversified Dynamics Corporation; *U.S. Private,* pg. 336
CAT PUMPS (UK) LTD.—See Diversified Dynamics Corporation; *U.S. Private,* pg. 336
CATALANA D'INICIATIVES, C.R., S.A.—See Telefonica de Espana, S.A.; *Int'l,* pg. 1372
CATALINA ASIA—See Catalina Lighting, Inc.; *U.S. Public,* pg. 314
CATALINA INDUSTRIAL, LTD.—See Catalina Lighting, Inc.; *U.S. Public,* pg. 314
CATALINA INDUSTRIES—See Catalina Lighting, Inc.; *U.S. Public,* pg. 314
CATALINA LIGHTING CANADA—See Catalina Lighting, Inc.; *U.S. Public,* pg. 314
CATALINA LIGHTING, INC.; *U.S. Public,* pg. 314
CATALINA LIGHTING MEXICO, S.A. DE C.V.—See Catalina Lighting, Inc.; *U.S. Public,* pg. 314
CATALINA MARKETING CORPORATION; *U.S. Public,* pg. 314
CATALINA REAL ESTATE TRUST, INC.—See Catalina Lighting, Inc.; *U.S. Public,* pg. 314
CATALINA YACHTS, INC.; *U.S. Private,* pg. 219
CATALOG RESOURCES, INC.—See LCS Industries, Inc.; *U.S. Public,* pg. 970
CATALYST RESOURCES, INC—See Mallinckrodt Inc.; *U.S. Public,* pg. 1039
CATALYSTS & CHEMICALS—See Johnson Matthey Public Limited Company; *Int'l,* pg. 713
CATAMARAN CRUISERS LTD./BATEAUX LONDON—See Sodexho S.A.; *Int'l,* pg. 1274
CATAMOUNT ENERGY CORPORATION—See Central Vermont Public Service Corporation; *U.S. Public,* pg. 328
CATAMOUNT INVESTMENT CORPORATION—See Central Vermont Public Service Corporation; *U.S. Public,* pg. 328
CATAMOUNT PETROLEUM; *U.S. Private,* pg. 220
CATAWBA INSURANCE CO.—See The Seibels Bruce Group, Inc.; *U.S. Public,* pg. 1454
CATELLUS DEVELOPMENT CORPORATION; *U.S. Public,* pg. 314
CATELLUS RESIDENTIAL GROUP—See Catellus Development Corporation; *U.S. Public,* pg. 315
CATERPILLAR ADMINISTRACAO E PARTICIPACOES LTDA.—See Caterpillar Inc.; *U.S. Public,* pg. 316
CATERPILLAR (AFRICA) (PROPRIETARY) LIMITED—See Caterpillar Inc.; *U.S. Public,* pg. 317
CATERPILLAR AMERICAS CO.—See Caterpillar Inc.; *U.S. Public,* pg. 315
CATERPILLAR ASIA LIMITED—See Caterpillar Inc.; *U.S. Public,* pg. 317
CATERPILLAR ASIA PACIFIC HOLDING INC.—See Caterpillar Inc.; *U.S. Public,* pg. 315
CATERPILLAR ASIA PTE. LTD.—See Caterpillar Inc.; *U.S. Public,* pg. 316
CATERPILLAR BELGIUM S.A.—See Caterpillar Inc.; *U.S. Public,* pg. 317
CATERPILLAR BRASIL S.A.—See Caterpillar Inc.; *U.S. Public,* pg. 316
CATERPILLAR CAPITAL COMPANY, INC.—See Caterpillar Inc.; *U.S. Public,* pg. 315
CATERPILLAR CHINA LIMITED—See Caterpillar Inc.; *U.S. Public,* pg. 317
CATERPILLAR COMMERCIAL A/O—See Caterpillar Inc.; *U.S. Public,* pg. 316
CATERPILLAR COMMERCIAL APS—See Caterpillar Inc.; *U.S. Public,* pg. 317
CATERPILLAR COMMERCIAL N.V.—See Caterpillar Inc.; *U.S. Public,* pg. 316
CATERPILLAR COMMERCIAL S.A.R.L.—See Caterpillar Inc.; *U.S. Public,* pg. 317
CATERPILLAR COMMERCIAL SERVICES LTD.—See Caterpillar Inc.; *U.S. Public,* pg. 316
CATERPILLAR COMMERCIALE S.R.L.—See Caterpillar Inc.; *U.S. Public,* pg. 317
CATERPILLAR EXPORT LIMITED—See Caterpillar Inc.; *U.S. Public,* pg. 315
CATERPILLAR FINANCE FRANCE S.A.—See Caterpillar Inc.; *U.S. Public,* pg. 315
CATERPILLAR FINANCIAL AUSTRALIA LTD.—See Caterpillar Inc.; *U.S. Public,* pg. 315
CATERPILLAR FINANCIAL LEASING, S.A.—See Caterpillar Inc.; *U.S. Public,* pg. 315

MASTER INDEX TO COMPANY NAMES
CELTITE
Company Index

CATERPILLAR FINANCIAL NORDIC SERVICES A.B.—See Caterpillar Inc.; *U.S. Public*, pg. 315
CATERPILLAR FINANCIAL RECEIVABLES INC.—See Caterpillar Inc.; *U.S. Public*, pg. 315
CATERPILLAR FINANCIAL SERVICES CORPORATION—See Caterpillar Inc.; *U.S. Public*, pg. 315
CATERPILLAR FINANCIAL SERVICES HOLDING GMBH—See Caterpillar Inc.; *U.S. Public*, pg. 315
CATERPILLAR FINANCIAL SERVICES LIMITED—See Caterpillar Inc.; *U.S. Public*, pg. 315
CATERPILLAR FINANCIAL SERVICES NORWAY A/S—See Caterpillar Inc.; *U.S. Public*, pg. 315
CATERPILLAR FINANCIAL SERVICES N.V.—See Caterpillar Inc.; *U.S. Public*, pg. 316
CATERPILLAR FINANCIAL SERVICES (U.K.) LIMITED—See Caterpillar Inc.; *U.S. Public*, pg. 315
CATERPILLAR FRANCE S.A.—See Caterpillar Inc.; *U.S. Public*, pg. 317
CATERPILLAR INC.; *U.S. Public*, pg. 315
CATERPILLAR INDUSTRIAL INC.—See Caterpillar Inc.; *U.S. Public*, pg. 315
CATERPILLAR INDUSTRIAL PRODUCTS, INC.—See Caterpillar Inc.; *U.S. Public*, pg. 316
CATERPILLAR INSURANCE CO., LTD.—See Caterpillar Inc.; *U.S. Public*, pg. 316
CATERPILLAR INSURANCE SERVICES CORPORATION—See Caterpillar Inc.; *U.S. Public*, pg. 316
CATERPILLAR INVESTMENT MANAGEMENT LTD.—See Caterpillar Inc.; *U.S. Public*, pg. 316
CATERPILLAR LEASING GMBH (ISMANING)—See Caterpillar Inc.; *U.S. Public*, pg. 315
CATERPILLAR LEASING GMBH (LEIPZIG)—See Caterpillar Inc.; *U.S. Public*, pg. 315
CATERPILLAR LOGISTICS SERVICES BELGIUM N.V.—See Caterpillar Inc.; *U.S. Public*, pg. 316
CATERPILLAR LOGISTICS SERVICES, INC.—See Caterpillar Inc.; *U.S. Public*, pg. 316
CATERPILLAR LOGISTICS SERVICES LIMITED—See Caterpillar Inc.; *U.S. Public*, pg. 317
CATERPILLAR LOGISTICS SERVICES SPAIN S.A.—See Caterpillar Inc.; *U.S. Public*, pg. 316
CATERPILLAR MATERIELS ROUTIERS—See Caterpillar Inc.; *U.S. Public*, pg. 316
CATERPILLAR MEXICO S.A. DE C.V.—See Caterpillar Inc.; *U.S. Public*, pg. 316
CATERPILLAR MHI MARKETING LTD.—See Caterpillar Inc.; *U.S. Public*, pg. 317
CATERPILLAR OF AUSTRALIA LTD.—See Caterpillar Inc.; *U.S. Public*, pg. 316
CATERPILLAR OF CANADA—See Caterpillar Inc.; *U.S. Public*, pg. 316
CATERPILLAR OF DELAWARE, INC.—See Caterpillar Inc.; *U.S. Public*, pg. 316
CATERPILLAR OVERSEAS CREDIT CORPORATION S.A.—See Caterpillar Inc.; *U.S. Public*, pg. 316
CATERPILLAR PAVING PRODUCTS INC.—See Caterpillar Inc.; *U.S. Public*, pg. 316
CATERPILLAR RISK MANAGEMENT SERVICES LTD.—See Caterpillar Inc.; *U.S. Public*, pg. 316
CATERPILLAR SECURITIES INC.—See Caterpillar Inc.; *U.S. Public*, pg. 316
CATERPILLAR SERVICES LIMITED—See Caterpillar Inc.; *U.S. Public*, pg. 316
CATERPILLAR SHANGHAI ENGINE COMPANY, LTD.—See Caterpillar Inc.; *U.S. Public*, pg. 316
CATERPILLAR (U.K.) LIMITED—See Caterpillar Inc.; *U.S. Public*, pg. 317
CATERPILLAR WORLD TRADING CORPORATION—See Caterpillar Inc.; *U.S. Public*, pg. 316
CATERPILLAR XUZHOU LTD.—See Caterpillar Inc.; *U.S. Public*, pg. 316
CATHAY FINANCE INTERNATIONAL (HOLDINGS) LIMITED—See The International Commercial Bank of China; *Int'l*, pg. 684
CATHERINES STORES CORPORATION; *U.S. Public*, pg. 317
CATHODIC PROTECTION SERVICES COMPANY—See Michael Curran & Associates; *U.S. Private*, pg. 297
CATHODIC PROTECTION SERVICES COMPANY—See Offshore Logistics, Inc.; *U.S. Public*, pg. 1213
CATHOLIC DIGEST; *U.S. Private*, pg. 220
CATHOLIC ORDER OF FORESTERS; *U.S. Private*, pg. 220
CATHOLIC RELIEF SERVICES; *U.S. Private*, pg. 220
THE CATO CORPORATION; *U.S. Public*, pg. 318
CATO OIL & GREASE CO.—See Petroleos de Venezuela S.A.; *Int'l*, pg. 1045
CATSKILL SAVINGS BANK; *U.S. Public*, pg. 318
CATTLE FEEDING DIV.—See Continental Grain Company; *U.S. Private*, pg. 268
CATTLEMAN'S, INC.; *U.S. Public*, pg. 318
CAUDAL S.A. DE SEGUROS Y REASEGUROS—See Zurich Insurance Company; *Int'l*, pg. 1531
CAUSA PUBLICIDAD—See Leo Burnett Company, Inc.; *U.S. Private*, pg. 184
JIM CAUSLEY PONTIAC GMC INC.; *U.S. Private*, pg. 220
CAVALIER ACCEPTANCE CORPORATION—See Cavalier Homes, Inc.; *U.S. Public*, pg. 318
CAVALIER CORPORATION; *U.S. Private*, pg. 220
CAVALIER HOMES, INC.; *U.S. Public*, pg. 318
CAVALIER HOTEL CORP.—See Kyanite Mining Corporation; *U.S. Private*, pg. 638
CAVALIER INDUSTRIES, INC.—See Cavalier Homes, Inc.; *U.S. Public*, pg. 318
CAVALIER INSURANCE AGENCY, INC.—See Cavalier Homes, Inc.; *U.S. Public*, pg. 318
CAVALIER MANUFACTURING, INC.—See Cavalier Homes, Inc.; *U.S. Public*, pg. 318
CAVCO INDUSTRIES, INC.—See Centex Corporation; *U.S. Public*, pg. 323
CAVE CITY CHEVROLET—See Don Massey Cadillac Inc.; *U.S. Private*, pg. 712
CAVENHAM FOREST INDUSTRIES INC.—See Hanson PLC; *Int'l*, pg. 593
CAVEXSA—See Magellan International Trading; *U.S. Private*, pg. 694
CAVEXSA NORTH AMERICA—See Magellan International Trading; *U.S. Private*, pg. 694
CAVIS S.R.L.—See Fiat Auto SpA; *Int'l*, pg. 482
CAVIS S.R.L.—See Labinal SA; *Int'l*, pg. 785
CAXTON DISTRIBUTORS LTD.—See KPN Koninklyke PTT Nederland NV; *Int'l*, pg. 720
CAXTON FORESTS LIMITED—See International Paper Company; *U.S. Public*, pg. 905
THE CAXTON GROUP OF COMPANIES—See International Paper Company; *U.S. Public*, pg. 905
CAXTON PAPER LIMITED—See International Paper Company; *U.S. Public*, pg. 905
THE CAXTON PRINTERS LTD.; *U.S. Private*, pg. 220
CAXTON PRODUCTS LIMITED—See International Paper Company; *U.S. Public*, pg. 905
CAXTON SERVICES COMPANY PTE. LTD.—See KPN Koninklyke PTT Nederland NV; *Int'l*, pg. 720
CAYE STEEL & WIRE CO.—See W.C. Caye & Company, Inc.; *U.S. Private*, pg. 220
W.C. CAYE & CO.—See W.C. Caye & Company, Inc.; *U.S. Private*, pg. 220
W.C. CAYE & COMPANY, INC.; *U.S. Private*, pg. 220
W.C. CAYE & CO.—See W.C. Caye & Company, Inc.; *U.S. Private*, pg. 220
CAYELI BAKIR ISLETMELERI—See Metallgesellschaft AG; *Int'l*, pg. 862
CAYMADRID INTERNATIONAL LIMITED—See Caja de Madrid Group; *Int'l*, pg. 252
CBC BANCORP, LTD.—See Banco Popular de Puerto Rico; *U.S. Public*, pg. 176
CBM AMERICA CORP.—See CBM America Corp.; *U.S. Private*, pg. 192
CE DE CANDY, INC.; *U.S. Private*, pg. 220
CEAG SICHERHEITSTECHNIK GMBH—See Cooper Industries, Inc.; *U.S. Public*, pg. 444
CEALCO C.A.—See FMC Corporation; *U.S. Public*, pg. 606
CEATRON TECHNOLOGY LTD.—See Auto-trol Technology Corporation; *U.S. Public*, pg. 148
CEBAL ENTEC S.A.—See Pechiney S.A.; *Int'l*, pg. 1030
CEBAL ITALIANA—See Pechiney S.A.; *Int'l*, pg. 1030
CEBAL PRINTAL OY—See Pechiney S.A.; *Int'l*, pg. 1030
CEBAL S.A.—See Pechiney S.A.; *Int'l*, pg. 1028
CEBAL VERPACKUNGEN GMBH & CO. KG—See Pechiney S.A.; *Int'l*, pg. 1030
CEBAS B.V.—See Royal Begemann Group; *Int'l*, pg. 1133
CEBAS IMMOBILIENENTWICKLUNGS GESELLSCHAFT MBH—See Royal Begemann Group; *Int'l*, pg. 1134
CEBCOR (CONSOLIDATED EMPLOYMENT BENEFITS CORP.); *U.S. Private*, pg. 220
S.A. CEBELOR—See Axel Johnson AB; *Int'l*, pg. 710
CEBRACE—See Saint-Gobain; *Int'l*, pg. 1177
CEBRACE CRISTAL PLANO LTDA.—See Pilkington Plc; *Int'l*, pg. 1057
CEBRIS S.P.A.—See Bristol-Myers Squibb Company; *U.S. Public*, pg. 256
CEBU MINING OPERATION—See Atlas Consolidated Mining & Development Corporation; *Int'l*, pg. 95
CECA S.A.—See Elf Aquitane; *Int'l*, pg. 445
CECO BUILDING SYSTEMS; *U.S. Private*, pg. 221
CECO BUILDING SYSTEMS-EASTERN REGION—See Ceco Building Systems; *U.S. Private*, pg. 221
CECO BUILDING SYSTEMS-MIDWESTERN REGION—See Ceco Building Systems; *U.S. Private*, pg. 221
CECO BUILDING SYSTEMS-SOUTHERN REGION—See Ceco Building Systems; *U.S. Private*, pg. 221
CECO CONCRETE CONSTRUCTION LLC—See Pettibone Corporation; *U.S. Private*, pg. 859
CECO DOOR PRODUCTS—See United Dominion Industries, Ltd.; *U.S. Public*, pg. 1676
CECOS INTERNATIONAL, INC.—See Browning-Ferris Industries, Inc.; *U.S. Public*, pg. 264
CEDAR CREEK PROPERTIES INC.—See Ash Grove Cement Company; *U.S. Private*, pg. 88
CEDAR CREEK REALTY CO., INC.—See Ash Grove Cement Company; *U.S. Private*, pg. 88
CEDAR CREST—See Paragon Health Network, Inc.; *U.S. Public*, pg. 1256
CEDAR FAIR, L.P.; *U.S. Public*, pg. 319
CEDAR FARMS COMPANY, INC.; *U.S. Private*, pg. 221
CEDAR HEIGHTS CLAY—See Resco Products, Inc.; *U.S. Private*, pg. 924
CEDAR POINT—See Cedar Fair, L.P.; *U.S. Public*, pg. 319
THE CEDAR POINT BRIDGE CO.—See Cedar Fair, L.P.; *U.S. Public*, pg. 319
THE CEDAR POINT TRANSPORTATION CO.—See Cedar Fair, L.P.; *U.S. Public*, pg. 319
CEDARAPIDS, INC.—See Raytheon Company; *U.S. Public*, pg. 1365
THE CEDARS—See Paragon Health Network, Inc.; *U.S. Public*, pg. 1256
CEDARS MEDICAL CENTER VICTORIA PAVILLION—See Columbia/HCA Healthcare Corporation; *U.S. Public*, pg. 404
CEDARTONE SPECIALTIES—See E.R. Probyn Ltd.; *Int'l*, pg. 1071
THE CEDARWOOD CONSTRUCTION COMPANY; *U.S. Private*, pg. 221
G CEDERHOLMS VERKSTAD AB—See Charter plc; *Int'l*, pg. 281
CEDERROTH INTERNATIONAL AB—See Alberto-Culver Company; *U.S. Public*, pg. 38
CEDEST CIMENTS—See Lafarge S.A.; *Int'l*, pg. 788
CEDIGRAPH S.A.—See Bobst S.A.; *Int'l*, pg. 198
CEDIMAT S.A.—See La Meridionale des Bois et Materiaux; *Int'l*, pg. 784
CEDOSA—See Thomson S.A.; *Int'l*, pg. 1384
CEDRALA TRANSPORT LIMITED—See The East Asiatic Company Ltd. A/S; *Int'l*, pg. 431
CEFEMO—See Thomson S.A.; *Int'l*, pg. 1381
CEGEDUR PECHINEY—See Pechiney S.A.; *Int'l*, pg. 1028
CEGELEC—See Alcatel Alsthom Compagnie Generale D'Electricite; *Int'l*, pg. 52
CEGELEC AEG AUTOMATION SYSTEMS CORP.—See Alcatel Alsthom Compagnie Generale D'Electricite; *Int'l*, pg. 52
CEGELEC DE MEXICO—See Alcatel Alsthom Compagnie Generale D'Electricite; *Int'l*, pg. 53
CEGELEC ENGENHARIA S.A.—See Alcatel Alsthom Compagnie Generale D'Electricite; *Int'l*, pg. 53
CEGELEC ENTREPRISES, INC.—See Alcatel Alsthom Compagnie Generale D'Electricite; *Int'l*, pg. 53
CEGELEC GMBH—See Alcatel Alsthom Compagnie Generale D'Electricite; *Int'l*, pg. 53
CEGELEC (M) SDN BHD—See Alcatel Alsthom Compagnie Generale D'Electricite; *Int'l*, pg. 53
CEGRAM S.A.—See Pechiney S.A.; *Int'l*, pg. 1030
CEILCOTE COMPANY—See Viag AG; *Int'l*, pg. 1465
CEILCOTE KORROSIONSTECHNIK G.M.B.H.—See Novartis AG; *Int'l*, pg. 975
CEILING & PARTITIONS, INC.; *U.S. Private*, pg. 221
CEITRONICS, INC.—See Synergism, Inc.; *U.S. Private*, pg. 1060
CEKAN/CDT—See Cable Design Technologies Corporation; *U.S. Public*, pg. 287
CELANESE CANADA, INC.—See Hoechst Aktiengesellschaft; *Int'l*, pg. 625
CELANESE CELLULOSICS—See Hoechst Aktiengesellschaft; *Int'l*, pg. 625
CELANESE INC.—See Hoechst Aktiengesellschaft; *Int'l*, pg. 624
CELBI SA—See Stora Kopparbergs Bergslags AB; *Int'l*, pg. 1303
CELEBRATION ARTS GROUP LIMITED—See American Greetings Corporation; *U.S. Public*, pg. 78
CELEBRITY CRUISES, INC.—See Royal Caribbean Cruises Ltd.; *U.S. Public*, pg. 1410
CELEBRITY INCORPORATED; *U.S. Public*, pg. 319
CELEGEC AUTOMATION—See Alcatel Alsthom Compagnie Generale D'Electricite; *Int'l*, pg. 53
CELEGEC AUTOMATION PROJECTS INC.—See Alcatel Alsthom Compagnie Generale D'Electricite; *Int'l*, pg. 53
CELENTANO BROS. INC.; *U.S. Private*, pg. 221
CELERITEK, INC.; *U.S. Public*, pg. 319
CELERON CORPORATION—See The Goodyear Tire & Rubber Company; *U.S. Public*, pg. 753
CELESTIAL BEVERAGES, INC.—See Celestial Seasonings; *U.S. Public*, pg. 320
CELESTIAL SEASONINGS; *U.S. Public*, pg. 319
CELFORTEC INC.—See Jannock Limited; *Int'l*, pg. 698
CELIKORD A.S.—See Pirelli S.p.A.; *Int'l*, pg. 1059
CELITE CORPORATION—See Alleghany Corporation; *U.S. Public*, pg. 42
CELIV—See Lagardere Groupe; *Int'l*, pg. 792
CELLA'S CONFECTIONS, INC.—See Tootsie Roll Industries, Inc.; *U.S. Public*, pg. 1621
CELLATEX—See Rhone-Poulenc S.A.; *Int'l*, pg. 1109
CELLCOR—See Cytogen Corporation; *U.S. Public*, pg. 471
AB CELLECO—See Tetra Laval Group; *Int'l*, pg. 1378
CELLECO HEDEMORA—See Tetra Laval Group; *Int'l*, pg. 1378
CELLEX MANUFACTURING, INC.—See Thermon Manufacturing Company; *U.S. Private*, pg. 1080
CELLNET SOLUTIONS LIMITED—See British Telecommunications plc; *Int'l*, pg. 222
CELLO BAG COMPANY, INC.—See Amcor Limited; *Int'l*, pg. 72
CELLOGLAS IRELAND LTD.—See Alusuisse-Lonza Holding Ltd.; *Int'l*, pg. 68
CELLOGLAS LIMITED—See Alusuisse-Lonza Holding Ltd.; *Int'l*, pg. 69
CELLPHONE SALES LTD.—See Telefonaktiebolaget LM Ericsson; *Int'l*, pg. 1365
CELLPRO, INCORPORATED; *U.S. Public*, pg. 320
CELLULAR ONE ALBANY TELEPHONE COMPANY—See SBC Communications Inc.; *U.S. Public*, pg. 1415
CELLULAR ONE BUFFALO—See SBC Communications Inc.; *U.S. Public*, pg. 1415
CELLULAR ONE GENESEE TELEPHONE COMPANY—See SBC Communications Inc.; *U.S. Public*, pg. 1415
CELLULARVISION CANADA LTD.—See WIC Western International Communications Ltd.; *Int'l*, pg. 1482
CELNOR, INC.—See Motorola, Inc.; *U.S. Public*, pg. 1137
CELOTEX CORPORATION; *U.S. Private*, pg. 221
CELSIUS AB; *Int'l*, pg. 276
CELSIUS ENERGY COMPANY—See Questar Corporation; *U.S. Public*, pg. 1352
AB CELSIUS FINANCE—See Celsius AB; *Int'l*, pg. 276
CELSIUS INC.—See Celsius AB; *Int'l*, pg. 278
CELSIUS INDUSTRIES CORP.—See Celsius AB; *Int'l*, pg. 276
CELSIUS INDUSTRIES CORPORATION EUROPEAN AFFAIRS OFFICE—See Celsius AB; *Int'l*, pg. 278
CELSIUS INFORMATION SYSTEM AB—See Celsius AB; *Int'l*, pg. 276
CELSIUS INVEST AB—See Celsius AB; *Int'l*, pg. 276
CELSIUS MATERIALTEKNIK AB—See Celsius AB; *Int'l*, pg. 276
CELSIUS MATERIALTEKNIK KARLSKOGA AB—See Celsius AB; *Int'l*, pg. 276
CELSIUSTECH AB—See Celsius AB; *Int'l*, pg. 276
CELSIUSTECH AUSTRALIA PTY LTD—See Celsius AB; *Int'l*, pg. 278
CELSIUSTECH ELECTRONICS AB—See Celsius AB; *Int'l*, pg. 276
CELSIUSTECH INC.—See Celsius AB; *Int'l*, pg. 278
CELSIUSTECH IT AB—See Celsius AB; *Int'l*, pg. 277
CELSIUSTECH NEW ZEALAND—See Celsius AB; *Int'l*, pg. 278
CELSIUSTECH SYSTEMS AB—See Celsius AB; *Int'l*, pg. 277
CELSIUSTECH SYSTEMS AB FAR EAST BRANCH—See Celsius AB; *Int'l*, pg. 278
CELTE S.P.A.—See Telefonaktiebolaget LM Ericsson; *Int'l*, pg. 1365
CELTIC INTERNATIONAL—See Eureko B.V.; *Int'l*, pg. 464
CELTITE INC.—See Burmah Castrol plc; *Int'l*, pg. 234

CELTONA B.V.—See Fort James Corporation; *U.S. Public*, pg. 672
CELULOSA Y DERIVADOS, S.A. DE C.V.—See CYDSA S.A.; *Int'l*, pg. 246
CELULOSAS DE ASTURIAS—See Groupe Saint Louis; *Int'l*, pg. 567
CEMAC COMMERCIAL INTERIORS LTD.—See International Paper Company; *U.S. Public*, pg. 905
CEMENLAND S.A.—See Lafarge S.A.; *Int'l*, pg. 790
CEMENT BOHEMIA PRAHA A.S.—See Heidelberger Zement A.G.; *Int'l*, pg. 605
CEMENT EQUIPMENT COMPANY S.A.—See FLS Industries A/S; *Int'l*, pg. 475
CEMENT TRANSIT CO.—See Medusa Corporation; *U.S. Public*, pg. 1084
CEMENTA AB—See Scancem AB; *Int'l*, pg. 1198
CEMENTA AB (DEGERHAMN)—See Scancem AB; *Int'l*, pg. 1199
CEMENTA AB (MALMO)—See Scancem AB; *Int'l*, pg. 1198
CEMENTA AB (SKOVDE)—See Scancem AB; *Int'l*, pg. 1199
CEMENTA AB (SLITE)—See Scancem AB; *Int'l*, pg. 1199
CEMENTA AB (STOCKHOLM)—See Scancem AB; *Int'l*, pg. 1198
CEMENTARNY A VAPENKY MOKRA—See Heidelberger Zement A.G.; *Int'l*, pg. 605
CEMENTATION MINING LIMITED—See Kvaerner a.s.a.; *Int'l*, pg. 772
CEMENTERIA DI MERONE S.P.A.—See Holderbank Financiere Glaris Ltd.; *Int'l*, pg. 629
CEMENTIA ENGINEERING & CONSULTING LTD.—See Lafarge S.A.; *Int'l*, pg. 791
CEMENTIA HOLDING AG—See Lafarge S.A.; *Int'l*, pg. 790
CEMENTIA PLANUNGS UND BERATUNGS AG—See Lafarge S.A.; *Int'l*, pg. 790
CEMENTIA TRADING—See Lafarge S.A.; *Int'l*, pg. 790
CEMENTO POLPAICO S.A.—See Holderbank Financiere Glaris Ltd.; *Int'l*, pg. 629
CEMENTOS ASLAND S.A.—See Lafarge S.A.; *Int'l*, pg. 790
CEMENTOS BOYACA S.A.—See Holderbank Financiere Glaris Ltd.; *Int'l*, pg. 629
CEMENTOS CARIBE C.A.—See Holderbank Financiere Glaris Ltd.; *Int'l*, pg. 629
CEMENTOS HISPANIA S.A.—See Dyckerhoff AG; *Int'l*, pg. 423
CEMENTOS MARROQUIES—See Lafarge S.A.; *Int'l*, pg. 790
CEMENTOS NOLINS FINANCERA MINERA—See Ciments Francais; *Int'l*, pg. 292
CEMENTOS PEYLAND S.A.—See Lafarge S.A.; *Int'l*, pg. 790
CEMENTOS TANGER—See Lafarge S.A.; *Int'l*, pg. 791
CEMENTOWNIA GORAZDZE S.A.—See Heidelberger Zement A.G.; *Int'l*, pg. 605
CEMENTOWNIA STRZELCE OPOLSKIE S.A.—See Heidelberger Zement A.G.; *Int'l*, pg. 605
CEMEX, S.A. DE C.V.; *Int'l*, pg. 278
CEMINDIA COMPANY LIMITED—See Kvaerner a.s.a.; *Int'l*, pg. 774
CEMIT DIRECT MEDIA S.P.A.—See Arnoldo Mondadori Editore S.p.A.; *Int'l*, pg. 888
CEMLAND INVESTMENT AG—See Lafarge S.A.; *Int'l*, pg. 790
CEMSTO—See Vendex International N.V.; *Int'l*, pg. 1463
CEMSTOBEL—See Vendex International N.V.; *Int'l*, pg. 1463
CENCAR LIMITED—See Carrefour; *Int'l*, pg. 273
CENDANT CORPORATION; *U.S. Public*, pg. 320
CENEX, INC.; *U.S. Private*, pg. 221
CENEX/LAND O'LAKES, INC.—See CENEX, Inc.; *U.S. Private*, pg. 222
CENGO CONSTRUCTION CORPORATION—See Golub Corporation; *U.S. Private*, pg. 463
CENTAINE INVESTMENTS LTD.—See Pasco Corporation; *Int'l*, pg. 1024
CENTAL CAROLINA BANK & TRUST COMPANY—See CCB Financial Corporation; *U.S. Public*, pg. 276
CENTEC ROLL CORPORATION—See Park Corp.; *U.S. Private*, pg. 839
CENTENARIO S.A.—See Nestle S.A.; *Int'l*, pg. 919
CENTENNIAL CELLULAR CORP.—See Century Communications Corp.; *U.S. Public*, pg. 329
CENTENNIAL ENERGY HOLDINGS, INC.—See MDU Resources Group, Inc.; *U.S. Public*, pg. 1025
CENTENNIAL FEDERAL SAVINGS BANK F.S.B.—See Zions Bancorporation; *U.S. Public*, pg. 1793
CENTENNIAL HOMES INC.—See Weyerhaeuser Company; *U.S. Public*, pg. 1764
CENTENNIAL INSURANCE CO.—See Atlantic Mutual Companies; *U.S. Private*, pg. 95
CENTENNIAL TECHNOLOGIES, INC.; *U.S. Public*, pg. 322
CENTENNIAL TRANSPORTATION INDUSTRIES, L.P.—See Union City Body Company, L.P.; *U.S. Private*, pg. 1119
CENTEON, L.L.C.—See Hoechst Aktiengesellschaft; *Int'l*, pg. 626
CENTEON, L.L.C.—See Rhone-Poulenc S.A.; *Int'l*, pg. 1110
CENTER CAFE—See Ark Restaurants Corp.; *U.S. Public*, pg. 130
CENTER FIXTURE OPERATIONS—See Hallmark Cards, Inc.; *U.S. Private*, pg. 496
CENTER FOR COMPREHENSIVE EXAMINATIONS—See Vencor, Inc.; *U.S. Public*, pg. 1715
CENTER LABORATORIES, INC.—See Heska Corporation; *U.S. Public*, pg. 813
CENTER LINE—See Crane Co.; *U.S. Public*, pg. 457
CENTER PARCS N.V.—See Scottish & Newcastle plc; *Int'l*, pg. 1212
CENTER PARTNERS MANAGEMENT LLC; *U.S. Private*, pg. 222
CENTEX AMERICAN GYPSUM CO.—See Centex Corporation; *U.S. Public*, pg. 322
CENTEX CONSTRUCTION COMPANY—See Centex Corporation; *U.S. Public*, pg. 322

CENTEX CONSTRUCTION GROUP, INC.—See Centex Corporation; *U.S. Public*, pg. 322
CENTEX CONSTRUCTION PRODUCTS, INC.—See Centex Corporation; *U.S. Public*, pg. 322
CENTEX CORPORATION; *U.S. Public*, pg. 322
CENTEX FORCUM-LANNOM, INC.—See Centex Corporation; *U.S. Public*, pg. 322
CENTEX MATERIALS, INC.—See Centex Corporation; *U.S. Public*, pg. 322
CENTEX REAL ESTATE CORP./CENTEX HOMES—See Centex Corporation; *U.S. Public*, pg. 323
CENTEX-RODGERS CONSTRUCTION COMPANY—See Centex Corporation; *U.S. Public*, pg. 322
CENTEX-ROONEY CONSTRUCTION CO., INC.—See Centex Corporation; *U.S. Public*, pg. 322
CENTIGRAM COMMUNICATIONS CORPORATION; *U.S. Public*, pg. 323
CENTIMARK CORPORATION; *U.S. Private*, pg. 222
CENTIN CORPORATION—See Irex Corporation; *U.S. Public*, pg. 913
CENTOCOR B.V.—See Centocor, Inc.; *U.S. Public*, pg. 323
CENTOCOR DIAGNOSTICS DIV.—See Centocor, Inc.; *U.S. Public*, pg. 323
CENTOCOR, INC.; *U.S. Public*, pg. 323
CENTOCOR PARTNERS III, L.P.—See Centocor, Inc.; *U.S. Public*, pg. 323
CENTOCOR PHARMACEUTICAL DIVISION—See Centocor, Inc.; *U.S. Public*, pg. 323
CENTRA GAS ALBERTA INC.—See Westcoast Energy Inc.; *Int'l*, pg. 1492
CENTRA GAS BRITISH COLUMBIA INC.—See Westcoast Energy Inc.; *Int'l*, pg. 1492
CENTRA GAS INC.—See Westcoast Energy Inc.; *Int'l*, pg. 1492
CENTRA GAS MANITOBA INC.—See Westcoast Energy Inc.; *Int'l*, pg. 1492
CENTRA GAS ONTARIO INC.—See Westcoast Energy Inc.; *Int'l*, pg. 1492
CENTRA 2000, INC.—See Auto-trol Technology Corporation; *U.S. Public*, pg. 148
CENTRACHIM SARL—See Novartis AG; *Int'l*, pg. 975
CENTRAL—See Accor S.A.; *Int'l*, pg. 21
CENTRAL ADVERTISING AGENCY; *U.S. Private*, pg. 222
CENTRAL ALL PRO—See Republic Automotive Parts, Inc.; *U.S. Public*, pg. 1377
CENTRAL ALLIED ENTERPRISES; *U.S. Private*, pg. 222
CENTRAL AND SOUTH WEST CORPORATION; *U.S. Public*, pg. 324
CENTRAL AND SOUTH WEST SERVICES, INC.—See Central and South West Corporation; *U.S. Public*, pg. 324
CENTRAL ARIZONA DETENTION CENTER—See Corrections Corporation of America; *U.S. Public*, pg. 450
CENTRAL AUTOMOTIVE PRODUCTS, LTD.; *Int'l*, pg. 278
CENTRAL BANK—See Firstbank of Illinois Co.; *U.S. Public*, pg. 643
CENTRAL BANK, N.A.—See Compass Bancshares, Inc.; *U.S. Public*, pg. 418
CENTRAL BANK OF MONROE—See First Commerce Corporation; *U.S. Public*, pg. 629
CENTRAL BEAUTY EQUIPMENT—See Smith Investment Company; *U.S. Public*, pg. 1008
CENTRAL BLOCKS LIMITED—See RMC Group p.l.c.; *Int'l*, pg. 1079
CENTRAL CALIFORNIA TRACTION CO.—See Union Pacific Corporation; *U.S. Public*, pg. 1668
CENTRAL CAROLINA BANK—See CCB Financial Corporation; *U.S. Public*, pg. 276
CENTRAL CASTINGS CORPORATION—See Central Sprinkler Corporation; *U.S. Public*, pg. 327
CENTRAL COALFIELDS LIMITED—See Coal India Limited; *Int'l*, pg. 298
CENTRAL COCA-COLA BOTTLING COMPANY, INC.; *U.S. Private*, pg. 222
CENTRAL COMMISSARY, INC.—See Cornucopia, Inc.; *U.S. Private*, pg. 276
CENTRAL CPVC CORPORATION—See Central Sprinkler Corporation; *U.S. Public*, pg. 327
CENTRAL DATA CORPORATION; *U.S. Private*, pg. 222
CENTRAL DE CERVEJAS-BELAS FACTORY—See Central de Cervejas, S.A.; *Int'l*, pg. 279
CENTRAL DE CERVEJAS-LORETO FACTORY—See Central de Cervejas, S.A.; *Int'l*, pg. 279
CENTRAL DE CERVEJAS-PORTO SUPPLY CENTER—See Central de Cervejas, S.A.; *Int'l*, pg. 279
CENTRAL DE CERVEJAS-PRIOR VELHO SUPPLY CENTER—See Central de Cervejas, S.A.; *Int'l*, pg. 279
CENTRAL DE CERVEJAS, S.A.; *Int'l*, pg. 279
CENTRAL DE CERVEJAS-VIALONGA FACTORY—See Central de Cervejas, S.A.; *Int'l*, pg. 279
CENTRAL DE INDUSTRIAS, S.A.—See Lear Corporation; *U.S. Public*, pg. 982
CENTRAL DISTRIBUTORS, INC.—See Golub Corporation; *U.S. Private*, pg. 463
CENTRAL DUPAGE HEALTH SYSTEM; *U.S. Private*, pg. 223
CENTRAL DUPAGE HOSPITAL ASSOCIATION—See Central DuPage Health System; *U.S. Private*, pg. 223
CENTRAL-EUROPEAN INTERNATIONAL BANK LTD. (CIB)—See Bayerische Vereinsbank Group; *Int'l*, pg. 181
CENTRAL-EUROPEAN INTERNATIONAL BANK LTD. (CIB)—See The Long-Term Credit Bank of Japan, Limited; *Int'l*, pg. 816
CENTRAL FLORIDA PIPELINE CORP.—See GATX Corporation; *U.S. Public*, pg. 692
CENTRAL FLORIDA PRESS L.C.—See Cadmus Communications Corporation; *U.S. Public*, pg. 291
CENTRAL FREIGHT LINES, INC.; *U.S. Private*, pg. 223
CENTRAL GOULET SUPPLY—See Granite Group Wholesale LLC; *U.S. Public*, pg. 469
CENTRAL GROCERS CO-OP; *U.S. Private*, pg. 223

CENTRAL GULF LINES, INC.—See International Shipholding Corporation; *U.S. Public*, pg. 907
CENTRAL HISPANO GENERALI, HOLDING DE ENTIDADES DE SEGUROS, S.A.—See Assicurazioni Generali S.p.A.; *Int'l*, pg. 90
CENTRAL HUDSON COGENERATION, INC.—See Central Hudson Gas & Electric Corporation; *U.S. Public*, pg. 325
CENTRAL HUDSON ENTERPRISES—See Central Hudson Gas & Electric Corporation; *U.S. Public*, pg. 325
CENTRAL HUDSON GAS & ELECTRIC CORPORATION; *U.S. Public*, pg. 324
CENTRAL HUDSON RESOURCES INC.—See Central Hudson Gas & Electric Corporation; *U.S. Public*, pg. 325
CENTRAL ILLINOIS LIGHT COMPANY—See CILCORP Inc.; *U.S. Public*, pg. 367
CENTRAL ILLINOIS PERIODICALS, INC.—See The Chas. Levy Company; *U.S. Private*, pg. 664
CENTRAL ILLINOIS STEEL COMPANY; *U.S. Private*, pg. 223
CENTRAL INSURANCE CORP. OF TALLAHASSEE—See Killearn Properties, Inc.; *U.S. Public*, pg. 956
CENTRAL JAPAN RAILWAY COMPANY; *Int'l*, pg. 279
CENTRAL KENTUCKY NEWS-JOURNAL—See Landmark Communications, Inc.; *U.S. Private*, pg. 648
CENTRAL KRANKENVERSICHERUNG AG—See AMB Aachener und Muenchener Beteiligungs-AG; *Int'l*, pg. 15
CENTRAL LEWMAR; *U.S. Private*, pg. 223
CENTRAL LEWMAR INTERNATIONAL—See Central Lewmar; *U.S. Private*, pg. 223
CENTRAL LINCOLN PEOPLE'S UTILITY DISTRICT; *U.S. Private*, pg. 223
CENTRAL LOUISIANA ELECTRIC COMPANY, INC.; *U.S. Public*, pg. 325
CENTRAL MAINE NEWSPAPERS—See Guy Gannett Communications; *U.S. Private*, pg. 439
CENTRAL MAINE POWER COMPANY; *U.S. Public*, pg. 325
CENTRAL MARYLAND SURGERY CENTER—See Healthsouth Corporation; *U.S. Public*, pg. 803
CENTRAL MINE PLANNING & DESIGN INSTITUTE LIMITED—See Coal India Limited; *Int'l*, pg. 298
CENTRAL MUTUAL INSURANCE CO.; *U.S. Private*, pg. 223
CENTRAL NATIONAL BANK OF MATTOON—See Firstbank of Illinois Co.; *U.S. Public*, pg. 643
CENTRAL NATIONAL ESPANOLA S.A.—See Norske Skogindustrier A.S; *Int'l*, pg. 966
CENTRAL NATIONAL-GOTTESMAN INC.; *U.S. Private*, pg. 224
CENTRAL NATIONAL-GOTTESMAN INC.—See Central National-Gottesman Inc.; *U.S. Private*, pg. 224
THE CENTRAL NATIONAL LIFE INSURANCE CO. OF OMAHA, INC.—See Beneficial Corporation; *U.S. Public*, pg. 211
CENTRAL NEW YORK BOTTLE CO.—See Philip Morris Companies Inc.; *U.S. Public*, pg. 1289
CENTRAL NEWSPAPERS, INC.; *U.S. Public*, pg. 326
CENTRAL NUCLEAR VANDELLOS II A.I.E.—See SEPI; *Int'l*, pg. 1224
CENTRAL OF GEORGIA RAILROAD COMPANY—See Norfolk Southern Corporation; *U.S. Public*, pg. 1191
CENTRAL OHIO COAL CO.—See American Electric Power Company, Inc.; *U.S. Public*, pg. 73
CENTRAL OPERATING CO.—See American Electric Power Company, Inc.; *U.S. Public*, pg. 72
CENTRAL PACIFIC BANK—See CPB Inc.; *U.S. Public*, pg. 283
CENTRAL PARK SOUTH, INC.—See Lennar Corporation; *U.S. Public*, pg. 987
CENTRAL PARKING CORP.; *U.S. Public*, pg. 326
CENTRAL PENNSYLVANIA INVESTMENT CO.—See Omega Financial Corporation; *U.S. Public*, pg. 1222
CENTRAL PENNSYLVANIA LIFE INSURANCE CO.—See Omega Financial Corporation; *U.S. Public*, pg. 1222
CENTRAL PLAINS STEEL CO.—See Owen Industries, Inc.; *U.S. Private*, pg. 824
CENTRAL PLANTS, INC.—See Pacific Enterprises; *U.S. Public*, pg. 1249
CENTRAL POINT LUMBER CO.—See WTD Industries, Inc.; *U.S. Public*, pg. 1729
CENTRAL POWER AND LIGHT COMPANY—See Central and South West Corporation; *U.S. Public*, pg. 324
THE CENTRAL PRESS OF MIAMI, INC.—See Wallace Computer Services, Inc.; *U.S. Public*, pg. 1735
CENTRAL PRODUCTS COMPANY, INC.—See Lynch Corporation; *U.S. Public*, pg. 1022
CENTRAL PROPERTY & CASUALTY INSURANCE COMPANY—See Preferred Risk Mutual Insurance; *U.S. Private*, pg. 880
CENTRAL REGION SALES—See Televideo, Inc.; *U.S. Public*, pg. 1572
CENTRAL REGISTRATION HONG KONG LTD.—See HSBC Holdings plc; *Int'l*, pg. 581
CENTRAL RESEARCH LABORATORIES—See Dover Corporation; *U.S. Public*, pg. 521
CENTRAL RESERVE CORPORATION; *U.S. Public*, pg. 326
CENTRAL RESERVE LIFE OF NORTH AMERICA INSURANCE CO.—See Central Reserve Life Corporation; *U.S. Public*, pg. 326
CENTRAL RUBBER COMPANY—See Woodhead Industries, Inc.; *U.S. Public*, pg. 1776
P.T. CENTRAL SARI FINANCE CORPORATION (CSF)—See The Long-Term Credit Bank of Japan, Limited; *Int'l*, pg. 816
CENTRAL SECURITIES CORPORATION; *U.S. Public*, pg. 326
CENTRAL SECURITY GUARDS, INC.—See Tyco International Ltd.; *U.S. Public*, pg. 1649
CENTRAL SERVICE GROUP BV—See N.V. Koninklijke KNP BT; *Int'l*, pg. 756

CENTRAL/SHIPPEE, INC.; *U.S. Private*, pg. 224

CENTRAL/SOUTHERN DIVISION—See Diageo Plc; *Int'l*, pg. 412

CENTRAL SOYA COMPANY, INC.—See Compart SpA; *Int'l*, pg. 324

CENTRAL SPRAYSAFE COMPANY PTE LTD—See Central Sprinkler Corporation; *U.S. Public*, pg. 327

CENTRAL SPRINK INC.—See Central Sprinkler Corporation; *U.S. Public*, pg. 327

CENTRAL SPRINKLER COMPANY—See Central Sprinkler Corporation; *U.S. Public*, pg. 327

CENTRAL SPRINKLER CORPORATION; *U.S. Public*, pg. 327

CENTRAL STATE BANK—See Union Planters Corporation; *U.S. Public*, pg. 1669

CENTRAL STATE TELEPHONE CO.—See Telephone and Data Systems, Inc.; *U.S. Public*, pg. 1571

CENTRAL STATES CAN CO.—See Crown Cork & Seal Company, Inc.; *U.S. Public*, pg. 463

CENTRAL STATES CAN CO.-COMPOSITE OPERATIONS—See Crown Cork & Seal Company, Inc.; *U.S. Public*, pg. 463

CENTRAL STATES CAN CO. OF PUERTO RICO, INC.—See Crown Cork & Seal Company, Inc.; *U.S. Public*, pg. 463

CENTRAL STATES DIVERSIFIED, INC.; *U.S. Private*, pg. 224

CENTRAL STATES ENTERPRISES, INC.; *U.S. Private*, pg. 225

CENTRAL STATES MULTIPLEX—See Adams Investment Company; *U.S. Private*, pg. 16

CENTRAL STEEL & WIRE COMPANY; *U.S. Public*, pg. 327

CENTRAL SUPPLY CO., INC.; *U.S. Private*, pg. 225

CENTRAL TERMICA LITORAL DE ALMERIA A.I.E.—See SEPI; *Int'l*, pg. 1224

CENTRAL TRACTOR FARM & COUNTRY, INC.—See J.W. Childs Associates, L.P.; *U.S. Private*, pg. 237

CENTRAL TRANSPORT; *U.S. Private*, pg. 225

CENTRAL UNITED LIFE INSURANCE CO.; *U.S. Private*, pg. 225

CENTRAL U.S.—See Supertex, Inc.; *U.S. Public*, pg. 1540

CENTRAL VALLEY PUBLISHING; *U.S. Private*, pg. 225

CENTRAL VERMONT PUBLIC SERVICE CORPORATION; *U.S. Public*, pg. 327

CENTRAL VERMONT RAILWAY, INC.—See Canadian National Railway Company; *Int'l*, pg. 258

CENTRAL WISCONSIN DEVELOPMENT CORPORATION—See Madison Gas and Electric Company; *U.S. Public*, pg. 1033

CENTRALE DE MLOTY—See Tractebel; *Int'l*, pg. 1415

S.A. CENTRALE ELECTRIQUE DE ZEEBRUGGE—See Cockerill Sambre; *Int'l*, pg. 301

CENTRALE G—See Commerzbank AG; *Int'l*, pg. 312

CENTRALE H—See Commerzbank AG; *Int'l*, pg. 312

CENTRALEBOUW COMBINATIE B.V.—See Royal Begemann Group; *Int'l*, pg. 1133

CENTRALIA MINING COMPANY—See PacifiCorp; *U.S. Public*, pg. 1251

AB CENTRALSUG—See Celsius AB; *Int'l*, pg. 276

CENTRE COURT TRAVEL—See Western Gas Resources, Inc.; *U.S. Public*, pg. 1758

CENTRE DAILY TIMES, INC.—See Knight-Ridder, Inc.; *U.S. Public*, pg. 964

CENTRE DE COORDINATION HACHETTE DISTRIBUTION SERVICES—See Lagardere Groupe; *Int'l*, pg. 795

CENTRE DE FORMATION—See Coop Switzerland; *Int'l*, pg. 329

CENTRE DE PRODUCTION ALIMENTAIRE—See Groupe Air France; *Int'l*, pg. 560

CENTRE DE RECHERCHE DE L'INSTITUT MERIEUX—See Rhone-Poulenc S.A.; *Int'l*, pg. 1109

S.A. CENTRE D'ENFOUISSEMENT TECHNIQUE DE MONT-SAINT-GUIBERT C.E.TE.M.—See Cockerill Sambre; *Int'l*, pg. 301

CENTRE D'IMPORTATION ET DE COURTAGE ALIMENTAIRE—See IRI Istituto Ricostruzione Industriale; *Int'l*, pg. 655

CENTRE EST VITRAGE—See Saint-Gobain; *Int'l*, pg. 1172

CENTRE FOUNDRY & MACHINE CO.—See The Dyson-Kissner-Moran Corporation; *U.S. Private*, pg. 351

CENTRE INTERNATIONAL DE PAIEMENTS EUROP ASSISTANCE S.C.—See Assicurazioni Generali S.p.A.; *Int'l*, pg. 90

CENTRE INVESTMENT SERVICES LTD.—See Zurich Insurance Company; *Int'l*, pg. 1531

CENTRE LUDIC DIAGONAL—See Caixa d'Estalvis de Catalunya; *Int'l*, pg. 250

CENTRE REINSURANCE (BERMUDA) LTD.—See Zurich Insurance Company; *Int'l*, pg. 1531

CENTRE REINSURANCE COMPANY OF NEW YORK—See Zurich Insurance Company; *Int'l*, pg. 1530

CENTRE REINSURANCE INTERNATIONAL COMPANY—See Zurich Insurance Company; *Int'l*, pg. 1531

CENTRE REINSURANCE REPRESENTATIVE LIMITED—See Zurich Insurance Company; *Int'l*, pg. 1530

CENTRE SUITE HOTEL LTD.—See Confederation Life Insurance Company; *Int'l*, pg. 325

CENTREX CORPORATION; *U.S. Private*, pg. 225

CENTRIA; *U.S. Private*, pg. 225

CENTRIC CLUTCH CO.—See Zurn Industries, Inc.; *U.S. Public*, pg. 1794

CENTRICA PLC; *Int'l*, pg. 279

CENTRIFUGAL & MECHANICAL INDUSTRIES—See Elgin National Industries, Inc.; *U.S. Private*, pg. 370

CENTRIFUGAL SERVICES—See Elgin National Industries, Inc.; *U.S. Private*, pg. 370

CENTRILIFT—See Baker Hughes Incorporated; *U.S. Public*, pg. 167

CENTRIS GROUP INC.; *U.S. Public*, pg. 328

CENTRO DE IDIOMAS BERLITZ DE VENEZUELA—See Berlitz International, Inc.; *U.S. Public*, pg. 222

CENTRO DE INFORMACION Y SERVICIOS DEL MERCADO INMOBILIARIO, S.A.—See Caja de Madrid Group; *Int'l*, pg. 251

CENTRO DE SERVICIO DE COMPUTO, S.A. DE C.V.—See Hewlett-Packard Company; *U.S. Public*, pg. 816

CENTRO DE TRATAMEINTO DE LA DOCUMENTACION, S.A.—See Caja de Madrid Group; *Int'l*, pg. 252

CENTRO INMOBILIARIO CAJA DE MADRID, S.A.—See Caja de Madrid Group; *Int'l*, pg. 251

CENTRO INTERNATIONALE HANDELSBANK AG (CENTROBANK)—See Dresdner Bank AG; *Int'l*, pg. 420

CENTRO MEDICO DE CHEQUEOS DE MAPFRE VIDA—See Corporacion MAPFRE, Compania Internacional de Reaseguros, S.A.; *Int'l*, pg. 334

CENTRO RICERCHE FIAT—See Fiat Auto SpA; *Int'l*, pg. 480

CENTRO RICERCHE S.P.A.—See Fiat Auto SpA; *Int'l*, pg. 480

CENTRO SCIENTIFICO INTERNAZIONALE—See Waverly, Inc.; *U.S. Public*, pg. 1748

CENTRO SUPERIOR DE MARKETING, S.A.—See Caja de Madrid Group; *Int'l*, pg. 252

CENTROBANCO (PANAMA), S.A.—See Banco Central Hispanoamericano S.A.; *Int'l*, pg. 140

CENTRONIC INC.—See Morgan Crucible Co. Plc; *Int'l*, pg. 892

CENTRONIC LIMITED—See Morgan Crucible Co. Plc; *Int'l*, pg. 892

CENTRORIENTE—See Transcanada Pipelines Limited; *Int'l*, pg. 1417

CENTROS COMMERCIALES PRYCA—See Carrefour; *Int'l*, pg. 273

CENTRUM SOUTH PARTNERS—See Cigna Corp.; *U.S. Public*, pg. 361

CENTRUM WARENHAUS DRESDEN GMBH—See Karstadt Aktiengesellschaft; *Int'l*, pg. 724

CENTRUM WARENHAUS GORLITZ GMBH—See Karstadt Aktiengesellschaft; *Int'l*, pg. 724

CENTRUM WARENHAUS HALLE GMBH—See Karstadt Aktiengesellschaft; *Int'l*, pg. 724

CENTRUM WARENHAUS HOYERSWERDA GMBH—See Karstadt Aktiengesellschaft; *Int'l*, pg. 724

CENTRUM WARENHAUSER LEIPZIG GMBH—See Karstadt Aktiengesellschaft; *Int'l*, pg. 724

CENTURA BANKS, INC.; *U.S. Public*, pg. 328

CENTURY ALUMINUM COMPANY; *U.S. Public*, pg. 328

CENTURY AMERICA CORPORATION; *U.S. Private*, pg. 225

CENTURY AREA LONG LINES INC.—See Century Telephone Enterprises, Inc.; *U.S. Public*, pg. 330

CENTURY BANCSHARES, INC.; *U.S. Public*, pg. 328

CENTURY BUSINESS CREDIT CORPORATION; *U.S. Private*, pg. 225

CENTURY CELLULARNET—See Century Telephone Enterprises, Inc.; *U.S. Public*, pg. 330

CENTURY CELLULARNET FOR EAU CLAIRE MSA, INC.—See Century Telephone Enterprises, Inc.; *U.S. Public*, pg. 330

CENTURY CELLULARNET FOR LACROSSE MSA, INC.—See Century Telephone Enterprises, Inc.; *U.S. Public*, pg. 330

CENTURY CELLUNET, INC.—See Century Telephone Enterprises, Inc.; *U.S. Public*, pg. 330

CENTURY CHEMICAL WORKS SDN. BHD.—See Takeda Chemical Industries, Ltd.; *Int'l*, pg. 1350

CENTURY COMMUNICATIONS CORP.; *U.S. Public*, pg. 329

CENTURY CONCRETE, INC.—See Ash Grove Cement Company; *U.S. Private*, pg. 88

CENTURY CONTRACTORS WEST INC.—See Kenetech Corp.; *U.S. Public*, pg. 950

CENTURY CREDIT LIFE INSURANCE COMPANY—See Bancorp South Inc.; *U.S. Public*, pg. 176

CENTURY DATA SERVICES, INC.—See Century Business Credit Corporation; *U.S. Private*, pg. 226

CENTURY DATA SYSTEMS, INCORPORATED; *U.S. Private*, pg. 226

CENTURY DIALYSIS CORPORATION—See Zeneca Group Plc; *Int'l*, pg. 1525

CENTURY DOOR U.S.A. INC.—See Premdor Inc.; *Int'l*, pg. 1067

CENTURY EMPLOYERS LIFE ASSURANCE COMPANY LIMITED—See Invesco Group Asset Management Ltd.; *Int'l*, pg. 685

CENTURY ENKA LTD.—See Akzo Nobel N.V.; *Int'l*, pg. 46

CENTURY FENCE COMPANY; *U.S. Private*, pg. 226

CENTURY FURNITURE INDUSTRIES; *U.S. Private*, pg. 226

CENTURY INDEMNITY COMPANY—See Cigna Corp.; *U.S. Public*, pg. 365

CENTURY LABS, INC.—See Lady Baltimore Foods, Inc.; *U.S. Public*, pg. 975

CENTURY LEASING & LIQUIDATING, INC.—See National Presto Industries, Inc.; *U.S. Public*, pg. 1159

CENTURY LUBRICANTS CO.—See Fuchs Petrolub AG Oel + Chemie; *Int'l*, pg. 518

CENTURY MANUFACTURING—See Pentair, Inc.; *U.S. Public*, pg. 1273

CENTURY OILS (CANADA), INC.—See Fuchs Petrolub AG Oel + Chemie; *Int'l*, pg. 518

CENTURY OILS (DEUTSCHLAND) GMBH—See Fuchs Petrolub AG Oel + Chemie; *Int'l*, pg. 517

CENTURY OILS HELLAS A.B.E.E.—See Fuchs Petrolub AG Oel + Chemie; *Int'l*, pg. 517

CENTURY OILS HOLDINGS (NEDERLAND) B.V.—See Fuchs Petrolub AG Oel + Chemie; *Int'l*, pg. 517

CENTURY OILS INDUSTRIES N.V.—See Fuchs Petrolub AG Oel + Chemie; *Int'l*, pg. 517

CENTURY OILS LTD.—See Fuchs Petrolub AG Oel + Chemie; *Int'l*, pg. 518

CENTURY OILS N.V.—See Fuchs Petrolub AG Oel + Chemie; *Int'l*, pg. 517

CENTURY PRINTING & PUBLISHING CO.—See Century Telephone Enterprises, Inc.; *U.S. Public*, pg. 330

CENTURY PRODUCTS CO.; *U.S. Private*, pg. 226

CENTURY PRODUCTS CO.—See Acme Canvas Co., Inc.; *U.S. Private*, pg. 13

CENTURY PUBLISHING COMPANY; *U.S. Private*, pg. 226

CENTURY REINSURANCE COMPANY—See Cigna Corp.; *U.S. Public*, pg. 365

CENTURY SUPPLY CORP.—See Richton International Corporation; *U.S. Public*, pg. 1389

CENTURY TELEPHONE COMPANY—See Century Telephone Enterprises, Inc.; *U.S. Public*, pg. 329

CENTURY TELEPHONE CO. OF COLORADO—See Century Telephone Enterprises, Inc.; *U.S. Public*, pg. 330

CENTURY TELEPHONE CO. OF NORTHERN WISCONSIN—See Century Telephone Enterprises, Inc.; *U.S. Public*, pg. 330

CENTURY TELEPHONE ENTERPRISES, INC.; *U.S. Public*, pg. 329

CENTURY TELEPHONE OF ARKANSAS, INC.—See Century Telephone Enterprises, Inc.; *U.S. Public*, pg. 329

CENTURY TELEPHONE OF CENTRAL LOUISIANA, INC.—See Century Telephone Enterprises, Inc.; *U.S. Public*, pg. 329

CENTURY TELEPHONE OF CLAIBORNE, INC.—See Century Telephone Enterprises, Inc.; *U.S. Public*, pg. 330

CENTURY TELEPHONE OF EVANGELINE, INC.—See Century Telephone Enterprises, Inc.; *U.S. Public*, pg. 329

CENTURY TELEPHONE OF IDAHO, INC.—See Century Telephone Enterprises, Inc.; *U.S. Public*, pg. 329

CENTURY TELEPHONE OF LAKE DALLAS, INC.—See Century Telephone Enterprises, Inc.; *U.S. Public*, pg. 329

CENTURY TELEPHONE OF MICHIGAN, INC.—See Century Telephone Enterprises, Inc.; *U.S. Public*, pg. 329

CENTURY TELEPHONE OF MOUNTAIN HOME—See Century Telephone Enterprises, Inc.; *U.S. Public*, pg. 330

CENTURY TELEPHONE OF NORTH LA, INC.—See Century Telephone Enterprises, Inc.; *U.S. Public*, pg. 329

CENTURY TELEPHONE OF WISCONSIN, INC.—See Century Telephone Enterprises, Inc.; *U.S. Public*, pg. 329

CENTURY TELEPHONE, REGION IV—See Century Telephone Enterprises, Inc.; *U.S. Public*, pg. 329

CENTURY 21 AGMONT REAL ESTATE, INC.; *U.S. Private*, pg. 226

CENTURY 21 REAL ESTATE CORP.—See Cendant Corporation; *U.S. Public*, pg. 321

CEPE—See Thomson S.A.; *Int'l*, pg. 1381

CEPROVIP SPA—See Lafarge S.A.; *Int'l*, pg. 790

CERADYNE, INC; *U.S. Public*, pg. 330

CERAMATEC—See Elkem ASA; *Int'l*, pg. 448

CERAMCO LTD.—See Dentsply International Inc.; *U.S. Public*, pg. 499

CERAMCO MANUFACTURING CO.—See Dentsply International Inc.; *U.S. Public*, pg. 499

CERAMIC COOLING TOWER CO.—See Amsted Industries Incorporated; *U.S. Private*, pg. 68

CERAMICA DOLOMITE S.P.A.—See Blue Circle Industries PLC; *Int'l*, pg. 198

CERAMICA SYRE S.A.—See Lafarge S.A.; *Int'l*, pg. 790

CERAMICAS TERMICAS DE GUATEMALA S.A.—See Morgan Crucible Co. Plc; *Int'l*, pg. 894

CERAMTEC AG—See Metallgesellschaft AG; *Int'l*, pg. 860

CERAMTEC NORTH AMERICA—See Metallgesellschaft AG; *Int'l*, pg. 860

CERAMTEC NORTH AMERICA APPLICATIONS, INC.—See Metallgesellschaft AG; *Int'l*, pg. 860

CERAPASTA-PASTAS PARA CERAMICA LDA.—See Watts Blake Bearne & Co. Plc; *Int'l*, pg. 1488

CERAS ALEX S.A.—See Henkel KGaA; *Int'l*, pg. 611

CERAS JOHNSON DE PORTUGAL, LDA.—See S.C. Johnson & Son, Inc.; *U.S. Private*, pg. 592

CERAS JOHNSON LTDA.—See S.C. Johnson & Son, Inc.; *U.S. Private*, pg. 593

CERASIV GMBH—See Metallgesellschaft AG; *Int'l*, pg. 861

CERATONIA S.A.—See Hercules Incorporated; *U.S. Public*, pg. 810

CERBAY COMPANY—See Saint-Gobain; *Int'l*, pg. 1171

CERBCO, INC.; *U.S. Public*, pg. 330

CERBERUS AB—See Siemens AG; *Int'l*, pg. 1246

CERBERUS AG—See Siemens AG; *Int'l*, pg. 1246

CERBERUS A/S—See Siemens AG; *Int'l*, pg. 1246

CERBERUS AS—See Siemens AG; *Int'l*, pg. 1246

CERBERUS DATI S.P.A.—See Siemens AG; *Int'l*, pg. 1246

CERBERUS-ENGENHARIA DE SEGURANCA LDA.—See Siemens AG; *Int'l*, pg. 1246

CERBERUS FINLAND OY AB—See Siemens AG; *Int'l*, pg. 1246

CERBERUS GUINARD SA—See Siemens AG; *Int'l*, pg. 1246

CERBERUS HONG KONG LTD.—See Siemens AG; *Int'l*, pg. 1246

CERBERUS HUNGARIA KLT.—See Siemens AG; *Int'l*, pg. 1246

CERBERUS LTD.—See Siemens AG; *Int'l*, pg. 1246

CERBERUS LTDA.—See Siemens AG; *Int'l*, pg. 1246

CERBERUS POLAND S.P.Z.O.O.—See Siemens AG; *Int'l*, pg. 1246

CERBERUS PROTECCION SA—See Siemens AG; *Int'l*, pg. 1246

CERBERUS PYROTRONICS INC.—See Siemens AG; *Int'l*, pg. 1246

CERBERUS RISTOW GMBH & CO.—See Siemens AG; *Int'l*, pg. 1246

N.V. CERBERUS SA—See Siemens AG; *Int'l*, pg. 1246

CERBERUS SINGAPORE PTE. LTD.—See Siemens AG; *Int'l*, pg. 1246
CERBERUS S.P.A.—See Siemens AG; *Int'l*, pg. 1246
CERBERUS S.R.O.—See Siemens AG; *Int'l*, pg. 1246
CERBEX AG—See Siemens AG; *Int'l*, pg. 1246
AB CERBO—See Trelleborg AB; *Int'l*, pg. 1423
CERCA—See Framatome SA; *Int'l*, pg. 503
CERDEC CORPORATION—See Ciba Specialty Chemicals Holding Inc.; *Int'l*, pg. 292
CEREAL INDUSTRIES GROUP—See Associated British Foods plc; *Int'l*, pg. 92
CEREAL PARTNERS WORLDWIDE—See General Mills, Inc.; *U.S. Public*, pg. 718
CEREAL PARTNERS WORLDWIDE—See Nestle S.A.; *Int'l*, pg. 916
CEREAL WANDER—See Novartis AG; *Int'l*, pg. 975
CEREBOS AUSTRALIA LIMITED—See Suntory Ltd.; *Int'l*, pg. 1322
CEREBOS PACIFIC LTD.—See Suntory Ltd.; *Int'l*, pg. 1322
CERENEX PHARMACEUTICALS—See Glaxo Wellcome plc; *Int'l*, pg. 553
CEREOL—See Compart SpA; *Int'l*, pg. 324
CERES—See Sodexho S.A.; *Int'l*, pg. 1274
CERESIT GMBH—See Henkel KGaA; *Int'l*, pg. 609
CERESTAR HOLDING B.V.—See Compart SpA; *Int'l*, pg. 324
CERIDIAN CORPORATION; *U.S. Public*, pg. 330
CERIDIAN EMPLOYER SERVICES—See Ceridian Corporation; *U.S. Public*, pg. 331
CERIDIAN PERFORMANCE PARTNERS—See Ceridian Corporation; *U.S. Public*, pg. 331
CERNER ARABIA LTD.—See Cerner Corporation; *U.S. Public*, pg. 331
CERNER CORPORATION; *U.S. Public*, pg. 331
CERNER CORPORATION -GREAT LAKES REGION—See Cerner Corporation; *U.S. Public*, pg. 331
CERNER CORPORATION -MID-ATLANTIC REGION—See Cerner Corporation; *U.S. Public*, pg. 331
CERNER CORPORATION -MIDWEST REGION—See Cerner Corporation; *U.S. Public*, pg. 331
CERNER CORPORATION -NORTHEAST REGION—See Cerner Corporation; *U.S. Public*, pg. 331
CERNER CORPORATION -NORTHWEST REGION—See Cerner Corporation; *U.S. Public*, pg. 331
CERNER CORPORATION PTY LTD—See Cerner Corporation; *U.S. Public*, pg. 331
CERNER CORPORATION -SOUTH CENTRAL REGION—See Cerner Corporation; *U.S. Public*, pg. 331
CERNER CORPORATION -SOUTHEAST REGION—See Cerner Corporation; *U.S. Public*, pg. 331
CERNER CORPORATION -SOUTHWEST REGION—See Cerner Corporation; *U.S. Public*, pg. 331
CERNER SINGAPORE PTE LTD—See Cerner Corporation; *U.S. Public*, pg. 331
CERNER SOLUTIONS CENTER -SNI HEALTH SOLUTIONS DIV.—See Cerner Corporation; *U.S. Public*, pg. 331
THE CERPLEX GROUP, INC.; *U.S. Public*, pg. 332
CERPLEX LTD.—See The Cerplex Group, Inc.; *U.S. Public*, pg. 332
CERPLEX MASS. INC.—See The Cerplex Group, Inc.; *U.S. Public*, pg. 332
CERPROBE CORPORATION; *U.S. Public*, pg. 332
CERRAP—See GIB Group; *Int'l*, pg. 534
CERRITOS FORD, INC.; *U.S. Private*, pg. 226
CERRO MATOSO—See Royal Dutch/Shell Group of Companies; *Int'l*, pg. 1141
CERTAINTEED CORPORATION—See Saint-Gobain; *Int'l*, pg. 1170
CERTAINTEED CORPORATION FOUNDATION—See Saint-Gobain; *Int'l*, pg. 1171
CERTAINTEED FOREIGN SALES CORP.—See Saint-Gobain; *Int'l*, pg. 1171
CERTAINTEED INTERNATIONAL, INC.—See Saint-Gobain; *Int'l*, pg. 1171
CERTAINTEED MANATEE INSULATION LTD.—See Saint-Gobain; *Int'l*, pg. 1176
CERTAINTEED VENTURES, INC.—See Saint-Gobain; *Int'l*, pg. 1171
CERTAINTEED WEAVING CORP.—See Saint-Gobain; *Int'l*, pg. 1171
CERTANIUM ALLOYS & RESEARCH—See Premier Farnell plc; *Int'l*, pg. 1068
CERTANIUM B.V.—See Premier Farnell plc; *Int'l*, pg. 1068
N.V. CERTANIUM SERVICES S.A.—See Premier Farnell plc; *Int'l*, pg. 1068
CERTAS AG—See Siemens AG; *Int'l*, pg. 1246
CERTECH, INC.—See Carpenter Technology Corporation; *U.S. Public*, pg. 307
CERTECH INTERNATIONAL LTD.—See Carpenter Technology Corporation; *U.S. Public*, pg. 308
CERTIFIED ALLOY PRODUCTS, INC.—See Vickers PLC; *Int'l*, pg. 1467
CERTIFIED APPAREL SERVICES OF HONDURAS, S.A.—See Kleinert's, Inc.; *U.S. Private*, pg. 625
CERTIFIED BAKERS—See Fleming Companies, Inc.; *U.S. Public*, pg. 653
CERTIFIED FOOD SERVICE OF GA., INC.—See Sun City Industries, Inc.; *U.S. Public*, pg. 1529
CERTIFIED FOOD SERVICE OF PA, INC.—See Sun City Industries, Inc.; *U.S. Public*, pg. 1529
CERTIFIED GROCERS MIDWEST, INC.; *U.S. Private*, pg. 226
CERTIFIED GROCERS OF CALIFORNIA; *U.S. Private*, pg. 226
CERTIFIED LABS—See NCH Corporation; *U.S. Public*, pg. 1145
CERTIFIED LIFE INSURANCE—See Conseco Inc.; *U.S. Public*, pg. 433
CERTIFIED POULTRY & EGG CO., INC.—See Sun City Industries, Inc.; *U.S. Public*, pg. 1529
CERTIFIED WHOLESALERS INC.—See Associated Grocers of New England, Inc.; *U.S. Private*, pg. 91

CERTINA GEBR. KURTH AG—See SMH Swiss Corporation for Micro Electronics & Watchmaking Indus. Ltd.; *Int'l*, pg. 1160
CERVEJARIAS KAISER BRASIL LTDA.; *Int'l*, pg. 279
CERWIN VEGA, INC.; *U.S. Private*, pg. 227
CESA S.P.A.—See Compagnie des Machines Bull; *Int'l*, pg. 318
CESELSA-INISEL, S.A.—See SEPI; *Int'l*, pg. 1224
CESIWID ELEKTROWARME GMBH—See Kanthal AB; *Int'l*, pg. 723
CESIWID REFRACTORIES J.S.C.—See Kanthal AB; *Int'l*, pg. 723
CESKA REKLAMNI/TBWA—See TBWA Chiat/Day; *U.S. Private*, pg. 1062
THE CESSNA AIRCRAFT CO.—See Textron Inc.; *U.S. Public*, pg. 1589
CESSNA FINANCE CORP.—See Textron Inc.; *U.S. Public*, pg. 1589
CESTIDUR INDUSTRIES S.A.—See DSM N.V.; *Int'l*, pg. 354
CESVIBRASIL, S.A. CENTRO DE EXPERIMENTO E SEGURANZA VIANA—See Corporacion MAPFRE, Compania Internacional de Reaseguros, S.A.; *Int'l*, pg. 333
CESVIMAP INTERNACIONAL, S.A.—See Corporacion MAPFRE, Compania Internacional de Reaseguros, S.A.; *Int'l*, pg. 333
CETA-BEVER BV—See Akzo Nobel N.V.; *Int'l*, pg. 43
CETEC CORPORATION—See Mark IV Industries Inc.; *U.S. Public*, pg. 1045
CETECO N.V.; *Int'l*, pg. 279
CETIA—See Thomson S.A.; *Int'l*, pg. 1381
CETIA INC.—See Thomson S.A.; *Int'l*, pg. 1383
CETRA METAAL B.V.—See Schuttersveld Holding N.V.; *Int'l*, pg. 1210
CETRK USA—See Teleflex Incorporated; *U.S. Public*, pg. 1569
CETRON ELECTRONICS MANUFACTURING DIVISION—See Richardson Electronics, Ltd.; *U.S. Public*, pg. 1388
CETUS ONCOLOGY—See Chiron Corporation; *U.S. Public*, pg. 350
CEVA PRACHOVICE A.S.—See Holderbank Financiere Glaris Ltd.; *Int'l*, pg. 629
CEYLON NUTRITIONAL FOODS LTD.—See Nestle S.A.; *Int'l*, pg. 919
CEYLON OXYGEN LIMITED—See Norsk Hydro a.s; *Int'l*, pg. 961
CEYLON TOBACCO CO. LTD.—See B.A.T Industries P.L.C.; *Int'l*, pg. 111
CEZUS—See Framatome SA; *Int'l*, pg. 503
CEZUS—See Pechiney S.A.; *Int'l*, pg. 1029
CHACE PRECISION METALS, INC.—See Technitrol, Inc.; *U.S. Public*, pg. 1564
CHACO ENERGY CO.—See Texas Utilities Company; *U.S. Public*, pg. 1587
CHAD THERAPEUTICS; *U.S. Public*, pg. 332
CHADA THONG CONSULTANTS CO., LTD.—See Siam City Bank Public Company Limited; *Int'l*, pg. 1239
CHADA THONG PROPERTIES CO., LTD.—See Siam City Bank Public Company Limited; *Int'l*, pg. 1239
CHADWICK-HELMUTH COMPANY, INC.; *U.S. Private*, pg. 227
CHADWICK-MILLER INC.—See CMI Holding Corp.; *U.S. Private*, pg. 195
CHADWICK-MILLER INTL. LTD.—See CMI Holding Corp.; *U.S. Private*, pg. 195
CHADWICK'S OF BOSTON—See The Limited, Inc.; *U.S. Public*, pg. 996
CHAGRIN BEACHWOOD INC.—See Forest City Enterprises, Inc.; *U.S. Public*, pg. 668
CHAITRA LEO BURNETT PRIVATE LTD.—See Leo Burnett Company, Inc.; *U.S. Private*, pg. 184
CHALLENGE INDUSTRIES—See Electrolux, AB; *Int'l*, pg. 438
THE CHALLENGE MACHINERY CO.; *U.S. Private*, pg. 227
CHALLENGE PROPERTIES LIMITED—See Fletcher Challenge Limited; *Int'l*, pg. 495
CHALLENGER ELECTRICAL EQUIPMENT CORP.—See Eaton Corporation; *U.S. Public*, pg. 558
CHALLENGER MINERALS INC.—See Global Marine Inc.; *U.S. Public*, pg. 748
CHALMETTE MEDICAL CENTER—See Universal Health Services, Inc.; *U.S. Public*, pg. 1697
THE CHAMBERLAIN GROUP, INC.—See Duchossois Industries, Inc.; *U.S. Private*, pg. 344
CHAMBERLAIN JOHN DEERE PTY. LTD.—See Deere & Company; *U.S. Public*, pg. 492
CHAMBERLAIN MANUFACTURING CORP.—See Duchossois Industries, Inc.; *U.S. Private*, pg. 344
HERB CHAMBERS COS.; *U.S. Private*, pg. 227
M.S. CHAMBERS ENGRAVING GROUP—See The Dyson-Kissner-Moran Corporation; *U.S. Private*, pg. 351
CHAMBERS MEDICAL TECHNOLOGIES, INC.—See USA Waste Services, Inc.; *U.S. Public*, pg. 1686
CHAMBERS PACKAGING—See BPB Industries PLC; *Int'l*, pg. 123
CHAMBERS USA WASTE, INC.—See USA Waste Services, Inc.; *U.S. Public*, pg. 1686
CHAMBOURCY FOOD CO. LTD.—See Nestle S.A.; *Int'l*, pg. 920
CHAMBOURCY ROCHE AUX FEES & CIE—See Nestle S.A.; *Int'l*, pg. 920
CHAMBOURCY S.A.—See Nestle S.A.; *Int'l*, pg. 920
CHAMP/PIK-A-NUT SERVICE LINE—See Standard Motor Products Inc.; *U.S. Public*, pg. 1503
CHAMPAGNE CANARD-DUCHENE—See LVMH Moet Hennessy Louis Vuitton; *Int'l*, pg. 779
CHAMPAGNE MERCIER—See LVMH Moet Hennessy Louis Vuitton; *Int'l*, pg. 779
CHAMPAGNE MOET & CHANDON—See LVMH Moet Hennessy Louis Vuitton; *Int'l*, pg. 779
CHAMPAGNE POMMERY & GRENO—See LVMH Moet Hennessy Louis Vuitton; *Int'l*, pg. 780
CHAMPAGNE POMMERY S.A.—See LVMH Moet Hennessy Louis Vuitton; *Int'l*, pg. 780

CHAMPAGNE RUINART—See LVMH Moet Hennessy Louis Vuitton; *Int'l*, pg. 780
CHAMPAGNES ET SPIRITUEUX ASSOCIES—See LVMH Moet Hennessy Louis Vuitton; *Int'l*, pg. 780
CHAMPAIGN LANDMARK, INC.; *U.S. Private*, pg. 227
CHAMPAIGN-URBANA COMMUNICATIONS, INC.—See Time Warner Inc.; *U.S. Public*, pg. 1610
CHAMPION ALUMINUM WINDOW CORPORATION; *U.S. Private*, pg. 227
CHAMPION AVIATION PRODUCTS—See Cooper Industries, Inc.; *U.S. Public*, pg. 443
CHAMPION BOXED BEEF; *U.S. Private*, pg. 228
CHAMPION BUSINESS FORMS; *U.S. Private*, pg. 228
CHAMPION DAIRYPAK DIV.—See Champion International Corp.; *U.S. Public*, pg. 334
CHAMPION DIRECT MAIL PRINTING—See Champion Business Forms; *U.S. Private*, pg. 228
CHAMPION ENTERPRISES, INC.; *U.S. Public*, pg. 332
CHAMPION HEALTHCARE CORPORATION; *U.S. Public*, pg. 333
CHAMPION HOME BUILDERS CO.—See Champion Enterprises, Inc.; *U.S. Public*, pg. 332
CHAMPION IGNITION PRODUCTS—See Cooper Industries, Inc.; *U.S. Public*, pg. 442
CHAMPION, INC.; *U.S. Private*, pg. 228
CHAMPION INDUSTRIES; *U.S. Public*, pg. 333
CHAMPION INTERNATIONAL CORP.; *U.S. Public*, pg. 333
CHAMPION INT'L. CORP.—See Champion International Corp.; *U.S. Public*, pg. 334
CHAMPION INTERNATIONAL CORP., PAPER DIV.—See Champion International Corp.; *U.S. Public*, pg. 334
CHAMPION INTERNATIONAL CORP., WOOD PRODUCTS DIV.—See Champion International Corp.; *U.S. Public*, pg. 334
CHAMPION INT'L. CORP.—See Champion International Corp.; *U.S. Public*, pg. 334
CHAMPION/JOGBRA—See Sara Lee Corporation; *U.S. Public*, pg. 1433
CHAMPION LABORATORIES, INC.—See UIS, Inc.; *U.S. Private*, pg. 1113
CHAMPION MODULAR RESTAURANT COMPANY—See Checkers Drive-In Restaurants, Inc.; *U.S. Public*, pg. 343
CHAMPION MOTOR COACH, INC.—See Champion Enterprises, Inc.; *U.S. Public*, pg. 332
CHAMPION MOTORS (1975) PTE. LTD.—See Inchcape PLC; *Int'l*, pg. 672
CHAMPION PAPEL E CELULOSE, S.A.—See Champion International Corp.; *U.S. Public*, pg. 334
CHAMPION PARTS (CANADA) LTD.—See Champion Parts, Inc.; *U.S. Public*, pg. 335
CHAMPION PARTS, INC.; *U.S. Public*, pg. 334
CHAMPION PNEUMATIC MACHINERY CO., INC.; *U.S. Private*, pg. 228
CHAMPION PRODUCTS—See Sara Lee Corporation; *U.S. Public*, pg. 1433
CHAMPION PRODUCTS INC.—See Sara Lee Corporation; *U.S. Public*, pg. 1433
CHAMPION REALTY, INC.—See Oriole Homes Corp.; *U.S. Public*, pg. 1231
CHAMPION RECYCLING CORPORATION—See Champion International Corp.; *U.S. Public*, pg. 334
CHAMPION STATIONARY MANUFACTURING COMPANY LTD.—See General Binding Corporation; *U.S. Public*, pg. 707
CHAMPION VALLEY FARMS—See H.J. Heinz Company; *U.S. Public*, pg. 806
CHAMPIONS—See Young & Rubicam Inc.; *U.S. Private*, pg. 1199
CHAMPION'S RESIDENTIAL TREATMENT CENTER—See Columbia/HCA Healthcare Corporation; *U.S. Public*, pg. 404
CHAMPLAIN CABLE CORP.—See Huber & Suhner AG; *Int'l*, pg. 637
CHAMPLAIN PRODUCTIONS INC.—See CFCF Inc.; *Int'l*, pg. 241
CHAMPPS ENTERTAINMENT, INC.—See Compass Group plc; *Int'l*, pg. 1777
CHAMPS—See Woolworth Corporation; *U.S. Public*, pg. 1777
CHAMPSSPORTS—See Woolworth Corporation; *U.S. Public*, pg. 1777
CHANCE COACH, INC.—See Chance Industries, Inc.; *U.S. Private*, pg. 228
CHANCE INDUSTRIES, INC.; *U.S. Private*, pg. 228
CHANCELLOR ASSET CORPORATION—See Chancellor Corporation; *U.S. Public*, pg. 335
CHANCELLOR CORPORATION; *U.S. Public*, pg. 335
CHANCELLOR DATACOMM, INC.—See Chancellor Corporation; *U.S. Public*, pg. 335
CHANCELLOR FINANCIAL SALES & SERVICES, INC.—See Chancellor Corporation; *U.S. Public*, pg. 335
CHANCELLOR FLEET CORPORATION—See Chancellor Corporation; *U.S. Public*, pg. 335
CHANCELLOR MANAGEMENT CORPORATION—See Chancellor Corporation; *U.S. Public*, pg. 335
CHANCELLOR MEDIA CORPORATION; *U.S. Public*, pg. 335
CHANCELLOR RADIO BROADCASTING CO.—See Chancellor Media Corporation; *U.S. Public*, pg. 335
CHANDELEUR HOMES, INC.—See Champion Enterprises, Inc.; *U.S. Public*, pg. 332
CHANDELEUR PIPE LINE CO.—See Chevron Corporation; *U.S. Public*, pg. 348
CHANDLER ATTWOOD LIMITED—See HON Industries Inc.; *U.S. Public*, pg. 772
CHANDLER EVANS CONTROL SYSTEMS DIVISION—See Coltec Holdings Inc; *U.S. Public*, pg. 401
CHANDLER PRODUCTS, INC.—See Elgin National Industries, Inc.; *U.S. Private*, pg. 370
CHANDLERS PRINTERS LTD.—See Wolseley Plc.; *Int'l*, pg. 1511
M. CHANDON DO BRASIL LTDA.—See LVMH Moet Hennessy Louis Vuitton; *Int'l*, pg. 782

CHANDON S.A.—See LVMH Moet Hennessy Louis Vuitton; *Int'l*, pg. 782
CHANDON SEKTKELLEREI GMBH—See LVMH Moet Hennessy Louis Vuitton; *Int'l*, pg. 782
CHANG CHENG-TAKENAKA CONSTRUCTION CO., LTD.—See Takenaka Corporation; *Int'l*, pg. 1351
CHANG JIANG FLOAT GLASS CO., LTD.—See Taiwan Glass Industry Corp.; *Int'l*, pg. 1348
CHANG SHING ELECTRIC CO., LTD.—See Fuji Electric Co., Ltd.; *Int'l*, pg. 522
CHANGCHUN SANYO ELECTRONICS (SHEKOU) CO., LTD.—See Sanyo Electric Co., Ltd.; *Int'l*, pg. 1191
CHANGE-O-MATIC/WESCO—See Steiner Corporation; *U.S. Private*, pg. 1039
CHANGZHOU HURAI NEW MATERIAL CO., LTD.—See Dainippon Ink & Chemicals, Inc.; *Int'l*, pg. 371
CHANNEL INDUSTRIES GAS CO.—See Tenneco Inc.; *U.S. Public*, pg. 1579
CHANNEL INDUSTRIES, INC.—See Channel Technologies, Inc.; *U.S. Private*, pg. 228
CHANNEL MASTER; *U.S. Private*, pg. 228
CHANNEL MASTER (UK) LIMITED—See Channel Master; *U.S. Private*, pg. 228
CHANNEL 1—See Lagardere Groupe; *Int'l*, pg. 792
CHANNEL ONE COMMUNICATIONS—See Primedia Inc.; *U.S. Private*, pg. 1328
CHANNEL PRODUCTS, INC.—See Channel Technologies, Inc.; *U.S. Private*, pg. 228
CHANNEL TECHNOLOGIES, INC.; *U.S. Private*, pg. 228
THE CHANNEL TUNNEL GROUP LIMITED—See The Eurotunnel Group; *Int'l*, pg. 466
CHANNELLOCK, INC.; *U.S. Private*, pg. 229
CHANTIERS MODERNES—See Lyonnaise des Eaux S.A.; *Int'l*, pg. 823
CHANTILLY PARTNERS—See Cigna Corp.; *U.S. Public*, pg. 361
THE CHANTLAND COMPANY DIVISION—See Magna International Inc.; *Int'l*, pg. 830
CHANTRE & CIE GMBH—See Eckes AG; *Int'l*, pg. 433
CHANTRE & CIE KG MIT BESCHRANKTER HAFTUNG—See Eckes AG; *Int'l*, pg. 433
CHAO PHAYA FINANCE & SECURITIES CO., LTD.—See Siam City Bank Public Company Limited; *Int'l*, pg. 1239
CHAPARRAL BOATS—See RPC Incorporated; *U.S. Public*, pg. 1356
CHAPARRAL STEEL CO.—See Texas Industries, Inc.; *U.S. Public*, pg. 1585
CHAPELLE DARBLAY GRAND COURONNE—See UPM-Kymmene Corporation; *Int'l*, pg. 1428
CHAPELLE DARBLAY GRAND COURONNE S.A.—See UPM-Kymmene Corporation; *Int'l*, pg. 1430
CHAPELLE DARBLAY SAINT ETIENNE S.A.—See UPM-Kymmene Corporation; *Int'l*, pg. 1430
CHAPELLIER BOIS-MATERIAUX-QUINCAILLERIE—See La Meridionale des Bois et Materiaux; *Int'l*, pg. 784
CHAPLEAU FOREST PRODUCTS—See MacMillan Bloedel Limited; *Int'l*, pg. 828
THE CHAPMAN AGENCY—See Young & Rubicam Inc.; *U.S. Private*, pg. 1197
CHAPMAN AUTOMOTIVE GROUP INC.; *U.S. Private*, pg. 229
CHAPMAN EQUIPMENT COMPANY—See Dimeo Construction Company; *U.S. Private*, pg. 334
CHAPMAN INDUSTRIES PLC—See Trelleborg AB; *Int'l*, pg. 1420
CHAPMAN MANAGEMENT GROUP; *U.S. Private*, pg. 229
CHAPMAN SECURITY SYSTEMS, INC.—See Code-Alarm, Inc.; *U.S. Public*, pg. 394
CHAPMAN WARWICK INC.—See Warwick Baker O'Neill; *U.S. Private*, pg. 1152
CHAPPARAL PARTNERS—See Cigna Corp.; *U.S. Public*, pg. 365
CHAPPELL AGENCY INC.—See Klockner-Moeller GmbH; *Int'l*, pg. 736
CHAPS BY RALPH LAUREN—See Warnaco Inc.; *U.S. Public*, pg. 1738
CHAPTER ONE GROUP LIMITED; *Int'l*, pg. 280
CHAPTERS INC.; *Int'l*, pg. 280
CHAR YONG GARDENS—See Scotts Holdings Limited; *Int'l*, pg. 1212
CHARAN INDUSTRIES, INC.; *U.S. Private*, pg. 229
CHARAN REALTY GROUP—See Charan Industries, Inc.; *U.S. Private*, pg. 229
CHARBONNAGES DE FRANCE; *Int'l*, pg. 280
CHARCON TUNNELS—See Costain Group PLC; *Int'l*, pg. 336
CHARCUTERIE LA TOUR EIFFEL INC.—See McCain Foods Limited; *Int'l*, pg. 850
CHARDON ELECTRICAL COMPONENTS, INC.—See The Chardon Rubber Co.; *U.S. Private*, pg. 229
THE CHARDON RUBBER CO.; *U.S. Private*, pg. 229
CHARGEURS; *Int'l*, pg. 280
CHARGEURS FABRICS—See Chargeurs; *Int'l*, pg. 280
CHARGEURS INTERLINING—See Chargeurs; *Int'l*, pg. 280
CHARGEURS PROTECTIVE FILMS—See Chargeurs; *Int'l*, pg. 280
CHARGEURS WOOL—See Chargeurs; *Int'l*, pg. 280
CHARGEX LTD./CHARGEX LTEE—See Canadian Imperial Bank of Commerce; *Int'l*, pg. 257
THE CHARIHO TIMES—See Journal Register Company; *U.S. Public*, pg. 934
CHARLES-ANDRE S.A.—See Saint-Gobain; *Int'l*, pg. 1172
CHARLES ATLAS, LTD.; *U.S. Private*, pg. 229
CHARLES CHURCH—See Beazer Group Plc; *Int'l*, pg. 182
CHARLES CURTAIN COMPANY, INC.; *U.S. Private*, pg. 229
CHARLES DUNN COMPANY, INC.; *U.S. Private*, pg. 229
CHARLES MACHINE WORKS, INC.; *U.S. Private*, pg. 230
CHARLES OF THE RITZ GROUP LTD.—See MacAndrews & Forbes Holdings Inc.; *U.S. Private*, pg. 689
CHARLES RIVER BIOTECHNICAL SERVICES, INC.—See Bausch & Lomb Incorporated; *U.S. Public*, pg. 194
CHARLES RIVER BREEDING LABS—See Bausch & Lomb Incorporated; *U.S. Public*, pg. 194

CHARLES RIVER CANADA, INC.—See Bausch & Lomb Incorporated; *U.S. Public*, pg. 195
CHARLES RIVER DATA SYSTEMS, INC.; *U.S. Private*, pg. 230
CHARLES RIVER ESPANA S.A.—See Bausch & Lomb Incorporated; *U.S. Public*, pg. 195
CHARLES RIVER FOODS, INC.; *U.S. Private*, pg. 230
CHARLES RIVER FRANCE S.A.—See Bausch & Lomb Incorporated; *U.S. Public*, pg. 195
CHARLES RIVER ITALIA S.P.A.—See Bausch & Lomb Incorporated; *U.S. Public*, pg. 195
CHARLES RIVER JAPAN, INC.—See Bausch & Lomb Incorporated; *U.S. Public*, pg. 195
CHARLES RIVER LABORATORIES, INC.—See Bausch & Lomb Incorporated; *U.S. Public*, pg. 194
CHARLES RIVER U.K., LTD.—See Bausch & Lomb Incorporated; *U.S. Public*, pg. 195
CHARLES RIVER WIGA G.M.B.H.—See Bausch & Lomb Incorporated; *U.S. Public*, pg. 195
CHARLES SCRIBNER'S SONS REFERENCE—See National Amusements, Inc.; *U.S. Private*, pg. 777
CHARLES TOWN RACES—See Penn National Gaming, Inc.; *U.S. Public*, pg. 1270
CHARLES WINN (VALVES) LIMITED—See Tyco International Ltd.; *U.S. Public*, pg. 1651
CHARLESTON BOTTOMS RURAL ELECTRIC—See East Kentucky Power Co-op; *U.S. Private*, pg. 357
CHARLESTON CONTAINERS SHOPS INC.—See Sea Containers Ltd.; *Int'l*, pg. 1214
CHARLESTON DIVISION—See Champion Industries; *U.S. Public*, pg. 333
CHARLESTON FINANCIAL SERVICES, INC.—See First Financial Holdings, Inc.; *U.S. Public*, pg. 634
CHARLESTON INDUSTRIES—See Petersen Aluminum Corporation; *U.S. Private*, pg. 856
CHARLESTON INSURANCE COMPANY—See Selective Insurance Group, Inc; *U.S. Public*, pg. 1455
CHARLESTON SUPPLY—See Associated Industrial Supply, Inc.; *U.S. Private*, pg. 91
CHARLESTON TELEVISION, INC.—See Media General, Inc.; *U.S. Public*, pg. 1078
CHARLESTON TOOL SERVICES—See Cummins Engine Company, Inc.; *U.S. Public*, pg. 468
CHARLIE BROWN'S & THE OFFICE RESTAURANT GROUP—See Castle-Harlan; *U.S. Private*, pg. 219
CHARLIE'S SPECIALTIES INC.—See Byrnes & Kiefer Company; *U.S. Private*, pg. 191
CHARLIO'S—See National Restaurant Management, Inc.; *U.S. Private*, pg. 786
CHARLOTTE COMMUNITY HOSPITAL—See Columbia/HCA Healthcare Corporation; *U.S. Public*, pg. 404
CHARLOTTE LABORATORY—See Pace Analytical Services; *U.S. Private*, pg. 829
CHARLOTTE MEDICAL SUPPLY, INC.—See Integrated Health Services, Inc.; *U.S. Public*, pg. 884
CHARLOTTE MOTOR SPEEDWAY—See Speedway Motorsports, Inc.; *U.S. Public*, pg. 1498
THE CHARLOTTE OBSERVER—See Knight-Ridder, Inc.; *U.S. Public*, pg. 964
CHARLOTTE-SOUTHERN CORPORATION—See Norfolk Southern Corporation; *U.S. Public*, pg. 1190
CHARLOTTETOWN, INC.—See The Rouse Company; *U.S. Public*, pg. 1407
CHARLOTTETOWN NORTH, INC.—See The Rouse Company; *U.S. Public*, pg. 1407
CHARLWOOD ALLIANCE HOLDINGS LTD.—See The Peninsular and Oriental Steam Navigation Company; *Int'l*, pg. 1034
CHARMER INDUSTRIES; *U.S. Private*, pg. 230
CHARMILLES DEUTSCHLAND MASCHINEN GES. MBH—See Georg Fischer Ltd.; *Int'l*, pg. 489
CHARMILLES TAIWAN ENGINEERING SERVICES CO., LTD.—See Georg Fischer Ltd.; *Int'l*, pg. 489
CHARMILLES TECHNOLOGIES CORP.—See Georg Fischer Ltd.; *Int'l*, pg. 489
CHARMILLES TECHNOLOGIES (FRANCE) S.A.—See Georg Fischer Ltd.; *Int'l*, pg. 489
CHARMILLES TECHNOLOGIES IBERICA S.A.—See Georg Fischer Ltd.; *Int'l*, pg. 489
CHARMILLES TECHNOLOGIES (ITALIA) SRL.—See Georg Fischer Ltd.; *Int'l*, pg. 489
CHARMILLES TECHNOLOGIES (JAPAN) LTD.—See Georg Fischer Ltd.; *Int'l*, pg. 489
CHARMILLES TECHNOLOGIES LTD.—See Georg Fischer Ltd.; *Int'l*, pg. 489
CHARMILLES TECHNOLOGIES LTD. SPB ST. PETERSBURG—See Georg Fischer Ltd.; *Int'l*, pg. 489
CHARMILLES TECHNOLOGIES MANUFACTURING CORP.—See Georg Fischer Ltd.; *Int'l*, pg. 489
CHARMILLES TECHNOLOGIES MASCHINENBAU AG—See Georg Fischer Ltd.; *Int'l*, pg. 489
CHARMILLES TECHNOLOGIES SA—See Georg Fischer Ltd.; *Int'l*, pg. 489
CHARMILLES TECHNOLOGIES (SOUTH EAST ASIA) PTE. LTD.—See Georg Fischer Ltd.; *Int'l*, pg. 489
CHARMING SHOPPES, INC.; *U.S. Public*, pg. 335
CHARMS COMPANY—See Tootsie Roll Industries, Inc.; *U.S. Public*, pg. 1621
CHARNAUX GES.M.B.H.—See Hesta Tex AG; *Int'l*, pg. 618
CHARNOS PLC; *Int'l*, pg. 280
CHAROEN SEEDS COMPANY LTD.—See Dekalb Genetics Corporation; *U.S. Public*, pg. 493
CHART INDUSTRIES, INC.; *U.S. Public*, pg. 336
CHARTER ALVARADO BEHAVIORAL HEALTH SYSTEMS, INC.—See Magellan Health Services, Inc.; *U.S. Public*, pg. 1033
CHARTER APPALACHIAN HALL BEHAVIORAL HEALTH SYSTEM, INC.—See Magellan Health Services, Inc.; *U.S. Public*, pg. 1033
CHARTER ARBOR INDY BEHAVIORAL HEALTH SYSTEM, INC.—See Magellan Health Services, Inc.; *U.S. Public*, pg. 1033

CHARTER AUGUSTA BEHAVIORAL HEALTH SYSTEM, INC.—See Magellan Health Services, Inc.; *U.S. Public*, pg. 1033
CHARTER BAY HARBOR BEHAVIORAL HEALTH SYSTEM, INC.—See Magellan Health Services, Inc.; *U.S. Public*, pg. 1033
CHARTER BEACON BEHAVIORAL HEALTH SYSTEM, INC.—See Magellan Health Services, Inc.; *U.S. Public*, pg. 1033
CHARTER BEHAVIORAL HEALTH OF PUERTO RICO, INC.—See Magellan Health Services, Inc.; *U.S. Public*, pg. 1033
CHARTER BEHAVIORAL HEALTH SYSTEM AT FAIR OAKS, INC.—See Magellan Health Services, Inc.; *U.S. Public*, pg. 1033
CHARTER BEHAVIORAL HEALTH SYSTEM AT HIDDEN BROOK, INC.—See Magellan Health Services, Inc.; *U.S. Public*, pg. 1033
CHARTER BEHAVIORAL HEALTH SYSTEM AT LOS ALTOS, INC.—See Magellan Health Services, Inc.; *U.S. Public*, pg. 1033
CHARTER BEHAVIORAL HEALTH SYSTEM AT MANATEE ADOLESCENT TREATMENT SERVICES, INC.—See Magellan Health Services, Inc.; *U.S. Public*, pg. 1033
CHARTER BEHAVIORAL HEALTH SYSTEM AT POTOMAC RIDGE, INC.—See Magellan Health Services, Inc.; *U.S. Public*, pg. 1033
CHARTER BEHAVIORAL HEALTH SYSTEM OF ATHENS, INC.—See Magellan Health Services, Inc.; *U.S. Public*, pg. 1033
CHARTER BEHAVIORAL HEALTH SYSTEM OF AUSTIN, INC.—See Magellan Health Services, Inc.; *U.S. Public*, pg. 1033
CHARTER BEHAVIORAL HEALTH SYSTEM OF BAYWOOD, INC.—See Magellan Health Services, Inc.; *U.S. Public*, pg. 1033
CHARTER BEHAVIORAL HEALTH SYSTEM OF BRADENTON, INC.—See Magellan Health Services, Inc.; *U.S. Public*, pg. 1033
CHARTER BEHAVIORAL HEALTH SYSTEM OF CENTRAL GEORGIA, INC.—See Magellan Health Services, Inc.; *U.S. Public*, pg. 1033
CHARTER BEHAVIORAL HEALTH SYSTEM OF CENTRAL VIRGINIA, INC.—See Magellan Health Services, Inc.; *U.S. Public*, pg. 1033
CHARTER BEHAVIORAL HEALTH SYSTEM OF CHARLESTON, INC.—See Magellan Health Services, Inc.; *U.S. Public*, pg. 1033
CHARTER BEHAVIORAL HEALTH SYSTEM OF CHARLOTTESVILLE, INC.—See Magellan Health Services, Inc.; *U.S. Public*, pg. 1033
CHARTER BEHAVIORAL HEALTH SYSTEM OF CHICAGO, INC.—See Magellan Health Services, Inc.; *U.S. Public*, pg. 1033
CHARTER BEHAVIORAL HEALTH SYSTEM OF CHULA VISTA, INC.—See Magellan Health Services, Inc.; *U.S. Public*, pg. 1034
CHARTER BEHAVIORAL HEALTH SYSTEM OF COLUMBIA, INC.—See Magellan Health Services, Inc.; *U.S. Public*, pg. 1034
CHARTER BEHAVIORAL HEALTH SYSTEM OF CORPUS CHRISTI, INC.—See Magellan Health Services, Inc.; *U.S. Public*, pg. 1034
CHARTER BEHAVIORAL HEALTH SYSTEM OF DALLAS, INC.—See Magellan Health Services, Inc.; *U.S. Public*, pg. 1034
CHARTER BEHAVIORAL HEALTH SYSTEM OF DELMARVA—See Magellan Health Services, Inc.; *U.S. Public*, pg. 1034
CHARTER BEHAVIORAL HEALTH SYSTEM OF EVANSVILLE, LLC—See Magellan Health Services, Inc.; *U.S. Public*, pg. 1034
CHARTER BEHAVIORAL HEALTH SYSTEM OF FORT WORTH, INC.—See Magellan Health Services, Inc.; *U.S. Public*, pg. 1034
CHARTER BEHAVIORAL HEALTH SYSTEM OF JACKSON, INC.—See Magellan Health Services, Inc.; *U.S. Public*, pg. 1034
CHARTER BEHAVIORAL HEALTH SYSTEM OF JACKSONVILLE, INC.—See Magellan Health Services, Inc.; *U.S. Public*, pg. 1034
CHARTER BEHAVIORAL HEALTH SYSTEM OF JEFFERSON, INC.—See Magellan Health Services, Inc.; *U.S. Public*, pg. 1034
CHARTER BEHAVIORAL HEALTH SYSTEM OF KANSAS CITY, INC.—See Magellan Health Services, Inc.; *U.S. Public*, pg. 1034
CHARTER BEHAVIORAL HEALTH SYSTEM OF LAFAYETTE, INC.—See Magellan Health Services, Inc.; *U.S. Public*, pg. 1034
CHARTER BEHAVIORAL HEALTH SYSTEM OF LAKE CHARLES, INC.—See Magellan Health Services, Inc.; *U.S. Public*, pg. 1034
CHARTER BEHAVIORAL HEALTH SYSTEM OF MICHIGAN CITY, INC.—See Magellan Health Services, Inc.; *U.S. Public*, pg. 1034
CHARTER BEHAVIORAL HEALTH SYSTEM OF MOBILE, INC.—See Magellan Health Services, Inc.; *U.S. Public*, pg. 1034
CHARTER BEHAVIORAL HEALTH SYSTEM OF NASHUA, INC.—See Magellan Health Services, Inc.; *U.S. Public*, pg. 1034
CHARTER BEHAVIORAL HEALTH SYSTEM OF NEVADA, INC.—See Magellan Health Services, Inc.; *U.S. Public*, pg. 1034
CHARTER BEHAVIORAL HEALTH SYSTEM OF NEW MEXICO, INC.—See Magellan Health Services, Inc.; *U.S. Public*, pg. 1034
CHARTER BEHAVIORAL HEALTH SYSTEM OF NORTHERN CALIFORNIA, INC.—See Magellan Health Services, Inc.; *U.S. Public*, pg. 1034
CHARTER BEHAVIORAL HEALTH SYSTEM OF NORTHWEST ARKANSAS, INC.—See Magellan Health Services, Inc.; *U.S. Public*, pg. 1034

Company Index

CHARTER | DIRECTORY OF CORPORATE AFFILIATIONS

CHARTER BEHAVIORAL HEALTH SYSTEM OF NORTHWEST INDIANA, INC.—See Magellan Health Services, Inc.; *U.S. Public*, pg. 1034
CHARTER BEHAVIORAL HEALTH SYSTEM OF PADUCAH, INC.—See Magellan Health Services, Inc.; *U.S. Public*, pg. 1034
CHARTER BEHAVIORAL HEALTH SYSTEM OF SAN JOSE, INC.—See Magellan Health Services, Inc.; *U.S. Public*, pg. 1034
CHARTER BEHAVIORAL HEALTH SYSTEM OF SAVANNAH, INC.—See Magellan Health Services, Inc.; *U.S. Public*, pg. 1034
CHARTER BEHAVIORAL HEALTH SYSTEM OF TEXARKANA, INC.—See Magellan Health Services, Inc.; *U.S. Public*, pg. 1034
CHARTER BEHAVIORAL HEALTH SYSTEM OF THE INLAND EMPIRE, INC.—See Magellan Health Services, Inc.; *U.S. Public*, pg. 1034
CHARTER BEHAVIORAL HEALTH SYSTEM OF TOLEDO, INC.—See Magellan Health Services, Inc.; *U.S. Public*, pg. 1034
CHARTER BEHAVIORAL HEALTH SYSTEM OF TUCSON, INC.—See Magellan Health Services, Inc.; *U.S. Public*, pg. 1034
CHARTER BEHAVIORAL HEALTH SYSTEM OF VISALIA, INC.—See Magellan Health Services, Inc.; *U.S. Public*, pg. 1034
CHARTER BEHAVIORAL HEALTH SYSTEM OF WAVERLY, INC.—See Magellan Health Services, Inc.; *U.S. Public*, pg. 1034
CHARTER BEHAVIORAL HEALTH SYSTEM OF WINSTON-SALEM, INC.—See Magellan Health Services, Inc.; *U.S. Public*, pg. 1034
CHARTER BEHAVIORAL HEALTH SYSTEM OF YORBA LINDA, INC.—See Magellan Health Services, Inc.; *U.S.* Public, pg. 1034
CHARTER BEHAVIORAL HEALTH SYSTEMS OF ATLANTA, INC.—See Magellan Health Services, Inc.; *U.S. Public*, pg. 1034
CHARTER BRAWNER BEHAVIORAL HEALTH SYSTEM, INC.—See Magellan Health Services, Inc.; *U.S. Public*, pg. 1034
CHARTER BUILDERS, INC.—See John Mowlem & Company plc; *Int'l*, pg. 896
CHARTER BY-THE-SEA BEHAVIORAL HEALTH SYSTEM, INC.—See Magellan Health Services, Inc.; *U.S. Public*, pg. 1034
CHARTER CANYON BEHAVIORAL HEALTH SYSTEN, INC.—See Magellan Health Services, Inc.; *U.S. Public*, pg. 1034
CHARTER CANYON SPRINGS BEHAVIORAL HEALTH SYSTEMS, INC.—See Magellan Health Services, Inc.; *U.S. Public*, pg. 1034
CHARTER CENTENNIAL PEAKS BEHAVIORAL HEALTH SYSTEM, INC.—See Magellan Health Services, Inc.; *U.S. Public*, pg. 1034
CHARTER CLINIC NIGHTINGALE—See Magellan Health Services, Inc.; *U.S. Public*, pg. 1036
CHARTER COMMUNICATIONS, INC.; *U.S. Private*, pg. 230
CHARTER COMMUNITY HOSPITAL, INC.—See Magellan Health Services, Inc.; *U.S. Public*, pg. 1034
CHARTER CONTRACT SERVICES, INC.—See Magellan Health Services, Inc.; *U.S. Public*, pg. 1034
CHARTER COVE FORGE BEHAVIORAL HEALTH SYSTEM, INC.—See Magellan Health Services, Inc.; *U.S. Public*, pg. 1034
CHARTER FAIRMOUNT BEHAVIORAL HEALTH SYSTEM, INC.—See Magellan Health Services, Inc.; *U.S. Public*, pg. 1034
CHARTER FENWICK HALL BEHAVIORAL HEALTH SYSTEM, INC.—See Magellan Health Services, Inc.; *U.S. Public*, pg. 1034
CHARTER FINANCIAL OFFICES, INC.—See Magellan Health Services, Inc.; *U.S. Public*, pg. 1034
CHARTER FOREST BEHAVIORAL HEALTH SYSTEM, INC.—See Magellan Health Services, Inc.; *U.S. Public*, pg. 1034
CHARTER GRAPEVINE BEHAVIORAL HEALTH SYSTEM, INC.—See Magellan Health Services, Inc.; *U.S. Public*, pg. 1034
CHARTER GREENSBORO BEHAVIORAL HEALTH SYSTEM, INC.—See Magellan Health Services, Inc.; *U.S. Public*, pg. 1034
THE CHARTER GROUP, INC.—See Skandia Insurance Company Limited; *Int'l*, pg. 1257
CHARTER GROUP, INC.—See Skandia Insurance Company Limited; *Int'l*, pg. 1257
CHARTER HEALTH MANAGEMENT OF TEXAS, INC.—See Magellan Health Services, Inc.; *U.S. Public*, pg. 1034
CHARTER HOSPITAL OF COLUMBUS, INC.—See Magellan Health Services, Inc.; *U.S. Public*, pg. 1034
CHARTER HOSPITAL OF DENVER, INC.—See Magellan Health Services, Inc.; *U.S. Public*, pg. 1034
CHARTER HOSPITAL OF FT. COLLINS, INC.—See Magellan Health Services, Inc.; *U.S. Public*, pg. 1034
CHARTER HOSPITAL OF LAREDO, INC.—See Magellan Health Services, Inc.; *U.S. Public*, pg. 1034
CHARTER HOSPITAL OF MIAMI, INC.—See Magellan Health Services, Inc.; *U.S. Public*, pg. 1034
CHARTER HOSPITAL OF MOBILE, INC.—See Magellan Health Services, Inc.; *U.S. Public*, pg. 1034
CHARTER HOSPITAL OF ST. LOUIS, INC.—See Magellan Health Services, Inc.; *U.S. Public*, pg. 1034
CHARTER HOSPITAL OF SANTA TERESA, INC.—See Magellan Health Services, Inc.; *U.S. Public*, pg. 1034
CHARTER HOSPITAL OF TORRANCE, INC.—See Magellan Health Services, Inc.; *U.S. Public*, pg. 1034
CHARTER HOUSE INCORPORATED—See Stainless Incorporated; *U.S. Private*, pg. 1029
CHARTER INDIANA BHS HOLDING, INC.—See Magellan Health Services, Inc.; *U.S. Public*, pg. 1034
CHARTER INDIANAPOLIS BEHAVIORAL HEALTH SYSTEM, INC.—See Magellan Health Services, Inc.; *U.S. Public*, pg. 1034
CHARTER LAFAYETTE BEHAVIORAL HEALTH SYSTEM, INC.—See Magellan Health Services, Inc.; *U.S. Public*, pg. 1034
CHARTER LAKEHURST BEHAVIORAL HEALTH SYSTEM, INC.—See Magellan Health Services, Inc.; *U.S. Public*, pg. 1034
CHARTER LAKESIDE BEHAVIORAL HEALTH SYSTEM, INC.—See Magellan Health Services, Inc.; *U.S. Public*, pg. 1034
CHARTER LAUREL HEIGHTS BEHAVIORAL HEALTH SYSTEM, INC.—See Magellan Health Services, Inc.; *U.S. Public*, pg. 1034
CHARTER LINDEN OAKS BEHAVIORAL HEALTH SYSTEM, INC.—See Magellan Health Services, Inc.; *U.S. Public*, pg. 1035
CHARTER LITTLE ROCK BEHAVIORAL HEALTH SYSTEM, INC.—See Magellan Health Services, Inc.; *U.S. Public*, pg. 1035
CHARTER LOUISIANA BEHAVIORAL HEALTH SYSTEM, INC.—See Magellan Health Services, Inc.; *U.S. Public*, pg. 1035
CHARTER LOUISVILLE BEHAVIORAL HEALTH SYSTEM, INC.—See Magellan Health Services, Inc.; *U.S. Public*, pg. 1035
CHARTER MEADOWS BEHAVIORAL HEALTH SYSTEM, INC.—See Magellan Health Services, Inc.; *U.S. Public*, pg. 1035
CHARTER MEDICAL-CALIFORNIA, INC.—See Magellan Health Services, Inc.; *U.S. Public*, pg. 1035
CHARTER MEDICAL (CAYMAN ISLANDS) LTD.—See Magellan Health Services, Inc.; *U.S. Public*, pg. 1036
CHARTER MEDICAL-CLAYTON COUNTY, INC.—See Magellan Health Services, Inc.; *U.S. Public*, pg. 1035
CHARTER MEDICAL-CLEVELAND, INC.—See Magellan Health Services, Inc.; *U.S. Public*, pg. 1035
CHARTER MEDICAL-DALLAS, INC.—See Magellan Health Services, Inc.; *U.S. Public*, pg. 1035
CHARTER MEDICAL EXECUTIVE CORPORATION—See Magellan Health Services, Inc.; *U.S. Public*, pg. 1035
CHARTER MEDICAL INFORMATION SERVICES, INC.—See Magellan Health Services, Inc.; *U.S. Public*, pg. 1035
CHARTER MEDICAL INTERNATIONAL, INC—See Magellan Health Services, Inc.; *U.S. Public*, pg. 1036
CHARTER MEDICAL INTERNATIONAL, S.A., INC.—See Magellan Health Services, Inc.; *U.S. Public*, pg. 1035
CHARTER MEDICAL-LONG BEACH, INC.—See Magellan Health Services, Inc.; *U.S. Public*, pg. 1035
CHARTER MEDICAL MANAGEMENT COMPANY—See Magellan Health Services, Inc.; *U.S. Public*, pg. 1035
CHARTER MEDICAL-NEW YORK, INC.—See Magellan Health Services, Inc.; *U.S. Public*, pg. 1035
CHARTER MEDICAL OF EAST VALLEY, INC.—See Magellan Health Services, Inc.; *U.S. Public*, pg. 1035
CHARTER MEDICAL OF ENGLAND LTD.—See Magellan Health Services, Inc.; *U.S. Public*, pg. 1036
CHARTER MEDICAL OF FLORIDA, INC.—See Magellan Health Services, Inc.; *U.S. Public*, pg. 1035
CHARTER MEDICAL OF NORTH PHOENIX, INC.—See Magellan Health Services, Inc.; *U.S. Public*, pg. 1035
CHARTER MEDICAL OF PUERTO RICO, INC.—See Magellan Health Services, Inc.; *U.S. Public*, pg. 1035
CHARTER MILWAUKEE BEHAVIORAL HEALTH SYSTEM, INC.—See Magellan Health Services, Inc.; *U.S. Public*, pg. 1035
CHARTER MISSION VIEJO BEHAVIORAL HEALTH SYSTEM, INC.—See Magellan Health Services, Inc.; *U.S. Public*, pg. 1035
CHARTER MOB OF CHARLOTTESVILLE, INC.—See Magellan Health Services, Inc.; *U.S. Public*, pg. 1035
CHARTER NATIONAL LIFE INSURANCE CO.—See Leucadia National Corporation; *U.S. Public*, pg. 990
CHARTER NORTH BEHAVIORAL HEALTH SYSTEM, INC.—See Magellan Health Services, Inc.; *U.S. Public*, pg. 1035
CHARTER NORTH COUNSELING CENTER, INC.—See Magellan Health Services, Inc.; *U.S. Public*, pg. 1035
CHARTER NORTHBROOKE BEHAVIORAL HEALTH SYSTEM, INC.—See Magellan Health Services, Inc.; *U.S. Public*, pg. 1035
CHARTER OAK BEHAVIORAL HEALTH SYSTEM, INC.—See Magellan Health Services, Inc.; *U.S. Public*, pg. 1035
CHARTER OAK ENERGY, INC.—See Northeast Utilities; *U.S. Public*, pg. 1194
THE CHARTER OAK FIRE INSURANCE CO.—See Travelers Group; *U.S. Public*, pg. 1633
CHARTER OAK VENTURES—See Cigna Corp.; *U.S. Public*, pg. 361
CHARTER OF ALABAMA, INC.—See Magellan Health Services, Inc.; *U.S. Public*, pg. 1035
CHARTER ONE BANK—See Charter One Financial, Inc.; *U.S. Public*, pg. 336
CHARTER ONE FINANCIAL, INC.; *U.S. Public*, pg. 336
CHARTER PALMS BEHAVIORAL HEALTH SYSTEM, INC.—See Magellan Health Services, Inc.; *U.S. Public*, pg. 1035
CHARTER PEACHFORD BEHAVIORAL HEALTH SYSTEM, INC.—See Magellan Health Services, Inc.; *U.S. Public*, pg. 1035
CHARTER PETERSBURG BEHAVIORAL HEALTH SYSTEM, INC.—See Magellan Health Services, Inc.; *U.S. Public*, pg. 1035
CHARTER PINES BEHAVIORAL HEALTH SYSTEM, INC.—See Magellan Health Services, Inc.; *U.S. Public*, pg. 1035
CHARTER PLAINS BEHAVIORAL HEALTH SYSTEM, INC.—See Magellan Health Services, Inc.; *U.S. Public*, pg. 1035
CHARTER PLC; *Int'l*, pg. 280
CHARTER-PROVO SCHOOL, INC.—See Magellan Health Services, Inc.; *U.S. Public*, pg. 1035
CHARTER PSYCHIATRIC HOSPITALS, INC.—See Magellan Health Services, Inc.; *U.S. Public*, pg. 1035
CHARTER REAL BEHAVIORAL HEALTH SYSTEM, INC.—See Magellan Health Services, Inc.; *U.S. Public*, pg. 1035
CHARTER REGIONAL MEDICAL CENTER, INC.—See Magellan Health Services, Inc.; *U.S. Public*, pg. 1035
CHARTER RIDGE BEHAVIORAL HEALTH SYSTEM, INC.—See Magellan Health Services, Inc.; *U.S. Public*, pg. 1035
CHARTER RIVERS BEHAVIORAL HEALTH SYSTEM, INC.—See Magellan Health Services, Inc.; *U.S. Public*, pg. 1035
CHARTER ROCKFORD BEHAVIORAL HEALTH SYSTEM, INC.—See Magellan Health Services, Inc.; *U.S. Public*, pg. 1035
CHARTER SAN DIEGO BEHAVIORAL HEALTH SYSTEM, INC.—See Magellan Health Services, Inc.; *U.S. Public*, pg. 1035
CHARTER SIOUX FALLS BEHAVIORAL HEALTH SYSTEM, INC.—See Magellan Health Services, Inc.; *U.S. Public*, pg. 1035
CHARTER SOUTH BEND BEHAVIORAL HEALTH SYSTEM, INC.—See Magellan Health Services, Inc.; *U.S. Public*, pg. 1035
CHARTER SPRINGS BEHAVIORAL HEALTH SYSTEM, INC.—See Magellan Health Services, Inc.; *U.S. Public*, pg. 1035
CHARTER SPRINGWOOD BEHAVIORAL HEALTH SYSTEM, INC.—See Magellan Health Services, Inc.; *U.S. Public*, pg. 1035
CHARTER SUBURBAN HOSPITAL OF MESQUITE, INC.—See Magellan Health Services, Inc.; *U.S. Public*, pg. 1035
CHARTER TERRE HAUTE BEHAVIORAL HEALTH SYSTEM, INC.—See Magellan Health Services, Inc.; *U.S. Public*, pg. 1035
CHARTER THOUSAND OAKS BEHAVIORAL HEALTH SYSTEM, INC.—See Magellan Health Services, Inc.; *U.S. Public*, pg. 1035
CHARTER TREATMENT CENTER OF MICHIGAN, INC.—See Magellan Health Services, Inc.; *U.S. Public*, pg. 1035
CHARTER WESTBROOK BEHAVIORL HEALTH SYSTEM, INC.—See Magellan Health Services, Inc.; *U.S. Public*, pg. 1035
CHARTER WHITE OAK BEHAVIORAL HEALTH SYSTEM, INC.—See Magellan Health Services, Inc.; *U.S. Public*, pg. 1035
CHARTER WICHITA BEHAVIORAL HEALTH SYSTEM, INC.—See Magellan Health Services, Inc.; *U.S. Public*, pg. 1035
CHARTER WOODS BEHAVIORAL HEALTH SYSTEM, INC.—See Magellan Health Services, Inc.; *U.S. Public*, pg. 1035
CHARTERED TRUST PLC.—See Standard Chartered Bank PLC; *Int'l*, pg. 1296
CHARTERHOUSE BANK LTD.—See Credit Commercial de France; *Int'l*, pg. 342
CHARTERHOUSE GROUP INTERNATIONAL, INC.; *U.S. Private*, pg. 230
CHARTERHOUSE INC.—See Credit Commercial de France; *Int'l*, pg. 342
CHARTERWAYS TRANSPORTATION LIMITED—See Scott's Restaurants Inc.; *Int'l*, pg. 1213
CHARTWELL ADVISERS LIMITED—See Chartwell Re Corporation; *U.S. Public*, pg. 337
CHARTWELL HOLDINGS LIMITED—See Chartwell Re Corporation; *U.S. Public*, pg. 337
CHARTWELL LAND PLC.—See Kingfisher plc; *Int'l*, pg. 733
CHARTWELL LEISURE—See Goldman, Sachs & Co.; *U.S. Private*, pg. 462
CHARTWELL PARTNERS; *U.S. Private*, pg. 230
CHARTWELL RE CORPORATION; *U.S. Public*, pg. 336
CHARTWELL REINSURANCE COMPANY—See Chartwell Re Corporation; *U.S. Public*, pg. 336
CHARTWELLS DINING SERVICES—See Compass Group plc; *Int'l*, pg. 324
CHARWELL PHARMACEUTICALS LIMITED—See Pfizer Inc.; *U.S. Public*, pg. 1283
CHASE ACCESS SERVICES CORP.—See The Chase Manhattan Corporation; *U.S. Public*, pg. 337
CHASE & SANBORN COFFEE, INC.—See Nestle S.A.; *Int'l*, pg. 917
CHASE & SONS-WEBSTER BRANCH—See Chase Corporation; *U.S. Public*, pg. 337
CHASE AUTO FINANCE CORPORATION—See The Chase Manhattan Corporation; *U.S. Public*, pg. 337
CHASE AUTOMATED CLEARING HOUSE, INC.—See The Chase Manhattan Corporation; *U.S. Public*, pg. 337
CHASE BANK & TRUST CO. (C.I.), LTD.—See The Chase Manhattan Corporation; *U.S. Public*, pg. 339
CHASE BANK INTERNATIONAL—See The Chase Manhattan Corporation; *U.S. Public*, pg. 338
CHASE BANK (IRELAND) PLC—See The Chase Manhattan Corporation; *U.S. Public*, pg. 339
CHASE BANK NV—See The Chase Manhattan Corporation; *U.S. Public*, pg. 339
CHASE BANK OF ARIZONA—See The Chase Manhattan Corporation; *U.S. Public*, pg. 338
CHASE BANK OF FLORIDA, N.A.—See The Chase Manhattan Corporation; *U.S. Public*, pg. 338
CHASE BANK OF MARYLAND—See The Chase Manhattan Corporation; *U.S. Public*, pg. 338
CHASE CANADA—See Chase Corporation; *U.S. Public*, pg. 337
CHASE CHEVROLET CO., INC.; *U.S. Private*, pg. 230
CHASE CORPORATION; *U.S. Public*, pg. 337
CHASE EDUCATION FINANCE—See The Chase Manhattan Corporation; *U.S. Public*, pg. 338
CHASE EQUIPMENT LEASING, INC.—See The Chase Manhattan Corporation; *U.S. Public*, pg. 338

CHASE EQUITY INCORPORATED—See The Chase Manhattan Corporation; *U.S. Public,* pg. 338
CHASE EXPORT CORPORATION—See Chase Corporation; *U.S. Public,* pg. 337
F.H. CHASE, INC.; *U.S. Private,* pg. 230
CHASE FINANCIAL MANAGEMENT CORP.—See The Chase Manhattan Corporation; *U.S. Public,* pg. 338
CHASE FUTURES & OPTIONS, INC.—See The Chase Manhattan Corporation; *U.S. Public,* pg. 341
CHASE GLOBAL FUNDS SERVICE COMPANY—See The Chase Manhattan Corporation; *U.S. Public,* pg. 338
CHASE HOME MORTGAGE CORPORATION—See The Chase Manhattan Corporation; *U.S. Public,* pg. 338
CHASE INSTITUTIONAL TRUST SYS.—See The Chase Manhattan Corporation; *U.S. Public,* pg. 338
CHASE INVEST A/S—See The Chase Manhattan Corporation; *U.S. Public,* pg. 339
CHASE INVESTIMENTI MOBILIARI S.P.A.—See The Chase Manhattan Corporation; *U.S. Public,* pg. 339
CHASE INVESTMENT BANK HOLDINGS LIMITED—See The Chase Manhattan Corporation; *U.S. Public,* pg. 339
CHASE INVESTMENT BANK LIMITED—See The Chase Manhattan Corporation; *U.S. Public,* pg. 339
P.T. CHASE LEASING INDONESIA—See The Chase Manhattan Corporation; *U.S. Public,* pg. 339
CHASE LEASING (JAPAN) LIMITED—See The Chase Manhattan Corporation; *U.S. Public,* pg. 339
CHASE LEASING LIMITED—See The Chase Manhattan Corporation; *U.S. Public,* pg. 339
CHASE LEASING (S.A.E.)—See The Chase Manhattan Corporation; *U.S. Public,* pg. 339
CHASE MANHATTAN ADMINISTRACAO E SERVICIOS, S.A.—See The Chase Manhattan Corporation; *U.S. Public,* pg. 339
THE CHASE MANHATTAN BANK—See The Chase Manhattan Corporation; *U.S. Public,* pg. 338
CHASE MANHATTAN BANK (AUSTRIA), A.G.—See The Chase Manhattan Corporation; *U.S. Public,* pg. 340
CHASE MANHATTAN BANK DELAWARE—See The Chase Manhattan Corporation; *U.S. Public,* pg. 338
CHASE MANHATTAN BANK ESPANA S.A.—See The Chase Manhattan Corporation; *U.S. Public,* pg. 340
CHASE MANHATTAN BANK LUXEMBOURG, S.A.—See The Chase Manhattan Corporation; *U.S. Public,* pg. 340
THE CHASE MANHATTAN BANK, N.A.—See The Chase Manhattan Corporation; *U.S. Public,* pg. 340
THE CHASE MANHATTAN BANK OF CANADA—See The Chase Manhattan Corporation; *U.S. Public,* pg. 340
THE CHASE MANHATTAN BANK OF CONNECTICUT—See The Chase Manhattan Corporation; *U.S. Public,* pg. 338
CHASE MANHATTAN BANK (SWITZERLAND)—See The Chase Manhattan Corporation; *U.S. Public,* pg. 340
THE CHASE MANHATTAN BANK (USA), NA—See The Chase Manhattan Corporation; *U.S. Public,* pg. 338
CHASE MANHATTAN CAPITAL MARKETS (U.K.) LTD.—See The Chase Manhattan Corporation; *U.S. Public,* pg. 339
THE CHASE MANHATTAN CORPORATION; *U.S. Public,* pg. 337
CHASE MANHATTAN EQUITIES LIMITED—See The Chase Manhattan Corporation; *U.S. Public,* pg. 339
CHASE MANHATTAN FINANCIAL CENTER, INC.—See The Chase Manhattan Corporation; *U.S. Public,* pg. 338
CHASE MANHATTAN FINANCIAL SERVICES (HONG KONG) LTD.—See The Chase Manhattan Corporation; *U.S. Public,* pg. 340
CHASE MANHATTAN FINANCIAL SERVICES, INC.—See The Chase Manhattan Corporation; *U.S. Public,* pg. 338
CHASE MANHATTAN FUTURES CORP.—See The Chase Manhattan Corporation; *U.S. Public,* pg. 341
CHASE MANHATTAN FUTURES (U.K.)—See The Chase Manhattan Corporation; *U.S. Public,* pg. 341
CHASE MANHATTAN GILTS LTD.—See The Chase Manhattan Corporation; *U.S. Public,* pg. 339
CHASE MANHATTAN INVESTMENT HOLDINGS, INC.—See The Chase Manhattan Corporation; *U.S. Public,* pg. 338
CHASE MANHATTAN INVESTMENT SERVICES (HONG KONG) LTD.—See The Chase Manhattan Corporation; *U.S. Public,* pg. 340
CHASE MANHATTAN LEASING—See The Chase Manhattan Corporation; *U.S. Public,* pg. 338
CHASE MANHATTAN LEASING GMBH—See The Chase Manhattan Corporation; *U.S. Public,* pg. 339
CHASE MANHATTAN MILBANK, LTD.—See The Chase Manhattan Corporation; *U.S. Public,* pg. 339
CHASE MANHATTAN MORTGAGE CORPORATION—See The Chase Manhattan Corporation; *U.S. Public,* pg. 338
CHASE MANHATTAN OF UTAH—See The Chase Manhattan Corporation; *U.S. Public,* pg. 338
CHASE MANHATTAN OVERSEAS BANKING CORPORATION—See The Chase Manhattan Corporation; *U.S. Public,* pg. 338
CHASE MANHATTAN OVERSEAS CORPORATION—See The Chase Manhattan Corporation; *U.S. Public,* pg. 340
CHASE MANHATTAN OVERSEAS FINANCE CORPORATION, N.V.—See The Chase Manhattan Corporation; *U.S. Public,* pg. 340
CHASE MANHATTAN, S.A.—See The Chase Manhattan Corporation; *U.S. Public,* pg. 340
CHASE MANHATTAN, S.A. CREDITO FINANCIAMENTO INVESTIMENTO—See The Chase Manhattan Corporation; *U.S. Public,* pg. 340
CHASE MANHATTAN, S.A. DISTRIBUIDORA DE TITULOS E VALORES MOBILIARIOS—See The Chase Manhattan Corporation; *U.S. Public,* pg. 340
CHASE MANHATTAN SECURITIES (JAPAN)—See The Chase Manhattan Corporation; *U.S. Public,* pg. 340

CHASE MANHATTAN SECURITIES S.A.—See The Chase Manhattan Corporation; *U.S. Public,* pg. 340
CHASE MANHATTAN SERVICE CORPORATION—See The Chase Manhattan Corporation; *U.S. Public,* pg. 338
CHASE MANHATTAN TRADING S.A.—See The Chase Manhattan Corporation; *U.S. Public,* pg. 340
CHASE MANHATTAN TRUST AND BANKING COMPANY (JAPAN) LIMITED—See The Chase Manhattan Corporation; *U.S. Public,* pg. 340
CHASE MANHATTAN TRUST CAYMAN LTD.—See The Chase Manhattan Corporation; *U.S. Public,* pg. 340
CHASE MANHATTAN TRUST COMPANY (HONG KONG) LTD.—See The Chase Manhattan Corporation; *U.S. Public,* pg. 340
THE CHASE MANHATTAN TRUST CO. OF CALIFORNIA, N.A.—See The Chase Manhattan Corporation; *U.S. Public,* pg. 338
THE CHASE MANHATTAN TRUST CORPORATION LIMITED—See The Chase Manhattan Corporation; *U.S. Public,* pg. 341
CHASE MANHATTAN TRUSTEES, LTD.—See The Chase Manhattan Corporation; *U.S. Public,* pg. 339
CHASE NATIONAL CORPORATE SERVICES, INC.—See The Chase Manhattan Corporation; *U.S. Public,* pg. 338
CHASE NETTING (U.K.) LTD.—See The Chase Manhattan Corporation; *U.S. Public,* pg. 341
CHASE SECURITIES, INC.—See The Chase Manhattan Corporation; *U.S. Public,* pg. 338
CHASE TRADE FINANCE, LTD.—See The Chase Manhattan Corporation; *U.S. Public,* pg. 339
CHASE TRADE, INC.—See The Chase Manhattan Corporation; *U.S. Public,* pg. 338
CHASE TRUST BANK—See The Chase Manhattan Corporation; *U.S. Public,* pg. 341
CHASE U.S. CONSUMER SERVICES—See The Chase Manhattan Corporation; *U.S. Public,* pg. 338
CHASEFIN-CHASE FINANZIARA, S.P.A.—See The Chase Manhattan Corporation; *U.S. Public,* pg. 341
CHASSIS OVERSEAS CORP.—See General Motors Corporation; *U.S. Public,* pg. 723
CHATAS GLASS CO., INC.—See Publicker Industries Inc.; *U.S. Public,* pg. 1341
CHATEAU BEAUMONT—See Suntory Ltd.; *Int'l,* pg. 1322
CHATEAU BEYCHEVELLE—See Suntory Ltd.; *Int'l,* pg. 1322
CHATEAU COMMUNITIES, INC.; *U.S. Public,* pg. 341
CHATEAU DE BLIGNY—See Suntory Ltd.; *Int'l,* pg. 1322
CHATEAU LAGRANGE S.A.—See Suntory Ltd.; *Int'l,* pg. 1322
CHATEAU ST. JEAN WINERY—See Suntory Ltd.; *Int'l,* pg. 1321
CHATEAUNEUF-LES-BAINS S.A.—See Nestle S.A.; *Int'l,* pg. 918
THE CHATHAM DAILY NEWS—See Hollinger Inc.; *Int'l,* pg. 631
CHATHAM IMPORTS, INC.—See Peerless Importers, Inc.; *U.S. Private,* pg. 847
CHATHAM TELEPHONE CO.—See Telephone and Data Systems, Inc.; *U.S. Public,* pg. 1571
CHATHAM TOWING COMPANY, INC.—See Colonial Oil Industries; *U.S. Private,* pg. 254
CHATHAM VENTURES, INC.—See The Chase Manhattan Corporation; *U.S. Public,* pg. 338
CHATSWORTH DATA CORPORATION; *U.S. Private,* pg. 231
CHATTAHOOCHEE INDUSTRIAL RAILROAD—See Georgia-Pacific Corporation; *U.S. Public,* pg. 736
CHATTANOOGA CABLE T.V. COMPANY—See The E.W. Scripps Company; *U.S. Public,* pg. 1447
CHATTANOOGA CHOO-CHOO HOLIDAY INN— *U.S. Private,* pg. 231
CHATTANOOGA GROUP, INC.; *U.S. Private,* pg. 231
CHATTANOOGA PAPERBOARD CORPORATION—See Caraustar Industries, Inc.; *U.S. Public,* pg. 303
CHATTEM (CANADA) INC.—See Chattem, Inc.; *U.S. Public,* pg. 342
CHATTEM, INC.; *U.S. Public,* pg. 341
CHATTEM, INC., CONSUMER PRODUCTS DIVISION—See Chattem, Inc.; *U.S. Public,* pg. 341
CHATTEM (U.K.) LTD.—See Chattem, Inc.; *U.S. Public,* pg. 342
CHATWINS GROUP, INC.; *U.S. Private,* pg. 231
BERNARD CHAUS, INC.; *U.S. Public,* pg. 342
CHAUSSEM—See Lagardere Groupe; *Int'l,* pg. 795
CHAUSSURES BALLY-FRANCE S.A.—See Oerlikon-Buhrle Holding AG; *Int'l,* pg. 997
CHAUSSURES BALLY MOULINS SA—See Oerlikon-Buhrle Holding AG; *Int'l,* pg. 997
S.A. CHAUSSURES BALLY SCHOENEN N.V.—See Oerlikon-Buhrle Holding AG; *Int'l,* pg. 997
CHAUSSURES BALLY VILLEURBANNE SA—See Oerlikon-Buhrle Holding AG; *Int'l,* pg. 997
CHAUVCO RESOURCES LTD.—See Trimac Corporation; *Int'l,* pg. 1424
CHAUX DE CONTERN S.A.—See Dyckerhoff AG; *Int'l,* pg. 423
CHAVANNE KETTIN—See Groupe Usinor; *Int'l,* pg. 571
CHAVENEAU BERNIS—See SNCF; *Int'l,* pg. 1163
CHECK CONSULTANTS INCORPORATED—See First Tennessee National Corporation; *U.S. Public,* pg. 639
CHECK POINT SOFTWARE TECHNOLOGIES (AUSTRALIA) LTD.—See Check Point Software Technologies Ltd.; *U.S. Public,* pg. 342
CHECK POINT SOFTWARE TECHNOLOGIES GMBH—See Check Point Software Technologies Ltd.; *U.S. Public,* pg. 342
CHECK POINT SOFTWARE TECHNOLOGIES INC.—See Check Point Software Technologies Ltd.; *U.S. Public,* pg. 342
CHECK POINT SOFTWARE TECHNOLOGIES (JAPAN) LTD.—See Check Point Software Technologies Ltd.; *U.S. Public,* pg. 342

CHECK POINT SOFTWARE TECHNOLOGIES LTD.; *U.S. Public,* pg. 342
CHECK POINT SOFTWARE TECHNOLOGIES LTD.—See Check Point Software Technologies Ltd.; *U.S. Public,* pg. 342
CHECK POINT SOFTWARE TECHNOLOGIES SARL—See Check Point Software Technologies Ltd.; *U.S. Public,* pg. 342
CHECK POINT SOFTWARE TECHNOLOGIES (SINGAPORE) LTD.—See Check Point Software Technologies Ltd.; *U.S. Public,* pg. 342
CHECK POINT SOFTWARE TECHNOLOGIES (UK) LTD.—See Check Point Software Technologies Ltd.; *U.S. Public,* pg. 342
THE CHECK STORE—See John H. Harland Company; *U.S. Public,* pg. 785
CHECK TECHNOLOGY CORPORATION; *U.S. Public,* pg. 342
CHECKERS DRIVE-IN RESTAURANTS, INC.; *U.S. Public,* pg. 342
CHECKMARK COMMUNICATIONS; *U.S. Private,* pg. 231
CHECKPOINT CANADA—See Checkpoint Systems Inc.; *U.S. Public,* pg. 343
CHECKPOINT CARRIBEAN—See Checkpoint Systems Inc.; *U.S. Public,* pg. 343
CHECKPOINT COMMUNICATIONS—See Rogers Communications, Inc.; *Int'l,* pg. 1123
CHECKPOINT DE MEXICO—See Checkpoint Systems Inc.; *U.S. Public,* pg. 343
CHECKPOINT SYSTEMS AUSTRALIA PTY LTD.—See Checkpoint Systems Inc.; *U.S. Public,* pg. 343
CHECKPOINT SYSTEMS BELGIUM NV—See Checkpoint Systems Inc.; *U.S. Public,* pg. 343
CHECKPOINT SYSTEMS DEUTSCHLAND GMGH—See Checkpoint Systems Inc.; *U.S. Public,* pg. 343
CHECKPOINT SYSTEMS FRANCE SARL—See Checkpoint Systems Inc.; *U.S. Public,* pg. 343
CHECKPOINT SYSTEMS INC.; *U.S. Public,* pg. 343
CHECKPOINT SYSTEMS, INC. PUERTO RICO—See Checkpoint Systems Inc.; *U.S. Public,* pg. 343
CHECKPOINT SYSTEMS NEDERLAND BV—See Checkpoint Systems Inc.; *U.S. Public,* pg. 343
CHECKPOINT SYSTEMS S.A.—See Checkpoint Systems Inc.; *U.S. Public,* pg. 343
CHECKPOINT SYSTEMS SCANDINAVIA AB—See Checkpoint Systems Inc.; *U.S. Public,* pg. 343
CHECKPOINT SYSTEMS UK LIMITED—See Checkpoint Systems Inc.; *U.S. Public,* pg. 343
CHECKRITE INTERNATIONAL—See Data Broadcasting Corporation; *U.S. Public,* pg. 484
CHEESECAKE FACTORY INCORPORATED; *U.S. Public,* pg. 343
CHEFARO ESPANOLA SA—See Akzo Nobel N.V.; *Int'l,* pg. 44
CHEFARO INTERNATIONAL B.V.—See Akzo Nobel N.V.; *Int'l,* pg. 44
CHEFARO NEDERLAND B.V.—See Akzo Nobel N.V.; *Int'l,* pg. 44
CHEFARO NV—See Akzo Nobel N.V.; *Int'l,* pg. 44
CHEFARO PROPS LTD.—See Akzo Nobel N.V.; *Int'l,* pg. 44
CHEFS INTERNATIONAL, INC.; *U.S. Public,* pg. 343
CHEGUTU CANNERS (PVT) LTD.—See H.J. Heinz Company; *U.S. Public,* pg. 807
CHEIL CIBA-GEIGY CO, LTD—See Novartis AG; *Int'l,* pg. 975
CHEIL COMMUNICATIONS, INC.—See Hakuhodo Incorporated; *Int'l,* pg. 588
CHEIL FOODS & CHEMICALS INC.—See Samsung Group; *Int'l,* pg. 1181
CHEIL INDUSTRIES INC.—See Samsung Group; *Int'l,* pg. 1181
CHEIL SYNTHETICS INC.—See Samsung Group; *Int'l,* pg. 1181
CHEKIANG FIRST BANK LTD.—See The Dai-Ichi Kangyo Bank, Limited; *Int'l,* pg. 361
CHELSEA GROUP—See Horizon Enterprises Group LLC; *U.S. Private,* pg. 539
CHELSEA HARBOUR LTD.—See The Peninsular and Oriental Steam Navigation Company; *Int'l,* pg. 1034
CHELSEA INDUSTRIES, INC.; *U.S. Private,* pg. 231
CHELSEA MILLING CO.; *U.S. Private,* pg. 231
CHELSEA STATE BANK; *U.S. Private,* pg. 231
CHELTENHAM & GLOUCESTER PLC; *Int'l,* pg. 283
CHELTENHAM NURSING & REHABILITATION CENTER—See Genesis Health Ventures, Inc.; *U.S. Public,* pg. 729
CHELTENHAM-YORK ROAD NURSING & REHABILITATION CENTER—See Genesis Health Ventures, Inc.; *U.S. Public,* pg. 729
CHEM FREE CORPORATION—See Intelligent Systems Corp.; *U.S. Public,* pg. 888
CHEM-PLAST S.P.A.—See Henkel KGaA; *Int'l,* pg. 611
CHEM-TAINER INDUSTRIES; *U.S. Private,* pg. 231
CHEM-TREND INCORPORATED—See Burmah Castrol plc; *Int'l,* pg. 235
CHEM-TRONICS, INC.—See The Interlake Corporation; *U.S. Public,* pg. 893
CHEMA BALCKE-DURR VERFAHRENSTECHNIK GMBH RUDISLEBEN—See Deutsche Babcock AG; *Int'l,* pg. 399
CHEMAG AKTIENGESELLSCHAFT—See BASF AG; *Int'l,* pg. 104
CHEMAG CHEMIKALIEN-HANDELS GES M.B.H.—See BASF AG; *Int'l,* pg. 107
CHEMAG IBERICA S.A.—See BASF AG; *Int'l,* pg. 107
CHEMAG SOUTH AFRICA LTD.—See BASF AG; *Int'l,* pg. 107
CHEMAIUS SAWMILL DIVISION—See MacMillan Bloedel Limited; *Int'l,* pg. 828
CHEMAP—See Tetra Laval Group; *Int'l,* pg. 1380
CHEMAP, INC.—See Tetra Laval Group; *Int'l,* pg. 1378
CHEMARKETING INTERNATIONAL, INC.—See Bayer AG; *Int'l,* pg. 173

CHEMBANK DIRECTORY OF CORPORATE AFFILIATIONS
Company Index

CHEMBANK DEPOSITORY NOMINEES, LTD.—See The Chase Manhattan Corporation; *U.S. Public*, pg. 341
CHEMBANK NOMINEES LIMITED—See The Chase Manhattan Corporation; *U.S. Public*, pg. 341
CHEMCENTRAL/ATLANTA—See CHEMCENTRAL Corporation; *U.S. Private*, pg. 232
CHEMCENTRAL/BUFFALO—See CHEMCENTRAL Corporation; *U.S. Private*, pg. 232
CHEMCENTRAL/CHICAGO—See CHEMCENTRAL Corporation; *U.S. Private*, pg. 232
CHEMCENTRAL/CINCINNATI—See CHEMCENTRAL Corporation; *U.S. Private*, pg. 232
CHEMCENTRAL/CLEVELAND—See CHEMCENTRAL Corporation; *U.S. Private*, pg. 232
CHEMCENTRAL CORPORATION; *U.S. Private*, pg. 231
CHEMCENTRAL/DALLAS—See CHEMCENTRAL Corporation; *U.S. Private*, pg. 232
CHEMCENTRAL/DETROIT—See CHEMCENTRAL Corporation; *U.S. Private*, pg. 232
CHEMCENTRAL/FORT WAYNE—See CHEMCENTRAL Corporation; *U.S. Private*, pg. 232
CHEMCENTRAL/GRAND RAPIDS—See CHEMCENTRAL Corporation; *U.S. Private*, pg. 232
CHEMCENTRAL/GREENSBORO—See CHEMCENTRAL Corporation; *U.S. Private*, pg. 232
CHEMCENTRAL/HOUSTON—See CHEMCENTRAL Corporation; *U.S. Private*, pg. 232
CHEMCENTRAL/INDIANAPOLIS—See CHEMCENTRAL Corporation; *U.S. Private*, pg. 232
CHEMCENTRAL/KANSAS CITY—See CHEMCENTRAL Corporation; *U.S. Private*, pg. 232
CHEMCENTRAL/LOS ANGELES—See CHEMCENTRAL Corporation; *U.S. Private*, pg. 232
CHEMCENTRAL/LOUISVILLE—See CHEMCENTRAL Corporation; *U.S. Private*, pg. 232
CHEMCENTRAL/MILWAUKEE—See CHEMCENTRAL Corporation; *U.S. Private*, pg. 232
CHEMCENTRAL/MINNESOTA—See CHEMCENTRAL Corporation; *U.S. Private*, pg. 232
CHEMCENTRAL/NEW ORLEANS—See CHEMCENTRAL Corporation; *U.S. Private*, pg. 232
CHEMCENTRAL/ODESSA—See CHEMCENTRAL Corporation; *U.S. Private*, pg. 232
CHEMCENTRAL/OKLAHOMA CITY—See CHEMCENTRAL Corporation; *U.S. Private*, pg. 232
CHEMCENTRAL/ORLANDO—See CHEMCENTRAL Corporation; *U.S. Private*, pg. 232
CHEMCENTRAL/PHILADELPHIA—See CHEMCENTRAL Corporation; *U.S. Private*, pg. 232
CHEMCENTRAL/PITTSBURGH—See CHEMCENTRAL Corporation; *U.S. Private*, pg. 232
CHEMCENTRAL/PORTLAND—See CHEMCENTRAL Corporation; *U.S. Private*, pg. 232
CHEMCENTRAL/ST. LOUIS—See CHEMCENTRAL Corporation; *U.S. Private*, pg. 232
CHEMCENTRAL/SALT LAKE CITY—See CHEMCENTRAL Corporation; *U.S. Private*, pg. 232
CHEMCENTRAL/SAN ANTONIO—See CHEMCENTRAL Corporation; *U.S. Private*, pg. 232
CHEMCENTRAL/SAN FRANCISCO—See CHEMCENTRAL Corporation; *U.S. Private*, pg. 232
CHEMCENTRAL/SEATTLE—See CHEMCENTRAL Corporation; *U.S. Private*, pg. 232
CHEMCENTRAL/SPOKANE—See CHEMCENTRAL Corporation; *U.S. Private*, pg. 232
CHEMCENTRAL/TOLEDO—See CHEMCENTRAL Corporation; *U.S. Private*, pg. 232
CHEMCENTRAL/TULSA—See CHEMCENTRAL Corporation; *U.S. Private*, pg. 232
CHEMCO EQUIPMENT FINANCE LIMITED—See The Chase Manhattan Corporation; *U.S. Public*, pg. 341
CHEMCO ITALIA S.P.A.—See Dainippon Ink & Chemicals, Inc.; *Int'l*, pg. 370
CHEMCO TECHNOLOGIES NORTH S.R.L.—See Dainippon Ink & Chemicals, Inc.; *Int'l*, pg. 371
CHEMDAL CORPORATION—See AMCOL International Corp.; *U.S. Public*, pg. 64
CHEMDESIGN CORPORATION—See Bayer AG; *Int'l*, pg. 173
CHEMDEX, INC.—See Polydex Pharmaceuticals Limited; *Int'l*, pg. 1063
CHEMED CORPORATION; *U.S. Public*, pg. 343
CHEMETALL GMBH GESELLSCHAFT FUER CHEMISCH TECHNISCHE VERFAHREN—See Metallgesellschaft AG; *Int'l*, pg. 861
CHEMETICS INTERNATIONAL COMPANY LTD VANCOUVER OPERATIONS—See Kvaerner a.s.a.; *Int'l*, pg. 774
CHEMETRONICS CARIBE INC.—See Williams Holdings Plc; *Int'l*, pg. 1500
CHEMFAB CORPORATION; *U.S. Public*, pg. 344
CHEMFERM INDUSTRIAL PHARMACEUTICALS S.A.—See Royal Gist-Brocades N.V.; *Int'l*, pg. 1143
CHEMFERM VOF—See DSM N.V.; *Int'l*, pg. 354
CHEMFERM VOF—See Royal Gist-Brocades N.V.; *Int'l*, pg. 1143
CHEMFIRST INC.; *U.S. Public*, pg. 344
CHEMFIX INTERNATIONAL, INC.—See Advanced Remediation Inc. (ARM); *U.S. Private*, pg. 22
CHEMGRAPHICS SYSTEMS, INC.—See The Chase Manhattan Corporation; *U.S. Public*, pg. 338
CHEMI-TROL CHEMICAL CO.; *U.S. Public*, pg. 345
CHEMIA GMBH—See Bayer AG; *Int'l*, pg. 175
CHEMICAL ADMINISTRACAO E CONSULTORIA ECONOMICO FINANCEIRA LTDA.—See The Chase Manhattan Corporation; *U.S. Public*, pg. 341
CHEMICAL ASIA LTD.—See The Chase Manhattan Corporation; *U.S. Public*, pg. 341
CHEMICAL BANK & TRUST COMPANY—See Chemical Financial Corporation; *U.S. Public*, pg. 345
CHEMICAL BANK BAY AREA—See Chemical Financial Corporation; *U.S. Public*, pg. 345
CHEMICAL BANK CENTRAL—See Chemical Financial Corporation; *U.S. Public*, pg. 345
CHEMICAL BANK (GUERNSEY) LIMITED—See The Chase Manhattan Corporation; *U.S. Public*, pg. 341
CHEMICAL BANK KEY STATE—See Chemical Financial Corporation; *U.S. Public*, pg. 345
CHEMICAL BANK MICHIGAN—See Chemical Financial Corporation; *U.S. Public*, pg. 345
CHEMICAL BANK MONTCALM—See Chemical Financial Corporation; *U.S. Public*, pg. 345
CHEMICAL BANK NORTH—See Chemical Financial Corporation; *U.S. Public*, pg. 345
CHEMICAL BANK PENSION PLAN TRUSTEE, LTD.—See The Chase Manhattan Corporation; *U.S. Public*, pg. 341
CHEMICAL BANK SOUTH—See Chemical Financial Corporation; *U.S. Public*, pg. 345
CHEMICAL BANK THUMB AREA—See Chemical Financial Corporation; *U.S. Public*, pg. 345
CHEMICAL BANK WEST—See Chemical Financial Corporation; *U.S. Public*, pg. 345
CHEMICAL CATALYSTS—See Engelhard Corporation; *U.S.* Public, pg. 582
CHEMICAL COATINGS, INC.—See RPM, Inc.; *U.S. Public*, pg. 1357
CHEMICAL COMPANY OF MALAYSIA BERHAD—See Imperial Chemical Industries PLC; *Int'l*, pg. 664
CHEMICAL CONSTRUCTION PRODUCTS—See Illinois Tool Works Inc.; *U.S. Public*, pg. 867
CHEMICAL ENGINEERING—See The McGraw-Hill Companies; *U.S. Public*, pg. 1071
CHEMICAL EXCHANGE INDUSTRIES; *U.S. Private*, pg. 232
CHEMICAL FABRICS LIMITED—See Chemfab Corporation; *U.S. Public*, pg. 344
CHEMICAL FINANCIAL CORPORATION; *U.S. Public*, pg. 345
CHEMICAL INSURANCE COMPANY LIMITED—See Novartis AG; *Int'l*, pg. 975
CHEMICAL LEAMAN CORPORATION; *U.S. Private*, pg. 233
CHEMICAL LEAMAN TANK LINES, INC.—See Chemical Leaman Corporation; *U.S. Private*, pg. 233
CHEMICAL PROPERTIES, INC.—See Chemical Leaman Corporation; *U.S. Private*, pg. 233
CHEMICAL SECURITIES LIMITED—See The Chase Manhattan Corporation; *U.S. Public*, pg. 341
CHEMICAL SPECIALTIES, INC.—See Laporte plc; *Int'l*, pg. 802
CHEMICAL SPECIALTIES MANUFACTURING CORP.—See RPM, Inc.; *U.S. Public*, pg. 1357
CHEMIE LINZ BENELUX B.V.—See DSM N.V.; *Int'l*, pg. 356
CHEMIE LINZ FRANCE S.A.R.L.—See DSM N.V.; *Int'l*, pg. 356
CHEMIE LINZ JAPAN LTD.—See DSM N.V.; *Int'l*, pg. 356
CHEMIE LINZ PRAG S.R.O.—See DSM N.V.; *Int'l*, pg. 356
CHEMIE LINZ UK LTD.—See DSM N.V.; *Int'l*, pg. 356
CHEMIE-WERK WEINSHEIM GMBH—See Ruetgers A.G.; *Int'l*, pg. 1148
CHEMIEWERK NUNCHRITZ GMBH—See Veba AG; *Int'l*, pg. 1454
CHEMIFAX—See Namico, Inc.; *U.S. Private*, pg. 774
CHEMIFORWARD GENERAL TRADING CO.—See Sinochem International Petroleum Co. Ltd.; *Int'l*, pg. 1255
CHEMINEER, INC.—See Robbins & Myers, Inc.; *U.S. Public*, pg. 1393
CHEMING A.S.—See Tractebel; *Int'l*, pg. 1415
CHEMIONICS CORPORATION—See Chessco Industries, Inc.; *U.S. Private*, pg. 234
CHEMIPRO FINE CHEMICAL KAISHA LIMITED—See Novartis AG; *Int'l*, pg. 975
CHEMISCHE BETRIEBE PLUTO GMBH—See Veba AG; *Int'l*, pg. 1460
CHEMISCHE FABRIK AUBING GMBH—See Ruetgers A.G.; *Int'l*, pg. 1148
CHEMISCHE FABRIK GRUNAU GMBH—See Henkel KGaA; *Int'l*, pg. 609
CHEMISCHE FABRIK KALK GMBH—See BASF AG; *Int'l*, pg. 104
CHEMISCHE FABRIK LEHRTE DR. ANDREAS KOSSEL GMBH—See Veba AG; *Int'l*, pg. 1458
CHEMISCHE FABRIK PROMONTA GMBH—See Altana AG; *Int'l*, pg. 66
CHEMISCHE FABRIK WIBARCO GMBH—See BASF AG; *Int'l*, pg. 104
CHEMISOLV—See Serv-Tech, Inc.; *U.S. Public*, pg. 1460
CHEMLAND INDUSTRIES, INC.—See Lakeland Industries, Inc.; *U.S. Public*, pg. 975
CHEMO-TECHNISCHE MANUFACTURING, INC.—See Wella Group; *Int'l*, pg. 1490
CHEMOFLON GMBH—See Martin Merkel GmbH & Co. KG; *Int'l*, pg. 859
CHEMOIL; *U.S. Private*, pg. 233
CHEMOL CO., INC.—See Siga, Inc.; *U.S. Private*, pg. 999
CHEMOLDANZAS GMBH—See Danzas Holding Ltd.; *Int'l*, pg. 382
CHEMONICS FIRE-TROL, INC.—See Erly Industries, Inc.; *U.S. Public*, pg. 591
CHEMONICS INDUSTRIES (CANADA) LTD.—See Erly Industries, Inc.; *U.S. Public*, pg. 591
CHEMONICS INTERNATIONAL-CONSULTING DIV.—See Erly Industries, Inc.; *U.S. Public*, pg. 591
CHEMOXY INTERNATIONAL PLC—See Ascot Holdings Plc; *Int'l*, pg. 88
CHEMPLAST, INC.—See Saint-Gobain; *Int'l*, pg. 1174
CHEMPOWER, INC.—See American Eco Corporation; *Int'l*, pg. 74
CHEMPUMP—See Crane Co.; *U.S. Public*, pg. 456
CHEMREX INC.—See Viag AG; *Int'l*, pg. 1465
CHEMRICH, INC.—See Albright & Wilson plc; *Int'l*, pg. 49
CHEMRITE SOUTHERN AFRICA (PTY) LTD.—See RPM, Inc.; *U.S. Public*, pg. 1358
CHEMROCK CORPORATION—See RGP Holding, Inc.; *U.S.* Private, pg. 903
CHEMSERV INDUSTRIE SERVICE GES.M.B.H.—See DSM N.V.; *Int'l*, pg. 356
CHEMSTONE CORP.; *U.S. Private*, pg. 233
CHEM-TECH, INC.—See Smith International, Inc.; *U.S. Public*, pg. 1478
CHEMTECH PRODUCTS INC.—See Allied Industrial Group, Inc.; *U.S. Private*, pg. 39
CHEMTEX ENGINEERING—See Mitsubishi Corporation; *Int'l*, pg. 872
CHEMTEX FIBERS EXPORT, INC.—See Mitsubishi Corporation; *Int'l*, pg. 872
CHEMTEX FIBERS INC.—See Mitsubishi Corporation; *Int'l*, pg. 872
CHEMTEX INTERNATIONAL, INC.—See Mitsubishi Corporation; *Int'l*, pg. 872
CHEMTEX OVERSEAS, INC.—See Mitsubishi Corporation; *Int'l*, pg. 872
CHEMTRONICS AB—See Spectra-Physics AB; *Int'l*, pg. 1289
CHEMTRONICS INC.—See Morgan Crucible Co. Plc; *Int'l*, pg. 892
CHEMUNG FORD, INC.; *U.S. Private*, pg. 233
CHEMVIRON CARBON—See Calgon Carbon Corporation; *U.S. Public*, pg. 293
CHEMVIRON CARBON GMBH—See Calgon Carbon Corporation; *U.S. Public*, pg. 293
CHEMVIRON SPECIALTY CHEMICALS—See Merck & Co., Inc.; *U.S. Public*, pg. 1091
CHEMWEST CORP.—See Corporacion Grupo Quimico, S.A.C.A.; *Int'l*, pg. 332
CHEONAN TECHNICAL CENTER—See Advantest Corporation; *Int'l*, pg. 25
CHEP AUSTRALIA—See Brambles Industries Limited; *Int'l*, pg. 211
CHEP CANADA INC.—See Brambles Industries Limited; *Int'l*, pg. 212
CHEP EUROP S.A.—See Brambles Industries Limited; *Int'l*, *pg. 212*
CHEP FRANCE SA—See Brambles Industries Limited; *Int'l*, *pg. 212*
CHEP IN EUROPE—See Brambles Industries Limited; *Int'l*, pg. 212
CHEP UK LIMITED—See Brambles Industries Limited; *Int'l*, pg. 212
CHEP USA—See Brambles Industries Limited; *Int'l*, pg. 211
CHEP USA—See GKN plc; *Int'l*, pg. 535
CHEQUE REPAS LUXEMBOURG S.A.—See Sodexho S.A.; *Int'l*, pg. 1274
CHEQUE RESTAURANT—See Sodexho S.A.; *Int'l*, pg. 1274
CHERASIA LIMITED—See Cherry Electrical Products Corporation; *U.S. Public*, pg. 346
CHERAW PLANT—See Cooper Industries, Inc.; *U.S. Public*, *pg. 444*
CHERAW YARN MILLS, INC.; *U.S. Private*, pg. 233
CHERNIN'S SHOE OUTLET—See Chernin's Shoes, Inc.; *U.S. Private*, pg. 233
CHERNIN'S SHOES, INC.; *U.S. Private*, pg. 233
CHEROKEE BRICK & TILE CO.; *U.S. Private*, pg. 233
CHEROKEE INC.; *U.S. Public*, pg. 345
CHEROKEE INTERNATIONAL LLC; *U.S. Private*, pg. 233
CHEROKEE NATIONAL LIFE INSURANCE CO.—See CNL Financial Corp.; *U.S. Public*, pg. 282
CHERRY AUSTRALIA PTY. LTD.—See Cherry Electrical Products Corporation; *U.S. Public*, pg. 346
CHERRY AUTOMOTIVE-JAPAN—See Cherry Electrical Products Corporation; *U.S. Public*, pg. 346
CHERRY CENTRAL COOPERATIVE; *U.S. Private*, pg. 233
CHERRY CREEK GOLF—See Millstein Industries; *U.S. Private*, pg. 749
CHERRY CREEK VILLAGE NURSING CENTER—See Horizon/CMS Healthcare Corporation; *U.S. Public*, pg. 837
CHERRY CREEK VILLAGE RETIREMENT CENTER—See Horizon/CMS Healthcare Corporation; *U.S. Public*, pg. 837
CHERRY ELECTRICAL PRODUCTS—See Cherry Electrical Products Corporation; *U.S. Public*, pg. 346
CHERRY ELECTRICAL PRODUCTS CORPORATION; *U.S.* Public, pg. 346
CHERRY HILL CENTER, INC.—See The Rouse Company; *U.S. Public*, pg. 1408
CHERRY MIKROSCHALTER GMBH—See Cherry Electrical Products Corporation; *U.S. Public*, pg. 346
CHERRY SARL—See Cherry Electrical Products Corporation; *U.S. Public*, pg. 346
CHERRY SEMICONDUCTOR CORP.—See Cherry Electrical Products Corporation; *U.S. Public*, pg. 346
CHERRY SRO—See Cherry Electrical Products Corporation; *U.S. Public*, pg. 346
CHESAPEAKE BAGEL BAKERY—See AFC Enterprises; *U.S. Private*, pg. 5
CHESAPEAKE CORPORATION; *U.S. Public*, pg. 346
CHESAPEAKE DISPLAY AND PACKAGING CO.—See Chesapeake Corporation; *U.S. Public*, pg. 346
CHESAPEAKE FOREST PRODUCTS CO.—See Chesapeake Corporation; *U.S. Public*, pg. 346
CHESAPEAKE INSURANCE DIVISION—See W.R. Berkley Corporation; *U.S. Public*, pg. 215
CHESAPEAKE INVESTMENT CO.—See Chesapeake Utilities Corporation; *U.S. Public*, pg. 347
THE CHESAPEAKE LIFE INSURANCE CO.—See United Insurance Companies, Inc.; *U.S. Public*, pg. 1679
CHESAPEAKE PACKAGING CO.—See Chesapeake Corporation; *U.S. Public*, pg. 346
CHESAPEAKE PACKAGING CO./BALTIMORE—See Chesapeake Corporation; *U.S. Public*, pg. 346
CHESAPEAKE PACKAGING CO./BINGHAMTON—See Chesapeake Corporation; *U.S. Public*, pg. 346
CHESAPEAKE PACKAGING CO./LEROY—See Chesapeake Corporation; *U.S. Public*, pg. 346
CHESAPEAKE PACKAGING CO./LOUISVILLE—See Chesapeake Corporation; *U.S. Public*, pg. 346

CHESAPEAKE PACKAGING CO./MADISON—See Chesapeake Corporation; *U.S. Public,* pg. 347
CHESAPEAKE PACKAGING CO./NORTH TONAWANDA—See Chesapeake Corporation; *U.S. Public,* pg. 347
CHESAPEAKE PACKAGING CO./RICHMOND—See Chesapeake Corporation; *U.S. Public,* pg. 347
CHESAPEAKE PACKAGING CO./ROANOKE—See Chesapeake Corporation; *U.S. Public,* pg. 347
CHESAPEAKE PACKAGING CO./SCOTIA—See Chesapeake Corporation; *U.S. Public,* pg. 347
CHESAPEAKE PACKAGING CO./SCRANTON—See Chesapeake Corporation; *U.S. Public,* pg. 347
CHESAPEAKE PAPER PRODUCTS CO.—See Chesapeake Corporation; *U.S. Public,* pg. 347
CHESAPEAKE SERVICES COMPANY—See Chesapeake Utilities Corporation; *U.S. Public,* pg. 347
CHESAPEAKE UTILITIES CORPORATION; *U.S. Public,* pg. 347
CHESAPEAKE WESTERN RAILWAY—See Norfolk Southern Corporation; *U.S. Public,* pg. 1191
CHESEBROUGH POND'S—See Unilever Plc; *Int'l,* pg. 1435
CHESEBROUGH-POND'S MFG. CO.—See Unilever Plc; *Int'l,* 1435
CHESEBROUGH-POND'S INC.—See Unilever Plc; *Int'l,* pg. 1436
CHESEBROUGH-POND'S USA CO.—See Unilever Plc; *Int'l,* 1435
CHESHIRE—See The General Electric Company, p.l.c.; *Int'l,* pg. 545
CHESHIRE WHOLEFOODS PLC—See Koninklijke BolsWessanen nv; *Int'l,* pg. 752
CHESSCO INDUSTRIES, INC.; *U.S. Private,* pg. 234
CHESSWOOD PRODUCE LTD.—See Tomkins PLC; *Int'l,* pg. 1396
CHESTER SPRINGS DISTRIBUTION POINT—See Cloister Pure Spring Water Co., Inc.; *U.S. Private,* pg. 247
CHESTERFIELD DIVISION—See Springs Industries, Inc.; *U.S. Public,* pg. 1500
CHESTERFIELD INDUSTRIAL PARK, INC.—See Watlow Electric Manufacturing Company; *U.S. Private,* pg. 1153
A.W. CHESTERTON CO.; *U.S. Private,* pg. 234
CHESTERTON BINSWANGER CAPITAL ADVISORS—See Binswanger; *U.S. Private,* pg. 144
THE CHESTERTOWN BANK OF MARYLAND—See Mercantile Bankshares Corporation; *U.S. Public,* pg. 1088
CHESTNUT HILL NATIONAL BANK—See National Penn Bancshares, Inc.; *U.S. Public,* pg. 1159
CHEVROLET MOTOR DIV. GENERAL MOTORS CORP.—See General Motors Corporation; *U.S. Public,* pg. 720
CHEVROLET, PONTIAC, GM OF CANADA GROUP—See General Motors Corporation; *U.S. Public,* pg. 720
CHEVRON CANADA LIMITED—See Chevron Corporation; *U.S. Public,* pg. 348
CHEVRON CANADA RESOURCES LIMITED—See Chevron Corporation; *U.S. Public,* pg. 348
CHEVRON CAPITAL U.S.A. INC.—See Chevron Corporation; *U.S. Public,* pg. 348
CHEVRON CHEMICAL COMPANY—See Chevron Corporation; *U.S. Public,* pg. 348
CHEVRON CHEMICAL S.A.—See Chevron Corporation; *U.S. Public,* pg. 348
CHEVRON CORPORATION; *U.S. Public,* pg. 347
CHEVRON INTERNATIONAL TRADING COMPANY-WEST AFRICA—See Chevron Corporation; *U.S. Public,* pg. 348
CHEVRON LAND & DEVELOPMENT COMPANY—See Chevron Corporation; *U.S. Public,* pg. 348
CHEVRON OIL COMPANY OF NETHERLANDS—See Chevron Corporation; *U.S. Public,* pg. 348
CHEVRON OIL FINANCE COMPANY—See Chevron Corporation; *U.S. Public,* pg. 348
CHEVRON OVERSEAS PETROLEUM, INC.—See Chevron Corporation; *U.S. Public,* pg. 348
CHEVRON OVERSEAS PETROLEUM LIMITED—See Chevron Corporation; *U.S. Public,* pg. 348
CHEVRON PETROLEUM COMPANY OF COLOMBIA—See Chevron Corporation; *U.S. Public,* pg. 348
CHEVRON PIPE LINE COMPANY—See Chevron Corporation; *U.S. Public,* pg. 348
CHEVRON RESEARCH AND TECHNOLOGY COMPANY—See Chevron Corporation; *U.S. Public,* pg. 348
CHEVRON SHALE OIL CO.—See Chevron Corporation; *U.S. Public,* pg. 348
CHEVRON SHIPPING CO.—See Chevron Corporation; *U.S. Public,* pg. 348
CHEVRON STANDARD LIMITED—See Chevron Corporation; *U.S. Public,* pg. 348
CHEVRON STATIONS, INC.—See Chevron Corporation; *U.S. Public,* pg. 348
CHEVRON TCI INC.—See Chevron Corporation; *U.S. Public,* pg. 348
CHEVRON (U.K.) LTD.—See Chevron Corporation; *U.S. Public,* pg. 348
CHEVRON U.S.A. INC.—See Chevron Corporation; *U.S. Public,* pg. 348
CHEVRON USA PRODUCTION CO.—See Chevron Corporation; *U.S. Public,* pg. 348
CHEVRON USA PRODUCTS CO.—See Chevron Corporation; *U.S. Public,* pg. 348
CHEVY CHASE CARS & GEO; *U.S. Private,* pg. 234
CHEVY CHASE, INC.—See Borden, Inc.; *U.S. Private,* pg. 158
CHEXSYSTEMS, INC.—See Deluxe Corporation; *U.S. Public,* pg. 498
CHEYENNE—See Computer Associates International, Inc.; *U.S. Public,* pg. 420
CHEYENNE LIGHT, FUEL & POWER CO.—See New Century Energies, Inc.; *U.S. Public,* pg. 1170
CHEYENNE OUTFITTERS, INC.; *U.S. Private,* pg. 234
CHI-CHI'S INC.—See Family Restaurants, Inc.; *U.S. Private,* pg. 393
CHI SYSTEMS DIVISION—See Superior Consultant Holdings Corp.; *U.S. Public,* pg. 1539

CHIA LUNG CHEMICAL INDUSTRIAL CORP.—See Dainippon Ink & Chemicals, Inc.; *Int'l,* pg. 371
CHIAPHUA SHINKO COPPER ALLOY CO., LTD.—See Kobe Steel, Ltd.; *Int'l,* pg. 741
CHIAPHUA SHINKO COPPER ALLOY CO., LTD.—See Nissho Iwai Corporation; *Int'l,* pg. 946
THE CHIBA BANK, LTD.-INTERNATIONAL DIVISON—See The Chiba Bank, Ltd.; *Int'l,* pg. 283
THE CHIBA BANK, LTD.-NEW YORK BRANCH—See The Chiba Bank, Ltd.; *Int'l,* pg. 283
THE CHIBA BANK, LTD.; *Int'l,* pg. 283
CHIBA BANK, LTD.-HONG KONG BRANCH—See The Chiba Bank, Ltd.; *Int'l,* pg. 283
CHIBA BANK, LTD.-LONDON BRANCH—See The Chiba Bank, Ltd.; *Int'l,* pg. 283
CHIBA BANK, LTD.-LOS ANGELES AGENCY—See The Chiba Bank, Ltd.; *Int'l,* pg. 283
CHIBA GENERAL LEASE CO., LTD.—See Chiba Kogyo Bank; *Int'l,* pg. 283
CHIBA GUARANTEE SERVICE CO., LTD.—See Chiba Kogyo Bank; *Int'l,* pg. 283
CHIBA INTERNATIONAL LTD.—See The Chiba Bank, Ltd.; *Int'l,* pg. 283
CHIBA KOGIN BUSINESS SERVICE CO., LTD.—See Chiba Kogyo Bank; *Int'l,* pg. 284
CHIBA KOGIN COMPUTER SOFT CO., LTD.—See Chiba Kogyo Bank; *Int'l,* pg. 284
CHIBA KOGIN FINANCE CO., LTD.—See Chiba Kogyo Bank; *Int'l,* pg. 284
CHIBA KOGIN STAFF SERVICES CO., LTD.—See Chiba Kogyo Bank; *Int'l,* pg. 284
CHIBA KOGIN UC CARD CO., LTD.—See Chiba Kogyo Bank; *Int'l,* pg. 284
CHIBA KOGYO BANK; *Int'l,* pg. 283
CHIBA KOGYO INTERNATIONAL DIV.—See Chiba Kogyo Bank; *Int'l,* pg. 283
CHIBA KOGYO-NEW YORK—See Chiba Kogyo Bank; *Int'l,* pg. 284
CHIBA TOYOPET CO., LTD.—See Toyota Motor Corporation; *Int'l,* pg. 1412
CHIBA TOYOTA MOTOR CO., LTD.—See Toyota Motor Corporation; *Int'l,* pg. 1412
CHIC—See Conseco Inc.; *U.S. Public,* pg. 433
CHICAGO ASSET MANAGEMENT COMPANY—See United Asset Management Corporation; *U.S. Public,* pg. 1672
CHICAGO AUTOWERKS, INC.—See Stamford Capital; *U.S. Private,* pg. 1030
CHICAGO BAKING CO.—See Lewis Brothers Bakeries, Inc.; *U.S. Private,* pg. 665
CHICAGO BOAT YARD, INC.—See CFB Industries, Inc.; *U.S. Private,* pg. 194
CHICAGO CONSOLIDATED—See Holberg Industries, Inc.; *U.S. Private,* pg. 533
CHICAGO CREATIVE PARTNERSHIP; *U.S. Private,* pg. 234
CHICAGO CUTLERY ETC. INC.—See General Housewares Corp.; *U.S. Public,* pg. 716
CHICAGO CUTLERY, INC.—See General Housewares Corp.; *U.S. Public,* pg. 716
CHICAGO EXTRUDED METALS CO.; *U.S. Private,* pg. 234
THE CHICAGO FAUCET CO.; *U.S. Private,* pg. 234
CHICAGO FINANCIAL PRINTING DIVISION—See R.R. Donnelley & Sons Company; *U.S. Public,* pg. 518
CHICAGO FIRE BRICK CO.—See CFB Industries, Inc.; *U.S. Private,* pg. 194
CHICAGO FIRE BRICK OF DELAWARE, INC.—See CFB Industries, Inc.; *U.S. Private,* pg. 194
CHICAGO HEIGHTS STEEL; *U.S. Private,* pg. 234
CHICAGO HOLDINGS, INC.; *U.S. Private,* pg. 234
CHICAGO INTERMODAL CO.—See Illinois Central Corporation; *U.S. Public,* pg. 865
CHICAGO LASER SYSTEMS—See Electro Scientific Industries, Inc.; *U.S. Public,* pg. 569
CHICAGO LOCK COMPANY; *U.S. Private,* pg. 235
CHICAGO MACHINE TOOL COMPANY; *U.S. Private,* pg. 235
CHICAGO MAGAZINE—See Primedia Inc.; *U.S. Public,* pg. 1328
CHICAGO MAGNET WIRE CORP.—See Philips Electronics N.V.; *Int'l,* pg. 1054
CHICAGO MEDICAL SCHOOL HOSPITAL, INC.—See Columbia/HCA Healthcare Corporation; *U.S. Public,* pg. 404
CHICAGO MERCANTILE EXCHANGE; *U.S. Private,* pg. 235
CHICAGO NATIONAL LEAGUE BALL CLUB, INC. (CHICAGO CUBS)—See Tribune Company; *U.S. Public,* pg. 1635
CHICAGO PAPER BOARD CORPORATION—See Caraustar Industries, Inc.; *U.S. Public,* pg. 303
CHICAGO PLANT—See Cooper Industries, Inc.; *U.S. Public,* pg. 443
CHICAGO PNEUMATIC TOOL COMPANY—See Atlas Copco AB; *Int'l,* pg. 96
CHICAGO RAIL LINK—See Broe Companies; *U.S. Private,* pg. 171
CHICAGO RAWHIDE—See AB SKF; *Int'l,* pg. 1157
CHICAGO READER, INC.; *U.S. Private,* pg. 235
CHICAGO RIVET & MACHINE CO.-AUTOMATED ASSEMBLY SYSTEMS—See Chicago Rivet & Machine Company; *U.S. Public,* pg. 349
CHICAGO RIVET & MACHINE COMPANY; *U.S. Public,* pg. 348
CHICAGO SHOW PRINTING CO.; *U.S. Private,* pg. 235
CHICAGO SOUTH FINANCIAL CENTER—See Northern Trust Corporation; *U.S. Public,* pg. 1196
CHICAGO STEEL TAPE; *U.S. Private,* pg. 235
CHICAGO STEEL & WIRE—See MCM Enterprises, Inc.; *U.S. Private,* pg. 686
CHICAGO SUN TIMES—See Hollinger Inc.; *Int'l,* pg. 632
CHICAGO TITLE & TRUST CO.—See Alleghany Corporation; *U.S. Public,* pg. 42
CHICAGO TITLE INSURANCE CO.—See Alleghany Corporation; *U.S. Public,* pg. 42

CHICAGO TRANSIT AUTHORITY—See Regional Transportation Authority (RTA); *U.S. Private,* pg. 919
CHICAGO TRIBUNE CO.—See Tribune Company; *U.S. Public,* pg. 1635
CHICAGO TRIBUNE DIRECT—See Tribune Company; *U.S. Public,* pg. 1635
CHICAGO TUBE & IRON CO.; *U.S. Private,* pg. 235
CHICAGO TUBE & IRON COMPANY OF MINNESOTA—See Chicago Tube & Iron Co.; *U.S. Private,* pg. 235
CHICAGO UNION STATION COMPANY—See Amtrak-National Railroad Passenger Corp.; *U.S. Private,* pg. 69
CHICAGO WEST PULLMAN & SOUTHERN RAILROAD—See Broe Companies; *U.S. Private,* pg. 171
CHICAGO WEST PULLMAN CORPORATION; *U.S. Private,* pg. 235
CHICAGO WEST PULLMAN FINANCIAL CORPORATION—See Chicago West Pullman Corporation; *U.S. Private,* pg. 236
CHICAGO WEST PULLMAN HEAVY INDUSTRIES—See Chicago West Pullman Corporation; *U.S. Private,* pg. 236
CHICAGO WHITE METAL CASTING, INC.; *U.S. Private,* pg. 236
CHICHIBU ONODA CEMENT CORPORATION; *Int'l,* pg. 284
CHICHIBU ONODA CEMENT CORPORATION-AUSTRALIA—See Chichibu Onoda Cement Corporation; *Int'l,* pg. 284
CHICHIBU ONODA CEMENT CORPORATION-BANGKOK—See Chichibu Onoda Cement Corporation; *Int'l,* pg. 284
CHICHIBU ONODA CEMENT CORPORATION-BEIJING—See Chichibu Onoda Cement Corporation; *Int'l,* pg. 284
CHICHIBU ONODA CEMENT CORPORATION-DALIAN—See Chichibu Onoda Cement Corporation; *Int'l,* pg. 284
CHICHIBU ONODA CEMENT CORPORATION-NANJING—See Chichibu Onoda Cement Corporation; *Int'l,* pg. 284
CHICHIBU ONODA CEMENT CORPORATION-UNITED KINGDOM—See Chichibu Onoda Cement Corporation; *Int'l,* pg. 284
CHICKASHA COTTON OIL CO.—See Tomen Corporation; *Int'l,* pg. 1395
CHICK-FIL-A, INC.; *U.S. Private,* pg. 236
CHICLE ADAMS S.A.—See Warner-Lambert Company; *U.S. Public,* pg. 1739
CHICLE ADAMS, S.A. DE C.V.—See Warner-Lambert Company; *U.S. Public,* pg. 1739
CHICOPEE—See BBA Group plc; *Int'l,* pg. 113
CHICOPEE INC.—See BBA Group plc; *Int'l,* pg. 113
CHICO'S FAS INC; *U.S. Public,* pg. 349
CHIEF AGRI/INDUSTRIAL DIVISION—See Chief Industries, Inc.; *U.S. Private,* pg. 236
CHIEF AUTO PARTS; *U.S. Private,* pg. 236
CHIEF CONSTRUCTION—See Chief Industries, Inc.; *U.S. Private,* pg. 236
CHIEF E-Z BREAKER, INC.—See Chief Industries, Inc.; *U.S. Private,* pg. 236
CHIEF ETHANOL FUELS, INC.—See Chief Industries, Inc.; *U.S. Private,* pg. 236
CHIEF FINANCIAL SERVICES—See Chief Industries, Inc.; *U.S. Private,* pg. 236
CHIEF INDUSTRIES, INC.; *U.S. Private,* pg. 236
CHIEF INDUSTRIES, INC.- FABRICATION DIV.—See Chief Industries, Inc.; *U.S. Private,* pg. 236
CHIEF INDUSTRIES UK LTD.—See Chief Industries, Inc.; *U.S. Private,* pg. 236
CHIEF INDUSTRIES UK LTD—See Chief Industries, Inc.; *U.S. Private,* pg. 236
CHIEFTAIN DEVELOPMENT CO. LTD.—See Alberta Energy Company, Ltd.; *Int'l,* pg. 49
CHIEFTAIN EXPLORATION (U.K.) LTD.—See Chieftain International, Inc.; *Int'l,* pg. 284
CHIEFTAIN INTERNATIONAL, INC.; *Int'l,* pg. 284
CHIEFTAIN INTERNATIONAL NORTH SEA LIMITED—See Chieftain International, Inc.; *Int'l,* pg. 284
CHIEFTAIN INTERNATIONAL (U.S.) INC.—See Chieftain International, Inc.; *Int'l,* pg. 284
CHIGASAKI PLANT—See Mitsubishi Chemical Corporation; *Int'l,* pg. 871
CHILD MAGAZINE—See Bertelsmann AG; *Int'l,* pg. 190
CHILDCRAFT EDUCATION CORPORATION—See The Walt Disney Company; *U.S. Public,* pg. 513
CHILDREN'S BETTER HEALTH INSTITUTE—See Benjamin Franklin Literary & Medical Society, Inc.; *U.S. Private,* pg. 133
CHILDREN'S BUSINESS—See The Walt Disney Company; *U.S. Public,* pg. 513
THE CHILDREN'S HOSPITAL OF PHILADELPHIA; *U.S. Private,* pg. 236
CHILDREN'S NURSING SERVICES, LTD.—See The Care Group, Inc.; *U.S. Public,* pg. 305
THE CHILDREN'S PLACE RETAIL STORES, INC.; *U.S. Private,* pg. 237
CHILDRENS PRESS INC.—See Lagardere Groupe; *Int'l,* pg. 794
CHILDRENS WORLD—See Storehouse PLC; *Int'l,* pg. 1304
J.W. CHILDS ASSOCIATES, L.P.; *U.S. Private,* pg. 237
CHILE COPPER LTD.—See CODELCO Chile (Corporacion Nacional Del Cobre De Chile); *Int'l,* pg. 303
CHILEBRAS METAIS LTDA.—See CODELCO Chile (Corporacion Nacional Del Cobre De Chile); *Int'l,* pg. 303
CHILENA CONSOLIDADA SEGUROS DE VIDA S.A.—See Zurich Insurance Company; *Int'l,* pg. 1531
CHILENA CONSOLIDADA SEGUROS GENERALES S.A.—See Zurich Insurance Company; *Int'l,* pg. 1531
CHILI PEPPER OF ROCKY POINT, INC.—See Specialty Restaurants Corporation; *U.S. Private,* pg. 1023
CHILLICOTHE NEWSPAPERS—See Gannett Company, Inc.; *U.S. Public,* pg. 700
CHILTEM GROUP SAM—See Alpha Omikron Limited; *Int'l,* pg. 65
CHILTON ELECTRIC—See The Glen Dimplex Group; *Int'l,* pg. 554

CHILTON RESEARCH SERVICES—See Reed Elsevier plc; *Int'l*, pg. 1096
CHIMIQUE DE LA MEDITERRANEE—See Royal Dutch/ Shell Group of Companies; *Int'l*, pg. 1138
CHINA AIRLINES LTD.; *Int'l*, pg. 284
CHINA AMERICAN PETROCHEMICAL CO., LTD.—See Amoco Corporation; *U.S. Public*, pg. 102
CHINA BEKAERT STEEL CORD CO., LTD.—See N.V. Bekaert S.A.; *Int'l*, pg. 185
CHINA CENTURY CEMENT LTD.—See Heidelberger Zement A.G.; *Int'l*, pg. 605
CHINA COMPUTERWORLD—See International Data Group; *U.S. Private*, pg. 569
CHINA COMPUTERWORLD/PC WORLD CHINA—See International Data Group; *U.S. Private*, pg. 569
CHINA ECOTEK CORPORATION—See China Steel Corporation; *Int'l*, pg. 285
CHINA HEWLETT-PACKARD CO., LTD.—See Hewlett-Packard Company; *U.S. Public*, pg. 816
CHINA HI-MENT CORP.—See China Steel Corporation; *Int'l*, pg. 285
CHINA INFOWORLD—See International Data Group; *U.S. Private*, pg. 569
CHINA INTERNATIONAL FINANCE COMPANY LIMITED (SHENZHEN)—See The Sumitomo Bank, Limited; *Int'l*, pg. 1310
CHINA INTERNATIONAL PETROLEUM & CHEMICALS UNITED CO. Ltd.; *Int'l*—See Sinochem International Petroleum Co. Ltd.; *Int'l*, pg. 1254
CHINA JIANGSU SUNTORY FOODS CO., LTD.—See Suntory Ltd.; *Int'l*, pg. 1322
CHINA JINSHAN ASSOCIATED TRADING CORPORATION—See Sinochem International Petroleum Co. Ltd.; *Int'l*, pg. 1254
CHINA KANG FU INTERNATIONAL LEASING CO., LTD.—See The Fuji Bank, Limited; *Int'l*, pg. 521
CHINA LIAOHUA UNITED FOREIGN TRADE CO. LTD.—See Sinochem International Petroleum Co. Ltd.; *Int'l*, pg. 1254
CHINA MANAGEMENT SYSTEMS (CMS)—See Marcam Solutions, Inc.; *U.S. Public*, pg. 1043
CHINA NATIONAL CEREALS, OILS & FOODSTUFFS CORPORATION (COFCO); *Int'l*, pg. 285
CHINA NATIONAL TECHNICAL IMPORT & EXPORT CORPORATION (CNTIC); *Int'l*, pg. 285
CHINA ORIENT LEASING CO., LTD.—See Orix Corporation; *Int'l*, pg. 1009
CHINA OTSUKA PHARMACEUTICAL CO., LTD.—See Otsuka Pharmaceutical Co., Ltd.; *Int'l*, pg. 1014
CHINA PROSPERING BUILDING DESIGN JOINT VENTURE CORPORATION LTD.—See Shimizu Corporation; *Int'l*, pg. 1233
CHINA SCHINDLER ELEVATOR CO. LTD.—See Schindler Holding AG; *Int'l*, pg. 1205
CHINA STEEL CHEMICAL CORP.—See China Steel Corporation; *Int'l*, pg. 286
CHINA STEEL CORPORATION; *Int'l*, pg. 285
CHINA STEEL EXPRESS CORPORATION—See China Steel Corporation; *Int'l*, pg. 285
CHINA STEEL GLOBAL TRADING CORPORATION—See China Steel Corporation; *Int'l*, pg. 285
CHINA STEEL STRUCTURE CO., LTD.—See China Steel Corporation; *Int'l*, pg. 286
CHINA SYNTHETIC RUBBER CORPORATION; *Int'l*, pg. 286
CHINA THREAD DEVELOPMENT CO. LTD.—See Coats Viyella plc; *Int'l*, pg. 299
CHINA UNITED INTERNATIONAL LEASING CO., LTD.—See The Sakura Bank, Limited; *Int'l*, pg. 1180
CHINA UNITED PETROLEUM CO.—See Sinochem International Petroleum Co. Ltd.; *Int'l*, pg. 1254
CHINA UNIVERSAL LEASING CO., LTD.—See The Sanwa Bank Limited; *Int'l*, pg. 1190
CHINA YANSHAN UNITED FOREIGN TRADE CO. LTD.—See Sinochem International Petroleum Co. Ltd.; *Int'l*, pg. 1254
CHINA YINGKOU-FUCHS OIL COMPANY LTD.—See Fuchs Petrolub AG Oel + Chemie; *Int'l*, pg. 518
THE CHINESE AMERICAN BANK—See The International Commercial Bank of China; *Int'l*, pg. 683
CHINESE PETROLEUM CORPORATION; *Int'l*, pg. 286
THE CHINET CO.—See Royal Packaging Industries Van Leer B.V.; *Int'l*, pg. 1146
CHINO MINES COMPANY—See Phelps Dodge Corporation; *U.S. Public*, pg. 1287
CHINON INDUSTRIES INC.; *Int'l*, pg. 286
CHIP SUPPLY INC.; *U.S. Private*, pg. 237
CHIPBOARD MILL BRASKEREIDFOSS—See Norske Skogindustrier A/S; *Int'l*, pg. 965
CHIPBOARD MILL KVAM—See Norske Skogindustrier A.S; *Int'l*, pg. 965
CHIPICO PICKLES—See Vienna Sausage Mfg. Co.; *U.S. Private*, pg. 1140
CHIPMAN-UNION, INC.; *U.S. Private*, pg. 237
CHIPMILL—See Anthony Forest Products Co., Inc.; *U.S. Private*, pg. 76
CHIPS AND TECHNOLOGIES, INC.; *U.S. Public*, pg. 349
CHIPS AND TECHNOLOGIES, INC.—See Chips and Technologies, Inc.; *U.S. Public*, pg. 349
CHIPS-OLW AB—See Novartis AG; *Int'l*, pg. 975
CHIPWICH INC.; *U.S. Private*, pg. 237
CHIQUITA BANANA NORTH AMERICA—See Chiquita Brands International, Inc.; *U.S. Public*, pg. 349
CHIQUITA BRANDS INTERNATIONAL, INC.; *U.S. Public*, pg. 349
CIA. CHIRICANA DE LECHE, S.A.—See Borden, Inc.; *U.S. Private*, pg. 159
CHIRON—See Chiron Corporation; *U.S. Public*, pg. 350
CHIRON ADATOMED—See Chiron Corporation; *U.S. Public*, pg. 350
CHIRON BEHRING GMBH & CO.—See Chiron Corporation; *U.S. Public*, pg. 350
CHIRON BEHRING GMBH & CO.—See Hoechst Aktiengesellschaft; pg. 624

CHIRON CORPORATION; *U.S. Public*, pg. 349
CHIRON DIAGNOSTICS—See Chiron Corporation; *U.S. Public*, pg. 350
CHIRON DOMILENS—See Chiron Corporation; *U.S. Public*, pg. 350
CHIRON FRANCE S.A.R.L.—See Chiron Corporation; *U.S. Public*, pg. 350
CHIRON GMBH—See Chiron Corporation; *U.S. Public*, pg. 350
CHIRON IBERIA S.A.—See Chiron Corporation; *U.S. Public*, pg. 350
CHIRON ITALIA S.R.L.—See Chiron Corporation; *U.S. Public*, pg. 350
CHIRON MIMOTOPES—See Chiron Corporation; *U.S. Public*, pg. 350
CHIRON MIMOTOPES PEPTIDE SYSTEMS—See Chiron Corporation; *U.S. Public*, pg. 350
CHIRON TECHNOLOGIES—See Chiron Corporation; *U.S. Public*, pg. 350
CHIRON THERAPEUTICS—See Chiron Corporation; *U.S. Public*, pg. 350
CHIRON U.K. LTD.—See Chiron Corporation; *U.S. Public*, pg. 350
CHIRON VIAGENE, INC.—See Chiron Corporation; *U.S. Public*, pg. 350
CHIRON VISION—See Chiron Corporation; *U.S. Public*, pg. 350
CHIRON VISION AUSTRALIA—See Chiron Corporation; *U.S. Public*, pg. 350
CHIRON VISION DOMILENS SPAIN—See Chiron Corporation; *U.S. Public*, pg. 350
CHIRON VISION SINGAPORE PTE LTD.—See Chiron Corporation; *U.S. Public*, pg. 350
CHIRON VISION UK—See Chiron Corporation; *U.S. Public*, pg. 350
CHISHOLM, BOYD & WHITE CO.—See Venturedyne, Ltd.; *U.S. Private*, pg. 1136
THE CHISHOLM-MINGO GROUP; *U.S. Private*, pg. 237
CHISWICK TRADING INC.; *U.S. Private*, pg. 237
CHITTENDEN & EASTMAN CO.; *U.S. Private*, pg. 237
CHITTENDEN BANK—See Chittenden Corporation; *U.S. Public*, pg. 350
CHITTENDEN CORPORATION; *U.S. Public*, pg. 350
CHIVAS PRODUCTS LTD.; *U.S. Private*, pg. 238
CHIYODA INVESTMENT CAYMAN LIMITED—See Chiyoda Mutual Life Insurance Company; *Int'l*, pg. 1321
CHIYODA KOGYO CO., LTD.—See Suntory Ltd.; *Int'l*, pg. 1321
CHIYODA LIFE EUROPE LIMITED—See Chiyoda Mutual Life Insurance Company; *Int'l*, pg. 287
CHIYODA LIFE INVESTMENT LUXEMBURG S.A.—See Chiyoda Mutual Life Insurance Company; *Int'l*, pg. 287
CHIYODA LIFE REALTY FRANCE S.A.—See Chiyoda Mutual Life Insurance Company; *Int'l*, pg. 287
CHIYODA LIFE REALTY OF AMERICA, INC.—See Chiyoda Mutual Life Insurance Company; *Int'l*, pg. 287
CHIYODA MUTUAL LIFE INSURANCE COMPANY; *Int'l*, pg. 286
CHLORIDE ELECTRONICS LTD.—See Chloride Group PLC; *Int'l*, pg. 287
CHLORIDE FRANCE SA—See Chloride Group PLC; *Int'l*, pg. 287
CHLORIDE GROUP PLC; *Int'l*, pg. 287
CHLORIDE GROUP PLC—See Chloride Group PLC; *Int'l*, pg. 287
CHLORIDE INDUSTRIAL BATTERIES LTD.—See BTR plc; *Int'l*, pg. 125
CHLORIDE PORTUGAL LIMITADA—See Chloride Group PLC; *Int'l*, pg. 287
CHLORIDE POWER ELECTRONICS INC.—See Chloride Group PLC; *Int'l*, pg. 287
CHLORIDE POWER ELECTRONICS PTY. LIMITED—See Chloride Group PLC; *Int'l*, pg. 287
CHLORIDE POWER ELECTRONICS (THAILAND) LTD.—See Chloride Group PLC; *Int'l*, pg. 287
CHLORURE DE VINYLE DE FOS—See Royal Dutch/Shell Group of Companies; *Int'l*, pg. 1138
CHO HUNG BANK; *Int'l*, pg. 287
CHO HUNG BANK, MUMBAI BRANCH—See Cho Hung Bank; *Int'l*, pg. 288
CHO HUNG FINANCE LIMITED—See Cho Hung Bank; *Int'l*, pg. 288
CHOCK FULL O' NUTS COFFEE COMPANY—See Chock Full O' Nuts Corporation; *U.S. Public*, pg. 351
CHOCK FULL O' NUTS CORPORATION; *U.S. Public*, pg. 351
CHOCOAMERICAN S.A.—See Midial S.A.; *Int'l*, pg. 865
CHOCOLAT FREY AG—See Migros; *Int'l*, pg. 865
CHOCOLATE PRODUCTS CO. LTD.—See George Weston Limited; *Int'l*, pg. 1495
CHOCOLATES NESTLE S.A.—See Nestle S.A.; *Int'l*, pg. 920
CHOCTAW ELECTRIC CO-OP; *U.S. Public*, pg. 238
CHOCTAW, INC.; *U.S. Private*, pg. 238
CHOICE HOTELS INTERNATIONAL, INC.; *U.S. Public*, pg. 351
CHOICE PUBLICATIONS LTD—See EMAP Plc; *Int'l*, pg. 451
CHOKWANG JOTUN LTD.—See Jotun A/S; *Int'l*, pg. 715
CHOMERICS EUROPE/U.K.—See Parker Hannifin Corporation; *U.S. Public*, pg. 1262
CHOMERICS INC.—See Parker Hannifin Corporation; *U.S. Public*, pg. 1262
CHONGQING TEKTRONIX ELECTRONIC INSTRUMENT CO., LTD.—See Tektronix, Inc.; *U.S. Public*, pg. 1567
CHONGQUING KANSAI PAINT CO., LTD.—See Kansai Paint Co., Ltd.; *Int'l*, pg. 723
CHONGQING SI YOU CONTINUOUS CASTING MACHINE TECHNICAL ENGINEERING CO., LTD.—See Mitsubishi Heavy Industries Ltd.; *Int'l*, pg. 874
CHONJU PAPER MFG. CO., LTD.—See Samsung Group; *Int'l*, pg. 1181
CHORE-TIME/BROCK INTERNATIONAL—See CTB International Corp.; *U.S. Public*, pg. 285

CHORE-TIME CAGE SYSTEMS—See CTB International Corp.; *U.S. Public*, pg. 285
CHORE-TIME EQUIPMENT—See CTB International Corp.; *U.S. Public*, pg. 285
CHORI AMERICA, INC.—See Chori Co., Ltd.; *Int'l*, pg. 288
CHORI CO., LTD.; *Int'l*, pg. 288
CHORUS LINE CORPORATION; *U.S. Private*, pg. 238
CHOTIN CARRIERS, INC.—See Kirby Corporation; *U.S. Public*, pg. 962
CHR. BROUWER SCHIFFAHRTS- UND BEFRACHTUNGSKONTOR GMBH—See Fried. Krupp AG; *Int'l*, pg. 515
CHR. HANSEN A/S—See Chr. Hansen Holding A/S; *Int'l*, pg. 288
CHR. HANSEN BIO SYSTEMS A/S—See Chr. Hansen Holding A/S; *Int'l*, pg. 288
CHR. HANSEN CZECH REPUBLIC, S.R.O.—See Chr. Hansen Holding A/S; *Int'l*, pg. 289
CHR. HANSEN DE MEXICO, S.A. DE CV—See Chr. Hansen Holding A/S; *Int'l*, pg. 289
CHR. HANSEN HOLDING A/S; *Int'l*, pg. 288
CHR. HANSEN INDUSTRIA E COMERCIO LTDA.—See Chr. Hansen Holding A/S; *Int'l*, pg. 289
CHR. HANSEN-LACTA S.L.—See Chr. Hansen Holding A/S; *Int'l*, pg. 289
CHRIS-CRAFT BOATS—See Greenway Partners, L.P.; *U.S. Private*, pg. 478
CHRIS-CRAFT INDUSTRIAL PRODUCTS, INC.—See Chris-Craft Industries, Inc.; *U.S. Public*, pg. 351
CHRIS-CRAFT INDUSTRIAL PRODUCTS, INC., MONO-SOL DIV.—See Chris-Craft Industries, Inc.; *U.S. Public*, pg. 351
CHRIS-CRAFT INDUSTRIES, INC.; *U.S. Public*, pg. 351
CHRISTAL RADIO—See Chancellor Media Corporation; *U.S. Public*, pg. 335
CHRISTENSEN DIAMOND PRODUCTS DEL PERU S.A.—See Saint-Gobain; *Int'l*, pg. 1174
CHRISTENSEN DRILLING SYSTEMS SDNN. BHD.—See Saint-Gobain; *Int'l*, pg. 1174
CHRISTENSEN GULF SERVICES (PRIVATE) LIMITED—See Saint-Gobain; *Int'l*, pg. 1174
CHRISTENSEN PRODUCTS—See Layne Christenson Co.; *U.S. Public*, pg. 981
CHRISTENSEN RÖDER ARGENTINA S.A.—See Saint-Gobain; *Int'l*, pg. 1174
CHRISTENSEN RÖDER PRODUCTOS DIAMANTADOS LTDA.—See Saint-Gobain; *Int'l*, pg. 1174
CHRISTENSEN RODER PRODUCTOS E SERVICOS DE PETROLEO LTDA.—See Saint-Gobain; *Int'l*, pg. 1174
CHRISTENSEN SAUDI ARABIA LIMITED—See Saint-Gobain; *Int'l*, pg. 1174
CHRISTENSON ELECTRIC, INC.; *U.S. Private*, pg. 238
CHRISTIAENSEN—See GIB Group; *Int'l*, pg. 534
CHRISTIAENSEN INTERNATIONAL—See GIB Group; *Int'l*, pg. 533
CHRISTIAN CHILDREN'S FUND, INC.; *U.S. Private*, pg. 238
CHRISTIAN DALLOZ—See Essilor International Compagnie Generale d'Optique; *Int'l*, pg. 462
CHRISTIAN DIOR PERFUMES INC.—See LVMH Moet Hennessy Louis Vuitton; *Int'l*, pg. 781
CHRISTIAN DIOR S.A.—See Au Bon Marche; *Int'l*, pg. 97
CHRISTIAN LACROIX INC.—See LVMH Moet Hennessy Louis Vuitton; *Int'l*, pg. 781
CHRISTIAN LACROIX MAROQUINERIE—See LVMH Moet Hennessy Louis Vuitton; *Int'l*, pg. 780
CHRISTIAN LACROIX SNC—See LVMH Moet Hennessy Louis Vuitton; *Int'l*, pg. 780
CHRISTIAN LACROIX U.K.—See LVMH Moet Hennessy Louis Vuitton; *Int'l*, pg. 782
CHRISTIAN MEMORIAL CULTURAL CENTER; *U.S. Private*, pg. 238
CHRISTIAN MUTUAL LIFE INSURANCE CO.—See Central United Life Insurance Co.; *U.S. Private*, pg. 225
CHRISTIANA COMMUNITY BUILDERS—See Christiana Companies, Inc.; *U.S. Public*, pg. 352
CHRISTIANA COMPANIES, INC.; *U.S. Public*, pg. 352
CHRISTIANIA BANK-COPENHAGEN REPRESENTATIVE OFFICE—See Christiania Bank og Kreditkasse ASA; *Int'l*, pg. 289
CHRISTIANIA BANK-LONDON BRANCH—See Christiania Bank og Kreditkasse ASA; *Int'l*, pg. 289
CHRISTIANIA BANK LUXEMBOURG S.A.—See Christiania Bank og Kreditkasse ASA; *Int'l*, pg. 289
CHRISTIANIA BANK LUXEMBOURG S.A.-REPRESENTACION EN ESPANA—See Christiania Bank og Kreditkasse ASA; *Int'l*, pg. 289
CHRISTIANIA BANK OG KREDITKASSE ASA; *Int'l*, pg. 289
CHRISTIANIA BANK-SINGAPORE BRANCH—See Christiania Bank og Kreditkasse ASA; *Int'l*, pg. 289
CHRISTIANIA BANK-STOCKHOLM BRANCH—See Christiania Bank og Kreditkasse ASA; *Int'l*, pg. 289
CHRISTIANIA BANK-HAMBURG REPRESENTATIVE OFFICE—See Christiania Bank og Kreditkasse ASA; *Int'l*, pg. 289
CHRISTIANITY TODAY, INC.; *U.S. Private*, pg. 238
CHRISTIANSBURG GARMENT CO. INC.—See Donnkenny, Inc.; *U.S. Public*, pg. 520
CHRISTIE DESIGN—See Recoton Corporation; *U.S. Public*, pg. 1369
CHRISTIE, MANSON & WOODS LIMITED—See Christies International plc; *Int'l*, pg. 290
AB AXEL CHRISTIERNSSON—See Axel Johnson AB; *Int'l*, pg. 708
CHRISTIE'S AMSTERDAM B.V.—See Christies International plc; *Int'l*, pg. 290
CHRISTIE'S AUSTRALIA PTY. LTD.—See Christies International plc; *Int'l*, pg. 290
CHRISTIE'S EAST—See Christies International plc; *Int'l*, pg. 290
CHRISTIE'S HELLAS LTD.—See Christies International plc; *Int'l*, pg. 290

CHRISTIE'S HONG KONG LTD.—See Christies International plc, pg. 290
CHRISTIE'S INC.—See Christies International plc; *Int'l*, pg. 290
CHRISTIES INTERNATIONAL PLC; *Int'l*, pg. 289
CHRISTIE'S (INTERNATIONAL) S.A.—See Christies International plc, *Int'l*, pg. 290
CHRISTIE'S INTERNATIONAL SINGAPORE PTE. LTD.— See Christies International plc; *Int'l*, pg. 290
CHRISTIE'S (ISRAEL) LTD.—See Christies International plc; *Int'l*, pg. 290
CHRISTIE'S MONACO S.A.M.—See Christies International plc; *Int'l*, pg. 290
CHRISTIE'S SCOTLAND LTD.—See Christies International plc; *Int'l*, pg. 290
CHRISTIE'S SOUTH KENSINGTON LIMITED— See Christies International plc; *Int'l*, pg. 290
CHRISTIE'S TAIWAN—See Christies International plc; *Int'l*, pg. 290
CHRISTOPH GMBH—See Fried. Krupp AG; *Int'l*, pg. 513
CHRISTY HALSEY OIL CO.—See Meenan Oil Co. L.P.; *U.S. Private*, pg. 729
CHRISTY'S MARKETS, INC.; *U.S. Private*, pg. 238
CHROMA CORPORATION; *U.S. Private*, pg. 238
CHROMA VIDEO, INC.—See Video Display Corporation; *U.S. Public*, pg. 1720
CHROMALLOY GAS TURBINE CORP.—See Sequa Corporation; *U.S. Public*, pg. 1458
CHROMALOX, S.A.—See Emerson Electric Co.; *U.S. Public*, pg. 576
CHROMA-TEK—See The Alpha Corporation Of Tennessee; *U.S. Private*, pg. 45
CHROMATIC TECHNOLOGIES, INC.—See Draka Kabel B.V.; *Int'l*, pg. 417
CHROMATOGRAPHY SYSTEMS—See Varian Associates, Inc.; *U.S. Public*, pg. 1710
CHROMAVISION MEDICAL SYSTEMS, INC.—See Safeguard Scientifics, Inc.; *U.S. Public*, pg. 1424
CHROMCRAFT CORPORATION—See Chromcraft Revington, Inc.; *U.S. Public*, pg. 352
CHROMCRAFT REVINGTON; *U.S. Public*, pg. 352
CHROME CHEMICALS (SOUTH AFRICA) (PTY.) LTD.— See Bayer AG; *Int'l*, pg. 175
CHROME CRANKSHAFT COMPANY—See Varlen Corporation; *U.S. Public*, pg. 1710
CHROME CRANKSHAFT OF ILLINOIS—See Varlen Corporation; *U.S. Public*, pg. 1710
CHROMIUM CORP.—See Elcor Corporation; *U.S. Public*, pg. 568
CHRONICLE PUBLISHING CO. INC.; *U.S. Private*, pg. 239
CHRONICLE SIT CO., LTD.—See Credit Commercial de France; *Int'l*, pg. 343
CHRONICLE-TRIBUNE—See Gannett Company, Inc.; *U.S. Public*, pg. 700
CHRONIMED INC.; *U.S. Public*, pg. 352
CHRONOS RICHARDSON—See Staveley Industries PLC; *Int'l*, pg. 1299
CHRONOS RICHARDSON GMBH—See Staveley Industries PLC; *Int'l*, pg. 1299
CHRONOS RICHARDSON LIMITED—See Staveley Industries PLC; *Int'l*, pg. 1299
CHRYSLER ADVANCE MANUFACTURING OPERATIONS—See Chrysler Corporation; *U.S. Public*, pg. 353
CHRYSLER CANADA LTD.—See Chrysler Corporation; *U.S. Public*, pg. 354
CHRYSLER CAPITAL CORP.—See Chrysler Corporation; *U.S. Public*, pg. 354
CHRYSLER COMERCIAL, S.A. DE C.V.—See Chrysler Corporation; *U.S. Public*, pg. 354
CHRYSLER CORPORATION; *U.S. Public*, pg. 352
CHRYSLER CREDIT CANADA LTD.—See Chrysler Corporation; *U.S. Public*, pg. 354
CHRYSLER CREDIT CORP.—See Chrysler Corporation; *U.S. Public*, pg. 354
CHRYSLER DE MEXICO S.A.—See Chrysler Corporation; *U.S. Public*, pg. 354
CHRYSLER FINANCIAL CORPORATION—See Chrysler Corporation; *U.S. Public*, pg. 354
CHRYSLER FIRST BUSINESS CREDIT CORPORATION— See Chrysler Corporation; *U.S. Public*, pg. 354
CHRYSLER INSURANCE CO.—See Chrysler Corporation; *U.S. Public*, pg. 354
CHRYSLER LIFE INSURANCE CO.—See Chrysler Corporation; *U.S. Public*, pg. 354
CHRYSLER OVERSEAS CAPITAL CORPORATION—See Chrysler Corporation; *U.S. Public*, pg. 354
CHRYSLER/PLYMOUTH DIVISION—See Chrysler Corporation; *U.S. Public*, pg. 353
CHRYSLER REALTY CORP.—See Chrysler Corporation; *U.S. Public*, pg. 354
CHRYSO—See Lafarge S.A.; *Int'l*, pg. 789
CHUANSHI CHRISTENSEN DIAMOND BIT COMPANY, LTD.—See Saint-Gobain; *Int'l*, pg. 1174
CHUBB & SON, INC.—See The Chubb Corporation; *U.S. Public*, pg. 355
THE CHUBB CORPORATION; *U.S. Public*, pg. 354
CHUBB CUSTOM INSURANCE COMPANY—See The Chubb Corporation; *U.S. Public*, pg. 355
CHUBB CUSTOM MARKET, INC.—See The Chubb Corporation; *U.S. Public*, pg. 355
CHUBB HONG KONG LTD.—See Jardine Matheson Holdings Limited; *Int'l*, pg. 705
THE CHUBB INSTITUTE—See The Chubb Corporation; *U.S. Public*, pg. 355
CHUBB INSURANCE CO. OF CANADA—See The Chubb Corporation; *U.S. Public*, pg. 355
CHUBB INSURANCE COMPANY OF EUROPE—See The Chubb Corporation; *U.S. Public*, pg. 355
CHUBB INSURANCE COMPANY OF NEW JERSEY— See The Chubb Corporation; *U.S. Public*, pg. 355
CHUBB LLOYDS INSURANCE CO. OF TX—See The Chubb Corporation; *U.S. Public*, pg. 355

CHUBB SINGAPORE PRIVATE LIMITED—See Sime Darby Berhad; *Int'l*, pg. 1250
CHUBBHEALTH NEW YORK/NEW JERSEY—See Cigna Corp.; *U.S. Public*, pg. 360
CHUBU CATERPILLAR MITSUBISHI CONSTRUCTION EQUIPMENT SALES, LTD.—See Caterpillar Inc.; *U.S. Public*, pg. 317
CHUBU CITIZEN CORPORATION—See Citizen Watch Company, Ltd.; *Int'l*, pg. 293
CHUBU ELECTRIC POWER CO., INC. (LONDON OFFICE)—See Chubu Electric Power Company, Inc.; *Int'l*, pg. 290
CHUBU ELECTRIC POWER CO., INC. (WASHINGTON OFFICE)—See Chubu Electric Power Company, Inc.; *Int'l*, pg. 290
CHUBU ELECTRIC POWER COMPANY, INC.; *Int'l*, pg. 290
CHUCKS DISPOSAL COMPANY—See Allied Waste Industries; *U.S. Public*, pg. 49
CHUDOVO-RWS—See UPM-Kymmene Corporation; *Int'l*, pg. 1429
CHUGAI BIOPHARMACEUTICALS, INC.—See Chugai Pharmaceutical Co., Ltd.; *Int'l*, pg. 291
CHUGAI BOYEKI CO., LTD.; *Int'l*, pg. 290
CHUGAI PHARMA EUROPE LTD.—See Chugai Pharmaceutical Co., Ltd.; *Int'l*, pg. 291
CHUGAI PHARMA U.K. LTD.—See Chugai Pharmaceutical Co., Ltd.; *Int'l*, pg. 291
CHUGAI PHARMA U.S.A.—See Chugai Pharmaceutical Co., Ltd.; *Int'l*, pg. 291
CHUGAI PHARMACEUTICAL CO., LTD.; *Int'l*, pg. 290
CHUGAI PHARMACEUTICAL CO., LTD.—See Chugai Pharmaceutical Co., Ltd.; *Int'l*, pg. 291
CHUGAI PHARMACEUTICAL CO. LTD.-BEIJING—See Chugai Pharmaceutical Co., Ltd.; *Int'l*, pg. 291
CHUGAI PHARMACEUTICAL CO., LTD.-SHANGHAI—See Chugai Pharmaceutical Co., Ltd.; *Int'l*, pg. 291
CHUGAI-RHONE-POULENC SNC—See Chugai Pharmaceutical Co., Ltd.; *Int'l*, pg. 291
CHUGOKU CITIZEN CORPORATION—See Citizen Watch Company, Ltd.; *Int'l*, pg. 293
THE CHUGOKU ELECTRIC POWER CO., INC.; *Int'l*, pg. 291
CHUN WANG INDUSTRIAL GASES, LIMITED—See Air Products and Chemicals, Inc.; *U.S. Public*, pg. 32
CHUNG HUEY PHARMACEUTICAL CO., LTD.—See Chugai Pharmaceutical Co., Ltd.; *Int'l*, pg. 291
CHUNGHWA PICTURE TUBES SDN. BHD.—See Tatung Corporation; *Int'l*, pg. 1357
CHUO SENKO ADVERTISING CO., LTD.; *Int'l*, pg. 291
CHUO SUBARU MOTORS CO., LTD.—See Fuji Heavy Industries; *Int'l*, pg. 522
CHUO TRUST & BANKING COMPANY (EUROPE) S.A.— See The Chuo Trust & Banking Co., Ltd.; *Int'l*, pg. 291
THE CHUO TRUST & BANKING CO., LTD.; *Int'l*, pg. 291
CHUO TRUST ASIA LIMITED—See The Chuo Trust & Banking Co., Ltd.; *Int'l*, pg. 291
CHUO TRUST INTERNATIONAL LIMITED—See The Chuo Trust & Banking Co., Ltd.; *Int'l*, pg. 291
THE CHUO WOOLLEN MILLS, LTD.—See Nissho Iwai Corporation; *Int'l*, pg. 946
CHUQUICAMATA DIVISION—See CODELCO Chile (Corporacion Nacional Del Cobre De Chile); *Int'l*, pg. 302
CHURCH & CHURCH INC.; *U.S. Private*, pg. 239
CHURCH & DWIGHT CO., INC.; *U.S. Public*, pg. 355
CHURCH & DWIGHT CO., LTD.—See Church & Dwight Co., Inc.; *U.S. Public*, pg. 356
CHURCH & DWIGHT SPECIALTY PRODUCTS DIVISION— See Church & Dwight Co., Inc.; *U.S. Public*, pg. 356
CHURCH MUTUAL INSURANCE CO.; *U.S. Private*, pg. 239
CHURCH STREET CLINIC, INC.—See Integrated Health Services, Inc.; *U.S. Public*, pg. 884
THE CHURCHILL COMPANIES; *U.S. Private*, pg. 239
CHURCHILL DOWNS, INC.; *U.S. Public*, pg. 356
CHURCHILL DOWNS MANAGEMENT CO.—See Churchill Downs, Inc.; *U.S. Public*, pg. 356
CHURCHILL PPS-KK—See Pearson plc; *Int'l*, pg. 1025
CHURCHILL WEAVERS, INC.—See Crown Crafts, Inc.; *U.S. Public*, pg. 465
CHURCH'S CHICKEN, INC.—See AFC Enterprises; *U.S. Private*, pg. 5
CHURNY COMPANY INC.—See Philip Morris Companies Inc.; *U.S. Public*, pg. 1288
CHURRASCO STEAK-RESTAURANT GMBH—See Whitbread PLC; *Int'l*, pg. 1499
CHURUBUSCO STATE BANK—See Fort Wayne National Corporation; *U.S. Public*, pg. 674
CHYRON CORP.—See Telefonica de Espana, S.A.; *Int'l*, pg. 1372
CIA ERICSSON DE CHILE S.A.—See Telefonaktiebolaget LM Ericsson; *Int'l*, pg. 1366
CIA ERICSSON URUGUAY S.A.—See Telefonaktiebolaget LM Ericsson; *Int'l*, pg. 1368
CIAP S.A.—See Oce-van der Grinten N.V.; *Int'l*, pg. 994
CIBA ADDITIVE GMBH—See Novartis AG; *Int'l*, pg. 975
CIBA ADDITIVES—See Novartis AG; *Int'l*, pg. 976
CIBA AGRICULTURE—See Novartis AG; *Int'l*, pg. 978
CIBA BUNTING LTD.—See Novartis AG; *Int'l*, pg. 975
CIBA CLAYTON—See Novartis AG; *Int'l*, pg. 975
CIBA CORNING CANADA INC.—See Novartis AG; *Int'l*, pg. 976
CIBA CORNING DIAGNOSTICS AG—See Novartis AG; *Int'l*, pg. 972
CIBA CORNING DIAGNOSTICS CORPORATION—See Novartis AG; *Int'l*, pg. 973
CIBA CORNING DIAGNOSTICS DE MEXICO, S.A. DE C.V.—See Novartis AG; *Int'l*, pg. 975
CIBA CORNING DIAGNOSTICS GMBH—See Novartis AG; *Int'l*, pg. 975
CIBA CORNING DIAGNOSTICS (HK) LTD.—See Novartis AG; *Int'l*, pg. 975
CIBA CORNING DIAGNOSTICS KK—See Novartis AG; *Int'l*, pg. 975

CIBA CORNING DIAGNOSTICS LIMITED—See Novartis AG; *Int'l*, pg. 978
S.A. CIBA CORNING DIAGNOSTICS NV—See Novartis AG; *Int'l*, pg. 975
CIBA CORNING DIAGNOSTICS S.A.—See Novartis AG; *Int'l*, pg. 975
CIBA CORNING DIAGNOSTICS SPA—See Novartis AG; *Int'l*, pg. 975
CIBA CORNING MARKETING SERVICES (HK) LIMITED KB—See Novartis AG; *Int'l*, pg. 975
CIBA CORNING MARKETING SERVICES (HK) LTD—See Novartis AG; *Int'l*, pg. 975
CIBA DYES & CHEMICALS—See Novartis AG; *Int'l*, pg. 975
CIBA-GEIGY AGRO D.O.O.—See Novartis AG; *Int'l*, pg. 976
CIBA-GEIGY AGRO INTERNATIONAL SRL—See Novartis AG; *Int'l*, pg. 976
N.V. CIBA-GEIGY AGRO S.A.—See Novartis AG; *Int'l*, pg. 976
CIBA-GEIGY ANIMAL HEALTH (TAIWAN) LIMITED—See Novartis AG; *Int'l*, pg. 976
CIBA-GEIGY ARGENTINA S.A.I.C. Y F., PHARMA PRODUCTION PLANT—See Novartis AG; *Int'l*, pg. 976
CIBA-GEIGY ARGENTINA S.A.I.C. Y F., ZARATE PLANT— See Novartis AG; *Int'l*, pg. 976
CIBA-GEIGY A/S—See Novartis AG; *Int'l*, pg. 976
CIBA-GEIGY (BANGLADESH) LIMITED-PESTICIDES PLANT—See Novartis AG; *Int'l*, pg. 976
CIBA-GEIGY (BANGLADESH) LIMITED-PHARMACEUTICALS PLANT—See Novartis AG; *Int'l*, pg. 976
CIBA-GEIGY BV—See Novartis AG; *Int'l*, pg. 976
CIBA-GEIGY CANADA LTD.—See Novartis AG; *Int'l*, pg. 976
CIBA-GEIGY CANADA LTD.-ELM RIVER RESEARCH FARM—See Novartis AG; *Int'l*, pg. 976
CIBA-GEIGY CANADA LTD.-HONEYWOOD RESEARCH FARM—See Novartis AG; *Int'l*, pg. 976
CIBA-GEIGY (CHINA) LIMITED—See Novartis AG; *Int'l*, pg. 976
CIBA-GEIGY (CHINA) LIMITED-GUANGZHOU BRANCH OFFICE—See Novartis AG; *Int'l*, pg. 976
CIBA-GEIGY (CHINA) LIMITED-QINGDAO OFFICE—See Novartis AG; *Int'l*, pg. 976
CIBA-GEIGY (CHINA) LIMITED-SHANGHAI BRANCH—See Novartis AG; *Int'l*, pg. 976
CIBA-GEIGY EGYPT SAE—See Novartis AG; *Int'l*, pg. 976
CIBA-GEIGY FINANCE & INVESTMENT LIMITED—See Novartis AG; *Int'l*, pg. 976
CIBA-GEIGY FOREIGN SALES CORPORATION LTD—See Novartis AG; *Int'l*, pg. 976
CIBA-GEIGY FORMULATED SYSTEMS GROUP (AUTOMOTIVE CENTER)—See Novartis AG; *Int'l*, pg. 973
CIBA-GEIGY GESELLSCHAFT MBH—See Novartis AG; *Int'l*, pg. 977
CIBA-GEIGY GMBH—See Novartis AG; *Int'l*, pg. 977
CIBA-GEIGY (HONG KONG) LIMITED—See Novartis AG; *Int'l*, pg. 977
CIBA-GEIGY (HONG KONG) LIMITED-BEIJING LIAISON OFFICE—See Novartis AG; *Int'l*, pg. 977
CIBA-GEIGY ILAC VE KIMYA URUNLERI SANAYII VE TICARET A.S.—See Novartis AG; *Int'l*, pg. 977
CIBA-GEIGY ILAC VE KIMYA URUNLERI SANAYI VE TICARET AS—See Novartis AG; *Int'l*, pg. 977
P.T. CIBA-GEIGY INDONESIA—See Novartis AG; *Int'l*, pg. 977
CIBA-GEIGY (INSURANCE SERVICES) LIMITED—See Novartis AG; *Int'l*, pg. 977
CIBA-GEIGY IRELAND LIMITED—See Novartis AG; *Int'l*, pg. 977
CIBA-GEIGY JAPAN LIMITED PHARMACEUTICALS DIVISION—See Novartis AG; *Int'l*, pg. 977
CIBA-GEIGY JAPAN LIMITED-SASAYAMA FACTORY—See Novartis AG; *Int'l*, pg. 977
CIBA-GEIGY JAPAN LIMITED-TOKYO BRANCH—See Novartis AG; *Int'l*, pg. 977
CIBA-GEIGY KOREA LTD.—See Novartis AG; *Int'l*, pg. 977
CIBA-GEIGY LIMITED-REPRESENTATIVE OFFICE—See Novartis AG; *Int'l*, pg. 977
CIBA-GEIGY LTD.-TECHNICAL ASSISTANCE OFFICE—See Novartis AG; *Int'l*, pg. 977
CIBA-GEIGY LTDA.—See Novartis AG; *Int'l*, pg. 978
CIBA-GEIGY MAASTRICHT B.V.—See Novartis AG; *Int'l*, pg. 978
CIBA-GEIGY (MALAYSIA) SDN. BHD.—See Novartis AG; *Int'l*, pg. 978
CIBA-GEIGY MARIENBERG GMBH—See Novartis AG; *Int'l*, pg. 977
CIBA-GEIGY MAROC SA—See Novartis AG; *Int'l*, pg. 978
CIBA-GEIGY MEXICANA SA DE CV—See Novartis AG; *Int'l*, pg. 978
CIBA-GEIGY (MPL) LIMITED—See Novartis AG; *Int'l*, pg. 978
CIBA-GEIGY NEW ZEALAND LTD.—See Novartis AG; *Int'l*, pg. 978
CIBA-GEIGY (PAKISTAN) LIMITED—See Novartis AG; *Int'l*, pg. 978
CIBA-GEIGY (PAKISTAN) LTD.—See Novartis AG; *Int'l*, pg. 978
CIBA-GEIGY PERUANA S.A.—See Novartis AG; *Int'l*, pg. 978
CIBA-GEIGY PHARMA MAROC SA—See Novartis AG; *Int'l*, pg. 978
CIBA-GEIGY PHARMACEUTICALS—See Novartis AG; *Int'l*, pg. 978
CIBA-GEIGY (PHILIPPINES) INC.—See Novartis AG; *Int'l*, pg. 978
CIBA-GEIGY PLASTICS (EGYPT) S.A.E.—See Novartis AG; *Int'l*, pg. 978
CIBA-GEIGY PLC—See Novartis AG; *Int'l*, pg. 978
CIBA-GEIGY POLAND SP. Z.O.O.—See Novartis AG; *Int'l*, pg. 978

Company Index

CIBA-GEIGY PORTUGUESA LDA.—See Novartis AG; *Int'l*, pg. 978

CIBA-GEIGY PORTUGUESA, LDA.—See Novartis AG; *Int'l*, pg. 978

CIBA-GEIGY (PTY) LIMITED—See Novartis AG; *Int'l*, pg. 979

CIBA-GEIGY QUIMICA S.A.—See Novartis AG; *Int'l*, pg. 979

CIBA-GEIGY REGIONAL CENTER—See Novartis AG; *Int'l*, pg. 979

CIBA-GEIGY S.A.—See Novartis AG; *Int'l*, pg. 979

CIBA-GEIGY SA—See Novartis AG; *Int'l*, pg. 979

CIBA-GEIGY SALES & DISTRIBUTION COMPANY LIMITED—See Novartis AG; *Int'l*, pg. 979

CIBA-GEIGY-SCIENTIFIC OFFICE PHARMACEUTICALS—See Novartis AG; *Int'l*, pg. 979

CIBA-GEIGY SCIENTIFIC PUBLICATIONS—See Novartis AG; *Int'l*, pg. 979

CIBA-GEIGY SE ASIA (PTE) LIMITED—See Novartis AG; *Int'l*, pg. 979

CIBA-GEIGY S.E. ASIA (PTE.) LTD.—See Novartis AG; *Int'l*, pg. 979

CIBA-GEIGY SERVICES AG—See Novartis AG; *Int'l*, pg. 979

CIBA-GEIGY SERVICES AG-TAO PLEVEN—See Novartis AG; *Int'l*, pg. 979

CIBA-GEIGY SERVICES AG-TAO RIGA—See Novartis AG; *Int'l*, pg. 979

CIBA-GEIGY SERVICES AG-TAO STARA ZAGORA—See Novartis AG; *Int'l*, pg. 979

CIBA-GEIGY SERVICES AG-TAO VILNIUS—See Novartis AG; *Int'l*, pg. 979

CIBA-GEIGY SERVICES AG-TECHNICAL ADVISORY OFFICE—See Novartis AG; *Int'l*, pg. 979

CIBA-GEIGY SERVICES LIMITED—See Novartis AG; *Int'l*, pg. 979

CIBA-GEIGY SERVICES LIMITED-ANIMAL HEALTH DIVISION—See Novartis AG; *Int'l*, pg. 979

CIBA-GEIGY SERVICES LIMITED-RESIDENT REPRESENTATIVE OFFICE—See Novartis AG; *Int'l*, pg. 979

CIBA-GEIGY SERVICES LIMITED-SCIENTIFIC & ADVISORY OFFICE—See Novartis AG; *Int'l*, pg. 980

CIBA-GEIGY SERVICES LIMITED-SCIENTIFIC OFFICE—See Novartis AG; *Int'l*, pg. 980

CIBA-GEIGY SERVICES LTD.—See Novartis AG; *Int'l*, pg. 979

REPRESENTATION OF CIBA-GEIGY SERVICES LTD.—See Novartis AG; *Int'l*, pg. 984

CIBA-GEIGY SERVICES S.A.—See Novartis AG; *Int'l*, pg. 980

CIBA-GEIGY SERVICES SA—See Novartis AG; *Int'l*, pg. 980

CIBA-GEIGY SERVICES SA-TECHNICAL ADVISORY OFFICE—See Novartis AG; *Int'l*, pg. 979

CIBA-GEIGY SERVILINE CO. LTD.—See Novartis AG; *Int'l*, pg. 980

CIBA-GEIGY SOCIEDAD ANONIMA DE VENTA Y DISTRIBUCION—See Novartis AG; *Int'l*, pg. 980

CIBA-GEIGY SPA-DIVISIONE ADDITIVI ITALIA—See Novartis AG; *Int'l*, pg. 980

CIBA-GEIGY SPA-SEEDS DIVISION—See Novartis AG; *Int'l*, pg. 980

CIBA-GEIGY TAO—See Novartis AG; *Int'l*, pg. 980

CIBA-GEIGY (THAILAND) LTD.—See Novartis AG; *Int'l*, pg. 980

CIBA-GEIGY TRADING AND MARKETING SERVICES CO. LTD.-REGIONAL OFFICE—See Novartis AG; *Int'l*, pg. 980

CIBA-GEIGY TRADING AND MARKETING SERVICES CO. LTD.—See Novartis AG; *Int'l*, pg. 980

CIBA-GEIGY TRADING AND MARKETING SERVICES CO LTD—See Novartis AG; *Int'l*, pg. 980

CIBA-GEIGY VERSICHERUNGSVERMITTLUNG GHBH—See Novartis AG; *Int'l*, pg. 980

CIBA-GEIGY ZIMBABWE (PRIVATE) LIMITED—See Novartis AG; *Int'l*, pg. 980

CIBA GRIMSBY—See Novartis AG; *Int'l*, pg. 980

CIBA HUNGARIA KFT.—See Novartis AG; *Int'l*, pg. 980

CIBA INDUSTRIAL MARKETING LTD—See Novartis AG; *Int'l*, pg. 972

REP. OF CIBA INDUSTRIAL MARKETING SERVICES LTD.—See Novartis AG; *Int'l*, pg. 984

CIBA INTER MARKETING—See Novartis AG; *Int'l*, pg. 980

CIBA KUBAN LTD—See Novartis AG; *Int'l*, pg. 981

CIBA PHARMA PURCHASE—See Novartis AG; *Int'l*, pg. 981

CIBA PHARMACEUTICALS—See Novartis AG; *Int'l*, pg. 981

CIBA PIGMENTS—See Ciba Specialty Chemicals Holding Inc.; *Int'l*, pg. 292

CIBA-PILATUS AERIAL SPRAYING CO. LTD.—See Oerlikon-Buhrle Holding AG; *Int'l*, pg. 998

CIBA POLYMERS—See Ciba Specialty Chemicals Holding Inc.; *Int'l*, pg. 292

CIBA SANTE ANIMALE—See Novartis AG; *Int'l*, pg. 981

CIBA SEEDS—See Novartis AG; *Int'l*, pg. 973

CIBA SEEDS(CIBA-GEIGY CANADA LTD.)—See Novartis AG; *Int'l*, pg. 976

CIBA SELF-MEDICATION, INC.—See Novartis AG; *Int'l*, pg. 973

CIBA SPECIALTY CHEMICALS—See Ciba Specialty Chemicals Holding Inc.; *Int'l*, pg. 291

CIBA SPECIALTY CHEMICALS HOLDING INC.; *Int'l*, pg. 291

CIBA SPECIALTY CHEMICALS-PERFORMANCE POLYMERS DIVISION—See Ciba Specialty Chemicals Holding Inc.; *Int'l*, pg. 291

CIBA TF/CH VERTRETUNG—See Novartis AG; *Int'l*, pg. 981

CIBA VISION—See Novartis AG; *Int'l*, pg. 981

CIBA VISION AB—See Novartis AG; *Int'l*, pg. 981

CIBA VISION AG—See Novartis AG; *Int'l*, pg. 972

CIBA VISION AG-HETTLINGEN—See Novartis AG; *Int'l*, pg. 972

CIBA VISION AUSTRALIA PTY LIMITED—See Novartis AG; *Int'l*, pg. 981

CIBA VISION AUSTRIA—See Novartis AG; *Int'l*, pg. 981

P.T. CIBA VISION BATAM—See Novartis AG; *Int'l*, pg. 981

S.A. CIBA VISION BENELUX NV—See Novartis AG; *Int'l*, pg. 981

CIBA VISION CARE AUSTRALIA—See Novartis AG; *Int'l*, pg. 981

CIBA VISION DANMARK A/S—See Novartis AG; *Int'l*, pg. 981

CIBA VISION FINLAND OY—See Novartis AG; *Int'l*, pg. 981

CIBA VISION GMBH—See Novartis AG; *Int'l*, pg. 981

CIBA VISION GROUP MANAGEMENT INC—See Novartis AG; *Int'l*, pg. 973

CIBA VISION HOLDING AG—See Novartis AG; *Int'l*, pg. 972

CIBA VISION (HONG KONG) LTD.—See Novartis AG; *Int'l*, pg. 981

CIBA VISION KONTAKTLINSEN-PFLEGEMITTEL GMBH—See Novartis AG; *Int'l*, pg. 981

CIBA VISION LENS CARE PRODUCTION LTD.—See Novartis AG; *Int'l*, pg. 981

CIBA VISION MALAYSIA—See Novartis AG; *Int'l*, pg. 981

CIBA VISION MANAGEMENT AG—See Novartis AG; *Int'l*, pg. 972

CIBA VISION MANAGEMENT INC.—See Novartis AG; *Int'l*, pg. 981

CIBA VISION NORGE A/S—See Novartis AG; *Int'l*, pg. 981

CIBA VISION OPHTHALMALICS GMBH—See Novartis AG; *Int'l*, pg. 981

CIBA VISION OPHTHALMICS—See Novartis AG; *Int'l*, pg. 981

CIBA VISION OPHTHALMICS GMBH—See Novartis AG; *Int'l*, pg. 981

CIBA VISION OPTICS B.V.—See Novartis AG; *Int'l*, pg. 981

CIBA VISION-RICKY LIMITED—See Novartis AG; *Int'l*, pg. 981

CIBA VISION S.A.—See Novartis AG; *Int'l*, pg. 981

CIBA VISION (SINGAPORE) PTE LTD—See Novartis AG; *Int'l*, pg. 981

CIBA VISION SRL—See Novartis AG; *Int'l*, pg. 981

CIBA VISION STERILE MANUFACTURING LTD.—See Novartis AG; *Int'l*, pg. 981

CIBA VISION TAIWAN CO LTD—See Novartis AG; *Int'l*, pg. 981

CIBA VISION (THAILAND) LIMITED—See Novartis AG; *Int'l*, pg. 981

CIBA VISION (UK) LTD.—See Novartis AG; *Int'l*, pg. 981

CIBA VISION VERTRIEBS GMBH—See Novartis AG; *Int'l*, pg. 981

CIBA VISION VERTRIEBS GMBH-EUROLOGISTICS—See Novartis AG; *Int'l*, pg. 981

CIBA-GEIGY SERVICES AG—See Novartis AG; *Int'l*, pg. 979

CIBATUL LTD.—See Novartis AG; *Int'l*, pg. 981

CIBER, INC.; *U.S. Public*, pg. 356

CID S.P.A.—See Otto Versand (GmbH & Co.); *Int'l*, pg. 1015

CIEMI—See Candy S.p.A.; *Int'l*, pg. 260

C.A. CIGARRERA BIGOTT, SUCS.—See B.A.T Industries P.L.C.; *Int'l*, pg. 111

CIGARRERA LA MODERNA, SA DE CV—See B.A.T Industries P.L.C.; *Int'l*, pg. 112

CIGARRERIA MORAZAN SA DE CV—See B.A.T Industries P.L.C.; *Int'l*, pg. 111

CIGARROS LA TABACCALERA MEXICANA SA DE CV—See Grupo Carso S.A. de C.V.; *Int'l*, pg. 572

CIGNA ADVISORY PARTNERS, INC.—See Cigna Corp.; *U.S. Public*, pg. 357

CIGNA ASSOCIATES, INC.—See Cigna Corp.; *U.S. Public*, pg. 358

CIGNA BENEFITS PROCESSING IRELAND LTD.—See Cigna Corp.; *U.S. Public*, pg. 358

CIGNA BOND SERVICES, INC.—See Cigna Corp.; *U.S. Public*, pg. 362

CIGNA BRASIL EMPREENDIMENTOS LTDA.—See Cigna Corp.; *U.S. Public*, pg. 363

CIGNA CAPITAL BROKERAGE, INC.—See Cigna Corp.; *U.S. Public*, pg. 357

CIGNA COMMUNITY CHOICE, INC.—See Cigna Corp.; *U.S. Public*, pg. 359

CIGNA COMPANIA DE SEGUROS (CHILE) S.A.—See Cigna Corp.; *U.S. Public*, pg. 363

CIGNA COMPANIA DE SEGUROS DE PANAMA S.A.—See Cigna Corp.; *U.S. Public*, pg. 364

CIGNA COMPANIA DE SEGUROS DE VIDA (CHILE) S.A.—See Cigna Corp.; *U.S. Public*, pg. 364

CIGNA CONFERENCE FACILITIES, INC.—See Cigna Corp.; *U.S. Public*, pg. 358

CIGNA CORP.; *U.S. Public*, pg. 356

CIGNA DE VENEZUELA INTERMEDIARIOS DE REASEGUROS, S.A.—See Cigna Corp.; *U.S. Public*, pg. 364

CIGNA DENTAL CARE OF ILLINOIS, INC.—See Cigna Corp.; *U.S. Public*, pg. 358

CIGNA DENTAL HEALTH, INC.—See Cigna Corp.; *U.S. Public*, pg. 358

CIGNA DENTAL HEALTH OF NEW JERSEY, INC.—See Cigna Corp.; *U.S. Public*, pg. 358

CIGNA DENTAL HEALTH OF OHIO, INC.—See Cigna Corp.; *U.S. Public*, pg. 358

CIGNA DENTAL HEALTH PLAN OF NEW MEXICO, INC.—See Cigna Corp.; *U.S. Public*, pg. 358

CIGNA DENTAL HEALTH PLAN OF NORTH CAROLINA, INC.—See Cigna Corp.; *U.S. Public*, pg. 358

CIGNA DIRECT MARKETING COMPANY, INC.—See Cigna Corp.; *U.S. Public*, pg. 362

CIGNA EMPLOYEE BENEFITS SERVICES, INC.—See Cigna Corp.; *U.S. Public*, pg. 358

CIGNA EMPLOYERS INSURANCE COMPANY—See Cigna Corp.; *U.S. Public*, pg. 366

CIGNA ENERGY PARTNERS 1985-A LTD. PARTNERSHIP—See Cigna Corp.; *U.S. Public*, pg. 359

CIGNA ENERGY PARTNERS 1986-A LTD. PARTNERSHIP—See Cigna Corp.; *U.S. Public*, pg. 358

CIGNA ENERGY PARTNERS 1986-B LTD. PARTNERSHIP—See Cigna Corp.; *U.S. Public*, pg. 358

CIGNA ENERGY RESOURCES, INC.—See Cigna Corp.; *U.S. Public*, pg. 358

CIGNA EXCESS & SURPLUS INSURANCE SERVICES, INC. (GA)—See Cigna Corp.; *U.S. Public*, pg. 362

CIGNA EXCESS & SURPLUS INSURANCE SERVICES, INC. (IL)—See Cigna Corp.; *U.S. Public*, pg. 363

CIGNA FINANCIAL ADVISORS, INC.—See Cigna Corp.; *U.S. Public*, pg. 358

CIGNA FINANCIAL FUTURES, INC.—See Cigna Corp.; *U.S. Public*, pg. 357

CIGNA FINANCIAL PARTNERS, INC.—See Cigna Corp.; *U.S. Public*, pg. 358

CIGNA FIRE UNDERWRITERS INSURANCE COMPANY—See Cigna Corp.; *U.S. Public*, pg. 365

CIGNA FOUNDATION—See Cigna Corp.; *U.S. Public*, pg. 367

CIGNA FUND MANAGERS LIMITED—See Cigna Corp.; *U.S. Public*, pg. 357

CIGNA FUNDING LIMITED PARTNERSHIP—See Cigna Corp.; *U.S. Public*, pg. 357

CIGNA G.B. HOLDINGS, LTD.—See Cigna Corp.; *U.S. Public*, pg. 363

CIGNA GUARANTY HOLDINGS, INC.—See Cigna Corp.; *U.S. Public*, pg. 357

CIGNA HEALTH CORPORATION—See Cigna Corp.; *U.S. Public*, pg. 359

CIGNA HEALTH NETWORK, INC.—See Cigna Corp.; *U.S. Public*, pg. 359

CIGNA HEALTHCARE BENEFITS, INC.—See Cigna Corp.; *U.S. Public*, pg. 359

CIGNA HEALTHCARE, INC.—See Cigna Corp.; *U.S. Public*, pg. 359

CIGNA HEALTHCARE MID-ATLANTIC, INC.—See Cigna Corp.; *U.S. Public*, pg. 359

CIGNA HEALTHCARE OF NORTH CAROLINA, INC.—See Cigna Corp.; *U.S. Public*, pg. 360

CIGNA HEALTHCARE OF OKLAHOMA, INC.—See Cigna Corp.; *U.S. Public*, pg. 360

CIGNA HEALTHCARE OF TENNESSEE, INC.—See Cigna Corp.; *U.S. Public*, pg. 360

CIGNA HEALTHCARE OF UTAH, INC.—See Cigna Corp.; *U.S. Public*, pg. 360

CIGNA HEALTHCARE OF VIRGINIA, INC.—See Cigna Corp.; *U.S. Public*, pg. 360

CIGNA HOLDINGS, INC.—See Cigna Corp.; *U.S. Public*, pg. 357

CIGNA HOSPITAL OF LOS ANGELES, INC.—See Cigna Corp.; *U.S. Public*, pg. 360

CIGNA HOTEL ASSOCIATES-I LIMITED PARTNERSHIP—See Cigna Corp.; *U.S. Public*, pg. 359

CIGNA INCOME REALTY-I LIMITED PARTNERSHIP—See Cigna Corp.; *U.S. Public*, pg. 359

CIGNA INFORMATION SERVICES, INC.—See Cigna Corp.; *U.S. Public*, pg. 357

CIGNA INSURANCE AUSTRALIA LIMITED—See Cigna Corp.; *U.S. Public*, pg. 365

CIGNA INSURANCE COMPANY—See Cigna Corp.; *U.S. Public*, pg. 365

CIGNA INSURANCE COMPANY (HELLAS) S.A.—See Cigna Corp.; *U.S. Public*, pg. 364

CIGNA INSURANCE COMPANY OF CANADA—See Cigna Corp.; *U.S. Public*, pg. 366

CIGNA INSURANCE COMPANY OF EUROPE, S.A.-N.V.—See Cigna Corp.; *U.S. Public*, pg. 364

CIGNA INSURANCE COMPANY OF ILLINOIS—See Cigna Corp.; *U.S. Public*, pg. 366

CIGNA INSURANCE COMPANY OF OHIO—See Cigna Corp.; *U.S. Public*, pg. 366

CIGNA INSURANCE COMPANY OF TEXAS—See Cigna Corp.; *U.S. Public*, pg. 365

CIGNA INSURANCE COMPANY OF THE MIDWEST—See Cigna Corp.; *U.S. Public*, pg. 365

CIGNA INSURANCE NEW ZEALAND LIMITED—See Cigna Corp.; *U.S. Public*, pg. 364

CIGNA INTERNATIONAL ASSET FUND LTD.—See Cigna Corp.; *U.S. Public*, pg. 364

CIGNA INTERNATIONAL BROKERS, LTD.—See Cigna Corp.; *U.S. Public*, pg. 364

CIGNA INTERNATIONAL FINANCE INC.—See Cigna Corp.; *U.S. Public*, pg. 357

CIGNA INTERNATIONAL FUND MANAGERS (CI) LTD.—See Cigna Corp.; *U.S. Public*, pg. 364

CIGNA INTERNATIONAL HOLDINGS, LTD.—See Cigna Corp.; *U.S. Public*, pg. 363

CIGNA INTERNATIONAL INSURANCE MANAGERS, LTD.—See Cigna Corp.; *U.S. Public*, pg. 364

CIGNA INTERNATIONAL INVESTMENT ADVISORS AUSTRALIA LIMITED—See Cigna Corp.; *U.S. Public*, pg. 357

CIGNA INTERNATIONAL INVESTMENT ADVISORS K.K.—See Cigna Corp.; *U.S. Public*, pg. 357

CIGNA INTERNATIONAL INVESTMENT ADVISORS, LTD.—See Cigna Corp.; *U.S. Public*, pg. 357

CIGNA INTERNATIONAL REINSURANCE COMPANY LTD.—See Cigna Corp.; *U.S. Public*, pg. 364

CIGNA INTERNATIONAL SPECIAL INVESTMENTS INC.—See Cigna Corp.; *U.S. Public*, pg. 357

CIGNA INTERNATIONAL STRATEGIC FUNDS, L.P.—See Cigna Corp.; *U.S. Public*, pg. 364

CIGNA INVESTMENT ADVISORY COMPANY, INC.—See Cigna Corp.; *U.S. Public*, pg. 357

CIGNA INVESTMENT GROUP, INC.—See Cigna Corp.; *U.S. Public*, pg. 357

CIGNA INVESTMENTS & PLACEMENTS COMPANY—See Cigna Corp.; *U.S. Public*, pg. 357

CIGNA INVESTMENTS, INC.—See Cigna Corp.; *U.S. Public*, pg. 357

CIGNA ITALY - SOCIETA A RESPONSABILITA LIMITATA—See Cigna Corp.; *U.S. Public*, pg. 364
CIGNA LEVERAGED CAPITAL FUND, INC.—See Cigna Corp.; *U.S. Public*, pg. 357
CIGNA LIFE INSURANCE AUSTRALIA LIMITED—See Cigna Corp.; *U.S. Public*, pg. 364
CIGNA LIFE INSURANCE COMPANY—See Cigna Corp.; *U.S. Public*, pg. 361
CIGNA LIFE INSURANCE COMPANY OF CANADA—See Cigna Corp.; *U.S. Public*, pg. 362
CIGNA LIFE INSURANCE COMPANY OF EUROPE S.A.-N.V.—See Cigna Corp.; *U.S. Public*, pg. 364
CIGNA LIFE INSURANCE NEW ZEALAND LIMITED—See Cigna Corp.; *U.S. Public*, pg. 364
CIGNA LLOYDS INSURANCE COMPANY—See Cigna Corp.; *U.S. Public*, pg. 364
CIGNA LOSS CONTROL SERVICES, INC.—See Cigna Corp.; *U.S. Public*, pg. 364
CIGNA MANAGED CARE BENEFITS COMPANY—See Cigna Corp.; *U.S. Public*, pg. 360
CIGNA MEZZANINE CAPITAL, INC.—See Cigna Corp.; *U.S. Public*, pg. 357
CIGNA MEZZANINE HOLDINGS, INC.—See Cigna Corp.; *U.S. Public*, pg. 357
CIGNA MEZZANINE PARTNERS III, INC.—See Cigna Corp.; *U.S. Public*, pg. 357
CIGNA MEZZANINE PARTNERS II, L.P.—See Cigna Corp.; *U.S. Public*, pg. 357
CIGNA MORTGAGE SECURITIES, INC.—See Cigna Corp.; *U.S. Public*, pg. 361
CIGNA OVERSEAS FINANCE N.V.—See Cigna Corp.; *U.S. Public*, pg. 364
CIGNA PROPERTIES, INC.—See Cigna Corp.; *U.S. Public*, pg. 358
CIGNA PROPERTY & CASUALTY INSURANCE COMPANY—See Cigna Corp.; *U.S. Public*, pg. 364
CIGNA RE CORPORATION—See Cigna Corp.; *U.S. Public*, pg. 360
CIGNA REAL ESTATE FUND S LTD. PARTNERSHIP—See Cigna Corp.; *U.S. Public*, pg. 361
CIGNA REAL ESTATE FUND T LTD. PARTNERSHIP—See Cigna Corp.; *U.S. Public*, pg. 365
CIGNA REAL ESTATE, INC.—See Cigna Corp.; *U.S. Public*, pg. 365
CIGNA REALTY RESOURCES, INC. - EIGHTH—See Cigna Corp.; *U.S. Public*, pg. 358
CIGNA REALTY RESOURCES, INC. - ELEVENTH—See Cigna Corp.; *U.S. Public*, pg. 358
CIGNA REALTY RESOURCES, INC. - FIFTEENTH—See Cigna Corp.; *U.S. Public*, pg. 359
CIGNA REALTY RESOURCES, INC. - FIFTH—See Cigna Corp.; *U.S. Public*, pg. 359
CIGNA REALTY RESOURCES, INC. - FOURTEENTH—See Cigna Corp.; *U.S. Public*, pg. 359
CIGNA REALTY RESOURCES, INC. - NINTH—See Cigna Corp.; *U.S. Public*, pg. 359
CIGNA REALTY RESOURCES, INC. - SEVENTH—See Cigna Corp.; *U.S. Public*, pg. 359
CIGNA REALTY RESOURCES, INC. - SIXTEENTH—See Cigna Corp.; *U.S. Public*, pg. 359
CIGNA REALTY RESOURCES, INC. - SIXTH—See Cigna Corp.; *U.S. Public*, pg. 359
CIGNA REALTY RESOURCES, INC. - TENTH—See Cigna Corp.; *U.S. Public*, pg. 359
CIGNA REALTY RESOURCES, INC. - TWELFTH—See Cigna Corp.; *U.S. Public*, pg. 359
CIGNA REASEGUROS, S.A.—See Cigna Corp.; *U.S. Public*, pg. 364
CIGNA REINSURANCE COMPANY—See Cigna Corp.; *U.S. Public*, pg. 365
CIGNA REINSURANCE COMPANY S.A.-N.V.—See Cigna Corp.; *U.S. Public*, pg. 365
CIGNA REINSURANCE COMPANY (U.K.) LIMITED—See Cigna Corp.; *U.S. Public*, pg. 363
CIGNA REINSURANCE NEW ZEALAND LIMITED—See Cigna Corp.; *U.S. Public*, pg. 363
CIGNA ROAD & TRAVEL CLUB, INC.—See Cigna Corp.; *U.S. Public*, pg. 362
CIGNA RUN-OFF SERVICES, INC.—See Cigna Corp.; *U.S. Public*, pg. 364
CIGNA SALUD ISAPRE S.A.—See Cigna Corp.; *U.S. Public*, pg. 360
CIGNA SECURITIES, INC.—See Cigna Corp.; *U.S. Public*, pg. 360
CIGNA SEGURADORA S.A.—See Cigna Corp.; *U.S. Public*, pg. 363
CIGNA SEGUROS DE COLOMBIA S.A.—See Cigna Corp.; *U.S. Public*, pg. 363
CIGNA SERVICES U.K. LIMITED—See Cigna Corp.; *U.S. Public*, pg. 363
CIGNA SICAV I—See Cigna Corp.; *U.S. Public*, pg. 364
CIGNA SPECIALTY INSURANCE COMPANY—See Cigna Corp.; *U.S. Public*, pg. 366
CIGNA STAFF PENSION INVESTMENTS LIMITED—See Cigna Corp.; *U.S. Public*, pg. 363
CIGNA SUPERANNUATION NOMINEES PTY LIMITED—See Cigna Corp.; *U.S. Public*, pg. 364
CIGNA THAI COMPANY LIMITED—See Cigna Corp.; *U.S. Public*, pg. 363
CIGNA/WILLOWBROOK ASSOCIATES LIMITED PARTNERSHIP—See Cigna Corp.; *U.S. Public*, pg. 359
CIGNA/WILLOWBROOK II ASSOCIATES LIMITED PARTNERSHIP—See Cigna Corp.; *U.S. Public*, pg. 359
CIGNA WORLDWIDE, INCORPORATED—See Cigna Corp.; *U.S. Public*, pg. 363
CIGNA WORLDWIDE INSURANCE COMPANY—See Cigna Corp.; *U.S. Public*, pg. 363
CIGNASA SIGORTA A.S.—See Cigna Corp.; *U.S. Public*, pg. 363
CIGNASA SIGORTA A.S.—See Sabanci Holding A.S.; *Int'l*, pg. 1167
CIL MIETKAUF GMBH—See Commerzbank AG; *Int'l*, pg. 309
CILAG AG—See Johnson & Johnson; *U.S. Public*, pg. 929

CILAG AG INTERNATIONAL—See Johnson & Johnson; *U.S. Public*, pg. 929
CILAG DE MEXICO, S.A. DE C.V.—See Johnson & Johnson; *U.S. Public*, pg. 929
CILCO ENERGY CORP.—See CILCORP Inc.; *U.S. Public*, pg. 367
CILCO EXPLORATION & DEVELOPMENT CO.—See CILCORP Inc.; *U.S. Public*, pg. 367
CILCORP INC.; *U.S. Public*, pg. 367
CILCORP INVESTMENT MANAGEMENT INC.—See CILCORP Inc.; *U.S. Public*, pg. 367
CILCORP VENTURES INC.—See CILCORP Inc.; *U.S. Public*, pg. 367
CIMATARN—See La Meridionale des Bois et Materiaux; *Int'l*, pg. 784
CIMATRIX GMBH—See Robotic Vision Systems, Inc.; *U.S. Public*, pg. 1395
CIMATRIX L.L.C.—See Robotic Vision Systems, Inc.; *U.S. Public*, pg. 1395
CIMATRIX LTD.—See Robotic Vision Systems, Inc.; *U.S. Public*, pg. 1395
CIMATRIX NV/SA—See Robotic Vision Systems, Inc.; *U.S. Public*, pg. 1395
CIMATRIX S.A.—See Robotic Vision Systems, Inc.; *U.S. Public*, pg. 1395
CIMBENIN S.A.—See Scancem AB; *Int'l*, pg. 1201
CIMCO—See Intesys Technologies; *U.S. Private*, pg. 574
CIME BOCUZE—See Pechiney S.A.; *Int'l*, pg. 1028
CIMELTA-JEUMONT—See Jeumont-Schneider Trenformeteurs; *Int'l*, pg. 706
CIMENTA, ADMON. DE FONDOS DE INVERSION, S.A.—See Corporacion MAPFRE, Compania Internacional de Reaseguros, S.A.; *Int'l*, pg. 335
CIMENTERIE NOUVELLE DE CASABLANCA-CINOUCA—See Lafarge S.A.; *Int'l*, pg. 790
S.A. CIMENTERIES CBR—See Heidelberger Zement A.G.; *Int'l*, pg. 605
CIMENTERIES DU CAMEROUN-CIMENCAM—See Lafarge S.A.; *Int'l*, pg. 790
CIMENTO MAUA S.A.—See Lafarge S.A.; *Int'l*, pg. 789
CIMENTS ARTIFICIELS DE MEKNES-CADEM—See Lafarge S.A.; *Int'l*, pg. 790
CIMENTS DE L'ADOUR—See Ciments Francais; *Int'l*, pg. 292
CIMENTS DU TOGO, S.A.—See Scancem AB; *Int'l*, pg. 1201
CIMENTS DUNAROC—See Ciments Francais; *Int'l*, pg. 292
CIMENTS FRANCAIS; *Int'l*, pg. 292
CIMENTS FRANCAIS DATA PROCESSING CENTER—See Ciments Francais; *Int'l*, pg. 292
CIMENTS LUXEMBOURGEOIS S.A.—See Arbed S.A.; *Int'l*, pg. 80
CIMEO PRECISION CO., LTD.—See Citizen Watch Company, Ltd.; *Int'l*, pg. 293
CIMEX-NOR S.A.—See Fried. Krupp AG; *Int'l*, pg. 515
CIMIANTO STH SA—See ETEX; *Int'l*, pg. 430
CIMINAS-CIMENTO NACIONAL DE MINAS S.A.—See Holderbank Financiere Glaris Ltd.; *Int'l*, pg. 629
CIMINELLI DEVELOPMENT COMPANY, INC.; *U.S. Private*, pg. 239
LOUIS P. CIMINELLI CONSTRUCTION CO. INC.; *U.S. Private*, pg. 239
CIMLINC INCORPORATED; *U.S. Private*, pg. 239
CINAMERICA SERVICE CORP.—See Cinamerica Theatres, L.P.; *U.S. Private*, pg. 239
CINAMERICA THEATRES, L.P.; *U.S. Private*, pg. 239
CINCH CONNECTOR DIVISION—See Labinal SA; *Int'l*, pg. 786
CINCH CONNECTORS GMBH—See Labinal SA; *Int'l*, pg. 786
CINCH CONNECTORS LTD.—See Labinal SA; *Int'l*, pg. 786
CINCH ITALIA SRL—See Labinal SA; *Int'l*, pg. 786
CINCH JAPAN KK—See Labinal SA; *Int'l*, pg. 786
CINCH MICROFITS PTE LTD.—See Labinal SA; *Int'l*, pg. 786
CINCINATTI LEARNING CENTER—See Berkshire Hathaway Inc.; *U.S. Public*, pg. 218
CINCINNATI BELL DIRECTORY INC.—See Cincinnati Bell Telephone; *U.S. Public*, pg. 367
CINCINNATI BELL INFORMATION SYSTEMS INC.—See Cincinnati Bell Telephone; *U.S. Public*, pg. 367
CINCINNATI BELL LONG DISTANCE INC.—See Cincinnati Bell Telephone; *U.S. Public*, pg. 367
CINCINNATI BELL SUPPLY COMPANY—See Cincinnati Bell Telephone; *U.S. Public*, pg. 367
CINCINNATI BELL TELEPHONE; *U.S. Public*, pg. 367
CINCINNATI BELL TELEPHONE COMPANY—See Cincinnati Bell Telephone; *U.S. Public*, pg. 367
CINCINNATI CASUALTY CO.—See Cincinnati Financial Corp.; *U.S. Public*, pg. 368
THE CINCINNATI CORDAGE & PAPER COMPANY; *U.S. Private*, pg. 239
CINCINNATI ELECTRONICS CORP.—See The General Electric Company, p.l.c.; *Int'l*, pg. 545
THE CINCINNATI ENQUIRER, INC.—See Gannett Company, Inc.; *U.S. Public*, pg. 700
CINCINNATI FINANCIAL CORP.; *U.S. Public*, pg. 368
CINCINNATI GEAR COMPANY; *U.S. Private*, pg. 240
CINCINNATI INCORPORATED; *U.S. Private*, pg. 240
CINCINNATI INDEMNITY COMPANY—See Cincinnati Financial Corp.; *U.S. Public*, pg. 368
CINCINNATI INDUSTRIAL MACHINERY DIV.—See Eagle-Picher Industries, Inc.; *U.S. Private*, pg. 355
CINCINNATI INSURANCE CO.—See Cincinnati Financial Corp.; *U.S. Public*, pg. 368
CINCINNATI LIFE INSURANCE CO.—See Cincinnati Financial Corp.; *U.S. Public*, pg. 368
CINCINNATI LIMOUSINE SERVICE INC.—See Beechmont Investments Inc.; *U.S. Private*, pg. 129
CINCINNATI MILACRON AUSTRIA AKTIENGESELLSCHAFT—See Cincinnati Milacron Inc.; *U.S. Public*, pg. 368

CINCINNATI MILACRON B.V.—See Cincinnati Milacron Inc.; *U.S. Public*, pg. 368
CINCINNATI MILACRON-CANADA LTD—See Cincinnati Milacron Inc.; *U.S. Public*, pg. 368
CINCINNATI MILACRON HOLDING GESELLSCHAFT MBH—See Cincinnati Milacron Inc.; *U.S. Public*, pg. 368
CINCINNATI MILACRON; *U.S. Public*, pg. 368
CINCINNATI MILACRON S.R.L.—See Cincinnati Milacron Inc.; *U.S. Public*, pg. 368
CINCINNATI MILACRON U.K. LIMITED—See Cincinnati Milacron Inc.; *U.S. Public*, pg. 368
THE CINCINNATI, NEW ORLEANS & TEXAS PACIFIC RAILWAY CO.—See Norfolk Southern Corporation; *U.S. Public*, pg. 1191
CINCINNATI PAPERBOARD CORPORATION—See Caraustar Industries, Inc.; *U.S. Public*, pg. 303
THE CINCINNATI POST—See The E.W. Scripps Company; *U.S. Public*, pg. 1447
CINCINNATI SALES—See Fairfield Communities, Inc.; *U.S. Public*, pg. 611
CINCINNATI SUB-ZERO PRODUCTS, INC.; *U.S. Private*, pg. 240
CINCINNATI THERMAL SPRAY, INC.; *U.S. Private*, pg. 240
CINCINNATI THERMAL SPRAY SOUTH—See Cincinnati Thermal Spray, Inc.; *U.S. Private*, pg. 240
CINCINNATI UNITED CONTRACTORS; *U.S. Private*, pg. 240
CINCOM SYSTEMS, INC.; *U.S. Private*, pg. 240
CINDU CHEMICALS B.V.—See Koninklijke Hoogovens N.V.; *Int'l*, pg. 754
CINE MAGNETICS, INC.; *U.S. Private*, pg. 240
CINEBOOKS, INC.—See The News Corporation Limited; *Int'l*, pg. 925
CINEMA ETOILE DIVISION—See Movie Star, Inc.; *U.S. Public*, pg. 1141
CINEMA INTERNATIONAL CORP., N.V.—See The Seagram Company Ltd.; *Int'l*, pg. 1216
CINEMAPRESSE AGENCE CONSEIL EN COMMUNICATION—See Young & Rubicam Inc.; *U.S. Private*, pg. 1198
CINEMARK USA, INC.; *U.S. Private*, pg. 240
CINEPLEX ODEON CORPORATION; *Int'l*, pg. 292
CINEPLEX ODEON CORPORATION—See Cineplex Odeon Corporation; *Int'l*, pg. 293
CINEPLEX ODEON CORPORATION -CALGARY—See Cineplex Odeon Corporation; *Int'l*, pg. 293
CINEPLEX ODEON CORPORATION -CHICAGO—See Cineplex Odeon Corporation; *Int'l*, pg. 293
CINEPLEX ODEON CORPORATION -LOS ANGELES—See Cineplex Odeon Corporation; *Int'l*, pg. 293
CINEPLEX ODEON CORPORATION -MONTREAL—See Cineplex Odeon Corporation; *Int'l*, pg. 293
CINEPLEX ODEON CORPORATION -NEW YORK—See Cineplex Odeon Corporation; *Int'l*, pg. 293
CINEPLEX ODEON CORPORATION -SEATTLE—See Cineplex Odeon Corporation; *Int'l*, pg. 293
CINEPLEX ODEON CORPORATION -VANCOUVER—See Cineplex Odeon Corporation; *Int'l*, pg. 293
CINEPONTO/LEO BURNETT PUBLICIDADE LDA.—See Leo Burnett Company, Inc.; *U.S. Private*, pg. 184
CINERGY CORP.; *U.S. Public*, pg. 369
CINERGY INVESTMENTS, INC.—See Cinergy Corp.; *U.S. Public*, pg. 369
CINERGY SERVICES, INC.—See Cinergy Corp.; *U.S. Public*, pg. 369
CINESTELLA S.P.A.—See Bastogi-S.p.A.; *Int'l*, pg. 170
CINET A/S—See Axel Johnson AB; *Int'l*, pg. 710
CINET DANMARK A/S—See Axel Johnson AB; *Int'l*, pg. 710
CINET PERIFERI A/S—See Axel Johnson AB; *Int'l*, pg. 710
CINEVIDEO ENTERPRISES BV—See KPN Koninklyke PTT Nederland NV; *Int'l*, pg. 720
CINRAM FRANCE—See Cinram Ltd.; *Int'l*, pg. 293
CINRAM FRANCE EAST—See Cinram Ltd.; *Int'l*, pg. 293
CINRAM FRANCE WEST—See Cinram Ltd.; *Int'l*, pg. 293
CINRAM INC.—See Cinram Ltd.; *Int'l*, pg. 293
CINRAM LATINO AMERICANA, S.A. DE C.V.—See Cinram Ltd.; *Int'l*, pg. 293
CINRAM LTD.; *Int'l*, pg. 293
THE CINRAM POP DVD CENTRE—See Cinram Ltd.; *Int'l*, pg. 293
CINRAM U.K. LTD.—See Cinram Ltd.; *Int'l*, pg. 293
CINRAM VIDEO CENTRE—See Cinram Ltd.; *Int'l*, pg. 293
CINTA COMPAGNIE INDEPENDANTE DES TABACS S.A.—See Reemtsma Cigarettenfabriken GmbH, Hamburg; *Int'l*, pg. 1101
CINTAS CORPORATION; *U.S. Public*, pg. 370
CINTI FAB—See Cincinnati Gear Company; *U.S. Private*, pg. 240
FRANCESCO CINZANO & C.IA SPA—See Diageo Plc; *Int'l*, pg. 409
CINZANO INTERNATIONAL—See Diageo Plc; *Int'l*, pg. 409
CIPA INDUSTRIES, INC.—See Itochu Corporation; *Int'l*, pg. 695
CIPRIANI KREMER DESIGN—See Arnold Communications, Inc.; *U.S. Private*, pg. 84
CIPRICO, INC.; *U.S. Public*, pg. 370
CIPRICO INTERTNATIONAL LTD.—See Ciprico, Inc.; *U.S. Public*, pg. 370
CIPSCO INVESTMENT COMPANY—See Ameren Corporation; *U.S. Public*, pg. 66
CIQUINE-COMPANHIA PETROQUIMICA—See Nissho Iwai Corporation; *Int'l*, pg. 947
CIRAL—See Carlyle Holding Corporation; *U.S. Private*, pg. 213
CIRCA PHARMACEUTICALS, INC.—See Watson Pharmaceuticals, Inc.; *U.S. Public*, pg. 1746
CIRCLE AIRFREIGHT INTERNATIONAL DE MEXICO S.A. DE C.V.—See Circle International Group, Inc.; *U.S. Public*, pg. 372

CIRCLE AIRFREIGHT INTERNATIONAL KOREA—See Circle International Group, Inc.; *U.S. Public*, pg. 372
CIRCLE AIRFREIGHT INTL. (TAIWAN) LTD.—See Circle International Group, Inc.; *U.S. Public*, pg. 372
CIRCLE AIRFREIGHT INTL. (THAILAND) LTD.—See Circle International Group, Inc.; *U.S. Public*, pg. 372
CIRCLE-ATS AG—See Circle International Group, Inc.; *U.S. Public*, pg. 372
CIRCLE A.W. PRODUCTS, CO.—See Sigma-Aldrich Corporation; *U.S. Public*, pg. 1471
CIRCLE BUSINESS CREDIT, INC.—See Xerox Corporation; *U.S. Public*, pg. 1785
CIRCLE ESPANA S.A.—See Circle International Group, Inc.; *U.S. Public*, pg. 372
CIRCLE FREIGHT INTERNATIONAL—See Circle International Group, Inc.; *U.S. Public*, pg. 372
CIRCLE FREIGHT INTERNATIONAL AGENCIA CHILENA—See Circle International Group, Inc.; *U.S. Public*, pg. 372
CIRCLE FREIGHT INTERNATIONAL ARGENTINA S.A.—See Circle International Group, Inc.; *U.S. Public*, pg. 372
CIRCLE FREIGHT INTERNATIONAL (BAHRAIN) LTD.—See Circle International Group, Inc.; *U.S. Public*, pg. 372
CIRCLE FREIGHT INTERNATIONAL (CANADA) LTD.—See Circle International Group, Inc.; *U.S. Public*, pg. 372
CIRCLE FREIGHT INTERNATIONAL DE PANAMA S.A.—See Circle International Group, Inc.; *U.S. Public*, pg. 372
CIRCLE FREIGHT INTERNATIONAL FRANCE, S.A.—See Circle International Group, Inc.; *U.S. Public*, pg. 372
CIRCLE FREIGHT INTERNATIONAL GREECE S.A.—See Circle International Group, Inc.; *U.S. Public*, pg. 372
CIRCLE FREIGHT INTERNATIONAL (H.K.)—See Circle International Group, Inc.; *U.S. Public*, pg. 372
CIRCLE FREIGHT INTERNATIONAL (HOLLAND) B.V.—See Circle International Group, Inc.; *U.S. Public*, pg. 372
CIRCLE FREIGHT INTERNATIONAL INDIA PVT. LTD.—See Circle International Group, Inc.; *U.S. Public*, pg. 372
P.T. CIRCLE FREIGHT INTERNATIONAL INDONESIA—See Circle International Group, Inc.; *U.S. Public*, pg. 372
CIRCLE FREIGHT INTERNATIONAL ITALIA-EUROLEVANT SRL—See Circle International Group, Inc.; *U.S. Public*, pg. 372
CIRCLE FREIGHT INTERNATIONAL JAPAN LTD.—See Circle International Group, Inc.; *U.S. Public*, pg. 372
CIRCLE FREIGHT INTERNATIONAL LLC—See Circle International Group, Inc.; *U.S. Public*, pg. 372
CIRCLE FREIGHT INTERNATIONAL (PHILIPPINES) LTD.—See Circle International Group, Inc.; *U.S. Public*, pg. 373
CIRCLE FREIGHT INTERNATIONAL (PORTUGAL) LTDA.—See Circle International Group, Inc.; *U.S. Public*, pg. 373
CIRCLE FREIGHT INTERNATIONAL PTE., LTD.—See Circle International Group, Inc.; *U.S. Public*, pg. 373
CIRCLE FREIGHT INTERNATIONAL (SAUDI ARABIA) LTD.—See Circle International Group, Inc.; *U.S. Public*, pg. 373
CIRCLE FREIGHT INTERNATIONAL SPEDITIONSGESELLSCHAFT MBH—See Circle International Group, Inc.; *U.S. Public*, pg. 373
CIRCLE FREIGHT INTERNATIONAL (U.S.A.)—See Circle International Group, Inc.; *U.S. Public*, pg. 373
CIRCLE FREIGHT INTERNATIONAL USA—See Circle International Group, Inc.; *U.S. Public*, pg. 370
CIRCLE FREIGHT INTERNATIONAL USA - FREE ZONE OFFICE—See Circle International Group, Inc.; *U.S. Public*, pg. 371
CIRCLE FREIGHT INTERNATIONAL USA - LATIN AMERICA—See Circle International Group, Inc.; *U.S. Public*, pg. 371
CIRCLE FREIGHT (MAYLAYSIA) SDN BHD—See Circle International Group, Inc.; *U.S. Public*, pg. 373
CIRCLE FREIGHT VENEZUELA S.A.—See Circle International Group, Inc.; *U.S. Public*, pg. 373
CIRCLE INTERNATIONAL—See Circle International Group, Inc.; *U.S. Public*, pg. 371
CIRCLE INTERNATIONAL GROUP, INC.; *U.S. Public*, pg. 370
CIRCLE INTERNATIONAL (N.Z.) LTD.—See Circle International Group, Inc.; *U.S. Public*, pg. 373
THE CIRCLE K COMPANY—See Tosco Corporation; *U.S. Public*, pg. 1624
CIRCLE LEMAN AIR FREIGHT—See Circle International Group, Inc.; *U.S. Public*, pg. 373
CIRCLE MACHINE CO.—See Kennametal Inc.; *U.S. Public*, pg. 950
CIRCLE PLASTICS PRODUCTS, INC.; *U.S. Private*, pg. 240
CIRCLE SEAL CONTROLS, INC.—See Watts Industries, Inc.; *U.S. Public*, pg. 1746
CIRCLE SERVICE CO.—See Andrew Corporation; *U.S. Public*, pg. 112
CIRCLE ZIEGLER S.A. AIRFREIGHT—See Circle International Group, Inc.; *U.S. Public*, pg. 373
CIRCON ACMI—See Circon Corporation; *U.S. Public*, pg. 373
CIRCON CORPORATION; *U.S. Public*, pg. 373
CIRCON GMBH—See Circon Corporation; *U.S. Public*, pg. 373
CIRCON VIDEO DIV.—See Circon Corporation; *U.S. Public*, pg. 373
CIRCUIT CITY CENTRAL DIV.—See Circuit City Stores, Inc.; *U.S. Public*, pg. 374
CIRCUIT CITY NORTHEAST DIVISION—See Circuit City Stores, Inc.; *U.S. Public*, pg. 374
CIRCUIT CITY SOUTHERN DIV.—See Circuit City Stores, Inc.; *U.S. Public*, pg. 374
CIRCUIT CITY STORES, INC.; *U.S. Public*, pg. 374

CIRCUIT CITY WESTERN DIV.—See Circuit City Stores, Inc.; *U.S. Public*, pg. 374
CIRCUIT FOIL JAPAN, LTD.—See Arbed S.A.; *Int'l*, pg. 80
CIRCUIT FOIL LUXEMBOURG S.A.—See Arbed S.A.; *Int'l*, pg. 80
CIRCUIT FOIL U.K. LTD.—See Arbed S.A.; *Int'l*, pg. 80
CIRCUIT FOIL USA INC.—See Arbed S.A.; *Int'l*, pg. 80
CIRCUIT SYSTEMS, INC.; *U.S. Public*, pg. 374
CIRCUIT-WISE, INC.; *U.S. Private*, pg. 240
CIRCUIT WORKS—See Liquid Controls LLC; *U.S. Private*, pg. 669
CIRCULO DE LECTORES S.A.—See Bertelsmann AG; *Int'l*, pg. 192
CIRCULO DE LEITORES—See Bertelsmann AG; *Int'l*, pg. 192
CIRCUS CIRCUS HOTEL CASINOS, INC.—See Circus Circus - Las Vegas; *U.S. Public*, pg. 374
CIRCUS CIRCUS - LAS VEGAS; *U.S. Public*, pg. 374
CIRCUS CIRCUS-LAS VEGAS HOTEL & CASINO—See Circus Circus - Las Vegas; *U.S. Public*, pg. 375
CIRCUS CIRCUS-RENO HOTEL & CASINO—See Circus Circus - Las Vegas; *U.S. Public*, pg. 375
CIREX BV—See Koninklijke Hoogovens N.V.; *Int'l*, pg. 753
CIREX MACHINING BV—See Koninklijke Hoogovens N.V.; *Int'l*, pg. 753
THE CIRIO CO. LTD.—See IRI Istituto Ricostruzione Industriale; *Int'l*, pg. 655
CIRMA ENTERPRISE—See Alcatel Alsthom Compagnie Generale D'Electricite; *Int'l*, pg. 53
CIRRUS DIAGNOSTICS INC.—See Diagnostic Products Corporation; *U.S. Public*, pg. 505
CIRRUS LOGIC, INC.; *U.S. Public*, pg. 375
CIRRUS LOGIC INTERNATIONAL LTD.—See Cirrus Logic, Inc.; *U.S. Public*, pg. 375
CIRRUS LOGIC K.K.—See Cirrus Logic, Inc.; *U.S. Public*, pg. 375
CIRRUS LOGIC (UK) LTD.—See Cirrus Logic, Inc.; *U.S. Public*, pg. 375
CISATOL—See Groupe Usinor; *Int'l*, pg. 571
CISCO SYSTEMS, INC.; *U.S. Public*, pg. 375
CISIGRAPH—See Lagardere Groupe; *Int'l*, pg. 792
CIT-CON OIL CORPORATION—See Petroleos de Venezuela S.A.; *Int'l*, pg. 1045
P.T. CITA SIMAS ARTHA—See CSA Holdings Ltd.; *Int'l*, pg. 243
THE CITADEL ASSURANCE COMPANIES—See Credit Suisse Group; *Int'l*, pg. 346
CITADEL BROADCASTING CO.—See Citadel Communications Corporation; *U.S. Private*, pg. 241
CITADEL BROADCASTING COMPANY—See Citadel Communications Corporation; *U.S. Private*, pg. 241
CITADEL COMMUNICATIONS CORPORATION; *U.S. Private*, pg. 241
CITADEL CORPORATION—See Obayashi Corporation; *Int'l*, pg. 995
CITADEL HOLDINGS CORP.—See Craig Corporation; *U.S. Public*, pg. 456
CITADEL REALTY, INC.—See Craig Corporation; *U.S. Public*, pg. 456
CITATION CORPORATION; *U.S. Public*, pg. 376
CITATION INSURANCE COMPANY—See Citation Insurance Group; *U.S. Public*, pg. 376
CITATION INSURANCE GROUP; *U.S. Public*, pg. 376
CITATION NATIONAL INSURANCE COMPANY—See Citation Insurance Group; *U.S. Public*, pg. 376
CITATION PLASTICS, CO.—See The West Company, Incorporated; *U.S. Public*, pg. 1755
CITAX KLEBETECHNIK GMBH—See Henkel KGaA; *Int'l*, pg. 609
CITENSY S.A.—See Tractebel; *Int'l*, pg. 1415
CITFED BANCORP, INC.; *U.S. Public*, pg. 376
CITFED MORTGAGE CORPORATION OF AMERICA—See CitFed Bancorp, Inc.; *U.S. Public*, pg. 376
CITGO CARIBBEAN CORPORATION—See Petroleos de Venezuela S.A.; *Int'l*, pg. 1045
CITGO PETROLEUM CORPORATION—See Petroleos de Venezuela S.A.; *Int'l*, pg. 1045
CITGO PIPELINE COMPANY—See Petroleos de Venezuela S.A.; *Int'l*, pg. 1045
CITIBANK A.G.—See Citicorp; *U.S. Public*, pg. 378
CITIBANK (AUSTRIA) A.G.—See Citicorp; *U.S. Public*, pg. 378
CITIBANK CANADA—See Citicorp; *U.S. Public*, pg. 378
CITIBANK (CHANNEL ISLANDS) LTD.—See Citicorp; *U.S. Public*, pg. 378
CITIBANK CREDIT CARD MARKETING—See Citicorp; *U.S. Public*, pg. 377
CITIBANK CREDITO, FINANCIAMENTO E INVESTIMENTO, S.A.—See Citicorp; *U.S. Public*, pg. 378
CITIBANK DELAWARE—See Citicorp; *U.S. Public*, pg. 377
CITIBANK ESPANA S.A.—See Citicorp; *U.S. Public*, pg. 377
CITIBANK (FLORIDA) N.A.—See Citicorp; *U.S. Public*, pg. 378
CITIBANK-MAGHREB—See Citicorp; *U.S. Public*, pg. 378
CITIBANK (MAINE) N.A.—See Citicorp; *U.S. Public*, pg. 377
CITIBANK N.A.—See Citicorp; *U.S. Public*, pg. 377
CITIBANK, N.A. BOGOTA—See Citicorp; *U.S. Public*, pg. 378
CITIBANK, N.A. LTD.—See Citicorp; *U.S. Public*, pg. 378
CITIBANK, N.A. NIGER S.A.—See Citicorp; *U.S. Public*, pg. 378
CITIBANK (NEVADA) N.A.—See Citicorp; *U.S. Public*, pg. 377
CITIBANK (NEW YORK STATE)—See Citicorp; *U.S. Public*, pg. 377
CITIBANK OY—See Citicorp; *U.S. Public*, pg. 378
CITIBANK SAVINGS—See Citicorp; *U.S. Public*, pg. 378
CITIBANK (SOUTH DAKOTA)—See Citicorp; *U.S. Public*, pg. 377
CITIBANK (ZAIRE) S.A.R.L.—See Citicorp; *U.S. Public*, pg. 379

CITIBANK ZAMBIA LTD.—See Citicorp; *U.S. Public*, pg. 378
CITIC GOLDEN TIGER GROUP CO., LTD.—See Gunze Sangyo, Inc.; *Int'l*, pg. 579
CITICARD S.A. COMERCIAL FINANCIERA Y DE SERVICIOS—See Citicorp; *U.S. Public*, pg. 378
CITICO REALTY CO.—See Norfolk Southern Corporation; *U.S. Public*, pg. 1191
CITICORP; *U.S. Public*, pg. 376
CITICORP ACCEPTANCE CO., INC.—See Citicorp; *U.S. Public*, pg. 378
CITICORP BANK (LUXEMBOURG) S.A.—See Citicorp; *U.S. Public*, pg. 378
CITICORP BANK (SWITZERLAND) AG—See Citicorp; *U.S. Public*, pg. 378
CITICORP BUSINESS CREDIT, INC.—See Citicorp; *U.S. Public*, pg. 378
CITICORP CAPITAL INVESTORS LTD.—See Citicorp; *U.S. Public*, pg. 378
CITICORP COMMUNITY DEVELOPMENT, INC.—See Citicorp; *U.S. Public*, pg. 377
CITICORP CREDIT—See Citicorp; *U.S. Public*, pg. 378
CITICORP CREDIT SERVICES, INC.—See Citicorp; *U.S. Public*, pg. 377
CITICORP DEL-LEASE, INC.—See Citicorp; *U.S. Public*, pg. 377
CITICORP GULF FINANCE LTD.—See Citicorp; *U.S. Public*, pg. 378
CITICORP INDUSTRIAL CREDIT, INC.—See Citicorp; *U.S. Public*, pg. 378
CITICORP INFO SYSTEMS RESEARCH—See Citicorp; *U.S. Public*, pg. 378
CITICORP INFORMATION RESOURCES, INC.—See Citicorp; *U.S. Public*, pg. 377
CITICORP INSURANCE GROUP—See Citicorp; *U.S. Public*, pg. 378
CITICORP INSURANCE SERVICES, INC.—See Citicorp; *U.S. Public*, pg. 377
CITICORP INTERNATIONAL BANK LTD.—See Citicorp; *U.S. Public*, pg. 378
CITICORP INTERNATIONAL BANK S.A.—See Citicorp; *U.S. Public*, pg. 378
CITICORP INTERNATIONAL LIMITED—See Citicorp; *U.S. Public*, pg. 378
CITICORP INTERNATIONAL TRADE INDEMNITY CO., INC.—See Citicorp; *U.S. Public*, pg. 377
CITICORP INVESTMENT BANK LTD.—See Citicorp; *U.S. Public*, pg. 379
CITICORP INVESTMENT BANK (SINGAPORE) LTD.—See Citicorp; *U.S. Public*, pg. 379
CITICORP LEASING INC.—See Citicorp; *U.S. Public*, pg. 377
CITICORP MORTGAGE, INC.—See Citicorp; *U.S. Public*, pg. 378
CITICORP, N.A.—See Citicorp; *U.S. Public*, pg. 377
CITICORP NATIONAL SYSTEM—See Citicorp; *U.S. Public*, pg. 378
CITICORP REAL ESTATE, INC.—See Citicorp; *U.S. Public*, pg. 378
CITICORP RETAIL SERVICES, INC.—See Citicorp; *U.S. Public*, pg. 377
CITICORP S.A.—See Citicorp; *U.S. Public*, pg. 379
CITICORP SAVINGS, A FEDERAL SAVINGS & LOAN ASSN.—See Citicorp; *U.S. Public*, pg. 378
CITICORP SAVINGS OF CALIFORNIA—See Citicorp; *U.S. Public*, pg. 377
CITICORP SAVINGS OF WASHINGTON, D.C.—See Citicorp; *U.S. Public*, pg. 377
CITICORP SCRIMGEOUR VICKERS—See Citicorp; *U.S. Public*, pg. 379
CITICORP SECURITIES MARKETS, INC.—See Citicorp; *U.S. Public*, pg. 377
CITICORP SELECT INVESTMENTS—See Citicorp; *U.S. Public*, pg. 377
CITICORP (USA), INC.—See Citicorp; *U.S. Public*, pg. 377
CITICORP VENTURE CAPITAL LTD.—See Citicorp; *U.S. Public*, pg. 379
CITILEASE INTERNACIONAL, S.A.—See Citicorp; *U.S. Public*, pg. 379
CITITRUST (BAHAMAS) LTD.—See Citicorp; *U.S. Public*, pg. 379
CITITRUST (CAYMAN) LTD.—See Citicorp; *U.S. Public*, pg. 379
CITIZEN AMERICA CORP.—See Citizen Watch Company, Ltd.; *Int'l*, pg. 294
CITIZEN COMPUTER PERIPHERALS G.M.B.H.—See Citizen Watch Company, Ltd.; *Int'l*, pg. 294
CITIZEN DE MEXICO, S.A. DE C.V.—See Citizen Watch Company, Ltd.; *Int'l*, pg. 294
CITIZEN ELECTRONICS CO., LTD.—See Citizen Watch Company, Ltd.; *Int'l*, pg. 293
CITIZEN IWATE CO., LTD.—See Citizen Watch Company, Ltd.; *Int'l*, pg. 293
CITIZEN KOHATSU CO., LTD.—See Citizen Watch Company, Ltd.; *Int'l*, pg. 293
CITIZEN LATINAMERICA CORP.—See Citizen Watch Company, Ltd.; *Int'l*, pg. 294
CITIZEN L.C. TEC CO., LTD.—See Citizen Watch Company, Ltd.; *Int'l*, pg. 293
CITIZEN MACHINERY EUROPE G.M.B.H.—See Citizen Watch Company, Ltd.; *Int'l*, pg. 294
CITIZEN MECHATRONICS CO., LTD.—See Citizen Watch Company, Ltd.; *Int'l*, pg. 293
CITIZEN OF KOREA CO., LTD.—See Citizen Watch Company, Ltd.; *Int'l*, pg. 294
CITIZEN PRECISION MACHINE CO., LTD.—See Citizen Watch Company, Ltd.; *Int'l*, pg. 293
CITIZEN PRECISION OF KOREA CO., LTD.—See Citizen Watch Company, Ltd.; *Int'l*, pg. 294
CITIZEN PUBLISHING CO.—See Gannett Company, Inc.; *U.S. Public*, pg. 700
CITIZEN SYSTEMS & PERIPHERALS EUROPE—See Citizen Watch Company, Ltd.; *Int'l*, pg. 294

CITIZEN TECHNO CO., LTD.—See Citizen Watch Company, Ltd.; *Int'l*, pg. 293
CITIZEN TOKUHAN (H.K.) CO., LTD.—See Citizen Watch Company, Ltd.; *Int'l*, pg. 294
CITIZEN TRADING CO., LTD.—See Citizen Watch Company, Ltd.; *Int'l*, pg. 293
CITIZEN UHRENFABRIK G.M.B.H.—See Citizen Watch Company, Ltd.; *Int'l*, pg. 294
CITIZEN WATCH (CHINA) CO., LTD.—See Citizen Watch Company, Ltd.; *Int'l*, pg. 294
CITIZEN WATCH COMPANY, LTD.; *Int'l*, pg. 293
CITIZEN WATCH CO. OF CANADA, LTD.—See Citizen Watch Company, Ltd.; *Int'l*, pg. 294
CITIZEN WATCH CO. OF AMERICA, INC.—See Citizen Watch Company, Ltd.; *Int'l*, pg. 294
CITIZEN WATCH ESPANA S.A.—See Citizen Watch Company, Ltd.; *Int'l*, pg. 294
CITIZEN WATCH EUROPE G.M.B.H.—See Citizen Watch Company, Ltd.; *Int'l*, pg. 294
CITIZEN WATCH FRANCE S.A.—See Citizen Watch Company, Ltd.; *Int'l*, pg. 294
CITIZEN WATCH ITALY S.P.A.—See Citizen Watch Company, Ltd.; *Int'l*, pg. 294
CITIZEN WATCH (SWITZERLAND) AG—See Citizen Watch Company, Ltd.; *Int'l*, pg. 294
CITIZEN WATCH (U.K.) LTD.—See Citizen Watch Company, Ltd.; *Int'l*, pg. 294
CITIZEN WATCHES AUSTRALIA PTY LTD.—See Citizen Watch Company, Ltd.; *Int'l*, pg. 294
CITIZEN WATCHES GULF CO.—See Citizen Watch Company, Ltd.; *Int'l*, pg. 294
CITIZEN WATCHES (H.K.) LTD.—See Citizen Watch Company, Ltd.; *Int'l*, pg. 294
CITIZEN WATCHES (INDIA) LTD.—See Citizen Watch Company, Ltd.; *Int'l*, pg. 294
CITIZEN WATCHES NEW ZEALAND LTD.—See Citizen Watch Company, Ltd.; *Int'l*, pg. 294
CITIZEN YOSHIMI CO., LTD.—See Citizen Watch Company, Ltd.; *Int'l*, pg. 294
CITIZENS BANC LEASING—See CNB Bancshares, Inc.; *U.S. Public*, pg. 280
THE CITIZENS BANK—See Synovus Financial Corp.; *U.S. Public*, pg. 1549
CITIZENS BANK & TRUST—See UMB Financial Corporation; *U.S. Public*, pg. 1654
CITIZENS BANK AND TRUST OF WEST GEORGIA—See Synovus Financial Corp.; *U.S. Public*, pg. 1549
CITIZENS BANK, GIBSON COUNTY REGION—See CNB Bancshares, Inc.; *U.S. Public*, pg. 281
CITIZENS BANK OF CENTRAL INDIANA—See CNB Bancshares, Inc.; *U.S. Public*, pg. 280
CITIZENS BANK OF CENTRAL INDIANA-BLOOMINGTON REGION—See CNB Bancshares, Inc.; *U.S. Public*, pg. 280
CITIZENS BANK OF CENTRAL INDIANA-CENTRAL REGION—See CNB Bancshares, Inc.; *U.S. Public*, pg. 280
CITIZENS BANK OF CENTRAL INDIANA-ORLEANS REGION—See CNB Bancshares, Inc.; *U.S. Public*, pg. 280
THE CITIZENS BANK OF COCHRAN—See Synovus Financial Corp.; *U.S. Public*, pg. 1549
CITIZENS BANK OF CONNECTICUT—See The Royal Bank of Scotland plc; *Int'l*, pg. 1132
CITIZENS BANK OF ILLINOIS—See CNB Bancshares, Inc.; *U.S. Public*, pg. 280
CITIZENS BANK OF JASPER—See CNB Bancshares, Inc.; *U.S. Public*, pg. 280
CITIZENS BANK OF KENTUCKY—See CNB Bancshares, Inc.; *U.S. Public*, pg. 280
CITIZENS BANK OF MASSACHUSETTS—See The Royal Bank of Scotland plc; *Int'l*, pg. 1132
CITIZENS BANK OF NORTHWEST ARKANSAS—See BOK Financial Corp.; *U.S. Public*, pg. 163
CITIZENS BANK OF WESTERN INDIANA—See CNB Bancshares, Inc.; *U.S. Public*, pg. 280
CITIZENS BANK, POSEY COUNTY REGION—See CNB Bancshares, Inc.; *U.S. Public*, pg. 281
CITIZENS BANK, VINCENNES REGION—See CNB Bancshares, Inc.; *U.S. Public*, pg. 281
CITIZENS BANKING CORPORATION; *U.S. Public*, pg. 379
CITIZENS COMMERCIAL & SAVINGS BANK—See Citizens Banking Corporation; *U.S. Public*, pg. 379
CITIZENS COMMUNICATIONS SERVICES, INC.—See Citizens Utilities Company; *U.S. Public*, pg. 380
CITIZENS FEDERAL BANK, F.S.B.—See CitFed Bancorp, Inc.; *U.S. Public*, pg. 376
CITIZENS FINANCIAL GROUP, INC.—See The Royal Bank of Scotland plc; *Int'l*, pg. 1132
CITIZENS FINANCIAL SERVICES CORPORATION—See The Royal Bank of Scotland plc; *Int'l*, pg. 1132
CITIZENS FIRST BANK—See First Commercial Corporation; *U.S. Public*, pg. 630
CITIZENS FIRST BANK—See Synovus Financial Corp.; *U.S. Public*, pg. 1549
CITIZENS FIRST STATE BANK—See First Financial Bancorp; *U.S. Public*, pg. 632
CITIZENS FUND INSURANCE COMPANY—See Meridian Insurance Group, Inc.; *U.S. Public*, pg. 1095
CITIZENS GAS & COKE UTILITY; *U.S. Private*, pg. 241
CITIZENS GAS FUEL COMPANY—See MCN Energy Group, Inc.; *U.S. Public*, pg. 1025
CITIZENS INFORMATION SYSTEMS, INC.—See CNB Bancshares, Inc.; *U.S. Public*, pg. 281
CITIZENS INSURANCE COMPANY OF AMERICA—See Allmerica Financial Corporation; *U.S. Public*, pg. 54
CITIZENS INSURANCE OF EVANSVILLE—See CNB Bancshares, Inc.; *U.S. Public*, pg. 280
CITIZENS LEASING CORPORATION—See The Royal Bank of Scotland plc; *Int'l*, pg. 1132
CITIZEN'S MANAGEMENT, INC.—See Allmerica Financial Corporation; *U.S. Public*, pg. 54
CITIZENS MORTGAGE CORPORATION—See The Royal Bank of Scotland plc; *Int'l*, pg. 1132

CITIZENS NATIONAL BANK—See CNB Bancshares, Inc.; *U.S. Public*, pg. 281
CITIZENS NATIONAL BANK OF LAKE GENEVA—See Firstar Corporation; *U.S. Public*, pg. 643
CITIZENS NATIONAL BANK OF SOUTHERN PENNSYLVANIA—See Susquehanna Bancshares, Inc.; *U.S. Public*, pg. 1542
THE CITIZENS NATIONAL BANK—See Mercantile Bankshares Corporation; *U.S. Public*, pg. 1089
CITIZENS RESOURCES COMPANY—See Citizens Utilities Company; *U.S. Public*, pg. 380
CITIZENS SAVINGS BANK—See The Royal Bank of Scotland plc; *Int'l*, pg. 1132
THE CITIZENS SAVINGS BANK COMPANY—See Rurban Financial Corp.; *U.S. Public*, pg. 1412
CITIZENS SECURITY MUTUAL INSURANCE—See Meridian Insurance Group, Inc.; *U.S. Public*, pg. 1095
THE CITIZENS STATE BANK—See Old National Bancorp; *U.S. Public*, pg. 1217
CITIZENS TELECOMMUNICATIONS—See Citizens Utilities Company; *U.S. Public*, pg. 380
CITIZENS TRUST COMPANY—See The Royal Bank of Scotland plc; *Int'l*, pg. 1132
CITIZENS TRUST COMPANY OF INDIANA, N.A.—See CNB Bancshares, Inc.; *U.S. Public*, pg. 280
CITIZENS UTILITIES COMPANY; *U.S. Public*, pg. 379
CITIZENS UTILITIES COMPANY OF CALIFORNIA—See Citizens Utilities Company; *U.S. Public*, pg. 380
CITIZENS UTILITIES COMPANY OF ILLINOIS—See Citizens Utilities Company; *U.S. Public*, pg. 380
CITIZENS UTILITIES COMPANY OF PENNSYLVANIA—See Citizens Utilities Company; *U.S. Public*, pg. 380
CITIZENS UTILITIES HOME WATER COMPANY—See Citizens Utilities Company; *U.S. Public*, pg. 380
CITIZENS UTILITIES WATER COMPANY OF PENNSYLVANIA—See Citizens Utilities Company; *U.S. Public*, pg. 380
CITO/CFCL-TV—See Baton Broadcasting Incorporated; *Int'l*, pg. 171
P.T. CITRAGUNA SARANATAMA(CIBA DISTRIBUTOR)—See Novartis AG; *Int'l*, pg. 981
S.A. CITRIQUE BELGE N.V.—See Roche Holding Ltd.; *Int'l*, pg. 1121
CITROEN HISPANA S.A.—See PSA Peugeot Citroen; *Int'l*, pg. 1020
CITROEN HISPANIA S.A.—See PSA Peugeot Citroen; *Int'l*, pg. 1020
CITROEN (SWITZERLAND)—See PSA Peugeot Citroen; *Int'l*, pg. 1020
CITRON HALIGMAN BEDECARRE; *U.S. Private*, pg. 241
CITRONAAS BV—See The Albert Fisher Group PLC; *Int'l*, pg. 491
CITRUS CORP.—See Enron Corp.; *U.S. Public*, pg. 585
CITRUS COUNTY CHRONICLE—See Landmark Communications, Inc.; *U.S. Private*, pg. 648
CITRUS COUNTY DETENTION FACILITY—See Corrections Corporation of America; *U.S. Public*, pg. 450
CITRUS MACHINERY ITALY, S.R.L.—See FMC Corporation; *U.S. Public*, pg. 606
CITRUS STATE DEVELOPMENT CORP.—See California State Bank; *U.S. Public*, pg. 294
CITRUS WORLD INC.; *U.S. Private*, pg. 241
CITY & SUBURBAN DELIVERY SYSTEMS, INC.—See The New York Times Company; *U.S. Public*, pg. 1175
CITY BLDG. KANRI CO., LTD.—See Matsuya Company Ltd.; *Int'l*, pg. 848
CITY CLUB OF CHARLOTTE—See Fairfield Communities, Inc.; *U.S. Public*, pg. 610
CITY COM B.V.—See Internatio-Muller N.V.; *Int'l*, pg. 681
CITY DEVELOPMENT DIVISION—See Tokyu Corporation; *Int'l*, pg. 1395
CITY FINANCE COMPANY—See Washington Mutual Inc.; *U.S. Public*, pg. 1741
CITY GAS COMPANY OF FLORIDA—See NUI Corporation; *U.S. Public*, pg. 1147
CITY LOOKS SALONS—See The Barbers, Hairstyling for Men & Women, Inc.; *U.S. Private*, pg. 115
CITY MACHINE & WHEEL CO.—See The Cypress Companies; *U.S. Private*, pg. 299
CITY MACHINE TOOL & DIE COMPANY, INC.; *U.S. Private*, pg. 241
CITY MEAT ALLIANT—See Clayton, Dubilier & Rice, Inc; *U.S. Private*, pg. 244
CITY MEATS & PROVISIONS CO.—See Clayton, Dubilier & Rice, Inc; *U.S. Private*, pg. 244
CITY MEATS & PROVISIONS - SAN DIEGO—See Clayton, Dubilier & Rice, Inc; *U.S. Private*, pg. 244
CITY NATIONAL BANK—See City National Corporation; *U.S. Public*, pg. 381
CITY NATIONAL BANK—See First Commerce Bancshares, Inc.; *U.S. Public*, pg. 629
CITY NATIONAL BANK—See UMB Financial Corporation; *U.S. Public*, pg. 1654
CITY NATIONAL BANK - FAIRFAX REGIONAL OFFICE—See City National Corporation; *U.S. Public*, pg. 381
CITY NATIONAL BANK OF BATON ROUGE—See First Commerce Corporation; *U.S. Public*, pg. 629
CITY NATIONAL BANK OF FORT SMITH—See First United Bancshares, Inc.; *U.S. Public*, pg. 641
CITY NATIONAL BANK - OLYMPIC PLAZA REGIONAL OFFICE—See City National Corporation; *U.S. Public*, pg. 381
CITY NATIONAL CORPORATION; *U.S. Public*, pg. 380
THE CITY OF LONDON REAL PROPERTY COMPANY LIMITED—See Land Securities Plc; *Int'l*, pg. 798
CITY POSTAL, INC.; *U.S. Public*, pg. 241
CITY RADIO—See Groupe Bruxelles Lambert S.A.; *Int'l*, pg. 561
CITY STORAGE & TRANSFER, INC.—See Norfolk Southern Corporation; *U.S. Public*, pg. 1191
CITY STORMARKNAD—See KF/Konsum Coop Group; *Int'l*, pg. 718

CITY TRUST BANKING CORP.—See Citicorp; *U.S. Public*, pg. 379
CITYWIDE TOWING—See Stamford Capital; *U.S. Private*, pg. 1030
CIVES CORPORATION; *U.S. Private*, pg. 241
CIVIC CENTER CORPORATION—See Anheuser-Busch Companies, Inc.; *U.S. Public*, pg. 114
CIVIL ENGINEERING INSTRUMENT CENTER—See Minebea Co., Ltd.; *Int'l*, pg. 868
CIVIL SERVICE EMPLOYEES INSURANCE CO.—See CSE Insurance Group; *U.S. Public*, pg. 197
CIZKOVICKA CEMENTARNA A VAPENICE, A.S.—See Lafarge S.A.; *Int'l*, pg. 790
CLADDING & DECKING (UK) LTD.—See Koninklijke Hoogovens N.V.; *Int'l*, pg. 754
CLADEN—See Groupe Casino; *Int'l*, pg. 563
CLADEVI—See Groupe Casino; *Int'l*, pg. 563
CLADWOOD DIV. (CENTRAL OFFICE)—See Jefferson Smurfit Group p.l.c.; *Int'l*, pg. 1270
CLAEYS SEMENCES—See Lafarge S.A.; *Int'l*, pg. 790
CLAIBORNE MENSWEAR DIV.—See Liz Claiborne, Inc.; *U.S. Public*, pg. 1006
CLAIBORNE TELEPHONE CO.—See Century Telephone Enterprises, Inc.; *U.S. Public*, pg. 330
CLAIMS SERVICE INTERNATIONAL, INC.—See UNUM Corporation; *U.S. Public*, pg. 1699
CLAIRE MANUFACTURING CO.—See Goldner Hawn Johnsons & Morrison Incorporated; *U.S. Private*, pg. 462
CLAIRE'S BOUTIQUES, INC.—See Claire's Stores Inc.; *U.S. Public*, pg. 381
CLAIRE'S STORES INC.; *U.S. Public*, pg. 381
CLAIROL CARIBE—See Bristol-Myers Squibb Company; *U.S. Public*, pg. 254
CLAIROL DISTRIBUTION CENTER—See Bristol-Myers Squibb Company; *U.S. Public*, pg. 255
CLAIROL DIVISION—See Bristol-Myers Squibb Company; *U.S. Public*, pg. 255
CLAIROL, INC.—See Bristol-Myers Squibb Company; *U.S. Public*, pg. 254
CLAIROL (TAIWAN) LTD.—See Bristol-Myers Squibb Company; *U.S. Public*, pg. 256
CLAIROL'S CONSUMER PRODUCTS DIVISION—See Bristol-Myers Squibb Company; *U.S. Public*, pg. 254
CLAIRSON INTERNATIONAL CORP.—See Emerson Electric Co.; *U.S. Public*, pg. 575
CLAM PETROLEUM CO.—See USX Corporation; *U.S. Public*, pg. 1662
CLANTON'S AUTO AUCTION—See Cox Enterprises, Inc.; *U.S. Private*, pg. 282
CLARCOR, INC.; *U.S. Public*, pg. 381
C.P. CLARE CORPORATION; *U.S. Public*, pg. 382
CLAREMONT FLOCK—See Claremont Flock Corporation; *U.S. Private*, pg. 242
CLAREMONT FLOCK CORPORATION; *U.S. Private*, pg. 241
CLAREMONT SERVICE CENTER—See CVB Financial Corp.; *U.S. Public*, pg. 287
CLARENDON IMPORTS INC.—See Rothmans UK Holdings Limited; *Int'l*, pg. 1130
CLARENDON INSURANCE AGENCY INC.—See Sun Life Assurance Company of Canada; *Int'l*, pg. 1319
CLARETTA & C.S.P.A.—See LVMH Moet Hennessy Louis Vuitton; *Int'l*, pg. 782
CLARIANT CORPORATION—See Hoechst Aktiengesellschaft; *Int'l*, pg. 624
CLARIANT INTERNATIONAL LTD.—See Hoechst Aktiengesellschaft; *Int'l*, pg. 624
CLARIANT (SCHWEIZ) AG—See Hoechst Aktiengesellschaft; *Int'l*, pg. 624
CLARICOM—See Bain Capital; *U.S. Private*, pg. 111
CLARIFY GMBH-GERMANY—See Clarify Inc.; *U.S. Public*, pg. 382
CLARIFY INC.; *U.S. Public*, pg. 382
CLARIFY INC.-AUSTRALIA/ASIA—See Clarify Inc.; *U.S. Public*, pg. 382
CLARIFY INC.-CANADA—See Clarify Inc.; *U.S. Public*, pg. 382
CLARIFY INC.-JAPAN—See Clarify Inc.; *U.S. Public*, pg. 382
CLARIFY LTD.-UNITED KINGDOM—See Clarify Inc.; *U.S. Public*, pg. 382
CLARIFY SARL-FRANCE—See Clarify Inc.; *U.S. Public*, pg. 382
CLARIN; *U.S. Private*, pg. 242
CLARINDA COLOR L.L.C.—See Capital Graphics Inc.; *U.S. Private*, pg. 206
THE CLARINDA COMPANY—See Capital Graphics Inc.; *U.S. Private*, pg. 206
CLARINS; *Int'l*, pg. 295
CLARINS B.V.—See Clarins; *Int'l*, pg. 295
CLARINS DE MEXICO SADE CV—See Clarins; *Int'l*, pg. 295
CLARINS INTERNATIONAL DIV.—See Clarins; *Int'l*, pg. 295
CLARINS LTD.—See Clarins; *Int'l*, pg. 295
CLARINS PRODUCTION FACILITIES—See Clarins; *Int'l*, pg. 295
CLARINS PTE LTD.—See Clarins; *Int'l*, pg. 295
CLARINS SDN BHD—See Clarins; *Int'l*, pg. 295
CLARINS USA INC.—See Clarins; *Int'l*, pg. 295
CLARION ASIA PTE. LTD.—See Clarion Co., Ltd.; *Int'l*, pg. 296
CLARION AUSTRALIA PTY., LTD.—See Clarion Co., Ltd.; *Int'l*, pg. 296
CLARION BOOKS—See Houghton Mifflin Company; *U.S. Public*, pg. 841
CLARION CANADA INC.—See Clarion Co., Ltd.; *Int'l*, pg. 296
CLARION CO., LTD.; *Int'l*, pg. 296
CLARION CORPORATION OF AMERICA—See Clarion Co., Ltd.; *Int'l*, pg. 296

Company Index

CLARION CORPORATION OF AMERICA, DETROIT ENGINEERING OFFICE—See Clarion Co., Ltd.; *Int'l*, pg. 296
CLARION CORPORATION OF AMERICA (EASTERN DIVISION)—See Clarion Co., Ltd.; *Int'l*, pg. 296
CLARION COSMETICS—See The Procter & Gamble Company; *U.S. Public*, pg. 1330
CLARION DEUTSCHLAND GMBH—See Clarion Co., Ltd.; *Int'l*, pg. 296
CLARION ELECTRONICS (S) PTE., LTD.—See Clarion Co., Ltd.; *Int'l*, pg. 296
CLARION EUROPA GMBH—See Clarion Co., Ltd.; *Int'l*, pg. 296
CLARION EUROPA GMBH FILLIALE ITALIANA—See Clarion Co., Ltd.; *Int'l*, pg. 296
CLARION EUROPA LIAISON OFFICE (NL)—See Clarion Co., Ltd.; *Int'l*, pg. 296
CLARION FRANCE S.A.—See Clarion Co., Ltd.; *Int'l*, pg. 296
CLARION (H.K.) CO., LTD.—See Clarion Co., Ltd.; *Int'l*, pg. 296
CLARION I.M.P. A/S—See DMB&B Communications; *U.S. Private*, pg. 303
THE CLARION-LEDGER—See Gannett Company, Inc.; *U.S. Public*, pg. 700
CLARION (MALAYSIA) SDN. BHD.—See Clarion Co., Ltd.; *Int'l*, pg. 296
CLARION MANUFACTURING CORP. OF AMERICA—See Clarion Co., Ltd.; *Int'l*, pg. 296
CLARION MANUFACTURING CORPORATION OF THE PHILIPPINES—See Clarion Co., Ltd.; *Int'l*, pg. 296
CLARION-MITSUWA PHILIPPINES, INC.—See Clarion Co., Ltd.; *Int'l*, pg. 296
CLARION NEDERLAND—See Clarion Co., Ltd.; *Int'l*, pg. 296
CLARION SALES CORPORATION—See Clarion Co., Ltd.; *Int'l*, pg. 296
CLARION SHOJI (U.K.) LTD.—See Clarion Co., Ltd.; *Int'l*, pg. 296
CLARION SVENSKA AB—See Clarion Co., Ltd.; *Int'l*, pg. 296
CLARION (TAIWAN) MANUFACTURING CO., LTD.—See Clarion Co., Ltd.; *Int'l*, pg. 296
CLARIS CORPORATION—See Apple Computer, Inc.; *U.S. Public*, pg. 121
CLARITAS, INC.—See VNU Verenigde Nederlandse Uitgeversbedrijven B.V.; *Int'l*, pg. 1447
CLARITY COVERDALE FURY ADVERTISING; *U.S. Private*, pg. 242
CLARITY VISION—See Highmark Inc.; *U.S. Private*, pg. 529
CLARK & WEINSTOCK—See Omnicom Group Inc.; *U.S. Public*, pg. 1223
CLARK CONSTRUCTION GROUP, INC.—See Clark Enterprises, Inc.; *U.S. Private*, pg. 242
CYRUS CLARK CO., INC.; *U.S. Private*, pg. 242
DAVID CLARK COMPANY INCORPORATED; *U.S. Private*, pg. 242
CLARK DETROIT-DIESEL ALLISON; *U.S. Private*, pg. 242
DICK CLARK CORPORATE PRODUCTIONS, INC.—See Dick Clark Productions, Inc.; *U.S. Public*, pg. 382
DICK CLARK MEDIA ARCHIVES—See Dick Clark Productions, Inc.; *U.S. Public*, pg. 382
DICK CLARK PRODUCTIONS, INC.; *U.S. Public*, pg. 382
DICK CLARK RESTAURANTS, INC.—See Dick Clark Productions, Inc.; *U.S. Public*, pg. 382
CLARK DISTRIBUTION SERVICES COMPANY—See Ingersoll-Rand Company; *U.S. Public*, pg. 876
CLARK DOOR, INC.; *U.S. Private*, pg. 242
CLARK ENTERPRISES, INC.; *U.S. Private*, pg. 242
CLARK FILTER—See CLARCOR, Inc.; *U.S. Public*, pg. 381
CLARK FOODSERVICE, INC.; *U.S. Private*, pg. 242
CLARK GRAVE VAULT CO.; *U.S. Private*, pg. 243
THE CLARK GROUP; *Int'l*, pg. 296
CLARK GUM COMPANY; *U.S. Private*, pg. 243
J.L. CLARK LANCASTER DIV.—See CLARCOR, Inc.; *U.S. Public*, pg. 381
J.L. CLARK TUBE DIV.—See CLARCOR, Inc.; *U.S. Public*, pg. 382
JOSLYN CLARK CONTROLS, INC.—See Danaher Corporation; *U.S. Public*, pg. 481
CLARK MATERIAL HANDLING COMPANY; *U.S. Private*, pg. 243
CLARK OIL & REFINING CORPORATION-BLUE ISLAND REFINERY—See Clark Refining & Marketing Inc.; *U.S. Private*, pg. 243
CLARK OIL & REFINING CORPORATION-WOOD RIVER REFINERY—See Clark Refining & Marketing Inc.; *U.S. Private*, pg. 243
CLARK OIL & REFINING CORP.-PORT ARTHUR REFINERY—See Clark Refining & Marketing Inc.; *U.S. Private*, pg. 243
CLARK OIL TRADING COMPANY—See Apex Oil Company, Inc.; *U.S. Public*, pg. 77
CLARK PACIFIC; *U.S. Private*, pg. 243
CLARK REFINING & MARKETING INC.; *U.S. Private*, pg. 243
CLARK SHOE CO.—See Clarks International; *Int'l*, pg. 297
CLARK SPECIALTY CO., INC.; *U.S. Private*, pg. 243
CLARKE AMERICAN CORP.—See Caradon Plc; *Int'l*, pg. 267
CLARKE CONTAINER COMPANY, INC.—See Mark IV Industries Inc.; *U.S. Public*, pg. 1045
CLARKE ELECTRONICS—See Video Display Corporation; *U.S. Public*, pg. 1720
J.M. CLARKE (ELECTRICAL ENGINEERS) LIMITED—See B. Elliott plc.; *Int'l*, pg. 448
CLARKE TRANSPORT—See Newfoundland Capital Corporation Limited; *Int'l*, pg. 924
P.J. CLARKE'S—See Lettuce Entertain You Enterprises, Inc.; *U.S. Private*, pg. 661
CLARKLIFT OF MINNESOTA, INC.; *U.S. Private*, pg. 243
CLARKLIFT OF NORTH DAKOTA—See Clarklift Of Minnesota, Inc.; *U.S. Private*, pg. 244
CLARKS COS. N.A.—See Clarks International; *Int'l*, pg. 297

CLARKS INTERNATIONAL; *Int'l*, pg. 296
CLARKSON CONSTRUCTION COMPANIES; *U.S. Private*, pg. 244
CLAROSTAT CENTERS & CONTROLS GROUP—See BTR plc; *Int'l*, pg. 127
CLASHFERN HOLDINGS LIMITED—See Avonmore Waterford Group plc; *Int'l*, pg. 102
CLASS ONE RESEARCH—See Clear Channel Communications, Inc.; *U.S. Public*, pg. 383
CLASSCO BENEFIT SERVICES LIMITED—See The Canada Life Assurance Company; *Int'l*, pg. 255
THE CLASSIC CARD COMPANY, LTD.—See Hallmark Cards, Inc.; *U.S. Private*, pg. 496
CLASSIC GMBH—See N.V. Koninklijke KNP BT; *Int'l*, pg. 757
CLASSIC MARKETS CORP.; *U.S. Private*, pg. 244
CLASSIC MOMENTS COMPANY—See Loews Corporation; *U.S. Public*, pg. 1010
CLASSIC NISSAN—See ASN Incorporated; *U.S. Private*, pg. 8
CLASSIC PAPERS LTD.—See Metsa-Serla Corporation; *Int'l*, pg. 864
CLASSIC RESIDENCE BY HYATT—See Hyatt Corporation; *U.S. Private*, pg. 551
CLASTER TELEVISION—See Hasbro, Inc.; *U.S. Public*, pg. 797
CLAUDIUS PETERS AG—See Babcock International Group PLC; *Int'l*, pg. 131
CLAUDIUS PETERS (IBERICA) S.A.—See Babcock International Group PLC; *Int'l*, pg. 131
CLAUDIUS PETERS INC.—See Babcock International Group PLC; *Int'l*, pg. 131
CLAUDIUS PETERS S.A.—See Babcock International Group PLC; *Int'l*, pg. 131
CLAUSE—See Lafarge S.A.; *Int'l*, pg. 790
CLAUSEN & BOSSE GMBH—See Georg von Holtzbrinck GmbH; *Int'l*, pg. 1478
CLAVIS MARIS FINLANDIAE OY—See Kvaerner a.s.a.; *Int'l*, pg. 771
CLAY FINLAY INC.—See United Asset Management Corporation; *U.S. Public*, pg. 1673
CLAY-PARK LABS, INC.—See Agis Industries Ltd.; *Int'l*, pg. 30
CLAYHITHE P.L.C.; *Int'l*, pg. 297
CLAYMORE CHEMICALS LTD.—See Raisio Group; *Int'l*, pg. 1086
CLAYORIENT LTD.—See Watts Blake Bearne & Co. Plc; *Int'l*, pg. 1488
CLAYS & MINERALS (THAILAND) LTD.—See Watts Blake Bearne & Co. Plc; *Int'l*, pg. 1488
CLAYSON KNITTING CO. INC.; *U.S. Private*, pg. 244
THE CLAYTON ANILINE COMPANY—See Novartis AG; *Int'l*, pg. 981
A.T. CLAYTON & COMPANY, INC.; *U.S. Private*, pg. 244
CLAYTON CORPORATION; *U.S. Private*, pg. 244
CLAYTON, DUBILIER & RICE, INC; *U.S. Private*, pg. 244
CLAYTON GROUP, INC.; *U.S. Private*, pg. 244
CLAYTON HOMES, INC.; *U.S. Public*, pg. 382
CLAYTON HOUSE HEALTHCARE—See Vencor, Inc.; *U.S. Public*, pg. 1712
CLAYTON INDUSTRIES CO.; *U.S. Private*, pg. 245
CLAYTON MANUFACTURING DIV., DYNAMIC EQUIPMENT—See Clayton Industries Co.; *U.S. Private*, pg. 245
CLAYTON-MARCUS COMPANY, INC.—See Ladd Furniture, Inc.; *U.S. Public*, pg. 975
CLAYTON METALS CORP.—See Clayton Corporation; *U.S. Private*, pg. 244
CLAYTON PLASTICS CORP.—See Clayton Corporation; *U.S. Private*, pg. 244
CLAYTON REINSURANCE, LTD.—See The Reliable Life Insurance Company; *U.S. Private*, pg. 1374
CLAYTON, WILLIAMS & SHERWOOD, INC.; *U.S. Private*, pg. 245
CLEAN ENERGY ENTERPRISE, INC.—See Public Service Company of North Carolina, Inc.; *U.S. Public*, pg. 1340
CLEAN HARBORS, INC.; *U.S. Public*, pg. 383
CLEANAWAY—See Brambles Industries Limited; *Int'l*, pg. 211
CLEANAWAY LIMITED—See Brambles Industries Limited; *Int'l*, pg. 212
CLEANAWAY LIMITED—See GKN plc; *Int'l*, pg. 535
CLEANERS HANGER CO.; *U.S. Private*, pg. 245
CLEANING SOLUTIONS GROUP/CELLO—See The Sherwin-Williams Company; *U.S. Public*, pg. 1466
CLEANING SPECIALTY COMPANY—See Ekco Group, Inc.; *U.S. Public*, pg. 566
CLEANROOM TECHNOLOGY—See Groupe Strafor Facom; *Int'l*, pg. 569
CLEAR CHANNEL COMMUNICATIONS, INC.; *U.S. Public*, pg. 383
CLEAR CHANNEL COMMUNICATIONS INTERNATIONAL—See Clear Channel Communications, Inc.; *U.S. Public*, pg. 383
CLEAR CHANNEL METROPLEX—See Clear Channel Communications, Inc.; *U.S. Public*, pg. 383
CLEAR CHANNEL RADIO, INC.—See Clear Channel Communications, Inc.; *U.S. Public*, pg. 383
CLEAR CHANNEL RADIO WORKS—See Clear Channel Communications, Inc.; *U.S. Public*, pg. 383
CLEAR CHANNEL TELEVISION, INC.—See Clear Channel Communications, Inc.; *U.S. Public*, pg. 383
CLEAR COMMUNICATIONS LIMITED—See British Telecommunications plc; *Int'l*, pg. 223
CLEAR RESULTS MARKETING—See Clear Channel Communications, Inc.; *U.S. Public*, pg. 383
CLEAR SHIELD NATIONAL, INC.—See Envirodyne Industries, Inc.; *U.S. Public*, pg. 586
CLEAR SPRINGS FOODS, INC.; *U.S. Private*, pg. 245
CLEARFIELD INSURANCE, LTD.—See Boise Cascade Corporation; *U.S. Public*, pg. 243
CLEARING-NIAGARA—See CNB International, Inc.; *U.S. Private*, pg. 196
CLEARLY CANADIAN BEVERAGE CORP.; *Int'l*, pg. 297

CLEARLY CANADIAN INTERNATIONAL—See Clearly Canadian Beverage Corp.; *Int'l*, pg. 297
CLEARPOINT ENTERPRISES; *U.S. Private*, pg. 245
CLEARWATER AUTO AUCTION INC.—See Tyco International Ltd.; *U.S. Public*, pg. 1648
CLEARWATER COMMODITY CORP.—See Potlatch Corporation; *U.S. Public*, pg. 1318
CLEARWATER FINE FOODS INC.; *Int'l*, pg. 297
CLEARWATER LOBSTER LIMITED—See Clearwater Fine Foods Inc.; *Int'l*, pg. 297
CLEARWATER MILL, INC.—See Fleming Companies, Inc.; *U.S. Public*, pg. 653
CLEARWATER PHILLIES—See The Phillies-A Limited Partnership; *U.S. Private*, pg. 861
CLEARWAYS DRILLING (M) SDN BHD—See Atwood Oceanics, Inc.; *U.S. Public*, pg. 146
CLECIM—See Kvaerner a.s.a.; *Int'l*, pg. 774
CLEMENS COUNTRY KITCHEN (CCK)—See Clemens Markets Inc.; *U.S. Private*, pg. 245
CLEMENS MARKETS INC.; *U.S. Private*, pg. 245
CLEMENS FOODS CO.; *U.S. Private*, pg. 245
CLEMENTS NUT CO.—See Clements Foods Co.; *U.S. Private*, pg. 245
CLEMENTS VINEGAR COMPANY—See Clements Foods Co.; *U.S. Private*, pg. 245
CLEMS READY-MIX—See Holderbank Financiere Glaris Ltd.; *Int'l*, pg. 629
CLEO INC.—See CSS Industries, Inc.; *U.S. Public*, pg. 284
CLERMONT SPECIALTY MANAGERS, LTD.—See W.R. Berkley Corporation; *U.S. Public*, pg. 215
CLESTRA GMBH—See Groupe Strafor Facom; *Int'l*, pg. 570
CLESTRA HAUSERMAN—See Groupe Strafor Facom; *Int'l*, pg. 569
CLESTRA HAUSERMAN A.G.—See Groupe Strafor Facom; *Int'l*, pg. 570
CLESTRA HAUSERMAN BELGIUM—See Groupe Strafor Facom; *Int'l*, pg. 570
CLESTRA HAUSERMAN B.V.—See Groupe Strafor Facom; *Int'l*, pg. 570
CLESTRA HAUSERMAN, INC.—See Groupe Strafor Facom; *Int'l*, pg. 569
CLESTRA HAUSERMAN KOREA—See Groupe Strafor Facom; *Int'l*, pg. 569
CLESTRA HAUSERMAN OVERSEAS—See Groupe Strafor Facom; *Int'l*, pg. 570
CLESTRA HAUSERMAN SCANDINAVIA—See Groupe Strafor Facom; *Int'l*, pg. 570
CLESTRA HOLDING AG—See Groupe Strafor Facom; *Int'l*, pg. 570
CLESTRA SRL—See Groupe Strafor Facom; *Int'l*, pg. 570
CLEVEDON RIVETS & TOOLS LTD.—See Clayhithe P.L.C.; *Int'l*, pg. 297
CLEVELAND BANK & TRUST COMPANY—See First Tennessee National Corporation; *U.S. Public*, pg. 639
CLEVELAND BROTHERS EQUIPMENT CO., INC.; *U.S. Private*, pg. 245
CLEVELAND CAPITAL HOLDINGS; *U.S. Private*, pg. 246
CLEVELAND CHAIR COMPANY—See Jackson Furniture Industries; *U.S. Private*, pg. 579
CLEVELAND CITY FORGE—See Park-Ohio Industries, Inc.; *U.S. Public*, pg. 1258
CLEVELAND-CLIFFS INC; *U.S. Public*, pg. 386
THE CLEVELAND-CLIFFS IRON COMPANY—See Cleveland-Cliffs Inc; *U.S. Public*, pg. 386
CLEVELAND CONTAINER SERVICE, INC.—See Republic Industries, Inc.; *U.S. Public*, pg. 1379
CLEVELAND COUNTY TELEPHONE COMPANY, INC.—See Telephone and Data Systems, Inc.; *U.S. Public*, pg. 1571
CLEVELAND DISTRICT COOLING CORP.—See Ipalco Enterprises, Inc.; *U.S. Public*, pg. 913
CLEVELAND ELECTRIC CO.—See Cleveland Group, Inc.; *U.S. Private*, pg. 246
CLEVELAND ELECTRIC COMPANY OF ARKANSAS—See Cleveland Group, Inc.; *U.S. Private*, pg. 246
THE CLEVELAND ELECTRIC ILLUMINATING COMPANY—See FirstEnergy Corp.; *U.S. Public*, pg. 645
CLEVELAND GROUP, INC.; *U.S. Private*, pg. 246
CLEVELAND PRE-RELEASE CENTER—See Corrections Corporation of America; *U.S. Public*, pg. 450
CLEVELAND PRECISION SYSTEMS GMBH—See Danaher Corporation; *U.S. Public*, pg. 482
CLEVELAND RANGE—See Berisford plc; *Int'l*, pg. 188
ROGER CLEVELAND GOLF COMPANY—See Rossignol S.A.; *Int'l*, pg. 1127
CLEVELAND SHIPREPAIR COMPANY—See The Manitowoc Company, Inc.; *U.S. Public*, pg. 1041
CLEVELAND STRUCTURAL ENGINEERING LIMITED—See Kvaerner a.s.a.; *Int'l*, pg. 772
CLEVELAND THERMAL ENERGY CORPORATION—See Ipalco Enterprises, Inc.; *U.S. Public*, pg. 913
CLEVELAND TWIST DRILL CANADA LIMITED—See Kennametal Inc.; *U.S. Public*, pg. 950
CLEVELAND WOOD PRODUCTS—See Berkshire Hathaway Inc.; *U.S. Public*, pg. 217
CLEVER S.A.—See Cardo AB; *Int'l*, pg. 269
CLEVITE DE MEXICO—See Tenneco Inc.; *U.S. Public*, pg. 1577
CLEWISTON SUGAR HOUSE—See United States Sugar Corporation; *U.S. Private*, pg. 1126
CLEXTRAL—See Framatome SA; *Int'l*, pg. 503
CLICQUOT, INC.—See LVMH Moet Hennessy Louis Vuitton; *Int'l*, pg. 781
CLIFFORD METAL—See Lapham-Hickey Steel Corp.; *U.S. Private*, pg. 651
CLIFFORD PAPER INC.; *U.S. Private*, pg. 246
CLIFFS DRILLING COMPANY; *U.S. Public*, pg. 386
CLIFFS MINING COMPANY—See Cleveland-Cliffs Inc; *U.S. Public*, pg. 386
CLIFFS NEDDRILL CENTRAL TURNKEY INTERNATIONAL—See Royal Nedlloyd Group N.V.; *Int'l*, pg. 1144

CLIFFS NEDDRILL TURNKEY INTERNATIONAL V.O.F.—See Royal Nedlloyd Group N.V.; *Int'l*, pg. 1144
CLIFFSIDE UTILITY CONTRACTORS—See BFC Construction Corporation; *Int'l*, pg. 118
CLIFTEX—See Woolworth Corporation; *U.S. Public*, pg. 1777
CLIFTON HOUSE REHABILITATION CENTER—See Horizon/CMS Healthcare Corporation; *U.S. Public*, pg. 836
CLIGGOTT PUBLISHING; *U.S. Private*, pg. 246
CLIMATEMASTER CORP.—See LSB Industries, Inc.; *U.S. Public*, pg. 970
CLIMATEMASTER INC.—See LSB Industries, Inc.; *U.S. Public*, pg. 970
THE CLIMATIC CORP.; *U.S. Private*, pg. 246
CLIMET INSTRUMENTS CO.—See Venturedyne, Ltd.; *U.S. Private*, pg. 1136
CLINCH RIVER CORP.—See Elgin National Industries, Inc.; *U.S. Private*, pg. 370
CLINE, DAVIS & MANN, INC.; *U.S. Private*, pg. 246
CLINICAL LABORATORY, INC.—See Integrated Health Services, Inc.; *U.S. Public*, pg. 884
CLINICAL RESEARCH CENTER, EUROPE—See Fujisawa Pharmaceutical Co. Ltd.; *Int'l*, pg. 525
CLINICAL-MANAGEMENT SYSTEMS, INC.—See Matria Healthcare, Inc.; *U.S. Public*, pg. 1057
CLINICARE SYSTEMS, INC.—See Gaymar Industries, Inc.; *U.S. Private*, pg. 442
CLINICON MANNHEIM GMBH—See Corange Limited; *Int'l*, pg. 331
THE CLINIPAD CORP.—See The Clinipad Corporation; *U.S. Private*, pg. 247
THE CLINIPAD CORPORATION; *U.S. Private*, pg. 246
CLINISHARE—See UniHealth; *U.S. Private*, pg. 1118
CLINT HURT DRILLING—See Key Energy Group Inc.; *U.S. Public*, pg. 953
CLINTOCK LIMITED—See Brown-Forman Corporation; *U.S. Public*, pg. 262
CLINTON GAS MARKETING—See Enron Corp.; *U.S. Public*, pg. 585
CLINTON MACHINERY AND SUPPLY—See Willcox & Gibbs, Inc.; *U.S. Private*, pg. 1177
THE CLINTON OIL COMPANY—See Enron Corp.; *U.S. Public*, pg. 585
CLINTON PLANT—See Belden Inc.; *U.S. Public*, pg. 201
CLINTON RECORDER—See Journal Register Company; *U.S. Public*, pg. 934
CLINTON STATE BANK—See First Commercial Corporation; *U.S. Public*, pg. 630
CLINTON STATE BANK—See Old National Bancorp; *U.S. Public*, pg. 1217
CLIPPER ABRASIVES INC.—See Saint-Gobain; *Int'l*, pg. 1174
CLIPPER BELT LACER COMPANY—See Flexible Steel Lacing Company; *U.S. Private*, pg. 413
CLIPPER EXXPRESS—See Arkansas Best Corporation; *U.S. Public*, pg. 130
CLIPSAL ASIA LIMITED—See GP Batteries International Ltd.; *Int'l*, pg. 537
THE CLOISTER—See Sea Island Company; *U.S. Private*, pg. 978
CLOISTER PURE SPRING WATER CO., INC.; *U.S. Private*, pg. 247
CLONETICS, INC.—See Cambrex Corporation; *U.S. Public*, pg. 297
CLOPAY CORPORATION—See Griffon Corp.; *U.S. Public*, pg. 766
CLOROX ARGENTINA S.A.—See The Clorox Company; *U.S. Public*, pg. 387
THE CLOROX COMPANY; *U.S. Public*, pg. 386
THE CLOROX COMPANY OF CANADA LTD.—See The Clorox Company; *U.S. Public*, pg. 387
THE CLOROX CO. OF PUERTO RICO—See The Clorox Company; *U.S. Public*, pg. 387
CLOROX DE MEXICO S.A. DE C.V.—See The Clorox Company; *U.S. Public*, pg. 387
THE CLOROX INTERNATIONAL CO.—See The Clorox Company; *U.S. Public*, pg. 387
CLOROX PROFESSIONAL PRODUCTS COMPANY—See The Clorox Company; *U.S. Public*, pg. 387
CLOTHESTIME STORES, INC.; *U.S. Public*, pg. 387
CLOUD CORPORATION; *U.S. Private*, pg. 247
CLOUDY BAY VINEYARDS LTD—See LVMH Moet Hennessy Louis Vuitton; *Int'l*, pg. 782
CLOUGH CHEMICAL CO., LTD.—See Dr. Th. Boehme KG Chem. Fabrik GmbH & Co.; *Int'l*, pg. 199
HERBERT CLOUGH, INC.—See General Re Corporation; *U.S. Public*, pg. 726
CLOUSTON FOODS CANADA—See Fishery Products International Ltd.; *Int'l*, pg. 492
CLOUSTON FOODS EURPOE—See Fishery Products International Ltd.; *Int'l*, pg. 492
CLOUTH GUMMIWERKE AG; *Int'l*, pg. 297
CLOVE DEVELOPMENT CORP.—See Orange and Rockland Utilities, Inc.; *U.S. Public*, pg. 1229
CLOVER CLUB FOODS, INC.—See Granny Goose Foods, Inc.; *U.S. Private*, pg. 469
CLOVER FINANCIAL CORPORATION; *U.S. Private*, pg. 247
CLOVER INSURANCE AGENCY, INC.—See Hilb, Rogal and Hamilton Company; *U.S. Public*, pg. 826
CLOVER PRODUCE LIMITED—See Empire Company Limited; *Int'l*, pg. 454
CLOVER SPRINGS—See Del Webb Corporation; *U.S. Public*, pg. 495
CLOVER YARNS INC.; *U.S. Private*, pg. 247
CLOVERDALE EQUIPMENT CO.; *U.S. Private*, pg. 247
CLOVERHILL BAKERY; *U.S. Private*, pg. 247
CLOVERLANES, INC.—See Great Lakes Realty Corp.; *U.S. Private*, pg. 475
CLOVERLEAF HEALTHCARE—See Vencor, Inc.; *U.S. Public*, pg. 1712
CLOVIS INDEPENDENT—See McClatchy Newspapers Inc.; *U.S. Public*, pg. 1065

CLOW VALVE DIV.—See McWane, Inc.; *U.S. Private*, pg. 725
CLOW WATER SYSTEMS CORP.—See McWane, Inc.; *U.S. Private*, pg. 725
CLUB ANDAMAN BEACH RESORT CO., LTD.—See Siam City Bank Public Company Limited; *Int'l*, pg. 1239
CLUB CAR, INC.—See Ingersoll-Rand Company; *U.S. Public*, pg. 877
CLUB CORP REALTY—See Club Corporation International; *U.S. Private*, pg. 247
CLUB CORPORATION INTERNATIONAL; *U.S. Private*, pg. 247
CLUB CORPORATION OF AMERICA—See Club Corporation International; *U.S. Private*, pg. 247
CLUB DEGLI EDITORI S.P.A.—See Arnoldo Mondadori Editore S.p.A.; *Int'l*, pg. 888
CLUB DEL MAR—See Groupe Air France; *Int'l*, pg. 560
CLUB MECH—See Club Mediterranee SA; *Int'l*, pg. 298
CLUB MED BOUTIQUE—See Club Mediterranee SA; *Int'l*, pg. 298
CLUB MED, INC.—See Club Mediterranee SA; *Int'l*, pg. 298
CLUB MED SALES, INC.—See Club Mediterranee SA; *Int'l*, pg. 298
CLUB MED S.R.L.—See Club Mediterranee SA; *Int'l*, pg. 298
CLUB MEDITERRANEE ASSOCIATION JAPAN CO. LTD.—See Club Mediterranee SA; *Int'l*, pg. 298
CLUB MEDITERRANEE AUSTRALIA PTY. LTD.—See Club Mediterranee SA; *Int'l*, pg. 298
CLUB MEDITERRANEE (BUREAU SUISSE) S.A.—See Club Mediterranee SA; *Int'l*, pg. 298
CLUB MEDITERRANEE INVESTISSEMENTS—See Club Mediterranee SA; *Int'l*, pg. 298
CLUB MEDITERRANEE ITALIA S.P.A.—See Club Mediterranee SA; *Int'l*, pg. 298
CLUB MEDITERRANEE K.K.—See Club Mediterranee SA; *Int'l*, pg. 298
CLUB MEDITERRANEE SA; *Int'l*, pg. 298
CLUB MEDITERRANEE S.A. BELGE—See Club Mediterranee SA; *Int'l*, pg. 298
CLUB MEDITERRANEE U.K. LTD.—See Club Mediterranee SA; *Int'l*, pg. 298
CLUB MONACO INC.; *Int'l*, pg. 298
CLUB RESORTS HOLDING, INC.—See Club Corporation International; *U.S. Private*, pg. 247
CLUB SA—See GIB Group; *Int'l*, pg. 533
CLUB VIDA AGENCIA DE VIAJES, S.A.—See Corporacion MAPFRE, Compania Internacional de Reaseguros, S.A.; *Int'l*, pg. 334
CLUBE DE SUCESSOS—See Philips Electronics N.V.; *Int'l*, pg. 1052
CLUETT INTERNATIONAL GROUP—See Bidermann International S.A.; *Int'l*, pg. 194
CLUETT, PEABODY CANADA INC.—See Bidermann International S.A.; *Int'l*, pg. 194
CLUNE CONSTRUCTION LIMITED; *U.S. Private*, pg. 247
CLUPAK, INC.—See Westvaco Corporation; *U.S. Public*, pg. 1762
O.C. CLUSS LUMBER CO.; *U.S. Private*, pg. 248
O.C. CLUSS LUMBER CO.—See O.C. Cluss Lumber Co.; *U.S. Private*, pg. 248
CLYDE CORPORATION—See Phillips Service Industries, Inc.; *U.S. Private*, pg. 862
CLYDE PETROLEUM - LONDON—See Gulf Canada Resources Ltd.; *Int'l*, pg. 578
CLYDE PETROLEUM - NETHERLANDS—See Gulf Canada Resources Ltd.; *Int'l*, pg. 578
CLYDE PETROLEUM PLC—See Gulf Canada Resources Ltd.; *Int'l*, pg. 577
CLYDE SAVINGS BANK COMPANY—See First Financial Bancorp; *U.S. Public*, pg. 632
CLYDESDALE BANK PLC—See National Australia Bank Limited; *Int'l*, pg. 906
CLYDESDALE ENGINEERING—See Caparo Group Ltd.; *Int'l*, pg. 265
CLYDESDALE FORGE CO.—See Caparo Group Ltd.; *Int'l*, pg. 265
CLYDESDALE JONES CO.—See Caparo Group Ltd.; *Int'l*, pg. 265
CLYDESDALE WALTON CO.—See Caparo Group Ltd.; *Int'l*, pg. 265
CLYDESDALE WHITEHOUSE & CO.—See Caparo Group Ltd.; *Int'l*, pg. 265
CMI INDUSTRIES, INC.—See CMI Industries, Inc.; *U.S. Private*, pg. 195
CMI INDUSTRIES, INC.—See Olsten Corporation; *U.S. Public*, pg. 1221
CO-JAC FINISHERS, INC.—See Barton Press, Inc.; *U.S. Private*, pg. 120
CO-OPERATIVE ANIMAL HEALTH LIMITED—See Avonmore Waterford Group plc; *Int'l*, pg. 102
CO-STEEL INC.; *Int'l*, pg. 298
COACH—See Sara Lee Corporation; *U.S. Public*, pg. 1433
COACH LABEL—See The Excellence Group; *U.S. Private*, pg. 387
COACH/MARK CROSS—See Sara Lee Corporation; *U.S. Public*, pg. 1433
COACHMEN AUTOMOTIVE—See Coachmen Industries, Inc.; *U.S. Public*, pg. 388
COACHMEN INDUSTRIES, INC.; *U.S. Public*, pg. 387
COACHMEN RECREATIONAL VEHICLE COMPANY—See Coachmen Industries, Inc.; *U.S. Public*, pg. 388
COACHMEN RECREATIONAL VEHICLE COMPANY OF GEORGIA—See Coachmen Industries, Inc.; *U.S. Public*, pg. 388
THE COAKLEY HEAGERTY ADVERTISING & PUBLIC RELATIONS CO.; *U.S. Private*, pg. 248
COAL INDIA LIMITED; *Int'l*, pg. 298
COAL VALLEY PROJECT—See Alberta Energy Company, Ltd.; *Int'l*, pg. 49
S.A. COAL WASTE ENGINEERING—See Cockerill Sambre; *Int'l*, pg. 301
THE COALINGA RECORD—See Pulitzer Publishing Company; *U.S. Public*, pg. 1343

COASIN, S.A.—See Hewlett-Packard Company; *U.S. Public*, pg. 817
COAST ASPHALT, INC.—See CalMat Co.; *U.S. Public*, pg. 295
COAST BUSINESS CREDIT—See Imperial Credit Industries, Inc.; *U.S. Public*, pg. 872
COAST CAST CORPORATION S.A.—See Coastcast Corporation; *U.S. Public*, pg. 391
THE COAST DISTRIBUTION SYSTEM; *U.S. Public*, pg. 388
COAST FED SERVICES—See Coast Savings Financial, Inc.; *U.S. Public*, pg. 389
COAST FEDERAL BANK FSB—See Coast Savings Financial, Inc.; *U.S. Public*, pg. 389
COAST GRAIN COMPANY, INC.; *U.S. Private*, pg. 248
COAST MANUFACTURING COMPANY; *U.S. Private*, pg. 248
COAST PACKING COMPANY; *U.S. Private*, pg. 248
COAST REFRIGERATED TRUCKING CO., INC.—See Thorn Apple Valley, Inc.; *U.S. Public*, pg. 1603
COAST RV, INC.—See The Coast Distribution System; *U.S. Public*, pg. 388
COAST SAVINGS FINANCIAL, INC.; *U.S. Public*, pg. 388
COAST STEEL FABRICATORS LTD.—See Agra Inc.; *Int'l*, pg. 31
COAST TO COAST CORPORATION—See Cigna Corp.; *U.S. Public*, pg. 366
THE COASTAL BANK OF GEORGIA—See Synovus Financial Corp.; *U.S. Public*, pg. 1549
COASTAL BELCHER PETROLEUM PTE. LTD.—See The Coastal Corporation; *U.S. Public*, pg. 390
COASTAL (BERMUDA) PETROLEUM LIMITED—See The Coastal Corporation; *U.S. Public*, pg. 390
COASTAL BORDER GAS SALES, INC.—See The Coastal Corporation; *U.S. Public*, pg. 390
THE COASTAL CORPORATION; *U.S. Public*, pg. 389
COASTAL DEVELOPMENT COMPANY—See The Coastal Corporation; *U.S. Public*, pg. 390
COASTAL FINANCIAL B.V.—See The Coastal Corporation; *U.S. Public*, pg. 390
COASTAL FUEL TERMINALS, INC.—See The Coastal Corporation; *U.S. Public*, pg. 390
COASTAL FUELS MARKETING, INC.—See The Coastal Corporation; *U.S. Public*, pg. 390
COASTAL FUELS OF PUERTO RICO, INC.—See The Coastal Corporation; *U.S. Public*, pg. 390
COASTAL GREAT LAKES, INC.—See The Coastal Corporation; *U.S. Public*, pg. 390
COASTAL JAVELINA, INC.—See The Coastal Corporation; *U.S. Public*, pg. 390
COASTAL LUMBER COMPANY; *U.S. Private*, pg. 248
COASTAL MARKETING INC.—See The Coastal Corporation; *U.S. Public*, pg. 390
COASTAL NATURAL GAS COMPANY—See The Coastal Corporation; *U.S. Public*, pg. 390
COASTAL OIL & GAS CORP.—See The Coastal Corporation; *U.S. Public*, pg. 390
COASTAL OIL CHELSEA, INC.—See The Coastal Corporation; *U.S. Public*, pg. 390
COASTAL OIL NEW ENGLAND, INC.—See The Coastal Corporation; *U.S. Public*, pg. 390
COASTAL OIL NEW YORK, INC.—See The Coastal Corporation; *U.S. Public*, pg. 390
COASTAL PETROLEUM (FAR EAST) PTE LTD.—See The Coastal Corporation; *U.S. Public*, pg. 390
COASTAL PHYSICIAN GROUP, INC.; *U.S. Public*, pg. 391
COASTAL POWER PRODUCTION COMPANY—See The Coastal Corporation; *U.S. Public*, pg. 390
COASTAL POWER REVERE COMPANY—See The Coastal Corporation; *U.S. Public*, pg. 390
COASTAL REFINING & MARKETING—See The Coastal Corporation; *U.S. Public*, pg. 390
COASTAL REMEDIATION COMPANY—See The Coastal Corporation; *U.S. Public*, pg. 390
COASTAL (ROTTERDAM) B.V.—See The Coastal Corporation; *U.S. Public*, pg. 390
COASTAL STATES ENERGY CO.—See The Coastal Corporation; *U.S. Public*, pg. 390
COASTAL STATES GAS TRANSMISSION COMPANY—See The Coastal Corporation; *U.S. Public*, pg. 390
COASTAL STATES MANAGEMENT CORP.—See The Coastal Corporation; *U.S. Public*, pg. 390
COASTAL STATES PETROLEUM (U.K.) LIMITED—See The Coastal Corporation; *U.S. Public*, pg. 391
COASTAL STATES TRADING, INC.—See The Coastal Corporation; *U.S. Public*, pg. 390
COASTAL STOCK CO., LTD.—See The Coastal Corporation; *U.S. Public*, pg. 390
COASTAL TELEPHONE & ELECTRONICS—See Century Telephone Enterprises, Inc.; *U.S. Public*, pg. 329
COASTAL TRAVEL MART, INC.—See The Coastal Corporation; *U.S. Public*, pg. 390
COASTAL TUG & BARGE, INC.—See The Coastal Corporation; *U.S. Public*, pg. 390
COASTAL UNILUBE, INC.—See The Coastal Corporation; *U.S. Public*, pg. 390
COASTAL WHOLESALE, INC.; *U.S. Private*, pg. 248
COASTAL WHOLESALE, INC.—See Hughes Supply, Inc.; *U.S. Public*, pg. 846
COASTAL WOOD PRODUCTS, INC.—See McConnell Cabinets, Inc.; *U.S. Private*, pg. 720
COASTALDRIL, INC.—See The Coastal Corporation; *U.S. Public*, pg. 390
COASTCAST CORPORATION; *U.S. Public*, pg. 391
COASTWISE TRADING COMPANY, INC.—See Amoco Corporation; *U.S. Public*, pg. 103
COATED & LAMINATED PRODUCTS—See Johns Manville Corporation; *U.S. Public*, pg. 927
COATED SPECIALTIES LTD.—See Hunt Corporation; *U.S. Public*, pg. 849
COATES BROTHERS PLC—See Total S.A.; *Int'l*, pg. 1409
COATES BROTHERS (SOUTH AFRICA) LTD.—See Total S.A.; *Int'l*, pg. 1409

COATES CHEMIE COMPOUNDS (PTY.) LTD.—See Total S.A.; *Int'l*, pg. 1410
COATS & CLARK INC.—See Coats Viyella plc; *Int'l*, pg. 300
COATS & CLARK INC. (SALES OFFICE)—See Coats Viyella plc; *Int'l*, pg. 300
COATS BELL—See Coats Viyella plc; *Int'l*, pg. 299
COATS CADENA SA—See Coats Viyella plc; *Int'l*, pg. 300
COATS CUCIRINI S.P.A.—See Coats Viyella plc; *Int'l*, pg. 300
COATS FABRA SA—See Coats Viyella plc; *Int'l*, pg. 300
COATS HARLANDER G.M.B.H—See Coats Viyella plc; *Int'l*, pg. 300
COATS LIMITED—See Coats Viyella plc; *Int'l*, pg. 299
COATS MEZ INDUSTRIEAHFADEN G.M.B.H.—See Coats Viyella plc; *Int'l*, pg. 300
COATS NATAL THREAD—See Coats Viyella plc; *Int'l*, pg. 300
COATS NORTH AMERICA—See Coats Viyella plc; *Int'l*, pg. 300
COATS PAKISTAN LIMITED—See Coats Viyella plc; *Int'l*, pg. 300
COATS PATONS—See Coats Viyella plc; *Int'l*, pg. 300
COATS PATONS (NORTH AMERICA) INC.—See Coats Viyella plc; *Int'l*, pg. 300
COATS PATONS PLC—See Coats Viyella plc; *Int'l*, pg. 299
COATS (TURKEY) IPLIK SANAYII AS—See Coats Viyella plc; *Int'l*, pg. 300
COATS VIYELLA PLC; *Int'l*, pg. 299
COAXIAL DYNAMICS INC.—See Kirkwood Industries, Inc.; *U.S. Private*, pg. 623
COBA VERMOEGENSVERWALTUNG GMBH—See Commerzbank AG; *Int'l*, pg. 309
COBAFI, COMPANHIA BAHIANA DE FIBRAS SA—See Akzo Nobel N.V.; *Int'l*, pg. 46
COBANK—See Federal Farm Credit Banks Funding Corporation; *U.S. Private*, pg. 398
THE COBB GROUP—See Softbank Corporation; *Int'l*, pg. 1276
COBB REPROGRAPHICS & OFFICE SUPPLY—See Wallace Computer Services, Inc.; *U.S. Public*, pg. 1735
COBB-VANTRESS, INC.—See Tyson Foods, Inc.; *U.S. Public*, pg. 1652
COBBS CREEK NURSING CENTER—See Genesis Health Ventures, Inc.; *U.S. Public*, pg. 729
COBDEN CHADWICK (UK) LTD.—See Firth-Rixson Plc; *Int'l*, pg. 488
COBE CARDIOVASCULAR INC.—See Incentive AB; *Int'l*, pg. 667
COBE DE MEXICO, S.A. DE C.V.—See Incentive AB; *Int'l*, pg. 667
COBE LAB. ITALIA S.R.L.—See Incentive AB; *Int'l*, pg. 667
COBE LABORATORIES, INC.—See Incentive AB; *Int'l*, pg. 667
COBELPLAST N.V.—See Schmalbach-Lubeca AG; *Int'l*, pg. 1207
COBELPLAST TRADING DEUTSCHLAND GMBH—See Schmalbach-Lubeca AG; *Int'l*, pg. 1206
COBELPLAST TRADING N.V.—See Schmalbach-Lubeca AG; *Int'l*, pg. 1207
COBELPLAST (U.K.) LTD.—See Schmalbach-Lubeca AG; *Int'l*, pg. 1207
COBHAM PLC; *Int'l*, pg. 301
COBOURG DAILY STAR—See Hollinger Inc.; *Int'l*, pg. 631
COBOURG PLANT—See Belden Inc.; *U.S. Public*, pg. 201
COBRA COMPONENTS—See Park Distributors, Inc.; *U.S. Private*, pg. 839
COBRA ELECTRONICS CORPORATION; *U.S. Public*, pg. 391
COBRA ELECTRONICS EUROPE—See Cobra Electronics Corporation; *U.S. Public*, pg. 391
COBRA ELECTRONICS INTERNATIONAL (HONG KONG) LTD.—See Cobra Electronics Corporation; *U.S. Public*, pg. 391
COBRA GOLF INCORPORATED—See Fortune Brands, Inc.; *U.S. Public*, pg. 675
COBRA-COMPUTADORES E SISTEMAS BRASILEIROS—See Banco do Brasil; *Int'l*, pg. 142
COBURN OPTICAL INDUSTRIES INC.; *U.S. Private*, pg. 248
COCA-COLA & SCHWEPPES BEVERAGES LTD.—See Coca-Cola Enterprises Inc.; *U.S. Public*, pg. 393
COCA-COLA BOTTLING CO. CONSOLIDATED; *U.S. Public*, pg. 391
COCA-COLA BOTTLING CO. CONSOLIDATED OF ARDEN—See Coca-Cola Bottling Co. Consolidated; *U.S. Public*, pg. 391
COCA-COLA BOTTLING CO. OF CHICAGO; *U.S. Private*, pg. 248
COCA-COLA BOTTLING CO. OF ELIZABETHTOWN; *U.S. Private*, pg. 248
COCA-COLA BOTTLING CO. OF JACKSON, INC.—See Coca-Cola Bottling Co. Consolidated; *U.S. Public*, pg. 391
THE COCA-COLA BOTTLING CO. OF MEMPHIS, TENNESSEE—See Coca-Cola Enterprises Inc.; *U.S. Public*, pg. 393
COCA-COLA BOTTLING CO. OF MOBILE, INC.—See Coca-Cola Bottling Co. Consolidated; *U.S. Public*, pg. 391
COCA-COLA BOTTLING CO. OF NEW ENGLAND—See Coca-Cola Enterprises Inc.; *U.S. Public*, pg. 393
THE COCA-COLA BOTTLING CO. OF NEW YORK, INC.—See Coca-Cola Enterprises Inc.; *U.S. Public*, pg. 393
THE COCA-COLA BOTTLING CO. OF NORTHERN OHIO—See Coca-Cola Enterprises Inc.; *U.S. Public*, pg. 393
COCA-COLA BOTTLING CO. OF ROANOKE—See Coca-Cola Bottling Co. Consolidated; *U.S. Public*, pg. 391
COCA-COLA BOTTLING CO. OF SHREVEPORT—See Coca-Cola Enterprises Inc.; *U.S. Public*, pg. 393
COCA-COLA BOTTLING CO. OF THE SOUTHWEST; *U.S. Private*, pg. 248

COCA-COLA BOTTLING CO. OF TEXARKANA—See Coca-Cola Enterprises Inc.; *U.S. Public*, pg. 393
COCA-COLA BOTTLING CO. OF WEST VIRGINIA, INC.—See Coca-Cola Bottling Co. Consolidated; *U.S. Public*, pg. 392
COCA-COLA BOTTLING CO. UNITED, INC.; *U.S. Private*, pg. 248
COCA-COLA BOTTLING WORKS OF COLUMBIA—See Coca-Cola Bottling Co. Consolidated; *U.S. Public*, pg. 392
THE COCA-COLA COMPANY; *U.S. Public*, pg. 392
COCA-COLA CONSOLIDATED—See Coca-Cola Bottling Co. Consolidated; *U.S. Public*, pg. 392
COCA-COLA/DR. PEPPER BOTTLING CO. OF SOUTH ARKANSAS—See Coca-Cola Enterprises Inc.; *U.S. Public*, pg. 393
COCA-COLA ENTERPRISES - EASTERN GROUP/SOUTHEAST REGION—See Coca-Cola Enterprises Inc.; *U.S. Public*, pg. 393
COCA-COLA ENTERPRISES INC.; *U.S. Public*, pg. 393
THE COCA-COLA EXPORT CORPORATION—See The Coca-Cola Company; *U.S. Public*, pg. 392
COCA-COLA FEMSA, S.A. DE CV—See Fomento Economico Mexicano, S.A. de CV; *Int'l*, pg. 496
COCA-COLA FINANCIAL CORPORATION—See The Coca-Cola Company; *U.S. Public*, pg. 392
COCA-COLA INTERAMERICAN CORP.—See The Coca-Cola Company; *U.S. Public*, pg. 392
COCA-COLA NORTHERN NEW ENGLAND, INC.—See Kirin Brewery Co., Ltd.; *Int'l*, pg. 736
COCA-COLA USA—See The Coca-Cola Company; *U.S. Public*, pg. 392
COCESA INGENIERIA Y CONSTRUCCION S.A.—See Sumitomo Electric Industries, Ltd.; *Int'l*, pg. 1313
COCETREL S.A.—See Tractebel; *Int'l*, pg. 1415
MAX COCHIUS GMBH—See Fried. Krupp AG; *Int'l*, pg. 514
MAX COCHIUS GMBH - GERMERING BRANCH—See Fried. Krupp AG; *Int'l*, pg. 514
COCHRANE FURNITURE CO., INC.—See Chromcraft Revington, Inc.; *U.S. Public*, pg. 352
COCHRANE, INC.—See Crane Co.; *U.S. Public*, pg. 456
COCHRAN/SYSCO FOOD SERVICES—See Sysco Corporation; *U.S. Public*, pg. 1550
COCIO CHOKOLADEMAELK—See Borden, Inc.; *U.S. Private*, pg. 159
BARTLETT COCKE, INC.; *U.S. Private*, pg. 249
S.A. COCKERILL FORGES AND RINGMILL C.F.R.—See Cockerill Sambre; *Int'l*, pg. 301
S.A. COCKERILL MECHANICAL INDUSTRIES C.M.I.—See Cockerill Sambre; *Int'l*, pg. 301
COCKERILL SAMBRE; *Int'l*, pg. 301
COCKERILL SAMBRE BETEILIGUNGS GMBH—See Cockerill Sambre; *Int'l*, pg. 302
S.A. COCKERILL SAMBRE FINANCES ET SERVICES C.S.F.S.—See Cockerill Sambre; *Int'l*, pg. 301
COCLER S.A.—See Coeclerici Group; *Int'l*, pg. 304
COCLISA S.A. DE C.V.—See Ford Motor Company; *U.S. Public*, pg. 665
COCO'S & CARROWS RESTAURANTS—See Advantica Restaurant Group, Inc.; *U.S. Public*, pg. 23
COCOS JAPAN—See Kasumi Co., Ltd.; *Int'l*, pg. 724
CODA—See Edison Brothers Stores, Inc.; *U.S. Public*, pg. 563
CODA ENERGY, INC.—See Enron Corp.; *U.S. Public*, pg. 584
CODAR TECHNOLOGY INC.—See NAI Technologies, Inc.; *U.S. Public*, pg. 1144
CODE-ALARM, INC.; *U.S. Public*, pg. 393
CODE ALARM SECURITY SYSTEMS—See Code-Alarm, Inc.; *U.S. Public*, pg. 394
CODE, HENNESSY & SIMMONS, INC.; *U.S. Private*, pg. 249
CODELCO-ASIA—See CODELCO Chile (Corporacion Nacional Del Cobre De Chile); *Int'l*, pg. 303
CODELCO CHILE (CORPORACION NACIONAL DEL COBRE DE CHILE); *Int'l*, pg. 302
CODELCO-FRANCE S.A.R.L.—See CODELCO Chile (Corporacion Nacional Del Cobre De Chile); *Int'l*, pg. 303
CODELCO-KUPFERHANDEL GMBH—See CODELCO Chile (Corporacion Nacional Del Cobre De Chile); *Int'l*, pg. 303
CODI INTERNATIONAL B.V.—See Fruit of the Loom, Inc.; *U.S. Public*, pg. 686
CODIC S.A.—See Dixons Group plc; *Int'l*, pg. 414
CODIMESA S.A.—See Rogers Communications, Inc.; *Int'l*, pg. 1123
CODITEL BRABANT S.A.—See Tractebel; *Int'l*, pg. 1415
CODVILLE DISTRIBUTORS—See The Oshawa Group Limited; *Int'l*, pg. 1012
CODY COMPANY; *U.S. Private*, pg. 249
CODY ENERGY, INC.—See Cody Company; *U.S. Private*, pg. 249
CODY GAS DIVISION—See Energy West Inc.; *U.S. Public*, pg. 581
COE & CLERICI, INC.—See Coeclerici Group; *Int'l*, pg. 304
COE MANUFACTURING CO—See The Coe Manufacturing Company; *U.S. Private*, pg. 249
THE COE MANUFACTURING COMPANY; *U.S. Private*, pg. 249
THE COE MFG. LTD.—See The Coe Manufacturing Company; *U.S. Private*, pg. 249
COECLERICI GROUP; *Int'l*, pg. 303
COECLERICI HOLDING INTERNATIONAL B.V.—See Coeclerici Group; *Int'l*, pg. 304
COECLERICI HOLDING OVERSEAS N.V.—See Coeclerici Group; *Int'l*, pg. 304
COECLERICI HOLDING S.P.A.—See Coeclerici Group; *Int'l*, pg. 304
COECLERICI LOGISTIC INTERNATIONAL B.V.—See Coeclerici Group; *Int'l*, pg. 304
COECLERICI LOGISTIC OVERSEAS N.V.—See Coeclerici Group; *Int'l*, pg. 304

COECLERICI SHIPPING N.V.—See Coeclerici Group; *Int'l*, pg. 304
COECLERICI SPEDIZIONI S.P.A.—See Coeclerici Group; *Int'l*, pg. 303
COECLERICI TRADING INTERNATIONAL B.V.—See Coeclerici Group; *Int'l*, pg. 304
COECLERICI TRADING OVERSEAS N.V.—See Coeclerici Group; *int'l*, pg. 304
COECLERICI TRADING S.P.A.—See Coeclerici Group; *Int'l*, pg. 303
COEMCO-SODEXHO—See Sodexho S.A.; *Int'l*, pg. 1274
COEMEA ANSALDO—See IRI Istituto Ricostruzione Industriale; *Int'l*, pg. 654
COEMSA—See IRI Istituto Ricostruzione Industriale; *Int'l*, pg. 654
COEUR D'ALENE MINES CORPORATION; *U.S. Public*, pg. 394
COEUR EXPLORATIONS, INC.—See Coeur D'Alene Mines Corporation; *U.S. Public*, pg. 394
COEUR INTERNATIONAL INC.—See Coeur D'Alene Mines Corporation; *U.S. Public*, pg. 394
COEUR ROCHESTER, INC.—See Coeur D'Alene Mines Corporation; *U.S. Public*, pg. 394
COFA COSMETIK-FABRIKATIONS GMBH—See Joh. A. Benckiser GmbH; *Int'l*, pg. 185
COFADE-SOCIEDADE FABRICADORA DE ELASTOMEROS LTDA.—See BASF AG; *Int'l*, pg. 107
COFAP-ARVIN SISTEMAS DE EXAUSTAO LTDA.—See Arvin Industries, Inc.; *U.S. Public*, pg. 137
COFASSUR VIE—See Groupe GAN; *Int'l*, pg. 564
COFATHEC—See Gaz de France; *Int'l*, pg. 541
COFATHEC - PARIS—See Gaz de France; *Int'l*, pg. 541
COFHYLUX SA—See Banque Generale du Luxembourg SA; *Int'l*, pg. 162
COFIDIS S.A.—See Otto Versand (GmbH & Co.); *Int'l*, pg. 1015
COFINA—See Allianz Aktiengesellschaft; *Int'l*, pg. 61
COFIRI SOCIETA AD INTERMEDIAZIONE MOBILIARE S.P.A.—See IRI Istituto Ricostruzione Industriale; *Int'l*, pg. 652
COFLEXIP & SERVICES INC.—See Coflexip S.A.; *Int'l*, pg. 304
COFLEXIP S.A.; *Int'l*, pg. 304
COFRAFER S.A.—See Arbed S.A.; *Int'l*, pg. 79
COGEMA AUSTRALIA PTY. LTD.—See COGEMA - Compagnie Generale des Matieres Nucleaires; *Int'l*, pg. 305
COGEMA CANADA LTEE. (CCI)—See COGEMA - Compagnie Generale des Matieres Nucleaires; *Int'l*, pg. 305
COGEMA - COMPAGNIE GENERALE DES MATIERES NUCLEAIRES; *Int'l*, pg. 304
COGEMA INC.—See COGEMA - Compagnie Generale des Matieres Nucleaires; *Int'l*, pg. 305
COGEMA JAPAN—See COGEMA - Compagnie Generale des Matieres Nucleaires; *Int'l*, pg. 305
COGEMA URAN SERVICES (DEUTSCHLAND) MBH & CO KG—See COGEMA - Compagnie Generale des Matieres Nucleaires; *Int'l*, pg. 305
COGENERATION TECHNOLOGIES INC.—See York Research Corporation; *U.S. Public*, pg. 1789
COGENTRIX INCORPORATED; *U.S. Private*, pg. 249
COGESAL S.A.—See Unilever Plc; *Int'l*, pg. 1436
COGGIN AUTOMOTIVE GROUP; *U.S. Private*, pg. 250
COGGIN PONTIAC-GMC INC.—See Coggin Automotive Group; *U.S. Private*, pg. 250
LESTER COGGINS TRUCKING; *U.S. Private*, pg. 250
COGIFER SA—See De Dietrich & Co.; *Int'l*, pg. 386
COGIN—See Groupe Casino; *Int'l*, pg. 563
COGITIEL—See Alcatel Alsthom Compagnie Generale D'Electricite; *Int'l*, pg. 53
COGNEX CORPORATION; *U.S. Public*, pg. 394
COGNEX K.K.—See Cognex Corporation; *U.S. Public*, pg. 394
COGNEX REGIONAL TECHNOLOGY CENTER—See Cognex Corporation; *U.S. Public*, pg. 394
COGNEX-FRANCE—See Cognex Corporation; *U.S. Public*, pg. 394
COGNEX-GERMANY—See Cognex Corporation; *U.S. Public*, pg. 394
COGNIS GESELLSCHAFT FUR BIOTECHNOLOGIE MBH—See Henkel KGaA; *Int'l*, pg. 609
COGNISEIS DEVELOPMENT, INC.—See Tech-Sym Corporation; *U.S. Public*, pg. 1563
COGNITRONICS CORPORATION; *U.S. Public*, pg. 394
COGNIZANT CORPORATION; *U.S. Public*, pg. 395
COGNIZANT ENTERPRISES, INC.—See Cognizant Corporation; *U.S. Public*, pg. 395
COGNIZANT TECHNOLOGY SOLUTIONS CORP.—See Cognizant Corporation; *U.S. Public*, pg. 395
COGNOS BARBADOS LTD.—See Cognos Inc.; *Int'l*, pg. 306
COGNOS B.V.—See Cognos Inc.; *Int'l*, pg. 306
COGNOS CORP.—See Cognos Inc.; *Int'l*, pg. 306
COGNOS ESPANA S.A.—See Cognos Inc.; *Int'l*, pg. 306
COGNOS FAR EAST PTE. LIMITED—See Cognos Inc.; *Int'l*, pg. 306
COGNOS GMBH—See Cognos Inc.; *Int'l*, pg. 306
COGNOS INC.; *Int'l*, pg. 305
COGNOS INC.-QUEBEC CITY SALES OFFICE—See Cognos Inc.; *Int'l*, pg. 306
COGNOS JAPAN KK—See Cognos Inc.; *Int'l*, pg. 306
COGNOS LTD.—See Cognos Inc.; *Int'l*, pg. 306
COGNOS PTY., LTD.—See Cognos Inc.; *Int'l*, pg. 306
COGNOS SARL—See Cognos Inc.; *Int'l*, pg. 306
COGRAMI S.A.E.—See Koninklijke BolsWessanen nv; *Int'l*, pg. 751
COGSDILL-NUNEATON, LTD.—See Cogsdill Tool Products, Inc.; *U.S. Private*, pg. 250
COGSDILL TOOL PRODUCTS, INC.; *U.S. Private*, pg. 250
COHART DE MEXICO, S.A. DE C.V.—See Waxman Industries, Inc.; *U.S. Public*, pg. 1749
COHASSET MARINER—See Gannett Company, Inc.; *U.S. Public*, pg. 700

A. COHEN & CO. P.L.C.; *Int'l*, pg. 306
COHEN FURNITURE COMPANY; *U.S. Private*, pg. 250
LOUIS COHEN AND SONS, INC.—See Medico Industries, Inc.; *U.S. Private*, pg. 728
COHERENT BENELUX—See Coherent, Inc.; *U.S. Public*, pg. 395
COHERENT COMMUNICATIONS SYSTEMS CORP.—See Safeguard Scientifics, Inc.; *U.S. Public*, pg. 1424
COHERENT GMBH—See Coherent, Inc.; *U.S. Public*, pg. 395
COHERENT, INC.; *U.S. Public*, pg. 395
COHERENT, INC.-AUBURN GROUP—See Coherent, Inc.; *U.S. Public*, pg. 395
COHERENT INC.-BEIJING—See Coherent, Inc.; *U.S. Public*, pg. 395
COHERENT, INC.-LASER GROUP—See Coherent, Inc.; *U.S. Public*, pg. 395
COHERENT, INC.-MEDICAL GROUP—See Coherent, Inc.; *U.S. Public*, pg. 395
COHERENT JAPAN CO., LTD.—See Coherent, Inc.; *U.S. Public*, pg. 395
COHERENT LUBECK—See Coherent, Inc.; *U.S. Public*, pg. 396
COHERENT OPTICS (EUROPE) LTD.—See Coherent, Inc.; *U.S. Public*, pg. 396
COHERENT PACIFIC—See Coherent, Inc.; *U.S. Public*, pg. 396
COHERENT S.A.—See Coherent, Inc.; *U.S. Public*, pg. 396
COHERENT SCANDINAVIA—See Coherent, Inc.; *U.S. Public*, pg. 396
COHERENT TUCSON RESEARCH CENTER—See Coherent, Inc.; *U.S. Public*, pg. 395
COHERENT (U.K.) LTD.—See Coherent, Inc.; *U.S. Public*, pg. 396
COHIBA—See BDDP Group; *Int'l*, pg. 117
COHN & WELLS—See Havas Advertising; *Int'l*, pg. 601
M.M. COHN CO., INC.—See The Dunlap Company; *U.S. Private*, pg. 346
SIGMUND COHN CORP.; *U.S. Private*, pg. 250
COHO ENERGY, INC.; *U.S. Public*, pg. 396
COHOES FASHIONS, INC.—See Burlington Coat Factory Warehouse Corporation; *U.S. Public*, pg. 268
COHU, INC.; *U.S. Public*, pg. 396
COHUTTA BANKING COMPANY—See Synovus Financial Corp.; *U.S. Public*, pg. 1549
COIL PLUS-ILLINOIS INC.—See Mitsubishi Corporation; *Int'l*, pg. 872
COIL-TEC CORPORATION—See Arbed S.A.; *Int'l*, pg. 79
COILCRAFT, INC.; *U.S. Private*, pg. 250
COISSA CORREDURIS INTERNACIONAL DE SUGUROS—See Volkswagen AG; *Int'l*, pg. 1475
COKEN COMPANY, INC.; *U.S. Private*, pg. 250
COKOLADOVNY—See Danone Group; *Int'l*, pg. 381
COKOLADOVNY—See Nestle S.A.; *Int'l*, pg. 922
COLAD GROUP INC.; *U.S. Private*, pg. 250
COLAS EAST AFRICA—See Royal Dutch/Shell Group of Companies; *Int'l*, pg. 1136
COLAS PRODUCTS LTD.—See Royal Dutch/Shell Group of Companies; *Int'l*, pg. 1139
TOM COBLEIGH PLC—See The Rank Group PLC; *Int'l*, pg. 1087
COLBOND BV—See Akzo Nobel N.V.; *Int'l*, pg. 45
COLBORN-DAWES AUSTRALIA (PTY.) LIMITED—See Roche Holding Ltd.; *Int'l*, pg. 1121
COLBORN-DAWES IBERICA S.A.—See Roche Holding Ltd.; *Int'l*, pg. 1121
COLBORN-DAWES IRELAND LTD.—See Roche Holding Ltd.; *Int'l*, pg. 1121
COLBORN-DAWES JAPAN LTD.—See Roche Holding Ltd.; *Int'l*, pg. 1121
COLBOURNE INSURANCE CO. LTD.—See The Coastal Corporation; *U.S. Public*, pg. 391
COLBY ENGINEERING PTY. LTD.—See Mannesmann A.G.; *Int'l*, pg. 838
COLCARGA TRANSPORTE INTERNACIONAL/UNION-TRANSPORT—See Union-Transport Corporation; *U.S. Private*, pg. 1120
COLD HEADING CO.; *U.S. Private*, pg. 250
COLD SPRING GRANITE (CANADA) LTD.—See Cold Spring Granite Company; *U.S. Private*, pg. 251
COLD SPRING GRANITE COMPANY; *U.S. Private*, pg. 250
COLD STORAGE WAREHOUSE AG ST. MARGRETHEN—See Migros; *Int'l*, pg. 866
COLDWATER CABLEVISION INC.—See Cable Michigan, Inc.; *U.S. Public*, pg. 287
COLDWATER CREEK; *U.S. Public*, pg. 396
COLDWATER REPORTER, INC.—See Media General, Inc.; *U.S. Public*, pg. 1077
COLDWATER SEAFOOD CORPORATION; *U.S. Private*, pg. 251
COLDWELL BANKER REAL ESTATE CORPORATION—See Cendant Corporation; *U.S. Public*, pg. 321
COLE CONSUMER PRODUCTS—See Vista 2000, Inc.; *U.S. Private*, pg. 1142
COLE ENGINEERING, INC.—See Giant Food Inc.; *U.S. Public*, pg. 741
COLE GIFT CENTERS, INC.—See Cole National Corporation; *U.S. Public*, pg. 396
COLE-HAAN—See Nike, Inc.; *U.S. Public*, pg. 1184
COLE HALL LUMBER CO.—See Lumber Group Inc.; *U.S. Private*, pg. 680
COLE HERSEE COMPANY; *U.S. Private*, pg. 251
COLE-LAYER-TRUMBLE COMPANY (CLT)—See Day & Zimmermann, Inc.; *U.S. Private*, pg. 317
COLE NATIONAL CORPORATION; *U.S. Public*, pg. 396
COLE PAPERS INC.; *U.S. Private*, pg. 251
COLE, SHERMAN & ASSOCIATES LTD.—See URS Corporation; *U.S. Public*, pg. 1657
COLE TAYLOR BANK—See Taylor Capital Group; *U.S. Private*, pg. 1070
COLEJON CORPORATION; *U.S. Private*, pg. 251
C.J. COLEMAN HOLDINGS LTD.; *Int'l*, pg. 306
COLEMAN CABLE SYSTEMS, INC.—See Kuhlman Corporation; *U.S. Public*, pg. 968

COLEMAN CADILLAC INC.; *U.S. Private*, pg. 251
THE COLEMAN COMPANY, INC.—See MacAndrews & Forbes Holdings Inc.; *U.S. Private*, pg. 690
COLEMAN DAIRY LLC; *U.S. Private*, pg. 251
COLEMAN (DEUTSCHLAND) GMBH—See MacAndrews & Forbes Holdings Inc.; *U.S. Private*, pg. 691
DON COLEMAN ADVERTISING, INC.; *U.S. Private*, pg. 251
COLEMAN HOLDING COMPANY—See Kuhlman Corporation; *U.S. Public*, pg. 968
COLEMAN JAPAN LTD.—See MacAndrews & Forbes Holdings Inc.; *U.S. Private*, pg. 691
COLEMAN OLDSMOBILE, INC.; *U.S. Private*, pg. 252
COLEMAN POWERMATE COMPRESSORS—See MacAndrews & Forbes Holdings Inc.; *U.S. Private*, pg. 691
COLEMAN POWERMATE, INC.—See MacAndrews & Forbes Holdings Inc.; *U.S. Private*, pg. 691
COLEMAN SPAS, INC.—See MacAndrews & Forbes Holdings Inc.; *U.S. Private*, pg. 691
COLEMAN U.K., INC.—See MacAndrews & Forbes Holdings Inc.; *U.S. Private*, pg. 691
COLEMAN WORLDWIDE—See MacAndrews & Forbes Holdings Inc.; *U.S. Private*, pg. 691
ROBERT F. COLEMAN, INC.—See Cigna Corp.; *U.S. Public*, pg. 366
COLES MYER LTD.; *Int'l*, pg. 306
COLEX INTERNATIONAL, LTD.—See NewAge Industries Inc.; *U.S. Private*, pg. 796
COLEY PORTER BELL—See WPP Group plc; *Int'l*, pg. 1482
COLFAX ENVELOPE CORPORATION; *U.S. Private*, pg. 252
COLFAX, INC.; *U.S. Private*, pg. 252
COLGATE-CLOROX (FAR EAST) LTD.—See The Clorox Company; *U.S. Public*, pg. 387
COLGATE ORAL PHARMACEUTICAL—See Colgate-Palmolive Company; *U.S. Public*, pg. 397
COLGATE-PALMOLIVE (ARKANSAS)—See Colgate-Palmolive Company; *U.S. Public*, pg. 397
COLGATE-PALMOLIVE CO., INSTITUTIONAL PRODUCTS DIV.—See Colgate-Palmolive Company; *U.S. Public*, pg. 397
COLGATE-PALMOLIVE COMPANY; *U.S. Public*, pg. 397
COLGATE-PALMOLIVE HOUSEHOLD PRODUCTS DIV.—See Colgate-Palmolive Company; *U.S. Public*, pg. 397
COLGATE-PALMOLIVE INTERNATIONAL DIV.—See Colgate-Palmolive Company; *U.S. Public*, pg. 397
COLGATE-PALMOLIVE IPD—See Colgate-Palmolive Company; *U.S. Public*, pg. 397
COLGATE-PALMOLIVE PERSONAL CARE PRODUCTS DIV.—See Colgate-Palmolive Company; *U.S. Public*, pg. 397
COLGATE-PALMOLIVE PURCHASING—See Colgate-Palmolive Company; *U.S. Public*, pg. 397
COLGATE U.S.A.—See Colgate-Palmolive Company; *U.S. Public*, pg. 397
COLIN BOOTH LTD.—See Simon Engineering plc; *Int'l*, pg. 1251
COLIN SERVICE SYSTEMS, INC.; *U.S. Private*, pg. 252
COLIN STEWART MINCHEM LIMITED—See Meristem plc; *Int'l*, pg. 858
COLINA INSURANCE COMPANY LIMITED—See Cigna Corp.; *U.S. Public*, pg. 363
COLINTA HOLDINGS PTY. LTD.—See M.I.M. Holdings Ltd.; *Int'l*, pg. 827
COLIVITA USA, INC.; *U.S. Private*, pg. 252
COLLAGEN CORPORATION; *U.S. Public*, pg. 399
THE COLLAPSIBLE TUBE CO. LIMITED—See Caradon Plc; *Int'l*, pg. 267
COLLE & McVOY, INC.; *U.S. Private*, pg. 252
COLLECTIBLES PLANT—See Fort James Corporation; *U.S. Public*, pg. 672
COLLECTION SERVICES, INC.—See Republic Industries, Inc.; *U.S. Public*, pg. 1379
COLLECTIVE BANK—See Summit Bancorp; *U.S. Public*, pg. 1528
COLLECTIVE MORTGAGE SERVICES, INC.—See Summit Bancorp; *U.S. Public*, pg. 1528
COLLEGE FOR FINANCIAL PLANNING—See Apollo Group, Inc.; *U.S. Public*, pg. 120
COLLEGEVILLE ADVERTISING—See Saatchi & Saatchi Advertising Worldwide; *Int'l*, pg. 1422
COLLEGEVILLE FLAG & MFG. COMPANY; *U.S. Private*, pg. 252
COLLEGEVILLE/IMAGINEERING L.P.—See Collegeville Flag & Mfg. Company; *U.S. Private*, pg. 252
COLLEGIATE CAP AND GOWN—See Herff Jones Inc.; *U.S. Private*, pg. 523
COLLEGIUM GLASHUTTEN ZENTRUM FUR KOMMUNIKATION GMBH—See Commerzbank AG; *Int'l*, pg. 312
COLLIER COUNTY PUBLISHING COMPANY—See The E.W. Scripps Company; *U.S. Public*, pg. 1447
E.D. COLLIER & SON—See Bateman Brothers Lumber Co., Inc.; *U.S. Private*, pg. 122
COLLIER-KEYWORTH COMPANY—See Leggett & Platt, Incorporated; *U.S. Public*, pg. 985
COLLIER-KEYWORTH, INC.—See Leggett & Platt, Incorporated; *U.S. Public*, pg. 985
P.F. COLLIER & SON LTD.—See Editorial Planeta - DeAgostini, S.A.; *Int'l*, pg. 433
P.F. COLLIER LP—See Editorial Planeta - DeAgostini, S.A.; *Int'l*, pg. 433
COLLIERIES DIVISION—See The Broken Hill Proprietary Company Limited; *Int'l*, pg. 226
COLLIERS JARDINE HOLDINGS LTD.—See Jardine Matheson Holdings Limited; *Int'l*, pg. 705
COLLIN STREET BAKERY; *U.S. Private*, pg. 252
COLLINGWOOD GRAIN, INC.—See Archer Daniels Midland Company (ADM); *U.S. Public*, pg. 128
COLLINS & AIKMAN CORPORATION; *U.S. Public*, pg. 399

COLLINS & AIKMAN FLOORCOVERINGS, INC.—See CAF Holding Company; *U.S. Public*, pg. 192
COLLINS & AIKMAN PRODUCTS CO.—See Collins & Aikman Corporation; *U.S. Public*, pg. 399
BILL COLLINS FORD INC.; *U.S. Private*, pg. 253
COLLINS BUS CORP.—See Collins Industries, Inc.; *U.S. Public*, pg. 400
COLLINS ELECTRIC COMPANY, INC.; *U.S. Private*, pg. 253
COLLINS INDUSTRIES, INC.; *U.S. Public*, pg. 399
COLLINS INTERNATIONAL SERVICE COMPANY—See Rockwell International Corporation; *U.S. Public*, pg. 1397
COLLINS OLDSMOBILE, INC.; *U.S. Private*, pg. 253
WARREN E. COLLINS, INC.; *U.S. Private*, pg. 253
COLLINSVILLE COAL CO. PTY. LTD.—See M.I.M. Holdings Ltd.; *Int'l*, pg. 827
COLLITEX SRL—See PAXAR Corporation; *U.S. Public*, pg. 1266
COLLMAN GRAPHICS, INC.; *U.S. Private*, pg. 253
COLLMARK-DIAGNOSTICS—See Zeneca Group Plc; *Int'l*, pg. 1524
COLLOID ENVIRONMENTAL TECHNOLOGIES COMPANY (CETCO)—See AMCOL International Corp.; *U.S. Public*, pg. 64
COLLOIDS CANADA INC.—See Rhone-Poulenc S.A.; *Int'l*, pg. 1113
COLLY COMPANY AB—See AB Industrivarden; *Int'l*, pg. 678
OY COLLY COMPANY AB—See AB Industrivarden; *Int'l*, pg. 678
COLMAIN PROPERTIES, INC.—See The Western and Southern Life Insurance Company; *U.S. Private*, pg. 1164
COLMAN MOTOR PRODUCTS, INC.—See Siebe plc; *Int'l*, pg. 1242
COLMAN OEM, INC.—See Siebe plc; *Int'l*, pg. 1242
CIA. COLOMBIANA DE ALIMENTOS LACETOS, S.A.—See Borden, Inc.; *U.S. Private*, pg. 159
COLOMBIANA KIMBERLY S.A.—See Kimberly-Clark Corporation; *U.S. Public*, pg. 959
COLOMBIANA UNIVERSAL DE PAPELES S.A.—See Kimberly-Clark Corporation; *U.S. Public*, pg. 959
COLOMET, INC.—See American Electric Power Company, Inc.; *U.S. Public*, pg. 72
COLONIAL AMERICAN CASUALTY AND SURETY COMPANY—See Zurich Insurance Company; *Int'l*, pg. 1530
THE COLONIAL BANCGROUP BUILDING CORPORATION—See The Colonial BancGroup, Inc.; *U.S. Public*, pg. 400
THE COLONIAL BANCGROUP, INC.; *U.S. Public*, pg. 400
COLONIAL BANK—See The Colonial BancGroup, Inc.; *U.S. Public*, pg. 400
COLONIAL BANK—See Firstbank of Illinois Co.; *U.S. Public*, pg. 643
COLONIAL BEEF CO.; *U.S. Private*, pg. 253
COLONIAL CAPITAL I—See The Colonial BancGroup, Inc.; *U.S. Public*, pg. 400
COLONIAL COMMERCIAL CORP.; *U.S. Public*, pg. 400
COLONIAL COMPANIES, INC.—See UNUM Corporation; *U.S. Public*, pg. 1699
COLONIAL DODGE, INC.; *U.S. Private*, pg. 253
COLONIAL DRILLING & EXPLORATION CORPORATION—See Colonial Oil Industries; *U.S. Private*, pg. 254
COLONIAL GAS COMPANY; *U.S. Public*, pg. 400
COLONIAL HOMES—See The Hearst Corporation; *U.S. Private*, pg. 517
COLONIAL INSURANCE COMPANY OF CALIFORNIA—See Nationwide Insurance Enterprise; *U.S. Private*, pg. 788
COLONIAL IRON WORKS—See Engineered Products, Inc.; *U.S. Private*, pg. 376
COLONIAL LIFE & ACCIDENT INSURANCE CO.—See UNUM Corporation; *U.S. Public*, pg. 1699
COLONIAL MANOR—See Horizon/CMS Healthcare Corporation; *U.S. Public*, pg. 838
COLONIAL MANOR NURSING & CONVALESCENT HOSPITAL—See Vencor, Inc.; *U.S. Public*, pg. 1712
COLONIAL MANOR OF DEER LODGE—See Horizon/CMS Healthcare Corporation; *U.S. Public*, pg. 837
COLONIAL MANOR OF WHITEFISH—See Horizon/CMS Healthcare Corporation; *U.S. Public*, pg. 837
COLONIAL MARINE INDUSTRIES, INC.—See Colonial Oil Industries; *U.S. Private*, pg. 254
COLONIAL METALS CO.; *U.S. Private*, pg. 253
COLONIAL MILLWORK, INC.—See Marmac Corporation; *U.S. Public*, pg. 706
COLONIAL MORTGAGE COMPANY—See The Colonial BancGroup, Inc.; *U.S. Public*, pg. 400
COLONIAL OIL INDUSTRIES; *U.S. Private*, pg. 253
COLONIAL PACIFIC LEASING CORP.—See Pitney Bowes Inc.; *U.S. Public*, pg. 1303
COLONIAL PENN GROUP, INC.—See Leucadia National Corporation; *U.S. Public*, pg. 990
COLONIAL PENN INSURANCE CO.—See General Electric Company; *U.S. Public*, pg. 712
COLONIAL PENN LIFE INSURANCE COMPANY—See Conseco Inc.; *U.S. Public*, pg. 433
COLONIAL PIPELINE CO.—See Texaco Inc.; *U.S. Public*, pg. 1584
COLONIAL PIPELINE COMPANY; *U.S. Private*, pg. 254
COLONIAL TERMINALS, INC.—See Colonial Oil Industries; *U.S. Private*, pg. 254
COLONIAL WILLIAMSBURG FOUNDATION; *U.S. Private*, pg. 254
COLONIE VENTURES, INC.—See Galesi Group; *U.S. Private*, pg. 438
COLONNA BROS., INC.; *U.S. Private*, pg. 254
COLONNADE ENTERPRISE CORPORATION—See Bacardi Limited; *Int'l*, pg. 132
COLONY GLASS—See Lancaster Colony Corporation; *U.S. Public*, pg. 976

COLONY HOUSE HEALTHCARE—See Vencor, Inc.; *U.S. Public*, pg. 1712
COLONY INSURANCE COMPANY—See Front Royal, Inc.; *U.S. Public*, pg. 430
COLONY LIQUOR DISTRIBUTORS, INC.; *U.S. Private*, pg. 254
COLONY MANAGEMENT SERVICES—See Front Royal, Inc.; *U.S. Public*, pg. 430
COLONY PAINTS—See The Valspar Corporation; *U.S. Public*, pg. 1707
COLONY PRINTING & LABELING—See Lancaster Colony Corporation; *U.S. Public*, pg. 976
COLOR ARTS, INC.; *U.S. Private*, pg. 254
COLOR-BOX, INC.—See Chesapeake Corporation; *U.S. Public*, pg. 347
COLOR CONTROL, INC.—See CGF Industries; *U.S. Private*, pg. 194
COLOR CORP. OF AMERICA—See The Valspar Corporation; *U.S. Public*, pg. 1707
COLOR COSMETICS GROUP—See Crown Cork & Seal Company, Inc.; *U.S. Public*, pg. 464
COLOR DATA EAST—See Schawk, Inc.; *U.S. Public*, pg. 1437
COLOR ME MINE, INC.—See Koo Koo Roo, Inc.; *U.S. Public*, pg. 966
COLOR MEDIA AG—See Fotolabo S.A.; *Int'l*, pg. 501
COLOR SPOT NURSERY, INC.; *U.S. Private*, pg. 254
COLOR TILE, INC.—See Investcorp International; *Int'l*, pg. 686
COLORADO—See Havas Advertising; *Int'l*, pg. 601
COLORADO AIR RESTAURANT CORP.—See Specialty Restaurants Corporation; *U.S. Private*, pg. 1023
COLORADO AUCTION SERVICES CORPORATION—See Cox Enterprises, Inc.; *U.S. Private*, pg. 282
COLORADO AVALANCHE—See Ascent Entertainment Group, Inc.; *U.S. Public*, pg. 138
COLORADO BELLE—See Circus Circus - Las Vegas; *U.S. Public*, pg. 375
COLORADO BOXED BEEF CO.; *U.S. Private*, pg. 254
COLORADO BUSINESS BANK—See Colorado Business Bankshares, Inc.; *U.S. Private*, pg. 255
COLORADO BUSINESS BANK OF LITTLETON, N.A.—See Colorado Business Bankshares, Inc.; *U.S. Private*, pg. 255
COLORADO BUSINESS BANKSHARES, INC.; *U.S. Private*, pg. 255
COLORADO BUSINESS LEASING, INC.—See Colorado Business Bankshares, Inc.; *U.S. Private*, pg. 255
COLORADO DATA SYSTEMS INC.—See Tektronix, Inc.; *U.S. Public*, pg. 1567
COLORADO INTERSTATE GAS CO.—See The Coastal Corporation; *U.S. Public*, pg. 390
COLORADO MEDTECH, INC.; *U.S. Public*, pg. 401
COLORADO NATIONAL BANK—See U.S. Bancorp; *U.S. Public*, pg. 1680
COLORADO NATIONAL BANK ASPEN—See U.S. Bancorp; *U.S. Public*, pg. 1680
COLORADO NATIONAL BANKSHARES, INC.—See U.S. Bancorp; *U.S. Public*, pg. 1680
COLORADO PLAINS MEDICAL CENTER—See Brim, Inc.; *U.S. Private*, pg. 169
COLORADO PRIME CORPORATION; *U.S. Private*, pg. 255
COLORADO SPRINGS AUTO AUCTION INC.—See Tyco International Ltd.; *U.S. Public*, pg. 1648
COLORADO SPRINGS CABLEVISION, INC.—See Time Warner Inc.; *U.S. Public*, pg. 1610
COLORBUS, INC.; *U.S. Private*, pg. 255
COLORCON—See Berwind Corporation; *U.S. Private*, pg. 139
COLORCON LTD.—See Berwind Corporation; *U.S. Private*, pg. 139
COLORFORMS—See Toy Biz, Inc.; *U.S. Public*, pg. 1625
COLORPROFIL N.V.—See Arbed S.A.; *Int'l*, pg. 79
COLORTYME, INC.; *U.S. Private*, pg. 228
COLOSO PORT MINE—See The Broken Hill Proprietary Company Limited; *Int'l*, pg. 228
COLOUR SERVICES—See Laporte plc; *Int'l*, pg. 803
COLOURINGS—See The Body Shop International; *Int'l*, pg. 199
COLPICK, INC.—See The Western and Southern Life Insurance Company; *U.S. Private*, pg. 1164
COLSTON—See Staveley Industries PLC; *Int'l*, pg. 1298
COLSTRIP COMMUNITY SERVICES COMPANY—See Montana Power Company; *U.S. Public*, pg. 1127
COLTEC AUTOMOTIVE DIVISION—See Coltec Holdings Inc; *U.S. Public*, pg. 401
COLTEC HOLDINGS INC; *U.S. Public*, pg. 401
COLTEC INDUSTRIES INC.—See Coltec Holdings Inc; *U.S. Public*, pg. 401
COLTEC PEABODY DIVISION—See Coltec Holdings Inc; *U.S. Public*, pg. 402
COLTELLERIE MONTANA S.R.L.—See Fiskars Oy AB; *Int'l*, pg. 492
COLUMBIA ANALYTICAL SERVICES, INC.—See EMCON; *U.S. Public*, pg. 571
COLUMBIA ATLANTIC TRADING CORPORATION—See Columbia Energy Group; *U.S. Public*, pg. 402
COLUMBIA BACK INSTITUTE—See Columbia/HCA Healthcare Corporation; *U.S. Public*, pg. 404
COLUMBIA-BAY AREA—See Columbia/HCA Healthcare Corporation; *U.S. Public*, pg. 404
COLUMBIA BEHAVIORAL CENTER—See Columbia/HCA Healthcare Corporation; *U.S. Public*, pg. 404
COLUMBIA BREWING COMPANY—See Interbrew S.A.; *Int'l*, pg. 679
COLUMBIA CEMENT CO. INC.—See Burmah Castrol plc; *Int'l*, pg. 235
COLUMBIA COAL GASIFICATION CORP.—See Columbia Energy Group; *U.S. Public*, pg. 402
COLUMBIA CORPORATION; *U.S. Private*, pg. 255
COLUMBIA COSMETICS GMBH—See Henkel KGaA; *Int'l*, pg. 609
COLUMBIA DIAGNOSTIC CENTER—See Columbia/HCA Healthcare Corporation; *U.S. Public*, pg. 404

COLUMBIA DIE MOLD—See Precision Plastics Inc.; *U.S. Private*, pg. 879
COLUMBIA ENERGY GROUP; *U.S. Public*, pg. 402
COLUMBIA ENERGY SERVICES CORPORATION—See Columbia Energy Group; *U.S. Public*, pg. 402
COLUMBIA EXECUTIVE ASSOCIATES—See Galesi Group; *U.S. Private*, pg. 438
COLUMBIA FALLS ALUMINUM COMPANY; *U.S. Public*, pg. 255
COLUMBIA FARMS DISTRIBUTION—See Columbia Farms Inc.; *U.S. Private*, pg. 255
COLUMBIA FARMS INC.; *U.S. Private*, pg. 255
COLUMBIA GAS DISTRIBUTION COMPANIES—See Columbia Energy Group; *U.S. Public*, pg. 402
COLUMBIA GAS OF KENTUCKY, INC.—See Columbia Energy Group; *U.S. Public*, pg. 403
COLUMBIA GAS OF MARYLAND, INC.—See Columbia Energy Group; *U.S. Public*, pg. 403
COLUMBIA GAS OF OHIO, INC.—See Columbia Energy Group; *U.S. Public*, pg. 403
COLUMBIA GAS OF PENNSYLVANIA, INC.—See Columbia Energy Group; *U.S. Public*, pg. 403
COLUMBIA GAS SYSTEM SERVICE CORP.—See Columbia Energy Group; *U.S. Public*, pg. 403
COLUMBIA GAS TRANSMISSION CORP.—See Columbia Energy Group; *U.S. Public*, pg. 403
COLUMBIA GRAIN, INC.—See Marubeni Corporation; *Int'l*, pg. 845
COLUMBIA GULF TRANSMISSION CO.—See Columbia Energy Group; *U.S. Public*, pg. 403
COLUMBIA/H.C.A.—See Columbia/HCA Healthcare Corporation; *U.S. Public*, pg. 404
COLUMBIA/HCA HEALTHCARE CORPORATION; *U.S. Public*, pg. 403
COLUMBIA HEALTH CARE, INC.—See Sun Healthcare Group Inc.; *U.S. Public*, pg. 1531
COLUMBIA HOUSE HEALTHCARE—See Vencor, Inc.; *U.S. Public*, pg. 1712
COLUMBIA HOUSE MUSIC CLUB—See Sony Corporation; *Int'l*, pg. 1281
COLUMBIA IRON & METAL CO.—See Columbia National Group, Inc.; *U.S. Private*, pg. 256
COLUMBIA LABORATORIES, INC.; *U.S. Public*, pg. 405
COLUMBIA LIFECARE CENTER—See Columbia/HCA Healthcare Corporation; *U.S. Public*, pg. 404
COLUMBIA LIGHTING, INC.—See U.S. Industries, Inc.; *U.S. Public*, pg. 1684
COLUMBIA LNG CORP.—See Columbia Energy Group; *U.S. Public*, pg. 403
COLUMBIA LUMBER & MANUFACTURING CO.; *U.S. Private*, pg. 255
COLUMBIA MALL, INC.—See The Rouse Company; *U.S. Public*, pg. 1407
COLUMBIA MANUFACTURING INC.; *U.S. Private*, pg. 255
COLUMBIA MEDICAL CENTER DALLAS SOUTHWEST—See Columbia/HCA Healthcare Corporation; *U.S. Public*, pg. 404
COLUMBIA MEDICAL CENTER-EAST—See Columbia/HCA Healthcare Corporation; *U.S. Public*, pg. 404
COLUMBIA MEDICAL CENTER-WEST—See Columbia/HCA Healthcare Corporation; *U.S. Public*, pg. 404
COLUMBIA MEDICAL, INC.—See Utah Medical Products, Inc.; *U.S. Public*, pg. 1700
COLUMBIA NATIONAL GROUP, INC.; *U.S. Private*, pg. 255
COLUMBIA NATURAL RESOURCES, INC.—See Columbia Energy Group; *U.S. Public*, pg. 403
COLUMBIA PAINT & COATINGS; *U.S. Private*, pg. 256
COLUMBIA PARCAR CORP.—See Flambeau Corporation; *U.S. Private*, pg. 409
COLUMBIA PICTURES—See Sony Corporation; *Int'l*, pg. 1281
COLUMBIA PICTURES EASTERN DIVISION—See Sony Corporation; *Int'l*, pg. 1281
COLUMBIA PICTURES INTERNATIONAL TELEVISION—See Sony Corporation; *Int'l*, pg. 1282
COLUMBIA PICTURES MERCHANDISING—See Sony Corporation; *Int'l*, pg. 1281
COLUMBIA PICTURES OF ARGENTINA, INC.—See Sony Corporation; *Int'l*, pg. 1282
COLUMBIA PICTURES SOUTHERN DIVISION—See Sony Corporation; *Int'l*, pg. 1281
COLUMBIA PICTURES TELEVISION—See Sony Corporation; *Int'l*, pg. 1282
COLUMBIA PICTURES TELEVISION PTY. LTD.—See Sony Corporation; *Int'l*, pg. 1282
COLUMBIA PICTURES WESTERN DIVISION—See Sony Corporation; *Int'l*, pg. 1281
COLUMBIA PIPE & SUPPLY COMPANY; *U.S. Private*, pg. 256
COLUMBIA PROPANE CORP.—See Columbia Energy Group; *U.S. Public*, pg. 403
COLUMBIA REG. ONCOLOGY—See Columbia/HCA Healthcare Corporation; *U.S. Public*, pg. 404
COLUMBIA SCIENTIFIC INDUSTRIES CORPORATION—See Williams Holdings Plc; *Int'l*, pg. 1500
COLUMBIA SERVICES, INC.—See Washington Mutual Inc.; *U.S. Public*, pg. 1742
COLUMBIA SPECIALTIES, INC.—See Fedders Corp.; *U.S. Public*, pg. 615
COLUMBIA SUPPLY—See Associated Industrial Supply, Inc.; *U.S. Private*, pg. 91
COLUMBIA SUPPLY, CONWAY—See Associated Industrial Supply, Inc.; *U.S. Private*, pg. 91
COLUMBIA SUPPLY, GREENWOOD—See Associated Industrial Supply, Inc.; *U.S. Private*, pg. 91
COLUMBIA TRAINING CENTER—See Corrections Corporation of America; *U.S. Public*, pg. 450
COLUMBIA TRI-STAR FILM DISTRIBUTORS INTERNATIONAL—See Sony Corporation; *Int'l*, pg. 1281
COLUMBIA TRI-STAR FILMS OF BRAZIL, INC.—See Sony Corporation; *Int'l*, pg. 1282

COLUMBIA TRI-STAR FILMS (UK)—See Sony Corporation; *Int'l*, pg. 1281
COLUMBIA TRI-STAR HOME VIDEO—See Sony Corporation; *Int'l*, pg. 1282
COLUMBIA TRI-STAR INTERNATIONAL RELEASING CORP.—See Sony Corporation; *Int'l*, pg. 1281
COLUMBIA TRI-STAR INTERNATIONAL TELEVISION—See Sony Corporation; *Int'l*, pg. 1281
COLUMBIA TRI-STAR TELEVISION DISTRIBUTION—See Sony Corporation; *Int'l*, pg. 1282
COLUMBIA TRI-STAR TELEVISION DISTRIBUTION - NEW YORK OFFICE—See Sony Corporation; *Int'l*, pg. 1282
COLUMBIA TRI-STAR TELEVISION DISTRIBUTION - CHICAGO OFFICE—See Sony Corporation; *Int'l*, pg. 1282
COLUMBIA TRI-STAR TELEVISION DISTRIBUTION - ATLANTA—See Sony Corporation; *Int'l*, pg. 1282
COLUMBIA TRI-STAR TELEVISION DISTRIBUTION - DALLAS—See Sony Corporation; *Int'l*, pg. 1282
COLUMBIA TRISTAR TELEVISION—See Sony Corporation; *Int'l*, pg. 1282
COLUMBIA UNIVERSAL LIFE INSURANCE COMPANY—See American Heritage Life Investment Corp.; *U.S. Public*, pg. 79
COLUMBIA WILLAMETTE DEVELOPMENT CO.—See Enron Corp.; *U.S. Public*, pg. 585
COLUMBIA WILLAMETTE LEASING, INC.—See Enron Corp.; *U.S. Public*, pg. 585
COLUMBIAN ADVERTISING INC.; *U.S. Private*, pg. 256
COLUMBIAN CHEMICALS COMPANY—See Phelps Dodge Corporation; *U.S. Public*, pg. 1286
COLUMBIAN LIFE INSURANCE COMPANY—See Columbian Mutual Life Insurance Co.; *U.S. Private*, pg. 256
COLUMBIAN MUTUAL LIFE INSURANCE CO.; *U.S. Private*, pg. 256
COLUMBIAN ROPE COMPANY; *U.S. Private*, pg. 256
COLUMBINA MEIJI S.A.—See Meiji Seika Kaisha, Ltd.; *Int'l*, pg. 856
COLUMBINE JDS SYSTEMS, INC.—See Big Flower Press Holdings, Inc.; *U.S. Public*, pg. 228
COLUMBUS BAKERY—See Ark Restaurants Corp.; *U.S. Public*, pg. 130
COLUMBUS BANK AND TRUST COMPANY—See Synovus Financial Corp.; *U.S. Public*, pg. 1549
COLUMBUS COCA-COLA BOTTLING CO.—See Coca-Cola Bottling Co. Consolidated; *U.S. Public*, pg. 392
COLUMBUS DIXON LTD.—See Electrolux, AB; *Int'l*, pg. 444
THE COLUMBUS LEDGER & ENQUIRER—See Knight-Ridder, Inc.; *U.S. Public*, pg. 964
COLUMBUS LIFE INSURANCE CO.—See The Western and Southern Life Insurance Company; *U.S. Public*, pg. 1164
COLUMBUS MCKINNON CORP.; *U.S. Public*, pg. 405
COLUMBUS MILLS, INC.; *U.S. Private*, pg. 256
COLUMBUS PIPE & EQUIPMENT COMPANY; *U.S. Private*, pg. 257
COLUMBUS RECYCLING, INC.—See Caraustar Industries, Inc.; *U.S. Public*, pg. 303
COLUMBUS SHOW CASE COMPANY; *U.S. Private*, pg. 257
COLUMBUS SHOWCASE, ASHLAND DIVISION—See Columbus Show Case Company; *U.S. Private*, pg. 257
COLUMBUS SOUTHERN POWER COMPANY—See American Electric Power Company, Inc.; *U.S. Public*, pg. 72
COLUMBUS SQUARE SHOPPING CENTER COMPANY—See Cigna Corp.; *U.S. Public*, pg. 361
COLUMBUS STEEL DRUM, INC.—See Evans Industries, Inc.; *U.S. Private*, pg. 385
COLUMBUS VERSICHERUNGS VERMITTLUNGS—See Nationwide Insurance Enterprise; *U.S. Private*, pg. 789
COLUMNA S.A.—See SMH Swiss Corporation for Micro Electronics & Watchmaking Indus. Ltd.; *Int'l*, pg. 1160
COLUSA COUNTY CANNING CO.—See Tomkins PLC; *Int'l*, pg. 1396
COLUSA ELEVATOR CO.; *U.S. Private*, pg. 257
COLUSON TECHNOLOGIES—See Strategic Distribution Inc.; *U.S. Public*, pg. 1523
COLWELL INDUSTRIES, INC.; *U.S. Private*, pg. 257
COLWOOD CO., INC.—See Columbia Lumber & Manufacturing Co.; *U.S. Private*, pg. 255
COM ALLOY INTERNATIONAL COMPANY—See A. Schulman, Inc.; *U.S. Public*, pg. 1441
COM CORP FACTORS, INC.—See Kennington Ltd., Inc.; *U.S. Private*, pg. 615
COMADUR S.A.—See SMH Swiss Corporation for Micro Electronics & Watchmaking Indus. Ltd.; *Int'l*, pg. 1161
COMAIR AVIATION ACADEMY, INC.—See Comair Holdings, Inc.; *U.S. Public*, pg. 406
COMAIR HOLDINGS, INC.; *U.S. Public*, pg. 406
COMAIR, INC.—See Comair Holdings, Inc.; *U.S. Public*, pg. 406
COMAIR INVESTMENT COMPANY—See Comair Holdings, Inc.; *U.S. Public*, pg. 406
COMAIR SERVICES, INC.—See Comair Holdings, Inc.; *U.S. Public*, pg. 406
COMALCO ALUMINIUM (BELL BAY) LIMITED—See Comalco Limited; *Int'l*, pg. 307
COMALCO-CHH ALUMINUM—See International Paper Company; *U.S. Public*, pg. 905
COMALCO FOUNDRY PRODUCTS—See Comalco Limited; *Int'l*, pg. 307
COMALCO LIMITED; *Int'l*, pg. 307
COMALCO MINERALS & ALUMINA—See Comalco Limited; *Int'l*, pg. 307
COMALCO NEW ZEALAND—See Comalco Limited; *Int'l*, pg. 307
COMALCO RESEARCH & TECHNOLOGY—See Comalco Limited; *Int'l*, pg. 307
COMALCO SMELTING—See Comalco Limited; *Int'l*, pg. 307

COMALCO (UK) LIMITED—See Comalco Limited; *Int'l*, pg. 307
COMALLOY INTERNATIONAL COMPANY—See A. Schulman, Inc.; *U.S. Public*, pg. 1441
COMARCO, INC.; *U.S. Public*, pg. 406
COMARCO STAFFING, INC.—See Comarco, Inc.; *U.S. Public*, pg. 406
COMARCO WIRELESS TECHNOLOGIES, INC.—See Comarco, Inc.; *U.S. Public*, pg. 406
COMARE PRODUCTS—See Windmere-Durable Holdings; *U.S. Public*, pg. 1771
COMARK; *U.S. Private*, pg. 257
COMARK COMMUNICATIONS, INC.—See Thomson S.A.; *Int'l*, pg. 1383
COMARK COMMUNICATIONS INC.—See Thomson S.A.; *Int'l*, pg. 1383
COMARSA S.A. AGNO—See IRI Istituto Ricostruzione Industriale; *Int'l*, pg. 655
COMATEL SRL—See Siebe plc; *Int'l*, pg. 1241
COMAU FINANZIARIA S.P.A.—See Fiat Auto SpA; *Int'l*, pg. 480
COMAU PRODUCTIVITY SYSTEMS, INC.—See Fiat Auto SpA; *Int'l*, pg. 483
COMAV—See SAFECO Corporation; *U.S. Public*, pg. 1423
COMAZAR (PTY) LTD.—See Transnet Ltd.; *Int'l*, pg. 1417
COMBAT SYSTEMS DIVISION—See Carlyle Holding Corporation; *U.S. Private*, pg. 213
COMBE INCORPORATED; *U.S. Private*, pg. 257
COMBI BLOCK, INC.—See PKL Verpackungssysteme GmbH; *Int'l*, pg. 1020
COMBI SHIPPING AB—See Korsnas AB; *Int'l*, pg. 759
COMBIBLOC INC.—See SIG Schweizersiche Industrie-Gesellschaft Holding AG; *Int'l*, pg. 1156
COMBIBLOC LTD.—See SIG Schweizersiche Industrie-Gesellschaft Holding AG; *Int'l*, pg. 1156
COMBIBLOC S.A.—See SIG Schweizersiche Industrie-Gesellschaft Holding AG; *Int'l*, pg. 1156
COMBIBLOC S.A.R.L.—See SIG Schweizersiche Industrie-Gesellschaft Holding AG; *Int'l*, pg. 1156
COMBIBLOC S.R.L.—See SIG Schweizersiche Industrie-Gesellschaft Holding AG; *Int'l*, pg. 1156
COMBINED INSURANCE COMPANY OF AMERICA—See AON Corporation; *U.S. Public*, pg. 118
COMBINED INSURANCE CO. OF AUSTRALIA, LTD.—See AON Corporation; *U.S. Public*, pg. 118
COMBINED INSURANCE COMPANY OF IRELAND LTD.—See AON Corporation; *U.S. Public*, pg. 118
COMBINED LIFE INSURANCE CO. OF AUSTRALIA, LTD.—See AON Corporation; *U.S. Public*, pg. 118
COMBINED LIFE INSURANCE CO. OF NEW YORK—See AON Corporation; *U.S. Public*, pg. 118
COMBINED TERMINALS AMSTERDAM V.O.F.—See Royal Nedlloyd Group N.V.; *Int'l*, pg. 1144
COMBITECH ELECTRONICS—See Investor AB; *Int'l*, pg. 686
COMBITRANS EESTI A.S.—See UPM-Kymmene Corporation; *Int'l*, pg. 1430
COMBITRANS OY—See UPM-Kymmene Corporation; *Int'l*, pg. 1428
COMBUSTHERM—See Eclipse Inc.; *U.S. Private*, pg. 361
COMBUSTION ENGINEERING-EUROPE—See ABB Asea Brown Boveri (Holding) Ltd.; *Int'l*, pg. 5
COMBUSTION ENGINEERING EUROPE S.A.R.L.—See ABB Asea Brown Boveri (Holding) Ltd.; *Int'l*, pg. 5
COMCAFE COMERCIAL DE CAFE, LTDA.—See Nestle S.A.; *Int'l*, pg. 920
COMCAST CABLE COMMUNICATIONS, INC.—See Comcast Corporation; *U.S. Public*, pg. 407
COMCAST CELLULAR COMMUNICATIONS, INC.—See Comcast Corporation; *U.S. Public*, pg. 407
COMCAST CORPORATION; *U.S. Public*, pg. 406
COMCO PIPE AND SUPPLY COMPANY—See Russel Metals Inc.; *Int'l*, pg. 1150
COMCOTEC, INC.—See Dynatech Corporation; *U.S. Public*, pg. 539
COMDATA CORPORATION—See Ceridian Corporation; *U.S. Public*, pg. 331
COMDATA SAUNDERS INCORPORATED—See Ceridian Corporation; *U.S. Public*, pg. 331
COMDATA TRANSCEIVER—See Ceridian Corporation; *U.S. Public*, pg. 331
OY COMDAX AB—See Axel Johnson AB; *Int'l*, pg. 710
COMDIAL CORPORATION; *U.S. Public*, pg. 407
COMDIAL ENTERPRISE SYSTEMS, INC.—See Comdial Corporation; *U.S. Public*, pg. 407
COMDIAL TELECOMMUNICATIONS INTERNATIONAL, INC.—See Comdial Corporation; *U.S. Public*, pg. 407
COMDIRECT BANK GMBH—See Commerzbank AG; *Int'l*, pg. 309
COMDISCO ASIA PTE. LTD.—See Comdisco, Inc.; *U.S. Public*, pg. 408
COMDISCO AUSTRALIA PTY. LTD.—See Comdisco, Inc.; *U.S. Public*, pg. 408
COMDISCO BELGIUM S.P.R.I.—See Comdisco, Inc.; *U.S. Public*, pg. 408
COMDISCO CANADA LTD.—See Comdisco, Inc.; *U.S. Public*, pg. 408
COMDISCO CONTINUITY SERVICES—See Comdisco, Inc.; *U.S. Public*, pg. 408
COMDISCO DEUTSCHLAND GMBH—See Comdisco, Inc.; *U.S. Public*, pg. 408
COMDISCO ELECTRONICS GROUP—See Comdisco, Inc.; *U.S. Public*, pg. 408
COMDISCO FINANCIAL SERVICES—See Comdisco, Inc.; *U.S. Public*, pg. 408
COMDISCO FRANCE S.A./PROMODATA—See Comdisco, Inc.; *U.S. Public*, pg. 408
COMDISCO HANDELSGESELLSCHAFT M.B.H. AUSTRIA—See Comdisco, Inc.; *U.S. Public*, pg. 408
COMDISCO HEALTHCARE AND SCIENTIFIC GROUP—See Comdisco, Inc.; *U.S. Public*, pg. 408
COMDISCO HEALTHCARE, INC.—See Comdisco, Inc.; *U.S. Public*, pg. 408

COMDISCO, INC.; *U.S. Public*, pg. 407
COMDISCO INTEGRATED SERVICES—See Comdisco, Inc.; *U.S. Public*, pg. 408
COMDISCO JAPAN INC.—See Comdisco, Inc.; *U.S. Public*, pg. 408
COMDISCO LABORATORY & SCIENTIFIC GROUP—See Comdisco, Inc.; *U.S. Public*, pg. 408
COMDISCO MEDICAL EXCHANGE, INC.—See Comdisco, Inc.; *U.S. Public*, pg. 408
COMDISCO NEDERLAND B.V.—See Comdisco, Inc.; *U.S. Public*, pg. 408
COMDISCO, S.A.—See Comdisco, Inc.; *U.S. Public*, pg. 408
COMDISCO SWEDEN AB—See Comdisco, Inc.; *U.S. Public*, pg. 408
COMDISCO SWITZERLAND S.A.—See Comdisco, Inc.; *U.S. Public*, pg. 408
COMDISCO TRADE, INC.—See Comdisco, Inc.; *U.S. Public*, pg. 408
COMDISCO UNITED KINGDOM LIMITED—See Comdisco, Inc.; *U.S. Public*, pg. 408
S.A. COMECI HOLDING—See Cockerill Sambre; *Int'l*, pg. 302
COMED—See Unicom Corporation; *U.S. Public*, pg. 1664
COMED COMMUNICATIONS, INC.—See Ted Thomas Associates Inc. Advertising; *U.S. Private*, pg. 1083
COMERCIAL ANGLO CHILENA—See Diageo Plc; *Int'l*, pg. 410
COMERCIAL NORTON, S.A.—See Saint-Gobain; *Int'l*, pg. 1174
COMERCIAL PAPELERA ALDI S.A.—See Mo och Domsjo AB; *Int'l*, pg. 886
COMERCIALIZADORA LA MODERNA DE TOLUCA, S.A. DE C.V.—See Tablex, S.a. de C.V.; *Int'l*, pg. 1346
COMERCIALIZADORA S.A. DE C.V.—See Leggett & Platt, Incorporated; *U.S. Public*, pg. 987
COMERCIO EXTERIOR DE CHILE LTDA.—See CODELCO Chile (Corporacion Nacional Del Cobre De Chile); *Int'l*, pg. 303
COMERICA ACCEPTANCE CORPORATION—See Comerica Incorporated; *U.S. Public*, pg. 409
COMERICA BANK CALIFORNIA—See Comerica Incorporated; *U.S. Public*, pg. 409
COMERICA BANK MICHIGAN—See Comerica Incorporated; *U.S. Public*, pg. 409
COMERICA BANK TEXAS—See Comerica Incorporated; *U.S. Public*, pg. 409
COMERICA INCORPORATED; *U.S. Public*, pg. 408
COMESTIBLES LA ROSA S.A.—See Nestle S.A.; *Int'l*, pg. 920
COMET—See Kingfisher plc; *Int'l*, pg. 733
COMET AMERICAN MARKETING—See Erly Industries, Inc.; *U.S. Public*, pg. 591
COMET ENTERPRISES, INC.—See Browning-Ferris Industries, Inc.; *U.S. Public*, pg. 264
COMET-PRESS NEWSPAPERS, INC.—See The New York Times Company; *U.S. Public*, pg. 1175
COMET RICE OF JAMAICA, LTD.—See Erly Industries, Inc.; *U.S. Public*, pg. 591
COMET RICE OF PUERTO RICO, INC.—See Erly Industries, Inc.; *U.S. Public*, pg. 591
COMET RICE, INC.-STUTTGART—See Erly Industries, Inc.; *U.S. Public*, pg. 591
COMET STEEL, INC.—See Commercial Metals Company; *U.S. Public*, pg. 412
COMET VENTURES, INC.—See Erly Industries, Inc.; *U.S. Public*, pg. 591
COMETALS, INC.—See Commercial Metals Company; *U.S. Public*, pg. 412
COMETALS CHINA, INC.—See Commercial Metals Company; *U.S. Public*, pg. 414
COMETRA OIL & GAS, INC.—See Groupe Bruxelles Lambert S.A.; *Int'l*, pg. 562
COMFORCE CORPORATION; *U.S. Public*, pg. 409
COMFORCE/UNIFORCE STAFFING SERVICES—See Comforce Corporation; *U.S. Public*, pg. 409
COMFORT FINANCIERINGEN NEDERLAND BV—See National Westminster Bank PLC; *Int'l*, pg. 911
COMFORT INC.—See Jannock Limited; *Int'l*, pg. 698
COMFORTABLE MORTGAGES, INC.—See NationsBank Corporation; *U.S. Public*, pg. 1163
COMFORTO GROUP—See Haworth, Inc.; *U.S. Private*, pg. 512
COMHLUCHT IASCAIREACHTA FANAD TEORANTA (FANAD FISHERIES)—See Norsk Hydro a.s; *Int'l*, pg. 961
COMIMET—See Imetal; *Int'l*, pg. 661
COMINCO ALASKA INCORPORATED—See Cominco, Ltd.; *Int'l*, pg. 308
COMINCO AMERICAN INCORPORATED—See Cominco, Ltd.; *Int'l*, pg. 308
COMINCO AMERICAN RESOURCES INCORPORATED, BUCKHORN OPERATIONS—See Cominco, Ltd.; *Int'l*, pg. 307
COMINCO JAPAN K.K.—See Cominco, Ltd.; *Int'l*, pg. 308
COMINCO LTD.-POLARIS OPERATIONS—See Cominco, Ltd.; *Int'l*, pg. 308
COMINCO, LTD.; *Int'l*, pg. 307
COMINCO LTD.—See Cominco, Ltd.; *Int'l*, pg. 308
COMINCO LTD. PRODUCT TECHNOLOGY CENTER—See Cominco, Ltd.; *Int'l*, pg. 308
COMINCO LTD.-RESEARCH DIV.—See Cominco, Ltd.; *Int'l*, pg. 308
COMINCO MADENCILIK SANAYI A.S.—See Cominco, Ltd.; *Int'l*, pg. 307
COMINCO METALS PTE. LTD.—See Cominco, Ltd.; *Int'l*, pg. 308
COMINCO (PERU) S.R.L.—See Cominco, Ltd.; *Int'l*, pg. 307
COMINCO RESOURCES (BOTSWANA) (PTY.) LTD.—See Cominco, Ltd.; *Int'l*, pg. 307
COMINCO RESOURCES EUROPE N.V.—See Cominco, Ltd.; *Int'l*, pg. 308
COMINCO RESOURCES INTERNATIONAL LIMITED—See Cominco, Ltd.; *Int'l*, pg. 308

COMING EVENT FASHIONS LTD.—See Shirmax Leasing Ltd.; *Int'l*, pg. 1235
COMLINEAR CORPORATION—See National Semiconductor Corporation; *U.S. Public*, pg. 1160
COMMAIR MECHANICAL SERVICES—See ABM Industries; *U.S. Public*, pg. 2
COMMAND, CONTROL & COMMUNICATIONS SYSTEMS—See Litton Industries, Inc.; *U.S. Public*, pg. 1002
COMMAND PLASTIC CORPORATION; *U.S. Private*, pg. 257
COMMAND SECURITY CORPORATION; *U.S. Public*, pg. 409
COMMAND WEB OFFSET CO.—See MacNaughton Einson Graphics; *U.S. Private*, pg. 693
COMMANDER OIL CORPORATION; *U.S. Private*, pg. 257
COMMCORP FINANCIAL SERVICES INC.—See Canadian Imperial Bank of Commerce; *Int'l*, pg. 256
COMMEMORATIVE BRANDS, INC.; *U.S. Private*, pg. 258
COMMENCEMENT BAY MILL COMPANY—See Simpson Investment Co.; *U.S. Private*, pg. 1003
COMMENDA BAUSTOFF A.G.—See Williams Holdings Plc; *Int'l*, pg. 1501
COMMENDA BAUSTOFFGESELLSCHAFT MBH—See Solvay S.A.; *Int'l*, pg. 1278
COMMENDA C.R. S.R.O.—See Williams Holdings Plc; *Int'l*, pg. 1501
COMMENDA HUNGARIA KPT.—See Williams Holdings Plc; *Int'l*, pg. 1501
COMMERCE—See FCA!BMZ; *Int'l*, pg. 470
COMMERCE & INDUSTRY INSURANCE CO.—See American International Group, Inc.; *U.S. Public*, pg. 84
COMMERCE & INDUSTRY INSURANCE CO. OF CANADA—See American International Group, Inc.; *U.S. Public*, pg. 85
COMMERCE BANCSHARES, INC.; *U.S. Public*, pg. 409
COMMERCE BANK—See MainStreet BankGroup Incorporated; *U.S. Public*, pg. 1038
COMMERCE BANK N.A.—See Commerce Bancshares, Inc.; *U.S. Public*, pg. 409
COMMERCE BANK, N.A.—See Commerce Bancshares, Inc.; *U.S. Public*, pg. 410
COMMERCE BROKERAGE SERVICES, INC.—See Commerce Bancshares, Inc.; *U.S. Public*, pg. 410
COMMERCE CAPITAL MANAGEMENT, INC.—See National Commerce Bancorporation; *U.S. Public*, pg. 1155
COMMERCE DRUG CANADA LTD.—See Del Laboratories, Inc.; *U.S. Public*, pg. 494
COMMERCE FINANCE COMPANY—See National Commerce Bancorporation; *U.S. Public*, pg. 1155
COMMERCE GENERAL CORPORATION—See National Commerce Bancorporation; *U.S. Public*, pg. 1155
COMMERCE GROUP CORP.; *U.S. Public*, pg. 410
COMMERCE INTERNATIONAL MERCHANT BANKERS BERHAD—See The Sanwa Bank Limited; *Int'l*, pg. 1190
COMMERCE INTERNATIONAL TRUST LIMITED—See Canadian Imperial Bank of Commerce; *Int'l*, pg. 257
COMMERCE INVESTMENT CORPORATION—See National Commerce Bancorporation; *U.S. Public*, pg. 1155
COMMERCE PROPERTY & CASUALTY AGENCY, INC.—See Commerce Bancshares, Inc.; *U.S. Public*, pg. 410
COMMERCE SERVICES GROUP—See Sterling Commerce, Inc.; *U.S. Public*, pg. 1516
COMMERCE/SANSEB—See Commerce Group Corp.; *U.S. Public*, pg. 410
COMMERCE/SANSEB JOINT VENTURE—See Commerce Group Corp.; *U.S. Public*, pg. 410
COMMERCIAL AIRCRAFT DIVISION—See Northrop Grumman Corporation; *U.S. Public*, pg. 1198
COMMERCIAL AIRCRAFT GROUP—See Israel Aircraft Industries Ltd.; *Int'l*, pg. 690
COMMERCIAL AND POLITICAL RISK CONSULTANTS—See Inchcape PLC; *Int'l*, pg. 671
THE COMMERCIAL APPEAL—See The E.W. Scripps Company; *U.S. Public*, pg. 1447
THE COMMERCIAL BANK; *U.S. Public*, pg. 410
COMMERCIAL BANK—See Synovus Financial Corp.; *U.S. Public*, pg. 1549
THE COMMERCIAL BANK-ALLENTOWN RD. BRANCH—See The Commercial Bank; *U.S. Public*, pg. 410
COMMERCIAL BANK AND TRUST COMPANY OF TROUP COUNTY—See Synovus Financial Corp.; *U.S. Public*, pg. 1549
COMMERCIAL BANK AT ALMA—See First United Bancshares, Inc.; *U.S. Public*, pg. 641
THE COMMERCIAL BANK-COLE ST. BRANCH—See The Commercial Bank; *U.S. Public*, pg. 410
THE COMMERCIAL BANK-GOMER BANKING CENTER—See The Commercial Bank; *U.S. Public*, pg. 410
THE COMMERCIAL BANK OF CEYLON LIMITED—See Standard Chartered Bank PLC; *Int'l*, pg. 1296
THE COMMERCIAL BANK OF NAMIBIA LIMITED—See Bank Brussels Lambert; *Int'l*, pg. 149
COMMERCIAL BANK OF SOLEURE—See Union Bank of Switzerland; *Int'l*, pg. 1440
COMMERCIAL CARE DIVISION—See 3M; *U.S. Public*, pg. 1605
COMMERCIAL COLD STORAGE, INC.—See Stone & Webster, Incorporated; *U.S. Public*, pg. 1519
COMMERCIAL CREDIT COMPANY—See Travelers Group; *U.S. Public*, pg. 1633
COMMERCIAL DESIGN ARCHITECTS/HEPY—See Harley Ellington Design; *U.S. Private*, pg. 503
COMMERCIAL ENVIRONMENTAL SYSTEMS GROUP, INC.—See Nortek, Inc.; *U.S. Public*, pg. 1193
COMMERCIAL FEDERAL BANK—See Commercial Federal Corporation; *U.S. Public*, pg. 411
COMMERCIAL FEDERAL CORPORATION; *U.S. Public*, pg. 411
COMMERCIAL FINANCIAL CORPORATION LIMITED—See BCE Inc.; *Int'l*, pg. 115

COMMERCIAL FORGED PRODUCTS—See Wozniak Industries, Inc.; *U.S. Private*, pg. 1192
COMMERCIAL GUARANTY INSURANCE COMPANY—See Ford Motor Company; *U.S. Public*, pg. 663
COMMERCIAL HENKEL S.A. (COHESA)—See Henkel KGaA; *Int'l*, pg. 611
COMMERCIAL HYDRAULICS KEELAVITE, LTD.—See Commercial Intertech Corp.; *U.S. Public*, pg. 411
COMMERCIAL HYDRAULICS KONTAK LTD.—See Commercial Intertech Corp.; *U.S. Public*, pg. 411
COMMERCIAL HYDRAULICS PTY. LTD.—See Commercial Intertech Corp.; *U.S. Public*, pg. 411
COMMERCIAL INTERIOR BUILDERS, INC.—See Irex Corporation; *U.S. Public*, pg. 913
COMMERCIAL INTERTECH CORP.; *U.S. Public*, pg. 411
COMMERCIAL INTERTECH DISTRIBUTION SERVICES—See Commercial Intertech Corp.; *U.S. Public*, pg. 411
COMMERCIAL INTERTECH DO BRASIL LTDA.—See Commercial Intertech Corp.; *U.S. Public*, pg. 411
COMMERCIAL INTERTECH LTD.—See Commercial Intertech Corp.; *U.S. Public*, pg. 411
COMMERCIAL INTERTECH S.A.—See Commercial Intertech Corp.; *U.S. Public*, pg. 411
COMMERCIAL-LEVIN—See Commercial Metals Company; *U.S. Public*, pg. 413
COMMERCIAL LIGHT COMPANY; *U.S. Private*, pg. 258
COMMERCIAL MARKETING SYSTEMS—See Royal & Sun Alliance Insurance Group plc; *Int'l*, pg. 1131
COMMERCIAL METALS COMPANY; *U.S. Public*, pg. 411
COMMERCIAL METALS COMPANY—See Commercial Metals Company; *U.S. Public*, pg. 412
COMMERCIAL METALS CO.-DALLAS TRADING DIV.—See Commercial Metals Company; *U.S. Public*, pg. 413
COMMERCIAL METALS DEUTSCHLAND GMBH—See Commercial Metals Company; *U.S. Public*, pg. 414
COMMERCIAL METALS (INTERNATIONAL) AG—See Commercial Metals Company; *U.S. Public*, pg. 414
COMMERCIAL NATIONAL BANK—See Deposit Guaranty Corp.; *U.S. Public*, pg. 500
COMMERCIAL NATIONAL BANK—See UMB Financial Corporation; *U.S. Public*, pg. 1654
COMMERCIAL NATIONAL BANK OF BERWYN—See Citizens Banking Corporation; *U.S. Public*, pg. 379
COMMERCIAL-NEWS—See Gannett Company, Inc.; *U.S. Public*, pg. 700
COMMERCIAL PLASTICS & SUPPLIES CORP.; *U.S. Private*, pg. 258
COMMERCIAL PRODUCTS INC.—See Bardon Group PLC; *Int'l*, pg. 166
COMMERCIAL PRODUCTS, INC.—See The Dickerson Group, Inc.; *U.S. Private*, pg. 331
COMMERCIAL REALTY & RESOURCES CORP.—See New Jersey Resources Corporation; *U.S. Public*, pg. 1172
COMMERCIAL RECORD CENTER—See Nelson Westerberg, Inc.; *U.S. Private*, pg. 1164
COMMERCIAL RISK PARTNERS LTD.—See SCOR; *Int'l*, pg. 1152
COMMERCIAL SEATING DIVISION—See Flexsteel Industries, Inc.; *U.S. Public*, pg. 654
COMMERCIAL SERVICE PRINTING—See Warner Press, Inc.; *U.S. Private*, pg. 1151
COMMERCIAL STEERING DIVISION—See TRW Inc.; *U.S. Public*, pg. 1558
COMMERCIAL SYSTEMS LIMITED—See Sanderson Technology Ltd.; *Int'l*, pg. 1184
COMMERCIAL TESTING & ENGINEERING CO.—See SGS Societe Generale de Surveillance Holding S.A.; *Int'l*, pg. 1153
COMMERCIAL TRAVELERS MUTUAL INSURANCE COMPANY; *U.S. Private*, pg. 258
COMMERCIAL UNION ASSURANCE COMPANY OF CANADA—See Commercial Union plc; *Int'l*, pg. 308
COMMERCIAL UNION CAPITAL CORPORATION—See Commercial Union plc; *Int'l*, pg. 308
COMMERCIAL UNION CORPORATION—See Commercial Union plc; *Int'l*, pg. 308
COMMERCIAL UNION INSURANCE COMPANY—See Commercial Union plc; *Int'l*, pg. 308
COMMERCIAL UNION LIFE ASSURANCE COMPANY OF CANADA—See Commercial Union plc; *Int'l*, pg. 308
COMMERCIAL UNION LIFE INSURANCE COMPANY OF AMERICA—See Commercial Union plc; *Int'l*, pg. 308
COMMERCIAL UNION OF CANADA HOLDINGS LTD—See Commercial Union plc; *Int'l*, pg. 308
COMMERCIAL UNION PLC; *Int'l*, pg. 308
COMMERCIAL VEHICLE DIV.—See Champion Enterprises, Inc.; *U.S. Public*, pg. 333
COMMERCIALE FINANZIARIA S.P.A.—See Fiat Auto SpA; *Int'l*, pg. 481
COMMERCIO INTL. LUSO ESPANSOL S.A.—See IRI Istituto Ricostruzione Industriale; *Int'l*, pg. 655
COMMERCIUM VERMOEGENSVERWALTUNG GMBH—See Commerzbank AG; *Int'l*, pg. 309
THE COMMERICAL BANK-MAIN STREET—See The Commercial Bank; *U.S. Public*, pg. 410
COMMERICAL E INDUSTRIAL DE PRODUCTOS QUIMICOS, S. A.—See FMC Corporation; *U.S. Public*, pg. 606
COMMERICAL ROOFERS INC.; *U.S. Private*, pg. 258
THE COMMERCIAL BANK-ELIDA—See The Commercial Bank; *U.S. Public*, pg. 410
COMMERZ ASSET MANAGEMENT ASIA LTD.—See Commerzbank AG; *Int'l*, pg. 312
COMMERZ ASSET MANAGEMENT (UK) PLC—See Commerzbank AG; *Int'l*, pg. 311
COMMERZ BAUCONTRACT GMBH—See Commerzbank AG; *Int'l*, pg. 309
COMMERZ BETEILIGUNGS GMBH—See Commerzbank AG; *Int'l*, pg. 309
COMMERZ FINANCIAL PRODUCTS GMBH—See Commerzbank AG; *Int'l*, pg. 309
COMMERZ FINANCIAL PRODUCTS S.A.—See Commerzbank AG; *Int'l*, pg. 309

COMMERZ FINANCIAL PRODUCTS USA INC.—See Commerzbank AG; *Int'l*, pg. 310
COMMERZ FINANZ-MANAGEMENT GMBH—See Commerzbank AG; *Int'l*, pg. 309
COMMERZ GRUNDBESITZ INVESTMENT GESELLSCHAFT MBH—See Commerzbank AG; *Int'l*, pg. 309
COMMERZ IMMOBILIEN GMBH—See Commerzbank AG; *Int'l*, pg. 309
COMMERZ IMMOBILIEN VERMIETUNGS GMBH—See Commerzbank AG; *Int'l*, pg. 309
COMMERZ INTERNATIONAL CAPITAL MANAGEMENT GMBH—See Commerzbank AG; *Int'l*, pg. 309
COMMERZ INTERNATIONAL CAPITAL MANAGEMENT (JAPAN) LTD.—See Commerzbank AG; *Int'l*, pg. 309
COMMERZ SECURITIES (JAPAN) COMPANY LTD.—See Commerzbank AG; *Int'l*, pg. 312
COMMERZ SERVICE GESELLSCHAFT FUR KUNDENBETREUUNG GMBH—See Commerzbank AG; *Int'l*, pg. 309
COMMERZ- UND INDUSTRIE-LEASING BERLIN GMBH—See Commerzbank AG; *Int'l*, pg. 309
COMMERZ- UND INDUSTRIE-LEASING GMBH—See Commerzbank AG; *Int'l*, pg. 309
COMMERZ UNTERNEHMENSBETEILIGUNGS AG—See Commerzbank AG; *Int'l*, pg. 309
COMMERZBANK AG; *Int'l*, pg. 308
COMMERZBANK AG—See Commerzbank AG; *Int'l*, pg. 311
COMMERZBANK AG VON 1870 I.L.—See Commerzbank AG; *Int'l*, pg. 309
COMMERZBANK AG-PRAGUE BRANCH—See Commerzbank AG; *Int'l*, pg. 311
COMMERZBANK CAPITAL MARKETS CORPORATION—See Commerzbank AG; *Int'l*, pg. 310
COMMERZBANK EUROPE (IRELAND)—See Commerzbank AG; *Int'l*, pg. 312
COMMERZBANK FUTURES CORPORATION—See Commerzbank AG; *Int'l*, pg. 310
COMMERZBANK INTERNATIONAL, S.A.—See Commerzbank AG; *Int'l*, pg. 311
COMMERZBANK INVESTMENT MANAGEMENT GMBH—See Commerzbank AG; *Int'l*, pg. 309
COMMERZBANK OVERSEAS FINANCE N.V.—See Commerzbank AG; *Int'l*, pg. 312
COMMERZBANK PROPERTIES SOUTH AFRICA PTY. LTD.—See Commerzbank AG; *Int'l*, pg. 312
COMMERZBANK RIO DE JANEIRO SERVICOS LTDA. REPRESENTATIVE OFFICE—See Commerzbank AG; *Int'l*, pg. 312
COMMERZBANK (SWITZERLAND) AG—See Commerzbank AG; *Int'l*, pg. 311
COMMERZBAUMANAGEMENT GMBH—See Commerzbank AG; *Int'l*, pg. 309
COMMERZKOMMUNALBAU GMBH—See Commerzbank AG; *Int'l*, pg. 309
COMMERZLEASING ANLAGEN-VERMIETUNGS GMBH—See Commerzbank AG; *Int'l*, pg. 309
COMMERZLEASING UND IMMOBILIEN GMBH—See Commerzbank AG; *Int'l*, pg. 309
COMMESTSA—See Bertrand Faure; *Int'l*, pg. 193
COMMETRO LEASING, INC.—See Citicorp; *U.S. Public*, pg. 377
COMMLINK—See Jack Henry & Associates, Inc.; *U.S. Public*, pg. 809
COMMNET CELLULAR INC.; *U.S. Public*, pg. 414
COMMODITY INFORMATION SERVICES GROUP—See The McGraw-Hill Companies; *U.S. Public*, pg. 1071
COMMODORE AVIATION—See Israel Aircraft Industries Ltd.; *Int'l*, pg. 690
COMMODORE FINANCIAL CORP.—See Marine Construction & Design Co.; *U.S. Private*, pg. 703
COMMODORE HOLDINGS; *U.S. Public*, pg. 414
COMMODORE NATIONAL LIFE—See CNL Financial Corp.; *U.S. Public*, pg. 282
COMMONWEALTH BANK-SHANGHAI—See Commonwealth Bank Group; *Int'l*, pg. 313
COMMONHEALTH USA—See WPP Group plc; *Int'l*, pg. 1483
COMMONWEALTH ALUMINUM-LEWISPORT—See Commonwealth Industries, Inc.; *U.S. Public*, pg. 415
COMMONWEALTH BANK-BEIJING—See Commonwealth Bank Group; *Int'l*, pg. 313
COMMONWEALTH BANK GROUP; *Int'l*, pg. 312
COMMONWEALTH BANK OF AUSTRALIA-BUSINESS BANKING—See Commonwealth Bank Group; *Int'l*, pg. 312
COMMONWEALTH BANK OF AUSTRALIA-INSTITUTIONAL BANKING—See Commonwealth Bank Group; *Int'l*, pg. 312
COMMONWEALTH BANK OF AUSTRALIA-PERSONAL BANKING—See Commonwealth Bank Group; *Int'l*, pg. 313
COMMONWEALTH BANK OF AUSTRALIA-TECHNOLOGY, OPERATIONS & PROPERTY—See Commonwealth Bank Group; *Int'l*, pg. 313
COMMONWEALTH BANK-VIETNAM—See Commonwealth Bank Group; *Int'l*, pg. 313
COMMONWEALTH BANK-JAKARTA—See Commonwealth Bank Group; *Int'l*, pg. 313
COMMONWEALTH COMMUNICATIONS—See RCN Corporation; *U.S. Public*, pg. 1354
COMMONWEALTH CONTROL, INC.—See Citicorp; *U.S. Public*, pg. 377
COMMONWEALTH DEVELOPMENT BANK—See Commonwealth Bank Group; *Int'l*, pg. 313
COMMONWEALTH EDISON COMPANY OF INDIANA, INC.—See Unicom Corporation; *U.S. Public*, pg. 1664
COMMONWEALTH ELECTRIC CO.—See Commonwealth Energy System; *U.S. Public*, pg. 415
COMMONWEALTH ENERGY SYSTEM; *U.S. Public*, pg. 414

COMMONWEALTH ENERGY SYSTEM, ELECTRIC DIVISION—See Commonwealth Energy System; *U.S. Public*, pg. 414
COMMONWEALTH ENERGY SYSTEM, GAS DIVISION—See Commonwealth Energy System; *U.S. Public*, pg. 414
COMMONWEALTH FINANCIAL SERVICES—See Commonwealth Bank Group; *Int'l*, pg. 313
COMMONWEALTH GAS CO.—See Commonwealth Energy System; *U.S. Public*, pg. 415
COMMONWEALTH GAS SERVICES, INC.—See Columbia Energy Group; *U.S. Public*, pg. 403
COMMONWEALTH INDONESIA—See Atkinson; *U.S. Public*, pg. 143
COMMONWEALTH INDUSTRIES—See Masco Corporation; *U.S. Public*, pg. 1054
COMMONWEALTH INDUSTRIES, INC.; *U.S. Public*, pg. 415
COMMONWEALTH INSURANCE MANAGERS—See Old Guard Insurance Group; *U.S. Public*, pg. 1216
COMMONWEALTH LAND TITLE INSURANCE COMPANY—See Reliance Group Holdings, Inc.; *U.S. Public*, pg. 1374
COMMONWEALTH METAL—See Commercial Metals Company; *U.S. Public*, pg. 412
THE COMMONWEALTH PLAN, INC.—See Citicorp; *U.S. Public*, pg. 377
COMMONWEALTH PROPANE, INC.—See Columbia Energy Group; *U.S. Public*, pg. 403
COMMONWEALTH RELOCATION SERVICES, INC.—See Reliance Group Holdings, Inc.; *U.S. Public*, pg. 1374
COMMONWEALTH RESEARCH CORP.—See Unicom Corporation; *U.S. Public*, pg. 1664
COMMONWEALTH STEEL CO. LTD.—See Australian National Industries Limited; *Int'l*, pg. 101
THE COMMONWEALTH SYSTEM, INC.—See Citicorp; *U.S. Public*, pg. 377
COMMONWEALTH TELEPHONE CO.—See Commonwealth Telephone Enterprises, Inc.; *U.S. Public*, pg. 415
COMMONWEALTH TELEPHONE ENTERPRISES, INC.; *U.S. Public*, pg. 415
COMMONWEALTH TOY & NOVELTY COMPANY; *U.S. Private*, pg. 258
COMMOX—See COGEMA - Compagnie Generale des Matieres Nucleaires; *Int'l*, pg. 305
COMMSCOPE, INC.; *U.S. Public*, pg. 415
COMMTEK COMMUNICATIONS, CORP.; *U.S. Private*, pg. 258
COMMUNAUTE BOULONNAISE DE DEVELOPPEMENT S.A.—See Etablissements Delhaize Freres Et Cie "Le Lion" S.A.; *Int'l*, pg. 463
COMMUNICACION CELULAR S.A. (COMCEL)—See BCE Inc.; *Int'l*, pg. 116
COMMUNICADE—See Omnicom Group Inc.; *U.S. Public*, pg. 1223
COMMUNICATIE & DESIGN—See TBWA GGK Zurick; *Int'l*, pg. 1335
COMMUNICATION CABLE (CCI)-SILER CITY—See Kuhlman Corporation; *U.S. Public*, pg. 968
COMMUNICATION CABLE, INC.—See Kuhlman Corporation; *U.S. Public*, pg. 968
COMMUNICATION GROUP—See Rhone-Poulenc S.A.; *Int'l*, pg. 1109
COMMUNICATION MICROWAVE CORP.—See Thomson S.A.; *Int'l*, pg. 1384
COMMUNICATION SERVICES NEDERLAND BV—See KPN Koninklyke PTT Nederland NV; *Int'l*, pg. 720
COMMUNICATION TECHNIQUES, INC.—See Dover Corporation; *U.S. Public*, pg. 521
COMMUNICATIONS & AUDIO SYSTEMS GROUP—See Sharp Corporation; *Int'l*, pg. 1228
COMMUNICATIONS & CABLEVISION, INC.—See Cable Michigan, Inc.; *U.S. Public*, pg. 287
COMMUNICATIONS CORP. OF INDIANA—See Telephone and Data Systems, Inc.; *U.S. Public*, pg. 1571
COMMUNICATIONS DATA SERVICES, INC.—See The Hearst Corporation; *U.S. Private*, pg. 517
COMMUNICATIONS DIVERSIFIED; *U.S. Private*, pg. 259
COMMUNICATIONS EQUIPMENT CO.—See CD Products, Inc.; *U.S. Public*, pg. 276
COMMUNICATIONS INSTRUMENTS INC.; *U.S. Private*, pg. 259
COMMUNICATIONS INTERNATIONAL (NY); *U.S. Private*, pg. 259
COMMUNICATIONS MACLEAN HUNTER INC.—See Rogers Communications, Inc.; *Int'l*, pg. 1123
COMMUNICATIONS SERVICES PTE. LTD.—See Telefonaktiebolaget LM Ericsson; *Int'l*, pg. 1365
COMMUNICATIONS SOFTWARE DIVISION—See Sterling Commerce, Inc.; *U.S. Public*, pg. 1516
COMMUNICATIONS SUPPLY CORPORATION; *U.S. Private*, pg. 259
COMMUNICATIONS SYSTEMS, INC.; *U.S. Public*, pg. 415
COMMUNICATIONS TECHNOLOGY (CANADA) LTD.—See Danaher Corporation; *U.S. Public*, pg. 480
COMMUNICATIONS TECHNOLOGY CORPORATION—See Danaher Corporation; *U.S. Public*, pg. 480
COMMUNICATIONS TECHNOLOGY GROUP—See Northrop Grumman Corporation; *U.S. Public*, pg. 1199
COMMUNICORP, INC.—See AFLAC Incorporated; *U.S. Public*, pg. 28
COMMUNITY—See Jasper Seating Co., Inc.; *U.S. Private*, pg. 583
COMMUNITY BANCORP; *U.S. Public*, pg. 416
COMMUNITY BANK & TRUST OF S.E. ALABAMA—See Synovus Financial Corp.; *U.S. Public*, pg. 1549
COMMUNITY BANK N.A.—See Community Bank System, Inc.; *U.S. Public*, pg. 416
COMMUNITY BANK OF THE ISLANDS—See NationsBank Corp.; *U.S. Public*, pg. 1162
COMMUNITY BANK SYSTEM, INC.; *U.S. Public*, pg. 416
COMMUNITY BIO-RESOURCES—See Baxter International Inc.; *U.S. Public*, pg. 196

COMMUNITY CARE HEALTH SOLUTIONS INC.—See Pfizer Inc.; *U.S. Public*, pg. 1282

COMMUNITY CASH STORES; *U.S. Private*, pg. 259

COMMUNITY CREDIT CO.—See Norwest Corporation; *U.S. Public*, pg. 1201

COMMUNITY CREDIT CORPORATION—See WSFS Financial Corporation; *U.S. Public*, pg. 1729

COMMUNITY ENERGY ALTERNATIVES INCORPORATED—See Public Service Enterprise Group Incorporated; *U.S. Public*, pg. 1340

COMMUNITY FINANCE CORPORATION—See St. Paul Bancorp, Inc.; *U.S. Public*, pg. 1428

COMMUNITY FIRST BANK & TRUST—See First Financial Bancorp; *U.S. Public*, pg. 633

COMMUNITY FIRST BANKSHARES, INC.; *U.S. Public*, pg. 416

COMMUNITY HEALTH SYSTEMS, INC.—See Forstmann Little & Co.; *U.S. Private*, pg. 419

COMMUNITY HOME OXYGEN, INC.—See Integrated Health Services, Inc.; *U.S. Public*, pg. 884

COMMUNITY HOSPITALS OF GALEN, INC.—See Columbia/HCA Healthcare Corporation; *U.S. Public*, pg. 404

COMMUNITY NATIONAL BANK—See Community Bancorp; *U.S. Public*, pg. 416

COMMUNITY NEWSDEALERS, INC.—See The New York Times Company; *U.S. Public*, pg. 701

COMMUNITY NEWSPAPER HOLDINGS INC.; *U.S. Private*, pg. 259

COMMUNITY NEWSPAPERS—See Gannett Company, Inc.; *U.S. Public*, pg. 701

COMMUNITY PSYCHIATRIC CENTERS OF ARKANSAS, INC.—See Vencor, Inc.; *U.S. Public*, pg. 1712

COMMUNITY PSYCHIATRIC CENTERS OF CALIFORNIA—See Vencor, Inc.; *U.S. Public*, pg. 1712

COMMUNITY PSYCHIATRIC CENTERS OF FLORIDA, INC.—See Vencor, Inc.; *U.S. Public*, pg. 1712

COMMUNITY PSYCHIATRIC CENTERS OF IDAHO, INC.—See Vencor, Inc.; *U.S. Public*, pg. 1712

COMMUNITY PSYCHIATRIC CENTERS OF INDIANA, INC.—See Vencor, Inc.; *U.S. Public*, pg. 1712

COMMUNITY PSYCHIATRIC CENTERS OF KANSAS, INC.—See Vencor, Inc.; *U.S. Public*, pg. 1712

COMMUNITY PSYCHIATRIC CENTERS OF LONDON (UNLIMITED)—See Vencor, Inc.; *U.S. Public*, pg. 1716

COMMUNITY PSYCHIATRIC CENTERS OF MISSISSIPPI, INC.—See Vencor, Inc.; *U.S. Public*, pg. 1712

COMMUNITY PSYCHIATRIC CENTERS OF MISSOURI, INC.—See Vencor, Inc.; *U.S. Public*, pg. 1712

COMMUNITY PSYCHIATRIC CENTERS OF NORTH CAROLINA, INC.—See Vencor, Inc.; *U.S. Public*, pg. 1712

COMMUNITY PSYCHIATRIC CENTERS OF OREGON, INC.—See Vencor, Inc.; *U.S. Public*, pg. 1712

COMMUNITY PSYCHIATRIC CENTERS OF UTAH, INC.—See Vencor, Inc.; *U.S. Public*, pg. 1712

COMMUNITY PSYCHIATRIC CENTERS PROPERTIES, INC.—See Vencor, Inc.; *U.S. Public*, pg. 1712

COMMUNITY RESEARCH & DEVELOPMENT, INC.—See The Rouse Company; *U.S. Public*, pg. 1407

COMNET CORPORATION; *U.S. Public*, pg. 416

COMO GRAIN CO.—See Tom Wade Co.; *U.S. Private*, pg. 1145

OWEN COMORA ASSOCIATES—See Serino Coyne Inc.; *U.S. Private*, pg. 985

COMP-AIRE—See Groupe Strafor Facom; *Int'l*, pg. 569

COMP-AIRE SYSTEMS INC.—See BTR plc; *Int'l*, pg. 126

COMP-U-CARD DIVISION—See Cendant Corporation; *U.S. Public*, pg. 320

COMPAC CORPORATION—See Masco Corporation; *U.S. Public*, pg. 1054

COMPACK DOUWE EGBERTS RT—See Sara Lee Corporation; *U.S. Public*, pg. 1434

COMPACTION AMERICA—See United Dominion Industries, Ltd.; *U.S. Public*, pg. 1676

COMPAGNIA DI GENOVA—See Allianz Aktiengesellschaft; *Int'l*, pg. 61

COMPAGNIA EURPOEA D'ASSICURAZIONE—See Allianz Aktiengesellschaft; *Int'l*, pg. 61

COMPAGNIA FINANZIAMENTI E. RIFINANZIAMENTI COFIRI S.P.A.—See IRI Istituto Ricostruzione Industriale; *Int'l*, pg. 652

COMPAGNIA GENERALE ELETTROMECCANICA S.P.A. (COGEMEC)—See The General Electric Company, p.l.c.; *Int'l*, pg. 545

COMPAGNIE AFRICAINE DE GEOPHYSIQUE—See CGG Group; *Int'l*, pg. 241

COMPAGNIE AFRICAINE DE PREPARATIONS ALIMENTAIRES CAPRAL NESTLE—See Nestle S.A.; *Int'l*, pg. 920

COMPAGNIE AUXILAIRE DE TELECOMMUNICATIONS—See France Telecom; *Int'l*, pg. 503

COMPAGNIE BRAND ET ASSOCIES S.A.—See Enso Oyj; *Int'l*, pg. 457

COMPAGNIE CII-HB INTERNATIONALE N.V.—See Compagnie des Machines Bull; *Int'l*, pg. 319

COMPAGNIE CONTINENTALE D'ASSURANCES S.A.—See Assicurazioni Generali S.p.A.; *Int'l*, pg. 90

COMPAGNIE COPPEE DE DEVELOPPEMENT INDUSTRIEL-CDI—See Lafarge S.A.; *Int'l*, pg. 790

COMPAGNIE D'ETUDES ET DE TRAITEMENT DE L'INFORMATION S.A.—See Halliburton Company; *U.S. Public*, pg. 776

COMPAGNIE DAKAR SAINT-LOUIS S.A.—See Assicurazioni Generali S.p.A.; *Int'l*, pg. 90

COMPAGNIE D'ASSURANCE DU QUEBEC—See Royal & Sun Alliance Insurance Group plc; *Int'l*, pg. 1131

COMPAGNIE DE CONSTRUCTION MECANIQUE SULZER—See Sulzer Ltd.; *Int'l*, pg. 1305

COMPAGNIE DE FAISCEAUX TUNISIAN INTERNATIONAL S.A.—See General Motors Corporation; *U.S. Public*, pg. 723

COMPAGNIE DE GESTION ET DE BANQUE GONET SA—See Generale de Banque S.A.; *Int'l*, pg. 548

COMPAGNIE DE PARTICIPATIONS BIOCHIMIQUES (COPABIO)—See Lafarge S.A.; *Int'l*, pg. 788

COMPAGNIE DE SAINT-GOBAIN-PONT-A MOUSSON—See Compagnie de Suez; *Int'l*, pg. 313

COMPAGNIE DE SAINT-GOBAIN SUCC. ZWEIGNIEDERLASSUNG DEUTSCHLAND—See Saint-Gobain; *Int'l*, pg. 1177

COMPAGNIE DE SUEZ; *Int'l*, pg. 313

COMPAGNIE DES ENTREPRISES CFE—See Lyonnaise des Eaux S.A.; *Int'l*, pg. 823

COMPAGNIE DES DISPOSITIFS SEMI-CONDUCTEURS WESTINGHOUSE—See Jeumont-Schneider Trenformeteurs; *Int'l*, pg. 706

COMPAGNIE DES GAZ DE PETROLE PRIMAGAZ S.A.—See SHV Holdings N.V.; *Int'l*, pg. 1155

COMPAGNIE DES IMMEUBLES DES LA PLAINE MONCEAU—See AXA-UAP; *Int'l*, pg. 18

COMPAGNIE DES MACHINES BULL; *Int'l*, pg. 315

COMPAGNIE DES MARGARINES, SAVONS ET COSMETIQUES AU ZAIRE S.A.R.L.—See Unilever Plc; *Int'l*, pg. 1436

COMPAGNIE DES MINES D-URANIUM DE FRANCEVILLE (COMUF)—See COGEMA - Compagnie Generale des Matieres Nucleaires; *Int'l*, pg. 305

S.A. COMPAGNIE DES PRODUITS INDUSTRIELS C.P.I.—See Cockerill Sambre; *Int'l*, pg. 302

S.A. COMPAGNIE DES PRODUITS SIDERURGIQUES COPROSID—See Cockerill Sambre; *Int'l*, pg. 301

COMPAGNIE DES SABLIERES DE LA SEINE—See Lafarge S.A.; *Int'l*, pg. 788

COMPAGNIE DES VERNIS VALENTINE SA—See Imperial Chemical Industries PLC; *Int'l*, pg. 664

COMPAGNIE EUROPEENNE DE DEZINGAGE "C.E.D." S.A.—See Koninklijke Hoogovens N.V.; *Int'l*, pg. 754

COMPAGNIE EUROPEENNE DE FINANCEMENT S.A.—See Tractebel; *Int'l*, pg. 1415

COMPAGNIE EUROPEENNE DES PEINTURES JULIEN SA—See Imperial Chemical Industries PLC; *Int'l*, pg. 664

COMPAGNIE FERMIERE DE L'ETABLISSEMENT THERMAL DE VICHY—See Nestle S.A.; *Int'l*, pg. 919

COMPAGNIE FINANCIERE DE LA COTE D'IVOIRE—See Bank Brussels Lambert; *Int'l*, pg. 149

COMPAGNIE FINANCIERE DE PARIBAS—See AXA-UAP; *Int'l*, pg. 319

COMPAGNIE FINANCIERE DE PARIS—See AXA-UAP; *Int'l*, pg. 18

COMPAGNIE FRANCAIS BUTTNER S.A.—See Deutsche Babcock AG; *Int'l*, pg. 399

COMPAGNIE FRANÇAISE D'INVESTISSEMENT—See Compagnie des Machines Bull; *Int'l*, pg. 319

COMPAGNIE FRANCAISE DE BOISSONS GAZEUSES—See Nestle S.A.; *Int'l*, pg. 918

COMPAGNIE FRANCAISE DE FORGES ET FONDRIES (C3F)—See Groupe Usinor; *Int'l*, pg. 571

COMPAGNIE FRANCAISE DE L'ETAIN—See Royal Dutch/Shell Group of Companies; *Int'l*, pg. 1138

COMPAGNIE FRANCAISE DE MANUTENTION—See Manitou BF; *Int'l*, pg. 834

COMPAGNIE FRANCAISE DE MOKTA (CFM)—See COGEMA - Compagnie Generale des Matieres Nucleaires; *Int'l*, pg. 305

COMPAGNIE FRANCAISE DES PETROLES (ALGERIE) CFP (A)—See Total S.A.; *Int'l*, pg. 1409

COMPAGNIE FRANCAISE PHILIPS—See Philips Electronics N.V.; *Int'l*, pg. 1055

COMPAGNIE GENERALE DE CHAUFFE—See Compagnie Generale Des Eaux; *Int'l*, pg. 321

COMPAGNIE GENERALE DE GEOPHYSIQUE—See CGG Group; *Int'l*, pg. 241

COMPAGNIE GENERALE DE GEOPHYSIQUE (FAR EAST)—See CGG Group; *Int'l*, pg. 241

COMPAGNIE GENERALE DE PREVOYANCE—See Allianz Aktiengesellschaft; *Int'l*, pg. 60

COMPAGNIE GENERALE DES EAUX; *Int'l*, pg. 321

COMPAGNIE GENERALE DES ETABLISSEMENTS MICHELIN; *Int'l*, pg. 322

COMPAGNIE GENERALE MARITIME—See Compagnie Generale Maritime et Financiere; *Int'l*, pg. 322

COMPAGNIE GENERALE MARITIME ET FINANCIERE; *Int'l*, pg. 322

COMPAGNIE HOBART, S.A.—See Premark International, Inc.; *U.S. Public*, pg. 1322

COMPAGNIE IBM FRANCE, S.A.—See International Business Machines Corporation; *U.S. Public*, pg. 897

COMPAGNIE IMMOBILIERE DE BELGIQUE S.A.—See Tractebel; *Int'l*, pg. 1415

COMPAGNIE INDUSTRIELLE DE MATERIELS DE MANUTENTION—See Manitou BF; *Int'l*, pg. 834

COMPAGNIE INGERSOLL-RAND S.A.—See Ingersoll-Rand Company; *U.S. Public*, pg. 878

COMPAGNIE INTERNATIONALE D'ASSURANCES ET REASSURANCES (CIAR)—See Corporacion MAPFRE, Compania Internacional de Reaseguros, S.A.; *Int'l*, pg. 335

COMPAGNIE INTERNATIONALE DES PRODUITS SANITAIRES (CIPS) JACOB DELAFON—See Kohler Company; *U.S. Private*, pg. 631

COMPAGNIE LAITIERE BESNIER; *Int'l*, pg. 322

COMPAGNIE MINIERE D'AKOUTA (COMINAK)—See COGEMA - Compagnie Generale des Matieres Nucleaires; *Int'l*, pg. 305

COMPAGNIE PARISIENNE DE REESCOMPTE—See Compagnie de Suez; *Int'l*, pg. 313

COMPAGNIE PHONOGRAPHIQUE FRANCAISE BARCLAY—See Philips Electronics N.V.; *Int'l*, pg. 1053

COMPAGNIE REUNIONAISE D'IMPORTATION DE CIMENT—See Lafarge S.A.; *Int'l*, pg. 788

COMPAGNIE UAP; *Int'l*, pg. 323

COMPAGNIE VERSAILLAISE DE TRANSPORTS—See Lagardere Groupe; *Int'l*, pg. 792

COMPAIN BOIS ET MATERIAUX—See La Meridionale des Bois et Materiaux; *Int'l*, pg. 784

COMPAIR LEROI—See Siebe plc; *Int'l*, pg. 1242

COMPAIR MAKO—See Siebe plc; *Int'l*, pg. 1242

COMPANHIA ADMINISTRADORA SAO LOURENCO—See Saint-Gobain; *Int'l*, pg. 1177

COMPANHIA ADRIATICA DE SEGUROS GERAIS—See Allianz Aktiengesellschaft; *Int'l*, pg. 61

COMPANHIA BRASILEIRA DE ESTIRENO—See Monsanto Company; *U.S. Public*, pg. 1125

COMPANHIA BRASILIERA CARBURETO DE CALCIO—See Solvay S.A.; *Int'l*, pg. 1278

COMPANHIA DE CONSTRUCAO E ENGENHARIA KIN SUN (MACAU)—See Bilfinger + Berger Bauaktiengesellschaft; *Int'l*, pg. 196

COMPANHIA DE SEGUROS METROPOLE S.A.—See Zurich Insurance Company; *Int'l*, pg. 1531

COMPANHIA EXPORTADORA DE MELACOS LTDA.—See Tate & Lyle PLC; *Int'l*, pg. 1357

COMPANHIA GOODYEAR DO BRASIL PRODUTOS DE BORRACHA—See The Goodyear Tire & Rubber Company; *U.S. Public*, pg. 753

COMPANHIA HOTELS PALACE—See Sea Containers Ltd.; *Int'l*, pg. 1214

COMPANHIA IBM PORTUGUESA, S.A.R.L.—See International Business Machines Corporation; *U.S. Public*, pg. 897

COMPANHIA INDUSTRIAL CELULOSE E PAPEL GUAIBA—See Melitta Unternehmensgruppe Bentz KG; *Int'l*, pg. 857

COMPANHIA METALLURGICA BARBARA—See Saint-Gobain; *Int'l*, pg. 1176

COMPANHIA NACIONAL DE CIMENTO PORTLAND (C.N.C.P.)—See Lafarge S.A.; *Int'l*, pg. 789

COMPANHIA NACIONAL DE OXIGENIO S.A.—See Praxair Inc.; *U.S. Public*, pg. 1320

COMPANHIA NIPO-BRASILEIRA DE PELOTIZACAO-NIBRASCO—See NKK Corporation; *Int'l*, pg. 903

COMPANHIA NIPO-BRASILEIRA DE PELOTIZACAO-NIBRASCO—See Nissho Iwai Corporation; *Int'l*, pg. 949

A.S. COMPANHIA PORTUGUESA DE SEGUROS—See La Fondiaria Assicurazioni S.p.A.; *Int'l*, pg. 784

COMPANHIA PRODUTORA DE ALIMENTOS S.A.—See Nestle S.A.; *Int'l*, pg. 920

COMPANHIA SIDERURGICA BELGO-MINEIRA—See Arbed S.A.; *Int'l*, pg. 79

COMPANHIA SIDERURGICA BELGO-MINEIRA—See Nissho Iwai Corporation; *Int'l*, pg. 949

COMPANHIA VIDRARIA SANTA MARINA—See Saint-Gobain; *Int'l*, pg. 1172

COMPANHIA VIDREIRA NACIONAL SA—See Saint-Gobain; *Int'l*, pg. 1172

COMPANIA ANONIMA DE SEGUROS "AVILA"—See Cigna Corp.; *U.S. Public*, pg. 364

COMPANIA ANONIMA ERICSSON—See Telefonaktiebolaget LM Ericsson; *Int'l*, pg. 1365

COMPANIA ANONIMA GOODYEAR DE VENEZUELA—See The Goodyear Tire & Rubber Company; *U.S. Public*, pg. 753

COMPANIA ANONIMA TOCARS—See Toyota Motor Corporation; *Int'l*, pg. 1413

COMPANIA ASEGURADORA ARGENTINA S.A.—See Allianz Aktiengesellschaft; *Int'l*, pg. 61

COMPANIA CASCO S.A. I.C.—See Borden, Inc.; *U.S. Private*, pg. 159

COMPANIA CELULAR COLOMBIA COCELCO, S.A.—See Telefonica de Espana, S.A.; *Int'l*, pg. 1373

COMPANIA COLOMBIANA DE FINANCIAMIENTOS, S.A.—See Citicorp; *U.S. Public*, pg. 379

COMPANIA COLOMBIANA DE GRASAS "COGRA-LEVER" S.A.—See Unilever Plc; *Int'l*, pg. 1436

COMPANIA DE ASISTENCIA DE LOS ANDES, S.A.—See Corporacion MAPFRE, Compania Internacional de Reaseguros, S.A.; *Int'l*, pg. 334

COMPANIA DE CHICLE ADAMS, INC.—See Warner-Lambert Company; *U.S. Public*, pg. 1739

COMPANIA DE FINANCIACION CASE, S.A.—See Tenneco Inc.; *U.S. Public*, pg. 1579

COMPANIA DE MOTORES DOMESTICOS, S.A. DE C.V.—See Emerson Electric Co.; *U.S. Public*, pg. 576

COMPANIA DE PETROLEO SHELL DEL PERU S.A.—See Royal Dutch/Shell Group of Companies; *Int'l*, pg. 1141

COMPANIA DE RADIOCOMUNICACIONES MOVILES S.A.—See BellSouth Corporation; *U.S. Public*, pg. 208

COMPANIA DE SEGURO ATLAS S.A.—See Assicurazioni Generali S.p.A.; *Int'l*, pg. 90

COMPANIA DE SEGUROS DE VIDA EUROAMERICA, S.A.—See Corporacion MAPFRE, Compania Internacional de Reaseguros, S.A.; *Int'l*, pg. 333

COMPANIA DE SEGUROS GENERALES EUROAMERICA S.A.—See Corporacion MAPFRE, Compania Internacional de Reaseguros, S.A.; *Int'l*, pg. 333

COMPANIA DE SEGUROS LA CHILENA CONSOLIDADA—See Zurich Insurance Company; *Int'l*, pg. 1531

COMPANIA DEL NORTE Y ORIENTE PARA INVERSIONES, S.A.—See Corporacion MAPFRE, Compania Internacional de Reaseguros, S.A.; *Int'l*, pg. 333

COMPANIA DISTRIBUIDORA DEL CENTRO S.A. DE C.V.—See Pfizer Inc.; *U.S. Public*, pg. 1283

COMPANIA DOMINICANA DE TELEFONOS, C. POR A.—See GTE Corporation; *U.S. Public*, pg. 697

COMPANIA DOWSON—See The Bank of New York Company, Inc.; *U.S. Public*, pg. 179

COMPAÑIA ECUATORIANA DE BALSA S.A.—See Baltek Corporation; *U.S. Public*, pg. 172

COMPANIA ERICSSON DE CHILE S.A.—See Telefonaktiebolaget LM Ericsson; *Int'l*, pg. 1365

COMPANIA ERICSSON S.A.—See Telefonaktiebolaget LM Ericsson; *Int'l*, pg. 1365

COMPANIA ERICSSON S.A.C.I.—See Telefonaktiebolaget LM Ericsson; *Int'l*, pg. 1365

COMPANIA ESPANOLA DE PETROLEOS, S.A. (CEPSA); *Int'l*, pg. 323

COMPANIA ESPANOLA DE TABACO EN RAMA, S.A.—See Tabacalera; *Int'l*, pg. 1346

COMPANIA ESPANOLA DE TECNOLOGIA, S.A.—See Telefonica de Espana, S.A.; *Int'l*, pg. 1371

COMPANIA ESPANOLA PARA LA FABRICACION DE ACERO INOXIDABLE S.A.—See Nissho Iwai Corporation; *Int'l*, pg. 947

COMPANIA FARMACEUTICA UPJOHN S.A.—See Pharmacia & Upjohn, Inc.; *Int'l*, pg. 1049

COMPANIA GENERAL DE ESENCIAS GRUPO FLORASYNTH S.A.—See Bayer AG; *Int'l*, pg. 173

COMPANIA GENERAL DE GEOFISICA S.A.—See CGG Group; *Int'l*, pg. 241

COMPANIA GENERAL DE TABACOS DE FILIPINAS, S.A.—See Tabacalera, S.A.; *Int'l*, pg. 1345

COMPANIA GESTORA DE SERVICIO MENSATEL, S.A.—See Telefonica de Espana, S.A.; *Int'l*, pg. 1372

COMPANIA GIVA S.A.—See The Gillette Company; *U.S. Public*, pg. 744

COMPANIA GOODYEAR DEL PERU, S.A.—See The Goodyear Tire & Rubber Company; *U.S. Public*, pg. 753

COMPANIA GRANADINA DE SEGUROS DE VIDA S.A.—See Assicurazioni Generali S.p.A.; *Int'l*, pg. 91

COMPANIA GRANADINA DE SEGUROS S.A.—See Assicurazioni Generali S.p.A.; *Int'l*, pg. 91

COMPANIA HALLIBOURTON DE CEMENTACION—See Halliburton Company; *U.S. Public*, pg. 776

COMPANIA HULERA GOODYEAR-OXO SOCIEDAD ANONIMA—See The Goodyear Tire & Rubber Company; *U.S. Public*, pg. 753

COMPANIA HULERA SULA, S.A. DE C.V.—See American Biltrite Inc.; *U.S. Public*, pg. 69

COMPANIA IMPORTADORA DE MAQUINAS COPLADORES SA—See N.V. Koninklijke KNP BT; *Int'l*, pg. 757

COMPANIA INDUSTRIAL DE SAN CRISTOBAL, S.A.—See Kimberly-Clark Corporation; *U.S. Public*, pg. 960

COMPANIA INGERSOLL ESPANOLA, S.A.—See Ingersoll-Rand Company; *U.S. Public*, pg. 878

COMPANIA INTERNACIONAL DE VENTAS, S.A.—See Borden, Inc.; *U.S. Private*, pg. 159

COMPANIA LATINOAMERICA DE SOFTWARE (LASC)—See Marcam Solutions, Inc.; *U.S. Public*, pg. 1043

COMPANIA LOGISTICA DE HIDROCARBUROS - CLH, S.A.—See Repsol S.A.; *Int'l*, pg. 1104

COMPANIA MEDICINAL LA CAMPANA, S.A. DE C.V.—See Warner-Lambert Company; *U.S. Public*, pg. 1739

COMPANIA MERCANTIL INTERCONTINENTAL, S.A. DE C.V.—See BASF AG; *Int'l*, pg. 107

COMPANIA MEXICANA DE GEOFISICA—See CGG Group; *Int'l*, pg. 241

COMPANIA MEXICANA TRI-SURE, S.A. DE C.V.—See Royal Packaging Industries Van Leer B.V.; *Int'l*, pg. 1146

COMPANIA MINERA AUTLAN S.A. DE C.V.; *Int'l*, pg. 324

COMPANIA MINERA CERRO COLORADO LIMITADA—See Rio Algom Limited; *Int'l*, pg. 1118

COMPANIA MINERA DISPUTADA DE LAS CONDES S.S.—See Exxon Corporation; *U.S. Public*, pg. 601

COMPANIA MINERA LAS CUEVAS S.A. DE C.V.—See Grupo Industrial Camesa S.A. de C.V.; *Int'l*, pg. 575

COMPANIA MINERA MANTOS DE ORO—See Placer Dome Inc.; *Int'l*, pg. 1060

COMPANIA MINERA RIOCHILEX S.A.—See Rio Algom Limited; *Int'l*, pg. 1118

COMPANIA MINERA ZALDIVAR—See Outokumpu Oyj; *Int'l*, pg. 1016

COMPANIA MINERA ZALDIVAR S.A.—See Outokumpu Oyj; *Int'l*, pg. 1016

COMPANIA MSA DE ARGENTINA, S.A.—See Mine Safety Appliances Co.; *U.S. Public*, pg. 1114

COMPANIA NACIONAL DE DIRECCIONES AUTOMOTRICES, S.A. DE C.V.—See General Motors Corporation; *U.S. Public*, pg. 724

COMPANIA NACIONAL DE HARINAS, S.A. DE C.V.—See Tablex, S.A. de C.V.; *Int'l*, pg. 1346

COMPANIA NACIONAL DE MINERACAO—See TVX Gold Inc.; *Int'l*, pg. 1345

COMPANIA NACIONAL DE MINERIA CNM LDA.—See TVX Gold Inc.; *Int'l*, pg. 1345

COMPANIA NACIONAL DE RENTAS—See Corporacion MAPFRE, Compania Internacional de Reaseguros, S.A.; *Int'l*, pg. 335

COMPANIA NHK CIMEBRA-COMERCIAL INDUSTRIAL E MECANICA BRASILEIRA—See Nissho Iwai Corporation; *Int'l*, pg. 947

COMPANIA PERUANA DE ALIMENTOS S.A.—See Nestle S.A.; *Int'l*, pg. 920

COMPANIA QUIMICA BORDEN, S.A.—See Borden, Inc.; *U.S. Private*, pg. 159

COMPANIA RADIO AEREA MARITIMA ESPANOLA, S.A.—See SAIT-RadioHolland Group S.A.; *Int'l*, pg. 1152

COMPANIA SCHOLL S.A.—See Scholl Plc; *Int'l*, pg. 1209

COMPANIA SHERWIN-WILLIAMS, S.A. DE C.V.—See The Sherwin-Williams Company; *U.S. Public*, pg. 1466

COMPANIA SIDERURGIA DE GUADALAJARA—See Grupo Sidek, S.A. de C.V.; *Int'l*, pg. 576

COMPANIA SUIZA DE REASEGUROS—See Swiss Reinsurance Company; *Int'l*, pg. 1333

COMPANIA TELEFONOS CHILE (C.T.C.)—See Telefonica de Espana, S.A.; *Int'l*, pg. 1373

COMPANION LIFE INSURANCE CO.—See Mutual of Omaha Insurance Company; *U.S. Private*, pg. 770

COMPANY STORE HOLDINGS, INC.—See Hanover Direct, Inc.; *U.S. Public*, pg. 782

COMPAQ CANADA, INC.—See COMPAQ Computer Corporation; *U.S. Public*, pg. 418

COMPAQ COMPUTER AG—See COMPAQ Computer Corporation; *U.S. Public*, pg. 418

COMPAQ COMPUTER A/S—See COMPAQ Computer Corporation; *U.S. Public*, pg. 418

COMPAQ COMPUTER ASIA PTE LTD.—See COMPAQ Computer Corporation; *U.S. Public*, pg. 418

COMPAQ COMPUTER B.V.—See COMPAQ Computer Corporation; *U.S. Public*, pg. 418

COMPAQ COMPUTER CORPORATION; *U.S. Public*, pg. 417

COMPAQ COMPUTER GMBH—See COMPAQ Computer Corporation; *U.S. Public*, pg. 418

COMPAQ COMPUTER HONG KONG LIMITED—See COMPAQ Computer Corporation; *U.S. Public*, pg. 418

COMPAQ COMPUTER JAPAN KK—See COMPAQ Computer Corporation; *U.S. Public*, pg. 418

COMPAQ COMPUTER LIMITED—See COMPAQ Computer Corporation; *U.S. Public*, pg. 418

COMPAQ COMPUTER MFG. LTD.—See COMPAQ Computer Corporation; *U.S. Public*, pg. 418

COMPAQ COMPUTER NEW ZEALAND LTD.—See COMPAQ Computer Corporation; *U.S. Public*, pg. 418

COMPAQ COMPUTER NORWAY A/S—See COMPAQ Computer Corporation; *U.S. Public*, pg. 418

COMPAQ COMPUTER N.V./S.A.—See COMPAQ Computer Corporation; *U.S. Public*, pg. 418

COMPAQ COMPUTER S.A.—See COMPAQ Computer Corporation; *U.S. Public*, pg. 418

COMPAQ COMPUTER S.A.R.L.—See COMPAQ Computer Corporation; *U.S. Public*, pg. 418

COMPAQ COMPUTER S.P.A.—See COMPAQ Computer Corporation; *U.S. Public*, pg. 418

COMPAR—See Antonio Puig SA; *Int'l*, pg. 1073

COMPAREX INFORMATION SYSTEMS B.V.—See BASF AG; *Int'l*, pg. 108

COMPAREX INFORMATION SYSTEMS S.A./N.V.—See BASF AG; *Int'l*, pg. 108

COMPAREX INFORMATIONSSYSTEME GES.M.B.H.—See BASF AG; *Int'l*, pg. 108

COMPAREX INFORMATIONSSYSTEME GMBH—See BASF AG; *Int'l*, pg. 105

COMPAREX SISTEMAS INFORMATICOS S.A.—See BASF AG; *Int'l*, pg. 108

COMPART SpA; pg. 324

COMPAS ELECTRONICS, INC.—See AIM Safety Company Inc.; *Int'l*, pg. 36

COMPASS BANCSHARES, INC.; *U.S. Public*, pg. 418

COMPASS BANK—See Compass Bancshares, Inc.; *U.S. Public*, pg. 418

COMPASS BANK DALLAS—See Compass Bancshares, Inc.; *U.S. Public*, pg. 419

COMPASS BANK HOUSTON—See Compass Bancshares, Inc.; *U.S. Public*, pg. 419

COMPASS BANK OF THE SOUTH, N.A.—See Compass Bancshares, Inc.; *U.S. Public*, pg. 419

COMPASS DESIGN AUTOMATION INC.—See VLSI Technology, Inc.; *U.S. Public*, pg. 1703

COMPASS DISTRIBUTION—See Paradigm Communications; *U.S. Private*, pg. 838

COMPASS FOODS, INC.—See Tengelmann Warenhandelsgesellschaft; *Int'l*, pg. 1375

COMPASS GROUP, INC.—See U.S. Bancorp; *U.S. Public*, pg. 1681

COMPASS GROUP, INTERNATIONAL—See Compass Group plc; *Int'l*, pg. 325

COMPASS GROUP PLC; *Int'l*, pg. 324

COMPASS GROUP-SCANDANAVIAN DIVISION—See Compass Group plc; *Int'l*, pg. 325

COMPASS GROUP-UK DIVISION—See Compass Group plc; *Int'l*, pg. 324

COMPASS GROUP-USA DIVISION—See Compass Group plc; *Int'l*, pg. 324

COMPASS INVESTMENT SERVICES—See North Fork Bancorporation, Inc.; *U.S. Public*, pg. 1194

COMPDATA SERVICES CORP.—See CDI Corp.; *U.S. Public*, pg. 277

COMPENDIUM SYSTEMS CORPORATION; *U.S. Private*, pg. 259

COMPETITIVE MEDIA REPORTING—See VNU Verenigde Nederlandse Uitgeversbedrijven B.V.; *Int'l*, pg. 1447

COMPHEALTH, INC.—See Horizon/CMS Healthcare Corporation; *U.S. Public*, pg. 839

COMPILERS PLUS INC.—See American Business Information, Inc.; *U.S. Public*, pg. 70

COMPLAN, INC.—See Citicorp; *U.S. Public*, pg. 377

COMPLAST, INC.; *U.S. Private*, pg. 259

COMPO EM—See G.T.C. Transcontinental Group Ltd.; *Int'l*, pg. 538

COMPO GMBH PRODUKTIONS UND VERTRIEBSGESELLSCHAFT—See BASF AG; *Int'l*, pg. 104

COMPOFLEX—See Senior Engineering Group, plc.; *Int'l*, pg. 1221

COMPONEDEX LTD.—See Telefonaktiebolaget LM Ericsson; *Int'l*, pg. 1365

COMPONENT OPERATIONS—See Chrysler Corporation; *U.S. Public*, pg. 353

COMPONENT PRODUCTS CO.—See Sony Corporation; *Int'l*, pg. 1281

COMPONENT PRODUCTS DIVISION—See Standard Microsystems Corporation; *U.S. Public*, pg. 1503

COMPONENTA BENELUX—See Svedala Industri AB; *Int'l*, pg. 1326

COMPONENTA BENELUX/BRANCH OFFICE BELGIUM—See Trelleborg AB; *Int'l*, pg. 1421

COMPONENTA BENELUX B.V.—See Trelleborg AB; *Int'l*, pg. 1421

COMPONENTA DYNAPAC AB—See Trelleborg AB; *Int'l*, pg. 1419

COMPONENTA GJUTERIER AB—See Trelleborg AB; *Int'l*, pg. 1419

COMPONENTA INDUSTRI—See Svedala Industri AB; *Int'l*, pg. 1323

COMPONENTA INTERNATIONAL A/S—See Trelleborg AB; *Int'l*, pg. 1421

COMPONENTA INTERNATIONAL B.V.—See Trelleborg AB; *Int'l*, pg. 1421

COMPONENTA INTERNATIONAL DEUTSCHLAND GMBH—See Trelleborg AB; *Int'l*, pg. 1421

COMPONENTA INTERNATIONAL FRANCE S.A.—See Trelleborg AB; *Int'l*, pg. 1421

COMPONENTA INTERNATIONAL GMBH—See Trelleborg AB; *Int'l*, pg. 1421

COMPONENTA INTERNATIONAL INC.—See Trelleborg AB; *Int'l*, pg. 1421

COMPONENTA INTERNATIONAL LTD.—See Trelleborg AB; *Int'l*, pg. 1421

COMPONENTA INTERNATIONAL MARKETING (F.E.) PTE. LTD.—See Trelleborg AB; *Int'l*, pg. 1421

COMPONENTA INTERNATIONAL SCANDINAVIA AB—See Trelleborg AB; *Int'l*, pg. 1421

COMPONENTA INTERNATIONAL S.P.A.—See Trelleborg AB; *Int'l*, pg. 1421

COMPONENTA KRANLYFT AB—See Trelleborg AB; *Int'l*, pg. 1419

COMPONENTA PARTS AB—See Trelleborg AB; *Int'l*, pg. 1421

COMPONENTA TOOLS AB—See Trelleborg AB; *Int'l*, pg. 1421

COMPONENTA TRANSPORT AB—See Trelleborg AB; *Int'l*, pg. 1420

COMPONENTA VAGSTAL AB—See Trelleborg AB; *Int'l*, pg. 1421

COMPONENTA WEAR PARTS—See Svedala Industri AB; *Int'l*, pg. 1323

COMPONENTES DELFA, C.A.—See General Motors Corporation; *U.S. Public*, pg. 724

COMPONENTES MECANICOS DE MATAMOROS S.A. DE C.V.—See General Motors Corporation; *U.S. Public*, pg. 721

COMPONENTS AND INDUSTRIAL PRODUCTS—See Litton Industries, Inc.; *U.S. Public*, pg. 1002

COMPONENTS CORPORATION OF AMERICA; *U.S. Private*, pg. 259

COMPONENTS DIVISION/BEDEK AVIATION GROUP—See Israel Aircraft Industries Ltd.; *Int'l*, pg. 690

COMPOOL CORPORATION—See Essef Corporation; *U.S. Public*, pg. 592

COMPOSITE PRODUCTS, INC.—See Masco Corporation; *U.S. Public*, pg. 1053

COMPOSITE RESEARCH & MANAGEMENT COMPANY—See Washington Mutual Inc.; *U.S. Public*, pg. 1742

COMPOSITE STRUCTURES INTERNATIONAL, INC.—See RPM, Inc.; *U.S. Public*, pg. 1357

COMPOSITE THREAD PROTECTORS, INC.—See Sammons Enterprises, Inc.; *U.S. Private*, pg. 963

COMPOSITES DISTRIBUTION CORP.—See GLS Corporation; *U.S. Private*, pg. 435

COMPREHENSIVE BEHAVIORAL CARE, INC.—See Comprehensive Care Corporation; *U.S. Public*, pg. 419

COMPREHENSIVE BENEFITS SERVICE CO., INC.—See First Health Group Corp.; *U.S. Public*, pg. 635

COMPREHENSIVE BUSINESS SERVICES INC.—See Franchise Services, Inc.; *U.S. Private*, pg. 423

COMPREHENSIVE CANCER CENTERS—See Zeneca Group Plc; *Int'l*, pg. 1525

COMPREHENSIVE CARE CORPORATION; *U.S. Public*, pg. 419

COMPREHENSIVE CARE INTEGRATION—See Comprehensive Care Corporation; *U.S. Public*, pg. 419

COMPREMEDX, INC.—See Continental Health Affiliates, Inc.; *U.S. Public*, pg. 440

COMPRESSOR SYSTEMS, INC.—See Pearson plc; *Int'l*, pg. 1027

COMPRINT, INC.—See The Washington Post Company; *U.S. Public*, pg. 1743

COMPSEE, INC.—See McRae Industries, Inc.; *U.S. Public*, pg. 1073

COMPSOLVEN CORPORATION—See Caterpillar Inc.; *U.S. Public*, pg. 316

COMPTEK FEDERAL SYSTEMS, INC.—See Comptek Research, Inc.; *U.S. Public*, pg. 419

COMPTEK RESEARCH, INC.; *U.S. Public*, pg. 419

COMPTOIR DES FERS ET METAUX SA—See Mannesmann A.G.; *Int'l*, pg. 838

S.A. COMPTOIR FINLANDAIS N.V.—See Enso Oyj; *Int'l*, pg. 457

COMPTOIR GENERAL DES GLACES (CGG)—See Saint-Gobain; *Int'l*, pg. 1172

COMPTOIR NORMAND DE PRODUITS VERRIERS (CNPV)—See Saint-Gobain; *Int'l*, pg. 1170

COMPTON PARTNERS—See Saatchi & Saatchi Advertising Worldwide; *U.S. Public*, pg. 1422

COMPU'TRAIN BV—See N.V. Koninklijke KNP BT; *Int'l*, pg. 756

COMPUCOM SYSTEMS, INC.—See Safeguard Scientifics, Inc.; *U.S. Public*, pg. 1424

COMPUDYNE CORPORATION; *U.S. Public*, pg. 419

COMPUGRAPHICS INTERNATIONAL LIMITED—See Laporte plc; *Int'l*, pg. 802

COMPU-MARK—See The Thomson Corporation; *U.S. Public*, pg. 1601

COMPUMOD PTY. LTD.—See The Macneal-Schwendler Corp.; *U.S. Public*, pg. 1031

COMPUMOTOR DIVISION—See Parker Hannifin Corporation; *U.S. Public*, pg. 1259

COMPUMUNDO—See Hewlett-Packard Company; *U.S. Public*, pg. 817

COMPUPRINT S.P.A.—See Compagnie des Machines Bull; *Int'l*, pg. 317

COMPUR-ELECTRONIC GMBH—See Bayer AG; *Int'l*, pg. 172

COMPUSA; *U.S. Public*, pg. 420

COMPUSERVE INTERACTIVE SERVICES, INC.—See America Online Incorporated; *U.S. Public*, pg. 66

COMPUTALOG DRILLING SERVICES INC.—See Computalog Ltd.; *Int'l*, pg. 325

COMPUTALOG HOLDINGS INC.—See Computalog Ltd.; *Int'l*, pg. 325

COMPUTALOG LTD.; *Int'l*, pg. 325

COMPUTALOG U.S.A., INC.—See Computalog Ltd.; *Int'l*, pg. 325

COMPUTASIA LIMITED—See Cable and Wireless plc; *Int'l*, pg. 247

MASTER INDEX TO COMPANY NAMES CONCORD

Company Index

COMPUTATION & MEASUREMENT SYSTEMS (C.M.S.) LTD.—See Motorola, Inc.; *U.S. Public*, pg. 1139
COMPUTATIONAL SYSTEMS INC.—See Emerson Electric Co.; *U.S. Public*, pg. 572
COMPUTATIONAL SYSTEMS, LTD.—See Emerson Electric Co.; *U.S. Public*, pg. 573
COMPUTE PX—See J.M. Smith Corp.; *U.S. Private*, pg. 1008
COMPUTER & ELECTRONIC DIVISION—See Abdulla Fouad Co. Ltd.; *Int'l*, pg. 501
COMPUTER & ENGINEERING BUREAU (CEB)—See Oracle Corporation; *U.S. Public*, pg. 1228
COMPUTER & MOBILE SYSTEMS—See Plantronics Inc.; *U.S. Public*, pg. 1308
COMPUTER ASSOCIATES INTERNATIONAL, INC.; *U.S. Public*, pg. 420
COMPUTER ASSOCIATES INTERNATIONAL, INC.—See Computer Associates International, Inc.; *U.S. Public*, pg. 420
COMPUTER CENTER-CINCINNATI—See Bell Industries, Inc.; *U.S. Public*, pg. 204
COMPUTER CENTER-INDIANAPOLIS—See Bell Industries, Inc.; *U.S. Public*, pg. 204
COMPUTER CENTER-LOUISVILLE—See Bell Industries, Inc.; *U.S. Public*, pg. 204
COMPUTER CENTER-MARYLAND—See Bell Industries, Inc.; *U.S. Public*, pg. 204
COMPUTER CENTER-N. INDIANAPOLIS—See Bell Industries, Inc.; *U.S. Public*, pg. 204
COMPUTER CENTRUM SITTARD—See Vendex International N.V.; *Int'l*, pg. 1463
COMPUTER CITY—See Tandy Corporation; *U.S. Public*, pg. 1560
COMPUTER COMMUNICATION COMPANY—See General Electric Company; *U.S. Public*, pg. 711
COMPUTER CORPORATION OF AMERICA; *U.S. Private*, pg. 260
COMPUTER CURRICULUM CORPORATION—See National Amusements, Inc.; *U.S. Private*, pg. 778
COMPUTER DATA SYSTEMS, INC.—See Affiliated Computer Services, Inc.; *U.S. Public*, pg. 28
COMPUTER DESIGN INC.—See Gores Technology Group; *U.S. Private*, pg. 465
COMPUTER DESIGN, INC.—See Masco Corporation; *U.S. Public*, pg. 1053
COMPUTER ENTERPRISES, INC.—See Technical Aid Corporation; *U.S. Private*, pg. 1072
COMPUTER FURNITURE & ACCESSORIES—See IAC Industries; *U.S. Private*, pg. 553
COMPUTER HORIZONS CORP.; *U.S. Public*, pg. 421
COMPUTER INFORMATION SYSTEMS—See Hewlett-Packard Company; *U.S. Public*, pg. 817
COMPUTER INTELLIGENCE—See Softbank Corporation; *Int'l*, pg. 1276
COMPUTER INTELLIGENCE INFOCORP—See Softbank Corporation; *Int'l*, pg. 1276
COMPUTER KNOWLEDGE—See Computer Horizons Corp.; *U.S. Public*, pg. 421
COMPUTER LANGUAGE RESEARCH, INC.; *U.S. Public*, pg. 421
COMPUTER MAINTENANCE CORPORATION LTD.—See Hewlett-Packard Company; *U.S. Public*, pg. 817
COMPUTER MAINTENANCE OF AUSTRALIA PTY. LTD.—See Compagnie des Machines Bull; *Int'l*, pg. 317
COMPUTER METHODS CORPORATION; *U.S. Private*, pg. 260
COMPUTER NETWORK SYSTEMS—See Knurr AG; *Int'l*, pg. 739
COMPUTER NETWORK TECHNOLOGY CORPORATION; *U.S. Public*, pg. 421
COMPUTER OPTICAL PRODUCTS INC.—See Hathaway Corporation; *U.S. Public*, pg. 799
THE COMPUTER PATCH OF JOPLIN—See Shivers Trading & Operating Co.; *U.S. Private*, pg. 995
COMPUTER POWER GROUP LIMITED; *Int'l*, pg. 325
COMPUTER POWER INCORPORATED; *U.S. Public*, pg. 421
COMPUTER POWER SUPPORT GROUP—See Emerson Electric Co.; *U.S. Public*, pg. 576
COMPUTER PRODUCTS—See Litton Industries, Inc.; *U.S. Public*, pg. 1002
COMPUTER PRODUCTS DIVISION—See Analog Devices, Inc.; *U.S. Public*, pg. 108
COMPUTER PRODUCTS, INC.; *U.S. Public*, pg. 422
COMPUTER PRODUCTS, NATIONAL ACCOUNTS DIVISION—See Computer Products, Inc.; *U.S. Public*, pg. 422
COMPUTER SALES INTERNATIONAL INC.; *U.S. Private*, pg. 260
COMPUTER SCIENCE PRESS, INC.—See Georg von Holtzbrinck GmbH; *Int'l*, pg. 1479
COMPUTER SCIENCES CORPORATION; *U.S. Public*, pg. 422
COMPUTER SERVICE COMPANY—See Steiny & Company, Inc.; *U.S. Private*, pg. 1040
COMPUTER SHOPPER—See Softbank Corporation; *Int'l*, pg. 1276
COMPUTER SPORTS WORLD—See Data Broadcasting Corporation; *U.S. Public*, pg. 484
COMPUTER STOCK FORMS, INC.—See Rotary Forms Press, Inc.; *U.S. Private*, pg. 947
COMPUTER SYSTEMS ADVISERS (M) BHD—See CSA Holdings Ltd.; *Int'l*, pg. 243
COMPUTER SYSTEMS AND APPLICATIONS INC.—See Severn Trent Plc; *Int'l*, pg. 1226
COMPUTER SYSTEMS RESEARCH, INC.—See The McGraw-Hill Companies; *U.S. Public*, pg. 1070
COMPUTER TASK GROUP EUROPE B.V.—See Computer Task Group, Inc. (CTG); *U.S. Public*, pg. 423
COMPUTER TASK GROUP, INC. (CTG); *U.S. Public*, pg. 423
COMPUTER TASK GROUP OF CANADA INC.—See Computer Task Group, Inc. (CTG); *U.S. Public*, pg. 423
COMPUTERIZED MEDICAL SYSTEMS, INC.; *U.S. Private*, pg. 260
COMPUTERIZED SECURITY SYSTEMS, INC.—See Masco Corporation; *U.S. Public*, pg. 1053
COMPUTERLAND CANADA—See SHL Systemhouse; *Int'l*, pg. 1154
COMPUTERS & CONTROLS—See Hewlett-Packard Company; *U.S. Public*, pg. 817
COMPUTERS & CONTROLS BARBADOS LTD.—See Hewlett-Packard Company; *U.S. Public*, pg. 817
COMPUTERS & CONTROLS LTD.—See Hewlett-Packard Company; *U.S. Public*, pg. 817
COMPUTERS, ETC.—See Storage Technology Corporation; *U.S. Public*, pg. 1522
COMPUTERSCOPE LTD.—See International Data Group; *U.S. Private*, pg. 569
COMPUTERWOCHE VERLAG GMBH—See International Data Group; *U.S. Private*, pg. 569
COMPUTERWORLD-COLUMBIA—See International Data Group; *U.S. Private*, pg. 569
COMPUTERWORLD DE BRAZIL—See International Data Group; *U.S. Private*, pg. 569
COMPUTERWORLD, INC.—See International Data Group; *U.S. Private*, pg. 569
COMPUTERWORLD KIEV COMIZDAT PUBLISHING COMPANY—See International Data Group; *U.S. Private*, pg. 569
COMPUTERWORLD VENEZUELA—See International Data Group; *U.S. Private*, pg. 569
COMPUTING DEVICES CO. LTD.—See Ceridian Corporation; *U.S. Public*, pg. 331
COMPUTING DEVICES INTERNATIONAL—See Ceridian Corporation; *U.S. Public*, pg. 331
COMPUTROL, INC.—See Armstrong International, Inc.; *U.S. Private*, pg. 83
COMPUWARE CORPORATION; *U.S. Public*, pg. 423
COMSAT CORPORATION; *U.S. Public*, pg. 424
COMSAT INTERNATIONAL VENTURES—See COMSAT Corporation; *U.S. Public*, pg. 425
COMSAT LABORATORIES—See COMSAT Corporation; *U.S. Public*, pg. 424
COMSAT MOBILE COMMUNICATIONS—See COMSAT Corporation; *U.S. Public*, pg. 424
COMSAT RSI, INC.—See COMSAT Corporation; *U.S. Public*, pg. 424
COMSAT WORLD SYSTEMS—See COMSAT Corporation; *U.S. Public*, pg. 424
COMSEARCH APPLIED TECHNOLOGY, INC.—See Allen Telecom, Inc.; *U.S. Public*, pg. 46
COMSEARCH, INC.—See Allen Telecom, Inc.; *U.S. Public*, pg. 46
COMSHARE, INCORPORATED; *U.S. Public*, pg. 425
COMSHARE LTD.—See Comshare, Incorporated; *U.S. Public*, pg. 425
COMSIP AUTOMACION S.A.—See Alcatel Alsthom Compagnie Generale D'Electricite; *Int'l*, pg. 53
COMSKILL LEARNING CENTERS, INC.—See ITC Learning Corp.; *U.S. Public*, pg. 859
COMSOF AG—See Bayerische Vereinsbank Group; *Int'l*, pg. 181
COMSONICS, INC.; *U.S. Private*, pg. 260
COMSOURCE, INC.—See SIGCORP, Inc.; *U.S. Public*, pg. 1471
COMSTOCK CANADA LTD.—See EMCOR Group, Inc.; *U.S. Public*, pg. 572
COMSTOCK FOODS—See Pro-Fac Cooperative, Inc.; *U.S. Private*, pg. 887
COMSTOCK MICHIGAN FRUIT—See Pro-Fac Cooperative, Inc.; *U.S. Private*, pg. 887
COMSTOR—See General Electric Company; *U.S. Public*, pg. 711
COMSTREAM, A SPAR COMPANY—See Spar Aerospace Limited; *Int'l*, pg. 1288
COMSTREAM CORPORATION—See Spar Aerospace Limited; *Int'l*, pg. 1288
COMSTRON DIVISION—See Aeroflex Incorporated; *U.S. Public*, pg. 24
COMTECH ANTENNA SYSTEMS, INC.—See Comtech Telecommunications Corp.; *U.S. Public*, pg. 425
COMTECH COMMUNICATIONS CORP.—See Comtech Telecommunications Corp.; *U.S. Public*, pg. 425
COMTECH PST CORP.—See Comtech Telecommunications Corp.; *U.S. Public*, pg. 425
COMTECH SYSTEMS, INC.—See Comtech Telecommunications Corp.; *U.S. Public*, pg. 425
COMTECH TELECOMMUNICATIONS CORP.; *U.S. Public*, pg. 425
COMTECO S.A.—See Sulzer Ltd.; *Int'l*, pg. 1306
COMTEST INSTRUMENTATION B.V.—See Thermo Electron Corporation; *U.S. Public*, pg. 1596
COMTEST ITALY—See Thermo Electron Corporation; *U.S. Public*, pg. 1596
COMTEST LIMITED—See Thermo Electron Corporation; *U.S. Public*, pg. 1596
COMTEXT INTERNATIONAL—See GN Great Nordic Ltd.; *Int'l*, pg. 537
COMTRADE INTERNATIONAL C.A.—See CODELCO Chile (Corporacion Nacional Del Cobre De Chile); *Int'l*, pg. 303
COMUNICA LEO BURNETT PANAMA, S.A.—See Leo Burnett Company, Inc.; *U.S. Private*, pg. 184
COMUNICACION Y PUBLICACIONES—See Lagardere Groupe; *Int'l*, pg. 795
COMUNICACIONES MTEL, S.A. DE C.V.—See Mobile Telecommunications Technologies Corp.; *U.S. Public*, pg. 1120
COMURHEX—See COGEMA - Compagnie Generale des Matieres Nucleaires; *Int'l*, pg. 305
COMVERSE NETWORK SYSTEMS—See Comverse Technology, Inc.; *U.S. Public*, pg. 425
COMVERSE TECHNOLOGY, INC.; *U.S. Public*, pg. 425
COMVIDEO SYSTEMS, INC./N.J.—See RCN Corporation; *U.S. Public*, pg. 1354
CON-CARRIERS LTD.—See Circle International Group, Inc.; *U.S. Public*, pg. 373
CON-WAY TRANSPORTATION SERVICES—See CNF Transportation Inc.; *U.S. Public*, pg. 281
CON-WAY TRUCKLOAD SERVICES—See CNF Transportation Inc.; *U.S. Public*, pg. 281
CON-WEB PRESS INC.—See Quebecor Inc.; *Int'l*, pg. 1076
CONAGRA AGRI-PRODUCTS CO.—See ConAgra, Inc.; *U.S. Public*, pg. 426
CONAGRA ASIA-PACIFIC—See ConAgra, Inc.; *U.S. Public*, pg. 429
CONAGRA BROILER CO.—See ConAgra, Inc.; *U.S. Public*, pg. 427
CONAGRA CONSUMER DIRECT, INC.—See ConAgra, Inc.; *U.S. Public*, pg. 426
CONAGRA DAIRY & FOOD OILS—See ConAgra, Inc.; *U.S. Public*, pg. 427
CONAGRA DIVERSIFIED PRODUCTS COMPANIES—See ConAgra, Inc.; *U.S. Public*, pg. 426
CONAGRA-EUROPE, INC.—See ConAgra, Inc.; *U.S. Public*, pg. 429
CONAGRA FEED CO.—See ConAgra, Inc.; *U.S. Public*, pg. 428
CONAGRA FEED INGREDIENT—See ConAgra, Inc.; *U.S. Public*, pg. 426
CONAGRA FEED INGREDIENT MERCHANDISING COMPANY—See ConAgra, Inc.; *U.S. Public*, pg. 428
CONAGRA FEED MILL—See ConAgra, Inc.; *U.S. Public*, pg. 427
CONAGRA FROZEN FOOD COMPANY—See ConAgra, Inc.; *U.S. Public*, pg. 427
CONAGRA FRUEN MILLING CO.—See ConAgra, Inc.; *U.S. Public*, pg. 428
CONAGRA GRAIN COMPANIES—See ConAgra, Inc.; *U.S. Public*, pg. 426
CONAGRA GROCERY PRODUCTS PACKAGING COMPANY—See ConAgra, Inc.; *U.S. Public*, pg. 428
CONAGRA, INC.; *U.S. Public*, pg. 425
CONAGRA INTERNATIONAL—See ConAgra, Inc.; *U.S. Public*, pg. 426
CONAGRA INTERNATIONAL PTE. LTD.—See ConAgra, Inc.; *U.S. Public*, pg. 429
CONAGRA NISSUI INC.—See ConAgra, Inc.; *U.S. Public*, pg. 429
CONAGRA POULTRY CO.—See ConAgra, Inc.; *U.S. Public*, pg. 427
CONAGRA POULTRY COMPANY—See ConAgra, Inc.; *U.S. Public*, pg. 427
CONAGRA POULTRY FOODSERVICE CO.—See ConAgra, Inc.; *U.S. Public*, pg. 427
CONAGRA PREPARED FOOD COMPANIES—See ConAgra, Inc.; *U.S. Public*, pg. 427
CONAGRA RED MEAT COMPANIES—See ConAgra, Inc.; *U.S. Public*, pg. 427
CONAGRA RETAIL COMPANIES—See ConAgra, Inc.; *U.S. Public*, pg. 426
CONAGRA SEAFOOD COMPANIES—See ConAgra, Inc.; *U.S. Public*, pg. 427
CONAGRA SHRIMP COMPANY—See ConAgra, Inc.; *U.S. Public*, pg. 427
CONAGRA SPAIN—See ConAgra, Inc.; *U.S. Public*, pg. 429
CONAGRA SPECIALTY GRAIN PRODUCTS CO.—See ConAgra, Inc.; *U.S. Public*, pg. 427
CONAGRA TRADING COMPANIES (CTC)—See ConAgra, Inc.; *U.S. Public*, pg. 428
CONAGRA TRADING & PROCESSING COMPANIES—See ConAgra, Inc.; *U.S. Public*, pg. 428
CONAGRA TURKEY COMPANY—See ConAgra, Inc.; *U.S. Public*, pg. 427
CONAIR CORPORATION; *U.S. Private*, pg. 261
THE CONAIR GROUP, INC.; *U.S. Private*, pg. 261
CONAIRE DIV.—See Tomkins PLC; *Int'l*, pg. 1398
CONAM INSPECTION—See Staveley Industries PLC; *Int'l*, pg. 1299
CONAP INC.; *U.S. Private*, pg. 261
CONASAN, S.A.—See ConAgra, Inc.; *U.S. Public*, pg. 429
CONATEL, S.A.—See Hewlett-Packard Company; *U.S. Public*, pg. 817
CONAX BUFFALO CORPORATION—See IMI Plc; *Int'l*, pg. 646
CONBRACO INDUSTRIES-APOLLO DIVISION—See Conbraco Industries Inc.; *U.S. Private*, pg. 261
CONBRACO INDUSTRIES INC.; *U.S. Private*, pg. 261
THE CONCENTRATE COMPANY OF IRELAND—See PepsiCo, Inc.; *U.S. Public*, pg. 1277
CONCENTRATE DIVISION—See Orange-Co., Inc.; *U.S. Public*, pg. 1229
CONCENTRIC DATA SYSTEMS—See Wall Data Incorporated; *U.S. Public*, pg. 1734
CONCEPT MANUFACTURING COMPANY, INC.—See Humphrey Products Company; *U.S. Private*, pg. 548
CONCEPTION ET COORDINATION LEOPOLD S.A.—See Tractebel; *Int'l*, pg. 1415
CONCERT COMMUNICATIONS COMPANY—See British Telecommunications plc; *Int'l*, pg. 223
CONCHEM—See Lafarge S.A.; *Int'l*, pg. 790
CONCO—See Columbus McKinnon Corp.; *U.S. Public*, pg. 405
CONCOMBER, LTD.—See Unicom Corporation; *U.S. Public*, pg. 1664
CONCORD ASSETS GROUP; *U.S. Private*, pg. 261
CONCORD CAMERA CORPORATION; *U.S. Public*, pg. 429
CONCORD COMMUNICATIONS, INC.; *U.S. Public*, pg. 429
CONCORD COMPUTING CORP.—See Concord EFS, Inc.; *U.S. Public*, pg. 429
CONCORD EFS, INC.; *U.S. Public*, pg. 429
CONCORD ELECTRIC COMPANY—See Unitil Corporation; *U.S. Public*, pg. 1692
CONCORD FABRICS INC.; *U.S. Public*, pg. 429
CONCORD FABRICS, LOS ANGELES—See Concord Fabrics Inc.; *U.S. Public*, pg. 430
CONCORD FOREIGN SALES CORP., INC.—See Concord Fabrics Inc.; *U.S. Public*, pg. 430

CONCORD GENERAL LIFE INSURANCE COMPANY—See American Heritage Life Investment Corp.; *U.S. Public*, pg. 79
CONCORD HOUSE DIVISION—See Concord Fabrics Inc.; *U.S. Public*, pg. 430
CONCORD LITHO CO., INC.; *U.S. Private*, pg. 261
CONCORD MINIATURES—See Cardinal Inc.; *U.S. Private*, pg. 209
CONCORD NATIONAL BANK, INC.—See Concord EFS, Inc.; *U.S. Public*, pg. 429
CONCORD SAVINGS BANK—See CFX Bank; *U.S. Public*, pg. 278
CONCORD SPECIALTY CORP.—See Buckeye Corrugated Inc.; *U.S. Private*, pg. 177
CONCORD TELEPHONE EXCHANGE—See Telephone and Data Systems, Inc.; *U.S. Public*, pg. 1571
THE CONCORD TRIBUNE, INC.—See Media General, Inc.; *U.S. Public*, pg. 1078
CONCORD WATCH COMPANY, S.A.—See Movado Group, Inc.; *U.S. Public*, pg. 1140
CONCORDE CAREER COLLEGES, INC.; *U.S. Public*, pg. 430
CONCORDE EXPRESS—See John Menzies plc; *Int'l*, pg. 707
CONCORDIA COMPANHIA DE SEGUROS—See The Kyoei Mutual Fire & Marine Insurance Company; *Int'l*, pg. 777
CONCORDIA CUSTOM YACHTS—See Sauer Industries, Inc.; *U.S. Private*, pg. 968
CONCORDIA PUBLISHING HOUSE; *U.S. Private*, pg. 261
CONCORP, INC.; *U.S. Private*, pg. 262
CONCOURSE DEVELOPMENT, INC.—See Forest City Enterprises; *U.S. Public*, pg. 668
CONCREBRAS S.A.—See Lafarge S.A.; *Int'l*, pg. 790
CONCRETE ACCESSORIES COMPANY, INC.—See Ritchie Corporation; *U.S. Private*, pg. 933
CONCRETE & STEEL PIPE GROUP (SOUTHERN DIV.)—See Ameron International Corporation; *U.S. Public*, pg. 99
CONCRETE INDUSTRIES SECTOR—See Fletcher Challenge Limited; *Int'l*, pg. 495
THE CONCRETE PRODUCTS AND AGGREGATE CO., LTD.—See The Siam Cement Public Company Limited; *Int'l*, pg. 1238
THE CONCRETE PRODUCTS AND AGGREGATE INDUSTRY CO., LTD.—See The Siam Cement Public Company Limited; *Int'l*, pg. 1237
CONCRETE PRODUCTS GROUP—See Southdown, Inc.; *U.S. Public*, pg. 1489
CONCRETE SERVICE CO.—See Bardon Group PLC; *Int'l*, pg. 166
CONCRETE TECHNOLOGY CORP.; *U.S. Private*, pg. 262
CONCURRENT COMPUTER CORPORATION; *U.S. Public*, pg. 430
CONCURRENT COMPUTER CORPORATION—See Concurrent Computer Corporation; *U.S. Public*, pg. 430
CONCURRENT INDUSTRIES GROUP, INC.; *U.S. Private*, pg. 262
CONDADO PLAZA HOTEL & CASINO—See Patriot American Hospitality; *U.S. Public*, pg. 1265
CONDAL CORNER, S.A.—See Assicurazioni Generali S.p.A.; *Int'l*, pg. 91
CONDAL DISTRIBUTORS INC.; *U.S. Private*, pg. 262
THE CONDE NAST PUBLICATIONS INC.—See Advance Publications Inc.; *U.S. Private*, pg. 20
CONDE NAST TRAVELER—See Advance Publications Inc.; *U.S. Private*, pg. 20
CONDEA AUGUSTA S.P.A.—See Condea Chemie GmbH; *Int'l*, pg. 325
CONDEA CHEMIE GMBH; *Int'l*, pg. 325
CONDEA CHIMICA D.A.C. S.P.A.—See Condea Chemie GmbH; *Int'l*, pg. 325
CONDEA NANJING CHEMICAL COMPANY—See Condea Chemie GmbH; *Int'l*, pg. 325
CONDEA VISTA COMPANY—See Condea Chemie GmbH; *Int'l*, pg. 325
CONDEPOLS S.A.—See Compania Espanola de Petroleos, S.A. (CEPSA); *Int'l*, pg. 323
CONDERE CORPORATION; *U.S. Private*, pg. 262
CONDO, HOTEL & RESORT MANAGEMENT—See The Hallwood Group Incorporated; *U.S. Public*, pg. 778
CONDON OIL COMPANY, INC.; *U.S. Private*, pg. 262
CONDON TV SYSTEMS, INC.—See Telephone and Data Systems, Inc.; *U.S. Public*, pg. 1571
CONDOR D.C. POWER SUPPLIES INC.—See SL Industries, Inc.; *U.S. Public*, pg. 1419
CONDOR FLUGDIENST GMBH—See Deutsche Lufthansa AG; *Int'l*, pg. 407
CONDOR MINE S.A.—See TVX Gold Inc.; *Int'l*, pg. 1345
CONDOR PACIFIC INDUSTRIES, INC.; *U.S. Public*, pg. 262
CONDOR TOOL & DIE, INC.—See Anchor Tool & Die Company; *U.S. Private*, pg. 71
CONDRECO PTY. LTD.—See Ballast Nedam NV; *Int'l*, pg. 135
CONDUCTORES COMPONENTES ELECTRICOS DE JUAREZ S.A. DE C.V.—See General Motors Corporation; *U.S. Public*, pg. 721
CONDUCTORES LATINCASA S.A. DE C.V.—See Telefonaktiebolaget LM Ericsson; *Int'l*, pg. 1365
CONDUPHON INDUSTRIA, COMERCIO, REPRESENTACAO E SERVICOS LTDA.—See The Furukawa Electric Co., Ltd.; *Int'l*, pg. 530
CONDURA, S.A. DE C.V.—See Eaton Corporation; *U.S. Public*, pg. 558
CONE-BLANCHARD MACHINE COMPANY; *U.S. Private*, pg. 262
CONE DECORATIVE FABRICS—See Cone Mills Corporation; *U.S. Public*, pg. 430
CONE DRIVE TEXTRON—See Textron Inc.; *U.S. Public*, pg. 1589
CONE FINISHING COMPANY—See Cone Mills Corporation; *U.S. Public*, pg. 430
CONE MILLS CORPORATION; *U.S. Public*, pg. 430
CONECTIV; *U.S. Public*, pg. 430

CONESTOGA CORPORATION; *U.S. Private*, pg. 262
CONESTOGA WOOD SPECIALTIES CORP.; *U.S. Private*, pg. 262
CONESVILLE COAL PREPARATION CO.—See American Electric Power Company, Inc.; *U.S. Public*, pg. 72
CONEX-SANBRA LTD.—See Delta plc; *Int'l*, pg. 390
CONEXIONADOS ELECTRICOS TARAZONA S.A.—See General Motors Corporation; *U.S. Public*, pg. 721
CONEXIONES TELEMATICAS IBERICA, S.A.—See Caja de Madrid Group; *Int'l*, pg. 252
CONFED ADMIN. SERVICES, INC.—See Confederation Life Insurance Company; *Int'l*, pg. 326
CONFED INVESTMENT COUNSELLING LIMITED—See Confederation Life Insurance Company; *Int'l*, pg. 325
CONFED MANAGED HEALTHCARE, INC.—See Confederation Life Insurance Company; *Int'l*, pg. 326
CONFEDERATION BANK (JERSEY) LIMITED—See Confederation Life Insurance Company; *Int'l*, pg. 326
CONFEDERATION DES CAISSES DES JARDINS; *Int'l*, pg. 325
CONFEDERATION FINANCIAL HOLDINGS, INC.—See Confederation Life Insurance Company; *Int'l*, pg. 326
CONFEDERATION FINANCIAL SERVICES (UK) LIMITED—See Sun Life Assurance Company of Canada; *Int'l*, pg. 1319
CONFEDERATION FINANCIAL SERVICES (U.S.) INC.—See Confederation Life Insurance Company; *Int'l*, pg. 326
CONFEDERATION LEASING (ALBERTA) LIMITED—See Confederation Life Insurance Company; *Int'l*, pg. 325
CONFEDERATION LIFE INSURANCE AND ANNUITY COMPANY—See Confederation Life Insurance Company; *Int'l*, pg. 326
CONFEDERATION LIFE INSURANCE COMPANY; *Int'l*, pg. 325
CONFEDERATION LIFE INSURANCE COMPANY (U.K.), LIMITED—See Sun Life Assurance Company of Canada; *Int'l*, pg. 1319
CONFEDERATION MORTGAGE SERVICES LIMITED—See Sun Life Assurance Company of Canada; *Int'l*, pg. 1319
CONFEDERATION PENSION INVESTMENT MANAGEMENT LIMITED—See Sun Life Assurance Company of Canada; *Int'l*, pg. 1319
CONFEDERATION TRUST COMPANY—See Confederation Life Insurance Company; *Int'l*, pg. 326
CONFERTECH CANADA INC.—See Frontier Corporation; *U.S. Public*, pg. 683
CONFERTECH INTERNATIONAL—See Frontier Corporation; *U.S. Public*, pg. 683
CONFORAMA—See Au Bon Marche; *Int'l*, pg. 98
CONGAREE CONSTRUCTION CO., INC.; *U.S. Private*, pg. 263
CONGEN PROPERTIES, INC.—See Cigna Corp.; *U.S. Public*, pg. 365
CONGLETON BOARD—See BPB Industries PLC; *Int'l*, pg. 123
CONGOLEUM CORPORATION—See American Biltrite Inc.; *U.S. Public*, pg. 69
CONGRESS FINANCIAL CORP.—See CoreStates Financial Corp.; *U.S. Public*, pg. 447
CONGRESS FINANCIAL (NORTHWEST)—See CoreStates Financial Corp.; *U.S. Public*, pg. 447
CONGRESS LIFE INSURANCE COMPANY—See Security American Financial Enterprises, Inc.; *U.S. Private*, pg. 980
CONGRESSIONAL INFORMATION SERVICE (CIS)—See Reed Elsevier plc; *Int'l*, pg. 1096
CONGRESSIONAL QUARTERLY—See The Times Publishing Co.; *U.S. Private*, pg. 1088
CONIDA FARMS—See Macristy Industries, Inc.; *U.S. Private*, pg. 693
P.T. CONIPLANT INDONESIA—See Bilfinger + Berger Bauaktiengesellschaft; *Int'l*, pg. 196
CONKLIN CO. INC.; *U.S. Private*, pg. 263
CONKLIN INSTRUMENT CORPORATION; *U.S. Private*, pg. 263
CONLEY FROG/SWITCH & FORGE CO.; *U.S. Private*, pg. 263
CONMED ANDOVER MEDICAL, INC.—See Conmed Corporation; *U.S. Public*, pg. 431
CONMED CORPORATION; *U.S. Public*, pg. 431
CONNAUGHT LABORATORIES, INC.—See Rhone-Poulenc S.A.; *Int'l*, pg. 1109
CONNAUGHT LABORATORIES LIMITED—See Rhone-Poulenc S.A.; *Int'l*, pg. 1109
CONNAUGHT NOVO NORDISK INC.—See Novo Nordisk A/S; *Int'l*, pg. 987
CONNECT COMPUTER—See Norstan, Inc.; *U.S. Public*, pg. 1192
CONNECTEURS CINCH S.A.—See Labinal SA; *Int'l*, pg. 786
CONNECTICUT-AMERICAN WATER CO.—See American Water Works Company, Inc.; *U.S. Public*, pg. 95
CONNECTICUT CONTAINER CORPORATION; *U.S. Private*, pg. 263
CONNECTICUT DRIVE SHAFT, INC.; *U.S. Private*, pg. 263
CONNECTICUT DRIVESHAFT—See Connecticut Drive Shaft, Inc.; *U.S. Private*, pg. 263
CONNECTICUT ENERGY CORPORATION; *U.S. Public*, pg. 431
CONNECTICUT GENERAL BENEFIT PAYMENTS, INC.—See Cigna Corp.; *U.S. Public*, pg. 360
CONNECTICUT GENERAL CORPORATION—See Cigna Corp.; *U.S. Public*, pg. 358
CONNECTICUT GENERAL EQUITY PROPERTIES-I LIMITED PARTNERSHIP—See Cigna Corp.; *U.S. Public*, pg. 359
CONNECTICUT GENERAL FIRE & CASUALTY INSURANCE COMPANY—See Cigna Corp.; *U.S. Public*, pg. 365
CONNECTICUT GENERAL LIFE INSURANCE COMPANY—See Cigna Corp.; *U.S. Public*, pg. 360

CONNECTICUT GENERAL PENSION SERVICES, INC.—See Cigna Corp.; *U.S. Public*, pg. 362
CONNECTICUT GENERAL REALTY INVESTORS LIMITED PARTNERSHIP—See Cigna Corp.; *U.S. Public*, pg. 359
CONNECTICUT GENERAL REALTY INVESTORS-III LIMITED PARTNERSHIP—See Cigna Corp.; *U.S. Public*, pg. 359
CONNECTICUT GENERAL REALTY INVESTORS-II LIMITED PARTNERSHIP—See Cigna Corp.; *U.S. Public*, pg. 359
CONNECTICUT GENERAL REALTY RESOURCES, INC.—See Cigna Corp.; *U.S. Public*, pg. 359
CONNECTICUT GENERAL REALTY RESOURCES, INC. - FOURTH—See Cigna Corp.; *U.S. Public*, pg. 359
CONNECTICUT GENERAL REALTY RESOURCES, INC. - SECOND—See Cigna Corp.; *U.S. Public*, pg. 359
CONNECTICUT GENERAL REALTY RESOURCES, INC. - THIRD—See Cigna Corp.; *U.S. Public*, pg. 359
THE CONNECTICUT INDEMNITY CO.—See Orion Capital Corporation; *U.S. Public*, pg. 1231
THE CONNECTICUT LIGHT & POWER CO.—See Northeast Utilities; *U.S. Public*, pg. 1194
CONNECTICUT NATURAL GAS CORPORATION—See CTG Resources, Inc.; *U.S. Public*, pg. 285
CONNECTICUT SPECIALTY INSURANCE COMPANY—See Orion Capital Corporation; *U.S. Public*, pg. 1231
CONNECTICUT SPRING & STAMPING CORPORATION; *U.S. Private*, pg. 263
CONNECTICUT VALLEY ELECTRIC CO., INC.—See Central Vermont Public Service Corporation; *U.S. Public*, pg. 328
THE CONNECTICUT WATER COMPANY—See Connecticut Water Service, Inc.; *U.S. Public*, pg. 431
CONNECTICUT WATER SERVICE, INC.; *U.S. Public*, pg. 431
CONNECTICUT YANKEE ATOMIC POWER CO.—See Central Maine Power Company; *U.S. Public*, pg. 325
CONNECTING POINT COMPUTER SERVICES—See Graphic Enterprises of Ohio, Inc.; *U.S. Public*, pg. 471
CONNECTIX CORPORATION; *U.S. Private*, pg. 264
CONNECTOR DIVISION—See Methode Electronics Inc.; *U.S. Public*, pg. 1101
CONNECTOR DIVISION AMERICA AND ASIA—See Labinal SA; *Int'l*, pg. 786
CONNECTOR MANUFACTURING COMPANY; *U.S. Private*, pg. 264
AB CONNECTORS LIMITED—See TT Group PLC; *Int'l*, pg. 1344
CONNECTWARE, INC. LLC—See AMP Incorporated; *U.S. Public*, pg. 8
CONNELL CO.; *U.S. Private*, pg. 264
CONNELL COMMUNICATIONS—See International Data Group; *U.S. Private*, pg. 569
CONNELL LIMITED PARTNERSHIP; *U.S. Private*, pg. 264
CONNELLY CONTAINERS, INC.; *U.S. Private*, pg. 264
CONNELLY PAPER MILL—See Connelly Containers, Inc.; *U.S. Private*, pg. 264
CONNELLY SKIS, INC.—See Thyssen AG; *Int'l*, pg. 1388
CONNEX TRAVEL (PTY) LTD.—See Transnet Ltd.; *Int'l*, pg. 1417
CONNING—See General American Life Insurance Co.; *U.S. Private*, pg. 443
CONNOLLY TOOL & MACHINE CO.—See Ennis Business Forms, Inc.; *U.S. Public*, pg. 583
CONNOR CORPORATION; *U.S. Private*, pg. 264
CONNOR CORPORATION—See Connor Corporation; *U.S. Private*, pg. 264
CONNOR FOREST INDUSTRIES, INC.—See Bridgewater Resources Corporation; *U.S. Private*, pg. 168
CONNOR PLASTIC TECHNOLOGIES—See Connor Corporation; *U.S. Private*, pg. 264
CONNORS BROS. LIMITED—See George Weston Limited; *Int'l*, pg. 1495
CONNORS BRUNSWICK, INC.; *U.S. Private*, pg. 264
CONOCO—See Du Pont (E.I. Du Pont De Nemours & Co.); *U.S. Public*, pg. 531
CONOCO INC.—See Du Pont (E.I. Du Pont De Nemours & Co.); *U.S. Public*, pg. 531
CONOCO IRELAND LTD.—See Du Pont (E.I. Du Pont De Nemours & Co.); *U.S. Public*, pg. 531
CONOCO MINERALOEL GMBH—See Du Pont (E.I. Du Pont De Nemours & Co.); *U.S. Public*, pg. 531
CONOCO NORWAY, INC.—See Du Pont (E.I. Du Pont De Nemours & Co.); *U.S. Public*, pg. 531
CONOCO OIL REFINERY—See Du Pont (E.I. Du Pont De Nemours & Co.); *U.S. Public*, pg. 531
CONOCO (UK) LTD.—See Du Pont (E.I. Du Pont De Nemours & Co.); *U.S. Public*, pg. 531
CONQUEST EUROPE—See WPP Group plc; *Int'l*, pg. 1483
CONRAC DISPLAY PRODUCTS; *U.S. Private*, pg. 264
MICHAEL CONRAD & LEO BURNETT GMBH—See Leo Burnett Company, Inc.; *U.S. Private*, pg. 184
CONRAD TACK KOMMANDITGESELLSCHAFT—See Freudenberg & Company; *Int'l*, pg. 506
CONRAIL DIRECT—See Conrail, Inc.; *U.S. Public*, pg. 432
CONRAIL, INC.; *U.S. Public*, pg. 431
CONRAN OCTOPUS LIMITED—See Reed Elsevier plc; *Int'l*, pg. 1093
CONROY'S FLOWERS—See 800-FLOWERS, Inc.; *U.S. Private*, pg. 366
CONSECO CAPITAL MANAGEMENT, INC.—See Conseco Inc.; *U.S. Public*, pg. 433
CONSECO CAPITAL PARTNERS II, L.P.—See Conseco Inc.; *U.S. Public*, pg. 432
CONSECO INC.; *U.S. Public*, pg. 432
CONSECO LIFE OF NEW YORK—See Conseco Inc.; *U.S. Public*, pg. 433
CONSECO RISK MANAGEMENT, INC.—See Conseco Inc.; *U.S. Public*, pg. 433
CONSERVENFABRIK EUGEN LACROIX GMBH—See Campbell Soup Company; *U.S. Public*, pg. 299
CONSERVERIFABRIEK L.P. UGTTEWAAD BV—See The Albert Fisher Group PLC; *Int'l*, pg. 491
CONSERVES ESTAVAYER S.A.—See Migros; *Int'l*, pg. 865

CONSHU HOLDINGS LTD.—See South African Breweries, Ltd.; *Int'l*, pg. 1287

CONSIDAR EUROPE S.A.—See Arbed S.A.; *Int'l*, pg. 79

CONSILIUM BULK - BABCOCK ATLANTA INC.—See Babcock International Group PLC; *Int'l*, pg. 131

CONSILIUM BULK-BABCOCK, KVANUM AB—See Babcock International Group PLC; *Int'l*, pg. 131

CONSILIUM BULK OY—See Babcock International Group PLC; *Int'l*, pg. 131

CONSILIUM CMH-BABCOCK AB—See Babcock International Group PLC; *Int'l*, pg. 131

CONSILIUM CLAUDIUS PETERS BABCOCK (HK) LTD— See Babcock International Group PLC; *Int'l*, pg. 131

CONSILIUM, INC.; *U.S. Public*, pg. 434

CONSO GROUP—See Conso Products Company; *U.S. Public*, pg. 434

CONSO PRODUCTS CO.—See Conso Products Company; *U.S. Public*, pg. 434

CONSO PRODUCTS COMPANY; *U.S. Public*, pg. 434

CONSOL—See Du Pont (E.I. Du Pont De Nemours & Co.); *U.S. Public*, pg. 531

CONSOL—See RWE AG; *Int'l*, pg. 1081

CONSOL OF KENTUCKY, INC.—See Du Pont (E.I. Du Pont De Nemours & Co.); *U.S. Public*, pg. 531

CONSOLIDACION COMERCIAL INFRA, S.A. DE C.V.—See Air Products and Chemicals, Inc.; *U.S. Public*, pg. 32

CONSOLIDATED ACCEPTANCE CORP., INC.—See Green Tree Financial Corporation; *U.S. Public*, pg. 762

CONSOLIDATED AMERICAN INSURANCE CO.—See The Seibels Bruce Group, Inc.; *U.S. Public*, pg. 1454

CONSOLIDATED BEVERAGES, INC.; *U.S. Private*, pg. 264

CONSOLIDATED BISCUIT CO.; *U.S. Private*, pg. 265

CONSOLIDATED CARGO CARRIERS—See Consolidated Systems, Inc.; *U.S. Private*, pg. 266

CONSOLIDATED CARMA CORPORATION—See Brookfield Properties Corporation; *Int'l*, pg. 229

CONSOLIDATED CIGAR CORP.—See MacAndrews & Forbes Holdings Inc.; *U.S. Private*, pg. 690

CONSOLIDATED CIGAR CORPORATION—See MacAndrews & Forbes Holdings Inc.; *U.S. Private*, pg. 690

CONSOLIDATED COAL CO.—See Du Pont (E.I. Du Pont De Nemours & Co.); *U.S. Public*, pg. 531

CONSOLIDATED COATINGS CORP.—See RPM, Inc.; *U.S. Public*, pg. 1357

CONSOLIDATED COMMUNICATIONS—See McLeodUSA Incorporated; *U.S. Public*, pg. 1073

CONSOLIDATED COMMUNICATIONS DIRECTORIES, INC.—See McLeodUSA Incorporated; *U.S. Public*, pg. 1073

CONSOLIDATED COMMUNICATIONS MOBILE SERVICES, INC.—See McLeodUSA Incorporated; *U.S. Public*, pg. 1073

CONSOLIDATED COMMUNICATIONS OPERATOR SERVICES, INC.—See McLeodUSA Incorporated; *U.S. Public*, pg. 1073

CONSOLIDATED COMMUNICATIONS PUBLIC SERVICES, INC.—See McLeodUSA Incorporated; *U.S. Public*, pg. 1073

CONSOLIDATED COMPANIES INC. (CONCO); *U.S. Private*, pg. 265

CONSOLIDATED CONVERTING CO.—See Cubic Corporation; *U.S. Public*, pg. 466

CONSOLIDATED DEVICE INC.—See Snap-On Tools Corporation; *U.S. Public*, pg. 1481

CONSOLIDATED DISTILLED PRODUCTS—See NWS Inc.; *U.S. Private*, pg. 772

CONSOLIDATED EDISON COMPANY OF NEW YORK, INC.; *U.S. Public*, pg. 434

CONSOLIDATED ELECTRIC SUPPLY, INC.—See Rexel, S.A.; *Int'l*, pg. 1107

CONSOLIDATED ELECTRICAL DISTRIBUTORS; *U.S. Private*, pg. 265

CONSOLIDATED ENGRAVERS-EAST, INC.—See The Dyson-Kissner-Moran Corporation; *U.S. Private*, pg. 351

CONSOLIDATED FASTFRATE—See Russel Metals Inc.; *Int'l*, pg. 1150

CONSOLIDATED FOOTWEAR CO., LTD.—See Itochu Corporation; *Int'l*, pg. 695

CONSOLIDATED FOUNDRIES; *U.S. Private*, pg. 265

CONSOLIDATED FREIGHTWAYS CORP.; *U.S. Public*, pg. 435

CONSOLIDATED FURNITURE CORPORATION; *U.S. Private*, pg. 265

CONSOLIDATED GRAIN & BARGE CO.—See Itochu Corporation; *Int'l*, pg. 694

CONSOLIDATED GRAPHIC COMMUNICATIONS—See Champion Industries; *U.S. Public*, pg. 333

CONSOLIDATED GRAPHICS, INC.; *U.S. Private*, pg. 265

CONSOLIDATED GROUP, INC.—See The Dyson-Kissner-Moran Corporation; *U.S. Private*, pg. 351

CONSOLIDATED INDUSTRIAL GASES INC.—See The BOC Group plc; *Int'l*, pg. 122

CONSOLIDATED INDUSTRIAL GASES, INC.—See Hewlett-Packard Company; *U.S. Public*, pg. 817

CONSOLIDATED INDUSTRIES CORP.—See Berisford plc; *Int'l*, pg. 188

CONSOLIDATED INDUSTRIES, INC.; *U.S. Private*, pg. 265

CONSOLIDATED LUMBER CO.; *U.S. Private*, pg. 265

CONSOLIDATED MARKET RESPONSE—See McLeodUSA Incorporated; *U.S. Public*, pg. 1073

CONSOLIDATED MEDICAL EQUIPMENT INTERNATIONAL, INC.—See Conmed Corporation; *U.S. Public*, pg. 431

CONSOLIDATED METAL PRODUCTS, INC.; *U.S. Private*, pg. 265

CONSOLIDATED METCO, INC.—See Varlen Corporation; *U.S. Public*, pg. 1710

CONSOLIDATED MIDWEST, INC.; *U.S. Private*, pg. 265

CONSOLIDATED NATURAL GAS COMPANY; *U.S. Public*, pg. 435

CONSOLIDATED NATURAL GAS SERVICE CO., INC.— See Consolidated Natural Gas Company; *U.S. Public*, pg. 435

CONSOLIDATED NETWORK, INC.—See McLeodUSA Incorporated; *U.S. Public*, pg. 1073

CONSOLIDATED ORIX LEASING AND FINANCE CORPORATION—See Orix Corporation; *Int'l*, pg. 1009

CONSOLIDATED PAPER CO.—See Paper Enterprises, Inc.; *U.S. Private*, pg. 838

CONSOLIDATED PAPERS, INC.; *U.S. Public*, pg. 436

CONSOLIDATED PIPE & SUPPLY COMPANY; *U.S. Private*, pg. 266

CONSOLIDATED PRODUCTS, INC.; *U.S. Public*, pg. 436

CONSOLIDATED PUBLISHING COMPANY; *U.S. Private*, pg. 266

CONSOLIDATED SCREEN-MAKERS, INC.—See The Dyson-Kissner-Moran Corporation; *U.S. Private*, pg. 351

CONSOLIDATED SHARE REGISTERS LIMITED—See Anglo American Corporation of South Africa Limited; *Int'l*, pg. 77

CONSOLIDATED SPECIALTY RESTAURANT—See Consolidated Products, Inc.; *U.S. Public*, pg. 436

CONSOLIDATED STORES CORP.; *U.S. Public*, pg. 437

CONSOLIDATED SYSTEMS, INC.; *U.S. Private*, pg. 266

CONSOLIDATED-TOMOKA LAND CO.; *U.S. Public*, pg. 437

CONSOLIDATED VISCOUNT RESOURCES LTD.; *Int'l*, pg. 326

CONSOLIDATED WATER CO.—See Avatar Holdings Inc.; *U.S. Public*, pg. 151

CONSOLIDATED WATER POWER CO.—See Consolidated Papers, Inc.; *U.S. Public*, pg. 436

CONSOLIDATED WHOLESALE LUMBER CO.—See Calcasieu Lumber Company; *U.S. Private*, pg. 200

CONSOLIDATED WOOL SERVICES PTY. LTD.—See Brambles Industries Limited; *Int'l*, pg. 211

CONSOLIDATED X-RAY SERVICE CORPORATION—See Costain Group PLC; *Int'l*, pg. 337

CONSOLIDATION COAL CO.-EASTERN REGION—See Du Pont (E.I. Du Pont De Nemours & Co.); *U.S. Public*, pg. 531

CONSOLIDATION COAL CO.-MID-CONTINENT REGION— See Du Pont (E.I. Du Pont De Nemours & Co.); *U.S. Public*, pg. 531

CONSOLIDATION COAL CO., REND LAKE MINE—See Du Pont (E.I. Du Pont De Nemours & Co.); *U.S. Public*, pg. 531

CONSOLIDATION COAL RESEARCH & DEVELOPMENT— See Du Pont (E.I. Du Pont De Nemours & Co.); *U.S. Public*, pg. 531

CONSOLTEX GROUP INC.; *Int'l*, pg. 326

CONSORCIO G. GRUPO DINA, S.A. DE C.V.; *Int'l*, pg. 326

CONSORCIO INDUSTRIAL PACKSA, S.A. DE C.V.—See Royal Packaging Industries Van Leer B.V.; *Int'l*, pg. 1146

CONSORCIO INTERMEX S.A. DE C.V.—See CYDSA S.A.; *Int'l*, pg. 246

CONSORCIO NACIONAL FORD LTDA.—See Ford Motor Company; *U.S. Public*, pg. 665

CONSORTIUM VINICOLE DE BORDEAUX ET DE LA GIRONDE S.A.—See Koninklijke BolsWessanen nv; *Int'l*, pg. 752

CONSORZIO CONSAC—See Compagnie des Machines Bull; *Int'l*, pg. 317

CONSORZIO CORESIA—See Compagnie des Machines Bull; *Int'l*, pg. 317

CONSORZIO GESPIMV—See Compagnie des Machines Bull; *Int'l*, pg. 317

CONSORZIO INFORMATICA A.T.—See Compagnie des Machines Bull; *Int'l*, pg. 318

CONSORZIO INFORSUD—See Compagnie des Machines Bull; *Int'l*, pg. 317

CONSORZIO INFORTURISM—See Compagnie des Machines Bull; *Int'l*, pg. 318

CONSORZIO PER LO SVILUPPO—See Compagnie des Machines Bull; *Int'l*, pg. 318

CONSORZIO PINACOS—See Compagnie des Machines Bull; *Int'l*, pg. 318

CONSORZIO RESOURCE SOCIETY—See Compagnie des Machines Bull; *Int'l*, pg. 318

CONSORZIO SATSCA—See Compagnie des Machines Bull; *Int'l*, pg. 318

CONSORZIO SIMT—See Compagnie des Machines Bull; *Int'l*, pg. 318

CONSTAR INC.—See Heidelberger Zement A.G.; *Int'l*, pg. 605

CONSTAR INTERNATIONAL, INC.—See Crown Cork & Seal Company, Inc.; *U.S. Public*, pg. 463

CONSTEL S.A.—See Telefonaktiebolaget LM Ericsson; *Int'l*, pg. 1365

CONSTELLATION ENERGY PROJECTS & SERVICES, INC.—See Baltimore Gas and Electric Company; *U.S. Public*, pg. 172

CONSTELLATION ENERGY SOURCE, INC.—See Baltimore Gas and Electric Company; *U.S. Public*, pg. 172

CONSTELLATION HOLDINGS, INC.—See Baltimore Gas and Electric Company; *U.S. Public*, pg. 172

CONSTELLATION INVESTMENTS, INC.—See Baltimore Gas and Electric Company; *U.S. Public*, pg. 172

CONSTELLATION POWER, INC.—See Baltimore Gas and Electric Company; *U.S. Public*, pg. 172

CONSTELLATION REAL ESTATE GROUP INC.—See Baltimore Gas and Electric Company; *U.S. Public*, pg. 172

CONSTITUTION HOLDING INC.—See Exor Group; *Int'l*, pg. 467

CONSTITUTION LIFE INSURANCE CO.—See Southwestern Financial Corporation; *U.S. Private*, pg. 1018

CONSTITUTION RE CORP.—See Exor Group; *Int'l*, pg. 467

CONSTITUTION REINSURANCE CORPORATION—See Exor Group; *Int'l*, pg. 467

CONSTRUCCIONES AERONAUTICAS, SA—See The Boeing Company; *U.S. Public*, pg. 242

CONSTRUCCIONES AERONAUTICAS, S.A. (CASA)—See Northrop Grumman Corporation; *U.S. Public*, pg. 1199

CONSTRUCCIONES AGROMETALICAS LEVANTE, S.A. (CALSA)—See Tenneco Inc.; *U.S. Public*, pg. 1579

CONSTRUCCIONES CAPITAL LTDA.—See Corporacion MAPFRE, Compania Internacional de Reaseguros, S.A.; *Int'l*, pg. 333

CONSTRUCCIONES INSTALACIONES BABCOCK S.A. DE C.V.—See FKI Plc; *Int'l*, pg. 474

CONSTRUCCIONES PITT-DES MOINES VENEZUELA, C.A.—See Pitt-Des Moines, Inc.; *U.S. Public*, pg. 1304

CONSTRUCCIONES RADIO ELECTRO MECANICAS S.A.—See Caparo Group Ltd.; *Int'l*, pg. 265

CONSTRUCCIONES TELEFONICAS S.A.—See Telefonaktiebolaget LM Ericsson; *Int'l*, pg. 1365

CONSTRUCTION & ENGINEERING UNDERWRITERS (PTY.) LTD.—See Assicurazioni Generali S.p.A.; *Int'l*, pg. 91

CONSTRUCTION & HOME IMPROVEMENT MARKETS DIVISION—See 3M; *U.S. Public*, pg. 1605

CONSTRUCTION & MINING INC.—See The Danis Companies; *U.S. Private*, pg. 310

CONSTRUCTION COUNSELLORS, INC.; *U.S. Private*, pg. 266

CONSTRUCTION DEVELOPERS INC.—See Dillard's, Inc.; *U.S. Public*, pg. 509

CONSTRUCTION EQUIPMENT GROUP—See Ingersoll-Rand Company; *U.S. Public*, pg. 876

CONSTRUCTION LENDING CORPORATION OF AMERICA-BUILDER DIVISION—See INMC Mortgage Holdings, Inc.; *U.S. Public*, pg. 857

CONSTRUCTION LOANS—See CVB Financial Corp.; *U.S. Public*, pg. 287

CONSTRUCTION MANAGEMENT SERVICE; *U.S. Private*, pg. 266

CONSTRUCTION MECANIQUE ET HYDRAULIQUE DE VENDEE—See Jeumont-Schneider Trenformeteurs; *Int'l*, pg. 706

CONSTRUCTION RESEARCH COMMUNICATIONS—See EMAP Plc; *Int'l*, pg. 451

CONSTRUCTION SERVICES—See Canadian Erectors Ltd.; *Int'l*, pg. 256

CONSTRUCTION SPECIALTIES, INC.; *U.S. Private*, pg. 266

CONSTRUCTION SPECIALTIES OF CALIFORNIA—See Construction Specialties, Inc.; *U.S. Private*, pg. 266

CONSTRUCTIONS ENTREPRISES GENERALES, IMPREFER S.A.—See Fiat Auto SpA; *Int'l*, pg. 482

CONSTRUCTIONS FERROVIAIRES DU MANS (CFM)— See Jeumont-Schneider Trenformeteurs; *Int'l*, pg. 706

CONSTRUCTIONS GENERALES ELECTRIQUES ER GAZIERES COGEGAZ S.A.—See Ruhrgas Aktiengesellschaft; *Int'l*, pg. 1149

CONSTRUCTIVE COMMUNICATIONS, INC.—See Tyco International Ltd.; *U.S. Public*, pg. 1649

CONSTRUCTORA ALMEX S.A.—See Dyckerhoff & Widmann AG; *Int'l*, pg. 424

CONSTRUCTORA DUMEZ DE CHILE—See Lyonnaise des Eaux S.A.; *Int'l*, pg. 823

CONSTRUCTORA VENEZOLANO DE VEHICULOS, C.A.— See General Motors Corporation; *U.S. Public*, pg. 723

CONSTRUCTORA DUMEZ-GTM LTDA—See Lyonnaise des Eaux S.A.; *Int'l*, pg. 823

CONSTRUTORA SHIMIZU DO BRASIL LTDA.-MANAUS OFFICE—See Shimizu Corporation; *Int'l*, pg. 1233

CONSTRUTORA SHIMIZU DO BRASIL LTDA.-RIO DE JANEIRO OFFICE—See Shimizu Corporation; *Int'l*, pg. 1233

CONSTRUTORA SHIMIZU DO BRASIL LTDA.-SAO PAULO OFFICE—See Shimizu Corporation; *Int'l*, pg. 1233

CONSTRUTORA SHIMIZU DO BRASIL LTDA.-VITORIA OFFICE—See Shimizu Corporation; *Int'l*, pg. 1233

CONSTRUZIONI FERROVIARIE DI COLLEFERRO S.P.A.— See Fiat Auto SpA; *Int'l*, pg. 481

CONSUL S.A.—See Whirlpool Corporation; *U.S. Public*, pg. 1765

CONSULAB MANNHEIM GMBH FUR LABORBERATUNG—See Corange Limited; *Int'l*, pg. 331

CONSULTA CHEMIE GMBH—See Burmah Castrol plc; *Int'l*, pg. 236

N.V. CONSULTANTS & ASSISTANTS "CONSULTASS"— See ABN-AMRO Holding N.V.; *Int'l*, pg. 9

CONSULTEC, INC.—See General American Life Insurance Co.; *U.S. Private*, pg. 443

CONSULTING AND ENGINEERING AGROBER COMPANY—See Heidemij N.V.; *Int'l*, pg. 607

CONSULTING & SYSTEMS INTEGRATION—See Computer Sciences Corporation; *U.S. Public*, pg. 422

CONSULTING ENGINEERS GRABOWSKY & POORT BV— See Heidemij N.V.; *Int'l*, pg. 607

CONSULTING INFORMATICO S.A. (CINSA)—See Marcam Solutions, Inc.; *U.S. Public*, pg. 1043

CONSULTORA ACTUARIAL Y DE PENSIONES MAPFRE VIDA, S.A.—See Corporacion MAPFRE, Compania Internacional de Reaseguros, S.A.; *Int'l*, pg. 334

CONSULTORES DE PENSIONES, S.R.L.—See Assicurazioni Generali S.p.A.; *Int'l*, pg. 91

CONSULTORES OCCIDENTALES, S.A. (COSA)—See Agra Inc.; *Int'l*, pg. 31

CONSUMER & INFORMATION SERVICE DIVISION—See Tokyu Corporation; *Int'l*, pg. 1395

CONSUMER AND SMALL BUSINESS MARKETS—See Sprint Corporation; *U.S. Public*, pg. 1501

CONSUMER AUDIO & VIDEO SALES—See Hitachi, Ltd.; *Int'l*, pg. 622

CONSUMER AUDIO PRODUCTS CO.—See Sony Corporation; *Int'l*, pg. 1281

CONSUMER DISPLAY PRODUCTS CO.—See Sony Corporation; *Int'l*, pg. 1281

CONSUMER FINANCE GROUP—See Washington Mutual Inc.; *U.S. Public*, pg. 1741

CONSUMER FOODS GROUP—See Goodman Fielder Limited; *Int'l*, pg. 555

CONSUMER GROUP SPECIAL MARKETS—See National Amusements, Inc.; *U.S. Private*, pg. 777

Company Index

CONSUMER IMAGING DIVISION—See Eastman Kodak Company; *U.S. Public,* pg. 555
CONSUMER MARKETING SERVICES, INC.—See First Chicago NBD Corporation; *U.S. Public,* pg. 628
CONSUMER PRODUCTS BUSINESS—See Fort James Corporation; *U.S. Public,* pg. 671
CONSUMER PRODUCTS COMPANY—See Alltrista Corporation; *U.S. Public,* pg. 56
CONSUMER PRODUCTS (PRIVATE) LTD.—See Unilever Plc; *Int'l,* pg. 1436
CONSUMER SALES PRODUCTS CO.—See Sony Corporation; *Int'l,* pg. 1281
CONSUMER SERVICES GROUP—See Sprint Corporation; *U.S. Public,* pg. 1501
CONSUMER SUPPORT SERVICES, INC.—See Torchmark Corporation; *U.S. Public,* pg. 1623
CONSUMER VIDEO PRODUCTS CO.—See Sony Corporation; *Int'l,* pg. 1281
CONSUMERS CAR CARE CORPORATION—See Consumers Financial Corporation; *U.S. Public,* pg. 438
CONSUMERS ENERGY—See CMS Energy Corporation; *U.S. Public,* pg. 280
CONSUMERS FINANCIAL CORPORATION; *U.S. Public,* pg. 437
THE CONSUMERS' GAS COMPANY LTD.—See IPL Energy Inc.; *Int'l,* pg. 652
CONSUMERS ILLINOIS WATER CO.—See Consumers Water Company; *U.S. Public,* pg. 438
CONSUMERS LIFE INSURANCE COMPANY—See Consumers Financial Corporation; *U.S. Public,* pg. 438
CONSUMERS MAINE WATER—See Consumers Water Company; *U.S. Public,* pg. 438
CONSUMERS MARKETS INC.—See Fleming Companies, Inc.; *U.S. Public,* pg. 653
CONSUMERS MINING COMPANY—See WHX Corporation; *U.S. Public,* pg. 1726
CONSUMERS NEW HAMPSHIRE WATER CO.—See Consumers Water Company; *U.S. Public,* pg. 438
CONSUMERS NEW JERSEY WATER COMPANY—See Consumers Water Company; *U.S. Public,* pg. 438
CONSUMERS OHIO WATER COMPANY—See Consumers Water Company; *U.S. Public,* pg. 438
CONSUMERS PACKAGING INC.; *Int'l,* pg. 326
CONSUMERS REINSURANCE COMPANY—See Consumers Financial Corporation; *U.S. Public,* pg. 438
CONSUMERS SERVICE COMPANY—See Consumers Water Company; *U.S. Public,* pg. 439
CONSUMERS WATER COMPANY; *U.S. Public,* pg. 438
CONTABILIDAD MECANIZADA, SOCIEDAD ANONIMA—See Cigna Corp.; *U.S. Public,* pg. 364
CONTADINA DALLA CASA BUITONI—See Nestle S.A.; *Int'l,* pg. 916
CONTADINA FRESH—See Nestle S.A.; *Int'l,* pg. 918
CONTADINA/LIBBY/TRENTON DIV.—See Nestle S.A.; *Int'l,* pg. 916
CONTAINER CARE INTERNATIONAL; *U.S. Private,* pg. 266
CONTAINER CARE INTERNATIONAL—See Container Care International; *U.S. Private,* pg. 267
CONTAINER GRAPHICS CORPORATION; *U.S. Private,* pg. 267
CONTAINER PORT GROUP—See World Shipping, Inc.; *U.S. Private,* pg. 1191
B.V. CONTAINER SERVICE—See Royal Nedlloyd Group N.V.; *Int'l,* pg. 1144
CONTAINER STRAPPING—See Illinois Tool Works Inc.; *U.S. Public,* pg. 867
CONTAINER TOOLING CORPORATION—See Federal Signal Corporation; *U.S. Public,* pg. 617
CONTAMINANT RECOVERY SYSTEMS—See Essef Corporation; *U.S. Public,* pg. 592
CONTASSUR ASSISTANCE-CONSEIL S.A.—See Tractebel; *Int'l,* pg. 1415
CONTASSUR S.A.—See Electrabel S.A.; *Int'l,* pg. 1273
CONTE S.A.—See Societe BIC S.A.; *Int'l,* pg. 1273
CONTEC LIMITED PARTNERSHIP—See Manhattan Partners L.P.; *U.S. Private,* pg. 699
CONTECH CONSTRUCTION PRODUCTS INC.; *U.S. Private,* pg. 267
CONTECH DIV. (KALAMAZOO)—See SPX Corporation; *U.S. Public,* pg. 1421
CONTEMPO CASUALS—See The Wet Seal, Inc.; *U.S. Public,* pg. 1763
CONTEMPO COLORS; *U.S. Private,* pg. 267
CONTEMPORARY COMMUNICATIONS CORPORATION—See Motorola, Inc.; *U.S. Public,* pg. 1137
CONTEMPORARY DIGITAL SERVICES, INC.—See Motorola, Inc.; *U.S. Public,* pg. 1137
CONTEMPORARY GROUP, INC.—See Motorola, Inc.; *U.S. Public,* pg. 1137
CONTEMPRI HOMES, INC.; *U.S. Public,* pg. 439
CONTENANTS GREIF INC.—See Greif Brothers Corporation; *U.S. Public,* pg. 764
CONTEX PREPRESS SYSTEMS—See Xyvision, Inc.; *U.S. Public,* pg. 1787
CONTICO CONTAINER COMPANY—See Contico International, Inc.; *U.S. Private,* pg. 267
CONTICO INTERNATIONAL, INC.; *U.S. Private,* pg. 267
CONTIFINANCIAL CORPORATION; *U.S. Public,* pg. 439
CONTIFINANCIAL SERVICES CORPORATION—See ContiFinancial Corporation; *U.S. Public,* pg. 439
CONTIMORTGAGE CORPORATION—See ContiFinancial Corporation; *U.S. Public,* pg. 439
CONTINENTAL AG; *Int'l,* pg. 327
CONTINENTAL AIRLINE HOLDINGS, INC.—See Scandinavian Airlines System (SAS); *Int'l,* pg. 1202
CONTINENTAL AIRLINES; *U.S. Public,* pg. 439
CONTINENTAL AMERICAN CORP.; *U.S. Private,* pg. 267
CONTINENTAL ASSURANCE COMPANY; *U.S. Private,* pg. 267
CONTINENTAL AUXILIARY COMPANY TRUSTEE—See BankAmerica Corporation; *U.S. Public,* pg. 181
CONTINENTAL AVIATION UNDERWRITERS, INC.—See Reliance Group Holdings, Inc.; *U.S. Public,* pg. 1374

CONTINENTAL BANK NEW YORK TRUST COMPANY—See BankAmerica Corporation; *U.S. Public,* pg. 181
CONTINENTAL BISCUITS LIMITED—See Danone Group; *Int'l,* pg. 380
CONTINENTAL CAN CO.; *U.S. Public,* pg. 439
CONTINENTAL CAN COMPANY LTD.—See Schmalbach-Lubeca AG; *Int'l,* pg. 1207
CONTINENTAL CAN COMPANY OF EUROPE B.V.—See Schmalbach-Lubeca AG; *Int'l,* pg. 1207
CONTINENTAL CAN COMPANY (WREXHAM) LTD.—See Schmalbach-Lubeca AG; *Int'l,* pg. 1207
CONTINENTAL CAN DISTRIBUTION S.A.R.L.—See Schmalbach-Lubeca AG; *Int'l,* pg. 1207
CONTINENTAL CAN EUROPE BETEILIGUNGSGESELLSCHAFT MBH—See Schmalbach-Lubeca AG; *Int'l,* pg. 1207
CONTINENTAL CAN EUROPE GMBH HOLDING—See Viag AG; *Int'l,* pg. 1464
CONTINENTAL CAN EUROPE SERVICE CENTER N.V.—See Schmalbach-Lubeca AG; *Int'l,* pg. 1207
CONTINENTAL CAN EUROPE SERVICES B.V.—See Schmalbach-Lubeca AG; *Int'l,* pg. 1207
CONTINENTAL CAN EUROPE VERPACKUNGSGESELLSCHAFT HERMSDORF MBH—See Schmalbach-Lubeca AG; *Int'l,* pg. 1206
CONTINENTAL CAN EUROPEAN INDUSTRIES N.V.—See Schmalbach-Lubeca AG; *Int'l,* pg. 1207
CONTINENTAL CAN FRANCE S.A.—See Schmalbach-Lubeca AG; *Int'l,* pg. 1207
CONTINENTAL CAN G.I.E.—See Schmalbach-Lubeca AG; *Int'l,* pg. 1207
CONTINENTAL CAN OF SAUDI ARABIA—See Crown Cork & Seal Company, Inc.; *U.S. Public,* pg. 465
CONTINENTAL CAN POLSKA SP.ZO.O.—See Schmalbach-Lubeca AG; *Int'l,* pg. 1207
CONTINENTAL CAN UK HOLDING COMPANY LTD.—See Schmalbach-Lubeca AG; *Int'l,* pg. 1207
CONTINENTAL CAOUTCHOUC (SUISSE) S.A.—See Continental AG; *Int'l,* pg. 327
CONTINENTAL CARBON COMPANY—See China Synthetic Rubber Corporation; *Int'l,* pg. 286
CONTINENTAL CATALINA, INC.—See Continental Materials Corporation; *U.S. Public,* pg. 441
CONTINENTAL CEMENT CO. INC.—See Scancem AB; *Int'l,* pg. 1201
CONTINENTAL CEMENT CO. OF FLORIDA INC.—See Scancem AB; *Int'l,* pg. 1201
CONTINENTAL CIRCUITS CORP.; *U.S. Public,* pg. 440
CONTINENTAL COFFEE—See The Quaker Oats Company; *U.S. Public,* pg. 1348
CONTINENTAL COIN CORPORATION; *U.S. Private,* pg. 267
CONTINENTAL COMMUNITY DEVELOPMENT CORP.—See BankAmerica Corporation; *U.S. Public,* pg. 181
CONTINENTAL CONAIR, LTD.—See Conair Corporation; *U.S. Private,* pg. 261
CONTINENTAL CONVEYOR & EQUIPMENT COMPANY—See NESCO; *U.S. Private,* pg. 791
CONTINENTAL COPPER, INC.—See Continental Materials Corporation; *U.S. Public,* pg. 441
THE CONTINENTAL CORPORATION—See Loews Corporation; *U.S. Public,* pg. 1011
CONTINENTAL DATA CENTER—See Loews Corporation; *U.S. Public,* pg. 1011
CONTINENTAL DIVIDE INSURANCE CO.—See Berkshire Hathaway Inc.; *U.S. Public,* pg. 221
CONTINENTAL DYNAMICS, INC.—See Analysis & Technology, Inc.; *U.S. Public,* pg. 110
CONTINENTAL EAGLE CORPORATION; *U.S. Private,* pg. 267
CONTINENTAL EAGLE VISALIA, CA—See Continental Eagle Corporation; *U.S. Private,* pg. 267
CONTINENTAL ELECTRIC—See Maclean-Fogg Co.; *U.S. Private,* pg. 692
CONTINENTAL ELECTRONICS CORPORATION—See Tech-Sym Corporation; *U.S. Public,* pg. 1563
CONTINENTAL ENERGY SERVICES, INC.—See Montana Power Company; *U.S. Public,* pg. 1127
CONTINENTAL EUROPE—See United Biscuits (Holdings) Plc; *Int'l,* pg. 1442
CONTINENTAL EUROPEAN REPRESENTATIVE OFFICE—See GATX Corporation; *U.S. Public,* pg. 692
CONTINENTAL EXPRESS—See Continental Airlines; *U.S. Public,* pg. 439
CONTINENTAL FEDERAL SAVING & LOAN—See Banc One Corporation; *U.S. Public,* pg. 174
CONTINENTAL FEMCSOMAGOLO MAGYARORSZAG KFT.—See Schmalbach-Lubeca AG; *Int'l,* pg. 1207
CONTINENTAL FORGE COMPANY; *U.S. Private,* pg. 268
CONTINENTAL GENERAL CORPORATION—See The Western and Southern Life Insurance Company; *U.S. Private,* pg. 1164
CONTINENTAL GENERAL INSURANCE COMPANY—See The Western and Southern Life Insurance Company; *U.S. Private,* pg. 1164
CONTINENTAL GENERAL TIRE, INC.—See Continental AG; *Int'l,* pg. 327
CONTINENTAL GENERAL TIRE INC.—See Continental AG; *Int'l,* pg. 327
CONTINENTAL GISLAVED DACK—See Continental AG; *Int'l,* pg. 327
CONTINENTAL GRAIN COMPANY; *U.S. Private,* pg. 268
CONTINENTAL GRAPHICS CORPORATION—See Continental Graphics Holdings, Inc.; *U.S. Private,* pg. 268
CONTINENTAL GRAPHICS HOLDINGS, INC.; *U.S. Private,* pg. 268
CONTINENTAL HEALTH AFFILIATES, INC.; *U.S. Public,* pg. 440
CONTINENTAL HOLDINGS INC.—See Loews Corporation; *U.S. Public,* pg. 1011
CONTINENTAL HOMES HOLDING CORP.; *U.S. Public,* pg. 440

CONTINENTAL HOMES, INC.—See Continental Homes Holding Corp.; *U.S. Public,* pg. 440
CONTINENTAL HOMES OF AUSTIN, L.P.—See Continental Homes Holding Corp.; *U.S. Public,* pg. 441
CONTINENTAL HOMES OF CALIFORNIA—See Continental Homes Holding Corp.; *U.S. Public,* pg. 441
CONTINENTAL HOMES OF DALLAS, L.P.—See Continental Homes Holding Corp.; *U.S. Public,* pg. 441
CONTINENTAL HOMES OF DENVER—See Continental Homes Holding Corp.; *U.S. Public,* pg. 441
CONTINENTAL HOMES OF MIAMI—See Continental Homes Holding Corp.; *U.S. Public,* pg. 441
CONTINENTAL HOMES OF SAN ANTONIO, L.P.—See Continental Homes Holding Corp.; *U.S. Public,* pg. 441
CONTINENTAL ILLINOIS VENTURE CORP.—See BankAmerica Corporation; *U.S. Public,* pg. 181
CONTINENTAL INDUSTRIEAS DEL CAUCHO SA—See Continental AG; *Int'l,* pg. 328
CONTINENTAL INDUSTRIES INC.—See Handy & Harman; *U.S. Public,* pg. 780
THE CONTINENTAL INSURANCE CO.—See Loews Corporation; *U.S. Public,* pg. 1011
CONTINENTAL INSURANCE CO. (U.K.) LTD.—See Loews Corporation; *U.S. Public,* pg. 1011
CONTINENTAL INTERNATIONAL LIFE INSURANCE CO.—See UNUM Corporation; *U.S. Public,* pg. 1700
CONTINENTAL ITALIA S.P.A.—See Continental AG; *Int'l,* pg. 328
CONTINENTAL LEBENSVERSICHERUNGSGESELLSCHAFT—See Allianz Aktiengesellschaft; *Int'l,* pg. 61
CONTINENTAL-LENSA S.A.—See Tech-Sym Corporation; *U.S. Public,* pg. 1563
CONTINENTAL LIFE INSURANCE COMPANY—See Conseco Inc.; *U.S. Public,* pg. 433
CONTINENTAL LIFE INSURANCE PLC—See Loews Corporation; *U.S. Public,* pg. 1011
CONTINENTAL LUMBER—See Fleetwood Enterprises, Inc.; *U.S. Public,* pg. 651
CONTINENTAL MABOR INDUSTRIA DE ANEUS S.A.—See Continental AG; *Int'l,* pg. 328
CONTINENTAL MACHINES, INC.; *U.S. Private,* pg. 268
CONTINENTAL MATERIALS CORPORATION; *U.S. Public,* pg. 441
CONTINENTAL MEDICAL SYSTEMS, INC.—See Horizon/CMS Healthcare Corporation; *U.S. Public,* pg. 839
CONTINENTAL MG PLAST A.S.—See Schmalbach-Lubeca AG; *Int'l,* pg. 1207
CONTINENTAL MICROWAVE (HOLDINGS) PLC—See Spectra-Physics AB; *Int'l,* pg. 1289
CONTINENTAL MICROWAVE LTD.—See Spectra-Physics AB; *Int'l,* pg. 1289
CONTINENTAL MICROWAVE TECHNOLOGY, INC.—See Spectra-Physics AB; *Int'l,* pg. 1289
CONTINENTAL MICROWAVE TECHNOLOGY LTD.—See Spectra-Physics AB; *Int'l,* pg. 1289
CONTINENTAL/MIDLAND, INC.; *U.S. Private,* pg. 268
CONTINENTAL MILLS, INC.; *U.S. Private,* pg. 269
CONTINENTAL MORTGAGE AND EQUITY TRUST; *U.S. Public,* pg. 441
CONTINENTAL NATIONAL LIFE INSURANCE CO.—See UNUM Corporation; *U.S. Public,* pg. 1700
CONTINENTAL NETHERLANDS OIL COMPANY—See Du Pont (E.I. Du Pont De Nemours & Co.); *U.S. Public,* pg. 532
CONTINENTAL PAPER & SUPPLY CO.; *U.S. Private,* pg. 269
CONTINENTAL PAPER RECYCLING LLC; *U.S. Private,* pg. 269
CONTINENTAL PARTNERS GROUP, INC.—See BankAmerica Corporation; *U.S. Public,* pg. 181
CONTINENTAL PET DEUTSCHLAND GMBH—See Schmalbach-Lubeca AG; *Int'l,* pg. 1206
CONTINENTAL PET ESPANA S.A.—See Schmalbach-Lubeca AG; *Int'l,* pg. 1207
CONTINENTAL PET EUROPE GMBH—See Schmalbach-Lubeca AG; *Int'l,* pg. 1206
CONTINENTAL PET FRANCE S.A.—See Schmalbach-Lubeca AG; *Int'l,* pg. 1207
CONTINENTAL PIR COMMUNICATIONS, INC.—See Shandwick International Plc; *Int'l,* pg. 1226
CONTINENTAL PLASTIC CARD CO.; *U.S. Private,* pg. 269
CONTINENTAL PLASTIC CONTAINERS, INC.—See Continental Can Co.; *U.S. Public,* pg. 440
CONTINENTAL PRINT & PHOTO CO.—See The Western and Southern Life Insurance Company; *U.S. Private,* pg. 1164
CONTINENTAL PROMOTION GROUP; *U.S. Private,* pg. 269
CONTINENTAL QUICKSILVER, INC.—See Continental Materials Corporation; *U.S. Public,* pg. 441
CONTINENTAL RANCH, INC.—See Continental Homes Holding Corp.; *U.S. Public,* pg. 441
CONTINENTAL REINSURANCE CORP.—See Loews Corporation; *U.S. Public,* pg. 1011
CONTINENTAL TELEPHONE CO.—See Telephone and Data Systems, Inc.; *U.S. Public,* pg. 1571
CONTINENTAL TYRE & RUBBER GROUP LTD.—See Continental AG; *Int'l,* pg. 328
CONTINENTAL URANIUM, INC.—See Continental Materials Corporation; *U.S. Public,* pg. 441
CONTINENTAL WATER COMPANY; *U.S. Private,* pg. 269
CONTINENTAL WEB PRESS, INC.; *U.S. Private,* pg. 269
CONTINENTAL WEB PRESS OF KENTUCKY—See Continental Web Press, Inc.; *U.S. Private,* pg. 269
CONTINENTAL WESTERN INSURANCE COMPANY—See W.R. Berkley Corporation; *U.S. Public,* pg. 215
CONTINENTAL WOOD PRESERVERS, INC.—See Nortek, Inc.; *U.S. Public,* pg. 1193
CONTINENTALE ALLGEMEINE VERSICHERUNGS-AG—See Allianz Aktiengesellschaft; *Int'l,* pg. 61
CONTINENTALE FINANZ GESELLSCHAFT A. ASMUSSEN GMBH & CO.—See Bayerische Vereinsbank Group; *Int'l,* pg. 179

CONTINUUM ASIA—See Computer Sciences Corporation; *U.S. Public*, pg. 423

CONTINUUM AUSTRALIA LIMITED—See Computer Sciences Corporation; *U.S. Public*, pg. 423

THE CONTINUUM COMPANY (FRANCE)—See Computer Sciences Corporation; *U.S. Public*, pg. 423

THE CONTINUUM COMPANY, INC.—See Computer Sciences Corporation; *U.S. Public*, pg. 422

THE CONTINUUM COMPANY, INC. (CANADA)—See Computer Sciences Corporation; *U.S. Public*, pg. 423

THE CONTINUUM COMPANY, INC. (DENMARK)—See Computer Sciences Corporation; *U.S. Public*, pg. 423

THE CONTINUUM COMPANY, INC. (EUROPE)—See Computer Sciences Corporation; *U.S. Public*, pg. 423

THE CONTINUUM COMPANY, INC. (NETHERLANDS)—See Computer Sciences Corporation; *U.S. Public*, pg. 423

THE CONTINUUM COMPANY, INC. (NORWAY)—See Computer Sciences Corporation; *U.S. Public*, pg. 423

THE CONTINUUM COMPANY, INC. (PORTUGAL)—See Computer Sciences Corporation; *U.S. Public*, pg. 423

THE CONTINUUM COMPANY, INC. (SWITZERLAND)—See Computer Sciences Corporation; *U.S. Public*, pg. 423

THE CONTINUUM COMPANY (JAPAN), LTD.—See Computer Sciences Corporation; *U.S. Public*, pg. 423

THE CONTINUUM COMPANY, LTD.—See Computer Sciences Corporation; *U.S. Public*, pg. 423

CONTINUUM (DEUTSCHLAND) GMBH—See Computer Sciences Corporation; *U.S. Public*, pg. 423

CONTINUUM (FRANCE) SARL—See Computer Sciences Corporation; *U.S. Public*, pg. 423

CONTINUUM (NZ) LIMITED—See Computer Sciences Corporation; *U.S. Public*, pg. 423

CONTITECH AGES S.P.A.—See Continental AG; *Int'l*, pg. 328

CONTITRADE SERVICES L.L.C.—See ContiFinancial Corporation; *U.S. Public*, pg. 439

CONTRA COSTA NEWSPAPERS, INC.—See Knight-Ridder, Inc.; *U.S. Public*, pg. 964

CONTRA COSTA TIMES—See Knight-Ridder, Inc.; *U.S. Public*, pg. 964

CONTRACT FREIGHTERS, INC.; *U.S. Private*, pg. 270

CONTRACT INTERIORS, INC.; *U.S. Private*, pg. 270

CONTRACT PAPERS (HOLDINGS) LTD—See N.V. Koninklijke KNP BT; *Int'l*, pg. 757

CONTRACT PAPERS LIMITED—See N.V. Koninklijke KNP BT; *Int'l*, pg. 757

CONTRACT TRANSPORTATION SYSTEMS CO.—See The Sherwin-Williams Company; *U.S. Public*, pg. 1466

CONTRACTOR EQUIPMENT SUPPLY COMPANY (CESCO)—See Lombardi Holdings Inc.; *U.S. Private*, pg. 673

CONTRACTORS MACHINERY & EQUIPMENT—See Hanson PLC; *Int'l*, pg. 594

CONTRACTORS STEEL COMPANY; *U.S. Private*, pg. 270

CONTRACTORS SUPPLIES, INC.; *U.S. Private*, pg. 270

CONTRACTORS SUPPLY COMPANY, INC.; *U.S. Private*, pg. 270

CONTRAN CORPORATION; *U.S. Private*, pg. 270

CONTRANS CORPORATION; *Int'l*, pg. 328

CONTRAVES ADVANCED DEVICES, SDN. BHD.—See Oerlikon-Buhrle Holding AG; *Int'l*, pg. 998

CONTRAVES GMBH—See Oerlikon-Buhrle Holding AG; *Int'l*, pg. 998

CONTRAVES INC.—See Oerlikon-Buhrle Holding AG; *Int'l*, pg. 998

CONTROL & INFORMATION GROUP—See Rockwell International Corporation; *Int'l*, pg. 1397

CONTROL COMPONENTS, INC.—See IMI Plc; *Int'l*, pg. 646

CONTROL DATA SYSTEMS, INC.; *U.S. Public*, pg. 441

CONTROL DYNAMICS DIVISION—See bd Systems, Inc; *U.S. Private*, pg. 106

CONTROL ENGINEERING CO.—See Jervis B. Webb Company; *U.S. Private*, pg. 1156

CONTROL EQUIPMENT CO.—See Eclipse Inc.; *U.S. Private*, pg. 360

CONTROL INSTRUMENTS (M) SDN. BHD—See Eclipse Inc.; *U.S. Private*, pg. 361

CONTROL LASER CORPORATION—See Excel Technology, Inc.; *U.S. Public*, pg. 599

CONTROL MODULE, INC.; *U.S. Private*, pg. 271

CONTROL NETWORK COMMUNICATIONS—See General Electric Company; *U.S. Public*, pg. 711

CONTROL SYSTEMS DIV.-MILITARY—See Parker Hannifin Corporation; *U.S. Public*, pg. 1262

CONTROL SYSTEMS DIVISION-COMMERCIAL—See Parker Hannifin Corporation; *U.S. Public*, pg. 1262

CONTROL SYSTEMS INC.; *U.S. Private*, pg. 271

CONTROL TECHNIQUE LIMITED—See Emerson Electric Co.; *U.S. Public*, pg. 576

CONTROL TRANSFORMER CORP.—See BBA Group plc; *Int'l*, pg. 113

CONTROLADORA COMERCIAL MEXICANA, S.A. DE C.V.; *Int'l*, pg. 328

CONTROLE BAILEY DIVISION—See Alcatel Alsthom Compagnie Generale D'Electricite; *Int'l*, pg. 52

CONTROLLED POWER (CPC)—See American Eco Corporation; *U.S. Public*, pg. 74

CONTROLLED SYSTEMS OF WISCONSIN, INC.; *U.S. Private*, pg. 271

CONTROLMATIC GMBH—See Hepworth Plc; *Int'l*, pg. 615

CONTRONIC DEVELOPMENT AB—See Perstorp AB; *Int'l*, pg. 1039

CONUS COMMUNICATION COMPANY LIMITED PARTNERSHIP—See Hubbard Broadcasting, Inc.; *U.S. Private*, pg. 544

CONVAIR COOLER CORP.; *U.S. Private*, pg. 271

CONVAIR DIV.—See General Dynamics Corporation; *U.S. Public*, pg. 709

CONVALESCENT CENTER OF THE PALM BEACHES—See Vencor, Inc.; *U.S. Public*, pg. 1712

CONVENIENCE PLUS PARTNERS LTD.; *U.S. Private*, pg. 271

CONVENIENCE PRODUCTS, INC.—See Clayton Corporation; *U.S. Private*, pg. 244

CONVENIENCE STORES DISTRIBUTORS—See Marsh Supermarkets, Inc.; *U.S. Public*, pg. 1049

CONVENIENT FOOD MART, INC.; *U.S. Private*, pg. 271

CONVENTRY HOMES OF PHOENIX—See Del Webb Corporation; *U.S. Public*, pg. 495

CONVERFLEX AB—See UPM-Kymmene Corporation; *Int'l*, pg. 1429

CONVERGENT, INC.—See Unisys Corporation; *U.S. Public*, pg. 1671

CONVERSE INC.; *U.S. Public*, pg. 441

CONVERSE LAND TITLE COMPANY—See The First American Financial Corporation; *U.S. Public*, pg. 625

THE CONVERSE PROFESSIONAL GROUP, INC.; *U.S. Private*, pg. 271

CONVERSION SYSTEMS, INC.—See EnviroSource, Inc.; *U.S. Public*, pg. 587

CONVERT VLIESVEREDELUNG GMBH—See Freudenberg & Company; *Int'l*, pg. 506

CONVERT VLIESVEREDELUNG GMBH & CO. KG—See Freudenberg & Company; *Int'l*, pg. 505

CONVERTER POWER, INC.—See ILC Technology, Inc.; *U.S. Public*, pg. 856

CONVERTING DIV.—See Consolidated Papers, Inc.; *U.S. Public*, pg. 436

CONVERTORS/CUSTOM STERILE—See Allegiance Healthcare Corp.; *U.S. Public*, pg. 44

CONVESCO VEHICLE SALES GMBH—See General Motors Corporation; *U.S. Public*, pg. 724

CONVEX TECHNOLOGY CENTER - HEWLETT-PACKARD—See Hewlett-Packard Company; *U.S. Public*, pg. 815

CONWAY CORPORATION; *U.S. Private*, pg. 271

CONWAY IMPORT CO. INC.; *U.S. Private*, pg. 272

CON-WAY NOW—See CNF Transportation Inc.; *U.S. Public*, pg. 281

CONWED PLASTICS—See Leucadia National Corporation; *U.S. Public*, pg. 990

CONWED PLASTICS/N.V. S.A.—See Leucadia National Corporation; *U.S. Public*, pg. 990

CONWELL CORP.—See Frozen Food Express Industries, Inc.; *U.S. Public*, pg. 685

CONWOOD COMPANY L.P.; *U.S. Private*, pg. 272

CONYERS—See Vencor, Inc.; *U.S. Public*, pg. 1715

THE COOK BATES DIVISION—See London International Group plc; *Int'l*, pg. 714

C. LEE COOK DIV.—See Dover Corporation; *U.S. Public*, pg. 521

COOK CHOCOLATE CANADA LTD.—See World's Finest Chocolate, Inc.; *U.S. Private*, pg. 1191

COOK COMMUNICATION MINISTRIES; *U.S. Private*, pg. 272

COOK COMPOSITES & POLYMERS INC.—See Total S.A.; *Int'l*, pg. 1409

E.J. COOK SCD PARTNERSHIP—See Costain Group PLC; *Int'l*, pg. 336

COOK FAMILY FOODS, LTD.—See ConAgra, Inc.; *U.S. Public*, pg. 428

JOAN COOK—See Initio, Inc.; *U.S. Public*, pg. 879

L.G. COOK DISTRIBUTOR, INC.—See Distribution America; *U.S. Private*, pg. 335

COOK MANLEY—See Dover Corporation; *U.S. Public*, pg. 521

COOK MANUFACTURING CORPORATION; *U.S. Private*, pg. 272

COOK MOVING SYSTEMS, INC.; *U.S. Private*, pg. 272

COOK MOVING SYSTEMS, INC. (FLORIDA CORPORATION)—See Cook Moving Systems, Inc.; *U.S. Private*, pg. 273

COOK MOVING SYSTEMS, INC. (ILLINOIS CORPORATION)—See Cook Moving Systems, Inc.; *U.S. Private*, pg. 273

COOK/SARASOTA MOVING SYSTEMS INC.—See Cook Moving Systems, Inc.; *U.S. Private*, pg. 273

TED COOK TOURS ISLANDS IN THE SUN—See Accor S.A.; *Int'l*, pg. 21

THE WILLIAM COOK AGENCY, INC.; *U.S. Private*, pg. 273

WILLIAM COOK DIRECT MARKETING, INC.—See The William Cook Agency, Inc.; *U.S. Private*, pg. 273

COOKE & BIELER, INC.—See United Asset Management Corporation; *U.S. Public*, pg. 1673

BENJAMIN COOKE ASSOCIATES—See Cigna Corp.; *U.S. Public*, pg. 361

JACK KENT COOKE, INC.; *U.S. Private*, pg. 273

COOKE MEDIA GROUP, INC.—See Jack Kent Cooke, Inc.; *U.S. Private*, pg. 273

COOKER RESTAURANT CORPORATION; *U.S. Public*, pg. 442

COOKIE TREE INC.; *U.S. Private*, pg. 273

COOKSON AMERICA INC.—See Cookson Group plc; *Int'l*, pg. 328

COOKSON GROUP PLC; *Int'l*, pg. 328

COOKSON MATTHEY (AUSTRALIA)—See Johnson Matthey Public Limited Company; *Int'l*, pg. 714

COOKSON MATTHEY B.V.—See Johnson Matthey Public Limited Company; *Int'l*, pg. 714

COOKSON MATTHEY CERAMICS PLC—See Johnson Matthey Public Limited Company; *Int'l*, pg. 713

COOKSON MATTHEY PRINT—See Johnson Matthey Public Limited Company; *Int'l*, pg. 713

COOKSON MATTHEY SPA—See Johnson Matthey Public Limited Company; *Int'l*, pg. 714

COOLEY, INC.; *U.S. Private*, pg. 273

COOLIDGE GLASS CO., INC.; *U.S. Private*, pg. 273

H A COOMBS LIMITED—See SLD Holdings Ltd.; *Int'l*, pg. 1160

THE COON-DE VISSER CO.; *U.S. Private*, pg. 273

COOP AARGAU—See Coop Switzerland; *Int'l*, pg. 329

COOP BANK—See Coop Switzerland; *Int'l*, pg. 329

COOP BASEL—See Coop Switzerland; *Int'l*, pg. 329

COOP BERN—See Coop Switzerland; *Int'l*, pg. 329

COOP BERN OBERLAND—See Coop Switzerland; *Int'l*, pg. 329

COOP BILDUNGSZENTRUM—See Coop Switzerland; *Int'l*, pg. 330

COOP BROYE-FRIBOURG-MOLESON—See Coop Switzerland; *Int'l*, pg. 329

COOP GENEVE—See Coop Switzerland; *Int'l*, pg. 329

COOP GRAUBUNDEN-SARGANSERLAND—See Coop Switzerland; *Int'l*, pg. 329

COOP HOSTELLERIE AG—See Coop Switzerland; *Int'l*, pg. 330

COOP LA CHAUX-DE-FONDS—See Coop Switzerland; *Int'l*, pg. 329

COOP LEBENSVERSICHERUNGS GENOSSENSCHAFT—See Coop Switzerland; *Int'l*, pg. 330

COOP NEUCHATEL—See Coop Switzerland; *Int'l*, pg. 329

COOP OBERAARGAU-THAL/GAU—See Coop Switzerland; *Int'l*, pg. 329

COOP OSTSCHWEIZ—See Coop Switzerland; *Int'l*, pg. 329

COOP RECHTSSCHUTZ—See Coop Switzerland; *Int'l*, pg. 330

COOP SWITZERLAND; *Int'l*, pg. 329

COOP SWITZERLAND FAR EAST LTD.—See Coop Switzerland; *Int'l*, pg. 330

COOP TICINO—See Coop Switzerland; *Int'l*, pg. 329

COOP VALAIS/WALLIS—See Coop Switzerland; *Int'l*, pg. 329

COOP VAUD CHABLAIS VALAISAN—See Coop Switzerland; *Int'l*, pg. 329

COOP VERSICHERUNGS-GESELLSCHAFT—See Coop Switzerland; *Int'l*, pg. 330

COOP WINTERTHUR—See Coop Switzerland; *Int'l*, pg. 329

COOP ZENTRALSCHWEIZ—See Coop Switzerland; *Int'l*, pg. 329

COOP ZURICH—See Coop Switzerland; *Int'l*, pg. 329

COOP ZURICHSEE-LINTH—See Coop Switzerland; *Int'l*, pg. 329

COOPER & BEATTY—See Jannock Limited; *Int'l*, pg. 698

COOPER AUTOMOTIVE DIVISION—See Cooper Industries, Inc.; *U.S. Public*, pg. 443

COOPER BEARINGS—See Kaydon Corporation; *U.S. Public*, pg. 946

COOPER COMMUNITIES, INC.; *U.S. Private*, pg. 273

THE COOPER COMPANIES, INC.; *U.S. Public*, pg. 442

COOPER HAND TOOLS—See Cooper Industries, Inc.; *U.S. Public*, pg. 444

COOPER INDUSTRIES (CANADA) INC.—See Cooper Industries, Inc.; *U.S. Public*, pg. 444

COOPER INDUSTRIES FOUNDATION—See Cooper Industries, Inc.; *U.S. Public*, pg. 444

COOPER INDUSTRIES, INC.; *U.S. Public*, pg. 442

COOPER INSTRUMENT CORP.; *U.S. Private*, pg. 274

COOPER LIGHTING DIVISION—See Cooper Industries, Inc.; *U.S. Public*, pg. 443

COOPER, MCDOUGALL & ROBERTSON LTD.—See Glaxo Wellcome plc; *Int'l*, pg. 552

COOPER POWER SYSTEMS—See Cooper Industries, Inc.; *U.S. Public*, pg. 443

COOPER POWER TOOLS DIVISION—See Cooper Industries, Inc.; *U.S. Public*, pg. 444

COOPER RIVER CONVALESCENT CENTER—See Genesis Health Ventures, Inc.; *U.S. Public*, pg. 729

COOPER ROLLER BEARING CO., LTD.—See Kaydon Corporation; *U.S. Public*, pg. 946

COOPER SMITH, INC.—See The Earthgrains Company; *U.S. Public*, pg. 557

COOPER TIRE & RUBBER COMPANY; *U.S. Public*, pg. 444

COOPER TIRE & RUBBER COMPANY, ALBANY PLANT—See Cooper Tire & Rubber Company; *U.S. Public*, pg. 445

COOPER TIRE & RUBBER COMPANY, AUBURN PLANT—See Cooper Tire & Rubber Company; *U.S. Public*, pg. 445

COOPER TIRE & RUBBER COMPANY, BOWLING GREEN PLANT—See Cooper Tire & Rubber Company; *U.S. Public*, pg. 445

COOPER TIRE & RUBBER COMPANY, CLARKSDALE PLANT—See Cooper Tire & Rubber Company; *U.S. Public*, pg. 445

COOPER TIRE & RUBBER COMPANY, EL DORADO PLANT—See Cooper Tire & Rubber Company; *U.S. Public*, pg. 445

COOPER TIRE & RUBBER COMPANY, FINDLAY PLANT—See Cooper Tire & Rubber Company; *U.S. Public*, pg. 445

COOPER TIRE & RUBBER COMPANY, MT. STERLING PLANT—See Cooper Tire & Rubber Company; *U.S. Public*, pg. 445

COOPER TIRE & RUBBER COMPANY, TEXARKANA PLANT—See Cooper Tire & Rubber Company; *U.S. Public*, pg. 445

COOPER TIRE & RUBBER COMPANY, TUPELO PLANT—See Cooper Tire & Rubber Company; *U.S. Public*, pg. 445

THE COOPER TIRE COMPANY—See Cooper Tire & Rubber Company; *U.S. Public*, pg. 445

COOPER TOOLS—See Cooper Industries, Inc.; *U.S. Public*, pg. 444

COOPER VENTURES, INC.—See Cooper Communities, Inc.; *U.S. Private*, pg. 274

THE COOPERAGE—See Greif Brothers Corporation; *U.S. Public*, pg. 763

COOPERATIVE CENTRAL BANK LTD.-INSURANCE DEPT.—See Allianz Aktiengesellschaft; *Int'l*, pg. 60

COOPERATIVE FEDEREE DE QUEBEC; *Int'l*, pg. 330

THE COOPERATIVE FINANCE ASSN., INC.—See Farmland Industries, Inc.; *U.S. Private*, pg. 396

COOPERATIVE MOTORS LTD.—See Harris Scarfe Holdings Limited; *Int'l*, pg. 597

COOPERATIVE SERVICE CO.—See Nationwide Insurance Enterprise; *U.S. Private*, pg. 789

COOPER-AVON TYRES, LTD.—See Cooper Tire & Rubber Company; *U.S. Public*, pg. 445

COOPERMEX—See Cooper Tire & Rubber Company; *U.S. Public*, pg. 445

COOPERS DIRECTORY OF CORPORATE AFFILIATIONS

Company Index

COOPERS & LYBRAND; *U.S. Private*, pg. 274
COOPERS PAYEN LTD.—See T & N Plc; *Int'l*, pg. 1334
COOPERSURGICAL INC.—See The Cooper Companies, Inc.; *U.S. Public*, pg. 442
COORDINATE MEASURING MACHINE DIV.—See The L.S. Starrett Company; *U.S. Public*, pg. 1511
COORDINATED HEALTHCARE SYSTEMS—See Cigna Corp.; *U.S. Public*, pg. 361
COORDINATION CENTER VOLKSWAGEN S.A.—See Volkswagen AG; *Int'l*, pg. 1475
ADOLPH COORS COMPANY; *U.S. Public*, pg. 445
COORS BREWING COMPANY—See Adolph Coors Company; *U.S. Public*, pg. 445
COORS CERAMICS COMPANY—See ACX Technologies Inc.; *U.S. Public*, pg. 3
COORS DISTRIBUTING CO.—See Adolph Coors Company; *U.S. Public*, pg. 445
COORS ENERGY CO.—See Adolph Coors Company; *U.S. Public*, pg. 446
H.F. COORS CHINA CO.—See Standex International Corporation; *U.S. Public*, pg. 1506
COPAIS FOOD & BEVERAGE COMPANY S.A.—See H.J. Heinz Company; *U.S. Public*, pg. 806
COPAL—See Pechiney S.A.; *Int'l*, pg. 1028
COPAMEX INDUSTRIAS S.A. DE C.V.; *Int'l*, pg. 330
COPAMEX PAPER—See Copamex Industrias S.A. de C.V.; *Int'l*, pg. 330
COPAP—See Enso Oyj; *Int'l*, pg. 457
COPART, INC.; *U.S. Public*, pg. 446
COPCO—See Wilton Industries, Inc.; *U.S. Private*, pg. 1182
COPCO STEEL CO.—See Russel Metals Inc.; *Int'l*, pg. 1150
COPELAND CANADA, LTD.—See Emerson Electric Co.; *U.S. Public*, pg. 576
COPELAND CORPORATION—See Emerson Electric Co.; *U.S. Public*, pg. 573
COPELAND LUMBER YARD, INC.; *U.S. Private*, pg. 274
COPELCO FINANCIAL SERVICES GROUP INC.—See Itochu Corporation; *Int'l*, pg. 694
COPEM COMPAGNIE DE PARTICIPATION EUROPEENNE MEINL B.V.—See Julius Meinl AG; *Int'l*, pg. 856
COPENHAGEN PECTIN A/S—See Hercules Incorporated; *U.S. Public*, pg. 810
JOHN COPES FOOD PRODUCTS, INC.; *U.S. Private*, pg. 274
COPES-VULCAN INC.; *U.S. Private*, pg. 274
COPETRO, S.A.—See Horsehead Industries, Inc.; *U.S. Private*, pg. 540
COPIER SYSTEMS/PITNEY BOWES OFFICE SYSTEMS—See Pitney Bowes Inc.; *U.S. Public*, pg. 1303
COPIJN BELGIE BOOMCHIRURGEN BVBA—See Heidemij N.V.; *Int'l*, pg. 608
COPIJN UTRECHT HOLDING BV—See Heidemij N.V.; *Int'l*, pg. 607
COPLAND FABRICS, INC.; *U.S. Private*, pg. 274
COPLEY PHARMACEUTICALS, INC.; *U.S. Public*, pg. 446
THE COPLEY PRESS, INC.; *U.S. Private*, pg. 275
COPPEE ENGINEERING A.S.—See SNC-Lavalin Group Inc.; *Int'l*, pg. 1162
COPPEE INDUSTRIES INC.—See Lafarge S.A.; *Int'l*, pg. 788
COPPEL S.A. DE C.V.; *Int'l*, pg. 330
COPPER & BRASS SALES, INC.—See Thyssen AG; *Int'l*, pg. 1389
COPPER MOUNTAIN RESORT—See Intrawest Corporation; *Int'l*, pg. 685
COPPER RANGE COMPANY—See Metallgesellschaft AG; *Int'l*, pg. 862
COPPERMOL S.A.—See CODELCO Chile (Corporacion Nacional Del Cobre De Chile); *Int'l*, pg. 303
COPPERWELD—See Imetal; *Int'l*, pg. 662
COPPERWELD BIMETALLICS PRODUCTS CO.—See Imetal; *Int'l*, pg. 662
COPPERWELD BIRMINGHAM DIVISION—See Imetal; *Int'l*, pg. 662
COPPERWELD CHICAGO DIVISION—See Imetal; *Int'l*, pg. 662
COPPERWELD FAYETTEVILLE DIVISION—See Imetal; *Int'l*, pg. 662
COPPERWELD INTERNATIONAL CO.—See Imetal; *Int'l*, pg. 662
COPPERWELD METALLON DIV.—See Imetal; *Int'l*, pg. 662
COPPERWELD MIAMI DIVISION—See Imetal; *Int'l*, pg. 662
COPPERWELD MIAMI INDUSTRIES—See Imetal; *Int'l*, pg. 662
COPPERWELD SHELBY DIVISION—See Imetal; *Int'l*, pg. 662
COPPERWELD TUBING—See Imetal; *Int'l*, pg. 662
THE COPPS CORP.; *U.S. Private*, pg. 275
COPPUS MURRAY GROUP, TUTHILL CORPORATION—See Tuthill Corporation; *U.S. Private*, pg. 1110
COPYER CO., LTD.—See Canon Inc.; *Int'l*, pg. 261
COPYGRAPHIC HARRIS LTD—See N.V. Koninklijke KNP BT; *Int'l*, pg. 757
COPYHOLDER DIVISION—See Fellowes Manufacturing Co.; *U.S. Private*, pg. 400
COR SAM GLASS TEC RESEARCH & DEVELOPMENT CENTER—See Corning Incorporated; *U.S. Public*, pg. 449
CORA TEXAS MANUFACTURING CO., INC.; *U.S. Private*, pg. 275
CORAFIN S.A.C.I.F.A.—See Cigna Corp.; *U.S. Public*, pg. 363
CORAL OIL & GAS INC.; *U.S. Private*, pg. 275
CORAL RACING LTD.—See Bass PLC; *Int'l*, pg. 170
CORAM HEALTHCARE CORPORATION; *U.S. Public*, pg. 446
CORANGE LIMITED; *Int'l*, pg. 330
CORANGE U.S. HOLDINGS, INC—See Corange Limited; *Int'l*, pg. 331
CORBERO S.A.—See Electrolux, AB; *Int'l*, pg. 443
CORBETT CANYON VINEYARDS—See The Wine Group; *U.S. Private*, pg. 1183
CORBETT HEALTHCONNECT, A FRANK J. CORBETT, INC., COMPANY—See Omnicom Group Inc.; *U.S. Public*, pg. 1223
CORBIN RUSSWIN, INC.—See Williams Holdings Plc; *Int'l*, pg. 1499
CORCOM FAR EAST LTD.—See Corcom, Inc.; *U.S. Public*, pg. 446
CORCOM GMBH—See Corcom, Inc.; *U.S. Public*, pg. 446
CORCOM, INC.; *U.S. Public*, pg. 446
CORCOM S.A. DE CV—See Corcom, Inc.; *U.S. Public*, pg. 446
CORCORAN TRUCKING COMPANY; *U.S. Private*, pg. 275
CORD LOGISTICS—See Cardinal Health Inc.; *U.S. Public*, pg. 304
CORDES & CO. GMBH—See Henkel KGaA; *Int'l*, pg. 609
CORDEX EXPLORATION CO.—See Rayrock Yellowknife Resources Inc.; *Int'l*, pg. 1089
CORDIS, A JOHNSON & JOHNSON COMPANY—See Johnson & Johnson; *U.S. Public*, pg. 928
CORDIS, A JOHNSON & JOHNSON COMPANY EUROPA N.V.—See Johnson & Johnson; *U.S. Public*, pg. 928
CORDLEY TEMPRITE—See Elkay Manufacturing Company; *U.S. Private*, pg. 372
CORE LABORATORIES-CANADA LTD.—See Litton Industries, Inc.; *U.S. Public*, pg. 1004
CORE LABORATORIES (NETHERLANDS)—See Litton Industries, Inc.; *U.S. Public*, pg. 1004
CORE LABORATORIES (SCOTLAND)—See Litton Industries, Inc.; *U.S. Public*, pg. 1004
CORE LABORATORIES (SINGAPORE)—See Litton Industries, Inc.; *U.S. Public*, pg. 1004
CORE LABORATORIES (UK)—See Litton Industries, Inc.; *U.S. Public*, pg. 1004
CORE-MARK INTERNATIONAL; *U.S. Private*, pg. 275
CORE RESEARCH, INC.—See Litton Industries, Inc.; *U.S. Public*, pg. 1003
COREGIS GROUP—See General Electric Company; *U.S. Public*, pg. 711
COREL CORPORATION; *Int'l*, pg. 331
COREL CORPORATION—See Corel Corporation; *Int'l*, pg. 331
CORENSO UNITED OY LTD.—See Enso Oyj; *Int'l*, pg. 456
COREPRO B.V.—See Forbo Holding SA; *Int'l*, pg. 497
COREQ, INC.—See The Chase Manhattan Corporation; *U.S. Public*, pg. 338
CORESTATES BANK—See CoreStates Financial Corp.; *U.S. Public*, pg. 446
CORESTATES BANK INTERNATIONAL—See CoreStates Financial Corp.; *U.S. Public*, pg. 446
CORESTATES BANK, N.A.—See CoreStates Financial Corp.; *U.S. Public*, pg. 446
CORESTATES BANK OF DELAWARE NA—See CoreStates Financial Corp.; *U.S. Public*, pg. 447
CORESTATES CAPITAL CORP.—See CoreStates Financial Corp.; *U.S. Public*, pg. 446
CORESTATES CAPITAL MARKETS GROUP—See CoreStates Financial Corp.; *U.S. Public*, pg. 446
CORESTATES FINANCIAL CORP.; *U.S. Public*, pg. 446
CORESTATES HOLDING, INC.—See CoreStates Financial Corp.; *U.S. Public*, pg. 447
CORESTATES SECURITIES CORP.—See CoreStates Financial Corp.; *U.S. Public*, pg. 447
COREX TECHNOLOGY (HK) LTD.—See IPC Corporation Ltd.; *Int'l*, pg. 651
COREX TECHNOLOGY (S) PTE LTD.—See IPC Corporation Ltd.; *Int'l*, pg. 651
CORFINA S.P.A.—See Freudenberg & Company; *Int'l*, pg. 507
CORGI BOOKS LTD.—See Bertelsmann AG; *Int'l*, pg. 191
CORIGAN PLANT, WOOD PRODUCTS DIV.—See Champion International Corp.; *U.S. Public*, pg. 334
CORINTHIAN MEDIA, INC.; *U.S. Private*, pg. 275
CORIS CO., LTD.—See Kanebo, Ltd.; *Int'l*, pg. 722
CORIS-MOBIUM CREATIVE GROUP—See R.R. Donnelley & Sons Company; *U.S. Public*, pg. 518
CORIS-POWERBASE TECHNOLOGY GROUP—See R.R. Donnelley & Sons Company; *U.S. Public*, pg. 518
CORKEN, INC.—See IDEX Corporation; *U.S. Public*, pg. 862
CORMAGIC N.V.—See Koninklijke BolsWessanen nv; *Int'l*, pg. 751
CORMETECH INC.—See Corning Incorporated; *U.S. Public*, pg. 449
CORMIER CHEVROLET COMPANY, INC.; *U.S. Private*, pg. 276
CORMIER RICE MILLING COMPANY, INC.; *U.S. Private*, pg. 276
CORMORANT CORP.—See Northern States Power Company; *U.S. Public*, pg. 1195
CORN PRODUCTS CO. (INDIA) LTD.—See Bestfoods; *U.S. Public*, pg. 224
CORN PRODUCTS INTERNATIONAL, INC.; *U.S. Public*, pg. 447
CORN PRODUCTS NORTH AMERICA DIV.—See Corn Products International, Inc.; *U.S. Public*, pg. 448
CORN STATES HYBRID SERVICE, INC.—See Monsanto Company; *U.S. Public*, pg. 1124
CORNEALENT WAICON DE BRASIL INDUSTRIA E COMERCIO LTDA.—See Bausch & Lomb Incorporated; *U.S. Public*, pg. 195
THE CORNELIUS COMPANY—See IMI Plc; *Int'l*, pg. 646
CORNELL DUBILIER ELECTRONICS—See Kaplan Electronics; *U.S. Private*, pg. 607
CORNELL FORGE COMPANY; *U.S. Private*, pg. 276
CORNELL IRON WORKS, INC.; *U.S. Private*, pg. 276
CORNELL MANUFACTURING COMPANY—See Jupiter Industries, Inc.; *U.S. Private*, pg. 602
CORNELL STOREFRONT SYSTEMS, INC.—See Cornell Iron Works, Inc.; *U.S. Private*, pg. 276
CORNER BROOK PULP & PAPER LIMITED—See Kruger Inc.; *Int'l*, pg. 761
CORNERCROFT ENGINEERING LIMITED—See Caparo Group Ltd.; *Int'l*, pg. 265
CORNERSTONE CONSTRUCTION & MATERIALS, INC.—See Hanson PLC; *Int'l*, pg. 593
CORNERSTONE HEALTH MANAGEMENT—See Paragon Health Network, Inc.; *U.S. Public*, pg. 1257
CORNERSTONE NATURAL GAS, INC.—See El Paso Natural Gas Co.; *U.S. Public*, pg. 567
CORNERSTONE NATURAL GAS, INC.-PITTSBURGH—See El Paso Natural Gas Co.; *U.S. Public*, pg. 567
CORNERSTONE NATURAL GAS, INC.-SHREVEPORT—See El Paso Natural Gas Co.; *U.S. Public*, pg. 567
CORNERSTONE PIPELINE CO.—See El Paso Natural Gas Co.; *U.S. Public*, pg. 567
CORNERSTONE PROPANE G.P. INC.—See Northwestern Public Service; *U.S. Public*, pg. 1201
CORNERSTONE REAL ESTATE—See Massachusetts Mutual Life Insurance Co.; *U.S. Private*, pg. 712
CORNERSTONE TITLE COMPANY—See The Ryland Group, Inc.; *U.S. Public*, pg. 1414
CORNHILL INSURANCE PLC—See Allianz Aktiengesellschaft; *Int'l*, pg. 60
CORNHUSKER CASUALTY CO.—See Berkshire Hathaway Inc.; *U.S. Public*, pg. 221
CORNING ASAHI VIDEO PRODUCTS COMPANY—See Corning Incorporated; *U.S. Public*, pg. 449
CORNING AUSTRALIA PTY. LIMITED—See Corning Incorporated; *U.S. Public*, pg. 448
CORNING CONSUMER LIMITED—See Corning Incorporated; *U.S. Public*, pg. 448
CORNING CONSUMER PRODUCTS COMPANY—See Corning Incorporated; *U.S. Public*, pg. 448
CORNING COSTAR CORPORATION—See Corning Incorporated; *U.S. Public*, pg. 448
CORNING ENTERPRISES INC.—See Corning Incorporated; *U.S. Public*, pg. 448
CORNING EUROPE INC.—See Corning Incorporated; *U.S. Public*, pg. 449
CORNING INCORPORATED; *U.S. Public*, pg. 448
CORNING INTERNATIONAL CORPORATION—See Corning Incorporated; *U.S. Public*, pg. 448
CORNING INTERNATIONAL K.K.—See Corning Incorporated; *U.S. Public*, pg. 449
CORNING TRADING (SINGAPORE) PTE. LTD.—See Corning Incorporated; *U.S. Public*, pg. 448
CORNUCOPIA, INC.; *U.S. Private*, pg. 276
THE CORNWALL & PATTERSON CO.—See Pratt-Read Corporation; *U.S. Private*, pg. 879
CORNWALL & STEVENS CO., INC.—See MSI Insurance Companies; *U.S. Private*, pg. 688
COROI MAURICE LTEE.—See BASF AG; *Int'l*, pg. 108
COROI-NEGOCE—See BASF AG; *Int'l*, pg. 108
CORON VERLAG MONIKA SCHOELLER & CO.—See Georg von Holtzbrinck GmbH; *Int'l*, pg. 1479
CORONA CLIPPER—See Harrow Industries; *U.S. Private*, pg. 506
CORONA ENGINEERING CORPORATION—See Westmoreland Coal Co.; *U.S. Public*, pg. 1761
CORONADO PAINT COMPANY—See Wattyl; *Int'l*, pg. 1488
CORONET COMMUNICATIONS—See Lynch Corporation; *U.S. Public*, pg. 1021
CORONET/MTI—See The Phoenix Learning Group, Inc.; *U.S. Private*, pg. 863
COROWAN TAIWAN CORPORATION—See Clarion Co., Ltd.; *Int'l*, pg. 296
COROX CONTROLS INC.—See Siebe plc; *Int'l*, pg. 1243
CORPAK INC.—See Thermo Electron Corporation; *U.S. Public*, pg. 1592
CORPORACION CEMENTERA ARGENTINA S.A. (CORCEMAR)—See Holderbank Financiere Glaris Ltd.; *Int'l*, pg. 629
CORPORACION DEL COBRE (U.S.A.), INC.—See CODELCO Chile (Corporacion Nacional Del Cobre De Chile); *Int'l*, pg. 303
CORPORACION E.G., S.A. DE C.V.—See Derlan Industries Limited; *Int'l*, pg. 395
CORPORACION ELECTRONICA METROPOLITANA S.A.—See Sanyo Electric Co., Ltd.; *Int'l*, pg. 1192
CORPORACION FINANCIERA ALBA S.A.—See Banca March S.A.; *Int'l*, pg. 136
CORPORACION FINANCIERA CAJA DE MADRID, S.A.—See Caja de Madrid Group; *Int'l*, pg. 251
CORPORACION GRUPO QUIMICO, S.A.C.A.; *Int'l*, pg. 331
CORPORACION INDUSTRIAL SANLUIS; *Int'l*, pg. 332
CORPORACION INTERNACIONAL DE AVIACION (CINTRA); *Int'l*, pg. 332
CORPORACION MAPFRE, COMPANIA INTERNACIONAL DE REASEGUROS, S.A.; *Int'l*, pg. 332
CORPORACION MICROSOFT DEL ECUADOR—See Microsoft Corporation; *U.S. Public*, pg. 1108
CORPORATE CASH MANAGEMENT DIV.—See Imperial Bancorp; *U.S. Public*, pg. 871
THE CORPORATE COMMUNICATIONS GROUP; *U.S. Private*, pg. 276
CORPORATE COMPUTERS (MID) PLC—See N.V. Koninklijke KNP BT; *Int'l*, pg. 757
CORPORATE COMPUTERS PLC—See N.V. Koninklijke KNP BT; *Int'l*, pg. 757
CORPORATE ENGINEERING—See Emerson Electric Co.; *U.S. Public*, pg. 575
CORPORATE EXPRESS DELIVERY SYSTEMS—See Corporate Express, Inc.; *U.S. Public*, pg. 449
CORPORATE EXPRESS DELIVERY SYSTEMS SOUTHWEST, INC.—See Corporate Express, Inc.; *U.S. Public*, pg. 449
CORPORATE EXPRESS, INC.; *U.S. Public*, pg. 449
CORPORATE EXPRESS OFFICE PRODUCTS—See Corporate Express, Inc.; *U.S. Public*, pg. 449
CORPORATE FINANCE MAGAZINE—See Financial World Partners; *U.S. Private*, pg. 405
CORPORATE FOODS LTD.—See Maple Leaf Foods Inc.; *Int'l*, pg. 841
CORPORATE HEALTH ADMINISTRATORS, INC.—See Aetna Inc.; *U.S. Public*, pg. 26
CORPORATE LOGISTICS SERVICES—See Kimball International, Inc.; *U.S. Public*, pg. 957

CORPORATE MARKETING AND SERVICES—See C.R. Bard, Inc.; *U.S. Public*, pg. 189
CORPORATE NATIONAL ACCOUNTS MIDWEST—See MCI Communications Corp.; *U.S. Public*, pg. 1024
CORPORATE NATIONAL ACCOUNTS NORTHEAST—See MCI Communications Corp.; *U.S. Public*, pg. 1024
CORPORATE NATIONAL ACCOUNTS PACIFIC SOUTHWEST—See MCI Communications Corp.; *U.S. Public*, pg. 1024
CORPORATE NATIONAL ACCOUNTS SOUTHEAST—See MCI Communications Corp.; *U.S. Public*, pg. 1024
CORPORATE NEW BUSINESS DEVELOPMENT DIV.—See Royal Gist-Brocades N.V.; *Int'l*, pg. 1142
CORPORATE PRODUCT INTEGRITY—See The Gillette Company; *U.S. Public*, pg. 744
CORPORATE SERVICES DIV.—See Imperial Bancorp; *U.S. Public*, pg. 519
CORPORATE SERVICES INTERNATIONAL, INC.—See Mantex, S.A.C.A.; *Int'l*, pg. 840
CORPORATE SOFTWARE LTD., KK—See R.R. Donnelley & Sons Company; *U.S. Public*, pg. 1142
CORPORATE TRAVEL SERVICES; *U.S. Private*, pg. 276
CORPORATION MS 90 DE VENEZUELA S.A.—See Microsoft Corporation; *U.S. Public*, pg. 1108
S.C. CORPORATIONS EFFICIENCY GROWTH THROUGH INFORMATION SYSTEMS CEGIS—See Cockerill Sambre; *Int'l*, pg. 301
CORPORATIVO TABLEX, S.A. DE C.V.—See Tablex, S.A. de C.V.; *Int'l*, pg. 1346
CORPOREX COMPANIES, INC.; *U.S. Private*, pg. 276
CORPOREX DEVELOPMENT—See Corporex Companies, Inc.; *U.S. Private*, pg. 276
CORPOREX PROPERTIES INC.—See Corporex Companies, Inc.; *U.S. Private*, pg. 276
CORPOVEN, S.A.—See Petroleos de Venezuela S.A.; *Int'l*, pg. 1045
CORPUS CHRISTI CALLER-TIMES—See Harte-Hanks Communications, Inc.; *U.S. Public*, pg. 793
R.J. CORR NATURALS, INC.; *U.S. Private*, pg. 276
CORRAL COIN, INC.—See Jackpot Enterprises, Inc.; *U.S. Public*, pg. 920
CORRAL UNITED, INC.—See Jackpot Enterprises, Inc.; *U.S. Public*, pg. 920
CORRECT CRAFT, INC.; *U.S. Private*, pg. 276
CORRECTA GMBH—See Bayer AG; *Int'l*, pg. 172
CORRECTIONAL BEHAVIORAL SOLUTIONS, INC.—See Magellan Health Services, Inc.; *U.S. Public*, pg. 1035
CORRECTIONAL BEHAVIORAL SOLUTIONS OF INDIANA, INC.—See Magellan Health Services, Inc.; *U.S. Public*, pg. 1035
CORRECTIONAL BEHAVIORAL SOLUTIONS OF NEW JERSEY, INC.—See Magellan Health Services, Inc.; *U.S. Public*, pg. 1035
CORRECTIONAL BEHAVIORAL SOLUTIONS OF OHIO, INC.—See Magellan Health Services, Inc.; *U.S. Public*, pg. 1035
CORRECTIONAL FOODSERVICES MANAGEMENT—See The Wackenhut Corporation; *U.S. Public*, pg. 1731
CORRECTIONAL SERVICES CORPORATION; *U.S. Public*, pg. 450
CORRECTIONAL TREATMENT FACILITY—See Corrections Corporation of America; *U.S. Public*, pg. 450
CORRECTIONS CORPORATION OF AMERICA; *U.S. Public*, pg. 450
CORRIGAN BROS., INC.; *U.S. Private*, pg. 277
CORRIGAN COMPANY MECHANICAL CONTRACTORS—See Corrigan Bros., Inc.; *U.S. Private*, pg. 277
CORRO CLARK COATINGS LTD.—See Jotun A/S; *Int'l*, pg. 715
CORRO-COAT A/S—See Jotun A/S; *Int'l*, pg. 714
CORRO-COAT (CZ) A.S.—See Jotun A/S; *Int'l*, pg. 715
CORRO-COAT EGYPT LTD.—See Jotun A/S; *Int'l*, pg. 715
CORRO-COAT (MALAYSIA) SDN. BHD.—See Jotun A/S; *Int'l*, pg. 715
CORRO-COAT (THAILAND) LTD.—See Jotun A/S; *Int'l*, pg. 715
CORRO-COAT TOZ BOYA SAN.VE TIC. A.S.—See Jotun A/S; *Int'l*, pg. 715
CORRO-COAT U.A.E. LTD.—See Jotun A/S; *Int'l*, pg. 715
CORRO-COAT SAUDI ARABIA LTD.—See Jotun A/S; *Int'l*, pg. 715
CORROSION TECHNOLOGIES INTL.—See Global Industrial Technologies; *U.S. Public*, pg. 748
CORRPRO COMPANIES, INC.; *U.S. Public*, pg. 451
CORRUGATED EUROPE BV—See N.V. Koninklijke KNP BT; *Int'l*, pg. 756
CORRUGATED METALS, INC.; *U.S. Private*, pg. 277
CORRUGATED PRODUCTS DIVISION—See Greif Brothers Corporation; *U.S. Public*, pg. 763
CORRYHIEBERT CORPORATION—See HON Industries Inc.; *U.S. Public*, pg. 772
CORSE COMPOSITES AERONAUTIQUES—See SNECMA - Societe Nationale d'Etude et de Construction de Moteurs d'Aviation; *Int'l*, pg. 1166
CORSE SUD EXPRESS—See SNCF; *Int'l*, pg. 1163
CORSO HANDELSGESELLSCHAFT MBH—See Otto Versand (GmbH & Co.); *Int'l*, pg. 1014
CORSON LIME COMPANY—See United States Lime & Minerals; *U.S. Public*, pg. 1685
CORT BUSINESS SERVICES CORPORATION; *U.S. Public*, pg. 451
CORTAULDS PACKAGING LTD.—See Courtaulds plc; *Int'l*, pg. 339
CORTEC COMPANY—See Crane Co.; *U.S. Public*, pg. 456
CORTEC GROUP; *U.S. Private*, pg. 277
CORTLAND LINE CO., INC.; *U.S. Private*, pg. 277
CORTLAND PLANT—See Cooper Industries, Inc.; *U.S. Public*, pg. 444
CORVALLIS GAZETTE-TIMES—See Lee Enterprises, Incorporated; *U.S. Public*, pg. 983
CORVEL CORPORATION; *U.S. Public*, pg. 451
CORVITA CANADA, INC.—See Pfizer Inc.; *U.S. Public*, pg. 1282

CORVITA CORPORATION—See Pfizer Inc.; *U.S. Public*, pg. 1281
CORVITA EUROPE S.A.—See Pfizer Inc.; *U.S. Public*, pg. 1282
CORY BROTHERS SHIPPING LIMITED—See Powell Duffryn PLC; *Int'l*, pg. 1065
COS-MAR, INC.—See Petrofina S.A.; *Int'l*, pg. 1044
COSAN CHEMICAL CORP.—See Cambrex Corporation; *U.S. Public*, pg. 297
COSBEL PETROLEUM CORP.—See The Coastal Corporation; *U.S. Public*, pg. 390
COSCAN ADLER LIMITED PARTNERSHIP—See Brookfield Properties Corporation; *Int'l*, pg. 228
COSCAN LAND, INC.—See Brookfield Properties Corporation; *Int'l*, pg. 228
COSCAN STEWART LIMITED PARTNERSHIP—See Brookfield Properties Corporation; *Int'l*, pg. 228
COSCAN WASHINGTON, INC.—See Brookfield Properties Corporation; *Int'l*, pg. 228
COSCAN WATERWAYS, INC.—See Brookfield Properties Corporation; *Int'l*, pg. 228
COSCIENT-ASTRAL DISTRIBUTION—See Coscient Group Inc.; *Int'l*, pg. 335
COSCIENT GROUP INC.; *Int'l*, pg. 335
COSCO FIRE PROTECTION INC.—See Zurn Industries, Inc.; *U.S. Public*, pg. 1795
COSCO, INC.; *U.S. Public*, pg. 278
COSCO INDUSTRIES; *U.S. Private*, pg. 277
COSCOL MARINE CORP.—See The Coastal Corporation; *U.S. Public*, pg. 390
COSCOL PETROLEUM CORP.—See The Coastal Corporation; *U.S. Public*, pg. 390
COSHOCTON L.D. CORP.—See Forest City Enterprises, Inc.; *U.S. Public*, pg. 668
COSID GMBH—See Ruetgers A.G.; *Int'l*, pg. 1148
COSKY CO. LTD.—See Selas Corporation of America; *U.S. Public*, pg. 1455
COSMA INTERNATIONAL INC.—See Magna International Inc.; *Int'l*, pg. 829
COSMAIR CANADA INC.—See L'Oreal S.A.; *Int'l*, pg. 819
COSMAIR, INC.—See L'Oreal S.A.; *Int'l*, pg. 818
COSMAIR, INC., RALPH LAUREN FRAGRANCE DIVISION—See L'Oreal S.A.; *Int'l*, pg. 818
COSMAR CORP.—See Renaissance Cosmetics, Inc.; *U.S. Private*, pg. 922
COSMED-PRODUKTIONS GMBH—See Beiersdorf Group; *Int'l*, pg. 182
THE COSMETIC CENTER INC.—See MacAndrews & Forbes Holdings Inc.; *U.S. Private*, pg. 689
COSMETIC GROUP, U.S.A.; *U.S. Private*, pg. 277
COSMETIC PRODUCTS PTY, LTD.—See Wella Group; *Int'l*, pg. 1490
COSMETICOS ASTOR S.A.—See Joh. A. Benckiser GmbH; *Int'l*, pg. 186
COSMETICOS AVON, LTDA.—See Avon Products, Inc.; *U.S. Public*, pg. 156
COSMETICOS AVON, S.A.C.I.—See Avon Products, Inc.; *U.S. Public*, pg. 156
COSMETICOS, S.A.—See Unilever Plc; *Int'l*, pg. 1436
COSMETIQUE, INC.; *U.S. Private*, pg. 277
COSMETIQUES DE FRANCE PTE. LTD.—See L'Oreal S.A.; *Int'l*, pg. 819
COSMEUROP S.A.—See Clarins; *Int'l*, pg. 295
COSMOHOGAR, S.A.—See Stanhome Inc.; *U.S. Public*, pg. 1508
COSMICAR LENS DIV.—See Asahi Optical Co., Ltd.; *Int'l*, pg. 85
COSMITAL S.A.—See Wella Group; *Int'l*, pg. 1490
COSMO COMMUNICATIONS CORPORATION; *U.S. Public*, pg. 451
COSMO OIL CO., LTD.; *Int'l*, pg. 335
COSMO OIL OF U.S.A. INC.—See Cosmo Oil Co., Ltd.; *Int'l*, pg. 335
COSMO SECURITIES CO., LTD.; *Int'l*, pg. 335
COSMOFERM B.V.—See Royal Gist-Brocades N.V.; *Int'l*, pg. 1143
COSMOFLEX, INC.—See The Goodyear Tire & Rubber Company; *U.S. Public*, pg. 753
COSMOLAB DIV.—See Koh-I-Noor, Inc.; *U.S. Private*, pg. 629
COSMOPOLITAN—See The Hearst Corporation; *U.S. Private*, pg. 517
COSMOS BROADCASTING CORP.—See Liberty Corporation; *U.S. Public*, pg. 992
COSMOS COMMUNICATIONS, INC.; *U.S. Private*, pg. 278
COSMOS KRANKENVERSICHERUNG AG—See AMB Aachener und Muenchener Beteiligungs-AG; *Int'l*, pg. 15
COSMOS LEBENSVERSICHERUNG AG—See AMB Aachener und Muenchener Beteiligungs-AG; *Int'l*, pg. 15
COSMOS VERSICHERUNG AG—See AMB Aachener und Muenchener Beteiligungs-AG; *Int'l*, pg. 15
COSSETTE COMMUNICATION MARKETING; *Int'l*, pg. 335
COSSETTE COMMUNICATION-MARKETING (MONTREAL) INC.—See Cossette Communication Marketing; *Int'l*, pg. 336
COSSETTE COMMUNICATION-MARKETING (QUEBEC) INC.—See Cossette Communication Marketing; *Int'l*, pg. 336
COSSETTE COMMUNICATION-MARKETING (TORONTO) INC.—See Cossette Communication Marketing; *Int'l*, pg. 336
COSSETTE COMMUNICATION-MARKETING (VANCOUVER) INC.—See Cossette Communication Marketing; *Int'l*, pg. 336
A.C. COSSOR ELECTRONICS, LIMITED—See Raytheon Company; *U.S. Public*, pg. 1366
COST CARE, INC.—See John Hancock Mutual Life Insurance Company; *U.S. Private*, pg. 589
COST CUTTERS—See The Barbers, Hairstyling for Men & Women, Inc.; *U.S. Private*, pg. 115
COST MANAGEMENT SERVICES—See Allegiance Healthcare Corp.; *U.S. Public*, pg. 44

COSTA CONTAINER LINES S.P.A.; *Int'l*, pg. 336
COSTA CRUISE LINES, N.V.; *U.S. Private*, pg. 278
COSTAIN (AFRICA) LIMITED—See Costain Group PLC; *Int'l*, pg. 337
COSTAIN BUILDING & CIVIL ENGINEERING LIMITED—See Costain Group PLC; *Int'l*, pg. 336
COSTAIN BUILDING PRODUCTS LIMITED—See Costain Group PLC; *Int'l*, pg. 336
COSTAIN CIVIL ENGINEERING LTD.—See Costain Group PLC; *Int'l*, pg. 336
COSTAIN COAL INC.—See Costain Group PLC; *Int'l*, pg. 337
COSTAIN CONSTRUCTION LIMITED—See Costain Group PLC; *Int'l*, pg. 336
COSTAIN DEVELOPMENTS SA—See Costain Group PLC; *Int'l*, pg. 337
COSTAIN DOW MAC—See Costain Group PLC; *Int'l*, pg. 336
COSTAIN ENGINEERING & CONSTRUCTION LIMITED—See Costain Group PLC; *Int'l*, pg. 336
COSTAIN ENVIRONMENTAL SERVICES LIMITED—See Costain Group PLC; *Int'l*, pg. 336
COSTAIN GROUP PLC; *Int'l*, pg. 336
COSTAIN HOLDINGS, INC.—See Costain Group PLC; *Int'l*, pg. 337
COSTAIN HOMES INC.—See Costain Group PLC; *Int'l*, pg. 337
COSTAIN HOMES LIMITED—See Costain Group PLC; *Int'l*, pg. 336
COSTAIN INTERNATIONAL LIMITED—See Costain Group PLC; *Int'l*, pg. 336
COSTAIN MARINE INTERNATIONAL LIMITED—See Costain Group PLC; *Int'l*, pg. 336
COSTAIN MIDDLE EAST—See Costain Group PLC; *Int'l*, pg. 337
COSTAIN MINING LIMITED—See Costain Group PLC; *Int'l*, pg. 336
COSTAIN OIL, GAS & PROCESS LIMITED PROCESS CONTRACTING DIVISION—See Costain Group PLC; *Int'l*, pg. 336
COSTAIN OIL, GAS & PROCESS LIMITED PIPELINE & OFFSHORE DIVISION—See Costain Group PLC; *Int'l*, pg. 336
COSTAIN PROCESS INC.—See Costain Group PLC; *Int'l*, pg. 337
COSTAIN SOUTH EAST ASIA—See Costain Group PLC; *Int'l*, pg. 337
COSTAIN URBAN ENTERPRISES LIMITED—See Costain Group PLC; *Int'l*, pg. 337
COSTAIN (WEST AFRICA) LTD.—See Costain Group PLC; *Int'l*, pg. 337
COSTAR EUROPE, LTD.—See Corning Incorporated; *U.S. Public*, pg. 448
COSTAR GMBH—See Corning Incorporated; *U.S. Public*, pg. 448
COSTAR ITALIA, S.R.L.—See Corning Incorporated; *U.S. Public*, pg. 448
COSTAR UK LTD.—See Corning Incorporated; *U.S. Public*, pg. 448
COSTCO WHOLESALE; *U.S. Public*, pg. 451
COSTECH—See Plastek Group; *U.S. Private*, pg. 870
CO-STEEL SAYREVILLE INC.—See Co-Steel Inc.; *Int'l*, pg. 298
COSTIGAN PLANT, WOOD PRODUCTS DIV.—See Champion International Corp.; *U.S. Public*, pg. 334
COSWORTH CASTINGS LTD.—See Vickers PLC; *Int'l*, pg. 1467
COSWORTH ENGINEERING INC.—See Vickers PLC; *Int'l*, pg. 1468
COSWORTH ENGINEERING LTD.—See Vickers PLC; *Int'l*, pg. 1466
COSWORTH ENGINEERING, WELLINGBOROUGH PLANT—See Vickers PLC; *Int'l*, pg. 1467
COTE D'OR S.A.—See Philip Morris Companies Inc.; *U.S. Public*, pg. 1288
THE COTEAU PROPERTIES CO.—See NACCO Industries, Inc.; *U.S. Public*, pg. 1149
COTO WABASH—See The Dyson-Kissner-Moran Corporation; *U.S. Private*, pg. 351
COTT BENELUX—See Cott Corporation; *Int'l*, pg. 338
COTT BEVERAGES ISRAEL LIMITED—See Cott Corporation; *Int'l*, pg. 338
COTT CORPORATION; *Int'l*, pg. 337
COTT CORPORATION - ATLANTIC CANADA REGION—See Cott Corporation; *Int'l*, pg. 337
COTT CORPORATION - CENTRAL DIVISION—See Cott Corporation; *Int'l*, pg. 337
COTT CORPORATION INTERNATIONAL OPERATIONS—See Cott Corporation; *Int'l*, pg. 338
COTT CORPORATION - MID-ATLANTIC REGION—See Cott Corporation; *Int'l*, pg. 338
COTT CORPORATION - NORTH CENTRAL REGION—See Cott Corporation; *Int'l*, pg. 338
COTT CORPORATION - NORTH CENTRAL REGION (SIKESTON)—See Cott Corporation; *Int'l*, pg. 337
COTT CORPORATION - NORTH EAST DIVISION—See Cott Corporation; *Int'l*, pg. 337
COTT CORPORATION - NORTH EAST REGION (ONTARIO)—See Cott Corporation; *Int'l*, pg. 337
COTT CORPORATION - NORTH EAST US REGION—See Cott Corporation; *Int'l*, pg. 338
COTT CORPORATION - PACIFIC CENTRAL REGION—See Cott Corporation; *Int'l*, pg. 338
COTT CORPORATION - PACIFIC NORTH WEST REGION (CALGARY)—See Cott Corporation; *Int'l*, pg. 337
COTT CORPORATION - PACIFIC NORTH WEST REGION (SURREY)—See Cott Corporation; *Int'l*, pg. 338
COTT CORPORATION - PACIFIC SOUTH WEST REGION—See Cott Corporation; *Int'l*, pg. 338
COTT CORPORATION - SOUTH CENTRAL REGION—See Cott Corporation; *Int'l*, pg. 338
COTT CORPORATION - SOUTH EAST REGION—See Cott Corporation; *Int'l*, pg. 338

COTT DIRECTORY OF CORPORATE AFFILIATIONS

Company Index

COTT EUROPE (CASTLEFORD)—See Cott Corporation; *Int'l*, pg. 338
COTT EUROPE (LONDON)—See Cott Corporation; *Int'l*, pg. 338
COTT EUROPE (PONTEFRACT)—See Cott Corporation; *Int'l*, pg. 338
COTT VENDING—See Cott Corporation; *Int'l*, pg. 338
COTTAGE GROVE SENTINEL—See Lee Enterprises, Incorporated; *U.S. Public*, pg. 983
COTTEE'S FOODS—See Cadbury Schweppes p.l.c.; *Int'l*, pg. 248
COTTER ACCEPTANCE CO., INC.—See TruServ Corporation; *U.S. Private*, pg. 1108
COTTER CORP.—See Unicom Corporation; *U.S. Public*, pg. 1664
COTTMAN TRANSMISSION SYSTEMS, INC.; *U.S. Private*, pg. 278
COTTO COPERTURE S.P.A.—See Redland PLC; *Int'l*, pg. 1092
COTTON ELECTRIC CO-OP; *U.S. Private*, pg. 278
COTTONS BREAD BAKERIES—See Interstate Bakeries Corporation; *U.S. Public*, pg. 909
COTUPLAS S.A.—See Pechiney S.A.; *Int'l*, pg. 1028
COTY AUSTRALIA PTY. LTD.—See Joh. A. Benckiser GmbH; *Int'l*, pg. 186
COTY CANADA—See Joh. A. Benckiser GmbH; *Int'l*, pg. 186
COTY INC.—See Joh. A. Benckiser GmbH; *Int'l*, pg. 185
F.X. COUGHLIN CO.; *U.S. Private*, pg. 278
COUGLE COMMISSION COMPANY, INC.; *U.S. Private*, pg. 278
COUNCE FINANCE CORPORATION—See Tenneco Inc.; *U.S. Public*, pg. 1578
COUNSEL CORPORATION; *Int'l*, pg. 338
COUNTDOWN CLEAN SYSTEMS LIMITED—See Laporte plc; *Int'l*, pg. 802
COUNTEC RECYCLING SYSTEMS DIVISION—See Portec, Inc.; *U.S. Public*, pg. 1318
COUNTERMEASURES & COMBAT SYSTEMS DIVISION—See Tracor, Inc.; *U.S. Public*, pg. 1627
COUNTRY AMERICA MAGAZINE—See Meredith Corporation; *U.S. Public*, pg. 1094
COUNTRY CASUALTY INSURANCE COMPANY—See Country Life Insurance Company; *U.S. Private*, pg. 279
COUNTRY CLASSIC DAIRIES, INC.; *U.S. Private*, pg. 278
COUNTRY CLUB INN, INC.—See Avatar Holdings Inc.; *U.S. Public*, pg. 151
COUNTRY COACH, INC.—See National R.V., Inc.; *U.S. Public*, pg. 1159
COUNTRY DELITE—See Suiza Foods Corporation; *U.S. Public*, pg. 1526
COUNTRY FRESH, INC.—See Suiza Foods Corporation; *U.S. Public*, pg. 1526
COUNTRY GENERAL STORES—See J.W. Childs Associates, L.P.; *U.S. Private*, pg. 237
COUNTRY HOME BAKERY, INC.; *U.S. Private*, pg. 278
COUNTRY HOME MAGAZINE—See Meredith Corporation; *U.S. Public*, pg. 1094
COUNTRY INVESTORS LIFE ASSURANCE COMPANY—See Country Life Insurance Company; *U.S. Private*, pg. 279
COUNTRY KITCHEN INTERNATIONAL, INC.—See Kitchen Investment Group; *U.S. Private*, pg. 624
COUNTRY LIFE INSURANCE COMPANY; *U.S. Private*, pg. 278
COUNTRY LIVING—See The Hearst Corporation; *U.S. Private*, pg. 517
COUNTRY MUTUAL INSURANCE COMPANY—See Country Life Insurance Company; *U.S. Private*, pg. 279
COUNTRY MUTUAL NORTHWEST REGIONAL OFFICE—See Country Life Insurance Company; *U.S. Private*, pg. 279
COUNTRY 103.5—See Groupe Bruxelles Lambert S.A.; *Int'l*, pg. 561
COUNTRY PREFERRED INSURANCE COMPANY—See Country Life Insurance Company; *U.S. Private*, pg. 279
COUNTRY PRODUCTS GROUP—See Agway, Inc.; *U.S. Private*, pg. 27
COUNTRY SAMPLER STORE—See Sampler Publications Inc.; *U.S. Private*, pg. 963
COUNTRY SKILLET CATFISH CO.—See ConAgra, Inc.; *U.S. Public*, pg. 428
COUNTRY WEEKLY, INC.—See American Media, Inc.; *U.S. Public*, pg. 87
COUNTRYMARK COOPERATIVE, INC.; *U.S. Private*, pg. 279
COUNTRYMARK FEED PLANT—See Countrymark Cooperative, Inc.; *U.S. Private*, pg. 279
COUNTRYWIDE AGENCY, INC.—See Countrywide Home Loans Inc.; *U.S. Public*, pg. 452
COUNTRYWIDE ASSET MANAGEMENT CORPORATION—See Countrywide Home Loans Inc.; *U.S. Public*, pg. 452
COUNTRYWIDE CAPITAL MARKETS, INC.—See Countrywide Home Loans Inc.; *U.S. Public*, pg. 453
COUNTRYWIDE CORPORATION—See Countrywide Home Loans Inc.; *U.S. Public*, pg. 453
COUNTRYWIDE FUNDING CORPORATION—See Countrywide Home Loans Inc.; *U.S. Public*, pg. 453
COUNTRYWIDE HOME LOANS INC.; *U.S. Public*, pg. 452
COUNTRYWIDE PARTNERSHIP INVESTMENTS, INC.—See Countrywide Home Loans Inc.; *U.S. Public*, pg. 453
COUNTRYWIDE PORTER/NOVELLI—See Omnicom Group Inc.; *U.S. Public*, pg. 1225
COUNTRYWIDE SECURITIES CORPORATION—See Countrywide Home Loans Inc.; *U.S. Public*, pg. 453
COUNTRYWIDE SERVICES CORP.—See Nationwide Insurance Enterprise; *U.S. Private*, pg. 789
COUNTRYWIDE SERVICING EXCHANGE—See Countrywide Home Loans Inc.; *U.S. Public*, pg. 453
COUNTRYWIDE TITLE CORPORATION—See Countrywide Home Loans Inc.; *U.S. Public*, pg. 453
COUNTY & DISTRICT PROPERTIES LIMITED—See Costain Group PLC; *Int'l*, pg. 337
COUNTY BANKING & TRUST COMPANY—See Mercantile Bankshares Corporation; *U.S. Public*, pg. 1089
COUNTY DATA CORP.—See American Business Information, Inc.; *U.S. Public*, pg. 70
COUNTY NATWEST AUSTRALIA INVESTMENT—See National Westminster Bank PLC; *Int'l*, pg. 911
COUNTY NATWEST AUSTRALIA LIMITED—See National Westminster Bank PLC; *Int'l*, pg. 911
COUNTY NATWEST CORPORATE FINANCE AUSTRALIA LIMITED—See National Westminster Bank PLC; *Int'l*, pg. 911
COUNTY NATWEST LIMITED—See National Westminster Bank PLC; *Int'l*, pg. 910
COUNTY NATWEST SECURITIES AUSTRALIA LIMITED—See National Westminster Bank PLC; *Int'l*, pg. 911
COUNTY REALTY CORP.—See Commerce Bancshares, Inc.; *U.S. Public*, pg. 409
COUNTY SEAT STORES, INC.; *U.S. Private*, pg. 279
COUNTY TOOL & ABRASIVE—See Buck Knives, Inc.; *U.S. Private*, pg. 177
COURBEVOIE-CONSUMER PRODUCTS DIVISION—See Fort James Corporation; *U.S. Public*, pg. 673
COURBU VITRAGE—See Saint-Gobain; *Int'l*, pg. 1172
COURI CARPET CO.—See Couristan Inc.; *U.S. Private*, pg. 279
COURI-MURAD & CO.—See Couristan Inc.; *U.S. Private*, pg. 279
COURIER COMPANIES, INC.—See Courier Corporation; *U.S. Public*, pg. 453
COURIER CONNECTION, INC.—See Courier Corporation; *U.S. Public*, pg. 453
COURIER CORPORATION; *U.S. Public*, pg. 453
COURIER DISPATCH DIVISION—See Corporate Express, Inc.; *U.S. Public*, pg. 450
COURIER INTERNATIONAL, LTD.—See Courier Corporation; *U.S. Public*, pg. 453
THE COURIER JOURNAL—See The E.W. Scripps Company; *U.S. Public*, pg. 1447
THE COURIER-JOURNAL LOUISVILLE TIMES CO.—See Gannett Company, Inc.; *U.S. Public*, pg. 700
COURIER KENDALLVILLE, INC.—See Courier Corporation; *U.S. Public*, pg. 453
COURIER-NEWS CO.—See Gannett Company, Inc.; *U.S. Public*, pg. 700
COURIER-POST—See Gannett Company, Inc.; *U.S. Public*, pg. 700
COURIER STOUGHTON, INC.—See Courier Corporation; *U.S. Public*, pg. 453
COURIER WESTFORD, INC.—See Courier Corporation; *U.S. Public*, pg. 453
COURISTAN INC.; *U.S. Private*, pg. 279
THE COURT COMPANY; *U.S. Private*, pg. 279
COURT GALVANIZING LIMITED—See Jannock Limited; *Int'l*, pg. 698
COURTAULDS AEROSPACE—See Courtaulds plc; *Int'l*, pg. 338
COURTAULDS AEROSPACE INC.—See Courtaulds plc; *Int'l*, pg. 339
COURTAULDS (CANADA) INC.—See Courtaulds plc; *Int'l*, pg. 339
COURTAULDS COATINGS INC.—See Courtaulds plc; *Int'l*, pg. 338
COURTAULDS COATINGS LTD.—See Courtaulds plc; *Int'l*, pg. 338
COURTAULDS ENGINEERING LTD.—See Courtaulds plc; *Int'l*, pg. 339
COURTAULDS ESPANA S.A.—See Courtaulds plc; *Int'l*, pg. 339
COURTAULDS EUROPEAN FIBRES—See Courtaulds plc; *Int'l*, pg. 339
COURTAULDS EUROPEAN FIBRES—See Hoechst Aktiengesellschaft; *Int'l*, pg. 626
COURTAULDS FIBERS INC.—See Courtaulds plc; *Int'l*, pg. 339
COURTAULDS FIBRES LTD.—See Courtaulds plc; *Int'l*, pg. 339
COURTAULDS FIBRES LTD.—See Hoechst Aktiengesellschaft; *Int'l*, pg. 626
COURTAULDS FILMS HOLDINGS LTD.—See Courtaulds plc; *Int'l*, pg. 339
COURTAULDS NIPPON PAINT AB—See Nippon Paint Company Ltd.; *Int'l*, pg. 937
COURTAULDS NIPPON PAINT LIMITED—See Nippon Paint Company Ltd.; *Int'l*, pg. 937
COURTAULDS PERFORMANCE FILMS INC.—See Courtaulds plc; *Int'l*, pg. 339
COURTAULDS PLC; *Int'l*, pg. 338
COURTAULDS STRUCTURAL COMPOSITES INC.—See Courtaulds plc; *Int'l*, pg. 338
COURTAULDS TEXTILES PLC; *Int'l*, pg. 339
COURTAULDS U.S. DEVELOPMENTS INC.—See Courtaulds plc; *Int'l*, pg. 339
COURTESY CHEVROLET & IMPORTS INC.; *U.S. Private*, pg. 279
COURTLAND MILL, CHAMPION INTERNATIONAL CORPORATION—See Champion International Corp.; *U.S. Public*, pg. 334
COURTYARD BY MARRIOTT—See Marriott International, Inc.; *U.S. Public*, pg. 1048
COURTYARD NURSING CARE, INC.—See The Western and Southern Life Insurance Company; *U.S. Private*, pg. 1165
COUSINS PROPERTIES INCORPORATED; *U.S. Public*, pg. 453
COUSINS SUBMARINES; *U.S. Private*, pg. 280
COUSINS SUBS SYSTEMS, INC.—See Cousins Submarines; *U.S. Private*, pg. 280
COUTANT ELECTRONIQUE SA—See Siebe plc; *Int'l*, pg. 1241
COUTANT LAMBDA LIMITED—See Siebe plc; *Int'l*, pg. 1241
COUTTS & CO.—See National Westminster Bank PLC; *Int'l*, pg. 910
COUTTS & CO (USA) INTERNATIONAL LIMITED—See National Westminster Bank PLC; *Int'l*, pg. 911
THE JEAN COUTU GROUP (PJC) INC.; *Int'l*, pg. 340
COVA FINANCIAL SERVICES LIFE INSURANCE CO.—See General American Life Insurance Co.; *U.S. Private*, pg. 443
COVADONGA S.A. DE SEGUROS Y REASEGUROS—See Assicurazioni Generali S.p.A.; *Int'l*, pg. 91
COVANCE, INC.; *U.S. Public*, pg. 453
COVANCE INC.—See Covance, Inc.; *U.S. Public*, pg. 454
COVANCE LABORATORIES—See Covance, Inc.; *U.S. Public*, pg. 454
COVANCE RESEARCH PRODUCTS, INC.—See Covance, Inc.; *U.S. Public*, pg. 454
COVE HAVEN, INC.—See Starwood Hotels & Resorts; *U.S. Public*, pg. 1512
COVE PETROLEUM—See Anchor Gasoline Corporation; *U.S. Private*, pg. 71
COVE SHOE COMPANY—See Berkshire Hathaway Inc.; *U.S. Public*, pg. 217
COVENTRY CORPORATION; *U.S. Public*, pg. 454
THE COVENTRY COURIER—See Journal Register Company; *U.S. Public*, pg. 934
COVENTRY HEALTH & LIFE INSURANCE—See Coventry Corporation; *U.S. Public*, pg. 454
COVENTRY HOMES OF COLORADO—See Del Webb Corporation; *U.S. Public*, pg. 495
COVENTRY HOMES OF LAS VEGAS—See Del Webb Corporation; *U.S. Public*, pg. 495
COVENTRY HOMES OF NEVADA, INC.—See Del Webb Corporation; *U.S. Public*, pg. 495
COVENTRY HOMES OF SOUTHERN CALIFORNIA—See Del Webb Corporation; *U.S. Public*, pg. 495
COVENTRY HOMES OF TUCSON, INC.—See Del Webb Corporation; *U.S. Public*, pg. 495
COVER GIRL COSMETICS—See The Procter & Gamble Company; *U.S. Public*, pg. 1330
COVERLAND S.A.—See Redland PLC; *Int'l*, pg. 1092
COVIA, LLC—See UAL Corporation; *U.S. Public*, pg. 1653
COVIGAL SA—See Novartis AG; *Int'l*, pg. 981
COVINGTON FOODS, INC.; *U.S. Private*, pg. 280
COVINGTON INDUSTRIES; *U.S. Private*, pg. 280
COVINGTON SPECIALTY PRINT—See John H. Harland Company; *U.S. Public*, pg. 786
COW & GATE NUTRICIA (IRELAND) LTD.—See Nutricia BV; *Int'l*, pg. 991
COW & GATE NUTRICIA LTD.—See Nutricia BV; *Int'l*, pg. 991
COW PROOFINGS LIMITED—See BTR plc; *Int'l*, pg. 124
COWARD-MCCANN, INC.—See Pearson plc; *Int'l*, pg. 1027
COWBOY OIL COMPANY; *U.S. Private*, pg. 280
COWDEN METAL-SAN JOSE—See Cowden Metal Specialties, Inc.; *U.S. Private*, pg. 280
COWDEN METAL SPECIALTIES, INC.; *U.S. Private*, pg. 280
COWELL'S BINGO—See Arrow International; *U.S. Private*, pg. 85
COWEN & COMPANY; *U.S. Private*, pg. 280
COWIN & COMPANY, INC.; *U.S. Private*, pg. 280
COWLES BUSINESS MEDIA, INC.—See Cowles Media Company; *U.S. Private*, pg. 281
COWLES ENTHUSIAST MEDIA, INC.—See Cowles Media Company; *U.S. Private*, pg. 281
COWLES HISTORY GROUP, INC.—See Cowles Media Company; *U.S. Private*, pg. 281
COWLES MEDIA COMPANY; *U.S. Private*, pg. 280
COWLES SYNDICATE, INC.—See The Hearst Corporation; *U.S. Private*, pg. 518
COWTOWN BOOT COMPANY; *U.S. Private*, pg. 281
COX & COMPANY, INC.; *U.S. Private*, pg. 281
COX CABLE GREATER OCALA, INC.—See Cox Communications, Inc.; *U.S. Public*, pg. 455
COX CABLE HAMPTON ROADS, INC.—See Cox Communications, Inc.; *U.S. Public*, pg. 455
COX CABLE UNIVERSITY CITY, INC.—See Cox Communications, Inc.; *U.S. Public*, pg. 455
COX COMMUNICATIONS-AMHERST—See Cox Communications, Inc.; *U.S. Public*, pg. 454
COX COMMUNICATIONS-ASHLAND—See Cox Communications, Inc.; *U.S. Public*, pg. 454
COX COMMUNICATIONS-BAKERSFIELD—See Cox Communications, Inc.; *U.S. Public*, pg. 454
COX COMMUNICATIONS-CEDAR RAPIDS—See Cox Communications, Inc.; *U.S. Public*, pg. 454
COX COMMUNICATIONS-CLEVELAND—See Cox Communications, Inc.; *U.S. Public*, pg. 454
COX COMMUNICATIONS-COSHOCTON—See Cox Communications, Inc.; *U.S. Public*, pg. 454
COX COMMUNICATIONS-DEFIANCE—See Cox Communications, Inc.; *U.S. Public*, pg. 454
COX COMMUNICATIONS-GAINESVILLE/OCALA—See Cox Communications, Inc.; *U.S. Public*, pg. 454
COX COMMUNICATIONS-GREATER HARTFORD—See Cox Communications, Inc.; *U.S. Public*, pg. 454
COX COMMUNICATIONS-HUMBOLDT BAY—See Cox Communications, Inc.; *U.S. Public*, pg. 454
COX COMMUNICATIONS, INC.—See Cox Enterprises, Inc.; *U.S. Private*, pg. 282
COX COMMUNICATIONS, INC.; *U.S. Public*, pg. 454
COX COMMUNICATIONS-JEFFERSON PARISH OFFICE—See Cox Communications, Inc.; *U.S. Public*, pg. 455
COX COMMUNICATIONS-LAFAYETTE—See Cox Communications, Inc.; *U.S. Public*, pg. 455
COX COMMUNICATIONS-LUBBOCK—See Cox Communications, Inc.; *U.S. Public*, pg. 455
COX COMMUNICATIONS-MERIDEN—See Cox Communications, Inc.; *U.S. Public*, pg. 455
COX COMMUNICATIONS-MIDDLE GEORGIA—See Cox Communications, Inc.; *U.S. Public*, pg. 455
COX COMMUNICATIONS-MIDLAND—See Cox Communications, Inc.; *U.S. Public*, pg. 455

COX COMMUNICATIONS-MYRTLE BEACH—See Cox Communications, Inc.; *U.S. Public*, pg. 455
COX COMMUNICATIONS-NEW ORLEANS—See Cox Communications, Inc.; *U.S. Public*, pg. 455
COX COMMUNICATIONS-NEWARK—See Cox Communications, Inc.; *U.S. Public*, pg. 455
COX COMMUNICATIONS-OKLAHOMA CITY—See Cox Communications, Inc.; *U.S. Public*, pg. 455
COX COMMUNICATIONS-OMAHA—See Cox Communications, Inc.; *U.S. Public*, pg. 455
COX COMMUNICATIONS-ORANGE COUNTY—See Cox Communications, Inc.; *U.S. Public*, pg. 455
COX COMMUNICATIONS-PALOS VERDES—See Cox Communications, Inc.; *U.S. Public*, pg. 455
COX COMMUNICATIONS-PENSACOLA/FT. WALTON—See Cox Communications, Inc.; *U.S. Public*, pg. 455
COX COMMUNICATIONS-PHOENIX—See Cox Communications, Inc.; *U.S. Public*, pg. 455
COX COMMUNICATIONS-PROVIDENCE/WEYMOUTH—See Cox Communications, Inc.; *U.S. Public*, pg. 455
COX COMMUNICATIONS-QUAD CITIES—See Cox Communications, Inc.; *U.S. Public*, pg. 455
COX COMMUNICATIONS-RHODE ISLAND—See Cox Communications, Inc.; *U.S. Public*, pg. 455
COX COMMUNICATIONS-ROANOKE—See Cox Communications, Inc.; *U.S. Public*, pg. 455
COX COMMUNICATIONS-SAGINAW—See Cox Communications, Inc.; *U.S. Public*, pg. 455
COX COMMUNICATIONS-SAN DIEGO—See Cox Communications, Inc.; *U.S. Public*, pg. 455
COX COMMUNICATIONS-SANTA BARBARA—See Cox Communications, Inc.; *U.S. Public*, pg. 455
COX COMMUNICATIONS-SPOKANE—See Cox Communications, Inc.; *U.S. Public*, pg. 455
COX COMMUNICATIONS-SPRINGFIELD—See Cox Communications, Inc.; *U.S. Public*, pg. 455
COX COMMUNICATIONS-VISTA—See Cox Communications, Inc.; *U.S. Public*, pg. 455
COX COMMUNICATIONS-WASHINGTON—See Cox Communications, Inc.; *U.S. Public*, pg. 455
COX COMMUNICATIONS-WILLIAMSPORT—See Cox Communications, Inc.; *U.S. Public*, pg. 455
COX ENTERPRISES, INC.; *U.S. Private*, pg. 281
COX FURNITURE; *U.S. Private*, pg. 283
COX LUMBER CO.; *U.S. Private*, pg. 283
P C COX (NEWBURY) LTD.—See BBA Group plc; *Int'l*, pg. 113
COX TEXAS PUBLICATIONS, INC.—See Cox Enterprises, Inc.; *U.S. Private*, pg. 281
COX WOOD PRESERVING CO.; *U.S. Private*, pg. 283
J.B. COXWELL CONTRACT, INC.; *U.S. Private*, pg. 283
COYNE & BELLIER S.A.—See Tractebel; *Int'l*, pg. 1416
COYNE BEAHM INC.; *U.S. Private*, pg. 283
COYNE BEAHM INC.—See Coyne Beahm Inc.; *U.S. Private*, pg. 283
COYOTE NETWORK SYSTEMS, INC.; *U.S. Public*, pg. 455
COYOTE RESTAURANT CORP.—See Specialty Restaurants Corporation; *U.S. Private*, pg. 1022
COZ PLASTICS INC.—See PMC, Inc.; *U.S. Private*, pg. 827
CPM/PACIFIC PRIVATE LTD.—See Gencor Industries, Inc.; *U.S. Public*, pg. 705
CRAB RUN GAS CO.—See Washington Gas Light Co.; *U.S. Public*, pg. 1740
CRABAR BUSINESS SYSTEMS; *U.S. Private*, pg. 283
CRABLE SPORTSWEAR, INC.—See The Midland Company; *U.S. Public*, pg. 1111
CRABTREE ELECTRICAL INDUSTRIES LIMITED—See Hanson PLC; *Int'l*, pg. 592
CRABTREE PREMIUM FINANCE—See United Fire & Casualty Company; *U.S. Public*, pg. 1677
CRACKEN, HARKEY, STREET & CO., LLC; *U.S. Private*, pg. 283
CRACKER BARREL OLD COUNTRY STORE, INC.; *U.S. Public*, pg. 455
CRACKER JACK DIVISION—See Borden, Inc.; *U.S. Private*, pg. 157
CRACKIN' GOOD BAKERS—See Winn-Dixie Stores, Inc.; *U.S. Public*, pg. 1772
CRADDOCK-TERRY INC.; *U.S. Private*, pg. 284
CRAFCO, INC.—See Ergon, Inc.; *U.S. Private*, pg. 381
CRAFT-CO ENTERPRISES INC.—See Noma Industries Limited; *Int'l*, pg. 955
CRAFTEX MILLS INC. OF PENNSYLVANIA; *U.S. Private*, pg. 284
CRAFTLITE—See The Genlyte Group Incorporated; *U.S. Public*, pg. 730
CRAFTMATIC INDUSTRIES, INC.; *U.S. Private*, pg. 284
CRAFTMATIC ORGANIZATION, INC.—See Craftmatic Industries, Inc.; *U.S. Private*, pg. 284
CRAFTS TECHNOLOGY, INC.—See Carpenter Technology Corporation; *U.S. Public*, pg. 307
CRAFTSMAN PRINTING COMPANY—See Wallace Computer Services, Inc.; *U.S. Public*, pg. 1735
CRAFTWAYS CORP.—See Meredith Corporation; *U.S. Public*, pg. 1094
CRAFTWELL CONTAINERS & PACKAGING LIMITED—See Kruger Inc.; *Int'l*, pg. 761
CRAFTY BEAVER HOME CENTER; *U.S. Private*, pg. 284
CRAGAR INDUSTRIES, INC.; *U.S. Public*, pg. 456
CRAIG CORPORATION; *U.S. Public*, pg. 456
CRAIG SYSTEMS; *U.S. Private*, pg. 284
CRAIN ASSOCIATED ENTERPRISES—See Crain Communications, Inc.; *U.S. Private*, pg. 285
CRAIN BROADCASTING—See Crain Communications, Inc.; *U.S. Private*, pg. 285
CRAIN COMMUNICATIONS, DALLAS—See Crain Communications, Inc.; *U.S. Private*, pg. 285
CRAIN COMMUNICATIONS, INC.; *U.S. Private*, pg. 284
CRAIN COMMUNICATIONS, LOS ANGELES—See Crain Communications, Inc.; *U.S. Private*, pg. 285
CRAIN COMMUNICATIONS, NASHVILLE—See Crain Communications, Inc.; *U.S. Private*, pg. 285
CRAIN COMMUNICATIONS, WASHINGTON, D.C.—See Crain Communications, Inc.; *U.S. Private*, pg. 285

CRAIN'S CHICAGO BUSINESS—See Crain Communications, Inc.; *U.S. Private*, pg. 285
CRAIN'S CLEVELAND BUSINESS—See Crain Communications, Inc.; *U.S. Private*, pg. 285
CRAIN'S DETROIT BUSINESS—See Crain Communications, Inc.; *U.S. Private*, pg. 285
CRAIN'S NEW YORK BUSINESS—See Crain Communications, Inc.; *U.S. Private*, pg. 285
CRAMER COMPANY—See Owosso Corporation; *U.S. Public*, pg. 1238
CRAMER INC.; *U.S. Private*, pg. 285
CRAMER-KRASSELT; *U.S. Private*, pg. 285
CRAMER-KRASSELT—See Cramer-Krasselt; *U.S. Private*, pg. 286
CRAMER-KRASSELT PUBLIC RELATIONS—See Cramer-Krasselt; *U.S. Private*, pg. 286
CRAMERTON AUTOMOTIVE PRODUCTS, L.P.—See Trace International Holdings, Inc.; *U.S. Private*, pg. 1095
CRAMIQUES TECHNIQUES DESMARQUEST—See Pechiney S.A.; *Int'l*, pg. 1028
CRANBERRY PIPELINE CORPORATION—See Cabot Oil & Gas Corporation; *U.S. Public*, pg. 289
CRANE & CO., INC.; *U.S. Private*, pg. 286
CRANE AUSTRALIA PTY. LTD.—See Crane Co.; *U.S. Public*, pg. 457
CRANE CANADA INC.—See Crane Co.; *U.S. Public*, pg. 457
CRANE CARRIER COMPANY; *U.S. Private*, pg. 286
CRANE CO.; *U.S. Public*, pg. 456
CRANE CONSTRUCTION CO.; *U.S. Private*, pg. 286
CRANE CREEK CEDAR—See E.R. Probyn Ltd.; *Int'l*, pg. 1071
CRANE DEFENSE SYSTEMS—See Crane Co.; *U.S. Public*, pg. 456
CRANE DEMING PUMPS—See Crane Co.; *U.S. Public*, pg. 457
CRANE GROUP LIMITED; *Int'l*, pg. 340
CRANE INSPECTION & CERTIFICATION BUREAU—See SGS Societe Generale de Surveillance Holding S.A.; *Int'l*, pg. 1153
JOHN CRANE AUSTRALIA PTY, LTD.—See TI Group plc; *Int'l*, pg. 1339
JOHN CRANE BELFAB—See TI Group plc; *Int'l*, pg. 1339
S.A. JOHN CRANE BELGIUM N.V.—See TI Group plc; *Int'l*, pg. 1339
JOHN CRANE BRASIL—See TI Group plc; *Int'l*, pg. 1340
JOHN CRANE BRASIL INDUSTRIAL LTDA.—See TI Group plc; *Int'l*, pg. 1339
JOHN CRANE CANADA, INC.—See TI Group plc; *Int'l*, pg. 1339
JOHN CRANE GMBH—See TI Group plc; *Int'l*, pg. 1339
JOHN CRANE GROUP—See TI Group plc; *Int'l*, pg. 1338
JOHN CRANE IBERICA S.A.—See TI Group plc; *Int'l*, pg. 1339
JOHN CRANE ITALIA SPA—See TI Group plc; *Int'l*, pg. 1339
JOHN CRANE (JAPAN), INC.—See TI Group plc; *Int'l*, pg. 1339
JOHN CRANE (KOREA) CO., LTD.—See TI Group plc; *Int'l*, pg. 1339
JOHN CRANE KUWAIT—See TI Group plc; *Int'l*, pg. 1339
JOHN CRANE LEMCO—See TI Group plc; *Int'l*, pg. 1339
JOHN CRANE LTD.—See TI Group plc; *Int'l*, pg. 1339
JOHN CRANE MARINE USA—See TI Group plc; *Int'l*, pg. 1339
JOHN CRANE MECHANICAL SEALS—See TI Group plc; *Int'l*, pg. 1339
JOHN CRANE SAUDI ARABIA LTD.—See TI Group plc; *Int'l*, pg. 1339
JOHN CRANE SINGAPORE PTE. LTD.—See TI Group plc; *Int'l*, pg. 1339
JOHN CRANE (TAIWAN) CO. LTD.—See TI Group plc; *Int'l*, pg. 1339
JOHN CRANE UK LTD.—See TI Group plc; *Int'l*, pg. 1338
CRANE LEAR ROMEC CORP.—See Crane Co.; *U.S. Public*, pg. 457
CRANE LIMITED U.K.—See Crane Co.; *U.S. Public*, pg. 458
CRANE MANUFACTURING; *U.S. Private*, pg. 286
CRANE NATIONAL VENDORS CO., LTD.—See Crane Co.; *U.S. Public*, pg. 456
CRANE PLASTICS COMPANY; *U.S. Private*, pg. 286
CRANE PUMPS & SYSTEMS INC.—See Crane Co.; *U.S. Public*, pg. 457
CRANE RESISTOFLEX/DEFENSE—See Crane Co.; *U.S. Public*, pg. 457
CRANE RESISTOFLEX/INDUSTRIAL—See Crane Co.; *U.S. Public*, pg. 457
CRANE VALVES/NORTH AMERICAN—See Crane Co.; *U.S. Public*, pg. 457
CRANER GMBH—See Freudenberg & Company; *Int'l*, pg. 506
CRANFORD JOHNSON ROBINSON WOODS; *U.S. Private*, pg. 287
CRANKSHAFT MACHINE GROUP—See Avis Industrial Corporation; *U.S. Private*, pg. 102
CRANSTON PRINT WORKS COMPANY; *U.S. Private*, pg. 286
CRAVENS, DARGAN & COMPANY, PACIFIC COAST—See Cigna Corp.; *U.S. Public*, pg. 365
CRAVENS, DARGAN & COMPANY, PACIFIC COAST OF ILLINOIS, INC.—See Cigna Corp.; *U.S. Public*, pg. 366
CRAVENS, DARGAN & COMPANY, PACIFIC COAST OF NEW YORK, INC.—See Cigna Corp.; *U.S. Public*, pg. 366
CRAVEY, GREEN & WAHLEN, INCORPORATED; *U.S. Private*, pg. 287
DAVID CRAVIT & ASSOCIATES ADVERTISING; *U.S. Private*, pg. 287
CRAWAL—See Buckeye Corrugated Inc.; *U.S. Private*, pg. 177
CRAWFORD & COMPANY; *U.S. Public*, pg. 458
CRAWFORD & COMPANY INSURANCE ADJUSTERS LTD.—See Crawford & Company; *U.S. Public*, pg. 458

CRAWFORD & COMPANY INTERNATIONAL, INC.—See Crawford & Company; *U.S. Public*, pg. 458
CRAWFORD & CRAWFORD, INC.—See Adair Feed & Grain Company; *U.S. Private*, pg. 16
CRAWFORD DOOR FORSALJNINGS AB—See Cardo AB; *Int'l*, pg. 269
CRAWFORD DOOR S.A.—See Cardo AB; *Int'l*, pg. 269
CRAWFORD DOOR S.R.L.—See Cardo AB; *Int'l*, pg. 269
CRAWFORD GARAGE DOOR SYSTEMS AB—See Cardo AB; *Int'l*, pg. 269
THE CRAWFORD GROUP; *U.S. Private*, pg. 287
CRAWFORD INDUSTRIES—See American Trading and Production Corporation; *U.S. Private*, pg. 64
CRAWFORD TOR GES.M.B.H.—See Cardo AB; *Int'l*, pg. 269
CRAWFORDSVILLE DOCUMENTATION DIVISION—See R.R. Donnelley & Sons Company; *U.S. Public*, pg. 518
CRAWFORDSVILLE MANUFACTURING DIVISION—See R.R. Donnelley & Sons Company; *U.S. Public*, pg. 518
CRAWFORDSVILLE TELEMARKETING—See R.R. Donnelley & Sons Company; *U.S. Public*, pg. 518
CRAWLER SYSTEMS—See Fried. Krupp AG; *Int'l*, pg. 511
CRAWMATOR AB—See Cardo AB; *Int'l*, pg. 269
CRAY RESEARCH—See Silicon Graphics, Inc.; *U.S. Public*, pg. 1473
CRAY VALLEY PRODUCTS—See Total S.A.; *Int'l*, pg. 1410
CRAYOLA PRODUCTS DIV.—See Hallmark Cards, Inc.; *U.S. Private*, pg. 496
CREACIONAL/DMB&B—See DMB&B Communications; *U.S. Private*, pg. 303
CREAM O'WEBER DAIRY INC.—See Dean Foods Company; *U.S. Public*, pg. 490
THE CREAMETTE CO. OF CANADA LTD.—See Borden, Inc.; *U.S. Private*, pg. 159
CREAMLAND DAIRIES, INC.—See Dean Foods Company; *U.S. Public*, pg. 490
JAMES CREAN HOLDINGS (UK) LTD.—See James Crean PLC; *Int'l*, pg. 341
JAMES CREAN PLC; *Int'l*, pg. 340
CREATION WINDOWS OF INDIANA, INC.; *U.S. Private*, pg. 287
CREATIONS AROMATIQUES, INC.—See Bayer AG; *Int'l*, pg. 173
CREATIVE ALLIANCE, INC.; *U.S. Private*, pg. 287
CREATIVE CARD CO.—See American Pad and Paper Company; *U.S. Public*, pg. 89
CREATIVE COMPUTERS, INC.; *U.S. Public*, pg. 458
CREATIVE COMPUTERS, INC.—See Creative Computers, Inc.; *U.S. Public*, pg. 458
CREATIVE DATA SYSTEMS DIVISIONS—See Sterling Software, Inc.; *U.S. Public*, pg. 1516
CREATIVE GROUP INC.; *U.S. Private*, pg. 287
CREATIVE HAIRDRESSERS; *U.S. Private*, pg. 287
CREATIVE MARKETING INTERNATIONAL CORP.; *U.S. Private*, pg. 287
CREATIVE MEDIA PRODUCTS—See Superior Label Systems, Inc.; *U.S. Private*, pg. 1055
CREATIVE PLAYTHINGS LTD.; *U.S. Private*, pg. 287
CREATIVE PROCESS, INC.—See United Grocers Inc.; *U.S. Private*, pg. 1122
CREATIVE PRODUCTIONS; *U.S. Private*, pg. 288
CREATIVE PUBLICATIONS; *U.S. Private*, pg. 288
CREATIVE PUBLICATIONS—See Creative Publications; *U.S. Private*, pg. 288
THE CREATIVE SERVICES INC.—See Proudfoot plc; *Int'l*, pg. 1072
CREATIVITY—See Testa International; *Int'l*, pg. 1377
CREATIVITY/YOUNG & RUBICAM ASOCIADOS—See Young & Rubicam Inc.; *U.S. Private*, pg. 1200
CRECSPAN, S.A.—See Borden, Inc.; *U.S. Private*, pg. 159
CREDA LTD.—See The General Electric Company, p.l.c.; *Int'l*, pg. 543
CREDIET EN EFFECTEN BANK—See ING Groep N.V.; *Int'l*, pg. 647
CREDIOP-CREDITO PER LE IMPRESE E LE OPERE PUBBLICHE SPA; *Int'l*, pg. 341
CREDIOP OVERSEAS BANK LTD.—See Crediop-Credito Per Le Imprese e le Opere Pubbliche SpA; *Int'l*, pg. 341
CREDIT ADMINISTRATION CENTER—See Pacific Capital Bancorp; *U.S. Public*, pg. 1248
CREDIT AGRICOLE; *Int'l*, pg. 341
CREDIT AGRICOLE ASSET MANAGEMENT - SOUTHEAST ASIA—See Credit Agricole; *Int'l*, pg. 341
CREDIT AGRICOLE (CNCA) LONDON—See Credit Agricole; *Int'l*, pg. 341
CREDIT AGRICOLE (CNCA) LUXEMBOURG—See Credit Agricole; *Int'l*, pg. 341
CREDIT AGRICOLE (CNCA) MADRID—See Credit Agricole; *Int'l*, pg. 341
CREDIT AGRICOLE (CNCA) MILAN—See Credit Agricole; *Int'l*, pg. 341
CREDIT AGRICOLE (CNCA) REPRESENTATIVE OFFICE-RIO DE JANEIRO—See Credit Agricole; *Int'l*, pg. 341
CREDIT AGRICOLE (CNCA) REPRESENTATIVE OFFICE-TOKYO—See Credit Agricole; *Int'l*, pg. 341
CREDIT AGRICOLE (CNCA) REPRESENTATIVE OFFICE-BANGKOK—See Credit Agricole; *Int'l*, pg. 341
CREDIT AGRICOLE (CNCA) REPRESENTATIVE OFFICE-BEIJING—See Credit Agricole; *Int'l*, pg. 341
CREDIT AGRICOLE (CNCA) SAN FRANCISCO—See Credit Agricole; *Int'l*, pg. 341
CREDIT AGRICOLE (CNCA) U.S.A. (CHICAGO)—See Credit Agricole; *Int'l*, pg. 341
CREDIT AGRICOLE (CNCA) U.S.A. (NEW YORK)—See Credit Agricole; *Int'l*, pg. 341
CREDIT AGRICOLE (DEUTSCHLAND) AG HANDELSBERATUNG—See Credit Agricole; *Int'l*, pg. 341
CREDIT & RISK MANAGEMENT ASSOCIATES—See Fair, Isaac and Company, Inc.; *U.S. Public*, pg. 610
THE CREDIT BUREAU, INC. OF GEORGIA—See Equifax Inc.; *U.S. Public*, pg. 588

Company Index
CREDIT DIRECTORY OF CORPORATE AFFILIATIONS

CREDIT CARD SENTINEL—See Montgomery Ward & Co., Inc.; *U.S. Private*, pg. 759
CREDIT COMMERCIAL DE FRANCE; *Int'l*, pg. 341
CREDIT COMMUNAL DE BELGIQUE SA; *Int'l*, pg. 343
CREDIT CORPORATION (MALAYSIA) BERHAD—See Standard Chartered Bank PLC; *Int'l*, pg. 1297
CREDIT CORPORATION (SINGAPORE) LTD.—See Standard Chartered Bank PLC; *Int'l*, pg. 1297
CREDIT DE LA BOURSE S.A.—See Swiss Bank Corporation; *Int'l*, pg. 1330
CREDIT EUROPEEN—See Bank Brussels Lambert; *Int'l*, pg. 148
CREDIT FORD S.A.—See Ford Motor Company; *U.S. Public*, pg. 666
CREDIT INDUSTRIEL D'ALSACE ET DE LORRAINE—See Groupe GAN; *Int'l*, pg. 564
CREDIT INDUSTRIEL DE L'OUEST—See Groupe GAN; *Int'l*, pg. 564
CREDIT INDUSTRIEL DE NORMANDIE—See Groupe GAN; *Int'l*, pg. 564
CREDIT INDUSTRIEL ET COMMERCIAL—See Compagnie de Suez; *Int'l*, pg. 313
CREDIT INSURANCE ASSOCIATION—See Inchcape PLC; *Int'l*, pg. 671
CREDIT INTERNATIONAL D'EGYPTE—See Credit Commercial de France; *Int'l*, pg. 343
CREDIT LYONNAIS BELGIUM—See Credit Lyonnais S.A.; *Int'l*, pg. 344
CREDIT LYONNAIS CAPITAL MARKETS PLC—See Credit Lyonnais S.A.; *Int'l*, pg. 344
CREDIT LYONNAIS ESPANA SA—See Credit Lyonnais S.A.; *Int'l*, pg. 344
CREDIT LYONNAIS HONG-KONG—See Credit Lyonnais S.A.; *Int'l*, pg. 344
CREDIT LYONNAIS JAPAN—See Credit Lyonnais S.A.; *Int'l*, pg. 344
CREDIT LYONNAIS S.A.; *Int'l*, pg. 343
CREDIT LYONNAIS SINGAPORE—See Credit Lyonnais S.A.; *Int'l*, pg. 344
CREDIT LYONNAIS SUISSE SA—See Credit Lyonnais S.A.; *Int'l*, pg. 344
CREDIT MUTUEL; *Int'l*, pg. 344
CREDIT NATIONALE; *Int'l*, pg. 344
CREDIT SAISON CO., LTD.—See The Saison Group; *Int'l*, pg. 1178
CREDIT SUISSE—See Credit Suisse Group; *Int'l*, pg. 345
CREDIT SUISSE FINANCIAL PRODUCTS—See Credit Suisse Group; *Int'l*, pg. 345
CREDIT SUISSE FINANCIAL PRODUCTS—See Swiss Reinsurance Company; *Int'l*, pg. 1333
CREDIT SUISSE FIRST BOSTON—See Credit Suisse Group; *Int'l*, pg. 345
CREDIT SUISSE FIRST BOSTON, INC.—See Credit Suisse Group; *Int'l*, pg. 345
CREDIT SUISSE GROUP; *Int'l*, pg. 345
CREDIT UNION BENEFITS SERVICES, INC.—See Credit Union National Association; *U.S. Private*, pg. 288
CREDIT UNION FOUNDATION—See Credit Union National Association; *U.S. Private*, pg. 288
CREDIT UNION NATIONAL ASSOCIATION; *U.S. Private*, pg. 288
CREDIT UNION OF CENTRAL CANADA—See Raiffeisen Zentralbank Osterreich; *Int'l*, pg. 1085
CREDITANSTALT AMERICAN CORPORATION—See Creditanstalt-Bankverein; *Int'l*, pg. 347
CREDITANSTALT A.S.—See Creditanstalt-Bankverein; *Int'l*, pg. 348
CREDITANSTALT-BANKVEREIN; *Int'l*, pg. 346
CREDITANSTALT BANKVEREIN AG—See Creditanstalt-Bankverein; *Int'l*, pg. 348
CREDITANSTALT-BANKVEREIN, ATLANTA REPRESENTATIVE OFFICE—See Creditanstalt-Bankverein; *Int'l*, pg. 347
CREDITANSTALT-BULINVEST LTD.—See Creditanstalt-Bankverein; *Int'l*, pg. 348
CREDITANSTALT EXPORT FINANCE LTD.—See Creditanstalt-Bankverein; *Int'l*, pg. 348
CREDITANSTALT FINANCE INC.- NEW YORK—See Creditanstalt-Bankverein; *Int'l*, pg. 347
CREDITANSTALT FINANZIARIA S.P.A.—See Creditanstalt-Bankverein; *Int'l*, pg. 348
CREDITANSTALT INVESTMENT BANK AG—See Creditanstalt-Bankverein; *Int'l*, pg. 347
CREDITANSTALT RT.—See Creditanstalt-Bankverein; *Int'l*, pg. 348
CREDITANSTALT (SINGAPORE) LTD.—See Creditanstalt-Bankverein; *Int'l*, pg. 348
CREDITCAPITAL FINANCE CORP., LTD.—See Union Bank of Switzerland; *Int'l*, pg. 1440
CREDITCORP DIV.—See Imperial Bancorp; *U.S. Public*, pg. 871
CREDITO ITALIANO—See IRI Istituto Ricostruzione Industriale; *Int'l*, pg. 652
CREDITOR RESOURCES, INC.—See AEGON N.V.; *Int'l*, pg. 27
CREED CO.—See NCH Corporation; *U.S. Public*, pg. 1145
CREEKSIDE INDUSTRIAL; *U.S. Private*, pg. 288
CREEP—See Young & Rubicam Inc.; *U.S. Private*, pg. 1199
CREGELUX SA—See Banque Generale du Luxembourg SA; *Int'l*, pg. 162
CREHALET POUGET POUSSIELGUES—See Warwick Baker O'Neill; *U.S. Private*, pg. 1152
CREMAR SA—See Mannesmann A.G.; *Int'l*, pg. 838
CRENLO, INC.; *U.S. Private*, pg. 288
CREO INTERNATIONAL—See Martin/Williams Advertising Inc.; *U.S. Private*, pg. 710
CREO/YOUNG & RUBICAM—See Young & Rubicam Inc.; *U.S. Private*, pg. 1199
CRES-COR; *U.S. Private*, pg. 288
CRESA ASEGURADORA Y REASEGURADORA IBERICA S.A.—See Allianz Aktiengesellschaft; *Int'l*, pg. 61
CRESAN, S.A.—See Caja de Madrid Group; *Int'l*, pg. 252
CRESAN II, S.A.—See Caja de Madrid Group; *Int'l*, pg. 252
CRESCENT BRICK-CLEARFIELD DIVISION—See Resco Products, Inc.; *U.S. Private*, pg. 924
CRESCENT BRICK DIVISION-EAST CANTON—See Resco Products, Inc.; *U.S. Private*, pg. 924
CRESCENT ELECTRIC SUPPLY CO.; *U.S. Private*, pg. 289
CRESCENT GENLYTE—See The Genlyte Group Incorporated; *U.S. Public*, pg. 730
CRESCENT MANUFACTURING COMPANY; *U.S. Private*, pg. 289
CRESCENT RESOURCES, INC.—See Duke Energy Corporation; *U.S. Public*, pg. 534
CRESCENT/XCELITE—See Cooper Industries, Inc.; *U.S. Public*, pg. 444
CRESCIVE DIE & TOOL, INC.; *U.S. Private*, pg. 289
CRESIVE MILAN DIVISION—See Crescive Die & Tool, Inc.; *U.S. Private*, pg. 289
CRESLINE PLASTIC PIPE CO. INC.; *U.S. Private*, pg. 289
CRESPIM S.P.A.—See Assicurazioni Generali S.p.A.; *Int'l*, pg. 90
CRESSWELL LIGHTING LIMITED—See Emess PLC; *Int'l*, pg. 453
CREST ARABIA LTD.—See ABB Asea Brown Boveri (Holding) Ltd.; *Int'l*, pg. 5
CREST CADILLAC COMPANY; *U.S. Private*, pg. 289
CREST CADILLAC, INC.—See Don Massey Cadillac Inc.; *U.S. Private*, pg. 712
CREST ENGINEERING (MALAYSIA) SBN. BHD.—See ABB Asea Brown Boveri (Holding) Ltd.; *Int'l*, pg. 5
CREST ENGINEERING OVERSEAS, INC.—See ABB Asea Brown Boveri (Holding) Ltd.; *Int'l*, pg. 5
CREST-FOAM CORPORATION—See Leggett & Platt, Incorporated; *U.S. Public*, pg. 986
CREST FRUIT CO.—See Standex International Corporation; *U.S. Public*, pg. 1506
CREST-HOOD FOAM COMPANY, INC.—See Leggett & Platt, Incorporated; *U.S. Public*, pg. 986
CREST NETHERLANDS INC.—See ABB Asea Brown Boveri (Holding) Ltd.; *Int'l*, pg. 5
CREST RIDGE HOMES, INC.—See Champion Enterprises, Inc.; *U.S. Public*, pg. 333
CREST STEEL CORP.—See Marubeni Corporation; *Int'l*, pg. 845
CREST VENEZUELA INC.—See ABB Asea Brown Boveri (Holding) Ltd.; *Int'l*, pg. 5
CRESTAR BANK—See Crestar Financial Corporation; *U.S. Public*, pg. 458
CRESTAR FINANCIAL CORPORATION; *U.S. Public*, pg. 458
CRESTAR FOOD PRODUCTS, INC.—See H.J. Heinz Company; *U.S. Public*, pg. 805
CRESTAR FOODS INC.—See H.J. Heinz Company; *U.S. Public*, pg. 805
CRESTAR INSURANCE AGENCY INCORPORATED—See Crestar Financial Corporation; *U.S. Public*, pg. 458
CRESTAR MORTGAGE CORPORATION—See Crestar Financial Corporation; *U.S. Public*, pg. 458
CRESTAR SECURITIES CORPORATION—See Crestar Financial Corporation; *U.S. Public*, pg. 458
CRESTBROOK FOREST INDUSTRIES LTD.; *Int'l*, pg. 348
CRESTBROOK FOREST INDUSTRIES LTD. - VANCOUVER—See Crestbrook Forest Industries Ltd.; *Int'l*, pg. 348
CRESTED BUTTE MARRIOTT RESORT—See Crested Butte Mountain Resort, Inc.; *U.S. Private*, pg. 289
CRESTED BUTTE MOUNTAIN RESORT, INC.; *U.S. Private*, pg. 289
CRESTLINE DISTRIBUTION FACILITY—See Nortek, Inc.; *U.S. Public*, pg. 1193
CRESTLINE DIV.—See Swank, Inc.; *U.S. Public*, pg. 1543
CRESTLINER, INC.—See Genmar Holdings, Inc.; *U.S. Private*, pg. 447
CRESTVIEW—See Genesis Health Ventures, Inc.; *U.S. Public*, pg. 729
CRESTWOOD BAKERY—See Fleming Companies, Inc.; *U.S. Public*, pg. 653
CRESTWOOD CARE CENTER—See Horizon/CMS Healthcare Corporation; *U.S. Public*, pg. 838
CRESWELL, MUNSELL, FULTZ & ZIRBEL—See Young & Rubicam Inc.; *U.S. Private*, pg. 1197
CRESWELL, MUNSELL, FULTZ & ZIRBEL, L.P.—See Young & Rubicam Inc.; *U.S. Private*, pg. 1197
CRETAN PAPERMILL S.A.—See Metsa-Serla Corporation; *Int'l*, pg. 864
CRETE CARRIER CORP.; *U.S. Private*, pg. 289
THE CRETEX COMPANIES; *U.S. Private*, pg. 289
CREUSOT-LOIRE INDUSTRIE—See Groupe Usinor; *Int'l*, pg. 571
CRICKET LANE—See Kellwood Company; *U.S. Public*, pg. 948
CRIIMI MAE; *U.S. Public*, pg. 459
CRINUM MINE—See The Broken Hill Proprietary Company Limited; *Int'l*, pg. 224
CRIOSBANC S.P.A.—See Linde AG; *Int'l*, pg. 810
CRISMATEC—See Saint-Gobain; *Int'l*, pg. 1174
THE CRISPIN COMPANY; *U.S. Private*, pg. 290
CRISPIN PORTER & BOGUSKY; *U.S. Private*, pg. 290
CRISPIN PORTER & BOGUSKY ADVERTISING—See Crispin Porter & Bogusky; *U.S. Private*, pg. 290
CRISSON SECURITIES NV—See Ricoh Company, Ltd.; *Int'l*, pg. 1115
CRISTALERIA ESPANOLA SA—See Saint-Gobain; *Int'l*, pg. 1172
CRISTALERIA ESPANOLA S.A.—See Saint-Gobain; *Int'l*, pg. 1176
CRITCHLEY, SHARP & TETLOW—See Carclo Engineering Group plc; *Int'l*, pg. 268
CRITERION CATALYST COMPANY L.P.—See Royal Dutch/Shell Group of Companies; *Int'l*, pg. 1136
CRITERION LIFE INSURANCE CO.—See Berkshire Hathaway Inc.; *U.S. Public*, pg. 219
CRITERION SOFTWARE LTD.—See Canon Inc.; *Int'l*, pg. 262
CRITESA S.A.—See BASF AG; *Int'l*, pg. 108
CRITICARE SYSTEMS, INC.; *U.S. Public*, pg. 459
CRITICARE SYSTEMS, INC.-EUROPE—See Criticare Systems, Inc.; *U.S. Public*, pg. 459
CRITICARE SYSTEMS, INC.-JAPAN—See Criticare Systems, Inc.; *U.S. Public*, pg. 459
CRITICS' CHOICE VIDEO, INC.—See Playboy Enterprises, Inc.; *U.S. Public*, pg. 1310
H.S. CROCKER CO., INC.; *U.S. Private*, pg. 290
CROCK'IN SA—See GIB Group; *Int'l*, pg. 533
CRODO SUD S.P.A.—See Koninklijke BolsWessanen nv; *Int'l*, pg. 751
CROFT & COMPANHIA LIMITADA—See Diageo Plc; *Int'l*, pg. 409
CROFT JEREZ SA—See Diageo Plc; *Int'l*, pg. 409
CROFT METALS, INC.; *U.S. Private*, pg. 290
CROFT METALS, INC. OF NC—See Croft Metals, Inc.; *U.S. Private*, pg. 290
CROFT SHERRY—See Diageo Plc; *Int'l*, pg. 409
CROKLAAN B.V.—See Unilever Plc; *Int'l*, pg. 1436
CROLL-REYNOLDS COMPANY, INC.; *U.S. Private*, pg. 290
CROMDANE STEEL & ENGINEERING LIMITED—See Australian National Industries Limited; *Int'l*, pg. 101
CROMPTON & KNOWLES CORPORATION; *U.S. Public*, pg. 459
CROMPTON & KNOWLES INTL. S.A.R.L.—See Crompton & Knowles Corporation; *U.S. Public*, pg. 460
CROMPTON & KNOWLES OF CANADA, LTD.—See Crompton & Knowles Corporation; *U.S. Public*, pg. 460
CROMPTON & KNOWLES TERTRE B.V.—See Crompton & Knowles Corporation; *U.S. Public*, pg. 460
CROMPTON & KNOWLES TERTRE SA—See Crompton & Knowles Corporation; *U.S. Public*, pg. 460
CROMPTON INSTRUMENTS LTD.—See BTR plc; *Int'l*, pg. 125
CROMPTON LIGHTING LTD.—See BTR plc; *Int'l*, pg. 124
CROMPTON METERMASTER INC.—See BTR plc; *Int'l*, pg. 125
CROMPTON MODUTEC INC.—See BTR plc; *Int'l*, pg. 125
CRONATRON WELDING SYSTEMS, INC.—See Lawson Products, Inc.; *U.S. Public*, pg. 980
CRONER PUBLICATIONS, LTD.—See Wolters Kluwer N.V.; *Int'l*, pg. 1514
CRONER-TYCO TOYS PTY. LTD.—See Mattel, Inc.; *U.S. Public*, pg. 1059
CRONES CO. GMBH—See Illinois Tool Works Inc.; *U.S. Public*, pg. 867
CRONOS/DMB&B—See DMB&B Communications; *U.S. Private*, pg. 303
CROP GROWERS INSURANCE—See Allianz Aktiengesellschaft; *Int'l*, pg. 59
CROSBIE & COMPANY INC.; *Int'l*, pg. 348
CROSBY & OVERTON, INC.; *U.S. Private*, pg. 290
BING CROSBY PRODUCTIONS, INC.—See Cox Enterprises, Inc.; *U.S. Private*, pg. 282
CROSBY CANADA LTD.—See FKI Plc; *Int'l*, pg. 473
THE CROSBY GROUP INC.—See FKI Plc; *Int'l*, pg. 473
CROSBY-NATIONAL SWAGE CO.—See FKI Plc; *Int'l*, pg. 473
PHILIP CROSBY ASSOCIATES, INC.—See Proudfoot plc; *Int'l*, pg. 1072
CROSCILL, INC.; *U.S. Private*, pg. 290
CROSCILL OUTLET STORE CORP.—See Croscill, Inc.; *U.S. Private*, pg. 291
CROSFIELD ELECTRONICS LIMITED—See Du Pont (E.I. Du Pont De Nemours & Co.); *U.S. Public*, pg. 532
JOSEPH CROSFIELD & SONS LTD.—See Unilever Plc; *Int'l*, pg. 1434
CROSLAND FILTERS BV—See Labinal SA; *Int'l*, pg. 786
CROSLAND FILTERS LTD.—See Labinal SA; *Int'l*, pg. 785
CROSLAND PLANT—See Labinal SA; *Int'l*, pg. 786
CROSLENE CHEMICAL INDUSTRIES, LTD.—See Takeda Chemical Industries, Ltd.; *Int'l*, pg. 1350
CROSMAN AIRGUNS—See Crosman Corp.; *U.S. Private*, pg. 291
CROSMAN CORP.; *U.S. Private*, pg. 291
A.T. CROSS CO.; *U.S. Public*, pg. 460
A.T. CROSS EXPORT CO.—See A.T. Cross Co.; *U.S. Public*, pg. 461
CROSS-COUNTRY LIFE INSURANCE COMPANY—See AEGON N.V.; *Int'l*, pg. 27
CROSS CREEK APPAREL, INC.—See Russell Corporation; *U.S. Public*, pg. 1413
CROSS HULLER—See Thyssen AG; *Int'l*, pg. 1389
CROSS MOTORS CORP.; *U.S. Private*, pg. 291
CROSS POINTE PAPER CORPORATION—See EdperBrascan Corporation; *Int'l*, pg. 434
W.W. CROSS, INC.—See D.D. Bean & Sons Co.; *U.S. Private*, pg. 127
CROSSAIR LTD.—See The Swissair Group; *Int'l*, pg. 1334
CROSSFIELD CHEMICAL—See Unilever Plc; *Int'l*, pg. 1435
THE CROSSINGS ASSOCIATES—See Cigna Corp.; *U.S. Public*, pg. 361
CROSSKEYS SYSTEMS CORPORATION—See Newbridge Networks Corporation; *Int'l*, pg. 924
CROSSMANN COMMUNITIES, INC.; *U.S. Public*, pg. 461
CROSSROADS PRESS, INC.—See Advance Publications Inc.; *U.S. Private*, pg. 19
CROSSVILLE CERAMICS COMPANY—See Curran Group, Inc.; *U.S. Private*, pg. 297
CROTON WATCH COMPANY & NATIONWIDE TIME; *U.S. Private*, pg. 291
CROUCH SUPPLY COMPANY, INC.; *U.S. Private*, pg. 291
CROUSE-HINDS—See Cooper Industries, Inc.; *U.S. Public*, pg. 444
CROUSE-HINDS (AUSTRALIA) PTY. LTD.—See Cooper Industries, Inc.; *U.S. Public*, pg. 445
CROUSE-HINDS MOLDED PRODUCTS—See Cooper Industries, Inc.; *U.S. Public*, pg. 444
CROUZET AUTOMATISMES—See Thomson S.A.; *Int'l*, pg. 1381
CROVEN CRYSTALS LIMITED—See Oak Industries Inc.; *U.S. Public*, pg. 1209
CROW-O.C. FUND T—See Cigna Corp.; *U.S. Public*, pg. 365

CROW RIVER INDUSTRIES INCORPORATED—See Mallinckrodt Inc.; *U.S. Private*, pg. 1040

CROW WOOD GLEN ASSOCIATES—See Cigna Corp.; *U.S. Public*, pg. 361

CROWCON DETECTION INSTRUMENTS LIMITED—See Halma p.l.c.; *Int'l*, pg. 589

CROWCON INSTRUMENTS B.V.—See Halma p.l.c.; *Int'l*, pg. 590

CROWDER CONSTRUCTION CO.; *U.S. Private*, pg. 291

CROWE ROPE INDUSTRIES L.L.C.; *U.S. Private*, pg. 291

CROWELL, WEEDON & CO.; *U.S. Private*, pg. 291

CROWLEY FOODS, INC.—See Koninklijke BolsWessanen nv; *Int'l*, pg. 752

CROWLEY FROZEN DESSERTS, INC.—See Koninklijke BolsWessanen nv; *Int'l*, pg. 752

CROWLEY GALVANIZING DIV.—See Aztec Manufacturing Co.; *U.S. Public*, pg. 159

CROWLEY MARITIME CORPORATION; *U.S. Private*, pg. 292

CROWLEY, MILNER & COMPANY; *U.S. Public*, pg. 461

CROWLEY TUBING DIV.—See Aztec Manufacturing Co.; *U.S. Public*, pg. 159

CROWN ADVERTISING LTD.—See DMB&B Communications; *U.S. Private*, pg. 303

CROWN AMERICA LIFE INSURANCE COMPANY—See Extendicare Inc.; *Int'l*, pg. 468

CROWN AMERICAN REALTY TRUST; *U.S. Public*, pg. 461

CROWN ANDERSEN INC.; *U.S. Public*, pg. 462

N.V. CROWN-BAELE S. A.—See Crown Cork & Seal Company, Inc.; *U.S. Public*, pg. 464

CROWN BOOKS CORPORATION—See Dart Group Corporation; *U.S. Public*, pg. 484

CROWN BOOKS EAST CORPORATION—See Dart Group Corporation; *U.S. Public*, pg. 484

CROWN BUICK, INC.; *U.S. Private*, pg. 292

CROWN CAN HONG KONG LTD.—See Crown Cork & Seal Company, Inc.; *U.S. Public*, pg. 464

CROWN CENTRAL HOLDING CORP.—See Crown Central Petroleum Corporation; *U.S. Public*, pg. 462

CROWN CENTRAL PETROLEUM CORPORATION; *U.S. Public*, pg. 462

CROWN CENTRAL PETROLEUM FOUNDATION—See Crown Central Petroleum Corporation; *U.S. Public*, pg. 462

CROWN CENTRAL PIPE LINE CO.—See Crown Central Petroleum Corporation; *U.S. Public*, pg. 462

CROWN CHEMICAL CORPORATION—See Veba AG; *Int'l*, pg. 1458

CROWN COAL & COKE CO. INC.; *U.S. Private*, pg. 292

CROWN COAT, INC.—See Spectrum Industries; *U.S. Private*, pg. 1024

THE CROWN COMPANY (SINGAPORE) LTD.—See Crown Cork & Seal Company, Inc.; *U.S. Public*, pg. 464

CROWN CONFECTIONERY CO., LTD.; *Int'l*, pg. 348

CROWN CORK & SEAL, AMERICAS DIVISION—See Crown Cork & Seal Company, Inc.; *U.S. Public*, pg. 463

CROWN CORK & SEAL, ASIA-PACIFIC DIVISION—See Crown Cork & Seal Company, Inc.; *U.S. Public*, pg. 464

CROWN CORK & SEAL CANADA, INC.—See Crown Cork & Seal Company, Inc.; *U.S. Public*, pg. 464

CROWN CORK & SEAL COMPANY, INC.; *U.S. Public*, pg. 462

CROWN CORK & SEAL COMPANY, INC.-CORPORATE TECHNOLOGIES—See Crown Cork & Seal Company, Inc.; *U.S. Public*, pg. 463

CROWN CORK & SEAL COMPANY, INC.-SUBSIDIARIES DIVISION—See Crown Cork & Seal Company, Inc.; *U.S. Public*, pg. 463

CROWN CORK & SEAL COMPANY (NIGERIA) LTD.—See Crown Cork & Seal Company, Inc.; *U.S. Public*, pg. 464

CROWN CORK & SEAL, EUROPEAN DIVISION—See Crown Cork & Seal Company, Inc.; *U.S. Public*, pg. 464

CROWN CORK & SEAL (PORTUGAL) S.A.—See Crown Cork & Seal Company, Inc.; *U.S. Public*, pg. 464

CROWN CORK COMPANY (GERMANY) G.M.B.H.—See Crown Cork & Seal Company, Inc.; *U.S. Public*, pg. 464

CROWN CORK COMPANY S.A. (PTY.) LTD.—See Crown Cork & Seal Company, Inc.; *U.S. Public*, pg. 464

CROWN CORK COORDINATION CENTER N.V.—See Crown Cork & Seal Company, Inc.; *U.S. Public*, pg. 464

CROWN CORK DE CHILE S.A.—See Crown Cork & Seal Company, Inc.; *U.S. Public*, pg. 464

CROWN CORK DE GUATEMALA, S.A.—See Crown Cork & Seal Company, Inc.; *U.S. Public*, pg. 464

CROWN CORK DE MEXICO, S.A.—See Crown Cork & Seal Company, Inc.; *U.S. Public*, pg. 464

CROWN CORK DE PUERTO RICO, INC.—See Crown Cork & Seal Company, Inc.; *U.S. Public*, pg. 463

CROWN CORK DO BRASIL S.A.—See Crown Cork & Seal Company, Inc.; *U.S. Public*, pg. 464

CROWN CORK OF CANADA LTD.—See Crown Cork & Seal Company, Inc.; *U.S. Public*, pg. 464

CROWN CORK & SEAL COMPANY, INC.-CORPORATE TECHNOLOGIES—See Crown Cork & Seal Company, Inc.; *U.S. Public*, pg. 464

CROWN CORNING LTD.—See BTR plc; *Int'l*, pg. 128

CROWN CRAFTS HOME FURNISHINGS, INC.—See Crown Crafts, Inc.; *U.S. Public*, pg. 465

CROWN CRAFTS HOME FURNISHINGS OF ILLINOIS, INC.—See Crown Crafts, Inc.; *U.S. Public*, pg. 465

CROWN CRAFTS, INC.; *U.S. Public*, pg. 465

CROWN CRYSTAL GLASS—See BTR plc; *Int'l*, pg. 129

THE CROWN DIVISIONS—See TransPro, Inc.; *U.S. Public*, pg. 1631

CROWN DOOR CORP.—See Premdor Inc.; *Int'l*, pg. 1067

CROWN ENGINEERING CO., LTD.—See Crown Confectionery Co., Ltd.; *Int'l*, pg. 348

CROWN EQUIPMENT CORPORATION; *U.S. Private*, pg. 292

CROWN FENCE CO.; *U.S. Private*, pg. 292

CROWN FINANCIAL MANAGEMENT LIMITED—See Extendicare Inc.; *Int'l*, pg. 468

CROWN FINE ARTS—See Carolina Mirror Company; *U.S. Private*, pg. 214

CROWN FOODS INC.; *U.S. Private*, pg. 292

CROWN GOLD, INC.—See Crown Central Petroleum Corporation; *U.S. Public*, pg. 462

CROWN GROCERS, INC.—See Certified Grocers of California; *U.S. Public*, pg. 227

THE CROWN GROUP-DETROIT PLANT—See The Crown Group, Inc.; *U.S. Public*, pg. 292

THE CROWN GROUP ECORSE PLANT—See The Crown Group, Inc.; *U.S. Public*, pg. 292

THE CROWN GROUP-FORT WAYNE PLANT—See The Crown Group, Inc.; *U.S. Public*, pg. 292

THE CROWN GROUP, INC.; *U.S. Public*, pg. 292

THE CROWN GROUP-LIVONIA PLANT—See The Crown Group, Inc.; *U.S. Public*, pg. 292

THE CROWN GROUP PORT HURON PLANT—See The Crown Group, Inc.; *U.S. Public*, pg. 292

THE CROWN GROUP-PORTLAND PLANT—See The Crown Group, Inc.; *U.S. Public*, pg. 293

CROWN HOLDINGS, INC.; *U.S. Private*, pg. 293

CROWN INTERNATIONAL, INC.; *U.S. Private*, pg. 293

CROWN IRON WORKS COMPANY—See Crown Holdings, Inc.; *U.S. Private*, pg. 293

CROWN LANCE, INC.—See Bolliger, Inc.; *U.S. Private*, pg. 155

CROWN LANCE ITALIA SRL—See Bolliger, Inc.; *U.S. Private*, pg. 155

CROWN LIFE INVESTMENT MANAGEMENT COMPANY (CLIMCO)—See Extendicare Inc.; *Int'l*, pg. 468

CROWN LITOMETAL, S.A.—See Crown Cork & Seal Company, Inc.; *U.S. Public*, pg. 465

CROWN MANUFACTURING CORP.—See Nippon Sanso Corporation; *Int'l*, pg. 939

CROWN MFG. INC.—See Owens Corning; *U.S. Public*, pg. 1237

CROWN MOVING & STORAGE INC.—See Wheaton Van Lines, Inc.; *U.S. Private*, pg. 1171

CROWN MOVING & STORAGE INC., OF ILLINOIS—See Wheaton Van Lines, Inc.; *U.S. Private*, pg. 1171

CROWN NIGERIA, INC.—See Crown Central Petroleum Corporation; *U.S. Public*, pg. 462

CROWN OBRIST AG—See Crown Cork & Seal Company, Inc.; *U.S. Public*, pg. 465

THE CROWN OIL & GAS CO.—See Crown Central Petroleum Corporation; *U.S. Public*, pg. 462

CROWN POWER & REDEVELOPMENT CORP.—See Hallmark Cards, Inc.; *U.S. Private*, pg. 496

CROWN PRINCE, INC. (CA); *U.S. Private*, pg. 293

CROWN PRODUCTS—See Sommer Metalcraft Corporation; *U.S. Private*, pg. 1014

CROWN PUBLISHERS, INC.—See Advance Publications Inc.; *U.S. Private*, pg. 21

CROWN-RANCHO PIPE LINE CORP.—See Crown Central Petroleum Corporation; *U.S. Public*, pg. 462

CROWN SACKS & SYSTEMS (AINTREE) LTD.—See Korsnas AB; *Int'l*, pg. 759

CROWN SACKS & SYSTEMS (HOLDINGS) LTD. U.K.—See Korsnas AB; *Int'l*, pg. 759

CROWN SHOE COMPANY, L.L.C.—See Tober Industries, Inc.; *U.S. Private*, pg. 1089

CROWN SNACK CO., LTD.—See Crown Confectionery Co., Ltd.; *Int'l*, pg. 348

CROWN STATIONS, INC.—See Crown Central Petroleum Corporation; *U.S. Public*, pg. 462

CROWN VANTAGE, INC.; *U.S. Public*, pg. 465

CROWN WALLCOVERINGS FRANCE, S.A.—See Borden, Inc.; *U.S. Private*, pg. 159

CROWN YOUNG INDUSTRIES LTD.—See Citizen Watch Company, Ltd.; *Int'l*, pg. 259

CROWNCEN INTL. N.V.—See Crown Central Petroleum Corporation; *U.S. Public*, pg. 462

CROWNGAP CONSTRUCTION LTD.—See The Peninsular and Oriental Steam Navigation Company; *Int'l*, pg. 1033

CROWNTUFT MANUFACTURING CO.—See Kellwood Company; *U.S. Public*, pg. 948

CROWS NEST RESOURCES LIMITED—See Royal Dutch/Shell Group of Companies; *Int'l*, pg. 1138

CRUCIBLE MATERIALS CORP.; *U.S. Private*, pg. 293

CRUISE AMERICA, INC.—See Budget Group, Inc.; *U.S. Private*, pg. 178

CRUISE CANADA, INC.—See Budget Group, Inc.; *U.S. Private*, pg. 178

CRUISE HOLDINGS LTD.; *U.S. Private*, pg. 293

CRUISES ONLY INC.; *U.S. Private*, pg. 293

CRUISING EQUIPMENT COMPANY—See Valley Forge Corporation; *U.S. Public*, pg. 1705

CRUM & FORSTER UNDERWRITERS CO. OF OHIO—See Xerox Corporation; *U.S. Public*, pg. 1784

CRUM ELECTRIC SUPPLY CO., INC.; *U.S. Private*, pg. 293

CRUM & FORSTER MANAGERS CORPORATION (NY)—See Xerox Corporation; *U.S. Public*, pg. 1784

CRUSADER COMPANY (GHANA) LIMITED—See Cigna Corp.; *U.S. Public*, pg. 363

CRUSADER INSURANCE COMPANY (GHANA) LIMITED—See Cigna Corp.; *U.S. Public*, pg. 364

CRUSADER INSURANCE COMPANY OF AUSTRALIA LIMITED—See Cigna Corp.; *U.S. Public*, pg. 364

CRUSADER MARINE ENGINES—See Thermo Electron Corporation; *U.S. Public*, pg. 1591

CRUSH INTERNATIONAL—See Cadbury Schweppes p.l.c.; *Int'l*, pg. 248

CRUSH INTERNATIONAL (OVERSEAS)—See Cadbury Schweppes p.l.c.; *Int'l*, pg. 248

CRUSH U.S.A.—See Cadbury Schweppes p.l.c.; *Int'l*, pg. 248

CRUSPI S.A.; *Int'l*, pg. 348

CRUSTACEA CORPORATION—See Baltek Corporation; *U.S. Public*, pg. 172

CRUSTBUSTER, INC.; *U.S. Private*, pg. 293

CRUSTEEL LTD.—See Crucible Materials Corp.; *U.S. Private*, pg. 293

CRUZ VERDE-LEGRAIN—See Sara Lee Corporation; *U.S. Public*, pg. 1434

CRYCO QUARTZ, INC.—See Tosoh Corporation; *Int'l*, pg. 1408

CRYCO TWENTY TWO, INC.—See Tosoh Corporation; *Int'l*, pg. 1408

CRYOGENIC STRUCTURES CORPORATION—See Baltek Corporation; *U.S. Public*, pg. 172

CRYOINFRA S.A. DE C.V.—See Air Products and Chemicals, Inc.; *U.S. Public*, pg. 32

CRYOSTAR FRANCE SA—See The BOC Group plc; *Int'l*, pg. 122

CRYOTECHNOLOGIES S.A.—See Thomson S.A.; *Int'l*, pg. 1381

CRYOTECHNOLOGIES SA—See Thomson S.A.; *Int'l*, pg. 1383

CRYSTAL BIOTECH, INC.—See Matec Corporation; *U.S. Public*, pg. 1056

CRYSTAL CABINET WORKS, INC.; *U.S. Private*, pg. 293

CRYSTAL CLEAR INDUSTRIES; *U.S. Private*, pg. 293

CRYSTAL CREAM & BUTTER COMPANY; *U.S. Private*, pg. 294

CRYSTAL CRUISES, INC.—See Nippon Yusen K.K.; *Int'l*, pg. 941

CRYSTAL EURASIA OIL CO.—See Crystal Oil Company; *U.S. Public*, pg. 466

CRYSTAL EXPLORATION & PRODUCTION CO.—See Crystal Oil Company; *U.S. Public*, pg. 466

CRYSTAL FLASH PETROLEUM CORP.; *U.S. Private*, pg. 294

CRYSTAL GEYSER; *U.S. Private*, pg. 294

CRYSTAL GEYSER ROXANE WATER L.P.—See Otsuka Pharmaceutical Co., Ltd.; *Int'l*, pg. 1013

CRYSTAL GEYSER WATER COMPANY—See Otsuka Pharmaceutical Co., Ltd.; *Int'l*, pg. 1013

CRYSTAL OIL COMPANY; *U.S. Public*, pg. 466

CRYSTAL PARK CASINO—See Hollywood Park, Inc.; *U.S. Public*, pg. 831

CRYSTAL PRECISION (M) SDN. BHD.—See Clarion Co., Ltd.; *Int'l*, pg. 296

CRYSTAL PROGRAM LTD., INC.—See Crystal Oil Company; *U.S. Public*, pg. 466

CRYSTAL SEMICONDUCTOR CORPORATION—See Cirrus Logic, Inc.; *U.S. Public*, pg. 375

THE CRYSTAL TISSUE CO.; *U.S. Private*, pg. 294

CTR MANUFACTURING, INC.—See Blount International, Inc.; *U.S. Public*, pg. 238

CUB FOODS STORES—See SuperValu, Inc.; *U.S. Public*, pg. 1541

CUBA CITY TELEPHONE EXCHANGE CO.—See Lynch Corporation; *U.S. Public*, pg. 1022

CUBAN ELECTRIC CO.—See Boise Cascade Corporation; *U.S. Public*, pg. 243

CUBIC APPLICATIONS, INC.—See Cubic Corporation; *U.S. Public*, pg. 466

CUBIC COMMUNICATIONS—See Cubic Corporation; *U.S. Public*, pg. 466

CUBIC CORPORATION; *U.S. Public*, pg. 466

CUBIC DEFENSE SYSTEMS—See Cubic Corporation; *U.S. Public*, pg. 466

CUBIC WORLDWIDE TECHNICAL SERVICES, INC.—See Cubic Corporation; *U.S. Public*, pg. 466

CUBIX CORPORATION; *U.S. Private*, pg. 294

CUCINA CLASSICA ITALIANA, INC.—See Saratoga Brands, Inc.; *U.S. Public*, pg. 1435

PATRICK CUDAHY INC.—See Smithfield Foods, Inc.; *U.S. Public*, pg. 1479

CUDD PRESSURE CONTROL, INC.—See RPC Incorporated; *U.S. Public*, pg. 1356

CUES—See ELXSI Corporation; *U.S. Public*, pg. 545

CUISINART INC.—See Conair Corporation; *U.S. Private*, pg. 261

CUISINE SOLUTIONS, INC.; *U.S. Public*, pg. 466

CULBRO LAND RESOURCES, INC.—See General Cigar Holdings Inc; *U.S. Public*, pg. 708

CULCO, INC.—See Randalls Food Markets, Inc.; *U.S. Private*, pg. 909

CULINAR INC.; *Int'l*, pg. 348

CULINARY FOODS GROUP—See Nestle S.A.; *Int'l*, pg. 917

CULINARY FOODS—See Tyson Foods, Inc.; *U.S. Public*, pg. 1652

CULLEN/FROST BANKERS, INC.; *U.S. Public*, pg. 467

CULLIGAN—See Culligan International Company; *U.S. Public*, pg. 467

CULLIGAN, C.I. DIV.—See Culligan International Company; *U.S. Public*, pg. 467

CULLIGAN INTERNATIONAL COMPANY; *U.S. Public*, pg. 467

CULLMAN PRODUCTS CORPORATION; *U.S. Private*, pg. 294

CULLMAN SUPPLY COMPANY—See Greif Brothers Corporation; *U.S. Public*, pg. 763

CULLMAN VENTURES, INC.; *U.S. Private*, pg. 294

CULLMAN VENTURES, INC.—See Cullman Ventures, Inc.; *U.S. Private*, pg. 295

CULLUM DEVELOPMENT CO.—See Randalls Food Markets, Inc.; *U.S. Private*, pg. 909

CULLUM DISTRIBUTION CENTER, INC.—See Randalls Food Markets, Inc.; *U.S. Private*, pg. 909

CULP, INC.; *U.S. Public*, pg. 467

CULTAROM—See Cultor Ltd.; *Int'l*, pg. 349

CULTOR FOOD SCIENCE INC.—See Cultor Ltd.; *Int'l*, pg. 349

CULTOR FOOD SERVICE—See Cultor Ltd.; *Int'l*, pg. 349

CULTOR LTD.; *Int'l*, pg. 349

CULVER STUDIOS—See Sony Corporation; *Int'l*, pg. 1283

CULVERDALE INVESTMENTS LIMITED—See Jardine Matheson Holdings Limited; *Int'l*, pg. 703

CUMBERLAND ENG. DIV.—See Kvaerner a.s.a.; *Int'l*, pg. 773

CUMBERLAND ENGINEERING—See Kvaerner a.s.a.; *Int'l*, pg. 774

Company Index

CUMBERLAND DIRECTORY OF CORPORATE AFFILIATIONS

Company Index

CUMBERLAND ENGINEERING-EUROPE—See Kvaerner a.s.a.; *Int'l*, pg. 774
CUMBERLAND FARMS, INC.; *U.S. Private*, pg. 295
CUMBERLAND GRAPHICS LTD.—See Fortune Brands, Inc.; *U.S. Public*, pg. 674
CUMBERLAND LEASING CO.—See Illinois Tool Works Inc.; *U.S. Public*, pg. 865
CUMBERLAND LIFE ASSURANCE CO. LIMITED—See Ford Motor Company; *U.S. Public*, pg. 665
CUMBERLAND PACKING CORP.; *U.S. Private*, pg. 295
CUMBERLAND SECURITIES CORP.—See Central Maine Power Company; *U.S. Public*, pg. 325
CUMBRIAN STORAGE LTD.—See Simon Engineering plc; *Int'l*, pg. 1251
CUMIS GENERAL INSURANCE COMPANY—See CUNA Mutual Insurance Society; *U.S. Private*, pg. 296
CUMIS INSURANCE SOCIETY, INC.—See CUNA Mutual Insurance Society; *U.S. Private*, pg. 296
CUMMINGS INC.; *U.S. Private*, pg. 295
CUMMINGS-MOORE GRAPHITE CO.—See Asbury Carbons, Inc.; *U.S. Private*, pg. 87
CUMMINS-ALLISON CORP.; *U.S. Private*, pg. 295
CUMMINS BRASIL S.A.—See Cummins Engine Company, Inc.; *U.S. Public*, pg. 468
CUMMINS CORPORATION—See Cummins Engine Company, Inc.; *U.S. Public*, pg. 468
CUMMINS CUMBERLAND INC.; *U.S. Private*, pg. 295
CUMMINS DE MEXICO S.A.—See Cummins Engine Company, Inc.; *U.S. Public*, pg. 468
CUMMINS DIESEL N.V.—See Cummins Engine Company, Inc.; *U.S. Public*, pg. 468
CUMMINS ENGINE COMPANY, INC.; *U.S. Public*, pg. 467
CUMMINS ENGINE COMPANY, LTD.—See Cummins Engine Company, Inc.; *U.S. Public*, pg. 469
CUMMINS INTERMOUNTAIN DIESEL; *U.S. Private*, pg. 295
CUMMINS KOMATSU ENGINE COMPANY—See Cummins Engine Company, Inc.; *U.S. Public*, pg. 468
CUMMINS KOMATSU ENGINE COMPANY—See Komatsu Ltd.; *Int'l*, pg. 744
CUMMINS KOREA LTD.—See Cummins Engine Company, Inc.; *U.S. Public*, pg. 469
CUMMINS MID-SOUTH, INC.; *U.S. Private*, pg. 295
CUMMINS NATURAL GAS ENGINES, INC.—See Cummins Engine Company, Inc.; *U.S. Public*, pg. 468
CUMMINS SOUTHWEST INC.; *U.S. Private*, pg. 296
CUNA MORTGAGE CORPORATION—See CUNA Mutual Insurance Society; *U.S. Private*, pg. 296
CUNA MUTUAL GROUP-AFRICA—See CUNA Mutual Insurance Society; *U.S. Private*, pg. 296
CUNA MUTUAL GROUP-ASIA/AFRICA—See CUNA Mutual Insurance Society; *U.S. Private*, pg. 296
CUNA MUTUAL GROUP-AUSTRALIA—See CUNA Mutual Insurance Society; *U.S. Private*, pg. 296
CUNA MUTUAL GROUP-DOMINICAN REPUBLIC—See CUNA Mutual Insurance Society; *U.S. Private*, pg. 296
CUNA MUTUAL GROUP-GREAT BRITAIN—See CUNA Mutual Insurance Society; *U.S. Private*, pg. 296
CUNA MUTUAL GROUP-HONG KONG—See CUNA Mutual Insurance Society; *U.S. Private*, pg. 296
CUNA MUTUAL GROUP-INDONESIA—See CUNA Mutual Insurance Society; *U.S. Private*, pg. 297
CUNA MUTUAL GROUP-JAMAICA—See CUNA Mutual Insurance Society; *U.S. Private*, pg. 297
CUNA MUTUAL GROUP-KOREA—See CUNA Mutual Insurance Society; *U.S. Private*, pg. 297
CUNA MUTUAL GROUP-LATIN AMERICA—See CUNA Mutual Insurance Society; *U.S. Private*, pg. 297
CUNA MUTUAL GROUP-NETHERLANDS ANTILLES—See CUNA Mutual Insurance Society; *U.S. Private*, pg. 297
CUNA MUTUAL GROUP-PUERTO RICO—See CUNA Mutual Insurance Society; *U.S. Private*, pg. 296
CUNA MUTUAL GROUP-TAIWAN—See CUNA Mutual Insurance Society; *U.S. Private*, pg. 297
CUNA MUTUAL GROUP-THAILAND—See CUNA Mutual Insurance Society; *U.S. Private*, pg. 297
CUNA MUTUAL INSURANCE AGENCY, INC.—See CUNA Mutual Insurance Society; *U.S. Private*, pg. 296
CUNA MUTUAL INSURANCE SOCIETY; *U.S. Private*, pg. 296
CUNA MUTUAL INVESTMENT CORPORATION—See CUNA Mutual Insurance Society; *U.S. Private*, pg. 296
CUNA MUTUAL LIFE INSURANCE CO.—See CUNA Mutual Insurance Society; *U.S. Private*, pg. 296
CUNA SERVICE GROUP, INC.—See Credit Union National Association; *U.S. Private*, pg. 288
CUNARD LINE LTD.—See Kvaerner a.s.a.; *Int'l*, pg. 773
THE CUNARD STEAM-SHIP COMPANY P.L.C.—See Kvaerner a.s.a.; *Int'l*, pg. 772
CUNNINGHAM-LIMP DEVELOPMENT CO.; *U.S. Private*, pg. 297
CUO, INC.—See USCS International, Inc.; *U.S. Public*, pg. 1659
CUPERTINO ELECTRIC, INC.—See Synergism, Inc.; *U.S. Private*, pg. 1060
CUPLEX, INC.; *U.S. Private*, pg. 297
CUPPLES PRODUCTS, INC.; *U.S. Private*, pg. 297
CUPRALEX—See Pechiney S.A.; *Int'l*, pg. 1028
CUPRINOL LIMITED—See Williams Holdings Plc; *Int'l*, pg. 1501
CURACAO OIL TERMINAL—See Royal Dutch/Shell Group of Companies; *Int'l*, pg. 1141
CURACAO TRADING COMPANY (DOMINICANA) C. POR A.—See Ceteco N.V.; *Int'l*, pg. 280
CURACARE, INC.—See American Shared Hospital Services; *U.S. Public*, pg. 91
CURAMIK ELECTRONICS GMBH—See Bowthorpe plc; *Int'l*, pg. 209
CURATIO VERSIGHERUNGS-VERMITTLUNGS GMBH—See Solvay S.A.; *Int'l*, pg. 1278
CURATIVE HEALTH SERVICES; *U.S. Public*, pg. 469
CURRAGH COAL—See BTR plc; *Int'l*, pg. 128
CURRAN CONTRACTING COMPANY—See Curran Group, Inc.; *U.S. Private*, pg. 297
CURRAN GROUP, INC.; *U.S. Private*, pg. 297
MICHAEL CURRAN & ASSOCIATES; *U.S. Private*, pg. 297
CURRAN PLANT—See Fort James Corporation; *U.S. Public*, pg. 672
CURRENT, INC.—See Deluxe Corporation; *U.S. Public*, pg. 498
CURRENT TECHNOLOGY, INC.—See Danaher Corporation; *U.S. Public*, pg. 480
CURRIES COMPANY—See Assa Abloy AB; *Int'l*, pg. 18
CURRIN & ASSOCIATES, INC.—See Chesapeake Utilities Corporation; *U.S. Public*, pg. 347
THE CURRY CORPORATION; *U.S. Private*, pg. 297
CURRYS GROUP PLC—See Dixons Group plc; *Int'l*, pg. 414
CURTAGIL LTD.—See Fuchs Petrolub AG Oel + Chemie; *Int'l*, pg. 519
CURTICE BURNS FOODS—See Pro-Fac Cooperative, Inc.; *U.S. Private*, pg. 887
CURTIN & PEASE/PENECO, INC—See Pittway Corporation; *U.S. Public*, pg. 1306
CURTIS BAY INSURANCE CO. LTD.—See Hercules Incorporated; *U.S. Public*, pg. 810
CURTIS BAY TOWING COMPANY OF PENNSYLVANIA—See Moran Transporation Company; *U.S. Private*, pg. 760
CURTIS BAY TOWING COMPANY OF VIRGINIA—See Moran Transporation Company; *U.S. Private*, pg. 760
CURTIS CIRCULATION COMPANY—See Lagardere Groupe; *Int'l*, pg. 794
CURTIS EQUIPMENT CO., INC.—See Hale-Halsell Company; *U.S. Private*, pg. 494
L.N. CURTIS & SONS; *U.S. Private*, pg. 297
CURTIS LUMBER COMPANY; *U.S. Private*, pg. 297
CURTIS MEDIA GROUP; *U.S. Private*, pg. 297
CURTIS 1000 EUROPE GMBH—See American Business Products, Inc.; *U.S. Public*, pg. 70
CURTIS 1000, INC.—See American Business Products, Inc.; *U.S. Public*, pg. 70
THE CURTIS PUBLISHING COMPANY—See Servaas, Inc.; *U.S. Private*, pg. 986
CURTIS SCREW CO., INC.; *U.S. Private*, pg. 298
CURTIS-TOLEDO, INC.; *U.S. Private*, pg. 298
CURTISS-WRIGHT CORP.; *U.S. Public*, pg. 469
CURTISS-WRIGHT FLIGHT SYSTEMS, INC.—See Curtiss-Wright Corp.; *U.S. Public*, pg. 469
CURTMAN DIVISION—See Uncas Manufacturing Company; *U.S. Private*, pg. 1116
CURVER B.V.—See DSM N.V.; *Int'l*, pg. 352
CURVER CONSUMER PRODUCTS LTD.—See DSM N.V.; *Int'l*, pg. 353
CURVER DEUTSCHLAND GMBH—See DSM N.V.; *Int'l*, pg. 353
CURVER KFT—See DSM N.V.; *Int'l*, pg. 353
CURVER (OSTERREICH) GMBH—See DSM N.V.; *Int'l*, pg. 353
CURVER RODEX S.A.—See DSM N.V.; *Int'l*, pg. 353
CURVER (SCHWEIZ) AG—See DSM N.V.; *Int'l*, pg. 353
CURWOOD, INC.—See Bemis Company, Inc.; *U.S. Public*, pg. 210
CURWOOD PACKAGING (CANADA) LTD.—See Bemis Company, Inc.; *U.S. Public*, pg. 210
T.F. CUSHING, INC.—See Astrex, Inc.; *U.S. Public*, pg. 141
CUSHMAN & WAKEFIELD—See Mitsubishi Estate Co., Ltd.; *Int'l*, pg. 873
CUSHMAN & WAKEFIELD, ATLANTA OFFICE—See Mitsubishi Estate Co., Ltd.; *Int'l*, pg. 873
CUSHMAN & WAKEFIELD, INC.—See Mitsubishi Estate Co., Ltd.; *Int'l*, pg. 873
CUSSONS GROUP LTD.—See Paterson Zochonis Plc; *Int'l*, pg. 1024
CUSSONS INTERNATIONAL LTD.—See Paterson Zochonis Plc; *Int'l*, pg. 1024
CUSSONS (U.K.) LTD.—See Paterson Zochonis Plc; *Int'l*, pg. 1024
CUSTER PHARMACY—See Seaway Food Town, Inc.; *U.S. Public*, pg. 1453
AB CUSTODIA—See Carnegie Holding AB; *Int'l*, pg. 272
CUSTODIAL TRUST COMPANY—See The Bear Stearns Companies Inc.; *U.S. Public*, pg. 198
CUSTODIS-COTTRELL, INC.—See Air & Water Technologies Corporation; *U.S. Public*, pg. 29
CUSTODIS-ECODYNE—See Air & Water Technologies Corporation; *U.S. Public*, pg. 29
CUSTOM ACCESSORIES ASIA LTD.—See Custom Accessories Inc.; *U.S. Private*, pg. 298
CUSTOM ACCESSORIES EUROPE LTD.—See Custom Accessories Inc.; *U.S. Private*, pg. 298
CUSTOM ACCESSORIES INC.; *U.S. Private*, pg. 298
CUSTOM ACCESSORIES SCANDINAVIA OY—See Custom Accessories Inc.; *U.S. Private*, pg. 298
CUSTOM BRANDS DIV.—See The Goodyear Tire & Rubber Company; *U.S. Public*, pg. 753
CUSTOM BUILDER—See Bertelsmann AG; *Int'l*, pg. 190
CUSTOM CASTING—See Esco Corporation; *U.S. Private*, pg. 383
CUSTOM CHEQUES OF CANADA—See Quebecor Inc.; *Int'l*, pg. 1077
CUSTOM CHROME INC.—See Global Motor Sport Group, Inc.; *U.S. Public*, pg. 748
CUSTOM COLORANTS, INC.—See Martin Color-Fi; *U.S. Public*, pg. 1052
CUSTOM CONCRETE—See Holderbank Financiere Glaris Ltd.; *Int'l*, pg. 629
CUSTOM CONTROL SENSORS, INC.; *U.S. Private*, pg. 298
CUSTOM DECOR, INC.; *U.S. Private*, pg. 298
CUSTOM DIRECT INC.—See Quebecor Inc.; *Int'l*, pg. 1076
CUSTOM EXTRUSIONS—See Interlock Industries, Inc.; *U.S. Private*, pg. 567
CUSTOM FARM SEED—See Unilever Plc; *Int'l*, pg. 1435
CUSTOM FOOD PRODUCTS INC.—See Griffith Laboratories Worldwide, Inc.; *U.S. Private*, pg. 481
CUSTOM FOODS LIMITED—See H.J. Heinz Company; *U.S. Public*, pg. 806
CUSTOM HEALTH CARE, INC.—See Lander Co., Inc.; *U.S. Private*, pg. 647
CUSTOM HOISTS, INC.—See Standex International Corporation; *U.S. Public*, pg. 1506
CUSTOM LAMINATES, INC.—See Sun Coast Industries, Inc; *U.S. Public*, pg. 1530
CUSTOM LIGHTS, INC.—See Group Dekko; *U.S. Private*, pg. 484
CUSTOM LUMBER MFG. CO.—See Lumber Group Inc.; *U.S. Private*, pg. 680
CUSTOM-MADE PACKAGING, INC.—See Norse Dairy Systems; *U.S. Private*, pg. 803
CUSTOM PAK, INC.; *U.S. Private*, pg. 298
CUSTOM PIPE & COUPLING CO.—See Wolseley Plc.; *Int'l*, pg. 1512
CUSTOM PROCESS—See Burke Industries, Inc.; *U.S. Private*, pg. 183
CUSTOM PRODUCTS CORPORATION—See Bolt Technology Corporation; *U.S. Public*, pg. 244
CUSTOM SERVO MOTORS—See MTS Systems Corporation; *U.S. Public*, pg. 1029
CUSTOM SHOP SHIRTMAKERS INC.—See HC Holdings; *U.S. Private*, pg. 490
CUSTOM SOURCE REALTY CORPORATION—See St. Paul Bancorp, Inc.; *U.S. Public*, pg. 1429
CUSTOMEDIX CORPORATION; *U.S. Private*, pg. 298
CUSTOMER DEVELOPMENT CORPORATION; *U.S. Private*, pg. 298
CUSTOMER DEVELOPMENT CORPORATION—See Customer Development Corporation; *U.S. Private*, pg. 298
CUSTOMER SERVICE & BRAND STRATEGY—See Motorola, Inc.; *U.S. Public*, pg. 1137
CUSTOMER SERVICE CENTER OF F.N.B., L.L.C.—See F.N.B. Corporation; *U.S. Public*, pg. 607
CUSTOMER SERVICES DIVISION—See The Boeing Company; *U.S. Public*, pg. 240
CUSTOMER SUPPORT COMMERCIAL DIVISION—See Parker Hannifin Corporation; *U.S. Public*, pg. 1262
CUSTOMIZED TRANSPORTATION, INC.—See CSX Corporation; *U.S. Public*, pg. 284
CUTCO INDUSTRIES, INC.; *U.S. Public*, pg. 470
CUTLER HAMMER AUSTRALIA PTY. LTD.—See Eaton Corporation; *U.S. Public*, pg. 558
CUTLER-HAMMER EATON CORPORATION—See Eaton Corporation; *U.S. Public*, pg. 556
CUTLER HAMMER MEXICANA, S.A.—See Eaton Corporation; *U.S. Public*, pg. 558
CUTLER-HAMMER NEW ZEALAND LIMITED—See Eaton Corporation; *U.S. Public*, pg. 558
CUTLER-HAMMER NIGERIA LIMITED—See Eaton Corporation; *U.S. Public*, pg. 558
CUTLER-HAMMER PRODUCTS—See Eaton Corporation; *U.S. Public*, pg. 556
CUTLER MANUFACTURING CORPORATION; *U.S. Private*, pg. 298
CUTLER-HAMMER PUERTO RICO—See Eaton Corporation; *U.S. Public*, pg. 556
CUTTER AVIATION—See Cutter Aviation Albuquerque, Inc; *U.S. Private*, pg. 299
CUTTER AVIATION ALBUQUERQUE, INC; *U.S. Private*, pg. 298
CUTTER BEECHCRAFT—See Cutter Aviation Albuquerque, Inc; *U.S. Private*, pg. 299
CUTTER BIOLOGICALS—See Bayer AG; *Int'l*, pg. 174
CUTTER DEER VALLEY—See Cutter Aviation Albuquerque, Inc; *U.S. Private*, pg. 299
CUTTER LABORATORIES INC.—See Bayer AG; *Int'l*, pg. 174
CUTTING EDGES PTY. LTD.—See Delta plc; *Int'l*, pg. 391
CUYK MILL—See Fort James Corporation; *U.S. Public*, pg. 672
CYANAMID AUSTRALIA, PTY., LTD.—See American Home Products Corporation; *U.S. Public*, pg. 80
CYANAMID CANADA INC.—See American Home Products Corporation; *U.S. Public*, pg. 80
CYANAMID CHILE LTDA.—See American Home Products Corporation; *U.S. Public*, pg. 80
CYANAMID DE ARGENTINA S.A.I.C.—See American Home Products Corporation; *U.S. Public*, pg. 80
CYANAMID DE COLUMBIA SA—See American Home Products Corporation; *U.S. Public*, pg. 80
CYANAMID DE VENEZUELA CA—See American Home Products Corporation; *U.S. Public*, pg. 80
CYANAMID (FAR EAST) LTD.—See American Home Products Corporation; *U.S. Public*, pg. 80
CYANAMID FRANCE—See American Home Products Corporation; *U.S. Public*, pg. 81
CYANAMID GMBH—See American Home Products Corporation; *U.S. Public*, pg. 81
CYANAMID IBERICA, S.A.—See American Home Products Corporation; *U.S. Public*, pg. 81
CYANAMID INDIA LTD.—See American Home Products Corporation; *U.S. Public*, pg. 81
CYANAMID INTER-AMERICAN CORPORATION—See American Home Products Corporation; *U.S. Public*, pg. 81
CYANAMID ITALIA S.P.A—See American Home Products Corporation; *U.S. Public*, pg. 81
CYANAMID (JAPAN) LTD.—See American Home Products Corporation; *U.S. Public*, pg. 81
CYANAMID-KETJEN KATALYSATOR BV—See Akzo Nobel N.V.; *Int'l*, pg. 47
CYANAMID KOREA, INC.—See American Home Products Corporation; *U.S. Public*, pg. 81
CYANAMID MEXICO—See American Home Products Corporation; *U.S. Public*, pg. 81
CYANAMID OF GREAT BRITAIN LTD.—See American Home Products Corporation; *U.S. Public*, pg. 81
CYANAMID PERUANA SA—See American Home Products Corporation; *U.S. Public*, pg. 81
CYANAMID PHILIPPINES, INC.—See American Home Products Corporation; *U.S. Public*, pg. 81

CYANAMID PORTUGAL LTD.—See American Home
  Products Corporation; *U.S. Public*, pg. 81
CYANAMID QUIMICA DO BRASIL LTDA.—See American
  Home Products Corporation; *U.S. Public*, pg. 81
CYANAMID TAIWAN CORP.—See American Home
  Products Corporation; *U.S. Public*, pg. 81
CYANCO—See Mining Services International, Inc.; *U.S.
  Public*, pg. 1115
CYANTEK CORPORATION—See Laporte plc; *Int'l*, pg. 802
CYBER SYSTEMS, INC.; *U.S. Private*, pg. 299
CYBEREX, INC.—See Danaher Corporation; *U.S. Public*,
  pg. 481
CYBERGUARD CORPORATION; *U.S. Public*, pg. 470
CYBEROPTICS CORPORATION; *U.S. Public*, pg. 470
CYBERTEK CORPORATION—See Policy Management
  Systems Corporation; *U.S. Public*, pg. 1314
CYBEX INTERNATIONAL, INC.—See U.M. Holding Limited;
  U.S. Private, pg. 1114
CYBORG SYSTEMS ASIA, LTD.—See Cyborg Systems,
  Inc.; *U.S. Private*, pg. 299
CYBORG SYSTEMS, INC.; *U.S. Private*, pg. 299
CYBORG SYSTEMS OF CANADA—See Cyborg Systems,
  Inc.; *U.S. Private*, pg. 299
CYBORG SYSTEMS SOUTH AFRICA, LTD.—See Cyborg
  Systems, Inc.; *U.S. Private*, pg. 299
CYBORG SYSTEMS (UK) LTD.—See Cyborg Systems, Inc.;
  U.S. Private, pg. 299
CYBUS CAPITAL MARKETS—See The Mutual Life
  Insurance Company of New York; *U.S. Private*, pg. 769
CYCLAM SA—See TI Group plc; *Int'l*, pg. 1339
CYCLE & CARRIAGE INDUSTRIES (1986) PTE. LIMITED;
  Int'l, pg. 350
CYCLEAN, INC.—See Caterpillar Inc.; *U.S. Public*, pg. 316
CYCLES EUROPE; *Int'l*, pg. 350
CYCLOPS COMMUNICATIONS (INTERACTIVE)—See
  Romann & Tannenholz Advertising, Inc.; *U.S. Private*,
  pg. 942
CYCOM COMPUTER PRODUCTS LTD.—See Oracle
  Corporation; *U.S. Public*, pg. 1228
CYDATA, INC.—See HBOC; *U.S. Public*, pg. 770
CYDSA S.A. CHEMICAL DIV.—See CYDSA S.A.; *Int'l*,
  pg. 246
CYDSA S.A. FIBERS DIV.—See CYDSA S.A.; *Int'l*, pg. 246
CYDSA S.A. PACKAGING DIV.—See CYDSA S.A.; *Int'l*,
  pg. 246
CYDSA S.A. TREAMENT DIV.—See CYDSA S.A.; *Int'l*,
  pg. 246
CYLINDER DIV., PARKER HANNIFIN PLC—See Parker
  Hannifin Corporation; *U.S. Public*, pg. 1263
CYLINDER DIVISION—See Parker Hannifin Corporation;
  U.S. Public, pg. 1262
CYLINK CORP.—See Pittway Corporation; *U.S. Public*,
  pg. 1306
CYNTHIANA DEMOCRAT—See Landmark
  Communications, Inc.; *U.S. Private*, pg. 648
CYNTHIANA HOME HEALTH CARE, INC.—See Integrated
  Health Services, Inc.; *U.S. Public*, pg. 884
CYPRESS ACQUISITION, INC.—See Stewart & Stevenson
  Services, Inc.; *U.S. Public*, pg. 1517
THE CYPRESS COMPANIES; *U.S. Private*, pg. 299
THE CYPRESS GROUP LLC; *U.S. Private*, pg. 300
CYPRESS SEMICONDUCTOR CORPORATION; *U.S.
  Public*, pg. 470
CYPRUS AMAX COAL CO.—See Cyprus Amax Minerals
  Company; *U.S. Public*, pg. 470
CYPRUS AMAX COAL SALES CORPORATION—See
  Cyprus Amax Minerals Company; *U.S. Public*, pg. 471
CYPRUS AMAX MINERALS COMPANY; *U.S. Public*,
  pg. 470
CYPRUS BAGDAD COPPER CORPORATION—See Cyprus
  Amax Minerals Company; *U.S. Public*, pg. 470
CYPRUS CEMENT COMPANY LTD.—See Holderbank
  Financiere Glaris Ltd.; *Int'l*, pg. 629
CYPRUS CLIMAX METALS COMPANY—See Cyprus Amax
  Minerals Company; *U.S. Public*, pg. 471
CYPRUS CUMBERLAND COAL CORPORATION—See
  Cyprus Amax Minerals Company; *U.S. Public*, pg. 471
CYPRUS EMERALD RESOURCES CORPORATION—See
  Cyprus Amax Minerals Company; *U.S. Public*, pg. 471
CYPRUS EMPIRE CORPORATION—See Cyprus Amax
  Minerals Company; *U.S. Public*, pg. 471
CYPRUS EXPLORATION & DEVELOPMENT
  CORPORATION—See Cyprus Amax Minerals
  Company; *U.S. Public*, pg. 471
CYPRUS FOOTE MINERAL CO.—See Cyprus Amax
  Minerals Company; *U.S. Public*, pg. 471
CYPRUS KANAWHA CORPORATION—See Cyprus Amax
  Minerals Company; *U.S. Public*, pg. 471
CYPRUS MIAMI MINING CORPORATION—See Cyprus Amax
  Minerals Company; *U.S. Public*, pg. 471
CYPRUS MINES CORP.—See Cyprus Amax Minerals
  Company; *U.S. Public*, pg. 471
CYPRUS MOUNTAIN COALS CORPORATION—See
  Cyprus Amax Minerals Company; *U.S. Public*, pg. 471
CYPRUS PLATEAU MINING CORPORATION—See Cyprus
  Amax Minerals Company; *U.S. Public*, pg. 471
THE CYPRUS POPULAR BANK LTD.—See HSBC Holdings
  plc; *Int'l*, pg. 581
CYPRUS ROD CHICAGO CORPORATION—See Cyprus
  Amax Minerals Company; *U.S. Public*, pg. 471
CYPRUS SHOSHONE COAL CORPORATION—See Cyprus
  Amax Minerals Company; *U.S. Public*, pg. 471
CYPRUS SIERRITA—See Cyprus Amax Minerals Company;
  U.S. Public, pg. 471
CYPRUS TOHONO CORPORATION—See Cyprus Amax
  Minerals Company; *U.S. Public*, pg. 471
CYRIX CORPORATION—See National Semiconductor
  Corporation; *U.S. Public*, pg. 1160
CYTEC FIBERITE EUROPE GMBH—See Cytec Industries
  Inc.; *U.S. Public*, pg. 471
CYTEC FIBERITE INC.—See Cytec Industries Inc.; *U.S.
  Public*, pg. 471
CYTEC INDUSTRIES INC.; *U.S. Public*, pg. 471
CYTOGEN CORPORATION; *U.S. Public*, pg. 471

CZECHIA SUPERHOBBY SYSTEMOVA CENTRALA
  S.R.O.—See OBI Bau-und Heimwerkermaerkte GmbH
  & Co. KG; *Int'l*, pg. 993

D

D&Z MICROELECTRONICS—See Day & Zimmermann,
  Inc.; *U.S. Private*, pg. 317
D&Z UTILITY SERVICES—See Day & Zimmermann, Inc.;
  U.S. Private, pg. 317
D INTERNATIONAL INC.—See The Daiei, Inc.; *Int'l*,
  pg. 364
D-A LUBRICANT CO., INC.—See Premier Farnell plc; *Int'l*,
  pg. 1068
D&A TECHNOLOGY—See Asahi Glass Co., Ltd.; *Int'l*,
  pg. 85
D & B ENTERPRISES INC.—See The Dun & Bradstreet
  Corporation; *U.S. Public*, pg. 535
D & B ZIMBABWE (PVT) LTD.—See The Dun & Bradstreet
  Corporation; *U.S. Public*, pg. 536
D & D SALADS—See Hy-Vee Food Stores Incorporated;
  U.S. Private, pg. 551
D & D TOLHURST LTD.—See Canadian Imperial Bank of
  Commerce; *Int'l*, pg. 257
D&H DISTRIBUTING COMPANY; *U.S. Private*, pg. 300
D & H PIPING—See Dombrowski & Holmes, Inc.; *U.S.
  Private*, pg. 338
D & H TOOL AND DIE—See United States Ceramic Tile
  Co.; *U.S. Private*, pg. 1124
D & K HEALTHCARE RESOURCES DIVISION—See D & K
  Healthcare Resources, Inc.; *U.S. Public*, pg. 472
D & K HEALTHCARE RESOURCES, INC.; *U.S. Public*,
  pg. 471
D & K HEALTHCARE RESOURCES-LEXINGTON
  DIVISION—See D & K Healthcare Resources, Inc.;
  U.S. Public, pg. 472
D & K HEALTHCARE RESOURCES-MINNEAPOLIS
  DIVISION—See D & K Healthcare Resources, Inc.;
  U.S. Public, pg. 472
D & N BANK—See D & N Financial Corporation; *U.S.
  Public*, pg. 472
D & N CAPITAL CORPORATION—See D & N Financial
  Corporation; *U.S. Public*, pg. 472
D & N FINANCIAL CORPORATION; *U.S. Public*, pg. 472
D & N MORTGAGE CORPORATION—See D & N Financial
  Corporation; *U.S. Public*, pg. 472
D & S MARKETING—See Bel-Art Products; *U.S. Private*,
  pg. 130
D & S PLASTICS INTERNATIONAL—See Solvay S.A.; *Int'l*,
  pg. 1277
D & W CAPITAL CORP.—See Dyckerhoff & Widmann AG;
  Int'l, pg. 424
D & W FOOD CENTERS, INC.; *U.S. Private*, pg. 300
D&Z CONSTRUCTION SERVICES—See Day &
  Zimmermann, Inc.; *U.S. Private*, pg. 317
D/B CAMERAS MICROCHECK DIVISION—See AEI
  Holding Co., Inc.; *U.S. Private*, pg. 5
D-GRUPPEN AB—See Axel Johnson AB; *Int'l*, pg. 708
D H FOOD CO.—See The Procter & Gamble Company;
  U.S. Public, pg. 1331
D-M-E COMPANY—See Cincinnati Milacron Inc.; *U.S.
  Public*, pg. 368
DA DEUTSCHE ALLGEMEINE LEBEN VERSICHERUNG
  AKTIENGESELLSCHAFT—See Zurich Insurance
  Company; *Int'l*, pg. 1531
DA DEUTSCHE ALLGEMEINE VERSICHERUNGS-
  AKTIENGELLSCHAFT—See Zurich Insurance
  Company; *Int'l*, pg. 1531
DAB DENTAL AB—See Axel Johnson AB; *Int'l*, pg. 708
DAB ORTODONTI AB—See Axel Johnson AB; *Int'l*,
  pg. 711
DAB-SILKEBORG A/S; *Int'l*, pg. 350
D.A.C. SYSTEMS/MICROS FRANCE—See Micros Systems
  Inc.; *U.S. Public*, pg. 1106
DAF TRUCKS N.V.—See Paccar Inc.; *U.S. Public*, pg. 1247
DAQ ELECTRONICS INC.; *U.S. Private*, pg. 300
DAV—See Labinal SA; *Int'l*, pg. 785
DAVC INC.—See Daiko Advertising, Inc.; *Int'l*, pg. 366
DAVR - DEUTSCHE ALUMINIUM VERPACKUNG
  RECYCLING GMBH—See Alusuisse-Lonza Holding
  Ltd.; *Int'l*, pg. 68
DB (BELGIUM) FINANCE S.A./N.V.—See Deutsche Bank
  AG; *Int'l*, pg. 403
DB CAPITAL MARKETS (ASIA) LTD. (HONG KONG)—See
  Deutsche Bank AG; *Int'l*, pg. 404
DB CAPITAL MARKETS (ASIA) LTD. (TOKYO)—See
  Deutsche Bank AG; *Int'l*, pg. 404
DB EXPORT LEASING G.M.B.H.—See Deutsche Bank AG;
  Int'l, pg. 402
DB RECLAME SERVICES—See De Bussy Harms N.V.;
  Int'l, pg. 386
DB U.K. FINANCE P.L.C.—See Deutsche Bank AG; *Int'l*,
  pg. 404
DBA SYSTEMS, INC.; *U.S. Public*, pg. 472
DBC EUROPE—See Data Broadcasting Corporation; *U.S.
  Public*, pg. 485
DBC WEST—See Data Broadcasting Corporation; *U.S.
  Public*, pg. 484
DBD INVESTMENT MANAGEMENT COMPANY—See
  Diebold, Incorporated; *U.S. Public*, pg. 506
DBF BUNDELFUNK GMBH & CO. BETRIEBS KG—See
  Geotek Communications; *U.S. Public*, pg. 740
DBLE—See Lyonnaise des Eaux S.A.; *Int'l*, pg. 822
DBM HATCH, INC.; *U.S. Private*, pg. 300
DBP - DAIWA SECURITIES (PHILIPPINES), INC.—See
  Daiwa Securities Co. Ltd.; *Int'l*, pg. 375
DBS ASIA CAPITAL LTD.—See DBS Bank Ltd.; *Int'l*,
  pg. 351
DBS ASIA LTD.—See DBS Bank Ltd.; *Int'l*, pg. 351
DBS ASSET MANAGEMENT LTD.—See DBS Bank Ltd.;
  Int'l, pg. 350
DBS ASSET MANAGEMENT (UNITED STATES) PTE.
  LTD.—See DBS Bank Ltd.; *Int'l*, pg. 350

DBS BANK LTD.; *Int'l*, pg. 350
DBS CAPITAL INVESTMENTS LTD.—See DBS Bank Ltd.;
  Int'l, pg. 350
DBS-CAPITAL TRUST SECURITIES INDIA PVT. LTD.—See
  DBS Bank Ltd.; *Int'l*, pg. 351
DBS CARD CENTRE PTE. LTD.—See DBS Bank Ltd.; *Int'l*,
  pg. 350
DBS CHINA SQUARE LTD.—See DBS Bank Ltd.; *Int'l*,
  pg. 350
DBS CO., LTD.—See Briggs & Stratton Corporation; *U.S.
  Public*, pg. 253
DBS COMPUTER SERVICES PTE. LTD.—See DBS Bank
  Ltd.; *Int'l*, pg. 350
DBS DEUTSCHE BAUSPARKASSE AG—See Assicurazioni
  Generali S.p.A.; *Int'l*, pg. 89
DBS EIGENHEIMBAU G.M.B.H.—See Assicurazioni
  Generali S.p.A.; *Int'l*, pg. 89
DBS FACTORS PTE. LTD.—See DBS Bank Ltd.; *Int'l*,
  pg. 350
DBS FINANCE LTD.—See DBS Bank Ltd.; *Int'l*, pg. 350
DBS FINANCE NOMINEES PTE. LTD.—See DBS Bank
  Ltd.; *Int'l*, pg. 350
DBS FUTURES HONG KONG LTD.—See DBS Bank Ltd.;
  Int'l, pg. 351
DBS INVESTMENT RESEARCH PTE. LTD.—See DBS
  Bank Ltd.; *Int'l*, pg. 350
DBS NOMINEES PTE. LTD.—See DBS Bank Ltd.; *Int'l*,
  pg. 350
DBS PTE. LTD.—See DBS Bank Ltd.; *Int'l*, pg. 351
DBS SECURITIES HOLDING PTE. LTD.—See DBS Bank
  Ltd.; *Int'l*, pg. 351
DBS SECURITIES HONG KONG LTD.—See DBS Bank
  Ltd.; *Int'l*, pg. 351
DBS SECURITIES MALAYSIA PTE LTD.—See DBS Bank
  Ltd.; *Int'l*, pg. 351
DBS SECURITIES NOMINEES (HK) LTD.—See DBS Bank
  Ltd.; *Int'l*, pg. 351
DBS SECURITIES NOMINEES PTE. LTD.—See DBS Bank
  Ltd.; *Int'l*, pg. 351
DBS SECURITIES PHILIPPINES, INC.—See DBS Bank
  Ltd.; *Int'l*, pg. 351
DBS SECURITIES SINGAPORE PTE. LTD.—See DBS
  Bank Ltd.; *Int'l*, pg. 351
DBS SECURITIES UK LTD.—See DBS Bank Ltd.; *Int'l*,
  pg. 351
DBS TRADING PTE. LTD.—See DBS Bank Ltd.; *Int'l*,
  pg. 351
DBS TRUSTEE LTD.—See DBS Bank Ltd.; *Int'l*, pg. 351
DBSF HOLDINGS PTE LTD.—See DBS Bank Ltd.; *Int'l*,
  pg. 351
DBSF INVESTMENTS PTE. LTD.—See DBS Bank Ltd.;
  Int'l, pg. 351
DBT ONLINE, INC.; *U.S. Public*, pg. 472
DBV-WINTERTHUR AG—See Commerzbank AG; *Int'l*,
  pg. 310
D.C. BRANCH OFFICE—See U.S. Home Corporation; *U.S.
  Public*, pg. 1683
D.C. CHARTERED HEALTH PLAN—See PHP Healthcare
  Corporation; *U.S. Public*, pg. 1241
DC COMICS, INC.—See Time Warner Inc.; *U.S. Public*,
  pg. 1614
DC COMPANY—See Klockner-Moeller GmbH; *Int'l*, pg. 736
D.C. SERVICES (ELECTRICAL)—See McKechnie PLC; *Int'l*,
  pg. 851
D.C. TAYLOR CO.; *U.S. Private*, pg. 300
DCA ADVERTISING, INC.—See Dentsu Inc.; *Int'l*, pg. 393
DCA AT BANYAN TREE, INC.—See Lennar Corporation;
  U.S. Public, pg. 987
DCA AT BOCA DEL MAR INC.—See Lennar Corporation;
  U.S. Public, pg. 987
DCA AT BOCA DEL MAR NO. 5, INC.—See Lennar
  Corporation; *U.S. Public*, pg. 987
DCA AT BOCA DEL MAR NO. 4, INC.—See Lennar
  Corporation; *U.S. Public*, pg. 987
DCA AT BOCA DEL MAR NO. 3, INC.—See Lennar
  Corporation; *U.S. Public*, pg. 987
DCA AT BOCA DEL MAR NO. 2, INC.—See Lennar
  Corporation; *U.S. Public*, pg. 987
DCA AT CARMEL PLACE, INC.—See Lennar Corporation;
  U.S. Public, pg. 987
DCA AT HACIENDAS, INC.—See Lennar Corporation; *U.S.
  Public*, pg. 987
DCA AT PALM PLACE INC.—See Lennar Corporation; *U.S.
  Public*, pg. 987
DCA AT PEMBROKE POINTS, INC.—See Lennar
  Corporation; *U.S. Public*, pg. 987
DCA AT PINE LAKES, INC.—See Lennar Corporation; *U.S.
  Public*, pg. 987
DCA AT THE CALIFORNIA CLUB, INC.—See Lennar
  Corporation; *U.S. Public*, pg. 987
DCA AT WATERSIDE, INC.—See Lennar Corporation; *U.S.
  Public*, pg. 988
DCA AT WATERSIDE NO. 2, INC.—See Lennar
  Corporation; *U.S. Public*, pg. 988
DCA AT WELLEBY INC.—See Lennar Corporation; *U.S.
  Public*, pg. 988
DCA AT WEST KENDALL, INC.—See Lennar Corporation;
  U.S. Public, pg. 988
DCA AT WESTCHESTER, INC.—See Lennar Corporation;
  U.S. Public, pg. 988
DCA FINANCIAL CORP.—See Lennar Corporation; *U.S.
  Public*, pg. 988
DCA GENERAL CONTRACTORS, INC.—See Lennar
  Corporation; *U.S. Public*, pg. 988
DCA HOMES, INC.—See Lennar Corporation; *U.S. Public*,
  pg. 988
DCA HOMES WEST, INC.—See Lennar Corporation; *U.S.
  Public*, pg. 988
DCA-INSTRUMENTS OY—See Rautaruukki Oy; *Int'l*,
  pg. 1088
DCA OF BROWARD COUNTY, INC.—See Lennar
  Corporation; *U.S. Public*, pg. 988
DCA OF CALIFORNIA, INC.—See Lennar Corporation; *U.S.
  Public*, pg. 988

DCA DIRECTORY OF CORPORATE AFFILIATIONS

Company Index

DCA OF DADE CITY—See Lennar Corporation; *U.S. Public*, pg. 988
DCA OF GOLDEN GATE, INC.—See Lennar Corporation; *U.S. Public*, pg. 988
DCA OF HIALEAH, INC.—See Lennar Corporation; *U.S. Public*, pg. 988
DCA OF HOMESTEAD INC.—See Lennar Corporation; *U.S. Public*, pg. 988
DCA OF KENDALL INC.—See Lennar Corporation; *U.S. Public*, pg. 988
DCA OF LAKE WORTH INC.—See Lennar Corporation; *U.S. Public*, pg. 988
DCA OF LAKESHORE, INC.—See Lennar Corporation; *U.S. Public*, pg. 988
DCA OF NEVADA, INC.—See Lennar Corporation; *U.S. Public*, pg. 988
DCA OF NEW JERSEY, INC.—See Lennar Corporation; *U.S. Public*, pg. 988
DCA OF PALM BEACH CITY—See Lennar Corporation; *U.S. Public*, pg. 988
DCA OF SAN FRANCISCO INC.—See Lennar Corporation; *U.S. Public*, pg. 988
DCA OF TEXAS, INC.—See Lennar Corporation; *U.S. Public*, pg. 988
DCA OF THE HAMMOCKS, INC.—See Lennar Corporation; *U.S. Public*, pg. 988
DCA OF WEST FLORIDA—See Lennar Corporation; *U.S. Public*, pg. 988
DCA OF WEST VIRGINIA, INC.—See Lennar Corporation; *U.S. Public*, pg. 988
DCA OIL & GAS ONE, INC.—See Lennar Corporation; *U.S. Public*, pg. 988
DCA PROPERTIES, INC.—See Lennar Corporation; *U.S. Public*, pg. 988
DCA REALTY INC.—See Lennar Corporation; *U.S. Public*, pg. 988
DCA SERVICES, INC.—See Lennar Corporation; *U.S. Public*, pg. 988
DCD (BELGIUM) N.V.—See Hapag-Lloyd AG; *Int'l*, pg. 596
DCD (SCHWIEZ) GMBH—See Hapag-Lloyd AG; *Int'l*, pg. 596
DCD (U.K.) CONTAINER SERVICES LTD.—See Hapag-Lloyd AG; *Int'l*, pg. 596
DCE GROUP—See BTR plc; *Int'l*, pg. 125
DCG PRECISION MANUFACTURING CORPORATION; *U.S. Private*, pg. 301
D.C.I., INC.; *U.S. Private*, pg. 301
DCI KIDS—See Durlacher & Co., Inc.; *U.S. Private*, pg. 348
DCI OF UTAH INC.—See D.C.I., Inc.; *U.S. Private*, pg. 301
DCM MANUFACTURING, INC.—See Dreison International, Inc.; *U.S. Private*, pg. 342
DCV INC.; *U.S. Private*, pg. 301
DDB NEEDHAM WORLDWIDE INC.—See Daehong Advertising Inc.; *Int'l*, pg. 357
DDB NEEDHAM WORLDWIDE INC.—See Omnicom Group Inc.; *U.S. Public*, pg. 1223
DDD ENERGY—See Seitel, Inc.; *U.S. Public*, pg. 1454
DDF DENTAL DEPOTET FLEX A/S—See Axel Johnson AB; *Int'l*, pg. 710
DDL ELECTRONICS, INC.; *U.S. Public*, pg. 473
DDL ELECTRONICS LTD.—See DDL Electronics, Inc.; *U.S. Public*, pg. 473
DDL EUROPE LTD.—See DDL Electronics, Inc.; *U.S. Public*, pg. 473
DE BRUSH COMPANY—See Dunn-Edwards Corporation; *U.S. Private*, pg. 347
DEA GMBH—See IRI Istituto Ricostruzione Industriale; *Int'l*, pg. 654
DEA IBERICA—See IRI Istituto Ricostruzione Industriale; *Int'l*, pg. 654
DEA KK—See IRI Istituto Ricostruzione Industriale; *Int'l*, pg. 654
DEA UK—See IRI Istituto Ricostruzione Industriale; *Int'l*, pg. 654
DEC AG—See DEC International, Inc.; *U.S. Private*, pg. 301
DEC ALKAR DIV.—See DEC International, Inc.; *U.S. Private*, pg. 301
DEC INTERNATIONAL, INC.; *U.S. Private*, pg. 301
DEGI DEUTSCHE GESELLSCHAFT FUR IMMOBILENFONDS MBH—See Dresdner Bank AG; *Int'l*, pg. 418
DEI DIVISION—See Alcatel Alsthom Compagnie Generale D'Electricite; *Int'l*, pg. 52
DEJ DATENTECHNIK GMBH—See Compagnie des Machines Bull; *Int'l*, pg. 317
DEUMU DEUTSCHE ERZ- UND METALL-UNION GMBH—See Preussag AG; *Int'l*, pg. 1069
DFA DEGGENDORFER FREIHAFEN ANSIEDLUNGS GMBH & CO. GRUNDSTUCKS KG—See Bayerische Vereinsbank Group; *Int'l*, pg. 178
DFA DEGGENDORFER FREIHAFEN ANSIEDLUNGS GMBH—See Bayerische Vereinsbank Group; *Int'l*, pg. 178
DFC CERAMICS INC.—See Morgan Crucible Co. Plc; *Int'l*, pg. 893
DFC TRANSPORTATION CO.—See Dean Foods Company; *U.S. Public*, pg. 490
DFI/INFLIGHT, INC.—See BAA plc; *Int'l*, pg. 103
DFM/TATHAM—See Havas Advertising; *Int'l*, pg. 601
D.F.S. AUSTRALIA PTY. LTD.—See Fortune Communication Holdings Ltd.; *Int'l*, pg. 500
DFTG - DEUTSCHE FLUSSIGERDAS TERMINAL GESELLSCHAFT MBH—See Ruhrgas Aktiengesellschaft; *Int'l*, pg. 1148
DG BANK; *Int'l*, pg. 351
DG EUROPEAN SECURITIES CORPORATION—See DG Bank; *Int'l*, pg. 352
DG FINANCE COMPANY B.V.—See DG Bank; *Int'l*, pg. 352
DG FOODS, LLC; *U.S. Private*, pg. 301
DG SECURITIES-TOKYO BRANCH—See DG Bank; *Int'l*, pg. 352
DG TRIM PRODUCTS DIV.—See Indian Head Industries Inc.; *U.S. Private*, pg. 560
DH COMPOUNDING CO.—See M.A. Hanna Company; *U.S. Public*, pg. 781
DHB-COMPONENTES AUTOMOTIVOS, S.A.—See General Motors Corporation; *U.S. Public*, pg. 724
DHC SOLVENT CHEMIE GMBH—See Veba AG; *Int'l*, pg. 1461
DHL AIRWAYS, INC.—See DHL Worldwide Express; *U.S. Private*, pg. 302
DHL INTERNATIONAL EXPRESS LTD.—See DHL Worldwide Express; *U.S. Private*, pg. 302
DHL INTERNATIONAL (HONG KONG) LTD.—See DHL Worldwide Express; *U.S. Private*, pg. 302
DHL INTERNATIONAL (SINGAPORE) PTE. LTD.—See DHL Worldwide Express; *U.S. Private*, pg. 302
DHL WORLDWIDE EXPRESS; *U.S. Private*, pg. 301
DHP LIMITED PARTNERSHIP; *U.S. Private*, pg. 302
DI INTERNATIONAL, INC.—See Grey Wolf, Inc.; *U.S. Public*, pg. 765
D.I.A.L. DIFFUSION INTERNATIONALE D'ARTS ET LOISIRS S.A.—See Philips Electronics N.V.; *Int'l*, pg. 1052
DIAX TELEKOMM A/S—See Telefonaktiebolaget LM Ericsson; *Int'l*, pg. 1365
DIC AMERICAS, INC.—See Dainippon Ink & Chemicals, Inc.; *Int'l*, pg. 369
P.T. DIC ASTRA CHEMICALS—See Dainippon Ink & Chemicals, Inc.; *Int'l*, pg. 371
D.I.C. AUSTRALIA PTY. LTD.—See Dainippon Ink & Chemicals, Inc.; *Int'l*, pg. 371
DIC BERLIN GMBH R & D LABORATORY—See Dainippon Ink & Chemicals, Inc.; *Int'l*, pg. 371
DIC COLOUR (HK) LTD.—See Dainippon Ink & Chemicals, Inc.; *Int'l*, pg. 371
DIC COMPOUNDS (MALAYSIA) SDN. BHD.—See Dainippon Ink & Chemicals, Inc.; *Int'l*, pg. 371
DIC DIGITAL SUPPLY CORP.—See Dainippon Ink & Chemicals, Inc.; *Int'l*, pg. 369
DIC ENTERTAINMENT—See The Walt Disney Company; *U.S. Public*, pg. 513
DIC EUROPE GMBH—See Dainippon Ink & Chemicals, Inc.; *Int'l*, pg. 371
DIC EXPRESS CO., LTD.—See Dainippon Ink & Chemicals, Inc.; *Int'l*, pg. 372
DIC FRANCE S.A.R.L.—See Dainippon Ink & Chemicals, Inc.; *Int'l*, pg. 372
PT DIC INDONESIA—See Dainippon Ink & Chemicals, Inc.; *Int'l*, pg. 372
DIC KOREA CORP.—See Dainippon Ink & Chemicals, Inc.; *Int'l*, pg. 372
DIC (MALAYSIA) SDN. BHD.—See Dainippon Ink & Chemicals, Inc.; *Int'l*, pg. 372
DIC POLYMER & CHEMICALS ASIA, PTE., LTD.—See Dainippon Ink & Chemicals, Inc.; *Int'l*, pg. 372
DIC (TAIWAN) LTD.—See Dainippon Ink & Chemicals, Inc.; *Int'l*, pg. 372
DIC TRADING CO., LTD.—See Dainippon Ink & Chemicals, Inc.; *Int'l*, pg. 372
DIC TRADING (USA) INC.—See Dainippon Ink & Chemicals, Inc.; *Int'l*, pg. 369
D.I.C. (UK) LTD.—See Dainippon Ink & Chemicals, Inc.; *Int'l*, pg. 372
DIMA—See Saint-Gobain; *Int'l*, pg. 1172
DIMC, INC.—See The Sherwin-Williams Company; *U.S. Public*, pg. 1465
DIN-S. BAKELAS—See GESTRA GmbH; *Int'l*, pg. 550
D.I.W.S.—See Olivetti SpA; *Int'l*, pg. 1002
D.J. TABLEWARE, INC.—See Oneida Ltd.; *U.S. Public*, pg. 1226
DK PUBLISHING—See Dorling Kindersley Holdings plc; *Int'l*, pg. 417
DKB & PARTNERS—See DKB & Partners, Inc.; *U.S. Private*, pg. 302
DKB & PARTNERS, INC.; *U.S. Private*, pg. 302
DKB ASIA LIMITED—See The Dai-Ichi Kangyo Bank, Limited; *Int'l*, pg. 361
DKB DATA SERVICES (USA) INC.—See The Dai-Ichi Kangyo Bank, Limited; *Int'l*, pg. 360
DKB FINANCE (ARUBA) A.E.C.—See The Dai-Ichi Kangyo Bank, Limited; *Int'l*, pg. 361
DKB FINANCE (BERLIN)—See The Dai-Ichi Kangyo Bank, Limited; *Int'l*, pg. 361
DKB FINANCE (DUSSELDORF)—See The Dai-Ichi Kangyo Bank, Limited; *Int'l*, pg. 361
DKB FINANCE (FRANKFURT)—See The Dai-Ichi Kangyo Bank, Limited; *Int'l*, pg. 361
DKB FINANCE (MUNICH)—See The Dai-Ichi Kangyo Bank, Limited; *Int'l*, pg. 361
DKB FINANCIAL FUTURES CORP.—See The Dai-Ichi Kangyo Bank, Limited; *Int'l*, pg. 360
DKB FINANCIAL PRODUCTS (HONG KONG) LIMITED—See The Dai-Ichi Kangyo Bank, Limited; *Int'l*, pg. 361
DKB FINANCIAL PRODUCTS, INC.—See The Dai-Ichi Kangyo Bank, Limited; *Int'l*, pg. 360
DKB FINANCIAL PRODUCTS (UK) LIMITED—See The Dai-Ichi Kangyo Bank, Limited; *Int'l*, pg. 361
DKB FUTURES (SINGAPORE) PTE LTD.—See The Dai-Ichi Kangyo Bank, Limited; *Int'l*, pg. 361
DKB INTERNATIONAL PUBLIC LIMITED COMPANY—See The Dai-Ichi Kangyo Bank, Limited; *Int'l*, pg. 361
DKB INVESTMENT MANAGEMENT INTERNATIONAL LIMITED—See The Dai-Ichi Kangyo Bank, Limited; *Int'l*, pg. 362
DKB LEASING (THAILAND) CO., LTD.—See The Dai-Ichi Kangyo Bank, Limited; *Int'l*, pg. 362
DKB MERCHANT BANK (SINGAPORE) LIMITED—See The Dai-Ichi Kangyo Bank, Limited; *Int'l*, pg. 361
DKB SECURITIES CORPORATION—See The Dai-Ichi Kangyo Bank, Limited; *Int'l*, pg. 360
DLJ CAPITAL CORP.—See The Equitable Companies Incorporated; *U.S. Public*, pg. 589
DLJ MERCHANT BANKING PARTNERS, L.P.—See The Equitable Companies Incorporated; *U.S. Public*, pg. 589
DM MANAGEMENT COMPANY; *U.S. Public*, pg. 473
DMB&B ASIA PACIFIC NORTH—See DMB&B Communications; *U.S. Private*, pg. 303
DMB&B BEIJING—See DMB&B Communications; *U.S. Private*, pg. 303
DMB&B/BUDAPEST—See DMB&B Communications; *U.S. Private*, pg. 303
DMB&B CENTRAL AND REGIONAL IT SERVICES—See DMB&B Communications; *U.S. Private*, pg. 302
DMB&B CHILE S.A.—See DMB&B Communications; *U.S. Private*, pg. 303
DMB&B COMMUNICATIONS; *U.S. Private*, pg. 302
DMB&B DUSSELDORF—See DMB&B Communications; *U.S. Private*, pg. 303
DMB&B EGYPT LTD.—See DMB&B Communications; *U.S. Private*, pg. 303
DMB&B GUANGZHOU—See DMB&B Communications; *U.S. Private*, pg. 303
DMB&B/HONG KONG—See DMB&B Communications; *U.S. Private*, pg. 303
DMB&B LISBON—See DMB&B Communications; *U.S. Private*, pg. 304
DMB&B LLC/KIEV—See DMB&B Communications; *U.S. Private*, pg. 304
DMB&B LOS ANGELES—See DMB&B Communications; *U.S. Private*, pg. 303
DMB&B/MIAMI—See DMB&B Communications; *U.S. Private*, pg. 304
DMB&B MONTREAL—See DMB&B Communications; *U.S. Private*, pg. 304
DMB&B PARIS—See DMB&B Communications; *U.S. Private*, pg. 304
DMB&B PRAGUE—See DMB&B Communications; *U.S. Private*, pg. 304
DMB&B PUBLIC RELATIONS—See DMB&B Communications; *U.S. Private*, pg. 303
DMB&B S.A. DE C.V.—See DMB&B Communications; *U.S. Private*, pg. 304
DMB&B ST. PETERSBURG—See DMB&B Communications; *U.S. Private*, pg. 304
DMB&B SHANGHAI—See DMB&B Communications; *U.S. Private*, pg. 304
DMB&B TAIWAN—See DMB&B Communications; *U.S. Private*, pg. 304
DMB&B/WARSAW—See DMB&B Communications; *U.S. Private*, pg. 304
DMB&B/WEEKES MORRIS OSBORN—See DMB&B Communications; *U.S. Private*, pg. 304
DMB&B/WORLDWIDE COMMUNICATIONS—See DMB&B Communications; *U.S. Private*, pg. 304
DMB&B/YELLOW PAGES—See DMB&B Communications; *U.S. Private*, pg. 303
DMC DE MEXICO, S.A. DE C.V.—See Digital Microwave Corporation; *U.S. Public*, pg. 508
DMC DRESDNER MANAGEMENT CONSULT GMBH—See Dresdner Bank AG; *Int'l*, pg. 418
DMC TELECOM CANADA INC.—See Digital Microwave Corporation; *U.S. Public*, pg. 508
DMC TELECOM U.K. LTD.—See Digital Microwave Corporation; *U.S. Public*, pg. 508
DMC TOYOTA LIMITED—See Toyota Motor Corporation; *Int'l*, pg. 1413
DMG BUSINESS MEDIA LTD.—See Daily Mail & General Trust PLC; *Int'l*, pg. 366
DMG EXHIBITION GROUP LTD.—See Daily Mail & General Trust PLC; *Int'l*, pg. 366
DMI FURNITURE INC.; *U.S. Public*, pg. 473
DMI FURNITURE, INC.—See DMI Furniture Inc.; *U.S. Public*, pg. 473
DMI, INC.; *U.S. Private*, pg. 305
DML INDUSTRIAL DIV.—See Emerson Electric Co.; *U.S. Public*, pg. 575
DML PRODUCTS—See Emerson Electric Co.; *U.S. Public*, pg. 575
DMR CONSULTING GROUP, INC.—See Fujitsu Limited; *Int'l*, pg. 527
DMR GROEP B.V.—See Fujitsu Limited; *Int'l*, pg. 528
DMR GROUP AUSTRALIA PTY. LTD.—See Fujitsu Limited; *Int'l*, pg. 528
DMR GROUP (BELGIUM) S.A.-N.V.—See Fujitsu Limited; *Int'l*, pg. 528
DMR GROUP, INC.—See Fujitsu Limited; *Int'l*, pg. 527
DMR GROUP LIMITED—See Fujitsu Limited; *Int'l*, pg. 528
DMR GROUP NEW ZEALAND LTD.—See Fujitsu Limited; *Int'l*, pg. 528
DMR GRUPPE AG—See Fujitsu Limited; *Int'l*, pg. 528
DMR GRUPPE GMBH—See Fujitsu Limited; *Int'l*, pg. 528
DMS-10 DIV.—See Northern Telecom Limited; *Int'l*, pg. 969
DMT DANSK MOBILTELEFON I/S—See BellSouth Corporation; *U.S. Public*, pg. 209
DMV INTERNATIONAL—See Campina Melkunie BV; *Int'l*, pg. 254
DNA PLANT TECHNOLOGY CORP.—See Empressa La Moderna SA de CV; *Int'l*, pg. 454
DNAP HOLDING CORP.—See Empressa La Moderna SA de CV; *Int'l*, pg. 454
DNE SYSTEMS, INC.—See The Alpine Group, Inc.; *U.S. Public*, pg. 58
DNN GALVANIZING CORPORATION—See DoFasco, Inc.; *Int'l*, pg. 414
DNN GALVANIZING CORPORATION—See NKK Corporation; *Int'l*, pg. 903
DNP (AMERICA), INC.—See Dai Nippon Printing Co., Ltd.; *Int'l*, pg. 363
DNP DENMARK A/S—See Dai Nippon Printing Co., Ltd.; *Int'l*, pg. 363
D.O.C. OPTICS CORPORATION; *U.S. Private*, pg. 305
DOD ELECTRONICS CORPORATION—See Harman International Industries, Inc.; *U.S. Public*, pg. 787
DOM AG SICHERHEITSTECHNIK—See The Black & Decker Corporation; *U.S. Public*, pg. 233
D.O.M. LTD.—See Caterpillar Inc.; *U.S. Public*, pg. 317
DOM S.A.R.L.—See The Black & Decker Corporation; *U.S. Public*, pg. 233

DOM-SICHERHEITSTECHNIK GMBH & CO. KG—See The Black & Decker Corporation; *U.S. Public*, pg. 233
DOWC OST-WEST-CONSULT AG—See Dresdner Bank AG; *Int'l*, pg. 418
D.P.&L. COMMUNITY URBAN REDEVELOPMENT CORP.—See DPL Inc.; *U.S. Public*, pg. 473
DPL INC.; *U.S. Public*, pg. 473
DPR CONSTRUCTION, INC., *U.S. Private*, pg. 305
DPSA DEUTSCHE PERSONENSUCH-ANLAGEN GMBH—See Telefonaktiebolaget LM Ericsson; *Int'l*, pg. 1365
DPZ—See DPZ-Duailibi, Petit, Zaragoza, Propaganda S.A.; *Int'l*, pg. 352
DPZ-DUAILIBI, PETIT, ZARAGOZA, PROPAGANDA S.A.; *Int'l*, pg. 352
DQE ENERGY SERVICES—See DQE Inc.; *U.S. Public*, pg. 474
DQE INC.; *U.S. Public*, pg. 474
D.Q.F., INC.—See Berkshire Hathaway Inc.; *U.S. Public*, pg. 220
DRG CARTONS LTD.—See Johns Manville Corporation; *U.S. Public*, pg. 927
DRI EUROPE, INC.—See The McGraw-Hill Companies; *U.S. Public*, pg. 1072
DRI EUROPE (U.K.) LTD.—See The McGraw-Hill Companies; *U.S. Public*, pg. 1072
DRI/MCGRAW-HILL—See The McGraw-Hill Companies; *U.S. Public*, pg. 1071
DRS AHEAD TECHNOLOGY, INC.—See DRS Technologies, Inc.; *U.S. Public*, pg. 475
DRS ELECTRONIC SYSTEMS, INC.—See DRS Technologies, Inc.; *U.S. Public*, pg. 474
DRS LAUREL TECHNOLOGIES—See DRS Technologies, Inc.; *U.S. Public*, pg. 475
DRS MEDICAL SYSTEMS—See DRS Technologies, Inc.; *U.S. Public*, pg. 475
DRS OPTRONICS, INC.—See DRS Technologies, Inc.; *U.S. Public*, pg. 474
DRS PHOTRONICS, INC.—See DRS Technologies, Inc.; *U.S. Public*, pg. 474
DRS PRECISION ECHO, INC.—See DRS Technologies, Inc.; *U.S. Public*, pg. 474
D.R.S. RESTAURANT SCHECK SODEXHO GMBH—See Sodexho S.A.; *Int'l*, pg. 1274
D.R.S. RESTAURANT SCHECK-SODEXHO GMBH—See Sodexho S.A.; *Int'l*, pg. 1274
DRS TECHNOLOGIES, INC.; *U.S. Public*, pg. 474
D.S., INC.—See Bell Atlantic Corporation; *U.S. Public*, pg. 203
DS INDUSTRIES APS—See The East Asiatic Company Ltd. A/S; *Int'l*, pg. 430
DSB-DRESDNER BANK—See Dresdner Bank AG; *Int'l*, pg. 419
DSC—See DSC Communications Corporation; *U.S. Public*, pg. 475
DSC COMMUNICATIONS CORPORATION; *U.S. Public*, pg. 475
DSC LTD.; *U.S. Private*, pg. 305
DSC LOGISTICS, INC.; *U.S. Private*, pg. 306
DSD DILLINGER STAHLBAU GMBH—See Commerzbank AG; *Int'l*, pg. 310
DSD INTERNATIONAL CONTRACTORS S.A.R.L.—See Commerzbank AG; *Int'l*, pg. 310
DSG-MECMAN TRAINING SYSTEMS GMBH—See Mannesmann A.G.; *Int'l*, pg. 838
DSI—See British Steel Plc; *Int'l*, pg. 221
DSI DYWIDAG -SYSTEMS INTERNATIONAL GES. M.B.H.—See Dyckerhoff & Widmann AG; *Int'l*, pg. 424
DSI DYWIDAG-SYSTEMS INTERNATIONAL GMBH—See Dyckerhoff & Widmann AG; *Int'l*, pg. 423
DSI GROUP—See Alcatel Alsthom Compagnie Generale D'Electricite; *Int'l*, pg. 52
DSI STAFF CONNXIONS SOUTHWEST—See Digital Solutions, Inc.; *U.S. Public*, pg. 508
DSI TRANSPORTS—See Sophus Berendsen A/S; *Int'l*, pg. 1285
DSI TRANSPORTS, INC.—See Sophus Berendsen A/S; *Int'l*, pg. 1285
DSL SERVICE CO.—See Downey Financial Corp.; *U.S. Public*, pg. 527
DSM AGARHANDELEN GMBH—See DSM N.V.; *Int'l*, pg. 355
DSM AGRO BV—See DSM N.V.; *Int'l*, pg. 353
DSM ANDENO B.V.—See DSM N.V.; *Int'l*, pg. 353
DSM ANDENO GMBH—See DSM N.V.; *Int'l*, pg. 355
DSM ANDENO MAARSSEN B.V.—See DSM N.V.; *Int'l*, pg. 353
DSM ANDENO S.A.—See DSM N.V.; *Int'l*, pg. 355
DSM BELGIUM N.V.—See DSM N.V.; *Int'l*, pg. 355
DSM CENTRAL EUROPE—See DSM N.V.; *Int'l*, pg. 355
DSM CHEMICALS & FERTILIZERS—See DSM N.V.; *Int'l*, pg. 353
DSM CHEMICALS NORTH AMERICA, INC.—See DSM N.V.; *Int'l*, pg. 354
DSM CHEMICALS ROTTERDAM—See DSM N.V.; *Int'l*, pg. 353
DSM CHEMICALS SALES GMBH—See DSM N.V.; *Int'l*, pg. 353
DSM CHEMIE LINZ GMBH—See DSM N.V.; *Int'l*, pg. 353
DSM CHEMIE LINZ GMBH—See OMV AG; *Int'l*, pg. 995
DSM CHEMIE LINZ NORTH AMERICA INC.—See DSM N.V.; *Int'l*, pg. 356
DSM CHINA—See DSM N.V.; *Int'l*, pg. 355
DSM COMPOUNDS GMBH—See DSM N.V.; *Int'l*, pg. 355
DSM COMPOUNDS UK LTD.—See DSM N.V.; *Int'l*, pg. 355
DSM COPOLYMER, INC.—See DSM N.V.; *Int'l*, pg. 354
DSM DESOTECH B.V.—See DSM N.V.; *Int'l*, pg. 353
DSM DESOTECH, INC.—See DSM N.V.; *Int'l*, pg. 354
DSM DEUTSCHLAND GMBH & CO.—See DSM N.V.; *Int'l*, pg. 356
DSM EASTERN EUROPE—See DSM N.V.; *Int'l*, pg. 355
DSM ELASTOMERS—See DSM N.V.; *Int'l*, pg. 353
DSM ELASTOMERS ASIA LTD.—See DSM N.V.; *Int'l*, pg. 354

DSM ELASTOMERS ASIA PACIFIC PTE LTD.—See DSM N.V.; *Int'l*, pg. 354
DSM ELASTOMERS ASIA PACIFIC PTE. LTD.—See DSM N.V.; *Int'l*, pg. 355
DSM ELASTOMERS EUROPE B.V.—See DSM N.V.; *Int'l*, pg. 353
DSM ENERGIE B.V.—See DSM N.V.; *Int'l*, pg. 353
DSM ENERGY (U.K.) LTD.—See DSM N.V.; *Int'l*, pg. 354
DSM ENGINEERING PLASTIC PRODUCTS—See DSM N.V.; *Int'l*, pg. 354
DSM ENGINEERING PLASTIC PRODUCTS BV—See DSM N.V.; *Int'l*, pg. 353
DSM ENGINEERING PLASTIC PRODUCTS FRANCE—See DSM N.V.; *Int'l*, pg. 354
DSM ENGINEERING PLASTIC PRODUCTS S.A.—See DSM N.V.; *Int'l*, pg. 354
DSM ENGINEERING PLASTICS—See Akzo Nobel N.V.; *Int'l*, pg. 46
DSM ENGINEERING PLASTICS INC.—See DSM N.V.; *Int'l*, pg. 354
DSM ENGRAIS FRANCE SA—See DSM N.V.; *Int'l*, pg. 355
DSM EPP UK LTD.—See DSM N.V.; *Int'l*, pg. 354
DSM ESPANA, S.A.—See DSM N.V.; *Int'l*, pg. 355
DSM FINE CHEMICALS—See DSM N.V.; *Int'l*, pg. 353
DSM FINE CHEMICALS USA INC.—See DSM N.V.; *Int'l*, pg. 355
DSM FRANCE SA—See DSM N.V.; *Int'l*, pg. 355
DSM HIGH PERFORMANCE FIBERS B.V.—See DSM N.V.; *Int'l*, pg. 353
DSM HYDROCARBONS—See DSM N.V.; *Int'l*, pg. 353
DSM HYDROCARBONS AMERICAS, INC.—See DSM N.V.; *Int'l*, pg. 353
DSM IDEMITSU CORP. LTD.—See DSM N.V.; *Int'l*, pg. 356
DSM ITALIA—See DSM N.V.; *Int'l*, pg. 355
DSM ITALIA SRL—See DSM N.V.; *Int'l*, pg. 355
DSM JAPAN KK—See DSM N.V.; *Int'l*, pg. 355
P.T. DSM KALTIM MELAMINE—See DSM N.V.; *Int'l*, pg. 354
DSM KENKYO EPP LTD.—See DSM N.V.; *Int'l*, pg. 354
DSM KUNSTHARZE GMBH—See DSM N.V.; *Int'l*, pg. 355
DSM KUNSTSTOFFEN B.V.—See DSM N.V.; *Int'l*, pg. 353
DSM LIMBURG B.V.—See DSM N.V.; *Int'l*, pg. 353
DSM MELAMINE AMERICAS, INC.—See DSM N.V.; *Int'l*, pg. 355
DSM MELAMINE LIMBURG—See DSM N.V.; *Int'l*, pg. 353
DSM MESTSTOFFEN B.V.—See DSM N.V.; *Int'l*, pg. 353
DSM MOREELS NV—See DSM N.V.; *Int'l*, pg. 355
DSM N.V.; *Int'l*, pg. 352
DSM PLASTIC PRODUCTS—See DSM N.V.; *Int'l*, pg. 353
DSM POLAND SP.Z.O.O.—See DSM N.V.; *Int'l*, pg. 355
DSM POLYMERS—See DSM N.V.; *Int'l*, pg. 353
DSM POLYMERS INTERNATIONAL—See DSM N.V.; *Int'l*, pg. 353
DSM RESEARCH B.V.—See DSM N.V.; *Int'l*, pg. 353
DSM RESINS BELGIUM N.V.—See DSM N.V.; *Int'l*, pg. 355
DSM RESINS BENELUX B.V.—See DSM N.V.; *Int'l*, pg. 353
DSM RESINS B.V.—See DSM N.V.; *Int'l*, pg. 353
DSM RESINS ESPANA SA—See DSM N.V.; *Int'l*, pg. 355
DSM RESINS ESPANA S.A.—See DSM N.V.; *Int'l*, pg. 355
DSM RESINS (FAR EAST) LTD.—See DSM N.V.; *Int'l*, pg. 355
DSM RESINS FRANCE S.A.—See DSM N.V.; *Int'l*, pg. 355
DSM RESINS INTERNATIONAL B.V.—See DSM N.V.; *Int'l*, pg. 355
DSM RESINS US, INC.—See DSM N.V.; *Int'l*, pg. 355
DSM RIM NYLON, INC.—See DSM N.V.; *Int'l*, pg. 355
DSM RIM NYLON VOF—See DSM N.V.; *Int'l*, pg. 353
DSM SCANDINAVIA AB—See DSM N.V.; *Int'l*, pg. 355
DSM SHEFFIELD PLASTICS—See DSM N.V.; *Int'l*, pg. 354
DSM SPECIAL PRODUCTS B.V.—See DSM N.V.; *Int'l*, pg. 353
DSM SPECIALTY COMPOUNDS NV—See DSM N.V.; *Int'l*, pg. 355
DSM THERMOPLASTIC ELASTOMERS B.V.—See DSM N.V.; *Int'l*, pg. 353
DSM THERMOPLASTIC ELASTOMERS INC.—See DSM N.V.; *Int'l*, pg. 354
DSM TRANSPORT MAATSCHAPPIJ B.V.—See DSM N.V.; *Int'l*, pg. 353
DSM TRANSPORTMAATSCHAPPIJ BV—See DSM N.V.; *Int'l*, pg. 354
DSM UNITED KINGDOM LIMITED—See DSM N.V.; *Int'l*, pg. 354
DSM VERKOOPKANTOOR POLYMEREN NEDERLAND—See DSM N.V.; *Int'l*, pg. 353
DSP COMMUNICATIONS INC.; *U.S. Public*, pg. 475
D.S.P. LTD.—See Daiko Advertising, Inc.; *Int'l*, pg. 366
DSP TECHNOLOGY INC.; *U.S. Public*, pg. 475
DSS ENGINEERS, INC.—See Stone & Webster, Incorporated; *U.S. Public*, pg. 1519
DST REALTY, INC.—See Kansas City Southern Industries, Inc.; *U.S. Public*, pg. 943
DST SECURITIES, INC.—See Kansas City Southern Industries, Inc.; *U.S. Public*, pg. 943
DST SYSTEMS, INC.—See Kansas City Southern Industries, Inc.; *U.S. Public*, pg. 943
DSU LEASING, INC.—See D.S.U.-Peterbilt & GMC, Inc.; *U.S. Private*, pg. 306
D.S.U.-PETERBILT & GMC, INC.; *U.S. Private*, pg. 306
DT INDUSTRIES INC.; *U.S. Public*, pg. 475
DTC COMMUNICATIONS, INC.; *U.S. Private*, pg. 306
DTC - DYNAMIC TEST CENTER—See Oerlikon-Buhrle Holding AG; *Int'l*, pg. 998
DTE ENERGY COMPANY; *U.S. Public*, pg. 475
DTK COMPUTER INC.; *U.S. Private*, pg. 306
DTV INTERNATIONAL—See Lagardere Groupe; *Int'l*, pg. 792
DTZ ZADELHOFF GMBH—See Landesbank Rheinland-Pfalz; *Int'l*, pg. 799
D.V.F. INC.—See MacAndrews & Forbes Holdings Inc.; *U.S. Private*, pg. 690
DVI BUSINESS CREDIT, INC.—See DVI, Inc.; *U.S. Public*, pg. 476

DVI FINANCIAL SERVICES INC.—See DVI, Inc.; *U.S. Public*, pg. 476
DVI, INC.; *U.S. Public*, pg. 476
DVM DATENVERARBEITUNGSMASCHINEN UND TIME-SHARE GMBH—See Compagnie des Machines Bull; *Int'l*, pg. 317
DVM GMBH—See Compagnie des Machines Bull; *Int'l*, pg. 318
DVO-DATENVERABEITUNGS-SERVICE OBERHAUSEN GMBH—See Deutsche Babcock AG; *Int'l*, pg. 401
D.W. CLOSE COMPANY—See MYR Group Inc.; *U.S. Public*, pg. 1029
DWF OF ALBUQUERQUE—See Denver Wholesale Florists Company; *U.S. Private*, pg. 326
DWF OF GAYLORD—See Denver Wholesale Florists Company; *U.S. Private*, pg. 326
D.W.M COPELAND G.M.B.H.—See Emerson Electric Co.; *U.S. Public*, pg. 576
DX COMMUNICATIONS, INC.—See Itochu Corporation; *Int'l*, pg. 694
DYD CO.—See Bacardi Limited; *Int'l*, pg. 132
DYWIDAG SPEZIALTIEFBAU GES.M.B.H.—See Dyckerhoff & Widmann AG; *Int'l*, pg. 424
DYWIDAG SYSTEMS INTERNATIONAL, USA, INC., EASTERN DIV.—See Dyckerhoff & Widmann AG; *Int'l*, pg. 424
DYWIDAG SYSTEMS INTERNATIONAL, USA, INC.—See Dyckerhoff & Widmann AG; *Int'l*, pg. 424
DZIC—See Day & Zimmermann, Inc.; *U.S. Private*, pg. 317
DA CAPO PRESS, INC.—See Plenum Publishing Corporation; *U.S. Public*, pg. 1311
DA GAMA TEXTILE COMPANY—See South African Breweries, Ltd.; *Int'l*, pg. 1287
DA-LITE SCREEN COMPANY, INC.; *U.S. Private*, pg. 306
DAARBERG-OEKOTECHNIK GMBH—See Saarbergwerke Aktiengesellschaft; *Int'l*, pg. 1167
D'AC—See Luxo A/S; *Int'l*, pg. 821
DAC CITY CO., LTD.—See Mycal, Corp.; *Int'l*, pg. 898
DAC INTERNATIONAL, INC.—See Banner Aerospace, Inc.; *U.S. Public*, pg. 187
DACAM CORP.—See Old Dominion Box Co., Inc.; *U.S. Private*, pg. 814
DACCO, INC.—See Jordan Industries, Inc.; *U.S. Private*, pg. 598
DACEM S.A.R.L.—See Kingfisher plc; *Int'l*, pg. 734
DACHSER GMBH & CO.; *Int'l*, pg. 356
DACHSER TRANSPORT OF AMERICA INC.—See Dachser GmbH & Co.; *Int'l*, pg. 357
DACON ELECTRONICS PLC.—See Cognitronics Corporation; *U.S. Public*, pg. 395
DACOR CORPORATION; *U.S. Private*, pg. 306
DACOR UK LIMITED—See Fortune Brands, Inc.; *U.S. Public*, pg. 674
DACRAL EUROPE—See Akzo Nobel N.V.; *Int'l*, pg. 43
DACTYLO—See Vendex International N.V.; *Int'l*, pg. 1463
DADA DADA & CIA S.A. DE C.V.—See Telefonaktiebolaget LM Ericsson; *Int'l*, pg. 1365
DADE BEHRING—See Bain Capital; *U.S. Private*, pg. 110
DADE BEHRING INC.—See Bain Capital; *U.S. Private*, pg. 110
DADE BEHRING INC.—See Hoechst Aktiengesellschaft; *Int'l*, pg. 626
DADE BEHRING-MICROSCAN DIV.—See Bain Capital; *U.S. Private*, pg. 110
DADE COUNTY LAND HOLDING CO.—See St. Joe Corp.; *U.S. Public*, pg. 1427
DADE LEASE MANAGEMENT, INC.—See Dollar General Corporation; *U.S. Public*, pg. 515
DAD'S PRODUCTS CO., INC.; *U.S. Private*, pg. 306
DAEDAL DIVISION—See Parker Hannifin Corporation; *U.S. Public*, pg. 1259
DAEHAN CHEMICAL MACHINERY MFG. CO., LTD.—See Kobe Steel, Ltd.; *Int'l*, pg. 741
DAEHAN SPECIALTY CHEMICALS COMPANY, LTD.—See Solvay S.A.; *Int'l*, pg. 1279
DAEHONG ADVERTISING INC.; *Int'l*, pg. 357
DAEKKO PRESENNING KOMPAGNI A/S—See Electrolux, AB; *Int'l*, pg. 441
DAEWOO AMERICA DEVELOPMENT, INC.—See Daewoo Corporation; *Int'l*, pg. 358
DAEWOO AUSTRALIA PTY. LIMITED—See Daewoo Corporation; *Int'l*, pg. 357
DAEWOO AUTOMOTIVE COMPONENTS, LTD.—See Daewoo Corporation; *Int'l*, pg. 357
DAEWOO BANK (HUNGARY) LTD.—See Daewoo Securities Co., Ltd.; *Int'l*, pg. 359
DAEWOO CANADA LTD.—See Daewoo Corporation; *Int'l*, pg. 357
DAEWOO CAPITAL MANAGEMENT CO., LTD.—See Daewoo Securities Co., Ltd.; *Int'l*, pg. 359
DAEWOO CHILE S.A.—See Daewoo Corporation; *Int'l*, pg. 358
DAEWOO CORP. - MADRID—See Daewoo Corporation; *Int'l*, pg. 358
DAEWOO CORP. - MONTEVIDEO—See Daewoo Corporation; *Int'l*, pg. 358
DAEWOO CORPORATION; *Int'l*, pg. 357
DAEWOO CORP. AMSTERDAM B.V.—See Daewoo Corporation; *Int'l*, pg. 358
DAEWOO CORP. - JOHANNESBURG—See Daewoo Corporation; *Int'l*, pg. 358
DAEWOO CORP. - KARACHI—See Daewoo Corporation; *Int'l*, pg. 357
DAEWOO CORP. - KHARTOUM—See Daewoo Corporation; *Int'l*, pg. 358
DAEWOO CORP. - LUANDA—See Daewoo Corporation; *Int'l*, pg. 358
DAEWOO CORP. - MEXICO—See Daewoo Corporation; *Int'l*, pg. 358
DAEWOO CORP. - MOSCOW—See Daewoo Corporation; *Int'l*, pg. 358

DAEWOO CORP. - NAGOYA—See Daewoo Corporation; *Int'l*, pg. 358
DAEWOO CORP.- NAIROBI—See Daewoo Corporation; *Int'l*, pg. 358
DAEWOO CORP. - OSLO—See Daewoo Corporation; *Int'l*, pg. 358
DAEWOO CORP. - PRAGUE—See Daewoo Corporation; *Int'l*, pg. 358
DAEWOO CORP. - QINGDAO—See Daewoo Corporation; *Int'l*, pg. 358
DAEWOO CORP. - SANAA—See Daewoo Corporation; *Int'l*, pg. 358
DAEWOO CORP. - SHANGHAI—See Daewoo Corporation; *Int'l*, pg. 358
DAEWOO CORP. - SLOVENIA—See Daewoo Corporation; *Int'l*, pg. 358
DAEWOO CORP. - SOFIA—See Daewoo Corporation; *Int'l*, pg. 358
DAEWOO CORP. - TAIWAN—See Daewoo Corporation; *Int'l*, pg. 358
DAEWOO CORP. - TEHRAN—See Daewoo Corporation; *Int'l*, pg. 358
DAEWOO CORP. - TRIPOLI—See Daewoo Corporation; *Int'l*, pg. 358
DAEWOO CORP. - VANCOUVER—See Daewoo Corporation; *Int'l*, pg. 358
DAEWOO CORP. - VIENNA—See Daewoo Corporation; *Int'l*, pg. 358
DAEWOO CORP. - WARSAW—See Daewoo Corporation; *Int'l*, pg. 358
DAEWOO INC (DALIAN) OFFICE—See Daewoo Corporation; *Int'l*, pg. 358
DAEWOO DO BRAZIL IMP EXP. LTD.—See Daewoo Corporation; *Int'l*, pg. 358
DAEWOO ELECTRIC MOTOR INDUSTRIES, LTD.—See Daewoo Corporation; *Int'l*, pg. 357
DAEWOO ELECTRONICS CO., LTD.—See Daewoo Corporation; *Int'l*, pg. 357
DAEWOO ENGINEERING COMPANY—See Daewoo Corporation; *Int'l*, pg. 357
DAEWOO FRANCE S.A.R.L.—See Daewoo Corporation; *Int'l*, pg. 358
DAEWOO FUKUOKA CORP.—See Daewoo Corporation; *Int'l*, pg. 358
DAEWOO HANDELS GMBH—See Daewoo Corporation; *Int'l*, pg. 358
DAEWOO HEAVY INDUSTRIES, LTD.—See Daewoo Corporation; *Int'l*, pg. 357
DAEWOO HONG KONG LTD.—See Daewoo Corporation; *Int'l*, pg. 358
DAEWOO INTERNATIONAL AMERICA CORP. - CHICAGO—See Daewoo Corporation; *Int'l*, pg. 357
DAEWOO INTERNATIONAL AMERICA CORP. - DALLAS—See Daewoo Corporation; *Int'l*, pg. 357
DAEWOO INTERNATIONAL AMERICA CORP. - DETROIT—See Daewoo Corporation; *Int'l*, pg. 357
DAEWOO INTERNATIONAL AMERICA CORP. - LOS ANGELES—See Daewoo Corporation; *Int'l*, pg. 357
DAEWOO INTERNATIONAL AMERICA CORP. - MIAMI—See Daewoo Corporation; *Int'l*, pg. 357
DAEWOO INTERNATIONAL AMERICA CORP. - NEW YORK—See Daewoo Corporation; *Int'l*, pg. 357
DAEWOO INTERNATIONAL AMERICA CORP. - RIDGEFIELD—See Daewoo Corporation; *Int'l*, pg. 357
DAEWOO INTERNATIONAL AMERICA CORP. - SANTA CLARA—See Daewoo Corporation; *Int'l*, pg. 357
DAEWOO INTERNATIONAL AMERICA CORP. - SEATTLE—See Daewoo Corporation; *Int'l*, pg. 357
DAEWOO INTERNATIONAL - CARACAS—See Daewoo Corporation; *Int'l*, pg. 358
DAEWOO INTERNATIONAL - COLON—See Daewoo Corporation; *Int'l*, pg. 358
DAEWOO INTERNATIONAL (JAPAN) CORP.—See Daewoo Corporation; *Int'l*, pg. 358
DAEWOO INTERNATIONAL (PANAMA) S.A.—See Daewoo Corporation; *Int'l*, pg. 358
DAEWOO ITALIA S.R.L.—See Daewoo Corporation; *Int'l*, pg. 358
DAEWOO (LATIN AMERICA) LTD.—See Daewoo Corporation; *Int'l*, pg. 358
DAEWOO METAL CO., LTD.—See Daewoo Corporation; *Int'l*, pg. 357
DAEWOO MOTOR CHILE S.A.—See Daewoo Corporation; *Int'l*, pg. 358
DAEWOO MOTOR COMPANY, LTD.—See Daewoo Corporation; *Int'l*, pg. 357
DAEWOO NIGERIA LIMITED—See Daewoo Corporation; *Int'l*, pg. 358
DAEWOO NIGERIA LTD.—See Daewoo Corporation; *Int'l*, pg. 358
DAEWOO PRECISION INDUSTRIES, LTD.—See Daewoo Corporation; *Int'l*, pg. 357
DAEWOO RESEARCH INSTITUTE—See Daewoo Securities Co., Ltd.; *Int'l*, pg. 359
DAEWOO SANG SA—See Daewoo Corporation; *Int'l*, pg. 357
DAEWOO SECURITIES (AMERICA) INC.—See Daewoo Securities Co., Ltd.; *Int'l*, pg. 359
DAEWOO SECURITIES CO., LTD.; *Int'l*, pg. 358
DAEWOO SECURITIES (EUROPE) LTD.—See Daewoo Securities Co., Ltd.; *Int'l*, pg. 359
DAEWOO SECURITIES (HONG KONG) LTD.—See Daewoo Securities Co., Ltd.; *Int'l*, pg. 359
DAEWOO SECURITIES - SHANGHAI REPRESENTATIVE OFFICE—See Daewoo Securities Co., Ltd.; *Int'l*, pg. 359
DAEWOO SECURITIES - SINGAPORE REPRESENTATIVE OFFICE—See Daewoo Securities Co., Ltd.; *Int'l*, pg. 359
DAEWOO SECURITIES - TOKYO REPRESENTATIVE OFFICE—See Daewoo Securities Co., Ltd.; *Int'l*, pg. 359

DAEWOO SECURITIES - ZURICH REPRESENTATIVE OFFICE—See Daewoo Securities Co., Ltd.; *Int'l*, pg. 359
DAEWOO SHIPBUILDING & HEAVY MACHINERY, LTD.—See Daewoo Corporation; *Int'l*, pg. 357
DAEWOO SINGAPORE PTE. LTD.—See Daewoo Corporation; *Int'l*, pg. 358
DAEWOO TELECOM CO., LTD.—See Daewoo Corporation; *Int'l*, pg. 357
DAEWOO TELECOM CO. (NEWTON)—See Daewoo Corporation; *Int'l*, pg. 358
DAEWOO UK LTD.—See Daewoo Corporation; *Int'l*, pg. 358
DAGAB SNABBGROSS AB—See Axel Johnson AB; *Int'l*, pg. 708
DAGBLADET BOERSEN A/S; *Int'l*, pg. 359
DAGENS NAERINGSLIV A/S—See The A/S Norges Handels og Sjoefartstidende Group; *Int'l*, pg. 958
OY DAGMAR AB; *Int'l*, pg. 359
DAGMARKT—See Vendex International N.V.; *Int'l*, pg. 1463
D'AGOSTINO SUPERMARKETS INC.; *U.S. Private*, pg. 306
DAHER GOLDEN EAGLE—See Golden Eagle Group, Inc.; *U.S. Public*, pg. 749
DAHL BROTHERS LTD.—See Dahl International AB; *Int'l*, pg. 359
DAHL INTERNATIONAL AB; *Int'l*, pg. 359
DAHL SVERIGE—See Dahl International AB; *Int'l*, pg. 359
DAHLBERG, INC.—See Bausch & Lomb Incorporated; *U.S. Public*, pg. 194
DAHLBERG INC. RETAIL STORES DIV.—See Bausch & Lomb Incorporated; *U.S. Public*, pg. 194
DAHLBERG SCIENCES, LTD.—See Bausch & Lomb Incorporated; *U.S. Public*, pg. 194
DAHLBUSCH AG—See Pilkington Plc; *Int'l*, pg. 1056
DAHLEM COMPANY, INC., *U.S. Private*, pg. 306
DAHLSTEN TRUCK LINE, INC., *U.S. Private*, pg. 306
DAI-ICHI KANGYO AUSTRALIA LIMITED—See The Dai-Ichi Kangyo Bank, Limited; *Int'l*, pg. 361
THE DAI-ICHI KANGYO BANK, LIMITED; *Int'l*, pg. 359
DAI-ICHI KANGYO BANK, LTD.-ATLANTA—See The Dai-Ichi Kangyo Bank, Limited; *Int'l*, pg. 359
DAI-ICHI KANGYO BANK, LTD.-BERLIN—See The Dai-Ichi Kangyo Bank, Limited; *Int'l*, pg. 361
DAI-ICHI KANGYO BANK, LTD.-BRUSSELS—See The Dai-Ichi Kangyo Bank, Limited; *Int'l*, pg. 361
DAI-ICHI KANGYO BANK, LTD.-CHICAGO—See The Dai-Ichi Kangyo Bank, Limited; *Int'l*, pg. 359
DAI-ICHI KANGYO BANK, LTD.-HOUSTON—See The Dai-Ichi Kangyo Bank, Limited; *Int'l*, pg. 359
DAI-ICHI KANGYO BANK, LTD.-KAOHSIUNG BRANCH—See The Dai-Ichi Kangyo Bank, Limited; *Int'l*, pg. 360
DAI-ICHI KANGYO BANK, LTD.-LOS ANGELES—See The Dai-Ichi Kangyo Bank, Limited; *Int'l*, pg. 359
DAI-ICHI KANGYO BANK, LTD.-NEW YORK—See The Dai-Ichi Kangyo Bank, Limited; *Int'l*, pg. 359
DAI-ICHI KANGYO BANK, LTD.-SAN FRANCISCO—See The Dai-Ichi Kangyo Bank, Limited; *Int'l*, pg. 359
DAI-ICHI KANGYO BANK, LTD.-XIAMEN—See The Dai-Ichi Kangyo Bank, Limited; *Int'l*, pg. 361
DAI-ICHI KANGYO BANK OF CALIFORNIA-LOS ANGELES—See The Dai-Ichi Kangyo Bank, Limited; *Int'l*, pg. 360
DAI-ICHI KANGYO BANK OF CALIFORNIA-SAN JOSE—See The Dai-Ichi Kangyo Bank, Limited; *Int'l*, pg. 360
DAI-ICHI KANGYO BANK OF CALIFORNIA-TORRANCE—See The Dai-Ichi Kangyo Bank, Limited; *Int'l*, pg. 360
P.T. DAI-ICHI KANGYO PANIN LEASING—See The Dai-Ichi Kangyo Bank, Limited; *Int'l*, pg. 362
DAI-ICHI KANGYO TRUST COMPANY OF NEW YORK—See The Dai-Ichi Kangyo Bank, Limited; *Int'l*, pg. 360
DAI-ICHI KIKAKU CO. LTD.—See Daehong Advertising Inc.; *Int'l*, pg. 357
DAI-ICHI LIFE INSURANCE AGENCY EUROPE LIMITED—See Dai-ichi Mutual Life Insurance Company; *Int'l*, pg. 362
DAI-ICHI LIFE INSURANCE AGENCY (U.S.A.) INC.—See Dai-ichi Mutual Life Insurance Company; *Int'l*, pg. 362
DAI-ICHI LIFE INSURANCE AGENCY (U.S.A.), INC.-LOS ANGELES—See Dai-ichi Mutual Life Insurance Company; *Int'l*, pg. 362
DAI-ICHI LIFE INTERNATIONAL (AUSTRALIA) LIMITED—See Dai-ichi Mutual Life Insurance Company; *Int'l*, pg. 362
DAI-ICHI LIFE INTERNATIONAL (CANADA), INC.—See Dai-ichi Mutual Life Insurance Company; *Int'l*, pg. 362
DAI-ICHI LIFE INTERNATIONAL (H.K.) LIMITED—See Dai-ichi Mutual Life Insurance Company; *Int'l*, pg. 362
DAI-ICHI LIFE INTERNATIONAL LIMITED-PARIS—See Dai-ichi Mutual Life Insurance Company; *Int'l*, pg. 362
DAI-ICHI LIFE INTERNATIONAL LIMITED-SINGAPORE—See Dai-ichi Mutual Life Insurance Company; *Int'l*, pg. 362
DAI-ICHI LIFE INTERNATIONAL LIMITED-TAIPEI—See Dai-ichi Mutual Life Insurance Company; *Int'l*, pg. 362
DAI-ICHI LIFE INTERNATIONAL (U.K.) LIMITED—See Dai-ichi Mutual Life Insurance Company; *Int'l*, pg. 362
DAI-ICHI LIFE INVESTMENT MANAGEMENT (U.S.A.), INC.—See Dai-ichi Mutual Life Insurance Company; *Int'l*, pg. 362
DAI-ICHI LIFE PROPERTY (LONDON) LIMITED—See Dai-ichi Mutual Life Insurance Company; *Int'l*, pg. 362
DAI-ICHI MUTUAL LIFE INSURANCE COMPANY; *Int'l*, pg. 362
THE DAI-ICHI MUTUAL LIFE INSURANCE (OI OFFICE)—See Dai-ichi Mutual Life Insurance Company; *Int'l*, pg. 362
DAI-ICHI SEIMEI AMERICA CORP.—See Dai-ichi Mutual Life Insurance Company; *Int'l*, pg. 362
DAI NIPPON BOOK BINDING CO., LTD.—See Dai Nippon Printing Co., Ltd.; *Int'l*, pg. 363
DAI NIPPON PRINTING CO. (AUSTRALIA) PTY. LTD.—See Dai Nippon Printing Co., Ltd.; *Int'l*, pg. 363

DAI NIPPON PRINTING CO. (HONG KONG) LTD.—See Dai Nippon Printing Co., Ltd.; *Int'l*, pg. 363
DAI NIPPON PRINTING CO., LTD.; *Int'l*, pg. 363
DAI NIPPON PRINTING CO. (SINGAPORE) PTE. LTD.—See Dai Nippon Printing Co., Ltd.; *Int'l*, pg. 363
DAI NIPPON PRINTING CO. (UK) LTD.—See Dai Nippon Printing Co., Ltd.; *Int'l*, pg. 363
DAI NIPPON PRINTING (EUROPA) GMBH—See Dai Nippon Printing Co., Ltd.; *Int'l*, pg. 363
P.T. DAI NIPPON PRINTING INDONESIA—See Dai Nippon Printing Co., Ltd.; *Int'l*, pg. 363
DAI NIPPON SHOJI CO., LTD.—See Dai Nippon Printing Co., Ltd.; *Int'l*, pg. 363
DAIASIA MOTOR CO., LTD.—See Daihatsu Motor Corporation, Ltd.; *Int'l*, pg. 365
DAICEL CHEMICAL INDUSTRIES LTD.—See Mitsui & Co., Ltd.; *Int'l*, pg. 877
DAICEL HULS LTD.—See Veba AG; *Int'l*, pg. 1455
DAICOLOR-POPE, INC.—See Dainichiseika Colour & Chemicals Mfg. Co., Ltd.; *Int'l*, pg. 369
DAIDO HERR ENGINEERING—See Salem Group, Inc.; *U.S. Private*, pg. 962
DAIDO HOXAN INC.; *Int'l*, pg. 363
DAIDO INTERNATIONAL INC.—See Daido Life Insurance Company; *Int'l*, pg. 364
DAIDO LIFE EUROPE LTD.—See Daido Life Insurance Company; *Int'l*, pg. 364
DAIDO LIFE INSURANCE COMPANY; *Int'l*, pg. 363
DAIDO STEEL CO., LTD.; *Int'l*, pg. 364
DAIDO STEEL CO., LTD.-TOKYO HEAD OFFICE—See Daido Steel Co., Ltd.; *Int'l*, pg. 364
DAIDONE ELECTRICAL INC., *U.S. Private*, pg. 307
THE DAIEI, INC.; *Int'l*, pg. 364
DAIG CORPORATION—See St. Jude Medical, Inc.; *U.S. Public*, pg. 1428
DAIGLE OIL CO.; *U.S. Private*, pg. 307
DAIHAN SWISS CHEMICAL CORPORATION—See Ciba Specialty Chemicals Holding Inc.; *Int'l*, pg. 292
DAIHATSU AMERICA, INC.—See Daihatsu Motor Corporation, Ltd.; *Int'l*, pg. 365
DAIHATSU AUSTRALIA PTY. LTD.—See Daihatsu Motor Corporation, Ltd.; *Int'l*, pg. 365
DAIHATSU AUTOHANDELSGES M.B.H.—See Daihatsu Motor Corporation, Ltd.; *Int'l*, pg. 365
DAIHATSU DEUTSCHLAND GMBH—See Daihatsu Motor Corporation, Ltd.; *Int'l*, pg. 365
DAIHATSU DIESEL (EUROPE) LTD.—See Daihatsu Diesel Mfg. Co., Ltd.; *Int'l*, pg. 364
DAIHATSU DIESEL MFG. CO., LTD.; *Int'l*, pg. 364
DAIHATSU DIESEL MFG. CO., LTD.—See Daihatsu Diesel Mfg. Co., Ltd.; *Int'l*, pg. 364
DAIHATSU DIESEL (SINGAPORE) PTE. LTD.—See Daihatsu Diesel Mfg. Co., Ltd.; *Int'l*, pg. 364
DAIHATSU DIESEL (U.S.A.), INC.—See Daihatsu Diesel Mfg. Co., Ltd.; *Int'l*, pg. 364
DAIHATSU DIESEL (U.S.A.), INC.—See Nissho Iwai Corporation; *Int'l*, pg. 947
DAIHATSU HOLLAND B.V.—See Daihatsu Motor Corporation, Ltd.; *Int'l*, pg. 365
DAIHATSU MALAYSIA SDN. BND.—See Daihatsu Motor Corporation, Ltd.; *Int'l*, pg. 365
DAIHATSU MOTOR CO., LTD.—See Daihatsu Motor Corporation, Ltd.; *Int'l*, pg. 365
DAIHATSU MOTOR CORPORATION, LTD.; *Int'l*, pg. 364
DAIHATSU MOTOR (H.K.) LTD.—See Daihatsu Motor Corporation, Ltd.; *Int'l*, pg. 365
DAIHATSU NEW ZEALAND LTD.—See Daihatsu Motor Corporation, Ltd.; *Int'l*, pg. 365
DAIHATSU-PHRANAKORN MOTOR CO., LTD.—See Daihatsu Motor Corporation, Ltd.; *Int'l*, pg. 365
DAIICHI FINE CHEMICALS—See Mitsui & Co., Ltd.; *Int'l*, pg. 879
DAIICHI FORGING CO., LTD.—See Fuji Heavy Industries, Ltd.; *Int'l*, pg. 522
DAI-ICHI KANGYO BANK, LTD.-KUALA LUMPUR—See The Dai-Ichi Kangyo Bank, Limited; *Int'l*, pg. 360
DAI-ICHI KANGYO BANK, LTD.-LABUAN—See The Dai-Ichi Kangyo Bank, Limited; *Int'l*, pg. 360
DAI-ICHI LIFE BAHAMA LIMITED—See Dai-ichi Mutual Life Insurance Company; *Int'l*, pg. 362
DAI-ICHI LIFE LUXEMBOURG S.A.—See Dai-ichi Mutual Life Insurance Company; *Int'l*, pg. 363
DAIKIN AIRCONDITIONING (HONG KONG) LTD.—See Daikin Industries, Ltd.; *Int'l*, pg. 365
DAIKIN AMERICA, INC.—See Daikin Industries, Ltd.; *Int'l*, pg. 365
DAIKIN AUSTRALIA PTY. LTD.—See Daikin Industries, Ltd.; *Int'l*, pg. 365
DAIKIN EUROPE N.V.—See Daikin Industries, Ltd.; *Int'l*, pg. 365
DAIKIN INDUSTRIES, LTD.; *Int'l*, pg. 365
DAIKIN INDUSTRIES LTD. -TOKYO OFFICE—See Daikin Industries, Ltd.; *Int'l*, pg. 365
DAIKIN INDUSTRIES (THAILAND) LTD.—See Daikin Industries, Ltd.; *Int'l*, pg. 365
DAIKIN U.S. CORPORATION—See Daikin Industries, Ltd.; *Int'l*, pg. 365
DAIKO ADVERTISING, INC.; *Int'l*, pg. 365
DAIKO AGENCY INC.—See Daiko Advertising, Inc.; *Int'l*, pg. 366
DAIKO DENSHI TSUSHIN, LTD.—See Daiwa Securities Co. Ltd.; *Int'l*, pg. 374
DAIKO: HIMEJI—See Daiko Advertising, Inc.; *Int'l*, pg. 365
DAIKO: HIROSHIMA BUSINESS DIVISION—See Daiko Advertising, Inc.; *Int'l*, pg. 365
DAIKO: HOKKAIDO—See Daiko Advertising, Inc.; *Int'l*, pg. 365
DAIKO: HOKURIN INC.—See Daiko Advertising, Inc.; *Int'l*, pg. 365
DAIKO: HOKURIKU—See Daiko Advertising, Inc.; *Int'l*, pg. 366
DAIKO HWG ADVERTISING CORP.—See Daiko Advertising, Inc.; *Int'l*, pg. 366

DAIKO INTELLECT INC.—See Daiko Advertising, Inc.; *Int'l*, pg. 366
DAIKO: KOCHI—See Daiko Advertising, Inc.; *Int'l*, pg. 365
DAIKO: MATSUYAMA—See Daiko Advertising, Inc.; *Int'l*, pg. 365
DAIKO MEDIAX INC.—See Daiko Advertising, Inc.; *Int'l*, pg. 366
DAIKO: MINAMI-KYUSHU—See Daiko Advertising, Inc.; *Int'l*, pg. 365
DAIKO: MIO—See Daiko Advertising, Inc.; *Int'l*, pg. 365
DAIKO: NARA—See Daiko Advertising, Inc.; *Int'l*, pg. 365
DAIKO: NIIGATA—See Daiko Advertising, Inc.; *Int'l*, pg. 366
DAIKO: OKAYAMA—See Daiko Advertising, Inc.; *Int'l*, pg. 366
DAIKO P.C.A. INC.—See Daiko Advertising, Inc.; *Int'l*, pg. 366
DAIKO SEIHAN INC.—See Daiko Advertising, Inc.; *Int'l*, pg. 366
DAIKO: SENDAI—See Daiko Advertising, Inc.; *Int'l*, pg. 366
DAIKO: TAKAMATSU—See Daiko Advertising, Inc.; *Int'l*, pg. 366
DAIKO: TOKUSHIMA—See Daiko Advertising, Inc.; *Int'l*, pg. 366
DAIKO: WAKAYAMA—See Daiko Advertising, Inc.; *Int'l*, pg. 366
DAIKUMA CO., LTD.—See Ito-Yokado Co., Ltd.; *Int'l*, pg. 693
DAIKYO SEIKO CO., LTD.—See The West Company, Incorporated; *U.S. Public*, pg. 1756
DAILEY & ASSOCIATES—See The Interpublic Group of Companies, Inc.; *U.S. Public*, pg. 909
THE DAILY & SUNDAY OKLAHOMAN—See Oklahoma Publishing Company; *U.S. Private*, pg. 813
THE DAILY BREEZE—See The Copley Press; *U.S. Private*, pg. 275
THE DAILY CHRONICLE—See Pulitzer Publishing Company; *U.S. Public*, pg. 1343
THE DAILY COMET—See The New York Times Company; *U.S. Public*, pg. 1175
DAILY COURIER-NEWS—See The Copley Press, Inc.; *U.S. Private*, pg. 275
DAILY EXPRESS, INC.; *U.S. Private*, pg. 307
THE DAILY HERALD—See Pulitzer Publishing Company; *U.S. Public*, pg. 1343
DAILY HERALD CO.—See The Washington Post Company; *U.S. Public*, pg. 1743
THE DAILY JOURNAL—See Pulitzer Publishing Company; *U.S. Public*, pg. 1343
THE DAILY JOURNAL (NJ)—See Gannett Company, Inc.; *U.S. Public*, pg. 700
THE DAILY LOCAL NEWS—See Journal Register Company; *U.S. Public*, pg. 934
DAILY MAIL & GENERAL TRUST PLC; *Int'l*, pg. 366
THE DAILY NEWS—See Hollinger Inc.; *Int'l*, pg. 631
DAILY NEWS—See Hollinger Inc.; *Int'l*, pg. 632
THE DAILY NEWS—See Newfoundland Capital Corporation Limited; *Int'l*, pg. 924
THE DAILY NEWS—See Pulitzer Publishing Company; *U.S. Public*, pg. 1343
THE DAILY NEWS LEADER—See Gannett Company, Inc.; *U.S. Public*, pg. 699
DAILY NEWS RECORD—See The Walt Disney Company; *U.S. Public*, pg. 513
THE DAILY PRESS—See Hollinger Inc.; *Int'l*, pg. 631
THE DAILY PRESS, INCORPORATED—See Tribune Company; *U.S. Public*, pg. 1635
DAILY PRESS LEADER—See Pulitzer Publishing Company; *U.S. Public*, pg. 1343
DAILY RACING FORM, INC.—See Primedia Inc.; *U.S. Public*, pg. 1327
THE DAILY SENTINEL—See Gannett Company, Inc.; *U.S. Public*, pg. 699
THE DAILY SOUTHTOWN—See Hollinger Inc.; *Int'l*, pg. 632
THE DAILY TIDINGS—See Lee Enterprises, Incorporated; *U.S. Public*, pg. 983
THE DAILY WORLD—See The New York Times Company; *U.S. Public*, pg. 1175
DAILYCER BV—See Koninklijke BolsWessanen nv; *Int'l*, pg. 751
DAIMLER-AEROSPACE AG MILITARY AIRCRAFT—See Daimler-Benz Aktiengesellschaft; *Int'l*, pg. 367
DAIMLER-BENZ AEROSPACE AG—See Daimler-Benz Aktiengesellschaft; *Int'l*, pg. 367
DAIMLER-BENZ AEROSPACE AG DYNAMICS—See Daimler-Benz Aktiengesellschaft; *Int'l*, pg. 367
DAIMLER-BENZ AEROSPACE AG SENSOR—See Daimler-Benz Aktiengesellschaft; *Int'l*, pg. 367
DAIMLER-BENZ AEROSPACE AIRBUS—See Daimler-Benz Aktiengesellschaft; *Int'l*, pg. 367
DAIMLER-BENZ AKTIENGESELLSCHAFT; *Int'l*, pg. 366
DAIMLER-BENZ CAPITAL INC.—See Daimler-Benz Aktiengesellschaft; *Int'l*, pg. 368
DAIMLER-BENZ INTERSERVICES (DEBIS) AG—See Daimler-Benz Aktiengesellschaft; *Int'l*, pg. 367
DAIMLER-BENZ LUFT-UND RAUMFAHRT HOLDING AG—See Daimler-Benz Aktiengesellschaft; *Int'l*, pg. 367
DAIMLER-BENZ NORTH AMERICA CORPORATION—See Daimler-Benz Aktiengesellschaft; *Int'l*, pg. 368
DAIN RAUSCHER CORPORATION; *U.S. Public*, pg. 476
DAIN RAUSCHER INCORPORATED—See Dain Rauscher Corporation; *U.S. Public*, pg. 476
DAINICHISEIKA COLOUR & CHEMICALS MFG. CO., LTD.; *Int'l*, pg. 369
DAINIPPON INK & CHEMICALS (HK) LTD.—See Dainippon Ink & Chemicals, Inc.; *Int'l*, pg. 372
DAINIPPON INK & CHEMICALS, INC.; *Int'l*, pg. 369
DAINIPPON INK & CHEMICALS, INC.—See Dainippon Ink & Chemicals, Inc.; *Int'l*, pg. 372
DAINIPPON INK & CHEMICALS SINGAPORE PTE., LTD.—See Dainippon Ink & Chemicals, Inc.; *Int'l*, pg. 372
DAINIPPON INK & CHEMICALS (THAILAND) CO., LTD.—See Dainippon Ink & Chemicals, Inc.; *Int'l*, pg. 372
DAIO PAPER CORPORATION; *Int'l*, pg. 372

DAIRY DELL, INC.—See The Penn Traffic Company; *U.S. Public*, pg. 1271
DAIRY EXPORT CO., INC.—See Darigold, Inc.; *U.S. Private*, pg. 311
THE DAIRY FARM COMPANY, LIMITED—See Jardine Matheson Holdings Limited; *Int'l*, pg. 703
DAIRY FARM INTERNATIONAL FINANCE LIMITED—See Jardine Matheson Holdings Limited; *Int'l*, pg. 703
DAIRY FARM INTERNATIONAL HOLDINGS LIMITED—See Jardine Matheson Holdings Limited; *Int'l*, pg. 703
DAIRY FARM MANAGEMENT LIMITED—See Jardine Matheson Holdings Limited; *Int'l*, pg. 703
DAIRY FARM MANAGEMENT SERVICES LIMITED—See Jardine Matheson Holdings Limited; *Int'l*, pg. 703
DAIRY FARMERS OF AMERICA, INC.; *U.S. Private*, pg. 307
DAIRY FRESH CORP.; *U.S. Private*, pg. 307
DAIRY FRESH ICE CREAM—See Dairy Fresh Corp.; *U.S. Private*, pg. 307
DAIRY FRESH, INC.—See Suiza Foods Corporation; *U.S. Public*, pg. 1527
DAIRY INDUSTRIES (JAMAICA) LTD.—See New Zealand Dairy Board; *Int'l*, pg. 923
DAIRY INGREDIENTS GROUP—See Cultor Ltd.; *Int'l*, pg. 349
DAIRY MART CONVENIENCE STORES, INC.; *U.S. Public*, pg. 476
DAIRY MART EAST, INC.—See Dairy Mart Convenience Stores, Inc.; *U.S. Public*, pg. 476
DAIRY MART FARMS, INC.—See Dairy Mart Convenience Stores, Inc.; *U.S. Public*, pg. 476
DAIRY MART, INC.—See Dairy Mart Convenience Stores, Inc.; *U.S. Public*, pg. 476
DAIRY MART SOUTHEAST—See Dairy Mart Convenience Stores, Inc.; *U.S. Public*, pg. 476
DAIRY PROJECTS BV—See Koninklijke BolsWessanen nv; *Int'l*, pg. 751
DAIRY QUEEN CANADA, INC.—See Berkshire Hathaway Inc.; *U.S. Public*, pg. 220
DAIRY QUEEN CORPORATE STORE—See Berkshire Hathaway Inc.; *U.S. Public*, pg. 220
DAIRY QUEEN OF GEORGIA, INC.—See Berkshire Hathaway Inc.; *U.S. Public*, pg. 220
DAIRY SUPPLIES HEREFORD LTD.—See Tetra Laval Group; *Int'l*, pg. 1380
DAIRY VALE CO-OP. LTD.; *Int'l*, pg. 372
DAIRYLAND COUNTY MUTUAL INSURANCE CO.—See Sentry Insurance, A Mutual Company; *U.S. Private*, pg. 985
DAIRYLAND GREYHOUND PARK, INC.; *U.S. Private*, pg. 307
DAIRYLAND INSURANCE CO.—See Sentry Insurance, A Mutual Company; *U.S. Private*, pg. 985
DAIRYLAND MARKETING SERVICES, INC.—See Dairyland Greyhound Park, Inc.; *U.S. Private*, pg. 307
DAIRYLAND POWER COOPERATIVE; *U.S. Private*, pg. 307
DAIRYLEA COOPERATIVE INC.; *U.S. Private*, pg. 307
THE DAISHI ASSOCIATED FINANCE CO. LTD.—See The Daishi Bank, Ltd.; *Int'l*, pg. 372
THE DAISHI BANK, LTD.; *Int'l*, pg. 372
THE DAISHI CASH BUSINESS CO. LTD.—See The Daishi Bank, Ltd.; *Int'l*, pg. 372
THE DAISHI COMPUTER SERVICE CO. LTD.—See The Daishi Bank, Ltd.; *Int'l*, pg. 372
THE DAISHI CREDIT SERVICE CO. LTD.—See The Daishi Bank, Ltd.; *Int'l*, pg. 372
THE DAISHI DC CARD CO. LTD.—See The Daishi Bank, Ltd.; *Int'l*, pg. 372
THE DAISHI FACTORS LTD.—See The Daishi Bank, Ltd.; *Int'l*, pg. 372
THE DAISHI GUARANTY CO. LTD.—See The Daishi Bank, Ltd.; *Int'l*, pg. 372
THE DAISHI INFORMATION SYSTEMS SERVICE CO. LTD.—See The Daishi Bank, Ltd.; *Int'l*, pg. 372
THE DAISHI INVESTMENT MANAGEMENT CO. LTD.—See The Daishi Bank, Ltd.; *Int'l*, pg. 373
THE DAISHI LEASE CO. LTD.—See The Daishi Bank, Ltd.; *Int'l*, pg. 373
THE DAISHI STAFF SERVICE CO. LTD.—See The Daishi Bank, Ltd.; *Int'l*, pg. 372
DAISHOWA PAPER MFG. CO., LTD.; *Int'l*, pg. 373
DAISY DE VENEZUELA C.A.—See Fruit of the Loom, Inc.; *U.S. Public*, pg. 686
DAISY MANUFACTURING COMPANY, INC.; *U.S. Private*, pg. 308
DAISYTEK AUSTRALIA PTY. LTD.—See Daisytek International Corporation; *U.S. Public*, pg. 477
DAISYTEK (CANADA) INC.—See Daisytek International Corporation; *U.S. Public*, pg. 477
DAISYTEK DE MEXICO S.A. DE C.V.—See Daisytek International Corporation; *U.S. Public*, pg. 477
DAISYTEK INCORPORATED—See Daisytek International Corporation; *U.S. Public*, pg. 477
DAISYTEK INTERNATIONAL CORPORATION; *U.S. Public*, pg. 477
DAISYTEK LATIN AMERICA—See Daisytek International Corporation; *U.S. Public*, pg. 477
DAIWA ASSET MANAGEMENT (AMERICA) LTD.—See Daiwa Securities Co. Ltd.; *Int'l*, pg. 374
DAIWA ASSET MANAGEMENT CO. LTD.—See Daiwa Securities Co. Ltd.; *Int'l*, pg. 374
DAIWA ASSET MANAGEMENT (H.K.) LTD.—See Daiwa Securities Co. Ltd.; *Int'l*, pg. 374
DAIWA ASSET MANAGEMENT (SINGAPORE) LTD.—See Daiwa Securities Co. Ltd.; *Int'l*, pg. 374
DAIWA ASSET MANAGEMENTS (EUROPE) LTD.—See Daiwa Securities Co. Ltd.; *Int'l*, pg. 374
DAIWA BANK-BANGKOK—See The Daiwa Bank Limited; *Int'l*, pg. 374
DAIWA BANK-BEIJING—See The Daiwa Bank Limited; *Int'l*, pg. 373
DAIWA BANK CANADA—See The Daiwa Bank Limited; *Int'l*, pg. 373

DAIWA BANK-CAYMAN BRANCH—See The Daiwa Bank Limited; *Int'l*, pg. 373
DAIWA BANK (DEUTSCHLAND) GMBH—See The Daiwa Bank Limited; *Int'l*, pg. 373
DAIWA BANK-GUANGZHOU—See The Daiwa Bank Limited; *Int'l*, pg. 373
DAIWA BANK-HO CHI MINH CITY—See The Daiwa Bank Limited; *Int'l*, pg. 373
DAIWA BANK-HONG KONG—See The Daiwa Bank Limited; *Int'l*, pg. 373
DAIWA BANK INTERNATIONAL BUSINESS DIVISION-HEAD OFFICE—See The Daiwa Bank Limited; *Int'l*, pg. 373
DAIWA BANK-INTERNATIONAL DIVISION—See The Daiwa Bank Limited; *Int'l*, pg. 373
DAIWA BANK-INTERNATIONAL TREASURY DIVISION—See The Daiwa Bank Limited; *Int'l*, pg. 373
DAIWA BANK-JAKARTA—See The Daiwa Bank Limited; *Int'l*, pg. 373
DAIWA BANK-KUALA LUMPUR—See The Daiwa Bank Limited; *Int'l*, pg. 373
THE DAIWA BANK LIMITED; *Int'l*, pg. 373
DAIWA BANK-LONDON—See The Daiwa Bank Limited; *Int'l*, pg. 373
DAIWA BANK-MADRID—See The Daiwa Bank Limited; *Int'l*, pg. 373
DAIWA BANK-MEXICO—See The Daiwa Bank Limited; *Int'l*, pg. 374
DAIWA BANK-PARIS—See The Daiwa Bank Limited; *Int'l*, pg. 374
DAIWA BANK-SAO PAULO—See The Daiwa Bank Limited; *Int'l*, pg. 373
DAIWA BANK (SCHWEIZ) AG—See The Daiwa Bank Limited; *Int'l*, pg. 373
DAIWA BANK-SEOUL—See The Daiwa Bank Limited; *Int'l*, pg. 373
DAIWA BANK-SHANGHAI—See The Daiwa Bank Limited; *Int'l*, pg. 373
DAIWA BANK-SINGAPORE—See The Daiwa Bank Limited; *Int'l*, pg. 374
DAIWA BANK-SYDNEY—See The Daiwa Bank Limited; *Int'l*, pg. 374
DAIWA BANK-UNITED CENTRE BRANCH—See The Daiwa Bank Limited; *Int'l*, pg. 374
DAIWA BK FINANCIAL FUTURES SINGAPORE PTE. LTD.—See The Daiwa Bank Limited; *Int'l*, pg. 373
THE DAIWA BUILDING CO., LTD.—See Daiwa Securities Co. Ltd.; *Int'l*, pg. 374
DAIWA BUSINESS TOURIST CO. LTD.—See Daiwa Securities Co. Ltd.; *Int'l*, pg. 374
DAIWA DO BRASIL TEXTIL LTDA.—See Nissho Iwai Corporation; *Int'l*, pg. 947
DAIWA EUROPE BANK PLC—See Daiwa Securities Co. Ltd.; *Int'l*, pg. 375
DAIWA EUROPE BANK PLC-DUBLIN BRANCH—See Daiwa Securities Co. Ltd.; *Int'l*, pg. 375
DAIWA EUROPE (DEUTSCHLAND) GMBH—See Daiwa Securities Co. Ltd.; *Int'l*, pg. 375
DAIWA EUROPE (FRANCE) S.A.—See Daiwa Securities Co. Ltd.; *Int'l*, pg. 375
DAIWA EUROPE (GILTS) LIMITED—See Daiwa Securities Co. Ltd.; *Int'l*, pg. 375
DAIWA EUROPE (ITALIA) SIM P.A.—See Daiwa Securities Co. Ltd.; *Int'l*, pg. 375
DAIWA EUROPE LIMITED—See Daiwa Securities Co. Ltd.; *Int'l*, pg. 375
DAIWA EUROPE LIMITED - AMSTERDAM—See Daiwa Securities Co. Ltd.; *Int'l*, pg. 375
DAIWA EUROPE (SPAIN) SOCIEDAD DE VALORES S.A.—See Daiwa Securities Co. Ltd.; *Int'l*, pg. 375
DAIWA FINANCE AUSTRALIA LIMITED—See The Daiwa Bank Limited; *Int'l*, pg. 373
DAIWA FINANCE CO. LTD.—See Daiwa Securities Co. Ltd.; *Int'l*, pg. 374
DAIWA FINANCE DIFFUSION S.A.—See Daiwa Securities Co. Ltd.; *Int'l*, pg. 375
DAIWA FRANCE GESTION S.A.—See Daiwa Securities Co. Ltd.; *Int'l*, pg. 375
DAIWA FUTURES (ASIA) LTD—See Daiwa Securities Co. Ltd.; *Int'l*, pg. 375
DAIWA FUTURES PTE LTD—See Daiwa Securities Co. Ltd.; *Int'l*, pg. 375
DAIWA HOUSE (AUSTRALIA) PTY. LTD.—See Daiwa House Industry Co., Ltd.; *Int'l*, pg. 374
DAIWA HOUSE CORPORATION—See Daiwa House Industry Co., Ltd.; *Int'l*, pg. 374
DAIWA HOUSE INDUSTRY CO., LTD.; *Int'l*, pg. 374
DAIWA HOUSE INDUSTRY CO., LTD.-NAGOYA OFFICE—See Daiwa House Industry Co., Ltd.; *Int'l*, pg. 374
DAIWA HOUSE INDUSTRY CO., LTD.-TOKYO HEAD OFFICE—See Daiwa House Industry Co., Ltd.; *Int'l*, pg. 374
P.T. DAIWA INDONESIA SECURITIES—See Daiwa Securities Co. Ltd.; *Int'l*, pg. 375
DAIWA INSTITUTE OF RESEARCH AMERICA INC.—See Daiwa Securities Co. Ltd.; *Int'l*, pg. 375
DAIWA INSTITUTE OF RESEARCH EUROPE LTD.—See Daiwa Securities Co. Ltd.; *Int'l*, pg. 375
DAIWA INSTITUTE OF RESEARCH HONG KONG LTD.—See Daiwa Securities Co. Ltd.; *Int'l*, pg. 374
DAIWA INSTITUTE OF RESEARCH LTD.—See Daiwa Securities Co. Ltd.; *Int'l*, pg. 374
DAIWA INSTITUTE OF RESEARCH SINGAPORE PTE LTD—See Daiwa Securities Co. Ltd.; *Int'l*, pg. 375
DAIWA INTERNATIONAL CAPITAL MANAGEMENT CO., LTD.—See Daiwa Securities Co. Ltd.; *Int'l*, pg. 375
DAIWA INTERNATIONAL CAPITAL MANAGEMENT CORP.—See Daiwa Securities Co. Ltd.; *Int'l*, pg. 375
DAIWA INTERNATIONAL CAPITAL MANAGEMENT (H.K.) LIMITED—See Daiwa Securities Co. Ltd.; *Int'l*, pg. 375
DAIWA INTERNATIONAL CAPITAL MANAGEMENT (SINGAPORE) LIMITED—See Daiwa Securities Co. Ltd.; *Int'l*, pg. 375

DAIWA INTERNATIONAL CAPITAL MANAGEMENT (U.K.) LIMIED—See Daiwa Securities Co.; *Int'l*, pg. 375
DAIWA INTERNATIONAL TRUST BANK LIMITED—See Daiwa Securities Co. Ltd.; *Int'l*, pg. 375
P.T. DAIWA LIPPO LEASING CORPORATION—See The Daiwa Bank Limited; *Int'l*, pg. 374
DAIWA MERCHANT BANK (SINGAPORE) LIMITED—See The Daiwa Bank Limited; *Int'l*, pg. 373
DAIWA MIDDLE EAST E.C.—See Daiwa Securities Co. Ltd.; *Int'l*, pg. 375
DAIWA-MKB (HUNGARY) INVESTMENT AND SECURITIES CO. LTD.—See Daiwa Securities Co. Ltd.; *Int'l*, pg. 376
DAIWA OVERSEAS FINANCE LTD.—See The Daiwa Bank Limited; *Int'l*, pg. 373
P.T. DAIWA PERDANIA BANK—See The Daiwa Bank Limited; *Int'l*, pg. 374
DAIWA PRECIOUS METALS CO., LTD.—See Daiwa Securities Co. Ltd.; *Int'l*, pg. 375
THE DAIWA REAL ESTATE CO., LTD.—See Daiwa Securities Co. Ltd.; *Int'l*, pg. 375
DAIWA SANKO CO., LTD.—See Daiwa Securities Co. Ltd.; *Int'l*, pg. 375
DAIWA SECURITIES ADVISER SDN. BHD.—See Daiwa Securities Co. Ltd.; *Int'l*, pg. 375
DAIWA SECURITIES (ASIA) LTD—See Daiwa Securities Co. Ltd.; *Int'l*, pg. 375
DAIWA SECURITIES BUSINESS CENTER CO. LTD.—See Daiwa Securities Co. Ltd.; *Int'l*, pg. 375
DAIWA SECURITIES CO. LTD.—See'l; *Int'l*, pg. 374
DAIWA SECURITIES (SEOUL)—See Daiwa Securities Co. Ltd.; *Int'l*, pg. 376
DAIWA SECURITIES (SINGAPORE) PTE LTD—See Daiwa Securities Co. Ltd.; *Int'l*, pg. 376
DAIWA SECURITIES (TAIPEI)—See Daiwa Securities Co. Ltd.; *Int'l*, pg. 376
DAIWA SECURITIES TRUST COMPANY—See Daiwa Securities Co. Ltd.; *Int'l*, pg. 376
DAIWA SINGAPORE LIMITED—See Daiwa Securities Co. Ltd.; *Int'l*, pg. 376
DAIWA SOFTWARE RESEARCH CO., LTD.—See Daiwa Securities Co. Ltd.; *Int'l*, pg. 375
DAKCO DISTRIBUTORS, INC.; *U.S. Private*, pg. 308
DAKOTA CASE INC.—See Krofam Inc.; *U.S. Private*, pg. 636
DAKOTA COAL COMPANY—See Basin Electric Power Cooperative; *U.S. Private*, pg. 121
DAKOTA DRUG, INC.—See Dakco Distributors, Inc.; *U.S. Private*, pg. 308
DAKOTA ELECTRIC ASSOCIATION; *U.S. Private*, pg. 308
DAKOTA ENERGY ALTERNATIVES, INC.—See Dakota Electric Association; *U.S. Private*, pg. 308
DAKOTA FARMS CHEESE, INC.—See Land O'Lakes, Inc.; *U.S. Private*, pg. 646
DAKOTA GASIFICATION CO.—See Basin Electric Power Cooperative; *U.S. Private*, pg. 121
DAKOTA MINING CORPORATION; *U.S. Public*, pg. 477
DAKOTA PORK INDUSTRIES—See American Foods Group, Inc.; *U.S. Private*, pg. 54
DAKOTA SPECIALTY INSURANCE COMPANY—See Chartwell Re Corporation; *U.S. Public*, pg. 337
DAKOTAH, INC.; *U.S. Public*, pg. 477
DAKTRONICS, INC.; *U.S. Public*, pg. 478
DAL KEYSTONE—See Dal-Tile International; *U.S. Private*, pg. 308
DAL-TILE CORP.—See Dal-Tile International; *U.S. Private*, pg. 308
DAL-TILE INTERNATIONAL; *U.S. Private*, pg. 308
DALA SANERING AB—See Incentive AB; *Int'l*, pg. 669
DALE CARNEGIE TRAINING; *U.S. Private*, pg. 308
DALE ELECTRONICS, EL PASO DIV.—See Vishay Intertechnology, Inc.; *U.S. Public*, pg. 1722
DALE ELECTRONICS GMBH—See Vishay Intertechnology, Inc.; *U.S. Public*, pg. 1722
DALE ELECTRONICS, INC.—See Vishay Intertechnology, Inc.; *U.S. Public*, pg. 1722
DALE ELECTRONICS RESISTOR NETWORK—See Vishay Intertechnology, Inc.; *U.S. Public*, pg. 1722
DALE ELECTRONICS, TECHRO—See Vishay Intertechnology, Inc.; *U.S. Public*, pg. 1722
DALE ELECTRONICS, TEMPE DIV.—See Vishay Intertechnology, Inc.; *U.S. Public*, pg. 1722
DALE ELECTRONICS, YANKTON DIVISION—See Vishay Intertechnology, Inc.; *U.S. Public*, pg. 1722
DALE FARM DAIRIES LTD.—See Northern Foods plc; *Int'l*, pg. 968
DALE FOODS—See DG Foods, LLC; *U.S. Private*, pg. 301
DALE INDUSTRIES INC.; *U.S. Private*, pg. 308
DALE POWER SYSTEMS PLC—See TT Group PLC; *Int'l*, pg. 1344
DALE WOOD MANUFACTURING—See Kimball International, Inc.; *U.S. Public*, pg. 957
DALEVILLE LEARNING CENTER—See Berkshire Hathaway Inc.; *U.S. Public*, pg. 218
DALFORT AEROSPACE—See Singapore Technologies Pte. Ltd.; *Int'l*, pg. 1253
DALGETY AGRICULTURE, LIMITED—See Dalgety Plc; *Int'l*, pg. 376
DALGETY FOOD INGREDIENTS LTD.—See Dalgety Plc; *Int'l*, pg. 376
DALGETY PLC; *Int'l*, pg. 376
DALGETY SPILLERS FOODS LTD.—See Dalgety Plc; *Int'l*, pg. 376
DALIAN CIVIL AVIATION HOTEL CO., LTD.—See Daiwa House Industry Co.; *Int'l*, pg. 374
DALIAN DALI STEEL WORKS CO., LTD.—See Hitachi Zosen Corporation; *Int'l*, pg. 629
DALIAN ERICSSON COMMUNICATION COMPANY LTD.—See Telefonaktiebolaget LM Ericsson; *Int'l*, pg. 1365
DALIAN FUJI ELECTRIC MOTOR CO., LTD.—See Fuji Electric Co., Ltd.; *Int'l*, pg. 522
DALIAN MORGAN REFRACTORY MATERIALS LIMITED—See Morgan Crucible Co. Plc; *Int'l*, pg. 894
DALIAN NISSAN GUANGMING GAS CO., LTD.—See Nippon Sanso Corporation; *Int'l*, pg. 939

DALKEITH KNITWEAR LIMITED—See Coats Viyella plc; *Int'l*, pg. 299
DALLA VERA—See Bouygues; *Int'l*, pg. 206
DALLAS AEROSPACE, INC.—See Banner Aerospace, Inc.; *U.S. Public*, pg. 187
DALLAS AIRLINE LEARNING CENTER—See Berkshire Hathaway Inc.; *U.S. Public*, pg. 218
DALLAS AUTO AUCTION INC.—See Tyco International Ltd.; *U.S. Public*, pg. 1648
DALLAS FLOWER MARKET, INC.—See Denver Wholesale Florists Company; *U.S. Private*, pg. 326
DALLAS-FT. WORTH SUBURBAN NEWSPAPERS, INC.—See A.H. Belo Corporation; *U.S. Public*, pg. 209
DALLAS GLOBAL TRAVEL—See Dallas Gold & Silver Exchange, Inc.; *U.S. Public*, pg. 478
DALLAS GOLD & SILVER EXCHANGE, INC.; *U.S. Public*, pg. 478
THE DALLAS MORNING NEWS, INC.—See A.H. Belo Corporation; *U.S. Public*, pg. 209
DALLAS MOVING SYSTEM INC.—See Wheaton Van Lines, Inc.; *U.S. Private*, pg. 1171
DALLAS PETERBILT, INC.; *U.S. Private*, pg. 309
DALLAS PRINTING—See Champion Industries; *U.S. Public*, pg. 333
DALLAS SEMICONDUCTOR CORPORATION; *U.S. Public*, pg. 478
DALLAS STARS; *U.S. Private*, pg. 309
DALLAS TERMINAL RAILWAY AND UNION DEPOT CO.—See Union Pacific Corporation; *U.S. Public*, pg. 1668
DALTEX GENERAL AGENCY—See Cullen/Frost Bankers, Inc.; *U.S. Public*, pg. 467
DALTON & CO. (SYNTHETIC PRODUCTS) LTD.—See Fuchs Petrolub AG Oel + Chemie; *Int'l*, pg. 519
DALTON HOLDINGS LTD.—See Bristol-Myers Squibb Company; *U.S. Public*, pg. 256
DALTRADING LIMITED—See Commercial Metals Company; *U.S. Public*, pg. 414
DALWORTH CONCRETE PRODUCTS, INC.—See For Better Living, Inc.; *U.S. Private*, pg. 417
LEO A. DALY COMPANY; *U.S. Private*, pg. 309
M.J. DALY & SONS, INC.; *U.S. Private*, pg. 309
DAMARK FINANCIAL SERVICES, INC.—See Damark International, Inc.; *U.S. Public*, pg. 478
DAMARK INTERNATIONAL, INC.; *U.S. Public*, pg. 478
DAMART—See Damart S.A.; *Int'l*, pg. 376
DAMART S.A.; *Int'l*, pg. 376
DAMART SERVIPOSTE S.A.—See Damart S.A.; *Int'l*, pg. 376
DAMASCUS BISHOP TUBE CO.—See Marcegaglia SpA; *Int'l*, pg. 842
DAMCO INTERMODAL SYSTEMS (TAIWAN) INC.—See Royal Nedlloyd Group N.V.; *Int'l*, pg. 1144
DAMCO MARITIME (BELGIUM) N.V.—See Royal Nedlloyd Group N.V.; *Int'l*, pg. 1144
DAMCO MARITIME B.V.—See Royal Nedlloyd Group N.V.; *Int'l*, pg. 1144
DAMCO MARITIME FRANCE S.A.R.L.—See Royal Nedlloyd Group N.V.; *Int'l*, pg. 1144
DAMCO MARITIME GMBH—See Royal Nedlloyd Group N.V.; *Int'l*, pg. 1144
DAMCO MARITIME (HK) LTD.—See Royal Nedlloyd Group N.V.; *Int'l*, pg. 1144
DAMCO MARITIME INTERNATIONAL B.V.—See Royal Nedlloyd Group N.V.; *Int'l*, pg. 1144
DAMCO MARITIME PTE. LTD.—See Royal Nedlloyd Group N.V.; *Int'l*, pg. 1144
DAMES & MOORE INC.—See Hochtief AG; *Int'l*, pg. 624
DAMIXA ARMATUREN, GMBH—See Masco Corporation; *U.S. Public*, pg. 1054
DAMIXA LTD.—See Masco Corporation; *U.S. Public*, pg. 1055
DAMIXA S.A.—See Masco Corporation; *U.S. Public*, pg. 1054
DAMM AGENTUR FUR MARKETING UND WERBUNG—See Warwick Baker O'Neill; *U.S. Private*, pg. 1152
DAMPA A/S—See FLS Industries A/S; *Int'l*, pg. 475
DAMPERS IBERICA, S.A.—See Cummins Engine Company, Inc.; *U.S. Public*, pg. 469
DAMPIER SALT LTD.—See Nissho Iwai Corporation; *Int'l*, pg. 947
DAMSMITH CORP.; *U.S. Private*, pg. 309
DAN-CO BAKERY, INC.—See Flowers Industries, Inc.; *U.S. Public*, pg. 657
DAN MERCHANT LIMITED—See The East Asiatic Company Ltd. A/S; *Int'l*, pg. 431
DAN RIVER COTTON CO., INC.—See Dan River Inc.; *U.S. Public*, pg. 479
DAN RIVER DANVILLE MFG. DIV.—See Dan River Inc.; *U.S. Public*, pg. 479
DAN RIVER, INC.; *U.S. Public*, pg. 478
DAN RIVER, INC.—See Dan River Inc.; *U.S. Public*, pg. 479
DAN RIVER INC.-HOME FURNISHINGS & RELATED PRODS., DIV. I—See Dan River Inc.; *U.S. Public*, pg. 479
DAN RIVER SPINDALE INC.—See Dan River Inc.; *U.S. Public*, pg. 479
DAN TEGL TAG A/S—See Redland PLC; *Int'l*, pg. 1092
DANA ASIA/PACIFIC—See Dana Corporation; *U.S. Public*, pg. 480
DANA BUCHMAN DIV.—See Liz Claiborne, Inc.; *U.S. Public*, pg. 1006
DANA CANADA INC.—See Dana Corporation; *U.S. Public*, pg. 480
DANA COMMERCIAL CREDIT CORP. (OHIO)—See Dana Corporation; *U.S. Public*, pg. 479
DANA COMMERCIAL CREDIT CORPORATION—See Dana Corporation; *U.S. Public*, pg. 479
DANA COMMERCIAL CREDIT SMALL TKT—See Dana Corporation; *U.S. Public*, pg. 480
DANA CORPORATION; *U.S. Public*, pg. 479
DANA DESIGN—See K2 Inc.; *U.S. Public*, pg. 940
DANA DISTRIBUTION U.K.—See Dana Corporation; *U.S. Public*, pg. 480

DANA EUROPE INDUSTRIAL—See Dana Corporation; *U.S. Public*, pg. 480
DANA LIGHTING, INC.—See Catalina Lighting, Inc.; *U.S. Public*, pg. 314
DANA PERFUMES CORP.—See Renaissance Cosmetics, Inc.; *U.S. Private*, pg. 922
DANA SOUTH AMERICAN OPERATIONS—See Dana Corporation; *U.S. Public*, pg. 480
DANA WORLD TRADE DIV.—See Dana Corporation; *U.S. Public*, pg. 479
DANAFILMS, INC.; *U.S. Private*, pg. 309
DANAHER CONTROLS—See Danaher Corporation; *U.S. Public*, pg. 480
DANAHER CORPORATION; *U.S. Public*, pg. 480
DANAHER TOOL GROUP—See Danaher Corporation; *U.S. Public*, pg. 480
DANAHER TOOL GROUP-WEST HARTFORD OPERATIONS—See Danaher Corporation; *U.S. Public*, pg. 481
DANAPAK A.M.B.A.—See MD Foods; *Int'l*, pg. 826
DANBEER AG—See Feldschlosschen Hurlimann Holding; *Int'l*, pg. 479
DANBEL INDUSTRIES INC.—See Noma Industries Limited; *Int'l*, pg. 955
DANBRAND PRODUCTS AUSTRALASIA—See International Paper Company; *U.S. Public*, pg. 904
DANBURY PHARMACAL INC.—See Schein Pharmaceutical, Inc.; *U.S. Private*, pg. 969
DANBURY PHARMACAL PUERTO RICO INC.—See Schein Pharmaceutical, Inc.; *U.S. Private*, pg. 969
DANCALL TELECOM A/S—See Robert Bosch GmbH; *Int'l*, pg. 206
DANCE FRANCE LTD.—See Danskin Inc.; *U.S. Public*, pg. 483
DANCHEM AG—See Danzas Holding Ltd.; *Int'l*, pg. 382
DANCKER, SELLEW & DOUGLAS, INC.; *U.S. Private*, pg. 309
DANCO PRODUCTS—See NCH Corporation; *U.S. Public*, pg. 1145
DANEK MEDICAL INC.—See Sofamor Danek Group, Inc.; *U.S. Public*, pg. 1482
DANEK SALES CORPORATION—See Sofamor Danek Group, Inc.; *U.S. Public*, pg. 1482
DANET—See Science Applications International Corp.; *U.S. Private*, pg. 976
JOHN W. DANFORTH CO.; *U.S. Private*, pg. 309
DANFOSS AB—See Danfoss A/S; *Int'l*, pg. 377
DANFOSS AB PLUMBING CONTROLS DIV.—See Danfoss A/S; *Int'l*, pg. 377
DANFOSS A/S; *Int'l*, pg. 376
DANFOSS A/S AUTOMATIC CONTROLS DIV.—See Danfoss A/S; *Int'l*, pg. 377
DANFOSS A/S BUILDING CONTROLS DIV.—See Danfoss A/S; *Int'l*, pg. 377
DANFOSS A/S BURNER CONTROLS DIV.—See Danfoss A/S; *Int'l*, pg. 377
DANFOSS A/S COMFORT DIV.—See Danfoss A/S; *Int'l*, pg. 377
DANFOSS A/S HOUSEHOLD COMPRESSORS DIV.—See Danfoss A/S; *Int'l*, pg. 377
DANFOSS A/S INSTRUMENTATION—See Danfoss A/S; *Int'l*, pg. 377
DANFOSS A/S MOBILE HYDRAULICS DIV.—See Danfoss A/S; *Int'l*, pg. 377
DANFOSS A/S TINGLEV FABRIKKEN—See Danfoss A/S; *Int'l*, pg. 377
DANFOSS A/S VIBY FABRIKKEN—See Danfoss A/S; *Int'l*, pg. 377
DANFOSS AUTOMATIC CONTROLS—See Danfoss A/S; *Int'l*, pg. 377
DANFOSS COMPRESSORS D.O.O.—See Danfoss A/S; *Int'l*, pg. 377
DANFOSS COMPRESSORS GMBH—See Danfoss A/S; *Int'l*, pg. 377
DANFOSS COMPRESSORS S.A. DE C.V.—See Danfoss A/S; *Int'l*, pg. 377
DANFOSS DRIVES A/S—See Danfoss A/S; *Int'l*, pg. 377
DANFOSS ELECTRONIC DRIVES—See Danfoss A/S; *Int'l*, pg. 377
DANFOSS ESCO AS—See Danfoss A/S; *Int'l*, pg. 377
DANFOSS FLOWMETERING LIMITED—See Danfoss A/S; *Int'l*, pg. 377
DANFOSS FLUID POWER—See Danfoss A/S; *Int'l*, pg. 377
DANFOSS FLUID POWER - MINI STEERING UNITS DIV.—See Danfoss A/S; *Int'l*, pg. 377
DANFOSS FLUID POWER A/S—See Danfoss A/S; *Int'l*, pg. 377
DANFOSS FLUIDTECHNIK GMBH—See Danfoss A/S; *Int'l*, pg. 377
DANFOSS INC.—See Danfoss A/S; *Int'l*, pg. 377
DANFOSS POLAND SP. Z.O.O.—See Danfoss A/S; *Int'l*, pg. 377
DANFOSS (PTY) LTD.—See Danfoss A/S; *Int'l*, pg. 377
DANFOSS RANDALL LIMITED—See Danfoss A/S; *Int'l*, pg. 377
DANFOSS S.A.R.L.—See Danfoss A/S; *Int'l*, pg. 377
DANFOSS SCHLESWIG—See Danfoss A/S; *Int'l*, pg. 377
DANFOSS S.R.L. CLIMATIC DIV.—See Danfoss A/S; *Int'l*, pg. 377
DANFOSS SYSTEM AUTOMATIK—See Danfoss A/S; *Int'l*, pg. 377
DANFOSS SYSTEM HYDRAULIK A/S—See Danfoss A/S; *Int'l*, pg. 377
DANFOSS (TIANJIN) LTD.—See Danfoss A/S; *Int'l*, pg. 377
DANFOSS TRATA D.D.—See Danfoss A/S; *Int'l*, pg. 377
DANFOSS VIDEK—See Danfoss A/S; *Int'l*, pg. 377
DANI MICHAELS, INC.; *U.S. Private*, pg. 309
DANI-TECH A/S—See Bondioli & Pavesi S.p.A.; *Int'l*, pg. 201
DANIEL AUTOMATION COMPANY—See Daniel Industries, Inc.; *U.S. Public*, pg. 483

DANIEL CANADA—See Daniel Industries, Inc.; U.S. Public, pg. 483
DANIEL CARON SPORTSWEAR; U.S. Private, pg. 309
DANIEL FLOW PRODUCTS, INC.—See Daniel Industries, Inc.; U.S. Public, pg. 483
DANIEL INDUSTRIES, INC.; U.S. Public, pg. 482
DANIEL INDUSTRIES LTD.—See Daniel Industries, Inc.; U.S. Public, pg. 483
DANIEL VALVE COMPANY—See Daniel Industries, Inc.; U.S. Public, pg. 483
DANIELLI & C. FAR EAST—See Danielli & C. Officine Meccaniche S.p.A.; Int'l, pg. 378
DANIELLI & C. OFFICINE MECCANICHE S.P.A.; Int'l, pg. 378
DANIELLI BURO DEUTSCHLAND—See Danielli & C. Officine Meccaniche S.p.A.; Int'l, pg. 378
DANIELLI MORGARDSHAMMAR SA—See Danielli & C. Officine Meccaniche S.p.A.; Int'l, pg. 378
DANIELLI OF AMERICA—See Danielli & C. Officine Meccaniche S.p.A.; Int'l, pg. 378
C.R. DANIELS, INC.; U.S. Private, pg. 310
DANIELS MANUFACTURING CORPORATION; U.S. Private, pg. 310
DANIELS PRINTING COMPANY; U.S. Private, pg. 310
DANIELSON HOLDING CORPORATION; U.S. Public, pg. 483
DANIELSON INDEMNITY COMPANY—See Danielson Holding Corporation; U.S. Public, pg. 483
DANIELSON INSURANCE COMPANY—See Danielson Holding Corporation; U.S. Public, pg. 483
DANIELSON NATIONAL INSURANCE COMPANY—See Danielson Holding Corporation; U.S. Public, pg. 483
DANIELSON REINSURANCE CORPORATION—See Danielson Holding Corporation; U.S. Public, pg. 483
DANIS CLARKCO LANDFILL COMPANY—See The Danis Companies; U.S. Private, pg. 310
THE DANIS COMPANIES; U.S. Private, pg. 310
DANIS ENVIRONMENTAL MANAGEMENT CO.—See The Danis Companies; U.S. Private, pg. 310
DANIS HEAVY CONSTRUCTION CO.—See The Danis Companies; U.S. Private, pg. 310
DANISCO A/S; Int'l, pg. 378
DANISCO DISTILLERS—See Danisco A/S; Int'l, pg. 378
DANISCO FINANCE PLC—See Danisco A/S; Int'l, pg. 378
DANISCO FLEXIBLE—See Danisco A/S; Int'l, pg. 378
DANISCO FOODS—See Danisco A/S; Int'l, pg. 378
DANISCO INGREDIENTS—See Danisco A/S; Int'l, pg. 378
DANISCO INGREDIENTS CANADA INC.—See Danisco A/S; Int'l, pg. 378
DANISCO INGREDIENTS USA, INC.—See Danisco A/S; Int'l, pg. 378
DANISCO PACK LTD.—See Danisco A/S; Int'l, pg. 378
DANISCO PAPER—See Danisco A/S; Int'l, pg. 378
DANISCO SEED—See Danisco A/S; Int'l, pg. 378
DANISCO SUGAR—See Danisco A/S; Int'l, pg. 378
DANISCO SUGAR AB—See Danisco A/S; Int'l, pg. 378
DANISCO SUGAR GMBH—See Danisco A/S; Int'l, pg. 378
DANISH AEROTECH A/S—See FLS Industries A/S; Int'l, pg. 475
DANISH BACON COMPANY PLC—See ESS-Food; Int'l, pg. 429
DANISH CREAMERY ASSOCIATION; U.S. Private, pg. 310
DANISH FREEZE-DRYING APS—See The East Asiatic Company Ltd. A/S; Int'l, pg. 430
DANISH PACK—See Danisco A/S; Int'l, pg. 378
DANKA BUSINESS SYSTEMS—See Danka Business Systems PLC; Int'l, pg. 379
DANKA BUSINESS SYSTEMS LTD.—See Danka Business Systems PLC; Int'l, pg. 379
DANKA BUSINESS SYSTEMS PLC; Int'l, pg. 379
DANKA EUROPE LTD.—See Danka Business Systems PLC; Int'l, pg. 379
DANKA OFFICE IMAGING—See Eastman Kodak Company; U.S. Public, pg. 551
DANKO GIDA TICARET A.S.—See Chr. Hansen Holding A/S; Int'l, pg. 288
DAN-LOC BOLT & GASKET, INC.—See The Flexitallic Group, Inc.; U.S. Private, pg. 413
DANLY DIE SET DIVISION—See Connell Limited Partnership; U.S. Private, pg. 264
DANMARK PROTEIN A/S—See Solvay S.A.; Int'l, pg. 1279
DANN DEE DISPLAY FIXTURES; U.S. Private, pg. 310
THE DANNON CO.—See Danone Group; Int'l, pg. 379
DANOMEX, S.A. DE C.V.—See The Dexter Corporation; U.S. Public, pg. 505
DANONE—See Danone Group; Int'l, pg. 379
DANONE AUSTRIA—See Danone Group; Int'l, pg. 379
DANONE BRANDS (SINGAPORE) PTE. LTD.—See Danone Group; Int'l, pg. 380
DANONE B.V.—See Danone Group; Int'l, pg. 379
DANONE DE MEXICO—See Danone Group; Int'l, pg. 379
DANONE GROUP; Int'l, pg. 379
DANONE PORTUGAL, S.A.—See Danone Group; Int'l, pg. 379
DANONE S.A.—See Danone Group; Int'l, pg. 379
DANONE S.P.A.—See Danone Group; Int'l, pg. 379
DANREC—See Imetal; Int'l, pg. 662
DAN'S SUPREME SUPER MARKETS INC.; U.S. Private, pg. 310
DANSK INDUSTRI SYNDIKAT A/S; Int'l, pg. 381
DANSK INTERNATIONAL DESIGNS LTD.—See Brown-Forman Corporation; U.S. Public, pg. 261
DANSK KENRAL A.P.S.—See Pharmacia & Upjohn, Inc.; Int'l, pg. 1049
DANSK ORRETODFER A.S.—See Norsk Hydro a.s; Int'l, pg. 961
DANSK SALT I/S—See Akzo Nobel N.V.; Int'l, pg. 44
A/S DANSK SHELL—See Royal Dutch/Shell Group of Companies; Int'l, pg. 1138
DANSK SIGNAL INDUSTRI A/S—See Telefonaktiebolaget LM Ericsson; Int'l, pg. 1365
DANSK SLURRY SEAL I/S—See Icopal a.s; Int'l, pg. 658
DANSK STYROPACK—See Royal Dutch/Shell Group of Companies; Int'l, pg. 1138

DANSK TRAEEMBALLAGE A/S—See FLS Industries A/S; Int'l, pg. 476
DANSK UNI-CARDAN A/S—See GKN plc; Int'l, pg. 535
DANSK VEJRENOVERING I/S—See Icopal a/s; Int'l, pg. 658
DANSKE LANDMAEND K/S—See MD Foods; Int'l, pg. 826
DANSKIN—See Danskin Inc.; U.S. Public, pg. 483
DANSKIN INC.; U.S. Public, pg. 483
DANTAS HOLDINGS LTD.—See Jardine Matheson Holdings Limited; Int'l, pg. 704
DANTEK HOLSTEBRO A.P.S.—See Freudenberg & Company; Int'l, pg. 506
DANTRANSPORT A/S—See FLS Industries A/S; Int'l, pg. 476
DANTRANSPORT HOLDING A/S—See FLS Industries A/S; Int'l, pg. 476
DANTRANSPORT INTERNATIONAL CORPORATION—See FLS Industries A/S; Int'l, pg. 476
DANUBIA HOLDING AG—See Lafarge S.A.; Int'l, pg. 790
DANUBIO COMPAGNIA DI ASSICURAZIONI E RIASSICURAZIONI GENERALI S.P.A.—See Zurich Insurance Company; Int'l, pg. 1531
DANUSER MACHINE CO.; U.S. Private, pg. 310
DANVALVE A/S—See Danfoss A/S; Int'l, pg. 377
DANVILLE DIV.—See Curt Bullock Builders, Inc.; U.S. Private, pg. 180
DANVILLE MFG. DIVISION—See R.R. Donnelley & Sons Company; U.S. Public, pg. 518
DANY CLUB SANDWICH GMBH & CO. VERTRIEBS KG—See Nestle S.A.; Int'l, pg. 920
DANZAS—See SNCF; Int'l, pg. 1163
DANZAS AB—See Danzas Holding Ltd.; Int'l, pg. 382
DANZAS A.E.—See Danzas Holding Ltd.; Int'l, pg. 382
DANZAS AG—See Danzas Holding Ltd.; Int'l, pg. 382
DANZAS ARGENTINA S.A.—See Danzas Holding Ltd.; Int'l, pg. 382
DANZAS BULGARIA—See Danzas Holding Ltd.; Int'l, pg. 382
DANZAS B.V.—See Danzas Holding Ltd.; Int'l, pg. 382
DANZAS (CANADA) LTD.—See Danzas Holding Ltd.; Int'l, pg. 382
DANZAS CHILE S.A.—See Danzas Holding Ltd.; Int'l, pg. 382
DANZAS CHINA LTD.—See Danzas Holding Ltd.; Int'l, pg. 382
DANZAS CORPORATION—See Danzas Holding Ltd.; Int'l, pg. 382
DANZAS DELEGATION—See Danzas Holding Ltd.; Int'l, pg. 382
DANZAS FREIGHT (H.K.) LTD.—See Danzas Holding Ltd.; Int'l, pg. 382
DANZAS FREIGHT (INDIA) PVT. LTD.—See Danzas Holding Ltd.; Int'l, pg. 382
DANZAS HOLDING GMBH—See Danzas Holding Ltd.; Int'l, pg. 382
DANZAS HOLDING LTD.; Int'l, pg. 382
DANZAS K.K.—See Danzas Holding Ltd.; Int'l, pg. 382
DANZAS LDA—See Danzas Holding Ltd.; Int'l, pg. 382
DANZAS LTDA—See Danzas Holding Ltd.; Int'l, pg. 382
DANZAS MANAGEMENT LATIN AMERICA, INC.—See Danzas Holding Ltd.; Int'l, pg. 382
DANZAS MANAGEMENT LTD.—See Danzas Holding Ltd.; Int'l, pg. 382
DANZAS MAROC SA—See Danzas Holding Ltd.; Int'l, pg. 382
DANZAS N.V.—See Danzas Holding Ltd.; Int'l, pg. 382
DANZAS PTY. LTD.—See Danzas Holding Ltd.; Int'l, pg. 382
DANZAS ROMANIA—See Danzas Holding Ltd.; Int'l, pg. 382
DANZAS SA—See Danzas Holding Ltd.; Int'l, pg. 382
DANZAS SAS—See Danzas Holding Ltd.; Int'l, pg. 382
P.T. DANZAS SARANAPERKASA—See Danzas Holding Ltd.; Int'l, pg. 382
DANZAS (SINGAPORE) PTE LTD.—See Danzas Holding Ltd.; Int'l, pg. 382
DANZAS (SOUTHERN AFRICA) TRANSPORT (PTY) LTD.—See Danzas Holding Ltd.; Int'l, pg. 383
DANZAS S.P.A.—See Danzas Holding Ltd.; Int'l, pg. 383
DANZAS SPA—See Danzas Holding Ltd.; Int'l, pg. 383
DANZAS SP.Z.O.O.—See Danzas Holding Ltd.; Int'l, pg. 383
DANZAS TAIWAN LTD.—See Danzas Holding Ltd.; Int'l, pg. 383
DANZAS (THAILAND) LIMITED—See Danzas Holding Ltd.; Int'l, pg. 383
DANZAS (UK) LTD.—See Danzas Holding Ltd.; Int'l, pg. 383
DANZAS UNITED ARAB EMIRATES—See Danzas Holding Ltd.; Int'l, pg. 383
C.A. DANZAS VENEZOLANA—See Danzas Holding Ltd.; Int'l, pg. 383
DANZAS VIETNAM—See Danzas Holding Ltd.; Int'l, pg. 383
DANZAS VOYAGES—See Danzas Holding Ltd.; Int'l, pg. 383
DANZASMAL SDN. BHD.—See Danzas Holding Ltd.; Int'l, pg. 383
DANZASMEX S.A.—See Danzas Holding Ltd.; Int'l, pg. 383
DANZER INDUSTRIES INC.—See Global Environmental Corp.; U.S. Public, pg. 747
DAP INC.—See Wassall Plc; Int'l, pg. 1486
DARBY GROUP OF COS.; U.S. Private, pg. 311
DARCHEM ENGINEERING LTD.—See Weir Group PLC; Int'l, pg. 1489
DARCI PHARMA SA—See UCB, S.A.; Int'l, pg. 1427
D'ARCY MASIUS BENTON & BOWLES, S.A.—See DMB&B Communications; U.S. Private, pg. 304
D'ARCY MASIUS BENTON & BOWLES COMMUNICATIONS—See DMB&B Communications; U.S. Private, pg. 303

DARDANEL MADENCILIK SANAYI VE TICARET S.A.—See Inco Limited; Int'l, pg. 672
DARDEN RESTAURANTS, INC.; U.S. Public, pg. 483
DARE FOODS LIMITED; Int'l, pg. 383
DAREX PUERTO RICO, INC.—See W.R. Grace & Co.; U.S. Public, pg. 755
DARIGOLD, INC.; U.S. Private, pg. 311
DARK HORSE COMICS, INC.; U.S. Private, pg. 311
DARLENE JEWELRY MANUFACTURING COMPANY; U.S. Private, pg. 311
DARLING ENVELOPE CORPORATION; U.S. Private, pg. 311
DARLING INTERNATIONAL, INC; U.S. Public, pg. 484
DARLING'S; U.S. Private, pg. 311
DARLINGTON VENEER COMPANY; U.S. Private, pg. 311
D'ARMIGENE DESIGN CENTER—See Superior Surgical Mfg. Co., Inc.; U.S. Public, pg. 1539
RUSS DARROW GROUP; U.S. Private, pg. 311
DARSA GADITANA, S.A.—See Telefonica de Espana, S.A.; Int'l, pg. 1372
DART CONTAINER CORP.; U.S. Private, pg. 311
DAVID DART—See Kellwood Company; U.S. Public, pg. 948
DART GROUP CORPORATION; U.S. Public, pg. 484
DART GROUP FINANCIAL CORP.—See Dart Group Corporation; U.S. Public, pg. 484
DART REALTY CO. LTD.—See Brodart Company; U.S. Private, pg. 170
DART TRANSIT COMPANY; U.S. Private, pg. 311
DART TRUCKING COMPANY, INC.—See American Waste Services, Inc.; U.S. Public, pg. 94
DARTAMERICA, INC.—See American Waste Services, Inc.; U.S. Public, pg. 94
DARTFORD PARTNERSHIP; U.S. Private, pg. 312
DARTINGTON CRYSTAL—See BTR plc; Int'l, pg. 124
THE DARTNELL CORPORATION; U.S. Private, pg. 312
DARTY ALSACE LORRAINE—See Kingfisher plc; Int'l, pg. 734
DARTY PROVINCE MEDITERRANNE—See Kingfisher plc; Int'l, pg. 734
DARTY RHONE-ALPES—See Kingfisher plc; Int'l, pg. 734
DARVEL REALTY TRUST—See Commonwealth Energy System; U.S. Public, pg. 415
DARWIN BAKERY PTY. LTD.—See Q.U.F. Industries Ltd.; Int'l, pg. 1074
DARWIN BREWERY—See Foster's Brewing Group Limited; Int'l, pg. 501
DARWIN DIGITAL—See Saatchi & Saatchi Advertising Worldwide; U.S. Public, pg. 1422
DARWIN GLASS—See BTR plc; Int'l, pg. 129
DARWISH CONSULTING ENGINEERS—See Heidemij N.V.; Int'l, pg. 606
DARWISH TRADING COMPANY—See GESTRA GmbH; Int'l, pg. 550
P.T. DARYA-VARIA LABORATORIA—See First Pacific Company Limited; Int'l, pg. 487
DAS BESTE AUS READER'S DIGEST AG—See The Reader's Digest Association, Inc.; U.S. Public, pg. 1368
DASSAS COMMUNICATION; Int'l, pg. 383
DASSAULT AVIATION GROUP; Int'l, pg. 383
DASSAULT FALCON JET CORP.—See Dassault Aviation Group; Int'l, pg. 383
DASSAULT SYSTEMES—See Dassault Aviation Group; Int'l, pg. 383
DATA AIRE, INC.—See Construction Specialties, Inc.; U.S. Private, pg. 266
DATA ARCHITECTURE & ENGINEERING—See MCI Communications Corp.; U.S. Public, pg. 1024
DATA BASE S.P.A.—See BASF AG; Int'l, pg. 108
DATA BROADCASTING CORPORATION; U.S. Public, pg. 484
DATA BUSINESS FORMS—See Data Business Forms Limited; Int'l, pg. 384
DATA BUSINESS FORMS LIMITED; Int'l, pg. 384
DATA COM—See SSE Telecom, Inc.; U.S. Public, pg. 1421
DATA COMMAND SYSTEMS—See Litton Industries, Inc.; U.S. Public, pg. 1002
DATA COMMUNICATIONS—See The McGraw-Hill Companies; U.S. Public, pg. 1070
DATA CONTROL SYSTEMS—See CompuDyne Corporation; U.S. Public, pg. 420
DATA DIMENSIONS, INC.; U.S. Public, pg. 485
DATA DISC SYSTEMS GMBH—See Mannesmann A.G.; Int'l, pg. 836
DATA DOCUMENTS HOLDINGS, INC.—See Corporate Express, Inc.; U.S. Public, pg. 449
DATA DOCUMENTS, INC.—See Corporate Express, Inc.; U.S. Public, pg. 449
DATA FORTH—See Burr-Brown Corporation; U.S. Public, pg. 270
DATA GENERAL CORPORATION; U.S. Public, pg. 485
DATA GENERAL CORP. TRAVEL—See Data General Corporation; U.S. Public, pg. 485
DATA GENERAL CUSTOMER SERVICE DIVISION—See Data General Corporation; U.S. Public, pg. 485
DATA GENERAL INTERNATIONAL, INC.—See Data General Corporation; U.S. Public, pg. 485
DATA GENERAL INTERNATIONAL SALES CORPORATION—See Data General Corporation; U.S. Public, pg. 485
DATA GENERAL INVESTMENT CORPORATION—See Data General Corporation; U.S. Public, pg. 485
DATA GENERAL MANUFACTURING DIVISION—See Data General Corporation; U.S. Public, pg. 485
DATA GENERAL PUERTO RICO, INC.—See Data General Corporation; U.S. Public, pg. 485
DATA GENERAL SALES & MARKETING DIVISION—See Data General Corporation; U.S. Public, pg. 485
DATA GENERAL SERVICES—See Data General Corporation; U.S. Public, pg. 485
DATA GENERAL SYSTEMS DEVELOPMENT DIVISION—See Data General Corporation; U.S. Public, pg. 485
DATA I/O CANADA CORPORATION—See Data I/O Corporation; U.S. Public, pg. 486

DATA I/O CORPORATION; *U.S. Public*, pg. 486
DATA I/O GMBH—See Data I/O Corporation; *U.S. Public*, pg. 486
DATA I/O JAPAN CO., LTD.—See Data I/O Corporation; *U.S. Public*, pg. 486
DATA I/O (MANUFACTURING AUTOMATION DIV.)—See Data I/O Corporation; *U.S. Public*, pg. 486
DATA I/O (SALES & SERVICE)—See Data I/O Corporation; *U.S. Public*, pg. 486
DATA IMAGES—See Litton Industries, Inc.; *U.S. Public*, pg. 1004
DATA INDUSTRIAL CORPORATION—See Datamarine International, Inc.; *U.S. Public*, pg. 487
DATA INSTRUMENTS, INC.; *U.S. Private*, pg. 312
DATA MANAGEMENT SERVICES (DMS)—See Oracle Corporation; *U.S. Public*, pg. 1228
DATA MEDIA CORPORATION—See Axent Technologies; *U.S. Public*, pg. 157
DATA NATIONAL—See Volt Information Sciences, Inc.; *U.S. Public*, pg. 1724
DATA RENTAL/SALES, DIVISION—See Electro Rent Corporation; *U.S. Public*, pg. 568
DATA RETRIEVAL CORP. OF AMERICA—See The Thomson Corporation; *U.S. Public*, pg. 1602
DATA SERWIS SP. Z.O.O.—See Compagnie des Machines Bull; *Int'l*, pg. 317
DATA SOURCES—See The Thomson Corporation; *U.S. Public*, pg. 1600
DATA STORAGE CENTER—See The Suddath Companies; *U.S. Private*, pg. 1049
DATA SYSTEMS AND SERVICES DIVISION—See Northrop Grumman Corporation; *U.S. Public*, pg. 1198
DATA SYSTEMS CONSULTING CO., LTD.—See CSA Holdings Ltd.; *Int'l*, pg. 243
DATA SYSTEMS GROUP—See DRS Technologies, Inc.; *U.S. Public*, pg. 474
DATA TRACK ACCOUNT SERVICES, INC.—See National Fuel Gas Company; *U.S. Public*, pg. 1156
DATA TRANSLATION GMBH—See Media 100, Inc.; *U.S. Public*, pg. 1079
DATA TRANSLATION LTD.—See Media 100, Inc.; *U.S. Public*, pg. 1079
DATA TRANSLATION NETWORKING LIMITED—See Media 100, Inc.; *U.S. Public*, pg. 1079
DATA TRANSLATION S.R.L.—See Media 100, Inc.; *U.S. Public*, pg. 1079
DATA TRANSMISSION NETWORK CORPORATION; *U.S. Public*, pg. 486
DATA-TRONICS CORP.—See Arkansas Best Corporation; *U.S. Public*, pg. 130
DATABASE AMERICA COMPANIES—See American Business Information, Inc.; *U.S. Public*, pg. 70
DATABASE AMERICA COMPANIES; *U.S. Private*, pg. 312
DATACARD CANADA INC.—See DataCard Corporation; *U.S. Private*, pg. 312
DATACARD-CLEVELAND—See DataCard Corporation; *U.S. Private*, pg. 312
DATACARD CORPORATION; *U.S. Private*, pg. 312
DATACARD EQUIPMENT—See DataCard Corporation; *U.S. Private*, pg. 312
DATACARD EUROPE LTD.—See DataCard Corporation; *U.S. Private*, pg. 312
DATACARD FRANCE S.A.—See DataCard Corporation; *U.S. Private*, pg. 313
DATACARD GERMANY GMBH—See DataCard Corporation; *U.S. Private*, pg. 313
DATACARD JAPAN LTD—See DataCard Corporation; *U.S. Private*, pg. 313
DATACARD PLASTIC CARD SERVICES—See DataCard Corporation; *U.S. Private*, pg. 312
DATACARD SERVICE—See DataCard Corporation; *U.S. Private*, pg. 312
DATACARD SWEDEN AB—See DataCard Corporation; *U.S. Private*, pg. 313
DATACOLOR AG—See Brauerei Eichhof; *Int'l*, pg. 213
DATACOMM DE MEXICO, S.A. DE C.V.—See Genicom Corporation; *U.S. Public*, pg. 729
DATACOMM LEASING CORP.—See General Datacomm Industries, Inc.; *U.S. Public*, pg. 708
DATACOR/ISM (INFORMATION SYSTEMS MANAGEMENT ATLANTIC CORP.)—See Bruncor, Inc.; *Int'l*, pg. 230
DATAFAST AB—See Celsius AB; *Int'l*, pg. 277
DATAFLEX CORPORATION; *U.S. Private*, pg. 313
DATAFORMS, INC.—See The Reynolds and Reynolds Company; *U.S. Public*, pg. 1385
DATAGEN, INC.—See Data General Corporation; *U.S. Public*, pg. 485
DATALINER AB—See Spectra-Physics AB; *Int'l*, pg. 1289
DATALINK SYSTEMS, LLC—See Fiserv, Inc.; *U.S. Public*, pg. 647
DATAMARINE INTERNATIONAL AUSTRALIA PTY., LTD.—See Datamarine International, Inc.; *U.S. Public*, pg. 487
DATAMARINE INTERNATIONAL, INC.; *U.S. Public*, pg. 486
DATAMAT SPA—See Oracle Corporation; *U.S. Public*, pg. 1228
DATAMATE DIVISION—See Methode Electronics Inc.; *U.S. Public*, pg. 1101
DATAMATE PRODUCTS GROUP—See Methode Electronics Inc.; *U.S. Public*, pg. 1101
DATAMAX INTERNATIONAL CORPORATION; *U.S. Private*, pg. 313
DATAMETRICS CORPORATION; *U.S. Public*, pg. 487
DATAPOINT CORPORATION; *Int'l*, pg. 384
DATAPOINT DEVELOPMENT CENTER, INC.—See Datapoint Corporation; *Int'l*, pg. 384
DATAPOINT-DISC, INC.—See Datapoint Corporation; *Int'l*, pg. 384
DATAPOINT S.A.—See Datapoint Corporation; *Int'l*, pg. 384
DATAPOINT (SCHWEIZ) AG—See Datapoint Corporation; *Int'l*, pg. 384
DATAPOINT (U.K.) LTD.—See Datapoint Corporation; *Int'l*, pg. 384

DATAPRO INFORMATION SERVICES GRP.—See The McGraw-Hill Companies; *U.S. Public*, pg. 1070
DATAPRO SERVICES—See The McGraw-Hill Companies; *U.S. Public*, pg. 1072
DATAPRODUCTS CORPORATION—See Hitachi Koki Co., Ltd.; *Int'l*, pg. 620
DATAPRODUCTS (DUBLIN) LTD.—See Hitachi Koki Co., Ltd.; *Int'l*, pg. 621
DATAPRODUCTS GMBH—See Hitachi Koki Co., Ltd.; *Int'l*, pg. 621
DATAPRODUCTS HANDELSGESELLSCHAFT M.B.H.—See Hitachi Koki Co., Ltd.; *Int'l*, pg. 621
DATAPRODUCTS (HONG KONG), LTD.—See Hitachi Koki Co., Ltd.; *Int'l*, pg. 621
DATAPRODUCTS INTERNATIONAL LTD.—See Hitachi Koki Co., Ltd.; *Int'l*, pg. 621
DATAPRODUCTS LTD.—See Hitachi Koki Co., Ltd.; *Int'l*, pg. 621
DATAPRODUCTS NEW ENGLAND, INC.—See Hitachi Koki Co., Ltd.; *Int'l*, pg. 621
DATAPRODUCTS S.A.R.L.—See Hitachi Koki Co., Ltd.; *Int'l*, pg. 621
DATAPRODUCTS SUPPLIES DIV.—See Hitachi Koki Co., Ltd.; *Int'l*, pg. 621
DATAQUEST INCORPORATED—See The Dun & Bradstreet Corporation; *U.S. Public*, pg. 535
DATARAM CORPORATION; *U.S. Public*, pg. 487
DATARAM INTERNATIONAL SALES CORP.—See Dataram Corporation; *U.S. Public*, pg. 487
DATARANGE COMMUNICATIONS PLC—See SFA, Inc.; *U.S. Private*, pg. 956
DATASCAN SERVICES CO.—See Alpha One Exchange; *U.S. Private*, pg. 45
DATASCAN TECHNOLOGY—See Alpha One Exchange; *U.S. Private*, pg. 45
DATASCHALT GESELLSCHAFT FUR INDUSTRIELLE DATEN-MESS-UND ANTRIEBSTECHNIK MGH—See FKI Plc; *Int'l*, pg. 473
DATASCOPE B.V.—See Datascope Corp.; *U.S. Public*, pg. 488
DATASCOPE CARDIAC ASSIST DIVISION—See Datascope Corp.; *U.S. Public*, pg. 487
DATASCOPE COLLAGEN PRODUCTS DIVISION—See Datascope Corp.; *U.S. Public*, pg. 487
DATASCOPE CORP.; *U.S. Public*, pg. 487
DATASCOPE FSC, LTD.—See Datascope Corp.; *U.S. Public*, pg. 487
DATASCOPE GMBH—See Datascope Corp.; *U.S. Public*, pg. 488
DATASCOPE HOLDING CORP.—See Datascope Corp.; *U.S. Public*, pg. 487
DATASCOPE INVESTMENT CORP.—See Datascope Corp.; *U.S. Public*, pg. 487
DATASCOPE MEDICAL CO., LTD.—See Datascope Corp.; *U.S. Public*, pg. 488
DATASCOPE PATIENT MONITORING DIVISION—See Datascope Corp.; *U.S. Public*, pg. 487
DATASCOPE SARL—See Datascope Corp.; *U.S. Public*, pg. 488
DATASERV COMPUTER MAINTENANCE, INC.—See Wang Laboratories, Inc.; *U.S. Public*, pg. 1737
DATASOUTH COMPUTER CORPORATION—See Bull Run Corporation; *U.S. Public*, pg. 267
DATASPHERE, INC.—See Construction Specialties, Inc.; *U.S. Private*, pg. 266
DATASTREAM INTERNATIONAL (FRANKFURT) LTD.—See Primark Corporation; *U.S. Public*, pg. 1326
DATASTREAM INTERNATIONAL (HONG KONG) LIMITED—See Primark Corporation; *U.S. Public*, pg. 1326
DATASTREAM INTERNATIONAL, INC.—See Primark Corporation; *U.S. Public*, pg. 1325
DATASTREAM INTERNATIONAL (JAPAN) KK—See Primark Corporation; *U.S. Public*, pg. 1326
DATASTREAM INTERNATIONAL LTD.—See Primark Corporation; *U.S. Public*, pg. 1325
DATASTREAM INTERNATIONAL LIMITED—See Primark Corporation; *U.S. Public*, pg. 1326
DATASTREAM INTERNATIONAL (LUXEMBOURG) LTD.—See Primark Corporation; *U.S. Public*, pg. 1326
DATASTREAM INTERNATIONAL (MILAN) LTD.—See Primark Corporation; *U.S. Public*, pg. 1326
DATASTREAM INTERNATIONAL (PARIS) LTD.—See Primark Corporation; *U.S. Public*, pg. 1326
DATASTREAM INTERNATIONAL (SCOTLAND) LTD.—See Primark Corporation; *U.S. Public*, pg. 1326
DATASTREAM INTERNATIONAL (SYDNEY)—See Primark Corporation; *U.S. Public*, pg. 1326
DATASTREAM INTERNATIONAL (ZURICH) LTD.—See Primark Corporation; *U.S. Public*, pg. 1326
DATASYSTEM S.A.—See Compagnie des Machines Bull; *Int'l*, pg. 317
DATATEAM DANMARK A/S—See Axel Johnson AB; *Int'l*, pg. 710
DATATEAM NORGE A/S—See Axel Johnson AB; *Int'l*, pg. 712
DATATEAM SVERIGE AB—See Axel Johnson AB; *Int'l*, pg. 708
DATATEL, INC.—See Seitel, Inc.; *U.S. Public*, pg. 1454
DATATROL TRANSACTION TERMINALS—See DataCard Corporation; *U.S. Private*, pg. 312
DATAVIEWS—See Dynatech Corporation; *U.S. Public*, pg. 539
DATAWATCH CORPORATION; *U.S. Public*, pg. 488
DATEC—See Groupe Usinor; *Int'l*, pg. 571
DATEL TECHNOLOGIES LTD.; *Int'l*, pg. 384
DATELINE, C.A.—See Hewlett-Packard Company; *U.S. Public*, pg. 817
DATEO IMPORT S.P.A.; *Int'l*, pg. 385
DATRON INCORPORATED; *U.S. Public*, pg. 313
DATUM—See Oracle Corporation; *U.S. Public*, pg. 1228
DATUM INC.; *U.S. Public*, pg. 488
DATURA DEVELOPMENT LABORATORY—See Platinum Technology, Inc.; *U.S. Public*, pg. 1309

DAUBERT CHEMICAL COMPANY, INC.—See Daubert Industries, Inc.; *U.S. Private*, pg. 313
DAUBERT COATED PRODUCTS, INC.—See Daubert Industries, Inc.; *U.S. Private*, pg. 313
DAUBERT INDUSTRIES, INC.; *U.S. Private*, pg. 313
MIKE DAUGHERTY'S CHEVROLET GEO, INC.; *U.S. Private*, pg. 313
DAUMAN DISPLAYS, INC.—See Continental Graphics Holdings, Inc.; *U.S. Private*, pg. 268
DAUPHIN DEPOSIT BANK AND TRUST COMPANY—See Allied Irish Banks, p.l.c.; *Int'l*, pg. 64
DAV-EL SERVICES, INC.—See Dav-El Worldwide; *U.S. Private*, pg. 314
DAV-EL WASHINGTON DC INC.—See Dav-El Worldwide; *U.S. Private*, pg. 314
DAV-EL WEST—See Dav-El Worldwide; *U.S. Private*, pg. 314
DAV-EL WORLDWIDE; *U.S. Private*, pg. 314
DAVAL NEDERLAND—See Groupe Usinor; *Int'l*, pg. 572
DAVALL GROUP LTD.—See EIS Group Plc; *Int'l*, pg. 426
DAVAO CENTRAL CHEMICAL CORPORATION—See Takeda Chemical Industries, Ltd.; *Int'l*, pg. 1350
DAVAO UNION CEMENT CORPORATION—See FLS Industries A/S; *Int'l*, pg. 475
DAVCO DIV.—See United States Filter Corporation; *U.S. Public*, pg. 1682
DAVCO EQUIPMENT, INC.—See Flowserve Corporation; *U.S. Public*, pg. 658
DAVCO RESTAURANTS INC.; *U.S. Public*, pg. 488
DAVCO SERVICE, INC.—See Lombardi Holdings Inc.; *U.S. Private*, pg. 673
DAVCO SERVICES—See Laporte plc; *Int'l*, pg. 803
DAVE & BUSTER'S; *U.S. Public*, pg. 488
DAVEL COMMUNICATIONS GROUP, INC.; *U.S. Public*, pg. 488
DAVENPORT INSULATION, INC; *U.S. Private*, pg. 314
J.T. DAVENPORT & SONS, INC.; *U.S. Private*, pg. 314
DAVENPORT MACHINE TOOL DIV.—See Dover Corporation; *U.S. Public*, pg. 520
DAVENPORT MAMMOET HEAVY TRANSPORT INC.—See Royal Nedlloyd Group N.V.; *Int'l*, pg. 1144
DAVENTRY INTERNATIONAL RAIL FREIGHT TERMINAL—See Severn Trent Plc; *Int'l*, pg. 1226
THE DAVEY TREE EXPERT COMPANY; *U.S. Private*, pg. 314
DAVEY TREE SURGERY CO.—See The Davey Tree Expert Company; *U.S. Private*, pg. 314
DAVID—See Harman International Industries, Inc.; *U.S. Public*, pg. 787
DAVID & SONS—See Nestle S.A.; *Int'l*, pg. 917
DAVID & CHARLES PLC—See The Reader's Digest Association, Inc.; *U.S. Public*, pg. 1368
DAVID CORPORATION—See Platinum Equity Holdings, LLC; *U.S. Private*, pg. 872
DAVID MANUFACTURING COMPANY (DMC)—See The GSI Group, Inc.; *U.S. Private*, pg. 436
DAVIDE CAMPARI; *Int'l*, pg. 385
DAVIDSON & ASSOCIATES, INC.—See Cendant Corporation; *U.S. Public*, pg. 320
D.A. DAVIDSON & CO.; *U.S. Private*, pg. 314
DAVIDSON COSCAN PARTNERS—See Brookfield Properties Corporation; *Int'l*, pg. 228
DAVIDSON COUNTY JUVENILE DETENTION CENTER—See Corrections Corporation of America; *U.S. Public*, pg. 450
DAVIDSON NURSING CENTER, INC.—See Vencor, Inc.; *U.S. Public*, pg. 1712
DAVIDSON PRINTING COMPANY; *U.S. Private*, pg. 314
DAVIDSONS WASTE PAPER—See BPB Industries PLC; *Int'l*, pg. 123
DAVIE INDUSTRIES INC.; *Int'l*, pg. 385
K.B. DAVIES & CO. (ZAMBIA) LTD.—See Unilever Plc; *Int'l*, pg. 1436
DAVIES MOLDING CO.—See Pettibone Corporation; *U.S. Private*, pg. 859
DAVIES SHEPHARD PTY. LTD.—See ABB Asea Brown Boveri (Holding) Ltd.; *Int'l*, pg. 2
THEO. H. DAVIES & CO., LTD—See Jardine Matheson Holdings Limited; *Int'l*, pg. 704
DAVIGEL S.A.—See Nestle S.A.; *Int'l*, pg. 920
DAVINCI B.V.—See De Bussy Harms N.V.; *Int'l*, pg. 386
DAVINCI SYSTEMS, INC.—See Dynatech Corporation; *U.S. Public*, pg. 539
DAVIS & HENDERSON LIMITED—See Data Business Forms Limited; *Int'l*, pg. 384
BUD DAVIS CADILLAC, INC.; *U.S. Private*, pg. 314
DAVIS COMPANIES; *U.S. Private*, pg. 315
DAVIS CORRECTIONAL FACILITY—See Corrections Corporation of America; *U.S. Public*, pg. 450
DAVIS ELECTRIC—See Siebe plc; *Int'l*, pg. 1240
DAVIS ELECTRICAL CONSTRUCTORS, INC.; *U.S. Private*, pg. 315
JIMMY DAVIS ENTERPRISES, INC.; *U.S. Private*, pg. 315
JOSEPH DAVIS, INC.; *U.S. Private*, pg. 315
DAVIS INDUSTRIES INC.; *U.S. Private*, pg. 315
DAVIS METER & SUPPLY DIV.—See United States Filter Corporation; *U.S. Public*, pg. 1682
DAVIS MINING & MANUFACTURING; *U.S. Private*, pg. 315
DAVIS-MOORE OLDSMOBILE, INC.; *U.S. Private*, pg. 315
DAVIS PAINT COMPANY; *U.S. Private*, pg. 315
DAVIS PROCESS DIV.—See United States Filter Corporation; *U.S. Public*, pg. 1682
DAVIS SELECTED ADVISORS, L.P.; *U.S. Private*, pg. 315
THE DAVIS SERVICE GROUP PLC.; *Int'l*, pg. 385
DAVIS TOOL & ENGINEERING CO.—See Davis Industries Inc.; *U.S. Private*, pg. 315
DAVIS WIRE CORP.—See Pettibone Corporation; *U.S. Private*, pg. 859
DAVIS WOOD PRODUCTS, INC.; *U.S. Private*, pg. 315
DAVIS WOOD PRODUCTS, INC.-MISSISSIPPI DIV.—See Davis Wood Products, Inc.; *U.S. Private*, pg. 316

DAVIS WOOD PRODUCTS, INC.-SOUTH CAROLINA DIV.—See Davis Wood Products, Inc.; *U.S. Private*, pg. 316
DAVISELEN ADVERTISING, INC.; *U.S. Private*, pg. 316
DAVISELEN ADVERTISING, INC.—See DavisElen Advertising, Inc.; *U.S. Private*, pg. 316
DAVOL INC.—See C.R. Bard, Inc.; *U.S. Public*, pg. 189
DAVOX CORP.; *U.S. Public*, pg. 488
DAVUM-ARMATURES—See Groupe Usinor; *Int'l*, pg. 571
DAVUM STAHL—See Groupe Usinor; *Int'l*, pg. 572
DAVY DRAVO DIVISION—See Kvaerner a.s.a.; *Int'l*, pg. 774
DAVY INTERNATIONAL—See Kvaerner a.s.a.; *Int'l*, pg. 773
DAVY INTERNATIONAL, CANADA—See Kvaerner a.s.a.; *Int'l*, pg. 775
DAVY INTERNATIONAL, SAN FRANCISCO—See Kvaerner a.s.a.; *Int'l*, pg. 774
DAVY JOHN BROWN PTY LIMITED—See Kvaerner a.s.a.; *Int'l*, pg. 775
DAVY MCKEE CHILE LTDA.—See Kvaerner a.s.a.; *Int'l*, pg. 775
DAVY MCKEE ENGENHARIA S/A—See Kvaerner a.s.a.; *Int'l*, pg. 775
DAVY PITTSBURGH—See Kvaerner a.s.a.; *Int'l*, pg. 774
THE DAVY ROLL CO. LTD.—See Kvaerner a.s.a.; *Int'l*, pg. 773
DAW TECHNOLOGIES, INC.; *U.S. Public*, pg. 489
DAWAHARES, INC.; *U.S. Private*, pg. 316
DAWMEC LIMITED—See Ascot Holdings Plc; *Int'l*, pg. 88
DAWN DISTRIBUTORS—See Thomas Nelson Inc.; *U.S. Public*, pg. 1168
DAWN FOOD PRODUCTS, INC.; *U.S. Private*, pg. 316
DAWN JOY FASHIONS, INC.; *U.S. Private*, pg. 316
DAWSON CONSTRUCTION CO., INC.; *U.S. Private*, pg. 316
DAWSON FUR FABRICS LTD—See Dawson International PLC; *Int'l*, pg. 385
DAWSON GEOPHYSICAL COMPANY; *U.S. Public*, pg. 489
DAWSON HOLDINGS PLC; *Int'l*, pg. 385
DAWSON INTERNATIONAL INVESTMENTS (KINROSS) INC—See Dawson International PLC; *Int'l*, pg. 386
DAWSON INTERNATIONAL PLC; *Int'l*, pg. 385
JOSEPH DAWSON LTD—See Dawson International PLC; *Int'l*, pg. 385
DAWSON-KEITH LIMITED—See TT Group PLC; *Int'l*, pg. 1344
DAWSON'S HANDY ANDY HOME IMPROVEMENT CENTERS—See GIB Group; *Int'l*, pg. 533
DAY & ROSS INC.—See McCain Foods Limited; *Int'l*, pg. 850
DAY & ZIMMERMAN INFRASTRUCTURE, INC.—See Day & Zimmermann, Inc.; *U.S. Private*, pg. 317
DAY & ZIMMERMANN HAWTHORNE CORPORATION—See Day & Zimmermann, Inc.; *U.S. Private*, pg. 317
DAY & ZIMMERMANN, INC.; *U.S. Private*, pg. 316
DAY & ZIMMERMANN INFORMATION SOLUTIONS—See Day & Zimmermann, Inc.; *U.S. Private*, pg. 317
DAY & ZIMMERMANN INTERNATIONAL, INC.—See Day & Zimmermann, Inc.; *U.S. Private*, pg. 317
DAY & ZIMMERMANN LLC—See Day & Zimmermann, Inc.; *U.S. Private*, pg. 317
DAY & ZIMMERMANN SERVICES—See Day & Zimmermann, Inc.; *U.S. Private*, pg. 317
DAY-GLO COLOR CORP.—See RPM, Inc.; *U.S. Public*, pg. 1357
DAY INDUSTRIES—See Powers Fastening, Inc.; *U.S. Private*, pg. 878
DAY INTERNATIONAL PRINTING PRODUCTS CO.—See American Industrial Partners; *U.S. Private*, pg. 56
DAY INTERNATIONAL TEXTILE PRODUCTS—See American Industrial Partners; *U.S. Private*, pg. 56
DAY-LEE FOODS INC.—See Nippon Meat Packers, Inc.; *Int'l*, pg. 936
DAY-LEE FOODS (SAN FRANCISCO), INC.—See Nippon Meat Packers, Inc.; *Int'l*, pg. 936
DAY TECH INDUSTRIES—See Davis Industries Inc.; *U.S. Private*, pg. 315
DAY-TIMERS, INC.—See Fortune Brands, Inc.; *U.S. Public*, pg. 674
DAY & ZIMMERMAN CONSTRUCTION INC.—See Day & Zimmermann, Inc.; *U.S. Private*, pg. 317
DAYCO EUROPE AB—See Mark IV Industries Inc.; *U.S. Public*, pg. 1045
DAYCO MOLDED PRODUCTS—See Mark IV Industries Inc.; *U.S. Public*, pg. 1045
DAYCO PRODUCTS INC.—See Mark IV Industries Inc.; *U.S. Public*, pg. 1045
DAYCO PTI, INC.—See Mark IV Industries Inc.; *U.S. Public*, pg. 1045
DAYCO RUBBER INDUSTRIAL SALES DIVISION—See Mark IV Industries Inc.; *U.S. Public*, pg. 1045
DAYCO RUBBER PRODUCTS CO.—See Mark IV Industries Inc.; *U.S. Public*, pg. 1045
DAYCO SWAN CORPORATION—See Mark IV Industries Inc.; *U.S. Public*, pg. 1045
DAYCON PRODUCTS COMPANY, INC.; *U.S. Private*, pg. 317
DAYEH TAKASHIMAYA DEPARTMENT STORE, INC.—See Takashimaya Company, Limited; *Int'l*, pg. 1350
DAYFLEX PLASTICS—See Mark IV Industries Inc.; *U.S. Public*, pg. 1045
DAYFLEX WORLDWIDE—See Mark IV Industries Inc.; *U.S. Public*, pg. 1045
DAYS INNS OF AMERICA, INC.—See Cendant Corporation; *U.S. Public*, pg. 321
DAY-TIMERS OF CANADA, LIMITED—See Fortune Brands, Inc.; *U.S. Public*, pg. 674
DAYTON HUDSON CORPORATION; *U.S. Public*, pg. 489
DAYTON NEWSPAPERS, INC.—See Cox Enterprises, Inc.; *U.S. Private*, pg. 281
DAYTON OPERATIONS—See IDB Holding Corporation; *Int'l*, pg. 644
DAYTON PARTS, INC.—See JPE, Inc.; *U.S. Public*, pg. 919

DAYTON POWER & LIGHT CO.—See DPL Inc.; *U.S. Public*, pg. 473
DAYTON PRECISION CO.—See Kirkwood Industries, Inc.; *U.S. Private*, pg. 623
DAYTON PROCESS B.V.—See Indivers B.V.; *Int'l*, pg. 673
DAYTON PROGRESS CORPORATION—See Federal Signal Corporation; *U.S. Public*, pg. 617
DAYTON PROGRESS INTL.—See Federal Signal Corporation; *U.S. Public*, pg. 617
DAYTON PROGRESS OF CANADA—See Federal Signal Corporation; *U.S. Public*, pg. 617
DAYTON PROGRESS OF JAPAN—See Federal Signal Corporation; *U.S. Public*, pg. 617
DAYTON ROGERS MFG. CO.; *U.S. Private*, pg. 318
DAYTON ROGERS OF CALIFORNIA—See Dayton Rogers Mfg. Co.; *U.S. Private*, pg. 318
DAYTON ROGERS OF FLORIDA—See Dayton Rogers Mfg. Co.; *U.S. Private*, pg. 318
DAYTON ROGERS OF NEW YORK—See Dayton Rogers Mfg. Co.; *U.S. Private*, pg. 318
DAYTON ROGERS OF OHIO—See Dayton Rogers Mfg. Co.; *U.S. Private*, pg. 318
DAYTON ROGERS OF TEXAS—See Dayton Rogers Mfg. Co.; *U.S. Private*, pg. 318
DAYTON SUPERIOR CANADA LTD.—See Ripplewood Holdings L.L.C.; *U.S. Private*, pg. 932
DAYTON SUPERIOR CORPORATION—See Ripplewood Holdings L.L.C.; *U.S. Private*, pg. 931
DAYTON THERMAL PRODUCTS DIV.—See Chrysler Corporation; *U.S. Public*, pg. 353
DAYTON TIRE COMPANY—See Bridgestone Corporation; *Int'l*, pg. 213
DAYTON TIRE COMPANY-OKLAHOMA CITY—See Bridgestone Corporation; *Int'l*, pg. 214
DAYTRONIC CORPORATION—See BTR plc; *Int'l*, pg. 126
J.L. DE BALL CANADA INC.—See Girmes GmbH; *Int'l*, pg. 552
J.L. DE BALL-GIRMES OF AMERICA, INC.—See Girmes GmbH; *Int'l*, pg. 552
J.L. DE BALL OF AMERICA LTD. APPAREL DIV.—See Girmes GmbH; *Int'l*, pg. 552
H. ALBERT DE BARY & CO. N.V. (AMSTERDAM)—See Deutsche Bank AG; *Int'l*, pg. 404
DE BEERS CENTENARY AG—See Anglo American Corporation of South Africa Limited; *Int'l*, pg. 77
DE BEERS CENTRAL SELLING ORGANIZATION—See Anglo American Corporation of South Africa Limited; *Int'l*, pg. 77
DE BEERS CONSOLIDATED MINES LIMITED—See Anglo American Corporation of South Africa Limited; *Int'l*, pg. 76
DE BEERS INDUSTRIAL DIAMOND DIVISION (PROPRIETARY) LIMITED—See Anglo American Corporation of South Africa Limited; *Int'l*, pg. 77
DE BES' INSURANCE LTD.—See Weyerhaeuser Company; *U.S. Public*, pg. 1764
ETABLISSEMENT DE BIARRITZ—See Dassault Aviation Group; *Int'l*, pg. 383
DE BIJENKORF B.V.—See N.V. Koninklijke Bijenkorf Beheer KBB; *Int'l*, pg. 750
DE BOO BEHEER B.V.—See Scancem AB; *Int'l*, pg. 1200
DE BUSSY—See De Bussy Harms N.V.; *Int'l*, pg. 386
DE BUSSY HARMS N.V.; *Int'l*, pg. 386
DE BUSSY PARTICIPATIES—See De Bussy Harms N.V.; *Int'l*, pg. 386
DE BUSSY UITGEVERIJ—See De Bussy Harms N.V.; *Int'l*, pg. 386
DE CLERCK N.V.—See Schmalbach-Lubeca AG; *Int'l*, pg. 1207
DE DÄNSKE MEJERIERS FAELLESINDKEB AMBA—See MD Foods; *Int'l*, pg. 826
DE DIETRICH & CO.; *Int'l*, pg. 386
B.V. DE FACTORIJ, FACTORBEDRIJF ALGEMENE VAN DE BANK NEDERLAND—See ABN-AMRO Holding N.V.; *Int'l*, pg. 9
DE GEILLUSTREERDE PERS BV—See VNU Verenigde Nederlandse Uitgeversbedrijven B.V.; *Int'l*, pg. 1445
DE GEILLUSTREERDE PERS/MC—See VNU Verenigde Nederlandse Uitgeversbedrijven B.V.; *Int'l*, pg. 1445
DE GLOBE BV—See Koninklijke Hoogovens N.V.; *Int'l*, pg. 753
DE GRAAF'S BAKKERIJEN BV—See Koninklijke BolsWessanen nv; *Int'l*, pg. 752
C. DE GROOT HOUTAGENTUREN—See Norske Skogindustrier A.S.; *Int'l*, pg. 966
DE HAES HOLLAND B.V.—See Blydenstein-Willink N.V.; *Int'l*, pg. 198
DE HALLEN-KORTRIJK S.V.—See Tractebel; *Int'l*, pg. 1415
DE HAVILLAND INC.—See Bombardier Inc.; *Int'l*, pg. 200
DE KORTRIJKSE VERZEKERING—See AXA-UAP; *Int'l*, pg. 19
MICHAEL DE KRETSER CONSULTANTS—See BDDP Group; *Int'l*, pg. 11
DE LA CRUZ & ASSOCIATES; *U.S. Private*, pg. 318
DE LA MA/TBWA—See TBWA Chiat/Day; *U.S. Private*, pg. 1062
DE LA RUE CARD TECHNOLOGY LIMITED—See De La Rue plc; *Int'l*, pg. 387
DE LA RUE CASH HANDLING PRODUCT GROUP—See De La Rue plc; *Int'l*, pg. 387
DE LA RUE FARADAY—See De La Rue plc; *Int'l*, pg. 387
DE LA RUE FARADAY - MIDWEST—See De La Rue plc; *Int'l*, pg. 387
DE LA RUE FARADAY - WEST—See De La Rue plc; *Int'l*, pg. 387
DE LA RUE FORTRONIC GMBH—See De La Rue plc; *Int'l*, pg. 387
DE LA RUE FORTRONIC LIMITED—See De La Rue plc; *Int'l*, pg. 387
DE LA RUE HOLOGRAPHICS LIMITED—See De La Rue plc; *Int'l*, pg. 387
DE LA RUE IDENTITY SYSTEMS LIMITED—See De La Rue plc; *Int'l*, pg. 387

DE LA RUE INTER INNOVATION AB—See De La Rue plc; *Int'l*, pg. 387
DE LA RUE LERCHUNDI PERSONALIZACION SA—See De La Rue plc; *Int'l*, pg. 386
DE LA RUE LERCHUNDI SA—See De La Rué plc; *Int'l*, pg. 386
DE LA RUE PAYMENT SYSTEMS DIVISION—See De La Rue plc; *Int'l*, pg. 387
DE LA RUE PLC; *Int'l*, pg. 386
DE LA RUE SECURITY PRINTING—See De La Rue plc; *Int'l*, pg. 386
DE LA RUE SERVICES (MALAYSIA) SDN BHD—See De La Rue plc; *Int'l*, pg. 387
DE LA RUE SMURFIT LIMITED—See De La Rue plc; *Int'l*, pg. 386
DE LA RUE SMURFIT (NI) LTD.—See De La Rue plc; *Int'l*, pg. 386
DE LA RUE SYSTEMS AB—See De La Rue plc; *Int'l*, pg. 387
DE LA RUE SYSTEMS ASIA PACIFIC LIMITED—See De La Rue plc; *Int'l*, pg. 387
DE LA RUE SYSTEMS BV—See De La Rue plc; *Int'l*, pg. 387
DE LA RUE SYSTEMS GMBH—See De La Rue plc; *Int'l*, pg. 387
DE LA RUE SYSTEMS IMPORTS PTY LIMITED—See De La Rue plc; *Int'l*, pg. 387
DE LA RUE SYSTEMS IRELAND LTD.—See De La Rue plc; *Int'l*, pg. 387
DE LA RUE SYSTEMS (LATIN AMERICA)—See De La Rue plc; *Int'l*, pg. 387
DE LA RUE SYSTEMS LIMITED—See De La Rue plc; *Int'l*, pg. 387
DE LA RUE SYSTEMS LTD.—See De La Rue plc; *Int'l*, pg. 387
DE LA RUE SYSTEMS SA—See De La Rue plc; *Int'l*, pg. 387
DE LA RUE SYSTEMS (UK)—See De La Rue plc; *Int'l*, pg. 387
THOMAS DE LA RUE AND COMPANY LIMITED—See De La Rue plc; *Int'l*, pg. 386
THOMAS DE LA RUE (HONG KONG) LIMITED—See De La Rue plc; *Int'l*, pg. 386
THOMAS DE LA RUE (KENYA) LIMITED—See De La Rue plc; *Int'l*, pg. 387
THOMAS DE LA RUE (KENYA) LIMITED—See De La Rue plc; *Int'l*, pg. 386
THOMAS DE LA RUE LANKA (PTE) LIMITED—See De La Rue plc; *Int'l*, pg. 386
THOMAS DE LA RUE (MALTA) LIMITED—See De La Rue plc; *Int'l*, pg. 386
THOMAS DE LA RUE (SINGAPORE) PTE. LIMITED—See De La Rue plc; *Int'l*, pg. 386
DE LA RUE TRANSACTION SYSTEMS DIVISION—See De La Rue plc; *Int'l*, pg. 387
DE LAGE LANDEN FACTORS N.V.—See Rabobank Nederland; *Int'l*, pg. 1082
DE LAGE LANDEN LEASING N.V.—See Rabobank Nederland; *Int'l*, pg. 1082
DE LAMPENIER—See N.V. Koninklijke Bijenkorf Beheer KBB; *Int'l*, pg. 750
DE LENDRECIE'S—See Mercantile Stores Company, Inc.; *U.S. Public*, pg. 1090
CIA. DE LINHA COATS & CLARK LDA.—See Coats Viyella plc; *Int'l*, pg. 300
ETABLISSEMENT DE MARTIGNAS—See Dassault Aviation Group; *Int'l*, pg. 383
DE MATTOS & SULLIVAN LIMITED—See BASF AG; *Int'l*, pg. 108
ETABLISSEMENT DE MERIGNAC—See Dassault Aviation Group; *Int'l*, pg. 383
DE NEUFLIZE, SCHLUMBERGER, MALLET S.A.—See ABN-AMRO Holding N.V.; *Int'l*, pg. 12
DE NOOYER CHEVROLET INC.; *U.S. Private*, pg. 318
CIA. DE PAPEL E PAPELAO PEDRAS BRANCAS—See S.A. Industrias Votorantim; *Int'l*, pg. 677
ETABLISSEMENT DE POITIERS—See Dassault Aviation Group; *Int'l*, pg. 383
DE PRETTO-ESCHER WYSS S.R.L.—See Sulzer Ltd.; *Int'l*, pg. 1305
ETABLISSEMENT DE SAINT-CLOUD—See Dassault Aviation Group; *Int'l*, pg. 383
ETABLISSEMENT DE SECLIN—See Dassault Aviation Group; *Int'l*, pg. 383
CIA. DE SEGUROS AMERICA DO SUL YASUDA—See The Fuji Bank, Limited; *Int'l*, pg. 521
DIANA DE SILVA COSMETIQUES S.P.A.—See Bracco S.p.A.; *Int'l*, pg. 210
DE-STA-CO, A DOVER RESOURCES CO.—See Dover Corporation; *U.S. Public*, pg. 521
DE SURINAAMSCHE BANK N.V.—See ABN-AMRO Holding N.V.; *Int'l*, pg. 12
DE VADERLANDSCHE INSURANCE—See ING Groep N.V.; *Int'l*, pg. 648
DE VADERLANDSCHE SPAARBANK N.V.—See ING Groep N.V.; *Int'l*, pg. 648
ETABLISSEMENT DE VELIZY—See Dassault Aviation Group; *Int'l*, pg. 383
DE VEREENIGDE BLIKFABRIEKEN B.V.—See Schmalbach-Lubeca AG; *Int'l*, pg. 1207
DE VONS JEWELERS; *U.S. Private*, pg. 318
ANDRE DE VRIENDT SA—See N.V. Koninklijke KNP BT; *Int'l*, pg. 757
DE WITTE-LIETAER INDUSTRIES N.V.—See Gamma Holding N.V.; *Int'l*, pg. 540
DE ZAAN FAR EAST PTE. LTD.—See Archer Daniels Midland Company (ADM); *U.S. Public*, pg. 128
DEAD RIVER COMPANY; *U.S. Private*, pg. 318
DEAD RIVER PETROLEUM CO.—See Dead River Company; *U.S. Private*, pg. 318
DEAD RIVER PROPERTIES—See Dead River Company; *U.S. Private*, pg. 318

Company Index

DEAD RIVER TRANSPORT—See Dead River Company; *U.S. Private*, pg. 318
DEAKTOR/SYSCO FOOD SERVICES CO.—See Sysco Corporation; *U.S. Public*, pg. 1551
DEALERS AUTO AUCTION OF PHOENIX INC.—See Tyco International Ltd.; *U.S. Public*, pg. 1648
DEALERS AUTO AUCTION OF SANFORD, INC.—See Tyco International Ltd.; *U.S. Public*, pg. 1649
DEALERS ELECTRICAL SUPPLY CO.; *U.S. Private*, pg. 318
DEALERS MANUFACTURING COMPANY; *U.S. Private*, pg. 318
DEALERS TRUCK EQUIPMENT—See Manning Equipment, Inc.; *U.S. Private*, pg. 700
DEAN DAIRY PRODUCTS CO.—See Dean Foods Company; *U.S. Public*, pg. 490
DEAN FOOD PRODUCTS DIVISION—See Dean Foods Company; *U.S. Public*, pg. 490
DEAN FOODS—See Dean Foods Company; *U.S. Public*, pg. 490
DEAN FOODS COMPANY; *U.S. Public*, pg. 489
DEAN FOODS/MCDONALD'S SALES DIVISION—See Dean Foods Company; *U.S. Public*, pg. 490
DEAN FOODS SPECIALTY PRODUCTS—See Dean Foods Company; *U.S. Public*, pg. 490
DEAN FOODS VEGETABLE CO.—See Dean Foods Company; *U.S. Public*, pg. 490
DEAN FOODS VEGETABLE COMPANY—See Dean Foods Company; *U.S. Public*, pg. 490
DEAN INDUSTRIES, INC.—See Berisford plc; *Int'l*, pg. 188
DEAN OPERATIONS INC.; *U.S. Private*, pg. 318
DEAN PICKLE & SPECIALTY PRODUCTS—See Dean Foods Company; *U.S. Public*, pg. 490
DEAN PICKLE & SPECIALTY PRODUCTS CO.—See Dean Foods Company; *U.S. Public*, pg. 490
DEAN PICKLES & SPECIALTY PRODUCTS—See Dean Foods Company; *U.S. Public*, pg. 490
DEAN WITTER, DISCOVER & CO.—See Morgan Stanley Dean Witter & Co.; *U.S. Public*, pg. 1132
DEAN'S GRAND CANYON PHOTOS—See Dean's Photo Service; *U.S. Private*, pg. 319
DEAN'S PHOTO SERVICE; *U.S. Private*, pg. 319
DEARBORN CAPITAL CORPORATION—See Ford Motor Company; *U.S. Public*, pg. 663
DEARBORN FABRICATING & ENGINEERING CO.—See Tomkins PLC; *Int'l*, pg. 1397
DEARBORN GAGE COMPANY; *U.S. Private*, pg. 319
THE DEARBORN GROUP; *U.S. Private*, pg. 319
DEARDEN'S; *U.S. Private*, pg. 319
DEARDORFF-JACKSON COMPANY; *U.S. Private*, pg. 319
DEASUNG-HENKEL CHEMICAL CO., LTD.—See Henkel KGaA; *Int'l*, pg. 614
DEB SHOPS, INC.; *U.S. Public*, pg. 491
THE EDWARD J. DEBARTOLO CORPORATION; *U.S. Private*, pg. 319
DEBIS ASSEKURANZ VERMITTLUNGS GMBH—See Daimler-Benz Aktiengesellschaft; *Int'l*, pg. 368
DEBIS FINANZDIENSTLEISTUNGEN—See Daimler-Benz Aktiengesellschaft; *Int'l*, pg. 368
DEBIS GESELLSCHAFT FUR POTSDAMER PLATZ PROJEKT UND IMMOBILIENMANAGEMENT—See Daimler-Benz Aktiengesellschaft; *Int'l*, pg. 368
DEBIS HANDEL—See Daimler-Benz Aktiengesellschaft; *Int'l*, pg. 368
DEBIS INDUSTRIEHANDEL GMBH—See Daimler-Benz Aktiengesellschaft; *Int'l*, pg. 368
DEBIS INTERNATIONAL TRADING—See Daimler-Benz Aktiengesellschaft; *Int'l*, pg. 368
DEBIS MARKETING SERVICES GMBH—See Daimler-Benz Aktiengesellschaft; *Int'l*, pg. 368
DEBIS SYSTEMHAUS—See CAP Gemini S.A.; *Int'l*, pg. 264
DEBIS SYSTEMHAUS—See Daimler-Benz Aktiengesellschaft; *Int'l*, pg. 369
DEBIS SYSTEMHAUS GMBH—See Daimler-Benz Aktiengesellschaft; *Int'l*, pg. 368
DEBITEL KOMMUNIKATIONSTECHNIK GMBH & CO. KG—See Daimler-Benz Aktiengesellschaft; *Int'l*, pg. 368
DEBOER'S FABRIEKEN B.V.—See Hanson PLC; *Int'l*, pg. 594
DEBORAH SERVICES—See Sophus Berendsen A/S; *Int'l*, pg. 1285
DEBRUCE GRAIN INC.; *U.S. Private*, pg. 319
DECATUR HERALD & REVIEW—See Lee Enterprises, Incorporated; *U.S. Public*, pg. 983
DECATUR TELEPHONE COMPANY—See Telephone and Data Systems, Inc.; *U.S. Public*, pg. 1571
DECCA—See Litton Industries, Inc.; *U.S. Public*, pg. 1003
DECCA INTERNATIONAL—See Philips Electronics N.V.; *Int'l*, pg. 1053
DECCO DIV.—See Elf Aquitane; *Int'l*, pg. 446
DECIBEL PRODUCTS, INC.—See Allen Telecom, Inc.; *U.S. Public*, pg. 46
DECISION DATA—See IIS Intelligent Information Systems Ltd.; *Int'l*, pg. 645
DECISION DATA U.K. LTD.—See IIS Intelligent Information Systems Ltd.; *Int'l*, pg. 645
DECISION SYSTEMS INTERNATIONAL SPA—See Olivetti SpA; *Int'l*, pg. 1002
DECISIONMARK—See The Gazette Company; *U.S. Private*, pg. 442
DECISIONS & DESIGN, INC.—See Comarco, Inc.; *U.S. Public*, pg. 406
DECK HOUSE INC.; *U.S. Private*, pg. 320
DECKERS OUTDOOR CORPORATION; *U.S. Public*, pg. 491
DECO PRODUCTS CO.; *U.S. Private*, pg. 320
DECOFLEX LIMITED—See Moore Corporation Limited; *Int'l*, pg. 889
DECOLLETAGE S.A. ST.-MAURICE—See AMP Incorporated; *U.S. Public*, pg. 9
DECOMA INTERNATIONAL INC.—See Magna International Inc.; *Int'l*, pg. 829
DECORA—See Alusuisse-Lonza Holding Ltd.; *Int'l*, pg. 67

DECORA'—See Fortune Brands, Inc.; *U.S. Public*, pg. 675
DECORATIVE CRAFTS, INC.; *U.S. Private*, pg. 320
DECORATOR INDUSTRIES, INC.; *U.S. Public*, pg. 491
DECOREL INCORPORATED—See Newell Co.; *U.S. Public*, pg. 1177
DECORP—See Kellwood Company; *U.S. Public*, pg. 948
DECORPORT LTD.—See BTR plc; *Int'l*, pg. 124
DECOSTEEL N.V.—See Arbed S.A.; *Int'l*, pg. 79
DECOUPAGE MOULAGE DE SAVOIE S.A.—See Molex Incorporated; *U.S. Public*, pg. 1122
DECRA A/S—See Icopal a/s; *Int'l*, pg. 658
DECRA ROOF SYSTEMS (U.K.) LTD.—See Icopal a/s; *Int'l*, pg. 658
DEDERT CORPORATION; *U.S. Private*, pg. 320
DEDERT EUROPE HOLDING CO—See Dedert Corporation; *U.S. Private*, pg. 320
DEE GOLD MINING CO.—See Rayrock Yellowknife Resources Inc.; *Int'l*, pg. 1089
THE DEE HOWARD—See IRI Istituto Ricostruzione Industriale; *Int'l*, pg. 653
DEE PAPER COMPANY; *U.S. Private*, pg. 320
DEE ZEE MFG., INC.—See Lancaster Colony Corporation; *U.S. Public*, pg. 976
DEECO INDUSTRIES; *U.S. Private*, pg. 320
DEEKO PLC—See Fort James Corporation; *U.S. Public*, pg. 672
DEEN WHOLESALE MEAT COMPANY, INC.; *U.S. Private*, pg. 320
DEEP SEA CLAM COMPANY LIMITED—See National Sea Products Limited; *Int'l*, pg. 909
DEEP SEA SEALS LTD.—See TI Group plc; *Int'l*, pg. 1339
DEEP SOUTH PRODUCTS—See Winn-Dixie Stores, Inc.; *U.S. Public*, pg. 1772
DEEPWATER CHEMICALS, INC.—See Tomen Corporation; *Int'l*, pg. 1395
DEEPWATER OPERATING CO.—See Conectiv; *U.S. Public*, pg. 430
DEER PARK FEDERAL SAVINGS AND LOAN ASSOCIATION—See Ameriana Bancorp; *U.S. Public*, pg. 66
DEER PARK SPRING WATER, INC.—See Nestle S.A.; *Int'l*, pg. 919
DEERE & COMPANY; *U.S. Public*, pg. 491
DEERE CREDIT, INC.—See Deere & Company; *U.S. Public*, pg. 492
DEERE CREDIT SERVICES, INC.—See Deere & Company; *U.S. Public*, pg. 492
JOHN DEERE—See Deere & Company; *U.S. Public*, pg. 492
JOHN DEERE CAPITAL CORPORATION—See Deere & Company; *U.S. Public*, pg. 492
JOHN DEERE COMMERCIAL PRODUCTS, INC.—See Deere & Company; *U.S. Public*, pg. 492
JOHN DEERE COMPANY—See Deere & Company; *U.S. Public*, pg. 492
JOHN DEERE CREDIT COMPANY—See Deere & Company; *U.S. Public*, pg. 492
JOHN DEERE DAVENPORT WORKS—See Deere & Company; *U.S. Public*, pg. 492
JOHN DEERE DES MOINES WORKS—See Deere & Company; *U.S. Public*, pg. 492
JOHN DEERE DUBUQUE WORKS—See Deere & Company; *U.S. Public*, pg. 492
JOHN DEERE ENGINE WORKS—See Deere & Company; *U.S. Public*, pg. 492
JOHN DEERE FINANCE LIMITED—See Deere & Company; *U.S. Public*, pg. 492
JOHN DEERE FINANCE LIMITED - ALBERTA—See Deere & Company; *U.S. Public*, pg. 492
JOHN DEERE HARVESTER WORKS—See Deere & Company; *U.S. Public*, pg. 492
JOHN DEERE HEALTH CARE, INC.—See Deere & Company; *U.S. Public*, pg. 492
JOHN DEERE HORICON WORKS—See Deere & Company; *U.S. Public*, pg. 492
JOHN DEERE IBERICA S.A.—See Deere & Company; *U.S. Public*, pg. 493
JOHN DEERE INDUSTRIAL EQUIPMENT COMPANY—See Deere & Company; *U.S. Public*, pg. 492
JOHN DEERE INSURANCE COMPANY—See Deere & Company; *U.S. Public*, pg. 492
JOHN DEERE-LANZ VERWALTUNGS A.G.—See Deere & Company; *U.S. Public*, pg. 493
JOHN DEERE POWER PRODUCTS, INC.—See Deere & Company; *U.S. Public*, pg. 493
JOHN DEERE (PTY.) LTD.—See Deere & Company; *U.S. Public*, pg. 493
JOHN DEERE RECEIVABLES, INC.—See Deere & Company; *U.S. Public*, pg. 492
JOHN DEERE S.A. DE C.V.—See Deere & Company; *U.S. Public*, pg. 493
JOHN DEERE TECHNOLOGIES INTERNATIONAL, INC.—See Deere & Company; *U.S. Public*, pg. 492
JOHN DEERE WATERLOO WORKS—See Deere & Company; *U.S. Public*, pg. 492
DEERE MARKETING SERVICES, INC.—See Deere & Company; *U.S. Public*, pg. 492
DEERFIELD HOMES, INC.—See The Rouse Company; *U.S. Public*, pg. 1409
DEERFIELD URETHANE, INC.—See Bayer AG; *Int'l*, pg. 173
DEERING ICE CREAM, INC.—See FieldBrook Farms, Inc.; *U.S. Private*, pg. 403
DEERSKIN TRADING POST—See Initio, Inc.; *U.S. Public*, pg. 879
DEFA S.A.—See Suspa Compart AG; *Int'l*, pg. 1322
DEFABCO INSTALLATION—See Tomkins PLC; *Int'l*, pg. 1397
DEFAG DEUTSCHE FLUGZEUGV. AG & CO. KG—See Hapag-Lloyd AG; *Int'l*, pg. 596
DEFENDER SERVICES, INC.; *U.S. Private*, pg. 320
DEFENSE & AMMUNITION SEGMENT—See Olin Corporation; *U.S. Public*, pg. 1219

DEFENSE & LAUNCH VEHICLES DIVISION—See Thiokol Corporation; *U.S. Public*, pg. 1597
DEFENSE CIVILE—See AXA-UAP; *Int'l*, pg. 18
DEFENSE CREDIT UNION COUNCIL—See Credit Union National Association; *U.S. Private*, pg. 288
DEFENSE PRODUCTS DIVISION—See California Microwave, Inc.; *U.S. Public*, pg. 293
DEFENSE TECHNOLOGY GROUP—See Northrop Grumman Corporation; *U.S. Public*, pg. 1199
DEFERIET MILL, CHAMPION INTERNATIONAL CORP.—See Champion International Corp.; *U.S. Public*, pg. 334
DEFEX, S.A.—See SEPI; *Int'l*, pg. 1224
DEFIANCE, INC.; *U.S. Public*, pg. 493
DEFIANCE PRECISION PRODUCTS, INC.—See Defiance, Inc.; *U.S. Public*, pg. 493
DEFIANCE TESTING & ENGINEERING SERVICES—See Defiance, Inc.; *U.S. Public*, pg. 493
DEFONTAINE IBERICA S.A.—See Fried. Krupp AG; *Int'l*, pg. 509
DEFONTAINE ITALIA S.R.L.—See Fried. Krupp AG; *Int'l*, pg. 509
DEFONTAINE S.A.—See Fried. Krupp AG; *Int'l*, pg. 509
DEFONTAINE TUNISIE—See Fried. Krupp AG; *Int'l*, pg. 509
DEFONTAINE U.K. LTD—See Fried. Krupp AG; *Int'l*, pg. 509
DEFONTAINE/INC.—See Fried. Krupp AG; *Int'l*, pg. 509
DEFOVER, S.A.—See SEPI; *Int'l*, pg. 1224
DEGA S.R.L.—See H.J. Heinz Company; *U.S. Public*, pg. 807
DEGAZ—See Gaz de France; *Int'l*, pg. 541
DEGELMAN INDUSTRIES LTD.; *Int'l*, pg. 388
DEGGENDORFER WERFT UND EISENBAU GMBH—See MAN Aktiengesellschaft; *Int'l*, pg. 824
J.L. DEGRAFFENREID & SONS, INC.—See DG Foods, LLC; *U.S. Private*, pg. 301
DEGREMONT INC.—See Lyonnaise des Eaux S.A.; *Int'l*, pg. 822
DEGUSSA AG; *Int'l*, pg. 388
DEGUSSA CORPORATION—See Degussa AG; *Int'l*, pg. 388
DEGUSSA CORP., DENTAL DEPT.—See Degussa AG; *Int'l*, pg. 388
DEILMANN-HANIEL GMBH—See Preussag AG; *Int'l*, pg. 1069
DEIND—See Petrobras - Petroleo Brasileiro S.A.; *Int'l*, pg. 1041
DEITEC S.A.—See NewsEdge Corporation; *U.S. Public*, pg. 1180
DEITERMANN CHEMIEWERK GMBH & CO. K.G.—See Heidelberger Zement A.G.; *Int'l*, pg. 606
DEITSCH PLASTIC EXPORT CO.—See Deitsch Plastics Company; *U.S. Private*, pg. 321
DEITSCH PLASTICS COMPANY; *U.S. Private*, pg. 320
DEKALB ARGENTINA, S.A.—See Dekalb Genetics Corporation; *U.S. Public*, pg. 493
DEKALB CANADA INC.—See Dekalb Genetics Corporation; *U.S. Public*, pg. 493
DEKALB CONCRETE PRODUCTS, INC.—See For Better Living, Inc.; *U.S. Private*, pg. 417
DEKALB GENETICS CORPORATION; *U.S. Public*, pg. 493
DEKALB ITALIA, S.P.A.—See Dekalb Genetics Corporation; *U.S. Public*, pg. 493
DEKALB SWINE BREEDERS, INC.—See Dekalb Genetics Corporation; *U.S. Public*, pg. 493
MARCEL DEKKER, INC.; *U.S. Private*, pg. 321
DEKKO AUTOMOTIVE TECHNOLOGIES IOWA ASSEMBLIES DIV.—See Group Dekko; *U.S. Private*, pg. 484
DEKKO HEATING TECHNOLOGIES, INC.—See Group Dekko; *U.S. Private*, pg. 484
DEKKO TECHNICAL CENTER—See Group Dekko; *U.S. Private*, pg. 484
DEKORON DIVISION—See Furon Company; *U.S. Public*, pg. 689
DEKORON/UNITHERM DIVISION—See Furon Company; *U.S. Public*, pg. 689
DEKORON WIRE & CABLE DIVISION—See Furon Company; *U.S. Public*, pg. 689
DEL AMERICAN PROPERTIES, INC.; *U.S. Private*, pg. 321
DEL AMO HOSPITAL—See Universal Health Services, Inc.; *U.S. Public*, pg. 1697
DEL BOSCO & C.S.R.L.—See CODELCO Chile (Corporacion Nacional Del Cobre De Chile); *Int'l*, pg. 303
DEL GLOBAL TECHNOLOGIES; *U.S. Public*, pg. 493
DEL INTERNATIONAL—See Del Laboratories, Inc.; *U.S. Public*, pg. 494
DEL LABORATORIES (CANADA) LTD.—See Del Laboratories, Inc.; *U.S. Public*, pg. 494
DEL LABORATORIES, INC.; *U.S. Public*, pg. 494
DEL MAR AVIONICS; *U.S. Private*, pg. 321
DEL MONTE FOODS; *U.S. Public*, pg. 321
DEL MONTE FOODS INTERNATIONAL LIMITED—See Del Monte Royal Corporation; *Int'l*, pg. 388
DEL MONTE ROYAL CORPORATION; *Int'l*, pg. 388
DEL PHARMACEUTICALS, INC.—See Del Laboratories, Inc.; *U.S. Public*, pg. 494
DEL-PRIME, INC.—See Prime Bancorp, Inc.; *U.S. Public*, pg. 1326
DEL REY RESTAURANT CORP.—See Specialty Restaurants Corporation; *U.S. Private*, pg. 1022
DEL RIVERO MESSIANU ADVERTISING, LTD.; *U.S. Private*, pg. 321
DEL TACO, INC.; *U.S. Private*, pg. 321
DEL-VEST INC.—See PNC Bank Corp.; *U.S. Public*, pg. 1243
DEL WEBB CALIFORNIA CORPORATION—See Del Webb Corporation; *U.S. Public*, pg. 495
DEL WEBB CORPORATION; *U.S. Public*, pg. 494
DEL WEBB HOMES, INC.—See Del Webb Corporation; *U.S. Public*, pg. 495
DEL WEBB'S COVENTRY HOMES—See Del Webb Corporation; *U.S. Public*, pg. 495

DELA—See Groupe Strafor Facom; *Int'l*, pg. 570
DELAFORCE SONS & CA VINHOS LDA.—See Diageo Plc; *Int'l*, pg. 409
DELAGRA CORPORATION; *U.S. Private*, pg. 321
DELAIR GROUP, L.L.C.—See Aluminum Shapes, LLC; *U.S. Private*, pg. 47
DELAMINE B.V.—See Tosoh Corporation; *Int'l*, pg. 1408
DELAMINE B.V.-DELFZIJL PLANT—See Tosoh Corporation; *Int'l*, pg. 1408
DELANO ENERGY COMPANY, INC.—See Thermo Electron Corporation; *U.S. Public*, pg. 1591
DELARUE SYSTEMS LIMITED PLC; *Int'l*, pg. 388
DELAVAN COMMERCIAL PRODUCTS DIVISION—See Coltec Holdings Inc; *U.S. Public*, pg. 401
DELAVAN GAS TURBINE PRODUCTS DIVISION—See Coltec Holdings Inc; *U.S. Public*, pg. 401
DELAVAN, INC.—See Coltec Holdings Inc; *U.S. Public*, pg. 401
DELAVEST, INC.—See Wendy's International Inc.; *U.S. Public*, pg. 1754
DELAWARE AMERICAN LIFE INSURANCE CO.—See American International Group, Inc.; *U.S. Public*, pg. 84
DELAWARE CHARTER GUARANTEE & TRUST CO.—See The Principal Financial Group; *U.S. Private*, pg. 885
DELAWARE COCA-COLA BOTTLING COMPANY, INC.—See Coca-Cola Enterprises Inc.; *U.S. Public*, pg. 393
DELAWARE COMPUTING DEUTSCHLAND GMBH—See N.V. Bekaert S.A.; *Int'l*, pg. 184
DELAWARE COMPUTING NEDERLAND B.V.—See N.V. Bekaert S.A.; *Int'l*, pg. 184
DELAWARE COMPUTING SERVICES INC.—See N.V. Bekaert S.A.; *Int'l*, pg. 184
DELAWARE COMPUTING ZWEVEGEM—See N.V. Bekaert S.A.; *Int'l*, pg. 183
DELAWARE ELECTRIC CO-OP; *U.S. Private*, pg. 321
DELAWARE INDUSTRIAL SERVICES N.V.—See N.V. Bekaert S.A.; *Int'l*, pg. 183
DELAWARE MANAGEMENT HOLDINGS, INC.—See Lincoln National Corporation; *U.S. Public*, pg. 997
DELAWARE NORTH COMPANIES, INC.; *U.S. Private*, pg. 321
DELAWARE REINSURANCE COMPANY—See Cigna Corp.; *U.S. Public*, pg. 363
DELAWARE RIBBON MANUFACTURERS, INC.; *U.S. Private*, pg. 322
DELAWARE VALLEY WOOL SCOURING CO.—See Mohawk Industries, Inc.; *U.S. Public*, pg. 1121
GEORGES DELBARD S.A.—See LVMH Moet Hennessy Louis Vuitton; *Int'l*, pg. 780
DELCAL ENTERPRISES, INC.; *U.S. Private*, pg. 322
DELCAR DIGITAL—See True North Diversified Companies; *U.S. Public*, pg. 1642
DELCHAMPS, INC.—See Jitney-Jungle Stores of America, Inc.; *U.S. Private*, pg. 588
DELCHESTER OIL CO. INC.—See Heating Oil Partners L.P.; *U.S. Private*, pg. 518
DELCO ELECTRONICS CORPORATION—See General Motors Corporation; *U.S. Public*, pg. 720
DELCO-ELECTRONICS CUSTOMER SUPPORT—See General Motors Corporation; *U.S. Public*, pg. 720
DELCO MORAINE NDH DIVISION—See General Motors Corporation; *U.S. Public*, pg. 724
DELCO PRODUCTS DIVISION—See General Motors Corporation; *U.S. Public*, pg. 724
DELCO REMI-COMPONENTES ELECTRONICOS, LDA.—See General Motors Corporation; *U.S. Public*, pg. 721
DELCO REMY AMERICA, INC.—See Delco Remy International, Inc.; *U.S. Public*, pg. 495
DELCO REMY DIVISION—See General Motors Corporation; *U.S. Public*, pg. 721
DELCO REMY INTERNATIONAL, INC.; *U.S. Public*, pg. 495
DELCO SYSTEMS OPERATION—See General Motors Corporation; *U.S. Public*, pg. 720
DELEGUE DE LA BAYERISCHE VEREINSBANK AUPRES DU CREDIT DU NORD—See Bayerische Vereinsbank Group; *Int'l*, pg. 181
DELESTO BV—See Akzo Nobel N.V.; *Int'l*, pg. 43
DELEUW, CATHER & COMPANY—See Parsons Corporation; *U.S. Private*, pg. 841
DELEUW, CATHER INTERNATIONAL LTD.—See Parsons Corporation; *U.S. Private*, pg. 842
DELEVAN DIV.—See American Precision Industries Inc.; *U.S. Public*, pg. 90
DELFIA, INC.—See Monsanto Company; *U.S. Public*, pg. 1124
DELFIELD COMPANY—See Scotsman Industries, Inc.; *U.S. Public*, pg. 1445
DELFOS/Y&R—See Young & Rubicam Inc.; *U.S. Private*, pg. 1200
BV DELFT ELECTRONIC PRODUCTS—See Delft Instruments N.V.; *Int'l*, pg. 388
DELFT INSTRUMENTS - BRD GMBH—See Delft Instruments N.V.; *Int'l*, pg. 389
DELFT INSTRUMENTS DEFENSE BV—See Delft Instruments N.V.; *Int'l*, pg. 388
DELFT INSTRUMENTS ELECTRO-OPTICS B.V.—See Delft Instruments N.V.; *Int'l*, pg. 389
DELFT INSTRUMENTS FAR EAST, LTD.—See Delft Instruments N.V.; *Int'l*, pg. 389
DELFT INSTRUMENTS INTERNATIONAL B.V.—See Delft Instruments N.V.; *Int'l*, pg. 389
DELFT INSTRUMENTS NEDERLAND B.V.—See Delft Instruments N.V.; *Int'l*, pg. 389
DELFT INSTRUMENTS N.V.; *Int'l*, pg. 388
DELGASCO, INC.—See Delta Natural Gas Company, Inc.; *U.S. Public*, pg. 497
DELHAIZE "LE LION" FRANCE S.A.—See Etablissements Delhaize Freres Et Cie "Le Lion" S.A.; *Int'l*, pg. 463
DELHAIZE THE LION AMERICA, INC.—See Etablissements Delhaize Freres Et Cie "Le Lion" S.A.; *Int'l*, pg. 463

DELHAIZE THE LION COORDINATION CENTER S.A.—See Etablissements Delhaize Freres Et Cie "Le Lion" S.A.; *Int'l*, pg. 463
DELHAIZE "THE LION" NEDERLAND B.V.—See Etablissements Delhaize Freres Et Cie "Le Lion" S.A.; *Int'l*, pg. 463
DELHI INDUSTRIES INC.—See Russel Metals Inc.; *Int'l*, pg. 1150
DELHI PETROLEUM PTY. LTD.—See Exxon Corporation; *U.S. Public*, pg. 601
DELHOME S.A.—See Etablissements Delhaize Freres Et Cie "Le Lion" S.A.; *Int'l*, pg. 463
N.V. DELI-UNIVERSAL—See Universal Corporation; *U.S. Public*, pg. 1695
DELICATO VINEYARDS; *U.S. Private*, pg. 322
DELICIA B.V.—See Koninklijke BolsWessanen nv; *Int'l*, pg. 752
DELIMMO S.A.—See Etablissements Delhaize Freres Et Cie "Le Lion" S.A.; *Int'l*, pg. 463
DELINVEST, INC.—See Etablissements Delhaize Freres Et Cie "Le Lion" S.A.; *Int'l*, pg. 463
DELISLE FOODS LTD.—See Danone Group; *Int'l*, pg. 380
DELKOR BATTERY COMPANY—See General Motors Corporation; *U.S. Public*, pg. 724
DELL ASIA PACIFIC LTD.—See Dell Computer Corporation; *U.S. Public*, pg. 495
DELL ASIA PACIFIC SDN.—See Dell Computer Corporation; *U.S. Public*, pg. 495
DELL BALER—See Carclo Engineering Group plc; *Int'l*, pg. 268
DELL COMPUTER AB—See Dell Computer Corporation; *U.S. Public*, pg. 496
DELL COMPUTER AS—See Dell Computer Corporation; *U.S. Public*, pg. 496
DELL COMPUTER A.S. DENMARK—See Dell Computer Corporation; *U.S. Public*, pg. 496
DELL COMPUTER ASIA LTD.—See Dell Computer Corporation; *U.S. Public*, pg. 496
DELL COMPUTER ASIA PTE LTD.—See Dell Computer Corporation; *U.S. Public*, pg. 496
DELL COMPUTER BV—See Dell Computer Corporation; *U.S. Public*, pg. 496
DELL COMPUTER CO., LTD.—See Dell Computer Corporation; *U.S. Public*, pg. 496
DELL COMPUTER CORPORATION; *U.S. Public*, pg. 495
DELL COMPUTER CORPORATION—See Dell Computer Corporation; *U.S. Public*, pg. 496
DELL COMPUTER CORPORATION LTD.—See Dell Computer Corporation; *U.S. Public*, pg. 496
DELL COMPUTER DE MEXICO S.A. DE C.V.—See Dell Computer Corporation; *U.S. Public*, pg. 496
DELL COMPUTER GES.M.B.H—See Dell Computer Corporation; *U.S. Public*, pg. 496
DELL COMPUTER GMBH—See Dell Computer Corporation; *U.S. Public*, pg. 496
DELL COMPUTER JAPAN—See Dell Computer Corporation; *U.S. Public*, pg. 496
DELL COMPUTER K.K.—See Dell Computer Corporation; *U.S. Public*, pg. 496
DELL COMPUTER LTD.—See Dell Computer Corporation; *U.S. Public*, pg. 496
DELL COMPUTER OY—See Dell Computer Corporation; *U.S. Public*, pg. 496
DELL COMPUTER POLAND—See Dell Computer Corporation; *U.S. Public*, pg. 496
DELL COMPUTER PTY. LTD.—See Dell Computer Corporation; *U.S. Public*, pg. 496
DELL COMPUTER S.A.—See Dell Computer Corporation; *U.S. Public*, pg. 496
DELL COMPUTER SA—See Dell Computer Corporation; *U.S. Public*, pg. 496
N.V. DELL COMPUTER S.A.—See Dell Computer Corporation; *U.S. Public*, pg. 496
DELL COMPUTER SRO—See Dell Computer Corporation; *U.S. Public*, pg. 496
DELL ESPANA S.A.—See Dell Computer Corporation; *U.S. Public*, pg. 496
DELL MARKETING CORPORATION—See Dell Computer Corporation; *U.S. Public*, pg. 495
DELL PRODUCTS (ASIA) B.V.—See Dell Computer Corporation; *U.S. Public*, pg. 496
DELL PRODUCTS (EUROPE) B.V.—See Dell Computer Corporation; *U.S. Public*, pg. 496
DELL PUBLISHING—See Bertelsmann AG; *Int'l*, pg. 191
DELMAR—See Herff Jones Inc.; *U.S. Private*, pg. 523
DELMAR PHOTOGRAPHIC AND PRINTING COMPANY—See Continental Graphics Holdings, Inc.; *U.S. Private*, pg. 268
DELMAR PUBLISHERS INC.—See The Thomson Corporation; *U.S. Public*, pg. 1600
DELMAR STUDIOS—See Continental Graphics Holdings, Inc.; *U.S. Private*, pg. 268
DELMARVA CAPITAL INVESTMENTS, INC.—See Conectiv; *U.S. Public*, pg. 431
DELMARVA ENERGY COMPANY—See Conectiv; *U.S. Public*, pg. 431
DELMARVA INDUSTRIES, INC.—See Conectiv; *U.S. Public*, pg. 431
DELMARVA POWER & LIGHT COMPANY—See Conectiv; *U.S. Public*, pg. 430
DELMARVA PROPERTIES, INC.—See Chesapeake Corporation; *U.S. Public*, pg. 347
DELMARVA SERVICES CO.—See Conectiv; *U.S. Public*, pg. 431
DELMEX DE JUAREZ S.A. DE C.V.—See General Motors Corporation; *U.S. Public*, pg. 721
DELMON READY MIXED CONCRETE & PRODUCTS CO. W.L.L. (BAHRAIN)—See Redland PLC; *Int'l*, pg. 1092
DELMONICO FOODS—See Hershey Foods Corporation; *U.S. Public*, pg. 812
DELNEMO A.S.—See Etablissements Delhaize Freres Et Cie "Le Lion" S.A.; *Int'l*, pg. 463
DELNOR CORP.—See Preussag AG; *Int'l*, pg. 1070

DELNOSA, S.A. DE C.V.—See General Motors Corporation; *U.S. Public*, pg. 721
DELOITTE & TOUCHE LLP; *U.S. Private*, pg. 322
DELORE—See American International Industries; *U.S. Private*, pg. 57
DELOS DEUTSCHER LLOYD SCHULUNGSZENTRUM G.M.B.H.—See Assicurazioni Generali S.p.A.; *Int'l*, pg. 89
DELPANAMA S.A.—See Cigna Corp.; *U.S. Public*, pg. 364
DELPHAX SYSTEMS—See Avery Dennison Corporation; *U.S. Public*, pg. 153
DELPHI AUTOMOTIVE SYSTEMS—See General Motors Corporation; *U.S. Public*, pg. 719
DELPHI CAPITAL MANAGEMENT, INC.—See Delphi Financial Group, Inc.; *U.S. Public*, pg. 496
DELPHI CHASSIS SYSTEMS—See General Motors Corporation; *U.S. Public*, pg. 719
DELPHI ENERGY & ENGINE MANAGEMENT SYSTEMS—See General Motors Corporation; *U.S. Public*, pg. 719
DELPHI FINANCIAL GROUP, INC.; *U.S. Public*, pg. 496
DELPHI HARRISON THERMAL SYSTEMS—See General Motors Corporation; *U.S. Public*, pg. 719
DELPHI PACKARD ELECTRIC SYSTEMS—See General Motors Corporation; *U.S. Public*, pg. 719
DELPHI SAGINAW STEERING SYSTEMS—See General Motors Corporation; *U.S. Public*, pg. 719
DELREDO S.A. DE C.V.—See General Motors Corporation; *U.S. Public*, pg. 721
DELREST, INC.—See Etablissements Delhaize Freres Et Cie "Le Lion" S.A.; *Int'l*, pg. 463
DELRIEU BOIS ET MATERIAUX—See La Meridionale des Bois et Materiaux; *Int'l*, pg. 784
DELROYD WORM GEAR—See IMO Industries Inc.; *U.S. Public*, pg. 857
DELSEY A/S—See Bertrand Faure; *Int'l*, pg. 192
DELSEY ESPANA SA—See Bertrand Faure; *Int'l*, pg. 192
DELSEY GMBH—See Bertrand Faure; *Int'l*, pg. 192
DELSEY ITALIA SPA—See Bertrand Faure; *Int'l*, pg. 192
DELSEY LUGGAGE INC.—See Bertrand Faure; *Int'l*, pg. 192
DELSEY LUGGAGE LTD.—See Bertrand Faure; *Int'l*, pg. 192
DELSEY NV—See Bertrand Faure; *Int'l*, pg. 192
DELSEY SA—See Bertrand Faure; *Int'l*, pg. 192
DELSHOP S.A.—See Etablissements Delhaize Freres Et Cie "Le Lion" S.A.; *Int'l*, pg. 463
DELTA AIR LINES FRANKFURT—See Delta Air Lines, Inc.; *U.S. Public*, pg. 497
DELTA AIR LINES, INC.; *U.S. Public*, pg. 497
DELTA AIR LINES MARKETING—See Delta Air Lines, Inc.; *U.S. Public*, pg. 497
DELTA AIR LINES MARKETING OFFICER—See Delta Air Lines, Inc.; *U.S. Public*, pg. 497
DELTA AIR LINES MUNICH—See Delta Air Lines, Inc.; *U.S. Public*, pg. 497
DELTA AIR LINES TOKYO—See Delta Air Lines, Inc.; *U.S. Public*, pg. 497
DELTA AIR LINES UK—See Delta Air Lines, Inc.; *U.S. Public*, pg. 497
DELTA AIR TRANSPORT N.V.—See Sabena; *Int'l*, pg. 1166
DELTA AMERICA INC.—See Delta plc; *Int'l*, pg. 391
DELTA & PINE LAND COMPANY; *U.S. Public*, pg. 497
DELTA APPAREL—See Delta Woodside Industries, Inc.; *U.S. Public*, pg. 498
DELTA BIOLOGICALS, S.R.L.—See IVAX Corporation; *U.S. Public*, pg. 915
DELTA-BOUW BV—See Heidemij N.V.; *Int'l*, pg. 607
DELTA CABLES HOLDINGS LTD.—See Delta plc; *Int'l*, pg. 390
DELTA CAPILLARY PRODUCTS—See Delta plc; *Int'l*, pg. 390
DELTA CIRCUIT PROTECTION & CONTROLS LTD.—See Delta plc; *Int'l*, pg. 390
DELTA CONSOLIDATED INDUSTRIES, INC.—See Danaher Corporation; *U.S. Public*, pg. 481
DELTA CONSOLIDATED INDUSTRIES, INC. (CO. HEADQUARTERS)—See Danaher Corporation; *U.S. Public*, pg. 481
DELTA CONTRACTOR EQUIPMENT RENTAL, INC.—See Lombardi Holdings Inc.; *U.S. Private*, pg. 673
DELTA CORRECTIONAL FACILITY—See Corrections Corporation of America; *U.S. Public*, pg. 450
DELTA COUNTY TELE-COMM., INC.—See Telephone and Data Systems, Inc.; *U.S. Public*, pg. 1571
DELTA CROMPTON CABLES LTD.—See Delta plc; *Int'l*, pg. 390
DELTA CROMPTON HOLDINGS LTD.—See Delta plc; *Int'l*, pg. 390
DELTA/CYKLOP STRAPPING—See Illinois Tool Works Inc.; *U.S. Public*, pg. 865
DELTA - DESGASIFICACION Y LIMPIEZA DE TANGQUES, S.A.—See SEPI; *Int'l*, pg. 1223
DELTA DESIGN, INC.—See Cohu, Inc.; *U.S. Public*, pg. 396
DELTA DISTRIBUTORS, INC.—See Veba AG; *Int'l*, pg. 1458
DELTA EDUCATION, INC.—See Torstar Corporation; *Int'l*, pg. 1402
DELTA ELECTRICAL & ENGINEERING SERVICES LTD.—See Delta plc; *Int'l*, pg. 390
DELTA ELECTRICAL INDUSTRIES LTD.—See Delta plc; *Int'l*, pg. 392
DELTA ELECTRICAL SYSTEMS LTD.—See Delta plc; *Int'l*, pg. 390
DELTA EMS LTD.—See Delta plc; *Int'l*, pg. 391
DELTA ENCON LTD.—See Delta plc; *Int'l*, pg. 391
DELTA ENFIELD CABLES (HOLDINGS) LTD.—See Delta plc; *Int'l*, pg. 390
DELTA ENFIELD LTD.—See Delta plc; *Int'l*, pg. 390
DELTA ENFIELD METALS LTD.—See Delta plc; *Int'l*, pg. 390
DELTA ENFIELD WIRES LTD.—See Delta plc; *Int'l*, pg. 390

DELTA DIRECTORY OF CORPORATE AFFILIATIONS
Company Index

DELTA ENGINEERING HOLDING LTD.—See Delta plc; *Int'l*, pg. 390
DELTA EXTRUDED METALS CO. LTD.—See Delta plc; *Int'l*, pg. 391
DELTA FASTENERS PTY. LTD.—See Delta plc; *Int'l*, pg. 391
DELTA FAUCET CORPORATION—See Masco Corporation; *U.S. Public*, pg. 1053
DELTA FAUCET OF CANADA—See Masco Corporation; *U.S. Public*, pg. 1053
DELTA FAUCET OF OKLAHOMA, INC.—See Masco Corporation; *U.S. Public*, pg. 1053
DELTA FLUID PRODUCTS LTD.—See Delta plc; *Int'l*, pg. 391
DELTA FOREMOST CHEMICAL CORP.; *U.S. Private*, pg. 322
DELTA GOLD N.L.; *Int'l*, pg. 389
DELTA GROUP AUSTRALIA PTY. LTD.—See Delta plc; *Int'l*, pg. 391
DELTA INDUSTRIES; *U.S. Private*, pg. 322
DELTA INSURANCE SERVICES CORP.—See Associated Grocers, Inc.; *U.S. Private*, pg. 91
DELTA INTERNATIONAL MACHINERY CORP.—See Pentair, Inc.; *U.S. Public*, pg. 1273
DELTA INTERNATIONAL MACHINERY CORP. (TUPELO)—See Pentair, Inc.; *U.S. Public*, pg. 1273
DELTA LIFE & ANNUITY CO.—See American Mutual Life Holding Co.; *U.S. Private*, pg. 59
DELTA LIFE CORPORATION—See American Mutual Life Holding Co.; *U.S. Private*, pg. 59
DELTA LITHOGRAPH CO.—See Bertelsmann AG; *Int'l*, pg. 191
DELTA (MANGANESE BRONZE) LTD.—See Delta plc; *Int'l*, pg. 391
DELTA MILLS MARKETING COMPANY—See Delta Woodside Industries, Inc.; *U.S. Public*, pg. 498
DELTA NATURAL GAS COMPANY, INC.; *U.S. Public*, pg. 497
DELTA PLC; *Int'l*, pg. 389
DELTA POWER CO.; *U.S. Private*, pg. 322
DELTA PRECISION LTD.—See Delta plc; *Int'l*, pg. 391
DELTA PRIDE CATFISH, INC.; *U.S. Private*, pg. 322
DELTA REPETITION COMPONENTS LTD.—See Delta plc; *Int'l*, pg. 391
DELTA RESINS & REFRACTORIES, INC.; *U.S. Private*, pg. 323
DELTA RESOURCES, INC.—See Delta Natural Gas Company, Inc.; *U.S. Public*, pg. 497
DELTA RUBBER COMPANY; *U.S. Private*, pg. 323
DELTA S.A. (PTY.) LTD.—See Delta plc; *Int'l*, pg. 392
DELTA SCHOELLER—See Delta plc; *Int'l*, pg. 390
DELTA STEEL INC.—See Preussag AG; *Int'l*, pg. 1070
DELTA SUPRENANT WIRE & CABLE INC.—See Delta plc; *Int'l*, pg. 391
DELTA TRADING CO. LTD.—See Olivetti SpA; *Int'l*, pg. 1003
DELTA-UNIBUS CORP.—See Powell Industries, Inc.; *U.S. Public*, pg. 1319
DELTA V TECHNOLOGIES, INC.—See Presstek, Inc.; *U.S. Public*, pg. 1324
DELTA WELDING EQUIPMENT LTD.—See Delta plc; *Int'l*, pg. 390
DELTA WEST PTY. LTD.—See Pharmacia & Upjohn, Inc.; *Int'l*, pg. 1049
DELTA WOODSIDE INDUSTRIES, INC.; *U.S. Public*, pg. 497
DELTAFINA S.P.A.—See Universal Corporation; *U.S. Public*, pg. 1695
DELTAIR U.K. INVESTMENTS LTD.—See Delta Air Lines, Inc.; *U.S. Public*, pg. 497
DELTAK INC.—See Jason Incorporated; *U.S. Public*, pg. 924
DELTAVEN S.A.—See Petroleos de Venezuela S.A.; *Int'l*, pg. 1045
DELTEC—See BTR plc; *Int'l*, pg. 126
DELTEC CORPORATION—See Fiskars Oy AB; *Int'l*, pg. 492
DELTEC S.A.—See Fiskars Oy AB; *Int'l*, pg. 492
DELTIC TIMBER CORPORATION; *U.S. Public*, pg. 498
DELTRAN DIV.—See American Precision Industries Inc.; *U.S. Public*, pg. 90
DELTRAN, INC.—See Delta Natural Gas Company, Inc.; *U.S. Public*, pg. 497
DELTRONICOS DE MATAMOROS S.A. DE C.V.—See General Motors Corporation; *U.S. Public*, pg. 721
DELUXAIR INCORPORATED—See Emco Limited; *Int'l*, pg. 453
DELUXE BUSINESS SYSTEMS DIVISION—See Deluxe Corporation; *U.S. Public*, pg. 498
DELUXE CORPORATION; *U.S. Public*, pg. 498
DELUXE HOMES OF PA., INC.; *U.S. Private*, pg. 323
DELUXE LABORATORIES, INC.—See The Rank Group PLC; *Int'l*, pg. 1087
DELUXE SPECIALTIES MFG. CO.—See Triumph Group, Inc.; *U.S. Public*, pg. 1640
DELUXE STORAGE SYSTEMS, INC.; *U.S. Private*, pg. 323
DELUXE TORONTO LIMITED—See The Rank Group PLC; *Int'l*, pg. 1087
DELVAG LUFTFAHRTVERSICHERUNGS-AG—See Deutsche Lufthansa AG; *Int'l*, pg. 407
DELVITA A.S.—See Etablissements Delhaize Freres Et Cie "Le Lion" S.A.; *Int'l*, pg. 463
DEMAG-BRANDENBURG ENGINEERING—See Mannesmann A.G.; *Int'l*, pg. 837
DEMAG DELAVAL TURBINE—See Mannesmann A.G.; *Int'l*, pg. 837
DEMAG-JUNGHEINRICH FAHRERLOSE TRANSPORTSYSTEMS GMBH—See Mannesmann A.G.; *Int'l*, pg. 837
DEMAG KOMATSU GMBH—See Komatsu Ltd.; *Int'l*, pg. 745
DEMAG KUNSTSTOFFTECHNIK GMBH—See Mannesmann A.G.; *Int'l*, pg. 837
DEMAG SCHRADER GMBH—See Mannesmann A.G.; *Int'l*, pg. 837
DEMAG TECHNICA GMBH—See Mannesmann A.G.; *Int'l*, pg. 837
DEMAG UNTERSTUTZUNGSKASSE GMBH—See Mannesmann A.G.; *Int'l*, pg. 837
DEMARIA BUILDING CO. INC.; *U.S. Private*, pg. 323
DEMARS PROGRAM MANAGEMENT, INC.—See Geupel DeMars, Inc.; *U.S. Private*, pg. 450
DEMCO INC.; *U.S. Private*, pg. 323
DEMERARA TOBACCO CO. LTD.—See B.A.T Industries P.L.C.; *Int'l*, pg. 111
DEMERT & DOUGHERTY, INC.; *U.S. Private*, pg. 323
DEMETER, INC.—See Archer Daniels Midland Company (ADM); *U.S. Public*, pg. 127
DEMINEX ALBANIA PETROLEUM GMBH—See Veba AG; *Int'l*, pg. 1461
DEMINEX ARGENTINA SA—See Veba AG; *Int'l*, pg. 1461
DEMINEX (CANADA) LTD.—See Veba AG; *Int'l*, pg. 1461
DEMINEX-DEUTSCHE GMBH—See Veba AG; *Int'l*, pg. 1460
DEMINEX EGYPT—See Veba AG; *Int'l*, pg. 1461
DEMINEX INDONESIA—See Veba AG; *Int'l*, pg. 1461
DEMINEX MOSCOW OFFICE—See Veba AG; *Int'l*, pg. 1461
DEMINEX NORGE AS—See Veba AG; *Int'l*, pg. 1461
DEMINEX SYRIA GMBH—See Veba AG; *Int'l*, pg. 1461
DEMINEX UK OIL AND GAS LTD.—See Veba AG; *Int'l*, pg. 1461
DEMIX BETON/AGREGATS—See Holderbank Financiere Glaris Ltd.; *Int'l*, pg. 629
DEMIX CONSTRUCTION—See Holderbank Financiere Glaris Ltd.; *Int'l*, pg. 629
JACK DEMMER FORD, INC.; *U.S. Private*, pg. 323
DEMNER, MERLICEK & BERGMANN WERBEGESELLSCHAFT MBH; *Int'l*, pg. 392
DEMOCRAT & CHRONICLE—See Gannett Company, Inc.; *U.S. Public*, pg. 699
DEMOCRAT NEWS—See Pulitzer Publishing Company; *U.S. Public*, pg. 1343
DEMOCRAT PRINTING & LITHOGRAPH COMPANY; *U.S. Private*, pg. 323
DEMOCRATIC NATIONAL COMMITTEE; *U.S. Private*, pg. 324
DEMONAX COMPUTER SERVICES LIMITED—See HSBC Holdings plc; *Int'l*, pg. 581
DEMOULAS MARKET BASKET; *U.S. Private*, pg. 324
DEMPSEY & SIDERS INSURANCE AGENCY—See American Financial Group; *U.S. Public*, pg. 75
DEMPSTER EQUIPMENT—See Toccoa Metal Technologies, Inc.; *U.S. Private*, pg. 1089
DEMPSTER INDUSTRIES INC.; *U.S. Private*, pg. 324
DEMSTAR LTD.—See Hewlett-Packard Company; *U.S. Public*, pg. 817
DEN HERTOG B.V.—See Koninklijke BolsWessanen nv; *Int'l*, pg. 752
DEN-MAT CORPORATION; *U.S. Private*, pg. 324
DEN NORSKE BANK—See Den norske Bank ASA; *Int'l*, pg. 392
DEN NORSKE BANK AS, LONDON BRANCH—See Den norske Bank ASA; *Int'l*, pg. 392
DEN NORSKE BANK AS, SINGAPORE BRANCH—See Den norske Bank ASA; *Int'l*, pg. 392
DEN NORSKE BANK ASA; *Int'l*, pg. 392
DEN NORSKE BANK - CENTRAL NORWAY—See Den norske Bank ASA; *Int'l*, pg. 392
DEN NORSKE BANK (LUXEMBOURG) S.A.—See Den norske Bank ASA; *Int'l*, pg. 392
DEN NORSKE BANK, NEW YORK BRANCH—See Den norske Bank ASA; *Int'l*, pg. 392
DEN NORSKE BANK - NORTHERN NORWAY—See Den norske Bank ASA; *Int'l*, pg. 392
DEN NORSKE BANK - SOUTHERN NORWAY—See Den norske Bank ASA; *Int'l*, pg. 392
DENA CORPORATION; *U.S. Private*, pg. 324
DENAK KK—See Akzo Nobel N.V.; *Int'l*, pg. 44
DENAMERICA CORP.; *U.S. Public*, pg. 498
DENCO LTD.—See AMEC Plc; *Int'l*, pg. 16
DENGYOSHA MACHINE WORKS CORPORATION—See Toshiba Corporation; *Int'l*, pg. 1402
DENI DISTRIBUTIECENTRUM B.V.—See Royal Nedlloyd Group N.V.; *Int'l*, pg. 1144
DENISE LINGERIE—See House of Ronnie, Inc.; *U.S. Private*, pg. 542
DENISON COLOUR LIMITED—See American Greetings Corporation; *U.S. Public*, pg. 78
DENISON HYDRAULICS, INC.; *U.S. Private*, pg. 324
T.S. DENISON & COMPANY—See Creative Publications; *U.S. Private*, pg. 288
DENKI KAGAKU KOGYO KABUSHIKI KAISHA—See Mitsui & Co., Ltd.; *Int'l*, pg. 877
DENLINGER, INC.; *U.S. Private*, pg. 324
DENMARK PLANT—See Cooper Industries, Inc.; *U.S. Public*, pg. 443
DENNIS CHEMICAL CO., INC.; *U.S. Private*, pg. 324
DENNISON DATA SYSTEMS DIV.—See Avery Dennison Corporation; *U.S. Public*, pg. 152
DENNISON DO BRAZIL COMMERCIAL LTDA.—See Avery Dennison Corporation; *U.S. Public*, pg. 153
DENNISON FASTENER DIV.—See Avery Dennison Corporation; *U.S. Public*, pg. 152
DENNISON IMAGING SYSTEMS DIV.—See Avery Dennison Corporation; *U.S. Public*, pg. 152
DENNISON INTERNATIONAL CO.—See Avery Dennison Corporation; *U.S. Public*, pg. 153
DENNISON MANUFACTURING CANADA, INC.—See Avery Dennison Corporation; *U.S. Public*, pg. 153
DENNISON MARKING SYSTEMS, PTY. LTD.—See Avery Dennison Corporation; *U.S. Public*, pg. 153
DENNISON PANAMERICANA, INC.—See Avery Dennison Corporation; *U.S. Public*, pg. 152
DENNISON PLC—See Avery Dennison Corporation; *U.S. Public*, pg. 153
DENNISON SPECIALTY PRODUCTS DIV.—See Avery Dennison Corporation; *U.S. Public*, pg. 152
DENNISON STATIONERY PRODUCTS COMPANY—See Avery Dennison Corporation; *U.S. Public*, pg. 153
DENNISON THERIMAGE DIV.—See Avery Dennison Corporation; *U.S. Public*, pg. 152
DENNISON TRADING HONG KONG LTD.—See Avery Dennison Corporation; *U.S. Public*, pg. 153
DENNISON TRANSOCEANIC CORPORATION—See Avery Dennison Corporation; *U.S. Public*, pg. 152
DENNY MENHOLT FRONTIER CHEVROLET; *U.S. Private*, pg. 324
DENNY'S, INC.—See Advantica Restaurant Group, Inc.; *U.S. Public*, pg. 23
DENNY'S JAPAN CO., LTD.—See Ito-Yokado Co., Ltd.; *Int'l*, pg. 693
DENNY'S OF CANADA—See Advantica Restaurant Group, Inc.; *U.S. Public*, pg. 23
A/S DENOFA OG LILLEBORG FABRIKER—See Orkla A.S.A.; *Int'l*, pg. 1010
DENPLAN LIMITED—See PPP hc; *Int'l*, pg. 1020
DENSHI GIKEN CO., LTD.—See Honda Motor Co., Ltd.; *Int'l*, pg. 634
DENSO SALES CALIFORNIA—See Toyota Motor Corporation; *Int'l*, pg. 1412
DENSTREE CORPORATION LTD.—See Jardine Matheson Holdings Limited; *Int'l*, pg. 703
DENT-X DIVISION—See AFP Imaging Corporation; *U.S. Public*, pg. 6
DENTAL HEALTH ALLIANCE, L.L.C.—See Fortis; *Int'l*, pg. 499
DENTAL PRODUCTS DIVISION—See 3M; *U.S. Public*, pg. 1605
DENTCO, INC.—See Block Drug Company, Inc.; *U.S. Public*, pg. 237
DENTEX RESEARCH DEVELOPMENT, INC.—See Fried. Krupp AG; *Int'l*, pg. 510
DENTICARE OF CALIFORNIA, INC.—See Foundation Health Systems, Inc.; *U.S. Public*, pg. 678
DENTON CONCRETE SERVICES INC.—See Denton Enterprises Inc.; *U.S. Private*, pg. 325
DENTON ENTERPRISES INC.; *U.S. Private*, pg. 325
DENTSPLY ARGENTINA S.A.C.I.—See Dentsply International Inc.; *U.S. Public*, pg. 499
DENTSPLY ASH—See Dentsply International Inc.; *U.S. Public*, pg. 499
DENTSPLY ASIA—See Dentsply International Inc.; *U.S. Public*, pg. 499
DENTSPLY AUSTRALIA—See Dentsply International Inc.; *U.S. Public*, pg. 499
DENTSPLY (AUSTRALIA) PTY. LTD.—See Dentsply International Inc.; *U.S. Public*, pg. 499
DENTSPLY BRAZIL—See Dentsply International Inc.; *U.S. Public*, pg. 499
DENTSPLY CANADA—See Dentsply International Inc.; *U.S. Public*, pg. 499
DENTSPLY CAVITRON—See Dentsply International Inc.; *U.S. Public*, pg. 499
DENTSPLY CAVITRON PLANT—See Dentsply International Inc.; *U.S. Public*, pg. 499
DENTSPLY CERAMCO—See Dentsply International Inc.; *U.S. Public*, pg. 499
DENTSPLY DENTAL (TIANJIN) CO., LTD.—See Dentsply International Inc.; *U.S. Public*, pg. 499
DENTSPLY GENDEX DIVISION—See Dentsply International Inc.; *U.S. Public*, pg. 499
DENTSPLY GMBH—See Dentsply International Inc.; *U.S. Public*, pg. 499
DENTSPLY/IMPLANT DIVISION—See Dentsply International Inc.; *U.S. Public*, pg. 499
DENTSPLY INDIA—See Dentsply International Inc.; *U.S. Public*, pg. 499
DENTSPLY INTERNATIONAL—See Dentsply International Inc.; *U.S. Public*, pg. 499
DENTSPLY INTERNATIONAL INC.; *U.S. Public*, pg. 498
DENTSPLY ITALIA—See Dentsply International Inc.; *U.S. Public*, pg. 499
DENTSPLY JAPAN—See Dentsply International Inc.; *U.S. Public*, pg. 499
DENTSPLY LATIN AMERICAN EXPORT—See Dentsply International Inc.; *U.S. Public*, pg. 499
DENTSPLY MAILLEFER—See Dentsply International Inc.; *U.S. Public*, pg. 499
DENTSPLY MEXICO, S.A. DE C.V.—See Dentsply International Inc.; *U.S. Public*, pg. 499
DENTSPLY NEW IMAGE—See Dentsply International Inc.; *U.S. Public*, pg. 499
DENTSPLY PHILIPPINES—See Dentsply International Inc.; *U.S. Public*, pg. 500
DENTSPLY RANSOM & RANDOLPH—See Dentsply International Inc.; *U.S. Public*, pg. 499
DENTSPLY STOMADENT—See Dentsply International Inc.; *U.S. Public*, pg. 500
DENTSPLY SWITZERLAND—See Dentsply International Inc.; *U.S. Public*, pg. 500
DENTSPLY (THAILAND) LIMITED—See Dentsply International Inc.; *U.S. Public*, pg. 500
DENTSPLY TRUBYTE—See Dentsply International Inc.; *U.S. Public*, pg. 499
DENTSPLY TULSA—See Dentsply International Inc.; *U.S. Public*, pg. 499
DENTSU BURSON MARSTELLER, INC.—See Dentsu Inc.; *Int'l*, pg. 393
DENTSU BURSON MARSTELLER, INC. LOS ANGELES OFFICE—See Dentsu Inc.; *Int'l*, pg. 393
DENTSU-CADENCE CANADA, INC.—See Dentsu Inc.; *Int'l*, pg. 393
DENTSU COMMUNICATIONS INC.—See Dentsu Inc.; *Int'l*, pg. 393
DENTSU CORPORATION OF AMERICA, LOS ANGELES OFFICE—See Dentsu Inc.; *Int'l*, pg. 393
DENTSU EAST JAPAN INC.—See Dentsu Inc.; *Int'l*, pg. 393
DENTSU ESPANA S.A.—See Dentsu Inc.; *Int'l*, pg. 393

DENTSU EUROPE-AMSTERDAM—See Dentsu Inc.; *Int'l*, pg. 393
DENTSU EUROPE-DUSSELDORF—See Dentsu Inc.; *Int'l*, pg. 393
DENTSU EUROPE LTD.-LONDON—See Dentsu Inc.; *Int'l*, pg. 393
DENTSU HOLDINGS B.V.—See Dentsu Inc.; *Int'l*, pg. 393
DENTSU INC.; *Int'l*, pg. 392
DENTSU INC. SEOUL OFFICE—See Dentsu Inc.; *Int'l*, pg. 393
DENTSU INC. TAIPEI—See Dentsu Inc.; *Int'l*, pg. 393
DENTSU MANDATE (MALAYSIA) SDN. BHD.—See Dentsu Inc.; *Int'l*, pg. 393
DENTSU MANDATE SINGAPORE PTE. LTD.—See Dentsu Inc.; *Int'l*, pg. 393
DENTSU MOSCOW OFFICE—See Dentsu Inc.; *Int'l*, pg. 393
DENTSU, SUDLER & HENNESSEY INC.—See Dentsu Young & Rubicam Partnerships; *U.S. Private*, pg. 325
DENTSU (TAIWAN) INC.—See Dentsu Inc.; *Int'l*, pg. 393
DENTSU TOHOKU INC.—See Dentsu Inc.; *Int'l*, pg. 393
DENTSU USA-ATLANTA OFFICE—See Dentsu Inc.; *Int'l*, pg. 393
DENTSU WEST JAPAN INC.—See Dentsu Inc.; *Int'l*, pg. 393
DENTSU YOUNG & RUBICAM ADVERTISING CO., LTD. (BEIJING)—See Dentsu Young & Rubicam Partnerships; *U.S. Private*, pg. 325
DENTSU YOUNG & RUBICAM ADVERTISING CO., LTD. (GUANGZHOU)—See Dentsu Young & Rubicam Partnerships; *U.S. Private*, pg. 325
DENTSU YOUNG & RUBICAM ADVERTISING CO., LTD. (SHANGHAI)—See Dentsu Young & Rubicam Partnerships; *U.S. Private*, pg. 325
DENTSU YOUNG & RUBICAM-ALCANTARA INC. (MANILA)—See Dentsu Young & Rubicam Partnerships; *U.S. Private*, pg. 325
DENTSU YOUNG & RUBICAM BRAND COMMUNICATIONS (NETWORK CENTER)—See Dentsu Young & Rubicam Partnerships; *U.S. Private*, pg. 325
DENTSU YOUNG & RUBICAM INC. (TOKYO)—See Dentsu Young & Rubicam Partnerships; *U.S. Private*, pg. 325
P.T. DENTSU YOUNG & RUBICAM INDONESIA (JAKARTA)—See Dentsu Young & Rubicam Partnerships; *U.S. Private*, pg. 325
DENTSU YOUNG & RUBICAM LIMITED (HONG KONG)—See Dentsu Young & Rubicam Partnerships; *U.S. Private*, pg. 325
DENTSU YOUNG & RUBICAM LTD. (BANGKOK)—See Dentsu Young & Rubicam Partnerships; *U.S. Private*, pg. 325
DENTSU YOUNG & RUBICAM PARTNERSHIPS; *U.S. Private*, pg. 325
DENTSU YOUNG & RUBICAM SDN. BHD. (KUALA LUMPUR)—See Dentsu Young & Rubicam Partnerships; *U.S. Private*, pg. 325
DENTSU YOUNG & RUBICAM/SEOUL—See Dentsu Young & Rubicam Partnerships; *U.S. Private*, pg. 325
DENTSU YOUNG & RUBICAM/SINGAPORE—See Dentsu Young & Rubicam Partnerships; *U.S. Private*, pg. 325
DENTSU YOUNG & RUBICAM/TAIPEI—See Dentsu Young & Rubicam Partnerships; *U.S. Private*, pg. 325
DENTURES AND DENTAL SERVICES—See Sharpe Dry Goods Co., Inc.; *U.S. Private*, pg. 990
DENVER AUTO AUCTION—See Cox Enterprises, Inc.; *U.S. Private*, pg. 282
DENVER AUTOMETRICS—See Svedala Industri AB; *Int'l*, pg. 1325
DENVER BABY DOE'S REST. CORP.—See Specialty Restaurants Corporation; *U.S. Private*, pg. 1023
THE DENVER BUSINESS JOURNAL, LLC—See Advance Publications Inc.; *U.S. Private*, pg. 19
DENVER CHEMICAL (PR) INC.—See Carter-Wallace, Inc.; *U.S. Public*, pg. 310
DENVER DISTRICT OFFICE—See Micros Systems Inc.; *U.S. Public*, pg. 1106
DENVER EQUIPMENT PTY., LTD.—See Svedala Industri AB; *Int'l*, pg. 1326
DENVER FREEWAY RESTAURANT CORP.—See Specialty Restaurants Corporation; *U.S. Private*, pg. 1023
DENVER MOVING & STORAGE CO.—See Johnson Storage Moving Co; *U.S. Private*, pg. 594
DENVER NUGGETS LIMITED PARTNERSHIP—See Ascent Entertainment Group, Inc.; *U.S. Public*, pg. 138
DENVER PROCESS EQUIPMENT, LTD.—See Svedala Industri AB; *Int'l*, pg. 1326
THE DENVER PUBLISHING COMPANY—See The E.W. Scripps Company; *U.S. Public*, pg. 1447
DENVER RECYCLING CENTER—See Republic Group Incorporated; *U.S. Public*, pg. 1378
DENVER TECHNOLOGICAL CENTER—See The Peninsular and Oriental Steam Navigation Company; *Int'l*, pg. 1035
DENVER THOMAS, INC.—See Svedala Industri AB; *Int'l*, pg. 1325
DENVER WHOLESALE FLORISTS COMPANY; *U.S. Private*, pg. 326
DEP CORPORATION; *U.S. Public*, pg. 500
DEP INTERNATIONAL, LTD.—See Dep Corporation; *U.S. Public*, pg. 500
DEPARTMENT 56 INC.; *U.S. Public*, pg. 500
THE DEPARTMENT STORE DIVISION OF DAYTON HUDSON CORPORATION—See Dayton Hudson Corporation; *U.S. Public*, pg. 489
DEPARTURES—See American Express Company; *U.S. Public*, pg. 74
DEPENDABLE COURIER—See Corporate Express, Inc.; *U.S. Public*, pg. 450
DEPEW DEVELOPMENT INC.; *U.S. Private*, pg. 326
DEPOSIT GUARANTY CORP.; *U.S. Public*, pg. 500
DEPOSIT GUARANTY INVESTMENTS, INC.—See Deposit Guaranty Corp.; *U.S. Public*, pg. 501

DEPOSIT GUARANTY MORTGAGE CO.—See Deposit Guaranty Corp.; *U.S. Public*, pg. 501
DEPOSIT GUARANTY NATIONAL BANK—See Deposit Guaranty Corp.; *U.S. Public*, pg. 500
DEPOSIT GUARANTY NATIONAL BANK OF LOUISIANA—See Deposit Guaranty Corp.; *U.S. Public*, pg. 500
DEPOSITION TECHNOLOGIES, INC.—See Material Sciences Corporation; *U.S. Public*, pg. 1056
DEPUY, INC.—See Corange Limited; *Int'l*, pg. 331
DERBY CYCLE CORPORATION—See Derby International Corporation S.A.; *Int'l*, pg. 394
DERBY CYCLE WERKE GMBH—See Derby International Corporation S.A.; *Int'l*, pg. 394
DERBY INDUSTRIES (PTY.) LTD.—See Derby International Corporation S.A.; *Int'l*, pg. 394
DERBY INTERNATIONAL CORPORATION S.A.; *Int'l*, pg. 394
DERBYSHIRE BUILDING SOCIETY; *Int'l*, pg. 394
THE DERBYSHIRE (ISLE OF MAN) LTD.—See Derbyshire Building Society; *Int'l*, pg. 395
THE DERBYSHIRE (PREMISES) LTD.—See Derbyshire Building Society; *Int'l*, pg. 395
DERBYSHIRE-ALFRETON BRANCH—See Derbyshire Building Society; *Int'l*, pg. 394
DERBYSHIRE-LIVERPOOL BRANCH—See Derbyshire Building Society; *Int'l*, pg. 394
DERBYSHIRE-SHEFFIELD BRANCH—See Derbyshire Building Society; *Int'l*, pg. 394
A.N. DERINGER, INC.; *U.S. Private*, pg. 326
DERIVADOS ACRILICOS, S.A. DE C.V.—See CYDSA S.A.; *Int'l*, pg. 246
DERIVADOS DEL FLUOR, S.A.—See Bayer AG; *Int'l*, pg. 175
DERIVADOS DEL PROPILENO, S.A. (DERPROSA)—See Compania Espanola de Petroleos, S.A. (CEPSA); *Int'l*, pg. 323
DERIVADOS LACTEOS Y ALIMENTICIOS S.A.—See Nestle S.A.; *Int'l*, pg. 920
DERLAN AEROSPACE CANADA LIMITED—See Derlan Industries Limited; *Int'l*, pg. 395
DERLAN INC./PHOENIX FACILITY—See Derlan Industries Limited; *Int'l*, pg. 395
DERLAN INC./SANTA ANA FACILITY—See Derlan Industries Limited; *Int'l*, pg. 395
DERLAN INDUSTRIES LIMITED; *Int'l*, pg. 395
DERLY, S.A.—See Eli Lilly and Company; *U.S. Public*, pg. 993
DERMAL MANAGEMENT SYS.—See Medline Industries, Inc.; *U.S. Private*, pg. 728
DERMIK LABORATORIES, INC.—See Rhone-Poulenc S.A.; *Int'l*, pg. 1110
DERST BAKING COMPANY, INC.; *U.S. Private*, pg. 326
DERWENT INSURANCE LIMITED—See Severn Trent Plc; *Int'l*, pg. 1226
DERWENT PUBLICATIONS LTD.—See The Thomson Corporation; *U.S. Public*, pg. 1601
S.A. DES CIMENTS LUXEMBOURGEOIS—See Dyckerhoff AG; *Int'l*, pg. 423
DES MOINES MFG. DIVISION—See R.R. Donnelley & Sons Company; *U.S. Public*, pg. 518
DES MOINES REGISTER & TRIBUNE CO.—See Gannett Company, Inc.; *U.S. Public*, pg. 700
DES MOINES TIRE—See Rott-Keller Supply Co.; *U.S. Private*, pg. 947
S.A. DES PAPETERIES DE BEGLES—See Lafarge S.A.; *Int'l*, pg. 789
AB S.A. DES ROULEMENTS A BILLES SUEDOIS SKF—See AB SKF; *Int'l*, pg. 1158
S.A. DES VIGNOBLES HENRIOT—See LVMH Moet Hennessy Louis Vuitton; *Int'l*, pg. 780
DESA INTERNATIONAL; *U.S. Private*, pg. 326
DESAI CAPITAL MANAGEMENT INCORPORATED; *U.S. Private*, pg. 326
DESAROLLO DEL VIDRIO (DEVISA)—See Saint-Gobain; *Int'l*, pg. 1172
DESARROLLO DE SISTEMAS DE INFORMACION, S.A.—See Assicurazioni Generali S.p.A.; *Int'l*, pg. 91
DESARROLLO Y COMERCIALIZACION DE INMUEBLES, S.A.—See Caja de Madrid Group; *Int'l*, pg. 251
DESARROLLOS MULTIPLES INSULARES, INC.—See Puerto Rican Cement Co., Inc.; *U.S. Public*, pg. 1342
DESARROLLOS URBANOS CI., S.A.—See Corporacion MAPFRE, Compania Internacional de Reaseguros, S.A.; *Int'l*, pg. 334
DESC, S.A. DE C.V.; *Int'l*, pg. 395
DESCENTE AMERICA INC.—See Descente Ltd.; *Int'l*, pg. 395
DESCENTE CANADA INC.—See Descente Ltd.; *Int'l*, pg. 395
DESCENTE LTD.; *Int'l*, pg. 395
DESCO ADVERTISING & MARKETING—See Desco Corporation; *U.S. Private*, pg. 327
DESCO CORPORATION; *U.S. Private*, pg. 326
DESCO DE SCHULTHESS LTD.; *Int'l*, pg. 396
DESENCRAGE C.M.D. INC.—See The Cascades Group; *Int'l*, pg. 273
DESERET BOOK CO.—See Deseret Management Corporation; *U.S. Private*, pg. 327
DESERET MANAGEMENT CORPORATION; *U.S. Private*, pg. 327
DESERET NEWS—See Deseret Management Corporation; *U.S. Private*, pg. 327
DESERT HAVEN NURSING CENTER—See Paragon Health Network, Inc.; *U.S. Public*, pg. 1256
DESERT LANE CARE CENTER—See Horizon/CMS Healthcare Corporation; *U.S. Public*, pg. 837
DESERT PALACE, INC.—See Starwood Hotels & Resorts; *U.S. Public*, pg. 1512
DESERT PRODUCTION CENTER—See MAC America Communications, Inc.; *U.S. Private*, pg. 685
DESERT SPRINGS HOSPITAL, INC.—See Magellan Health Services, Inc.; *U.S. Public*, pg. 1035
THE DESERT SUN—See Gannett Company, Inc.; *U.S. Public*, pg. 700

DESERT TERRACE NURSING CENTER—See Paragon Health Network, Inc.; *U.S. Public*, pg. 1256
DESERT TURBINE SERVICES, INC.—See Mesa Air Group; *U.S. Public*, pg. 1099
DESFOSSES INTERNATIONAL—See LVMH Moet Hennessy Louis Vuitton; *Int'l*, pg. 780
DESIGN-BUILD WEST—See RNL Facilities Corporation; *U.S. Private*, pg. 905
DESIGN CENTER—See Del Webb Corporation; *U.S. Public*, pg. 495
DESIGN CONCEPTS INTEGRATION, INC.—See International Research & Evaluation; *U.S. Private*, pg. 572
DESIGN/CRAFT FABRIC CORP.—See RPM, Inc.; *U.S. Public*, pg. 1357
DESIGN DATA, INC.—See Data General Corporation; *U.S. Public*, pg. 485
DESIGN ELECTRICAL MANUFACTURING—See Noma Industries Limited; *Int'l*, pg. 955
DESIGN PERFORMANCE GROUP—See Plasti-Line, Inc.; *U.S. Public*, pg. 1309
DESIGN PROFESSIONAL INSURANCE CO.—See Orion Capital Corporation; *U.S. Public*, pg. 1231
DESIGN SECURITY INC.—See Detex Corporation; *U.S. Private*, pg. 328
DESIGN SERVICES GROUP—See SuperValu, Inc.; *U.S. Public*, pg. 1541
DESIGN SYSTEMS INC.—See AGA AB; *Int'l*, pg. 13
DESIGN SYSTEMS INC.—See FMC Corporation; *U.S. Public*, pg. 606
DESIGN-TUFT DT GMBH—See Forbo Holding SA; *Int'l*, pg. 497
DESIGN USA—See Jacmar Companies, Inc.; *U.S. Private*, pg. 580
DESIGNATRONICS; *U.S. Private*, pg. 327
DESIGNED & ENGINEERED SYSTEMS—See AFA Protective Systems, Inc.; *U.S. Public*, pg. 6
DESIGNERS KNITTING MILLS—See Hampshire Group, Ltd.; *U.S. Public*, pg. 778
DESIGNS, INC.; *U.S. Public*, pg. 501
THE DESIGNS/OLS PARTNERSHIP—See Designs, Inc.; *U.S. Public*, pg. 501
DESJARDINS-LAURENTIAN FINANCIAL CORPORATION; *Int'l*, pg. 396
DESJARDINS LAURENTIAN LIFE ASSURANCE—See Desjardins-Laurentian Financial Corporation; *Int'l*, pg. 396
DESKTOP GRAPHICS—See Evans & Sutherland Computer Corporation; *U.S. Public*, pg. 596
DESKTOP NETWORKS BUSINESS UNIT—See Standard Microsystems Corp.; *U.S. Public*, pg. 1503
DESOBRY S.A.—See Sara Lee Corporation; *U.S. Public*, pg. 1435
DESOTO INC.—See Keystone Consolidated Industries, Inc.; *U.S. Public*, pg. 956
DESOTO MILLS, INC.—See Russell Corporation; *U.S. Public*, pg. 1413
DESOUTTER BROTHERS (HOLDINGS) PLC—See Atlas Copco AB; *Int'l*, pg. 96
DESOUTTER, INC.—See Atlas Copco AB; *Int'l*, pg. 96
DESOWAG-BAYER HOLZSCHUTZ GMBH—See Bayer AG; *Int'l*, pg. 172
DESOWAG GMBH—See Williams Holdings Plc; *Int'l*, pg. 1501
DESPATCH INDUSTRIES; *U.S. Private*, pg. 327
DESTEC ENERGY, INC.—See NGC Corporation; *U.S. Public*, pg. 1146
DESTINATION PRODUCTS INTERNATIONAL, INC.—See Cott Corporation; *Int'l*, pg. 338
DESTINY INDUSTRIES INC.—See Oakwood Homes Corporation; *U.S. Public*, pg. 1209
DET BESTE A/S—See The Reader's Digest Association, Inc.; *U.S. Public*, pg. 1368
DET NORSKE VERITAS; *Int'l*, pg. 396
DET NORSKE VERITAS (ASIA PACIFIC)—See Det Norske Veritas; *Int'l*, pg. 398
DET NORSKE VERITAS EIENDOM A/S—See Det Norske Veritas; *Int'l*, pg. 396
DET NORSKE VERITAS INDUSTRY—See Det Norske Veritas; *Int'l*, pg. 396
DET NORSKE VERITAS/RUSS LARKIN & ASSOCIATES—See Det Norske Veritas; *Int'l*, pg. 398
DETACLAD DIVISION—See Dynamic Materials Corporation; *U.S. Public*, pg. 539
DETAILS—See Steelcase Inc.; *U.S. Private*, pg. 1038
DETAILS MAGAZINE—See Advance Publications Inc.; *U.S. Private*, pg. 20
DETALJINVEST/VIVO-FAVOR—See Carnegie Holding AB; *Int'l*, pg. 272
DETE IMMOBILIEN, DEUTSCHE TELEKOM IMMOBILIEN UND SERVICE GMBH—See Deutsche Telekom AG; *Int'l*, pg. 407
DETEC INTERNATIONAL OY—See Tamrock Corp.; *Int'l*, pg. 1352
DETECTAR DESENVOL TECNICAS Y ADMON. DE RIESGOS—See Corporacion MAPFRE, Compania Internacional de Reaseguros, S.A.; *Int'l*, pg. 334
DETECTION SYSTEMS, INC.; *U.S. Public*, pg. 501
DETECTO SCALE COMPANY—See Cardinal Scale Manufacturing Company; *U.S. Private*, pg. 209
DETECTOR ELECTRONICS CORPORATION—See Williams Holdings Plc; *Int'l*, pg. 1500
DETECTORS, INC.—See Media Recovery, Inc.; *U.S. Private*, pg. 727
DETELINE DEUTSCHE TELEKOM KOMMUNIKATIONSNETZE GMBH—See Deutsche Telekom AG; *Int'l*, pg. 407
DETERGENTS DIVISION, ALBRIGHT & WILSON LIMITED—See Albright & Wilson plc; *Int'l*, pg. 49
DETEX CORPORATION; *U.S. Private*, pg. 327
DETOX, INC.—See American Ecology Corporation; *U.S. Public*, pg. 71
DETREX AUTOMATION DIV.—See Detrex Corporation; *U.S. Public*, pg. 501

Company Index

DETREX CORPORATION; *U.S. Public*, pg. 501
DETREX EQUIPMENT DIV.—See Detrex Corporation; *U.S. Public*, pg. 501
DETREX GENERAL CHEMICALS & SOLVENTS DIV.—See Detrex Corporation; *U.S. Public*, pg. 501
DETREX INDUSTRIAL CHEMICAL SPECIALTIES DIV.—See Detrex Corporation; *U.S. Public*, pg. 502
DETREY DENTSPLY AG—See Dentsply International Inc.; *U.S. Public*, pg. 500
DETREY DENTSPLY S.A.—See Dentsply International Inc.; *U.S. Public*, pg. 500
DETREY/DENTSPLY S.R.L.—See Dentsply International Inc.; *U.S. Public*, pg. 500
DETRICK BELGE—See Lafarge S.A.; *Int'l*, pg. 789
DETRICK REFRACTORY FIBERS, INC.—See A.P. Green Industries, Inc.; *U.S. Public*, pg. 761
DETROIT AXLE DIV.—See Chrysler Corporation; *U.S. Public*, pg. 353
DETROIT CITY DAIRY, INC.; *U.S. Private*, pg. 328
DETROIT COIL COMPANY; *U.S. Private*, pg. 328
DETROIT DIESEL - ALISON CANADA—See Wajax Limited; *Int'l*, pg. 1485
DETROIT DIESEL CORP.—See Penske Corporation; *U.S. Private*, pg. 850
DETROIT DIVISION—See Time Warner Inc.; *U.S. Public*, pg. 1613
DETROIT DOWNTOWN DEVELOPMENT CORPORATION—See Ford Motor Company; *U.S. Public*, pg. 664
DETROIT ELECTRO-COATINGS CO. LLC; *U.S. Private*, pg. 328
DETROIT FREE PRESS—See Knight-Ridder, Inc.; *U.S. Public*, pg. 965
DETROIT GASKET—See Indian Head Industries Inc.; *U.S. Private*, pg. 560
THE DETROIT MEDICAL CENTER; *U.S. Private*, pg. 328
DETROIT MONTHLY—See Crain Communications, Inc.; *U.S. Private*, pg. 285
THE DETROIT NEWS—See Gannett Company, Inc.; *U.S. Public*, pg. 700
DETROIT NEWSPAPERS—See Knight-Ridder, Inc.; *U.S. Public*, pg. 965
DETROIT STOKER CO.—See United Industrial Corporation; *U.S. Public*, pg. 1679
DETTELBACH PESTICIDE CORP.—See Rollins, Inc.; *U.S. Public*, pg. 1405
DETTRA FLAG COMPANY; *U.S. Private*, pg. 328
B. D'ETUDES MOULINEX—See Moulinex S.A.; *Int'l*, pg. 896
DEUER MANUFACTURING, INC.—See Selas Corporation of America; *U.S. Public*, pg. 1455
DEUNA ZEMENT GMBH—See Dyckerhoff AG; *Int'l*, pg. 422
DEUTAG MARKETING & TECHNICAL SERVICES INC.—See Preussag AG; *Int'l*, pg. 1069
THE DEUTSCH COMPANY; *U.S. Private*, pg. 328
DEUTSCH ENGINEERED CONNECTING DEVICES CO.—See The Deutsch Company; *U.S. Private*, pg. 328
DEUTSCH, INC.; *U.S. Private*, pg. 328
DEUTSCH INDUSTRIAL PRODUCT DIVISION—See The Deutsch Company; *U.S. Private*, pg. 328
DEUTSCH LA—See Deutsch, Inc.; *U.S. Private*, pg. 328
DEUTSCH METAL COMPONENTS—See The Deutsch Company; *U.S. Private*, pg. 328
DEUTSCH-SUDAMERIKANISCHE BANK AG—See Dresdner Bank AG; *Int'l*, pg. 418
DEUTSCHE AEROSPACE AIRBUS GMBH—See Daimler-Benz Aktiengesellschaft; *Int'l*, pg. 367
DEUTSCHE ASPHALT GMBH—See Philipp Holzmann AG; *Int'l*, pg. 632
DEUTSCHE ASSET MANAGEMENT G.M.B.H.—See Deutsche Bank AG; *Int'l*, pg. 402
DEUTSCHE AUTOMOBILGESELLSCHAFT MBH—See Volkswagen AG; *Int'l*, pg. 1473
DEUTSCHE BABCOCK AG; *Int'l*, pg. 398
DEUTSCHE BABCOCK ANLAGEN GMBH—See Deutsche Babcock AG; *Int'l*, pg. 398
DEUTSCHE BABCOCK ARGENTINA S.A.—See Deutsche Babcock AG; *Int'l*, pg. 398
DEUTSCHE BABCOCK BALCKE-DURR LTD.—See Deutsche Babcock AG; *Int'l*, pg. 401
DEUTSCHE BABCOCK BAU GMBH—See Deutsche Babcock AG; *Int'l*, pg. 401
DEUTSCHE BABCOCK-BETEILIGUNG GMBH—See Deutsche Babcock AG; *Int'l*, pg. 401
DEUTSCHE BABCOCK BORSIG AG—See Deutsche Babcock AG; *Int'l*, pg. 399
DEUTSCHE BABCOCK-BORSIG LTD.—See Deutsche Babcock AG; *Int'l*, pg. 401
DEUTSCHE BABCOCK ENERGIE-UND UMWELTTECHNIK AG—See Deutsche Babcock AG; *Int'l*, pg. 398
DEUTSCHE BABCOCK HANDEL GMBH—See Deutsche Babcock AG; *Int'l*, pg. 401
DEUTSCHE BABCOCK INDUSTRIE UND SYSTEMTECHNIK AG—See Deutsche Babcock AG; *Int'l*, pg. 399
DEUTSCHE BABCOCK INTERNATIONAL VETRIEBS-GMBH—See Deutsche Babcock AG; *Int'l*, pg. 401
DEUTSCHE BABCOCK ITALIANA S.P.A.—See Deutsche Babcock AG; *Int'l*, pg. 398
DEUTSCHE BABCOCK LIMITED—See Deutsche Babcock AG; *Int'l*, pg. 401
DEUTSCHE BABCOCK (NIGERIA) LTD.—See Deutsche Babcock AG; *Int'l*, pg. 399
DEUTSCHE BABCOCK-RILEY INTERNATIONAL INC.—See Deutsche Babcock AG; *Int'l*, pg. 401
DEUTSCHE BABCOCK S.A.—See Deutsche Babcock AG; *Int'l*, pg. 398
DEUTSCHE BABCOCK (S.A.) (PTY.) LTD.—See Deutsche Babcock AG; *Int'l*, pg. 399
DEUTSCHE BABCOCK TECHNOLOGIES, INC.—See Deutsche Babcock AG; *Int'l*, pg. 401
DEUTSCHE BAHN; *Int'l*, pg. 401
DEUTSCHE BANK AG; *Int'l*, pg. 401

DEUTSCHE BANK AG (ANTWERP)—See Deutsche Bank AG; *Int'l*, pg. 403
DEUTSCHE BANK AG (BAHRAIN)—See Deutsche Bank AG; *Int'l*, pg. 404
DEUTSCHE BANK AG (BANGKOK)—See Deutsche Bank AG; *Int'l*, pg. 404
DEUTSCHE BANK AG (BIELEFELD)—See Deutsche Bank AG; *Int'l*, pg. 402
DEUTSCHE BANK AG (BOMBAY)—See Deutsche Bank AG; *Int'l*, pg. 404
DEUTSCHE BANK AG (BREMEN)—See Deutsche Bank AG; *Int'l*, pg. 402
DEUTSCHE BANK AG (BRUSSELS)—See Deutsche Bank AG; *Int'l*, pg. 403
DEUTSCHE BANK AG (BUDAPEST)—See Deutsche Bank AG; *Int'l*, pg. 404
DEUTSCHE BANK AG (CAIRO)—See Deutsche Bank AG; *Int'l*, pg. 404
DEUTSCHE BANK AG (CAMPINAS)—See Deutsche Bank AG; *Int'l*, pg. 404
DEUTSCHE BANK AG (CANADA)—See Deutsche Bank AG; *Int'l*, pg. 404
DEUTSCHE BANK AG (CHINA)—See Deutsche Bank AG; *Int'l*, pg. 404
DEUTSCHE BANK AG (COLOGNE)—See Deutsche Bank AG; *Int'l*, pg. 402
DEUTSCHE BANK AG (COLUMBO, SRI LANKA)—See Deutsche Bank AG; *Int'l*, pg. 404
DEUTSCHE BANK AG (DUSSELDORF)—See Deutsche Bank AG; *Int'l*, pg. 402
DEUTSCHE BANK AG (ESSEN)—See Deutsche Bank AG; *Int'l*, pg. 402
DEUTSCHE BANK AG (FRANKFURT)—See Deutsche Bank AG; *Int'l*, pg. 402
DEUTSCHE BANK AG (FREIBURG)—See Deutsche Bank AG; *Int'l*, pg. 402
DEUTSCHE BANK AG (HAMBURG)—See Deutsche Bank AG; *Int'l*, pg. 402
DEUTSCHE BANK AG (HANNOVER)—See Deutsche Bank AG; *Int'l*, pg. 402
DEUTSCHE BANK AG (HONG KONG)—See Deutsche Bank AG; *Int'l*, pg. 404
DEUTSCHE BANK AG (ISTANBUL)—See Deutsche Bank AG; *Int'l*, pg. 404
DEUTSCHE BANK AG (JAKARTA)—See Deutsche Bank AG; *Int'l*, pg. 404
DEUTSCHE BANK AG (KARACHI)—See Deutsche Bank AG; *Int'l*, pg. 404
DEUTSCHE BANK AG (KUALA LUMPUR)—See Deutsche Bank AG; *Int'l*, pg. 404
DEUTSCHE BANK AG (LAHORE)—See Deutsche Bank AG; *Int'l*, pg. 404
DEUTSCHE BANK AG (MACAU)—See Deutsche Bank AG; *Int'l*, pg. 404
DEUTSCHE BANK AG (MADRID)—See Deutsche Bank AG; *Int'l*, pg. 404
DEUTSCHE BANK AG (MAINZ)—See Deutsche Bank AG; *Int'l*, pg. 402
DEUTSCHE BANK AG (MANCHESTER)—See Deutsche Bank AG; *Int'l*, pg. 404
DEUTSCHE BANK AG (MANILA)—See Deutsche Bank AG; *Int'l*, pg. 404
DEUTSCHE BANK AG (MANNHEIM)—See Deutsche Bank AG; *Int'l*, pg. 402
DEUTSCHE BANK AG (MEXICO)—See Deutsche Bank AG; *Int'l*, pg. 404
DEUTSCHE BANK AG (MOSCOW)—See Deutsche Bank AG; *Int'l*, pg. 404
DEUTSCHE BANK AG (MUNICH)—See Deutsche Bank AG; *Int'l*, pg. 402
DEUTSCHE BANK AG (NAGOYA)—See Deutsche Bank AG; *Int'l*, pg. 404
DEUTSCHE BANK AG (NEW DELHI)—See Deutsche Bank AG; *Int'l*, pg. 404
DEUTSCHE BANK AG (NIGERIA) LTD.—See Deutsche Bank AG; *Int'l*, pg. 404
DEUTSCHE BANK AG (OSAKA)—See Deutsche Bank AG; *Int'l*, pg. 404
DEUTSCHE BANK AG (PARIS)—See Deutsche Bank AG; *Int'l*, pg. 404
DEUTSCHE BANK AG (PORTO ALEGRE)—See Deutsche Bank AG; *Int'l*, pg. 404
DEUTSCHE BANK AG (PRAGUE)—See Deutsche Bank AG; *Int'l*, pg. 404
DEUTSCHE BANK AG (PUSAN)—See Deutsche Bank AG; *Int'l*, pg. 404
DEUTSCHE BANK AG (SAO PAULO)—See Deutsche Bank AG; *Int'l*, pg. 404
DEUTSCHE BANK AG (SEOUL)—See Deutsche Bank AG; *Int'l*, pg. 404
DEUTSCHE BANK AG (SINGAPORE)—See Deutsche Bank AG; *Int'l*, pg. 404
DEUTSCHE BANK AG (STRASBOURG)—See Deutsche Bank AG; *Int'l*, pg. 405
DEUTSCHE BANK AG (STUTTGART)—See Deutsche Bank AG; *Int'l*, pg. 402
DEUTSCHE BANK AG (SURABAYA)—See Deutsche Bank AG; *Int'l*, pg. 405
DEUTSCHE BANK AG (TAIPEI)—See Deutsche Bank AG; *Int'l*, pg. 405
DEUTSCHE BANK AG (TEHRAN)—See Deutsche Bank AG; *Int'l*, pg. 405
DEUTSCHE BANK AG (TOKYO)—See Deutsche Bank AG; *Int'l*, pg. 405
DEUTSCHE BANK AG (VIENNA)—See Deutsche Bank AG; *Int'l*, pg. 405
DEUTSCHE BANK AG (WUPPERTAL)—See Deutsche Bank AG; *Int'l*, pg. 402
DEUTSCHE BANK (ASIA PACIFIC) LTD.—See Deutsche Bank AG; *Int'l*, pg. 405
DEUTSCHE BANK AUSTRALIA LTD.—See Deutsche Bank AG; *Int'l*, pg. 405
DEUTSCHE BANK AUSTRALIA LTD. (SYDNEY)—See Deutsche Bank AG; *Int'l*, pg. 405

DEUTSCHE BANK BERLIN AG—See Deutsche Bank AG; *Int'l*, pg. 402
DEUTSCHE BANK CAPITAL CORPORATION—See Deutsche Bank AG; *Int'l*, pg. 403
DEUTSCHE BANK DE INVESTIMENTO, S.A. (LISBON)—See Deutsche Bank AG; *Int'l*, pg. 405
DEUTSCHE BANK DE INVESTIMENTO, S.A. (PORTO)—See Deutsche Bank AG; *Int'l*, pg. 405
DEUTSCHE BANK FINANCE N.V.—See Deutsche Bank AG; *Int'l*, pg. 405
DEUTSCHE BANK GOVERNMENT SECURITIES, INC.—See Deutsche Bank AG; *Int'l*, pg. 403
DEUTSCHE BANK-KREDITBANK AG—See Deutsche Bank AG; *Int'l*, pg. 402
DEUTSCHE BANK-KREDITBANK AG (BERLIN)—See Deutsche Bank AG; *Int'l*, pg. 402
DEUTSCHE BANK-KREDITBANK AG (CHEMNITZ)—See Deutsche Bank AG; *Int'l*, pg. 402
DEUTSCHE BANK-KREDITBANK AG (DRESDEN)—See Deutsche Bank AG; *Int'l*, pg. 402
DEUTSCHE BANK-KREDITBANK AG (ERFURT)—See Deutsche Bank AG; *Int'l*, pg. 402
DEUTSCHE BANK-KREDITBANK AG (HALLE)—See Deutsche Bank AG; *Int'l*, pg. 402
DEUTSCHE BANK-KREDITBANK AG (LEIPZIG)—See Deutsche Bank AG; *Int'l*, pg. 402
DEUTSCHE BANK-KREDITBANK AG (MAGDEBURG)—See Deutsche Bank AG; *Int'l*, pg. 402
DEUTSCHE BANK-KREDITBANK AG (ROSTOCK)—See Deutsche Bank AG; *Int'l*, pg. 402
DEUTSCHE BANK LUBECK AG—See Deutsche Bank AG; *Int'l*, pg. 402
DEUTSCHE BANK LUXEMBOURG S.A.—See Deutsche Bank AG; *Int'l*, pg. 405
DEUTSCHE BANK SAAR AG—See Deutsche Bank AG; *Int'l*, pg. 402
DEUTSCHE BANK (SCHWEIZ) AG (ZURICH)—See Deutsche Bank AG; *Int'l*, pg. 405
DEUTSCHE BANK (SVIZZERA) S.A. (LUGANO)—See Deutsche Bank AG; *Int'l*, pg. 405
DEUTSCHE BANK (SWISS) S.A.—See Deutsche Bank AG; *Int'l*, pg. 405
DEUTSCHE BARYT-INDUSTRIE DR. RUDOLF ALBERTI & CO.—See Solvay S.A.; *Int'l*, pg. 1278
DEUTSCHE BAU-UND SIEDLUNGS-GESELLSCHAFT MBH—See Hochtief AG; *Int'l*, pg. 623
DEUTSCHE CARBONE AG—See Pechiney S.A.; *Int'l*, pg. 1030
DEUTSCHE CASTROL INDUSTRIEOLE GMBH—See Burmah Castrol plc; *Int'l*, pg. 236
DEUTSCHE CASTROL VMBH—See Burmah Castrol plc; *Int'l*, pg. 236
DEUTSCHE CHEFARO PHARMA GMBH—See Akzo Nobel N.V.; *Int'l*, pg. 44
DEUTSCHE CREDIT CORPORATION—See Deutsche Bank AG; *Int'l*, pg. 403
DEUTSCHE DUNI GMBH—See Duni AB; *Int'l*, pg. 421
DEUTSCHE FATA GMBH—See FKI Plc; *Int'l*, pg. 474
DEUTSCHE FERNSPRECHER GMBH (DFG)—See Lagardere Groupe; *Int'l*, pg. 795
DEUTSCHE FIAT AG—See Fiat Auto SpA; *Int'l*, pg. 484
DEUTSCHE FINANCIAL SERVICES CORPORATION—See Deutsche Bank AG; *Int'l*, pg. 403
DEUTSCHE FLUGZEUGVERMIETUNGS AG—See Hapag-Lloyd AG; *Int'l*, pg. 596
DEUTSCHE GAMMA GMBH—See Gamma Holding N.V.; *Int'l*, pg. 540
DEUTSCHE GARDNER-DENVER GMBH & CO.—See Cooper Industries, Inc.; *U.S. Public*, pg. 444
DEUTSCHE GES. FUER IMMOBILIENANLAGEN "AMERICA" MBH—See Commerzbank AG; *Int'l*, pg. 310
DEUTSCHE GIROZENTRALE-DEUTSCHE KOMMUNALBANK; *Int'l*, pg. 406
DEUTSCHE GIROZENTRALE-DEUTSCHE KOMMUNALBANK—See Deutsche Girozentrale-Deutsche Kommunalbank; *Int'l*, pg. 406
DEUTSCHE GIROZENTRALE-DEUTSCHE KOMMUNALBANK (LUXEMBOURG)—See Deutsche Girozentrale-Deutsche Kommunalbank; *Int'l*, pg. 406
DEUTSCHE GIROZENTRALE INTERNATIONAL S.A.—See Deutsche Girozentrale-Deutsche Kommunalbank; *Int'l*, pg. 407
DEUTSCHE GOODYEAR GMBH—See The Goodyear Tire & Rubber Company; *U.S. Public*, pg. 753
DEUTSCHE GRAMMOPHON GESELLSCHAFT MBH—See Philips Electronics N.V.; *Int'l*, pg. 1052
DEUTSCHE HERAKLITH A.G.—See RGP Holding, Inc.; *U.S. Private*, pg. 903
DEUTSCHE HEY'DI CHEMISCHE GMBH—See Laporte plc; *Int'l*, pg. 803
DEUTSCHE HUSQVARNA GMBH—See Electrolux, AB; *Int'l*, pg. 442
DEUTSCHE HYPOTHEKENBANK (ACTIEN-GESELLSCHAFT)—See BHF-BANK AG; *Int'l*, pg. 119
DEUTSCHE HYPOTHEKENBANK FRANKFURTAG—See Dresdner Bank AG; *Int'l*, pg. 418
DEUTSCHE ICI GMBH—See Imperial Chemical Industries PLC; *Int'l*, pg. 664
DEUTSCHE INDUSTRIE-VERSICHERUNGSSTELLE GMBH—See Viag AG; *Int'l*, pg. 1464
DEUTSCHE INDUSTRIEANLAGENGESELLSCHAFT MBH—See MAN Aktiengesellschaft; *Int'l*, pg. 824
DEUTSCHE KRANKENVERSICHERUNG AG—See Allianz Aktiengesellschaft; *Int'l*, pg. 58
DEUTSCHE KRANKENVERSICHERUNG AG—See Munchener Ruckversicherungs-Gesellschaft; *Int'l*, pg. 897
DEUTSCHE LEBENSVERSICHERUNGS-AG—See Allianz Aktiengesellschaft; *Int'l*, pg. 58
DEUTSCHE LIBBY GMBH—See Nestle S.A.; *Int'l*, pg. 920
DEUTSCHE LUFTHANSA AG; *Int'l*, pg. 407
DEUTSCHE NYCO GMBH—See Fuchs Petrolub AG Oel + Chemie; *Int'l*, pg. 517

MASTER INDEX TO COMPANY NAMES DIAMOND

Company Index

DEUTSCHE OWENS-CORNING GLASSWOOL GMBH—See Owens Corning; *U.S. Public*, pg. 1237
DEUTSCHE POST AG; *Int'l*, pg. 407
DEUTSCHE POST BETEILIGUNGEN GMBH—See Deutsche Post AG; *Int'l*, pg. 407
DEUTSCHE POST WOHNBAU GMBH—See Deutsche Post AG; *Int'l*, pg. 407
DEUTSCHE POSTCONSULT—See Deutsche Post AG; *Int'l*, *pg. 407*
DEUTSCHE RANCO GMBH—See Siebe plc; *Int'l*, pg. 1243
DEUTSCHE SB-KAUF AG—See Metro AG; *Int'l*, pg. 863
DEUTSCHE SCHIFFSBANK AG—See Commerzbank AG; *Int'l*, pg. 310
DEUTSCHE SCHLAUCHBOOTFABRIK HANS SCHEIBERT GMBH & CO.—See Continental AG; *Int'l*, pg. 327
DEUTSCHE SHELL AG—See Royal Dutch/Shell Group of Companies; *Int'l*, pg. 1138
DEUTSCHE SINOCHEM GMBH—See Sinochem International Petroleum Co. Ltd.; *Int'l*, pg. 1255
DEUTSCHE SPEZIALGLAS AG—See Carl-Zeiss-Stiftung; *Int'l*, pg. 1523
DEUTSCHE STAR GMBH—See Mannesmann A.G.; *Int'l*, pg. 838
DEUTSCHE TELEKOM AG; *Int'l*, pg. 407
DEUTSCHE TELEKOM MEDIEN GMBH—See Deutsche Telekom AG; *Int'l*, pg. 407
DEUTSCHE TIEFBOHR AG—See Preussag AG; *Int'l*, pg. 1069
DEUTSCHE UNILEVER GMBH—See Unilever Plc; *Int'l*, pg. 1436
DEUTSCHE VAN RIETSCHOTEN & HOUWENS GMBH—See Internatio-Muller N.V.; *Int'l*, pg. 682
DEUTSCHE VEEDOL GMBH—See Burmah Castrol plc; *Int'l*, pg. 236
DEUTSCHE VERSICHERUNGS-AG—See Allianz Aktiengesellschaft; *Int'l*, pg. 58
DEUTSCHE WAGNISFINANZIERUNGS-GESELLSCHAFT MBH—See Bayerische Vereinsbank Group; *Int'l*, pg. 179
DEUTSCHE WRIGLEY G.M.B.H—See Wm. Wrigley Jr. Company; *U.S. Public*, pg. 1781
DEUTSCHER CONTAINER-DIENST GES. MBH—See Hapag-Lloyd AG; *Int'l*, pg. 596
DEUTSCHER CONTAINER-DIENST GMBH—See Hapag-Lloyd AG; *Int'l*, pg. 596
DEUTSCHER INVESTMENT-TRUST GESELLSCHAFT FUR WERTPAPIERANLAGEN MBH—See Dresdner Bank AG; *Int'l*, pg. 418
DEUTSCHER LLOYD LEBENSVERSICHERUNG AG—See Assicurazioni Generali S.p.A.; *Int'l*, pg. 89
DEUTSCHER LLOYD VERSICHERUNGS AG—See Assicurazioni Generali S.p.A.; *Int'l*, pg. 89
DEUTSCHER PRESS VERTRIEB BUCH-HANSA GMBH—See Bertelsmann AG; *Int'l*, pg. 190
DEUTSCHER STRASSEN-DIENST GMBH—See BASF AG; *Int'l*, pg. 104
DEUTSCHMANN & ROELANTS BV—See N.V. Koninklijke KNP BT; *Int'l*, pg. 756
DEUTSCH-SUDAMERIKANISCHE BANK AG, MIAMI AGENCY—See Dresdner Bank AG; *Int'l*, pg. 418
W.A. DEUTSHER PTY. LTD.—See Illinois Tool Works Inc.; *U.S. Public*, pg. 867
DEUTZ AG; *Int'l*, pg. 407
DEUTZ CORPORATION—See Deutz AG; *Int'l*, pg. 408
DEVA A.S.—See Nutricia BV; *Int'l*, pg. 991
DEVARRIEUX VILLARET—See Havas Advertising; *Int'l*, pg. 600
DEVAULT FOODS; *U.S. Private*, pg. 329
DEVCO LAND CORP.—See Lennar Corporation; *U.S. Public*, pg. 988
DEVCO OF ORLANDO, INC.—See Lennar Corporation; *U.S. Public*, pg. 988
DEVCON CROWN BAY CORP.—See Devcon International Corp.; *U.S. Public*, pg. 502
DEVCON DE MEXICO, S.A.—See Illinois Tool Works Inc.; *U.S. Public*, pg. 867
DEVCON INTERNATIONAL CORP.; *U.S. Public*, pg. 502
DEVCON LTD.—See Illinois Tool Works Inc.; *U.S. Public*, pg. 867
DEVE HYDRAULIC LIFTS PTY. LTD.—See Schindler Holding AG; *Int'l*, pg. 1205
DEVE SCHINDLER AB—See Schindler Holding AG; *Int'l*, pg. 1205
DEVELOPERS DIVERSIFIED REALTY CORPORATION; *U.S. Public*, pg. 502
DEVELOPERS INVESTORS, INC.—See W.C. Bradley Co.; *U.S. Private*, pg. 164
DEVELOPMENT AND MANUFACTURING—See Xerox Corporation; *U.S. Public*, pg. 1784
DEVELOPMENT ASSOCIATION, INC.—See Tandycrafts, Inc.; *U.S. Public*, pg. 1561
DEVELOPMENT COMPANY FOR TV-PROGRAM GMBH—See Dentsu Inc.; *Int'l*, pg. 394
DEVELOPMENT CORPORATION OF AMERICA—See Lennar Corporation; *U.S. Public*, pg. 987
DEVELOPMENT CORP. OF DELRAY, INC.—See Lennar Corporation; *U.S. Public*, pg. 988
DEVELOPMENTAL RESEARCH LABORATORIES—See Shionogi & Co., Ltd.; *Int'l*, pg. 1235
DEVELOPMENTAL SCIENCES CORP.—See The General Electric Company, p.l.c.; *Int'l*, pg. 544
DEVILBISS AUTOMOTIVE REFINISHING PRODUCTS—See Illinois Tool Works Inc.; *U.S. Public*, pg. 865
DEVILBISS COMPRESSOR PRODUCTS—See Illinois Tool Works Inc.; *U.S. Public*, pg. 867
DEVILBISS DISTRIBUTED PRODUCTS DIVISION—See Illinois Tool Works Inc.; *U.S. Public*, pg. 867
DEVILBISS HEALTH CARE (EUROPE) GMBH—See Sunrise Medical, Inc.; *U.S. Public*, pg. 1536
DEVILBISS RANSBURG BRAZIL—See Illinois Tool Works Inc.; *U.S. Public*, pg. 867
DEVILBISS RANSBURG INDUSTRIAL COATING EQUIPMENT—See Illinois Tool Works Inc.; *U.S. Public*, *pg. 865*
DEVILBISS RANSBURG INDUSTRIAL LIQUID SYSTEMS (IN)—See Illinois Tool Works Inc.; *U.S. Public*, pg. 865
DEVILBISS RANSBURG INDUSTRIAL LIQUID SYSTEMS (OH)—See Illinois Tool Works Inc.; *U.S. Public*, pg. 866
DEVILBISS RANSBURG MEXICO—See Illinois Tool Works Inc.; *U.S. Public*, pg. 868
DEVILBISS RANSBURG SPRAY EQUIPMENT—See Illinois Tool Works Inc.; *U.S. Public*, pg. 868
DEVILBISS SPRAY BOOTH DIV.—See Illinois Tool Works Inc.; *U.S. Public*, pg. 866
DEVILBISS SPRAY BOOTH PRODUCTS—See Illinois Tool Works Inc.; *U.S. Public*, pg. 868
DEVILLE DUMPING & CONTAINERISATION PTY. LTD.—See The East Asiatic Company Ltd. A/S; *Int'l*, pg. 431
DEVILLE (NSW) PTY. LTD.—See The East Asiatic Company Ltd. A/S; *Int'l*, pg. 431
DEVILS LAKE JOURNAL—See Media General, Inc.; *U.S. Public*, pg. 1078
DEVIMCO—See Accor S.A.; *Int'l*, pg. 20
DEVIMCO LTD.—See Accor S.A.; *Int'l*, pg. 21
THE DEVINEY COMPANY INC.—See MasTec, Inc.; *U.S. Public*, pg. 1056
H.B. DEVINEY CO.—See J.M. Smucker Company; *U.S. Public*, pg. 1480
DEVLIEG-BULLARD INC.; *U.S. Public*, pg. 502
DEVLIEG-BULLARD SERVICES GROUP—See DeVlieg-Bullard Inc.; *U.S. Public*, pg. 502
DEVLIEG-BULLARD TOOLING SYSTEMS DIVISION—See DeVlieg-Bullard Inc.; *U.S. Public*, pg. 502
DEVLIN ELECTRONICS LIMITED—See Bowthorpe plc; *Int'l*, pg. 207
DEVOE & RAYNOLDS—See Imperial Chemical Industries PLC; *Int'l*, pg. 663
DEVOE COATINGS, B.V.—See Imperial Chemical Industries PLC; *Int'l*, pg. 663
DEVOE COATINGS CO.—See Imperial Chemical Industries PLC; *Int'l*, pg. 663
DEVOE PAINT—See Imperial Chemical Industries PLC; *Int'l*, pg. 663
DEVON CAPITAL CORP.—See Colonial Commercial Corp.; *U.S. Public*, pg. 400
DEVON DIRECT MARKETING & ADVERTISING, INC.; *U.S. Private*, pg. 329
DEVON ENERGY CANADA CORPORATION—See Devon Energy Corporation; *U.S. Public*, pg. 503
DEVON ENERGY CORPORATION; *U.S. Public*, pg. 503
DEVON GROUP, INC.; *U.S. Public*, pg. 503
DEVON PUBLISHING GROUP—See Devon Group, Inc.; *U.S. Public*, pg. 503
DEVRO INTERNATIONAL PLC; *Int'l*, pg. 408
DEVRO-TEEPAK, INC.—See Devro International Plc; *Int'l*, pg. 408
DEVRY INSTITUTE OF TECHNOLOGY—See DeVry Institutes; *U.S. Public*, pg. 504
DEVRY INSTITUTES; *U.S. Public*, pg. 503
DEWBERRY & DAVIS; *U.S. Private*, pg. 329
DEWBERRY DESIGN GROUP—See Dewberry & Davis; *U.S. Private*, pg. 329
DEWCO CHICAGO—See Don E. Williams Co.; *U.S. Private*, *pg. 1178*
DEWCO MILWAUKEE SALES—See Don E. Williams Co.; *U.S. Private*, pg. 1178
DEWE ROGERSON LIMITED; *Int'l*, pg. 408
DEWEY AND ALMY COMPANY—See W.R. Grace & Co.; *U.S. Public*, pg. 755
DEWEY CORPORATION; *U.S. Private*, pg. 329
DEWEY SQUARE INVESTORS CORPORATION—See United Asset Management Corporation; *U.S. Public*, pg. 1673
DEWITT MEDIA, INC.; *U.S. Private*, pg. 329
DEWOLFE & FISKE INC.—See CMI Holding Corp.; *U.S. Private*, pg. 195
DEXION (AUSTRALIA) PTY. LTD.—See The Interlake Corporation; *U.S. Public*, pg. 893
DEXION GMBH—See The Interlake Corporation; *U.S. Public*, pg. 893
DEXION GROUP PLC—See The Interlake Corporation; *U.S. Public*, pg. 893
DEXION LTD.—See The Interlake Corporation; *U.S. Public*, pg. 893
DEXION LTD.-STORAGE DIV.—See The Interlake Corporation; *U.S. Public*, pg. 893
S.A. DEXION REDIRACK—See The Interlake Corporation; *U.S. Public*, pg. 893
DEXOL—See Ringer Corporation; *U.S. Public*, pg. 1390
S.A. D'EXPLOITATION DE SABLIERES A MONT-SAINT-GUIBERT—See Cockerill Sambre; *Int'l*, pg. 301
DEXT COMPANY—See Scope Industries; *U.S. Public*, pg. 1444
DEXT COMPANY OF AZ—See Scope Industries; *U.S. Public*, pg. 1444
DEXT COMPANY OF CO—See Scope Industries; *U.S. Public*, pg. 1444
DEXT COMPANY OF IL—See Scope Industries; *U.S. Public*, pg. 1444
DEXT COMPANY OF MD—See Scope Industries; *U.S. Public*, pg. 1444
DEXT COMPANY OF NJ—See Scope Industries; *U.S. Public*, pg. 1444
DEXT COMPANY OF TX—See Scope Industries; *U.S. Public*, pg. 1444
P.T. DEXTAM CONTRACTORS—See Shimizu Corporation; *Int'l*, pg. 1233
DEXTER AEROSPACE MATERIALS DIVISION—See The Dexter Corporation; *U.S. Public*, pg. 504
DEXTER ASIA PACIFIC LIMITED—See The Dexter Corporation; *U.S. Public*, pg. 505
DEXTER AXLE DIV.—See Tomkins PLC; *Int'l*, pg. 1396
DEXTER CHEMICAL CORP.; *U.S. Private*, pg. 329
DEXTER COMPANY; *U.S. Private*, pg. 329
THE DEXTER CORPORATION; *U.S. Public*, pg. 504
DEXTER ELECTRONIC MATERIALS—See The Dexter Corporation; *U.S. Public*, pg. 505
DEXTER EUROPE—See The Dexter Corporation; *U.S. Public*, pg. 505
DEXTER GMBH—See The Dexter Corporation; *U.S. Public*, *pg. 505*
DEXTER MAGNETIC MATERIALS—See The Dexter Corporation; *U.S. Public*, pg. 504
DEXTER MAGNETIC MATERIALS GMBH—See The Dexter Corporation; *U.S. Public*, pg. 505
DEXTER MIDLAND CO. LTD.—See The Dexter Corporation; *U.S. Public*, pg. 505
DEXTER NONWOVENS AB—See The Dexter Corporation; *U.S. Public*, pg. 505
DEXTER NONWOVENS DIVISION—See The Dexter Corporation; *U.S. Public*, pg. 504
DEXTER PACKAGING PRODUCTS DIV.—See The Dexter Corporation; *U.S. Public*, pg. 505
DEXTER S.A.—See The Dexter Corporation; *U.S. Public*, pg. 505
DEXTER SHOE COMPANY—See Berkshire Hathaway Inc.; *U.S. Public*, pg. 217
DEXTER SPECIALTY MATERIALS, LTD.—See The Dexter Corporation; *U.S. Public*, pg. 505
DEXTER, U.K. LTD.—See The Dexter Corporation; *U.S. Public*, pg. 505
DEXTRAN PRODUCTS LIMITED—See Polydex Pharmaceuticals Limited; *Int'l*, pg. 1063
DEY LABORATORIES INC.—See Lipha Chemicals S.A.; *Int'l*, pg. 812
DEZURIK—See General Signal Corporation; *U.S. Public*, pg. 726
DEZURIK-FRANCE S.A.R.L.—See General Signal Corporation; *U.S. Public*, pg. 727
DEZURIK INTERNATIONAL LTD.—See General Signal Corporation; *U.S. Public*, pg. 727
DEZURIK-MEXICO, S.A. DE C.V.—See General Signal Corporation; *U.S. Public*, pg. 727
DEZURIK OF AUSTRALIA PTY., LTD.—See General Signal Corporation; *U.S. Public*, pg. 727
DHALENNE BERGUETTE S.C.I.—See Etablissements Delhaize Freres Et Cie "Le Lion" S.A.; *Int'l*, pg. 463
DHALENNE S.A.—See Etablissements Delhaize Freres Et Cie "Le Lion" S.A.; *Int'l*, pg. 463
DHARMALA MANULIFE—See Manulife Financial (The Manufacturers Life Insurance Company); *Int'l*, pg. 841
DI GIORGIO CORPORATION; *U.S. Private*, pg. 330
DIA RENTAL HOKIRIKU CO., LTD.—See Caterpillar Inc.; *U.S. Public*, pg. 317
DIAB DATA INC.—See Compagnie des Machines Bull; *Int'l*, *pg. 317*
DIABETES SHOPPE—See AmeriSource Health Corp.; *U.S. Public*, pg. 97
DIABLO RESEARCH CORPORATION—See Safeguard Scientifics, Inc.; *U.S. Public*, pg. 1424
DIABOLO-MANUS S.A.—See Tetra Laval Group; *Int'l*, pg. 1379
DIACHEM PACIFIC NORTHWEST INC.—See Raisio Group; *Int'l*, pg. 1086
DIADORA AMERICA, INC.; *U.S. Private*, pg. 330
DIAGEO PLC; *Int'l*, pg. 408
DIAGNOSTIC IMAGING OF ATLANTA, L.P.—See Vencor, Inc.; *U.S. Public*, pg. 1715
DIAGNOSTIC PRODUCTS CORPORATION; *U.S. Public*, pg. 505
DIAGONAL SARRIA, S.A.—See Caja de Madrid Group; *Int'l*, pg. 251
DIAGRAPH CORPORATION; *U.S. Private*, pg. 330
DIAL A HAMPER LIMITED—See Campbells/Bewley Group; *Int'l*, pg. 254
DIAL A MATTRESS USA; *U.S. Private*, pg. 330
DIAL BANK—See Norwest Corporation; *U.S. Public*, pg. 1202
THE DIAL CORPORATION; *U.S. Public*, pg. 505
DIAL FORSAKRINGS AB—See Skandia Insurance Company Limited; *Int'l*, pg. 1256
DIAL FORSIKRING A/S—See Skandia Insurance Company Limited; *Int'l*, pg. 1257
DIALIGHT CORPORATION—See The Roxboro Group PLC; *Int'l*, pg. 1130
DIALOG AB—See Celsius AB; *Int'l*, pg. 277
THE DIALOG CORPORATION—See The Dialog Corporation plc; *Int'l*, pg. 412
THE DIALOG CORPORATION PLC; *Int'l*, pg. 412
DIALOG CRS AB—See Celsius AB; *Int'l*, pg. 277
DIALOG LEBENSVERSICHERUNGS AG—See Assicurazioni Generali S.p.A.; *Int'l*, pg. 89
DIALOG VERSICHERUNGS AG—See Assicurazioni Generali S.p.A.; *Int'l*, pg. 89
DIALOGOS, INC.—See Black Rogers Sullivan Goodnight, Inc.; *U.S. Private*, pg. 147
DIALYSIS CORPORATION OF AMERICA—See Medicore Inc.; *U.S. Public*, pg. 1080
DIALYSIS CORPORATION OF HARRISBURG—See Medicore Inc.; *U.S. Public*, pg. 1080
DIALYSIS SERVICE OF FLORIDA—See Medicore Inc.; *U.S. Public*, pg. 1080
DIAMEDIX CORPORATION—See IVAX Corporation; *U.S. Public*, pg. 914
DIAMETER PAPER CO.—See Bradner Central Company; *U.S. Private*, pg. 165
DIAMONAIR—See Litton Industries, Inc.; *U.S. Public*, pg. 1003
DIAMOND ADVERTISING LTD.—See Saatchi & Saatchi Advertising Worldwide; *U.S. Public*, pg. 1422
DIAMOND BRANDS, INC.; *U.S. Private*, pg. 330
DIAMOND CHAIN COMPANY—See Amsted Industries Incorporated; *U.S. Private*, pg. 68
DIAMOND CHEMICAL CO., INC.; *U.S. Private*, pg. 330
DIAMOND COMIC DISTRIBUTORS, INC.; *U.S. Private*, pg. 330
DIAMOND CRYSTAL SPECIALTY FOODS, INC.; *U.S. Private*, pg. 330
DIAMOND ELECTRONICS, INC.—See Ultrak Inc.; *U.S. Public*, pg. 1663

DIAMOND ENERGY OPERATING CO.—See Enron Corp.; *U.S. Public,* pg. 584

DIAMOND FILM DIVISION—See Saint-Gobain; *Int'l,* pg. 1171

DIAMOND FINANCIAL HOLDINGS, INC.—See Dana Corporation; *U.S. Public,* pg. 480

DIAMOND FORECAST—See The Genlyte Group Incorporated; *U.S. Public,* pg. 730

DIAMOND HILL PLYWOOD COMPANY—See Darlington Veneer Company; *U.S. Private,* pg. 311

DIAMOND LEASE CO., LTD.; *Int'l,* pg. 413

DIAMOND MOTORS INC.; *U.S. Private,* pg. 330

DIAMOND MULTIMEDIA SYSTEMS, INC.; *U.S. Public,* pg. 505

DIAMOND OFFSHORE DRILLING, INC.—See Loews Corporation; *U.S. Public,* pg. 1011

DIAMOND P SPORTS—See Hubbard Broadcasting, Inc.; *U.S. Private,* pg. 544

DIAMOND PAPER CORPORATION—See Gould Paper Corporation; *U.S. Private,* pg. 467

DIAMOND POWER SPECIALTY CO.—See McDermott International, Inc.; *U.S. Public,* pg. 1068

DIAMOND POWER SPECIALTY LTD.—See FKI Plc; *Int'l,* pg. 472

DIAMOND PRODUCTIONS, INC.; *U.S. Private,* pg. 330

DIAMOND PRODUCTS COMPANY—See Havatampa, Inc.; *U.S. Private,* pg. 510

DIAMOND SHAMROCK CREDIT CARD CENTER—See Ultramar Diamond Shamrock Corporation; *U.S. Public,* pg. 1663

DIAMOND STAR MOTORS—See Mitsubishi Motors Corporation; *Int'l,* pg. 875

DIAMOND STATIONERY EST.—See BASF AG; *Int'l,* pg. 108

DIAMOND TECHNOLOGY PARTNERS—See Safeguard Scientifics, Inc.; *U.S. Public,* pg. 1424

T.L. DIAMOND COMPANY; *U.S. Private,* pg. 330

DIAMOND VISION, INC.—See Mitsubishi Electric Corporation; *Int'l,* pg. 873

DIAMOND WALNUT GROWERS, INC.—See Sun Diamond Growers of California; *U.S. Private,* pg. 1051

DIAMONITE PLANT—See Ferro Corporation; *U.S. Public,* pg. 618

DIANA—See Coop Switzerland; *Int'l,* pg. 330

DIANON SYSTEMS, INC.; *U.S. Public,* pg. 506

DIANTUS WATCH SA—See SMH Swiss Corporation for Micro Electronics & Watchmaking Indus. Ltd.; *Int'l,* pg. 1160

DIASONICS CREDIT CORPORATION—See IDB Holding Corporation; *Int'l,* pg. 644

DIASONICS PTY. LTD.—See IDB Holding Corporation; *Int'l,* pg. 644

DIASONICS ULTRA SOUND, INC.—See IDB Holding Corporation; *Int'l,* pg. 644

DIATOM VERKTOJ A/S—See AB Industrivarden; *Int'l,* pg. 678

DIAVIA S.P.A.—See United Technologies Corporation; *U.S. Public,* pg. 1691

DICALITE CORPORATION—See RGP Holding, Inc.; *U.S. Private,* pg. 903

DICALITE HOLDING B.V.—See RGP Holding, Inc.; *U.S. Private,* pg. 903

DICALITE HOLDINGS, INC.—See RGP Holding, Inc.; *U.S. Private,* pg. 903

DICASER S.A. DE C.V.—See RGP Holding, Inc.; *U.S. Private,* pg. 903

A.B. DICK COMPANY—See NESCO, Inc.; *U.S. Private,* pg. 791

A.B. DICK COMPANY OF CANADA, LTD.—See NESCO, Inc.; *U.S. Private,* pg. 791

A.B. DICK HOLLAND B.V.—See NESCO, Inc.; *U.S. Private,* pg. 791

A.B. DICK-ITEK—See NESCO, Inc.; *U.S. Private,* pg. 791

A.B. DICK/ITEK GRAPHIX INTERNATIONAL DIVISION DISTRIBUTOR OPERATIONS-FAR EAST—See NESCO, Inc.; *U.S. Private,* pg. 791

A.B. DICK S.A.—See NESCO, Inc.; *U.S. Private,* pg. 791

DICK CORPORATION; *U.S. Private,* pg. 331

SAM DICK INDUSTRIES, INC.—See Eclipse Inc.; *U.S. Private,* pg. 360

DICKERSON CAROLINA, INC.—See The Dickerson Group, Inc.; *U.S. Private,* pg. 331

THE DICKERSON GROUP, INC.; *U.S. Private,* pg. 331

DICKERSON, INC.—See The Dickerson Group, Inc.; *U.S. Private,* pg. 331

DICKERSON REALTY CORP.—See The Dickerson Group, Inc.; *U.S. Private,* pg. 331

DICKERSON REALTY FLORIDA, INC.—See The Dickerson Group, Inc.; *U.S. Private,* pg. 331

DICKIES OPERATIONAL WEAR—See Williamson-Dickie Mfg. Co.; *U.S. Private,* pg. 1179

DICKINSON CONTROL SYSTEMS, LTD.—See Brunel Holdings Plc; *Int'l,* pg. 231

W.H. DICKINSON ENGINEERING LTD.—See Brunel Holdings Plc; *Int'l,* pg. 231

THE DICKINSON FAMILY, INC.—See J.M. Smucker Company; *U.S. Public,* pg. 1480

DICKINSON PRESS, INC.; *U.S. Private,* pg. 331

WALTER DICKINSON INC.; *U.S. Private,* pg. 331

DICKSON ELBERTON MILLS INC.; *U.S. Public,* pg. 331

DICKTEN & MASCH MANUFACTURING CO.; *U.S. Private,* pg. 331

DICKURSBY FARG AB—See Kemira Oy; *Int'l,* pg. 729

DICO—See Petrobras - Petroleo Brasileiro S.A.; *Int'l,* pg. 1043

DICTAPHONE CANADA LTD.-LTEE.—See Stonington Partners Inc.; *U.S. Private,* pg. 1045

DICTAPHONE CO. U.K. LTD—See Stonington Partners Inc.; *U.S. Private,* pg. 1045

DICTAPHONE CORP.—See Stonington Partners Inc.; *U.S. Private,* pg. 1045

DICTAPHONE INTERNATIONAL AG—See Stonington Partners Inc.; *U.S. Private,* pg. 1045

DIDDE CORPORATION; *U.S. Private,* pg. 331

DIDDE WEB PRESS—See Didde Corporation; *U.S. Private,* pg. 331

DIDIER-ANLAGENTECHNIK HOLDING GMBH—See Viag AG; *Int'l,* pg. 1464

DIDIER MISCH- UND TRENNTECHNIK MUT GMBH—See Viag AG; *Int'l,* pg. 1464

DIDIER SAUREBAU GMBH—See Viag AG; *Int'l,* pg. 1464

DIE BETONKNACKER—See Rothenberger Group GmbH; *Int'l,* pg. 1128

DIE BETONKNACKER GMBH—See Rothenberger Group GmbH; *Int'l,* pg. 1128

DIE HAGER—See The Lowe Group; *U.S. Private,* pg. 678

DIEBEL MANUFACTURING CO.; *U.S. Private,* pg. 331

DIEBELS PRIVATE BREWERY; *Int'l,* pg. 413

DIEBOLD CREDIT CORP.—See Diebold, Incorporated; *U.S. Public,* pg. 506

DIEBOLD DEUTSCHLAND GMBH—See Daimler-Benz Aktiengesellschaft; *Int'l,* pg. 368

DIEBOLD FINANCE COMPANY, INC.—See Diebold, Incorporated; *U.S. Public,* pg. 506

DIEBOLD FINANCIAL EQUIPMENT COMPANY, LTD.—See Diebold, Incorporated; *U.S. Public,* pg. 506

DIEBOLD FOREIGN SALES CORP.—See Diebold, Incorporated; *U.S. Public,* pg. 506

DIEBOLD, INCORPORATED; *U.S. Public,* pg. 506

DIEBOLD INTERNATIONAL LIMITED—See Diebold, Incorporated; *U.S. Public,* pg. 506

DIEBOLD INVESTMENT CO.—See Diebold, Incorporated; *U.S. Public,* pg. 506

DIEBOLD LATIN AMERICA HOLDING COMPANY, INC.—See Diebold, Incorporated; *U.S. Public,* pg. 506

DIEBOLD MEXICO HOLDING COMPANY, INC.—See Diebold, Incorporated; *U.S. Public,* pg. 506

DIEBOLD MEXICO, S.A. DE C.V.—See Diebold, Incorporated; *U.S. Public,* pg. 506

DIEBOLD OF NEVADA, INC.—See Diebold, Incorporated; *U.S. Public,* pg. 506

DIEBOLD PACIFIC, LIMITED—See Diebold, Incorporated; *U.S. Public,* pg. 506

N.V. DIEETCENTRUM-WANDER S.A.—See Novartis AG; *Int'l,* pg. 981

J. DIEFFENBACHER GMBH & CO.; *Int'l,* pg. 413

DIEFFENBACHER NORTH AMERICA—See J. Dieffenbacher GmbH & Co.; *Int'l,* pg. 413

DIEFFENBACHER TORONTO—See J. Dieffenbacher GmbH & Co.; *Int'l,* pg. 413

DIEHL & EAGLE-PICHER GMBH—See Eagle-Picher Industries, Inc.; *U.S. Private,* pg. 355

DIEHL INC.; *U.S. Private,* pg. 332

DIEHL MACHINES—See Katy Industries, Inc.; *U.S. Public,* pg. 944

DIEHL SPECIALTIES INTERNATIONAL—See Diehl Inc.; *U.S. Private,* pg. 332

DIELECTRIC COMMUNICATIONS—See General Signal Corporation; *U.S. Public,* pg. 727

DIELECTRIC LABORATORIES—See Dover Corporation; *U.S. Public,* pg. 521

DIELECTRIC POLYMERS, INC.—See Park Electrochemical Corporation; *U.S. Public,* pg. 1258

DIELINK—See Synergis Technologies Group; *U.S. Private,* pg. 1060

DIEMAKERS, INC.; *U.S. Private,* pg. 332

DIEMOLDING CORP.; *U.S. Private,* pg. 332

DIEPAL-N.S.A.—See Danone Group; *Int'l,* pg. 380

DIERBERGS MARKETS INC.; *U.S. Private,* pg. 332

THE WILLIAM DIERICKX COMPANY—See Ikon Office Solutions, Inc.; *U.S. Public,* pg. 863

DIESEL MARINE NORSHIPCO—See Norfolk Shipbuilding & Drydock Corporation; *U.S. Public,* pg. 802

DIESEL RECON—See Cummins Engine Company, Inc.; *U.S. Public,* pg. 468

DIESEL RECON AUSTRALIA—See Cummins Engine Company, Inc.; *U.S. Public,* pg. 469

DIESEL TECHNOLOGY COMPANY—See Robert Bosch GmbH; *Int'l,* pg. 205

DIET CENTER WORLDWIDE, INC.—See Physicians Weight Loss Centers, Inc.; *U.S. Public,* pg. 864

DIETER HAFEMEISTER ERDBAU GMBH & CO.—See Hochtief AG; *Int'l,* pg. 623

DIETER HASE BV—See Bayerische Vereinsbank Group; *Int'l,* pg. 181

DIETERLE EDELSTAHL GMBH—See British Steel Plc; *Int'l,* pg. 222

DIETIKER AG—See Migros; *Int'l,* pg. 865

DIETISA S.A.—See Novartis AG; *Int'l,* pg. 981

DIETITIQUE ET SANTE S.A.—See Novartis AG; *Int'l,* pg. 981

DIETRICH'S MILK PRODUCTS, INC.; *U.S. Private,* pg. 332

DIETZGEN CORPORATION; *U.S. Private,* pg. 332

DIETZGEN DE MEXICO S.A. DE C.V.—See Dietzgen Corporation; *U.S. Private,* pg. 332

DIFEO AUTOMOTIVE NETWORK—See Trace International Holdings, Inc.; *U.S. Private,* pg. 1095

J.D. DIFFENBAUGH, INC.; *U.S. Private,* pg. 332

DIFFUCAP-EURAND S.A.—See American Home Products Corporation; *U.S. Public,* pg. 81

DIFFULIVRE—See Lagardere Groupe; *Int'l,* pg. 795

DIFFUSION ASSURANCE CONSEIL S.R.L.—See Assicurazioni Generali S.p.A.; *Int'l,* pg. 91

DIFFUSION PAYOT—See Lagardere Groupe; *Int'l,* pg. 795

DIGA GEBAUDE - UND ROHRTECHNIK GMBH—See Ruhrgas Aktiengesellschaft; *Int'l,* pg. 1148

DIGA VERSORGUNGSTECHNIK HOLDING GMBH—See Ruhrgas Aktiengesellschaft; *Int'l,* pg. 1148

DIGI INTERNATIONAL—See Digi International Inc.; *U.S. Public,* pg. 507

DIGI INTERNATIONAL FEDERAL SYSTEMS—See Digi International Inc.; *U.S. Public,* pg. 507

DIGI INTERNATIONAL INC.; *U.S. Public,* pg. 506

DIGICOM CIA. LTDA.—See Hewlett-Packard Company; *U.S. Public,* pg. 817

DIGICOURSE, INC.—See The Laitram Corporation; *U.S. Private,* pg. 643

DIGIPHONIC SYSTEMS PTE. LTD.—See Oki Electric Industry Company, Ltd.; *Int'l,* pg. 1000

DIGITAL—See Digital Equipment Corporation; *U.S. Public,* pg. 507

PT DIGITAL ASTRA NUSANTARA—See Digital Equipment Corporation; *U.S. Public,* pg. 507

DIGITAL AUDIO DISC CORP.—See Sony Corporation; *Int'l,* pg. 1284

DIGITAL COMMUNICATIONS OF AMERICA, INC.—See Platinum Equity Holdings, LLC; *U.S. Private,* pg. 872

DIGITAL COMPUTER CONTROLS, INC.—See Data General Corporation; *U.S. Public,* pg. 485

DIGITAL COURIER INTERNATIONAL INC.; *Int'l,* pg. 413

DIGITAL EQUIPMENT ALGERIA—See Digital Equipment Corporation; *U.S. Public,* pg. 507

DIGITAL EQUIPMENT (BCFI) AB—See Digital Equipment Corporation; *U.S. Public,* pg. 507

DIGITAL EQUIPMENT BULGARIA—See Digital Equipment Corporation; *U.S. Public,* pg. 507

DIGITAL EQUIPMENT CHINA INCORPORATED—See Digital Equipment Corporation; *U.S. Public,* pg. 507

DIGITAL EQUIPMENT CO., LIMITED—See Digital Equipment Corporation; *U.S. Public,* pg. 507

DIGITAL EQUIPMENT CORPORATION; *U.S. Public,* pg. 507

DIGITAL EQUIPMENT CORPORATION—See Digital Equipment Corporation; *U.S. Public,* pg. 507

DIGITAL EQUIPMENT CORPORATION AG—See Digital Equipment Corporation; *U.S. Public,* pg. 507

DIGITAL EQUIPMENT CORP. A/S—See Digital Equipment Corporation; *U.S. Public,* pg. 507

DIGITAL EQUIPMENT CORPORATION A/S—See Digital Equipment Corporation; *U.S. Public,* pg. 507

DIGITAL EQUIPMENT CORPORATION (AUSTRALIA) PTY. LIMITED—See Digital Equipment Corporation; *U.S. Public,* pg. 507

DIGITAL EQUIPMENT CORPORATION ESPANA S.A.—See Digital Equipment Corporation; *U.S. Public,* pg. 507

DIGITAL EQUIPMENT CORPORATION GMBH—See Digital Equipment Corporation; *U.S. Public,* pg. 507

DIGITAL EQUIPMENT CORPORATION JAPAN—See Digital Equipment Corporation; *U.S. Public,* pg. 507

DIGITAL EQUIPMENT CORPORATION (NEW ZEALAND) LTD.—See Digital Equipment Corporation; *U.S. Public,* pg. 507

DIGITAL EQUIPMENT CORPORATION OY—See Digital Equipment Corporation; *U.S. Public,* pg. 507

DIGITAL EQUIPMENT CORPORATION, TAIWAN—See Digital Equipment Corporation; *U.S. Public,* pg. 507

DIGITAL EQUIPMENT CORPORATION (THAILAND) LIMITED—See Digital Equipment Corporation; *U.S. Public,* pg. 507

DIGITAL EQUIPMENT DE MEXICO S.A. DE C.V.—See Digital Equipment Corporation; *U.S. Public,* pg. 507

DIGITAL EQUIPMENT DE VENEZUELA—See Digital Equipment Corporation; *U.S. Public,* pg. 508

DIGITAL EQUIPMENT (DEC) LIMITED—See Digital Equipment Corporation; *U.S. Public,* pg. 508

DIGITAL EQUIPMENT DO BRASIL LTDA.—See Digital Equipment Corporation; *U.S. Public,* pg. 508

DIGITAL EQUIPMENT FILIPINAS INC.—See Digital Equipment Corporation; *U.S. Public,* pg. 508

DIGITAL EQUIPMENT FRANCE—See Digital Equipment Corporation; *U.S. Public,* pg. 508

DIGITAL EQUIPMENT G.M.B.H.—See Digital Equipment Corporation; *U.S. Public,* pg. 508

DIGITAL EQUIPMENT HELLAS LTD.—See Digital Equipment Corporation; *U.S. Public,* pg. 508

DIGITAL EQUIPMENT (HOLDINGS) B.V.—See Digital Equipment Corporation; *U.S. Public,* pg. 508

DIGITAL EQUIPMENT HONG KONG LIMITED—See Digital Equipment Corporation; *U.S. Public,* pg. 508

DIGITAL EQUIPMENT HUNGARY LTD.—See Digital Equipment Corporation; *U.S. Public,* pg. 508

DIGITAL EQUIPMENT (ICELAND)—See Digital Equipment Corporation; *U.S. Public,* pg. 508

DIGITAL EQUIPMENT (INDIA) LTD.—See Digital Equipment Corporation; *U.S. Public,* pg. 508

DIGITAL EQUIPMENT IRELAND LIMITED—See Digital Equipment Corporation; *U.S. Public,* pg. 508

DIGITAL EQUIPMENT KOREA INC.—See Digital Equipment Corporation; *U.S. Public,* pg. 508

DIGITAL EQUIPMENT (MALAYSIA) SDN BHD—See Digital Equipment Corporation; *U.S. Public,* pg. 508

DIGITAL EQUIPMENT N.V./S.A.—See Digital Equipment Corporation; *U.S. Public,* pg. 508

DIGITAL EQUIPMENT PORTUGAL, LDA—See Digital Equipment Corporation; *U.S. Public,* pg. 508

DIGITAL EQUIPMENT ROMANIA S.R.L.—See Digital Equipment Corporation; *U.S. Public,* pg. 508

DIGITAL EQUIPMENT SINGAPORE (PTE) LIMITED—See Digital Equipment Corporation; *U.S. Public,* pg. 508

DIGITAL EQUIPMENT S.P.A.—See Digital Equipment Corporation; *U.S. Public,* pg. 508

DIGITAL EQUIPMENT S.R.O.—See Digital Equipment Corporation; *U.S. Public,* pg. 508

DIGITAL FUEL INJECTION, INC.—See Echlin Inc.; *U.S. Public,* pg. 560

DIGITAL HOUSE, LTD.—See Emulex Corporation; *U.S. Public,* pg. 579

DIGITAL INSURANCE SERVICES—See Digital Solutions, Inc.; *U.S. Public,* pg. 508

DIGITAL LINK CORPORATION; *U.S. Public,* pg. 508

DIGITAL LINK CORPORATION—See Digital Link Corporation; *U.S. Public,* pg. 508

DIGITAL LINK DEUTSCHLAND GMBH—See Digital Link Corporation; *U.S. Public,* pg. 508

DIGITAL LINK U.K. LIMITED—See Digital Link Corporation; *U.S. Public,* pg. 508

DIGITAL MEDIA CENTER—See R.R. Donnelley & Sons Company; *U.S. Public,* pg. 518

DIGITAL MICROWAVE CORPORATION; *U.S. Public,* pg. 508

DIGITAL MICROWAVE DE VENEZUELA, C.A.—See Digital Microwave Corporation; *U.S. Public*, pg. 508
DIGITAL SIGNAL PROCESSING DIVISION—See Motorola, Inc.; *U.S. Public*, pg. 1137
DIGITAL SOLUTIONS, INC.; *U.S. Public*, pg. 508
DIGITAL SOUND CORPORATION; *U.S. Public*, pg. 508
DIGITAL STAFF CONNXIONS—See Digital Solutions, Inc.; *U.S. Public*, pg. 508
DIGITAL STATION—See Griffin Bacal Inc.; *U.S. Private*, pg. 480
DIGITAL TYPEFACE CORPORATION—See LaserMaster Technologies, Inc.; *U.S. Public*, pg. 979
DIGITALE KARTSYSTEMER—See Kvaerner a.s.a.; *Int'l*, pg. 766
DIGITREE, INC.—See The Thomson Corporation; *U.S. Public*, pg. 1600
DIGITRON INC.—See Digitron Tool Co., Inc.; *U.S. Private*, pg. 332
DIGITRON KETTERING—See Digitron Tool Co., Inc.; *U.S. Private*, pg. 333
DIGITRON TOOL CO., INC.; *U.S. Private*, pg. 332
DIGNITAS S.A.—See Cigna Corp.; *U.S. Public*, pg. 364
DIHURST HOLDINGS LTD.—See Wolseley Plc.; *Int'l*, pg. 1511
A/S DIKEMA NORGE—See Cockerill Sambre; *Int'l*, pg. 302
A/S DIKEMA STAL—See Cockerill Sambre; *Int'l*, pg. 302
DILIGENTIA BUSINESS PRESS NV—See VNU Verenigde Nederlandse Uitgeversbedrijven B.V.; *Int'l*, pg. 1445
DILKS STAMP CO.—See American Marking Systems; *U.S. Private*, pg. 58
DILLARD, A RESOURCENET INTERNATIONAL COMPANY—See International Paper Company; *U.S. Public*, pg. 901
DILLARD INVESTMENT CO. INC.—See Dillard's, Inc.; *U.S. Public*, pg. 509
DILLARD NATIONAL BANK—See Dillard's, Inc.; *U.S. Public*, pg. 509
DILLARD PAPER CO. OF GREENSBORO—See International Paper Company; *U.S. Public*, pg. 902
DILLARD PAPER CO. OF JACKSONVILLE—See International Paper Company; *U.S. Public*, pg. 902
DILLARD PAPER CO. OF MIAMI—See International Paper Company; *U.S. Public*, pg. 902
DILLARD PAPER CO. OF ORLANDO—See International Paper Company; *U.S. Public*, pg. 902
DILLARD PAPER CO. OF TAMPA—See International Paper Company; *U.S. Public*, pg. 902
DILLARD'S, INC.; *U.S. Public*, pg. 509
DER DILLINGER HUETTENWERKE AG—See Groupe Usinor; *Int'l*, pg. 572
DILLINGHAM CONSTRUCTION CORPORATION; *U.S. Private*, pg. 333
DILLINGHAM CONSTRUCTION N.A., INC.—See Dillingham Construction Corporation; *U.S. Private*, pg. 333
DILLINGHAM CONSTRUCTION PACIFIC, LTD.—See Dillingham Construction Corporation; *U.S. Private*, pg. 333
DILLON COMPANIES, INC.—See The Kroger Co.; *U.S. Public*, pg. 967
EDWARD DILLON & CO LTD—See LVMH Moet Hennessy Louis Vuitton; *Int'l*, pg. 782
DIM, S.A.—See Sara Lee Corporation; *U.S. Public*, pg. 1434
DIMARK, INC.—See Harte-Hanks Communications, Inc.; *U.S. Public*, pg. 793
DIMCO-GRAY COMPANY; *U.S. Private*, pg. 333
THE DIME SAVINGS BANK OF NEW YORK; *U.S. Public*, pg. 509
DIMELING, SCHREIBER & PARK; *U.S. Private*, pg. 333
DIMEMN, S.A.—See Hewlett-Packard Company; *U.S. Public*, pg. 817
DIMENSIONAL MERCHANDISING, INC.; *U.S. Private*, pg. 333
DIMENSIONAL STONE LIMITED—See RMC Group p.l.c.; *Int'l*, pg. 1081
DIMENSIONS INC.—See Coats Viyella plc; *Int'l*, pg. 300
DIMEO CONSTRUCTION COMPANY; *U.S. Private*, pg. 333
DIMEQ MEDIZINELECTRONIK GMBH—See Delft Instruments N.V.; *Int'l*, pg. 389
DIMEQ NV—See Delft Instruments N.V.; *Int'l*, pg. 389
DIMEQ SOUTH EAST ASIA LTD.—See Delft Instruments N.V.; *Int'l*, pg. 389
DIMERIC DEVELOPMENT LABORTORY—See Platinum Technology, Inc.; *U.S. Public*, pg. 1309
P.T. DIMET INDONESIA—See BTR plc; *Int'l*, pg. 129
DIMET (THAILAND) LTD.—See BTR plc; *Int'l*, pg. 129
DIMETRICS, INC.—See Carpenter Technology Corporation; *U.S. Public*, pg. 308
DIMON, INCORPORATED; *U.S. Public*, pg. 509
DIMON, INTERNATIONAL, INC.—See DIMON, Incorporated; *U.S. Public*, pg. 510
DIMOND INDUSTRIES—See Fletcher Challenge Limited; *Int'l*, pg. 495
DIMPLEX NORTH AMERICA—See The Glen Dimplex Group; *Int'l*, pg. 554
DIMPLEX UK—See The Glen Dimplex Group; *Int'l*, pg. 554
DINAGRAPHICS, INC.—See Jefferson Smurfit Group p.l.c.; *Int'l*, pg. 1270
DINAIRE CORP.; *U.S. Private*, pg. 334
DINERS CLUB AUSTRIA AG—See Creditanstalt-Bankverein; *Int'l*, pg. 347
DINERS CLUB INC.—See Citicorp; *U.S. Public*, pg. 377
DINERS CLUB NORDIC A/S—See Scandinavian Airlines System (SAS); *Int'l*, pg. 1202
DINGS DYNAMICS CO.—See Venturedyne, Ltd.; *U.S. Private*, pg. 1136
DINGS MAGNETIC CO.—See Venturedyne, Ltd.; *U.S. Private*, pg. 1136
P.T. DINO INDONESIA INDUSTRIAL LTD.—See Kao Corporation; *Int'l*, pg. 717
DINOL AB—See Novartis AG; *Int'l*, pg. 981
DINOL AUSTRALIA PTY. LTD.—See Novartis AG; *Int'l*, pg. 981
DINOL FRANCE S.A.R.L.—See Novartis AG; *Int'l*, pg. 981
DINOL GMBH—See Novartis AG; *Int'l*, pg. 982

DINOL INDUSTRIAL CANADA INC.—See Novartis AG; *Int'l*, pg. 982
DINOL JAPAN—See Novartis AG; *Int'l*, pg. 982
DINOL KOREA LTD.—See Novartis AG; *Int'l*, pg. 982
DINOL NORGE A/S—See Novartis AG; *Int'l*, pg. 982
DINOL OY—See Novartis AG; *Int'l*, pg. 982
DINOL-SHROFF (INDIA) PVT. LTD.—See Novartis AG; *Int'l*, pg. 982
DIODES CO. LTD.—See Diodes Incorporated; *U.S. Public*, pg. 510
DIODES INCORPORATED; *U.S. Public*, pg. 510
DIONEX B.V.—See Dionex Corporation; *U.S. Public*, pg. 510
DIONEX CANADA LTD.—See Dionex Corporation; *U.S. Public*, pg. 510
DIONEX CORPORATION; *U.S. Public*, pg. 510
DIONEX GMBH—See Dionex Corporation; *U.S. Public*, pg. 510
DIONEX N.V.—See Dionex Corporation; *U.S. Public*, pg. 510
DIONEX S.A.—See Dionex Corporation; *U.S. Public*, pg. 510
DIONEX S.R.L.—See Dionex Corporation; *U.S. Public*, pg. 510
DIONEX (SWITZERLAND) AG—See Dionex Corporation; *U.S. Public*, pg. 510
DIONEX (U.K.) LTD.—See Dionex Corporation; *U.S. Public*, pg. 510
J.B. DIONNE LTD.—See Purdel, Cooperative Agro-Alimentaire; *Int'l*, pg. 1074
DIORFIL S.A.—See LVMH Moet Hennessy Louis Vuitton; *Int'l*, pg. 782
DIOSYNTH BV—See Akzo Nobel N.V.; *Int'l*, pg. 44
DIOSYNTH FRANCE SA—See Akzo Nobel N.V.; *Int'l*, pg. 44
DIOSYNTH, INC.—See Akzo Nobel N.V.; *Int'l*, pg. 48
DIOSYNTH INTERNATIONAL BV—See Akzo Nobel N.V.; *Int'l*, pg. 44
DIOSYNTH SCANDINAVIA—See Akzo Nobel N.V.; *Int'l*, pg. 44
DIOSYNTH VERTRIEBSGESELLSCHAFT MBH—See Akzo Nobel N.V.; *Int'l*, pg. 44
DIPLAC—See Petrobras - Petroleo Brasileiro S.A.; *Int'l*, pg. 1041
S.A. DIRAME—See Axel Johnson AB; *Int'l*, pg. 710
A/S DIRECT—See Philips Electronics N.V.; *Int'l*, pg. 1052
DIRECT ASSURANCE—See AXA-UAP; *Int'l*, pg. 18
DIRECT DENTAL SUPPLY CO.—See Patterson Dental Company; *U.S. Public*, pg. 604
DIRECT FUELS, L.P.—See FFP Marketing Company, Inc.; *U.S. Public*, pg. 604
DIRECT LINE INSURANCE PLC—See The Royal Bank of Scotland plc; *Int'l*, pg. 1132
DIRECT PRESS MODERN LITHO CORPORATION; *U.S. Private*, pg. 334
DIRECT SCRIPT—See Oxford Health Plans Inc.; *U.S. Public*, pg. 1239
DIRECT TOOL INC.—See Cold Heading Co.; *U.S. Private*, pg. 250
DIRECTIONAL FURNITURE—See CF Group; *U.S. Private*, pg. 193
DIRECTORY DISTRIBUTING ASSOCIATES, INC.; *U.S. Private*, pg. 334
DIRECTORY SERVICES GROUP—See Liggett-Stashower, Inc.; *U.S. Private*, pg. 667
DIRECTV INC.—See General Motors Corporation; *U.S. Public*, pg. 720
DIRECTVIEW BV—See VNU Verenigde Nederlandse Uitgeversbedrijven B.V.; *Int'l*, pg. 1445
DIRKSEN HOUSE HEALTHCARE—See Vencor, Inc.; *U.S. Public*, pg. 1712
DISABILITY CLAIM SERVICES, INC.—See Cigna Corp.; *U.S. Public*, pg. 362
DISATEC S.A.—See Norsk Hydro a.s; *Int'l*, pg. 961
DISC MANUFACTURING CINRAM—See Cinram Ltd.; *Int'l*, pg. 293
DISCLOSURE INCORPORATED—See Primark Corporation; *U.S. Public*, pg. 1325
DISCO CORPORATION; *Int'l*, pg. 413
DISCO HI-TEC AMERICA INC.—See Disco Corporation; *Int'l*, pg. 413
DISCO HI-TEC EUROPE GMBH—See Disco Corporation; *Int'l*, pg. 413
DISCO HI-TEC FRANCE SARL—See Disco Corporation; *Int'l*, pg. 413
DISCO HI-TEC (SINGAPORE) PTE, LTD.—See Disco Corporation; *Int'l*, pg. 413
DISCO HI-TEC U.K LTD.—See Disco Corporation; *Int'l*, pg. 413
DISCOS DE CENTRO AMERICA—See Philips Electronics N.V.; *Int'l*, pg. 1052
DISCOUNT AUTO PARTS, INC.; *U.S. Public*, pg. 510
DISCOUNT DRUG MART INC.; *U.S. Private*, pg. 334
DISCOUNT INVESTMENT CORPORATION LTD.—See IDB Holding Corporation; *Int'l*, pg. 644
DISCOUNT LABELS, INC.—See American Business Products, Inc.; *U.S. Public*, pg. 70
DISCOUNT TIRE; *U.S. Private*, pg. 334
DISCOVER—See The Walt Disney Company; *U.S. Public*, pg. 513
THE DISCOVERY CHANNEL—See TSN Communications; *Int'l*, pg. 1343
DISCOVERY COMMUNICATIONS, INC.; *U.S. Private*, pg. 334
DISCOVERY NETWORKS, INC.—See Discovery Communications, Inc.; *U.S. Private*, pg. 334
DISCOVERY PLASTICS, INC.—See RHC/Spacemaster Corporation; *U.S. Private*, pg. 904
DISCOVISION ASSOCIATES—See Pioneer Electronic Corporation; *Int'l*, pg. 1057
DISCUS ELECTRONIC TRAINING—See Eastman Kodak Company; *U.S. Public*, pg. 551
DISCWASHER—See Recoton Corporation; *U.S. Public*, pg. 1369

DISEASE MANAGEMENT—See Medpartners Inc.; *U.S. Public*, pg. 1082
DISEASE MANAGEMENT SCIENCES INC.—See Pfizer Inc.; *U.S. Public*, pg. 1282
DISEL (DISENO E INGENIERIA DE SISTEMAS ELECTRONICOS S.A.)—See The Macneal-Schwendler Corp.; *U.S. Public*, pg. 1032
DISKO FACTORING FINANZ GMBH—See Dresdner Bank AG; *Int'l*, pg. 418
DISKOMAT AB—See Cardo AB; *Int'l*, pg. 270
DISKUS AG—See Rothenberger Group GmbH; *Int'l*, pg. 1128
THE DISNEY CHANNEL—See The Walt Disney Company; *U.S. Public*, pg. 513
DISNEY EDUCATIONAL PRODUCTIONS—See The Walt Disney Company; *U.S. Public*, pg. 513
DISNEY PUBLISHING GROUP—See The Walt Disney Company; *U.S. Public*, pg. 511
WALT DISNEY ATTRACTIONS DIVISION—See The Walt Disney Company; *U.S. Public*, pg. 511
WALT DISNEY ATTRACTIONS-WALT DISNEY WORLD—See The Walt Disney Company; *U.S. Public*, pg. 513
THE WALT DISNEY COMPANY; *U.S. Public*, pg. 511
THE WALT DISNEY COMPANY (CANADA)—See The Walt Disney Company; *U.S. Public*, pg. 514
THE WALT DISNEY COMPANY (FRANCE) S.A.—See The Walt Disney Company; *U.S. Public*, pg. 514
THE WALT DISNEY COMPANY (GERMANY) GMBH—See The Walt Disney Company; *U.S. Public*, pg. 514
THE WALT DISNEY COMPANY (ITALIA)—See The Walt Disney Company; *U.S. Public*, pg. 514
THE WALT DISNEY COMPANY LTD.—See The Walt Disney Company; *U.S. Public*, pg. 514
WALT DISNEY CONSUMER PRODUCTS—See The Walt Disney Company; *U.S. Public*, pg. 511
WALT DISNEY ENTERPRISES OF JAPAN LTD.—See The Walt Disney Company; *U.S. Public*, pg. 514
WALT DISNEY IMAGINEERING—See The Walt Disney Company; *U.S. Public*, pg. 513
WALT DISNEY MUSIC CO.—See The Walt Disney Company; *U.S. Public*, pg. 513
WALT DISNEY NETWORK TELEVISION—See The Walt Disney Company; *U.S. Public*, pg. 511
WALT DISNEY PICTURES AND TELEVISION—See The Walt Disney Company; *U.S. Public*, pg. 513
WALT DISNEY TRAVEL CO., INC.—See The Walt Disney Company; *U.S. Public*, pg. 513
DISNEYLAND—See The Walt Disney Company; *U.S. Public*, pg. 511
DISNEYLAND HOTEL—See The Walt Disney Company; *U.S. Public*, pg. 513
DISOGRIN MEXICANA S.A. DE C.V.—See Freudenberg & Co.; *Int'l*, pg. 505
DISPATCH CONSUMER SERVICES—See The Dispatch Printing Company; *U.S. Private*, pg. 335
THE DISPATCH PRINTING COMPANY; *U.S. Private*, pg. 335
THE DISPATCH PUBLISHING COMPANY, INC.—See The New York Times Company; *U.S. Public*, pg. 1175
DISPATCH SERVICES, INC.—See Viad Corp; *U.S. Public*, pg. 1719
DISPERSA AG—See Novartis AG; *Int'l*, pg. 972
DISPERSA GMBH—See Novartis AG; *Int'l*, pg. 982
DISPLAY TECHNOLOGIES ELECTROHOME INC.—See Electrohome Ltd.; *Int'l*, pg. 438
DISPLAY TECHNOLOGIES, INC.—See Toshiba Corporation; *Int'l*, pg. 1402
DISPORT—See GIB Group; *Int'l*, pg. 534
DISPORT INTERNATIONAL—See GIB Group; *Int'l*, pg. 533
DISPOSABLE SAFETY WEAR INC.—See Eastco Industrial Safety Corp.; *U.S. Public*, pg. 548
DISPOSAL SPECIALISTS, INC.—See Browning-Ferris Industries, Inc.; *U.S. Public*, pg. 264
DISPOSAL SYSTEMS, INC.—See The GNI Group, Inc.; *U.S. Public*, pg. 694
DISPOSAL URBAN MAINTENANCE PROCESSION CO., INC.—See Republic Industries, Inc.; *U.S. Public*, pg. 1380
DISPOSITIVOS DE PRECISION ELECTRONICA, S.A. DE C.V.—See Clarion Co., Ltd.; *Int'l*, pg. 296
THE DISSTON CO.—See Kennametal Inc.; *U.S. Public*, pg. 950
DISTA PRODUCTS CO.—See Eli Lilly and Company; *U.S. Public*, pg. 993
DISTA PRODUCTS LTD.—See Eli Lilly and Company; *U.S. Public*, pg. 993
DISTA, S.A.—See Eli Lilly and Company; *U.S. Public*, pg. 993
DISTEX IND. INC.—See Echlin Inc.; *U.S. Public*, pg. 560
DISTILERIA BAGO, INC. (DBI)—See La Tondena Distillers, Inc.; *Int'l*, pg. 785
DISTILLATION PRODUCTS INDUSTRIES—See Eastman Kodak Company; *U.S. Public*, pg. 551
DISTILLEERDERIJEN ERVEN LUCAS BOLS BV—See Koninklijke BolsWessanen nv; *Int'l*, pg. 751
B.V. DISTILLERDERIJ 'DE FRANSCHE KROON' V/H HARTEVELT EN ZOON—See Koninklijke BolsWessanen nv; *Int'l*, pg. 751
DISTILLERIE DE LA GROIE—See LVMH Moet Hennessy Louis Vuitton; *Int'l*, pg. 780
DISTILLERS CORPORATION S.A.—See Rothmans UK Holdings Limited; *Int'l*, pg. 1129
DISTINCT HOME HEALTH CARE, INC.—See Integrated Health Services, Inc.; *U.S. Public*, pg. 884
DISTRECO—See Groupe Casino; *Int'l*, pg. 563
DISTRIBUCION QUELLE, S.A. Y CIA SEC—See Tabacalera, S.A.; *Int'l*, pg. 1346
DISTRIBUIDORA DE MANUFACTURAS CENTRO-AMERICANAS, S.A.—See Kimberly-Clark Corporation; *U.S. Public*, pg. 959
CIA. DISTRIBUIDORA DE PETROLEOS, S.A. (CEDIPSA)—See Compania Espanola de Petroleos, S.A. (CEPSA); *Int'l*, pg. 323

Company Index

DISTRIBUIDORA DE PRODUCTOS PETROLIFEROS, S.A. (DISPESA)—See Compania Espanola de Petroleos, S.A. (CEPSA); *Int'l*, pg. 323
DISTRIBUIDORA DE PRODUCTOS SANDOZ S.A.—See Novartis AG; *Int'l*, pg. 982
DISTRIBUIDORA SHELL DE EL SALVADOR SA—See Royal Dutch/Shell Group of Companies; *Int'l*, pg. 1141
DISTRIBUIDORA TOYOTA CHILE LTDA.—See Mitsui & Co., *Int'l*, pg. 879
DISTRIBUIDORES CONCESIONARIOS S.A.—See Hepworth Plc; *Int'l*, pg. 615
DISTRIBUPRO, INC.—See Computer Associates International, Inc.; *U.S. Public*, pg. 420
DISTRIBUTED SYSTEMS DIVISION—See Storage Technology Corporation; *U.S. Public*, pg. 1522
DISTRIBUTION—See Allegiance Healthcare Corp.; *U.S. Public*, pg. 44
DISTRIBUTION AB DAGAB—See Carnegie Holding AB; *Int'l*, pg. 272
DISTRIBUTION AMERICA; *U.S. Private*, pg. 335
DISTRIBUTION CONTROL SYSTEMS, INC. (DCS)—See ESCO Electronics Corporation; *U.S. Public*, pg. 546
DISTRIBUTION PUBLICITAIRE ESTRIE—See G.T.C. Transcontinental Group Ltd.; *Int'l*, pg. 539
DISTRIBUTION SERVICES—See National Amusements, Inc.; *U.S. Private*, pg. 777
DISTRIBUTION SERVICES, INC.—See American Media, Inc.; *U.S. Public*, pg. 87
DISTRIBUTION SYSTEMS DIVISION—See ABB Asea Brown Boveri (Holding) Ltd.; *Int'l*, pg. 4
DISTRIBUTION UNLIMITED, INC.—See Galesi Group; *U.S. Private*, pg. 438
DISTRIBUTOR CONCEPTS—See King Group, Inc.; *U.S. Private*, pg. 620
DISTRIBUTOREN INTERELKO A/S—See Axel Johnson AB; *Int'l*, pg. 710
DISTRIBUTORS OIL COMPANY, INC.; *U.S. Private*, pg. 336
DISTRICT PETROLEUM PRODUCTS, INC.; *U.S. Private*, pg. 336
DISTRIGAS CORP.—See Cabot Corporation; *U.S. Public*, pg. 289
DISTRIGAS OF MASSACHUSETTS CORPORATION—See Cabot Corporation; *U.S. Public*, pg. 289
DISTRIGAZ SA SOC. DE DISTRIBUTION DU GAZ—See Royal Dutch/Shell Group of Companies; *Int'l*, pg. 1138
DISTRILEASE B.S.E.T.—See GIB Group; *Int'l*, pg. 533
DISTRIMEDIA SERVICES B.V.—See The Reader's Digest Association, Inc.; *U.S. Public*, pg. 1368
DISTRIPIPE S.A.—See Tractebel; *Int'l*, pg. 1416
DISTRIREST—See GIB Group; *Int'l*, pg. 533
DISTRISERVICE—See Lagardere Groupe; *Int'l*, pg. 792
SARL DISTRISID—See Cockerill Sambre; *Int'l*, pg. 302
DISTRISUD—See Lagardere Groupe; *Int'l*, pg. 795
DISTRIWAX S.A.—See Gamma Holding N.V.; *Int'l*, pg. 540
DIT HARRIS S.A.—See Technip; *Int'l*, pg. 1361
DITEP—See Petrobras - Petroleo Brasileiro S.A.; *Int'l*, pg. 1042
DITEQ—See Petrobras - Petroleo Brasileiro S.A.; *Int'l*, pg. 1042
DITTMAN & NEUHAUS GMBH—See Fried. Krupp AG; *Int'l*, pg. 508
DIVAL—See Allianz Aktiengesellschaft; *Int'l*, pg. 61
DIVANE BROS. ELECTRIC CO.; *U.S. Private*, pg. 336
DIVERSA-VERSICHERUNGSKONTOR GMBH—See Viag AG; *Int'l*, pg. 1464
DIVERSCO, INC.; *U.S. Private*, pg. 336
DIVERSEY LEVER—See Unilever Plc; *Int'l*, pg. 1437
DIVERSEY WATER TECHNOLOGIES—See Nalco Chemical Company; *U.S. Public*, pg. 1150
DIVERSIFIED BUSINESS CREDIT, INC.—See National City Bancorp; *U.S. Public*, pg. 1154
DIVERSIFIED COMMUNICATIONS; *U.S. Private*, pg. 336
DIVERSIFIED COMPOUNDERS—See Dennis Chemical Co., Inc.; *U.S. Private*, pg. 324
DIVERSIFIED DYNAMICS CORPORATION; *U.S. Private*, pg. 336
DIVERSIFIED GROUP—See The Gillette Company; *U.S. Public*, pg. 743
DIVERSIFIED GROUP, INC.; *U.S. Private*, pg. 336
DIVERSIFIED INSURANCE AGENCY, INC.—See Cigna Corp.; *U.S. Public*, pg. 366
DIVERSIFIED PARCELS FREIGHT DIVISION—See SNCF; *Int'l*, pg. 1163
DIVERSIFIED PHARMACEUTICAL SERVICES, INC.—See SmithKline Beecham plc; *Int'l*, pg. 1265
DIVERSIFIED STAINLESS STEEL OF CANADA—See Carpenter Technology Corporation; *U.S. Public*, pg. 308
DIVERSION—See The Hearst Corporation; *U.S. Private*, pg. 516
DIVERSITECH, INC.—See Chr. Hansen Holding A/S; *Int'l*, pg. 288
DIVI HOTELS, INC.; *U.S. Private*, pg. 336
DIVINO AG—See Feldschlosschen Hurlimann Holding; *Int'l*, pg. 479
DIVISIONE AMBIENTE—See IRI Istituto Ricostruzione Industriale; *Int'l*, pg. 653
DIVISIONE ELETTRONICA DI POTENZA E MACCHINE—See IRI Istituto Ricostruzione Industriale; *Int'l*, pg. 653
DIVISIONE NUCLEARE—See IRI Istituto Ricostruzione Industriale; *Int'l*, pg. 653
DIX & EATON INCORPORATED; *U.S. Private*, pg. 336
DIXIE BEARINGS, INC.—See Applied Industrial Technologies; *U.S. Public*, pg. 122
DIXIE BENDERS LIMITED—See Fort James Corporation; *U.S. Public*, pg. 672
DIXIE BREWING CO., INC.; *U.S. Private*, pg. 336
DIXIE BUILDING SUPPLIES, INC.—See Walter Industries, Inc.; *U.S. Public*, pg. 1736
DIXIE BULK TRANSPORT, INC.—See Kirby Corporation; *U.S. Public*, pg. 962
DIXIE CANAL GROUP—See Kirby Corporation; *U.S. Public*, pg. 961

DIXIE CARRIERS, INC.—See Kirby Corporation; *U.S. Public*, pg. 962
DIXIE CRYSTALS BRANDS, INC.—See Imperial Holly Corporation; *U.S. Public*, pg. 872
DIXIE DAIRY COMPANY; *U.S. Private*, pg. 337
DIXIE ELECTRIC COOPERATIVE; *U.S. Private*, pg. 337
DIXIE EXPRESS, INC.—See Torchmark Corporation; *U.S. Public*, pg. 1622
DIXIE FOODSERVICE—See Fort James Corporation; *U.S. Public*, pg. 671
DIXIE FUELS LIMITED—See Kirby Corporation; *U.S. Public*, pg. 962
DIXIE FUELS II LIMITED—See Kirby Corporation; *U.S. Public*, pg. 962
DIXIE FUELS II, LIMITED—See Kirby Corporation; *U.S. Public*, pg. 962
THE DIXIE GROUP, INC.; *U.S. Public*, pg. 514
DIXIE INDUSTRIES, INC.—See Columbus McKinnon Corp.; *U.S. Public*, pg. 406
DIXIE INSURANCE COMPANY—See American Financial Group; *U.S. Public*, pg. 75
DIXIE LINEHAUL GROUP—See Kirby Corporation; *U.S. Public*, pg. 961
DIXIE MARINE, INC.—See Kirby Corporation; *U.S. Public*, pg. 962
DIXIE-NARCO, INC.—See Maytag Corporation; *U.S. Public*, pg. 1065
DIXIE NATIONAL LIFE INSURANCE COMPANY—See Standard Management Corporation; *U.S. Public*, pg. 1502
DIXIE OIL COMPANY; *U.S. Private*, pg. 337
DIXIE PACKERS—See Winn-Dixie Stores, Inc.; *U.S. Public*, pg. 1772
DIXIE REEL & BOX CO.—See Lone Star Corrugated Container Corporation; *U.S. Private*, pg. 674
DIXIE RIVER TOW GROUP—See Kirby Corporation; *U.S. Public*, pg. 961
DIXIE ROYAL HOMES, INC.—See Family Inns of America, Inc.; *U.S. Private*, pg. 392
DIXIE SYNTHETIC YARN GROUP—See The Dixie Group, Inc.; *U.S. Public*, pg. 514
DIXIE TYPE & SUPPLY CO., INC.—See PrimeSource Corporation; *U.S. Public*, pg. 1329
DIXIE UNION VERPACKUNGEN GMBH—See Continental Can Co.; *U.S. Public*, pg. 440
DIXIELAND FOOD STORES INC.; *U.S. Private*, pg. 337
DIXON INDUSTRIES, INC.—See Blount International, Inc.; *U.S. Public*, pg. 238
DIXON PAPER CO.—See International Paper Company; *U.S. Public*, pg. 902
T.H. DIXON & CO. LTD.—See Brunel Holdings Plc; *Int'l*, pg. 231
DIXON TICONDEROGA COMPANY; *U.S. Public*, pg. 515
DIXON TICONDEROGA COMPANY DE MEXICO, S.A. DE C.V.—See Dixon Ticonderoga Company; *U.S. Public*, pg. 515
DIXON TICONDEROGA INC.—See Dixon Ticonderoga Company; *U.S. Public*, pg. 515
DIXON WEAREVER INC.—See Dixon Ticonderoga Company; *U.S. Public*, pg. 515
DIXONS—See Vendex International N.V.; *Int'l*, pg. 1462
DIXONS FINANCE PLC—See Dixons Group plc; *Int'l*, pg. 414
DIXONS GROUP PLC; *Int'l*, pg. 413
DIXONS STORES GROUP (FAR EAST) LIMITED—See Dixons Group plc; *Int'l*, pg. 414
DIXONS STORES GROUP LTD.—See Dixons Group plc; *Int'l*, pg. 414
DIXONWEB PRINTING COMPANY—See Sleepeck Printing Company; *U.S. Private*, pg. 1005
D'JESCO, INC.—See AJC International, Inc.; *U.S. Private*, pg. 6
DO IT ALL—See The Boots Company PLC; *Int'l*, pg. 203
DOAK DERMATOLOGICS—See Bradley Pharmaceuticals; *U.S. Public*, pg. 250
DOALL COMPANY; *U.S. Private*, pg. 337
DOANE PRODUCTS CO.; *U.S. Private*, pg. 337
DOBBINS JEWLERS INC.—See Zale Corporation; *U.S. Public*, pg. 1789
DOBBS BROTHERS MANAGEMENT; *U.S. Private*, pg. 337
DOBBS INTERNATIONAL SERVICES, INC.—See Viad Corp.; *U.S. Public*, pg. 1718
DOBER CHEMICAL CORP.; *U.S. Private*, pg. 337
DOBSON & JOHNSON, INC.; *U.S. Private*, pg. 337
DOBSON PARK INDUSTRIES PLC—See Harnischfeger Industries, Inc.; *U.S. Public*, pg. 789
DOC FRANCOIS—See Auchan S.A.; *Int'l*, pg. 98
DOCAP (1985) CORPORATION—See The Ivaco Group; *Int'l*, pg. 695
DOCK FOUNDRY COMPANY; *U.S. Private*, pg. 337
KELLEY DOCK SYSTEMS—See Kelley Company, Inc.; *U.S. Private*, pg. 612
DOCKERS BRAND—See Levi Strauss & Co.; *U.S. Private*, pg. 663
DOCKERS FOOTWEAR—See Genesco Inc.; *U.S. Public*, pg. 728
DOCKS DE FRANCE S.A.—See Auchan S.A.; *Int'l*, pg. 98
DOCTOR DESIGN—See Integrated Systems, Inc.; *U.S. Public*, pg. 886
DR. MANN PHARMA—See Bausch & Lomb Incorporated; *U.S. Public*, pg. 196
DOCTORS HOSPITAL OF SHREVEPORT—See Universal Health Services, Inc.; *U.S. Public*, pg. 1697
DOCUCORP INTERNATIONAL—See Safeguard Scientifics, Inc.; *U.S. Public*, pg. 1425
DOCUMENTATION SERVICES-CIM LAB—See R.R. Donnelley & Sons Company; *U.S. Public*, pg. 518
DODGE CAR/TRUCK DIVISION—See Chrysler Corporation; *U.S. Public*, pg. 353
DODGE CITY DAILY GLOBE—See Shivers Trading & Operating Co.; *U.S. Private*, pg. 995
DODGE CITY SHOPPER'S WEEKLY—See Shivers Trading & Operating Co.; *U.S. Private*, pg. 995

DODGE DIVISION—See Rockwell International Corporation; *U.S. Public*, pg. 1398
F.W. DODGE GROUP—See The McGraw-Hill Companies; *U.S. Public*, pg. 1070
DODGE MECHANICAL GROUP—See Rockwell International Corporation; *U.S. Public*, pg. 1398
DODGE OF WINTER PARK; *U.S. Private*, pg. 337
DODGE REGUPOL; *U.S. Private*, pg. 337
DODI S.P.A.—See Bang & Olufsen A/S; *Int'l*, pg. 146
DODSON GROUP; *U.S. Private*, pg. 338
THE DOE RUN COMPANY—See Renco Group; *U.S. Private*, pg. 922
DOEHLER-JARVIS, INC.—See Harvard Industries, Inc.; *U.S. Public*, pg. 796
DOERNER PRODUCTS LTD—See Leggett & Platt, Incorporated; *U.S. Public*, pg. 986
DOFASCO, INC.; *Int'l*, pg. 414
DOFASCO USA, INC.—See DoFasco, Inc.; *Int'l*, pg. 414
DOG BREEDER'S INSURANCE COMPANY LTD.—See Assicurazioni Generali S.p.A.; *Int'l*, pg. 90
THE F. DOHMEN COMPANY; *U.S. Private*, pg. 338
F. DOHMEN COMPANY—See The F. Dohmen Company; *U.S. Private*, pg. 338
DOHMEN S.A.—See Fried. Krupp AG; *Int'l*, pg. 514
DOHNAN SHOKUHIN CO., LTD.—See Meiji Seika Kaisha, Ltd.; *Int'l*, pg. 855
DOLAN NORTHWEST LLC; *U.S. Private*, pg. 338
DOLD FOODS—See Hormel Foods Corp.; *U.S. Public*, pg. 844
DOLE ASIA—See Dole Food Company, Inc.; *U.S. Public*, pg. 515
DOLE CITRUS & DOLE DECIDUOUS—See Dole Food Company, Inc.; *U.S. Public*, pg. 515
DOLE EUROPE, S.A.—See Dole Food Company, Inc.; *U.S. Public*, pg. 515
DOLE FOOD COMPANY, INC.; *U.S. Public*, pg. 515
DOLE FRESH FRUIT COMPANY—See Dole Food Company, Inc.; *U.S. Public*, pg. 515
DOLE HAWAII—See Dole Food Company, Inc.; *U.S. Public*, pg. 515
DOLE LATIN AMERICA—See Dole Food Company, Inc.; *U.S. Public*, pg. 515
DOLE NORTHWEST—See Dole Food Company, Inc.; *U.S. Public*, pg. 515
DOLE PACKAGED FOOD COMPANY—See Dole Food Company, Inc.; *U.S. Public*, pg. 515
DOLET HILLS MINING VENTURE—See Costain Group PLC; *Int'l*, pg. 337
DOLGENCORP, INC.—See Dollar General Corporation; *U.S. Public*, pg. 515
DOLISOS—See Groupe Limagrain; *Int'l*, pg. 566
DOLLAND & AITCHISON LTD.; *Int'l*, pg. 414
DOLLAND & AITCHISON SERVICES LTD.—See Dolland & Aitchison Ltd.; *Int'l*, pg. 414
DOLLAND & AITCHISON - SOUTH EAST (LONDON) LTD.—See Dolland & Aitchison Ltd.; *Int'l*, pg. 414
DOLLANDS PHOTOGRAPHIC HOLDINGS LTD.—See Dolland & Aitchison Ltd.; *Int'l*, pg. 414
DOLLAR GENERAL CORP.; *U.S. Private*, pg. 338
DOLLAR GENERAL CORPORATION; *U.S. Public*, pg. 515
DOLLAR RENT A CAR—See Chrysler Corporation; *U.S. Public*, pg. 354
DOLLINGER/TECHNOLAB—See United Dominion Industries, Ltd.; *U.S. Public*, pg. 1676
DOLLY MADISON BAKERIES—See Interstate Bakeries Corporation; *U.S. Public*, pg. 909
DOLMAR GMBH—See Makita Corporation; *Int'l*, pg. 831
DOLOMITWERKE GMBH—See Thyssen AG; *Int'l*, pg. 1388
THE DOLPHIN—See Journal Register Company; *U.S. Public*, pg. 934
DOLPHIN & BRADBURY, INC.; *U.S. Private*, pg. 338
DOLPHIN CONSTRUCTION CO.—See Texas Industries, Inc.; *U.S. Public*, pg. 1585
DOLPHIN, INC.—See Karsten Manufacturing Corporation; *U.S. Private*, pg. 608
DOM SEMENTI S.R.L.—See Assicurazioni Generali S.p.A.; *Int'l*, pg. 90
DOMAIN ARGENTINA S.A.—See Domain Energy Corporation; *U.S. Public*, pg. 516
DOMAIN ENERGY CORPORATION; *U.S. Public*, pg. 515
DOMAIN ENERGY FINANCE CORPORATION—See Domain Energy Corporation; *U.S. Public*, pg. 516
DOMAIN ENERGY INTERNATIONAL CORPORATION—See Domain Energy Corporation; *U.S. Public*, pg. 516
DOMAIN ENERGY PRODUCTION CORPORATION—See Domain Energy Corporation; *U.S. Public*, pg. 516
DOMAIN ENERGY VENTURES CORPORATION—See Domain Energy Corporation; *U.S. Public*, pg. 516
DOMAINE CARNEROS—See Taittinger; *Int'l*, pg. 1348
DOMAINE CHANDON AUSTRALIA PTY LTD—See LVMH Moet Hennessy Louis Vuitton; *Int'l*, pg. 782
DOMAINE CHANDON, INC.—See LVMH Moet Hennessy Louis Vuitton; *Int'l*, pg. 781
DOMAINES CODEM S.A.—See Exor Group; *Int'l*, pg. 467
DOMAINES MICHEL BERNARD SA—See Koninklijke BolsWessanen nv; *Int'l*, pg. 752
DOMAN INDUSTRIES LIMITED; *Int'l*, pg. 414
DOMAR S.A.—See Electrolux, AB; *Int'l*, pg. 443
DOMBROWSKI & HOLMES, INC.; *U.S. Private*, pg. 338
DOMBURY INVESTMENTS LIMITED—See Manulife Financial (The Manufacturers Life Insurance Company); *Int'l*, pg. 840
DOMCO—See Domco Inc.; *Int'l*, pg. 415
DOMCO INC.; *Int'l*, pg. 415
DOMCO INC. FLOOR PRODUCTS (ALABAMA)—See Domco Inc.; *Int'l*, pg. 415
DOMCO INC. FLOOR PRODUCTS (TEXAS)—See Domco Inc.; *Int'l*, pg. 415
DOMCOR - ALBERTA—See Domco Inc.; *Int'l*, pg. 415
DOMCOR U.S.A.—See Domco Inc.; *Int'l*, pg. 415
DOMECQ IMPORTERS INC.—See Allied Domecq PLC; *Int'l*, pg. 63
DOMESTIC CIGARS—See MacAndrews & Forbes Holdings Inc.; *U.S. Private*, pg. 690

DOMESTIC LIABILITY UNDERWRITERS (PTY.) LTD.—See Assicurazioni Generali S.p.A.; *Int'l*, pg. 91
DOMESTIC LICENSING—See Wolverine World Wide, Inc.; *U.S. Public*, pg. 1775
DOMESTIC UNIFORM RENTAL—See Domestic Uniform Rental Co.; *U.S. Private*, pg. 338
DOMESTIC UNIFORM RENTAL CO.; *U.S. Private*, pg. 338
THE DOMETIC CORPORATION—See Electrolux, AB; *Int'l*, pg. 440
DOMGROUP LTD.—See Hollinger Inc.; *Int'l*, pg. 631
DOMIBAIL—See Credit Nationale; *Int'l*, pg. 344
DOMICILE MANAGEMENT SERVICES, INC.—See UAL Corporation; *U.S. Public*, pg. 1653
DOMICILIO CONOCIDO HERCULES—See Grupo Acerero del Norte S.A. de C.V. (GAN); *Int'l*, pg. 572
DOMIEQUIPEMENT—See Credit Nationale; *Int'l*, pg. 344
DOMILENS AB—See Chiron Corporation; *U.S. Public*, pg. 350
DOMILENZ—See Essilor International Compagnie Generale d'Optique; *Int'l*, pg. 462
DOMINGUEZ SERVICES CORPORATION; *U.S. Public*, pg. 516
DOMINGUEZ WATER COMPANY—See Dominguez Services Corporation; *U.S. Public*, pg. 516
THE DOMINIC GROUP LTD.—See Whitbread PLC; *Int'l*, pg. 1499
DOMINICK & DOMINICK FUTURES, INC.—See Dominick & Dominick, Incorporated; *U.S. Private*, pg. 339
DOMINICK & DOMINICK, INCORPORATED; *U.S. Private*, pg. 338
DOMINICK'S FINER FOODS—See The Yucaipa Companies; *U.S. Public*, pg. 1202
DOMINION BANKSHARE CORPORATION—See First Union Corporation; *U.S. Public*, pg. 640
DOMINION CAPITAL, INC.—See Dominion Resources, Inc.; *U.S. Public*, pg. 516
DOMINION CONTROLS COMPANY—See FKI Plc; *Int'l*, pg. 473
DOMINION ENERGY, INC.—See Dominion Resources, Inc.; *U.S. Public*, pg. 516
DOMINION ENERGY SERVICES COMPANY—See Dominion Resources, Inc.; *U.S. Public*, pg. 516
DOMINION ENTERTAINMENT, INC.—See K-Tel International, Inc.; *U.S. Public*, pg. 938
DOMINION FINANCING, INC.—See Dominion Resources, Inc.; *U.S. Public*, pg. 516
DOMINION HOMES; *U.S. Public*, pg. 516
DOMINION INDUSTRIAL FABRICS COMPANY—See Dominion Textile Inc.; *Int'l*, pg. 415
DOMINION INSURANCE LTD.—See La Fondiaria Assicurazioni S.p.A.; *Int'l*, pg. 784
DOMINION LANDS, INC.—See Dominion Resources, Inc.; *U.S. Public*, pg. 516
DOMINION MACHINERY CO. LTD.—See Brunel Holdings Plc; *Int'l*, pg. 231
DOMINION NONWOVENS SUDAMERICANA—See Dominion Textile Inc.; *Int'l*, pg. 415
DOMINION PAPER PRODUCTS—See International Paper Company; *U.S. Public*, pg. 905
THE DOMINION REALTY COMPANY LIMITED—See Canadian Imperial Bank of Commerce; *Int'l*, pg. 256
DOMINION RESOURCES, INC.; *U.S. Public*, pg. 516
DOMINION SEAL LTD.—See BTR plc; *Int'l*, pg. 129
DOMINION SEMICONDUCTOR, L.L.C.—See Toshiba Corporation; *Int'l*, pg. 1405
DOMINION STORES—See Tengelmann Warenhandelsgesellschaft; *Int'l*, pg. 1375
DOMINION STORES, INC.—See Tultex Corporation; *U.S. Public*, pg. 1644
DOMINION TELEVISION RENTALS LIMITED—See Thorn plc; *Int'l*, pg. 1386
DOMINION TEXTILE INC.; *Int'l*, pg. 415
DOMINION TEXTILE INTERNATIONAL B.V.—See Dominion Textile Inc.; *Int'l*, pg. 415
DOMINION TEXTILE MAURITIUS INC.—See Dominion Textile Inc.; *Int'l*, pg. 415
DOMINION TEXTILE (USA) INC.—See Dominion Textile Inc.; *Int'l*, pg. 415
DOMINION VERTRIEBS, G.M.B.H.—See K-Tel International, Inc.; *U.S. Public*, pg. 938
DOMINIQUE DUTSCHER, S.A.—See Corning Incorporated; *U.S. Public*, pg. 448
DOMINO; *Int'l*, pg. 415
DOMINO SUGAR CORPORATION—See Tate & Lyle PLC; *Int'l*, pg. 1356
DOMINO'S PIZZA DISTRIBUTION CORP.—See Domino's Pizza Inc.; *U.S. Private*, pg. 339
DOMINO'S PIZZA INC.; *U.S. Private*, pg. 339
DOMINO'S PIZZA INTERNATIONAL, INC.—See Domino's Pizza Inc.; *U.S. Private*, pg. 339
DOMORE CORPORATION; *U.S. Private*, pg. 339
DOMSJO MILLS—See Mo och Domsjo AB; *Int'l*, pg. 886
DOMSJO SAWMILL—See Mo och Domsjo AB; *Int'l*, pg. 886
DOMTAR FOREST PRODUCTS—See Domtar Inc.; *Int'l*, pg. 416
DOMTAR INC.; *Int'l*, pg. 416
DOMTAR PACKAGING DIVISION—See Domtar Inc.; *Int'l*, pg. 416
DOMTECH HOLDINGS, INC.—See Leucadia National Corporation; *U.S. Public*, pg. 990
DOMUS FORSIKRINGSAKTIESELSKABET A/S—See Allianz Aktiengesellschaft; *Int'l*, pg. 61
DON ALLESON, INC.; *U.S. Private*, pg. 339
DON AND CHARLIE'S—See Lettuce Entertain You Enterprises, Inc.; *U.S. Private*, pg. 661
DON CE SAR RESORT HOTEL LTD.—See Cigna Corp.; *U.S. Public*, pg. 361
EDWARD DON & COMPANY; *U.S. Private*, pg. 339
DON JUAN SPORTSWEAR, INC.—See Marubeni Corporation; *Int'l*, pg. 845
DON MIGUEL MEXICAN FOODS, INC.; *U.S. Private*, pg. 339

DONAHUE SCHRIBER—See Cambridge Shopping Centres Limited; *Int'l*, pg. 253
JON DONAIRE DESSERTS, INC.—See Suiza Foods Corporation; *U.S. Public*, pg. 1527
DONALDSON AUSTRALASIA (PTY.) LTD.—See Donaldson Company, Inc.; *U.S. Public*, pg. 517
DONALDSON COMPANY, INC.; *U.S. Public*, pg. 517
DONALDSON COORDINATION CENTER, N.V.—See Donaldson Company, Inc.; *U.S. Public*, pg. 517
DONALDSON DO BRASIL, LTDA.—See Donaldson Company, Inc.; *U.S. Public*, pg. 517
DONALDSON EUROPE N.V.—See Donaldson Company, Inc.; *U.S. Public*, pg. 517
DONALDSON FAR EAST LTD.—See Donaldson Company, Inc.; *U.S. Public*, pg. 517
DONALDSON FILTER COMPONENTS LTD.—See Donaldson Company, Inc.; *U.S. Public*, pg. 517
DONALDSON FILTER SYSTEMS PVT. LTD.—See Donaldson Company, Inc.; *U.S. Public*, pg. 517
DONALDSON FILTRATION SYSTEMS (PTY.) LTD.—See Donaldson Company, Inc.; *U.S. Public*, pg. 517
DONALDSON FRANCE, S.A.—See Donaldson Company, Inc.; *U.S. Public*, pg. 517
DONALDSON GESELLSCHAFT M.B.H.—See Donaldson Company, Inc.; *U.S. Public*, pg. 517
DONALDSON ITALIA S.R.L.—See Donaldson Company, Inc.; *U.S. Public*, pg. 517
DONALDSON, LUFKIN, & JENRETTE, INC.—See The Equitable Companies Incorporated; *U.S. Public*, pg. 589
DONALDSON, LUFKIN & JENRETTE SECURITIES CORP.—See The Equitable Companies Incorporated; *U.S. Public*, pg. 589
DONALDSON MICRO PORE S.A. DE C.V.—See Donaldson Company, Inc.; *U.S. Public*, pg. 517
DONALDSON TORIT.—See Donaldson Company, Inc.; *U.S. Public*, pg. 517
DONAU CHEMIE AG—See Rhone-Poulenc S.A.; *Int'l*, pg. 1112
DONAX J/V—See Axel Johnson AB; *Int'l*, pg. 710
DONCASTERS PLC; *Int'l*, pg. 416
DONG-A OTSUKA CO., LTD.—See Otsuka Pharmaceutical Co., Ltd.; *Int'l*, pg. 1014
DONG BANG COMMUNICATIONS—See BDDP Group; *Int'l*, pg. 117
DONG BU INSURANCE CO.; *Int'l*, pg. 416
DONG HOO TRADING CO. LTD.—See GESTRA GmbH; *Int'l*, pg. 550
DONG-MYUNG INDUSTRIAL CO., LTD.—See Meiji Seika Kaisha, Ltd.; *Int'l*, pg. 856
DONG-SUH FOODS CORPORATION; *Int'l*, pg. 416
DONG YANG ELANCO CO., LTD.—See Eli Lilly and Company; *U.S. Public*, pg. 993
DONGBANG HEALTHCARE PRODUCTS CO. LTD.—See Hewlett-Packard Company; *U.S. Public*, pg. 817
DONGBO EXPRESS CO. LTD.—See Danzas Holding Ltd.; *Int'l*, pg. 383
DONGBU AETNA LIFE INSURANCE CO., LTD.—See Aetna Inc.; *U.S. Public*, pg. 27
DONGGUAN CHAO BA BATTERIES CO.—See GP Batteries International Ltd.; *Int'l*, pg. 537
DONGGUAN PULSE ELECTRONICS CO. LTD.—See Technitrol, Inc.; *U.S. Public*, pg. 1564
DONGGUAN SANXING SOCKS CO., LTD.—See Gunze Sangyo, Inc.; *Int'l*, pg. 579
DONGGUAN YINFEA BATTERY PRODUCTS CO. LTD.—See GP Batteries International Ltd.; *Int'l*, pg. 537
DONGSEONG EXPRESS TOURISTS CO., LTD.—See Ssangyong Business Group; *Int'l*, pg. 1292
DONHAD ARMCO PTY. LTD.—See Delta plc; *Int'l*, pg. 391
DONIHE GRAPHICS—See Champion Industries; *U.S. Public*, pg. 333
DONKENNY APPAREL, INC.—See Donnkenny, Inc.; *U.S. Public*, pg. 520
DONLEE TECHNOLOGIES INC.; *U.S. Private*, pg. 339
DONLEN CORP.; *U.S. Private*, pg. 340
DONLEY'S, INC.; *U.S. Private*, pg. 340
DONNA KARAN; *U.S. Public*, pg. 517
DONNELLEY BUSINESS CENTERS—See R.R. Donnelley & Sons Company; *U.S. Public*, pg. 518
DONNELLEY INFORMATION PUBLISHING, INC.—See The Dun & Bradstreet Corporation; *U.S. Public*, pg. 535
DONNELLEY LOGISTIC SERVICES—See R.R. Donnelley & Sons Company; *U.S. Public*, pg. 518
R.R. DONNELLEY & SONS COMPANY; *U.S. Public*, pg. 517
R.R. DONNELLEY BARBADOS—See R.R. Donnelley & Sons Company; *U.S. Public*, pg. 519
R.R. DONNELLEY FAR EAST LIMITED—See R.R. Donnelley & Sons Company; *U.S. Public*, pg. 519
R.R. DONNELLEY, LIMITED-YORK—See R.R. Donnelley & Sons Company; *U.S. Public*, pg. 519
R.R. DONNELLEY NORWEST DIV.-GREELEY—See R.R. Donnelley & Sons Company; *U.S. Public*, pg. 518
R.R. DONNELLEY SEYMOUR INC.—See R.R. Donnelley & Sons Company; *U.S. Public*, pg. 518
THE REUBEN H. DONNELLEY CORPORATION—See The Dun & Bradstreet Corporation; *U.S. Public*, pg. 535
DONNELLY CORPORATION; *U.S. Public*, pg. 519
DONNELLY ELECTRONICS—See Donnelly Corporation; *U.S. Public*, pg. 519
DONNELLY EURO GLAS SYSTEMS—See Donnelly Corporation; *U.S. Public*, pg. 519
DONNELLY MIRRORS, LIMITED—See Donnelly Corporation; *U.S. Public*, pg. 519
DONNELLY OPTICS CORPORATION—See Donnelly Corporation; *U.S. Public*, pg. 519
DONNELLY VISION SYSTEMS EUROPE LTD.—See Donnelly Corporation; *U.S. Public*, pg. 519
DONNELLY YANTAI ELECTRONICS CORP. LTD.—See Donnelly Corporation; *U.S. Public*, pg. 519
DONNKENNY, INC.; *U.S. Public*, pg. 519
THE DONOHOE COMPANIES, INC.; *U.S. Private*, pg. 340
DONOHOE LIFT ENGINEERING SYSTEMS LTD.—See Schindler Holding AG; *Int'l*, pg. 1205

DONOHUE INC.—See Quebecor Inc.; *Int'l*, pg. 1075
DONOHUE MALBAIE, INC.—See The New York Times Company; *U.S. Public*, pg. 1174
DONOHUE MATANE, INC.—See Quebecor Inc.; *Int'l*, pg. 1075
DONOHUE NORMICK INC.—See Quebecor Inc.; *Int'l*, pg. 1075
DONOHUE PAPER SALES CORPORATION—See Quebecor Inc.; *Int'l*, pg. 1075
DONOHUE PULP & PAPER SALES CORP.—See Quebecor Inc.; *Int'l*, pg. 1075
DONOHUE RECYCLING INC.—See Quebecor Inc.; *Int'l*, pg. 1075
DONRUSS TRADING CARD CO.—See Pinnacle Brands, Inc.; *U.S. Private*, pg. 866
DONTECH—See Ameritech Corporation; *U.S. Public*, pg. 98
DONTECH—See The Dun & Bradstreet Corporation; *U.S. Public*, pg. 535
DONUTS COMERCIO DE PRODUTAS ALIMENTICIOS, LTDA.—See Allied Domecq PLC; *Int'l*, pg. 64
DONZI MARINE CORPORATION—See American Marine Holdings Inc.; *U.S. Private*, pg. 58
DOODLE ART DIV.—See The Seagram Company Ltd.; *Int'l*, pg. 1215
DOOLEY EQUIPMENT CORP.—See Browning-Ferris Industries, Inc.; *U.S. Public*, pg. 264
DOONAN & SONS, INC.; *U.S. Private*, pg. 340
DOOR STORE, INC.—See Furniture In Parts, Inc.; *U.S. Private*, pg. 432
DOORCRAFT & CHALLENGE—See Jeld-Wen, Inc.; *U.S. Private*, pg. 585
DOOSAN CROWN CAN MFG. CO. LTD.—See Crown Cork & Seal Company, Inc.; *U.S. Public*, pg. 465
DORAL HOTEL & RESORTS MANAGEMENT CO.; *U.S. Private*, pg. 340
ACE DORAN HAULING & RIGGING COMPANY; *U.S. Private*, pg. 340
DORBYL LIMITED; *Int'l*, pg. 416
DORCHESTER—See The Jaydor Corporation; *U.S. Private*, pg. 584
DORCHESTER TRANSPORT SERVICES (LEE LINE COMMERCIALS)—See Franz Haniel & Cie, GmbH; *Int'l*, pg. 591
DOREMUS & COMPANY—See Omnicom Group Inc.; *U.S. Public*, pg. 1223
DORET S.A.—See Avery Dennison Corporation; *U.S. Public*, pg. 154
DORFER DIALOGUE GMBH—See DMB&B Communications; *U.S. Private*, pg. 304
DORFILE COMPANY—See Newell Co.; *U.S. Public*, pg. 1177
DORINCO REINSURANCE CO.—See The Dow Chemical Company; *U.S. Public*, pg. 517
DORING INDUSTRIETECHNIK BMBH—See Freudenberg & Company; *Int'l*, pg. 506
DORION S.A. EMPREENDIMENTOS E PARTICIPACOES—See Bayer AG; *Int'l*, pg. 175
DORLING KINDERSLEY HOLDINGS PLC; *Int'l*, pg. 416
DORLING KINDERSLEY LTD.—See Dorling Kindersley Holdings plc; *Int'l*, pg. 417
DORMAN & WILSON, INC.—See Legg Mason, Inc.; *U.S. Public*, pg. 985
DORMER TOOLS AB—See Sandvik AB; *Int'l*, pg. 1185
DORMER TOOLS B.V.—See Sandvik AB; *Int'l*, pg. 1186
DORMER TOOLS GMBH—See Sandvik AB; *Int'l*, pg. 1186
DORMER TOOLS, INC.—See Sandvik AB; *Int'l*, pg. 1188
DORMER TOOLS LTD.—See Sandvik AB; *Int'l*, pg. 1186
DORMER TOOLS N.V./S.A.—See Sandvik AB; *Int'l*, pg. 1186
DORMER TOOLS S.A.S.—See Sandvik AB; *Int'l*, pg. 1186
DORMER TOOLS (SHEFFIELD) LTD.—See Sandvik AB; *Int'l*, pg. 1186
DORMER TOOLS S.P.A.—See Sandvik AB; *Int'l*, pg. 1186
DORMEYER INDUSTRIES; *U.S. Private*, pg. 340
ERNST W. DORN CO., INC.; *U.S. Private*, pg. 340
DORNBIRNER SPARKASSE; *Int'l*, pg. 417
DORNE & MARGOLIN, INC.—See United Capital Corp.; *U.S. Public*, pg. 1675
DORNER MANUFACTURING CORP.; *U.S. Private*, pg. 340
DORNEY PARK & WILDWATER KINGDOM—See Cedar Fair, L.P.; *U.S. Public*, pg. 319
DORNIER GMBH—See Daimler-Benz Aktiengesellschaft; *Int'l*, pg. 367
DORNIER GMBH INFORMATION & COMMUNICATION—See Daimler-Benz Aktiengesellschaft; *Int'l*, pg. 367
DORNIER MEDICAL SYSTEMS, INC.—See Daimler-Benz Aktiengesellschaft; *Int'l*, pg. 368
DORNIER MEDIZINTECHNIK GMBH—See Daimler-Benz Aktiengesellschaft; *Int'l*, pg. 368
DORON PRECISION SYSTEMS, INC.; *U.S. Private*, pg. 341
DORR-OLIVER INCORPORATED—See Mannesmann A.G.; *Int'l*, pg. 839
DORRIES GMBH—See J.M. Voith, GmbH; *Int'l*, pg. 1473
THE DORRIS LUMBER & MOULDING CO.; *U.S. Private*, pg. 341
DORSCH CONSULT GMBH—See Texas Utilities Company; *U.S. Public*, pg. 1587
DORSET CHILLED FOOD PRODUCTS LTD.—See Northern Foods plc; *Int'l*, pg. 968
DORSEY TRAILERS, INC.; *U.S. Public*, pg. 520
DORSEY TRAILERS, INC.—See Dorsey Trailers, Inc.; *U.S. Public*, pg. 520
DORTMUNDER EISENHANDEL CELLER GMBH—See Fried. Krupp AG; *Int'l*, pg. 513
DORTMUNDER SHREDDER GMBH—See Fried. Krupp AG; *Int'l*, pg. 513
DOS:PUNTOS—See DMB&B Communications; *U.S. Private*, pg. 304
DOSAPRO-MILTON ROY S.A.—See Sundstrand Corporation; *U.S. Public*, pg. 1534
THE DOO CORP.—See BTR plc; *Int'l*, pg. 124
DOSCO OVERSEAS ENGINEERING LIMITED—See Hawker Siddeley Canada Inc.; *Int'l*, pg. 604

DOSIMETER CORPORATION OF AMERICA—See Morgan Crucible Co. Plc; *Int'l*, pg. 892
DOT PRINTER, INC.; *U.S. Private*, pg. 341
DOTCO—See Cooper Industries, Inc.; *U.S. Public*, pg. 444
DOTCOM AB—See Celsius AB; *Int'l*, pg. 277
DOTHAN APPAREL, INC.—See Host Apparel, Inc.; *U.S. Private*, pg. 540
DOTHAN AUTO AUCTION—See Tyco International Ltd.; *U.S. Public*, pg. 1649
DOTHAN LEARNING CENTER—See Berkshire Hathaway Inc.; *U.S. Public*, pg. 218
DOTRONIX, INC.; *U.S. Public*, pg. 520
DOTTO MAG MEZOGAZDASAGI ES KERESKEDELMI KFT.—See Assicurazioni Generali S.p.A.; *Int'l*, pg. 91
DOTY LABORATORIES, INC.—See Inchcape PLC; *Int'l*, pg. 671
DOUBLE AA BUILDERS, LTD.; *U.S. Private*, pg. 341
DOUBLE-COLA CO.-USA; *U.S. Private*, pg. 341
DOUBLE H BOOT CO.—See Berkshire Hathaway Inc.; *U.S. Public*, pg. 217
DOUBLE H WEST SHOE WHOLESALE—See Berkshire Hathaway Inc.; *U.S. Public*, pg. 217
DOUBLECOAT, L.L.C.—See Consolidated Systems, Inc.; *U.S. Private*, pg. 266
DOUBLEDAY AUSTRALIA PTY. LTD.—See Bertelsmann AG; *Int'l*, pg. 192
DOUBLEDAY BOOK CLUB—See Bertelsmann AG; *Int'l*, pg. 191
DOUBLEDAY BOOK SHOPS, INC.—See Barnes & Noble Inc.; *U.S. Public*, pg. 189
DOUBLEDAY BROS. & CO.—See Standex International Corporation; *U.S. Public*, pg. 1506
DOUBLEDAY CANADA LTD.—See Bertelsmann AG; *Int'l*, pg. 192
DOUBLEDAY DIRECT—See Bertelsmann AG; *Int'l*, pg. 191
DOUBLEDAY NEW ZEALAND LTD.—See Bertelsmann AG; *Int'l*, pg. 192
DOUBLEDAY PUBLISHING COMPANY—See Bertelsmann AG; *Int'l*, pg. 191
DOUBLETREE CORPORATION—See Promus Hotel Corporation; *U.S. Public*, pg. 1335
DOUCET, INC.—See Henry Birks & Sons (1993) Inc.; *Int'l*, pg. 197
DOUGLAS & LOMASON COMPANY—See Magna International Inc.; *Int'l*, pg. 830
DOUGLAS DYNAMICS, INC.—See Armco Inc.; *U.S. Public*, pg. 131
DOUGLAS ELLIMAN; *U.S. Private*, pg. 341
DOUGLAS KANE HARDWARE—See McKechnie PLC; *Int'l*, pg. 851
DOUGLAS MANAGEMENT COMPANY—See Lynden Incorporated; *U.S. Private*, pg. 683
DOUGLAS PRODUCTS DIVISION—See Tecumseh Products Company; *U.S. Public*, pg. 1565
DOUGLAS/QUIKUT—See Berkshire Hathaway Inc.; *U.S. Public*, pg. 217
DOUGLAS-RANDALL, INC.—See Publicker Industries Inc.; *U.S. Public*, pg. 1341
THE DOUGLAS STEAM SAW MILL AND TIMBER COMPANY LIMITED—See RMC Group p.l.c.; *Int'l*, pg. 1079
DOUGLAS STEEL FABRICATING CORPORATION; *U.S. Private*, pg. 341
DOUGLAS STEPHEN PLASTICS, INC.; *U.S. Private*, pg. 341
DOUGLAS Y LOMASON DE COAHUILA S.A. DE C.V.—See Magna International Inc.; *Int'l*, pg. 830
DOUGLAS Y LOMASON DE MEXICO S.A. DE C.V.—See Magna International Inc.; *Int'l*, pg. 830
DOUGLASTON ELECTRIC—See Turtle & Hughes, Inc.; *U.S. Private*, pg. 1110
PT DOULTON MULTIFORTUNA—See Royal Doulton Plc.; *Int'l*, pg. 1135
DOUR—See GIB Group; *Int'l*, pg. 533
DOURTHE FRERES AG—See Koninklijke BolsWessanen nv; *Int'l*, pg. 752
DOUSSAN INC.—See Nippon Sanso Corporation; *Int'l*, pg. 938
DOUWE EGBERTS COFFEE SYSTEMS AMERICAS—See Sara Lee Corporation; *U.S. Public*, pg. 1433
DOVATECH, LTD.—See Dover Corporation; *U.S. Public*, pg. 520
DOVE EUROPE—See Mars, Incorporated; *U.S. Private*, pg. 707
DOVER CHEMICAL CORP.—See ICC Industries, Inc.; *U.S. Private*, pg. 553
DOVER CORPORATION; *U.S. Public*, pg. 520
DOVER CORP. (CANADA) LTD.—See Dover Corporation; *U.S. Public*, pg. 522
DOVER CORPORATION (CANADA) LTD.-INDUSTRIAL DIV.—See Dover Corporation; *U.S. Public*, pg. 522
DOVER CORPORATION (CANADA) LTD.-TURNBULL ELEVATOR DIV.—See Dover Corporation; *U.S. Public*, pg. 522
DOVER DIVERSIFIED—See Dover Corporation; *U.S. Public*, pg. 521
DOVER ELEVATOR INTERNATIONAL, INC.—See Dover Corporation; *U.S. Public*, pg. 521
DOVER ELEVATOR SYSTEMS, INC.—See Dover Corporation; *U.S. Public*, pg. 521
DOVER EXPLORATION COMPANY—See Chesapeake Utilities Corporation; *U.S. Public*, pg. 347
DOVER FLOUR MILLS—See Dover Industries Limited; *Int'l*, pg. 417
DOVER HANDBAG CO., INC.—See Michael Stevens Ltd.; *U.S. Private*, pg. 1042
DOVER HOUSE HEALTHCARE—See Vencor, Inc.; *U.S. Public*, pg. 1712
DOVER INDUSTRIES, INC.—See Dover Corporation; *U.S. Public*, pg. 520
DOVER INDUSTRIES LIMITED; *Int'l*, pg. 417
DOVER MILLS LIMITED—See Dover Industries Limited; *Int'l*, pg. 417

DOVER RESOURCES INC.—See Dover Corporation; *U.S. Public*, pg. 521
DOVER TECHNOLOGIES—See Dover Corporation; *U.S. Public*, pg. 521
THE DOVERCOURT MOTOR CO. LTD.—See Lonrho plc; *Int'l*, pg. 817
DOW BENELUX (NEDERLAND) B.V.—See The Dow Chemical Company; *U.S. Public*, pg. 523
DOW CHEM CO.- FRESNO PLANT—See The Dow Chemical Company; *U.S. Public*, pg. 523
DOW CHEMICAL (AUSTRALIA) LTD.—See The Dow Chemical Company; *U.S. Public*, pg. 523
DOW CHEMICAL AUSTRIA GESELLSCHAFT MBH—See The Dow Chemical Company; *U.S. Public*, pg. 523
DOW CHEMICAL BELGIUM NV/SA—See The Dow Chemical Company; *U.S. Public*, pg. 523
DOW CHEMICAL CANADA, INC.—See The Dow Chemical Company; *U.S. Public*, pg. 523
DOW CHEMICAL CO. LTD.—See The Dow Chemical Company; *U.S. Public*, pg. 523
THE DOW CHEMICAL COMPANY; *U.S. Public*, pg. 522
DOW CHEMICAL EXPORT S.A.—See The Dow Chemical Company; *U.S. Public*, pg. 523
DOW CHEMICAL IBERICA S.A.—See The Dow Chemical Company; *U.S. Public*, pg. 524
DOW CHEMICAL INTERNATIONAL LTD.—See The Dow Chemical Company; *U.S. Public*, pg. 523
DOW CHEMICAL JAPAN LTD.—See The Dow Chemical Company; *U.S. Public*, pg. 523
DOW CHEMICAL NORTH AMERICA—See The Dow Chemical Company; *U.S. Public*, pg. 522
DOW CHEMICAL (N.Z.) LIMITED—See The Dow Chemical Company; *U.S. Public*, pg. 523
DOW CHEMICAL PACIFIC LIMITED—See The Dow Chemical Company; *U.S. Public*, pg. 523
DOW CORNING CORPORATION—See The Dow Chemical Company; *U.S. Public*, pg. 523
DOW CORNING S.T.I.—See The Dow Chemical Company; *U.S. Public*, pg. 523
DOW CORNING TORAY SILICON CO., LTD.—See Toray Industries, Inc.; *Int'l*, pg. 1400
DOW CORNING WRIGHT—See The Dow Chemical Company; *U.S. Public*, pg. 523
DOW CREDIT CORPORATION—See The Dow Chemical Company; *U.S. Public*, pg. 522
DOW ELANCO—See The Dow Chemical Company; *U.S. Public*, pg. 522
DOW EUROPE SA—See The Dow Chemical Company; *U.S. Public*, pg. 523
DOW FRANCE S.A.—See The Dow Chemical Company; *U.S. Public*, pg. 524
DOW HELLAS—See The Dow Chemical Company; *U.S. Public*, pg. 524
DOW HICKAM PHARMACEUTICALS INC.—See Mylan Laboratories, Inc.; *U.S. Public*, pg. 1143
DOW ITALIA S.P.A.—See The Dow Chemical Company; *U.S. Public*, pg. 524
DOW JONES & COMPANY, INC.; *U.S. Public*, pg. 524
DOW JONES (BAHAMAS) LIMITED—See Dow Jones & Company, Inc.; *U.S. Public*, pg. 525
DOW JONES CANADA, INC.—See Dow Jones & Company, Inc.; *U.S. Public*, pg. 525
DOW JONES COURRIER, B.V.—See Dow Jones & Company, Inc.; *U.S. Public*, pg. 525
DOW JONES FINANCIAL NEWS SERVICES—See Dow Jones & Company, Inc.; *U.S. Public*, pg. 524
DOW JONES INTERACTIVE—See Dow Jones & Company, Inc.; *U.S. Public*, pg. 524
DOW JONES INTERACTIVE PUBLISHING—See Dow Jones & Company, Inc.; *U.S. Public*, pg. 524
DOW JONES INTERNATIONAL MARKETING SERVICES GMBH—See Dow Jones & Company, Inc.; *U.S. Public*, pg. 525
DOW JONES INTERNATIONAL MARKETING SERVICES (U.K.) LTD.—See Dow Jones & Company, Inc.; *U.S. Public*, pg. 525
DOW JONES MARKETS—See Dow Jones & Company, Inc.; *U.S. Public*, pg. 525
DOW JONES MARKETS (ASIA PACIFIC) LIMITED—See Dow Jones & Company, Inc.; *U.S. Public*, pg. 525
DOW JONES MARKETS (ASIA PACIFIC) SINGAPORE PTE LTD.—See Dow Jones & Company, Inc.; *U.S. Public*, pg. 525
DOW JONES MARKETS (AUSTRALIA) PTY LIMITED—See Dow Jones & Company, Inc.; *U.S. Public*, pg. 525
DOW JONES MARKETS BELGIUM SA—See Dow Jones & Company, Inc.; *U.S. Public*, pg. 525
DOW JONES MARKETS CANADA, INC.—See Dow Jones & Company, Inc.; *U.S. Public*, pg. 525
DOW JONES MARKETS CYPRUS LIMITED—See Dow Jones & Company, Inc.; *U.S. Public*, pg. 525
DOW JONES MARKETS DANMARK A/S—See Dow Jones & Company, Inc.; *U.S. Public*, pg. 525
DOW JONES MARKETS DE VENEZUELA, C.A.—See Dow Jones & Company, Inc.; *U.S. Public*, pg. 525
DOW JONES MARKETS ESPANA S.A.—See Dow Jones & Company, Inc.; *U.S. Public*, pg. 525
DOW JONES MARKETS FINANCIAL INFORMATION SERVICES, INC.—See Dow Jones & Company, Inc.; *U.S. Public*, pg. 525
DOW JONES MARKETS FINANSAL SISTEMLER A.S.—See Dow Jones & Company, Inc.; *U.S. Public*, pg. 525
DOW JONES MARKETS FINLAND OY—See Dow Jones & Company, Inc.; *U.S. Public*, pg. 525
DOW JONES MARKETS FRANCE SA—See Dow Jones & Company, Inc.; *U.S. Public*, pg. 525
DOW JONES MARKETS GES.M.B.H.—See Dow Jones & Company, Inc.; *U.S. Public*, pg. 525
DOW JONES MARKETS G.M.B.H.—See Dow Jones & Company, Inc.; *U.S. Public*, pg. 525
DOW JONES MARKETS (HONG KONG) LIMITED—See Dow Jones & Company, Inc.; *U.S. Public*, pg. 525

DOW JONES MARKETS INFORMACAO FINANCEIRA, LDA.—See Dow Jones & Company, Inc.; *U.S. Public*, pg. 525
DOW JONES MARKETS IRELAND LIMITED—See Dow Jones & Company, Inc.; *U.S. Public*, pg. 525
DOW JONES MARKETS LIMITED—See Dow Jones & Company, Inc.; *U.S. Public*, pg. 525
DOW JONES MARKETS LUXEMBOURG SARL—See Dow Jones & Company, Inc.; *U.S. Public*, pg. 525
DOW JONES MARKETS NETHERLANDS BV—See Dow Jones & Company, Inc.; *U.S. Public*, pg. 525
DOW JONES MARKETS (NEW ZEALAND) LTD.—See Dow Jones & Company, Inc.; *U.S. Public*, pg. 525
DOW JONES MARKETS NORWAY AS—See Dow Jones & Company, Inc.; *U.S. Public*, pg. 525
DOW JONES MARKETS (PANAMA) INC.—See Dow Jones & Company, Inc.; *U.S. Public*, pg. 525
DOW JONES MARKETS (SINGAPORE) PTE LTD.—See Dow Jones & Company, Inc.; *U.S. Public*, pg. 525
DOW JONES MARKETS (SOUTH AFRICA) (PTY) LIMITED—See Dow Jones & Company, Inc.; *U.S. Public*, pg. 525
DOW JONES MARKETS SWEDEN AB—See Dow Jones & Company, Inc.; *U.S. Public*, pg. 525
DOW JONES MARKETS (SWITZERLAND) AG—See Dow Jones & Company, Inc.; *U.S. Public*, pg. 525
DOW JONES MARKETS SYSTEMS, INC.—See Dow Jones & Company, Inc.; *U.S. Public*, pg. 525
DOW JONES MARKETS TECHNICAL SERVICES LIMITED—See Dow Jones & Company, Inc.; *U.S. Public*, pg. 525
DOW JONES MARKETS (THAILAND) LTD.—See Dow Jones & Company, Inc.; *U.S. Public*, pg. 525
DOW JONES PRINTING COMPANY (ASIA) INC.—See Dow Jones & Company, Inc.; *U.S. Public*, pg. 525
DOW JONES PUBLISHING CO. (ASIA), INC.—See Dow Jones & Company, Inc.; *U.S. Public*, pg. 525
DOW JONES PUBLISHING COMPANY (EUROPE) INC.—See Dow Jones & Company, Inc.; *U.S. Public*, pg. 525
DOW JONES TELERATE HOLDINGS, INC.—See Dow Jones & Company, Inc.; *U.S. Public*, pg. 525
DOW JONES TELERATE PUERTO RICO, INC.—See Dow Jones & Company, Inc.; *U.S. Public*, pg. 525
DOW KAKOH KABASHIKI KAISHA—See The Dow Chemical Company; *U.S. Public*, pg. 524
DOW PLASTICS DEVELOPMENT AG—See The Dow Chemical Company; *U.S. Public*, pg. 524
DOW QUIMICA CHILENA S.A.—See The Dow Chemical Company; *U.S. Public*, pg. 524
DOW SUOMI OY—See The Dow Chemical Company; *U.S. Public*, pg. 524
DOW SVERIGE AB—See The Dow Chemical Company; *U.S. Public*, pg. 524
DOW UNITED TECHNOLOGIES—See The Dow Chemical Company; *U.S. Public*, pg. 524
DOW VENEZUELA CA—See The Dow Chemical Company; *U.S. Public*, pg. 524
DOW VERTRIEBSGES.MBH—See The Dow Chemical Company; *U.S. Public*, pg. 524
DOWBRANDS, L.P.—See The Dow Chemical Company; *U.S. Public*, pg. 524
DOWDALL, O'MAHONEY & COMPANY LIMITED—See Philip Morris Companies Inc.; *U.S. Public*, pg. 1290
DOWELL SCHLUMBERGER CANADA INC.—See Schlumberger Limited; *U.S. Public*, pg. 1439
DOWELL SCHLUMBERGER CORPORATION—See Schlumberger Limited; *U.S. Public*, pg. 1439
DOWLING TEXTILE MANUFACTURING CO.; *U.S. Private*, pg. 341
DOWN RIVER FOREST PRODUCTS, INC.—See Greif Brothers Corporation; *U.S. Public*, pg. 763
DOWN RIVER INTERNATIONAL, INC.—See Greif Brothers Corporation; *U.S. Public*, pg. 763
DOWNEY DESIGNS INTERNATIONAL; *U.S. Private*, pg. 342
DOWNEY FINANCIAL CORP.; *U.S. Public*, pg. 525
DOWNEY, INC.—See K & G of Wisconsin; *U.S. Private*, pg. 602
DOWNEY PRINTING; *U.S. Private*, pg. 342
DOWNEY SAVINGS & LOAN ASSOCIATION, F.A.—See Downey Financial Corp.; *U.S. Public*, pg. 526
DOWNHOLE SEISMIC SERVICES—See Litton Industries, Inc.; *U.S. Public*, pg. 1003
TONY DOWNS FOODS COMPANY; *U.S. Private*, pg. 342
DOWNTOWN COGENERATION ASSOCIATES—See CTG Resources, Inc.; *U.S. Public*, pg. 285
DOWTY AEROSPACE—See TI Group plc; *Int'l*, pg. 1337
DOWTY AEROSPACE AVIATION SERVICES—See TI Group plc; *Int'l*, pg. 1337
DOWTY AEROSPACE AVIATION SERVICES PTE LTD—See TI Group plc; *Int'l*, pg. 1337
DOWTY AEROSPACE HYDRAULICS, CHELTENHAM—See TI Group plc; *Int'l*, pg. 1337
DOWTY AEROSPACE, ISLE OF MAN—See TI Group plc; *Int'l*, pg. 1337
DOWTY AEROSPACE, LOS ANGELES—See TI Group plc; *Int'l*, pg. 1337
DOWTY AEROSPACE MARKETING—See TI Group plc; *Int'l*, pg. 1337
DOWTY AEROSPACE NORTH AMERICA—See TI Group plc; *Int'l*, pg. 1337
DOWTY AEROSPACE PROPELLERS—See TI Group plc; *Int'l*, pg. 1337
DOWTY AEROSPACE TURBINE ENGINE COMPONENTS GROUP—See TI Group plc; *Int'l*, pg. 1337
DOWTY AEROSPACE, WOLVERHAMPTON—See TI Group plc; *Int'l*, pg. 1337
DOWTY AEROSPACE YAKIMA—See TI Group plc; *Int'l*, pg. 1337
DOWTY AUTOMOTIVE GASKETS—See TI Group plc; *Int'l*, pg. 1338
DOWTY BONDED SEALS—See TI Group plc; *Int'l*, pg. 1338
DOWTY GROUP—See TI Group plc; *Int'l*, pg. 1340

DOWTY O RINGS & ACTUATION POLYMERS—See TI Group plc; *Int'l*, pg. 1338
DOWTY O RINGS NORTH AMERICA—See TI Group plc; *Int'l*, pg. 1338
DOWTY O RINGS NORTH AMERICA - CHARLESTON—See TI Group plc; *Int'l*, pg. 1338
DOWTY PALMER-CHENARD—See TI Group plc; *Int'l*, pg. 1338
DOWTY POLYPAC SPA—See TI Group plc; *Int'l*, pg. 1338
DOWTY SAS—See TI Group plc; *Int'l*, pg. 1338
DOWTY SILCOFAB—See TI Group plc; *Int'l*, pg. 1338
DOWTY TECMOLD—See TI Group plc; *Int'l*, pg. 1338
DOWTY WOODVILLE POLYMER—See TI Group plc; *Int'l*, pg. 1338
DOYON MINE—See Barrick Gold Corporation; *Int'l*, pg. 169
DR. BECK & CO. (INDIA) LTD.—See BASF AG; *Int'l*, pg. 108
DR. D.A. DELIS AG—See BASF AG; *Int'l*, pg. 108
DR. GENTHE GMBH & CO. KG—See Carl-Zeiss-Stiftung; *Int'l*, pg. 1523
DR. MULLER FEINDRAHT AG—See Kulicke & Soffa Industries, Inc.; *U.S. Public*, pg. 969
DR. PEPPER CO.—See Cadbury Schweppes p.l.c.; *Int'l*, pg. 248
DR PEPPER/SEVEN UP NO. AMERICA—See Cadbury Schweppes p.l.c.; *Int'l*, pg. 248
DR. PEPPER/SEVEN-UP FOUNTAIN FOODSERVICE—See Cadbury Schweppes p.l.c.; *Int'l*, pg. 248
DR. RITTER GMBH & CO.—See Nestle S.A.; *Int'l*, pg. 920
DR. SCHOLL'S SPA—See Scholl Plc; *Int'l*, pg. 1209
DR. TIGGES GESCHAFTSREISEN GMBH—See Fried. Krupp AG; *Int'l*, pg. 515
DR. TIGGES INCENTIVES—See Fried. Krupp AG; *Int'l*, pg. 515
DR. WOLMANN GMBH—See BASF AG; *Int'l*, pg. 104
DRAAD NIJMEGEN B.V.—See Royal Begemann Group; *Int'l*, pg. 1133
DRACO LAKEMEDEL AB/TIKA LAKEMEDEL AB—See Astra AB; *Int'l*, pg. 93
DRAGON INTERNATIONAL—See Bugle Boy Industries, Inc.; *U.S. Private*, pg. 179
DRAKA KABEL B.V.; *Int'l*, pg. 417
DRAKA POLVA B.V.—See Solvay S.A.; *Int'l*, pg. 1278
DRAKA U.S.A.—See Draka Kabel B.V.; *Int'l*, pg. 417
DRAKE & SCULL ENGINEERING LTD.—See EMCOR Group, Inc.; *U.S. Public*, pg. 572
DRAKE BAKERIES, INC.—See Culinar Inc.; *Int'l*, pg. 349
DRAKE BEAM MORIN, INC.—See Harcourt General, Inc.; *U.S. Public*, pg. 783
DRAKE CONSTRUCTION COMPANY—See Dunn Industries Inc.; *U.S. Private*, pg. 347
DRAKE PETROLEUM COMPANY, INC.—See Warren Equities Inc.; *U.S. Private*, pg. 1151
DRALORIC ELECTRONIC GMBH—See Vishay Intertechnology, Inc.; *U.S. Public*, pg. 1722
DRANETZ-BMI—See WPT, Inc.; *U.S. Private*, pg. 1144
DRANKENHANDEL DE GRAAFSCHAP B.V.—See Grolsch N.V.; *Int'l*, pg. 559
DRAPER TEXMACO, INC.; *U.S. Private*, pg. 342
G. DRAUZ GMBH & CO.—See Fried. Krupp AG; *Int'l*, pg. 507
DRAUZ INGENIEURBETRIEB GMBH—See Fried. Krupp AG; *Int'l*, pg. 508
DRAVO CORPORATION; *U.S. Public*, pg. 527
DRAVO LEASING CO.—See Dravo Corporation; *U.S. Public*, pg. 527
DRAVO LIME COMPANY—See Dravo Corporation; *U.S. Public*, pg. 527
DRAW-TITE, INC.—See Masco Corporation; *U.S. Public*, pg. 1054
DRAYCOTT PARTNERS, LTD.—See Metropolitan Life Insurance Co.; *U.S. Private*, pg. 738
DRAYTON CONTROL (ENGINEERING) LIMITED—See Siebe plc; *Int'l*, pg. 1241
DREAM MAKERS, INC.—See Leggett & Platt, Incorporated; *U.S. Public*, pg. 986
DREAMLAND APPLIANCES LIMITED—See Newmond PLC; *Int'l*, pg. 925
DREAMPORT, INC.—See GTECH Corporation; *U.S. Public*, pg. 767
DREAMWORKS INTERACTIVE—See DreamWorks SKG; *U.S. Private*, pg. 342
DREAMWORKS SKG; *U.S. Private*, pg. 342
DREIS & KRUMP MANUFACTURING COMPANY; *U.S. Private*, pg. 342
DREISON INTERNATIONAL, INC.; *U.S. Private*, pg. 342
DREMEL—See Emerson Electric Co.; *U.S. Public*, pg. 574
DRESDNER-ABD SECURITIES LTD.—See Dresdner Bank AG; *Int'l*, pg. 419
DRESDNER ASSET MANAGEMENT IRELAND LTD.—See Dresdner Bank AG; *Int'l*, pg. 419
DRESDNER ASSET MANAGEMENT (SCHWEIZ) AG—See Dresdner Bank AG; *Int'l*, pg. 419
DRESDNER BANK AG; *Int'l*, pg. 417
DRESDNER BANK CANADA—See Dresdner Bank AG; *Int'l*, pg. 419
DRESDNER BANK (IRELAND) PLC—See Dresdner Bank AG; *Int'l*, pg. 419
DRESDNER BANK KREDITBANK AG—See Dresdner Bank AG; *Int'l*, pg. 418
DRESDNER BANK LATEINAMERICA—See Dresdner Bank AG; *Int'l*, pg. 418
DRESDNER BANK LUXEMBOURG S.A.—See Dresdner Bank AG; *Int'l*, pg. 419
DRESDNER BANK MEXICO S.A.—See Dresdner Bank AG; *Int'l*, pg. 419
DRESDNER BANK (SWITZERLAND) LTD.—See Dresdner Bank AG; *Int'l*, pg. 419
DRESDNER BAUSPAR AG—See Dresdner Bank AG; *Int'l*, pg. 418
DRESDNER FORFAITIERUNGS AKTIENGESELLSCHAFT—See Dresdner Bank AG; *Int'l*, pg. 419

DRESDNER INTERNATIONAL FINANCE PLC—See Dresdner Bank AG; *Int'l*, pg. 419
DRESDNER INTERNATIONAL FINANCIAL MARKETS (AUSTRALIA) LTD.—See Dresdner Bank AG; *Int'l*, pg. 419
DRESDNER-NY INC.—See Dresdner Bank AG; *Int'l*, pg. 418
DRESDNER (S.E. ASIA) LTD.—See Dresdner Bank AG; *Int'l*, pg. 420
DRESDNER SECURITIES (ASIA) LTD.—See Dresdner Bank AG; *Int'l*, pg. 420
DRESDNER SECURITIES (USA) INC.—See Dresdner Bank AG; *Int'l*, pg. 418
DRESDNER VERMOGENSBERATUNGS-GESELLSCHAFT MBH—See Dresdner Bank AG; *Int'l*, pg. 418
DRESDNERBANK ASSET MANAGEMENT S.A.—See Dresdner Bank AG; *Int'l*, pg. 420
DRESDNERBANK INVESTMENT MANAGEMENT KAPITALANLAGEGESELLSCHAFT MBH—See Dresdner Bank AG; *Int'l*, pg. 418
DRESHER, INC.—See Leggett & Platt, Incorporated; *U.S. Public*, pg. 986
THE DRESS BARN, INC.; *U.S. Public*, pg. 528
DRESSER CANADA, INC.—See Dresser Industries, Inc.; *U.S. Public*, pg. 529
DRESSER DRILLING & PRODUCTION SERVICES—See Dresser Industries, Inc.; *U.S. Public*, pg. 529
DRESSER INDUSTRIES, INC.; *U.S. Public*, pg. 528
DRESSER INDUSTRIES WAYNE DIVISION—See Dresser Industries, Inc.; *U.S. Public*, pg. 528
DRESSER OIL TOOLS—See Dresser Industries, Inc.; *U.S. Public*, pg. 528
DRESSER-RAND CO.—See Dresser Industries, Inc.; *U.S. Public*, pg. 529
DRESSER-RAND CO.—See Ingersoll-Rand Company; *U.S. Public*, pg. 877
DRESSER-RAND CO. (OLEAN)—See Dresser Industries, Inc.; *U.S. Public*, pg. 529
DRESSER-RAND CO. (PAINTED POST)—See Dresser Industries, Inc.; *U.S. Public*, pg. 529
DRESSER-RAND CO. (WELLSVILLE)—See Dresser Industries, Inc.; *U.S. Public*, pg. 529
DRESSER-RAND GMBH—See Ingersoll-Rand Company; *U.S. Public*, pg. 877
DRESSER-RAND SALES—See Dresser Industries, Inc.; *U.S. Public*, pg. 529
DRESSER VALVE & CONTROLS DIV.—See Dresser Industries, Inc.; *U.S. Public*, pg. 528
DRESSER WHEATLEY DIVISION—See Dresser Industries, Inc.; *U.S. Public*, pg. 529
DRESSIN KOSMETIK-U. PHARMA GMBH—See The Procter & Gamble Company; *U.S. Public*, pg. 1333
ALEXANDER DREW & SONS LTD.—See Lamont Holdings Plc; *Int'l*, pg. 798
DREW INDUSTRIAL—See Ashland, Inc.; *U.S. Public*, pg. 139
DREW INDUSTRIES INCORPORATED; *U.S. Public*, pg. 529
JAMES H. DREW CORP.—See Medusa Corporation; *U.S. Public*, pg. 1084
DREW PRIMARY CARE CLINIC, INC.—See Integrated Health Services, Inc.; *U.S. Public*, pg. 884
DREXEL HERITAGE FURNISHINGS INC.—See Furnishings International, Inc.; *U.S. Private*, pg. 432
DREYER'S GRAND ICE CREAM, INC.; *U.S. Public*, pg. 529
DREYER'S GRAND ICE CREAM, INC.—See Dreyer's Grand Ice Cream, Inc.; *U.S. Public*, pg. 529
DREYER'S NEW ENGLAND DIVISION—See Dreyer's Grand Ice Cream, Inc.; *U.S. Public*, pg. 529
DREYER'S NORTHERN CALIFORNIA REGION—See Dreyer's Grand Ice Cream, Inc.; *U.S. Public*, pg. 529
DREYER'S NORTHWEST DIVISION—See Dreyer's Grand Ice Cream, Inc.; *U.S. Public*, pg. 529
DREYER'S ROCKY MOUNTAIN REGION—See Dreyer's Grand Ice Cream, Inc.; *U.S. Public*, pg. 529
DREYER'S SOUTHERN CALIFORNIA REGION—See Dreyer's Grand Ice Cream, Inc.; *U.S. Public*, pg. 529
DREYER'S SOUTHWEST DIVISION—See Dreyer's Grand Ice Cream, Inc.; *U.S. Public*, pg. 529
THE DREYFUS CORPORATION—See Mellon Bank Corporation; *U.S. Public*, pg. 1085
DREYFUS INVESTMENT SERVICES CORP.—See Mellon Bank Corporation; *U.S. Public*, pg. 1085
L.A. DREYFUS CO.—See Wm. Wrigley Jr. Company; *U.S. Public*, pg. 1781
LOUIS DREYFUS CORPORATION; *U.S. Private*, pg. 342
DREYFUS RETIREMENT SERVICES—See Mellon Bank Corporation; *U.S. Public*, pg. 1085
DREYFUS SERVICE CORP.—See Mellon Bank Corporation; *U.S. Public*, pg. 1085
DRI MARK PRODUCTS, INC.; *U.S. Private*, pg. 342
DRI-PRINT FOILS INC.; *U.S. Private*, pg. 343
DRIBECK IMPORTERS, INC.; *U.S. Private*, pg. 343
DRIEHOEK—See Sara Lee Corporation; *U.S. Public*, pg. 1435
DRILL AND BLAST (AUSTRALIA) PTY LIMITED—See Imperial Chemical Industries PLC; *Int'l*, pg. 664
DRILLERS INC.—See Grey Wolf, Inc.; *U.S. Public*, pg. 765
DRILLERS INC., DI DE VENEZUELA—See Grey Wolf, Inc.; *U.S. Public*, pg. 765
DRILLERS INTERNATIONAL S.A.—See Grey Wolf, Inc.; *U.S. Public*, pg. 765
DRILTECH INC.—See Tamrock Corp.; *Int'l*, pg. 1352
L.F. DRISCOLL CO.; *U.S. Private*, pg. 343
DRIV-LOK, INC.; *U.S. Private*, pg. 343
DRIVE MEDIUM R & D COMPANY N.V.—See Royal Begemann Group; *Int'l*, pg. 1134
DRIVE TRAIN INDUSTRIES; *U.S. Private*, pg. 343
DRIVER-HARRIS ALLOYS, INC.—See Driver-Harris Company; *U.S. Public*, pg. 530
DRIVER-HARRIS AUSTRALIA—See Kanthal AB; *Int'l*, pg. 723
DRIVER-HARRIS COMPANY; *U.S. Public*, pg. 530

DRIVER-HARRIS ITALIANA, S.P.A.—See Kanthal AB; *Int'l*, pg. 723
DRIVER-HARRIS, S.A.—See Kanthal AB; *Int'l*, pg. 723
ROBERT F. DRIVER CO., INC.; *U.S. Private*, pg. 343
DRIVES & METALS SYSTEMS DIVISION—See ABB Asea Brown Boveri (Holding) Ltd.; *Int'l*, pg. 4
DRIVETRAIN SERVICE DIV.—See Dana Corporation; *U.S. Public*, pg. 479
DROEMERSCHE VERLAGSANSTALT TH. KNAUR NACHF. GMBH & CO.—See Georg von Holtzbrinck GmbH; *Int'l*, pg. 1478
A/S DROMMEKJOKKENET—See Electrolux, AB; *Int'l*, pg. 443
DROSTE B.V.—See CSM N.V.; *Int'l*, pg. 243
DROTT AB—See Skanska AB; *Int'l*, pg. 1260
DROYHURST LIMITED—See James Crean PLC; *Int'l*, pg. 341
DRS TECHNICAL SERVICES—See DRS Technologies, Inc.; *U.S. Public*, pg. 474
DRU INDUSTRIAL PRODUCTS & SERVICES BV—See Schuttersveld Holding N.V.; *Int'l*, pg. 1210
DRU STAINLESS STEEL PRODUCTS B.V.—See Schuttersveld Holding N.V.; *Int'l*, pg. 1210
DRU VERWARMING B.V.—See Schuttersveld Holding N.V.; *Int'l*, pg. 1210
DRUG EMPORIUM, INC.; *U.S. Public*, pg. 530
DRUG EMPORIUM OF ARIZONA; *U.S. Private*, pg. 343
DRUG GUILD DIV.—See Neuman Distributors, Inc.; *U.S. Public*, pg. 1169
DRUG HOUSES OF AUSTRALIA (ASIA) PTE. LTD.—See Haw Par Brothers International Limited; *Int'l*, pg. 603
DRUGASAR LTD.—See Schuttersveld Holding N.V.; *Int'l*, pg. 1210
DRUKKERIJ JACOB VAN CAMPEN—See De Bussy Harms N.V.; *Int'l*, pg. 386
DRUKKERIJEN DE BUSSY ELLERMAN HARMS—See De Bussy Harms N.V.; *Int'l*, pg. 386
DRUKKERJ VAN ROESSEL—See De Bussy Harms N.V.; *Int'l*, pg. 386
DRUMHELLER BAG & SUPPLY—See Norfoods, Inc.; *U.S. Private*, pg. 802
DRUMM & ASSOCIATES, INC.; *U.S. Private*, pg. 343
DRUMMOND COMPANY, INC.; *U.S. Private*, pg. 343
DRUMMOND MCCALL INC.—See Russel Metals Inc.; *Int'l*, pg. 1150
DRUMS LTD.—See Royal Packaging Industries Van Leer B.V.; *Int'l*, pg. 1146
DRY HOLE OIL & GAS CORPORATION—See Torchmark Corporation; *U.S. Public*, pg. 1623
DRYDEN & PALMER COMPANY—See Gravymaster Inc.; *U.S. Private*, pg. 471
DRYDEN OIL COMPANY, INC.—See Burmah Castrol plc; *Int'l*, pg. 235
DRYDEN OIL OF NEW ENGLAND—See Burmah Castrol plc; *Int'l*, pg. 235
THE DRYDEN PRESS, A DIVISION OF HOLT, RINEHART AND WINSTON COLLEGE DIVISION—See Harcourt General, Inc.; *U.S. Public*, pg. 783
DRYPER'S CORP.; *U.S. Private*, pg. 344
DRYVIT SYSTEMS, INC.—See RPM, Inc.; *U.S. Public*, pg. 1357
DU MOULIN S.C.I.—See Etablissements Delhaize Freres Et Cie "Le Lion" S.A.; *Int'l*, pg. 463
DU PONT AGRICULTURAL PRODUCTS—See Du Pont (E.I. Du Pont De Nemours & Co.); *U.S. Public*, pg. 531
DU PONT ASIA PACIFIC LTD.—See Du Pont (E.I. Du Pont De Nemours & Co.); *U.S. Public*, pg. 532
DU PONT (AUSTRALIA) LTD.—See Du Pont (E.I. Du Pont De Nemours & Co.); *U.S. Public*, pg. 532
DU PONT AUTOMOTIVE PRODUCTS—See Du Pont (E.I. Du Pont De Nemours & Co.); *U.S. Public*, pg. 531
DU PONT BELLE PLANT—See Du Pont (E.I. Du Pont De Nemours & Co.); *U.S. Public*, pg. 531
DU PONT CANADA-AJAX—See Du Pont (E.I. Du Pont De Nemours & Co.); *U.S. Public*, pg. 532
DU PONT CANADA-BURNABY—See Du Pont (E.I. Du Pont De Nemours & Co.); *U.S. Public*, pg. 532
DU PONT CANADA-CALGARY—See Du Pont (E.I. Du Pont De Nemours & Co.); *U.S. Public*, pg. 532
DU PONT CANADA-CALGARY DISTRIBUTION—See Du Pont (E.I. Du Pont De Nemours & Co.); *U.S. Public*, pg. 532
DU PONT CANADA-GIBBONS—See Du Pont (E.I. Du Pont De Nemours & Co.); *U.S. Public*, pg. 532
DU PONT CANADA INC.—See Du Pont (E.I. Du Pont De Nemours & Co.); *U.S. Public*, pg. 532
DU PONT CANADA-KINGSTON RESEARCH—See Du Pont (E.I. Du Pont De Nemours & Co.); *U.S. Public*, pg. 532
DU PONT CANADA-KINGSTON WORKS—See Du Pont (E.I. Du Pont De Nemours & Co.); *U.S. Public*, pg. 532
DU PONT CANADA-MAITLAND—See Du Pont (E.I. Du Pont De Nemours & Co.); *U.S. Public*, pg. 532
DU PONT CANADA-MONTREAL—See Du Pont (E.I. Du Pont De Nemours & Co.); *U.S. Public*, pg. 532
DU PONT CANADA-POINTE CLAIRE—See Du Pont (E.I. Du Pont De Nemours & Co.); *U.S. Public*, pg. 532
DU PONT CANADA-ST. CLAIR RIVER—See Du Pont (E.I. Du Pont De Nemours & Co.); *U.S. Public*, pg. 532
DU PONT CANADA-SCARBOROUGH—See Du Pont (E.I. Du Pont De Nemours & Co.); *U.S. Public*, pg. 532
DU PONT CANADA-WHITBY—See Du Pont (E.I. Du Pont De Nemours & Co.); *U.S. Public*, pg. 532
DU PONT CHAMBERS WORKS—See Du Pont (E.I. Du Pont De Nemours & Co.); *U.S. Public*, pg. 531
DU PONT DE COLOMBIA S.A.—See Du Pont (E.I. Du Pont De Nemours & Co.); *U.S. Public*, pg. 532
DU PONT DE NEMOURS (BELGIUM) S.A.—See Du Pont (E.I. Du Pont De Nemours & Co.); *U.S. Public*, pg. 532
DU PONT DE NEMOURS (DEUTSCHLAND) GMBH—See Du Pont (E.I. Du Pont De Nemours & Co.); *U.S. Public*, pg. 532
DU PONT DE NEMOURS (DEUTSCHLAND) GMBH, PLANT UENTROP—See Du Pont (E.I. Du Pont De Nemours & Co.); *U.S. Public*, pg. 532

DU PONT DE NEMOURS (DEUTSCHLAND) GMBH, PLANT NEU-ISENBURG—See Du Pont (E.I. Du Pont De Nemours & Co.); *U.S. Public*, pg. 532
DU PONT DE NEMOURS (FRANCE) S.A.—See Du Pont (E.I. Du Pont De Nemours & Co.); *U.S. Public*, pg. 532
DU PONT DE NEMOURS INTERNATIONAL S.A.—See Du Pont (E.I. Du Pont De Nemours & Co.); *U.S. Public*, pg. 532
DU PONT DE NEMOURS ITALIANA SP.A.—See Du Pont (E.I. Du Pont De Nemours & Co.); *U.S. Public*, pg. 532
DU PONT DE NEMOURS (LUXEMBOURG) S.A.—See Du Pont (E.I. Du Pont De Nemours & Co.); *U.S. Public*, pg. 532
DU PONT DE NEMOURS (NEDERLAND) B.V.—See Du Pont (E.I. Du Pont De Nemours & Co.); *U.S. Public*, pg. 532
DU PONT DE VENEZUELA C.A.—See Du Pont (E.I. Du Pont De Nemours & Co.); *U.S. Public*, pg. 532
DU PONT DO BRASIL S.A.—See Du Pont (E.I. Du Pont De Nemours & Co.); *U.S. Public*, pg. 532
DU PONT (E.I. DU PONT DE NEMOURS & CO.); *U.S. Public*, pg. 530
DU PONT ELECTRONICS INFORMATION STORAGE DIVISION—See Du Pont (E.I. Du Pont De Nemours & Co.); *U.S. Public*, pg. 531
DU PONT FAR EAST INC.—See Du Pont (E.I. Du Pont De Nemours & Co.); *U.S. Public*, pg. 532
DU PONT IBERICA S.A.—See Du Pont (E.I. Du Pont De Nemours & Co.); *U.S. Public*, pg. 532
DU PONT INTERNATIONAL—See Du Pont (E.I. Du Pont De Nemours & Co.); *U.S. Public*, pg. 531
DU PONT INTERNATIONAL SALES CORP.—See Du Pont (E.I. Du Pont De Nemours & Co.); *U.S. Public*, pg. 531
DU PONT JAPAN LTD.—See Du Pont (E.I. Du Pont De Nemours & Co.); *U.S. Public*, pg. 531
DU PONT MATERIALS & LOGISTICS DIVISION—See Du Pont (E.I. Du Pont De Nemours & Co.); *U.S. Public*, pg. 531
THE DU PONT MERCK PHARMACEUTICAL COMPANY—See Du Pont (E.I. Du Pont De Nemours & Co.); *U.S. Public*, pg. 531
THE DU PONT MERCK PHARMACEUTICAL COMPANY—See Merck & Co., Inc.; *U.S. Public*, pg. 1091
DU PONT MITSUI FLUOROCHEMICALS CO., LTD.—See Du Pont (E.I. Du Pont De Nemours & Co.); *U.S. Public*, pg. 533
DU PONT MITSUI POLYCHEMICALS CO., LTD.—See Du Pont (E.I. Du Pont De Nemours & Co.); *U.S. Public*, pg. 533
DU PONT NDT SYSTEMS—See Du Pont (E.I. Du Pont De Nemours & Co.); *U.S. Public*, pg. 531
DU PONT NDT SYSTEMS INC.—See Du Pont (E.I. Du Pont De Nemours & Co.); *U.S. Public*, pg. 531
DU PONT (NEW ZEALAND) LTD.—See Du Pont (E.I. Du Pont De Nemours & Co.); *U.S. Public*, pg. 533
DU PONT PHARMACEUTICALS—See Du Pont (E.I. Du Pont De Nemours & Co.); *U.S. Public*, pg. 531
DU PONT PHOTOLUX S.A.—See Du Pont (E.I. Du Pont De Nemours & Co.); *U.S. Public*, pg. 533
DU PONT PHOTOMASKS—See Du Pont (E.I. Du Pont De Nemours & Co.); *U.S. Public*, pg. 531
DU PONT PRINTING & PUBLISHING—See Du Pont (E.I. Du Pont De Nemours & Co.); *U.S. Public*, pg. 531
DU PONT PROTEIN TECHNOLOGIES INTERNATIONAL—See Du Pont (E.I. Du Pont De Nemours & Co.); *U.S. Public*, pg. 531
DU PONT, S.A. DE C.V.—See Du Pont (E.I. Du Pont De Nemours & Co.); *U.S. Public*, pg. 531
DU PONT, S.A. DE C.V. DIV. PIGMENTOS Y PRODUCTOS QUIMICOS—See Du Pont (E.I. Du Pont De Nemours & Co.); *U.S. Public*, pg. 531
DU PONT SCANDINAVIA AB—See Du Pont (E.I. Du Pont De Nemours & Co.); *U.S. Public*, pg. 533
DU PONT/SHELL—See Du Pont (E.I. Du Pont De Nemours & Co.); *U.S. Public*, pg. 531
DU PONT-SHOWA DENKO CO., LTD.—See Du Pont (E.I. Du Pont De Nemours & Co.); *U.S. Public*, pg. 533
DU PONT (SINGAPORE) ELECTRONICS PVT. LTD.—See Du Pont (E.I. Du Pont De Nemours & Co.); *U.S. Public*, pg. 531
DU PONT SRP—See Du Pont (E.I. Du Pont De Nemours & Co.); *U.S. Public*, pg. 531
DU PONT TAIWAN LIMITED—See Du Pont (E.I. Du Pont De Nemours & Co.); *U.S. Public*, pg. 533
DU PONT TAIWAN LIMITED-HSIEN PLANT—See Du Pont (E.I. Du Pont De Nemours & Co.); *U.S. Public*, pg. 533
DU PONT-TORAY COMPANY, LTD.—See Du Pont (E.I. Du Pont De Nemours & Co.); *U.S. Public*, pg. 533
DU PONT (U.K.) LTD.—See Du Pont (E.I. Du Pont De Nemours & Co.); *U.S. Public*, pg. 533
DU PONT-KANSAI AUTOMOTIVE COATINGS, INC.—See Kansai Paint Co., Ltd.; *Int'l*, pg. 723
S.A. DU TRAIN UNIVERSEL DE LONGWY—See Arbed S.A.; *Int'l*, pg. 79
DUAL-LITE—See General Signal Corporation; *U.S. Public*, pg. 726
DUAL MANUFACTURING & ENGINEERING, INC.—See Furnishings International, Inc.; *U.S. Private*, pg. 432
DUALITE INC.; *U.S. Private*, pg. 344
DUALITE SALES & SERVICE, INC.—See Dualite Inc.; *U.S. Private*, pg. 344
DUALL PLASTICS, INC.—See Bunzl PLC; *Int'l*, pg. 233
DUBACH GAS COMPANY—See El Paso Natural Gas Co.; *U.S. Public*, pg. 567
DUBAI PETROLEUM COMPANY—See Du Pont (E.I. Du Pont De Nemours & Co.); *U.S. Public*, pg. 533
DUBBERS MALDEN GROEP B.V.—See Philipp Holzmann AG; *Int'l*, pg. 633
DUBEK LTD.; *Int'l*, pg. 421
DUBEK TRADE LTD.—See Dubek Ltd.; *Int'l*, pg. 421
DUBIN-CLARK & COMPANY; *U.S. Private*, pg. 344
DUBOIS CHEMICALS—See Unilever Plc; *Int'l*, pg. 1437
DUBOIS COUNTY BANK—See Old National Bancorp; *U.S. Public*, pg. 1217

DUBOIS MATERIAUX—See Castorama Dubois Investissements S.C.A.; *Int'l*, pg. 275
DUBOIS MATERIAUX RHONE ALPES—See Castorama Dubois Investissements S.C.A.; *Int'l*, pg. 275
DUBREUIL FOREST PRODUCTS, LTD.—See Fort James Corporation; *U.S. Public*, pg. 672
DUCHEM LABORATORIES LIMITED—See Pfizer Inc.; *U.S. Public*, pg. 1282
DUCHESNE BANK—See Firstbank of Illinois Co.; *U.S. Public*, pg. 643
DUCHOSSOIS COMMUNICATIONS, INC.—See Duchossois Industries, Inc.; *U.S. Private*, pg. 344
DUCHOSSOIS INDUSTRIES, INC.; *U.S. Private*, pg. 344
DUCILO S.A.—See Du Pont (E.I. Du Pont De Nemours & Co.); *U.S. Public*, pg. 533
DUCK HEAD APPAREL—See Delta Woodside Industries, Inc.; *U.S. Public*, pg. 498
DUCK RIVER COMPANY—See Saint-Gobain; *Int'l*, pg. 1174
DUCKBACK PRODUCTS—See Katy Industries, Inc.; *U.S. Public*, pg. 944
DUCKWALL-ALCO STORES, INC.; *U.S. Public*, pg. 533
DUCOA L.P.—See DCV Inc.; *U.S. Private*, pg. 301
DUCOMMUN INCORPORATED; *U.S. Public*, pg. 533
DUCOST ENGINEERING LTD.—See Haden Maclellan Holdings plc; *Int'l*, pg. 585
A. DUDA & SONS INC.; *U.S. Private*, pg. 344
DUDEK & BOCK SPRING MANUFACTURING COMPANY; *U.S. Private*, pg. 344
DUDLEY SPORTS CO. DIVISION—See Kohlberg Kravis Roberts & Co.; *U.S. Private*, pg. 629
DUEL SYSTEMS—See Methode Electronics Inc.; *U.S. Public*, pg. 1101
DUELLMAN ELECTRIC SUPPLY, INC.—See Rexel, S.A.; *Int'l*, pg. 1107
DUESBURY'S—See Brambles Industries Limited; *Int'l*, pg. 211
DUESSE—See Saint-Gobain; *Int'l*, pg. 1172
DUEWAG AG—See Siemens AG; *Int'l*, pg. 1244
DUFALCO NV—See Koninklijke Hoogovens N.V.; *Int'l*, pg. 755
DUFAYLITE DEVELOPMENTS LIMITED—See SLD Holdings Ltd.; *Int'l*, pg. 1160
DUFERCO INTL. INVESTMENT HOLDING LTD.—See IRI Istituto Ricostruzione Industriale; *Int'l*, pg. 654
DUFERCO STEEL INC.; *U.S. Private*, pg. 345
DUFF & PHELPS UTILITIES INCOME INC.; *U.S. Public*, pg. 534
DUFF-NORTON—See Columbus McKinnon Corp.; *U.S. Public*, pg. 406
DUFFERIN AGGREGATES—See Holderbank Financiere Glaris Ltd.; *Int'l*, pg. 628
DUFFERIN CONSTRUCTION—See Holderbank Financiere Glaris Ltd.; *Int'l*, pg. 628
DUFFERIN-CUSTOM CONCRETE GROUP—See Holderbank Financiere Glaris Ltd.; *Int'l*, pg. 628
DUFFORD MARKETING; *U.S. Private*, pg. 345
DUFFY TOOL & STAMPING, INC.—See Brittany Corporation; *U.S. Private*, pg. 169
DUGAN/FARLEY COMMUNICATIONS—See True North Diversified Companies; *U.S. Public*, pg. 1642
DUGAN & MEYERS CONSTRUCTION CO.—See Dugan & Meyers Interests, Inc.; *U.S. Private*, pg. 345
DUGAN & MEYERS INTERESTS, INC.; *U.S. Private*, pg. 345
DUGAN PRODUCTION CORP.; *U.S. Private*, pg. 345
DUGAN VALVA CONTESS-CHICAGO—See Dugan Valva Contess Inc.; *U.S. Private*, pg. 345
DUGAN VALVA CONTESS-DALLAS—See Dugan Valva Contess Inc.; *U.S. Private*, pg. 345
DUGAN VALVA CONTESS INC.; *U.S. Private*, pg. 345
DUGGAN INDUSTRIES, INC.; *U.S. Private*, pg. 345
DUIF CONVENIENCE FOODS BV—See Koninklijke BolsWessanen nv; *Int'l*, pg. 751
DUISBURG BRANCH—See Deutsche Babcock AG; *Int'l*, pg. 401
DUKANE CANADA LTD.—See Dukane Corporation; *U.S. Private*, pg. 346
DUKANE CORPORATION; *U.S. Private*, pg. 345
DUKANE CSDIT DIV.—See Dukane Corporation; *U.S. Private*, pg. 346
DUKE ENERGY CORPORATION; *U.S. Public*, pg. 534
DUKE ENERGY FIELD SERVICES, INC.—See Duke Energy Corporation; *U.S. Public*, pg. 534
DUKE ENERGY INTERNATIONAL, L.L.C.—See Duke Energy Corporation; *U.S. Public*, pg. 534
DUKE ENGINEERING & SERVICES, INC.—See Duke Energy Corporation; *U.S. Public*, pg. 534
DUKE/FLUOR DANIEL—See Duke Energy Corporation; *U.S. Public*, pg. 535
DUKE/FLUOR DANIEL—See Fluor Corporation; *U.S. Public*, pg. 660
DUKE MANUFACTURING CO.; *U.S. Private*, pg. 346
DUKE POWER CO. MCGUIRE NUCLEAR—See Duke Energy Corporation; *U.S. Public*, pg. 534
DUKE POWER OCONEE NUCLEAR STATION—See Duke Energy Corporation; *U.S. Public*, pg. 534
DUKE REALTY INVESTMENTS, INC.; *U.S. Public*, pg. 535
DUKHAN SERVICE—See Royal Dutch/Shell Group of Companies; *Int'l*, pg. 1141
DULMISON INC.—See Morgan Crucible Co. Plc; *Int'l*, pg. 894
DULMISON (NZ) LIMITED—See Morgan Crucible Co. Plc; *Int'l*, pg. 893
DULMISON PTY. LIMITED—See Morgan Crucible Co. Plc; *Int'l*, pg. 893
DULMISON (THAILAND) CO. LTD.—See Morgan Crucible Co. Plc; *Int'l*, pg. 893
DULMISON (U.K.) LIMITED—See Morgan Crucible Co. Plc; *Int'l*, pg. 893
DULUTH & NORTHEASTERN RAILROAD CO.—See Potlatch Corporation; *U.S. Public*, pg. 1318
DULUTH NEWS-TRIBUNE—See Knight-Ridder, Inc.; *U.S. Public*, pg. 964

DULUTH, WINNIPEG & PACIFIC RAILWAY CO.—See Canadian National Railway Company; *Int'l*, pg. 258
DULUX PAPUA NEW GUINEA PTY LTD—See Imperial Chemical Industries PLC; *Int'l*, pg. 664
DUMEZ CALEDONIA—See Lyonnaise des Eaux S.A.; *Int'l*, pg. 823
DUMEZ CONSTRUCTION—See Lyonnaise des Eaux S.A.; *Int'l*, pg. 823
DUMEZ-GTM—See Lyonnaise des Eaux S.A.; *Int'l*, pg. 823
DUMEZ-GTM—See Lyonnaise des Eaux S.A.; *Int'l*, pg. 823
DUMEZ-GTM—See Lyonnaise des Eaux S.A.; *Int'l*, pg. 823
DUMEZ-GTM CAMBODGE—See Lyonnaise des Eaux S.A.; *Int'l*, pg. 823
DUMEZ-GTM CHINE—See Lyonnaise des Eaux S.A.; *Int'l*, pg. 823
DUMEZ-GTM HONG KONG—See Lyonnaise des Eaux S.A.; *Int'l*, pg. 823
DUMEZ-GTM JAKARTA—See Lyonnaise des Eaux S.A.; *Int'l*, pg. 823
DUMEZ-GTM PORTUGAL—See Lyonnaise des Eaux S.A.; *Int'l*, pg. 823
DUMEZ-GTM REPRESENTATIVE OFFICE—See Lyonnaise des Eaux S.A.; *Int'l*, pg. 823
DUMEZ-GTM TOKYO—See Lyonnaise des Eaux S.A.; *Int'l*, pg. 823
DUMEZ GUYANE—See Lyonnaise des Eaux S.A.; *Int'l*, pg. 823
DUMEZ-JAYA SDN BHD—See Lyonnaise des Eaux S.A.; *Int'l*, pg. 823
DUMEZ MESA—See Lyonnaise des Eaux S.A.; *Int'l*, pg. 823
DUMEZ MOSCOU—See Lyonnaise des Eaux S.A.; *Int'l*, pg. 823
DUMEZ S.A. EMIRATES—See Lyonnaise des Eaux S.A.; *Int'l*, pg. 823
DUMORE CORPORATION; *U.S. Private*, pg. 346
DUN & BRADSTREET (AUSTRALIA) PTY. LTD.—See The Dun & Bradstreet Corporation; *U.S. Public*, pg. 536
DUN & BRADSTREET BUSINESS EDUCATION SERVICES—See The Dun & Bradstreet Corporation; *U.S. Public*, pg. 536
DUN & BRADSTREET B.V.—See The Dun & Bradstreet Corporation; *U.S. Public*, pg. 536
DUN & BRADSTREET CANADA LTD.—See The Dun & Bradstreet Corporation; *U.S. Public*, pg. 536
DUN & BRADSTREET CIS—See The Dun & Bradstreet Corporation; *U.S. Public*, pg. 536
THE DUN & BRADSTREET CORPORATE FOUNDATION—See The Dun & Bradstreet Corporation; *U.S. Public*, pg. 535
THE DUN & BRADSTREET CORPORATION; *U.S. Public*, pg. 535
DUN & BRADSTREET DANMARK A/S—See The Dun & Bradstreet Corporation; *U.S. Public*, pg. 536
DUN & BRADSTREET DEUTSCHLAND GMBH—See The Dun & Bradstreet Corporation; *U.S. Public*, pg. 536
DUN & BRADSTREET DO BRASIL LTDA—See The Dun & Bradstreet Corporation; *U.S. Public*, pg. 536
DUN & BRADSTREET EURINFORM SA-NV—See The Dun & Bradstreet Corporation; *U.S. Public*, pg. 536
DUN & BRADSTREET FINLAND OY—See The Dun & Bradstreet Corporation; *U.S. Public*, pg. 536
DUN & BRADSTREET FRANCE SA—See The Dun & Bradstreet Corporation; *U.S. Public*, pg. 536
DUN & BRADSTREET HUNGARIA KFT.—See The Dun & Bradstreet Corporation; *U.S. Public*, pg. 536
DUN & BRADSTREET (INDIA) PVT. LTD.—See The Dun & Bradstreet Corporation; *U.S. Public*, pg. 536
DUN & BRADSTREET INFORMATION SERVICES (M) SDN. BHD.—See The Dun & Bradstreet Corporation; *U.S. Public*, pg. 536
DUN & BRADSTREET INTERNATIONAL CONSULTANT (SHANGHAI) LTD.—See The Dun & Bradstreet Corporation; *U.S. Public*, pg. 536
DUN & BRADSTREET INTERNATIONAL, LTD. TAIWAN BRANCH—See The Dun & Bradstreet Corporation; *U.S. Public*, pg. 536
DUN & BRADSTREET INTERNATIONAL LTD., KOREA BRANCH—See The Dun & Bradstreet Corporation; *U.S. Public*, pg. 536
DUN & BRADSTREET (ISRAEL) LTD.—See The Dun & Bradstreet Corporation; *U.S. Public*, pg. 536
DUN & BRADSTREET JAPAN LTD.—See The Dun & Bradstreet Corporation; *U.S. Public*, pg. 536
DUN & BRADSTREET KOSMOS SPA—See The Dun & Bradstreet Corporation; *U.S. Public*, pg. 536
DUN & BRADSTREET LATIN AMERICA & CARIBBEAN—See The Dun & Bradstreet Corporation; *U.S. Public*, pg. 536
DUN & BRADSTREET LTD.—See The Dun & Bradstreet Corporation; *U.S. Public*, pg. 536
DUN & BRADSTREET (NEW ZEALAND) LTD.—See The Dun & Bradstreet Corporation; *U.S. Public*, pg. 536
DUN & BRADSTREET NORGE AS—See The Dun & Bradstreet Corporation; *U.S. Public*, pg. 536
DUN & BRADSTREET PENSION SERVICES, INC.—See The Dun & Bradstreet Corporation; *U.S. Public*, pg. 536
DUN & BRADSTREET POLAND SP. Z.O.O.—See The Dun & Bradstreet Corporation; *U.S. Public*, pg. 536
DUN & BRADSTREET PORTUGAL LDA.—See The Dun & Bradstreet Corporation; *U.S. Public*, pg. 536
DUN & BRADSTREET SA—See The Dun & Bradstreet Corporation; *U.S. Public*, pg. 536
DUN & BRADSTREET S.A. DE C.V.—See The Dun & Bradstreet Corporation; *U.S. Public*, pg. 537
DUN & BRADSTREET SCHIMMELPFENG GMBH—See The Dun & Bradstreet Corporation; *U.S. Public*, pg. 537
DUN & BRADSTREET SCHWEIZ AG—See The Dun & Bradstreet Corporation; *U.S. Public*, pg. 537
DUN & BRADSTREET (SINGAPORE) PTE. LTD.—See The Dun & Bradstreet Corporation; *U.S. Public*, pg. 537
DUN & BRADSTREET SOLIDITET AB—See The Dun & Bradstreet Corporation; *U.S. Public*, pg. 537

MASTER INDEX TO COMPANY NAMES DURR

Company Index

DUN & BRADSTREET SPOL S.R.O.—See The Dun & Bradstreet Corporation; *U.S. Public*, pg. 537
DUN & BRADSTREET SVERIGE AB—See The Dun & Bradstreet Corporation; *U.S. Public*, pg. 537
DUN & BRADSTREET SOFTWARE SERVICES—See Geac Computer Corporation Limited; *Int'l*, pg. 532
DUNA-DRAVA CEMENT-ES MESZMUVEK KFT.—See Heidelberger Zement A.G.; *Int'l*, pg. 605
DUNABEST KFT.—See Maresi Markenartikelvertrieb Aktiengesellschaft; *Int'l*, pg. 842
DUNASTYR POLYSTYR. MANUFACTURING CO. LTD.—See ENI S.p.A.; *Int'l*, pg. 429
DUNAVANT ENTERPRISES, INC.; *U.S. Private*, pg. 346
DUNBAR SALES INC.—See Video Display Corporation; *U.S. Public*, pg. 1720
DUNBARTON CORPORATION—See CGF Industries; *U.S. Private*, pg. 194
DUNBRIK (ULSTER) LIMITED—See RMC Group p.l.c.; *Int'l*, pg. 1079
DUNCAN & HILL DIVISION—See Ha-Lo Industries, Inc.; *U.S. Public*, pg. 773
DUNCAN CREEK INC.—See Mason Shoe Mfg. Co.; *U.S. Private*, pg. 712
DUNCAN EQUIPMENT COMPANY; *U.S. Private*, pg. 346
DUNCAN FLOCKHART & CO. LIMITED—See Glaxo Wellcome plc; *Int'l*, pg. 552
DUNCAN TOYS COMPANY—See Flambeau Corporation; *U.S. Private*, pg. 409
DUNCANSON & HOLT—See UNUM Corporation; *U.S. Public*, pg. 1699
DUNDEE CEMENT CO.—See Holderbank Financiere Glaris Ltd.; *Int'l*, pg. 628
DUNDRIDGE COLLEGE LIMITED—See The General Electric Company, p.l.c.; *Int'l*, pg. 544
DUNE—See Groupe Casino; *Int'l*, pg. 563
DUNEARN DISTRIBUTION SERVICES PRIVATE LIMITED—See Sime Darby Berhad; *Int'l*, pg. 1250
DUNGARVAN CRYSTAL LTD.—See Waterford Wedgwood Plc; *Int'l*, pg. 1487
DUNGEY & ASSOCIATES—See FirstCity Financial Corporation; *U.S. Public*, pg. 644
DUNHAM'S ATHLEISURE CORPORATION; *U.S. Private*, pg. 346
ALFRED DUNHILL COGNAC S.A.—See Diageo Plc; *Int'l*, pg. 409
DUNHILL PERSONNEL SYSTEM, INC.—See Watsco, Inc.; *U.S. Public*, pg. 1746
DUNHILL SCOTCH WHISKY SALES LIMITED—See Diageo Plc; *Int'l*, pg. 409
DUNI AB; *Int'l*, pg. 421
DUNI AB-FINESS FORSALJNING—See Duni AB; *Int'l*, pg. 421
DUNI AB-NORDIC DIVISION—See Duni AB; *Int'l*, pg. 421
DUNI AG—See Duni AB; *Int'l*, pg. 421
DUNI A/S—See Duni AB; *Int'l*, pg. 421
DUNI BELGIUM NV—See Duni AB; *Int'l*, pg. 421
DUNI/FINESS HYGIENE—See Duni AB; *Int'l*, pg. 421
DUNI GMBH—See Duni AB; *Int'l*, pg. 421
DUNI IBERICA S.L.—See Duni AB; *Int'l*, pg. 421
DUNI INC.—See Duni AB; *Int'l*, pg. 421
DUNI LTD.—See Duni AB; *Int'l*, pg. 421
DUNI NEDERLAND B.V.—See Duni AB; *Int'l*, pg. 421
DUNI SARL—See Duni AB; *Int'l*, pg. 421
DUNKERQUE ELECTROMETALLURGIE—See Pechiney S.A.; *Int'l*, pg. 1028
P.T. DUNKIN DO LESTARI—See Allied Domecq PLC; *Int'l*, pg. 64
DUNKIN' DONUTS (BAHAMAS) LTD.—See Allied Domecq PLC; *Int'l*, pg. 63
DUNKIN' DONUTS INCORPORATED—See Allied Domecq PLC; *Int'l*, pg. 63
DUNKIN' DONUTS U.K. LIMITED—See Allied Domecq PLC; *Int'l*, pg. 63
DUNKIN' DONUTS VENEZUELA—See Allied Domecq PLC; *Int'l*, pg. 63
DUNKIN' VENTURES CORPORATION—See Allied Domecq PLC; *Int'l*, pg. 63
DUNKLEY INTL.—See Cherry Central Cooperative; *U.S. Private*, pg. 234
DUNLAP & CO. INC.; *U.S. Private*, pg. 346
THE DUNLAP COMPANY; *U.S. Private*, pg. 346
DUNLAP DIVISION—See Tecumseh Products Company; *U.S. Public*, pg. 1565
DUNLAP MANUFACTURING CO.—See The Vernon Company; *U.S. Private*, pg. 1137
DUNLITE POWER GENERATION PTY. LTD.—See Cummins Engine Company, Inc.; *U.S. Public*, pg. 469
DUNLOP ADHESIVES—See BTR plc; *Int'l*, pg. 125
DUNLOP AEROSPACE GROUP—See BTR plc; *Int'l*, pg. 125
DUNLOP AIRCRAFT TYRES DIV.—See BTR plc; *Int'l*, pg. 125
DUNLOP AUTOMOTIVE COMPOSITES (UK) LIMITED—See Ford Motor Company; *U.S. Public*, pg. 665
DUNLOP AUTOMOTIVE UK—See BTR plc; *Int'l*, pg. 125
DUNLOP AVIATION DIV.—See BTR plc; *Int'l*, pg. 125
DUNLOP FRANCE S.A.—See Sumitomo Rubber Industries Ltd.; *Int'l*, pg. 1317
DUNLOP GMBH—See Sumitomo Rubber Industries Ltd.; *Int'l*, pg. 1317
DUNLOP HIFLEX LTD.—See BTR plc; *Int'l*, pg. 125
DUNLOP HOLDINGS PLC—See BTR plc; *Int'l*, pg. 124
DUNLOP INDUSTRIAL HOSE LTD.—See BTR plc; *Int'l*, pg. 125
DUNLOP INTERNATIONAL PROJECTS—See BTR plc; *Int'l*, pg. 126
DUNLOP MARINE SAFETY LTD.—See BTR plc; *Int'l*, pg. 126
DUNLOP PRECISION RUBBER DIVISION—See BTR plc; *Int'l*, pg. 125
DUNLOP SKEGA—See Svedala Industri AB; *Int'l*, pg. 1323
DUNLOP TIRE CORPORATION—See Sumitomo Rubber Industries Ltd.; *Int'l*, pg. 1317
DUNLOP TYRES UK LTD.—See Sumitomo Rubber Industries Ltd.; *Int'l*, pg. 1317
DUNMORE CORPORATION; *U.S. Private*, pg. 346
DUNMORE CORPORATION/BREWSTER—See Dunmore Corporation; *U.S. Private*, pg. 347
DUNN-EDWARDS CORPORATION; *U.S. Private*, pg. 347
DUNN INDUSTRIES INC.; *U.S. Private*, pg. 347
DUNN INVESTMENT CO.; *U.S. Private*, pg. 347
J.E. DUNN CONSTRUCTION CO.—See Dunn Industries Inc.; *U.S. Private*, pg. 347
J.E. DUNN EQUITIES, INC.—See Dunn Industries Inc.; *U.S. Private*, pg. 347
DUNN NURSING HOME—See Paragon Health Network, Inc.; *U.S. Public*, pg. 1256
DUNN NUTRATECH—See Archer Daniels Midland Company (ADM); *U.S. Public*, pg. 128
DUNN REALITY, INC.—See Dunn Industries Inc.; *U.S. Private*, pg. 347
DUNN REBER GLENN MARZ; *U.S. Private*, pg. 347
DUNN REBER GLENN MARZ/LAS VEGAS—See Dunn Reber Glenn Marz; *U.S. Private*, pg. 347
DUNNINGTON-BEACH TOBACCO CO.—See Universal Corporation; *U.S. Public*, pg. 1694
DUNPHY HOLDING PTY. LTD.—See Shimano Inc.; *Int'l*, pg. 1232
DUNSGATE—See The Dun & Bradstreet Corporation; *U.S. Public*, pg. 535
DUNSTON LEATHERS, INC.—See United States Luggage Company; *U.S. Private*, pg. 1125
DUO-FAST CORPORATION; *U.S. Private*, pg. 347
DUO-FORM OF MICHIGAN, INC.—See Kevco, Inc.; *U.S. Public*, pg. 953
DUPERIAL 9 DE JULIO S.A.I.C.—See Imperial Chemical Industries PLC; *Int'l*, pg. 664
DUPERIAL S.A.I.C.—See Imperial Chemical Industries PLC; *Int'l*, pg. 664
DUPEY MANAGEMENT CORP.; *U.S. Private*, pg. 348
DUPHAR & CIE S.N.C.—See Solvay S.A.; *Int'l*, pg. 1277
DUPHAR LABORATORIES LTD.—See Solvay S.A.; *Int'l*, pg. 1278
DUPLEX ENVELOPE CO.—See International Paper Company; *U.S. Public*, pg. 903
DUPLI-COLOR PRODUCTS COMPANY—See The Sherwin-Williams Company; *U.S. Public*, pg. 1466
DUPLI-FAX, INC.—See Canon Inc.; *Int'l*, pg. 262
DUPONT-BEDU—See SNCF; *Int'l*, pg. 1163
DUPONT MERCK—See Merck & Co., Inc.; *U.S. Public*, pg. 1091
DUPONT MERCK PHARM—See Merck & Co., Inc.; *U.S. Public*, pg. 1091
DUPONT MERCK PHARM CO.—See Merck & Co., Inc.; *U.S. Public*, pg. 1091
DUPPS COMPANY; *U.S. Private*, pg. 348
DUQUE DE CAXIAS REFINERY—See Petrobras - Petroleo Brasileiro S.A.; *Int'l*, pg. 1042
DUQUESNE ENTERPRISES—See DQE Inc.; *U.S. Public*, pg. 474
DUQUESNE LIGHT COMPANY—See DQE Inc.; *U.S. Public*, pg. 474
DUQUESNE-PURINA S.A.—See Ralston Purina Company; *U.S. Public*, pg. 1360
DURA AUTOMOTIVE SYSTEMS, INC.; *U.S. Public*, pg. 537
DURA CONVERTIBLE SYSTEMS, INC.—See Collins & Aikman Corporation; *U.S. Public*, pg. 399
DURA-LINE CORP.—See Jordan Industries, Inc.; *U.S. Private*, pg. 598
DURA-VENT—See Smiths Industries plc; *Int'l*, pg. 1267
DURABLE ELECTRICAL METAL FACTORY, LTD.—See Windmere-Durable Holdings; *U.S. Public*, pg. 1771
DURABLE SPECIALTIES DIVISION—See FiberMark Inc.; *U.S. Public*, pg. 620
DURACELL AG—See The Gillette Company; *U.S. Public*, pg. 743
DURACELL ARGENTINA S.A.—See The Gillette Company; *U.S. Public*, pg. 743
DURACELL AUSTRALIA PTY. LIMITED—See The Gillette Company; *U.S. Public*, pg. 743
DURACELL BATTERIES LIMITED—See The Gillette Company; *U.S. Public*, pg. 743
N.V. DURACELL BATTERIES, S.A.—See The Gillette Company; *U.S. Public*, pg. 743
DURACELL BATTERY JAPAN, LTD.—See The Gillette Company; *U.S. Public*, pg. 743
S.A. DURACELL BENELUX N.V.—See The Gillette Company; *U.S. Public*, pg. 743
DURACELL CANADA INC.—See The Gillette Company; *U.S. Public*, pg. 743
DURACELL CHILE LTDA.—See The Gillette Company; *U.S. Public*, pg. 743
DURACELL-DAIMON SVENSKA—See The Gillette Company; *U.S. Public*, pg. 743
DURACELL DE MEXICO S.A. DE C.V.—See The Gillette Company; *U.S. Public*, pg. 743
DURACELL DO BRASIL INDUSTRIA & COMERCIO LTDA.—See The Gillette Company; *U.S. Public*, pg. 743
DURACELL HOLDINGS B.V.—See The Gillette Company; *U.S. Public*, pg. 744
DURACELL INC. ENVIRONMENTAL—See The Gillette Company; *U.S. Public*, pg. 743
DURACELL INTERNATIONAL INC.—See The Gillette Company; *U.S. Public*, pg. 743
DURACELL NEW ZEALAND LIMITED—See The Gillette Company; *U.S. Public*, pg. 744
DURACELL PRODUCTS CO.—See The Gillette Company; *U.S. Public*, pg. 743
DURACELL SCANDINAVIA APS—See The Gillette Company; *U.S. Public*, pg. 744
DURACELL (S.E.A.) PTE. LTD.—See The Gillette Company; *U.S. Public*, pg. 744
DURACELL SOUTH AFRICA (PROPRIETARY) LIMITED—See The Gillette Company; *U.S. Public*, pg. 744
DURACELL U.S.A.—See The Gillette Company; *U.S. Public*, pg. 743
DURACELL USA TN PACKAGING—See The Gillette Company; *U.S. Public*, pg. 743
DURACO PRODUCTS, INC.; *U.S. Private*, pg. 348
DURACO PRODUCTS INC. OF SOUTH CAROLINA—See Duraco Products, Inc.; *U.S. Private*, pg. 348
DURAFLAME, INC.; *U.S. Private*, pg. 348
DURAKON INDUSTRIES, INC.; *U.S. Public*, pg. 537
DURAKON MEXICANA, S.A. DE C.V.—See Durakon Industries, Inc.; *U.S. Public*, pg. 537
DURAKUT INTERNATIONAL CORP.—See Kobe Steel, Ltd.; *Int'l*, pg. 740
DURAL LEEDS PTY. LTD.—See Hunter Douglas N.V.; *Int'l*, pg. 639
DURALAM, INC.—See Sargento Foods Inc.; *U.S. Private*, pg. 966
DURALAY ACCESSORIES—See BBA Group plc; *Int'l*, pg. 113
DURALAY LTD.—See BBA Group plc; *Int'l*, pg. 113
DURALINER U.S.A.—See Durakon Industries, Inc.; *U.S. Public*, pg. 537
DURALOY TECHNOLOGIES—See Park Corp.; *U.S. Private*, pg. 839
DURAMETALLIC CORP.—See Flowserve Corporation; *U.S. Public*, pg. 658
DURAND INC.—See L & D Group; *U.S. Private*, pg. 638
DURANT ELECTRONICS, INC.—See Strombecker Corporation; *U.S. Private*, pg. 1047
DURATEC—See ETEX; *Int'l*, pg. 430
DURATEK CORPORATION—See GP Strategies Corporation; *U.S. Public*, pg. 694
DURAY, INC.—See Newell Co.; *U.S. Public*, pg. 1177
DURAY/J.F. DUNCAN INDUSTRIES, INC.; *U.S. Private*, pg. 348
DURBIN-DURCO—See Columbus McKinnon Corp.; *U.S. Public*, pg. 406
DURCO AGENCY, INC.—See AEGON N.V.; *Int'l*, pg. 27
DURCO B.V.—See Flowserve Corporation; *U.S. Public*, pg. 659
S.A. DURCO EUROPE N.V.—See Flowserve Corporation; *U.S. Public*, pg. 659
DURCO EUROPE S.R.L.—See Flowserve Corporation; *U.S. Public*, pg. 659
DURCO FRANCE S.A.R.L.—See Flowserve Corporation; *U.S. Public*, pg. 659
DURCO GMBH ATOMAC DIVISION—See Flowserve Corporation; *U.S. Public*, pg. 659
DURCO PROCESS EQUIPMENT LTD.—See Flowserve Corporation; *U.S. Public*, pg. 659
DURCO-VALTEK (ASIA PACIFIC) PTE. LTD.—See Flowserve Corporation; *U.S. Public*, pg. 659
DUREL CORPORATION—See Rogers Corporation; *U.S. Public*, pg. 1403
DUREX CONSUMER PRODUCTS—See London International Group plc; *Int'l*, pg. 815
DURHAM CHEMICALS LTD.—See Harrisons & Crosfield plc; *Int'l*, pg. 598
DURHAM TRANSPORTATION, INC.; *U.S. Private*, pg. 348
DURHAM TRANSPORTATION INC.—See Durham Transportation, Inc.; *U.S. Private*, pg. 348
DURHAM TUBE—See Senior Engineering Group, plc.; *Int'l*, pg. 1221
DURISOL RAALTE B.V.—See Ballast Nedam NV; *Int'l*, pg. 134
DURKOPP ADLER AG—See FAG Group; *Int'l*, pg. 468
DURKOPP ADLER AMERICA INC.—See FAG Group; *Int'l*, pg. 468
DURKOPP ADLER AUSTRIA GMBH—See FAG Group; *Int'l*, pg. 469
DURKOPP ADLER CR S.R.O.—See FAG Group; *Int'l*, pg. 469
DURKOPP ADLER FAR EAST LTD.—See FAG Group; *Int'l*, pg. 469
DURKOPP ADLER FRANCE S.A.—See FAG Group; *Int'l*, pg. 469
DURKOPP ADLER ITALIA S.R.L.—See FAG Group; *Int'l*, pg. 469
DURKOPP ADLER MEXICO S.A. DE C.V.—See FAG Group; *Int'l*, pg. 469
DURKOPP ADLER POLSKA SPOLKA ZO.O.—See FAG Group; *Int'l*, pg. 469
DURKOPP ADLER R. LTD.—See FAG Group; *Int'l*, pg. 469
DURKOPP ADLER (UK) LTD.—See FAG Group; *Int'l*, pg. 469
DURKOPP ADLER UKRAINE LTD.—See FAG Group; *Int'l*, pg. 469
DURKOPP MASCHINEBAU GMBH—See FAG Group; *Int'l*, pg. 468
DURKOPP SYSTEMTECHNIK GMBH—See FAG Group; *Int'l*, pg. 468
DURLACHER & CO., INC.; *U.S. Private*, pg. 348
A.K. DURNIN CHRYSLER PLYMOUTH, INC.; *U.S. Private*, pg. 348
DURO BAG MANUFACTURING CO.; *U.S. Private*, pg. 348
DURO DYNE CORPORATION; *U.S. Private*, pg. 349
DURO-LAST ROOFING, INC.; *U.S. Private*, pg. 349
DURO-LITE INTERNATIONAL; *U.S. Private*, pg. 349
DURO-TEST CANADA—See Duro-Lite International; *U.S. Private*, pg. 349
DURO-TEST CORPORATION—See Duro-Lite International; *U.S. Private*, pg. 349
DURO-TEST DE MEXICO, S.A.—See Duro-Lite International; *U.S. Private*, pg. 349
DURO-TEST INTL. CORP.—See Duro-Lite International; *U.S. Private*, pg. 349
DUROFORM-J. FRITZ GMBH & CO KG—See Alusuisse-Lonza Holding Ltd.; *Int'l*, pg. 68
DUROL OIL CO. (PTY.) LTD.—See Burmah Castrol plc; *Int'l*, pg. 236
DURON, INC.; *U.S. Private*, pg. 349
DUROX BUILDING PRODUCTS LIMITED—See RMC Group p.l.c.; *Int'l*, pg. 1080
DURR AG; *Int'l*, pg. 421
DURR ANLAGENBAU GES.M.B.H.—See Durr AG; *Int'l*, pg. 422

Company Index

DURR AUTOMATION, INC.—See Durr AG; *Int'l*, pg. 421
DURR CONTROL SYSTEMS LTD.—See Durr AG; *Int'l*, pg. 422
DURR DE MEXICO S.A. DE C.V.—See Durr AG; *Int'l*, pg. 422
DURR DO BRASIL S.A.—See Durr AG; *Int'l*, pg. 422
DURR GMBH SHANGHAI OFFICE—See Durr AG; *Int'l*, pg. 422
DURR INDUSTRIES, INC.—See Durr AG; *Int'l*, pg. 421
DURR LTD.—See Durr AG; *Int'l*, pg. 422
DURRETT-SHEPPARD STEEL CO., INC.; *U.S. Private*, pg. 349
DURRIESSCHARMANN, AG—See Metallgesellschaft AG; *Int'l*, pg. 860
DURRPOL SP.Z.O.O.—See Durr AG; *Int'l*, pg. 422
DURST CORPORATION; *U.S. Private*, pg. 349
DURST DIV.—See Regal-Beloit Corporation; *U.S. Public*, pg. 1370
DURUM (AUSTRALIA) PTY. LTD.—See Durum Energy Corp.; *Int'l*, pg. 422
DURUM ENERGY CORP.; *Int'l*, pg. 422
DURUM ENERGY CORP., SUCURSAL DEL PERU—See Durum Energy Corp.; *Int'l*, pg. 422
DUSA ENDUSTRIYEL IPLIK SANAYI VE TICARET A.S.—See Du Pont (E.I. Du Pont De Nemours & Co.); *U.S. Public*, pg. 533
DUSA ENDUSTRIYEL IPLIK SANAYI VE TICARET A.S.—See Sabanci Holding A.S.; *Int'l*, pg. 1167
DUSENBERY EUROPE LTD.—See John Dusenbery Co., Inc.; *U.S. Private*, pg. 350
JOHN DUSENBERY CO., INC.; *U.S. Private*, pg. 349
DUSKIN CO., LTD.; *Int'l*, pg. 422
DUSKIN USA, INC.—See Duskin Co., Ltd.; *Int'l*, pg. 422
DUSOLIER—See SNCF; *Int'l*, pg. 1163
DUSSEK BROS. (SA) LTD.—See Burmah Castrol plc; *Int'l*, pg. 236
DUSSEK CAMPBELL (DEUTSCHLAND) GMBH—See Burmah Castrol plc; *Int'l*, pg. 236
DUSSEK CAMPBELL, INC.—See Burmah Castrol plc; *Int'l*, pg. 234
DUSSEK CAMPBELL LTD.—See Burmah Castrol plc; *Int'l*, pg. 234
DUSSEK CAMPBELL PTY LTD.—See Burmah Castrol plc; *Int'l*, pg. 236
DUSSELDORF-MUENCHENER BETEILIGUNGS-GESELLSCHAFT MBH—See Bayerische Vereinsbank Group; *Int'l*, pg. 179
DUTA LTD.—See Durr AG; *Int'l*, pg. 422
DUTCH HOUSING, INC.—See Champion Enterprises, Inc.; *U.S. Public*, pg. 333
DUTCH MILL BAKING COMPANY—See Tasty Baking Company; *U.S. Public*, pg. 1561
DUTCH PARCEL DISTRIBUTION ZUID B.V.—See Royal Nedlloyd Group N.V.; *Int'l*, pg. 1145
DUTCH PARKING INC.—See Allright Corporation; *U.S. Private*, pg. 43
DUTCHESS QUARRY & SUPPLY CO. INC.; *U.S. Private*, pg. 350
DUTCHMEN FOLD DOWN CAMPER DIVISION—See Thor Industries, Inc.; *U.S. Public*, pg. 1602
DUTCHMEN MANUFACTURING, INC.—See Thor Industries, Inc.; *U.S. Public*, pg. 1602
DUTTON-FORSHAW (LAND MACHINERY) LTD.—See Lonrho plc; *Int'l*, pg. 817
DUTTON-LAINSON CO.; *U.S. Private*, pg. 350
DUTTON PARTNERS—See Cigna Corp.; *U.S. Public*, pg. 361
DUTY FREE INTERNATIONAL, INC.—See BAA plc; *Int'l*, pg. 103
DUVERGER—See SNCF; *Int'l*, pg. 1163
DWIGHT ASSET MANAGEMENT COMPANY—See United Asset Management Corporation; *U.S. Public*, pg. 1673
DWIGHT MFG. DIVISION—See R.R. Donnelley & Sons Company; *U.S. Public*, pg. 518
THE DWYER GROUP, INC.; *U.S. Public*, pg. 537
DWYER INSTRUMENTS; *U.S. Private*, pg. 350
DYAS B.V.—See SHV Holdings N.V.; *Int'l*, pg. 1155
DYCKERHOFF AG; *Int'l*, pg. 422
DYCKERHOFF & WIDMANN AG; *Int'l*, pg. 423
DYCKERHOFF & WIDMANN AG & CO. GRUNDSTUCKS OHG—See Dyckerhoff & Widmann AG; *Int'l*, pg. 423
DYCKERHOFF & WIDMANN AG SUCURSAL BUENOS AIRES—See Dyckerhoff & Widmann AG; *Int'l*, pg. 424
DYCKERHOFF & WIDMANN BAUGESELLSCHAFT MBH—See Dyckerhoff & Widmann AG; *Int'l*, pg. 423
DYCKERHOFF & WIDMANN BERLIN GMBH—See Dyckerhoff & Widmann AG; *Int'l*, pg. 423
DYCKERHOFF & WIDMANN GESELLSCHAFT M.B.H.—See Dyckerhoff & Widmann AG; *Int'l*, pg. 424
DYCKERHOFF & WIDMANN SACHSEN/THURINGEN GMBH—See Dyckerhoff & Widmann AG; *Int'l*, pg. 423
DYCKERHOFF AUSBAUPRODUKTE—See Dyckerhoff AG; *Int'l*, pg. 422
DYCKERHOFF AUSTRIA AUSBAUPRODUKTE GES.MBH—See Dyckerhoff AG; *Int'l*, pg. 423
EDUARD DYCKERHOFF GMBH—See Dyckerhoff AG; *Int'l*, pg. 422
DYCKERHOFF SOPRO GMBH—See Dyckerhoff AG; *Int'l*, pg. 422
DYCKERHOFF TRANSPORTBETON ELBE GMBH—See Dyckerhoff AG; *Int'l*, pg. 422
DYCKERHOFF TRANSPORTBETON GMBH—See Dyckerhoff AG; *Int'l*, pg. 422
DYCKERHOFF TRANSPORTBETON GOTHA GMBH & CO. KG—See Dyckerhoff AG; *Int'l*, pg. 422
DYCKERHOFF TRANSPORTBETON LAUSITZ GMBH & CO. KG—See Dyckerhoff AG; *Int'l*, pg. 422
DYCKERHOFF TRANSPORTBETON OSTSACHSEN GMBH & CO. KG—See Dyckerhoff AG; *Int'l*, pg. 422
DYCKERHOFF TRANSPORTBETON SACHSEN GMBH—See Dyckerhoff & Widmann AG; *Int'l*, pg. 422
DYCKERHOFF TRANSPORTBETON ZWICKAU GMBH & CO. KG—See Dyckerhoff AG; *Int'l*, pg. 422

DYCKERHOFF ZEMENT INTERNATIONAL GMBH—See Dyckerhoff AG; *Int'l*, pg. 422
DYCOM INDUSTRIES, INC.; *U.S. Public*, pg. 538
DYER GRAIN CO.—See Tom Wade Co.; *U.S. Private*, pg. 1145
DYER-LAUDERDALE FARMERS CO-OP—See Tennessee Farmers Co-op; *U.S. Private*, pg. 1076
THOMAS K. DYER, INC.—See HNTB Corporation; *U.S. Private*, pg. 492
DYERSBURG CORPORATION; *U.S. Public*, pg. 538
DYERSBURG FABRIC—See Dyersburg Corporation; *U.S. Public*, pg. 538
DYGERT SEATING—See Flexsteel Industries, Inc.; *U.S. Public*, pg. 654
DYKE INDUSTRY, INC.; *U.S. Public*, pg. 350
DYKEM COMPANY—See Illinois Tool Works Inc.; *U.S. Public*, pg. 866
DYLEX LIMITED; *Int'l*, pg. 425
DYNA-PAK DIV.—See Package Machinery Co.; *U.S. Private*, pg. 832
DYNA S.A.—See Nestle S.A.; *Int'l*, pg. 916
DYNA SYSTEMS—See NCH Corporation; *U.S. Public*, pg. 1145
DYNA TECHNOLOGY INCORPORATED; *U.S. Public*, pg. 350
DYNABILT PRODUCTS—See Burtman Iron Works, Inc.; *U.S. Private*, pg. 188
DYNAC CO.—See Suntory Ltd.; *Int'l*, pg. 1321
DYNACARE, INC.; *Int'l*, pg. 425
DYNACARE-ALBERTA—See Dynacare, Inc.; *Int'l*, pg. 425
DYNACARE-ONTARIO—See Dynacare, Inc.; *Int'l*, pg. 425
DYNACARE-WASHINGTON—See Dynacare, Inc.; *Int'l*, pg. 425
DYNACARE-WYOMING—See Dynacare, Inc.; *Int'l*, pg. 425
DYNACAST—See Coats Viyella plc; *Int'l*, pg. 300
DYNACAST DE MEXICO, S.A. DE C.V.—See Coats Viyella plc; *Int'l*, pg. 300
DYNACAST DEUTSCHLAND GMBH—See Coats Viyella plc; *Int'l*, pg. 300
DYNACAST DO BRAZIL LTDA.—See Coats Viyella plc; *Int'l*, pg. 301
DYNACAST INTERNATIONAL LIMITED—See Coats Viyella plc; *Int'l*, pg. 299
DYNACHEM SINGAPORE PTE. LTD.—See Morton International Inc.; *U.S. Public*, pg. 1135
DYNACOR DIV.—See Medline Industries, Inc.; *U.S. Private*, pg. 728
DYNACRAFT—See Paccar Inc.; *U.S. Public*, pg. 1246
DYNADRO BV—See Internatio-Muller N.V.; *Int'l*, pg. 681
DYNAGEAR INC.; *U.S. Private*, pg. 350
DYNAGEAR OIL PUMPS, INC.—See Dynagear Inc.; *U.S. Private*, pg. 350
DYNAGEN INC.—See Continental AG; *Int'l*, pg. 327
DYNALCO CONTROLS CORPORATION—See Crane Co.; *U.S. Public*, pg. 457
DYNALECTRIC COMPANY—See EMCOR Group, Inc.; *U.S. Public*, pg. 571
DYNAMAR INTERNATIONAL LTD.—See Hewlett-Packard Company; *U.S. Public*, pg. 817
DYNAMARK, INC.—See Fair, Isaac and Company, Inc.; *U.S. Public*, pg. 610
DYNAMEC—See Bertrand Faure; *Int'l*, pg. 193
DYNAMET INC.—See Carpenter Technology Corporation; *U.S. Public*, pg. 307
DYNAMEX EXPRESS—See Air Canada; *Int'l*, pg. 36
DYNAMIC GRAPHICS INC.—See Bertelsmann AG; *Int'l*, pg. 191
DYNAMIC HOMES, INC.; *U.S. Public*, pg. 538
DYNAMIC HOMES OF DAKOTA—See Dynamic Homes, Inc.; *U.S. Public*, pg. 539
DYNAMIC HOMES OF FARGO-MOORHEAD—See Dynamic Homes, Inc.; *U.S. Public*, pg. 539
DYNAMIC MATERIALS CORPORATION; *U.S. Public*, pg. 539
DYNAMIC METAL PRODUCTS COMPANY; *U.S. Private*, pg. 350
DYNAMIC S.A.—See Amer Group Ltd.; *Int'l*, pg. 73
DYNAMICS CORPORATION OF AMERICA—See CTS Corporation; *U.S. Public*, pg. 286
DYNAMICS RESEARCH CORPORATION; *U.S. Public*, pg. 539
DYNAMIT NOBEL AG—See Metallgesellschaft AG; *Int'l*, pg. 861
DYNAMIX, INC.—See Cendant Corporation; *U.S. Public*, pg. 321
DYNAPAC AB—See Trelleborg AB; *Int'l*, pg. 1420
DYNAPAC A/S—See Trelleborg AB; *Int'l*, pg. 1420
DYNAPAC CONCRETE EQUIPMENT AB—See Trelleborg AB; *Int'l*, pg. 1420
DYNAPAC CONSTRUCTION EQUIPMENT LTD.—See Trelleborg AB; *Int'l*, pg. 1420
DYNAPAC EQUIPAMENTOS INDUSTRIAIS LTD.—See Trelleborg AB; *Int'l*, pg. 1420
DYNAPAC FAR EAST LTD.—See Trelleborg AB; *Int'l*, pg. 1420
DYNAPAC GMBH—See Trelleborg AB; *Int'l*, pg. 1420
DYNAPAC HEAVY EQUIPMENT AB—See Trelleborg AB; *Int'l*, pg. 1420
DYNAPAC HITACHI CONSTRUCTION MACHINERY—See Svedala Industri AB; *Int'l*, pg. 1326
DYNAPAC HITACHI PLANT—See Svedala Industri AB; *Int'l*, pg. 1326
DYNAPAC KENKI KK—See Trelleborg AB; *Int'l*, pg. 1420
DYNAPAC LIGHT EQUIPMENT AB—See Trelleborg AB; *Int'l*, pg. 1420
DYNAPAC LTD.—See Trelleborg AB; *Int'l*, pg. 1420
DYNAPAC MFG. INC.—See Trelleborg AB; *Int'l*, pg. 1420
DYNAPAC NORDEN AB—See Trelleborg AB; *Int'l*, pg. 1420
DYNAPAC S.A.—See Trelleborg AB; *Int'l*, pg. 1420
DYNAPAC S.P.A.—See Trelleborg AB; *Int'l*, pg. 1420
DYNAPAC (UK) LTD.—See Trelleborg AB; *Int'l*, pg. 1420
DYNAPERT INC.—See Dover Corporation; *U.S. Public*, pg. 522

DYNAPERT JAPAN LTD.—See The Black & Decker Corporation; *U.S. Public*, pg. 233
DYNAPERT LIMITED—See The Black & Decker Corporation; *U.S. Public*, pg. 234
DYNAPOWER/STRATOPOWER—See Aeroquip-Vickers, Inc.; *U.S. Public*, pg. 24
DYNAPRESSE—See Lagardere Groupe; *Int'l*, pg. 795
DYNARAD CORPORATION—See Del Global Technologies; *U.S. Public*, pg. 494
DYNARAY INCORPORATED—See Kaufel Group Ltd.; *Int'l*, pg. 725
DYNARIC, INC.—See Dainippon Ink & Chemicals, Inc.; *Int'l*, pg. 369
DYNARTAIL BV—See Internatio-Muller N.V.; *Int'l*, pg. 681
DYNASONICS—See Racine Federated, Inc.; *U.S. Private*, pg. 906
DYNATECH CORPORATION; *U.S. Public*, pg. 539
DYNATECH DATA COMMUNICATIONS LTD.—See Thermo Electron Corporation; *U.S. Public*, pg. 1591
DYNAVAC—See Tenney Environmental; *U.S. Private*, pg. 1076
DYNCORP; *U.S. Private*, pg. 351
DYNECOL, INC.—See PVS Chemicals, Inc.; *U.S. Private*, pg. 828
DYNETCOM; *Int'l*, pg. 425
DYNETCOM—See DynetCom; *Int'l*, pg. 425
DYNETCOM GMBH—See DynetCom; *Int'l*, pg. 425
DYNEX TECHNOLOGIES—See Thermo Electron Corporation; *U.S. Public*, pg. 1591
DYNEX TECHNOLOGIES GMBH—See Thermo Electron Corporation; *U.S. Public*, pg. 1591
DYNEX TECHNOLOGIES, INC.—See Thermo Electron Corporation; *U.S. Public*, pg. 1591
DYNEX TECHNOLOGIES LTD. (U.K.)—See Thermo Electron Corporation; *U.S. Public*, pg. 1591
DYNISCO GERATE G.M.B.H.—See Berwind Corporation; *U.S. Private*, pg. 139
DYNISCO, INC.—See Berwind Corporation; *U.S. Private*, pg. 138
DYNISCO INSTRUMENT SARL.—See Berwind Corporation; *U.S. Private*, pg. 139
DYNISCO S.R.L.—See Berwind Corporation; *U.S. Private*, pg. 139
DYNISCO (U.K.) LIMITED—See Berwind Corporation; *U.S. Private*, pg. 139
DYNMARK PLASTICS INC.—See Tomkins PLC; *Int'l*, pg. 1397
DYNO MERCHANDISE CORP.—See ConAgra, Inc.; *U.S. Public*, pg. 428
THE DYSON-KISSNER-MORAN CORPORATION; *U.S. Private*, pg. 351
DYSTAR TEXTILFARBEN GMBH—See Bayer AG; *Int'l*, pg. 174
DYSTAR TEXTILFARBEN GMBH—See Hoechst Aktiengesellschaft; *Int'l*, pg. 626
DYTEL INC.—See Syntellect, Inc.; *U.S. Public*, pg. 1550
DYWIBEL N.V.—See Dyckerhoff & Widmann AG; *Int'l*, pg. 424
DYWIDAG AQUASCHUTZ B.V.—See Dyckerhoff & Widmann AG; *Int'l*, pg. 424
DYWIDAG BETON-UND UMWELTPRODUKTE GMBH—See Dyckerhoff & Widmann AG; *Int'l*, pg. 423
DYWIDAG CAMEROUN S.A.R.L.—See Dyckerhoff & Widmann AG; *Int'l*, pg. 424
DYWIDAG NIGERIA LTD.—See Dyckerhoff & Widmann AG; *Int'l*, pg. 424
DYWIDAG-SYSTEMEN NEDERLAND B.V.—See Dyckerhoff & Widmann AG; *Int'l*, pg. 424
DYWIDAG-SYSTEMS INTERNATIONAL S.A.R.L.—See Dyckerhoff & Widmann AG; *Int'l*, pg. 424
DYWIDAG-SYSTEMS INTERNATIONAL A/S—See Dyckerhoff & Widmann AG; *Int'l*, pg. 424
DYWIDAG-SYSTEMS INTERNATIONAL CANADA LTD.—See Dyckerhoff & Widmann AG; *Int'l*, pg. 424
DYWIDAG-SYSTEMS INTERNATIONAL CO., LTD.—See Dyckerhoff & Widmann AG; *Int'l*, pg. 424
DYWIDAG-SYSTEMS INTERNATIONAL CO., LTD.—See Dyckerhoff & Widmann AG; *Int'l*, pg. 424
DYWIDAG-SYSTEMS INTERNATIONAL FAR EAST, LTD.—See Dyckerhoff & Widmann AG; *Int'l*, pg. 424
DYWIDAG-SYSTEMS INTERNATIONAL N.V.—See Dyckerhoff & Widmann AG; *Int'l*, pg. 424
DYWIDAG-SYSTEMS INTERNATIONAL S.A.—See Dyckerhoff & Widmann AG; *Int'l*, pg. 424
DYWIDAG SYSTEMS NORGE A/S—See Dyckerhoff & Widmann AG; *Int'l*, pg. 424
DYWIDAG SYSTEMS TAIWAN CO. LTD.—See Dyckerhoff & Widmann AG; *Int'l*, pg. 425
DYWIDAG-SYSTEMS (U.K.) LTD.—See Dyckerhoff & Widmann AG; *Int'l*, pg. 425
DYWIDAG UMWELTSCHUTZTECHNIK GMBH—See Dyckerhoff & Widmann AG; *Int'l*, pg. 423
DYWIT S.P.A.—See Dyckerhoff & Widmann AG; *Int'l*, pg. 425

E

E & A ENVIRONMENTAL CONSULTANTS, INC.—See EMCON; *U.S. Public*, pg. 571
E & A INDUSTRIES, INC.; *U.S. Private*, pg. 352
E & A INVESTORS, L.P.—See E & A Industries, Inc.; *U.S. Private*, pg. 352
E & B MARINE INCORPORATED—See West Marine, Inc.; *U.S. Public*, pg. 1756
E & B MARINE SUPPLY, INC.—See West Marine, Inc.; *U.S. Public*, pg. 1756
E & D GRAIN MARKETING CO—See EDI International, Inc.; *U.S. Private*, pg. 353
E & D TAYLOR (INSURANCE BROKERS) LIMITED—See Taylor Woodrow plc; *Int'l*, pg. 1358
E & E STEEL, INC.—See Rolled Steel Products Corporation; *U.S. Private*, pg. 941
E & G FOODS; *U.S. Private*, pg. 352

E & J DISTILLERS BRANDY—See E. & J. Gallo Winery; U.S. Private, pg. 438
E & L ENGINEERING—See Texas Utilities Company; U.S. Public, pg. 1587
E & M LAMORT—See Thermo Electron Corporation; U.S. Public, pg. 1596
E&P RESEARCH—See Petrobras - Petroleo Brasileiro S.A.; Int'l, pg. 1042
E&S INSULATION—See Egan Cos.; U.S. Private, pg. 366
E-C APPARATUS CORP.—See Thermo Electron Corporation; U.S. Public, pg. 1595
E FOR M CORP.—See Marquette Medical Systems, Inc.; U.S. Public, pg. 1047
E-L PRODUCTS COMPANY—See Astronics Corporation; U.S. Public, pg. 142
E. MISSEL GMBH—See Masco Corporation; U.S. Public, pg. 1055
E-P CONSULTING GROUP AB—See Telefonaktiebolaget LM Ericsson; Int'l, pg. 1363
E-PLUS MOBILFUNK GMBH—See Veba AG; Int'l, pg. 1461
E PRIME, INC.—See New Century Energies, Inc.; U.S. Public, pg. 1170
E'TOWN CORPORATION; U.S. Public, pg. 540
E'TOWN PROPERTIES INC.—See E'Town Corporation; U.S. Public, pg. 540
E-Z BOWZ, INC.; U.S. Private, pg. 352
E-Z-EM CANADA INC.—See E-Z-Em, Inc.; U.S. Public, pg. 540
E-Z-EM CARIBE, INC.—See E-Z-Em, Inc.; U.S. Public, pg. 540
E-Z-EM IMAGING PRODUCTS DIVISION—See E-Z-Em, Inc.; U.S. Public, pg. 540
E-Z-EM, INC.; U.S. Public, pg. 540
E-Z-EM LTD.—See E-Z-Em, Inc.; U.S. Public, pg. 540
E-Z-EM NEDERLAND, B.V.—See E-Z-Em, Inc.; U.S. Public, pg. 540
E-Z-GO TEXTRON—See Textron Inc.; U.S. Public, pg. 1589
E Z LOADER BOAT TRAILERS, INC.—See E Z Loader Corporate; U.S. Private, pg. 353
E Z LOADER CORPORATE; U.S. Private, pg. 352
E-Z LOK—See TCI Aluminum; U.S. Private, pg. 1063
E-Z MART STORES, INC.; U.S. Private, pg. 353
E-Z SERVE CONVENIENCE STORES, INC.—See E-Z Serve Corp.; U.S. Public, pg. 540
E-Z SERVE CONVENIENCE STORES, INC.-CENTRAL ZONE OFFICE—See E-Z Serve Corp.; U.S. Public, pg. 540
E-Z SERVE CONVENIENCE STORES, INC.-PANAMA CITY MARKET—See E-Z Serve Corp.; U.S. Public, pg. 540
E-Z SERVE CORP.; U.S. Public, pg. 540
EA EISATZBETREUUNGS UND AUSLANDSDIENSTE GMBH—See Assicurazioni Generali S.p.A.; Int'l, pg. 89
EA ENGINEERING, SCIENCE & TECHNOLOGY, INC.; U.S. Public, pg. 540
EA ENGINEERING, SCIENCE & TECHNOLOGY DE MEXICO, S.A. DE C.V.—See EA Engineering, Science & Technology, Inc.; U.S. Public, pg. 541
EA ENGINEERING, SCIENCE & TECHNOLOGY, INC.—See EA Engineering, Science & Technology, Inc.; U.S. Public, pg. 541
EA FINANCIAL, INC.—See EA Engineering, Science & Technology, Inc.; U.S. Public, pg. 541
EA - GENERALI AG—See Assicurazioni Generali S.p.A.; Int'l, pg. 89
EA-GENERALI AG—See Assicurazioni Generali S.p.A.; Int'l, pg. 91
EA-GENERALI EPITO ES TERVEZO KFT.—See Assicurazioni Generali S.p.A.; Int'l, pg. 91
EA-GENERALI MANAGEMENT-CONSULTING AG—See Assicurazioni Generali S.p.A.; Int'l, pg. 89
EA GENERALI RISK CONSULT GMBH—See Assicurazioni Generali S.p.A.; Int'l, pg. 89
EA GENERALI VERMOGENSBERATUNGS GMBH—See Assicurazioni Generali S.p.A.; Int'l, pg. 89
EA GLOBAL, INC.—See EA Engineering, Science & Technology, Inc.; U.S. Public, pg. 541
EA INDUSTRIES; U.S. Public, pg. 541
EA LABORATORIES—See EA Engineering, Science & Technology, Inc.; U.S. Public, pg. 541
EA RECHTSSCHUTZ VERSICHERUNGS AG—See Assicurazioni Generali S.p.A.; Int'l, pg. 89
EAB DEUTSCHLAND INDUSTRIE-TV ANGLEN GMBH—See Rothenberger Group GmbH; Int'l, pg. 1129
EAB ELECTRONIC APPARATEBAU GMBH—See Rothenberger Group GmbH; Int'l, pg. 1129
EAC CORPORATION; U.S. Private, pg. 353
EAC DATE APS—See The East Asiatic Company Ltd. A/S; Int'l, pg. 430
EAC-EMBRAER AIRCRAFT CORPORATION—See Embraer-Empresa Brasileira de Aeronautica S.A.; Int'l, pg. 452
EAC GRAPHICS (NEW ZEALAND) LTD.—See The East Asiatic Company Ltd. A/S; Int'l, pg. 431
EAC GRAPHICS NORDIC AB—See The East Asiatic Company Ltd. A/S; Int'l, pg. 431
EAC GRAPHICS (S.A.) (PTY.) LTD.—See The East Asiatic Company Ltd. A/S; Int'l, pg. 431
EAC MARKETING SERVICES LTD. A/S—See The East Asiatic Company Ltd. A/S; Int'l, pg. 431
EAC SHIPPING LTD. A/S—See The East Asiatic Company Ltd. A/S; Int'l, pg. 431
EAC TIMBER (FRANCE) S.A.—See The East Asiatic Company Ltd. A/S; Int'l, pg. 431
EAC TIMBER LTD. A/S—See The East Asiatic Company Ltd. A/S; Int'l, pg. 431
EAC TIMBER (UK) LTD.—See The East Asiatic Company Ltd. A/S; Int'l, pg. 431
EAC TRANSPORT (UK) LIMITED—See The East Asiatic Company Ltd. A/S; Int'l, pg. 431
EAI-EMBRAER AVIATION INTERNATIONAL—See Embraer-Empresa Brasileira de Aeronautica S.A.; Int'l, pg. 452
EAMI HORNOS INDUSTRIAIES, S.A.—See Eclipse Inc.; U.S. Private, pg. 361

EAO FAR EAST—See Elektro-Apparatebau Olten AG; Int'l, pg. 444
EAO-HIGHLAND—See Elektro-Apparatebau Olten AG; Int'l, pg. 444
EAO SWITCH CORPORATION—See Elektro-Apparatebau Olten AG; Int'l, pg. 444
EAS TECHNOLOGIES, INC.—See Ceridian Corporation; U.S. Public, pg. 331
EASAMS (AUSTRALIA) LTD.—See The General Electric Company, p.l.c.; Int'l, pg. 543
EASAMS LTD.—See The General Electric Company, p.l.c.; Int'l, pg. 543
EASAMS SYSTEMS ENGINEERING GMBH—See The General Electric Company; Int'l, pg. 543
EB5 CORPORATION; U.S. Private, pg. 353
EB INSTALLASJON A/S—See ABB Åsea Brown Boveri (Holding) Ltd.; Int'l, pg. 3
EBC ECZACIBASI-BEIERSDORF—See Beiersdorf Group; Int'l, pg. 183
EBC AMRO BANK LTD.—See ABN-AMRO Holding N.V.; Int'l, pg. 10
E/B/D/INTERPARTNERS—See Warwick Baker O'Neill; U.S. Private, pg. 1152
E/B/D-INTERPARTNERS BUDAPEST KFT—See Warwick Baker O'Neill; U.S. Private, pg. 1152
E/B/D/INTERPARTNERS - MOSCOW GMBH—See Warwick Baker O'Neill; U.S. Private, pg. 1152
E/B/D/INTERPARTNERS WARSZAWA—See Warwick Baker O'Neill; U.S. Private, pg. 1152
EBE EDELSTAHL-BAUELEMENTE GMBH—See Fried. Krupp AG; Int'l, pg. 508
EBEWE ARZNEIMITTEL GES.M.B.H.—See BASF AG; Int'l, pg. 108
EBG VERLAGS GMBH—See Bertelsmann AG; Int'l, pg. 190
EBI/AOA DIVISION—See Biomet, Inc.; U.S. Public, pg. 231
EBI CONSULTING SERVICES, INC.—See Orion Capital Corporation; U.S. Public, pg. 1231
E.B.I. FOODS LTD.—See Dean Foods Company; U.S. Public, pg. 491
EBI INDEMNITY COMPANY—See Orion Capital Corporation; U.S. Public, pg. 1231
EBI MEDICAL SYSTEMS, INC.—See Biomet, Inc.; U.S. Public, pg. 231
EBP LIFE INSURNACE CO.—See First Health Group Corp.; U.S. Public, pg. 635
EC ERDOLCHEMIE GMBH—See Bayer AG; Int'l, pg. 172
EC III—See EG & G, Inc.; U.S. Public, pg. 543
E.C.B. BROKERAGE—See E.C. Barton & Company; U.S. Private, pg. 119
ECC FINANCIAL GROUP—See Eaton Corporation; U.S. Public, pg. 558
ECC INTERNATIONAL INC.—See English China Clays Plc; Int'l, pg. 455
ECC INTERNATIONAL LTD.—See English China Clays Plc; Int'l, pg. 455
ECC OVERSEAS INVESTMENTS LIMITED—See English China Clays Plc; Int'l, pg. 455
ECCI EUROPE—See English China Clays Plc; Int'l, pg. 455
E.C.D., INC.; U.S. Private, pg. 353
E.C.E. DISTRIBUTION SERVICES—See Franz Haniel & Cie, GmbH; Int'l, pg. 591
ECI TELECOM AMERICAS INC.—See IDB Holding Corporation; Int'l, pg. 643
ECI TELECOM (ARGENTINA)—See IDB Holding Corporation; Int'l, pg. 643
ECI TELECOM CHINA—See IDB Holding Corporation; Int'l, pg. 643
ECI TELECOM GMBH—See IDB Holding Corporation; Int'l, pg. 643
ECI TELECOM (HK) LTD.—See IDB Holding Corporation; Int'l, pg. 643
ECI TELECOM INC.—See IDB Holding Corporation; Int'l, pg. 643
ECI TELECOM LTD.—See IDB Holding Corporation; Int'l, pg. 643
ECI TELECOM LTD.-ISRAEL—See IDB Holding Corporation; Int'l, pg. 643
ECI TELECOM (PHILIPPINES) LTD.—See IDB Holding Corporation; Int'l, pg. 643
ECI TELECOM (SINGAPORE)—See IDB Holding Corporation; Int'l, pg. 643
ECI TELECOM (UK) LIMITED—See IDB Holding Corporation; Int'l, pg. 644
ECI TELEMATICS INTERNATIONAL S.A.—See IDB Holding Corporation; Int'l, pg. 644
ECI TELEMATICS SARL—See IDB Holding Corporation; Int'l, pg. 644
ECIA-EQUIPMENTS ET COMPOSANTS POUR L'INDUSTRIE AUTOMOBILE—See PSA Peugeot Citroen; Int'l, pg. 1021
E.C.L.—See Pechiney S.A.; Int'l, pg. 1028
ECO KUNSTOFF GMBH—See Eldon AB; Int'l, pg. 436
ECO, YOUNG & RUBICAM S.A.—See Young & Rubicam Inc.; U.S. Private, pg. 1200
ECO RESOURCES, INC.—See Southwest Water Company; U.S. Public, pg. 1494
ECP - ENICHEM POLYMERS NETHERLANDS B.V.—See ENI S.p.A.; Int'l, pg. 429
ECP INCORPORATED—See Daubert Industries, Inc.; U.S. Private, pg. 313
ECRM; U.S. Private, pg. 353
ECW, INC.—See The Dow Chemical Company; U.S. Public, pg. 523
EDA—See Vendex International N.V.; Int'l, pg. 1463
EDC EUROPEAN EXCAVATOR DESIGN CENTER GMBH & CO. KG—See Caterpillar Inc.; U.S. Public, pg. 315
EDC EUROPEAN EXCAVATOR DESIGN CENTER VERWALTUNGS GMBH—See Caterpillar Inc.; U.S. Public, pg. 315
EDD-ATLANTA—See Bell Industries, Inc.; U.S. Public, pg. 204

EDD-BELLEVUE—See Bell Industries, Inc.; U.S. Public, pg. 204
EDD-BOSTON—See Bell Industries, Inc.; U.S. Public, pg. 204
EDD-CHICAGO—See Bell Industries, Inc.; U.S. Public, pg. 204
EDD-CLEVELAND - See Bell Industries, Inc.; U.S. Public, pg. 204
EDD-DALLAS—See Bell Industries, Inc.; U.S. Public, pg. 204
EDD-DAYTON—See Bell Industries, Inc.; U.S. Public, pg. 205
EDD-DAYTON GOVERNMENT—See Bell Industries, Inc.; U.S. Public, pg. 205
EDD-DENVER—See Bell Industries, Inc.; U.S. Public, pg. 205
EDD-FLORIDA—See Bell Industries, Inc.; U.S. Public, pg. 205
EDD-FT. WAYNE—See Bell Industries, Inc.; U.S. Public, pg. 205
EDD-HOUSTON—See Bell Industries, Inc.; U.S. Public, pg. 205
EDD-HUNTSVILLE—See Bell Industries, Inc.; U.S. Public, pg. 205
EDD-INDIANAPOLIS—See Bell Industries, Inc.; U.S. Public, pg. 205
EDD-LONG ISLAND—See Bell Industries, Inc.; U.S. Public, pg. 205
EDD-MARYLAND—See Bell Industries, Inc.; U.S. Public, pg. 205
EDD-MILWAUKEE—See Bell Industries, Inc.; U.S. Public, pg. 205
EDD-MINNESOTA—See Bell Industries, Inc.; U.S. Public, pg. 205
EDD-NEW JERSEY—See Bell Industries, Inc.; U.S. Public, pg. 205
EDD-NORTH CAROLINA—See Bell Industries, Inc.; U.S. Public, pg. 205
EDD-ORANGE COUNTY—See Bell Industries, Inc.; U.S. Public, pg. 205
EDD-PHILADELPHIA—See Bell Industries, Inc.; U.S. Public, pg. 205
EDD-PHOENIX—See Bell Industries, Inc.; U.S. Public, pg. 205
EDD-PORTLAND—See Bell Industries, Inc.; U.S. Public, pg. 205
EDD-SACRAMENTO—See Bell Industries, Inc.; U.S. Public, pg. 205
EDD-SALT LAKE CITY—See Bell Industries, Inc.; U.S. Public, pg. 205
EDD-SAN DIEGO—See Bell Industries, Inc.; U.S. Public, pg. 205
EDD-SUNNYVALE—See Bell Industries, Inc.; U.S. Public, pg. 205
EDD-VENTURA—See Bell Industries, Inc.; U.S. Public, pg. 205
EDE – EMBRAER EQUIPMENT DIVISION—See Embraer-Empresa Brasileira de Aeronautica S.A.; Int'l, pg. 452
EDF INTERNATIONAL NORTH AMERICA, INC.—See Electricite de France; Int'l, pg. 437
EDI—See Vendex International N.V.; Int'l, pg. 1463
EDI INTERNATIONAL, INC.; U.S. Private, pg. 353
EDI II—See Lagardere Groupe; Int'l, pg. 792
E.D.I.C.E.F.—See Lagardere Groupe; Int'l, pg. 792
EDL INDUSTRIES LTD.—See Luxo A/S; Int'l, pg. 821
EDO ACOUSTIC PRODUCTS—See EDO Corporation; U.S. Public, pg. 542
EDO CERAMICS—See EDO Corporation; U.S. Public, pg. 542
EDO COMBAT SYSTEMS—See EDO Corporation; U.S. Public, pg. 542
EDO CORPORATION; U.S. Public, pg. 541
EDO FIBER SCIENCE—See EDO Corporation; U.S. Public, pg. 542
EDO INDUSTRIAL PRODUCTS DIVISION—See EDO Corporation; U.S. Public, pg. 542
EDO MARINE & AIRCRAFT SYSTEMS—See EDO Corporation; U.S. Public, pg. 542
EDO MARINE AND AIRCRAFT SYSTEMS—See EDO Corporation; U.S. Public, pg. 542
EDO WASHINGTON OFFICE—See EDO Corporation; U.S. Public, pg. 542
EDP/TEMPS INC.—See Technical Aid Corporation; U.S. Private, pg. 1072
EDS, BUSINESS OPERATIONS GROUP—See Electronic Data Systems Corporation; U.S. Public, pg. 570
EDS FIDES—See Electronic Data Systems Corporation; U.S. Public, pg. 570
EDS, FINANCIAL AND INSURANCE GROUP—See Electronic Data Systems Corporation; U.S. Public, pg. 570
EDS, GOVERNMENT SYSTEMS GROUP—See Electronic Data Systems Corporation; U.S. Public, pg. 570
EDS, INTERNATIONAL, COMMERCIAL AND COMMUNICATIONS GROUPS—See Electronic Data Systems Corporation; U.S. Public, pg. 570
EDS OF CANADA LTD.—See Electronic Data Systems Corporation; U.S. Public, pg. 570
EDS (SWITZERLAND) LTD.—See Electronic Data Systems Corporation; U.S. Public, pg. 570
EECO, SWITCH—See Transico Incorporated; U.S. Public, pg. 1631
EEI-AUSTRALIA—See BTR plc; Int'l, pg. 126
EEI-CONSTRUCTION DIV.—See EEI Corporation; Int'l, pg. 426
EEI-CONSTRUCTION FABRICATION SHOP—See EEI Corporation; Int'l, pg. 426
EEI CORPORATION; Int'l, pg. 425
EEI LIMITED—See EEI Corporation; Int'l, pg. 426
EEI-MACHINERY DIVISION—See EEI Corporation; Int'l, pg. 426
EEI-MACHINERY DIVISION (CEBU REGIONAL OFFICE)—See EEI Corporation; Int'l, pg. 426
EEI-MARINE CORP.—See EEI Corporation; Int'l, pg. 426

Company Index

EEI POWER CORP.—See EEI Corporation; *Int'l*, pg. 426
EEI-TOEI ANIMATION CORPORATION—See EEI Corporation; *Int'l*, pg. 426
EES - ERDGAS-ENERGIESYSTEME GMBH—See Ruhrgas Aktiengesellschaft; *Int'l*, pg. 1148
EEV LTD.—See The General Electric Company, p.l.c.; *Int'l*, pg. 543
EEX CORPORATION; *U.S. Public*, pg. 542
EF DATA CORP.—See California Microwave, Inc.; *U.S. Public*, pg. 293
EFC PROPERTY MANAGEMENT, INC.—See Orion Capital Corporation; *U.S. Public*, pg. 1231
EFCO CORPORATION; *U.S. Private*, pg. 353
EFCO INC.; *U.S. Private*, pg. 353
EFEKA FRIEDRICH & KAUFMANN GMBH & CO.—See American Home Products Corporation; *Int'l*, pg. 81
EFG TECHNOLOGIES INC.—See United Insurance Companies, Inc.; *U.S. Public*, pg. 1679
EFI CORPORATION—See Racal Electronics Plc; *Int'l*, pg. 1082
EFI DIVISION—See Dynamic Materials Corporation; *U.S. Public*, pg. 539
EFS/SAN DIEGO SERVICE CORPORATION—See St. Paul Bancorp, Inc.; *U.S. Public*, pg. 1428
EFS SERVICE CORPORATION—See St. Paul Bancorp, Inc.; *U.S. Public*, pg. 1428
EG & G AEROSPACE & ENGINEERED PRODUCTS—See EG & G, Inc.; *U.S. Public*, pg. 542
EG & G ASTROPHYSICS—See EG & G, Inc.; *U.S. Public*, pg. 543
EG & G AUTOMOTIVE RESEARCH—See EG & G, Inc.; *U.S. Public*, pg. 544
EG & G BERTHOLD (HQ)—See EG & G, Inc.; *U.S. Public*, pg. 544
EG & G CANADA LIMITED INSTRUMENTS DIVISION—See EG & G, Inc.; *U.S. Public*, pg. 544
EG & G CANADA, LTD. OPTOELECTRONICS—See EG & G, Inc.; *U.S. Public*, pg. 544
EG & G CHINA REPRESENTATIVE OFFICE—See EG & G, Inc.; *U.S. Public*, pg. 544
EG & G DEFENSE MATERIALS DIVISION—See EG & G, Inc.; *U.S. Public*, pg. 543
EG & G DYNATREND—See EG & G, Inc.; *U.S. Public*, pg. 544
EG & G ENVIRONMENTAL, INC.—See EG & G, Inc.; *U.S. Public*, pg. 543
EG & G FIBER OPTICS—See EG & G, Inc.; *U.S. Public*, pg. 543
EG & G FLORIDA—See EG & G, Inc.; *U.S. Public*, pg. 544
EG & G FRANK HILL ASSOCIATES—See EG & G, Inc.; *U.S. Public*, pg. 543
EG & G GMBH INSTRUMENTS DIVISION—See EG & G, Inc.; *U.S. Public*, pg. 544
EG & G GMBH SEALOL—See EG & G, Inc.; *U.S. Public*, pg. 544
EG & G HEIMANN OPTO. GMBH—See EG & G, Inc.; *U.S. Public*, pg. 544
EG & G, INC.; *U.S. Public*, pg. 542
EG & G INSTRUMENTS—See EG & G, Inc.; *U.S. Public*, pg. 543
EG & G INSTRUMENTS APPLIED RESEARCH—See EG & G, Inc.; *U.S. Public*, pg. 543
EG & G INSTRUMENTS-PROCESS MEASUREMENTS/CHANDLER—See EG & G, Inc.; *U.S. Public*, pg. 543
EG & G IRELAND, INSTRUMENTS DIVISION—See EG & G, Inc.; *U.S. Public*, pg. 544
EG & G JAPAN—See EG & G, Inc.; *U.S. Public*, pg. 544
EG & G KT AEROFAB—See EG & G, Inc.; *U.S. Public*, pg. 542
EG & G MANAGEMENT SYSTEMS—See EG & G, Inc.; *U.S. Public*, pg. 543
EG & G MANAGEMENT SYSTEMS INC.- ALBUQUERQUE OPERATIONS—See EG & G, Inc.; *U.S. Public*, pg. 543
EG & G MISSOURI METALS—See EG & G, Inc.; *U.S. Public*, pg. 544
EG & G MOUND APPLIED TECHNOLOGIES—See EG & G, Inc.; *U.S. Public*, pg. 543
EG & G OPTOELECTRONICS-COVINA—See EG & G, Inc.; *U.S. Public*, pg. 543
EG & G OPTOELECTRONICS MONTGOMERYVILLE—See EG & G, Inc.; *U.S. Public*, pg. 543
EG & G OPTOELECTRONICS RETICON—See EG & G, Inc.; *U.S. Public*, pg. 543
EG & G OPTOELECTRONICS-ST. LOUIS—See EG & G, Inc.; *U.S. Public*, pg. 543
EG & G OPTOELECTRONICS-SALEM—See EG & G, Inc.; *U.S. Public*, pg. 543
EG & G ORTEC—See EG & G, Inc.; *U.S. Public*, pg. 543
EG & G RETICON—See EG & G, Inc.; *U.S. Public*, pg. 544
EG & G ROTRON—See EG & G, Inc.; *U.S. Public*, pg. 543
EG & G ROTRON INDUSTRIAL DIVISION—See EG & G, Inc.; *U.S. Public*, pg. 543
EG & G SEALOL-CALLISTO S.A.—See EG & G, Inc.; *U.S. Public*, pg. 544
EG & G SEALOL EAGLE—See EG & G, Inc.; *U.S. Public*, pg. 544
EG & G SEALOL ENGINEERED PRODUCTS DIVISION—See EG & G, Inc.; *U.S. Public*, pg. 542
EG & G SEALOL INC.—See EG & G, Inc.; *U.S. Public*, pg. 544
EG & G SEALOL-INDUSTRIAL DIVISION—See EG & G, Inc.; *U.S. Public*, pg. 543
EG & G SERVICES INFORMATION TECHNOLOGIES—See EG & G, Inc.; *U.S. Public*, pg. 544
EG & G S.P.A. INSTRUMENTS DIVISION—See EG & G, Inc.; *U.S. Public*, pg. 544
EG & G SPECIAL PROJECTS—See EG & G, Inc.; *U.S. Public*, pg. 543
EG & G STRUCTURAL KINEMATICS—See EG & G, Inc.; *U.S. Public*, pg. 544
EG & G TECHNICAL SERVICES OF WEST VIRGINIA—See EG & G, Inc.; *U.S. Public*, pg. 543

EG & G VENTURE MANAGEMENT—See EG & G, Inc.; *U.S. Public*, pg. 544
EG & G WALLAC OY—See EG & G, Inc.; *U.S. Public*, pg. 544
EG & G WRIGHT COMPONENTS—See EG & G, Inc.; *U.S. Public*, pg. 542
EGA—See Eldon AB; *Int'l*, pg. 436
EGE FERRO KIMYA SANAYI VE TICARRET—See Ferro Corporation; *Int'l*, pg. 619
EGT—See Lagardere Groupe; *Int'l*, pg. 795
EI ENERGY, INC.—See GPU, Inc.; *U.S. Public*, pg. 695
EI POWER, INC.—See GPU, Inc.; *U.S. Public*, pg. 695
EIB ATHENS BRANCH—See European Investment Bank; *Int'l*, pg. 465
EIB BRUSSELS BRANCH—See European Investment Bank; *Int'l*, pg. 465
EIB LISBON BRANCH—See European Investment Bank; *Int'l*, pg. 465
EIB MADRID BRANCH—See European Investment Bank; *Int'l*, pg. 465
EIB ROME BRANCH—See European Investment Bank; *Int'l*, pg. 465
EIBA—See Union Bank of Switzerland; *Int'l*, pg. 1440
EIJ IMTECH NV—See Internatio-Muller N.V.; *Int'l*, pg. 681
EIJ IMTECH N.V.—See Internatio-Muller N.V.; *Int'l*, pg. 682
EIP GROUP PLC; *Int'l*, pg. 426
EIP METALS LIMITED—See EIP Group plc; *Int'l*, pg. 426
EIS BRAKE MANUFACTURING, LTD.—See Standard Motor Products Inc.; *U.S. Public*, pg. 1503
EIS BRAKE PARTS DIV.—See Standard Motor Products Inc.; *U.S. Public*, pg. 1503
EIS GROUP PLC; *Int'l*, pg. 426
EIS, INC.—See Electrical Insulation Suppliers; *U.S. Private*, pg. 368
EIS INTERNATIONAL INC.; *U.S. Public*, pg. 544
E.J. FOOTWEAR CORP.—See U.S. Industries, Inc.; *U.S. Public*, pg. 1684
EJC SECOMA AFRICA LTD.—See Tamrock Corp.; *Int'l*, pg. 1353
EJL ADVERTISING/CHICAGO—See Lois/EJL Los Angeles; *U.S. Private*, pg. 673
EJL ADVERTISING/HOUSTON—See Lois/EJL Los Angeles; *U.S. Private*, pg. 673
EJL ADVERTISING/LOS ANGELES—See Lois/EJL Los Angeles; *U.S. Private*, pg. 673
EJP CORPORATION—See Promus Hotel Corporation; *U.S. Public*, pg. 1335
EKA NOBEL AB—See Akzo Nobel N.V.; *Int'l*, pg. 48
EKC TECHNOLOGY, INC.—See ChemFirst Inc.; *U.S. Public*, pg. 344
EKCO CLEANING, INC.—See Ekco Group, Inc.; *U.S. Public*, pg. 566
EKN BANK IN NIDWALDEN—See Union Bank of Switzerland; *Int'l*, pg. 1440
ELA MEDICAL INC.—See L'Oreal S.A.; *Int'l*, pg. 818
ELCO INSURANCE COMPANY LTD.—See Eli Lilly and Company; *U.S. Public*, pg. 993
ELCO MANAGEMENT CORPORATION—See Eli Lilly and Company; *U.S. Public*, pg. 993
ELE INTERNATIONAL, INC./SOILTEST—See South West Water PLC; *Int'l*, pg. 1287
ELECBRO - TERMOELECTRICA DEL EBRO, S.A.—See SEPI; *Int'l*, pg. 1224
ELG HANIEL GMBH—See Franz Haniel & Cie, GmbH; *Int'l*, pg. 591
ELM COMPUTER TECHNOLOGIES LIMITED—See CSA Holdings Ltd.; *Int'l*, pg. 243
ELX GROUP—See Electrolux, AB; *Int'l*, pg. 439
ELXSI CORPORATION; *U.S. Public*, pg. 545
EM MICROELECTRONIC-MARIN S.A.—See SMH Swiss Corporation for Micro Electronics & Watchmaking Indus. Ltd.; *Int'l*, pg. 1160
E.M.A.—See Hewlett-Packard Company; *U.S. Public*, pg. 817
EMA PUBLIC RELATIONS SERVICES, INC.—See Eric Mower and Associates, Inc.; *U.S. Private*, pg. 765
EMAB CANADA DIV.—See Electrolux, AB; *Int'l*, pg. 441
EMAP IMAGES—See EMAP Plc; *Int'l*, pg. 451
EMAP METRO—See EMAP Plc; *Int'l*, pg. 451
EMAP NATIONALS—See EMAP Plc; *Int'l*, pg. 451
EMAP RESPONSE LTD.—See EMAP Plc; *Int'l*, pg. 451
EMC-BELGIQUE—See Entreprise Miniere et Chimique; *Int'l*, pg. 459
EMC COMPUTER SYSTEMS—See EMC Corporation; *U.S. Public*, pg. 545
EMC CORPORATION; *U.S. Public*, pg. 545
EMC INSURANCE COMPANIES—See EMC Insurance Group, Inc.; *U.S. Public*, pg. 545
EMC INSURANCE GROUP, INC.; *U.S. Public*, pg. 545
EMC TEST SYSTEM, L.P.—See ESCO Electronics Corporation; *U.S. Public*, pg. 546
EME-NORLETT AB—See Electrolux, AB; *Int'l*, pg. 438
EMG EISEN-UND METALLGUSSWERK GMBH—See Deutsche Babcock AG; *Int'l*, pg. 400
EMI AUSTRIA GESMBH—See EMI Group plc; *Int'l*, pg. 427
EMI BELGIUM SA—See EMI Group plc; *Int'l*, pg. 427
EMI CAPITOL DE MEXICO SA DE CV—See EMI Group plc; *Int'l*, pg. 427
EMI COMPACT DISC (HOLLAND) BV—See EMI Group plc; *Int'l*, pg. 427
EMI ELECTROLA GMBH—See EMI Group plc; *Int'l*, pg. 427
OY EMI FINLAND AB—See EMI Group plc; *Int'l*, pg. 427
EMI FRANCE—See EMI Group plc; *Int'l*, pg. 427
EMI GROUP PLC; *Int'l*, pg. 426
EMI (HONG KONG) LTD.—See EMI Group plc; *Int'l*, pg. 427
EMI ITALIANA SPA—See EMI Group plc; *Int'l*, pg. 427
EMI (MALAYSIA) SDN BHD—See EMI Group plc; *Int'l*, pg. 428
EMI-MANHATTAN RECORDS—See EMI Group plc; *Int'l*, pg. 427
EMI-MEDLEY—See EMI Group plc; *Int'l*, pg. 427
EMI MUSIC—See EMI Group plc; *Int'l*, pg. 427

EMI MUSIC AUSTRALIA—See EMI Group plc; *Int'l*, pg. 427
EMI MUSIC GROUP—See EMI Group plc; *Int'l*, pg. 427
EMI MUSIC HOLLAND BV—See EMI Group plc; *Int'l*, pg. 427
EMI MUSIC INTERNATIONAL SERVICES LTD.—See EMI Group plc; *Int'l*, pg. 427
EMI MUSIC PUBLISHING—See EMI Group plc; *Int'l*, pg. 427
EMI MUSIC PUBLISHING (BELGIUM) SA—See EMI Group plc; *Int'l*, pg. 427
EMI MUSIC PUBLISHING (HOLLAND) B.V.—See EMI Group plc; *Int'l*, pg. 427
EMI MUSIC PUBLISHING (SWEDEN) AB—See EMI Group plc; *Int'l*, pg. 427
EMI MUSIC SOUTH AFRICA (PTY) LTD.—See EMI Group plc; *Int'l*, pg. 427
EMI (NEW ZEALAND) LTD.—See EMI Group plc; *Int'l*, pg. 427
EMI NORSK A/S—See EMI Group plc; *Int'l*, pg. 427
EMI ODEON CHILENA SA—See EMI Group plc; *Int'l*, pg. 427
EMI-ODEON SAIC—See EMI Group plc; *Int'l*, pg. 427
EMI RECORDS (INTERTON) AG—See EMI Group plc; *Int'l*, pg. 427
EMI RECORDS (IRELAND) LTD.—See EMI Group plc; *Int'l*, pg. 427
EMI RECORDS (SWITZERLAND) AG—See EMI Group plc; *Int'l*, pg. 427
EMI RECORDS (UK)—See EMI Group plc; *Int'l*, pg. 427
EMI RECORDS (UK), STUDIOS DIV.—See EMI Group plc; *Int'l*, pg. 427
EMI (SINGAPORE) PTE LTD.—See EMI Group plc; *Int'l*, pg. 427
EMI SVENSKA AB—See EMI Group plc; *Int'l*, pg. 427
EMI (THAILAND) LIMITED/AUDIOVISION LIMITED—See EMI Group plc; *Int'l*, pg. 427
E.M.I. TRAVEL CENTER, INC.—See Encore Marketing International, Inc.; *U.S. Public*, pg. 580
EMI-VALENTINI DE CARVALHO MUSICA LDA.—See EMI Group plc; *Int'l*, pg. 427
EMPI, INC.; *U.S. Public*, pg. 545
EMS ASIA PACIFIC—See Effective Management Systems; *U.S. Public*, pg. 566
EMS CENTRAL REGIONAL OFFICE (CORPORATE)—See Effective Management Systems; *U.S. Public*, pg. 565
EMS CHINA LIMITED—See Effective Management Systems; *U.S. Public*, pg. 566
EMS EASTERN REGIONAL OFFICE—See Effective Management Systems; *U.S. Public*, pg. 565
EMS-ILLINOIS—See Effective Management Systems; *U.S. Public*, pg. 565
EMS KURIERPOST GMBH—See Deutsche Post AG; *Int'l*, pg. 407
EMS SOUTHWEST REGION OFFICE—See Effective Management Systems; *U.S. Public*, pg. 565
EMS-TOGO—See Novartis AG; *Int'l*, pg. 981
EMS-WEST—See Effective Management Systems; *U.S. Public*, pg. 565
E.N. BAZAN DE CONSTRUCCIONES NAVALES MILITARES, S.A.—See SEPI; *Int'l*, pg. 1224
ENA LINE LIMITED—See Stena Line AB; *Int'l*, pg. 1300
E.N.C.—See Kellwood Company; *U.S. Public*, pg. 948
ENCASUR - E.N. CARBONIFERA DEL SUR, S.A.—See SEPI; *Int'l*, pg. 1224
ENCE - E.N. DE CELULOSAS, S.A.—See SEPI; *Int'l*, pg. 605
ENCI NEDERLAND B.V.—See Heidelberger Zement A.G.; *Int'l*, pg. 605
ENCI N.V.—See Heidelberger Zement A.G.; *Int'l*, pg. 605
ENDESA - EMPRESA NACIONAL DE ELECTRICIDAD, S.A.—See SEPI; *Int'l*, pg. 1224
ENGY, INC.—See EVI, Inc.; *U.S. Public*, pg. 547
ENHER - E.N. HIDROELECTRICA DEL RIBAGORZANA, S.A.—See SEPI; *Int'l*, pg. 1224
ENI; *U.S. Private*, pg. 354
ENI GAS SERVICES, INC.—See CTG Resources, Inc.; *U.S. Public*, pg. 285
ENI INTERNATIONAL HOLDING—See ENI S.p.A.; *Int'l*, pg. 429
ENI POWER SYSTEMS—See Emerson Electric Co.; *U.S. Public*, pg. 574
ENI S.P.A.; *Int'l*, pg. 428
ENPAC—See Essef Corporation; *U.S. Public*, pg. 592
ENS GROUP—See Alcatel Alsthom Compagnie Generale D'Electricite; *Int'l*, pg. 52
ENSA - EQUIPOS NUCLEARES, S.A.—See SEPI; *Int'l*, pg. 1224
ENSI, INC.—See ERD Waste Corp.; *U.S. Public*, pg. 546
ENSR; *U.S. Private*, pg. 354
ENUSA - E.N. DEL URANIO, S.A.—See SEPI; *Int'l*, pg. 1224
ENV SERVICES, INC.—See Donaldson Company, Inc.; *U.S. Public*, pg. 517
EOC FORMSYSTEM GMBH—See Anchor Lamina Inc.; *Int'l*, pg. 75
EOC FRANCE SARL—See Anchor Lamina Inc.; *Int'l*, pg. 75
EOC NORMALIEN AUSTRALIA PTY. LTD.—See Anchor Lamina Inc.; *Int'l*, pg. 75
EOC NORMALIEN BELGIUM N.V./S.A.—See Anchor Lamina Inc.; *Int'l*, pg. 75
EOC NORMALIEN GMBH & CO. KG—See Anchor Lamina Inc.; *Int'l*, pg. 75
EOC NORMALIEN (IRL) LTD.—See Anchor Lamina Inc.; *Int'l*, pg. 75
EOC NORMALIEN PRAHA S.R.O.—See Anchor Lamina Inc.; *Int'l*, pg. 75
EOC NORMALIEN PRODUKTIONS UND VERTRIEBS GMBH—See Anchor Lamina Inc.; *Int'l*, pg. 75
EOC NORMALIEN UND VERWALTUNGSGESELLSCHAFT MBH—See Anchor Lamina Inc.; *Int'l*, pg. 75
EOS GMBH ELECTRO OPTICAL SYSTEMS—See Carl-Zeiss-Stiftung; *Int'l*, pg. 1523
E.P. GRAPHICS, INC.; *U.S. Private*, pg. 354

MASTER INDEX TO COMPANY NAMES EAGLE

Company Index

EPAM CORPORATION—See Promus Hotel Corporation; *U.S. Public*, pg. 1335
EPCO, INC.—See Kvaerner a.s.a.; *Int'l*, pg. 773
EPEX GROUP—See Alcatel Alsthom Compagnie Generale D'Electricite; *Int'l*, pg. 52
EPFSA—See Lagardere Groupe; *Int'l*, pg. 795
EPG/TBWA—See TBWA Chiat/Day; *U.S. Private*, pg. 1062
E.P.I.—See Bouygues; *Int'l*, pg. 206
EPI/CLEVELAND—See Engineered Products, Inc.; *U.S. Private*, pg. 376
EPI WALL SYSTEMS—See Engineered Products, Inc.; *U.S. Private*, pg. 376
EPIC, INC.—See Masco Corporation; *U.S. Public*, pg. 1053
EPL PLANT & ACCESS—See John Laing PLC; *Int'l*, pg. 796
EPPC POLYPLASTIC S.A.—See The B.F. Goodrich Company; *U.S. Public*, pg. 752
EPS/ENTERTAINMENT PROGRAMMING SERVICES LTD.—See Sony Corporation; *Int'l*, pg. 1282
EPX; *U.S. Private*, pg. 354
EQE INTERNATIONAL; *U.S. Private*, pg. 354
ER-ELECTRIC A/S—See ABB Asea Brown Boveri (Holding) Ltd.; *Int'l*, pg. 3
ER-WE-PA USA LTD.—See Klockner-Werke AG; *Int'l*, pg. 737
ERA AVIATION, INC.—See Rowan Companies, Inc.; *U.S. Public*, pg. 1410
ERA RANGER MINE—See North Limited; *Int'l*, pg. 967
ERA REAL ESTATE—See Cendant Corporation; *U.S. Public*, pg. 321
ERAG ELEKTRIZITATSWERK RHEINAU AG—See Alusuisse-Lonza Holding Ltd.; *Int'l*, pg. 67
ERD ENVIRONMENTAL, INC.—See ERD Waste Corp.; *U.S. Public*, pg. 546
ERD WASTE CORP.; *U.S. Public*, pg. 546
ERE P DIVISION—See Alcatel Alsthom Compagnie Generale D'Electricite; *Int'l*, pg. 52
ERE T DIVISION—See Alcatel Alsthom Compagnie Generale D'Electricite; *Int'l*, pg. 52
ERI LABORATORIES—See Inverness Corp.; *U.S. Private*, pg. 574
ERI REALTY, INC.—See Equitable Resources, Inc.; *U.S. Public*, pg. 589
ERI SERVICES—See Equitable Resources, Inc.; *U.S. Public*, pg. 589
ERJ INSURANCE GROUP—See American Heritage Life Investment Corp.; *U.S. Public*, pg. 79
ERM-ENVIROCLEAN—See Environmental Resources Management; *U.S. Private*, pg. 379
ERO, INC.—See Hicks, Muse, Tate & Furst Inc.; *U.S. Private*, pg. 526
ERO INDUSTRIES, INC.—See Hicks, Muse, Tate & Furst Inc.; *U.S. Private*, pg. 526
ERZ - ELECTRICAS REUNIDAS DE ZARAGOZA, S.A.—See SEPI; *Int'l*, pg. 1224
ES+ES VERPAKKINGEN B.V.—See Royal Packaging Industries Van Leer B.V.; *Int'l*, pg. 1146
ESA, INC.; *U.S. Private*, pg. 354
ESA LABORATORIES—See ESA, Inc.; *U.S. Private*, pg. 354
ESA PORTUGAL—See Accor S.A.; *Int'l*, pg. 21
AS ESAB—See Charter plc; *Int'l*, pg. 281
ESAB AB—See Charter plc; *Int'l*, pg. 281
ESAB AG—See Charter plc; *Int'l*, pg. 282
ESAB A/S—See Charter plc; *Int'l*, pg. 282
ESAB ASIA/PACIFIC PTE LTD.—See Charter plc; *Int'l*, pg. 282
ESAB AUSTRALIA PTY. LTD.—See Charter plc; *Int'l*, pg. 282
ESAB AUTOMATION LTD.—See Charter plc; *Int'l*, pg. 282
ESAB BUREAU DE LIAISON—See Charter plc; *Int'l*, pg. 282
ESAB CONSUMABLES—See Charter plc; *Int'l*, pg. 281
ESAB-CSEPEL KFT—See Charter plc; *Int'l*, pg. 282
ESAB EGYPT—See Charter plc; *Int'l*, pg. 282
ESAB EQUIPMENT/AUTOMATION—See Charter plc; *Int'l*, pg. 281
ESAB FAR EAST REPRESENTATIVE OFFICE—See Charter plc; *Int'l*, pg. 282
ESAB FRANCE S.A.—See Charter plc; *Int'l*, pg. 282
ESAB GES.M.B.H—See Charter plc; *Int'l*, pg. 282
ESAB GMBH—See Charter plc; *Int'l*, pg. 282
ESAB GROUP CANADA, INC.—See Charter plc; *Int'l*, pg. 282
THE ESAB GROUP, INC.—See Charter plc; *Int'l*, pg. 281
ESAB GROUP (UK) LTD.—See Charter plc; *Int'l*, pg. 282
ESAB-HANCOCK GMBH—See Charter plc; *Int'l*, pg. 282
ESAB HOLDING S.P.A.—See Charter plc; *Int'l*, pg. 282
ESAB IBERICA S.A.—See Charter plc; *Int'l*, pg. 282
ESAB INDIA LTD.—See Charter plc; *Int'l*, pg. 282
ESAB INTERNATIONAL AB—See Charter plc; *Int'l*, pg. 281
ESAB INTERNATIONAL HOLDING B.V.—See Charter plc; *Int'l*, pg. 282
ESAB KFT—See Charter plc; *Int'l*, pg. 282
ESAB LDA.—See Charter plc; *Int'l*, pg. 282
ESAB (MALAYSIA) SDN, BHD—See Charter plc; *Int'l*, pg. 282
ESAB MIDDLE EAST—See Charter plc; *Int'l*, pg. 282
ESAB NEDERLAND B.V.—See Charter plc; *Int'l*, pg. 282
S.A. ESAB N.V.—See Charter plc; *Int'l*, pg. 282
ESAB OY—See Charter plc; *Int'l*, pg. 282
ESAB PRZEDSTAWICIELSTWO W. POLSCE—See Charter plc; *Int'l*, pg. 282
ESAB REPRESENTATIVE OFFICE—See Charter plc; *Int'l*, pg. 282
ESAB S.A. INDUSTRIA E COMERCIO—See Charter plc; *Int'l*, pg. 282
ESAB SALDATURA S.P.A.—See Charter plc; *Int'l*, pg. 282
ESAB SINGAPORE PTE. LTD.—See Charter plc; *Int'l*, pg. 282
ESAB SOLDADURA S.A.—See Charter plc; *Int'l*, pg. 282
ESAB S.R.O.—See Charter plc; *Int'l*, pg. 282
ESAB SVERIGE AB—See Charter plc; *Int'l*, pg. 281
ESAB TECH AB—See Charter plc; *Int'l*, pg. 281
ESAB TELE-COMP AB—See Charter plc; *Int'l*, pg. 281
ESAB (THAILAND) LTD.—See Charter plc; *Int'l*, pg. 282
ESAB TREASURY AB—See Charter plc; *Int'l*, pg. 281
ESAB VAMBERK A.S.—See Charter plc; *Int'l*, pg. 282
ESAB WELDING & CUTTING PRODUCTS—See Charter plc; *Int'l*, pg. 281
ESAB WELDING EQUIPMENT AB—See Charter plc; *Int'l*, pg. 281
ESC MEDICAL SYSTEMS LTD.; *Int'l*, pg. 429
ESCO ELECTRONICS CORPORATION; *U.S. Public*, pg. 546
ESH NETHERLANDS HOLDING B.V.—See Ebara Corporation; *Int'l*, pg. 432
ESI-AIR, INC.—See Harrah's Entertainment, Inc.; *U.S. Public*, pg. 790
ESI ENERGY, INC.—See FPL Group, Inc.; *U.S. Public*, pg. 608
ESI, INC.—See Browning-Ferris Industries, Inc.; *U.S. Public*, pg. 264
ESI MORTGAGE DEVELOPMENT CORPORATION—See Promus Hotel Corporation; *U.S. Public*, pg. 1335
ESI STAMPA MEDICA SRL—See Reed Elsevier plc; *Int'l*, pg. 1099
ESIS INTERNATIONAL ASESORIAS LIMITADA—See Cigna Corp.; *U.S. Public*, pg. 363
ESIS INTERNATIONAL, INC.—See Cigna Corp.; *U.S. Public*, pg. 366
ESJ HOTEL CORPORATION—See Patriot American Hospitality, Inc.; *U.S. Public*, pg. 1265
ESL, INC.—See Penn National Insurance; *U.S. Private*, pg. 850
ESL INC.—See TRW Inc.; *U.S. Public*, pg. 1558
ESL-NIPPON CO. LTD.—See Electro-Science Laboratories, Inc.; *U.S. Private*, pg. 369
ESL S.N.C.—See Electro-Science Laboratories, Inc.; *U.S. Private*, pg. 369
ESM II, INC.—See Viag AG; *Int'l*, pg. 1465
OY ESMI AB—See A. Ahlstrom Corporation; *Int'l*, pg. 32
ESMI A/S—See A. Ahlstrom Corporation; *Int'l*, pg. 33
ESMR, INC—See Motorola, Inc.; *U.S. Public*, pg. 1137
ESMR SUB, INC.—See Motorola, Inc.; *U.S. Public*, pg. 1137
E.S.P. EUROPESE STAALPREFABRICATLE N.V.—See Arbed S.A.; *Int'l*, pg. 79
ESPN HOLDING COMPANY, INC.—See The Walt Disney Company; *U.S. Public*, pg. 512
ESPN, INC.—See The Walt Disney Company; *U.S. Public*, pg. 512
ESS-FOOD; *Int'l*, pg. 429
ESS-FOOD CANADA, INC.—See ESS-Food; *Int'l*, pg. 429
ESS-FOOD ESPANA S.A.—See ESS-Food; *Int'l*, pg. 429
ESS-FOOD HANDELS-GMBH—See ESS-Food; *Int'l*, pg. 429
ESS-FOOD (H.K.) LTD.—See ESS-Food; *Int'l*, pg. 429
ESS-FOOD HUNGARIA LLC—See ESS-Food; *Int'l*, pg. 429
ESS-FOOD MEATIMEX S.A.—See ESS-Food; *Int'l*, pg. 429
ESS-FOOD S.A.—See ESS-Food; *Int'l*, pg. 429
ESS-FOOD UK LTD.—See ESS-Food; *Int'l*, pg. 430
ESS-FOOD USA INC.—See ESS-Food; *Int'l*, pg. 429
ESS-FOOD KOREA—See ESS-Food; *Int'l*, pg. 429
EST COMPANY OF TENNESSEE, INC.—See Leggett & Platt, Incorporated; *U.S. Public*, pg. 986
ESTA B.V.—See Charter plc; *Int'l*, pg. 282
ESTA FASTIGHETS AB—See Charter plc; *Int'l*, pg. 281
ESTA VASTGOED B.V.—See Charter plc; *Int'l*, pg. 283
E.S.T.E., S.A.—See Borden, Inc.; *U.S. Private*, pg. 159
ESTESA—See Charter plc; *Int'l*, pg. 283
ESW EXTEL SYSTEMS WEDEL—See Daimler-Benz Aktiengesellschaft; *Int'l*, pg. 367
ESY EXPORT CO., INC.—See Raytheon Company; *U.S. Public*, pg. 1365
ET STORAGE COMPANY—See Equitable Resources, Inc.; *U.S. Public*, pg. 590
ETA HOME HEALTH CARE, INC.—See Integrated Health Services, Inc.; *U.S. Public*, pg. 884
ETA INGENIEURS BV—See Heidemij N.V.; *Int'l*, pg. 607
ETA S.A. FABRIQUES D'EBAUCHES—See SMH Swiss Corporation for Micro Electronics & Watchmaking Indus. Ltd.; *Int'l*, pg. 1160
ETA (THAILAND) CO. LTD.—See SMH Swiss Corporation for Micro Electronics & Watchmaking Indus. Ltd.; *Int'l*, pg. 1161
ETA UHRENWERKE GMBH—See SMH Swiss Corporation for Micro Electronics & Watchmaking Indus. Ltd.; *Int'l*, pg. 1161
ETC SIMULATION GROUP—See Environmental Tectonics Corporation (ETC); *U.S. Public*, pg. 587
ETCD—See Lyonnaise des Eaux S.A.; *Int'l*, pg. 823
ETEX; *Int'l*, pg. 430
ETP TRANSMISSION AB—See AB Industrivarden; *Int'l*, pg. 678
ETS FRINGAND—See Siebe plc; *Int'l*, pg. 1240
ETV-EROTERV RT.—See Imatran Voima Oy; *Int'l*, pg. 661
EUA BIOTEN, INC.—See Eastern Utilities Associates; *U.S. Public*, pg. 549
EUA CITIZENS CONSERVATION SERVICES, INC.—See Eastern Utilities Associates; *U.S. Public*, pg. 549
EUA COGENEX CORPORATION—See Eastern Utilities Associates; *U.S. Public*, pg. 549
EUA COGENEX WEST—See Eastern Utilities Associates; *U.S. Public*, pg. 549
EUA DAY—See Eastern Utilities Associates; *U.S. Public*, pg. 549
EUA ENERGY INVESTMENT CORPORATION—See Eastern Utilities Associates; *U.S. Public*, pg. 549
EUA OCEAN STATE CORPORATION—See Eastern Utilities Associates; *U.S. Public*, pg. 549
EUA SERVICE CORPORATION—See Eastern Utilities Associates; *U.S. Public*, pg. 549
E.V. INTERNATIONAL, INC.—See Greenwich Street Capital Partners, Inc.; *U.S. Private*, pg. 479
EV PRODUCTS—See II-VI Incorporated; *U.S. Public*, pg. 1647
EVI, INC.; *U.S. Public*, pg. 547
EVI INTERNATIONAL, INC.—See EVI, Inc.; *U.S. Public*, pg. 547
EVM AG—See Veba AG; *Int'l*, pg. 1456
EVSCO PHARMACEUTICALS—See IGI, Inc.; *U.S. Public*, pg. 855
EWA LTD.—See WPP Group plc; *Int'l*, pg. 1482
EWE AKTIENGESELLSCHAFT—See Veba AG; *Int'l*, pg. 1456
EWU-AKTIENGESELLSCHAFT—See Rubbermaid Incorporated; *U.S. Public*, pg. 1411
EXAR CORP.-EUROPE—See EXAR Corporation; *U.S. Public*, pg. 598
EXAR JAPAN CORPORATION—See EXAR Corporation; *U.S. Public*, pg. 598
E.Z. EDITIONS ZURICH AG.—See Philip Morris Companies Inc.; *U.S. Public*, pg. 1288
EZ INTERNATIONAL—See Wm. E. Wright Limited Partnership; *U.S. Private*, pg. 1192
EZ PAINTR CANADA—See Newell Co.; *U.S. Public*, pg. 1178
EZ PAINTR CORP.—See Newell Co.; *U.S. Public*, pg. 1177
EZL HANSA GMBH ENTSORGUNGSZWISCHENLAGER—See Dyckerhoff & Widmann AG; *Int'l*, pg. 423
EA ENGINEERING, SCIENCE & TECHNOLOGY, INC.—See EA Engineering, Science & Technology, Inc.; *U.S. Public*, pg. 541
EAGER BEAVER; *U.S. Private*, pg. 354
EAGLE AFFILIATES, INC.—See APL Corporation; *U.S. Private*, pg. 7
EAGLE ASSET MANAGEMENT, INC.—See Raymond James Financial, Inc.; *U.S. Public*, pg. 923
EAGLE AVIATION LTD.—See Air New Zealand Ltd.; *Int'l*, pg. 38
EAGLE BUTTON CO., INC.; *U.S. Private*, pg. 354
EAGLE CONVERTING INC.—See Bradner Central Company; *U.S. Private*, pg. 165
EAGLE ELECTRIC MFG. CO., INC.; *U.S. Private*, pg. 354
EAGLE ELECTRONICS—See Lowrance Electronics, Inc.; *U.S. Public*, pg. 1016
EAGLE ENGINEERING & MANUFACTURING, INC.—See Dreison International, Inc.; *U.S. Private*, pg. 342
EAGLE FOOD CENTERS, INC.; *U.S. Public*, pg. 547
EAGLE FRIEGHT SERVICES—See Eagle USA Airfreight; *U.S. Public*, pg. 547
EAGLE GENERAL AGENCY—See Credit Suisse Group; *Int'l*, pg. 346
EAGLE ICE CREAM DIV.—See Giant Eagle, Inc.; *U.S. Private*, pg. 451
EAGLE INDUSTRIES, INC.—See Great American Management & Investment, Inc.; *U.S. Private*, pg. 473
EAGLE INDUSTRY, LTD.—See EG & G, Inc.; *U.S. Public*, pg. 544
EAGLE IRON WORKS; *U.S. Private*, pg. 354
EAGLE LINCOLN MERCURY INC.; *U.S. Private*, pg. 355
EAGLE MANAGED CARE—See Rite Aid Corporation; *U.S. Public*, pg. 1391
EAGLE MARINE SERVICES, LTD.—See Neptune Orient Lines Ltd.; *Int'l*, pg. 912
EAGLE MEXICO—See Eagle USA Airfreight; *U.S. Public*, pg. 547
EAGLE MOUNTAIN ENERGY, INC.—See Enron Corp.; *U.S. Public*, pg. 585
EAGLE MOUNTAIN RECLAMATION, INC.—See Kaiser Ventures, Inc.; *U.S. Public*, pg. 941
EAGLE OCEANICS, INC.—See Atwood Oceanics, Inc.; *U.S. Public*, pg. 146
EAGLE-OTTAWA LEATHER CO.—See Albert Trostel & Sons Co.; *U.S. Private*, pg. 1105
EAGLE PACKAGING CORP.—See SIG Schweizersiche Industrie-Gesellschaft Holding AG; *Int'l*, pg. 1156
EAGLE PACKAGING GROUP—See Package Machinery Co.; *U.S. Private*, pg. 832
EAGLE PERFORMANCE SYSTEMS—See Graham-Field Health Products, Inc.; *U.S. Public*, pg. 758
EAGLE-PICHER ESPANA, S.A.—See Eagle-Picher Industries, Inc.; *U.S. Private*, pg. 355
EAGLE-PICHER FAR EAST, INC.—See Eagle-Picher Industries, Inc.; *U.S. Private*, pg. 355
EAGLE-PICHER FLUID SYSTEMS LIMITED—See Eagle-Picher Industries, Inc.; *U.S. Private*, pg. 355
EAGLE-PICHER INDUSTRIES, INC.; *U.S. Private*, pg. 355
EAGLE-PICHER WOLVERINE GMBH—See Eagle-Picher Industries, Inc.; *U.S. Private*, pg. 355
EAGLE PROPERTIES, INC.—See The Western and Southern Life Insurance Company; *U.S. Private*, pg. 1164
EAGLE SIGNAL CONTROLS—See Danaher Corporation; *U.S. Public*, pg. 481
EAGLE STAR—See B.A.T Industries P.L.C.; *Int'l*, pg. 110
EAGLE STAR INSURANCE CO.—See B.A.T Industries P.L.C.; *Int'l*, pg. 110
EAGLE STAR VIE SA—See B.A.T Industries P.L.C.; *Int'l*, pg. 112
EAGLE TECH INC.—See Northrop Grumman Corporation; *U.S. Public*, pg. 1199
EAGLE TECHNOLOGY—See Microdyne Corporation; *U.S. Public*, pg. 1105
EAGLE TRANSPORTATION SERVICES—See Eagle USA Airfreight; *U.S. Public*, pg. 547
EAGLE USA AIRFREIGHT; *U.S. Public*, pg. 547
EAGLE USA AIRFREIGHT—See Eagle USA Airfreight; *U.S. Public*, pg. 547
EAGLE USA CHARTER SERVICES—See Eagle USA Airfreight; *U.S. Public*, pg. 547
EAGLE USA INFORMATION SERVICES—See Eagle USA Airfreight; *U.S. Public*, pg. 547
EAGLE USA INTERNATIONAL—See Eagle USA Airfreight; *U.S. Public*, pg. 547
EAGLE USA LOGISTICS SERVICES—See Eagle USA Airfreight; *U.S. Public*, pg. 547
EAGLE USA TRADSHOW SERVICES—See Eagle USA Airfreight; *U.S. Public*, pg. 547
EAGLE VALVE CO., INC.—See Watts Industries, Inc.; *U.S. Public*, pg. 1746

EAGLE WINDOW & DOOR, INC.—See American Architectural Products, Inc.; *U.S. Public*, pg. 67
EAGLE ZINC CO.—See T.L. Diamond Company; *U.S. Private*, pg. 331
EAGLEMARK FINANCIAL SERVICES, INC.—See Harley-Davidson, Inc.; *U.S. Public*, pg. 786
EAGLE'S LANDING COUNTRY CLUB, INC.—See Killearn Properties, Inc.; *U.S. Public*, pg. 956
EARL CONSTRUCTION COMPANY—See Sundt Corp.; *U.S. Private*, pg. 1051
EARL MAY SEED & NURSERY L.C.; *U.S. Private*, pg. 356
EARLE INDUSTRIES, INC.; *U.S. Private*, pg. 356
EARL'S COURT & OLYMPIA LTD.—See The Peninsular and Oriental Steam Navigation Company; *Int'l*, pg. 1033
EARLY CALIFORNIA FOODS—See Erly Industries, Inc.; *U.S. Public*, pg. 591
EARLY LEARNING CENTRE—See John Menzies plc; *Int'l*, pg. 707
EARLY TIMES DISTILLERS CO.—See Brown-Forman Corporation; *U.S. Public*, pg. 261
EARNHARDT'S MOTOR COMPANIES; *U.S. Private*, pg. 356
EARP DISTRIBUTION CENTER; *U.S. Private*, pg. 356
EARTH BIOCHEMICAL CO., LTD.—See Otsuka Pharmaceutical Co., Ltd.; *Int'l*, pg. 1013
EARTH CHEMICAL CO., LTD.—See Otsuka Pharmaceutical Co., Ltd.; *Int'l*, pg. 1013
EARTH DEVELOPMENT (S) PTE. LTD.—See Kobe Steel, Ltd.; *Int'l*, pg. 741
EARTH ENVIRONMENTAL SANITARY SERVICE CO., LTD.—See Otsuka Pharmaceutical Co., Ltd.; *Int'l*, pg. 1013
EARTH OBSERVATION SCIENCES LIMITED—See Orbital Sciences Corporation; *U.S. Public*, pg. 1230
EARTH SCIENCES CONSULTANTS, INC.—See American Waste Services, Inc.; *U.S. Public*, pg. 94
EARTH SCIENCES CONSULTANTS, INC. (OHIO OPERS.)—See American Waste Services, Inc.; *U.S. Public*, pg. 94
EARTH SCIENCES CONSULTANTS, INC. (OHIO VALLEY OPERS.)—See American Waste Services, Inc.; *U.S. Public*, pg. 94
EARTH SCIENCES CONSULTANTS, INC. (ROCKY MOUNTAIN OPERS.)—See American Waste Services, Inc.; *U.S. Public*, pg. 94
EARTH STATION DIV.—See Allen Telecom, Inc.; *U.S. Public*, pg. 46
EARTH TECHNOLOGY CORP.—See Tyco International Ltd.; *U.S. Public*, pg. 1648
EARTH TECHNOLOGY CORP. USA—See Tyco International Ltd.; *U.S. Public*, pg. 1648
EARTHGRAINS CO.—See The Earthgrains Company; *U.S. Public*, pg. 547
THE EARTHGRAINS COMPANY; *U.S. Public*, pg. 547
EARTHMOVING EQUIPMENT DIV.—See Esco Corporation; *U.S. Private*, pg. 383
EARTHRISE FARMS—See Dainippon Ink & Chemicals, Inc.; *Int'l*, pg. 369
EARTHRISE TRADING CO.—See Dainippon Ink & Chemicals, Inc.; *Int'l*, pg. 369
EASCO INC.; *U.S. Public*, pg. 548
EAST AFRICA INDUSTRIES LTD.—See Unilever Plc; *Int'l*, pg. 1436
EAST AFRICAN CABLES LTD.—See Delta plc; *Int'l*, pg. 390
EAST ASCENSION TELEPHONE COMPANY, INC.—See Eatelcorp Inc.; *U.S. Private*, pg. 358
EAST ASIA AETNA INSURANCE GROUP—See Aetna Inc.; *U.S. Public*, pg. 27
EAST ASIA HELLER LIMITED—See The Fuji Bank, Limited; *Int'l*, pg. 521
THE EAST ASIATIC CO. (AUSTRALIA) LIMITED—See The East Asiatic Company Ltd. A/S; *Int'l*, pg. 431
THE EAST ASIATIC CO. (NEW ZEALAND) LIMITED—See The East Asiatic Company Ltd. A/S; *Int'l*, pg. 431
THE EAST ASIATIC COMPANY (KOREA) LTD. APS—See The East Asiatic Company Ltd. A/S; *Int'l*, pg. 431
THE EAST ASIATIC COMPANY LTD. A/S; *Int'l*, pg. 430
THE EAST ASIATIC COMPANY (PRIVATE) LIMITED—See The East Asiatic Company Ltd. A/S; *Int'l*, pg. 431
THE EAST ASIATIC COMPANY (S.A.) (PTY.) LIMITED—See The East Asiatic Company Ltd. A/S; *Int'l*, pg. 431
THE EAST ASIATIC COMPANY UK (HOLDINGS) LIMITED—See The East Asiatic Company Ltd. A/S; *Int'l*, pg. 431
EAST ASIATIC INSURANCE BROKERS (UK) LIMITED—See The East Asiatic Company Ltd. A/S; *Int'l*, pg. 431
EAST ASIATIC TIMBER (HOLLAND) B.V.—See The East Asiatic Company Ltd. A/S; *Int'l*, pg. 431
EAST BRANCH IMPROVEMENT COMPANY—See Bangor Hydro-Electric Company; *U.S. Public*, pg. 178
EAST CAROLINA ENVIRONMENTAL, INC.—See Republic Industries, Inc.; *U.S. Public*, pg. 1379
EAST COAST STEEL, INC.; *U.S. Private*, pg. 356
THE EAST GREENWICH PENDULUM—See Journal Register Company; *U.S. Public*, pg. 934
EAST JAPAN RAILWAY COMPANY; *Int'l*, pg. 431
EAST JAPAN RAILWAY COMPANY - NEW YORK OFFICE—See East Japan Railway Company; *Int'l*, pg. 431
EAST JAPAN RAILWAY COMPANY - PARIS OFFICE—See East Japan Railway Company; *Int'l*, pg. 431
EAST JAPAN TOSHIBA DISTRIBUTOR CORPORATION—See Toshiba Corporation; *Int'l*, pg. 1402
EAST JORDAN IRON WORKS; *U.S. Private*, pg. 356
EAST KANTO CATERPILLAR MITSUBISHI CONSTRUCTION EQUIPMENT SALES, LTD.—See Caterpillar Inc.; *U.S. Public*, pg. 317
EAST KENTUCKY POWER CO-OP; *U.S. Private*, pg. 356

EAST LANCASHIRE CABLEVISION LIMITED—See Rogers Communications, Inc.; *Int'l*, pg. 1123
EAST LIVERPOOL LANDFILL, INC.—See American Waste Services, Inc.; *U.S. Public*, pg. 94
EAST MANOR MEDICAL CARE CENTER—See Vencor, Inc.; *U.S. Public*, pg. 1712
EAST MAUI IRRIGATION CO., LTD.—See Alexander & Baldwin, Inc.; *U.S. Public*, pg. 39
EAST MOLINE METAL PRODUCTS COMPANY; *U.S. Private*, pg. 357
EAST MOORE NURSING CENTER—See Horizon/CMS Healthcare Corporation; *U.S. Public*, pg. 839
THE EAST OHIO GAS CO.—See Consolidated Natural Gas Company; *U.S. Public*, pg. 435
EAST PENN MFG. CO.; *U.S. Private*, pg. 357
EAST RAND GOLD AND URANIUM MINING—See Anglo American Corporation of South Africa Limited; *Int'l*, pg. 77
EAST RIVER ELECTRIC COOPERATIVE; *U.S. Private*, pg. 357
EAST SMITHFIELD FARMS INC.—See Bongrain S.A.; *Int'l*, pg. 201
EAST STROUDSBURG PLANT—See Cooper Industries, Inc.; *U.S. Public*, pg. 443
EAST TENNESSEE INFUSION & RESPIRATORY, INC.—See Integrated Health Services, Inc.; *U.S. Public*, pg. 884
EAST TENNESSEE NATURAL GAS CO.—See El Paso Natural Gas Co.; *U.S. Public*, pg. 567
EAST-WEST CONSULTANTS GMBH—See Bayerische Vereinsbank Group; *Int'l*, pg. 179
EAST-WEST DESIGN GROUP—See The Buntin Group; *U.S. Private*, pg. 181
EASTALCO ALUMINUM COMPANY—See Alumax Inc.; *U.S. Public*, pg. 60
EASTBRIDGE ASSET MANAGEMENT INC.—See The Nippon Credit Bank, Ltd.; *Int'l*, pg. 933
EASTBRIDGE CAPITAL INC.—See The Nippon Credit Bank, Ltd.; *Int'l*, pg. 933
EASTBRIDGE HOLDINGS INC.—See The Nippon Credit Bank, Ltd.; *Int'l*, pg. 933
EASTCO GLOVE TECHNOLOGIES—See Eastco Industrial Safety Corp.; *U.S. Public*, pg. 548
EASTCO INDUSTRIAL SAFETY CORP.; *U.S. Public*, pg. 548
EASTERDAY JANITORIAL SUPPLY CO.—See ABM Industries; *U.S. Public*, pg. 2
EASTERN AIR DEVICES, INC.; *U.S. Private*, pg. 357
EASTERN AMERICAN ENERGY CORPORATION; *U.S. Private*, pg. 357
EASTERN ASSOCIATED COAL CORP.—See Hanson PLC; *Int'l*, pg. 594
EASTERN BOOK SERVICE—See Springer-Verlag GmbH & Co. KG; *Int'l*, pg. 1291
EASTERN BRANCH—See Deutsche Babcock AG; *Int'l*, pg. 401
EASTERN BULKCEM CO. LTD.—See Scancem AB; *Int'l*, pg. 1201
EASTERN CANVAS PRODUCTS, INC.; *U.S. Private*, pg. 357
EASTERN COALFIELDS LIMITED—See Coal India Limited; *Int'l*, pg. 298
EASTERN COLOR PRINTING COMPANY; *U.S. Private*, pg. 357
THE EASTERN COMPANY; *U.S. Public*, pg. 548
EASTERN DIVISION—See Costain Group PLC; *Int'l*, pg. 337
EASTERN DIV.-PLYMOUTH—See Crown Cork & Seal Company, Inc.; *U.S. Public*, pg. 463
EASTERN EDISON COMPANY—See Eastern Utilities Associates; *U.S. Public*, pg. 550
EASTERN ELEVATOR LIMITED—See Kone Corporation; *Int'l*, pg. 747
EASTERN ENGRAVING—See Standex International Corporation; *U.S. Public*, pg. 1506
EASTERN ENTERPRISES; *U.S. Public*, pg. 548
EASTERN ENVIRONMENTAL SERVICES, INC.; *U.S. Public*, pg. 549
EASTERN FINE PAPER; *U.S. Private*, pg. 357
EASTERN HARBOUR CROSSING CO., LTD.—See Kumagai Gumi Co., Ltd.; *Int'l*, pg. 764
EASTERN INDUSTRIES—See Stabler Companies, Inc.; *U.S. Private*, pg. 1028
EASTERN INSURANCE COMPANY LTD.—See Tenneco Inc.; *U.S. Public*, pg. 1579
EASTERN NEWS DISTRIBUTORS, INC.—See The Hearst Corporation; *U.S. Public*, pg. 517
EASTERN OIL WELL SERVICES—See PrimeEnergy Corporation; *U.S. Public*, pg. 1329
EASTERN PENNSYLVANIA DEVELOPMENT CO.—See PECO Energy Company; *U.S. Public*, pg. 1268
EASTERN PENNSYLVANIA EXPLORATION CO.—See PECO Energy Company; *U.S. Public*, pg. 1268
P.T. EASTERN POLYMER—See Tokuyama Corporation; *Int'l*, pg. 1394
EASTERN REGION SALES—See Televideo, Inc.; *U.S. Public*, pg. 1572
EASTERN RESEARCH, INC.—See Allen Organ Company; *U.S. Public*, pg. 45
EASTERN SEA LAEM CHABANG TERMINAL CO., LTD.—See Siam City Public Bank Public Company Limited; *Int'l*, pg. 1239
EASTERN SHORE MARKETS, INC.—See Camellia Food Stores, Inc.; *U.S. Private*, pg. 203
EASTERN SHORE NATURAL GAS COMPANY—See Chesapeake Utilities Corporation; *U.S. Public*, pg. 347
EASTERN SMELTING & REFINING CORPORATION; *U.S. Private*, pg. 357
EASTERN SOFTWOOD SAWMILL—See Georgia-Pacific Corporation; *U.S. Public*, pg. 738
EASTERN SUGAR—See Generale Suciere SNC; *Int'l*, pg. 549
EASTERN TECHNOLOGICAL SERVICES PTE. LTD.—See Hewlett-Packard Company; *U.S. Public*, pg. 817

EASTERN U.S.—See Supertex, Inc.; *U.S. Public*, pg. 1540
EASTERN UTILITIES ASSOCIATES; *U.S. Public*, pg. 549
P.T. EASTERNTEX—See Toray Industries, Inc.; *Int'l*, pg. 1400
EASTEX ENERGY INC.—See El Paso Natural Gas Co.; *U.S. Public*, pg. 567
EASTEX GAS PRODUCTION CO.—See El Paso Natural Gas Co.; *U.S. Public*, pg. 567
EASTEX GAS TRANSMISSION CO.—See El Paso Natural Gas Co.; *U.S. Public*, pg. 567
EASTEX HYDROCARBONS, INC.—See El Paso Natural Gas Co.; *U.S. Public*, pg. 567
EASTFIELD MALL, INC.—See The Rouse Company; *U.S. Public*, pg. 1408
EASTLAND NATIONAL BANK—See First Financial Bankshares, Inc.; *U.S. Public*, pg. 633
EASTLAND SHOE MANUFACTURING CORPORATION; *U.S. Private*, pg. 357
EASTMAN CHEMICAL COMPANY; *U.S. Public*, pg. 550
EASTMAN CHRISTENSEN (CAMEROON) S.A.R.L.—See Baker Hughes Incorporated; *U.S. Public*, pg. 167
EASTMAN CHRISTENSEN CANADA LTD.—See Baker Hughes Incorporated; *U.S. Public*, pg. 167
EASTMAN CHRISTENSEN (CHINA) LIMITED—See Baker Hughes Incorporated; *U.S. Public*, pg. 167
EASTMAN CHRISTENSEN DE ESPANA S.A.—See Baker Hughes Incorporated; *U.S. Public*, pg. 167
EASTMAN CHRISTENSEN GMBH—See Baker Hughes Incorporated; *U.S. Public*, pg. 167
EASTMAN CHRISTENSEN LTD.—See Baker Hughes Incorporated; *U.S. Public*, pg. 167
EASTMAN CHRISTENSEN (M) SDN. BDH—See Baker Hughes Incorporated; *U.S. Public*, pg. 167
EASTMAN FINE CHEMICALS—See Eastman Kodak Company; *U.S. Public*, pg. 550
EASTMAN GELATINE CORP.—See Eastman Kodak Company; *U.S. Public*, pg. 551
EASTMAN HOUSE OF ALABAMA, INC.—See Chittenden & Eastman Co.; *U.S. Private*, pg. 238
EASTMAN HOUSE OF CALIFORNIA, INC.—See Chittenden & Eastman Co.; *U.S. Private*, pg. 238
EASTMAN KODAK ADW INC.—See Eastman Kodak Company; *U.S. Public*, pg. 555
EASTMAN KODAK CO.—See Eastman Kodak Company; *U.S. Public*, pg. 550
EASTMAN KODAK COMPANY; *U.S. Public*, pg. 550
EASTMAN KODAK COMPANY DISTRIBUTION—See Eastman Kodak Company; *U.S. Public*, pg. 555
EASTMAN KODAK COMPANY-EUROPEAN REGION—See Eastman Kodak Company; *U.S. Public*, pg. 551
EASTMAN KODAK COMPANY-SINGAPORE—See Eastman Kodak Company; *U.S. Public*, pg. 552
EASTMAN KODAK HEALTH CARE INC.—See Eastman Kodak Company; *U.S. Public*, pg. 555
EASTMAN KODAK (JAPAN) LTD.—See Eastman Kodak Company; *U.S. Public*, pg. 552
EASTMAN KODAK (JAPAN) RESEARCH & DEVEL. CTR.—See Eastman Kodak Company; *U.S. Public*, pg. 552
EASTMAN KODAK KCD—See Eastman Kodak Company; *U.S. Public*, pg. 555
EASTMAN KODAK LIFE SCIENCES DIV.—See Eastman Kodak Company; *U.S. Public*, pg. 551
EASTMAN KODAK RIVERBEND—See Eastman Kodak Company; *U.S. Public*, pg. 555
EASTMAN RADIO—See Chancellor Media Corporation; *U.S. Public*, pg. 335
EASTMAN SAVINGS & LOAN ASSOCIATION—See Eastman Kodak Company; *U.S. Public*, pg. 551
EASTMAN SOFTWARE N.Y.—See Eastman Kodak Company; *U.S. Public*, pg. 555
EASTMAN SOFTWARE STORAGE MANAGEMENT GROUP, INC.—See Eastman Kodak Company; *U.S. Public*, pg. 555
EASTMAN TECHNOLOGY INC.—See Eastman Kodak Company; *U.S. Public*, pg. 551
EASTMAN WHIPSTOCK (CHINA) LIMITED—See Baker Hughes Incorporated; *U.S. Public*, pg. 167
EASTMAN WHIPSTOCK (FAR EAST) PTE. LTD.—See Baker Hughes Incorporated; *U.S. Public*, pg. 167
EASTMAN WORLDWIDE; *U.S. Private*, pg. 358
EASTON PRESS BOOKS—See MBI Inc.; *U.S. Private*, pg. 685
EASTON PRESS VIDEOS—See MBI Inc.; *U.S. Private*, pg. 685
EASTSIDE LINCOLN MERCURY—See Beechmont Investments Inc.; *U.S. Private*, pg. 129
THE EASTVILLE BANK—See Mercantile Bankshares Corporation; *U.S. Public*, pg. 1089
EASY DAY MANUFACTURING COMPANY; *U.S. Private*, pg. 358
EASY GARDENER INC.—See U.S. Home & Garden Inc.; *U.S. Public*, pg. 1682
EASY MOVE HANDLING & INDUSTRIAL EQUIPMENT LTD.—See Atlet AB; *Int'l*, pg. 97
EAT N PARK RESTAURANTS; *U.S. Private*, pg. 358
EATEL CONSTRUCTION CO., INC.—See Eatelcorp Inc.; *U.S. Private*, pg. 358
EATEL PUBLISHING INC.—See Eatelcorp Inc.; *U.S. Private*, pg. 358
EATEL TECHNOLOGY OUTLET—See Eatelcorp Inc.; *U.S. Private*, pg. 358
EATELCORP, INC.; *U.S. Private*, pg. 358
EATERIES, INC.; *U.S. Public*, pg. 555
EATON ADMINISTRATION CORP.—See Eaton Corporation; *U.S. Public*, pg. 558
EATON AUTOMOTIVE S.P.A. ENGINE COMPONENTS OPERATIONS—See Eaton Corporation; *U.S. Public*, pg. 558
EATON CONTROLES INDUSTRIALES, S.A.—See Eaton Corporation; *U.S. Public*, pg. 558
EATON CONTROLS S.P.A—See Eaton Corporation; *U.S. Public*, pg. 558
EATON CORPORATION; *U.S. Public*, pg. 555

EATON CORP., AEROSPACE & COMMERCIAL CONTROLS DIV.—See Eaton Corporation; *U.S. Public*, pg. 557

EATON CORPORATION AUTOMOTIVE CONTROLS DIVISION—See Eaton Corporation; *U.S. Public*, pg. 557

EATON CORPORATION COMMERCIAL CONTROLS DIVISION—See Eaton Corporation; *U.S. Public*, pg. 556

EATON CORPORATION, DEFENSE VALVE AND ACTUATOR DIVISION—See Eaton Corporation; *U.S. Public*, pg. 556

EATON CORP. DIV.—See Eaton Corporation; *U.S. Public*, pg. 556

EATON CORPORATION DO BRASIL ENGINE COMPONENTS OPERATIONS—See Eaton Corporation; *U.S. Public*, pg. 558

EATON CORPORATION, ELECTRIC DRIVES DIVISION—See Eaton Corporation; *U.S. Public*, pg. 556

EATON CORPORATION, ENGINE COMPONENTS DIVISION—See Eaton Corporation; *U.S. Public*, pg. 556

EATON CORPORATION, ENGINEERED FASTENERS DIVISION—See Eaton Corporation; *U.S. Public*, pg. 556

EATON CORP., FLUID POWER DIV.—See Eaton Corporation; *U.S. Public*, pg. 556

EATON CORPORATION-HEINEMANN PRODUCTS, COMMERCIAL CONTROLS DIVISION—See Eaton Corporation; *U.S. Public*, pg. 557

EATON CORPORATION, HYDRAULICS DIVISION—See Eaton Corporation; *U.S. Public*, pg. 557

EATON CORPORATION, PRESSURE SENSORS DIVISION—See Eaton Corporation; *U.S. Public*, pg. 557

EATON CORPORATION, SEMI-CONDUCTOR—See Eaton Corporation; *U.S. Public*, pg. 557

EATON CORPORATION SINGAPORE REPRESENTATIVE OFFICE—See Eaton Corporation; *U.S. Public*, pg. 558

EATON CORPORATION, SPECIALTIES DIVISION—See Eaton Corporation; *U.S. Public*, pg. 557

EATON CORPORATION, SPECIFIC INDUSTRY CONTROL DIVISION—See Eaton Corporation; *U.S. Public*, pg. 557

EATON CORP., SUPERCHARGER DIV.—See Eaton Corporation; *U.S. Public*, pg. 556

EATON CORPORATION, TORT CONTROL DIVISION—See Eaton Corporation; *U.S. Public*, pg. 557

EATON CORPORATION, TRUCK COMPONENTS OPERATIONS-NORTH AMERICA—See Eaton Corporation; *U.S. Public*, pg. 557

EATON CORPORATION, U.S. ENGINE VALVE CORPORATION—See Eaton Corporation; *U.S. Public*, pg. 557

EATON COUNTY ABSTRACT & TITLE COMPANY—See The First American Financial Corporation; *U.S. Public*, pg. 625

EATON EJES, S.A. DE C.V.—See Eaton Corporation; *U.S. Public*, pg. 558

EATON ENGINE LIFTERS S.P.A.—See Eaton Corporation; *U.S. Public*, pg. 558

EATON EST S.P.A. ENGINE COMPONENTS OPERATIONS—See Eaton Corporation; *U.S. Public*, pg. 558

EATON GMBH—See Eaton Corporation; *U.S. Public*, pg. 558

EATON GMBH CONTROLS DIV.-EUROPE—See Eaton Corporation; *U.S. Public*, pg. 558

EATON GMBH CONTROLS DIV.-EUROPE MARKETING CENTER—See Eaton Corporation; *U.S. Public*, pg. 558

EATON GMBH FLUID POWER OPERATIONS—See Eaton Corporation; *U.S. Public*, pg. 558

EATON HYDRAULICS LIMITED—See Eaton Corporation; *U.S. Public*, pg. 558

EATON I.C.S.A AXLE & FOUNDRY DIVISIONS—See Eaton Corporation; *U.S. Public*, pg. 558

EATON IDT—See Eaton Corporation; *U.S. Public*, pg. 558

EATON INTERNATIONAL CORP.—See Eaton Corporation; *U.S. Public*, pg. 558

EATON INTERNATIONAL CORPORATION, KOREA—See Eaton Corporation; *U.S. Public*, pg. 558

EATON JAPAN CO., LTD.—See Eaton Corporation; *U.S. Public*, pg. 558

EATON LEASING CORP.—See Eaton Corporation; *U.S. Public*, pg. 558

EATON LIMITED—See Eaton Corporation; *U.S. Public*, pg. 558

EATON LIMITED AEROSPACE & COMMERCIAL CONTROLS—See Eaton Corporation; *U.S. Public*, pg. 558

EATON LIMITED AXLE OPERATIONS—See Eaton Corporation; *U.S. Public*, pg. 559

EATON LIMITED COMMERCIAL & MILITARY CONTROLS OPERATIONS—See Eaton Corporation; *U.S. Public*, pg. 559

EATON LIMITED FORGE DIVISION—See Eaton Corporation; *U.S. Public*, pg. 559

EATON LIMITED TRANSMISSION DIVISION—See Eaton Corporation; *U.S. Public*, pg. 559

EATON MANUFACTURERA, S.A. DE C.V.—See Eaton Corporation; *U.S. Public*, pg. 559

EATON METAL PRODUCTS COMPANY; *U.S. Private*, pg. 358

EATON OFFICE SUPPLY CO., INC.; *U.S. Private*, pg. 358

EATON PTY. LTD. CONTROLS DIVISION—See Eaton Corporation; *U.S. Public*, pg. 559

EATON PTY. LTD.-TRUCK COMPONENTS OPERATIONS—See Eaton Corporation; *U.S. Public*, pg. 559

EATON S.A. AXLE DIV.—See Eaton Corporation; *U.S. Public*, pg. 559

EATON S.A. TRANSMISSION DIV.—See Eaton Corporation; *U.S. Public*, pg. 559

EATON S.A.M-CONTROLS DIV.-EUROPE—See Eaton Corporation; *U.S. Public*, pg. 559

EATON SVENSKA AB—See Eaton Corporation; *U.S. Public*, pg. 559

EATON TECHNOLOGIES INC.—See Eaton Corporation; *U.S. Public*, pg. 558

EATON TECHNOLOGIES LIMITED—See Eaton Corporation; *U.S. Public*, pg. 559

EATON VANCE CORP.; *U.S. Public*, pg. 559

EATON YALE LTD.-CONTROLS DIVISION—See Eaton Corporation; *U.S. Public*, pg. 559

EATON YALE LTD. ENGINEERED FASTENERS DIV.—See Eaton Corporation; *U.S. Public*, pg. 559

EATON YALE LTD. INDUSTRIAL CONTROL DIVISION—See Eaton Corporation; *U.S. Public*, pg. 559

EATON YALE LTD. SUSPENSION DIV.—See Eaton Corporation; *U.S. Public*, pg. 559

EAU ET FEU—See Williams Holdings Plc; *Int'l*, pg. 1500

EAU ET FORCE—See Lyonnaise des Eaux S.A.; *Int'l*, pg. 822

EAU MINERALE DE PLANCOET—See Nestle S.A.; *Int'l*, pg. 919

EAUX DE MARSEILLE—See Lyonnaise des Eaux S.A.; *Int'l*, pg. 823

EAUX DU NORD—See Lyonnaise des Eaux S.A.; *Int'l*, pg. 823

S.A. DES EAUX MINERALES DE RIBEAUVILLE—See Nestle S.A.; *Int'l*, pg. 922

EBAM—See GIB Group; *Int'l*, pg. 533

EBARA AMERICA CORPORATION—See Ebara Corporation; *Int'l*, pg. 431

EBARA-BENGUET, INC.—See Benguet Corporation; *Int'l*, pg. 187

EBARA-BENGUET, INC.—See Ebara Corporation; *Int'l*, pg. 432

EBARA CORPORATION; *Int'l*, pg. 431

EBARA DENSAN TAIWAN MANUFACTURING CO., LTD.—See Ebara Corporation; *Int'l*, pg. 432

EBARA - ELLIOTT SERVICE (TAIWAN) CO., LTD.—See Ebara Corporation; *Int'l*, pg. 432

EBARA ENGINEERING (MALAYSIA) SDN. BHD.—See Ebara Corporation; *Int'l*, pg. 432

EBARA ENGINEERING SINGAPORE PTE. LTD.—See Ebara Corporation; *Int'l*, pg. 432

EBARA ESPANA BOMBAS S.A.—See Ebara Corporation; *Int'l*, pg. 432

EBARA GERMANY GMBH—See Ebara Corporation; *Int'l*, pg. 432

EBARA HAI DUONG COMPANY LTD.—See Ebara Corporation; *Int'l*, pg. 432

P.T. EBARA INDONESIA—See Ebara Corporation; *Int'l*, pg. 432

EBARA INDUSTRIAS MECANICAS E COMERCIO LTDA.—See Ebara Corporation; *Int'l*, pg. 432

EBARA INTERNATIONAL CORP.—See Ebara Corporation; *Int'l*, pg. 431

EBARA ITALIA S.P.A.—See Ebara Corporation; *Int'l*, pg. 432

EBARA KAILAY ENVIRONMENTAL ENGINEERING CO., LTD.—See Ebara Corporation; *Int'l*, pg. 432

EBARA PRECISION MACHINERY KOREA INCORPORATED—See Ebara Corporation; *Int'l*, pg. 432

P.T. EBARA PRIMA INDONESIA—See Ebara Corporation; *Int'l*, pg. 432

EBARA PUMPEN GMBH—See Ebara Corporation; *Int'l*, pg. 432

EBARA PUMPS UNITED KINGDOM LIMITED—See Ebara Corporation; *Int'l*, pg. 432

EBARA QINGDAO CO. LTD.—See Ebara Corporation; *Int'l*, pg. 432

EBARA SOLAR, INC.—See Ebara Corporation; *Int'l*, pg. 432

EBARA TECHNOLOGIES INC.—See Ebara Corporation; *Int'l*, pg. 432

EBARA (THAILAND) LIMITED—See Ebara Corporation; *Int'l*, pg. 432

EBARA UK LTD.—See Ebara Corporation; *Int'l*, pg. 432

EBASCO ARABIA LIMITED—See Texas Utilities Company; *U.S. Public*, pg. 1587

EBASCO AUSTRALIA PTY. LIMITED—See Texas Utilities Company; *U.S. Public*, pg. 1587

EBASCO B.V.—See Texas Utilities Company; *U.S. Public*, pg. 1587

EBASCO CAYMAN LIMITED—See Texas Utilities Company; *U.S. Public*, pg. 1587

EBASCO CORPORATION—See Texas Utilities Company; *U.S. Public*, pg. 1587

EBASCO-CTCI CORPORATION—See Texas Utilities Company; *U.S. Public*, pg. 1587

EBASCO ENERGY A.G.—See Texas Utilities Company; *U.S. Public*, pg. 1587

EBASCO ESPANA, S.A.—See Texas Utilities Company; *U.S. Public*, pg. 1587

EBASCO ITALIA S.R.L.—See Texas Utilities Company; *U.S. Public*, pg. 1587

EBASCO SERVICES OF CANADA LIMITED—See Texas Utilities Company; *U.S. Public*, pg. 1587

EBASCO SERVICES SINGAPORE PTE. LTD.—See Texas Utilities Company; *U.S. Public*, pg. 1587

EBASCO V.I. INC.—See Texas Utilities Company; *U.S. Public*, pg. 1587

EBASINT INTERNATIONAL, INC.—See Boise Cascade Corporation; *U.S. Public*, pg. 243

EBCO AGRICOLAS, COMPANIA DE ALIMENTACION, S.A.—See Tabacalera, S.A.; *Int'l*, pg. 1346

EBELING & REUSS COMPANY; *U.S. Private*, pg. 358

EBERHARD HARDWARE MANUFACTURING LTD.—See The Eastern Company; *U.S. Public*, pg. 548

EBERHARD MANUFACTURING—See The Eastern Company; *U.S. Public*, pg. 548

EBERLINE INSTRUMENT COMPANY LTD.—See Thermo Electron Corporation; *U.S. Public*, pg. 1596

EBERLINE INSTRUMENT CORPORATION—See Thermo Electron Corporation; *U.S. Public*, pg. 1593

EBONY FASHIONS—See Johnson Publishing Company, Inc.; *U.S. Private*, pg. 592

EBSCO GRAPHICS—See EBSCO Industries, Inc.; *U.S. Private*, pg. 359

EBSCO INDUSTRIES, INC.; *U.S. Private*, pg. 358

EBSCO INVESTMENT SERVICES, INC.—See EBSCO Industries, Inc.; *U.S. Private*, pg. 359

EBTEC CORPORATION—See TI Group plc; *Int'l*, pg. 1337

EBY-BROWN CO.; *U.S. Private*, pg. 359

EBY BROWN CO.—See Eby-Brown Co.; *U.S. Private*, pg. 359

EBY-BROWN CO.—See Eby-Brown Co.; *U.S. Private*, pg. 359

EBY CORPORATION; *U.S. Private*, pg. 359

MARTIN K. EBY CONSTRUCTION COMPANY, INC.—See Eby Corporation; *U.S. Private*, pg. 359

E.C. ERNST SOUTH EAST—See The Philadelphia Bourse, Inc.; *U.S. Private*, pg. 861

ECARG, INC.—See W.R. Grace & Co.; *U.S. Public*, pg. 755

ECHELON INTERNATIONAL CORPORATION; *U.S. Public*, pg. 560

ECHELON MALL, INC.—See The Rouse Company; *U.S. Public*, pg. 1408

ECHELON URBAN CENTER, INC.—See The Rouse Company; *U.S. Public*, pg. 1408

ECHLIN ARGENTINA S.A.—See Echlin Inc.; *U.S. Public*, pg. 561

ECHLIN CANADA INC.—See Echlin Inc.; *U.S. Public*, pg. 560

ECHLIN CHARGER MFG. CO. (PTY.) LTD.—See Echlin Inc.; *U.S. Public*, pg. 561

ECHLIN DE VENEZUELA, C.A.—See Echlin Inc.; *U.S. Public*, pg. 561

ECHLIN DO BRASIL S.A.—See Echlin Inc.; *U.S. Public*, pg. 561

ECHLIN DOMINICANA, S.A.—See Echlin Inc.; *U.S. Public*, pg. 561

ECHLIN INC.; *U.S. Public*, pg. 560

ECHLIN MEXICANA S.A. DE C.V.—See Echlin Inc.; *U.S. Public*, pg. 561

ECHLIN-PONCE, INC.—See Echlin Inc.; *U.S. Public*, pg. 560

ECHO BAY ALASKA INC.—See Echo Bay Mines Ltd.; *U.S. Public*, pg. 562

ECHO BAY MINES LTD.; *U.S. Public*, pg. 561

ECHO BAY MINES-LUPIN OPERATIONS—See Echo Bay Mines Ltd.; *U.S. Public*, pg. 562

ECHO BAY MINING COMPANY—See Echo Bay Mines Ltd.; *U.S. Public*, pg. 562

ECHO COMMUNICATION—See Lagardere Groupe; *Int'l*, pg. 792

THE ECHO DESIGN GROUP, INC.; *U.S. Private*, pg. 359

ECHO FARMS GOLF & COUNTRY CLUB, INC.—See The Rouse Company; *U.S. Public*, pg. 1409

ECHOVISION DIVISION—See Armatron International, Inc.; *U.S. Public*, pg. 131

PAUL ECKE RANCH; *U.S. Private*, pg. 359

ECKERD CORPORATION—See JC Penney Company, Inc.; *U.S. Public*, pg. 917

ECKERD DRUG CO.—See JC Penney Company, Inc.; *U.S. Public*, pg. 917

ECKES AG; *Int'l*, pg. 432

ECKES-GRANINI GMBH & CO.—See Eckes AG; *Int'l*, pg. 433

ECKMAN CONSTRUCTION COMPANY; *U.S. Private*, pg. 359

ECLIPSE COMBUSTION—See Eclipse Inc.; *U.S. Private*, pg. 361

ECLIPSE COMBUSTION & INDUSTRIAL EQUIPMENT—See Eclipse Inc.; *U.S. Private*, pg. 361

ECLIPSE COMBUSTION B.V.—See Eclipse Inc.; *U.S. Private*, pg. 361

ECLIPSE COMBUSTION BV—See Eclipse Inc.; *U.S. Private*, pg. 361

ECLIPSE COMBUSTION CHINA LTD.—See Eclipse Inc.; *U.S. Private*, pg. 361

ECLIPSE COMBUSTION GMBH—See Eclipse Inc.; *U.S. Private*, pg. 361

ECLIPSE COMBUSTION, INC.—See Eclipse Inc.; *U.S. Private*, pg. 360

ECLIPSE COMBUSTION LTD.—See Eclipse Inc.; *U.S. Private*, pg. 361

ECLIPSE COMBUSTION S.A.—See Eclipse Inc.; *U.S. Private*, pg. 361

ECLIPSE COMBUSTION SARL—See Eclipse Inc.; *U.S. Private*, pg. 361

ECLIPSE COMBUSTION TAIWAN LTD.—See Eclipse Inc.; *U.S. Private*, pg. 361

ECLIPSE-DUNGS CONTROLS, L.P.—See Eclipse Inc.; *U.S. Private*, pg. 360

ECLIPSE INC.; *U.S. Private*, pg. 360

ECLIPSE MANUFACTURING COMPANY; *U.S. Private*, pg. 361

ECLIPSE MOBILE ELECTRONICS—See Fujitsu Limited; *Int'l*, pg. 526

ECOCONTAINER S.A.—See Royal Packaging Industries Van Leer B.V.; *Int'l*, pg. 1146

ECODYNE COOLING TOWER SERVICES—See Air & Water Technologies Corporation; *U.S. Public*, pg. 29

ECOGEST AIE—See Heidemij N.V.; *Int'l*, pg. 607

ECOLAB CANADA—See Ecolab Inc.; *U.S. Public*, pg. 562

ECOLAB INC.; *U.S. Public*, pg. 562

ECOLAB NEW ZEALAND LTD.—See Ecolab Inc.; *U.S. Public*, pg. 562

ECOLAB PTY. LTD.—See Ecolab Inc.; *U.S. Public*, pg. 562

ECOLE DE PILOTAGE AMAURY DE LA GRANGE—See Groupe Air France; *Int'l*, pg. 560

ECOLOGICAL CHEMICAL PRODUCTS CO.—See Du Pont (E.I. Du Pont De Nemours & Co.); *U.S. Public*, pg. 531

ECOLOGY AND ENVIRONMENT ENGINEERING, INC.—See Ecology and Environment, Inc.; *U.S. Public*, pg. 563

ECOLOGY AND ENVIRONMENT, INC.; *U.S. Public,* pg. 562
ECOM ET PARTENAIRE; *Int'l,* pg. 433
ECONO-CLAD BOOKS—See The American Companies, Inc.; *U.S. Public,* pg. 52
ECONOCOM-USA INC.; *U.S. Private,* pg. 361
ECONOLITE CANADA, INC.—See Econolite Control Products, Inc.; *U.S. Private,* pg. 362
ECONOLITE CONTROL PRODUCTS, INC.; *U.S. Private,* pg. 361
ECONOMATS DU CENTRE—See Auchan S.A.; *Int'l,* pg. 98
THE ECONOMICS PRESS, INC.; *U.S. Private,* pg. 362
THE ECONOMIST GROUP LIMITED.—See Pearson plc; *Int'l,* pg. 1026
ECONOMY FOLDING BOX CORP.; *U.S. Private,* pg. 362
ECONOMY INTERNATIONAL SERVICE INC.—See AJC International, Inc.; *U.S. Private,* pg. 6
ECONOMY MECHANICAL INDUSTRIES, INC.—See Jupiter Industries, Inc.; *U.S. Private,* pg. 602
ECOPHON AB—See Saint-Gobain; *Int'l,* pg. 1176
ECOPHON CERTAINTEED, INC.—See Saint-Gobain; *Int'l,* pg. 1171
ECOS GROUP, INC.; *U.S. Public,* pg. 563
ECOSCIENCE CORPORATION; *U.S. Public,* pg. 563
ECOTRANS OEM TRANSPORTATION—See Pacific Enterprises; *U.S. Public,* pg. 1249
ECOVA CORPORATION—See Amoco Corporation; *U.S. Public,* pg. 103
ECTONA FIBRES LIMITED—See Eastman Kodak Company; *U.S. Public,* pg. 552
ECUASISTEM—See International Data Group; *U.S. Private,* pg. 569
ECUATORIANA DE LUBRICANTES—See Royal Dutch/ Shell Group of Companies; *Int'l,* pg. 1141
ECUATORIANA DE PETROQUIMICOS PETROLITE S.A.— See Baker Hughes Incorporated; *U.S. Public,* pg. 166
ECUATORIANA DE SAL Y PRODUCTOS QUIMICOS C.A. (ECUASAL)—See Morton International Inc.; *U.S. Public,* pg. 1135
ECUAVIA ORIENTE S.A.—See Petroleum Helicopters, Inc.; *U.S. Public,* pg. 1281
ECUSTA AUSTRALIA PTY. LIMITED—See P.H. Glatfelter Company; *U.S. Public,* pg. 746
ECUSTA DIVISION—See P.H. Glatfelter Company; *U.S. Public,* pg. 746
ECUSTA FIBRES LTD.—See P.H. Glatfelter Company; *U.S. Public,* pg. 746
ED. AST & CO. BAUGESELLSCHAFT MBH—See Philipp Holzmann AG; *Int'l,* pg. 633
EDAH—See Vendex International N.V.; *Int'l,* pg. 1463
EDAX INTERNATIONAL, INC.—See Philips Electronics N.V.; *Int'l,* pg. 1053
EDDIE BAUER, INC.—See Spiegel, Inc.; *U.S. Public,* pg. 1499
EDDIE BAUER JAPAN INC.—See Otto Versand (GmbH & Co.); *Int'l,* pg. 1014
EDDIE BAUER MAIL ORDER DIVISION—See Spiegel, Inc.; *U.S. Public,* pg. 1499
EDDINS-WALCHER COMPANY; *U.S. Private,* pg. 362
E.B. EDDY FOREST PRODUCTS LTD.—See George Weston Limited; *Int'l,* pg. 1495
E.B. EDDY PAPER, INC.—See George Weston Limited; *Int'l,* pg. 1495
EDDY PAPER COMPANY LIMITED—See George Weston Limited; *Int'l,* pg. 1495
EDEKA ZENTRALE AG; *Int'l,* pg. 433
EDELBROCK CORP.; *U.S. Public,* pg. 563
DANIEL J. EDELMAN GMBH—See Edelman Public Relations Worldwide; *U.S. Private,* pg. 363
DANIEL J. EDELMAN IRELAND, LTD.—See Edelman Public Relations Worldwide; *U.S. Private,* pg. 363
DANIEL J. EDELMAN LTD.—See Edelman Public Relations Worldwide; *U.S. Private,* pg. 363
DANIEL J. EDELMAN PTY. LTD.—See Edelman Public Relations Worldwide; *U.S. Private,* pg. 363
DANIEL J. EDELMAN SDN. BHD.—See Edelman Public Relations Worldwide; *U.S. Private,* pg. 363
EDELMAN ESPANA S.A.—See Edelman Public Relations Worldwide; *U.S. Private,* pg. 363
EDELMAN EUROPE—See Edelman Public Relations Worldwide; *U.S. Private,* pg. 363
EDELMAN GRUPPO D'—See Edelman Public Relations Worldwide; *U.S. Private,* pg. 363
EDELMAN/HEUER & PARTNER, GMBH—See Edelman Public Relations Worldwide; *U.S. Private,* pg. 363
EDELMAN HOUSTON GROUP—See Edelman Public Relations Worldwide; *U.S. Private,* pg. 363
EDELMAN PR WORLDWIDE—See Edelman Public Relations Worldwide; *U.S. Private,* pg. 363
EDELMAN PUBLIC RELATIONS WORLDWIDE; *U.S. Private,* pg. 362
EDELMAN PUBLIC RELATIONS WORLDWIDE—See Edelman Public Relations Worldwide; *U.S. Private,* pg. 363
EDELMAN PUBLIC RELATIONS WORLDWIDE PTE. LTD.—See Edelman Public Relations Worldwide; *U.S. Private,* pg. 363
EDELMAN-ROUET FRANCE—See Edelman Public Relations Worldwide; *U.S. Private,* pg. 363
EDELMAN WORLDWIDE—See Hakuhodo Incorporated; *Int'l,* pg. 588
EDELMAN WORLDWIDE CHINA—See Edelman Public Relations Worldwide; *U.S. Private,* pg. 363
EDELMAN WORLDWIDE (HONG KONG) LIMITED—See Edelman Public Relations Worldwide; *U.S. Private,* pg. 363
EDELMAN WORLDWIDE, INC.—See Edelman Public Relations Worldwide; *U.S. Private,* pg. 362
EDELSON & SONS CORPORATION; *U.S. Private,* pg. 363
EDEN DETENTION CENTER—See Corrections Corporation of America; *U.S. Public,* pg. 450
EDEN NEWS—See Media General, Inc.; *U.S. Public,* pg. 1078
EDEN VALE—See Northern Foods plc; *Int'l,* pg. 968

EDEN VALE FOOD INGREDIENTS—See Northern Foods plc; *Int'l,* pg. 968
EDENS INDUSTRIAL PARK, INC.—See Continental Materials Corporation; *U.S. Public,* pg. 441
EDER INDUSTRIES, INC.—See Applied Power Inc.; *U.S. Public,* pg. 124
EDERER CRANES—See Ederer Inc.; *U.S. Private,* pg. 363
EDERER INC.; *U.S. Private,* pg. 363
EDERER SERVICES, INC.—See Ederer Inc.; *U.S. Private,* pg. 364
EDGARS STORES LTD.—See South African Breweries, Ltd.; *Int'l,* pg. 1287
EDGCOMB METALS—See Groupe Usinor; *Int'l,* pg. 572
EDGCUMBE INSTRUMENTS LTD.—See Bowthorpe plc; *Int'l,* pg. 207
EDGE SEMICONDUCTOR—See Semtech Corporation; *U.S. Public,* pg. 1456
EDGERTON FORGE, INC.—See Avis Industrial Corporation; *U.S. Public,* pg. 102
EDGEWATER CARE CENTER—See Paragon Health Network, Inc.; *U.S. Private,* pg. 1256
EDGEWATER HOTEL CORP.—See Circus Circus - Las Vegas; *U.S. Public,* pg. 375
EDGEWATER STEEL COMPANY; *U.S. Private,* pg. 364
EDGINGTON OIL COMPANY—See Apex Oil Company, Inc.; *U.S. Private,* pg. 77
EDICOM S.P.A.—See Assicurazioni Generali S.p.A.; *Int'l,* pg. 90
EDICON SYSTEMS—See Eastman Kodak Company; *U.S. Public,* pg. 551
EDIFICACIONES EN MADRID Y PROVINCIA, S.A.—See Vallehermoso, S.A.; *Int'l,* pg. 1447
EDIFICE DORCHESTER-COMMERCE, INC.—See Canadian Imperial Bank of Commerce; *Int'l,* pg. 256
EDIFICIOS AURORA—See Allianz Aktiengesellschaft; *Int'l,* pg. 61
EDILIT—See ETEX; *Int'l,* pg. 430
EDINBURGH—See National Westminster Bank PLC; *Int'l,* pg. 910
EDINBURGH TERMINAL—See GATX Corporation; *U.S. Public,* pg. 692
EDISA INFORMATICA S.A.—See Hewlett-Packard Company; *U.S. Public,* pg. 817
EDISA INFORMATICA S.A. (BELO HORIZONTE)—See Hewlett-Packard Company; *U.S. Public,* pg. 817
EDISA INFORMATICA S.A. (BRASILIA)—See Hewlett-Packard Company; *U.S. Public,* pg. 817
EDISA INFORMATICA S.A. (CAMPINAS)—See Hewlett-Packard Company; *U.S. Public,* pg. 817
EDISA INFORMATICA S.A. (CURITIBA)—See Hewlett-Packard Company; *U.S. Public,* pg. 817
EDISA INFORMATICA S.A. (FLORIANOPOLIS)—See Hewlett-Packard Company; *U.S. Public,* pg. 817
EDISA INFORMATICA S.A. (PORTO ALEGRE)—See Hewlett-Packard Company; *U.S. Public,* pg. 817
EDISA INFORMATICA S.A. (RECIFE)—See Hewlett-Packard Company; *U.S. Public,* pg. 817
EDISA INFORMATICA S.A. (RIO DE JANEIRO)—See Hewlett-Packard Company; *U.S. Public,* pg. 817
EDISA INFORMATICA S.A. (SALVADOR)—See Hewlett-Packard Company; *U.S. Public,* pg. 817
EDISA INFORMATICA S.A. (VITORIA)—See Hewlett-Packard Company; *U.S. Public,* pg. 817
EDISON BROTHERS STORES, INC.; *U.S. Public,* pg. 563
EDISON CAPITAL—See Edison International; *U.S. Public,* pg. 564
EDISON DEVELOPMENT CANADA, INC.—See Unicom Corporation; *U.S. Public,* pg. 1664
EDISON DIVISION—See The Genlyte Group Incorporated; *U.S. Public,* pg. 730
EDISON FOAM PROCESSING CORP.—See Leggett & Platt, Incorporated; *U.S. Public,* pg. 986
EDISON FUSE GEAR—See Cooper Industries, Inc.; *U.S. Public,* pg. 443
THE EDISON GROUP—See Martin/Williams Advertising Inc.; *U.S. Private,* pg. 710
EDISON HOMES-SOUTHEAST, INC.—See Columbia/HCA Healthcare Corporation; *U.S. Public,* pg. 404
THE EDISON ILLUMINATING CO. OF DETROIT—See DTE Energy Company; *U.S. Public,* pg. 476
EDISON INTERNATIONAL; *U.S. Public,* pg. 564
EDISON MISSION ENERGY—See Edison International; *U.S. Public,* pg. 564
EDISON MISSION ENERGY ASIA PTE. LTD.—See Edison International; *U.S. Public,* pg. 564
EDISON MISSION ENERGY HOLDINGS PTY. LTD.—See Edison International; *U.S. Public,* pg. 564
EDISON MISSION ENERGY INTERNATIONAL B.V.—See Edison International; *U.S. Public,* pg. 564
EDISON MISSION ENERGY LIMITED—See Edison International; *U.S. Public,* pg. 564
EDISON OPERATION—See Nozaki & Company Ltd.; *Int'l,* pg. 990
EDISON PARKING PROPERTIES, LLC; *U.S. Private,* pg. 364
EDISON PLASTICS CO.—See Williamson-Dickie Mfg. Co.; *U.S. Private,* pg. 1179
EDISON PLASTICS DIV.—See Williamson-Dickie Mfg. Co.; *U.S. Private,* pg. 1179
EDISON SAULT ELECTRIC COMPANY—See ESELCO, Inc.; *U.S. Public,* pg. 592
EDISON S.P.A.—See Compart SpA; *Int'l,* pg. 324
EDITECO S.A.—See Tractebel; *Int'l,* pg. 1415
EDITION N 1—See Lagardere Groupe; *Int'l,* pg. 792
EDITIONS BORDAS—See C.E.P. Communication Group; *Int'l,* pg. 239
EDITIONS D'ENSEIGNEMENTS-RELIGIEUX F.P.R. INC.— See Quebecor Inc.; *Int'l,* pg. 1077
EDITIONS DU JURIS-CLASSEUR—See Reed Elsevier plc; *Int'l,* pg. 1095
EDITIONS DU MONITEUR—See C.E.P. Communication Group; *Int'l,* pg. 239
EDITIONS EDOUARD PRIVAT SA—See C.E.P. Communication Group; *Int'l,* pg. 239

EDITIONS FRANCAISES INC.—See C.E.P. Communication Group; *Int'l,* pg. 240
EDITIONS FRANCOPHONES BELGES SA (EFB)—See VNU Verenigde Nederlandse Uitgeversbedrijven B.V.; *Int'l,* pg. 1447
EDITIONS GARNIER—See C.E.P. Communication Group; *Int'l,* pg. 239
EDITIONS GERARD DE VILLIERS—See Lagardere Groupe; *Int'l,* pg. 792
EDITIONS GRASSET-FASQUELLE—See Lagardere Groupe; *Int'l,* pg. 792
EDITIONS JEAN-CLAUDE LATTES—See Lagardere Groupe; *Int'l,* pg. 794
EDITIONS LAMY—See Wolters Kluwer N.V.; *Int'l,* pg. 1513
EDITIONS MUSICALES FRANCOIS I—See Lagardere Groupe; *Int'l,* pg. 792
EDITIONS ROMBALDI—See Lagardere Groupe; *Int'l,* pg. 792
EDITIONS SCIENTIFIQUES ET MEDICALES ELSEVIER— See Reed Elsevier plc; *Int'l,* pg. 1099
EDITIONS STOCK—See Lagardere Groupe; *Int'l,* pg. 792
EDITIONS WILSON & LAFLEUR, MARTEL LTEE—See Quebecor Inc.; *Int'l,* pg. 1077
EDITOR AG MULTIMEDIA UND DESIGN—See Impuls Advertising AG; *U.S. Public,* pg. 666
EDITORA CAMPUS LTDA.—See Reed Elsevier plc; *Int'l,* pg. 1100
EDITORIAL ALHAMBRA MEXICANA S.A. DE C.V.—See Pearson plc; *Int'l,* pg. 1025
EDITORIAL CARIBE INC.—See Thomas Nelson Inc.; *U.S. Public,* pg. 1168
EDITORIAL DIANA, S.A. DE C.V.—See Corporacion MAPFRE, Compania Internacional de Reaseguros, S.A.; *Int'l,* pg. 334
EDITORIAL MEDICA PANAMERICANA S.A.—See Waverly, Inc.; *U.S. Public,* pg. 1748
EDITORIAL PLANETA - DEAGOSTINI, S.A.; *Int'l,* pg. 433
EDITORIALE SORIT S.P.A.—See Arnoldo Mondadori Editore S.p.A.; *Int'l,* pg. 888
EDITORS PRESS, INC.—See The Kiplinger Washington Editors, Inc.; *U.S. Private,* pg. 623
EDITRICE ABITARE SEGESTA S.P.A.—See Arnoldo Mondadori Editore S.p.A.; *Int'l,* pg. 888
EDITRICE LA STAMPA S.P.A.—See Fiat Auto SpA; *Int'l,* pg. 482
EDITRICE PORTORIA S.R.L.—See Arnoldo Mondadori Editore S.p.A.; *Int'l,* pg. 888
EDIZIONI DI COMUNITA S.R.L.—See Arnoldo Mondadori Editore S.p.A.; *Int'l,* pg. 888
EDIZIONI FRASSINELLI S.R.L.—See Arnoldo Mondadori Editore S.p.A.; *Int'l,* pg. 888
EDLON PRODUCTS, INC.—See Robbins & Myers, Inc.; *U.S. Public,* pg. 1393
EDLUND COMPANY, INC.; *U.S. Private,* pg. 364
EDMESTON AB—See Sandvik AB; *Int'l,* pg. 1185
EDMONSON WHEAT GROWERS, INC.; *U.S. Private,* pg. 364
THE EDMONTON JOURNAL—See Hollinger Inc.; *Int'l,* pg. 631
EDMONTON PLANT—See Fort James Corporation; *U.S. Public,* pg. 672
THE EDMONTON SUN—See Sun Media Corporation; *Int'l,* pg. 1320
EDMUND SCIENTIFIC COMPANY; *U.S. Private,* pg. 364
EDON MACHINE DIV.—See Simpson Industries, Inc.; *U.S. Public,* pg. 1475
EDPERBRASCAN CORPORATION; *Int'l,* pg. 433
EDUCATION & ENTERTAINMENT—See Evans & Sutherland Computer Corporation; *U.S. Public,* pg. 596
THE EDUCATION PUBLISHING GROUP—See Pearson plc; *Int'l,* pg. 1026
THE EDUCATION SHOW—See EMAP Plc; *Int'l,* pg. 452
EDUCATIONAL & PROFESSIONAL PUBLISHING GROUP—See The McGraw-Hill Companies; *U.S. Public,* pg. 1070
EDUCATIONAL DEVELOPMENT CORPORATION; *U.S. Public,* pg. 564
EDUCATIONAL FINANCE GROUP—See United Insurance Companies, Inc.; *U.S. Public,* pg. 1679
EDUCATIONAL INSIGHTS, INC.; *U.S. Public,* pg. 565
EDUCATIONAL MANAGEMENT GROUP—See National Amusements, Inc.; *U.S. Private,* pg. 778
EDWAL SCIENTIFIC PRODUCTS DIV.—See Falcon Safety Products Inc.; *U.S. Private,* pg. 392
EDWARD DON & COMPANY-CLARKSTON BRANCH—See Edward Don & Company; *U.S. Private,* pg. 339
EDWARDS—See Imetal; *Int'l,* pg. 661
A.G. EDWARDS & SONS, INC.—See A.G. Edwards, Inc.; *U.S. Public,* pg. 565
A.G. EDWARDS, INC.; *U.S. Public,* pg. 565
A.G. EDWARDS TRUST COMPANY—See A.G. Edwards, Inc.; *U.S. Public,* pg. 565
EDWARDS ALTO VUOTO SPA—See The BOC Group plc; *Int'l,* pg. 122
EDWARDS & BROUGHTON COMPANY—See Wallace Computer Services, Inc.; *U.S. Public,* pg. 1735
EDWARDS & KELCEY CONSTRUCTION, INC.—See Edwards and Kelcey, Inc.; *U.S. Private,* pg. 364
EDWARDS & KELCEY ENGINEERS, INC.—See Edwards and Kelcey, Inc.; *U.S. Private,* pg. 364
EDWARDS AND KELCEY, INC.; *U.S. Private,* pg. 364
EDWARDS & KELCEY WIRELESS—See Edwards and Kelcey, Inc.; *U.S. Private,* pg. 364
EDWARDS BAKING CO.; *U.S. Private,* pg. 365
EDWARDS BROTHERS - CAROLINA—See Edwards Brothers, Inc.; *U.S. Private,* pg. 365
EDWARDS BROTHERS, INC.; *U.S. Private,* pg. 365
EDWARDS DUNLOP CO. PTY. LTD.—See Amcor Limited; *Int'l,* pg. 72
EDWARDS ENGINEERING CORPORATION; *U.S. Private,* pg. 365
EDWARDS HIGH VACUUM, INTERNATIONAL—See The BOC Group plc; *Int'l,* pg. 121

EDWARDS HIGH VACUUM INTERNATIONAL—See The BOC Group plc; *Int'l*, pg. 121
EDWARDS HOCHVAKUUM GMBH—See The BOC Group plc; *Int'l*, pg. 122
J.D. EDWARDS & COMPANY; *U.S. Private*, pg. 365
EDWARDS JAPAN LTD.—See The BOC Group plc; *Int'l*, pg. 122
K.R. EDWARDS LEAF TOBACCO CO., INC.—See Universal Corporation; *U.S. Public*, pg. 1694
EDWARDS SUPER FOOD STORES—See Koninklijke Ahold NV; *Int'l*, pg. 749
EDWARDS SUPER FOOD STORES, LONG ISLAND DIV.—See Koninklijke Ahold NV; *Int'l*, pg. 750
EDWARDS SYSTEMS TECH—See General Signal Corporation; *U.S. Public*, pg. 726
EDWARDS TELEPHONE CO.—See Telephone and Data Systems, Inc.; *U.S. Public*, pg. 1571
EDWARDSTONE & COMPANY, INC.; *U.S. Private*, pg. 365
EDWARDSVILLE INTELLIGENCER—See The Hearst Corporation; *U.S. Private*, pg. 517
EDY'S MID-ATLANTIC REGION—See Dreyer's Grand Ice Cream, Inc.; *U.S. Public*, pg. 529
EDY'S MIDWEST REGION—See Dreyer's Grand Ice Cream, Inc.; *U.S. Public*, pg. 529
EDY'S NORTHEAST REGION—See Dreyer's Grand Ice Cream, Inc.; *U.S. Public*, pg. 529
EDY'S SOUTHEAST REGION—See Dreyer's Grand Ice Cream, Inc.; *U.S. Public*, pg. 530
EEKLO MILL—See Fort James Corporation; *U.S. Public*, pg. 673
EERSTE SURINAAMS-NEDERLANDSE LEVENSVERZEKERING MAATSCHAPPIJ ENNA NV—See AEGON N.V.; *Int'l*, pg. 28
AS EESTI AGA—See AGA AB; *Int'l*, pg. 14
AS EESTI VARV—See Kemira Oy; *Int'l*, pg. 729
EFESIS SCHLEIFTECHNIK—See Saint-Gobain; *Int'l*, pg. 1174
EFFECTIVE MANAGEMENT SYSTEMS; *U.S. Public*, pg. 565
EFFECTONA A/S—See Wella Group; *Int'l*, pg. 1490
EFFEMS AG—See Mars, Incorporated; *U.S. Private*, pg. 707
EFFICIENT ENGINEERING CO.; *U.S. Private*, pg. 365
EFFINGHAM-CLAY SERVICE CO.; *U.S. Private*, pg. 365
EFFKA INFORMATION AB—See Axel Johnson AB; *Int'l*, pg. 708
EFFRON FUEL OIL CO., INC.—See Meenan Oil Co L.P.; *U.S. Private*, pg. 729
EFTHOR HOLDING BV—See Accor S.A.; *Int'l*, pg. 21
EGAN COS.; *U.S. Private*, pg. 365
EGAN EUROPE (JOHN BROWN PLASTICS MACHINERY LTD.)—See Kvaerner a.s.a.; *Int'l*, pg. 774
EGAN MACHINERY DIVISION—See Kvaerner a.s.a.; *Int'l*, pg. 774
EGAN MCKAY ELECTRICAL CONTRACTORS—See Egan Cos.; *U.S. Private*, pg. 366
EGAN MECHANICAL CONTRACTORS INC.—See Egan Cos.; *U.S. Private*, pg. 366
EGAZ—See Gaz de France; *Int'l*, pg. 541
EGGED ISRAEL TRANSPORT COOPERATIVE SOCIETY LTD.; *Int'l*, pg. 435
EGGHEAD, INC.; *U.S. Public*, pg. 566
EGGLAND'S BEST, INC.; *U.S. Private*, pg. 366
EGIS-NUTRICIA KFT—See Nutricia BV; *Int'l*, pg. 991
EGIZII ELECTRIC, INC.; *U.S. Private*, pg. 366
EGON LUCAS MEDIZIN TECHNIK GMBH—See Getinge Industrier AB; *Int'l*, pg. 551
EGUZKIA-NHK, S.A.—See NHK Spring Co., Ltd.; *Int'l*, pg. 902
EGYBRIT—See Atlet AB; *Int'l*, pg. 97
EGYPOR TRADE—See Hewlett-Packard Company; *U.S. Public*, pg. 817
EGYPT OTSUKA PHARMACEUTICAL CO., S.A.E.—See Otsuka Pharmaceutical Co., Ltd.; *Int'l*, pg. 1014
EGYPTIAN ALUMINIUM PRODUCTS COMPANY—See Reynolds Metals Company; *U.S. Public*, pg. 1386
EGYPTIAN BRITISH BANK S.A.E.—See HSBC Holdings plc; *Int'l*, pg. 581
EGYPTIAN FUND MANAGEMENT GROUP—See Credit Commercial de France; *Int'l*, pg. 343
EHIME KANZUME CO., LTD.—See Meiji Seika Kaisha, Ltd.; *Int'l*, pg. 855
EIBA LAUSANNE BRANCH—See Union Bank of Switzerland; *Int'l*, pg. 1440
EICHLER KG—See GESTRA GmbH; *Int'l*, pg. 550
EICKEL & SPINDELDREHER GMBH—See Schuttersveld Holding N.V.; *Int'l*, pg. 1210
EICKHOFF CORPORATION—See Gebr. Eickhoff Maschinenfabrik und Eisengiesserei mbH; *Int'l*, pg. 542
EIDESIGN TECHNOLOGIES, INC.—See Nippon Steel Corporation; *Int'l*, pg. 940
H. EIGENBRODT AB—See Axel Johnson AB; *Int'l*, pg. 708
800-FLOWERS, INC.; *U.S. Private*, pg. 366
EIGHT O'CLOCK COFFEE—See Tengelmann Warenhandelsgesellschaft; *Int'l*, pg. 1375
838 INVESTMENT GROUP, INC.—See WSFS Financial Corporation; *U.S. Public*, pg. 1729
1838 BOND-DEBENTURE TRADING FUND; *U.S. Public*, pg. 566
EIGHTY EIGHT OIL CO.—See True Companies; *U.S. Private*, pg. 1107
EIGHTY FOUR COAL CO.—See Rochester & Pittsburgh Coal Company; *U.S. Public*, pg. 1395
84 LUMBER COMPANY; *U.S. Private*, pg. 366
EIKIN LTD.—See Norske Skogindustrier A.S.; *Int'l*, pg. 966
EILER & RIEMEL - TESTA—See Testa International; *Int'l*, pg. 1377
EIMCO COAL MACHINERY INC.—See Tamrock Corp.; *Int'l*, pg. 1352
EIMCO ELECON (INDIA) LTD.—See Tamrock Corp.; *Int'l*, pg. 1353
EIMCO (GREAT BRITAIN) LTD.—See Tamrock Corp.; *Int'l*, pg. 1353

EIMCO PROCESS EQUIPMENT CO.—See Baker Hughes Incorporated; *U.S. Public*, pg. 166
GIULIO EINAUDI EDITORE S.P.A.—See Arnoldo Mondadori Editore S.p.A.; *Int'l*, pg. 888
EINLAGENSICHERUNG DER BANKEN UND BANKIERS GMBH—See Creditanstalt-Bankverein; *Int'l*, pg. 347
EINSON FREEMAN INC.—See WPP Group plc; *Int'l*, pg. 1483
EINSTEIN MOOMJY INC.; *U.S. Private*, pg. 366
EINSTEIN/NOAH BAGEL CORP.—See Boston Chicken, Inc.; *U.S. Public*, pg. 247
EIS, INC.—See Electrical Insulation Suppliers; *U.S. Private*, pg. 368
EISAI CO., LTD.; *Int'l*, pg. 435
HENRY EISEN ADV. AGENCY, INC.—See Tootsie Roll Industries, Inc.; *U.S. Public*, pg. 1621
EISEN LOTHRINGEN STAHLHANDEL GMBH (SSH)—See Veba AG; *Int'l*, pg. 1459
EISEN RIEG HAUSTECHNIK-HANDEL GMBH—See Mannesmann A.G.; *Int'l*, pg. 838
EISEN UND METALL GMBH—See Fried. Krupp AG; *Int'l*, pg. 514
EISEN- UND STEIN-GESELLSCHAFT MBH—See Fried. Krupp AG; *Int'l*, pg. 513
EISENBAHN-TRANSPORTMITTEL AG—See Brambles Industries Limited; *Int'l*, pg. 212
EISENBAHN VERKEHRSMITTEL A.G.—See Brambles Industries Limited; *Int'l*, pg. 212
EISENMETALL GESELLSCHAFT MBH—See Fried. Krupp AG; *Int'l*, pg. 514
EISENMETALL LAGER GMBH—See Fried. Krupp AG; *Int'l*, pg. 514
EISENMETALL LEGIERUNGEN GMBH—See Fried. Krupp AG; *Int'l*, pg. 513
EISENMETALL ROHR GMBH—See Fried. Krupp AG; *Int'l*, pg. 514
EISENMETALL ROHSTOFF GMBH—See Fried. Krupp AG; *Int'l*, pg. 513
EISENSTAHL GMBH—See Cockerill Sambre; *Int'l*, pg. 302
EISNER & ASSOCIATES, INC.; *U.S. Private*, pg. 366
EISNER, PETROU & ASSOCIATES, INC.—See Eisner & Associates, Inc.; *U.S. Private*, pg. 366
EISYS S.P.A.—See Thomson S.A.; *Int'l*, pg. 1385
EIVAL, S.A.—See Petrogal, s.a.; *Int'l*, pg. 1045
EIZAN CO., LTD.—See Yamanouchi Pharmaceutical Co. Ltd.; *Int'l*, pg. 1518
EJENDOMSSELSKABET TRETORN A/S—See Skandia Insurance Company Limited; *Int'l*, pg. 1257
EJEVEN S.A.—See Eaton Corporation; *U.S. Public*, pg. 559
EKCO CANADA, INC.—See Ekco Group, Inc.; *U.S. Public*, pg. 566
EKCO GROUP, INC.; *U.S. Public*, pg. 566
EKCO HOUSEWARES, INC.—See Ekco Group, Inc.; *U.S. Public*, pg. 566
EKCO INTERNATIONAL HOUSEWARES, LTD.—See Ekco Group, Inc.; *U.S. Public*, pg. 566
EKCO INTERNATIONAL, INC.—See Ekco Group, Inc.; *U.S. Public*, pg. 566
EKER—See Sodexho S.A.; *Int'l*, pg. 1274
EKLOW SCANDINAVIA A/S—See Axel Johnson AB; *Int'l*, pg. 710
EKLOW SCANDINAVIA GROUP AB—See Axel Johnson AB; *Int'l*, pg. 710
EKMEL LAFARGE BETON AS—See Lafarge S.A.; *Int'l*, pg. 790
EKOKONREM SPOLKA Z O.O.—See Heidemij N.V.; *Int'l*, pg. 566
EKOMAT SWEDEN AB—See Nestle S.A.; *Int'l*, pg. 920
EKOTECH—See Technip; *Int'l*, pg. 1360
EKTELON—See Prince Sports Group Inc.; *U.S. Private*, pg. 884
EL AGUILA S.A.—See Heineken N.V.; *Int'l*, pg. 608
EL AL AIRLINES LTD.; *Int'l*, pg. 435
EL AL ISRAEL AIRLINES, LTD.—See El Al Airlines Ltd.; *Int'l*, pg. 435
THE EL-BEE CHARGIT CORP.—See The Elder-Beerman Stores Corp.; *U.S. Private*, pg. 367
EL. BO. MEC. THERMALLOY SRL.—See Bowthorpe plc; *Int'l*, pg. 209
EL CAMINO RESOURCES, LTD.; *U.S. Private*, pg. 366
EL CAMPO ALUMINUM CO.—See Reynolds Metals Company; *U.S. Public*, pg. 1386
EL CHACO S.A. FINANCIERA—See Citicorp; *U.S. Public*, pg. 379
EL CHICO RESTAURANTS, INC.—See Cracken, Harkey, Street & Co., LLC; *U.S. Private*, pg. 283
EL CONQUISTADOR DEVELOPMENT CORP.—See Lennar Corporation; *U.S. Public*, pg. 988
EL CONQUISTADOR RESORT & COUNTRY CLUB—See Patriot American Hospitality, Inc.; *U.S. Public*, pg. 1265
EL CORTE INGLES SA; *Int'l*, pg. 435
EL DORADO CHEMICAL CO.—See LSB Industries, Inc.; *U.S. Public*, pg. 970
EL DORADO INVESTMENT COMPANY—See Pinnacle West Capital Corporation; *U.S. Public*, pg. 1298
EL DORADO NATIONAL—See Thor Industries, Inc.; *U.S. Public*, pg. 1602
EL DORADO TIRE CO.—See Sumitomo Corporation; *Int'l*, pg. 1312
EL INDIA AND TAMBO MINES—See Barrick Gold Corporation; *Int'l*, pg. 169
EL-MOHANDES JOTUN EGYPT—See Jotun A/S; *Int'l*, pg. 715
EL MOLINO FOODS, INC.—See Borden, Inc.; *U.S. Private*, pg. 158
EL PASO BAKING CO., INC.—See Flowers Industries, Inc.; *U.S. Public*, pg. 657
EL PASO ELECTRIC COMPANY; *U.S. Public*, pg. 567
EL PASO ENERGY—See El Paso Natural Gas Co.; *U.S. Public*, pg. 567
EL PASO HERALD-POST—See The E.W. Scripps Company; *U.S. Public*, pg. 1447
EL PASO NATURAL GAS CO.; *U.S. Public*, pg. 567

EL PASO RESTAURANT CORP.—See Specialty Restaurants Corporation; *U.S. Private*, pg. 1023
EL PASO TIMES, INC.—See Gannett Company, Inc.; *U.S. Public*, pg. 700
EL POLLO LOCO—See Advantica Restaurant Group, Inc.; *U.S. Public*, pg. 23
EL PUERTO DE LIVERPOOL S.A.; *Int'l*, pg. 435
EL RIO GRANDE—See Ark Restaurants Corp.; *U.S. Public*, pg. 130
EL SAN JUAN HOTEL & CASINO—See Patriot American Hospitality, Inc.; *U.S. Public*, pg. 1265
EL SOL COMPANIA DE SEGUROS GENERALES—See Allianz Aktiengesellschaft; *Int'l*, pg. 61
EL. TE. SICILIANA S.P.A.—See Telefonaktiebolaget LM Ericsson; *Int'l*, pg. 1365
EL TENIENTE DIVISION—See CODELCO Chile (Corporacion Nacional Del Cobre De Chile); *Int'l*, pg. 302
EL TORITO RESTAURANTS INC.—See Family Restaurants, Inc.; *U.S. Private*, pg. 393
ELABORADORA ARGENTINA DE CEREALES, S.A.—See The Quaker Oats Company; *U.S. Public*, pg. 1348
ELAN CLINICAL SERVICES LTD.—See Elan Corporation Plc; *Int'l*, pg. 436
ELAN CORPORATION PLC; *Int'l*, pg. 435
ELAN FOODS—See Grotech Capital Group, Inc.; *U.S. Private*, pg. 484
ELAN INSURANCE SERVICES, INC.—See Firstar Corporation; *U.S. Public*, pg. 643
ELAN INTERNATIONAL FINANCE LTD.—See Elan Corporation Plc; *Int'l*, pg. 436
ELAN INVESTMENT SERVICES, INC.—See Firstar Corporation; *U.S. Public*, pg. 643
ELAN LIFE INSURANCE COMPANY—See Firstar Corporation; *U.S. Public*, pg. 643
ELAN PHARMA GMBH—See Elan Corporation Plc; *Int'l*, pg. 436
ELAN PHARMA INC.—See Elan Corporation Plc; *Int'l*, pg. 436
ELAN PHARMA LTD.—See Elan Corporation Plc; *Int'l*, pg. 436
ELAN PHARMA PHILIPPINES, INC.—See Elan Corporation Plc; *Int'l*, pg. 436
ELAN PHARMACEUTICAL RESEARCH CORP.—See Elan Corporation Plc; *Int'l*, pg. 436
ELAN/PRI LTD.—See Elan Corporation Plc; *Int'l*, pg. 436
ELAN TITLE SERVICES, INC.—See Firstar Corporation; *U.S. Public*, pg. 643
ELAN TRANSDERMAL LTD.—See Elan Corporation Plc; *Int'l*, pg. 436
ELANCO—See Eli Lilly and Company; *U.S. Public*, pg. 993
ELANCO ANIMAL HEALTH—See Eli Lilly and Company; *U.S. Public*, pg. 993
ELANCO IHARA K. K.—See Eli Lilly and Company; *U.S. Public*, pg. 993
ELANCO INDUSTRIAL, S.A.—See Eli Lilly and Company; *U.S. Public*, pg. 993
ELANCO PREMEZCLAS, S.A.—See Eli Lilly and Company; *U.S. Public*, pg. 993
ELANCO PRODUCTS LIMITED—See Eli Lilly and Company; *U.S. Public*, pg. 993
ELANCO QUIMICA LIMITADA—See Eli Lilly and Company; *U.S. Public*, pg. 993
ELANCO S.A.—See Eli Lilly and Company; *U.S. Public*, pg. 993
ELANCO, VETERINARIA, S.A.—See Eli Lilly and Company; *U.S. Public*, pg. 993
ELAND-BRANDT, B.V.—See International Aluminum Corporation; *U.S. Public*, pg. 895
ELASCO AGENCY SALES, INC.—See Hughes Supply, Inc.; *U.S. Public*, pg. 846
ELASCO INTERNATIONAL CORP.—See Eclipse Inc.; *U.S. Private*, pg. 361
ELASTIC MATERIALS, INC.; *U.S. Private*, pg. 367
ELASTIMOLD CO.—See Thomas & Betts Corporation; *U.S. Public*, pg. 1598
ELASTOGRAN FRANCE S.A.—See BASF AG; *Int'l*, pg. 108
ELASTOGRAN GMBH—See BASF AG; *Int'l*, pg. 104
ELASTOGRAN HEADWAY URETHANES CO., LTD.—See BASF AG; *Int'l*, pg. 108
ELASTOGRAN ITALIA S.P.A.—See BASF AG; *Int'l*, pg. 108
ELASTOGRAN S.A.—See BASF AG; *Int'l*, pg. 108
ELASTOGRAN SCHWARZHEIDE GMBH—See BASF AG; *Int'l*, pg. 104
ELASTOGRAN UK LIMITED—See BASF AG; *Int'l*, pg. 108
ELASTOMER SEALS - NORTH AMERICA—See TI Group plc; *Int'l*, pg. 1338
ELASTOMERIC TECHNOLOGIES, INC.—See Thomas & Betts Corporation; *U.S. Public*, pg. 1598
ELBAR B.V.—See Imperial Chemical Industries B.V.; *Int'l*, pg. 673
ELBE-FLUGZEUGWERKE GMBH—See Daimler-Benz Aktiengesellschaft; *Int'l*, pg. 367
ELBE TRANSPORT G.M.B.H.—See Unilever Plc; *Int'l*, pg. 1436
ELBECO INCORPORATED; *U.S. Private*, pg. 367
ELBERTA CRATE & BOX COMPANY; *U.S. Private*, pg. 367
ELBERTON SOUTHERN RAILWAY CO.—See Norfolk Southern Corporation; *U.S. Public*, pg. 1191
ELBIT COMPUTERS LTD.—See IDB Holding Corporation; *Int'l*, pg. 644
ELBIT LTD.—See IDB Holding Corporation; *Int'l*, pg. 644
ELCALOR AG—See Electrolux, AB; *Int'l*, pg. 443
E.N. ELCANO DE LA MARINA MERCANTE, S.A.—See SEPI; *Int'l*, pg. 1224
ELCAT CORPORATION—See Electrocatalytic, Inc.; *U.S. Private*, pg. 369
ELCO CONSTRUCTION PRODUCTS DIVISION—See Textron Inc.; *U.S. Public*, pg. 1590
ELCO CONSUMER PRODUCTS CORP.—See Textron Inc.; *U.S. Public*, pg. 1590
THE ELCO CORP.—See Detrex Corporation; *U.S. Public*, pg. 502

ELCO CORPORATION—See Kyocera Corporation; *Int'l*, pg. 775
ELCO DOMINICANA, S.A.—See Eli Lilly and Company; *U.S. Public*, pg. 993
ELCO ELEKTRONIK GMBH—See Kyocera Corporation; *Int'l*, pg. 775
ELCO EURPOE GMBH—See Textron Inc.; *U.S. Public*, pg. 1590
ELCO INTERNATIONAL K.K.—See Kyocera Corporation; *Int'l*, pg. 775
ELCO INTERNATIONAL/SYNERGY DIVISION—See Textron Inc.; *U.S. Public*, pg. 1590
ELCO NV-SA—See Kyocera Corporation; *Int'l*, pg. 775
ELCO PRECISION FORMING DIV.—See Textron Inc.; *U.S. Public*, pg. 1590
ELCO PRECISION STAMPING DIV.—See Textron Inc.; *U.S. Public*, pg. 1590
ELCO SDD—See Textron Inc.; *U.S. Public*, pg. 1590
ELCO TEXTRON—See Textron Inc.; *U.S. Public*, pg. 1590
ELCOR CORPORATION; *U.S. Public*, pg. 567
ELCOTEL, INC.; *U.S. Public*, pg. 568
ELDAN ELECTRONICS—See Hewlett-Packard Company; *U.S. Public*, pg. 817
ELDEEN MANUFACTURING CORPORATION—See Recoton Corporation; *U.S. Public*, pg. 1369
THE ELDER-BEERMAN STORES CORP.; *U.S. Private*, pg. 367
ELDER MANUFACTURING COMPANY; *U.S. Private*, pg. 367
ELDER'S FINANCE GROUP—See Foster's Brewing Group Limited; *Int'l*, pg. 500
ELDERS LIMITED—See Foster's Brewing Group Limited; *Int'l*, pg. 500
ELDERS - NEW SOUTH WALES—See Foster's Brewing Group Limited; *Int'l*, pg. 501
ELDERS - QUEENSLAND—See Foster's Brewing Group Limited; *Int'l*, pg. 501
ELDERS - SOUTH AUSTRALIA—See Foster's Brewing Group Limited; *Int'l*, pg. 501
ELDERS - VICTORIA—See Foster's Brewing Group Limited; *Int'l*, pg. 501
ELDERS - WESTERN AUSTRALIA—See Foster's Brewing Group Limited; *Int'l*, pg. 501
ELDIM B.V.—See Indivers B.V.; *Int'l*, pg. 673
ELDIM INC.—See Indivers B.V.; *Int'l*, pg. 673
ELDON AB; *Int'l*, pg. 436
ELDON A/S—See Eldon AB; *Int'l*, pg. 436
ELDON CYPRUS—See Eldon AB; *Int'l*, pg. 436
ELDON ELECTRIC LTD.—See Eldon AB; *Int'l*, pg. 436
ELDON ELECTRONICS AB—See Eldon AB; *Int'l*, pg. 436
ELDON ELMATERIEL AB—See Eldon AB; *Int'l*, pg. 436
ELDON ESPANA S.A.—See Eldon AB; *Int'l*, pg. 436
ELDON FRANCE—See Eldon AB; *Int'l*, pg. 436
ELDON GMBH—See Eldon AB; *Int'l*, pg. 436
ELDON INTERNATIONAL S.A.—See Eldon AB; *Int'l*, pg. 436
ELDON LABORATORIES LIMITED—See Alliance UniChem PLC; *Int'l*, pg. 58
ELDON N.V.—See Eldon AB; *Int'l*, pg. 436
ELDON RENTAL TRAILER—See Eldon AB; *Int'l*, pg. 436
ELDON S.A.—See Eldon AB; *Int'l*, pg. 436
ELDORADO CHEMICAL COMPANY; *U.S. Private*, pg. 367
ELDORADO AT SANTA FE—See AMREP Corporation; *U.S. Public*, pg. 105
ELECOMP—See Kone Corporation; *Int'l*, pg. 746
ELECSYS INC.; *U.S. Private*, pg. 367
ELEC-TEL SUPPLY COMPANY—See Hughes Supply, Inc.; *U.S. Public*, pg. 847
ELECTRA COMMUNICATIONS—See IXC Communications, Inc.; *U.S. Private*, pg. 556
ELECTRA DE VIESGO, S.A.—See SEPI; *Int'l*, pg. 1224
ELECTRA-GEAR DIV.—See Regal-Beloit Corporation; *U.S. Public*, pg. 1370
ELECTRA INSURANCE LIMITED—See Telefonaktiebolaget LM Ericsson; *Int'l*, pg. 1365
ELECTRABEL S.A.; *Int'l*, pg. 436
ELECTRAFINA—See Groupe Bruxelles Lambert S.A.; *Int'l*, pg. 562
ELECTRI-CORD MANUFACTURING CO.—See Leucadia National Corporation; *U.S. Public*, pg. 990
ELECTRIC COMPONENT OF PTE. LTD.—See General Electric Company; *U.S. Public*, pg. 713
ELECTRIC ENERGY EXPORT CORP.—See Citizens Utilities Company; *U.S. Public*, pg. 380
ELECTRIC ENERGY, INC.—See Illinova Inc.; *U.S. Public*, pg. 870
ELECTRIC FUEL CORP.—See Florida Progress Corporation; *U.S. Public*, pg. 655
ELECTRIC FURNACE CO.; *U.S. Private*, pg. 367
ELECTRIC FURNACE FRANCE S.A.R.L.—See Electric Furnace Co.; *U.S. Private*, pg. 368
ELECTRIC FURNACE GERMANY, GMBH—See Electric Furnace Co.; *U.S. Private*, pg. 368
ELECTRIC INSURANCE CO.; *U.S. Private*, pg. 368
ELECTRIC LABORATORIES & SALES CORP.—See Hughes Supply, Inc.; *U.S. Public*, pg. 847
ELECTRIC MOTOR DEVELOPMENTS (HALSTEAD) LTD.—See Wolseley Plc.; *Int'l*, pg. 1511
ELECTRIC POWER EQUIPMENT CO.; *U.S. Private*, pg. 368
ELECTRIC PROTECTION SERVICES (EPS)—See Tyco International Ltd.; *U.S. Public*, pg. 1650
ELECTRIC RAILS LTD.—See Imatran Voima Oy; *Int'l*, pg. 660
ELECTRIC RESEARCH AND MANUFACTURING COOPERATIVE, INC. (ERMCO)—See Arkansas Electric Cooperatives Inc.; *U.S. Private*, pg. 82
ELECTRICAL CARBON LIMITED—See Morgan Crucible Co. Plc; *Int'l*, pg. 891
ELECTRICAL EQUIPMENT COMPANY; *U.S. Private*, pg. 368
ELECTRICAL EQUIPMENT COMPANY—See Electrical Equipment Company; *U.S. Private*, pg. 368

ELECTRICAL INSULATION SUPPLIERS; *U.S. Private*, pg. 368
ELECTRICAL PRODUCTS DIVISION—See 3M; *U.S. Public*, pg. 1605
ELECTRICAL WHOLESALE SUPPLY COMPANY, INC.; *U.S. Private*, pg. 368
ELECTRICAL WORLD—See The McGraw-Hill Companies; *U.S. Public*, pg. 1071
ELECTRICITE DE FRANCE; *Int'l*, pg. 437
ELECTRICITE DE FRANCE—See Electricite de France; *Int'l*, pg. 437
ELECTRICITE DE LA LIENNE SA-(LIENNE)—See Alusuisse-Lonza Holding Ltd.; *Int'l*, pg. 67
ELECTRICITE DE TAHITI—See Lyonnaise des Eaux S.A.; *Int'l*, pg. 824
ELECTRIFICATION CHARPENTE LEVAGE (E.C.L.)—See Pechiney S.A.; *Int'l*, pg. 1028
ELECTRO ALLOYS—See Park Corp.; *U.S. Public*, pg. 839
ELECTRO-BIOLOGY, INC.—See Biomet, Inc.; *U.S. Public*, pg. 231
ELECTRO BRAND, INC.; *U.S. Private*, pg. 368
ELECTRO-COATINGS, INC.; *U.S. Private*, pg. 368
ELECTRO CORPORATION—See BTR plc; *Int'l*, pg. 127
ELECTRO DYNAMICS CRYSTAL CORPORATION; *U.S. Private*, pg. 368
ELECTRO-JACOBS, GUCO, HEIJMANS, ROVATO AND VALKENBERG—See Vendex International N.V.; *Int'l*, pg. 1462
ELECTRO KINETICS DIV.—See Pacific Scientific Company; *U.S. Public*, pg. 1250
ELECTRO-MATIC PRODUCTS INC.; *U.S. Private*, pg. 369
ELECTRO MECHANICAL DESIGN SERVICES, INC.; *U.S. Private*, pg. 369
ELECTRO-MECHANICAL INSTRUMENTS DIV.—See AEI Holding Co., Inc.; *U.S. Private*, pg. 5
ELECTRO METHODS INC.; *U.S. Private*, pg. 369
ELECTRO METRICS, INC.; *U.S. Private*, pg. 369
ELECTRO-MOTIVE DIVISION—See General Motors Corporation; *U.S. Public*, pg. 719
ELECTRO NAVALE MOTEURS SAS—See Thrige-Titan Group; *Int'l*, pg. 1387
ELECTRO OPTICAL DIV.—See Kollmorgen Corporation; *U.S. Public*, pg. 965
ELECTRO OPTICAL IND.—See Channel Technologies, Inc.; *U.S. Private*, pg. 228
ELECTRO PARTES DE MATAMOROS, S.A. DE C.V.—See Zenith Electronics Corp.; *U.S. Public*, pg. 1790
ELECTRO PROTECTION SERVICES/CEPS—See Tyco International Ltd.; *U.S. Public*, pg. 1650
ELECTRO QUIMICA MEXICANA S.A. DE C.V.—See FMC Corporation; *U.S. Public*, pg. 606
ELECTRO RENT CORPORATION; *U.S. Public*, pg. 568
ELECTRO RENT CORPORATION-ESD, INC.—See Electro Rent Corporation; *U.S. Public*, pg. 568
ELECTRO-SCIENCE DEUTSCHLAND—See Electro-Science Laboratories, Inc.; *U.S. Private*, pg. 369
ELECTRO-SCIENCE LABORATORIES, INC.; *U.S. Private*, pg. 369
ELECTRO SCIENTIFIC INDUSTRIES B.V.—See Electro Scientific Industries, Inc.; *U.S. Public*, pg. 569
ELECTRO SCIENTIFIC INDUSTRIES GMBH—See Electro Scientific Industries, Inc.; *U.S. Public*, pg. 569
ELECTRO SCIENTIFIC INDUSTRIES, INC.; *U.S. Public*, pg. 568
ELECTRO SCIENTIFIC INDUSTRIES KK—See Electro Scientific Industries, Inc.; *U.S. Public*, pg. 569
ELECTRO SCIENTIFIC INDUSTRIES KOREA—See Electro Scientific Industries, Inc.; *U.S. Public*, pg. 569
ELECTRO SCIENTIFIC INDUSTRIES LTD.—See Electro Scientific Industries, Inc.; *U.S. Public*, pg. 569
ELECTRO SCIENTIFIC INDUSTRIES SARL—See Electro Scientific Industries, Inc.; *U.S. Public*, pg. 569
ELECTRO SCIENTIFIC INDUSTRIES TAIWAN—See Electro Scientific Industries, Inc.; *U.S. Public*, pg. 569
ELECTRO-TEC CORP.—See Kaydon Corporation; *U.S. Public*, pg. 946
ELECTRO-VOICE, INC.—See Greenwich Street Capital Partners, Inc.; *U.S. Private*, pg. 479
ELECTRO WEST B.V.—See Royal Begemann Group; *Int'l*, pg. 1133
ELECTROCATALYTIC, INC.; *U.S. Private*, pg. 369
ELECTROCHEMICAL INDUSTRIES (FRUTAROM) LTD.—See ICC Industries, Inc.; *U.S. Private*, pg. 553
ELECTROCLOR S.A.—See Imperial Chemical Industries PLC; *Int'l*, pg. 664
ELECTROCOM AUTOMATION L.P.—See Siemens AG; *Int'l*, pg. 1244
ELECTROCOMPONENTS—See CTS Corporation; *U.S. Public*, pg. 286
ELECTRODE/ORE—See Ralston Purina Company; *U.S. Public*, pg. 1360
ELECTRODOS MONTERREY S.A. DE C.V.—See Charter plc; *Int'l*, pg. 281
ELECTRODYNAMICS, INC.—See Carpenter Technology Corporation; *U.S. Public*, pg. 308
ELECTROFORM—See Thomas & Betts Corporation; *U.S. Public*, pg. 1598
ELECTROGLAS—See General Signal Corporation; *U.S. Public*, pg. 727
ELECTROHOME LTD.; *Int'l*, pg. 438
ELECTROHOME U.S.A. (1989), INC.—See Electrohome Ltd.; *Int'l*, pg. 438
ELECTROID CO.; *U.S. Private*, pg. 369
ELECTROLUX—See Electrolux, AB; *Int'l*, pg. 442
ELECTROLUX, AB; *Int'l*, pg. 438
OY ELECTROLUX AB-ASAB—See Electrolux, AB; *Int'l*, pg. 441
OY ELECTROLUX AB-ELEKTRO HELIOS—See Electrolux, AB; *Int'l*, pg. 441
OY ELECTROLUX AB-HUSQVARNA—See Electrolux, AB; *Int'l*, pg. 441
OY ELECTROLUX AB—See Electrolux, AB; *Int'l*, pg. 441
OY ELECTROLUX AB-PARTNER—See Electrolux, AB; *Int'l*, pg. 441

OY ELECTROLUX AB-TAMMERMATIC—See Electrolux, AB; *Int'l*, pg. 441
ELECTROLUX AG—See Electrolux, AB; *Int'l*, pg. 443
ELECTROLUX & CIE SNC—See Electrolux, AB; *Int'l*, pg. 441
ELECTROLUX A/S—See Electrolux, AB; *Int'l*, pg. 441
ELECTROLUX ATERFORSAKRINGS AB—See Electrolux, AB; *Int'l*, pg. 438
ELECTROLUX AUTOLIV—See Electrolux, AB; *Int'l*, pg. 439
ELECTROLUX BEDENPFLEGEGERATE VERTRIEBSGESELLSCHAFT GMBH—See Electrolux, AB; *Int'l*, pg. 440
C.A. ELECTROLUX—See Electrolux, AB; *Int'l*, pg. 441
ELECTROLUX CANADA—See Electrolux Corporation; *U.S. Private*, pg. 370
ELECTROLUX CANARIAS S.A.—See Electrolux, AB; *Int'l*, pg. 443
ELECTROLUX (CHILE) LTDA.—See Electrolux, AB; *Int'l*, pg. 443
ELECTROLUX CLEANING EQUIPMENT AB—See Electrolux, AB; *Int'l*, pg. 438
ELECTROLUX (COMMERCIAL EQUIPMENT) LTD.—See Electrolux, AB; *Int'l*, pg. 444
ELECTROLUX COMMERCIAL REFRIGERATION AB—See Electrolux, AB; *Int'l*, pg. 438
ELECTROLUX CONSTRUCTOR—See Electrolux, AB; *Int'l*, pg. 441
ELECTROLUX CONSTRUCTOR AB—See Electrolux, AB; *Int'l*, pg. 438
ELECTROLUX CONSTRUCTOR A/S—See Electrolux, AB; *Int'l*, pg. 443
ELECTROLUX CONSTRUCTOR B.V.—See Electrolux, AB; *Int'l*, pg. 443
ELECTROLUX-CONSTRUCTOR GMBH—See Electrolux, AB; *Int'l*, pg. 442
ELECTROLUX CORPORATION; *U.S. Private*, pg. 369
ELECTROLUX-CR GMBH—See Electrolux, AB; *Int'l*, pg. 442
ELECTROLUX-CRAMER GMBH—See Electrolux, AB; *Int'l*, pg. 442
ELECTROLUX ELMOTOR A/S—See Electrolux, AB; *Int'l*, pg. 441
ELECTROLUX (FAR EAST) LTD.—See Electrolux, AB; *Int'l*, pg. 442
ELECTROLUX GJUTERIPRODUKTER AB—See Electrolux, AB; *Int'l*, pg. 438
ELECTROLUX GMBH—See Electrolux, AB; *Int'l*, pg. 442
ELECTROLUX GROUP—See Electrolux, AB; *Int'l*, pg. 444
ELECTROLUX INDUSTRIER A/S—See Electrolux, AB; *Int'l*, pg. 443
ELECTROLUX INTERNATIONAL SALES AB—See Electrolux, AB; *Int'l*, pg. 438
ELECTROLUX INTERNATIONAL S.P.A.—See Electrolux, AB; *Int'l*, pg. 442
ELECTROLUX (JAPAN) LTD.—See Electrolux, AB; *Int'l*, pg. 443
ELECTROLUX JORDAN TRADING COMPANY LTD.—See Electrolux, AB; *Int'l*, pg. 443
ELECTROLUX KALTE-UND WARMETECHNIK GMBH—See Electrolux, AB; *Int'l*, pg. 442
ELECTROLUX KUCHENTECHNIK GMBH—See Electrolux, AB; *Int'l*, pg. 442
ELECTROLUX LAGARES C. POR A.—See Electrolux, AB; *Int'l*, pg. 441
ELECTROLUX LTD.—See Electrolux, AB; *Int'l*, pg. 443
ELECTROLUX LTDA.—See Electrolux, AB; *Int'l*, pg. 443
ELECTROLUX MALAYSIA SDN. BHD.—See Electrolux, AB; *Int'l*, pg. 443
ELECTROLUX-MARTIN S.A.—See Electrolux, AB; *Int'l*, pg. 441
ELECTROLUX MECATRONIK AB—See Electrolux, AB; *Int'l*, pg. 438
ELECTROLUX MIDDLE EAST S.A.R.L.—See Electrolux, AB; *Int'l*, pg. 443
ELECTROLUX MOTOR AB—See Electrolux, AB; *Int'l*, pg. 438
ELECTROLUX NEDERLAND B.V.—See Electrolux, AB; *Int'l*, pg. 443
ELECTROLUX PHILIPPINES, INC.—See Electrolux, AB; *Int'l*, pg. 443
ELECTROLUX PTY. LTD.—See Electrolux, AB; *Int'l*, pg. 440
ELECTROLUX RENGJO/RINGSMASKINER A/S—See Electrolux, AB; *Int'l*, pg. 443
ELECTROLUX S.A.—See Electrolux, AB; *Int'l*, pg. 441
ELECTROLUX S.A. DE C.V.—See Electrolux, AB; *Int'l*, pg. 443
ELECTROLUX SAN JOSE—See Electrolux, AB; *Int'l*, pg. 442
ELECTROLUX S.A.R.L.—See Electrolux, AB; *Int'l*, pg. 443
ELECTROLUX SAUDI SERVICES, LTD.—See Electrolux, AB; *Int'l*, pg. 443
ELECTROLUX S.E.A. PRIVATE LTD.—See Electrolux, AB; *Int'l*, pg. 443
ELECTROLUX-SERVICOS SOC. COMMERCIAL LTDA.—See Electrolux, AB; *Int'l*, pg. 441
ELECTROLUX SIEGEN GMBH—See Electrolux, AB; *Int'l*, pg. 442
ELECTROLUX STORKOK AB—See Electrolux, AB; *Int'l*, pg. 438
ELECTROLUX SVENSKA FORSALJININGS AB—See Electrolux, AB; *Int'l*, pg. 439
ELECTROLUX THAILAND CO. LTD.—See Electrolux, AB; *Int'l*, pg. 444
ELECTROLUX UTILITY SERVICES PTY. LTD.—See Electrolux, AB; *Int'l*, pg. 439
ELECTROLUX-WASCATOR AB—See Electrolux, AB; *Int'l*, pg. 439
ELECTROLUX-WASCATOR A/S—See Electrolux, AB; *Int'l*, pg. 441
ELECTROLUX-WASCATOR S.A.—See Electrolux, AB; *Int'l*, pg. 441
ELECTROLUX WASCHEREI UND SERVICE GMBH—See Electrolux, AB; *Int'l*, pg. 442

ELECTROMAGNETIC SCIENCES, INC.; U.S. Public, pg. 569
ELECTROMECH TECHNOLOGIES—See Western Sky Industries, Inc.; U.S. Private, pg. 1168
ELECTROMECHANICAL DIVISION—See Parker Hannifin Corporation; U.S. Public, pg. 1263
ELECTROMECHANICAL SYSTEMS, INC.—See COMSAT Corporation; U.S. Public, pg. 424
CIA. ELECTROMEDICA, S.A.—See Hewlett-Packard Company; U.S. Public, pg. 817
ELECTRON BEAM TECHNOLOGIES; U.S. Private, pg. 370
ELECTRON CORP.; U.S. Private, pg. 370
ELECTRONIA DALE DE MEXICO S.A. DE C.V.—See Vishay Intertechnology, Inc.; U.S. Public, pg. 1722
ELECTRONIC ARTS; U.S. Public, pg. 569
ELECTRONIC ARTS (CANADA) INC.—See Electronic Arts; U.S. Public, pg. 569
ELECTRONIC ARTS GMBH—See Electronic Arts; U.S. Public, pg. 569
ELECTRONIC ARTS PTY. LTD.—See Electronic Arts; U.S. Public, pg. 569
ELECTRONIC ARTS S.A.—See Electronic Arts; U.S. Public, pg. 569
ELECTRONIC ARTS VICTOR INC.—See Electronic Arts; U.S. Public, pg. 569
AB ELECTRONIC ASSEMBLIES LIMITED—See TT Group PLC; Int'l, pg. 1344
ELECTRONIC DATA MAGNETICS, INC.; U.S. Private, pg. 370
ELECTRONIC DATA SYSTEMS CORPORATION; U.S. Public, pg. 569
ELECTRONIC DEVICES AND MATERIALS—See Litton Industries, Inc.; U.S. Public, pg. 1003
ELECTRONIC DISPLAY SYSTEMS (KALLEGO)—See Chief Industries, Inc.; U.S. Private, pg. 236
ELECTRONIC DRIVES AND CONTROLS; U.S. Private, pg. 370
ELECTRONIC ENGINEERS MASTER—See The Hearst Corporation; U.S. Private, pg. 516
ELECTRONIC FORM SYSTEMS—See The Reynolds and Reynolds Company; U.S. Public, pg. 1385
ELECTRONIC HARNESSES (U.K.) LTD.—See Sumitomo Electric Industries, Ltd.; Int'l, pg. 1313
ELECTRONIC INTERCONNECT SYSTEMS INC.—See Noma Industries Limited; Int'l, pg. 955
AB ELECTRONIC LIMITED—See TT Group PLC; Int'l, pg. 1344
ELECTRONIC MATERIALS & REFRACTORY METALS DIV.—See Cabot Corporation; U.S. Public, pg. 289
ELECTRONIC MEASUREMENTS, INC.—See Berwind Corporation; U.S. Private, pg. 138
ELECTRONIC MEDIA—See Crain Communications, Inc.; U.S. Private, pg. 285
ELECTRONIC NAVIGATION INDUSTRIES—See Emerson Electric Co.; U.S. Public, pg. 574
ELECTRONIC PRINTING SYSTEMS—See Eastman Kodak Company; U.S. Public, pg. 551
ELECTRONIC PRODUCTS DIVISION—See 3M; U.S. Public, pg. 1605
ELECTRONIC PRODUCTS MAGAZINE—See The Hearst Corporation; U.S. Private, pg. 516
ELECTRONIC SENSORS & SYSTEMS DIVISION—See Northrop Grumman Corporation; U.S. Public, pg. 1198
ELECTRONIC SOLUTIONS—See Zero Corporation; U.S. Public, pg. 1791
ELECTRONIC SYSTEMS DIVISION—See The Boeing Company; U.S. Public, pg. 241
ELECTRONIC SYSTEMS DIVISION—See Tracor, Inc.; U.S. Public, pg. 1627
ELECTRONIC SYSTEMS GROUP—See DRS Technologies, Inc.; U.S. Public, pg. 474
ELECTRONIC SYSTEMS PACKAGING CORP.—See Electronics Stamping Corp.; U.S. Private, pg. 370
ELECTRONIC TAX SYSTEMS, INC.—See Computer Language Research, Inc.; U.S. Public, pg. 421
ELECTRONIC TELE-COMMUNICATIONS, INC.; U.S. Public, pg. 570
ELECTRONIC TELE-COMMUNICATIONS, INC.—See Electronic Tele-Communications, Inc.; U.S. Public, pg. 570
ELECTRONIC TRANSACTION CORPORATION—See Deluxe Corporation; U.S. Public, pg. 498
ELECTRONIC VOTING SYSTEMS, INC.—See H.M.G. Worldwide Corp.; U.S. Public, pg. 771
ELECTRONIC WARFARE SYSTEMS—See Litton Industries, Inc.; U.S. Public, pg. 1002
ELECTRONICA BASICA, S.A. (ELBASA)—See Northrop Grumman Corporation; U.S. Public, pg. 1199
ELECTRONICA CLARION, S.A. DE C.V.—See Clarion Co., Ltd.; Int'l, pg. 296
ELECTRONICA CONDOR DE MEXICO, S.A.—See SL Industries, Inc.; U.S. Public, pg. 1419
ELECTRONICA PANTERA, S.A. DE C.V.—See The JPM Company; U.S. Public, pg. 919
ELECTRONICO REPUBLICA, S.A.—See Hewlett-Packard Company; U.S. Public, pg. 817
ELECTRONICS & SYSTEMS INTEGRATION DIVISION—See Northrop Grumman Corporation; U.S. Public, pg. 1198
ELECTRONICS AND SYSTEMS INTEGRATION DIVISION—See Northrop Grumman Corporation; U.S. Public, pg. 1198
ELECTRONICS ARTS SOFTWARE S.A.—See Electronic Arts; U.S. Public, pg. 569
ELECTRONICS COMPONENTS GROUP—See Sharp Corporation; Int'l, pg. 1228
ELECTRONICS FOR IMAGING, INC.; U.S. Public, pg. 570
ELECTRONICS STAMPING CORP.; U.S. Private, pg. 370
ELECTRONICS SYSTEMS DIVISION—See Northrop Grumman Corporation; U.S. Public, pg. 1198
ELECTRONSKA INDUSTRIJA KFT.—See Compagnie des Machines Bull; Int'l, pg. 317
ELECTRO-OPTICAL SYSTEMS GROUP—See DRS Technologies, Inc.; U.S. Public, pg. 474

ELECTROSCON NETWORK ENGINEERING SDN. BHD.—See Telefonaktiebolaget LM Ericsson; Int'l, pg. 1366
ELECTROSPACE SYSTEMS, INC.—See Raytheon Company; U.S. Public, pg. 1365
ELECTROSTATIC TECHNOLOGY, INC.—See Nordson Corporation; U.S. Public, pg. 1189
ELECTROVERT—See Cookson Group plc; Int'l, pg. 328
ELECTROWATT LTD.—See Siemens AG; Int'l, pg. 1246
N.V. ELEFANT—See Freudenberg & Company; Int'l, pg. 506
ELEFANT N.V.I.L.—See Freudenberg & Company; Int'l, pg. 507
ELEFANTE PORTUGUESA LDA. INDUSTRIA DE CALCADO—See Freudenberg & Company; Int'l, pg. 505
ELEFANTEN-SCHUH-GES.M.B.H.—See Freudenberg & Company; Int'l, pg. 505
ELEFANTEN-SCHUH GMBH—See Freudenberg & Company; Int'l, pg. 505
ELEFANTEN-SLOWAKEI, SPOL.SR.O.—See Freudenberg & Company; Int'l, pg. 507
ELEKLUFT ELEKTRONIK-UND LUFTFAHRTGERATE GMBH—See Daimler-Benz Aktiengesellschaft; Int'l, pg. 367
ELEKLUFT GMBH—See Daimler-Benz Aktiengesellschaft; Int'l, pg. 367
AB ELEKRONIK GMBH—See TT Group PLC; Int'l, pg. 1344
ELEKTRA ENTERTAINMENT—See Time Warner Inc.; U.S. Public, pg. 1612
ELEKTRIC KOMURLERI ANONIM SIRKETI—See Pechiney S.A.; Int'l, pg. 1030
ELEKTRIZITAETS-AKTIENGESELLSCHAFT MITTELDEUTSCHLAND—See Veba AG; Int'l, pg. 1456
ELEKTRO-APPARATEBAU OLTEN AG; Int'l, pg. 444
ELEKTRO CHEMIE IBBENBUREN GMBH—See Akzo Nobel N.V.; Int'l, pg. 44
ELEKTRO CHEMIE IBBENBUREN GMBH—See Preussag AG; Int'l, pg. 1070
AB ELEKTRO HELIOS—See Electrolux, AB; Int'l, pg. 438
ELEKTRO METALL EXPORT GMBH—See Datron Incorporated; U.S. Private, pg. 313
ELEKTRODY BAILDON—See Charter plc; Int'l, pg. 282
AB ELEKTROKOPPAR—See ABB Asea Brown Boveri (Holding) Ltd.; Int'l, pg. 7
AB ELEKTROSERVICE—See Electrolux, AB; Int'l, pg. 439
ELEKTROWERK WEISWEILER GMBH—See Metallurg, Inc.; U.S. Private, pg. 735
ELEKTROWERKE GMBH HOLDING—See Viag AG; Int'l, pg. 1464
ELEMOND S.P.A.—See Arnoldo Mondadori Editore S.p.A.; Int'l, pg. 888
ELETTROLITICA DEL NERA SPA—See Morgan Crucible Co. Plc; Int'l, pg. 891
ELEVADORES KONE SABIEM S.A. DE C.V.—See Kone Corporation; Int'l, pg. 747
ELEVADORES OTIS S/A—See United Technologies Corporation; U.S. Public, pg. 1691
ELEVADORES OTIS, S.A. DE C.V.—See United Technologies Corporation; U.S. Public, pg. 1691
ELEVADORES SCHINDLER DO BRASIL S.A.—See Schindler Holding AG; Int'l, pg. 1205
ELEVADORES SCHINDLER SUWIS, S.A. DE C.V.—See Schindler Holding AG; Int'l, pg. 1205
ELEVATOR CAR SYSTEM—See Schindler Holding AG; Int'l, pg. 1205
ELEY AMERICAS INC.—See IMI Plc; Int'l, pg. 646
ELF AQUITAINE ANGOLA—See Elf Aquitaine; Int'l, pg. 444
ELF AQUITAINE ASPHALT, INC.—See Elf Aquitaine; Int'l, pg. 445
ELF AQUITAINE, INC.—See Elf Aquitaine; Int'l, pg. 445
ELF AQUITAINE NORGE A/S—See Elf Aquitaine; Int'l, pg. 445
ELF AQUITANE; Int'l, pg. 444
ELF ATOCHEM NORTH AMERICA, AGRICHEMICALS DIV.—See Elf Aquitane; Int'l, pg. 446
ELF ATOCHEM NORTH AMERICA, BASIC CHEMICALS DIV.—See Elf Aquitane; Int'l, pg. 446
ELF ATOCHEM NORTH AMERICA, FLUOROCHEMICAL DIV.—See Elf Aquitane; Int'l, pg. 446
ELF ATOCHEM NORTH AMERICA, INC.—See Elf Aquitane; Int'l, pg. 445
ELF ATOCHEM ORGANIC PEROXIDES PLANT—See Elf Aquitane; Int'l, pg. 446
ELF ATOCHEM ROTTERDAH B.V.—See Elf Aquitane; Int'l, pg. 446
ELF ATOCHEM S.A.—See Elf Aquitane; Int'l, pg. 445
ELF CONGO—See Elf Aquitane; Int'l, pg. 446
ELF ERDOEL UNDERDGAS DEUTSCHLAND GMBH—See Elf Aquitane; Int'l, pg. 446
ELF EXPLORATION INC.—See Elf Aquitane; Int'l, pg. 445
ELF FRANCE—See Elf Aquitane; Int'l, pg. 445
ELF GABON—See Elf Aquitane; Int'l, pg. 446
ELF IDROCARBURI ITALIANA SPA—See Elf Aquitane; Int'l, pg. 446
ELF LUBRICANTS—See Elf Aquitane; Int'l, pg. 445
ELF NIGERIA—See Elf Aquitane; Int'l, pg. 446
ELF PETROLAND—See Elf Aquitane; Int'l, pg. 446
ELF PETROLEUM U.K.—See Elf Aquitane; Int'l, pg. 446
ELF SANOFI INC.—See Elf Aquitane; Int'l, pg. 445
ELF SANOFI S.A.—See Elf Aquitane; Int'l, pg. 445
ELF SEREPCA—See Elf Aquitane; Int'l, pg. 446
ELF SUISSE S.A.—See Elf Aquitane; Int'l, pg. 446
ELF TRADING, INC.—See Elf Aquitane; Int'l, pg. 445
ELFAB LIMITED—See Halma plc; Int'l, pg. 589
ELGA RONAL S.R.L.—See LeaRonal, Inc.; U.S. Public, pg. 982
ELGAR CORPORATION—See Harnischfeger Industries, Inc.; U.S. Public, pg. 789
ELGIN BROTHER INDUSTRIAL LTDA.—See Brother Industries, Ltd.; Int'l, pg. 230
ELGIN DAIRY FOODS, INC.; U.S. Private, pg. 370

ELGIN DIGITAL COLORGRAPHIC SERVICE CENTER—See R.R. Donnelley & Sons Company; U.S. Public, pg. 518
ELGIN NATIONAL INDUSTRIES, INC.; U.S. Private, pg. 370
ELGIN SWEEPER COMPANY—See Federal Signal Corporation; U.S. Public, pg. 617
ELGIN WATCH COMPANY; U.S. Private, pg. 371
ELGOOD-MAYO CORP.—See Gannett Fleming Affiliates, Inc.; U.S. Private, pg. 439
ELGRO SP Z.O.O.—See Groschopp & Co. GmbH EMW Elektromotoren-Feinbauwerk; Int'l, pg. 559
ELIAS BROTHERS RESTAURANTS, INC.; U.S. Private, pg. 371
ELIDA COSMETIC AG—See Unilever Plc; Int'l, pg. 1437
ELIDA FABERGE—See Unilever Plc; Int'l, pg. 1437
ELIDA FABERGE (IRELAND) LTD.—See Unilever Plc; Int'l, pg. 1437
ELIDA FABERGE—See Unilever Plc; Int'l, pg. 1434
ELIDA-GIBBS G.M.B.H.—See Unilever Plc; Int'l, pg. 1437
ELIDA-GIBBS (PTY.) LTD.—See Unilever Plc; Int'l, pg. 1437
ELIMO VERMIETUNGS GMBH—See Commerzbank AG; Int'l, pg. 310
ELI'S CHEESE CAKE COMPANY; U.S. Private, pg. 371
ELISABETH DIVISION—See Liz Claiborne, Inc.; U.S. Public, pg. 1006
ELIT FONSTER AB—See Skanska AB; Int'l, pg. 1260
ELITE INFORMATION SYSTEMS, INC.—See Broadway & Seymour, Inc.; U.S. Public, pg. 258
ELITE LAMP, INC.; U.S. Private, pg. 371
ELITE PARFUMS, LTD.—See Jean Philippe Fragrances, Inc.; U.S. Public, pg. 924
ELITE PERSONALIZED CREATIONS—See American Pad and Paper Company; U.S. Public, pg. 89
ELITE SEWING MACHINE MFG. CO. LTD.—See Aisin Seiki Co. Ltd.; Int'l, pg. 39
ELITEC S.A.—See Woodhead Industries, Inc.; U.S. Public, pg. 1776
ELITFONSTER AB—See AB Industrivarden; Int'l, pg. 678
ELIXIR INDUSTRIES; U.S. Private, pg. 371
ELIZABETH ARDEN COMPANY—See Unilever Plc; Int'l, pg. 1435
ELIZABETH ARDEN DE MEXICO, S.A.—See Unilever Plc; Int'l, pg. 1437
ELIZABETH DETENTION CENTER—See Corrections Corporation of America; U.S. Public, pg. 450
ELIZABETHTON TWINS BASEBALL CLUB—See Minnesota Twins Baseball Club; U.S. Private, pg. 751
ELIZABETHTOWN GAS CO.—See NUI Corporation; U.S. Public, pg. 1147
ELIZABETHTOWN WATER COMPANY—See E'Town Corporation; U.S. Public, pg. 540
ELJAY DIVISION—See Raytheon Company; U.S. Public, pg. 1365
ELJER MANUFACTURING/HVAC GROUP—See Zurn Industries, Inc.; U.S. Public, pg. 1794
ELJER PLUMBINGWARE—See Zurn Industries, Inc.; U.S. Public, pg. 1794
ELJSSINK—See Vendex International N.V.; Int'l, pg. 1463
ELK CORP. OF ALABAMA—See Elcor Corporation; U.S. Public, pg. 568
ELK CORPORATION OF DALLAS—See Elcor Corporation; U.S. Public, pg. 568
ELK CORPORATION OF TEXAS—See Elcor Corporation; U.S. Public, pg. 568
ELK SUPPLY COMPANY; U.S. Private, pg. 371
ELKAY ELECTRICAL—See Smiths Industries plc; Int'l, pg. 1267
ELKAY MANUFACTURING COMPANY; U.S. Private, pg. 372
ELKAY PLASTICS CO., INC., STOCK SERVICE CENTER—See Elkay Plastics Company, Inc.; U.S. Private, pg. 372
ELKAY PLASTICS COMPANY, INC.; U.S. Private, pg. 372
ELKAY PRODUCTS, INC.; U.S. Private, pg. 372
ELKEM ALLOY—See Elkem ASA; Int'l, pg. 447
ELKEM ALUMINIUM ANS—See Elkem ASA; Int'l, pg. 446
ELKEM ALUMINIUM LISTA—See Elkem ASA; Int'l, pg. 446
ELKEM ALUMINIUM MOSJOEN—See Elkem ASA; Int'l, pg. 447
ELKEM-AMERICAN CARBIDE COMPANY (ASHTABULA)—See Airgas, Inc.; U.S. Public, pg. 33
ELKEM-AMERICAN CARBIDE COMPANY (PITTSBURGH)—See Airgas, Inc.; U.S. Public, pg. 33
ELKEM-AMERICAN CARBIDE COMPANY (PRYOR)—See Airgas, Inc.; U.S. Public, pg. 33
ELKEM ASA; Int'l, pg. 446
ELKEM ASA ENERGY—See Elkem ASA; Int'l, pg. 447
ELKEM ASA FERROSILICON DIVISION—See Elkem ASA; Int'l, pg. 448
ELKEM ASA MANGANESE/CHROME DIVISION—See Elkem ASA; Int'l, pg. 447
ELKEM ASHTABULA (CALCIUM CARBIDES)—See Elkem ASA; Int'l, pg. 447
ELKEM BENELUX S.A.—See Elkem ASA; Int'l, pg. 447
ELKEM BREMANGER—See Elkem ASA; Int'l, pg. 448
ELKEM CARBON—See Elkem ASA; Int'l, pg. 447
ELKEM CHARTERING—See Elkem ASA; Int'l, pg. 447
ELKEM CHICOUTIMI—See Elkem ASA; Int'l, pg. 448
ELKEM DANMARK A/S—See Elkem ASA; Int'l, pg. 448
ELKEM FISKAA SILICON—See Elkem ASA; Int'l, pg. 448
ELKEM GMBH—See Elkem ASA; Int'l, pg. 447
ELKEM INTERNATIONAL AS—See Elkem ASA; Int'l, pg. 447
ELKEM LTD.—See Elkem ASA; Int'l, pg. 447
ELKEM LTD. - MATERIALS—See Elkem ASA; Int'l, pg. 447
ELKEM MANGAN—See Elkem ASA; Int'l, pg. 447
ELKEM MANGAN PEA—See Elkem ASA; Int'l, pg. 447
ELKEM MANGAN SAUDA—See Elkem ASA; Int'l, pg. 447
ELKEM MARIETTA—See Elkem ASA; Int'l, pg. 447
ELKEM MATERIALS—See Elkem ASA; Int'l, pg. 447
ELKEM MATERIALS INC.—See Elkem ASA; Int'l, pg. 447
ELKEM MATERIALS JAPAN—See Elkem ASA; Int'l, pg. 447

ELKEM METALLURGY—See Elkem ASA; Int'l, pg. 447
ELKEM METALS COMPANY—See Elkem ASA; Int'l, pg. 447
ELKEM RANA—See Elkem ASA; Int'l, pg. 447
ELKEM REPRESENTATIVE OFFICE - BEIJING—See Elkem ASA; Int'l, pg. 447
ELKEM REPRESENTATIVE OFFICE - CZECH REPUBLIC—See Elkem ASA; Int'l, pg. 447
ELKEM REPRESENTATIVE OFFICE - HONG KONG—See Elkem ASA; Int'l, pg. 447
ELKEM REPRESENTATIVE OFFICE - RUSSIA—See Elkem ASA; Int'l, pg. 447
ELKEM RESEARCH—See Elkem ASA; Int'l, pg. 448
ELKEM SALES & MARKETING SERVICE—See Elkem ASA; Int'l, pg. 448
ELKEM SALTEN—See Elkem ASA; Int'l, pg. 448
ELKEM S.A.R.L.—See Elkem ASA; Int'l, pg. 447
ELKEM SAUDEFALDLNE—See Elkem ASA; Int'l, pg. 447
ELKEM S.R.L.—See Elkem ASA; Int'l, pg. 447
ELKEM SVERIGE—See Elkem ASA; Int'l, pg. 447
ELKEM TANA—See Elkem ASA; Int'l, pg. 448
ELKEM TECHNOLOGY SERVICES—See Elkem ASA; Int'l, pg. 448
ELKEM THAMSHAVN—See Elkem ASA; Int'l, pg. 448
ELKES BISCUITS—See Northern Foods plc; Int'l, pg. 968
ELKHART CAPITAL CORPORATION—See Schult Homes Corporation; U.S. Public, pg. 1442
ELKHART METALS DIVISION—See Sturgis Iron & Metal Company, Inc.; U.S. Private, pg. 1048
ELKHART PRODUCTS CORP.-PLUMBING DIVISION—See Amcast Industrial Corporation; U.S. Public, pg. 63
ELKHART PRODUCTS CORPORATION-INDUSTRIAL DIVISION—See Amcast Industrial Corporation; U.S. Public, pg. 63
ELKINS CONSTRUCTORS, INC.; U.S. Private, pg. 372
ELKINS-SINN, INC.-LEDERLE—See American Home Products Corporation; U.S. Public, pg. 79
ELKON GAS SERVICE—See NUI Corporation; U.S. Public, pg. 1148
ELKRO GAS S.P.A—See Ruhrgas Aktiengesellschaft; Int'l, pg. 1149
ELKRO S.P.R.L.—See Ruhrgas Aktiengesellschaft; Int'l, pg. 1149
ELKTON DLV OPERATIONS—See Thiokol Corporation; U.S. Public, pg. 1597
ELLAN ELETROMECANICA LTDA.—See Knurr AG; Int'l, pg. 739
ELLE HONG KONG—See Lagardere Groupe; Int'l, pg. 795
ELLE PUBLISHING, L.P.—See Lagardere Groupe; Int'l, pg. 795
ELLEMME S.R.L.—See Arnoldo Mondadori Editore S.p.A.; Int'l, pg. 888
ELLEN TRACY INC.; U.S. Private, pg. 372
ELLER MEDIA COMPANY—See Clear Channel Communications, Inc.; U.S. Public, pg. 383
ELLESMERE BRITANNIA LTD.—See Agra Inc.; Int'l, pg. 31
ELLESMERE DEVELOPMENTS LTD.—See Agra Inc.; Int'l, pg. 31
ELLICOTT MACHINE CORPORATION INTERNATIONAL; U.S. Private, pg. 372
ELLIOT GROVE ASSOCIATES—See Cigna Corp.; U.S. Public, pg. 361
B. ELLIOTT INC.—See B. Elliott plc.; Int'l, pg. 449
B. ELLIOTT PLC.; Int'l, pg. 448
ELLIOTT COMPANY; U.S. Private, pg. 373
ELLIOTT GROUP LIMITED—See The Davis Service Group Plc.; Int'l, pg. 385
ELLIOTT STATE BANK—See Firstbank of Illinois Co.; U.S. Public, pg. 643
ELLIOTT TURBOMACHINERY CANADA, INC.—See Elliott Company; U.S. Private, pg. 373
ELLIOTT TURBOMACHINERY LTD.—See Elliott Company; U.S. Private, pg. 373
ELLIOTT TURBOMACHINERY S.A.—See Elliott Company; U.S. Private, pg. 373
ELLIS & MCDOUGALL LIFTS LTD.—See Kone Corporation; Int'l, pg. 747
ELLIS & WATTS DIV.—See CTS Corporation; U.S. Public, pg. 286
ELLIS COMMUNICATIONS—See Raycom Media, Inc.; U.S. Private, pg. 912
ELLIS GRAIN RIVER TERMINAL—See Owensboro Grain Co., Inc.; U.S. Private, pg. 824
JAMES C. ELLIS GRAIN CO.—See Owensboro Grain Co., Inc.; U.S. Private, pg. 824
ELLISON GRAPHICS—See Herlin Press Inc.; U.S. Private, pg. 524
ELLME CO., LTD.—See Mycal, Corp.; Int'l, pg. 898
ELLOREE FOODS, INC. (SOUTH CAROLINA)—See WSMP, Inc.; U.S. Public, pg. 1729
ELLOS AB—See ICA Handlarnas AB; Int'l, pg. 643
ELLSON EQUIPMENT CO., INC.—See Eclipse Inc.; U.S. Private, pg. 360
ELLWOOD CITY FORGE—See Ellwood Group, Inc.; U.S. Private, pg. 373
ELLWOOD CRANKSHAFT & MACHINE COMPANY—See Ellwood Group, inc.; U.S. Private, pg. 373
ELLWOOD GROUP, INC.; U.S. Private, pg. 373
ELLWOOD TEXAS FORGE, INC.—See Ellwood Group, Inc.; U.S. Private, pg. 373
ELM CITY NEWSPAPER—See Journal Register Company; U.S. Public, pg. 934
ELMA ELECTRONIC—See Sulzer Ltd.; Int'l, pg. 1305
ELMA ELECTRONIC LTD.—See Sulzer Ltd.; Int'l, pg. 1305
ELMER'S PRODUCTS, INC.—See Borden, Inc.; U.S. Private, pg. 158
ELMER'S WEIGHTS—See Bollinger Industries Inc.; U.S. Public, pg. 243
ELMIRA STAR-GAZETTE—See Gannett Company, Inc.; U.S. Public, pg. 700
ELMO SEMICONDUCTEURS SARL—See Kimball International, Inc.; U.S. Public, pg. 958
ELMO SEMICONDUCTOR CORP.—See Kimball International, Inc.; U.S. Public, pg. 957

ELMS HAVEN CARE CENTER—See Horizon/CMS Healthcare Corporation; U.S. Public, pg. 836
ELMTUBE LTD.—See Wolseley Plc.; Int'l, pg. 1511
ELMWOOD SENSORS, INC.—See BTR plc; Int'l, pg. 125
ELNI, S.P.A.—See General Signal Corporation; U.S. Public, pg. 727
ELO TOUCHSYSTEMS, INC.—See Raychem Corporation; U.S. Public, pg. 836
ELOF HANSSON WOOD PRODUCTS, INC.—See Elof Hansson AB; Int'l, pg. 595
ELOMETA CORPORATION—See Treadwell Corporation; U.S. Private, pg. 1098
ELOPAK A/S—See Tiedemanns - Joh.H.Andresen ANS; Int'l, pg. 1389
ELOPAK, INC.—See Tiedemanns - Joh.H.Andresen ANS; Int'l, pg. 1390
ELOX CORPORATION—See Georg Fischer Ltd.; Int'l, pg. 490
ELOY DETENTION CENTER—See Corrections Corporation of America; U.S. Public, pg. 450
ELPRO S.A.—See Siemens AG; Int'l, pg. 1246
ELQUIBER, S.A.—See Eli Lilly and Company; U.S. Public, pg. 994
ELRICK & LAVIDGE, INC.—See Equifax Inc.; U.S. Public, pg. 588
ELRON ELECTRONIC INDUSTRIES LTD.—See IDB Holding Corporation; Int'l, pg. 644
ELRON TECHNOLOGIES INC.—See IDB Holding Corporation; Int'l, pg. 644
ELSAG—See IRI Istituto Ricostruzione Industriale; Int'l, pg. 654
ELSAG BAILEY (CANADA) INC.—See ELSAG Bailey Process Automation N.V.; Int'l, pg. 449
ELSAG BAILEY PROCESS AUTOMATION N.V.; Int'l, pg. 449
ELSAG BAILEY PTE. LTD.—See ELSAG Bailey Process Automation N.V.; Int'l, pg. 449
ELSAG BAILEY PTY LIMITED—See ELSAG Bailey Process Automation N.V.; Int'l, pg. 449
ELSAG BAILEY S.A.—See ELSAG Bailey Process Automation N.V.; Int'l, pg. 449
ELSAG INC.—See IRI Istituto Ricostruzione Industriale; Int'l, pg. 653
ELSCINT (ASIA PACIFIC) LTD.—See Elscint Ltd.; Int'l, pg. 450
ELSCINT (CANADA) LTD.—See Elscint Ltd.; Int'l, pg. 450
ELSCINT CENTRAL & EASTERN EUROPE—See Elscint Ltd.; Int'l, pg. 450
ELSCINT CRYOMAGNETICS LTD.—See Elscint Ltd.; Int'l, pg. 450
ELSCINT DE MEXICO S. DE R.L. DE C.V.—See Elscint Ltd.; Int'l, pg. 450
ELSCINT ESPANA S.A.—See Elscint Ltd.; Int'l, pg. 450
ELSCINT FRANCE S.A.—See Elscint Ltd.; Int'l, pg. 450
ELSCINT (GB) LIMITED—See Elscint Ltd.; Int'l, pg. 450
ELSCINT GMBH—See Elscint Ltd.; Int'l, pg. 450
ELSCINT INC.—See Elscint Ltd.; Int'l, pg. 450
ELSCINT ITALIA S.R.L.—See Elscint Ltd.; Int'l, pg. 450
ELSCINT LTD.; Int'l, pg. 450
ELSCINT MR INC.—See Elscint Ltd.; Int'l, pg. 450
ELSCINT NV/SA—See Elscint Ltd.; Int'l, pg. 450
ELSCINT (PTY) LTD.—See Elscint Ltd.; Int'l, pg. 450
ELSEVIER ADVANCED TECHNOLOGY—See Reed Elsevier plc; Int'l, pg. 1100
ELSEVIER BEDRIJFINFORMATIE B.V.—See Reed Elsevier plc; Int'l, pg. 1099
ELSEVIER BUSINESS INFORMATION—See Reed Elsevier plc; Int'l, pg. 1099
ELSEVIER EDITORIAL SERVICES—See Reed Elsevier plc; Int'l, pg. 1100
ELSEVIER ELECTRONIC PUBLISHING SERVICES—See Reed Elsevier plc; Int'l, pg. 1100
ELSEVIER GEO ABSTRACTS—See Reed Elsevier plc; Int'l, pg. 1100
ELSEVIER NV—See Reed Elsevier plc; Int'l, pg. 1093
ELSEVIER OPLEIDINGEN BV—See Reed Elsevier plc; Int'l, pg. 1094
ELSEVIER PRENSA SA—See Reed Elsevier plc; Int'l, pg. 1100
ELSEVIER REED FINANCE BV—See Reed Elsevier plc; Int'l, pg. 1093
ELSEVIER REED FINANCE IRELAND—See Reed Elsevier plc; Int'l, pg. 1093
ELSEVIER SA—See Reed Elsevier plc; Int'l, pg. 1093
ELSEVIER SCIENCE (INTERNATIONAL)—See Reed Elsevier plc; Int'l, pg. 1099
ELSEVIER SCIENCE (THE NETHERLANDS)—See Reed Elsevier plc; Int'l, pg. 1099
ELSEVIER THOMAS FACHVERLAG GMBH—See Reed Elsevier plc; Int'l, pg. 1100
ELSEVIER TRAINING BV—See Reed Elsevier plc; Int'l, pg. 1100
ELSEVIER TRENDS JOURNALS—See Reed Elsevier plc; Int'l, pg. 1100
ELSINORE CORPORATION; U.S. Public, pg. 570
ELSINORE SHORE ASSOCIATES—See Elsinore Corporation; U.S. Public, pg. 570
ELSLUX HOLDING SA—See Reed Elsevier plc; Int'l, pg. 1093
ELSTER AG MESS- UND REGELTECHNIK—See Ruhrgas Aktiengesellschaft; Int'l, pg. 1148
ELSTER GASTECHNIC PRODUKTIONS -UND VERTRIEBSGESELLSCHAFT M.B.H—See Ruhrgas Aktiengesellschaft; Int'l, pg. 1149
ELSTER-HANDEL G.M.B.H. MESS- UND REGELTECHNIK—See Ruhrgas Aktiengesellschaft; Int'l, pg. 1148
ELSTER PRODUKTION GMBH—See Ruhrgas Aktiengesellschaft; Int'l, pg. 1148
ELSTER (UK) LTD.—See Ruhrgas Aktiengesellschaft; Int'l, pg. 1149
ELSTREE COMPUTING LTD.—See John Laing PLC; Int'l, pg. 796

ELSUB CORPORATION—See Elsinore Corporation; U.S. Public, pg. 570
ELTA ELECTRONICS INDUSTRIES, LTD.—See Israel Aircraft Industries Ltd.; Int'l, pg. 690
ELTA PLASTICS LIMITED—See Nifco Inc.; Int'l, pg. 929
ELTIS PRECISION PRINTING LIMITED—See HSBC Holdings plc; Int'l, pg. 581
ELTS BV—See KPN Koninklyke PTT Nederland NV; Int'l, pg. 720
ELU MASKINER A/S—See The Black & Decker Corporation; U.S. Public, pg. 234
ELVIA ASSURANCES S.A.—See Allianz Aktiengesellschaft; Int'l, pg. 60
ELVIA ASSURANCES SIEGE SOCIAL—See Allianz Aktiengesellschaft; Int'l, pg. 60
ELVIA LEBEN—See Allianz Aktiengesellschaft; Int'l, pg. 60
ELVIA LEVENVERZEKERINGEN N.V.—See Allianz Aktiengesellschaft; Int'l, pg. 60
ELVIA REISEVERSICHERUNGEN—See Allianz Aktiengesellschaft; Int'l, pg. 60
ELVIA SCHADEVERZEKERINGEN N.V.—See Allianz Aktiengesellschaft; Int'l, pg. 60
ELVIA VERSICHERUNGEN—See Allianz Aktiengesellschaft; Int'l, pg. 60
ELVIASEG. S. A.—See Allianz Aktiengesellschaft; Int'l, pg. 60
ELVINS EQUIPMENT SALES LIMITED—See Wajax Limited; Int'l, pg. 1485
ELVY PTY. LTD.—See Philips Electronics N.V.; Int'l, pg. 1052
ELWELL-PARKER LIMITED; U.S. Private, pg. 373
ELWELL-PARKER, INC.—See Elwell-Parker Limited; U.S. Private, pg. 373
ELYO CORP.—See Lyonnaise des Eaux S.A.; Int'l, pg. 823
ELYRIA FOUNDRY COMPANY; U.S. Private, pg. 373
ELYRIA SAVINGS & TRUST NATIONAL BANK—See FirstMerit Corporation; U.S. Public, pg. 646
EMAIL LIMITED; Int'l, pg. 450
EMAIL LIMITED-BUILDING PRODUCTS GROUP—See Email Limited; Int'l, pg. 450
EMAIL LIMITED-INDUSTRIAL PRODUCTS GROUP—See Email Limited; Int'l, pg. 450
EMAIL LIMITED-METALS GROUP—See Email Limited; Int'l, pg. 450
EMAILS S.P.A.—See Bayer AG; Int'l, pg. 175
EMAP APEX—See EMAP Plc; Int'l, pg. 451
EMAP ARCHITECTURE LTD.—See EMAP Plc; Int'l, pg. 451
EMAP BUSINESS COMMUNICATIONS DIVISION—See EMAP Plc; Int'l, pg. 451
EMAP BUSINESS COMMUNICATIONS USA—See EMAP Plc; Int'l, pg. 451
EMAP BUSINESS INFORMATION/EMAP HEIGHWAY—See EMAP Plc; Int'l, pg. 451
EMAP BUSINESS INTERNATIONAL LTD.—See EMAP Plc; Int'l, pg. 451
EMAP COMPUTING LTD.—See EMAP Plc; Int'l, pg. 451
EMAP CONSUMER MAGAZINES—See EMAP Plc; Int'l, pg. 451
EMAP DIRECT—See EMAP Plc; Int'l, pg. 451
EMAP ELAN—See EMAP Plc; Int'l, pg. 451
EMAP ENTERPRISE EVENTS—See EMAP Plc; Int'l, pg. 451
EMAP FASHION LTD.—See EMAP Plc; Int'l, pg. 451
EMAP FINANCE & FREIGHT LTD.—See EMAP Plc; Int'l, pg. 451
EMAP FRANCE—See EMAP Plc; Int'l, pg. 451
EMAP MACLAREN—See EMAP Plc; Int'l, pg. 451
EMAP MEDIA—See EMAP Plc; Int'l, pg. 451
EMAP MEDIA LTD.—See EMAP Plc; Int'l, pg. 451
EMAP PLC; Int'l, pg. 451
EMAP PROPERTIES—See EMAP Plc; Int'l, pg. 451
EMAP PUBLISHING SRL—See EMAP Plc; Int'l, pg. 451
EMAP PURSUIT PUBLISHING—See EMAP Plc; Int'l, pg. 451
EMAP RADIO—See EMAP Plc; Int'l, pg. 451
EMBALAGENS DE PORTUGAL - VAN LEER, LTDA—See Royal Packaging Industries Van Leer B.V.; Int'l, pg. 1146
EMBALLAGES CASCADES DRUMMONDVILLE INC.—See The Cascades Group; Int'l, pg. 273
EMBALLAGES CASCADES P.A.T. INC.—See The Cascades Group; Int'l, pg. 273
EMBARC COMMUNICATION SERVICES, INC.—See Motorola, Inc.; U.S. Public, pg. 1137
EMBARE INDUSTRIAS ALIMENTICIAS—See Philip Morris Companies Inc.; U.S. Public, pg. 1290
EMBASSY DEVELOPMENT CORPORATION—See Promus Hotel Corporation; U.S. Public, pg. 1335
EMBASSY EQUITY DEVELOPMENT CORPORATION—See Promus Hotel Corporation; U.S. Public, pg. 1335
EMBASSY HOUSE HEALTHCARE—See Vencor, Inc.; U.S. Public, pg. 1712
EMBASSY INDUSTRIES, INC.—See P & F Industries, Inc.; U.S. Public, pg. 1240
EMBASSY PACIFIC EQUITY CORPORATION—See Promus Hotel Corporation; U.S. Public, pg. 1335
EMBASSY SUITES CLUB NO. 1, INC.—See Promus Hotel Corporation; U.S. Public, pg. 1335
EMBASSY SUITES CLUB NO. 2, INC.—See Promus Hotel Corporation; U.S. Public, pg. 1335
EMBASSY SUITES (PUERTO RICO), INC.—See Promus Hotel Corporation; U.S. Public, pg. 1335
EMBASSY SYRACUSE DEVELOPMENT CORPORATION—See Promus Hotel Corporation; U.S. Public, pg. 1335
EMBECON (NEW ZEALAND) LIMITED—See Novartis AG; Int'l, pg. 982
EMBEDDED PERFORMANCE, INC.; U.S. Private, pg. 373
EMBERS CHARCOAL COMPANY, INC.; U.S. Private, pg. 373
EMBOLTELLADORA DEL URUGUAY, S.A.—See PepsiCo, Inc.; U.S. Public, pg. 1277
EMBOTELLADORES DEL VALLE DE ANAHUAC S.A. DE C.V.; Int'l, pg. 452

MASTER INDEX TO COMPANY NAMES

EMTEC

Company Index

EMBRACO NORTH AMERICA, INC.—See Whirlpool Corporation; *U.S. Public*, pg. 1765
EMBRAER-EMPRESA BRASILEIRA DE AERONAUTICA S.A.; *Int'l*, pg. 452
EMBRATEL-EMPRESA BRASILIERA DE TELECOMUNICAGOES S.A.—See Telebras S.A.; *Int'l*, pg. 1362
EMCEE BROADCAST PRODUCTS, INC.; *U.S. Public*, pg. 570
EMCEE CELLULAR, INC.—See Emcee Broadcast Products, Inc.; *U.S. Public*, pg. 571
EMCO BUILDING PRODUCTS—See Emco Limited; *Int'l*, pg. 453
EMCO CUSTOM PRODUCTS GROUP—See Emco Limited; *Int'l*, pg. 453
EMCO DISTRIBUTION—See Emco Limited; *Int'l*, pg. 453
EMCO DISTRIBUTION GROUP WESTERN REGION—See Emco Limited; *Int'l*, pg. 453
EMCO LIMITED; *Int'l*, pg. 452
EMCO SUPPLY ATLANTIC DIVISION—See Emco Limited; *Int'l*, pg. 453
EMCO SUPPLY CENTRAL REGION—See Emco Limited; *Int'l*, pg. 453
EMCO SUPPLY EASTERN REGION—See Emco Limited; *Int'l*, pg. 453
EMCON; *U.S. Public*, pg. 571
EMCOR GROUP, INC.; *U.S. Public*, pg. 571
EMDEME SA—See Heidemij N.V.; *Int'l*, pg. 608
EMERALD COAST CABLE TELEVISION—See Cox Communications, Inc.; *U.S. Public*, pg. 455
EMERALD COAST CABLE TELEVISION—See Time Warner Inc.; *U.S. Public*, pg. 1610
EMERALD INDUSTRIES INC.—See Flowers Industries, Inc.; *U.S. Public*, pg. 657
EMERALD WAREHOUSE & DISTRIBUTION SERVICES—See Mail-Well Inc.; *U.S. Public*, pg. 1038
EMEREX S.A. DE C.V.—See Emerson Electric Co.; *U.S. Public*, pg. 576
EMERGE COMMUNICATIONS—See Black Entertainment Television Holdings Inc.; *U.S. Public*, pg. 235
EMERGE VISION SYSTEMS—See Safeguard Scientifics, Inc.; *U.S. Public*, pg. 1425
EMERGENCY LIGHTING DIV.—See General Signal Corporation; *U.S. Public*, pg. 726
EMERGENCY ONE, INC.—See Federal Signal Corporation; *U.S. Public*, pg. 617
EMERGI-LITE, INC.—See Kaufel Group Ltd.; *Int'l*, pg. 725
EMERGI-LITE LANDMARK INC.—See Kaufel Group Ltd.; *Int'l*, pg. 725
EMERGI-LITE SAFETY SYSTEMS LTD.—See Kaufel Group Ltd.; *Int'l*, pg. 725
EMERSON & CUMING SPECIALTY POLYMERS—See Unilever Plc; *Int'l*, pg. 1435
EMERSON ELECTRIC (ASIA)—See Emerson Electric Co.; *U.S. Public*, pg. 576
EMERSON ELECTRIC, C.A.—See Emerson Electric Co.; *U.S. Public*, pg. 576
EMERSON ELECTRIC CANADA LTD.—See Emerson Electric Co.; *U.S. Public*, pg. 576
EMERSON ELECTRIC CO.; *U.S. Public*, pg. 572
EMERSON ELECTRIC (FRANCE) S.A.—See Emerson Electric Co.; *U.S. Public*, pg. 576
EMERSON ELECTRIC GMBH—See Emerson Electric Co.; *U.S. Public*, pg. 576
EMERSON ELECTRIC IBERICA S.A.—See Emerson Electric Co.; *U.S. Public*, pg. 576
EMERSON ELECTRIC INDUS. CONTROLS LTD.—See Emerson Electric Co.; *U.S. Public*, pg. 576
EMERSON ELECTRIC INDUS. CONTROLS, S.A.—See Emerson Electric Co.; *U.S. Public*, pg. 576
EMERSON ELECTRIC IRELAND LIMITED—See Emerson Electric Co.; *U.S. Public*, pg. 576
EMERSON ELECTRIC NEDERLAND B.V.—See Emerson Electric Co.; *U.S. Public*, pg. 576
EMERSON ELECTRIC S.R.L.—See Emerson Electric Co.; *U.S. Public*, pg. 576
EMERSON ELECTRIC U.K. LTD.—See Emerson Electric Co.; *U.S. Public*, pg. 576
EMERSON EUROPA TRADING B.V.—See Emerson Electric Co.; *U.S. Public*, pg. 576
EMERSON JAPAN, LTD.—See Emerson Electric Co.; *U.S. Public*, pg. 576
EMERSON JAPAN, LTD., FUSITE DIVISION—See Emerson Electric Co.; *U.S. Public*, pg. 576
EMERSON MOTOR COMPANY—See Emerson Electric Co.; *U.S. Public*, pg. 573
EMERSON PACIFIC PTE. LTD.—See Emerson Electric Co.; *U.S. Public*, pg. 576
EMERSON POWER TRANSMISSION CO.—See Emerson Electric Co.; *U.S. Public*, pg. 573
EMERSON POWER TRANSMISSION CORPORATION—See Emerson Electric Co.; *U.S. Public*, pg. 573
EMERSON RADIO CORP.; *U.S. Public*, pg. 578
EMERSON RADIO HONG KONG LTD.—See Emerson Radio Corp.; *U.S. Public*, pg. 578
EMERSON TECHNOLOGY G.M.B.H.—See Emerson Electric Co.; *U.S. Public*, pg. 577
EMERY CUSTOMS BROKERS—See CNF Transportation Inc.; *U.S. Public*, pg. 281
EMERY EXPEDITE!—See CNF Transportation Inc.; *U.S. Public*, pg. 281
EMERY GLOBAL LOGISTICS—See CNF Transportation Inc.; *U.S. Public*, pg. 281
EMERY GROUP HENKEL CORP.—See Henkel KGaA; *Int'l*, pg. 611
EMERY OCEAN SERVICES—See CNF Transportation Inc.; *U.S. Public*, pg. 281
EMERY WATERHOUSE COMPANY; *U.S. Private*, pg. 373
EMERY WORLDWIDE—See CNF Transportation Inc.; *U.S. Public*, pg. 281
EMERY WORLDWIDE AIRLINES—See CNF Transportation Inc.; *U.S. Public*, pg. 281
EMESS LIGHTING INC.—See Emess PLC; *Int'l*, pg. 453
EMESS PLC; *Int'l*, pg. 453
EMESTA EMPRESSA ESPANOLA DE TABACOS S.L.—See Reemtsma Cigarettenfabriken GmbH, Hamburg; *Int'l*, pg. 1101
EMHART (ASIA) LTD.—See The Black & Decker Corporation; *U.S. Public*, pg. 233
EMHART AUSTRALIA PTY. LTD.—See The Black & Decker Corporation; *U.S. Public*, pg. 234
EMHART CORP.—See The Black & Decker Corporation; *U.S. Public*, pg. 233
EMHART DEUTSCHLAND GMBH—See The Black & Decker Corporation; *U.S. Public*, pg. 233
EMHART GES.M.B.H. (AUSTRIA)—See The Black & Decker Corporation; *U.S. Public*, pg. 233
EMHART GLASS S.A.—See The Black & Decker Corporation; *U.S. Public*, pg. 233
EMHART INTERNATIONAL LTD.—See The Black & Decker Corporation; *U.S. Public*, pg. 233
EMHART S.A.—See The Black & Decker Corporation; *U.S. Public*, pg. 233
EMHART SINGAPORE PTE. LTD.—See The Black & Decker Corporation; *U.S. Public*, pg. 233
EMHART S.R.L.—See The Black & Decker Corporation; *U.S. Public*, pg. 233
EMHART SWEDEN AKTIEBOLAG—See The Black & Decker Corporation; *U.S. Public*, pg. 233
EMHART TEKNIK AB MACHINERY DIVISION—See The Black & Decker Corporation; *U.S. Public*, pg. 233
EMHART (U.K.) LTD.—See The Black & Decker Corporation; *U.S. Public*, pg. 234
EMICH OLDSMOBILE, INC.; *U.S. Private*, pg. 373
EMIGRANT SAVINGS BANK; *U.S. Private*, pg. 373
EMIL MOESTUE AS—See Esselte AB; *Int'l*, pg. 460
EMINENCE SA—See Hesta Tex AG; *Int'l*, pg. 618
EMIRATES CAN COMPANY LTD.—See Crown Cork & Seal Company, Inc.; *U.S. Public*, pg. 465
EMIRATES TECHNOLOGY COMPANY (EMITAC)—See Hewlett-Packard Company; *U.S. Public*, pg. 817
EMITEC INC.—See GKN plc; *Int'l*, pg. 535
EMKAY, INC.; *U.S. Private*, pg. 374
EMMABODA GLAS AB—See Saint-Gobain; *Int'l*, pg. 1173
EMMERLING POST, INC.; *U.S. Private*, pg. 374
EMMETT POWER COMPANY—See Boise Cascade Corporation; *U.S. Public*, pg. 243
EMONS FINANCE CORP.—See Emons Transportation Group, Inc.; *U.S. Public*, pg. 578
EMONS FINANCE CORPORATION—See Emons Transportation Group, Inc.; *U.S. Public*, pg. 578
EMONS INDUSTRIES, INC.—See Emons Transportation Group, Inc.; *U.S. Public*, pg. 578
EMONS LOGISTICS SERVICES INC.—See Emons Transportation Group, Inc.; *U.S. Public*, pg. 578
EMONS RAILROAD GROUP, INC.—See Emons Transportation Group, Inc.; *U.S. Public*, pg. 578
EMONS TRANSPORTATION GROUP, INC.; *U.S. Public*, pg. 578
EMPACADORA ECUATORIANA-DANESA (ECUADASA) S.A.—See The East Asiatic Company Ltd. A/S; *Int'l*, pg. 431
EMPAQUES PONDEROSA SA—See Empressa La Moderna SA de CV; *Int'l*, pg. 454
EMPATICA AB—See Pharmacia & Upjohn, Inc.; *Int'l*, pg. 1047
EMPIRE AIRLINES; *U.S. Private*, pg. 374
EMPIRE BEROL U.S.A.—See Newell Co.; *U.S. Public*, pg. 1178
EMPIRE BLUE CROSS & BLUE SHIELD; *U.S. Private*, pg. 374
EMPIRE CANDLE, INC.—See Diamond Brands, Inc.; *U.S. Private*, pg. 330
EMPIRE CHEESE, INC.—See The Great Lakes Cheese Co.; *U.S. Private*, pg. 474
EMPIRE CLOTHING—See Excelled Sheepskin & Leather Coat Corporation; *U.S. Private*, pg. 387
EMPIRE COMMUNICATIONS CONSULTANTS, INC.—See Motorola, Inc.; *U.S. Public*, pg. 1137
EMPIRE COMPANY LIMITED; *Int'l*, pg. 453
EMPIRE DIAMOND CORPORATION; *U.S. Private*, pg. 374
THE EMPIRE DISTRICT ELECTRIC COMPANY; *U.S. Public*, pg. 579
EMPIRE DIVISION—See U.S. Industries, Inc.; *U.S. Public*, pg. 1684
EMPIRE ELECTRIC ASSOCIATION; *U.S. Private*, pg. 374
EMPIRE FIRE & MARINE INSURANCE CO.—See Zurich Insurance Company; *Int'l*, pg. 1530
EMPIRE FOUNDRY—See Crane Co.; *U.S. Public*, pg. 457
EMPIRE GENERAL LIFE ASSURANCE CORPORATION—See Protective Life Corporation; *U.S. Public*, pg. 1336
EMPIRE HYDRAULIC SERVICE—See Empire Southwest Co.; *U.S. Private*, pg. 374
EMPIRE INDEMNITY INSURANCE COMPANY—See Zurich Insurance Company; *Int'l*, pg. 1530
EMPIRE INDUSTRIES, INC.—See Empire of Carolina, Inc.; *U.S. Public*, pg. 579
EMPIRE INSURANCE GROUP—See Leucadia National Corporation; *U.S. Public*, pg. 990
EMPIRE KOSHER POULTRY, INC.; *U.S. Private*, pg. 374
EMPIRE LIFE INSURANCE COMPANY—See Washington Mutual Inc.; *U.S. Public*, pg. 1742
EMPIRE LIVESTOCK MARKETING INC.—See Dairylea Cooperative Inc.; *U.S. Private*, pg. 308
EMPIRE MACHINERY—See Empire Southwest Co.; *U.S. Private*, pg. 374
EMPIRE MACHINERY - CALIFORNIA—See Empire Southwest Co.; *U.S. Private*, pg. 375
EMPIRE MACHINERY - IMPERIAL—See Empire Southwest Co.; *U.S. Private*, pg. 375
EMPIRE MACHINERY - KINGMAN—See Empire Southwest Co.; *U.S. Private*, pg. 375
EMPIRE MACHINERY - PRESCOTT—See Empire Southwest Co.; *U.S. Private*, pg. 375
EMPIRE MACHINERY - SHOW LOW—See Empire Southwest Co.; *U.S. Private*, pg. 375
EMPIRE MACHINERY - TUCSON—See Empire Southwest Co.; *U.S. Private*, pg. 375
EMPIRE MACHINERY - YUMA—See Empire Southwest Co.; *U.S. Private*, pg. 375
EMPIRE METRO—See Empire Southwest Co.; *U.S. Private*, pg. 375
EMPIRE NATIONAL BANK; *U.S. Private*, pg. 374
EMPIRE OF CAROLINA, INC.; *U.S. Public*, pg. 579
EMPIRE OFFICE EQUIPMENT, INC.; *U.S. Private*, pg. 374
EMPIRE POWER SYSTEMS—See Empire Southwest Co.; *U.S. Private*, pg. 375
EMPIRE POWER SYSTEMS - TUCSON—See Empire Southwest Co.; *U.S. Private*, pg. 375
EMPIRE SOUTHWEST CO.; *U.S. Private*, pg. 374
EMPIRE STATE PIPELINE COMPANY—See The Coastal Corporation; *U.S. Public*, pg. 390
EMPIRE STEEL CASTINGS, INC.—See Atchison Casting Corporation; *U.S. Public*, pg. 142
EMPIRE THEATERS LIMITED—See Empire Company Limited; *Int'l*, pg. 454
EMPIRE TRANSPORT—See Empire Southwest Co.; *U.S. Private*, pg. 375
EMPLOYEE ASSISTANCE SERVICES, INC.—See Magellan Health Services, Inc.; *U.S. Public*, pg. 1035
EMPLOYEE BENEFIT PLAN ADMINISTRATION, INC.—See Cigna Corp.; *U.S. Public*, pg. 360
EMPLOYEE BENEFITS DIV.—See Anglo American Corporation of South Africa Limited; *Int'l*, pg. 77
EMPLOYEE BENEFITS INSURANCE COMPANY—See Orion Capital Corporation; *U.S. Public*, pg. 1231
EMPLOYEE SOLUTIONS, INC.; *U.S. Public*, pg. 579
EMPLOYERS HEALTH INSURANCE COMPANY—See Humana Inc.; *U.S. Public*, pg. 847
EMPLOYERS INSURANCE OF WAUSAU—See Nationwide Insurance Enterprise; *U.S. Private*, pg. 788
EMPLOYERS LIFE INS. CO. OF WAUSAU—See Nationwide Insurance Enterprise; *U.S. Private*, pg. 789
EMPLOYERS REINSURANCE CORP.—See General Electric Company; *U.S. Public*, pg. 711
EMPREENDIMENTOS AGRICOLA PIONEER LTDA.—See Pioneer Hi-Bred International, Inc.; *U.S. Public*, pg. 1299
EMPRESA AUXILIAR DE LA INDUSTRIA, AUXINI, S.A.—See SEPI; *Int'l*, pg. 1224
EMPRESA BRASILEIRA DE COMPRESSORES S.A. (EMBRACO)—See Whirlpool Corporation; *U.S. Public*, pg. 1765
EMPRESA DE REFRACTARIOS COLOMBIANOS S.A.—See RGP Holding, Inc.; *U.S. Private*, pg. 903
EMPRESA GUATEMALTICA CIGNA DE SEGUROS, SOCIEDAD ANONIMA—See Cigna Corp.; *U.S. Public*, pg. 364
EMPRESA TECNOLOGICA ERICSSON S.A. DE C.V.—See Telefonaktiebolaget LM Ericsson; *Int'l*, pg. 1366
EMPRESAS BRISTOL DE COSTA RICA, S.A.—See Bristol-Myers Squibb Company; *U.S. Public*, pg. 256
EMPRESAS FRISCO SA DE CV—See Grupo Carso S.A. de C.V.; *Int'l*, pg. 572
EMPRESAS ICA SOCIEDAD CONTROLADORA (ARGENTINA)—See Empresas ICA Sociedad Controladora S.A.C.V.; *Int'l*, pg. 454
EMPRESAS ICA SOCIEDAD CONTROLADORA (COLOMBIA)—See Empresas ICA Sociedad Controladora S.A.C.V.; *Int'l*, pg. 454
EMPRESAS ICA SOCIEDAD CONTROLADORA (EL SALVADOR)—See Empresas ICA Sociedad Controladora S.A.C.V.; *Int'l*, pg. 454
EMPRESAS ICA SOCIEDAD CONTROLADORA (HOUSTON)—See Empresas ICA Sociedad Controladora S.A.C.V.; *Int'l*, pg. 454
EMPRESAS ICA SOCIEDAD CONTROLADORA (MALAYSIA)—See Empresas ICA Sociedad Controladora S.A.C.V.; *Int'l*, pg. 454
EMPRESAS ICA SOCIEDAD CONTROLADORA (MIAMI)—See Empresas ICA Sociedad Controladora S.A.C.V.; *Int'l*, pg. 454
EMPRESAS ICA SOCIEDAD CONTROLADORA (PANAMA)—See Empresas ICA Sociedad Controladora S.A.C.V.; *Int'l*, pg. 454
EMPRESAS ICA SOCIEDAD CONTROLADORA (PERU)—See Empresas ICA Sociedad Controladora S.A.C.V.; *Int'l*, pg. 454
EMPRESAS ICA SOCIEDAD CONTROLADORA (PUERTO RICO)—See Empresas ICA Sociedad Controladora S.A.C.V.; *Int'l*, pg. 454
EMPRESAS ICA SOCIEDAD CONTROLADORA S.A.C.V.; *Int'l*, pg. 454
EMPRESS FOODS LTD.—See Safeway Inc.; *U.S. Public*, pg. 1426
EMPRESS HANDBAGS—See Jaclyn, Inc.; *U.S. Public*, pg. 920
EMPRESS INTERNATIONAL LTD.; *U.S. Private*, pg. 375
EMPRESSA LA MODERNA SA DE CV; *Int'l*, pg. 454
EMPTY CHAIR PRODUCTIONS, INC.—See The Walt Disney Company; *U.S. Public*, pg. 511
EMSLAND-RAISIO CHEMIE GMBH—See Raisio Group; *Int'l*, pg. 1086
EMSON, INC.; *U.S. Private*, pg. 375
EMTEC DA AMAZONIA S.A.—See KOHAP Group; *Int'l*, pg. 743
EMTEC MAGNETICS AUSTRALIA PTY. LTD.—See KOHAP Group; *Int'l*, pg. 743
EMTEC MAGNETICS BENELUX N.V.—See KOHAP Group; *Int'l*, pg. 743
EMTEC MAGNETICS CHINA LTD.—See KOHAP Group; *Int'l*, pg. 743
EMTEC MAGNETICS DATASOURCE MEDIA INC.—See KOHAP Group; *Int'l*, pg. 743
EMTEC MAGNETICS ECE GMBH—See KOHAP Group; *Int'l*, pg. 743
EMTEC MAGNETICS GMBH—See KOHAP Group; *Int'l*, pg. 743
EMTEC MAGNETICS IBERICA S.A.—See KOHAP Group; *Int'l*, pg. 743
EMTEC MAGNETICS ITALIA SPA—See KOHAP Group; *Int'l*, pg. 743

EMTEC MAGNETICS NORDIC A/S—See KOHAP Group; Int'l, pg. 743
EMTEC MAGNETICS POLSKA SP. Z.O.O.—See KOHAP Group; Int'l, pg. 743
EMTEC MAGNETICS PRO MEDIA INC.—See KOHAP Group; Int'l, pg. 743
EMTEC MAGNETICS (SCHWEIZ) GMBH—See KOHAP Group; Int'l, pg. 743
EMTEC MAGNETICS SINGAPORE PTY. LTD.—See KOHAP Group; Int'l, pg. 743
EMTEC MAGNETICS U.K. LIMITED—See KOHAP Group; Int'l, pg. 743
EMTEC PRODUCTS CORPORATION—See Kuhlman Corporation; U.S. Public, pg. 968
EMTEK HEALTH CARE SYSTEMS, INC.—See Motorola, Inc.; U.S. Public, pg. 1137
EMTEX LEASING CORP.—See Willcox & Gibbs, Inc.; U.S. Private, pg. 1177
EMULEX CARIBE INC.—See Emulex Corporation; U.S. Public, pg. 579
EMULEX CORPORATION; U.S. Public, pg. 579
EMULSIO AB—See Dainippon Ink & Chemicals, Inc.; Int'l, pg. 370
OY EMULSIO AB—See Dainippon Ink & Chemicals, Inc.; Int'l, pg. 370
ENAEX S.A.—See Mining Services International, Inc.; U.S. Public, pg. 1115
ENATOR AB—See Axel Johnson AB; Int'l, pg. 708
ENATOR A/S—See Celsius AB; Int'l, pg. 278
ENATOR DEUSTCHLAND GMBH—See Celsius AB; Int'l, pg. 278
ENATOR MALARDALEN AB—See Celsius AB; Int'l, pg. 277
ENATOR RYHMA OY—See Celsius AB; Int'l, pg. 278
ENATOR SYD AB—See Celsius AB; Int'l, pg. 277
ENATOR VAST AB—See Celsius AB; Int'l, pg. 277
ENAVAL—See Petrobras - Petroleo Brasileiro S.A.; Int'l, pg. 1041
ENCAP SYSTEMS, INC.—See Hayes, Seay, Mattern & Mattern, Inc.; U.S. Private, pg. 513
ENCARA—See AmeriSource Health Corp.; U.S. Public, pg. 97
ENCERATEC, INC.—See Toshiba Corporation; Int'l, pg. 1405
ENCIA S.P.A—See Nestle S.A.; Int'l, pg. 920
ENCO—See Jeumont-Schneider Trenformeteurs; Int'l, pg. 706
ENCO-GEORGIA—See Enco Materials, Inc.; U.S. Private, pg. 375
ENCO-JACKSON—See Enco Materials, Inc.; U.S. Private, pg. 375
ENCO-JOHNSON CITY DIVISION—See Enco Materials, Inc.; U.S. Private, pg. 375
ENCO-KNOXVILLE—See Enco Materials, Inc.; U.S. Private, pg. 375
ENCO MATERIALS, INC.; U.S. Private, pg. 375
ENCO-MEMPHIS—See Enco Materials, Inc.; U.S. Private, pg. 375
ENCOAT-NORTH ARLINGTON, INC.—See Lukens Inc.; U.S. Public, pg. 1020
ENCOMPASS EUROPE NV—See KPN Koninklyke PTT Nederland NV; Int'l, pg. 720
ENCON SAFETY PRODUCTS, INC.—See Vallen Corporation; U.S. Public, pg. 1705
ENCORE CLUBS, INC.—See Encore Marketing International, Inc.; U.S. Public, pg. 580
ENCORE COMPUTER (ASIA) LTD.—See Encore Computer Corporation; U.S. Public, pg. 580
ENCORE COMPUTER CORPORATION; U.S. Public, pg. 580
ENCORE COMPUTER ESPANA S.A.—See Encore Computer Corporation; U.S. Public, pg. 580
ENCORE COMPUTER GMBH—See Encore Computer Corporation; U.S. Public, pg. 580
ENCORE COMPUTER ITALIA S.P.A.—See Encore Computer Corporation; U.S. Public, pg. 580
ENCORE COMPUTER (UK) LTD.—See Encore Computer Corporation; U.S. Public, pg. 580
ENCORE GROUP, INC.—See Encore Marketing International, Inc.; U.S. Public, pg. 580
ENCORE HOME HEALTH CARE, INC.—See Integrated Health Services, Inc.; U.S. Public, pg. 884
ENCORE INFORMATIQUE LIMITEE—See Encore Computer Corporation; U.S. Public, pg. 580
ENCORE MARKETING INTERNATIONAL, INC.; U.S. Public, pg. 580
ENCORE SHOE CORPORATION; U.S. Private, pg. 375
ENCYCLE/TEXAS, INC.—See Asarco Incorporated; U.S. Public, pg. 138
ENCYCLOPAEDIA BRITANNICA DIRECT, INC.—See Encyclopaedia Britannica, Inc.; U.S. Private, pg. 375
ENCYCLOPAEDIA BRITANNICA, INC.; U.S. Private, pg. 375
ENDECOTTS LTD.—See Firth-Rixson Plc; Int'l, pg. 488
ENDEVCO CORPORATION—See Meggitt plc; Int'l, pg. 853
ENDEVCO FRANCE S.A.—See Meggitt plc; Int'l, pg. 854
ENDEVCO PRODUCING CO.—See El Paso Natural Gas Co.; U.S. Public, pg. 567
ENDEVCO UK LTD.—See Meggitt plc; Int'l, pg. 853
ENDEVCO VERTRIEBS GMBH—See Meggitt plc; Int'l, pg. 854
ENDLESS VACATION—See Cendant Corporation; U.S. Public, pg. 322
ENDO-SERVICES S.A.R.L.—See Olympus Optical Co., Ltd.; Int'l, pg. 1005
ENDURA SA—See SMH Swiss Corporation for Micro Electronics & Watchmaking Indus. Ltd.; Int'l, pg. 1160
ENDURO-NIAGARA LTD.—See J.H. Roberts Industries Inc.; U.S. Private, pg. 935
ENECO TECH GROUP; U.S. Private, pg. 376
ENER-TEK INTERNATIONAL CORPORATION; U.S. Private, pg. 376
ENERCO, INC.—See The Broken Hill Proprietary Company Limited; Int'l, pg. 225

ENERCOM INC.—See Nova Scotia Power Inc.; Int'l, pg. 971
ENERCON ENGINEERING PRIVATE LIMITED—See GESTRA GmbH; Int'l, pg. 550
ENERCOP GAS MARKETING—See KCS Energy Inc.; U.S. Public, pg. 938
ENERFAB INC.; U.S. Private, pg. 376
ENERFLEX LEASING—See Toromont Industries Ltd.; Int'l, pg. 1400
ENERFLEX SYSTEMS LTD.—See Toromont Industries Ltd.; Int'l, pg. 1400
ENERGAS COMPANY—See Atmos Energy Corporation; U.S. Public, pg. 145
ENERGAS GESELLSCHAFT ZUR ENERGIEGEWINNUNG AUS MULL UND KOHLE MBH—See Saarbergwerke Aktiengesellschaft; Int'l, pg. 1166
ENERGEN CORPORATION; U.S. Public, pg. 581
ENERGEX CORP.—See Eaton Vance Corp.; U.S. Public, pg. 559
ENERGIE-AKTIENGESELLSCHAFT MITTELDEUTSCHLAND EAM—See Veba AG; Int'l, pg. 1456
ENERGIE BEHEER NEDERLAND B.V.—See DSM N.V.; Int'l, pg. 353
ENERGIE UND UMWELT SERVICE GMBH—See Mannesmann A.G.; Int'l, pg. 836
ENERGIE- UND UMWELTTECHNIK GMBH—See Veba AG; Int'l, pg. 1460
ENERGIEOBJEKTGESELLSCHAFT MBH-EOG—See Veba AG; Int'l, pg. 1456
ENERGIEVERSORGUNG MURITZ-ODERHAFF AKTIENGESELLSCHAFT—See Veba AG; Int'l, pg. 1456
ENERGIEVERSORGUNG WESER-EMS AG—See Veba AG; Int'l, pg. 1456
ENERGIEWERKE FRANKFURT/ODER AG—See Veba AG; Int'l, pg. 1456
ENERGIEWERKE MAGDEBURG AG—See Veba AG; Int'l, pg. 1456
ENERGIEWERKE NORDTHURINGEN AG—See Veba AG; Int'l, pg. 1456
ENERGIEWERKE POTSDAM AG—See Veba AG; Int'l, pg. 1456
ENERGIEWERKE ROSTOCK AG—See Veba AG; Int'l, pg. 1456
ENERGIS RESOURCES INCORPORATED—See Public Service Enterprise Group Incorporated; U.S. Public, pg. 1340
ENERGIZER EVEREADY LTD.—See Ralston Purina Company; U.S. Public, pg. 1360
ENERGOSOFIN—See Tamrock Corp.; Int'l, pg. 1354
ENERGY ABSORPTION SYSTEMS, INC.—See Quixote Corporation; U.S. Public, pg. 1353
ENERGY ABSORPTION SYSTEMS, INC.-PELL CITY—See Quixote Corporation; U.S. Public, pg. 1353
ENERGY ABSORPTION SYSTEMS, INC.-ROCKLIN—See Quixote Corporation; U.S. Public, pg. 1353
ENERGY & ENVIRONMENTAL RESEARCH CORP.; U.S. Private, pg. 376
ENERGY & MINERALS, INC.—See South Jersey Industries, Inc.; U.S. Public, pg. 1488
ENERGY & PROCESS CORP.—See Wolseley Plc.; Int'l, pg. 1512
ENERGY BROKERS GUILD; U.S. Private, pg. 376
ENERGY COMPANIES OF ONEOK—See ONEOK Inc.; U.S. Public, pg. 1226
ENERGY CONTROL PRODUCTS—See TI Group plc; Int'l, pg. 1338
ENERGY CONVERSION DEVICES, INC.; U.S. Public, pg. 581
ENERGY DEVELOPMENT CORPORATION—See Noble Affiliates, Inc.; U.S. Public, pg. 1186
ENERGY DYNAMICS DIVISION—See Pacific Scientific Company; U.S. Public, pg. 1250
ENERGY INITIATIVES, INC.—See GPU, Inc.; U.S. Public, pg. 695
ENERGY INVESTORS MANAGEMENT, INC.—See John Hancock Mutual Life Insurance Company; U.S. Private, pg. 589
ENERGY LAND, INCORPORATED—See Minnesota Power; U.S. Public, pg. 1116
ENERGY LOGISTICS AZERBAIJAN LTD.—See Golden Eagle Group, Inc.; U.S. Public, pg. 749
ENERGY MFG. CO.—See CGF Industries; U.S. Private, pg. 194
ENERGY NATIONAL, INC.—See PacifiCorp; U.S. Public, pg. 1252
ENERGY NETWORKS, INC. (ENI)—See CTG Resources, Inc.; U.S. Public, pg. 285
ENERGY PACIFIC—See Enova Corp; U.S. Public, pg. 584
ENERGY PACIFIC—See Pacific Enterprises; U.S. Public, pg. 1249
ENERGY POWER SYSTEMS AUSTRALIA PTY. LIMITED—See Caterpillar Inc.; U.S. Public, pg. 316
ENERGY POWER SYSTEMS PNG PTY. LIMITED—See Caterpillar Inc.; U.S. Public, pg. 316
ENERGY REALTY, INC.—See Indiana Energy, Inc.; U.S. Public, pg. 875
ENERGY RESOURCES OF AUSTRALIA LTD.—See North Limited; Int'l, pg. 967
ENERGY SERVICES, INC.—See Edison International; U.S. Public, pg. 564
ENERGY SERVICES INTERNATIONAL LIMITED—See Caterpillar Inc.; U.S. Public, pg. 316
ENERGY SYSTEMS GROUP, INC.—See SIGCORP, Inc.; U.S. Public, pg. 1471
ENERGY SYSTEMS INDUSTRIES, INC.; U.S. Private, pg. 376
ENERGY TECHNOLOGY CO. LTD.—See GESTRA GmbH; Int'l, pg. 550
ENERGY USA—See Bay State Gas Company; U.S. Public, pg. 197
ENERGY VALVE DIVISION—See Dresser Industries, Inc.; U.S. Public, pg. 528

ENERGY VENTURES MID EAST, INC.—See EVI, Inc.; U.S. Public, pg. 604
ENERGY WEST INC.; U.S. Public, pg. 581
ENERGY WEST MINING COMPANY—See PacifiCorp; U.S. Public, pg. 1251
ENERGY WEST RESOURCES—See Energy West Inc.; U.S. Public, pg. 581
ENERGYLINE CORPORATION—See Rochester Gas And Electric Corporation; U.S. Public, pg. 1396
ENERGYNORTH, INC.; U.S. Public, pg. 581
ENERGYNORTH NATURAL GAS, INC.—See EnergyNorth, Inc.; U.S. Public, pg. 582
ENERGYNORTH PROPANE, INC.—See EnergyNorth, Inc.; U.S. Public, pg. 582
ENERGYNORTH REALTY, INC.—See EnergyNorth, Inc.; U.S. Public, pg. 582
ENERMARK INCOME FUND; Int'l, pg. 454
ENERMET LTD.—See Imatran Voima Oy; Int'l, pg. 660
ENERPAC LTD.—See Applied Power Inc.; U.S. Public, pg. 125
ENERPAC U.S.—See Applied Power Inc.; U.S. Public, pg. 124
ENERSTAT DIVISION- ERIE MANUFACTURING CO. (CANADA) LTD.—See Siebe plc; Int'l, pg. 1241
ENERTECH CAPITAL PARTNERS—See Safeguard Scientifics, Inc.; U.S. Public, pg. 1424
ENERTECH INDUSTRIES AB—See Trelleborg AB; Int'l, pg. 1422
ENESCO CORPORATION—See Stanhome Inc.; U.S. Public, pg. 1508
ENESCO IMPORT, GMBH—See Stanhome Inc.; U.S. Public, pg. 1508
ENESCO INTERNATIONAL (HONG KONG) LTD.—See Stanhome Inc.; U.S. Public, pg. 1508
ENESCO LIMITED—See Stanhome Inc.; U.S. Public, pg. 1508
ENFIELD CABLES (PVT) LTD.—See Delta plc; Int'l, pg. 390
ENFIELD DISTRIBUTION CENTER—See Hallmark Cards, Inc.; U.S. Private, pg. 496
ENFIELD ELECTRIC LTD.—See Delta plc; Int'l, pg. 390
ENFIELD ENGINEERS LIMITED—See Delta plc; Int'l, pg. 390
ENFIELD HOLDINGS LTD.—See Delta plc; Int'l, pg. 390
ENFIELD INDUSTRIAL CORP.—See Glynwed International PLC; Int'l, pg. 554
ENFIELD MANUFACTURING (PVT) LTD.—See Delta plc; Int'l, pg. 390
ENFIELD WINDING WIRES LTD. (ENAMEL & TEXTILE)—See Delta plc; Int'l, pg. 390
ENGEL & MEIER GMBH—See SAIT-RadioHolland Group S.A.; Int'l, pg. 1152
ENGELHARD CANADA LIMITED—See Engelhard Corporation; U.S. Public, pg. 582
ENGELHARD CATALYSTS GMBH—See Engelhard Corporation; U.S. Public, pg. 582
ENGELHARD CORPORATION; U.S. Public, pg. 582
ENGELHARD CORP. ENGINEERED MATERIALS AND PRECIOUS METALS MANAGEMENT—See Engelhard Corporation; U.S. Public, pg. 582
ENGELHARD CORP.-QUINCY OPERATIONS—See Engelhard Corporation; U.S. Public, pg. 582
ENGELHARD METALS AG—See Engelhard Corporation; U.S. Public, pg. 582
ENGELHARD METALS LTD.—See Engelhard Corporation; U.S. Public, pg. 582
ENGER-KRESS COMPANY; U.S. Private, pg. 376
ENGINE AND GEAR SERVICE DIVISION—See Tecumseh Products Company; U.S. Public, pg. 1565
ENGINE CONTROL SYSTEMS, LTD.—See The Lubrizol Corporation; U.S. Public, pg. 1016
ENGINEER CONTROL INTL.; U.S. Private, pg. 376
ENGINEERED CARBONS, INC.—See Ameripol Synpol Corp.; U.S. Private, pg. 66
ENGINEERED CONSTRUCTION-ATLANTA—See Pitt-Des Moines, Inc.; U.S. Public, pg. 1304
ENGINEERED CONSTRUCTION DIVISION—See Pitt-Des Moines, Inc.; U.S. Public, pg. 1304
ENGINEERED CONSTRUCTION-FULLERTON—See Pitt-Des Moines, Inc.; U.S. Public, pg. 1304
ENGINEERED CONSTRUCTION-NEW JERSEY—See Pitt-Des Moines, Inc.; U.S. Public, pg. 1304
ENGINEERED CONSTRUCTION-PITTSBURGH—See Pitt-Des Moines, Inc.; U.S. Public, pg. 1304
ENGINEERED CONSTRUCTION-SACRAMENTO—See Pitt-Des Moines, Inc.; U.S. Public, pg. 1304
ENGINEERED POLYMERS CORPORATION—See Cookson Group plc; Int'l, pg. 328
ENGINEERED PRODUCTS, INC.; U.S. Public, pg. 583
ENGINEERED SEALS—See TI Group plc; Int'l, pg. 1338
ENGINEERED SINTERED COMPONENTS COMPANY—See Eaton Corporation; U.S. Public, pg. 558
ENGINEERED SPECIALTY PLASTICS—See Engineered Support Systems Inc.; U.S. Public, pg. 583
ENGINEERED SUPPORT SYSTEMS INC.; U.S. Public, pg. 583
ENGINEERED SYSTEMS GROUP—See Aeroquip-Vickers, Inc.; U.S. Public, pg. 24
ENGINEERED SYSTEMS INC.—See Phillips Service Industries, Inc.; U.S. Private, pg. 862
ENGINEERING & MANUFACTURING DIV.—See Siebe plc; Int'l, pg. 1240
ENGINEERING & TECHNICAL SERVICES, INC.—See American Financial Group; U.S. Public, pg. 75
ENGINEERING CERAMIC TECHNOLOGIES, INC.—See Cummins Engine Company, Inc.; U.S. Public, pg. 469
ENGINEERING COMPANY—See Eclipse Inc.; U.S. Private, pg. 361
ENGINEERING DIVISION—See The Boeing Company; U.S. Public, pg. 240
ENGINEERING NEWS-RECORD MAGAZINE—See The McGraw-Hill Companies; U.S. Public, pg. 1070
ENGINEERING RESEARCH ASSOCIATES—See Raytheon Company; U.S. Public, pg. 1365

MASTER INDEX TO COMPANY NAMES ENTSORGUNG

ENGINEERING SERVICE, INC.; *U.S. Private*, pg. 376
ENGINEERING SERVICES (SEGEN)—See Petrobras - Petroleo Brasileiro S.A.; *Int'l*, pg. 1041
ENGINEERING-STAMICARBON—See DSM N.V.; *Int'l*, pg. 354
ENGINEERING SYSTEMS CO.—See Datron Incorporated; *U.S. Private*, pg. 313
ENGINEERING TECHNOLOGY LTD. (E.T.); *U.S. Private*, pg. 377
ENGINEERING TEST SERVICES—See Cummins Engine Company, Inc.; *U.S. Public*, pg. 468
ENGINEERS & FABRICATORS CO.; *U.S. Private*, pg. 377
ENGINES DIVISION/BEDEK AVIATION GROUP—See Israel Aircraft Industries Ltd.; *Int'l*, pg. 690
ENGINS TACTIQUES DIV.—See Aerospatiale; *Int'l*, pg. 29
ENGLAND/CORSAIR—See La-Z-Boy Incorporated; *U.S. Public*, pg. 972
ENGLE HOMES, INC.; *U.S. Public*, pg. 583
ENGLEFIELD, INC.; *U.S. Private*, pg. 377
ROBERT ENGLEKIRK, INC.; *U.S. Private*, pg. 377
ENGLEKIRK & SABOL, INC.—See Robert Englekirk, Inc.; *U.S. Private*, pg. 377
ENGLEWOOD COMMUNITY HOSPITAL, INC.—See Columbia/HCA Healthcare Corporation; *U.S. Public*, pg. 404
ENGLISH CARD CLOTHING CO. LIMITED—See Carclo Engineering Group plc; *Int'l*, pg. 268
ENGLISH CHINA CLAYS, INC.—See English China Clays Plc; *Int'l*, pg. 455
ENGLISH CHINA CLAYS PLC; *Int'l*, pg. 455
ENGRAIS BATTAILLE S.A.—See Kemira Oy; *Int'l*, pg. 728
ENGRANASA-BRAZIL—See Hermann Pfauter GmbH & Co.; *Int'l*, pg. 617
ENGRAPH MACHINE GROUP—See Sonoco Products Company; *U.S. Public*, pg. 1486
ENGRAPH PUERTO RICO—See Sonoco Products Company; *U.S. Public*, pg. 1486
ENIAC C.A.—See Marcam Solutions, Inc.; *U.S. Public*, pg. 1043
ENICHEM FINANCE (OVERSEAS) LTD.—See ENI S.p.A.; *Int'l*, pg. 429
ENICHEM INTERNATIONAL HOLDINGS B.V.—See ENI S.p.A.; *Int'l*, pg. 429
ENICHEM POLYURETHANE DEUTSCHLAND GMBH—See ENI S.p.A.; *Int'l*, pg. 429
ENICHEM S.P.A.—See ENI S.p.A.; *Int'l*, pg. 428
ENIDINE INCORPORATED; *U.S. Private*, pg. 377
ENIRICERCHE S.P.A.—See ENI S.p.A.; *Int'l*, pg. 428
ENKA AG—See Akzo Nobel N.V.; *Int'l*, pg. 46
ENKA BV—See Akzo Nobel N.V.; *Int'l*, pg. 45
ENKA DANMARK A/S—See Akzo Nobel N.V.; *Int'l*, pg. 46
ENKA DE COLOMBIA S.A.—See Akzo Nobel N.V.; *Int'l*, pg. 46
ENKA FRANCE SARL—See Akzo Nobel N.V.; *Int'l*, pg. 46
ENKA HELLAS LTD.—See Akzo Nobel N.V.; *Int'l*, pg. 46
ENKA HOUSEHOLD PRODUCTS B.V.—See Freudenberg & Company; *Int'l*, pg. 505
ENKA INTERNATIONAL BV—See Akzo Nobel N.V.; *Int'l*, pg. 45
ENKA ITALIANA SRL.—See Akzo Nobel N.V.; *Int'l*, pg. 46
ENKA OSTERREICH HANDELSGESELLSCHAFT MBH—See Akzo Nobel N.V.; *Int'l*, pg. 46
ENKA PORTUGUESA LDA—See Akzo Nobel N.V.; *Int'l*, pg. 46
ENKA (SCHWEIZ) GMBH—See Akzo Nobel N.V.; *Int'l*, pg. 46
ENKA SUOMI OY—See Akzo Nobel N.V.; *Int'l*, pg. 46
ENKA SVERIGE AB—See Akzo Nobel N.V.; *Int'l*, pg. 46
ENKA UK LTD.—See Akzo Nobel N.V.; *Int'l*, pg. 46
ENKADOR S.A.—See Akzo Nobel N.V.; *Int'l*, pg. 46
ENKEL CORPORATION—See Baldwin Technology Company, Inc.; *U.S. Public*, pg. 170
ENMARK STATIONS, INC.—See Colonial Oil Industries; *U.S. Private*, pg. 254
ENNIA CARIBE N.V.—See AEGON N.V.; *Int'l*, pg. 28
ENNIS BUSINESS FORMS, INC.; *U.S. Public*, pg. 583
ENNIS BUSINESS FORMS OF GEORGIA—See Ennis Business Forms, Inc.; *U.S. Public*, pg. 583
ENNIS BUSINESS FORMS OF KANSAS, INC.—See Ennis Business Forms, Inc.; *U.S. Public*, pg. 583
ENNIS BUSINESS FORMS OF OHIO, INC.—See Ennis Business Forms, Inc.; *U.S. Public*, pg. 583
ENNIS BUSINESS FORMS OF OREGON, INC.—See Ennis Business Forms, Inc.; *U.S. Public*, pg. 583
ENNIS BUSINESS FORMS TENN INC.—See Ennis Business Forms, Inc.; *U.S. Public*, pg. 583
ENNIS-TEXAS TAG—See Ennis Business Forms, Inc.; *U.S. Public*, pg. 583
ENOCELL OY—See Enso Oyj; *Int'l*, pg. 455
ENOGEX INC.—See OGE Energy Corp.; *U.S. Public*, pg. 1207
ENOVA CORP; *U.S. Public*, pg. 583
ENPAP KFT—See Enso Oyj; *Int'l*, pg. 457
ENPRO, INC.—See Delta Natural Gas Company, Inc.; *U.S. Public*, pg. 497
ENPROTECH CORP.—See Itochu Corporation; *Int'l*, pg. 694
ENRAF B.V.—See Delft Instruments N.V.; *Int'l*, pg. 389
ENRAF INC.—See Delft Instruments N.V.; *Int'l*, pg. 389
ENRAF-NONIUS B.V.—See Delft Instruments N.V.; *Int'l*, pg. 389
ENRAF-NONIUS COMPANY (LTD PTS)—See Delft Instruments N.V.; *Int'l*, pg. 389
ENRAF-NONIUS GMBH—See Delft Instruments N.V.; *Int'l*, pg. 389
ENRAF-NONIUS IBERICA S.A.—See Delft Instruments N.V.; *Int'l*, pg. 389
ENRAF-NONIUS LTD.—See Delft Instruments N.V.; *Int'l*, pg. 389
ENRAF NONIUS S.A.—See Delft Instruments N.V.; *Int'l*, pg. 389
ENRAF-NONIUS TANK INVENTORY SYSTEMS INC.—See Delft Instruments N.V.; *Int'l*, pg. 389
ENRAF SARL—See Delft Instruments N.V.; *Int'l*, pg. 389
ENRON ACESS—See Enron Corp.; *U.S. Public*, pg. 584
ENRON AMERICAS, INC.—See Enron Corp.; *U.S. Public*, pg. 584
ENRON CAPITAL & TRADE RESOURCES—See Enron Corp.; *U.S. Public*, pg. 584
ENRON CORP.; *U.S. Public*, pg. 584
ENRON LIQUID SERVICES CORP.—See Enron Corp.; *U.S. Public*, pg. 584
ENRON LIQUIDS SERVICES CORP.—See Enron Corp.; *U.S. Public*, pg. 584
ENRON OIL & GAS CO.—See Enron Corp.; *U.S. Public*, pg. 584
ENRON OIL TRADING & TRANSPORTATION CO.—See Enron Corp.; *U.S. Public*, pg. 584
ENRON OPERATIONS CORP.—See Enron Corp.; *U.S. Public*, pg. 584
ENROUTE CARD INC.—See Air Canada; *Int'l*, pg. 36
ENSABLADORA CENTROAMERICANA DE COSTA RICA S.A.—See Toyota Motor Corporation; *Int'l*, pg. 1413
ENSAMBLE DE CABLES Y COMPONENTES, S.A. DE C.V.—See General Motors Corporation; *U.S. Public*, pg. 721
ENSCO DRILLING (VENEZUELA), S.A.—See Ensco International Incorporated (ENSCO); *U.S. Public*, pg. 585
ENSCO INTERNATIONAL INCORPORATED (ENSCO); *U.S. Public*, pg. 585
ENSCO MARINE CO.—See Ensco International Incorporated (ENSCO); *U.S. Public*, pg. 585
ENSERCH CORPORATION—See Texas Utilities Company; *U.S. Public*, pg. 1587
ENSERCH DEVELOPMENT CORPORATION—See Texas Utilities Company; *U.S. Public*, pg. 1587
ENSERCH DEVELOPMENT INC.—See Texas Utilities Company; *U.S. Public*, pg. 1587
ENSERCH EXPLORATION (UK) LTD.—See Texas Utilities Company; *U.S. Public*, pg. 1587
ENSERCH FAR EAST LTD.—See Texas Utilities Company; *U.S. Public*, pg. 1587
ENSERCH FINANCE N.V.—See Texas Utilities Company; *U.S. Public*, pg. 1587
ENSERCH GAS CO.—See Texas Utilities Company; *U.S. Public*, pg. 1587
ENSERCH SHIRLEY—See Texas Utilities Company; *U.S. Public*, pg. 1587
ENSERV, INC.—See WPL Holdings, Inc.; *U.S. Public*, pg. 1728
ENSIGN-BICKFORD—See Sasol Limited; *Int'l*, pg. 1196
ENSIS CORPORATION INC.; *Int'l*, pg. 455
ENSKILDA (DEUTSCHLAND) GMBH—See Skandinaviska Enskilda Banken; *Int'l*, pg. 1259
ENSKILDA ESPANA S.A.—See Skandinaviska Enskilda Banken; *Int'l*, pg. 1259
ENSKILDA S.A.—See Skandinaviska Enskilda Banken; *Int'l*, pg. 1259
ENSKILDA SECURITIES—See Skandinaviska Enskilda Banken; *Int'l*, pg. 1259
ENSKILDA SECURITIES INC., NEW YORK—See Skandinaviska Enskilda Banken; *Int'l*, pg. 1259
ENSKILDA VENTURES LIMITED—See Skandinaviska Enskilda Banken; *Int'l*, pg. 1259
ENSLEY TOOL CO. INC.—See Rothenberger Group GmbH; *Int'l*, pg. 1129
ENSO AG—See Enso Oyj; *Int'l*, pg. 457
ENSO CARTONBOARDS OY LTD.—See Enso Oyj; *Int'l*, pg. 456
ENSO DANMARK A/S—See Enso Oyj; *Int'l*, pg. 457
ENSO (DEUTSCHLAND) GMBH—See Enso Oyj; *Int'l*, pg. 457
ENSO ESPANOLA, S.A.—See Enso Oyj; *Int'l*, pg. 458
ENSO-EUROCAN-BUMJIN CO. LTD.—See Enso Oyj; *Int'l*, pg. 457
ENSO-EUROCAN FAR EAST CO. LTD.—See Enso Oyj; *Int'l*, pg. 457
ENSO-EUROCAN (H.K.) LTD.—See Enso Oyj; *Int'l*, pg. 457
ENSO-EUROCAN HONG KONG LTD.—See Enso Oyj; *Int'l*, pg. 457
ENSO-EUROCAN SOUTH EAST ASIA PTE. LTD.—See Enso Oyj; *Int'l*, pg. 457
ENSO FINE PAPERS OY—See Enso Oyj; *Int'l*, pg. 456
ENSO FOREST DEVELOPMENT OY LTD.—See Enso Oyj; *Int'l*, pg. 455
ENSO FRANCE S.A.—See Enso Oyj; *Int'l*, pg. 457
ENSO (HOLLAND) B.V.—See Enso Oyj; *Int'l*, pg. 457
ENSO IBERICA S.A.—See Enso Oyj; *Int'l*, pg. 457
ENSO INTERNATIONAL, INC.—See Enso Oyj; *Int'l*, pg. 457
ENSO MARKETING CO. LTD.—See Enso Oyj; *Int'l*, pg. 457
ENSO (MIDDLE EAST)—See Enso Oyj; *Int'l*, pg. 457
ENSO (MOROCCO)—See Enso Oyj; *Int'l*, pg. 457
ENSO NORD TRANSPORTGESELLSCHAFT MBH—See Enso Oyj; *Int'l*, pg. 457
S.A. ENSO N.V. ENSO WEST—See Enso Oyj; *Int'l*, pg. 457
S.A. ENSO N.V.—See Enso Oyj; *Int'l*, pg. 457
ENSO OYJ; *Int'l*, pg. 455
ENSO PAPERIKEMIA OY—See Enso Oyj; *Int'l*, pg. 456
ENSO PAPIER FORMAT GMBH—See Enso Oyj; *Int'l*, pg. 458
ENSO (POLAND)—See Enso Oyj; *Int'l*, pg. 457
ENSO PORTUGAL LDA.—See Enso Oyj; *Int'l*, pg. 457
ENSO PRESSE DRUCK VERTRIEB GMBH—See Enso Oyj; *Int'l*, pg. 457
ENSO PUBLICATION PAPERS LIMITED—See Enso Oyj; *Int'l*, pg. 457
ENSO PUBLICATION PAPERS OY LTD.—See Enso Oyj; *Int'l*, pg. 457
ENSO SOUTH AFRICA—See Enso Oyj; *Int'l*, pg. 457
ENSO SURYA PTE. LTD.—See Enso Oyj; *Int'l*, pg. 457
ENSO TIMBER OY LTD.—See Enso Oyj; *Int'l*, pg. 456
ENSO TRADING AB—See Enso Oyj; *Int'l*, pg. 457
ENSO TRADING HANDELSGESELLSCHAFT MBH—See Enso Oyj; *Int'l*, pg. 457
ENSO-YHTEISPALVELUT OY—See Enso Oyj; *Int'l*, pg. 457
ENSONIQ; *U.S. Private*, pg. 377
ENSOPACK LTD.—See Enso Oyj; *Int'l*, pg. 458
ENSTAR, INC.; *U.S. Public*, pg. 585
ENSTAR NATURAL GAS CO.—See Seagull Energy Corporation; *U.S. Public*, pg. 1450
ENSTAR NETWORKING CORP.—See ENStar, Inc.; *U.S. Public*, pg. 585
ENSUENO-TYCO (MEXICO) S.A. DE C.V.—See Mattel, Inc.; *U.S. Public*, pg. 1059
ENTE NAZIONALE PER L'ENERGIA ELETTRICA SPA (ENEL); *Int'l*, pg. 458
ENTECH, INC.—See Montana Power Company; *U.S. Public*, pg. 1127
ENTERGY ARKANSAS, INC.—See Entergy Corporation; *U.S. Public*, pg. 586
ENTERGY CORPORATION; *U.S. Public*, pg. 585
ENTERGY GULF STATES, INC.—See Entergy Corporation; *U.S. Public*, pg. 586
ENTERGY LOUISIANA, INC.—See Entergy Corporation; *U.S. Public*, pg. 586
ENTERGY MISSISSIPPI, INC.—See Entergy Corporation; *U.S. Public*, pg. 586
ENTERGY NEW ORLEANS, INC.—See Entergy Corporation; *U.S. Public*, pg. 586
ENTERGY OPERATIONS, INC.—See Entergy Corporation; *U.S. Public*, pg. 586
ENTERIC PRODUCTS, INC.—See E-Z-Em, Inc.; *U.S. Public*, pg. 540
ENTERPRISE; *U.S. Private*, pg. 377
ENTERPRISE DIVERSIFIED HOLDINGS INCORPORATED—See Public Service Enterprise Group Incorporated; *U.S. Public*, pg. 1340
ENTERPRISE ELECTRONICS CORP.—See Tech-Sym Corporation; *U.S. Public*, pg. 1563
ENTERPRISE FINANCIAL MANAGEMENT GROUP—See Computer Associates International, Inc.; *U.S. Public*, pg. 420
ENTERPRISE GENERALE DE TELECOMMUNICATIONS—See France Telecom; *Int'l*, pg. 503
THE ENTERPRISE GROUP—See The Mutual Life Insurance Company of New York; *U.S. Private*, pg. 769
ENTERPRISE GROUP DEVELOPMENT CORPORATION—See Public Service Enterprise Group Incorporated; *U.S. Public*, pg. 1340
ENTERPRISE MANAGEMENT—See DynCorp; *U.S. Private*, pg. 351
ENTERPRISE NETWORKS BUSINESS UNIT—See Standard Microsystems Corp.; *U.S. Public*, pg. 1503
ENTERPRISE NEXUS COMMUNICATIONS—See The Lowe Group; *U.S. Private*, pg. 678
ENTERPRISE PRODUCTS COMPANY; *U.S. Private*, pg. 377
ENTERPRISE RENT-A-CAR COMPANY; *U.S. Private*, pg. 377
ENTERPRISE SERVICE SOLUTIONS—See Genicom Corporation; *U.S. Public*, pg. 729
ENTERPRISES INTERNATIONAL INC.; *U.S. Private*, pg. 377
ENTERPRISES MEDIA GROUP—See Coca-Cola Enterprises Inc.; *U.S. Public*, pg. 393
ENTERPRISING SERVICE SOLUTIONS CORPORATION—See Genicom Corporation; *U.S. Public*, pg. 729
ENTERRA COMPRESSIONS CO.—See Weatherford Enterra Incorporated; *U.S. Public*, pg. 1749
ENTERRA OIL FIELD SERVICES, LTD.—See Weatherford Enterra Incorporated; *U.S. Public*, pg. 1750
ENTERRA PETROLEUM EQUIPMENT GROUP, INC.—See Weatherford Enterra Incorporated; *U.S. Public*, pg. 1749
ENTERTAINMENT COMMUNICATIONS; *U.S. Private*, pg. 378
ENTERTAINMENT INDUSTRIES GROUP—See Imperial Bancorp; *U.S. Public*, pg. 871
ENTERTAINMENT PARTNERS—See IDC Services, Inc.; *U.S. Private*, pg. 554
ENTERTAINMENT PUBLICATIONS, INC.—See Cendant Corporation; *U.S. Public*, pg. 320
ENTERTAINMENT UK LTD.—See Kingfisher plc; *Int'l*, pg. 733
ENTERTAINMENT WEEKLY INC.—See Time Warner Inc.; *U.S. Public*, pg. 1613
ENTERWORKS.COM, INC.—See Telos Corporation; *U.S. Public*, pg. 1573
ENTEX—See Houston Industries Incorporated; *U.S. Public*, pg. 843
ENTEX INFORMATION SERVICES; *U.S. Private*, pg. 378
ENTHONE OMI-BRIDGEVIEW—See Asarco Incorporated; *U.S. Public*, pg. 138
ENTHONE-OMI, INC.—See Asarco Incorporated; *U.S. Public*, pg. 138
ENTHOVEN B.V.—See Goodman Fielder Limited; *Int'l*, pg. 555
ENTOLETER, INC.—See Lynch Corporation; *U.S. Public*, pg. 1022
ENTORES LTD.—See Imetal; *Int'l*, pg. 661
ENTRADA INDUSTRIES, INC.—See Questar Corporation; *U.S. Public*, pg. 1352
ENTREE CORPORATION—See Coyote Network Systems, Inc.; *U.S. Public*, pg. 455
ENTREMONT S.A.; *Int'l*, pg. 458
ENTREPOT IVRY—See Bazar de L'Hotel de Ville; *Int'l*, pg. 181
ENTREPRENEUR, INC.—See Worsley Companies Inc.; *U.S. Private*, pg. 1191
S.A. ENTREPRISE DE TRAVAUX ET DE CONSTRUCTIONS ENTRACON—See Cockerill Sambre; *Int'l*, pg. 301
ENTREPRISE MINIERE ET CHIMIQUE; *Int'l*, pg. 458
ENTREPRISE NOUEL—See Lafarge S.A.; *Int'l*, pg. 788
ENTRON INDUSTRIES LIMITED PARTNERSHIP; *U.S. Private*, pg. 378
ENTRUST HOME FINANCING—See Long Island Bancorp, Inc.; *U.S. Public*, pg. 1013
ENTSORGUNG DORTMUND GMBH—See Harpen AG; *Int'l*, pg. 597

Company Index

ENTSORGUNGSGESELLSCHAFT STEINFURT MBH—See Harpen AG; *Int'l*, pg. 597
ENTSORGUNGSWIRTSCHAFT SOEST GMBH—See Harpen AG; *Int'l*, pg. 597
THE ENTWISTLE COMPANY; *U.S. Private*, pg. 378
ENVASES DE ACERO, S.A. DE C.V.—See Air Products and Chemicals, Inc.; *U.S. Private*, pg. 32
ENVASES INDUSTRIALES DE COSTA RICA, S.A.—See Georgia-Pacific Corporation; *U.S. Public*, pg. 739
ENVASES INTERNACIONAL S.A.—See International Paper Company; *U.S. Public*, pg. 906
ENVASES MODERNOS (CHH) S.A.—See International Paper Company; *U.S. Public*, pg. 905
ENVASES MULTIPAC S.A. DE C.V.—See Illinois Tool Works Inc.; *U.S. Public*, pg. 868
ENVASES VALENCIANOS, S.A.—See Reynolds Metals Company; *U.S. Public*, pg. 1386
ENVASES Y ALIMENTACION MADRID, S.A.—See Reynolds Metals Company; *U.S. Public*, pg. 1386
ENVASES Y ALIMENTACION, S.A.—See Reynolds Metals Company; *U.S. Public*, pg. 1387
ENVIRAS—See Heidemij N.V.; *Int'l*, pg. 608
ENVIRCO CORPORATION—See Trion, Inc.; *U.S. Public*, pg. 1639
ENVIRCO TRANSPORTATION, INC.—See American Waste Services, Inc.; *U.S. Public*, pg. 94
ENVIRCO TRANSPORTATION MANAGEMENT, INC.—See American Waste Services, Inc.; *U.S. Public*, pg. 94
ENVIREX INC.—See Aluminum Company of America; *U.S. Public*, pg. 61
ENVIRODYNE INDUSTRIES, INC.; *U.S. Public*, pg. 586
ENVIRODYNE LIMITED—See Envirodyne Industries, Inc.; *U.S. Public*, pg. 586
ENVIROMENTAL PRODUCTS INC.—See The Will-Burt Company; *U.S. Private*, pg. 1177
ENVIRON CORPORATION—See Pharmaceutical Product Development, Inc.; *U.S. Public*, pg. 1285
ENVIRON, INC.—See Ford Motor Company; *U.S. Public*, pg. 664
ENVIRON INTERNATIONAL—See Pharmaceutical Product Development, Inc.; *U.S. Public*, pg. 1285
ENVIRON INTERNATIONAL CORPORATION-EMERYVILLE—See Pharmaceutical Product Development, Inc.; *U.S. Public*, pg. 1285
ENVIRONETX; *U.S. Private*, pg. 378
ENVIRONMENT/ONE CORPORATION; *U.S. Public*, pg. 586
ENVIRONMENTAL AIR SYSTEMS, INC.; *U.S. Private*, pg. 378
ENVIRONMENTAL & COMMERCIAL INSURANCE—See Frontier Insurance Group, Inc.; *U.S. Public*, pg. 684
ENVIRONMENTAL CONSTRUCTION, INC. (ECI)—See Heidemij N.V.; *Int'l*, pg. 607
ENVIRONMENTAL CONTROL INC.—See Allied Waste Industries; *U.S. Public*, pg. 49
ENVIRONMENTAL DEVELOPMENT CORP.—See Allied Waste Industries; *U.S. Public*, pg. 49
ENVIRONMENTAL ELEMENTS CORPORATION; *U.S. Public*, pg. 586
ENVIRONMENTAL ELEMENTS LIMITED—See Environmental Elements Corporation; *U.S. Public*, pg. 587
ENVIRONMENTAL FINANCIAL SERVICES CORP.—See OHM Corporation; *U.S. Public*, pg. 1208
ENVIRONMENTAL FRAGRANCE TECHNOLOGIES, LTD.—See MacAndrews & Forbes Holdings Inc.; *U.S. Private*, pg. 689
ENVIRONMENTAL/GOVERNMENT GROUP—See Morrison Knudsen Corporation; *U.S. Public*, pg. 1134
ENVIRONMENTAL HEALTH STRATEGIES—See The Failure Group, Inc.; *U.S. Public*, pg. 609
ENVIRONMENTAL INDUSTRIES, INC.; *U.S. Public*, pg. 378
ENVIRONMENTAL MEDIATION, INC.—See American Vanguard Corporation; *U.S. Public*, pg. 94
ENVIRONMENTAL RESORTS INC.—See Greenwood Mills, Inc.; *U.S. Private*, pg. 479
ENVIRONMENTAL RESOURCES MANAGEMENT; *U.S. Private*, pg. 378
ENVIRONMENTAL RESTORATION SYSTEMS, INC.—See Science Applications International Corp.; *U.S. Private*, pg. 976
ENVIRONMENTAL SERVICE INSURANCE CO.—See Quexco Incorporated; *U.S. Private*, pg. 900
ENVIRONMENTAL SERVICES OF AMERICA, INC.—See ERD Waste Corp.; *U.S. Public*, pg. 546
ENVIRONMENTAL SERVICES OF AMERICA-IN, INC.—See ERD Waste Corp.; *U.S. Public*, pg. 546
ENVIRONMENTAL SERVICES OF AMERICA-MO, INC.—See ERD Waste Corp.; *U.S. Public*, pg. 546
ENVIRONMENTAL SPECIALISTS, INC.—See Republic Industries, Inc.; *U.S. Public*, pg. 1379
ENVIRONMENTAL TECTONICS CORPORATION (ETC); *U.S. Public*, pg. 587
ENVIRONMENTAL TREATMENT & TECHNOLOGIES CORP.—See OHM Corporation; *U.S. Public*, pg. 1208
ENVIROPOWER—See Chemical Leaman Corporation; *U.S. Private*, pg. 233
ENVIROPOWER—See Tamrock Corp.; *Int'l*, pg. 1353
ENVIROPOWER RESEARCH & DEVELOPMENT—See Tamrock Corp.; *Int'l*, pg. 1353
ENVIROQ—See Insituform Technologies, Inc.; *U.S. Public*, pg. 881
ENVIROSAFE SERVICES, INC.—See EnviroSource, Inc.; *U.S. Public*, pg. 587
ENVIROSOURCE, INC.; *U.S. Public*, pg. 587
ENVIROSOURCE-INTERNATIONAL MILL SERVICE, INC.—See EnviroSource, Inc.; *U.S. Public*, pg. 587
ENVIROSOURCE TREATMENT & DISPOSAL SERVICES, INC.—See EnviroSource, Inc.; *U.S. Public*, pg. 587
ENVIROTECH CONTROLS, INC.—See Thermo Electron Corporation; *U.S. Public*, pg. 1594
ENVIROTECH EQUIPAMENTOS LTDA.—See Weir Group PLC; *Int'l*, pg. 1489

ENVIROTECH PUMPSYSTEMS—See Weir Group PLC; *Int'l*, pg. 1489
ENVIROTECH PUMPSYSTEMS NETHERLANDS BV—See Weir Group PLC; *Int'l*, pg. 1489
ENVIROTROL INC.—See Environmental Air Systems, Inc.; *U.S. Private*, pg. 378
ENVIROVAC, INC.—See Electrolux, AB; *Int'l*, pg. 439
ENVOY CORPORATION; *U.S. Public*, pg. 587
ENWAY INC.—See Skylark Co., Ltd.; *Int'l*, pg. 1262
ENZON, INC.; *U.S. Public*, pg. 587
ENZOPAC, INC.; *U.S. Private*, pg. 379
ENZYMATIX LTD.—See Genzyme Corporation; *U.S. Public*, pg. 733
ENZYME BIO-SYSTEMS, LTD.—See Corn Products International, Inc.; *U.S. Public*, pg. 448
EOMAG AG - ERSTE OSTERREICHISCHE MACHINGLASINDUSTRIE BRUNN AM GEBIRGE—See Pilkington Plc; *Int'l*, pg. 1056
EON LABS MANUFACTURING, INC.; *U.S. Private*, pg. 379
EONIC INC.—See Newcor, Inc.; *U.S. Public*, pg. 1176
EPACAR NV—See N.V. Koninklijke KNP BT; *Int'l*, pg. 757
EPEC, INC.; *U.S. Private*, pg. 379
EPIC EXPRESS—See Consolidated Freightways Corp.; *U.S. Public*, pg. 435
EPIPHARM GMBH—See Chr. Hansen Holding A/S; *Int'l*, pg. 288
EPIREZ CONSTRUCTION PRODUCTS PTY LIMITED—See Morgan Crucible Co. Plc; *Int'l*, pg. 892
EPITRONICS, INC.—See ATMI, Inc.; *U.S. Public*, pg. 12
EPOXYLITE CORPORATION-EQUIPMENT DIV.—See Epoxylite Corporation-Resin Div.; *U.S. Private*, pg. 379
EPOXYLITE CORPORATION-RESIN DIV.; *U.S. Private*, pg. 379
EPPENS SMITH CO.—See Chock Full O' Nuts Corporation; *U.S. Public*, pg. 351
EPPERSON WASTE DISPOSAL, INC.—See Republic Industries, Inc.; *U.S. Public*, pg. 1379
EPSILON—See American Express Company; *U.S. Public*, pg. 74
EPSILON HOME HEALTH CARE, INC.—See Integrated Health Services, Inc.; *U.S. Public*, pg. 884
EPSILON INDUSTRIAL—See Thermo Electron Corporation; *U.S. Public*, pg. 1593
EPSILON/WEST—See American Express Company; *U.S. Public*, pg. 74
EPSON AMERICA INC.—See Seiko Epson Corporation; *Int'l*, pg. 1219
EPSON AUSTRALIA PTY. LTD. (E.A.L.)—See Seiko Epson Corporation; *Int'l*, pg. 1219
EPSON CANADA LIMITED—See Seiko Epson Corporation; *Int'l*, pg. 1219
EPSON DEUTSCHLAND GMBH (E.D.G.)—See Seiko Epson Corporation; *Int'l*, pg. 1219
EPSON ELECTRONICS TRADING, LTD., TAIWAN BRANCH (E.T.T.)—See Seiko Epson Corporation; *Int'l*, pg. 1219
EPSON FRANCE S.A. (E.F.S.)—See Seiko Epson Corporation; *Int'l*, pg. 1219
EPSON HONG KONG LTD.—See Seiko Epson Corporation; *Int'l*, pg. 1219
EPSON MANUFACTURING LTD.—See Seiko Epson Corporation; *Int'l*, pg. 1219
EPSON PORTLAND INC.—See Seiko Epson Corporation; *Int'l*, pg. 1219
EPSON SINGAPORE PTE., LTD. (ESP)—See Seiko Epson Corporation; *Int'l*, pg. 1219
EPSON (U.K.) LTD. (E.U.L.)—See Seiko Epson Corporation; *Int'l*, pg. 1219
A. EPSTEIN AND SONS, INTL., INC.; *U.S. Private*, pg. 379
A. EPSTEIN & SONS (NEW YORK)—See A. Epstein and Sons, Intl., Inc.; *U.S. Private*, pg. 379
EPSTEIN CIVIL ENGINEERING, INC.—See A. Epstein and Sons, Intl., Inc.; *U.S. Private*, pg. 379
EPSTEIN CONSTRUCTION INC.—See A. Epstein and Sons, Intl., Inc.; *U.S. Private*, pg. 379
EPSTEIN ENGINEERING EXPORT, LTD.—See A. Epstein and Sons, Intl., Inc.; *U.S. Private*, pg. 379
EPSTEIN ENGINEERING EXPORT (WARSAW), LTD.—See A. Epstein and Sons, Intl., Inc.; *U.S. Private*, pg. 379
EPTISA SA—See Heidemij N.V.; *Int'l*, pg. 608
EPYSA—See Lafarge S.A.; *Int'l*, pg. 790
EQUATOR—See Havas Advertising; *Int'l*, pg. 602
EQUATOR ADVISORY SERVICES LIMITED—See HSBC Holdings plc; *Int'l*, pg. 580
EQUATOR BANK LIMITED—See HSBC Holdings plc; *Int'l*, pg. 580
EQUATOR HOLDINGS LTD.—See HSBC Holdings plc; *Int'l*, pg. 580
EQUATOR LIMITED—See HSBC Holdings plc; *Int'l*, pg. 580
EQUATOR TRADE SERVICES LIMITED—See HSBC Holdings plc; *Int'l*, pg. 580
EQUICOR-CIGNA CORPORATION—See Cigna Corp.; *U.S. Public*, pg. 362
EQUICOR HOLDINGS, INC.—See Cigna Corp.; *U.S. Public*, pg. 362
EQUICREDIT CORPORATION—See NationsBank Corporation; *U.S. Public*, pg. 1162
EQUIFAX CANADA—See Equifax Inc.; *U.S. Public*, pg. 588
EQUIFAX CENTER FOR INFORMATION RESEARCH—See Equifax Inc.; *U.S. Public*, pg. 588
EQUIFAX CHECK SERVICE—See Equifax Inc.; *U.S. Public*, pg. 588
EQUIFAX CONSUMER DIRECT—See Equifax Inc.; *U.S. Public*, pg. 588
EQUIFAX CREDIT MARKETING SERVICES, INC.—See Equifax Inc.; *U.S. Public*, pg. 588
EQUIFAX EUROPE—See Equifax Inc.; *U.S. Public*, pg. 588
EQUIFAX GOVERNMENT & SPECIAL SERVICES—See Equifax Inc.; *U.S. Public*, pg. 588
EQUIFAX INC.; *U.S. Public*, pg. 588
EQUIFAX INFORMATION TECHNOLOGY—See Equifax Inc.; *U.S. Public*, pg. 588

EQUIFAX INSURANCE SERVICES INC.—See Equifax Inc.; *U.S. Public*, pg. 588
EQUIFAX NATIONAL DECISION SYSTEMS—See Equifax Inc.; *U.S. Public*, pg. 588
EQUILUX S.A.—See Electrolux, AB; *Int'l*, pg. 441
EQUINOX CAPITAL (HK) LTD.—See Credit Commercial de France; *Int'l*, pg. 343
EQUINOX CAPITAL (SINGAPORE) LTD.—See Credit Commercial de France; *Int'l*, pg. 343
EQUINOX COMMUNICATIONS—See Warwick Baker O'Neill; *U.S. Public*, pg. 1152
EQUIPAMENTOS CIENTIFICOS INSTRON LTD.—See Instron Corporation; *U.S. Public*, pg. 883
EQUIPE—See Havas Advertising; *Int'l*, pg. 602
E'QUIPE, LTD.—See Kanebo, Ltd.; *Int'l*, pg. 722
EQUIPMENT ASSURANCE LTD.—See Bucyrus International; *U.S. Private*, pg. 177
EQUIPMENT ENGINEERS INC.—See EEI Corporation; *Int'l*, pg. 426
EQUIPMENT LEASING LIMITED—See Halliburton Company; *U.S. Public*, pg. 776
EQUIPMENT MANUFACTURING PLANT—See Bandag, Incorporated; *U.S. Public*, pg. 177
EQUIPMENT RESOURCES, INC.—See Builder Marts of America, Inc.; *U.S. Private*, pg. 180
EQUIPMENT SALES CO.—See Sterline Technologies Corporation; *U.S. Public*, pg. 594
EQUIPMENT SALES DIVISION—See Electro Rent Corporation; *U.S. Public*, pg. 568
EQUIPOS AGRICOLAS ALFA-LAVAL S.A.—See Tetra Laval Group; *Int'l*, pg. 1377
EQUIPOS DE ACUNA, S.A. DE C.V.—See Eagle-Picher Industries, Inc.; *U.S. Private*, pg. 356
EQUIPOS PERCOM, C.A.—See Hewlett-Packard Company; *U.S. Public*, pg. 817
EQUIS FINANCIAL GROUP; *U.S. Private*, pg. 379
EQUISCOT LIMITED—See Diageo Plc; *Int'l*, pg. 412
EQUITABLE BAG COMPANY, INC.; *U.S. Private*, pg. 380
THE EQUITABLE COMPANIES INCORPORATED; *U.S. Public*, pg. 588
EQUITABLE FINANCIAL CONSULTANTS, INC.—See The Equitable Companies Incorporated; *U.S. Public*, pg. 589
EQUITABLE GAS CO.—See Equitable Resources, Inc.; *U.S. Public*, pg. 589
EQUITABLE GAS-ENERGY CO.—See Equitable Resources, Inc.; *U.S. Public*, pg. 589
EQUITABLE HOLDING CORPORATION—See The Equitable Companies Incorporated; *U.S. Public*, pg. 589
EQUITABLE INVESTMENT CORPORATION—See The Equitable Companies Incorporated; *U.S. Public*, pg. 589
EQUITABLE LIFE INSURANCE COMPANY OF IOWA—See ING Groep N.V.; *Int'l*, pg. 647
EQUITABLE OF IOWA COMPANIES—See ING Groep N.V.; *Int'l*, pg. 647
EQUITABLE PIPELINE COMPANY—See Equitable Resources, Inc.; *U.S. Public*, pg. 589
EQUITABLE RESOURCES ENERGY COMPANY—See Equitable Resources, Inc.; *U.S. Public*, pg. 589
EQUITABLE RESOURCES EXPLORATION DIVISION—See Equitable Resources, Inc.; *U.S. Public*, pg. 589
EQUITABLE RESOURCES, INC.; *U.S. Public*, pg. 589
EQUITABLE RESOURCES MARKETING COMPANY—See Equitable Resources, Inc.; *U.S. Public*, pg. 590
EQUITABLE SAVINGS & LOAN ASSOCIATION; *U.S. Private*, pg. 380
EQUITABLE STORAGE COMPANY—See Equitable Resources, Inc.; *U.S. Public*, pg. 590
EQUITECH DIVISION—See Equitable Resources, Inc.; *U.S. Public*, pg. 590
EQUITRAC CORPORATION; *U.S. Public*, pg. 590
EQUITRANS, INC.—See Equitable Resources, Inc.; *U.S. Public*, pg. 590
EQUITY COUNTRY INC.—See Farmland Industries, Inc.; *U.S. Private*, pg. 396
EQUITY FC, LTD.—See The Principal Financial Group; *U.S. Private*, pg. 885
EQUITY FIRE & CASUALTY INSURANCE COMPANY—See Preferred Risk Mutual Insurance; *U.S. Private*, pg. 881
EQUITY FUND ADVISORS INC.; *U.S. Private*, pg. 380
EQUITY GROUP INVESTMENTS; *U.S. Private*, pg. 380
EQUITY OIL COMPANY; *U.S. Public*, pg. 590
EQUITY ONE, INC.—See Banco Popular de Puerto Rico; *U.S. Public*, pg. 176
EQUITY RESIDENTIAL PROPERTIES TRUST; *U.S. Public*, pg. 590
EQUITY SERVICES, INC.—See National Life Insurance Company; *U.S. Private*, pg. 785
EQUITY SUPPLY COMPANY; *U.S. Private*, pg. 380
ERAMET-SLN—See Imetal; *Int'l*, pg. 661
ERASMUS PRESS PUBLISHING KFT—See VNU Verenigde Nederlandse Uitgeversbedrijven B.V.; *Int'l*, pg. 1445
ERCON DEVELOPMENT CO.—See Gulfmark Offshore Inc.; *U.S. Public*, pg. 769
ERDGAS MARK BRANDENBURG GMBH - EMB—See Gaz de France; *Int'l*, pg. 541
ERDLE PERFORATING CO.; *U.S. Private*, pg. 380
ERDLE PERFORATING CO. LTD.—See Erdle Perforating Co.; *U.S. Private*, pg. 380
ERDLE PERFORATING OF CAROLINA—See Erdle Perforating Co.; *U.S. Private*, pg. 380
MARSHALL ERDMAN AND ASSOCIATES, INC.; *U.S. Private*, pg. 380
ERDOEL-RAFFINERIE NEUSTADT GMBH & CO., OHG—See Veba AG; *Int'l*, pg. 1461
ERDOL-ERDGAS GOMMERN GMBH (E.E.G.)—See Gaz de France; *Int'l*, pg. 541
ERGON, INC.; *U.S. Private*, pg. 380
OY ERHO AB—See Oy Algol AB; *Int'l*, pg. 15
ERICKSON OIL PRODUCTS, INC.; *U.S. Private*, pg. 381
ERICKSON TRANSPORT CORPORATION; *U.S. Private*, pg. 381
ERICKSON'S DIVERSIFIED CORP.; *U.S. Private*, pg. 381
ERICO INTERNATIONAL; *U.S. Private*, pg. 381

ERICOM SERVICES PTY. LTD.—See Telefonaktiebolaget LM Ericsson; *Int'l*, pg. 1366
ERICSON PACKARD ELECTRIC COMPONENTES S.A.—See General Motors Corporation; *U.S. Public*, pg. 724
ERICSSON AG—See Telefonaktiebolaget LM Ericsson; *Int'l*, pg. 1366
ERICSSON AMAZONIA S.A.—See Telefonaktiebolaget LM Ericsson; *Int'l*, pg. 1366
ERICSSON ANSLUTNINGSSYSTEM AB—See Telefonaktiebolaget LM Ericsson; *Int'l*, pg. 1363
ERICSSON A/S—See Telefonaktiebolaget LM Ericsson; *Int'l*, pg. 1366
ERICSSON AUSTRALIA PTY. LTD.—See Telefonaktiebolaget LM Ericsson; *Int'l*, pg. 1366
ERICSSON BUSINESS COMMUNICATIONS A/S—See Telefonaktiebolaget LM Ericsson; *Int'l*, pg. 1366
ERICSSON BUSINESS COMMUNICATIONS GMBH—See Telefonaktiebolaget LM Ericsson; *Int'l*, pg. 1366
ERICSSON BUSINESS COMMUNICATIONS, INC.—See Telefonaktiebolaget LM Ericsson; *Int'l*, pg. 1364
ERICSSON BUSINESS COMMUNICATIONS LTD.—See Telefonaktiebolaget LM Ericsson; *Int'l*, pg. 1366
ERICSSON BUSINESS COMMUNICATIONS NV/SA—See Telefonaktiebolaget LM Ericsson; *Int'l*, pg. 1366
ERICSSON BUSINESS MOBILE NETWORKS BV—See Telefonaktiebolaget LM Ericsson; *Int'l*, pg. 1366
ERICSSON BUSINESS NETWORKS AB—See Telefonaktiebolaget LM Ericsson; *Int'l*, pg. 1363
ERICSSON BUSINESS SYSTEMS AB - WARSAW BRANCH OFFICE—See Telefonaktiebolaget LM Ericsson; *Int'l*, pg. 1366
ERICSSON CABLES AB—See Telefonaktiebolaget LM Ericsson; *Int'l*, pg. 1363
ERICSSON CELLULAR LTD.—See Telefonaktiebolaget LM Ericsson; *Int'l*, pg. 1366
ERICSSON COMMUNICATIONS (HONG KONG) LTD.—See Telefonaktiebolaget LM Ericsson; *Int'l*, pg. 1366
ERICSSON COMMUNICATIONS, INC.—See Telefonaktiebolaget LM Ericsson; *Int'l*, pg. 1366
ERICSSON COMMUNICATIONS LTD.—See Telefonaktiebolaget LM Ericsson; *Int'l*, pg. 1366
ERICSSON COMMUNICATIONS (THAILAND) LTD.—See Telefonaktiebolaget LM Ericsson; *Int'l*, pg. 1366
ERICSSON COMPONENTS—See Telefonaktiebolaget LM Ericsson; *Int'l*, pg. 1366
ERICSSON COMPONENTS AB—See Telefonaktiebolaget LM Ericsson; *Int'l*, pg. 1363
ERICSSON COMPONENTS A/S—See Telefonaktiebolaget LM Ericsson; *Int'l*, pg. 1366
ERICSSON COMPONENTS EUROPE GMBH—See Telefonaktiebolaget LM Ericsson; *Int'l*, pg. 1366
ERICSSON COMPONENTS, INC.—See Telefonaktiebolaget LM Ericsson; *Int'l*, pg. 1364
ERICSSON COMPONENTS POWER DIVISION—See Telefonaktiebolaget LM Ericsson; *Int'l*, pg. 1363
ERICSSON COMPONENTS S.R.L.—See Telefonaktiebolaget LM Ericsson; *Int'l*, pg. 1366
ERICSSON COMPOSANTS S.A.—See Telefonaktiebolaget LM Ericsson; *Int'l*, pg. 1366
ERICSSON COMPUTER PRODUCTS—See Telefonaktiebolaget LM Ericsson; *Int'l*, pg. 1366
THE ERICSSON CORPORATION—See Telefonaktiebolaget LM Ericsson; *Int'l*, pg. 1366
ERICSSON CUKOROVA TELEKOM A.S.—See Telefonaktiebolaget LM Ericsson; *Int'l*, pg. 1366
ERICSSON DATA SERVICES NEDERLAND B.V.—See Telefonaktiebolaget LM Ericsson; *Int'l*, pg. 1366
ERICSSON DATA UK LTD.—See Telefonaktiebolaget LM Ericsson; *Int'l*, pg. 1366
ERICSSON DE COLOMBIA S.A.—See Telefonaktiebolaget LM Ericsson; *Int'l*, pg. 1366
ERICSSON DE COSTA RICA—See Telefonaktiebolaget LM Ericsson; *Int'l*, pg. 1366
ERICSSON DE GUATEMALA, S.A.—See Telefonaktiebolaget LM Ericsson; *Int'l*, pg. 1366
ERICSSON DE PORTUGAL, LDA—See Telefonaktiebolaget LM Ericsson; *Int'l*, pg. 1366
ERICSSON DEFENSE SYSTEMS PTY. LTD.—See Telefonaktiebolaget LM Ericsson; *Int'l*, pg. 1366
ERICSSON DO BRASIL COMERCIO E INDUSTRIA S.A.—See Telefonaktiebolaget LM Ericsson; *Int'l*, pg. 1366
ERICSSON ELECTRONIC DISTR. AB—See Telefonaktiebolaget LM Ericsson; *Int'l*, pg. 1363
ERICSSON ELECTRONIC SERVICES—See Telefonaktiebolaget LM Ericsson; *Int'l*, pg. 1363
ERICSSON EMERGENCY CONTROL SYSTEMS AB—See Telefonaktiebolaget LM Ericsson; *Int'l*, pg. 1363
ERICSSON EUROLAB DEUTSCHLAND GMBH—See Telefonaktiebolaget LM Ericsson; *Int'l*, pg. 1366
ERICSSON EUROPEAN SUPPORT CENTRE—See Telefonaktiebolaget LM Ericsson; *Int'l*, pg. 1366
ERICSSON FINANCE HOLDING B.V.—See Telefonaktiebolaget LM Ericsson; *Int'l*, pg. 1366
ERICSSON FINANZ AG—See Telefonaktiebolaget LM Ericsson; *Int'l*, pg. 1366
ERICSSON FUBA TELECOM GMBH—See Telefonaktiebolaget LM Ericsson; *Int'l*, pg. 1366
ERICSSON GE MOBILE COMMUNICATIONS CANADA, INC.—See Telefonaktiebolaget LM Ericsson; *Int'l*, pg. 1366
ERICSSON GE MOBILE COMMUNICATIONS DISTRIBUTION—See Telefonaktiebolaget LM Ericsson; *Int'l*, pg. 1364
ERICSSON GE MOBILE COMMUNICATIONS HOLDING INC.—See Telefonaktiebolaget LM Ericsson; *Int'l*, pg. 1365
ERICSSON GE MOBILE COMMUNICATIONS INC.—See Telefonaktiebolaget LM Ericsson; *Int'l*, pg. 1365
ERICSSON GE TELECOMMUNICATION INC.—See Telefonaktiebolaget LM Ericsson; *Int'l*, pg. 1366
ERICSSON GMBH—See Telefonaktiebolaget LM Ericsson; *Int'l*, pg. 1366

ERICSSON (HELLAS) TELECOMMUNICATIONS EQUIPMENT S.A.—See Telefonaktiebolaget LM Ericsson; *Int'l*, pg. 1366
ERICSSON HEWLETT-PACKARD TELECOMMUNICATIONS AB—See Telefonaktiebolaget LM Ericsson; *Int'l*, pg. 1363
ERICSSON HOLDING A/S—See Telefonaktiebolaget LM Ericsson; *Int'l*, pg. 1367
ERICSSON HOLDING INTERNATIONAL B.V.—See Telefonaktiebolaget LM Ericsson; *Int'l*, pg. 1367
ERICSSON HOLDING NEDERLAND B.V.—See Telefonaktiebolaget LM Ericsson; *Int'l*, pg. 1367
ERICSSON I.F.S.—See Telefonaktiebolaget LM Ericsson; *Int'l*, pg. 1367
ERICSSON, INC.—See Telefonaktiebolaget LM Ericsson; *Int'l*, pg. 1364
ERICSSON INDIA LTD.—See Telefonaktiebolaget LM Ericsson; *Int'l*, pg. 1367
ERICSSON INFOCOM CONSULTANTS—See Telefonaktiebolaget LM Ericsson; *Int'l*, pg. 1363
ERICSSON KOREA LTD.—See Telefonaktiebolaget LM Ericsson; *Int'l*, pg. 1367
ERICSSON LTD.—See Telefonaktiebolaget LM Ericsson; *Int'l*, pg. 1367
ERICSSON MESSAGING SYSTEMS INC.—See Telefonaktiebolaget LM Ericsson; *Int'l*, pg. 1365
ERICSSON MICROWAVE SYSTEMS-GOTHENBURG—See Telefonaktiebolaget LM Ericsson; *Int'l*, pg. 1363
ERICSSON MICROWAVE SYSTEMS-MOLNDAL—See Telefonaktiebolaget LM Ericsson; *Int'l*, pg. 1363
ERICSSON MOBILE COMMUNICATIONS—See Telefonaktiebolaget LM Ericsson; *Int'l*, pg. 1367
ERICSSON MOBILE COMMUNICATIONS AB—See Telefonaktiebolaget LM Ericsson; *Int'l*, pg. 1364
ERICSSON MOBILE DATA INC.—See Telefonaktiebolaget LM Ericsson; *Int'l*, pg. 1365
ERICSSON MOBILE NETWORKS B.V.—See Telefonaktiebolaget LM Ericsson; *Int'l*, pg. 1367
ERICSSON MOBILFUNK GMBH—See Telefonaktiebolaget LM Ericsson; *Int'l*, pg. 1367
ERICSSON NETWORK CONSTRUCTIONS AB—See Telefonaktiebolaget LM Ericsson; *Int'l*, pg. 1363
ERICSSON NETWORK ENGINEERING AB—See Telefonaktiebolaget LM Ericsson; *Int'l*, pg. 1367
ERICSSON NETWORK ENGINEERING (B) SDN BHD—See Telefonaktiebolaget LM Ericsson; *Int'l*, pg. 1367
ERICSSON NETWORK ENGINEERING LTD.—See Telefonaktiebolaget LM Ericsson; *Int'l*, pg. 1367
ERICSSON NETWORK ENGINEERING PTE. LTD.—See Telefonaktiebolaget LM Ericsson; *Int'l*, pg. 1367
ERICSSON NETWORK SYSTEMS, INC.—See Telefonaktiebolaget LM Ericsson; *Int'l*, pg. 1364
ERICSSON NETWORKS, INC.—See Telefonaktiebolaget LM Ericsson; *Int'l*, pg. 1367
ERICSSON NETZBAU GMBH—See Telefonaktiebolaget LM Ericsson; *Int'l*, pg. 1367
ERICSSON NORTH AMERICA, INC.—See Telefonaktiebolaget LM Ericsson; *Int'l*, pg. 1364
ERICSSON PAGING SYSTEMS AB—See Telefonaktiebolaget LM Ericsson; *Int'l*, pg. 1364
ERICSSON PAGING SYSTEMS INC.—See Telefonaktiebolaget LM Ericsson; *Int'l*, pg. 1365
ERICSSON PAGING SYSTEMS ZWEIGNIEDERLASSUNG DEUTSCHLAND—See Telefonaktiebolaget LM Ericsson; *Int'l*, pg. 1367
ERICSSON PRIVATE SYSTEMS GMBH—See Telefonaktiebolaget LM Ericsson; *Int'l*, pg. 1367
ERICSSON PROCOMP—See Telefonaktiebolaget LM Ericsson; *Int'l*, pg. 1363
ERICSSON PROGRAMATIC SWEDEN AB—See Telefonaktiebolaget LM Ericsson; *Int'l*, pg. 1363
ERICSSON PROJECT SERVICES (PTY) LTD.—See Telefonaktiebolaget LM Ericsson; *Int'l*, pg. 1367
ERICSSON PROPERTY COMPANY B.V.—See Telefonaktiebolaget LM Ericsson; *Int'l*, pg. 1367
ERICSSON RADAR A/S—See Telefonaktiebolaget LM Ericsson; *Int'l*, pg. 1367
ERICSSON RADAR ELECTRONICS AB—See Telefonaktiebolaget LM Ericsson; *Int'l*, pg. 1363
ERICSSON RADIO ACCESS AB—See Telefonaktiebolaget LM Ericsson; *Int'l*, pg. 1364
ERICSSON RADIO MESSAGING AB—See Telefonaktiebolaget LM Ericsson; *Int'l*, pg. 1364
ERICSSON RADIO, S.A.—See Telefonaktiebolaget LM Ericsson; *Int'l*, pg. 1367
ERICSSON RADIO SYSTEMER A/S—See Telefonaktiebolaget LM Ericsson; *Int'l*, pg. 1367
ERICSSON RADIO SYSTEMS—See Telefonaktiebolaget LM Ericsson; *Int'l*, pg. 1365
ERICSSON RADIO SYSTEMS AB—See Telefonaktiebolaget LM Ericsson; *Int'l*, pg. 1363
ERICSSON RADIO SYSTEMS A/S—See Telefonaktiebolaget LM Ericsson; *Int'l*, pg. 1367
ERICSSON RADIO SYSTEMS B.V.—See Telefonaktiebolaget LM Ericsson; *Int'l*, pg. 1367
ERICSSON RADIO SYSTEMS SVERIGE AB—See Telefonaktiebolaget LM Ericsson; *Int'l*, pg. 1364
OY ERICSSON RADIOPUHELIN AB—See Telefonaktiebolaget LM Ericsson; *Int'l*, pg. 1367
ERICSSON-RAYNET—See Telefonaktiebolaget LM Ericsson; *Int'l*, pg. 1365
ERICSSON REDES S.A.—See Telefonaktiebolaget LM Ericsson; *Int'l*, pg. 1367
ERICSSON REINSURANCE S.A.—See Telefonaktiebolaget LM Ericsson; *Int'l*, pg. 1367
ERICSSON RESEARCH CANADA—See Telefonaktiebolaget LM Ericsson; *Int'l*, pg. 1367
ERICSSON S.A.—See Telefonaktiebolaget LM Ericsson; *Int'l*, pg. 1367
ERICSSON SCHRACK AG—See Telefonaktiebolaget LM Ericsson; *Int'l*, pg. 1367
ERICSSON SIELTE-INTERNATIONAL S.P.A.—See Telefonaktiebolaget LM Ericsson; *Int'l*, pg. 1367

ERICSSON SIGNAL SYSTEMS AB—See Telefonaktiebolaget LM Ericsson; *Int'l*, pg. 1364
ERICSSON SISTEMAS AVANZADOS S.A.—See Telefonaktiebolaget LM Ericsson; *Int'l*, pg. 1367
ERICSSON SISTEMAS DE ENERGIA LTDA.—See Telefonaktiebolaget LM Ericsson; *Int'l*, pg. 1367
ERICSSON S.P.A.—See Telefonaktiebolaget LM Ericsson; *Int'l*, pg. 1367
ERICSSON STANDARD COMPONENTS—See Telefonaktiebolaget LM Ericsson; *Int'l*, pg. 1367
ERICSSON STANDARD COMPONENTS AB—See Telefonaktiebolaget LM Ericsson; *Int'l*, pg. 1363
ERICSSON SUC. URUGUAY—See Telefonaktiebolaget LM Ericsson; *Int'l*, pg. 1367
ERICSSON SYSTEMS EXPERTISE LTD.—See Telefonaktiebolaget LM Ericsson; *Int'l*, pg. 1367
ERICSSON TAIWAN LTD.—See Telefonaktiebolaget LM Ericsson; *Int'l*, pg. 1367
ERICSSON TECHNIKA KFT.—See Telefonaktiebolaget LM Ericsson; *Int'l*, pg. 1367
ERICSSON TELECOM AB—See Telefonaktiebolaget LM Ericsson; *Int'l*, pg. 1364
ERICSSON TELECOM A/S—See Telefonaktiebolaget LM Ericsson; *Int'l*, pg. 1367
ERICSSON TELECOMMUNICATIE B.V.—See Telefonaktiebolaget LM Ericsson; *Int'l*, pg. 1367
ERICSSON TELECOMMUNICATIONE S.P.A.—See Telefonaktiebolaget LM Ericsson; *Int'l*, pg. 1368
ERICSSON TELECOMMUNICATIONS, INC.—See Telefonaktiebolaget LM Ericsson; *Int'l*, pg. 1367
ERICSSON TELECOMMUNICATIONS PTE LTD.—See Telefonaktiebolaget LM Ericsson; *Int'l*, pg. 1368
ERICSSON TELECOMMUNICATIONS PVT. LTD.—See Telefonaktiebolaget LM Ericsson; *Int'l*, pg. 1368
ERICSSON TELECOMMUNICATIONS SDN BHD—See Telefonaktiebolaget LM Ericsson; *Int'l*, pg. 1368
ERICSSON TELECOMUNICACIONES S.A.—See Telefonaktiebolaget LM Ericsson; *Int'l*, pg. 1368
ERICSSON TELECOMUNICACOES S.A.—See Telefonaktiebolaget LM Ericsson; *Int'l*, pg. 1368
ERICSSON TELEKOM GMBH—See Telefonaktiebolaget LM Ericsson; *Int'l*, pg. 1368
ERICSSON TELEKOMUNIKASYON A.S.—See Telefonaktiebolaget LM Ericsson; *Int'l*, pg. 1368
ERICSSON TELEPHONE CORPORATION FAR EAST AB—See Telefonaktiebolaget LM Ericsson; *Int'l*, pg. 1368
ERICSSON TELEPHONE SALES (PVT) LTD.—See Telefonaktiebolaget LM Ericsson; *Int'l*, pg. 1368
ERICSSON TERMINALES MOVILES S.A.—See Telefonaktiebolaget LM Ericsson; *Int'l*, pg. 1368
ERICSSON THAI NETWORKS COMPANY LTD.—See Telefonaktiebolaget LM Ericsson; *Int'l*, pg. 1368
ERICSSON TOSHIBA TELECOMMUNICATION SYSTEMS K.K.—See Telefonaktiebolaget LM Ericsson; *Int'l*, pg. 1368
ERICSSON TRAFFIC SYSTEMS AB—See Telefonaktiebolaget LM Ericsson; *Int'l*, pg. 1364
ERICSSON TRANSMISSIONI S.P.A.—See Telefonaktiebolaget LM Ericsson; *Int'l*, pg. 1368
ERICSSON TREASURY AUSTRALIA PTY. LTD.—See Telefonaktiebolaget LM Ericsson; *Int'l*, pg. 1368
ERICSSON TREASURY IRELAND LTD.—See Telefonaktiebolaget LM Ericsson; *Int'l*, pg. 1368
ERICSSON TREASURY SERVICES AB—See Telefonaktiebolaget LM Ericsson; *Int'l*, pg. 1364
ERICSSON TUNISIE S.A.—See Telefonaktiebolaget LM Ericsson; *Int'l*, pg. 1368
ERICSSON UTVECKLINGS AB—See Telefonaktiebolaget LM Ericsson; *Int'l*, pg. 1364
ERIDANIA BEGHIN-SAY GROUP—See Compart SpA; *Int'l*, pg. 324
ERIE BRONZE & ALUMINUM CO.—See McInnes Steel Company; *U.S. Private*, pg. 722
ERIE COCA-COLA BOTTLING COMPANY—See Coca-Cola Enterprises Inc.; *U.S. Public*, pg. 393
ERIE CONTROLS EUROPE-NV—See Siebe plc; *Int'l*, pg. 1241
ERIE CONTROLS IBERICA S.A.—See Siebe plc; *Int'l*, pg. 1241
ERIE COUNTY CABLEVISION—See Blade Communications, Inc.; *U.S. Private*, pg. 147
ERIE FAMILY LIFE INSURANCE COMPANY; *U.S. Public*, pg. 590
ERIE INDEMNITY COMPANY—See Erie Family Life Insurance Company; *U.S. Public*, pg. 591
ERIE INSURANCE EXCHANGE—See Erie Family Life Insurance Company; *U.S. Public*, pg. 591
ERIE INSURANCE GROUP—See Erie Family Life Insurance Company; *U.S. Public*, pg. 591
ERIE MANUFACTURING CO.—See Siebe plc; *Int'l*, pg. 1241
ERIE MANUFACTURING CO. (CANADA) LTD.—See Siebe plc; *Int'l*, pg. 1241
ERIE PLASTICS; *U.S. Private*, pg. 381
ERIE PRESS SYSTEMS—See EFCO Inc.; *U.S. Private*, pg. 353
ERIE SCIENTIFIC CO.—See Sybron International Corporation; *U.S. Public*, pg. 1545
ERIEVIEW CARTAGE, INC.—See Alcan Aluminium Limited; *Int'l*, pg. 50
ERIEZ MAGNETICS; *U.S. Private*, pg. 381
ERIFIN SERVIZI FINANZIARI S.P.A.—See Telefonaktiebolaget LM Ericsson; *Int'l*, pg. 1368
ERIFOCAS AB—See Telefonaktiebolaget LM Ericsson; *Int'l*, pg. 1364
AB ERIFON KOREA BRANCH—See Telefonaktiebolaget LM Ericsson; *Int'l*, pg. 1368
ERIKSBERGS FORVALTNINGS AB—See Celsius AB; *Int'l*, pg. 277
ERIMA GMBH & CO.—See Adidas AG; *Int'l*, pg. 24
THE ERIN COMPANY; *U.S. Private*, pg. 381
ERINDO UTAMA P.T.—See Telefonaktiebolaget LM Ericsson; *Int'l*, pg. 1368

ERISCO, INC.—See Cognizant Corporation; *U.S. Public*, pg. 395
ERISOFT AB—See Telefonaktiebolaget LM Ericsson; *Int'l*, pg. 1364
ERISUD S.P.A.—See Telefonaktiebolaget LM Ericsson; *Int'l*, pg. 1368
ERITEL AB—See Telefonaktiebolaget LM Ericsson; *Int'l*, pg. 1364
ERITEL, S.A.—See Telefonica de Espana, S.A.; *Int'l*, pg. 1372
ERKA HANDELSGESELLSCHAFT MBH—See Karstadt Aktiengesellschaft; *Int'l*, pg. 724
ERLANG SYSTEMS AB—See Telefonaktiebolaget LM Ericsson; *Int'l*, pg. 1364
ERLANGER TUBULAR CORPORATION—See NS Group, Inc.; *U.S. Public*, pg. 1147
ERLEN GETRANKEDIENST AG—See Feldschlosschen Hurlimann Holding; *Int'l*, pg. 479
ERLING SANDE A/S—See Tiedemanns - Joh.H.Andresen ANS; *Int'l*, pg. 1390
ERLY INDUSTRIES, INC.; *U.S. Public*, pg. 591
ERMACO OY—See Brother Industries, Ltd.; *Int'l*, pg. 230
B.V. ERMAF—See Ruhrgas Aktiengesellschaft; *Int'l*, pg. 1149
ERMCO, INC.; *U.S. Private*, pg. 381
ERNEST LINSDELL LIMITED—See Cigna Corp.; *U.S. Public*, pg. 363
ERNEST PAPER PRODUCTS, INC.; *U.S. Private*, pg. 381
ERNIE'S—See Ark Restaurants Corp.; *U.S. Public*, pg. 130
ERNST & YOUNG, LLP; *U.S. Private*, pg. 861
E.C. ERNST, INC.—See The Philadelphia Bourse, Inc.; *U.S. Private*, pg. 861
ERNST MICHALKE GMBH—See Hoechst Aktiengesellschaft; *Int'l*, pg. 624
ERNST SIEGLING BETEILIGUNGS GMBH—See Forbo Holding SA; *Int'l*, pg. 497
ERNST SIEGLING GMBH & CO.—See Forbo Holding SA; *Int'l*, pg. 497
A/S ERNST VOSS FABRIK—See Electrolux, AB; *Int'l*, pg. 441
EROL'S INTERNET; *U.S. Private*, pg. 382
ERSA—See SNCF; *Int'l*, pg. 1164
ERSECO, INC.—See Erving Industries, Inc.; *U.S. Private*, pg. 382
ERSKINE HOUSE GROUP PLC—See Ikon Office Solutions, Inc.; *U.S. Public*, pg. 864
ERSKINE SYSTEMS LIMITED—See TT Group PLC; *Int'l*, pg. 1344
ERSTALLGES BETRIEBSKUCHE LANDSKRONGASSE GMBH—See Assicurazioni Generali S.p.A.; *Int'l*, pg. 89
ERSTE ALLGEMEINE VERSICHERUNGS AG—See Assicurazioni Generali S.p.A.; *Int'l*, pg. 89
ERSTE BANK DER OESTERREICHISCHEN SPARKASSEN AG; *Int'l*, pg. 459
ERSTE BANK - LONDON BRANCH—See Erste Bank der oesterreichischen Sparkassen AG; *Int'l*, pg. 459
ERSTE BANK - NEW YORK BRANCH—See Erste Bank der oesterreichischen Sparkassen AG; *Int'l*, pg. 459
ERSTE SALZBURGER GIPSWERKS-GESELLSCHAFT CHRISTIAN MOLDAN KG—See Heidelberger Zement A.G.; *Int'l*, pg. 606
ERTA (ARNOLD) UK LTD.—See DSM N.V.; *Int'l*, pg. 354
ERTA NV—See DSM N.V.; *Int'l*, pg. 354
ERTA PLASTICS GMBH—See DSM N.V.; *Int'l*, pg. 354
ERTAN J.V.-HONG KONG—See Lyonnaise des Eaux S.A.; *Int'l*, pg. 823
THE ERTL COMPANY, INC—See U.S. Industries, Inc.; *U.S. Public*, pg. 1684
ERTL DE MEXICO—See U.S. Industries, Inc.; *U.S. Public*, pg. 1684
ERTL (H.K.) LTD.—See U.S. Industries, Inc.; *U.S. Public*, pg. 1684
ERTL U.K. LTD.—See U.S. Industries, Inc.; *U.S. Public*, pg. 1684
ERVACO GRUPPEN AB; *Int'l*, pg. 459
ERVEN LUCAS BOLS ITALIA S.P.A.—See Koninklijke BolsWessanen nv; *Int'l*, pg. 751
ERVEN LUCAS BOLS S.A.—See Koninklijke BolsWessanen nv; *Int'l*, pg. 751
ERVIN AMASTEEL DIV.—See Ervin Industries, Inc.; *U.S. Private*, pg. 382
ERVIN INDUSTRIES, INC.; *U.S. Private*, pg. 382
ERVING INDUSTRIES, INC.; *U.S. Private*, pg. 382
ERVING PAPER MILLS, INC.—See Erving Industries, Inc.; *U.S. Private*, pg. 382
ERVING PAPER PRODUCTS, INC.—See Erving Industries, Inc.; *U.S. Private*, pg. 382
ERVINS GROUP—See Acme Mills Co. Inc.; *U.S. Private*, pg. 13
ERZ UND STAHL GMBH—See Veba AG; *Int'l*, pg. 1458
PT ESABINDO PRATAMA—See Charter plc; *Int'l*, pg. 282
ESACOMP—See Hewlett-Packard Company; *U.S. Public*, pg. 817
ESANDA FINANCE CORPORATION LIMITED—See Australia & New Zealand Banking Group Limited; *Int'l*, pg. 98
ESBJERG GLAS A/S—See Saint-Gobain; *Int'l*, pg. 1172
ESCA CORPORATION—See Alcatel Alsthom Compagnie Generale D'Electricite; *Int'l*, pg. 53
ESCALADE INTERNATIONAL LTD.—See Escalade Sports; *U.S. Public*, pg. 591
ESCALADE SPORTS; *U.S. Public*, pg. 591
ESCALADE SPORTS SALES & MARKETING—See Escalade Sports; *U.S. Public*, pg. 591
ESCANABA PAPER CO.—See The Mead Corporation; *U.S. Public*, pg. 1076
ESCAP LIMITED—See Eskom; *Int'l*, pg. 459
ESCAST, AUTOMATED EQUIPMENT & TOOLING DIV.—See Fansteel, Inc.; *U.S. Public*, pg. 612
ESCAST, INC.—See Fansteel, Inc.; *U.S. Public*, pg. 612
ESCHER HOLLAND B.V.—See Royal Begemann Group; *Int'l*, pg. 1133
ESCHMANN EQUIPMENT—See Smiths Industries plc; *Int'l*, pg. 1267

ESCO—See Esco Corporation; *U.S. Private*, pg. 383
ESCO CORPORATION; *U.S. Private*, pg. 382
ESCO ELEVATOR CORP.; *U.S. Private*, pg. 383
ESCO, EUROPE S.A.—See Esco Corporation; *U.S. Private*, pg. 383
ESCO INTERNATIONAL—See Esco Corporation; *U.S. Private*, pg. 383
ESCO LTD.—See Esco Corporation; *U.S. Private*, pg. 383
ESCO PEST CONTROL SERVICES—See ISS-International Service System A/S; *Int'l*, pg. 656
ESCO, S.A.—See Esco Corporation; *U.S. Private*, pg. 383
ESCOD INDUSTRIES—See Insilco Corporation; *U.S. Public*, pg. 881
ESCONDIDA MINE—See The Broken Hill Proprietary Company Limited; *Int'l*, pg. 228
ESCORT, INC.; *U.S. Private*, pg. 383
ESCOY SMELTING SENDIRIAN BHD.—See Preussag AG; *Int'l*, pg. 1071
ESCUELAS DE IDIOMAS BERLITZ DE ESPANA, S.A.—See Berlitz International, Inc.; *U.S. Public*, pg. 222
ESELCO, INC.; *U.S. Public*, pg. 591
DAVID ESHELBY LIMITED—See British Building & Engineering Appliances Plc; *Int'l*, pg. 219
ESHUIS BOUWMATERIALEN GROEP—See Veba AG; *Int'l*, pg. 1458
ESIS, INC.—See Cigna Corp.; *U.S. Public*, pg. 366
ESIS INTERNATIONAL (PUERTO RICO), INC.—See Cigna Corp.; *U.S. Public*, pg. 366
ESIX—See Insurance Management Associates; *U.S. Private*, pg. 565
ESKAY SCREW CORPORATION—See Masco Corporation; *U.S. Public*, pg. 1054
ESKAYEF LTD.—See SmithKline Beecham plc; *Int'l*, pg. 1265
ESKIMO EUROP S.A.R.L.—See Eskimo Pie Corporation; *U.S. Public*, pg. 592
ESKIMO FLAVORS—See Eskimo Pie Corporation; *U.S. Public*, pg. 592
ESKIMO PIE CORPORATION; *U.S. Public*, pg. 592
ESKIMOS, INC.—See Arctic Slope Regional Corporation; *U.S. Private*, pg. 80
ESKOM; *Int'l*, pg. 459
ESMACH SPA—See Groupe Strafor Facom; *Int'l*, pg. 570
ESPACE EXPANSION—See Unibail; *Int'l*, pg. 1431
ESPACE JARDIN—See Castorama Dubois Investissements S.C.A.; *Int'l*, pg. 276
S.A. ESPACE MOBILE INTERNATIONAL E.M.I.—See Cockerill Sambre; *Int'l*, pg. 301
ESPACE 96—See Lagardere Groupe; *Int'l*, pg. 792
ESPAN CORPORATION—See RPM, Inc.; *U.S. Public*, pg. 1358
CIA. ESPANOLA DE PETROLEOS ATLANTICO, S.A.—See Compania Espanola de Petroleos, S.A. (CEPSA); *Int'l*, pg. 323
ESPE OY—See Royal Dutch/Shell Group of Companies; *Int'l*, pg. 1138
ESPE WINDOW SYSTEMS LTD.—See Stora Kopparbergs Bergslags AB; *Int'l*, pg. 1302
ESPECIALIDADES ALIMENTICIAS S.A.—See Nestle S.A.; *Int'l*, pg. 920
ESPECIALIDADES DE REYNOSA S.A. DE C.V.—See Saint-Gobain; *Int'l*, pg. 1174
ESPECIALIDADES NUTRITIVAS S.A. DE C.V.—See Nestle S.A.; *Int'l*, pg. 920
ESPECIALIDADES QUIMICAS SA DE CV—See Rhone-Poulenc S.A.; *Int'l*, pg. 1113
ESPECIALIDADES QUIMICIAS GRACE DE MEXICO S.A. DE C.V.—See W.R. Grace & Co.; *U.S. Public*, pg. 755
ESPEY HUSTON ASSOCIATES, INC.—See The PBS&J Corporation; *U.S. Private*, pg. 826
ESPEY MFG. & ELECTRONICS CORP.; *U.S. Public*, pg. 592
ESPLA GMBH—See PMC, Inc.; *U.S. Private*, pg. 827
ESPLANADE LEOPOLD S.A.—See Tractebel; *Int'l*, pg. 1416
ESPRIT ACCESSORIES—See Esprit de Corp.; *U.S. Private*, pg. 383
ESPRIT DE CORP.; *U.S. Private*, pg. 383
ESPRIT KIDS—See Esprit de Corp.; *U.S. Private*, pg. 383
ESPRIT SPORT—See Esprit de Corp.; *U.S. Private*, pg. 383
ESPRIT SYSTEMS, INC.; *U.S. Private*, pg. 383
ESQUIRE—See The Hearst Corporation; *U.S. Private*, pg. 517
ESQUIRE CANADA, INC.—See Strombecker Corporation; *U.S. Private*, pg. 1047
ESQUIRE NOVELTY CO.—See Strombecker Corporation; *U.S. Private*, pg. 1047
ESQUIRE RADIO & ELECTRONICS INC.; *U.S. Private*, pg. 383
ESSEF CARIBBEAN, INCORPORATED—See Essef Corporation; *U.S. Public*, pg. 592
ESSEF CORPORATION; *U.S. Public*, pg. 592
ESSEF MANUFACTURING FSC, INC.—See Essef Corporation; *U.S. Public*, pg. 592
ESSELENPARK DEVELOPMENTS (PTY) LTD.—See Transnet Ltd.; *Int'l*, pg. 1417
ESSELTE—See Esselte AB; *Int'l*, pg. 460
ESSELTE AB; *Int'l*, pg. 459
ESSELTE A/S—See Esselte AB; *Int'l*, pg. 460
ESSELTE ASIA PACIFIC—See Esselte AB; *Int'l*, pg. 460
ESSELTE AUSTRALIA PTY. LTD.—See Esselte AB; *Int'l*, pg. 461
ESSELTE BV—See Esselte AB; *Int'l*, pg. 461
ESSELTE CHRONO AB—See Esselte AB; *Int'l*, pg. 459
ESSELTE CORPORATION—See Esselte AB; *Int'l*, pg. 460
ESSELTE DE MEXICO, S.A. DE C.V.—See Esselte AB; *Int'l*, pg. 461
ESSELTE EUROPE—See Esselte AB; *Int'l*, pg. 460
ESSELTE GMBH—See Esselte AB; *Int'l*, pg. 461
ESSELTE LTD.—See Esselte AB; *Int'l*, pg. 461
ESSELTE METO—See Esselte AB; *Int'l*, pg. 460
ESSELTE METO AB—See Esselte AB; *Int'l*, pg. 459
ESSELTE METO A-S—See Esselte AB; *Int'l*, pg. 461
ESSELTE METO A/S—See Esselte AB; *Int'l*, pg. 461

ESSELTE METO BV—See Esselte AB; *Int'l*, pg. 461
ESSELTE METO CANADA—See Esselte AB; *Int'l*, pg. 461
ESSELTE METO FINLAND—See Esselte AB; *Int'l*, pg. 461
ESSELTE METO GES MBH—See Esselte AB; *Int'l*, pg. 461
ESSELTE METO GMBH—See Esselte AB; *Int'l*, pg. 461
ESSELTE METO IND. E. COM. LTDA.—See Esselte AB; *Int'l*, pg. 461
ESSELTE METO INTERNATIONAL GMBH—See Esselte AB; *Int'l*, pg. 461
ESSELTE METO INTERNATIONAL PRODUKTIONS GMBH—See Esselte AB; *Int'l*, pg. 461
ESSELTE METO KIMBALL SYSTEMS—See Esselte AB; *Int'l*, pg. 460
ESSELTE METO LTD.—See Esselte AB; *Int'l*, pg. 461
ESSELTE METO (MALAYSIA) SDN BHD—See Esselte AB; *Int'l*, pg. 461
ESSELTE METO NV—See Esselte AB; *Int'l*, pg. 461
ESSELTE METO PORTUGAL LDA—See Esselte AB; *Int'l*, pg. 461
ESSELTE METO PTY. LTD.—See Esselte AB; *Int'l*, pg. 461
ESSELTE METO SDN BHD—See Esselte AB; *Int'l*, pg. 461
ESSELTE METO SNC—See Esselte AB; *Int'l*, pg. 461
ESSELTE NEW ZEALAND—See Esselte AB; *Int'l*, pg. 461
ESSELTE NV PRODUKTION—See Esselte AB; *Int'l*, pg. 461
ESSELTE OY—See Esselte AB; *Int'l*, pg. 461
ESSELTE PENDAFLEX CANADA, INC.—See Esselte AB; *Int'l*, pg. 460
ESSELTE POLSKA SP.Z.O.O.—See Esselte AB; *Int'l*, pg. 461
ESSELTE SA—See Esselte AB; *Int'l*, pg. 461
ESSELTE S.A.—See Esselte AB; *Int'l*, pg. 461
ESSELTE S.P.A.—See Esselte AB; *Int'l*, pg. 461
ESSELTE SVERIGE AB—See Esselte AB; *Int'l*, pg. 459
ESSELTE UK LTD.—See Esselte AB; *Int'l*, pg. 461
ESSELTE VERTRIEBSGES. MBH—See Esselte AB; *Int'l*, pg. 461
ESSELTE WENSBO AB—See Esselte AB; *Int'l*, pg. 459
ESSENCE COMMUNICATIONS, INC.; *U.S. Private*, pg. 383
ESSENER HOCHDRUCK-ROHRLEITUNGSBAU GMBH—See Mannesmann A.G.; *Int'l*, pg. 836
ESSENTIAL HOME HEALTH CARE, INC.—See Integrated Health Services, Inc.; *U.S. Public*, pg. 886
ESSEX CHEMICAL CORPORATION—See The Dow Chemical Company; *U.S. Public*, pg. 523
ESSEX CORPORATION—See Cendant Corporation; *U.S. Public*, pg. 320
ESSEX CORPORATION; *U.S. Public*, pg. 593
ESSEX COUNTY GAS COMPANY; *U.S. Public*, pg. 593
ESSEX ELECTRIC BV—See IPC Corporation Ltd.; *Int'l*, pg. 651
ESSEX GRAIN PRODUCTS, INC.; *U.S. Private*, pg. 383
ESSEX HOUSE LIMITED PARTNERSHIP—See Cooper Communities, Inc.; *U.S. Private*, pg. 274
ESSEX INDUSTRIAL CHEMICALS, INC.—See The Dow Chemical Company; *U.S. Public*, pg. 523
ESSEX INDUSTRIES—See Assa Abloy AB; *Int'l*, pg. 18
ESSEX INDUSTRIES, INC.—See Assa Abloy AB; *Int'l*, pg. 18
ESSEX INSURANCE CO.—See Markel Corporation; *U.S. Public*, pg. 1046
ESSEX INTERNATIONAL, INC.; *U.S. Public*, pg. 593
ESSEX, L.L.C.—See Friedman, Eisenstein, Raemer and Schwartz, LLP; *U.S. Private*, pg. 428
ESSEX MANUFACTURING—See Ford Motor Company; *U.S. Public*, pg. 665
ESSEX PLANT, BELDEN WIRE & CABLE—See Belden Inc.; *U.S. Public*, pg. 201
ESSEX POLYTECH, INC.—See The Dow Chemical Company; *U.S. Public*, pg. 523
ESSEX SPECIALTY PRODUCTS, INC.—See The Dow Chemical Company; *U.S. Public*, pg. 523
ESSEX SPECIALTY PRODUCTS, INC., CANADA—See The Dow Chemical Company; *U.S. Public*, pg. 523
ESSILOR CANADA LTEE.—See Essilor International Compagnie Generale d'Optique; *Int'l*, pg. 462
ESSILOR INTERNATIONAL COMPAGNIE GENERALE D'OPTIQUE; *Int'l*, pg. 462
ESSILOR IRELAND LTD.—See Essilor International Compagnie Generale d'Optique; *Int'l*, pg. 462
ESSILOR LIMITED—See Essilor International Compagnie Generale d'Optique; *Int'l*, pg. 462
ESSILOR OF AMERICA—See Essilor International Compagnie Generale d'Optique; *Int'l*, pg. 462
ESSKAY—See Smithfield Foods, Inc.; *U.S. Public*, pg. 1479
ESSO AKTIENGESELLSCHAFT—See Exxon Corporation; *U.S. Public*, pg. 601
ESSO AUSTRALIA RESOURCES LTD.—See Exxon Corporation; *U.S. Public*, pg. 602
ESSO BRASILEIRA DE PETROLEO LIMITADA—See Exxon Corporation; *U.S. Public*, pg. 602
ESSO EASTERN INC.—See Exxon Corporation; *U.S. Public*, pg. 601
ESSO EXPLORATION AND PRODUCTION UK LIMITED—See Exxon Corporation; *U.S. Public*, pg. 602
ESSO INC.—See Exxon Corporation; *U.S. Public*, pg. 602
ESSO INTERNATIONAL SHIPPING (BAHAMAS) CO. LIMITED—See Exxon Corporation; *U.S. Public*, pg. 601
ESSO ITALIANA S.P.A.—See Exxon Corporation; *U.S. Public*, pg. 602
ESSO MALAYSIA BERHAD—See Exxon Corporation; *U.S. Public*, pg. 602
ESSO NEDERLAND B.V.—See Exxon Corporation; *U.S. Public*, pg. 602
ESSO NORGE A.S.—See Exxon Corporation; *U.S. Public*, pg. 602
ESSO N.V./S.A.—See Exxon Corporation; *U.S. Public*, pg. 602
ESSO PETROLEUM COMPANY, LIMITED—See Exxon Corporation; *U.S. Public*, pg. 602
ESSO PRODUCTION MALAYSIA INC.—See Exxon Corporation; *U.S. Public*, pg. 602
ESSO SEKIYU KABUSHIKI KAISHA—See Exxon Corporation; *U.S. Public*, pg. 602

ESSO SINGAPORE PRIVATE LIMITED—See Exxon Corporation; *U.S. Public*, pg. 602
ESSO SOCIEDAD ANONIMA PETROLEUM ARGENTINA—See Exxon Corporation; *U.S. Public*, pg. 602
ESSO SOCIETE ANONYME FRANCAISE—See Exxon Corporation; *U.S. Public*, pg. 602
ESSO STANDARD OIL S.A. LIMITED—See Exxon Corporation; *U.S. Public*, pg. 602
ESSO STANDARD THAILAND LTD.—See Exxon Corporation; *U.S. Public*, pg. 602
ESSO TRADING COMPANY OF ABU DHABI—See Exxon Corporation; *U.S. Public*, pg. 602
ESSO UK PLC—See Exxon Corporation; *U.S. Public*, pg. 602
ESSPA-EDILIZIA SICILIANA S.P.A.—See Bastogi-S.p.A.; *Int'l*, pg. 170
ESSROC CANADA—See Ciments Francais; *Int'l*, pg. 292
ESSROC CEMENT, CORP.; *U.S. Private*, pg. 384
ESSROC MATERIALS INC.—See Ciments Francais; *Int'l*, pg. 292
ESSVE PRODUKTER AB—See Bergman & Beving AB; *Int'l*, pg. 188
ESTA BEHANG B.V.—See Gamma Holding N.V.; *Int'l*, pg. 540
ESTA GESELLSCHAFT FUR EDELSTAHLVERARBEITUNG MBH—See Fried. Krupp AG; *Int'l*, pg. 513
ESTABLIS. PLATT FRERES S.A.—See Carclo Engineering Group plc; *Int'l*, pg. 268
ESTABLISSEMENTS DARTY & FILS S.A.—See Kingfisher plc; *Int'l*, pg. 734
ESTACIONAMIENTOS SUBTERRANEOS MONTEVIDEO, S.A.—See Caja de Madrid Group; *Int'l*, pg. 252
ESTADO SOLIDO, S.A.—See Caja de Madrid Group; *Int'l*, pg. 252
ESTAMPACIONES NOROESTE S.A.—See Caparo Group Ltd.; *Int'l*, pg. 265
ESTE ASIATICO COMERCIO E INDUSTRIA LTDA.—See The East Asiatic Company Ltd. A/S; *Int'l*, pg. 431
ESTECH CORPORATION—See Structural Dynamics Research Corp.; *U.S. Public*, pg. 1525
ESTEE LAUDER—See Estee Lauder Companies Inc.; *U.S. Public*, pg. 594
ESTEE LAUDER COMPANIES INC.; *U.S. Public*, pg. 594
ESTELAR SA DE CV—See Sara Lee Corporation; *U.S. Public*, pg. 1434
ESTEREL—See Groupe Air France; *Int'l*, pg. 560
ESTERLINE TECHNOLOGIES CORPORATION; *U.S. Public*, pg. 594
ESTES EXPRESS LINES, INC.; *U.S. Private*, pg. 384
ESTEVAN BRICK DIVISION—See Jannock Limited; *Int'l*, pg. 698
ESTEVAN DIVISION—See MacMillan Bloedel Limited; *Int'l*, pg. 828
ESTEVENON—See GIB Group; *Int'l*, pg. 534
ESTIA TRADING S.A.—See Freudenberg & Company; *Int'l*, pg. 506
AS ESTIVO—See Imatran Voima Oy; *Int'l*, pg. 660
ESTONIAN TRANSOIL—See Neste Oy; *Int'l*, pg. 914
ESTRATEGIAS TELEFONICAS, S.A. (ESTRATEL)—See Telefonica de Espana, S.A.; *Int'l*, pg. 1371
ESTRAVEL—See FinnAir Oy; *Int'l*, pg. 486
ETABLISSEMENT CHARLES MONSEUR S.A.—See Axel Johnson AB; *Int'l*, pg. 710
ETABLISSEMENT D'ARGENTEUIL—See Dassault Aviation Group; *Int'l*, pg. 383
ETABLISSEMENT D'ARGONAY—See Dassault Aviation Group; *Int'l*, pg. 383
ETABLISSEMENT D'ISTRES—See Dassault Aviation Group; *Int'l*, pg. 383
ETABLISSEMENT ROBERT BELLANGER S.A.—See Tenneco Inc.; *U.S. Public*, pg. 1579
S.A. ETABLISSEMENTS A. LAFLEUR ET F. SICARD—See Cockerill Sambre; *Int'l*, pg. 302
S.A. ETABLISSEMENTS BELLUE—See Cockerill Sambre; *Int'l*, pg. 302
ETABLISSEMENTS BEZ S.A.—See Allied Colloids Group Plc.; *Int'l*, pg. 62
ETABLISSEMENTS CIBA-GEIGY SA—See Novartis AG; *Int'l*, pg. 982
ETABLISSEMENTS DEBRISE-DULAC & CIE—See LVMH Moet Hennessy Louis Vuitton; *Int'l*, pg. 780
ETABLISSEMENTS DELHAIZE FRERES ET CIE "LE LION" S.A.; *Int'l*, pg. 462
ETABLISSEMENTS HENRI PEIGNEN S.A.—See Schindler Holding AG; *Int'l*, pg. 1205
ETABLISSEMENTS JEAN SALLE—See Generale Sucriere SNC; *Int'l*, pg. 549
ETABLISSEMENTS RENE SALOMON—See Saint-Gobain; *Int'l*, pg. 1171
ETABLISSEMENTS VALLAROCHE (SA)—See SNECMA - Societe Nationale d'Etude et de Construction de Moteurs d'Aviation; *Int'l*, pg. 1165
ETABLISSEMENTS VAN RULLEN—See Williams Holdings Plc; *Int'l*, pg. 1499
ETABLISSEMENTS VENTEX SA—See Adidas AG; *Int'l*, pg. 25
ETEC SYSTEMS, INC.; *U.S. Public*, pg. 594
ETERBAS TECH LTDA.—See Saint-Gobain; *Int'l*, pg. 1171
ETERNIT BRESIL—See Saint-Gobain; *Int'l*, pg. 1171
ETERNIT INDUSTRIES—See ETEX; *Int'l*, pg. 430
ETERPLAST PLASTIK SANAYI—See ETEX; *Int'l*, pg. 430
GIE ETEX GESTION—See ETEX; *Int'l*, pg. 430
ETHAN ALLEN, INC.—See Ethan Allen Interiors Inc.; *U.S. Public*, pg. 595
ETHAN ALLEN INTERIORS INC.; *U.S. Public*, pg. 595
ETHEL M CHOCOLATES—See Mars, Incorporated; *U.S. Private*, pg. 707
ETHICAL NUTRIMENT, INC.—See Eggland's Best, Inc.; *U.S. Private*, pg. 366
ETHICON ENDO-SURGERY, INC.—See Johnson & Johnson; *U.S. Public*, pg. 928
ETHICON G.M.B.H. & CO. KG—See Johnson & Johnson; *U.S. Public*, pg. 929

ETHICON, INC.—See Johnson & Johnson; *U.S. Public*, pg. 928
ETHICON S.P.A.—See Johnson & Johnson; *U.S. Public*, pg. 929
ETHIKA AFJP—See The Principal Financial Group; *U.S. Private*, pg. 886
ETHIKA CORPORATION; *U.S. Public*, pg. 595
ETHIX MIDLANDS—See New York Life Insurance Company; *U.S. Private*, pg. 795
ETHNOR S.A.—See Johnson & Johnson; *U.S. Public*, pg. 929
ETHONE OMI-WARREN—See Asarco Incorporated; *U.S. Public*, pg. 138
ETHONE OMI-WEST HAVEN—See Asarco Incorporated; *U.S. Public*, pg. 138
ETHYL CANADA, INC.—See Ethyl Corporation; *U.S. Public*, pg. 595
ETHYL CORPORATION; *U.S. Public*, pg. 595
ETHYL EUROPE S.A.—See Ethyl Corporation; *U.S. Public*, pg. 595
ETHYL PETROLEUM ADDITIVES LTD.—See Ethyl Corporation; *U.S. Public*, pg. 595
ETIENNE AIGNER; *U.S. Private*, pg. 384
ETILAM-GRAVIGNY—See Groupe Usinor; *Int'l*, pg. 571
ETIQUETAS INTERNACIONALES, Inc.—See Bacardi Limited; *Int'l*, pg. 132
ETIREX S.A.—See Emerson Electric Co.; *U.S. Public*, pg. 577
ETITAS ELEKTRIK TECHIZATI—See Jeumont-Schneider Trenformeteurs; *Int'l*, pg. 706
A.J. ETKIN CONSTRUCTION CO.—See Alex J. Etkin, Inc.; *U.S. Private*, pg. 384
ALEX J. ETKIN, INC.; *U.S. Private*, pg. 384
ETMOFINA S.A.—See Petrofina S.A.; *Int'l*, pg. 1043
ETOILE BLEUE—See Havas Advertising; *Int'l*, pg. 600
ETONIC TRETORN—See Kohlberg Kravis Roberts & Co.; *U.S. Private*, pg. 629
ETOS BV—See Koninklijke Ahold NV; *Int'l*, pg. 749
ETOXYL, C.A.—See Olin Corporation; *U.S. Public*, pg. 1219
THE EUCLID CHEMICAL COMPANY—See RPM, Inc.; *U.S. Public*, pg. 1358
EUCLID HITACHI—See Hitachi, Ltd.; *Int'l*, pg. 622
EUCLID HITACHI—See AB Volvo; *Int'l*, pg. 1477
EUCLID TECHNOLOGIES PTE. LTD.—See Ssangyong Business Group; *Int'l*, pg. 1292
EUFAULA PLANT—See Cooper Industries, Inc.; *U.S. Public*, pg. 444
EUFIDIS—See GIB Group; *Int'l*, pg. 534
EUFRADIS SPRL—See GIB Group; *Int'l*, pg. 533
EUL & GUNTHER GMBH & CO KG—See Melitta Unternehmensgruppe Bentz KG; *Int'l*, pg. 857
EULER; *Int'l*, pg. 463
EURAD RSCG—See Havas Advertising; *Int'l*, pg. 602
EURAFRICAN BANK (TANZANIA) LTD.—See Generale de Banque S.A.; *Int'l*, pg. 548
EURAGRIND S.R.L.—See Banco Ambrosiano Veneto S.p.A.; *Int'l*, pg. 138
EURALLIANCE—See Fortis; *Int'l*, pg. 499
EURAND FRANCE S.A.—See American Home Products Corporation; *U.S. Private*, pg. 81
EURAND INTERNATIONAL S.P.A.—See American Home Products Corporation; *U.S. Private*, pg. 81
EURASEM B.V.—See Royal Begemann Group; *Int'l*, pg. 1133
EURASIA CONSULT—See Heidemij N.V.; *Int'l*, pg. 606
EURASPACE GESELLSCHAFT FUR RAUMFAHRTTECHNIK MBH—See Daimler-Benz Aktiengesellschaft; *Int'l*, pg. 367
EURATEC B.V.—See Royal Begemann Group; *Int'l*, pg. 1133
THE EUREKA COMPANY—See Electrolux, AB; *Int'l*, pg. 440
EUREKA MANUFACTURING CO., INC.—See Reed & Barton Corporation; *U.S. Private*, pg. 916
EUREKO BENEFITS SERVICE—See Eureko B.V.; *Int'l*, pg. 464
EUREKO B.V.; *Int'l*, pg. 464
EUREKO IRELAND HOLDINGS—See Eureko B.V.; *Int'l*, pg. 464
EUREKO RE—See Eureko B.V.; *Int'l*, pg. 464
EUREKO SALES SUPPORT—See Eureko B.V.; *Int'l*, pg. 464
EUREST BELGILUX SA—See Accor S.A.; *Int'l*, pg. 21
EUREST DEUTSCHLAND—See Accor S.A.; *Int'l*, pg. 21
EUREST DINING SERVICES—See Compass Group plc; *Int'l*, pg. 324
EUREST ESPAGNE—See Accor S.A.; *Int'l*, pg. 21
EUREST NEDERLAND BV—See Accor S.A.; *Int'l*, pg. 21
S.A. EURINBEL—See Cockerill Sambre; *Int'l*, pg. 301
EURO-ASPARTAME S.A.—See Ajinomoto Company Inc.; *Int'l*, pg. 41
EURO-BELL S.A.—See Bell Sports Corp.; *U.S. Public*, pg. 207
EURO GLOBAL TRAVEL INC.—See Assicurazioni Generali S.p.A.; *Int'l*, pg. 90
EURO-LLOYD TRAVEL—See Hapag-Lloyd AG; *Int'l*, pg. 596
EURO MAKITA CORPORATION B.V.—See Makita Corporation; *Int'l*, pg. 831
EURO REINSURANCE BROKERS S.A.—See Assicurazioni Generali S.p.A.; *Int'l*, pg. 91
EURO RSCG—See Havas Advertising; *Int'l*, pg. 602
EURO RSCG AUDIENCE—See Havas Advertising; *Int'l*, pg. 600
EURO RSCG BABINET, ERRA, TONG CUONG—See Havas Advertising; *Int'l*, pg. 600
EURO RSCG BARCELONA—See Havas Advertising; *Int'l*, pg. 603
EURO RSCG-BOMBAY—See Havas Advertising; *Int'l*, pg. 602
EURO RSCG COMMUNICANCE—See Havas Advertising; *Int'l*, pg. 600
EURO RSCG, COPENHAGEN—See Havas Advertising; *Int'l*, pg. 602

EURO RSCG D 10—See Havas Advertising; *Int'l*, pg. 600
EURO RSCG DAHLIN SMITH WHITE, LLC; *U.S. Private*, pg. 384
EURO RSCG ENSEMBLE—See Havas Advertising; *Int'l*, pg. 600
EURO RSCG EST—See Havas Advertising; *Int'l*, pg. 600
EURO RSCG FRANCE—See Havas Advertising; *Int'l*, pg. 601
EURO RSCG GRAFFITI—See Havas Advertising; *Int'l*, pg. 603
EURO RSCG GREGOIRE, BLACHERE, HUARD & ROUSSEL—See Havas Advertising; *Int'l*, pg. 601
EURO RSCG HEALTHCARE—See Havas Advertising; *Int'l*, pg. 603
EURO RSCG INSTITUTIONNEL—See Havas Advertising; *Int'l*, pg. 600
EURO RSCG KOREA—See Havas Advertising; *Int'l*, pg. 602
EURO RSCG MEDIA—See Havas Advertising; *Int'l*, pg. 603
EURO RSCG MEZZANO COSTANTINI MIGNANI—See Havas Advertising; *Int'l*, pg. 603
EURO RSCG NORD—See Havas Advertising; *Int'l*, pg. 601
EURO RSCG NORTON—See Havas Advertising; *Int'l*, pg. 603
EURO RSCG NOVATION—See Havas Advertising; *Int'l*, pg. 601
EURO RSCG OPINIONS—See Havas Advertising; *Int'l*, pg. 601
EURO RSCG PARTNERSHIP—See Havas Advertising; *Int'l*, pg. 602
EURO RSCG POLAND—See Havas Advertising; *Int'l*, pg. 603
EURO RSCG, PRAHA—See Havas Advertising; *Int'l*, pg. 602
EURO RSCG QUARTET—See Havas Advertising; *Int'l*, pg. 601
EURO RSCG SCHER, LEFARGE—See Havas Advertising; *Int'l*, pg. 601
EURO RSCG TATHAM—See Havas Advertising; *Int'l*, pg. 601
EURO RSCG-VENEZUELA—See Havas Advertising; *Int'l*, pg. 601
EURO RSCG WNEK GOSPER—See Havas Advertising; *Int'l*, pg. 603
EURO-SUITES—See Sunstone Hotel Investors, Inc.; *U.S. Public*, pg. 1537
EURO SYNERGIES MANAGEMENT SA—See Bayerische Vereinsbank Group; *Int'l*, pg. 181
EURO SYNERGIES MANAGEMENT SA—See Credit Nationale; *Int'l*, pg. 345
EUROBAYERNWERK GMBH—See Viag AG; *Int'l*, pg. 1464
EUROBULL OVERSEAS N.V.—See Compagnie des Machines Bull; *Int'l*, pg. 318
EUROC BETON AB—See Scancem AB; *Int'l*, pg. 1199
EUROC BETONG & BALLAST AB—See Scancem AB; *Int'l*, pg. 1200
EUROC BRICK LTD.—See Scancem AB; *Int'l*, pg. 1199
EUROC CAPITAL B.V.—See Scancem AB; *Int'l*, pg. 1200
EUROC RECYCLING AB—See Scancem AB; *Int'l*, pg. 1199
EUROC REINSURANCE S.A.—See Scancem AB; *Int'l*, pg. 1199
EUROC TRADE AB—See Scancem AB; *Int'l*, pg. 1199
EUROCAMP INDEPENDENT LIMITED—See Eurocamp Plc; *Int'l*, pg. 465
EUROCAMP PLC; *Int'l*, pg. 464
EUROCAMP TRAVEL LIMITED—See Eurocamp Plc; *Int'l*, pg. 465
EUROCARBON TILBURG B.V.—See DSM N.V.; *Int'l*, pg. 354
EUROCARD AB, STOCKHOLM—See Skandinaviska Enskilda Banken; *Int'l*, pg. 1259
EUROCERMEX N.V.—See Anheuser-Busch Companies, Inc.; *U.S. Public*, pg. 115
EUROCETUS—See Chiron Corporation; *U.S. Public*, pg. 290
EUROCHEM DIVISION—See Baker Hughes Incorporated; *U.S. Public*, pg. 166
EUROCLEAN—See Electrolux, AB; *Int'l*, pg. 440
EUROCLEAN AB—See Electrolux, AB; *Int'l*, pg. 439
EUROCLEAN A/S—See Electrolux, AB; *Int'l*, pg. 443
EUROCLEAN CANADA INC.—See Electrolux, AB; *Int'l*, pg. 441
EUROCLEAN WALLONIE S.A.—See Temco Service Industries; *U.S. Public*, pg. 1574
EUROCLEAR OPERATIONS CENTRE—See J.P. Morgan Co. Incorporated; *U.S. Public*, pg. 1130
EUROCOL B.V.—See Forbo Holding SA; *Int'l*, pg. 497
EUROCOM CONCATO DI PACE SRL—See Havas Advertising; *Int'l*, pg. 603
EUROCON—See Incentive AB; *Int'l*, pg. 667
EUROCONSULT BV—See Heidemij N.V.; *Int'l*, pg. 606
EUROCONSULT ENERGIE UND UMWELT BERATUNGS GMBH—See Creditanstalt-Bankverein; *Int'l*, pg. 347
EUROCONSULT PAKISTAN—See Heidemij N.V.; *Int'l*, pg. 606
EUROCOPTER DEUTSCHLAND GMBH—See Daimler-Benz Aktiengesellschaft; *Int'l*, pg. 369
EUROCOPTER FRANCE S.A.—See Aerospatiale; *Int'l*, pg. 29
EUROCOPTER HOLDING S.A.—See Aerospatiale; *Int'l*, pg. 29
EUROCOPTER S.A.—See Aerospatiale; *Int'l*, pg. 29
EUROCOUSTIC—See Saint-Gobain; *Int'l*, pg. 1176
EUROCOPTER PARTICIPATIONS S.A.—See Aerospatiale; *Int'l*, pg. 29
EURODIA INDUSTRIE S.A.—See Tokuyama Corporation; *Int'l*, pg. 1394
EURODIF SA—See COGEMA - Compagnie Generale des Matieres Nucleaires; *Int'l*, pg. 305
EURODIS AG—See Siemens AG; *Int'l*, pg. 1247
EURODIS BYTECH ELECTRONICS LIMITED—See Siemens AG; *Int'l*, pg. 1247
EURODIS BYTECH ONBOARD LIMITED—See Siemens AG; *Int'l*, pg. 1247

EURODIS ELECTRON GROUP—See Siemens AG; *Int'l*, pg. 1247
EURODIS ELECTRON PLC—See Siemens AG; *Int'l*, pg. 1247
EURODIS HB ELECTRONICS LIMITED—See Siemens AG; *Int'l*, pg. 1247
EUROFIGHTER JAGDFLUGZEUG GMBH—See British Aerospace p.l.c.; *Int'l*, pg. 218
EUROFINN SERVICES—See Enso Oyj; *Int'l*, pg. 458
EUROFIP (MADRID)—See Banque Nationale de Paris; *Int'l*, pg. 163
EUROFLAMM GMBH—See Deutsche Babcock AG; *Int'l*, pg. 400
EUROFLEX SCREEN PRINT SUPPLIES LTD.—See Flexible Products Company; *U.S. Private*, pg. 412
EUROFLOAT—See Saint-Gobain; *Int'l*, pg. 1172
EUROFOIL LTD.—See Illinois Tool Works Inc.; *U.S. Public*, pg. 868
EUROFORUM ESCORIAL, S.A.—See Caja de Madrid Group; *Int'l*, pg. 252
EUROFORUM TORREALTA, S.A.—See Caja de Madrid Group; *Int'l*, pg. 252
EUROGENETICS ITALIA SRL—See Tosoh Corporation; *Int'l*, pg. 1408
EUROGENETICS N.V.—See Tosoh Corporation; *Int'l*, pg. 1408
EUROGLASS—See Saint-Gobain; *Int'l*, pg. 1172
EUROGROUP ITALIA SRL—See GIB Group; *Int'l*, pg. 534
EUROGROUP SA—See Coop Switzerland; *Int'l*, pg. 330
EUROGROUP SA—See GIB Group; *Int'l*, pg. 533
EUROGUARD SA—See GIB Group; *Int'l*, pg. 533
EUROIPEX, S.P.A.—See Essef Corporation; *U.S. Public*, pg. 593
EUROJET TURBO GMBH—See Daimler-Benz Aktiengesellschaft; *Int'l*, pg. 367
EUROKASCO—See Bairnco Corporation; *U.S. Public*, pg. 165
EUROLATINA—See Heidemij N.V.; *Int'l*, pg. 606
EUROLEASE—See Generale de Banque S.A.; *Int'l*, pg. 547
EUROLEASE FACTOR SA—See Banque Generale du Luxembourg SA; *Int'l*, pg. 162
EUROLEASE-FACTOR (ELFA) SA—See Generale de Banque S.A.; *Int'l*, pg. 548
EUROLEC BV—See The General Electric Company, p.l.c.; *Int'l*, pg. 546
EUROLINERS—See Lafarge S.A.; *Int'l*, pg. 789
EUROLYSINE SA—See Ajinomoto Company Inc.; *Int'l*, pg. 41
EUROLYSINE S.A., PLANT—See Ajinomoto Company Inc.; *Int'l*, pg. 41
EUROMARKET DESIGNS, INC.; *U.S. Private*, pg. 384
EUROMARKETING—See Crain Communications, Inc.; *U.S. Private*, pg. 285
EUROMETAAL HOLDING N.V.—See Oerlikon-Buhrle Holding AG; *Int'l*, pg. 998
EUROMEZZANINE GESTION—See Credit Nationale; *Int'l*, pg. 344
EUROMISSLE DYNAMICS GROUP—See British Aerospace p.l.c.; *Int'l*, pg. 218
EURONORD WTM AB—See AB Industrivarden; *Int'l*, pg. 678
EURONOVA S.R.L.—See Otto Versand (GmbH & Co.); *Int'l*, pg. 1015
EUROP ASSISTANCE—See Assicurazioni Generali S.p.A.; *Int'l*, pg. 91
EUROP ASSISTANCE COMPANHIA PORTUGUESA DE SEGUROS DE ASSISTENCIA, S.A.—See Assicurazioni Generali S.p.A.; *Int'l*, pg. 91
EUROP ASSISTANCE ESPANA S.A.—See Assicurazioni Generali S.p.A.; *Int'l*, pg. 91
EUROP ASSISTANCE HOLDINGS LTD.—See Assicurazioni Generali S.p.A.; *Int'l*, pg. 91
EUROP ASSISTANCE INSURANCE LTD.—See Assicurazioni Generali S.p.A.; *Int'l*, pg. 91
EUROP ASSISTANCE INTERNATIONAL INC.—See Assicurazioni Generali S.p.A.; *Int'l*, pg. 90
EUROP ASSISTANCE (IRELAND) LTD.—See Assicurazioni Generali S.p.A.; *Int'l*, pg. 91
EUROP ASSISTANCE ITALIA S.P.A.—See Assicurazioni Generali S.p.A.; *Int'l*, pg. 90
EUROP ASSISTANCE LTD.—See Assicurazioni Generali S.p.A.; *Int'l*, pg. 90
EUROP ASSISTANCE S.A.—See Assicurazioni Generali S.p.A.; *Int'l*, pg. 91
EUROP ASSISTANCE SERVICE S.P.A.—See Assicurazioni Generali S.p.A.; *Int'l*, pg. 90
EUROP ASSISTANCE SERVICES S.A.—See Assicurazioni Generali S.p.A.; *Int'l*, pg. 91
EUROP ASSISTANCE SERVICIOS S.A.—See Assicurazioni Generali S.p.A.; *Int'l*, pg. 91
EUROP ASSISTANCE SERVICOS DE ASSISTENCIA PERSONALIZADOS, S.A.—See Assicurazioni Generali S.p.A.; *Int'l*, pg. 91
EUROP ASSISTANCE SOCIETE D'ASSISTANCE AUX VOYAGEURS S.A.—See Assicurazioni Generali S.p.A.; *Int'l*, pg. 91
EUROP ASSISTANCE TRADE S.P.A.—See Assicurazioni Generali S.p.A.; *Int'l*, pg. 90
EUROP ASSISTANCE U.S. HOLDINGS, INC.—See Assicurazioni Generali S.p.A.; *Int'l*, pg. 90
EUROP ASSISTANCE VERISCHERUNGS AG—See Assicurazioni Generali S.p.A.; *Int'l*, pg. 89
EUROP ASSISTANCE WORLDWIDE SERVICES (SOUTH AFRICA) LTD.—See Assicurazioni Generali S.p.A.; *Int'l*, pg. 91
EUROPA BANK AG—See Dresdner Bank AG; *Int'l*, pg. 420
EUROPA CARTON AG—See Abitibi-Consolidated Inc.; *Int'l*, pg. 20
EUROPA CRUISES CORPORATION; *U.S. Public*, pg. 595
EUROPA INSURANCE COMPANY LTD.—See Assicurazioni Generali S.p.A.; *Int'l*, pg. 90
EUROPA MANAGEMENT INC.—See Transco Inc.; *U.S. Private*, pg. 1096

EUROPA METALLI S.P.A.—See KM-Europa Metal Aktiengesellschaft; *Int'l*, pg. 719
EUROPA PLUS MEDIEN BETEILIGUNGS—See Lagardere Groupe; *Int'l*, pg. 795
EUROPAEA-ASSURANCE PROTECTION JURIDIQUE S.A.—See Assicurazioni Generali S.p.A.; *Int'l*, pg. 91
EUROPA-GAN BIZTOSITO—See Groupe GAN; *Int'l*, pg. 564
EUROPAISCHE HYPOTHEKENBANK DER DEUTSCHEN BANK—See Deutsche Bank AG; *Int'l*, pg. 405
EUROPAISCHE REISEVERSICHERUNGS AG—See Assicurazioni Generali S.p.A.; *Int'l*, pg. 89
EUROPARTNERS HOLDING S.A.—See Commerzbank AG; *Int'l*, pg. 312
EUROPAY AUSTRIA ZAHLUNGSVERKEHRSSYSTEME GMBH—See Creditanstalt-Bankverein; *Int'l*, pg. 347
EUROPAY BELGIUM S.C.—See Bank Brussels Lambert; *Int'l*, pg. 147
EUROPCAR AUTOVERMIETUNG GMBH—See Volkswagen AG; *Int'l*, pg. 1473
EUROPCAR INTERNATIONAL S.A.—See Volkswagen AG; *Int'l*, pg. 1475
EUROPE—See Supertex, Inc.; *U.S. Public*, pg. 1540
EUROPE AUDIOVISUEL—See Lagardere Groupe; *Int'l*, pg. 792
EUROPE AUTO EQUIPMENT—See Code-Alarm, Inc.; *U.S. Public*, pg. 394
EUROPE COMBINED TERMINALS B.V.—See Internatio-Muller N.V.; *Int'l*, pg. 682
EUROPE COMBINED TERMINALS B.V.—See Royal Nedlloyd Group N.V.; *Int'l*, pg. 1145
EUROPE CRAFT IMPORTS—See Aris Industries, Inc.; *U.S. Public*, pg. 129
EUROPE DEVELOPMENT INTERNATIONAL—See Lagardere Groupe; *Int'l*, pg. 792
EUROPE IMAGES CONSEIL—See Lagardere Groupe; *Int'l*, pg. 792
EUROPE LANGUAGE CENTER SRL—See Berlitz International, Inc.; *U.S. Public*, pg. 222
EUROPE NEWS—See Lagardere Groupe; *Int'l*, pg. 792
EUROPE 1 COMMUNICATION—See Lagardere Groupe; *Int'l*, pg. 792
EUROPE 1 IMMOBILIER—See Lagardere Groupe; *Int'l*, pg. 792
EUROPE 1 TELECOMPAGNIE—See Lagardere Groupe; *Int'l*, pg. 792
EUROPE PRESSE ET RADIO—See Lagardere Groupe; *Int'l*, pg. 792
EUROPE REGIES—See Lagardere Groupe; *Int'l*, pg. 792
EUROPE TAX-FREE SHOPPING LTD.—See Cendant Corporation; *U.S. Public*, pg. 320
EUROPE 2 COMMUNICATION—See Lagardere Groupe; *Int'l*, pg. 792
EUROPE 2 ENTREPRISES—See Lagardere Groupe; *Int'l*, pg. 792
EUROPE 2 PRAGUE—See Lagardere Groupe; *Int'l*, pg. 795
EUROPEAN AMERICAN BANK—See ABN-AMRO Holding N.V.; *Int'l*, pg. 9
EUROPEAN AMERICAN BANK & TRUST CO.—See ABN-AMRO Holding N.V.; *Int'l*, pg. 9
EUROPEAN AREA—See CNF Transportation Inc.; *U.S. Public*, pg. 281
EUROPEAN BAKERS, LTD—See Flowers Industries, Inc.; *U.S. Public*, pg. 657
EUROPEAN BRAZILIAN BANK LTD.—See BankAmerica Corporation; *U.S. Public*, pg. 183
EUROPEAN BUSINESS DEVELOPMENT—See Computer Sciences Corporation; *U.S. Public*, pg. 423
EUROPEAN CABLES CONTROLS DIV.—See FKI Plc; *Int'l*, pg. 472
EUROPEAN CATERING SERVICES—See Groupe Air France; *Int'l*, pg. 560
EUROPEAN CELLARS LTD.—See Whitbread PLC; *Int'l*, pg. 1499
EUROPEAN COFFEE CLASSICS—See Melitta Unternehmensgruppe Bentz KG; *Int'l*, pg. 857
EUROPEAN COMPUTER INDUSTRY RESEARCH CENTER GMBH—See Compagnie des Machines Bull; *Int'l*, pg. 318
EUROPEAN FINANCE REINSURANCE COMPANY LTD.—See Swiss Reinsurance Company; *Int'l*, pg. 1333
EUROPEAN GROUP—See Computer Sciences Corporation; *U.S. Public*, pg. 423
EUROPEAN INDUSTRIAL SERVICES—See Brunel Holdings Plc; *Int'l*, pg. 231
EUROPEAN INTERNATIONAL HOLDING—See Eureko B.V.; *Int'l*, pg. 464
EUROPEAN INTERNATIONAL REINSURANCE COMPANY LTD.—See Swiss Reinsurance Company; *Int'l*, pg. 1333
EUROPEAN INVESTMENT BANK; *Int'l*, pg. 465
EUROPEAN MAGAZINES LIMITED—See IPC Magazines Limited; *Int'l*, pg. 651
EUROPEAN OWENS-CORNING FIBERGLAS SA—See Owens Corning; *U.S. Public*, pg. 1237
EUROPEAN REINSURANCE COMPANY OF ZURICH—See Swiss Reinsurance Company; *Int'l*, pg. 1332
EUROPEAN REINSURANCE CORPORATION OF AMERICA—See Swiss Reinsurance Company; *Int'l*, pg. 1332
EUROPEAN RUBBER JOURNAL—See Crain Communications, Inc.; *U.S. Private*, pg. 285
EUROPEAN SAFETY & HEALTH CONSULTANTS (ESC)—See Willis Corroon Group PLC; *Int'l*, pg. 1503
EUROPEAN TECHNICAL CENTER—See General Motors Corporation; *U.S. Public*, pg. 721
EUROPEAN TECHNOLOGY CENTRE—See Oracle Corporation; *U.S. Public*, pg. 1228
EUROPEAN TELECOMMUNICATIONS SATELLITE ORGANIZATION (EUTELSAT)—See British Telecommunications plc; *Int'l*, pg. 223
EUROPEAN TURKISH MERCHANT BANK—See Generale de Banque S.A.; *Int'l*, pg. 548

EUROPEAN VACUUM INTERRUPTERS S.A.—See Toshiba Corporation; *Int'l*, pg. 1405
EUROPEAN VINYLS CORP. (HOLDINGS) B.V.—See ENI S.p.A.; *Int'l*, pg. 429
EUROPEENNE DE SURBOUCHAGE—See Pechiney S.A.; *Int'l*, pg. 1028
EUROPEENNE D'INTERMEDIATION FINANCIERE ET BOURSIERE—See Groupe GAN; *Int'l*, pg. 564
EUROPEISKA FORSAKRING (SWEDEN)—See Eureko B.V.; *Int'l*, pg. 464
EUROPENNE DE PROTECTION JURIDIQUE S.A.—See Assicurazioni Generali S.p.A.; *Int'l*, pg. 91
B.V. EUROPESE TABAK MAATSCHAPPIJ—See Universal Corporation; *U.S. Public*, pg. 1695
EUROPLAST—See ETEX; *Int'l*, pg. 430
EUROPTICS LIMITED—See The Furukawa Electric Co., Ltd.; *Int'l*, pg. 530
EURORESINS S.A.—See DSM N.V.; *Int'l*, pg. 355
EUROSEEL EQUIPAMENTOS METALICOS, SA—See Groupe Strafor Facom; *Int'l*, pg. 569
EUROSELECCORS-PUBLICACOES & ARTIGES PROMOCIONAS, LDA (PORTUGAL)—See The Reader's Digest Association, Inc.; *U.S. Public*, pg. 1368
EUROSOS—See Corporacion MAPFRE, Compania Internacional de Reaseguros, S.A.; *Int'l*, pg. 334
EUROSUD PUBLICITE—See Lagardere Groupe; *Int'l*, pg. 792
EUROTAPIJT NEDERLAND B.V.—See Gamma Holding N.V.; *Int'l*, pg. 540
EUROTEC SYSTEMTEILE GMBH—See Klockner-Werke AG; *Int'l*, pg. 737
EUROTEL BRATISLAVA LTD.—See Bell Atlantic Corporation; *U.S. Public*, pg. 204
EUROTEL PRAHA LTA—See Bell Atlantic Corporation; *U.S. Public*, pg. 204
EUROTHERM AB—See Eurotherm plc; *Int'l*, pg. 466
EUROTHERM ANTRIEBSTECHNIK GMBH—See Eurotherm plc; *Int'l*, pg. 466
EUROTHERM A/S—See Eurotherm plc; *Int'l*, pg. 466
EUROTHERM AUTOMATION SA—See Eurotherm plc; *Int'l*, pg. 466
EUROTHERM BV—See Eurotherm plc; *Int'l*, pg. 466
EUROTHERM BV (BELGIAN BRANCH)—See Eurotherm plc; *Int'l*, pg. 466
EUROTHERM CIRCUITS INC.—See Eurotherm plc; *Int'l*, pg. 466
EUROTHERM CONTROLS INC.—See Eurotherm plc; *Int'l*, pg. 466
EUROTHERM CONTROLS LTD.—See Eurotherm plc; *Int'l*, pg. 466
EUROTHERM DANMARK A/S—See Eurotherm plc; *Int'l*, pg. 466
EUROTHERM DRIVES INC.—See Eurotherm plc; *Int'l*, pg. 466
EUROTHERM DRIVES LTD.—See Eurotherm plc; *Int'l*, pg. 466
EUROTHERM DRIVES SPA—See Eurotherm plc; *Int'l*, pg. 466
EUROTHERM DRIVTEKNIK AB—See Eurotherm plc; *Int'l*, pg. 466
EUROTHERM ESPANA SA—See Eurotherm plc; *Int'l*, pg. 466
EUROTHERM GAUGING SYSTEMS INC.—See Eurotherm plc; *Int'l*, pg. 466
EUROTHERM GAUGING SYSTEMS LTD.—See Eurotherm plc; *Int'l*, pg. 466
EUROTHERM GMBH—See Eurotherm plc; *Int'l*, pg. 466
EUROTHERM INDIA LIMITED—See Eurotherm plc; *Int'l*, pg. 466
EUROTHERM IRELAND LTD.—See Eurotherm plc; *Int'l*, pg. 466
EUROTHERM (JAPAN) LIMITED—See Eurotherm plc; *Int'l*, pg. 466
EUROTHERM KOREA LTD.—See Eurotherm plc; *Int'l*, pg. 466
EUROTHERM LTD.—See Eurotherm plc; *Int'l*, pg. 466
EUROTHERM MESSDATENTECHNIK GMBH—See Eurotherm plc; *Int'l*, pg. 466
EUROTHERM MESURES SA—See Eurotherm plc; *Int'l*, pg. 466
EUROTHERM PLC; *Int'l*, pg. 465
EUROTHERM PROCESS AUTOMATION LTD.—See Eurotherm plc; *Int'l*, pg. 466
EUROTHERM PRODUKTE (SCHWIEZ) AG—See Eurotherm plc; *Int'l*, pg. 466
EUROTHERM PTY LTD.—See Eurotherm plc; *Int'l*, pg. 466
EUROTHERM RECORDERS INC.—See Eurotherm plc; *Int'l*, pg. 466
EUROTHERM RECORDERS LTD.—See Eurotherm plc; *Int'l*, pg. 466
EUROTHERM REGLER GMBH—See Eurotherm plc; *Int'l*, pg. 466
EUROTHERM SPA—See Eurotherm plc; *Int'l*, pg. 466
EUROTHERM SYSTEMES SA—See Eurotherm plc; *Int'l*, pg. 466
EUROTHERM VITESSE VARIABLE SA—See Eurotherm plc; *Int'l*, pg. 466
EUROTRON S.A.—See Sanyo Electric Co., Ltd.; *Int'l*, pg. 1192
EUROTUNNEL DEVELOPMENTS LIMITED—See The Eurotunnel Group; *Int'l*, pg. 466
EUROTUNNEL DEVELOPMENTS S.A.—See The Eurotunnel Group; *Int'l*, pg. 466
EUROTUNNEL FINANCE LIMITED—See The Eurotunnel Group; *Int'l*, pg. 466
THE EUROTUNNEL GROUP; *Int'l*, pg. 466
EUROTUNNEL SERVICES LIMITED—See The Eurotunnel Group; *Int'l*, pg. 466
EUROVIDA S.A. (ALLIANZ-RAS/BANCO POPULAR)—See Allianz Aktiengesellschaft; *Int'l*, pg. 60
EURYZA BV—See CSM N.V.; *Int'l*, pg. 243
EURYZA INTERNATIONAL AG—See CSM N.V.; *Int'l*, pg. 244
EURYZA REIS GMBH—See CSM N.V.; *Int'l*, pg. 244

EUTECH CYBERNETICS PTE. LTD.—See CSA Holdings Ltd.; *Int'l*, pg. 242
EVA-TONE INC.; *U.S. Private*, pg. 384
EVANA AUTOMATION SPECIALISTS; *U.S. Private*, pg. 384
EVANGELINE AIRMOTIVE, INC.—See Petroleum Helicopters, Inc.; *U.S. Public*, pg. 1281
EVANITE FIBER CORP.—See Hollingsworth & Vose Co.; *U.S. Private*, pg. 535
EVANS ADHESIVE CORP.; *U.S. Private*, pg. 384
EVANS & FITZGERALD ADVERTISING—See MARC; *U.S. Private*, pg. 701
EVANS & SUTHERLAND COMPUTER CORPORATION; *U.S. Public*, pg. 595
EVANS BALL BRASS & ALUMINUM FOUNDRY—See Evans Industries, Inc.; *U.S. Private*, pg. 385
EVANS-BLACK CARPET MILLS—See Shaw Industries, Inc.; *U.S. Public*, pg. 1464
BOB EVANS FARMS, INC.; *U.S. Public*, pg. 596
EVANS ENVIRONMENTAL & GEOLOGICAL SCIENCE AND MANAGEMENT INC.—See ECOS Group, Inc.; *U.S. Public*, pg. 563
EVANS, HARDY & YOUNG, INC.; *U.S. Private*, pg. 384
EVANS, INC.; *U.S. Public*, pg. 596
EVANS, INC. (MA)—See Evans, Inc.; *U.S. Public*, pg. 596
EVANS INDUSTRIES, INC.; *U.S. Private*, pg. 385
EVANS RULE CO., INC.—See The L.S. Starrett Company; *U.S. Public*, pg. 1511
EVANS ST. CLAIR—See Evans Industries, Inc.; *U.S. Private*, pg. 385
STU EVANS LINCOLN-MERCURY INC.; *U.S. Private*, pg. 385
EVANS TEMPCON INC.—See APL Corporation; *U.S. Private*, pg. 7
EVANSGROUP; *U.S. Private*, pg. 385
EVANSGROUP—See EvansGroup; *U.S. Private*, pg. 385
EVANSGROUP (PUBLIC RELATIONS)—See EvansGroup; *U.S. Private*, pg. 385
EVANSGROUP TECHNOLOGY—See EvansGroup; *U.S. Private*, pg. 385
EVANSTON BANK—See GreatBanc, Inc.; *U.S. Public*, pg. 760
EVANSTON INSURANCE COMPANY—See Markel Corporation; *U.S. Public*, pg. 1046
THE EVANSVILLE COURIER—See The E.W. Scripps Company; *U.S. Public*, pg. 1447
EVANSVILLE VENEER & LUMBER CO.—See Kimball International, Inc.; *U.S. Public*, pg. 957
EVART PRODUCTS CO.—See Chrysler Corporation; *U.S. Public*, pg. 353
EVCON INDUSTRIES—See York International Corporation; *U.S. Public*, pg. 1788
EVCON INDUSTRIES, INC.—See York International Corporation; *U.S. Public*, pg. 1788
EVCON SUPPLY, INC.—See York International Corporation; *U.S. Public*, pg. 1789
EVE RIVER DIVISION—See MacMillan Bloedel Limited; *Int'l*, pg. 828
EVELEC S.A.—See Electrabel S.A.; *Int'l*, pg. 437
EVELETH MINES—See Oglebay Norton Company; *U.S. Public*, pg. 1213
EVENFLO COMPANY, INC.—See Kohlberg Kravis Roberts & Co.; *U.S. Private*, pg. 629
EVENFLO MEXICO S.A.—See Kohlberg Kravis Roberts & Co.; *U.S. Private*, pg. 630
THE EVENING CALL PUBLISHING CO.-THE CALL—See Journal Register Company; *U.S. Public*, pg. 934
THE EVENING NEWS—See Hollinger Inc.; *Int'l*, pg. 631
EVENING POST PUBLISHING CO.; *U.S. Private*, pg. 385
THE EVENING TELEGRAM—See Hollinger Inc.; *Int'l*, pg. 631
EVENTS MARKETING LIMITED—See Air New Zealand Ltd.; *Int'l*, pg. 38
EVENWOOD ENGINEERING—See Brunel Holdings Plc; *Int'l*, pg. 231
EVER-SKI PROPERTIES, INC.—See Santa Fe Gaming Corporation; *U.S. Public*, pg. 1432
EVER-TITE COUPLING PRODUCTS—See Morris Coupling Co.; *U.S. Private*, pg. 762
EVERBRIGHT FASTENERS LTD.—See Haden Maclellan Holdings plc; *Int'l*, pg. 585
EVERBRITE, INC.; *U.S. Private*, pg. 386
EVERBRITE LACROSSE—See Everbrite, Inc.; *U.S. Private*, pg. 386
EVEREADY BATTERY CO.—See Ralston Purina Company; *U.S. Public*, pg. 1360
EVEREADY DE MÉXICO S.A. DE C.V.—See Ralston Purina Company; *U.S. Public*, pg. 1360
EVEREADY SINGAPORE PTE. LTD.—See Ralston Purina Company; *U.S. Public*, pg. 1360
EVEREN SECURITIES, INC.; *U.S. Public*, pg. 597
EVEREST—See Lettuce Entertain You Enterprises, Inc.; *U.S. Private*, pg. 661
EVEREST & JENNINGS DE MÉXICO S.A. DE C.V.—See Graham-Field Health Products, Inc.; *U.S. Public*, pg. 758
EVEREST & JENNINGS/GRAHAM-FIELD, CANADA—See Graham-Field Health Products, Inc.; *U.S. Public*, pg. 758
EVEREST & JENNINGS, INC.—See Graham-Field Health Products, Inc.; *U.S. Public*, pg. 758
EVEREST ENCLOSURES—See Applied Power Inc.; *U.S. Public*, pg. 124
EVEREST INDEMNITY INSURANCE COMPANY—See Everest Reinsurance Holdings; *U.S. Public*, pg. 597
EVEREST INSURANCE COMPANY OF CANADA—See Everest Reinsurance Holdings; *U.S. Public*, pg. 597
EVEREST NATIONAL INSURANCE CO.—See Everest Reinsurance Holdings; *U.S. Public*, pg. 597
EVEREST REINSURANCE CO.—See Everest Reinsurance Holdings; *U.S. Public*, pg. 597
EVEREST REINSURANCE HOLDINGS; *U.S. Public*, pg. 597

EVEREST REINSURANCE, LTD.—See Everest Reinsurance Holdings; *U.S. Public*, pg. 597
EVERETT/CHARLES AUTOMATION SYSTEMS, INC.—See Everett Charles Technologies; *U.S. Private*, pg. 386
EVERETT/CHARLES CONTACT PRODUCTS, INC.—See Everett Charles Technologies; *U.S. Private*, pg. 386
EVERETT CHARLES TECHNOLOGIES; *U.S. Private*, pg. 386
EVERETT/CHARLES TEST EQUIPMENT—See Everett Charles Technologies; *U.S. Private*, pg. 386
EVERETT DIVISION—See The Boeing Company; *U.S. Public*, pg. 240
EVEREX SYSTEMS INC.—See Formosa Plastics Corporation; *Int'l*, pg. 498
EVERFAST INC.; *U.S. Private*, pg. 386
EVERFRESH BEVERAGES INC.—See National Beverage Corp.; *U.S. Public*, pg. 1153
EVERGLADES PIPE LINE COMPANY, L.P.—See Buckeye Partners, L.P.; *U.S. Public*, pg. 266
EVERGLADES SUGAR REFINERY, INC.—See Imperial Holly Corporation; *U.S. Public*, pg. 873
EVERGOOD PRODUCTS CORPORATION; *U.S. Private*, pg. 386
EVERGREEN BUFFETS, INC.—See Buffets, Inc.; *U.S. Public*, pg. 267
EVERGREEN INTERNATIONAL AVIATION, INC.; *U.S. Private*, pg. 386
EVERGREEN MILLS INC.—See Varied Investments, Inc.; *U.S. Private*, pg. 1134
L.G. EVERIST INC.; *U.S. Private*, pg. 386
EVERITE S.A.—See Saint-Gobain; *Int'l*, pg. 1170
EVERLAST SPORTS MANUFACTURING CORP.—See Everlast World Boxing Corp.; *U.S. Private*, pg. 386
EVERLAST WORLD BOXING CORP.; *U.S. Private*, pg. 386
EVERLASTING VALVE CO.—See Armstrong International, Inc.; *U.S. Private*, pg. 83
EVERPURE INC.—See Culligan International Company; *U.S. Public*, pg. 467
EVERSHARP PEN CO.; *U.S. Private*, pg. 386
EVERT HEERE GMBH & CO.—See Fried. Krupp AG; *Int'l*, pg. 513
EVERT LARSSON INDUSTRI AB—See Electrolux, AB; *Int'l*, pg. 439
EVERYDAY LEARNING/CREATIVE PUBLICATIONS GROUP—See Tribune Company; *U.S. Public*, pg. 1635
EVESHAM FOODS—See Northern Foods plc; *Int'l*, pg. 968
EVIAN—See Danone Group; *Int'l*, pg. 381
EVOBUS GMBH—See Daimler-Benz Aktiengesellschaft; *Int'l*, pg. 368
EVOBUS GMBH SETRA OMNIBUSSE—See Daimler-Benz Aktiengesellschaft; *Int'l*, pg. 368
EVODE CLEAREX LTD.—See Laporte plc; *Int'l*, pg. 802
EVODE GROUP LTD.—See Laporte plc; *Int'l*, pg. 802
EVODE LTD.—See Laporte plc; *Int'l*, pg. 802
EVODE SPECIALTY ADHESIVES LTD.—See Laporte plc; *Int'l*, pg. 802
EVOLUON-PHILIPS COMPETENCE CENTRE—See Philips Electronics N.V.; *Int'l*, pg. 1051
EVY OF CALIFORNIA, INC.; *U.S. Private*, pg. 387
EWALD GLEBEL LUXEMBOURG G.M.B.H.—See Arbed S.A.; *Int'l*, pg. 79
EWING COLE CHERRY BROTT; *U.S. Private*, pg. 387
EWING TOWNSHIP-NEW JERSEY DIV.—See EAC Corporation; *U.S. Private*, pg. 353
EWOS AB—See Cultor Ltd.; *Int'l*, pg. 349
EWOS AQUA A.S.—See Cultor Ltd.; *Int'l*, pg. 349
EWOS AQUA A/S—See Cultor Ltd.; *Int'l*, pg. 349
EWOS AQUA A.S, FLORO—See Cultor Ltd.; *Int'l*, pg. 349
EWOS CANADA LTD.—See Cultor Ltd.; *Int'l*, pg. 349
EWOS CHILE S.A.—See Cultor Ltd.; *Int'l*, pg. 349
EWOS LTD.—See Cultor Ltd.; *Int'l*, pg. 349
EWOS POLFARM LTD.—See Cultor Ltd.; *Int'l*, pg. 349
EWOS S.A.—See Cultor Ltd.; *Int'l*, pg. 349
EWOTRA SA—See Accor S.A.; *Int'l*, pg. 21
EX LIBRIS AG—See Migros; *Int'l*, pg. 865
EX MACHINA—See Thomson S.A.; *Int'l*, pg. 1381
EXABYTE CORPORATION; *U.S. Public*, pg. 597
EXABYTE FSC LTD.—See Exabyte Corporation; *U.S. Public*, pg. 597
EXABYTE SCOTLAND LIMITED—See Exabyte Corporation; *U.S. Public*, pg. 597
EXACT EQUIPMENT CORPORATION; *U.S. Private*, pg. 387
EXACT LEVEL—See The L.S. Starrett Company; *U.S. Public*, pg. 1511
EXAR CORPORATION; *U.S. Public*, pg. 597
EXAR CORP.-SOUTHEAST—See EXAR Corporation; *U.S. Public*, pg. 598
EXAR CORP.-WEST—See EXAR Corporation; *U.S. Public*, pg. 598
EXCALIBUR TECHNOLOGIES CORPORATION; *U.S. Public*, pg. 598
EXCALIBUR TECHNOLOGIES INTERNATIONAL, LTD.—See Excalibur Technologies Corporation; *U.S. Public*, pg. 598
EXCAVATOR ENTERPRISES, INC.—See Tenneco Inc.; *U.S. Public*, pg. 1578
EXCEL CO-OP INC.; *U.S. Private*, pg. 387
EXCEL COMMUNICATIONS, INC.; *U.S. Public*, pg. 598
EXCEL CORP.—See Cargill; *U.S. Private*, pg. 210
EXCEL/DIGITRAN—See Microtel International Inc.; *U.S. Public*, pg. 1108
EXCEL INDUSTRIES, INC.; *U.S. Public*, pg. 598
EXCEL INDUSTRIES, INC.; *U.S. Private*, pg. 387
EXCEL OF STOCKTON—See Excel Industries, Inc.; *U.S. Public*, pg. 598
EXCEL TECHNOLOGY, INC.; *U.S. Public*, pg. 599
EXCELIS, INC.—See The First American Financial Corporation; *U.S. Public*, pg. 625
EXCELL MANUFACTURING COMPANY; *U.S. Private*, pg. 387
EXCELLED SHEEPSKIN & LEATHER COAT CORPORATION; *U.S. Private*, pg. 387
THE EXCELLENCE GROUP; *U.S. Private*, pg. 387

EXCELLON AUTOMATION CO.—See Esterline Technologies Corporation; *U.S. Public*, pg. 594
EXCELLON EUROPA GMBH—See Esterline Technologies Corporation; *U.S. Public*, pg. 594
EXCELLON JAPAN—See Esterline Technologies Corporation; *U.S. Public*, pg. 594
EXCELLON U.K.—See Esterline Technologies Corporation; *U.S. Public*, pg. 594
EXCELSIOR HOTEIS E INVESTIMENTOS LIMITADA—See Jardine Matheson Holdings Limited; *Int'l*, pg. 704
EXCELSIOR HOTEL GALLIA S.P.A.—See Granada Group PLC; *Int'l*, pg. 556
THE EXCELSIOR HOTEL, HONG KONG—See Jardine Matheson Holdings Limited; *Int'l*, pg. 704
EXCELSIOR INC.; *U.S. Public*, pg. 387
EXCELSIOR INFORMATIQUE SA—See VNU Verenigde Nederlandse Uitgeversbedrijven B.V.; *Int'l*, pg. 1445
EXCELSIOR MANUFACTURING & SUPPLY CORP.; *U.S. Private*, pg. 387
EXCELSIOR PRINTING CO.—See Crane & Co., Inc.; *U.S. Private*, pg. 286
EXCELSIOR PROCESS & ENGRAVING INC.—See Crane & Co., Inc.; *U.S. Private*, pg. 286
EXCENTRA GMBH HYDRAULISCHE ANTRIEBE—See Mannesmann A.G.; *Int'l*, pg. 838
EXCERPTA MEDICA INC.—See Reed Elsevier plc; *Int'l*, pg. 1100
EXCERPTA MEDICA MEDICAL COMMUNICATIONS BV—See Reed Elsevier plc; *Int'l*, pg. 1099
EXCHANGE BANK; *U.S. Public*, pg. 599
EXCHANGE BANK OF DUPAGE—See ABN-AMRO Holding N.V.; *Int'l*, pg. 10
EXCHANGE CAPITAL CORPORATION—See Robert Fleming Holdings Ltd.; *Int'l*, pg. 493
EXCHANGE INSURANCE COMPANY—See Selective Insurance Group, Inc; *U.S. Public*, pg. 1455
EXCITE, INC.; *U.S. Public*, pg. 599
EXCLAY SUOMI OY—See Scancem AB; *Int'l*, pg. 1200
EXCLUSIVE HEALTHCARE, INC.—See Mutual of Omaha Insurance Company; *U.S. Private*, pg. 770
EXCORIM AB—See Incentive AB; *Int'l*, pg. 667
EXECORP—See Aerospatiale; *Int'l*, pg. 29
EXECUTION SERVICES INCORPORATED—See The Industrial Bank of Japan, Limited; *Int'l*, pg. 675
EXECUTIVE AIRLINES—See AMR Corporation; *U.S. Public*, pg. 9
EXECUTIVE CAPITAL CORP.; *U.S. Private*, pg. 388
EXECUTIVE CAR LEASING COMPANY—See Executive Car Leasing, Inc.; *U.S. Private*, pg. 388
EXECUTIVE CAR LEASING, INC.; *U.S. Private*, pg. 388
EXECUTIVE COURIER, INC.—See Wallace Computer Services, Inc.; *U.S. Public*, pg. 1736
EXECUTIVE JET AVIATION, INC.; *U.S. Private*, pg. 388
EXECUTIVE MANAGEMENT AND CONSULTANT SERVICES, INC.—See AEGON N.V.; *Int'l*, pg. 27
EXECUTIVE PARK, INC.—See Cigna Corp.; *U.S. Public*, pg. 365
EXECUTIVE PRODUCTIVITY SYSTEMS, INC.; *U.S. Private*, pg. 388
EXECUTIVE RISK, INC.; *U.S. Public*, pg. 599
EXECUTIVE SOFTWARE; *U.S. Private*, pg. 388
EXECUTIVE SUPERINTENDENCY FOR EXPLORATION & PRODUCTION (SUEX)—See Petrobras - Petroleo Brasileiro S.A.; *Int'l*, pg. 1041
EXECUTONE INFORMATION SYSTEMS, INC.; *U.S. Public*, pg. 599
EXEL INSURANCE CO. LTD.; *U.S. Public*, pg. 467
EXEL LOGISTICS—See NFC plc; *Int'l*, pg. 901
EXEL LOGISTICS NORTH AMERICA—See NFC plc; *Int'l*, pg. 901
EXEL MICROELECTRONICS, INC.—See Rohm Co., Ltd.; *Int'l*, pg. 1125
EXEL ÖSTERREICH—See Neste Oy; *Int'l*, pg. 914
EXEL OY—See Neste Oy; *Int'l*, pg. 913
EXELKA S.A.—See Standard Commercial Corporation; *U.S. Public*, pg. 1502
EXETER & HAMPTON ELECTRIC CO.—See Unitil Corporation; *U.S. Public*, pg. 1692
EXETER REASSURANCE COMPANY, LTD.—See Metropolitan Life Insurance Co.; *U.S. Private*, pg. 738
EXHIBITGROUP/GILTSPUR—See Viad Corp; *U.S. Public*, pg. 1718
EXIDE CORPORATION; *U.S. Public*, pg. 600
EXIDE ELECTRONICS CANADA, INC.—See BTR plc; *Int'l*, pg. 126
EXIDE ELECTRONICS DE MEXICO—See BTR plc; *Int'l*, pg. 126
EXIDE ELECTRONICS GROUP, INC.—See BTR plc; *Int'l*, pg. 126
EXIDE ELECTRONICS INTERNATIONAL-GMBH—See BTR plc; *Int'l*, pg. 126
EXIDE ELECTRONICS INTERNATIONAL/IPM—See BTR plc; *Int'l*, pg. 126
EXIDE ELECTRONICS S.A.—See BTR plc; *Int'l*, pg. 126
EXISA CONSTRUCTIONES S.A.—See Lafarge S.A.; *Int'l*, pg. 790
EXLED WARENHANDELSGESELLSCHAFT MBH—See Freudenberg & Company; *Int'l*, pg. 506
EXOLON-ESK COMPANY; *U.S. Public*, pg. 600
THE EXOLON-ESK COMPANY OF CANADA LTD.—See Exolon-Esk Company; *U.S. Public*, pg. 600
EXOR AMERICA—See Exor Group; *Int'l*, pg. 467
EXOR GROUP; *Int'l*, pg. 467
EXOR S.A.—See Exor Group; *Int'l*, pg. 467
EXOTHERMICS-ECLIPSE, INC.—See Eclipse Inc.; *U.S. Private*, pg. 360
EXOTIC RUBBER & PLASTICS CORP.; *U.S. Private*, pg. 388
EXPAMET BUILDING PRODUCTS—See Expamet International Plc; *Int'l*, pg. 467
EXPAMET FENCING—See Expamet International Plc; *Int'l*, pg. 467
EXPAMET INTERNATIONAL PLC; *Int'l*, pg. 467

EXPANDED METAL INDUSTRIAL—See Expamet International Plc; *Int'l*, pg. 467
EXPANDITE S.A.—See Burmah Castrol plc; *Int'l*, pg. 236
EXPANDITES SECOMASTIC A/S—See Burmah Castrol plc; *Int'l*, pg. 236
EXPANSION VALVE DIVISION—See Parker Hannifin Corporation; *U.S. Public*, pg. 1260
EXPASA ANSTALT—See Sao Paulo Alpargatas S.A.; *Int'l*, pg. 1193
EXPECTING—See Bertelsmann AG; *Int'l*, pg. 190
EXPEDITIEBEDRIJF GAMEX B.V.—See Gamma Holding N.V.; *Int'l*, pg. 540
EXPEDITORS INTERNATIONAL OCEAN, INC.—See Expeditors International of Washington, Inc.; *U.S. Public*, pg. 600
EXPEDITORS INTERNATIONAL OF WASHINGTON, INC.; *U.S. Public*, pg. 600
EXPERIENCE IN SOFTWARE, INC.; *U.S. Public*, pg. 388
EXPERT BOIS ET MATERIAUX—See La Meridionale des Bois et Materiaux; *Int'l*, pg. 784
EXPERT SYSTEMS, INC.—See National Health Enhancement Systems, Inc.; *U.S. Public*, pg. 1157
EXPLO-MIDWEST, INC.—See Imperial Chemical Industries PLC; *Int'l*, pg. 663
EXPLOITATIEMAATSCHAPPIJ LELIEGRACHT B.V.—See Koninklijke BolsWessanen nv; *Int'l*, pg. 751
EXPLOITATIEMAATSCHAPPIJ ROZENGRACHT B.V.—See Koninklijke BolsWessanen nv; *Int'l*, pg. 751
EXPLOITATIEMAATSCHAPPIJ TRANSPORTBETON B.V.—See Ballast Nedam NV; *Int'l*, pg. 134
EXPLONOR, INC.—See Imperial Chemical Industries PLC; *Int'l*, pg. 664
EXPLORATION COMPUTING LIMITED—See Halliburton Company; *U.S. Public*, pg. 776
EXPLORATION COORDINATION & CONTROL (GECEX)—See Petrobras - Petroleo Brasileiro S.A.; *Int'l*, pg. 1041
EXPLORATION & PRODUCTION RESEARCH CENTER—See Chinese Petroleum Corporation; *Int'l*, pg. 286
EXPLORER PIPELINE CO.—See Texaco Inc.; *U.S. Public*, pg. 1584
EXPLOSIVES DIV.—See Nippon Kayaku Co. Ltd.; *Int'l*, pg. 934
EXPLOSIVOS MEXICANOS S.A. DE C.V.—See Imperial Chemical Industries PLC; *Int'l*, pg. 664
EXPLOTACION Y COMERCIALIZACION DE AGUAS MINERALES S.A.—See Nestle S.A.; *Int'l*, pg. 920
EXPO PARTES S.A. DE C.V.—See Varco International, Inc.; *U.S. Public*, pg. 1709
EXPOCHEM S.R.O.—See Enso Oyj; *Int'l*, pg. 458
EXPOPAK OY—See Enso Oyj; *Int'l*, pg. 458
EXPOPESCA—See EMAP Plc; *Int'l*, pg. 452
EXPORT FINANCE CORPORATION OF CANADA LIMITED—See Canadian Imperial Bank of Commerce; *Int'l*, pg. 257
THE EXPORT-IMPORT BANK OF KOREA; *Int'l*, pg. 467
EXPORT SALES & DISTRIBUTION—See Delta plc; *Int'l*, pg. 390
EXPORTADORA DE TABACO DE CEUTA Y MELILLA, S.A.—See Tabacalera, S.A.; *Int'l*, pg. 1345
EXPORTADORA DE TABACOS TRANS-CONTINENTAL LTDA.—See Standard Commercial Corporation; *U.S. Public*, pg. 1502
EXPORTSLACHTERIJ UDEMA B.V.—See Unilever Plc; *Int'l*, pg. 1437
THE EXPOSITOR—See Hollinger Inc.; *Int'l*, pg. 631
EXPOXIQUIM, C.A.—See Corporacion Grupo Quimico, S.A.C.A.; *Int'l*, pg. 332
EXPRESS—See The Limited, Inc.; *U.S. Public*, pg. 995
EXPRESS NEWSPAPERS PLC—See United News & Media plc; *Int'l*, pg. 1443
EXPRESS 1 STOP—See Sullivan Oil Company; *U.S. Private*, pg. 1050
EXPRESS SCRIPTS, INC.; *U.S. Public*, pg. 600
EXPRESS SCRIPTS VISION—See Express Scripts, Inc.; *U.S. Public*, pg. 601
EXPRESSVU INC.—See BCE Inc.; *Int'l*, pg. 115
EXQUISITE FORM BRASSIERE (GB) LTD.—See AGP Industrial Corporation; *Int'l*, pg. 14
EXSIL, INC.—See Laporte plc; *Int'l*, pg. 802
EXSOL, INC.—See Seitel, Inc.; *U.S. Public*, pg. 1454
EXTAND—See GEODIS; *Int'l*, pg. 549
EXTEL—See Pearson plc; *Int'l*, pg. 1025
EXTENDICARE (CANADA) INC.—See Extendicare Inc.; *Int'l*, pg. 468
EXTENDICARE INC.; *Int'l*, pg. 468
EXTENDICARE PROPERTIES, INC.—See Columbia/HCA Healthcare Corporation; *U.S. Public*, pg. 404
EXTENSIVE TRADING CO., LTD.—See GESTRA GmbH; *Int'l*, pg. 550
EXTERNA HANDELS- UND BETEILIGUNGSGESELLSCHAFT MBH—See Freudenberg & Company; *Int'l*, pg. 506
EXTERNA S.A.—See Freudenberg & Company; *Int'l*, pg. 507
EXTON SQUARE, INC.—See The Rouse Company; *U.S. Public*, pg. 1407
EXTRACT-OIL, A.S.—See Chr. Hansen Holding A/S; *Int'l*, pg. 288
EXTRATEC AS—See Norsk Hydro a.s; *Int'l*, pg. 959
EXTREMULTUS INDUSTRIA DE CORREIAS LTDA.—See Forbo Holding SA; *Int'l*, pg. 497
EXXON ASSET MANAGEMENT COMPANY—See Exxon Corporation; *U.S. Public*, pg. 601
EXXON BIOMEDICAL SCIENCES INC.—See Exxon Corporation; *U.S. Public*, pg. 601
EXXON CHEMICAL ASSET MANAGEMENT PARTNERSHIP—See Exxon Corporation; *U.S. Public*, pg. 601
EXXON CHEMICAL COMPANY—See Exxon Corporation; *U.S. Public*, pg. 601
EXXON CHEMICAL LIMITED—See Exxon Corporation; *U.S. Public*, pg. 602
EXXON CHEMICAL OLEFINS INC.—See Exxon Corporation; *U.S. Public*, pg. 602

EXXON CHEMICAL POLYMERES, SNC—See Exxon Corporation; *U.S. Public*, pg. 602
EXXON CHEMICAL POLYMERS, ENG.—See Exxon Corporation; *U.S. Public*, pg. 601
EXXON COAL AND MINERALS COMPANY—See Exxon Corporation; *U.S. Public*, pg. 601
EXXON COAL AUSTRALIA LTD.—See Exxon Corporation; *U.S. Public*, pg. 601
EXXON COMPANY INTERNATIONAL—See Exxon Corporation; *U.S. Public*, pg. 601
EXXON COMPANY, U.S.A.—See Exxon Corporation; *U.S. Public*, pg. 601
EXXON COMPUTING SERVICES COMPANY—See Exxon Corporation; *U.S. Public*, pg. 601
EXXON CORPORATION; *U.S. Public*, pg. 601
EXXON EXPLORATION COMPANY—See Exxon Corporation; *U.S. Public*, pg. 601
EXXON INSURANCE HOLDINGS, INC.—See Exxon Corporation; *U.S. Public*, pg. 602
EXXON PIPELINE COMPANY—See Exxon Corporation; *U.S. Public*, pg. 601
EXXON TRADING ASIA PACIFIC PRIVATE LIMITED—See Exxon Corporation; *U.S. Public*, pg. 602
EXXON UPSTREAM TECHNICAL COMPUTING COMPANY—See Exxon Corporation; *U.S. Public*, pg. 601
EXXON YEMEN INC.—See Exxon Corporation; *U.S. Public*, pg. 601
EYECARE (THAILAND) LIMITED—See Novartis AG; *Int'l*, pg. 982
EYELET IBERICA, S.A.—See Crown Cork & Seal Company, Inc.; *U.S. Public*, pg. 464
EYELET MEXICANA S.A. DE C.V.—See Crown Cork & Seal Company, Inc.; *U.S. Public*, pg. 464
EZON PRODUCTS, INC.; *U.S. Private*, pg. 388

F

F&B MANUFACTURING CO.; *U.S. Private*, pg. 388
F & E COMMUNITY DEVELOPERS OF FLORIDA, INC.—See Columbia/HCA Healthcare Corporation; *U.S. Public*, pg. 404
F&F FOODS; *U.S. Private*, pg. 388
F & F PRODUCTIONS, INC.—See Hubbard Broadcasting, Inc.; *U.S. Private*, pg. 544
F&G RE, INC.—See USF&G Corporation; *U.S. Public*, pg. 1659
F&P HOLDING, INC.—See ELSAG Bailey Process Automation N.V.; *Int'l*, pg. 449
F&S INCORPORATED—See Veba AG; *Int'l*, pg. 1458
F & W PUBLICATIONS, INC.; *U.S. Public*, pg. 388
F & Z BAUGESELLSCHAFT MBH—See Bilfinger + Berger Bauaktiengesellschaft; *Int'l*, pg. 195
FCB; *U.S. Private*, pg. 389
F C L GRAPHICS; *U.S. Private*, pg. 389
F-M TOWER COMPANY—See Nextel Communications; *U.S. Public*, pg. 1180
F-P ELECTRONICS—See Mark IV Industries Inc.; *U.S. Public*, pg. 1045
F.R. GROSS COMPANY—See Ampco-Pittsburgh Corporation; *U.S. Public*, pg. 103
F.A.A.—See Vendex International N.V.; *Int'l*, pg. 1463
FAB INDUSTRIES, INC.; *U.S. Public*, pg. 603
FABC (NEW YORK) GRP.—See Banque Nationale de Paris; *Int'l*, pg. 163
THE FACS GROUP—See Federated Department Stores, Inc.; *U.S. Public*, pg. 618
FACS RECORDS CENTRE INC.—See Western Corporate Enterprises Inc.; *Int'l*, pg. 1494
FAG AIRCRAFT/SUPER PRECISION BEARINGS, GMBH—See FAG Group; *Int'l*, pg. 468
FAG AUSTRALIA PTY. LTD.—See FAG Group; *Int'l*, pg. 469
FAG AUSTRIA WAELZLAGER AG—See FAG Group; *Int'l*, pg. 469
FAG AUTOMOBILTECHNIK AG—See FAG Group; *Int'l*, pg. 468
FAG BEARINGS CORPORATION—See FAG Group; *Int'l*, pg. 469
FAG BEARINGS LIMITED—See FAG Group; *Int'l*, pg. 469
FAG BELGIUM S.A. N.V.—See FAG Group; *Int'l*, pg. 469
FAG DANMARK A/S—See FAG Group; *Int'l*, pg. 469
FAG ESPANOLA S.A.—See FAG Group; *Int'l*, pg. 469
FAG FINLAND OY—See FAG Group; *Int'l*, pg. 469
FAG FRANCE—See FAG Group; *Int'l*, pg. 469
FAG GROUP; *Int'l*, pg. 468
FAG HOLDING CORPORATION—See FAG Group; *Int'l*, pg. 468
FAG INFORMATION SERVICES INC.—See FAG Group; *Int'l*, pg. 468
FAG INTERAMERICANA AG—See FAG Group; *Int'l*, pg. 469
FAG ITALIA S.P.A.—See FAG Group; *Int'l*, pg. 469
FAG JAPAN CO. LTD.—See FAG Group; *Int'l*, pg. 469
FAG KOMPONENTEN AG—See FAG Group; *Int'l*, pg. 468
FAG KUGELFISCHER GEORG SCHAFER AG—See FAG Group; *Int'l*, pg. 468
FAG NEDERLAND B.V.—See FAG Group; *Int'l*, pg. 469
FAG NORGE A/S—See FAG Group; *Int'l*, pg. 469
FAG OEM UND HANDEL AG—See FAG Group; *Int'l*, pg. 468
FAG PERSONALDIENSTE U. SERVICE GMBH—See FAG Group; *Int'l*, pg. 468
FAG S.A.—See Bobst S.A.; *Int'l*, pg. 198
FAG (SCHWEIZ)—See FAG Group; *Int'l*, pg. 469
FAG SOUTH AFRICA (PTY.) LTD.—See FAG Group; *Int'l*, pg. 469
FAG SOUTH EAST ASIA PTE. LTD.—See FAG Group; *Int'l*, pg. 469
FAG SVENSKA AB—See FAG Group; *Int'l*, pg. 469
FAG (UK) LIMITED—See FAG Group; *Int'l*, pg. 469
F.A.I. TRADING COMPANY—See H.B. Fuller Company; *U.S. Public*, pg. 686

F.A.O. SCHWARZ—See N.V. Koninklijke Bijenkorf Beheer KBB; *Int'l*, pg. 750
AB FAS LASFABRIK—See Assa Abloy AB; *Int'l*, pg. 17
FAW-VOLKSWAGEN AUTOMOTIVE COMPANY CO. LTD.—See Volkswagen AG; *Int'l*, pg. 1475
FBC HOLDINGS (PTY.) LTD.—See Schering AG; *Int'l*, pg. 1204
FBC FINANCE CO.—See Farmer Brothers Company; *U.S. Public*, pg. 613
FBFC—See Framatome SA; *Int'l*, pg. 503
FBOH CREDIT LIFE INSURANCE CO.—See FirstMerit Corporation; *U.S. Public*, pg. 647
FBS INFORMATION SERVICES CORPORATION—See U.S. Bancorp; *U.S. Public*, pg. 1681
FBS LIFE INSURANCE COMPANY—See U.S. Bancorp; *U.S. Public*, pg. 1681
FBT-FINANCE BY TRADE GMBH—See Bankgesellschaft Berlin; *Int'l*, pg. 159
F. C. BANKS—See Federal Farm Credit Banks Funding Corporation; *U.S. Private*, pg. 398
F.C. BURTON L.D. CORP.—See Forest City Enterprises, Inc.; *U.S. Public*, pg. 668
F.C. HEDGED MORTGAGE CO.—See Forest City Enterprises, Inc.; *U.S. Public*, pg. 668
F.C. LAUREL, INC.—See Forest City Enterprises, Inc.; *U.S. Public*, pg. 668
FC NEW YORK, INC.—See Nextel Communications; *U.S. Public*, pg. 1180
F.C. PARKLABREA TOWERS, INC.—See Forest City Enterprises, Inc.; *U.S. Public*, pg. 668
F.C. PROPERTIES CO.—See Forest City Enterprises, Inc.; *U.S. Public*, pg. 668
F.C. SOUTHRIDGE CORP.—See Forest City Enterprises, Inc.; *U.S. Public*, pg. 668
F.C. TEANECK, INC.—See Forest City Enterprises, Inc.; *U.S. Public*, pg. 668
FCA!—See FCA!BMZ; *Int'l*, pg. 470
FCA!BMZ; *Int'l*, pg. 469
FCA!BMZ—See FCA!BMZ; *Int'l*, pg. 470
FCA!BMZ AMSTERDAM—See FCA!BMZ; *Int'l*, pg. 470
FCA!BMZ BARCELONA—See FCA!BMZ; *Int'l*, pg. 470
FCA!BMZ CID; *Int'l*, pg. 469
FCA!BMZ CID BARCELONA—See FCA!BMZ CID; *Int'l*, pg. 469
FCA!BMZ CID BILBAO—See FCA!BMZ CID; *Int'l*, pg. 469
FCA!BMZ CID/VALENCIA—See FCA!BMZ CID; *Int'l*, pg. 469
FCA!BMZ FRANCE—See FCA!BMZ; *Int'l*, pg. 469
FCA!BMZ MADRID—See FCA!BMZ; *Int'l*, pg. 470
FCA!BMZ PARIS—See FCA!BMZ; *Int'l*, pg. 469
FCA!BMZ PARK—See FCA!BMZ; *Int'l*, pg. 470
FCA!BMZ SEVILLA—See FCA!BMZ; *Int'l*, pg. 470
FCA HOLDINGS, INC.—See FCA International Ltd.; *Int'l*, pg. 471
FCA INTERNATIONAL LTD.; *Int'l*, pg. 470
FCA TRANSACTION SERVICES, INC.—See FCA International Ltd.; *Int'l*, pg. 471
FCB BRUSSELS—See FCB; *U.S. Private*, pg. 389
FCB FREIZEIT-CLUB BETREUUNGS-GMBH & CO.—See Otto Versand (GmbH & Co.); *Int'l*, pg. 1014
FCB HEALTHCARE—See True North Communications Inc.; *U.S. Public*, pg. 1641
FCB SINGAPORE—See FCB; *U.S. Private*, pg. 389
FCC NATIONAL BANK—See First Chicago NBD Corporation; *U.S. Public*, pg. 627
F.C.D. PARMA LIMITED DIVIDEND CORP.—See Forest City Enterprises, Inc.; *U.S. Public*, pg. 668
FCI 900, INC.—See Nextel Communications; *U.S. Public*, pg. 1180
FCI SMR COMPANY—See Nextel Communications; *U.S. Public*, pg. 1180
FCM UNTERNEHMENSVERWALTUNGS-AG—See Schering AG; *Int'l*, pg. 1203
FCN CORPORATION—See KOHAP Group; *Int'l*, pg. 742
FCR (FRANCE CABLES ET RADIO)—See France Telecom; *Int'l*, pg. 503
FCS CURRENCY MANAGEMENT—See The British Land Company PLC; *Int'l*, pg. 219
FCW PUBLISHING CORP.—See International Data Group; *U.S. Private*, pg. 569
FDC REPORTS INC.—See Reed Elsevier plc; *Int'l*, pg. 1100
FDK TATUNG CO. LTD.—See Tatung Corporation; *Int'l*, pg. 1357
FDL FOODS, INC.—See Farmland Industries, Inc.; *U.S. Private*, pg. 396
FDP CORP.; *U.S. Public*, pg. 603
FDX CORPORATION; *U.S. Public*, pg. 603
FE MAGNET WIRE (MALAYSIA) SDN. BHD.—See Furukawa Electric Co., Ltd.; *Int'l*, pg. 530
FEB LTD.—See Novartis AG; *Int'l*, pg. 982
FEC CONSULT GES. F. MANAGEMENT- UND BETEILIGUNGSBERATUNG MBH—See Landesbank Hessen-Thuringen Girozentrale; *Int'l*, pg. 799
FEF CHEMICALS A/S—See Novo Nordisk A/S; *Int'l*, pg. 987
F.E.P. U.K. LIMITED—See Lagardere Groupe; *Int'l*, pg. 795
FFE TRANSPORTATION SERVICES, INC.—See Frozen Food Express Industries, Inc.; *U.S. Public*, pg. 685
FFG INVESTMENTS, INC.—See Firstbank of Illinois Co.; *U.S. Public*, pg. 644
FFG TRUST, INC.—See Firstbank of Illinois Co.; *U.S. Public*, pg. 644
FFI PRODUCTION OY—See Cultor Ltd.; *Int'l*, pg. 349
FFP FINANCIAL SERVICES, L.P.—See FFP Marketing Company, Inc.; *U.S. Public*, pg. 604
FFP MARKETING COMPANY, INC.; *U.S. Public*, pg. 604
FFV AEROTECH AB—See Celsius AB; *Int'l*, pg. 276
FFV AEROTECH INC.—See Celsius AB; *Int'l*, pg. 276
FFV AVIOCOMP AB—See Celsius AB; *Int'l*, pg. 276
FFV FINANCE INC.—See Celsius AB; *Int'l*, pg. 278
FFV JAPAN KK—See Celsius AB; *Int'l*, pg. 278
FFV MATTEKNIK AB—See Celsius AB; *Int'l*, pg. 277
FFV TEST SYSTEMS AB—See Celsius AB; *Int'l*, pg. 277

FGH BANK N.V.—See AEGON N.V.; *Int'l*, pg. 26
FGI INC.; *U.S. Private*, pg. 389
FGI NEW YORK—See FGI Inc.; *U.S. Private*, pg. 389
FGI RESEARCH, WASHINGTON—See FGI Inc.; *U.S. Private*, pg. 389
FH CENTER, INC.—See First Hawaiian, Inc.; *U.S. Public*, pg. 635
FHB PROPERTIES, INC.—See First Hawaiian, Inc.; *U.S. Public*, pg. 635
FHE SERVICES, INC.—See Kone Corporation; *Int'l*, pg. 746
FHI BENEFIT SYSTEMS, INC.—See Robert F. Driver Co., Inc.; *U.S. Private*, pg. 343
FHI INTERNATIONAL, INC.—See First Hawaiian, Inc.; *U.S. Public*, pg. 634
FHL LEASE HOLDING COMPANY, INC.—See First Hawaiian; *U.S. Public*, pg. 634
FHP DI R. FREUDENBERT S.A.S.—See Freudenberg & Company; *Int'l*, pg. 506
FHP EXPORT GMBH—See Freudenberg & Company; *Int'l*, pg. 506
FHP, FREUDENBERG HOUSEHOLD PRODUCTS AB—See Freudenberg & Company; *Int'l*, pg. 505
FHP, FREUDENBERG HOUSEHOLD PRODUCTS OY AB—See Freudenberg & Company; *Int'l*, pg. 506
FHP VILEDA S.A.—See Freudenberg & Company; *Int'l*, pg. 506
FHP VILEDA SP. Z.O.O.—See Freudenberg & Company; *Int'l*, pg. 506
FIAR-FABBRICA ITALIANA APPARECCHIATURE RADIOELECTTRICHE S.P.A.—See Telefonaktiebolaget LM Ericsson; *Int'l*, pg. 1368
FIDCO (FOOD INGREDIENT DEVELOPMENT COMPANY)—See Nestle S.A.; *Int'l*, pg. 917
FIL (U.S.) INC.—See Russel Metals Inc.; *Int'l*, pg. 1151
FIMA-PRODUCTOS ALIMENTARES, LDA; *Int'l*, pg. 471
F.I.R. FABBRICA ITALIANA RELE S.P.A.—See The General Electric Company, p.l.c.; *Int'l*, pg. 546
FISI MADISON FINANCIAL CORPORATION—See Cendant Corporation; *U.S. Public*, pg. 320
FKG OIL COMPANY—See Moto, Inc.; *U.S. Private*, pg. 764
FKI FAI KOMATSU INDUSTRIES, S.P.A.—See FKI Plc; *Int'l*, pg. 474
FKI FAI KOMATSU INDUSTRIES, S.P.A.—See Komatsu Ltd.; *Int'l*, pg. 745
FKI INDUSTRIES. INC.—See FKI Plc; *Int'l*, pg. 472
FKI PLC; *Int'l*, pg. 471
FKL DONG HWA LTD.—See Fujitsu Limited; *Int'l*, pg. 528
FLC SHOP AG—See Fotolabo S.A.; *Int'l*, pg. 501
FLO-TECH WELDING & CUTTING SYSTEMS LTD.—See Charter plc; *Int'l*, pg. 283
FLS AEROSPACE ENGINEERING LTD.—See FLS Industries A/S; *Int'l*, pg. 475
FLS AEROSPACE (LOVAUX) LTD.—See FLS Industries A/S; *Int'l*, pg. 475
FLS AEROSPACE LTD.—See FLS Industries A/S; *Int'l*, pg. 475
FLS AEROSPACE SUPPORT LTD.—See FLS Industries A/S; *Int'l*, pg. 475
FLS AUTOMATION A/S—See FLS Industries A/S; *Int'l*, pg. 475
FLS CEMENT INVESTMENTS A/S—See FLS Industries A/S; *Int'l*, pg. 476
FLS DATA A/S—See FLS Industries A/S; *Int'l*, pg. 476
FLS ENERGY A/S—See FLS Industries A/S; *Int'l*, pg. 476
FLS FINANCE A/S—See FLS Industries A/S; *Int'l*, pg. 476
FLS FRANCE S.A.R.L.—See FLS Industries A/S; *Int'l*, pg. 476
FLS INDUSTRIES A/S; *Int'l*, pg. 474
FLS JAPAN LTD.—See FLS Industries A/S; *Int'l*, pg. 475
FLS MASKINTEKNIK A/S—See FLS Industries A/S; *Int'l*, pg. 475
FLS MILJO A/S—See FLS Industries A/S; *Int'l*, pg. 475
FLS REAL ESTATE A/S—See FLS Industries A/S; *Int'l*, pg. 476
FM SERVICES CORPORATION—See Payco American Corporation; *U.S. Public*, pg. 1267
FMB S.A. - PRODUCTOS METALLURGICOS—See Fiat Auto SpA; *Int'l*, pg. 483
FMC AGROQUIMICA DE MEXICO SI DE R.L. DE C.V.—See FMC Corporation; *U.S. Public*, pg. 606
FMC ARGENTINA, S.A. C.I., Y.F.—See FMC Corporation; *U.S. Public*, pg. 606
FMC (AUSTRALIA) LIMITED—See FMC Corporation; *U.S. Public*, pg. 606
FMC CAMEROON SARL—See FMC Corporation; *U.S. Public*, pg. 606
FMC CORPORATION; *U.S. Public*, pg. 604
FMC CORP., AGRICULTURAL PRODUCTS GROUP—See FMC Corporation; *U.S. Public*, pg. 605
FMC CORP., LITHIUM DIVISION—See FMC Corporation; *U.S. Public*, pg. 605
FMC-CROSBY VALVE, INC.—See FMC Corporation; *U.S. Public*, pg. 605
FMC DO BRASIL, S.A.—See FMC Corporation; *U.S. Public*, pg. 606
FMC EUROPE NV—See FMC Corporation; *U.S. Public*, pg. 606
FMC EUROPE, S.A./N.V.—See FMC Corporation; *U.S. Public*, pg. 606
FMC FINANCE LIMITED—See FMC Corporation; *U.S. Public*, pg. 606
FMC FOOD INGREDIENTS DIV.—See FMC Corporation; *U.S. Public*, pg. 605
FMC FOOD MACHINERY EUROPE, S.A.—See FMC Corporation; *U.S. Public*, pg. 606
FMC FOOD MACHINERY FRANCE, S.A.—See FMC Corporation; *U.S. Public*, pg. 606
FMC FOOD MACHINERY (ITALY) S.P.A.—See FMC Corporation; *U.S. Public*, pg. 606
FMC FOODTECH/FRAN RICA—See FMC Corporation; *U.S. Public*, pg. 605
FMC GOLD CO.—See FMC Corporation; *U.S. Public*, pg. 605

FMC GUATEMALA, S.A.—See FMC Corporation; *U.S. Public*, pg. 606
FMC HELLAS EPE—See FMC Corporation; *U.S. Public*, pg. 606
FMC INSURANCE COMPANY LIMITED—See FMC Corporation; *U.S. Public*, pg. 606
FMC INTERNATIONAL, A.G.—See FMC Corporation; *U.S. Public*, pg. 606
FMC (IRELAND) LIMITED—See FMC Corporation; *U.S. Public*, pg. 606
FMC MACHINERY (GERMANY) GMBH—See FMC Corporation; *U.S. Public*, pg. 606
FMC MARINE COLLOIDS DIV.—See FMC Corporation; *U.S. Public*, pg. 605
FMC MATERIAL HANDLING SYSTEMS DIVISION—See FMC Corporation; *U.S. Public*, pg. 605
FMC NEDERLAND B.V.—See FMC Corporation; *U.S. Public*, pg. 606
FMC OF CANADA LIMITED—See FMC Corporation; *U.S. Public*, pg. 606
FMC PACKAGING MACHINERY, S.P.A.—See FMC Corporation; *U.S. Public*, pg. 606
FMC-SMITH METER CO.—See FMC Corporation; *U.S. Public*, pg. 605
FMC SOUTH AFRICA (PTY.) LIMITED—See FMC Corporation; *U.S. Public*, pg. 606
FMC SOUTHEAST ASIA PTE. LTD.—See FMC Corporation; *U.S. Public*, pg. 606
FMC S.P.A.—See FMC Corporation; *U.S. Public*, pg. 606
FMC WYOMING CORP.—See FMC Corporation; *U.S. Public*, pg. 605
F.M.K. CO., LTD.—See Caterpillar Inc.; *U.S. Public*, pg. 317
FMP-RAUMA COMPANY—See UPM-Kymmene Corporation; *Int'l*, pg. 1428
FMR CORP.—See Fidelity Investments (FMR Corp.); *U.S. Private*, pg. 403
FMS MANAGEMENT SYSTEMS, INC.; *U.S. Private*, pg. 389
FMU LTD.—See BBA Group plc; *Int'l*, pg. 113
F/N GROUP, INC.—See American International Group, Inc.; *U.S. Public*, pg. 84
FN HERSTAL S.A.—See Herstal S.A.; *Int'l*, pg. 617
F.N.B. BUILDING CORPORATION—See F.N.B. Corporation; *U.S. Public*, pg. 607
F.N.B. CORPORATION; *U.S. Public*, pg. 607
FNCB FINANCIAL, LTD.—See Citicorp; *U.S. Public*, pg. 379
FO-MAC DIVISION—See Furon Company; *U.S. Public*, pg. 689
F.O.S. FIBRE OTTICHE SUD S.P.A.—See Pirelli S.p.A.; *Int'l*, pg. 1058
FP CAMEOCOLOR, INC.—See Fleming Packaging Corp.; *U.S. Private*, pg. 411
FPA CORPORATION; *U.S. Public*, pg. 608
F.P.A., INC.; *U.S. Private*, pg. 389
FPA MEDICAL MANAGEMENT, INC.; *U.S. Public*, pg. 608
FPB BANK HOLDING COMPANY LIMITED—See First Pacific Company Limited; *Int'l*, pg. 487
FPB HOLDING AG—See Stora Kopparbergs Bergslags AB; *Int'l*, pg. 1303
FPC, INC.—See Eastman Kodak Company; *U.S. Public*, pg. 551
FPL GROUP, INC.; *U.S. Public*, pg. 608
FPS POWER SYSTEMS A/S—See Fiskars Oy AB; *Int'l*, pg. 492
FPS POWER SYSTEMS OY AB—See Fiskars Oy AB; *Int'l*, pg. 492
FRB CONNECTRON SA—See Smiths Industries plc; *Int'l*, pg. 1268
FRI KÖPENSKAP FORLAGS AB—See Axel Johnson AB; *Int'l*, pg. 708
FRL, INC.—See Cohu, Inc.; *U.S. Public*, pg. 396
FS CANADA, INC.—See Opal Concepts, Inc.; *U.S. Private*, pg. 818
FS CONCEPTS, INC.—See Opal Concepts, Inc.; *U.S. Private*, pg. 818
FSA REBUILDING OF VIRGINIA, INC.—See Varlen Corporation; *Int'l*, pg. 1711
FSE PTY. LTD.—See Rhone-Poulenc S.A.; *Int'l*, pg. 1111
FSEC, INC.—See Arctic Slope Regional Corporation; *U.S. Private*, pg. 80
FSF FINANCIAL CORP.; *U.S. Public*, pg. 608
FSG HOLDING GMBH—See Ruhrgas Aktiengesellschaft; *Int'l*, pg. 1148
FSI-MIDDLE EAST—See Williams Holdings Plc; *Int'l*, pg. 1500
FSP LABORATOIRES PHARMEUROP S.A.—See Unilever Plc; *Int'l*, pg. 1437
FSQ TAIWAN CO. LTD.—See AB SKF; *Int'l*, pg. 1157
FSSL LTD.—See Kvaerner a.s.a.; *Int'l*, pg. 772
FSW COATINGS LIMITED—See The Sherwin-Williams Company; *U.S. Public*, pg. 1466
FSW LTD.—See The Sherwin-Williams Company; *U.S. Public*, pg. 1466
FT INFORMATION—See Pearson plc; *Int'l*, pg. 1025
FT MORTGAGE—See First Tennessee National Corporation; *U.S. Public*, pg. 639
F.T. PUBLICATIONS INC.—See Pearson plc; *Int'l*, pg. 1026
FTD, INC./FLORISTS TRANSWORLD DELIVERY, INC.; *U.S. Private*, pg. 389
FTI-BANQUE FIDUCIARY TRUST—See Fiduciary Trust Company International; *U.S. Public*, pg. 621
FTI FOODTECH INTERNATIONAL INC.; *Int'l*, pg. 476
FTK HOLLAND B.V.—See Axel Johnson AB; *Int'l*, pg. 710
FTP SOFTWARE INC.; *U.S. Public*, pg. 609
FTSB BROADCASTING; *U.S. Private*, pg. 389
FTX, INC.—See Farah Incorporated; *U.S. Public*, pg. 613
FTZ INDUSTRIES, INC.—See Ilsco; *U.S. Private*, pg. 558
FW MANAGEMENT OPERATIONS LTD.—See Foster Wheeler Corporation; *U.S. Public*, pg. 677
FWD/SEAGRAVE FIRE APPARATUS, INC.; *U.S. Private*, pg. 390
FWI HOLDINGS INC.—See The Fuji Bank, Limited; *Int'l*, pg. 519

F.W.S.F. CORPORATION—See Firstar Corporation; *U.S. Public*, pg. 643
FZ CORPORATION—See Crown Central Petroleum Corporation; *U.S. Public*, pg. 462
FA HUA FRAGRANCE & COSMETIC CO LTD—See LVMH Moet Hennessy Louis Vuitton; *Int'l*, pg. 782
FAB INTERNATIONAL, LTD.—See Fab Industries, Inc.; *U.S. Public*, pg. 603
FABA VERMIETUNGSGESELLSCHAFT MBH—See Commerzbank AG; *Int'l*, pg. 309
FABBRICA ACCUMULATORI YORK S.P.A.—See Fiat Auto SpA; *Int'l*, pg. 482
FABCO AUTOMOTIVE—See Johnstown America Industries; *U.S. Public*, pg. 933
FABDEC LTD.—See DEC International, Inc.; *U.S. Private*, pg. 301
FABER, COE & GREGG, INC.; *U.S. Private*, pg. 390
FABER ENTERPRISES, INC.; *U.S. Private*, pg. 390
NEIL FABER MEDIA INC.; *U.S. Private*, pg. 390
FABIAN HOLDINGS BV—See Lagardere Groupe; *Int'l*, pg. 795
FABICK & COMPANY—See John Fabick Tractor Company; *U.S. Private*, pg. 390
FABICK BROTHERS EQUIPMENT—See John Fabick Tractor Company; *U.S. Private*, pg. 390
JOHN FABICK TRACTOR COMPANY; *U.S. Private*, pg. 390
FABICK MACHINERY—See John Fabick Tractor Company; *U.S. Private*, pg. 390
FABICK TRACTOR—See John Fabick Tractor Company; *U.S. Private*, pg. 390
FABREEKA INTERNATIONAL, INC.; *U.S. Private*, pg. 390
FABRI-CENTERS OF AMERICA, INC.; *U.S. Public*, pg. 609
THE FABRI-FORM COMPANY; *U.S. Private*, pg. 390
FABRIC KING—See House of Fabrics, Inc.; *U.S. Public*, pg. 842
FABRICA CARIOCA DE CATALISADORES—See Akzo Nobel N.V.; *Int'l*, pg. 47
FABRICA DE BOTES CASARI—See Altos Hornos de Mexico, S.A.; *Int'l*, pg. 66
FABRICA DE GALLETAS LA MODERNA, S.A. DE C.V.—See Tablex, S.A. de C.V.; *Int'l*, pg. 1346
FABRICA DE MOLDURAS Y CAJAS, S.A.—See UST Inc.; *U.S. Public*, pg. 1661
FABRICA DE PASTAS ALIMENTICIAS LA MODERNA, S.A. DE C.V.—See Tablex, S.A. de C.V.; *Int'l*, pg. 1346
FABRICA DE VALVULAS—See Fruit of the Loom, Inc.; *U.S. Public*, pg. 686
FABRICA NACIONAL DE CEMENTOS—See Lafarge S.A.; *Int'l*, pg. 791
FABRICACION NACIONAL DE COLORANTES, S.A.—See Bayer AG; *Int'l*, pg. 175
FABRICATION & OFFSHORE OPERATIONS—See McDermott International, Inc.; *U.S. Public*, pg. 1068
FABRICATION OPERATIONS EAST—See The Ivaco Group; *Int'l*, pg. 695
FABRICATION PLANT/CUSTOM PRODUCTS—See Newell Co.; *U.S. Public*, pg. 1177
FABRICATIONS MECANIQUES DE L'ATLANTIQUE (FAMAT SA)—See SNECMA - Societe Nationale d'Etude et de Construction de Moteurs d'Aviation; *Int'l*, pg. 1166
FABRICLAND, INC.—See House of Fabrics, Inc.; *U.S. Public*, pg. 842
FABRICON PRODUCTS—See Eagle-Picher Industries, Inc.; *U.S. Private*, pg. 355
M. FABRIKANT & SONS, INC.; *U.S. Private*, pg. 390
FABRIKEN ODIN AB—See Tetra Laval Group; *Int'l*, pg. 1378
FABRIMETAL S.A.—See Kone Corporation; *Int'l*, pg. 748
FABRIQUES DE TABAC REUNIS SA—See Philip Morris Companies Inc.; *U.S. Public*, pg. 1290
FABWEL INC.; *U.S. Private*, pg. 390
FACEMATE CORP.—See Facemate Corporation; *U.S. Private*, pg. 391
FACEMATE CORPORATION; *U.S. Private*, pg. 391
FACEY MEDICAL FOUNDATION—See UniHealth; *U.S. Private*, pg. 1118
FACILITY WORKS INC.—See TNP Enterprises, Inc.; *U.S. Public*, pg. 1557
FACOM—See Groupe Strafor Facom; *Int'l*, pg. 570
FACOM TOOLS INC.—See Groupe Strafor Facom; *Int'l*, pg. 570
FACOMEC S.A.—See Telefonaktiebolaget LM Ericsson; *Int'l*, pg. 1368
FACSIMILE SYSTEMS/PITNEY BOWES OFFICE SYSTEMS—See Pitney Bowes Inc.; *U.S. Public*, pg. 1313
FACTOFRANCE HELLER—See Compagnie de Suez; *Int'l*, pg. 313
FACTOR-BANK—See Creditanstalt-Bankverein; *Int'l*, pg. 347
FACTORAJE BANCOMER—See Bancomer, S.A.; *Int'l*, pg. 145
FACTORCAT, ESTABLECIMIENTO FINANCIERO DE CREDITO, S.A.—See Caixa d'Estalvis de Catalunya; *Int'l*, pg. 250
FACTORY 2-U—See Family Bargain Corporation; *U.S. Public*, pg. 612
FACTS ON FILE NEWS SERVICES—See Primedia Inc.; *U.S. Public*, pg. 1327
FACULTATIVE RESOURCES, INC.—See W.R. Berkley Corporation; *U.S. Public*, pg. 215
FADAL ENGINEERING COMPANY, INC.—See Thyssen AG; *Int'l*, pg. 1389
FADLER, INC.—See Hale-Halsell Company; *U.S. Private*, pg. 494
FAFNIR DIV. OF TORRINGTON CO.—See Ingersoll-Rand Company; *U.S. Public*, pg. 877
FAG-VRG SA—See N.V. Koninklijke KNP BT; *Int'l*, pg. 757
FAGERSTA STAINLESS AB; *Int'l*, pg. 476
FAHLGREN; *U.S. Private*, pg. 391
FAHLGREN—See Fahlgren; *U.S. Private*, pg. 391
FAHNESTOCK VINER HOLDINGS INC.; *Int'l*, pg. 476

Company Index

FAHRZEUGBAU GMBH—See Linde AG; *Int'l*, pg. 811
FAHRZEUGWERKE NORD GMBH—See MAN Aktiengesellschaft; *Int'l*, pg. 824
FAILURE ANALYSIS ASSOCIATES—See The Macneal-Schwendler Corp.; *U.S. Public*, pg. 1032
THE FAILURE GROUP, INC.; *U.S. Public*, pg. 609
FAIR GROUNDS CORPORATION; *U.S. Public*, pg. 609
FAIR, ISAAC AND COMPANY, INC.; *U.S. Public*, pg. 609
FAIRBANK BREARLEY—See Carclo Engineering Group plc; *Int'l*, pg. 268
FAIRBANKS MORSE ENGINE DIVISION—See Coltec Holdings Inc.; *U.S. Public*, pg. 401
FAIRCHILD AEROSPACE CORPORATION; *U.S. Private*, pg. 391
FAIRCHILD CONTROLS—See Lagardere Groupe; *Int'l*, pg. 794
THE FAIRCHILD CORPORATION; *U.S. Public*, pg. 610
FAIRCHILD DORNIER LUFTFAHRT GMBH—See Fairchild Aerospace Corporation; *U.S. Private*, pg. 391
FAIRCHILD DORNIER USA—See Fairchild Aerospace Corporation; *U.S. Private*, pg. 391
FAIRCHILD FASTENERS FRANCE—See The Fairchild Corporation; *U.S. Public*, pg. 610
FAIRCHILD PUBLICATIONS—See The Walt Disney Company; *U.S. Public*, pg. 513
FAIRCHILD TECHNOLOGIES GMBH—See The Fairchild Corporation; *U.S. Public*, pg. 610
FAIRCLOUGH HOMES LTD.—See AMEC Plc; *Int'l*, pg. 16
FAIRFAX BUILDING SYSTEMS—See Fairfax Lumber & Millwork Company Inc.; *U.S. Private*, pg. 391
FAIRFAX COMMUNITY NEWSPAPERS PTY. LIMITED—See John Fairfax Holdings Limited; *Int'l*, pg. 477
FAIRFAX COMMUNITY NEWSPAPERS PTY. LTD.—See John Fairfax Holdings Limited; *Int'l*, pg. 477
FAIRFAX FINANCIAL HOLDINGS LIMITED; *Int'l*, pg. 476
JOHN FAIRFAX HOLDINGS LIMITED; *Int'l*, pg. 477
JOHN FAIRFAX PUBLICATIONS PTY. LTD.—See John Fairfax Holdings Limited; *Int'l*, pg. 477
FAIRFAX LUMBER & MILLWORK COMPANY INC.; *U.S. Private*, pg. 391
FAIRFAX SAVINGS BANK—See Susquehanna Bancshares, Inc.; *U.S. Public*, pg. 1543
FAIRFIELD ACCEPTANCE CORPORATION—See Fairfield Communities, Inc.; *U.S. Public*, pg. 611
FAIRFIELD BAY—See Fairfield Communities, Inc.; *U.S. Public*, pg. 610
FAIRFIELD BRANSON—See Fairfield Communities, Inc.; *U.S. Public*, pg. 610
FAIRFIELD COMMUNITIES, INC.; *U.S. Public*, pg. 610
FAIRFIELD ELECTRIC COOPERATIVE; *U.S. Private*, pg. 391
FAIRFIELD FLAGSTAFF—See Fairfield Communities, Inc.; *U.S. Public*, pg. 611
FAIRFIELD GLADE—See Fairfield Communities, Inc.; *U.S. Public*, pg. 610
FAIRFIELD GROUP—See Legg Mason, Inc.; *U.S. Public*, pg. 985
FAIRFIELD HARBOUR—See Fairfield Communities, Inc.; *U.S. Public*, pg. 610
FAIRFIELD INDUSTRIES, INC.—See Fairfield Maxwell Ltd.; *U.S. Private*, pg. 391
FAIRFIELD INN—See Marriott International, Inc.; *U.S. Public*, pg. 1048
FAIRFIELD MAXWELL LTD.; *U.S. Private*, pg. 391
FAIRFIELD MOUNTAINS—See Fairfield Communities, Inc.; *U.S. Public*, pg. 611
FAIRFIELD MYRTLE BEACH, INC.—See Fairfield Communities, Inc.; *U.S. Public*, pg. 611
FAIRFIELD NASHVILLE—See Fairfield Communities, Inc.; *U.S. Public*, pg. 611
FAIRFIELD OCEAN RIDGE—See Fairfield Communities, Inc.; *U.S. Public*, pg. 610
FAIRFIELD ORLANDO AT CYPRUSS PALMS—See Fairfield Communities, Inc.; *U.S. Public*, pg. 611
FAIRFIELD PAGOSA—See Fairfield Communities, Inc.; *U.S. Public*, pg. 611
FAIRFIELD PLANTATION—See Fairfield Communities, Inc.; *U.S. Public*, pg. 611
FAIRFIELD PURCHASING & DESIGN, INC.—See Fairfield Communities, Inc.; *U.S. Public*, pg. 611
FAIRFIELD SAPPHIRE VALLEY—See Fairfield Communities, Inc.; *U.S. Public*, pg. 611
FAIRFIELD WILLIAMSBURG—See Fairfield Communities, Inc.; *U.S. Public*, pg. 611
FAIRLANE LIFE INSURANCE COMPANY—See Ford Motor Company; *U.S. Public*, pg. 664
FAIRLANES BOWL, INC.—See Great Lakes Realty Corp.; *U.S. Private*, pg. 475
FAIRMONT HOMES, INC.; *U.S. Private*, pg. 391
THE FAIRMONT HOTELS; *U.S. Private*, pg. 391
FAIRMONT MORTGAGE, INC.—See Del Webb Corporation; *U.S. Public*, pg. 495
FAIRMONT PRODUCTS—See Dean Foods Company; *U.S. Public*, pg. 490
FAIRMONT SNACK GROUP, INC.; *U.S. Private*, pg. 392
FAIRMONT TAMPER—See Harsco Corporation; *U.S. Public*, pg. 793
FAIRPRENE IND. PRODUCTS COMPANY—See BBA Group plc; *Int'l*, pg. 113
FAIRVIEW CARE CENTER OF BETHLEHEM PIKE—See Genesis Health Ventures, Inc.; *U.S. Public*, pg. 729
FAIRVIEW CARE CENTER OF PAPERMILL RD.—See Genesis Health Ventures, Inc.; *U.S. Public*, pg. 729
FAIRVIEW CONSTRUCTION, INC; *U.S. Private*, pg. 392
FAIRVIEW NURSING HOME—See Paragon Health Network, Inc.; *U.S. Public*, pg. 1256
FAIRVIEW PRINTING—See American Media, Inc.; *U.S. Public*, pg. 87
FAIRVIEW PROPERTIES, INC.—See The Kiplinger Washington Editors, Inc.; *U.S. Private*, pg. 864
FAIRVIEW WINE CO.—See White Rock Distilleries Inc.; *U.S. Private*, pg. 1173
FAIRWAY DISTRICT PRODUCTION OFFICE—See Hunt Oil Company; *U.S. Private*, pg. 548

FAIRWAY FOODS, INC.—See Holiday Companies; *U.S. Private*, pg. 534
FAIRWAY FORD, INC.; *U.S. Private*, pg. 392
FAIRWAY FORD OF ANDERSON—See Fairway Ford, Inc.; *U.S. Private*, pg. 392
FAIRWAY GROUP—See Hollinger Inc.; *Int'l*, pg. 631
FAIRWAYS AND SWINFORD (TRAVEL) LTD.—See Sea Containers Ltd.; *Int'l*, pg. 1214
FAIRWAYS & SWINFORD TRAVEL LTD.—See Sea Containers Ltd.; *Int'l*, pg. 1213
FAKTA—See KF/Konsum Coop Group; *Int'l*, pg. 718
FALCON-ANAHEIM—See Falcon Products, Inc.; *U.S. Public*, pg. 611
FALCON ASSOCIATES—See Air & Water Technologies Corporation; *U.S. Public*, pg. 29
FALCON-BELDING—See Falcon Products, Inc.; *U.S. Public*, pg. 611
FALCON-BELMONT—See Falcon Products, Inc.; *U.S. Public*, pg. 611
FALCON-CITY OF INDUSTRY—See Falcon Products, Inc.; *U.S. Public*, pg. 611
FALCON DE BAJA CALIFORNIA, S.A. DE C.V.—See Falcon Products, Inc.; *U.S. Public*, pg. 611
FALCON DE JUAREZ, S.A. DE C.V.—See Falcon Products, Inc.; *U.S. Public*, pg. 611
FALCON DRILLING COMPANY INC.—See R&B Falcon Corporation; *U.S. Public*, pg. 1354
FALCON FOAM CORPORATION—See Owens Corning; *U.S. Public*, pg. 1237
FALCON-LEWISVILLE—See Falcon Products, Inc.; *U.S. Public*, pg. 611
FALCON MIMON, A.S.—See Falcon Products, Inc.; *U.S. Public*, pg. 611
FALCON-NEWPORT—See Falcon Products, Inc.; *U.S. Public*, pg. 611
FALCON PRODUCTS, INC.; *U.S. Public*, pg. 611
FALCON SAFETY PRODUCTS INC.; *U.S. Private*, pg. 392
FALCONBRIDGE CHILE S.A.—See EdperBrascan Corporation; *Int'l*, pg. 434
FALCONBRIDGE DOMINICANA, C. POR A.—See EdperBrascan Corporation; *Int'l*, pg. 434
FALCONBRIDGE EUROPE S.A.—See EdperBrascan Corporation; *Int'l*, pg. 434
FALCONBRIDGE EXPLORATIONS—See EdperBrascan Corporation; *Int'l*, pg. 433
FALCONBRIDGE EXPLORATIONS (ZIMBABWE)—See EdperBrascan Corporation; *Int'l*, pg. 434
FALCONBRIDGE INTERNATIONAL LTD.—See EdperBrascan Corporation; *Int'l*, pg. 434
FALCONBRIDGE INTERNATIONAL RUSSIA—See EdperBrascan Corporation; *Int'l*, pg. 434
FALCONBRIDGE INTERNATIONAL S.A.—See EdperBrascan Corporation; *Int'l*, pg. 434
FALCONBRIDGE (JAPAN) LTD.—See EdperBrascan Corporation; *Int'l*, pg. 434
FALCONBRIDGE LIMITED—See EdperBrascan Corporation; *Int'l*, pg. 433
FALCONBRIDGE NIKKELVERK A/S—See EdperBrascan Corporation; *Int'l*, pg. 434
FALCONBRIDGE U.S. INC.—See EdperBrascan Corporation; *Int'l*, pg. 434
THE FALK CORPORATION—See Sundstrand Corporation; *U.S. Public*, pg. 1534
FALKEMA AB; *Int'l*, pg. 477
THE FALKIRK MINING CO.—See NACCO Industries, Inc.; *U.S. Public*, pg. 1149
FALKLAND PARTNERS—See Cigna Corp.; *U.S. Public*, pg. 361
FALL RIVER GAS APPLIANCE CO., INC.—See Fall River Gas Company; *U.S. Public*, pg. 612
FALL RIVER GAS COMPANY; *U.S. Public*, pg. 611
G.W. FALLAND & CO.—See Dairy Vale Co-op Ltd.; *Int'l*, pg. 372
FALLEK CHEMICAL COMPANY (UK) LTD.—See ICC Industries, Inc.; *U.S. Private*, pg. 553
FALLEK CHEMICAL JAPAN K.K.—See ICC Industries, Inc.; *U.S. Private*, pg. 553
FALLEK CHEMICAL S.A.—See ICC Industries, Inc.; *U.S. Private*, pg. 553
FALLEY'S INC.—See The Yucaipa Companies; *U.S. Private*, pg. 1202
FALLON COMMUNITY HEALTH PLAN; *U.S. Private*, pg. 392
FALLON CONVALESCENT CENTER—See Horizon/CMS Healthcare Corporation; *U.S. Public*, pg. 837
FALLS CHURCH DIV.—See Raytheon Company; *U.S. Public*, pg. 1365
FALMER PRESS LTD.—See Taylor & Francis Group Ltd.; *Int'l*, pg. 1358
FALSTRIA SERVICES COMPANY LIMITED—See The East Asiatic Company Ltd. A/S; *Int'l*, pg. 431
FALTEC BENELUX B.V.—See Cardo AB; *Int'l*, pg. 269
FALTEC DOORS LTD.—See Cardo AB; *Int'l*, pg. 269
FALTEC PORTE A/S—See Cardo AB; *Int'l*, pg. 269
FALTEC TORE GES.M.B.H.—See Cardo AB; *Int'l*, pg. 269
FALTEC TORE GMBH—See Cardo AB; *Int'l*, pg. 269
FAMA DE DURANGO, S.A. DE C.V.—See Farah Incorporated; *U.S. Public*, pg. 613
FAMA S.A.—See IRI Istituto Ricostruzione Industriale; *Int'l*, pg. 654
FAME—See Martin/Williams Advertising Inc.; *U.S. Private*, pg. 710
FAMESA S.A.—See Akzo Nobel N.V.; *Int'l*, pg. 43
FAMEX, INC.—See Allianz Aktiengesellschaft; *Int'l*, pg. 59
FAMIBANK S.A.—See Citicorp; *U.S. Public*, pg. 379
FAMICREDIT—See Citicorp; *U.S. Public*, pg. 379
FAMIL CO., LTD.—See Ito-Yokado Co., Ltd.; *Int'l*, pg. 693
FAMILIA LEBENSVERSICHERUNGS-GESELLSCHAFT—See Assicurazioni Generali S.p.A.; *Int'l*, pg. 91
FAMILIAN CORP.—See Wolseley Plc.; *Int'l*, pg. 1512
FAMILIAN PIPE & SUPPLY CO.—See Wolseley Plc.; *Int'l*, pg. 1512
FAMILIAN PIPE INC.—See Wolseley Plc.; *Int'l*, pg. 1512

FAMILIAN SOUTHWEST, INC.—See Wolseley Plc.; *Int'l*, pg. 1512
FAMILY BARGAIN CORPORATION; *U.S. Public*, pg. 612
FAMILY BUFFETS—See GIB Group; *Int'l*, pg. 533
FAMILY CARE SPECIALISTS, INC.—See Integrated Health Services, Inc.; *U.S. Public*, pg. 884
THE FAMILY CHANNEL INC.—See WIC Western International Communications Ltd.; *Int'l*, pg. 1482
THE FAMILY CIRCLE, INC.—See Bertelsmann AG; *Int'l*, pg. 190
FAMILY DOLLAR STORES, INC.; *U.S. Public*, pg. 612
FAMILY HEALTHCARE SERVICES, INC.—See Sierra Health Services, Inc.; *U.S. Public*, pg. 1469
FAMILY HOME HOSPICE, INC.—See Sierra Health Services, Inc.; *U.S. Public*, pg. 1469
FAMILY INNS OF AMERICA, INC.; *U.S. Private*, pg. 392
FAMILY INNS OF NEW ORLEANS, INC.—See Family Inns of America, Inc.; *U.S. Private*, pg. 392
THE FAMILY INSURANCE AGENCY, INC.—See The Troy Savings Bank; *U.S. Private*, pg. 1106
THE FAMILY INVESTMENT SERVICES CO., INC.—See The Troy Savings Bank; *U.S. Private*, pg. 1106
THE FAMILY MORTGAGE BANKING CO., INC.—See The Troy Savings Bank; *U.S. Private*, pg. 1106
FAMILY PHARMACY GENERAL OFFICE—See AmeriSource Health Corp.; *U.S. Public*, pg. 97
FAMILY READING PROGRAM CORP.—See The Reader's Digest Association, Inc.; *U.S. Public*, pg. 1367
FAMILY RESTAURANTS, INC.; *U.S. Private*, pg. 393
FAMILY SERVICE LIFE INSURANCE CO.—See Torchmark Corporation; *U.S. Public*, pg. 1622
FAMILY SMACKS, INC.; *U.S. Private*, pg. 393
FAMOUS-BARR—See The May Department Stores Company; *U.S. Public*, pg. 1063
FAMOUS FOOTWEAR—See Brown Group, Inc.; *U.S. Public*, pg. 262
FAMOUS MUSIC CORPORATION—See National Amusements, Inc.; *U.S. Private*, pg. 777
FAMOUS PLAYERS INC.—See National Amusements, Inc.; *U.S. Private*, pg. 779
FAMOUS RESTAURANTS INC.; *U.S. Private*, pg. 393
FAN BLADE ASSOCIATES, INC.—See SNECMA - Societe Nationale d'Etude et de Construction de Moteurs d'Aviation; *Int'l*, pg. 1166
FAN FUELER SPORTS MARKETING—See Action Performance Companies, Inc.; *U.S. Public*, pg. 17
FAN LING MACHINE & MECHANICAL CENTRE—See Nishimatsu Construction Co., Ltd.; *Int'l*, pg. 943
FANCHEM, LTD.—See PVS Chemicals, Inc.; *U.S. Private*, pg. 828
FANEUIL HALL MARKETPLACE, INC.—See The Rouse Company; *U.S. Public*, pg. 1408
FANNER-PLP—See Preformed Line Products; *U.S. Public*, pg. 1321
FANNIE MAY CANDY SHOPS, INC.—See The Jordan Company; *U.S. Private*, pg. 598
FANSTEEL, INC.; *U.S. Public*, pg. 612
FANSTEEL VR/WESSON-LEXINGTON—See Fansteel, Inc.; *U.S. Public*, pg. 612
FANSTEEL VR/WESSON-PLANTSVILLE—See Fansteel, Inc.; *U.S. Public*, pg. 612
FANTA FURNITURE—See All-Luminum Products, Inc.; *U.S. Private*, pg. 35
FANUC EUROPE GMBH—See Fanuc Ltd.; *Int'l*, pg. 478
FANUC FRANCE S.A.—See Fanuc Ltd.; *Int'l*, pg. 477
FANUC GE AUTOMATION INDIA LIMITED—See Fanuc Ltd.; *Int'l*, pg. 478
FANUC GE AUTOMATION INDIA LIMITED—See General Electric Company; *U.S. Public*, pg. 714
FANUC GE AUTOMATION SINGAPORE PTE. LTD.—See Fanuc Ltd.; *Int'l*, pg. 478
FANUC GE AUTOMATION SINGAPORE PTE. LTD.—See General Electric Company; *U.S. Public*, pg. 714
FANUC GERMANY GMBH—See Fanuc Ltd.; *Int'l*, pg. 477
FANUC HONG KONG LIMITED—See Fanuc Ltd.; *Int'l*, pg. 477
FANUC IBERIA, S.A.—See Fanuc Ltd.; *Int'l*, pg. 478
PT. FANUC INDONESIA—See Fanuc Ltd.; *Int'l*, pg. 478
FANUC ITALIA S.P.A.—See Fanuc Ltd.; *Int'l*, pg. 478
FANUC KOREA CORPORATION—See Fanuc Ltd.; *Int'l*, pg. 478
FANUC LTD.; *Int'l*, pg. 477
FANUC-MACHINEX LTD.—See Fanuc Ltd.; *Int'l*, pg. 478
FANUC MECHATRONICS (MALAYSIA) SDN. BHD.—See Fanuc Ltd.; *Int'l*, pg. 478
FANUC OCEANIA PTY. LTD.—See Fanuc Ltd.; *Int'l*, pg. 478
FANUC PHILIPPINES CORPORATION—See Fanuc Ltd.; *Int'l*, pg. 478
FANUC ROBOTICS EUROPE S.A.—See Fanuc Ltd.; *Int'l*, pg. 478
FANUC ROBOTICS NORTH AMERICA, INC.—See Fanuc Ltd.; *Int'l*, pg. 477
FANUC SINGAPORE PTE. LTD.—See Fanuc Ltd.; *Int'l*, pg. 478
FANUC TAIWAN LIMITED—See Fanuc Ltd.; *Int'l*, pg. 478
FANUC THAI LIMITED—See Fanuc Ltd.; *Int'l*, pg. 478
FANUC TURKEY LTD—See Fanuc Ltd.; *Int'l*, pg. 478
FANUC U.K. LIMITED—See Fanuc Ltd.; *Int'l*, pg. 478
FANUC USA CORP.—See Fanuc Ltd.; *Int'l*, pg. 477
FAR-BEN S.A. DE C.V.; *Int'l*, pg. 477
FAR EAST BANK AND TRUST COMPANY—See The Sakura Bank, Limited; *Int'l*, pg. 1180
FAR EASTERN ELECTRIC INDUSTRY CO., LTD.—See Oki Electric Industry Company, Ltd.; *Int'l*, pg. 1000
FAR FRANCE ALUMINIUM RECYCLAGE S.A.—See Alusuisse-Lonza Holding Ltd.; *Int'l*, pg. 68
FAR-MOR BIOCHEM—See Laporte plc; *Int'l*, pg. 802
FAR WEST INSURANCE COMPANY—See Amwest Insurance Group, Inc.; *U.S. Public*, pg. 106
FARADAY, INC.—See Siemens AG; *Int'l*, pg. 1246
FARAH AUSTRALIA PTY. LIMITED—See Farah Incorporated; *U.S. Public*, pg. 613

FARAH CLOTHING, INC.—See Farah Incorporated; *U.S. Public,* pg. 613

FARAH (EXPORTS) IRELAND—See Farah Incorporated; *U.S. Public,* pg. 613

FARAH (FAR EAST) LIMITED—See Farah Incorporated; *U.S. Public,* pg. 613

FARAH INCORPORATED; *U.S. Public,* pg. 612

FARAH INTERNATIONAL, INC.—See Farah Incorporated; *U.S. Public,* pg. 613

FARAH JAPAN LIMITED—See Farah Incorporated; *U.S. Public,* pg. 613

FARAH MFG. CO. OF NEW MEXICO—See Farah Incorporated; *U.S. Public,* pg. 613

FARAH MANUFACTURING SERVICES, INC.—See Farah Incorporated; *U.S. Public,* pg. 613

FARAH MANUFACTURING (U.K.) LIMITED—See Farah Incorporated; *U.S. Public,* pg. 613

FARAH SALES CORP.—See Farah Incorporated; *U.S. Public,* pg. 613

FARAH U.S.A., INC.—See Farah Incorporated; *U.S. Public,* pg. 613

FARALLON COMMUNICATIONS SARL—See Netopia, Inc.; *U.S. Public,* pg. 1168

FARBEST INC.—See Countrymark Cooperative, Inc.; *U.S. Private,* pg. 279

FARBEST INDUSTRIES LTD.—See Citizen Watch Company, Ltd.; *Int'l,* pg. 294

FARDEM BV—See DSM N.V.; *Int'l,* pg. 352

FARDEM INTERNATIONAL B.V.—See DSM N.V.; *Int'l,* pg. 352

FARDEM NV—See DSM N.V.; *Int'l,* pg. 353

FARDEM PACKAGING B.V.—See DSM N.V.; *Int'l,* pg. 352

FARDEM VERPACKUNGEN GMBH—See DSM N.V.; *Int'l,* pg. 353

FAREWAY STORES, INC.; *U.S. Private,* pg. 393

FARGO GLASS & PAINT CO—See Fargo Glass & Paint Company; *U.S. Private,* pg. 393

FARGO GLASS & PAINT CO.—See Fargo Glass & Paint Company; *U.S. Private,* pg. 393

FARGO GLASS & PAINT COMPANY; *U.S. Private,* pg. 393

FARIBAULT FOODS INC.; *U.S. Private,* pg. 393

FARIBAULT WOOLEN MILL CO.; *U.S. Private,* pg. 394

FARIBO WOOLENS, INC.—See Faribault Woolen Mill Co.; *U.S. Private,* pg. 394

FARINON CANADA LTD.—See Harris Corporation; *U.S. Public,* pg. 791

FARKEMO S.R.L.—See Pfizer Inc.; *U.S. Public,* pg. 1283

FARLEY CANDY COMPANY—See Favorite Brands International, Inc.; *U.S. Private,* pg. 397

FARLEY, INC.; *U.S. Private,* pg. 394

FARM & HOME OIL COMPANY; *U.S. Private,* pg. 394

FARM BUREAU BUILDING INC.—See Arkansas Farm Bureau Federation; *U.S. Private,* pg. 82

FARM BUREAU CASUALTY INSURANCE CO.—See Arkansas Farm Bureau Federation; *U.S. Private,* pg. 82

FARM BUREAU MUTUAL INSURANCE CO. OF ARKANSAS—See Arkansas Farm Bureau Federation; *U.S. Private,* pg. 82

FARM CREDIT BANK OF TEXAS—See Federal Farm Credit Banks Funding Corporation; *U.S. Private,* pg. 398

FARM CREDIT BANK OF WICHITA—See Federal Farm Credit Banks Funding Corporation; *U.S. Private,* pg. 398

FARM CREDIT COUNCIL SERVICES—See Federal Farm Credit Banks Funding Corporation; *U.S. Private,* pg. 398

FARM CREDIT LEASING SERVICES CORPORATION—See Federal Farm Credit Banks Funding Corporation; *U.S. Private,* pg. 398

FARM ELECTRIC SERVICES LTD.—See Transalta Corporation; *Int'l,* pg. 1416

FARM FAMILY CASUALTY INSURANCE CO.; *U.S. Private,* pg. 394

FARM FRESH, INC.—See Richfood Holdings, Inc.; *U.S. Public,* pg. 1388

FARM JOURNAL INC.; *U.S. Private,* pg. 394

FARM PLAN CORPORATION—See Deere & Company; *U.S. Public,* pg. 492

FARM PRESS—See Primedia Inc.; *U.S. Public,* pg. 1328

FARM PROGRESS PUBLICATIONS—See The Walt Disney Company; *U.S. Public,* pg. 513

FARM STORE NO. 1—See Steiner Corporation; *U.S. Private,* pg. 1039

FARM STORES; *U.S. Private,* pg. 394

FARMACAS B.V.—See Rohto Pharmaceutical Co.; *Int'l,* pg. 1126

FARMAN BROTHERS PICKLE COMPANY—See Pro-Fac Cooperative, Inc.; *U.S. Private,* pg. 887

FARMATIC RESEARCH, INC.; *Int'l,* pg. 478

FARMER BROTHERS COMPANY; *U.S. Public,* pg. 613

FARMER JACK SUPERMARKETS—See Tengelmann Warenhandelsgesellschaft; *Int'l,* pg. 1375

FARMERS & MERCHANTS BANK—See First Commercial Corporation; *U.S. Public,* pg. 630

FARMERS AND MERCHANTS BANK AND TRUST—See Susquehanna Bancshares, Inc.; *U.S. Public,* pg. 1542

FARMERS & MERCHANTS BANK-EASTERN SHORE—See Mercantile Bankshares Corporation; *U.S. Public,* pg. 1089

FARMERS AND MERCHANTS BANK OF CARLINVILLE—See Firstbank of Illinois Company; *U.S. Public,* pg. 644

FARMERS & MERCHANTS BANK OF CENTRAL CALIFORNIA; *U.S. Private,* pg. 394

FARMERS AND TRADERS LIFE INSURANCE CO.; *U.S. Private,* pg. 394

FARMERS BANK & TRUST CO.—See Old National Bancorp; *U.S. Public,* pg. 1217

FARMERS BANK OF MARYLAND—See First Virginia Banks, Inc.; *U.S. Public,* pg. 641

FARMERS CHEMICAL CO.—See Farmland Industries, Inc.; *U.S. Private,* pg. 396

FARMERS CO-OP MARKET INC.; *U.S. Private,* pg. 395

FARMER'S COOPERATIVE ASSOCIATION; *U.S. Private,* pg. 395

FARMERS COPPER & INDUSTRIAL SUPPLY—See Four Winds Investment Corp.; *U.S. Private,* pg. 422

FARMERS ELEVATORS, INC.—See Owensboro Grain Co., Inc.; *U.S. Private,* pg. 824

FARMERS FIRST BANK—See Susquehanna Bancshares, Inc.; *U.S. Public,* pg. 1542

FARMERS GROUP, INC.—See B.A.T Industries P.L.C.; *Int'l,* pg. 110

FARMERS INSURANCE GROUP—See B.A.T Industries P.L.C.; *Int'l,* pg. 111

FARMERS INVESTMENT COMPANY, INC.—See Bale Of Kentucky, Inc.; *U.S. Private,* pg. 112

FARMERS MARINE COPPER WORKS—See Four Winds Investment Corp.; *U.S. Private,* pg. 422

FARMERS MUTUAL HAIL INSURANCE CO. OF IOWA; *U.S. Private,* pg. 395

FARMERS NATIONAL BANK—See UMB Financial Corporation; *U.S. Public,* pg. 1654

FARMERS NATIONAL COMPANY—See Metropolitan Life Insurance Co.; *U.S. Private,* pg. 738

FARMERS NEW WORLD LIFE INSURANCE CO.—See B.A.T Industries P.L.C.; *Int'l,* pg. 110

FARMER'S PRIDE, INC.; *U.S. Private,* pg. 395

FARMERS STATE BANK—See First Financial Bancorp; *U.S. Public,* pg. 633

FARMERS TELEPHONE CO-OP; *U.S. Private,* pg. 395

FARMERS UNION CO-OPERATIVE INSURANCE COMPANY OF NEBRASKA—See Farmers Mutual Hail Insurance Co. of Iowa; *U.S. Private,* pg. 395

FARMERS UNION MARKETING & PROCESSING ASSOCIATION; *U.S. Private,* pg. 395

FARMINGTON HILLS HOLDING COMPANY; *U.S. Private,* pg. 395

FARMINGTON NATIONAL BANK—See Banknorth Group Inc.; *U.S. Public,* pg. 187

FARMINOVA PRODUTOS FARMACEUTICOS DE INOVACAO, LDA.—See Pfizer Inc.; *U.S. Public,* pg. 1283

FARMITALIA CARLO ERBA S.A.—See Pharmacia & Upjohn, Inc.; *Int'l,* pg. 1049

FARMITALIA CARLO ERBA S.R.L.—See Pharmacia & Upjohn, Inc.; *Int'l,* pg. 1049

FARMLAND DAIRIES; *U.S. Private,* pg. 395

FARMLAND HYDRO, L.P.—See Norsk Hydro a.s; *Int'l,* pg. 961

FARMLAND INDUSTRIES, INC.; *U.S. Private,* pg. 395

FARMLAND INDUSTRIES U.K. LTD.—See Farmland Industries, Inc.; *U.S. Private,* pg. 396

FARMLAND INSURANCE AGENCY, INC.—See Farmland Industries, Inc.; *U.S. Private,* pg. 396

FARMLAND MISSCHEM, LTD.—See Mississippi Chemical Corporation; *U.S. Public,* pg. 1117

FARMLAND MUTUAL INSURANCE COMPANY—See Nationwide Insurance Enterprise; *U.S. Private,* pg. 789

FARMLAND NATIONAL BEEF PACKING COMPANY, L.P.—See Farmland Industries, Inc.; *U.S. Private,* pg. 396

FARMLAND NATIONAL BEEF PACKING COMPANY, LP—See Farmland Industries, Inc.; *U.S. Private,* pg. 396

FARMSTEAD—See Farmland Industries, Inc.; *U.S. Private,* pg. 396

FARMWAY CO-OP INC.; *U.S. Private,* pg. 396

FARNAM COMPANIES, INC.; *U.S. Private,* pg. 396

FARNAM SEALING SYSTEMS DIVISION—See Coltec Holdings Inc; *U.S. Public,* pg. 401

FARNSWORTH COMPANIES; *U.S. Private,* pg. 397

FARNSWORTH DEVELOPMENT CO.—See Farnsworth Companies; *U.S. Private,* pg. 397

FARNSWORTH HOMES—See Farnsworth Companies; *U.S. Private,* pg. 397

FARO TECHNOLOGIES, INC.; *U.S. Public,* pg. 613

FAROUDJA, INC.; *U.S. Public,* pg. 613

FAROUK ADVERTISING—See DMB&B Communications; *U.S. Private,* pg. 304

FARR COMPANY; *U.S. Public,* pg. 613

FARR FILTRATION, LTD.—See Farr Company; *U.S. Public,* pg. 614

FARR INCORPORATED—See Farr Company; *U.S. Public,* pg. 614

FARRAND CONTROLS—See Ruhle Companies, Inc.; *U.S. Private,* pg. 951

FARRAR, STRAUS & GIROUX, INC.—See Georg von Holtzbrinck GmbH; *Int'l,* pg. 1479

FARREL CORPORATION; *U.S. Public,* pg. 614

FARREL LTD.—See Farrel Corporation; *U.S. Public,* pg. 614

FARRELL LINES INCORPORATED; *U.S. Private,* pg. 397

FARRELL WAKO GLOBAL INVESTMENT MANAGEMENT, INC.—See Wako Securities Co., Ltd.; *Int'l,* pg. 1485

FARREY'S WHOLESALE HARDWARE CO., INC.—See Distribution America; *U.S. Private,* pg. 335

FASCO CONTROLS CORPORATION—See BTR plc; *Int'l,* pg. 125

FASCO DC MOTORS—See BTR plc; *Int'l,* pg. 125

FASCO INDUSTRIES, INC.—See BTR plc; *Int'l,* pg. 125

FASCO SENSORS & CONTROLS DIVISION—See BTR plc; *Int'l,* pg. 127

FASERWERK KELHEIM GMBH—See Courtaulds plc; *Int'l,* pg. 339

FASHION BUG—See Charming Shoppes, Inc.; *U.S. Public,* pg. 336

FASHION BUG PLUS—See Charming Shoppes, Inc.; *U.S. Public,* pg. 336

FASHION HOUSE TRAIN—See Kosugi Sangyo Co., Ltd.; *Int'l,* pg. 759

FASHION SHOP OF KENTUCKY INC.; *U.S. Private,* pg. 397

FASHIONAIRE—See Hartmarx Corporation; *U.S. Public,* pg. 796

FASHIONS OUTLET OF AMERICA—See Polo/Ralph Lauren Corporation; *U.S. Private,* pg. 875

FASSON AB—See Avery Dennison Corporation; *U.S. Public,* pg. 154

FASSON ADHESIVE PRODUCTS, LTD.—See Avery Dennison Corporation; *U.S. Public,* pg. 154

FASSON A/S—See Avery Dennison Corporation; *U.S. Public,* pg. 154

FASSON DE MEXICO, S.A.—See Avery Dennison Corporation; *U.S. Public,* pg. 154

FASSON FILMS—See Avery Dennison Corporation; *U.S. Public,* pg. 153

FASSON FRANCE S.A.R.L.—See Avery Dennison Corporation; *U.S. Public,* pg. 154

FASSON GESELLSCHAFT GMBH—See Avery Dennison Corporation; *U.S. Public,* pg. 154

FASSON HANDELSGESELLSHAFT GMBH—See Avery Dennison Corporation; *U.S. Public,* pg. 154

N.V. FASSON INDUS. DIV.—See Avery Dennison Corporation; *U.S. Public,* pg. 154

FASSON INDUSTRIAL (U.S.) DIV.—See Avery Dennison Corporation; *U.S. Public,* pg. 153

FASSON IRELAND LTD.—See Avery Dennison Corporation; *U.S. Public,* pg. 154

FASSON ITALIA S.P.A.—See Avery Dennison Corporation; *U.S. Public,* pg. 154

FASSON (NEDERLAND) B.V.—See Avery Dennison Corporation; *U.S. Public,* pg. 154

FASSON NORGE A/S—See Avery Dennison Corporation; *U.S. Public,* pg. 154

FASSON PRODUCTEN VERKOOPMAATSHAPPIJ B.V.—See Avery Dennison Corporation; *U.S. Public,* pg. 154

FASSON PRODUCTS (PTY) LTD.—See Avery Dennison Corporation; *U.S. Public,* pg. 154

FASSON PRODUTOS ADESIVOS LTDA.—See Avery Dennison Corporation; *U.S. Public,* pg. 154

FASSON PTY. LTD.—See Avery Dennison Corporation; *U.S. Public,* pg. 154

FASSON ROLL DIV.—See Avery Dennison Corporation; *U.S. Public,* pg. 153

FASSON ROLL MATERIALS DIV.—See Avery Dennison Corporation; *U.S. Public,* pg. 154

FASSON-SANYO KOKUSAKU PULP CO. LTD.—See Avery Dennison Corporation; *U.S. Public,* pg. 154

FASSON TARRA OY—See Avery Dennison Corporation; *U.S. Public,* pg. 154

FASSON U.K. LTD.—See Avery Dennison Corporation; *U.S. Public,* pg. 154

FASSON VERTRIEBS, AG—See Avery Dennison Corporation; *U.S. Public,* pg. 154

FAST COMPANY MAGAZINE—See The Atlantic Monthly Magazine; *U.S. Public,* pg. 95

FAST FARE, INC.—See Crown Central Petroleum Corporation; *U.S. Public,* pg. 462

FAST FOOD MERCHANDISERS INC.—See CKE Restaurants Inc.; *U.S. Public,* pg. 278

FAST STATIC RAM DIVISION—See Motorola, Inc.; *U.S. Public,* pg. 1137

FAST-TAX—See Computer Language Research, Inc.; *U.S. Public,* pg. 421

FASTCUT TOOL CORPORATION—See Cincinnati Milacron Inc.; *U.S. Public,* pg. 368

FASTEC INDUSTRIAL; *U.S. Private,* pg. 397

FASTEC SW CORPORATION—See Fastec Industrial; *U.S. Private,* pg. 397

FASTENAL COMPANY; *U.S. Public,* pg. 614

FASTFOOD INTERNATIONAL BV—See Koninklijke BolsWessanen nv; *Int'l,* pg. 751

FASTIGHETS AB FUNDAMENT/REAL ESTATE OPERATIONS—See AB Industrivarden; *Int'l,* pg. 678

FASTIGHETSAKTIEBOLAGET HUFVUDSTADEN; *Int'l,* pg. 478

FASTRAC SYSTEMS, INC.—See National Insurance Group; *U.S. Public,* pg. 1158

FASTRAC SYSTEMS, INC.-INSURANCE AGENT & BROKER—See National Insurance Group; *U.S. Public,* pg. 1158

FATA EUROPEAN GROUP S.P.A.—See FKI Plc; *Int'l,* pg. 474

FATA INDUSTRIE S.A.—See FKI Plc; *Int'l,* pg. 474

FATA-NEW HUNTER ENGINEERING S.P.A.—See FKI Plc; *Int'l,* pg. 474

FATA PRODUCTION MACHINERY—See FKI Plc; *Int'l,* pg. 474

FATA SA—See FKI Plc; *Int'l,* pg. 474

FATA SUD—See FKI Plc; *Int'l,* pg. 474

FATA USSR—See FKI Plc; *Int'l,* pg. 474

FATALUMINIUM—See FKI Plc; *Int'l,* pg. 474

FATATI-BTR S.A.—See BTR plc; *Int'l,* pg. 130

FATE DO BRASIL LTDA.—See Fate S.A.; *Int'l,* pg. 478

FATE S.A.; *Int'l,* pg. 478

FATME SOC. PER AZ—See Telefonaktiebolaget LM Ericsson; *Int'l,* pg. 1368

FATTAL & COLLINS (F&C)—See Grey Advertising Inc.; *U.S. Public,* pg. 765

FATTY CHEMICAL (MALAYSIA) SDN., BHD.—See Kao Corporation; *Int'l,* pg. 717

FAUCHER INDUSTRIES INC.; *Int'l,* pg. 479

FAUGERE & JUTHEAU S.A.—See Marsh & McLennan Companies, Inc.; *U.S. Public,* pg. 1049

FAULKNER CADILLAC INC.; *U.S. Private,* pg. 397

FAULTLESS CASTER—See FKI Plc; *Int'l,* pg. 473

FAULTLESS NUTTING—See FKI Plc; *Int'l,* pg. 473

FAURE VADON FOREST—See Havas Advertising; *Int'l,* pg. 601

FAUSTO CARELLO S.P.A.—See Fiat Auto SpA; *Int'l,* pg. 482

FAVESA S.A. DE C.V., (MEXICO)—See Lear Corporation; *U.S. Public,* pg. 982

FAVORITE BRANDS INTERNATIONAL, INC.; *U.S. Private,* pg. 397

FAVORITE FOODS, INC.—See Suiza Foods Corporation; *U.S. Public,* pg. 1527

FAVORITE PRODUCTS CO.—See Oil-Dri Corporation of America; *U.S. Public,* pg. 1215

FAVORY CONVENIENCE FOOD BV—See Koninklijke BolsWessanen nv; *Int'l,* pg. 751
FAWCETT BOOKS—See Advance Publications Inc.; *U.S. Private,* pg. 21
FAWCETT MEMORIAL HOSPITAL, INC.—See Columbia/ HCA Healthcare Corporation; *U.S. Public,* pg. 404
FAWN INDUSTRIES, INC.; *U.S. Private,* pg. 397
FAXION B.V.—See Royal Nedlloyd Group N.V.; *Int'l,* pg. 1144
FAXION ITALY S.R.L.—See Royal Nedlloyd Group N.V.; *Int'l,* pg. 1144
FAXION-OESCHGER A.G.—See Royal Nedlloyd Group N.V.; *Int'l,* pg. 1144
THE FAXON COMPANY, INC.—See Dawson Holdings PLC; *Int'l,* pg. 385
FAY, SPOFFORD & THORNDIKE, INC.; *U.S. Private,* pg. 397
FAYETTE ENTERPRISES, INC.—See Furniture Brands International Inc.; *U.S. Public,* pg. 688
FAYGO BEVERAGES, INC.—See National Beverage Corp.; *U.S. Public,* pg. 1153
FCB/MEGACOM—See FCB; *U.S. Private,* pg. 389
FEATHER FINE SERVICES—See Pittway Corporation; *U.S. Public,* pg. 1306
FEATHERLITE BUILDING PRODUCTS OPERATION—See Justin Industries, Inc.; *U.S. Public,* pg. 936
FECHHEIMER BROS. CO.—See Berkshire Hathaway Inc.; *U.S. Public,* pg. 217
BRUNO FECHNER GMBH & CO. KG—See Veba AG; *Int'l,* pg. 1454
FEDCO AUTOMOTIVE COMPONENTS COMPANY, INC.— See Tomkins PLC; *Int'l,* pg. 1396
FEDCO, INC.; *U.S. Private,* pg. 398
FEDCO OMEGA, INC.—See Omega Environmental Inc.; *U.S. Private,* pg. 1222
FEDDERS ASIA PTE. LTD.—See Fedders Corp.; *U.S. Public,* pg. 615
FEDDERS CORP.; *U.S. Public,* pg. 614
FEDDERS INTERNATIONAL—See Fedders Corp.; *U.S. Public,* pg. 614
FEDDERS INTERNATIONAL, INC.—See Fedders Corp.; *U.S. Public,* pg. 614
FEDDERS NORTH AMERICA, INC.—See Fedders Corp.; *U.S. Public,* pg. 614
FEDERAL APD, INC.—See Federal Signal Corporation; *U.S. Public,* pg. 616
FEDERAL ASSIST—See Corporacion MAPFRE, Compania Internacional de Reaseguros, S.A.; *Int'l,* pg. 334
FEDERAL BEEF PROCESSORS NORTH—See GFI America; *U.S. Private,* pg. 435
FEDERAL BEEF PROCESSORS SOUTH—See GFI America; *U.S. Private,* pg. 435
FEDERAL BRONZE PRODUCTS INC.—See Metals USA, Inc.; *U.S. Public,* pg. 1100
FEDERAL BUSINESS PRODUCTS, INC.; *U.S. Private,* pg. 398
FEDERAL CARTRIDGE CO.—See Blount International, Inc.; *U.S. Public,* pg. 239
FEDERAL CHICAGO CORPORATION; *U.S. Private,* pg. 398
FEDERAL COMPRESS & WAREHOUSE COMPANY, INC.; *U.S. Private,* pg. 398
FEDERAL CONSTRUCTION CO.—See Kvaerner a.s.a.; *Int'l,* pg. 774
FEDERAL DATA CORPORATION; *U.S. Private,* pg. 398
FEDERAL DISTILLERS—See White Rock Distilleries Inc.; *U.S. Private,* pg. 1173
FEDERAL EXPRESS AVIATION SERVICES INC.—See FDX Corporation; *U.S. Public,* pg. 604
FEDERAL EXPRESS CANADA LTD.—See FDX Corporation; *U.S. Public,* pg. 604
FEDERAL EXPRESS EUROPE & CO.—See FDX Corporation; *U.S. Public,* pg. 604
FEDERAL EXPRESS (HONG KONG) LTD.—See FDX Corporation; *U.S. Public,* pg. 604
FEDERAL EXPRESS INTERNATIONAL, INC.—See FDX Corporation; *U.S. Public,* pg. 604
FEDERAL EXPRESS LEASING CORP.—See FDX Corporation; *U.S. Public,* pg. 604
FEDERAL EXPRESS LOGISTICS, INC.—See FDX Corporation; *U.S. Public,* pg. 604
FEDERAL EXPRESS REDEVELOPMENT CORP.—See FDX Corporation; *U.S. Public,* pg. 604
FEDERAL EXPRESS (U.K.) LTD.—See FDX Corporation; *U.S. Public,* pg. 604
FEDERAL FARM CREDIT BANKS FUNDING CORPORATION; *U.S. Private,* pg. 398
FEDERAL HOME LOAN BANK OF NEW YORK; *U.S. Private,* pg. 399
FEDERAL HOME LOAN MORTGAGE CORPORATION; *U.S. Public,* pg. 615
FEDERAL HOME LOAN MORTGAGE CORPORATION (FREDDIE MAC)-NORTHEAST REGION—See Federal Home Loan Mortgage Corporation; *U.S. Public,* pg. 615
FEDERAL HOME LOAN MORTGAGE CORPORATION (FREDDIE MAC)-NORTH CENTRAL REGION—See Federal Home Loan Mortgage Corporation; *U.S. Public,* pg. 615
FEDERAL HOME LOAN MORTGAGE CORPORATION (FREDDIE MAC)-SOUTHEAST/SOUTHERN REGION—See Federal Home Loan Mortgage Corporation; *U.S. Public,* pg. 615
FEDERAL HOME LOAN MORTGAGE CORPORATION (FREDDIE MAC)-WESTERN REGION—See Federal Home Loan Mortgage Corporation; *U.S. Public,* pg. 615
FEDERAL HOSE MANUFACTURING CORP.—See Flexfab Horizons International, Inc.; *U.S. Private,* pg. 412
FEDERAL INDUSTRIES CONSUMER GROUP, INC.—See Russel Metals Inc.; *Int'l,* pg. 1150
FEDERAL INDUSTRIES, INC.—See Standex International Corporation; *U.S. Public,* pg. 1506
FEDERAL INDUSTRIES INDUSTRIAL GROUP, INC.—See Russel Metals Inc.; *Int'l,* pg. 1150

FEDERAL INDUSTRIES TRANSPORT GROUP—See Russel Metals Inc.; *Int'l,* pg. 1150
FEDERAL INFORMATION SERVICES—See Dawson Holdings PLC; *Int'l,* pg. 385
FEDERAL INSURANCE CO.—See The Chubb Corporation; *U.S. Public,* pg. 355
FEDERAL INTEGRATED SYSTEMS CORP.—See Electronic Data Systems Corporation; *U.S. Public,* pg. 570
FEDERAL KEMPER LIFE ASSURANCE COMPANY—See Zurich Insurance Company; *Int'l,* pg. 1530
FEDERAL LABORATORIES, INC.—See Mace Security International, Inc.; *U.S. Public,* pg. 1030
FEDERAL-MOGUL CORPORATION; *U.S. Public,* pg. 615
FEDERAL-MOGUL SERVICES—See Kyowa Hakko Kogyo Company, Ltd.; *Int'l,* pg. 778
FEDERAL NATIONAL MORTGAGE ASSOCIATION (FANNIE MAE); *U.S. Public,* pg. 615
FEDERAL PACKAGING CORPORATION—See Caraustar Industries, Inc.; *U.S. Public,* pg. 303
FEDERAL PAPER BOARD COMPANY, INC.—See International Paper Company; *U.S. Public,* pg. 903
FEDERAL PARTS—See Standard Motor Products Inc.; *U.S. Public,* pg. 1503
FEDERAL PROCESS CORP.; *U.S. Private,* pg. 399
FEDERAL PRODUCTS CO.—See Esterline Technologies Corporation; *U.S. Public,* pg. 594
FEDERAL PRODUCTS U.K. LTD.—See Esterline Technologies Corporation; *U.S. Public,* pg. 594
FEDERAL REALTY INVESTMENT TRUST; *U.S. Public,* pg. 616
FEDERAL RESERVE BANK OF DALLAS; *U.S. Private,* pg. 399
FEDERAL SAVINGS BANK—See Kemmons Wilson, Inc.; *U.S. Private,* pg. 614
FEDERAL SCREW WORKS; *U.S. Public,* pg. 616
FEDERAL SIGNAL CORPORATION; *U.S. Public,* pg. 616
FEDERAL SIGNAL CORPORATION, SIGNAL DIV.—See Federal Signal Corporation; *U.S. Public,* pg. 616
FEDERAL SIGNAL INTERNATIONAL LTD.—See Federal Signal Corporation; *U.S. Public,* pg. 616
FEDERAL SYSTEMS GROUP—See Sterling Software, Inc.; *U.S. Public,* pg. 1516
FEDERAL SYSTEMS INTEGRATION CORPORATION— See Compagnie des Machines Bull; *Int'l,* pg. 316
FEDERATED BANK, S.S.B.—See Firstar Corporation; *U.S. Public,* pg. 643
FEDERATED-BLAIKIE LTD.—See Barlow Ltd.; *Int'l,* pg. 167
FEDERATED CORPORATE—See Federated Department Stores, Inc.; *U.S. Public,* pg. 618
FEDERATED CREDIT CORP.—See Lagardere Groupe; *Int'l,* pg. 794
FEDERATED DEPARTMENT STORES, INC.; *U.S. Public,* pg. 617
FEDERATED FRY METALS, INC.—See Cookson Group plc; *Int'l,* pg. 328
FEDERATED LOGISTICS—See Federated Department Stores, Inc.; *U.S. Public,* pg. 618
FEDERATED MERCHANDISING—See Federated Department Stores, Inc.; *U.S. Public,* pg. 618
FEDERATED METALS CORP.—See Asarco Incorporated; *U.S. Public,* pg. 138
FEDERATED MUTUAL INSURANCE COMPANY; *U.S. Private,* pg. 399
FEDERATED SYSTEMS GROUP—See Federated Department Stores, Inc.; *U.S. Public,* pg. 618
FEDERATION DES CAISSES POPULAIRES DESJARDINS; *Int'l,* pg. 479
FEDERATION INSURANCE COMPANY OF CANADA—See Assicurazioni Generali S.p.A.; *Int'l,* pg. 90
FEDEX CUSTOMS BROKERAGE CORP.—See FDX Corporation; *U.S. Public,* pg. 604
FEDEX INTERNATIONAL TRANSMISSION CORP.—See FDX Corporation; *U.S. Public,* pg. 604
FEDMET INTERNATIONAL INC.—See Russel Metals Inc.; *Int'l,* pg. 1150
FEDMET TUBULARS—See Russel Metals Inc.; *Int'l,* pg. 1150
C.R. FEDRICK, INC.—See Sundt Corp.; *U.S. Private,* pg. 1052
FEED SCREWS DIV.—See Ampco-Pittsburgh Corporation; *U.S. Public,* pg. 104
FEED SERVICE CORP.; *U.S. Private,* pg. 399
FEENY MANUFACTURING COMPANY—See Knape & Vogt Mfg. Co.; *U.S. Public,* pg. 963
J. FEGELY INC.; *U.S. Private,* pg. 399
OHG FEGRO/SELGROS GESELLSCHAFT FUR GROSSHANDEL MBH & CO.—See Otto Versand (GmbH & Co.); *Int'l,* pg. 1014
FEHR DEMAG AG—See Mannesmann A.G.; *Int'l,* pg. 837
HANS FEHR GMBH—See Mannesmann A.G.; *Int'l,* pg. 837
HANS FEIERABEND GMBH—See Robert Bosch GmbH; *Int'l,* pg. 204
FEINTOOL AG LYSS—See Feintool International Holding AG; *Int'l,* pg. 479
FEINTOOL CINCINNATI INC.—See Feintool International Holding AG; *Int'l,* pg. 479
FEINTOOL ENGINEERING CO. LTD.—See Feintool International Holding AG; *Int'l,* pg. 479
FEINTOOL EQUIPMENT CORP.—See Feintool International Holding AG; *Int'l,* pg. 479
FEINTOOL INTERNATIONAL HOLDING AG; *Int'l,* pg. 479
FEINTOOL JAPAN CO. LTD.—See Feintool International Holding AG; *Int'l,* pg. 479
FEINTOOL NEW YORK INC.—See Feintool International Holding AG; *Int'l,* pg. 479
FEINTOOL U.S. OPERATIONS INC.—See Feintool International Holding AG; *Int'l,* pg. 479
FEL-PRO INCORPORATED; *U.S. Private,* pg. 399
FELD PRODUCTIONS; *U.S. Private,* pg. 399
FELDMUHLE KYOCERA EUROPA ELEKTRONISCHE—See Kyocera Corporation; *Int'l,* pg. 776
FELDSCHLOSSCHEN HURLIMANN HOLDING; *Int'l,* pg. 479

THE FELDSPAR CORP.—See Zemex Corporation; *Int'l,* pg. 1523
FELGUERA-IHI S.A.—See Ishikawajima-Harima Heavy Industries Co., Ltd.; *Int'l,* pg. 689
FELICITACIONES NACIONALES S.A. DE C.V.—See American Greetings Corporation; *U.S. Public,* pg. 78
THE FELIXSTOWE DOCK & RAILWAY CO.—See The Peninsular and Oriental Steam Navigation Company; *Int'l,* pg. 1033
FELLOWES MANUFACTURING; *U.S. Private,* pg. 400
FELLOWS CORPORATION—See Goldman Financial Group; *U.S. Private,* pg. 461
FELS BAKU LTD.—See Keppel Corporation Limited; *Int'l,* pg. 731
FELS-WERKE GMBH—See Preussag AG; *Int'l,* pg. 1069
FELSTED DIVISION—See Furon Company; *U.S. Public,* pg. 689
THE FELTERS COMPANY; *U.S. Private,* pg. 400
FELTON BRUSH INC.; *U.S. Private,* pg. 400
FELTON WORLDWIDE LTD.—See Universal Foods Corporation; *U.S. Public,* pg. 1696
FELTRAX INTERNATIONAL, INC.—See BTR plc; *Int'l,* pg. 130
FEMCO MAGNET WIRE CORPORATION—See The Furukawa Electric Co., Ltd.; *Int'l,* pg. 530
FEMSA CERVEZA S.A. DE CV—See Fomento Economico Mexicano, S.A. de CV; *Int'l,* pg. 496
FEMSA EMPAQUE, S.A. DE CV—See Fomento Economico Mexicano, S.A. de CV; *Int'l,* pg. 496
FEMSA S.P.A.—See Charter plc; *Int'l,* pg. 283
FENCHURCH CAPITAL MANAGEMENT LIMITED—See Dresdner Bank AG; *Int'l,* pg. 420
FENCO MACLAREN INC.—See SNC-Lavalin Group Inc.; *Int'l,* pg. 1162
FENCOURT REINSURANCE CO. LTD.—See The Hartford Financial Services Group Inc.; *U.S. Public,* pg. 795
FENDER MUSICAL INSTRUMENTS; *U.S. Private,* pg. 400
FENLAND FOODS—See Northern Foods plc; *Int'l,* pg. 968
FENN MANUFACTURING—See United Dominion Industries, Ltd.; *U.S. Public,* pg. 1676
FENNER DRIVES; *U.S. Private,* pg. 400
OY FENNOFELT AB-FORMING & FABRICS DRYER PLANT—See Albany International Corp.; *U.S. Public,* pg. 37
OY FENNOFELT AB-PRESS FABRIC PLANT—See Albany International Corp.; *U.S. Public,* pg. 37
H.G. FENTON MATERIAL COMPANY; *U.S. Private,* pg. 400
FENTON HILL AMERICAN LIMITED—See BAA plc; *Int'l,* pg. 103
FENTON PRESS, INC.; *U.S. Private,* pg. 400
FENWAL ELECTRONICS, INC.—See Publicker Industries Inc.; *U.S. Public,* pg. 1341
FENWAY PARTNERS INC.; *U.S. Private,* pg. 401
J. FENWICK & CO. PTY. LTD.—See Brambles Industries Limited; *Int'l,* pg. 211
FENWICK KALMAR SA—See Trelleborg AB; *Int'l,* pg. 1421
FENWICK-LINDE S.A.R.L.—See Linde AG; *Int'l,* pg. 810
FERAG AG—See WRH Walter Reist Holding AG; *Int'l,* pg. 1484
FERAG INC.—See WRH Walter Reist Holding AG; *Int'l,* pg. 1484
FERALLOY CORP.—See Preussag AG; *Int'l,* pg. 1070
FERALLOY INDIANA CORP.—See Preussag AG; *Int'l,* pg. 1070
FERALLOY MIDWEST CORP.—See Preussag AG; *Int'l,* pg. 1070
FERALLOY NORTH AMERICAN STEEL CO. LTD. PARTNERSHIP—See Preussag AG; *Int'l,* pg. 1070
FERALLOY NORTH AMERICAN STEEL CORP.—See Preussag AG; *Int'l,* pg. 1070
FERALLOY PROCESSING COMPANY—See Preussag AG; *Int'l,* pg. 1070
FERALLOY RELIANCE COMPANY LTD. PARTNERSHIP— See Preussag AG; *Int'l,* pg. 1070
FERALLOY RELIANCE MANAGEMENT CORP.—See Preussag AG; *Int'l,* pg. 1070
FERALLOY WEST CORP.—See Preussag AG; *Int'l,* pg. 1070
FERDEE LIMITED—See Saint-Gobain; *Int'l,* pg. 1172
FEREMBAL S.A.—See Continental Can Co.; *U.S. Public,* pg. 440
FERGUSON ELECTRIC CONSTRUCTION CO., INC.; *U.S. Private,* pg. 401
FERGUSON ELECTRIC EQUIPMENT CORPORATION— See Ferguson Electric Construction Co., Inc.; *U.S. Private,* pg. 401
FERGUSON ELECTRIC SERVICE CO., INC.—See Ferguson Electric Construction Co., Inc.; *U.S. Private,* pg. 401
FERGUSON ENTERPRISES, INC.—See Wolseley Plc.; *Int'l,* pg. 1512
FERGUSON INTERNATIONAL HOLDINGS; *Int'l,* pg. 479
FERGUSON INTERNATIONAL, INC.; *U.S. Private,* pg. 401
FERGUSON LIMITED—See Thomson S.A.; *Int'l,* pg. 1384
FERGUSON LYON CONKLIN & COMPANY INC.—See Wolseley Plc.; *Int'l,* pg. 1512
FERGUSON MACHINE CO.—See Crane Co.; *U.S. Public,* pg. 457
FERGUSON MACHINE CO. S.A.—See Crane Co.; *U.S. Public,* pg. 457
FERGUSON MANUFACTURING & EQUIPMENT COMPANY, INC.; *U.S. Private,* pg. 401
FERGUSON PUBLISHING COMPANY; *U.S. Private,* pg. 401
THOMAS G. FERGUSON ASSOCIATES, INC.—See WPP Group plc; *Int'l,* pg. 1483
FERGUSSON, WILD & CO. LTD.—See Veba AG; *Int'l,* pg. 1458
FERIMPEX GMBH—See Cockerill Sambre; *Int'l,* pg. 302
FERMAN OLDSMOBILE; *U.S. Private,* pg. 401
FERMAR S.P.A.—See Coeclerici Group; *Int'l,* pg. 304
FERMEC HOLDINGS, LTD.—See Case Corporation; *U.S. Public,* pg. 312

FERMENTA AB; *Int'l,* pg. 480
FERMENTACIONES MEXICANAS, S.A. DE C.V. (FERMEX)—See Kyowa Hakko Kogyo Company, Ltd.; *Int'l,* pg. 778
GEORGE E. FERN COMPANY—See Budco Group Inc.; *U.S. Private,* pg. 178
FERNANDINA BEACH NEWS LEADER, INC.—See The New York Times Company; *U.S. Public,* pg. 1175
FERNANDO ROQUE TISA—See Royal Nedlloyd Group N.V.; *Int'l,* pg. 1145
FERNGAS NORDBAYERN GMBH—See Ruhrgas Aktiengesellschaft; *Int'l,* pg. 1148
FERNGAS SALZGITTER GMBH—See Ruhrgas Aktiengesellschaft; *Int'l,* pg. 1148
FERNWAERMEVERBUND SAAR GMBH—See Saarbergwerke Aktiengesellschaft; *Int'l,* pg. 1167
FERNWARMEVERSORGUNG HERNE GMBH—See Veba AG; *Int'l,* pg. 1460
FERODO LTD.—See T & N Plc; *Int'l,* pg. 1334
FEROLIE GROUP; *U.S. Private,* pg. 401
FERON DE CLERSATTEL—See SNCF; *Int'l,* pg. 1165
FEROX A.S.—See Air Products and Chemicals, Inc.; *U.S. Public,* pg. 32
FERRANTI AIR SYSTEMS LTD.—See Datel Technologies Ltd.; *Int'l,* pg. 384
FERRANTI GMBH—See Thomson S.A.; *Int'l,* pg. 1384
FERRANTI NAVAL—See The General Electric Company, p.l.c.; *Int'l,* pg. 544
FERRANTI SYSECA—See Thomson S.A.; *Int'l,* pg. 1384
FERRANTI TECHNOLOGIES LTD.; *Int'l,* pg. 480
FERRARI NORTH AMERICA, INC.—See Fiat Auto SpA; *Int'l,* pg. 483
FERRARIA OY AB—See Fiskars Oy AB; *Int'l,* pg. 492
FERRARIS PISTON SERVICES LTD.—See Tomkins PLC; *Int'l,* pg. 1395
FERRARRI FINANCIAL SERVICES, INC.—See Fiat Auto SpA; *Int'l,* pg. 483
FERRAS—See Pechiney S.A.; *Int'l,* pg. 1028
FERRAZ CORPORATION—See Pechiney S.A.; *Int'l,* pg. 1028
FERRE EXPORT CORP.—See Puerto Rican Cement Co., Inc.; *U.S. Public,* pg. 1342
FERRELLCALVILLO COMMUNICATIONS, INC.; *U.S. Private,* pg. 401
FERRELLGAS HOUSTON—See Ferrellgas Partners, L.P.; *U.S. Public,* pg. 618
FERRELLGAS PARTNERS, L.P.; *U.S. Public,* pg. 618
JAMES FERRERA & SONS, INC.; *U.S. Private,* pg. 401
FERRERO; *Int'l,* pg. 480
FERRERO INC.—See Ferrero; *Int'l,* pg. 480
FERRERO U.S.A., INC.—See Ferrero; *Int'l,* pg. 480
FERRIER LULLIN & CIE SA; *Int'l,* pg. 480
FERRIER LULLIN & CIE SA—See Ferrier Lullin & Cie SA; *Int'l,* pg. 480
FERRIER LULLIN BANK & TRUST (BAHAMAS) LIMITED— See Ferrier Lullin & Cie SA; *Int'l,* pg. 480
FERRIER LULLIN CAYMAN BANK & TRUST—See Ferrier Lullin & Cie SA; *Int'l,* pg. 480
FERRIKLOR AB—See Kemira Oy; *Int'l,* pg. 728
FERRO CORPORATION; *U.S. Public,* pg. 618
FERRO DE VENEZUELA, C.A.—See Ferro Corporation; *U.S. Public,* pg. 619
FERRO (DEUTSCHLAND) GMBH—See Ferro Corporation; *U.S. Public,* pg. 619
FERRO ECUATORIANA S.A.—See Ferro Corporation; *U.S. Public,* pg. 619
FERRO ENAMEL ARGENTINA, S.A.—See Ferro Corporation; *U.S. Public,* pg. 619
FERRO ENAMEL DO BRASIL I.C.L.—See Ferro Corporation; *U.S. Public,* pg. 619
FERRO ENAMEL ESPANOLA, S.A.—See Ferro Corporation; *U.S. Public,* pg. 619
FERRO ENAMELS (JAPAN) LTD.—See Ferro Corporation; *U.S. Public,* pg. 619
FERRO FAR EAST LTD.—See Ferro Corporation; *U.S. Public,* pg. 619
FERRO FRANCE-EUROSTAR—See Ferro Corporation; *U.S. Public,* pg. 619
FERRO FRANCE S.A.R.L.—See Ferro Corporation; *U.S. Public,* pg. 619
FERRO (HOLLAND) B.V.—See Ferro Corporation; *U.S. Public,* pg. 619
FERRO (ITALIA) S.R.L.—See Ferro Corporation; *U.S. Public,* pg. 619
P.T. FERRO MAS DINAMIKA—See Ferro Corporation; *U.S. Public,* pg. 619
FERRO METAL & CHEMICAL CORPORATION LTD.—See Philipp Brothers Chemicals, Inc.; *U.S. Private,* pg. 861
FERRO MEXICANA S.A. DE C.V.—See Ferro Corporation; *U.S. Public,* pg. 619
FERRO MSI—See Ferro Corporation; *U.S. Public,* pg. 619
FERRO ROSEMAR—See Ferro Corporation; *U.S. Public,* pg. 619
FERRO (THAILAND) CO. LTD.—See Ferro Corporation; *U.S. Public,* pg. 619
FERRO TOYO CO. LIMITED—See Ferro Corporation; *U.S. Public,* pg. 619
FERRO UNION, INC.; *U.S. Private,* pg. 402
FERRO UNION, INC., NORTHERN CALIFORNIA—See Ferro Union, Inc.; *U.S. Private,* pg. 402
FERROCARBON GMBH—See Veba AG; *Int'l,* pg. 1458
FERROFLUIDICS CORPORATION; *U.S. Public,* pg. 620
FERROFLUIDICS JAPAN CORPORATION—See Ferrofluidics Corporation; *U.S. Public,* pg. 620
AB FERROLEGERINGAR—See Metallurg, Inc.; *U.S. Private,* pg. 735
FERROLEGERINGAR AG—See Metallurg, Inc.; *U.S. Private,* pg. 735
OY FERROSAN AB—See Novo Nordisk A/S; *Int'l,* pg. 989
FERROSAN A/S—See Novo Nordisk A/S; *Int'l,* pg. 987
FERROSAN BENELUX B.V.—See Novo Nordisk A/S; *Int'l,* pg. 989
FERROSAN DANMARK A/S—See Novo Nordisk A/S; *Int'l,* pg. 987

FERROSAN HEALTHCARE LTD.—See Novo Nordisk A/S; *Int'l,* pg. 989
FERROSAN HEALTHCRAFTS NV/SA—See Novo Nordisk A/S; *Int'l,* pg. 989
FERROSAN INTERNATIONAL A/S—See Novo Nordisk A/S; *Int'l,* pg. 987
FERROSTAAL AKTIENGESELLSCHAFT—See MAN Aktiengesellschaft; *Int'l,* pg. 824
FERROUS PROCESSING & TRADING CO.; *U.S. Private,* pg. 402
FERRULMATIC—See Alliant Techsystems; *U.S. Public,* pg. 47
FERRUM INC.—See DoFasco, Inc.; *Int'l,* pg. 414
FERRUM INC.—See Jannock Limited; *Int'l,* pg. 699
FERRY-MORSE SEED COMPANY—See Groupe Limagrain; *Int'l,* pg. 566
FERRY MOUGIN—See SNCF; *Int'l,* pg. 1164
HERBERT FERRYMAN—See Franz Haniel & Cie, GmbH; *Int'l,* pg. 591
FERRYMASTERS LIMITED—See The Peninsular and Oriental Steam Navigation Company; *Int'l,* pg. 1033
FERS ET METAUX RECYCLES LTEE.—See Stelco Inc.; *Int'l,* pg. 1299
FERS PERSONAL FINANCIAL SERVICES, L.L.C.—See Friedman, Eisenstein, Raemer and Schwartz, LLP; *U.S. Private,* pg. 428
FERS TECHNOLOGY GROUP, L.L.C.—See Friedman, Eisenstein, Raemer and Schwartz, LLP; *U.S. Private,* pg. 428
FERSINSA GIST-BROCADES SA DE CV—See Royal Gist-Brocades N.V.; *Int'l,* pg. 1143
FERTILIZANTES DEL PACIFICO S.A.—See BASF AG; *Int'l,* pg. 108
FESLENTE BONIFACE S.A.—See Borden, Inc.; *U.S. Public,* pg. 159
FESTO AG & CO.; *Int'l,* pg. 480
FESTO CORPORATION—See Festo AG & Co.; *Int'l,* pg. 480
FETERL MFG. CO.—See United Dominion Industries, Ltd.; *U.S. Public,* pg. 1676
THE SCOTT FETZER COMPANY—See Berkshire Hathaway Inc.; *U.S. Public,* pg. 217
FETZER VINEYARDS CALIFORNIA WINES—See Brown-Forman Corporation; *U.S. Public,* pg. 261
DR. C. OTTO FEUERFEST GMBH—See Preussag AG; *Int'l,* pg. 1070
FEUMAS GMBH—See Icopal a/s; *Int'l,* pg. 659
FEVI-PROMAVENT—See Jeumont-Schneider Trenformeteurs; *Int'l,* pg. 706
FEY MFG. CO., INC.—See Wedgestone Financial Inc.; *U.S. Public,* pg. 1751
FIAMM-GS—See Fiamm S.p.A.; *Int'l,* pg. 480
FIAMM S.P.A.; *Int'l,* pg. 480
FIAMM TECHNOLOGIES INC.—See Fiamm S.p.A.; *Int'l,* pg. 480
FIANZAS MONTERREY S.A.—See Aetna Inc.; *U.S. Public,* pg. 27
F.I.A.P. DEUTSCHLAND GMBH—See AEP Industries, Inc.; *U.S. Public,* pg. 5
F.I.A.P. SPA—See AEP Industries, Inc.; *U.S. Public,* pg. 5
FIAT-ALLIS B.V.—See Fiat Auto SpA; *Int'l,* pg. 483
FIAT AUTO ESPANA S.A.—See Fiat Auto SpA; *Int'l,* pg. 481
FIAT AUTO IRELAND LTD.—See Fiat Auto SpA; *Int'l,* pg. 481
FIAT AUTO PORTUGUESA SA—See Fiat Auto SpA; *Int'l,* pg. 481
FIAT AUTO R&D—See Fiat Auto SpA; *Int'l,* pg. 483
FIAT AUTO SPA; *Int'l,* pg. 481
FIAT AUTO S.P.A.—See Fiat Auto SpA; *Int'l,* pg. 481
FIAT AUTO SUISSE SA—See Fiat Auto SpA; *Int'l,* pg. 481
FIAT AUTO SVERIGE AB—See Fiat Auto SpA; *Int'l,* pg. 481
FIAT AUTO (UK) LTD.—See Fiat Auto SpA; *Int'l,* pg. 483
FIAT AUTOMISVEIS S.A.—See Fiat Auto SpA; *Int'l,* pg. 483
FIAT AUTOMOBILE AG—See Fiat Auto SpA; *Int'l,* pg. 481
FIAT AVIAZIONE S.P.A.—See Fiat Auto SpA; *Int'l,* pg. 481
FIAT AVIO, INC.—See Fiat Auto SpA; *Int'l,* pg. 483
FIAT CHARIOTS ELEVATEURS FRANCE S.A.—See Linde AG; *Int'l,* pg. 811
FIAT COMPONENTI AUTOVEICOLISTI S.P.A.—See Fiat Auto SpA; *Int'l,* pg. 481
FIAT CONCORD S.A.—See Fiat Auto SpA; *Int'l,* pg. 483
FIAT CONCORD SAIC—See Fiat Auto SpA; *Int'l,* pg. 484
FIAT CREDIT INTERNATIONAL S.R.L.—See Fiat Auto SpA; *Int'l,* pg. 482
FIAT DEUTSCHLAND—See Fiat Auto SpA; *Int'l,* pg. 483
FIAT DO BRAZIL SA—See Fiat Auto SpA; *Int'l,* pg. 484
FIAT FERROVIARIA SAVIGLIANO S.P.A.—See Fiat Auto SpA; *Int'l,* pg. 481
FIAT FERROVIARIA S.P.A.—See Fiat Auto SpA; *Int'l,* pg. 481
FIAT FINANCE U.S.A., INC.—See Fiat Auto SpA; *Int'l,* pg. 483
FIAT FRANCE—See Fiat Auto SpA; *Int'l,* pg. 483
FIAT FRANCE SA—See Fiat Auto SpA; *Int'l,* pg. 484
FIAT IBERICA S.A.—See Fiat Auto SpA; *Int'l,* pg. 483
FIAT LUBRIFICANTI S.R.L.—See Fiat Auto SpA; *Int'l,* pg. 482
FIAT OM—See Linde AG; *Int'l,* pg. 811
FIAT OM CARRELLI ELEVATORI S.P.A.—See Linde AG; *Int'l,* pg. 811
FIAT OM PIMESPO FODERTECHNIK GMBH—See Linde AG; *Int'l,* pg. 811
FIAT SERVICES, INC.—See Fiat Auto SpA; *Int'l,* pg. 483
FIAT TRATTORI S.P.A.—See Fiat Auto SpA; *Int'l,* pg. 481
FIAT TTG S.P.A.—See Fiat Auto SpA; *Int'l,* pg. 481
FIAT USA INC.—See Fiat Auto SpA; *Int'l,* pg. 483
FIATALLIS NORTH AMERICA, INC.—See Fiat Auto SpA; *Int'l,* pg. 483
FIATGEOTECH S.P.A.—See Fiat Auto SpA; *Int'l,* pg. 484
FIATIMPRESIT S.P.A.—See Fiat Auto SpA; *Int'l,* pg. 481
FIATSAVA S.P.A.—See Fiat Auto SpA; *Int'l,* pg. 482
FIBELPAR S.A.—See Tractebel; *Int'l,* pg. 1416

FIBER CABLE, INC.—See Dycom Industries, Inc.; *U.S. Public,* pg. 538
FIBER KEMI A/S—See DSM N.V.; *Int'l,* pg. 355
FIBER MATERIALS, INC.; *U.S. Private,* pg. 402
FIBER OPTIC PRODUCTS DIVISION—See Methode Electronics Inc.; *U.S. Public,* pg. 1101
FIBER OPTIC SERVICES, INC.—See The Goldfield Corporation; *U.S. Public,* pg. 750
FIBER-RESIN CORPORATION—See H.B. Fuller Company; *U.S. Public,* pg. 686
FIBERCOTE INDUSTRIES, INC.—See Park Electrochemical Corporation; *U.S. Public,* pg. 1258
FIBERESIN INDUSTRIES INC.; *U.S. Private,* pg. 402
FIBERLOCK TECHNOLOGIES, INC.—See California Products Corp.; *U.S. Private,* pg. 201
FIBERLUX, INC.—See Tredegar Industries Inc.; *U.S. Public,* pg. 1634
FIBERMARK, INC.; *U.S. Public,* pg. 620
FIBERPACHS S.A.—See DSM N.V.; *Int'l,* pg. 355
FIBERTEX A/S—See The East Asiatic Company Ltd. A/S; *Int'l,* pg. 431
FIBERWEB NORTH AMERICA INC.—See BBA Group plc; *Int'l,* pg. 113
FIBERWEB WASHOUGAL INC.—See BBA Group plc; *Int'l,* pg. 113
A/S FIBO—See Scancem AB; *Int'l,* pg. 1200
FIBO EXCLAY EESTI AS—See Scancem AB; *Int'l,* pg. 1200
FIBO EXCLAY LTD.—See Scancem AB; *Int'l,* pg. 1200
FIBO EXCLAY POLSKA SP.Z.O.O.—See Scancem AB; *Int'l,* pg. 1200
FIBO-TRESPO—See Norske Skogindustrier A.S; *Int'l,* pg. 965
FIBO-TRESPO-LANGMOEN—See Norske Skogindustrier A.S; *Int'l,* pg. 966
FIBRAS ACOLCHABLES S.A. DE C.V.—See Leggett & Platt, Incorporated; *U.S. Public,* pg. 987
FIBRAS CERAMICAS, C.A.—See Morgan Crucible Co. Plc; *Int'l,* pg. 894
FIBRAS CERAMICAS, S.A.—See Morgan Crucible Co. Plc; *Int'l,* pg. 893
FIBRAS QUIMICAS SA—See Akzo Nobel N.V.; *Int'l,* pg. 46
FIBRE GLASS-EVERCOAT COMPANY—See Illinois Tool Works Inc.; *U.S. Public,* pg. 866
THE FIBRE-METAL PRODUCTS COMPANY; *U.S. Private,* pg. 402
FIBRE PRODUCTS NEW ZEALAND LIMITED— See International Paper Company; *U.S. Public,* pg. 905
FIBREBOND CORPORATION; *U.S. Private,* pg. 402
FIBRES INTERNATIONAL, INC.—See Continental Paper Recycling LLC; *U.S. Private,* pg. 269
FIBREWEB INTERNATIONAL, LTD.—See Gould Paper Corporation; *U.S. Private,* pg. 467
FIBRO FRICTION—See Standard Motor Products Inc.; *U.S. Public,* pg. 1503
FIBRO TAMBOR—See Sonoco Products Company; *U.S. Public,* pg. 1487
FIBROCO S.A.—See Telefonaktiebolaget LM Ericsson; *Int'l,* pg. 1368
FIBROLITH DAMMSTOFFE WILMS GMBH—See Lafarge S.A.; *Int'l,* pg. 791
FIC TRADING CORPORATION—See Fastec Industrial; *U.S. Private,* pg. 397
FICHTEL & SACHS & CO. VERWALTUNGSGESELLSCHAFT OHG— See Mannesmann A.G.; *Int'l,* pg. 835
FICHTEL & SACHS AG—See Mannesmann A.G.; *Int'l,* pg. 835
FICHTEL & SACHS AG & CO.—See Mannesmann A.G.; *Int'l,* pg. 835
FICHTEL & SACHS AUSTRIA GMBH—See Mannesmann A.G.; *Int'l,* pg. 835
FICHTEL & SACHS INDUSTRIES, INC.—See Mannesmann A.G.; *Int'l,* pg. 835
FICOMET S.A.R.L.—See AXIA Incorporated; *U.S. Private,* pg. 103
FICON CORPORATION—See American International Group, Inc.; *U.S. Public,* pg. 84
FICUT S.P.A.—See Oce-van der Grinten N.V.; *Int'l,* pg. 994
FIDABEL NV—See Almanij N.V.; *Int'l,* pg. 65
FIDCO—See Nestle S.A.; *Int'l,* pg. 916
FIDEICOMISOS—See Bancomer, S.A.; *Int'l,* pg. 145
FIDELIDAD—See Caixa Geral de Depositos; *Int'l,* pg. 250
FIDELIO AUSTRALIA (PTY) LTD.—See Micros Systems Inc.; *U.S. Public,* pg. 1106
FIDELIO INDIA PRIVATE LTD.—See Micros Systems Inc.; *U.S. Public,* pg. 1106
FIDELIO INDONESIA—See Micros Systems Inc.; *U.S. Public,* pg. 1106
FIDELIO ITALIA SRL.—See Micros Systems Inc.; *U.S. Public,* pg. 1106
FIDELIO-MICROS FRANCE S.A.—See Micros Systems Inc.; *U.S. Public,* pg. 1106
FIDELIO MICROS ISRAEL & FIDELIO LTD.—See Micros Systems Inc.; *U.S. Public,* pg. 1106
FIDELIO NORDIC NORGE A/S—See Micros Systems Inc.; *U.S. Public,* pg. 1106
FIDELIO NORDIC OY—See Micros Systems Inc.; *U.S. Public,* pg. 1106
FIDELIO NORDIC SVERIGE AB—See Micros Systems Inc.; *U.S. Public,* pg. 1106
FIDELIO PORTUGAL, LDA.—See Micros Systems Inc.; *U.S. Public,* pg. 1106
FIDELIO SOFTWARE CORPORATION—See Micros Systems Inc.; *U.S. Public,* pg. 1106
FIDELIO SOFTWARE GMBH—See Micros Systems Inc.; *U.S. Public,* pg. 1106
FIDELIO SOFTWARE LTD.—See Micros Systems Inc.; *U.S. Public,* pg. 1106
FIDELIO SOFTWARE U.K. LTD.—See Micros Systems Inc.; *U.S. Public,* pg. 1106
FIDELIO SOUTHERN AFRICA (PTY) LTD.—See Micros Systems Inc.; *U.S. Public,* pg. 1106

FIDELIO STP—See Micros Systems Inc.; *U.S. Public,* pg. 1106
FIDELIO TECHNOLOGIES, INC.—See Micros Systems Inc.; *U.S. Public,* pg. 1106
FIDELIO TECHNOLOGIES SUCURSAL ARGENTINA—See Micros Systems Inc.; *U.S. Public,* pg. 1106
FIDELIO THAILAND CO. LTD.—See Micros Systems Inc.; *U.S. Public,* pg. 1106
FIDELIS NV—See Almanij N.V.; *Int'l,* pg. 65
FIDELITAS NV—See Almanij N.V.; *Int'l,* pg. 65
FIDELITY AND CASUALTY CO. OF NEW YORK—See Loews Corporation; *U.S. Public,* pg. 1011
FIDELITY & DEPOSIT COMPANY OF MARYLAND—See Zurich Insurance Company; *Int'l,* pg. 1530
FIDELITY & GUARANTY LIFE INSURANCE CO.—See USF&G Corporation; *U.S. Public,* pg. 1659
FIDELITY & SURETY DIVISION—See W.R. Berkley Corporation; *U.S. Public,* pg. 215
THE FIDELITY BANK—See Mercantile Bankshares Corporation; *U.S. Public,* pg. 1089
FIDELITY CAPITAL—See Fidelity Investments (FMR Corp.); *U.S. Private,* pg. 402
FIDELITY EXPRESS MONEY ORDER COMPANY DIVISION—See GSC Enterprises, Inc.; *U.S. Private,* pg. 436
FIDELITY FEDERAL SAVINGS BANK—See First Financial Bancorp; *U.S. Public,* pg. 632
FIDELITY GAS SYSTEMS, INC.—See Cigna Corp.; *U.S. Public,* pg. 358
FIDELITY INVESTMENTS (FMR CORP.); *U.S. Private,* pg. 402
FIDELITY MUTUAL LIFE INSURANCE CO.; *U.S. Private,* pg. 403
FIDELITY NATIONAL FINANCIAL, INC.; *U.S. Public,* pg. 620
FIDELITY NATIONAL TITLE INSURANCE COMPANY—See Fidelity National Financial, Inc.; *U.S. Public,* pg. 620
FIDELITY NATIONAL TITLE INSURANCE COMPANY OF PENNSYLVANIA—See Fidelity National Financial, Inc.; *U.S. Public,* pg. 621
FIDELITY NATIONAL TITLE INSURANCE COMPANY OF TENNESSEE—See Fidelity National Financial, Inc.; *U.S. Public,* pg. 621
FIDELITY OIL CO.—See MDU Resources Group, Inc.; *U.S. Public,* pg. 1025
FIDELITY OIL HOLDINGS, INC.—See MDU Resources Group, Inc.; *U.S. Public,* pg. 1025
FIDELITY TIRE MFG. CO.—See Condere Corporation; *U.S. Private,* pg. 262
FIDENTA OY—See Merita Ltd.; *Int'l,* pg. 859
FIDES TRUST COMPANY LTD.—See Commerzbank AG; *Int'l,* pg. 312
FIDIS S.P.A.—See Fiat Auto SpA; *Int'l,* pg. 482
FIDIS S.P.A.-FINANZIARIA DI SVILUPPO—See Fiat Auto SpA; *Int'l,* pg. 482
FIDISCO NV—See Almanij N.V.; *Int'l,* pg. 65
FIDRAS—See Allianz Aktiengesellschaft; *Int'l,* pg. 61
FIDUCIARY FINANCIAL SERVICES CORP.—See Fiduciary Trust Company International; *U.S. Public,* pg. 621
FIDUCIARY INTERNATIONAL, INC.—See Fiduciary Trust Company International; *U.S. Public,* pg. 621
FIDUCIARY MANAGEMENT ASSOCIATES, INC.—See United Asset Management Corporation; *U.S. Public,* pg. 1673
FIDUCIARY SPECIAL SERVICES, INC.—See Fiduciary Trust Company International; *U.S. Public,* pg. 621
FIDUCIARY TRUST COMPANY INTERNATIONAL; *U.S. Public,* pg. 621
FIDUCIARY TRUST COMPANY INTERNATIONAL—See Fiduciary Trust Company International; *U.S. Public,* pg. 621
FIDUCIARY TRUST CO. OF NEW HAMPSHIRE—See Torchmark Corporation; *U.S. Public,* pg. 1623
FIDUCIARY TRUST INTERNATIONAL ASIA LIMITED—See Fiduciary Trust Company International; *U.S. Public,* pg. 621
FIDUCIARY TRUST INTERNATIONAL LIMITED—See Fiduciary Trust Company International; *U.S. Public,* pg. 621
FIDUCIARY TRUST INTERNATIONAL OF CALIFORNIA—See Fiduciary Trust Company International; *U.S. Public,* pg. 621
FIDUCIARY TRUST INTERNATIONAL OF THE SOUTH—See Fiduciary Trust Company International; *U.S. Public,* pg. 621
FIDUS INSTRUMENT CORP.—See Bunzl PLC; *Int'l,* pg. 233
FIELD & STREAM—See The Times Mirror Company; *U.S. Public,* pg. 1617
FIELD CONSOLIDATED (PRIVATE) LTD.—See Hewlett-Packard Company; *U.S. Public,* pg. 817
FIELD CONTAINER COMPANY, L.P.; *U.S. Private,* pg. 403
FIELD CONTROLS CO.—See Pettibone Corporation; *U.S. Private,* pg. 860
FIELD EFFECTS—See Intermagnetics General Corporation; *U.S. Public,* pg. 894
FIELD EFFECTS, INC.—See Intermagnetics General Corporation; *U.S. Public,* pg. 893
FIELD NORTON (PVT.) LIMITED—See Saint-Gobain; *Int'l,* pg. 1174
FIELD PACKING COMPANY; *U.S. Private,* pg. 403
FIELDALE CORPORATION; *U.S. Private,* pg. 403
FIELDBROOK FARMS, INC.; *U.S. Private,* pg. 403
FIELDCREST CANNON, INC.—See Pillowtex Corporation; *U.S. Public,* pg. 1296
FIELDFRESH FARMS INC.—See The Oshawa Group Limited; *Int'l,* pg. 1012
FIELDS & DEVEREAUX/HEPY, INC.—See Harley Ellington Design; *U.S. Private,* pg. 503
FIELDS FINANCIAL SERVICES, INC.—See Kaneb Services, Inc.; *U.S. Public,* pg. 942
FIELDS STORES—See Hudson's Bay Company; *Int'l,* pg. 637

FIELDSTONE CABINETRY INC.—See Masco Corporation; *U.S. Public,* pg. 1053
FIELDSTONE TRANSPORTATION COMPANY—See Masco Corporation; *U.S. Public,* pg. 1053
FIESTA MART INC.; *U.S. Private,* pg. 403
FIESTA RESTAURANTS—See Eateries, Inc.; *U.S. Public,* pg. 555
FIFED—See Lyonnaise des Eaux S.A.; *Int'l,* pg. 823
THE FIFTH & RACE COMPANY LIMITED PARTNERSHIP—See Cigna Corp.; *U.S. Public,* pg. 361
FIFTH AVENUE CONVALESCENT HOUSE—See Vencor, Inc.; *U.S. Public,* pg. 1712
FIFTH QUARTER—See Shoney's, Inc.; *U.S. Public,* pg. 1467
FIFTH THIRD BANCORP; *U.S. Public,* pg. 621
THE FIFTH THIRD BANK—See Fifth Third Bancorp; *U.S. Public,* pg. 622
FIFTH THIRD BANK OF CENTRAL INDIANA—See Fifth Third Bancorp; *U.S. Public,* pg. 621
THE FIFTH THIRD BANK OF COLUMBUS—See Fifth Third Bancorp; *U.S. Public,* pg. 621
THE FIFTH THIRD BANK OF KENTUCKY—See Fifth Third Bancorp; *U.S. Public,* pg. 621
THE FIFTH THIRD BANK OF KENTUCKY, LOUISVILLE—See Fifth Third Bancorp; *U.S. Public,* pg. 621
THE FIFTH THIRD BANK OF NORTHEASTERN OHIO—See Fifth Third Bancorp; *U.S. Public,* pg. 621
THE FIFTH THIRD BANK OF NORTHERN KENTUCKY—See Fifth Third Bancorp; *U.S. Public,* pg. 621
THE FIFTH THIRD BANK OF NORTHWESTERN OHIO, NATIONAL ASSOCIATION—See Fifth Third Bancorp; *U.S. Public,* pg. 622
THE FIFTH THIRD BANK OF SOUTHERN OHIO—See Fifth Third Bancorp; *U.S. Public,* pg. 622
THE FIFTH THIRD BANK OF WESTERN OHIO, NATIONAL ASSOCIATION—See Fifth Third Bancorp; *U.S. Public,* pg. 622
FIFTH-THIRD TRUST CO. & SAVINGS BANK, FSB—See Fifth Third Bancorp; *U.S. Public,* pg. 622
57TH FIGHTER GROUP OF ATLANTA, INC.—See Specialty Restaurants Corporation; *U.S. Private,* pg. 1023
5601 MEDICAL PLAZA—See Genesis Health Ventures, Inc.; *U.S. Public,* pg. 729
56TH FIGHTER GROUP OF LONG ISLAND, INC.—See Specialty Restaurants Corporation; *U.S. Private,* pg. 1023
5300 RICHMOND ROAD CORPORATION—See Giant Eagle, Inc.; *U.S. Private,* pg. 451
THE FIGARO COMPANY, INC.; *U.S. Private,* pg. 404
FIGARO ENGINEERING INC.—See Tokuyama Corporation; *Int'l,* pg. 1393
FIGGIE INTERNATIONAL INC.; *U.S. Public,* pg. 622
FIGGIE PROPERTIES INC.—See Figgie International Inc.; *U.S. Public,* pg. 622
FIGI'S, INC.—See Fingerhut Corp.; *U.S. Public,* pg. 623
FIGUEROA—See Imetal; *Int'l,* pg. 662
FIKE CANADA INC.—See Fike Corporation; *U.S. Private,* pg. 404
FIKE CORPORATION; *U.S. Private,* pg. 404
FIKE EUROPE N.V.—See Fike Corporation; *U.S. Private,* pg. 404
FIKE JAPAN CORPORATION—See Fike Corporation; *U.S. Private,* pg. 404
FIKE SOUTH EAST ASIA PTE LTD—See Fike Corporation; *U.S. Private,* pg. 404
FILA FITNESS LTD.—See MacAndrews & Forbes Holdings Inc.; *U.S. Private,* pg. 690
FILA SPORT S.P.A.; *Int'l,* pg. 484
FILA USA—See Fila Sport S.p.A.; *Int'l,* pg. 484
FILARC WELDING INDUSTRIES B.V.—See Charter plc; *Int'l,* pg. 283
FILBERT CORP.—See Vilter Manufacturing Corporation; *U.S. Private,* pg. 1140
FILCO, INC.; *U.S. Private,* pg. 404
FILENE RESEARCH INSTITUTE—See Credit Union National Association; *U.S. Private,* pg. 288
FILENE'S—See The May Department Stores Company; *U.S. Public,* pg. 1063
FILENE'S BASEMENT, INC.; *U.S. Public,* pg. 622
FILENE'T CORPORATION; *U.S. Public,* pg. 622
FILERGIE S.N.C.—See Pirelli S.p.A.; *Int'l,* pg. 1059
FILIPINAS-ISEKI CORP.—See Nissho Iwai Corporation; *Int'l,* pg. 947
FILLAUER, INC.—See Bergen Brunswig Corporation; *U.S. Public,* pg. 214
FILL-RITE DIVISION—See Tuthill Corporation; *U.S. Private,* pg. 1110
FILM PRODUCTS DIVISION—See General Binding Corporation; *U.S. Public,* pg. 707
FILMCO INDUSTRIES INC.—See Thermwell Products Co., Inc.; *U.S. Private,* pg. 1081
FILMS FOR THE HUMANITIES & SCIENCES, INC.—See Primedia Inc.; *U.S. Public,* pg. 1327
FILMS PARAMOUNT S.A.—See National Amusements, Inc.; *U.S. Private,* pg. 777
FILMTEC CORPORATION—See The Dow Chemical Company; *U.S. Public,* pg. 523
FILODORO—See Sara Lee Corporation; *U.S. Public,* pg. 1434
FILPAC, INC.—See Bunzl PLC; *Int'l,* pg. 233
FILTER DIVISION, PARKER HANNIFIN (U.K.) LTD.—See Parker Hannifin Corporation; *U.S. Public,* pg. 1260
FILTER MEDIA—See Hosokawa Micron Corporation; *Int'l,* pg. 636
FILTER PRODUCTS DIVISION—See FiberMark Inc.; *U.S. Public,* pg. 620
FILTERTEK INC.—See ESCO Electronics Corporation; *U.S. Public,* pg. 546
FILTERWERK MANN & HUMMEL GMBH—See Filterwerk Mann & Hummel GmbH; *Int'l,* pg. 484
FILTERWERK MANN & HUMMEL GMBH; *Int'l,* pg. 484
FILTRAN—See SPX Corporation; *U.S. Public,* pg. 1421

FILTRATION GROUP—See Parker Hannifin Corporation; *U.S. Public,* pg. 1260
FILTRATION SYSTEMS DIVISION—See Aqua Care Systems Inc.; *U.S. Public,* pg. 126
FILTROL CORPORATION—See Akzo Nobel N.V.; *Int'l,* pg. 47
FILTRONA RICHMOND COMPANY—See Bunzl PLC; *Int'l,* pg. 232
FILTROS MANN LTDA.—See Filterwerk Mann & Hummel GmbH; *Int'l,* pg. 484
FILTROS MANN S.A.—See Filterwerk Mann & Hummel GmbH; *Int'l,* pg. 484
FILTROS MANN S.A. DE C.V.—See Filterwerk Mann & Hummel GmbH; *Int'l,* pg. 484
FIMA METAL BOX HOLDINGS SENDIRIAN BERHAD—See Caradon Plc; *Int'l,* pg. 267
FIMACOM - FINANCIERE MATRA COMMUNICATION—See Lagardere Groupe; *Int'l,* pg. 792
FIMAGEST—See Generale de Banque S.A.; *Int'l,* pg. 548
FIMAGROUP SA—See GIB Group; *Int'l,* pg. 533
FIMASER—See GIB Group; *Int'l,* pg. 533
FIMBEL DOOR CORPORATION; *U.S. Private,* pg. 404
FIMEUSE S.A.—See Tractebel; *Int'l,* pg. 1415
FIN.CO-ALGERIA—See IRI Istituto Ricostruzione Industriale; *Int'l,* pg. 654
FIN.CO BUDAPEST—See IRI Istituto Ricostruzione Industriale; *Int'l,* pg. 654
FIN.CO-CROATIA—See IRI Istituto Ricostruzione Industriale; *Int'l,* pg. 654
FIN.CO-MOSCOW—See IRI Istituto Ricostruzione Industriale; *Int'l,* pg. 654
FINA ANTWERP OLEFINS N.V.—See Petrofina S.A.; *Int'l,* pg. 1043
FINA AVIATION-CHEMICALS S.A.—See Petrofina S.A.; *Int'l,* pg. 1043
FINA BP BURUNDI S.A.R.L.—See Petrofina S.A.; *Int'l,* pg. 1044
FINA CHEMICALS—See Petrofina S.A.; *Int'l,* pg. 1044
FINA CHEMICALS ANTWERPEN N.V.—See Petrofina S.A.; *Int'l,* pg. 1043
FINA CHEMICALS FELUY S.A.—See Petrofina S.A.; *Int'l,* pg. 1043
FINA CONGO S.A.R.L.—See Petrofina S.A.; *Int'l,* pg. 1044
FINA DEUTSCHLAND GMBH—See Petrofina S.A.; *Int'l,* pg. 1043
FINA EUROPE S.A.—See Petrofina S.A.; *Int'l,* pg. 1043
FINA EXPLORATION LIBYA S.A.—See Petrofina S.A.; *Int'l,* pg. 1044
FINA EXPLORATION LTD.—See Petrofina S.A.; *Int'l,* pg. 1044
FINA EXPLORATION MINH HAI B.V.—See Petrofina S.A.; *Int'l,* pg. 1044
FINA EXPLORATION NORWAY, S.A. (FEN SA)—See Petrofina S.A.; *Int'l,* pg. 1043
FINA EXPLORATION NORWAY, SCA (FENSCA)—See Petrofina S.A.; *Int'l,* pg. 1043
FINA FAR EAST PTE. LTD.—See Petrofina S.A.; *Int'l,* pg. 1043
FINA FRANCE S.A.—See Petrofina S.A.; *Int'l,* pg. 1043
FINA GMBH—See Petrofina S.A.; *Int'l,* pg. 1043
FINA HOLDING DEUTSCHLAND GMBH—See Petrofina S.A.; *Int'l,* pg. 1043
FINA IBERICA S.A.—See Petrofina S.A.; *Int'l,* pg. 1043
FINA, INC.—See Petrofina S.A.; *Int'l,* pg. 1044
FINA INSURANCE S.A.—See Petrofina S.A.; *Int'l,* pg. 1043
FINA INTERNATIONAL N.V.—See Petrofina S.A.; *Int'l,* pg. 1044
FINA ITALIANA SPA—See Petrofina S.A.; *Int'l,* pg. 1043
FINA LIFE S.A.—See Petrofina S.A.; *Int'l,* pg. 1043
FINA MARINE S.A.—See Petrofina S.A.; *Int'l,* pg. 1043
FINA NEDERLAND B.V.—See Petrofina S.A.; *Int'l,* pg. 1043
FINA OIL & CHEMICAL CO. (BIG SPRING)—See Petrofina S.A.; *Int'l,* pg. 1044
FINA OIL & CHEMICAL CO. (DALLAS)—See Petrofina S.A.; *Int'l,* pg. 1044
FINA OIL & CHEMICAL CO. (PORT ARTHUR)—See Petrofina S.A.; *Int'l,* pg. 1043
FINA OLEOCHEMICALS N.V.—See Petrofina S.A.; *Int'l,* pg. 1043
FINA PETROLEOS DE ANGOLA, S.A.R.L.—See Petrofina S.A.; *Int'l,* pg. 1043
FINA PLC—See Petrofina S.A.; *Int'l,* pg. 1043
FINA PORTUGUESA-OLEOS E CARBURANTES, S.A.—See Petrofina S.A.; *Int'l,* pg. 1043
FINA RAFFINADERIJ ANTWERPEN N.V.—See Petrofina S.A.; *Int'l,* pg. 1044
FINA REP S.P.R.L.—See Petrofina S.A.; *Int'l,* pg. 1044
FINA RESEARCH S.A.—See Petrofina S.A.; *Int'l,* pg. 1043
FINA ROAD SERVICES—See Petrofina S.A.; *Int'l,* pg. 1043
FINACTA—See Groupe Air France; *Int'l,* pg. 561
FINADIS S.A.—See Otto Versand (GmbH & Co.); *Int'l,* pg. 1015
FINAGRAIN, CIE COMMERCIALE AGRICOLE ET FINANCIERE S.A.—See Continental Grain Company; *U.S. Private,* pg. 268
THE FINALS, INC.; *U.S. Private,* pg. 404
FINAMBRA IMPE. E. COM. EQUIPAMENTOS, LTDA.—See Selas Corporation of America; *U.S. Public,* pg. 1455
FINANCE CORPORATION OF BAHAMAS LIMITED—See Royal Bank of Canada; *Int'l,* pg. 1131
FINANCE ONE PUBLIC COMPANY LIMITED; *Int'l,* pg. 484
FINANCES CONSEIL INTERNTIONAL S.A.—See Assicurazioni Generali S.p.A.; *Int'l,* pg. 91
FINANCIAL AIMS CORPORATION—See D.A. Davidson & Co.; *U.S. Private,* pg. 314
FINANCIAL ASSET MANAGEMENT CORPORATION—See M.D.C. Holdings, Inc.; *U.S. Public,* pg. 1025
FINANCIAL ASSOCIATES; *U.S. Private,* pg. 404
FINANCIAL COLLECTION AGENCIES (INTERNATIONAL) INC.—See FCA International Ltd.; *Int'l,* pg. 471
FINANCIAL COLLECTION AGENCIES (1990) INC.—See FCA International Ltd.; *Int'l,* pg. 471
FINANCIAL COLLECTION AGENCIES OF PENNSYLVANIA INC—See FCA International Ltd.; *Int'l,* pg. 471

Company Index

FINANCIAL COLLECTION AGENCIES (UK) LIMITED—See FCA International Ltd.; *Int'l*, pg. 471
FINANCIAL DATA PLANNING CORP.—See FDP Corp.; *U.S. Public*, pg. 603
FINANCIAL DYNAMICS LTD.—See BDDP Group; *Int'l*, pg. 117
FINANCIAL EXCHANGE, INC.—See American Bankers Insurance Group, Inc.; *U.S. Public*, pg. 67
FINANCIAL INDEMNITY—See Unitrin, Inc.; *U.S. Public*, pg. 1694
FINANCIAL INDUSTRIES CORP.; *U.S. Public*, pg. 622
FINANCIAL INSTITUTIONS DIV.—See Imperial Bancorp; *U.S. Public*, pg. 871
FINANCIAL INSURANCE MARKETING GROUP—See Equifax Inc.; *U.S. Public*, pg. 588
FINANCIAL LEASING CORP.—See Citicorp; *U.S. Public*, pg. 377
FINANCIAL LIFE ASSURANCE CO. OF CANADA—See American General Corporation; *U.S. Public*, pg. 77
FINANCIAL LIFE COMPANIES, INC.; *U.S. Private*, pg. 404
FINANCIAL LIFE INSURANCE CO. OF GEORGIA—See Wachovia Corporation; *U.S. Public*, pg. 1730
FINANCIAL MANAGEMENT—See BankAmerica Corporation; *U.S. Public*, pg. 181
FINANCIAL NETWORK INVESTMENT CORP; *U.S. Private*, pg. 404
FINANCIAL OPPORTUNITIES, INC.—See Dairy Mart Convenience Stores, Inc.; *U.S. Public*, pg. 477
THE FINANCIAL POST—See Sun Media Corporation; *Int'l*, pg. 1320
FINANCIAL PROTECTION MARKETING INC.—See Protective Life Corporation; *U.S. Public*, pg. 1336
FINANCIAL REASSURANCE COMPANY, LTD.—See Ford Motor Company; *U.S. Public*, pg. 665
FINANCIAL RECOVERY CORPORATION OF AMERICA—See National Auto Credit Inc.; *U.S. Public*, pg. 1153
FINANCIAL RESEARCH ASSOCIATES—See First Financial Building Corporation; *U.S. Private*, pg. 407
FINANCIAL SECURITY ASSURANCE HOLDINGS LTD.; *U.S. Public*, pg. 622
FINANCIAL SECURITY ASSURANCE INC.—See Financial Security Assurance Holdings Ltd.; *U.S. Public*, pg. 623
FINANCIAL SECURITY ASSURANCE (U.K.) LIMITED—See Financial Security Assurance Holdings Ltd.; *U.S. Public*, pg. 623
THE FINANCIAL TIMES LTD.—See Pearson plc; *Int'l*, pg. 1025
FINANCIAL TRAINING COMPANY—See Wolters Kluwer N.V.; *Int'l*, pg. 1514
FINANCIAL TRUST CORP—See Keystone Financial Inc.; *U.S. Public*, pg. 956
FINANCIAL WORLD PARTNERS; *U.S. Private*, pg. 404
FINANCIERA BAMERICAL S.A.—See BankAmerica Corporation; *U.S. Public*, pg. 183
FINANCIERA FUSA, S.A.—See Corporacion MAPFRE, Compania Internacional de Reaseguros, S.A.; *Int'l*, pg. 335
FINANCIERE ATLAS S.A.—See BHF-BANK AG; *Int'l*, pg. 120
FINANCIERE EQUIPMENT S.A.; *Int'l*, pg. 485
FINANCIERE INDOSUEZ INC.—See Compagnie de Suez; *Int'l*, pg. 314
FINANCIERE LAFARGE COPPEE—See Lafarge S.A.; *Int'l*, pg. 788
FINANCIERE RYSSEN—See Generale Sucriere SNC; *Int'l*, pg. 549
FINANCIERE SAINT DOMINIQUE—See Credit Nationale; *Int'l*, pg. 344
FINANCIERINGS MAATSCHAPPIJ NEDASFIMIJ B.V.—See Assicurazioni Generali S.p.A.; *Int'l*, pg. 91
FINANMADRID ENTIDAD DE FINANCIACION, S.A.—See Caja de Madrid Group; *Int'l*, pg. 251
FINANSSKANDIC AB—See Skandinaviska Enskilda Banken; *Int'l*, pg. 1259
FINANZ CHARTERHOUSE IBERICA, SA—See Credit Commercial de France; *Int'l*, pg. 343
FINANZIARIA BTB S.P.A.—See Banco Ambrosiano Veneto S.p.A.; *Int'l*, pg. 138
FINANZIARIA INDOSUEZ ITALIA SIM S.P.A.—See Compagnie de Suez; *Int'l*, pg. 314
FINANZIARIA MEDIA ITALIA—See La Fondiaria Assicurazioni S.p.A.; *Int'l*, pg. 784
FINANZIARIA SUMITOMO (ITALIA) S.P.A.—See The Sumitomo Bank, Limited; *Int'l*, pg. 1310
FINAST—See Koninklijke Ahold NV; *Int'l*, pg. 750
FINATA BANK N.V.—See ABN-AMRO Holding N.V.; *Int'l*, pg. 9
FINAXA—See AXA-UAP; *Int'l*, pg. 18
FINBOW OY—See Valmet Corporation; *Int'l*, pg. 1449
FINCH, PRUYN & CO., INC.; *U.S. Private*, pg. 405
FINCO-LONDON—See IRI Istituto Ricostruzione Industriale; *Int'l*, pg. 654
FINCOMAU S.P.A.—See Fiat Auto SpA; *Int'l*, pg. 482
FINCOR ELECTRONICS—See IMO Industries Inc.; *U.S. Public*, pg. 857
FINCRAL - FINANZIAMENTI AL LAVORO S.P.A.—See Assicurazioni Generali S.p.A.; *Int'l*, pg. 90
FINCRAL LEASING S.P.A.—See Assicurazioni Generali S.p.A.; *Int'l*, pg. 90
FIND/SVP PUBLISHED PRODUCTS, INC.—See Find/SVP, Inc.; *U.S. Public*, pg. 623
WALLY FINDLAY GALLERIES INTERNATIONAL; *U.S. Private*, pg. 405
J.H. FINDORFF & SON, INC.; *U.S. Private*, pg. 405
FIND/SVP, INC.; *U.S. Public*, pg. 623
AB FINDUS—See Nestle S.A.; *Int'l*, pg. 920
A/S FINDUS—See Nestle S.A.; *Int'l*, pg. 920
FINE ART DEVELOPMENTS PLC; *Int'l*, pg. 485
FINE ART GRAPHICS LTD.—See Fine Art Developments plc; *Int'l*, pg. 485
FINE CARE CO. LTD.—See Wella Group; *Int'l*, pg. 1490
FINE CHEMICALS—See Alpharma Inc.; *U.S. Public*, pg. 58
FINE INORGANIC CHEMICALS—See Rhone-Poulenc S.A.; *Int'l*, pg. 1109

FINE LINE FEATURES—See Time Warner Inc.; *U.S. Public*, pg. 1615
M. FINE & SONS MANUFACTURING CO., INC.; *U.S. Private*, pg. 405
FINE ORGANICS LIMITED—See Laporte plc; *Int'l*, pg. 802
FINE PAPER DIV.—See The Mead Corporation; *U.S. Public*, pg. 1074
FINE PITCH TECHNOLOGY, INC.—See Solectron Corporation; *U.S. Public*, pg. 1483
FINERO B.V.—See Outokumpu Oyj; *Int'l*, pg. 1018
FINES SPECIALITES—See LVMH Moet Hennessy Louis Vuitton; *Int'l*, pg. 780
FINETECH CO., LTD.—See Skylark Co., Ltd.; *Int'l*, pg. 1262
FINEX ESPANA, E.F., S.A.—See Corporacion MAPFRE, Compania Internacional de Reaseguros, S.A.; *Int'l*, pg. 332
FINGER FURNITURE COMPANY, INC.; *U.S. Private*, pg. 405
FINGER LAKES PRINTING COMPANY—See Independent Publications, Inc.; *U.S. Private*, pg. 559
FINGERHUT CORP.; *U.S. Public*, pg. 623
FINGERLE LUMBER CO.; *U.S. Private*, pg. 405
FINGERMA S.P.A.—See Volkswagen AG; *Int'l*, pg. 1475
FININVEST—See Compagnie de Suez; *Int'l*, pg. 313
FINISH LINE, INC.; *U.S. Public*, pg. 623
FINISHLINE INDUSTRIES INC. OF GEORGIA—See John S. Frey Enterprises; *U.S. Public*, pg. 428
FINISHMASTER INC.—See LDI, Ltd.; *U.S. Private*, pg. 639
FINITE FILTER DIV.—See Parker Hannifin Corporation; pg. 1260
FINKEL OUTDOOR PRODUCTS, INC.—See Trace International Holdings, Inc.; *U.S. Private*, pg. 1094
A. FINKL & SONS CO.; *U.S. Private*, pg. 405
FINLAND TRAVEL BUREAU LTD.—See FinnAir Oy; *Int'l*, pg. 485
FINLAND VAKANTIES WESTERMAN—See FinnAir Oy; *Int'l*, pg. 485
FINLAY ENTERPRISES, INC.; *U.S. Public*, pg. 623
FINLAY FINE JEWELRY CORPORATION—See Finlay Enterprises, Inc.; *U.S. Public*, pg. 624
FINLEY FARMERS GRAIN & ELEVATOR COMPANY; *U.S. Private*, pg. 405
FINMARE—See IRI Istituto Ricostruzione Industriale; *Int'l*, pg. 652
FINMARE-UK—See IRI Istituto Ricostruzione Industriale; *Int'l*, pg. 655
FINMECCANICA S.P.A.—See IRI Istituto Ricostruzione Industriale; *Int'l*, pg. 654
FINMECCANICA-BELGIUM—See IRI Istituto Ricostruzione Industriale; *Int'l*, pg. 654
FINMECCANICA-JAPAN—See IRI Istituto Ricostruzione Industriale; *Int'l*, pg. 654
FINNAIR—See FinnAir Oy; *Int'l*, pg. 485
FINNAIR GATEWAY RAVINTOLAT OY—See FinnAir Oy; *Int'l*, pg. 485
FINNAIR OY; *Int'l*, pg. 485
FINNAIR TRAVEL SERVICES OY—See FinnAir Oy; *Int'l*, pg. 485
FINNAREN & HALEY, INC.; *U.S. Private*, pg. 405
FINNAVIATION OY—See FinnAir Oy; *Int'l*, pg. 485
FINNBEND OY—See British Steel Plc; *Int'l*, pg. 222
FINNCATERING OY—See FinnAir Oy; *Int'l*, pg. 485
FINNEWOS AQUA OY—See Cultor Ltd.; *Int'l*, pg. 349
FINNFEEDS INTERNATIONAL LTD.—See Cultor Ltd.; *Int'l*, pg. 349
FINNIGAN CORPORATION—See Thermo Electron Corporation; *U.S. Public*, pg. 1591
FINNIGAN MAT—See Thermo Electron Corporation; *U.S. Public*, pg. 1591
FINNIGAN MAT AB—See Thermo Electron Corporation; *U.S. Public*, pg. 1596
FINNIGAN MAT BENELUX—See Thermo Electron Corporation; *U.S. Public*, pg. 1596
FINNIGAN MAT CHINA, INC.—See Thermo Electron Corporation; *U.S. Public*, pg. 1596
FINNIGAN MAT GMBH—See Thermo Electron Corporation; *U.S. Public*, pg. 1596
FINNIGAN MAT INSTITUTE—See Thermo Electron Corporation; *U.S. Public*, pg. 1591
FINNIGAN MAT INSTRUMENTS, INC.—See Thermo Electron Corporation; *U.S. Public*, pg. 1596
FINNIGAN MAT LTD.—See Thermo Electron Corporation; *U.S. Public*, pg. 1596
FINNIGAN MAT S.A.R.L.—See Thermo Electron Corporation; *U.S. Public*, pg. 1596
FINNIGAN MAT S.R.L.—See Thermo Electron Corporation; *U.S. Public*, pg. 1596
FINNIGAN PROPERTIES, INC.—See Thermo Electron Corporation; *U.S. Public*, pg. 1591
FINNISH CHEMICALS OY—See UPM-Kymmene Corporation; *Int'l*, pg. 1430
FINNISH FIBREBOARD LTD.—See UPM-Kymmene Corporation; *Int'l*, pg. 1428
OY FINNISH PEROXIDES AB—See UPM-Kymmene Corporation; *Int'l*, pg. 1430
FINNISH RICH COFFEE LTD.—See Kesko Ltd.; *Int'l*, pg. 732
OY FINNMATKAT-FINNTOURS LTD.—See FinnAir Oy; *Int'l*, pg. 485
FINNSEMENTTI OY AB—See Scancem AB; *Int'l*, pg. 1198
FINNSTEEL INC.—See Rautaruukki Oy; *Int'l*, pg. 1089
FINNSUGAR BIOPRODUCTS—See Cultor Ltd.; *Int'l*, pg. 349
FINNSUGAR LTD.—See Cultor Ltd.; *Int'l*, pg. 349
OY FINNTERMINALS AB—See UPM-Kymmene Corporation; *Int'l*, pg. 1428
FINOP—See GIB Group; *Int'l*, pg. 533
FINORA COMPANY, INC.—See Norfoods, Inc.; *U.S. Private*, pg. 802
FINOVA CAPITAL CORPORATION—See The FINOVA Group Inc.; *U.S. Public*, pg. 624
THE FINOVA GROUP INC.; *U.S. Public*, pg. 624
FINPIPE G.I.E.—See Tractebel; *Int'l*, pg. 1416
FINS VERKOOPKANTOOR—See Enso Oyj; *Int'l*, pg. 458

FINSERVIZI S.P.A.—See Bastogi-S.p.A.; *Int'l*, pg. 170
FINSIEL—See IRI Istituto Ricostruzione Industriale; *Int'l*, pg. 654
FINSTAR FINANCE INC.—See FCA International Ltd.; *Int'l*, pg. 471
FINTECNA - SOC. PER L'IMPIANTISTICA INDUSTRIALE L'ASSETTO DEL TERRITORIO S.P.A.—See IRI Istituto Ricostruzione Industriale; *Int'l*, pg. 654
FINWOOD PAPERS (PTY.) LTD.—See N.V. Koninklijke KNP BT; *Int'l*, pg. 757
FIONIA (C.I.PROPERTIES) LIMITED—See The East Asiatic Company Ltd. A/S; *Int'l*, pg. 431
FIORENTINA GAS S.P.A.—See ENI S.p.A.; *Int'l*, pg. 428
FIOS E CABOS PLASTICOS DO BRASIL S.A.—See Telefonaktiebolaget LM Ericsson; *Int'l*, pg. 1368
FIOTEC, INC.—See Itochu Corporation; *Int'l*, pg. 694
THE FIRE & CASUALTY CO. OF CONNECTICUT—See Orion Capital Corporation; *U.S. Public*, pg. 1231
FIRE BURGLARY INSTRUMENTS, INC.—See Pittway Corporation; *U.S. Public*, pg. 1306
FIRE CONTROL INSTRUMENTS, INC.; *U.S. Private*, pg. 406
FIRE CONTROLS INSTRUMENTS—See Pittway Corporation; *U.S. Public*, pg. 1306
FIRE, EQUITY & GENERAL INSURANCE COMPANY LIMITED—See Cigna Corp.; *U.S. Public*, pg. 363
FIRE KING INTERNATIONAL, INC.; *U.S. Private*, pg. 406
FIRE LITE ALARMS, INC./NOTIFIER CO.—See Pittway Corporation; *U.S. Public*, pg. 1306
FIRE PROTECTION INDUSTRIES, INC.—See Compagnie Generale Des Eaux; *Int'l*, pg. 321
FIRE UNDERWRITERS ASSOCIATION—See B.A.T Industries P.L.C.; *Int'l*, pg. 110
FIREARMS TRAINING SYSTEMS, INC.—See Center Partners Management LLC; *U.S. Private*, pg. 222
FIREFIN SRL—See Williams Holdings Plc; *Int'l*, pg. 1500
FIRELAND INDUSTRIES, INC.—See Lakeland Industries, Inc.; *U.S. Public*, pg. 975
FIRELANDS TOOL RENTAL—See Jennings & Churella Construction Company; *U.S. Private*, pg. 586
FIREMAN'S FUND INDEMNITY CORPORATION—See Allianz Aktiengesellschaft; *Int'l*, pg. 59
FIREMAN'S FUND INSURANCE CO. OF GEORGIA—See Allianz Aktiengesellschaft; *Int'l*, pg. 59
FIREMAN'S FUND INSURANCE CO. OF HAWAII, INC.—See Allianz Aktiengesellschaft; *Int'l*, pg. 59
FIREMAN'S FUND INSURANCE CO. OF IOWA—See Allianz Aktiengesellschaft; *Int'l*, pg. 59
FIREMAN'S FUND INSURANCE CO. OF LOUISIANA—See Allianz Aktiengesellschaft; *Int'l*, pg. 59
FIREMAN'S FUND INSURANCE CO. OF NEW JERSEY—See Allianz Aktiengesellschaft; *Int'l*, pg. 59
FIREMAN'S FUND INSURANCE CO. OF OHIO—See Allianz Aktiengesellschaft; *Int'l*, pg. 59
FIREMAN'S FUND INSURANCE CO. OF TEXAS—See Allianz Aktiengesellschaft; *Int'l*, pg. 59
FIREMAN'S FUND INSURANCE CO. OF WISCONSIN—See Allianz Aktiengesellschaft; *Int'l*, pg. 59
FIREMAN'S FUND INSURANCE COMPANY—See Allianz Aktiengesellschaft; *Int'l*, pg. 58
FIREMAN'S FUND RISK MANAGEMENT SERVICES, INC.—See Allianz Aktiengesellschaft; *Int'l*, pg. 59
FIREMEN'S INSURANCE CO. OF NEWARK, N.J.—See Loews Corporation; *U.S. Public*, pg. 1011
FIREMEN'S INSURANCE COMPANY OF WASHINGTON, D.C.—See W.R. Berkley Corporation; *U.S. Public*, pg. 215
FIRESIDE BOOKS—See National Amusements, Inc.; *U.S. Private*, pg. 777
FIRESIDE THRIFT—See Unitrin, Inc.; *U.S. Public*, pg. 1694
FIRESTONE AGRICULTURAL TIRE COMPANY—See Bridgestone Corporation; *Int'l*, pg. 214
FIRESTONE AGRICULTURAL TIRE COMPANY-DES MOINES—See Bridgestone Corporation; *Int'l*, pg. 214
FIRESTONE BUILDING PRODUCTS COMPANY—See Bridgestone Corporation; *Int'l*, pg. 214
FIRESTONE BUILDING PRODUCTS COMPANY-BEECH GROVE—See Bridgestone Corporation; *Int'l*, pg. 214
FIRESTONE BUILDING PRODUCTS COMPANY-KINGSTREE PLANT—See Bridgestone Corporation; *Int'l*, pg. 214
FIRESTONE BUILDING PRODUCTS COMPANY-PRESCOTT—See Bridgestone Corporation; *Int'l*, pg. 214
FIRESTONE FIBERS & TEXTILES CO.—See Bridgestone Corporation; *Int'l*, pg. 214
FIRESTONE FIBERS & TEXTILES COMPANY-GASTONIA—See Bridgestone Corporation; *Int'l*, pg. 214
FIRESTONE FIBERS & TEXTILES COMPANY-KINGS MOUNTAIN—See Bridgestone Corporation; *Int'l*, pg. 214
FIRESTONE FIBERS & TEXTILES COMPANY-WOODSTOCK PLANT—See Bridgestone Corporation; *Int'l*, pg. 214
FIRESTONE FINANCIAL—See UST Corporation; *U.S. Public*, pg. 1660
FIRESTONE FRANCE S.A.—See Bridgestone Corporation; *Int'l*, pg. 214
FIRESTONE INDUSTRIAL PRODUCTS CO.—See Bridgestone Corporation; *Int'l*, pg. 214
FIRESTONE INDUSTRIAL PRODUCTS COMPANY-DYERSBURG—See Bridgestone Corporation; *Int'l*, pg. 214
FIRESTONE INDUSTRIAL PRODUCTS COMPANY-NOBLESVILLE PLANT—See Bridgestone Corporation; *Int'l*, pg. 214
FIRESTONE INDUSTRIAL PRODUCTS COMPANY-WILLIAMSBURG—See Bridgestone Corporation; *Int'l*, pg. 214
SUE FIRESTONE & ASSOC.; *U.S. Private*, pg. 406
FIRESTONE SYNTHETIC RUBBER & LATEX CO.—See Bridgestone Corporation; *Int'l*, pg. 214

FIRESTONE SYNTHETIC RUBBER & LATEX COMPANY-LAKE CHARLES—See Bridgestone Corporation; *Int'l*, pg. 214

FIRESTONE SYNTHETIC RUBBER & LATEX COMPANY-ORANGE—See Bridgestone Corporation; *Int'l*, pg. 214

FIRESTONE TEXTILES COMPANY—See Bridgestone Corporation; *Int'l*, pg. 214

FIRESTONE TIRE & RUBBER CO. OF NEW ZEALAND, LTD.—See Bridgestone Corporation; *Int'l*, pg. 214

FIRESTONE TIRE & RUBBER COMPANY OF NEW ZEALAND LIMITED—See Bridgestone Corporation; *Int'l*, pg. 214

FIRESTONE TUBE COMPANY—See Bridgestone Corporation; *Int'l*, pg. 214

FIRESTONE TUBE COMPANY-RUSSELLVILLE PLANT—See Bridgestone Corporation; *Int'l*, pg. 214

C.A. FIRESTONE VENEZOLANA—See Bridgestone Corporation; *Int'l*, pg. 215

THE FIRESTONE VINEYARD—See Suntory Ltd.; *Int'l*, pg. 1321

FIRET, B.V.—See Fruit of the Loom, Inc.; *U.S. Public*, pg. 686

FIRETROL PROTECTION SYSTEMS, INC.—See Zurn Industries, Inc.; *U.S. Public*, pg. 1795

FIREYE, INC.—See Williams Holdings Plc; *Int'l*, pg. 1500

FIRMA E. LUCAS MED. TECHNIK GMBH—See Getinge Industrier AB; *Int'l*, pg. 551

FIRMENICH—See Firmenich S.A.; *Int'l*, pg. 486

FIRMENICH INCORPORATED—See Firmenich S.A.; *Int'l*, pg. 486

FIRMENICH S.A.; *Int'l*, pg. 486

FIROILLO A. CO. INC.—See Seaboard Corporation; *U.S. Public*, pg. 1449

FIRST ALERT, INC.; *U.S. Private*, pg. 406

FIRST ALERT PROFESSIONAL—See Pittway Corporation; *U.S. Public*, pg. 1306

FIRST ALLMERICA FINANCIAL LIFE INSURANCE COMPANY—See Allmerica Financial Corporation; *U.S. Public*, pg. 54

FIRST AMERICAN ABSTRACT & TITLE CO.—See The First American Financial Corporation; *U.S. Public*, pg. 625

FIRST AMERICAN APPRAISAL SERVICES—See The First American Financial Corporation; *U.S. Public*, pg. 625

FIRST AMERICAN BANK METRO—See Bremer Financial Corporation; *U.S. Private*, pg. 167

FIRST AMERICAN BANK SOUTHWEST—See Bremer Financial Corporation; *U.S. Private*, pg. 167

FIRST AMERICAN BANK VALLEY—See Bremer Financial Corporation; *U.S. Private*, pg. 167

FIRST AMERICAN BANK WEST—See Bremer Financial Corporation; *U.S. Private*, pg. 167

FIRST AMERICAN BANK WISCONSIN—See Bremer Financial Corporation; *U.S. Private*, pg. 167

FIRST AMERICAN CAPITAL MANAGEMENT, INC.—See The First American Financial Corporation; *U.S. Public*, pg. 625

FIRST AMERICAN CO. OF ALASKA—See The First American Financial Corporation; *U.S. Public*, pg. 625

FIRST AMERICAN CORPORATION; *U.S. Public*, pg. 624

FIRST AMERICAN CREDCO—See The First American Financial Corporation; *U.S. Public*, pg. 625

FIRST AMERICAN EQUITY LOAN SERVICES—See The First American Financial Corporation; *U.S. Public*, pg. 625

FIRST AMERICAN FEDERAL SAVINGS BANK—See First American Corporation; *U.S. Public*, pg. 624

FIRST AMERICAN FIELD SERVICES—See The First American Financial Corporation; *U.S. Public*, pg. 625

FIRST AMER. FINANCE CORP.—See The Marcus Corporation; *U.S. Public*, pg. 1044

THE FIRST AMERICAN FINANCIAL CORPORATION; *U.S. Public*, pg. 624

FIRST AMERICAN FLOOD DATA SERVICES—See The First American Financial Corporation; *U.S. Public*, pg. 625

FIRST AMERICAN HOME BUYERS PROTECTION CORP.—See The First American Financial Corporation; *U.S. Public*, pg. 625

FIRST AMERICAN INSURANCE AGENCIES, INC.—See Bremer Financial Corporation; *U.S. Private*, pg. 167

FIRST AMERICAN METRO CORP.—See First Union Corporation; *U.S. Public*, pg. 640

FIRST AMERICAN NATIONAL BANK—See First American Corporation; *U.S. Public*, pg. 624

FIRST AMERICAN REAL ESTATE INFORMATION SERVICES, INC.—See The First American Financial Corporation; *U.S. Public*, pg. 625

FIRST AMERICAN REAL ESTATE TAX SERVICE, INC.—See The First American Financial Corporation; *U.S. Public*, pg. 625

FIRST AMERICAN RECORDS MANAGEMENT—See The First American Financial Corporation; *U.S. Public*, pg. 625

FIRST AMERICAN TAX VALUATION—See The First American Financial Corporation; *U.S. Public*, pg. 625

FIRST AMERICAN TITLE CO. OF BELLINGHAM—See The First American Financial Corporation; *U.S. Public*, pg. 625

FIRST AMERICAN TITLE CO. OF CLARK COUNTY—See The First American Financial Corporation; *U.S. Public*, pg. 625

FIRST AMERICAN TITLE CO. OF FLORIDA, INC.—See The First American Financial Corporation; *U.S. Public*, pg. 625

FIRST AMERICAN TITLE CO. OF HAWAII, INC.—See The First American Financial Corporation; *U.S. Public*, pg. 625

FIRST AMERICAN TITLE CO. OF IDAHO—See The First American Financial Corporation; *U.S. Public*, pg. 625

FIRST AMERICAN TITLE CO. OF LOS ANGELES—See The First American Financial Corporation; *U.S. Public*, pg. 625

FIRST AMERICAN TITLE CO. OF MENDOCINO COUNTY—See The First American Financial Corporation; *U.S. Public*, pg. 625

FIRST AMERICAN TITLE CO. OF NEVADA—See The First American Financial Corporation; *U.S. Public*, pg. 625

FIRST AMERICAN TITLE CO. OF NEW MEXICO—See The First American Financial Corporation; *U.S. Public*, pg. 625

FIRST AMERICAN TITLE CO. OF SPOKANE—See The First American Financial Corporation; *U.S. Public*, pg. 625

FIRST AMERICAN TITLE CO. OF ST. LUCIE COUNTY, INC.—See The First American Financial Corporation; *U.S. Public*, pg. 625

FIRST AMERICAN TITLE CO. OF THURSTON COUNTY—See The First American Financial Corporation; *U.S. Public*, pg. 625

FIRST AMERICAN TITLE CO. OF UTAH—See The First American Financial Corporation; *U.S. Public*, pg. 625

FIRST AMERICAN TITLE GUARANTY CO.—See The First American Financial Corporation; *U.S. Public*, pg. 625

FIRST AMERICAN TITLE INSURANCE CO.—See The First American Financial Corporation; *U.S. Public*, pg. 625

FIRST AMERICAN TITLE INSURANCE CO. OF N.Y.—See The First American Financial Corporation; *U.S. Public*, pg. 626

FIRST AMERICAN TITLE INSURANCE CO. OF OREGON—See The First American Financial Corporation; *U.S. Public*, pg. 626

FIRST AMERICAN TITLE INSURANCE CO. OF TEXAS, INC.—See The First American Financial Corporation; *U.S. Public*, pg. 626

FIRST AMERICAN TRUST CO.—See The First American Financial Corporation; *U.S. Public*, pg. 626

FIRST AMERICAN TRUST COMPANY OF MINNESOTA—See Bremer Financial Corporation; *U.S. Private*, pg. 167

FIRST AMERITAS LIFE INSURANCE CORP. OF NEW YORK—See Ameritas Life Insurance Corp.; *U.S. Private*, pg. 65

FIRST ASIA SECURITIES LIMITED—See Finance One Public Company Limited; *Int'l*, pg. 485

FIRST ATLANTIC BUILDING CORP.—See Lennar Corporation; *U.S. Public*, pg. 988

FIRST BANK & TRUST—See UMB Financial Corporation; *U.S. Public*, pg. 1654

FIRST BANK MONTANA, NATIONAL ASSOCIATION—See U.S. Bancorp; *U.S. Public*, pg. 1680

FIRST BANK N.A.—See U.S. Bancorp; *U.S. Public*, pg. 1680

FIRST BANK NATIONAL ASSOCIATION—See U.S. Bancorp; *U.S. Public*, pg. 1681

FIRST BANK OF ARKANSAS—See First Commercial Corporation; *U.S. Public*, pg. 630

FIRST BANK OF CALIFORNIA—See First Banks America, Inc.; *U.S. Public*, pg. 626

FIRST BANK OF NIGERIA PLC—See Standard Chartered Bank PLC; *Int'l*, pg. 1296

THE FIRST BANK OF OAK PARK; *U.S. Private*, pg. 406

FIRST BANK OF STUART—See MainStreet BankGroup Incorporated; *U.S. Public*, pg. 1039

FIRST BANKS AMERICA, INC.; *U.S. Public*, pg. 626

FIRST BANKS, INC.—See First Banks America, Inc.; *U.S. Public*, pg. 626

FIRST BOWRING INSURANCE BROKERS HOLDINGS (PTY.) LTD.—See First National Bank Holdings Limited; *Int'l*, pg. 487

FIRST BRANDS AFRICA (PTY) LTD.—See First Brands Corporation; *U.S. Public*, pg. 627

FIRST BRANDS ASIA—See First Brands Corporation; *U.S. Public*, pg. 627

FIRST BRANDS AUSTRALIA—See First Brands Corporation; *U.S. Public*, pg. 627

FIRST BRANDS (CANADA) CORP.—See First Brands Corporation; *U.S. Public*, pg. 627

FIRST BRANDS CORPORATION; *U.S. Public*, pg. 626

FIRST BRANDS (EUROPE) LTD.—See First Brands Corporation; *U.S. Public*, pg. 627

FIRST BRANDS PHILIPPINES—See First Brands Corporation; *U.S. Public*, pg. 627

FIRST BRANDS PUERTO RICO—See First Brands Corporation; *U.S. Public*, pg. 627

FIRST CAPITAL CORP. OF CHICAGO—See First Chicago NBD Corporation; *U.S. Public*, pg. 628

FIRST CAPITAL FINANCIAL CORP.—See Great American Management & Investment, Inc.; *U.S. Public*, pg. 473

FIRST CASH, INC.; *U.S. Public*, pg. 627

FIRST CENTRAL FINANCIAL CORPORATION; *U.S. Private*, pg. 406

FIRST CENTRAL INSURANCE CO.—See First Central Financial Corporation; *U.S. Private*, pg. 406

FIRST CHARTER CORPORATION; *U.S. Public*, pg. 627

FIRST CHARTER NATIONAL BANK—See First Charter Corporation; *U.S. Public*, pg. 627

FIRST CHEMICAL CORP.—See ChemFirst Inc.; *U.S. Public*, pg. 344

FIRST CHICAGO AUSTRALIA LTD.—See First Chicago NBD Corporation; *U.S. Public*, pg. 628

FIRST CHICAGO AUSTRALIA SECURITY LTD.—See First Chicago NBD Corporation; *U.S. Public*, pg. 628

FIRST CHICAGO CREDIT CORP.—See First Chicago NBD Corporation; *U.S. Public*, pg. 628

FIRST CHICAGO FINANCIAL CORP.—See First Chicago NBD Corporation; *U.S. Public*, pg. 628

FIRST CHICAGO FUTURES, INC.—See First Chicago NBD Corporation; *U.S. Public*, pg. 628

FIRST CHICAGO INVESTMENT CORP.—See First Chicago NBD Corporation; *U.S. Public*, pg. 628

FIRST CHICAGO LEASING CORP.—See First Chicago NBD Corporation; *U.S. Public*, pg. 628

FIRST CHICAGO LIMITED—See First Chicago NBD Corporation; *U.S. Public*, pg. 628

FIRST CHICAGO NBD CORPORATION; *U.S. Public*, pg. 627

FIRST CHICAGO TRADING CO.—See First Chicago NBD Corporation; *U.S. Public*, pg. 628

FIRST CHOICE—See The Langer Biomechanics Group, Inc.; *U.S. Public*, pg. 978

FIRST CHURCH FINANCING CORPORATION—See The Ziegler Companies, Inc.; *U.S. Public*, pg. 1792

FIRST CITIZENS BANC SHARES, INC.; *U.S. Public*, pg. 628

FIRST CITIZENS BANK & TRUST CO.—See First Citizens Banc Shares, Inc.; *U.S. Public*, pg. 629

FIRST CITIZENS BANK & TRUST COMPANY-WEST VIRGINIA—See First Citizens Banc Shares, Inc.; *U.S. Public*, pg. 629

FIRST CITIZENS BANK & TRUST COMPANY-WHITE SULPHUR SPRINGS—See First Citizens Banc Shares, Inc.; *U.S. Public*, pg. 629

FIRST CITIZENS BANK OF HOHENWALD—See Union Planters Corporation; *U.S. Public*, pg. 1669

FIRST CITIZENS BANK OF VIRGINIA CORPORATION—See First Citizens Banc Shares, Inc.; *U.S. Public*, pg. 629

FIRST CITIZENS INVESTOR SERVICES, INC.—See First Citizens Banc Shares, Inc.; *U.S. Public*, pg. 629

FIRST CITIZENS STATE BANK—See First Financial Corporation; *U.S. Public*, pg. 634

FIRST COAST COMMUNITY BANK & TRUST—See Synovus Financial Corp.; *U.S. Public*, pg. 1549

FIRST COLONIAL INSURANCE COMPANY—See American Heritage Life Investment Corp.; *U.S. Public*, pg. 79

FIRST COLONY LIFE INSURANCE CO.—See General Electric Company; *U.S. Public*, pg. 711

FIRST COLORADO BANKSHARES INSURANCE CO.—See Banc One Corporation; *U.S. Public*, pg. 173

FIRST COLUMBIA ESCROW, INC.—See Washington Mutual Inc.; *U.S. Public*, pg. 1742

FIRST COMMERCE BANCSHARES, INC.; *U.S. Public*, pg. 629

FIRST COMMERCE CORPORATION; *U.S. Public*, pg. 629

FIRST COMMERCE INVESTORS—See First Commerce Bancshares, Inc.; *U.S. Public*, pg. 629

FIRST COMMERCE MORTGAGE COMPANY—See First Commerce Bancshares, Inc.; *U.S. Public*, pg. 629

FIRST COMMERCE TECHNOLOGIES—See First Commerce Bancshares, Inc.; *U.S. Public*, pg. 629

FIRST COMMERCIAL BANK—See Synovus Financial Corp.; *U.S. Public*, pg. 1549

FIRST COMMERCIAL BANK, N.A.—See First Commercial Corporation; *U.S. Public*, pg. 630

FIRST COMMERCIAL BANK, N.A. OF MEMPHIS—See First Commercial Corporation; *U.S. Public*, pg. 630

FIRST COMMERCIAL CORPORATION; *U.S. Public*, pg. 630

FIRST COMMERCIAL MORTGAGE CO.—See First Commercial Corporation; *U.S. Public*, pg. 630

FIRST COMMONWEALTH CORPORATION; *U.S. Private*, pg. 406

FIRST COMMONWEALTH CORPORATION—See First Commonwealth Corporation; *U.S. Private*, pg. 406

FIRST COMMUNITY BANK—See MainStreet BankGroup Incorporated; *U.S. Public*, pg. 1039

FIRST COMMUNITY BANK OF SALTVILLE—See MainStreet BankGroup Incorporated; *U.S. Public*, pg. 1039

FIRST COMMUNITY BANK OF TIFTON—See Synovus Financial Corp.; *U.S. Public*, pg. 1549

FIRST COMPUTER CORPORATION; *U.S. Private*, pg. 406

FIRST CONSOLIDATED HOLDINGS (PROPRIETARY) LIMITED—See Anglo American Corporation of South Africa Limited; *Int'l*, pg. 77

FIRST CONSUMERS NATIONAL BANK—See Spiegel, Inc.; *U.S. Public*, pg. 1499

FIRST COUNTY BANK—See F.N.B. Corporation; *U.S. Public*, pg. 607

FIRST CRAWFORD STATE BANK—See First Financial Corporation; *U.S. Public*, pg. 634

FIRST DATA CORPORATION; *U.S. Public*, pg. 630

FIRST DATA RESOURCES—See First Data Corporation; *U.S. Public*, pg. 631

FIRST DATABANK—See The Hearst Corporation; *U.S. Private*, pg. 515

FIRST DEPOSIT NATIONAL BANK—See Providian Financial Corporation; *U.S. Public*, pg. 1338

FIRST DISTRICT ASSOCIATION; *U.S. Private*, pg. 406

FIRST ELECTRIC COOPERATIVE, CORP.; *U.S. Private*, pg. 407

FIRST EMPIRE STATE CORPORATION; *U.S. Public*, pg. 631

FIRST EQUICOR LIFE INSURANCE COMPANY—See Cigna Corp.; *U.S. Public*, pg. 361

FIRST FAMILY FINANCIAL SERVICES—See Ford Motor Company; *U.S. Public*, pg. 663

FIRST FARMERS & MERCHANTS NATIONAL BANK; *U.S. Private*, pg. 407

FIRST FARMERS STATE BANK—See First Financial Corporation; *U.S. Public*, pg. 634

FIRST FEDERAL BANK OF CALIFORNIA, FSB—See FirstFed Financial Corp.; *U.S. Public*, pg. 646

FIRST FEDERAL CAPITAL CORP.; *U.S. Public*, pg. 632

FIRST FEDERAL FINANCE CORPORATION—See Firstbank Puerto Rico; *U.S. Public*, pg. 644

FIRST FEDERAL FSB—See FSF Financial Corp.; *U.S. Public*, pg. 608

FIRST FEDERAL OF MICHIGAN—See Charter One Financial, Inc.; *U.S. Public*, pg. 336

FIRST FEDERAL SAVINGS; *U.S. Public*, pg. 632

FIRST FEDERAL SAVINGS—See First Federal Savings; *U.S. Public*, pg. 632

FIRST FEDERAL SAVINGS & LOAN ASSOCIATION OF CHARLESTON—See First Financial Holdings, Inc.; *U.S. Public*, pg. 634

FIRST FEDERAL SAVINGS & LOAN OF AMERICA—See Pacific Century Financial Corporation; *U.S. Public*, pg. 1248

FIRST FEDERAL SAVINGS BANK LA CROSSE-MADISON—See First Federal Capital Corp.; *U.S. Public*, pg. 632

FIRST FINANCE MORTGAGE COMPANY—See First Financial Bancorp; *U.S. Public*, pg. 633

FIRST FINANCIAL BANCORP; *U.S. Public*, pg. 632

FIRST FINANCIAL BANK, FSB—See Associated Banc-Corp; *U.S. Public*, pg. 140

FIRST FINANCIAL BANKSHARES, INC.; *U.S. Public*, pg. 633

FIRST FINANCIAL BUILDING CORPORATION; *U.S. Private*, pg. 407

FIRST FINANCIAL CORPORATION; *U.S. Public*, pg. 633

FIRST FINANCIAL CORPORATION—See Associated Banc-Corp; *U.S. Public*, pg. 140

FIRST FINANCIAL GROUP, INC.; *U.S. Private*, pg. 407

FIRST FINANCIAL HOLDINGS, INC.; *U.S. Public*, pg. 634

FIRST FLORIDA EQUITIES, INC.; *U.S. Private*, pg. 407

FIRST FRANKLIN FINANCIAL CORP.; *U.S. Private*, pg. 407

FIRST GIBRALTAR BANK—See BankAmerica Corporation; *U.S. Public*, pg. 181

FIRST GRAY LINE CORPORATION; *U.S. Private*, pg. 407

FIRST HAWAIIAN BANK—See First Hawaiian, Inc.; *U.S. Public*, pg. 634

FIRST HAWAIIAN CAPITAL 1—See First Hawaiian, Inc.; *U.S. Public*, pg. 635

FIRST HAWAIIAN CREDITCORP, INC.—See First Hawaiian, Inc.; *U.S. Public*, pg. 635

FIRST HAWAIIAN, INC.; *U.S. Public*, pg. 634

FIRST HAWAIIAN INSURANCE, INC.—See First Hawaiian, Inc.; *U.S. Public*, pg. 635

FIRST HAWAIIAN LEASING, INC.—See First Hawaiian, Inc.; *U.S. Public*, pg. 635

FIRST HEALTH CENTER—See Columbia/HCA Healthcare Corporation; *U.S. Public*, pg. 404

FIRST HEALTH GROUP CORP.; *U.S. Public*, pg. 635

FIRST HEALTH SERVICES—See First Health Group Corp.; *U.S. Public*, pg. 635

FIRST HEALTH STRATEGIES—See First Health Group Corp.; *U.S. Public*, pg. 635

FIRST IMAGE MANAGEMENT CO.—See First Data Corporation; *U.S. Public*, pg. 631

FIRST INDEPENDENCE NATIONAL BANK; *U.S. Public*, pg. 635

FIRST INDIANA BANK, A FEDERAL SAVINGS BANK—See The Somerset Group, Inc.; *U.S. Public*, pg. 1484

FIRST INDIANA CORPORATION—See The Somerset Group, Inc.; *U.S. Public*, pg. 1484

FIRST INSURANCE AGENCY, INC.—See Washington Federal Savings; *U.S. Public*, pg. 1740

FIRST INSURANCE CO. OF HAWAII, LTD.—See Loews Corporation; *U.S. Public*, pg. 1011

FIRST INTERNATIONAL BANCORP, INC.; *U.S. Public*, pg. 635

FIRST INTERNATIONAL REINSURANCE COMPANY—See Geneve Corporation; *U.S. Private*, pg. 446

FIRST INTERSTATE BANK OF ARIZONA, N.A.—See Wells Fargo & Company; *U.S. Public*, pg. 1753

FIRST INTERSTATE BANK OF CALIFORNIA—See Wells Fargo & Company; *U.S. Public*, pg. 1753

FIRST INTERSTATE BANK OF ENGLEWOOD, N.A.—See Wells Fargo & Company; *U.S. Public*, pg. 1753

FIRST INTERSTATE BANK OF IDAHO, N.A.—See Wells Fargo & Company; *U.S. Public*, pg. 1753

FIRST INTERSTATE BANK OF MONTANA, N.A.—See Wells Fargo & Company; *U.S. Public*, pg. 1753

FIRST INTERSTATE BANK OF NEVADA, N.A.—See Wells Fargo & Company; *U.S. Public*, pg. 1753

FIRST INTERSTATE BANK OF NEW MEXICO N.A.—See Wells Fargo & Company; *U.S. Public*, pg. 1753

FIRST INTERSTATE BANK OF OREGON, N.A.—See Wells Fargo & Company; *U.S. Public*, pg. 1753

FIRST INTERSTATE BANK OF TEXAS N.A.—See Wells Fargo & Company; *U.S. Public*, pg. 1753

FIRST INTERSTATE BANK OF UTAH, N.A.—See Wells Fargo & Company; *U.S. Public*, pg. 1753

FIRST INTERSTATE BANK OF WASHINGTON, N.A.—See Wells Fargo & Company; *U.S. Public*, pg. 1753

FIRST INTERSTATE BANK OF WYOMING N.A.—See Wells Fargo & Company; *U.S. Public*, pg. 1753

FIRST KITCHEN CO., LTD.—See Suntory Ltd.; *Int'l*, pg. 1321

FIRST LEASING & RENTAL CORPORATION—See Firstbank Puerto Rico; *U.S. Public*, pg. 644

FIRST LOUISIANA ACCEPTANCE CORP.—See BankBoston Corporation; *U.S. Public*, pg. 184

1ST MAIN LINE BANK—See National Penn Bancshares, Inc.; *U.S. Public*, pg. 1159

FIRST MARATHON BANK GMBH—See First Marathon Inc.; *Int'l*, pg. 487

FIRST MARATHON INC.; *Int'l*, pg. 486

FIRST MARATHON SECURITIES LIMITED—See First Marathon Inc.; *Int'l*, pg. 486

FIRST MARYLAND ANNUITIES AGENCY CORPORATION—See Allied Irish Banks, p.l.c.; *Int'l*, pg. 64

FIRST MARYLAND BANCORP—See Allied Irish Banks, p.l.c.; *Int'l*, pg. 64

FIRST MARYLAND BROKERAGE CORPORATION—See Allied Irish Banks, p.l.c.; *Int'l*, pg. 64

FIRST MARYLAND CREDIT CORP.—See Allied Irish Banks, p.l.c.; *Int'l*, pg. 64

FIRST MARYLAND INTL. BANKING CORP.—See Allied Irish Banks, p.l.c.; *Int'l*, pg. 64

FIRST MARYLAND LEASECORP—See Allied Irish Banks, p.l.c.; *Int'l*, pg. 64

FIRST MARYLAND LIFE INSURANCE COMPANY—See Allied Irish Banks, p.l.c.; *Int'l*, pg. 64

FIRST MASSACHUSETTS BANK, N.A.—See Banknorth Group Inc.; *U.S. Public*, pg. 187

FIRST MEDICAL GROUP INC.; *U.S. Public*, pg. 636

FIRST MIDWEST AUTO PARK, INC.—See Northern States Power Company; *U.S. Public*, pg. 1195

FIRST MIDWEST BANCORP, INC.; *U.S. Public*, pg. 636

FIRST MIDWEST BANK, N.A.—See First Midwest Bancorp, Inc.; *U.S. Public*, pg. 636

FIRST MIDWEST MORTGAGE CORPORATION—See First Midwest Bancorp, Inc.; *U.S. Public*, pg. 636

FIRST MIDWEST TRUST COMPANY, N.A.—See First Midwest Bancorp, Inc.; *U.S. Public*, pg. 636

FIRST MORTGAGE CORPORATION—See Deposit Guaranty Corp.; *U.S. Public*, pg. 501

FIRST MOUNT JOY CORPORATION; *U.S. Private*, pg. 407

FIRST MUTUAL OF BOSTON—See BankBoston Corporation; *U.S. Public*, pg. 184

FIRST NATIONAL ASSET MANAGEMENT & TRUST COMPANY (PTY) LTD.—See First National Bank Holdings Limited; *Int'l*, pg. 487

FIRST NATIONAL BANK—See First Commerce Bancshares, Inc.; *U.S. Public*, pg. 629

FIRST NATIONAL BANK—See Synovus Financial Corp.; *U.S. Public*, pg. 1549

FIRST NATIONAL BANK (ASIA) LTD.—See First National Bank Holdings Limited; *Int'l*, pg. 487

FIRST NATIONAL BANK HOLDINGS (BOTSWANA) LTD.—See First National Bank Holdings Limited; *Int'l*, pg. 487

FIRST NATIONAL BANK HOLDINGS LIMITED; *Int'l*, pg. 487

FIRST NATIONAL BANK IN CHICAGO HEIGHTS—See GreatBanc, Inc.; *U.S. Public*, pg. 760

FIRST NATIONAL BANK IN CLEBURNE—See First Financial Bankshares, Inc.; *U.S. Public*, pg. 633

FIRST NATIONAL BANK IN MARLINTON—See Horizon Bancorp, Inc.; *U.S. Public*, pg. 836

FIRST NATIONAL BANK IN MASSILLON—See FirstMerit Corporation; *U.S. Public*, pg. 646

FIRST NATIONAL BANK, NASHVILLE—See First Commercial Corporation; *U.S. Public*, pg. 630

FIRST NATIONAL BANK OF ABILENE—See First Financial Bankshares, Inc.; *U.S. Public*, pg. 633

FIRST NATIONAL BANK OF BLUE ISLAND—See Great Lakes Financial Resources, Inc.; *U.S. Private*, pg. 474

THE FIRST NATIONAL BANK OF BOSTON (GUERNSEY) LIMITED—See BankBoston Corporation; *U.S. Public*, pg. 185

FIRST NATIONAL BANK OF CENTRAL CALIFORNIA—See Pacific Capital Bancorp; *U.S. Public*, pg. 1248

FIRST NATIONAL BANK OF CENTRAL ILLINOIS—See Firstbank of Illinois Co.; *U.S. Public*, pg. 644

FIRST NATIONAL BANK OF CHICAGO—See First Chicago NBD Corporation; *U.S. Public*, pg. 627

FIRST NATIONAL BANK OF CLIFTON FORGE—See MainStreet BankGroup Incorporated; *U.S. Public*, pg. 1039

FIRST NATIONAL BANK OF COMMERCE—See First Commerce Corporation; *U.S. Public*, pg. 629

FIRST NATIONAL BANK OF CONWAY—See First Commercial Corporation; *U.S. Public*, pg. 630

FIRST NATIONAL BANK OF CROSSVILLE—See Union Planters Corporation; *U.S. Public*, pg. 1669

FIRST NATIONAL BANK OF EAST GRAND FORKS—See U.S. Bancorp; *U.S. Public*, pg. 1681

FIRST NATIONAL BANK OF EDMOND—See Banc One Corporation; *U.S. Public*, pg. 174

FIRST NATIONAL BANK OF EL DORADO—See First United Bancshares, Inc.; *U.S. Public*, pg. 641

FIRST NATIONAL BANK OF FORT MYERS—See F.N.B. Corporation; *U.S. Public*, pg. 608

FIRST NATIONAL BANK OF HUNTINGTON—See Fort Wayne National Corporation; *U.S. Public*, pg. 674

FIRST NATIONAL BANK OF JENKS—See Banc One Corporation; *U.S. Public*, pg. 174

THE FIRST NATIONAL BANK OF LAFAYETTE—See First Commerce Corporation; *U.S. Public*, pg. 629

THE FIRST NATIONAL BANK OF LAKE CHARLES—See First Commerce Corporation; *U.S. Public*, pg. 629

FIRST NATIONAL BANK OF MAGNOLIA—See First United Bancshares, Inc.; *U.S. Public*, pg. 641

FIRST NATIONAL BANK OF MARSHALL—See First Financial Corporation; *U.S. Public*, pg. 634

FIRST NATIONAL BANK OF MARYLAND—See Allied Irish Banks, p.l.c.; *Int'l*, pg. 64

FIRST NATIONAL BANK OF NAMBIA LTD.—See First National Bank Holdings Limited; *Int'l*, pg. 487

FIRST NATIONAL BANK OF NAPLES—See F.N.B. Corporation; *U.S. Public*, pg. 607

FIRST NATIONAL BANK OF NEW ENGLAND—See First International Bancorp, Inc.; *U.S. Public*, pg. 636

FIRST NATIONAL BANK OF OHIO—See FirstMerit Corporation; *U.S. Public*, pg. 646

THE FIRST NATIONAL BANK OF OTTAWA—See Rurban Financial Corp.; *U.S. Public*, pg. 1413

FIRST NATIONAL BANK OF PENNSYLVANIA—See F.N.B. Corporation; *U.S. Public*, pg. 607

FIRST NATIONAL BANK OF RUSSELLVILLE—See First Commercial Corporation; *U.S. Public*, pg. 630

THE FIRST NATIONAL BANK OF ST. MARY'S—See Mercantile Bankshares Corporation; *U.S. Public*, pg. 1089

FIRST NATIONAL BANK OF SAXTON—See Omega Financial Corporation; *U.S. Public*, pg. 1222

FIRST NATIONAL BANK OF SEARCY—See First Commercial Corporation; *U.S. Public*, pg. 630

FIRST NATIONAL BANK OF SOUTHWESTERN OHIO—See First Financial Bancorp; *U.S. Public*, pg. 633

FIRST NATIONAL BANK OF SPRINGDALE—See First Tennessee National Corporation; *U.S. Public*, pg. 639

FIRST NATIONAL BANK OF SWEETWATER—See First Financial Bankshares, Inc.; *U.S. Public*, pg. 633

FIRST NATIONAL BANK OF WARSAW—See Fort Wayne National Corporation; *U.S. Public*, pg. 674

FIRST NATIONAL BANK, PALESTINE—See First Commercial Corporation; *U.S. Public*, pg. 630

FIRST NATIONAL CINCINNATI CORPORATION—See Starbanc Corporation; *U.S. Public*, pg. 1510

FIRST NATIONAL INSURANCE CO. OF AMERICA—See SAFECO Corporation; *U.S. Public*, pg. 1423

FIRST NATIONAL MORTGAGE CORPORATION—See Allied Irish Banks, p.l.c.; *Int'l*, pg. 64

FIRST NATIONAL NIPPON SHINPAN CO., LTD.—See Citicorp; *U.S. Public*, pg. 379

FIRST NATIONWIDE ASSURANCE CORPORATION—See Zurich Insurance Company; *Int'l*, pg. 1532

FIRST NET (PTY.) LTD.—See First National Bank Holdings Limited; *Int'l*, pg. 487

FIRST NH INVESTMENT SERVICES CORPORATION—See Bank of Ireland; *Int'l*, pg. 153

FIRST NH MORTGAGE CORP.—See Bank of Ireland; *Int'l*, pg. 153

FIRST NORTHERN CAPITAL CORP.; *U.S. Public*, pg. 636

FIRST OF AMERICA BANK CORPORATION; *U.S. Public*, pg. 636

FIRST OF AMERICA BANK FLORIDA—See First of America Bank Corporation; *U.S. Public*, pg. 636

FIRST OF AMERICA BANK-ILLINOIS, N.A.—See First of America Bank Corporation; *U.S. Public*, pg. 636

FIRST OF AMERICA BANK, N.A.—See First of America Bank Corporation; *U.S. Public*, pg. 636

FIRST OF AMERICA BROKERAGE SERVICES, INC.—See First of America Bank Corporation; *U.S. Public*, pg. 636

FIRST OF AMERICA COMMUNITY DEVELOPMENT CORPORATION—See First of America Bank Corporation; *U.S. Public*, pg. 637

FIRST OF AMERICA - FLORIDA—See First of America Bank Corporation; *U.S. Public*, pg. 636

FIRST OF AMERICA INSURANCE COMPANY—See First of America Bank Corporation; *U.S. Public*, pg. 637

FIRST OF AMERICA INVESTMENT CORP.—See First of America Bank Corporation; *U.S. Public*, pg. 637

FIRST OF AMERICA SECURITIES, INC.—See First of America Bank Corporation; *U.S. Public*, pg. 637

FIRST OF AMERICA TRUST COMPANY—See First of America Bank Corporation; *U.S. Public*, pg. 637

FIRST OKLAHOMA BANK & TRUST COMPANY OF EDMOND—See Banc One Corporation; *U.S. Public*, pg. 174

FIRST OMNI BANK, N.A.—See Allied Irish Banks, p.l.c.; *Int'l*, pg. 65

FIRST PACIFIC ADVISORS, INC.—See United Asset Management Corporation; *U.S. Public*, pg. 1673

FIRST PACIFIC BANK—See First Pacific Company Limited; *Int'l*, pg. 487

FIRST PACIFIC COMPANY LIMITED; *Int'l*, pg. 487

FIRST PACIFIC DAVIES LIMITED—See First Pacific Company Limited; *Int'l*, pg. 487

FIRST PARKE STATE BANK—See First Financial Corporation; *U.S. Public*, pg. 634

FIRST PENN-PACIFIC LIFE INSURANCE CO.—See Lincoln National Corporation; *U.S. Public*, pg. 998

FIRST PHILIPPINE INDUSTRIAL CORP.—See Royal Dutch/Shell Group of Companies; *Int'l*, pg. 1140

FIRST PROTECTIVE INSURANCE GROUP—See Protective Life Corporation; *U.S. Public*, pg. 1336

FIRST QUADRANT CORPORATION—See Xerox Corporation; *U.S. Public*, pg. 1784

FIRST RATE BUREAU DE CHANGE LIMITED—See Bank of Ireland; *Int'l*, pg. 152

FIRST-RE LIFE INSURANCE COMPANY—See AEGON N.V.; *Int'l*, pg. 27

FIRST RECOVERY—See Ashland, Inc.; *U.S. Public*, pg. 139

THE FIRST REPUBLIC BUILDING CORP.—See The First Republic Corporation of America; *U.S. Public*, pg. 637

THE FIRST REPUBLIC CORPORATION OF AMERICA; *U.S. Public*, pg. 637

FIRST RIDGE FARM STATE BANK—See First Financial Corporation; *U.S. Public*, pg. 634

FIRST SAFECO NATIONAL LIFE INSURANCE COMPANY OF NEW YORK—See SAFECO Corporation; *U.S. Public*, pg. 1423

FIRST SECURITY BANK OF NEVADA—See First Security Corporation; *U.S. Public*, pg. 637

FIRST SECURITY BANK OF NEW MEXICO—See First Security Corporation; *U.S. Public*, pg. 637

FIRST SECURITY CORPORATION; *U.S. Public*, pg. 637

FIRST SECURITY INFORMATION TECHNOLOGY, INC.—See First Security Corporation; *U.S. Public*, pg. 637

FIRST SECURITY INVESTMENT MANAGEMENT, INC.—See First Security Corporation; *U.S. Public*, pg. 638

FIRST SECURITY PROCESSING SERVICES, INC.—See First Security Corporation; *U.S. Public*, pg. 638

FIRST SECURITY THRIFT—See The First American Financial Corporation; *U.S. Public*, pg. 626

FIRST SIGNATURE BANK & TRUST CO.—See John Hancock Mutual Life Insurance Company; *U.S. Private*, pg. 589

1ST SOURCE BANK CONSOLIDATED—See 1st Source Corporation; *U.S. Public*, pg. 638

1ST SOURCE CAPITAL CORPORATION—See 1st Source Corporation; *U.S. Public*, pg. 638

1ST SOURCE CORPORATION; *U.S. Public*, pg. 638

FIRST SOURCE FINANCIAL, INC—See Household International, Inc.; *U.S. Public*, pg. 842

1ST SOURCE INSURANCE—See 1st Source Corporation; *U.S. Public*, pg. 638

1ST SOURCE LEASING—See 1st Source Corporation; *U.S. Public*, pg. 638

FIRST SOURCE YELLOW PAGES—See Arnold Communications; *U.S. Private*, pg. 84

FIRST SOUTHEAST INSURANCE AGENCY—See First Financial Holdings, Inc.; *U.S. Public*, pg. 634

FIRST SOUTHWEST COMPANY; *U.S. Private*, pg. 407

FIRST STATE BANK—See First Financial Corporation; *U.S. Public*, pg. 634

FIRST STATE BANK—See Union Planters Corporation; *U.S. Public*, pg. 1669

FIRST STATE BANK AND TRUST COMPANY—See Synovus Financial Corp.; *U.S. Public*, pg. 1549

FIRST STATE BANK N.A., ABILENE—See Independent Bankshares, Inc.; *U.S. Public*, pg. 874

Company Index

FIRST STATE BANK OF FAYETTE CO.—See Union Planters Corporation; *U.S. Public*, pg. 1669
FIRST STATE COMPUTING PTY LTD—See British Telecommunications plc; *Int'l*, pg. 222
FIRST STATE INSURANCE COMPANY—See The Hartford Financial Services Group Inc.; *U.S. Public*, pg. 794
FIRST STATE PAPER, INC.—See Central Lewmar; *U.S. Private*, pg. 223
FIRST STRATEGIC GROUP—See National Health Enhancement Systems, Inc.; *U.S. Public*, pg. 1157
FIRST STUTTGART BANK & TRUST—See First United Bancshares, Inc.; *U.S. Public*, pg. 641
FIRST SUNAMERICA LIFE INSURANCE COMPANY—See SunAmerica Inc.; *U.S. Public*, pg. 1533
FIRST TEAM SPORTS INC.; *U.S. Public*, pg. 638
FIRST TENNESSEE BANK - LEBANON—See First Tennessee National Corporation; *U.S. Public*, pg. 639
FIRST TENNESSEE BANK - MEMPHIS—See First Tennessee National Corporation; *U.S. Public*, pg. 639
FIRST TENNESSEE BANK NATIONAL ASSOCIATION—See First Tennessee National Corporation; *U.S. Public*, pg. 639
FIRST TENNESSEE BANK NATIONAL ASSOCIATION MISSISSIPPI—See First Tennessee National Corporation; *U.S. Public*, pg. 639
FIRST TENNESSEE BROKERAGE, INC.—See First Tennessee National Corporation; *U.S. Public*, pg. 639
FIRST TENNESSEE CAPITAL ASSETS CORPORATION—See First Tennessee National Corporation; *U.S. Public*, pg. 639
FIRST TENNESSEE NATIONAL CORPORATION; *U.S. Public*, pg. 638
FIRST TRANSAMERICA LIFE INSURANCE COMPANY—See Transamerica Corporation; *U.S. Public*, pg. 1630
FIRST TRAVELCORP INC.; *U.S. Private*, pg. 408
FIRST TRUST AND SAVINGS BANK OF TAYLORVILLE—See Firstbank of Illinois Co.; *U.S. Public*, pg. 644
FIRST TRUST COMPANY OF MONTANA, NATIONAL ASSOCIATION—See U.S. Bancorp; *U.S. Public*, pg. 1681
FIRST TRUST COMPANY OF NORTH DAKOTA, NATIONAL ASSOCIATION—See U.S. Bancorp; *U.S. Public*, pg. 1681
FIRST TRUST CORPORATION—See Fiserv, Inc.; *U.S. Public*, pg. 647
FIRST TRUST NATIONAL ASSOCIATION—See U.S. Bancorp; *U.S. Public*, pg. 1681
FIRST TRUST OF CALIFORNIA, NATIONAL ASSOCIATION—See U.S. Bancorp; *U.S. Public*, pg. 1681
FIRST UNION BROKERAGE SERVICES, INC.—See First Union Corporation; *U.S. Public*, pg. 640
FIRST UNION COMMERCIAL CORP.—See First Union Corporation; *U.S. Public*, pg. 640
FIRST UNION CORPORATION; *U.S. Public*, pg. 639
FIRST UNION HOME EQUITY CORPORATION—See First Union Corporation; *U.S. Public*, pg. 640
FIRST UNION INSURANCE GROUP, INC.—See First Union Corporation; *U.S. Public*, pg. 640
FIRST UNION MANAGEMENT, INC.—See First Union Real Estate Investments; *U.S. Public*, pg. 641
FIRST UNION MORTGAGE CORPORATION—See First Union Corporation; *U.S. Public*, pg. 640
FIRST UNION NATIONAL BANK OF CONNECTICUT—See First Union Corporation; *U.S. Public*, pg. 640
FIRST UNION NATIONAL BANK OF FLORIDA—See First Union Corporation; *U.S. Public*, pg. 640
FIRST UNION NATIONAL BANK OF GEORGIA—See First Union Corporation; *U.S. Public*, pg. 640
FIRST UNION NATIONAL BANK OF MARYLAND—See First Union Corporation; *U.S. Public*, pg. 640
FIRST UNION NATIONAL BANK OF NORTH CAROLINA—See First Union Corporation; *U.S. Public*, pg. 640
FIRST UNION NATIONAL BANK OF SOUTH CAROLINA—See First Union Corporation; *U.S. Public*, pg. 640
FIRST UNION NATIONAL BANK OF TENNESSEE—See First Union Corporation; *U.S. Public*, pg. 640
FIRST UNION NATIONAL BANK OF VIRGINIA—See First Union Corporation; *U.S. Public*, pg. 640
FIRST UNION NATIONAL BANK OF WASHINGTON—See First Union Corporation; *U.S. Public*, pg. 640
FIRST UNION REAL ESTATE INVESTMENTS; *U.S. Public*, pg. 640
FIRST UNION SECURITIES INC.—See First Union Corporation; *U.S. Public*, pg. 640
FIRST UNITED AMERICAN LIFE INSURANCE COMPANY—See Torchmark Corporation; *U.S. Public*, pg. 1623
FIRST UNITED BANCSHARES, INC.; *U.S. Public*, pg. 641
FIRST UNITED SMALL BUSINESS INVESTMENT CO.—See James Ferrera & Sons, Inc.; *U.S. Private*, pg. 402
FIRST UNUM LIFE INSURANCE COMPANY—See UNUM Corporation; *U.S. Public*, pg. 1699
FIRST USA BANK—See Banc One Corporation; *U.S. Public*, pg. 174
FIRST USA CAPITAL MARKETS, INC.—See Banc One Corporation; *U.S. Public*, pg. 174
FIRST USA FEDERAL SAVINGS BANK—See Banc One Corporation; *U.S. Public*, pg. 174
FIRST USA FINANCIAL SERVICES, INC.—See Banc One Corporation; *U.S. Public*, pg. 174
FIRST USA, INC.—See Banc One Corporation; *U.S. Public*, pg. 174
FIRST USA PAYMENTECH, INC.—See Banc One Corporation; *U.S. Public*, pg. 174
FIRST VALLEY CORPORATION—See Summit Bancorp; *U.S. Public*, pg. 1528
FIRST VALLEY LEASING, INC.—See Summit Bancorp; *U.S. Public*, pg. 1528
FIRST VALLEY LIFE INSURANCE COMPANY—See Summit Bancorp; *U.S. Public*, pg. 1528
FIRST VANTAGE-TENNESSEE—See First Virginia Banks, Inc.; *U.S. Public*, pg. 641

FIRST VERMONT BANK & TRUST COMPANY—See Banknorth Group Inc.; *U.S. Public*, pg. 187
FIRST VIRGINIA BANK—See First Virginia Banks, Inc.; *U.S. Public*, pg. 641
FIRST VIRGINIA BANK-COLONIAL—See First Virginia Banks, Inc.; *U.S. Public*, pg. 641
FIRST VIRGINIA BANK-COMMONWEALTH—See First Virginia Banks, Inc.; *U.S. Public*, pg. 641
FIRST VIRGINIA BANK-MARYLAND—See First Virginia Banks, Inc.; *U.S. Public*, pg. 642
FIRST VIRGINIA BANK-MOUNTAIN EMPIRE—See First Virginia Banks, Inc.; *U.S. Public*, pg. 642
FIRST VIRGINIA BANK-SOUTHWEST—See First Virginia Banks, Inc.; *U.S. Public*, pg. 642
FIRST VIRGINIA BANKS, INC.; *U.S. Public*, pg. 641
FIRST VIRGINIA INSURANCE SERVICES, INC.—See First Virginia Banks, Inc.; *U.S. Public*, pg. 642
FIRST VIRGINIA LIFE INSURANCE COMPANY—See First Virginia Banks, Inc.; *U.S. Public*, pg. 642
FIRST VIRGINIA MORTGAGE COMPANY—See First Virginia Banks, Inc.; *U.S. Public*, pg. 642
FIRST WESTERN BANCORP, INC.; *U.S. Public*, pg. 642
FIRST WESTERN BANK, NATIONAL ASSOCIATION—See First Western Bancorp, Inc.; *U.S. Public*, pg. 642
FIRST WESTERN TRUST SERVICES CO.—See First Western Bancorp, Inc.; *U.S. Public*, pg. 642
FIRST WISCONSIN ASSET MANAGEMENT, INC.—See Firstar Corporation; *U.S. Public*, pg. 643
FIRST WISCONSIN TRUST COMPANY OF FLORIDA—See Firstar Corporation; *U.S. Public*, pg. 643
FIRST WORTHING COMPANY; *U.S. Private*, pg. 408
THE FIRST YEARS INC.; *U.S. Public*, pg. 642
FIRSTAFF, INC.—See AccuStaff Incorporated; *U.S. Public*, pg. 15
FIRSTAR BANK OF MINNESOTA—See Firstar Corporation; *U.S. Public*, pg. 643
FIRSTAR CAPITAL MARKETS GROUP—See Firstar Corporation; *U.S. Public*, pg. 643
FIRSTAR COMMUNITY INVESTMENT CORP.—See Firstar Corporation; *U.S. Public*, pg. 643
FIRSTAR CORPORATION; *U.S. Public*, pg. 642
FIRSTAR CORPORATION ARIZONA—See Firstar Corporation; *U.S. Public*, pg. 643
FIRSTAR CORPORATION ILLINOIS—See Firstar Corporation; *U.S. Public*, pg. 643
FIRSTAR CORPORATION-IOWA—See Firstar Corporation; *U.S. Public*, pg. 643
FIRSTAR CORPORATION OF MINNESOTA—See Firstar Corporation; *U.S. Public*, pg. 643
FIRSTAR DEVELOPMENT CORPORATION—See Firstar Corporation; *U.S. Public*, pg. 643
FIRSTAR EXPORT CREDIT LIMITED—See Firstar Corporation; *U.S. Public*, pg. 643
FIRSTAR INFORMATION SERVICES CORPORATION—See Firstar Corporation; *U.S. Public*, pg. 643
FIRSTAR LEASING CORPORATION—See Firstar Corporation; *U.S. Public*, pg. 643
FIRSTAR MORTGAGE CORPORATION—See Firstar Corporation; *U.S. Public*, pg. 643
FIRSTAR REAL ESTATE SERVICES, INC.—See Firstar Corporation; *U.S. Public*, pg. 643
FIRSTAR WISCONSIN RAPIDS—See Firstar Corporation; *U.S. Public*, pg. 643
FIRSTATE SERVICES, INC.—See FSF Financial Corp.; *U.S. Public*, pg. 608
FIRSTBANK—See First United Bancshares, Inc.; *U.S. Public*, pg. 641
FIRSTBANK OF ILLINOIS CO.; *U.S. Public*, pg. 643
FIRSTBANK PUERTO RICO; *U.S. Public*, pg. 644
FIRSTCITY FINANCIAL CORPORATION; *U.S. Public*, pg. 644
FIRSTCOM MARKETING INC.—See Young & Rubicam Inc.; *U.S. Private*, pg. 1200
FIRSTCORP; *U.S. Public*, pg. 408
FIRSTCORP—See Firstcorp; *U.S. Private*, pg. 408
FIRSTCORP MERCHANT BANK LIMITED—See First National Bank Holdings Limited; *Int'l*, pg. 487
FIRSTENERGY CORP.; *U.S. Public*, pg. 644
FIRSTFED FINANCIAL CORP.; *U.S. Public*, pg. 645
FIRSTMERIT CORPORATION; *U.S. Public*, pg. 646
FIRSTMISS STEEL, INC.—See ChemFirst Inc.; *U.S. Public*, pg. 344
FIRTH-RIXSON CASTINGS LTD.—See Firth-Rixson Plc; *Int'l*, pg. 487
FIRTH-RIXSON FORGINGS—See Firth-Rixson Plc; *Int'l*, pg. 487
FIRTH-RIXSON MONROE—See Firth-Rixson Plc; *Int'l*, pg. 488
FIRTH-RIXSON PLC; *Int'l*, pg. 487
FIRTH-RIXSON RINGS LTD.—See Firth-Rixson Plc; *Int'l*, pg. 488
FIRTH-RIXSON SUPERALLOYS LTD.—See Firth-Rixson Plc; *Int'l*, pg. 488
FIRTH-RIXSON VIKING—See Firth-Rixson Plc; *Int'l*, pg. 488
FISAT S.P.A.—See Dainippon Ink & Chemicals, Inc.; *Int'l*, pg. 371
FISAX—See AXIA Incorporated; *U.S. Private*, pg. 103
FISCA OIL CO., INC.; *U.S. Private*, pg. 408
FISCAMBI FACTORING S.P.A.—See Banco Ambrosiano Veneto S.p.A.; *Int'l*, pg. 138
FISCAMBI LEASING S.P.A.—See Banco Ambrosiano Veneto S.p.A.; *Int'l*, pg. 138
FISCAMBI LEASING SUD S.P.A.—See Banco Ambrosiano Veneto S.p.A.; *Int'l*, pg. 138
FISCHBACH & DOUGHERTY, INC.; *U.S. Private*, pg. 408
FISCHBACH & MOORE, INC.—See American International Group, Inc.; *U.S. Public*, pg. 84
FISCHBACH & MOORE INTERNATIONAL CORP.—See American International Group, Inc.; *U.S. Public*, pg. 84
FISCHBACH CORPORATION—See American International Group, Inc.; *U.S. Public*, pg. 84
FISCHBEIN CO.—See AXIA Incorporated; *U.S. Private*, pg. 103

FISCHER & FORTER AB—See ELSAG Bailey Process Automation N.V.; *Int'l*, pg. 449
FISCHER & FORTER (CANADA) LTD.—See ELSAG Bailey Process Automation N.V.; *Int'l*, pg. 449
FISCHER & FORTER ITALIANA S.P.A.—See ELSAG Bailey Process Automation N.V.; *Int'l*, pg. 449
FISCHER & FORTER LTD.—See ELSAG Bailey Process Automation N.V.; *Int'l*, pg. 449
FISCHER COMPANIES; *U.S. Private*, pg. 408
GEORG FISCHER AB—See Georg Fischer Ltd.; *Int'l*, pg. 489
GEORG FISCHER AG & CO.—See Georg Fischer Ltd.; *Int'l*, pg. 491
GEORG FISCHER AMASTEEL S.A.—See Ervin Industries, Inc.; *U.S. Private*, pg. 382
GEORG FISCHER ANLAGENBAU HOLDING AG—See Georg Fischer Ltd.; *Int'l*, pg. 490
GEORG FISCHER A/S—See Georg Fischer Ltd.; *Int'l*, pg. 489
GEORG FISCHER A.S.—See Georg Fischer Ltd.; *Int'l*, pg. 489
GEORG FISCHER AUTOMOBILGUSS GES.M.B.H.—See Georg Fischer Ltd.; *Int'l*, pg. 488
GEORG FISCHER AUTOMOBILGUSS GMBH—See Georg Fischer Ltd.; *Int'l*, pg. 488
GEORG FISCHER AUTOMOTIVE PRODUCTS INC.—See Georg Fischer Ltd.; *Int'l*, pg. 488
GEORG FISCHER BETEILIGUNGS GMBH—See Georg Fischer Ltd.; *Int'l*, pg. 491
GEORG FISCHER CASTINGS—See Georg Fischer Ltd.; *Int'l*, pg. 489
GEORG FISCHER CORPORATION—See Georg Fischer Ltd.; *Int'l*, pg. 491
GEORG FISCHER DISA AG—See Georg Fischer Ltd.; *Int'l*, pg. 488
GEORG FISCHER DISA A/S—See Georg Fischer Ltd.; *Int'l*, pg. 489
GEORG FISCHER DISA ENGINEERING AG—See Georg Fischer Ltd.; *Int'l*, pg. 488
GEORG FISCHER DISA ENGINEERING LTD.—See Georg Fischer Ltd.; *Int'l*, pg. 489
GEORG FISCHER DISA GMBH—See Georg Fischer Ltd.; *Int'l*, pg. 489
GEORG FISCHER DISA GOFF INC.—See Georg Fischer Ltd.; *Int'l*, pg. 488
GEORG FISCHER DISA HOLDING AG—See Georg Fischer Ltd.; *Int'l*, pg. 488
GEORG FISCHER DISA HOLDING CORP.—See Georg Fischer Ltd.; *Int'l*, pg. 488
GEORG FISCHER DISA INC.—See Georg Fischer Ltd.; *Int'l*, pg. 488
GEORG FISCHER DISA, INC.—See Georg Fischer Ltd.; *Int'l*, pg. 490
GEORG FISCHER DISA K.K.—See Georg Fischer Ltd.; *Int'l*, pg. 489
GEORG FISCHER DISA LTD.—See Georg Fischer Ltd.; *Int'l*, pg. 489
GEORG FISCHER DISA SARL—See Georg Fischer Ltd.; *Int'l*, pg. 489
GEORG FISCHER DISA S.R.O.—See Georg Fischer Ltd.; *Int'l*, pg. 489
GEORG FISCHER FAHRZEUGTECHNIK AG—See Georg Fischer Ltd.; *Int'l*, pg. 488
GEORG FISCHER FITTINGS GMBH—See Georg Fischer Ltd.; *Int'l*, pg. 489
GEORG FISCHER FORWARDING LOGISTICS LTD.—See Georg Fischer Ltd.; *Int'l*, pg. 490
GEORG FISCHER GESCHAFTSFUHRUNGS GMBH—See Georg Fischer Ltd.; *Int'l*, pg. 491
GEORG FISCHER GMBH—See Georg Fischer Ltd.; *Int'l*, pg. 488
GEORG FISCHER (GREAT BRITAIN) LTD.—See Georg Fischer Ltd.; *Int'l*, pg. 491
GEORG FISCHER HOLDING (N.V.)—See Georg Fischer Ltd.; *Int'l*, pg. 489
GEORG FISCHER IMMOBILIEN AG—See Georg Fischer Ltd.; *Int'l*, pg. 491
GEORG FISCHER, INC.—See Georg Fischer Ltd.; *Int'l*, pg. 488
GEORG FISCHER INC.—See Georg Fischer Ltd.; *Int'l*, pg. 489
GEORG FISCHER JAPAN LTD.—See Georg Fischer Ltd.; *Int'l*, pg. 490
GEORG FISCHER KUNSTSTOFFARMATUREN AG—See Georg Fischer Ltd.; *Int'l*, pg. 489
GEORG FISCHER LEICHTMETALL AG—See Georg Fischer Ltd.; *Int'l*, pg. 490
GEORG FISCHER LTD.; *Int'l*, pg. 488
GEORG FISCHER (LINCOLN) LTD.—See Georg Fischer Ltd.; *Int'l*, pg. 488
GEORG FISCHER LOGIMATICS LTD.—See Georg Fischer Ltd.; *Int'l*, pg. 490
GEORG FISCHER N.V.—See Georg Fischer Ltd.; *Int'l*, pg. 489
GEORG FISCHER NV-SA—See Georg Fischer Ltd.; *Int'l*, pg. 489
GEORG FISCHER PIPING SYSTEMS LTD.—See Georg Fischer Ltd.; *Int'l*, pg. 489
GEORG FISCHER PLASTICS LTD.—See Georg Fischer Ltd.; *Int'l*, pg. 490
GEORG FISCHER PLASTIK A.G.—See Georg Fischer Ltd.; *Int'l*, pg. 489
GEORG FISCHER PTE. LTD.—See Georg Fischer Ltd.; *Int'l*, pg. 490
GEORG FISCHER PTY LTD.—See Georg Fischer Ltd.; *Int'l*, pg. 488
GEORG FISCHER REAL ESTATE SERVICES LTD.—See Georg Fischer Ltd.; *Int'l*, pg. 490
GEORG FISCHER RISK MANAGEMENT LTD.—See Georg Fischer Ltd.; *Int'l*, pg. 491
GEORG FISCHER ROHRLEITUNGSSYSTEME (SCHWEIZ) A.G.—See Georg Fischer Ltd.; *Int'l*, pg. 489
GEORG FISCHER ROHRLEITUNGSSYSTEMS GMBH—See Georg Fischer Ltd.; *Int'l*, pg. 490

GEORG FISCHER ROHRVERBINDUNGSTECHNIK GMBH—See Georg Fischer Ltd.; *Int'l*, pg. 490
GEORG FISCHER S.A.—See Georg Fischer Ltd.; *Int'l*, pg. 490
GEORG FISCHER SALES LTD.—See Georg Fischer Ltd.; *Int'l*, pg. 490
GEORG FISCHER SLOANE INC.—See Georg Fischer Ltd.; *Int'l*, pg. 490
GEORG FISCHER TRENTON LTD.—See Georg Fischer Ltd.; *Int'l*, pg. 490
GEORG FISCHER TREUHAND A.G.—See Georg Fischer Ltd.; *Int'l*, pg. 490
GEORG FISCHER VERKEHRSTECHNIK AG—See Georg Fischer Ltd.; *Int'l*, pg. 488
GEORG FISCHER VERKEHRSTECHNIK GMBH—See Georg Fischer Ltd.; *Int'l*, pg. 488
GEORG FISCHER WAGA N.V.—See Georg Fischer Ltd.; *Int'l*, pg. 490
GEORG FISCHER WOHNBAU GMBH & CO.—See Georg Fischer Ltd.; *Int'l*, pg. 491
GEORG FISCHER DISA INC.—See Dansk Industri Syndikat A/S; *Int'l*, pg. 382
GIORGIO FISCHER S.P.A.—See Georg Fischer Ltd.; *Int'l*, pg. 490
GUSTAV FISCHER VERLAG GMBH & CO. KG—See Georg von Holtzbrinck GmbH; *Int'l*, pg. 1478
GUSTAV FISCHER VERLAG JENA GMBH—See Georg von Holtzbrinck GmbH; *Int'l*, pg. 1478
FISCHER IMAGING AUSTRALIA PTY, LTD.—See Fischer Imaging Corporation; *U.S. Public*, pg. 647
FISCHER IMAGING CHINA—See Fischer Imaging Corporation; *U.S. Public*, pg. 647
FISCHER IMAGING CORPORATION; *U.S. Public*, pg. 647
FISCHER IMAGING CORPORATION, RMS MANUFACTURING DIVISION—See Fischer Imaging Corporation; *U.S. Public*, pg. 647
FISCHER IMAGING EUROPE—See Fischer Imaging Corporation; *U.S. Public*, pg. 647
FISCHER PACKING CO.—See Bongrain S.A.; *Int'l*, pg. 201
S. FISCHER VERLAG GMBH—See Georg von Holtzbrinck GmbH; *Int'l*, pg. 1478
FISCHER TASCHENBUCH VERLAG GMBH—See Georg von Holtzbrinck GmbH; *Int'l*, pg. 1478
FISERV (ASPAC), PTE. LTD.—See Fiserv, Inc.; *U.S. Public*, pg. 647
FISERV CIR, INC.—See Fiserv, Inc.; *U.S. Public*, pg. 647
FISERV EUROPE LIMITED—See Fiserv, Inc.; *U.S. Public*, pg. 647
FISERV FRESNO, INC.—See Fiserv, Inc.; *U.S. Public*, pg. 647
FISERV, INC.; *U.S. Public*, pg. 647
FISH INTERNATIONAL CO.—See KTI Fish; *U.S. Private*, pg. 604
FISH INTERNATIONAL ENGINEERS—See KTI Fish; *U.S. Private*, pg. 604
FISH SERVICE CORPORATION—See KTI Fish; *U.S. Private*, pg. 604
THE ALBERT FISHER GROUP PLC; *Int'l*, pg. 491
ALBERT FISHER NORTH AMERICA—See The Albert Fisher Group PLC; *Int'l*, pg. 491
FISHER & LUDLOW—See Harris Steel Group Inc.; *Int'l*, pg. 598
FISHER BROADCASTING INC.—See Fisher Companies Inc.; *U.S. Public*, pg. 648
FISHER CHILLED FOODS—See The Albert Fisher Group PLC; *Int'l*, pg. 491
FISHER COMPANIES INC.; *U.S. Public*, pg. 647
FISHER CONTROLS INTERNATIONAL, INC.—See Emerson Electric Co.; *U.S. Public*, pg. 573
FISHER FROZEN FOODS LIMITED—See The Albert Fisher Group PLC; *Int'l*, pg. 491
FISHER GAUGE INC./FISHERCAST DIV.—See Fisher Gauge Inc.; *Int'l*, pg. 492
FISHER GAUGE LIMITED; *Int'l*, pg. 491
FISHER GRAPHIC INDUSTRIES—See Container Graphics Corporation; *U.S. Private*, pg. 267
FISHER MILLS, INC.—See Fisher Companies Inc.; *U.S. Public*, pg. 648
FISHER PIERCE DIVISION—See Pacific Scientific Company; *U.S. Public*, pg. 1250
FISHER-PRICE HOUSE—See Mattel, Inc.; *U.S. Public*, pg. 1058
FISHER-PRICE, INC.—See Mattel, Inc.; *U.S. Public*, pg. 1058
FISHER-PRICE SPIELWAREN GMBH—See Mattel, Inc.; *U.S. Public*, pg. 1058
FISHER PROPERTIES, INC.—See Giant Eagle, Inc.; *U.S. Private*, pg. 451
FISHER PROPERTIES INC.—See Fisher Companies Inc.; *U.S. Public*, pg. 648
FISHER QUALITY FOODS LIMITED—See The Albert Fisher Group PLC; *Int'l*, pg. 491
FISHER SCIENTIFIC COMPANY—See Thomas H. Lee Co.; *U.S. Private*, pg. 658
FISHER SCIENTIFIC INTERNATIONAL—See Thomas H. Lee Co.; *U.S. Private*, pg. 658
FISHER SEAFOODS (GROSFORTH) LTD.—See The Albert Fisher Group PLC; *Int'l*, pg. 491
FISHER SKYLIGHTS, INC.; *U.S. Private*, pg. 408
FISHERCAST—See Fisher Gauge Limited; *Int'l*, pg. 491
FISHERIES SUPPLY COMPANY; *U.S. Private*, pg. 408
FISHERTECH—See Fisher Gauge Limited; *Int'l*, pg. 491
FISHERY FOODS GMBH—See Fishery Products International Ltd.; *Int'l*, pg. 492
FISHERY PRODUCTS INTERNATIONAL LTD.; *Int'l*, pg. 492
FISHERY PRODUCTS INTERNATIONAL USA—See Fishery Products International Ltd.; *Int'l*, pg. 492
FISHING TACKLE RETAILER—See B.A.S.S., Inc.; *U.S. Private*, pg. 105
FISHING UK—See EMAP Plc; *Int'l*, pg. 486
FISHKING PROCESSORS, INC.—See Nippon Suisan Kaisha, Ltd.; *Int'l*, pg. 940
FISHMAN & TOBIN, INC.; *U.S. Private*, pg. 408

FISK ELECTRIC COMPANY—See AMEC Plc; *Int'l*, pg. 16
FISKARS CANADA INC.—See Fiskars Oy AB; *Int'l*, pg. 492
FISKARS CONSUMER OY AB—See Fiskars Oy AB; *Int'l*, pg. 492
FISKARS DANMARK A/S—See Fiskars Oy AB; *Int'l*, pg. 492
FISKARS ELECTRONICS LTD.—See Fiskars Oy AB; *Int'l*, pg. 492
FISKARS-GERBER—See Fiskars Oy AB; *Int'l*, pg. 492
FISKARS HAND TOOL DIVISION—See Fiskars Oy AB; *Int'l*, pg. 492
FISKARS INC.—See Fiskars Oy AB; *Int'l*, pg. 492
FISKARS INC.-LATIN AMERICA—See Fiskars Oy AB; *Int'l*, pg. 492
FISKARS INC.-POWER SENTRY DIVISION—See Fiskars Oy AB; *Int'l*, pg. 492
FISKARS INC.-SPECIAL MARKETS—See Fiskars Oy AB; *Int'l*, pg. 492
FISKARS INC.-WALLACE DIV.—See Fiskars Oy AB; *Int'l*, pg. 492
FISKARS KONSUMENTPRODUKTER AB—See Fiskars Oy AB; *Int'l*, pg. 492
FISKARS NORGE A/S—See Fiskars Oy AB; *Int'l*, pg. 492
FISKARS OY AB; *Int'l*, pg. 492
FISKARS POWER SYSTEMS—See BTR plc; *Int'l*, pg. 127
FISKARS POWER SYSTEMS—See Fiskars Oy AB; *Int'l*, pg. 493
FISKARS POWER SYSTEMS AB—See Fiskars Oy AB; *Int'l*, pg. 492
FISKARS POWER SYSTEMS A/S—See Fiskars Oy AB; *Int'l*, pg. 492
FISKARS POWER SYSTEMS GMBH—See Fiskars Oy AB; *Int'l*, pg. 492
FISKARS S.A.R.L.—See Fiskars Oy AB; *Int'l*, pg. 492
FISKARS SVERIGE AB—See Fiskars Oy AB; *Int'l*, pg. 492
FISKARS UK LTD.—See Fiskars Oy AB; *Int'l*, pg. 493
FISKE BROTHERS REFINING COMPANY; *U.S. Private*, pg. 408
FISONS AG—See Rhone-Poulenc S.A.; *Int'l*, pg. 1111
FISONS ARZNEIMITTEL GMBH—See Rhone-Poulenc S.A.; *Int'l*, pg. 1111
FISONS A/S—See Rhone-Poulenc S.A.; *Int'l*, pg. 1111
FISONS (BANGLADESH) LIMITED—See Rhone-Poulenc S.A.; *Int'l*, pg. 1111
FISONS BV—See Rhone-Poulenc S.A.; *Int'l*, pg. 1111
FISONS CONSUMER HEALTH PLC—See Rhone-Poulenc S.A.; *Int'l*, pg. 1110
FISONS CORPORATION LIMITED—See Rhone-Poulenc S.A.; *Int'l*, pg. 1111
FISONS FARMACEUTICI S.P.A.—See Rhone-Poulenc S.A.; *Int'l*, pg. 1111
FISONS HORTICULTURE—See Rhone-Poulenc S.A.; *Int'l*, pg. 1110
FISONS INSTRUMENTS—See Rhone-Poulenc S.A.; *Int'l*, pg. 1111
FISONS INSTRUMENTS USA—See Rhone-Poulenc S.A.; *Int'l*, pg. 1111
FISONS PTY. LIMITED—See Rhone-Poulenc S.A.; *Int'l*, pg. 1111
FISONS WESTERN CORPORATION—See Rhone-Poulenc S.A.; *Int'l*, pg. 1111
FIT CONTAINER AG—See Alusuisse-Lonza Holding Ltd.; *Int'l*, pg. 67
FITCH FOOD SERVICES LTD.—See Booker PLC; *Int'l*, pg. 202
FITCHBURG GAS AND ELECTRIC LIGHT CO.—See Unitil Corporation; *U.S. Public*, pg. 1692
FITEL LUCENT—See The Furukawa Electric Co., Ltd.; *Int'l*, pg. 530
FITEL PHOTOMATRIX INC.—See The Furukawa Electric Co., Ltd.; *Int'l*, pg. 530
FITNESS—See Bertelsmann AG; *Int'l*, pg. 190
THE FITNESS INSTITUTE—See H.J. Heinz Company; *U.S. Public*, pg. 806
FITTINGS TRAISEN GMBH—See Georg Fischer Ltd.; *Int'l*, pg. 490
FITTON & PITTMAN, INC.—See MasTec, Inc.; *U.S. Public*, pg. 1056
FITUR S.P.A.—See Fiat Auto SpA; *Int'l*, pg. 482
FITZ & FLOYD; *U.S. Private*, pg. 409
FITZGERALD & CO.; *U.S. Private*, pg. 409
G.P. FITZGERALD & CO. LTD.—See Harris Scarfe Holdings Limited; *Int'l*, pg. 597
FITZPATRICK & WELLER, INC.; *U.S. Private*, pg. 409
FITZSIMONS MANUFACTURING CO.—See Mark IV Industries Inc.; *U.S. Public*, pg. 1045
FIVE CROWNS—See Lawry's Restaurants, Inc.; *U.S. Private*, pg. 654
5 RUBBER CORPORATION—See The Standard Products Company; *U.S. Public*, pg. 1504
FIVE STAR BEEF LTD.—See Itoham Foods Inc.; *Int'l*, pg. 695
FIVE STAR FOODS INCORPORATED; *U.S. Private*, pg. 409
A FIVE STAR FORWARDING, INC.—See Norfolk Southern Corporation; *U.S. Public*, pg. 1191
FIVE STAR GROUP, INC.—See GP Strategies Corporation; *U.S. Public*, pg. 694
FIX AB—See Assa Abloy AB; *Int'l*, pg. 17
FIXTURES FURNITURE—See Jami, Inc.; *U.S. Private*, pg. 581
FJARFESTINGARFELAGID SKANDIA HF—See Skandia Insurance Company Limited; *Int'l*, pg. 1257
FJELDHAMMERTAK NORD A/S—See Icopal a/s; *Int'l*, pg. 659
FJELDHAMMERTAK OST A/S—See Icopal a/s; *Int'l*, pg. 659
FJELDHAMMERTAK SOR A/S—See Icopal a/s; *Int'l*, pg. 659
FJELDHAMMERTAK VEST A/S—See Icopal a/s; *Int'l*, pg. 659
FLACHFORM STAHL GMBH—See Arbed S.A.; *Int'l*, pg. 79
FLACHGLAS AG—See Pilkington Plc; *Int'l*, pg. 1056

FLACHGLAS TORGAU GMBH—See Saint-Gobain; *Int'l*, pg. 1172
FLAGEUL—See SNCF; *Int'l*, pg. 1164
FLAGG BRASS—See Amcast Industrial Corporation; *U.S. Public*, pg. 63
FLAGSHIP—See Landmark Communications, Inc.; *U.S. Private*, pg. 649
FLAGSHIP AIRLINES—See AMR Corporation; *U.S. Public*, pg. 9
FLAGSHIP BANK & TRUST COMPANY—See Chittenden Corporation; *U.S. Public*, pg. 351
FLAGSHIP CITY INSURANCE COMPANY—See Erie Family Life Insurance Company; *U.S. Public*, pg. 591
FLAIR CORPORATION—See United Dominion Industries, Ltd.; *U.S. Public*, pg. 1676
FLAKT AB—See ABB Asea Brown Boveri (Holding) Ltd.; *Int'l*, pg. 7
FLAKT, S.A. DE C.V.—See ABB Asea Brown Boveri (Holding) Ltd.; *Int'l*, pg. 5
FLAMBEAU AIRMOLD CORPORATION—See Flambeau Corporation; *U.S. Private*, pg. 409
FLAMBEAU CORPORATION; *U.S. Private*, pg. 409
FLAMBEAU CORPORATION—See Flambeau Corporation; *U.S. Private*, pg. 409
FLAMBEAU MICRO CO.—See Flambeau Corporation; *U.S. Private*, pg. 409
FLAMBEAU MILL—See EdperBrascan Corporation; *Int'l*, pg. 434
FLAMBEAU PLASTICS CO.—See Flambeau Corporation; *U.S. Private*, pg. 409
FLAMBEAU PRODUCTS CORP.—See Flambeau Corporation; *U.S. Private*, pg. 409
FLAMBEAU SOUTHEAST CO.—See Flambeau Corporation; *U.S. Private*, pg. 409
FLAMINGO PRODUCTS, INC.—See Erving Industries, Inc.; *U.S. Private*, pg. 382
FLANAGAN BROS. TRUCKING CO.—See Pro-Fac Cooperative, Inc.; *U.S. Private*, pg. 887
FLANDERS AIR SEAL FILTERS HOUSINGS INC.—See Flanders Corp.; *U.S. Public*, pg. 648
FLANDERS AIRPURE PRODUCTS CO., LLC—See Flanders Corp.; *U.S. Public*, pg. 648
FLANDERS CORP.; *U.S. Public*, pg. 648
FLANDERS CSC CORP.—See Flanders Corp.; *U.S. Public*, pg. 648
FLANDERS FILTERS, INC.—See Flanders Corp.; *U.S. Public*, pg. 648
FLANDERS INDUSTRIES, INC.; *U.S. Private*, pg. 410
FLANDERS PRECISIONAIRE—See Flanders Corp.; *U.S. Public*, pg. 648
FLANDRIA GARDEN N.V.—See Proventus AB; *Int'l*, pg. 1072
FLANIGAN'S ENTERPRISES, INC.; *U.S. Public*, pg. 648
FLANIGAN'S ENTERPRISES, INC.—See Flanigan's Enterprises, Inc.; *U.S. Public*, pg. 648
FLANIGAN'S LOUNGE 648
FLANIGAN'S MANAGEMENT SERVICES, INC.—See Flanigan's Enterprises, Inc.; *U.S. Public*, pg. 648
FLASHMEDIA ADVERTISING INC.—See Quebecor Inc.; *Int'l*, pg. 1076
FLASKAMP GMBH; *Int'l*, pg. 493
FLASKAMP GMBH—See Flaskamp GmbH; *Int'l*, pg. 493
THE FLATLEY COMPANY; *U.S. Private*, pg. 410
FLAVOR HOUSE PRODUCTS, INC.; *U.S. Private*, pg. 410
FLAVORING AB—See Cultor Ltd.; *Int'l*, pg. 349
FLAVORITE LABORATORIES—See A.M. Todd Company; *U.S. Private*, pg. 1090
FLECK CONTROLS—See Pentair, Inc.; *U.S. Public*, pg. 1273
FLECK MANUFACTURING INC.—See Noma Industries Limited; *Int'l*, pg. 955
THE FLECTO CO., INC.; *U.S. Private*, pg. 410
FRANK H. FLEER CORP.—See Marvel Entertainment Group; *U.S. Public*, pg. 1052
FLEER-SKYBOX INTERNATIONAL INC.—See Marvel Entertainment Group; *U.S. Public*, pg. 1052
FLEET BANK—See Fleet Financial Group, Inc.; *U.S. Public*, pg. 649
FLEET BANK, F.S.B.—See Fleet Financial Group, Inc.; *U.S. Public*, pg. 649
FLEET BANK, N.A.—See Fleet Financial Group, Inc.; *U.S. Public*, pg. 649
FLEET BANK-NH—See Fleet Financial Group, Inc.; *U.S. Public*, pg. 649
FLEET BANK NH—See Fleet Financial Group, Inc.; *U.S. Public*, pg. 649
FLEET BANK OF MAINE—See Fleet Financial Group, Inc.; *U.S. Public*, pg. 649
FLEET BANK OF MASSACHUSETTS, N.A.—See Fleet Financial Group, Inc.; *U.S. Public*, pg. 649
FLEET BROKERAGE SECURITIES CORP.—See Fleet Financial Group, Inc.; *U.S. Public*, pg. 649
C. B. FLEET CO., INC.; *U.S. Private*, pg. 410
FLEET CALL CORPORATION—See Nextel Communications; *U.S. Public*, pg. 1180
FLEET CALL OF TEXAS, INC.—See Nextel Communications; *U.S. Public*, pg. 1180
FLEET CALL OF UTAH, INC.—See Nextel Communications; *U.S. Public*, pg. 1180
FLEET CAPITAL CORPORATION—See Fleet Financial Group, Inc.; *U.S. Public*, pg. 649
FLEET CAPITAL LEASING—See Fleet Financial Group, Inc.; *U.S. Public*, pg. 650
FLEET CREDIT CORPORATION—See Fleet Financial Group, Inc.; *U.S. Public*, pg. 650
FLEET ENGINEERS, INC.; *U.S. Private*, pg. 410
FLEET EQUITY PARTNERS—See Fleet Financial Group, Inc.; *U.S. Public*, pg. 650
FLEET FINANCE, INC.—See Fleet Financial Group, Inc.; *U.S. Public*, pg. 650
FLEET FINANCIAL GROUP, INC.; *U.S. Public*, pg. 648
FLEET INDUSTRIES—See Magellan Aerospace Corporation; *Int'l*, pg. 829

FLEET INSURANCE MANAGEMENT, INC.—See Norfolk Southern Corporation; *U.S. Public*, pg. 1191
FLEET INVESTMENT ADVISORS, INC.—See Fleet Financial Group, Inc.; *U.S. Public*, pg. 650
FLEET INVESTMENT SERVICES—See Fleet Financial Group, Inc.; *U.S. Public*, pg. 650
FLEET LEASING DIVISION—See Ford Motor Company; *U.S. Public*, pg. 663
FLEET MORTGAGE GROUP, INC.—See Fleet Financial Group, Inc.; *U.S. Public*, pg. 650
FLEET NATIONAL BANK—See Fleet Financial Group, Inc.; *U.S. Public*, pg. 649
FLEET NATIONAL BANK OF CONNECTICUT—See Fleet Financial Group, Inc.; *U.S. Public*, pg. 649
FLEET NATIONAL BANK OF MASSACHUSETTS—See Fleet Financial Group, Inc.; *U.S. Public*, pg. 649
FLEET PR LTD.—See Shandwick International Plc; *Int'l*, pg. 1227
FLEET PRECIOUS METALS, INC.—See Fleet Financial Group, Inc.; *U.S. Public*, pg. 650
FLEET REAL ESTATE, INC.—See Fleet Financial Group, Inc.; *U.S. Public*, pg. 650
FLEET SECURITIES, INC.—See Fleet Financial Group, Inc.; *U.S. Public*, pg. 650
FLEET SERVICES CORP.—See Fleet Financial Group, Inc.; *U.S. Public*, pg. 650
FLEET SUPPORT CENTER—See Analysis & Technology, Inc.; *U.S. Public*, pg. 110
FLEET TRUST CO. OF FLORIDA, N.A.—See Fleet Financial Group, Inc.; *U.S. Public*, pg. 650
FLEETFOOT LTD.—See Pentland Group PLC; *Int'l*, pg. 1035
FLEETGUARD INC.—See Cummins Engine Company, Inc.; *U.S. Public*, pg. 468
FLEETGUARD INTERNATIONAL CORPORATION—See Cummins Engine Company, Inc.; *U.S. Public*, pg. 469
FLEETWOOD ALUMINUM PRODUCTS; *U.S. Private*, pg. 410
FLEETWOOD CANADA LTD.—See Fleetwood Enterprises, Inc.; *U.S. Public*, pg. 651
FLEETWOOD CREDIT CORP.—See Ford Motor Company; *U.S. Public*, pg. 663
FLEETWOOD ENTERPRISES, INC.; *U.S. Public*, pg. 650
FLEETWOOD FOLDING TRAILERS, INC.—See Fleetwood Enterprises, Inc.; *U.S. Public*, pg. 651
FLEETWOOD HOMES OF ALABAMA, INC.—See Fleetwood Enterprises, Inc.; *U.S. Public*, pg. 651
FLEETWOOD HOMES OF ARIZONA, INC.—See Fleetwood Enterprises, Inc.; *U.S. Public*, pg. 651
FLEETWOOD HOMES OF FLORIDA, INC.-AUBURNDALE—See Fleetwood Enterprises, Inc.; *U.S. Public*, pg. 651
FLEETWOOD HOMES OF GEORGIA, INC.-ALMA—See Fleetwood Enterprises, Inc.; *U.S. Public*, pg. 651
FLEETWOOD HOMES OF GEORGIA, INC. 651
FLEETWOOD HOMES OF GEORGIA, INC.-SOUTHWEST-INDUSTRIAL PARK—See Fleetwood Enterprises, Inc.; *U.S. Public*, pg. 651
FLEETWOOD HOMES OF INDIANA, INC.—See Fleetwood Enterprises, Inc.; *U.S. Public*, pg. 651
FLEETWOOD HOMES OF NORTH CAROLINA, INC.-LUMBERTON—See Fleetwood Enterprises, Inc.; *U.S. Public*, pg. 651
FLEETWOOD HOMES OF NORTH CAROLINA, INC./MOORESVILLE—See Fleetwood Enterprises, Inc.; *U.S. Public*, pg. 651
FLEETWOOD HOMES OF PENNSYLVANIA, INC.-ELIZABETHTOWN—See Fleetwood Enterprises, Inc.; *U.S. Public*, pg. 651
FLEETWOOD HOMES OF TENNESSEE, INC./WESTMORELAND PLANT/PLEASANT GROVE—See Fleetwood Enterprises, Inc.; *U.S. Public*, pg. 651
FLEETWOOD HOMES OF TEXAS—See Fleetwood Enterprises, Inc.; *U.S. Public*, pg. 651
FLEETWOOD HOMES OF TEXAS, INC.—See Fleetwood Enterprises, Inc.; *U.S. Public*, pg. 651
FLEETWOOD HOMES OF TEXAS, INC.-WACO/GHOLSON RD.—See Fleetwood Enterprises, Inc.; *U.S. Public*, pg. 651
FLEETWOOD HOMES OF VIRGINIA, INC.—See Fleetwood Enterprises, Inc.; *U.S. Public*, pg. 651
FLEETWOOD MOTOR HOMES OF INDIANA, INC.-DECATUR PLANT—See Fleetwood Enterprises, Inc.; *U.S. Public*, pg. 651
FLEETWOOD MOTOR HOMES OF CALIFORNIA, INC./CHICO—See Fleetwood Enterprises, Inc.; *U.S. Public*, pg. 651
FLEETWOOD MOTOR HOMES OF CALIFORNIA, INC.-RIVERSIDE PLANT/VIA RICARDO—See Fleetwood Enterprises, Inc.; *U.S. Public*, pg. 651
FLEETWOOD SYSTEMS, INC.; *U.S. Private*, pg. 410
FLEETWOOD TRAVEL TRAILERS OF CALIFORNIA, INC.-RUBIDOUX—See Fleetwood Enterprises, Inc.; *U.S. Public*, pg. 652
FLEISCHER MANUFACTURING, INC.; *U.S. Private*, pg. 410
FLEISCHLI OIL COMPANY, INC.; *U.S. Private*, pg. 410
FLEISCHMANN COMPANY—See RJR Nabisco Holdings Corp.; *U.S. Public*, pg. 1355
FLEISCHMANN MALTING COMPANY, INC.—See Archer Daniels Midland Company (ADM); *U.S. Public*, pg. 128
FLEISCHMANN'S YEAST—See Burns, Philp & Company Limited; *Int'l*, pg. 237
FLEISCHMANN'S YEAST CONSUMER PRODUCTS DIV.—See Burns, Philp & Company Limited; *Int'l*, pg. 237
FLEISHMAN-HILLARD—See Fleishman-Hillard Inc.; *U.S. Private*, pg. 411
FLEISHMAN-HILLARD BRUSSELS—See Fleishman-Hillard Inc.; *U.S. Private*, pg. 411
FLEISHMAN-HILLARD CARIBBEAN—See Fleishman-Hillard Inc.; *U.S. Private*, pg. 411
FLEISHMAN-HILLARD EUROPE—See Fleishman-Hillard Inc.; *U.S. Private*, pg. 411

FLEISHMAN-HILLARD FRANCE—See Fleishman-Hillard Inc.; *U.S. Private*, pg. 411
FLEISHMAN-HILLARD GERMANY—See Fleishman-Hillard Inc.; *U.S. Private*, pg. 411
FLEISHMAN-HILLARD INC.; *U.S. Private*, pg. 411
FLEISHMAN-HILLARD, INC.—See Fleishman-Hillard Inc.; *U.S. Private*, pg. 411
FLEISHMAN-HILLARD, ITALY—See Fleishman-Hillard Inc.; *U.S. Private*, pg. 411
FLEISHMAN-HILLARD, MEXICO, S.A. DE C.V.—See Fleishman-Hillard Inc.; *U.S. Private*, pg. 411
FLEISHMAN-HILLARD SAUNDERS LIMITED—See Fleishman-Hillard Inc.; *U.S. Private*, pg. 411
FLEISHMAN-HILLARD U.K. LIMITED—See Fleishman-Hillard Inc.; *U.S. Private*, pg. 411
FLEISSNER GMBH & CO. MASCHINENFABRIK; *Int'l*, pg. 493
FLEMING ASSET MANAGEMENT LIMITED—See Robert Fleming Holdings Ltd.; *Int'l*, pg. 493
FLEMING CANADA PARTNERS INC.—See Robert Fleming Holdings Ltd.; *Int'l*, pg. 493
FLEMING CAPITAL MANAGEMENT—See Robert Fleming Holdings Ltd.; *Int'l*, pg. 493
FLEMING CO. OF NEBRASKA, INC.—See Fleming Companies, Inc.; *U.S. Public*, pg. 653
FLEMING COMPANIES, INC.; *U.S. Public*, pg. 652
FLEMING COMPANY—See Fleming Companies, Inc.; *U.S. Public*, pg. 653
FLEMING FINANCE CORP.—See Fleming Companies, Inc.; *U.S. Public*, pg. 653
FLEMING FINANCE S.A.—See Robert Fleming Holdings Ltd.; *Int'l*, pg. 493
FLEMING FOODS OF ALABAMA, INC.—See Fleming Companies, Inc.; *U.S. Public*, pg. 653
FLEMING FOODS OF MISSOURI, INC.—See Fleming Companies, Inc.; *U.S. Public*, pg. 653
FLEMING FOODS OF OHIO, INC.—See Fleming Companies, Inc.; *U.S. Public*, pg. 653
FLEMING FOODS OF PENNSYLVANIA, INC.—See Fleming Companies, Inc.; *U.S. Public*, pg. 653
FLEMING FOODS OF TENNESSEE, INC.—See Fleming Companies, Inc.; *U.S. Public*, pg. 653
FLEMING FOODS OF TEXAS, INC.—See Fleming Companies, Inc.; *U.S. Public*, pg. 653
FLEMING FOODS WEST—See Fleming Companies, Inc.; *U.S. Public*, pg. 653
FLEMING FOODS WEST - FRESNO DIV.—See Fleming Companies, Inc.; *U.S. Public*, pg. 653
FLEMING FOODS WEST - SACRAMENTO DIV.—See Fleming Companies, Inc.; *U.S. Public*, pg. 653
FLEMING FUND MANAGEMENT (LUXEMBOURG) S.A.—See Robert Fleming Holdings Ltd.; *Int'l*, pg. 493
FLEMING INTERNATIONAL FIXED INTEREST MANAGEMENT LIMITED—See Robert Fleming Holdings Ltd.; *Int'l*, pg. 493
FLEMING INVESTMENT TRUST MANAGEMENT LIMITED—See Robert Fleming Holdings Ltd.; *Int'l*, pg. 493
FLEMING INVESTMENTS LIMITED—See Robert Fleming Holdings Ltd.; *Int'l*, pg. 493
FLEMING MARTIN INC.—See Robert Fleming Holdings Ltd.; *Int'l*, pg. 493
FLEMING MARTIN LIMITED—See Robert Fleming Holdings Ltd.; *Int'l*, pg. 493
FLEMING PACKAGING CORP.; *U.S. Private*, pg. 411
FLEMING-POTTER CO.—See Fleming Packaging Corp.; *U.S. Private*, pg. 411
FLEMING-POTTER FAST PRINTING—See Fleming Packaging Corp.; *U.S. Private*, pg. 411
FLEMING-POTTER WEBKOTE—See Fleming Packaging Corp.; *U.S. Private*, pg. 411
FLEMING PRIVATE ASSET MANAGEMENT LIMITED—See Robert Fleming Holdings Ltd.; *Int'l*, pg. 493
ROBERT FLEMING & CO. LIMITED—See Robert Fleming Holdings Ltd.; *Int'l*, pg. 493
ROBERT FLEMING ASSET MANAGEMENT LIMITED—See Robert Fleming Holdings Ltd.; *Int'l*, pg. 493
ROBERT FLEMING (DEUTSCHLAND) GMBH—See Robert Fleming Holdings Ltd.; *Int'l*, pg. 493
ROBERT FLEMING (FRANCE) S.A.—See Robert Fleming Holdings Ltd.; *Int'l*, pg. 494
ROBERT FLEMING HOLDINGS LIMITED—See Robert Fleming Holdings Ltd.; *Int'l*, pg. 494
ROBERT FLEMING HOLDINGS LTD.; *Int'l*, pg. 493
ROBERT FLEMING, INC.—See Robert Fleming Holdings Ltd.; *Int'l*, pg. 493
ROBERT FLEMING INSURANCE BROKERS LIMITED—See Robert Fleming Holdings Ltd.; *Int'l*, pg. 493
ROBERT FLEMING (ISLE OF MAN) LIMITED—See Robert Fleming Holdings Ltd.; *Int'l*, pg. 493
ROBERT FLEMING ITALIA SPA—See Robert Fleming Holdings Ltd.; *Int'l*, pg. 494
ROBERT FLEMING MANAGEMENT (JERSEY) LIMITED—See Robert Fleming Holdings Ltd.; *Int'l*, pg. 493
ROBERT FLEMING MANAGEMENT SERVICES LIMITED—See Robert Fleming Holdings Ltd.; *Int'l*, pg. 493
ROBERT FLEMING SECURITIES LIMITED—See Robert Fleming Holdings Ltd.; *Int'l*, pg. 493
ROBERT FLEMING (SOUTH AFRICA) (PTY) LIMITED—See Robert Fleming Holdings Ltd.; *Int'l*, pg. 494
ROBERT FLEMING SPAIN SA—See Robert Fleming Holdings Ltd.; *Int'l*, pg. 494
ROBERT FLEMING (STOCK LENDING) LIMITED—See Robert Fleming Holdings Ltd.; *Int'l*, pg. 493
ROBERT FLEMING (SWITZERLAND) A.G.—See Robert Fleming Holdings Ltd.; *Int'l*, pg. 494
ROBERT FLEMING (SWITZERLAND) S.A.—See Robert Fleming Holdings Ltd.; *Int'l*, pg. 494
FLEMINGS (JERSEY) LIMITED—See Robert Fleming Holdings Ltd.; *Int'l*, pg. 493
A. FRIEDRICH FLENDER AG—See Deutsche Babcock AG; *Int'l*, pg. 400
FLENDER-ATB-LOHER SYSTEMTECHNIK GMBH—See Deutsche Babcock AG; *Int'l*, pg. 400

FLENDER (AUSTRALIA) PTY. LTD.—See Deutsche Babcock AG; *Int'l*, pg. 400
FLENDER AUSTRIA ANTRIEBSTECHNIK AG—See Deutsche Babcock AG; *Int'l*, pg. 400
NV FLENDER BELGE S.A.—See Deutsche Babcock AG; *Int'l*, pg. 400
FLENDER BRASIL LTDA.—See Deutsche Babcock AG; *Int'l*, pg. 400
FLENDER-CIGALA S.P.A.—See Deutsche Babcock AG; *Int'l*, pg. 400
FLENDER CORPORATION—See Deutsche Babcock AG; *Int'l*, pg. 400
FLENDER DE MEXICO, S.A. DE C.V.—See Deutsche Babcock AG; *Int'l*, pg. 400
FLENDER ENGINEERING & SERVICE ANTRIEBSTECHNIK GMBH—See Deutsche Babcock AG; *Int'l*, pg. 400
FLENDER GES. M.B.H.—See Deutsche Babcock AG; *Int'l*, pg. 400
FLENDER GETRIEBEWERK PENIG GMBH—See Deutsche Babcock AG; *Int'l*, pg. 400
FLENDER-GRAFFENSTADEN S.A.—See Deutsche Babcock AG; *Int'l*, pg. 400
FLENDER GUSS GMBH—See Deutsche Babcock AG; *Int'l*, pg. 400
FLENDER-HIMMELWERK GMBH—See Deutsche Babcock AG; *Int'l*, pg. 400
FLENDER IBERICA S.A.—See Deutsche Babcock AG; *Int'l*, pg. 400
FLENDER ISHIBASHI CO. LTD.—See Deutsche Babcock AG; *Int'l*, pg. 400
FLENDER MACNEILL GEARS LTD.—See Deutsche Babcock AG; *Int'l*, pg. 401
FLENDER NEDERLAND B.V.—See Deutsche Babcock AG; *Int'l*, pg. 400
FLENDER OY—See Deutsche Babcock AG; *Int'l*, pg. 400
FLENDER POWER TRANSMISSION INC.—See Deutsche Babcock AG; *Int'l*, pg. 400
FLENDER POWER TRANSMISSION LTD.—See Deutsche Babcock AG; *Int'l*, pg. 400
FLENDER POWER TRANSMISSION (PTY.) LTD.—See Deutsche Babcock AG; *Int'l*, pg. 400
FLENDER S.A.R.L.—See Deutsche Babcock AG; *Int'l*, pg. 400
FLENDER SINGAPORE PTE. LTD.—See Deutsche Babcock AG; *Int'l*, pg. 401
FLENDER SVENKA AB—See Deutsche Babcock AG; *Int'l*, pg. 401
FLETCHER CHALLENGE AUSTRALIA LIMITED—See Fletcher Challenge Limited; *Int'l*, pg. 495
FLETCHER CHALLENGE CANADA LIMITED—See Fletcher Challenge Limited; *Int'l*, pg. 495
FLETCHER CHALLENGE LIMITED; *Int'l*, pg. 494
FLETCHER CHALLENGE METHANOL LIMITED—See Fletcher Challenge Limited; *Int'l*, pg. 495
FLETCHER CHALLENGE PETROLEUM INC.—See Fletcher Challenge Limited; *Int'l*, pg. 495
FLETCHER CHALLENGE PETROLEUM LIMITED—See Fletcher Challenge Limited; *Int'l*, pg. 495
FLETCHER COBRE TIRE CO. INC.; *U.S. Private*, pg. 411
THE FLETCHER CONSTRUCTION COMPANY LIMITED—See Fletcher Challenge Limited; *Int'l*, pg. 495
FLETCHER HOMES LIMITED—See Fletcher Challenge Limited; *Int'l*, pg. 495
J.H. FLETCHER & CO.; *U.S. Private*, pg. 412
FLETCHER MERCHANTS LIMITED—See Fletcher Challenge Limited; *Int'l*, pg. 495
FLETCHER PACIFIC CONSTRUCTION COMPANY LIMITED—See Fletcher Challenge Limited; *Int'l*, pg. 495
FLETCHER SMITH LTD.—See Booker PLC; *Int'l*, pg. 202
FLETCHER WOOD PANELS LIMITED—See Fletcher Challenge Limited; *Int'l*, pg. 495
FLEURBOURG—See LVMH Moet Hennessy Louis Vuitton; *Int'l*, pg. 780
FLEURSEILLE—See LVMH Moet Hennessy Louis Vuitton; *Int'l*, pg. 780
FLEURTEUIL—See LVMH Moet Hennessy Louis Vuitton; *Int'l*, pg. 780
FLEURUS BOUTIQUE SA—See LVMH Moet Hennessy Louis Vuitton; *Int'l*, pg. 780
FLEX-FAB—See Flexfab Horizons International, Inc.; *U.S. Private*, pg. 412
FLEX-KEY CORPORATION—See Astronics Corporation; *U.S. Public*, pg. 142
FLEX-KLEEN CORPORATION—See Air & Water Technologies Corporation; *U.S. Public*, pg. 29
FLEX-LINK SYSTEMS AB—See AB SKF; *Int'l*, pg. 1157
FLEX-O-FILM PLASTIC DIV.—See Flex-O-Glass, Inc.; *U.S. Private*, pg. 412
FLEX-O-GLASS, INC.; *U.S. Private*, pg. 412
FLEX PRODUCTS, INC.—See Optical Coating Laboratory, Inc.; *U.S. Public*, pg. 1227
FLEXA FABRIEKEN B.V.—See Akzo Nobel N.V.; *Int'l*, pg. 43
FLEXA SPA—See Chargeurs; *Int'l*, pg. 280
THE FLEXAUST CO.—See Coeur D'Alene Mines Corporation; *U.S. Public*, pg. 394
FLEXAUST G.M.B.H.—See Coeur D'Alene Mines Corporation; *U.S. Public*, pg. 394
FLEXCON CO., INC.; *U.S. Private*, pg. 412
FLEXFAB HORIZONS INTERNATIONAL, INC.; *U.S. Private*, pg. 412
FLEXI-VAN LEASING, INC.—See Flexi-Van Leasing, Inc.; *U.S. Private*, pg. 413
FLEXI-VAN UNITED KINGDOM—See Flexi-Van Leasing, Inc.; *U.S. Private*, pg. 413
FLEXIBLE CIRCUIT PRODUCTS DIVISION—See Parlex Corporation; *U.S. Public*, pg. 1264
FLEXIBLE DUCTING LIMITED—See Smiths Industries plc; *Int'l*, pg. 1267
FLEXIBLE FLYER TOYS; *U.S. Private*, pg. 412
FLEXIBLE LAMPS LTD.—See UIS, Inc.; *U.S. Private*, pg. 1113

FLEXIBLE PRODUCTS COMPANY; *U.S. Private*, pg. 412
FLEXIBLE STEEL LACING COMPANY; *U.S. Private*, pg. 413
FLEXIBLE TECHNOLOGIES INC.—See Smiths Industries plc; *Int'l*, pg. 1267
FLEXIBOX GMBH—See EIS Group Plc; *Int'l*, pg. 426
FLEXIBOX LTD.—See EIS Group Plc; *Int'l*, pg. 426
FLEXIDER S.P.A.—See Anamet Inc.; *U.S. Private*, pg. 70
FLEXIPLAS SA—See Smiths Industries plc; *Int'l*, pg. 1268
THE FLEXITALLIC GROUP, INC.; *U.S. Private*, pg. 413
FLEXITALLIC LP—See The Flexitallic Group, Inc.; *U.S. Private*, pg. 413
FLEXITALLIC LTD—See The Flexitallic Group, Inc.; *U.S. Private*, pg. 413
FLEXI-VAN LEASING, INC.; *U.S. Private*, pg. 413
FLEXLINE HOSE CO.—See Williams Holdings Plc; *Int'l*, pg. 1500
FLEXMAG INDUSTRIES—See SPS Technologies, Inc.; *U.S. Public*, pg. 1420
FLEXMEDICS CORPORATION—See Phillips Plastics Corporation; *U.S. Private*, pg. 862
FLEXONICS AUTOMOTIVE—See Senior Engineering Group, plc.; *Int'l*, pg. 1220
FLEXONICS EXPANSION JOINTS—See Senior Engineering Group, plc.; *Int'l*, pg. 1222
FLEXONICS HOSE—See Senior Engineering Group, plc.; *Int'l*, pg. 1222
FLEXONICS OEM PRODUCTS—See Senior Engineering Group, plc.; *Int'l*, pg. 1222
FLEXRX—See Merck & Co., Inc.; *U.S. Public*, pg. 1091
FLEXSCHLAUCH PRODUKTIONS GMBH—See Smiths Industries plc; *Int'l*, pg. 1268
FLEXSTEEL DIVISION—See Flexsteel Industries, Inc.; *U.S. Public*, pg. 654
FLEXSTEEL INDUSTRIES, INC.; *U.S. Public*, pg. 653
FLEXTECH P.L.C.; *Int'l*, pg. 495
W.A. FLICK & CO. PTY. LIMITED; *Int'l*, pg. 207
THE FLIGHT DATA COMPANY LTD.—See Bowthorpe plc; *Int'l*, pg. 207
FLIGHT INTERNATIONAL AVIATION, INC.—See The Flight International Group, Inc.; *U.S. Public*, pg. 654
THE FLIGHT INTERNATIONAL GROUP, INC.; *U.S. Public*, pg. 654
FLIGHT INTERNATIONAL, INC.—See The Flight International Group, Inc.; *U.S. Public*, pg. 654
FLIGHT OPERATIONS/BEDEK AVIATION GROUP—See Israel Aircraft Industries Ltd.; *Int'l*, pg. 703
FLIGHTSAFETY ACADEMY—See Berkshire Hathaway Inc.; *U.S. Public*, pg. 218
FLIGHTSAFETY INTERNATIONAL INC.—See Berkshire Hathaway Inc.; *U.S. Public*, pg. 218
FLIGHTSAFETY SERVICES CORPORATION—See Berkshire Hathaway Inc.; *U.S. Public*, pg. 218
FLIGHTSAFETY WASHINGTON OFFICE—See Berkshire Hathaway Inc.; *U.S. Public*, pg. 219
FLIK FLAK—See SMH Swiss Corporation for Micro Electronics & Watchmaking Indus. Ltd.; *Int'l*, pg. 1160
FLIK INTERNATIONAL—See Compass Group plc; *Int'l*, pg. 324
FLINN & DREFFEIN ENGINEERING CO.; *U.S. Private*, pg. 413
FLINT & WALLING INDUSTRIES, INC.—See Masco Corporation; *U.S. Public*, pg. 1053
FLINT INK CORP.; *U.S. Private*, pg. 413
FLINT MANUFACTURING CO.; *U.S. Private*, pg. 413
FLINT RIVER—See Galesi Group; *U.S. Private*, pg. 437
FLINT RIVER MILLS; *U.S. Private*, pg. 413
FLIR SYSTEMS, INC.; *U.S. Public*, pg. 654
FLO-CON ITALIANA S.R.L.—See Zimmermann & Jansen GmbH; *Int'l*, pg. 1529
FLO CONTROL, INC.; *U.S. Private*, pg. 414
FLO JAPON CO., LTD.—See Skylark Co., Ltd.; *Int'l*, pg. 1262
FLO-LINE FILTERS, INC.—See Perry Equipment Corporation; *U.S. Private*, pg. 855
FLO-LITE OPTICAL CORP.—See Essilor International Compagnie Generale d'Optique; *Int'l*, pg. 462
FLO-PAC CORPORATION; *U.S. Private*, pg. 414
FLO-PAC MIDWEST—See Flo-Pac Corporation; *U.S. Private*, pg. 414
FLO-PAC PACIFIC—See Flo-Pac Corporation; *U.S. Private*, pg. 414
FLO-PAC SOUTHEAST—See Flo-Pac Corporation; *U.S. Private*, pg. 414
THE FLOATING TECHNOLOGY CO—See Taylor Woodrow plc; *Int'l*, pg. 1358
FLOBEND—See Trinity Industries Inc.; *U.S. Public*, pg. 1639
FLOJET CORPORATION; *U.S. Private*, pg. 414
FLOMATIC CORPORATION—See Danfoss A/S; *Int'l*, pg. 377
THE FLOOD COMPANY; *U.S. Private*, pg. 414
FLOOR COVERING WEEKLY—See The Hearst Corporation; *U.S. Private*, pg. 516
FLOORDRESS REINIGUNGSGERATE GMBH—See Henkel KGaA; *Int'l*, pg. 609
FLOORDRESS REINIGUNGSMASCHINEN AG—See Henkel KGaA; *Int'l*, pg. 611
FLOQUIL-POLLY S COLOR CORP.—See RPM, Inc.; *U.S. Public*, pg. 1357
FLORAFAX INTERNATIONAL, INC.; *U.S. Public*, pg. 654
FLORAL GLASS & MIRROR, INC.; *U.S. Private*, pg. 414
FLORALA TELEPHONE CO.—See St. Joe Corp.; *U.S. Public*, pg. 1427
FLORASYNTH AUSTRALASIA PTY. LTD.—See Bayer AG; *Int'l*, pg. 173
FLORASYNTH CANADA, INC.—See Bayer AG; *Int'l*, pg. 173
FLORASYNTH FRAGANCIAS Y AROMAS LTDA.—See Bayer AG; *Int'l*, pg. 173
FLORASYNTH GMBH—See Bayer AG; *Int'l*, pg. 173
FLORASYNTH INC.—See Bayer AG; *Int'l*, pg. 173
FLORASYNTH ITALIA S.R.L.—See Bayer AG; *Int'l*, pg. 173

FLORASYNTH-LAUTIER K.K.—See Bayer AG; *Int'l*, pg. 173
FLORASYNTH LIMITED—See Bayer AG; *Int'l*, pg. 173
FLORASYNTH LTDA.—See Bayer AG; *Int'l*, pg. 173
FLORASYNTH S.A.—See Bayer AG; *Int'l*, pg. 174
FLORASYNTH S.A. DE C.V.—See Bayer AG; *Int'l*, pg. 174
FLORASYNTH SINGAPORE PTE LTD.—See Bayer AG; *Int'l*, pg. 174
FLORENCE CORPORATION; *U.S. Private*, pg. 414
FLORENCE DEPOSIT BANK—See Banc One Corporation; *U.S. Public*, pg. 173
FLORENCE INDUSTRIAL SUPPLY—See Associated Industrial Supply, Inc.; *U.S. Private*, pg. 91
LEONARD FLORENCE ASSOCIATES—See Syratech Corporation; *U.S. Private*, pg. 1061
FLORI CORP.; *U.S. Private*, pg. 414
FLORIBILIS—See LVMH Moet Hennessy Louis Vuitton; *Int'l*, pg. 780
FLORIDA ASSOCIATED SERVICES, INC.—See American Heritage Life Investment Corp.; *U.S. Public*, pg. 79
FLORIDA AUTO AUCTION OF ORLANDO, INC.—See Cox Enterprises, Inc.; *U.S. Private*, pg. 282
FLORIDA CAPITAL PARTNERS; *U.S. Private*, pg. 414
FLORIDA CASH AMERICA, INC.—See Cash America International, Inc.; *U.S. Public*, pg. 312
FLORIDA CITIES WATER CO.—See Avatar Holdings Inc.; *U.S. Public*, pg. 151
FLORIDA COCA-COLA BOTTLING COMPANY—See Coca-Cola Enterprises Inc.; *U.S. Public*, pg. 393
FLORIDA CRUSHED STONE COMPANY; *U.S. Private*, pg. 414
FLORIDA EAST COAST DELIVERIES, INC.—See St. Joe Corp.; *U.S. Public*, pg. 1427
FLORIDA EAST COAST HIGHWAY DISPATCH CO.—See St. Joe Corp.; *U.S. Public*, pg. 1427
FLORIDA EAST COAST INDUSTRIES INC.—See St. Joe Corp.; *U.S. Public*, pg. 1427
FLORIDA EAST COAST INSPECTIONS, INC.—See St. Joe Corp.; *U.S. Public*, pg. 1427
FLORIDA EAST COAST RAILWAY CO.—See St. Joe Corp.; *U.S. Public*, pg. 1427
FLORIDA EXPRESS CARRIER INC.—See St. Joe Corp.; *U.S. Public*, pg. 1427
FLORIDA FARM BUREAU CASUALTY INSURANCE COMPANY—See Southern Farm Bureau Casualty Insurance Company; *U.S. Private*, pg. 1016
FLORIDA FAVORITE FERTILIZER—See Potash Corporation of Saskatchewan Inc.; *Int'l*, pg. 1064
FLORIDA GAS TRANSMISSION CO.—See Enron Corp.; *U.S. Public*, pg. 585
FLORIDA HARDWARE COMPANY—See Distribution America; *U.S. Private*, pg. 335
FLORIDA HEALTH FACILITIES, INC.—See Magellan Health Services, Inc.; *U.S. Public*, pg. 1035
FLORIDA HEAT PUMP—See Harrow Industries; *U.S. Private*, pg. 506
FLORIDA HOME FINDERS—See Atlantic Gulf Communities Corporation; *U.S. Public*, pg. 144
FLORIDA HOMES TITLE—See Lennar Corporation; *U.S. Public*, pg. 988
FLORIDA INTERNATIONAL FRUCHTSAFTGETRAENKE GMBH—See PepsiCo, Inc.; *U.S. Public*, pg. 1277
FLORIDA LIME CORP.—See Puerto Rican Cement Co., Inc.; *U.S. Public*, pg. 1342
FLORIDA MEDICAL CENTER SOUTH—See Tenet Healthcare Corporation; *U.S. Public*, pg. 1577
FLORIDA MEDICAL COLLECTION SERVICES, INC.—See Columbia/HCA Healthcare Corporation; *U.S. Public*, pg. 404
FLORIDA MINING & MATERIALS CONCRETE CORP.—See Southdown, Inc.; *U.S. Public*, pg. 1489
FLORIDA OUTLET MARTS, INC.—See The Western and Southern Life Insurance Company; *U.S. Private*, pg. 1164
FLORIDA PANTHERS HOLDINGS, INC.; *U.S. Public*, pg. 654
FLORIDA PIPE & SUPPLY COMPANY—See Hughes Supply, Inc.; *U.S. Public*, pg. 847
FLORIDA PNEUMATIC MFG. CORP.—See P & F Industries, Inc.; *U.S. Public*, pg. 1240
FLORIDA POWER & LIGHT COMPANY—See FPL Group, Inc.; *U.S. Public*, pg. 608
FLORIDA POWER CORPORATION—See Florida Progress Corporation; *U.S. Public*, pg. 655
FLORIDA PROGRESS CORPORATION; *U.S. Public*, pg. 655
FLORIDA PUBLIC UTILITIES COMPANY; *U.S. Public*, pg. 655
FLORIDA RESIDENTIAL TREATMENT CENTERS, INC.—See Magellan Health Services, Inc.; *U.S. Public*, pg. 1035
FLORIDA ROCK INDUSTRIES, INC.; *U.S. Public*, pg. 655
FLORIDA SUN PUBLICATIONS, INC.—See Pearson plc; *Int'l*, pg. 1026
FLORIDA TILE INDUSTRIES, INC.—See Premark International, Inc.; *U.S. Public*, pg. 1322
FLORIDA TOWING COMPANY—See Moran Transporation Company; *U.S. Private*, pg. 760
FLORIDA TREND MAGAZINE—See The Times Publishing Co.; *U.S. Private*, pg. 1088
FLORIDOR S.A.—See Novartis AG; *Int'l*, pg. 972
FLORIG EQUIPMENT COMPANY, INC.; *U.S. Private*, pg. 415
FLORIGENE BV—See Novartis AG; *Int'l*, pg. 982
FLORIMEX WORLDWIDE GMBH—See DIMON, Incorporated; *U.S. Public*, pg. 510
FLORIMEX WORLDWIDE, INC.—See DIMON, Incorporated; *U.S. Public*, pg. 510
FLORISLOANE LTD.—See LVMH Moet Hennessy Louis Vuitton; *Int'l*, pg. 782
FLORIST DISTRIBUTING—See Hy-Vee Food Stores Incorporated; *U.S. Private*, pg. 551
THE FLORISTS ASSN. OF GREATER CLEVELAND, INC.; *U.S. Private*, pg. 415

FLORISTS' MUTUAL INSURANCE CO.; *U.S. Private*, pg. 415
FLORIXELLES—See LVMH Moet Hennessy Louis Vuitton; *Int'l*, pg. 782
FLORSHEIM GROUP INC.; *U.S. Public*, pg. 656
FLORSHEIM, INC.—See Florsheim Group Inc.; *U.S. Public*, pg. 656
FLOTTWEG GMBH—See Mannesmann A.G.; *Int'l*, pg. 836
FLOTTWEG IBERICA SL—See Mannesmann A.G.; *Int'l*, pg. 836
FLOURO-PRECISION COATINGS—See TI Group plc; *Int'l*, pg. 1338
FLOW ASIA—See Flow International Corporation; *U.S. Public*, pg. 656
FLOW CONTROL DIVISION—See Raven Industries, Inc.; *U.S. Public*, pg. 1361
FLOW CONTROL EQUIPMENT—See Robbins & Myers, Inc.; *U.S. Public*, pg. 1393
FLOW EUROPE—See Flow International Corporation; *U.S. Public*, pg. 656
FLOW INTERNATIONAL CORPORATION; *U.S. Public*, pg. 656
FLOWERS BAKING CO. OF BATON ROUGE, INC.—See Flowers Industries, Inc.; *U.S. Public*, pg. 657
FLOWERS BAKING CO. OF BRADENTON, INC.—See Flowers Industries, Inc.; *U.S. Public*, pg. 657
FLOWERS BAKING CO. OF FOUNTAIN INN, INC.—See Flowers Industries, Inc.; *U.S. Public*, pg. 657
FLOWERS BAKING CO. OF GADSDEN, INC.—See Flowers Industries, Inc.; *U.S. Public*, pg. 657
FLOWERS BAKING CO. OF JACKSONVILLE, INC.—See Flowers Industries, Inc.; *U.S. Public*, pg. 657
FLOWERS BAKING CO. OF JAMESTOWN, INC.—See Flowers Industries, Inc.; *U.S. Public*, pg. 657
FLOWERS BAKING CO. OF LYNCHBURG, INC.—See Flowers Industries, Inc.; *U.S. Public*, pg. 657
FLOWERS BAKING CO. OF MIAMI, INC.—See Flowers Industries, Inc.; *U.S. Public*, pg. 657
FLOWERS BAKING CO. OF MORRISTOWN—See Flowers Industries, Inc.; *U.S. Public*, pg. 657
FLOWERS BAKING CO. OF NORFOLK, INC.—See Flowers Industries, Inc.; *U.S. Public*, pg. 657
FLOWERS BAKING CO. OF OPELIKA, INC.—See Flowers Industries, Inc.; *U.S. Public*, pg. 657
FLOWERS BAKING CO. OF SOUTH CAROLINA, INC.—See Flowers Industries, Inc.; *U.S. Public*, pg. 657
FLOWERS BAKING CO. OF THOMASVILLE, INC.—See Flowers Industries, Inc.; *U.S. Public*, pg. 657
FLOWERS BAKING CO. OF TYLER, INC.—See Flowers Industries, Inc.; *U.S. Public*, pg. 657
FLOWERS BAKING CO. OF WEST VIRGINIA—See Flowers Industries, Inc.; *U.S. Public*, pg. 657
FLOWERS INDUSTRIES, INC.; *U.S. Public*, pg. 656
FLOWERS OF HAWAII; *U.S. Private*, pg. 415
FLOWERS SPECIALTY FOODS OF MONTGOMERY, INC.—See Flowers Industries, Inc.; *U.S. Public*, pg. 657
FLOWERS USA; *U.S. Private*, pg. 415
FLOWING WELLS, INC.—See Citizens Utilities Company; *U.S. Public*, pg. 380
FLOWMATRIX CORPORATION—See Inamed Corporation; *U.S. Public*, pg. 874
FLOWMAX S.A.—See Axel Johnson AB; *Int'l*, pg. 710
FLOWMOLE EXPORT SALES CORPORATION—See UTILX Corporation; *U.S. Public*, pg. 1701
FLOWMOLE LIMITED—See UTILX Corporation; *U.S. Public*, pg. 1701
FLOW-QUIP TEXAS, INC.—See Bovaird Supply Co.; *U.S. Private*, pg. 162
FLOWSEAL—See Crane Co.; *U.S. Public*, pg. 457
FLOWSERVE CORPORATION; *U.S. Public*, pg. 658
FLOWSERVE CORPORATION—See Flowserve Corporation; *U.S. Public*, pg. 658
FLOWSERVE CORPORATION, ENGINEERED PLASTIC PRODUCTS DIV—See Flowserve Corporation; *U.S. Public*, pg. 658
FLOWSERVE CORPORATION, VALVE DIV—See Flowserve Corporation; *U.S. Public*, pg. 658
FLOWSERVE DURIRON CANADA—See Flowserve Corporation; *U.S. Public*, pg. 659
FLOWSERVE DURIRON CANADA INC.—See Flowserve Corporation; *U.S. Public*, pg. 659
FLOWTITE OFFSHORE SERVICES LTD.—See Owens Corning; *U.S. Public*, pg. 1237
FLOWTRON/GALAXIE DIVISION—See Armatron International, Inc.; *U.S. Public*, pg. 131
FLOYD THEATRES, INC.—See MasTec, Inc.; *U.S. Public*, pg. 1056
FLUBB-UND SCHWERSPATWERKE PFORZHEIM GMBH—See Bayer AG; *Int'l*, pg. 172
FLUGZEUGWERFT DRESDEN GMBH—See Daimler-Benz Aktiengesellschaft; *Int'l*, pg. 367
FLUID CONNECTORS GROUP—See Parker Hannifin Corporation; *U.S. Public*, pg. 1260
FLUID CONNECTORS GROUP, CANADA—See Parker Hannifin Corporation; *U.S. Public*, pg. 1261
FLUID CONNECTORS GROUP, PARKER HANNIFIN (U.K.) LTD.—See Parker Hannifin Corporation; *U.S. Public*, pg. 1261
FLUID CONSERVATION SYSTEMS INC.—See Halma p.l.c.; *Int'l*, pg. 590
FLUID MANAGEMENT, INC.—See IDEX Corporation; *U.S. Public*, pg. 862
FLUID POLYMERS—See Chase Corporation; *U.S. Public*, pg. 337
FLUID POWER DIV—See Quanex Corporation; *U.S. Public*, pg. 1350
FLUID PRODUCT SALES DIV—See Dana Corporation; *U.S. Public*, pg. 479
FLUID RECYCLING SERVICES COMPANY, L.L.C.—See Quaker Chemical Corporation; *U.S. Public*, pg. 1346
FLUID REGULATORS CO.—See Esterline Technologies Corporation; *U.S. Public*, pg. 594
FLUIDEX DIV.—See Parker Hannifin Corporation; *U.S. Public*, pg. 1260

FLUIDISED COMBUSTION CONTRACTORS LTD.—See FKI Plc; *Int'l*, pg. 472
FLUIDRIVE INC.; *U.S. Private*, pg. 415
FLUIDTEC ENGINEER PRODUCTS—See Coltec Holdings Inc; *U.S. Public*, pg. 401
FLUKA CHEMIE AG—See Sigma-Aldrich Corporation; *U.S. Public*, pg. 1472
FLUKE CORPORATION; *U.S. Public*, pg. 659
FLUKE ELECTRONICS CANADA INC.—See Fluke Corporation; *U.S. Public*, pg. 659
FLUKE, INC.—See Fluke Corporation; *U.S. Public*, pg. 659
FLUKE INTERNATIONAL CORPORATION—See Fluke Corporation; *U.S. Public*, pg. 659
FLUOR CONSTRUCTORS INTERNATIONAL, INC.—See Fluor Corporation; *U.S. Public*, pg. 660
FLUOR CORPORATION; *U.S. Public*, pg. 659
FLUOR DANIEL ARABIA LIMITED—See Fluor Corporation; *U.S. Public*, pg. 660
FLUOR DANIEL AUSTRALIA LIMITED—See Fluor Corporation; *U.S. Public*, pg. 660
FLUOR DANIEL B.V. HAARLEM—See Fluor Corporation; *U.S. Public*, pg. 660
FLUOR DANIEL CANADA INC.—See Fluor Corporation; *U.S. Public*, pg. 660
FLUOR DANIEL CHILE, S.A.—See Fluor Corporation; *U.S. Public*, pg. 660
FLUOR DANIEL CHINA, INC.—See Fluor Corporation; *U.S. Public*, pg. 660
FLUOR DANIEL EASTERN, INC.—See Fluor Corporation; *U.S. Public*, pg. 660
FLUOR DANIEL ENGINEERS & CONSTRUCTORS, LTD.—See Fluor Corporation; *U.S. Public*, pg. 660
FLUOR DANIEL GMBH—See Fluor Corporation; *U.S. Public*, pg. 660
FLUOR DANIEL GTI, INC.—See Fluor Corporation; *U.S. Public*, pg. 660
FLUOR DANIEL HOUSTON—See Fluor Corporation; *U.S. Public*, pg. 660
FLUOR DANIEL INC.—See Fluor Corporation; *U.S. Public*, pg. 660
FLUOR DANIEL (JAPAN) INC.—See Fluor Corporation; *U.S. Public*, pg. 660
FLUOR DANIEL LIMITED—See Fluor Corporation; *U.S. Public*, pg. 660
FLUOR DANIEL (MALAYSIA) SDN. BHD.—See Fluor Corporation; *U.S. Public*, pg. 660
FLUOR DANIEL PACIFIC, INC.—See Fluor Corporation; *U.S. Public*, pg. 660
FLUOR DANIEL THAILAND LTD.—See Fluor Corporation; *U.S. Public*, pg. 660
FLUOR DANIEL WILLIAMS BROTHERS—See Fluor Corporation; *U.S. Public*, pg. 660
FLUOR DANIEL WRIGHT LIMITED—See Fluor Corporation; *U.S. Public*, pg. 660
FLUOROSCAN IMAGING SYSTEMS, INC.—See Hologic, Inc.; *U.S. Public*, pg. 831
FLUORPLAST NEDERLAND B.V.—See Saint-Gobain; *Int'l*, pg. 1174
THE FLXIBLE CORP.—See General Automotive Corporation; *U.S. Private*, pg. 444
FLYING FOOD FARE, INC.; *U.S. Private*, pg. 415
FLYING J. INC.; *U.S. Private*, pg. 415
FLYMO GMBH—See Electrolux, AB; *Int'l*, pg. 442
FLYMO-HUSQVARNA SNC—See Electrolux, AB; *Int'l*, pg. 441
FLYMO LTD.—See Electrolux, AB; *Int'l*, pg. 444
FLYMO S.R.L.—See Electrolux, AB; *Int'l*, pg. 442
W.J. FLYTE CORPORATION—See Allied Waste Industries; *U.S. Public*, pg. 49
FOAM CRAFT, INC.—See Future Foam, Inc.; *U.S. Private*, pg. 433
FOAM MOLDING CORP.—See FMC Corporation; *U.S. Public*, pg. 605
FOAM PLUS LIMITED—See James Crean PLC; *Int'l*, pg. 341
FOAM PRO MANUFACTURING; *U.S. Private*, pg. 415
FOAMEX—See Trace International Holdings, Inc.; *U.S. Private*, pg. 1094
FOAMEX INTERNATIONAL-CONSUMER PRODUCTS DIVISION—See Trace International Holdings, Inc.; *U.S. Private*, pg. 1094
FOAMEX INTERNATIONAL INC.—See Trace International Holdings, Inc.; *U.S. Private*, pg. 1094
FOAMEX, L.P.—See Trace International Holdings, Inc.; *U.S. Private*, pg. 1094
FOARSA FORJAS Y ACEROS DE REINOSA, S.A.—See SEPI; *Int'l*, pg. 1225
FOCAS—See Cookson Group plc; *Int'l*, pg. 329
FOCKE & CO. (GMBH & CO.) VERPACKUNGSMASCHINER; *Int'l*, pg. 496
FOCKE & CO., INC.—See Focke & Co. (GmbH & Co.) Verpackungsmaschiner; *Int'l*, pg. 496
THE FOCUS AGENCY, INC.—See Omnicom Group Inc.; *U.S. Public*, pg. 1224
FOCUS MAGAZIN VERLAG—See Burda Holding GmbH & Co., KG; *Int'l*, pg. 233
FOCUS MEDIA; *U.S. Private*, pg. 415
FOCUS MEDIA—See Focus Media; *U.S. Private*, pg. 415
FOCUS TRAVEL—See Air New Zealand Ltd.; *Int'l*, pg. 38
FOCUS2020, INC.; *U.S. Private*, pg. 415
FODOR'S TRAVEL PUBLICATIONS, INC.—See Advance Publications Inc.; *U.S. Private*, pg. 21
FOGA SYSTEM INTERNATIONAL AB; *Int'l*, pg. 496
FOGA SYSTEMS—See Foga System International AB; *Int'l*, pg. 496
FOGARTY KLEIN & PARTNERS; *U.S. Private*, pg. 415
FOGARTY KLEIN & PARTNERS—See Fogarty Klein & Partners; *U.S. Private*, pg. 416
FOGARTY KLEIN & PARTNERS DIRECT—See Fogarty Klein & Partners; *U.S. Private*, pg. 416
FOGARTY KLEIN & PARTNERS PUBLIC RELATIONS—See Fogarty Klein & Partners; *U.S. Private*, pg. 416
FOGARTY KLEIN & PARTNERS YELLOW PAGES, INC.—See Fogarty Klein & Partners; *U.S. Private*, pg. 416

FOGELSTA INDUSTRI AB—See Eldon AB; *Int'l*, pg. 436
FOKAB AB—See Axel Johnson AB; *Int'l*, pg. 708
FOKKER AIRCRAFT SERVICES B.V.—See Stork N.V.; *Int'l*, pg. 1304
FOKUS BANK A/S; *Int'l*, pg. 496
FOKUSZ MARKETING KOMMUNIKACIO KFT.—See TBWA Chiat/Day; *U.S. Private*, pg. 1062
FOLAND'S JEWELRY BROKERS; *U.S. Private*, pg. 416
FOLEY-BELSAW COMPANY; *U.S. Private*, pg. 416
FOLEY HOLDING COMPANY, INC.; *U.S. Private*, pg. 416
FOLEY MARTENS COMPANY—See Foley-Belsaw Company; *U.S. Private*, pg. 416
FOLEY-PLP COMPANY—See Foley-Belsaw Company; *U.S. Private*, pg. 416
STEVE FOLEY CADILLAC; *U.S. Private*, pg. 416
FOLEY TRACTOR COMPANY, INC.—See Foley Holding Company, Inc.; *U.S. Private*, pg. 416
FOLEY'S—See The May Department Stores Company; *U.S. Public*, pg. 1063
FOLGER ADAM SECURITY INC.; *U.S. Private*, pg. 416
THE FOLGER COFFEE COMPANY—See The Procter & Gamble Company; *U.S. Public*, pg. 1331
FOLGER NOLAN FLEMING DOUGLAS; *U.S. Private*, pg. 416
FOLIO PRODUCTS GROUP—See Open Market, Inc.; *U.S. Public*, pg. 1227
FOLLA CTMP A/S—See Norske Skogindustrier A.S; *Int'l*, pg. 966
FOLLDAL GJENRINNING A/S—See Icopal a/s; *Int'l*, pg. 659
FOLLETT CAMPUS RESOURCES—See Follett Corporation; *U.S. Private*, pg. 417
FOLLETT COLLEGE STORES CORP.—See Follett Corporation; *U.S. Private*, pg. 417
FOLLETT COLLEGIATE GRAPHICS—See Follett Corporation; *U.S. Private*, pg. 417
FOLLETT CORPORATION; *U.S. Private*, pg. 416
FOLLETT EDUCATIONAL SERVICES—See Follett Corporation; *U.S. Private*, pg. 417
FOLLETT LIBRARY RESOURCES—See Follett Corporation; *U.S. Private*, pg. 417
FOLLETT SOFTWARE COMPANY—See Follett Corporation; *U.S. Private*, pg. 417
FOLLUM FABRIKKER—See Norske Skogindustrier A.S; *Int'l*, pg. 965
FOLMAR & ASSOCIATES; *U.S. Private*, pg. 417
FOMENTO DE OBRAS URBANAS EUROPEAS, S.A.—See Caja de Madrid Group; *Int'l*, pg. 252
FOMENTO ECONOMICO MEXICANO, S.A. DE CV; *Int'l*, pg. 496
FONAR CORPORATION; *U.S. Public*, pg. 661
FONCIERE CASAMADRID—See Caja de Madrid Group; *Int'l*, pg. 252
THE FONDA GROUP, INC.—See Four M Corporation, Inc.; *U.S. Private*, pg. 421
FONDARGE (PTY.) LTD.—See Lafarge S.A.; *Int'l*, pg. 790
FONDARGE PTY. LTD.—See Lafarge S.A.; *Int'l*, pg. 791
FONDIARIA S.P.A.; *Int'l*, pg. 496
FONDITEL ENTIDAD GESTORA DE FONDOS DE PENSIONES, S.A.—See Telefonica de Espana, S.A.; *Int'l*, pg. 1371
FONDO EDUCATIVO INTERAMERICANO—See Pearson plc; *Int'l*, pg. 1027
FONDO EDUCATIVO INTERAMERICANO FEI C.A.—See Pearson plc; *Int'l*, pg. 1027
FONE AMERICA, INC.; *U.S. Public*, pg. 661
FONOGRAM S.A.—See Philips Electronics N.V.; *Int'l*, pg. 1052
FONT VELLA—See Danone Group; *Int'l*, pg. 381
FONTANA—See The Genlyte Group Incorporated; *U.S. Public*, pg. 730
FONTANA CENTRO—See Saint-Gobain; *Int'l*, pg. 1172
FONTANA SARDA—See Saint-Gobain; *Int'l*, pg. 1172
FONTANA SUD SRL—See Saint-Gobain; *Int'l*, pg. 1172
FONTANA WATER RESOURCES, INC.—See Kaiser Ventures, Inc.; *U.S. Public*, pg. 941
FOOD & BEVERAGE—See Ecolab Inc.; *U.S. Public*, pg. 562
FOOD & GAS, INC.; *U.S. Private*, pg. 417
FOOD & NUTRITIONAL PRODUCTS (PTY.) LTD.—See Nestle S.A.; *Int'l*, pg. 920
FOOD AND SNACK HOLDINGS (SINGAPORE)—See Borden, Inc.; *U.S. Private*, pg. 159
FOOD & WINE—See American Express Company; *U.S. Public*, pg. 74
FOOD CARRIER, INC.—See Imperial Holly Corporation; *U.S. Public*, pg. 872
FOOD DIVISION—See Nestle S.A.; *Int'l*, pg. 916
THE FOOD EMPORIUM—See Tengelmann Warenhandelsgesellschaft; *Int'l*, pg. 1375
FOOD 4 LESS, INC.—See The Yucaipa Companies; *U.S. Private*, pg. 1202
FOOD HAULERS, INC.—See Wakefern Food Corporation; *U.S. Public*, pg. 1146
FOOD INGREDIENTS—See FMC Corporation; *U.S. Public*, pg. 606
FOOD INGREDIENTS (PHILLIPINES) INC.—See FMC Corporation; *U.S. Public*, pg. 606
FOOD INGREDIENTS SPECIALTIES S.A.—See Nestle S.A.; *Int'l*, pg. 916
FOOD LIFE—See Lettuce Entertain You Enterprises, Inc.; *U.S. Private*, pg. 661
FOOD LION, INC.—See Etablissements Delhaize Freres Et Cie "Le Lion" S.A.; *Int'l*, pg. 463
FOOD OILS CORPORATION—See Trinidad/Benham Corp.; *U.S. Private*, pg. 1103
FOOD PREMIER, S.A.—See Tabacalera, S.A.; *Int'l*, pg. 1345
FOOD PRODUCTS MANAGEMENT BV—See Koninklijke BolsWessanen nv; *Int'l*, pg. 751
FOOD SERVICES DIVISION—See Nestle S.A.; *Int'l*, pg. 917
FOOD SERVICES OF AMERICA—See Services Group of America; *U.S. Private*, pg. 987

FOOD SPECIALTIES GHANA LTD.—See Nestle S.A.; *Int'l*, pg. 920
P.T. FOOD SPECIALTIES INDONESIA—See Nestle S.A.; *Int'l*, pg. 920
FOOD SPECIALTIES JAMAICA LTD.—See Nestle S.A.; *Int'l*, pg. 920
FOOD SPECIALTIES LTD.—See Nestle S.A.; *Int'l*, pg. 920
FOOD SPECIALTIES (NIGERIA) LTD.—See Nestle S.A.; *Int'l*, pg. 920
FOOD SPECIALTIES (PVT.) LTD.—See Nestle S.A.; *Int'l*, pg. 920
FOOD TECHNOLOGY CORPORATION—See General Kinetics Incorporated; *U.S. Public*, pg. 717
FOOD TOWN SUPERMARKETS DIVISION—See Seaway Food Town, Inc.; *U.S. Public*, pg. 1453
FOODANE A/S—See Vestjyske Slagterier; *Int'l*, pg. 1464
FOODARAMA SUPERMARKETS, INC.; *U.S. Public*, pg. 661
FOODBRANDS AMERICA, INC.—See IBP, Inc.; *U.S. Public*, pg. 852
FOODCORP LIMITED; *Int'l*, pg. 496
FOODIE OY—See Raisio Group; *Int'l*, pg. 1085
FOODLAND DISTRIBUTORS—See SuperValu, Inc.; *U.S. Public*, pg. 1541
FOODLAND, INC.—See Hale-Halsell Company; *U.S. Private*, pg. 494
FOODMAKER, INC.; *U.S. Public*, pg. 661
FOODSERVICE DIRECTOR—See VNU Verenigde Nederlandse Uitgeversbedrijven B.V.; *Int'l*, pg. 1446
FOODTOWN, INC.—See Hale-Halsell Company; *U.S. Private*, pg. 494
FOOT LOCKER—See Woolworth Corporation; *U.S. Public*, pg. 1777
FOOT LOCKER EUROPE B.V.—See Woolworth Corporation; *U.S. Public*, pg. 1778
S.B. FOOT TANNING CO.—See Red Wing Shoe Co., Inc.; *U.S. Private*, pg. 915
FOOTACTION USA—See Footstar Inc.; *U.S. Public*, pg. 661
BRAD FOOTE GEAR WORKS, INC.; *U.S. Private*, pg. 417
FOOTE-JONES/ILLINOIS GEAR—See Regal-Beloit Corporation; *U.S. Public*, pg. 1370
THE FOOTHILL GROUP, INC.—See Norwest Corporation; *U.S. Public*, pg. 1201
FOOTHILL INVESTMENT COMPANY—See Lewis Homes Management Corp.; *U.S. Private*, pg. 665
FOOTHILLS TRADER, INC.—See Journal Register Company; *U.S. Public*, pg. 934
FOOTQUARTERS—See Woolworth Corporation; *U.S. Public*, pg. 1777
FOOTSTAR INC.; *U.S. Public*, pg. 661
FOOTWEAR NEWS—See The Walt Disney Company; *U.S. Public*, pg. 513
FOR BETTER LIVING, INC.; *U.S. Private*, pg. 417
FOR EYES PLC—See Dolland & Aitchison Ltd.; *Int'l*, pg. 414
FORA INTERNATIONAL CORP.—See Acer Incorporated; *Int'l*, pg. 22
FORAL SERVICE PROPRIETARY LIMITED—See Ford Motor Company; *U.S. Public*, pg. 665
FORASOL S.A.; *Int'l*, pg. 496
FORATEX INC.—See Forasol S.A.; *Int'l*, pg. 496
FORBES, INC.; *U.S. Private*, pg. 417
FORBES INVESTORS ADVISORY INSTITUTE, INC.—See Forbes, Inc.; *U.S. Private*, pg. 418
FORBES MAGAZINE DIVISION—See Forbes, Inc.; *U.S. Private*, pg. 417
OY FORBO AB—See Forbo Holding SA; *Int'l*, pg. 497
FORBO AMERICA INC.—See Forbo Holding SA; *Int'l*, pg. 497
FORBO A/S—See Forbo Holding SA; *Int'l*, pg. 497
FORBO AUSTRALIA PTY. LTD.—See Forbo Holding SA; *Int'l*, pg. 497
FORBO BETEILIGUNGEN GMBH—See Forbo Holding SA; *Int'l*, pg. 497
FORBO BONAPARTE B.V.—See Forbo Holding SA; *Int'l*, pg. 497
FORBO CONTEL HANDELSGESELLSCHAFT MBH—See Forbo Holding SA; *Int'l*, pg. 497
FORBO CONTRACT FABRICS LTD.—See Forbo Holding SA; *Int'l*, pg. 497
FORBO CP LTD.—See Forbo Holding SA; *Int'l*, pg. 497
FORBO CTU SA—See Forbo Holding SA; *Int'l*, pg. 497
FORBO DECOR S.A.—See Forbo Holding SA; *Int'l*, pg. 497
FORBO ERFURT GMBH—See Forbo Holding SA; *Int'l*, pg. 497
FORBO FINANZ SA—See Forbo Holding SA; *Int'l*, pg. 497
FORBO FORSHAGA AB—See Forbo Holding SA; *Int'l*, pg. 497
FORBO GENDEREN B.V.—See Forbo Holding SA; *Int'l*, pg. 497
FORBO-GIUBIASCO SA—See Forbo Holding SA; *Int'l*, pg. 497
FORBO GLAWO GMBH—See Forbo Holding SA; *Int'l*, pg. 497
FORBO HELMITIN GMBH—See Forbo Holding SA; *Int'l*, pg. 497
FORBO HOLDING SA; *Int'l*, pg. 496
FORBO IMMOB SA—See Forbo Holding SA; *Int'l*, pg. 497
FORBO INDUSTRIEPRODUKTE GES.M.B.H.—See Forbo Holding SA; *Int'l*, pg. 497
FORBO INDUSTRIES INC.—See Forbo Holding SA; *Int'l*, pg. 497
FORBO INTERNATIONAL SA—See Forbo Holding SA; *Int'l*, pg. 497
FORBO INVEST LTD.—See Forbo Holding SA; *Int'l*, pg. 497
FORBO IRELAND LTD.—See Forbo Holding SA; *Int'l*, pg. 497
FORBO KROMMENIE B.V.—See Forbo Holding SA; *Int'l*, pg. 497
FORBO KROMMENIE S.A.—See Forbo Holding SA; *Int'l*, pg. 497

FORBO LANCASTER LTD.—See Forbo Holding SA; *Int'l*, pg. 497
FORBO MURS SA—See Forbo Holding SA; *Int'l*, pg. 497
FORBO NAIRN LTD.—See Forbo Holding SA; *Int'l*, pg. 497
FORBO NL HOLDING B.V.—See Forbo Holding SA; *Int'l*, pg. 497
FORBO NOVILON GMBH—See Forbo Holding SA; *Int'l*, pg. 497
FORBO NOVILON PRODUKTIEBEDRIJVEN BV—See Forbo Holding SA; *Int'l*, pg. 497
FORBO PARADE TAPIJT B.V.—See Forbo Holding SA; *Int'l*, pg. 497
FORBO PARKETT AB—See Forbo Holding SA; *Int'l*, pg. 497
FORBO PARQUET SA—See Forbo Holding SA; *Int'l*, pg. 498
FORBO PARTICIPATIONS SA—See Forbo Holding SA; *Int'l*, pg. 498
FORBO PAVIMENTOS SA—See Forbo Holding SA; *Int'l*, pg. 498
FORBO PERGOL REVESTIMENTOS SA—See Forbo Holding SA; *Int'l*, pg. 498
FORBO RESILIENTI S.R.L.—See Forbo Holding SA; *Int'l*, pg. 498
FORBO SARLINO SA—See Forbo Holding SA; *Int'l*, pg. 498
FORBO SCANACHROME GMBH—See Forbo Holding SA; *Int'l*, pg. 498
FORBO SCANACHROME LTD.—See Forbo Holding SA; *Int'l*, pg. 498
FORBO SIEGLING SINGAPORE PTE. LTD.—See Forbo Holding SA; *Int'l*, pg. 498
FORBO S.R.O.—See Forbo Holding SA; *Int'l*, pg. 498
FORBO-STAMOID AG—See Forbo Holding SA; *Int'l*, pg. 497
FORBO STAMOID B.V.—See Forbo Holding SA; *Int'l*, pg. 498
FORBO TAPIJT N.V.—See Forbo Holding SA; *Int'l*, pg. 498
FORBO TAPIS S.A.R.L.—See Forbo Holding SA; *Int'l*, pg. 498
FORBO TEPPICHWERKE SA—See Forbo Holding SA; *Int'l*, pg. 497
FORBO 2MA SA—See Forbo Holding SA; *Int'l*, pg. 498
FORBO ULI-CHEMIE GMBH—See Forbo Holding SA; *Int'l*, pg. 498
FORBO UK LTD.—See Forbo Holding SA; *Int'l*, pg. 498
FORBO WALLCOVERINGS INC.—See Forbo Holding SA; *Int'l*, pg. 497
FORBO WALLCOVERINGS LTD.—See Forbo Holding SA; *Int'l*, pg. 498
FORBO WERKE GMBH—See Forbo Holding SA; *Int'l*, pg. 498
FORBO WIENER TEPPICHFABRIK GMBH—See Forbo Holding SA; *Int'l*, pg. 498
FORCE V CORPORATION—See The E.W. Scripps Company; *U.S. Public*, pg. 1447
FORCE IMAGING TECHNOLOGIES—See Breed Technologies, Inc.; *U.S. Public*, pg. 251
FORCE 10 MARINE LTD.—See Valley Forge Corporation; *U.S. Public*, pg. 1705
FORCHEM GMBH—See Enso Oyj; *Int'l*, pg. 458
FORCHEM LIMITED—See Enso Oyj; *Int'l*, pg. 458
FORCHEM OY—See Enso Oyj; *Int'l*, pg. 456
FORCHEM OY - VALKEAKOSKI—See Enso Oyj; *Int'l*, pg. 456
OY FORD AB—See Ford Motor Company; *U.S. Public*, pg. 665
FORD & SLATER GROUP LTD.—See Unilever Plc; *Int'l*, pg. 1434
FORD ASIA-PACIFIC, INC.—See Ford Motor Company; *U.S. Public*, pg. 664
FORD AUTO CLUB, INC.—See Ford Motor Company; *U.S. Public*, pg. 663
FORD AUTOMOTIVE LEASING LIMITED—See Ford Motor Company; *U.S. Public*, pg. 665
FORD, BACON & DAVIS COMPANIES INC.—See Deutsche Babcock AG; *Int'l*, pg. 401
FORD, BACON & DAVIS COMPANIES, INC.—See Deutsche Babcock AG; *Int'l*, pg. 401
FORD BANK AG—See Ford Motor Company; *U.S. Public*, pg. 665
FORD BANK AKTIENGESELLSCHAFT (AUSTRIA)—See Ford Motor Company; *U.S. Public*, pg. 665
FORD BODY & ASSEMBLY OPERATIONS—See Ford Motor Company; *U.S. Public*, pg. 662
FORD BODY ENGINEERING—See Ford Motor Company; *U.S. Public*, pg. 662
FORD CASTING DIVISION—See Ford Motor Company; *U.S. Public*, pg. 662
CHARLES E. FORD, LIMITED—See Tate & Lyle PLC; *Int'l*, pg. 1356
FORD CLIMATE CONTROL DIVISION—See Ford Motor Company; *U.S. Public*, pg. 662
FORD COLORADO PROPERTIES, INC.—See Ford Motor Company; *U.S. Public*, pg. 663
FORD COMMUNICATIONS, INC.—See Ford Motor Company; *U.S. Public*, pg. 664
FORD CONSUMER DISCOUNT COMPANY—See Ford Motor Company; *U.S. Public*, pg. 664
FORD CONSUMER FINANCE COMPANY, INC.—See Ford Motor Company; *U.S. Public*, pg. 664
FORD CREDIT AB—See Ford Motor Company; *U.S. Public*, pg. 666
FORD CREDIT A/S—See Ford Motor Company; *U.S. Public*, pg. 666
FORD CREDIT AUSTRALIA LIMITED—See Ford Motor Company; *U.S. Public*, pg. 665
FORD CREDIT AUSTRALIA WHOLESALE LIMITED—See Ford Motor Company; *U.S. Public*, pg. 665
FORD CREDIT AUTO RECEIVABLES CORPORATION—See Ford Motor Company; *U.S. Public*, pg. 663
FORD CREDIT B.V.—See Ford Motor Company; *U.S. Public*, pg. 665

FORD CREDIT CANADA LTD.—See Ford Motor Company; *U.S. Public*, pg. 665
FORD CREDIT FUNDING PLC—See Ford Motor Company; *U.S. Public*, pg. 665
FORD CREDIT N.V.—See Ford Motor Company; *U.S. Public*, pg. 666
FORD CREDIT OVERSEAS FINANCE N.V.—See Ford Motor Company; *U.S. Public*, pg. 666
FORD CREDIT S.A.—See Ford Motor Company; *U.S. Public*, pg. 666
FORD CREDIT SPA—See Ford Motor Company; *U.S. Public*, pg. 666
FORD DESIGN STAFF—See Ford Motor Company; *U.S. Public*, pg. 663
FORD DEVELOPMENT CORPORATION; *U.S. Private*, pg. 418
FORD DIRECT MARKETS, INCORPORATED—See Ford Motor Company; *U.S. Public*, pg. 664
FORD DISTRIBUIDORA DE PRODUTOS DE PETROLEO LTDA.—See Ford Motor Company; *U.S. Public*, pg. 665
FORD DIVISION—See Ford Motor Company; *U.S. Public*, pg. 662
FORD ELECTRONICA PORTUGUESA, LTD.—See Ford Motor Company; *U.S. Public*, pg. 665
FORD ELECTRONICS & REFRIGERATION CORP.—See Ford Motor Company; *U.S. Public*, pg. 664
FORD ELECTRONICS DIVISION—See Ford Motor Company; *U.S. Public*, pg. 662
FORD ELECTRONICS MANUFACTURING CORPORATION—See Ford Motor Company; *U.S. Public*, pg. 662
FORD ENGINE DIVISION—See Ford Motor Company; *U.S. Public*, pg. 662
FORD ENSITE INTERNATIONAL INC. (CANADIAN)—See Ford Motor Company; *U.S. Public*, pg. 665
FORD ENTERPRISE COMPANY TAIWAN, LTD.—See Ford Motor Company; *U.S. Public*, pg. 665
FORD ENVIRONMENTAL & SAFETY ENGINEERING STAFF—See Ford Motor Company; *U.S. Public*, pg. 663
FORD ESPANA S.A.—See Ford Motor Company; *U.S. Public*, pg. 665
FORD EXPORT SERVICES B.V.—See Ford Motor Company; *U.S. Public*, pg. 665
FORD FINANCE COMPANY OF JAPAN, LIMITED—See Ford Motor Company; *U.S. Public*, pg. 666
FORD FINANCIAL SERVICES INC.—See Ford Motor Company; *U.S. Public*, pg. 663
FORD FINANCIAL TRUST LIMITED—See Ford Motor Company; *U.S. Public*, pg. 666
FORD FLEET FINANCING LIMITED—See Ford Motor Company; *U.S. Public*, pg. 666
FORD FRANCE S.A.—See Ford Motor Company; *U.S. Public*, pg. 666
FORD GLASS & METAL, INC.—See Ford Motor Company; *U.S. Public*, pg. 664
FORD GRAPHICS; *U.S. Private*, pg. 418
HENRY FORD & SON (FINANCE) LIMITED—See Ford Motor Company; *U.S. Public*, pg. 665
HENRY FORD & SON, LIMITED—See Ford Motor Company; *U.S. Public*, pg. 665
HENRY FORD & SON (SALES) LIMITED—See Ford Motor Company; *U.S. Public*, pg. 665
FORD HOLDINGS INC.—See Ford Motor Company; *U.S. Public*, pg. 663
FORD INDUSTRIA E COMERCIO LTDA.—See Ford Motor Company; *U.S. Public*, pg. 666
FORD INTERNATIONAL CAPITAL CORPORATION—See Ford Motor Company; *U.S. Public*, pg. 664
FORD INTERNATIONAL EXPORT SALES (ASIA-PACIFIC REGION) INCORPORATED—See Ford Motor Company; *U.S. Public*, pg. 664
FORD INTERNATIONAL SERVICES, INC.—See Ford Motor Company; *U.S. Public*, pg. 664
FORD INVESTITIONS GMBH & CO. OHG—See Ford Motor Company; *U.S. Public*, pg. 664
FORD INVESTMENT PARTNERSHIP—See Ford Motor Company; *U.S. Public*, pg. 664
FORD ITALIANA S.P.A.—See Ford Motor Company; *U.S. Public*, pg. 666
FORD LEASE FINANCING LIMITED—See Ford Motor Company; *U.S. Public*, pg. 666
FORD LEASING DEVELOPMENT CO.—See Ford Motor Company; *U.S. Public*, pg. 664
FORD LEASING S.A.—See Ford Motor Company; *U.S. Public*, pg. 665
FORD LEASING SPA—See Ford Motor Company; *U.S. Public*, pg. 666
FORD LIFE INSURANCE COMPANY—See SunAmerica Inc.; *U.S. Public*, pg. 1533
FORD LIO HO MOTOR CO., LTD.—See Ford Motor Company; *U.S. Public*, pg. 665
FORD LUSITANA—See Ford Motor Company; *U.S. Public*, pg. 666
FORD MANUFACTURING OPERATIONS—See Ford Motor Company; *U.S. Public*, pg. 662
FORD MARKETING STAFF—See Ford Motor Company; *U.S. Public*, pg. 663
FORD METER BOX COMPANY; *U.S. Private*, pg. 418
FORD MICROELECTRONICS, INC.—See Ford Motor Company; *U.S. Public*, pg. 664
FORD MOTOR COMPANIA COMMERCIAL, S.A. DE C.V.—See Ford Motor Company; *U.S. Public*, pg. 666
FORD MOTOR COMPANY; *U.S. Public*, pg. 661
FORD MOTOR CO. AKTIEBOLAG—See Ford Motor Company; *U.S. Public*, pg. 666
FORD MOTOR COMPANY A/S—See Ford Motor Company; *U.S. Public*, pg. 666
FORD MOTOR CO. (AUSTRIA) KG—See Ford Motor Company; *U.S. Public*, pg. 666
FORD MOTOR COMPANY (BELGIUM) N.V.—See Ford Motor Company; *U.S. Public*, pg. 666
FORD MOTOR COMPANY (JAPAN) LTD.—See Ford Motor Company; *U.S. Public*, pg. 666

FORD MOTOR COMPANY LIMITED—See Ford Motor Company; *U.S. Public*, pg. 666
FORD MOTOR CO. OF AUSTRALIA LTD.—See Ford Motor Company; *U.S. Public*, pg. 666
FORD MOTOR CO. OF CANADA LTD—See Ford Motor Company; *U.S. Public*, pg. 666
FORD MOTOR CO. OF NEW ZEALAND LTD.—See Ford Motor Company; *U.S. Public*, pg. 666
FORD MOTOR COMPANY S.A. DE C.V., (MEXICO)—See Ford Motor Company; *U.S. Public*, pg. 666
FORD MOTOR CO. (SWITZERLAND) S.A.—See Ford Motor Company; *U.S. Public*, pg. 666
FORD MOTOR CREDIT COMPANY—See Ford Motor Company; *U.S. Public*, pg. 663
FORD MOTOR CREDIT COMPANY INTERNATIONAL—See Ford Motor Company; *U.S. Public*, pg. 664
FORD MOTOR CREDIT COMPANY OF NEW ZEALAND LIMITED—See Ford Motor Company; *U.S. Public*, pg. 663
FORD MOTOR CREDIT COMPANY OF PUERTO RICO INC.—See Ford Motor Company; *U.S. Public*, pg. 664
FORD MOTOR CREDIT S.A.—See Ford Motor Company; *U.S. Public*, pg. 666
FORD MOTOR DE VENEZUELA, S.A.—See Ford Motor Company; *U.S. Public*, pg. 666
FORD MOTOR DEALERSHIP FACILITIES CO.—See Ford Motor Company; *U.S. Public*, pg. 664
FORD MOTOR LAND DEVELOPMENT CORPORATION—See Ford Motor Company; *U.S. Public*, pg. 663
FORD MOTOR NORGE A/S—See Ford Motor Company; *U.S. Public*, pg. 666
FORD NEW HOLLAND—See Fiat Auto SpA; *Int'l*, pg. 483
FORD NEW HOLLAND CREDIT COMPANY—See Ford Motor Company; *U.S. Public*, pg. 664
FORD NEW HOLLAND CREDIT, INC.—See Fiat Auto SpA; *Int'l*, pg. 483
FORD NORTH AMERICAN AUTOMOTIVE OPERATION—See Ford Motor Company; *U.S. Public*, pg. 662
FORD NORTH AMERICAN DESIGN—See Ford Motor Company; *U.S. Public*, pg. 662
FORD OF EUROPE, INCORPORATED—See Ford Motor Company; *U.S. Public*, pg. 664
FORD PARTS AND SERVICE DIV.—See Ford Motor Company; *U.S. Public*, pg. 662
FORD PERSONAL IMPORT EXPORT LTD.—See Ford Motor Company; *U.S. Public*, pg. 666
FORD PLASTIC & TRIM PRODUCTS INTERNATIONAL, INC.—See Ford Motor Company; *U.S. Public*, pg. 662
FORD PRODUCT ASSURANCE—See Ford Motor Company; *U.S. Public*, pg. 662
FORD PURCHASING & SUPPLY STAFF—See Ford Motor Company; *U.S. Public*, pg. 664
FORD RESEARCH STAFF—See Ford Motor Company; *U.S. Public*, pg. 664
FORD SALES COMPANY OF AUSTRALIA LIMITED—See Ford Motor Company; *U.S. Public*, pg. 666
FORD STEEL CO., INC.; *U.S. Private*, pg. 418
FORD TECHNICAL AFFAIRS & OPERATING STAFFS—See Ford Motor Company; *U.S. Public*, pg. 662
FORD TRANSMISSION AND CHASSIS DIV.—See Ford Motor Company; *U.S. Public*, pg. 662
FORD TRUCK OPERATIONS—See Ford Motor Company; *U.S. Public*, pg. 662
FORD VAGNSKADEGARANTI AB—See Ford Motor Company; *U.S. Public*, pg. 666
FORD VERSICHERUNGS-VERMITTLUNGS GMBH—See Ford Motor Company; *U.S. Public*, pg. 666
FORD-VERSORGUNGS-UND UNTERSTÜTZUNGSEINRICHTUNG GMBH—See Ford Motor Company; *U.S. Public*, pg. 666
FORD-WERKE AG & CO.—See Ford Motor Company; *U.S. Public*, pg. 666
FORD WERKE AG - GENK BRANCH—See Ford Motor Company; *U.S. Public*, pg. 666
FORDATH S.A. DE CV—See Hepworth Plc; *Int'l*, pg. 615
FORDING COAL LTD.—See Canadian Pacific Limited; *Int'l*, pg. 259
FORDSON COAL COMPANY—See Ford Motor Company; *U.S. Public*, pg. 664
FORDYCE CONCRETE CO., INC.—See Ash Grove Cement Company; *U.S. Private*, pg. 88
FORDYCE & PRINCETON R.R. CO.—See Georgia-Pacific Corporation; *U.S. Public*, pg. 736
FORE LINE SECURITY—See Reeves Southeastern Corporation; *U.S. Private*, pg. 917
FORE SYSTEMS, INC.; *U.S. Public*, pg. 667
FORECAST GROUP; *U.S. Private*, pg. 418
FORECAST INTERNATIONAL—See Groupe Usinor; *Int'l*, pg. 571
THE FOREIGN CANDY CO., INC.; *U.S. Private*, pg. 418
FOREIGN TRADE DIVISION—See Nestle S.A.; *Int'l*, pg. 917
FOREM S.P.A.—See Allen Telecom, Inc.; *U.S. Public*, pg. 46
L.P. FOREMAN & SONS LTD.—See The General Electric Company, p.l.c.; *Int'l*, pg. 543
FOREMOST CORPORATION OF AMERICA; *U.S. Public*, pg. 667
FOREMOST FARMS USA COOPERATIVE; *U.S. Private*, pg. 418
FOREMOST FINANCIAL SERVICES CORP.—See Foremost Corporation of America; *U.S. Public*, pg. 667
FOREMOST INGREDIENT GROUP—See Foremost Farms USA Cooperative; *U.S. Private*, pg. 418
FOREMOST INSURANCE CO.—See Foremost Corporation of America; *U.S. Public*, pg. 667
FOREMOST PROPERTY & CASUALTY INSURANCE COMPANY—See Foremost Corporation of America; *U.S. Public*, pg. 667
FOREMOST SIGNATURE INSURANCE CO.—See Foremost Corporation of America; *U.S. Public*, pg. 667
FORESIGHT SOFTWARE, INC.—See Platinum Equity Holdings, LLC; *U.S. Private*, pg. 872

Company Index

FOREST BAY, INC.—See Forest City Enterprises, Inc.; *U.S. Public*, pg. 668
FOREST CITY ANTELOPE VALLEY, INC.—See Forest City Enterprises, Inc.; *U.S. Public*, pg. 668
FOREST CITY APARTMENT MNGMT. DIV.—See Forest City Enterprises, Inc.; *U.S. Public*, pg. 668
FOREST CITY AUTO PARTS—See Tyler Corporation; *U.S. Public*, pg. 1652
FOREST CITY BAYSIDE CORPORATION—See Forest City Enterprises, Inc.; *U.S. Public*, pg. 668
FOREST CITY BURBANK, INC.—See Forest City Enterprises, Inc.; *U.S. Public*, pg. 668
FOREST CITY CAMBRIDGE INC.—See Forest City Enterprises, Inc.; *U.S. Public*, pg. 668
FOREST CITY CAPITAL CORPORATION—See Forest City Enterprises, Inc.; *U.S. Public*, pg. 668
FOREST CITY COMMERCIAL CONSTRUCTION COMPANY, INC.—See Forest City Enterprises, Inc.; *U.S. Public*, pg. 668
FOREST CITY COMMERCIAL MNGMT. DIV.—See Forest City Enterprises, Inc.; *U.S. Public*, pg. 668
FOREST CITY CONTRACT LUMBER, INC.—See Forest City Enterprises, Inc.; *U.S. Public*, pg. 668
FOREST CITY CREDIT CORPORATION—See Forest City Enterprises, Inc.; *U.S. Public*, pg. 668
FOREST CITY ENTERPRISES, INC.; *U.S. Public*, pg. 667
FOREST CITY EUREKA, INC.—See Forest City Enterprises, Inc.; *U.S. Public*, pg. 668
FOREST CITY GRAND TERRACE, INC.—See Forest City Enterprises, Inc.; *U.S. Public*, pg. 668
FOREST CITY INTERNATIONAL PLAZA CORPORATION—See Forest City Enterprises, Inc.; *U.S. Public*, pg. 668
FOREST CITY KENT, INC.—See Forest City Enterprises, Inc.; *U.S. Public*, pg. 668
FOREST CITY LAND GROUP—See Forest City Enterprises, Inc.; *U.S. Public*, pg. 668
FOREST CITY METROTECH CORP.—See Forest City Enterprises, Inc.; *U.S. Public*, pg. 668
FOREST CITY PALMDALE, INC.—See Forest City Enterprises, Inc.; *U.S. Public*, pg. 668
FOREST CITY PARK MANOR, INC.—See Forest City Enterprises, Inc.; *U.S. Public*, pg. 668
FOREST CITY PARKLABREA, INC.—See Forest City Enterprises, Inc.; *U.S. Public*, pg. 668
FOREST CITY PIERREPONT, INC.—See Forest City Enterprises, Inc.; *U.S. Public*, pg. 668
FOREST CITY PROPERTIES CORPORATION—See Forest City Enterprises, Inc.; *U.S. Public*, pg. 668
FOREST CITY RENTAL PROPERTIES CORPORATION—See Forest City Enterprises, Inc.; *U.S. Public*, pg. 668
FOREST CITY RENTAL PROPERTIES OF NEVADA, INC.—See Forest City Enterprises, Inc.; *U.S. Public*, pg. 669
FOREST CITY RESIDENTIAL DEVELOPMENT INC.—See Forest City Enterprises, Inc.; *U.S. Public*, pg. 669
FOREST CITY ROLLING ACRES, INC.—See Forest City Enterprises, Inc.; *U.S. Public*, pg. 669
FOREST CITY SAN VICENTE CORP.—See Forest City Enterprises, Inc.; *U.S. Public*, pg. 669
FOREST CITY S.I.A.C. BUILDING, INC.—See Forest City Enterprises, Inc.; *U.S. Public*, pg. 669
FOREST CITY SOUTHPARK CORP.—See Forest City Enterprises, Inc.; *U.S. Public*, pg. 668
FOREST CITY SOUTHPARK TWO, INC.—See Forest City Enterprises, Inc.; *U.S. Public*, pg. 669
FOREST CITY 38 SIDNEY STREET, INC.—See Forest City Enterprises, Inc.; *U.S. Public*, pg. 669
FOREST CITY TRADING GROUP, INC.—See Forest City Enterprises, Inc.; *U.S. Public*, pg. 669
FOREST CITY VINEYARD VILLAGE, INC.—See Forest City Enterprises, Inc.; *U.S. Public*, pg. 669
FOREST FASTENERS—See Caparo Group Ltd.; *Int'l*, pg. 265
THE FOREST HILL STATE BANK—See Mercantile Bankshares Corporation; *U.S. Public*, pg. 1089
FOREST INDUSTRIES FLYING TANKERS LIMITED—See MacMillan Bloedel Limited; *Int'l*, pg. 828
FOREST INDUSTRIES, INC.—See Saunders Brothers; *U.S. Private*, pg. 968
FOREST KRAFT COMPANY—See The Mead Corporation; *U.S. Public*, pg. 1076
FOREST LABORATORIES CARIBE, INC.—See Forest Laboratories, Inc.; *U.S. Public*, pg. 670
FOREST LABORATORIES, INC.; *U.S. Public*, pg. 670
FOREST LAKE TRAVEL SERVICE, INC.—See The Seibels Bruce Group; *U.S. Public*, pg. 1454
FOREST LINES INC.—See International Shipholding Corporation; *U.S. Public*, pg. 907
FOREST OIL CORPORATION; *U.S. Public*, pg. 670
FOREST OIL NEW VENTURES—See Forest Oil Corporation; *U.S. Public*, pg. 670
FOREST OIL OFFSHORE PRODUCTION OFFICE—See Forest Oil Corporation; *U.S. Public*, pg. 670
FOREST PHARMACEUTICALS, INC.—See Forest Laboratories, Inc.; *U.S. Public*, pg. 670
FOREST PLACE ASSOCIATES—See Cigna Corp.; *U.S. Public*, pg. 361
FOREST PRODUCTS S.A.—See Enso Oyj; *Int'l*, pg. 458
FOREST SIDING SUPPLY, INC.—See Thermal Technology Industries; *U.S. Private*, pg. 1080
FOREST S.P.A.—See Coeclerici Group; *Int'l*, pg. 303
FOREST VIEW PSYCHIATRIC HOSPITAL—See Universal Health Services, Inc.; *U.S. Public*, pg. 1697
FORESTVILLE TELEPHONE, INC.—See Century Telephone Enterprises, Inc.; *U.S. Public*, pg. 330
FORET, S.A.—See FMC Corporation; *U.S. Public*, pg. 606
THE FORETHOUGHT GROUP, INC.—See Hillenbrand Industries, Inc.; *U.S. Public*, pg. 828
FOREVER LIVING PRODUCTS INTERNATIONAL, INC.; *U.S. Private*, pg. 418
FORGEAL—See Pechiney S.A.; *Int'l*, pg. 1028
FORGED PRODUCTS—See The Cypress Companies; *U.S. Private*, pg. 299

FORGES DE BOLOGNE—See Aluminum Company of America; *U.S. Public*, pg. 62
FORIND AVIO ELETTRONICA SPA—See Knurr AG; *Int'l*, pg. 739
FORJACERO—See Altos Hornos de Mexico, S.A.; *Int'l*, pg. 66
BUCK FORKARDT, INC.—See Wagon Industrial Holdings PLC; *Int'l*, pg. 1484
FORKARDT INTERNATIONAL GMBH—See Wagon Industrial Holdings PLC; *Int'l*, pg. 1484
FORLAGET DET BESTE A/S—See The Reader's Digest Association, Inc.; *U.S. Public*, pg. 1368
FORM FITTINGS LTD.—See Wolseley Plc.; *Int'l*, pg. 1511
FORM FLOW, INC.—See Secom General Corporation; *U.S. Public*, pg. 1453
FORM-YOU-3 INTERNATIONAL, INC.; *U.S. Private*, pg. 418
FORMA SCIENTIFIC INC.—See Thermo Electron Corporation; *U.S. Public*, pg. 1595
FORMAN BROTHERS, INC.; *U.S. Private*, pg. 418
FORMATION, INC.; *U.S. Private*, pg. 419
FORMAX, INC.—See Tetra Laval Group; *Int'l*, pg. 1378
FORMECA OY—See Enso Oyj; *Int'l*, pg. 456
FORMEMBAU UND KUNSTSTOFFTECHMIK GMBH—See Freudenberg & Company; *Int'l*, pg. 505
FORMEX, INC. - PERMANENT STEEL FORMS—See Omega Environmental; *U.S. Public*, pg. 1222
FORMFLO LIMITED—See Caradon Plc; *Int'l*, pg. 267
FORMICA ASIA LIMITED—See BTR plc; *Int'l*, pg. 129
FORMICA CANADA, INC.—See BTR plc; *Int'l*, pg. 129
FORMICA CORPORATION—See BTR plc; *Int'l*, pg. 129
FORMICA ESPANOLA S.A.—See BTR plc; *Int'l*, pg. 129
FORMICA ITALIA S.R.1.—See BTR plc; *Int'l*, pg. 129
FORMICA LIMITED—See BTR plc; *Int'l*, pg. 129
FORMICA NEDERLAND B.V.—See BTR plc; *Int'l*, pg. 129
FORMICA SWITZERLAND AG—See BTR plc; *Int'l*, pg. 129
FORMICA TAIWAN CORPORATION—See BTR plc; *Int'l*, pg. 130
FORMICA VERTRIEBS GMBH—See BTR plc; *Int'l*, pg. 130
FORMOSA PLASTICS CORPORATION; *Int'l*, pg. 498
FORMOSA PLASTICS CORP., U.S.A.—See Formosa Plastics Corporation; *Int'l*, pg. 498
FORMS & SUPPLY, INC.; *U.S. Private*, pg. 419
FORMTEK—See Lockheed Martin Corporation; *U.S. Public*, pg. 1008
FORMULARIOS MOORE DE COSTA RICA S.A. DE CV—See Moore Corporation Limited; *Int'l*, pg. 889
FORMULARIOS MOORE DE GUATEMALA, S.A.—See Moore Corporation Limited; *Int'l*, pg. 889
FORMULARIOS MOORE DE NICARAGUA S.A.—See Moore Corporation Limited; *Int'l*, pg. 890
FORMULARIOS Y PROCEDIMIENTOS MOORE S.A.—See Moore Corporation Limited; *Int'l*, pg. 890
FORMULES D'AFFAIRES DATA—See Data Business Forms Limited; *Int'l*, pg. 384
AB FORMVERKTYG—See Electrolux, AB; *Int'l*, pg. 439
FORMWELD FITTINGS—See Canadian Erectors Ltd.; *Int'l*, pg. 256
FORNEY CORPORATION—See Williams Holdings Plc; *Int'l*, pg. 1500
FORON INTERNATIONAL SALES CORP.—See Doron Precision Systems, Inc.; *U.S. Private*, pg. 341
FORSAKRINGSAKTIEBOLAGET ALLIANZ NORDEUROPA (RAS)—See Allianz Aktiengesellschaft; *Int'l*, pg. 60
FORSAKRINGSAKTIEBOLAGET SIRIUS—See ABB Asea Brown Boveri (Holding) Ltd.; *Int'l*, pg. 7
FORSAKRINGSAKTIEBOLAGET VOLVIA—See AB Volvo; *Int'l*, pg. 1476
R.H. FORSCHNER DIVISION—See Swiss Army Brands, Inc.; *U.S. Public*, pg. 1544
FORSIKRINGSAKSJESELSKAPET ALLIANZ NORDEUROPA—See Allianz Aktiengesellschaft; *Int'l*, pg. 60
FORSIKRINGSAKTIESELSKABET (RAS) ALLIANZ NORDEUROPA—See Allianz Aktiengesellschaft; *Int'l*, pg. 60
FORSLID AB—See Telefonaktiebolaget LM Ericsson; *Int'l*, pg. 1363
FORSLID A/S—See Telefonaktiebolaget LM Ericsson; *Int'l*, pg. 1368
FORSMARKS KRAFTGRUPP AB—See Vattenfall AB; *Int'l*, pg. 1453
FORSS-PARATOR—See Trelleborg AB; *Int'l*, pg. 330
FORSTER, INC.—See Diamond Brands, Inc.; *U.S. Private*, pg. 330
FORSTMANN & COMPANY, INC.; *U.S. Public*, pg. 670
FORSTMANN LITTLE & CO.; *U.S. Private*, pg. 419
FORSVARSMEDIA AB—See Celsius AB; *Int'l*, pg. 277
FORT BEND UTILITIES CO.—See Imperial Holly Corporation; *U.S. Public*, pg. 872
FORT COLLINS NEWSPAPERS, INC.—See Gannett Company, Inc.; *U.S. Public*, pg. 700
FORT DEARBORN COMPANY; *U.S. Private*, pg. 419
FORT DODGE ANIMAL HEALTH—See American Home Products Corporation; *U.S. Public*, pg. 79
FORT JAMES CANADA, INC.—See Fort James Corporation; *U.S. Public*, pg. 672
FORT JAMES CORPORATION; *U.S. Public*, pg. 670
FORT JAMES CORPORATION—See Fort James Corporation; *U.S. Public*, pg. 672
FORT JAMES-MARATHON, LTD.—See Fort James Corporation; *U.S. Public*, pg. 672
FORT JAMES TIMBER CORP.—See Fort James Corporation; *U.S. Public*, pg. 672
FORT JAMES WESTERN TRANSPORTATION—See Fort James Corporation; *U.S. Public*, pg. 672
FORT LOCK CORPORATION; *U.S. Private*, pg. 419
FORT LOCK UK, LTD.—See Fort Lock Corporation; *U.S. Private*, pg. 419
FORT MYERS BRANCH OFFICE—See U.S. Home Corporation; *U.S. Public*, pg. 1683
FORT MYERS MIRACLE—See Minnesota Twins Baseball Club; *U.S. Private*, pg. 751

FORT ORANGE PAPER CO., INC.—See Relm Wireless Corp.; *U.S. Public*, pg. 1376
FORT PITT ACQUISITIONS, INC.; *U.S. Private*, pg. 419
FORT SECURITE—See Fort Lock Corporation; *U.S. Private*, pg. 419
FORT WASHINGTON INVESTMENT ADVISORS, INC.—See The Western and Southern Life Insurance Company; *U.S. Private*, pg. 1164
FORT WAYNE NATIONAL BANK—See Fort Wayne National Corporation; *U.S. Public*, pg. 674
FORT WAYNE NATIONAL CORPORATION; *U.S. Public*, pg. 673
FORT WAYNE NEWSPAPER AGENCY—See Knight-Ridder, Inc.; *U.S. Public*, pg. 964
FORT WAYNE NEWSPAPERS, INC.—See Knight-Ridder, Inc.; *U.S. Public*, pg. 964
FORT WAYNE VEHICLE AUCTION INC.—See Tyco International Ltd.; *U.S. Public*, pg. 1649
FORT WAYNE WIZARDS—See Minnesota Twins Baseball Club; *U.S. Private*, pg. 751
FORT WORTH AUTO AUCTION—See Cox Enterprises, Inc.; *U.S. Private*, pg. 283
FORT WORTH COMMUNICATIONS, INC.—See Nextel Communications; *U.S. Public*, pg. 1180
FORT WORTH LEARNING CENTER—See Berkshire Hathaway Inc.; *U.S. Public*, pg. 218
FORT WORTH LUMBER COMPANY; *U.S. Private*, pg. 419
FORTE (BERMUDA) LIMITED—See Granada Group PLC; *Int'l*, pg. 556
FORTE FINANCE N.V.—See Granada Group PLC; *Int'l*, pg. 556
FORTE FRANCE S.A.—See Granada Group PLC; *Int'l*, pg. 556
FORTE HOLDINGS IRELAND LIMITED—See Granada Group PLC; *Int'l*, pg. 556
FORTE HOTELS (DEUTSCHLAND) GMBH—See Granada Group PLC; *Int'l*, pg. 556
FORTE HOTELS (UK) LIMITED—See Granada Group PLC; *Int'l*, pg. 556
FORTE ITALIA SPA—See Granada Group PLC; *Int'l*, pg. 556
FORTEK OY—See Enso Oyj; *Int'l*, pg. 456
FORTIFIBER CORPORATION; *U.S. Private*, pg. 419
FORTINO'S SUPERMARKETS LTD.—See George Weston Limited; *Int'l*, pg. 1495
FORTINOX S.A.—See Fried. Krupp AG; *Int'l*, pg. 515
FORTIS; *Int'l*, pg. 498
FORTIS ADVISERS, INC.—See Fortis; *Int'l*, pg. 499
FORTIS BENEFITS INSURANCE COMPANY—See Fortis; *Int'l*, pg. 499
FORTIS FINANCIAL GROUP—See Fortis; *Int'l*, pg. 499
FORTIS, INC.—See Fortis; *Int'l*, pg. 499
FORTIS INTERNATIONAL N.V.—See Fortis; *Int'l*, pg. 499
FORTIS LIFE—See Fortis; *Int'l*, pg. 499
FORTIS LONG TERM CARE—See Fortis; *Int'l*, pg. 499
FORTIS SALES—See Fortis; *Int'l*, pg. 499
FORTIS (U.K.) LIMITED—See Fortis; *Int'l*, pg. 499
FORTNUM & MASON (EXPORT)—See Fortnum & Mason PLC; *Int'l*, pg. 500
FORTNUM & MASON PLC; *Int'l*, pg. 500
FORTON B.V.—See DSM N.V.; *Int'l*, pg. 354
FORTRESS INTERLOCKS LIMITED—See Halma p.l.c.; *Int'l*, pg. 589
FORTRESS SCIENTIFIC LIMITED—See MDS Inc.; *Int'l*, pg. 826
FORTRESS SECURITY PTY LIMITED—See Halma p.l.c.; *Int'l*, pg. 590
FORTUNE—See Time Warner Inc.; *U.S. Public*, pg. 1613
FORTUNE BRANDS, INC.; *U.S. Public*, pg. 674
FORTUNE BRANDS INTERNATIONAL CORPORATION—See Fortune Brands, Inc.; *U.S. Public*, pg. 675
FORTUNE COMMUNICATION HOLDINGS LTD.; *Int'l*, pg. 500
FORTUNE FASHION INC.; *U.S. Private*, pg. 419
FORTUNE PRODUCTS, INC.—See Windmere-Durable Holdings; *U.S. Public*, pg. 1771
FORTUNOFF; *U.S. Private*, pg. 420
FORTWAY FINANCE LIMITED—See HSBC Holdings plc; *Int'l*, pg. 581
4520 CORP., INC.—See Blount International, Inc.; *U.S. Public*, pg. 239
40 FORT EYE ASSOCIATES; *U.S. Private*, pg. 420
FORUM ASIA LTD.—See The Forum Corporation; *U.S. Private*, pg. 420
FORUM COMMUNICATIONS COMPANY; *U.S. Private*, pg. 420
THE FORUM CORPORATION; *U.S. Private*, pg. 420
FORUM CORPORATION OF CANADA, LTD.—See The Forum Corporation; *U.S. Private*, pg. 420
FORUM EUROPE LTD.—See The Forum Corporation; *U.S. Private*, pg. 420
FORUM (HOLDINGS) LTD.—See Ajinomoto Company Inc.; *Int'l*, pg. 41
FORUM LEOPOLD S.A.—See Tractebel; *Int'l*, pg. 1416
FORVALTNINGS AB RATOS; *Int'l*, pg. 500
FORWARD INSURANCE BROKERS LIMITED—See Britax International plc; *Int'l*, pg. 216
FORWARD TRUST GROUP LIMITED—See HSBC Holdings plc; *Int'l*, pg. 579
FORWEST INC.—See Forasol S.A.; *Int'l*, pg. 496
FOSBEL, INC.—See Burmah Castrol plc; *Int'l*, pg. 234
FOSECO HOLDING INC.—See Burmah Castrol plc; *Int'l*, pg. 234
FOSECO INC.—See Burmah Castrol plc; *Int'l*, pg. 234
FOSECO PLC.—See Burmah Castrol plc; *Int'l*, pg. 234
FOSECO (SINGAPORE) PTE. LTD.—See Burmah Castrol plc; *Int'l*, pg. 234
FOSHAN CROWN CAN COMPANY LTD.—See Crown Cork & Seal Company, Inc.; *U.S. Public*, pg. 465
FOSHAN EASY-OPENING END COMPANY LTD.—See Crown Cork & Seal Company, Inc.; *U.S. Public*, pg. 465
FOSHAN HUA NAN BUNDY TUBING CO LTD.—See TI Group plc; *Int'l*, pg. 1341

FOSROC EXPANDITE (AUSTRALIA) PTY. LTD.—See Burmah Castrol plc; *Int'l*, pg. 236
FOSROC EXPANDITE LTD.—See Burmah Castrol plc; *Int'l*, pg. 234
FOSROC EXPANDITE (PRIVATE) LTD.—See Burmah Castrol plc; *Int'l*, pg. 236
FOSROC EXPANDITE (PTE) LTD.—See Burmah Castrol plc; *Int'l*, pg. 236
FOSROC EXPANDITE SB—See Burmah Castrol plc; *Int'l*, pg. 236
FOSROC INC.—See Burmah Castrol plc; *Int'l*, pg. 234
FOSS MANUFACTURING COMPANY INCORPORATED; *U.S. Private*, pg. 420
FOSS MARITIME CO.—See Totem Resources Corporation; *U.S. Private*, pg. 1092
FOSSIL INC.; *U.S. Private*, pg. 420
FOSTAFIL FIBERS INC.—See Akzo Nobel N.V.; *Int'l*, pg. 46
FOSTER & GALLAGHER, INC.; *U.S. Private*, pg. 420
FOSTER ELECTRIC CO., LTD.; *Int'l*, pg. 500
FOSTER ELECTRIC CO. (TAIWAN), LTD.—See Foster Electric Co., Ltd.; *Int'l*, pg. 500
FOSTER ELECTRIC (EUROPE) GMBH—See Foster Electric Co., Ltd.; *Int'l*, pg. 500
FOSTER ELECTRIC (SINGAPORE) PTE. LTD.—See Foster Electric Co., Ltd.; *Int'l*, pg. 500
FOSTER ELECTRIC (U.S.A.) INC.—See Foster Electric Co., Ltd.; *Int'l*, pg. 500
FOSTER FARMS; *U.S. Private*, pg. 421
L.B. FOSTER COMPANY; *U.S. Public*, pg. 675
L.B. FOSTER COMPANY-BEDFORD PLANT—See L.B. Foster Company; *U.S. Public*, pg. 676
L.B. FOSTER COMPANY-BIRMINGHAM PLANT—See L.B. Foster Company; *U.S. Public*, pg. 676
L.B. FOSTER COMPANY-DORAVILLE YARD/COATED PIPE—See L.B. Foster Company; *U.S. Public*, pg. 676
L.B. FOSTER COMPANY-DORAVILLE YARD/FABRICATION SHOP—See L.B. Foster Company; *U.S. Public*, pg. 676
L.B. FOSTER COMPANY-EPHRATA PLANT—See L.B. Foster Company; *U.S. Public*, pg. 676
L.B. FOSTER COMPANY-LANGFIELD YARD—See L.B. Foster Company; *U.S. Public*, pg. 676
L.B. FOSTER COMPANY-NEWPORT PLANT—See L.B. Foster Company; *U.S. Public*, pg. 676
L.B. FOSTER COMPANY-NILES PLANT—See L.B. Foster Company; *U.S. Public*, pg. 676
L.B. FOSTER COMPANY-PARKERSBURG PLANT—See L.B. Foster Company; *U.S. Public*, pg. 676
L.B. FOSTER COMPANY-POMEROY PLANT—See L.B. Foster Company; *U.S. Public*, pg. 676
L.B. FOSTER COMPANY-SENECA YARD—See L.B. Foster Company; *U.S. Public*, pg. 676
L.B. FOSTER COMPANY-STOCKTON YARD—See L.B. Foster Company; *U.S. Public*, pg. 676
FOSTER MANAGEMENT CO.; *U.S. Private*, pg. 421
FOSTER-MILLER, INC.; *U.S. Private*, pg. 421
FOSTER MORTGAGE CORPORATION—See United Companies Financial Corporation; *U.S. Public*, pg. 1675
FOSTER PONTIAC, INC.; *U.S. Private*, pg. 421
FOSTER PRODUCTS CORPORATION—See H.B. Fuller Company; *U.S. Public*, pg. 686
FOSTER REFRIGERATOR CORPORATION; *U.S. Private*, pg. 421
FOSTER WHEELER ANDINA, S.A.—See Foster Wheeler Corporation; *U.S. Public*, pg. 677
FOSTER WHEELER ARABIA, LTD.—See Foster Wheeler Corporation; *U.S. Public*, pg. 677
FOSTER WHEELER ASIA—See Foster Wheeler Corporation; *U.S. Public*, pg. 677
FOSTER WHEELER AUSTRALIA PTY. LTD.—See Foster Wheeler Corporation; *U.S. Public*, pg. 677
FOSTER WHEELER BIMAS—See Foster Wheeler Corporation; *U.S. Public*, pg. 677
FOSTER WHEELER CARIBE CORPORATION, C.A.—See Foster Wheeler Corporation; *U.S. Public*, pg. 677
FOSTER WHEELER CHILE, S.A.—See Foster Wheeler Corporation; *U.S. Public*, pg. 677
FOSTER WHEELER CONSTRUCTORS, INC.—See Foster Wheeler Corporation; *U.S. Public*, pg. 677
FOSTER WHEELER CORPORATION; *U.S. Public*, pg. 676
FOSTER WHEELER DEVELOPMENT CORP.—See Foster Wheeler Corporation; *U.S. Public*, pg. 676
FOSTER WHEELER EASTERN PRIVATE LIMITED—See Foster Wheeler Corporation; *U.S. Public*, pg. 677
FOSTER WHEELER ENERGIA OY—See Foster Wheeler Corporation; *U.S. Public*, pg. 677
FOSTER WHEELER ENERGIA, S.A.—See Foster Wheeler Corporation; *U.S. Public*, pg. 677
FOSTER WHEELER ENERGY CORPORATION—See Foster Wheeler Corporation; *U.S. Public*, pg. 676
FOSTER WHEELER ENERGY FAKOP, LTD.—See Foster Wheeler Corporation; *U.S. Public*, pg. 677
FOSTER WHEELER ENERGY INTERNATIONAL, INC.—See Foster Wheeler Corporation; *U.S. Public*, pg. 676
FOSTER WHEELER ENERGY LIMITED—See Foster Wheeler Corporation; *U.S. Public*, pg. 677
FOSTER WHEELER ENERGY SERVICES, INC.—See Foster Wheeler Corporation; *U.S. Public*, pg. 677
FOSTER WHEELER ENVIRONMENTAL CORPORATION—See Foster Wheeler Corporation; *U.S. Public*, pg. 677
FOSTER WHEELER FACILITIES MANAGEMENT, INC.—See Foster Wheeler Corporation; *U.S. Public*, pg. 677
FOSTER WHEELER FRANCE S.A.—See Foster Wheeler Corporation; *U.S. Public*, pg. 677
FOSTER WHEELER IBERIA S.A.—See Foster Wheeler Corporation; *U.S. Public*, pg. 677
FOSTER WHEELER INTERNATIONAL CORPORATION—See Foster Wheeler Corporation; *U.S. Public*, pg. 677
FOSTER WHEELER ITALIANA S.P.A. (ITALY)—See Foster Wheeler Corporation; *U.S. Public*, pg. 677
FOSTER WHEELER K.K.—See Foster Wheeler Corporation; *U.S. Public*, pg. 677

FOSTER WHEELER LTD. (CANADA)—See Foster Wheeler Corporation; *U.S. Public*, pg. 677
FOSTER WHEELER LTD. (ENGLAND)—See Foster Wheeler Corporation; *U.S. Public*, pg. 677
FOSTER WHEELER MARTINEZ—See Foster Wheeler Corporation; *U.S. Public*, pg. 677
FOSTER WHEELER PETROLEUM DEVELOPMENT CORP., LTD. (ENGLAND)—See Foster Wheeler Corporation; *U.S. Public*, pg. 677
FOSTER WHEELER POWER SYSTEMS, INC.—See Foster Wheeler Corporation; *U.S. Public*, pg. 677
FOSTER WHEELER REAL ESTATE DEVELOPMENT CORP.—See Foster Wheeler Corporation; *U.S. Public*, pg. 677
FOSTER WHEELER (THAILAND) LIMITED—See Foster Wheeler Corporation; *U.S. Public*, pg. 677
FOSTER WHEELER TRADING CO., LTD.—See Foster Wheeler Corporation; *U.S. Public*, pg. 677
FOSTER WHEELER USA CORPORATION—See Foster Wheeler Corporation; *U.S. Public*, pg. 677
FOSTER WHEELER WORLD SERVICES CORP.—See Foster Wheeler Corporation; *U.S. Public*, pg. 677
FOSTER WHEELER ZACK, INC.—See Foster Wheeler Corporation; *U.S. Public*, pg. 677
FOSTER'S BREWING GROUP—See Foster's Brewing Group Limited; *Int'l*, pg. 501
FOSTER'S BREWING GROUP LIMITED; *Int'l*, pg. 500
FOSTER'S CHINA—See Foster's Brewing Group Limited; *Int'l*, pg. 501
FOSTER'S FINANCE EUROPEAN REGION—See Foster's Brewing Group Limited; *Int'l*, pg. 500
FOSTERS FREEZE INTERNATIONAL, INC.; *U.S. Public*, pg. 501
FOSTER'S LANDING—See BRE Properties, Inc.; *U.S. Public*, pg. 163
FOSTORIA INDUSTRIES, INC.; *U.S. Private*, pg. 421
FOTO INTERAMERICANA DE VENEZUELA S.A.—See Eastman Kodak Company; *U.S. Public*, pg. 552
FOTO INTERNACIONAL, S.A.—See Hewlett-Packard Company; *U.S. Public*, pg. 817
FOTOBALL USA, INC.; *U.S. Public*, pg. 678
FOTOGRABADO INDUSTRIAL CENTRO-AMERICANO S.A.—See Takagi Chokoku Co., Ltd.; *Int'l*, pg. 1349
FOTOLAB LIMITED—See Tie Rack plc; *Int'l*, pg. 1389
FOTOLABO CLUB BV—See Fotolabo S.A.; *Int'l*, pg. 501
FOTOLABO CLUB (FRANCE) S.A.—See Fotolabo S.A.; *Int'l*, pg. 501
FOTOLABO CLUB S.A.—See Fotolabo S.A.; *Int'l*, pg. 501
FOTOLABO S.A.; *Int'l*, pg. 501
ABDULLA FOUAD AUCTIONEERS—See Abdulla Fouad Co. Ltd.; *Int'l*, pg. 502
ABDULLA FOUAD CO. LTD.; *Int'l*, pg. 501
ABDULLA FOUAD IMPALLOY LTD. CO.—See Abdulla Fouad Co. Ltd.; *Int'l*, pg. 502
ABDULLA FOUAD-TESTRADE MIDDLE EAST—See Abdulla Fouad Co. Ltd.; *Int'l*, pg. 502
FOUAD & TOUFIC FADEL & CO.—See Enso Oyj; *Int'l*, pg. 458
FOUAD SUPPLY & SERVICES DIVISION—See Abdulla Fouad Co. Ltd.; *Int'l*, pg. 502
FOUAD TRAVEL & CARGO AGENCY—See Abdulla Fouad Co. Ltd.; *Int'l*, pg. 502
FOULDS INC.; *U.S. Private*, pg. 421
FOUNDATION BUILDING WEST INC.—See BFC Construction Corporation; *Int'l*, pg. 118
THE FOUNDATION COMPANY—See BFC Construction Corporation; *Int'l*, pg. 118
THE FOUNDATION COMPANY - HALIFAX—See BFC Construction Corporation; *Int'l*, pg. 118
FOUNDATION HEALTH SYSTEMS, INC.; *U.S. Public*, pg. 678
FOUNDATION INSURANCE COMPANY—See Foundation Health Systems, Inc.; *U.S. Public*, pg. 678
FOUNDATION NUCLEAR MANAGERS—See BFC Construction Corporation; *Int'l*, pg. 118
FOUNTAIN HEAD BREWERY—See Scottish & Newcastle plc; *Int'l*, pg. 1212
FOUNTAIN POWERBOAT INDUSTRIES, INC.; *U.S. Public*, pg. 678
FOUNTAIN SPORTSWEAR—See Fountain Powerboat Industries, Inc.; *U.S. Public*, pg. 679
FOUNTAIN SQUARE MANAGEMENT CO.—See Fifth Third Bancorp; *U.S. Public*, pg. 622
THE FOUNTAINS—See Paragon Health Network, Inc.; *U.S. Public*, pg. 1256
4C FOODS CORPORATION; *U.S. Private*, pg. 421
FOUR CORNERS AVIATION, INC.—See Mesa Air Group; *U.S. Public*, pg. 1099
4DAY TIRE STORES; *U.S. Private*, pg. 421
FOUR-F NUTRITION—See Tate & Lyle PLC; *Int'l*, pg. 1356
FOUR M CORPORATION, INC.; *U.S. Private*, pg. 421
FOUR MEDIA COMPANIES; *U.S. Private*, pg. 422
4P EMBALLAGES FRANCE—See Royal Packaging Industries Van Leer B.V.; *Int'l*, pg. 1146
4P FOLIE FORCHHEIM GMBH—See Royal Packaging Industries Van Leer B.V.; *Int'l*, pg. 1146
4P NICOLAUS KEMPTEN GMBH—See Royal Packaging Industries Van Leer B.V.; *Int'l*, pg. 1146
4P RUBE GOTTINGEN GMBH—See Royal Packaging Industries Van Leer B.V.; *Int'l*, pg. 1146
4P RUBE POLSKA—See Royal Packaging Industries Van Leer B.V.; *Int'l*, pg. 1146
4P VERPACKUNGEN RONSBERG GMBH—See Royal Packaging Industries Van Leer B.V.; *Int'l*, pg. 1146
4P VERPACKUNGSGRUPPE B.V.—See Royal Packaging Industries Van Leer B.V.; *Int'l*, pg. 1146
FOUR-PHASE OVERSEAS CORP.—See Motorola, Inc.; *U.S. Public*, pg. 1139
FOUR-PHASE SYSTEMS INTERNATIONAL, INC.—See Motorola, Inc.; *U.S. Public*, pg. 1137
FOUR QUEENS INC.—See Elsinore Corporation; *U.S. Public*, pg. 570
FOUR-S BAKING COMPANY; *U.S. Private*, pg. 422

FOUR SEASONS AIR CONDITIONING DIV.—See Standard Motor Products Inc.; *U.S. Public*, pg. 1503
FOUR SEASONS CLIFT HOTEL—See Four Seasons Hotels Inc.; *Int'l*, pg. 502
FOUR SEASONS HOTELS & RESORTS—See Four Seasons Hotels Inc.; *Int'l*, pg. 502
FOUR SEASONS HOTELS INC.; *Int'l*, pg. 502
FOUR SEASONS OLYMPIC HOTEL—See Four Seasons Hotels Inc.; *Int'l*, pg. 502
FOUR SEASONS RESORTS—See Four Seasons Hotels Inc.; *Int'l*, pg. 502
FOUR SEASONS SOLAR PRODUCTS CORP.; *U.S. Private*, pg. 422
FOUR SEASONS WASHINGTON—See Four Seasons Hotels Inc.; *Int'l*, pg. 502
FOUR STAR HOLDINGS CORP.—See MacAndrews & Forbes Holdings Inc.; *U.S. Private*, pg. 689
FOUR STARS INSURANCE COMPANY—See UAL Corporation; *U.S. Public*, pg. 1653
FOUR-TEN CORP.—See Wm. Wrigley Jr. Company; *U.S. Public*, pg. 1781
FOUR WIND INTERNATIONAL CORP.—See Thor Industries, Inc.; *U.S. Public*, pg. 1602
FOUR WINDS INVESTMENT CORP.; *U.S. Private*, pg. 422
FOUR WINNS, INC.—See Greenway Partners, L.P.; *U.S. Private*, pg. 478
FOURCO GLASS CO.—See Asahi Glass Co., Ltd.; *Int'l*, pg. 84
SALLY FOURMY & ASSOCIATES—See Angelica Corporation; *U.S. Public*, pg. 113
FOURNEX N.V.—See SmithKline Beecham plc; *Int'l*, pg. 1265
FOURNIER FURNITURE; *U.S. Private*, pg. 422
S.C. FOURS A CHAUX DE BEN-AHIN—See Cockerill Sambre; *Int'l*, pg. 301
1480 WELTON, INC.—See New Century Energies, Inc.; *U.S. Public*, pg. 1170
FOURTH GENERATION TECHNOLOGY INC.—See Northrop Grumman Corporation; *U.S. Public*, pg. 1199
FOVA, INC.—See Grey Advertising Inc.; *U.S. Public*, pg. 764
FRED V. FOWLER COMPANY, INC.; *U.S. Private*, pg. 422
FOWLER TOOLS OF CANADA—See Fred V. Fowler Company, Inc.; *U.S. Private*, pg. 422
FOWNES BROTHERS & CO., INC.; *U.S. Private*, pg. 422
FOX BROADCASTING COMPANY (FBC)—See The News Corporation Limited; *Int'l*, pg. 926
FOX, INC.—See The News Corporation Limited; *Int'l*, pg. 926
FOX INTERNATIONAL LTD., INC.—See Video Display Corporation; *U.S. Public*, pg. 1720
FOX KIDS WORLDWIDE—See The News Corporation Limited; *Int'l*, pg. 927
FOX-KNAPP—See David Peyser Sportswear Inc.; *U.S. Private*, pg. 860
FOX NET—See The News Corporation Limited; *Int'l*, pg. 926
FOX PHOTO, INC.—See CPI Corp.; *U.S. Public*, pg. 283
FOX PHOTO, INC.—See Eastman Kodak Company; *U.S. Public*, pg. 551
FOX RIDGE HOMES—See NVR, Inc.; *U.S. Public*, pg. 1148
FOX RIVER PAPER COMPANY—See Fox Valley Corporation; *U.S. Private*, pg. 422
FOX TELEVISION STATIONS INC.—See The News Corporation Limited; *Int'l*, pg. 926
FOX VALLEY & WESTERN LTD.—See Wisconsin Central Transportation Corporation; *U.S. Public*, pg. 1772
FOX VALLEY CORPORATION; *U.S. Private*, pg. 422
FOX VALLEY STEEL & WIRE CO.—See Keystone Consolidated Industries, Inc.; *U.S. Public*, pg. 956
FOX VIDEO COMPANY—See The News Corporation Limited; *Int'l*, pg. 926
THE FOXBORO COMPANY—See Siebe plc; *Int'l*, pg. 1243
FOXBORO GREAT BRITAIN LIMITED—See Siebe plc; *Int'l*, pg. 1243
FOXBORO NEDERLAND N.V.—See Siebe plc; *Int'l*, pg. 1243
FOXBORO, S.A.—See Siebe plc; *Int'l*, pg. 1243
FOX'S BISCUITS LTD.—See Northern Foods plc; *Int'l*, pg. 968
FOXVIDEO (ESPANOLA) S.A.—See The News Corporation Limited; *Int'l*, pg. 926
FOXVIDEO (FAR EAST) K.K.—See The News Corporation Limited; *Int'l*, pg. 926
FOXVIDEO (FRANCE) S.A.—See The News Corporation Limited; *Int'l*, pg. 926
FOXVIDEO (GERMANY) G.M.B.H.—See The News Corporation Limited; *Int'l*, pg. 926
FOXVIDEO LIMITED—See The News Corporation Limited; *Int'l*, pg. 926
FOXVIDEO (NEW ZEALAND) LIMITED—See The News Corporation Limited; *Int'l*, pg. 926
FOXVIDEO (SOUTH PACIFIC) PTY., LTD.—See The News Corporation Limited; *Int'l*, pg. 926
FOXWORTH-GALBRAITH LUMBER CO.; *U.S. Private*, pg. 423
FRADIS FRANCE DISTRIBUTIQUE—See Lagardere Groupe; *Int'l*, pg. 792
FRAENKEL COMPANY; *U.S. Private*, pg. 423
FRAGEMA—See Framatome SA; *Int'l*, pg. 503
FRAGOL INDUSTRIESCHIMIERSTOFF GMBH—See Fuchs Petrolub AG Oel + Chemie; *Int'l*, pg. 517
FRAGRANCE RESOURCES, INC.; *U.S. Private*, pg. 423
FRAGRANCE SERVICES PTY. LTD.—See Unilever Plc; *Int'l*, pg. 1436
FRAKTARNA AB—See FLS Industries A/S; *Int'l*, pg. 476
FRAM EUROPE A.B.—See AlliedSignal Inc.; *U.S. Public*, pg. 53
FRAM EUROPE LTD.—See AlliedSignal Inc.; *U.S. Public*, pg. 53
FRAM FILTER S.P.A.—See AlliedSignal Inc.; *U.S. Public*, pg. 53
FRAMATOME COGEMA FUELS—See Framatome SA; *Int'l*, pg. 503

FRAMATOME CONNECTORS—See Framatome SA; *Int'l*, pg. 503
FRAMATOME CONNECTORS BELGIUM N.V.—See Framatome SA; *Int'l*, pg. 503
FRAMATOME CONNECTORS ESPANA S.A.—See Framatome SA; *Int'l*, pg. 503
FRAMATOME CONNECTORS INTERNATIONAL—See Framatome SA; *Int'l*, pg. 503
FRAMATOME CONNECTORS NEDERLAND B.V.—See Framatome SA; *Int'l*, pg. 503
FRAMATOME CONNECTORS SCHWEIZ A.G.—See Framatome SA; *Int'l*, pg. 503
FRAMATOME CONNECTORS S.P.A.—See Framatome SA; *Int'l*, pg. 503
FRAMATOME CONNECTORS SWEDEN AB—See Framatome SA; *Int'l*, pg. 503
FRAMATOME CONNECTORS U.K. LTD.—See Framatome SA; *Int'l*, pg. 503
FRAMATOME ET CIE—See Alcatel Alsthom Compagnie Generale D'Electricite; *Int'l*, pg. 52
FRAMATOME JAPAN; *Int'l*—See Framatome SA; *Int'l*, pg. 503
FRAMATOME-MEXICO S.A. DE C.V.—See Framatome SA; *Int'l*, pg. 503
FRAMATOME SA; *Int'l*, pg. 502
FRAMES UNLIMITED INC.—See Zimdar Enterprises/ Frames Unlimited; *U.S. Private*, pg. 1206
FRAMESI USA, INC./ROFFLER INDUSTRIES, INC./CASA DI COLORE, INC.—See Fort Pitt Acquisitions, Inc.; *U.S. Private*, pg. 419
FRAMETAL S.A.R.L.—See Coeclerici Group; *Int'l*, pg. 304
FRAMLINGTON ASSET MANAGEMENT MAGHREB—See Credit Commercial de France; *Int'l*, pg. 343
FRAMLINGTON ASSET MANAGEMENT RUSSIA—See Credit Commercial de France; *Int'l*, pg. 343
FRANCAISE D'ALIMENTATION ET DE BOISSONS S.A.— See Unilever Plc; *Int'l*, pg. 1437
FRANCAISE DE MECANIQUE—See PSA Peugeot Citroen; *Int'l*, pg. 1021
FRANCAISE DE MECANIQUE—See Renault; *Int'l*, pg. 1102
FRANCE ASSISTANCE—See Corporacion MAPFRE, Compania Internacional de Reaseguros, S.A.; *Int'l*, pg. 334
FRANCE CHAMPAGNE—See LVMH Moet Hennessy Louis Vuitton; *Int'l*, pg. 780
FRANCE COMPRESSOR PRODUCTS DIVISION—See Coltec Holdings Inc; *U.S. Public*, pg. 402
FRANCE DIV.—See Berkshire Hathaway Inc.; *U.S. Public*, pg. 217
FRANCE GLACES-FINDUS S.A.—See Nestle S.A.; *Int'l*, pg. 920
FRANCE JARDINERIES—See Castorama Dubois Investissements S.C.A.; *Int'l*, pg. 276
FRANCE LOISIRS—See C.E.P. Communication Group; *Int'l*, pg. 239
FRANCE MANCHE S.A.—See The Eurotunnel Group; *Int'l*, pg. 466
FRANCE QUICK—See GIB Group; *Int'l*, pg. 534
FRANCE ST.-YORRE—See Nestle S.A.; *Int'l*, pg. 919
FRANCE TELECOM; *Int'l*, pg. 503
FRANCE TELECOM INC.—See France Telecom; *Int'l*, pg. 504
FRANCE TRANSFO—See Jeumont-Schneider Trentormeteurs; *Int'l*, pg. 706
FRANCESCO CINZANO & C.IA SPA—See Diageo Plc; *Int'l*, pg. 409
FRANCESCO PARISI GES.M.B.H.—See Francesco Parisi S.p.A.; *Int'l*, pg. 504
FRANCESCO PARISI G.M.B.H.—See Francesco Parisi S.p.A.; *Int'l*, pg. 504
FRANCESCO PARISI S.A.G.L.—See Francesco Parisi S.p.A.; *Int'l*, pg. 504
FRANCESCO PARISI S.P.A.; *Int'l*, pg. 504
FRANCHISE FINANCE CORP. OF AMERICA; *U.S. Public*, pg. 679
FRANCHISE MORTGAGE ACCEPTANCE COMPANY—See Imperial Credit Industries, Inc.; *U.S. Public*, pg. 872
FRANCHISE SERVICES, INC.; *U.S. Private*, pg. 423
FRANCIA-LOTUS S.A.—See Fort James Corporation; *U.S. Public*, pg. 672
FRANCO-BELGE DE FABRICATION DE COMBUSTIBLES (FBFC)—See COGEMA - Compagnie Generale des Matieres Nucleaires; *Int'l*, pg. 305
FRANCO-PACIFIC VIETNAM CO., LTD.—See Credit Commercial de France; *Int'l*, pg. 343
FRANCOMET S.A.—See CODELCO Chile (Corporacion Nacional del Cobre De Chile); *Int'l*, pg. 303
FRANCON-LAFARGE—See Lafarge S.A.; *Int'l*, pg. 791
FRANCORAIL—See Jeumont-Schneider Trenformeteurs; *Int'l*, pg. 706
FRANCOSTEEL CORPORATION—See Groupe Usinor; *Int'l*, pg. 572
FRANDISCO LIFE INSURANCE CO.—See First Franklin Financial Corp.; *U.S. Private*, pg. 407
FRANDISCO PROPERTY & CASUALTY INSURANCE—See First Franklin Financial Corp.; *U.S. Private*, pg. 407
MARTY FRANICH AUTO CENTER; *U.S. Private*, pg. 423
FRANK & SCHULTE GMBH—See Veba AG; *Int'l*, pg. 1458
FRANK CONSOLIDATED ENTERPRISES INC.; *U.S. Private*, pg. 423
FRANK FAIR INDUSTRIES LTD.—See Consorcio G. Grupo Dina, S.A. de C.V.; *Int'l*, pg. 326
FRANK INDUSTRIES, INC.; *U.S. Private*, pg. 423
FRANK IX & SONS, INC.; *U.S. Private*, pg. 423
FRANK IX & SONS, INC.—See Frank Ix & Sons, Inc.; *U.S. Private*, pg. 423
FRANK PAXTON LUMBER COMPANY—See Jeld-Wen, Inc.; *U.S. Private*, pg. 585
S.M. FRANK & CO., INC.; *U.S. Private*, pg. 423
FRANK SMYTHSON INC.—See John Menzies plc; *Int'l*, pg. 707
FRANKE GMBH—See Delft Instruments N.V.; *Int'l*, pg. 389

HANS FRANKE NE-METALLHANDEL GMBH—See Fried. Krupp AG; *Int'l*, pg. 514
FRANKE SYSTEMTECHNIK GMBH—See Delft Instruments N.V.; *Int'l*, pg. 389
FRANKEL & COMPANY; *U.S. Private*, pg. 424
FRANKEL & COMPANY—See Frankel & Company; *U.S. Private*, pg. 424
FRANKEL METAL COMPANY—See Metallurg, Inc.; *U.S. Private*, pg. 735
FRANKEN ROHSTOFF GMBH—See Fried. Krupp AG; *Int'l*, pg. 513
FRANKEN WKV BANK GMBH—See Bayerische Vereinsbank Group; *Int'l*, pg. 179
FRANKFORD ABSTRACT CO.—See Keystone Financial Inc.; *U.S. Public*, pg. 956
FRANKFURT BALKIND PARTNERS; *U.S. Private*, pg. 424
FRANKFURT BALKIND PARTNERS—See Frankfurt Balkind Partners; *U.S. Private*, pg. 424
FRANKFURT CONSULT GMBH—See BHF-BANK AG; *Int'l*, pg. 119
FRANKFURT-TRUST INVESTMENT GMBH—See BHF-BANK AG; *Int'l*, pg. 119
FRANKFURTER HANDMANDLUNG GMBH—See Swiss Bank Corporation; *Int'l*, pg. 1330
FRANKFURTER SPARKASSE; *Int'l*, pg. 504
FRANKFURTER VERSICHERUNGS-AG—See Allianz Aktiengesellschaft; *Int'l*, pg. 58
FRANKI GRUNDBAU GMBH—See Philipp Holzmann AG; *Int'l*, pg. 632
FRANKLIN ADVISERS, INC.—See Franklin Resources, Inc.; *U.S. Public*, pg. 680
FRANKLIN BAKING CO., INC.; *U.S. Public*, pg. 424
FRANKLIN BANK—See Franklin Resources, Inc.; *U.S. Public*, pg. 680
FRANKLIN BRINE TREATMENT CORPORATION—See Cabot Oil & Gas Corporation; *U.S. Public*, pg. 289
FRANKLIN BRUSH DIVISION—See Crown Cork & Seal Company, Inc.; *U.S. Public*, pg. 463
FRANKLIN-BURLINGTON PLASTICS—See Spartech Corporation; *U.S. Public*, pg. 1496
FRANKLIN COAL—See Zeigler Coal Holding Company; *U.S. Public*, pg. 1790
FRANKLIN COVEY; *U.S. Public*, pg. 679
FRANKLIN ELECTRIC CO., INC.; *U.S. Public*, pg. 679
FRANKLIN ELECTRIC EUROPA, GMBH—See Franklin Electric Co., Inc.; *U.S. Public*, pg. 679
FRANKLIN ELECTRIC SOUTH AFRICA—See Franklin Electric Co., Inc.; *U.S. Public*, pg. 679
FRANKLIN ELECTRONIC PUBLISHERS, INC.; *U.S. Public*, pg. 679
FRANKLIN FIRST SAVINGS BANK—See First Empire State Corporation; *U.S. Public*, pg. 632
FRANKLIN HOUSE HEALTHCARE—See Vencor, Inc.; *U.S. Public*, pg. 1712
THE FRANKLIN INSTITUTE; *U.S. Private*, pg. 424
FRANKLIN-LAMOILLE BANK—See Banknorth Group Inc.; *U.S. Public*, pg. 187
THE FRANKLIN LIFE INSURANCE COMPANY—See American General Corporation; *U.S. Public*, pg. 76
THE FRANKLIN MINT—See Roll International Corporation; *U.S. Private*, pg. 941
FRANKLIN OIL CORP.—See Morgan Crucible Co. Plc; *Int'l*, pg. 892
FRANKLIN PARK MALL, INC.—See The Rouse Company; *U.S. Public*, pg. 1408
FRANKLIN PLANT, BELDEN DIVISION—See Belden Inc.; *U.S. Public*, pg. 201
FRANKLIN PORTFOLIO ASSOCIATES TRUST—See Mellon Bank Corporation; *U.S. Public*, pg. 1085
FRANKLIN PRESS—See Continental Graphics Holdings, Inc.; *U.S. Private*, pg. 268
FRANKLIN PROPERTIES, INC.—See Franklin Resources, Inc.; *U.S. Public*, pg. 680
FRANKLIN PROPERTY CO.—See Saul Centers Inc.; *U.S. Public*, pg. 1435
FRANKLIN REAL ESTATE CO.—See American Electric Power Company, Inc.; *U.S. Public*, pg. 72
FRANKLIN RESOURCES, INC.; *U.S. Public*, pg. 679
FRANKLIN RIVER DIVISION—See MacMillan Bloedel Limited; *Int'l*, pg. 828
FRANKLIN SHOE CO.—See Shaer Shoe Corporation; *U.S. Private*, pg. 988
FRANKLIN SPORTS, INC.; *U.S. Private*, pg. 424
FRANKLIN/TEMPLETON DISTRIBUTORS, INC.—See Franklin Resources, Inc.; *U.S. Public*, pg. 680
FRANKLIN TEMPLETON INVESTOR SERVICES, INC.— See Franklin Resources, Inc.; *U.S. Public*, pg. 680
FRANKLIN TEMPLETON TRUST COMPANY—See Franklin Resources, Inc.; *U.S. Public*, pg. 680
FRANKLINS HOLDINGS LTD.—See Jardine Matheson Holdings Limited; *Int'l*, pg. 703
FRANKLINS LIMITED—See Jardine Matheson Holdings Limited; *Int'l*, pg. 703
LYNNE FRANKS LTD.—See BDDP Group; *Int'l*, pg. 117
FRANK'S NURSERY & CRAFTS, INC.—See General Host Corporation; *U.S. Public*, pg. 715
FRANKULIN TOOL & MFG. CO.—See Wrought Washer Mfg., Inc.; *U.S. Public*, pg. 1192
FRANSABANK (FRANCE) S.A.—See Credit Agricole; *Int'l*, pg. 341
FRANSEN TRANSPORT B.V.—See Royal Nedlloyd Group N.V.; *Int'l*, pg. 1144
FRANSHIN COMPANY LTD.—See Sinochem International Petroleum Co. Ltd.; *Int'l*, pg. 1255
FRANTOUR GROUP—See SNCF; *Int'l*, pg. 1165
FRANZ BAKERY—See United States Bakery; *U.S. Private*, pg. 1124
FRANZ KASSECKER GMBH—See Bilfinger + Berger Bauaktiengesellschaft; *Int'l*, pg. 195
FRANZ POHL METALL- UND KUNSTSTOFFWARENFABRIK GMBH—See Freudenberg & Company; *Int'l*, pg. 506
FRANZ SEATTLE—See United States Bakery; *U.S. Private*, pg. 1124

FRANZIA BROTHERS WINERY—See The Wine Group; *U.S. Private*, pg. 1183
A.W. FRASER—See McKechnie PLC; *Int'l*, pg. 852
FRASER PAPERS, INC.—See EdperBrascan Corporation; *Int'l*, pg. 434
FRASER VALLEY FOREST INC.—See Premdor Inc.; *Int'l*, pg. 1067
FRASER VALLEY FOREST PRODUCTS LIMITED—See Premdor Inc.; *Int'l*, pg. 1067
FRASER VALLEY FOREST PRODUCTS LIMITED-FLUSH DOOR PLANT—See Premdor Inc.; *Int'l*, pg. 1067
FRAZEE INDUSTRIES INC.—See Williams Holdings Plc; *Int'l*, pg. 1501
FRAZER & JONES DIV.—See The Eastern Company; *U.S. Public*, pg. 548
S.A. FRECOLUX—See Cockerill Sambre; *Int'l*, pg. 302
FRED PERRY SPORTSWEAR LTD.—See Hit Union Company Ltd.; *Int'l*, pg. 620
FRED S.A.—See LVMH Moet Hennessy Louis Vuitton; *Int'l*, pg. 780
FRED WEBER, INC.; *U.S. Private*, pg. 424
FREDERIC PRINTING COMPANY—See Consolidated Graphics, Inc.; *U.S. Private*, pg. 265
FREDERICK & VALENZUELA/TBWA—See TBWA Chiat/ Day; *U.S. Private*, pg. 1062
FREDERICK GAS CO., INC.—See Washington Gas Light Co.; *U.S. Public*, pg. 1740
FREDERICK MANUFACTURING CO.—See SFA, Inc.; *U.S. Private*, pg. 956
FREDERICK MANUFACTURING CORPORATION—See Blount International, Inc.; *U.S. Public*, pg. 238
FREDERICK TRADING COMPANY—See Distribution America; *U.S. Private*, pg. 335
FREDERICK'S OF HOLLYWOOD, INC.; *U.S. Private*, pg. 424
FREDERICKTOWN BANK & TRUST CO.—See Mercantile Bankshares Corporation; *U.S. Public*, pg. 1089
FREDERICTON BUSINESS PARK LTD.—See Bruncor, Inc.; *Int'l*, pg. 230
FREDESTEIN BANDEN; *Int'l*, pg. 504
FREDONIA SEED CO.—See Novartis AG; *Int'l*, pg. 974
FRED'S INC.; *U.S. Public*, pg. 680
THE FREE LANCE-STAR PUBLISHING CO.; *U.S. Private*, pg. 424
THE FREE PRESS—See National Amusements, Inc.; *U.S. Private*, pg. 777
FREE SERVICE TIRE COMPANY, INC.; *U.S. Private*, pg. 425
FREE TIME—See GIB Group; *Int'l*, pg. 534
S. FREEDMAN & SONS, INC.; *U.S. Private*, pg. 425
FREEDOM CHEMICAL COMPANY; *U.S. Private*, pg. 425
FREEDOM COMMUNICATION INC.; *U.S. Private*, pg. 425
FREEDOM FORGE CORPORATION; *U.S. Private*, pg. 425
FREEDOM INVESTMENT—See Fahnestock Viner Holdings Inc.; *Int'l*, pg. 476
FREEDOM TEXTILES CHEMICALS CO.—See Freedom Chemical Company; *U.S. Private*, pg. 425
FREEDOM VALU CENTERS, INC.—See Erickson Oil Products, Inc.; *U.S. Private*, pg. 381
FREEMAN ASSOCIATES, INC.; *U.S. Private*, pg. 425
CARL M. FREEMAN ASSOCIATES, INC.; *U.S. Private*, pg. 426
CLIFF FREEMAN & PARTNERS—See Saatchi & Saatchi Advertising Worldwide; *U.S. Public*, pg. 1422
FREEMAN COSMETIC CORP.; *U.S. Private*, pg. 426
FREEMAN DECORATING CO.; *U.S. Private*, pg. 426
FREEMAN DISTRIBUTION LTD.—See DSM N.V.; *Int'l*, pg. 355
FREEMAN ENERGY CORPORATION—See General Dynamics Corporation; *U.S. Public*, pg. 709
FREEMAN EXHIBIT CO.—See Freeman Decorating Co.; *U.S. Private*, pg. 426
H. FREEMAN & SON, INC.; *U.S. Private*, pg. 426
J.R. FREEMAN & SON LIMITED—See Gallaher Limited; *Int'l*, pg. 539
FREEMAN MANUFACTURING & SUPPLY COMPANY; *U.S. Private*, pg. 426
FREEMAN PRODUCTS—See Trophy Holdings Inc.; *U.S. Private*, pg. 1105
W.H. FREEMAN & CO.—See Georg von Holtzbrinck GmbH; *Int'l*, pg. 1479
WILLIAM FREEMAN LIMITED—See Arnotts plc; *Int'l*, pg. 81
FREEPORT-MCMORAN COPPER & GOLD, INC.— See Freeport-McMoRan Inc.; *U.S. Public*, pg. 680
FREEPORT-MCMORAN INC.; *U.S. Public*, pg. 680
FREEPORT-MCMORAN RESOURCE PARTNERS, LTD.— See Freeport-McMoRan Inc.; *U.S. Public*, pg. 681
FREESIA—See Dairy Vale Co-op. Ltd.; *Int'l*, pg. 372
FREEWAY CORPORATION; *U.S. Private*, pg. 426
FREEWAY ROCKFORD—See Freeway Corporation; *U.S. Private*, pg. 426
FREEZER QUEEN FOODS INC.—See James Crean PLC; *Int'l*, pg. 340
FREGA VERMOGENSVERWALTUNGS GMBH—See Commerzbank AG; *Int'l*, pg. 310
FREIHER CONSTRUCTION COMPANY, INC.; *U.S. Private*, pg. 426
FREIGHT-TRANS INTERNATIONAL CO., LTD.—See Jardine Matheson Holdings Limited; *Int'l*, pg. 704
FREIGHTLINER CORP.—See Daimler-Benz Aktiengesellschaft; *Int'l*, pg. 368
FREIGHTLINER ENTERPRISE CORP.—See Daimler-Benz Aktiengesellschaft; *Int'l*, pg. 368
FREIGHTLINER OF CANADA, LTD.—See Daimler-Benz Aktiengesellschaft; *Int'l*, pg. 368
FREIGHTLINER TRUCK MFG. PLANT—See Daimler-Benz Aktiengesellschaft; *Int'l*, pg. 368
FREINRAIL S.A.—See Knorr-Bremse AG; *Int'l*, pg. 738
FREIOS KNORR SISTEMAS FERROVIARIAS LDTA.— See Knorr-Bremse AG; *Int'l*, pg. 738
FREIOS VARGA S/A—See LucasVarity plc; *Int'l*, pg. 820
THE FREMONT CO.; *U.S. Private*, pg. 426

FREMONT COUNTY TITLE COMPANY—See The First American Financial Corporation; *U.S. Public,* pg. 626
FREMONT DIVISION—See R.R. Donnelley & Sons Company; *U.S. Public,* pg. 518
FREMONT FINANCIAL CORPORATION—See Fremont General Corporation; *U.S. Public,* pg. 681
FREMONT GENERAL CORPORATION; *U.S. Public,* pg. 681
THE FREMONT GROUP; *U.S. Private,* pg. 427
FREMONT INDEMNITY CO./MEDICAL PROFESSIONAL LIAB. DIV.—See Fremont General Corporation; *U.S. Public,* pg. 681
FREMONT INDEMNITY CORP.—See Fremont General Corporation; *U.S. Public,* pg. 681
FREMONT INVESTMENT & LOAN—See Fremont General Corporation; *U.S. Public,* pg. 681
FREMONT LIFE INSURANCE CO.—See Fremont General Corporation; *U.S. Public,* pg. 681
FREMONT MANNOR NURSING & CONVALESCENT HOME—See Vencor, Inc.; *U.S. Public,* pg. 1712
FREMONT MFG.—See The Oilgear Company; *U.S. Public,* pg. 1215
FREMONT MFG. DIV.—See Simpson Industries, Inc.; *U.S. Public,* pg. 1475
FREMONT NEWS-MESSENGER—See Gannett Company, Inc.; *U.S. Public,* pg. 700
FREMONT PREMIUM FINANCE CORP.—See Fremont General Corporation; *U.S. Public,* pg. 681
FRENCH & BEAN—See Associated Grocers of New England, Inc.; *U.S. Private,* pg. 91
FRENCH DIVISION—See Computer Sciences Corporation; *U.S. Public,* pg. 423
FRENCH FRAGRANCES, INC.; *U.S. Public,* pg. 681
I.H. FRENCH & CO. INC.; *U.S. Private,* pg. 427
FRENCH LICK FURNITURE—See Kimball International, Inc.; *U.S. Public,* pg. 957
FRENCH RAILWAYS LTD.—See SNCF; *Int'l,* pg. 1165
FRENCKEN DE BRUYN B.V.—See DSM N.V.; *Int'l,* pg. 354
FRENOS LUSAC S.A. DE C.V.—See Echlin Inc.; *U.S. Public,* pg. 561
FRENSISTEMI S.R.L.—See Knorr-Bremse AG; *Int'l,* pg. 738
FREQUENCE PLUS—See Groupe Air France; *Int'l,* pg. 560
FREQUENCY AND TIME SYSTEMS, INC.—See Datum Inc.; *U.S. Public,* pg. 488
FREQUENCY ELECTRONICS, INC.; *U.S. Public,* pg. 681
FREQUENCY ENGINEERING LABORATORIES; *U.S. Private,* pg. 427
FRERE-BOURGEOIS UK LTD—See Cockerill Sambre; *Int'l,* pg. 302
FRESARD COMPOSANTS S.A.—See SMH Swiss Corporation for Micro Electronics & Watchmaking Indus. Ltd.; *Int'l,* pg. 1161
JIM FRESARD PONTIAC BUICK, INC.; *U.S. Private,* pg. 427
FRESE & WOLFF WERBEAGENTUR—See DMB&B Communications; *U.S. Private,* pg. 304
FRESENIUS AG; *Int'l,* pg. 505
FRESENIUS MEDICAL CARE, INC.—See Fresenius AG; *Int'l,* pg. 505
FRESH AMERICA CORP.; *U.S. Public,* pg. 681
FRESH CHOICE, INC.; *U.S. Public,* pg. 682
FRESH FOOD, INC.; *U.S. Private,* pg. 427
FRESH JUICE COMPANY; *U.S. Private,* pg. 427
FRESH-LINE DISTRIBUTORS, INC.—See Bozzuto's Inc.; *U.S. Public,* pg. 249
FRESH MARK, INC.; *U.S. Private,* pg. 427
FRESH MATSUYA CO., LTD.—See Matsuya Company Ltd.; *Int'l,* pg. 848
FRESH SKYLARK CO., LTD.—See Skylark Co., Ltd.; *Int'l,* pg. 1262
FRESH WESTERN INTERNATIONAL—See The Albert Fisher Group PLC; *Int'l,* pg. 491
FRESH WORLD—See Empressa La Moderna SA de CV; *Int'l,* pg. 454
FRESINBRA INDUS. S.A.—See American Standard Inc.; *U.S. Public,* pg. 92
FRESNO AUTO DEALERS AUCTION—See Cox Enterprises, Inc.; *U.S. Private,* pg. 282
THE FRESNO BEE—See McClatchy Newspapers Inc.; *U.S. Public,* pg. 1065
SARL ROBERT FRET—See Cockerill Sambre; *Int'l,* pg. 302
FREUDENBERG A.B.—See Freudenberg & Company; *Int'l,* pg. 506
FREUDENBERG & COMPANY; *Int'l,* pg. 505
FREUDENBERG & VILENE INT. LTD.—See Freudenberg & Company; *Int'l,* pg. 507
FREUDENBERG ANGUS LP—See Freudenberg & Company; *Int'l,* pg. 505
FREUDENBERG ANLAGEN-UND WERKZEUGTECHNIK KG—See Freudenberg & Company; *Int'l,* pg. 505
FREUDENBERG A/S—See Freudenberg & Company; *Int'l,* pg. 506
FREUDENBERG BETEILIGUNGSGESELLSCHAFT MBH—See Freudenberg & Company; *Int'l,* pg. 506
FREUDENBERG BUILDING SYSTEMS A.S.—See Freudenberg & Company; *Int'l,* pg. 506
FREUDENBERG BUILDING SYSTEMS INC.—See Freudenberg & Company; *Int'l,* pg. 506
CARL FREUDENBERG—See Freudenberg & Company; *Int'l,* pg. 505
CARL FREUDENBERG GMBH—See Freudenberg & Company; *Int'l,* pg. 506
CARL FREUDENBERG WOHNBAUHILFE GMBH—See Freudenberg & Company; *Int'l,* pg. 506
FREUDENBERG COMPONENTES LTDA.—See Freudenberg & Company; *Int'l,* pg. 505
FREUDENBERG DANMARK A.S.—See Freudenberg & Company; *Int'l,* pg. 506
FREUDENBERG DICHTUNGS- UND SCHWINGUNGSTECHNIK GMBH—See Freudenberg & Company; *Int'l,* pg. 505
FREUDENBERG ENGINEERING LTD.—See Freudenberg & Company; *Int'l,* pg. 505

FREUDENBERG ESPANA S.A.—See Freudenberg & Company; *Int'l,* pg. 507
FREUDENBERG FAR EASTERN SPUNWEB COMP. LTD.—See Freudenberg & Company; *Int'l,* pg. 505
FREUDENBERG HAUSHALTSPRODUKTE AUGSBURG GMBH & CO, KG—See Freudenberg & Company; *Int'l,* pg. 505
FREUDENBERG HAUSHALTSPRODUKTE KG—See Freudenberg & Company; *Int'l,* pg. 506
FREUDENBERG HAUSHALTSPRODUKTE SCS—See Freudenberg & Company; *Int'l,* pg. 507
FREUDENBERG HAUSHALTSPRODUKTE VERWALTUNGS-BMBH—See Freudenberg & Company; *Int'l,* pg. 506
FREUDENBERG HOLDINGS LTD.—See Freudenberg & Company; *Int'l,* pg. 507
FREUDENBERG HOUSEHOLD PRODUCTS EVICI KULLANIM ARAGLARI TICARET A.S.—See Freudenberg & Company; *Int'l,* pg. 506
FREUDENBERG HOUSEHOLD PRODUCTS LP—See Freudenberg & Company; *Int'l,* pg. 505
FREUDENBERG IBERICA S.A.—See Freudenberg & Company; *Int'l,* pg. 505
FREUDENBERG IBERICA S.A., S.EN C.—See Freudenberg & Company; *Int'l,* pg. 506
FREUDENBERG LIMITED—See Freudenberg & Company; *Int'l,* pg. 507
FREUDENBERG LM PLAST S.A.S.—See Freudenberg & Company; *Int'l,* pg. 506
FREUDENBERG LP—See Freudenberg & Company; *Int'l,* pg. 506
FREUDENBERG NAO TECIDOS LTDA.—See Freudenberg & Company; *Int'l,* pg. 507
FREUDENBERG NAO-TECIDOS LTDA. & CIA.—See Freudenberg & Company; *Int'l,* pg. 505
FREUDENBERG NH CO. LTD.—See Freudenberg & Company; *Int'l,* pg. 507
FREUDENBERG-NOK; *U.S. Private,* pg. 427
FREUDENBERG NOK—See Freudenberg & Company; *Int'l,* pg. 507
FREUDENBERG NONWOVENS—See Freudenberg & Company; *Int'l,* pg. 507
FREUDENBERG NONWOVENS INC.—See Freudenberg & Company; *Int'l,* pg. 507
FREUDENBERG NONWOVENS LTD.—See Freudenberg & Company; *Int'l,* pg. 507
FREUDENBERG NONWOVENS LIMITED PARTNERSHIP—See Freudenberg & Company; *Int'l,* pg. 505
FREUDENBERG NONWOVENS (PTY.) LTD.—See Freudenberg & Company; *Int'l,* pg. 505
FREUDENBERG NORTH AMERICA LIMITED PARTNERSHIP—See Freudenberg & Company; *Int'l,* pg. 507
FREUDENBERG OY—See Freudenberg & Company; *Int'l,* pg. 506
FREUDENBERG PELLON CORPORATION—See Freudenberg & Company; *Int'l,* pg. 507
FREUDENBERG PROPERTIES AND SERVICES LTD.—See Freudenberg & Company; *Int'l,* pg. 507
FREUDENBERG PTY. LTD.—See Freudenberg & Company; *Int'l,* pg. 506
FREUDENBERG S.A.—See Freudenberg & Company; *Int'l,* pg. 505
FREUDENBERG S.A. TELAS SIN TEJER—See Freudenberg & Company; *Int'l,* pg. 505
FREUDENBERG SIMRIT A.B.—See Freudenberg & Company; *Int'l,* pg. 506
FREUDENBERG SIMRIT AG—See Freudenberg & Company; *Int'l,* pg. 506
FREUDENBERG SIMRIT A.S.—See Freudenberg & Company; *Int'l,* pg. 506
FREUDENBERG SIMRIT B.V.—See Freudenberg & Company; *Int'l,* pg. 506
FREUDENBERG SIMRIT KUFSTEIN GES.M.B.H.—See Freudenberg & Company; *Int'l,* pg. 507
FREUDENBERG SIMRIT KUFSTEIN GES.M.B.H. & CO. KG—See Freudenberg & Company; *Int'l,* pg. 506
FREUDENBERG S.P.A.—See Freudenberg & Company; *Int'l,* pg. 506
FREUDENBERG SPUNWEB CO.—See Freudenberg & Company; *Int'l,* pg. 507
FREUDENBERG SPUNWEB S.A.—See Freudenberg & Company; *Int'l,* pg. 505
FREUDENBERG TECHNICAL PRODUCTS LTD.—See Freudenberg & Company; *Int'l,* pg. 507
FREUDENBERG TELAS SIN TEJER S.A.—See Freudenberg & Company; *Int'l,* pg. 505
FREUDENBERG TELAS SIN TEJER S.A. DE C.V.—See Freudenberg & Company; *Int'l,* pg. 507
FREUDENBERG TRADING (HONG KONG) LTD.—See Freudenberg & Company; *Int'l,* pg. 507
FREUDENBERG TRADING PORTUGUESA LDA.—See Freudenberg & Company; *Int'l,* pg. 506
FREUDENBERG VERSICHERUNGSVERMITTLUNGS-GMBH—See Freudenberg & Company; *Int'l,* pg. 506
FREUDENBERG VERTRIEB EINLAGESTOFFE KG—See Freudenberg & Company; *Int'l,* pg. 506
FREUDENBERG VERTRIEBS-KG IN AUSTRIA—See Freudenberg & Company; *Int'l,* pg. 506
FREUDENBERG VILEDA LTD.—See Freudenberg & Company; *Int'l,* pg. 507
FREUDENBERG VILENE SP. Z.O.O.—See Freudenberg & Company; *Int'l,* pg. 506
FREUDENBERG-NOK DE MEXICO—See Freudenberg-NOK; *U.S. Private,* pg. 428
JOHN S. FREY ENTERPRISES; *U.S. Private,* pg. 428
FRIALATOR INTERNATIONAL—See Maytag Corporation; *U.S. Public,* pg. 1065
FRICK COMPANY—See York International Corporation; *U.S. Public,* pg. 1788
FRICKE GMBH & CO. KG—See KM-Europa Metal Aktiengesellschaft; *Int'l,* pg. 719
FRICTION INC.—See Echlin Inc.; *U.S. Public,* pg. 560

FRIDEN ALCATEL—See Alcatel Alsthom Compagnie Generale D'Electricite; *Int'l,* pg. 55
FRIED. KRUPP AG; *Int'l,* pg. 507
FRIEDLAND JACOBS COMMUNICATIONS; *U.S. Private,* pg. 428
FRIEDMAN, EISENSTEIN, RAEMER AND SCHWARTZ, LLP; *U.S. Private,* pg. 428
FRIEDMAN INDUSTRIES, INC.; *U.S. Public,* pg. 682
FRIENDLY CHEVROLET CO. INC.; *U.S. Private,* pg. 428
FRIENDLY HOLIDAYS INC.; *U.S. Private,* pg. 428
FRIENDLY HOLIDAYS INC.-WEST—See Friendly Holidays Inc.; *U.S. Private,* pg. 429
FRIENDLY ICE CREAM CORP.; *U.S. Public,* pg. 682
FRIENDS PROVIDENT—See Eureko B.V.; *Int'l,* pg. 464
FRIENDS PROVIDENT IRELAND—See Eureko B.V.; *Int'l,* pg. 464
FRIENDSHIP DAIRIES, INC.; *U.S. Private,* pg. 429
FRIENDSHIP DAIRIES, INC.—See Friendship Dairies, Inc.; *U.S. Private,* pg. 429
FRIENDSHIP MACOMB SC, INC.—See Giant Food Inc.; *U.S. Public,* pg. 741
FRIENDSWOOD DEVELOPMENT COMPANY—See Lennar Corporation; *U.S. Public,* pg. 988
MICHAEL FRIESS GMBH (SSH)—See Veba AG; *Int'l,* pg. 1459
FRIGID COIL WEST—See York International Corporation; *U.S. Public,* pg. 1789
FRIGIDAIRE COMMERCIAL REFRIGERATION—See Electrolux, AB; *Int'l,* pg. 439
FRIGIDAIRE COMPANY DISHWASHER PRODUCTS—See Electrolux, AB; *Int'l,* pg. 439
FRIGIDAIRE COMPANY RANGE PRODUCTS—See Electrolux, AB; *Int'l,* pg. 439
FRIGIDAIRE HOME PRODUCTS—See Electrolux, AB; *Int'l,* pg. 439
FRIGIDAIRE HOME PRODUCTS-FREEZER PRODUCTS—See Electrolux, AB; *Int'l,* pg. 440
FRIGIDAIRE HOME PRODUCTS-HOME COMFORT PRODUCTS—See Electrolux, AB; *Int'l,* pg. 440
FRIGIDAIRE HOME PRODUCTS-LAUNDRY PRODUCTS—See Electrolux, AB; *Int'l,* pg. 440
FRIGIDAIRE HOME PRODUCTS-REFRIGERATOR PRODUCTS—See Electrolux, AB; *Int'l,* pg. 440
FRIGIDAIRE HOME PRODUCTS-SPECIALTY POWER EQUIPMENT—See Electrolux, AB; *Int'l,* pg. 440
FRIGO S.A.—See Unilever Plc; *Int'l,* pg. 1437
FRIGOBRAS COMPANHIA BRASILEIRA DE FRIGORIFICOS—See Sadia Group; *Int'l,* pg. 1168
FRIGOREX AG FUR KALTETECHNIK—See Sulzer Ltd.; *Int'l,* pg. 1306
FRIGORIFERI DI TAVAZZANO S.P.A.—See FMC Corporation; *U.S. Public,* pg. 606
FRIGOSCANDIA AB—See FMC Corporation; *U.S. Public,* pg. 606
FRIGOSCANDIA A/S—See FMC Corporation; *U.S. Public,* pg. 606
FRIGOSCANDIA FOOD PROCESS SYSTEMS AB—See FMC Corporation; *U.S. Public,* pg. 606
FRIGOSCANDIA FOOD PROCESS SYSTEMS AB, JAPAN BRANCH—See FMC Corporation; *U.S. Public,* pg. 606
FRIGOSCANDIA FOOD PROCESS SYSTEMS GMBH—See FMC Corporation; *U.S. Public,* pg. 606
FRIGOSCANDIA FOOD PROCESS SYSTEMS INC.—See FMC Corporation; *U.S. Public,* pg. 607
FRIGOSCANDIA FOOD PROCESS SYSTEMS INTERNATIONAL AB—See FMC Corporation; *U.S. Public,* pg. 607
FRIGOSCANDIA FOOD PROCESS SYSTEMS LTD.—See FMC Corporation; *U.S. Public,* pg. 607
FRIGOSCANDIA FOOD PROCESS SYSTEMS PTY LTD—See FMC Corporation; *U.S. Public,* pg. 607
FRIGOSCANDIA FOOD PROCESS SYSTEMS S.A.—See FMC Corporation; *U.S. Public,* pg. 607
FRIGOSCANDIA FOOD PROCESS SYSTEMS S.R.L.—See FMC Corporation; *U.S. Public,* pg. 607
FRIGOSCANDIA GMBH—See FMC Corporation; *U.S. Public,* pg. 607
FRIGOSCANDIA LTD.—See FMC Corporation; *U.S. Public,* pg. 607
FRIGOSCANDIA NORTH AMERICA INC.—See FMC Corporation; *U.S. Public,* pg. 606
FRIGOSCANDIA SVENSKA AB—See FMC Corporation; *U.S. Public,* pg. 606
FRIGOSCANDIA TRANSPORT B.V.—See FMC Corporation; *U.S. Public,* pg. 607
FRIGOSCANDIA WINNER FOOD PROCESS SYSTEMS PVT LTD—See FMC Corporation; *U.S. Public,* pg. 607
FRIGUIA—See Pechiney S.A.; *Int'l,* pg. 1030
LEWIS FRIMEL—See Donnkenny, Inc.; *U.S. Public,* pg. 519
FRIMONT, S.P.A.—See Scotsman Industries, Inc.; *U.S. Public,* pg. 1445
FRIONA AGRICULTURE CREDIT CORP.—See Friona Industries, L.P.; *U.S. Private,* pg. 429
FRIONA FEED YARD—See Friona Industries, L.P.; *U.S. Private,* pg. 429
FRIONA INDUSTRIES, L.P.; *U.S. Private,* pg. 429
FRIONOR A/S; *Int'l,* pg. 516
FRIONOR ASIA PACIFIC PTE. LTD.—See Frionor A/S; *Int'l,* pg. 516
FRIONOR C.R. A.S.—See Frionor A/S; *Int'l,* pg. 516
FRIONOR DANMARK A/S—See Frionor A/S; *Int'l,* pg. 516
FRIONOR FABRIKKER A/S—See Frionor A/S; *Int'l,* pg. 516
FRIONOR FRANCE SARL—See Frionor A/S; *Int'l,* pg. 516
FRIPPIAT S.A.—See Etablissements Delhaize Freres Et Cie "Le Lion" S.A.; *Int'l,* pg. 463
FRISBY P.M.C. INCORPORATED—See Intermet Corporation; *U.S. Public,* pg. 894
FRISCH-BETON AEGIDIENBERG GMBH & CO. KG—See Dyckerhoff AG; *Int'l,* pg. 422
FRISCH FLORIDA, INC.—See Frisch's Restaurants, Inc.; *U.S. Public,* pg. 682
FRISCH GERMANTOWN ROAD, INC.—See Frisch's Restaurants, Inc.; *U.S. Public,* pg. 682

FRISCH INDIANA, INC.—See Frisch's Restaurants, Inc.; U.S. Public, pg. 682
FRISCH KENTUCKY, INC.—See Frisch's Restaurants, Inc.; U.S. Public, pg. 682
FRISCH OHIO, INC.—See Frisch's Restaurants, Inc.; U.S. Public, pg. 682
FRISCHMUTH & FREITAG GMBH—See Rothenberger Group GmbH; Int'l, pg. 1128
FRISCH'S RESTAURANTS, INC.; U.S. Public, pg. 682
FRISCO-FINDUS AG—See Nestle S.A.; Int'l, pg. 916
FRISKIES PET CARE PTY. LTD.—See Nestle S.A.; Int'l, pg. 920
FRISKIES PETCARE DIV.—See Nestle S.A.; Int'l, pg. 917
FRISKIES SERVICE MERCHANDISING—See Nestle S.A.; Int'l, pg. 920
FRISMAT AG—See Nestle S.A.; Int'l, pg. 916
FRIT DIVISION—See Ferro Corporation; U.S. Public, pg. 619
FRITO-LAY COMPANY—See PepsiCo, Inc.; U.S. Public, pg. 1277
FRITO-LAY FINANCE N.V.—See PepsiCo, Inc.; U.S. Public, pg. 1277
FRITZ AIR FREIGHT—See Fritz Companies, Inc.; U.S. Public, pg. 683
FRITZ CO. INC.; U.S. Private, pg. 429
FRITZ COMPANIES, INC.; U.S. Public, pg. 683
FRITZ CULVER, INC.—See Halter Marine Group, Inc.; U.S. Public, pg. 778
FRITZ INDUSTRIES INC.; U.S. Private, pg. 429
PHILIP FRITZE & SONS, INC.; U.S. Private, pg. 429
FRITZI OF CALIFORNIA MANUFACTURING CORP.; U.S. Private, pg. 429
FRIUL-VENEZIA GIULIA ASSICURAZIONI—See Assicurazioni Generali S.p.A.; Int'l, pg. 90
FROG SWITCH & MANUFACTURING COMPANY; U.S. Private, pg. 429
CARL FROH GMBH & CO.—See Rautaruukki Oy; Int'l, pg. 1088
JOSEPH FROHLEN PAPIERGROSSHANDLUNG GMBH—See N.V. Koninklijke KNP BT; Int'l, pg. 757
FROLIC FOOTWEAR DIV.—See Wolverine World Wide, Inc.; U.S. Public, pg. 1775
FROMAGERIE DES CHAUMES S.A.—See Bongrain S.A.; Int'l, pg. 201
FROMAGERIE PERRAULT S.A.—See Bongrain S.A.; Int'l, pg. 201
FROMAGERIE RAMBOL S.A.—See Bongrain S.A.; Int'l, pg. 201
FROMARSAC SARL—See Bongrain S.A.; Int'l, pg. 201
FROMM, MAYER-BASS GMBH—See Viag AG; Int'l, pg. 1464
FROMMELT INDUSTRIES—See Rite-Hite Corporation; U.S. Private, pg. 933
FRONAPE—See Petrobras - Petroleo Brasileiro S.A.; Int'l, pg. 1043
FRONT ROYAL, INC.; U.S. Private, pg. 430
FRONT ROYAL INSURANCE COMPANY—See Front Royal, Inc.; U.S. Private, pg. 430
FRONTEC CORPORATION—See ATCO Group Co.; Int'l, pg. 95
FRONTEC LOGISTICS CORPORATION—See ATCO Group Co.; Int'l, pg. 95
FRONTEL COMMUNICATIONS SERVICES—See Frontier Corporation; U.S. Public, pg. 684
FRONTIER CELLULAR—See Frontier Corporation; U.S. Public, pg. 683
FRONTIER COMMUNICATION OF LAMAR COUNTY, INC.—See Frontier Corporation; U.S. Public, pg. 683
FRONTIER COMMUNICATIONS-LAKESHORE, INC.—See Frontier Corporation; U.S. Public, pg. 683
FRONTIER COMMUNICATIONS-LAKESIDE, INC.—See Frontier Corporation; U.S. Public, pg. 683
FRONTIER COMMUNICATIONS-LAKEWOOD, INC.—See Frontier Corporation; U.S. Public, pg. 683
FRONTIER COMMUNICATIONS-MIDLAND, INC.—See Frontier Corporation; U.S. Public, pg. 683
FRONTIER COMMUNICATIONS NORTH CENTRAL, INC.—See Frontier Corporation; U.S. Public, pg. 683
FRONTIER COMMUNICATIONS OF ALABAMA, INC.—See Frontier Corporation; U.S. Public, pg. 683
FRONTIER COMMUNICATIONS OF AUSABLE VALLEY—See Frontier Corporation; U.S. Public, pg. 683
FRONTIER COMMUNICATIONS OF BREEZEWOOD, INC.—See Frontier Corporation; U.S. Public, pg. 683
FRONTIER COMMUNICATIONS OF CANTON, INC.—See Frontier Corporation; U.S. Public, pg. 683
FRONTIER COMMUNICATIONS OF DEPUE, INC.—See Frontier Corporation; U.S. Public, pg. 683
FRONTIER COMMUNICATIONS OF FAIRMOUNT, INC.—See Frontier Corporation; U.S. Public, pg. 683
FRONTIER COMMUNICATIONS OF GEORGIA, INC.—See Frontier Corporation; U.S. Public, pg. 683
FRONTIER COMMUNICATIONS OF ILLINOIS, INC.—See Frontier Corporation; U.S. Public, pg. 683
FRONTIER COMMUNICATIONS OF INDIANA, INC.—See Frontier Corporation; U.S. Public, pg. 683
FRONTIER COMMUNICATIONS OF IOWA, INC.—See Frontier Corporation; U.S. Public, pg. 683
FRONTIER COMMUNICATIONS OF MICHIGAN, INC.—See Frontier Corporation; U.S. Public, pg. 683
FRONTIER COMMUNICATIONS OF MINNESOTA, INC.—See Frontier Corporation; U.S. Public, pg. 684
FRONTIER COMMUNICATIONS OF MISSISSIPPI, INC.—See Frontier Corporation; U.S. Public, pg. 684
FRONTIER COMMUNICATIONS OF MONDOVI, INC.—See Frontier Corporation; U.S. Public, pg. 684
FRONTIER COMMUNICATIONS OF MT. PULASKI, INC.—See Frontier Corporation; U.S. Public, pg. 684
FRONTIER COMMUNICATIONS OF NEW ENGLAND, INC.—See Frontier Corporation; U.S. Public, pg. 684
FRONTIER COMMUNICATIONS OF NEW YORK, INC.—See Frontier Corporation; U.S. Public, pg. 684
FRONTIER COMMUNICATIONS OF ORION, INC.—See Frontier Corporation; U.S. Public, pg. 684

FRONTIER COMMUNICATIONS OF PENNSYLVANIA, INC.—See Frontier Corporation; U.S. Public, pg. 684
FRONTIER COMMUNICATIONS OF SENECA GORHAM, INC.—See Frontier Corporation; U.S. Public, pg. 684
FRONTIER COMMUNICATIONS OF SLYVAN LAKE, INC.—See Frontier Corporation; U.S. Public, pg. 684
FRONTIER COMMUNICATIONS OF THE MID ATLANTIC, INC.—See Frontier Corporation; U.S. Public, pg. 683
FRONTIER COMMUNICATIONS OF THE SOUTH, INC.—See Frontier Corporation; U.S. Public, pg. 684
FRONTIER COMMUNICATIONS OF THE WEST, INC.—See Frontier Corporation; U.S. Public, pg. 684
FRONTIER COMMUNICATIONS OF THORNTOWN, INC.—See Frontier Corporation; U.S. Public, pg. 684
FRONTIER COMMUNICATIONS OF VIROQUA, INC.—See Frontier Corporation; U.S. Public, pg. 684
FRONTIER COMMUNICATIONS OF WISCONSIN, INC.—See Frontier Corporation; U.S. Public, pg. 684
FRONTIER COMMUNICATIONS-OSWAYO RIVER, INC.—See Frontier Corporation; U.S. Public, pg. 684
FRONTIER COMMUNICATIONS-PRAIRIE INC.—See Frontier Corporation; U.S. Public, pg. 684
FRONTIER COMMUNICATIONS-SCHUYLER, INC.—See Frontier Corporation; U.S. Public, pg. 684
FRONTIER COMMUNICATIONS SERVICES—See Frontier Corporation; U.S. Public, pg. 684
FRONTIER COMMUNICATIONS-ST. CROIX, INC.—See Frontier Corporation; U.S. Public, pg. 684
FRONTIER CORPORATION; U.S. Public, pg. 683
FRONTIER FOUNDRY, INC.; U.S. Private, pg. 430
FRONTIER HOLDINGS INC.—See Wainoco Oil Corporation; U.S. Public, pg. 1732
FRONTIER INFORMATION TECHNOLOGIES—See Frontier Corporation; U.S. Public, pg. 684
FRONTIER INFOSERVICES—See Frontier Corporation; U.S. Public, pg. 684
FRONTIER INSURANCE COMPANY OF NEW YORK—See Frontier Insurance Group, Inc.; U.S. Public, pg. 685
FRONTIER INSURANCE GROUP, INC.; U.S. Public, pg. 684
FRONTIER NETWORK SYSTEMS, INC.—See Frontier Corporation; U.S. Public, pg. 684
FRONTIER OIL & REFINING COMPANY—See Wainoco Oil Corporation; U.S. Public, pg. 1732
FRONTIER OIL CORPORATION—See Wainoco Oil Corporation; U.S. Public, pg. 1732
FRONTIER PACIFIC INSURANCE COMPANY—See Frontier Insurance Group, Inc.; U.S. Public, pg. 685
FRONTIER PIPELINE INC.—See Wainoco Oil Corporation; U.S. Public, pg. 1732
FRONTIER REFINING, INC.—See Wainoco Oil Corporation; U.S. Public, pg. 1732
FRONTIER TRANSPORT CORPORATION—See Vitran Corporation Inc.; Int'l, pg. 1469
FRONTLINE—See BBC Magazines; Int'l, pg. 114
FRONTLINE—See EMAP Plc; Int'l, pg. 452
FRONTLINE- DISTRIBUTION DIVISION—See EMAP Plc; Int'l, pg. 451
FRONTLINE LTD.—See BBC Magazines; Int'l, pg. 114
FROSST LABORATORIES, INC.—See Merck & Co., Inc.; U.S. Public, pg. 1091
FROST & SULLIVAN; U.S. Private, pg. 430
FROST BROKERAGE SERVICES, INC.—See Cullen/Frost Bankers, Inc.; U.S. Public, pg. 467
FROST COMPANY; U.S. Private, pg. 430
FROST INC.; U.S. Private, pg. 430
FROST NATIONAL BANK—See Cullen/Frost Bankers, Inc.; U.S. Public, pg. 467
FROST WIRE PRODUCTS, LTD.—See Stelco Inc.; Int'l, pg. 1299
FROUDE CONSINE—See FKI Plc; Int'l, pg. 472
FROUDE CONSINE INC.—See FKI Plc; Int'l, pg. 473
FROZEN FOOD EXPRESS INDUSTRIES, INC.; U.S. Public, pg. 685
FROZEN SPECIALTIES, INC.—See Citicorp; U.S. Public, pg. 378
FROZFRUIT CORPORATION; U.S. Private, pg. 430
FRU-CON CONSTRUCTION CORPORATION—See Bilfinger + Berger Bauaktiengesellschaft; Int'l, pg. 196
FRUEHAUF FINANCE COMPANY—See Ford Motor Company; U.S. Public, pg. 663
FRUEHLING COSMETICS CO. LTD.—See Wella Group; Int'l, pg. 1490
FRUEN OAT MILLING CO.—See ConAgra, Inc.; U.S. Public, pg. 430
FRUISEC S.A.—See Bongrain S.A.; Int'l, pg. 201
FRUIT GROWERS SUPPLY CO.; U.S. Private, pg. 430
FRUIT OF THE LOOM, INC.; U.S. Public, pg. 685
FRUIT OF THE LOOM LIMITED—See Fruit of the Loom, Inc.; U.S. Public, pg. 686
FRUITASOL BV—See The Albert Fisher Group PLC; Int'l, pg. 491
FRUTAROM LTD.—See ICC Industries, Inc.; U.S. Private, pg. 553
FRUTAROM MEER CORPORATION—See ICC Industries, Inc.; U.S. Private, pg. 554
FRUTERA COLOMBIANA S.A.—See Corn Products International, Inc.; U.S. Public, pg. 447
THE FRYE COMPANY; U.S. Private, pg. 430
FRYETECH, INC.; U.S. Private, pg. 430
THE FRYMASTER CORP.—See Berisford plc; Int'l, pg. 188
FRY'S ELECTRONICS, INC.; U.S. Private, pg. 430
FTCI-CAYMAN LTD.—See Fiduciary Trust Company International; U.S. Public, pg. 621
FUBON INSURANCE CO. LTD.—See Allianz Aktiengesellschaft; Int'l, pg. 60
FUCHS & VOSS GMBH CO. KG.—See Rothenberger Group GmbH; Int'l, pg. 1128
FUCHS ARGENTINA S.A.—See Fuchs Petrolub AG Oel + Chemie; Int'l, pg. 517
FUCHS AUSTRALIA PTY.—See Fuchs Petrolub AG Oel + Chemie; Int'l, pg. 518
FUCHS CHEMICALS PTE. LTD.—See Fuchs Petrolub AG Oel + Chemie; Int'l, pg. 517

FUCHS CHEMICALS TRADING SDN.BHD.—See Fuchs Petrolub AG Oel + Chemie; Int'l, pg. 517
FUCHS FINANZSERVICE GMBH—See Fuchs Petrolub AG Oel + Chemie; Int'l, pg. 517
H. FUCHS DO BRAZIL S.A.—See Fuchs Petrolub AG Oel + Chemie; Int'l, pg. 517
FUCHS HELLAS S.A.—See Fuchs Petrolub AG Oel + Chemie; Int'l, pg. 517
FUCHS INTERLUB GMBH—See Fuchs Petrolub AG Oel + Chemie; Int'l, pg. 517
FUCHS INTEROIL GMBH—See Fuchs Petrolub AG Oel + Chemie; Int'l, pg. 517
FUCHS-JANOS—See Fuchs Petrolub AG Oel + Chemie; Int'l, pg. 517
FUCHS JAPAN K.K.—See Fuchs Petrolub AG Oel + Chemie; Int'l, pg. 517
FUCHS LUBRICANTES S.A.—See Fuchs Petrolub AG Oel + Chemie; Int'l, pg. 518
FUCHS LUBRICANTS, MIDLANTIC DIV.—See Fuchs Petrolub AG Oel + Chemie; Int'l, pg. 518
FUCHS LUBRICANTS (S.A) PTY., LTD.—See Fuchs Petrolub AG Oel + Chemie; Int'l, pg. 518
FUCHS LUBRICANTS TAIWAN CORP.—See Fuchs Petrolub AG Oel + Chemie; Int'l, pg. 517
FUCHS LUBRICANTS (THAILAND) LTD.—See Fuchs Petrolub AG Oel + Chemie; Int'l, pg. 517
FUCHS LUBRIFICANTES LDA.—See Fuchs Petrolub AG Oel + Chemie; Int'l, pg. 518
FUCHS LUBRIFICANTI S.R.L.—See Fuchs Petrolub AG Oel + Chemie; Int'l, pg. 517
FUCHS LUBRIFICANTS INDUSTRIE S.A.—See Fuchs Petrolub AG Oel + Chemie; Int'l, pg. 517
FUCHS MAZIVA D.O.O.—See Fuchs Petrolub AG Oel + Chemie; Int'l, pg. 517
FUCHS MINERALOELWERKE GMBH—See Fuchs Petrolub AG Oel + Chemie; Int'l, pg. 517
FUCHS-MONTGOMERY COMPANY, INC.—See Fuchs Petrolub AG Oel + Chemie; Int'l, pg. 518
FUCHS NE-METALLHANDEL GMBH—See Fried. Krupp AG; Int'l, pg. 514
FUCHS OIL CO. (CZ) SPOL. S R.O.—See Fuchs Petrolub AG Oel + Chemie; Int'l, pg. 518
FUCHS OIL CO. (PL) SP Z.O.O.—See Fuchs Petrolub AG Oel + Chemie; Int'l, pg. 518
FUCHS-PETROCHEMA SPOL, S.R.O.—See Fuchs Petrolub AG Oel + Chemie; Int'l, pg. 518
FUCHS PETROLEUM S.A.R.L.—See Fuchs Petrolub AG Oel + Chemie; Int'l, pg. 517
FUCHS PETROLUB AG—See Fuchs Petrolub AG Oel + Chemie; Int'l, pg. 517
FUCHS PETROLUB AG OEL + CHEMIE; Int'l, pg. 517
FUCHS REINER SCHMIERMITTEL GES. M.B.H.—See Fuchs Petrolub AG Oel + Chemie; Int'l, pg. 519
FUCHS' SCHE TONGRUBEN GMBH & CO. LTD.—See Watts Blake Bearne & Co. Plc; Int'l, pg. 1488
FUCHS (UK) P.L.C.—See Fuchs Petrolub AG Oel + Chemie; Int'l, pg. 518
FUCHUNJIANG FUJI ELECTRIC CO., LTD.—See Fuji Electric Co., Ltd.; Int'l, pg. 325
FUDDRUCKERS, INC.—See Compass Group plc; Int'l, pg. 325
FUDICKAR METALL GMBH—See Fried. Krupp AG; Int'l, pg. 514
FUEL SOUTH, INC.—See Jones Company, Inc.; U.S. Public, pg. 596
FUEL SYSTEMS TEXTRON INC.—See Textron Inc.; U.S. Public, pg. 1589
FUGAZY INTERNATIONAL CORPORATION; U.S. Private, pg. 430
FUGAZY LIMOUSINES—See Fugazy International Corporation; U.S. Private, pg. 430
FUGAZY TRAVEL—See Fugazy International Corporation; U.S. Private, pg. 430
FUGRO GROUP COMPANIES; U.S. Private, pg. 430
FUGRO HONG KONG, LTD.—See Fugro Group Companies; U.S. Private, pg. 430
FUGRO-MIDDLE EAST—See Fugro Group Companies; U.S. Private, pg. 430
FUGRO PENINSULAR GEOTECHNICAL SERVICES—See Fugro Group Companies; U.S. Private, pg. 431
FUGRO UNITED KINGDOM, LTD.—See Fugro Group Companies; U.S. Private, pg. 431
FUJASAWA RESEARCH INSTITUTE OF AMERICA—See Fujisawa Pharmaceutical Co. Ltd.; Int'l, pg. 525
THE FUJI BANK & TRUST CO.—See The Fuji Bank, Limited; Int'l, pg. 519
FUJI BANK, BERLIN REPRESENTATIVE OFFICE—See The Fuji Bank, Limited; Int'l, pg. 520
FUJI BANK CANADA—See The Fuji Bank, Limited; Int'l, pg. 521
FUJI BANK CANADA (MONTREAL BRANCH)—See The Fuji Bank, Limited; Int'l, pg. 521
FUJI BANK (DEUTSCHLAND) AG—See The Fuji Bank, Limited; Int'l, pg. 521
FUJI BANK, HANOI BRANCH—See The Fuji Bank, Limited; Int'l, pg. 520
FUJI BANK INTERNATIONAL, INC.—See The Fuji Bank, Limited; Int'l, pg. 519
P.T. FUJI BANK INTERNATIONAL INDONESIA—See The Fuji Bank, Limited; Int'l, pg. 521
FUJI BANK, LABUAN OFFICE—See The Fuji Bank, Limited; Int'l, pg. 520
THE FUJI BANK, LIMITED; Int'l, pg. 519
FUJI BANK (LUXEMBOURG) S.A.—See The Fuji Bank, Limited; Int'l, pg. 521
FUJI BANK (MEXICO) S.A.—See The Fuji Bank, Limited; Int'l, pg. 521
FUJI BANK, MUMBAI BRANCH—See The Fuji Bank, Limited; Int'l, pg. 520
FUJI BANK NEDERLAND N.V.—See The Fuji Bank, Limited; Int'l, pg. 521
FUJI BANK (SCHWEIZ) AG—See The Fuji Bank, Limited; Int'l, pg. 521

MASTER INDEX TO COMPANY NAMES FUKOKU
Company Index

FUJI BONDSTRAND CO., LTD.—See Ameron International Corporation; *U.S. Public*, pg. 99
FUJI CAPITAL HOLDINGS INC.—See The Fuji Bank, Limited; *Int'l*, pg. 519
FUJI CAPITAL MARKETS CORPORATION—See The Fuji Bank, Limited; *Int'l*, pg. 519
FUJI CAPITAL MARKETS (HK) LIMITED—See The Fuji Bank, Limited; *Int'l*, pg. 521
FUJI CAPITAL MARKETS (U.K.) LIMITED—See The Fuji Bank, Limited; *Int'l*, pg. 521
FUJI COMPUTER MEDIA DIV.—See Fuji Photo Film Co., Ltd.; *Int'l*, pg. 524
P.T. FUJI DHARMA ELECTRIC—See Fuji Electric Co., Ltd.; *Int'l*, pg. 522
FUJI ELECTRIC (ASIA) CO., LTD.—See Fuji Electric Co., Ltd.; *Int'l*, pg. 522
FUJI ELECTRIC CO., LTD.; *Int'l*, pg. 522
FUJI ELECTRIC CORP. OF AMERICA—See Fuji Electric Co., Ltd.; *Int'l*, pg. 522
FUJI ELECTRIC DALIAN CO., LTD.—See Fuji Electric Co., Ltd.; *Int'l*, pg. 522
FUJI ELECTRIC DO BRASIL INDUSTRIA E COMERCIO LTDA.—See Fuji Electric Co., Ltd.; *Int'l*, pg. 522
FUJI ELECTRIC FRANCE S.A.—See Fuji Electric Co., Ltd.; *Int'l*, pg. 522
FUJI ELECTRIC GMBH—See Fuji Electric Co., Ltd.; *Int'l*, pg. 522
FUJI ELECTRIC KOREA CO., LTD.—See Fuji Electric Co., Ltd.; *Int'l*, pg. 522
FUJI ELECTRIC (MALAYSIA) SDN. BHD.—See Fuji Electric Co., Ltd.; *Int'l*, pg. 522
FUJI ELECTRIC NORDESTE S.A.—See Fuji Electric Co., Ltd.; *Int'l*, pg. 522
FUJI ELECTRIC PHILIPPINES, INC.—See Fuji Electric Co., Ltd.; *Int'l*, pg. 522
FUJI ELECTRIC (SCOTLAND) LTD.—See Fuji Electric Co., Ltd.; *Int'l*, pg. 522
FUJI ELECTRIC SINGAPORE PRIVATE LTD.—See Fuji Electric Co., Ltd.; *Int'l*, pg. 522
FUJI ELECTRIC TECHNOLOGY AND SERVICE (SHENZHEN) CO., LTD.—See Fuji Electric Co., Ltd.; *Int'l*, pg. 522
FUJI ELECTRIC (U.K.) LTD.—See Fuji Electric Co., Ltd.; *Int'l*, pg. 522
FUJI ELECTROCHEMICAL CO., LTD.—See Fujitsu Limited; *Int'l*, pg. 526
FUJI FILM ESPANA, S.A.—See Fuji Photo Film Co., Ltd.; *Int'l*, pg. 524
FUJI FILM SVERIGE AB—See Axel Johnson AB; *Int'l*, pg. 708
THE FUJI FUTURES (SINGAPORE) PTE., LIMITED—See The Fuji Bank, Limited; *Int'l*, pg. 521
FUJI/GE PRIVATE LTD.—See Fuji Electric Co., Ltd.; *Int'l*, pg. 522
FUJI/GE PTE LTD.—See General Electric Company; *U.S. Public*, pg. 713
FUJI/GE (TAIWAN) CO., LTD.—See Fuji Electric Co., Ltd.; *Int'l*, pg. 522
FUJI GRAPHIC ARTS DIV.—See Fuji Photo Film Co., Ltd.; *Int'l*, pg. 524
FUJI GRAPHIC SYSTEMS CANADA INC.—See Fuji Photo Film Co., Ltd.; *Int'l*, pg. 524
FUJI HEAVY INDUSTRIES, LTD.; *Int'l*, pg. 522
FUJI HEAVY INDUSTRIES, LTD., AIRCRAFT DIV.—See Fuji Heavy Industries, Ltd.; *Int'l*, pg. 522
FUJI HEAVY INDUSTRIES, LTD., AUTOMOBILE DIV.—See Fuji Heavy Industries, Ltd.; *Int'l*, pg. 522
FUJI HEAVY INDUSTRIES, LTD., BUS. DIV.—See Fuji Heavy Industries, Ltd.; *Int'l*, pg. 523
FUJI HEAVY INDUSTRIES, LTD., ENGINE & MACHINERY DIV.—See Fuji Heavy Industries, Ltd.; *Int'l*, pg. 523
FUJI HEAVY INDUSTRIES, LTD., MITAKA PLANT—See Fuji Heavy Industries, Ltd.; *Int'l*, pg. 523
FUJI HEAVY INDUSTRIES, LTD., NORTH PLANT—See Fuji Heavy Industries, Ltd.; *Int'l*, pg. 523
FUJI HEAVY INDUSTRIES, LTD., OIZUMI PLANT—See Fuji Heavy Industries, Ltd.; *Int'l*, pg. 523
FUJI HEAVY INDUSTRIES, LTD., OMIYA PARTS CENTER—See Fuji Heavy Industries, Ltd.; *Int'l*, pg. 523
FUJI HEAVY INDUSTRIES, LTD., ROLLING STOCK DIV.—See Fuji Heavy Industries, Ltd.; *Int'l*, pg. 523
FUJI HEAVY INDUSTRIES, LTD., TRANSPORTATION EQUIPMENT DIV.—See Fuji Heavy Industries, Ltd.; *Int'l*, pg. 522
FUJI HEAVY INDUSTRIES, LTD., YAJIMA PLANT—See Fuji Heavy Industries, Ltd.; *Int'l*, pg. 523
FUJI HEAVY INDUSTRIES USA, INC.—See Fuji Heavy Industries, Ltd.; *Int'l*, pg. 523
FUJI HI-TECH, INC.—See Fuji Electric Co., Ltd.; *Int'l*, pg. 522
FUJI-HUNT ELECTRONICS TECHNOLOGY CO., LTD.—See Olin Corporation; *U.S. Public*, pg. 1219
FUJI HUNT PHOTOGRAPHIC CHEMICALS (DEUTSCHLAND) GMBH—See Fuji Photo Film Co., Ltd.; *Int'l*, pg. 524
FUJI HUNT PHOTOGRAPHIC CHEMICALS (FRANCE) S.A.R.L.—See Fuji Photo Film Co., Ltd.; *Int'l*, pg. 524
FUJI HUNT PHOTOGRAPHIC CHEMICALS, INC.—See Fuji Photo Film Co., Ltd.; *Int'l*, pg. 524
FUJI HUNT PHOTOGRAPHIC CHEMICALS (ITALIA) SRL—See Fuji Photo Film Co., Ltd.; *Int'l*, pg. 524
FUJI HUNT PHOTOGRAPHIC CHEMICALS, N.V.—See Fuji Photo Film Co., Ltd.; *Int'l*, pg. 524
FUJI HUNT PHOTOGRAPHIC CHEMICALS PTE. LTD.—See Fuji Photo Film Co., Ltd.; *Int'l*, pg. 524
FUJI HUNT PHOTOGRAPHIC CHEMICALS (SVERIGE) AB—See Fuji Photo Film Co., Ltd.; *Int'l*, pg. 524
FUJI HUNT PHOTOGRAPHIC CHEMICALS (U.K.) LTD.—See Fuji Photo Film Co., Ltd.; *Int'l*, pg. 524
FUJI INDUSTRIAL PHOTO PRODUCTS DIV.—See Fuji Photo Film Co., Ltd.; *Int'l*, pg. 524
FUJI INTERNATIONAL FINANCE (AUSTRALIA) LIMITED—See The Fuji Bank, Limited; *Int'l*, pg. 521
FUJI INTERNATIONAL FINANCE (HK) LIMITED—See The Fuji Bank, Limited; *Int'l*, pg. 521
FUJI INTERNATIONAL FINANCE PLC—See The Fuji Bank, Limited; *Int'l*, pg. 521
FUJI INVESTMENT MANAGEMENT COMPANY (EUROPE) LIMITED—See The Fuji Bank, Limited; *Int'l*, pg. 521
FUJI KIKO CO., LTD.—See Nissan Motor Co., Ltd.; *Int'l*, pg. 944
FUJI KISEN KAISHA, LTD.—See Mitsui & Co., Ltd.; *Int'l*, pg. 878
FUJI LEASING (DEUTSCHLAND) GMBH—See The Fuji Bank, Limited; *Int'l*, pg. 521
FUJI LEASING (UK) LIMITED—See The Fuji Bank, Limited; *Int'l*, pg. 521
FUJI MAGNETIC PRODUCTS DIV.—See Fuji Photo Film Co., Ltd.; *Int'l*, pg. 524
FUJI MAGNETICS GMBH—See Fuji Photo Film Co., Ltd.; *Int'l*, pg. 524
FUJI MEDICAL SYSTEMS BENELUX N.V.—See Fuji Photo Film Co., Ltd.; *Int'l*, pg. 524
FUJI MEDICAL SYSTEMS USA, INC.—See Fuji Photo Film Co., Ltd.; *Int'l*, pg. 524
FUJI MICROGRAPHICS DIV.—See Fuji Photo Film Co., Ltd.; *Int'l*, pg. 524
FUJI PHOTO FILM B.V.—See Fuji Photo Film Co., Ltd.; *Int'l*, pg. 524
FUJI PHOTO FILM CANADA, INC.—See Fuji Photo Film Co., Ltd.; *Int'l*, pg. 524
FUJI PHOTO FILM CO., LTD.; *Int'l*, pg. 523
FUJI PHOTO FILM CO., LTD., BEIJING REPRESENTATIVE OFFICE—See Fuji Photo Film Co., Ltd.; *Int'l*, pg. 524
FUJI PHOTO FILM CO., LTD., DUBAI OFFICE—See Fuji Photo Film Co., Ltd.; *Int'l*, pg. 524
FUJI PHOTO FILM CO., LTD., HO CHI MINH OFFICE—See Fuji Photo Film Co., Ltd.; *Int'l*, pg. 525
FUJI PHOTO FILM CO., LTD., HONG KONG OFFICE—See Fuji Photo Film Co., Ltd.; *Int'l*, pg. 525
FUJI PHOTO FILM CO., LTD., SEOUL OFFICE—See Fuji Photo Film Co., Ltd.; *Int'l*, pg. 525
FUJI PHOTO FILM CO., LTD., SYDNEY OFFICE—See Fuji Photo Film Co., Ltd.; *Int'l*, pg. 525
FUJI PHOTO FILM CO., LTD., TAIPEI OFFICE—See Fuji Photo Film Co., Ltd.; *Int'l*, pg. 525
FUJI PHOTO FILM DO BRASIL LTDA.—See Fuji Photo Film Co., Ltd.; *Int'l*, pg. 524
FUJI PHOTO FILM (EUROPE) GMBH—See Fuji Photo Film Co., Ltd.; *Int'l*, pg. 524
FUJI PHOTO FILM HAWAII, INC.—See Fuji Photo Film Co., Ltd.; *Int'l*, pg. 524
FUJI PHOTO FILM, INC.—See Fuji Photo Film Co., Ltd.; *Int'l*, pg. 524
FUJI PHOTO FILM (MALAYSIA) SDN. BHD.—See Fuji Photo Film Co., Ltd.; *Int'l*, pg. 524
FUJI PHOTO FILM (SINGAPORE) PTE. LTD.—See Fuji Photo Film Co., Ltd.; *Int'l*, pg. 524
FUJI PHOTO FILM (THAILAND) LTD.—See Fuji Photo Film Co., Ltd.; *Int'l*, pg. 525
FUJI PHOTO FILM (U.K.), LTD.—See Fuji Photo Film Co., Ltd.; *Int'l*, pg. 524
FUJI PHOTO FILM U.S.A., INC.—See Fuji Photo Film Co., Ltd.; *Int'l*, pg. 524
FUJI PHOTOGRAPHIC PRODUCTS DIV.—See Fuji Photo Film Co., Ltd.; *Int'l*, pg. 524
FUJI ROBIN INDUSTRIES, LTD.—See Fuji Heavy Industries, Ltd.; *Int'l*, pg. 523
FUJI SECURITIES INC.-CHICAGO—See The Fuji Bank, Limited; *Int'l*, pg. 519
FUJI SECURITIES INC.-NEW YORK—See The Fuji Bank, Limited; *Int'l*, pg. 519
FUJI SEITO CO., LTD.—See Nissho Iwai Corporation; *Int'l*, pg. 947
FUJI XEROX COMPANY LTD.—See Xerox Corporation; *U.S. Public*, pg. 1785
FUJIAN INTERNATIONAL LEASING COMPANY LIMITED—See The Asahi Bank, Ltd.; *Int'l*, pg. 83
FUJICONE—See Recoton Corporation; *U.S. Public*, pg. 1369
FUJIFILM MICRODISKS U.S.A., INC.—See Fuji Photo Film Co., Ltd.; *Int'l*, pg. 524
FUJIKURA AMERICA INC.—See Fujikura Ltd.; *Int'l*, pg. 525
FUJIKURA LTD.; *Int'l*, pg. 525
FUJILEASE CORPORATION—See The Fuji Bank, Limited; *Int'l*, pg. 519
FUJISAWA BEIJING—See Fujisawa Pharmaceutical Co. Ltd.; *Int'l*, pg. 525
FUJISAWA EUROPE GMBH—See Fujisawa Pharmaceutical Co. Ltd.; *Int'l*, pg. 525
FUJISAWA FISONS KK—See Rhone-Poulenc S.A.; *Int'l*, pg. 1111
FUJISAWA GMBH—See Fujisawa Pharmaceutical Co. Ltd.; *Int'l*, pg. 525
FUJISAWA HOLLAND B.V.—See Fujisawa Pharmaceutical Co. Ltd.; *Int'l*, pg. 525
FUJISAWA IRELAND LIMITED—See Fujisawa Pharmaceutical Co. Ltd.; *Int'l*, pg. 525
FUJISAWA KASHIMA—See Fujisawa Pharmaceutical Co. Ltd.; *Int'l*, pg. 525
FUJISAWA LTD.—See Fujisawa Pharmaceutical Co. Ltd.; *Int'l*, pg. 525
FUJISAWA PHARM KOREA LTD.—See Fujisawa Pharmaceutical Co. Ltd.; *Int'l*, pg. 525
FUJISAWA PHARMACEUTICAL CO. LTD.; *Int'l*, pg. 525
FUJISAWA SA—See Fujisawa Pharmaceutical Co. Ltd.; *Int'l*, pg. 525
FUJISAWA SARL—See Fujisawa Pharmaceutical Co. Ltd.; *Int'l*, pg. 525
FUJISAWA SRL—See Fujisawa Pharmaceutical Co. Ltd.; *Int'l*, pg. 525
FUJISAWA SYNTHELABO K.K.—See L'Oreal S.A.; *Int'l*, pg. 818
FUJISAWA TOKYO—See Fujisawa Pharmaceutical Co. Ltd.; *Int'l*, pg. 525
FUJISAWA U.S.A.—See Fujisawa Pharmaceutical Co. Ltd.; *Int'l*, pg. 525
FUJISAWA U.S.A. INC.—See Fujisawa Pharmaceutical Co. Ltd.; *Int'l*, pg. 525
FUJITSU AMD SEMI-CONDUCTOR, LTD.—See Advanced Micro Devices, Inc.; *U.S. Public*, pg. 21
FUJITSU AMERICA, INC.—See Fujitsu Limited; *Int'l*, pg. 526
FUJITSU AMERICA - INFORMATION SYSTEMS GROUP—See Fujitsu Limited; *Int'l*, pg. 526
FUJITSU AMERICA - SUPER COMPUTER GROUP—See Fujitsu Limited; *Int'l*, pg. 526
FUJITSU AUSTRALIA LTD.—See Fujitsu Limited; *Int'l*, pg. 528
FUJITSU BUSINESS COMMUNICATION SYSTEMS—See Fujitsu Limited; *Int'l*, pg. 526
FUJITSU BUSINESS COMMUNICATION SYSTEMS, INC. - SALES & MARKETING—See Fujitsu Limited; *Int'l*, pg. 526
FUJITSU BUSINESS SYSTEMS LTD.—See Fujitsu Limited; *Int'l*, pg. 526
FUJITSU CANADA, INC.—See Fujitsu Limited; *Int'l*, pg. 527
FUJITSU COMPONENT (MALAYSIA) SDN. BHD.—See Fujitsu Limited; *Int'l*, pg. 528
FUJITSU COMPOUND SEMICONDUCTOR, INC.—See Fujitsu Limited; *Int'l*, pg. 526
FUJITSU COMPUTER PACKAGING TECHNOLOGIES, INC.—See Fujitsu Limited; *Int'l*, pg. 526
FUJITSU COMPUTER PRODUCTS OF AMERICA, INC.—See Fujitsu Limited; *Int'l*, pg. 526
FUJITSU COMPUTER PRODUCTS OF AMERICA - MFG.—See Fujitsu Limited; *Int'l*, pg. 526
FUJITSU COMPUTER PRODUCTS OF AMERICA - RESEARCH & DEVELOPMENT—See Fujitsu Limited; *Int'l*, pg. 526
FUJITSU DENSO LTD.—See Fujitsu Limited; *Int'l*, pg. 526
FUJITSU DEUTSCHLAND GMBH—See Fujitsu Limited; *Int'l*, pg. 528
FUJITSU DO BRASIL COMUNICA CAO ELECTRONICA MAQINAS E SEVICOS LIMITADA—See Fujitsu Limited; *Int'l*, pg. 528
FUJITSU ESPANA, S.A.—See Fujitsu Limited; *Int'l*, pg. 528
FUJITSU EUROPE LTD.—See Fujitsu Limited; *Int'l*, pg. 528
FUJITSU GENERAL AMERICA CORP.—See Fujitsu Limited; *Int'l*, pg. 526
FUJITSU GENERAL LTD.—See Fujitsu Limited; *Int'l*, pg. 526
FUJITSU ICL AUSTRALIA PTY. LIMITED—See Fujitsu Limited; *Int'l*, pg. 529
FUJITSU ITALIA S.P.A.—See Fujitsu Limited; *Int'l*, pg. 528
FUJITSU KIDEN LTD.—See Fujitsu Limited; *Int'l*, pg. 526
FUJITSU KOREA LTD.—See Fujitsu Limited; *Int'l*, pg. 528
FUJITSU LABORATORIES LTD.—See Fujitsu Limited; *Int'l*, pg. 526
FUJITSU LABORATORIES OF AMERICA, INC.—See Fujitsu Limited; *Int'l*, pg. 526
FUJITSU LIMITED; *Int'l*, pg. 525
FUJITSU MICRODEVICES LTD.—See Fujitsu Limited; *Int'l*, pg. 526
FUJITSU MICROELECTRONICS, INC.—See Fujitsu Limited; *Int'l*, pg. 527
FUJITSU MICROELECTRONICS IRELAND LTD.—See Fujitsu Limited; *Int'l*, pg. 528
FUJITSU MICROELECTRONICS LTD.—See Fujitsu Limited; *Int'l*, pg. 528
FUJITSU MICROELECTRONICS - MFG.—See Fujitsu Limited; *Int'l*, pg. 527
FUJITSU MIKROELEKTRONIK GMBH—See Fujitsu Limited; *Int'l*, pg. 528
FUJITSU NETWORK SWITCHING OF AMERICA, INC.—See Fujitsu Limited; *Int'l*, pg. 526
FUJITSU NETWORK TRANSMISSION SYSTEMS INC.—See Fujitsu Limited; *Int'l*, pg. 526
FUJITSU NETWORKS INDUSTRIES—See Fujitsu Limited; *Int'l*, pg. 529
FUJITSU NEW ZEALAND LTD.—See Fujitsu Limited; *Int'l*, pg. 528
FUJITSU NORDIC AB—See Fujitsu Limited; *Int'l*, pg. 528
FUJITSU OPEN SYSTEMS SOLUTIONS, INC.—See Fujitsu Limited; *Int'l*, pg. 526
FUJITSU PERSONAL SYSTEMS, INC.—See Fujitsu Limited; *Int'l*, pg. 526
FUJITSU (SINGAPORE) PTE. LTD.—See Fujitsu Limited; *Int'l*, pg. 528
FUJITSU SYSTEMS BUSINESS OF AMERICA, INC.—See Fujitsu Limited; *Int'l*, pg. 526
FUJITSU SYSTEMS BUSINESS OF CANADA - CUSTOMER SUPPORT—See Fujitsu Limited; *Int'l*, pg. 527
FUJITSU SYSTEMS BUSINESS OF CANADA, INC.—See Fujitsu Limited; *Int'l*, pg. 527
FUJITSU SYSTEMS OF AMERICA, INC.—See Fujitsu Limited; *Int'l*, pg. 526
FUJITSU TEN CORP. OF AMERICA—See Fujitsu Limited; *Int'l*, pg. 526
FUJITSU TEN CORP. OF AMERICA/INDIANAPOLIS—See Fujitsu Limited; *Int'l*, pg. 526
FUJITSU TEN CORP. OF AMERICA/MICHIGAN—See Fujitsu Limited; *Int'l*, pg. 526
FUJITSU TEN CORP. OF AMERICA/RUSHVILLE—See Fujitsu Limited; *Int'l*, pg. 526
FUJITSU TEN LTD.—See Fujitsu Limited; *Int'l*, pg. 526
FUJITSU VITORIA COMPUTADORES E SERVICOS, LTDA.—See Fujitsu Limited; *Int'l*, pg. 528
FUJIURA BUTSURYU CENTER CO., LTD.—See Pohang Iron & Steel Co., Ltd.; *Int'l*, pg. 1062
FUJI-WOLFENSOHN INTERNATIONAL—See The Fuji Bank, Limited; *Int'l*, pg. 519
FUKADA-KIDDE CO., LTD.—See Hanson PLC; *Int'l*, pg. 594
THE FUKOKU MUTUAL LIFE INSURANCE CO.-OSAKA KITA BRANCH—See Fukoku Mutual Life Insurance Company; *Int'l*, pg. 529
FUKOKU MUTUAL LIFE INSURANCE COMPANY; *Int'l*, pg. 529

FUKUSHIMA HAKUHODO INC.—See Hakuhodo Incorporated; *Int'l*, pg. 587
FUKUSHIMA HAKUHODO, INC.—See Hakuhodo Incorporated; *Int'l*, pg. 587
FUKUSHIMA SANKEN CO., LTD.—See Sanken Electric Co., Ltd.; *Int'l*, pg. 1188
FUKUTAKE PUBLISHING CO. LTD.—See Berlitz International, Inc.; *U.S. Public*, pg. 222
FUKUYAMA ASAHI ORIKOMI CENTER—See Daiko Advertising, Inc.; *Int'l*, pg. 366
FUKUYAMA INTEGRATED CIRCUITS GROUP—See Sharp Corporation; *Int'l*, pg. 1228
FULFLO SPECIALTIES—See Gusher Pumps, Inc.; *U.S. Private*, pg. 488
FULL CIRCLE—See CENEX, Inc.; *U.S. Private*, pg. 222
FULL CIRCLE TRANSPORT, INC.—See Hughes Supply, Inc.; *U.S. Public*, pg. 847
FULL HOUSE SPORTS & ENTERTAINMENT—See The Ackerley Group; *U.S. Public*, pg. 16
FULL SERVICE BEVERAGE COMPANY—See All American Bottling Corp.; *U.S. Private*, pg. 34
FULL SERVICE BEVERAGE COMPANY OF COLORADO—See All American Bottling Corp.; *U.S. Private*, pg. 34
THE FULLER BRUSH COMPANY—See CPAC, Inc.; *U.S. Public*, pg. 282
FULLER COMPANY—See FLS Industries A/S; *Int'l*, pg. 475
FULLER COMPANY (ALLENTOWN)—See FLS Industries A/S; *Int'l*, pg. 475
FULLER COMPANY (CATASAUQUA)—See FLS Industries A/S; *Int'l*, pg. 475
FULLER COMPANY (MANHEIM)—See FLS Industries A/S; *Int'l*, pg. 475
FULLER-F.L. SMIDTH CANADA LIMITED—See FLS Industries A/S; *Int'l*, pg. 475
FULLER-F.L. SMIDTH (PTY) LTD.—See FLS Industries A/S; *Int'l*, pg. 475
FULLER-F.L. SMIDTH S.A.—See FLS Industries A/S; *Int'l*, pg. 475
H.B. FULLER ARGENTINA S.A.I.C—See H.B. Fuller Company; *U.S. Public*, pg. 687
H.B. FULLER AUSTRIA GESMBH—See H.B. Fuller Company; *U.S. Public*, pg. 687
H.B. FULLER AUTOMOTIVE PRODUCTS—See H.B. Fuller Company; *U.S. Public*, pg. 687
H.B. FULLER BELGIUM N.V./S.A.—See H.B. Fuller Company; *U.S. Public*, pg. 687
H.B. FULLER, CANADA INC.—See H.B. Fuller Company; *U.S. Public*, pg. 687
H.B. FULLER CHILE, S.A.—See H.B. Fuller Company; *U.S. Public*, pg. 687
H.B. FULLER (CHINA) ADHESIVES, LTD.—See H.B. Fuller Company; *U.S. Public*, pg. 687
H.B. FULLER COATINGS LTD.—See H.B. Fuller Company; *U.S. Public*, pg. 686
H.B. FULLER COMPANY; *U.S. Public*, pg. 686
H.B. FULLER CO. AUSTRALIA PTY., LTD.—See H.B. Fuller Company; *U.S. Public*, pg. 687
H.B. FULLER CO. (N.Z.) LTD.—See H.B. Fuller Company; *U.S. Public*, pg. 687
H.B. FULLER DOMINICANA, S.A.—See H.B. Fuller Company; *U.S. Public*, pg. 687
H.B. FULLER ECUADOR, S.A.—See H.B. Fuller Company; *U.S. Public*, pg. 687
H.B. FULLER EUROPE—See H.B. Fuller Company; *U.S. Public*, pg. 687
H.B. FULLER FRANCE—See H.B. Fuller Company; *U.S. Public*, pg. 687
H.B. FULLER GMBH—See H.B. Fuller Company; *U.S. Public*, pg. 687
H.B. FULLER INTERNATIONAL INC.—See H.B. Fuller Company; *U.S. Public*, pg. 687
H.B. FULLER INTERNATIONAL, INC.—See H.B. Fuller Company; *U.S. Public*, pg. 687
H.B. FULLER JAPAN CO. LTD.—See H.B. Fuller Company; *U.S. Public*, pg. 687
H.B. FULLER MEXICO, S.A. DE C.V.—See H.B. Fuller Company; *U.S. Public*, pg. 687
H.B. FULLER NETHERLANDS B.V.—See H.B. Fuller Company; *U.S. Public*, pg. 687
H.B. FULLER (PHILIPPINES) INC.—See H.B. Fuller Company; *U.S. Public*, pg. 687
H.B. FULLER SVERIGE AB—See H.B. Fuller Company; *U.S. Public*, pg. 687
H.B. FULLER U.K., LTD.—See H.B. Fuller Company; *U.S. Public*, pg. 687
FULLER-K.C.P. LIMITED—See FLS Industries A/S; *Int'l*, pg. 475
FULLER-KOVAKO CORPORATION—See FLS Industries A/S; *Int'l*, pg. 475
FULLER OFFSHORE FINANCE CORP., B.V.—See FLS Industries A/S; *Int'l*, pg. 475
FULLER, SMITH & TURNER PLC; *Int'l*, pg. 529
FULLER-F.L. SMIDTH (PACIFIC) PTY. LTD.—See FLS Industries A/S; *Int'l*, pg. 475
FULLERTON METALS CO.; *U.S. Private*, pg. 431
FULMER COMPANY, INC.—See Morgan Crucible Co. Plc; *Int'l*, pg. 891
FULMER SUPERMARKETS, INC.; *U.S. Private*, pg. 431
FULTON CONTAINER DIV.—See Philip Morris Companies Inc.; *U.S. Public*, pg. 1289
FULTON FINANCIAL CORP.; *U.S. Public*, pg. 687
FULTON INDUSTRIES INC.; *U.S. Public*, pg. 687
FUN RADIO—See Groupe Bruxelles Lambert S.A.; *Int'l*, pg. 561
FUN STORES—See GIB Group; *Int'l*, pg. 533
FUNAI CORPORATION—See Funai Electric Co., Ltd.; *Int'l*, pg. 530
FUNAI ELECTRIC CO., LTD.; *Int'l*, pg. 529
FUNAI ELECTRIC (EUROPE) GMBH—See Funai Electric Co., Ltd.; *Int'l*, pg. 530
FUNAI ELECTRIC RESEARCH INSTITUTE CO., LTD.—See Funai Electric Co., Ltd.; *Int'l*, pg. 529

FUNAI ELECTRIC SILICON VALLEY—See Funai Electric Co., Ltd.; *Int'l*, pg. 530
FUNAI ELECTRIC TRADING (EUROPE) GMBH—See Funai Electric Co., Ltd.; *Int'l*, pg. 530
FUNCO, INC.; *U.S. Public*, pg. 688
FUND AMERICAN ENTERPRISES HOLDINGS, INC.; *U.S. Public*, pg. 688
FUNDACAO IOCHPE—See Iochpe-Maxion S.A.; *Int'l*, pg. 688
FUNDACION GCN S.A.—See Marcam Solutions, Inc.; *U.S. Public*, pg. 1043
FUNDAMENTAL MANAGEMENT, INC.—See Industrial Wire Products Corporation; *U.S. Private*, pg. 561
FUNDIA AB—See Rautaruukki Oy; *Int'l*, pg. 1088
FUNDICIONES METALICAS, S.A.—See Siebe plc; *Int'l*, pg. 1244
FUNDIMO—See Caixa Geral de Depositos; *Int'l*, pg. 250
FUNDING SERVICES INC.—See Danka Business Systems PLC; *Int'l*, pg. 379
FUNDINOX LTDA.—See Sulzer Ltd.; *Int'l*, pg. 1305
FUNDITUBO—See Saint-Gobain; *Int'l*, pg. 1176
FUNDO ALUMINIUM AB—See Norsk Hydro a.s; *Int'l*, pg. 962
FUNDUS GESELLSCHAFT FUR GRUNDBESITZ UND BETEILIGUNGEN MBH—See Bayerische Vereinsbank Group; *Int'l*, pg. 179
FUNERAL SECURITY PLANS, INC.—See D.W. Newcomer's Sons, Inc.; *U.S. Private*, pg. 796
FUNG YONG CO., LTD.—See Toyota Motor Corporation; *Int'l*, pg. 1413
FUNK ALUMINUM GMBH—See Fried. Krupp AG; *Int'l*, pg. 514
KALKWERK D. FUNK GMBH & CO. KG—See Heidelberger Zement A.G.; *Int'l*, pg. 606
FUNK MANUFACTURING CO.—See Deere & Company; *U.S. Public*, pg. 607
FUNSOFT HOLDING GMBH—See John Menzies plc; *Int'l*, pg. 707
FURMAN FOODS, INC.; *U.S. Private*, pg. 431
FURMAN LUMBER COMPANY, INC.; *U.S. Private*, pg. 431
FURMAN SELZ HOLDING CORPORATION—See Xerox Corporation; *U.S. Public*, pg. 1785
FURMANITE WORLDWIDE, INC.—See Kaneb Services, Inc.; *U.S. Public*, pg. 942
FURNESS BV; *Int'l*, pg. 530
FURNESS NORTH AMERICA INC.—See Furness BV; *Int'l*, pg. 530
FURNISHINGS INTERNATIONAL, INC.; *U.S. Private*, pg. 431
FURNITURE BRANDS INTERNATIONAL INC.; *U.S. Public*, pg. 688
FURNITURE CONSULTANTS—See U.S. Office Products Company; *U.S. Public*, pg. 1686
FURNITURE GROUP INDUSTRIES; *U.S. Private*, pg. 432
FURNITURE IN PARTS, INC.; *U.S. Private*, pg. 432
FURNIVAL/STATE MACHINERY CO.—See Komatsu Ltd.; *Int'l*, pg. 744
FURON COMPANY; *U.S. Public*, pg. 688
FURON FLUORGLAS PRODUCTS—See Furon Company; *U.S. Public*, pg. 689
FURON LTD.—See Furon Company; *U.S. Public*, pg. 689
FURON S.A./N.V.—See Furon Company; *U.S. Public*, pg. 689
FURR'S/BISHOPS, INC.; *U.S. Public*, pg. 689
FURR'S SUPERMARKETS; *U.S. Private*, pg. 432
FURST-MCNESS COMPANY; *U.S. Private*, pg. 432
FURUKAWA ALUMINUM CO., LTD.—See The Furukawa Electric Co., Ltd.; *Int'l*, pg. 530
THE FURUKAWA BATTERY CO., LTD.—See The Furukawa Electric Co., Ltd.; *Int'l*, pg. 530
FURUKAWA ELECTRIC AMERICA INC. (FEA)—See The Furukawa Electric Co., Ltd.; *Int'l*, pg. 530
FURUKAWA ELECTRIC CABLES (MALAYSIA) SDN. BHD.—See The Furukawa Electric Co., Ltd.; *Int'l*, pg. 530
THE FURUKAWA ELECTRIC CO., LTD.; *Int'l*, pg. 530
FURUKAWA ELECTRIC COMPOSITE INSULATORS CO., LTD.—See The Furukawa Electric Co., Ltd.; *Int'l*, pg. 530
FURUKAWA ELECTRIC INSTITUTE OF TECHNOLOGY—See The Furukawa Electric Co., Ltd.; *Int'l*, pg. 530
FURUKAWA ELECTRIC SINGAPORE PTE. LTD.—See The Furukawa Electric Co., Ltd.; *Int'l*, pg. 530
FURUKAWA ELECTRIC TECHNOLOGIES INC. (FET)—See The Furukawa Electric Co., Ltd.; *Int'l*, pg. 530
FURUKAWA FINANCE NETHERLANDS B.V.—See The Furukawa Electric Co., Ltd.; *Int'l*, pg. 531
FURUKAWA INDUSTRIAL S.A. PRODUTOS ELETRICOS (FISA)—See The Furukawa Electric Co., Ltd.; *Int'l*, pg. 531
FURUKAWA METAL (THAILAND) CO., LTD.—See The Furukawa Electric Co., Ltd.; *Int'l*, pg. 531
FURUKAWA RESEARCH & ENGINEERING EUROPE LTD.—See The Furukawa Electric Co., Ltd.; *Int'l*, pg. 531
FURUKAWA SANGYO KAISHA, LTD.—See The Furukawa Electric Co., Ltd.; *Int'l*, pg. 530
FURUKAWA SAUDI ARABIA, LTD. (FSA)—See The Furukawa Electric Co., Ltd.; *Int'l*, pg. 531
THE FUSCO CORPORATION; *U.S. Private*, pg. 432
FUSHIKI MILL—See Nippon Paper Industries Company Limited; *Int'l*, pg. 938
FUSHIMAN CO. LTD.—See GESTRA GmbH; *Int'l*, pg. 550
FUSION METERS LIMITED—See Severn Trent Plc; *Int'l*, pg. 1226
FUSITE, B.V.—See Emerson Electric Co.; *U.S. Public*, pg. 577
FUSITE JAPAN—See Emerson Electric Co.; *U.S. Public*, pg. 577
LOU FUSZ AUTOMOTIVE NETWORK; *U.S. Private*, pg. 432
LOU FUSZ MOTOR COMPANY—See Lou Fusz Automotive Network; *U.S. Private*, pg. 432
FUTABA CORPORATION; *Int'l*, pg. 531

FUTABA CORPORATION OF AMERICA—See Futaba Corporation; *Int'l*, pg. 531
FUTRONIX SYSTEMS—See Kent Electronics Corp.; *U.S. Public*, pg. 951
FUTTER LUMBER CORPORATION; *U.S. Private*, pg. 432
FUTTY & COMPANY—See NCH Corporation; *U.S. Public*, pg. 1145
FUTURE FOAM, INC.; *U.S. Private*, pg. 433
FUTURE TECHNOLOGY WORLDWIDE L.L.C.—See SASIB SpA; *Int'l*, pg. 1194
FUTURES PERSONNEL SERVICES; *U.S. Private*, pg. 433
FUTUREWORKS—See EvansGroup; *U.S. Private*, pg. 385
FUYO GENERAL LEASE CO. LTD.—See Citicorp; *U.S. Public*, pg. 379
JOHN FYFE LTD.—See Bardon Group PLC; *Int'l*, pg. 166
FYRNETICS, INC.—See Williams Holdings Plc; *Int'l*, pg. 1499

G

THE G&C FOUNDRY COMPANY—See Atchison Casting Corporation; *U.S. Public*, pg. 142
G & G SHOPS, INC.—See Petrie Retail, Inc.; *U.S. Private*, pg. 858
G & H CASTINGS CORPORATION—See ITT Industries, Inc.; *U.S. Public*, pg. 861
G&H PRODUCTS CORP.—See Tetra Laval Group; *Int'l*, pg. 1378
G & H TECHNOLOGY, INC.—See American Financial Group; *U.S. Public*, pg. 75
G&K SERVICES, INC.; *U.S. Public*, pg. 690
THE G & O MANUFACTURING CO.—See TransPro, Inc.; *U.S. Public*, pg. 1631
G&P STARKE DIEKSTRA BV—See Heidemij N.V.; *Int'l*, pg. 607
G & W ELECTRIC CO.; *U.S. Private*, pg. 433
G & W LIFE INSURANCE CO.—See Deposit Guaranty Corp.; *U.S. Public*, pg. 501
G-B MILLER—See Miller Advertising Agency Inc.; *U.S. Private*, pg. 746
G B STORES—See Schottenstein Stores Corporation; *U.S. Private*, pg. 972
G-I HOLDINGS INC.—See GAF Corporation; *U.S. Private*, pg. 433
G INDUSTRIES CORPORATION—See GAF Corporation; *U.S. Private*, pg. 433
G-NET CORPORATION; *Int'l*, pg. 531
G-P CONFEDERATION, INC.—See Confederation Life Insurance Company; *Int'l*, pg. 326
G-SECURITIES—See Generale de Banque S.A.; *Int'l*, pg. 547
G-III APPAREL GROUP, LTD.; *U.S. Public*, pg. 690
G-2 OFFICE FURNITURE MARKET—See Goodmans, Inc.; *U.S. Private*, pg. 464
GA FERAL AB—See Norsk Hydro a.s; *Int'l*, pg. 962
GA INSURANCE SERVICES—See H.W. Kaufman Financial Group, Inc.; *U.S. Private*, pg. 609
GA LTD.—See Hollandsche Beton Groep NV; *Int'l*, pg. 630
GA LINDBERG AB—See AB Industrivarden; *Int'l*, pg. 678
GAB ROBINS NORTH AMERICA, INC.—See SGS Societe Generale de Surveillance Holding S.A.; *Int'l*, pg. 1153
GAC COLOR GRAPHICS—See Mail-Well Inc.; *U.S. Public*, pg. 1038
GACC HOLDING COMPANY—See American Financial Group; *U.S. Public*, pg. 75
GAF CORPORATION; *U.S. Private*, pg. 433
GAF-HULS CHEMIE GMBH—See Veba AG; *Int'l*, pg. 1454
GAF MATERIALS CORPORATION—See GAF Corporation; *U.S. Private*, pg. 433
GAF PREMIUM PRODUCTS, INC.—See GAF Corporation; *U.S. Private*, pg. 433
GAI CONSULTANTS, INC.; *U.S. Private*, pg. 433
GAI CONSULTANTS-SOUTHEAST, INC.—See GAI Consultants, Inc.; *U.S. Private*, pg. 434
GATX CAPITAL CORPORATION—See GATX Corporation; *U.S. Public*, pg. 690
GATX CONTRACT CARRIERS, INC.—See GATX Corporation; *U.S. Public*, pg. 691
GATX CORPORATION; *U.S. Public*, pg. 690
GATX FINANCE (UK) LTD.—See GATX Corporation; *U.S. Public*, pg. 691
GATX FINANCIAL SERVICES—See GATX Corporation; *U.S. Public*, pg. 690
GATX FINANCIAL SERVICES (AUSTRALIA) PTY. LIMITED—See GATX Corporation; *U.S. Public*, pg. 691
GATX FINANCIAL SERVICES GMBH—See GATX Corporation; *U.S. Public*, pg. 691
GATX FREIGHT SYSTEMS-CALIFORNIA—See GATX Corporation; *U.S. Public*, pg. 691
GATX LAS VEGAS CORPORATION—See GATX Corporation; *U.S. Public*, pg. 692
GATX LEASING (PACIFIC) LTD.—See GATX Corporation; *U.S. Public*, pg. 691
GATX LOGISTICS DE MEXICO, S.A. DE C.V.—See GATX Corporation; *U.S. Public*, pg. 692
GATX LOGISTICS (DWC), INC.—See GATX Corporation; *U.S. Public*, pg. 691
GATX LOGISTICS, INC.—See GATX Corporation; *U.S. Public*, pg. 691
GATX LOGISTICS, INC.-CALIFORNIA (KELLOGG)—See GATX Corporation; *U.S. Public*, pg. 691
GATX LOGISTICS, INC.-FLORIDA; *U.S. Public*, pg. 691
GATX LOGISTICS, INC.-GEORGIA—See GATX Corporation; *U.S. Public*, pg. 691
GATX LOGISTICS, INC.-ILLINOIS—See GATX Corporation; *U.S. Public*, pg. 691
GATX LOGISTICS, INC.-N.Y.—See GATX Corporation; *U.S. Public*, pg. 691
GATX LOGISTICS, INC.-UTAH—See GATX Corporation; *U.S. Public*, pg. 692
GATX LOGISTICS (JMH), INC.—See GATX Corporation; *U.S. Public*, pg. 691

GATX LOGISTICS (LWD), INC.—See GATX Corporation; U.S. Public, pg. 691
GATX LOGISTICS NORPACK, INC.—See GATX Corporation; U.S. Public, pg. 691
GATX LOGISTICS PROPERTIES, INC.—See GATX Corporation; U.S. Public, pg. 691
GATX NATIONAL LEASING, LTD.—See GATX Corporation; U.S. Public, pg. 691
GATX PIPELINE COMPANY—See GATX Corporation; U.S. Public, pg. 692
GATX PRIVATE LTD.—See GATX Corporation; U.S. Public, pg. 692
GATX TERMINALS CORPORATION—See GATX Corporation; U.S. Public, pg. 692
GATX TERMINALS LTD.—See GATX Corporation; U.S. Public, pg. 693
GATX TERMINALS (PTE.) LTD.—See GATX Corporation; U.S. Public, pg. 693
GB DISTRIBUTION LLC—See The Bartell Drug Company; U.S. Private, pg. 118
GB ELECTRICAL, INC.—See Applied Power Inc.; U.S. Public, pg. 124
GB! GRIFFIN BACAL PROMOTIONS—See Griffin Bacal Inc.; U.S. Private, pg. 480
GB HOLDINGS; Int'l, pg. 531
GB INTERNATIONAL—See GIB Group; Int'l, pg. 534
GB LEX—See Groupe Bruxelles Lambert S.A.; Int'l, pg. 562
GB PAPERS LIMITED—See Fort James Corporation; U.S. Public, pg. 672
GB UNIC SA—See GIB Group; Int'l, pg. 533
SARL GB ZAIRE—See GIB Group; Int'l, pg. 534
GB ZAIRE SARL—See GIB Group; Int'l, pg. 534
GBB GEWERBEBAU-BERATUNG GMBH—See Commerzbank AG; Int'l, pg. 310
GBC/VELOBLIND—See General Binding Corporation; U.S. Public, pg. 707
GBR LEIPZIGER STRASSE/QUARTIER 108—See Commerzbank AG; Int'l, pg. 309
GC & CO.-MOBILE FIELD SHOP & GARAGE—See Unitel Video, Inc.; U.S. Public, pg. 1692
GC COMPANIES, INC.; U.S. Public, pg. 693
GC INTERNATIONAL, INC.—See GC Companies, Inc.; U.S. Public, pg. 693
G.C. PHARMACEUTICAL (SINGAPORE) LTD.—See The Green Cross Corporation; Int'l, pg. 558
G.C.A.—See Bouygues; Int'l, pg. 206
GCC FAR EAST, INC.—See Bell Atlantic Corporation; U.S. Public, pg. 203
GCC INVESTMENTS, INC.—See GC Companies, Inc.; U.S. Public, pg. 693
GCE—See AGA AB; Int'l, pg. 14
GCE-GAS CONTROL EQUIPMENT AB—See Charter plc; Int'l, pg. 281
GCH ACQUISITION CORP.—See Taisei Corporation; Int'l, pg. 1347
GCI BOSTON, INC.—See Granum Communications; U.S. Private, pg. 470
GCI DALLAS, INC/GCI TEXAS, INC—See Granum Communications; U.S. Private, pg. 470
GCI GROUP INC.—See Grey Advertising Inc.; U.S. Public, pg. 764
GCI HOLDINGS CORPORATION; U.S. Private, pg. 434
GCI LOWELL INC/WZYZ F.M.—See Granum Communications; U.S. Private, pg. 470
GCI ORANGE, INC/GCI ORLANDO, INC.—See Granum Communications; U.S. Private, pg. 470
GCMP (THAILAND) LTD.—See BASF AG; Int'l, pg. 108
GCO MINERALS CO.—See International Paper Company; U.S. Public, pg. 902
GD EXPRESS WORLDWIDE NV—See TNT Limited; Int'l, pg. 1343
GD-GÖLVDEPAN I SVERIGE AB—See Forbo Holding SA; Int'l, pg. 498
G.D. INTERNATIONAL, LTD.—See Olin Corporation; U.S. Public, pg. 1219
GD NET BV—See KPN Koninklyke PTT Nederland NV; Int'l, pg. 720
G.D. PACKAGING MACHINERY INC.—See G.D. S.p.A.; Int'l, pg. 531
G.D. S.p.A.; Int'l, pg. 531
GDC FEDERAL SYSTEMS, INC.—See General Datacomm Industries, Inc.; U.S. Public, pg. 708
GDE SYSTEMS, INC.—See Tracor, Inc.; U.S. Public, pg. 1627
GDIVC (GLAVNI DEMONSTRATCIONO-ISPYTALELNJY VYCHESLITEINJY CENTER)—See Hewlett-Packard Company; U.S. Public, pg. 817
GDRU, LTD.—See Genzyme Corporation; U.S. Public, pg. 733
G.E. AIRCRAFT ENGINES—See General Electric Company; U.S. Public, pg. 710
G.E. AMERICAN COMMUNICATIONS, INC.—See General Electric Company; U.S. Public, pg. 711
G.E. APPLIANCES—See General Electric Company; U.S. Public, pg. 710
G.E. ASIA—See General Electric Company; U.S. Public, pg. 713
G.E. CANADA, PETERBOROUGH—See General Electric Company; U.S. Public, pg. 713
G.E. CANADA POWER SYSTEMS—See General Electric Company; U.S. Public, pg. 713
G.E. CAPITAL ASSURANCE—See General Electric Company; U.S. Public, pg. 710
G.E. CAPITAL COMMERCIAL REAL ESTATE FINANCING—See General Electric Company; U.S. Public, pg. 712
G.E. CAPITAL FLEET SERVICES—See General Electric Company; U.S. Public, pg. 710
G.E. CAPITAL/IT SOLUTIONS—See General Electric Company; U.S. Public, pg. 711
G.E. CAPITAL MORTGAGE SERVICES—See General Electric Company; U.S. Public, pg. 712
G.E. CAPITAL VENDOR FINANCIAL SERVICES—See General Electric Company; U.S. Public, pg. 712

G.E. FANUC AUTOMATION CANADA—See General Electric Company; Int'l, pg. 713
GE FANUC AUTOMATION CORPORATION—See Fanuc Ltd.; Int'l, pg. 477
GE FANUC AUTOMATION CORPORATION—See General Electric Company; U.S. Public, pg. 711
GE FANUC AUTOMATION EUROPE S.A.—See Fanuc Ltd.; Int'l, pg. 478
GE FANUC AUTOMATION NORTH AMERICA, INC.—See Fanuc Ltd.; Int'l, pg. 477
GE/FUJI ELECTRIC CO., LTD.—See Fuji Electric Co., Ltd.; Int'l, pg. 522
G.E. HARRIS ENERGY CONTROL SYSTEMS, LLC—See General Electric Company; U.S. Public, pg. 712
G.E. HARRIS ENERGY CONTROL SYSTEMS, LLC—See Harris Corporation; U.S. Public, pg. 792
G.E.-HITACHI HVB INC.—See Hitachi, Ltd.; Int'l, pg. 622
GE IMMOBILIENVERWALTUNGS GMBH—See Bayerische Vereinsbank Group; Int'l, pg. 178
GE IMMOBILIENVERWALTUNGS GMBH & CO. GRUNDSTUCKS KG—See Bayerische Vereinsbank Group; Int'l, pg. 178
G.E. INDUSTRIAL & POWER SYSTEMS SALES—See General Electric Company; U.S. Public, pg. 711
G.E. INFORMATION SERVICES—See General Electric Company; U.S. Public, pg. 710
G.E. LIGHTING DIVISION—See General Electric Company; U.S. Public, pg. 710
G.E. LIGHTING EUROPE—See General Electric Company; U.S. Public, pg. 713
G.E. LIGHTING (IRELAND) LTD.—See General Electric Company; U.S. Public, pg. 713
G.E. LIGHTING LTD.—See General Electric Company; U.S. Public, pg. 713
G.E. LIGHTING LIMITED—See General Electric Company; U.S. Public, pg. 713
G.E. MEDICAL SYSTEMS—See General Electric Company; U.S. Public, pg. 710
GE MEDICAL SYSTEMS ASIA LTD.—See General Electric Company; U.S. Public, pg. 713
G.E. NUCLEAR ENERGY—See General Electric Company; U.S. Public, pg. 711
G.E. PLASTIC CANADA—See General Electric Company; U.S. Public, pg. 710
G.E. PLASTICS—See General Electric Company; U.S. Public, pg. 710
G.E. PLASTICS-AMERICA—See General Electric Company; U.S. Public, pg. 710
G.E. PLASTICS EUROPE—See General Electric Company; U.S. Public, pg. 713
G.E. PLASTICS PACIFIC LTD.—See General Electric Company; U.S. Public, pg. 713
G.E. POWER SYSTEMS—See General Electric Company; U.S. Public, pg. 710
G.E. SILICONES—See General Electric Company; U.S. Public, pg. 711
G.E. SPACENET CORPORATION—See General Electric Company; U.S. Public, pg. 711
G.E. SPECIALTY CHEMICALS—See General Electric Company; U.S. Public, pg. 711
G.E. SUPERABRASIVES—See General Electric Company; U.S. Public, pg. 711
G.E. TECHNICAL SERVICES—See General Electric Company; U.S. Public, pg. 713
G.E.-THORN LAMPS PRESSCAPS DIVISION—See General Electric Company; U.S. Public, pg. 713
GE TOSHIBA APPLIANCES COMPANY PTE. LTD.—See Toshiba Corporation; Int'l, pg. 1405
G.E. TOSHIBA LIGHTING CORPORATION—See General Electric Company; U.S. Public, pg. 710
G.E. TUNGSTRAM CO.—See General Electric Company; U.S. Public, pg. 713
G.E. (U.S.A.) AVIATION SERVICE OPERATION PTE. LTD.—See General Electric Company; U.S. Public, pg. 713
GEAC COMPUTER CORPORATION LIMITED; Int'l, pg. 532
GEC AEROSPACE LTD.—See The General Electric Company, p.l.c.; Int'l, pg. 543
GEC ALSTHOM—See Alcatel Alsthom Compagnie Generale D'Electricite; Int'l, pg. 52
GEC ALSTHOM-INTERMAGNETICS S.A.—See Alcatel Alsthom Compagnie Generale D'Electricite; Int'l, pg. 56
GEC ALSTHOM N.V.—See Alcatel Alsthom Compagnie Generale D'Electricite; Int'l, pg. 56
GEC AUSTRALIA LTD.—See The General Electric Company, p.l.c.; Int'l, pg. 546
GEC AVERY LTD.—See The General Electric Company, p.l.c.; Int'l, pg. 543
GEC AVIONICS INC.—See The General Electric Company, p.l.c.; Int'l, pg. 544
GEC AVIONICS LTD.—See The General Electric Company, p.l.c.; Int'l, pg. 543
GEC BRUNEI SDN. BHD.—See The General Electric Company, p.l.c.; Int'l, pg. 546
GEC CARD TECHNOLOGY LTD.—See The General Electric Company, p.l.c.; Int'l, pg. 544
GEC COMPOSANTS S.A.—See The General Electric Company, p.l.c.; Int'l, pg. 544
GEC COMPUTER SERVICES LTD.—See The General Electric Company, p.l.c.; Int'l, pg. 544
GEC DISTRIBUTORS (IRELAND) LTD.—See The General Electric Company, p.l.c.; Int'l, pg. 546
GEC DYNAMICS LIMITED-MISSILES & ORDNANCE—See The General Electric Company, p.l.c.; Int'l, pg. 544
GEC EDUCATION LIAISON—See The General Electric Company, p.l.c.; Int'l, pg. 544
GEC ELECTRICAL PROJECTS LTD.—See Alcatel Alsthom Compagnie Generale D'Electricite; Int'l, pg. 53
GEC ENGINEERING (ACCRINGTON) LTD.—See The General Electric Company, p.l.c.; Int'l, pg. 544
GEC ESTATES DEPARTMENT—See The General Electric Company, p.l.c.; Int'l, pg. 544

GEC FERRANTI DEFENCE SYSTEMS LTD.—See The General Electric Company, p.l.c.; Int'l, pg. 544
GEC-GENERAL SIGNAL LTD.—See General Signal Corporation; U.S. Public, pg. 727
GEC INDUSTRIAL CONTROLS LTD.—See Alcatel Alsthom Compagnie Generale D'Electricite; Int'l, pg. 53
GEC MANAGEMENT COLLEGE—See The General Electric Company, p.l.c.; Int'l, pg. 544
GEC-MARCONI COMMUNICATION NETWORKS LTD.—See The General Electric Company, p.l.c.; Int'l, pg. 544
GEC-MARCONI COMMUNICATIONS LTD.—See The General Electric Company, p.l.c.; Int'l, pg. 544
GEC-MARCONI DYNAMICS LTD.—See The General Electric Company, p.l.c.; Int'l, pg. 544
GEC-MARCONI ELECTRONIC SYSTEMS CORP.—See The General Electric Company, p.l.c.; Int'l, pg. 544
GEC-MARCONI HAZELTINE CORPORATION—See The General Electric Company, p.l.c.; Int'l, pg. 544
GEC-MARCONI LTD.—See The General Electric Company, p.l.c.; Int'l, pg. 544
GEC-MARCONI MATERIALS TECHNOLOGY LTD.—See The General Electric Company, p.l.c.; Int'l, pg. 544
GEC-MARCONI PROJECTS (MALAYSIA) SDN. BHD.—See The General Electric Company, p.l.c.; Int'l, pg. 544
GEC-MARCONI RESEARCH CENTRE—See The General Electric Company, p.l.c.; Int'l, pg. 544
GEC-MARCONI SYSTEMS PTY. LTD.—See The General Electric Company, p.l.c.; Int'l, pg. 546
GEC NAVAL SYSTEMS LTD.—See The General Electric Company, p.l.c.; Int'l, pg. 544
GEC (NEW ZEALAND) LTD.—See The General Electric Company, p.l.c.; Int'l, pg. 546
GEC PLESSEY NAVAL SYSTEMS INC.—See The General Electric Company, p.l.c.; Int'l, pg. 545
GEC PLESSEY SEMICONDUCTORS—See The General Electric Company, p.l.c.; Int'l, pg. 544
GEC POWER INSTRUMENTATION & CONTROL LTD.—See Alcatel Alsthom Compagnie Generale D'Electricite; Int'l, pg. 53
GEC PRECISION CORP.—See The General Electric Company, p.l.c.; Int'l, pg. 545
GEC REINFORCED PLASTICS LTD.—See The General Electric Company, p.l.c.; Int'l, pg. 544
GEC SENSORS LTD.—See The General Electric Company, p.l.c.; Int'l, pg. 544
GEC SOUTH AFRICA (PTY) LTD.—See The General Electric Company, p.l.c.; Int'l, pg. 546
GEC (UK) AEROSPACE INC.—See The General Electric Company, p.l.c.; Int'l, pg. 545
GEC ZAMBIA LTD.—See The General Electric Company, p.l.c.; Int'l, pg. 546
GEC ZIMBABWE (PVT) LTD.—See The General Electric Company, p.l.c.; Int'l, pg. 546
GECC GROUP—See Alcatel Alsthom Compagnie Generale D'Electricite; Int'l, pg. 53
GECI (GROUPE D'ETUDES ET CONSEILS EN INGENIERIE)—See The Macneal-Schwendler Corp.; U.S. Public, pg. 1032
GEFCO—See PSA Peugeot Citroen; Int'l, pg. 1021
GEFIL GESELLSCHAFT FUR INTERNATIONALEN LABORSERVICE MBH—See Bayer AG; Int'l, pg. 174
GEHE AG—See Franz Haniel & Cie, GmbH; Int'l, pg. 591
GEKE AG—See Mannesmann A.G.; Int'l, pg. 836
G.E.O.S. FREIBERG INGENIEURGESELLSCHAFT MBH—See Philipp Holzmann AG; Int'l, pg. 632
GES—See Groupe Casino; Int'l, pg. 563
GES ENVIRONMENTAL, INC.—See Omega Environmental Inc.; U.S. Public, pg. 1222
GES EXPOSITION SERVICES, INC.—See Viad Corp; U.S. Public, pg. 1718
GES INC.; U.S. Private, pg. 434
GESA - GAS Y ELECTRICIDAD, S.A.—See SEPI; Int'l, pg. 1224
GESTRA ESPANOLA S.A.—See GESTRA GmbH; Int'l, pg. 550
PZ GESTRA POLONIA SP. Z O.O.—See GESTRA GmbH; Int'l, pg. 550
GETCO GENERAL ENTERPRISES AND TRADING CORP.—See GESTRA GmbH; Int'l, pg. 550
GF FOOD SERVICES—See Goodman Fielder Limited; Int'l, pg. 555
GF INDUSTRIES, INC.; U.S. Private, pg. 434
GF INTERNATIONAL LIMITED—See Goodman Fielder Limited; Int'l, pg. 555
GF MCLEAN SHOPPING CENTER—See Giant Food Inc.; U.S. Public, pg. 741
GF OFFICE FURNITURE LTD.; U.S. Private, pg. 434
GF PACIFIC EXPORTS (NZ) LTD.—See Goodman Fielder Limited; Int'l, pg. 556
GF PROPERTIES, INC.—See GF Industries, Inc.; U.S. Private, pg. 434
GFA BRANDS, INC.; U.S. Private, pg. 435
G.F.C.—See Bouygues; Int'l, pg. 206
GFE EICHERHEIT FUHRUNGSGESELLSCHAFT MBH—See Veba AG; Int'l, pg. 1457
GFG CORPORATION—See Derlan Industries Limited; Int'l, pg. 395
GFI AMERICA; U.S. Private, pg. 435
GFI-GENFARE—See General Signal Corporation; U.S. Public, pg. 727
GFI INC.—See Kaufel Group Ltd.; Int'l, pg. 725
GFI TB LA MONDIALE BULL—See Compagnie des Machines Bull; Int'l, pg. 318
GFS REALTY, INC.—See Giant Food Inc.; U.S. Public, pg. 741
GFW GESELLSCHAFT ZUR FORDERUNG VON WOHNEIGENTUM MBH—See Commerzbank AG; Int'l, pg. 310
GG WS GROSS—See Dahl International AB; Int'l, pg. 359
GGK ATHENS—See TBWA GGK Zurich; Int'l, pg. 1335
GGK BARCELONA—See TBWA GGK Zurich; Int'l, pg. 1335
GGK BASEL—See TBWA GGK Zurich; Int'l, pg. 1335
GGK BRUSSELS—See TBWA GGK Zurich; Int'l, pg. 1335
GGK BUDAPEST—See TBWA GGK Zurich; Int'l, pg. 1335

GGK COMMUNICATIONS—See TBWA GGK Zurick; *Int'l*, pg. 1335
GGK COPENHAGEN—See TBWA GGK Zurick; *Int'l*, pg. 1335
GGK DUBLIN—See TBWA GGK Zurick; *Int'l*, pg. 1335
GGK DUSSELDORF—See TBWA GGK Zurick; *Int'l*, pg. 1335
GGK EUROPE—See TBWA GGK Zurick; *Int'l*, pg. 1335
GGK INTERNATIONAL'S EXECUTIVE BOARD—See TBWA GGK Zurick; *Int'l*, pg. 1335
GGK LONDON LTD.—See TBWA GGK Zurick; *Int'l*, pg. 1335
GGK MADRID—See TBWA GGK Zurick; *Int'l*, pg. 1335
GGK OCCIDENTAL—See TBWA GGK Zurick; *Int'l*, pg. 1335
GGK OCCIDENTAL HOLDING AG—See TBWA GGK Zurick; *Int'l*, pg. 1335
GGK OSLO—See TBWA GGK Zurick; *Int'l*, pg. 1335
GGK PARIS—See TBWA GGK Zurick; *Int'l*, pg. 1335
GGK SALZBURG—See TBWA GGK Zurick; *Int'l*, pg. 1335
GGK SAO PAULO—See TBWA GGK Zurick; *Int'l*, pg. 1335
GGK TEL AVIV—See TBWA GGK Zurick; *Int'l*, pg. 1336
GGK VIENNA—See TBWA GGK Zurick; *Int'l*, pg. 1336
GGK WARSAW—See TBWA GGK Zurick; *Int'l*, pg. 1336
GGK WIEN WERBEAGENTUR GMBH—See TBWA GGK Zurick; *Int'l*, pg. 1336
GGK ZURICH—See TBWA GGK Zurick; *Int'l*, pg. 1335
GGP/HOMART, INC.—See General Growth Properties Inc.; *U.S. Public*, pg. 715
GGRI, INC.—See Griffin Group Inc.; *U.S. Private*, pg. 480
GGT ADVERTISING LTD.; *Int'l*, pg. 532
GGT DIRECT ADVERTISING; *Int'l*, pg. 532
GGT DIRECT MANCHESTER—See GGT Direct Advertising; *Int'l*, pg. 532
GH HENSLEY INDUSTRIES, INC.—See Galveston-Houston Company; *U.S. Private*, pg. 435
GHH BORSIG TURBOMASCHINEN GMBH—See MAN Aktiengesellschaft; *Int'l*, pg. 824
GHM INDUSTRIES, INC.; *U.S. Private*, pg. 435
GHN—See Everbrite, Inc.; *U.S. Private*, pg. 386
G.I. JOE'S INC.; *U.S. Private*, pg. 435
G.I. PLASTEK; *U.S. Private*, pg. 435
G.I. TRUCKING CO.—See Arkansas Best Corporation; *U.S. Public*, pg. 131
GI-YAMANOUCHI, INC.—See Yamanouchi Pharmaceutical Co. Ltd.; *Int'l*, pg. 1518
GIAG-GLASINDUSTRIE AG—See Saint-Gobain; *Int'l*, pg. 1172
GIB COORDINATION CENTER—See GIB Group; *Int'l*, pg. 533
GIB GROUP; *Int'l*, pg. 532
GIEE BRICO INTERNATIONAL—See GIB Group; *Int'l*, pg. 533
GIP GEWERBE IM PARK GMBH—See Philipp Holzmann AG; *Int'l*, pg. 632
GIS MUNSTERS B.V.—See Royal Begemann Group; *Int'l*, pg. 1133
GIT GESELLSCHAFT FUR INGENIEUER-TECHNIK MBH—See Mannesmann A.G.; *Int'l*, pg. 836
GIT, LTD.—See Gibraltar Steel Corp.; *U.S. Public*, pg. 742
GIW INDUSTRIES, INC.—See KSB Aktiengesellschaft; *Int'l*, pg. 721
GK FINANCE CORPORATION—See Gold Kist, Inc.; *U.S. Private*, pg. 459
GK FINANCING, LLC—See American Shared Hospital Services; *U.S. Public*, pg. 91
GK GESELLSCHAFT FUER KOHLEVERFLUESSIGUNG MBH—See Saarbergwerke Aktiengesellschaft; *Int'l*, pg. 1166
GK STORES INC.—See Gold Kist, Inc.; *U.S. Private*, pg. 459
GKI ELECTRONIC ENCLOSURE DIVISION-JOHNSTOWN—See General Kinetics Incorporated; *U.S. Public*, pg. 717
GKI ELECTRONIC ENCLOSURE DIVISION-ORLANDO—See General Kinetics Incorporated; *U.S. Public*, pg. 717
GKK AUTOMOTIVE—See GenCorp Inc.; *U.S. Public*, pg. 706
GKK PLASTICS LTD.—See Brother Industries, Ltd.; *Int'l*, pg. 230
GKN AUTOMOTIVE INC.—See GKN plc; *Int'l*, pg. 535
GKN AUTOMOTIVE INTERNATIONAL GMBH—See GKN plc; *Int'l*, pg. 535
GKN AUTOMOTIVE LTD.—See GKN plc; *Int'l*, pg. 534
GKN AYRA CARDAN SA—See GKN plc; *Int'l*, pg. 535
GKN AYRA DUREX SA—See GKN plc; *Int'l*, pg. 535
GKN BIRFIELD SPA—See GKN plc; *Int'l*, pg. 535
GKN BOUND BROOK LTD.—See GKN plc; *Int'l*, pg. 534
GKN-BRAMBLES ENTERPRISES, LTD.—See Brambles Industries Limited; *Int'l*, pg. 212
GKN-BRAMBLES ENTERPRISES, LTD.—See GKN plc; *Int'l*, pg. 535
GKN CHEP SA (PTY) LTD.—See GKN plc; *Int'l*, pg. 536
GKN COMERCIAL LIMITADA—See GKN plc; *Int'l*, pg. 536
GKN COMPONENTI FIRENZE SPA—See GKN plc; *Int'l*, pg. 536
GKN COMPUTER SERVICES LTD.—See GKN plc; *Int'l*, pg. 534
GKN DEFENCE LTD.—See GKN plc; *Int'l*, pg. 534
GKN DISTRIBUTION GMBH—See GKN plc; *Int'l*, pg. 536
GKN DRIVELINE LTD.—See GKN plc; *Int'l*, pg. 534
GKN DRIVESHAFTS LTD.—See GKN plc; *Int'l*, pg. 534
GKN DRIVETECH LTD.—See GKN plc; *Int'l*, pg. 534
GKN FLORANGE SARL—See GKN plc; *Int'l*, pg. 536
GKN FORJAS DE PRECISION DE LEGAZPIA SA—See GKN plc; *Int'l*, pg. 536
GKN FREIGHT SERVICES LTD.—See GKN plc; *Int'l*, pg. 534
GKN GELENKWELLENBAU GMBH—See GKN plc; *Int'l*, pg. 536
GKN GELENKWELLENWERK KIEL GMBH—See GKN plc; *Int'l*, pg. 536
GKN GELENKWELLENWERK MOSEL GMBH—See GKN plc; *Int'l*, pg. 535

GKN GLAENZER CARDAN SA—See GKN plc; *Int'l*, pg. 536
GKN GLAENZER SPICER SA—See GKN plc; *Int'l*, pg. 536
GKN HARDY SPICER LTD.—See GKN plc; *Int'l*, pg. 534
GKN INDUGASA SA—See GKN plc; *Int'l*, pg. 536
GKN INFORMATIK GMBH—See GKN plc; *Int'l*, pg. 536
GKN JAPAN LTD.—See GKN plc; *Int'l*, pg. 536
GKN NORDISKA KARDAN AB—See GKN plc; *Int'l*, pg. 536
GKN NORTH AMERICA SERVICES INC.—See GKN plc; *Int'l*, pg. 535
GKN PLC; *Int'l*, pg. 534
GKN POWDER METALLURGY DIVISION—See GKN plc; *Int'l*, pg. 534
GKN REMANUFACTURING GMBH—See GKN plc; *Int'l*, pg. 536
GKN RIBEMONT SARL—See GKN plc; *Int'l*, pg. 536
GKN SANKEY ENGINEERING PRODUCTS—See GKN plc; *Int'l*, pg. 535
GKN SANKEY INDUSTRIAL PRODUCTS—See GKN plc; *Int'l*, pg. 535
GKN SANKEY LTD.—See GKN plc; *Int'l*, pg. 534
GKN SERVICE-AUSTRIA GMBH—See GKN plc; *Int'l*, pg. 536
GKN SERVICE GMBH—See GKN plc; *Int'l*, pg. 536
GKN SHEEPBRIDGE STOKES LTD.—See GKN plc; *Int'l*, pg. 535
GKN SINTER METALS INC.—See GKN plc; *Int'l*, pg. 535
GKN SQUEEZEFORM—See GKN plc; *Int'l*, pg. 534
GKN TECHNOLOGY LTD.—See GKN plc; *Int'l*, pg. 535
GKN TECHNOLOGY US—See GKN plc; *Int'l*, pg. 535
GKN WALTERSCHEID GMBH—See GKN plc; *Int'l*, pg. 535
GKN WALTERSCHEID INC.—See GKN plc; *Int'l*, pg. 536
GKN WALTERSCHEID PRESSWERK GMBH—See GKN plc; *Int'l*, pg. 536
GKN WESTLAND AEROSPACE LIMITED—See GKN plc; *Int'l*, pg. 535
GKN WESTLAND AEROSPACE NORTH AMERICA INC.—See GKN plc; *Int'l*, pg. 535
GKN WESTLAND HELICOPTERS LIMITED—See GKN plc; *Int'l*, pg. 535
GKN WESTLAND INDUSTRIAL PRODUCTS LTD.—See GKN plc; *Int'l*, pg. 535
GKN WESTLAND TECHNOLOGIES LIMITED—See GKN plc; *Int'l*, pg. 535
GKN WHEELS—See GKN plc; *Int'l*, pg. 535
GKN WHEELS NAGBOL A/S—See GKN plc; *Int'l*, pg. 535
GL DIRECT—See Great Lakes Lithograph Co.; *U.S. Private*, pg. 475
G.L.G. CORPORATION—See NHK Spring Co., Inc.; *Int'l*, pg. 901
GLI HOLDING COMPANY—See Greyhound Lines, Inc.; *U.S. Public*, pg. 765
GLI VENTURE COMPANY—See Greyhound Lines, Inc.; *U.S. Public*, pg. 765
GLS CORPORATION; *U.S. Private*, pg. 435
GLS GESELLSCHAFT FUR LOGISTISCHEN SERVICE MBH—See Mannesmann A.G.; *Int'l*, pg. 836
N.V. GLS LOGISTICAL SERVICE SA—See Mannesmann A.G.; *Int'l*, pg. 836
GLS OF INDIANA—See GLS Corporation; *U.S. Private*, pg. 435
GM ALLISON JAPAN LIMITED—See General Motors Corporation; *U.S. Public*, pg. 721
G.M. KENKI LEASE CO.—See Caterpillar Inc.; *U.S. Public*, pg. 317
GM POWERTRAIN GROUP—See General Motors Corporation; *U.S. Public*, pg. 719
GMAC MORTGAGE CORPORATION—See General Motors Corporation; *U.S. Public*, pg. 720
GMAC MORTGAGE CORPORATION OF IOWA—See General Motors Corporation; *U.S. Public*, pg. 720
GMAC MORTGAGE CORPORATION OF PENNSYLVANIA—See General Motors Corporation; *U.S. Public*, pg. 720
GMB SALES—See Video Display Corporation; *U.S. Public*, pg. 1720
GME GENERALI-MIDI EXPANSION B.V.—See Assicurazioni Generali S.p.A.; *Int'l*, pg. 91
GMO LAND COMPANY—See Illinois Central Corporation; *U.S. Public*, pg. 865
GMOC JAPAN—See General Motors Corporation; *U.S. Public*, pg. 723
GMP REAL ESTATE CORP.—See Green Mountain Power Corporation; *U.S. Public*, pg. 761
THE GMR GROUP—See Omnicom Group Inc.; *U.S. Public*, pg. 1224
GMS CORPORATION; *U.S. Private*, pg. 435
GMSI, INC.—See Geotek Communications; *U.S. Public*, pg. 740
GN DANAVOX A/S—See GN Great Nordic Ltd.; *Int'l*, pg. 537
GN EJENDOMME—See GN Great Nordic Ltd.; *Int'l*, pg. 537
GN GREAT NORDIC LTD.; *Int'l*, pg. 536
GN GREAT NORTHERN TELEGRAPH COMPANY—See GN Great Nordic Ltd.; *Int'l*, pg. 537
GN NETCOM A/S—See GN Great Nordic Ltd.; *Int'l*, pg. 537
GN NETTEST, DATACOM DIVISION—See GN Great Nordic Ltd.; *Int'l*, pg. 536
GN NETTEST FIBER OPTIC DIVISION—See GN Great Nordic Ltd.; *Int'l*, pg. 536
GN NETTEST HOLDING—See GN Great Nordic Ltd.; *Int'l*, pg. 536
GN NETTEST, TELECOM DIVISION—See GN Great Nordic Ltd.; *Int'l*, pg. 536
GN RATHDOWN—See GN Great Nordic Ltd.; *Int'l*, pg. 537
GNA CORP.—See General Electric Company; *U.S. Public*, pg. 712
GNB TECHNOLOGIES—See Pacific Dunlop Limited; *Int'l*, pg. 1021
GNC CORP—See Goshen Rubber Co., Inc.; *U.S. Private*, pg. 466

GNI CHEMICAL CORPORATION—See The GNI Group, Inc.; *U.S. Public*, pg. 693
THE GNI GROUP, INC.; *U.S. Public*, pg. 693
GNL, CORP.—See Mirage Resorts Incorporated; *U.S. Public*, pg. 1116
GNLV, CORP.—See Mirage Resorts Incorporated; *U.S. Public*, pg. 1117
GNWC WIRE, CABLE & NETWORK PRODUCTS—See Communications Supply Corporation; *U.S. Private*, pg. 259
GO INTERNATIONAL DE ARGENTINA S.A.—See Halliburton Company; *U.S. Public*, pg. 776
GO INTERNATIONAL DE VENEZUELA, S.A.—See Halliburton Company; *U.S. Public*, pg. 776
GO INTERNATIONAL SERVICES ELECTRO-DIGITAL DE BRAZIL, LTDA.—See Halliburton Company; *U.S. Public*, pg. 776
GO INTERNATIONAL SOUTH AMERICA, S.A.—See Halliburton Company; *U.S. Public*, pg. 776
GO WELL SERVICES, INC.—See Halliburton Company; *U.S. Public*, pg. 776
GP BATTERIES (CHINA) LTD.—See GP Batteries International Ltd.; *Int'l*, pg. 537
GP BATTERIES INTERNATIONAL LTD.; *Int'l*, pg. 537
GP BATTERIES (MALAYSIA) SDN. BHD.—See GP Batteries International Ltd.; *Int'l*, pg. 537
GP BATTERY MARKETING (HK) LTD.—See GP Batteries International Ltd.; *Int'l*, pg. 537
GP BATTERY MARKETING (SINGAPORE) PTE LTD.—See GP Batteries International Ltd.; *Int'l*, pg. 537
GP BATTERY MARKETING (TAIWAN) LTD.—See GP Batteries International Ltd.; *Int'l*, pg. 537
GP ELECTRONICS LIMITED—See GP Batteries International Ltd.; *Int'l*, pg. 537
GP INSTRUMENT SERVICES—See GP Strategies Corporation; *U.S. Public*, pg. 694
GP STRATEGIES CORPORATION; *U.S. Public*, pg. 694
GP TAURIO, INC.—See GP Strategies Corporation; *U.S. Public*, pg. 694
GPA GROUP PLC—See Air Canada; *Int'l*, pg. 37
GPA PLAST AB—See AB Industrivarden; *Int'l*, pg. 678
GPA PLAST A/S—See AB Industrivarden; *Int'l*, pg. 678
GPC COMMUNICATIONS (CALGARY)—See Omnicom Group Inc.; *U.S. Public*, pg. 1225
GPC COMMUNICATIONS (MONTREAL)—See Omnicom Group Inc.; *U.S. Public*, pg. 1225
GPC COMMUNICATIONS (ONTARIO)—See Omnicom Group Inc.; *U.S. Public*, pg. 1225
GPC CONNECT (LONDON)—See Omnicom Group Inc.; *U.S. Public*, pg. 1225
GPC GOVERNMENT POLICY CONSULTANTS (CALGARY)—See Omnicom Group Inc.; *U.S. Public*, pg. 1225
GPC GOVERNMENT POLICY CONSULTANTS (EDMONTON)—See Omnicom Group Inc.; *U.S. Public*, pg. 1225
GPC GOVERNMENT POLICY CONSULTANTS (FEDERAL)—See Omnicom Group Inc.; *U.S. Public*, pg. 1225
GPC GOVERNMENT POLICY CONSULTANTS (ONTARIO)—See Omnicom Group Inc.; *U.S. Public*, pg. 1225
GPC GOVERNMENT POLICY CONSULTANTS (QUEBEC)—See Omnicom Group Inc.; *U.S. Public*, pg. 1225
GPC GOVERNMENT POLICY CONSULTANTS (VANCOUVER)—See Omnicom Group Inc.; *U.S. Public*, pg. 1225
GPC GOVERNMENT POLICY CONSULTANTS (VICTORIA)—See Omnicom Group Inc.; *U.S. Public*, pg. 1225
GPC INTERNATIONAL HOLDINGS—See Omnicom Group Inc.; *U.S. Public*, pg. 1225
GPC MARKET ACCESS EUROPE—See Omnicom Group Inc.; *U.S. Public*, pg. 1225
GPC MARKET ACCESS SCOTLAND—See Omnicom Group Inc.; *U.S. Public*, pg. 1225
GPD/EMBRACO NORTH AMERICA, INC.—See Whirlpool Corporation; *U.S. Public*, pg. 1765
GPI INTERNATIONAL LIMITED—See GP Batteries International Ltd.; *Int'l*, pg. 537
GPI (JAPAN) LIMITED—See GP Batteries International Ltd.; *Int'l*, pg. 537
GPM GAS CORPORATION—See Phillips Petroleum Company; *U.S. Public*, pg. 1291
GPM GAS GATHERING L.L.C.—See Cigna Corp.; *U.S. Public*, pg. 362
GPRI—See Groupe Usinor; *Int'l*, pg. 571
GPT HOLDINGS LTD.—See Siemens AG; *Int'l*, pg. 1248
GPT LTD.—See The General Electric Company, p.l.c.; *Int'l*, pg. 544
GPU ELECTRIC, INC.—See GPU, Inc.; *U.S. Public*, pg. 695
GPU ENERGY—See GPU, Inc.; *U.S. Public*, pg. 695
GPU GENERATION CORPORATION—See GPU, Inc.; *U.S. Public*, pg. 695
GPU, INC.; *U.S. Public*, pg. 695
GPU INTERNATIONAL, INC.—See GPU, Inc.; *U.S. Public*, pg. 695
GPU NUCLEAR CORP.—See GPU, Inc.; *U.S. Public*, pg. 695
GPU POWER, INC.—See GPU, Inc.; *U.S. Public*, pg. 695
GPU SERVICE CORP.—See GPU, Inc.; *U.S. Public*, pg. 695
GR DO MEXICO—See Accor S.A.; *Int'l*, pg. 21
GRC HOLDING, INC.—See RGP Holding, Inc.; *U.S. Private*, pg. 903
GRC INTERNATIONAL, INC.; *U.S. Public*, pg. 695
GRC REALTY CORP.—See General Re Corporation; *U.S. Public*, pg. 725
GRN CORP.—See Goshen Rubber Co., Inc.; *U.S. Private*, pg. 466
GRP RECORDS—See The Seagram Company Ltd.; *Int'l*, pg. 1215

MASTER INDEX TO COMPANY NAMES GALVESTON-HOUSTON

Company Index

GS BATTERY (U.S.A.), INC.—See Japan Storage Battery Co., Ltd.; *Int'l*, pg. 702
GS-EE CO., LTD.—See BTR plc; *Int'l*, pg. 126
GS ELECTRIC—See General Signal Corporation; *U.S. Public*, pg. 726
GS INDUSTRIES, INC.; *U.S. Private*, pg. 435
GS SOCIETA GENERALE SUPERMERCATI—See Benetton Group S.p.A.; *Int'l*, pg. 186
GS SOCIETA GENERALE SUPERMERCATI—See IRI Istituto Ricostruzione Industriale; *Int'l*, pg. 655
GSB INVESTMENT MANAGEMENT, INC.—See United Asset Management Corporation; *U.S. Public*, pg. 1673
GSC ENTERPRISES, INC.; *U.S. Private*, pg. 436
GSD&M; *U.S. Private*, pg. 436
GSE, INC.—See United Dominion Industries, Ltd.; *U.S. Public*, pg. 1676
GSE LIVING TECHNOLOGY, INC.—See Gundle/SLT Environmental, Inc.; *U.S. Public*, pg. 770
GSF ENERGY INC.—See Air Products and Chemicals, Inc.; *U.S. Public*, pg. 31
GSF VERPAKKINGEN—See N.V. Koninklijke KNP BT; *Int'l*, *pg. 756*
GSG SIEDLUNGSGESELLSCHAFT FUER WOHNUNGS- UND STAEDTEBAU MBH—See Landesbank Hessen-Thuringen Girozentrale; *Int'l*, pg. 799
GSH CORP.—See Goshen Rubber Co., Inc.; *U.S. Private*, pg. 466
GSI (BEIJING) HOSIERY CO., LTD.—See Gunze Sangyo, Inc.; *Int'l*, pg. 579
GSI ENGINEERING, INC.—See Worthington Industries, Inc.; *U.S. Public*, pg. 1780
GSI EUROPE-IMPORT & EXPORT GMBH—See Gunze Sangyo, Inc.; *Int'l*, pg. 579
GSI EXIM AMERICA INC.—See Gunze Sangyo, Inc.; *Int'l*, pg. 578
THE GSI GROUP, INC.; *U.S. Private*, pg. 436
GSI DE MEXICO S.A. DE C.V.—See Halliburton Company; *U.S. Public*, pg. 776
GSI OF CALIFORNIA—See Gulf States, Inc.; *U.S. Private*, pg. 487
GSI TRADING HONG KONG LIMITED—See Gunze Sangyo, Inc.; *Int'l*, pg. 579
GSL SOLAR CONSULTANTS & ADVISORS, INC.—See Harris Chemical Group, Inc.; *U.S. Private*, pg. 505
GSM—See Ciments Francais; *Int'l*, pg. 292
GSP MARKETING SERVICES, INC.; *U.S. Private*, pg. 436
GST INDUSTRIES, INC.—See Summa Industries; *U.S. Public*, pg. 1527
GSW HEATING PRODUCTS COMPANY—See GSW Inc.; *Int'l*, pg. 538
GSW INC.; *Int'l*, pg. 538
GSW JACKES-EVANS MANUFACTURING CO.—See GSW Inc.; *Int'l*, pg. 538
GSW PUMP COMPANY—See GSW Inc.; *Int'l*, pg. 538
GSW THERMOPLASTICS COMPANY—See GSW Inc.; *Int'l*, *pg. 538*
GSW THERMOPLASTICS - MICHIGAN—See GSW Inc.; *Int'l*, pg. 538
GSW WATER HEATING COMPANY—See GSW Inc.; *Int'l*, pg. 538
GT BICYCLES, INC.; *U.S. Public*, pg. 695
GT GLOBAL FONDSSERVICE GMBH—See Liechtenstein Global Trust Limited; *Int'l*, pg. 809
G.T. GLOBAL FUND MANAGEMENT LTD.—See Liechtenstein Global Trust Limited; *Int'l*, pg. 809
G.T. GLOBAL, INC.—See Liechtenstein Global Trust Limited; *Int'l*, pg. 809
GT INTERACTIVE SOFTWARE CORP.; *U.S. Public*, pg. 696
G.T. MANAGEMENT (DEUTSCHLAND) GMBH—See Liechtenstein Global Trust Limited; *Int'l*, pg. 809
G.T. MANAGEMENT PLC ZURICH—See Liechtenstein Global Trust Limited; *Int'l*, pg. 809
GTA AGENCY, INC.—See Green Tree Financial Corporation; *U.S. Public*, pg. 762
G.T.C. TRANSCONTINENTAL GROUP LTD.; *Int'l*, pg. 538
GTCO CORPORATION; *U.S. Private*, pg. 436
GTE AIRFONE INCORPORATED—See GTE Corporation; *U.S. Public*, pg. 696
GTE ALASKA INCORPORATED—See GTE Corporation; *U.S. Public*, pg. 697
GTE CALIFORNIA INCORPORATED—See GTE Corporation; *U.S. Public*, pg. 697
GTE CORPORATION; *U.S. Public*, pg. 696
GTE DATA SERVICES INCORPORATED—See GTE Corporation; *U.S. Public*, pg. 696
GTE FLORIDA INCORPORATED—See GTE Corporation; *U.S. Public*, pg. 697
GTE GOVERNMENT SYSTEMS CORPORATION—See GTE Corporation; *U.S. Public*, pg. 696
GTE HAWAIIAN TELEPHONE COMPANY INCORPORATED—See GTE Corporation; *U.S. Public*, pg. 697
GTE INFORMATION SERVICES INCORPORATED—See GTE Corporation; *U.S. Public*, pg. 696
GTE INTERNETWORKING—See GTE Corporation; *U.S. Public*, pg. 696
GTE INTERNETWORKING GMBH—See GTE Corporation; *U.S. Public*, pg. 696
GTE INTERNETWORKING UK LIMITED—See GTE Corporation; *U.S. Public*, pg. 696
GTE LABORATORIES INCORPORATED—See GTE Corporation; *U.S. Public*, pg. 697
GTE LEASING CORPORATION—See GTE Corporation; *U.S. Public*, pg. 696
GTE MOBILE COMMUNICATIONS INCORPORATED—See GTE Corporation; *U.S. Public*, pg. 696
GTE MOBILNET INCORPORATED—See GTE Corporation; *U.S. Public*, pg. 696
GTE NORTH INCORPORATED—See GTE Corporation; *U.S. Public*, pg. 696
GTE NORTHWEST INCORPORATED—See GTE Corporation; *U.S. Public*, pg. 697
GTE REINSURANCE COMPANY LIMITED—See GTE Corporation; *U.S. Public*, pg. 697
GTE SOUTH INCORPORATED—See GTE Corporation; *U.S. Public*, pg. 697
GTE SOUTHWEST INCORPORATED—See GTE Corporation; *U.S. Public*, pg. 697
GTE SUPPLY—See GTE Corporation; *U.S. Public*, pg. 697
G.T.F.C.—See Bouygues; *Int'l*, pg. 206
GTL TRUCK LINES, INC.—See Nash Finch Company; *U.S. Public*, pg. 1152
GTM CARAIBES—See Lyonnaise des Eaux S.A.; *Int'l*, pg. 823
GTM CONSTRUCTION—See Lyonnaise des Eaux S.A.; *Int'l*, pg. 823
GTM GUADELOUPE—See Lyonnaise des Eaux S.A.; *Int'l*, pg. 823
GTM WAN SOON PTE LTD.—See Lyonnaise des Eaux S.A.; *Int'l*, pg. 823
GTMI (M) SDN BHD—See Lyonnaise des Eaux S.A.; *Int'l*, pg. 823
GTS INDUSTRIES—See Groupe Usinor; *Int'l*, pg. 571
GTY TIRE CO.—See Continental AG; *Int'l*, pg. 327
GTY TIRE CO.—See Toyo Tire & Rubber Co., Ltd.; *Int'l*, pg. 1411
GTY TIRE CO.—See The Yokohama Rubber Co., Ltd.; *Int'l*, *pg. 1521*
GUD HOLDINGS LIMITED; *Int'l*, pg. 539
GV EMISSION TECHNOLOGY AB—See Celsius AB; *Int'l*, pg. 277
GV NESTLE GMBH FUR GROSSVERBRAUCHERZENGNISSE—See Nestle S.A.; *Int'l*, pg. 920
GVA CONSULTANTS AB—See Celsius AB; *Int'l*, pg. 277
GVA INDUSTRISERVICE AB—See Celsius AB; *Int'l*, pg. 276
GVA MATERIALVERKSTADER AB—See Celsius AB; *Int'l*, pg. 277
GVG JAPAN, LTD.—See Tektronix, Inc.; *U.S. Public*, pg. 1567
GVG LIMITED—See Tektronix, Inc.; *U.S. Public*, pg. 1567
GVT GESELLSCHAFT FUER VERSORGUNGSTECHNIK MBH—See Saarbergwerke Aktiengesellschaft; *Int'l*, pg. 1167
GW SERVICES, INC.—See Glacier Water Services Inc.; *U.S. Public*, pg. 745
GWC HEALTH, INC.; *U.S. Private*, pg. 436
GWC PROPERTIES, INC.—See McCall Oil & Chemical Corp.; *U.S. Private*, pg. 719
GWL PROPERTIES INC.—See The Great-West Life Assurance Company; *Int'l*, pg. 558
GWL REALTY ADVISORS CO.—See The Great-West Life Assurance Company; *Int'l*, pg. 558
GWP, INC.; *U.S. Private*, pg. 437
G.Y. INDUSTRIES, INC.—See American Pad and Paper Company; *U.S. Public*, pg. 89
GZA DRILLING, INC.—See GZA GeoEnvironmental Technologies, Inc.; *U.S. Public*, pg. 697
GZA GEOENVIRONMENTAL, INC.—See GZA GeoEnvironmental Technologies, Inc.; *U.S. Public*, pg. 697
GZA GEOENVIRONMENTAL TECHNOLOGIES, INC.; *U.S. Public*, pg. 697
GABBERT'S, INC.; *U.S. Private*, pg. 437
GABLE HOUSE ESTATES LTD.—See Ladbroke Group Plc; *Int'l*, pg. 787
GACHOT S.A.—See Tyco International Ltd.; *U.S. Public*, pg. 1650
GACO LTD.—See Freudenberg & Company; *Int'l*, pg. 507
THE GADSDEN TIMES—See The New York Times Company; *U.S. Public*, pg. 1175
GAEART KUMAGAI CO., LTD.—See Kumagai Gumi Co., Ltd.; *Int'l*, pg. 763
GAFFNEY-KROESE ELECTRICAL SUPPLY CORP.; *U.S. Private*, pg. 437
GAFSEN LIMITED—See Saint-Gobain; *Int'l*, pg. 1172
GAGE ADISTRA CORP.—See Gage Marketing Group; *U.S. Private*, pg. 437
THE GAGE COMPANY; *U.S. Private*, pg. 437
GAGE FOOD PRODUCTS COMPANY—See DG Foods, LLC; *U.S. Private*, pg. 301
GAGE MARKETING GROUP; *U.S. Private*, pg. 437
GAGE MARKETING GROUP-WEST COAST—See Gage Marketing Group; *U.S. Private*, pg. 437
GAGGENAU USA CORPORATION; *U.S. Private*, pg. 437
GAGGIANO S.R.L.—See Allianz Aktiengesellschaft; *Int'l*, pg. 61
GAI-TRONICS CORPORATION—See Salient 3 Communications, Inc.; *U.S. Public*, pg. 1430
GAICO—See Parsons Corporation; *U.S. Private*, pg. 841
GAILEY & ROBERTS LTD.—See Unilever Plc; *Int'l*, pg. 1437
GAILEY & ROBERTS (UGANDA) LTD.—See Unilever Plc; *Int'l*, pg. 1437
J. GORDON GAINES INSURANCE SERVICES, INC.—See Torchmark Corporation; *U.S. Public*, pg. 1622
J. GORDON GAINES OF TEXAS, INC.—See Torchmark Corporation; *U.S. Public*, pg. 1623
GAINESVILLE SUN PUBLISHING COMPANY—See The New York Times Company; *U.S. Public*, pg. 1175
GAINS INVESTMENT CORPORATION—See China Steel Corporation; *Int'l*, pg. 285
GAI'S NORTHWEST BAKERIES—See United States Bakery; *U.S. Private*, pg. 1124
GAJRIA ELECTRONICS—See BASF AG; *Int'l*, pg. 108
GAL CORP.—See Silcorp Limited; *Int'l*, pg. 1249
GALA LEISURE LTD.—See Bass PLC; *Int'l*, pg. 170
GALAMBA METALS, INC.—See Galamet, Inc.; *U.S. Private*, *pg. 437*
GALAMET, INC.; *U.S. Private*, pg. 437
GALARDI GROUP, INC.; *U.S. Private*, pg. 437
GALAVISION—See Chartwell Partners; *U.S. Private*, pg. 230
GALAXY CARPET MILLS, INC.—See Mohawk Industries, Inc.; *U.S. Public*, pg. 1121
GALAXY FOOD COMPANY; *U.S. Public*, pg. 697
GALBANI—See Danone Group; *Int'l*, pg. 380
GALCO INTERNATIONAL TOYS, N.V.—See Galoob Toys, Inc.; *U.S. Public*, pg. 698
GALDERMA LABORATORIES, INC.—See L'Oreal S.A.; *Int'l*, pg. 819
GALDERMA LABORATORIES, INC.—See Nestle S.A.; *Int'l*, *pg. 918*
GALE RESEARCH INC.—See The Thomson Corporation; *U.S. Public*, pg. 1600
GALEN ALASKA REALTY, INC.—See Columbia/HCA Healthcare Corporation; *U.S. Public*, pg. 404
GALEN BH, INC.—See Columbia/HCA Healthcare Corporation; *U.S. Public*, pg. 404
GALEN HOSPITAL-ALASKA—See Columbia/HCA Healthcare Corporation; *U.S. Public*, pg. 404
GALEN HOSPITAL CORPORATION, INC.—See Columbia/HCA Healthcare Corporation; *U.S. Public*, pg. 404
GALEN HOSPITAL ILLINOIS, INC.—See Columbia/HCA Healthcare Corporation; *U.S. Public*, pg. 404
GALEN HOSPITAL OF BAYTOWN, INC.—See Columbia/HCA Healthcare Corporation; *U.S. Public*, pg. 404
GALEN INTERNATIONAL HOLDINGS, INC.—See Columbia/HCA Healthcare Corporation; *U.S. Public*, pg. 404
GALEN MEDICAL CORPORATION—See Columbia/HCA Healthcare Corporation; *U.S. Public*, pg. 404
GALEN OF ARIZONA, INC.—See Columbia/HCA Healthcare Corporation; *U.S. Public*, pg. 404
GALEN OF FLORIDA, INC.—See Columbia/HCA Healthcare Corporation; *U.S. Public*, pg. 404
GALEN OF ILLINOIS, INC.—See Columbia/HCA Healthcare Corporation; *U.S. Public*, pg. 404
GALEN OF KANSAS, INC.—See Columbia/HCA Healthcare Corporation; *U.S. Public*, pg. 404
GALEN OF KENTUCKY, INC.—See Columbia/HCA Healthcare Corporation; *U.S. Public*, pg. 404
GALEN OF LOUISIANA, INC.—See Columbia/HCA Healthcare Corporation; *U.S. Public*, pg. 404
GALEN OF MISSISSIPPI, INC.—See Columbia/HCA Healthcare Corporation; *U.S. Public*, pg. 404
GALEN OF NORTH CAROLINA, INC.—See Columbia/HCA Healthcare Corporation; *U.S. Public*, pg. 404
GALEN OF TENNESSEE, INC.—See Columbia/HCA Healthcare Corporation; *U.S. Public*, pg. 404
GALEN OF VIRGINIA, INC.—See Columbia/HCA Healthcare Corporation; *U.S. Public*, pg. 404
GALEN OF WEST VIRGINIA, INC.—See Columbia/HCA Healthcare Corporation; *U.S. Public*, pg. 404
GALEN VIRGINIA HOSPITAL CORPORATION—See Columbia/HCA Healthcare Corporation; *U.S. Public*, pg. 404
GALENCO LTD.—See Nutricia BV; *Int'l*, pg. 991
N.V. GALENCO—See Nutricia BV; *Int'l*, pg. 991
GALENUS CHEMICALS GMBH—See Corange Limited; *Int'l*, pg. 331
GALENUS MANNHEIM GMBH—See Corange Limited; *Int'l*, *pg. 331*
GALESI ENTERPRISES—See Galesi Group; *U.S. Private*, pg. 437
GALESI GROUP; *U.S. Private*, pg. 437
GALEX METALL GMBH—See Axel Johnson AB; *Int'l*, pg. 710
GALILEO CANADA DISTRIBUTION SYSTEMS INC.—See Air Canada; *Int'l*, pg. 36
GALILEO CORP.; *U.S. Public*, pg. 698
GALILEO HELLAS—See Olympic Airways, S.A.; *Int'l*, pg. 1004
GALL & GALL—See Koninklijke Ahold NV; *Int'l*, pg. 749
ARTHUR J. GALLAGHER & CO.; *U.S. Public*, pg. 698
GALLAGHER-KAISER CORP.; *U.S. Private*, pg. 438
R.J. GALLAGHER CO.; *U.S. Private*, pg. 438
GALLAHER (DUBLIN) LTD.—See Gallaher Limited; *Int'l*, pg. 539
GALLAHER INTERNATIONAL LIMITED—See Gallaher Limited; *Int'l*, pg. 539
GALLAHER INVESTMENTS LIMITED—See Gallaher Limited; *Int'l*, pg. 539
GALLAHER LIMITED; *Int'l*, pg. 539
GALLAHER OVERSEAS LIMITED—See Gallaher Limited; *Int'l*, pg. 539
GALLAHER TOBACCO LTD.—See Gallaher Limited; *Int'l*, pg. 539
GALLATIN STEEL COMPANY—See DoFasco, Inc.; *Int'l*, pg. 414
GALLE—See SNCF; *Int'l*, pg. 1164
GALLEON LTD.—See BBC Magazines; *Int'l*, pg. 114
GALLERY FURNITURE; *U.S. Private*, pg. 438
GALLES CHEVROLET; *U.S. Private*, pg. 438
GALLINA BLANCA PURINA—See Borden, Inc.; *U.S. Private*, pg. 159
GALLINA BLANCA S.A.—See Borden, Inc.; *U.S. Private*, pg. 159
GALLINO PLASTURGIA S.R.L.—See Breed Technologies, Inc.; *U.S. Public*, pg. 251
GALLIPOLIS DAILY TRIBUNE—See Gannett Company, Inc.; *U.S. Public*, pg. 699
E & J GALLO—See E. & J. Gallo Winery; *U.S. Private*, pg. 438
E. & J. GALLO WINERY; *U.S. Private*, pg. 438
GALLO/GALILEO SALAME—See Sara Lee Corporation; *U.S. Public*, pg. 1433
GALOOB TOYS, INC.; *U.S. Public*, pg. 698
GALP INTERNATIONAL CORPORATION—See Petrogal, s.a.; *Int'l*, pg. 1045
GALPGESTE, LDA.—See Petrogal, s.a.; *Int'l*, pg. 1045
GALPIN MOTORS; *U.S. Private*, pg. 438
GALSTAFF INDUSTRIE CHEMICHE S.P.A.—See Hickson International Plc; *Int'l*, pg. 619
GALTEC N.V.—See Arbed S.A.; *Int'l*, pg. 79
GALVAK S.A.—See Alfa, S.A. de C.V.; *Int'l*, pg. 56
GALVALANGE S.A.R.L.—See Arbed S.A.; *Int'l*, pg. 79
GALVANO DIVISION—See The Ivaco Group; *Int'l*, pg. 696
GALVESTON-HOUSTON COMPANY; *U.S. Private*, pg. 438

GALYAN'S
DIRECTORY OF CORPORATE AFFILIATIONS
Company Index

GALYAN'S TRADING CO.—See The Limited, Inc.; *U.S. Public*, pg. 995
GAM/DMB&B BEIRUT—See DMB&B Communications; *U.S. Private*, pg. 304
GAMA SERVICES—See Lagardere Groupe; *Int'l*, pg. 792
GAMATEX N.V—See GATX Corporation; *U.S. Public*, pg. 692
AG GAMBRINUS—See Feldschlosschen Hurlimann Holding; *Int'l*, pg. 479
GAMBRO AB—See Incentive AB; *Int'l*, pg. 666
GAMBRO AB OY—See Incentive AB; *Int'l*, pg. 667
GAMBRO AG—See Incentive AB; *Int'l*, pg. 667
GAMBRO A/S—See Incentive AB; *Int'l*, pg. 667
GAMBRO B.V.—See Incentive AB; *Int'l*, pg. 667
GAMBRO CHINA LTD—See Incentive AB; *Int'l*, pg. 667
GAMBRO DIALYSATOREN GMBH & CO KG—See Incentive AB; *Int'l*, pg. 667
GAMBRO ENGSTROM AB—See Incentive AB; *Int'l*, pg. 667
GAMBRO HEALTHCARE—See Incentive AB; *Int'l*, pg. 667
GAMBRO INDIA—See Incentive AB; *Int'l*, pg. 667
GAMBRO JR. CHINA LTD.—See Incentive AB; *Int'l*, pg. 667
GAMBRO KFT—See Incentive AB; *Int'l*, pg. 667
GAMBRO K.K.—See Incentive AB; *Int'l*, pg. 668
GAMBRO KOREA CO., LTD—See Incentive AB; *Int'l*, pg. 668
GAMBRO LDA.—See Incentive AB; *Int'l*, pg. 668
GAMBRO LTD.—See Incentive AB; *Int'l*, pg. 668
GAMBRO MEDICAL K.K.—See Incentive AB; *Int'l*, pg. 668
GAMBRO MEDICAL PRODUCTS CO. LTD. SHANGHAI—See Incentive AB; *Int'l*, pg. 668
GAMBRO MEDICOTEKNIK A/S—See Incentive AB; *Int'l*, pg. 668
GAMBRO MEDIZINTECHNIK GMBH—See Incentive AB; *Int'l*, pg. 668
GAMBRO N.V./S.A.—See Incentive AB; *Int'l*, pg. 668
GAMBRO POLAND SP. Z.O.O.—See Incentive AB; *Int'l*, pg. 668
GAMBRO PTY LTD.—See Incentive AB; *Int'l*, pg. 668
GAMBRO PTY. LTD.—See Incentive AB; *Int'l*, pg. 668
GAMBRO S.A.—See Incentive AB; *Int'l*, pg. 668
GAMBRO SALES AB—See Incentive AB; *Int'l*, pg. 667
GAMBRO S.P.A.—See Incentive AB; *Int'l*, pg. 668
GAMBRO SVENSKA FORSALJNINGS AB—See Incentive AB; *Int'l*, pg. 667
GAMBRO TAIWAN LTD.—See Incentive AB; *Int'l*, pg. 668
GAMBRO VERTRIEBSGESELLSCHAFT M.B.H.—See Incentive AB; *Int'l*, pg. 668
GAMBRO-MEOPTA S.R.O.—See Incentive AB; *Int'l*, pg. 668
GAMBRO-SHIMIZU—See Incentive AB; *Int'l*, pg. 668
W. GAMBY & CO.; *U.S. Private*, pg. 439
GAMCO PRODUCTS CO.—See Masco Corporation; *U.S. Public*, pg. 1053
THE GAME INC.—See Russell Corporation; *U.S. Public*, pg. 1413
GAME TIME, INC.—See Swing-N-Slide Corp.; *U.S. Public*, pg. 1543
GAMEPRO—See International Data Group; *U.S. Private*, pg. 569
THE GAMES—See John Menzies plc; *Int'l*, pg. 707
GAMESCAPE, INC.—See GTECH Corporation; *U.S. Public*, pg. 767
GAMKO HOLDINGS—See Specialty Equipment Companies Inc.; *U.S. Public*, pg. 1497
GAMMA BIOLOGICALS, B.V.—See Gamma Biologicals Inc.; *U.S. Public*, pg. 698
GAMMA BIOLOGICALS INC.; *U.S. Public*, pg. 698
GAMMA-F CORPORATION—See Vertex Communications Corporation; *U.S. Public*, pg. 1718
GAMMA HOLDING BELGIE N.V.—See Gamma Holding N.V.; *Int'l*, pg. 540
GAMMA HOLDING NEDERLAND N.V.—See Gamma Holding N.V.; *Int'l*, pg. 540
GAMMA HOLDING N.V.; *Int'l*, pg. 539
GAMMA HOLDING (UK) LTD.—See Gamma Holding N.V.; *Int'l*, pg. 540
GAMMA INAC, INC.—See Cigna Corp.; *U.S. Public*, pg. 365
GAMMA ONE, INC.—See Big Flower Press Holdings, Inc.; *U.S. Public*, pg. 228
GAMMON CONSTRUCTION LTD.—See Kvaerner a.s.a.; *Int'l*, pg. 775
GAN CANADA INSURANCE COMPANY—See Groupe GAN; *Int'l*, pg. 564
GAN CAPITALISATION—See Groupe GAN; *Int'l*, pg. 564
THE GAN COMPANY OF CANADA LTD.—See Groupe GAN; *Int'l*, pg. 564
GAN ESPANA SEGUROS GENERALES Y VIDA—See Groupe GAN; *Int'l*, pg. 564
GAN GENERAL INSURANCE COMPANY—See Groupe GAN; *Int'l*, pg. 564
GAN HOLDING PACIFIQUE—See Groupe GAN; *Int'l*, pg. 564
GAN INCENDIE ACCIDENTS—See Groupe GAN; *Int'l*, pg. 564
GAN INCENDIE ACCIDENTS GUADELOUPE—See Groupe GAN; *Int'l*, pg. 564
GAN INCENDIE ACCIDENTS HONG KONG—See Groupe GAN; *Int'l*, pg. 564
GAN INCENDIE ACCIDENTS JAPAN—See Groupe GAN; *Int'l*, pg. 564
GAN INCENDIE ACCIDENTS MARTINIQUE—See Groupe GAN; *Int'l*, pg. 564
GAN INCENDIE ACCIDENTS SWITZERLAND—See Groupe GAN; *Int'l*, pg. 564
GAN INSURANCE COMPANY LIMITED—See Groupe GAN; *Int'l*, pg. 565
GAN INTERNATIONAL—See Groupe GAN; *Int'l*, pg. 564
GAN ITALIA S.P.A.—See Groupe GAN; *Int'l*, pg. 564
GAN ITALIA VITA S.P.A.—See Groupe GAN; *Int'l*, pg. 564
GAN LIFE AND PENSIONS PLC—See Groupe GAN; *Int'l*, pg. 565
GAN NATIONAL INSURANCE CO.—See Groupe GAN; *Int'l*, pg. 564
GAN NORTH AMERICA INC.—See Groupe GAN; *Int'l*, pg. 564
GAN PACIFIQUE IARD—See Groupe GAN; *Int'l*, pg. 564
GAN PACIFIQUE VIE—See Groupe GAN; *Int'l*, pg. 564
GAN PORTUGAL SEGUROS—See Groupe GAN; *Int'l*, pg. 564
GAN PORTUGAL VIDA—See Groupe GAN; *Int'l*, pg. 564
GAN SA—See Groupe GAN; *Int'l*, pg. 565
GAN S.A. CHINA—See Groupe GAN; *Int'l*, pg. 565
GAN S.A. VIETNAM—See Groupe GAN; *Int'l*, pg. 565
GAN SANTE—See Groupe GAN; *Int'l*, pg. 565
GAN UK PLC—See Groupe GAN; *Int'l*, pg. 565
GAN VIE—See Groupe GAN; *Int'l*, pg. 565
GAN VIE GUADELOUPE—See Groupe GAN; *Int'l*, pg. 565
GAN VIE MARTINIQUE—See Groupe GAN; *Int'l*, pg. 565
GANAHL LUMBER COMPANY; *U.S. Private*, pg. 439
GANDALF CANADA LTD.—See Gandalf Technologies Inc.; *Int'l*, pg. 540
GANDALF DIGITAL COMMUNICATIONS LTD.—See Gandalf Technologies Inc.; *Int'l*, pg. 540
GANDALF INTERNATIONAL LTD.—See Gandalf Technologies Inc.; *Int'l*, pg. 540
GANDALF NEDERLAND B.V.—See Gandalf Technologies Inc.; *Int'l*, pg. 540
GANDALF S.A.—See Gandalf Technologies Inc.; *Int'l*, pg. 541
GANDALF SYSTEMS BELGIUM, S.A.—See Gandalf Technologies Inc.; *Int'l*, pg. 541
GANDALF SYSTEMS CORPORATION—See Gandalf Technologies Inc.; *Int'l*, pg. 540
GANDALF TECHNOLOGIES INC.; *Int'l*, pg. 540
GANDER MOUNTAIN RETAIL—See Holiday Companies; *U.S. Private*, pg. 534
GANFLEC CORPORATION—See Gannett Fleming Affiliates, Inc.; *U.S. Private*, pg. 439
GANIN TIRE CO., INC.; *U.S. Private*, pg. 439
GANNETT COMPANY, INC.; *U.S. Public*, pg. 698
GANNETT DIRECT MARKETING SERVICES—See Gannett Company, Inc.; *U.S. Public*, pg. 699
GANNETT FLEMING AFFILIATES, INC.; *U.S. Private*, pg. 439
GANNETT FLEMING, INC.—See Gannett Fleming Affiliates, Inc.; *U.S. Private*, pg. 439
GANNETT FLEMING INVESTMENT CORPORATION—See Gannett Fleming Affiliates, Inc.; *U.S. Private*, pg. 439
GANNETT FLEMING VALUATION AND RATE CONSULTANTS, INC.—See Gannett Fleming Affiliates, Inc.; *U.S. Private*, pg. 439
GUY GANNETT COMMUNICATIONS; *U.S. Private*, pg. 439
GANNETT MEDIA TECHNOLOGIES INTERNATIONAL—See Gannett Company, Inc.; *U.S. Public*, pg. 699
GANNETT OFFSET-SPRINGFIELD PLANT—See Gannett Company, Inc.; *U.S. Public*, pg. 700
GANNETT SATELLITE INFORMATION NETWORK, INC.—See Gannett Company, Inc.; *U.S. Public*, pg. 700
GANNETT SUBURBAN NEWSPAPERS—See Gannett Company, Inc.; *U.S. Public*, pg. 700
GANNETT SUPPLY CORP.—See Gannett Company, Inc.; *U.S. Public*, pg. 699
GANNETT TELEMARKETING INC.—See Gannett Company, Inc.; *U.S. Public*, pg. 699
GANS INK & SUPPLY COMPANY, INC.; *U.S. Private*, pg. 440
GANT—See Phillips-Van Heusen Corporation; *U.S. Public*, pg. 1291
JAMES GANT & COMPANY LIMITED—See Fine Art Developments plc; *Int'l*, pg. 485
GANT RETAIL—See Phillips-Van Heusen Corporation; *U.S. Public*, pg. 1292
GANTON HOUSE INVESTMENTS LIMITED—See Ladbroke Group Plc; *Int'l*, pg. 787
GANTOS INC.; *U.S. Public*, pg. 702
GANTOS, INC.—See Gantos Inc.; *U.S. Public*, pg. 702
THE GAP, INC.; *U.S. Public*, pg. 702
GAP STORES DIVISION—See The Gap, Inc.; *U.S. Public*, pg. 702
GAPKIDS DIVISION—See The Gap, Inc.; *U.S. Public*, pg. 702
GARAN, INCORPORATED; *U.S. Public*, pg. 703
GARAN MANUFACTURING CORP.—See Garan, Incorporated; *U.S. Public*, pg. 703
GARANIMALS—See Garan, Incorporated; *U.S. Public*, pg. 703
GARANTI-KOZA INSAAT—See Hochtief AG; *Int'l*, pg. 624
GARANTIAS Y CREDITO DE CHILE S.A.—See Corporacion MAPFRE, Compania Internacional de Reaseguros, S.A.; *Int'l*, pg. 335
GARBARSKI EURO RSCG—See Havas Advertising; *Int'l*, pg. 603
THE GARBER COMPANY—See Caraustar Industries, Inc.; *U.S. Public*, pg. 303
GARCIA'S MEXICAN RESTAURANTS—See Famous Restaurants Inc.; *U.S. Private*, pg. 393
GARDEN CITY COMPLEX—See Sunflower Electric Power Corporation; *U.S. Private*, pg. 1052
GARDEN HOTEL SHANGHAI MITSUKOSHI—See Mitsukoshi, Ltd.; *Int'l*, pg. 884
GARDEN INSURANCE COMPANIES—See Elixir Industries; *U.S. Private*, pg. 371
THE GARDEN ISLAND—See Pulitzer Publishing Company; *U.S. Public*, pg. 1343
GARDEN STATE CABLE—See Comcast Corporation; *U.S. Public*, pg. 407
GARDEN STATE CONVERTERS—See Triangle Marketing Corp.; *U.S. Private*, pg. 1102
GARDEN STATE LIFE INSURANCE COMPANY—See American National Insurance Company; *U.S. Public*, pg. 88
GARDEN STATE NEWSPAPERS, INC.—See MediaNews Group Inc.; *U.S. Private*, pg. 727
GARDEN STATE PAPER CO., INC.—See Media General, Inc.; *U.S. Public*, pg. 1078
GARDEN STATE PAPER MILL/GARFIELD MILL—See Media General, Inc.; *U.S. Public*, pg. 1078
GARDEN STATE RACE TRACK, INC.—See International Thoroughbred Breeders, Inc.; *U.S. Public*, pg. 908
GARDEN WAY, INC.; *U.S. Private*, pg. 440
GARDENER'S EDEN, INC.—See Williams-Sonoma, Inc.; *U.S. Public*, pg. 1770
GARDENWOOD LIMITED PARTNERSHIP—See Cooper Communities, Inc.; *U.S. Private*, pg. 274
GARDNER AVON—See Texas Holdings Ltd.; *Int'l*, pg. 1381
GARDNER CRYOGENICS—See Air Products and Chemicals, Inc.; *U.S. Public*, pg. 32
GARDNER DENVER MACHINERY INC.; *U.S. Public*, pg. 703
L. GARDNER & SONS LTD.—See Texas Holdings Ltd.; *Int'l*, pg. 1381
L. GARDNER GROUP PLC—See Texas Holdings Ltd.; *Int'l*, pg. 1381
GARDNER PUBLICATIONS, INC.; *U.S. Private*, pg. 440
GARED SPORTS INC.—See Nixdorff Krein Industries Inc.; *U.S. Private*, pg. 799
GARELICK FARMS, INC.—See Suiza Foods Corporation; *U.S. Public*, pg. 1527
GARGIULO INC.—See Monsanto Company; *U.S. Public*, pg. 1124
GARIBOLDI PARISI VERGA/INTERAD—See The Lowe Group; *U.S. Private*, pg. 678
GARLAND COMMERCIAL INDUSTRIES, INC.—See Berisford plc; *Int'l*, pg. 188
GARLAND OPERATIONS—See BTR plc; *Int'l*, pg. 126
GARLOCK BEARINGS DIVISION—See Coltec Holdings Inc; *U.S. Public*, pg. 402
GARLOCK SEALING TECHNOLOGIES—See Coltec Holdings Inc; *U.S. Public*, pg. 402
GARLOCK VALVES & INDUSTRIAL PLASTICS—See Coltec Holdings Inc; *U.S. Public*, pg. 402
GARMENT CENTER REGION—See Imperial Bancorp; *U.S. Public*, pg. 872
GARNAC GRAIN CO., INC.—See Norfoods, Inc.; *U.S. Private*, pg. 802
GARNEY COMPANIES, INC.—See Garney Holding Company, Inc.; *U.S. Private*, pg. 440
GARNEY HOLDING COMPANY, INC.; *U.S. Private*, pg. 440
GARNY AG—See De La Rue plc; *Int'l*, pg. 387
GARNY SICHERHEITSTECHNIK GMBH—See De La Rue plc; *Int'l*, pg. 387
RENE GARRAUD S.A.—See Wella Group; *Int'l*, pg. 1490
GARRETSON EQUIPMENT CO., INC.—See Pioneer Natural Resources Co.; *U.S. Public*, pg. 1300
GARRETT AIRLINE SERVICES DIVISION—See AlliedSignal Inc.; *U.S. Public*, pg. 50
GARRETT PRODUCTS, INC.—See Group Dekko; *U.S. Private*, pg. 484
GARRIDO Y COMPANIA—See Suiza Foods Corporation; *U.S. Public*, pg. 1527
GARRISON BREWER—See Champion Industries; *U.S. Public*, pg. 333
GARRY ELECTRONICS—See Wire-Pro Inc.; *U.S. Private*, pg. 1184
GARRY PRECISION SCREW MACHINE—See Wire-Pro Inc.; *U.S. Private*, pg. 1184
GARRYSON-INSLEY LTD.—See B. Elliott plc.; *Int'l*, pg. 448
GARSITE, INC.—See TSI Holdings, Inc.; *U.S. Private*, pg. 1066
GARST SEED COMPANY—See Zeneca Group Plc; *Int'l*, pg. 1524
GARTELL LIMITED—See Avonmore Waterford Group plc; *Int'l*, pg. 102
GARTEN UND HEIM GMBH—See Philipp Holzmann AG; *Int'l*, pg. 632
GARTENHILFE GES.M.B.H.—See DSM N.V.; *Int'l*, pg. 356
GARVENS AUTOMATION GMBH—See Novartis AG; *Int'l*, pg. 982
GARVEY INDUSTRIES, INC.; *U.S. Private*, pg. 440
GARVEY INTERNATIONAL, INC.—See Garvey Industries, Inc.; *U.S. Private*, pg. 440
GARY CONCRETE PRODUCTS INC.—See Zurn Industries, Inc.; *U.S. Public*, pg. 1795
GARY STEEL CO., INC.—See Primac Corp.; *U.S. Private*, pg. 884
GARY-WILLIAMS ENERGY CORPORATION; *U.S. Private*, pg. 440
GARY-WILLIAMS ENERGY CORPORATION—See Gary-Williams Energy Corporation; *U.S. Private*, pg. 440
GAS CONTROL POLYMETRON AG—See Hesta Tex AG; *Int'l*, pg. 618
GAS DRIVE SYSTEMS—See Toromont Industries Ltd.; *Int'l*, pg. 1401
GAS ENERGIA S.P.A.—See ENI S.p.A.; *Int'l*, pg. 428
GAS ENERGY INC.—See Calpine Corporation; *U.S. Public*, pg. 296
GAS EQUIPMENT COMPANY, INC.; *U.S. Private*, pg. 440
GAS-FIRED PRODUCTS, INC.; *U.S. Private*, pg. 440
GAS-FIRED PRODUCTS (U.K.) LTD.—See Gas-Fired Products, Inc.; *U.S. Private*, pg. 440
GAS SPRINGS DIVISION—See The Fairchild Corporation; *U.S. Public*, pg. 610
GAS SYSTEMS, FINLAND OY—See Eclipse Inc.; *U.S. Private*, pg. 361
GAS TECH—See Thermo Electron Corporation; *U.S. Public*, pg. 1593
GAS TECH INSTRUMENT CANADA, LTD.—See Thermo Electron Corporation; *U.S. Public*, pg. 1593
GAS TURBINE FUEL SYSTEMS DIV.—See Parker Hannifin Corporation; *U.S. Public*, pg. 1262
GAS-UNION GMBH—See Ruhrgas Aktiengesellschaft; *Int'l*, pg. 1148
GASBETRIEBE GMBH—See Veba AG; *Int'l*, pg. 1456
GASBOY INTERNATIONAL, INC.—See Tokheim Corporation; *U.S. Public*, pg. 1620
GASCO, INC.—See The Broken Hill Proprietary Company Limited; *Int'l*, pg. 225
GASEBA S.A.—See Gaz de France; *Int'l*, pg. 541
GASELL PROFIL AB—See Rautaruukki Oy; *Int'l*, pg. 1088

GASELL PROFIL AS—See Rautaruukki Oy; *Int'l*, pg. 1088
GASELWEST—See Electrabel S.A.; *Int'l*, pg. 437
GASLINE S.R.L.—See Compagnie des Machines Bull; *Int'l*, pg. 318
GASONICS INTERNATIONAL; *U.S. Public*, pg. 703
GASPOL SP. Z O.O.—See SHV Holdings N.V.; *Int'l*, pg. 1155
GAST MFG. CORP.; *U.S. Private*, pg. 440
GASTECHNIC PRODUKTIONS UND VERTRIEBSGESELLSCHAFT M.B.H.—See Ruhrgas Aktiengesellschaft; *Int'l*, pg. 1148
GASTON COUNTY DYEING MACHINE CO.; *U.S. Private*, pg. 441
GASTRA SPOL. S.R.O.—See Huhtamaki Oy; *Int'l*, pg. 638
GASUM OY—See Neste Oy; *Int'l*, pg. 913
GASWERK PHILIPPSBURG GMBH—See Ruhrgas Aktiengesellschaft; *Int'l*, pg. 1148
GASZTRO-LANC KFT—See Sodexho S.A.; *Int'l*, pg. 1274
GATE CITY BEVERAGE DISTRIBUTORS; *U.S. Private*, pg. 441
GATE CITY EQUIPMENT COMPANY, INC.—See The Lubrizol Corporation; *U.S. Public*, pg. 1016
GATE CITY MEDICAL EQUIPMENT, INC.—See Integrated Health Services, Inc.; *U.S. Public*, pg. 884
THE GATE DEVELOPMENT CORP.—See Lennar Corporation; *U.S. Public*, pg. 988
GATE PETROLEUM COMPANY; *U.S. Private*, pg. 441
GATEFIELD CORPORATION; *U.S. Public*, pg. 703
GATES CANADA INC.—See Tomkins PLC; *Int'l*, pg. 1396
THE GATES CORPORATION—See Tomkins PLC; *Int'l*, pg. 1396
GATES DO BRASIL IND. E COM. LTDA.—See Tomkins PLC; *Int'l*, pg. 1396
GATES EUROPE—See Tomkins PLC; *Int'l*, pg. 1396
GATES FORMED-FIBRE PRODUCTS—See Tomkins PLC; *Int'l*, pg. 1396
GATES HYDRAULICS LTD.—See Tomkins PLC; *Int'l*, pg. 1397
GATES LAND CO.—See Cody Company; *U.S. Private*, pg. 249
GATES, MCDONALD & CO.—See Nationwide Insurance Enterprise; *U.S. Private*, pg. 789
GATES RUBBER CO. INC.—See Tomkins PLC; *Int'l*, pg. 1396
THE GATES RUBBER COMPANY LIMITED—See Tomkins PLC; *Int'l*, pg. 1397
GATES RUBBER DE MEXICO—See Tomkins PLC; *Int'l*, pg. 1397
GATES SPAIN AUTOMOTIVE PRODUCTS DIVISION—See Tomkins PLC; *Int'l*, pg. 1397
GATEWAY ADDITIVE COMPANY—See The Lubrizol Corporation; *U.S. Public*, pg. 1016
GATEWAY APPAREL, INC.; *U.S. Private*, pg. 441
GATEWAY COMMUNICATIONS—See Macromedia Incorporated; *U.S. Public*, pg. 693
GATEWAY LAND PRIVATE LIMITED—See Singapore Land Limited; *Int'l*, pg. 1253
GATEWAY PRESS, INC.; *U.S. Private*, pg. 441
GATEWAY 2000; *U.S. Public*, pg. 703
GATINEAU OFFICE—See The Cascades Group; *Int'l*, pg. 274
GATOR FREIGHTWAYS, INC.; *U.S. Private*, pg. 441
GATOR INDUSTRIES INC.; *U.S. Private*, pg. 441
GATORADE WORLDWIDE DIVISION—See The Quaker Oats Company; *U.S. Public*, pg. 1347
GAULT DISTRIBUTORS, INC.; *Int'l*, pg. 541
GAUSS DIV.—See Greenwich Street Capital Partners, Inc.; *U.S. Private*, pg. 479
GAVINO SANNA ASSOCIATI—See DMB&B Communications; *U.S. Private*, pg. 304
GAVIOTA RE, S.A.—See Repsol S.A.; *Int'l*, pg. 1104
GAYFERS—See Mercantile Stores Company, Inc.; *U.S. Public*, pg. 1090
GAYLE SUPPLY INC.—See Hughes Supply, Inc.; *U.S. Public*, pg. 847
GAYLORD BROADCASTING CO.—See Gaylord Entertainment Co.; *U.S. Public*, pg. 704
GAYLORD CHEMICAL CORPORATION—See Gaylord Container Corporation; *U.S. Public*, pg. 704
GAYLORD CONTAINER CORPORATION; *U.S. Public*, pg. 704
GAYLORD ENTERTAINMENT CO.; *U.S. Public*, pg. 704
GAYLORD ENTERTAINMENT/OPRYLAND USA—See Gaylord Entertainment Co.; *U.S. Public*, pg. 704
GAYLORD PRINTING, INC.; *U.S. Private*, pg. 441
GAYMAR INDUSTRIES, INC.; *U.S. Private*, pg. 442
GAYNES ENGINEERING CO.—See Noonan Machine Co.; *U.S. Private*, pg. 801
GAZ DE FRANCE; *Int'l*, pg. 541
GAZ DE FRANCE DEUTSCHLAND GMBH—See Gaz de France; *Int'l*, pg. 541
GAZ ET THERMIQUE CONTROLE S.A.R.L.—See Ruhrgas Aktiengesellschaft; *Int'l*, pg. 1149
GAZ METROPOLITAIN & COMPANY; *Int'l*, pg. 541
GAZ METROPOLITAIN, INC.-ABITIBI-TEMISCAMINGUE—See Gaz Metropolitain & Company; *Int'l*, pg. 541
GAZ METROPOLITAIN, INC.-EASTERN TOWNSHIPS—See Gaz Metropolitain & Company; *Int'l*, pg. 541
GAZ METROPOLITAIN, INC.-LAURENTIANS—See Gaz Metropolitain & Company; *Int'l*, pg. 541
GAZ METROPOLITAIN, INC.-MAURICIE—See Gaz Metropolitain & Company; *Int'l*, pg. 541
GAZ METROPOLITAIN, INC.-MONTEREGIE—See Gaz Metropolitain & Company; *Int'l*, pg. 541
GAZ METROPOLITAIN, INC.-QUEBEC—See Gaz Metropolitain & Company; *Int'l*, pg. 541
GAZ METROPOLITAIN, INC.-SAGUENAY/LAC ST.-JEAN—See Gaz Metropolitain & Company; *Int'l*, pg. 541
GAZ METROPOLITAIN - VAL D'OR—See Gaz Metropolitain & Company; *Int'l*, pg. 541
THE GAZETTE—See Hollinger Inc.; *Int'l*, pg. 631
THE GAZETTE—See Landmark Communications, Inc.; *U.S. Private*, pg. 648
THE GAZETTE COMPANY; *U.S. Private*, pg. 442

THE GAZETTE MARKETING—See The Gazette Company; *U.S. Private*, pg. 442
THE GAZETTE NEWSPAPERS, INC.—See The Washington Post Company; *U.S. Public*, pg. 1743
GAZETTE TELEGRAPH—See Freedom Communication Inc.; *U.S. Private*, pg. 425
GAZNAT SA (GAZNAT)—See Alusuisse-Lonza Holding Ltd.; *Int'l*, pg. 67
GAZODUC SA—See Alusuisse-Lonza Holding Ltd.; *Int'l*, pg. 67
GAZZONI 1907 S.R.L.—See Novartis AG; *Int'l*, pg. 982
GCI CABLE, INC.—See General Communication, Inc.; *U.S. Public*, pg. 708
G.E. CAPITAL MODULAR SPACE—See General Electric Company; *U.S. Public*, pg. 712
GEAR HEADQUARTERS INC.—See Bearing Headquarters Co.; *U.S. Private*, pg. 127
GEAR PRODUCTS INC.—See Blount International, Inc.; *U.S. Public*, pg. 238
GEAR RESEARCH INCORPORATED—See Jordan Industries, Inc.; *U.S. Private*, pg. 598
GEARBOX DEL PRAT, S.A.—See Volkswagen AG; *Int'l*, pg. 1475
GEARHART AUSTRALIA LIMITED—See Halliburton Company; *U.S. Public*, pg. 776
GEARHART FINANCE N.V.—See Halliburton Company; *U.S. Public*, pg. 776
GEARHART FRANCE S.A.R.L.—See Halliburton Company; *U.S. Public*, pg. 776
GEARHART GEO CONSULTANTS LIMITED—See Halliburton Company; *U.S. Public*, pg. 776
GEARHART GEODATA SERVICES (OVERSEAS) LIMITED—See Halliburton Company; *U.S. Public*, pg. 776
GEARHART INDUSTRIES ASIA, INC.—See Halliburton Company; *U.S. Public*, pg. 776
GEARHART (MALAYSIA) SDN. BHD.—See Halliburton Company; *U.S. Public*, pg. 776
GEARHART M.E. HOLDINGS, INC.—See Halliburton Company; *U.S. Public*, pg. 776
GEARHART MIDDLE EAST S.A.—See Halliburton Company; *U.S. Public*, pg. 776
GEARHART NIGERIA LIMITED—See Halliburton Company; *U.S. Public*, pg. 776
GEARHART TESEL LIMITED—See Halliburton Company; *U.S. Public*, pg. 776
GEARHART (UNITED KINGDOM) LIMITED—See Halliburton Company; *U.S. Public*, pg. 776
GEARHART WEST AFRICA S.A.—See Halliburton Company; *U.S. Public*, pg. 776
GEARHART WIRELINE SERVICES, LTD.—See Halliburton Company; *U.S. Public*, pg. 776
GEARS & SPROCKETTS, INC.—See Bearing Headquarters Co.; *U.S. Private*, pg. 127
GEBAUER AG—See Schindler Holding AG; *Int'l*, pg. 1204
GEBHARDT SARL—See Masco Corporation; *U.S. Public*, pg. 1054
GEBHARDT VENTILATOREN, GMBH—See Masco Corporation; *U.S. Public*, pg. 1054
GEBHARDT VENTILATOREN VERWALTUNGS GMBH—See Masco Corporation; *U.S. Public*, pg. 1055
W. GEBHART, AKTIEBOLAG—See Masco Corporation; *U.S. Public*, pg. 1054
GEBO DISTRIBUTING CO., INC.; *U.S. Private*, pg. 442
GEBR. BECKER SPORTANLAGENBAU GMBH—See Heidemij N.V.; *Int'l*, pg. 608
GEBR. EICKHOFF MASCHINENFABRIK UND EISENGIESSEREI MBH; *Int'l*, pg. 542
GEBR. EIJFFINGER B.V.—See Gamma Holding N.V.; *Int'l*, pg. 540
GEBR. E. & O. KRAUSE GMBH—See Freudenberg & Company; *Int'l*, pg. 506
GEBR. HEIMER GMBH—See Mannesmann A.G.; *Int'l*, pg. 838
GEBRUDER BOHLER & CO. AG—See Voest-Alpine Stahl AG; *Int'l*, pg. 1471
GEBRUDER DAHL GMBH—See Dahl International AB; *Int'l*, pg. 359
GEBRUDER DIPPE SAATZUCHT G.M.B.H.—See Novartis AG; *Int'l*, pg. 982
GEBRUDER GROSS GES.M.B.H.—See Julius Meinl AG; *Int'l*, pg. 856
GEBRUDER HAAKE GMBH—See Rhone-Poulenc S.A.; *Int'l*, pg. 1111
GEBRUDER SULZER GESELLSCHQAFT MBH, ANLAGEN- UND GEBAUDETECHNIK—See Sulzer Ltd.; *Int'l*, pg. 1306
GEBRUDER SULZER HOLDING GMBH—See Sulzer Ltd.; *Int'l*, pg. 1308
GEBRUDER SULZER-ESCHER WYSS-KALTETECHNIK GMBH—See Sulzer Ltd.; *Int'l*, pg. 1306
GEBRUEDER KEMMER GMBH—See Philipp Holzmann AG; *Int'l*, pg. 632
GECO A.S.—See Schlumberger Limited; *U.S. Public*, pg. 1439
GECONSULT LTD.—See The General Electric Company, p.l.c.; *Int'l*, pg. 544
GECOTEC—See GIB Group; *Int'l*, pg. 533
GECOTEC SA—See GIB Group; *Int'l*, pg. 533
GEDAS NV—See Heidemij N.V.; *Int'l*, pg. 608
GEDDES GRANT SPROSTONS INDUS., LTD.—See Alcan Aluminium Limited; *Int'l*, pg. 52
GEDY IBERICA—See Gedy S.p.A.; *Int'l*, pg. 542
GEDY S.p.A.; *Int'l*, pg. 542
GEE, JEFFERY & PARTNERS ADVERTISING INC.; *Int'l*, pg. 542
GEELONG ROD MILL—See The Broken Hill Proprietary Company Limited; *Int'l*, pg. 227
GEELONG WIRE MILL—See The Broken Hill Proprietary Company Limited; *Int'l*, pg. 226
GEERS GROSS ADVERTISING LIMITED; *Int'l*, pg. 542
GEESINK B.V.—See Powell Duffryn PLC; *Int'l*, pg. 1066
GEEST PLC; *Int'l*, pg. 542

GEESTEMUNDER BANK AG—See Bayerische Vereinsbank Group; *Int'l*, pg. 179
GEESTEMUNDER VERWALTUNGS- UND BETEILIGUNGSGES MBH—See Bayerische Vereinsbank Group; *Int'l*, pg. 179
GEFFEN RECORDS—See The Seagram Company Ltd.; *Int'l*, pg. 1215
GEFINA—See Assicurazioni Generali S.p.A.; *Int'l*, pg. 90
GEFINA DUE S.P.A.—See Assicurazioni Generali S.p.A.; *Int'l*, pg. 90
GEFINA INTERNATIONAL LTD.—See Assicurazioni Generali S.p.A.; *Int'l*, pg. 91
GEFINA INTERNATIONAL N.V.—See Assicurazioni Generali S.p.A.; *Int'l*, pg. 91
GEFINOR FINANCE S.A.—See Gefinor S.A. Luxembourg; *Int'l*, pg. 542
GEFINOR S.A. LUXEMBOURG; *Int'l*, pg. 542
GEFINOR U.S.A., INC.—See Gefinor S.A. Luxembourg; *Int'l*, pg. 542
GEHL COMPANY; *U.S. Public*, pg. 704
GEHL POWER PRODUCTS, INC.—See Gehl Company; *U.S. Public*, pg. 704
GEICO CASUALTY COMPANY—See Berkshire Hathaway Inc.; *U.S. Public*, pg. 219
GEICO CORPORATION—See Berkshire Hathaway Inc.; *U.S. Public*, pg. 219
GEICO FACILITIES CORPORATION—See Berkshire Hathaway Inc.; *U.S. Public*, pg. 219
GEICO GENERAL INSURANCE CO.—See Berkshire Hathaway Inc.; *U.S. Public*, pg. 219
GEICO INDEMNITY COMPANY—See Berkshire Hathaway Inc.; *U.S. Public*, pg. 220
GEICO INVESTMENT SERVICES CO.—See Berkshire Hathaway Inc.; *U.S. Public*, pg. 220
GEICO PROPERTIES, INC.—See Berkshire Hathaway Inc.; *U.S. Public*, pg. 220
GEICO WASHINGTON PROPERTIES, INC.—See Berkshire Hathaway Inc.; *U.S. Public*, pg. 220
GEIGER BROTHERS; *U.S. Private*, pg. 442
GEINP—See Petrobras - Petroleo Brasileiro S.A.; *Int'l*, pg. 1041
GEKA, S.A.—See Vishay Intertechnology, Inc.; *U.S. Public*, pg. 1722
GEKRU B.V.—See Gamma Holding N.V.; *Int'l*, pg. 540
GELALP—See Groupe Casino; *Int'l*, pg. 563
GELAZUR SA—See ConAgra, Inc.; *U.S. Public*, pg. 429
GELCO INFORMATION NETWORK, INC.; *U.S. Private*, pg. 442
GELDER ADVERTISING—See Warwick Baker O'Neill; *U.S. Private*, pg. 1152
GELDERLANDER FLEISCHWAREN GMBH—See Koninklijke BolsWessanen nv; *Int'l*, pg. 752
GELDNET BV—See KPN Koninklyke PTT Nederland NV; *Int'l*, pg. 720
GELLATLY HANKEY MARINE SERVICES—See Inchcape PLC; *Int'l*, pg. 672
GELLER NESSIS/DMB&B TEL AVIV—See DMB&B Communications; *U.S. Private*, pg. 304
GELMAN IRELAND LTD.—See Pall Corporation; *U.S. Public*, pg. 1253
GELMAN ITALY S.R.L.—See Pall Corporation; *U.S. Public*, pg. 1253
GELMAN SCIENCES (DEUTSCHLAND) GMBH—See Pall Corporation; *U.S. Public*, pg. 1253
GELMAN SCIENCES, INC.—See Pall Corporation; *U.S. Public*, pg. 1253
GELMAN SCIENCES, INC. (CANADA)—See Pall Corporation; *U.S. Public*, pg. 1253
GELMAN SCIENCES JAPAN LIMITED—See Pall Corporation; *U.S. Public*, pg. 1253
GELMAN SCIENCES, LTD.—See Pall Corporation; *U.S. Public*, pg. 1253
GELMAN SCIENCES PTY. LTD.—See Pall Corporation; *U.S. Public*, pg. 1253
GELMAN SCIENCES S.A.—See Pall Corporation; *U.S. Public*, pg. 1253
ANDRE GELOT ET CIE. S.R.L.—See Assicurazioni Generali S.p.A.; *Int'l*, pg. 91
GELSENWASSER AG—See Veba AG; *Int'l*, pg. 1456
GELSON'S MARKETS—See Arden Group, Inc.; *U.S. Public*, pg. 129
GEM—See Havatampa, Inc.; *U.S. Private*, pg. 510
GEM—See Groupe Casino; *Int'l*, pg. 563
GEM-DANDY, INC.; *U.S. Private*, pg. 442
GEM INDUSTRIES FINANCE CORPORATION; *U.S. Private*, pg. 442
GEM INDUSTRIES NE INC.—See Gem Industries Finance Corporation; *U.S. Private*, pg. 442
GEM SOUTHEAST, INC.—See Gem Industries Finance Corporation; *U.S. Private*, pg. 443
GEM STATE UTILITIES CORPORATION—See PacifiCorp; *U.S. Public*, pg. 1252
GEM TECH—See Katy Industries, Inc.; *U.S. Public*, pg. 944
GEM TOP MFG., INC.; *U.S. Private*, pg. 443
GEMA—See Illinois Tool Works Inc.; *U.S. Public*, pg. 866
GEMA S.A.—See Novartis AG; *Int'l*, pg. 982
GEMA VOLSTATIC INDUSTRIAL POWDER SYSTEMS (SWITZERLAND)—See Illinois Tool Works Inc.; *U.S. Public*, pg. 868
GEMA VOLSTATIC INDUSTRIAL POWDER SYSTEMS (ITALY)—See Illinois Tool Works Inc.; *U.S. Public*, pg. 868
GEMAIRE DISTRIBUTORS, INC.—See Watsco, Inc.; *U.S. Public*, pg. 1746
GEMCHEM, INC.—See American Vanguard Corporation; *U.S. Public*, pg. 94
GEMEAZ—See Accor S.A.; *Int'l*, pg. 21
GEMEINNUTZIGE WOHNUNGS - GES.MBH—See Bayer AG; *Int'l*, pg. 172
GEMEINSCHAFTSKERNKRAFTWERK GROHNDE GMBH—See Veba AG; *Int'l*, pg. 1456
GEMEINSCHAFTSKRAFTWERK KIEL GMBH—See Veba AG; *Int'l*, pg. 1456

GEMEINSCHAFTSKRAFTWERK WEST GBR—See Harpen AG; *Int'l*, pg. 597
GEMEINSCHAFTSUNTERNEHMEN PETROVOITH—See J.M. Voith, GmbH; *Int'l*, pg. 1473
GEMEY DIV.—See L'Oreal S.A.; *Int'l*, pg. 819
GEMINI ALUMINUM CORPORATION; *U.S. Private*, pg. 443
GEMINI BAKERY EQUIPMENT CO.—See Fried. Krupp AG; *Int'l*, pg. 511
GEMINI CONSULTING—See CAP Gemini S.A.; *Int'l*, pg. 264
THE GEMINI GROUP LIMITED PARTNERSHIP—See Air Canada; *Int'l*, pg. 36
GEMINI SCIENCE, INC.—See Kirin Brewery Co., Ltd.; *Int'l*, pg. 736
GEMISA S.A. DE C.V.—See Henkel KGaA; *Int'l*, pg. 614
GEMS SENSORS—See Danaher Corporation; *U.S. Public*, pg. 481
GEMSTAR INTERNATIONAL GROUP LIMITED; *U.S. Public*, pg. 705
GEMSTONE GASKET CO.—See Dana Corporation; *U.S. Public*, pg. 480
GEMTRON CORPORATION—See Carl-Zeiss-Stiftung; *Int'l*, pg. 1523
GEN CORP INC.—See Toyo Tire & Rubber Co., Ltd.; *Int'l*, pg. 1411
GEN-EA BEFEKTETESI ES TANACSADO KFT.—See Assicurazioni Generali S.p.A.; *Int'l*, pg. 91
GEN-PROBE INC.—See Chugai Pharmaceutical Co., Ltd.; *Int'l*, pg. 291
GEN TRAC—See Jones Medical Industries Inc.; *U.S. Public*, pg. 934
GENAGRICOLA S.P.A.—See Assicurazioni Generali S.p.A.; *Int'l*, pg. 90
GENAMERICA MANAGEMENT CORPORATION—See Assicurazioni Generali S.p.A.; *Int'l*, pg. 90
GENCAB OF CANADA LTD.—See American Financial Group; *U.S. Public*, pg. 75
GENCO DISTRIBUTING DIV.—See Genovese Drug Stores, Inc.; *U.S. Public*, pg. 730
GENCON SERVICES, INC.—See George W. Auch Co.; *U.S. Private*, pg. 98
GENCONSULTORIA—See Generale de Banque S.A.; *Int'l*, pg. 547
GENCOR ACP LTD.—See Gencor Industries, Inc.; *U.S. Public*, pg. 705
GENCOR INDUSTRIES, INC.; *U.S. Public*, pg. 705
GENCORP DECORATIVE PRODUCT MANUFACTURING DIV.—See GenCorp Inc.; *J.S. Public*, pg. 706
GENCORP INC.; *U.S. Public*, pg. 705
GENCORP PRINTWORLD—See GenCorp Inc.; *U.S. Public*, pg. 706
GENCORP SPECIALTY PRODUCT DIV.—See GenCorp Inc.; *U.S. Public*, pg. 706
GENCORP VEHICLE SEALING DIV.—See GenCorp Inc.; *U.S. Public*, pg. 706
GENDEX-DEL MEDICAL IMAGING CORP.—See Del Global Technologies; *U.S. Public*, pg. 494
GENDEX DENTAL SYSTEMS—See Dentsply International Inc.; *U.S. Public*, pg. 500
GENDEX DENTAL SYSTEMS GMBH—See Dentsply International Inc.; *U.S. Public*, pg. 500
GENDEX DENTAL SYSTEMS S.R.L.—See Dentsply International Inc.; *U.S. Public*, pg. 500
GENDIS INC.; *Int'l*, pg. 542
GENELCO, INC.—See General American Life Insurance Co.; *U.S. Private*, pg. 443
GENENCOR INTERNATIONAL B.V.—See Cultor Ltd.; *Int'l*, pg. 349
GENENCOR INTERNATIONAL EUROPE OY—See Cultor Ltd.; *Int'l*, pg. 349
GENENCOR INTERNATIONAL, INC.—See Cultor Ltd.; *Int'l*, pg. 349
GENENCOR INTERNATIONAL N.V.—See Cultor Ltd.; *Int'l*, pg. 349
GENENTECH CANADA INC.—See Roche Holding Ltd.; *Int'l*, pg. 1120
GENENTECH EUROPE LIMITED—See Roche Holding Ltd.; *Int'l*, pg. 1120
GENENTECH, INC.—See Roche Holding Ltd.; *Int'l*, pg. 1120
GENENTECH, LTD.-JAPAN—See Roche Holding Ltd.; *Int'l*, pg. 1120
GENERA TECHNOLOGIES LIMITED—See Severn Trent Plc; *Int'l*, pg. 1226
GENERAL ACCIDENT FIRE AND LIFE ASSURANCE CORPORATION P.L.C.; *Int'l*, pg. 542
GENERAL ACCIDENT INSURANCE—See General Accident Fire and Life Assurance Corporation p.l.c.; *Int'l*, pg. 543
GENERAL ALUM & CHEMICAL; *U.S. Private*, pg. 443
GENERAL ALUM - NEW ENGLAND—See General Alum & Chemical; *U.S. Private*, pg. 443
GENERAL AMERICAN DOOR COMPANY—See Merchant Capital Group Ltd.; *U.S. Private*, pg. 732
GENERAL AMERICAN INVESTORS COMPANY, INC.; *U.S. Public*, pg. 706
GENERAL AMERICAN LIFE INSURANCE CO.; *U.S. Private*, pg. 443
GENERAL AMERICAN TRANSPORTATION CORPORATION—See GATX Corporation; *U.S. Public*, pg. 692
GENERAL AQUATICS CORPORATION—See Essef Corporation; *U.S. Public*, pg. 592
GENERAL ASSURANCE COMPANY—See General Accident Fire and Life Assurance Corporation p.l.c.; *Int'l*, pg. 543
GENERAL ASSURANCE INSURANCE COMPANY OF NEW YORK—See General Accident Fire and Life Assurance Corporation p.l.c.; *Int'l*, pg. 543
GENERAL ATOMICS; *U.S. Private*, pg. 443
GENERAL ATOMICS—See General Dynamics Corporation; *U.S. Public*, pg. 709
GENERAL ATOMICS, AERONAUTICS—See General Dynamics Corporation; *U.S. Public*, pg. 709

GENERAL AUTOMATION, INC.; *U.S. Public*, pg. 706
GENERAL AUTOMOTIVE CORPORATION; *U.S. Private*, pg. 443
GENERAL BEARING CORP.; *U.S. Public*, pg. 706
GENERAL BINDING CORPORATION; *U.S. Public*, pg. 707
GENERAL BISCUITS BELGIE N.V.—See Danone Group; *Int'l*, pg. 380
GENERAL BISCUITS ESPANA (GBE)—See Danone Group; *Int'l*, pg. 381
GENERAL BISCUITS GMBH (GBG)—See Danone Group; *Int'l*, pg. 381
GENERAL BISCUITS NEDERLAND (GBNL)—See Danone Group; *Int'l*, pg. 381
GENERAL BISCUITS OSTERREICH (GBO)—See Danone Group; *Int'l*, pg. 381
THE GENERAL BUILDING SUPPLY COMPANY—See Fidelity Investments (FMR Corp.); *U.S. Private*, pg. 403
GENERAL BUSINESS FORMS LTD.—See Data Business Forms Limited; *Int'l*, pg. 384
GENERAL BUSINESS SERVICES, INC.—See The Dwyer Group, Inc.; *U.S. Private*, pg. 538
GENERAL CABLE APPARATUS DIVISION—See Wassall Plc; *Int'l*, pg. 1487
GENERAL CABLE CO.—See Wassall Plc; *Int'l*, pg. 1487
GENERAL CABLE CORPORATION—See Wassall Plc; *Int'l*, pg. 1486
GENERAL CABLE GUARDIAN PRODUCTS DIVISION—See Wassall Plc; *Int'l*, pg. 1487
GENERAL CASUALTY COMPANY OF ILLINOIS—See Credit Suisse Group; *Int'l*, pg. 346
GENERAL CASUALTY COMPANY OF WISCONSIN—See Credit Suisse Group; *Int'l*, pg. 345
GENERAL CERAMICS, INC.—See Tokuyama Corporation; *Int'l*, pg. 1394
GENERAL CHEMICAL CORPORATION—See The General Chemical Group, Inc.; *U.S. Public*, pg. 707
THE GENERAL CHEMICAL GROUP, INC.; *U.S. Public*, pg. 707
GENERAL CHEMICAL (SODA ASH) PARTNERS—See Tosoh Corporation; *Int'l*, pg. 1407
GENERAL CIGAR COMPANY, INC.—See General Cigar Holdings Inc.; *U.S. Public*, pg. 708
GENERAL CIGAR HOLDINGS INC; *U.S. Public*, pg. 707
GENERAL CINEMA THEATRES, INC.—See GC Companies, Inc.; *U.S. Public*, pg. 693
GENERAL COACH—See Thor Industries, Inc.; *U.S. Public*, pg. 1360
GENERAL COMBUSTION CORPORATION—See Gencor Industries, Inc.; *U.S. Public*, pg. 705
GENERAL COMBUSTION LTD.—See Gencor Industries, Inc.; *U.S. Public*, pg. 705
GENERAL COMMERCIAL PACKAGING, INC.—See The Suddath Companies; *U.S. Private*, pg. 1049
GENERAL COMMUNICATION, INC.; *U.S. Public*, pg. 708
GENERAL CONNECTOR—See Wire-Pro Inc.; *U.S. Private*, pg. 1184
GENERAL COSMETICS B.V.—See Joh. A. Benckiser GmbH; *Int'l*, pg. 186
GENERAL DATACOM INDUSTRIES, INC.—See General Datacomm Industries, Inc.; *U.S. Public*, pg. 708
GENERAL DATACOMM, INC.—See General Datacomm Industries, Inc.; *U.S. Public*, pg. 708
GENERAL DATACOMM INDUSTRIES, INC.; *U.S. Public*, pg. 708
GENERAL DATACOMM INTL. CORP.—See General Datacomm Industries, Inc.; *U.S. Public*, pg. 708
GENERAL DATACOMM LTD.—See General Datacomm Industries, Inc.; *U.S. Public*, pg. 708
GENERAL DE BAZAR—See GIB Group; *Int'l*, pg. 534
GENERAL DRUG CO.—See C.D. Smith Drug Company; *U.S. Private*, pg. 1007
GENERAL DYNAMICS—See Lockheed Martin Corporation; *U.S. Public*, pg. 1006
GENERAL DYNAMICS, ABILENE FACILITY—See General Dynamics Corporation; *U.S. Public*, pg. 709
GENERAL DYNAMICS ARMAMENT SYSTEMS—See General Dynamics Corporation; *U.S. Public*, pg. 709
GENERAL DYNAMICS CORPORATION; *U.S. Public*, pg. 708
GENERAL DYNAMICS DEFENSE SYSTEMS—See General Dynamics Corporation; *U.S. Public*, pg. 709
GENERAL DYNAMICS HARLINGEN—See General Dynamics Corporation; *U.S. Public*, pg. 709
GENERAL DYNAMICS INTERNATIONAL CORPORATION—See General Dynamics Corporation; *U.S. Public*, pg. 709
GENERAL DYNAMICS LAND SYSTEMS DIV.—See General Dynamics Corporation; *U.S. Public*, pg. 709
GENERAL DYNAMICS SERVICES CO.—See General Dynamics Corporation; *U.S. Public*, pg. 709
GENERAL ELECTRIC CAPITAL AVIATION SERVICES—See General Electric Company; *U.S. Public*, pg. 712
GENERAL ELECTRIC CAPITAL RAILCAR SERVICES—See General Electric Company; *U.S. Public*, pg. 712
GENERAL ELECTRIC CAPITAL SERVICES, INC.—See General Electric Company; *U.S. Public*, pg. 711
GENERAL ELECTRIC COMPANY; *U.S. Public*, pg. 709
THE GENERAL ELECTRIC COMPANY OF BANGLADESH LTD.—See The General Electric Company, p.l.c.; *Int'l*, pg. 546
THE GENERAL ELECTRIC COMPANY OF HONG KONG LTD.—See The General Electric Company, p.l.c.; *Int'l*, pg. 546
THE GENERAL ELECTRIC COMPANY OF MALAYSIA SDN. BHD.—See The General Electric Company, p.l.c.; *Int'l*, pg. 546
THE GENERAL ELECTRIC CO. OF SINGAPORE PRIVATE LTD.—See The General Electric Company, p.l.c.; *Int'l*, pg. 546
THE GENERAL ELECTRIC COMPANY, P.L.C.; *Int'l*, pg. 543
GENERAL ELECTRIC DE MEXICO, S.A. DE C.V.—See General Electric Company; *U.S. Public*, pg. 713

GENERAL ELECTRIC DO BRAZIL, S.A.—See General Electric Company; *U.S. Public*, pg. 713
G.E. FINANCIAL ASSURANCE—See General Electric Company; *U.S. Public*, pg. 712
GENERAL ELECTRIC INTERNATIONAL OPERATIONS—See General Electric Company; *U.S. Public*, pg. 713
GENERAL ELECTRIC INVESTMENT CORP.—See General Electric Company; *U.S. Public*, pg. 712
GENERAL ELECTRIC PHILIPPINES INC.—See General Electric Company; *U.S. Public*, pg. 713
GENERAL ELECTRIC PLASTICS GMBH—See General Electric Company; *U.S. Public*, pg. 713
GENERAL ELECTRIC RAILCAR REPAIR SERVICES CORP.—See General Electric Company; *U.S. Public*, pg. 712
GENERAL ELECTRIC (USA) ASIA CO.—See General Electric Company; *U.S. Public*, pg. 713
GENERAL ELECTRIC (USA) AVIATION SERVICE OPERATION PTE.—See General Electric Company; *U.S. Public*, pg. 714
GENERAL ELECTRIC (USA) CHINA COMPANY, LTD.—See General Electric Company; *U.S. Public*, pg. 713
GENERAL ELECTRIC (USA) CONSUMER ELECTRONICS (PTE) LTD.—See General Electric Company; *U.S. Public*, pg. 714
GENERAL ELECTRIC (USA) HERMETIC MOTOR OPERATION (PTE) LTD.—See General Electric Company; *U.S. Public*, pg. 714
GENERAL EMPLOYMENT ENTERPRISES—See General Employment Enterprises, Inc.; *U.S. Public*, pg. 714
GENERAL EMPLOYMENT ENTERPRISES, INC.; *U.S. Public*, pg. 714
GENERAL EMPLOYMENT ENTERPRISES, INC.—See General Employment Enterprises, Inc.; *U.S. Public*, pg. 715
GENERAL ENGINEERS LIMITED—See IDB Holding Corporation; *Int'l*, pg. 645
GENERAL FELT INDUSTRIES, INC.—See Trace International Holdings, Inc.; *U.S. Private*, pg. 1094
GENERAL FILTERS, INC.; *U.S. Private*, pg. 444
GENERAL FINDINGS—See Leach & Garner Company; *U.S. Private*, pg. 655
GENERAL GENERIC TRUCKING DIV.—See Accra Pac Group; *U.S. Private*, pg. 11
GENERAL GRAPHICS, INC.—See Cigna Corp.; *U.S. Public*, pg. 362
GENERAL GROWTH MANAGEMENT, INC.—See General Growth Properties Inc.; *U.S. Public*, pg. 715
GENERAL GROWTH PROPERTIES INC.; *U.S. Public*, pg. 715
GENERAL HARDWARE DISTRIBUTORS—See Alaska Industrial Hardware Inc.; *U.S. Private*, pg. 31
GENERAL HOLDINGS LIMITED—See CoreStates Financial Corp.; *U.S. Public*, pg. 447
GENERAL HOMES CORPORATION; *U.S. Private*, pg. 444
GENERAL HOSPITAL—See Brim, Inc.; *U.S. Private*, pg. 169
GENERAL HOSPITALS OF GALEN, INC.—See Columbia/HCA Healthcare Corporation; *U.S. Public*, pg. 404
GENERAL HOST CORPORATION; *U.S. Public*, pg. 715
GENERAL HOUSEWARES CORP.; *U.S. Public*, pg. 715
GENERAL IMPLEMENT DISTRIBUTORS—See Arnold Machinery Company; *U.S. Private*, pg. 84
GENERAL INSTRUMENT CORPORATION; *U.S. Public*, pg. 716
GENERAL INSTRUMENT CORPORATION—See General Instrument Corporation; *U.S. Public*, pg. 716
GENERAL INSTRUMENT OF CANADA LTD.—See General Instrument Corporation; *U.S. Public*, pg. 716
GENERAL INSURANCE CO. OF AMERICA—See SAFECO Corporation; *U.S. Public*, pg. 1423
GENERAL IONICS—See Ionics, Incorporated; *U.S. Public*, pg. 912
GENERAL KINETICS INCORPORATED; *U.S. Public*, pg. 716
GENERAL LATEX & CHEMICAL CORPORATION; *U.S. Private*, pg. 444
GENERAL LIFE INSURANCE COMPANY OF AMERICA—See General American Life Insurance Co.; *U.S. Private*, pg. 443
GENERAL MACHINERY CO.—See Alusuisse-Lonza Holding Ltd.; *Int'l*, pg. 68
GENERAL MAGNAPLATE CALIFORNIA—See General Magnaplate Corporation; *U.S. Public*, pg. 717
GENERAL MAGNAPLATE CANADA—See General Magnaplate Corporation; *U.S. Public*, pg. 717
GENERAL MAGNAPLATE CORPORATION; *U.S. Public*, pg. 717
GENERAL MAGNAPLATE TEXAS—See General Magnaplate Corporation; *U.S. Public*, pg. 717
GENERAL MAGNAPLATE WISCONSIN—See General Magnaplate Corporation; *U.S. Public*, pg. 717
GENERAL MAGNETIC—See Recoton Corporation; *U.S. Public*, pg. 1369
GENERAL MANAGEMENT CO.—See Management Dynamics; *U.S. Public*, pg. 1040
GENERAL MANUFACTURING DIV.—See FKI Plc; *Int'l*, pg. 472
GENERAL MARBLE CORPORATION—See Leucadia National Corporation; *U.S. Public*, pg. 990
GENERAL MEDIA AUTOMOTIVE GROUP INC.—See General Media International Inc.; *U.S. Private*, pg. 444
GENERAL MEDIA COMMUNICATIONS GROUP INC.—See General Media International Inc.; *U.S. Private*, pg. 444
GENERAL MEDIA ENTERTAINMENT GROUP INC.—See General Media International Inc.; *U.S. Private*, pg. 444
GENERAL MEDIA FILMS GROUP INC.—See General Media International Inc.; *U.S. Private*, pg. 444
THE GENERAL MEDIA GROUP INC.—See General Media International Inc.; *U.S. Private*, pg. 444
GENERAL MEDIA INTERNATIONAL INC.; *U.S. Private*, pg. 444
GENERAL MEDICAL CORP.—See McKesson Corporation; *U.S. Public*, pg. 1073

GENERAL MEDICAL EQUIPMENT—See Graham-Field Health Products, Inc.; *U.S. Public,* pg. 758

GENERAL MERCHANDISE DISTRIBUTORS, INC.—See Fleming Companies, Inc.; *U.S. Public,* pg. 653

GENERAL METAL PRODUCTS—See Wozniak Industries, Inc.; *U.S. Private,* pg. 1192

GENERAL MICROCIRCUITS CORPORATION—See General Microwave Corporation; *U.S. Public,* pg. 717

GENERAL MICROCIRCUITS, INC.—See Microsemi Corporation; *U.S. Public,* pg. 1107

GENERAL MICROWAVE CORPORATION; *U.S. Public,* pg. 717

GENERAL MILLS CANADA INC.—See General Mills, Inc.; *U.S. Public,* pg. 718

GENERAL MILLS, CONSUMER FOODS SALES DIV.—See General Mills, Inc.; *U.S. Public,* pg. 718

GENERAL MILLS EUROPE LIMITED—See General Mills, Inc.; *U.S. Public,* pg. 718

GENERAL MILLS, INC.; *U.S. Public,* pg. 717

GENERAL MILLS, MARKETING SERVICES DIV.—See General Mills, Inc.; *U.S. Public,* pg. 718

GENERAL MILLS OPERATIONS, INC.—See General Mills, Inc.; *U.S. Public,* pg. 718

GENERAL MILLS SALES, INC.—See General Mills, Inc.; *U.S. Public,* pg. 718

GENERAL MOTORS ACCEPTANCE CORPORATION (GMAC)—See General Motors Corporation; *U.S. Public,* pg. 719

GENERAL MOTORS ACCEPTANCE CORPORATION OF CANADA LIMITED—See General Motors Corporation; *U.S. Public,* pg. 720

GENERAL MOTORS CANADA COMPONENTS DIV.—See General Motors Corporation; *U.S. Public,* pg. 722

GENERAL MOTORS CANADA DIESEL DIV.—See General Motors Corporation; *U.S. Public,* pg. 722

GENERAL MOTORS CANADA ENGINE DIV.—See General Motors Corporation; *U.S. Public,* pg. 722

GENERAL MOTORS CANADA FOUNDRY DIV.—See General Motors Corporation; *U.S. Public,* pg. 722

GENERAL MOTORS CANADA STE. THERESE DIV.—See General Motors Corporation; *U.S. Public,* pg. 722

GENERAL MOTORS CANADA TRANSMISSION DIV.—See General Motors Corporation; *U.S. Public,* pg. 722

GENERAL MOTORS COLMOTORES, S.A.—See General Motors Corporation; *U.S. Public,* pg. 722

GENERAL MOTORS CORPORATION; *U.S. Public,* pg. 718

GENERAL MOTORS CORPORATION-AUTOMOTIVE COMPONENTS GRP. WORLDWIDE—See General Motors Corporation; *U.S. Public,* pg. 719

GENERAL MOTORS DE MEXICO, S.A. DE C.V.—See General Motors Corporation; *U.S. Public,* pg. 722

GENERAL MOTORS DEL ECUADOR S.A.—See General Motors Corporation; *U.S. Public,* pg. 722

GENERAL MOTORS EGYPT S.A.E.—See Isuzu Motors Limited; *Int'l,* pg. 692

GENERAL MOTORS EGYPT S.A.E.—See General Motors Corporation; *U.S. Public,* pg. 724

GENERAL MOTORS FRANCE AUTOMOBILES S.A.—See General Motors Corporation; *U.S. Public,* pg. 722

GENERAL MOTORS-HOLDEN'S AUTOMOTIVE LIMITED—See General Motors Corporation; *U.S. Public,* pg. 723

GENERAL MOTORS HUNGARY—See General Motors Corporation; *U.S. Public,* pg. 722

GENERAL MOTORS HUNGARY (DISTRIBUTION) LTD.—See General Motors Corporation; *U.S. Public,* pg. 722

GENERAL MOTORS HUNGARY (MANUFACTURING) LTD.—See General Motors Corporation; *U.S. Public,* pg. 722

GENERAL MOTORS MARKETING SERVICES HELLAS AEE—See General Motors Corporation; *U.S. Public,* pg. 722

GENERAL MOTORS OF CANADA LTD.—See General Motors Corporation; *U.S. Public,* pg. 722

GENERAL MOTORS OVERSEAS CORP.—See General Motors Corporation; *U.S. Public,* pg. 722

GENERAL MOTORS TAIWAN, INC.—See General Motors Corporation; *U.S. Public,* pg. 723

GENERAL MOTORS TURKIYE LIMITED SIRKETI—See General Motors Corporation; *U.S. Public,* pg. 723

GENERAL MOTORS VENEZOLANA, C.A.—See General Motors Corporation; *U.S. Public,* pg. 723

GENERAL NUTRITION CENTERS—See General Nutrition, Inc.; *U.S. Public,* pg. 725

GENERAL NUTRITION FRANCHISING, INC.—See General Nutrition, Inc.; *U.S. Public,* pg. 725

GENERAL NUTRITION, INC.; *U.S. Public,* pg. 725

GENERAL NUTRITION PRODUCTS, INC.—See General Nutrition, Inc.; *U.S. Public,* pg. 725

GENERAL NUTRITION SERVICES, INC.—See General Nutrition, Inc.; *U.S. Public,* pg. 725

GENERAL OFFICE ENVIRONMENTS INC.; *U.S. Private,* pg. 445

GENERAL PAINT LTD.—See Williams Holdings Plc; *Int'l,* pg. 1501

GENERAL PARTS, INC.; *U.S. Private,* pg. 445

GENERAL PHYSICS CORPORATION—See GP Strategies Corporation; *U.S. Public,* pg. 694

GENERAL PHYSICS FINANCE INC.—See GP Strategies Corporation; *U.S. Public,* pg. 694

GENERAL PHYSICS MOHAWK CORPORATION—See GP Strategies Corporation; *U.S. Public,* pg. 694

GENERAL PHYSICS NIAGARA CORPORATION—See GP Strategies Corporation; *U.S. Public,* pg. 694

GENERAL PHYSICS OHIO CORPORATION—See GP Strategies Corporation; *U.S. Public,* pg. 694

GENERAL PHYSICS PHILADELPHIA CORPORATION—See GP Strategies Corporation; *U.S. Public,* pg. 694

GENERAL PORTFOLIOS CORP.—See GPU, Inc.; *U.S. Public,* pg. 695

GENERAL POWER SYSTEMS, INC.—See Components Corporation Of America; *U.S. Private,* pg. 260

GENERAL PRECISION TOOL & DIE DIVISION—See Leggett & Platt, Incorporated; *U.S. Public,* pg. 986

GENERAL PRINTING INK—See Dainippon Ink & Chemicals, Inc.; *Int'l,* pg. 370

GENERAL PROCESSORS, INC.—See Standard Commercial Corporation; *U.S. Public,* pg. 1502

THE GENERAL PUBLISHING GROUP—See Pearson plc; *Int'l,* pg. 1026

GENERAL RAILWAY SIGNAL CORP.—See SASIB SpA; *Int'l,* pg. 1194

GENERAL RE CORPORATION; *U.S. Public,* pg. 725

GENERAL RE EUROPE LIMITED—See General Re Corporation; *U.S. Public,* pg. 726

GENERAL REINSURANCE CORP.—See General Re Corporation; *U.S. Public,* pg. 726

GENERAL SCIENCES CORP.—See Science Applications International Corp.; *U.S. Public,* pg. 1405

GENERAL SEATING OF AMERICA INC.—See NHK Spring Co., Ltd.; *Int'l,* pg. 902

GENERAL SEATING OF CANADA LIMITED—See NHK Spring Co., Ltd.; *Int'l,* pg. 902

GENERAL SECURITIES CORPORATION OF NORTH AMERICA—See Assicurazioni Generali S.p.A.; *Int'l,* pg. 90

GENERAL SEKIYU K.K.—See Exxon Corporation; *U.S. Public,* pg. 602

GENERAL SEMICONDUCTOR, INC.; *U.S. Public,* pg. 726

GENERAL SERVICES CORPORATION; *U.S. Private,* pg. 445

GENERAL SHALE PRODUCTS CORP.—See Marley PLC; *Int'l,* pg. 843

THE GENERAL SHOE WAREHOUSE—See Genesco Inc.; *U.S. Public,* pg. 728

GENERAL SIGNAL CORPORATION; *U.S. Public,* pg. 726

GENERAL SIGNAL NETWORKS—See General Signal Corporation; *U.S. Public,* pg. 727

GENERAL SIGNAL THINFILM COMPANY—See General Signal Corporation; *U.S. Public,* pg. 727

GENERAL SLICING/RED GOAT DISPOSERS—See Standex International Corporation; *U.S. Public,* pg. 1506

GENERAL SPRING, INC.; *U.S. Private,* pg. 445

GENERAL STAR MANAGEMENT COMPANY—See General Re Corporation; *U.S. Public,* pg. 725

GENERAL STEEL CORPORATION—See Pitt-Des Moines, Inc.; *U.S. Public,* pg. 1305

GENERAL SURETY & GUARANTEE LTD.—See Zurich Insurance Company; *Int'l,* pg. 1531

GENERAL TECHNICAL SERVICES, INC.—See GP Strategies Corporation; *U.S. Public,* pg. 695

GENERAL TEXTILES; *U.S. Private,* pg. 445

GENERAL TIME CORP.; *U.S. Private,* pg. 445

GENERAL TIRE & RUBBER CO. OF MOROCCO—See Continental AG; *Int'l,* pg. 327

GENERAL TIRE INTL. CO.—See Continental AG; *Int'l,* pg. 327

GENERAL TOOLS MFG., CO. INC.; *U.S. Public,* pg. 445

GENERAL TOURS INC.; *U.S. Private,* pg. 445

GENERAL TRADE ASSOCIATES—See Georgia Tent & Awning Co.; *U.S. Private,* pg. 448

GENERAL TRADING & CHEMICALS CO.—See BASF AG; *Int'l,* pg. 108

GENERAL TRADING CO.; *U.S. Private,* pg. 445

GENERAL TRAVEL SERVICES, INC.—See Washington Mutual Inc.; *U.S. Public,* pg. 1742

GENERAL TRUST INVESTMENT FUNDS LTD.—See National Bank of Canada; *Int'l,* pg. 907

GENERAL TRUST OF CANADA—See National Bank of Canada; *Int'l,* pg. 907

GENERAL TYRE EAST AFRICA LTD.—See Continental AG; *Int'l,* pg. 327

GENERAL VALVE—See Parker Hannifin Corporation; *U.S. Public,* pg. 1262

GENERAL WHOLESALE COMPANY—See General Wholesale Company, Inc.; *U.S. Private,* pg. 446

GENERAL WHOLESALE COMPANY, INC.; *U.S. Private,* pg. 445

GENERAL WIG MANUFACTURERS, INC.—See MacAndrews & Forbes Holdings Inc.; *U.S. Private,* pg. 690

GENERALA ASIIGURARI S.A.—See Assicurazioni Generali S.p.A.; *Int'l,* pg. 91

GENERALE BANK—See Generale de Banque S.A.; *Int'l,* pg. 547

GENERALE BANK & CO.—See Generale de Banque S.A.; *Int'l,* pg. 548

GENERALE BANK & CO.—See Generale de Banque S.A.; *Int'l,* pg. 548

GENERALE BANK - BANCO BELGA—See Generale de Banque S.A.; *Int'l,* pg. 547

GENERALE BANK - BREDA—See Generale de Banque S.A.; *Int'l,* pg. 547

GENERALE BANK - EINDHOVEN—See Generale de Banque S.A.; *Int'l,* pg. 547

GENERALE BANK - LISBOA—See Generale de Banque S.A.; *Int'l,* pg. 547

GENERALE BANK - LONDON—See Generale de Banque S.A.; *Int'l,* pg. 547

GENERALE BANK - MAASTRICHT—See Generale de Banque S.A.; *Int'l,* pg. 547

GENERALE BANK - MILANO—See Generale de Banque S.A.; *Int'l,* pg. 547

GENERALE BANK NEDERLAND—See Generale de Banque S.A.; *Int'l,* pg. 548

GENERALE BANK OVERSEAS (BELGIUM) - BELGIAN BANK—See Generale de Banque S.A.; *Int'l,* pg. 548

GENERALE BANK - PORTO—See Generale de Banque S.A.; *Int'l,* pg. 547

GENERALE BANK - UTRECHT—See Generale de Banque S.A.; *Int'l,* pg. 547

GENERALE BELGIAN BANK—See Generale de Banque S.A.; *Int'l,* pg. 547

GENERALE DE BANQUE BELGE (FRANCE) SA—See Generale de Banque S.A.; *Int'l,* pg. 548

GENERALE DE BANQUE DE MAURITANIE POUR L'INVESTISSEMENT ET LE COMMERCE—See Generale de Banque S.A.; *Int'l,* pg. 548

GENERALE DE BANQUE - GENERALE BANK—See Generale de Banque S.A.; *Int'l,* pg. 546

GENERALE DE BANQUE S.A.; *Int'l,* pg. 546

GENERALE DE GRANDES SOURCES—See Nestle S.A.; *Int'l,* pg. 920

GENERALE FINANCE LUXEMBOURG SA—See Banque Generale du Luxembourg SA; *Int'l,* pg. 162

GENERALE INVESTMENT BANKING CORPORATION—See Generale de Banque S.A.; *Int'l,* pg. 547

GENERALE SUCRIERE SNC; *Int'l,* pg. 548

GENERALE TRAITEUR—See Danone Group; *Int'l,* pg. 380

GENERALI ALLGEMEINE LEBENSVERSICHERUNG AG—See Assicurazioni Generali S.p.A.; *Int'l,* pg. 89

GENERALI - AUSTRIA—See Assicurazioni Generali S.p.A.; *Int'l,* pg. 89

GENERALI BELGIUM HOLDING S.A.—See Assicurazioni Generali S.p.A.; *Int'l,* pg. 91

GENERALI BELGIUM INVEST S.A.—See Assicurazioni Generali S.p.A.; *Int'l,* pg. 91

GENERALI BELGIUM S.A.—See Assicurazioni Generali S.p.A.; *Int'l,* pg. 91

GENERALI BUDAPEST BIZTOSITO RT.—See Assicurazioni Generali S.p.A.; *Int'l,* pg. 91

GENERALI DO BRASIL COMPANHIA NACIONAL DE SEGUROS—See Assicurazioni Generali S.p.A.; *Int'l,* pg. 91

GENERALI FINANCES S.A.—See Assicurazioni Generali S.p.A.; *Int'l,* pg. 91

S.N.C. GENERALI FRANCE ET CIE—See Assicurazioni Generali S.p.A.; *Int'l,* pg. 91

GENERALI FRANCE S.A.—See Assicurazioni Generali S.p.A.; *Int'l,* pg. 91

GENERALI GERANCE S.A.—See Assicurazioni Generali S.p.A.; *Int'l,* pg. 91

GENERALI - GERMANY—See Assicurazioni Generali S.p.A.; *Int'l,* pg. 89

GENERALI GESTION S.A.—See Assicurazioni Generali S.p.A.; *Int'l,* pg. 91

GENERALI HELLAS A.E. ASFALISEON ZIMION—See Assicurazioni Generali S.p.A.; *Int'l,* pg. 91

GENERALI - ITALY—See Assicurazioni Generali S.p.A.; *Int'l,* pg. 89

GENERALI KRANKENVERSICHERUNG AG—See Assicurazioni Generali S.p.A.; *Int'l,* pg. 89

GENERALI LEVENSVERZEKERING MIJ. N.V.—See Assicurazioni Generali S.p.A.; *Int'l,* pg. 91

GENERALI LIFE A.E. ASFALISEON ZOIS—See Assicurazioni Generali S.p.A.; *Int'l,* pg. 91

GENERALI MUNCHEN LEBENSVERSICHERUNG AG—See Assicurazioni Generali S.p.A.; *Int'l,* pg. 89

GENERALI - NORTH AMERICA—See Assicurazioni Generali S.p.A.; *Int'l,* pg. 90

GENERALI PROPERTIES (1977) LTD.—See Assicurazioni Generali S.p.A.; *Int'l,* pg. 91

GENERALI RUCKVERSICHERUNG AG—See Assicurazioni Generali S.p.A.; *Int'l,* pg. 89

GENERALI SCHADEVERZEKERING MAATSCHAPPIJ N.V.—See Assicurazioni Generali S.p.A.; *Int'l,* pg. 91

GENERALI SIGORTA A.S.—See Assicurazioni Generali S.p.A.; *Int'l,* pg. 91

GENERALI - U.K.—See Assicurazioni Generali S.p.A.; *Int'l,* pg. 90

GENERALI UNDERWRITERS, INC.—See Assicurazioni Generali S.p.A.; *Int'l,* pg. 91

GENERALI VERZEKERINGSGROEP N.V.—See Assicurazioni Generali S.p.A.; *Int'l,* pg. 91

GENERALI VIDA COMPANHIA DE SEGUROS S.A.—See Assicurazioni Generali S.p.A.; *Int'l,* pg. 91

GENERALI WORLDWIDE INSURANCE COMPANY COMPANY—See Assicurazioni Generali S.p.A.; *Int'l,* pg. 91

GENERALIFE—See Generale de Banque S.A.; *Int'l,* pg. 548

GENERATION METALS CORP.; *U.S. Private,* pg. 446

GENERATIONS GOLD—See Leon Shaffer Golnick Advertising, Inc.; *U.S. Private,* pg. 463

THE GENERRA COMPANY; *U.S. Private,* pg. 446

GENESCO INC.; *U.S. Public,* pg. 728

GENESEE A & B, INC.—See Genesee Metal Stampings, Inc.; *U.S. Private,* pg. 446

THE GENESEE BREWING COMPANY, INC.—See Genesee Corporation; *U.S. Public,* pg. 728

GENESEE CORPORATION; *U.S. Public,* pg. 728

GENESEE METAL STAMPINGS, INC.; *U.S. Private,* pg. 446

GENESEE PRECISION FABRICATING—See Genesee Metal Stampings, Inc.; *U.S. Private,* pg. 446

GENESEE STAMPING—See Genesee Metal Stampings, Inc.; *U.S. Private,* pg. 446

GENESEE VENTURES, INC.—See Genesee Corporation; *U.S. Public,* pg. 728

GENESEE WESTER—See Genesee Metal Stampings, Inc.; *U.S. Private,* pg. 446

GENESIS ELDERCARE—See Genesis Health Ventures, Inc.; *U.S. Public,* pg. 728

GENESIS HEALTH VENTURES, INC.; *U.S. Public,* pg. 728

GENESIS UNDERWRITING MANAGEMENT COMPANY—See General Re Corporation; *U.S. Public,* pg. 725

GENESYS COMBUSTION—See Eclipse Inc.; *U.S. Private,* pg. 360

GENETIC DESIGN INC.—See Genzyme Corporation; *U.S. Public,* pg. 733

GENETIC SYSTEMS CORPORATION—See Elf Aquitane; *U.S. Public,* pg. 445

GENETIC THERAPY, INC.—See Novartis AG; *Int'l,* pg. 973

GENETICS INSTITUTE, INC.—See American Home Products Corporation; *U.S. Public,* pg. 79

GENETICS INSTITUTE INC. OF JAPAN.—See American Home Products Corporation; *U.S. Public,* pg. 80

GENETRACE SYSTEMS, INC.—See SRI International; *U.S. Private,* pg. 958

GENEVA CORPORATION; U.S. Private, pg. 446
GENEVA GENERAL INSURANCE COMPANY—See Zurich Insurance Company; Int'l, pg. 1529
GENEVA LIFE INSURANCE COMPANY—See Zurich Insurance Company; Int'l, pg. 1529
GENEVA PHARMACEUTICALS, INC.—See Novartis AG; Int'l, pg. 973
GENEVA STEEL; U.S. Public, pg. 729
GENEVAD CELLPLAST—See Scancem AB; Int'l, pg. 1199
GENEVE CAPITAL GROUP INC.—See Geneve Corporation; U.S. Private, pg. 446
GENEVE CORPORATION; U.S. Private, pg. 446
GENFOOT INC.; Int'l, pg. 549
GENICOM CANADA, INC.—See Genicom Corporation; U.S. Public, pg. 729
GENICOM CORPORATION; U.S. Public, pg. 729
GENICOM ESSC—See Genicom Corporation; U.S. Public, pg. 729
GENICOM GMBH—See Genicom Corporation; U.S. Public, pg. 729
GENICOM LIMITED—See Genicom Corporation; U.S. Public, pg. 729
GENICOM PTY. LTD.—See Genicom Corporation; U.S. Public, pg. 729
GENICOM S.A.—See Genicom Corporation; U.S. Public, pg. 729
GENICOM SPA—See Genicom Corporation; U.S. Public, pg. 729
THE GENIE COMPANY—See Overhead Door Corporation; U.S. Private, pg. 823
GENIE MECHANIQUE ZAIROISE, S.A.R.L—See General Motors Corporation; U.S. Public, pg. 724
GENIMOBIL S.P.A.—See Assicurazioni Generali S.p.A.; Int'l, pg. 90
GENINVER S.A.—See Assicurazioni Generali S.p.A.; Int'l, pg. 91
THE GENLYTE GROUP INCORPORATED; U.S. Public, pg. 729
GENMAR HOLDINGS, INC.; U.S. Private, pg. 447
GENMARK, INC.—See General American Life Insurance Co.; U.S. Private, pg. 443
GENOME THERAPEUTICS CORPORATION; U.S. Public, pg. 730
GENOSA—See Pechiney S.A.; Int'l, pg. 1030
GENOVA PRODUCTS, INC.; U.S. Private, pg. 447
GENOVA-NEVADA—See Genova Products, Inc.; U.S. Private, pg. 447
GENOVESE DRUG STORES, INC.; U.S. Public, pg. 730
GENRAD (ADS), MANCHESTER—See GenRad, Inc.; U.S. Public, pg. 731
GENRAD, INC.; U.S. Public, pg. 731
GENSEGUR, AGENCIA DE SEGUROS GRUPO GENERALI, S.A.—See Assicurazioni Generali S.p.A.; Int'l, pg. 91
GENSTAR DEVELOPMENT COMPANY—See B.A.T Industries P.L.C.; Int'l, pg. 112
GENSYM—See Gensym Corporation; U.S. Public, pg. 731
GENSYM B.V.—See Gensym Corporation; U.S. Public, pg. 731
GENSYM CANADA LTD.—See Gensym Corporation; U.S. Public, pg. 731
GENSYM CORPORATION; U.S. Public, pg. 731
GENSYM GMBH—See Gensym Corporation; U.S. Public, pg. 731
GENSYM LTD.—See Gensym Corporation; U.S. Public, pg. 731
GENSYM S.A.—See Gensym Corporation; U.S. Public, pg. 731
GENTECH INTERNATIONAL LTD.—See Wolseley Plc.; Int'l, pg. 1511
GENTEX CORPORATION; U.S. Public, pg. 731
GENTEX GMBH—See Gentex Corporation; U.S. Public, pg. 732
GENTEX OPTICS, INC.—See Essilor International Compagnie Generale d'Optique; Int'l, pg. 462
GENTLEMAN GIVENCHY S.A.—See LVMH Moet Hennessy Louis Vuitton; Int'l, pg. 780
GENTLEMEN'S QUARTERLY—See Advance Publications Inc.; U.S. Private, pg. 20
GENTY—See Groupe Casino; Int'l, pg. 563
GENUARDI FAMILY MARKETS INC.; U.S. Private, pg. 447
GENUINE PARTS COMPANY; U.S. Public, pg. 732
GENUINE PARTS LTD.—See Genuine Parts Company; U.S. Public, pg. 732
GENUS EUROPA GMBH—See Genus Inc.; U.S. Public, pg. 733
GENUS EUROPA LTD.—See Genus Inc.; U.S. Public, pg. 733
GENUS EUROPA SARL—See Genus Inc.; U.S. Public, pg. 733
GENUS EUROPA S.R.L.—See Genus Inc.; U.S. Public, pg. 733
GENUS INC.; U.S. Public, pg. 732
GENUS, INC.—See Genus Inc.; U.S. Public, pg. 732
GENUS INC.-ION TECHNOLOGY PRODUCTS—See Genus Inc.; U.S. Public, pg. 732
GENUS KK—See Genus Inc.; U.S. Public, pg. 733
GENUS KOREA, LTD.—See Genus Inc.; U.S. Public, pg. 733
GENXON POWER SYSTEMS LLC—See Woodward Governor Company; U.S. Public, pg. 1776
GENZYME BIOCHEMICALS LTD.—See Genzyme Corporation; U.S. Public, pg. 733
GENZYME B.V.—See Genzyme Corporation; U.S. Public, pg. 733
GENZYME CORPORATION; U.S. Public, pg. 733
GENZYME DIAGNOSTICS, MEDIX BIOTECH—See Genzyme Corporation; U.S. Public, pg. 733
GENZYME FINE CHEMICALS—See Genzyme Corporation; U.S. Public, pg. 733
GENZYME GENETICS DIV.—See Genzyme Corporation; U.S. Public, pg. 733
GENZYME JAPAN—See Genzyme Corporation; U.S. Public, pg. 733
GENZYME TRANSGENICS—See Genzyme Corporation; U.S. Public, pg. 733
GEO- AMBIENTAL CONSULTORES CIA LTDA.—See GAI Consultants, Inc.; U.S. Private, pg. 434
GEO-CENTERS, INC.; U.S. Private, pg. 447
GEO-CENTERS, INC.—See Geo-Centers, Inc.; U.S. Private, pg. 447
GEO-CON, INC.—See URS Corporation; U.S. Public, pg. 1657
GEO-MARKTPROFIEL BV—See KPN Koninklyke PTT Nederland NV; Int'l, pg. 720
GEO-YOUNG & RUBICAM—See Young & Rubicam Inc.; U.S. Private, pg. 1199
GEOCENTER VERLAGSVERTRIEB GMBH—See Bertelsmann AG; Int'l, pg. 190
GEODESY (GEODES)—See Petrobras - Petroleo Brasileiro S.A.; Int'l, pg. 1041
GEODIMETER GMBH—See Spectra-Physics AB; Int'l, pg. 1290
GEODIMETER HANDELS GESMBH—See Spectra-Physics AB; Int'l, pg. 1290
GEODIMETER OF AUSTRALIA PTY. LTD.—See Spectra-Physics AB; Int'l, pg. 1290
GEODIMETER OF CANADA LTD.—See Spectra-Physics AB; Int'l, pg. 1290
GEODIS; Int'l, pg. 549
GEOGRAPHIA LTD.—See The News Corporation Limited; Int'l, pg. 927
GEOLOGISCHE FORSCHUNG UND ERKUNDUNG - GFE GMBH—See Harpen AG; Int'l, pg. 597
GEOMET TECHNOLOGIES, INC.—See Versar Inc.; U.S. Public, pg. 1717
GEOMINERALS INSURANCE COMPANY, INC. (NY)—See Asarco Incorporated; U.S. Public, pg. 138
THE GEON COMPANY; U.S. Public, pg. 733
GEONEX—See Geonex Corporation; U.S. Private, pg. 448
GEONEX CORPORATION; U.S. Private, pg. 447
GEONOR A.S.—See Norsk Hydro a.s; Int'l, pg. 959
GEOPHYSICAL ACQUISITION TECHNOLOGY (GETAG)—See Petrobras - Petroleo Brasileiro S.A.; Int'l, pg. 1041
GEOPHYSICAL PROCESSING (GEPROG)—See Petrobras - Petroleo Brasileiro S.A.; Int'l, pg. 1041
GEOPHYSICAL SURVEY SYSTEMS, INC.—See OYO Corporation; Int'l, pg. 1019
GEOREX INC.—See CGG Group; Int'l, pg. 241
GEORG JENSEN S.A.R.L.—See Royal Copenhagen A/S; Int'l, pg. 1134
GEORG JENSEN SILVER—See Royal Copenhagen A/S; Int'l, pg. 1134
GEORG JENSEN SILVER AB—See Royal Copenhagen A/S; Int'l, pg. 1134
GEORG JENSEN SILVER LTD.—See Royal Copenhagen A/S; Int'l, pg. 1134
GEORG JENSEN SILVER (NSW) PTY. LTD—See Royal Copenhagen A/S; Int'l, pg. 1134
GEORG JENSEN SILVERSMITHY LTD.—See Royal Copenhagen A/S; Int'l, pg. 1134
GEORGE & LYNCH, INC.; U.S. Private, pg. 448
GEORGE & THOMAS CONE CO.; U.S. Private, pg. 448
GEORGE LITHOGRAPH; U.S. Private, pg. 448
GEORGET S.A.—See Dainippon Ink & Chemicals, Inc.; Int'l, pg. 371
GEORGETOWN JET CENTER, INC.—See Banner Aerospace, Inc.; U.S. Public, pg. 187
GEORGETOWN PARTNERS, INC.—See Gould Investors, L.P.; U.S. Private, pg. 466
GEORGIA-BONDED FIBERS, INC.; U.S. Public, pg. 734
GEORGIA CASH AMERICA, INC.—See Cash America International, Inc.; U.S. Public, pg. 312
GEORGIA CASUALTY & SURETY COMPANY—See Atlantic American Corporation; U.S. Public, pg. 143
GEORGIA CROWN DISTRIBUTING; U.S. Private, pg. 448
GEORGIA DEALERS AUTO AUCTION—See Cox Enterprises, Inc.; U.S. Private, pg. 282
GEORGIA DUCK & CORDAGE MILLS; U.S. Private, pg. 448
GEORGIA/DURANGO BOOT COMPANY—See U.S. Industries, Inc.; U.S. Public, pg. 1684
GEORGIA FEDERAL BANK, FSB—See First Union Corporation; U.S. Public, pg. 640
GEORGIA GULF CORPORATION; U.S. Public, pg. 734
THE GEORGIA MARBLE COMPANY; U.S. Private, pg. 448
THE GEORGIA MIDLAND RAILWAY CO.—See Norfolk Southern Corporation; U.S. Public, pg. 1191
GEORGIA PACIFIC—See Georgia-Pacific Corporation; U.S. Public, pg. 736
GEORGIA-PACIFIC BUILDING MATERIALS SALES, LTD.—See Georgia-Pacific Corporation; U.S. Public, pg. 739
GEORGIA-PACIFIC CORPORATION; U.S. Public, pg. 735
GEORGIA-PACIFIC FINANCE N.V.—See Georgia-Pacific Corporation; U.S. Public, pg. 739
GEORGIA-PACIFIC GMBH—See Georgia-Pacific Corporation; U.S. Public, pg. 739
GEORGIA PACIFIC HARDBOARD—See Georgia-Pacific Corporation; U.S. Public, pg. 736
GEORGIA-PACIFIC INDUSTRIAL WOOD PRODUCTS DIV.—See Georgia-Pacific Corporation; U.S. Public, pg. 735
GEORGIA-PACIFIC INTERNATIONAL CORP.—See Georgia-Pacific Corporation; U.S. Public, pg. 739
GEORGIA-PACIFIC MID-CONTINENT WOOD PRODS. MFG. DIV.—See Georgia-Pacific Corporation; U.S. Public, pg. 735
GEORGIA-PACIFIC NEKOOSA OPERATIONS—See Georgia-Pacific Corporation; U.S. Public, pg. 736
GEORGIA-PACIFIC PORT EDWARDS OPERATIONS—See Georgia-Pacific Corporation; U.S. Public, pg. 736
GEORGIA-PACIFIC PULP & PAPER DIVISION—See Georgia-Pacific Corporation; U.S. Public, pg. 735
GEORGIA-PACIFIC S.A.—See Georgia-Pacific Corporation; U.S. Public, pg. 739
GEORGIA POWER CO.—See Southern Company; U.S. Public, pg. 1490
GEORGIA PRODUCTION SITE—See Northrop Grumman Corporation; U.S. Public, pg. 1198
GEORGIA SOUTHERN & FLORIDA RAILWAY CO.—See Norfolk Southern Corporation; U.S. Public, pg. 1191
GEORGIA STONE INDUSTRIES, INC.—See New England Stone Industries, Inc.; U.S. Private, pg. 793
GEORGIA TELEVISION COMPANY—See Cox Enterprises, Inc.; U.S. Private, pg. 282
GEORGIA TENT & AWNING INC.; U.S. Private, pg. 448
GEORGIA TRANSMISSION CORPORATION; U.S. Private, pg. 448
GEORGIA WOODLANDS RAILROAD CO.—See Broe Companies; U.S. Private, pg. 171
GEORGIA WSMP, INC. (GEORGIA)—See WSMP, Inc.; U.S. Public, pg. 1729
GEORGIE BOY MANUFACTURING, INC.—See Coachmen Industries, Inc.; U.S. Public, pg. 388
GEOSAFE CORPORATION—See Battelle Memorial Institute; U.S. Private, pg. 123
GEOSISMO S.A.—See Halliburton Company; U.S. Public, pg. 777
GEOSOURCE (ANTILLES) N.V.—See Halliburton Company; U.S. Public, pg. 777
GEOSOURCE ARGENTINA S.A.—See Halliburton Company; U.S. Public, pg. 777
GEOSOURCE CO. (CAYMAN) LTD.—See Halliburton Company; U.S. Public, pg. 777
GEOSOURCE EPIG SERVICES CO LTD.—See Halliburton Company; U.S. Public, pg. 777
GEOSOURCE (FAR EAST) PTE., LTD.—See Halliburton Company; U.S. Public, pg. 777
GEOSOURCE INDUSTRIA E COMMERCIO LTDA.—See Halliburton Company; U.S. Public, pg. 777
GEOSOURCE INTERNATIONAL (NEDERLAND) B.V.—See Halliburton Company; U.S. Public, pg. 777
GEOSOURCE NIGERIA LTD.—See Halliburton Company; U.S. Public, pg. 777
GEOSOURCE S.A.R.L.—See Halliburton Company; U.S. Public, pg. 777
GEOSOURCE U.K. LIMITED—See Halliburton Company; U.S. Public, pg. 777
GEOSTR CORPORATION—See Kumagai Gumi Co., Ltd.; Int'l, pg. 763
GEOSYSTEMS DIVISION—See R.R. Donnelley & Sons Company; U.S. Public, pg. 518
GEOTEK COMMUNICATIONS; U.S. Public, pg. 739
GEOTEK COMMUNICATIONS, INC.—See Geotek Communications; U.S. Public, pg. 740
GEOTEK EUROPE—See Geotek Communications; U.S. Public, pg. 740
GEOTEK ISRAEL—See Geotek Communications; U.S. Public, pg. 740
GEOTEK TECHNOLOGIES ISRAEL LTD.—See Geotek Communications; U.S. Public, pg. 740
GEOTEK USA/POWERSPECTRUM—See Geotek Communications; U.S. Public, pg. 740
S.A. GEOTER—See Cockerill Sambre; Int'l, pg. 301
GEOTHERMAL EXPLORATION CO., INC.—See Barnwell Industries, Inc.; U.S. Public, pg. 191
GEOTRANS, INC.—See Tetra Tech, Inc.; U.S. Public, pg. 1582
GEOTRONICS AB—See Spectra-Physics AB; Int'l, pg. 1290
GEOTRONICS ITALIA S.P.A.—See Spectra-Physics AB; Int'l, pg. 1290
GEOTRONICS LTD.—See Spectra-Physics AB; Int'l, pg. 1290
GEOTRONICS OF NORTH AMERICA, INC.—See Spectra-Physics AB; Int'l, pg. 1289
GEOTRONICS S.A.—See Spectra-Physics AB; Int'l, pg. 1290
GEOTRONICS S.A.R.L.—See Spectra-Physics AB; Int'l, pg. 1290
GEOTRONICS SCANDINAVIA AB—See Spectra-Physics AB; Int'l, pg. 1289
GERAGHTY & MILLER, INC.—See Heidemij N.V.; Int'l, pg. 607
GERAGHTY & MILLER ENVIRONMENTAL EQUIPMENT—See Heidemij N.V.; Int'l, pg. 607
GERALD GROUP INC.; U.S. Private, pg. 448
GERBER AGRI INC.—See Gerber International Inc.; U.S. Private, pg. 449
GERBER ARGENTINA—See Novartis AG; Int'l, pg. 973
GERBER AUSTRALIA, LTD.—See Novartis AG; Int'l, pg. 973
GERBER CANADA—See Novartis AG; Int'l, pg. 973
GERBER CHILE, S.A.—See Novartis AG; Int'l, pg. 973
GERBER COLOMBIA—See Novartis AG; Int'l, pg. 973
GERBER CS LTD.—See Novartis AG; Int'l, pg. 973
GERBER DE VENEZUELA—See Novartis AG; Int'l, pg. 973
GERBER FINANCE CO.—See Novartis AG; Int'l, pg. 973
GERBER FRANCE—See Novartis AG; Int'l, pg. 973
GERBER GARMENT TECHNOLOGY, INC.—See Gerber Scientific, Inc.; U.S. Public, pg. 740
GERBER HUNGARY BABY PRODUCTS TRADING—See Novartis AG; Int'l, pg. 973
GERBER INTERNATIONAL INC.; U.S. Private, pg. 448
GERBER ITALY, SRL.—See Novartis AG; Int'l, pg. 973
J. GERBER & CO. INC.—See Gerber International Inc.; U.S. Private, pg. 449
GERBER LIFE INSURANCE CO.—See Novartis AG; Int'l, pg. 973
GERBER OPTICAL, INC.—See Gerber Scientific, Inc.; U.S. Public, pg. 740
GERBER PLUMBING FIXTURES CORPORATION; U.S. Private, pg. 449
GERBER POLSKA—See Novartis AG; Int'l, pg. 973
GERBER PRODUCTS CO SINGAPORE—See Novartis AG; Int'l, pg. 973
GERBER PRODUCTS COMPANY—See Novartis AG; Int'l, pg. 973
GERBER PRODUCTS COMPANY OF PUERTO RICO, INC.—See Novartis AG; Int'l, pg. 973

GERBER PRODUCTS DIVISION-BABY CARE—See Novartis AG; *Int'l*, pg. 973
GERBER PRODUCTS OVERSEAS—See Novartis AG; *Int'l*, pg. 973
GERBER PRODUCTS, S.A. DE C.V.—See Novartis AG; *Int'l*, pg. 973
GERBER SCIENTIFIC, INC.; *U.S. Public*, pg. 740
GERBIG, SNELL/WEISHEIMER & ASSOC., INC.; *U.S. Private*, pg. 449
GEREMIA ELECTRIC CO., INC.—See ACMAT Corporation; *U.S. Public*, pg. 16
GERESA—See Accor S.A.; *Int'l*, pg. 21
GERHARD COLLARDIN GMBH—See Henkel KGaA; *Int'l*, pg. 609
GERHARD PRAHM GMBH & CO.—See Spar Handels AG; *Int'l*, pg. 1288
GERIS—See Thomson S.A.; *Int'l*, pg. 1382
GERLACH & CO. GMBH—See Royal Nedlloyd Group N.V.; *Int'l*, pg. 1144
GERLACH & CO. INTERNATIONALE EXPEDITEURS B.V.—See Royal Nedlloyd Group N.V.; *Int'l*, pg. 1144
GERLACH & CO. N.V.—See Royal Nedlloyd Group N.V.; *Int'l*, pg. 1144
GERLACH ART PACKERS & SHIPPERS B.V.—See Royal Nedlloyd Group N.V.; *Int'l*, pg. 1144
GERLACH SPOL SRO—See Royal Nedlloyd Group N.V.; *Int'l*, pg. 1144
GERLACH-WERKE GMBH—See Fried. Krupp AG; *Int'l*, pg. 508
GERLAND CORP.; *U.S. Private*, pg. 449
GERMAN BULK CHARTERING GMBH—See BASF AG; *Int'l*, pg. 104
P.T. GERMAN MOTOR MFG.—See Daimler-Benz Aktiengesellschaft; *Int'l*, pg. 368
GERMANTOWN—See Lagardere Groupe; *Int'l*, pg. 794
GERMANTOWN INTERNATIONAL—See Goodman Fielder Limited; *Int'l*, pg. 555
GERMANTOWN (USA) CO.—See Goodman Fielder Limited; *Int'l*, pg. 555
GERMAPHARM GMBH, IMPORT, EXPORT SPEDITION—See Schering AG; *Int'l*, pg. 1203
GERMINAL—See Groupe Casino; *Int'l*, pg. 563
A.J. GERRARD AND COMPANY; *U.S. Private*, pg. 449
GERRARD-OVALSTRAPPING—See Enterprises International Inc.; *U.S. Private*, pg. 378
GERRARD SIGNODE PTE. LTD.—See Illinois Tool Works Inc.; *U.S. Public*, pg. 868
GERRER—See Saint-Gobain; *Int'l*, pg. 1172
GERRESHEIMER GLAS AG—See Viag AG; *Int'l*, pg. 1464
GERRY BABY PRODUCTS COMPANY—See Kohlberg Kravis Roberts & Co.; *U.S. Private*, pg. 629
GERRY SPORTSWEAR COMPANY; *U.S. Private*, pg. 449
GERSON & GERSON, INC.; *U.S. Private*, pg. 449
THE GERSTENSLAGER COMPANY—See Worthington Industries, Inc.; *U.S. Public*, pg. 1780
GERTRUDE HAWK CHOCOLATES, INC.; *U.S. Private*, pg. 449
ROTH GERUSTE AG—See Plettac AG; *Int'l*, pg. 1061
GERVAIS DANONE AG—See Danone Group; *Int'l*, pg. 380
GERVAIS DANONE AUSTRIA—See Danone Group; *Int'l*, pg. 380
GES INC.—See GES Inc.; *U.S. Private*, pg. 434
GESBANSANDER—See Banco Santander; *Int'l*, pg. 143
GESCAT, ENTIDAD GESTORA DE FONDOS DE PENSIONES, S.A.—See Caixa d'Estalvis de Catalunya; *Int'l*, pg. 250
GESCHÄFTSBEREICH DER ALLIEDSIGNAL (DEUTSCHLAND) GMBH (ENEVCO GERMANY)—See AlliedSignal Inc.; *U.S. Public*, pg. 53
GESCHÄFTSBEREICH SCHIESS-WOTAN—See Metallgesellschaft AG; *Int'l*, pg. 861
GESCHÄFTSHAUS SEILBAHN AG—See Feldschlosschen Hurlimann Holding; *Int'l*, pg. 479
GESCHÄFTSSTELLE BAUTZEN—See Bilfinger + Berger Bauaktiengesellschaft; *Int'l*, pg. 194
GESCHÄFTSSTELLE BERLIN—See Knurr AG; *Int'l*, pg. 739
GESCHÄFTSSTELLE BOCHUM—See Bilfinger + Berger Bauaktiengesellschaft; *Int'l*, pg. 194
GESCHÄFTSSTELLE COLOGNE—See Knurr AG; *Int'l*, pg. 739
GESCHÄFTSSTELLE DARMSTADT—See Bilfinger + Berger Bauaktiengesellschaft; *Int'l*, pg. 194
GESCHÄFTSSTELLE FRANKFURT—See Knurr AG; *Int'l*, pg. 739
GESCHÄFTSSTELLE GERA—See Bilfinger + Berger Bauaktiengesellschaft; *Int'l*, pg. 194
GESCHÄFTSSTELLE GIESSEN—See Bilfinger + Berger Bauaktiengesellschaft; *Int'l*, pg. 194
GESCHÄFTSSTELLE HAMBURG—See Knurr AG; *Int'l*, pg. 739
GESCHÄFTSSTELLE HANNOVER—See Knurr AG; *Int'l*, pg. 739
GESCHÄFTSSTELLE IDAR-OBERSTEIN—See Bilfinger + Berger Bauaktiengesellschaft; *Int'l*, pg. 194
GESCHÄFTSSTELLE LEIPZIG—See Knurr AG; *Int'l*, pg. 739
GESCHÄFTSSTELLE NURNBERG—See Knurr AG; *Int'l*, pg. 739
GESCHÄFTSSTELLE QUEDLINBURG—See Bilfinger + Berger Bauaktiengesellschaft; *Int'l*, pg. 194
GESCHÄFTSSTELLE STUTTGART—See Knurr AG; *Int'l*, pg. 739
GESCO INTERNATIONAL—See C.R. Bard, Inc.; *U.S. Public*, pg. 189
GESCON 30 S.R.L.—See Freudenberg & Company; *Int'l*, pg. 507
GESELLSCHAFT FUER MARKT- UND ABSATZFORSCHUNG MBH—See Wuestenrot Holding GmbH; *Int'l*, pg. 1514
GESELLSCHAFT FUR DIE VERWERTUND INDUSTRIELLER RESTSTOFFE MBH—See Fried. Krupp AG; *Int'l*, pg. 513

GESELLSCHAFT FUR ELEKTROMETALLURGIE M.B.H.—See Metallurg, Inc.; *U.S. Private*, pg. 735
GESELLSCHAFT FUR ENERGIEBETEILIGUNG MBH—See Veba AG; *Int'l*, pg. 1460
GESELLSCHAFT FUR GEROTEBAU MBH—See Hanson PLC; *Int'l*, pg. 594
GESELLSCHAFT FUR INDUSTRIEBETEILIGUNGGEN MBH—See Bayerische Vereinsbank Group; *Int'l*, pg. 179
GESELLSCHAFT FUR KOHLE-TECHNOLOGIE MBH—See Fried. Krupp AG; *Int'l*, pg. 511
GESELLSCHAFT FUR NUKLEAR-SERVICE MBH-GNS—See Veba AG; *Int'l*, pg. 1457
GESELLSCHAFT FUR WERTPAPIERANLAGEN MBH—See Dresdner Bank AG; *Int'l*, pg. 418
GESELLSCHAFT FUR WOHNEN DATTELN MBH--See Veba AG; *Int'l*, pg. 1460
GESELLSCHAFT ZUR VERMITTLUNG VON BAUVERSICHERUNGEN MBH—See Hochtief AG; *Int'l*, pg. 623
GESFO GEMEINNUTIZIGE BAU- UND SIEDLUNGS GMBH—See Creditanstalt-Bankverein; *Int'l*, pg. 347
GESMADRID PATRIMONIOS, S.G.C., S.A.—See Caja de Madrid Group; *Int'l*, pg. 251
GESMADRID S.G.I.I.C., S.A.—See Caja de Madrid Group; *Int'l*, pg. 251
GESSNER/MILLER CORPORATION—See GHM Industries, Inc.; *U.S. Private*, pg. 435
GESTAO E PUBLICIDADE—See Lagardere Groupe; *Int'l*, pg. 795
GESTETNER AB—See Ricoh Company, Ltd.; *Int'l*, pg. 1115
GESTETNER A/S—See Ricoh Company, Ltd.; *Int'l*, pg. 1115
GESTETNER ASIA PACIFIC LIMITED—See Ricoh Company, Ltd.; *Int'l*, pg. 1114
GESTETNER AUSTRALASIA LIMITED—See Ricoh Company, Ltd.; *Int'l*, pg. 1115
GESTETNER BANGLADESH LTD.—See Ricoh Company, Ltd.; *Int'l*, pg. 1115
GESTETNER BUROMASCHINEN-VERKAUFSGESELLSCHAFT M.B.H.—See Ricoh Company, Ltd.; *Int'l*, pg. 1115
GESTETNER CHILE S.A.—See Ricoh Company, Ltd.; *Int'l*, pg. 1115
GESTETNER COLOMBIA S.A.—See Ricoh Company, Ltd.; *Int'l*, pg. 1115
GESTETNER CORPORATION—See Ricoh Company, Ltd.; *Int'l*, pg. 1115
GESTETNER DO BRASIL, S.A. SISTEMAS REPROGRAPHICOS—See Ricoh Company, Ltd.; *Int'l*, pg. 1115
GESTETNER HOLDING BV—See Ricoh Company, Ltd.; *Int'l*, pg. 1115
GESTETNER HOLDINGS PLC—See Ricoh Company, Ltd.; *Int'l*, pg. 1114
GESTETNER INVESTMENTS LIMITED—See Ricoh Company, Ltd.; *Int'l*, pg. 1114
GESTETNER (ISRAEL) LIMITED—See Ricoh Company, Ltd.; *Int'l*, pg. 1115
GESTETNER ITALIA SPA—See Ricoh Company, Ltd.; *Int'l*, pg. 1115
GESTETNER LIMITED—See Ricoh Company, Ltd.; *Int'l*, pg. 1115
GESTETNER MALAYSIA SDN BHD—See Ricoh Company, Ltd.; *Int'l*, pg. 1115
GESTETNER MANUFACTURING LIMITED—See Ricoh Company, Ltd.; *Int'l*, pg. 1114
GESTETNER OFFICE EQUIPMENT (CHINA) CO. LTD.—See Ricoh Company, Ltd.; *Int'l*, pg. 1115
GESTETNER OFFICE SYSTEM (HK) LTD.—See Ricoh Company, Ltd.; *Int'l*, pg. 1115
GESTETNER OFFICE SYSTEMS NEW ZEALAND LIMITED—See Ricoh Company, Ltd.; *Int'l*, pg. 1115
GESTETNER (PRIVATE) LIMITED—See Ricoh Company, Ltd.; *Int'l*, pg. 1115
GESTETNER REGIONAL SERVICES INC. (USA)—See Ricoh Company, Ltd.; *Int'l*, pg. 1115
GESTETNER S.A.—See Ricoh Company, Ltd.; *Int'l*, pg. 1115
GESTETNER SECURITIES B.V.—See Ricoh Company, Ltd.; *Int'l*, pg. 1115
GESTETNER SERVICES S.A.—See Ricoh Company, Ltd.; *int'l*, pg. 1115
GESTION DE CENTROS CULTURALES, S.A.—See Caja de Madrid Group; *Int'l*, pg. 251
GESTION ET PATRIMOINE—See AXA-UAP; *Int'l*, pg. 19
GESTION MODA SHOPPING S.A.—See Corporacion MAPFRE, Compania Internacional de Reaseguros, S.A.; *Int'l*, pg. 334
GESTIONE FONDI INVESTIMENTO MILANO SPA—See Banca Popolare di Milano; *Int'l*, pg. 137
GESTIRAS—See Allianz Aktiengesellschaft; *Int'l*, pg. 61
GESTORA DE SEGUROS DE MAPFRE DIVERSOS, SOCIEDAD DE AGENCIA, S.A.—See Corporacion MAPFRE, Compania Internacional de Reaseguros, S.A.; *Int'l*, pg. 332
GESTRA GMBH; *Int'l*, pg. 549
GESTRA, INC.—See GESTRA GmbH; *Int'l*, pg. 549
GESTRA PORTUGUESA VALVULAS LDA.—See GESTRA GmbH; *Int'l*, pg. 550
GESTRA PORTUGUESA VALVULAS LTDA.—See GESTRA GmbH; *Int'l*, pg. 550
GESTRA S.A.—See GESTRA GmbH; *Int'l*, pg. 550
GESTRA (U.K.) LTD.—See GESTRA GmbH; *Int'l*, pg. 550
GETAC INSTRUMENTEBAU GMBH—See Rhone-Poulenc S.A.; *Int'l*, pg. 1112
GETCHELL GOLD CORP.; *U.S. Public*, pg. 740
GETI WILBA GMBH—See Sudzucker AG Mannheim/Ochsenfurt; *Int'l*, pg. 1305
GETINGE AB—See Getinge Industrier AB; *Int'l*, pg. 551
GETINGE AB BEIJING—See Getinge Industrier AB; *Int'l*, pg. 551
GETINGE AB ITALIA—See Getinge Industrier AB; *Int'l*, pg. 551

GETINGE AB JAPAN—See Getinge Industrier AB; *Int'l*, pg. 551
OY GETINGE AB—See Getinge Industrier AB; *Int'l*, pg. 551
GETINGE AUSTRALIA PTY. LTD.—See Getinge Industrier AB; *Int'l*, pg. 551
GETINGE/CASTLE ASIA LIMITED—See Getinge Industrier AB; *Int'l*, pg. 551
GETINGE/CASTLE CANADA LIMITED—See Getinge Industrier AB; *Int'l*, pg. 551
GETINGE/CASTLE, INC.; *U.S. Private*, pg. 449
GETINGE/CASTLE INC.—See Getinge Industrier AB; *Int'l*, pg. 551
GETINGE/CASTLE INTERNATIONAL LIMITED—See Getinge Industrier AB; *Int'l*, pg. 551
GETINGE DISINFECTION INC.—See Getinge Industrier AB; *Int'l*, pg. 551
GETINGE GMBH—See Getinge Industrier AB; *Int'l*, pg. 551
GETINGE HONG KONG LTD.—See Getinge Industrier AB; *Int'l*, pg. 551
GETINGE INDUSTRIER AB; *Int'l*, pg. 551
GETINGE INTERNATIONAL INC.—See Getinge Industrier AB; *Int'l*, pg. 551
GETINGE POLAND SP.ZO.O.—See Getinge Industrier AB; *Int'l*, pg. 551
GETINGE SKARHAMM AB—See Getinge Industrier AB; *Int'l*, pg. 551
GETINGE STERILIZING EQUIPMENT INC.—See Getinge Industrier AB; *Int'l*, pg. 552
GETINGE VAXJO A/S—See Getinge Industrier AB; *Int'l*, pg. 552
GETINGE-D.S.E. BV—See Getinge Industrier AB; *Int'l*, pg. 551
GETINGE-D.S.E. NV—See Getinge Industrier AB; *Int'l*, pg. 551
GETKO GROUP INC.—See Cendant Corporation; *U.S. Public*, pg. 320
GETOFLEX METZLER INDUSTRIA E COMMERCIO LTDA.—See BTR plc; *Int'l*, pg. 130
GETRAN—See Petrobras - Petroleo Brasileiro S.A.; *Int'l*, pg. 1041
GETRANKE-DIENST AG—See Feldschlosschen Hurlimann Holding; *Int'l*, pg. 479
GIE GETTINOR—See Castorama Dubois Investissements S.C.A.; *Int'l*, pg. 276
GETTY OIL EXPLORATION CO.—See Texaco Inc.; *U.S. Public*, pg. 1583
GETTY PETROLEUM MARKETING INC.; *U.S. Public*, pg. 740
GETTY TERMINALS, INC.—See Getty Petroleum Marketing Inc.; *U.S. Public*, pg. 741
GEUPEL DEMARS, INC.; *U.S. Private*, pg. 449
GEUPEL DEMARS, INC.—See Geupel DeMars, Inc.; *U.S. Private*, pg. 450
GEVETEX TEXTILGLAS GMBH—See Saint-Gobain; *Int'l*, pg. 1177
GEWERKSCHAFT BRIGITTA—See Royal Dutch/Shell Group of Companies; *Int'l*, pg. 1138
GEWERKSCHAFT DEURAG-NERAG—See Royal Dutch/Shell Group of Companies; *Int'l*, pg. 1138
GEWERKSCHAFT ELWERATH—See Royal Dutch/Shell Group of Companies; *Int'l*, pg. 1138
GEYER-MCALLISTER PUBLICATIONS, INC.; *U.S. Private*, pg. 450
GEYSER CREATION INC.—See Cossette Communication Marketing; *Int'l*, pg. 336
GEYTENBEEK B.V.—See Royal Nedlloyd Group N.V.; *Int'l*, pg. 1144
GHACEM, LTD.—See Scancem AB; *Int'l*, pg. 1201
GHAFARI ASSOCIATES, INC.; *U.S. Private*, pg. 450
GHAFARI ASSOCIATES, INC.—See Ghafari Associates, Inc.; *U.S. Private*, pg. 450
GHANA CEMENT CO. LTD.—See Scancem AB; *Int'l*, pg. 1201
GHANA SANYO CO., LTD.—See Sanyo Electric Co., Ltd.; *Int'l*, pg. 1192
GHENT MANUFACTURING, INC.; *U.S. Private*, pg. 450
GHIA, INC.—See Ford Motor Company; *U.S. Public*, pg. 664
GHIA, S.P.A.—See Ford Motor Company; *U.S. Public*, pg. 666
GHISALBA S.P.A.—See Eaton Corporation; *U.S. Public*, pg. 559
GIANETTINO & MEREDITH ADVERTISING; *U.S. Private*, pg. 450
GIANT AUTOMATIC MONEY SYSTEMS—See Giant Food Inc.; *U.S. Public*, pg. 741
GIANT CEMENT COMPANY—See Giant Cement Holding Inc.; *U.S. Public*, pg. 741
GIANT CEMENT HOLDING INC.; *U.S. Public*, pg. 741
GIANT CONSTRUCTION CO., INC.—See Giant Food Inc.; *U.S. Public*, pg. 741
GIANT EAGLE, INC.; *U.S. Private*, pg. 450
GIANT EAGLE MARKET CO.—See Giant Eagle, Inc.; *U.S. Private*, pg. 450
GIANT EXPLORATION & PRODUCTION CO.—See Giant Industries Inc.; *U.S. Public*, pg. 742
GIANT FOOD INC.; *U.S. Public*, pg. 750
GIANT FOOD STORES INC.—See Koninklijke Ahold NV; *Int'l*, pg. 750
GIANT INDUSTRIES; *U.S. Private*, pg. 451
GIANT INDUSTRIES ARIZONA, INC.—See Giant Industries Inc.; *U.S. Public*, pg. 742
GIANT INDUSTRIES INC.; *U.S. Public*, pg. 741
GIANT MINE—See Royal Oak Mines Inc.; *U.S. Public*, pg. 1411
GIANT OF CHERRY HILL, INC.—See Giant Food Inc.; *U.S. Public*, pg. 741
GIANT OF MARYLAND, INC.—See Giant Food Inc.; *U.S. Public*, pg. 741
GIANT OF SALISBURY, INC.—See Giant Food Inc.; *U.S. Public*, pg. 741
GIANT OF TALBOT COUNTY, INC.—See Giant Food Inc.; *U.S. Public*, pg. 741

GIANT REFINING COMPANY—See Giant Industries Inc.; *U.S. Public*, pg. 742
GIANT RESOURCE RECOVERY COMPANY (GRRI)—See Giant Cement Holding Inc.; *U.S. Public*, pg. 741
ROBERT GIBB & SONS, INC.; *U.S. Private*, pg. 451
GIBBONS & REED COMPANY—See Granite Construction Incorporated; *U.S. Public*, pg. 759
JAMES GIBBONS FORMAT LIMITED—See TT Group PLC; *Int'l*, pg. 1344
GIBBS AB—See Unilever Plc; *Int'l*, pg. 1437
GIBBS DIE CASTING CORP.—See George Koch Sons, Inc.; *U.S. Private*, pg. 628
GIBBS GULF INSURANCE CONSULTANTS LIMITED—See HSBC Holdings plc; *Int'l*, pg. 581
GIBBS WIRE & STEEL COMPANY, INC.; *U.S. Private*, pg. 451
GIBBS WIRE & STEEL COMPANY OF CANADA LTD.—See Gibbs Wire & Steel Company, Inc.; *U.S. Private*, pg. 451
GIBCO/BIO-CULT DIAGNOSTICS, LTD.—See The Dexter Corporation; *U.S. Public*, pg. 505
GIBRALTAR CASUALTY CO.—See The Prudential Insurance Company of America; *U.S. Public*, pg. 892
GIBRALTAR CORP. OF AMERICA—See Summit Bancorp; *U.S. Public*, pg. 1528
GIBRALTAR LOCK CO. LTD.—See Masco Corporation; *U.S. Public*, pg. 1054
GIBRALTAR SAVINGS—See BankAmerica Corporation; *U.S. Public*, pg. 181
GIBRALTAR STEEL CORP.; *U.S. Public*, pg. 742
GIBRALTAR STEEL CORPORATION OF TENNESSEE—See Gibraltar Steel Corp.; *U.S. Public*, pg. 742
GIBRALTAR STRIP STEEL, INC.—See Gibraltar Steel Corp.; *U.S. Public*, pg. 742
GIBRALTAR TELECOMMUNICATIONS INTERNATIONAL LIMITED—See British Telecommunications plc; *Int'l*, pg. 223
GIBRALTAR TELEPHONE COMPANY—See Bell Atlantic Corporation; *U.S. Public*, pg. 204
GIBSON APPLIANCES—See Electrolux, AB; *Int'l*, pg. 439
C.R. GIBSON CO.—See Thomas Nelson Inc.; *U.S. Public*, pg. 1168
GIBSON CONTAINER DIVISION—See Weston Paper & Manufacturing Co.; *U.S. Private*, pg. 1170
GIBSON COUNTY BANK—See Old National Bancorp; *U.S. Public*, pg. 1217
GIBSON GREETINGS, INC.; *U.S. Public*, pg. 742
GIBSON GREETINGS INTERNATIONAL LIMITED—See Gibson Greetings, Inc.; *U.S. Public*, pg. 742
THE GIBSON GROUP INC.; *U.S. Private*, pg. 451
GIBSON-HOMAS—See The Gibson-Homans Company; *U.S. Private*, pg. 451
THE GIBSON-HOMANS COMPANY; *U.S. Private*, pg. 451
JOHN GIBSON (PLASTICS) LTD.—See DSM N.V.; *Int'l*, pg. 355
GIBSON MUSICAL INSTRUMENTS, INC.; *U.S. Private*, pg. 451
GIBSON WINE COMPANY; *U.S. Private*, pg. 452
GIBSON'S DISCOUNT CENTERS INC.; *U.S. Private*, pg. 452
GICEL—See Compagnie des Machines Bull; *Int'l*, pg. 316
GICQUEL—See Groupe Casino; *Int'l*, pg. 563
GIDDINGS & LEWIS AUTOMATION TECHNOLOGY—See Thyssen AG; *Int'l*, pg. 1389
GIDDINGS & LEWIS CASTING TECHNOLOGY—See Thyssen AG; *Int'l*, pg. 1389
GIDDINGS & LEWIS, INC.—See Thyssen AG; *Int'l*, pg. 1389
GIDDINGS & LEWIS LTD—See Thyssen AG; *Int'l*, pg. 1389
GIDDINGS & LEWIS SHEFFIELD MEASUREMENT SYSTEMS—See Thyssen AG; *Int'l*, pg. 1389
GIEN MILL—See Fort James Corporation; *U.S. Public*, pg. 673
GIESECKE & DEVRIENT ENGINEERING, INC.; *U.S. Private*, pg. 452
GIFFELS ASSOCIATES, INC.; *U.S. Private*, pg. 452
GIFFELS HOYEM BASSO, INC.—See Giffels Associates, Inc.; *U.S. Private*, pg. 452
GIFFELS STRATEGIC CONSULTANTS, L.L.C.—See Giffels Associates, Inc.; *U.S. Private*, pg. 452
GIFFELS TECHNOLOGIES INC.—See Giffels Associates, Inc.; *U.S. Private*, pg. 452
GIFFORD-HILL-AMERICAN, INC.—See Ameron International Corporation; *U.S. Public*, pg. 99
GIFFORD-HILL CEMENT COMPANY OF SOUTH CAROLINA—See Hanson PLC; *Int'l*, pg. 593
GIFFORD-HILL COMPANY—See Hanson PLC; *Int'l*, pg. 593
GIFFORD-HILL CONCRETE PRODUCTS INC.—See Hanson PLC; *Int'l*, pg. 593
GIGA-TRONICS INCORPORATED; *U.S. Public*, pg. 742
GIGALEX CO., LTD.—See Rohm Co., Ltd.; *Int'l*, pg. 1125
GIGAMAX—See Tai-II Media Co.; *Int'l*, pg. 1347
GIGANTE VERTE S.A.—See Diageo Plc; *Int'l*, pg. 409
GIGI—See American International Industries; *U.S. Private*, pg. 57
GIKEN ENGINEERING CORPORATION—See Kenwood Corporation; *Int'l*, pg. 730
GILARDINI S.P.A.—See Fiat Auto SpA; *Int'l*, pg. 482
GILBANE BUILDING COMPANY; *U.S. Private*, pg. 452
GILBANE PROPERTIES, INC.—See Gilbane Building Company; *U.S. Private*, pg. 452
GILBARCO AUSTRALIA LTD.—See The General Electric Company, p.l.c.; *Int'l*, pg. 545
GILBARCO CANADA LTD.—See The General Electric Company, p.l.c.; *Int'l*, pg. 545
GILBARCO GMBH—See The General Electric Company, p.l.c.; *Int'l*, pg. 545
GILBARCO INC.—See The General Electric Company, p.l.c.; *Int'l*, pg. 545
GILBARCO LTD.—See The General Electric Company, p.l.c.; *Int'l*, pg. 545
GILBARCO USA—See The General Electric Company, p.l.c.; *Int'l*, pg. 545

GILBERT & BENNETT MANUFACTURING COMPANY; *U.S. Private*, pg. 453
GILBERT/COMMONWEALTH INTERNATIONAL, INC.—See Parsons Corporation; *U.S. Private*, pg. 841
THE GILBERT COMPANIES, INC.; *U.S. Private*, pg. 453
GILBERT PAPER—See The Mead Corporation; *U.S. Public*, pg. 1074
GILBEY CANADA INC.—See Diageo Plc; *Int'l*, pg. 409
GILBEY'S OF IRELAND—See Diageo Plc; *Int'l*, pg. 409
GILBEYS OF IRELAND—See Diageo Plc; *Int'l*, pg. 409
GILCREST STORAGE—See The Fred W. Albrecht Grocery Co.; pg. 32
GILCRON CORPORATION—See ITT Industries, Inc.; *U.S. Public*, pg. 860
GILES & RANSOME, INC.; *U.S. Private*, pg. 453
GILETTE FOOD FLAVORINGS, INC.; *U.S. Private*, pg. 453
M.C. GILL CORPORATION; *U.S. Private*, pg. 453
GILLESPIE; *U.S. Private*, pg. 453
GILLESPIE PUBLIC RELATIONS—See Gillespie; *U.S. Private*, pg. 454
GILLETTE ARGENTINA S.A.—See The Gillette Company; *U.S. Public*, pg. 744
GILLETTE (AUSTRALIA) PTY., LIMITED—See The Gillette Company; *U.S. Public*, pg. 744
GILLETTE BOSPHORUS SANAYI A.S.—See The Gillette Company; *U.S. Public*, pg. 744
GILLETTE CANADA INC.—See The Gillette Company; *U.S. Public*, pg. 744
GILLETTE CO.-PARKER PEN USA—See The Gillette Company; *U.S. Public*, pg. 745
THE GILLETTE COMPANY; *U.S. Public*, pg. 743
THE GILLETTE COMPANY, GILLETTE GROOMING PRODUCTS, USA—See The Gillette Company; *U.S. Public*, pg. 744
THE GILLETTE COMPANY, PERSONAL CARE GROUP—See The Gillette Company; *U.S. Public*, pg. 744
GILLETTE DA AMAZONIA S/A—See The Gillette Company; *U.S. Public*, pg. 744
GILLETTE DAIRY OF THE BLACK HILLS, INC.—See Nash Finch Company; *U.S. Public*, pg. 1152
GILLETTE DE MEXICO S.A. DE C.V.—See The Gillette Company; *U.S. Public*, pg. 744
GILLETTE DE PERU S.C.—See The Gillette Company; *U.S. Public*, pg. 744
GILLETTE DE VENEZUELA S.A.—See The Gillette Company; *U.S. Public*, pg. 744
GILLETTE DEUTSCHLAND G.M.B.H.—See The Gillette Company; *U.S. Public*, pg. 744
GILLETTE DO BRASIL & CIA—See The Gillette Company; *U.S. Public*, pg. 744
GILLETTE ESPANOLA, S.A.—See The Gillette Company; *U.S. Public*, pg. 744
GILLETTE EUROPE—See The Gillette Company; *U.S. Public*, pg. 744
GILLETTE FAR EAST TRADING LIMITED—See The Gillette Company; *U.S. Public*, pg. 744
GILLETTE FINANCE B.V.—See The Gillette Company; *U.S. Public*, pg. 744
GILLETTE FRANCE, S.A.—See The Gillette Company; *U.S. Public*, pg. 744
GILLETTE GROUP ITALY S.R.L.—See The Gillette Company; *U.S. Public*, pg. 745
GILLETTE (HONG KONG) LIMITED—See The Gillette Company; *U.S. Public*, pg. 745
GILLETTE INDUSTRIES, LTD.—See The Gillette Company; *U.S. Public*, pg. 745
GILLETTE INTERNILE S.A.E.—See The Gillette Company; *U.S. Public*, pg. 745
GILLETTE (JAPAN) INC.—See The Gillette Company; *U.S. Public*, pg. 745
GILLETTE (PHILIPPINES), INC.—See The Gillette Company; *U.S. Public*, pg. 745
GILLETTE PRODUCTS DIVISION-EUROPE AMEE—See The Gillette Company; *U.S. Public*, pg. 745
GILLETTE RESEARCH INSTITUTE—See The Gillette Company; *U.S. Public*, pg. 744
GILLETTE SOUTH AFRICA LIMITED—See The Gillette Company; *U.S. Public*, pg. 745
GILLETTE (SWITZERLAND) AG—See The Gillette Company; *U.S. Public*, pg. 745
GILLETTE UK LTD.—See The Gillette Company; *U.S. Public*, pg. 745
GILLIAM CANDY BRANDS; *U.S. Private*, pg. 454
GILLOGLY CHEVROLET & GEO, INC.; *U.S. Private*, pg. 454
GILL'S CABLES LIMITED—See Carclo Engineering Group plc; *Int'l*, pg. 268
GILMAN—See Thyssen AG; *Int'l*, pg. 1389
GILMAN BUILDING PRODUCTS CO.—See Gilman Investment Company, Inc.; *U.S. Private*, pg. 454
GILMAN INVESTMENT COMPANY, INC.; *U.S. Private*, pg. 454
GILMAN PAPER CO.—See Gilman Investment Company, Inc.; *U.S. Private*, pg. 454
GILMAN WALLCOVERING DIV.—See Jones Blair Company; *U.S. Private*, pg. 596
GILMORE BROS., INC.; *U.S. Private*, pg. 454
GILMORE ENVELOPE CORP.; *U.S. Private*, pg. 454
GILMOUR HOSE COMPANY—See Emerson Electric Co.; *U.S. Public*, pg. 575
GILMOUR MANUFACTURING CO.—See Emerson Electric Co.; *U.S. Public*, pg. 575
GILPATRICK CONSTRUCTION COMPANY, INC; *U.S. Private*, pg. 454
GILRICHCO, INC.; *U.S. Private*, pg. 454
GILROY DISPATCH—See Central Valley Publishing; *U.S. Private*, pg. 225
GILROY ENERGY COMPANY—See Calpine Corporation; *U.S. Public*, pg. 296
GILROY FOODS, INC.—See ConAgra, Inc.; *U.S. Public*, pg. 428
GILSTER MARY LEE CORP.; *U.S. Private*, pg. 455
GILT EDGE MINE—See Dakota Mining Corporation; *U.S. Public*, pg. 477

GILTEX HOSIERY—See Sara Lee Corporation; *U.S. Public*, pg. 1434
GILVIN-TERRILL INC.; *U.S. Private*, pg. 455
GINGISS FORMALWEAR, INC.—See Gingiss International; *U.S. Private*, pg. 455
GINGISS INTERNATIONAL; *U.S. Private*, pg. 455
GINN & CO. LIMITED—See Reed Elsevier plc; *Int'l*, pg. 1094
GINO'S EAST/ROLLING MEADOWS—See Lettuce Entertain You Enterprises, Inc.; *U.S. Private*, pg. 661
GINSBERG'S INSTITUTIONAL FOODS, INC.; *U.S. Private*, pg. 455
GIORGIO BEVERLY HILLS—See The Procter & Gamble Company; *U.S. Public*, pg. 1331
GIPSWERK SCHOLVEN GMBH—See Veba AG; *Int'l*, pg. 1460
GIRARD POINT REFINERY—See Sun Company, Inc.; *U.S. Public*, pg. 1530
MARITHE AND FRANCOIS GIRBAUD N.A.—See VF Corporation; *U.S. Public*, pg. 1702
GIRDLESTONE PUMPS LIMITED—See North Limited; *Int'l*, pg. 967
GIRGENTI, HUGHES, BUTLER & MCDOWELL; *U.S. Private*, pg. 455
GIRL'S DIVISION—See Fruit of the Loom, Inc.; *U.S. Public*, pg. 686
GIRMES GMBH; *Int'l*, pg. 552
GIRO SPORTS DESIGN, INC.—See Bell Sports Corp.; *U.S. Public*, pg. 207
GIROBANK—See Alliance Leicester Building Society; *Int'l*, pg. 57
GIRPI—See ETEX; *Int'l*, pg. 430
GISEBO VAGNINDUSTRI AB—See Eldon AB; *Int'l*, pg. 436
GISH BIOMEDICAL, INC.; *U.S. Public*, pg. 745
GISH INTERNATIONAL, INC.—See Gish Biomedical, Inc.; *U.S. Public*, pg. 745
GIST-BROCADES AB—See Royal Gist-Brocades N.V.; *Int'l*, pg. 1142
GIST-BROCADES BENELUX B.V.—See Royal Gist-Brocades N.V.; *Int'l*, pg. 1143
GIST-BROCADES BENELUX N.V.—See Royal Gist-Brocades N.V.; *Int'l*, pg. 1142
GIST-BROCADES BIO-SPECIALTIES GMBH—See Royal Gist-Brocades N.V.; *Int'l*, pg. 1142
GIST-BROCADES B.V.—See Royal Gist-Brocades N.V.; *Int'l*, pg. 1142
GIST-BROCADES CHILI S.A.—See Royal Gist-Brocades N.V.; *Int'l*, pg. 1142
GIST-BROCADES EGYPT S.A.E.—See Royal Gist-Brocades N.V.; *Int'l*, pg. 1142
GIST-BROCADES FOOD SPECIALTIES—See Royal Gist-Brocades N.V.; *Int'l*, pg. 1142
GIST-BROCADES FOOD SPECIALTIES MEXICANA S.A. DE C.V.—See Royal Gist-Brocades N.V.; *Int'l*, pg. 1142
GIST-BROCADES FRANCE S.A.—See Royal Gist-Brocades N.V.; *Int'l*, pg. 1143
GIST-BROCADES HOLDING A.G.—See Royal Gist-Brocades N.V.; *Int'l*, pg. 1142
GIST-BROCADES, INC.—See Royal Gist-Brocades N.V.; *Int'l*, pg. 1143
GIST-BROCADES INDUSTRIAL PHARMACEUTICALS MEXICANA—See Royal Gist-Brocades N.V.; *Int'l*, pg. 1143
GIST-BROCADES INTERNATIONAL BV—See Royal Gist-Brocades N.V.; *Int'l*, pg. 1142
GIST-BROCADES IPPD LTD.—See Royal Gist-Brocades N.V.; *Int'l*, pg. 1142
GIST-BROCADES ITALY S.P.A.—See Royal Gist-Brocades N.V.; *Int'l*, pg. 1143
GIST-BROCADES, LDA.—See Royal Gist-Brocades N.V.; *Int'l*, pg. 1143
GIST-BROCADES MEXICANA, S.A. DE CV—See Royal Gist-Brocades N.V.; *Int'l*, pg. 1142
GIST-BROCADES N.V.—See Royal Gist-Brocades N.V.; *Int'l*, pg. 1142
GIST-BROCADES S.A.—See Royal Gist-Brocades N.V.; *Int'l*, pg. 1142
GIST-BROCADES SAVOURY B.V.—See Royal Gist-Brocades N.V.; *Int'l*, pg. 1142
GIST-BROCADES SP. Z O.O.—See Royal Gist-Brocades N.V.; *Int'l*, pg. 1143
GIST-BROCADES S.P.A.—See Royal Gist-Brocades N.V.; *Int'l*, pg. 1142
GIST-BROCADES FRANCE S.A.—See Royal Gist-Brocades N.V.; *Int'l*, pg. 1142
P.T. GIST-BROCADES INDONESIA—See Royal Gist-Brocades N.V.; *Int'l*, pg. 1143
GIT N GO, INC.—See Hale-Halsell Company; *U.S. Private*, pg. 494
GITAM/BBDO; *Int'l*, pg. 552
GITANO FASHIONS LTD.—See Fruit of the Loom, Inc.; *U.S. Public*, pg. 686
GITANO MEN'S DIVISION—See Fruit of the Loom, Inc.; *U.S. Public*, pg. 686
GITS MANUFACTURING COMPANY, INC.—See Valley Forge Corporation; *U.S. Public*, pg. 1705
GIUFFRE EDITORE SPA—See Reed Elsevier plc; *Int'l*, pg. 1095
GIULINI PHARMA GMBH—See Solvay S.A.; *Int'l*, pg. 1278
GIUMARRA VINEYARDS; *U.S. Private*, pg. 455
GIVAUDAN-ROURE CORPORATION—See Roche Holding Ltd.; *Int'l*, pg. 1120
GIVAUDAN-ROURE CORPORATION-FLAVORS DIVISION—See Roche Holding Ltd.; *Int'l*, pg. 1119
GIVAUDAN-ROURE, CORPORATION-FRAGRANCES DIV.—See Roche Holding Ltd.; *Int'l*, pg. 1120
GIVAUDAN-ROURE DO BRAZIL LTDA—See Roche Holding Ltd.; *Int'l*, pg. 1120
GIVAUDAN-ROURE FLAVOURS LTD.—See Roche Holding Ltd.; *Int'l*, pg. 1119
GIVAUDAN-ROURE GMBH—See Roche Holding Ltd.; *Int'l*, pg. 1120
GIVAUDAN-ROURE INC.—See Roche Holding Ltd.; *Int'l*, pg. 1120

GIVAUDAN-ROURE (INDIA) PVT LTD.—See Roche Holding Ltd.; *Int'l*, pg. 1120
GIVAUDAN-ROURE (INTERNATIONAL) S.A.—See Roche Holding Ltd.; *Int'l*, pg. 1119
GIVAUDAN-ROURE K.K.—See Roche Holding Ltd.; *Int'l*, pg. 1120
GIVAUDAN-ROURE LTD.—See Roche Holding Ltd.; *Int'l*, pg. 1120
P.T. GIVAUDAN-ROURE PTE. LTD.—See Roche Holding Ltd.; *Int'l*, pg. 1120
GIVAUDAN-ROURE PTY. LTD.—See Roche Holding Ltd.; *Int'l*, pg. 1120
GIVAUDAN-ROURE (PTY.) LTD.—See Roche Holding Ltd.; *Int'l*, pg. 1120
GIVAUDAN-ROURE RESEARCH LTD.—See Roche Holding Ltd.; *Int'l*, pg. 1119
GIVAUDAN-ROURE S.A.—See Roche Holding Ltd.; *Int'l*, pg. 1119
GIVAUDAN-ROURE, S.A. DE C.V.—See Roche Holding Ltd.; *Int'l*, pg. 1120
GIVAUDAN-ROURE S.P.A.—See Roche Holding Ltd.; *Int'l*, pg. 1120
GIVAUDAN-ROURE LTD.—See Roche Holding Ltd.; *Int'l*, pg. 1120
GIVENCHY CORP. (USA)—See LVMH Moet Hennessy Louis Vuitton; *Int'l*, pg. 780
GIVENCHY KK (JAPAN)—See LVMH Moet Hennessy Louis Vuitton; *Int'l*, pg. 782
GIVENCHY S.A.—See LVMH Moet Hennessy Louis Vuitton; *Int'l*, pg. 780
GLACAUTO—See Saint-Gobain; *Int'l*, pg. 1172
GLACERIES DE SAINT-ROCH—See Saint-Gobain; *Int'l*, pg. 1172
GLACIER GAS COMPANY—See Montana Power Company; *U.S. Public*, pg. 1127
THE GLACIER METAL CO. LTD.—See T & N Plc; *Int'l*, pg. 1334
GLACIER PARK, INC.—See Viad Corp; *U.S. Public*, pg. 1718
GLACIER VANDERVELL, INC.—See T & N Plc; *Int'l*, pg. 1334
GLACIER WATER SERVICES INC.; *U.S. Public*, pg. 745
GLADDING BRAIDED PRODUCTS LLC—See Crowe Rope Industries L.L.C.; *U.S. Private*, pg. 291
GLADWIN MACHINE PRODUCTS DIV.—See Simpson Industries, Inc.; *U.S. Public*, pg. 1475
GLAENZER-SEURRE NV/SA—See GKN plc; *Int'l*, pg. 536
GLAMORIE FOUNDATIONS, INC.; *U.S. Private*, pg. 455
GLAMOUR—See Advance Publications Inc.; *U.S. Private*, pg. 20
GLAMOURETTE FASHION MILLS—See Hampshire Group, Ltd.; *U.S. Private*, pg. 779
GLANFORD BRIGG GENERATING STATION—See Imatran Voima Oy; *Int'l*, pg. 660
GLASFABRIK SAS VAN GENT B.V.—See Saint-Gobain; *Int'l*, pg. 1173
MARY GLASGOW PUBLICATIONS LTD.—See Wolters Kluwer N.V.; *Int'l*, pg. 1514
GLASGOW MFG. DIVISION—See R.R. Donnelley & Sons Company; *U.S. Public*, pg. 518
GLASGOW TERMINAL—See GATX Corporation; *U.S. Public*, pg. 693
GLASHUSET I KARLSTAD AB—See Saint-Gobain; *Int'l*, pg. 1173
GLASHUSET UDDEVALLA AB PARTICIPACOES LTDA.—See Saint-Gobain; *Int'l*, pg. 1173
GLASKONTOR MULLHEIM GMBH—See Carl-Zeiss-Stiftung; *Int'l*, pg. 1523
GLASS BLOCK—See Mercantile Stores Company, Inc.; *U.S. Public*, pg. 1090
THE GLASS DEPOT, INC.—See Apogee Enterprises, Inc.; *U.S. Public*, pg. 120
GLASS PRODUCTS, INC.—See Asahi Glass Co., Ltd.; *Int'l*, pg. 84
GLASS ROCK PLANT—See Oglebay Norton Company; *U.S. Public*, pg. 1213
GLASSEAL PRODUCTS, INC.—See HCC Industries; *U.S. Private*, pg. 490
GLASSMASTER COMPANY; *U.S. Public*, pg. 745
GLASSMASTER CONTROLS COMPANY, INC.—See Glassmaster Company; *U.S. Public*, pg. 746
GLASSTITE, INC.—See Raven Industries, Inc.; *U.S. Public*, pg. 1361
GLASTEEL INDUSTRIAL LAMINATES—See The Alpha Corporation of Tennessee; *U.S. Private*, pg. 45
GLASTEEL TENNESSEE, INC.—See The Alpha Corporation of Tennessee; *U.S. Private*, pg. 45
GLASTIC CORPORATION—See Kobe Steel, Ltd.; *Int'l*, pg. 740
GLASTRON BOATS—See Genmar Holdings, Inc.; *U.S. Private*, pg. 447
GLASULD A/S—See Saint-Gobain; *Int'l*, pg. 1176
GLASURIT DE ARGENTINA S.A.—See BASF AG; *Int'l*, pg. 105
P.H. GLATFELTER COMPANY; *U.S. Public*, pg. 746
THE GLATFELTER PULP WOOD CO.—See P.H. Glatfelter Company; *U.S. Public*, pg. 746
GLAVERBEL S.A.—See Asahi Glass Co., Ltd.; *Int'l*, pg. 85
GLAXO DANMARK A/S—See Glaxo Wellcome plc; *Int'l*, pg. 553
GLAXO DERMATOLOGY—See Glaxo Wellcome plc; *Int'l*, pg. 553
GLAXO DEVELOPMENT PTE. LTD.—See Glaxo Wellcome plc; *Int'l*, pg. 553
GLAXO FAR EAST PTE. LTD.—See Glaxo Wellcome plc; *Int'l*, pg. 553
GLAXO LABORATORIES LIMITED—See Glaxo Wellcome plc; *Int'l*, pg. 552
GLAXO PHARMACEUTICALS—See Glaxo Wellcome plc; *Int'l*, pg. 552
GLAXO PHARMACEUTICALS UK LTD.—See Glaxo Wellcome plc; *Int'l*, pg. 552

GLAXO TECHNICAL OPERATIONS—See Glaxo Wellcome plc; *Int'l*, pg. 552
GLAXO WELLCOME AB—See Glaxo Wellcome plc; *Int'l*, pg. 553
GLAXO WELLCOME AUSTRALIA LTD.—See Glaxo Wellcome plc; *Int'l*, pg. 553
GLAXO WELLCOME BELGIUM S.A.—See Glaxo Wellcome plc; *Int'l*, pg. 553
GLAXO WELLCOME CHINA LTD.—See Glaxo Wellcome plc; *Int'l*, pg. 553
GLAXO WELLCOME GMBH—See Glaxo Wellcome plc; *Int'l*, pg. 553
GLAXO WELLCOME HONG KONG LTD.—See Glaxo Wellcome plc; *Int'l*, pg. 553
GLAXO WELLCOME INC.—See Glaxo Wellcome plc; *Int'l*, pg. 552
GLAXO WELLCOME PHARMA GMBH—See Glaxo Wellcome plc; *Int'l*, pg. 553
GLAXO WELLCOME PLC; *Int'l*, pg. 552
GLAXO WELLCOME SINGAPORE PTE. LTD.—See Glaxo Wellcome plc; *Int'l*, pg. 553
GLAXOCHEM LTD.—See Glaxo Wellcome plc; *Int'l*, pg. 552
GLAXOCHEM PTE. LTD.—See Glaxo Wellcome plc; *Int'l*, pg. 553
GLAZER'S WHOLESALE DRUG CO. INC.; *U.S. Private*, pg. 455
GLEACHER MORGAN GRENFELL INC.—See Deutsche Bank AG; *Int'l*, pg. 405
GLEASON/CALISE/ASSOCIATES, INC.; *U.S. Private*, pg. 455
GLEASON CORPORATION; *U.S. Public*, pg. 746
GLEASON CORPORATION SALES—See Gleason Corporation; *U.S. Public*, pg. 746
GLEASON-HURTH—See Gleason Corporation; *U.S. Public*, pg. 746
GLEASON MILANO—See Gleason Corporation; *U.S. Public*, pg. 746
THE GLEASON WORKS—See Gleason Corporation; *U.S. Public*, pg. 746
GLEASON WORKS LTD.—See Gleason Corporation; *U.S. Public*, pg. 746
GLEISBAU HILBIG UND VENTZKE GMBH & CO. KG—See Philipp Holzmann AG; *Int'l*, pg. 632
GLEITMOLYBDAN SCHMIERSTOFFE GMBH—See Fuchs Petrolub AG Oel + Chemie; *Int'l*, pg. 517
GLEN ALSACE WATER COMPANY—See Citizens Utilities Company; *U.S. Public*, pg. 380
THE GLEN DIMPLEX GROUP; *Int'l*, pg. 553
GLEN ELECTRIC—See The Glen Dimplex Group; *Int'l*, pg. 554
GLEN ELLEN WINERY; *U.S. Private*, pg. 455
GLEN FALLS NATIONAL BANK & TRUST COMPANY—See Arrow Financial Corporation; *U.S. Public*, pg. 135
GLEN-GERY CORPORATION—See Ibstock Plc; *Int'l*, pg. 658
GLEN OAKS HOSPITAL—See Universal Health Services, Inc.; *U.S. Public*, pg. 1697
GLEN OAKS INDUSTRIES, INC.; *U.S. Private*, pg. 456
GLEN RAVEN MARKETING CORPORATION—See Glen Raven Mills, Inc.; *U.S. Private*, pg. 456
GLEN RAVEN MILLS, INC.; *U.S. Private*, pg. 456
GLEN RAVEN MILLS, INC.-FILAMENT FABRICS DIVISION—See Glen Raven Mills, Inc.; *U.S. Private*, pg. 456
GLEN RAVEN MILLS, INC.-GLEN TOUCH PLANT—See Glen Raven Mills, Inc.; *U.S. Private*, pg. 456
GLEN RAVEN MILLS, INC.-GLENSPUN DIVISION—See Glen Raven Mills, Inc.; *U.S. Private*, pg. 456
GLEN RAVEN MILLS, INC.-KINSTON PLANT—See Glen Raven Mills, Inc.; *U.S. Private*, pg. 456
GLEN RAVEN MILLS, INC.-NORLINA PLANT—See Glen Raven Mills, Inc.; *U.S. Private*, pg. 456
GLEN RAVEN MILLS, INC.-TEXTURED MILLS GROUP-GLEN TOUCH DIV.—See Glen Raven Mills, Inc.; *U.S. Private*, pg. 456
GLEN RAVEN MILLS, INC.-TEXTURED YARN GROUP-GLEN TOUCH DIVISION—See Glen Raven Mills, Inc.; *U.S. Private*, pg. 456
GLEN RAVEN MILLS, INC.-TRANSPORTATION DIVISION—See Glen Raven Mills, Inc.; *U.S. Private*, pg. 456
GLEN RAVEN MILLS, INC.-ULTRASPUN PLANT—See Glen Raven Mills, Inc.; *U.S. Private*, pg. 456
GLEN RAVEN MILLS, INC.-PARK AVE. DIVISION—See Glen Raven Mills, Inc.; *U.S. Private*, pg. 456
GLENAYRE ELECTRONICS, INC.—See Glenayre Technologies, Inc.; *U.S. Public*, pg. 747
GLENAYRE TECHNOLOGIES, INC.; *U.S. Public*, pg. 746
GLENBOROUGH REALTY TRUST INCORPORATED; *U.S. Public*, pg. 747
GLENBROOK NICKEL COMPANY—See Cominco Ltd.; *Int'l*, pg. 307
GLENCO SA—See GKN plc; *Int'l*, pg. 536
GLENCOE MC-GRAW HILL—See The McGraw-Hill Companies, U.S. Public, pg. 1070
GLENCRAFT LINGERIE, INC.; *U.S. Private*, pg. 456
GLENDALE ASSOCIATES—See Cigna Corp.; *U.S. Public*, pg. 361
GLENDALE FEDERAL BANK, F.S.B.; *U.S. Public*, pg. 747
GLENDALE LIMITED PARTNERSHIP ASSOCIATES - II—See Cigna Corp.; *U.S. Public*, pg. 361
GLENDALE MEMORIAL HOSPITAL AND MEDICAL CENTER—See UniHealth; *U.S. Private*, pg. 1118
GLENDALE OHRBACH'S ASSOCIATES—See Cigna Corp.; *U.S. Public*, pg. 365
GLENDINNING MARINE PRODUCTS, INC.—See Valley Forge Corporation; *U.S. Public*, pg. 1705
THE GLENEAGLES HOTEL—See Diageo Plc; *Int'l*, pg. 412
GLENFED BROKERAGE SERVICES—See Glendale Federal Bank, F.S.B.; *U.S. Public*, pg. 747
GLENFED INSURANCE SERVICES, INC.—See Glendale Federal Bank, F.S.B.; *U.S. Public*, pg. 747

GLENGARRY AND STORMONT RAILWAY COMPANY—See Sun Life Assurance Company of Canada; *Int'l*, pg. 1319
GLENGLASSAUGH DISTILLERY—See The Highland Distilleries Company plc; *Int'l*, pg. 619
GLENOIT MILLS, INC.; *U.S. Private*, pg. 456
GLENROCK COAL COMPANY—See PacifiCorp; *U.S. Public*, pg. 1251
GLENROTHES DISTILLERY—See The Highland Distilleries Company plc; *Int'l*, pg. 619
GLENROY CONSTRUCTION CO. INC.; *U.S. Private*, pg. 456
GLENS FALLS CEMENT CO.—See Dyckerhoff AG; *Int'l*, pg. 423
GLENSHAW GLASS CO. INC.—See Glenshaw Glass Co. Inc.; *U.S. Private*, pg. 457
GLENSHAW GLASS CO. INC.; *U.S. Private*, pg. 457
GLENTEL INC.—See TCG International Inc.; *Int'l*, pg. 1336
GLENTURRET DISTILLERY LIMITED—See The Highland Distilleries Company plc; *Int'l*, pg. 619
GLENVIEW STATE BANK—See Cummins-Allison Corp.; *U.S. Private*, pg. 295
GLENWOOD POST—See Shivers Trading & Operating Co.; *U.S. Private*, pg. 995
GENE B. GLICK COMPANY, INC.; *U.S. Private*, pg. 457
THE GLIDDEN COMPANY (CANADA) LIMITED—See Imperial Chemical Industries PLC; *Int'l*, pg. 664
GLIDE LUMBER PRODUCTS CO.—See WTD Industries, Inc.; *U.S. Public*, pg. 1729
GLINES & RHODES, INC.; *U.S. Private*, pg. 457
GLIT—See Katy Industries, Inc.; *U.S. Public*, pg. 944
GLITSCH INTERNATIONAL—See Koch Industries, Incorporated; *U.S. Private*, pg. 628
GLO SPA—See MascoTech, Inc.; *U.S. Public*, pg. 1055
MATTHEW GLOAG & SON LIMITED—See The Highland Distilleries Company plc; *Int'l*, pg. 619
GLOBAL ADVANCED TECHNOLOGY CORP.—See Yamaichi Securities Co., Ltd.; *Int'l*, pg. 1517
GLOBAL ATMOSPHERICS, INC.—See Sankosha Corporation; *Int'l*, pg. 1189
GLOBAL BEVERAGE CO.; *U.S. Private*, pg. 457
GLOBAL BUSINESSES—See Texaco Inc.; *U.S. Public*, pg. 1583
GLOBAL DIRECT MAIL CORP; *U.S. Public*, pg. 747
GLOBAL ENVIRONMENTAL CORP.; *U.S. Public*, pg. 747
GLOBAL ERECTORS—See American Eco Corporation; *Int'l*, pg. 74
GLOBAL FOOD CORPORATION—See Basic Food International Inc.; *U.S. Public*, pg. 121
GLOBAL INDUSTRIAL TECHNOLOGIES; *U.S. Public*, pg. 747
GLOBAL INDUSTRIES, LTD.; *U.S. Public*, pg. 748
GLOBAL MARINE DRILLING CO.—See Global Marine Inc.; *U.S. Public*, pg. 748
GLOBAL MARINE INC.; *U.S. Public*, pg. 748
GLOBAL MARKETING RESOURCES (GMR); *U.S. Private*, pg. 457
GLOBAL MOTOR SPORT GROUP; *U.S. Public*, pg. 748
GLOBAL MOVING & STORAGE, INC.—See Global Van Lines, Inc.; *U.S. Private*, pg. 458
GLOBAL MOVING SYSTEMS, INC.—See Global Van Lines, Inc.; *U.S. Private*, pg. 458
GLOBAL ONE—See Sprint Corporation; *U.S. Public*, pg. 1501
GLOBAL PETROLEUM CORP.; *U.S. Private*, pg. 457
GLOBAL PIPELINE SURVEYS—See T.D. Williamson, Inc.; *U.S. Private*, pg. 1180
GLOBAL POWER COMPANY—See American Eco Corporation; *Int'l*, pg. 74
GLOBAL PRECISION, INC.—See AptarGroup, Inc.; *U.S. Public*, pg. 125
GLOBAL PROCESSING & RECYCLING GROUP, SHIED-TECH CAMBRIDGE—See Global Industrial Technologies; *U.S. Public*, pg. 748
GLOBAL RENTAL CORPORATION—See Orix Corporation; *Int'l*, pg. 1009
GLOBAL SOFTWARE, INC.; *U.S. Private*, pg. 457
GLOBAL SOLAR ENERGY—See UniSource Energy Corporation; *U.S. Public*, pg. 1670
GLOBAL SOURCING, INC.—See Fruit of the Loom, Inc.; *U.S. Public*, pg. 686
GLOBAL SPECIAL RISKS, INC. HOLDINGS—See Willis Corroon Group PLC; *Int'l*, pg. 1503
GLOBAL SPECIAL RISKS, INC. OF HOUSTON—See Willis Corroon Group PLC; *Int'l*, pg. 1503
GLOBAL SPECIAL RISKS, INC. OF NEW YORK—See Willis Corroon Group PLC; *Int'l*, pg. 1503
GLOBAL SPECIAL RISKS, INC. OF TEXAS—See Willis Corroon Group PLC; *Int'l*, pg. 1503
GLOBAL SPECIAL RISKS INSURANCE SERVICES CALIFORNIA—See Willis Corroon Group PLC; *Int'l*, pg. 1503
GLOBAL STEEL PRODUCTS CORPORATION; *U.S. Private*, pg. 457
GLOBAL TH—See Tesco PLC; *Int'l*, pg. 1376
GLOBAL TRADING LTD—See Iochpe-Maxion S.A.; *Int'l*, pg. 688
GLOBAL TRAVEL COMPUTER HOLDINGS LTD.—See Air Canada; *Int'l*, pg. 36
GLOBAL TURNKEY SYSTEMS INC.; *U.S. Private*, pg. 457
GLOBAL VAN & STORAGE CO.—See Global Van Lines, Inc.; *U.S. Private*, pg. 458
GLOBAL VAN LINES, INC.; *U.S. Private*, pg. 458
GLOBAL VILLAGE COMMUNICATION; *U.S. Public*, pg. 748
GLOBALSTAR—See Loral Space & Communications; *U.S. Public*, pg. 1014
GLOBE-AMERADA GLASS COMPANY; *U.S. Private*, pg. 458
GLOBE BUSINESS FURNITURE, INC.—See Haworth, Inc.; *U.S. Private*, pg. 512
GLOBE FASTENERS CORP.—See Itochu Corporation; *Int'l*, pg. 694

GLOBE FURNITURE RENTALS; *U.S. Private*, pg. 458
GLOBE-GAZETTE—See Lee Enterprises, Incorporated; *U.S. Public*, pg. 983
GLOBE INDEMNITY CO.—See Royal & Sun Alliance Insurance Group plc; *Int'l*, pg. 1130
GLOBE INSURANCE AGENCY, INC.—See Torchmark Corporation; *U.S. Public*, pg. 1622
GLOBE LIFE AND ACCIDENT INSURANCE CO.—See Torchmark Corporation; *U.S. Public*, pg. 1622
GLOBE LIFE AND ACCIDENT INSURANCE CO. OF OKLAHOMA, INC.—See Torchmark Corporation; *U.S. Public*, pg. 1622
GLOBE-MEAT IMPORTERS CO., LTD.—See ESS-Food; *Int'l*, pg. 430
GLOBE MORTGAGE AMERICA, LLC.; *U.S. Private*, pg. 458
GLOBE MOTORS DIVISION—See Labinal SA; *Int'l*, pg. 787
GLOBE NEWSPAPER COMPANY—See The New York Times Company; *U.S. Public*, pg. 1175
GLOBE SPECIALTY PRODUCTS, INC.—See The New York Times Company; *U.S. Public*, pg. 1175
GLOBE SPRING & CUSHION CO., LTD.—See Leggett & Platt, Incorporated; *U.S. Public*, pg. 987
GLOBE VALVE CORPORAT ON—See Gerber Plumbing Fixtures Corporation; *U.S. Private*, pg. 449
GLOBELLE CORPORATION; *Int'l*, pg. 554
GLOBUS & COSMOS; *U.S. Private*, pg. 458
GLOBUS-TEPPICH-FABRIK WALTER POSER GMBH—See Gamma Holding N.V.; *Int'l*, pg. 540
GLOBUS VERSICHERUNGS AG—See Allianz Aktiengesellschaft; *Int'l*, pg. 58
GLORIA JEAN'S AND COFFEE PLANTATION—See Cara Operations Limited; *Int'l*, pg. 266
GLORIA S.A.—See Nestle S.A.; *Int'l*, pg. 920
GLORY KAWASAKI MOTORS CO., LTD.—See Nissho Iwai Corporation; *Int'l*, pg. 947
GLORY LTD.; *Int'l*, pg. 554
GLORY USA, INC.—See Glory Ltd.; *Int'l*, pg. 554
GLOUCESTER NEW COMMUNITIES—See W.R. Grace & Co.; *U.S. Public*, pg. 755
GLOUCESTER RAILWAY CARRIAGE & WAGON COMPANY LTD.—See FKI Plc; *Int'l*, pg. 473
GLOVER WEBB LTD.—See GKN plc; *Int'l*, pg. 535
GLUCKSELE GESELLSCHAFT MBH—See Nestle S.A.; *Int'l*, pg. 920
GLUCONA VOF—See Akzo Nobel N.V.; *Int'l*, pg. 47
GLYNWED CONSUMER & CONSTRUCTION PRODUCTS LTD.—See Glynwed International PLC; *Int'l*, pg. 554
GLYNWED ENGINEERING LTD.—See Glynwed International PLC; *Int'l*, pg. 554
GLYNWED INTERNATIONAL PLC; *Int'l*, pg. 554
GLYNWED METAL SERVICES LTD.—See Glynwed International PLC; *Int'l*, pg. 554
GLYNWED PIPE SYSTEMS—See Glynwed International PLC; *Int'l*, pg. 554
GLYNWED STEEL TUBES LTD.—See Glynwed International PLC; *Int'l*, pg. 554
GMAC INSURANCE HOLDINGS—See General Motors Corporation; *U.S. Public*, og. 719
GNOMI ADVERTISING—See DMB&B Communications; *U.S. Private*, pg. 304
GO/DAN INDUSTRIES—See TransPro, Inc.; *U.S. Public*, pg. 1631
GO JO INDUSTRIES; *U.S. Private*, pg. 458
GO MANUFACTURING—See TransPro, Inc.; *U.S. Public*, pg. 1631
GO SPORT—See Kingfisher plc; *Int'l*, pg. 734
GO-VIDEO, INC.; *U.S. Public*, pg. 748
GO VOYAGES—See Groupe Air France; *Int'l*, pg. 560
GODDESS BRA COMPANY; *U.S. Private*, pg. 458
GODFATHER'S PIZZA, INC.; *U.S. Private*, pg. 751
GODFREY ENGINEERING—See The B.F. Goodrich Company; *U.S. Public*, pg. 751
GODIVA CHOCOLATIER, INC.—See Campbell Soup Company; *U.S. Public*, pg. 299
GODREJ MAKRO PVT LTD.—See SHV Holdings N.V.; *Int'l*, pg. 1155
H.J. GODWIN LTD.—See Wolseley Plc.; *Int'l*, pg. 1511
GODWINS, BOOKE & DICKENSON, INC.—See AON Corporation; *U.S. Public*, pg. 117
GODWINS LIMITED—See AON Corporation; *U.S. Public*, pg. 119
GOEDECKE A.G.—See Warner-Lambert Company; *U.S. Public*, pg. 1739
OTTO GOEDECKE, INC.; *U.S. Private*, pg. 458
GOER MANUFACTURING CO —See RHC/Spacemaster Corporation; *U.S. Private*, pg. 904
GOETHE MANAGEMENT LTD.—See Banque Generale du Luxembourg SA; *Int'l*, pg. 162
GOETZE CORP. OF AMERICA—See T & N Plc; *Int'l*, pg. 1335
AE GOETZE GMBH—See T & N Plc; *Int'l*, pg. 1334
GOFF DIVISION GEORG FISCHER—See Georg Fischer Ltd.; *Int'l*, pg. 490
GO-GRO INDUSTRIES, LTD.—See Catalina Lighting, Inc.; *U.S. Public*, pg. 314
GOHMANN ASPHALT & CONSTRUCTION INC.; *U.S. Private*, pg. 459
GOHMANN ASPHALT & CONSTRUCTION OF KY., INC.—See Gohmann Asphalt & Construction Inc.; *U.S. Private*, pg. 459
GOINBRAS INDUSTRIA E COMERCIA DO BRASIL, LTDA.—See Halliburton Company; *U.S. Public*, pg. 777
GOL-PAK CORP.—See CKE Restaurants Inc.; *U.S. Public*, pg. 278
GOL TRELAST—See Norske Skogindustrier A.S; *Int'l*, pg. 965
GOLD CIRCLE INSURANCE CO.—See The Great-West Life Assurance Company; *Int'l*, pg. 558
GOLD COAST MILK PTY. LTD.—See Q.U.F. Industries Ltd.; *Int'l*, pg. 1074
GOLD EAGLE COMPANY; *U.S. Private*, pg. 459
GOLD KEY INSURANCE AGENCY—See The Progressive Corporation; *U.S. Public*, pg. 1334

GOLD KIST, INC.; *U.S. Private*, pg. 459
GOLD LANCE, INC.—See Town & Country Corporation; *U.S. Public*, pg. 1625
GOLD MEDAL BEVERAGE CORP.—See All American Bottling Corp.; *U.S. Private*, pg. 34
GOLD MEDAL DIV.—See General Mills, Inc.; *U.S. Public*, pg. 718
GOLD MEDAL INSURANCE CO.—See General Mills, Inc.; *U.S. Public*, pg. 718
GOLD MEDAL PRODUCTS CO.; *U.S. Private*, pg. 459
GOLD'N PLUMP POULTRY—See JFC Inc.; *U.S. Private*, pg. 577
GOLD PEAK INDUSTRIES (HOLDINGS) LIMITED—See GP Batteries International Ltd.; *Int'l*, pg. 537
GOLD PEAK INDUSTRIES (TAIWAN) LTD.—See GP Batteries International Ltd.; *Int'l*, pg. 537
GOLD SHIELD FIBERGLASS, INC.—See Fleetwood Enterprises, Inc.; *U.S. Public*, pg. 652
GOLDBERG MOSER O'NEILL; *U.S. Private*, pg. 459
GOLDBERGER DOLL MFG. COMPANY, INC.; *U.S. Private*, pg. 459
GOLDBERGS MARINE DISTRIBUTORS—See West Marine, Inc.; *U.S. Public*, pg. 1756
GOLDBLATT'S DEPARTMENT STORES—See JG Industries, Inc.; *U.S. Public*, pg. 917
GOLDCORP INC.—See CSA Management Inc.; *Int'l*, pg. 243
GOLDEN ALASKA SEAFOODS, INC.—See Nichiro Corporation; *Int'l*, pg. 928
GOLDEN BAY CEMENT LTD.—See Fletcher Challenge Limited; *Int'l*, pg. 495
GOLDEN BOOKS FAMILY ENTERTAINMENT INC.; *U.S. Public*, pg. 749
GOLDEN BOOKS PUBLISHING—See Golden Books Family Entertainment Inc.; *U.S. Public*, pg. 749
GOLDEN CARE INC.—See Sun Healthcare Group Inc.; *U.S. Public*, pg. 1531
GOLDEN CAT CORPORATION—See Ralston Purina Company; *U.S. Public*, pg. 1360
GOLDEN CORRAL CORPORATION—See Investors Management Corp.; *U.S. Private*, pg. 575
GOLDEN DONUTS, INC.—See Allied Domecq PLC; *Int'l*, pg. 63
GOLDEN DONUTS SBN. BHD.—See Allied Domecq PLC; *Int'l*, pg. 63
GOLDEN EAGLE DISTRIBUTORS, INC.; *U.S. Private*, pg. 460
GOLDEN EAGLE GROUP, INC.; *U.S. Public*, pg. 749
GOLDEN EAGLE SYSTEMS—See Sanmina Corporation; *U.S. Public*, pg. 1431
GOLDEN ENTERPRISES INC.; *U.S. Public*, pg. 749
GOLDEN FLEECE OUTERWEAR CO.—See I. Spiewak & Sons, Inc.; *U.S. Private*, pg. 1025
GOLDEN GATE AUTO AUCTION INC.—See Tyco International Ltd.; *U.S. Public*, pg. 1649
GOLDEN GEM GROWERS INC.; *U.S. Private*, pg. 460
GOLDEN GRAIN COMPANY—See The Quaker Oats Company; *U.S. Public*, pg. 1348
GOLDEN ISLES ASSURANCE CO., LTD.—See Magellan Health Services, Inc.; *U.S. Public*, pg. 1036
GOLDEN PATRICIA MINE—See Barrick Gold Corporation; *Int'l*, pg. 169
GOLDEN PEANUT COMPANY—See Gold Kist, Inc.; *U.S. Private*, pg. 459
GOLDEN PLAINS CARE CENTER—See Horizon/CMS Healthcare Corporation; *U.S. Public*, pg. 837
GOLDEN REWARD MINE—See CSA Management Inc.; *Int'l*, pg. 243
GOLDEN REWARD MINE—See Dakota Mining Corporation; *U.S. Public*, pg. 477
GOLDEN STAR INC.; *U.S. Private*, pg. 460
GOLDEN STATE/CAS, INC.—See EMCON; *U.S. Public*, pg. 571
GOLDEN STATE FOODS; *U.S. Private*, pg. 460
GOLDEN STATE FOODS-OAK BROOK—See Golden State Foods; *U.S. Private*, pg. 460
GOLDEN STATE FOODS-SOUTH CAROLINA DIVISION—See Golden State Foods; *U.S. Private*, pg. 461
GOLDEN STATE FOODS-SUFFOLK—See Golden State Foods; *U.S. Private*, pg. 461
GOLDEN STATE MUTUAL LIFE INSURANCE COMPANY; *U.S. Private*, pg. 461
GOLDEN SUN FEEDS, INC.—See Purina Mills, Inc.; *U.S. Private*, pg. 895
GOLDEN TIGER—See Windsor Quality Food Co., Ltd.; *U.S. Private*, pg. 1182
THE GOLDEN TOUCH DIVISION—See Gold Eagle Company; *U.S. Private*, pg. 459
GOLDEN VALLEY MICROWAVE FOODS, INC.—See ConAgra, Inc.; *U.S. Public*, pg. 427
GOLDEN WEST BASEBALL CLUB—See Golden West Broadcasters; *U.S. Private*, pg. 461
GOLDEN WEST BROADCASTERS; *U.S. Private*, pg. 461
GOLDEN WEST FINANCIAL CORPORATION; *U.S. Public*, pg. 750
GOLDEN WEST HOMES—See Oakwood Homes Corporation; *U.S. Public*, pg. 1209
GOLDEN WEST REFINING COMPANY—See Thrifty Oil Co.; *U.S. Private*, pg. 1084
GOLDENBERG CANDY COMPANY; *U.S. Private*, pg. 461
GOLDENBERG GROUP, INC.—See Nortek, Inc.; *U.S. Public*, pg. 1193
THE GOLDFIELD CONSOLIDATED MINES CO.—See The Goldfield Corporation; *U.S. Public*, pg. 750
THE GOLDFIELD CORPORATION; *U.S. Public*, pg. 750
THE GOLDHIRSH GROUP; *U.S. Public*, pg. 461
GOLDMAN FINANCIAL GROUP; *U.S. Private*, pg. 461
G.B. GOLDMAN PAPER CO.—See Bunzl PLC; *Int'l*, pg. 233
S.I. GOLDMAN CO.; *U.S. Private*, pg. 461
GOLDMAN, SACHS & CO.—See Goldman, Sachs & Co.; *U.S. Public*, pg. 462
GOLDMAN, SACHS & CO.; *U.S. Private*, pg. 462

GOLDMAN, SACHS & COMPANHIA—See Goldman, Sachs & Co.; *U.S. Private*, pg. 462
GOLDMAN, SACHS & CO. BANK—See Goldman, Sachs & Co.; *U.S. Private*, pg. 462
GOLDMAN, SACHS & CO. OHG MESSETURM—See Goldman, Sachs & Co.; *U.S. Private*, pg. 462
GOLDMAN SACHS (ASIA) LIMITED—See Goldman, Sachs & Co.; *U.S. Private*, pg. 462
GOLDMAN SACHS AUSTRALIA L.L.C.—See Goldman, Sachs & Co.; *U.S. Private*, pg. 462
GOLDMAN SACHS CANADA—See Goldman, Sachs & Co.; *U.S. Private*, pg. 462
GOLDMAN SACHS (CAYMAN) TRUST, LIMITED—See Goldman, Sachs & Co.; *U.S. Private*, pg. 462
GOLDMAN SACHS (CHINA) L.L.C.—See Goldman, Sachs & Co.; *U.S. Private*, pg. 462
GOLDMAN SACHS INTERNATIONAL—See Goldman, Sachs & Co.; *U.S. Private*, pg. 462
GOLDMAN SACHS INTERNATIONAL LIMITED—See Goldman, Sachs & Co.; *U.S. Private*, pg. 462
GOLDMAN SACHS (JAPAN)—See Goldman, Sachs & Co.; *U.S. Private*, pg. 462
GOLDMAN SACHS MEXICO CASA DE BOLSA, S.A. DE C.V.—See Goldman, Sachs & Co.; *U.S. Private*, pg. 462
GOLDMAN SACHS PARIS INC. ET CIE.—See Goldman, Sachs & Co.; *U.S. Private*, pg. 462
GOLDMAN SACHS S.I.M. SPA—See Goldman, Sachs & Co.; *U.S. Private*, pg. 462
GOLDMAN SACHS (SINGAPORE) PTE.—See Goldman, Sachs & Co.; *U.S. Private*, pg. 462
WILHELM GOLDMANN VERLAG GMBH—See Bertelsmann AG; *Int'l*, pg. 190
GOLD'N PLUMP POULTRY, INC.—See JFC Inc.; *U.S. Private*, pg. 577
GOLDNER HAWN JOHNSONS & MORRISON INCORPORATED; *U.S. Private*, pg. 462
GOLDSACK HARRIS THOMPSON ADVERTISING—See Leo Burnett Company, Inc.; *U.S. Private*, pg. 184
GOLDSBORO MILLING COMPANY; *U.S. Private*, pg. 462
GOLDSBORO PLANT—See Cooper Industries, Inc.; *U.S. Public*, pg. 443
GOLDSHIELD FIBERGLASS OF INDIANA, INC.—See Fleetwood Enterprises, Inc.; *U.S. Public*, pg. 652
GOLDSMITH/JEFFREY INC.; *U.S. Private*, pg. 462
GOLDSMITHS, INC.; *U.S. Private*, pg. 462
P.T. GOLDSTAR ASTRA—See LG Group; *Int'l*, pg. 779
GOLDSTAR CABLE CO. LTD.—See LG Group; *Int'l*, pg. 778
GOLDSTAR CANADA LTD.—See LG Group; *Int'l*, pg. 779
GOLDSTAR CO. LTD.—See LG Group; *Int'l*, pg. 778
GOLDSTAR COLLINS PHILS INC.—See LG Group; *Int'l*, pg. 779
GOLDSTAR DEUTSCHLAND GMBH—See LG Group; *Int'l*, pg. 779
GOLDSTAR EGYPT ELECTRONICS S.A.E.—See LG Group; *Int'l*, pg. 779
GOLDSTAR ELECTRIC CO. LTD.—See LG Group; *Int'l*, pg. 779
GOLDSTAR ELECTRIC U.K. LTD.—See LG Group; *Int'l*, pg. 779
GOLDSTAR ELECTRONICS (THAILAND) CO., LTD.—See LG Group; *Int'l*, pg. 779
GOLDSTAR EUROPE GMBH—See LG Group; *Int'l*, pg. 779
GOLDSTAR FRANCE S.A.R.L.—See LG Group; *Int'l*, pg. 779
GOLDSTAR IBERNA ITALY S.R.L.—See LG Group; *Int'l*, pg. 779
GOLDSTAR INSTRUMENT & ELECTRIC CO. LTD.—See LG Group; *Int'l*, pg. 779
GOLDSTAR JAPAN—See LG Group; *Int'l*, pg. 779
GOLDSTAR JAPAN C/S—See LG Group; *Int'l*, pg. 779
GOLDSTAR MAGYAR KFT—See LG Group; *Int'l*, pg. 779
GOLDSTAR MEXICANA, S.A. DE C.V.—See LG Group; *Int'l*, pg. 779
GOLDSTAR MEXICO S.A. DE C.V.—See LG Group; *Int'l*, pg. 779
GOLDSTAR MIDDLE EAST CO., LTD.—See LG Group; *Int'l*, pg. 779
GOLDSTAR MITR CO. LTD.—See LG Group; *Int'l*, pg. 779
GOLDSTAR OF AMERICA, INC.—See LG Group; *Int'l*, pg. 779
GOLDSTAR PANAMA S.A.—See LG Group; *Int'l*, pg. 779
GOLDSTAR PHILS. SALES CO., LTD.—See LG Group; *Int'l*, pg. 779
GOLDSTAR PRECISION INDUSTRIES LTD.—See LG Group; *Int'l*, pg. 779
GOLDSTAR SEMICONDUCTOR LTD.—See LG Group; *Int'l*, pg. 779
GOLDSTAR TELECOMMUNICATIONS CO. LTD.—See LG Group; *Int'l*, pg. 779
GOLDSTAR UNITED KINGDOM—See LG Group; *Int'l*, pg. 779
GOLDSTRIKE HOTEL—See Circus Circus - Las Vegas; *U.S. Public*, pg. 375
GOLDSTRIKE MINE—See Barrick Gold Corporation; *Int'l*, pg. 169
GOLDWAY LTD.—See The Chase Manhattan Corporation; *U.S. Public*, pg. 341
GOLDWELL A.G.—See Kao Corporation; *Int'l*, pg. 717
GOLDWELL COSMETICS (USA) INC.—See Kao Corporation; *Int'l*, pg. 717
GOLDWIN INC.—See Orkla A.S.A.; *Int'l*, pg. 1010
THE SAMUEL GOLDWYN COMPANY; *U.S. Private*, pg. 577
GOLF DE LA LARGUR MANAGEMENT AG—See Bayerische Vereinsbank Group; *Int'l*, pg. 181
GOLF DIGEST INFORMATION SYSTEMS, INC.—See The New York Times Company; *U.S. Public*, pg. 1174
GOLF FOR WOMEN—See Meredith Corporation; *U.S. Public*, pg. 1094
GOLF HOST RESORTS, INC.—See Starwood Capital Group LLC; *U.S. Private*, pg. 1036

Company Index

GOLF HOSTS, INC.—See Starwood Capital Group LLC; U.S. Private, pg. 1036
GOLF MAGAZINE—See The Times Mirror Company; U.S. Public, pg. 1617
GOLF SHOP OPERATIONS—See The New York Times Company; U.S. Public, pg. 1174
GOLF SOPHISTICATES—See Maruzen Company Limited; Int'l, pg. 846
GOLF WORLD—See The New York Times Company; U.S. Public, pg. 1174
GOLFKARTONFABRIEK VAN DAM B.V.—See N.V. Koninklijke KNP BT; Int'l, pg. 756
GOLIN/HARRIS COMMUNICATIONS, INC.—See Shandwick International Plc; Int'l, pg. 1226
GOLIN/HARRIS TECHNOLOGIES—See Shandwick International Plc; Int'l, pg. 1227
LEON SHAFFER GOLNICK ADVERTISING, INC.; U.S. Private, pg. 463
GOLUB & CO.; U.S. Private, pg. 463
GOLUB CORPORATION; U.S. Private, pg. 463
GOLUB SERVICE STATIONS, INC.—See Golub Corporation; U.S. Private, pg. 463
GOMALA IMTECH NV—See Internatio-Muller N.V.; Int'l, pg. 681
AB GÖMAN-PRODUKTER—See KF/Konsum Coop Group; Int'l, pg. 718
GOMAR MANUFACTURING CO., INC.—See AlliedSignal Inc.; U.S. Public, pg. 51
GOMIYA USA, INC.—See G-Net Corporation; Int'l, pg. 531
GONNELLA BAKING CO.; U.S. Private, pg. 463
GONZALEZ Y GONZALEZ—See Ark Restaurants Corp.; U.S. Public, pg. 130
GOOCH FOODS, INC.—See Archer Daniels Midland Company (ADM); U.S. Public, pg. 128
GOOCH PACKING CO., INC.—See Randalls Food Markets, Inc.; U.S. Private, pg. 909
GOOD COMPANIES; U.S. Private, pg. 463
GOOD FOOD MAGAZINE—See The News Corporation Limited; Int'l, pg. 925
THE GOOD GUYS, INC.; U.S. Public, pg. 750
GOOD HOUSEKEEPING—See The Hearst Corporation; U.S. Private, pg. 517
GOOD HUMOR/BREYERS ICE CREAM—See Unilever Plc; Int'l, pg. 1435
SHELDON GOOD & CO.; U.S. Private, pg. 463
SHELDON GOOD & COMPANY-COLORADO—See Sheldon Good & Company; U.S. Private, pg. 464
GOOD TIME LTD.—See Kosugi Sangyo Co., Ltd.; Int'l, pg. 759
GOODALL RUBBER COMPANY—See Trelleborg AB; Int'l, pg. 1423
GOODALL TRANSPORTATION CO.—See Trelleborg AB; Int'l, pg. 1423
GOODBODY STOCKBROKERS—See Allied Irish Banks, p.l.c.; Int'l, pg. 64
GOODBY, SILVERSTEIN & PARTNERS—See Omnicom Group Inc.; U.S. Public, pg. 1224
GOODHEART-WILLCOX PUBLISHER; U.S. Private, pg. 464
GOODKIND & O'DEA, INC.—See Dewberry & Davis; U.S. Private, pg. 329
GOODLASS NEROLAC PAINTS LTD.—See Kansai Paint Co., Ltd.; Int'l, pg. 723
A. GOODMAN & SONS, INC.—See Borden, Inc.; U.S. Private, pg. 158
GOODMAN EQUIPMENT CORP.; U.S. Private, pg. 464
GOODMAN FIELDER ASIA HOLDINGS LTD.—See Goodman Fielder Limited; Int'l, pg. 555
GOODMAN FIELDER LIMITED; Int'l, pg. 555
GOODMAN FIELDER MILLING & BAKING GROUP—See Goodman Fielder Limited; Int'l, pg. 555
GOODMAN FIELDER MILLS LTD.—See Goodman Fielder Limited; Int'l, pg. 555
GOODMAN FIELDER MILLS (NZ) LTD.—See Goodman Fielder Limited; Int'l, pg. 556
GOODMAN FIELDER NEW ZEALAND—See Goodman Fielder Limited; Int'l, pg. 555
GOODMAN KNITTING COMPANY—See Kellwood Company; U.S. Private, pg. 948
GOODMAN MANUFACTURING; U.S. Private, pg. 464
GOODMANS, INC.; U.S. Private, pg. 464
GOODMARK FOODS, INC.; U.S. Public, pg. 751
GOODPASTURE, INC.; U.S. Private, pg. 464
B.F. GOODRICH AEROSPACE—See The B.F. Goodrich Company; U.S. Public, pg. 751
BF GOODRICH AVIONIC SYSTEMS, INC.—See The B.F. Goodrich Company; U.S. Public, pg. 751
B.F. GOODRICH CHEMICAL EUROPE—See The B.F. Goodrich Company; U.S. Public, pg. 752
THE B.F. GOODRICH COMPANY; U.S. Public, pg. 751
B.F. GOODRICH COMPONENT SERVICES, LTD.—See The B.F. Goodrich Company; U.S. Public, pg. 752
BF GOODRICH FLIGHT SYSTEMS, INC.—See The B.F. Goodrich Company; U.S. Public, pg. 752
GOODRING INTERNATIONAL INC.—See Sinochem International Petroleum Co. Ltd.; Int'l, pg. 1255
GOODRINGTON CO., LTD.—See Citizen Watch Company, Ltd.; Int'l, pg. 295
GOODTIMES ENTERTAINMENT CO.; U.S. Private, pg. 464
GOODWAY TECHNOLOGIES CORPORATION; U.S. Private, pg. 464
GOODWILL INDUSTRIES INTERNATIONAL; U.S. Private, pg. 464
GOODWIN WEAVERS, INC.—See Crown Crafts, Inc.; U.S. Public, pg. 465
GOODY CANADA LIMITED—See Newell Co.; U.S. Public, pg. 1177
GOODY PRODUCTS, INC.—See Newell Co.; U.S. Public, pg. 1177
GOODYEAR DE CHILE S.A./C.—See The Goodyear Tire & Rubber Company; U.S. Public, pg. 753
GOODYEAR DE COLOMBIA S.A.—See The Goodyear Tire & Rubber Company; U.S. Public, pg. 753

GOODYEAR HELLAS S.A.I.C.—See The Goodyear Tire & Rubber Company; U.S. Public, pg. 753
GOODYEAR-INDIA LTD.—See The Goodyear Tire & Rubber Company; U.S. Public, pg. 753
P.T. GOODYEAR INDONESIA—See The Goodyear Tire & Rubber Company; U.S. Public, pg. 753
GOODYEAR ITALIANA S.P.A.—See The Goodyear Tire & Rubber Company; U.S. Public, pg. 753
GOODYEAR JAMAICA LIMITED—See The Goodyear Tire & Rubber Company; U.S. Public, pg. 753
GOODYEAR LASTIKLERI TURK ANONIM SIRKETI—See The Goodyear Tire & Rubber Company; U.S. Public, pg. 753
GOODYEAR-LUXEMBOURG—See The Goodyear Tire & Rubber Company; U.S. Public, pg. 753
GOODYEAR MALAYSIA BERHAD—See The Goodyear Tire & Rubber Company; U.S. Public, pg. 753
GOODYEAR MAROC S.A.—See The Goodyear Tire & Rubber Company; U.S. Public, pg. 753
GOODYEAR PHILIPPINES INC.—See The Goodyear Tire & Rubber Company; U.S. Public, pg. 753
GOODYEAR RUBBER PLANTATIONS—See The Goodyear Tire & Rubber Company; U.S. Public, pg. 753
GOODYEAR S.A.—See The Goodyear Tire & Rubber Company; U.S. Public, pg. 753
GOODYEAR (SWITZERLAND) S.A.—See The Goodyear Tire & Rubber Company; U.S. Public, pg. 753
GOODYEAR TAIWAN LIMITED—See The Goodyear Tire & Rubber Company; U.S. Public, pg. 753
GOODYEAR-THAILAND LTD.—See The Goodyear Tire & Rubber Company; U.S. Public, pg. 753
THE GOODYEAR TIRE & RUBBER COMPANY; U.S. Public, pg. 752
GOODY'S FAMILY CLOTHING, INC.; U.S. Public, pg. 753
J.E. GOOLD & COMPANY—See Bindley Western Industries, Inc.; U.S. Public, pg. 229
GOONYELLA MINE—See The Broken Hill Proprietary Company Limited; Int'l, pg. 223
GORCY S.A.—See Danone Group; Int'l, pg. 380
GORDON & FERGUSON OF DELAWARE, INC.; U.S. Private, pg. 465
GORDON BROTHERS PARTNERS INC.; U.S. Private, pg. 465
GORDON FOOD SERVICE INC.; U.S. Private, pg. 465
GORDON FRASER GALLERY—See Hallmark Cards, Inc.; U.S. Private, pg. 496
KENNETH GORDON IAG, INC.—See Tom James Company; U.S. Private, pg. 581
GORDON PUBLICATIONS, INC.—See Reed Elsevier plc; Int'l, pg. 1096
GORDON'S INC.—See Furniture Brands International Inc.; U.S. Public, pg. 688
GORDY'S, INC.; U.S. Private, pg. 465
W.L. GORE & ASSOCIATES, INC.; U.S. Private, pg. 465
GORES TECHNOLOGY GROUP; U.S. Private, pg. 465
GORGES/QUIK-TO-FIX FOODS; U.S. Private, pg. 465
GORICON METALLURGICAL SERVICES LTD.—See Veba AG; Int'l, pg. 1459
THE GORMAN-RUPP COMPANY; U.S. Public, pg. 754
GORMAN-RUPP INDUSTRIES DIV.—See The Gorman-Rupp Company; U.S. Public, pg. 754
THE GORMAN-RUPP INTERNATIONAL CO.—See The Gorman-Rupp Company; U.S. Public, pg. 754
GORMAN-RUPP OF CANADA LTD.—See The Gorman-Rupp Company; U.S. Public, pg. 754
GORO NICKEL S.A.—See Inco Limited; Int'l, pg. 672
THE GORTON GROUP—See Unilever Plc; Int'l, pg. 1434
GORUD—See Assa Abloy AB; Int'l, pg. 18
GORVI S.A.—See Solvay S.A.; Int'l, pg. 1278
GOSCHEN HOPPEN - HOME MUTUAL INSURANCE CO.—See Old Guard Insurance Group; U.S. Public, pg. 1216
GOSHEN COUNTY ABSTRACT & TITLE—See The First American Financial Corporation; U.S. Public, pg. 626
GOSHEN RUBBER COMPANY, INC.; U.S. Private, pg. 465
GOSHEN RUBBER OF CANADA LTD.—See Goshen Rubber Co., Inc.; U.S. Private, pg. 465
GOSHEN TELEPHONE COMPANY, INC.—See Telephone and Data Systems, Inc.; U.S. Public, pg. 1571
GOSIGER INC.; U.S. Private, pg. 466
GOSNELL BUILDERS—See Pointe Group Ltd.; U.S. Private, pg. 873
GOSS GRAPHIC SYSTEMS; U.S. Private, pg. 466
GOSS GRAPHIC SYSTEMS INC.—See Goss Graphic Systems; U.S. Private, pg. 466
GOSS GRAPHIC SYSTEMS-JAPAN CORPORATION—See Goss Graphic Systems; U.S. Private, pg. 466
GOSS GRAPHIC SYSTEMS LTD.—See Goss Graphic Systems; U.S. Private, pg. 466
AB GOSTA BACKSTROM—See Telefonaktiebolaget LM Ericsson; Int'l, pg. 1363
GOTAVERKEN ARENDAL AB—See Celsius AB; Int'l, pg. 277
GOTAVERKEN ARENDAL INC.—See Celsius AB; Int'l, pg. 278
GOTAVERKEN CITYVARVET AB—See Celsius AB; Int'l, pg. 277
GOTAVERKEN ENERGY AB—See Kvaerner a.s.a.; Int'l, pg. 771
GOTAVERKEN ENERGY DO BRASIL—See Kvaerner a.s.a.; Int'l, pg. 771
GOTAVERKEN ENERGY SYSTEMS INC.—See Kvaerner a.s.a.; Int'l, pg. 770
GOTAVERKEN ENERGY SYSTEMS LTD.—See Kvaerner a.s.a.; Int'l, pg. 771
GOTAVERKEN MILJO AB—See Celsius AB; Int'l, pg. 276
GOTAVERKEN MOTOR AB—See Celsius AB; Int'l, pg. 276
GOTAVERKEN OY—See Kvaerner a.s.a.; Int'l, pg. 771
GOTEK GMBH—See Metallgesellschaft AG; Int'l, pg. 861
GOTHAM INCORPORATED—See The Lowe Group; U.S. Private, pg. 677
GOTHIA PULP & PAPER AB—See Axel Johnson AB; Int'l, pg. 708
GOTHIA-WELLMABOLAGEN AB—See Axel Johnson AB; Int'l, pg. 708

GOTLANDS ENERGIVERK AB—See Vattenfall AB; Int'l, pg. 1453
GOTSU MILL—See Nippon Paper Industries Company Limited; Int'l, pg. 938
GOTTLIEB TESCH GMBH BAUUNTERNEHMUNG—See Bilfinger + Berger Bauaktiengesellschaft; Int'l, pg. 195
GOTTLIEB TESCH STRASSEN-UND LEITUNGSBAU GMBH—See Bilfinger + Berger Bauaktiengesellschaft; Int'l, pg. 195
GOTTSCHALKS INC.; U.S. Public, pg. 754
GOUGLER INDUSTRIES, INC.; U.S. Private, pg. 466
GOULD ELECTRONICS (CANADA) LTD., SHAWMUT DIV.—See Thermo Electron Corporation; U.S. Public, pg. 1592
GOULD ELECTRONICS GMBH FOIL DIVISION—See Thermo Electron Corporation; U.S. Public, pg. 1592
GOULD ELECTRONICS INC.—See Thermo Electron Corporation; U.S. Public, pg. 1592
GOULD ELECTRONICS INC., FIBER OPTICS—See Thermo Electron Corporation; U.S. Public, pg. 1592
GOULD ELECTRONICS INC., FOIL DIVISION—See Thermo Electron Corporation; U.S. Public, pg. 1592
GOULD ELECTRONICS INC., SHAWMUT CIRCUIT PROTECTION DIVISION—See Thermo Electron Corporation; U.S. Public, pg. 1592
GOULD ELECTRONICS LTD., CIRCUIT PROTECTION—See Thermo Electron Corporation; U.S. Public, pg. 1592
GOULD ELECTRONICS LTD., FOIL DIV.—See Thermo Electron Corporation; U.S. Public, pg. 1592
GOULD INSTRUMENT SYSTEMS, INC.—See Thermo Electron Corporation; U.S. Public, pg. 1592
GOULD INSTRUMENT SYSTEMS, LTD.—See Thermo Electron Corporation; U.S. Public, pg. 1592
GOULD INSTRUMENT SYSTEMS, S.A.—See Thermo Electron Corporation; U.S. Public, pg. 1592
GOULD INVESTORS, L.P.; U.S. Private, pg. 466
GOULD MIDWEST, INC.—See Stephen Gould Paper Co., Inc.; U.S. Private, pg. 467
GOULD PACKAGING, INC.; U.S. Private, pg. 466
GOULD PAPER CORPORATION -BALTIMORE/WASHINGTON—See Gould Paper Corporation; U.S. Private, pg. 467
GOULD PAPER CORPORATION; U.S. Private, pg. 466
GOULD PAPER CORPORATION-NJ—See Gould Paper Corporation; U.S. Private, pg. 466
GOULD PAPER CORPORATION OF NEW YORK, INC.—See Stephen Gould Paper Co., Inc.; U.S. Private, pg. 467
GOULD PAPER CORPORATION-MID ATLANTIC—See Gould Paper Corporation; U.S. Private, pg. 467
GOULD PAPER INC/MIDHUDSON DIV.—See Stephen Gould Paper Co., Inc.; U.S. Private, pg. 467
GOULD PAPER OF FLORIDA, INC.—See Stephen Gould Paper Co., Inc.; U.S. Private, pg. 467
GOULD SOUTHERN—See Stephen Gould Paper Co., Inc.; U.S. Private, pg. 467
STEPHEN GOULD, INC./LA—See Stephen Gould Paper Co., Inc.; U.S. Private, pg. 467
STEPHEN GOULD OF ALABAMA, INC.—See Stephen Gould Paper Co., Inc.; U.S. Private, pg. 467
STEPHEN GOULD OF ARIZONA, INC.—See Stephen Gould Paper Co., Inc.; U.S. Private, pg. 467
STEPHEN GOULD OF CALIFORNIA—See Stephen Gould Paper Co., Inc.; U.S. Private, pg. 467
STEPHEN GOULD OF CAROLINA, INC.—See Stephen Gould Paper Co., Inc.; U.S. Private, pg. 467
STEPHEN GOULD OF CAROLINA, INC./CHARLOTTE DIV.—See Stephen Gould Paper Co., Inc.; U.S. Private, pg. 467
STEPHEN GOULD OF COLORADO, INC.—See Stephen Gould Paper Co., Inc.; U.S. Private, pg. 467
STEPHEN GOULD OF CONNECTICUT CORP.—See Stephen Gould Paper Co., Inc.; U.S. Private, pg. 467
STEPHEN GOULD OF ILLINOIS, INC.—See Stephen Gould Paper Co., Inc.; U.S. Private, pg. 467
STEPHEN GOULD OF INDIANA, INC.—See Stephen Gould Paper Co., Inc.; U.S. Private, pg. 467
STEPHEN GOULD OF MARYLAND, INC.—See Stephen Gould Paper Co., Inc.; U.S. Private, pg. 467
STEPHEN GOULD OF MICHIGAN, INC.—See Stephen Gould Paper Co., Inc.; U.S. Private, pg. 467
STEPHEN GOULD OF NEW ENGLAND, INC.—See Stephen Gould Paper Co., Inc.; U.S. Private, pg. 467
STEPHEN GOULD OF OHIO, CORP.—See Stephen Gould Paper Co., Inc.; U.S. Private, pg. 467
STEPHEN GOULD OF PENNSYLVANIA CORP.—See Stephen Gould Paper Co., Inc.; U.S. Private, pg. 467
STEPHEN GOULD OF PUERTO RICO, INC.—See Stephen Gould Paper Co., Inc.; U.S. Private, pg. 468
STEPHEN GOULD OF TENNESSEE, INC.—See Stephen Gould Paper Co., Inc.; U.S. Private, pg. 468
STEPHEN GOULD OF TEXAS, INC.—See Stephen Gould Paper Co., Inc.; U.S. Private, pg. 468
STEPHEN GOULD PAPER CO., INC.; U.S. Private, pg. 467
GOULD'S PAPER HOUSE, INC.—See Gould Paper Corporation; U.S. Private, pg. 467
GOULDS PUMPS CANADA, INC.—See ITT Industries, Inc.; U.S. Public, pg. 861
GOULDS PUMPS EUROPE B.V.—See ITT Industries, Inc.; U.S. Public, pg. 861
GOULDS PUMPS, INCORPORATED—See ITT Industries, Inc.; U.S. Public, pg. 860
GOULDS PUMPS (PHIL.) INC.—See ITT Industries, Inc.; U.S. Public, pg. 861
GOULDS PUMPS SINGAPORE PTE. LTD.—See ITT Industries, Inc.; U.S. Public, pg. 861
GOULDS PUMPS U.K. LTD.—See ITT Industries, Inc.; U.S. Public, pg. 861
GOURMET—See Advance Publications Inc.; U.S. Private, pg. 20
GOURMET FOODS, INC.—See Koninklijke BolsWessanen nv; Int'l, pg. 752

Company Index

GOURMET MENU-SERVICE GMBH & CO KG—See Maresi Markenartikelvertrieb Aktiengesellschaft; *Int'l*, pg. 842
GOURMET POPPING CORN CO.—See The Scoular Company; *U.S. Private*, pg. 977
GOVERNAIR CORPORATION—See Nortek, Inc.; *U.S. Public*, pg. 1193
GOVERNALE CO., INC.—See Burnham; *U.S. Public*, pg. 270
GOVERNING MAGAZINE—See The Times Publishing Co.; *U.S. Private*, pg. 1088
GOVERNMENT AEROSPACE SYSTEMS DIVISION-ORLANDO OPERATIONS—See Harris Corporation; *U.S. Public*, pg. 792
GOVERNMENT COMMUNICATIONS SYSTEMS DIVISION—See California Microwave, Inc.; *U.S. Public*, pg. 293
GOVERNMENT ELECTRONICS DIV.—See California Microwave, Inc.; *U.S. Public*, pg. 293
GOVERNMENT EMPLOYEES FINANCIAL CORPORATION—See Berkshire Hathaway Inc.; *U.S. Public*, pg. 220
GOVERNMENT EMPLOYEES INSURANCE CO. (GEICO)—See Berkshire Hathaway Inc.; *U.S. Public*, pg. 220
GOVERNMENT FORMS & SYSTEMS, INC.—See National Fiberstock Corporation; *U.S. Private*, pg. 782
GOVERNOR'S SQUARE, INC.—See The Rouse Company; *U.S. Public*, pg. 1408
GOWAN, INC.—See EMCOR Group, Inc.; *U.S. Public*, pg. 572
GOWLAND/ADD—See Young & Rubicam; *U.S. Private*, pg. 1200
GOWLAND PUBLICIDAD S.A.—See True North Diversified Companies; *U.S. Public*, pg. 1642
GOYA FOODS, INC.; *U.S. Private*, pg. 468
GOYA FOODS OF FLORIDA—See Goya Foods, Inc.; *U.S. Private*, pg. 468
GOYEN CONTROLS DIVISION—See Southcorp Holdings Ltd.; *Int'l*, pg. 1287
GRA-GAR INC.—See Werner Enterprises, Inc.; *U.S. Public*, pg. 1755
GRABER-ROGG, INC.; *U.S. Private*, pg. 468
GRABNER PACIFIC CO.—See Bradner Central Company; *U.S. Private*, pg. 165
GRABOWSKY & POORT BV—See Heidemij N.V.; *Int'l*, pg. 607
GRABOWSKY & POORT CARIBBEAN NV—See Heidemij N.V.; *Int'l*, pg. 607
GRABOWSKY & POORT ETA INGENIEURS—See Heidemij N.V.; *Int'l*, pg. 607
GRABOWSKY & POORT HAMELEERS BV—See Heidemij N.V.; *Int'l*, pg. 607
GRABOWSKY & POORT INTERNATIONAL CONSULTANTS—See Heidemij N.V.; *Int'l*, pg. 607
GRABOWSKY & POORT SCHIEBROECK-STRUIK BV—See Heidemij N.V.; *Int'l*, pg. 607
GRABOWSKY & POORT ZUID BV—See Heidemij N.V.; *Int'l*, pg. 607
GRACE A-B INC.—See W.R. Grace & Co.; *U.S. Public*, pg. 755
GRACE & ROTHSCHILD; *U.S. Private*, pg. 468
GRACE ARGENTINA S.A.—See W.R. Grace & Co.; *U.S. Public*, pg. 755
GRACE BROADCASTING LIMITED PARTNERSHIP—See Cigna Corp.; *U.S. Public*, pg. 362
GRACE B.V.—See W.R. Grace & Co.; *U.S. Public*, pg. 755
GRACE CENTRAL AMERICA—See W.R. Grace & Co.; *U.S. Public*, pg. 755
GRACE CHEMICAL COMPANY OF CUBA—See W.R. Grace & Co.; *U.S. Public*, pg. 755
GRACE CHINA LTD.—See W.R. Grace & Co.; *U.S. Public*, pg. 755
GRACE COCOA/AMBROSIA CHOCOLATE—See Archer Daniels Midland Company (ADM); *U.S. Public*, pg. 128
GRACE COCOA/MERCKENS—See Archer Daniels Midland Company (ADM); *U.S. Public*, pg. 128
GRACE COLOMBIA S.A.—See W.R. Grace & Co.; *U.S. Public*, pg. 755
GRACE COMMUNICATIONS, INC.—See W.R. Grace & Co.; *U.S. Public*, pg. 755
GRACE CONSTRUCTION PRODUCTS—See W.R. Grace & Co.; *U.S. Public*, pg. 755
GRACE DAVISON—See W.R. Grace & Co.; *U.S. Public*, pg. 755
W.M. GRACE DEVELOPMENT; *U.S. Private*, pg. 468
GRACE ENVIRONMENTAL INC.—See W.R. Grace & Co.; *U.S. Public*, pg. 755
GRACE ESPECIALIDADES QUIMICOS E PLASTICAS—See W.R. Grace & Co.; *U.S. Public*, pg. 755
GRACE EXPRESS—See Brambles Industries Limited; *Int'l*, pg. 211
GRACE G.M.B.H.—See W.R. Grace & Co.; *U.S. Public*, pg. 755
GRACE H-G INC.—See W.R. Grace & Co.; *U.S. Public*, pg. 755
GRACE HELLAS INDUSTRIAL & COMMERCIAL L.L.C.—See W.R. Grace & Co.; *U.S. Public*, pg. 756
GRACE HOTEL SERVICES CORP.—See W.R. Grace & Co.; *U.S. Public*, pg. 755
GRACE ITALIANA S.P.A.—See W.R. Grace & Co.; *U.S. Public*, pg. 756
GRACE JAPAN K.K.—See W.R. Grace & Co.; *U.S. Public*, pg. 756
GRACE KOREA, INC.—See W.R. Grace & Co.; *U.S. Public*, pg. 756
GRACE LOGISTICS SERVICES—See W.R. Grace & Co.; *U.S. Public*, pg. 755
GRACE NANBU LTD.—See Kosugi Sangyo Co., Ltd.; *Int'l*, pg. 759
GRACE PACKAGING—See W.R. Grace & Co.; *U.S. Public*, pg. 755
GRACE PAR CORPORATION—See W.R. Grace & Co.; *U.S. Public*, pg. 755
GRACE PORTUGUESA LDA.—See W.R. Grace & Co.; *U.S. Public*, pg. 756

GRACE QUIMICA CIA. LTDA.—See W.R. Grace & Co.; *U.S. Public*, pg. 756
GRACE REMOVALS—See Brambles Industries Limited; *Int'l*, pg. 211
GRACE, S.A.—See W.R. Grace & Co.; *U.S. Public*, pg. 756
GRACE S.A.—See W.R. Grace & Co.; *U.S. Public*, pg. 756
GRACE SILICA N.V.—See W.R. Grace & Co.; *U.S. Public*, pg. 756
GRACE (SWEDEN) AB—See W.R. Grace & Co.; *U.S. Public*, pg. 756
GRACE TAIWAN, INC.—See W.R. Grace & Co.; *U.S. Public*, pg. 756
GRACE VENEZUELA S.A.—See W.R. Grace & Co.; *U.S. Public*, pg. 756
GRACE (WA) PTY. LIMITED—See Brambles Industries Limited; *Int'l*, pg. 211
GRACE WASHINGTON INC.—See W.R. Grace & Co.; *U.S. Public*, pg. 755
W.R. GRACE AB—See W.R. Grace & Co.; *U.S. Public*, pg. 755
W.R. GRACE & CO.; *U.S. Public*, pg. 754
W.R. GRACE & CO.-CONN.—See W.R. Grace & Co.; *U.S. Public*, pg. 755
W.R. GRACE & CO. OF CANADA LTD., GRACE CONSTRUCTION PRODUCTS—See W.R. Grace & Co.; *U.S. Public*, pg. 755
W.R. GRACE A/S—See W.R. Grace & Co.; *U.S. Public*, pg. 755
W.R. GRACE AUSTRALIA LTD.—See W.R. Grace & Co.; *U.S. Public*, pg. 755
W.R. GRACE CAPITAL—See W.R. Grace & Co.; *U.S. Public*, pg. 755
W.R. GRACE (HONG KONG) LTD.—See W.R. Grace & Co.; *U.S. Public*, pg. 756
W.R. GRACE LAND CORPORATION—See W.R. Grace & Co.; *U.S. Public*, pg. 755
W.R. GRACE LTD.—See W.R. Grace & Co.; *U.S. Public*, pg. 756
W.R. GRACE (MALAYSIA) SDN. BHD.—See W.R. Grace & Co.; *U.S. Public*, pg. 756
W.R. GRACE (N.Z.) LTD.—See W.R. Grace & Co.; *U.S. Public*, pg. 756
W.R. GRACE OY—See W.R. Grace & Co.; *U.S. Public*, pg. 756
W.R. GRACE (PHILIPPINES) INC.—See W.R. Grace & Co.; *U.S. Public*, pg. 756
W.R. GRACE (SINGAPORE) PTE. LTD.—See W.R. Grace & Co.; *U.S. Public*, pg. 756
W.R. GRACE (THAILAND) LTD.—See W.R. Grace & Co.; *U.S. Public*, pg. 756
GRACO CANADA INC.—See Graco Inc.; *U.S. Public*, pg. 757
GRACO COMMUNICATIONS CENTER—See Graco Inc.; *U.S. Public*, pg. 757
GRACO CONTRACTOR EQUIPMENT DIV.—See Graco Inc.; *U.S. Public*, pg. 757
GRACO GMBH—See Graco Inc.; *U.S. Public*, pg. 757
GRACO (HK) LIMITED—See Graco Inc.; *U.S. Public*, pg. 757
GRACO HONG KONG LIMITED (TAIWAN LIAISON OFFICE)—See Graco Inc.; *U.S. Public*, pg. 757
GRACO HONG KONG LTD.—See Graco Inc.; *U.S. Public*, pg. 757
GRACO INC.; *U.S. Public*, pg. 756
GRACO INDUSTRIAL/AUTOMOTIVE EQUIPMENT DIVISION—See Graco Inc.; *U.S. Public*, pg. 757
GRACO K.K.—See Graco Inc.; *U.S. Public*, pg. 757
GRACO KOREA—See Graco Inc.; *U.S. Public*, pg. 757
GRACO NORGE A.S.—See Graco Inc.; *U.S. Public*, pg. 757
GRACO N.V.—See Graco Inc.; *U.S. Public*, pg. 757
GRACO S.A.—See Graco Inc.; *U.S. Public*, pg. 757
GRACO S.A. SUCCURSALE ESPAGNOLE—See Graco Inc.; *U.S. Public*, pg. 757
GRACO SOUTHEAST REGIONAL SALES & DISTRIBUTION CENTER—See Graco Inc.; *U.S. Public*, pg. 757
GRACO S.R.L.—See Graco Inc.; *U.S. Public*, pg. 757
GRACO UK LIMITED—See Graco Inc.; *U.S. Public*, pg. 757
GRACO WESTERN REGIONAL SALES & DISTRIBUTION CENTER—See Graco Inc.; *U.S. Public*, pg. 757
GRADCO (JAPAN), LTD.—See Gradco Systems, Inc.; *U.S. Public*, pg. 757
GRADCO SYSTEMS, INC.; *U.S. Public*, pg. 757
GRADCO (USA), INC.—See Gradco Systems, Inc.; *U.S. Public*, pg. 757
GRADISON DIVISION—See McDonald & Company Investments, Inc.; *U.S. Public*, pg. 1068
GRADMANN & HOLLER & GMBH—See Marsh & McLennan Companies, Inc.; *U.S. Public*, pg. 1049
GRAFFITI/DMB&B—See DMB&B Communications; *U.S. Private*, pg. 304
GRAFFITI OFFICE SUPPLIERS AND PAPER MARKETING LTD.—See American Israeli Paper Mills Ltd.; *Int'l*, pg. 75
GRAFIBA SOCIEDAD ANONIMA—See Reynolds Metals Company; *U.S. Public*, pg. 1387
GRAFICAS MONTE ALBAN, S.A.—See Quebecor Inc.; *Int'l*, pg. 1078
GRAFISKT PAPER & NORDEN AB—See Metsa-Serla Corporation; *Int'l*, pg. 864
GRAFITO SUPERIOR SA—See Superior Graphite Co.; *U.S. Private*, pg. 1055
GRAFO COLLOIDS DIVISION—See Fuchs Petrolub AG Oel + Chemie; *Int'l*, pg. 518
GRAFTELE—See Gores Technology Group; *U.S. Private*, pg. 465
GRAFTON FRASER INC.; *Int'l*, pg. 556
GRAHAM—See Danfoss A/S; *Int'l*, pg. 377
GRAHAM BUILDERS MERCHANTS LIMITED—See BTR plc; *Int'l*, pg. 124
GRAHAM CONSTRUCTION CORP.—See Graham Group, Inc.; *U.S. Private*, pg. 468
GRAHAM CORPORATION; *U.S. Public*, pg. 757

GRAHAM-FIELD HEALTH PRODUCTS, INC.; *U.S. Public*, pg. 757
GRAHAM GREGORY BOZELL, INC.—See True North Diversified Companies; *U.S. Public*, pg. 1642
GRAHAM GROUP, INC.; *U.S. Private*, pg. 468
GRAHAM MANUFACTURING CO.—See Assa Abloy AB; *Int'l*, pg. 18
GRAHAM MANUFACTURING CO., INC.—See Graham Corporation; *U.S. Public*, pg. 757
GRAHAM MILLER GROUP LIMITED—See Crawford & Company; *U.S. Public*, pg. 458
GRAHAM PAINT AND VARNISH COMPANY; *U.S. Private*, pg. 468
GRAHAM PRECISION PUMPS LTD.—See Graham Corporation; *U.S. Public*, pg. 757
GRAHAM TRANSMISSIONS INC/GRAHAM GEAR SYSTEMS, INC.—See Danfoss A/S; *Int'l*, pg. 377
GRAHAM & TROTMAN—See Wolters Kluwer N.V.; *Int'l*, pg. 1513
GRAHAM VACUUM & HEAT TRANSFER LTD.—See Graham Corporation; *U.S. Public*, pg. 757
GRAIN D'OR—See Northern Foods plc; *Int'l*, pg. 968
GRAIN FLOUR MILLING CO.—See ConAgra, Inc.; *U.S. Public*, pg. 428
GRAIN PROCESSING CORP.—See Varied Investments, Inc.; *U.S. Private*, pg. 1134
GRAIN SYSTEMS DIVISION—See Butler Manufacturing Company; *U.S. Public*, pg. 271
GRAINES FRANCO-SUEDOISES S.A.—See Novartis AG; *Int'l*, pg. 982
GRAINGER—See W.W. Grainger, Inc.; *U.S. Public*, pg. 758
W.W. GRAINGER, INC.; *U.S. Public*, pg. 758
GRAKO OY—See American Greetings Corporation; *U.S. Public*, pg. 78
GRALEX S.A.—See Heidelberger Zement A.G.; *Int'l*, pg. 605
GRALI, SERVICIOS CONTABLES Y ADMINISTRATIVOS, S.A.—See Assicurazioni Generali S.p.A.; *Int'l*, pg. 91
GRAMERCY ASSETS CORPORATION—See Consolidated Edison Company of New York, Inc.; *U.S. Public*, pg. 435
GRAMERCY PICTURES; *U.S. Private*, pg. 468
GRAMEX CORPORATION; *U.S. Private*, pg. 468
GRAMMOPHON SPEZIALHAUS SCHALLPLATTEN-EINZELHANDELS-GESELLSCHAFT MBH—See Philips Electronics N.V.; *Int'l*, pg. 1052
GRAN AUTO EXPRESS, SA DE C.V.—See Volkswagen AG; *Int'l*, pg. 1475
GRAN CENTRAL CORPORATION—See St. Joe Corp.; *U.S. Public*, pg. 1427
GRAN CIRCULO DE MADRID, S.A.—See Caja de Madrid Group; *Int'l*, pg. 251
GRAN DISTRIBUCION AVANZADA ESPANOLA S.A.—See Otto Versand (GmbH & Co.); *Int'l*, pg. 1015
GRAN INDUSTRIA DE NEUMATICOS CENTROAMERICANA, S.A.—See The Goodyear Tire & Rubber Company; *U.S. Public*, pg. 753
GRANADA GROUP PLC.; *Int'l*, pg. 556
GRANADA REALTY SERVICES, INC.—See California State Bank; *U.S. Public*, pg. 294
GRANCOL, ASESORAMIENTO Y SERVICIOS LTDA.—See Cigna Corp.; *U.S. Public*, pg. 364
GRAND & TOY LIMITED—See Boise Cascade Corporation; *U.S. Public*, pg. 243
GRAND BANKS YACHTS, LTD.—See GB Holdings; *Int'l*, pg. 531
GRAND BANKS YACHTS SDN. BHD.—See GB Holdings; *Int'l*, pg. 531
GRAND CASINOS, INC.; *U.S. Public*, pg. 758
GRAND DETOUR PLOW COMPANY—See Tenneco Inc.; *U.S. Public*, pg. 1578
GRAND FORKS HERALD, INCORPORATED—See Knight-Ridder, Inc.; *U.S. Public*, pg. 964
GRAND GENERALE ASIA LTD.—See Generale de Banque S.A.; *Int'l*, pg. 548
GRAND HOLDINGS; *U.S. Private*, pg. 468
GRAND ILLUSION SPORTSWEAR—See Signal Apparel Company, Inc.; *U.S. Public*, pg. 1472
GRAND ISLAND CONTRACT CARRIERS & BROKERAGE, INC.—See Chief Industries, Inc.; *U.S. Private*, pg. 350
THE GRAND ISLAND DAILY INDEPENDENT—See Shivers Trading & Operating Co.; *U.S. Private*, pg. 995
GRAND JUNCTION NEWSPAPERS, INC.—See Cox Enterprises, Inc.; *U.S. Private*, pg. 281
GRAND METROPOLITAN COMMUNITY RELATIONS—See Diageo Plc; *Int'l*, pg. 408
GRAND METROPOLITAN COMMUNITY SERVICES-USA—See Diageo Plc; *Int'l*, pg. 408
GRAND METROPOLITAN CORPORATE PROPERTY—See Diageo Plc; *Int'l*, pg. 408
GRAND METROPOLITAN ESTATES LTD.—See Diageo Plc; *Int'l*, pg. 408
GRAND METROPOLITAN FINANCE PLC—See Diageo Plc; *Int'l*, pg. 408
GRAND METROPOLITAN FOODSERVICE INC.—See Diageo Plc; *Int'l*, pg. 408
GRAND METROPOLITAN INFORMATION SERVICES LTD.—See Diageo Plc; *Int'l*, pg. 408
GRAND METROPOLITAN PLC—See Diageo Plc; *Int'l*, pg. 408
GRAND METROPOLITAN PLC-GROUP INTERNAL AUDIT:LONDON—See Diageo Plc; *Int'l*, pg. 408
GRAND PRAIRIE CO-OP, INC.; *U.S. Private*, pg. 468
THE GRAND PUB COMPANY LIMITED—See The Nomura Securities Co., Ltd.; *Int'l*, pg. 956
GRAND RAPIDS DIE CASTING CORP.—See Park Electrochemical Corporation; *U.S. Public*, pg. 1258
GRAND RIVER INFRASTRUCTURE, INC.—See Premarc Corporation; *U.S. Private*, pg. 881
GRAND TRUNK CORPORATION (GTC)—See Canadian National Railway Company; *Int'l*, pg. 258
GRAND TRUNK WESTERN RAILROAD, INC.—See Canadian National Railway Company; *Int'l*, pg. 258
THE GRAND UNION COMPANY; *U.S. Public*, pg. 758

MASTER INDEX TO COMPANY NAMES GRAYSTONE

Company Index

GRANDE DISTRIBUZIONE AVANZATA S.P.A.—See Otto Versand (GmbH & Co.); *Int'l*, pg. 1015
GRANDE SEMOULERIE DE L'OUEST A GOND-PONTOUVRE—See Grands Moulins de Paris S.A.; *Int'l*, *pg. 556*
GRANDES LIGNES INTERNATIONAL—See SNCF; *Int'l*, pg. 1165
GRANDES MARCAS SA—See Diageo Plc; *Int'l*, pg. 409
GRANDETEL TECHNOLOGIES INC.; *Int'l*, pg. 556
GRANDMA FOOD PRODUCTS LIMITED—See Crompton & Knowles Corporation; *U.S. Public*, pg. 460
GRANDMET FOODS EUROPE—See Diageo Plc; *Int'l*, pg. 408
GRANDMET FOODS FRANCE—See Diageo Plc; *Int'l*, pg. 408
GRANDMET FOODS GMBH—See Diageo Plc; *Int'l*, pg. 409
GRANDMET FOODS SOUTHERN EUROPE—See Diageo Plc; *Int'l*, pg. 409
GRANDMET FOODS UK—See Diageo Plc; *Int'l*, pg. 408
THE GRANDOE CORP.; *U.S. Private*, pg. 469
GRANDS MILLESIMES DE FRANCE S.A.—See Suntory Ltd.; *Int'l*, pg. 1322
GRANDS MOULINS DE PARIS S.A.; *Int'l*, pg. 556
GRANDS TERROIRS ASSOCIES BV—See Koninklijke BolsWessanen nv; *Int'l*, pg. 751
GRANDVIEW SURGERY CENTER—See Healthsouth Corporation; *U.S. Public*, pg. 803
GRANDVILLE PRINTING COMPANY; *U.S. Private*, pg. 469
GRANDY'S, INC.—See American Restaurant Group, Inc.; *U.S. Private*, pg. 61
GRANER GMBH—See Freudenberg & Company; *Int'l*, pg. 506
GRANER GMBH & CO.—See Freudenberg & Company; *Int'l*, pg. 506
GRANFORD MANUFACTURING, INC.—See The Goodyear Tire & Rubber Company; *U.S. Public*, pg. 753
GRANGE GLAZING LIMITED—See Saint-Gobain; *Int'l*, pg. 1173
GRANGER COMPANIES; *U.S. Private*, pg. 469
GRANGER CONSTRUCTION CO.; *U.S. Private*, pg. 469
GRANGER CONTAINER SERVICE—See Granger Companies; *U.S. Private*, pg. 469
GRANGER LAND DEVELOPMENT CO.—See Granger Companies; *U.S. Private*, pg. 469
GRANGER WASTE MANAGEMENT CO.—See Granger Companies; *U.S. Private*, pg. 469
GRANGES AB—See Electrolux, AB; *Int'l*, pg. 439
GRANGES ALUMINIUM AB—See Electrolux, AB; *Int'l*, pg. 439
GRANGES ALUMINIUM GMBH—See Electrolux, AB; *Int'l*, pg. 442
GRANGES ALUMINIUM S.A.—See Electrolux, AB; *Int'l*, pg. 441
GRANGES AUTOMOTIVE (UK) LTD.—See Electrolux, AB; *Int'l*, pg. 444
GRANGES DANMARK A/S—See Electrolux, AB; *Int'l*, pg. 441
GRANGES ESSEM IBERICA S.A.—See Electrolux, AB; *Int'l*, pg. 443
GRANGES HEDLUND AB—See Electrolux, AB; *Int'l*, pg. 439
GRANGES INTERNATIONAL MINING—See Electrolux, AB; *Int'l*, pg. 439
GRANGES METALL GMBH—See Electrolux, AB; *Int'l*, pg. 442
GRANGES METALLHANDELS-GES. GMBH—See Electrolux, AB; *Int'l*, pg. 440
GRANGES METALOCK AB—See Electrolux, AB; *Int'l*, pg. 439
GRANGES METALOCK A/S—See Electrolux, AB; *Int'l*, pg. 441
GRANGES METALOCK GMBH—See Electrolux, AB; *Int'l*, pg. 442
GRANGES NIGERIA LTD.—See Electrolux, AB; *Int'l*, pg. 443
GRANIT-BRONZ, INC.—See Cold Spring Granite Company; *U.S. Private*, pg. 251
GRANITE BROADCASTING CORPORATION; *U.S. Public*, pg. 759
GRANITE CONSTRUCTION INC.-ARIZONA DIV.—See Granite Construction Incorporated; *U.S. Public*, pg. 759
GRANITE CONSTRUCTION INC.-BAKERSFIELD DIV.—See Granite Construction Incorporated; *U.S. Public*, pg. 759
GRANITE CONSTRUCTION INC.-CENTRAL VALLEY DIV.—See Granite Construction Incorporated; *U.S. Public*, pg. 759
GRANITE CONSTRUCTION INC.-HEAVY CONSTRUCTION DIV.—See Granite Construction Incorporated; *U.S. Public*, pg. 759
GRANITE CONSTRUCTION INC.-MONTEREY BAY DIV.—See Granite Construction Incorporated; *U.S. Public*, pg. 759
GRANITE CONSTRUCTION INC.-NEVADA DIV.—See Granite Construction Incorporated; *U.S. Public*, pg. 759
GRANITE CONSTRUCTION INC.-SACRAMENTO DIV.—See Granite Construction Incorporated; *U.S. Public*, pg. 759
GRANITE CONSTRUCTION INC.-SAN JOSE DIV.—See Granite Construction Incorporated; *U.S. Public*, pg. 759
GRANITE CONSTRUCTION INC.-SANTA BARBARA DIV.—See Granite Construction Incorporated; *U.S. Public*, pg. 759
GRANITE CONSTRUCTION INC.-SOUTHERN CALIFORNIA REG. DIV.—See Granite Construction Incorporated; *U.S. Public*, pg. 759
GRANITE CONSTRUCTION INC.-STOCKTON DIV.—See Granite Construction Incorporated; *U.S. Public*, pg. 759
GRANITE CONSTRUCTION INCORPORATED; *U.S. Public*, *pg. 759*
GRANITE FURNITURE CO.; *U.S. Private*, pg. 469
GRANITE GROUP WHOLESALE LLC; *U.S. Private*, pg. 469
GRANITE SAVINGS BANK & TRUST COMPANY—See Banknorth Group Inc.; *U.S. Public*, pg. 187
GRANITE STATE ELECTRIC CO.—See New England Electric System; *U.S. Public*, pg. 1171
GRANITE STATE ENERGY, INC.—See New England Electric System; *U.S. Public*, pg. 1171
GRANITE STATE GAS TRANSMISSION, INC.—See Bay State Gas Company; *U.S. Public*, pg. 197
GRANITE STATE INSURANCE CO.—See American International Group, Inc.; *U.S. Public*, pg. 84
GRANITE STATE MANUFACTURING CO.—See Allard Industries; *U.S. Private*, pg. 36
GRANITEVILLE COMPANY—See Avondale Incorporated; *U.S. Private*, pg. 103
GRANJA CASTELLO S.A.—See Nestle S.A.; *Int'l*, pg. 920
GRANJAS PORCINAS DEL ECUADOR (GRANPORSA) S.A.—See The East Asiatic Company Ltd. A/S; *Int'l*, pg. 431
GRANNY GOOSE FOODS—See Granny Goose Foods, Inc.; *U.S. Private*, pg. 469
GRANNY GOOSE FOODS, INC.; *U.S. Private*, pg. 469
GRANNY SMITH JOINT VENTURE—See Placer Dome Inc.; *Int'l*, pg. 1060
GRANPLEX, INC.—See Nichimen Corporation; *Int'l*, pg. 927
GRANPLEX, INC., PORTLAND BRANCH—See Nichimen Corporation; *Int'l*, pg. 927
GRANT CENTER OF DEERING—See Columbia/HCA Healthcare Corporation; *U.S. Public*, pg. 405
GRANT CHEMICAL DIV.—See Ferro Corporation; *U.S. Public*, pg. 618
GRANT COUNTY NEWS—See Landmark Communications, Inc.; *U.S. Private*, pg. 648
GRANT GEOPHYSICAL INC.; *U.S. Private*, pg. 470
GRANT, INC.—See Northwestern Public Service; *U.S. Public*, pg. 1201
GRANT/JACOBY, INC.; *U.S. Private*, pg. 470
GRANT-LYDICK BEVERAGE CO.; *U.S. Private*, pg. 470
GRANT MARKETING COMMUNICATIONS; *U.S. Private*, pg. 470
GRANT PRIDECO, INC.—See EVI, Inc.; *U.S. Public*, pg. 547
GRANT STEEL CORP.—See Columbia National Group, Inc.; *U.S. Private*, pg. 256
GRANT THORNTON LLP; *U.S. Private*, pg. 470
WILLIAM GRANT & SONS DISTILLERS LTD.; *Int'l*, pg. 557
GRANTHAM DISTRIBUTING COMPANY, INC.; *U.S. Private*, pg. 470
GRANTHAM ROAD SERVICES—See Franz Haniel & Cie, GmbH; *Int'l*, pg. 591
GRANUM COMMUNICATIONS; *U.S. Private*, pg. 470
GRANZOW A/S—See AB Industrivarden; *Int'l*, pg. 678
GRAPHEME INC.—See Cossette Communication Marketing; *Int'l*, pg. 336
GRAPHIC ARTS DIVISION—See Fort Dearborn Company; *U.S. Private*, pg. 419
GRAPHIC ARTS MUTUAL INSURANCE CO.—See Utica Mutual Insurance Company; *U.S. Private*, pg. 1130
GRAPHIC ARTS SUPPLY DIVISION—See Bell Industries, Inc.; *U.S. Public*, pg. 205
GRAPHIC CONTROLS CORPORATION; *U.S. Private*, pg. 470
GRAPHIC DIRECT, INC.—See Wallace Computer Services, Inc.; *U.S. Public*, pg. 1735
GRAPHIC DIRECT, INC.-ILLINOIS—See Wallace Computer Services, Inc.; *U.S. Public*, pg. 1735
GRAPHIC ENTERPRISES OF OHIO, INC.; *U.S. Private*, pg. 471
GRAPHIC INDUSTRIES, INC.—See Wallace Computer Services, Inc.; *U.S. Public*, pg. 1735
GRAPHIC INSTRUMENTS—See Danaher Corporation; *U.S. Public*, pg. 481
GRAPHIC JACKETS—See PPG Inc.; *U.S. Private*, pg. 827
GRAPHIC LEARNING—See Abrams & Co. Publishing Inc.; *U.S. Private*, pg. 10
GRAPHIC LEASE—See ING Groep N.V.; *Int'l*, pg. 647
GRAPHIC PACKAGING CORPORATION—See ACX Technologies Inc.; *U.S. Public*, pg. 3
GRAPHIC RESEARCH, INC.—See Methode Electronics Inc.; *U.S. Public*, pg. 1101
GRAPHIC RESOURCES, INC.—See Sonoco Products Company; *U.S. Public*, pg. 1486
GRAPHIC TECHNOLOGY, INC.—See Nitto Denko Corporation; *Int'l*, pg. 950
GRAPHICS ARTS CENTER—See Mail-Well Inc.; *U.S. Public*, pg. 1038
GRAPHICS MANAGEMENT—See R.R. Donnelley & Sons Company; *U.S. Public*, pg. 518
GRAPHICS SYSTEMS DIVISION—See Avery Dennison Corporation; *U.S. Public*, pg. 153
GRAPHISCHER MASCHINENBAU—See Koenig & Bauer-Albert AG; *Int'l*, pg. 742
GRAPHIT-PRODUKTE DOHNA GMBH—See Fuchs Petrolub AG Oel + Chemie; *Int'l*, pg. 517
GRAPHITE & SPECIALTY PRODUCTS, INC.—See Morgan Crucible Co. Plc; *Int'l*, pg. 891
GRAPHITWERK KROPFMUEHL AG—See Viag AG; *Int'l*, pg. 1464
GRAPHLINE INC.; *U.S. Private*, pg. 471
GRASEBY ALLEN LTD.—See Smiths Industries plc; *Int'l*, pg. 1267
GRASEBY ANDERSEN—See Smiths Industries plc; *Int'l*, pg. 1268
GRASEBY ANDERSEN LTD.—See Smiths Industries plc; *Int'l*, pg. 1267
GRASEBY BEST LTD.—See Smiths Industries plc; *Int'l*, pg. 1267
GRASEBY DYNAMICS LTD.—See Smiths Industries plc; *Int'l*, pg. 1267
GRASEBY GK INTEREST LTD.—See Smiths Industries plc; *Int'l*, pg. 1267
GRASEBY GMW—See Smiths Industries plc; *Int'l*, pg. 1268
GRASEBY GORING KERR CANADA INC.—See Smiths Industries plc; *Int'l*, pg. 1268
GRASEBY GORING KERR INC.—See Smiths Industries plc; *Int'l*, pg. 1268
GRASEBY GORING KERR LTD.—See Smiths Industries plc; *Int'l*, pg. 1267
GRASEBY GORING KERR (N2) LTD.—See Smiths Industries plc; *Int'l*, pg. 1268
GRASEBY IONICS—See Smiths Industries plc; *Int'l*, pg. 1268
GRASEBY IONICS LTD.—See Smiths Industries plc; *Int'l*, pg. 1267
GRASEBY MEDICAL BV—See Smiths Industries plc; *Int'l*, pg. 1268
GRASEBY MEDICAL LTD.—See Smiths Industries plc; *Int'l*, *pg. 1267*
GRASEBY MICROSYSTEMS LTD.—See Smiths Industries plc; *Int'l*, pg. 1267
GRASEBY SECURITY LTD.—See Smiths Industries plc; *Int'l*, pg. 1267
GRASEBY SPECAC LTD.—See Smiths Industries plc; *Int'l*, pg. 1267
GRASEBY STI—See Smiths Industries plc; *Int'l*, pg. 1268
GRASS ROOTS GROUP PLC—See WPP Group plc; *Int'l*, pg. 1482
GRASSLAND EQUIPMENT & IRRIGATION CORP.; *U.S. Private*, pg. 471
GRASSLAND EQUIPMENT & IRRIGATION CORP.—See Grassland Equipment & Irrigation Corp.; *U.S. Private*, pg. 471
GRASSLAND FERTILISERS (KILKENNY) LIMITED—See Avonmore Waterford Group plc; *Int'l*, pg. 102
GRATTAN PLC—See Otto Versand (GmbH & Co.); *Int'l*, pg. 1015
GRAU GMBH—See Echlin Inc.; *U.S. Public*, pg. 561
GRAU LIMITED—See Echlin Inc.; *U.S. Public*, pg. 561
GRAU WERKZEUG-UND FORMENBAU GMBH & CO.—See Koninklijke Hoogovens N.V.; *Int'l*, pg. 755
GRAV & SCHAKT VASTERAS AB—See Scancem AB; *Int'l*, *pg. 1200*
GRAVER TANK & MFG. CO., INC.—See ITEQ, Inc.; *U.S. Public*, pg. 914
EARL G. GRAVES, LTD.; *U.S. Private*, pg. 471
EARL G. GRAVES PUBLISHING CO., INC.—See Earl G. Graves, Ltd.; *U.S. Private*, pg. 471
GRAVEY S.A.—See La Meridionale des Bois et Materiaux; *Int'l*, pg. 784
GRAVYMASTER INC.; *U.S. Private*, pg. 471
GRAY & COMPANY—See Portland Food Products Company; *U.S. Private*, pg. 876
GRAY COMMUNICATIONS SYSTEMS, INC.; *U.S. Public*, pg. 759
P.T. GRAY INDONESIA—See ABB Asea Brown Boveri (Holding) Ltd.; *Int'l*, pg. 5
JACK GRAY TRANSPORT, INC.; *U.S. Private*, pg. 471
JAMES N. GRAY CONSTRUCTION CO., INC.; *U.S. Private*, pg. 472
GRAY KIRK/VANSANT ADVERTISING, INC.; *U.S. Private*, *pg. 472*
GRAY LINE OF ALASKA—See Carnival Corporation; *U.S. Public*, pg. 306
GRAY LINE OF SEATTLE—See Carnival Corporation; *U.S. Public*, pg. 306
GRAY PRINTING CO.; *U.S. Private*, pg. 472
GRAY REAL ESTATE & DEVELOPMENT CO.—See Gray Communications Systems, Inc.; *U.S. Public*, pg. 759
GRAY SERVICE CO., A.G.—See ABB Asea Brown Boveri (Holding) Ltd.; *Int'l*, pg. 5
GRAY TOOL CO. DE VENEZUELA CA.—See ABB Asea Brown Boveri (Holding) Ltd.; *Int'l*, pg. 5
GRAY TOOL CO. (EUROPE)—See ABB Asea Brown Boveri (Holding) Ltd.; *Int'l*, pg. 5
GRAY TOOL CO. (NORWAY) A/S—See ABB Asea Brown Boveri (Holding) Ltd.; *Int'l*, pg. 5
GRAY TOOL COMPANY—See ABB Asea Brown Boveri (Holding) Ltd.; *Int'l*, pg. 5
GRAY TOOL CO. (EUROPE)—See ABB Asea Brown Boveri (Holding) Ltd.; *Int'l*, pg. 5
GRAY TOOL CO. (NORWAY) A/S—See ABB Asea Brown Boveri (Holding) Ltd.; *Int'l*, pg. 5
GRAY TOOL INTERNATIONAL—See ABB Asea Brown Boveri (Holding) Ltd.; *Int'l*, pg. 6
GRAY TOOL INTERNATIONAL CORPORATION—See ABB Asea Brown Boveri (Holding) Ltd.; *Int'l*, pg. 6
GRAY TOOL INTERNATIONAL, INC.—See ABB Asea Brown Boveri (Holding) Ltd.; *Int'l*, pg. 6
GRAYBAR ELECTRIC COMPANY, INC.; *U.S. Private*, pg. 472
GRAYBAR INTERNATIONAL, INC.—See Graybar Electric Company, Inc.; *U.S. Private*, pg. 472
GRAYCOR BLASTING COMPANY INC.—See Graycor Operating Companies; *U.S. Private*, pg. 472
GRAYCOR CONSTRUCTION COMPANY INC.—See Graycor Operating Companies; *U.S. Private*, pg. 472
GRAYCOR INDUSTRIAL CONSTRUCTORS INC.—See Graycor Operating Companies; *U.S. Private*, pg. 472
GRAYCOR INTERNATIONAL INC.—See Graycor Operating Companies; *U.S. Private*, pg. 472
GRAYCOR OPERATING COMPANIES; *U.S. Private*, pg. 472
GRAYLINE HOUSEWARES; *U.S. Private*, pg. 472
GRAYLING STATE BANK—See Citizens Banking Corporation; *U.S. Public*, pg. 379
GRAYMILLS CORP.; *U.S. Private*, pg. 473
GRAYS TERMINAL—See GATX Corporation; *U.S. Public*, pg. 693
GRAYSON CONTROLS DIV.—See Siebe plc; *Int'l*, pg. 1243
GRAYSON ELECTRONICS CORPORATION—See Allen Telecom, Inc.; *U.S. Public*, pg. 46
GRAYSONIA, NASHVILLE & ASHDOWN RAILROAD CO.—See Holderbank Financiere Glaris Ltd.; *Int'l*, pg. 628
GRAYSTON, WHITE & SPARROW LTD.—See Sophus Berendsen A/S; *Int'l*, pg. 1285
GRAYSTONE CORPORATION—See Northern States Power Company; *U.S. Public*, pg. 1195
GRAYSTONE PLC; *Int'l*, pg. 557

GREASE MONKEY INTERNATIONAL INC.; U.S. Public, pg. 759
GREAT AMERICAN HOLDING CORPORATION—See American Financial Group; U.S. Public, pg. 74
GREAT AMERICAN INDUSTRIES, INC.; U.S. Private, pg. 473
GREAT AMERICAN INSURANCE COMPANY—See American Financial Group; U.S. Public, pg. 74
GREAT AMERICAN KNITTING MILLS—See Bidermann International S.A.; Int'l, pg. 194
GREAT AMERICAN MANAGEMENT & INVESTMENT, INC.; U.S. Private, pg. 473
GREAT AMERICAN MANAGEMENT SERVICES, INC.—See American Financial Group; U.S. Public, pg. 75
GREAT AMERICAN OAK, INC.—See Cowden Metal Specialties, Inc.; U.S. Private, pg. 280
GREAT AMERICAN RESERVE INSURANCE COMPANY—See Conseco Inc.; U.S. Public, pg. 433
THE GREAT ATLANTIC & PACIFIC COMPANY OF CANADA LIMITED—See Tengelmann Warenhandelsgesellschaft; Int'l, pg. 1375
THE GREAT ATLANTIC & PACIFIC TEA COMPANY, INC.—See Tengelmann Warenhandelsgesellschaft; Int'l, pg. 1375
GREAT ATLANTIC HOSPITALITY CO. INC.—See The Great Atlantic Management Company; U.S. Private, pg. 473
GREAT ATLANTIC MANAGEMENT CO. INC.—See The Great Atlantic Management Company; U.S. Private, pg. 473
THE GREAT ATLANTIC MANAGEMENT COMPANY; U.S. Private, pg. 473
THE GREAT AUSTRALIAN PIE COMPANY PTY. LTD.—See Q.U.F. Industries Ltd.; Int'l, pg. 1074
GREAT BARRINGTON HEALTHCARE—See Vencor, Inc.; U.S. Public, pg. 1712
GREAT BEAR SPRING COMPANY—See Nestle S.A.; Int'l, pg. 919
GREAT BRANDS OF EUROPE—See Danone Group; Int'l, pg. 381
GREAT CLIPS, INC.; U.S. Private, pg. 473
GREAT! COMMUNICATIONS—See Grey Advertising Inc.; U.S. Public, pg. 764
GREAT DANE LOS ANGELES, INC.—See Stamford Capital; U.S. Private, pg. 1030
GREAT DANE TRAILERS-NEBRASKA, INC.—See Stamford Capital; U.S. Private, pg. 1030
GREAT DANE TRAILERS TENNESSEE, INC.—See Stamford Capital; U.S. Private, pg. 1030
GREAT DIVIDE INSURANCE COMPANY—See W.R. Berkley Corporation; U.S. Public, pg. 216
GREAT EARTH DISTRIBUTION—See Evergood Products Corporation; U.S. Private, pg. 386
THE GREAT EASTERN INSURANCE COMPANY—See The Hartford Financial Services Group Inc.; U.S. Public, pg. 794
GREAT EASTERN LIFE ASSURANCE COMPANY—See The Great Eastern Life Assurance Company Limited; Int'l, pg. 557
GREAT EASTERN LIFE ASSURANCE COMPANY-ALOR SETAR—See The Great Eastern Life Assurance Company Limited; Int'l, pg. 557
GREAT EASTERN LIFE ASSURANCE COMPANY-BRUNEI—See The Great Eastern Life Assurance Company Limited; Int'l, pg. 557
GREAT EASTERN LIFE ASSURANCE COMPANY-IPOH—See The Great Eastern Life Assurance Company Limited; Int'l, pg. 557
GREAT EASTERN LIFE ASSURANCE COMPANY-JOHOR BAHRU—See The Great Eastern Life Assurance Company Limited; Int'l, pg. 557
GREAT EASTERN LIFE ASSURANCE COMPANY-KELUANG—See The Great Eastern Life Assurance Company Limited; Int'l, pg. 557
GREAT EASTERN LIFE ASSURANCE COMPANY-KLUANG—See The Great Eastern Life Assurance Company Limited; Int'l, pg. 557
GREAT EASTERN LIFE ASSURANCE COMPANY-KOTA BHARU—See The Great Eastern Life Assurance Company Limited; Int'l, pg. 557
GREAT EASTERN LIFE ASSURANCE COMPANY-KUANTAN—See The Great Eastern Life Assurance Company Limited; Int'l, pg. 557
THE GREAT EASTERN LIFE ASSURANCE COMPANY LIMITED; Int'l, pg. 557
GREAT EASTERN LIFE ASSURANCE COMPANY-MALAYSIA—See The Great Eastern Life Assurance Company Limited; Int'l, pg. 557
GREAT EASTERN LIFE ASSURANCE COMPANY-MELAKA—See The Great Eastern Life Assurance Company Limited; Int'l, pg. 557
GREAT EASTERN LIFE ASSURANCE COMPANY-PENANG—See The Great Eastern Life Assurance Company Limited; Int'l, pg. 557
GREAT EASTERN LIFE ASSURANCE COMPANY-SEREMBAN—See The Great Eastern Life Assurance Company Limited; Int'l, pg. 557
GREAT FALLS NORTH AMERICAN, INC.—See Norfolk Southern Corporation; U.S. Public, pg. 1191
GREAT FALLS TRIBUNE—See Gannett Company, Inc.; U.S. Public, pg. 700
GREAT FINANCIAL BANK FSB; U.S. Private, pg. 473
THE GREAT FRAME UP SYSTEMS, INC.; U.S. Private, pg. 473
GREAT LAKES BANCORP—See TCF Financial Corp.; U.S. Public, pg. 1554
GREAT LAKES BIOCHEMICAL CO., INC.—See Laporte plc; Int'l, pg. 802
GREAT LAKES CARBON CORP.—See Horsehead Industries, Inc.; U.S. Private, pg. 540
GREAT LAKES CASTINGS CORPORATION—See Brittany Corporation; U.S. Private, pg. 169
THE GREAT LAKES CHEESE CO.; U.S. Private, pg. 473

GREAT LAKES CHEESE OF LA CROSSE WISCONSIN, INC.—See The Great Lakes Cheese Co.; U.S. Private, pg. 474
GREAT LAKES CHEESE OF NEW YORK, INC.—See The Great Lakes Cheese Co.; U.S. Private, pg. 474
GREAT LAKES CHEMICAL CORPORATION; U.S. Public, pg. 760
GREAT LAKES CHEMICAL (EUROPE) LTD.—See Great Lakes Chemical Corporation; U.S. Public, pg. 760
GREAT LAKES COAL AND DOCK COMPANY—See Ashland, Inc.; U.S. Public, pg. 139
GREAT LAKES CONFECTIONERY—See Midial S.A.; Int'l, pg. 865
GREAT LAKES CONSTRUCTION CO.; U.S. Private, pg. 474
GREAT LAKES DREDGE & DOCK CO.; U.S. Private, pg. 474
GREAT LAKES-EGLINTON—See United Dominion Industries, Ltd.; U.S. Public, pg. 1676
GREAT LAKES ENERGY CORP.—See Madison Gas and Electric Company; U.S. Public, pg. 1033
GREAT LAKES ENVIRONMENTAL SERVICES, INC.—See Research Environmental Industries, Inc.; U.S. Private, pg. 924
GREAT LAKES FILTER—See Acme Mills Co. Inc.; U.S. Private, pg. 13
GREAT LAKES FINANCIAL RESOURCES, INC.; U.S. Private, pg. 474
GREAT LAKES GAS TRANSMISSION CO.—See Transcanada Pipelines Limited; Int'l, pg. 1417
GREAT LAKES KRAUT CO.—See Pro-Fac Cooperative, Inc.; U.S. Private, pg. 887
GREAT LAKES KRAUT CO., L.L.C.—See Pro-Fac Cooperative, Inc.; U.S. Private, pg. 887
GREAT LAKES LITHOGRAPH CO.; U.S. Private, pg. 474
GREAT LAKES MEDIA, INC.—See The Walt Disney Company; U.S. Public, pg. 513
GREAT LAKES OF WISCONSIN—See The Great Lakes Cheese Co.; U.S. Private, pg. 474
GREAT LAKES PETERBILT, GMC; U.S. Private, pg. 475
GREAT LAKES POWER INC.—See EdperBrascan Corporation; Int'l, pg. 433
GREAT LAKES REALTY CORP.; U.S. Private, pg. 475
GREAT LAKES REGION—See MCI Communications Corp.; U.S. Public, pg. 1024
GREAT LAKES SUGAR COMPANY—See Imperial Holly Corporation; U.S. Public, pg. 873
GREAT LAKES TECHNOLOGIES CORP.; U.S. Private, pg. 475
GREAT LAKES TERMINAL & TRANSPORT OF PENNSYLVANIA—See GLS Corporation; U.S. Private, pg. 435
GREAT LAKES WHOLESALE DRUGS; U.S. Private, pg. 475
GREAT LAKES WINDOW, INC.—See Nortek, Inc.; U.S. Public, pg. 1193
GREAT MILLS (CENTRAL) LIMITED—See RMC Group p.l.c.; Int'l, pg. 1080
GREAT MILLS (NORTH) LIMITED—See RMC Group p.l.c.; Int'l, pg. 1080
GREAT MILLS (SOUTH) LIMITED—See RMC Group p.l.c.; Int'l, pg. 1080
GREAT NECK SAW MANUFACTURERS, INC.; U.S. Private, pg. 475
GREAT NORTH RADIO—See EMAP Plc; Int'l, pg. 451
GREAT NORTHERN INSURANCE CO.—See The Chubb Corporation; U.S. Public, pg. 355
GREAT NORTHERN IRON ORE—See Great Northern Iron Ore Properties; U.S. Public, pg. 760
GREAT NORTHERN IRON ORE PROPERTIES; U.S. Public, pg. 760
GREAT NORTHERN MORTGAGE COMPANY—See Associated Banc-Corp; U.S. Public, pg. 141
GREAT NORTHERN PAPER, INC.—See Bowater Incorporated; U.S. Public, pg. 248
GREAT OAKS INSURANCE COMPANY—See Harleysville Group; U.S. Public, pg. 786
GREAT PACIFIC ENTERPRISES INC.; Int'l, pg. 557
GREAT PACIFIC INSURANCE COMPANY—See National Insurance Group; U.S. Public, pg. 1158
GREAT PLAINS COMPANIES, INC.; U.S. Private, pg. 475
GREAT PLAINS CORRECTIONAL FACILITY—See Corrections Corporation of America; U.S. Public, pg. 450
GREAT PLAINS GRAIN DRILLS—See Great Plains Manufacturing, Inc.; U.S. Private, pg. 475
GREAT PLAINS MANUFACTURING, INC.; U.S. Private, pg. 475
GREAT RIVER INSURANCE COMPANY—See W.R. Berkley Corporation; U.S. Public, pg. 215
GREAT RIVER OIL & GAS CORP.—See Georgia Gulf Corporation; U.S. Public, pg. 735
GREAT SALT LAKE MINERALS CORP.—See Harris Chemical Group, Inc.; U.S. Private, pg. 505
GREAT SCOTT ADVERTISING CO. INC.; U.S. Private, pg. 475
GREAT SCOTT ADVERTISING CO., INC.—See Great Scott Advertising Co. Inc.; U.S. Private, pg. 476
GREAT SCOTT FOOD MARKETS, INC.—See James Ferrera & Sons, Inc.; U.S. Private, pg. 402
GREAT SOURCE EDUCATION GROUP—See Houghton Mifflin Company; U.S. Public, pg. 841
GREAT SOUTHWEST TELEPHONE CORP.—See ALLTEL Corporation; U.S. Public, pg. 56
GREAT STATES—See PacifiCare Health Systems, Inc.; U.S. Public, pg. 1251
GREAT UNIVERSAL CAPITAL CORP.—See Lee National Corporation; U.S. Private, pg. 658
THE GREAT UNIVERSAL STORES P.L.C.; Int'l, pg. 557
GREAT VACATIONS INTERNATIONAL—See New Mexico & Arizona Land Co.; U.S. Public, pg. 1172
GREAT WATERS OF FRANCE—See Nestle S.A.; Int'l, pg. 919

GREAT WEST CASUALTY COMPANY—See Old Republic International Corporation; U.S. Public, pg. 1218
GREAT-WEST LIFE & ANNUITY INSURANCE CO.—See The Great-West Life Assurance Company; Int'l, pg. 558
THE GREAT-WEST LIFE ASSURANCE COMPANY; Int'l, pg. 557
GREAT-WEST REALTY INVESTMENTS, INC.—See The Great-West Life Assurance Company; Int'l, pg. 558
GREAT WESTERN BANK—See Washington Mutual Inc.; U.S. Public, pg. 1741
GREAT WESTERN CONSUMER FINANCE GROUP—See Washington Mutual Inc.; U.S. Public, pg. 1741
GREAT WESTERN FINANCIAL CORPORATION—See Washington Mutual Inc.; U.S. Public, pg. 1741
GREAT WESTERN FINANCIAL SECURITIES—See Washington Mutual Inc.; U.S. Public, pg. 1742
GREAT WESTERN INDUSTRIAL MACHINERY CO.-GWIM—See LSB Industries, Inc.; U.S. Public, pg. 970
GREAT WESTERN MALTING CO.—See ConAgra, Inc.; U.S. Public, pg. 428
GREAT WESTERN METALS INC.—See Four Winds Investment Corp.; U.S. Public, pg. 422
GREAT WESTERN MORTGAGE CORPORATION—See Washington Mutual Inc.; U.S. Public, pg. 1742
GREAT WESTERN STEEL—See Triumph Group, Inc.; U.S. Public, pg. 1640
GREAT YEAR TRADING CO. LTD.—See The Green Cross Corporation; Int'l, pg. 558
GREAT YORKSHIRE GOLD—See EMAP Plc; Int'l, pg. 451
GREATBANC, INC.; U.S. Public, pg. 760
GREATBANC TRUST COMPANY—See GreatBanc, Inc.; U.S. Public, pg. 760
GREATE BAY CASINO CORPORATION; U.S. Public, pg. 760
GREATE BAY HOTEL & CASINO—See Greate Bay Casino Corporation; U.S. Public, pg. 761
GREATE BAY PROPERTY FUNDING—See Greate Bay Casino Corporation; U.S. Public, pg. 761
GREATER CHICAGO AUTO AUCTION—See Cox Enterprises, Inc.; U.S. Private, pg. 282
GREATER CONSTRUCTION CORP.; U.S. Private, pg. 476
GREATER NEW YORK BOX CO.; U.S. Private, pg. 476
GREATER NEW YORK MUTUAL INSURANCE COMPANY; U.S. Private, pg. 476
GREATER PHILADELPHIA/WILMINGTON—See Berkshire Hathaway Inc.; U.S. Public, pg. 218
GREATER TAMPA BAY AUTO AUCTION—See Cox Enterprises, Inc.; U.S. Private, pg. 282
GREATER WASHINGTON INVESTMENTS, INC.—See Johnston Industries, Inc.; U.S. Public, pg. 933
GREDE FOUNDRIES, INC.; U.S. Private, pg. 476
GREDE-PRYOR, INC.—See Grede Foundries, Inc.; U.S. Private, pg. 476
GREDE TRANSPORT, INC.—See Grede Foundries, Inc.; U.S. Private, pg. 476
GREEK SALT INDUSTRIAL COMMERCIAL EPE—See Akzo Nobel N.V.; Int'l, pg. 44
GREELEY GAS CO.—See Atmos Energy Corporation; U.S. Public, pg. 145
A.P. GREEN INDUSTRIES, INC.; U.S. Public, pg. 761
GREEN & CLEAR LAKES—See New Century Energies, Inc.; U.S. Public, pg. 1170
B. GREEN & CO.; U.S. Private, pg. 476
GREEN BAY DRESSED BEEF COMPANY—See American Foods Group, Inc.; U.S. Private, pg. 54
GREEN BAY PACKAGING INC.; U.S. Private, pg. 476
GREEN BAY PRESS-GAZETTE—See Gannett Company, Inc.; U.S. Public, pg. 700
GREEN BAY SUPPLY CO., INC.—See Carpenter Technology Corporation; U.S. Public, pg. 307
GREEN BUS HOLDING—See Green Bus Lines, Inc.; U.S. Private, pg. 477
GREEN BUS LINES, INC.; U.S. Private, pg. 476
THE GREEN CROSS CORP.-NEW YORK REPRESENTATIVE OFFICE—See The Green Cross Corporation; Int'l, pg. 558
THE GREEN CROSS CORPORATION; Int'l, pg. 558
GREEN CROSS (U.S.A.), INC.—See The Green Cross Corporation; Int'l, pg. 558
GREEN CROSS GUANGZHOU PHARMACEUTICAL CO.—See The Green Cross Corporation; Int'l, pg. 558
DANIEL GREEN CO.; U.S. Private, pg. 477
GREEN EQUITY INVESTORS II, L.P.—See Leonard Green & Partners; U.S. Private, pg. 477
GREEN EQUITY INVESTORS L.P.—See Leonard Green & Partners; U.S. Private, pg. 477
GREEN FLOUR MILLS LIMITED—See Harrisons & Crosfield plc; Int'l, pg. 598
GREEN FOODS SERVICE CO., LTD.—See Matsuya Company Ltd.; Int'l, pg. 848
GREEN FOREST LUMBER CORPORATION—See MacMillan Bloedel Limited; Int'l, pg. 828
GREEN GIANT COMPANY—See Diageo Plc; Int'l, pg. 411
GREEN GIANT INTERNATIONAL, INC.—See Diageo Plc; Int'l, pg. 411
GREEN ISLE LTD.—See Northern Foods plc; Int'l, pg. 968
JOHN E. GREEN CO.; U.S. Private, pg. 477
LEONARD GREEN & PARTNERS; U.S. Private, pg. 477
GREEN LINE INVESTOR SERVICE—See The Toronto Dominion Bank; Int'l, pg. 1401
GREEN MEADOWS, LTD.—See Pioneer Hi-Bred International, Inc.; U.S. Public, pg. 1299
GREEN MOUNTAIN COFFEE ROASTERS, INC.; U.S. Public, pg. 761
GREEN MOUNTAIN POWER CORPORATION; U.S. Public, pg. 761
GREEN MOUNTAIN PROPANE GAS CO.—See Green Mountain Power Corporation; U.S. Public, pg. 761
GREEN MOUNTAIN STEEL ERECTORS INC.—See Bennington Iron Works, Inc.; U.S. Private, pg. 133
GREEN OAKS PARK HOTEL—See Sunstone Hotel Investors, Inc.; U.S. Public, pg. 1537
GREEN SEED CO.; U.S. Private, pg. 477
GREEN SPOT PACKAGING INC.; U.S. Private, pg. 477
THOMAS L. GREEN & CO., INC.; U.S. Private, pg. 477

GREEN TREE ACCEPTANCE, INC.—See Green Tree Financial Corporation; *U.S. Public,* pg. 762
GREEN TREE ACCEPTANCE OF ALABAMA, INC.—See Green Tree Financial Corporation; *U.S. Public,* pg. 762
GREEN TREE ACCEPTANCE OF KENTUCKY, INC.—See Green Tree Financial Corporation; *U.S. Public,* pg. 762
GREEN TREE ACCEPTANCE OF LOUISIANA, INC.—See Green Tree Financial Corporation; *U.S. Public,* pg. 762
GREEN TREE ACCEPTANCE OF MISSISSIPPI, INC.—See Green Tree Financial Corporation; *U.S. Public,* pg. 762
GREEN TREE ACCEPTANCE OF MONTANA, INC.—See Green Tree Financial Corporation; *U.S. Public,* pg. 762
GREEN TREE ACCEPTANCE OF NORTH CAROLINA, INC.—See Green Tree Financial Corporation; *U.S. Public,* pg. 762
GREEN TREE ACCEPTANCE OF OHIO, INC.—See Green Tree Financial Corporation; *U.S. Public,* pg. 762
GREEN TREE ACCEPTANCE OF TEXAS, INC.—See Green Tree Financial Corporation; *U.S. Public,* pg. 762
GREEN TREE AGENCY, INC.—See Green Tree Financial Corporation; *U.S. Public,* pg. 763
GREEN TREE AGENCY OF NEVADA, INC.—See Green Tree Financial Corporation; *U.S. Public,* pg. 763
GREEN TREE CONSUMER DISCOUNT COMPANY—See Green Tree Financial Corporation; *U.S. Public,* pg. 763
GREEN TREE CREDIT CORP.—See Green Tree Financial Corporation; *U.S. Public,* pg. 763
GREEN TREE FINANCE CORP.-ONE—See Green Tree Financial Corporation; *U.S. Public,* pg. 763
GREEN TREE FINANCIAL CORPORATION; *U.S. Public,* pg. 761
GREEN TREE LIFE INSURANCE CO.—See Green Tree Financial Corporation; *U.S. Public,* pg. 763
GREEN VALLEY ENVIRONMENTAL, INC.—See Republic Industries, Inc.; *U.S. Public,* pg. 1379
THE GREENALLS GROUP PLC; *Int'l,* pg. 558
GREENAWAY-HARRISON LTD. D/B/A GREENAWAYS—See Lonrho plc; *Int'l,* pg. 817
GREENBERG FINANCIAL INSURANCE SERVICES, INC.—See The Progressive Corporation; *U.S. Public,* pg. 1334
GREENBRIAR TERRACE HEALTHCARE—See Vencor, Inc.; *U.S. Public,* pg. 1712
THE GREENBRIER—See CSX Corporation; *U.S. Public,* pg. 284
GREENBRIER VALLEY NATIONAL BANK—See Horizon Bancorp, Inc.; *U.S. Public,* pg. 836
GREENBULL INC.; *U.S. Private,* pg. 477
GREENE COUNTY REALTY COMPANY—See O'Reilly Automotive, Inc.; *U.S. Public,* pg. 1230
GREENE MANOR COAL CO.—See PP&L Resources; *U.S. Public,* pg. 1244
GREENE POINT DEVELOPMENT CORP.—See Central Hudson Gas & Electric Corporation; *U.S. Public,* pg. 325
M.H. GREENEBAUM, INC.; *U.S. Private,* pg. 477
GREENERY EXTENDED CARE CENTER—See Horizon/CMS Healthcare Corporation; *U.S. Public,* pg. 836
GREENERY EXTENDED CARE CENTER AT CHESHIRE—See Horizon/CMS Healthcare Corporation; *U.S. Public,* pg. 836
GREENERY EXTENDED CARE CENTER AT DANVERS—See Horizon/CMS Healthcare Corporation; *U.S. Public,* pg. 836
GREENERY EXTENDED CARE CENTER AT FARMINGTON—See Horizon/CMS Healthcare Corporation; *U.S. Public,* pg. 837
GREENERY EXTENDED CARE CENTER OF BEVERLY—See Horizon/CMS Healthcare Corporation; *U.S. Public,* pg. 836
GREENERY EXTENDED CARE CENTER OF NORTH ANDOVER—See Horizon/CMS Healthcare Corporation; *U.S. Public,* pg. 837
GREENERY HEALTH CARE CENTER—See Horizon/CMS Healthcare Corporation; *U.S. Public,* pg. 837
GREENERY HEALTH CARE CENTER AT CLARKSTON—See Horizon/CMS Healthcare Corporation; *U.S. Public,* pg. 837
GREENERY NEUROLOGICAL REHABILITATION—See Horizon/CMS Healthcare Corporation; *U.S. Public,* pg. 837
GREENERY REHAB - WATERBURY—See Horizon/CMS Healthcare Corporation; *U.S. Public,* pg. 836
GREENERY REHABILITATION & SKILLED NURSING CENTER—See Horizon/CMS Healthcare Corporation; *U.S. Public,* pg. 837
GREENERY REHABILITATION CENTER—See Horizon/CMS Healthcare Corporation; *U.S. Public,* pg. 837
GREENEVILLE METAL MANUFACTURING, INC.—See Newport News Shipbuilding, Inc.; *U.S. Public,* pg. 1180
ALBERT M. GREENFIELD & COMPANY; *U.S. Private,* pg. 477
GREENFIELD INDUSTRIES INC.—See Kennametal Inc.; *U.S. Public,* pg. 950
GREENFIELD PROPERTIES, INC.—See Ford Motor Company; *U.S. Public,* pg. 663
GREENFIELDS WOOLSCOUR PTY. LTD.—See The East Asiatic Company Ltd. A/S; *Int'l,* pg. 431
GREENGATE MALL, INC.—See The Rouse Company; *U.S. Public,* pg. 1407
GREENHAM CONSTRUCTION MATERIALS LIMITED—See Taylor Woodrow plc; *Int'l,* pg. 1358
GREENHAM TRADING LIMITED—See Taylor Woodrow plc; *Int'l,* pg. 1358
GREENHORNE & O'MARA, INC.; *U.S. Private,* pg. 477
GREENING DONALD CO. LTD.—See Thyssen AG; *Int'l,* pg. 1389
GREENLEE LIGHTING INC.—See LSI Industries, Inc.; *U.S. Public,* pg. 971
GREENLEE TEXTRON—See Textron Inc.; *U.S. Public,* pg. 1589
GREENLUX A/S—See Electrolux, AB; *Int'l,* pg. 441
GREENOCK ENGINEERING BV—See N.V. Koninklijke KNP BT; *Int'l,* pg. 756

GREENS CREEK UNIT—See Hecla Mining Company; *U.S. Public,* pg. 804
GREENSBORO SALES—See Fairfield Communities, Inc.; *U.S. Public,* pg. 611
GREENSBURG MANUFACTURING—See Kimball International, Inc.; *U.S. Public,* pg. 957
GREENSPOINT MARRIOTT RESTAURANT CORPORATION—See Cigna Corp.; *U.S. Public,* pg. 361
GREENSTONE ROBERTS ADVERTISING; *U.S. Public,* pg. 763
GREENSTONE ROBERTS/FLORIDA—See Greenstone Roberts Advertising; *U.S. Public,* pg. 763
GREENVILLE DIVISION—See Consumers Water Company; *U.S. Public,* pg. 438
GREENVILLE FOOD SYSTEMS, INC.—See WSMP, Inc.; *U.S. Public,* pg. 1729
GREENVILLE MFG. DIV.—See Simpson Industries, Inc.; *U.S. Public,* pg. 1475
THE GREENVILLE NEWS—See Gannett Company, Inc.; *U.S. Public,* pg. 699
GREENVILLE PRIMARY CARE CLINIC, INC.—See Integrated Health Services, Inc.; *U.S. Public,* pg. 884
GREENVILLE TUBE CO.—See Chart Industries, Inc.; *U.S. Public,* pg. 336
GREENWALD INDUSTRIES, INC.—See Publicker Industries Inc.; *U.S. Public,* pg. 1341
GREENWAY CO-OP SERVICE; *U.S. Private,* pg. 478
GREENWAY CORPORATION—See Williams Industries, Inc.; *U.S. Public,* pg. 1770
GREENWAY PARTNERS, L.P.; *U.S. Private,* pg. 478
GREENWAYS LANDFILL—See Hanson PLC; *Int'l,* pg. 592
GREENWICH AIR SERVICES—See General Electric Company; *U.S. Public,* pg. 710
GREENWICH CAPITAL MARKETS, INC.—See National Westminster Bank PLC; *Int'l,* pg. 911
GREENWICH INSURANCE COMPANY—See NAC Re Corp.; *U.S. Public,* pg. 1144
GREENWICH STREET CAPITAL PARTNERS, INC.; *U.S. Private,* pg. 479
GREENWICH TIMES—See The Times Mirror Company; *U.S. Public,* pg. 1616
GREENWICH WATER SYSTEM, INC.—See American Water Works Company, Inc.; *U.S. Public,* pg. 95
GREENWILLOW BOOKS—See The Hearst Corporation; *U.S. Private,* pg. 515
GREENWOOD DEVELOPMENT CO.—See Greenwood Mills, Inc.; *U.S. Private,* pg. 479
GREENWOOD MILLS, INC.; *U.S. Private,* pg. 479
GREENWOOD MULTI-SPECIALTY CLINIC, INC.—See Integrated Health Services, Inc.; *U.S. Public,* pg. 885
GREENWOOD PLANT—See Cooper Industries, Inc.; *U.S. Public,* pg. 443
GREENWOOD PLANT—See Stoneridge, Inc.; *U.S. Private,* pg. 1044
GREENWOOD PUBLISHING GROUP INC.—See Reed Elsevier plc; *Int'l,* pg. 1094
GREENWOOD WAREHOUSE CO.—See Greenwood Mills, Inc.; *U.S. Private,* pg. 479
AUTRY GREER & SONS, INC.; *U.S. Private,* pg. 479
GERARD L. GREER CO.—See Morgan Crucible Co. Plc; *Int'l,* pg. 891
GREER LIMESTONE CO.—See Greer Steel Co.; *U.S. Private,* pg. 479
GREER STEEL CO.; *U.S. Private,* pg. 479
GREER STEEL COMPANY FERNDALE MICHIGAN SERVICE CENTER—See Greer Steel Co.; *U.S. Private,* pg. 479
GREFCO, INC.—See RGP Holding, Inc.; *U.S. Private,* pg. 903
GREGERSEN MALE-OG PROSESSTEKNIKK A/S—See Axel Johnson AB; *Int'l,* pg. 710
GREGG APPLIANCES INC.; *U.S. Private,* pg. 479
GREGG FOODS OF GARDEN GROVE, INC.—See Borden, Inc.; *U.S. Private,* pg. 158
GREGG FOODS OF PORTLAND, INC.—See Borden, Inc.; *U.S. Private,* pg. 158
GREGG INDUSTRIES, INC.; *U.S. Private,* pg. 480
GREGG INTERIM—See Vendex International N.V.; *Int'l,* pg. 1463
GREGG KNOWHOW—See Vendex International N.V.; *Int'l,* pg. 1463
GREGORY MINE—See The Broken Hill Proprietary Company Limited; *Int'l,* pg. 223
GREIF BOARD CORPORATION—See Greif Brothers Corporation; *U.S. Public,* pg. 763
GREIF BROS. CORPORATION—See Greif Brothers Corporation; *U.S. Public,* pg. 763
GREIF BROTHERS CORPORATION; *U.S. Public,* pg. 763
GREIF CONTAINERS, INC.—See Greif Brothers Corporation; *U.S. Public,* pg. 764
GREIF DIVISION—See Greif Brothers Corporation; *U.S. Public,* pg. 763
GREITER AG—See Johnson & Johnson; *U.S. Public,* pg. 929
GREMAC INC.—See Macromedia Incorporated; *U.S. Private,* pg. 693
GRENADA DOCTORS CLINIC, INC.—See Integrated Health Services, Inc.; *U.S. Public,* pg. 885
GRENADA FAMILY DOCTORS, INC.—See Integrated Health Services, Inc.; *U.S. Public,* pg. 885
GRENADIER REALTY CORP.—See Starrett HRH; *U.S. Private,* pg. 1035
GRENLAND INDUSTRIUTVIKLING A/S—See Norsk Hydro a.s; *Int'l,* pg. 959
GRENOBLE MILL—See Fort James Corporation; *U.S. Public,* pg. 673
GRESHAM OUTLOOK—See Lee Enterprises, Incorporated; *U.S. Public,* pg. 983
GRESS FOODS INC.; *U.S. Private,* pg. 480
GRESSER N.V.—See Brunel Holdings Plc; *Int'l,* pg. 231
DON GRESSWELL LTD.—See U.S. Office Products Company; *U.S. Public,* pg. 1687

GRETAGMACBETH AG—See Kollmorgen Corporation; *U.S. Public,* pg. 966
GRETAGMACBETH GMBH—See Kollmorgen Corporation; *U.S. Public,* pg. 966
GRETAGMACBETH LLC—See Kollmorgen Corporation; *U.S. Public,* pg. 965
GRETAGMACBETH (UK) LTD.—See Kollmorgen Corporation; *U.S. Public,* pg. 966
GRETOBA, S.A.—See Universal Corporation; *U.S. Public,* pg. 1695
GREY ADVERTISING INC.; *U.S. Public,* pg. 764
GREY ADVERTISING INC., WESTERN DIV.—See Grey Advertising Inc.; *U.S. Public,* pg. 764
GREY ASIA PACIFIC—See Grey Advertising Inc.; *U.S. Public,* pg. 765
GREY DAIKO ADVERTISING, INC.—See Daiko Advertising, Inc.; *Int'l,* pg. 366
GREY DESIGN & PROMOTION—See Grey Advertising Inc.; *U.S. Public,* pg. 764
GREY DIRECT—See Grey Advertising Inc.; *U.S. Public,* pg. 764
GREY DIRECTORY MARKETING INC.—See Grey Advertising Inc.; *U.S. Public,* pg. 764
GREY EAGLE DISTRIBUTORS INC.; *U.S. Private,* pg. 480
GREY ENTERTAINMENT INC.—See Grey Advertising Inc.; *U.S. Public,* pg. 765
GREY EUROPE/BRUSSELS—See Grey Advertising Inc.; *U.S. Public,* pg. 765
GREY EUROPE/DUSSELDORF—See Grey Advertising Inc.; *U.S. Public,* pg. 765
GREY EUROPE/LONDON—See Grey Advertising Inc.; *U.S. Public,* pg. 765
GREY HEALTHCARE GROUP—See Grey Advertising Inc.; *U.S. Public,* pg. 765
GREY INTERACTIVE—See Grey Advertising Inc.; *U.S. Public,* pg. 764
GREY WOLF, INC.; *U.S. Public,* pg. 765
GREYHOUND LEISURE SERVICES, INC.—See Viad Corp; *U.S. Public,* pg. 1718
GREYHOUND LINES, INC.; *U.S. Public,* pg. 765
GREYHOUND LINES OF CANADA LTD.; *Int'l,* pg. 559
GREYLAND BUSINESS PARK, PHASE I—See Cigna Corp.; *U.S. Public,* pg. 361
GREYLANDS BUSINESS PARK, PHASE 2—See Cigna Corp.; *U.S. Public,* pg. 361
GREYSTONE REALTY CORPORATION—See New York Life Insurance Company; *U.S. Private,* pg. 795
GREYVEST CAPITOL INC.; *Int'l,* pg. 559
GREYVEST TECHNOLOGY INC.—See Greyvest Capitol Inc.; *Int'l,* pg. 559
GRIBETZ INTERNATIONAL, INC.—See Leggett & Platt, Incorporated; *U.S. Public,* pg. 986
GRIBETZ THREADS, INC.—See Leggett & Platt, Incorporated; *U.S. Public,* pg. 986
GRIDWELD—See N.V. Bekaert S.A.; *Int'l,* pg. 185
THE GRIEVE CORPORATION; *U.S. Private,* pg. 480
GRIFFIN BACAL INC.; *U.S. Private,* pg. 480
GRIFFIN BACAL INTERNATIONAL B.V.—See Griffin Bacal Inc.; *U.S. Private,* pg. 480
GRIFFIN BACAL LTD.—See Griffin Bacal Inc.; *U.S. Private,* pg. 480
GRIFFIN BACAL PUBLICIDAD—See Griffin Bacal Inc.; *U.S. Private,* pg. 480
GRIFFIN BACAL VOLNY—See Griffin Bacal Inc.; *U.S. Private,* pg. 480
GRIFFIN CANADA INC.—See Amsted Industries Incorporated; *U.S. Private,* pg. 68
GRIFFIN CORPORATION; *U.S. Private,* pg. 480
GRIFFIN CREDIT SERVICES—See HSBC Holdings plc; *Int'l,* pg. 579
GRIFFIN ENVELOPE, INC.—See Mail-Well Inc.; *U.S. Public,* pg. 1038
GRIFFIN FINANCIAL SERVICES—See H.F. Ahmanson & Co.; *U.S. Public,* pg. 29
GRIFFIN GROUP, INC.; *U.S. Private,* pg. 480
GRIFFIN INDUSTRIES, INC.; *U.S. Private,* pg. 480
GRIFFIN MANUFACTURING CO.; *U.S. Private,* pg. 481
MERV GRIFFIN ENTERPRISES—See Sony Corporation; *Int'l,* pg. 1282
GRIFFIN PIPE PRODUCTS CO.—See Amsted Industries Incorporated; *U.S. Private,* pg. 68
GRIFFIN TECHNOLOGY INC., AMSEC DIV.—See Diebold, Incorporated; *U.S. Public,* pg. 506
GRIFFIN TECHNOLOGY INCORPORATED—See Diebold, Incorporated; *U.S. Public,* pg. 506
GRIFFIN TRANSPORT SERVICES, INC.; *U.S. Private,* pg. 481
GRIFFIN WHEEL CO.—See Amsted Industries Incorporated; *U.S. Private,* pg. 68
GRIFFINE SA—See Solvay S.A.; *Int'l,* pg. 1278
GRIFFINS FOODS LTD.—See Danone Group; *Int'l,* pg. 381
GRIFFITH COLOMBIA S.A.—See Griffith Laboratories Worldwide, Inc.; *U.S. Private,* pg. 481
GRIFFITH LABORATORIES (H.K.) LTD.—See Griffith Laboratories Worldwide, Inc.; *U.S. Private,* pg. 481
GRIFFITH LABORATORIES IBERIA S.A.—See Griffith Laboratories Worldwide, Inc.; *U.S. Private,* pg. 481
GRIFFITH LABORATORIES IRELAND LIMITED—See Griffith Laboratories Worldwide, Inc.; *U.S. Private,* pg. 481
GRIFFITH LABORATORIES ITALIA S.R.L.—See Griffith Laboratories Worldwide, Inc.; *U.S. Private,* pg. 481
GRIFFITH LABORATORIES, K.K.—See Griffith Laboratories Worldwide, Inc.; *U.S. Private,* pg. 481
GRIFFITH LABORATORIES (PHILS.) INC.—See Griffith Laboratories Worldwide, Inc.; *U.S. Private,* pg. 481
N.V. GRIFFITH LABORATORIES S.A.—See Griffith Laboratories Worldwide, Inc.; *U.S. Private,* pg. 481
GRIFFITH LABORATORIES WORLDWIDE—See Griffith Laboratories Worldwide, Inc.; *U.S. Private,* pg. 481
GRIFFITH LABORATORIES WORLDWIDE, INC.; *U.S. Private,* pg. 481

GRIFFITH MICRO SCIENCE INTERNATIONAL INC.—See Griffith Laboratories Worldwide, Inc.; *U.S. Private,* pg. 481
GRIFFITH PANAMA S.A.—See Griffith Laboratories Worldwide, Inc.; *U.S. Private,* pg. 481
GRIFFON CORP.; *U.S. Public,* pg. 766
JACK GRIGGS INC.; *U.S. Private,* pg. 482
GRIJALBO MONDADORI S.A.—See Arnoldo Mondadori Editore S.p.A.; *Int'l,* pg. 888
GRILLO-WERKE AG—See Metallgesellschaft AG; *Int'l,* pg. 861
GRIMA QUIMICA, S.A.—See Eli Lilly and Company; *U.S. Public,* pg. 994
B. GRIMM—See General Electric Company; *U.S. Public,* pg. 713
GRIMMER REALTY CO. INC.; *U.S. Private,* pg. 482
GRINDEX AB—See ITT Industries, Inc.; *U.S. Public,* pg. 860
GRINDING MACHINE-U.K.—See Litton Industries, Inc.; *U.S. Public,* pg. 1005
GRINDLAYS BAHRAIN BANK B.S.C. (C)—See Australia & New Zealand Banking Group Limited; *Int'l,* pg. 100
GRINDMASTER CORPORATION; *U.S. Private,* pg. 482
GRINDWELL NORTON LTD.—See Saint-Gobain; *Int'l,* pg. 1174
GRINNELL ASIA PACIFIC PTY LIMITED—See Tyco International Ltd.; *U.S. Public,* pg. 1651
GRINNELL CANADA LTD.—See Tyco International Ltd.; *U.S. Public,* pg. 1651
GRINNELL CORPORATION—See Tyco International Ltd.; *U.S. Public,* pg. 1651
GRINNELL EUROPE S.A./N.V.—See Tyco International Ltd.; *U.S. Public,* pg. 1651
GRINNELL FIRE PROTECTION SYSTEMS—See Thorn Security Group, Ltd.; *Int'l,* pg. 1386
GRINNELL FIRE PROTECTION SYSTEMS—See Tyco International Ltd.; *U.S. Public,* pg. 1647
GRINNELL FLOW CONTROL—See Tyco International Ltd.; *U.S. Public,* pg. 1650
GRINNELL SISTEMAS DE PROTECCION CONTRA INCENDIO S.A. DE C.V.—See Tyco International Ltd.; *U.S. Public,* pg. 1651
GRINNELL SUPPLY SALES ASIA PTE LTD.—See Tyco International Ltd.; *U.S. Public,* pg. 1651
GRINNELL SUPPLY SALES DIVISION—See Tyco International Ltd.; *U.S. Public,* pg. 1648
GRISANTI, INC.; *U.S. Private,* pg. 482
GRISEZ WAREHOUSE CO. INC.—See ConAgra, Inc.; *U.S. Public,* pg. 428
GRIST MILL COMPANY; *U.S. Public,* pg. 766
GRISWOLD INDUSTRIES, INC.; *U.S. Private,* pg. 482
GRIZZARD; *U.S. Private,* pg. 482
GRIZZARD—See Grizzard; *U.S. Private,* pg. 482
GRIZZARD/LOS ANGELES—See Grizzard; *U.S. Private,* pg. 482
GRIZZARD (SALES OFFICE)—See Grizzard; *U.S. Private,* pg. 482
GROCERS AND MERCHANTS INSURANCE, INC.—See Certified Grocers of California; *U.S. Private,* pg. 227
GROCERS & MERCHANTS MANAGEMENT CO.—See Certified Grocers of California; *U.S. Private,* pg. 227
GROCERS BAKING CO.; *U.S. Private,* pg. 482
GROCERS CAPITAL CO.—See Certified Grocers of California; *U.S. Private,* pg. 227
GROCERS DEVELOPMENT CO.—See Certified Grocers of California; *U.S. Private,* pg. 227
GROCERS EQUIPMENT CO.—See Certified Grocers of California; *U.S. Private,* pg. 227
GROCERS GENERAL MERCHANDISE CO.—See Certified Grocers of California; *U.S. Private,* pg. 227
GROCERS SPECIALTY CO.—See Certified Grocers of California; *U.S. Private,* pg. 227
GROCERS SUPPLY CO. INC.; *U.S. Private,* pg. 483
GROCERS SUPPLY CONVENIENCE STORES—See Grocers Supply Co. Inc.; *U.S. Private,* pg. 483
GROCERS SUPPLY INTERNATIONAL—See Grocers Supply Co. Inc.; *U.S. Private,* pg. 483
GROCERS SUPPLY PRODUCE—See Grocers Supply Co. Inc.; *U.S. Private,* pg. 483
GROCERY SUPPLY COMPANY DIVISION—See GSC Enterprises, Inc.; *U.S. Private,* pg. 436
GROCERY SUPPLY COMPANY-SAN ANTONIO—See GSC Enterprises, Inc.; *U.S. Private,* pg. 436
GROCERY SUPPLY OF DALLAS—See GSC Enterprises, Inc.; *U.S. Private,* pg. 436
GROCERY SUPPLY OF EL PASO—See GSC Enterprises, Inc.; *U.S. Private,* pg. 436
GROCERY SUPPLY OF JEFFERSON CITY—See GSC Enterprises, Inc.; *U.S. Private,* pg. 436
GROCERY SUPPLY OF OKLAHOMA CITY—See GSC Enterprises, Inc.; *U.S. Private,* pg. 436
GROCERY SUPPLY OF PADUCAH—See GSC Enterprises, Inc.; *U.S. Private,* pg. 436
GROEN, A DOVER INDUSTRIES CO.—See Dover Corporation; *U.S. Public,* pg. 521
GROENDYK, INC.—See American Industrial Partners; *U.S. Private,* pg. 56
GROENDYKE TRANSPORTS, INC.; *U.S. Private,* pg. 483
GROESBECK LUMBER & SUPPLY, INC.; *U.S. Private,* pg. 483
GROHE AMERICA, INC.—See Friedrich Grohe Armaturenfabrik GmbH & Co.; *Int'l,* pg. 559
FRIEDRICH GROHE ARMATURENFABRIK GMBH & CO.; *Int'l,* pg. 559
GROLIER AUSTRALIA PTY LIMITED—See Lagardere Groupe; *Int'l,* pg. 795
GROLIER EDUCATIONAL CORPORATION—See Lagardere Groupe; *Int'l,* pg. 794
GROLIER ELECTRONIC PUBLISHING, INC.—See Lagardere Groupe; *Int'l,* pg. 794
GROLIER ENTERPRISES CORPORATION—See Lagardere Groupe; *Int'l,* pg. 794
GROLIER ENTERPRISES INC.—See Lagardere Groupe; *Int'l,* pg. 794

GROLIER HACHETTE GESTIONE CLIENTI SRL—See Lagardere Groupe; *Int'l,* pg. 795
GROLIER HACHETTE INTERNATIONAL—See Lagardere Groupe; *Int'l,* pg. 795
GROLIER INC.—See Lagardere Groupe; *Int'l,* pg. 794
GROLIER INTERNATIONAL, INC.—See Lagardere Groupe; *Int'l,* pg. 794
GROLIER INTERNATIONAL LIMITED—See Lagardere Groupe; *Int'l,* pg. 795
GROLIER INTERSTATE, INC.—See Lagardere Groupe; *Int'l,* pg. 794
GROLIER LIMITED—See Lagardere Groupe; *Int'l,* pg. 794
GROLIER LIMITED CANADA—See Lagardere Groupe; *Int'l,* pg. 795
GROLIER LIMITED NEW ZEALAND—See Lagardere Groupe; *Int'l,* pg. 795
GROLIER OVERSEAS INC.—See Lagardere Groupe; *Int'l,* pg. 794
GROLIER PUBLISHING INC.—See Lagardere Groupe; *Int'l,* pg. 794
GROLIER READING PROGRAMS, INC.—See Lagardere Groupe; *Int'l,* pg. 794
GROLIER TELEMARKETING, INC.—See Lagardere Groupe; *Int'l,* pg. 794
GROLIER YEAR BOOK, INC.—See Lagardere Groupe; *Int'l,* pg. 794
GROLSCH IMPORTERS INC.—See Grolsch N.V.; *Int'l,* pg. 559
GROLSCH N.V.; *Int'l,* pg. 559
GROLSCH (UK) LTD.—See Grolsch N.V.; *Int'l,* pg. 559
GRONA KONSUM STOCKHOLM AB—See KF/Konsum Coop Group; *Int'l,* pg. 718
GRONINGER INDUSTRIEELE CREDIET BANK N.V.—See ABN-AMRO Holding N.V.; *Int'l,* pg. 9
GROOTE EYLANDT MINING COMPANY—See The Broken Hill Proprietary Company Limited; *Int'l,* pg. 224
GROOTVERBRUIK BV—See Koninklijke Ahold NV; *Int'l,* pg. 749
GROSCHOPP & CO. GMBH EMW ELEKTROMOTOREN-FEINBAUWERK; *Int'l,* pg. 559
GROSCHOPP, INC.—See Groschopp & Co. GmbH EMW Elektromotoren-Feinbauwerk; *Int'l,* pg. 559
JOHN GROSS & CO.; *U.S. Private,* pg. 483
GROSSENBURG CONCRETE—See Grossenburg Implements, Incorporated; *U.S. Private,* pg. 483
GROSSENBURG IMPLEMENTS, INCORPORATED; *U.S. Private,* pg. 483
GROSSET & DUNLAP, INC.—See Pearson plc; *Int'l,* pg. 1027
GROSSKRAFTWERK FRANKEN AG—See Viag AG; *Int'l,* pg. 1464
GROSSMAN IRON & STEEL COMPANY; *U.S. Private,* pg. 483
M. GROSSMAN & SON, INC.; *U.S. Private,* pg. 483
GROSSMAN'S, INC.—See Jeld-Wen, Inc.; *U.S. Private,* pg. 585
GROSSMONT BANK—See Zions Bancorporation; *U.S. Public,* pg. 1793
GROSVENOR CASINOS LTD.—See The Rank Group PLC; *Int'l,* pg. 1086
GROSVENOR MARKETING LTD.—See Associated British Foods plc; *Int'l,* pg. 92
GROSVENOR THEATRICAL PRODUCTIONS LTD.—See Granada Group PLC; *Int'l,* pg. 556
GROTE INDUSTRIES; *U.S. Private,* pg. 483
GROTECH CAPITAL GROUP, INC.; *U.S. Private,* pg. 483
GROTHUSEN GES.M.B.H.—See Knurr AG; *Int'l,* pg. 739
THE JOHN C. GROUB COMPANY INC.; *U.S. Private,* pg. 484
GROUND FLAT STOCK DIV.—See The L.S. Starrett Company; *U.S. Public,* pg. 1511
GROUND ROUND INC.; *U.S. Public,* pg. 766
GROUND SYSTEMS GROUP—See Raytheon Company; *U.S. Public,* pg. 1364
GROUND WATER ASSOCIATES, INC.—See Hydro Group, Inc.; *U.S. Private,* pg. 552
GROUND ZERO; *U.S. Private,* pg. 484
GROUNDWATER TECHNOLOGY GOVERNMENT SERVICES, INC.—See Fluor Corporation; *U.S. Public,* pg. 660
GROUP ACCOR ESPANA—See Accor S.A.; *Int'l,* pg. 21
GROUP DEKKO; *U.S. Private,* pg. 484
GROUP FABRICOM S.A.—See Tractebel; *Int'l,* pg. 1415
GROUP HEALTH PLAN, INC.—See Coventry Corporation; *U.S. Public,* pg. 454
GROUP INSURANCE INC. OF LOUISIANA; *U.S. Private,* pg. 484
GROUP INSURANCE OF COLORADO—See Group Insurance Inc. of Louisiana; *U.S. Private,* pg. 484
GROUP INSURANCE OF JACKSON—See Group Insurance Inc. of Louisiana; *U.S. Private,* pg. 484
GROUP INSURANCE OF SHREVEPORT—See Group Insurance Inc. of Louisiana; *U.S. Private,* pg. 484
GROUP LIFE & HEALTH INSURANCE COMPANY—See Blue Cross & Blue Shield of Texas, Inc.; *U.S. Private,* pg. 152
GROUP LOTUS LTD.—See Proton; *Int'l,* pg. 1071
GROUP MAINTENANCE AMERICA CORP.; *U.S. Public,* pg. 766
GROUP 1 AUTOMOTIVE, INC.; *U.S. Public,* pg. 767
GROUP 1 SOFTWARE, INC.—See COMNET Corporation; *U.S. Public,* pg. 417
GROUP 3 DESIGN—See GWP, Inc.; *U.S. Private,* pg. 437
GROUP W SATELLITE COMMUNICATIONS—See CBS Corporation; *U.S. Public,* pg. 275
GROUPACIER—See Groupe Usinor; *Int'l,* pg. 571
GROUPE ABILIS—See Vendex International N.V.; *Int'l,* pg. 1463
GROUPE ACCOR OF CANADA INC.—See Accor S.A.; *Int'l,* pg. 21
GROUPE ADA—See Hewlett-Packard Company; *U.S. Public,* pg. 817
GROUPE AIR FRANCE; *Int'l,* pg. 559

GROUPE BETON QUEBEC—See Holderbank Financiere Glaris Ltd.; *Int'l,* pg. 629
GROUPE BRENNTAG S.A.—See Veba AG; *Int'l,* pg. 1458
GROUPE BRUXELLES LAMBERT S.A.; *Int'l,* pg. 561
GROUPE CASINO; *Int'l,* pg. 562
GROUPE CONSTRUCTO—See G.T.C. Transcontinental Group Ltd.; *Int'l,* pg. 539
GROUPE DAFSA—See Primark Corporation; *U.S. Public,* pg. 1326
GROUPE DE LA CITE—See Alcatel Alsthom Compagnie Generale D'Electricite; *Int'l,* pg. 53
GROUPE DES ASSURANCES DE TUNISIE (GAT)—See Groupe GAN; *Int'l,* pg. 565
GROUPE DES CAISES D'EPARGNE; *Int'l,* pg. 563
GROUPE DMR S.A.—See Fujitsu Limited; *Int'l,* pg. 528
GROUPE ESAB S.A.—See Charter plc; *Int'l,* pg. 283
GROUPE GAN; *Int'l,* pg. 563
GROUPE GTM—See Lyonnaise des Eaux S.A.; *Int'l,* pg. 823
GROUPE LIMAGRAIN; *Int'l,* pg. 565
GROUPE L.S.A.—See C.E.P. Communication Group; *Int'l,* pg. 239
GROUPE MORROW INC.; *Int'l,* pg. 566
GROUPE ORIGNY S.A.—See Holderbank Financiere Glaris Ltd.; *Int'l,* pg. 629
GROUPE PERNOD RICARD; *Int'l,* pg. 566
GROUPE SAINT LOUIS; *Int'l,* pg. 567
GROUPE SEB; *Int'l,* pg. 568
GROUPE SEB ARGENTINA—See Groupe SEB; *Int'l,* pg. 568
GROUPE SEB CR—See Groupe SEB; *Int'l,* pg. 568
GROUPE SEB DO BRASIL—See Groupe SEB; *Int'l,* pg. 568
GROUPE SEB HUNGARY—See Groupe SEB; *Int'l,* pg. 568
GROUPE SEB POLSKA—See Groupe SEB; *Int'l,* pg. 568
GROUPE SEB SLOVENSKO—See Groupe SEB; *Int'l,* pg. 568
GROUPE SERVAIR (COMPAGNIE D'EXPLOITATION DES SERVICES AUXILIAIRIES AERIENS)—See Groupe Air France; *Int'l,* pg. 559
GROUPE STRAFOR FACOM; *Int'l,* pg. 569
GROUPE STRATEGIES—See Reed Elsevier plc; *Int'l,* pg. 1099
GROUPE SYSTRA—See SNCF; *Int'l,* pg. 1165
GROUPE USINOR; *Int'l,* pg. 570
GROUPE VERVIETOIS D'ASSUREURS S.A.—See Assicurazioni Generali S.p.A.; *Int'l,* pg. 91
GROUPE VOLKSWAGEN FRANCE S.A.—See Volkswagen AG; *Int'l,* pg. 1475
GROUPE ZODIAC; *Int'l,* pg. 572
S.C. GROUPEMENT IMMOBILIER GROUPIMO—See Cockerill Sambre; *Int'l,* pg. 301
GROUPO CAJA POSTAL—See Argentaria Corporacion Bancaria de Espana, S.A.; *Int'l,* pg. 81
GROUSE CREEK UNIT—See Hecla Mining Company; *U.S. Public,* pg. 804
GROVE COLES FRANCE, S.A.—See Hanson PLC; *Int'l,* pg. 594
GROVE COLES GMBH—See Hanson PLC; *Int'l,* pg. 594
GROVE DIVISION—See Orange-Co., Inc.; *U.S. Public,* pg. 1229
GROVE EUROPE—See Hanson PLC; *Int'l,* pg. 592
GROVE GEAR DIV.—See Regal-Beloit Corporation; *U.S. Public,* pg. 1370
GROVE HILL TELEPHONE CO.—See Telephone and Data Systems, Inc.; *U.S. Public,* pg. 1571
GROVE INSURANCE COMPANY LTD.—See Bristol-Myers Squibb Company; *U.S. Public,* pg. 256
GROVE VALVE & REGULATOR COMPANY; *U.S. Private,* pg. 484
GROVE WORLDWIDE—See Hanson PLC; *Int'l,* pg. 593
GROVENBERG—See Tenney Environmental; *U.S. Private,* pg. 1077
GROVER PISTON RING DIVISION—See Furon Company; *U.S. Public,* pg. 689
GROVE'S DICTIONARIES OF MUSIC INC.—See Georg von Holtzbrinck GmbH; *Int'l,* pg. 1479
SAMUEL GROVES & CO., LTD.—See Zero Corporation; *U.S. Public,* pg. 1791
GROW BIZ GAMES, INC.—See Grow Biz International, Inc.; *U.S. Public,* pg. 767
GROW BIZ INTERNATIONAL, INC.; *U.S. Public,* pg. 767
GROW FORCE AUSTRALIA LIMITED—See Imperial Chemical Industries PLC; *Int'l,* pg. 664
GROW GROUP CANADA LTD.—See Imperial Chemical Industries PLC; *Int'l,* pg. 663
GROW GROUP, INC.—See Imperial Chemical Industries PLC; *Int'l,* pg. 663
GROWMARK, INC.; *U.S. Private,* pg. 484
GROWTH MANAGEMENT CORP.—See Family Inns of America, Inc.; *U.S. Private,* pg. 392
GRUBB & ELLIS COMPANY; *U.S. Public,* pg. 767
GRUBB & ELLIS MANAGEMENT SERVICES, INC.—See Grubb & Ellis Company; *U.S. Public,* pg. 767
GRUBER'S FOOD TOWN—See Seaway Food Town, Inc.; *U.S. Public,* pg. 1453
MAX GRUENHUT CHILE—See Circle International Group, Inc.; *U.S. Public,* pg. 373
MAX GRUENHUT, GMBH & CO.—See Circle International Group, Inc.; *U.S. Public,* pg. 373
MAX GRUENHUT INTERNATIONAL CANADA INC—See Circle International Group, Inc.; *U.S. Public,* pg. 373
MAX GRUENHUT INTERNATIONAL, INC.—See Circle International Group, Inc.; *U.S. Public,* pg. 372
GRUMMAN OHIO CORP.—See Northrop Grumman Corporation; *U.S. Public,* pg. 1198
GRUMMAN OLSON DIVISION—See Northrop Grumman Corporation; *U.S. Public,* pg. 1198
GRUN + BILFINGER—See Bilfinger + Berger Bauaktiengesellschaft; *Int'l,* pg. 196
GRUNAU ILLERTISSEN GMBH—See Henkel KGaA; *Int'l,* pg. 609
GRUND- UND PFAHLBAU GMBH—See Bilfinger + Berger Bauaktiengesellschaft; *Int'l,* pg. 195

GRUNDSTUCKE- UND GEBAUDEVERWALTUNGS GMBH—See Creditanstalt-Bankverein; *Int'l*, pg. 347
GRUNDSTUCKS- UND VERMOGENSVERWALTUNGSGESELLSCHAFT GERETSRIED MBH—See Commerzbank AG; *Int'l*, pg. 309
BV GRUNDSTUCKSENTWICKLUNGS GMBH & CO. JOTA KG—See Bayerische Vereinsbank Group; *Int'l*, pg. 178
GRUNDSTUCKSGESELLSCHAFT GEETBANK-HAUS—See Bayerische Vereinsbank Group; *Int'l*, pg. 179
GRUNDSTUCKSGESELLSCHAFT JUNGFERNSTIEG MBH—See Bayerische Vereinsbank Group; *Int'l*, pg. 179
GRUNDSTUCKSGESELLSCHAFT SIMON BESCHRANKT HAFTENDE KOMMANDIGESEELLSCHAFT—See Bayerische Vereinsbank Group; *Int'l*, pg. 179
GRUNDSTUCKSVERWALTUNG LBH GMBH & CO.—See Ruhrgas Aktiengesellschaft; *Int'l*, pg. 1148
GRUNDSTUCKSVERWALTUNGSGESELLSCHAFT RUHRGAS AG & CO.—See Ruhrgas Aktiengesellschaft; *Int'l*, pg. 1148
GRUNDY WORLDWIDE—See Pearson plc; *Int'l*, pg. 1025
GRUNER + JAHR AG & CO.—See Bertelsmann AG; *Int'l*, pg. 190
GRUNER + JAHR AG & CO. DRUCK UND VERLAGSHAUS—See Bertelsmann AG; *Int'l*, pg. 190
GRUNER + JAHR AG (SCHWEIZ)—See Bertelsmann AG; *Int'l*, pg. 190
GRUNER + JAHR (ESPANA) DISTRIBUIDORA S.A.—See Bertelsmann AG; *Int'l*, pg. 190
GRUNER + JAHR INTERNATIONAL MARKETING- AND MEDIA SERVICES, INC.—See Bertelsmann AG; *Int'l*, pg. 190
GRUNER + JAHR OF THE UK—See Bertelsmann AG; *Int'l*, pg. 190
GRUNER + JAHR USA PUBLISHING, INC.—See Bertelsmann AG; *Int'l*, pg. 190
GRUNER + JAHR VERLAGS-GMBH—See Bertelsmann AG; *Int'l*, pg. 191
MAX GRUNHUT GMBH—See The Peninsular and Oriental Steam Navigation Company; *Int'l*, pg. 1033
R.J. GRUNTS/CHICAGO—See Lettuce Entertain You Enterprises, Inc.; *U.S. Private*, pg. 661
GRUNZWEIG & HARTMANN UND GLASFASER AG—See Saint-Gobain; *Int'l*, pg. 1176
GRUPO ACERERO DEL NORTE S.A. DE C.V. (GAN); *Int'l*, pg. 572
GRUPO AGROGEN S.A. DE C.V., MEXICO—See Dekalb Genetics Corporation; *U.S. Public*, pg. 493
GRUPO BANCO EXTERIOR—See Argentaria Corporacion Bancaria de Espana, S.A.; *Int'l*, pg. 80
GRUPO BARRO TESTA—See Testa International; *Int'l*, pg. 1377
GRUPO CARPENTER S.A. DE C.V.—See Carpenter Technology Corporation; *U.S. Public*, pg. 308
GRUPO CARSO S.A. DE C.V.; *Int'l*, pg. 572
GRUPO CASA AUTREY; *Int'l*, pg. 573
GRUPO CELANESE—See Hoechst Aktiengesellschaft; *Int'l*, pg. 625
GRUPO CEMENTOS DE CHIHUAHUA S.A. DE C.V.; *Int'l*, pg. 573
GRUPO COMERCIAL CHEDRAUI S.A. DE C.V.; *Int'l*, pg. 573
GRUPO CONDUMEX—See Grupo Carso S.A. de C.V.; *Int'l*, pg. 572
GRUPO CONTINENTAL S.A.; *Int'l*, pg. 573
GRUPO CRUZCAMPO S.A.—See Diageo Plc; *Int'l*, pg. 412
GRUPO CYDSA, S.A. DE C.V.—See CYDSA S.A.; *Int'l*, pg. 246
GRUPO ECA S.A. DE C.V.—See Eclipse Inc.; *U.S. Private*, pg. 361
GRUPO ECHLIN AUTOMOTRIZ—See Echlin Inc.; *U.S. Public*, pg. 561
GRUPO ELEKTRA S.A. DE C.V.; *Int'l*, pg. 573
GRUPO EMBOTELLADORAS UNIDAS SA DE CV; *Int'l*, pg. 574
GRUPO FINANCIERO BANAMEX/ACCIVAL, S.A. DE C.V.; *Int'l*, pg. 574
GRUPO FINANCIERO SANTANDER MEXICO—See Banco Santander; *Int'l*, pg. 144
GRUPO GIGANTE S.A. DE C.V.; *Int'l*, pg. 574
GRUPO GRIFOLS, S.A.—See The Green Cross Corporation; *Int'l*, pg. 558
GRUPO IBERIA; *Int'l*, pg. 574
GRUPO IBERPHONE INVERSIONES, S.A.—See Caja de Madrid Group; *Int'l*, pg. 252
GRUPO ICI DE MEXICO, S.A. DE C.V.—See Imperial Chemical Industries PLC; *Int'l*, pg. 664
GRUPO IMSA S.A. DE C.V.; *Int'l*, pg. 575
GRUPO INDUSTRIAL BIMBO S.A. DE C.V.; *Int'l*, pg. 575
GRUPO INDUSTRIAL CAMESA S.A. DE C.V.; *Int'l*, pg. 575
GRUPO INDUSTRIAL DURANGO S.A. DE C.V.; *Int'l*, pg. 575
GRUPO INDUSTRIAL MINERA MEXICO, S.A. DE C.V.—See Asarco Incorporated; *U.S. Public*, pg. 138
GRUPO INDUSTRIAL MORGAN, S.A. DE C.V.—See Morgan Crucible Co. Plc; *Int'l*, pg. 891
GRUPO INDUSTRIAL SALTILLO—See Vitromex, S.A.; *Int'l*, pg. 1469
GRUPO INMOBILIARIO CAISSE—See Caisse de depot et placement du Quebec; *Int'l*, pg. 249
GRUPO IUSACELL SA DE CV—See Bell Atlantic Corporation; *Int'l*, pg. 204
GRUPO MEXICANO DE DESARROLLO; *Int'l*, pg. 575
GRUPO MEXICO S.A. DE C.V.—See Asarco Incorporated; *U.S. Public*, pg. 138
GRUPO MODELO S.A.—See Anheuser-Busch Companies, Inc.; *U.S. Public*, pg. 115
GRUPO PALACIO DE HIERRO S.A. DE C.V.; *Int'l*, pg. 576
GRUPO POSADAS S.A. DE C.V.; *Int'l*, pg. 576
GRUPO PROTEXA S.A. DE C.V.; *Int'l*, pg. 576
GRUPO SANTANDER—See Banco Santander; *Int'l*, pg. 144
GRUPO SIDEK, S.A. DE C.V.; *Int'l*, pg. 576

GRUPO SIEMENS S.A. DE C.V.—See Siemens AG; *Int'l*, pg. 1247
GRUPO SIMEC, S.A. DE C.V.—See Grupo Sidek, S.A. de C.V.; *Int'l*, pg. 576
GRUPO SITRA, S.A. DE C.V.—See Kvaerner a.s.a.; *Int'l*, pg. 775
GRUPO SITUR SA DE CV—See Grupo Sidek, S.A. de C.V.; *Int'l*, pg. 576
GRUPO SYNKRO, S.A. DE C.V.; *Int'l*, pg. 576
GRUPO SYR, S.A. DE C.V.; *Int'l*, pg. 576
GRUPO TABAQUERO CANARIO, S.A.—See Tabacalera, S.A.; *Int'l*, pg. 1346
GRUPO TELEVISA, S.A. DE C.V.; *Int'l*, pg. 576
GRUPO TERMOINDUSTRIAL ECA, S.A. DE C.V.—See Eclipse Inc.; *U.S. Private*, pg. 361
GRUPO TRIBASA S.A. DE C.V.; *Int'l*, pg. 577
GRUPO VIDEO VISA S.A. DE C.V.; *Int'l*, pg. 577
GRUPPO DOLCIARIO ITALIANO S.P.A.—See Nestle S.A.; *Int'l*, pg. 920
GRUPPO EDITORIALE JACKSON SRL—See VNU Verenigde Nederlandse Uitgeversbedrijven B.V.; *Int'l*, pg. 1445
GRUPPO LEPETIT S.P.A.—See The Dow Chemical Company; *U.S. Public*, pg. 524
GRYBAUSKAS BEATRICE; *U.S. Private*, pg. 485
GTECH CORPORATION; *U.S. Public*, pg. 767
GTI CORPORATION; *U.S. Public*, pg. 767
GUAM PUBLICATIONS, INC.—See Gannett Company, Inc.; *U.S. Public*, pg. 702
GUANGDONG ERICSSON ENGINEERING COMPANY LTD.—See Telefonaktiebolaget LM Ericsson; *Int'l*, pg. 1368
GUANGDONG NORTEL TELECOMMUNICATIONS SWITCHING EQUIPMENT LIMITED—See Northern Telecom Limited; *Int'l*, pg. 970
GUANGDONG OTSUKA PHARMACEUTICAL CO., LTD.—See Otsuka Pharmaceutical Co., Ltd.; *Int'l*, pg. 1014
GUANGDONG SANYO AIR CONDITIONERS SYSTEM MANUFACTURING LTD.—See Sanyo Electric Co., Ltd.; *Int'l*, pg. 1192
GUANGDONG SHUNDE NISSIN FOODS CO., LTD.—See Nissin Food Products Co., Ltd.; *Int'l*, pg. 950
GUANGZHOU CHIA TAI MAKRO (JIAJING) CO. LTD.—See SHV Holdings N.V.; *Int'l*, pg. 1155
GUANGZHOU HENKEL CHEMICAL PRODUCTS CO. LTD.—See Henkel KGaA; *Int'l*, pg. 611
GUANGZHOU REPRESENTATIVE OFFICE—See Komatsu Ltd.; *Int'l*, pg. 744
GUANO-WERKE H GMBH—See BASF AG; *Int'l*, pg. 104
GUARANTEE AMERICAN LIFE COMPANY—See Guarantee Life Insurance Co.; *U.S. Public*, pg. 768
GUARANTEE ELECTRICAL COMPANY; *U.S. Private*, pg. 485
GUARANTEE LIFE INSURANCE CO.; *U.S. Public*, pg. 768
GUARANTEE NATIONAL INSURANCE COMPANY—See Orion Capital Corporation; *U.S. Public*, pg. 1231
GUARANTEE TITLE & TRUST CO.; *U.S. Private*, pg. 485
GUARANTY ASSET PROTECTION SERVICES, INC.—See INMC Mortgage Holdings, Inc.; *U.S. Public*, pg. 857
GUARANTY BROADCASTING—See Guaranty Corporation; *U.S. Private*, pg. 485
GUARANTY CORPORATION; *U.S. Private*, pg. 485
GUARANTY F.S.B.—See Temple-Inland Inc.; *U.S. Public*, pg. 1575
GUARANTY INCOME LIFE INSURANCE CO.—See Guaranty Corporation; *U.S. Private*, pg. 485
GUARD PUBLISHING COMPANY; *U.S. Private*, pg. 485
THE GUARDIAN—See Hollinger Inc.; *Int'l*, pg. 631
GUARDIAN ALARM CO.; *U.S. Private*, pg. 485
GUARDIAN ALARM OF CLEVELAND—See Guardian Alarm Co.; *U.S. Private*, pg. 485
GUARDIAN & OBSERVER—See Guardian Media Group plc; *Int'l*, pg. 577
GUARDIAN AUTOMOTIVE—See Guardian Industries Corp.; *U.S. Private*, pg. 486
GUARDIAN BAILLIE GIFFORD, LTD.—See The Guardian Life Insurance Company of America; *U.S. Private*, pg. 486
GUARDIAN CARE OF AHOSKIE—See Vencor, Inc.; *U.S. Public*, pg. 1712
GUARDIAN CARE OF BURGAW—See Vencor, Inc.; *U.S. Public*, pg. 1712
GUARDIAN CARE OF ELIZABETH CITY—See Vencor, Inc.; *U.S. Public*, pg. 1712
GUARDIAN CARE OF ELKIN—See Vencor, Inc.; *U.S. Public*, pg. 1712
GUARDIAN CARE OF FARMVILLE—See Vencor, Inc.; *U.S. Public*, pg. 1712
GUARDIAN CARE OF GASTONIA—See Vencor, Inc.; *U.S. Public*, pg. 1712
GUARDIAN CARE OF GOLDSBORO—See Vencor, Inc.; *U.S. Public*, pg. 1712
GUARDIAN CARE OF HENDERSON—See Vencor, Inc.; *U.S. Public*, pg. 1712
GUARDIAN CARE OF KENANSVILLE—See Vencor, Inc.; *U.S. Public*, pg. 1712
GUARDIAN CARE OF KINSTON—See Vencor, Inc.; *U.S. Public*, pg. 1712
GUARDIAN CARE OF MONROE—See Vencor, Inc.; *U.S. Public*, pg. 1712
GUARDIAN CARE OF NEW BERN—See Vencor, Inc.; *U.S. Public*, pg. 1713
GUARDIAN CARE OF ROANOKE RAPIDS—See Vencor, Inc.; *U.S. Public*, pg. 1713
GUARDIAN CARE OF ROCKY MOUNT—See Vencor, Inc.; *U.S. Public*, pg. 1713
GUARDIAN CARE OF SCOTLAND NECK—See Vencor, Inc.; *U.S. Public*, pg. 1713
GUARDIAN CARE OF WALNUT COVE—See Vencor, Inc.; *U.S. Public*, pg. 1713
GUARDIAN CARE OF ZEBULON—See Vencor, Inc.; *U.S. Public*, pg. 1713
GUARDIAN ESPANOLA S.A.—See Pechiney S.A.; *Int'l*, pg. 1030

GUARDIAN INDUSTRIES CORP.; *U.S. Private*, pg. 485
GUARDIAN INSPECTION, S.A. DE C.V.—See Shaw Industries Ltd.; *Int'l*, pg. 1231
THE GUARDIAN INSURANCE & ANNUITY CO. (GIAC)—See The Guardian Life Insurance Company of America; *U.S. Private*, pg. 486
GUARDIAN INVESTOR SERVICES CORP.—See The Guardian Life Insurance Company of America; *U.S. Private*, pg. 486
THE GUARDIAN LIFE INSURANCE COMPANY OF AMERICA; *U.S. Private*, pg. 486
GUARDIAN MEDIA GROUP PLC; *Int'l*, pg. 577
GUARDIAN OILFIELD SERVICES—See Shaw Industries Ltd.; *Int'l*, pg. 1231
GUARDIAN PRODUCTS/CAPITAL WIRE—See Wassall Plc; *Int'l*, pg. 1487
GUARDIAN PRODUCTS, INC.—See Sunrise Medical, Inc.; *U.S. Public*, pg. 1535
GUARDIAN PTS LTD—See Shaw Industries Ltd.; *Int'l*, pg. 1231
GUARDIAN ROYAL EXCHANGE PLC; *Int'l*, pg. 577
GUARDIAN TRANSPORTATION CORP.—See Guardian Industries Corp.; *U.S. Private*, pg. 485
GUARDSMAN CONSUMER PRODUCTS DIV.—See Lilly Industries, Inc.; *U.S. Public*, pg. 995
GUARDSMARK, INC.; *U.S. Private*, pg. 486
GUATEMALTECA SHELL SA—See Royal Dutch/Shell Group of Companies; *Int'l*, pg. 1141
GUAY, BLOUIN, & ASSOCIATES, INC.—See Willis Corroon Group PLC; *Int'l*, pg. 1509
GUAYAMA CORRECTIONAL CENTER—See Corrections Corporation of America; *U.S. Public*, pg. 450
THE GUBER PETERS ENTERTAINMENT COMPANY—See Sony Corporation; *Int'l*, pg. 1283
THE GUBER PETERS ENTERTAINMENT COMPANY (BURBANK)—See Sony Corporation; *Int'l*, pg. 1283
THE GUBER PETERS ENTERTAINMENT COMPANY (NEW YORK)—See Sony Corporation; *Int'l*, pg. 1283
GUCCI AMERICA INC.—See Investcorp International; *Int'l*, pg. 686
GUCCIO GUCCI S.P.A.—See Investcorp International; *Int'l*, pg. 686
GUDEBROD, INC.; *U.S. Private*, pg. 486
GUELPH PRODUCTS—See Chrysler Corporation; *U.S. Public*, pg. 354
GUERIN S.A.—See Pirelli S.p.A.; *Int'l*, pg. 1059
OY GUERLAIN AB—See LVMH Moet Hennessy Louis Vuitton; *Int'l*, pg. 780
GUERLAIN (ASIA PACIFIC) LTD.—See LVMH Moet Hennessy Louis Vuitton; *Int'l*, pg. 780
GUERLAIN (ASIA PACIFIC) LTD.-NEW ZEALAND BRANCH—See LVMH Moet Hennessy Louis Vuitton; *Int'l*, pg. 780
GUERLAIN BENELUX S.A.—See LVMH Moet Hennessy Louis Vuitton; *Int'l*, pg. 780
GUERLAIN CANADA LTD. LTEE—See LVMH Moet Hennessy Louis Vuitton; *Int'l*, pg. 780
GUERLAIN DE MEXICO S.A.—See LVMH Moet Hennessy Louis Vuitton; *Int'l*, pg. 780
GUERLAIN DE PORTUGAL—See LVMH Moet Hennessy Louis Vuitton; *Int'l*, pg. 780
GUERLAIN FAR EAST—See LVMH Moet Hennessy Louis Vuitton; *Int'l*, pg. 780
GUERLAIN GMBH—See LVMH Moet Hennessy Louis Vuitton; *Int'l*, pg. 780
GUERLAIN, INC.—See LVMH Moet Hennessy Louis Vuitton; *Int'l*, pg. 780
GUERLAIN KK—See LVMH Moet Hennessy Louis Vuitton; *Int'l*, pg. 780
GUERLAIN LTD.—See LVMH Moet Hennessy Louis Vuitton; *Int'l*, pg. 780
GUERLAIN (MALAYSIA) SDN BHD—See LVMH Moet Hennessy Louis Vuitton; *Int'l*, pg. 780
GUERLAIN PARFUMEUR GMBH—See LVMH Moet Hennessy Louis Vuitton; *Int'l*, pg. 780
GUERLAIN PUERTO RICO INC.—See LVMH Moet Hennessy Louis Vuitton; *Int'l*, pg. 780
GUERLAIN S.A.—See LVMH Moet Hennessy Louis Vuitton; *Int'l*, pg. 780
GUERLAIN S.A.E.—See LVMH Moet Hennessy Louis Vuitton; *Int'l*, pg. 780
GUERLAIN SPA—See LVMH Moet Hennessy Louis Vuitton; *Int'l*, pg. 780
GUERLAIN TAIWAN CO. LTD.—See LVMH Moet Hennessy Louis Vuitton; *Int'l*, pg. 780
GUERLAIN WESTERN HEMISPHERE CO. LTD.—See LVMH Moet Hennessy Louis Vuitton; *Int'l*, pg. 780
GUERNSEY INTERNATIONAL FUND MANAGERS LIMITED—See ING Groep N.V.; *Int'l*, pg. 648
GUERNSEY INTERNATIONAL INVESTMENT MANAGEMENT LIMITED—See The Bank of Bermuda Limited; *Int'l*, pg. 151
GUESS ?, INC.; *U.S. Public*, pg. 768
GUEST COMPUTER SERVICES LTD.—See Assicurazioni Generali S.p.A.; *Int'l*, pg. 90
GUEST INTERNATIONAL (CANADA) LTD.—See Guest Supply, Inc.; *U.S. Public*, pg. 768
GUEST INTERNATIONAL (ENGLAND) LTD.—See Guest Supply, Inc.; *U.S. Public*, pg. 768
GUEST INTERNATIONAL (NEW ZEALAND) LTD.—See Guest Supply, Inc.; *U.S. Public*, pg. 768
GUEST SERVICES, INC.; *U.S. Private*, pg. 486
GUEST SUPPLY, INC.; *U.S. Public*, pg. 768
GUESTINFORMANT, INC.—See AT&T Corporation; *U.S. Public*, pg. 11
GUHL IKEBANA GMBH—See Kao Corporation; *Int'l*, pg. 718
GUIDANCE & CONTROL SYSTEMS DIV.—See Litton Industries, Inc.; *U.S. Public*, pg. 1002
GUIDANT CORPORATION; *U.S. Public*, pg. 768
GUIDANT CORPORATION-CARDIAC & VASCULAR SURGERY GROUP—See Guidant Corporation; *U.S. Public*, pg. 768

GUIDANT CORPORATION-CARDIAC RHYTHM MANAGEMENT GROUP—See Guidant Corporation; *U.S. Public*, pg. 768
GUIDANT CORPORATION-VASCULAR INTERVENTION GROUP—See Guidant Corporation; *U.S. Public*, pg. 768
GUIDEPOSTS ASSOCIATES, INC.; *U.S. Private*, pg. 487
GUIGOZ FRANCE S.A.—See Nestle S.A.; *Int'l*, pg. 920
GUIGOZ S.A.—See Nestle S.A.; *Int'l*, pg. 916
GUIGUES S.A.—See Technip; *Int'l*, pg. 1361
GUILD MOLDERS DIVISION—See Crown Cork & Seal Company, Inc.; *U.S. Public*, pg. 463
GUILD MUSIC DIVISION—See Fender Musical Instruments; *U.S. Public*, pg. 400
GUILFORD EUROPE, LTD.—See Guilford Mills, Inc.; *U.S. Public*, pg. 769
GUILFORD KAPWOOD GMBH—See Guilford Mills, Inc.; *U.S. Public*, pg. 769
GUILFORD MILLS (APPAREL, HOME & INDUSTRIAL FABRICS)—See Guilford Mills, Inc.; *U.S. Public*, pg. 769
GUILFORD MILLS (AUTOMOTIVE & UPHOLSTERY FABRICS)—See Guilford Mills, Inc.; *U.S. Public*, pg. 769
GUILFORD MILLS (FIBERS)—See Guilford Mills, Inc.; *U.S. Public*, pg. 769
GUILFORD MILLS, INC.; *U.S. Public*, pg. 768
GUILFORD OF MAINE, INC.—See Interface Inc.; *U.S. Public*, pg. 889
GUILFORD RAIL SYSTEM—See Guilford Transportation Industries Inc.; *U.S. Private*, pg. 487
GUILFORD TEXLA N.V.—See Guilford Mills, Inc.; *U.S. Public*, pg. 769
GUILFORD TRANSPORTATION INDUSTRIES INC.; *U.S. Private*, pg. 487
GUILIN HENKEL DETERGENTS & CLEANING PRODUCTS CO. LTD.—See Henkel KGaA; *Int'l*, pg. 611
GUILIN-NOKIA TELECOM LTD.—See Oy Nokia Ab/Nokia Group; *Int'l*, pg. 954
GUINESS FINANCE AUSTRALIA LIMITED—See Diageo Plc; *Int'l*, pg. 412
GUINESS KENYA LIMITED—See Diageo Plc; *Int'l*, pg. 412
GUINESS BREWING WORLDWIDE LTD.—See Diageo Plc; *Int'l*, pg. 412
GUINESS ENTERPRISES LTD.—See Diageo Plc; *Int'l*, pg. 412
GUINESS IMPORT COMPANY—See Diageo Plc; *Int'l*, pg. 412
GUINESS IRELAND (HOLDINGS) LTD.—See Diageo Plc; *Int'l*, pg. 412
GUINESS MAHON HOLDINGS PLC—See Bank of Yokohama; *Int'l*, pg. 159
GUINESS NORTHERN IRELAND LIMITED—See Diageo Plc; *Int'l*, pg. 412
GUINESS PLC—See Diageo Plc; *Int'l*, pg. 412
GUINESS PUBLISHING LTD.—See Diageo Plc; *Int'l*, pg. 412
GUINESS YOKOHAMA LEASING LIMITED—See Bank of Yokohama; *Int'l*, pg. 159
GULDSMEDSHYTTE BRUKS AB—See Sandvik AB; *Int'l*, pg. 1185
GULF ASIA INTERNATIONAL CORPORATION—See EEI Corporation; *Int'l*, pg. 426
GULF ASIA TRAVEL CORPORATION—See EEI Corporation; *Int'l*, pg. 426
GULF ASSIST E.C.—See Corporacion MAPFRE, Compania Internacional de Reaseguros, S.A.; *Int'l*, pg. 334
GULF CANADA RESOURCES - JAKARTA—See Gulf Canada Resources Ltd; *Int'l*, pg. 577
GULF CANADA RESOURCES LTD.; *Int'l*, pg. 577
GULF CANADA RESOURCES - SINGAPORE—See Gulf Canada Resources Ltd; *Int'l*, pg. 577
GULF COAST DISTRICT—See American Financial Group; *U.S. Public*, pg. 75
GULF COAST EAP SERVICES, INC.—See Magellan Health Services, Inc.; *U.S. Public*, pg. 1036
GULF COAST FOOD SERVICE INC.—See Sun City Industries, Inc.; *U.S. Public*, pg. 1529
GULF COAST GALVANIZING INC.—See Aztec Manufacturing Co.; *U.S. Public*, pg. 159
GULF COAST LEAGUE TWINS—See Minnesota Twins Baseball Club; *U.S. Private*, pg. 751
GULF COAST RECYCLING; *U.S. Private*, pg. 487
GULF CONFERENCE—See EMAP Plc; *Int'l*, pg. 452
GULF ENERGY DEVELOPMENT CORP.—See Royal Dutch/Shell Group of Companies; *Int'l*, pg. 1136
GULF ENERGY GATHERING & PROCESSING CORP.—See Royal Dutch/Shell Group of Companies; *Int'l*, pg. 1136
GULF ENERGY MARKETING CO.—See Royal Dutch/Shell Group of Companies; *Int'l*, pg. 1136
GULF ENERGY PIPELINE CO.—See Royal Dutch/Shell Group of Companies; *Int'l*, pg. 1136
GULF INSURANCE COMPANY—See Travelers Group; *U.S. Public*, pg. 1633
GULF LINE BROKERAGE—See US 1 Industries Inc.; *U.S. Public*, pg. 1687
GULF LINE TRANSPORTATION—See US 1 Industries Inc.; *U.S. Public*, pg. 1687
GULF LUMBER COMPANY, INC.; *U.S. Private*, pg. 487
GULF MARINE FAR EAST PTE. LTD.—See Gulfmark Offshore Inc.; *U.S. Public*, pg. 769
GULF OF SUEZ PETROLEUM COMPANY—See Amoco Corporation; *U.S. Public*, pg. 102
GULF OFFSHORE DO BRASIL—See Gulfmark Offshore Inc.; *U.S. Public*, pg. 769
GULF OFFSHORE MARINE—See Gulfmark Offshore Inc.; *U.S. Public*, pg. 769
GULF OFFSHORE MARINE INTERNATIONAL, INC.—See Gulfmark Offshore Inc.; *U.S. Public*, pg. 769
GULF OFFSHORE N.S. LTD.—See Gulfmark Offshore Inc.; *U.S. Public*, pg. 769
GULF OIL—See Cumberland Farms, Inc.; *U.S. Private*, pg. 295

GULF OIL LIMITED PARTNERSHIP; *U.S. Private*, pg. 487
GULF PETROCHEMICAL INDUSTRIES CO.—See Kuwait Petroleum Corporation; *Int'l*, pg. 766
GULF POWER COMPANY—See Southern Company; *U.S. Public*, pg. 1490
GULF PUBLISHING COMPANY, INC.—See Knight-Ridder, Inc.; *U.S. Public*, pg. 964
GULF SOUTH MEDICAL SUPPLY—See Physician Sales and Services Inc.; *U.S. Public*, pg. 1294
GULF SOUTH MEDICAL SUPPLY, INC.—See Physician Sales and Services Inc.; *U.S. Public*, pg. 1294
GULF STATE MORTGAGE, INC.—See The Royal Bank of Scotland plc; *Int'l*, pg. 1133
GULF STATE SPECIALTIES, INC.—See Gulf States Asphalt Company, Inc.; *U.S. Private*, pg. 487
GULF STATES ASPHALT COMPANY, INC.; *U.S. Private*, pg. 487
GULF STATES, INC.; *U.S. Private*, pg. 487
GULF STATES MANUFACTURERS, INC.—See Jannock Limited; *Int'l*, pg. 699
GULF STATES PAPER CORPORATION; *U.S. Private*, pg. 487
GULF STATES STEEL, INC.; *U.S. Private*, pg. 488
GULF STATES TOYOTA, INC.; *U.S. Private*, pg. 488
GULF TELEPHONE CO.—See St. Joe Corp.; *U.S. Public*, pg. 1427
GULFCO INVESTMENT, INC.—See Mercury Finance Co.; *U.S. Public*, pg. 1093
GULFMARK ENERGY INC.—See Adams Resources & Energy, Inc.; *U.S. Public*, pg. 19
GULFMARK OFFSHORE INC.; *U.S. Public*, pg. 769
GULFPORT CONVALESCENT CENTER MANOR—See Vencor, Inc.; *U.S. Public*, pg. 1713
GULFSTAR ENERGY, INC.—See Domain Energy Corporation; *U.S. Public*, pg. 516
GULFSTREAM AEROSPACE CORPORATION—See Forstmann Little & Co.; *U.S. Private*, pg. 419
GULFSTREAM LEASING CORPORATION—See NationsBank Corporation; *U.S. Public*, pg. 1162
GULIO GALAVOTTI BV—See Bayerische Vereinsbank Group; *Int'l*, pg. 181
GULL ELECTRONIC SYSTEMS DIV.—See Parker Hannifin Corporation; *U.S. Public*, pg. 1262
GULLFIBER AB—See Saint-Gobain; *Int'l*, pg. 1176
GUMACO INDUSTRIA E COMERCIO LTDA.—See Gencor Industries, Inc.; *U.S. Public*, pg. 705
GUMMIWERKE FULDA—See The Goodyear Tire & Rubber Company; *U.S. Public*, pg. 753
GUMOUT DIVISION—See Pennzoil Company; *U.S. Public*, pg. 1273
GUMP'S—See Hanover Direct, Inc.; *U.S. Public*, pg. 782
GUMP'S BY MAIL, INC.—See Hanover Direct, Inc.; *U.S. Public*, pg. 782
GUNDLE/SLT ENVIRONMENTAL, INC.; *U.S. Public*, pg. 769
GUNES SIGORTA—See Groupe GAN; *Int'l*, pg. 565
GUNITE CORPORATION—See Johnstown America Corporation; *U.S. Public*, pg. 933
THE GUNLOCKE COMPANY—See HON Industries Inc.; *U.S. Public*, pg. 772
GUNMA FACTORY—See Advantest Corporation; *Int'l*, pg. 25
CURTIS C. GUNN, INC.; *U.S. Private*, pg. 488
GUNN PONTIAC GMC, INC.—See Curtis C. Gunn, Inc.; *U.S. Private*, pg. 488
GUNNAR OLSSON TRANSPORTKONSULT AB—See Norske Skogindustrier A.S; *Int'l*, pg. 966
GUNNEBO A/S—See Gunnebo Industrier AB; *Int'l*, pg. 578
GUNNEBO BALTIC SP Z O O—See Gunnebo Industrier AB; *Int'l*, pg. 578
GUNNEBO CORPORATION—See Gunnebo Industrier AB; *Int'l*, pg. 578
GUNNEBO DO BRASIL LTDA—See Gunnebo Industrier AB; *Int'l*, pg. 578
GUNNEBO ENTRANCE CONTROL SARL—See Gunnebo Industrier AB; *Int'l*, pg. 578
GUNNEBO FASTENING CORP.; *U.S. Private*, pg. 488
GUNNEBO FASTENING CORPORATION—See Gunnebo Industrier AB; *Int'l*, pg. 578
GUNNEBO GMBH—See Gunnebo Industrier AB; *Int'l*, pg. 578
GUNNEBO INDUSTRIER AB; *Int'l*, pg. 578
GUNNEBO IRELAND LTD.—See Gunnebo Industrier AB; *Int'l*, pg. 578
GUNNEBO JOHNSON CORPORATION—See Gunnebo Industrier AB; *Int'l*, pg. 578
GUNNEBO LTD.—See Gunnebo Industrier AB; *Int'l*, pg. 578
GUNNEBO MAYOR LTD.—See Gunnebo Industrier AB; *Int'l*, pg. 578
GUNONG PRINTING INK (M) SDN. BHD.—See Dainippon Ink & Chemicals, Inc.; *Int'l*, pg. 372
GUNSAN EXPORTADORA E IMPORTADORA LTDA.—See Gunze Sangyo, Inc.; *Int'l*, pg. 579
GUNSTONES BAKERY—See Northern Foods plc; *Int'l*, pg. 968
GUNTHER & CO. GMBH—See Sandvik AB; *Int'l*, pg. 1186
GUNTHER MELE LIMITED; *Int'l*, pg. 578
GUNTHER MELE PACKAGING, INC.—See Gunther Mele Limited; *Int'l*, pg. 578
GUNTHER S.A.—See Sandvik AB; *Int'l*, pg. 1186
GUNVER MANUFACTURING CO.; *U.S. Private*, pg. 488
GUNZE SANGYO (FUKUOKA)—See Gunze Sangyo, Inc.; *Int'l*, pg. 578
GUNZE SANGYO (HIDAKA)—See Gunze Sangyo, Inc.; *Int'l*, pg. 578
GUNZE SANGYO (HOKURIKU)—See Gunze Sangyo, Inc.; *Int'l*, pg. 578
GUNZE SANGYO, INC.; *Int'l*, pg. 578
GUNZE SANGYO (KYOTO)—See Gunze Sangyo, Inc.; *Int'l*, pg. 578
GUNZE SANGYO (OSAKA)—See Gunze Sangyo, Inc.; *Int'l*, pg. 578
GURLEY MOTOR COMPANY; *U.S. Private*, pg. 488

GURTEC GMBH & CO., KG—See Tamrock Corp.; *Int'l*, pg. 1353
GUSAB STAINLESS AB—See Sandvik AB; *Int'l*, pg. 1185
GUSHER PUMPS, INC.; *U.S. Private*, pg. 488
GUSSCO MANUFACTURING, INC.; *U.S. Private*, pg. 488
AB GUST CARLSSON & CO.—See The East Asiatic Company Ltd. A/S; *Int'l*, pg. 431
AB GUSTAF KAHR—See Skanska AB; *Int'l*, pg. 1260
GUSTAFSON, INC.—See Crompton & Knowles Corporation; *U.S. Public*, pg. 460
GUSTAV WAGNER MASCHINENFABRIK GMBH; *Int'l*, pg. 579
GUSTO GELEEN B.V.—See Royal Begemann Group; *Int'l*, pg. 1133
GUTH LIGHTING COMPANY—See Luxo A/S; *Int'l*, pg. 821
GUTHRIE CANADIAN INVESTMENTS LIMITED—See BBA Group plc; *Int'l*, pg. 113
THE GUTHRIE CORPORATION, PLC—See BBA Group plc; *Int'l*, pg. 113
GUTHRIE INTERNATIONAL—See BBA Group plc; *Int'l*, pg. 113
GUTHRIE NORTH AMERICA, INC.—See BBA Group plc; *Int'l*, pg. 113
GUTHY-RENKER CORP.; *U.S. Private*, pg. 488
GUTHY-RENKER CORP.—See Guthy-Renker Corp.; *U.S. Private*, pg. 488
WERNER GÜTTGES GMBH—See Mannesmann A.G.; *Int'l*, pg. 838
THE GUTTMAN GROUP; *U.S. Private*, pg. 488
GUTTMAN OIL, INC.—See The Guttman Group; *U.S. Private*, pg. 489
GUYERZELLER BANK AG—See HSBC Holdings plc; *Int'l*, pg. 582
GUYOT-HICKS-ANDERSON & ASSOCIATES—See Old Kent Financial Corporation; *U.S. Public*, pg. 1217
GUZZLER MANUFACTURING, INC.—See Federal Signal Corporation; *U.S. Public*, pg. 616
GWALTNEY OF SMITHFIELD, LTD.—See Smithfield Foods, Inc.; *U.S. Public*, pg. 1479
GWENT STEEL LTD.—See Fried. Krupp AG; *Int'l*, pg. 512
GWINNETT IMMEDIATE CARE CENTER, INC.—See Magellan Health Services, Inc.; *U.S. Public*, pg. 1036
GWYNEDD PARTNERS—See Cigna Corp.; *U.S. Public*, pg. 361
GYMBOREE CORPORATION; *U.S. Public*, pg. 770
GYODA R&D CENTER—See Advantest Corporation; *Int'l*, pg. 25
GYPROC AB—See BPB Industries PLC; *Int'l*, pg. 122
GYPROC AB—See Scancem AB; *Int'l*, pg. 1200
GYPROC A/S—See Scancem AB; *Int'l*, pg. 1200
GYPROC BALSTA PLANT—See Scancem AB; *Int'l*, pg. 1200
GYPROC GIPSPLATEFABRIKK A/S—See Scancem AB; *Int'l*, pg. 1200
GYPROC INSULATION LTD.—See BPB Industries PLC; *Int'l*, pg. 123
GYPROC OY—See Scancem AB; *Int'l*, pg. 1200
GYPSUM INDUSTRIES PLC—See BPB Industries PLC; *Int'l*, pg. 123
GYYR, INC.—See Odetics Inc.; *U.S. Public*, pg. 1212

H

H. SALT OF SOUTHERN CALIFORNIA, INC.; *U.S. Private*, pg. 489
H.A.C. CORP.—See Cade Industries, Inc.; *U.S. Public*, pg. 290
H&C CEREALES S.A.—See Koninklijke BolsWessanen nv; *Int'l*, pg. 752
H&C, LEO BURNETT—See Leo Burnett Company, Inc.; *U.S. Private*, pg. 184
H & C TIMBER & BUILDING SUPPLIES LTD.—See Harrisons & Crosfield plc; *Int'l*, pg. 598
H & D GRAPHICS—See American Bankers Insurance Group, Inc.; *U.S. Public*, pg. 68
H & D STEEL SERVICE, INC.; *U.S. Private*, pg. 489
H & H DISTRIBUTING COMPANY, INC.; *U.S. Private*, pg. 489
H & H HOBBY-UND MODELLBAUPRODUKTE GMBH—See Borden, Inc.; *U.S. Private*, pg. 159
H & H REFRIGERATION CO.—See Pentland Group PLC; *Int'l*, pg. 1035
H & H TUBE & MANUFACTURING CO.; *U.S. Private*, pg. 489
H&K AMERICA INC.—See Klockner-Werke AG; *Int'l*, pg. 737
H&K HOLDINGS, INC.—See Klockner-Werke AG; *Int'l*, pg. 737
H&K MACHINES, INC.—See Klockner-Werke AG; *Int'l*, pg. 737
H & L TOOL CO.—See Chicago Rivet & Machine Company; *U.S. Public*, pg. 349
H & M MEXICO, INC.—See Henkels & McCoy, Inc.; *U.S. Private*, pg. 522
H & R BLOCK, INC.; *U.S. Public*, pg. 770
H&Y COMMUNICATIONS INC.—See Hakuhodo Incorporated; *Int'l*, pg. 588
H-C INDUSTRIES, INC.—See Aluminum Company of America; *U.S. Public*, pg. 60
H C PRODUCTS CO.—See Aluminum Company of America; *U.S. Public*, pg. 61
H-D MICHIGAN, INC.—See Harley-Davidson, Inc.; *U.S. Public*, pg. 786
H F SECURITE S.A.—See Halma p.l.c.; *Int'l*, pg. 590
H M K ENTERPRISES, INC.; *U.S. Private*, pg. 489
H-PARTNERS—See Vendex International N.V.; *Int'l*, pg. 1463
H S DIE & ENGINEERING, INC.; *U.S. Private*, pg. 489
H. VENTURE CORP.—See Hughes Supply, Inc.; *U.S. Public*, pg. 847
HAB MERCATOR—See Axel Johnson AB; *Int'l*, pg. 708
HAC CATHERWOOD & SONS (BELFAST) LIMITED—See RMC Group p.l.c.; *Int'l*, pg. 1080

HAM, HOLLANDSCHE AANNEMING MAATSCHAPPIJ B.V.—See Hollandsche Beton Groep NV; *Int'l*, pg. 630

HAWA GRUNDSTICKS GMBH & CO. OHG IMMOBILIENVERWALTUNG—See Bayerische Vereinsbank Group; *Int'l*, pg. 179

HAWA GRUNDSTUECKS GMBH U. CO. OHG HOTELVERWALTUNG—See Bayerische Vereinsbank Group; *Int'l*, pg. 179

HB ENTERTAINMENT CO.—See Time Warner Inc.; *U.S. Public*, pg. 1615

HB ICE CREAM LTD.—See Unilever Plc; *Int'l*, pg. 1437

HBA INSURANCE LTD.—See Chattem, Inc.; *U.S. Public*, pg. 342

HBC INFORMATIONAL AND INSTRUCTIONAL SERVICES, INC.—See Harcourt General, Inc.; *U.S. Public*, pg. 783

HBC INSURANCE GROUP—See Horizon Bancorp; *U.S. Private*, pg. 539

HBD INDUSTRIES, INC.; *U.S. Private*, pg. 489

HBE ADAM'S RIB—See HBE Corporation/Design Build Divisions; *U.S. Private*, pg. 489

HBE BANK FACILITIES—See HBE Corporation/Design Build Divisions; *U.S. Private*, pg. 489

HBE CORPORATION/DESIGN BUILD DIVISIONS; *U.S. Private*, pg. 489

HBE GRUNDBESITZVERWALTUNGS- UND VERWERTUNGS GMBH—See Commerzbank AG; *Int'l*, pg. 310

HBE MEDICAL BUILDINGS—See HBE Corporation/Design Build Divisions; *U.S. Private*, pg. 489

H.B.L., INC.—See Lantzsch-Andreas Enterprises, Inc.; *U.S. Private*, pg. 650

HBM, HOLLANDSCHE BETON MAATSCHAPPIJ BV—See Hollandsche Beton Groep NV; *Int'l*, pg. 630

HBO & COMPANY CANADA LTD.—See HBOC; *U.S. Public*, pg. 770

HBO & COMPANY/CYCARE BUSINESS GROUP—See HBOC; *U.S. Public*, pg. 770

HBO & COMPANY OF GEORGIA—See HBOC; *U.S. Public*, pg. 770

HBO & COMPANY (UK) LIMITED—See HBOC; *U.S. Public*, pg. 770

HBO & COMPANY (VI), INC.—See HBOC; *U.S. Public*, pg. 770

HBO FILM MANAGEMENT, INC.—See Time Warner Inc.; *U.S. Public*, pg. 1612

HBO PICTURES, INC.—See Time Warner Inc.; *U.S. Public*, pg. 1612

HBO SATELLITES, INC.—See Time Warner Inc.; *U.S. Public*, pg. 1612

HBO VIDEO, INC.—See Time Warner Inc.; *U.S. Public*, pg. 1612

HBOC; *U.S. Public*, pg. 770

HBS MARKETING (ASIA) LIMITED—See GP Batteries International Ltd.; *Int'l*, pg. 537

HBS MARKETING (ASIA) LIMITED TAIPEI BRANCH OFFICE—See GP Batteries International Ltd.; *Int'l*, pg. 537

HBW, HOLLANDSCHE BETON EN WATERBOUW B.V.—See Hollandsche Beton Groep NV; *Int'l*, pg. 630

HC ABBRUCH UND RECYCLING GMBH—See Fried. Krupp AG; *Int'l*, pg. 513

HC&D DIV.—See Ameron International Corporation; *U.S. Public*, pg. 99

HC HOLDINGS; *U.S. Private*, pg. 489

HCA-CLUSTER—See Columbia/HCA Healthcare Corporation; *U.S. Public*, pg. 403

HCA-FLORIDA GROUP—See Columbia/HCA Healthcare Corporation; *U.S. Public*, pg. 403

HCA INTERNATIONAL CO.—See Columbia/HCA Healthcare Corporation; *U.S. Public*, pg. 405

HCA PSYCHIATRIC CO.—See Columbia/HCA Healthcare Corporation; *U.S. Public*, pg. 405

HCBECK; *U.S. Private*, pg. 490

HCC INC.; *U.S. Private*, pg. 490

HCC INDUSTRIES; *U.S. Private*, pg. 490

HCG INDUSTRIESERVICE BV—See Hollandsche Beton Groep NV; *Int'l*, pg. 630

HCI CHEMTECH; *U.S. Private*, pg. 490

HCL LTD.—See Hewlett-Packard Company; *U.S. Public*, pg. 817

HCM INTERCOAL GMBH IMPORT, EXPORT, TRANSIT—See Veba AG; *Int'l*, pg. 1454

HCO ENERGY LTD.—See HarCor Energy, Inc.; *U.S. Public*, pg. 782

HCS, INC.—See Magellan Health Services, Inc.; *U.S. Public*, pg. 1036

HCW OIL INCOME FUND (DEVONIAN)—See Cigna Corp.; *U.S. Public*, pg. 361

HD VEST FINANCIAL SERVICES; *U.S. Public*, pg. 770

HDA FORGINGS LTD.—See BTR plc; *Int'l*, pg. 126

HDF SECURITIES PVT LIMITED—See Robert Fleming Holdings Ltd.; *Int'l*, pg. 494

H.D.H. LTD.—See Lagardere Groupe; *Int'l*, pg. 795

HDM, HOLLANDSCHE DELFSTOFFEN MAATSCHAPPIJ BV—See Hollandsche Beton Groep NV; *Int'l*, pg. 630

HDR ARCHITECTURE—See Bouygues; *Int'l*, pg. 206

HDR ENGINEERING, INC.—See Bouygues; *Int'l*, pg. 207

HDR INC.—See Bouygues; *Int'l*, pg. 206

HDR TECHSERV INC.—See Bouygues; *Int'l*, pg. 206

HDS SERVICES; *U.S. Private*, pg. 490

H.D.S. UK LTD.—See Lagardere Groupe; *Int'l*, pg. 795

HDV HAMBURGER DATENVERARBEITUNGS GMBH—See Bayerische Vereinsbank Group; *Int'l*, pg. 179

HDW ELECTRONICS—See Preussag AG; *Int'l*, pg. 1070

HDW, INCORPORATED—See Distribution America; *U.S. Private*, pg. 335

HDW-NOBISKRUG GMBH—See Preussag AG; *Int'l*, pg. 1069

HEC, INC.—See Northeast Utilities; *U.S. Public*, pg. 1194

HEG HOPFENEXTRAKTION GMBH—See Viag AG; *Int'l*, pg. 1464

HEI DIVERSIFIED, INC.—See Hawaiian Electric Industries, Inc.; *U.S. Public*, pg. 800

HEI, INC.; *U.S. Public*, pg. 770

HEI INVESTMENT CORP.—See Hawaiian Electric Industries, Inc.; *U.S. Public*, pg. 800

HEI POWER CORP.—See Hawaiian Electric Industries, Inc.; *U.S. Public*, pg. 800

H.E.S. INTERNATIONAL, INC.—See Oak Industries Inc.; *U.S. Public*, pg. 1209

H.F.&P. MUNCHEN GMBH—See Dentsu Inc.; *Int'l*, pg. 394

HFC BANK PLC—See Household International, Inc.; *U.S. Public*, pg. 842

HFC ESTAMFOR—See Groupe Usinor; *Int'l*, pg. 570

HFC TRUST & SAVINGS LTD.—See Household International, Inc.; *U.S. Public*, pg. 842

HFS INC.—See Compagnie des Machines Bull; *Int'l*, pg. 316

HFS, INCORPORATED—See Cendant Corporation; *U.S. Public*, pg. 321

HFS MOBILITY SERVICES—See Cendant Corporation; *U.S. Public*, pg. 321

HGC BANK—See Bank of Montreal; *Int'l*, pg. 154

HHH, INC.—See Hughes Supply, Inc.; *U.S. Public*, pg. 847

H.H.U.K., INC.—See Columbia/HCA Healthcare Corporation; *U.S. Public*, pg. 405

HI PRODUCTS INC.—See Hofmann Industries, Inc.; *U.S. Private*, pg. 533

HI PROPERTY, INC.—See Home Interiors & Gifts, Inc.; *U.S. Private*, pg. 537

HIAC/ROYCO DIVISION—See Pacific Scientific Company; *U.S. Public*, pg. 1250

HIG CAPITAL MANAGEMENT; *U.S. Private*, pg. 490

HIG HOLZLEIMBAU-INDUSTRIE GMBH—See Philipp Holzmann AG; *Int'l*, pg. 632

HIH AMERICA—See Blue Shield of California; *U.S. Private*, pg. 153

HIII—See Alcatel Alsthom Compagnie Generale D'Electricite; *Int'l*, pg. 53

HISALBA - HORNOS IBERICOS ALBA S.A.—See Holderbank Financiere Glaris Ltd.; *Int'l*, pg. 629

HK ASSET PARTICIPATION GMBH—See Rothenberger Group GmbH; *Int'l*, pg. 1128

H.K. INTERNATIONAL, INC.; *U.S. Private*, pg. 491

HK SYSTEMS—See HK Systems, Inc.; *U.S. Private*, pg. 491

HK SYSTEMS, INC.; *U.S. Private*, pg. 491

HKS HOOGOVENS KLOCKNER SCRAP METALS BV—See Koninklijke Hoogovens N.V.; *Int'l*, pg. 754

HL FARM CORP.—See Liebherr-International AG; *Int'l*, pg. 808

HL-NIW, INC.—See Browning-Ferris Industries, Inc.; *U.S. Public*, pg. 264

HLA ENVIROSCIENCES PTY. LTD.—See Harding Lawson Associates Group, Inc.; *U.S. Public*, pg. 785

HLB COMMUNICATIONS, INC.; *U.S. Private*, pg. 491

HLPB—See Testa International; *Int'l*, pg. 1377

HLS CORP.—See WPP Group plc; *Int'l*, pg. 1483

HLW INTERNATIONAL LLP; *U.S. Private*, pg. 491

HLW INTERNATIONAL SERVICES CORPORATION—See HLW International LLP; *U.S. Private*, pg. 491

HLW SERVICES CORPORATION—See HLW International LLP; *U.S. Private*, pg. 491

HM INTERNATIONAL; *U.S. Private*, pg. 491

HM1, HEUSER, MAYER & PARTNER DIRECT MARKETING GMBH; *Int'l*, pg. 579

HMC DIVISION—See McKechnie PLC; *Int'l*, pg. 851

HMG INSTORE MARKETING INC.—See H.M.G. Worldwide Corp.; *U.S. Public*, pg. 771

HMG INTERMARK MANUFACTURING INC.—See H.M.G. Worldwide Corp.; *U.S. Public*, pg. 771

H.M.G. WORLDWIDE CORP.; *U.S. Public*, pg. 771

HMI ACCEPTANCE CORP.—See HMI Industries; *U.S. Public*, pg. 771

HMI ELECTRIC—See Heavy Machines, Inc.; *U.S. Private*, pg. 518

HMI, HOLLANDSCHE MAATSCHAPPIJ INSTALLATIETECHNIEK BV—See Hollandsche Beton Groep NV; *Int'l*, pg. 630

HMI INCORPORATED—See HMI Industries; *U.S. Public*, pg. 771

HMI INDUSTRIES; *U.S. Public*, pg. 771

HMO OREGON—See Regence BlueCross BlueShield of Oregon; *U.S. Private*, pg. 918

HMO TEXAS, L.C.—See Sierra Health Services, Inc.; *U.S. Public*, pg. 1470

HMS/CINCINNATI—See HMS Partners; *U.S. Private*, pg. 492

HMS DIRECT—See HMS Partners; *U.S. Private*, pg. 492

HMS-DIRECT COLUMBUS—See HMS Partners; *U.S. Private*, pg. 492

HMS/MEMPHIS—See HMS Partners; *U.S. Private*, pg. 492

HMS PARTNERS; *U.S. Private*, pg. 491

HMS PARTNERS-COLUMBUS—See HMS Partners; *U.S. Private*, pg. 492

HMS PARTNERS-TALLAHASSEE—See HMS Partners; *U.S. Private*, pg. 492

HMT INC.—See ITEQ, Inc.; *U.S. Public*, pg. 914

HMT INSPECTION & ENGINEERING SERVICES—See ITEQ, Inc.; *U.S. Public*, pg. 914

HMT RUBBER GLAS LTD.—See ITEQ, Inc.; *U.S. Public*, pg. 914

HMT SENTRY SYSTEMS, INC.—See ITEQ, Inc.; *U.S. Public*, pg. 914

HMT TECHNOLOGY CORPORATION; *U.S. Public*, pg. 771

HMT TONKAWA TANK COMPANY, INC.—See ITEQ, Inc.; *U.S. Public*, pg. 914

HMV LIMITED—See EMI Group plc; *Int'l*, pg. 427

H.M.Z. BELGIUM N.V.—See Royal Begemann Group; *Int'l*, pg. 1134

H.M.Z. FRANCE S.A.R.L.—See Royal Begemann Group; *Int'l*, pg. 1134

H.M.Z. U.K. LTD.—See Royal Begemann Group; *Int'l*, pg. 1134

HND CORPORATION—See Hitachi Koki Co., Ltd.; *Int'l*, pg. 620

HNTB CORPORATION; *U.S. Private*, pg. 492

HNTB DESIGN & BUILD—See HNTB Corporation; *U.S. Private*, pg. 492

HODY BV—See Koninklijke Hoogovens N.V.; *Int'l*, pg. 754

HOH ARCHITECTS, INC.—See The HOH Organizations; *U.S. Private*, pg. 492

HOH ENGINEERS, INC.—See The HOH Organizations; *U.S. Private*, pg. 492

THE HOH ORGANIZATIONS; *U.S. Private*, pg. 492

THE HON CO.—See HON Industries Inc.; *U.S. Public*, pg. 772

THE HON CO. SYSTEMS FURNITURE PLANT—See HON Industries Inc.; *U.S. Public*, pg. 772

HON EXPORT LIMITED—See HON Industries Inc.; *U.S. Public*, pg. 772

HON INDUSTRIES INC.; *U.S. Public*, pg. 772

HP FOODS—See Danone Group; *Int'l*, pg. 380

HP SALES MALAYSIA SDN BHD—See Hewlett-Packard Company; *U.S. Public*, pg. 818

H.P.E.—See The Gibson Group Inc.; *U.S. Private*, pg. 451

HPI HOLDING S.A.; *Int'l*, pg. 579

HPM CORPORATION; *U.S. Private*, pg. 492

HPS, INC.; *U.S. Private*, pg. 492

HR HUTTENWERKSENSORGUNG GMBH—See Fried. Krupp AG; *Int'l*, pg. 513

HR INDUSTRIEMONTAGE GMBH—See Fried. Krupp AG; *Int'l*, pg. 513

HR SCHLACKENAUFBEREITUNG GMBH—See Fried. Krupp AG; *Int'l*, pg. 513

HR SCHROTTAUFBEREITUNG GMBH—See Fried. Krupp AG; *Int'l*, pg. 513

HR TEXTRON—See Textron Inc.; *U.S. Public*, pg. 1589

HRB SYSTEMS—See Raytheon Company; *U.S. Public*, pg. 1365

HRH/ATLAS CONSTRUCTION INC.—See Starrett HRH; *U.S. Private*, pg. 1035

HRH CONSTRUCTION CORP.—See Starrett HRH; *U.S. Private*, pg. 1035

HRH CONSTRUCTION INTERIORS, INC.—See Starrett HRH; *U.S. Private*, pg. 1035

HRH INSURANCE SERVICES OF NORTHERN CALIFORNIA, INC.—See Hilb, Rogal and Hamilton Company; *U.S. Public*, pg. 827

HRH INSURANCE SERVICES OF THE COACHELLA VALLEY, INC.—See Hilb, Rogal and Hamilton Company; *U.S. Public*, pg. 826

HRI HOSPITAL—See Universal Health Services, Inc.; *U.S. Public*, pg. 1697

HRR ENTERPRISES, INC.—See Kane-Miller Corp.; *U.S. Private*, pg. 607

H.S. PROCESSING—See Heidtman Steel Products, Inc.; *U.S. Private*, pg. 519

HS RESOURCES; *U.S. Public*, pg. 772

HSB ENGINEERING INSURANCE LIMITED—See The Hartford Steam Boiler Inspection & Insurance Co.; *U.S. Public*, pg. 795

HSB RELIABILITY TECHNOLOGIES—See The Hartford Steam Boiler Inspection & Insurance Co.; *U.S. Public*, pg. 795

HSBC AMERICAS—See HSBC Holdings plc; *Int'l*, pg. 580

HSBC ASSET MANAGEMENT AMERICAS, INC.—See HSBC Holdings plc; *Int'l*, pg. 581

HSBC ASSET MANAGEMENT AMERICAS INC.—See HSBC Holdings plc; *Int'l*, pg. 581

HSBC ASSET MANAGEMENT LIMITED—See HSBC Holdings plc; *Int'l*, pg. 582

HSBC CAPITAL (ASIA) PTE LIMITED—See HSBC Holdings plc; *Int'l*, pg. 582

HSBC CAPITAL LIMITED—See HSBC Holdings plc; *Int'l*, pg. 582

HSBC CORPORATE FINANCE LIMITED—See HSBC Holdings plc; *Int'l*, pg. 582

HSBC FINANCE & SECURITIES (THAILAND) LIMITED—See HSBC Holdings plc; *Int'l*, pg. 582

HSBC FINANCE (MALAYSIA) BERHAD—See HSBC Holdings plc; *Int'l*, pg. 582

HBSC FORFAITING ASIA PTE. LIMITED—See HSBC Holdings plc; *Int'l*, pg. 582

HSBC FORFAITING LTD.—See HSBC Holdings plc; *Int'l*, pg. 579

HSBC FUTURES, INC.—See HSBC Holdings plc; *Int'l*, pg. 581

HSBC FUTURES (SINGAPORE) PTE LIMITED—See HSBC Holdings plc; *Int'l*, pg. 582

HSBC GIBBS BENEFIT CONSULTANTS LIMITED—See HSBC Holdings plc; *Int'l*, pg. 579

HSBC GIBBS HARNETT AND RICHARDSON LIMITED—See HSBC Holdings plc; *Int'l*, pg. 582

HSBC GIBBS LTD.—See HSBC Holdings plc; *Int'l*, pg. 579

HSBC GIBBS SINGAPORE PTE LTD—See HSBC Holdings plc; *Int'l*, pg. 582

HSBC GREENWELL—See HSBC Holdings plc; *Int'l*, pg. 580

HSBC HOLDINGS BV—See HSBC Holdings plc; *Int'l*, pg. 582

HSBC HOLDINGS INC.—See HSBC Holdings plc; *Int'l*, pg. 581

HSBC HOLDINGS PLC; *Int'l*, pg. 579

HSBC INSURANCE HOLDINGS LIMITED—See HSBC Holdings plc; *Int'l*, pg. 580

HSBC INSURANCE LIMITED—See HSBC Holdings plc; *Int'l*, pg. 582

HSBC INTERNATIONAL TRADE FINANCE LTD—See HSBC Holdings plc; *Int'l*, pg. 580

HSBC INTERNATIONAL INSURANCE LIMITED—See HSBC Holdings plc; *Int'l*, pg. 580

HSBC INTERNATIONAL TRUSTEE (SINGAPORE) LIMITED—See HSBC Holdings plc; *Int'l*, pg. 582

HSBC INVESTMENT BANK ASIA LTD.—See HSBC Holdings plc; *Int'l*, pg. 582

HSBC INVESTMENT BANK LIMITED—See HSBC Holdings plc; *Int'l*, pg. 580

HSBC INVESTMENT FUNDS AUSTRALIA LIMITED—See HSBC Holdings plc; *Int'l*, pg. 582

HSBC INVESTMENT SERVICES LIMITED—See HSBC Holdings plc; *Int'l*, pg. 580
HSBC (KUALA LUMPUR) NOMINEES SDN BHD—See HSBC Holdings plc; *Int'l*, pg. 580
HSBC (MALAYSIA) TRUSTEE BERHAD—See HSBC Holdings plc; *Int'l*, pg. 582
HSBC MARKETS LIMITED—See HSBC Holdings plc; *Int'l*, pg. 582
HSBC NOMINEES ASIA LIMITED—See HSBC Holdings plc; *Int'l*, pg. 582
HSBC NOMINEES (JERSEY) LIMITED—See HSBC Holdings plc; *Int'l*, pg. 580
HSBC PRIVATE BANKING (C.I.) LIMITED—See HSBC Holdings plc; *Int'l*, pg. 580
HSBC PRIVATE EQUITY EUROPE LIMITED—See HSBC Holdings plc; *Int'l*, pg. 580
HSBC PRIVATE EQUITY MANAGEMENT LIMITED—See HSBC Holdings plc; *Int'l*, pg. 583
HSBC ROBERTS S.A.—See HSBC Holdings plc; *Int'l*, pg. 583
HSBC SECURITIES, INC.—See HSBC Holdings plc; *Int'l*, pg. 581
HSBC (SINGAPORE) NOMINEES PRIVATE LIMITED—See HSBC Holdings plc; *int'l*, pg. 583
HSBC TRUSTEE (JERSEY) LIMITED—See HSBC Holdings plc; *Int'l*, pg. 580
HSBC UNIT TRUST MANAGEMENT LIMITED—See HSBC Holdings plc; *Int'l*, pg. 580
H.S.C. CANADA INC.—See Harris Chemical Group, Inc.; *U.S. Private*, pg. 505
HSC CONTROLS—See Woodward Governor Company; *U.S. Public*, pg. 1776
HSC EXPORT CORPORATION—See Imperial Holly Corporation; *U.S. Public*, pg. 872
HSC SECURITIES CORPORATION—See The Hallwood Group Incorporated; *U.S. Public*, pg. 778
HSG-HOLZMANN TECHNISCHER SERVICE GMBH—See Philipp Holzmann AG *Int'l*, pg. 632
HSI AVIATION, INC.—See Huntco Inc.; *U.S. Public*, pg. 849
HSI CORP.—See Hughes Supply, Inc.; *U.S. Public*, pg. 847
HSI INTERNATIONAL—See Haydon Switch & Instrument, Inc.; *U.S. Private*, pg. 513
HSMM FACILITIES, INC.—See Hayes, Seay, Mattern & Mattern, Inc.; *U.S. Private*, pg. 513
HSN INSURANCE, INC.—See USA Networks, Inc.; *U.S. Public*, pg. 1685
HSN LIFEWAY HEALTH PRODUCTS, INC.—See USA Networks, Inc.; *U.S. Public*, pg. 1685
HSN MAIL ORDER—See USA Networks, Inc.; *U.S. Public*, pg. 1685
HSN MAIL ORDER, INC.—See USA Networks, Inc.; *U.S. Public*, pg. 1685
HSN TELECOMMUNICATIONS, INC.—See USA Networks, Inc.; *U.S. Public*, pg. 1685
HSS HIRE SERVICE GROUP PLC—See The Davis Service Group Plc.; *Int'l*, pg. 385
HSS RECRUITING, INC.—See Hospital Staffing Services, Inc.; *U.S. Public*, pg. 840
HSSI MANAGEMENT COMPANY, INC.—See Hospital Staffing Services, Inc.; *U.S. Public*, pg. 840
HSSI MEDICARE HOME OFFICE, INC.—See Hospital Staffing Services, Inc.; *U.S. Public*, pg. 840
HSSI TRAVEL NURSE OPERATION—See Hospital Staffing Services, Inc.; *U.S. Public*, pg. 840
HT&T COMPANY, INC.—See Buyco, Inc.; *U.S. Private*, pg. 190
HT TROPLAST—See Ruetgers A.G.; *Int'l*, pg. 1148
HTD VERZEKERINGS & TRANSPORT BV—See Koninklijke Hoogovens N.V.; *Int'l*, pg. 753
HTH HAUSTECHNISCHE HANDELS GES M.B.H—See Masco Corporation; *U.S. Public*, pg. 1054
HTH KEITTIOT OY—See Stora Kopparbergs Bergslags AB; *Int'l*, pg. 1302
HTH KOKKENER A/S—See Stora Kopparbergs Bergslags AB; *Int'l*, pg. 1302
HTI EXPORT LTD.—See Hutchinson Technology Inc.; *U.S. Public*, pg. 851
HTL/KIN-TECH DIVISION—See Pacific Scientific Company; *U.S. Public*, pg. 1250
HTM ONROEREND GOED B.V.—See Gamma Holding N.V.; *Int'l*, pg. 540
HTS INSPECTION SYSTEMS BV—See Koninklijke Hoogovens N.V.; *Int'l*, pg. 753
HTV GESELLSCHAFT FUR HOCHTEMPERATURVERBRENNUNG MBH—See Veba AG; *Int'l*, pg. 1460
HUNOSA - E.N. HULLERAS DEL NORTE, S.A.—See SEPI; *Int'l*, pg. 1224
HVCL LTD.—See Hewlett-Packard Company; *U.S. Public*, pg. 818
THE HVR COMPANY—See The Clorox Company; *U.S. Public*, pg. 387
HVR/BMZ LA HAYE—See FCA!BMZ; *Int'l*, pg. 470
HWC DISTRIBUTION CORP.—See ALLTEL Corporation; *U.S. Public*, pg. 55
HWC EXPORT SALES CORPORATION—See Hein-Werner Corporation; *U.S. Public*, pg. 805
HWI BUILDING CORP.—See Hardware Wholesalers, Inc.; *U.S. Private*, pg. 502
HWZ, HOLLANDSCHE WEGENBOUW ZANEN B.V.—See Hollandsche Beton Groep NV; *Int'l*, pg. 630
HY MARKETING INC.—See Hakuhodo Incorporated; *Int'l*, pg. 588
HA-LO INDUSTRIES, INC.; *U.S. Public*, pg. 773
HA-LO MARKETING & PROMOTIONS—See Ha-Lo Industries, Inc.; *U.S. Public*, pg. 773
HAAGEN-DAZS—See Diageo Plc; *Int'l*, pg. 411
THE HAAGEN-DAZS COMPANY INC.—See Diageo Plc; *Int'l*, pg. 411
HAAGEN-DAZS EUROPE—See Diageo Plc; *Int'l*, pg. 411
HAAGEN-DAZS FRANCE—See Diageo Plc; *Int'l*, pg. 411
HAAGEN-DAZS JAPAN, INC.—See Diageo Plc; *Int'l*, pg. 409

HAAGEN-DAZS JAPAN, INC.—See Suntory Ltd.; *Int'l*, pg. 1321
HAAPAVESI POWER PLANT—See Imatran Voima Oy; *Int'l*, pg. 660
HAARMAN & REIMER AROMA CHEMICALS—See Bayer AG; *Int'l*, pg. 173
HAARMANN & REIMER CORP.—See Bayer AG; *Int'l*, pg. 173
HAARMANN & REIMER FOOD INGREDIENTS DIV.—See Bayer AG; *Int'l*, pg. 173
HAARMANN & REIMER GMBH—See Bayer AG; *Int'l*, pg. 174
HAARTZ-MASON, INC.—See RPM, Inc.; *U.S. Public*, pg. 1358
HAAS PUBLISHING COMPANIES, INC.—See Primedia Inc.; *U.S. Public*, pg. 1327
HAAS, WHEAT & PARTNERS; *U.S. Private*, pg. 492
THE HABAND CO.; *U.S. Private*, pg. 492
THE HABEGGER CORPORATION; *U.S. Private*, pg. 492
HABETAS HAZIR BETON SAN. VE TIC. A.S.—See Lafarge S.A.; *Int'l*, pg. 791
HABIB BANK LTD.; *Int'l*, pg. 584
HABIB BANK LIMITED—See Habib Bank Ltd.; *Int'l*, pg. 584
HABIB CREDIT & EXCHANGE BANK LTD.—See Habib Bank Ltd.; *Int'l*, pg. 584
HABIB NIGERIA BANK LTD.—See Habib Bank Ltd.; *Int'l*, pg. 584
HABISAT GLOBE INC.—See Habisat Svergie AB; *Int'l*, pg. 585
HABISAT SVERGIE AB; *Int'l*, pg. 585
HABITAT FRANCE SA—See Ikea Holdings AB; *Int'l*, pg. 659
HABITAT GROUP—See Ikea Holdings AB; *Int'l*, pg. 660
HABITAT INTERNATIONAL—See Ikea Holdings AB; *Int'l*, pg. 659
HABITS, INC.—See Saul Bros. & Company, Inc.; *U.S. Private*, pg. 968
HACH COMPANY; *U.S. Public*, pg. 773
HACH EUROPE, S.A./N.V.—See Hach Company; *U.S. Public*, pg. 773
HACH FRANCE, S.A.—See Hach Company; *U.S. Public*, pg. 773
HACH INTERNATIONAL FOREIGN SALES CO., INC.—See Hach Company; *U.S. Public*, pg. 773
HACH INTERNATIONAL, INC.—See Hach Company; *U.S. Public*, pg. 773
HACH SALES & SERVICE CANADA LTD.—See Hach Company; *U.S. Public*, pg. 773
HACHETTE CANADA—See Lagardere Groupe; *Int'l*, pg. 795
HACHETTE CONSOLIDATED AUSTRALIA—See Lagardere Groupe; *Int'l*, pg. 795
HACHETTE DISTRIBUTION INC.—See Lagardere Groupe; *Int'l*, pg. 794
HACHETTE DISTRIBUTION SERVICES—See Lagardere Groupe; *Int'l*, pg. 792
HACHETTE FILIPACCHI AUSTRALIA—See Lagardere Groupe; *Int'l*, pg. 795
HACHETTE FILIPACCHI JAPAN—See Lagardere Groupe; *Int'l*, pg. 795
HACHETTE FILIPACCHI MAGAZINES INC.—See Lagardere Groupe; *Int'l*, pg. 794
HACHETTE FILIPACCHI PRESSE—See Lagardere Groupe; *Int'l*, pg. 794
HACHETTE FILIPACCHI PUBLICACOES—See Lagardere Groupe; *Int'l*, pg. 795
HACHETTE FILIPACCHI SA—See Lagardere Groupe; *Int'l*, pg. 794
HACHETTE FILIPACCHI USA—See Lagardere Groupe; *Int'l*, pg. 792
HACHETTE 5—See Lagardere Groupe; *Int'l*, pg. 792
HACHETTE INTERCULTURE INC.—See Lagardere Groupe; *Int'l*, pg. 795
HACHETTE INTERDECO SA—See Lagardere Groupe; *Int'l*, pg. 795
HACHETTE LATINO AMERICA S.A. DE C.V.—See Lagardere Groupe; *Int'l*, pg. 796
HACHETTE LIVRE—See Lagardere Groupe; *Int'l*, pg. 792
HACHETTE MAGAZINE HOUSE H.K. LTD.—See Lagardere Groupe; *Int'l*, pg. 795
HACHETTE MAGAZINE VDB—See Lagardere Groupe; *Int'l*, pg. 795
HACHETTE PREMIERE SNC—See Lagardere Groupe; *Int'l*, pg. 792
HACHETTE SVERIGE HB—See Lagardere Groupe; *Int'l*, pg. 795
HACIENDA DE SALUD - BLOOMFIELD—See Horizon/CMS Healthcare Corporation; *U.S. Public*, pg. 838
HACIENDA DE SALUD - ESPANOLA—See Horizon/CMS Healthcare Corporation; *U.S. Public*, pg. 838
HACIENDA HAWAIIAN PROPERTIES, INC.—See Santa Fe Gaming Corporation; *U.S. Public*, pg. 1432
HACIENDA HOTEL INC.—See Santa Fe Gaming Corporation; *U.S. Public*, pg. 1432
J. LEE HACKETT CO.; *U.S. Private*, pg. 492
HACKNEY AND SONS, INC.—See Transportation Technologies, Inc.; *U.S. Private*, pg. 1097
THE H.T. HACKNEY CO.; *U.S. Private*, pg. 493
HACKNEY INC.—See Trinity Industries Inc.; *U.S. Public*, pg. 1639
HACKNEY INTERNATIONAL—See Transportation Technologies, Inc.; *U.S. Private*, pg. 1097
HACKNEY PETROLEUM, INC.—See The H.T. Hackney Co.; *U.S. Private*, pg. 493
HACO N.V.; *Int'l*, pg. 585
HACOBA-TEXTILMASCHINEN GMBH & CO. KG—See Deutsche Babcock AG; *Int'l*, pg. 399
HADAR INSURANCE COMPANY LTD.—See Groupe GAN; *Int'l*, pg. 565
HADCO CORPORATION; *U.S. Public*, pg. 773
HADCO CORPORATION—See Hadco Corporation; *U.S. Public*, pg. 773
HADDON CRAFTSMEN, INC.—See R.R. Donnelley & Sons Company; *U.S. Public*, pg. 518

HADELER LAW MEDIA MANAGEMENT—See Hadeler Sullivan Ewing; *U.S. Private*, pg. 493
HADELER SULLIVAN EWING; *U.S. Private*, pg. 493
HADELER WHITE PUBLIC RELATIONS—See Hadeler Sullivan Ewing; *U.S. Private*, pg. 493
HADEN DRYSYS ENVIRONMENTAL LTD.—See Haden Maclellan Holdings plc; *Int'l*, pg. 585
HADEN DRYSYS GMBH—See Haden Maclellan Holdings plc; *Int'l*, pg. 586
HADEN DRYSYS INTERNATIONAL LTD.—See Haden Maclellan Holdings plc; *Int'l*, pg. 585
HADEN DRYSYS LTD.—See Haden Maclellan Holdings plc; *Int'l*, pg. 585
HADEN ENGINEERING PTY—See Haden Maclellan Holdings plc; *Int'l*, pg. 586
HADEN ENVIRONMENTAL CORPORATION—See Haden Maclellan Holdings plc; *Int'l*, pg. 586
HADEN FRANCE S.A.—See Haden Maclellan Holdings plc; *Int'l*, pg. 586
HADEN GMBH—See Haden Maclellan Holdings plc; *Int'l*, pg. 586
HADEN, INC.—See Haden Maclellan Holdings plc; *Int'l*, pg. 586
HADEN KING LIMITED—See Haden Maclellan Holdings plc; *Int'l*, pg. 585
HADEN MACLELLAN HOLDINGS PLC; *Int'l*, pg. 585
HADEN MANAGEMENT CORPORATION—See Haden Maclellan Holdings plc; *Int'l*, pg. 586
HADEN RESEARCH & DEVELOPMENT CORPORATION—See Haden Maclellan Holdings plc; *Int'l*, pg. 586
HADEN SCHWEITZER CANADA INC.—See Haden Maclellan Holdings plc; *Int'l*, pg. 586
HADEN SCHWEITZER CORPORATION—See Haden Maclellan Holdings plc; *Int'l*, pg. 586
HADEN TECHNICAL SERVICES CORPORATION—See Haden Maclellan Holdings plc; *Int'l*, pg. 586
HADRON, INC.; *U.S. Public*, pg. 773
HADSON CORPORATION—See Apache Corporation; *U.S. Public*, pg. 119
HADSYS, INC.—See Honda Motor Co., Ltd.; *Int'l*, pg. 634
HAEGER INDUSTRIES, INC.; *U.S. Private*, pg. 493
HAEGER POTTERIES, INC.—See Haeger Industries, Inc.; *U.S. Private*, pg. 493
HAEGER POTTERIES OF MACOMB, INC.—See Haeger Industries, Inc.; *U.S. Private*, pg. 493
HAEGLE IMMOBILIEN-OST INGATLANFORGALMI KFT.—See Commerzbank AG; *Int'l*, pg. 310
HAEMONETICS CORPORATION; *U.S. Public*, pg. 773
HAGEMEYER N.V.—See First Pacific Company Limited; *Int'l*, pg. 487
HAGER MODULAIRE S.A.—See ABB Asea Brown Boveri (Holding) Ltd.; *Int'l*, pg. 3
HAGERSTOWN CEMENT PLANT INDEPENDENT CEMENT CORP.—See Holderbank Financiere Glaris Ltd.; *Int'l*, pg. 629
HAGFORS MEKANISKA VERKSTADS AB—See Voest-Alpine Stahl AG; *Int'l*, pg. 1471
HAGFORS TOOLING AB—See Voest-Alpine Stahl AG; *Int'l*, pg. 1471
HAGGAR CORPORATION; *U.S. Public*, pg. 774
HAGGEN, INC.; *U.S. Private*, pg. 493
HAGGLUNDS CHINA LTD.—See Incentive AB; *Int'l*, pg. 670
HAGGLUNDS DRIVES AB—See Incentive AB; *Int'l*, pg. 669
HAGGLUNDS DRIVES A/S—See Incentive AB; *Int'l*, pg. 670
HAGGLUNDS DRIVES GMBH—See Incentive AB; *Int'l*, pg. 670
HAGGLUNDS DRIVES INC.—See Incentive AB; *Int'l*, pg. 670
HAGGLUNDS DRIVES LTD.—See Incentive AB; *Int'l*, pg. 670
HAGGLUNDS DRIVES OY—See Incentive AB; *Int'l*, pg. 670
HAGGLUNDS DRIVES PTY LTD—See Incentive AB; *Int'l*, pg. 670
HAGGLUNDS DRIVES SARL—See Incentive AB; *Int'l*, pg. 670
HAGGLUNDS DRIVES SRL—See Incentive AB; *Int'l*, pg. 670
HAGGLUNDS HYDRAULIC DRIVES (INDIA) PVT. LTD.—See Incentive AB; *Int'l*, pg. 670
HAGGLUNDS LIDAN AB—See Incentive AB; *Int'l*, pg. 670
HAGGLUNDS LTD. DEPT. DRIVES—See Incentive AB; *Int'l*, pg. 670
HAGIE MANUFACTURING CO.; *U.S. Private*, pg. 493
HAGLER, MASTROVITA & HEWITT, INC.—See United Asset Management Corporation; *U.S. Public*, pg. 1673
JOHN HAGLEY COMMUNICATIONS—See BDDP Group; *Int'l*, pg. 117
C.F. HAGLIN & SONS; *U.S. Private*, pg. 493
HAHN AUTOMOTIVE WAREHOUSE, INC.; *U.S. Public*, pg. 774
HAHN EQUIPMENT CO.—See The Toro Company; *U.S. Public*, pg. 1624
ERNEST W. HAHN INC.—See Brookfield Properties Corporation; *Int'l*, pg. 229
HAHN SYSTEMS, INC.; *U.S. Private*, pg. 493
HAI SUN HUP GROUP LTD.; *Int'l*, pg. 586
W.L. HAILEY & COMPANY, INC.; *U.S. Private*, pg. 494
THE HAIN FOOD GROUP INC.; *U.S. Public*, pg. 774
HAINDL PAPIER GMBH; *Int'l*, pg. 586
HAINES & CO., INC.; *U.S. Private*, pg. 494
HAINES CITY CITRUS GROWERS ASSOCIATION; *U.S. Private*, pg. 494
HAINES CITY HERALD & RIDGE SHOPPER—See Shivers Trading & Operating Co.; *U.S. Private*, pg. 995
HAINES KIBBLEHOUSE; *U.S. Private*, pg. 494
HAINES RECRUITMENT ADVERTISING—See FCB; *U.S. Private*, pg. 389
THE HAIR CUTTERY—See Creative Hairdressers; *U.S. Private*, pg. 287
HAIRCUTS PLUS, INC.—See Opal Concepts, Inc.; *U.S. Private*, pg. 818

HAITSMA BETON B.V.—See Ballast Nedam NV; *Int'l*, pg. 134
HAJDUTEJ TEJIPARI RT.—See Nutricia BV; *Int'l*, pg. 991
HAJOCA CORP.; *U.S. Private*, pg. 494
HAK B.V.—See CSM N.V.; *Int'l*, pg. 244
HAKING ENTERPRISES; *Int'l*, pg. 586
HAKING INTERNATIONAL—See Haking Enterprises; *Int'l*, pg. 587
HAKO MINUTEMAN LTD.(CANADA)—See Hako-Werke GmbH & Co.; *Int'l*, pg. 587
HAKO-WERKE GMBH & CO.; *Int'l*, pg. 587
HAKON GRUPPEN AS—See ICA Handlarnas AB; *Int'l*, pg. 643
HAKUHODO COMMUNICATIONS, INC.—See Hakuhodo Incorporated; *Int'l*, pg. 588
HAKUHODO ADVERTISING AMERICA INC.—See Hakuhodo Incorporated; *Int'l*, pg. 588
HAKUHODO AUSTRALIA PTY. LTD.—See Hakuhodo Incorporated; *Int'l*, pg. 588
HAKUHODO BANGKOK CO., LTD.—See Hakuhodo Incorporated; *Int'l*, pg. 588
HAKUHODO CAPCO, INC.—See Hakuhodo Incorporated; *Int'l*, pg. 587
HAKUHODO CORPORATE SOUND DESIGN CO., LTD.—See Hakuhodo Incorporated; *Int'l*, pg. 587
HAKUHODO CREATIVE & DEVELOPMENT, INC.—See Hakuhodo Incorporated; *Int'l*, pg. 588
HAKUHODO DEUTSCHLAND GMBH—See Hakuhodo Incorporated; *Int'l*, pg. 588
HAKUHODO ERG INC.—See Hakuhodo Incorporated; *Int'l*, pg. 588
HAKUHODO FOODS SERVICES CO., LTD.—See Hakuhodo Incorporated; *Int'l*, pg. 588
HAKUHODO FRANCE S.A.—See Hakuhodo Incorporated; *Int'l*, pg. 588
HAKUHODO HONG KONG LTD.—See Hakuhodo Incorporated; *Int'l*, pg. 588
HAKUHODO I.O. CO. LTD.—See Hakuhodo Incorporated; *Int'l*, pg. 588
HAKUHODO INC.—See Hakuhodo Incorporated; *Int'l*, pg. 587
HAKUHODO INCENTIVE PROMOTIONS INC.—See Hakuhodo Incorporated; *Int'l*, pg. 588
HAKUHODO INCORPORATED; *Int'l*, pg. 587
HAKUHODO INSTITUTE OF LIFE AND LIVING—See Hakuhodo Incorporated; *Int'l*, pg. 588
HAKUHODO LINTAS—See Hakuhodo Incorporated; *Int'l*, pg. 587
HAKUHODO MALAYSIA SDN. BHD.—See Hakuhodo Incorporated; *Int'l*, pg. 588
HAKUHODO OFFICE SERVICES CO., LTD.—See Hakuhodo Incorporated; *Int'l*, pg. 588
HAKUHODO PHOTO CREATIVE INC.—See Hakuhodo Incorporated; *Int'l*, pg. 588
HAKUHODO PRO'S, INC.—See Hakuhodo Incorporated; *Int'l*, pg. 588
HAKUHODO SERVICES CO., LTD.—See Hakuhodo Incorporated; *Int'l*, pg. 588
HAKUHODO SINGAPORE PTE. LTD.—See Hakuhodo Incorporated; *Int'l*, pg. 588
HAKUHODO U.K. LTD.—See Hakuhodo Incorporated; *Int'l*, pg. 588
HAKUSHIAN CO., LTD.—See Skylark Co., Ltd.; *Int'l*, pg. 1262
HAKUYO CONSTRUCTION SDN. BHD.—See Obayashi Corporation; *Int'l*, pg. 996
HAL COMPUTER SYSTEMS, INC.—See Fujitsu Limited; *Int'l*, pg. 526
HALBA AG—See Coop Switzerland; *Int'l*, pg. 330
HALBERGERHUTTE GMBH—See Saint-Gobain; *Int'l*, pg. 1176
HALCYON INSURANCE CO.—See The Progressive Corporation; *U.S. Public*, pg. 1335
HALCYON UNDERWRITERS—See Poe & Brown, Inc.; *U.S. Public*, pg. 1312
HALE BROTHERS, INC.—See Performance Food Group Company; *U.S. Public*, pg. 1278
HALE ENGINEERING LTD.—See Axel Johnson AB; *Int'l*, pg. 711
HALE-HALSELL COMPANY; *U.S. Private*, pg. 494
HALE OIL FIELD PRODUCTS CO.—See Watts Industries, Inc.; *U.S. Public*, pg. 1746
HALE PRODUCTS INC.—See IDEX Corporation; *U.S. Public*, pg. 862
HALESA LTD.—See Novartis AG; *Int'l*, pg. 982
HALEX DIV.—See Berkshire Hathaway Inc.; *U.S. Public*, pg. 217
HALEYVILLE DRAPERY—See Decorator Industries, Inc.; *U.S. Public*, pg. 491
HALEYVILLE DRAPERY MANUFACTURING DIVISION—See Decorator Industries, Inc.; *U.S. Public*, pg. 491
HALEYVILLE MANUFACTURING—See Decorator Industries, Inc.; *U.S. Public*, pg. 491
HALEYVILLE MANUFACTURING OF ELKHART—See Decorator Industries, Inc.; *U.S. Public*, pg. 491
HALEYVILLE OFFICE—See Pinnacle Bank; *U.S. Public*, pg. 1297
ROBERT HALF—See Robert Half International Inc.; *U.S. Public*, pg. 775
ROBERT HALF INTERNATIONAL INC.; *U.S. Public*, pg. 774
HALFORDS, LTD.—See The Boots Company PLC; *Int'l*, pg. 203
HALI-BUROMOBEL VERTRIEBS GESMBH; *Int'l*, pg. 589
HALIFAX CORPORATION; *U.S. Public*, pg. 775
HALIFAX ENGINEERING, INC.—See Halifax Corporation; *U.S. Public*, pg. 775
THE HALIFAX INSURANCE COMPANY—See ING Groep N.V.; *Int'l*, pg. 648
HALIFAX PLC.; *Int'l*, pg. 589
HALIFAX PORT CORPORATION—See Canada Ports Corporation; *Int'l*, pg. 255

HALIFAX RACK & SCREW CUTTING CO., LTD.—See B. Elliott plc.; *Int'l*, pg. 448
HALIFAX TECHNICAL SERVICES—See Halifax Corporation; *U.S. Public*, pg. 775
HALIFAX TECHNOLOGY SERVICES COMPANY—See Halifax Corporation; *U.S. Public*, pg. 775
HALL AGGREGATES (SOUTH COAST) LIMITED—See RMC Group p.l.c.; *Int'l*, pg. 1079
HALL AGGREGATES (SOUTH EAST) LIMITED—See RMC Group p.l.c.; *Int'l*, pg. 1079
HALL & CEDERQUIST, INC.—See Young & Rubicam Inc.; *U.S. Private*, pg. 1197
HALL & CO. LIMITED, CENTRAL REGION—See RMC Group p.l.c.; *Int'l*, pg. 1079
HALL & CO. LIMITED, MIDLANDS & NORTH REGION—See RMC Group p.l.c.; *Int'l*, pg. 1079
HALL & CO. LIMITED, SOUTHERN REGION—See RMC Group p.l.c.; *Int'l*, pg. 1079
HALL & CEDERQUIST/YOUNG & RUBICAM—See Young & Rubicam Inc.; *U.S. Private*, pg. 1198
HALL BROTHERS (WHITEFIELD) LIMITED—See Warner-Lambert Company; *U.S. Public*, pg. 1739
THE HALL CHEMICAL COMPANY—See Goldman Financial Group; *U.S. Private*, pg. 461
THE HALL CHINA COMPANY; *U.S. Private*, pg. 494
HALL CONTRACTING CORP.; *U.S. Private*, pg. 495
THE C.P. HALL COMPANY; *U.S. Private*, pg. 495
HALL FINANCIAL GROUP, INC.; *U.S. Private*, pg. 495
HALL & KAY FIRE—See Staveley Industries PLC; *Int'l*, pg. 1298
HALL-MARK COMPUTER PRODUCTS—See Avnet, Inc.; *U.S. Public*, pg. 155
MATTHEW HALL & CO.—See AMEC Plc; *Int'l*, pg. 16
HALL SIGN, INC.; *U.S. Private*, pg. 495
HALL SURGICAL DIVISION—See Bristol-Myers Squibb Company; *U.S. Public*, pg. 254
HALL SYSTEMS, INC.—See The E.W. Scripps Company; *U.S. Public*, pg. 1447
HALLAM FM—See EMAP Plc; *Int'l*, pg. 451
AB HALLEVIKS ROKERI—See Nestle S.A.; *Int'l*, pg. 920
HALLIBURTON ARGENTINA S.A.—See Halliburton Company; *U.S. Public*, pg. 777
HALLIBURTON COMPANY; *U.S. Public*, pg. 775
HALLIBURTON COMPANY GERMANY GMBH—See Halliburton Company; *U.S. Public*, pg. 777
HALLIBURTON DE MEXICO S.A. DE C.V.—See Halliburton Company; *U.S. Public*, pg. 777
HALLIBURTON ENERGY SERVICES—See Halliburton Company; *U.S. Public*, pg. 776
HALLIBURTON ENERGY SERVICES, INC.—See Halliburton Company; *U.S. Public*, pg. 776
HALLIBURTON ENVIRONMENTAL TECHNOLOGIES, INC.—See Halliburton Company; *U.S. Public*, pg. 776
HALLIBURTON ITALIANA S.P.A.—See Halliburton Company; *U.S. Public*, pg. 777
HALLIBURTON MFG. & SERVICES LTD.—See Halliburton Company; *U.S. Public*, pg. 777
HALLIBURTON NIGERIA LTD.—See Halliburton Company; *U.S. Public*, pg. 777
HALLIBURTON SERVICES, LTD.—See Halliburton Company; *U.S. Public*, pg. 777
HALLIBURTON TRINIDAD LTD.—See Halliburton Company; *U.S. Public*, pg. 777
HALLIDIE MACHINERY COMPANY, INC.; *U.S. Private*, pg. 495
HALLMAN & LORBER, INC.—See Harcourt General, Inc.; *U.S. Public*, pg. 783
HALLMARK ART PRODUCTS & INTERNATIONAL DIV.—See Hallmark Cards, Inc.; *U.S. Private*, pg. 496
HALLMARK ASIA/PACIFIC REGION—See Hallmark Cards, Inc.; *U.S. Private*, pg. 496
HALLMARK CARDS AUSTRALIA LTD.—See Hallmark Cards, Inc.; *U.S. Private*, pg. 496
HALLMARK CARDS CANADA—See Hallmark Cards, Inc.; *U.S. Private*, pg. 496
HALLMARK CARDS IBERICA, S.A.—See Hallmark Cards, Inc.; *U.S. Private*, pg. 496
HALLMARK CARDS, INC.; *U.S. Private*, pg. 495
HALLMARK CARDS LTD.—See Hallmark Cards, Inc.; *U.S. Private*, pg. 496
HALLMARK CARDS NEDERLAND, B.V.—See Hallmark Cards, Inc.; *U.S. Private*, pg. 496
HALLMARK CARDS NEW ZEALAND LTD.—See Hallmark Cards, Inc.; *U.S. Private*, pg. 496
HALLMARK EDUCATIONAL PRODUCTS DIV.—See Hallmark Cards, Inc.; *U.S. Private*, pg. 496
HALLMARK ENTERTAINMENT, INC.—See Hallmark Cards, Inc.; *U.S. Private*, pg. 496
HALLMARK GROUP FRANCE, S.A.—See Hallmark Cards, Inc.; *U.S. Private*, pg. 496
HALLMARK INTERNATIONAL—See Hallmark Cards, Inc.; *U.S. Private*, pg. 496
HALLMARK MEXICANA, S. DE R.I. DE C.V.—See Hallmark Cards, Inc.; *U.S. Private*, pg. 496
HALLMARK PUERTO RICO, INC.—See Hallmark Cards, Inc.; *U.S. Private*, pg. 496
HALLS MERCHANDISING INC.—See Hallmark Cards, Inc.; *U.S. Private*, pg. 496
HALLSMITH-SYSCO FOOD SERVICES—See Sysco Corporation; *U.S. Public*, pg. 1550
HALLSTA PAPER MILL—See Mo och Domsjo AB; *Int'l*, pg. 885
HALLWOOD COMMERCIAL REAL ESTATE, INC.—See The Hallwood Group Incorporated; *U.S. Public*, pg. 778
HALLWOOD ENERGY PARTNERS, L.P.—See The Hallwood Group Incorporated; *U.S. Public*, pg. 778
THE HALLWOOD GROUP INCORPORATED; *U.S. Public*, pg. 777
HALLWOOD HOTELS INC.—See The Hallwood Group Incorporated; *U.S. Public*, pg. 778
HALLWOOD REALTY CORPORATION—See The Hallwood Group Incorporated; *U.S. Public*, pg. 778
HALLWOOD REALTY INVESTORS INC.—See The Hallwood Group Incorporated; *U.S. Public*, pg. 778

HALLWOOD REALTY PARTNERS, L.P.—See The Hallwood Group Incorporated; *U.S. Public*, pg. 778
HALM INDUSTRIES COMPANY, INCORPORATED; *U.S. Private*, pg. 496
HALM INDUSTRIES INTERNATIONAL—See Halm Industries Company, Incorporated; *U.S. Private*, pg. 496
HALMA ASIA PTE. LIMITED—See Halma p.l.c.; *Int'l*, pg. 590
HALMA HOLDINGS INC.—See Halma p.l.c.; *Int'l*, pg. 590
HALMA P.L.C.; *Int'l*, pg. 589
HALMODE APPAREL, INC.—See Kellwood Company; *U.S. Public*, pg. 948
HALO LIGHTING—See Cooper Industries, Inc.; *U.S. Public*, pg. 443
HALOCARBON PRODUCTS CORP.; *U.S. Private*, pg. 496
HALOGEN INSULATOR & SEAL CORP.—See Saint-Gobain; *Int'l*, pg. 1174
HALOTRON, INC.—See American Pacific Corporation; *U.S. Public*, pg. 88
HALPER BROS.—See Reliable Knitting Works; *U.S. Private*, pg. 920
HALSEY DRUG COMPANY; *U.S. Private*, pg. 496
HALSTEAD INDUSTRIAL PRODS. DIV.—See Halstead Industries, Inc.; *U.S. Private*, pg. 497
HALSTEAD INDUSTRIES, INC.; *U.S. Private*, pg. 496
HALSTON ENTERPRISES, INC.—See MacAndrews & Forbes Holdings Inc.; *U.S. Private*, pg. 690
HALTEN GMBH & CO. KG—See Franz Haniel & Cie, GmbH; *Int'l*, pg. 592
HALTER MARINE GROUP, INC.; *U.S. Public*, pg. 778
HALTERM CONTAINER TERMINAL—See Newfoundland Capital Corporation Limited; *Int'l*, pg. 924
HALTERMANN AG; *Int'l*, pg. 590
HALTERMANN LTD.—See Haltermann AG; *Int'l*, pg. 590
HALVIC KUNSTSTOFFWERKE GMBH—See Solvay S.A.; *Int'l*, pg. 1278
HAMAMATSU CORP.; *U.S. Private*, pg. 497
HAMAMATSU KOHAN KAKO CO., LTD.—See Nissho Iwai Corporation; *Int'l*, pg. 946
HAMAOKA TOSHIBA ELECTRONICS CORP.—See Toshiba Corporation; *Int'l*, pg. 1402
HAMBLEDON STUDIOS LTD.—See Fine Art Developments plc; *Int'l*, pg. 485
HAMBLIN CONTACT LENSES—See Dolland & Aitchison Ltd.; *Int'l*, pg. 414
HAMBLIN OPTICAL SERVICES LTD.—See Dolland & Aitchison Ltd.; *Int'l*, pg. 414
HAMBRECHT & QUIST LLC.; *U.S. Public*, pg. 778
HAMBURG BROTHERS; *U.S. Private*, pg. 497
HAMBURGER ABENDBLATT/DIE WELT REISEBURO GMBH—See Axel Springer Verlag AG; *Int'l*, pg. 102
HAMBURGER ALUMINIUM-WERK GESELLSCHAFT MIT BESCHRANKTER HAFTUNG—See Reynolds Metals Company; *U.S. Public*, pg. 1387
HAMBURGER SPARKASSE; *Int'l*, pg. 590
HAMBURGISCHE GRUNDSTUECKS GESELLSCHAFT MBH—See Commerzbank AG; *Int'l*, pg. 310
HAMCO, INC.—See Crown Crafts, Inc.; *U.S. Public*, pg. 465
HAMDEN CHRONICLE—See Journal Register Company; *U.S. Public*, pg. 935
HAMEENLINNA TUBE WORKS—See Rautaruukki Oy; *Int'l*, pg. 1088
HAMEENLINNA WORKS—See Rautaruukki Oy; *Int'l*, pg. 1088
HAMER GUITARS—See Kaman Corporation; *U.S. Public*, pg. 942
HAMER PROPERTIES, INC.—See Walter Industries, Inc.; *U.S. Public*, pg. 1736
HAMILTON, ALLEN & ASSOCIATES, INC.—See United Asset Management Corporation; *U.S. Public*, pg. 1673
HAMILTON ARMS NURSING & REHABILITATION CENTER—See Genesis Health Ventures, Inc.; *U.S. Public*, pg. 729
HAMILTON BEACH/PROCTOR-SILEX, INC.—See NACCO Industries, Inc.; *U.S. Public*, pg. 1149
HAMILTON BONADUZ AG—See Hamilton Co., Inc.; *U.S. Private*, pg. 497
THE HAMILTON COLLECTION—See Bradford Exchange Ltd.; *U.S. Private*, pg. 163
HAMILTON COMMUNICATIONS GROUP, INC.; *U.S. Private*, pg. 497
THE HAMILTON COMMUNICATIONS GROUP—See Hamilton Communications Group, Inc.; *U.S. Private*, pg. 497
HAMILTON CO., INC.; *U.S. Private*, pg. 497
HAMILTON DIVISION—See Stevens International, Inc.; *U.S. Public*, pg. 1517
HAMILTON EQUIPMENT, INC.; *U.S. Private*, pg. 497
HAMILTON FINANCIAL SERVICES CORP.—See FirstCity Financial Corporation; *U.S. Public*, pg. 644
THE HAMILTON GROUP LIMITED, INC.—See Bradford Exchange Ltd.; *U.S. Private*, pg. 163
HAMILTON HALLMARK—See Avnet, Inc.; *U.S. Public*, pg. 155
HAMILTON HALLMARK (CANADA) LTD.—See Avnet, Inc.; *U.S. Public*, pg. 155
HAMILTON LAMP CORP.—See RDM Sports Group; *U.S. Public*, pg. 1354
HAMILTON/LIVINGSTON—See Brammer plc; *Int'l*, pg. 212
HAMILTON MACHINING CENTER—See Stevens International, Inc.; *U.S. Public*, pg. 1517
HAMILTON MARINE & ENGINEERING LTD.—See Canadian Shipbuilding & Engineering Ltd.; *Int'l*, pg. 259
HAMILTON MILL, CHAMPION INTERNATIONAL CORPORATION—See Champion International Corp.; *U.S. Public*, pg. 334
HAMILTON MUTUAL INSURANCE COMPANY OF CINCINNATI; *U.S. Private*, pg. 497
HAMILTON PAVILION HEALTHCARE—See Vencor, Inc.; *U.S. Public*, pg. 1713
HAMILTON PRECISION METALS—See Katy Industries, Inc.; *U.S. Public*, pg. 944
HAMILTON SPECIALTY BAR—See Slater Industries Inc.; *Int'l*, pg. 1262

HAMILTON STANDARD—See United Technologies Corporation; *U.S. Public,* pg. 1690
HAMILTON STORES, INC.; *U.S. Private,* pg. 497
HAMILTON WORLDWIDE DIRECT RESPONSE GROUP— See Bradford Exchange Ltd.; *U.S. Private,* pg. 163
HAMILTONS OF MELBOURNE PTY. LTD.—See Porsche AG; *Int'l,* pg. 1063
HAMILTONS PTY. LTD.—See Porsche AG; *Int'l,* pg. 1063
HAMLET GROUP, INC.—See Koo Koo Roo, Inc.; *U.S. Public,* pg. 966
HAMLIN, INC.—See Breed Technologies, Inc.; *U.S. Public,* pg. 251
HAMLIN STEEL PRODUCTS—See The Cypress Companies; *U.S. Private,* pg. 299
HAMLYN/OCTOPUS—See Reed Elsevier plc; *Int'l,* pg. 1093
JERRY HAMM CHEVROLET INC.; *U.S. Private,* pg. 497
HAMMACHER, SCHLEMMER & CO., INC.; *U.S. Private,* pg. 497
HAMMARY FURNITURE CO.—See La-Z-Boy Incorporated; *U.S. Public,* pg. 973
HAMMEL, GREEN & ABRAHAMSON, INC.; *U.S. Private,* pg. 497
THE HAMMERBLOW CORP.; *U.S. Private,* pg. 498
HAMMERITE PRODUCTOS ESPECIALES—See Williams Holdings Plc; *Int'l,* pg. 1501
HAMMERITE PRODUCTS LIMITED—See Williams Holdings Plc; *Int'l,* pg. 1501
HAMMERLI GMBH—See SIG Schweizerische Industrie-Gesellschaft Holding AG; *Int'l,* pg. 1156
HAMMERLI LTD.—See SIG Schweizerische Industrie-Gesellschaft Holding AG; *Int'l,* pg. 1156
HAMMERMILL PAPER GMBH—See International Paper Company; *U.S. Public,* pg. 905
HAMMERMILL PAPERS—See International Paper Company; *U.S. Public,* pg. 902
J.L. HAMMETT COMPANY; *U.S. Private,* pg. 498
HAMMOND GROUP INC.; *U.S. Private,* pg. 498
HAMPEL/STEFANIDES; *U.S. Private,* pg. 498
HAMPEL/STEFANIDES—See Hampel/Stefanides; *U.S. Private,* pg. 498
HAMPSHIRE CHEMICAL CORP.; *U.S. Private,* pg. 498
HAMPSHIRE CHEMICAL GMBH—See Hampshire Chemical Corp.; *U.S. Private,* pg. 498
HAMPSHIRE CHEMICAL LTD.—See Hampshire Chemical Corp.; *U.S. Private,* pg. 498
HAMPSHIRE DESIGNERS INC.—See Hampshire Group, Ltd.; *U.S. Public,* pg. 778
HAMPSHIRE GAS CO.—See Washington Gas Light Co.; *U.S. Public,* pg. 1740
HAMPSHIRE GROUP, LTD.; *U.S. Public,* pg. 778
HAMPSHIRE HOTEL—See Taj International Hotels; *U.S. Private,* pg. 1067
HAMPTON INDUSTRIES, INC.; *U.S. Public,* pg. 779
HAMPTON INNS, INC.—See Promus Hotel Corporation; *U.S. Public,* pg. 1335
HAMPTON LAKES ASSOCIATES—See Cigna Corp.; *U.S. Public,* pg. 361
HAMPTON PRINT WORKS, INC.; *U.S. Private,* pg. 498
HAMPTON RESOURCES, INC.; *U.S. Private,* pg. 498
HAMPTON ROADS LAND CO., LTD—See Moran Transporation Company; *U.S. Private,* pg. 760
HAMPTON TRUST PLC; *Int'l,* pg. 591
THE HAMPTON WATER WORKS CO.—See American Water Works Company, Inc.; *U.S. Public,* pg. 95
HAMPTONS RESIDENTIAL—See Bristol & West Building Society; *Int'l,* pg. 216
HAMSVEDP INDUSTRIES, INC.—See Hardings, Inc.; *U.S. Private,* pg. 502
HAMWORTHY ALLWEILLER LIMITED—See Powell Duffryn PLC; *Int'l,* pg. 1065
HAMWORTHY COMBUSTION EQUIPMENT LIMITED—See Powell Duffryn PLC; *In'l,* pg. 1065
HAMWORTHY COMBUSTION SYSTEMS LIMITED—See Powell Duffryn PLC; *In'l,* pg. 1065
HAMWORTHY COMPRESSOR SYSTEMS LIMITED—See Powell Duffryn PLC; *In'l,* pg. 1065
HAMWORTHY ENGINEERING LIMITED—See Powell Duffryn PLC; *Int'l,* pg. 1065
HAMWORTHY HEATING LIMITED—See Powell Duffryn PLC; *Int'l,* pg. 1065
HAMWORTHY INDUSTRAMAR LIMITED—See Powell Duffryn PLC; *Int'l,* pg. 1065
HAMWORTHY MARINE LIMITED—See Powell Duffryn PLC; *Int'l,* pg. 1065
HAMWORTHY PUMPS AND COMPRESSORS LIMITED—See Powell Duffryn PLC; *Int'l,* pg. 1065
HAMWORTHY USA, INC.—See Powell Duffryn PLC; *Int'l,* pg. 1066
HAN RYUK ELECTRONICS CO., LTD.—See Hokuriku Electric Industry Co., Ltd.; *Int'l,* pg. 628
HAN WHA PHARMA CO. LTD.—See Akzo Nobel N.V.; *Int'l,* pg. 44
HANA SEMICONDUCTOR (BKK) CO., LTD.—See Nishimatsu Construction Co., Ltd.; *Int'l,* pg. 943
HANA SEMICONDUCTOR (HI-TECH) PLANT—See Nishimatsu Construction Co., Ltd.; *Int'l,* pg. 943
HANAWA SEIKI, INC.—See Canon Inc.; *Int'l,* pg. 261
HANCO A/S—See Axel Johnson AB; *Int'l,* pg. 711
HANCOCK FABRICS, INC.; *U.S. Public,* pg. 779
JOHN W. HANCOCK JR., INC.—See Roanoke Electric Steel Corporation; *U.S. Public,* pg. 1392
HANCOCK LUMBER, INC.; *U.S. Private,* pg. 498
HANCOCK MANUFACTURING—See The Cypress Companies; *U.S. Private,* pg. 299
HANCOCK PEANUT COMPANY—See Morven Partners LP; *U.S. Private,* pg. 763
LOUIS HAND DIV.—See Trace International Holdings, Inc.; *U.S. Private,* pg. 1094
HANDAR, INC.—See TSI Incorporated; *U.S. Public,* pg. 1559
HANS HUTH HANDEL GMBH—See Mannesmann A.G.; *Int'l,* pg. 838

HANS HUTH HANDEL GMBH & CO. KG—See Mannesmann A.G.; *Int'l,* pg. 838
HANDEL UND FINANZ WARMOND AG—See Internatio-Muller N.V.; *Int'l,* pg. 682
HANDELMAATSCHAPPIJ NOORDA B.V.—See Unilever Plc; *Int'l,* pg. 1437
HANDELSBANK NATWEST—See National Westminster Bank PLC; *Int'l,* pg. 911
HANDELSBANKEN COPENHANGEN—See Svenska Handelsbanken; *Int'l,* pg. 1327
HANDELSBANKEN FINANS—See Svenska Handelsbanken; *Int'l,* pg. 1327
HANDELSBANKEN FONDER AB—See Svenska Handelsbanken; *Int'l,* pg. 1327
HANDELSBANKEN HYPOTEK—See Svenska Handelsbanken; *Int'l,* pg. 1327
HANDELSBANKEN LIV—See Svenska Handelsbanken; *Int'l,* pg. 1327
HANDELSBANKEN MARKETS—See Svenska Handelsbanken; *Int'l,* pg. 1327
HANDELSBANKEN MARKETS FRANCE S.A.—See Svenska Handelsbanken; *Int'l,* pg. 1328
HANDELSBANKEN OSLO—See Svenska Handelsbanken; *Int'l,* pg. 1327
HANDELSBETEILIGUNGS GMBH—See Creditanstalt-Bankverein; *Int'l,* pg. 347
HANDELSBLATT-DOW JONES GMBH—See Georg von Holtzbrinck GmbH; *Int'l,* pg. 1479
HANDELSFINANZ-CCF BANK—See Credit Commercial de France; *Int'l,* pg. 343
HANDELSFINANZ-CCF BANK (INTERNATIONAL)—See Credit Commercial de France; *Int'l,* pg. 343
HANDELSGESELLSCHAFT HEINRICH HEINE GMBH—See Otto Versand (GmbH & Co.); *Int'l,* pg. 1014
HANDELSGEST S.A.R.L.—See Commerzbank AG; *Int'l,* pg. 312
HANDELSMAATSCHAPPIJ V/H KORTMAN B.V.—See Schmalbach-Lubeca AG; *Int'l,* pg. 1207
HANDEX ENVIRONMENTAL INC.; *U.S. Private,* pg. 498
HANDEX ENVIRONMENTAL INC.—See Handex Environment Inc.; *U.S. Private,* pg. 499
HANDEX OF FLORIDA, INC.—See Handex Environment Inc.; *U.S. Private,* pg. 499
HANDEX OF MARYLAND, INC.—See Handex Environment Inc.; *U.S. Private,* pg. 499
HANDEX OF NEW ENGLAND, INC.—See Handex Environment Inc.; *U.S. Private,* pg. 499
HANDEX OF NEW JERSEY, INC.—See Handex Environment Inc.; *U.S. Private,* pg. 499
HANDGARDS INC.; *U.S. Private,* pg. 499
HANDI THOMSON—See Thomson S.A.; *Int'l,* pg. 1382
HANDLEMAN COMPANY; *U.S. Public,* pg. 779
HANDLEMAN COMPANY OF CANADA LTD.—See Handleman Company; *U.S. Public,* pg. 780
HANDLING SYSTEMS ENGINEERING; *U.S. Private,* pg. 499
HANDLOWY-HELLER S.A.—See The Fuji Bank, Limited; *Int'l,* pg. 521
HANDSCHY INDUSTRIES—See Field Container Company, L.P.; *U.S. Private,* pg. 403
HANDSOME REWARDS—See Starcrest Products of California; *U.S. Private,* pg. 1035
HANDY & HARMAN; *U.S. Public,* pg. 780
HANDY & HARMAN ELECTRONIC MATERIALS CORP.—See Handy & Harman; *U.S. Public,* pg. 780
HANDY & HARMAN (EUROPE) LTD.—See Handy & Harman; *U.S. Public,* pg. 780
HANDY & HARMAN INTERNATIONAL, LTD.—See Handy & Harman; *U.S. Public,* pg. 780
HANDY & HARMAN MANUFACTURING (SINGAPORE) PTE. LTD.—See Handy & Harman; *U.S. Public,* pg. 780
HANDY & HARMAN OF CANADA LTD.—See Handy & Harman; *U.S. Public,* pg. 780
HANDY & HARMAN PRECIOUS METALS PRODUCTS DIVISION—See Handy & Harman; *U.S. Public,* pg. 780
HANDY & HARMAN TUBE CO., INC.—See Handy & Harman; *U.S. Public,* pg. 780
HANDY ANDY HELPING HANDS—See GIB Group; *Int'l,* pg. 533
HANDY ANDY HOLDING CO.—See GIB Group; *Int'l,* pg. 533
HANDY ANDY REALTY CO.—See GIB Group; *Int'l,* pg. 533
HANDY STORE FIXTURES, INC.; *U.S. Private,* pg. 499
HANEL LUMBER CO., INC.—See Hood Lumber Co.; *U.S. Private,* pg. 538
HANEL, S.A.—See Hewlett-Packard Company; *U.S. Public,* pg. 818
HANES COMPANIES, INC.—See Leggett & Platt, Incorporated; *U.S. Public,* pg. 986
HANES FABRICS COMPANY, INC.—See Leggett & Platt, Incorporated; *U.S. Public,* pg. 986
HANES HOLDING COMPANY—See Leggett & Platt, Incorporated; *U.S. Public,* pg. 986
HANES HOSIERY, INC.—See Sara Lee Corporation; *U.S. Public,* pg. 1434
HANEY SEED CO.—See ConAgra, Inc.; *U.S. Public,* pg. 428
THE HANFORD SENTINEL—See Pulitzer Publishing Company; *U.S. Public,* pg. 1343
HANFT BYRNE RABOY ABRAMS & PARTNERS, INC.; *U.S. Private,* pg. 499
HANG SENG BANK LIMITED—See HSBC Holdings plc; *Int'l,* pg. 583
HANG SENG BANK LTD.—See HSBC Holdings plc; *Int'l,* pg. 583
HANG SENG LIFE LTD.—See HSBC Holdings plc; *Int'l,* pg. 583
HANG TEN—See Genfoot Inc.; *Int'l,* pg. 549
HANGUKE GENSYM—See Gensym Corporation; *U.S. Public,* pg. 731
HANGZHI MACHINERY & ELECTRONICS CO., LTD.—See Toshiba Corporation; *Int'l,* pg. 1405
HANIEL BAUSTOFF-INDUSTRIE GMBH—See Franz Haniel & Cie, GmbH; *Int'l,* pg. 592

HANIEL BAUSTOFF-INDUSTRIE GMBH—See Philipp Holzmann AG; *Int'l,* pg. 633
HANIEL ENVIRSERVICE GMBH—See Franz Haniel & Cie, GmbH; *Int'l,* pg. 592
FRANZ HANIEL & CIE, GMBH; *Int'l,* pg. 591
HANIEL REEDEREI HOLDING GMBH—See Franz Haniel & Cie, GmbH; *Int'l,* pg. 592
HANIL CAN CO., LTD.—See Pechiney S.A.; *Int'l,* pg. 1029
HANIL DEVELOPMENT CO. LTD.—See Hanjin Shipping Company Ltd.; *Int'l,* pg. 592
HANIL LEASING COMPANY LIMITED—See The Tokai Bank, Limited; *Int'l,* pg. 1391
HANIMEX (FIJI) LIMITED—See Ricoh Company, Ltd.; *Int'l,* pg. 1115
HANIMEX (FRANCE) S.A.—See Ricoh Company, Ltd.; *Int'l,* pg. 1115
HANIMEX (NZ) LIMITED—See Ricoh Company, Ltd.; *Int'l,* pg. 1116
HANIMEX PTY. LIMITED—See Ricoh Company, Ltd.; *Int'l,* pg. 1115
HANIMEX VIVITAR (H.K.) LTD.—See Plaza Create; *Int'l,* pg. 1061
HANIMEX VIVITAR JAPAN K.K.—See Plaza Create; *Int'l,* pg. 1061
HANJIN CO., LTD.—See Hanjin Shipping Company Ltd.; *Int'l,* pg. 592
HANJIN SHIPPING COMPANY LTD.; *Int'l,* pg. 592
HANJIN TRANSPORTATION CO. LTD.—See Hanjin Shipping Company Ltd.; *Int'l,* pg. 592
PT HANKEN INDONESIA—See Komatsu Ltd.; *Int'l,* pg. 745
HANKINS LUMBER COMPANY, INC.; *U.S. Private,* pg. 499
HANKOOK ILBO TIME-LIFE LTD.—See Time Warner Inc.; *U.S. Public,* pg. 1615
HANKOOK OTIS ELEVATOR COMPANY—See United Technologies Corporation; *U.S. Public,* pg. 1691
HANKUK SAFETY GLASS LIMITED—See Pilkington Plc; *Int'l,* pg. 1057
HANLEY & BELFUS, INC.—See Georg von Holtzbrinck GmbH; *Int'l,* pg. 1479
HANNA—See Genfoot Inc.; *Int'l,* pg. 549
HANNA-BARBERA PRODUCTIONS, INC.—See Time Warner Inc.; *U.S. Public,* pg. 1614
HANNA CORPORATION—See Chatwins Group, Inc.; *U.S. Private,* pg. 231
HANNA HAMILTON HOLDINGS CO.—See M.A. Hanna Company; *U.S. Public,* pg. 781
HANNA INSURANCE SERVICES DIVISION—See M.A. Hanna Company; *U.S. Public,* pg. 781
M.A. HANNA COLOR—See M.A. Hanna Company; *U.S. Public,* pg. 781
M.A. HANNA COMPANY; *U.S. Public,* pg. 780
M.A. HANNA ENGINEERED MATERIALS—See M.A. Hanna Company; *U.S. Public,* pg. 781
M.A. HANNA RESIN DISTRIBUTION—See M.A. Hanna Company; *U.S. Public,* pg. 781
M.A. HANNA RUBBER COMPOUNDING—See M.A. Hanna Company; *U.S. Public,* pg. 781
HANNA MARINE SERVICES—See M.A. Hanna Company; *U.S. Public,* pg. 781
HANNA-SHERMAN INTERNATIONAL, INC.; *U.S. Private,* pg. 499
HANNAFORD BROS. CO.; *U.S. Public,* pg. 781
HANNAFORD SEEDMASTER SERVICES AUSTRALIA (PTY) LTD.—See Crompton & Knowles Corporation; *U.S. Public,* pg. 460
HANNAY REELS; *U.S. Private,* pg. 499
THE HANNIBAL COURIER-POST—See Shivers Trading & Operating Co.; *U.S. Private,* pg. 995
HANNOVER-BRAUNSCHWEIGISCHE STROMVERSORGUNGS-AG—See Veba AG; *Int'l,* pg. 1456
HANO DOCUMENT PRINTERS, INC.—See U.S. Office Products Company; *U.S. Public,* pg. 1686
HANOI RESIDENT REPRESENTATIVE OFFICE—See Nishimatsu Construction Co., Ltd.; *Int'l,* pg. 942
HANORA SPINNING, INC.—See The First Republic Corporation of America; *U.S. Public,* pg. 637
THE HANOVER AMERICAN INSURANCE COMPANY—See Allmerica Financial Corporation; *U.S. Public,* pg. 54
HANOVER BANK—See MainStreet BankGroup Incorporated; *U.S. Public,* pg. 1039
HANOVER DIRECT, INC.; *U.S. Public,* pg. 782
HANOVER DIRECT PENNSYLVANIA, INC.—See Hanover Direct, Inc.; *U.S. Public,* pg. 782
HANOVER DIRECT VIRGINIA, INC.—See Hanover Direct, Inc.; *U.S. Public,* pg. 782
HANOVER FOODS—See Hanover Foods Corporation; *U.S. Private,* pg. 499
HANOVER FOODS CORPORATION; *U.S. Private,* pg. 499
THE HANOVER INSURANCE COMPANY—See Allmerica Financial Corporation; *U.S. Public,* pg. 54
HANOVER LLOYD'S INSURANCE COMPANY—See Allmerica Financial Corporation; *U.S. Public,* pg. 54
HANOVER MANUFACTURING CORPORATION—See Reynolds Metals Company; *U.S. Public,* pg. 1386
HANOVER MARINER—See Gannett Company, Inc.; *U.S. Public,* pg. 701
HANOVER SHOE CO.—See Clarks International; *Int'l,* pg. 297
HANOVER SQUARE CORPORATION—See W.R. Grace & Co.; *U.S. Public,* pg. 755
HANOVER STORES—See Clarks International; *Int'l,* pg. 297
HANOVER TERRACE HEALTHCARE—See Vencor, Inc.; *U.S. Public,* pg. 1713
HANOVER TEXAS INSURANCE MANAGEMENT COMPANY, INC.—See Allmerica Financial Corporation; *U.S. Public,* pg. 54
HANOVER WIRE CLOTH—See CCX, Inc.; *U.S. Private,* pg. 193
HANOVIA COLIGHT—See ARC International Corporation; *Int'l,* pg. 17
HANOVIA LIMITED—See Halma p.l.c.; *Int'l,* pg. 589

HANSA BETEILIGUNGSGESELLSCHAFT MBH—See Bayer AG; *Int'l*, pg. 172
HANSA INDUSTRIAL INSURANCE N.V.—See Trygg-Hansa; *Int'l*, pg. 1425
HANSA KINDLUSTUS—See Trygg-Hansa; *Int'l*, pg. 1425
HANSA LTDA.—See BASF AG; *Int'l*, pg. 108
HANSA MELASSE HANDELS GMBH—See Tate & Lyle PLC; *Int'l*, pg. 1357
HANSA-NORDLUX MANAGEMENTGESELLSCHAFT—See Bayerische Vereinsbank Group; *Int'l*, pg. 181
HANSA RE & MARINE INSURANCE CO., (UK) LTD.—See Trygg-Hansa; *Int'l*, pg. 1425
HANSA ROHSTOFF GMBH - ILA TRADING SECTOR—See Fried. Krupp AG; *Int'l*, pg. 513
HANSA ROHSTOFFE GMBH—See Fried. Krupp AG; *Int'l*, pg. 513
HANSAPORT HAFENBETRIEBSGESELLSCHAFT MBH—See Preussag AG; *Int'l*, pg. 1069
HANSBERGER PRECISION GOLF INC.; *U.S. Private*, pg. 499
HANSEATIC BANK GMBH & CO.—See Otto Versand (GmbH & Co.); *Int'l*, pg. 1014
HANSEATIC VERSICHERUNGS-DIENST GMBH—See Otto Versand (GmbH & Co.); *Int'l*, pg. 1014
HANSEATISCHE ENERGIEVERSORGUNG AKTIENGESELLACHAFT ROSTOCK—See Veba AG; *Int'l*, pg. 1456
HANSEATISCHE INVESTITIONS BANK GMBH—See Bayerische Vereinsbank Group; *Int'l*, pg. 179
HANSEATISCHE LEASING GMBH—See Bayerische Vereinsbank Group; *Int'l*, pg. 179
OTTO HANSEL GMBH—See Klockner-Werke AG; *Int'l*, pg. 737
A.L. HANSEN MANUFACTURING CO.; *U.S. Private*, pg. 500
CHR. HANSEN AB—See Chr. Hansen Holding A/S; *Int'l*, pg. 288
CHR. HANSEN ARGENTINA S.A.I.C.—See Chr. Hansen Holding A/S; *Int'l*, pg. 289
CHR. HANSEN AS—See Chr. Hansen Holding A/S; *Int'l*, pg. 289
CHR. HANSEN BIOSYSTEMS S.P.A.—See Chr. Hansen Holding A/S; *Int'l*, pg. 289
CHR. HANSEN FRANCE S.A.—See Chr. Hansen Holding A/S; *Int'l*, pg. 289
CHR. HANSEN G.M.B.H.—See Chr. Hansen Holding A/S; *Int'l*, pg. 289
CHR. HANSEN GMBH NIEDERLASSUNG FUR OSTERREICH—See Chr. Hansen Holding A/S; *Int'l*, pg. 289
CHR. HANSEN, INC.—See Chr. Hansen Holding A/S; *Int'l*, pg. 288
CHR. HANSEN IRELAND LIMITED—See Chr. Hansen Holding A/S; *Int'l*, pg. 289
CHR. HANSEN LIMITED (CANADA)—See Chr. Hansen Holding A/S; *Int'l*, pg. 288
CHR. HANSEN POLAND SP. Z.O.O.—See Chr. Hansen Holding A/S; *Int'l*, pg. 289
CHR. HANSEN PTY. LTD.—See Chr. Hansen Holding A/S; *Int'l*, pg. 289
CHR. HANSEN S.P.A.—See Chr. Hansen Holding A/S; *Int'l*, pg. 289
CHR. HANSEN (UK) LTD.—See Chr. Hansen Holding A/S; *Int'l*, pg. 289
HANSEN CORPORATION—See Minebea, Ltd.; *Int'l*, pg. 868
HANSEN COUPLING DIVISION—See Tuthill Corporation; *U.S. Private*, pg. 1110
HANSEN FAR EAST LTD.—See Royal Nedlloyd Group N.V.; *Int'l*, pg. 1144
HANS HANSEN—See Norske Skogindustrier A.S.; *Int'l*, pg. 966
HANSEN HELLAS ABEE—See Chr. Hansen Holding A/S; *Int'l*, pg. 289
HANSEN MECHANICAL CONTRACTORS, INC.—See EMCOR Group, Inc.; *U.S. Public*, pg. 572
HANSEN PLASTICS DIVISION—See Tuthill Corporation; *U.S. Private*, pg. 1110
A. HANSEN'S AMAGERFROE A/S—See Novartis AG; *Int'l*, pg. 982
HANSEO FOOD CO. LTD.—See Nestle S.A.; *Int'l*, pg. 920
HANSON AMALGAMATED INDUSTRIES—See Hanson PLC; *Int'l*, pg. 592
HANSON BANK LTD.—See Hanson PLC; *Int'l*, pg. 592
HANSON BUILDING DIVISION—See Hanson PLC; *Int'l*, pg. 593
HANSON ENGINEERS—See Hanson Engineers Inc.; *U.S. Private*, pg. 500
HANSON ENGINEERS INC.; *U.S. Private*, pg. 500
HANSON INVESTMENT MANAGEMENT COMPANY—See United Asset Management Corporation; *U.S. Public*, pg. 1673
HANSON NORTH AMERICA—See Hanson PLC; *Int'l*, pg. 593
HANSON OVERSEAS FINANCE—See Hanson PLC; *Int'l*, pg. 594
HANSON PLC; *Int'l*, pg. 592
HANSON PROPERTIES LIMITED—See Hanson PLC; *Int'l*, pg. 593
HANSON WHITE LTD.—See Pentland Group PLC; *Int'l*, pg. 1035
ELOF HANSSON AB; *Int'l*, pg. 595
ELOF HANSSON INC.—See Elof Hansson AB; *Int'l*, pg. 595
ELOF HANSSON PAPER & BOARD, INC.—See Elof Hansson AB; *Int'l*, pg. 595
ELOF HANSSON PULP, INC.—See Elof Hansson AB; *Int'l*, pg. 595
HANWA AMERICAN CORP.—See Hanwa Co., Ltd.; *Int'l*, pg. 595
HANWA AMERICAN CORP., SEATTLE BRANCH—See Hanwa Co., Ltd.; *Int'l*, pg. 595
HANWA CO., LTD.; *Int'l*, pg. 595

HANWA CO., LTD.-BANGKOK BRANCH—See Hanwa Co., Ltd.; *Int'l*, pg. 595
HANWA CO., LTD.-BEIJING BRANCH—See Hanwa Co., Ltd.; *Int'l*, pg. 595
HANWA CO., LTD.-BOGATA BRANCH—See Hanwa Co., Ltd.; *Int'l*, pg. 595
HANWA CO., LTD.-BOMBAY BRANCH—See Hanwa Co., Ltd.; *Int'l*, pg. 595
HANWA CO., LTD.-HONG KONG BRANCH—See Hanwa Co., Ltd.; *Int'l*, pg. 595
HANWA CO., LTD.-JAKARTA BRANCH—See Hanwa Co., Ltd.; *Int'l*, pg. 595
HANWA CO., LTD.-JEDDAH BRANCH—See Hanwa Co., Ltd.; *Int'l*, pg. 595
HANWA CO., LTD.-KOTA KINABALU BRANCH—See Hanwa Co., Ltd.; *Int'l*, pg. 595
HANWA CO., LTD.-KUALA LUMPUR BRANCH—See Hanwa Co., Ltd.; *Int'l*, pg. 595
HANWA CO., LTD.-KUWAIT BRANCH—See Hanwa Co., Ltd.; *Int'l*, pg. 595
HANWA CO., LTD.-KYUSHU BRANCH—See Hanwa Co., Ltd.; *Int'l*, pg. 595
HANWA CO., LTD.-LAS PALMAS BRANCH—See Hanwa Co., Ltd.; *Int'l*, pg. 595
HANWA CO., LTD.-LONDON BRANCH—See Hanwa Co., Ltd.; *Int'l*, pg. 595
HANWA CO., LTD.-NAGOYA BRANCH—See Hanwa Co., Ltd.; *Int'l*, pg. 595
HANWA CO., LTD-OSAKA BRANCH—See Hanwa Co., Ltd.; *Int'l*, pg. 595
HANWA CO., LTD.-RIYADH BRANCH—See Hanwa Co., Ltd.; *Int'l*, pg. 595
HANWA CO., LTD.-SHANGHAI BRANCH—See Hanwa Co., Ltd.; *Int'l*, pg. 595
HANWA CO., LTD.-SINGAPORE BRANCH—See Hanwa Co., Ltd.; *Int'l*, pg. 595
HANWA CO., LTD.-TAIPEI BRANCH—See Hanwa Co., Ltd.; *Int'l*, pg. 595
HANWA CO., LTD.-TEHERAN BRANCH—See Hanwa Co., Ltd.; *Int'l*, pg. 595
HANWA CO., LTD.-TOHOKU BRANCH—See Hanwa Co., Ltd.; *Int'l*, pg. 596
HANWA CO., LTD.-TOKYO BRANCH—See Hanwa Co., Ltd.; *Int'l*, pg. 595
HANWA CO., LTD.-VANCOUVER BRANCH—See Hanwa Co., Ltd.; *Int'l*, pg. 596
HANWA-NSK PRECISION CO., LTD.—See NSK Ltd.; *Int'l*, pg. 903
HANYU SANYO ELECTRONICS CO., LTD.—See Sanyo Electric Co., Ltd.; *Int'l*, pg. 1191
THE HAOKKAIDO TAKUSHOKU SECURITIES CO. (SAPPORO)—See The Hokkaido Takushoku Bank, Ltd.; *Int'l*, pg. 626
HAPAG-LLOYD AG; *Int'l*, pg. 596
HAPAG-LLOYD (AMERICA), INC.—See Hapag-Lloyd AG; *Int'l*, pg. 596
HAPAG-LLOYD (ASIA) PTE. LTD.—See Hapag-Lloyd AG; *Int'l*, pg. 596
HAPAG-LLOYD (AUSTRALIA) PTE. LTD.—See Hapag-Lloyd AG; *Int'l*, pg. 596
HAPAG-LLOYD AUSTRIA GES. MBH—See Hapag-Lloyd AG; *Int'l*, pg. 596
HAPAG-LLOYD BELGIUM N.V.—See Hapag-Lloyd AG; *Int'l*, pg. 596
HAPAG-LLOYD FLUGGESELLSCHAFT GMBH—See Hapag-Lloyd AG; *Int'l*, pg. 596
HAPAG-LLOYD FLUGGESELLSCHAFT MBH—See Hapag-Lloyd AG; *Int'l*, pg. 596
HAPAG-LLOYD (FRANCE) S.A.—See Hapag-Lloyd AG; *Int'l*, pg. 596
HAPAG-LLOYD HOLDING PTE. LTD.—See Hapag-Lloyd AG; *Int'l*, pg. 596
HAPAG-LLOYD INTERNATIONAL S.A.—See Hapag-Lloyd AG; *Int'l*, pg. 596
HAPAG-LLOYD (ITALY) S.R.I.—See Hapag-Lloyd AG; *Int'l*, pg. 596
HAPAG-LLOYD (JAPAN) LTD.—See Hapag-Lloyd AG; *Int'l*, pg. 596
HAPAG-LLOYD KREUZFAHRTEN GMBH—See Hapag-Lloyd AG; *Int'l*, pg. 596
HAPAG-LLOYD NEDERLAND B.V.—See Hapag-Lloyd AG; *Int'l*, pg. 596
HAPAG-LLOYD REISEBURO GMBH—See Hapag-Lloyd AG; *Int'l*, pg. 596
HAPAG-LLOYD REISEBURO GMBH KOLN—See Hapag-Lloyd AG; *Int'l*, pg. 596
HAPAG-LLOYD (SCHWEIZ) AG—See Hapag-Lloyd AG; *Int'l*, pg. 596
HAPAG-LLOYD (SINGAPORE) PTE. LTD.—See Hapag-Lloyd AG; *Int'l*, pg. 596
HAPAG-LLOYD (TAIWAN) SHIPPING AGENCIES LTD.—See Hapag-Lloyd AG; *Int'l*, pg. 596
HAPAG-LLOYD TOURS GMBH—See Hapag-Lloyd AG; *Int'l*, pg. 596
HAPAG-LLOYD TRANSPORT & SERVICE GMBH—See Hapag-Lloyd AG; *Int'l*, pg. 596
HAPAG-LLOYD (U.K.) HOLDINGS LTD.—See Hapag-Lloyd AG; *Int'l*, pg. 596
HAPAG-LLOYD (U.K.) LTD.—See Hapag-Lloyd AG; *Int'l*, pg. 596
HAPAG-LLOYD VERWALTUNGS-GESELLSCHAFT MBH—See Hapag-Lloyd AG; *Int'l*, pg. 596
HAPAM-GOLDBACH B.V.—See Internatio-Muller N.V.; *Int'l*, pg. 681
HAPCO/AMERICAN DIV.—See The Dyson-Kissner-Moran Corporation; *U.S. Private*, pg. 351
HAPOALIM (LATIN AMERICA) S.A.—See Bank Hapoalim; *Int'l*, pg. 150
HAPPILAND SINGAPORE PRIVATE LTD.—See Namco Ltd.; *Int'l*, pg. 905
HAPPY HOLIDAY TREE FARMS—See Color Spot Nursery, Inc.; *U.S. Private*, pg. 254
MARTIN HARALDSTAD A/S—See Icopal a/s; *Int'l*, pg. 659

HARBAUER GMBH & CO. KG—See Philipp Holzmann AG; *Int'l*, pg. 632
HARBERT CORPORATION; *U.S. Private*, pg. 500
HARBINGER CARPET—See Mohawk Industries, Inc.; *U.S. Public*, pg. 1121
HARBISON-WALKER REFRACTORIES—See Global Industrial Technologies; *U.S. Public*, pg. 748
HARBOR ELECTRIC ENERGY COMPANY—See Boston Edison Company; *U.S. Public*, pg. 247
HARBOR FINANCIAL MORTGAGE CORP.—See FirstCity Financial Corporation; *U.S. Public*, pg. 644
HARBOR FINANCIAL/NEW AMERICA—See FirstCity Financial Corporation; *U.S. Public*, pg. 644
HARBOR FINANCIAL PROPERTY MANAGEMENT INC.—See FirstCity Financial Corporation; *U.S. Public*, pg. 644
HARBOR FINANCIAL SERVICES—See Sterling Financial Corporation; *U.S. Public*, pg. 1516
HARBOR VIEW CARE CENTER—See Horizon/CMS Healthcare Corporation; *U.S. Public*, pg. 839
HARBORLITE CORPORATION—See Alleghany Corporation; *U.S. Public*, pg. 42
HARBORPLACE—See The Rouse Company; *U.S. Public*, pg. 1407
HARBOUR CONTRACTORS, INC.; *U.S. Private*, pg. 500
HARBOUR GROUP LTD.; *U.S. Private*, pg. 500
HARBOUR ISLAND, INC.—See Beneficial Corporation; *U.S. Public*, pg. 211
HARBOUR WATER CORPORATION—See NIPSCO Industries, Inc.; *U.S. Public*, pg. 1185
HARCO—See Banner Aerospace, Inc.; *U.S. Public*, pg. 187
HARCO INSURANCE SERVICES, INC.—See Navistar International Corporation; *U.S. Public*, pg. 1167
HARCO LEASING CO., INC.—See Navistar International Corporation; *U.S. Public*, pg. 1167
HARCOR ENERGY, INC.; *U.S. Public*, pg. 782
HARCOURT-BRACE—See Harcourt General, Inc.; *U.S. Public*, pg. 783
HARCOURT BRACE & COMPANY - ELEMENTARY DIV.—See Harcourt General, Inc.; *U.S. Public*, pg. 783
HARCOURT BRACE & COMPANY FARM PUBLICATIONS INC.—See Harcourt General, Inc.; *U.S. Public*, pg. 783
HARCOURT BRACE & COMPANY INTL. CORP.—See Harcourt General, Inc.; *U.S. Public*, pg. 783
HARCOURT BRACE & COMPANY LEGAL AND PROFESSIONAL PUBLICATIONS, INC.—See Harcourt General, Inc.; *U.S. Public*, pg. 783
HARCOURT BRACE & COMPANY MEDIA SYSTEMS CORPORATION—See Harcourt General, Inc.; *U.S. Public*, pg. 783
HARCOURT BRACE & COMPANY REAL PROPERTIES CORPORATION—See Harcourt General, Inc.; *U.S. Public*, pg. 783
HARCOURT GENERAL, INC.; *U.S. Public*, pg. 782
HARCREST INTERNATIONAL, LTD.; *U.S. Private*, pg. 500
HARCROS CHEMICALS—See Harrisons & Crosfield plc; *Int'l*, pg. 599
HARCROS CHEMICALS INC.—See Harrisons & Crosfield plc; *Int'l*, pg. 598
HARCROS TIMBER AUSTRALIA PTY. LTD.—See Harrisons & Crosfield plc; *Int'l*, pg. 599
HARD ROCK CAFE INTERNATIONAL INC.—See The Rank Group PLC; *Int'l*, pg. 1087
THE HARDAWAY COMPANY; *U.S. Private*, pg. 501
HARDAWAY CONCRETE CO., INC.; *U.S. Private*, pg. 501
HARDAWAY CONSTRUCTION CORP. OF TENNESSEE, INC.; *U.S. Private*, pg. 501
HARDEE'S EQUIPMENT DEPARTMENT—See CKE Restaurants Inc.; *U.S. Public*, pg. 278
HARDEE'S FOOD SYSTEMS, INC.—See CKE Restaurants Inc.; *U.S. Public*, pg. 278
HARDEL BUILDERS CENTER—See Hardel Mutual Plywood Corporation; *U.S. Private*, pg. 501
HARDEL MUTUAL PLYWOOD CORPORATION; *U.S. Private*, pg. 501
HARDEMAN CO. CORRECTIONAL FACILITY—See Corrections Corporation of America; *U.S. Public*, pg. 450
HARDEN FURNITURE COMPANY; *U.S. Private*, pg. 501
HARDEN INDUSTRIES, INC.; *U.S. Private*, pg. 501
JAMES HARDIE BUILDING PRODUCTS—See James Hardie Industries Ltd.; *Int'l*, pg. 597
JAMES HARDIE BUILDING PRODUCTS INC.—See James Hardie Industries Ltd.; *Int'l*, pg. 597
JAMES HARDIE BUILDING SERVICES—See James Hardie Industries Ltd.; *Int'l*, pg. 597
JAMES HARDIE GYPSUM WASHINGTON—See James Hardie Industries Ltd.; *Int'l*, pg. 597
JAMES HARDIE INDUSTRIES LTD.; *Int'l*, pg. 596
JAMES HARDIE PLUMBING & PIPELINES—See James Hardie Industries Ltd.; *Int'l*, pg. 597
JAMES HARDIE USA—See James Hardie Industries Ltd.; *Int'l*, pg. 597
HARDIN CONSTRUCTION GROUP, INC.; *U.S. Private*, pg. 501
HARDIN COUNTY GAS COMPANY—See Atrion Corporation; *U.S. Public*, pg. 146
HARDING LAWSON ASSOCIATES—See Harding Lawson Associates Group, Inc.; *U.S. Public*, pg. 785
HARDING LAWSON ASSOCIATES GROUP, INC.; *U.S. Public*, pg. 785
HARDING LAWSON ASSOCIATES, INFRASTRUCTURE, INC.—See Harding Lawson Associates Group, Inc.; *U.S. Public*, pg. 785
HARDINGS, INC.; *U.S. Private*, pg. 502
HARDINGS MACHINE TOOLS, LTD.—See Hardings, Inc.; *U.S. Private*, pg. 502
HARDIN'S BAKERY, INC.—See Flowers Industries, Inc.; *U.S. Public*, pg. 657
HARDIN'S-SYSCO FOOD SERVICES, INC.—See Sysco Corporation; *U.S. Public*, pg. 1551
HARDMAN DIVISION OF HARCROS CHEMICALS, INC.—See Harrisons & Crosfield plc; *Int'l*, pg. 598

Company Index

HARDWARE & COMPONENTS OPERATION—See Newell Co.; *U.S. Public*, pg. 1177
HARDWARE CITY ROCK CATS—See Minnesota Twins Baseball Club; *U.S. Private*, pg. 751
HARDWARE MANUFACTURING—See McKechnie PLC; *Int'l*, pg. 851
HARDWARE WHOLESALERS, INC.; *U.S. Private*, pg. 502
HARDWICK CLOTHES INC.; *U.S. Private*, pg. 502
HARDWOODS OF MICHIGAN, INC.; *U.S. Private*, pg. 502
HARDY & CO PRIVATBANKIERS—See Dresdner Bank AG; *Int'l*, pg. 418
HARFORD SYSTEMS, INC.—See Lab Products, Inc.; *U.S. Private*, pg. 641
HARGRO ENTERPRISES, INC.; *U.S. Private*, pg. 502
HARIG GRINDERS—See Bridgeport Machines, Inc.; *U.S. Public*, pg. 252
HARIMA M.I.D., INC.—See The Mead Corporation; *U.S. Public*, pg. 1077
HARINERA LA MONTANA, S.A. DE C.V.—See Tablex, S.A. de C.V.; *Int'l*, pg. 1345
HARINERA LOS PIRINEOS, S.A. DE C.V.—See Tablex, S.A. de C.V.; *Int'l*, pg. 1346
HARKEN BAHRAIN OIL COMPANY—See Harken Energy Corporation; *U.S. Public*, pg. 785
HARKEN ENERGY CORPORATION; *U.S. Public*, pg. 785
HARKEN EXPLORATION COMPANY—See Harken Energy Corporation; *U.S. Public*, pg. 785
HARKEN RESOURCE MANAGEMENT COMPANY—See Harken Energy Corporation; *U.S. Public*, pg. 785
HARKER'S DISTRIBUTION, INC.; *U.S. Private*, pg. 502
HARKINS BUILDERS, INC.; *U.S. Private*, pg. 502
THE HARLAN DAILY ENTERPRISE—See Hollinger Inc.; *Int'l*, pg. 632
HARLAN ELECTRIC CO.—See MYR Group Inc.; *U.S. Public*, pg. 1029
JOHN H. HARLAND COMPANY; *U.S. Public*, pg. 785
JOHN H. HARLAND CO. OF PUERTO RICO—See John H. Harland Company; *U.S. Public*, pg. 785
HARLEQUIN ENTERPRISES LTD.—See Torstar Corporation; *Int'l*, pg. 1402
HARLEQUIN MONDADORI S.P.A.—See Arnoldo Mondadori Editore S.p.A.; *Int'l*, pg. 888
HARLEY-DAVIDSON, INC.; *U.S. Public*, pg. 786
HARLEY-DAVIDSON MOTOR COMPANY—See Harley-Davidson, Inc.; *U.S. Public*, pg. 786
HARLEY ELLINGTON DESIGN; *U.S. Private*, pg. 503
HARLEY GAUGE & INSTRUMENT CO.—See Innovative Valve Technology, Inc.; *U.S. Public*, pg. 880
HARLEY INDUSTRIES, INC.—See Innovative Valve Technology, Inc.; *U.S. Public*, pg. 880
HARLEY VALVE & INSTRUMENT CO.—See Innovative Valve Technology, Inc.; *U.S. Public*, pg. 880
HARLEYSVILLE ATLANTIC INSURANCE COMPANY—See Harleysville Group; *U.S. Public*, pg. 786
HARLEYSVILLE-GARDEN STATE INSURANCE CO.—See Harleysville Group; *U.S. Public*, pg. 787
HARLEYSVILLE GROUP; *U.S. Public*, pg. 786
HARLEYSVILLE INSURANCE COMPANY OF NEW JERSEY—See Harleysville Group; *U.S. Public*, pg. 787
HARLEYSVILLE LIFE INSURANCE CO.—See Harleysville Group; *U.S. Public*, pg. 787
HARLEYSVILLE MUTUAL INSURANCE—See Harleysville Group; *U.S. Public*, pg. 787
HARLEYSVILLE SERVICES INC—See Harleysville Group; *U.S. Public*, pg. 787
HARMAG, INC.—See Pfizer Inc.; *U.S. Public*, pg. 1282
HARMAN AUDIO—See Harman International Industries, Inc.; *U.S. Public*, pg. 787
HARMAN AUTOMOTIVE—See Harvard Industries, Inc.; *U.S. Public*, pg. 796
HARMAN CONSUMER GROUP—See Harman International Industries, Inc.; *U.S. Public*, pg. 787
HARMAN DEUTSCHLAND GMBH—See Harman International Industries, Inc.; *U.S. Public*, pg. 787
HARMAN ELECTRONICS, INC.—See Harman International Industries, Inc.; *U.S. Public*, pg. 787
HARMAN FRANCE—See Harman International Industries, Inc.; *U.S. Public*, pg. 787
HARMAN INTERACTIVE GROUP—See Harman International Industries, Inc.; *U.S. Public*, pg. 787
HARMAN INTERNATIONAL INDUSTRIES, INC.; *U.S. Public*, pg. 787
HARMAN JAPAN—See Harman International Industries, Inc.; *U.S. Public*, pg. 787
HARMAN MOTIVE LTD—See Harman International Industries, Inc.; *U.S. Public*, pg. 787
HARMAN SPEAKER MANUFACTURING—See Harman International Industries, Inc.; *U.S. Public*, pg. 787
HARMO INDUSTRIES, LTD.—See Tenneco Inc.; *U.S. Public*, pg. 1579
HARMON CITY, INC.; *U.S. Private*, pg. 503
HARMON CONTRACT GLAZING, INC.—See Apogee Enterprises, Inc.; *U.S. Public*, pg. 120
HARMON GLASS COMPANY—See Apogee Enterprises, Inc.; *U.S. Public*, pg. 120
HARMON GLASS OF FLORIDA, INC.—See Apogee Enterprises, Inc.; *U.S. Public*, pg. 120
HARMON INDUSTRIES-GRAIN VALLEY—See Harmon Industries, Inc.; *U.S. Public*, pg. 788
HARMON INDUSTRIES, INC.; *U.S. Public*, pg. 788
HARMON INDUSTRIES-LEES SUMMIT—See Harmon Industries, Inc.; *U.S. Public*, pg. 788
HARMON INDUSTRIES-RIVERSIDE—See Harmon Industries, Inc.; *U.S. Public*, pg. 788
HARMON INDUSTRIES-JACKSONVILLE—See Harmon Industries, Inc.; *U.S. Public*, pg. 788
HARMON PUBLISHING—See United News & Media plc; *Int'l*, pg. 1443
HARMONIC LIGHTWAVES; *U.S. Public*, pg. 788
HARMONIC LIGHTWAVES (ISRAEL) LTD—See Harmonic Lightwaves; *U.S. Public*, pg. 788
HARMONY BOOKS—See Advance Publications Inc.; *U.S. Private*, pg. 21

HARMONY ENGINEERING CORPORATION; *U.S. Private*, pg. 503
HARMONY FOODS CORPORATION; *U.S. Private*, pg. 503
HARMONY HOUSE RECORDS & TAPES; *U.S. Private*, pg. 503
HARMSWORTH MEDIA LTD.—See Daily Mail & General Trust PLC; *Int'l*, pg. 366
HARNISCHFEGER CORP.—See Kobe Steel, Ltd.; *Int'l*, pg. 740
HARNISCHFEGER INDUSTRIES, INC.; *U.S. Public*, pg. 788
THE HARODITE FINISHING COMPANY INC.; *U.S. Private*, pg. 503
HAROWE SERVO CONTROLS—See American Precision Industries Inc.; *U.S. Public*, pg. 90
THE HARP LAGER CO. LTD.—See Diageo Plc; *Int'l*, pg. 412
HARPEN AG; *Int'l*, pg. 597
HARPEN AG & CO. GEWERBEIMMOBILIEN KG—See Harpen AG; *Int'l*, pg. 597
HARPEN AG & CO. HOTELBAUTEN KG—See Harpen AG; *Int'l*, pg. 597
HARPEN AG & CO. INDUSTRIEPARK KG—See Harpen AG; *Int'l*, pg. 597
HARPEN AG & CO. VERBRAUCHERMARKTE KG—See Harpen AG; *Int'l*, pg. 597
HARPEN IMMOBILIEN VERW.U. BETEILIG GES.MBH—See Harpen AG; *Int'l*, pg. 597
HARPEN TRANSPORT AG—See Harpen AG; *Int'l*, pg. 597
HARPER AUDIO—See The News Corporation Limited; *Int'l*, pg. 926
HARPER BROS., INC.; *U.S. Public*, pg. 504
HARPER FREIGHT INTERNATIONAL—See Circle International Group, Inc.; *U.S. Public*, pg. 373
HARPER FREIGHT INTERNATIONAL (SWEDEN) AB—See Circle International Group, Inc.; *U.S. Public*, pg. 373
HARPER INDUSTRIES, INC.—See Harcrest International, Ltd.; *U.S. Private*, pg. 501
HARPER MECHANICAL CORPORATION—See Compagnie Generale Des Eaux; *Int'l*, pg. 322
HARPER REFERENCE—See The News Corporation Limited; *Int'l*, pg. 927
HARPER-WYMAN CO.—See Oak Industries Inc.; *U.S. Public*, pg. 926
HARPERCOLLINS ADULT TRADE DIVISION—See The News Corporation Limited; *Int'l*, pg. 926
HARPERCOLLINS JUNIOR BOOKS DIVISION—See The News Corporation Limited; *Int'l*, pg. 927
HARPERCOLLINS PUBLISHERS—See The News Corporation Limited; *Int'l*, pg. 926
HARPERCOLLINS SAN FRANCISCO—See The News Corporation Limited; *Int'l*, pg. 927
HARPER'S BAZAAR—See The Hearst Corporation; *U.S. Private*, pg. 517
HARPERS MANUFACTURING—See Kimball International, Inc.; *U.S. Public*, pg. 957
HARPERS SALES—See Kimball International, Inc.; *U.S. Public*, pg. 957
HARPO ENTERTAINMENT GROUP; *U.S. Private*, pg. 504
HARP'S FOOD STORES, INC.; *U.S. Private*, pg. 504
HARRAH'S ALBERTA INVESTMENT CORPORATION—See Harrah's Entertainment, Inc.; *U.S. Public*, pg. 790
HARRAH'S ARIZONA CORPORATION—See Harrah's Entertainment, Inc.; *U.S. Public*, pg. 790
HARRAH'S ATLANTIC CITY, INC.—See Harrah's Entertainment, Inc.; *U.S. Public*, pg. 790
HARRAH'S CALIFORNIA CORPORATION—See Harrah's Entertainment, Inc.; *U.S. Public*, pg. 790
HARRAH'S CALIFORNIA SSR CORPORATION—See Harrah's Entertainment, Inc.; *U.S. Public*, pg. 790
HARRAH'S COLORADO INVESTMENT CORPORATION—See Harrah's Entertainment, Inc.; *U.S. Public*, pg. 790
HARRAH'S ENTERTAINMENT, INC.; *U.S. Public*, pg. 790
HARRAH'S HOLIDAY INNS OF NEW JERSEY INC.—See Harrah's Entertainment, Inc.; *U.S. Public*, pg. 790
HARRAH'S ILLINOIS CORPORATION—See Harrah's Entertainment, Inc.; *U.S. Public*, pg. 790
HARRAH'S LAS VEGAS—See Harrah's Entertainment, Inc.; *U.S. Public*, pg. 790
HARRAH'S LAUGHLIN, INC.—See Harrah's Entertainment, Inc.; *U.S. Public*, pg. 790
HARRAH'S MANAGEMENT CO.—See Harrah's Entertainment, Inc.; *U.S. Public*, pg. 790
HARRAH'S NEW JERSEY, INC.—See Harrah's Entertainment, Inc.; *U.S. Public*, pg. 790
HARRAH'S OPERATING COMPANY, INC.—See Harrah's Entertainment, Inc.; *U.S. Public*, pg. 790
HARRAH'S PTY. LIMITED—See Harrah's Entertainment, Inc.; *U.S. Public*, pg. 790
HARRAH'S RENO HOLDING COMPANY—See Harrah's Entertainment, Inc.; *U.S. Public*, pg. 791
HARRAH'S SOUTH SHORE CORP.—See Harrah's Entertainment, Inc.; *U.S. Public*, pg. 791
HARRICROS CHEMICALS PTE. LTD.—See Harrisons & Crosfield plc; *Int'l*, pg. 599
HARRIET & HENDERSON YARNS, INC.; *U.S. Private*, pg. 504
HARRIMAN RECORD—See Landmark Communications, Inc.; *U.S. Private*, pg. 648
HARRINGTON & KING; *U.S. Private*, pg. 504
HARRINGTON & KING, SOUTH, INC.—See Harrington & King; *U.S. Private*, pg. 504
HARRINGTON & KING SOUTH, INC.—See Harrington & King; *U.S. Private*, pg. 504
HARRINGTON HOISTS, INC.; *U.S. Private*, pg. 504
HARRINGTON INDUSTRIAL PLASTICS INC.—See Glynwed International PLC; *Int'l*, pg. 554
HARRINGTON INTERNATIONAL INSURANCE LTD.—See Swiss Reinsurance Company; *Int'l*, pg. 1333
HARRINGTON'S OF VERMONT, INC.; *U.S. Private*, pg. 504
HARRIS ADACOM NETWORK SERVICES—See Genicom Corporation; *U.S. Public*, pg. 729

HARRIS AIR SYSTEMS COMPANY—See Harris Contracting Co.; *U.S. Private*, pg. 505
HARRIS ALLIED SYSTEMS—See Harris Corporation; *U.S. Public*, pg. 791
HARRIS & DIXON (INSURANCE BROKERS) LTD.—See Assicurazioni Generali S.p.A.; *Int'l*, pg. 90
HARRIS & DIXON (INSURANCE BROKERS) PTY. LTD.—See Assicurazioni Generali S.p.A.; *Int'l*, pg. 90
HARRIS & DIXON INSURANCE HOLDINGS LTD.—See Assicurazioni Generali S.p.A.; *Int'l*, pg. 90
HARRIS & DIXON REINSURANCE BROKERS LTD.—See Assicurazioni Generali S.p.A.; *Int'l*, pg. 90
HARRIS/ARIZONA REBAR INC.—See Harris Steel Group Inc.; *Int'l*, pg. 598
HARRIS, BAIO & MCCULLOUGH INC.; *U.S. Private*, pg. 504
HARRIS & BANK—See Bank of Montreal; *Int'l*, pg. 154
HARRIS BANK ARLINGTON-MEADOWS—See Bank of Montreal; *Int'l*, pg. 154
HARRIS BANK AURORA, N.A.—See Bank of Montreal; *Int'l*, pg. 154
HARRIS BANK BARTLETT—See Bank of Montreal; *Int'l*, pg. 154
HARRIS BANK CARY-GROVE—See Bank of Montreal; *Int'l*, pg. 154
HARRIS BANK ELK GROVE, N.A.—See Bank of Montreal; *Int'l*, pg. 154
HARRIS BANK HOFFMAN-SCHAUMBURG—See Bank of Montreal; *Int'l*, pg. 154
HARRIS BANK HUNTLEY—See Bank of Montreal; *Int'l*, pg. 154
HARRIS BANK INTERNATIONAL CORP.—See Bank of Montreal; *Int'l*, pg. 154
HARRIS BANK MARENGO—See Bank of Montreal; *Int'l*, pg. 154
HARRIS BANK OAKBROOK TERRACE—See Bank of Montreal; *Int'l*, pg. 154
HARRIS BANK PALATINE, N.A.—See Bank of Montreal; *Int'l*, pg. 154
HARRIS BANK WESTCHESTER—See Bank of Montreal; *Int'l*, pg. 154
HARRIS BANK WOODSTOCK—See Bank of Montreal; *Int'l*, pg. 154
HARRIS BANKCORP, INC.—See Bank of Montreal; *Int'l*, pg. 154
HARRIS BROADCAST DIVISION—See Harris Corporation; *U.S. Public*, pg. 791
HARRIS BUILDING SERVICES CORPORATION—See Bank of Montreal; *Int'l*, pg. 154
HARRIS CHEMICAL GROUP, INC.; *U.S. Private*, pg. 505
HARRIS CONTRACTING CO.; *U.S. Private*, pg. 505
HARRIS CORP. B.V.—See Harris Corporation; *U.S. Public*, pg. 791
HARRIS CORP., DIGITAL TELEPHONE SYSTEMS DIV.—See Harris Corporation; *U.S. Public*, pg. 791
HARRIS CORP., RF COMMUNICATIONS GROUP MARKETING DIVISION—See Harris Corporation; *U.S. Public*, pg. 792
HARRIS CORPORATION; *U.S. Public*, pg. 791
HARRIS DATA SERVICES CORPORATION—See Harris Corporation; *U.S. Public*, pg. 791
HARRIS DRURY COHEN; *U.S. Private*, pg. 505
HARRIS ENTERPRISES INC.; *U.S. Private*, pg. 505
HARRIS EUROPA, S.P.A.—See Emerson Electric Co.; *U.S. Public*, pg. 577
HARRIS FARMS, INC.; *U.S. Private*, pg. 505
HARRIS FEEDING CO.—See Harris Farms, Inc.; *U.S. Private*, pg. 505
HARRIS FORD, INC.; *U.S. Private*, pg. 506
HARRIS FUTURES CORPORATION—See Bank of Montreal; *Int'l*, pg. 154
HARRIS GMBH—See Harris Corporation; *U.S. Public*, pg. 791
HARVEY HARRIS & CO. LTD.—See Dolland & Aitchison Ltd.; *Int'l*, pg. 414
HARRIS INVESTMENT MANAGEMENT, INC.—See Bank of Montreal; *Int'l*, pg. 154
HARRIS INVESTORS DIRECT, INC.—See Bank of Montreal; *Int'l*, pg. 154
HARRIS ITALIANA, INC.—See Harris Corporation; *U.S. Public*, pg. 791
HARRIS-KAYOT, INC.; *U.S. Private*, pg. 506
HARRIS LANIER AUSTRALIA—See Harris Corporation; *U.S. Public*, pg. 791
HARRIS LIFE INSURANCE COMPANY—See Bank of Montreal; *Int'l*, pg. 154
HARRIS METALS—See Lindberg Corporation; *U.S. Public*, pg. 999
HARRIS METALS-ARROW ACME CO.—See Lindberg Corporation; *U.S. Public*, pg. 999
HARRIS MORAN SEED COMPANY—See Lafarge S.A.; *Int'l*, pg. 789
HARRIS-NESBITT THOMSON SECURITIES, INC.—See Bank of Montreal; *Int'l*, pg. 155
HARRIS NETWORK SUPPORT SYSTEMS—See Harris Corporation; *U.S. Public*, pg. 792
HARRIS NOVATEL—See Harris Corporation; *U.S. Public*, pg. 792
PAUL HARRIS STORES, INC.; *U.S. Public*, pg. 792
PAUL HARRIS STORES OF VIRGINIA, INC.—See Paul Harris Stores, Inc.; *U.S. Public*, pg. 792
HARRIS PROTOCALL, INC.—See Harris Corporation; *U.S. Public*, pg. 792
HARRIS PUBLISHING SYSTEMS CORPORATION—See Harris Corporation; *U.S. Public*, pg. 791
HARRIS RANCH BEEF CO.—See Harris Farms, Inc.; *U.S. Private*, pg. 505
HARRIS RANCH RESTAURANT—See Harris Farms, Inc.; *U.S. Private*, pg. 506
HARRIS REBAR—See Harris Steel Group Inc.; *Int'l*, pg. 598
HARRIS REBAR ATLANTIC, INC.—See Harris Steel Group Inc.; *Int'l*, pg. 598

HARRIS REBAR BOSTON, INC.—See Harris Steel Group Inc.; *Int'l*, pg. 598
HARRIS REBAR OAKLAND, INC.—See Harris Steel Group Inc.; *Int'l*, pg. 598
HARRIS REBAR SEATTLE, INC.—See Harris Steel Group Inc.; *Int'l*, pg. 598
HARRIS SARL-SCIENTIFIC CALCULATIONS—See Harris Corporation; *U.S. Public*, pg. 791
HARRIS SAUDI ARABIA LTD.—See Harris Corporation; *U.S. Public*, pg. 791
HARRIS SCARFE HOLDINGS LIMITED; *Int'l*, pg. 597
HARRIS SCARFE LTD.—See Harris Scarfe Holdings Limited; *Int'l*, pg. 597
HARRIS SEMICONDUCTOR—See Harris Corporation; *U.S. Public*, pg. 792
HARRIS SEMICONDUCTOR MICROELECTRONICS CENTER—See Harris Corporation; *U.S. Public*, pg. 792
HARRIS SPACE SYSTEMS CORP.—See Harris Corporation; *U.S. Public*, pg. 791
HARRIS SPECIALTY CHEMICAL—See Harris Chemical Group, Inc.; *U.S. Private*, pg. 505
HARRIS STEEL CO.; *U.S. Public*, pg. 506
HARRIS STEEL GROUP INC.; *Int'l*, pg. 597
HARRIS SYSTEMS LTD.—See Harris Corporation; *U.S. Public*, pg. 791
HARRIS TECHNICAL SERVICES CORP.—See Harris Corporation; *U.S. Public*, pg. 792
HARRIS TEETER, INC.—See Ruddick Corporation; *U.S. Public*, pg. 1412
HARRIS TRADING ADVISORY CORPORATION—See Bank of Montreal; *Int'l*, pg. 154
HARRIS TRUST BANK OF ARIZONA—See Bank of Montreal; *Int'l*, pg. 155
HARRIS TRUST COMPANY OF CALIFORNIA—See Bank of Montreal; *Int'l*, pg. 155
HARRIS TRUST COMPANY OF FLORIDA—See Bank of Montreal; *Int'l*, pg. 155
HARRIS TRUST COMPANY OF NEW YORK—See Bank of Montreal; *Int'l*, pg. 155
HARRIS WASHINGTON OPERATIONS—See Harris Corporation; *U.S. Public*, pg. 792
HARRIS WASTE MGMT. GROUP, INC.—See FKI Plc; *Int'l*, pg. 473
HARRISBURG STAMP CO.—See American Marking Systems; *U.S. Private*, pg. 59
HARRISBURG TELEVISION, INC—See Perpetual Corporation; *U.S. Private*, pg. 854
HARRISCORP CAPITAL CORPORATION—See Bank of Montreal; *Int'l*, pg. 155
HARRISCORP FINANCE, INC.—See Bank of Montreal; *Int'l*, pg. 155
HARRISCORP LEASING, INC.—See Bank of Montreal; *Int'l*, pg. 155
HARRISON & SONS LTD.—See Lonrho plc; *Int'l*, pg. 817
HARRISON & STAR—See Harrison & Star, Inc.; *U.S. Private*, pg. 506
HARRISON & STAR, INC.; *U.S. Private*, pg. 506
HARRISON BAKING CO.—See Amerifoods Inc.; *U.S. Private*, pg. 65
HARRISON CONSTRUCTION CORP.; *U.S. Private*, pg. 506
HARRISON DRAPE—See McKechnie PLC; *Int'l*, pg. 851
HARRISON ELECTRIC CO., LTD.—See Toshiba Corporation; *Int'l*, pg. 1402
HARRISON PAINT CORP.; *U.S. Private*, pg. 506
HARRISON RADIATOR DIVISION—See General Motors Corporation; *U.S. Public*, pg. 725
HARRISON WILSON & ASSOCIATES—See Omnicom Group Inc.; *U.S. Public*, pg. 1224
HARRISON, YOUNG, PESONEN & NEWELL INC.; *Int'l*, pg. 598
HARRISONBURG AUTO AUCTION—See Cox Enterprises, Inc.; *U.S. Private*, pg. 282
HARRISONS & CROSFIELD PLC; *Int'l*, pg. 598
HARRISONS & CROSFIELD (AUSTRALIA) LTD.—See Harrisons & Crosfield plc; *Int'l*, pg. 599
HARRISONS & CROSFIELD (CANADA) LTD.—See Harrisons & Crosfield plc; *Int'l*, pg. 599
HARRISONS & CROSFIELD (HONG KONG) LTD.—See Harrisons & Crosfield plc; *Int'l*, pg. 599
HARRISONS & CROSFIELD (N.Z.) LTD.—See Harrisons & Crosfield plc; *Int'l*, pg. 599
HARRISS & COVINGTON HOSIERY MILLS; *U.S. Private*, pg. 506
HARROD DEVITT SOCIEDAD ANONIMA—See The Prudential Insurance Company of America; *U.S. Private*, pg. 893
HARRODSBURG HEALTH CARE—See Vencor, Inc.; *U.S. Public*, pg. 1713
HARROP INDUSTRIES, INC.; *U.S. Private*, pg. 506
HARROW INDUSTRIES; *U.S. Private*, pg. 506
HARROWSTON CAPITAL CORPORATION—See Harrowston Corporation; *Int'l*, pg. 599
HARROWSTON CORPORATION; *Int'l*, pg. 599
HARROWSTON DEVELOPMENTS CORPORATION—See Harrowston Corporation; *Int'l*, pg. 599
HARRY AND DAVID—See Yamanouchi Pharmaceutical Co. Ltd.; *Int'l*, pg. 1518
HARRY ROSEN INC.—See Dylex Limited; *Int'l*, pg. 425
HARRY'S BAR LTD.—See Sea Containers Ltd.; *Int'l*, pg. 1213
HARSCO CORPORATION; *U.S. Public*, pg. 792
HARSHAW FILTROL—See Akzo Nobel N.V.; *Int'l*, pg. 46
ARTHUR HART WEBBING—See Bridport-Gundry p.l.c.; *Int'l*, pg. 215
HART CROWSER, INC.; *U.S. Public*, pg. 507
HART DISTRIBUTION SERVICES—See Hart Graphics Inc.; *U.S. Private*, pg. 507
HART ENGINEERING CORPORATION; *U.S. Private*, pg. 507
HART, FENTON & CO. LTD.—See Sea Containers Ltd.; *Int'l*, pg. 1214
HART FORMS & SERVICES—See Hart Graphics Inc.; *U.S. Private*, pg. 507
HART GRAPHICS INC.; *U.S. Private*, pg. 507

HART HOLDING COMPANY, INC.; *U.S. Private*, pg. 507
HART INDUSTRIAL SUPPLY CO.—See LSB Industries, Inc.; *U.S. Public*, pg. 970
HART MACHINERY SALES CO.—See LSB Industries, Inc.; *U.S. Public*, pg. 970
HART SCHAFFNER & MARX CLOTHES—See Hartmarx Corporation; *U.S. Public*, pg. 795
HARTA WANGSA SDN. BHD.—See Ssangyong Business Group; *Int'l*, pg. 1293
HARTCO FLOORING COMPANY—See Premark International, Inc.; *U.S. Public*, pg. 1322
HARTE-HANKS—See Harte-Hanks Communications, Inc.; *U.S. Public*, pg. 793
HARTE-HANKS COMMUNICATIONS, INC.; *U.S. Public*, pg. 793
HARTE-HANKS COMMUNITY NEWSPAPERS, INC.—See Harte-Hanks Communications, Inc.; *U.S. Public*, pg. 793
HARTE-HANKS DATA TECHNOLOGIES—See Harte-Hanks Communications, Inc.; *U.S. Public*, pg. 794
HARTE-HANKS DIRECT MAIL/CALIFORNIA—See Harte-Hanks Communications, Inc.; *U.S. Public*, pg. 794
HARTE-HANKS DIRECT MARKETING CINCINNATI—See Harte-Hanks Communications, Inc.; *U.S. Public*, pg. 794
HARTE-HANKS DIRECT MARKETING MARYLAND—See Harte-Hanks Communications, Inc.; *U.S. Public*, pg. 794
HARTE-HANKS MARKETING SERVICES—See Harte-Hanks Communications, Inc.; *U.S. Public*, pg. 794
HARTE HANKS SHOPPER DALLAS FORT WORTH—See Harte-Hanks Communications, Inc.; *U.S. Public*, pg. 794
HARTE-HANKS SHOPPER MIAMI—See Harte-Hanks Communications, Inc.; *U.S. Public*, pg. 794
HARTE-HANKS SHOPPERS—See Harte-Hanks Communications, Inc.; *U.S. Public*, pg. 794
HARTE HANKS SHOPPERS—See Harte-Hanks Communications, Inc.; *U.S. Public*, pg. 794
HARTE-HANKS TELEVISION, INC. (KENS-TV)—See Harte-Hanks Communications, Inc.; *U.S. Public*, pg. 794
HARTEK BEVERAGE HANDLING GMBH—See Scotsman Industries, Inc.; *U.S. Public*, pg. 1445
HARTELL DIV.—See Sundstrand Corporation; *U.S. Public*, pg. 1534
HARTER—See Jami, Inc.; *U.S. Private*, pg. 581
HARTEREI VTN WITTEN GMBH—See Ruhrgas Aktiengesellschaft; *Int'l*, pg. 1149
HARTFORD BAKERY, INC.—See Lewis Brothers Bakeries, Inc.; *U.S. Private*, pg. 665
HARTFORD CARE CENTER—See Horizon/CMS Healthcare Corporation; *U.S. Public*, pg. 840
THE HARTFORD COURANT COMPANY—See The Times Mirror Company; *U.S. Public*, pg. 1616
HARTFORD DISTRIBUTORS INC.; *U.S. Private*, pg. 507
HARTFORD DISTRICT OFFICE—See Micros Systems Inc.; *U.S. Public*, pg. 1106
HARTFORD EUROPE, INC.—See The Hartford Financial Services Group Inc.; *U.S. Public*, pg. 795
THE HARTFORD FINANCIAL SERVICES GROUP INC.; *U.S. Public*, pg. 794
HARTFORD FIRE INSURANCE CO.—See The Hartford Financial Services Group Inc.; *U.S. Public*, pg. 794
THE HARTFORD FIRE INSURANCE COMPANY—See The Hartford Financial Services Group Inc.; *U.S. Public*, pg. 794
HARTFORD INSURANCE GROUP OF CANADA—See The Hartford Financial Services Group Inc.; *U.S. Public*, pg. 794
HARTFORD INTERNATIONAL INSURANCE COMPANY—See The Hartford Financial Services Group Inc.; *U.S. Public*, pg. 795
HARTFORD LIFE & ACCIDENT INSURANCE COMPANY—See The Hartford Financial Services Group Inc.; *U.S. Public*, pg. 795
THE HARTFORD LIFE INSURANCE COMPANY—See The Hartford Financial Services Group Inc.; *U.S. Public*, pg. 794
THE HARTFORD STEAM BOILER INSPECTION & INSURANCE CO.; *U.S. Public*, pg. 795
HARTFORD STEAM CO.—See CTG Resources, Inc.; *U.S. Public*, pg. 285
HARTFORD-WOOD RIVER TERMINAL—See Piasa Motor Fuels Inc.; *U.S. Private*, pg. 864
HARTGER & WILLARD MORTGAGE ASSOCIATES, INC.—See Old Kent Financial Corporation; *U.S. Public*, pg. 1216
HARTLAND DIVISION—See Consumers Water Company; *U.S. Public*, pg. 438
HARTLAND & ST. ALBANS TELEPHONE CO.—See Telephone and Data Systems, Inc.; *U.S. Public*, pg. 1572
ALBERT HARTLEY LIMITED—See Coats Viyella plc; *Int'l*, pg. 299
HARTLEY COURSEWARE—See Jostens Learning Corporation; *U.S. Public*, pg. 601
HARTLEY PLATINUM MINE—See The Broken Hill Proprietary Company Limited; *Int'l*, pg. 224
HARTMANN & BRAUN AG—See Mannesmann A.G.; *Int'l*, pg. 835
HARTMANN & BRAUN AUSTRIA—See Mannesmann A.G.; *Int'l*, pg. 835
HARTMANN & BRAUN DO BRASIL CONTROLE E INSTRUMENTACAP LTDA.—See Mannesmann A.G.; *Int'l*, pg. 835
HARTMANN & BRAUN FRANCE SA—See Mannesmann A.G.; *Int'l*, pg. 835
HARTMANN & BRAUN ITALIA SPA—See Mannesmann A.G.; *Int'l*, pg. 835
HARTMANN & BRAUN LEIPZIG GMBH—See Mannesmann A.G.; *Int'l*, pg. 835
HARTMANN & BRAUN MONTAGE GMBH—See Mannesmann A.G.; *Int'l*, pg. 835

HARTMANN & BRAUN NEDERLAND BV—See Mannesmann A.G.; *Int'l*, pg. 835
HARTMANN & BRAUN (PTY.) LTD.—See Mannesmann A.G.; *Int'l*, pg. 835
HARTMANN & BRAUN SA—See Mannesmann A.G.; *Int'l*, pg. 835
HARTMANN & BRAUN (UK) LTD.—See Mannesmann A.G.; *Int'l*, pg. 835
HARTMANN & CIE GMBH & CO KG—See N.V. Koninklijke KNP BT; *Int'l*, pg. 757
HARTMANN & FLINSCH GMBH—See N.V. Koninklijke KNP BT; *Int'l*, pg. 757
HARTMANN & BRAUN AG—See Mannesmann A.G.; *Int'l*, pg. 835
HARTMANN D.O.O.—See Dainippon Ink & Chemicals, Inc.; *Int'l*, pg. 371
HARTMANN DRUCKFARBEN GMBH—See Dainippon Ink & Chemicals, Inc.; *Int'l*, pg. 371
HARTMANN LUGGAGE & LEATHER GOODS GROUP—See Brown-Forman Corporation; *U.S. Public*, pg. 261
HARTMANN-SUN CHEMICAL LTD.—See Dainippon Ink & Chemicals, Inc.; *Int'l*, pg. 371
HARTMANN TRYCKFARGER AB—See Dainippon Ink & Chemicals, Inc.; *Int'l*, pg. 371
HARTMARX CORPORATION; *U.S. Public*, pg. 795
S.A. HARTOG N.V.—See Unilever Plc; *Int'l*, pg. 1437
HARTOG RAHIL FOODS, INC.; *U.S. Private*, pg. 508
HARTONS GROUP PLC.—See Schuttersveld Holding N.V.; *Int'l*, pg. 1210
THE HARTSTONE GROUP PLC; *Int'l*, pg. 599
HARTTUNG FASTENERS A/S—See The Black & Decker Corporation; *U.S. Public*, pg. 233
HARTUNG, KUHN, & CO., MASCHINENFABRIK GMBH—See Fried. Krupp AG; *Int'l*, pg. 511
HARTWELL COMMERCIAL DIVISION—See Western Sky Industries, Inc.; *U.S. Private*, pg. 1168
HARTWELL CORPORATION—See Western Sky Industries, Inc.; *U.S. Private*, pg. 1168
HARTZ GROUP—See The Hartz Mountain Corp.; *U.S. Private*, pg. 508
JACOB HARTZ SEED COMPANY, INC.—See Monsanto Company; *U.S. Public*, pg. 1125
THE HARTZ MOUNTAIN CORP.; *U.S. Private*, pg. 508
HARTZ MOUNTAIN INDUSTRIES—See The Hartz Mountain Corp.; *U.S. Private*, pg. 508
HARUNDALE MALL—See The Rouse Company; *U.S. Public*, pg. 1407
HARVARD INDUSTRIES, INC.; *U.S. Public*, pg. 796
HARVARD INTERIORS MANUFACTURING CO.—See Harvard Industries, Inc.; *U.S. Public*, pg. 796
HARVARD SPORTS, INC.—See Escalade Sports; *U.S. Public*, pg. 591
HARVE BENARD LTD.; *U.S. Private*, pg. 508
HARVE BENARD LTD.—See Harve Benard Ltd.; *U.S. Private*, pg. 508
HARVEL PLASTICS, INC.—See Detrex Corporation; *U.S. Public*, pg. 502
HARVEST BRANDS, INC.—See Altair Corporation; *U.S. Private*, pg. 46
HARVEST INDUSTRIES, INC.—See Altair Corporation; *U.S. Private*, pg. 46
HARVEST PARTNERS, INC.; *U.S. Private*, pg. 508
HARVEST PRODUCTS PTY. LTD.—See Internatio-Muller N.V.; *Int'l*, pg. 682
HARVEST STATE FEED, INC.—See Harvest States Cooperatives; *U.S. Private*, pg. 508
HARVEST STATES COOPERATIVES; *U.S. Private*, pg. 508
HARVEY & THOMPSON LTD.—See Cash America International, Inc.; *U.S. Public*, pg. 312
HARVEY ELECTRONICS—See Harvey Electronics, Inc.; *U.S. Public*, pg. 796
HARVEY ELECTRONICS, INC.; *U.S. Public*, pg. 796
HARVEY INDUSTRIES, INC.; *U.S. Private*, pg. 508
J.H. HARVEY COMPANY; *U.S. Private*, pg. 508
LEX HARVEY LTD.; *Int'l*, pg. 599
HARVEY PLANT LIMITED—See National Westminster Bank PLC; *Int'l*, pg. 910
HARVEY TITANIUM LTD.—See Metals USA, Inc.; *U.S. Public*, pg. 1100
HARVEYS OF BRISTOL LIMITED—See Allied Domecq PLC; *Int'l*, pg. 63
HARWICK STANDARD DISTRIBUTION CORPORATION; *U.S. Private*, pg. 509
THE HARWOOD COMPANIES, INC.—See Sara Lee Corporation; *U.S. Public*, pg. 1433
HARZ-KALK GMBH—See Preussag AG; *Int'l*, pg. 1069
HARZA ENGINEERING CO.; *U.S. Private*, pg. 509
HARZA ENGINEERING COMPANY OF CALIFORNIA—See Harza Engineering Co.; *U.S. Private*, pg. 509
HARZA ENVIRONMENTAL SERVICES, INC.—See Harza Engineering Co.; *U.S. Private*, pg. 509
HARZA-HIDROBRASILEIRA ENGENHARIA E PROJETOS LTDA—See Harza Engineering Co.; *U.S. Private*, pg. 509
HARZA NORTHEAST, INC.—See Harza Engineering Co.; *U.S. Private*, pg. 509
HARZA NORTHWEST, INC.—See Harza Engineering Co.; *U.S. Private*, pg. 509
HASBRO—See Hasbro, Inc.; *U.S. Public*, pg. 797
HASBRO BRADLEY FAR EAST (1987) LTD.—See Hasbro, Inc.; *U.S. Public*, pg. 797
HASBRO BRADLEY UK LIMITED—See Hasbro, Inc.; *U.S. Public*, pg. 797
HASBRO CANADA INC.—See Hasbro, Inc.; *U.S. Public*, pg. 797
HASBRO EUROPE UK LIMITED—See Hasbro, Inc.; *U.S. Public*, pg. 797
HASBRO FOREIGN SALES CORP.—See Hasbro, Inc.; *U.S. Public*, pg. 797
HASBRO, INC.; *U.S. Public*, pg. 797
HASBRO INTERNATIONAL, INC.—See Hasbro, Inc.; *U.S. Public*, pg. 797
HASBRO-MB S.A.—See Hasbro, Inc.; *U.S. Public*, pg. 797

HASBRO DIRECTORY OF CORPORATE AFFILIATIONS

Company Index

HASBRO S.A.—See Hasbro, Inc.; *U.S. Public*, pg. 797
HASBRO TOY DIVISION—See Hasbro, Inc.; *U.S. Public*, pg. 797
HASEKO (CALIFORNIA) INC.—See Haseko Corporation; *Int'l*, pg. 600
HASEKO COMMUNITY INC.—See Haseko Corporation; *Int'l*, pg. 600
HASEKO CORP.-KANSAI OFFICE—See Haseko Corporation; *Int'l*, pg. 600
HASEKO CORPORATION; *Int'l*, pg. 599
HASEKO DEVELOPMENT INC.—See Haseko Corporation; *Int'l*, pg. 600
HASEKO (HAWAII) INC.—See Haseko Corporation; *Int'l*, pg. 600
HASEKO LIVENET INC.—See Haseko Corporation; *Int'l*, pg. 600
HASEKO (NEW YORK) INC.—See Haseko Corporation; *Int'l*, pg. 600
HASEKO REAL ESTATE INC.—See Haseko Corporation; *Int'l*, pg. 600
HASEKO REALTY (CALIFORNIA), INC.—See Haseko Corporation; *Int'l*, pg. 600
HASEKO REALTY INC.—See Haseko Corporation; *Int'l*, pg. 600
HASEKO URBAN CO., LTD.—See Haseko Corporation; *Int'l*, pg. 600
HASEKO URBEST INC.—See Haseko Corporation; *Int'l*, pg. 600
HASEKO (USA) CORPOFATION—See Haseko Corporation; *Int'l*, pg. 600
HASELDONCKX SA—See Groupe Saint Louis; *Int'l*, pg. 567
HASEN-BRAU AG—See Bayerische Vereinsbank Group; *Int'l*, pg. 179
HASK TOILETRIES; *U.S. Private*, pg. 509
HASKEL CONTROL—See Haskel International, Inc.; *U.S. Public*, pg. 798
HASKEL ENERGY SYSTEMS LTD.—See Haskel International, Inc.; *U.S. Public*, pg. 798
HASKEL INTERNATIONAL, INC.; *U.S. Public*, pg. 798
HASLIMANN TAYLOR—See Shandwick International Plc; *Int'l*, pg. 1226
HASPER EQUIPMENT CO.—See Cloverdale Equipment Co.; *U.S. Private*, pg. 247
JOHN HASSALL, INC.; *U.S. Private*, pg. 509
CARL HASSE & WREDE GMBH—See Knorr-Bremse AG; *Int'l*, pg. 738
HASSELBLAD BELGIUM S.A. NV—See Victor Hasselblad AB; *Int'l*, pg. 1468
HASSELBLAD BV—See Victor Hasselblad AB; *Int'l*, pg. 1468
HASSELBLAD FRANCE S.A.—See Victor Hasselblad AB; *Int'l*, pg. 1468
HASSELBLAD SVENSKA AB—See Victor Hasselblad AB; *Int'l*, pg. 1468
HASSELBLAD (UK) LTD.—See Victor Hasselblad AB; *Int'l*, pg. 1468
HASSELBLAD USA, INC.—See Victor Hasselblad AB; *Int'l*, pg. 1468
HASSELBLAD USA INC.—See Victor Hasselblad AB; *Int'l*, pg. 1468
HASSELBLAD VERTRIEBSGESELLSCHAFT M.B.H—See Victor Hasselblad AB; *Int'l*, pg. 1468
THE HASSINGER COMPANIES HOFFMAN HOMES; *U.S. Private*, pg. 510
HASSLE LAKEMEDEL AB—See Astra AB; *Int'l*, pg. 93
HASSLOCHER ENTERPRISES, INC.; *U.S. Private*, pg. 510
HASTINGS CO-OP CREAMERY COMPANY; *U.S. Private*, pg. 510
HASTINGS DEERING (AUSTRALIA) LIMITED—See Sime Darby Berhad; *Int'l*, pg. 1250
HASTINGS FILTERS—See CLARCOR, Inc.; *U.S. Public*, pg. 382
HASTINGS, INC.—See Hastings Manufacturing Company; *U.S. Public*, pg. 798
HASTINGS MANUFACTURING COMPANY; *U.S. Public*, pg. 798
HASTRA AKTIENGESELLACHAFT—See Veba AG; *Int'l*, pg. 1456
CHARLES HASWELL AND PARTNERS LIMITED—See Severn Trent Plc; *Int'l* pg. 1226
HAT DANCE—See Lettuce Entertain You Enterprises, Inc.; *U.S. Private*, pg. 661
HATBORO MANOR PROFESSIONAL CONDOMINIUMS—See Prime Bancorp, Inc.; *U.S. Public*, pg. 1326
HATCO, INC.; *U.S. Private*, pg. 510
HATEMA CONTRACT B.V.—See Gamma Holding N.V.; *Int'l*, pg. 540
HATEMA-DISTRIBUTIE B.V.—See Gamma Holding N.V.; *Int'l*, pg. 540
HATEMA LTD.—See Gamma Holding N.V.; *Int'l*, pg. 540
HATEMA RETAIL BEHEER B.V.—See Gamma Holding N.V.; *Int'l*, pg. 540
HATFIELD AUTO AUCTION—See Tyco International Ltd.; *U.S. Public*, pg. 1649
HATFIELD QUALITY MEATS; *U.S. Private*, pg. 510
HATHAWAY ADVANCED POWER LIMITED—See Hathaway Corporation; *U.S. Public*, pg. 799
C.F. HATHAWAY; *U.S. Private*, pg. 510
HATHAWAY CORPORATION; *U.S. Public*, pg. 798
HATHAWAY INDUSTRIAL AUTOMATION, INC.—See Hathaway Corporation; *U.S. Public*, pg. 799
HATHAWAY INSTRUMENTS LIMITED—See Hathaway Corporation; *U.S. Public*, pg. 799
HATHAWAY MOTION CONTROL DIVISION—See Hathaway Corporation; *U.S. Public*, pg. 799
HATHAWAY MOTORS & INSTRUMENTS DIVISION—See Hathaway Corporation; *U.S. Public*, pg. 799
HATHAWAY PROCESS INSTRUMENTATION—See Hathaway Corporation; *U.S. Public*, pg. 799
HATHAWAY SYSTEMS CORPORATION—See Hathaway Corporation; *U.S. Public*, pg. 799
HATHAWAY SYSTEMS NORTHWEST—See Hathaway Corporation; *U.S. Public*, pg. 799
A.C. HATRICK CHEMICALS PTY. LIMITED—See Hercules Incorporated; *U.S. Public*, pg. 811
A.C. HATRICK (N.Z.) LTD.—See Hercules Incorporated; *U.S. Public*, pg. 811
HATRIUM GRUNDSTUCKS BETEILIGUNGS GMBH—See Bayerische Vereinsbank Group; *Int'l*, pg. 180
HATRIUM GRUNDSTUCKS GMBH & CO. KG—See Bayerische Vereinsbank Group; *Int'l*, pg. 180
HATTERAS YACHTS—See Genmar Holdings, Inc.; *U.S. Private*, pg. 447
HATTIESBURG AMERICAN—See Gannett Company, Inc.; *U.S. Public*, pg. 701
HATTIESBURG GAS STORAGE, INC.—See Crystal Oil Company; *U.S. Public*, pg. 466
HATTON ET COOKSON S.A.—See Unilever Plc; *Int'l*, pg. 1437
HATTORI OVERSEAS HONG KONG LTD.—See Seiko Corporation; *Int'l*, pg. 1218
HATZEL & BUEHLER, INC.—See Construction Management Service; *U.S. Private*, pg. 266
HAUCK MFG. CO.; *U.S. Private*, pg. 510
HAUCK MANUFACTURING COMPANY INC.—See Ruhrgas Aktiengesellschaft; *Int'l*, pg. 1149
HAUENSTEIN & BURMEISTER, INC.; *U.S. Private*, pg. 510
WM. HAUGHTON & CO. LTD.—See Foster's Brewing Group Limited; *Int'l*, pg. 501
HAUMONT MESTSOFFEN N.V.—See Kemira Oy; *Int'l*, pg. 728
C.D. HAUPT PAPIER-UND PAPPENFABRIK GMBH & CO., K.G.—See Jefferson Smurfit Group p.l.c.; *Int'l*, pg. 1271
HAUPTNIEDERLASSUNG BADEN-WURTTEMBERG NIEDERLASSUNG STUTTGART—See Bilfinger + Berger Bauaktiengesellschaft; *Int'l*, pg. 194
HAUPTNIEDERLASSUNG BERLIN-BRANDENBURG NIEDERLASSUNG BERLIN—See Bilfinger + Berger Bauaktiengesellschaft; *Int'l*, pg. 194
HAUPTNIEDERLASSUNG ESSEN/NIEDERLASSUNG ESSEN/NIEDERLASSUNG WAREHAUSBAU ESSEN—See Bilfinger + Berger Bauaktiengesellschaft; *Int'l*, pg. 194
HAUPTNIEDERLASSUNG KOLN NIEDERLASSUNG KOLN—See Bilfinger + Berger Bauaktiengesellschaft; *Int'l*, pg. 194
HAUPTNIEDERLASSUNG MUNCHEN NIEDERLASSUNG MUNCHEN NEIDERLASSUNG TUNNELBAU MUNCHEN—See Bilfinger + Berger Bauaktiengesellschaft; *Int'l*, pg. 194
HAUPTNIEDERLASSUNG NORD NIEDERLASSUNG HAMBURG—See Bilfinger + Berger Bauaktiengesellschaft; *Int'l*, pg. 194
HAUPTNIEDERLASSUNG RHEIN-MAIN NIEDERLASSUNG FRANKFURT NIEDERLASSUNG TIED-UND INDUSTRIEBAU—See Bilfinger + Berger Bauaktiengesellschaft; *Int'l*, pg. 194
HAUPTNIEDERLASSUNG SACHSEN NEIDERLASSUNG DRESDEN GESCHAFTSSTELLE SPEZIALTIEFBAU—See Bilfinger + Berger Bauaktiengesellschaft; *Int'l*, pg. 194
HAUS CRAMER GASTSTATTEN MANAGEMENT GMBH & CO. KG—See Warsteiner Brauerei Haus Cramer GmbH & Co.; *Int'l*, pg. 1486
HAUS CRAMER GMBH & CO. IMMOBILIEN MANAGEMENT K.G.—See Warsteiner Brauerei Haus Cramer GmbH & Co.; *Int'l*, pg. 1486
HAUSBAU WUESTENROT GMBH—See Wuestenrot Holding GmbH; *Int'l*, pg. 1514
HAUSER LAKE LUMBER OPERATION, INC.—See Fleetwood Enterprises, Inc.; *U.S. Public*, pg. 652
HAUSMAN BUS SALES, INC.—See Consorcio G. Grupo Dina, S.A. de C.V.; *Int'l*, pg. 326
HAUSMANN TRANSPORT AG—See Panalpina Welttransport (Holding) AG; *Int'l*, pg. 1022
HAUTE-PROVENCE EXPRESS—See SNCF; *Int'l*, pg. 1164
HAVAS ADVERTISING; *Int'l*, pg. 600
HAVASU WATER COMPANY—See Citizens Utilities Company; *U.S. Public*, pg. 380
HAVATAMPA, INC.; *U.S. Private*, pg. 510
HAVELLANDISCHE MASCHINENBAU GMBH—See Hako-Werke GmbH & Co.; *Int'l*, pg. 587
HAVELOCK LIME DIV.—See CSA Management Inc.; *Int'l*, pg. 243
HAVEN COMMODITIES LLC—See Mid-Kansas Co-op Association; *U.S. Private*, pg. 743
HAVENS ERECTORS—See Havens Steel Co.; *U.S. Private*, pg. 511
HAVENS STEEL CO.; *U.S. Private*, pg. 510
THE HAVERHILL GAZETTE—See Pulitzer Publishing Company; *U.S. Public*, pg. 1343
HAVERTY FURNITURE COMPANIES, INC.; *U.S. Public*, pg. 799
HAVICO N.V.—See Plettac AG; *Int'l*, pg. 1061
HAVILAND CANDY INC.—See UIS, Inc.; *U.S. Private*, pg. 1113
HAVILAND CONSUMER PRODUCTS, INC.—See Haviland Enterprises; *U.S. Private*, pg. 511
HAVILAND ENTERPRISES; *U.S. Private*, pg. 511
HAVILAND PRODUCTS—See Haviland Enterprises; *U.S. Private*, pg. 511
HAVILAND TELEPHONE COMPANY, INC.—See Lynch Corporation; *U.S. Public*, pg. 1021
HAW PAR BROTHERS INTERNATIONAL LIMITED; *Int'l*, pg. 603
HAW PAR INTERNATIONAL LIMITED—See Haw Par Brothers International Limited; *Int'l*, pg. 604
HAW PAR LAND (MALAYSIA) SDN. BHD.—See Haw Par Brothers International Limited; *Int'l*, pg. 604
HAW PAR LEISURE INTERNATIONAL PTE. LTD.—See Haw Par Brothers International Limited; *Int'l*, pg. 604
HAW PAR PROPERTIES (SINGAPORE) PRIVATE LIMITED—See Haw Par Brothers International Limited; *Int'l*, pg. 604
HAW PAR SECURITIES (PRIVATE) LIMITED—See Haw Par Brothers International Limited; *Int'l*, pg. 604
HAWA MUNTERS CO. LTD.—See Incentive AB; *Int'l*, pg. 669
HAWAII ELECTRIC LIGHT CO., INC.—See Hawaiian Electric Industries, Inc.; *U.S. Public*, pg. 800
HAWAII INDEPENDENT REFINERY—See The Broken Hill Proprietary Company Limited; *Int'l*, pg. 225
HAWAII NEWSPAPER AGENCY, INC.—See Gannett Company, Inc.; *U.S. Public*, pg. 701
HAWAII PIZZA HUT INC.—See Jardine Matheson Holdings Limited; *Int'l*, pg. 704
HAWAII SERVICE CENTER—See Pace Analytical Services; *U.S. Private*, pg. 829
HAWAIIAN ADVERTISING & PUBLIC RELATIONS, INC.—See Servco Pacific Inc.; *U.S. Private*, pg. 986
HAWAIIAN AIRLINES, INC.; *U.S. Public*, pg. 799
HAWAIIAN AIRLINES, INC.—See Hawaiian Airlines, Inc.; *U.S. Public*, pg. 799
HAWAIIAN BITUMULS & PAVING COMPANY—See Dillingham Construction Corporation; *U.S. Private*, pg. 333
HAWAIIAN COMMERCIAL & SUGAR CO.—See Alexander & Baldwin, Inc.; *U.S. Public*, pg. 39
HAWAIIAN DREDGING & CONSTRUCTION COMPANY—See Dillingham Construction Corporation; *U.S. Private*, pg. 333
HAWAIIAN ELECTRIC COMPANY, INC.—See Hawaiian Electric Industries, Inc.; *U.S. Public*, pg. 800
HAWAIIAN ELECTRIC INDUSTRIES, INC.; *U.S. Public*, pg. 799
HAWAIIAN FRUIT SPECIALTIES CO., LTD.—See Buyco, Inc.; *U.S. Private*, pg. 190
HAWAIIAN INDEPENDENT REFINERY, INC.—See The Broken Hill Proprietary Company Limited; *Int'l*, pg. 225
HAWAIIAN PACIFIC ELEVATOR COMPANY—See Dover Corporation; *U.S. Public*, pg. 521
HAWAIIAN TUG & BARGE CORP.—See Hawaiian Electric Industries, Inc.; *U.S. Public*, pg. 800
GLENN O. HAWBAKER, INC.; *U.S. Private*, pg. 511
HAWE HOLDING B.V.—See Royal Begemann Group; *Int'l*, pg. 1133
HAWG HAULING & DISPOSAL, INC.—See Columbia Energy Group; *U.S. Public*, pg. 403
HAWK CORP.; *U.S. Private*, pg. 511
HAWK MANAGEMENT & FINANCIAL SERVICES INC.—See Hawk Management Corporation; *U.S. Private*, pg. 511
HAWK MANAGEMENT CORPORATION; *U.S. Private*, pg. 511
HAWKE CABLE GLANDS—See McKechnie PLC; *Int'l*, pg. 851
HAWKER DE HAVILLAND LTD.—See BTR plc; *Int'l*, pg. 128
HAWKER INSTRUMENTS LTD.—See BTR plc; *Int'l*, pg. 125
HAWKER PACIFIC PTY. LTD.—See BTR plc; *Int'l*, pg. 128
HAWKER SIDDELEY CANADA INC.; *Int'l*, pg. 604
HAWKEYE CONSTRUCTION, INC.—See MYR Group Inc.; *U.S. Public*, pg. 1029
HAWKEYE HOLDING, INC.—See AEGON N.V.; *Int'l*, pg. 27
HAWKEYE LEASING CORPORATION—See Mercantile Bancorporation Inc.; *U.S. Public*, pg. 1087
HAWKEYE QUALITY SERVICE CORPORATION—See Mercantile Bancorporation Inc.; *U.S. Public*, pg. 1087
HAWKEYE-SECURITY INSURANCE CO.—See General Accident Fire and Life Assurance Corporation p.l.c.; *Int'l*, pg. 543
HAWKEYE SECURITY INSURANCE COMPANY—See General Accident Fire and Life Assurance Corporation p.l.c.; *Int'l*, pg. 543
HAWKEYE STEEL PRODUCTS, INC.; *U.S. Private*, pg. 511
HAWKINS CHEMICAL, INC.; *U.S. Public*, pg. 800
HAWKINS MARKETS—See SuperValu, Inc.; *U.S. Public*, pg. 1540
HAWKINS STRUCTURES—See Canadian Erectors Ltd.; *Int'l*, pg. 256
HAWKINS TERMINAL I—See Hawkins Chemical, Inc.; *U.S. Public*, pg. 800
HAWKINS WATER TREATMENT GROUP, INC.—See Hawkins Chemical, Inc.; *U.S. Public*, pg. 800
HAWKS NEST MINE—See The Broken Hill Proprietary Company Limited; *Int'l*, pg. 224
HAWLEY & HAZEL CHEMICAL CO., (HONG KONG) LTD.—See Colgate-Palmolive Company; *U.S. Public*, pg. 399
HAWORTH GROUP INC.; *U.S. Private*, pg. 511
THE HAWORTH GROUP, INC.—See Haworth Group Inc.; *U.S. Private*, pg. 511
HAWORTH, INC.; *U.S. Private*, pg. 511
HAWORTH PORTUGAL-CORTAL—See Haworth, Inc.; *U.S. Private*, pg. 512
HAWORTH THAILAND COMPANY LTD.—See Haworth, Inc.; *U.S. Private*, pg. 512
HAWORTH U.K. LTD.—See Haworth, Inc.; *U.S. Private*, pg. 512
HAWS DRINKING FAUCET CO.; *U.S. Private*, pg. 512
HAWTHORNE ABE—See Hawthorne Corp.; *U.S. Private*, pg. 512
HAWTHORNE ADV., INC.; *U.S. Private*, pg. 512
HAWTHORNE AIRPORT SERVICES, INC.—See Hawthorne Corp.; *U.S. Private*, pg. 512
HAWTHORNE AVIATION—See Hawthorne Corp.; *U.S. Private*, pg. 512
HAWTHORNE COMMUNICATIONS, INC.; *U.S. Private*, pg. 512
HAWTHORNE COMMUNICATIONS, INC.-WESTERN REGIONAL OFFICE—See Hawthorne Communications, Inc.; *U.S. Private*, pg. 512
HAWTHORNE CORP.; *U.S. Private*, pg. 512
HAWTHORNE LAKELAND, INC.—See Hawthorne Corp.; *U.S. Private*, pg. 512
HAWTHORNE LIFT SYSTEMS—See Hawthorne Machinery Company; *U.S. Private*, pg. 513
HAWTHORNE MACHINERY COMPANY; *U.S. Private*, pg. 512

MASTER INDEX TO COMPANY NAMES HEATH

Company Index

HAWTHORNE OCALA—See Hawthorne Corp.; *U.S. Private, pg. 512*
HAWTHORNE POWER SYSTEMS—See Hawthorne Machinery Company; *U.S. Private*, pg. 513
HAWTHORNE PROPERTIES, INC.—See Hawthorne Corp.; *U.S. Private*, pg. 512
HAWTHORNE SERVICES, INC.—See Hawthorne Corp.; *U.S. Private*, pg. 512
HAY POINT EXPORT TERMINAL—See The Broken Hill Proprietary Company Limited; *Int'l*, pg. 223
HAYDEN—See Standard Motor Products Inc.; *U.S. Public*, pg. 1503
HAYDON SWITCH & INSTRUMENT, INC.; *U.S. Private*, pg. 513
HAYES-ALBION—See Harvard Industries, Inc.; *U.S. Public*, pg. 796
HAYES AXLE, INC.—See The Cypress Companies; *U.S. Private*, pg. 299
HAYES BRAKE—See The Cypress Companies; *U.S. Private*, pg. 299
C.I. HAYES, INC.; *U.S. Private*, pg. 513
HAYES CORPORATION; *U.S. Public*, pg. 800
HAYES CORPORATION, REGIONAL OFFICE—See Hayes Corporation; *U.S. Public*, pg. 801
HAYES-DANA FILTER, FITTING & GASKET DIV.—See Dana Corporation; *U.S. Public*, pg. 480
HAYES-DANA SERVICE PARTS DIV.—See Dana Corporation; *U.S. Public*, pg. 480
HAYES LAMINATE GLASS CO. LTD.—See Saint-Gobain; *Int'l*, pg. 1173
HAYES MICROCOMPUTER PRODUCTS (CANADA) LTD.—See Hayes Corporation; *U.S. Public*, pg. 801
HAYES MICROCOMPUTER PRODUCTS, INC.—See Hayes Corporation; *U.S. Public*, pg. 801
HAYES MICROCOMPUTER PRODUCTS LTD.—See Hayes Corporation; *U.S. Public*, pg. 801
HAYES, SEAY, MATTERN & MATTERN, INC.; *U.S. Private*, pg. 513
HAYES WHEELS INTERNATIONAL, INC.; *U.S. Private*, pg. 513
HAYHURST ELIAS DUDEK, INC.—See Hilb, Rogal and Hamilton Company; *U.S. Public*, pg. 827
HAYMARKET EXHIBITIONS LTD.—See BBC Magazines; *Int'l*, pg. 114
HAYNES INTERNATIONAL, INC.; *U.S. Public*, pg. 801
HAYS FLUID CONTROLS-DIVISION OF ROMAC INDUSTRIES—See Romac Industries, Inc.; *U.S. Private*, pg. 942
HAYSELTON ENTERPRISES LIMITED—See Jardine Matheson Holdings Limited; *Int'l*, pg. 703
HAYSSEN—See Barry-Wehmiller Company; *U.S. Private*, pg. 118
HAYSTACK SKI RESORT AT MOUNT SNOW—See American Skiing Company; *U.S. Private*, pg. 61
HAYWARD INDUSTRIAL PRODUCTS—See Hayward Industries, Inc.; *U.S. Private*, pg. 513
HAYWARD INDUSTRIAL PRODUCTS-PLASTICS DIV.—See Hayward Industries, Inc.; *U.S. Private*, pg. 513
HAYWARD INDUSTRIAL PRODUCTS-STRAINER DIV.—See Hayward Industries, Inc.; *U.S. Private*, pg. 513
HAYWARD INDUSTRIES, INC.; *U.S. Private*, pg. 513
HAYWARD LABORATORIES—See E.T. Browne Drug Co., Inc.; *U.S. Private*, pg. 175
HAYWARD POOL PRODUCTS, INC.—See Hayward Industries, Inc.; *U.S. Private*, pg. 513
HAYWARD S.A.—See Hayward Industries, Inc.; *U.S. Private*, pg. 514
HAYWIN TEXTILE PRODUCTS, INC.; *U.S. Private*, pg. 514
HAZARD CENTER ASSOCIATES—See Cigna Corp.; *U.S. Public*, pg. 361
HAZCO CANADA, INC.—See Mine Safety Appliances Co.; *U.S. Public*, pg. 1114
HAZEL BISHOP INTERNATIONAL; *U.S. Private*, pg. 514
HAZELNUT GROWERS OF OREGON—See Sun Diamond Growers of California; *U.S. Private*, pg. 1051
HAZELTINE OCEAN SYSTEMS—See The General Electric Company, p.l.c.; *Int'l*, pg. 544
HAZELWOOD FARMS BAKERIES, INC.—See SuperValu, Inc.; *U.S. Public*, pg. 1541
HAZEN & SAWYER; *U.S. Private*, pg. 514
HAZEN PAPER COMPANY; *U.S. Private*, pg. 514
HAZLETON PUMPS INC.—See North Limited; *Int'l*, pg. 967
THE HE-RO GROUP, LTD.; *U.S. Public*, pg. 801
HEAD DISTRIBUTING CO.; *U.S. Private*, pg. 514
HEAD OFFICE REFERENCE LABORATORY, LTD.—See Seafield Capital Corporation; *U.S. Public*, pg. 1449
HEAD USA, INC.; *U.S. Private*, pg. 514
HEADACHE AND PAIN MANAGEMENT CENTER, INC.—See Integrated Health Services, Inc.; *U.S. Public*, pg. 885
HEADACHE CENTER OF THE WEST COAST—See Integrated Health Services, Inc.; *U.S. Public*, pg. 885
HEADACHE MANAGEMENT OF AMERICA, INC.—See Integrated Health Services, Inc.; *U.S. Public*, pg. 885
HEADCO MACHINE WORKS, INC.—See Bearing Headquarters Co.; *U.S. Private*, pg. 127
HEADER PRODUCTS INC.; *U.S. Private*, pg. 514
HEADLAMP FACILITY—See Cooper Industries, Inc.; *U.S. Public*, pg. 442
HEADLEY READING LTD.—See Alusuisse-Lonza Holding Ltd.; *Int'l*, pg. 68
HEADS & THREADS—See Alleghany Corporation; *U.S. Public*, pg. 42
J.H. HEAFNER CO. INC.; *U.S. Private*, pg. 514
A HEALD LIMITED—See Avonmore Waterford Group plc; *Int'l*, pg. 102
HEALD COLLEGES; *U.S. Private*, pg. 514
HEALDS AG—See Avonmore Waterford Group plc; *Int'l*, pg. 102
HEALTH ACQUISITION CORP.—See National Home Health Care Corp.; *U.S. Public*, pg. 1157
HEALTH & LIFE INSURANCE CO. OF AMERICA—See Conseco Inc.; *U.S. Public*, pg. 434
HEALTH & MEDICATIONS AT HOME, INC.—See Integrated Health Services, Inc.; *U.S. Public*, pg. 885
HEALTH AND RETIREMENT PROPERTIES TRUST; *U.S. Public*, pg. 801
HEALTH & SCIENCES RESEARCH, INC.—See Genzyme Corporation; *U.S. Public*, pg. 733
HEALTH AT HOME—See Integrated Health Services, Inc.; *U.S. Public*, pg. 885
HEALTH CARE & RETIREMENT CORPORATION; *U.S. Public*, pg. 801
HEALTH CARE, INC.—See Accra Pac Group; *U.S. Private*, pg. 11
HEALTH CARE INSTITUTIONAL SERVICES—See National Data Corporation; *U.S. Public*, pg. 1156
HEALTH CARE MANAGEMENT CORP., INC.—See Columbia/HCA Healthcare Corporation; *U.S. Public*, pg. 405
HEALTH CARE MICROSYSTEMS, INC.—See Health Management Systems, Inc.; *U.S. Public*, pg. 802
HEALTH CARE PROPERTY INVESTORS, INC.; *U.S. Public*, pg. 801
HEALTH CARE SERVICES OF MISSISSIPPI, INC.—See Integrated Health Services, Inc.; *U.S. Public*, pg. 885
HEALTH CARE VENTURES INC.—See Pfizer Inc.; *U.S. Public*, pg. 1282
HEALTH-CHEM CORPORATION; *U.S. Public*, pg. 802
HEALTH ECONOMICS CORPORATION—See Equifax Inc.; *U.S. Public*, pg. 588
HEALTH EDUCATION CENTER INC.—See Highmark Inc.; *U.S. Private*, pg. 529
HEALTH EDUCATION TECHNOLOGIES (HET) DIV.—See Omnicom Group Inc.; *U.S. Public*, pg. 1224
HEALTH MAINTENANCE OREGON—See Regence BlueCross BlueShield of Oregon; *U.S. Private*, pg. 918
HEALTH MAINTENANCE ORGANIZATION OF NEW JERSEY, INC.—See Aetna Inc.; *U.S. Public*, pg. 26
HEALTH MANAGEMENT ASSOCIATES, INC.; *U.S. Public*, pg. 802
HEALTH MANAGEMENT, INC.—See Counsel Corporation; *Int'l*, pg. 338
HEALTH MANAGEMENT SYSTEMS, INC.; *U.S. Public*, pg. 802
HEALTH-MOR ACCEPTANCE CORP.—See HMI Industries; *U.S. Public*, pg. 771
HEALTH-MOR B.V.—See HMI Industries; *U.S. Public*, pg. 771
HEALTH-MOR MEXICANA S.A. DE C.V.—See HMI Industries; *U.S. Public*, pg. 771
HEALTH 'N' HOME CORPORATION—See American Stores Company; *U.S. Public*, pg. 93
HEALTH PLAN OF NEVADA, INC.—See Sierra Health Services, Inc.; *U.S. Public*, pg. 1469
HEALTH PRODUCTS CORPORATION; *U.S. Private*, pg. 514
HEALTH PROFESSIONALS, INC.; *U.S. Public*, pg. 802
HEALTH RESOURCES INTERNATIONAL; *U.S. Private*, pg. 514
HEALTH SCIENCE COMMUNICATIONS—See Harrison & Star, Inc.; *U.S. Private*, pg. 506
HEALTH VENTURES—See MeritCare Health System; *U.S. Private*, pg. 733
HEALTHAMERICA OF CENTRAL PENNSYLVANIA—See Coventry Corporation; *U.S. Public*, pg. 454
HEALTHAMERICA PENNSYLVANIA, INC.—See Coventry Corporation; *U.S. Public*, pg. 454
HEALTHCARE ACCESSORIES—See MeritCare Health System; *U.S. Private*, pg. 733
HEALTHCARE AMERICA, INC.; *U.S. Private*, pg. 515
HEALTHCARE BUSINESS SOLUTIONS, INC.—See Integrated Health Services, Inc.; *U.S. Public*, pg. 885
HEALTHCARE CLAIMS RECOVERY, INC.—See Integrated Health Services, Inc.; *U.S. Public*, pg. 885
THE HEALTHCARE CONNECTION—See Saatchi & Saatchi Advertising Worldwide; *U.S. Public*, pg. 1422
HEALTHCARE DIAGNOSTICS CENTERS—See Columbia/HCA Healthcare Corporation; *U.S. Public*, pg. 405
HEALTHCARE GROUP—See The Hearst Corporation; *U.S. Private*, pg. 515
HEALTHCARE MANAGEMENT GROUP—See The McGraw-Hill Companies; *U.S. Public*, pg. 1071
HEALTHCARE PRESCRIPTION SERVICES, INC.—See Columbia/HCA Healthcare Corporation; *U.S. Public*, pg. 405
HEALTHCARE SERVICES DIVISION—See Keane, Inc.; *U.S. Public*, pg. 946
HEALTHCARE SERVICES GROUP, INC.; *U.S. Public*, pg. 803
HEALTHCARE STAFFING SOLUTIONS, INC.—See RehabCare Group, Inc.; *U.S. Public*, pg. 1373
HEALTHCARE USA—See Coventry Corporation; *U.S. Public*, pg. 454
HEALTHGATE DATA CORP.—See Nichols Research Corporation; *U.S. Public*, pg. 1182
HEALTHGUARD OF LANCASTER—See Highmark Inc.; *U.S. Private*, pg. 529
HEALTH-MOR ACCEPTANCE PTY LTD.—See HMI Industries; *U.S. Public*, pg. 771
HEALTHSOURCE ARKANSAS, INC.—See Cigna Corp.; *U.S. Public*, pg. 360
HEALTHSOURCE CONNECTICUT—See Cigna Corp.; *U.S. Public*, pg. 360
HEALTHSOURCE GEORGIA—See Cigna Corp.; *U.S. Public*, pg. 360
HEALTHSOURCE, INC.—See Cigna Corp.; *U.S. Public*, pg. 360
HEALTHSOURCE INDIANA—See Cigna Corp.; *U.S. Public*, pg. 360
HEALTHSOURCE INDIANA MANAGED CARE PLAN, INC.—See Cigna Corp.; *U.S. Public*, pg. 360
HEALTHSOURCE KENTUCKY—See Cigna Corp.; *U.S. Public*, pg. 360
HEALTHSOURCE MAINE, INC.—See Cigna Corp.; *U.S. Public*, pg. 360
HEALTHSOURCE NEW HAMPSHIRE, INC.—See Cigna Corp.; *U.S. Public*, pg. 360
HEALTHSOURCE NEW YORK—See Cigna Corp.; *U.S. Public*, pg. 360
HEALTHSOURCE NORTH CAROLINA, INC.—See Cigna Corp.; *U.S. Public*, pg. 360
HEALTHSOURCE NORTH TEXAS, INC.—See Cigna Corp.; *U.S. Public*, pg. 360
HEALTHSOURCE SAVANNAH, INC.—See Cigna Corp.; *U.S. Public*, pg. 360
HEALTHSOURCE SOUTH CAROLINA, INC.—See Cigna Corp.; *U.S. Public*, pg. 360
HEALTHSOURCE TENNESSEE, INC.—See Cigna Corp.; *U.S. Public*, pg. 360
HEALTHSOUTH CORPORATION; *U.S. Public*, pg. 803
HEALTHSOUTH CORPORATION—See Healthsouth Corporation; *U.S. Public*, pg. 803
HEALTHTEX—See VF Corporation; *U.S. Public*, pg. 1702
HEALTHWISE OF AMERICA—See United HealthCare Corporation; *U.S. Public*, pg. 1678
S.A. HEALY COMPANY—See Fiat Auto SpA; *Int'l*, pg. 483
BILL HEARD ENTERPRISES, INC.; *U.S. Private*, pg. 515
HEARST-ARGYLE TELEVISION INCORPORATED—See The Hearst Corporation; *U.S. Private*, pg. 516
HEARST BOOK GROUP—See The Hearst Corporation; *U.S. Private*, pg. 515
HEARST BOOKS/BUSINESS PUBLISHING GROUP—See The Hearst Corporation; *U.S. Private*, pg. 515
HEARST BUSINESS PUBLISHING, INC./UTP DIVISION—See The Hearst Corporation; *U.S. Private*, pg. 515
THE HEARST CORPORATION; *U.S. Private*, pg. 515
HEARST ENTERPRISES DIVISION—See The Hearst Corporation; *U.S. Private*, pg. 516
HEARST ENTERTAINMENT—See The Hearst Corporation; *U.S. Private*, pg. 516
HEARST ENTERTAINMENT & SYNDICATION—See The Hearst Corporation; *U.S. Private*, pg. 516
HEARST ENTERTAINMENT PRODUCTIONS, INC.—See The Hearst Corporation; *U.S. Private*, pg. 516
HEARST MAGAZINES DIVISION—See The Hearst Corporation; *U.S. Private*, pg. 516
HEARST MAGAZINES INTERNATIONAL—See The Hearst Corporation; *U.S. Private*, pg. 517
HEARST MARINE BOOKS—See The Hearst Corporation; *U.S. Private*, pg. 515
HEARST NEW MEDIA & TECHNOLOGY—See The Hearst Corporation; *U.S. Private*, pg. 517
HEARST NEWSPAPERS—See The Hearst Corporation; *U.S. Private*, pg. 517
HEARST REAL ESTATE DIVISION—See The Hearst Corporation; *U.S. Private*, pg. 518
HEARST REALTY DEVELOPMENT CO., INC.—See The Hearst Corporation; *U.S. Private*, pg. 515
HEART INTERFACE CORPORATION—See Valley Forge Corporation; *U.S. Public*, pg. 1705
HEARTHSONG, INC.—See Foster & Gallagher, Inc.; *U.S. Private*, pg. 421
HEARTHSTONE OF NORTHERN NEVADA—See Horizon/CMS Healthcare Corporation; *U.S. Public*, pg. 837
HEARTLAND BUILDING PRODUCTS, INC.—See Jannock Limited; *Int'l*, pg. 699
HEARTLAND DEVELOPMENT CORPORATION—See WPL Holdings, Inc.; *U.S. Public*, pg. 1728
HEARTLAND ENERGY GROUP, INC.—See WPL Holdings, Inc.; *U.S. Public*, pg. 1728
HEARTLAND ENERGY SERVICES, INC.—See WPL Holdings, Inc.; *U.S. Public*, pg. 1728
HEARTLAND EQUIPMENT, INC.—See Heartland Express, Inc.; *U.S. Public*, pg. 803
HEARTLAND EXPRESS, INC.; *U.S. Public*, pg. 803
HEARTLAND EXPRESS, INC., OF IOWA—See Heartland Express, Inc.; *U.S. Public*, pg. 803
HEARTLAND HOME CARE, INC.—See Integrated Health Services, Inc.; *U.S. Public*, pg. 885
HEARTLAND LIVESTOCK SERVICES—See Saskatchewan Wheat Pool; *Int'l*, pg. 1195
HEARTLAND LYSINE INC.—See Ajinomoto Company Inc.; *Int'l*, pg. 40
HEARTLAND LYSINE, INC.—See Ajinomoto Company Inc.; *Int'l*, pg. 40
HEARTLAND LYSINE INC.—See Lafarge S.A.; *Int'l*, pg. 790
HEARTLAND PANTRY—See Hy-Vee Food Stores Incorporated; *U.S. Private*, pg. 551
HEARTLAND PROPERTIES, INC.—See WPL Holdings, Inc.; *U.S. Public*, pg. 1728
HEAT & CONTROL, INC.; *U.S. Private*, pg. 518
HEAT BATH PARK METALLURGICAL CORP.; *U.S. Private*, pg. 518
HEAT BATH PARK METALLURGICAL PRODUCTS—See Heat Bath Park Metallurgical Corp.; *U.S. Private*, pg. 518
HEAT CONTAINMENT INDUSTRIES LIMITED—See Morgan Crucible Co. Plc; *Int'l*, pg. 894
HEAT CONTAINMENT INDUSTRIES PTY. LIMITED—See Morgan Crucible Co. Plc; *Int'l*, pg. 894
HEAT CONTROLLER, INC.; *U.S. Private*, pg. 518
HEAT PROCESS & CONTROL—See Eclipse Inc.; *U.S. Private*, pg. 360
HEAT TRANSFER SYSTEMS—See Eclipse Inc.; *U.S. Private*, pg. 360
HEAT TRANSFER TONDER—See Norsk Hydro a.s; *Int'l*, pg. 962
HEATEC, INC.—See Astec Industries, Inc.; *U.S. Public*, pg. 141
HEATER UTILITIES, INCORPORATED—See Minnesota Power; *U.S. Public*, pg. 1116
HEATH COMPANY—See Compagnie des Machines Bull; *Int'l*, pg. 317
HEATH CONSULTANTS INCORPORATED; *U.S. Private*, pg. 518
JOHN HEATH & CO. LIMITED—See American Trading and Production Corporation; *U.S. Private*, pg. 64

Company Index

HEATH SPRING COMPANY LTD—See Peterson American Corp.; *U.S. Private*, pg. 857
W. HEATH & CO.—See American International Group, Inc.; *U.S. Public*, pg. 84
HEATILATOR INC.—See HON Industries Inc.; *U.S. Public*, pg. 772
HEATING AND COOLING SUPPLY INC.—See Watsco, Inc.; *U.S. Public*, pg. 1746
HEATING OIL PARTNERS L.P.; *U.S. Private*, pg. 518
HEATING REPLACEMENT PARTS AND CONTROLS LTD.—See Wolseley Plc; *Int'l*, pg. 1511
HEATRIC LTD.—See Meggitt plc; *Int'l*, pg. 853
HEAVY CIVIL CONSTRUCTION—See Morrison Knudsen Corporation; *U.S. Public*, pg. 1134
HEAVY MACHINES, INC.; *U.S. Private*, pg. 518
HEAVYLIFT CARGO AIRLINES LIMITED—See Kvaerner a.s.a.; *Int'l*, pg. 773
HEBCO PRODUCTS—See MascoTech, Inc.; *U.S. Public*, pg. 1055
HEBDO MAG. INC.—See Cendant Corporation; *U.S. Public*, pg. 321
HEBRA PROMOCION E INVERSIONES, S.A.—See Tabacalera, S.A.; *Int'l*, pg. 1345
HEBREW NATIONAL KOSHER FOODS DIV.—See ConAgra, Inc.; *U.S. Public*, pg. 429
HEBRON S.A.—See Otsuka Pharmaceutical Co., Ltd.; *Int'l*, pg. 1014
HECHINGER COMPANY INVESTORS II, L.P.—See Leonard Green & Partners; *U.S. Private*, pg. 477
HECHT'S—See The May Department Stores Company; *U.S. Public*, pg. 1063
HECK CELLARS WINERY—See F. Korbel Bros. Inc.; *U.S. Private*, pg. 632
HECK INDUSTRIES; *U.S. Private*, pg. 519
HECKERT CHEMNITZER WERZEUGMASCHINEN GMBH—See Traub AG; *Int'l*, pg. 1419
HECKETHORN MFG. COMPANY, INC.; *U.S. Private*, pg. 519
HECKETT MULTISERV—See Harsco Corporation; *U.S. Public*, pg. 793
HECKETT MULTISERV-EASTERN REGION—See Harsco Corporation; *U.S. Public*, pg. 793
HECKLER & KOCH GMBH—See British Aerospace p.l.c.; *Int'l*, pg. 217
HECLA MINING COMPANY; *U.S. Public*, pg. 803
HECTOR & CO. A.B.—See RGP Holding, Inc.; *U.S. Private*, pg. 904
HEDEMORA AB—See NCC AB; *Int'l*, pg. 898
HEDINN SCHINDLER LYFTUR HF.—See Schindler Holding AG; *Int'l*, pg. 1205
HEDLAND—See Racine Federated, Inc.; *U.S. Private*, pg. 906
HEDLUND-MARTIN INC.—See Gehl Company; *U.S. Public*, pg. 704
HEDSORBOARD LTD.—See Metsa-Serla Corporation; *Int'l*, pg. 864
HEDSTROM CANADA—See Hicks, Muse, Tate & Furst Inc.; *U.S. Private*, pg. 526
HEDSTROM CORP.—See Hicks, Muse, Tate & Furst Inc.; *U.S. Private*, pg. 526
HEDSTROM CORPORATION—See Hicks, Muse, Tate & Furst Inc.; *U.S. Private*, pg. 526
HEDSTROM HOLDING CO.—See Hicks, Muse, Tate & Furst Inc.; *U.S. Private*, pg. 526
HEDWIN CORPORATION—See Solvay S.A.; *Int'l*, pg. 1278
HEE SUNG CO. LTD.—See LG Group; *Int'l*, pg. 779
HEERY INTERNATIONAL INC.; *U.S. Private*, pg. 519
HEFELE GMBH—See Fried. Krupp AG; *Int'l*, pg. 511
HARRY O. HEFTER-ASSOCIATES, INC.—See The HOH Organizations; *U.S. Private*, pg. 492
HEHR GLASS COMPANY INC.—See Hehr International Inc.; *U.S. Private*, pg. 519
HEHR INTERNATIONAL INC.; *U.S. Private*, pg. 519
HEHR POWER SYSTEMS—See Hehr International Inc.; *U.S. Private*, pg. 519
HEICO AEROSPACE CORPORATION—See HEICO Corporation; *U.S. Public*, pg. 804
HEICO CHEMICALS, INC.—See Cambrex Corporation; *U.S. Public*, pg. 297
HEICO CORPORATION; *U.S. Public*, pg. 804
HEIDELBERG CANADA GRAPHIC EQUIPMENT LTD.—See Heidelberger Druckmaschinen A.G.; *Int'l*, pg. 605
HEIDELBERG CEMENT INC.—See Heidelberger Zement A.G.; *Int'l*, pg. 605
HEIDELBERG FINISHING SYSTEMS—See Heidelberger Druckmaschinen A.G.; *Int'l*, pg. 604
HEIDELBERG GRAPHIC EQUIPMENT LTD.-HEIDELBERG AUSTRALIA—See Heidelberger Druckmaschinen A.G.; *Int'l*, pg. 605
HEIDELBERG GRAPHIC EQUIPMENT LTD.-HEIDELBERG NEW ZEALAND—See Heidelberger Druckmaschinen A.G.; *Int'l*, pg. 605
HEIDELBERG GRAPHIC EQUIPMENT LTD.-HEIDELBERG UK—See Heidelberger Druckmaschinen A.G.; *Int'l*, pg. 605
HEIDELBERG HARRIS S.A.—See Heidelberger Druckmaschinen A.G.; *Int'l*, pg. 605
HEIDELBERG USA, INC.—See Heidelberger Druckmaschinen A.G.; *Int'l*, pg. 604
HEIDELBERG WEB PRESS, INC.—See Heidelberger Druckmaschinen A.G.; *Int'l*, pg. 604
HEIDELBERGER BAUSTOFFTECHNIK GMBH—See Heidelberger Zement A.G.; *Int'l*, pg. 605
HEIDELBERGER DAEMMSYSTEME GMBH—See Heidelberger Zement A.G.; *Int'l*, pg. 606
HEIDELBERGER DRUCKMASCHINEN A.G.; *Int'l*, pg. 604
HEIDELBERGER ZEMENT A.G.; *Int'l*, pg. 605
HEIDELBERGER ZEMENT - CEMENT EUROPE EAST—See Heidelberger Zement A.G.; *Int'l*, pg. 606
HEIDELBERGER ZEMENT INTERNATIONAL HOLDING GMBH—See Heidelberger Zement A.G.; *Int'l*, pg. 605
HEIDEMIJ ADVIES BV—See Heidemij N.V.; *Int'l*, pg. 607
HEIDEMIJ COMPUTER SERVICES—See Heidemij N.V.; *Int'l*, pg. 607

HEIDEMIJ DEUTSCHLAND GMBH—See Heidemij N.V.; *Int'l*, pg. 607
HEIDEMIJ EUROPE BV—See Heidemij N.V.; *Int'l*, pg. 607
HEIDEMIJ NEDERLAND BV—See Heidemij N.V.; *Int'l*, pg. 607
HEIDEMIJ N.V.; *Int'l*, pg. 606
HEIDEMIJ REALISATIE BV—See Heidemij N.V.; *Int'l*, pg. 607
HEIDEMIJ REALISATIE LELYSTAD BV—See Heidemij N.V.; *Int'l*, pg. 607
HEIDEMIJ REALISIERUNG GMBH—See Heidemij N.V.; *Int'l*, pg. 608
HEIDTMAN STEEL PRODUCTS, INC.; *U.S. Private*, pg. 519
HEIGHTS HEATING & COOLING; *U.S. Private*, pg. 519
ALBERT HEIJN B.V.—See Koninklijke Ahold NV; *Int'l*, pg. 749
H.E.I.L.—See Dover Corporation; *U.S. Public*, pg. 521
HEIL-BRICE RETAIL ADVERTISING; *U.S. Private*, pg. 519
HEIL ENVIRONMENTAL INDUSTRIES—See Dover Corporation; *U.S. Public*, pg. 520
HEIL ENVIRONMENTAL INDUSTRIES (H.E.I.L.)—See Dover Corporation; *U.S. Public*, pg. 520
HEIL EUROPE—See Dover Corporation; *U.S. Public*, pg. 521
HEIL STEEL FABRICATING, INC.—See Dover Corporation; *U.S. Public*, pg. 521
HEIL TRAILER INTERNATIONAL—See Dover Corporation; *U.S. Public*, pg. 520
HEIL-UND MINERALQUELLEN GMBH—See Nestle S.A.; *Int'l*, pg. 920
HEIL WEST, INC.—See Dover Corporation; *U.S. Public*, pg. 521
HEIL-BRICE RETAIL ADVERTISING, INC.—See Heil-Brice Retail Advertising; *U.S. Private*, pg. 519
HEILIG-MEYERS COMPANY; *U.S. Public*, pg. 804
HEILIG MEYERS FURNITURE CO.—See Heilig-Meyers Company; *U.S. Public*, pg. 804
HEIMBS & SOHN GMBH & CO KG—See Nestle S.A.; *Int'l*, pg. 920
HEIMSOETH—See Borland International, Inc.; *U.S. Public*, pg. 246
HEIN DE WINDT B.V.—See Fuchs Petrolub AG Oel + Chemie; *Int'l*, pg. 517
HEIN, LEHMANN AG—See Arbed S.A.; *Int'l*, pg. 80
HEIN-WERNER CORPORATION; *U.S. Public*, pg. 805
HEINEKEN ITALIA S.P.A.—See Heineken N.V.; *Int'l*, pg. 608
HEINEKEN NEDERLAND BV—See Heineken N.V.; *Int'l*, pg. 608
HEINEKEN N.V.; *Int'l*, pg. 608
HEINEKEN USA INC.—See Heineken N.V.; *Int'l*, pg. 608
HEINEMANN EDUCATIONAL PUBLISHING—See Reed Elsevier plc; *Int'l*, pg. 1094
HEINEMANN ELECTRIC CANADA LTD.—See Eaton Corporation; *U.S. Public*, pg. 557
HEINEMANN ELECTRIC PTY. LTD.—See Eaton Corporation; *U.S. Public*, pg. 557
HEINEMANN ELT-BRAZIL—See Georg von Holtzbrinck GmbH; *Int'l*, pg. 1479
HEINEMANN ELT-TURKEY—See Georg von Holtzbrinck GmbH; *Int'l*, pg. 1479
HEINEMANN ENGLISH LANGUAGE TEACHING—See Georg von Holtzbrinck GmbH; *Int'l*, pg. 1479
HEINEMANN HELLAS—See Reed Elsevier plc; *Int'l*, pg. 1094
HEINEMANN IBERIA SA—See Reed Elsevier plc; *Int'l*, pg. 1094
HEINEMANN JAPAN—See Reed Elsevier plc; *Int'l*, pg. 1094
HEINEMANN LE MONNIER—See Reed Elsevier plc; *Int'l*, pg. 1095
HEINEMANN PUBLISHERS (PTY) LTD.—See Reed Elsevier plc; *Int'l*, pg. 1094
HEINEMANN USA—See Reed Elsevier plc; *Int'l*, pg. 1094
HEINEN'S INC.; *U.S. Private*, pg. 519
HEINKEL FILTERING SYSTEMS INC.—See Heinkel Industriezentrifugen GmbH & Co.; *Int'l*, pg. 609
HEINKEL INDUSTRIEZENTRIFUGEN GMBH & CO.; *Int'l*, pg. 608
HEINOLA MILL—See UPM-Kymmene Corporation; *Int'l*, pg. 1428
HEINRICH HEINE HANDELSGESELLSCHAFT AG—See Otto Versand (GmbH & Co.); *Int'l*, pg. 1014
HEINRICH INDUSTRIE-UND HANDELS-AKTIENGESELLSCHAFT—See Harpen AG; *Int'l*, pg. 597
HEINRICH MACK NACHF.—See Pfizer Inc.; *U.S. Public*, pg. 1283
HEINS TELEPHONE COMPANY—See ALLTEL Corporation; *U.S. Public*, pg. 56
HEINTZELMAN'S TRUCK CENTER INC.; *U.S. Private*, pg. 519
HEIN-WERNER OF CANADA, LTD.—See Hein-Werner Corporation; *U.S. Public*, pg. 805
HEINZ BAKERY PRODUCTS—See H.J. Heinz Company; *U.S. Public*, pg. 806
HEINZ ESSMAN GMBH—See Skanska AB; *Int'l*, pg. 1261
HEINZ FOOD SERVICE S.R.L.—See H.J. Heinz Company; *U.S. Public*, pg. 806
H.J. HEINZ (BOTSWANA) (PROPRIETARY) LTD.—See H.J. Heinz Company; *U.S. Public*, pg. 806
H.J. HEINZ BRANCH BELGIUM—See H.J. Heinz Company; *U.S. Public*, pg. 806
H.J. HEINZ B.V.—See H.J. Heinz Company; *U.S. Public*, pg. 806
H.J. HEINZ CENTRAL EUROPE S.A.—See H.J. Heinz Company; *U.S. Public*, pg. 806
H.J. HEINZ COMPANY; *U.S. Public*, pg. 805
H.J. HEINZ COMPANY AUSTRALIA LTD.—See H.J. Heinz Company; *U.S. Public*, pg. 807
H.J. HEINZ COMPANY (IRELAND) LIMITED—See H.J. Heinz Company; *U.S. Public*, pg. 806

H.J. HEINZ COMPANY, LIMITED—See H.J. Heinz Company; *U.S. Public*, pg. 806
H.J. HEINZ CO. OF CANADA LTD.—See H.J. Heinz Company; *U.S. Public*, pg. 806
H.J. HEINZ GMBH—See H.J. Heinz Company; *U.S. Public*, pg. 806
H.J. HEINZ SARL—See H.J. Heinz Company; *U.S. Public*, pg. 806
HEINZ IBERICA, S.A.—See H.J. Heinz Company; *U.S. Public*, pg. 806
HEINZ JAPAN LTD.—See H.J. Heinz Company; *U.S. Public*, pg. 806
HEINZ PET PRODUCTS COMPANY—See H.J. Heinz Company; *U.S. Public*, pg. 806
HEINZ PLASMON DIETETCI ALIMENTARI S.P.A.—See H.J. Heinz Company; *U.S. Public*, pg. 806
HEINZ POLSKA SP.—See H.J. Heinz Company; *U.S. Public*, pg. 806
HEINZ-UFE LTD.—See H.J. Heinz Company; *U.S. Public*, pg. 807
HEINZ U.S.A. DIV.—See H.J. Heinz Company; *U.S. Public*, pg. 805
HEINZ WIN CHANCE LTD.—See H.J. Heinz Company; *U.S. Public*, pg. 807
RICHARD HEINZE KUNSTSTOFF SPRITZGIESSWERKE GMBH & CO.—See Schuttersveld Holding N.V.; *Int'l*, pg. 1210
HEINZ-WATTIE'S AUSTRALASIA—See H.J. Heinz Company; *U.S. Public*, pg. 807
C.H. HEIST CORP.; *U.S. Public*, pg. 807
HEITA BELGIQUE S.A.—See Nestle S.A.; *Int'l*, pg. 920
HEITMAN FINANCIAL LTD.—See United Asset Management Corporation; *U.S. Public*, pg. 1673
HEIWA TOKEI MANUFACTURING CO., LTD.—See Citizen Watch Company, Ltd.; *Int'l*, pg. 294
HEIZKRAFTWERK GLUCKSTADT GMBH—See Veba AG; *Int'l*, pg. 1456
HEIZOL-HANDELSGESELLSCHAFT MBH—See Veba AG; *Int'l*, pg. 1461
HEKIMIAN LABORATORIES, INC.—See Axel Johnson AB; *Int'l*, pg. 146
HELABA DUBLIN-LANDESBANK INTERNATIONAL—See Landesbank Hessen-Thuringen Girozentrale; *Int'l*, pg. 799
HELABA INTERNATIONAL FINANCE PLC—See Landesbank Hessen-Thuringen Girozentrale; *Int'l*, pg. 799
HELABA INVEST KAPITALANLAGEGESELLSCHAFT MBH—See Landesbank Hessen-Thuringen Girozentrale; *Int'l*, pg. 799
HELABA LUXEMBOURG LANDESBANK HESSEN-THURINGEN INTERNATIONAL S.A.—See Landesbank Hessen-Thuringen Girozentrale; *Int'l*, pg. 799
HELABA SWITZERLAND LTD.—See Landesbank Hessen-Thuringen Girozentrale; *Int'l*, pg. 799
HELABA TRUST BERATUNGS-UND MANAGEMENT GESELLSCHAFT MBH—See Landesbank Hessen-Thuringen Girozentrale; *Int'l*, pg. 799
HELADOS BORDEN, S.A.—See Borden, Inc.; *U.S. Private*, pg. 159
HELEN OF TROY (CAYMAN) LTD.—See Helen of Troy Corporation; *U.S. Public*, pg. 807
HELEN OF TROY, CONSUMER PRODUCTS DIV.—See Helen of Troy Corporation; *U.S. Public*, pg. 807
HELEN OF TROY CORPORATION; *U.S. Public*, pg. 807
HELEN OF TROY (FAR EAST) LTD.—See Helen of Troy Corporation; *U.S. Public*, pg. 807
HELEN OF TROY, PROFESSIONAL SALON DIV.—See Helen of Troy Corporation; *U.S. Public*, pg. 807
HELENA CHEMICAL COMPANY—See Marubeni Corporation; *U.S. Public*, pg. 845
HELENA LABORATORIES CORPORATION; *U.S. Private*, pg. 519
HELENA SPORTSWEAR CO.—See Hartmarx Corporation; *U.S. Public*, pg. 795
HELENE CURTIS AUSTRALIA PTY. LTD.—See Unilever Plc; *Int'l*, pg. 1434
HELENE CURTIS EUROPA B.V.—See Unilever Plc; *Int'l*, pg. 1434
HELENE CURTIS INDUSTRIES, INC.—See Unilever Plc; *Int'l*, pg. 1434
HELENE CURTIS INTERNATIONAL ITALIA S.P.A.—See Unilever Plc; *Int'l*, pg. 1434
HELENE CURTIS JAPAN INC.—See Unilever Plc; *Int'l*, pg. 1434
HELENE CURTIS LTD./LTEE.—See Unilever Plc; *Int'l*, pg. 1434
HELENE CURTIS MEXICO—See Unilever Plc; *Int'l*, pg. 1434
HELENE CURTIS NEW ZEALAND LTD.—See Unilever Plc; *Int'l*, pg. 1434
HELENE CURTIS NORTH AMERICA—See Unilever Plc; *Int'l*, pg. 1434
HELENE CURTIS SCANDINAVIA AB—See Unilever Plc; *Int'l*, pg. 1434
HELENE CURTIS UK, INC.—See Unilever Plc; *Int'l*, pg. 1434
HELIAN ASC OF NORTHRIDGE, INC.—See Vencor, Inc.; *U.S. Public*, pg. 1715
HELIAN HEALTH GROUP, INC.—See Vencor, Inc.; *U.S. Public*, pg. 1715
HELIAN HEALTH GROUP OF FRESNO, INC.—See Vencor, Inc.; *U.S. Public*, pg. 1715
HELIAN OCCUPATIONAL-CENTRAL—See Vencor, Inc.; *U.S. Public*, pg. 1715
HELIAN OCCUPATIONAL-NORTH—See Vencor, Inc.; *U.S. Public*, pg. 1715
HELIAN OCCUPATIONAL-SOUTH—See Vencor, Inc.; *U.S. Public*, pg. 1715
HELIAN RECOVERY CORP.—See Vencor, Inc.; *U.S. Public*, pg. 1715
HELICEUTA, S.A.—See Caja de Madrid Group; *Int'l*, pg. 252
HELICOFLEX CO.—See Pechiney S.A.; *Int'l*, pg. 1028

HELICOID GAUGE DIV.—See FKI Plc; *Int'l*, pg. 473
HELIKON FURNITURE CO., INC.; *U.S. Private*, pg. 520
HELIOS CAPITAL CORPORATION—See Sun Company, Inc.; *U.S. Public*, pg. 1530
HELIOZOID OCE REPROGRAPHIC (CYPRUS) LTD.—See Oce-van der Grinten N.V.; *Int'l*, pg. 995
HELIX/HI-TEMP CABLES, INC.—See Draka Kabel B.V.; *Int'l*, pg. 417
HELIX TECHNOLOGY CORP.; *U.S. Public*, pg. 808
HELLAMAT—See Lafarge S.A.; *Int'l*, pg. 791
HELLAMCO—See Hewlett-Packard Company; *U.S. Public*, pg. 818
HELLAMCO-MICHAEL COTOYANNIS—See Hewlett-Packard Company; *U.S. Public*, pg. 818
HELLAS CAN S.A.—See Caradon Plc; *Int'l*, pg. 267
HELLENCI STEEL CO.—See IRI Istituto Ricostruzione Industriale; *Int'l*, pg. 654
HELLER BANK A.G.—See The Fuji Bank, Limited; *Int'l*, pg. 521
HELLER BROS. PACKING CORP.; *U.S. Private*, pg. 520
HELLER FACTORING ANONIM SIRKETI—See The Fuji Bank, Limited; *Int'l*, pg. 521
HELLER FACTORING ESPANOLA, S.A.—See The Fuji Bank, Limited; *Int'l*, pg. 521
HELLER FACTORING (M) SDN. BHD.—See The Fuji Bank, Limited; *Int'l*, pg. 521
HELLER FACTORING PORTUGUESA S.A.—See The Fuji Bank, Limited; *Int'l*, pg. 521
HELLER FACTORING (SINGAPORE) LTD.—See The Fuji Bank, Limited; *Int'l*, pg. 521
HELLER FINANCIAL, INC.—See The Fuji Bank, Limited; *Int'l*, pg. 519
HELLER FINANCIAL (MEXICO), S.A. DE CV—See The Fuji Bank, Limited; *Int'l*, pg. 521
HELLER FINANCIAL SERVICES LIMITED—See The Fuji Bank, Limited; *Int'l*, pg. 521
HELLER INTERNATIONAL, *U.S. Private*, pg. 520
HELLER INTERNATIONAL CORPORATION—See The Fuji Bank, Limited; *Int'l*, pg. 519
HELLER INTERNATIONAL GROUP, INC.—See The Fuji Bank, Limited; *Int'l*, pg. 519
HELLER NET-SUD—See The Fuji Bank, Limited; *Int'l*, pg. 521
HELLER SEASONINGS & INGREDIENTS, INC.; *U.S. Private*, pg. 520
HELLER-SUD SERVICIOS FINANCIEROS S.A.—See The Fuji Bank, Limited; *Int'l*, pg. 521
HELLERMAN ELETTRO SRL—See Bowthorpe plc; *Int'l*, pg. 207
HELLERMANN ELECTRIC—See Bowthorpe plc; *Int'l*, pg. 207
HELLERMANN FINLAND—See Bowthorpe plc; *Int'l*, pg. 209
HELLERMANN FRANCE SA—See Bowthorpe plc; *Int'l*, pg. 209
HELLERMANN INSULOID—See Bowthorpe plc; *Int'l*, pg. 207
HELLERMANN IRELAND—See Bowthorpe plc; *Int'l*, pg. 208
HELLERMANN NORGE A/S—See Bowthorpe plc; *Int'l*, pg. 209
PAUL HELLERMANN GMBH—See Bowthorpe plc; *Int'l*, pg. 209
HELLERMANN SCANDINAVIA AB—See Bowthorpe plc; *Int'l*, pg. 209
HELLINE BETEILIGUNGS GMBH—See Otto Versand (GmbH & Co.); *Int'l*, pg. 1014
HELLION S.A.—See Pechiney S.A.; *Int'l*, pg. 1028
HELLMA GASTRONOMIE-SERVICE GMBH—See Sudzucker AG Mannheim/Ochsenfurt; *Int'l*, pg. 1305
J. HELLMAN FROZEN, INC.—See J. Hellman Produce, Inc.; *U.S. Private*, pg. 520
J. HELLMAN PRODUCE, INC.; *U.S. Private*, pg. 520
HELLMAN, JORDAN MANAGEMENT COMPANY, INC.—See United Asset Management Corporation; *U.S. Public*, pg. 1673
HELLMUTH, OBATA & KASSABAUM, INC.; *U.S. Private*, pg. 520
HELLY-HANSEN AB—See Orkla A.S.A.; *Int'l*, pg. 1010
HELLY-HANSEN A/S—See Orkla A.S.A.; *Int'l*, pg. 1010
HELLY-HANSEN CANADA LTD.—See Orkla A.S.A.; *Int'l*, pg. 1010
HELLY-HANSEN CONFECCOES LDA.—See Orkla A.S.A.; *Int'l*, pg. 1010
HELLY-HANSEN DISTRIBUTIE B.V.—See Orkla A.S.A.; *Int'l*, pg. 1010
HELLY-HANSEN (FAR EAST) LTD.—See Orkla A.S.A.; *Int'l*, pg. 1010
HELLY-HANSEN FRANCE—See Orkla A.S.A.; *Int'l*, pg. 1011
HELLY-HANSEN GMBH—See Orkla A.S.A.; *Int'l*, pg. 1011
HELLY-HANSEN SPESIALPRODUKTER AS—See Orkla A.S.A.; *Int'l*, pg. 1010
HELLY-HANSEN (SUISSE) SA—See Orkla A.S.A.; *Int'l*, pg. 1011
HELLY-HANSEN (UK) LTD.—See Orkla A.S.A.; *Int'l*, pg. 1011
HELLY-HANSEN VERAKUFS G.M.B.H.—See Orkla A.S.A.; *Int'l*, pg. 1011
HELLY-HANSEN (US), INC.—See Orkla A.S.A.; *Int'l*, pg. 1010
HELM BEAN & SEED WAREHOUSE, INC.—See ConAgra, Inc.; *U.S. Public*, pg. 428
HELM, INC.; *U.S. Private*, pg. 520
HELM RESOURCES INC.; *U.S. Public*, pg. 808
HELMERICH & PAYNE (COLOMBIA) DRILLING CO.—See Helmerich & Payne, Inc.; *U.S. Public*, pg. 808
HELMERICH & PAYNE DE VENEZUELA C.A.—See Helmerich & Payne, Inc.; *U.S. Public*, pg. 808
HELMERICH & PAYNE DEL ECUADOR, INC.—See Helmerich & Payne, Inc.; *U.S. Public*, pg. 808
HELMERICH & PAYNE FINCO—See Helmerich & Payne, Inc.; *U.S. Public*, pg. 808

HELMERICH & PAYNE (GABON)—See Helmerich & Payne, Inc.; *U.S. Public*, pg. 808
HELMERICH & PAYNE, INC.; *U.S. Public*, pg. 808
HELMERICH & PAYNE INTERNATIONAL DRILLING CO.—See Helmerich & Payne, Inc.; *U.S. Public*, pg. 808
HELMERICH & PAYNE INVEST CO.—See Helmerich & Payne, Inc.; *U.S. Public*, pg. 808
HELMERICH & PAYNE PROPERTIES, INC.—See Helmerich & Payne, Inc.; *U.S. Public*, pg. 808
HELMERICH & PAYNE RASCO INC.—See Helmerich & Payne, Inc.; *U.S. Public*, pg. 808
HELMICX CORPORATION; *U.S. Private*, pg. 520
HELMITIN SA—See Forbo Holding SA; *Int'l*, pg. 498
HELMKE-FEUERSTEIN PAKETOGISTIK GMBH—See Hapag-Lloyd AG; *Int'l*, pg. 596
EDD HELMS ELECTRICAL CONTRACTING; *U.S. Private*, pg. 520
EDD HELMS ELECTRICAL SERVICE, INC.—See Edd Helms Electrical Contracting; *U.S. Private*, pg. 521
ED HELMS MCDONALD AIR CONDITIONING, INC.—See Edd Helms Electrical Contracting; *U.S. Private*, pg. 521
HELMSLEY ENTERPRISES, INC.; *U.S. Private*, pg. 521
HELMSLEY-NOYES CO., INC.—See Helmsley Enterprises, Inc.; *U.S. Private*, pg. 521
HELMSLEY-SPEAR INC.—See Helmsley Enterprises, Inc.; *U.S. Private*, pg. 521
HELMSMAN MANAGEMENT SERVICES, INC.—See Liberty Mutual Insurance Co.; *U.S. Private*, pg. 666
HELOX AS—See Orkla A.S.A.; *Int'l*, pg. 1010
HELP USA INC.—See Hawk Management Corporation; *U.S. Private*, pg. 511
JOAN & DAVID HELPERN, INC.; *U.S. Private*, pg. 521
OY HELSINGEN HUUTTOKAUPPAKAMARI—See Merita Ltd.; *Int'l*, pg. 859
HELSINGEN PANTTI-OSAKEYHTIO—See Merita Ltd.; *Int'l*, pg. 859
HELUVA GOOD CHEESE INC.—See Koninklijke BolsWessanen nv; *Int'l*, pg. 752
HELVETIA COAL CO.—See Rochester & Pittsburgh Coal Company; *U.S. Public*, pg. 1395
HELWIG CARBON PRODUCTS, INC.; *U.S. Private*, pg. 521
HELZBERG'S DIAMOND SHOPS, INC.—See Berkshire Hathaway Inc.; *U.S. Public*, pg. 220
HEMA B.V.—See N.V. Koninklijke Bijenkorf Beheer KBB; *Int'l*, pg. 750
HEMISPHERE-LEO BURNETT, INC.—See Leo Burnett Company, Inc.; *U.S. Private*, pg. 184
J.S. HEMKOPSKEDJAN AB—See Carnegie Holding AB; *Int'l*, pg. 272
HEMLOCK SEMICONDUCTOR CO.—See The Dow Chemical Company; *U.S. Public*, pg. 523
PAUL HEMMER CONSTRUCTION COMPANY; *U.S. Private*, pg. 521
HEMOCUE AB—See Mallinckrodt Inc.; *U.S. Public*, pg. 1040
HEMOMAK EXPORT-IMPORT C.O.—See BASF AG; *Int'l*, pg. 108
HEMOSTATIX—See Telegenix Inc.; *U.S. Private*, pg. 1073
HEMPT BROTHERS, INC.; *U.S. Private*, pg. 521
HEN TRE—See Norske Skogindustrier A.S; *Int'l*, pg. 965
HENCO, INC.; *U.S. Private*, pg. 521
HENDERSON ADMINISTRATION GROUP PLC; *Int'l*, pg. 609
HENDERSON ADMINISTRATION (GUERNSEY) LIMITED—See Henderson Administration Group PLC; *Int'l*, pg. 609
HENDERSON AUCTIONS—See JAH Enterprises, Inc.; *U.S. Private*, pg. 577
HENDERSON CONVALESCENT HOSPITAL—See Horizon/CMS Healthcare Corporation; *U.S. Public*, pg. 837
HENDERSON ELECTRIC CO., INC.; *U.S. Private*, pg. 521
HENDERSON FINANCIAL MANAGEMENT (JERSEY) LIMITED—See Henderson Administration Group PLC; *Int'l*, pg. 609
HENDERSON HARDWARE LTD.—See Hepworth Plc; *Int'l*, pg. 615
HENDERSON INTERNATIONAL EUROPE BV—See Henderson Administration Group PLC; *Int'l*, pg. 609
HENDERSON INTERNATIONAL JAPAN KK—See Henderson Administration Group PLC; *Int'l*, pg. 609
HENDERSON INTERNATIONAL LUXEMBORG SA—See Henderson Administration Group PLC; *Int'l*, pg. 609
JOSEPH J. HENDERSON & SON, INC.; *U.S. Private*, pg. 521
HENDERSON (NEDERLAND) BV—See Hepworth Plc; *Int'l*, pg. 615
P.C. HENDERSON (IRELAND) LTD.—See Hepworth Plc; *Int'l*, pg. 615
P.C. HENDERSON LIMITED—See Hepworth Plc; *Int'l*, pg. 615
HENDERSON UNIT TRUST MANAGEMENT LIMITED—See Henderson Administration Group PLC; *Int'l*, pg. 609
HENDERSONVILLE NEWSPAPER CORPORATION—See The New York Times Company; *U.S. Public*, pg. 1175
HENDRICK AUTOMOTIVE GROUP; *U.S. Private*, pg. 522
HENDRICK IMPORTS—See Hendrick Automotive Group; *U.S. Private*, pg. 522
HENDRICK MOTORSPORTS—See Hendrick Automotive Group; *U.S. Private*, pg. 522
HENDRICKSON INTERNATIONAL—See Boler Company; *U.S. Private*, pg. 155
HENDRICKSON STAMPING—See Boler Company; *U.S. Private*, pg. 155
HENDRIK VEDER B.V.—See Royal Nedlloyd Group N.V.; *Int'l*, pg. 1144
HENDRIX WIRE & CABLE—See Thomas & Betts Corporation; *U.S. Public*, pg. 1598
HENEBRYS—See Reliable Stores, Inc.; *U.S. Private*, pg. 921
HENKEL ADHESIVES CORPORATION—See Henkel KGaA; *Int'l*, pg. 610
HENKEL & CIE AG—See Henkel KGaA; *Int'l*, pg. 611
HENKEL & CIE GMBH—See Henkel KGaA; *Int'l*, pg. 609

HENKEL ARGENTINA S.A.—See Henkel KGaA; *Int'l*, pg. 611
HENKEL ASIA-PACIFIC LTD.—See Henkel KGaA; *Int'l*, pg. 611
HENKEL AUSTRALIA PTY. LTD.—See Henkel KGaA; *Int'l*, pg. 611
HENKEL AUSTRIA GROUP—See Henkel KGaA; *Int'l*, pg. 611
HENKEL BARNANGEN A/S—See Henkel KGaA; *Int'l*, pg. 611
HENKEL BAUTECHNIK GMBH—See Henkel KGaA; *Int'l*, pg. 609
HENKEL BELGIUM S.A.—See Henkel KGaA; *Int'l*, pg. 612
HENKEL BENELUX GRUPPE—See Henkel KGaA; *Int'l*, pg. 612
HENKEL BUDAPEST CHEMISCHE GESELLSCHAFT MBH—See Henkel KGaA; *Int'l*, pg. 612
HENKEL CANADA LTD.—See Henkel KGaA; *Int'l*, pg. 612
HENKEL CENTROAMERICANA S.A.—See Henkel KGaA; *Int'l*, pg. 612
HENKEL CHEMICAL SPECIALTIES DIV.—See Henkel KGaA; *Int'l*, pg. 610
HENKEL CHEMICALS (BARBADOS) LTD.—See Henkel KGaA; *Int'l*, pg. 614
HENKEL CHEMICALS (CARIBBEAN) LTD.—See Henkel KGaA; *Int'l*, pg. 614
HENKEL CHEMICALS EAST AFRICA LTD.—See Henkel KGaA; *Int'l*, pg. 612
HENKEL CHEMICALS (H.K) LTD.—See Henkel KGaA; *Int'l*, pg. 612
HENKEL CHEMICALS (INDIA) LTD.—See Henkel KGaA; *Int'l*, pg. 614
HENKEL CHEMICALS (IRELAND) LTD.—See Henkel KGaA; *Int'l*, pg. 612
HENKEL CHEMICALS LTD.—See Henkel KGaA; *Int'l*, pg. 612
HENKEL CHEMICALS (MALAYSIA) SDN. BHD.—See Henkel KGaA; *Int'l*, pg. 612
HENKEL CHEMICALS (NIGERIA) LTD.—See Henkel KGaA; *Int'l*, pg. 614
HENKEL CHEMICALS (SINGAPORE) PTE. LTD.—See Henkel KGaA; *Int'l*, pg. 612
HENKEL CHILE S.A.—See Henkel KGaA; *Int'l*, pg. 612
HENKEL CHIMICA S.P.A.—See Henkel KGaA; *Int'l*, pg. 612
HENKEL (CHINA) INVESTMENT CO. LTD.—See Henkel KGaA; *Int'l*, pg. 612
HENKEL CHINA LTD.—See Henkel KGaA; *Int'l*, pg. 612
HENKEL COLOMBIANA S.A.—See Henkel KGaA; *Int'l*, pg. 612
HENKEL COMERCIAL SA DE C.V.—See Henkel KGaA; *Int'l*, pg. 612
HENKEL COORDINATION CENTER N.V., S.A.—See Henkel KGaA; *Int'l*, pg. 612
HENKEL CORP. - PROCESS CHEMICALS—See Henkel KGaA; *Int'l*, pg. 611
HENKEL CORPORATION - CHEMICALS GROUP—See Henkel KGaA; *Int'l*, pg. 610
HENKEL CORPORATION FINE CHEMICALS DIV.—See Henkel KGaA; *Int'l*, pg. 610
HENKEL CORPORATION FUNCTIONAL PRODUCTS DIV.—See Henkel KGaA; *Int'l*, pg. 610
HENKEL CORPORATION MINERALS INDUSTRY DIV.—See Henkel KGaA; *Int'l*, pg. 610
HENKEL CORPORATION POLYMERS DIVISION—See Henkel KGaA; *Int'l*, pg. 610
HENKEL CORPORATION TEXTILE CHEMICALS—See Henkel KGaA; *Int'l*, pg. 610
HENKEL COSMETIC GMBH—See Henkel KGaA; *Int'l*, pg. 609
HENKEL COSMETICS CHINA LTD.—See Henkel KGaA; *Int'l*, pg. 612
HENKEL COSMETICS GES.MBH—See Henkel KGaA; *Int'l*, pg. 612
HENKEL COSMETICS ZHAOQUING LTD.—See Henkel KGaA; *Int'l*, pg. 612
HENKEL CR, S.R.O.—See Henkel KGaA; *Int'l*, pg. 612
HENKEL CROATIA D.O.O.—See Henkel KGaA; *Int'l*, pg. 612
HENKEL-DAESUNG CO.—See Henkel KGaA; *Int'l*, pg. 612
HENKEL-ECOLAB GMBH & CO.—See Henkel KGaA; *Int'l*, pg. 610
HENKEL ENTRETIEN S.A.—See Henkel KGaA; *Int'l*, pg. 612
HENKEL-EYTESA S.A.—See Henkel KGaA; *Int'l*, pg. 612
HENKEL FRANCE S.A.—See Henkel KGaA; *Int'l*, pg. 612
HENKEL FUNCTIONAL PRODUCTS DIV.—See Henkel KGaA; *Int'l*, pg. 610
HENKEL GENTHIN GMBH—See Henkel KGaA; *Int'l*, pg. 610
HENKEL HAKUSUI CORPORATION—See Henkel KGaA; *Int'l*, pg. 610
HENKEL HARTOL GMBH—See Henkel KGaA; *Int'l*, pg. 610
HENKEL HELLAS—See Henkel KGaA; *Int'l*, pg. 612
HENKEL HELLAS, S.A.—See Henkel KGaA; *Int'l*, pg. 612
HENKEL IBERICA S.A.—See Henkel KGaA; *Int'l*, pg. 612
P.T. HENKEL INDONESIA—See Henkel KGaA; *Int'l*, pg. 614
HENKEL INDUSTRIE AG—See Henkel KGaA; *Int'l*, pg. 612
HENKEL (IRELAND) LTD.—See Henkel KGaA; *Int'l*, pg. 612
HENKEL IRELAND LTD.—See Henkel KGaA; *Int'l*, pg. 612
HENKEL ITALIANA S.P.A.—See Henkel KGaA; *Int'l*, pg. 613
HENKEL-KEMENG COSMETICS LTD.—See Henkel KGaA; *Int'l*, pg. 613
HENKEL KEMI AB—See Henkel KGaA; *Int'l*, pg. 613
HENKEL KENORD AS—See Henkel KGaA; *Int'l*, pg. 613
HENKEL KENYA LTD.—See Henkel KGaA; *Int'l*, pg. 613
HENKEL KGAA; *Int'l*, pg. 609
HENKEL KIMIANIKA (M) SDN. BHD.—See Henkel KGaA; *Int'l*, pg. 614
HENKEL KOREA LTD.—See Henkel KGaA; *Int'l*, pg. 613

HENKEL LEATHER CHEMICALS DIV.—See Henkel KGaA; *Int'l*, pg. 610
HENKEL LTD.—See Herkel KGaA; *Int'l*, pg. 613
HENKEL MAGYARORSZAG KFT.—See Henkel KGaA; *Int'l*, pg. 613
HENKEL MAROC S.A.—See Henkel KGaA; *Int'l*, pg. 613
HENKEL MEXICANA S.A. DE C.V.—See Henkel KGaA; *Int'l*, pg. 614
HENKEL NEDERLAND B.V.—See Henkel KGaA; *Int'l*, pg. 613
HENKEL NEW ZEALAND LTD.—See Henkel KGaA; *Int'l*, pg. 613
HENKEL NOPCO AB—See Henkel KGaA; *Int'l*, pg. 613
HENKEL NOPCO AG—See Henkel KGaA; *Int'l*, pg. 613
HENKEL NOPCO A/S—See Henkel KGaA; *Int'l*, pg. 613
HENKEL NOPCO LTD.—See Henkel KGaA; *Int'l*, pg. 613
HENKEL NOPCO OY—See Henkel KGaA; *Int'l*, pg. 614
HENKEL NOPCO S/A—See Henkel KGaA; *Int'l*, pg. 613
HENKEL NOPCO TAIWAN—See Henkel KGaA; *Int'l*, pg. 613
HENKEL NORDEN AB—See Henkel KGaA; *Int'l*, pg. 613
HENKEL NORGE A/S—See Henkel KGaA; *Int'l*, pg. 613
HENKEL OLEOCHEMICALS (MALAYSIA) SND. BHD.—See Henkel KGaA; *Int'l*, pg. 613
HENKEL OLEOCHEMICALS NEDERLAND B.V.—See Henkel KGaA; *Int'l*, pg. 613
HENKEL ORGANIC PRODUCTS DIV.—See Henkel KGaA; *Int'l*, pg. 610
HENKEL-PALMA SPOL, S.R.O.—See Henkel KGaA; *Int'l*, pg. 613
HENKEL PHILIPPINES INC.—See Henkel KGaA; *Int'l*, pg. 614
HENKEL POLSKA S.A.—See Henkel KGaA; *Int'l*, pg. 613
HENKEL PORTUGUESA PRODUCTOS QUIMICOS LDA.—See Henkel KGaA; *Int'l*, pg. 613
HENKEL RIKA (M) SDN. BHD.—See Henkel KGaA; *Int'l*, pg. 613
HENKEL ROMANIA SRL—See Henkel KGaA; *Int'l*, pg. 613
HENKEL S/A. INDUSTRIAS QUIMICAS—See Henkel KGaA; *Int'l*, pg. 613
HENKEL SINGAPORE PTE., LTD.—See Henkel KGaA; *Int'l*, pg. 613
HENKEL SOUTH AFRICA (PTY.) LTD.—See Henkel KGaA; *Int'l*, pg. 614
HENKEL SPA—See Henkel KGaA; *Int'l*, pg. 613
HENKEL SUD S.P.A.—See Henkel KGaA; *Int'l*, pg. 613
HENKEL SURFACE TECHNOLOGIES—See Henkel KGaA; *Int'l*, pg. 610
HENKEL TAIWAN LTD.—See Henkel KGaA; *Int'l*, pg. 613
HENKEL TEROSON GMBH—See Henkel KGaA; *Int'l*, pg. 610
HENKEL THAI LTD.—See Henkel KGaA; *Int'l*, pg. 613
HENKEL TURYAG A.S.—See Henkel KGaA; *Int'l*, pg. 613
HENKEL VENEZOLANA S.A.—See Henkel KGaA; *Int'l*, pg. 614
HENKEL WASCHMITTEL GMBH—See Henkel KGaA; *Int'l*, pg. 610
HENKEL ZIMBABWE (PVT) LTD.—See Henkel KGaA; *Int'l*, pg. 613
HENKEL ZLATOROG D.O.O.—See Henkel KGaA; *Int'l*, pg. 613
HENKELS & McCOY EQUIPMENT CO., INC.—See Henkels & McCoy, Inc.; *U.S. Private*, pg. 522
HENKELS & McCOY, INC.; *U.S. Private*, pg. 522
HENKES-HARMON INDUSTRIES, PTY. LTD.—See Harmon Industries, Inc.; *U.S. Public*, pg. 788
WILL HENKO BV—See Henkel KGaA; *Int'l*, pg. 614
HENKOMAR S.A.—See Henkel KGaA; *Int'l*, pg. 614
HENKOS COSMETIC GMBH—See Henkel KGaA; *Int'l*, pg. 610
THE HENLEY CENTRE—See WPP Group plc; *Int'l*, pg. 1482
HENLEY HEALTHCARE—See Maxxim Medical, Inc.; *U.S. Public*, pg. 1063
HENLEY PAPER COMPANY; *U.S. Private*, pg. 522
W.T. HENLEY'S—See TT Group PLC; *Int'l*, pg. 1344
THE HENNEGAN COMPANY; *U.S. Private*, pg. 522
HENNELLS, INC.; *U.S. Private*, pg. 522
HENNESEYS—See Mercantile Stores Company, Inc.; *U.S. Public*, pg. 1090
JA. HENNESSY & CO.—See LVMH Moet Hennessy Louis Vuitton; *Int'l*, pg. 780
JA. HENNESSY & CO LTD—See LVMH Moet Hennessy Louis Vuitton; *Int'l*, pg. 782
HENNESSY/COATS DIVISION—See Danaher Corporation; *U.S. Public*, pg. 481
HENNESSY INDUSTRIES, INC.—See Danaher Corporation; *U.S. Public*, pg. 481
JA. HENNESSY (FAR EAST) LTD—See LVMH Moet Hennessy Louis Vuitton; *Int'l*, pg. 782
HENNESSY U.K. LTD—See LVMH Moet Hennessy Louis Vuitton; *Int'l*, pg. 782
HENNIGES-VEHICLE SEALING DIV.—See GenCorp Inc.; *U.S. Public*, pg. 706
HENNINGSEN FOODS, INC.—See Q.P. Corporation; *Int'l*, pg. 1074
HENNINGSEN NEDERLAND B.V.—See Q.P. Corporation; *Int'l*, pg. 1074
HENNINGSEN-VAN DEN BURG—See Q.P. Corporation; *Int'l*, pg. 1074
HENNINGSEN-VAN DEN BURG—See Unilever Plc; *Int'l*, pg. 1434
HENNINGSON, DURHAM & RICHARDSON INC.—See Bouygues; *Int'l*, pg. 207
HENREDON FURNITURE INDUSTRIES, INC.—See Furnishings International, Inc.; *U.S. Private*, pg. 432
HENREDON UPHOLSTERY—See Furnishings International, Inc.; *U.S. Private*, pg. 432
HENRI BENDEL—See The Limited, Inc.; *U.S. Public*, pg. 995
HENRIJEAN & CIE. S.A.—See Marsh & McLennan Companies, Inc.; *U.S. Public*, pg. 1049
HENRIOT DISTRIBUTION—See LVMH Moet Hennessy Louis Vuitton; *Int'l*, pg. 780

HENRY & HENRY, INC.—See CSM N.V.; *Int'l*, pg. 244
HENRY COUNTY LOCAL—See Landmark Communications, Inc.; *U.S. Private*, pg. 648
E.P. HENRY CORPORATION; *U.S. Private*, pg. 522
JACK HENRY & ASSOCIATES, INC.; *U.S. Public*, pg. 808
JACK HENRY INTERNATIONAL—See Jack Henry & Associates, Inc.; *U.S. Public*, pg. 809
HENSCHEL CORP.—See SPD Technologies; *U.S. Private*, pg. 957
HENSEL PHELPS CONSTRUCTION CO.; *U.S. Private*, pg. 523
HENSLEY & CO.; *U.S. Private*, pg. 523
M. HENSOLDT & SOHNE WETZLAR, OPTISCHE WERKE AG—See Carl-Zeiss-Stiftung; *Int'l*, pg. 1523
HENSON TIMBER PRODUCTS CORP.—See Stonecutter Mills Corp.; *U.S. Private*, pg. 1044
HEPARDIMPEX S.R.L.—See Hewlett-Packard Company; *U.S. Public*, pg. 818
HEPWORTH BUILDING PRODUCTS INTERNATIONAL—See Hepworth Plc; *Int'l*, pg. 615
HEPWORTH BUILDING PRODUCTS LIMITED—See Hepworth Plc; *Int'l*, pg. 615
HEPWORTH CERAMIC OVERSEAS LTD.—See Hepworth Plc; *Int'l*, pg. 615
HEPWORTH HEATING LTD.—See Hepworth Plc; *Int'l*, pg. 615
HEPWORTH HOME PRODUCTS LIMITED—See Hepworth Plc; *Int'l*, pg. 615
HEPWORTH INDUSTRIAL PLASTICS LTD.—See Hepworth Plc; *Int'l*, pg. 615
HEPWORTH MINERALIEN UND CHEMICALIEN GMBH—See Hepworth Plc; *Int'l*, pg. 615
HEPWORTH MINERALS AND CHEMICALS B.V.—See Hepworth Plc; *Int'l*, pg. 615
HEPWORTH MINERALS AND CHEMICALS LIMITED—See Hepworth Plc; *Int'l*, pg. 615
HEPWORTH MINERALS AND CHEMICALS S.A.—See Hepworth Plc; *Int'l*, pg. 615
BV HEPWORTH-NGI—See Hepworth Plc; *Int'l*, pg. 615
HEPWORTH PLC; *Int'l*, pg. 614
HEPWORTH REFRACTORIES (BELGIUM) S.A.—See Hepworth Plc; *Int'l*, pg. 615
HEPWORTH REFRACTORIES (CANADA) LIMITED—See Hepworth Plc; *Int'l*, pg. 615
HEPWORTH REFRACTORIES INC.—See Hepworth Plc; *Int'l*, pg. 615
HEPWORTH REFRACTORIES ITALIANA SRL—See Hepworth Plc; *Int'l*, pg. 615
HEPWORTH REFRACTORIES LTD.—See Hepworth Plc; *Int'l*, pg. 615
HERAEUS AMERSIL INC.—See Heraeus Holding GmbH; *Int'l*, pg. 616
HERAEUS DE NORA INC.—See Heraeus Holding GmbH; *Int'l*, pg. 616
HERAEUS ELECTRO-NITE CO.—See Heraeus Holding GmbH; *Int'l*, pg. 616
HERAEUS ELECTRO-NITE INTERNATIONAL N.V.—See Heraeus Holding GmbH; *Int'l*, pg. 616
HERAEUS HOLDING GMBH; *Int'l*, pg. 616
HERAEUS INC.—See Heraeus Holding GmbH; *Int'l*, pg. 616
HERAEUS INSTRUMENTS GMBH—See Heraeus Holding GmbH; *Int'l*, pg. 616
HERAEUS INSTRUMENTS INC.—See Heraeus Holding GmbH; *Int'l*, pg. 616
HERAEUS INVESTMENT CORPORATION—See Heraeus Holding GmbH; *Int'l*, pg. 616
HERAEUS KULZER GMBH—See Heraeus Holding GmbH; *Int'l*, pg. 616
HERAEUS/KULZER, INC. - DENTAL PRODUCTS DIV.—See Heraeus Holding GmbH; *Int'l*, pg. 616
HERAEUS/KULZER, INC. - KULZER DIV.—See Heraeus Holding GmbH; *Int'l*, pg. 616
HERAEUS MED GMBH—See Heraeus Holding GmbH; *Int'l*, pg. 616
HERAEUS PRECIOUS METALS MANAGEMENT INC.—See Heraeus Holding GmbH; *Int'l*, pg. 616
HERAEUS QUARZGLAS GMBH—See Heraeus Holding GmbH; *Int'l*, pg. 616
HERAEUS SHIN-ETSU AMERICA INC.—See Heraeus Holding GmbH; *Int'l*, pg. 616
W.C. HERAEUS GMBH—See Heraeus Holding GmbH; *Int'l*, pg. 616
THE HERALD—See Journal Register Company; *U.S. Public*, pg. 935
THE HERALD-DISPATCH—See Gannett Company, Inc.; *U.S. Public*, pg. 701
HERALD-NEWS—See The Copley Press, Inc.; *U.S. Private*, pg. 275
HERALD VOICE—See Pulitzer Publishing Company; *U.S. Public*, pg. 1343
THE HERALD & WEEKLY TIMES LTD.—See The News Corporation Limited; *Int'l*, pg. 925
HERAULT MINING DIVISION—See COGEMA - Compagnie Generale des Matieres Nucleaires; *Int'l*, pg. 305
HERBALIFE AUSTRALASIA PTY. LTD.—See Herbalife International of America, Inc.; *U.S. Public*, pg. 809
HERBALIFE DENMARK APS—See Herbalife International of America, Inc.; *U.S. Public*, pg. 809
HERBALIFE DOMINICANA, S.A.—See Herbalife International of America, Inc.; *U.S. Public*, pg. 809
HERBALIFE INTERNATIONAL ARGENTINA, S.A.—See Herbalife International of America, Inc.; *U.S. Public*, pg. 809
HERBALIFE INTERNATIONAL BELGIUM S.A./N.V.—See Herbalife International of America, Inc.; *U.S. Public*, pg. 809
HERBALIFE INTERNATIONAL-CZECHOSLOVAKIA—See Herbalife International of America, Inc.; *U.S. Public*, pg. 809
HERBALIFE INTERNATIONAL DE MEXICO, S.A.D.C.V.—See Herbalife International of America, Inc.; *U.S. Public*, pg. 809

HERBALIFE INTERNATIONAL DEUTSCHLAND GMBH—See Herbalife International of America, Inc.; *U.S. Public*, pg. 809
HERBALIFE INTERNATIONAL ESPANA, S.A.—See Herbalife International of America, Inc.; *U.S. Public*, pg. 809
HERBALIFE INTERNATIONAL FRANCE, S.A.—See Herbalife International of America, Inc.; *U.S. Public*, pg. 809
HERBALIFE INTERNATIONAL-HONG KONG—See Herbalife International of America, Inc.; *U.S. Public*, pg. 809
HERBALIFE INTERNATIONAL ISRAEL (1990) LTD.—See Herbalife International of America, Inc.; *U.S. Public*, pg. 809
HERBALIFE INTERNATIONAL (NETHERLANDS) B.V.—See Herbalife International of America, Inc.; *U.S. Public*, pg. 809
HERBALIFE INTERNATIONAL OF AMERICA, INC.; *U.S. Public*, pg. 809
HERBALIFE INTERNATIONAL OF AMERICA, INC.—See Herbalife International of America, Inc.; *U.S. Public*, pg. 809
HERBALIFE INTERNATIONAL PHILIPPINES—See Herbalife International of America, Inc.; *U.S. Public*, pg. 809
HERBALIFE INTERNATIONAL, S.A.-PORTUGAL—See Herbalife International of America, Inc.; *U.S. Public*, pg. 809
HERBALIFE ITALIA S.P.A.—See Herbalife International of America, Inc.; *U.S. Public*, pg. 809
HERBALIFE (N.Z.) LIMITED—See Herbalife International of America, Inc.; *U.S. Public*, pg. 809
HERBALIFE OF CANADA LTD.—See Herbalife International of America, Inc.; *U.S. Public*, pg. 809
HERBALIFE OF JAPAN K.K.—See Herbalife International of America, Inc.; *U.S. Public*, pg. 809
HERBALIFE POLSKA SP.Z.O.O—See Herbalife International of America, Inc.; *U.S. Public*, pg. 809
HERBALIFE SWEDEN AB—See Herbalife International of America, Inc.; *U.S. Public*, pg. 809
HERBALIFE (UK) LIMITED—See Herbalife International of America, Inc.; *U.S. Public*, pg. 809
G.R. HERBERGER'S, INC.—See Proffitt's, Inc.; *U.S. Public*, pg. 1333
HERBERTS GMBH—See Hoechst Aktiengesellschaft; *Int'l*, pg. 625
HERBERTS-O'BRIEN INC.—See Hoechst Aktiengesellschaft; *Int'l*, pg. 626
HERBOL FARBEN & LACKE AG—See BASF AG; *Int'l*, pg. 108
OY HERCOFINN AB—See Hercules Incorporated; *U.S. Public*, pg. 810
HERCON ENVIRONMENTAL CORPORATION—See Health-Chem Corporation; *U.S. Public*, pg. 802
HERCON LABORATORIES CORP.—See Health-Chem Corporation; *U.S. Public*, pg. 802
HERCULES AB—See Hercules Incorporated; *U.S. Public*, pg. 810
HERCULES AEROSPACE ESPANA, S.A.—See Hercules Incorporated; *U.S. Public*, pg. 810
HERCULES BELGIUM N.V.—See Hercules Incorporated; *U.S. Public*, pg. 810
HERCULES B.V.—See Hercules Incorporated; *U.S. Public*, pg. 810
HERCULES CANADA INC.—See Hercules Incorporated; *U.S. Public*, pg. 810
HERCULES CHEMICAL CO., INC.; *U.S. Private*, pg. 523
HERCULES CHEMICALS INVESTMENTS PTY. LTD.—See Hercules Incorporated; *U.S. Public*, pg. 811
HERCULES CREDIT, INC.—See Hercules Incorporated; *U.S. Public*, pg. 811
HERCULES DO BRASIL PRODUTOS QUIMICOS LTDA.—See Hercules Incorporated; *U.S. Public*, pg. 811
HERCULES ENERGY CORP.—See LSB Industries, Inc.; *U.S. Public*, pg. 970
HERCULES ENGINE COMPANY; *U.S. Private*, pg. 523
S.A. HERCULES EUROPE N.V.—See Hercules Incorporated; *U.S. Public*, pg. 811
HERCULES FOOD & FUNCTIONAL PRODUCTS CO.—See Hercules Incorporated; *U.S. Public*, pg. 810
HERCULES FRANCE, S.A.—See Hercules Incorporated; *U.S. Public*, pg. 811
HERCULES GMBH—See Hercules Incorporated; *U.S. Public*, pg. 811
HERCULES GRANDLAGGNING AB—See NCC AB; *Int'l*, pg. 899
HERCULES INCORPORATED; *U.S. Public*, pg. 809
HERCULES INC., ABSORBENT & TEXTILE PRODUCTS GROUP—See Hercules Incorporated; *U.S. Public*, pg. 810
HERCULES INC.-BRUNSWICK—See Hercules Incorporated; *U.S. Public*, pg. 810
HERCULES INC.-JEFFERSON—See Hercules Incorporated; *U.S. Public*, pg. 810
HERCULES INC.-MAGNA—See Hercules Incorporated; *U.S. Public*, pg. 810
HERCULES INC.-OXFORD—See Hercules Incorporated; *U.S. Public*, pg. 810
HERCULES INCORPORATED GRAPHITE FIBERS—See Hercules Incorporated; *U.S. Public*, pg. 810
HERCULES INTERNATIONAL TRADE CORP., LTD. (HINTCO)—See Hercules Incorporated; *U.S. Public*, pg. 811
HERCULES ITALIA S.P.A.—See Hercules Incorporated; *U.S. Public*, pg. 811
HERCULES JAPAN LTD.—See Hercules Incorporated; *U.S. Public*, pg. 811
HERCULES KOREA CHEMICAL CO. LTD.—See Hercules Incorporated; *U.S. Public*, pg. 811
HERCULES LIMITED—See Hercules Incorporated; *U.S. Public*, pg. 811
P.T. HERCULES MAS INDONESIA—See Hercules Incorporated; *U.S. Public*, pg. 811

MASTER INDEX TO COMPANY NAMES HEWLETT-PACKARD
Company Index

HERCULES OIL GESELLSCHAFT FUR HOCHLEISTUNGSSCHMIER-STOFFE MBH—See Fuchs Petrolub AG Oel + Chemie; *Int'l*, pg. 517
HERCULES OVERSEAS CORPORATION—See Hercules Incorporated; *U.S. Public*, pg. 810
HERCULES-SANYO, INC.—See Hercules Incorporated; *U.S. Public*, pg. 810
HERCULES SINGAPORE PTE LTD.—See Hercules Incorporated; *U.S. Public*, pg. 811
THE HERCULES TIRE & RUBBER COMPANY; *U.S. Private*, pg. 523
HERCULES TRADING CORP.—See Hercules Incorporated; *U.S. Public*, pg. 810
HERCULITE PRODUCTS, INC.—See Health-Chem Corporation; *U.S. Public*, pg. 802
HERDILLIA UNIMERS LTD.—See Crompton & Knowles Corporation; *U.S. Public*, pg. 460
HEREFORD STATE BANK—See First Financial Bankshares, Inc.; *U.S. Public*, pg. 633
HERESITE PROTECTIVE COATINGS INC.; *U.S. Private*, pg. 523
HERFF JONES, FINE PAPERS—See Herff Jones Inc.; *U.S. Private*, pg. 523
HERFF JONES INC.; *U.S. Private*, pg. 523
HERFF JONES, JEWLERY—See Herff Jones Inc.; *U.S. Private*, pg. 523
HERFF JONES OF CANADA—See Herff Jones Inc.; *U.S. Private*, pg. 524
HERFF JONES PHOTOGRAPHY—See Herff Jones Inc.; *U.S. Private*, pg. 523
HERFF JONES YEARBOOKS—See Herff Jones Inc.; *U.S. Private*, pg. 524
HERIDER FARMS, INC.—See Campbell Soup Company; *U.S. Public*, pg. 299
HERITABLE GROUP, PLC—See CoreStates Financial Corp.; *U.S. Public*, pg. 447
HERITAGE AIR SYSTEMS, INC.—See EMCOR Group, Inc.; *U.S. Public*, pg. 572
HERITAGE ASSET MANAGEMENT, INC.—See Raymond James Financial, Inc.; *U.S. Public*, pg. 923
HERITAGE CABLEVISION, INC.—See TCI Communications, Inc.; *U.S. Public*, pg. 1555
HERITAGE CARE CENTER—See Horizon/CMS Healthcare Corporation; *U.S. Public*, pg. 838
HERITAGE CO-OP; *U.S. Private*, pg. 524
HERITAGE COUNTRY MANOR—See Horizon/CMS Healthcare Corporation; *U.S. Public*, pg. 839
HERITAGE CUTLERY, INC.—See Rogers, Lunt & Bowlen Co.; *U.S. Private*, pg. 940
HERITAGE ESTATES—See Horizon/CMS Healthcare Corporation; *U.S. Public*, pg. 839
HERITAGE FOREST LANE—See Horizon/CMS Healthcare Corporation; *U.S. Public*, pg. 839
HERITAGE GARDENS—See Horizon/CMS Healthcare Corporation; *U.S. Public*, pg. 839
HERITAGE HILLHAVEN NURSING HOME—See Vencor, Inc.; *U.S. Public*, pg. 1713
HERITAGE HILLS—See Kimball International, Inc.; *U.S. Public*, pg. 957
HERITAGE INKS INTERNATIONAL; *U.S. Private*, pg. 524
HERITAGE LINCOLN-MERCURY—See Fairway Ford, Inc.; *U.S. Private*, pg. 392
HERITAGE MANOR CANTON—See Horizon/CMS Healthcare Corporation; *U.S. Public*, pg. 839
HERITAGE MANOR LONGVIEW—See Horizon/CMS Healthcare Corporation; *U.S. Public*, pg. 839
HERITAGE MANOR PLANO—See Horizon/CMS Healthcare Corporation; *U.S. Public*, pg. 839
HERITAGE MERCHANDISING CO., INC.—See Pennzoil Company; *U.S. Public*, pg. 1272
HERITAGE NATIONAL HEALTHPLAN OF TENNESSEE, INC.—See Deere & Company; *U.S. Public*, pg. 492
HERITAGE OAKS—See Horizon/CMS Healthcare Corporation; *U.S. Public*, pg. 839
HERITAGE PARK—See Horizon/CMS Healthcare Corporation; *U.S. Public*, pg. 839
HERITAGE PLACE—See Horizon/CMS Healthcare Corporation; *U.S. Public*, pg. 839
HERITAGE PRESS, INC.—See Wallace Computer Services, Inc.; *U.S. Public*, pg. 1735
HERITAGE SPORTSWEAR—See Signal Apparel Company, Inc.; *U.S. Public*, pg. 1472
HERITAGE VILLAGE—See Horizon/CMS Healthcare Corporation; *U.S. Public*, pg. 839
HERITAGE WESTERN HILLS—See Horizon/CMS Healthcare Corporation; *U.S. Public*, pg. 839
HERKULESSTEINE GMBH—See Dyckerhoff & Widmann AG; *Int'l*, pg. 423
HERLEY INDUSTRIES, INC.; *U.S. Public*, pg. 811
HERLEY VEGA INDUSTRY—See Herley Industries, Inc.; *U.S. Public*, pg. 811
HERLEY-MDI—See Herley Industries, Inc.; *U.S. Public*, pg. 811
HERLIN PRESS INC.; *U.S. Private*, pg. 524
HERLITZ AKTIENGESELLSCHAFT PRODUKTION—See Herlitz PBS Aktiengesellschaft; *Int'l*, pg. 616
HERLITZ AKTIENSGESELLSCHAFT VERSAND—See Herlitz PBS Aktiengesellschaft; *Int'l*, pg. 616
HERLITZ BENELUX BV—See Herlitz PBS Aktiengesellschaft; *Int'l*, pg. 616
HERLITZ FALKENHOH GMBH—See Herlitz PBS Aktiengesellschaft; *Int'l*, pg. 616
HERLITZ GES.M.B.H.—See Herlitz PBS Aktiengesellschaft; *Int'l*, pg. 616
HERLITZ HUNGARIA—See Herlitz PBS Aktiengesellschaft; *Int'l*, pg. 616
HERLITZ INTERNATIONAL TRADING AG—See Herlitz PBS Aktiengesellschaft; *Int'l*, pg. 616
HERLITZ OY AB—See Herlitz PBS Aktiengesellschaft; *Int'l*, pg. 616
HERLITZ PBS AKTIENGESELLSCHAFT; *Int'l*, pg. 616
HERLITZ S.A.—See Herlitz PBS Aktiengesellschaft; *Int'l*, pg. 616
HERLITZ SPOL. S.R.O.—See Herlitz PBS Aktiengesellschaft; *Int'l*, pg. 616
HERLITZ SPOLKA Z.O.O.—See Herlitz PBS Aktiengesellschaft; *Int'l*, pg. 616
HERMAL KURT HERRMANN & CO.; *Int'l*, pg. 616
A.D. HERMAN CONSTRUCTION CO.—See Starrett HRH; *U.S. Private*, pg. 1035
JOS. M. HERMAN SHOE CO.; *U.S. Private*, pg. 524
HERMAN MILLER, INC.—See Herman Miller, Inc.; *U.S. Public*, pg. 1112
HERMAN MILLER ITALIA SPA—See Herman Miller, Inc.; *U.S. Public*, pg. 1112
HERMAN MILLER MEXICO—See Herman Miller, Inc.; *U.S. Public*, pg. 1112
HERMAN MILLER MEXICO, PUEBLA OFFICE—See Herman Miller, Inc.; *U.S. Public*, pg. 1112
HERMANN BERSTORFF MASCHINENBAU GMBH; *Int'l*, pg. 617
HERMANN BOHLER GMBH—See Herlitz PBS Aktiengesellschaft; *Int'l*, pg. 616
HERMANN H.C. STARCK BERLIN GBMH & CO. KG—See Bayer AG; *Int'l*, pg. 174
HERMANN LEIST GMBH & CO. KG—See Veba AG; *Int'l*, pg. 1459
HERMANN LUDWIG GMBH & CO.—See SNCF; *Int'l*, pg. 1165
HERMANN PFAUTER GMBH & CO.; *Int'l*, pg. 617
HERMANN WAGNER, GMBH—See Transworld Interweaving AG (TIAG); *Int'l*, pg. 1418
HERMANS GROEP B.V.—See Tengelmann Warenhandelsgesellschaft; *Int'l*, pg. 1375
HERMEDICO BV—See Novo Nordisk A/S; *Int'l*, pg. 987
HERMES—See Hewlett-Packard Company; *U.S. Public*, pg. 818
HERMES ELECTRONICS, INC.—See Ultra Electronics Holdings plc; *Int'l*, pg. 1431
HERMES INTERNATIONAL; *Int'l*, pg. 617
HERMES PRECISA AUSTRALIA PTY LTD.—See HPI Holding S.A.; *Int'l*, pg. 579
HERMES TECHNISCHER KUNDENDIENST GMBH & CO.—See Otto Versand (GmbH & Co.); *Int'l*, pg. 1014
HERMES VERSAND SERVICE BERLIN GMBH—See Otto Versand (GmbH & Co.); *Int'l*, pg. 1014
KG HERMES VERSAND SERVICE GMBH & CO.—See Otto Versand (GmbH & Co.); *Int'l*, pg. 1014
HERMETIC SEAL CORP.—See HCC Industries; *U.S. Private*, pg. 490
HERMETITE CORP.—See HCC Industries; *U.S. Private*, pg. 490
HERMI INGENIERIA DE S.A. DE C.V.—See Mitsubishi Heavy Industries Ltd.; *Int'l*, pg. 874
HERMISTON FOODS, INC.—See Norpac Foods, Inc.; *U.S. Private*, pg. 802
HERMLE AG—See Traub AG; *Int'l*, pg. 1419
HERNANDO COUNTY JAIL—See Corrections Corporation of America; *U.S. Public*, pg. 450
HERO; *Int'l*, pg. 617
HERO EQUIPAMENTOS INDUSTRIAS LTDA.—See North Limited; *Int'l*, pg. 967
HERON INDUSTRIES LIMITED—See Russel Metals Inc.; *Int'l*, pg. 1150
THE HERONHILL CORPORATION—See Taylor Woodrow plc; *Int'l*, pg. 1359
HERPU S.A.—See Akzo Nobel N.V.; *Int'l*, pg. 43
HERR-VOSS CORP.—See Salem Group, Inc.; *U.S. Private*, pg. 961
HERR VOSS LTD.—See Salem Group, Inc.; *U.S. Private*, pg. 962
HERRAMIENTAS CLEVELAND, S.A.—See Kennametal Inc.; *U.S. Public*, pg. 950
HERRAMIENTAS KLEIN S.A. DE C.V.—See Klein Tools Inc.; *U.S. Private*, pg. 625
HERRAMIENTAS SNAP-ON DE MEXICO, S.A.—See Snap-On Tools Corporation; *U.S. Public*, pg. 1481
HERRAMIENTAS VARCO S.A.C.V.—See Varco International, Inc.; *U.S. Public*, pg. 1709
HERRING NEWMAN; *U.S. Private*, pg. 524
HERRMIDIFIER CO., INC.—See Trion, Inc.; *U.S. Public*, pg. 1639
HERSCHEL ADAMS—See Alamo Group, Inc.; *U.S. Public*, pg. 35
HERSHEY CANADA INC.—See Hershey Foods Corporation; *U.S. Public*, pg. 812
HERSHEY CANADA INC.-SMITH FALLS PLANT—See Hershey Foods Corporation; *U.S. Public*, pg. 812
HERSHEY CHOCOLATE U.S.A.—See Hershey Foods Corporation; *U.S. Public*, pg. 812
HERSHEY CREAMERY COMPANY; *U.S. Private*, pg. 524
HERSHEY FOODS CORPORATION; *U.S. Public*, pg. 811
HERSHEY INTERNATIONAL—See Hershey Foods Corporation; *U.S. Public*, pg. 812
HERSHEY JAPAN CO., LTD.—See Hershey Foods Corporation; *U.S. Public*, pg. 812
HERSHEY PASTA AND GROCERY GROUP—See Hershey Foods Corporation; *U.S. Public*, pg. 812
HERSHEY PASTA GROUP WINCHESTER, INC.—See Hershey Foods Corporation; *U.S. Public*, pg. 812
HERSTAL S.A.; *Int'l*, pg. 617
HERTA S.A.—See Nestle S.A.; *Int'l*, pg. 920
HERTA (U.K.) LTD.—See Nestle S.A.; *Int'l*, pg. 920
HERTECANT N.V.—See British Steel Plc; *Int'l*, pg. 222
HERTFORDSHIRE BTR LTD.—See BTR plc; *Int'l*, pg. 126
HERTIE WAREN-UND KAUFHAUS GMBH—See Karstadt Aktiengesellschaft; *Int'l*, pg. 724
HERTWICH ENGINEERING GMBH—See Mannesmann A.G.; *Int'l*, pg. 837
HERTZ CLAIM MANAGEMENT—See Ford Motor Company; *U.S. Public*, pg. 664
HERTZ CORPORATION—See Ford Motor Company; *U.S. Public*, pg. 664
THE HERTZ CORPORATION—See Ford Motor Company; *U.S. Public*, pg. 664
HERTZ EQUIPMENT RENTAL CORP.—See Ford Motor Company; *U.S. Public*, pg. 664
HERTZ RENT-A-CAR—See Ford Motor Company; *U.S. Public*, pg. 664
HERZBERGER PAPIERFABRIK LUDWIG OSTHUSHANRICH GMBH & CO. KG—See N.V. Koninklijke KNP BT; *Int'l*, pg. 757
HERZOG COILEX GMBH—See Fried. Krupp AG; *Int'l*, pg. 512
WALTER HERZOG G.M.B.H.—See Varlen Corporation; *U.S. Public*, pg. 1711
HESCO, INC.—See Hesco Parts Corporation; *U.S. Private*, pg. 524
HESCO PARTS CORPORATION; *U.S. Private*, pg. 524
HESCO SUPPLY CO., INC.—See The Hearst Corporation; *U.S. Private*, pg. 518
HESKA CORPORATION; *U.S. Public*, pg. 812
HESS & CLARK COMPANY—See ConAgra, Inc.; *U.S. Public*, pg. 426
HESS ENGINEERING AG—See Hess Engineering Inc.; *U.S. Private*, pg. 524
HESS ENGINEERING INC.; *U.S. Private*, pg. 524
HESS OIL VIRGIN ISLANDS CORP.—See Amerada Hess Corporation; *U.S. Public*, pg. 65
HESSCON GMBH WALZLAGER UND INDUSTRIEBEDARF—See Freudenberg & Company; *Int'l*, pg. 506
HESSE NEWMAN & CO.—See Banca Nazionale del Lavoro Sj.A.; *Int'l*, pg. 137
HESSE, RHINELAND-PALATINATE & SAAR BRANCH—See IKB Deutsche Industriebank AG; *Int'l*, pg. 645
HESTA TEX AG; *Int'l*, pg. 617
HESTIA-PHARMA GMBH—See Corange Limited; *Int'l*, pg. 331
HETZEL GMBH—See Fortune Brands, Inc.; *U.S. Public*, pg. 675
HEUBLEIN DO BRASIL—See Diageo Plc; *Int'l*, pg. 410
HEUBLEIN INC.—See Diageo Plc; *Int'l*, pg. 410
HEUBLEIN, INC.—See Diageo Plc; *Int'l*, pg. 410
HEUDEBERT—See Danone Group; *Int'l*, pg. 380
HEURIKON CORPORATION—See Computer Products, Inc.; *U.S. Public*, pg. 422
F. HEUSSER AG—See Sulzer Ltd.; *Int'l*, pg. 1306
HEVEA B.V.—See Vredestein N.V.; *Int'l*, pg. 1481
HEVI-DUTY/DOWZER—See General Signal Corporation; *U.S. Public*, pg. 726
HEVI-DUTY ELECTRIC—See General Signal Corporation; *U.S. Public*, pg. 726
HEWITT ASSOCIATES LLC; *U.S. Private*, pg. 524
HEWITT SOAP CO.—See The Jordan Company; *U.S. Private*, pg. 597
HEWLETT-PACKARD & CONTROL LTD.—See Hewlett-Packard Company; *U.S. Public*, pg. 818
HEWLETT-PACKARD A/S—See Hewlett-Packard Company; *U.S. Public*, pg. 818
HEWLETT PACKARD AVONDALE—See Hewlett-Packard Company; *U.S. Public*, pg. 816
HEWLETT PACKARD-BOISE—See Hewlett-Packard Company; *U.S. Public*, pg. 816
HEWLETT-PACKARD CESKOSLOVENSKO SPOL.S.R.O.—See Hewlett-Packard Company; *U.S. Public*, pg. 818
HEWLETT-PACKARD COMPANY; *U.S. Public*, pg. 813
HEWLETT-PACKARD DE MEXICO, S.A. DE C.V.—See Hewlett-Packard Company; *U.S. Public*, pg. 819
HEWLETT-PACKARD DE VENEZUELA, C.A.—See Hewlett-Packard Company; *U.S. Public*, pg. 819
HEWLETT-PACKARD ESPANOLA, S.A.—See Hewlett-Packard Company; *U.S. Public*, pg. 819
HEWLETT-PACKARD FINLAND FIELD OY—See Hewlett-Packard Company; *U.S. Public*, pg. 819
HEWLETT-PACKARD FRANCE—See Hewlett-Packard Company; *U.S. Public*, pg. 819
HEWLETT-PACKARD GES.M.B.H.—See Hewlett-Packard Company; *U.S. Public*, pg. 820
HEWLETT-PACKARD GMBH—See Hewlett-Packard Company; *U.S. Public*, pg. 820
HEWLETT-PACKARD HELLAS—See Hewlett-Packard Company; *U.S. Public*, pg. 820
HEWLETT-PACKARD HELLAS SERVICE CENTER—See Hewlett-Packard Company; *U.S. Public*, pg. 820
HEWLETT-PACKARD ICELAND—See Hewlett-Packard Company; *U.S. Public*, pg. 820
HEWLETT-PACKARD INDIA PVT. LTD.—See Hewlett-Packard Company; *U.S. Public*, pg. 820
HEWLETT-PACKARD IRELAND LTD.—See Hewlett-Packard Company; *U.S. Public*, pg. 820
HEWLETT-PACKARD ITALIANA S.P.A.—See Hewlett-Packard Company; *U.S. Public*, pg. 820
HEWLETT-PACKARD LIMITED—See Hewlett-Packard Company; *U.S. Public*, pg. 821
HEWLETT-PACKARD NEDERLAND B.V.—See Hewlett-Packard Company; *U.S. Public*, pg. 821
HEWLETT-PACKARD (NEW ENGLAND)—See Hewlett-Packard Company; *U.S. Public*, pg. 815
HEWLETT-PACKARD NORGE A/S—See Hewlett-Packard Company; *U.S. Public*, pg. 821
HEWLETT-PACKARD (N.Z.) LTD.—See Hewlett-Packard Company; *U.S. Public*, pg. 821
HEWLETT-PACKARD OY—See Hewlett-Packard Company; *U.S. Public*, pg. 821
HEWLETT-PACKARD POLSKA SP.Z.O.O.—See Hewlett-Packard Company; *U.S. Public*, pg. 821
HEWLETT PACKARD PRODUCT DIVISION—See Hewlett-Packard Company; *U.S. Public*, pg. 816
HEWLETT-PACKARD PUERTO RICO—See Hewlett-Packard Company; *U.S. Public*, pg. 816
HEWLETT PACKARD, RESEARCH & DEVELOPMENT—See Hewlett-Packard Company; *U.S. Public*, pg. 816
HEWLETT-PACKARD SALES (MALAYSIA) SDN. BHD.—See Hewlett-Packard Company; *U.S. Public*, pg. 821
HEWLETT-PACKARD (SCHWEIZ) AG—See Hewlett-Packard Company; *U.S. Public*, pg. 821
HEWLETT-PACKARD SINGAPORE PTE. LTD.—See Hewlett-Packard Company; *U.S. Public*, pg. 822
HEWLETT-PACKARD SINGAPORE (SALES) PTE., LTD.—See Hewlett-Packard Company; *U.S. Public*, pg. 822

HEWLETT-PACKARD SVERIGE AB—See Hewlett-Packard Company; *U.S. Public,* pg. 822

HEWLETT-PACKARD TAIWAN LTD.—See Hewlett-Packard Company; *U.S. Public,* pg. 822

HEWLETT-PACKARD (THAILAND) LTD.—See Hewlett-Packard Company; *U.S. Public,* pg. 822

HEWLETT-PACKARD TRADING S.A.—See Hewlett-Packard Company; *U.S. Public,* pg. 822

HEWLETT-PACKARD VORARLBERG—See Hewlett-Packard Company; *U.S. Public,* pg. 822

HEXAQUIMIA SA—See Akzo Nobel N.V.; *Int'l,* pg. 47

HEXCEL CHEMICAL PRODUCTS DIV.—See Hexcel Corporation; *U.S. Public,* pg. 824

HEXCEL CORPORATION; *U.S. Public,* pg. 824

HEXCEL, FAR EAST—See Hexcel Corporation; *U.S. Public,* pg. 824

HEXCEL-FYFE COMPANY, INC.—See Hexcel Corporation; *U.S. Public,* pg. 824

HEXCEL KNYTEX—See Hexcel Corporation; *U.S. Public,* pg. 824

HEXCEL (LYON) S.A.—See Hexcel Corporation; *U.S. Public,* pg. 824

HEXCEL, S.A.—See Hexcel Corporation; *U.S. Public,* pg. 824

HEXCEL, U.K.—See Hexcel Corporation; *U.S. Public,* pg. 824

HEXFET AMERICA—See International Rectifier Corporation; *U.S. Public,* pg. 906

HEXZA-NESTE CHEMICALS SDN. BHD.—See Neste Oy; *Int'l,* pg. 914

D.C. HEY COMPANY—See Ikon Office Solutions, Inc.; *U.S. Public,* pg. 863

HEYMAN CORPORATION; *U.S. Private,* pg. 524

HEYWOOD WILLIAMS GROUP PLC; *Int'l,* pg. 618

THE HI-DAIEI TRADING CO., LTD.—See The Daiei, Inc.; *Int'l,* pg. 364

HI-EISAI PHARMACEUTICALS, INC.—See Eisai Co., Ltd.; *Int'l,* pg. 435

HI/LO AUTOMOTIVE, INC.—See O'Reilly Automotive Inc.; *U.S. Public,* pg. 1230

HI NABOR SUPERMARKET INC.; *U.S. Private,* pg. 525

HI-P TOOL & DIE PTE. LTD.—See Molex Incorporated; *U.S. Public,* pg. 1122

HI PERFORMANCE SYSTEMS (PTY.) LTD.—See Hewlett-Packard Company; *U.S. Public,* pg. 822

HI-PRO ANIMAL HEALTH—See Friona Industries, L.P.; *U.S. Private,* pg. 429

HI-PRO FEED—See Friona Industries, L.P.; *U.S. Private,* pg. 429

HI-PROFIT DISTRIBUTORS, INC.—See Koninklijke BolsWessanen nv; *Int'l,* pg. 752

HI-PURE CHEMICALS, INC.—See Olin Corporation; *U.S. Public,* pg. 1219

HI-SHEAR CORP.—See Hi-Shear Industries Inc.; *U.S. Public,* pg. 825

HI-SHEAR INDUSTRIES INC.; *U.S. Public,* pg. 824

HI-SPEED CHECKWEIGHER CO., INC.—See Novartis AG; *Int'l,* pg. 973

HI-TECH PHARMACAL CO., INC.; *U.S. Public,* pg. 825

HI-TEMP MATERIALS, INC.—See Chemfab Corporation; *U.S. Public,* pg. 344

HIABA PTY LIMITED—See Britax International plc; *Int'l,* pg. 217

HIBARI KAIHATSU CO., LTD.—See Skylark Co., Ltd.; *Int'l,* pg. 1262

C.G. HIBBERT LTD.—See Allied Domecq PLC; *Int'l,* pg. 63

THE HIBBERT COMPANY; *U.S. Private,* pg. 525

HIBERNIA ALPHA BETEILIGUNGS GMBH—See Commerzbank AG; *int'l,* pg. 310

HIBERNIA BETA BETEILIGUNGS GMBH—See Commerzbank AG; *int'l,* pg. 310

HIBERNIA CORPORATION; *U.S. Public,* pg. 825

HIBERNIA DELTA BETEILIGUNGS GMBH—See Commerzbank AG; *int'l,* pg. 310

HIBERNIA ETA BETEILIGUNGS GMBH—See Commerzbank AG; *int'l,* pg. 310

HIBERNIA GAMMA BETEILIGUNGS GMBH—See Commerzbank AG; *int'l,* pg. 310

HIBERNIA NATIONAL BANK—See Hibernia Corporation; *U.S. Public,* pg. 825

HIBERNIA NATIONAL BANK OF TEXAS—See Hibernia Corporation; *U.S. Public,* pg. 825

HIBERNIA OMEGA BETEILIGUNGS GMBH—See Commerzbank AG; *int'l,* pg. 310

HIBERNIA SIGMA BETEILIGUNGS GMBH—See Commerzbank AG; *int'l,* pg. 310

HIBERNIA ZETA BETEILIGUNGS GMBH—See Commerzbank AG; *int'l,* pg. 310

HIBINO REAL ESTATE LTD.—See Suntory Ltd.; *Int'l,* pg. 1321

HIBRIDOS PIONEER DE MEXICO S.A. DE C.V.—See Pioneer Hi-Bred International, Inc.; *U.S. Public,* pg. 1299

HIBRIVEN HIBRIDOS VENEZOLANOS S.A.—See Pioneer Hi-Bred International, Inc.; *U.S. Public,* pg. 1299

HICHEM DIAGNOSTICS B.V.—See Elan Corporation Plc; *Int'l,* pg. 436

HICHEM DIAGNOSTICS, INC.—See Elan Corporation Plc; *Int'l,* pg. 436

HICKEY-FREEMAN/BOBBY JONES—See Hartmarx Corporation; *U.S. Public,* pg. 795

HICKHAM INDUSTRIES INC.—See Sulzer Ltd.; *Int'l,* pg. 1305

HICKING PENTECOST PLC; *Int'l,* pg. 618

HICKMAN, WILLIAMS & COMPANY OF KENTUCKY—See Hickman, Williams & Co. Inc.; *U.S. Private,* pg. 525

HICKMAN, WILLIAMS & CO. INC.; *U.S. Private,* pg. 525

HICKMAN, WILLIAMS CANADA, INC.—See Hickman, Williams & Co. Inc.; *U.S. Private,* pg. 525

HICKMAN, WILLIAMS DE MEXICO S.A. DE C.V.—See Hickman, Williams & Co. Inc.; *U.S. Private,* pg. 525

HICKOK INCORPORATED; *U.S. Public,* pg. 525

HICKORY CAPITAL CORPORATION—See First Tennessee National Corporation; *U.S. Public,* pg. 639

HICKORY CHAIR DIV.—See Furniture Brands International Inc.; *U.S. Public,* pg. 688

HICKORY CONSTRUCTION COMPANY; *U.S. Private,* pg. 525

HICKORY FARMS CATALOGUES OF AMERICA, INC.—See Hickory Farms, Inc.; *U.S. Private,* pg. 525

HICKORY FARMS, INC.; *U.S. Private,* pg. 525

HICKORY FURNITURE COMPANY—See R D I S Corporation; *U.S. Private,* pg. 903

HICKORY FURNITURE MART—See Conso Products Company; *U.S. Public,* pg. 434

HICKORY HILL FURNITURE CORPORATION—See Norwalk Furniture Corporation; *U.S. Private,* pg. 808

HICKORY POINT BANK & TRUST—See Archer Daniels Midland Company (ADM); *U.S. Public,* pg. 128

HICKORY PRINTING GROUP, INC.; *U.S. Private,* pg. 525

HICKORY SPECIALTIES, INC.—See Bob Evans Farms, Inc.; *U.S. Public,* pg. 596

HICKORY VENTURE CAPITAL CORPORATION—See First Tennessee National Corporation; *U.S. Public,* pg. 639

HICKS & ASSOCIATES INC.—See Science Applications International Corp.; *U.S. Private,* pg. 976

HICKS, MUSE, TATE & FURST INC.; *U.S. Private,* pg. 526

HICKS OIL-HICKS GAS, INC.; *U.S. Private,* pg. 526

HICKSON & WELCH LTD.—See Hickson International Plc; *Int'l,* pg. 619

HICKSON COATINGS HOLLAND BV—See Hickson International Plc; *Int'l,* pg. 619

HICKSON CORPORATION—See Hickson International Plc; *Int'l,* pg. 619

HICKSON DANCHEM CORPORATION—See Hickson International Plc; *Int'l,* pg. 619

HICKSON-GARANTOR NEDERLAND BV—See Hickson International Plc; *Int'l,* pg. 619

HICKSON INTERNATIONAL PLC; *Int'l,* pg. 618

HICKSON MANRO LTD.—See Hickson International Plc; *Int'l,* pg. 619

HICKSON PHARMACHEM LTD.—See Hickson International Plc; *Int'l,* pg. 619

HICKSON PHARMACHEM LTD.—See Hickson International Plc; *Int'l,* pg. 619

HICKSON TIMBER PRODUCTS LTD.—See Hickson International Plc; *Int'l,* pg. 619

HIDDEN VALLEY COAL COMPANY—See CalMat Co.; *U.S. Public,* pg. 296

HIDDEN VALLEY RESORT—See Kettler Brothers, Inc.; *U.S. Private,* pg. 617

HIDEPITO—See Lyonnaise des Eaux S.A.; *Int'l,* pg. 823

HIDRO NITRO ESPANOLA—See Pechiney S.A.; *Int'l,* pg. 1030

HIGASHI-MATSUYAMA CENTRAL KITCHEN—See Skylark Co., Ltd.; *Int'l,* pg. 1262

HIGASHIMATSUYAMA MILL—See Nippon Paper Industries Company Limited; *Int'l,* pg. 938

IRA HIGDON GROCERY, INC.; *U.S. Private,* pg. 527

HIGGINBOTHAM-BARTLETT CO.; *U.S. Private,* pg. 527

J.C. HIGGINS CORP.—See EMCOR Group, Inc.; *U.S. Public,* pg. 572

J.E. HIGGINS LUMBER COMPANY—See J.E. Higgins Lumber Co.; *U.S. Private,* pg. 527

J.E. HIGGINS LUMBER CO.; *U.S. Private,* pg. 527

HIGGINS REDDING—See J.E. Higgins Lumber Co.; *U.S. Private,* pg. 527

HIGGINS VENTURA—See J.E. Higgins Lumber Co.; *U.S. Private,* pg. 527

HIGH INDUSTRIES, INC.; *U.S. Private,* pg. 528

HIGH-LITES, INC.—See Luxo A/S; *Int'l,* pg. 821

HIGH PLAINS COMPANY; *U.S. Public,* pg. 825

HIGH POINT CHEMICAL CORPORATION—See Kao Corporation; *Int'l,* pg. 717

HIGH POINT FINANCIAL CORP.; *U.S. Public,* pg. 826

HIGH POINT OIL CO.; *U.S. Private,* pg. 528

HIGH POINT, RANDLEMAN, ASHEBORO AND SOUTHERN RAILROAD CO.—See Norfolk Southern Corporation; *U.S. Public,* pg. 1191

HIGH PROFORMANCE INDUSTRIAL DOORS—See Albany International Corp.; *U.S. Public,* pg. 36

HIGH RIDGE CO. LTD.—See General Signal Corporation; *U.S. Public,* pg. 727

HIGH STATE/INVESTORS GUARANTY—See B.A.T Industries P.L.C.; *Int'l,* pg. 110

HIGH VOLTAGE ENGINEERING B.V.—See High Voltage Engineering Corporation; *U.S. Private,* pg. 528

HIGH VOLTAGE ENGINEERING CORPORATION; *U.S. Private,* pg. 528

HIGHER EDUCATION DIVISION—See National Amusements, Inc.; *U.S. Private,* pg. 778

HIGHER EDUCATION LOAN PROGRAM OF KANSAS—See Hawk Management Corporation; *U.S. Private,* pg. 511

HIGHFIELD MANUFACTURING CO.—See BTR plc; *Int'l,* pg. 127

HIGHLAND CAPITAL MANAGEMENT CORPORATION—See First Tennessee National Corporation; *U.S. Public,* pg. 639

THE HIGHLAND DISTILLERIES COMPANY PLC; *Int'l,* pg. 619

HIGHLAND HYDRAULICS, INC.—See Bearing Headquarters Co.; *U.S. Private,* pg. 127

HIGHLAND INDUSTRIES INC.; *U.S. Private,* pg. 528

HIGHLAND INTERNATIONAL, INC.—See Lakeland Industries, Inc.; *U.S. Public,* pg. 975

HIGHLAND LAND MINERALS, INC.—See National Fuel Gas Company; *U.S. Public,* pg. 1156

HIGHLAND MALT DISTILLING LIMITED—See The Highland Distilleries Company plc; *Int'l,* pg. 619

HIGHLAND MANOR NURSING HOME—See Paragon Health Network, Inc.; *U.S. Public,* pg. 1257

HIGHLAND MANUFACTURING—See Illinois Tool Works Inc.; *U.S. Public,* pg. 866

HIGHLAND MILLS INC.; *U.S. Private,* pg. 528

HIGHLAND NEWS-LEADER—See Knight-Ridder, Inc.; *U.S. Public,* pg. 964

HIGHLAND PARK BANK & TRUST—See UMB Financial Corporation; *U.S. Public,* pg. 1654

HIGHLAND PARK FINANCIAL CENTER—See Northern Trust Corporation; *U.S. Public,* pg. 1196

HIGHLAND PROPANE COMPANY—See Roanoke Gas Company; *U.S. Public,* pg. 1393

HIGHLAND VALLEY COPPER—See Cominco, Ltd.; *Int'l,* pg. 308

HIGHLAND VALLEY COPPER—See Rio Algom Limited; *Int'l,* pg. 1118

HIGHLANDS AT BRIARCLIFF LIMITED PARTNERSHIP—See Cooper Communities, Inc.; *U.S. Private,* pg. 274

HIGHLANDS INSURANCE CO.; *U.S. Public,* pg. 826

HIGHLIGHTS FOR CHILDREN, INC.; *U.S. Private,* pg. 528

HIGHLINE FINANCIAL SERVICES, INC.—See Xerox Corporation; *U.S. Public,* pg. 1785

HIGHMARK INC.; *U.S. Private,* pg. 528

HIGH-TECH NACHRICHTENTECHNISCHE ANLAGEN GMBH—See Motorola, Inc.; *U.S. Public,* pg. 1139

HIGHVELD STEEL & VANADIUM CORPORATION—See Anglo American Corporation of South Africa Limited; *Int'l,* pg. 76

HIGHWAY EQUIPMENT COMPANY; *U.S. Private,* pg. 529

HIGHWAY ONE COMMUNICATIONS, INTEGRATED MARKETING SERVICES—See DMB&B Communications; *U.S. Private,* pg. 303

HIGHWAY TOLL SYSTEMS SDN. BHD. (HTS)—See Mitsubishi Heavy Industries Ltd.; *Int'l,* pg. 874

HIGHWOOD RESOURCES LTD.—See Royal Oak Mines Inc.; *U.S. Public,* pg. 1411

HIJOS DE J. BARRERAS, S.A.—See SEPI; *Int'l,* pg. 1224

HIKAMI MANUFACTURING CO., INC.—See Shizuki Electric Corporation; *Int'l,* pg. 1236

HIKARI CORPORATION—See N.V. Bekaert S.A.; *Int'l,* pg. 185

HIKO BYGGPLAST A/S—See Perstorp AB; *Int'l,* pg. 1037

HILANA C.A.—See Nissho Iwai Corporation; *Int'l,* pg. 947

HILAND DAIRY COMPANY—See Prairie Farms Dairy, Inc.; *U.S. Private,* pg. 879

HILB, ROGAL AND HAMILTON COMPANY; *U.S. Public,* pg. 826

HILB, ROGAL & HAMILTON COMPANY OF AMARILLO—See Hilb, Rogal and Hamilton Company; *U.S. Public,* pg. 827

HILB, ROGAL AND HAMILTON COMPANY OF CANADA, LIMITED—See Hilb, Rogal and Hamilton Company; *U.S. Public,* pg. 828

HILB, ROGAL AND HAMILTON COMPANY OF CORPUS CHRISTI—See Hilb, Rogal and Hamilton Company; *U.S. Public,* pg. 827

HILB, ROGAL AND HAMILTON COMPANY OF DENVER—See Hilb, Rogal and Hamilton Company; *U.S. Public,* pg. 827

HILB, ROGAL AND HAMILTON COMPANY OF FORT LAUDERDALE—See Hilb, Rogal and Hamilton Company; *U.S. Public,* pg. 827

HILB, ROGAL & HAMILTON COMPANY OF MCALLEN—See Hilb, Rogal and Hamilton Company; *U.S. Public,* pg. 827

HILB, ROGAL AND HAMILTON COMPANY OF PORT HURON—See Hilb, Rogal and Hamilton Company; *U.S. Public,* pg. 827

HILB, ROGAL & HAMILTON COMPANY OF THE QUAD CITIES—See Hilb, Rogal and Hamilton Company; *U.S. Public,* pg. 827

HILB, ROGAL AND HAMILTON INSURANCE SERVICES OF ORANGE COUNTY, INC.—See Hilb, Rogal and Hamilton Company; *U.S. Public,* pg. 827

HILB, ROGAL AND HAMILTON INSURANCE SERVICES OF CENTRAL CALIFORNIA, INC.—See Hilb, Rogal and Hamilton Company; *U.S. Public,* pg. 827

HILCO, INC.—See Bank of Ireland; *Int'l,* pg. 153

HILDEGUND LTD.—See Commerzbank AG; *Int'l,* pg. 312

HILER INDUSTRIES; *U.S. Private,* pg. 529

HILL & GRIFFITH COMPANY; *U.S. Private,* pg. 529

HILL AND KNOWLTON, INC.—See WPP Group plc; *Int'l,* pg. 1483

HILL & WANG—See Georg von Holtzbrinck GmbH; *Int'l,* pg. 1479

HILL-BEHAN LUMBER COMPANY; *U.S. Private,* pg. 529

HILL GRAHAM CONTROLS—See IRI Istituto Ricostruzione Industriale; *Int'l,* pg. 654

HILL, HOLIDAY, CONNORS, COSMOPULOS, INC.—See Hill, Holliday, Connors, Cosmopulos, Inc.; *U.S. Private,* pg. 529

HILL, HOLLIDAY/ALTSCHILLER—See Hill, Holliday, Connors, Cosmopulos, Inc.; *U.S. Private,* pg. 529

HILL, HOLLIDAY, CONNORS, COSMOPULOS, INC.; *U.S. Private,* pg. 529

HILL INTERNATIONAL INC.; *U.S. Private,* pg. 529

HILL-LOMA, INC.—See Golden Corporation Group; *U.S. Private,* pg. 461

HILL PHOENIX—See Dover Corporation; *U.S. Public,* pg. 521

HILL-ROM COMPANY, INC.—See Hillenbrand Industries, Inc.; *U.S. Public,* pg. 828

HILL-ROM/LE COUVIOUR S.A.—See Hillenbrand Industries, Inc.; *U.S. Public,* pg. 828

HILL SAMUEL INC.—See Lloyds TSB Group PLC; *Int'l,* pg. 813

HILL SAMUEL INTERNATIONAL BANKING CORP.—See Lloyds TSB Group PLC; *Int'l,* pg. 813

HILLAND DAIRY COMPANY—See Prairie Farms Dairy, Inc.; *U.S. Private,* pg. 879

HILLARD SCOTCHBROOK COMMUNICATIONS PTE. LTD.—See Fleishman-Hillard Inc.; *U.S. Private,* pg. 411

HILLCREST CENTER—See Genesis Health Ventures, Inc.; *U.S. Public,* pg. 729

HILLCREST HEALTH CARE, INC.—See Vencor, Inc.; *U.S. Public,* pg. 1713

HILLCROSS PHARMACEUTICALS—See Franz Haniel & Cie, GmbH; *Int'l,* pg. 591

HILLE & MULLER—See Koninklijke Hoogovens N.V.; *Int'l,* pg. 754

HILLE HANDEL GMBH—See Mannesmann A.G.; *Int'l,* pg. 838

HILLEN & ROOSEN B.V.—See Philipp Holzmann AG; *Int'l*, pg. 633
HILLENBRAND INDUSTRIES, INC.; *U.S. Public*, pg. 828
HILLERICH & BRADSBY CO.; *U.S. Private*, pg. 530
HILLESHOG AB—See Novartis AG; *Int'l*, pg. 982
HILLESHOG FORESTRY AB—See Novartis AG; *Int'l*, pg. 982
HILLESHOG G.M.B.H.—See Novartis AG; *Int'l*, pg. 973
HILLESHOG MONO-HY INC.—See Novartis AG; *Int'l*, pg. 982
HILLESHOG NK S.A.—See Novartis AG; *Int'l*, pg. 982
HILLESHOG NK S.P.A.—See Novartis AG; *Int'l*, pg. 982
HILLESHOG RESEARCH AB—See Novartis AG; *Int'l*, pg. 982
HILLESHOG SKOGAR AB—See Novartis AG; *Int'l*, pg. 982
HILLESHOG SUGAR BEET SEED AB—See Novartis AG; *Int'l*, pg. 982
HILLHAVEN EXTENDED CARE—See Vencor, Inc.; *U.S. Public*, pg. 1713
HILLHAVEN HEALTHCARE, PHOENIX—See Vencor, Inc.; *U.S. Public*, pg. 1713
HILLHAVEN HIGHLAND HOUSE—See Vencor, Inc.; *U.S. Public*, pg. 1713
HILLHAVEN-LASALLE NURSING CENTER—See Vencor, Inc.; *U.S. Public*, pg. 1713
HILLHAVEN REHABILITATION & CONVALESCENT HOSPITAL—See Vencor, Inc.; *U.S. Public*, pg. 1713
HILLIARD CORPORATION; *U.S. Private*, pg. 530
THE HILLMAN COMPANY; *U.S. Private*, pg. 530
HILLS COLGATE JAPAN LTD.—See Colgate-Palmolive Company; *U.S. Public*, pg. 399
HILLS DEPARTMENT STORE COMPANY—See Hills Stores Co.; *U.S. Public*, pg. 828
HILLS MATERIALS CO.—See Northwestern Engineering Co.; *U.S. Private*, pg. 806
HILL'S PET NUTRITION—See Colgate-Palmolive Company; *U.S. Public*, pg. 397
HILLS PHARMACEUTICALS—See Franz Haniel & Cie, GmbH; *Int'l*, pg. 591
HILLS PRECISION COMPONENTS LTD.—See PSA Peugeot Citroen; *int'l*, pg. 1021
HILLS STORES CO.; *U.S. Public*, pg. 828
THE HILLS—See Paragon Health Network, Inc.; *U.S. Public*, pg. 1257
HILLSDALE DAILY NEWS—See Shivers Trading & Operating Co.; *U.S. Private*, pg. 995
HILLSDALE TOOL & MFG. CO.—See Eagle-Picher Industries, Inc.; *U.S. Private*, pg. 355
HILLSDOWN HOLDINGS PLC; *Int'l*, pg. 619
HILLSDOWN LTD.—See Hillsdown Holdings Plc; *Int'l*, pg. 619
HILLSHIRE FARM & KAHN'S—See Sara Lee Corporation; *U.S. Public*, pg. 1433
HILLSHIRE FARM COMPANY—See Sara Lee Corporation; *U.S. Public*, pg. 1433
HILLSHOG ESPAÑOLA S.A.—See Novartis AG; *Int'l*, pg. 982
HILLSHOG HOLLAND B.V.—See Novartis AG; *Int'l*, pg. 982
HILLSHOG (UNITED KINGDOM) LTD.—See Novartis AG; *Int'l*, pg. 346
HILLSIDE CAPITAL INCORPORATED; *U.S. Private*, pg. 530
HILLSIDE INDUSTRIES, INC.—See Hillside Capital Incorporated; *U.S. Private*, pg. 530
HILLSIDE MANOR CONVALESCENT HOSPITAL—See Vencor, Inc.; *U.S. Public*, pg. 1714
HILLTOP VILLAGE—See Paragon Health Network, Inc.; *U.S. Public*, pg. 1257
HILOS MAGIC H.M. DE VENEZUELA CA—See Mantex, S.A.C.A.; *Int'l*, pg. 840
HILROY—See Abitibi-Consolidated Inc.; *Int'l*, pg. 20
THE HILSINGER CO. L.P.; *U.S. Private*, pg. 530
HILTI AG; *Int'l*, pg. 619
HILTI INC.—See Hilti AG; *Int'l*, pg. 620
HILTI LATIN AMERICA—See Hilti AG; *Int'l*, pg. 620
HILTON ACTIVE APPAREL—See K2 Inc.; *U.S. Public*, pg. 940
HILTON CANADA INC.—See Ladbroke Group Plc; *Int'l*, pg. 788
HILTON EQUIPMENT CORP.—See Hilton Hotels Corporation; *U.S. Public*, pg. 829
HILTON HEAD ISLAND PACKET—See McClatchy Newspapers Inc.; *U.S. Public*, pg. 1065
HILTON HOTELS CORPORATION; *U.S. Public*, pg. 828
HILTON HOTELS, GAMING DIV.—See Hilton Hotels Corporation; *U.S. Public*, pg. 829
HILTON INNS, INC.—See Hilton Hotels Corporation; *U.S. Public*, pg. 829
HILTON INTERNATIONAL CO.—See Ladbroke Group Plc; *Int'l*, pg. 787
HILTON INTERNATIONAL HOTELS (U.K.) LTD.—See Ladbroke Group Plc; *Int'l*, pg. 787
HILTON INTERNATIONAL (SWITZERLAND) AG—See Ladbroke Group Plc; *Int'l*, pg. 788
HILTON RESERVATIONS WORLDWIDE—See Hilton Hotels Corporation; *U.S. Public*, pg. 829
HILTON WORKS—See Stelco Inc.; *Int'l*, pg. 1299
HIMEJI ASAHI ORIKOMI CENTER, LTD.—See Daiko Advertising, Inc.; *Int'l*, pg. 366
HIMEJI TOSHIBA E.P. CORPORATION—See Toshiba Corporation; *Int'l*, pg. 1402
HIMMELWERK GMBH & CO.—See Deutsche Babcock AG; *Int'l*, pg. 400
HIMOLENE CORP.—See First Brands Corporation; *U.S. Public*, pg. 627
HINCKLEY & SCHMITT, INC.—See Suntory Ltd.; *Int'l*, pg. 1322
HINDERLITER HEAT TREATING, INC.; *U.S. Private*, pg. 530
HINDITRON TEKTRONIX INSTRUMENTS LTD.—See Tektronix, Inc.; *U.S. Public*, pg. 1568
HINDITRON TEKTRONIX INSTRUMENTS LTD.-BANGALORE—See Tektronix, Inc.; *U.S. Public*, pg. 1568

HINDITRON TEKTRONIX INSTRUMENTS LTD.-BOMBAY—See Tektronix, Inc.; *U.S. Public*, pg. 1568
HINDITRON TEKTRONIX INSTRUMENTS LTD.-CALCUTTA—See Tektronix, Inc.; *U.S. Public*, pg. 1568
HINDITRON TEKTRONIX INSTRUMENTS LTD.-MADRAS—See Tektronix, Inc.; *U.S. Public*, pg. 1568
HINDITRON TEKTRONIX INSTRUMENTS LTD.-SECUNDERABAD—See Tektronix, Inc.; *U.S. Public*, pg. 1568
HINDUSTAN CIBA-GEIGY LIMITED—See Novartis AG; *Int'l*, pg. 982
HINDUSTAN CIBA-GEIGY LIMITED-ANIMAL HEALTH DIVISION—See Novartis AG; *Int'l*, pg. 982
HINDUSTAN CIBA-GEIGY LIMITED-RESEARCH CENTRE—See Novartis AG; *Int'l*, pg. 982
HINDUSTAN CIBA-GEIGY LIMITED—See Novartis AG; *Int'l*, pg. 982
HINDUSTAN GUM & CHEMICALS LTD.—See Rhone-Poulenc S.A.; *Int'l*, pg. 1113
HINDUSTAN LEVER LTD.—See Unilever Plc; *Int'l*, pg. 1437
HINDUSTAN POWERPLUS LIMITED—See Caterpillar Inc.; *U.S. Public*, pg. 316
HINE PACIFIC—See LVMH Moet Hennessy Louis Vuitton; *Int'l*, pg. 782
THOMAS HINE & CIE—See LVMH Moet Hennessy Louis Vuitton; *Int'l*, pg. 780
HINE U.K.—See LVMH Moet Hennessy Louis Vuitton; *Int'l*, pg. 782
EDWARD HINES LUMBER CO.; *U.S. Private*, pg. 530
HINES-PARK FOODS, INC.—See The Procter & Gamble Company; *U.S. Public*, pg. 1331
HINGHAM MARINER—See Gannett Company, Inc.; *U.S. Public*, pg. 701
HINIKER COMPANY; *U.S. Private*, pg. 530
HINKLE EASTER PRODUCTS—See Life-Like Products, Inc.; *U.S. Private*, pg. 666
HINKLEY LIGHTING INC.; *U.S. Private*, pg. 530
HINO DIESEL TRUCKS (U.S.A.), INC.—See Hino Motors, Ltd.; *Int'l*, pg. 620
HINO MOTORS, LTD.; *Int'l*, pg. 620
HIPOTEBANSA—See Banco Santander; *Int'l*, pg. 143
HIPOTRONICS, INC.—See Hubbell Incorporated; *U.S. Public*, pg. 844
HIPPOCRENE HOLDINGS—See Pegasus Gold Corporation; *U.S. Public*, pg. 1269
HIRAKAWA SINGAPORE PTE. LTD.—See The Furukawa Electric Co., Ltd.; *Int'l*, pg. 531
HIRAM WALKER—See Allied Domecq PLC; *Int'l*, pg. 63
HIRAM WALKER & SONS LIMITED—See Allied Domecq PLC; *Int'l*, pg. 63
HIRANO PLANT—See Sharp Corporation; *Int'l*, pg. 1228
HIRAYAMA MANUFACTURING LTD.—See Sulzer Ltd.; *Int'l*, pg. 1306
HIROCEM A.S.—See Holderbank Financiere Glaris Ltd.; *Int'l*, pg. 629
HIROSAKI SEIKI, INC.—See Canon Inc.; *Int'l*, pg. 261
HIROSE CHERRY PRECISION COMPANY LTD.—See Cherry Electrical Products Corporation; *U.S. Public*, pg. 346
HIROSE ELECTRIC CO., LTD.; *Int'l*, pg. 620
HIROSE ELECTRIC GMBH—See Hirose Electric Co., Ltd.; *Int'l*, pg. 620
HIROSE ELECTRIC UK LTD.—See Hirose Electric Co., Ltd.; *Int'l*, pg. 620
HIROSE ELECTRIC (U.S.A.), INC.—See Hirose Electric Co., Ltd.; *Int'l*, pg. 620
HIROSE KOREA CO. LTD.—See Hirose Electric Co., Ltd.; *Int'l*, pg. 620
THE HIROSHIMA BANK, LTD.; *Int'l*, pg. 620
HIRSCH INTERNATIONAL CORP.; *U.S. Public*, pg. 829
WALTER HIRSCH ADM—See BASF AG; *Int'l*, pg. 108
HIRSCHFELD, INC.; *U.S. Private*, pg. 530
HIRSCHFELD STEEL COMPANY, INC.—See Hirschfeld, Inc.; *U.S. Private*, pg. 531
HIRSCHMANN ESPANA S.A.—See Rheinmetall Group; *Int'l*, pg. 1108
R. HIRSCHMANN ELECTRONICS UK LTD.—See Rheinmetall Group; *Int'l*, pg. 1108
RICHARD HIRSCHMANN ÉLECTRONIQUE SA—See Rheinmetall Group; *Int'l*, pg. 1108
RICHARD HIRSCHMANN GMBH & CO.—See Rheinmetall Group; *Int'l*, pg. 1108
RICHARD HIRSCHMANN OF AMERICA, INC.—See Rheinmetall Group; *Int'l*, pg. 1108
HIRSH COMPANY—See Knape & Vogt Mfg. Co.; *U.S. Public*, pg. 963
HIRST RESEARCH CENTRE—See The General Electric Company, p.l.c.; *Int'l*, pg. 544
HIRTLER GMBH—See Beiersdorf Group; *Int'l*, pg. 182
HISPACEMENT S.A.—See Lafarge S.A.; *Int'l*, pg. 790
HISPALAND, S.A.—See Vallehermoso, S.A.; *Int'l*, pg. 1447
HISPAN CORP.—See Hercules Incorporated; *U.S. Public*, pg. 810
HISPANO COMMERZBANK (GIBRALTAR LTD.)—See Banco Central Hispanoamericano S.A.; *Int'l*, pg. 140
HISPANO COMMERZBANK (GIBRALTAR LTD.)—See Commerzbank AG; *Int'l*, pg. 312
HISPANO OLIVETTI OFFICE—See Olivetti SpA; *Int'l*, pg. 1003
HISPANO SUECA DE SOLDADURA S.A. (HISSOL)—See Charter plc; *Int'l*, pg. 283
HISPANO-SUIZA S.A.—See SNECMA - Societe Nationale d'Etude et de Construction de Moteurs d'Aviation; *Int'l*, pg. 1165
HISPANO-SUIZA DO BRASIL EQUIPAMENTOS LIMITADA—See SNECMA - Societe Nationale d'Etude et de Construction de Moteurs d'Aviation; *Int'l*, pg. 1165
HISPASAT, S.A.—See Telefonica de Espana, S.A.; *Int'l*, pg. 1372
HISPAVIC INDUSTRIAL S.A.—See Solvay S.A.; *Int'l*, pg. 1278
HISSI-ALA OY—See Kone Corporation; *Int'l*, pg. 746

HISTOCENTER-SKANDINAVISKT CENTRUM FOR HISTOTEKNIK AB—See Axel Johnson AB; *Int'l*, pg. 708
HISTORY BOOK CLUB, INC.—See Time Warner Inc.; *U.S. Public*, pg. 1612
THE HISTORY CHANNEL—See The Walt Disney Company; *U.S. Public*, pg. 512
HIT OR MISS, INC.; *U.S. Private*, pg. 531
HIT PROMOTIONAL PRODUCTS INC.—See Cosco Industries; *U.S. Private*, pg. 277
HIT UNION COMPANY LTD.; *Int'l*, pg. 620
HITACHI AMERICA, LTD.—See Hitachi, Ltd.; *Int'l*, pg. 622
HITACHI-BORDEN CHEMICAL PRODUCTS, INC.—See AEP Industries, Inc.; *U.S. Public*, pg. 5
HITACHI-BORDEN CHEMICAL PRODUCTS, INC.—See Hitachi, Ltd.; *Int'l*, pg. 622
HITACHI CABLE, LTD.—See Hitachi, Ltd.; *Int'l*, pg. 621
HITACHI CHEMICAL CO. AMERICA LTD.—See Hitachi, Ltd.; *Int'l*, pg. 622
HITACHI CHEMICAL CO., LTD.—See Hitachi, Ltd.; *Int'l*, pg. 621
HITACHI CONSTRUCTION MACHINERY CO., LTD.—See Hitachi, Ltd.; *Int'l*, pg. 621
HITACHI CONSUMER PRODUCTS DE MEXICO—See Hitachi, Ltd.; *Int'l*, pg. 622
HITACHI CONSUMER PRODUCTS OF AMERICA, INC.—See Hitachi, Ltd.; *Int'l*, pg. 622
HITACHI DATA SYSTEMS CORPORATION—See Hitachi, Ltd.; *Int'l*, pg. 622
HITACHI DATA SYSTEMS INC.—See Hitachi, Ltd.; *Int'l*, pg. 622
HITACHI DATA SYSTEMS INC.—See Sand Technology Systems; *Int'l*, pg. 1184
HITACHI DENSHI, LTD.—See Hitachi, Ltd.; *Int'l*, pg. 621
HITACHI ELECTRONICS ENGINEERING CO., LTD.—See Hitachi, Ltd.; *Int'l*, pg. 621
HITACHI HEATING APPLIANCES CO., LTD.—See Hitachi, Ltd.; *Int'l*, pg. 621
HITACHI HOME ELECTRONICS—See Hitachi, Ltd.; *Int'l*, pg. 621
HITACHI HOME ELECTRONICS (AMERICA) INC.—See Hitachi, Ltd.; *Int'l*, pg. 622
HITACHI HOME ELECTRONICS, EASTERN REGION—See Hitachi, Ltd.; *Int'l*, pg. 622
HITACHI HOME ELECTRONICS, WESTERN REGION—See Hitachi, Ltd.; *Int'l*, pg. 622
HITACHI INSTRUMENTS, INC.—See Hitachi, Ltd.; *Int'l*, pg. 622
HITACHI KENKI DYNAPAC KK—See Trelleborg AB; *Int'l*, pg. 1420
HITACHI KIDEN KOGYO, LTD.—See Hitachi, Ltd.; *Int'l*, pg. 621
HITACHI KOKI CO., LTD.; *Int'l*, pg. 620
HITACHI KOKI U.S.A. LTD.—See Hitachi Koki Co., Ltd.; *Int'l*, pg. 620
HITACHI LIGHTING, LTD.—See Hitachi, Ltd.; *Int'l*, pg. 621
HITACHI, LTD.; *Int'l*, pg. 621
HITACHI MACHINERY & ENGINEERING, LTD.—See Hitachi, Ltd.; *Int'l*, pg. 621
HITACHI MAXELL, LTD.—See Hitachi, Ltd.; *Int'l*, pg. 621
HITACHI MEDICAL CORPORATION—See Hitachi, Ltd.; *Int'l*, pg. 621
HITACHI METALS, LTD.—See Hitachi, Ltd.; *Int'l*, pg. 621
HITACHI OHIRA INDUSTRIAL CO., LTD.—See Hitachi, Ltd.; *Int'l*, pg. 621
HITACHI POWER ENGINEERING CO., LTD.—See Hitachi, Ltd.; *Int'l*, pg. 621
HITACHI SALES CORP.—See Hitachi, Ltd.; *Int'l*, pg. 622
HITACHI SEIKO, LTD.—See Hitachi, Ltd.; *Int'l*, pg. 622
HITACHI SEMICONDUCTOR (AMERICA), INC.—See Hitachi, Ltd.; *Int'l*, pg. 622
HITACHI TELECOM TECHNOLOGIES CO., LTD.—See Hitachi, Ltd.; *Int'l*, pg. 622
HITACHI TELEVISION (TAIWAN) LTD.—See Hitachi, Ltd.; *Int'l*, pg. 622
HITACHI ZONSEN TOKYO—See Hitachi Zosen Corporation; *Int'l*, pg. 622
HITACHI ZOSEN BANGKOK—See Hitachi Zosen Corporation; *Int'l*, pg. 623
HITACHI ZOSEN BEIJING—See Hitachi Zosen Corporation; *Int'l*, pg. 623
HITACHI ZOSEN CHIKKO—See Hitachi Zosen Corporation; *Int'l*, pg. 623
HITACHI ZOSEN COMPANY (HK), LTD.—See Hitachi Zosen Corporation; *Int'l*, pg. 623
HITACHI ZOSEN CORPORATION; *Int'l*, pg. 622
HITACHI ZOSEN DUSSELDORF—See Hitachi Zosen Corporation; *Int'l*, pg. 623
HITACHI ZOSEN ENGINEERING SINGAPORE (PTE.) LTD.—See Hitachi Zosen Corporation; *Int'l*, pg. 623
HITACHI ZOSEN EUROPE LTD.—See Hitachi Zosen Corporation; *Int'l*, pg. 623
HITACHI ZOSEN FUKUOKA—See Hitachi Zosen Corporation; *Int'l*, pg. 623
HITACHI ZOSEN HIROSHIMA—See Hitachi Zosen Corporation; *Int'l*, pg. 623
HITACHI ZOSEN HO CHI MINH CITY OFFICE—See Hitachi Zosen Corporation; *Int'l*, pg. 623
HITACHI ZOSEN JAKARTA—See Hitachi Zosen Corporation; *Int'l*, pg. 623
HITACHI ZOSEN KOBE—See Hitachi Zosen Corporation; *Int'l*, pg. 623
HITACHI ZOSEN METALMECANICA LTDA.—See Nissho Iwai Corporation; *Int'l*, pg. 947
HITACHI ZOSEN NAGOYA—See Hitachi Zosen Corporation; *Int'l*, pg. 623
HITACHI ZOSEN NIIGATA—See Hitachi Zosen Corporation; *Int'l*, pg. 623
HITACHI ZOSEN SAPPORO—See Hitachi Zosen Corporation; *Int'l*, pg. 622
HITACHI ZOSEN SENDAI—See Hitachi Zosen Corporation; *Int'l*, pg. 622
HITACHI ZOSEN SEOUL—See Hitachi Zosen Corporation; *Int'l*, pg. 623

Company Index

HITACHI ZOSEN SHANGHAI—See Hitachi Zosen Corporation; *Int'l*, pg. 623
HITACHI ZOSEN SINGAPORE LIMITED—See Hitachi Zosen Corporation; *Int'l*, pg. 623
HITACHI ZOSEN SYSTEMS, INC—See Effective Management Systems; *U.S. Public*, pg. 566
HITACHI ZOSEN TAIWAN OFFICE—See Hitachi Zosen Corporation; *Int'l*, pg. 623
HITACHI ZOSEN TAKAMATSU—See Hitachi Zosen Corporation; *Int'l*, pg. 622
HITACHI ZOSEN U.S.A. LTD.—See Hitachi Zosen Corporation; *Int'l*, pg. 623
HITACHI ZOSEN U.S.A. LTD.-CHICAGO—See Hitachi Zosen Corporation; *Int'l*, pg. 623
HITCHCOCK AUTOMOTIVE RESOURCES; *U.S. Private*, pg. 531
HITCHCOCK CHAIR COMPANY LTD; *U.S. Private*, pg. 531
HITCHCOCK INDUSTRIES, INC.; *U.S. Private*, pg. 531
HITCHINER MANUFACTURING COMPANY, INC.; *U.S. Private*, pg. 531
HITCO—See John Hassall, Inc.; *U.S. Private*, pg. 509
THE HITE COMPANY; *U.S. Private*, pg. 531
HITEK PRODUCT FINISHING, INC.—See Cowden Metal Specialties, Inc.; *U.S. Private*, pg. 280
HITMA BV—See AB Industrivarden; *Int'l*, pg. 678
HITOX CORPORATION OF AMERICA; *U.S. Public*, pg. 829
HIVEC-IRELAND—See High Voltage Engineering Corporation; *U.S. Private*, pg. 528
H.J. HEINZ COMPANY C.I.S.—See H.J. Heinz Company; *U.S. Public*, pg. 806
H.J. HEINZ FOODSERVICE—See H.J. Heinz Company; *U.S. Public*, pg. 806
H.J. HEINZ NORTHERN EUROPE—See H.J. Heinz Company; *U.S. Public*, pg. 806
HO CHI MINH CITY REPRESENTATIVE OFFICE—See The Asahi Bank, Ltd.; *Int'l*, pg. 83
HO CHI MINH REPRESENTATIVE OFFICE—See The Fuji Bank, Limited; *Int'l*, pg. 520
HOAK CAPITAL; *U.S. Private*, pg. 531
HOARE GOVETT LIMITED—See BankAmerica Corporation; *U.S. Public*, pg. 183
HOBAN FOODS, INC.; *U.S. Private*, pg. 531
HOBART BREWERY—See Foster's Brewing Group Limited; *Int'l*, pg. 501
HOBART BROTHERS CO.—See Illinois Tool Works Inc.; *U.S. Public*, pg. 866
HOBART CORPORATION—See Premark International, Inc.; *U.S. Public*, pg. 1322
HOBART/MCINTOSH PAPER COMPANY—See Amer Group Ltd.; *Int'l*, pg. 72
HOBBS CORPORATION—See BTR plc; *Int'l*, pg. 127
HOBBS HEALTHCARE CENTER—See Horizon/CMS Healthcare Corporation; *U.S. Public*, pg. 838
HOBBY HALL—See OY Stockmann AB; *Int'l*, pg. 1301
HOBIE CAT COMPANY; *U.S. Private*, pg. 531
HOBOKEN FLOORS-A.S.T. DIVISION—See Hoboken Wood Flooring Corporation; *U.S. Private*, pg. 532
HOBOKEN FLOORS-ADIRONDACK DIVISION—See Hoboken Wood Flooring Corporation; *U.S. Private*, pg. 532
HOBOKEN FLOORS-CAPITOL DIVISION—See Hoboken Wood Flooring Corporation; *U.S. Private*, pg. 532
HOBOKEN FLOORS-CONNECTICUT DIV.—See Hoboken Wood Flooring Corporation; *U.S. Private*, pg. 532
HOBOKEN FLOORS-EASTERN FLOORING DIVISION—See Hoboken Wood Flooring Corporation; *U.S. Private*, pg. 532
HOBOKEN FLOORS-NEW ENGLAND DIVISION—See Hoboken Wood Flooring Corporation; *U.S. Private*, pg. 532
HOBOKEN WOOD FLOORING CORPORATION; *U.S. Private*, pg. 532
HOBOURN AUTOMOTIVE LIMITED—See Echlin Inc.; *U.S. Public*, pg. 561
HOBOURN-EATON STEERING LTD.—See Eaton Corporation; *U.S. Public*, pg. 559
HOCHBAU HALLE-SEEBEN GMBH—See Bilfinger + Berger Bauaktiengesellschaft; *Int'l*, pg. 195
HOCHE FRIEDLAND—See C.E.P. Communication Group; *Int'l*, pg. 239
HOCHIKI AMERICA CORPORATION—See Hochiki Corporation; *Int'l*, pg. 623
HOCHIKI CORPORATION; *Int'l*, pg. 623
HOCHIKI EUROPE U.K. LTD.—See Hochiki Corporation; *Int'l*, pg. 623
HOCHTEMPERATUR-REAKTORBAU GMBH—See ABB Asea Brown Boveri (Holding) Ltd.; *Int'l*, pg. 2
HOCHTIEF AG; *Int'l*, pg. 623
HOCHTIEF AKTIENGESELLSCHAFT VORM. GEBR. HELFMANN GES.M.B.H.—See Hochtief AG; *Int'l*, pg. 624
HOCHTIEF LIMITED—See Hochtief AG; *Int'l*, pg. 624
BERNARD HODES GROUP—See Omnicom Group Inc.; *U.S. Public*, pg. 1224
HODGES DIVISION—See Leggett & Platt, Incorporated; *U.S. Public*, pg. 985
HODGSON MILL, INC.—See Siemer Milling Company; *U.S. Private*, pg. 998
HODIOS (IRELAND) LTD.—See Proventus AB; *Int'l*, pg. 1072
HOECHST AKTIENGESELLSCHAFT; *Int'l*, pg. 624
HOECHST AUSTRALIA LTD.—See Hoechst Aktiengesellschaft; *Int'l*, pg. 626
HOECHST CELANESE ADVANCED MATERIALS—See Hoechst Aktiengesellschaft; *Int'l*, pg. 624
HOECHST CELANESE ADVANCED TECHNOLOGY—See Hoechst Aktiengesellschaft; *Int'l*, pg. 625
HOECHST CELANESE CORP. SPUNBOND PRODUCTS—See Hoechst Aktiengesellschaft; *Int'l*, pg. 626
HOECHST CELANESE FILM & FIBER INTERMEDIATES GROUP—See Hoechst Aktiengesellschaft; *Int'l*, pg. 626

HOECHST-MARION-ROUSELL—See Hoechst Aktiengesellschaft; *Int'l*, pg. 625
HOECHST MARION ROUSSEL AG—See Hoechst Aktiengesellschaft; *Int'l*, pg. 624
HOECHST MARION ROUSSEL, INC.—See Hoechst Aktiengesellschaft; *Int'l*, pg. 624
HOECHST MARION ROUSSEL ITALY—See Hoechst Aktiengesellschaft; *Int'l*, pg. 625
HOECHST MARION ROUSSEL NORTH AMERICA—See Hoechst Aktiengesellschaft; *Int'l*, pg. 625
HOECHST MARION ROUSSEL RESEARCH—See Hoechst Aktiengesellschaft; *Int'l*, pg. 625
HOECHST-PERSTORP AB—See Perstorp AB; *Int'l*, pg. 1039
HOECHST ROUSSEL VET GMBH—See Hoechst Aktiengesellschaft; *Int'l*, pg. 626
HOECHST SPECIALTY PRODUCTS GROUP—See Hoechst Aktiengesellschaft; *Int'l*, pg. 625
HOECHST TRESPAPHAN—See Courtaulds plc; *Int'l*, pg. 339
HOECHST TRESPAPHAN—See Hoechst Aktiengesellschaft; *Int'l*, pg. 624
HOECHST TREVIRA GMBH & CO. KG—See Hoechst Aktiengesellschaft; *Int'l*, pg. 626
HOECHST VETERINAR GMBH—See Hoechst Aktiengesellschaft; *Int'l*, pg. 626
HOECHSTETTER PRINTING COMPANY, INC.—See Wallace Computer Services, Inc.; *U.S. Public*, pg. 1735
HOEGANAES CORP.—See The Interlake Corporation; *U.S. Public*, pg. 893
HOEI ELECTRONICS (S) PRIVATE LTD.—See Fuji Electric Co., Ltd.; *Int'l*, pg. 522
HOEK LOOS NV—See Linde AG; *Int'l*, pg. 811
NV W.A. HOEK'S MACHINE- EN ZUURSTOFFABRIEK—See Linde AG; *Int'l*, pg. 811
HOESCH ARGENTINA S.A.I.Y.C.—See Fried. Krupp AG; *Int'l*, pg. 508
HOESCH BAUSYSTEME GMBH—See Fried. Krupp AG; *Int'l*, pg. 508
HOESCH FEDERN GMBH—See Fried. Krupp AG; *Int'l*, pg. 508
HOESCH HOHENLIMBURG GMBH—See Fried. Krupp AG; *Int'l*, pg. 508
HOESCH INDUSTRIA DE MOLAS LTDA.—See Fried. Krupp AG; *Int'l*, pg. 508
HOESCH INDUSTRIA ESPANOLA DE SUSPENSIONES S.A.—See Fried. Krupp AG; *Int'l*, pg. 508
HOESCH LIMITED—See Fried. Krupp AG; *Int'l*, pg. 515
HOESCH PLATINEN GMBH—See Fried. Krupp AG; *Int'l*, pg. 512
HOESCH RENOVA GMBH—See Fried. Krupp AG; *Int'l*, pg. 508
HOESCH ROTHE ERDE AG—See Fried. Krupp AG; *Int'l*, pg. 509
HOESCH ROTHE ERDE GESELLSCHAFT—See Fried. Krupp AG; *Int'l*, pg. 509
HOESCH ROTHE ERDE GMBH—See Fried. Krupp AG; *Int'l*, pg. 509
HOESCH SIEGERLANDWERKE GMBH—See Fried. Krupp AG; *Int'l*, pg. 508
HOESCH SPUNDWAND UND PROFIL GMBH—See Fried. Krupp AG; *Int'l*, pg. 512
HOESCH STAHLHANDEL GMBH—See Fried. Krupp AG; *Int'l*, pg. 515
HOESCH SUSPENSIONES AUTOMOTRICES S.A. DE C.V.—See Fried. Krupp AG; *Int'l*, pg. 508
HOESCH SUSPENSIONS INC.—See Fried. Krupp AG; *Int'l*, pg. 508
HOESCH SYSTEMES BATIMENT S.A.R.L.—See Fried. Krupp AG; *Int'l*, pg. 508
HOESCH WOODHEAD LTD.—See Fried. Krupp AG; *Int'l*, pg. 508
HOF TEXTILES INC.—See Neuebaum Woll-Spinnerei Und Weberei Hof A.G.; *Int'l*, pg. 923
HOFFCO/COMET INDUSTRIES, INC.; *U.S. Private*, pg. 532
HOFFER PLASTICS CORPORATION; *U.S. Private*, pg. 532
HOFFER'S GLASS FAB—See The Churchill Companies; *U.S. Private*, pg. 239
HOFFER'S INC.—See The Churchill Companies; *U.S. Private*, pg. 239
A.H. HOFFMAN, INC.; *U.S. Private*, pg. 532
HOFFMAN CONSTRUCTION COMPANY OF ALASKA—See Hoffman Corporation; *U.S. Private*, pg. 532
HOFFMAN CONSTRUCTION COMPANY OF OREGON—See Hoffman Corporation; *U.S. Private*, pg. 532
HOFFMAN CONSTRUCTION COMPANY OF WASHINGTON—See Hoffman Corporation; *U.S. Private*, pg. 532
HOFFMAN CORPORATION; *U.S. Private*, pg. 532
HOFFMAN ENGINEERING COMPANY—See Pentair, Inc.; *U.S. Public*, pg. 1273
HOFFMAN IMPORT AND DISTRIBUTION COMPANY—See The Jaydor Corporation; *U.S. Private*, pg. 584
HOFFMAN LACES, LTD.—See Guilford Mills, Inc.; *U.S. Public*, pg. 769
HOFFMAN/LEWIS; *U.S. Private*, pg. 532
HOFFMAN MECHANICAL CORPORATION—See Hoffman Corporation; *U.S. Private*, pg. 532
HOFFMAN-MILLER ENGINEERS, INC.—See Parsons Corporation; *U.S. Private*, pg. 842
HOFFMAN PRODUCTS—See Premier Farnell plc; *Int'l*, pg. 1068
HOFFMAN SEEDS, INC.—See A.H. Hoffman, Inc.; *U.S. Private*, pg. 532
HOFFMAN STRUCTURES, INC.—See Hoffman Corporation; *U.S. Private*, pg. 532
HOFFMANN-LA ROCHE AG—See Roche Holding Ltd.; *Int'l*, pg. 1121
F. HOFFMANN-LA ROCHE LTD.—See Roche Holding Ltd.; *Int'l*, pg. 1119
HOFFMANN-LA ROCHE INC.—See Roche Holding Ltd.; *Int'l*, pg. 1120

HOFFMANN-LA ROCHE LTD.—See Roche Holding Ltd.; *Int'l*, pg. 1121
HOFFMANN-LA ROCHE WIEN GMBH—See Roche Holding Ltd.; *Int'l*, pg. 1121
HOFLEY MANUFACTURING COMPANY; *U.S. Private*, pg. 532
HOFMANN INDUSTRIES, INC.; *U.S. Private*, pg. 533
HOGAMED S.A.—See Incentive AB; *Int'l*, pg. 668
HOGAN SYSTEMS AUSTRALIA—See Computer Sciences Corporation; *U.S. Public*, pg. 422
HOGAN SYSTEMS EUROPE—See Computer Sciences Corporation; *U.S. Public*, pg. 422
HOGAN SYSTEMS, INC.—See Computer Sciences Corporation; *U.S. Public*, pg. 422
MICHAEL HOGG-YOUNG & RUBICAM (PVT.) LTD.—See Young & Rubicam Inc.; *U.S. Private*, pg. 1198
HOGLA-KIMBERLY LTD.—See American Israeli Paper Mills Ltd.; *Int'l*, pg. 75
HOGLA-KIMBERLY LTD.—See Kimberly-Clark Corporation; *U.S. Public*, pg. 959
GUNNAR F. HOGLUND AB—See Axel Johnson AB; *Int'l*, pg. 708
HOHENBERG BROS. COMPANY—See Cargill; *U.S. Private*, pg. 210
HOHN & HOHN GMBH—See American Home Products Corporation; *U.S. Public*, pg. 81
HOHNER/HSS INC.; *U.S. Private*, pg. 533
HOKKAIDO AMADA CO., LTD.—See Amada Co., Ltd.; *Int'l*, pg. 70
HOKKAIDO CATERPILLAR MITSUBISHI CONSTRUCTION EQUIPMENT SALES, MITSUBISHI—See Caterpillar Inc.; *U.S. Public*, pg. 317
HOKKAIDO CITIZEN CORPORATION—See Citizen Watch Company, Ltd.; *Int'l*, pg. 294
HOKKAIDO COCA-COLA BOTTLING CO., LTD.—See Dai Nippon Printing Co., Ltd.; *Int'l*, pg. 363
HOKKAIDO COLLIERY & STEAMSHIP CO., LTD.—See Mitsui & Co., Ltd.; *Int'l*, pg. 877
HOKKAIDO SHANNON CO., LTD.—See Tokuyama Corporation; *Int'l*, pg. 1393
HOKKAIDO SNOW BRAND SALES CO., LTD.—See Snow Brand Milk Products Co. Ltd.; *Int'l*, pg. 1272
THE HOKKAIDO TAKUSHOKU BANK, LTD.; *Int'l*, pg. 626
THE HOKKAIDO TAKUSHOKU BANK, LTD. (BANGKOK)—See The Hokkaido Takushoku Bank, Ltd.; *Int'l*, pg. 627
THE HOKKAIDO TAKUSHOKU BANK, LTD. (BEIJING)—See The Hokkaido Takushoku Bank, Ltd.; *Int'l*, pg. 627
THE HOKKAIDO TAKUSHOKU BANK, LTD. (HONG KONG)—See The Hokkaido Takushoku Bank, Ltd.; *Int'l*, pg. 627
THE HOKKAIDO TAKUSHOKU BANK, LTD. (JAKARTA)—See The Hokkaido Takushoku Bank, Ltd.; *Int'l*, pg. 627
THE HOKKAIDO TAKUSHOKU BANK, LTD.-LOS ANGELES AGENCY—See The Hokkaido Takushoku Bank, Ltd.; *Int'l*, pg. 627
THE HOKKAIDO TAKUSHOKU BANK, LTD. (SHENZHEN)—See The Hokkaido Takushoku Bank, Ltd.; *Int'l*, pg. 627
THE HOKKAIDO TAKUSHOKU BANK, LTD. (SINGAPORE)—See The Hokkaido Takushoku Bank, Ltd.; *Int'l*, pg. 627
THE HOKKAIDO TAKUSHOKU BANK, LTD. (VANCOUVER)—See The Hokkaido Takushoku Bank, Ltd.; *Int'l*, pg. 627
THE HOKKAIDO TAKUSHOKU SECURITIES CO., LTD.—See The Hokkaido Takushoku Bank, Ltd.; *Int'l*, pg. 626
HOKUETSU CATERPILLAR MITSUBISHI CONSTRUCTION EQUIPMENT SALES, LTD.—See Caterpillar Inc.; *U.S. Public*, pg. 317
THE HOKURIKU BANK, LTD.; *Int'l*, pg. 627
THE HOKURIKU BANK, LTD.-FRANKFURT REPRESENTATIVE OFFICE—See The Hokuriku Bank, Ltd.; *Int'l*, pg. 627
THE HOKURIKU BANK, LTD.-HONG KONG—See The Hokuriku Bank, Ltd.; *Int'l*, pg. 627
THE HOKURIKU BANK, LTD.-INTERNATIONAL DEPT.—See The Hokuriku Bank, Ltd.; *Int'l*, pg. 627
THE HOKURIKU BANK, LTD.-LONDON—See The Hokuriku Bank, Ltd.; *Int'l*, pg. 627
THE HOKURIKU BANK, LTD.-NEW YORK—See The Hokuriku Bank, Ltd.; *Int'l*, pg. 627
HOKURIKU CATERPILLAR MITSUBISHI CONSTRUCTION EQUIPMENT SALES, LTD.—See Caterpillar Inc.; *U.S. Public*, pg. 317
HOKURIKU ELECTRIC INDUSTRY CO., LTD.; *Int'l*, pg. 627
HOKURIKU FINANCE (H.K.) LIMITED—See The Hokuriku Bank, Ltd.; *Int'l*, pg. 627
HOKURIKU (MALAYSIA), SDN. BHD.—See Hokuriku Electric Industry Co., Ltd.; *Int'l*, pg. 628
HOKURIKU (SINGAPORE) PTE., LTD.—See Hokuriku Electric Industry Co., Ltd.; *Int'l*, pg. 628
PT HOKURIKU UNITED FORGING INDUSTRIES—See Komatsu Ltd.; *Int'l*, pg. 745
HOKURIKU U.S.A. CO., LTD.—See Hokuriku Electric Industry Co., Ltd.; *Int'l*, pg. 628
HOKURYU CEMENT CORP.—See Ssangyong Business Group; *Int'l*, pg. 1291
HOKUTO ELECTRONICS CO., LTD.—See Toshiba Corporation; *Int'l*, pg. 1402
HOLAD HOLDING & ADMINISTRATION INC.—See Volkswagen AG; *Int'l*, pg. 1475
HOLADAY INDUSTRIES, INC.—See Bowthorpe plc; *Int'l*, pg. 208
HOLANTSE BANK-UNI—See ABN-AMRO Holding N.V.; *Int'l*, pg. 12
HOLBERG INDUSTRIES, INC.; *U.S. Private*, pg. 533
HOLBORN OIL TRADING LTD.—See The Coastal Corporation; *U.S. Public*, pg. 390
HOLBROOK LUMBER COMPANY; *U.S. Private*, pg. 533
THE HOLBROOK SUN—See Gannett Company, Inc.; *U.S. Public*, pg. 701
HOLCOMB & HOKE MFG. COMPANY, INC.; *U.S. Private*, pg. 533

HOLCOMB BRIDGE IMMEDIATE CARE CENTER, INC.—See Magellan Health Services, Inc.; *U.S. Public*, pg. 1036
J.I. HOLCOMB MFG.—See Premier Farnell plc; *Int'l*, pg. 1068
HOLCOMB STATION—See Sunflower Electric Power Corporation; *U.S. Private*, pg. 1052
HOLD EVERYTHING, INC.—See Williams-Sonoma, Inc.; *U.S. Public*, pg. 1770
ARTHUR HOLDEN & SONS PLC—See Imperial Chemical Industries PLC; *Int'l*, pg. 663
THE HOLDEN GROUP—See EdperBrascan Corporation; *Int'l*, pg. 435
HOLDEN'S ENGINE PRODUCTS OVERSEAS CORPORATION—See General Motors Corporation; *U.S. Public*, pg. 723
HOLDER CONSTRUCTION COMPANY—See Holder Corporation; *U.S. Private*, pg. 534
HOLDER CORPORATION; *U.S. Private*, pg. 533
HOLDERBANK CEMENT & BETON—See Holderbank Financiere Glaris Ltd.; *Int'l*, pg. 628
HOLDERBANK FINANCIERE GLARIS LTD.; *Int'l*, pg. 628
HOLDERBANK MANAGEMENT & CONSULTING LTD.—See Holderbank Financiere Glaris Ltd.; *Int'l*, pg. 628
HOLDERBANK UNGARN GMBH—See Holderbank Financiere Glaris Ltd.; *Int'l*, pg. 629
HOLDERCHEM LTD—See Holderbank Financiere Glaris Ltd.; *Int'l*, pg. 628
HOLDERNESS SUPPLIES; *U.S. Private*, pg. 534
HOLDUX BETEILIGUNGSGESELLSCHAFT—See Assicurazioni Generali S.p.A.; *Int'l*, pg. 91
HOLDUX CURACAO N.V.—See Assicurazioni Generali S.p.A.; *Int'l*, pg. 91
HOLEC MACHINES & APPARATEN B.V.—See Royal Begemann Group; *Int'l*, pg. 1133
HOLEC PROJECTS B.V.—See Royal Begemann Group; *Int'l*, pg. 1133
HOLGA INC.—See HON Industries Inc.; *U.S. Public*, pg. 772
HOLIDAY COMPANIES; *U.S. Private*, pg. 534
HOLIDAY HOUSE, INC.—See Washington Mutual Inc.; *U.S. Public*, pg. 1742
HOLIDAY INN—See Benson's, Inc.; *U.S. Private*, pg. 134
HOLIDAY INN DOWNTOWN—See Sunstone Hotel Investors, Inc.; *U.S. Public*, pg. 1537
THE HOLIDAY INN LANCASTER HOST HOTEL & CONFERENCE CENTER; *U.S. Private*, pg. 534
HOLIDAY INN WORLDWIDE—See Bass PLC; *Int'l*, pg. 170
HOLIDAY RAMBLER—See Monaco Coach Corporation; *U.S. Public*, pg. 1123
HOLIDAY RV RENTAL/LEASING, INC.—See Holiday RV Superstores, Inc.; *U.S. Public*, pg. 829
HOLIDAY RV SUPERSTORES, INC.; *U.S. Public*, pg. 829
HOLIDAY RV SUPERSTORES OF NEW MEXICO INC.—See Holiday RV Superstores, Inc.; *U.S. Public*, pg. 830
HOLIDAY RV SUPERSTORES WEST, INC.—See Holiday RV Superstores, Inc.; *U.S. Public*, pg. 830
HOLIDAY STATION STORES, INC.—See Holiday Companies; *U.S. Private*, pg. 534
HOLLAND AMERICA LINE WESTOURS—See Carnival Corporation; *U.S. Public*, pg. 306
HOLLAND COMPANY—See Curran Group, Inc.; *U.S. Private*, pg. 297
THE HOLLAND HITCH COMPANY; *U.S. Private*, pg. 534
JOHN HOLLAND CONSTRUCTIONS PTY LTD.—See John Holland Group Pty. Ltd.; *Int'l*, pg. 630
JOHN HOLLAND ENGINEERING PTY LTD.—See John Holland Group Pty. Ltd.; *Int'l*, pg. 630
JOHN HOLLAND GROUP PTY. LTD.; *Int'l*, pg. 630
HOLLAND MARK MARTIN; *U.S. Private*, pg. 534
HOLLAND MEDICAL SERVICES, INC.—See Integrated Health Services, Inc.; *U.S. Public*, pg. 885
HOLLAND NOVOCHEM B.V.—See Norsk Hydro a.s; *Int'l*, pg. 962
THE HOLLAND SENTINEL—See Shivers Trading & Operating Co.; *U.S. Private*, pg. 995
HOLLAND SWEETENER COMPANY—See Tosoh Corporation; *Int'l*, pg. 1408
HOLLAND SWEETENER COMPANY V.O.F.—See Tosoh Corporation; *Int'l*, pg. 1408
HOLLAND SWEETENER NORTH AMERICA, INC.—See Tosoh Corporation; *Int'l*, pg. 1407
WALTER HOLLAND & SON—See Northern Foods plc; *Int'l*, pg. 968
HOLLANDALE PRIMARY CARE, INC.—See Integrated Health Services, Inc.; *U.S. Public*, pg. 885
HOLLANDIA WEATHERSHIELDS LIMITED—See Vermeulen Hollandia BV; *Int'l*, pg. 1463
HOLLANDSCHE BETON GROEP NV; *Int'l*, pg. 630
HOLLANDSE DISCONTERINGSMAATSCHAPPIJ MUNDUS N.V.—See ABN-AMRO Holding N.V.; *Int'l*, pg. 9
HOLLANDSE SIGNAALAPPARATEN B.V.—See Thomson S.A.; *Int'l*, pg. 1384
ROGER HOLLER CHEVROLET & GEO CO.; *U.S. Private*, pg. 534
HOLLEY REPLACEMENT PARTS DIVISION—See Coltec Holdings Inc; *U.S. Public*, pg. 402
HOLLIDAYSBURG TRUST COMPANY—See Omega Financial Corporation; *U.S. Public*, pg. 1222
HOLLINDE & BOUDON GMBH (SSH)—See Veba AG; *Int'l*, pg. 1459
HOLLINGER INC.; *Int'l*, pg. 630
HOLLINGER INTERNATIONAL INC.—See Hollinger Inc.; *Int'l*, pg. 632
HOLLINGSWORTH & VOSE CO.; *U.S. Private*, pg. 534
HOLLINGSWORTH & VOSE U.K. LTD.—See Hollingsworth & Vose Co.; *U.S. Private*, pg. 535
HOLLINGSWORTH & VOSE EUROPE NV—See Hollingsworth & Vose Co.; *U.S. Private*, pg. 535
HOLLINGSWORTH OIL CO. INC.; *U.S. Private*, pg. 535
HOLLINGSWORTH SACO LOWELL CORPORATION, INC.; *U.S. Private*, pg. 535
HOLLIS & EASTERN RAILROAD CO.—See Republic Group Incorporated; *U.S. Public*, pg. 1378

HOLLISTER ADVERTISING; *U.S. Public*, pg. 830
HOLLISTER FREE LANCE—See Central Valley Publishing; *U.S. Private*, pg. 225
HOLLISTER INCORPORATED; *U.S. Private*, pg. 535
HOLLISTER MEDIA—See Hollister Advertising; *U.S. Public*, pg. 830
HOLLISTER MEDICAL SYSTEMS DIVISION—See Hollister Incorporated; *U.S. Private*, pg. 535
HOLLOW SPHERES BUSINESS—See PQ Corporation; *U.S. Private*, pg. 827
HOLLOWAY WHITE ALLOM LTD.—See John Laing PLC; *Int'l*, pg. 796
HOLLY CORPORATION; *U.S. Public*, pg. 830
HOLLY MUSIC—See Handleman Company; *U.S. Public*, pg. 780
HOLLY PETROLEUM, INC.—See Holly Corporation; *U.S. Public*, pg. 830
HOLLY SPRINGS BRICK AND TILE, INC.—See Jannock Limited; *Int'l*, pg. 699
HOLLY SUGAR CORPORATION—See Imperial Holly Corporation; *U.S. Public*, pg. 872
HOLLYBANK BLEACH & DYE WORKS LTD.—See Lamont Holdings Plc; *Int'l*, pg. 798
HOLLYBANK ENGINEERING COMPANY LIMITED—See Hawker Siddeley Canada Inc.; *Int'l*, pg. 604
HOLLYMATIC CORPORATION; *U.S. Private*, pg. 535
HOLLY'S INC.; *U.S. Private*, pg. 535
HOLLYTEX CARPET MILLS, INC.; *U.S. Private*, pg. 535
HOLLYWOOD CASINO CORP; *U.S. Public*, pg. 830
HOLLYWOOD ENTERTAINMENT CORP.; *U.S. Public*, pg. 535
HOLLYWOOD PARK CASINO—See Hollywood Park, Inc.; *U.S. Public*, pg. 831
HOLLYWOOD PARK, INC.; *U.S. Public*, pg. 830
HOLLYWOOD PARK OPERATING COMPANY—See Hollywood Park, Inc.; *U.S. Public*, pg. 831
THE HOLLYWOOD REPORTER—See VNU Verenigde Nederlandse Uitgeversbedrijven B.V.; *Int'l*, pg. 1446
HOLLYWOOD SUPPLY COMPANY—See The Todd-AO Corporation; *U.S. Public*, pg. 1619
HOLM INDUSTRIES, INC.—See The Standard Products Company; *U.S. Public*, pg. 1504
HOLMAN BOILER WORKS, INC.—See Copes-Vulcan Inc.; *U.S. Private*, pg. 274
HOLMAN ENTERPRISES; *U.S. Private*, pg. 535
HOLMATRO, INC.—See Holmatro Industrial & Rescue Equipment; *Int'l*, pg. 632
HOLMATRO INDUSTRIAL & RESCUE EQUIPMENT; *Int'l*, pg. 632
HOLMEGAARDS GLASS—See Royal Copenhagen A/S; *Int'l*, pg. 1134
HOLMEN BELGIUM NV/SA—See Mo och Domsjo AB; *Int'l*, pg. 885
HOLMEN ESPANA S.A. (MODO IBERICA SA)—See Mo och Domsjo AB; *Int'l*, pg. 885
HOLMEN MD S.R.L—See Mo och Domsjo AB; *Int'l*, pg. 885
HOLMEN NEDERLAND B.V.—See Mo och Domsjo AB; *Int'l*, pg. 885
HOLMEN PAPER AB—See Mo och Domsjo AB; *Int'l*, pg. 885
HOLMEN PAPER LTD.—See Mo och Domsjo AB; *Int'l*, pg. 885
HOLMEN PAPERS—See Mo och Domsjo AB; *Int'l*, pg. 885
HOLMEN (SCHWEIZ) AG—See Mo och Domsjo AB; *Int'l*, pg. 885
HOLMENS BRUK G.M.B.H.—See Mo och Domsjo AB; *Int'l*, pg. 885
G.D. HOLMES LIMITED—See Laporte plc; *Int'l*, pg. 802
HOLMES PRODUCTS CORP.—See Pentland Group PLC; *Int'l*, pg. 1035
HOLMES PROTECTION GROUP, INC.—See Tyco International Ltd.; *U.S. Public*, pg. 1649
HOLMES PROTECTION OF LONG ISLAND, INC.—See Tyco International Ltd.; *U.S. Public*, pg. 1649
HOLMES PROTECTION OF NEW JERSEY, INC.—See Tyco International Ltd.; *U.S. Public*, pg. 1649
HOLMES PROTECTION OF NEW YORK, INCORPORATED—See Tyco International Ltd.; *U.S. Public*, pg. 1649
HOLMES PROTECTION OF PHILADELPHIA, INC.—See Tyco International Ltd.; *U.S. Public*, pg. 1649
HOLMES TUTTLE FORD, INC.; *U.S. Private*, pg. 535
HOLMQUIST GRAIN & LUMBER CO.; *U.S. Private*, pg. 535
HOLNAM INC.—See Holderbank Financiere Glaris Ltd.; *Int'l*, pg. 628
HOLOGIC EUROPE N.V.—See Hologic, Inc.; *U.S. Public*, pg. 831
HOLOGIC FRANCE—See Hologic, Inc.; *U.S. Public*, pg. 831
HOLOGIC, INC.; *U.S. Public*, pg. 831
HOLOPHANE, S.A. DE C.V.—See McNeel International Corp.; *U.S. Private*, pg. 725
HOLOUBEK INC.; *U.S. Private*, pg. 536
HOLOX INC.—See Linde AG; *Int'l*, pg. 811
HOLPA—See Lagardere Groupe; *Int'l*, pg. 792
HOLPART—See Saint-Gobain; *Int'l*, pg. 1171
HOLSET BRAZIL—See Cummins Engine Company, Inc.; *U.S. Public*, pg. 469
HOLSET ENGINEERING CO. INC.—See Cummins Engine Company, Inc.; *U.S. Public*, pg. 468
HOLSET ENGINEERING CO. LTD.—See Cummins Engine Company, Inc.; *U.S. Public*, pg. 469
HOLSET KOREA, LTD.—See Cummins Engine Company, Inc.; *U.S. Public*, pg. 469
HOLSON BURNES GROUP—See Newell Co.; *U.S. Public*, pg. 1177
HOLSTEIN AND KAPPERT GMBH—See Klockner-Werke AG; *Int'l*, pg. 737
HOLSTEIN ASSOCIATION USA, INC.; *U.S. Private*, pg. 536
HOLSUM BAKERY, INC.; *U.S. Private*, pg. 536

HOLSUM BREAD BAKERIES—See Interstate Bakeries Corporation; *U.S. Public*, pg. 909
HOLSUM OF FORT WAYNE, INC.—See Lewis Brothers Bakeries, Inc.; *U.S. Private*, pg. 665
HENRY HOLT & CO. PUBLISHING—See Georg von Holtzbrinck GmbH; *Int'l*, pg. 1479
HOLT HOSIERY MILLS, INC.; *U.S. Private*, pg. 536
JOHN HOLT GROUP LTD.—See Lonrho plc; *Int'l*, pg. 817
HOLT-MCDERMOTT MINE—See Barrick Gold Corporation; *Int'l*, pg. 169
HOLT, RINEHART AND WINSTON COLLEGE DIVISION—See Harcourt General, Inc.; *U.S. Public*, pg. 783
HOLT, RINEHART AND WINSTON, INC.—See Harcourt General, Inc.; *U.S. Public*, pg. 783
HOLT, RINEHART AND WINSTON SCHOOL DIVISION—See Harcourt General, Inc.; *U.S. Public*, pg. 783
HOLTER GROUP—See Australian National Industries Limited; *Int'l*, pg. 101
FRANK HOLTON CO.—See G. Leblanc Corporation; *U.S. Private*, pg. 657
HOLTON MACHINERY LIMITED—See Outokumpu Oyj; *Int'l*, pg. 1017
HOLTZMAN'S LITTLE FOLK SHOP, INC.—See Woolworth Corporation; *U.S. Public*, pg. 1777
HOLY CROSS ELECTRIC ASSOCIATION, INC.; *U.S. Private*, pg. 536
HOLYOKE FOOD MART, INC.—See Tengelmann Warenhandelsgesellschaft; *Int'l*, pg. 1375
HOLYOKE LITHOGRAPH CO., INC.—See Quebecor Inc.; *Int'l*, pg. 1078
HOLYOKE POWER AND ELECTRIC CO.—See Northeast Utilities; *U.S. Public*, pg. 1195
HOLYOKE WATER POWER CO.—See Northeast Utilities; *U.S. Public*, pg. 1195
HOLY'S EXCLUSIVE HERRENMODEN GMBH—See Hugo Boss AG; *Int'l*, pg. 637
HOLZ-HER U.S. INC.—See Karl M. Reich Maschinenfabrik GmbH; *Int'l*, pg. 1101
HOLZ RUBBER INC.—See BBA Group plc; *Int'l*, pg. 113
HOLZINDUSTRIE BRUCHSAL GMBH—See Daimler-Benz Aktiengesellschaft; *Int'l*, pg. 368
HOLZMANN GLEISBAU GMBH—See Philipp Holzmann AG; *Int'l*, pg. 632
PHILIPP HOLZMANN AG; *Int'l*, pg. 632
PHILIPP HOLZMANN-HELD & FRANCKE BAUAKTIENGESELLSCHAFT—See Philipp Holzmann AG; *Int'l*, pg. 632
PHILIPP HOLZMANN IBERICA, S.A.—See Philipp Holzmann AG; *Int'l*, pg. 633
PHILIPP HOLZMANN (NIGERIA) LTD—See Philipp Holzmann AG; *Int'l*, pg. 634
PHILIPP HOLZMANN (THAI) LTD—See Philipp Holzmann AG; *Int'l*, pg. 634
PHILIPP HOLZMANN USA, LTD.—See Philipp Holzmann AG; *Int'l*, pg. 633
HOMAN LUMBER MART, INC.; *U.S. Private*, pg. 536
HOMASOTE COMPANY; *U.S. Public*, pg. 831
HOMBURGER PAPIERFABRIK WILHELM GELDMACHER GMBH & CO. KG—See A. Ahlstrom Corporation; *Int'l*, pg. 35
HOME & GARDEN SHOW PLACE—See TruServ Corporation; *U.S. Private*, pg. 1108
HOME & GARDEN TELEVISION—See The E.W. Scripps Company; *U.S. Public*, pg. 1447
HOME AUTOMATION GROUP LTD.—See Delta plc; *Int'l*, pg. 390
HOME BENEFICIAL CORPORATION—See American General Corporation; *U.S. Public*, pg. 76
HOME BENEFICIAL LIFE INSURANCE CO.—See American General Corporation; *U.S. Public*, pg. 77
HOME BOX OFFICE COMMUNICATIONS, INC.—See Time Warner Inc.; *U.S. Public*, pg. 1612
HOME BOX OFFICE, INC.—See Time Warner Inc.; *U.S. Public*, pg. 1612
HOME BOX OFFICE INTERNATIONAL, INC.—See Time Warner Inc.; *U.S. Public*, pg. 1612
HOME BOX OFFICE SERVICES, INC.—See Time Warner Inc.; *U.S. Public*, pg. 1612
HOME BREWERY PLC—See Scottish & Newcastle plc; *Int'l*, pg. 1211
HOME CARE P.R.N., INC.—See Technical Aid Corporation; *U.S. Private*, pg. 1072
HOME CARE SOLUTIONS OF MURRAY, INC.—See Integrated Health Services, Inc.; *U.S. Public*, pg. 885
HOME COMPUTER SOFTWARE DIV.—See Handleman Company; *U.S. Public*, pg. 779
HOME CURTAIN CORPORATION—See Home Innovations, Inc.; *U.S. Private*, pg. 536
HOME DEPOT CANADA—See The Home Depot, Inc.; *U.S. Public*, pg. 832
THE HOME DEPOT, INC.; *U.S. Public*, pg. 831
HOME ELECTRONICS CO., LTD.—See The Siam Cement Public Company Limited; *Int'l*, pg. 1239
HOME FASHIONS—See The Walt Disney Company; *U.S. Public*, pg. 513
HOME FEDERAL BANK—See First Financial Bancorp; *U.S. Public*, pg. 633
HOME FURNISHING LEDERLAND—See Vendex International N.V.; *Int'l*, pg. 1463
HOME FURNISHINGS DAILY—See The Walt Disney Company; *U.S. Public*, pg. 513
HOME FURNISHINGS SEGMENT—See Springs Industries, Inc.; *U.S. Public*, pg. 1500
HOME INNOVATIONS, INC.; *U.S. Private*, pg. 536
HOME INTERIORS & GIFTS, INC.; *U.S. Private*, pg. 536
HOME JUICE CO.; *U.S. Private*, pg. 537
HOME JUICE COMPANY OF FLORIDA—See Home Juice Co.; *U.S. Private*, pg. 537
HOME MAGAZINE PUBLISHING CORP.—See Lagardere Groupe; *Int'l*, pg. 795
HOME MEDICAL SYSTEMS, INC.—See Integrated Health Services, Inc.; *U.S. Public*, pg. 885
HOME-OWNERS INSURANCE CO.—See Auto-Owners Insurance; *U.S. Private*, pg. 100

HOME OWNERS LIFE INSURANCE CO.—See Old Republic International Corporation; *U.S. Public,* pg. 1218
HOME PRODUCTS INC.—See American Home Products Corporation; *U.S. Public,* pg. 81
HOME PRODUCTS INTERNATIONAL, INC.; *U.S. Public,* pg. 832
HOME PRODUCTS ITALIANA SPA—See American Home Products Corporation; *U.S. Public,* pg. 81
HOME SAVINGS OF AMERICA, FSB—See H.F. Ahmanson & Co.; *U.S. Public,* pg. 29
HOME SERVICE PUBLICATIONS, INC.—See The Reader's Digest Association, Inc.; *U.S. Public,* pg. 1367
HOME SHOPPING CLUB, INC.—See USA Networks, Inc.; *U.S. Public,* pg. 1685
HOME SHOPPING NETWORK, INC.—See USA Networks, Inc.; *U.S. Public,* pg. 1685
HOME SHOWCASE PRODUCTS—See Tri Tech Laboratories, Inc.; *U.S. Private,* pg. 1101
HOME TELEPHONE CO.—See Telephone and Data Systems, Inc.; *U.S. Public,* pg. 1571
HOME TELEPHONE CO., INC.—See Telephone and Data Systems, Inc.; *U.S. Public,* pg. 1571
HOME TELEPHONE CO. OF PITTSBORO, INC.—See Telephone and Data Systems, Inc.; *U.S. Public,* pg. 1571
HOMEADD FINANCIAL CORPORATION—See RSI Holdings Inc.; *U.S. Public,* pg. 1358
HOMEAMERICAN MORTGAGE CORP.—See M.D.C. Holdings, Inc.; *U.S. Public,* pg. 1025
HOMEBASE, INC.; *U.S. Public,* pg. 832
HOMEBASE LTD—See GIB Group; *Int'l,* pg. 534
HOMEBASE LTD—See J. Sainsbury plc; *Int'l,* pg. 1170
HOMEBUYER'S MORTGAGE, INC.—See Washington Homes, Inc.; *U.S. Public,* pg. 1741
HOMEBYER'S PREFERRED, INC.—See Landauer, Inc.; *U.S. Public,* pg. 977
HOMEFED TRUST—See Washington Mutual Inc.; *U.S. Public,* pg. 1742
HOMEGOODS—See The TJX Companies, Inc.; *U.S. Public,* pg. 1557
HOMELAND HOLDING CORP.; *U.S. Public,* pg. 832
HOMELAND STORES, INC.—See Homeland Holding Corp.; *U.S. Public,* pg. 832
HOMEOWNERS GROUP, INC.; *U.S. Public,* pg. 832
HOMEOWNERS MARKETING SERVICES, INC.—See Homeowners Group, Inc.; *U.S. Public,* pg. 832
HOMEOWNERS MARKETING SERVICES INTERNATIONAL, INC.—See Homeowners Group, Inc.; *U.S. Public,* pg. 832
HOMES & SON CONTRACTORS, INC.; *U.S. Private,* pg. 537
HOMES BY DAVE BROWN; *U.S. Private,* pg. 537
HOMES OF MERIT INC.; *U.S. Private,* pg. 537
HOMESHIELD FABRICATED PRODUCTS—See Quanex Corporation; *U.S. Public,* pg. 1350
HOMESIDE LENDING COMPANY—See National Australia Bank Limited; *Int'l,* pg. 906
HOMESPAN REALTY CO., INC.—See Commerce Group Corp.; *U.S. Public,* pg. 410
HOMESTAKE CANADA INC.—See Homestake Mining Company; *U.S. Public,* pg. 833
HOMESTAKE GOLD OF AUSTRALIA LIMITED—See Homestake Mining Company; *U.S. Public,* pg. 833
HOMESTAKE MINE—See Homestake Mining Company; *U.S. Public,* pg. 833
HOMESTAKE MINING COMPANY; *U.S. Public,* pg. 832
HOMESTEAD HOMES—See Cavalier Homes, Inc.; *U.S. Public,* pg. 318
HOMESTEAD HOUSE INC.; *U.S. Private,* pg. 537
THE HOMESTEAD L.C.—See Club Corporation International; *U.S. Private,* pg. 247
HOMESTEAD PUBLISHING—See The Times Mirror Company; *U.S. Public,* pg. 1616
HOMETOWN COMMUNICATIONS NETWORK, INC.; *U.S. Private,* pg. 537
HOMETOWN PUBLICATIONS—See Journal Communications Inc.; *U.S. Private,* pg. 601
HOMETTE CORPORATION—See Skyline Corporation; *U.S. Public,* pg. 1476
HOMEWOOD CORPORATION; *U.S. Private,* pg. 537
HOMEWORTHY FURNITURE LTD.—See Silentnight Holdings Plc; *Int'l,* pg. 1249
THE HON CO., LOUISBURG PLANT—See HON Industries Inc.; *U.S. Public,* pg. 772
THE HON CO., OWENSBORO PLANT—See HON Industries Inc.; *U.S. Public,* pg. 772
THE HON CO., SULPHUR SPRINGS PLANT—See HON Industries Inc.; *U.S. Public,* pg. 772
THE HON CO., WILLIAMSPORT PLANT—See HON Industries Inc.; *U.S. Public,* pg. 772
THE HON CO., WINNSBORO PLANT—See HON Industries Inc.; *U.S. Public,* pg. 772
HONAM OIL REFINERY CO. LTD.—See LG Group; *Int'l,* pg. 779
HONDA ACCESS CORP.—See Honda Motor Co., Ltd.; *Int'l,* pg. 634
HONDA ACCESS SALES CORP.—See Honda Motor Co., Ltd.; *Int'l,* pg. 634
HONDA AUSTRALIA PTY., LTD.—See Honda Motor Co., Ltd.; *Int'l,* pg. 635
HONDA AUSTRIA G.M.B.H.—See Honda Motor Co., Ltd.; *Int'l,* pg. 635
HONDA AUTOMOBILI ITALIA S.P.A.—See Honda Motor Co., Ltd.; *Int'l,* pg. 635
HONDA CANADA INC.—See Honda Motor Co., Ltd.; *Int'l,* pg. 635
HONDA CLIO SHIN TOKYO CO., LTD.—See Honda Motor Co., Ltd.; *Int'l,* pg. 634
HONDA DE MEXICO, S.A. DE C.V.—See Honda Motor Co., Ltd.; *Int'l,* pg. 635
HONDA DEUTSCHLAND GMBH—See Honda Motor Co., Ltd.; *Int'l,* pg. 635

HONDA ENGINEERING CO., LTD.—See Honda Motor Co., Ltd.; *Int'l,* pg. 634
HONDA EUROPE N.V.—See Honda Motor Co., Ltd.; *Int'l,* pg. 635
HONDA FINANCE CO., LTD.—See Honda Motor Co., Ltd.; *Int'l,* pg. 634
HONDA FOUNDRY CO., LTD.—See Honda Motor Co., Ltd.; *Int'l,* pg. 634
HONDA FRANCE S.A.—See Honda Motor Co., Ltd.; *Int'l,* pg. 635
HONDA INTERNATIONAL SALES CORP.—See Honda Motor Co., Ltd.; *Int'l,* pg. 634
HONDA LEASING CORPORATION—See Honda Motor Co., Ltd.; *Int'l,* pg. 634
HONDA LOCK MFG., CO., LTD.—See Honda Motor Co., Ltd.; *Int'l,* pg. 634
HONDA MOTOR CO., LTD.; *Int'l,* pg. 634
HONDA MOTOR DO BRASIL LTDA.—See Honda Motor Co., Ltd.; *Int'l,* pg. 635
HONDA MOTOR EUROPE LTD—See Honda Motor Co., Ltd.; *Int'l,* pg. 635
HONDA MOTOR PARTS SERVICE CO., LTD.—See Honda Motor Co., Ltd.; *Int'l,* pg. 634
HONDA NEDERLAND B.V.—See Honda Motor Co., Ltd.; *Int'l,* pg. 635
HONDA NORTH AMERICA INC.—See Honda Motor Co., Ltd.; *Int'l,* pg. 635
HONDA PARTS SALES CO., LTD.—See Honda Motor Co., Ltd.; *Int'l,* pg. 634
HONDA POWER EQUIPMENT MANUFACTURING, INC.—See Honda Motor Co., Ltd.; *Int'l,* pg. 635
HONDA RACING CORPORATION—See Honda Motor Co., Ltd.; *Int'l,* pg. 634
HONDA R&D CO., LTD.—See Honda Motor Co., Ltd.; *Int'l,* pg. 634
HONDA R&D NORTH AMERICA, INC.—See Honda Motor Co., Ltd.; *Int'l,* pg. 634
HONDA SOGO TATEMONO CO., LTD.—See Honda Motor Co., Ltd.; *Int'l,* pg. 634
HONDA TRADING CORP.—See Honda Motor Co., Ltd.; *Int'l,* pg. 634
THE HONDO COMPANY—See Lonrho plc; *Int'l,* pg. 818
HONDO OIL & GAS COMPANY—See Lonrho plc; *Int'l,* pg. 818
HONEY FASHIONS LTD.; *U.S. Private,* pg. 537
HONEYMEAD PRODUCTS CO.; *U.S. Private,* pg. 537
HONEYWELL—See Honeywell Inc.; *U.S. Public,* pg. 834
HONEYWELL AB—See Honeywell Inc.; *U.S. Public,* pg. 834
HONEYWELL AG—See Honeywell Inc.; *U.S. Public,* pg. 834
HONEYWELL & CO. OMAN LLC—See Honeywell Inc.; *U.S. Public,* pg. 835
HONEYWELL A/S—See Honeywell Inc.; *U.S. Public,* pg. 834
HONEYWELL AS—See Honeywell Inc.; *U.S. Public,* pg. 834
HONEYWELL ASIA PACIFIC INC.—See Honeywell Inc.; *U.S. Public,* pg. 834
HONEYWELL AUSTRALIA LIMITED—See Honeywell Inc.; *U.S. Public,* pg. 834
HONEYWELL AUSTRIA GMBH—See Honeywell Inc.; *U.S. Public,* pg. 834
HONEYWELL BUCHAREST—See Honeywell Inc.; *U.S. Public,* pg. 834
HONEYWELL BULL AB—See Compagnie des Machines Bull; *Int'l,* pg. 318
OY HONEYWELL BULL AB—See Compagnie des Machines Bull; *Int'l,* pg. 318
HONEYWELL BULL AE—See Compagnie des Machines Bull; *Int'l,* pg. 318
HONEYWELL BULL AG—See Compagnie des Machines Bull; *Int'l,* pg. 318
HONEYWELL BULL A/S—See Compagnie des Machines Bull; *Int'l,* pg. 318
HONEYWELL BULL DO BRAZIL S.A.—See Compagnie des Machines Bull; *Int'l,* pg. 318
HONEYWELL BULL MADAGASCAR S.A.—See Compagnie des Machines Bull; *Int'l,* pg. 318
HONEYWELL BULL MAROC S.A.—See Compagnie des Machines Bull; *Int'l,* pg. 318
HONEYWELL BULL S.A.—See Compagnie des Machines Bull; *Int'l,* pg. 318
HONEYWELL BULL SAL—See Compagnie des Machines Bull; *Int'l,* pg. 318
HONEYWELL BULL (SCHWEIZ) A/G—See Compagnie des Machines Bull; *Int'l,* pg. 318
HONEYWELL BV—See Honeywell Inc.; *U.S. Public,* pg. 834
HONEYWELL, C.A.—See Honeywell Inc.; *U.S. Public,* pg. 834
HONEYWELL CHINA INC.—See Honeywell Inc.; *U.S. Public,* pg. 834
HONEYWELL DEFENSE AVIONICS SYSTEMS—See Honeywell Inc.; *U.S. Public,* pg. 834
HONEYWELL DO BRASIL & CIA.—See Honeywell Inc.; *U.S. Public,* pg. 834
HONEYWELL EGYPT LTD.—See Honeywell Inc.; *U.S. Public,* pg. 834
HONEYWELL EOOD—See Honeywell Inc.; *U.S. Public,* pg. 834
HONEYWELL EUROPE S.A.—See Honeywell Inc.; *U.S. Public,* pg. 834
HONEYWELL GMBH—See Honeywell Inc.; *U.S. Public,* pg. 834
HONEYWELL HOME & BUIIDING CONTROL—See Honeywell Inc.; *U.S. Public,* pg. 834
HONEYWELL INC.; *U.S. Public,* pg. 833
HONEYWELL, INC.—See Honeywell Inc.; *U.S. Public,* pg. 834
HONEYWELL INTERNATIONAL—See Honeywell Inc.; *U.S. Public,* pg. 835
HONEYWELL KFT—See Honeywell Inc.; *U.S. Public,* pg. 835
HONEYWELL KUWAIT KSC—See Honeywell Inc.; *U.S. Public,* pg. 835

HONEYWELL LDA—See Honeywell Inc.; *U.S. Public,* pg. 835
HONEYWELL LEEDS & NORTHRUP AUSTRALIA PTY. LTD.—See Honeywell Inc.; *U.S. Public,* pg. 834
HONEYWELL LEEDS & NORTHRUP INTERNATIONAL—See Honeywell Inc.; *U.S. Public,* pg. 834
HONEYWELL LIMITED—See Honeywell Inc.; *U.S. Public,* pg. 835
HONEYWELL LTD.—See Honeywell Inc.; *U.S. Public,* pg. 835
HONEYWELL-MEASUREX AG—See Honeywell Inc.; *U.S. Public,* pg. 833
HONEYWELL-MEASUREX B.V.—See Honeywell Inc.; *U.S. Public,* pg. 833
HONEYWELL-MEASUREX CORPORATION—See Honeywell Inc.; *U.S. Public,* pg. 833
HONEYWELL-MEASUREX CREDIT CORPORATION—See Honeywell Inc.; *U.S. Public,* pg. 833
HONEYWELL-MEASUREX DEVRON—See Honeywell Inc.; *U.S. Public,* pg. 833
HONEYWELL-MEASUREX DO BRAZIL CONTROLES DE PROCESSAMENTO LTDA.—See Honeywell Inc.; *U.S. Public,* pg. 833
HONEYWELL-MEASUREX FOREIGN SALES CORPORATION—See Honeywell Inc.; *U.S. Public,* pg. 833
HONEYWELL-MEASUREX G.M.B.H.—See Honeywell Inc.; *U.S. Public,* pg. 833
HONEYWELL-MEASUREX, INC.—See Honeywell Inc.; *U.S. Public,* pg. 833
HONEYWELL-MEASUREX INTERNATIONAL GMBH—See Honeywell Inc.; *U.S. Public,* pg. 833
HONEYWELL-MEASUREX INTERNATIONAL SYSTEMS LTD.—See Honeywell Inc.; *U.S. Public,* pg. 833
HONEYWELL-MEASUREX (IRELAND) FINANCE UNLIMITED—See Honeywell Inc.; *U.S. Public,* pg. 833
HONEYWELL-MEASUREX (IRELAND) LIMITED—See Honeywell Inc.; *U.S. Public,* pg. 833
HONEYWELL-MEASUREX (IRELAND) SERVICE LTD.—See Honeywell Inc.; *U.S. Public,* pg. 833
HONEYWELL-MEASUREX ITALIA S.R.L.—See Honeywell Inc.; *U.S. Public,* pg. 833
HONEYWELL-MEASUREX JAPAN, LTD.—See Honeywell Inc.; *U.S. Public,* pg. 833
HONEYWELL-MEASUREX MANAGEMENT SYSTEMS DIVISION (MSD)—See Honeywell Inc.; *U.S. Public,* pg. 833
HONEYWELL-MEASUREX NORWAY A/S—See Honeywell Inc.; *U.S. Public,* pg. 833
HONEYWELL-MEASUREX OY—See Honeywell Inc.; *U.S. Public,* pg. 833
HONEYWELL-MEASUREX (PORTUGAL) SISTEMAS DE CONTROLE LTDA.—See Honeywell Inc.; *U.S. Public,* pg. 833
HONEYWELL-MEASUREX PTY. LTD.—See Honeywell Inc.; *U.S. Public,* pg. 834
HONEYWELL-MEASUREX S.A. DE C.V.—See Honeywell Inc.; *U.S. Public,* pg. 834
HONEYWELL-MEASUREX S.A.R.L.—See Honeywell Inc.; *U.S. Public,* pg. 834
HONEYWELL-MEASUREX SWEDEN AB—See Honeywell Inc.; *U.S. Public,* pg. 834
HONEYWELL-MEASUREX SYSTEMS INC.—See Honeywell Inc.; *U.S. Public,* pg. 833
HONEYWELL-MEASUREX SYSTEMS N.Z. LTD.—See Honeywell Inc.; *U.S. Public,* pg. 834
HONEYWELL MIDDLE EAST LTD.—See Honeywell Inc.; *U.S. Public,* pg. 835
HONEYWELL OY—See Honeywell Inc.; *U.S. Public,* pg. 835
HONEYWELL PTE. LTD.—See Honeywell Inc.; *U.S. Public,* pg. 835
HONEYWELL SA—See Honeywell Inc.; *U.S. Public,* pg. 835
HONEYWELL S.A.—See Honeywell Inc.; *U.S. Public,* pg. 835
HONEYWELL S.A. DE C.V.—See Honeywell Inc.; *U.S. Public,* pg. 835
HONEYWELL S.A.I.C.—See Honeywell Inc.; *U.S. Public,* pg. 835
HONEYWELL SOUTHERN AFRICA LTD.—See Honeywell Inc.; *U.S. Public,* pg. 835
HONEYWELL SPA—See Honeywell Inc.; *U.S. Public,* pg. 835
HONEYWELL SSRO—See Honeywell Inc.; *U.S. Public,* pg. 835
HONEYWELL STERCH INDUSTRIAL AUTOMATION—See Honeywell Inc.; *U.S. Public,* pg. 835
HONEYWELL SYSTEMS (THAILAND) LTD.—See Honeywell Inc.; *U.S. Public,* pg. 835
HONEYWELL TAIWAN LIMITED—See Honeywell Inc.; *U.S. Public,* pg. 835
HONEYWELL TURKI ARABIA LTD.—See Honeywell Inc.; *U.S. Public,* pg. 835
HONEYWELL'S MICRO SWITCH DIVISION—See Honeywell Inc.; *U.S. Public,* pg. 834
HONG FOK CORPORATION LTD.; *Int'l,* pg. 635
HONG FOK LAND PTE. LTD.—See Hong Fok Corporation Ltd.; *Int'l,* pg. 635
HONG KONG AIR TERMINAL SERVICES LTD.—See Jardine Matheson Holdings Limited; *Int'l,* pg. 705
HONG KONG CONVENIENCE STORES LIMITED—See Jardine Matheson Holdings Limited; *Int'l,* pg. 704
HONG KONG FUJIDENKI CO., LTD.—See Fuji Electric Co., *Int'l,* pg. 522
THE HONG KONG LAND PROPERTY COMPANY LTD.—See Jardine Matheson Holdings Limited; *Int'l,* pg. 704
HONG KONG LTD.—See Wolters Kluwer N.V.; *Int'l,* pg. 1513
HONG KONG OFFICE—See Yamaichi Securities Co., Ltd.; *Int'l,* pg. 1517
HONG KONG OXYGEN & ACETYLENE CO. LTD.—See The BOC Group plc; *Int'l,* pg. 122
HONG KONG SECURITY LTD.—See Jardine Matheson Holdings Limited; *Int'l,* pg. 704

HONG KONG TELECOM CSL LIMITED—See Cable and Wireless plc; *Int'l*, pg. 247
HONG KONG TELECOM INTERNATIONAL LIMITED—See Cable and Wireless plc; *Int'l*, pg. 247
HONG KONG TELECOMMUNICATIONS LIMITED—See Cable and Wireless plc; *Int'l*, pg. 247
HONG KONG TELEPHONE COMPANY LTD.—See Cable and Wireless plc; *Int'l*, pg. 247
HONG KONG YAMAZAKI BAKING CO., LTD.—See Yamazaki Baking Co., Ltd.; *Int'l*, pg. 1519
HONG LEONG ASSURANCE SDN. BHD. (NON-LIFE DIV)—See Allianz Aktiengesellschaft; *Int'l*, pg. 60
HONGGROUP NOMINEES LIMITED—See HSBC Holdings plc; *Int'l*, pg. 580
THE HONGKONG AND SHANGHAI BANKING CORPORATION LIMITED (HONGKONGBANK)—See HSBC Holdings plc; *Int'l*, pg. 583
HONGKONG AND SHANGHAI THOMAS COOK LTD.—See HSBC Holdings plc; *Int'l*, pg. 583
HONGKONG BANK (BAHAMAS) LIMITED—See HSBC Holdings plc; *Int'l*, pg. 583
HONGKONG BANK MALAYSIA BERHAD—See HSBC Holdings plc; *Int'l*, pg. 583
HONGKONG BANK OF CANADA—See HSBC Holdings plc; *Int'l*, pg. 583
HONGKONG INTERNATIONAL TRADE FINANCE (JAPAN) KK—See HSBC Holdings plc; *Int'l*, pg. 583
HONGKONG LAND HOLDINGS LIMITED—See Jardine Matheson Holdings Limited; *Int'l*, pg. 704
HONGKONGBANK OF AUSTRALIA LIMITED—See HSBC Holdings plc; *Int'l*, pg. 583
HONICKMAN AFFILIATES; *U.S. Private*, pg. 537
HONIG FOODS-B.V.—See CSM N.V.; *Int'l*, pg. 244
HONIG MERKARTIKELEN B.V.—See CSM N.V.; *Int'l*, pg. 244
HONOLULU FUELING FACILITIES CORP.—See Japan Airlines Company, Ltd.; *Int'l*, pg. 700
HONORIS COMPANIA DE SEGUROS DE VIDA S.A.—See Cigna Corp.; *U.S. Public*, pg. 364
HOOD & COMPANY—See Groupe Usinor; *Int'l*, pg. 572
HOOD COMMUNICATIONS, INC.—See Lombardi Holdings Inc.; *U.S. Private*, pg. 673
HOOD CORPORATION—See Lombardi Holdings Inc.; *U.S. Private*, pg. 673
HOOD INDUSTRIES INC.—See The Carpenter Group; *U.S. Private*, pg. 215
HOOD LUMBER CO.; *U.S. Private*, pg. 538
HOOGOVENS ALUMINIUM BAUSYSTEME GMBH—See Koninklijke Hoogovens N.V.; *Int'l*, pg. 755
HOOGOVENS ALUMINIUM BUILDING SYSTEMS LTD.—See Koninklijke Hoogovens N.V.; *Int'l*, pg. 755
HOOGOVENS ALUMINIUM BUILDING SYSTEMS NV—See Koninklijke Hoogovens N.V.; *Int'l*, pg. 755
HOOGOVENS ALUMINIUM BV—See Koninklijke Hoogovens N.V.; *Int'l*, pg. 753
HOOGOVENS ALUMINIUM CORP.—See Koninklijke Hoogovens N.V.; *Int'l*, pg. 755
HOOGOVENS ALUMINIUM DANMARK A/S—See Koninklijke Hoogovens N.V.; *Int'l*, pg. 755
HOOGOVENS ALUMINIUM ESPANA SA—See Koninklijke Hoogovens N.V.; *Int'l*, pg. 755
HOOGOVENS ALUMINIUM EUROPE SRL—See Koninklijke Hoogovens N.V.; *Int'l*, pg. 755
HOOGOVENS ALUMINIUM FRANCE SA—See Koninklijke Hoogovens N.V.; *Int'l*, pg. 755
HOOGOVENS ALUMINIUM GMBH—See Koninklijke Hoogovens N.V.; *Int'l*, pg. 754
HOOGOVENS ALUMINIUM HUTTENWERK GMBH—See Koninklijke Hoogovens N.V.; *Int'l*, pg. 755
HOOGOVENS ALUMINIUM INTERNATIONAL NV—See Koninklijke Hoogovens N.V.; *Int'l*, pg. 755
HOOGOVENS ALUMINIUM ITALIA SPA—See Koninklijke Hoogovens N.V.; *Int'l*, pg. 755
HOOGOVENS ALUMINIUM JAPAN LTD.—See Koninklijke Hoogovens N.V.; *Int'l*, pg. 755
HOOGOVENS ALUMINIUM METALL GMBH—See Koninklijke Hoogovens N.V.; *Int'l*, pg. 755
HOOGOVENS ALUMINIUM NV—See Koninklijke Hoogovens N.V.; *Int'l*, pg. 755
HOOGOVENS ALUMINIUM NV FILIAL SVERIGE—See Koninklijke Hoogovens N.V.; *Int'l*, pg. 755
HOOGOVENS ALUMINIUM NV PROFIEL CENTRUM—See Koninklijke Hoogovens N.V.; *Int'l*, pg. 755
HOOGOVENS ALUMINIUM PORTUGAL LDA.—See Koninklijke Hoogovens N.V.; *Int'l*, pg. 755
HOOGOVENS ALUMINIUM PRIMARY PRODUCTS—See Koninklijke Hoogovens N.V.; *Int'l*, pg. 753
HOOGOVENS ALUMINIUM PROFILTECHNIK BITTERFELD GMBH—See Koninklijke Hoogovens N.V.; *Int'l*, pg. 755
HOOGOVENS ALUMINIUM PROFILTECHNIK GMBH—See Koninklijke Hoogovens N.V.; *Int'l*, pg. 755
HOOGOVENS ALUMINIUM QUEBEC AND COMPANY LTD.—See Koninklijke Hoogovens N.V.; *Int'l*, pg. 755
HOOGOVENS ALUMINIUM SALES BV—See Koninklijke Hoogovens N.V.; *Int'l*, pg. 753
HOOGOVENS ALUMINIUM SERVICE CENTER NV—See Koninklijke Hoogovens N.V.; *Int'l*, pg. 755
HOOGOVENS ALUMINIUM SIDAL GMBH—See Koninklijke Hoogovens N.V.; *Int'l*, pg. 755
HOOGOVENS ALUMINIUM U.K. LTD.—See Koninklijke Hoogovens N.V.; *Int'l*, pg. 755
HOOGOVENS ALUMINIUM VERKAUF GMBH—See Koninklijke Hoogovens N.V.; *Int'l*, pg. 755
HOOGOVENS ALUMINIUM WALZPRODUKTE GMBH—See Koninklijke Hoogovens N.V.; *Int'l*, pg. 755
HOOGOVENS BEHEERMAATSCHAPPIJ INDUSTRIELE PRODUKTEN BV—See Koninklijke Hoogovens N.V.; *Int'l*, pg. 753
HOOGOVENS BUIZEN B.V.—See Koninklijke Hoogovens N.V.; *Int'l*, pg. 754
HOOGOVENS BV—See Koninklijke Hoogovens N.V.; *Int'l*, pg. 754
HOOGOVENS CORPORATE SERVICES BV—See Koninklijke Hoogovens N.V.; *Int'l*, pg. 753

HOOGOVENS GROEP B.V.—See Koninklijke Hoogovens N.V.; *Int'l*, pg. 753
HOOGOVENS HANDEL BV—See Koninklijke Hoogovens N.V.; *Int'l*, pg. 754
HOOGOVENS HYLITE BV—See Koninklijke Hoogovens N.V.; *Int'l*, pg. 753
HOOGOVENS IJMUIDEN—See Koninklijke Hoogovens N.V.; *Int'l*, pg. 753
HOOGOVENS IJMUIDEN VERKOOPKANTOOR B.V.—See Koninklijke Hoogovens N.V.; *Int'l*, pg. 753
HOOGOVENS ITALIA SRL—See Koninklijke Hoogovens N.V.; *Int'l*, pg. 754
HOOGOVENS METALS BV—See Koninklijke Hoogovens N.V.; *Int'l*, pg. 754
HOOGOVENS PACKAGING STEEL—See Koninklijke Hoogovens N.V.; *Int'l*, pg. 756
HOOGOVENS RESEARCH & DEVELOPMENT—See Koninklijke Hoogovens N.V.; *Int'l*, pg. 754
HOOGOVENS SCRAP PROCESSING BV—See Koninklijke Hoogovens N.V.; *Int'l*, pg. 753
HOOGOVENS STAAL BV—See Koninklijke Hoogovens N.V.; *Int'l*, pg. 754
HOOGOVENS STAALVERWERKING EN HANDEL BV—See Koninklijke Hoogovens N.V.; *Int'l*, pg. 754
HOOGOVENS STEEL PRIMARY PRODUCTS—See Koninklijke Hoogovens N.V.; *Int'l*, pg. 756
HOOGOVENS STEEL PRODUCTS—See Koninklijke Hoogovens N.V.; *Int'l*, pg. 756
HOOGOVENS STEEL SERVICE CENTER LTD.—See Koninklijke Hoogovens N.V.; *Int'l*, pg. 754
HOOGOVENS STEEL STRIP MILL PRODUCTS—See Koninklijke Hoogovens N.V.; *Int'l*, pg. 754
HOOGOVENS TECHNICAL SERVICE DO BRASIL LTDA.—See Koninklijke Hoogovens N.V.; *Int'l*, pg. 755
HOOGOVENS TECHNICAL SERVICES BV—See Koninklijke Hoogovens N.V.; *Int'l*, pg. 754
HOOGOVENS TECHNICAL SERVICES CHINA—See Koninklijke Hoogovens N.V.; *Int'l*, pg. 755
HOOGOVENS TECHNICAL SERVICES ENERGY & ENVIRONMENT BV—See Koninklijke Hoogovens N.V.; *Int'l*, pg. 755
HOOGOVENS TECHNICAL SERVICES INSPECTION SYSTEMS BV—See Koninklijke Hoogovens N.V.; *Int'l*, pg. 753
HOOGOVENS TECHNICAL SERVICES IRON & STEEL BV—See Koninklijke Hoogovens N.V.; *Int'l*, pg. 755
HOOGOVENS TECHNICAL SERVICES POLAND—See Koninklijke Hoogovens N.V.; *Int'l*, pg. 755
HOOGOVENS TECHNICAL SERVICES TECHNOLOGICAL & OPERATIONAL ASSISTANCE BV—See Koninklijke Hoogovens N.V.; *Int'l*, pg. 755
HOOGOVENS TECHNICAL SERVICES TECHNOLOGICAL & OPERATIONAL ASSISTANCE INC.—See Koninklijke Hoogovens N.V.; *Int'l*, pg. 755
HOOGOVENS TECHNICAL SERVICES USA, INC.—See Koninklijke Hoogovens N.V.; *Int'l*, pg. 755
HOOGOVENS TECHNISCHE DIENSTVERLENING BV—See Koninklijke Hoogovens N.V.; *Int'l*, pg. 754
HOOGOVENS (UK) LTD.—See Koninklijke Hoogovens N.V.; *Int'l*, pg. 754
HOOGOVENS WAPENINGSSTAAL BV—See Koninklijke Hoogovens N.V.; *Int'l*, pg. 754
J.G. HOOK ENTERPRISES, INC.—See J.G. Hook, Inc.; *U.S. Private*, pg. 538
J.G. HOOK, INC.; *U.S. Private*, pg. 538
V.B. HOOK & CO., INC.; *U.S. Private*, pg. 538
HOOKER FURNITURE CORPORATION; *U.S. Private*, pg. 538
HOOKER INDUSTRIES; *U.S. Public*, pg. 538
HOOPER HOLMES CORPORATION; *U.S. Public*, pg. 835
AB HOORS PLAT—See Electrolux, AB; *Int'l*, pg. 439
HOOSIER INSURANCE COMPANY—See Credit Suisse Group; *Int'l*, pg. 346
HOOSIER PARK LTD.—See Churchill Downs, Inc.; *U.S. Public*, pg. 356
HOOSIER WIRE, INC.—See Hicks, Muse, Tate & Furst Inc.; *U.S. Private*, pg. 526
HOOVER CANADA INC.—See Maytag Corporation; *U.S. Public*, pg. 1065
HOOVER COMPANY—See Maytag Corporation; *U.S. Public*, pg. 1065
HOOVER ELECTRICA PORTUGUESA LTDA.—See Candy S.p.A.; *Int'l*, pg. 260
HOOVER GROUP, INC.; *U.S. Private*, pg. 538
HOOVER HANES COMPANY—See American Industrial Partners; *U.S. Private*, pg. 56
HOOVER LTD.-WHITE GOODS MANUFACTURING FACILITY—See Candy S.p.A.; *Int'l*, pg. 260
HOOVER LTD.-FLOOR CARE MANUFACTURING FACILITY—See Candy S.p.A.; *Int'l*, pg. 260
HOOVER MAJOR APPLIANCES—See Candy S.p.A.; *Int'l*, pg. 260
HOOVER MEXICANA S.A. DE C.V.—See Maytag Corporation; *U.S. Public*, pg. 1065
HOOVER STAINLESS PTE LTD.—See Superior Metal Printing Limited; *Int'l*, pg. 1322
HOOVER TREATED WOOD PRODUCTS, INC.—See Nortek, Inc.; *U.S. Public*, pg. 1193
HOPE BROOK MINE—See Royal Oak Mines Inc.; *U.S. Public*, pg. 1411
HOPE GAS, INC.—See Consolidated Natural Gas Company; *U.S. Public*, pg. 435
HOPE'S ARCHITECTURAL PRODUCTS INC.; *U.S. Private*, pg. 538
HOP-IN MICHIGAN, INC.—See Silcorp Limited; *Int'l*, pg. 1249
HOPKINS & BAILEY LTD.—See Shandwick International Plc; *Int'l*, pg. 1226
HOPKINSONS LTD.—See Weir Group PLC; *Int'l*, pg. 1489
HOPKINSVILLE ELEVATOR COMPANY, INC.; *U.S. Private*, pg. 538
HOPKINSVILLE MILLING CO.; *U.S. Private*, pg. 538
HOPKINTON LNG CORP.—See Commonwealth Energy System; *U.S. Public*, pg. 415

HOPPER SOLIDAY & CO., INC.—See Allied Irish Banks, p.l.c.; *Int'l*, pg. 65
HOPPE'S A BRUNSWICK COMPANY—See Brunswick Corporation; *U.S. Public*, pg. 266
HOPPLE PLASTICS, INC.; *U.S. Private*, pg. 538
HORACE MANN EDUCATORS CORPORATION; *U.S. Public*, pg. 835
HORACE MANN INSURANCE COMPANY—See Horace Mann Educators Corporation; *U.S. Public*, pg. 836
HORACE MANN LIFE INSURANCE COMPANY—See Horace Mann Educators Corporation; *U.S. Public*, pg. 836
HORACE SMALL APPAREL COMPANY—See Horace Small Apparel PLC; *Int'l*, pg. 635
HORACE SMALL APPAREL PLC; *Int'l*, pg. 635
HORAN GOLDMAN COMPANIES INC.—See Jardine Matheson Holdings Limited; *Int'l*, pg. 705
HOPDA PACKINGSINDUSTRI AB—See Trelleborg AB; *Int'l*, pg. 1422
HORIKIRI SPRING MFG. CO., LTD.—See NHK Spring Co., Ltd.; *Int'l*, pg. 901
HORIZON AEROSPACE LLC; *U.S. Private*, pg. 538
HORIZON AIR INDUSTRIES—See Alaska Air Group, Inc.; *U.S. Public*, pg. 35
HORIZON ALUMINIUM PRODS. LTD.—See Alcan Aluminium Limited; *Int'l*, pg. 51
HORIZON BANCORP; *U.S. Private*, pg. 538
HORIZON BANCORP, INC.; *U.S. Public*, pg. 836
HORIZON BANK—See Horizon Bancorp; *U.S. Private*, pg. 539
HORIZON CARPET—See Mohawk Industries, Inc.; *U.S. Public*, pg. 1121
HORIZON/CMS HEALTHCARE CORPORATION; *U.S. Public*, pg. 836
HORIZON COAL SERVICES, INC.—See Montana Power Company; *U.S. Public*, pg. 1127
HORIZON COMMUNICATIONS SYSTEMS LIMITED—See Telefonaktiebolaget LM Ericsson; *Int'l*, pg. 1368
HORIZON DISTRIBUTION INC.; *U.S. Private*, pg. 539
HORIZON ENTERPRISES GROUP LLC; *U.S. Private*, pg. 539
HORIZON HEALTHCARE & SPECIALTY CENTER—See Horizon/CMS Healthcare Corporation; *U.S. Public*, pg. 836
HORIZON INITIATIVES—See Computer Sciences Corporation; *U.S. Public*, pg. 423
HORIZON INTERNATIONAL—See The Oshawa Group Limited; *Int'l*, pg. 1012
HORIZON INVESTMENT CORP.—See Schindler Holding AG; *Int'l*, pg. 1205
HORIZON INVESTMENT GROUP—See Horizon Enterprises Group LLC; *U.S. Private*, pg. 539
HORIZON MEADOWS—See Horizon/CMS Healthcare Corporation; *U.S. Public*, pg. 838
HORIZON PAPER CO., INC.; *U.S. Private*, pg. 539
HORIZON PLACE ASSOCIATES—See Cigna Corp.; *U.S. Public*, pg. 361
HORIZON PROPERTIES—See Horizon Enterprises Group LLC; *U.S. Private*, pg. 539
HORIZON SPECIALTY CENTER OF PENSACOLA—See Horizon/CMS Healthcare Corporation; *U.S. Public*, pg. 836
HORIZON SPECIALTY HOSPITAL—See Horizon/CMS Healthcare Corporation; *U.S. Public*, pg. 839
HORIZON SPECIALTY HOSPITAL - ALBUQUERQUE—See Horizon/CMS Healthcare Corporation; *U.S. Public*, pg. 838
HORIZON SPECIALTY HOSPITAL - CORPUS CHRISTI—See Horizon/CMS Healthcare Corporation; *U.S. Public*, pg. 839
HORIZON SPECIALTY HOSPITAL - EL PASO—See Horizon/CMS Healthcare Corporation; *U.S. Public*, pg. 839
HORIZON SPECIALTY HOSPITAL - KANSAS CITY—See Horizon/CMS Healthcare Corporation; *U.S. Public*, pg. 837
HORIZON SPECIALTY HOSPITAL - LAS VEGAS—See Horizon/CMS Healthcare Corporation; *U.S. Public*, pg. 837
HORIZON SPECIALTY HOSPITAL - LUBBOCK—See Horizon/CMS Healthcare Corporation; *U.S. Public*, pg. 839
HORIZON SPECIALTY HOSPITAL - SAN ANTONIO—See Horizon/CMS Healthcare Corporation; *U.S. Public*, pg. 839
HORIZON SPECIALTY HOSPITAL - WICHITA—See Horizon/CMS Healthcare Corporation; *U.S. Public*, pg. 837
HORIZON SPECIALTY & REHABILITATION CENTER OF KISSIMMEE—See Horizon/CMS Healthcare Corporation; *U.S. Public*, pg. 836
HORIZON TECHNOLOGY GROUP - JACKSON DIVISION—See Horizon Enterprises Group LLC; *U.S. Private*, pg. 539
HORIZON TECHNOLOGY GROUP LLC—See Horizon Enterprises Group LLC; *U.S. Private*, pg. 539
HORIZON TECHNOLOGY GROUP - TAYLOR DIVISION—See Horizon Enterprises Group LLC; *U.S. Private*, pg. 539
HORIZON TECHNOLOGY GROUP - TIFFIN DIVISION—See Horizon Enterprises Group LLC; *U.S. Private*, pg. 539
HORIZON VILLAGE NURSING & REHABILITATION—See Horizon/CMS Healthcare Corporation; *U.S. Public*, pg. 838
HORIZON'S BAYSIDE MANOR—See Horizon/CMS Healthcare Corporation; *U.S. Public*, pg. 836
HORIZONS CONSULTING INC.—See Computer Horizons Corp.; *U.S. Public*, pg. 421
HORMEL FOODS CORP.; *U.S. Public*, pg. 840
HORMEL FROZEN FOODS DIV—See Hormel Foods Corp.; *U.S. Public*, pg. 840
HORMEL INTERNATIONAL CORPORATION—See Hormel Foods Corp.; *U.S. Public*, pg. 840

HORMOQUIMICA DE CHILE LTDA.—See Akzo Nobel N.V.; *Int'l*, pg. 44
HORN PACKAGING CORPORATION; *U.S. Private*, pg. 539
HORNADY AMMUNITION—See Hornady Manufacturing Company; *U.S. Private*, pg. 540
HORNADY MANUFACTURING COMPANY; *U.S. Private*, pg. 539
HORNBACHERS—See SuperValu, Inc.; *U.S. Public*, pg. 1541
HORNE & PITFIELD—See The Oshawa Group Limited; *Int'l*, pg. 1012
ROBERT HORNE GROUP PLC—See N.V. Koninklijke KNP BT; *Int'l*, pg. 757
ROBERT HORNE PAPER COMPANY LIMITED—See N.V. Koninklijke KNP BT; *Int'l*, pg. 757
ROBERT HORNE PAPER (IRELAND) LIMITED—See N.V. Koninklijke KNP BT; *Int'l*, pg. 757
ROBERT HORNE PAPER (SCOTLAND) LIMITED—See N.V. Koninklijke KNP BT; *Int'l*, pg. 757
FRANK W. HORNER INC. (CANADA)—See Carter-Wallace, Inc.; *U.S. Public*, pg. 310
HORNER RAUSCH OPTICAL COMPANY EAST, INC.; *U.S. Private*, pg. 540
HORNOR, TOWNSEND & KENT—See The Penn Mutual Life Insurance Company; *U.S. Private*, pg. 849
HOROWITZ SALVAGE—See Commercial Metals Company; *U.S. Public*, pg. 412
HORRIGAN AMERICAN INC.—See ABN-AMRO Holding N.V.; *Int'l*, pg. 9
HORSEHEAD INDUSTRIES, INC.; *U.S. Private*, pg. 540
HORSEHEAD RESOURCE DEVELOPMENT CO., INC.—See Metallgesellschaft AG; *Int'l*, pg. 860
HORSEHEAD RESOURCE DEVELOPMENT COMPANY, INC.—See Horsehead Industries, Inc.; *U.S. Private*, pg. 540
HORSFALL & BICKHAM LIMITED—See Carclo Engineering Group plc; *Int'l*, pg. 268
HORST BREVER GMBH—See Masco Corporation; *U.S. Public*, pg. 1055
HORST & SONS FORLAG A/S—See B.H. Blackwell Ltd.; *Int'l*, pg. 197
HORSTMAN TIMERS & CONTROLS LIMITED—See Clayhithe P.L.C.; *Int'l*, pg. 297
HORTICOM BV—See Reed Elsevier plc; *Int'l*, pg. 1099
HORTON AUTOMATICS DIV.—See Overhead Door Corporation; *U.S. Private*, pg. 823
HORTON AUTOMATICS, LTD.—See Overhead Door Corporation; *U.S. Private*, pg. 823
D.R. HORTON, INC.; *U.S. Public*, pg. 840
HORTON HOMES, INC.; *U.S. Private*, pg. 540
THE LEWIS HORWITZ ORGANIZATION; *U.S. Private*, pg. 540
HOSE PRODUCTS DIV. PLANT—See Parker Hannifin Corporation; *U.S. Public*, pg. 1260
HOSHO AMERICA INC.—See Kibun Co. Ltd.; *Int'l*, pg. 733
HOSIDEN CORPORATION; *Int'l*, pg. 635
HOSKINS MFG. CO.—See Armada Corporation; *U.S. Private*, pg. 83
HOSKINS THERMAL SYSTEMS, INC.—See Armada Corporation; *U.S. Private*, pg. 83
HOSKYNS GROUP PLC—See CAP Gemini S.A.; *Int'l*, pg. 264
HOSOFT GMBH—See Gores Technology Group; *U.S. Private*, pg. 465
HOSOKAWA MICRON AUSTRALIA PTY. LTD.—See Hosokawa Micron Corporation; *Int'l*, pg. 636
HOSOKAWA MICRON B.V.—See Hosokawa Micron Corporation; *Int'l*, pg. 636
HOSOKAWA MICRON CORPORATION; *Int'l*, pg. 635
HOSOKAWA MICRON ESPANA S.A.—See Hosokawa Micron Corporation; *Int'l*, pg. 636
HOSOKAWA MICRON INTERNATIONAL B.V.—See Hosokawa Micron Corporation; *Int'l*, pg. 636
HOSOKAWA MICRON INTERNATIONAL INC.—See Hosokawa Micron Corporation; *Int'l*, pg. 635
HOSOKAWA MICRON LTD.—See Hosokawa Micron Corporation; *Int'l*, pg. 636
HOSOKAWA MICRON POWDER SYSTEMS—See Hosokawa Micron Corporation; *Int'l*, pg. 636
HOSOKAWA MIKROPUL GMBH—See Hosokawa Micron Corporation; *Int'l*, pg. 636
HOSPAL B.V.—See Incentive AB; *Int'l*, pg. 668
HOSPAL-COBE RENAL N.V.—See Incentive AB; *Int'l*, pg. 668
HOSPAL DASCO S.P.A.—See Incentive AB; *Int'l*, pg. 668
HOSPAL-GAMBRO LIMITEE—See Incentive AB; *Int'l*, pg. 668
HOSPAL INDUSTRIE S.A.—See Incentive AB; *Int'l*, pg. 668
HOSPAL INTERNATIONAL MARKETING—See Incentive AB; *Int'l*, pg. 668
HOSPAL LTD.—See Incentive AB; *Int'l*, pg. 668
HOSPAL MED TECH GMBH—See Incentive AB; *Int'l*, pg. 668
HOSPAL MEDIZINTECHNISCHE PRODUKTE GES.M.B.H—See Incentive AB; *Int'l*, pg. 668
HOSPAL S.A.—See Incentive AB; *Int'l*, pg. 668
HOSPAL S.P.A.—See Incentive AB; *Int'l*, pg. 668
HOSPITAL AFFILIATES DEVELOPMENT CORPORATION; *U.S. Private*, pg. 540
HOSPITAL BUILDING & EQUIPMENT CO.—See HBE Corporation/Design Build Divisions; *U.S. Private*, pg. 489
HOSPITAL DATA PROCESSING—See Columbia/HCA Healthcare Corporation; *U.S. Public*, pg. 405
HOSPITAL DEVELOPMENT CO.—See Columbia/HCA Healthcare Corporation; *U.S. Public*, pg. 405
HOSPITAL GROUP OF AMERICA—See The Cooper Companies; *U.S. Public*, pg. 442
HOSPITAL INVESTORS, INC.—See Magellan Health Services, Inc.; *U.S. Public*, pg. 1036
HOSPITAL MANAGEMENT & SUPPLIES LIMITED—See Alliance UniChem PLC; *Int'l*, pg. 58
HOSPITAL STAFFING SERVICES, INC.; *U.S. Public*, pg. 840

HOSPITAL STAFFING SERVICES OF CALIFORNIA, INC.—See Hospital Staffing Services, Inc.; *U.S. Public*, pg. 840
HOSPITAL STAFFING SERVICES OF MASSACHUSETTS, INC.—See Hospital Staffing Services, Inc.; *U.S. Public*, pg. 840
HOSPITAL STAFFING SERVICES OF TENNESEE, INC.—See Hospital Staffing Services, Inc.; *U.S. Public*, pg. 840
THE HOSPITAL TRUST LEASING CORPORATION—See BankBoston Corporation; *U.S. Public*, pg. 184
HOSPITALITY—See Sodexho S.A.; *Int'l*, pg. 1274
HOSPITALITY DESIGN—See VNU Verenigde Nederlandse Uitgeversbedrijven B.V.; *Int'l*, pg. 1446
HOSPITALITY INT. THAILANDE—See Accor S.A.; *Int'l*, pg. 21
HOSPITALITY MANAGEMENT SYSTEMS, INC.—See Sulcus Computer Corp.; *U.S. Public*, pg. 1527
HOSPITALITY PROCUREMENT DIVISION—See Carlson Companies, Inc.; *U.S. Private*, pg. 212
HOSPITALITY WORLDWIDE SERVICES, INC.; *U.S. Public*, pg. 841
HOST APPAREL, INC.; *U.S. Private*, pg. 540
HOST FOR HER—See Host Apparel, Inc.; *U.S. Private*, pg. 540
HOST INTERNATIONAL, INC.—See Host Marriott Services Corporation; *U.S. Public*, pg. 841
HOST MARRIOTT CORPORATION; *U.S. Public*, pg. 841
HOST MARRIOTT SERVICES CORPORATION; *U.S. Public*, pg. 841
HOSTALEN POLYETHYLEN—See Hoechst Aktiengesellschaft AG; *Int'l*, pg. 626
HOSTESS FRITO-LAY CO.—See PepsiCo, Inc.; *U.S. Public*, pg. 1277
HOSTMARK MANAGEMENT GROUP; *U.S. Private*, pg. 541
HOSTRA BETEILIGUNGS GMBH—See Commerzbank AG; *Int'l*, pg. 310
HOT'N NOW—See Tricon Global Restaurants, Inc.; *U.S. Public*, pg. 1637
HOT SHOPPES CAFETERIAS & RESTAURANTS—See Marriott International, Inc.; *U.S. Public*, pg. 1048
HOT SHOT DELIVERY INC.; *U.S. Private*, pg. 541
HOTEC—See Accor S.A.; *Int'l*, pg. 20
HOTEL CIPRIANI S.P.A.—See Sea Containers Ltd.; *Int'l*, pg. 1213
HOTEL CORPORATION OF AMERICA; *U.S. Private*, pg. 541
HOTEL INTER-CONTINENTAL—See The Saison Group; *Int'l*, pg. 1178
HOTEL LOWEN SCHRUNS GMBH—See Liebherr-International AG; *Int'l*, pg. 808
HOTEL MEAD CORP.—See Consolidated Papers, Inc.; *U.S. Public*, pg. 436
HOTEL NASSAUER HOF GMBH—See Veba AG; *Int'l*, pg. 1459
HOTEL NIKKO SAN FRANCISCO—See Japan Airlines Company, Ltd.; *Int'l*, pg. 700
HOTEL PLAZA LIMITED—See United Overseas Land Limited; *Int'l*, pg. 1443
HOTEL RITZ MADRID S.A.—See Granada Group PLC; *Int'l*, pg. 556
HOTEL SHILLA CO. LTD.—See Nissho Iwai Corporation; *Int'l*, pg. 947
HOTEL SPLENDIDO—See Sea Containers Ltd.; *Int'l*, pg. 1213
HOTEL ZURICH AG—See Oerlikon-Buhrle Holding AG; *Int'l*, pg. 996
HOTELPLAN INTERNATIONAL TRAVEL ORGANIZATION AG—See Migros; *Int'l*, pg. 865
HOTELTOUR—See Club Mediterranee SA; *Int'l*, pg. 298
HOTPAC RESERVATIONS (NZ) LTD.—See Air New Zealand Ltd.; *Int'l*, pg. 38
HOTPOINT LTD.—See The General Electric Company, p.l.c.; *Int'l*, pg. 544
THE HOTSY CORPORATION—See Harbour Group Ltd.; *U.S. Private*, pg. 500
HOUCHENS INDUSTRIES INC.; *U.S. Private*, pg. 541
HOUCHENS MARKETS—See Houchens Industries Inc.; *U.S. Private*, pg. 541
HOUCHIN AEROSPACE LIMITED—See TT Group PLC; *Int'l*, pg. 1344
HOUCK INDUSTRIES, INC.; *U.S. Private*, pg. 541
HOUGEN MANUFACTURING INC.; *U.S. Private*, pg. 541
HOUGET DUESBERG BOSSON—See N. Schlumberger & Cie; *Int'l*, pg. 1206
HOUGHTON A.G. SWITZERLAND—See Houghton International Inc.; *U.S. Private*, pg. 541
HOUGHTON-BENELUX B.V.—See Houghton International Inc.; *U.S. Private*, pg. 541
HOUGHTON BRAZIL LTDA.—See Houghton International Inc.; *U.S. Private*, pg. 541
HOUGHTON CANADA INC.—See Houghton International Inc.; *U.S. Private*, pg. 541
HOUGHTON INTERNATIONAL INC.; *U.S. Private*, pg. 541
HOUGHTON ITALIA S.P.A.—See Houghton International Inc.; *U.S. Private*, pg. 541
HOUGHTON MIFFLIN COLLEGE DIV.—See Houghton Mifflin Company; *U.S. Public*, pg. 841
HOUGHTON MIFFLIN COMPANY; *U.S. Public*, pg. 841
HOUGHTON MIFFLIN INTERACTIVE CORP.—See Houghton Mifflin Company; *U.S. Public*, pg. 841
HOUGHTON MIFFLIN SCHOOL DIVISION—See Houghton Mifflin Company; *U.S. Public*, pg. 841
HOUGHTON MIFFLIN TRADE & REFERENCE DIV.—See Houghton Mifflin Company; *U.S. Public*, pg. 841
HOUGHTON VAUGHN PLC—See Houghton International Inc.; *U.S. Private*, pg. 541
HOUILLERES DE BASSIN DU CENTRE ET DU MIDI—See Charbonnages de France; *Int'l*, pg. 280
HOULIHAN'S RESTAURANT GROUP; *U.S. Public*, pg. 841
THE HOUMA COURIER NEWSPAPER CORPORATION—See The New York Times Company; *U.S. Public*, pg. 1175

HOUNDOUVILLE MILL—See Fort James Corporation; *U.S. Public*, pg. 673
HOUSATONIC CORPORATION—See Yankee Energy System, Inc.; *U.S. Public*, pg. 1787
HOUSE BEAUTIFUL—See The Hearst Corporation; *U.S. Private*, pg. 517
HOUSE-HASSON HARDWARE CO.—See Distribution America; *U.S. Private*, pg. 335
HOUSE OF BANFI—See Banfi Vintners; *U.S. Private*, pg. 113
HOUSE OF BIANCHI, INC.; *U.S. Private*, pg. 541
HOUSE OF CRAVEN LTD.—See Rothmans UK Holdings Limited; *Int'l*, pg. 1130
HOUSE OF FABRICS, INC.; *U.S. Public*, pg. 842
HOUSE OF FULLER, S.A. DE C.V.—See Sara Lee Corporation; *U.S. Public*, pg. 1434
HOUSE OF LLOYD JAPAN, INC.—See Duskin Co., Ltd.; *Int'l*, pg. 422
HOUSE OF PERFECTION, INC.; *U.S. Private*, pg. 542
HOUSE OF RAEFORD FARMS, INC.; *U.S. Private*, pg. 542
HOUSE OF RONNIE, INC.; *U.S. Private*, pg. 542
THE HOUSE OF SEAGRAM—See The Seagram Company Ltd.; *Int'l*, pg. 1217
HOUSE OF TRADE & CONSTRUCTION CO.—See GESTRA GmbH; *Int'l*, pg. 550
HOUSE OF WHITE BIRCHES, INC.; *U.S. Private*, pg. 542
HOUSEHOLD BANK F.S.B.—See Household International, Inc.; *U.S. Public*, pg. 842
HOUSEHOLD BANK, N.A.—See Household International, Inc.; *U.S. Public*, pg. 842
HOUSEHOLD CREDIT SERVICES—See Household International, Inc.; *U.S. Public*, pg. 842
HOUSEHOLD FINANCE CORPORATION—See Household International, Inc.; *U.S. Public*, pg. 842
HOUSEHOLD FINANCE INTL. N.V.—See Household International, Inc.; *U.S. Public*, pg. 842
HOUSEHOLD FINANCE LTD.—See Household International, Inc.; *U.S. Public*, pg. 842
HOUSEHOLD FINANCIAL CORPORATION LIMITED—See Household International, Inc.; *U.S. Public*, pg. 842
HOUSEHOLD INTERNATIONAL, INC.; *U.S. Public*, pg. 842
HOUSEHOLD INTL. (U.K.) LTD.—See Household International, Inc.; *U.S. Public*, pg. 842
HOUSEHOLD LIFE INSURANCE CO.—See Household International, Inc.; *U.S. Public*, pg. 842
HOUSEHOLD PRODUCTS CO.—See The Clorox Company; *U.S. Public*, pg. 387
HOUSEHOLD RENTAL SYSTEMS—See HMI Industries; *U.S. Public*, pg. 771
HOUSEHOLD RETAIL SERVICES, INC.—See Household International, Inc.; *U.S. Public*, pg. 842
HOUSEWARES HOLDING COMPANY—See NACCO Industries, Inc.; *U.S. Public*, pg. 1149
HOUSTON ATLAS—See Thermo Electron Corporation; *U.S. Public*, pg. 1593
HOUSTON CELLULAR TELEPHONE CO.—See AT&T Corporation; *U.S. Public*, pg. 11
HOUSTON CHRONICLE—See The Hearst Corporation; *U.S. Private*, pg. 517
HOUSTON CONTRACTING COMPANY-ALASKA, LTD.—See Arctic Slope Regional Corporation; *U.S. Private*, pg. 80
HOUSTON DIVISION—See Albertson's, Inc.; *U.S. Public*, pg. 38
HOUSTON DIVISION—See U.S. Home Corporation; *U.S. Public*, pg. 1683
HOUSTON ENGINEERS—See Wilson Industries Inc.; *U.S. Private*, pg. 1181
THE HOUSTON EXPLORATION COMPANY—See Brooklyn Union; *U.S. Public*, pg. 259
HOUSTON FEARLESS 76 INC.; *U.S. Private*, pg. 542
HOUSTON FOODS COMPANY; *U.S. Private*, pg. 542
HOUSTON GENERAL INSURANCE CO.—See The Tokio Marine & Fire Insurance Company, Ltd.; *Int'l*, pg. 1392
HOUSTON HELM AND COMPANY—See Houston Herstek Favat; *U.S. Private*, pg. 542
HOUSTON HERSTEK FAVAT; *U.S. Private*, pg. 542
HOUSTON INDUSTRIES ENERGY, INC.—See Houston Industries Incorporated; *U.S. Public*, pg. 843
HOUSTON INDUSTRIES INCORPORATED; *U.S. Public*, pg. 842
HOUSTON INTERNATIONAL MINERALS CORP.—See Tenneco Inc.; *U.S. Public*, pg. 1578
HOUSTON LABORATORY—See Pace Analytical Services; *U.S. Private*, pg. 829
HOUSTON LEARNING CENTER—See Berkshire Hathaway Inc.; *U.S. Public*, pg. 218
HOUSTON LIGHTING & POWER COMPANY—See Houston Industries Incorporated; *U.S. Public*, pg. 843
HOUSTON MARINE CONTAINERS INC.—See Sea Containers Ltd.; *Int'l*, pg. 1214
HOUSTON OIL & MINERALS EXPLORATION CO.—See Tenneco Inc.; *U.S. Public*, pg. 1578
HOUSTON PIPE LINE CO.—See Enron Corp.; *U.S. Public*, pg. 584
HOUSTON PROCESSING CENTER—See Corrections Corporation of America; *U.S. Public*, pg. 450
HOUSTON PRODUCTS—See American Eco Corporation; *Int'l*, pg. 74
HOUSTON STEEL SERVICE COMPANY OF TEXAS—See Commercial Metals Company; *U.S. Public*, pg. 412
HOUSTON VENTURE—See Drug Emporium, Inc.; *U.S. Public*, pg. 530
HOUSTON WARWICK INC.—See Royal Begemann Group; *Int'l*, pg. 1134
HOUTOPSLAG MAATSCHAPPIJ VLISSINGEN B.V.—See The East Asiatic Company Ltd. A/S; *Int'l*, pg. 431
HOVANES B.V.—See Schindler Holding Ltd.; *Int'l*, pg. 1205
HOVELMANN & CO. EISENGROSSHANDLUNG GMBH—See Friedr. Krupp AG; *Int'l*, pg. 514
HOVERSPEED LTD.—See Sea Containers Ltd.; *Int'l*, pg. 1214
HOVNANIAN ENTERPRISES, INC.; *U.S. Public*, pg. 843

MASTER INDEX TO COMPANY NAMES HUFFY

Company Index

K. HOVNANIAN COMPANIES NORTHEAST, INC.—See Hovnanian Enterprises, Inc.; U.S. Public, pg. 843
K. HOVNANIAN COMPANIES OF FLORIDA, INC.—See Hovnanian Enterprises, Inc.; U.S. Public, pg. 843
K. HOVNANIAN INVESTMENT PROPERTIES, INC.—See Hovnanian Enterprises, Inc.; U.S. Public, pg. 843
HOVOMEX S.A. DE C.V.—See Hollingsworth & Vose Co.; U.S. Private, pg. 535
HOW GROUP LIMITED; Int'l, pg. 636
HOWALDTSWERKE-DEUTSCHE WERFT AG—See Preussag AG; Int'l, pg. 1069
HOWARD—See Thrige-Titan Group; Int'l, pg. 1387
HOWARD AUSTRALIA PTY. LTD.—See Thrige-Titan Group; Int'l, pg. 1387
THE HOWARD BANK, N.A.—See Banknorth Group Inc.; U.S. Public, pg. 187
HOWARD CARPET MILLS, INC.—See Shaw Industries, Inc.; U.S. Public, pg. 1464
THE DEE HOWARD COMPANY; U.S. Private, pg. 542
HOWARD ENGINEERING LTD.—See Thrige-Titan Group; Int'l, pg. 1387
HOWARD HUGHES CORPORATION—See The Rouse Company; U.S. Public, pg. 1407
HOWARD JOHNSON—See Taj International Hotels; U.S. Private, pg. 1067
HOWARD MACHINERY (PTY.) LTD.—See Thrige-Titan Group; Int'l, pg. 1387
HOWARD MANUFACTURING—See Greenbull Inc.; U.S. Private, pg. 477
HOWARD MASCHINENFABRIK GMBH—See Thrige-Titan Group; Int'l, pg. 1387
HOWARD, MERRELL & PARTNERS, INC.; U.S. Private, pg. 542
HOWARD PACIFIC LTD.—See Thrige-Titan Group; Int'l, pg. 1387
HOWARD PRODUCTS—See United Receptical, Inc.; U.S. Private, pg. 1124
HOWARD ROTAVATOR CO.—See Thrige-Titan Group; Int'l, pg. 1387
HOWARD S.A.—See Thrige-Titan Group; Int'l, pg. 1387
HOWARD WEIL LABOUISSE FRIEDRICHS, INC.—See Legg Mason, Inc.; U.S. Public, pg. 985
HOWARD'S ELECTRONICS—See Video Display Corporation; U.S. Public, pg. 1720
HOWARDS TV & APPLIANCES, INC.; U.S. Private, pg. 543
HOWDEN AIRDYNAMICS GROUP LIMITED—See Howden Group Plc; Int'l, pg. 636
HOWDEN COMPRESSORS—See Howden Group Plc; Int'l, pg. 636
THE HOWDEN FAN CO.; U.S. Private, pg. 543
HOWDEN FLUID SYSTEMS—See Mark IV Industries Inc.; U.S. Public, pg. 1045
HOWDEN GERMANY—See Howden Group Plc; Int'l, pg. 636
HOWDEN GROUP AUSTRALIA PTY LIMITED—See Howden Group Plc; Int'l, pg. 636
HOWDEN GROUP CANADA LIMITED—See Howden Group Plc; Int'l, pg. 636
HOWDEN GROUP EUROPE B.V.—See Howden Group Plc; Int'l, pg. 637
HOWDEN GROUP PLC; Int'l, pg. 636
HOWDEN GROUP SOUTH AFRICA LIMITED—See Howden Group Plc; Int'l, pg. 637
JAMES HOWDEN AMERICA INC.—See Howden Group Plc; Int'l, pg. 636
JAMES HOWDEN GROUP LIMITED—See Howden Group Plc; Int'l, pg. 636
NOAH HOWDEN, INC.—See Howden Group Plc; Int'l, pg. 636
HOWDEN SIROCCO, FLUID DRIVE DEPARTMENT—See Howden Group Plc; Int'l, pg. 636
HOWDEN SIROCCO, INC.—See Howden Group Plc; Int'l, pg. 636
HOWDEN SOUTH EAST ASIA—See Howden Group Plc; Int'l, pg. 637
HOWE AGRA LIMITED—See Agra Inc.; Int'l, pg. 31
HOWE FURNITURE CORPORATION; U.S. Private, pg. 543
HOWE (INDIA) PRIVATE LTD.—See Agra Inc.; Int'l, pg. 31
HOWE MONENCO INC.—See Agra Inc.; Int'l, pg. 31
HOWE SCALE—See Staveley Industries PLC; Int'l, pg. 1299
HOWE SOUND PULP & PAPER LIMITED—See Canfor Corporation; Int'l, pg. 260
HOWELL CORPORATION; U.S. Public, pg. 843
E.W. HOWELL COMPANY, INC.—See Obayashi Corporation; Int'l, pg. 995
HOWELL GAS MANAGEMENT CO.—See Howell Corporation; U.S. Public, pg. 844
HOWELL HENRY CHALDECOTT LURY & PARTNERS; Int'l, pg. 637
HOWELL INDUSTRIAL CLINIC—See Vencor, Inc.; U.S. Public, pg. 1715
HOWELL INSTRUMENTS INC.; U.S. Private, pg. 543
HOWELL MEDICAL CENTER—See Vencor, Inc.; U.S. Public, pg. 1715
HOWELL METAL COMPANY—See Commercial Metals Company; U.S. Public, pg. 413
HOWELL PACKAGING—See Dover Industries Limited; Int'l, pg. 417
HOWELL PETROLEUM CORP.—See Howell Corporation; U.S. Public, pg. 844
HOWER CORP.—See Forest City Enterprises, Inc.; U.S. Public, pg. 669
HOWES LEATHER CORPORATION; U.S. Private, pg. 543
HOWMEDICA FRANCE S.A.—See Pfizer Inc.; U.S. Public, pg. 1283
HOWMEDICA G.M.B.H.—See Pfizer Inc.; U.S. Public, pg. 1282
HOWMEDICA IBERICA S.A.—See Pfizer Inc.; U.S. Public, pg. 1283
HOWMEDICA, INC.—See Pfizer Inc.; U.S. Public, pg. 1282
HOWMEDICA INTERNATIONAL, INC.—See Pfizer Inc.; U.S. Public, pg. 1282
HOWMEDICA INTERNATIONAL LIMITED—See Pfizer Inc.; U.S. Public, pg. 1283
HOWMEDICA INVESTMENTS PTY. LTD.—See Pfizer Inc.; U.S. Public, pg. 1282
HOWMEDICA LEIBINGER G.M.B.H.—See Pfizer Inc.; U.S. Public, pg. 1282
HOWMEDICA LEIBINGER INC.—See Pfizer Inc.; U.S. Public, pg. 1282
HOWMET-CERCAST INC.—See Carlyle Holding Corporation; U.S. Private, pg. 213
HOWMET CORPORATION—See Carlyle Holding Corporation; U.S. Private, pg. 213
HOWMET CORPORATION—See Thiokol Corporation; U.S. Public, pg. 1597
HOWMET EXETER CASTING—See Carlyle Holding Corporation; U.S. Private, pg. 213
HOWMET-TEMPCRAFT, INC.—See Carlyle Holding Corporation; U.S. Private, pg. 213
HOWMET TURBINE COMPONENT CORPORATION—See Carlyle Holding Corporation; U.S. Private, pg. 213
HOWTEK, INC.; U.S. Public, pg. 844
HOXAN AMERICA INCORPORATED—See Daido Hoxan Inc.; Int'l, pg. 363
O.G. HOYER A/S—See Tetra Laval Group; Int'l, pg. 1378
O.G. HOYER INC.—See Tetra Laval Group; Int'l, pg. 1378
HOYLE PRODUCTS—See Brown & Bigelow, Inc.; U.S. Private, pg. 172
HOYT DEVELOPMENT; U.S. Private, pg. 543
HOYT HOME IMPROVEMENT; U.S. Private, pg. 543
HSBC JAMES CAPEL JAPAN LIMITED—See HSBC Holdings plc; Int'l, pg. 582
HSIN CHONG-PHILIPP HOLZMANN CIVIL ENGINEERING COMPANY LIMITED—See Philipp Holzmann AG; Int'l, pg. 634
HSIN-FENG CHEMICAL CORP.—See Jason Incorporated; U.S. Public, pg. 924
HUA TONG INTERNATIONAL LEASING CO., LTD.—See The Sakura Bank, Limited; Int'l, pg. 1181
HUA YAN BUNDY TUBING CORPORATION—See TI Group plc; Int'l, pg. 1341
HUAGIANG SANYO ELECTRONICS CO., LTD.—See Sanyo Electric Co., Ltd.; Int'l, pg. 1192
HUAMING PHARMACEUTICALS CO. LTD. OF SHANTOU, S.E.Z.—See Meiji Seika Kaisha, Ltd.; Int'l, pg. 856
HUB CITY FOODS—See Fleming Companies, Inc.; U.S. Public, pg. 653
HUB CITY, INC.—See Regal-Beloit Corporation; U.S. Public, pg. 1371
HUB FURNITURE STORE—See Reliable Stores, Inc.; U.S. Private, pg. 920
HUB GROUP, INC.; U.S. Public, pg. 844
HUBACHER, CADILLAC & LANDROVER INC.; U.S. Private, pg. 543
HUBBARD BROADCASTING, INC.; U.S. Private, pg. 543
HUBBARD COMMUNICATIONS—See Hubbard Broadcasting, Inc.; U.S. Private, pg. 544
HUBBARD CONSTRUCTION CO.; U.S. Private, pg. 544
HUBBARD EUROPA B.V.—See Merck & Co., Inc.; U.S. Public, pg. 1091
HUBBARD FARMS, INC.—See Merck & Co., Inc.; U.S. Public, pg. 1092
HUBBARD FEEDS INC.—See Ridley Canada Limited; Int'l, pg. 1116
HUBBARD HALL INC.; U.S. Private, pg. 544
HUBBARD MILLING COMPANY—See Windy Hill Pet Food Co.; U.S. Private, pg. 1182
HUBBARD PETFOOD—See Ridley Canada Limited; Int'l, pg. 1116
HUBBARD SCIENTIFIC—See American Educational Products; U.S. Public, pg. 71
HUBBELL CANADA INC.—See Hubbell Incorporated; U.S. Public, pg. 845
HUBBELL INCORPORATED; U.S. Public, pg. 844
HUBBELL INDUSTRIAL CONTROLS, INC.—See Hubbell Incorporated; U.S. Public, pg. 844
HUBBELL LIGHTING INC.—See Hubbell Incorporated; U.S. Public, pg. 844
HUBBELL, LTD.—See Hubbell Incorporated; U.S. Public, pg. 845
HUBBELL PLASTICS, INC.—See Hubbell Incorporated; U.S. Public, pg. 844
HUBBELL PREMISE WIRING, INC.—See Hubbell Incorporated; U.S. Public, pg. 844
HUBBELL STEEL CORPORATION—See Gibraltar Steel Corp.; U.S. Public, pg. 742
HUBCO, INC.; U.S. Public, pg. 845
HUBER & SUHNER AG; Int'l, pg. 637
HUBER & SUHNER AG—See Huber & Suhner AG; Int'l, pg. 637
HUBER & SUHNER FRANCE—See Huber & Suhner AG; Int'l, pg. 637
HUBER & SUHNER INC.—See Huber & Suhner AG; Int'l, pg. 637
HUBER, HUNT & NICHOLS, INC.—See The Hunt Corporation; U.S. Private, pg. 548
J.M. HUBER, CALCIUM CARBONATE DIVISION—See J.M. Huber Corporation; U.S. Private, pg. 545
J.M. HUBER, CHEMICALS DIVISION—See J.M. Huber Corporation; U.S. Private, pg. 545
J.M. HUBER, CLAY DIV.—See J.M. Huber Corporation; U.S. Private, pg. 545
J.M. HUBER CORPORATION; U.S. Private, pg. 544
J.M. HUBER, OIL & GAS DIV.—See J.M. Huber Corporation; U.S. Private, pg. 545
J.M. HUBER, SOLEM DIV.—See J.M. Huber Corporation; U.S. Private, pg. 545
J.M. HUBER, WOOD PRODUCTS DIV.—See J.M. Huber Corporation; U.S. Private, pg. 545
JOSEPH HUBER BREWING CO., INC.; U.S. Private, pg. 545
HUBER S.A.I.C.—See AB SKF; Int'l, pg. 1157
HUBER & SUHNER (AUSTRALIA) PTY. LTD.—See Huber & Suhner AG; Int'l, pg. 637
HUBER & SUHNER (FAR EAST)—See Huber & Suhner AG; Int'l, pg. 637
HUBER & SUHNER (SINGAPORE) PTE. LTD.—See Huber & Suhner AG; Int'l, pg. 637
HUBERT COMPANY; U.S. Private, pg. 545
HUBLER CHEVROLET INC.; U.S. Private, pg. 545
HUBNER-GRAY GES. M.B.H.—See ABB Asea Brown Boveri (Holding) Ltd.; Int'l, pg. 6
HUCK BRENNSTOFFE GMBH—See Fried. Krupp AG; Int'l, pg. 513
HUCK, EUROPE—See Thiokol Corporation; U.S. Public, pg. 1597
HUCK INTERNATIONAL AEROSPACE FASTENER DIVISION—See Thiokol Corporation; U.S. Public, pg. 1597
HUCK INTERNATIONAL, INC.—See Thiokol Corporation; U.S. Public, pg. 1597
HUCK INTERNATIONAL INDUSTRIAL FASTENER DIVISION—See Thiokol Corporation; U.S. Public, pg. 1597
HUCK INTERNATIONAL INSTALLATION SYSTEMS DIVISION—See Thiokol Corporation; U.S. Public, pg. 1597
HUDEPOHL-SCHOENLING BREWING COMPANY; U.S. Private, pg. 545
HUDON ET DEAUDELIN LTEE—See The Oshawa Group Limited; Int'l, pg. 1012
HUDSON AVIATION SERVICES INC., CALIFORNIA—See Hudson General Corporation; U.S. Public, pg. 845
HUDSON AVIATION SERVICES INC., DELAWARE—See Hudson General Corporation; U.S. Public, pg. 845
THE HUDSON CORPORATION—See Nature's Bounty Inc.; U.S. Public, pg. 1166
HUDSON COUNTY NEWS COMPANY; U.S. Private, pg. 545
HUDSON DEMAND SERVICES—See R.R. Donnelley & Sons Company; U.S. Public, pg. 518
HUDSON ELMS NURSING HOME—See Horizon/CMS Healthcare Corporation; U.S. Public, pg. 838
HUDSON ENGINEERING & PROJECT MANAGEMENT SERVICES—See McDermott International, Inc.; U.S. Public, pg. 1068
HUDSON ENGINEERING CORP.—See McDermott International, Inc.; U.S. Public, pg. 1068
HUDSON GENERAL AVIATION SERVICES INC.—See Hudson General Corporation; U.S. Public, pg. 846
HUDSON GENERAL COACH LINES, INC.—See Hudson General Corporation; U.S. Public, pg. 845
HUDSON GENERAL CORPORATION; U.S. Public, pg. 845
H.D. HUDSON MANUFACTURING COMPANY; U.S. Private, pg. 545
HUDSON INSURANCE COMPANY—See Skandia Insurance Company Limited; Int'l, pg. 1258
JIM HUDSON, PONTIAC, OLDSMOBILE GMC; U.S. Private, pg. 545
HUDSON KOHALA INC.—See Hudson General Corporation; U.S. Public, pg. 845
HUDSON LIFE REASSURANCE CORPORATION—See Skandia Insurance Company Limited; Int'l, pg. 1257
HUDSON MFG. DIVISION—See R.R. Donnelley & Sons Company; U.S. Public, pg. 518
HUDSON PRECAST PROPERTIES, INC.—See Forest City Enterprises, Inc.; U.S. Public, pg. 669
HUDSON, RCI; U.S. Private, pg. 546
HUDSON REINSURANCE COMPANY LIMITED—See Skandia Insurance Company Limited; Int'l, pg. 1257
ROBERT HUDSON (MACHINERY SALE & SERVICE) LTD.—See Lonrho plc; Int'l, pg. 817
HUDSON STREET PARTNERS—See Saatchi & Saatchi Advertising Worldwide; U.S. Public, pg. 1422
HUDSON UNDERWRITING LTD.—See Skandia Insurance Company Limited; Int'l, pg. 1257
HUDSON UNITED BANK-CEDAR GROVE—See Hubco, Inc.; U.S. Public, pg. 845
HUDSON UNITED BANK-CLIFFSIDE PARK—See Hubco, Inc.; U.S. Public, pg. 845
HUDSON UNITED BANK-CLIFTON—See Hubco, Inc.; U.S. Public, pg. 845
HUDSON UNITED BANK-DUNELLEN—See Hubco, Inc.; U.S. Public, pg. 845
HUDSON UNITED BANK-FAIRVIEW—See Hubco, Inc.; U.S. Public, pg. 845
HUDSON UNITED BANK-HOBOKEN—See Hubco, Inc.; U.S. Public, pg. 845
HUDSON UNITED BANK-NORTH BERGEN—See Hubco, Inc.; U.S. Public, pg. 845
HUDSON UNITED BANK-UNION CITY—See Hubco, Inc.; U.S. Public, pg. 845
HUDSON UNITED BANK-WEST NEW YORK—See Hubco, Inc.; U.S. Public, pg. 845
HUDSON VALLEY PAPER COMPANY; U.S. Private, pg. 546
HUDSON'S BAY COMPANY; Int'l, pg. 637
HUDSON'S BAY COMPANY ACCEPTANCE LTD.—See Hudson's Bay Company; Int'l, pg. 637
HUELLER HILLE CORPORATION—See Thyssen AG; Int'l, pg. 1387
HUEPPE GMBH—See Masco Corporation; U.S. Public, pg. 1055
HUEPPE SARL—See Masco Corporation; U.S. Public, pg. 1054
S.A. HEURBEL—See Cockerill Sambre; Int'l, pg. 301
HUFFMAN KOOS; U.S. Private, pg. 546
NEIL HUFFMAN CHRYSLER PLYMOUTH DODGE—See Neil Huffman Nissan Inc.; U.S. Private, pg. 546
NEIL HUFFMAN NISSAN INC.; U.S. Private, pg. 546
NEIL HUFFMAN VOLKSWAGON MAZDA SUBURU—See Neil Huffman Nissan Inc.; U.S. Private, pg. 546
S.E. HUFFMAN CORP.; U.S. Private, pg. 546
HUFFY CORPORATION; U.S. Public, pg. 846
HUFFY SERVICE FIRST, INC.—See Huffy Corporation; U.S. Public, pg. 846
HUFFY SPORTS COMPANY—See Huffy Corporation; U.S. Public, pg. 846

HUFVUDSTADEN FRANCE S.A.—See Fastighetsaktiebolaget Hufvudstaden; *Int'l*, pg. 478
HUFVUDSTADEN NEDERLAND B.V.—See Fastighetsaktiebolaget Hufvudstaden; *Int'l*, pg. 478
HUFVUDSTADEN (U.K.) LTD.—See Fastighetsaktiebolaget Hufvudstaden; *Int'l*, pg. 478
HUGHES ACQUISITION CORP.—See Hughes Supply, Inc.; *U.S. Public*, pg. 847
HUGHES & SPENCER STEEL LTD.—See Arbed S.A.; *Int'l*, pg. 79
HUGHES CHRISTENSEN—See Baker Hughes Incorporated; *U.S. Public*, pg. 166
HUGHES CHRISTENSEN CO.—See Baker Hughes Incorporated; *U.S. Public*, pg. 166
HUGHES COMMUNICATIONS, INC.—See General Motors Corporation; *U.S. Public*, pg. 721
HUGHES CONSTRUCTION, INC.; *U.S. Private*, pg. 546
HUGHES DAIRY LTD.—See Avonmore Waterford Group plc; *Int'l*, pg. 102
HUGHES ELECTRONICS CORPORATION—See General Motors Corporation; *U.S. Public*, pg. 720
HUGHES FAMILY MARKETS, INC.—See Quality Food Centers, Inc.; *U.S. Public*, pg. 1349
HUGHES GROUP; *U.S. Private*, pg. 546
JOE D. HUGHES, INC.—See Halliburton Company; *U.S. Public*, pg. 776
HUGHES-JVC TECHNOLOGY CORP.—See Matsushita Electric Industrial Co., Ltd.; *Int'l*, pg. 846
HUGHES LEITZ OPTICAL TECHNOLOGIES, LTD.—See General Motors Corporation; *U.S. Public*, pg. 722
HUGHES MICROELECTRONICS EUROPA ESPANA S.A.—See General Motors Corporation; *U.S. Public*, pg. 725
HUGHES-PETERS, INC.; *U.S. Private*, pg. 546
R.S. HUGHES CO., INC.; *U.S. Private*, pg. 547
HUGHES RESEARCH LABORATORIES—See General Motors Corporation; *U.S. Public*, pg. 721
HUGHES SPACE & COMMUNICATIONS GROUP—See General Motors Corporation; *U.S. Public*, pg. 721
HUGHES SUPPLY CORP.; *U.S. Private*, pg. 547
HUGHES SUPPLY, INC.; *U.S. Public*, pg. 846
HUGHES-TREITLER MANUFACTURING CORPORATION; *U.S. Private*, pg. 547
HUGO BOSS AG; *Int'l*, pg. 637
HUGO BOSS AUSTRALIA PTY. LTD.—See Hugo Boss AG; *Int'l*, pg. 638
HUGO BOSS CANADA INC.—See Hugo Boss AG; *Int'l*, pg. 638
HUGO BOSS DO BRASIL LTDA.—See Hugo Boss AG; *Int'l*, pg. 638
HUGO BOSS FASHIONS INC.—See Hugo Boss AG; *Int'l*, pg. 637
HUGO BOSS FRANCE S.A.R.L.—See Hugo Boss AG; *Int'l*, pg. 638
HUGO BOSS HOLDING (BRASIL) LTDA.—See Hugo Boss AG; *Int'l*, pg. 638
HUGO BOSS HOLDINGS PTY. LTD.—See Hugo Boss AG; *Int'l*, pg. 638
HUGO BOSS HONG KONG LTD.—See Hugo Boss AG; *Int'l*, pg. 638
HUGO BOSS, INC.—See Hugo Boss AG; *Int'l*, pg. 637
HUGO BOSS ITALIA S.P.A.—See Hugo Boss AG; *Int'l*, pg. 638
HUGO BOSS K.K.—See Hugo Boss AG; *Int'l*, pg. 638
HUGO BOSS USA, INC.—See Hugo Boss AG; *Int'l*, pg. 637
HUGO FASSBENDER KG—See Freudenberg & Company; *Int'l*, pg. 505
HUGO NEU-PROLER CO.—See Schnitzer Steel Industries, Inc.; *U.S. Public*, pg. 1440
HUGOTON CAPITAL LIMITED PARTNERSHIP (HCLP)—See Pioneer Natural Resources Co.; *U.S. Public*, pg. 1300
HUGUENOT-FENAL—See Imetal; *Int'l*, pg. 661
HUHTAMAKI FINANCE B.V.—See Huhtamaki Oy; *Int'l*, pg. 638
HUHTAMAKI FINANCE OY—See Huhtamaki Oy; *Int'l*, pg. 638
HUHTAMAKI OY; *Int'l*, pg. 638
HUHTAMAKI OY—See Huhtamaki Oy; *Int'l*, pg. 638
HUITT-ZOLLARS, INC.; *U.S. Private*, pg. 547
HUIZHOU ADVANCE BATTERY TECHNOLOGY CO. LTD.—See GP Batteries International Ltd.; *Int'l*, pg. 537
HUIZHOU POWER PACK CO. LTD.—See GP Batteries International Ltd.; *Int'l*, pg. 537
HULL CORPORATION; *U.S. Private*, pg. 547
D.M. HULL & CO. PTY. LTD.—See Delta plc; *Int'l*, pg. 391
HULL-THOMSON LIMITED—See Russel Metals Inc.; *Int'l*, pg. 1150
HULLERAS DEL NORTE, S.A. (HUNOSA); *Int'l*, pg. 639
HULL/FINMAC, INC.—See Hull Corporation; *U.S. Private*, pg. 547
HULMAN & COMPANY; *U.S. Private*, pg. 547
HULS AG—See Veba AG; *Int'l*, pg. 1454
HULS AMERICA INC.—See Veba AG; *Int'l*, pg. 1455
HULS AMERICA PLASTICS DIVISION—See Veba AG; *Int'l*, pg. 1455
HULS AUSTRIA GMBH-ZAGREB OFFICE—See Veba AG; *Int'l*, pg. 1455
HULS NORDIC AB—See Veba AG; *Int'l*, pg. 1455
HULS NORDIC AB-DENMARK BRANCH OFFICE—See Veba AG; *Int'l*, pg. 1455
HULS SILICONE GMBH—See Veba AG; *Int'l*, pg. 1454
HULS SOUTHERN AFRICA (PTY.) LTD.—See Veba AG; *Int'l*, pg. 1455
HUMAN AFFAIRS INTERNATIONAL INC.—See Magellan Health Services, Inc.; *U.S. Public*, pg. 1036
HUMAN SCIENCES PRESS, INC.—See Plenum Publishing Corporation; *U.S. Public*, pg. 1311
HUMANA HEALTH CHICAGO, INC.—See Humana Inc.; *U.S. Public*, pg. 847
HUMANA HEALTH INSURANCE OF NEVADA, INC.—See Humana Inc.; *U.S. Public*, pg. 847
HUMANA HEALTH PLAN, INC.—See Humana Inc.; *U.S. Public*, pg. 848

HUMANA HEALTH PLAN OF ALABAMA, INC.—See Humana Inc.; *U.S. Public*, pg. 848
HUMANA HEALTH PLAN OF GEORGIA, INC.—See Humana Inc.; *U.S. Public*, pg. 848
HUMANA HEALTH PLAN OF OHIO, INC.—See Humana Inc.; *U.S. Public*, pg. 848
HUMANA HEALTH PLAN OF TEXAS, INC.—See Humana Inc.; *U.S. Public*, pg. 848
HUMANA HEALTH PLAN OF UTAH, INC.—See Humana Inc.; *U.S. Public*, pg. 848
HUMANA INC.; *U.S. Public*, pg. 847
HUMANA INSURANCE COMPANY—See Humana Inc.; *U.S. Public*, pg. 848
HUMANA MEDICAL PLAN INC.-JACKSONVILLE—See Humana Inc.; *U.S. Public*, pg. 848
HUMANA WISCONSIN HEALTH ORGANIZATION INSURANCE CORPORATION—See Humana Inc.; *U.S. Public*, pg. 848
HUMANASEGUR SA—See Willis Corroon Group PLC; *Int'l*, pg. 1502
HUMANPHARMAKOLOGISCHES INSTITUT CIBA-GEIGY GMBH—See Novartis AG; *Int'l*, pg. 982
HUMBERSIDE HOLDINGS LTD—See Powell Duffryn PLC; *Int'l*, pg. 1065
HUMBOLDT WEDAG DIVISION—See Deutz AG; *Int'l*, pg. 408
HUMBROL LIMITED—See Borden, Inc.; *U.S. Private*, pg. 159
HUME INDUSTRIES (MALAYSIA) BERHAD—See FLS Industries A/S; *Int'l*, pg. 475
HUMISEAL DIV.—See Chase Corporation; *U.S. Public*, pg. 337
A.C. HUMKO—See Associated British Foods plc; *Int'l*, pg. 92
HUMMINGBIRD SPECIALIZED SOLUTIONS—See Hamilton Communications Group, Inc.; *U.S. Private*, pg. 497
THE HUMPHREY CHEMICAL COMPANY, INC.—See Cambrex Corporation; *U.S. Public*, pg. 297
HUMPHREY CO., LTD.—See Carl-Zeiss-Stiftung; *Int'l*, pg. 1523
HUMPHREY FLUID POWER LTD.—See Humphrey Products Company; *U.S. Private*, pg. 548
HUMPHREY, INC.—See Remec, Inc.; *U.S. Public*, pg. 1376
HUMPHREY INSTRUMENTS GMBH—See Carl-Zeiss-Stiftung; *Int'l*, pg. 1523
HUMPHREY PRODUCTS COMPANY; *U.S. Private*, pg. 547
HUMPHREYS & GLASGOW (ATLANTIC) LIMITED—See Texas Utilities Company; *U.S. Public*, pg. 1587
HUMPHREYS & GLASGOW (CANADA) LIMITED C/O MCTAGGART, STONE, WINTERS & HERRIDGE—See Texas Utilities Company; *U.S. Public*, pg. 1587
HUMPHREYS & GLASGOW CONSULTANTS PRIVATE LIMITED—See Texas Utilities Company; *U.S. Public*, pg. 1587
HUMPHREYS & GLASGOW EUROPE LIMITED—See Texas Utilities Company; *U.S. Public*, pg. 1587
HUMPHREYS & GLASGOW INTERNATIONAL PLC—See Texas Utilities Company; *U.S. Public*, pg. 1587
HUMPHREYS & GLASGOW (MALAYSIA) SDN. BHD.—See Texas Utilities Company; *U.S. Public*, pg. 1587
HUMPHREYS & GLASGOW (OVERSEAS) LIMITED—See Texas Utilities Company; *U.S. Public*, pg. 1587
HUMPHREYS & GLASGOW PACIFIC PTY. LIMITED C/O FESLER RUSSELL & CO.—See Texas Utilities Company; *U.S. Public*, pg. 1587
HUMPHREYS MINERAL INDUSTRIES, INC.—See Reunion Industries, Inc.; *U.S. Public*, pg. 1383
HUNAN KANSAI AUTOMOTIVE COATINGS CO., LTD.—See Kansai Paint Co., Ltd.; *Int'l*, pg. 723
HUNAN RESUN-ALBRIGHT & WILSON INDUSTRIAL CO. LTD.—See Albright & Wilson plc; *Int'l*, pg. 50
WALTER HUNDHAUSEN GMBH & CO. KG—See Fried. Krupp AG; *Int'l*, pg. 508
HUNDO MAGDALENA OIL & GAS LTD.—See Lonrho plc; *Int'l*, pg. 818
HUNGARIA BIZTOSITO RT.—See Allianz Aktiengesellschaft; *Int'l*, pg. 60
HUNGAROFERT CHEMIKALIEN HANDELSGESMBH—See DSM N.V.; *Int'l*, pg. 356
HUNGARY OBI BARKACSARUHAZ—See OBI Bau-und Heimwerkermaerkte GmbH & Co. KG; *Int'l*, pg. 993
HUNGER DFE GMBH; *Int'l*, pg. 639
HUNGER HYDRAULICS, LIMITED—See Hunger DFE GmbH; *Int'l*, pg. 639
HUNKEMOLLER—See Vendex International N.V.; *Int'l*, pg. 1462
HUNT BUILDING CORPORATION; *U.S. Private*, pg. 548
HUNT CANADA—See Hunt Corporation; *U.S. Public*, pg. 849
CAROLINE HUNT TRUST ESTATE; *U.S. Private*, pg. 548
HUNT CORPORATION; *U.S. Public*, pg. 848
THE HUNT CORPORATION; *U.S. Private*, pg. 548
HUNT FOREIGN INVESTMENT CORP.—See Olin Corporation; *U.S. Public*, pg. 1219
HUNT INTERNATIONAL—See The Hunt Corporation; *U.S. Private*, pg. 548
HUNT INTERNATIONAL DIV.—See Hunt Corporation; *U.S. Public*, pg. 849
J.B. HUNT TRANSPORT, INC.—See J.B. Hunt Transport Services, Inc.; *U.S. Public*, pg. 849
J.B. HUNT TRANSPORT SERVICES, INC.; *U.S. Public*, pg. 849
HUNT LASCARIS/TBWA—See TBWA Chiat/Day; *U.S. Private*, pg. 1062
HUNT LASCARIS/TBWA DURBAN—See TBWA Chiat/Day; *U.S. Private*, pg. 1062
HUNT OIL CENTRAL EXPLORATION DIVISION—See Hunt Oil Company; *U.S. Private*, pg. 548
HUNT OIL COMPANY; *U.S. Private*, pg. 548
HUNT OIL COTTON VALLEY DISTRICT—See Hunt Oil Company; *U.S. Private*, pg. 548
HUNT OIL GULF COAST EXPLORATION DIVISION—See Hunt Oil Company; *U.S. Private*, pg. 548

HUNT OIL LAFAYETTE LAND OFFICE—See Hunt Oil Company; *U.S. Private*, pg. 548
THE HUNT PAVING COMPANY, INC.—See The Hunt Corporation; *U.S. Private*, pg. 548
HUNT REFINING COMPANY—See Hunt Oil Company; *U.S. Private*, pg. 548
RODNEY HUNT COMPANY; *U.S. Private*, pg. 549
HUNT-SECO ENGINEERING LTD.—See Hunt Valve; *U.S. Private*, pg. 549
HUNT SPORTS—See The Hunt Corporation; *U.S. Private*, pg. 548
HUNT VALVE; *U.S. Private*, pg. 549
HUNT-WESSON CONSUMER ADVERTISING DIV.—See ConAgra, Inc.; *U.S. Public*, pg. 428
HUNT-WESSON FOODSERVICE DIVISION—See ConAgra, Inc.; *U.S. Public*, pg. 428
HUNT-WESSON GROCERY SALES DIVISION—See ConAgra, Inc.; *U.S. Public*, pg. 428
HUNT-WESSON, INC.—See ConAgra, Inc.; *U.S. Public*, pg. 428
HUNT-WESSON MARKETING SERVICES DIVISION—See ConAgra, Inc.; *U.S. Public*, pg. 428
HUNT-WESSON REFRIGERATED FOODS DIV.—See ConAgra, Inc.; *U.S. Public*, pg. 426
HUNT-WESSON TOMATO PRODUCTS DIVISION—See ConAgra, Inc.; *U.S. Public*, pg. 428
HUNTCO INC.; *U.S. Public*, pg. 849
HUNTCO NEVADA, INC.—See Huntco Inc.; *U.S. Public*, pg. 849
HUNTCO STEEL CO.—See Huntco Inc.; *U.S. Public*, pg. 849
HUNTER CONTRACTING COMPANY; *U.S. Private*, pg. 549
HUNTER CORP.; *U.S. Private*, pg. 549
HUNTER DOUGLAS ARCHITECTURAL PRODUCTS INC.—See Hunter Douglas N.V.; *Int'l*, pg. 639
HUNTER DOUGLAS CANADA INC.—See Hunter Douglas N.V.; *Int'l*, pg. 639
HUNTER DOUGLAS DO BRAZIL LTDA.—See Hunter Douglas N.V.; *Int'l*, pg. 640
HUNTER DOUGLAS FABRICATION COMPANY—See Hunter Douglas N.V.; *Int'l*, pg. 639
HUNTER DOUGLAS HOLDINGS LTD.—See Hunter Douglas N.V.; *Int'l*, pg. 640
HUNTER DOUGLAS, INC.—See Hunter Douglas N.V.; *Int'l*, pg. 639
HUNTER DOUGLAS LTD.—See Hunter Douglas N.V.; *Int'l*, pg. 640
HUNTER DOUGLAS LTD.-SYDNEY—See Hunter Douglas N.V.; *Int'l*, pg. 640
HUNTER DOUGLAS METALS—See Hunter Douglas N.V.; *Int'l*, pg. 639
HUNTER DOUGLAS N.V.; *Int'l*, pg. 639
HUNTER DOUGLAS PLEATED SHADE CORP.—See Hunter Douglas N.V.; *Int'l*, pg. 639
HUNTER DOUGLAS SINGAPORE PTE. LTD.—See Hunter Douglas N.V.; *Int'l*, pg. 640
HUNTER DOUGLAS VERTICALS—See Hunter Douglas N.V.; *Int'l*, pg. 639
HUNTER ENGINEERING CO., INC.—See FKI Plc; *Int'l*, pg. 474
HUNTER FAN COMPANY; *U.S. Private*, pg. 549
HUNTER/KREY FOODS—See American Financial Group; *U.S. Public*, pg. 75
HUNTER MARINE CORPORATION; *U.S. Private*, pg. 549
HUNTER PLASTICS LTD.—See ETEX; *Int'l*, pg. 430
THE HUNTERSKIL HOWARD GROUP PLC.—See Wolseley Plc.; *Int'l*, pg. 1511
HUNTING PLC; *Int'l*, pg. 640
THE HUNTINGTON ACCEPTANCE COMPANY—See Huntington Bancshares Inc.; *U.S. Public*, pg. 850
HUNTINGTON BANCSHARES INC.; *U.S. Public*, pg. 849
HUNTINGTON BANCSHARES INDIANA, INC.—See Huntington Bancshares Inc.; *U.S. Public*, pg. 850
HUNTINGTON BANCSHARES MICHIGAN, INC.—See Huntington Bancshares Inc.; *U.S. Public*, pg. 850
HUNTINGTON BEACH CO.—See Chevron Corporation; *U.S. Public*, pg. 348
HUNTINGTON CLOTHIERS, INC.—See HC Holdings; *U.S. Private*, pg. 490
HUNTINGTON DIVISION—See Champion Industries; *U.S. Public*, pg. 333
THE HUNTINGTON INVESTMENT COMPANY—See Huntington Bancshares Inc.; *U.S. Public*, pg. 850
HUNTINGTON INVESTMENT MANAGEMENT CO.—See Huntington Bancshares Inc.; *U.S. Public*, pg. 850
THE HUNTINGTON MORTGAGE COMPANY—See Huntington Bancshares Inc.; *U.S. Public*, pg. 850
HUNTINGTON NATIONAL BANK—See Huntington Bancshares Inc.; *U.S. Public*, pg. 850
THE HUNTINGTON NATIONAL LIFE INSURANCE COMPANY—See Huntington Bancshares Inc.; *U.S. Public*, pg. 850
HUNTINGTON PROVIDER MANAGEMENT SERVICES—See UniHealth; *U.S. Private*, pg. 1118
THE HUNTINGTON SERVICE COMPANY—See Huntington Bancshares Inc.; *U.S. Public*, pg. 850
HUNTINGTON TILE, INC.—See Pacific Holding Corporation; *U.S. Private*, pg. 831
THE HUNTINGTON TRUST CO. N.A.—See Huntington Bancshares Inc.; *U.S. Public*, pg. 850
THE HUNTINGTON TRUST COMPANY OF FLORIDA, N.A.—See Huntington Bancshares Inc.; *U.S. Public*, pg. 850
HUNTMIX, INC.—See CalMat Co.; *U.S. Public*, pg. 296
HUNTSMAN CORPORATION; *U.S. Private*, pg. 549
HUNTSMAN CORPORATION—See Huntsman Corporation; *U.S. Private*, pg. 549
HUNTSVILLE ELECTRONICS DIV.—See Chrysler Corporation; *U.S. Public*, pg. 353
HUNTSVILLE SPACE OPERATIONS—See Thiokol Corporation; *U.S. Public*, pg. 1597
HUNTSVILLE TIMES—See Advance Publications Inc.; *U.S. Private*, pg. 20

MASTER INDEX TO COMPANY NAMES HYDRO

Company Index

HUONEISTOKESKUS OY—See Merita Ltd.; *Int'l*, pg. 858
HUONEISTOMARKKINOINTI OY—See Merita Ltd.; *Int'l*, pg. 858
HURCO COMPANIES, INC.; *U.S. Public*, pg. 850
HURCO MANUFACTURING COMPANY—See Hurco Companies, Inc.; *U.S. Public*, pg. 850
HURD LOCKS—See Avis Industrial Corporation; *U.S. Private*, pg. 102
HURD MILLWORK COMPANY, INC.—See UIS, Inc.; *U.S. Private*, pg. 1113
HUREL ARC—See Norsk Hydro a.s; *Int'l*, pg. 962
HURLETRON INC.—See Altair Corporation; *U.S. Private*, pg. 46
HURLIMANN IMMOBILIEN AG—See Feldschlosschen Hurlimann Holding; *Int'l*, pg. 479
NORMAN J. HURLL & CO.—See Eclipse Inc.; *U.S. Private*, pg. 361
HURON CAPITAL LIMITED—See Confederation Life Insurance Company; *Int'l*, pg. 326
HURON DAILY TRIBUNE—See The Hearst Corporation; *U.S. Private*, pg. 517
HURON - GRAFFENSTADEN S.A.—See Fiat Auto SpA; *Int'l*, pg. 481
HURON INSURANCE CO.—See Harleysville Group; *U.S. Public*, pg. 787
HURON MANUFACTURING DIV.—See U.S. Industries, Inc.; *U.S. Public*, pg. 1684
HURON VALLEY STEEL CORP.; *U.S. Private*, pg. 549
HURST MANUFACTURING—See Emerson Electric Co.; *U.S. Public*, pg. 573
HURTH BRANCH—See Deutsche Babcock AG; *Int'l*, pg. 401
HURUM PAPIRFABRIKK—See Norske Skogindustrier A.S; *Int'l*, pg. 965
HUSDJURFORSAKRINGS AB SLEIPNER—See Skandia Insurance Company Limited; *Int'l*, pg. 1256
HUSH PUPPIES COMPANY—See Wolverine World Wide, Inc.; *U.S. Public*, pg. 1775
HUSH PUPPIES RETAIL, INC.—See Wolverine World Wide, Inc.; *U.S. Public*, pg. 1775
AB HUSKVARNA ELEKTROLYTPOLERING—See British Steel Plc; *Int'l*, pg. 221
HUSKY OIL INTL. LTD.—See Husky Oil Ltd.; *Int'l*, pg. 640
HUSKY OIL LTD.; *Int'l*, pg. 640
HUSKY OIL MKTG. COMPANY—See Husky Oil Ltd.; *Int'l*, pg. 640
HUSKY OIL OPERATIONS LTD.—See Husky Oil Ltd.; *Int'l*, pg. 640
HUSMAN SNACK FOODS, CO.—See Pro-Fac Cooperative, Inc.; *U.S. Private*, pg. 887
HUSQVARNA AB—See Electrolux, AB; *Int'l*, pg. 439
HUSQVARNA A/S—See Electrolux, AB; *Int'l*, pg. 441
HUSQVARNA CHAINSAWS LTD.—See Electrolux, AB; *Int'l*, *pg. 443*
HUSQVARNA ELEKTRO A/S—See Electrolux, AB; *Int'l*, pg. 443
HUSQVARNA FOREST & GARDEN PRODUCTS—See Electrolux, AB; *Int'l*, pg. 440
HUSQVARNA GESELLSCHAFT GMBH—See Electrolux, AB; *Int'l*, pg. 441
HUSQVARNA LTD.—See Electrolux, AB; *Int'l*, pg. 444
HUSQVARNA PTY. LTD.—See Electrolux, AB; *Int'l*, pg. 440
HUSQVARNA SVENSKA FORSALJNINGS AB—See Electrolux, AB; *Int'l*, pg. 439
HUSQVARNA VERTRIEBS GMBH—See Electrolux, AB; *Int'l*, pg. 442
HUSSEY CORPORATION; *U.S. Private*, pg. 550
HUSSEY PLASTICS CO.—See Hussey Corporation; *U.S. Private*, pg. 550
HUSSEY PRODUCTS CO.—See Hussey Corporation; *U.S. Private*, pg. 550
HUSSEY SEATING CO. (CANADA) LTD.—See Hussey Corporation; *U.S. Private*, pg. 550
HUSSEY SEATING SYSTEMS (EUROPE) LTD.—See Hussey Corporation; *U.S. Private*, pg. 550
HUSSMANN CORP.—See Whitman Corporation; *U.S. Public*, pg. 1766
HUSUM MILLS—See Mo och Domsjo AB; *Int'l*, pg. 886
P.T. HUTAMA-TAKENAKA CORPORATION INDONESIA—See Takenaka Corporation; *Int'l*, pg. 1351
HUTCH SPORTS USA, INC.—See RDM Sports Group; *U.S. Public*, pg. 1354
HUTCHENS INDUSTRIES INC.; *U.S. Private*, pg. 550
HUTCHENSON SEAL CORPORATION; *U.S. Private*, pg. 550
HUTCHINS MANUFACTURING COMPANY; *U.S. Private*, pg. 550
HUTCHINS/YOUNG & RUBICAM—See Young & Rubicam Inc.; *U.S. Private*, pg. 1197
HUTCHINSON S.A.—See Total S.A.; *Int'l*, pg. 1409
HUTCHINSON TECHNOLOGY ASIA—See Hutchinson Technology Inc.; *U.S. Public*, pg. 851
HUTCHINSON TECHNOLOGY ASIA, INC.—See Hutchinson Technology Inc.; *U.S. Public*, pg. 850
HUTCHINSON TECHNOLOGY INC.; *U.S. Public*, pg. 850
HUTCHINSON TECHNOLOGY, INC., EAU CLAIRE—See Hutchinson Technology Inc.; *U.S. Public*, pg. 851
HUTCHINSON TECHNOLOGY INC., SIOUX FALLS—See Hutchinson Technology Inc.; *U.S. Public*, pg. 851
HUTCHINSON WIL-RICH MANUFACTURING CO.—See TIC United Corporation; *U.S. Private*, pg. 1063
HUTCHISON INFORMATION SERVICES LIMITED—See Motorola, Inc.; *U.S. Public*, pg. 1139
HUTCHISON MOBILE DATA LIMITED—See Motorola, Inc.; *U.S. Public*, pg. 1139
HUTCHISON PAGING HOLDINGS LTD.—See Motorola, Inc.; *U.S. Public*, pg. 1139
ROBERT HUTCHISON LIMITED—See Harrisons & Crosfield plc; *Int'l*, pg. 598
HUTCHISON TELECOMMUNICATIONS (UK) LIMITED—See British Aerospace p.l.c.; *Int'l*, pg. 218
HUTCHISON TELEPHONE COMPANY LTD.—See Motorola, Inc.; *U.S. Public*, pg. 1139
HUTEC HOLZMANN UMWELTTECHNIK GMBH—See Philipp Holzmann AG; *Int'l*, pg. 633
HUTTENWERKE KRUPP MANNESMANN GMBH—See Fried. Krupp AG; *Int'l*, pg. 512
HUTTER & SCHRANTZ AG—See Creditanstalt-Bankverein; *Int'l*, pg. 347
HUTTIG SASH & DOOR CO.—See Crane Co.; *U.S. Public*, pg. 457
CHUCK HUTTON CHEVROLET COMPANY; *U.S. Private*, pg. 550
HUVAL BAKERY, INC.—See Flowers Industries, Inc.; *U.S. Public*, pg. 657
HUWOOD ELECTRIC LTD.—See FKI Plc; *Int'l*, pg. 473
HUWOOD INTERNATIONAL—See FKI Plc; *Int'l*, pg. 473
HUWOOD MINING SUPPORTS LIMITED—See FKI Plc; *Int'l*, pg. 473
HUYCK LTD.—See BTR plc; *Int'l*, pg. 124
HVIDE MARINE INCORPORATED; *U.S. Public*, pg. 851
HWACHENG GENERAL CONTRACTOR CO., LTD.—See Taisei Corporation; *Int'l*, pg. 1347
HWACHING CONSTRUCTION CO., LTD.—See Shimizu Corporation; *Int'l*, pg. 1233
HWAN CHONG ENTERPRISE CO., LTD.—See Minebea Co., Ltd.; *Int'l*, pg. 868
HWANG-DBS ASSET MANAGEMENT (MALAYSIA) SDN. BHD.—See DBS Bank Ltd.; *Int'l*, pg. 351
HY-ALLOY STEELS CO.—See A.M. Castle & Co.; *U.S. Public*, pg. 313
HY-FORM PRODUCTS, INC.—See Defiance, Inc.; *U.S. Public*, pg. 493
HY-TEK MATERIAL HANDLING, INC.; *U.S. Private*, pg. 550
HY-VEE FOOD STORES INCORPORATED; *U.S. Private*, pg. 550
HY VEE WEITZ CONSTRUCTION, L.C.—See The Weitz Company, Inc.; *U.S. Private*, pg. 1161
HYATT AIR, INC.—See Hyatt Corporation; *U.S. Private*, pg. 551
HYATT CORPORATION; *U.S. Private*, pg. 551
HYATT HOTELS CORPORATION—See Hyatt Corporation; *U.S. Private*, pg. 551
HYATT INTERNATIONAL CORPORATION—See Hyatt Corporation; *U.S. Private*, pg. 551
HYATT REGENCY LAKE TAHOE RESORT & CASINO—See Hyatt Corporation; *U.S. Private*, pg. 551
HYBRID PRODUCTS—See Sony Corporation; *Int'l*, pg. 1283
HYBRINOVA—See Lafarge S.A.; *Int'l*, pg. 788
HYCALOG—See Camco International Inc.; *U.S. Public*, pg. 298
HYCAST A.S.—See Norsk Hydro a.s; *Int'l*, pg. 959
HYCLONE EUROPE—See Perstorp AB; *Int'l*, pg. 1037
HYCLONE EUROPE LTD.—See Perstorp AB; *Int'l*, pg. 1037
HYCLONE LABORATORIES INC.—See Perstorp AB; *Int'l*, pg. 1037
HYCON, INC.—See Pitt-Des Moines, Inc.; *U.S. Public*, pg. 1304
HYCOP AB—See Continental AG; *Int'l*, pg. 328
HYCOR BIOMEDICAL, INC.; *U.S. Public*, pg. 851
HYCROFT RESOURCES & DEVELOPMENT—See Vista Gold Corp.; *U.S. Public*, pg. 1723
HYDALU S.A.—See Norsk Hydro a.s; *Int'l*, pg. 962
HYDAP S.A.—See Sophus Berendsen A/S; *Int'l*, pg. 1285
A.L. HYDE COMPANY—See Danaher Corporation; *U.S. Public*, pg. 481
HYDE ATHLETIC INDUSTRIES, INC.; *U.S. Public*, pg. 851
HYDE INSURANCE AGENCY, INC.—See Fleming Companies, Inc.; *U.S. Public*, pg. 653
HYDE MANUFACTURING CO.; *U.S. Private*, pg. 551
HYDE PARK MARKETS—See Fleming Companies, Inc.; *U.S. Public*, pg. 653
HYDE PHARMACEUTICALS (PTY.) LTD.—See Rohto Pharmaceutical Co.; *Int'l*, pg. 1126
HYDELKO KS—See Norsk Hydro a.s; *Int'l*, pg. 959
HYDRA-SPORTS CORPORATION—See Greenway Partners, L.P.; *U.S. Private*, pg. 478
HYDRANAUTICS—See Nitto Denko Corporation; *Int'l*, pg. 950
HYDRAUDYNE BEHEER BV—See Mannesmann A.G.; *Int'l*, *pg. 838*
HYDRAUDYNE BRUINHOF BV—See Mannesmann A.G.; *Int'l*, pg. 838
HYDRAUDYNE CYLINDERS BV—See Mannesmann A.G.; *Int'l*, pg. 838
HYDRAUDYNE HYDRAULIEK BV—See Mannesmann A.G.; *Int'l*, pg. 838
HYDRAUDYNE PNEUMATIEK BV—See Mannesmann A.G.; *Int'l*, pg. 838
HYDRAUDYNE SYSTEMS & ENGINEERING BV—See Mannesmann A.G.; *Int'l*, pg. 838
HYDRAULIC VALVE DIV.—See Parker Hannifin Corporation; *U.S. Public*, pg. 1261
HYDRAULICS GROUP—See Parker Hannifin Corporation; *U.S. Public*, pg. 1261
HYDRAULICS INC.—See Echlin Inc.; *U.S. Public*, pg. 560
HYDRAULICS INTERNATIONAL, INC.; *U.S. Private*, pg. 551
HYDRAUTO AB—See AB Industrivarden; *Int'l*, pg. 678
HYDRIL COMPANY; *U.S. Private*, pg. 551
HYDRIL RUBBER OPERS.—See Hydril Company; *U.S. Private*, pg. 551
HYDRIL TECHNOLOGY CENTER—See Hydril Company; *U.S. Private*, pg. 551
HYDRITE CHEMICAL COMPANY; *U.S. Private*, pg. 551
HYDRO AGRI BELGIUM S.A.—See Norsk Hydro a.s; *Int'l*, pg. 962
HYDRO AGRI BENELUX B.V.—See Norsk Hydro a.s; *Int'l*, pg. 962
HYDRO AGRI BRUNSBUTTEL GMBH—See Norsk Hydro a.s; *Int'l*, pg. 962
HYDRO AGRI DULMEN GMBH—See Norsk Hydro a.s; *Int'l*, pg. 962
HYDRO AGRI ESPANA S.A.—See Norsk Hydro a.s; *Int'l*, pg. 962
HYDRO AGRI EUROPE LICENSING & ENGINEERING B.V.—See Norsk Hydro a.s; *Int'l*, pg. 962
HYDRO AGRI FRANCE—See Norsk Hydro a.s; *Int'l*, pg. 962
HYDRO AGRI FRANCE USINE DU HAVRE (S.N.A.)—See Norsk Hydro a.s; *Int'l*, pg. 962
HYDRO AGRI GLOMFJORD—See Norsk Hydro a.s; *Int'l*, pg. 959
HYDRO AGRI NORTH AMERICA—See Norsk Hydro a.s; *Int'l*, pg. 961
HYDRO AGRI ROSTOCK GMBH—See Norsk Hydro a.s; *Int'l*, pg. 962
HYDRO AGRI ROTTERDAM B.V.—See Norsk Hydro a.s; *Int'l*, pg. 962
HYDRO AGRI SAN FRANCISCO, INC.—See Norsk Hydro a.s; *Int'l*, pg. 961
HYDRO AGRI SLUISKIL B.V.—See Norsk Hydro a.s; *Int'l*, pg. 962
HYDRO AGRI SPECIALTIES FRANCE—See Norsk Hydro a.s; *Int'l*, pg. 962
HYDRO AGRI TRINIDAD LTD.—See Norsk Hydro a.s; *Int'l*, *pg. 962*
HYDRO AGRI (UK) LTD.—See Norsk Hydro a.s; *Int'l*, pg. 962
HYDRO AGRI-VANCOUVER—See Norsk Hydro a.s; *Int'l*, pg. 961
HYDRO AGRICOLTURA S.R.D.—See Norsk Hydro a.s; *Int'l*, pg. 962
HYDRO-AIRE—See Crane Co.; *U.S. Public*, pg. 457
HYDRO ALLUMINIO ATESSA S.P.A.—See Norsk Hydro a.s; *Int'l*, pg. 962
HYDRO ALLUMINIO LA ROCA S.A.—See Norsk Hydro a.s; *Int'l*, pg. 962
HYDRO ALLUMINIO ORNAGO S.P.A.—See Norsk Hydro a.s; *Int'l*, pg. 962
HYDRO ALUMINIUM—See Norsk Hydro a.s; *Int'l*, pg. 962
HYDRO ALUMINIUM ALUSERV A/S—See Norsk Hydro a.s; *Int'l*, pg. 959
HYDRO ALUMINIUM ARDAL VERK—See Norsk Hydro a.s; *Int'l*, pg. 959
HYDRO ALUMINIUM A/S—See Norsk Hydro a.s; *Int'l*, pg. 959
HYDRO ALUMINIUM A/S ROLLED PRODUCTS—See Norsk Hydro a.s; *Int'l*, pg. 959
HYDRO ALUMINIUM AUTOMOTIVE—See Norsk Hydro a.s; *Int'l*, pg. 962
HYDRO ALUMINIUM AUTOMOTIVE GMBH—See Norsk Hydro a.s; *Int'l*, pg. 962
HYDRO ALUMINIUM BELLENBERG GMBH—See Norsk Hydro a.s; *Int'l*, pg. 962
HYDRO ALUMINIUM CENTURY LTD.—See Norsk Hydro a.s; *Int'l*, pg. 962
HYDRO ALUMINIUM CHATEAUROUX S.N.C.—See Norsk Hydro a.s; *Int'l*, pg. 962
HYDRO ALUMINIUM DEUTSCHLAND GMBH—See Norsk Hydro a.s; *Int'l*, pg. 962
HYDRO ALUMINIUM EQUIPMENT A/S—See Norsk Hydro a.s; *Int'l*, pg. 959
HYDRO ALUMINIUM ETP HOLMESTRAND—See Norsk Hydro a.s; *Int'l*, pg. 959
HYDRO ALUMINIUM EXTRUSION SERVICES S.A.R.L.—See Norsk Hydro a.s; *Int'l*, pg. 962
HYDRO ALUMINIUM EXTRUSION TOOLS—See Norsk Hydro a.s; *Int'l*, pg. 959
HYDRO ALUMINIUM FORMTECH A/S—See Norsk Hydro a.s; *Int'l*, pg. 959
HYDRO ALUMINIUM FRANCE S.N.C.—See Norsk Hydro a.s; *Int'l*, pg. 962
HYDRO ALUMINIUM FUNDO A/S—See Norsk Hydro a.s; *Int'l*, pg. 959
HYDRO ALUMINIUM HOLMESTRAND LAQUERED PRODUCTS—See Norsk Hydro a.s; *Int'l*, pg. 959
HYDRO ALUMINIUM HOLMESTRAND ROLLING MILL—See Norsk Hydro a.s; *Int'l*, pg. 959
HYDRO ALUMINIUM HOYANGER VERK—See Norsk Hydro a.s; *Int'l*, pg. 960
HYDRO ALUMINIUM HYCAST A/S—See Norsk Hydro a.s; *Int'l*, pg. 960
HYDRO ALUMINIUM HYDAL—See Norsk Hydro a.s; *Int'l*, pg. 960
HYDRO ALUMINIUM HYDRO TRANS—See Norsk Hydro a.s; *Int'l*, pg. 960
HYDRO ALUMINIUM ITC S.N.C.—See Norsk Hydro a.s; *Int'l*, pg. 962
HYDRO ALUMINIUM KARMOY FABRIKKER—See Norsk Hydro a.s; *Int'l*, pg. 960
HYDRO ALUMINIUM KARMOY ROLLING MILL—See Norsk Hydro a.s; *Int'l*, pg. 960
HYDRO ALUMINIUM LOUISVILLE—See Norsk Hydro a.s; *Int'l*, pg. 961
HYDRO ALUMINIUM LUCE S.N.C.—See Norsk Hydro a.s; *Int'l*, pg. 962
HYDRO ALUMINIUM MAGNOR A/S—See Norsk Hydro a.s; *Int'l*, pg. 960
HYDRO ALUMINIUM METAL SALES S.A.—See Norsk Hydro a.s; *Int'l*, pg. 962
HYDRO ALUMINIUM MOSCOW—See Norsk Hydro a.s; *Int'l*, pg. 962
HYDRO ALUMINIUM NENZING GMBH—See Norsk Hydro a.s; *Int'l*, pg. 962
HYDRO ALUMINIUM NETHERLANDS—See Norsk Hydro a.s; *Int'l*, pg. 962
HYDRO ALUMINIUM NORDISK AVIATION PRODUCTS A/S—See Norsk Hydro a.s; *Int'l*, pg. 960
HYDRO ALUMINIUM NORDISK AVIATION PRODUCTS RUSSIA—See Norsk Hydro a.s; *Int'l*, pg. 962
HYDRO ALUMINIUM PACKAGING AB—See Norsk Hydro a.s; *Int'l*, pg. 962
HYDRO ALUMINIUM PACKAGING A/S—See Norsk Hydro a.s; *Int'l*, pg. 960
HYDRO ALUMINIUM PINON S.N.C.—See Norsk Hydro a.s; *Int'l*, pg. 963
HYDRO ALUMINIUM PRIMARY METAL SALES—See Norsk Hydro a.s; *Int'l*, pg. 963

Company Index

HYDRO ALUMINIUM PROFILER A/S—See Norsk Hydro a.s; *Int'l*, pg. 960
HYDRO ALUMINIUM PROFILER A/S KARMOY EXTRUSIONS—See Norsk Hydro a.s; *Int'l*, pg. 960
HYDRO ALUMINIUM PROLIFER UK LTD., WARWICK—See Norsk Hydro a.s; *Int'l*, pg. 963
S.A. HYDRO ALUMINIUM RAEREN N.V.—See Norsk Hydro a.s; *Int'l*, pg. 963
HYDRO ALUMINIUM ROLLED PRODUCTS—See Norsk Hydro a.s; *Int'l*, pg. 963
HYDRO ALUMINIUM ROLLED PRODUCTS LTD.—See Norsk Hydro a.s; *Int'l*, pg. 963
HYDRO ALUMINIUM S.A.—See Norsk Hydro a.s; *Int'l*, pg. 963
HYDRO ALUMINIUM SLUGFABRIKKEN—See Norsk Hydro a.s; *Int'l*, pg. 960
HYDRO ALUMINIUM STRUCTURES A.S.—See Norsk Hydro a.s; *Int'l*, pg. 960
HYDRO ALUMINIUM SUNNDAL VERK—See Norsk Hydro a.s; *Int'l*, pg. 960
HYDRO ALUMINIUM SUOMI OY—See Norsk Hydro a.s; *Int'l*, pg. 963
HYDRO ALUMINIUM SVERIGE AB—See Norsk Hydro a.s; *Int'l*, pg. 960
HYDRO ALUMINIUM SVERIGE AB (TYRESO)—See Norsk Hydro a.s; *Int'l*, pg. 963
HYDRO ALUMINIUM SYSTEMS HELLAS S.A.—See Norsk Hydro a.s; *Int'l*, pg. 963
HYDRO ALUMINIUM SYSTEMS IBERICA-DOMAL DIVISION—See Norsk Hydro a.s; *Int'l*, pg. 963
HYDRO ALUMINIUM SYSTEMS IBERICA-WICONA DIVISION—See Norsk Hydro a.s; *Int'l*, pg. 963
HYDRO ALUMINIUM SYSTEMS U.K.—See Norsk Hydro a.s; *Int'l*, pg. 963
HYDRO ALUMINIUM TONDER—See Norsk Hydro a.s; *Int'l*, pg. 963
HYDRO ALUMINIUM U.K. LTD.—See Norsk Hydro a.s; *Int'l*, pg. 963
HYDRO ALUMINIUM UPHUSEN GMBH—See Norsk Hydro a.s; *Int'l*, pg. 963
HYDRO ALUMINIUM VEKST—See Norsk Hydro a.s; *Int'l*, pg. 960
HYDRO ALUMINIUM VIK VERK A/S—See Norsk Hydro a.s; *Int'l*, pg. 960
HYDRO ALUMINUM BOHN, INC.—See Norsk Hydro a.s; *Int'l*, pg. 961
HYDRO BERGEN—See Norsk Hydro a.s; *Int'l*, pg. 960
HYDRO CHEMICALS BELGIUM—See Norsk Hydro a.s; *Int'l*, pg. 963
HYDRO CHEMICALS LTD.—See Norsk Hydro a.s; *Int'l*, pg. 963
HYDRO CHEMICALS NORGE A.S.—See Norsk Hydro a.s; *Int'l*, pg. 963
HYDRO CHEMTECH GMBH—See Norsk Hydro a.s; *Int'l*, pg. 963
HYDRO COATINGS LTD.—See Norsk Hydro a.s; *Int'l*, pg. 963
HYDRO CONDUIT CORP.—See CSR Limited; *Int'l*, pg. 245
HYDRO CZECHOSLOVAKIA S.R.O.—See Norsk Hydro a.s; *Int'l*, pg. 963
HYDRO ENERGI—See Norsk Hydro a.s; *Int'l*, pg. 960
HYDRO ENERGI ARDAL—See Norsk Hydro a.s; *Int'l*, pg. 960
HYDRO ENERGI HOYANGER—See Norsk Hydro a.s; *Int'l*, pg. 960
HYDRO ENERGI KRAFTVERK—See Norsk Hydro a.s; *Int'l*, pg. 960
HYDRO ENERGI ROLDAL-SULDAL—See Norsk Hydro a.s; *Int'l*, pg. 960
HYDRO ENERGI SOGN—See Norsk Hydro a.s; *Int'l*, pg. 960
HYDRO ENERGI TELEMARK—See Norsk Hydro a.s; *Int'l*, pg. 960
HYDRO ENERGY DEVELOPMENT CORP.—See Puget Sound Energy, Inc.; *U.S. Public*, pg. 1342
HYDRO FERTILIZANTED LTDA.—See Norsk Hydro a.s; *Int'l*, pg. 963
HYDRO FINANCE CONSULTANCY NV—See Almanij N.V.; *Int'l*, pg. 65
HYDRO GROUP, INC.; *U.S. Private*, pg. 552
HYDRO HAGEBRUK A.S.—See Norsk Hydro a.s; *Int'l*, pg. 963
HYDRO HARSTAD—See Norsk Hydro a.s; *Int'l*, pg. 960
HYDRO/KIRBY AGRI SERVICE, INC.; *U.S. Private*, pg. 552
HYDRO KRISTIANSUND—See Norsk Hydro a.s; *Int'l*, pg. 960
HYDRO MAGNESIUM—See Norsk Hydro a.s; *Int'l*, pg. 960
HYDRO MAGNESIUM JAPAN OFFICE—See Norsk Hydro a.s; *Int'l*, pg. 963
HYDRO MAGNESIUM LTD.—See Norsk Hydro a.s; *Int'l*, pg. 963
HYDRO MAGNESIUM MARKETING—See Norsk Hydro a.s; *Int'l*, pg. 963
HYDRO MAGNESIUM MARKETING GESELLSCHAFT MBH—See Norsk Hydro a.s; *Int'l*, pg. 963
HYDRO MAGNESIUM MARKETING GMBH—See Norsk Hydro a.s; *Int'l*, pg. 963
HYDRO MAGNESIUM NORGE—See Norsk Hydro a.s; *Int'l*, pg. 960
HYDRO-MILL CO.—See Triumph Group, Inc.; *U.S. Public*, pg. 1640
HYDRO NOTODDEN INDUSTRIPARK—See Norsk Hydro a.s; *Int'l*, pg. 960
HYDRO OLJE A/S—See Norsk Hydro a.s; *Int'l*, pg. 960
HYDRO PLAST AB—See Norsk Hydro a.s; *Int'l*, pg. 963
HYDRO PLAST OY—See Norsk Hydro a.s; *Int'l*, pg. 963
HYDRO POLAND SP.Z.O.O.—See Norsk Hydro a.s; *Int'l*, pg. 963
HYDRO POLYMER GMBH—See Norsk Hydro a.s; *Int'l*, pg. 963
HYDRO POLYMERS LTD.—See Norsk Hydro a.s; *Int'l*, pg. 963
HYDRO PORSGRUNN—See Norsk Hydro a.s; *Int'l*, pg. 960

HYDRO PRODUITS CHIMIQUES—See Norsk Hydro a.s; *Int'l*, pg. 963
HYDRO-QUEBEC; *Int'l*, pg. 640
HYDRO RAFNES—See Norsk Hydro a.s; *Int'l*, pg. 960
HYDRO RJUKAN NAERINGSPARK—See Norsk Hydro a.s; *Int'l*, pg. 960
HYDRO S.A.—See Norsk Hydro a.s; *Int'l*, pg. 963
HYDRO SEAFOOD A/S—See Norsk Hydro a.s; *Int'l*, pg. 960
HYDRO-STACK PRODUCTS—See The Oilgear Company; *U.S. Public*, pg. 1215
HYDRO SUPRA AB—See Norsk Hydro a.s; *Int'l*, pg. 963
HYDRO SUPRA CHEMICALS OY—See Norsk Hydro a.s; *Int'l*, pg. 963
HYDRO SUPRA KEMISERVICE AB—See Norsk Hydro a.s; *Int'l*, pg. 963
HYDRO SYDPLAST AB—See Norsk Hydro a.s; *Int'l*, pg. 963
HYDRO THAI LTD.—See Norsk Hydro a.s; *Int'l*, pg. 963
HYDROBUDOWA-6 S.A.—See Bilfinger + Berger Bauaktiengesellschaft; *Int'l*, pg. 196
HYDROCARBON & CHEMICAL PROCESSING DIVISION—See ABB Asea Brown Boveri (Holding) Ltd.; *Int'l*, pg. 4
HYDROCARBON DEVELOPMENT CORP.—See Royal Dutch/Shell Group of Companies; *Int'l*, pg. 1136
HYDROCARBONS INTERNATIONAL HOLDING CO.—See ENI S.p.A.; *Int'l*, pg. 429
HYDROCARE BV—See Mannesmann A.G.; *Int'l*, pg. 838
HYDROCHEM C.I.—See Norsk Hydro a.s; *Int'l*, pg. 963
HYDROCHIM, S.A.—See Olin Corporation; *U.S. Public*, pg. 1219
HYDROCORP, INC.—See Aquarion Company; *U.S. Public*, pg. 126
HYDROELECTRIC LIFT TRUCKS, INC.—See Clark Material Handling Company; *U.S. Private*, pg. 243
HYDROGAS A/S—See Norsk Hydro a.s; *Int'l*, pg. 960
HYDROGAS A/S MARKEDSSEKSJON—See Norsk Hydro a.s; *Int'l*, pg. 963
HYDROGAS DANMARK A.S—See Norsk Hydro a.s; *Int'l*, pg. 963
HYDROGAS FRANCE S.A.—See Norsk Hydro a.s; *Int'l*, pg. 963
HYDROGAS HOLLAND B.V.—See Norsk Hydro a.s; *Int'l*, pg. 963
HYDROGEN SUPPLY, INC.—See Praxair Inc.; *U.S. Public*, pg. 1320
HYDROGEO CANADA INC.—See SNC-Lavalin Group Inc.; *Int'l*, pg. 1162
HYDROLABS INC.—See Allied Colloids Group Plc.; *Int'l*, pg. 62
HYDROLECTRIC LIFT TRUCKS INC.—See Aluminum Company of America; *U.S. Public*, pg. 61
HYDROMARINE SRL—See Mannesmann A.G.; *Int'l*, pg. 839
HYDROMATIC PUMPS—See General Signal Corporation; *U.S. Public*, pg. 726
HYDROMATIK GMBH—See Mannesmann A.G.; *Int'l*, pg. 838
HYDROMATION FRANCE S.A.R.L.—See Filterwerk Mann & Hummel GmbH; *Int'l*, pg. 484
HYDROMECHANICS DIV.—See Zurn Industries, Inc.; *U.S. Public*, pg. 1794
HYDRO-MED SCIENCES—See GP Strategies Corporation; *U.S. Public*, pg. 695
HYDROMETRICS, INC.—See Asarco Incorporated; *U.S. Public*, pg. 138
HYDRON JAPAN K.K.—See GP Strategies Corporation; *U.S. Public*, pg. 695
HYDRO-QUEBEC INTERNATIONAL—See Hydro-Quebec; *Int'l*, pg. 640
HYDROSCIENCE, INC.; *U.S. Private*, pg. 552
HYDROSHIP A/S—See Norsk Hydro a.s; *Int'l*, pg. 960
HYDROTEX INC.—See Morgan Crucible Co. Plc; *Int'l*, pg. 892
HYDROWA B.V.—See Sophus Berendsen A/S; *Int'l*, pg. 1285
HYDURA PRODUCTS—See The Oilgear Company; *U.S. Public*, pg. 1215
HYE PRECISION CO.—See Amer Group Ltd.; *Int'l*, pg. 73
HYER INDUSTRIES INC./THAYER SCALE; *U.S. Private*, pg. 552
HYGEIA COCA-COLA BOTTLING COMPANY—See Coca-Cola Enterprises Inc.; *U.S. Public*, pg. 393
HYGEIA DAIRY CO., INC.; *U.S. Private*, pg. 552
HYGEIA SCIENCES, INC.—See Carter-Wallace, Inc.; *U.S. Public*, pg. 310
HYGIE FRANCE—See Fort James Corporation; *U.S. Public*, pg. 552
HYGIENIC SERVICE GEBAUDEREINIGUNG BETRIEBS-KG.—See Vorwerk & Co.; *Int'l*, pg. 1480
HYGIENIC SERVICE GEBAUDEREINIGUNG UND GEBAUDEDIENSTE KG.—See Vorwerk & Co.; *Int'l*, pg. 1480
HYGRADE FOOD PRODUCTS CORPORATION—See Sara Lee Corporation; *U.S. Public*, pg. 1433
HYGRADE METAL MOULDING MFG. CORP.; *U.S. Private*, pg. 552
HYLAR METAL PRODUCTS—See Degelman Industries Ltd.; *Int'l*, pg. 388
HYLSA BEKAERT—See Alfa, S.A. de C.V.; *Int'l*, pg. 56
HYLSA DAD—See N.V. Bekaert S.A.; *Int'l*, pg. 185
HYLSA S.A.-BAR AND ROD DIVISION—See Alfa, S.A. de C.V.; *Int'l*, pg. 56
HYLSA S.A.-FLAT ROLLED DIVISION—See Alfa, S.A. de C.V.; *Int'l*, pg. 56
HYLSA S.A.-MINING AND PELLETIING DIVISION—See Alfa, S.A. de C.V.; *Int'l*, pg. 56
HYLSA S.A.-NORTH PLANT—See Alfa, S.A. de C.V.; *Int'l*, pg. 56
HYLSA S.A.-TECHNOLOGY DIVISION—See Alfa, S.A. de C.V.; *Int'l*, pg. 56
HYLSA S.A.-TUBULAR DIVISION—See Alfa, S.A. de C.V.; *Int'l*, pg. 56

HYLSAMEX, S.A. DE C.V.—See Alfa, S.A. de C.V.; *Int'l*, pg. 56
HYMECA MANUTENTION S.A.—See Cardo AB; *Int'l*, pg. 269
HYNAUTIC—See IMO Industries Inc.; *U.S. Public*, pg. 857
HYNES INDUSTRIES INC.; *U.S. Private*, pg. 552
HYOGO TOYOTA MOTOR CO., LTD.—See Toyota Motor Corporation; *Int'l*, pg. 1412
HYOSUNG ASC—See ASC Incorporated; *U.S. Private*, pg. 8
HYOSUNG ALUMINUM CO., LTD.—See Hyosung Group; *Int'l*, pg. 640
HYOSUNG AMERICA, INC.—See Hyosung Group; *Int'l*, pg. 641
HYOSUNG-BASF CO., LTD.—See BASF AG; *Int'l*, pg. 108
HYOSUNG-EBARA COMPANY LTD.—See Ebara Corporation; *Int'l*, pg. 432
HYOSUNG-EBARA ENVIRONMENT ENGINEERING CO., LTD.—See Ebara Corporation; *Int'l*, pg. 432
HYOSUNG GROUP; *Int'l*, pg. 640
HYOSUNG INDUSTRIES CO., LTD.—See Hyosung Group; *Int'l*, pg. 640
HYOSUNG METAL PRODUCTS CO., LTD.—See Hyosung Group; *Int'l*, pg. 641
HYPERALLYE—See Groupe Casino; *Int'l*, pg. 563
HYPERION SOFTWARE; *U.S. Public*, pg. 851
HYPERMART USA—See Wal-Mart Stores, Inc.; *U.S. Public*, pg. 1733
HYPERMEDIA COMMUNICATIONS, INC.; *U.S. Public*, pg. 851
HYPERTAC LIMITED—See Smiths Industries plc; *Int'l*, pg. 1267
HYPERTRONICS CORPORATION—See Smiths Industries plc; *Int'l*, pg. 1268
HYPERVISION A/S—See Bang & Olufsen A/S; *Int'l*, pg. 146
HYPO PROPERTY FINANCE—See Bayerische Hypotheken-und Wechsel-Bank Aktiengesellschaft; *Int'l*, pg. 176
HYPO SECURITIES INC.—See Bayerische Hypotheken-und Wechsel-Bank Aktiengesellschaft; *Int'l*, pg. 176
HYPO TRADE FINANCE LTD.—See Bayerische Hypotheken-und Wechsel-Bank Aktiengesellschaft; *Int'l*, pg. 176
HYPOBANK INTERNATIONAL S.A.—See Bayerische Hypotheken-und Wechsel-Bank Aktiengesellschaft; *Int'l*, pg. 176
HYPONEX CORPORATION—See The Scotts Company; *U.S. Public*, pg. 1447
HYPOSWISS SCHWEIZERISCHE—See Union Bank of Switzerland; *Int'l*, pg. 1440
HYPOSWISS (SWISS MORTGAGE & COMMERCIAL BANK)—See Union Bank of Switzerland; *Int'l*, pg. 1440
HYPOTHEKENBANK IN ESSEN AG—See Commerzbank AG; *Int'l*, pg. 310
HYPOTHEKENBANK IN HAMBURG AG—See Dresdner Bank AG; *Int'l*, pg. 418
HYPOTHEQUES CDPQ—See Caisse de depot et placement du Quebec; *Int'l*, pg. 249
HYPRO CORPORATION—See WICOR, Inc.; *U.S. Public*, pg. 1767
HYRE ELECTRIC COMPANY OF INDIANA, INC.—See EMCOR Group, Inc.; *U.S. Public*, pg. 572
HYROLEC MANAGEMENT LIMITED—See The Lubrizol Corporation; *U.S. Public*, pg. 1016
HYSOL JAPAN LIMITED—See The Dexter Corporation; *U.S. Public*, pg. 505
HYSPAN PRECISION PRODUCTS, INC.; *U.S. Private*, pg. 552
HYSTER AUSTRALIA PTY. LTD.—See NACCO Industries, Inc.; *U.S. Public*, pg. 1149
HYSTER BRASIL LIMITADA—See NACCO Industries, Inc.; *U.S. Public*, pg. 1149
HYSTER B.V.—See NACCO Industries, Inc.; *U.S. Public*, pg. 1149
HYSTER EUROPE LTD.—See NACCO Industries, Inc.; *U.S. Public*, pg. 1149
HYSTER FRANCE—See NACCO Industries, Inc.; *U.S. Public*, pg. 1150
HYSTER INTERNATIONAL SALES CORPORATION—See NACCO Industries, Inc.; *U.S. Public*, pg. 1149
HYSTER ITALIA S.R.L.—See NACCO Industries, Inc.; *U.S. Public*, pg. 1149
HYSTER LTD.—See NACCO Industries, Inc.; *U.S. Public*, pg. 1150
HYSTER (NI) LTD.—See NACCO Industries, Inc.; *U.S. Public*, pg. 1150
HYSTER OVERSEAS CAPITAL CORPORATION—See NACCO Industries, Inc.; *U.S. Public*, pg. 1149
HYTEK FINISHES CO.—See Esterline Technologies Corporation; *U.S. Public*, pg. 594
HYUN DAI TERMINAL CO., LTD.—See Molex Incorporated; *U.S. Public*, pg. 1122
HYUNDAI ALUMINUM INDUSTRY CO., LTD.—See Hyundai Motor Company; *Int'l*, pg. 641
HYUNDAI AUTO CANADA INC.—See Hyundai Motor Company; *Int'l*, pg. 641
HYUNDAI CAR (UK) LTD—See Lex Service PLC; *Int'l*, pg. 807
HYUNDAI CONSTRUCTION EQUIPMENT INDUSTRIAL CO., LTD.—See Hyundai Motor Company; *Int'l*, pg. 641
HYUNDAI CONSTRUCTION EQUIPMENT SERVICE CO., LTD.—See Hyundai Motor Company; *Int'l*, pg. 641
HYUNDAI CORP., U.S.A.—See Hyundai Motor Company; *Int'l*, pg. 641
HYUNDAI ELECTRICAL ENGINEERING CO., LTD.—See Hyundai Motor Company; *Int'l*, pg. 641
HYUNDAI ELECTRONICS AMERICA—See Hyundai Motor Company; *Int'l*, pg. 641
HYUNDAI ELECTRONICS INDUSTRIES CO., LTD.—See Hyundai Motor Company; *Int'l*, pg. 641
HYUNDAI ELEVATOR CO., LTD.—See Hyundai Motor Company; *Int'l*, pg. 641

HYUNDAI ENGINEERING & CONSTRUCTION CO., LTD.—See Hyundai Motor Company; *Int'l*, pg. 641
HYUNDAI ENGINEERING CO., LTD.—See Hyundai Motor Company; *Int'l*, pg. 641
HYUNDAI HEAVY INDUSTRIES CO., LTD.—See Hyundai Motor Company; *Int'l*, pg. 641
HYUNDAI HOUSING & INDUSTRIAL DEVELOPMENT CO., LTD.—See Hyundai Motor Company; *Int'l*, pg. 641
HYUNDAI MARINE & FIRE INSURANCE CO., LTD.—See Hyundai Motor Company; *Int'l*, pg. 641
HYUNDAI MERCHANT MARINE CO., LTD.—See Hyundai Motor Company; *Int'l*, pg. 641
HYUNDAI MIPO DOCKYARD CO., LTD.—See Hyundai Motor Company; *Int'l*, pg. 641
HYUNDAI MOTOR AMERICA—See Hyundai Motor Company; *Int'l*, pg. 641
HYUNDAI MOTOR AMERICA EASTERN REGIONAL OFFICE—See Hyundai Motor Company; *Int'l*, pg. 641
HYUNDAI MOTOR AMERICA SOUTHERN REGIONAL OFFICE—See Hyundai Motor Company; *Int'l*, pg. 641
HYUNDAI MOTOR AMERICA WESTERN REGIONAL OFFICE—See Hyundai Motor Company; *Int'l*, pg. 641
HYUNDAI MOTOR COMPANY; *Int'l*, pg. 641
HYUNDAI MOTOR COMPANY—See Hyundai Motor Company; *Int'l*, pg. 641
HYUNDAI MOTOR SERVICE CO., LTD.—See Hyundai Motor Company; *Int'l*, pg. 641
HYUNDAI OIL REFINERY CO., LTD.—See Hyundai Motor Company; *Int'l*, pg. 642
HYUNDAI PETROCHEMICAL CO., LTD.—See Hyundai Motor Company; *Int'l*, pg. 642
HYUNDAI PIPE CO., LTD.—See Hyundai Motor Company; *Int'l*, pg. 642
HYUNDAI PRECISION & INDUSTRY CO., LTD.—See Hyundai Motor Company; *Int'l*, pg. 642
HYUNDAI SECURITIES CO., LTD.—See Hyundai Motor Company; *Int'l*, pg. 642
HYUNDAI STEEL INDUSTRIES INC.—See Hyundai Motor Company; *Int'l*, pg. 642
HYUNDAI WOOD INDUSTRIES CO., LTD.—See Hyundai Motor Company; *Int'l*, pg. 642

I

I&S CORPORATION (FUKUOKA BRANCH)—See I&S Corp.; *Int'l*, pg. 642
I&S CORPORATION (HIROSHIMA BRANCH)—See I&S Corp.; *Int'l*, pg. 642
I&S CORPORATION (KANSAI REGIONAL HEAD OFFICE)—See I&S Corp.; *Int'l*, pg. 642
I&S CORPORATION (NAGOYA REGIONAL HEAD OFFICE)—See I&S Corp.; *Int'l*, pg. 642
I&S CORPORATION (OKINAWA BRANCH)—See I&S Corp.; *Int'l*, pg. 642
I&S CORPORATION (SAPPORO BRANCH)—See I&S Corp.; *Int'l*, pg. 642
I&S CORPORATION (SENDAI BRANCH)—See I&S Corp.; *Int'l*, pg. 642
I CAN'T BELIEVE IT'S YOGURT—See Yogen Fruz Worldwide Inc.; *Int'l*, pg. 1520
I&S CORPORATION (HONG KONG OFFICE)—See I&S Corp.; *Int'l*, pg. 642
I & K DISTRIBUTORS, INC.; *U.S. Private*, pg. 552
I&S CORP.; *Int'l*, pg. 642
I&S CORPORATION (BEIJING OFFICE)—See I&S Corp.; *Int'l*, pg. 642
I&S CORPORATION (HONG KONG BRANCH)—See I&S Corp.; *Int'l*, pg. 642
I&S CORPORATION (KITA-KYUSHU BRANCH)—See I&S Corp.; *Int'l*, pg. 642
I&S CORPORATION (KYUSHU REGIONAL HEAD OFFICE)—See I&S Corp.; *Int'l*, pg. 642
I&S CORPORATION (SINGAPORE BRANCH)—See I&S Corp.; *Int'l*, pg. 642
I&S CORPORATION (TAIWAN BRANCH)—See I&S Corp.; *Int'l*, pg. 642
I-BIMSA ULUSLARARASI IS BILGI VEYONETIM SISTEMLERI A.S.—See International Business Machines Corporation; *U.S. Public*, pg. 898
I-BIMSA ULUSLARARASI IS BILGI VEYONETIM SISTEMLERI A.S.—See Sabanci Holding A.S.; *Int'l*, pg. 1167
I-BIMSA ULUSLARARASI IS BILGI VEYONETIM SISTEMLERI A.S.—See Westpac Banking Corporation; *Int'l*, pg. 1496
I-BUS DIVISION—See Maxwell Technologies, Inc.; *U.S. Public*, pg. 1062
I-FLOW CORPORATION; *U.S. Public*, pg. 851
I/N KOTE—See Inland Steel Industries, Inc.; *U.S. Public*, pg. 879
I/N TEK—See Inland Steel Industries, Inc.; *U.S. Public*, pg. 879
I-NET, INC.—See Wang Laboratories, Inc.; *U.S. Public*, pg. 1737
I-R EQUIPMENT SALES—See Ingersoll-Rand Company; *U.S. Public*, pg. 876
I-SPED INTERNATIONALE SPEDITION GMBH—See Korf-Transport-GmbH; *Int'l*, pg. 759
IA CONSTRUCTION CORP.; *U.S. Private*, pg. 552
IA CORPORATION; *U.S. Private*, pg. 553
IAC INDUSTRIES; *U.S. Private*, pg. 553
IAE INTERNATIONAL AERO ENGINES AG—See Daimler-Benz Aktiengesellschaft; *Int'l*, pg. 367
IAF BIOVAC INC.—See BioChem Pharma Inc.; *Int'l*, pg. 196
IAI-EUROPE-EAT-EUROPEAN ADVANCED TECHNOLOGIES A.S.—See Israel Aircraft Industries Ltd.; *Int'l*, pg. 690
IAV INGENIEURGESELLSCHAFT FUR AGGREGATETECHNIK UND VERKEHRSFAHRZEUGE MBH—See Volkswagen AG; *Int'l*, pg. 1473
I.B. DIFFUSION, LP; *U.S. Private*, pg. 553
IBC VEHICLES LTD.—See Isuzu Motors Limited; *Int'l*, pg. 693

IBCS-PRIMAX SOFTWARE LTD.—See Oracle Corporation; *U.S. Public*, pg. 1228
I.B.D.—See Lagardere Groupe; *Int'l*, pg. 795
IBD INFORMATIONSSYSTEME BETRIEBS- UND DIENSTLEISTUNGS GMBH—See Porsche AG; *Int'l*, pg. 1063
I/B/E/S INTERNATIONAL INC.—See VNU Verenigde Nederlandse Uitgeversbedrijven B.V.; *Int'l*, pg. 1446
IBI CORPORATE FINANCE LIMITED—See Bank of Ireland; *Int'l*, pg. 152
IBI INVESTMENT SERVICES LIMITED—See Bank of Ireland; *Int'l*, pg. 152
I.B.I.S.-S.P.A.; *Int'l*, pg. 642
IBJ ASIA LIMITED—See The Industrial Bank of Japan, Limited; *Int'l*, pg. 676
IBJ AUSTRALIA BANK LIMITED—See The Industrial Bank of Japan, Limited; *Int'l*, pg. 676
IBJ AUSTRALIA CORPORATION LIMITED—See The Industrial Bank of Japan, Limited; *Int'l*, pg. 676
IBJ AUSTRALIA NOMINEES LIMITED—See The Industrial Bank of Japan, Limited; *Int'l*, pg. 676
IBJ-CA CONSULT HANDELS-UND INVESTITIONSBERATUNGSGESELLSCHAFT M.B.H.—See Creditanstalt-Bankverein; *Int'l*, pg. 347
IBJ-CA CONSULT HANDELS-UND INVESTITIONSBERATUNGSGESELLSCHAFT M.B.H.—See The Industrial Bank of Japan, Limited; *Int'l*, pg. 676
IBJ ESPANA—See The Industrial Bank of Japan, Limited; *Int'l*, pg. 676
IBJ FUTURES PTE. LIMITED—See The Industrial Bank of Japan, Limited; *Int'l*, pg. 676
P.T. IBJ INDONESIA BANK—See The Industrial Bank of Japan, Limited; *Int'l*, pg. 676
IBJ INTERNATIONAL PLC—See The Industrial Bank of Japan, Limited; *Int'l*, pg. 676
IBJ MERCHANT BANK (SINGAPORE) LIMITED—See The Industrial Bank of Japan, Limited; *Int'l*, pg. 676
IBJ NW ASSET MANAGEMENT CO., LTD.—See Wako Securities Co., Ltd.; *Int'l*, pg. 1485
IBJ SCHRODER BANK & TRUST COMPANY—See The Industrial Bank of Japan, Limited; *Int'l*, pg. 674
IBJ SCHRODER BANK & TRUST COMPANY (CAYMAN BRANCH)—See The Industrial Bank of Japan, Limited; *Int'l*, pg. 675
IBJ SCHRODER BANK & TRUST COMPANY (MIDTOWN BRANCH)—See The Industrial Bank of Japan, Limited; *Int'l*, pg. 675
IBJ SCHRODER BANKING CORPORATION—See The Industrial Bank of Japan, Limited; *Int'l*, pg. 675
IBJ SCHRODER INTERNATIONAL BANK—See The Industrial Bank of Japan, Limited; *Int'l*, pg. 675
IBJ SCHRODER LEASING CORPORATION—See The Industrial Bank of Japan, Limited; *Int'l*, pg. 675
IBL (BALLSCREWS) LTD.—See FAG Group; *Int'l*, pg. 469
IBL LIMITED, INC.—See Accor S.A.; *Int'l*, pg. 21
IBL S.A.—See Accor S.A.; *Int'l*, pg. 21
IBM AFRICA MIDDLE EAST, S.A.—See International Business Machines Corporation; *U.S. Public*, pg. 897
IBM APPLICATION SOLUTIONS—See International Business Machines Corporation; *U.S. Public*, pg. 895
IBM ARGENTINA, S.A.—See International Business Machines Corporation; *U.S. Public*, pg. 896
IBM AUSTRALIA LIMITED—See International Business Machines Corporation; *U.S. Public*, pg. 896
IBM AUSTRALIA RENTALS PTY. LTD.—See International Business Machines Corporation; *U.S. Public*, pg. 896
IBM AUSTRALIA SERVICES PTY. LTD.—See International Business Machines Corporation; *U.S. Public*, pg. 896
IBM BAHAMAS LIMITED—See International Business Machines Corporation; *U.S. Public*, pg. 896
IBM BRASIL-INDUSTRIA MAQUINAS E SERVICOS LTDA.—See International Business Machines Corporation; *U.S. Public*, pg. 896
IBM CANADA LIMITED—See International Business Machines Corporation; *U.S. Public*, pg. 896
IBM CANADA PRODUCT DISTRIBUTION INC.-DISTRIBUTION DE PRODUITS IBM CANADA INCORPOREE—See International Business Machines Corporation; *U.S. Public*, pg. 896
IBM CREDIT CORPORATION—See International Business Machines Corporation; *U.S. Public*, pg. 896
IBM DANMARK A/S, DANISH DIV—See International Business Machines Corporation; *U.S. Public*, pg. 897
IBM DANMARK-PRODUKT DISTRIBUTION SELSKAB A/S, DANISH DIV—See International Business Machines Corporation; *U.S. Public*, pg. 898
IBM DE BOLIVIA, S.A—See International Business Machines Corporation; *U.S. Public*, pg. 897
IBM DE CHILE S.A.C—See International Business Machines Corporation; *U.S. Public*, pg. 897
IBM DE COLOMBIA, S.A.—See International Business Machines Corporation; *U.S. Public*, pg. 897
IBM DE COSTA RICA, S.A.—See International Business Machines Corporation; *U.S. Public*, pg. 897
IBM DE EXPORTACION Y SERVICIOS, S.A.—See International Business Machines Corporation; *U.S. Public*, pg. 897
IBM DE GUATEMALA, S.A.—See International Business Machines Corporation; *U.S. Public*, pg. 897
IBM DE HONDURAS, S.A.—See International Business Machines Corporation; *U.S. Public*, pg. 897
IBM DE MEXICO, S.A.—See International Business Machines Corporation; *U.S. Public*, pg. 897
IBM DE PANAMA, S.A.—See International Business Machines Corporation; *U.S. Public*, pg. 897
IBM DE VENEZUELA, S.A—See International Business Machines Corporation; *U.S. Public*, pg. 897
IBM DEL PERU, S.A.—See International Business Machines Corporation; *U.S. Public*, pg. 897
IBM DEL URUGUAY, S.A.—See International Business Machines Corporation; *U.S. Public*, pg. 897
IBM DEUTSCHLAND GMBH—See International Business Machines Corporation; *U.S. Public*, pg. 897

IBM DEUTSCHLAND KREDITBANK GMBH—See International Business Machines Corporation; *U.S. Public*, pg. 897
IBM DEUTSCHLAND PRODUKTVERTRIEB GMBH—See International Business Machines Corporation; *U.S. Public*, pg. 897
IBM DISTRIBUTION AND SUPPORT, S.A.—See International Business Machines Corporation; *U.S. Public*, pg. 897
IBM DEL ECUADOR, C.A.—See International Business Machines Corporation; *U.S. Public*, pg. 897
IBM ENTERPRISE SYSTEMS—See International Business Machines Corporation; *U.S. Public*, pg. 895
IBM ESPANA DISTRIBUIDORA DE PRODUCTOS, S.A.—See International Business Machines Corporation; *U.S. Public*, pg. 898
IBM EUROCOORDINATION, S.A.—See International Business Machines Corporation; *U.S. Public*, pg. 897
IBM EUROPE, S.A.—See International Business Machines Corporation; *U.S. Public*, pg. 897
IBM FOREIGN SALES CORPORATION, LTD.—See International Business Machines Corporation; *U.S. Public*, pg. 898
IBM FRANCE DIFFUSION, S.A—See International Business Machines Corporation; *U.S. Public*, pg. 897
IBM INFORMATION SERVICES LIMITED—See International Business Machines Corporation; *U.S. Public*, pg. 897
IBM IRELAND LIMITED—See International Business Machines Corporation; *U.S. Public*, pg. 897
IBM ISRAEL LTD.—See International Business Machines Corporation; *U.S. Public*, pg. 897
IBM ITALIA-DISTRIBUZIONE PRODOTTI S.R.L.—See International Business Machines Corporation; *U.S. Public*, pg. 897
IBM ITALIA S.P.A.—See International Business Machines Corporation; *U.S. Public*, pg. 897
IBM JAPAN, LTD.—See International Business Machines Corporation; *U.S. Public*, pg. 897
IBM JAPAN SALES COMPANY, LTD.—See International Business Machines Corporation; *U.S. Public*, pg. 897
IBM KOREA, INC.—See International Business Machines Corporation; *U.S. Public*, pg. 897
IBM KOREA SYSTEMS CORPORATION—See International Business Machines Corporation; *U.S. Public*, pg. 897
IBM LATIN AMERICAN REGION S.A.—See International Business Machines Corporation; *U.S. Public*, pg. 897
CIE. IBM MADAGASIKARA, S.A.—See International Business Machines Corporation; *U.S. Public*, pg. 897
IBM NEDERLAND N.V.—See International Business Machines Corporation; *U.S. Public*, pg. 897
IBM NEW ZEALAND LIMITED—See International Business Machines Corporation; *U.S. Public*, pg. 897
IBM NEW ZEALAND PRODUCT DISTRIBUTION COMPANY LIMITED—See International Business Machines Corporation; *U.S. Public*, pg. 897
IBM NORGE PRODUKT DISTRIBUSJON A/S—See International Business Machines Corporation; *U.S. Public*, pg. 898
IBM OESTERREICH, INTERNATIONALE BUEROMASCHINEN GESELLSCHAFT MBH—See International Business Machines Corporation; *U.S. Public*, pg. 897
IBM PERSONAL COMPUTER COMPANY—See International Business Machines Corporation; *U.S. Public*, pg. 896
IBM PERSONAL SYSTEMS—See International Business Machines Corporation; *U.S. Public*, pg. 895
IBM PHILIPPINES, INCORPORATED—See International Business Machines Corporation; *U.S. Public*, pg. 897
IBM PRODUKTVERTRIEB GESELLSCHAFT MBH—See International Business Machines Corporation; *U.S. Public*, pg. 897
IBM PROGRAMMING SYSTEMS—See International Business Machines Corporation; *U.S. Public*, pg. 895
IBM REAL ESTATE & CONSTRUCTION DIV.—See International Business Machines Corporation; *U.S. Public*, pg. 896
IBM RESEARCH DIV.—See International Business Machines Corporation; *U.S. Public*, pg. 896
IBM SINGAPORE PTE LTD.—See International Business Machines Corporation; *U.S. Public*, pg. 897
IBM SONDERSYSTEME GESELLSCHAFT MBH—See International Business Machines Corporation; *U.S. Public*, pg. 897
IBM SOUTHEAST ASIA SERVICES LTD.—See International Business Machines Corporation; *U.S. Public*, pg. 897
IBM SVENSKA AKTIEBOLAG—See International Business Machines Corporation; *U.S. Public*, pg. 897
IBM SVENSKA PRODUKT DISTRIBUTION AKTIEBOLAG—See International Business Machines Corporation; *U.S. Public*, pg. 897
IBM SWITZERLAND—See International Business Machines Corporation; *U.S. Public*, pg. 897
IBM SYSTEMS INTEGRATION DIV.—See International Business Machines Corporation; *U.S. Public*, pg. 896
IBM TAIWAN CORPORATION—See International Business Machines Corporation; *U.S. Public*, pg. 897
IBM TECHNOLOGY PRODUCTS—See International Business Machines Corporation; *U.S. Public*, pg. 896
IBM THAILAND COMPANY LIMITED—See International Business Machines Corporation; *U.S. Public*, pg. 897
IBM TRADE DEVELOPMENT, S.A.—See International Business Machines Corporation; *U.S. Public*, pg. 897
IBM UNITED KINGDOM HOLDINGS LIMITED—See International Business Machines Corporation; *U.S. Public*, pg. 897
IBM UNITED KINGDOM INTERNATIONAL PRODUCT SALES LIMITED—See International Business Machines Corporation; *U.S. Public*, pg. 897
IBM UNITED KINGDOM LABORATORIES LIMITED—See International Business Machines Corporation; *U.S. Public*, pg. 897

IBM UNITED KINGDOM LIMITED—See International Business Machines Corporation; *U.S. Public*, pg. 898
IBM UNITED KINGDOM PRODUCT SALES LIMITED—See International Business Machines Corporation; *U.S. Public*, pg. 898
IBM WORLD TRADE AMERICAS/FAR EAST CORPORATION—See International Business Machines Corporation; *U.S. Public*, pg. 896
IBM WORLD TRADE EUROPE/MIDDLE EAST/AFRICA CORP.—See International Business Machines Corporation; *U.S. Public*, pg. 896
IBP—See Delta plc; *Int'l*, pg. 391
IBP ARMATUREN GMBH—See Delta plc; *Int'l*, pg. 391
IBP, INC.; *U.S. Public*, pg. 852
IBP INSTALLFITTINGS SP ZOO—See Delta plc; *Int'l*, pg. 391
IBP LTD.—See Delta plc; *Int'l*, pg. 391
I.B.T. IDEAL-BEFESTIGUNGS-TECHNIK UND INDUSTRIEBEDARF GMBH—See Rothenberger Group GmbH; *Int'l*, pg. 1128
IBT, INC.; *U.S. Private*, pg. 553
S.A. I.B.T.—See Cockerill Sambre; *Int'l*, pg. 301
IC IMTECH NV—See Internatio-Muller N.V.; *Int'l*, pg. 681
IC INSURANCE LIMITED—See Zeneca Group Plc; *Int'l*, pg. 1524
I.C. SYSTEM, INC.; *U.S. Private*, pg. 553
ICA BANAN AB—See ICA Handlarnas AB; *Int'l*, pg. 643
ICA BUTIKSFINANS AB—See ICA Handlarnas AB; *Int'l*, pg. 643
ICA EKONOMIBYRA AB—See ICA Handlarnas AB; *Int'l*, pg. 643
ICA FASTIGHETS AB—See ICA Handlarnas AB; *Int'l*, pg. 643
ICA FÖRLAGET AB—See ICA Handlarnas AB; *Int'l*, pg. 643
ICA HANDLARNA MELLANSVERIGE AB—See ICA Handlarnas AB; *Int'l*, pg. 642
ICA HANDLARNA NORR AB—See ICA Handlarnas AB; *Int'l*, pg. 642
ICA HANDLARNA OST AB—See ICA Handlarnas AB; *Int'l*, pg. 642
ICA HANDLARNA SYD AB—See ICA Handlarnas AB; *Int'l*, pg. 642
ICA HANDLARNA SYDOST AB—See ICA Handlarnas AB; *Int'l*, pg. 643
ICA HANDLARNA VAST AB—See ICA Handlarnas AB; *Int'l*, pg. 643
ICA HANDLARNAS AB—See ICA Handlarnas AB; *Int'l*, pg. 642
ICA HANDLARNAS AB; *Int'l*, pg. 642
ICA KOPMANNATJANST AB—See ICA Handlarnas AB; *Int'l*, pg. 643
ICA KORT AB—See ICA Handlarnas AB; *Int'l*, pg. 643
ICA MENY FORETAGEN AB—See ICA Handlarnas AB; *Int'l*, pg. 643
ICA - RODIO—See Empresas ICA Sociedad Controladora S.A.C.V.; *Int'l*, pg. 454
ICA SPECIALVAROR AB—See ICA Handlarnas AB; *Int'l*, pg. 643
ICA UTBILDNINGAR AB—See ICA Handlarnas AB; *Int'l*, pg. 643
ICAT (INTEGRATING CADCAM)—See EMAP Plc; *Int'l*, pg. 452
ICB INGENIEURS CONSEILS—See SMH Swiss Corporation for Micro Electronics & Watchmaking Indus. Ltd.; *Int'l*, pg. 1160
ICBC (EUROPE) N.V.—See The International Commercial Bank of China; *Int'l*, pg. 684
ICC CHEMICAL (UK) LIMITED—See ICC Industries, Inc.; *U.S. Private*, pg. 554
ICC COMERCIO E INDUSTRIA LTDS.—See ICC Industries, Inc.; *U.S. Private*, pg. 554
ICC HANDELS AG—See ICC Industries, Inc.; *U.S. Private*, pg. 554
ICC (HONG KONG) LTD.—See ICC Industries, Inc.; *U.S. Private*, pg. 554
ICC IBERICA S.A.—See ICC Industries, Inc.; *U.S. Private*, pg. 554
ICC INDUSTRIES, B.V.—See ICC Industries, Inc.; *U.S. Private*, pg. 554
ICC INDUSTRIES, INC.; *U.S. Private*, pg. 553
ICC (ISRAEL) CHEMICALS LTD.—See ICC Industries, Inc.; *U.S. Private*, pg. 554
ICC ITALIA S.R.L.—See ICC Industries, Inc.; *U.S. Private*, pg. 554
ICC TRADING, INC.—See ICC Industries, Inc.; *U.S. Private*, pg. 553
ICC TRADING (TAIWAN) LTD.—See ICC Industries, Inc.; *U.S. Private*, pg. 554
ICD GROUP INTERNATIONAL INC.; *U.S. Private*, pg. 554
I.C.E. INTERNATIONAL CAPITAL EQUIPMENT, INC.—See International Capital Equipment Limited; *Int'l*, pg. 683
ICEE-USA CORP—See J & J Snack Foods Corporation; *U.S. Public*, pg. 916
ICF INCORPORATED—See ICF Kaiser International Inc.; *U.S. Public*, pg. 853
ICF INFORMATION TECHNOLOGY, INC.—See ICF Kaiser International Inc.; *U.S. Public*, pg. 853
ICF KAISER ENGINEERS—See ICF Kaiser International Inc.; *U.S. Public*, pg. 853
ICF KAISER ENGINEERS, INC.—See ICF Kaiser International Inc.; *U.S. Public*, pg. 853
ICF KAISER HANFORD COMPANY—See ICF Kaiser International Inc.; *U.S. Public*, pg. 853
ICF KAISER INTERNATIONAL INC.; *U.S. Public*, pg. 852
ICG DIRECT, INC.—See Carat ICG; *U.S. Private*, pg. 208
ICG MEDIA CONSULTANTS, INC—See Carat ICG; *U.S. Private*, pg. 208
ICG PROPANE INC.—See Petro-Canada; *Int'l*, pg. 1041
I.C.H. CORPORATION; *U.S. Public*, pg. 853
ICI ACRYLICS INC.—See Imperial Chemical Industries PLC; *Int'l*, pg. 663
ICI ADVANCED MATERIALS—See Imperial Chemical Industries PLC; *Int'l*, pg. 663

ICI AEROSPACE—See Imperial Chemical Industries PLC; *Int'l*, pg. 663
ICI AGRICULTURAL PRODUCTS—See Imperial Chemical Industries PLC; *Int'l*, pg. 663
ICI AGROCHEMICALS (MALAYSIA) SDN BHD—See Imperial Chemical Industries PLC; *Int'l*, pg. 664
ICI AMERICAN HOLDINGS INC.—See Imperial Chemical Industries PLC; *Int'l*, pg. 663
ICI AMERICAS, INC.—See Imperial Chemical Industries PLC; *Int'l*, pg. 663
ICI ASIATIC (AGRICULTURE) CO. LTD.—See Imperial Chemical Industries PLC; *Int'l*, pg. 664
ICI ASIATIC (AGRICULTURE) CO. LTD.—See Zeneca Group Plc; *Int'l*, pg. 1527
ICI ASIATIC CHEMICAL CO. LTD.—See Imperial Chemical Industries PLC; *Int'l*, pg. 664
ICI ATLANTIK GMBH—See Imperial Chemical Industries PLC; *Int'l*, pg. 664
ICI AUSTRALIA ENGINEERING PROPRIETARY LTD—See Imperial Chemical Industries PLC; *Int'l*, pg. 664
ICI AUSTRALIA HOSPITAL PRODUCTS PTY LTD—See Imperial Chemical Industries PLC; *Int'l*, pg. 664
ICI AUSTRALIA LTD.—See Zeneca Group Plc; *Int'l*, pg. 1525
ICI BANGLADESH LIMITED—See Imperial Chemical Industries PLC; *Int'l*, pg. 664
ICI C & P FRANCE S.A.—See Imperial Chemical Industries PLC; *Int'l*, pg. 664
ICI CANADA INC.—See Imperial Chemical Industries PLC; *Int'l*, pg. 664
ICI CHEMICALS & POLYMERS—See Imperial Chemical Industries PLC; *Int'l*, pg. 663
ICI CHEMICALS & POLYMERS LTD.—See Imperial Chemical Industries PLC; *Int'l*, pg. 663
ICI CHILE S.A.—See Imperial Chemical Industries PLC; *Int'l*, pg. 665
ICI COLORS—See Imperial Chemical Industries PLC; *Int'l*, pg. 663
ICI ESPANA SA—See Imperial Chemical Industries PLC; *Int'l*, pg. 665
ICI EXPLOSIVES—See Imperial Chemical Industries PLC; *Int'l*, pg. 664
ICI EXPLOSIVES USA INC.—See Imperial Chemical Industries PLC; *Int'l*, pg. 663
ICI EXPLOSIVES—See Imperial Chemical Industries PLC; *Int'l*, pg. 664
P.T. ICI FARMASI INDONESIA—See Imperial Chemical Industries PLC; *Int'l*, pg. 666
P.T. ICI FARMASI INDONESIA—See Zeneca Group Plc; *Int'l*, pg. 1527
ICI FERTILIZERS (MALAYSIA) SDN BERHAD—See Imperial Chemical Industries PLC; *Int'l*, pg. 665
ICI FIBERITE—See Imperial Chemical Industries PLC; *Int'l*, pg. 664
ICI FIJI LIMITED—See Imperial Chemical Industries PLC; *Int'l*, pg. 665
ICI FILMS—See Imperial Chemical Industries PLC; *Int'l*, pg. 664
ICI FINANCE PLC—See Imperial Chemical Industries PLC; *Int'l*, pg. 663
ICI FRANCE SA—See Imperial Chemical Industries PLC; *Int'l*, pg. 665
ICI INDIA LIMITED—See Imperial Chemical Industries PLC; *Int'l*, pg. 665
ICI INDUSTRIAL CHEMICALS (MALAYSIA) SDN BHD—See Imperial Chemical Industries PLC; *Int'l*, pg. 665
ICI INSTRUMENTS PTY LTD—See Imperial Chemical Industries PLC; *Int'l*, pg. 665
ICI (ISRAEL) LIMITED—See Imperial Chemical Industries PLC; *Int'l*, pg. 665
ICI ITALIA MILANO S.P.A.—See Imperial Chemical Industries PLC; *Int'l*, pg. 665
ICI JAPAN LIMITED—See Imperial Chemical Industries PLC; *Int'l*, pg. 665
ICI KATALCO—See Imperial Chemical Industries PLC; *Int'l*, pg. 664
ICI KOREA LTD.—See Imperial Chemical Industries PLC; *Int'l*, pg. 665
ICI LACKE FARBEN GMBH—See Imperial Chemical Industries PLC; *Int'l*, pg. 665
ICI-MEVISA, S.A.—See Imperial Chemical Industries PLC; *Int'l*, pg. 665
ICI NEW ZEALAND LIMITED—See Imperial Chemical Industries PLC; *Int'l*, pg. 665
ICI OESTERREICH GMBH—See Imperial Chemical Industries PLC; *Int'l*, pg. 665
ICI PACKAGING INKS—See Imperial Chemical Industries PLC; *Int'l*, pg. 664
ICI PAINTS—See Imperial Chemical Industries PLC; *Int'l*, pg. 664
ICI PAINTS (CANADA) INC.—See Imperial Chemical Industries PLC; *Int'l*, pg. 665
ICI PAINTS ESPANA SA—See Imperial Chemical Industries PLC; *Int'l*, pg. 665
ICI PAINTS (MALAYSIA) SDN BHD—See Imperial Chemical Industries PLC; *Int'l*, pg. 665
ICI PAINTS (SINGAPORE) PRIVATE LIMITED—See Imperial Chemical Industries PLC; *Int'l*, pg. 665
ICI (PERU) S.A.—See Imperial Chemical Industries PLC; *Int'l*, pg. 665
ICI (PHILIPPINES) INC.—See Imperial Chemical Industries PLC; *Int'l*, pg. 665
ICI POLYURETHANES GROUP—See Imperial Chemical Industries PLC; *Int'l*, pg. 664
ICI PRETECHNIK GGS FUER POLYURETHANE-ROHSTOFFE MBH—See Imperial Chemical Industries PLC; *Int'l*, pg. 665
ICI RESINS B.V.—See Imperial Chemical Industries PLC; *Int'l*, pg. 665
ICI RESINS CANADA INC.—See Imperial Chemical Industries PLC; *Int'l*, pg. 665
ICI RESINS SA—See Imperial Chemical Industries PLC; *Int'l*, pg. 665
ICI SEEDS—See Zeneca Group Plc; *Int'l*, pg. 1524

ICI (SINGAPORE) PRIVATE LIMITED—See Imperial Chemical Industries PLC; *Int'l*, pg. 665
ICI (SOUTH AFRICA) LIMITED—See Imperial Chemical Industries PLC; *Int'l*, pg. 665
ICI SPECIALTIES—See Imperial Chemical Industries PLC; *Int'l*, pg. 664
ICI SWIRE PAINTS LIMITED—See Imperial Chemical Industries PLC; *Int'l*, pg. 665
ICI (SWITZERLAND) AG—See Imperial Chemical Industries PLC; *Int'l*, pg. 665
ICI SYSTEMS S.A.R.L.—See Imperial Chemical Industries PLC; *Int'l*, pg. 665
ICI TAIWAN LIMITED—See Imperial Chemical Industries PLC; *Int'l*, pg. 665
ICI VALCHEM—See Zeneca Group Plc; *Int'l*, pg. 1525
ICI WILHELMSHAVEN GMBH & CO.—See Imperial Chemical Industries PLC; *Int'l*, pg. 665
ICI ZAMBIA LIMITED—See Imperial Chemical Industries PLC; *Int'l*, pg. 665
ICICI ASSET MANAGEMENT COMPANY LIMITED—See J.P. Morgan Co. Incorporated; *U.S. Public*, pg. 1130
ICICI SECURITIES & FINANCE COMPANY LIMITED—See J.P. Morgan Co. Incorporated; *U.S. Public*, pg. 1130
ICIS LOR-ASIA/PACIFIC—See Reed Elsevier plc; *Int'l*, pg. 1094
ICIS LOR-EUROPE—See Reed Elsevier plc; *Int'l*, pg. 1094
ICIS LOR-USA—See Reed Elsevier plc; *Int'l*, pg. 1094
ICL (BELGIUM) S.A.—See Fujitsu Limited; *Int'l*, pg. 529
ICL COMPUTADORES LIMITADA—See Fujitsu Limited; *Int'l*, pg. 529
ICL DATA AB—See Fujitsu Limited; *Int'l*, pg. 529
ICL DATA A/S—See Fujitsu Limited; *Int'l*, pg. 529
ICL DEUTSCHLAND INTERNATIONAL COMPUTERS GMBH—See Fujitsu Limited; *Int'l*, pg. 529
ICL ESPANA INTERNATIONAL COMPUTERS S.A.—See Fujitsu Limited; *Int'l*, pg. 529
ICL FINLAND OY—See Fujitsu Limited; *Int'l*, pg. 529
ICL (FRANCE) INTERNATIONAL COMPUTERS—See Fujitsu Limited; *Int'l*, pg. 529
ICL INTERNATIONAL COMPUTERS GMBH—See Fujitsu Limited; *Int'l*, pg. 529
ICL ITALIA INTERNATIONAL COMPUTERS SPA—See Fujitsu Limited; *Int'l*, pg. 529
ICL KENYA LIMITED—See Fujitsu Limited; *Int'l*, pg. 529
ICL LUXEMBOURG S.A.—See Fujitsu Limited; *Int'l*, pg. 529
ICL (MALAWI) LIMITED—See Fujitsu Limited; *Int'l*, pg. 529
ICL NEDERLAND B.V.—See Fujitsu Limited; *Int'l*, pg. 529
ICL NEW ZEALAND LIMITED—See Fujitsu Limited; *Int'l*, pg. 529
ICL PLC—See Fujitsu Limited; *Int'l*, pg. 528
ICL SINGAPORE PRIVATE LIMITED—See Fujitsu Limited; *Int'l*, pg. 529
ICL (SWITZERLAND) INTERNATIONAL COMPUTERS AG—See Fujitsu Limited; *Int'l*, pg. 529
ICL ZAMBIA LIMITED—See Fujitsu Limited; *Int'l*, pg. 529
ICL ZIMBABWE LIMITED—See Fujitsu Limited; *Int'l*, pg. 529
ICM ARTISTS, LTD.—See ICM Holdings Inc.; *U.S. Private*, pg. 554
ICM HOLDINGS INC.; *U.S. Private*, pg. 554
ICN PHARMACEUTICALS, INC.; *U.S. Public*, pg. 853
ICO, INC.—See Cigna Corp.; *U.S. Public*, pg. 361
ICO, INC.; *U.S. Public*, pg. 853
ICOMA PACKTECHNIK GMBH—See Korsnas AB; *Int'l*, pg. 759
ICOS SYSTEMS, GMBH—See IKOS Systems, Inc.; *U.S. Public*, pg. 864
ICS BUILDING SOCIETY—See Bank of Ireland; *Int'l*, pg. 152
ICS INTANGIBLES HOLDING COMPANY—See Harcourt General, Inc.; *U.S. Public*, pg. 783
ICS LEARNING SYSTEMS, INC.—See Harcourt General, Inc.; *U.S. Public*, pg. 783
ICSA (INGENIERIA Y COMPUTACION, S.A.)—See The Macneal-Schwendler Corp.; *U.S. Public*, pg. 1032
I.C.S.A. - INTERNACIONAL DE COMPOSITES, S.A.—See SEPI; *Int'l*, pg. 1224
ICV LIMITED—See Primark Corporation; *U.S. Public*, pg. 1326
ICW LIMITED—See Tech/Ops Sevcon, Inc.; *U.S. Public*, pg. 1563
ID SOLUTIONS—See Intelligent Controls Inc.; *U.S. Private*, pg. 566
IDA-WEST ENERGY COMPANY—See Idaho Power Company; *U.S. Public*, pg. 862
IDAB WAMAC INTERNATIONAL; *Int'l*, pg. 643
IDAB WAMAC PACIFIC LIMITED—See IDAB Wamac International; *Int'l*, pg. 643
IDAC BILFARGER SVENSKA AKTIEBOLAG—See Imperial Chemical Industries PLC; *Int'l*, pg. 665
IDAL-BENAVENTE—See H.J. Heinz Company; *U.S. Public*, pg. 807
IDAL(INDUSTRIAS DE ALIMENTACAO, LDA.)—See H.J. Heinz Company; *U.S. Public*, pg. 807
IDB DEVELOPMENT CORPORATION LIMITED—See IDB Holding Corporation; *Int'l*, pg. 644
IDB HOLDING CORPORATION; *Int'l*, pg. 643
IDB WORLDCOM—See WorldCom, Inc.; *U.S. Public*, pg. 1779
IDB WORLDCOM, INC.—See WorldCom, Inc.; *U.S. Public*, pg. 1779
IDC AFRICA—See International Data Group; *U.S. Private*, pg. 570
IDC ARGENTINA—See International Data Group; *U.S. Private*, pg. 570
IDC AUSTRALIA—See International Data Group; *U.S. Private*, pg. 570
IDC AUSTRIA—See International Data Group; *U.S. Private*, pg. 570
IDC BENELUX—See International Data Group; *U.S. Private*, pg. 570
IDC CANADA—See International Data Group; *U.S. Private*, pg. 570

IDC COLUMBIA/INVIARCO LTDA.—See International Data Group; *U.S. Private*, pg. 570
IDC DEUTSCHLAND GMBH—See International Data Group; *U.S. Private*, pg. 571
IDC FRANCE—See International Data Group; *U.S. Private*, pg. 571
IDC ITALIA S.R.L.—See International Data Group; *U.S. Private*, pg. 571
IDC MEXICO—See International Data Group; *U.S. Private*, pg. 571
IDC MULTI USER EXPERTISE CENTER—See International Data Group; *U.S. Private*, pg. 571
IDC NEDERLAND—See International Data Group; *U.S. Private*, pg. 571
IDC NEW ZEALAND—See International Data Group; *U.S. Private*, pg. 571
IDC NORGE—See International Data Group; *U.S. Private*, pg. 571
IDC RUSSIA—See International Data Group; *U.S. Private*, pg. 571
IDC SCANDINAVIA A/S—See International Data Group; *U.S. Private*, pg. 571
IDC SERVICES, INC.; *U.S. Private*, pg. 554
IDC SWITZERLAND—See International Data Group; *U.S. Private*, pg. 571
IDC THAILAND—See International Data Group; *U.S. Private*, pg. 571
IDC TURKEY—See International Data Group; *U.S. Private*, pg. 571
IDC UNITED KINGDOM—See International Data Group; *U.S. Private*, pg. 571
IDC VENEZUELA—See International Data Group; *U.S. Private*, pg. 571
IDD CO., LTD.—See Rohm Co., Ltd.; *Int'l*, pg. 1125
IDG BOOKS WORLDWIDE—See International Data Group; *U.S. Private*, pg. 569
IDG COMMUNICACIONES S.A. DE C.V.—See International Data Group; *U.S. Private*, pg. 570
IDG COMMUNICATIONS—See International Data Group; *U.S. Private*, pg. 569
IDG COMMUNICATIONS FRANCE—See International Data Group; *U.S. Private*, pg. 569
IDG COMMUNICATIONS/HUNGARY—See International Data Group; *U.S. Private*, pg. 570
IDG COMMUNICATIONS, INC.—See International Data Group; *U.S. Private*, pg. 570
IDG COMMUNICATIONS ITALIA SRL—See International Data Group; *U.S. Private*, pg. 570
IDG COMMUNICATIONS JAPAN—See International Data Group; *U.S. Private*, pg. 570
IDG COMMUNICATIONS LTD.—See International Data Group; *U.S. Private*, pg. 570
IDG COMMUNICATIONS NEDERLAND BV—See International Data Group, *U.S. Private*, pg. 570
IDG COMMUNICATIONS NORGE AS—See International Data Group; *U.S. Private*, pg. 570
IDG COMMUNICATIONS P/L—See International Data Group; *U.S. Private*, pg. 570
IDG COMMUNICATIONS PUBLISHING GROUP SRL—See International Data Group; *U.S. Private*, pg. 570
IDG COMMUNICATIONS RESEARCH—See International Data Group; *U.S. Private*, pg. 569
IDG COMMUNICATIONS, S.A.—See International Data Group; *U.S. Private*, pg. 570
IDG COMMUNICATIONS VERLAGSGES.MBH—See International Data Group; *U.S. Private*, pg. 570
IDG CZECHOSLOVAKIA—See International Data Group; *U.S. Private*, pg. 570
IDG DENMARK A/S—See International Data Group; *U.S. Private*, pg. 570
IDG INTERNATIONAL NEWS GROUP—See International Data Group; *U.S. Private*, pg. 569
IDG LIST SERVICES—See International Data Group; *U.S. Private*, pg. 569
IDG MAGYAROSZAGI LAPLADO KFT.—See International Data Group; *U.S. Private*, pg. 570
IDG POLAND S.A.—See International Data Group; *U.S. Private*, pg. 570
IDG SHENZHEN—See International Data Group; *U.S. Private*, pg. 570
IDG SWEDEN—See International Data Group; *U.S. Private*, pg. 570
IDG-TECHNIKA COMMUNICATIONS COMPANY—See International Data Group; *U.S. Private*, pg. 570
IDG/UFT—See International Data Group; *U.S. Private*, pg. 570
THE IDI GROUP COMPANIES; *U.S. Private*, pg. 554
IDM BANK N.V.—See ABN-AMRO Holding N.V.; *Int'l*, pg. 9
IDM CONTROLS; *U.S. Private*, pg. 554
I.D.M. ELECTRONICS LTD.—See Kaydon Corporation; *U.S. Public*, pg. 946
IDM EQUIPMENT COMPANY—See IDM Controls; *U.S. Private*, pg. 555
I.D.Q. CANADA, INC.—See Berkshire Hathaway Inc.; *U.S. Public*, pg. 220
IDS CERTIFICATE COMPANY—See American Express Company; *U.S. Public*, pg. 73
IDS DEPOSIT CORP.—See American Express Company; *U.S. Public*, pg. 73
IDS FINANCIAL SERVICES, INC.—See American Express Company; *U.S. Public*, pg. 73
IDS LIFE INSURANCE CO. OF NEW YORK—See American Express Company; *U.S. Public*, pg. 73
IDS PROPERTY CASUALTY INSURANCE COMPANY—See American Express Company; *U.S. Public*, pg. 73
IDS TRUST CO.—See American Express Company; *U.S. Public*, pg. 73
IDT ASIA, LTD.—See Integrated Device Technology, Inc.; *U.S. Public*, pg. 884
IDV AFRICA & LATIN AMERICA—See Diageo Plc; *Int'l*, pg. 409
IDV ASIA PACIFIC—See Diageo Plc; *Int'l*, pg. 409
IDV CENTRAL EUROPE—See Diageo Plc; *Int'l*, pg. 410
IDV CZECH REPUBLIC—See Diageo Plc; *Int'l*, pg. 410
IDV NORTH AMERICA—See Diageo Plc; *Int'l*, pg. 409
IDV OPERATIONS IRELAND LTD.—See Diageo Plc; *Int'l*, pg. 410
IDV POLAND—See Diageo Plc; *Int'l*, pg. 410
IDV FRANCE—See Diageo Plc; *Int'l*, pg. 410
IDV UK—See Diageo Plc; *Int'l*, pg. 409
IDX SYSTEMS CORPORATION; *U.S. Public*, pg. 854
IDX SYSTEMS CORPORATION-ATLANTA—See IDX Systems Corporation; *U.S. Public*, pg. 854
IDX SYSTEMS CORPORATION-BOSTON—See IDX Systems Corporation; *U.S. Public*, pg. 854
IDX SYSTEMS CORPORATION-CHICAGO—See IDX Systems Corporation; *U.S. Public*, pg. 854
IDX SYSTEMS CORPORATION-DALLAS—See IDX Systems Corporation; *U.S. Public*, pg. 854
IDX SYSTEMS CORPORATION-SAN DIEGO—See IDX Systems Corporation; *U.S. Public*, pg. 854
IDX SYSTEMS CORPORATION-SAN FRANCISCO—See IDX Systems Corporation; *U.S. Public*, pg. 854
IDX SYSTEMS CORPORATION-SEATTLE—See IDX Systems Corporation; *U.S. Public*, pg. 854
IE MANAGEMENT CONSULTANT PTY. LTD.—See Bourton Group; *U.S. Private*, pg. 162
IEA, INC.—See Aquarion Company; *U.S. Public*, pg. 126
IEA, INC.-MASSACHUSETTS—See Aquarion Company; *U.S. Public*, pg. 126
IEC ARAB ALABAMA OPERATIONS—See IEC Electronics Corp.; *U.S. Public*, pg. 855
IEC EDINBURG, TEXAS—See IEC Electronics Corp.; *U.S. Public*, pg. 855
IEC ELECTRONICS CORP.; *U.S. Public*, pg. 854
I.E.D. CO., LTD.—See Suntory Ltd.; *Int'l*, pg. 1321
I.E.H. S.C.—See Electrabel S.A.; *Int'l*, pg. 437
IEI INVESTMENTS, INC.—See Indiana Energy, Inc.; *U.S. Public*, pg. 875
IER DIVISION—See Furon Company; *U.S. Public*, pg. 689
IES INDUSTRIES INC.; *U.S. Public*, pg. 855
IES INVESTMENTS INC.—See IES Industries Inc.; *U.S. Public*, pg. 855
IES TRANSPORTATION, INC.—See IES Industries Inc.; *U.S. Public*, pg. 855
IES UTILITIES INC.—See IES Industries Inc.; *U.S. Public*, pg. 855
I.F.C. (FASTENERS) INC.—See The Ivaco Group; *Int'l*, pg. 696
IFC NON WOVENS—See Wyant Coporation; *U.S. Public*, pg. 1782
I.F.C. USA CORP.—See The Ivaco Group; *Int'l*, pg. 696
IFCT FINANCE & SECURITIES CO., LTD.—See The Industrial Finance Corporation of Thailand; *Int'l*, pg. 677
IFCT NOMURA/JAFCO HOLDINGS CO., LTD.—See The Industrial Finance Corporation of Thailand; *Int'l*, pg. 677
IFD—See AXA-UAP; *Int'l*, pg. 19
IFD PROPERTIES, INC.-FIRST—See Cigna Corp.; *U.S. Public*, pg. 359
IFF CONCENTRATES, INC.—See International Flavors & Fragrances, Inc.; *U.S. Public*, pg. 899
IFF FSC, INC.—See International Flavors & Fragrances, Inc.; *U.S. Public*, pg. 899
IFG ASSET MANAGEMENT SERVICES, INC.—See Dain Rauscher Corporation; *U.S. Public*, pg. 476
IFI OY—See Fotolabo S.A.; *Int'l*, pg. 501
IFI/PLENUM DATA CORPORATION—See Plenum Publishing Corporation; *U.S. Public*, pg. 1311
IFS AGENCY SERVICES, INC.—See The Western and Southern Life Insurance Company; *U.S. Private*, pg. 1165
IFS FINANCIAL SERVICES, INC.—See The Western and Southern Life Insurance Company; *U.S. Private*, pg. 1165
IFS INSURANCE AGENCY, INC.—See The Western and Southern Life Insurance Company; *U.S. Private*, pg. 1165
IFS SYSTEMS, INC.—See The Western and Southern Life Insurance Company; *U.S. Private*, pg. 1165
IG AUTOTRIM, INC.—See Rieter Holdings; *Int'l*, pg. 1117
IG LABORATORIES, INC.—See Genzyme Corporation; *U.S. Public*, pg. 733
I.G. TECHNOLOGIES LTD.—See Pechiney S.A.; *Int'l*, pg. 1030
IGA, INC. (INDEPENDENT GROCERS ALLIANCE); *U.S. Private*, pg. 555
IGAO—See Electrabel S.A.; *Int'l*, pg. 437
IGC ADVANCED SUPERCONDUCTORS, INC.—See Intermagnetics General Corporation; *U.S. Public*, pg. 893
IGC ENERGY, INC.—See Indiana Energy, Inc.; *U.S. Public*, pg. 875
IGH—See Electrabel S.A.; *Int'l*, pg. 437
IGI, INC.; *U.S. Public*, pg. 855
IGI RESOURCES, INC.—See Intermountain Industries, Inc.; *U.S. Private*, pg. 568
IGT-INTERNATIONAL CORP. DEVELOPMENT—See International Game Technology; *U.S. Public*, pg. 900
IGT-MONTANA, INCORPORATED—See International Game Technology; *U.S. Public*, pg. 900
IGT NORTH AMERICA—See International Game Technology; *U.S. Public*, pg. 900
IGV INDUSTRIE-GRUNDSTUCKSVERWALTUNGS GMBH—See Mannesmann A.G.; *Int'l*, pg. 837
IH-KUNNOSSAPITO OY—See Imatran Voima Oy; *Int'l*, pg. 660
IHC GROUP, INC.; *U.S. Private*, pg. 555
I.H.F. S.A.—See Fiat Auto SpA; *Int'l*, pg. 483
IHI ENGINEERING AUSTRALIA PTY. LTD.—See Ishikawajima-Harima Heavy Industries Co., Ltd.; *Int'l*, pg. 689
IHI EUROPE LTD.—See Ishikawajima-Harima Heavy Industries Co., Ltd.; *Int'l*, pg. 689
IHI (HK) LTD.—See Ishikawajima-Harima Heavy Industries Co., Ltd.; *Int'l*, pg. 689
IHI INC.—See Ishikawajima-Harima Heavy Industries Co., Ltd.; *Int'l*, pg. 689
IHI INTERNATIONAL INC.—See Ishikawajima-Harima Heavy Industries Co., Ltd.; *Int'l*, pg. 689
IHI MARINE B.V.—See Ishikawajima-Harima Heavy Industries Co., Ltd.; *Int'l*, pg. 689
IHI MARINE ENGINEERING (SINGAPORE) PTE. LTD.—See Ishikawajima-Harima Heavy Industries Co., Ltd.; *Int'l*, pg. 689
IIB FINANCE UNLTD.—See Kredietbank N.V.; *Int'l*, pg. 760
IIB INTERNATIONAL FINANCE UNLTD.—See Kredietbank N.V.; *Int'l*, pg. 760
IIRUC—See Hewlett-Packard Company; *U.S. Public*, pg. 822
IIS INTELLIGENT INFORMATION SYSTEMS LTD.; *Int'l*, pg. 645
IIT RESEARCH INSTITUTE; *U.S. Private*, pg. 555
IKB DEUTSCHE INDUSTRIEBANK AG; *Int'l*, pg. 645
IKB FINANCE B.V.—See IKB Deutsche Industriebank AG; *Int'l*, pg. 646
IKB LEASING BERLIN GMBH—See IKB Deutsche Industriebank AG; *Int'l*, pg. 645
IKG INDUSTRIES—See Harsco Corporation; *U.S. Public*, pg. 793
P.T. IKI INDAH KABEL INDONESIA—See Sumitomo Electric Industries, Ltd.; *Int'l*, pg. 1313
IKO INDUSTRIEKOHLE GMBH & CO. KG—See Veba AG; *Int'l*, pg. 1455
IKOS JAPAN—See IKOS Systems, Inc.; *U.S. Public*, pg. 864
IL INTERNATIONAL INC.; *U.S. Public*, pg. 855
IL RETURPAPPER; *Int'l*, pg. 646
IL (STRATFORD), INC.—See IL International Inc.; *U.S. Public*, pg. 856
IL USA, INC.—See IL International Inc.; *U.S. Public*, pg. 856
IL WASTEPAPER (UK) LTD—See Danisco A/S; *Int'l*, pg. 378
ILA FINANCIAL SERVICES, INC.—See Franklin Resources, Inc.; *U.S. Public*, pg. 680
ILC DATA DEVICE—See ILC Industries, Inc.; *U.S. Private*, pg. 555
ILC DOVER, INC.—See ILC Industries, Inc.; *U.S. Private*, pg. 555
ILC INDUSTRIES, INC.; *U.S. Private*, pg. 555
ILC TECHNOLOGY, INC.; *U.S. Public*, pg. 856
ILD COMMUNICATIONS, INC.—See Intellicall, Inc.; *U.S. Public*, pg. 887
I.L.D. DEVELOPMENT & CONSTRUCTION CO. LTD.—See The Israel Land Development Co., Ltd.; *Int'l*, pg. 691
I.L.D. INSURANCE CO. LTD.—See The Israel Land Development Co., Ltd.; *Int'l*, pg. 691
ILIS INTERNATIONAL LAND INFORMATION SERVICES CV—See Heidemij N.V.; *Int'l*, pg. 606
ILRO SRL; *Int'l*, pg. 646
ILS—See Ceridian Corporation; *U.S. Public*, pg. 331
ILSA-FRUTICULTURA E REFLORESTAMENTO LTDA.—See Iochpe-Maxion S.A.; *Int'l*, pg. 688
ILSE BERGBAU-GMBH—See Viag AG; *Int'l*, pg. 1464
ILV IMMOBILIEN-LEASING VERWALTUNGS GMBH—See Commerzbank AG; *Int'l*, pg. 310
ILX SYSTEMS, INC.—See The Thomson Corporation; *U.S. Public*, pg. 1601
IMA OF COLORADO INC.—See Insurance Management Associates; *U.S. Private*, pg. 565
IMA OF TOPEKA INC—See Insurance Management Associates; *U.S. Private*, pg. 565
IMA OF WICHITA INC.—See Insurance Management Associates; *U.S. Private*, pg. 565
IMASA—See BASF AG; *Int'l*, pg. 108
I.M.B. INGENIEURTECHNOLOGIEN FUR MATERIALPRUFUNG UND BAUWERKSERHALTUNG GMBH—See Dyckerhoff & Widmann AG; *Int'l*, pg. 423
IMC/A.K. FANS LTD.—See Minebea Co., Ltd.; *Int'l*, pg. 868
IMC AGRIBUSINESS—See IMC Global; *U.S. Public*, pg. 856
IMC ASSOCIATES, INC.—See Man Nen Sha Inc.; *Int'l*, pg. 834
IMC GLOBAL; *U.S. Public*, pg. 856
IMC MAGNETICS CORP.—See Minebea Co., Ltd.; *Int'l*, pg. 868
IMCO INVESTMENT COMPANY—See IMCO Recycling Inc.; *U.S. Public*, pg. 871
IMCO MANAGEMENT PARTNERSHIP L.P.—See IMCO Recycling Inc.; *U.S. Public*, pg. 871
IMCO RECYCLING OF ILLINOIS, INC.—See IMCO Recycling Inc.; *U.S. Public*, pg. 871
IMCO RECYCLING OF INDIANA INC.—See IMCO Recycling Inc.; *U.S. Public*, pg. 871
IMCO RECYCLING OF OHIO INC.—See IMCO Recycling Inc.; *U.S. Public*, pg. 871
IMD MICON BV—See Heidemij N.V.; *Int'l*, pg. 607
IMG; *U.S. Private*, pg. 555
IMG COMMUNICATIONS—See Integrated Marketing Group; *U.S. Private*, pg. 566
IMG INTERNATIONAL—See Integrated Marketing Group; *U.S. Private*, pg. 566
IMG SERVICES—See Integrated Marketing Group; *U.S. Private*, pg. 566
IMI CASH VALVE, INC.—See IMI Plc; *Int'l*, pg. 646
IMI CORNELIUS BRASIL—See IMI Plc; *Int'l*, pg. 646
IMI CORNELIUS CANADA—See IMI Plc; *Int'l*, pg. 646
IMI CORNELIUS, INC. (IA)—See IMI Plc; *Int'l*, pg. 646
IMI CORNELIUS INC. (MN)—See IMI Plc; *Int'l*, pg. 646
IMI MARSTON INC.—See IMI Plc; *Int'l*, pg. 646
IMI PLC; *Int'l*, pg. 646
IMI SYSTEMS INC.—See Olsten Corporation; *U.S. Public*, pg. 1221
I.M.I.B.J. S.P.A.—See The Industrial Bank of Japan, Limited; *Int'l*, pg. 676
IMO INDUSTRIES INC.; *U.S. Public*, pg. 856
IMO PUMP—See IMO Industries Inc.; *U.S. Public*, pg. 857
IMR FINANCE S.A.—See Pharmaceutical Marketing Services Inc.; *U.S. Public*, pg. 1284
IMS—See Groupe Usinor; *Int'l*, pg. 571

IMS DIVISION—See Cadence Design Systems, Inc.; *U.S. Public*, pg. 290
IMS INGENIEURGESELLSCHAFT MBH—See Philipp Holzmann AG; *Int'l*, pg. 633
IMS/INTERNATIONAL—See International Data Group; *U.S. Private*, pg. 569
IMSA S.A.—See Corn Products International, Inc.; *U.S. Public*, pg. 447
I.M.W.V. C.V.—See Electrabel S.A.; *Int'l*, pg. 437
INA CORPORATION—See Cigna Corp.; *U.S. Public*, pg. 362
INA COUNTY MUTUAL INSURANCE COMPANY—See Cigna Corp.; *U.S. Public*, pg. 366
INA FINANCIAL CORPORATION—See Cigna Corp.; *U.S. Public*, pg. 362
INA LIFE INSURANCE CO., LTD.—See Cigna Corp.; *U.S. Public*, pg. 362
INA LIFE INSURANCE COMPANY OF NEW YORK—See Cigna Corp.; *U.S. Public*, pg. 362
INA OVERSEAS PROPERTIES, LTD.—See Cigna Corp.; *U.S. Public*, pg. 363
INA SPECIAL RISK FACILITIES, INC.—See Cigna Corp.; *U.S. Public*, pg. 366
INA TAX BENEFITS REPORTING, INC.—See Cigna Corp.; *U.S. Public*, pg. 362
INA UNDERWRITING AGENCY LIMITED—See Cigna Corp.; *U.S. Public*, pg. 363
INAC CORP.—See Cigna Corp.; *U.S. Public*, pg. 366
INAC CORP. OF CALIFORNIA—See Cigna Corp.; *U.S. Public*, pg. 366
INAC INDUSTRIA NACIONAL DE PRODUTOS QUIMICOS LDA.—See Novartis AG; *Int'l*, pg. 982
INCA PRESSWOOD PALLETS, LTD.—See Inka Paletten GmbH; *Int'l*, pg. 678
INCOM J.V.—See Telefonaktiebolaget LM Ericsson; *Int'l*, pg. 1368
INESPAL - INDUSTRIA ESPANOLA DEL ALUMINIO, S.A.—See SEPI; *Int'l*, pg. 1225
IN.F.A. S.P.A.—See Electrolux, AB; *Int'l*, pg. 442
ING BANK ANTWERP—See ING Groep N.V.; *Int'l*, pg. 649
ING BANK ATHENS—See ING Groep N.V.; *Int'l*, pg. 648
ING BANK BANGKOK—See ING Groep N.V.; *Int'l*, pg. 648
ING BANK BEIJING—See ING Groep N.V.; *Int'l*, pg. 648
ING BANK BEIRUT—See ING Groep N.V.; *Int'l*, pg. 648
ING BANK BOGOTA—See ING Groep N.V.; *Int'l*, pg. 649
ING BANK BRATISLAVA—See ING Groep N.V.; *Int'l*, pg. 649
ING BANK BRNO—See ING Groep N.V.; *Int'l*, pg. 649
ING BANK BRUSSELS—See ING Groep N.V.; *Int'l*, pg. 649
ING BANK BUDAPEST—See ING Groep N.V.; *Int'l*, pg. 649
ING BANK BUENOS AIRES—See ING Groep N.V.; *Int'l*, pg. 649
ING BANK CARACAS—See ING Groep N.V.; *Int'l*, pg. 649
ING BANK CHONBURI—See ING Groep N.V.; *Int'l*, pg. 648
ING BANK EURASIA—See ING Groep N.V.; *Int'l*, pg. 649
ING BANK FRANKFURT—See ING Groep N.V.; *Int'l*, pg. 649
ING BANK GREATER CHINA—See ING Groep N.V.; *Int'l*, pg. 649
ING BANK GREECE—See ING Groep N.V.; *Int'l*, pg. 649
ING BANK HAMBURG—See ING Groep N.V.; *Int'l*, pg. 649
ING BANK HANOI—See ING Groep N.V.; *Int'l*, pg. 649
ING BANK HARARE—See ING Groep N.V.; *Int'l*, pg. 649
ING BANK HAVANA—See ING Groep N.V.; *Int'l*, pg. 649
ING BANK HO CHI MINH CITY—See ING Groep N.V.; *Int'l*, pg. 649
ING BANK HONG KONG—See ING Groep N.V.; *Int'l*, pg. 649
ING BANK HUNGARY—See ING Groep N.V.; *Int'l*, pg. 649
ING BANK ISTANBUL—See ING Groep N.V.; *Int'l*, pg. 649
ING BANK JAKARTA—See ING Groep N.V.; *Int'l*, pg. 649
ING BANK KIEV—See ING Groep N.V.; *Int'l*, pg. 649
ING BANK KOSICE—See ING Groep N.V.; *Int'l*, pg. 649
ING BANK LABUAN—See ING Groep N.V.; *Int'l*, pg. 649
ING BANK LIBEREC—See ING Groep N.V.; *Int'l*, pg. 649
ING BANK LONDON—See ING Groep N.V.; *Int'l*, pg. 650
ING BANK LUXEMBOURG—See ING Groep N.V.; *Int'l*, pg. 649
ING BANK PARIS—See ING Groep N.V.; *Int'l*, pg. 649
ING BANK PRAGUE—See ING Groep N.V.; *Int'l*, pg. 649
ING BANK QUITO—See ING Groep N.V.; *Int'l*, pg. 649
ING BANK SANTIAGO DE CHILE—See ING Groep N.V.; *Int'l*, pg. 649
ING BANK SAO PAULO—See ING Groep N.V.; *Int'l*, pg. 649
ING BANK SHANGHAI—See ING Groep N.V.; *Int'l*, pg. 649
ING BANK SHENYANG—See ING Groep N.V.; *Int'l*, pg. 649
ING BANK SHENZEN—See ING Groep N.V.; *Int'l*, pg. 649
ING BANK SOFIA—See ING Groep N.V.; *Int'l*, pg. 649
ING BANK VIENNA—See ING Groep N.V.; *Int'l*, pg. 649
ING BANK VLADIVOSTOK—See ING Groep N.V.; *Int'l*, pg. 649
ING BANK ZURICH—See ING Groep N.V.; *Int'l*, pg. 649
ING BARING ARGENTINA S.A.—See ING Groep N.V.; *Int'l*, pg. 649
ING BARING CORRETORA DE VALORES MOBILIAROS—See ING Groep N.V.; *Int'l*, pg. 649
ING BARING SECURITIES—See ING Groep N.V.; *Int'l*, pg. 649
ING BARING SECURITIES (ANDEAN PACT)—See ING Groep N.V.; *Int'l*, pg. 649
ING BARING SECURITIES ARGENTINA—See ING Groep N.V.; *Int'l*, pg. 649
ING BARING SECURITIES DO BRAZIL—See ING Groep N.V.; *Int'l*, pg. 649
ING BARING SECURITIES (FRANCE)—See ING Groep N.V.; *Int'l*, pg. 650
ING BARING SECURITIES INDONESIA—See ING Groep N.V.; *Int'l*, pg. 650
ING BARING SOCIEDAD DE BOLSA (ARGENTINA)—See ING Groep N.V.; *Int'l*, pg. 649
ING BARING (U.S.) HOLDINGS—See ING Groep N.V.; *Int'l*, pg. 647

ING BARING (U.S.) SECURITIES:—See ING Groep N.V.; *Int'l*, pg. 647
ING BARINGS—See ING Groep N.V.; *Int'l*, pg. 650
ING BARINGS CHILE LTDA.—See ING Groep N.V.; *Int'l*, pg. 650
ING BARINGS GREECE EPE—See ING Groep N.V.; *Int'l*, pg. 650
ING BARINGS INDIA PRIVATE EQUITY—See ING Groep N.V.; *Int'l*, pg. 650
ING BARINGS SECURITIES INTERNATIONAL—See ING Groep N.V.; *Int'l*, pg. 650
ING BARINGS SOUTHERN AFRICA (PROPRIETARY)—See ING Groep N.V.; *Int'l*, pg. 650
ING (BVI) TRUST—See ING Groep N.V.; *Int'l*, pg. 650
ING CANADA—See ING Groep N.V.; *Int'l*, pg. 650
ING CAPITAL—See ING Groep N.V.; *Int'l*, pg. 648
ING CAPITAL MARKETS (HONG KONG)—See ING Groep N.V.; *Int'l*, pg. 650
ING COMPANIA DE INVERSIONES Y SERVICIOS LTDA.—See ING Groep N.V.; *Int'l*, pg. 650
ING CONSULTANTS—See ING Groep N.V.; *Int'l*, pg. 649
ING FARM FINANCE—See ING Groep N.V.; *Int'l*, pg. 650
ING FINANCIAL SERVICES INTERNATIONAL ASIA—See ING Groep N.V.; *Int'l*, pg. 650
ING FINANZBERATUNGS- UND LEASING—See ING Groep N.V.; *Int'l*, pg. 650
ING FUTURES & OPTIONS—See ING Groep N.V.; *Int'l*, pg. 647
ING GROEP N.V.; *Int'l*, pg. 647
ING GUILDER—See ING Groep N.V.; *Int'l*, pg. 650
ING IMMOBILIER—See ING Groep N.V.; *Int'l*, pg. 650
ING INSURANCE—See ING Groep N.V.; *Int'l*, pg. 650
ING INSURANCE INDONESIA—See ING Groep N.V.; *Int'l*, pg. 650
ING INSURANCE INTERNATIONAL—See ING Groep N.V.; *Int'l*, pg. 650
ING INSURANCE MEXICO—See ING Groep N.V.; *Int'l*, pg. 650
ING INSURANCE SEGUROS DE VIDA—See ING Groep N.V.; *Int'l*, pg. 650
ING INVESTMENT MANAGEMENT INC.—See ING Groep N.V.; *Int'l*, pg. 648
ING LEASE—See ING Groep N.V.; *Int'l*, pg. 650
ING LEASE BELGIUM—See ING Groep N.V.; *Int'l*, pg. 650
ING LEASE DEUTSCHLAND—See ING Groep N.V.; *Int'l*, pg. 650
ING LEASE FRANCE—See ING Groep N.V.; *Int'l*, pg. 650
ING LEASE (UK)—See ING Groep N.V.; *Int'l*, pg. 650
ING LEASE VASTGOED—See ING Groep N.V.; *Int'l*, pg. 647
ING LEASING GMBH & CO. FOX OHG—See Porsche AG; *Int'l*, pg. 1063
ING LIFE INSURANCE COMPANY—See ING Groep N.V.; *Int'l*, pg. 650
ING (LONDON) FUTURES & OPTIONS—See ING Groep N.V.; *Int'l*, pg. 647
ING MERCANTILE MUTUAL BANK—See ING Groep N.V.; *Int'l*, pg. 650
ING REAL ESTATE—See ING Groep N.V.; *Int'l*, pg. 648
ING SERVICOS—See ING Groep N.V.; *Int'l*, pg. 649
ING TRUST COMPANY OF CANADA—See ING Groep N.V.; *Int'l*, pg. 650
ING TRUST (HONG KONG)—See ING Groep N.V.; *Int'l*, pg. 650
ING TRUST (JERSEY)—See ING Groep N.V.; *Int'l*, pg. 650
ING (U.S.) CAPITAL CORPORATION—See ING Groep N.V.; *Int'l*, pg. 648
ING (U.S.) CAPITAL HOLDINGS—See ING Groep N.V.; *Int'l*, pg. 648
ING (U.S.) SECURITIES CORP.—See ING Groep N.V.; *Int'l*, pg. 648
ING (U.S.) FINANCIAL SERVICES KK—See ING Groep N.V.; *Int'l*, pg. 648
ING VASTGOED SA—See ING Groep N.V.; *Int'l*, pg. 650
ING VERZEKERINGEN N.V.—See ING Groep N.V.; *Int'l*, pg. 647
INI MEDIOAMBIENTE, S.A.—See SEPI; *Int'l*, pg. 1225
INITEC - E.N. DE INGENIERIA Y TECNOLOGIA, S.A.—See SEPI; *Int'l*, pg. 1225
INMC MORTGAGE HOLDINGS, INC.; *U.S. Public*, pg. 857
INS COMMUNICATIONS PTE LTD.—See Singapore Reinsurance Corporation Limited; *Int'l*, pg. 1253
INS INVESTIGATIONS BUREAU, INC.—See SGS Societe Generale de Surveillance Holding S.A.; *Int'l*, pg. 1153
INT. VINTNERS—See The Jaydor Corporation; *U.S. Private*, pg. 584
INX CORPORATION—See Sumitomo Chemical Company, Ltd.; *Int'l*, pg. 1311
INX INTERNATIONAL—See Sumitomo Chemical Company, Ltd.; *Int'l*, pg. 1311
IP FOREST RESOURCES COMPANY—See International Paper Company; *U.S. Public*, pg. 904
IP GAS SUPPLY CO.—See Illinova Inc.; *U.S. Public*, pg. 869
IP TIMBERLANDS, LTD.—See International Paper Company; *U.S. Public*, pg. 904
IPAC, INC.; *U.S. Private*, pg. 555
I.P.C.—See Darling International, Inc; *U.S. Public*, pg. 484
IPC COMMUNICATION SERVICES—See Journal Communications Inc.; *U.S. Private*, pg. 601
IPC CORPORATION (AUSTRALIA) PTY LTD.—See IPC Corporation Ltd.; *Int'l*, pg. 651
IPC CORPORATION (FRANCE) S.A.—See IPC Corporation Ltd.; *Int'l*, pg. 651
IPC CORPORATION (GERMANY)—See IPC Corporation Ltd.; *Int'l*, pg. 651
IPC CORPORATION (HK) LTD.—See IPC Corporation Ltd.; *Int'l*, pg. 651
IPC CORPORATION (KOREA) LTD.—See IPC Corporation Ltd.; *Int'l*, pg. 651
IPC CORPORATION LTD.; *Int'l*, pg. 651
IPC CORPORATION RACUNALNIKI IN POS SISTEMI D.O.O.—See IPC Corporation Ltd.; *Int'l*, pg. 651

IPC CORPORATION SPOL.S.R.O—See IPC Corporation Ltd.; *Int'l*, pg. 651
IPC CORPORATION (UK) LTD.—See IPC Corporation Ltd.; *Int'l*, pg. 651
IPC DEVELOPMENT CO.—See Interstate Power Company; *U.S. Public*, pg. 910
IPC HOLDING CORP.—See Motorola, Inc.; *U.S. Public*, pg. 1137
IPC INFORMATION TECHNOLOGY (BEIJING)—See IPC Corporation Ltd.; *Int'l*, pg. 651
IPC INTERACTIVE, INC.—See IPC Corporation Ltd.; *Int'l*, pg. 651
IPC INTERACTIVE PTE LTD.—See IPC Corporation Ltd.; *Int'l*, pg. 651
IPC-INTERNATIONAL PARTS CORP.—See Whitman Corporation; *U.S. Public*, pg. 1766
IPC MAGAZINES LIMITED; *Int'l*, pg. 651
IPC PERIPHERALS—See IPC Corporation Ltd.; *Int'l*, pg. 651
IPC PERIPHERALS PTE LTD.—See IPC Corporation Ltd.; *Int'l*, pg. 651
IPC POWER RESISTORS INTERNATIONAL INC.—See Halma p.l.c.; *Int'l*, pg. 590
IPC RESISTORS INC.—See Halma p.l.c.; *Int'l*, pg. 590
IPC SYSTEMS (M) SDN BHD—See IPC Corporation Ltd.; *Int'l*, pg. 651
IPC TECHNOLOGIES, INC.—See IPC Corporation Ltd.; *Int'l*, pg. 651
IPCF PROPERTIES INC.—See George Weston Limited; *Int'l*, pg. 1495
PT IPCINDO SISKOMDATA—See IPC Corporation Ltd.; *Int'l*, pg. 651
IPD MARKETING SERVICES, INC.—See Protective Life Corporation; *U.S. Public*, pg. 1336
IPD PRINTING & DISTRIBUTING, INC.—See Wallace Computer Services, Inc.; *U.S. Public*, pg. 1735
IPEDEX—See Technip; *Int'l*, pg. 1361
IPI CORPORATION—See International Paper Company; *U.S. Public*, pg. 906
IPI SDN. BHD.—See BASF AG; *Int'l*, pg. 108
IPL ENERGY INC.; *Int'l*, pg. 651
IPL INTERNATIONAL—See IPL Energy Inc.; *Int'l*, pg. 652
IPM BEIJING OFFICE—See BTR plc; *Int'l*, pg. 126
IPM-ELYRIA OPERATIONS—See BTR plc; *Int'l*, pg. 126
IPM FEDERAL OPERS. GROUP—See BTR plc; *Int'l*, pg. 126
IPM GUANGZHOU OFFICE—See BTR plc; *Int'l*, pg. 126
IPM INC.—See Owens Corning; *U.S. Public*, pg. 1237
IPM NEW YORK—See BTR plc; *Int'l*, pg. 126
IPM PACIFIC, LTD.—See BTR plc; *Int'l*, pg. 126
IPM SHANGHAI LIASION OFFICE—See BTR plc; *Int'l*, pg. 126
IPM WEST COAST—See BTR plc; *Int'l*, pg. 126
IPOK—See Corn Products International, Inc.; *U.S. Public*, pg. 447
IPR PHARMACEUTICALS, INC.—See Zeneca Group Plc; *Int'l*, pg. 1524
IPSOA S.A.R.L.—See Wolters Kluwer N.V.; *Int'l*, pg. 1514
IPT DIVISION—See The Gorman-Rupp Company; *U.S. Public*, pg. 754
IPU - INTERNATIONAL—See GESTRA GmbH; *Int'l*, pg. 550
IQ SOFTWARE CORPORATION; *U.S. Public*, pg. 858
IQS INSTITUT FUR QUALITATSSICHERUNG—See Spar Handels AG; *Int'l*, pg. 1288
IQSOFT SZKI INTELLIGENS-SOFTWARE CO. LTD.—See Oracle Corporation; *U.S. Public*, pg. 1228
IR INTERNATIONAL HOLDINGS, INC.—See International Rectifier Corporation; *U.S. Public*, pg. 907
IRAD DEVELOPMENT LTD.—See Scientific Software-Intercomp, Inc.; *U.S. Public*, pg. 1444
IRD MECHANALYSIS, INC. (U.S.A.)—See Harnischfeger Industries, Inc.; *U.S. Public*, pg. 789
I.R.E. CORPORATION PTE. LTD.—See Nippon Paint Company Ltd.; *Int'l*, pg. 937
IRI INTERNATIONAL CORPORATION; *U.S. Public*, pg. 858
IRI ISTITUTO RICOSTRUZIONE INDUSTRIALE; *Int'l*, pg. 652
IRI SOFTWARE—See Information Resources, Inc.; *U.S. Public*, pg. 876
IRIBV-INTERNATIONAL REFRACTORY INVESTMENT B.V.—See Lafarge S.A.; *Int'l*, pg. 791
IRPC HINTON LIMITED—See Willis Corroon Group PLC; *Int'l*, pg. 1502
IRT MANAGEMENT COMPANY—See IRT Property Company; *U.S. Public*, pg. 858
IRT PROPERTY COMPANY; *U.S. Public*, pg. 858
IRT PROPERTY COMPANY—See IRT Property Company; *U.S. Public*, pg. 858
I.S. DE COSTA RICA, S.A.—See Hewlett-Packard Company; *U.S. Public*, pg. 822
IS-PLAN OY—See Imatran Voima Oy; *Int'l*, pg. 660
ISA INFORMATION SYSTEMS SERVICES—See Integrated Systems Analysts, Inc.; *U.S. Private*, pg. 566
ISA INTERNATIONALE SCHIFFAHRTS-AGENTUR GMBH—See Axel Johnson AB; *Int'l*, pg. 711
I.S.A. ISTITUTO ATESINO DI SVILUPPO S.P.A.—See Banco Ambrosiano Veneto S.p.A.; *Int'l*, pg. 138
ISAGA H.F.—See AGA AB; *Int'l*, pg. 14
ISAL ICELANDIC ALUMINIUM CO. LTD.—See Alusuisse-Lonza Holding Ltd.; *Int'l*, pg. 68
ISC CHEMICALS LTD.—See Rhone-Poulenc S.A.; *Int'l*, pg. 1113
ISC FUTURES CORPORATION—See Interstate/Johnson Lane, Inc.; *U.S. Public*, pg. 910
ISC REALTY CORPORATION—See Interstate/Johnson Lane, Inc.; *U.S. Public*, pg. 910
ISC SYSTEMS ASIA PACIFIC LTD.—See Olivetti SpA; *Int'l*, pg. 1003
ISG INGENIEURBAU + SCHALUNGS-BAUGESELLSCHAFT MBH—See Bilfinger + Berger Bauaktiengesellschaft; *Int'l*, pg. 195
ISI AS—See Celsius AB; *Int'l*, pg. 278

MASTER INDEX TO COMPANY NAMES ITW

Company Index

ISI INSORTEX—See Friedman, Eisenstein, Raemer and Schwartz, LLP; *U.S. Private*, pg. 428
ISI INSURANCE SERVICE—See Hapag-Lloyd AG; *Int'l*, pg. 596
ISI NORGEN—See IMI Plc; *Int'l*, pg. 646
ISI NORGEN, INC.—See IMI Plc; *Int'l*, pg. 646
ISI SYSTEMS INC.—See Teleglobe, Inc.; *Int'l*, pg. 1373
ISK BIOSCIENCES—See Ishihara Sangyo Kaisha, Ltd.; *Int'l*, *pg. 689*
ISK BIOTECH—See Ishihara Sangyo Kaisha, Ltd.; *Int'l*, pg. 689
ISK (EUROPE) S.A.—See Ishihara Sangyo Kaisha, Ltd.; *Int'l*, pg. 689
ISK SINGAPORE PTE. LTD.—See Ishihara Sangyo Kaisha, Ltd.; *Int'l*, pg. 689
ISK TAIWAN CO., LTD.—See Ishihara Sangyo Kaisha, Ltd.; *Int'l*, pg. 689
ISL MARKETING A.G.—See Dentsu Inc.; *Int'l*, pg. 394
ISM SOCCER INC.—See Dentsu Inc.; *Int'l*, pg. 393
ISO HOLDING, AG—See Armstrong World Industries, Inc.; *U.S. Public*, pg. 132
ISP CHEMICALS INC.—See ISP Holdings, Inc.; *U.S. Public*, *pg. 858*
ISP ENVIRONMENTAL SERVICES INC.—See ISP Holdings, Inc.; *U.S. Public*, pg. 858
ISP FILTERS INC.—See ISP Holdings, Inc.; *U.S. Public*, pg. 858
ISP GLOBAL TECHNOLOGIES INC.—See ISP Holdings, Inc.; *U.S. Public*, pg. 858
ISP HOLDINGS, INC.; *U.S. Public*, pg. 858
ISP INTERNATIONAL CORP.—See ISP Holdings, Inc.; *U.S.* Public, pg. 858
ISP INVESTMENTS INC.—See ISP Holdings, Inc.; *U.S. Public*, pg. 858
ISP MANAGEMENT COMPANY, INC.—See ISP Holdings, Inc.; *U.S. Public*, pg. 858
ISP MINERAL PRODUCTS INC.—See ISP Holdings, Inc.; *U.S. Public*, pg. 858
ISP MINERALS INC.—See ISP Holdings, Inc.; *U.S. Public*, pg. 858
ISP (PUERTO RICO) INC.—See ISP Holdings, Inc.; *U.S. Public*, pg. 858
ISP REAL ESTATE COMPANY, INC.—See ISP Holdings, Inc.; *U.S. Public*, pg. 858
ISP REALTY CORPORATION—See ISP Holdings, Inc.; *U.S.* Public, pg. 859
ISP TECHNOLOGIES INC.—See ISP Holdings, Inc.; *U.S. Public*, pg. 859
ISS AIRPORT SERVICES LTD.—See ISS-International Service System A/S; *Int'l*, pg. 657
ISS AIRPORT SERVICES S.A.-N.V.—See ISS-International Service System A/S; *Int'l*, pg. 657
ISS BUILDING MAINTENANCE, INC.—See ISS-International Service System A/S; *Int'l*, pg. 656
ISS CATERING A.S.—See ISS-International Service System A/S; *Int'l*, pg. 656
ISS CENTRAL EUROPE GESMBH—See ISS-International Service System A/S; *Int'l*, pg. 656
ISS CLEANING SERVICES GROUP, INC.—See ISS-International Service System A/S; *Int'l*, pg. 656
ISS CLEANING SERVICES LTD.—See ISS-International Service System A/S; *Int'l*, pg. 657
ISS CONTRACT CLEAN MIDLANDS LTD.—See ISS-International Service System A/S; *Int'l*, pg. 657
ISS CONTRACT CLEANERS LTD.—See ISS-International Service System A/S; *Int'l*, pg. 657
ISS CONTRACT CLEANING SERVICES (NORTH)—See ISS-International Service System A/S; *Int'l*, pg. 657
ISS CONTRACT CLEANING SERVICES (SOUTH)—See ISS-International Service System A/S; *Int'l*, pg. 657
ISS DARENAS AB—See ISS-International Service System A/S; *Int'l*, pg. 656
ISS DARENAS A.S.—See ISS-International Service System A/S; *Int'l*, pg. 656
ISS DARENAS INTERNATIONAL A/S—See ISS-International Service System A/S; *Int'l*, pg. 656
ISS DARENAS LTD.—See ISS-International Service System A/S; *Int'l*, pg. 657
ISS DATA A/S—See ISS-International Service System A/S; *Int'l*, pg. 656
ISS ENERGY SERVICES, INC.—See ISS-International Service System A/S; *Int'l*, pg. 656
ISS FINANS A/S—See ISS-International Service System A/S; *Int'l*, pg. 656
ISS FOOD B.V.—See ISS-International Service System A/S; *Int'l*, pg. 657
ISS FOOD HYGIENE LTD.—See ISS-International Service System A/S; *Int'l*, pg. 657
ISS FOOD HYGIENE S.A.-N.V.—See ISS-International Service System A/S; *Int'l*, pg. 657
ISS FOOD HYGIENE SERVICE GMBH—See ISS-International Service System A/S; *Int'l*, pg. 657
ISS FRANCE S.A.—See ISS-International Service System A/S; *Int'l*, pg. 656
ISS HASCO MANAGEMENT AG—See ISS-International Service System A/S; *Int'l*, pg. 657
ISS HEALTHCARE S.A.-N.V.—See ISS-International Service System A/S; *Int'l*, pg. 657
ISS HOLDING GMBH—See ISS-International Service System A/S; *Int'l*, pg. 657
ISS HOLDING S.A.—See ISS-International Service System A/S; *Int'l*, pg. 657
ISS HOLZL GMBH SERVISYSTEM—See ISS-International Service System A/S; *Int'l*, pg. 657
ISS HOSPITAL SERVICE AG—See ISS-International Service System A/S; *Int'l*, pg. 657
ISS HOSPITAL SERVICE A/S—See ISS-International Service System A/S; *Int'l*, pg. 656
ISS HOSPITAL SERVICE B.V.—See ISS-International Service System A/S; *Int'l*, pg. 657
ISS-INTERNATIONAL SERVICE SYSTEM A/S; *Int'l*, pg. 656
ISS INTERNATIONAL SERVICE SYSTEM, INC.—See ISS-International Service System A/S; *Int'l*, pg. 656
ISS LANDSCAPE MANAGEMENT SERVICES, INC.—See ISS-International Service System A/S; *Int'l*, pg. 656
ISS LONDON LTD.—See ISS-International Service System A/S; *Int'l*, pg. 657
ISS LUXEMBOURG S.A.—See ISS-International Service System A/S; *Int'l*, pg. 657
ISS MALL SERVICES, INC.—See ISS-International Service System A/S; *Int'l*, pg. 656
ISS MARISCHKA SPOL.S.R.O.—See ISS-International Service System A/S; *Int'l*, pg. 657
ISS MEDICLEAN LTD.—See ISS-International Service System A/S; *Int'l*, pg. 657
ISS NET INTER S.A.—See ISS-International Service System A/S; *Int'l*, pg. 657
ISS PJONUSTAN HF.—See ISS-International Service System A/S; *Int'l*, pg. 657
ISS RENGORINGSSERVICE—See ISS-International Service System A/S; *Int'l*, pg. 656
ISS SCANDINAVIA A/S—See ISS-International Service System A/S; *Int'l*, pg. 656
ISS SECURISYSTEM GESMBH—See Veba AG; *Int'l*, pg. 1458
ISS SERVISYSTEM—See ISS-International Service System A/S; *Int'l*, pg. 657
ISS SERVISYSTEM B.V.—See ISS-International Service System A/S; *Int'l*, pg. 657
ISS SERVISYSTEM COM. E. IND. LTDA.—See ISS-International Service System A/S; *Int'l*, pg. 657
ISS SERVISYSTEM D.O.O.—See ISS-International Service System A/S; *Int'l*, pg. 657
ISS SERVISYSTEM GESMBH—See ISS-International Service System A/S; *Int'l*, pg. 657
ISS SERVISYSTEM GMBH—See ISS-International Service System A/S; *Int'l*, pg. 657
ISS SERVISYSTEM KFT.—See ISS-International Service System A/S; *Int'l*, pg. 657
ISS SERVISYSTEM LTD.—See ISS-International Service System A/S; *Int'l*, pg. 657
ISS SERVISYSTEM LTDA.—See ISS-International Service System A/S; *Int'l*, pg. 657
ISS SERVISYSTEM S.A.—See ISS-International Service System A/S; *Int'l*, pg. 657
ISS SERVISYSTEM S.A.-N.V.—See ISS-International Service System A/S; *Int'l*, pg. 657
ISS SERVISYSTEM S.R.O.—See ISS-International Service System A/S; *Int'l*, pg. 657
ISS SOUTHERN MANAGEMENT COMPANY—See ISS-International Service System A/S; *Int'l*, pg. 656
ISS SPECIALSERVICE—See ISS-International Service System A/S; *Int'l*, pg. 656
ISS SULAMERICANA COMERCIAL LTDA.—See ISS-International Service System A/S; *Int'l*, pg. 657
ISS SUOMI OY—See ISS-International Service System A/S; *Int'l*, pg. 656
ISS SVERIGE AB—See ISS-International Service System A/S; *Int'l*, pg. 656
ISS TELE RESPONSE—See ISS-International Service System A/S; *Int'l*, pg. 656
ISS U.K. LTD.—See ISS-International Service System A/S; *Int'l*, pg. 657
ISS UNIVERSITY HOTEL—See ISS-International Service System A/S; *Int'l*, pg. 656
ISSCO LUXEMBOURG S.A.—See Arbed S.A.; *Int'l*, pg. 80
ISYS CORP.—See International Business Machines Corporation; *U.S. Public*, pg. 896
IT CORP.—See International Technology Corporation; *U.S. Public*, pg. 908
IT FORGING (THAILAND) CO., LTD.—See Isuzu Motors Limited; *Int'l*, pg. 693
IT MEDIA—See International Data Group; *U.S. Private*, pg. 570
ITA GROUP INC.; *U.S. Private*, pg. 555
ITAS S.P.A.—See Eclipse Inc.; *U.S. Private*, pg. 361
ITB CORPORATION—See Tabacalera, S.A.; *Int'l*, pg. 1346
ITC AUSTRALASIA PTY LTD.—See ITC Learning Corp.; *U.S. Public*, pg. 859
ITC FLAVOR & SEASONING DIV.—See Crompton & Knowles Corporation; *U.S. Public*, pg. 459
ITC INLAND TEKNIK OTO YAN SANAYI LIMITED SIRKETI—See General Motors Corporation; *U.S. Public*, pg. 723
ITC LEARNING CORP.; *U.S. Public*, pg. 859
ITEDI S.P.A.—See Fiat Auto SpA; *Int'l*, pg. 482
ITI MARKETING SERVICES, INC.; *U.S. Private*, pg. 555
ITK INTERNATIONAL, INC.; *U.S. Private*, pg. 556
ITK TELECOMMUNICATIONS, INC.—See ITK International, Inc.; *U.S. Private*, pg. 556
ITMI—See CAP Gemini S.A.; *Int'l*, pg. 263
ITOCHU AVIATION, INC.—See Itochu Corporation; *Int'l*, pg. 694
ITOCHU INDUSTRIAL MACHINERY, INC.—See Itochu Corporation; *Int'l*, pg. 695
ITOCHU INTERNATIONAL PETROLEUM CO., LTD.—See Itochu Corporation; *Int'l*, pg. 695
ITOCHU PIPE & TUBE, INC.—See Itochu Corporation; *Int'l*, *pg. 695*
ITOCHU SHOE CO., INC.—See Itochu Corporation; *Int'l*, pg. 695
ITOCHU TAKUMA RESOURCE SYSTEMS, INC.—See Itochu Corporation; *Int'l*, pg. 695
ITS AUSTRALIA PTY., LTD.—See International Lottery & Totalizator Systems, Inc.; *U.S. Public*, pg. 900
ITS GROUP—See Alcatel Alsthom Compagnie Generale D'Electricite; *Int'l*, pg. 53
ITT A-C PUMP/ITT MARLOW—See ITT Industries, Inc.; *U.S. Public*, pg. 860
ITT AEROSPACE/COMMUNICATIONS DIV.—See ITT Industries, Inc.; *U.S. Public*, pg. 859
ITT AUTOMOTIVE, INC.—See ITT Industries, Inc.; *U.S. Public*, pg. 859
ITT AVIONICS DIVISION—See ITT Industries, Inc.; *U.S. Public*, pg. 859
ITT BARTON INSTRUMENTS—See ITT Industries, Inc.; *U.S. Public*, pg. 860
ITT BELL & GOSSETT—See ITT Industries, Inc.; *U.S. Public*, pg. 860
ITT CANNON—See ITT Industries, Inc.; *U.S. Public*, pg. 859
ITT CANNON SEALECTRO—See ITT Industries, Inc.; *U.S. Public*, pg. 859
ITT CANNON SWITCH PRODUCTS, INC.—See ITT Industries, Inc.; *U.S. Public*, pg. 859
ITT CONTROLS & INSTRUMENTS DIVISION—See ITT Industries, Inc.; *U.S. Public*, pg. 860
ITT CORPORATION—See Starwood Hotels & Resorts; *U.S.* Public, pg. 1512
ITT DEFENSE & ELECTRONICS, INC.—See ITT Industries, Inc.; *U.S. Public*, pg. 859
ITT DOMESTIC PUMP—See ITT Industries, Inc.; *U.S. Public*, pg. 860
ITT EDUCATIONAL SERVICES, INC.—See Starwood Hotels & Resorts; *U.S. Public*, pg. 1512
ITT FEDERAL SERVICES CORPORATION—See ITT Industries, Inc.; *U.S. Public*, pg. 859
ITT FLUID HANDLING—See ITT Industries, Inc.; *U.S. Public*, pg. 860
ITT FLUID TECHNOLOGY CORPORATION—See ITT Industries, Inc.; *U.S. Public*, pg. 860
ITT FLUID TRANSFER DIVISION—See ITT Industries, Inc.; *U.S. Public*, pg. 860
ITT FLYGT—See ITT Industries, Inc.; *U.S. Public*, pg. 860
ITT FLYGT AB—See ITT Industries, Inc.; *U.S. Public*, pg. 860
ITT FLYGT A/S—See ITT Industries, Inc.; *U.S. Public*, pg. 860
ITT FLYGT CORPORATION—See ITT Industries, Inc.; *U.S. Public*, pg. 860
ITT FLYGT GMBH—See ITT Industries, Inc.; *U.S. Public*, pg. 860
ITT FLYGT KFT—See ITT Industries, Inc.; *U.S. Public*, pg. 860
ITT FLYGT LIMITED—See ITT Industries, Inc.; *U.S. Public*, pg. 860
ITT FLYGT LTD.—See ITT Industries, Inc.; *U.S. Public*, pg. 860
ITT FLYGT N.V./S.A.—See ITT Industries, Inc.; *U.S. Public*, *pg. 860*
ITT FLYGT S.A.—See ITT Industries, Inc.; *U.S. Public*, pg. 860
ITT FLYGT S.P.A.—See ITT Industries, Inc.; *U.S. Public*, pg. 860
ITT FLYGT SP.Z.O.O.—See ITT Industries, Inc.; *U.S. Public*, pg. 860
ITT FLYGT S.V.—See ITT Industries, Inc.; *U.S. Public*, pg. 860
ITT FLYGT WERK GMBH—See ITT Industries, Inc.; *U.S. Public*, pg. 860
ITT GALLIUM ARSENIDE TECHNOLOGY CENTER—See ITT Industries, Inc.; *U.S. Public*, pg. 859
ITT GILFILLAN—See ITT Industries, Inc.; *U.S. Public*, pg. 859
ITT HARTFORD LIFE & ANNUITY INSURANCE CORPORATION—See The Hartford Financial Services Group Inc.; *U.S. Public*, pg. 795
ITT HOFFMAN—See ITT Industries, Inc.; *U.S. Public*, pg. 860
ITT INDUSTRIES, INC.; *U.S. Public*, pg. 859
ITT INFORMATION SERVICES, INC.—See Starwood Hotels & Resorts; *U.S. Public*, pg. 1512
ITT JABSCO—See ITT Industries, Inc.; *U.S. Public*, pg. 860
ITT MCDONNELL & MILLER—See ITT Industries, Inc.; *U.S.* Public, pg. 860
ITT NIGHT VISION—See ITT Industries, Inc.; *U.S. Public*, pg. 860
ITT PAMONA—See ITT Industries, Inc.; *U.S. Public*, pg. 859
ITT PROMEDIA N.V.—See VNU Verenigde Nederlandse Uitgeversbedrijven B.V.; *Int'l*, pg. 1447
ITT SHERATON CORPORATION—See Starwood Hotels & Resorts; *U.S. Public*, pg. 1512
ITT SHERATON HOTELS—See Starwood Hotels & Resorts; *U.S. Public*, pg. 1512
ITT SHERATON INNS CANADA—See Starwood Hotels & Resorts; *U.S. Public*, pg. 1512
ITW ADHESIVES—See Illinois Tool Works Inc.; *U.S. Public*, *pg. 866*
ITW ANGLEBOARD—See Illinois Tool Works Inc.; *U.S. Public*, pg. 866
ITW ASIA (PTE) LTD.—See Illinois Tool Works Inc.; *U.S. Public*, pg. 868
ITW BASIC SWITCH PRODUCTS—See Illinois Tool Works Inc.; *U.S. Public*, pg. 866
ITW BEFESTIGUNGSSYSTEME (ANSBACH) GMBH—See Illinois Tool Works Inc.; *U.S. Public*, pg. 868
ITW BEFESTIGUNGSSYSTEME (HATTERSHEIM) GMBH—See Illinois Tool Works Inc.; *U.S. Public*, pg. 868
ITW BELGIUM S.A./N.V.—See Illinois Tool Works Inc.; *U.S.* Public, pg. 868
ITW BEVESTIGINGSSYSTEMEN B.V.—See Illinois Tool Works Inc.; *U.S. Public*, pg. 868
ITW BRAND MERCHANDISING—See Illinois Tool Works Inc.; *U.S. Public*, pg. 866
ITW BUILDEX—See Illinois Tool Works Inc.; *U.S. Public*, pg. 866
ITW CODING PRODUCTS—See Illinois Tool Works Inc.; *U.S. Public*, pg. 867
ITW COMPONENTS & TOOLS—See Illinois Tool Works Inc.; *U.S. Public*, pg. 866
ITW COMPULAR—See Illinois Tool Works Inc.; *U.S. Public*, *pg. 868*
ITW CONSTRUCTION PRODUCTS—See Illinois Tool Works Inc.; *U.S. Public*, pg. 868
ITW CORPORATE TECHNOLOGY—See Illinois Tool Works Inc.; *U.S. Public*, pg. 866
ITW DE FRANCE SA—See Illinois Tool Works Inc.; *U.S. Public*, pg. 868

ITW DELTAR—See Illinois Tool Works Inc.; *U.S. Public*, pg. 866
ITW DELTAR-FASTENERS—See Illinois Tool Works Inc.; *U.S. Public*, pg. 866
ITW DELTAR-INSERT MOLDED—See Illinois Tool Works Inc.; *U.S. Public*, pg. 866
ITW DELTAR-SPECIAL PRODUCTS—See Illinois Tool Works Inc.; *U.S. Public*, pg. 866
ITW DEVCON—See Illinois Tool Works Inc.; *U.S. Public*, pg. 868
ITW DEVCON ATECO GMBH—See Illinois Tool Works Inc.; *U.S. Public*, pg. 868
ITW DEVCON INDUSTRIAL—See Illinois Tool Works Inc.; *U.S. Public*, pg. 866
ITW DEVCON JAPAN—See Illinois Tool Works Inc.; *U.S. Public*, pg. 868
ITW DYNATEC—See Illinois Tool Works Inc.; *U.S. Public*, pg. 867
ITW DYNATEC KK—See Illinois Tool Works Inc.; *U.S. Public*, pg. 868
ITW DYNATEC-MACON—See Illinois Tool Works Inc.; *U.S. Public*, pg. 868
ITW ELECTRONIC COMPONENT PACKAGING—See Illinois Tool Works Inc.; *U.S. Public*, pg. 866
ITW ENGINEERED POLYMERS—See Illinois Tool Works Inc.; *U.S. Public*, pg. 868
ITW ENGINEERED POLYMERS BUSINESSES—See Illinois Tool Works Inc.; *U.S. Public*, pg. 866
ITW ESPANA, S.A.—See Illinois Tool Works Inc.; *U.S. Public*, pg. 868
ITW ESPANA S.A. SPIT—See Illinois Tool Works Inc.; *U.S. Public*, pg. 868
ITW FASTEX—See Illinois Tool Works Inc.; *U.S. Public*, pg. 866
ITW FASTEX ITALIA, SPA—See Illinois Tool Works Inc.; *U.S. Public*, pg. 868
ITW FINISHING SYSTEMS & PRODUCTS—See Illinois Tool Works Inc.; *U.S. Public*, pg. 866
ITW FINISHING SYSTEMS & PRODUCTS-NORTH AMERICA—See Illinois Tool Works Inc.; *U.S. Public*, pg. 866
ITW FINISHING SYSTEMS & PRODUCTS PTY. LTD.—See Illinois Tool Works Inc.; *U.S. Public*, pg. 868
ITW FINISHING SYSTEMS & PRODUCTS-SOUTHERN EUROPE—See Illinois Tool Works Inc.; *U.S. Public*, pg. 868
ITW FIXATIONS—See Illinois Tool Works Inc.; *U.S. Public*, pg. 868
ITW FIXFAST AB—See Illinois Tool Works Inc.; *U.S. Public*, pg. 868
ITW FIXLOCK AB—See Illinois Tool Works Inc.; *U.S. Public*, pg. 868
ITW FLUID PRODUCTS GROUP—See Illinois Tool Works Inc.; *U.S. Public*, pg. 866
ITW GUNTHER—See Illinois Tool Works Inc.; *U.S. Public*, pg. 868
ITW HEARTLAND COMPONENTS—See Illinois Tool Works Inc.; *U.S. Public*, pg. 866
ITW HEISTRAP GMBH—See Illinois Tool Works Inc.; *U.S. Public*, pg. 868
ITW HI-CONE—See Illinois Tool Works Inc.; *U.S. Public*, pg. 866
ITW HI-CONE LTD.—See Illinois Tool Works Inc.; *U.S. Public*, pg. 868
ITW INDUSTRY CO., LTD.—See Illinois Tool Works Inc.; *U.S. Public*, pg. 868
ITW IRATHANE—See Illinois Tool Works Inc.; *U.S. Public*, pg. 866
ITW IRATHANE INTL. LTD.—See Illinois Tool Works Inc.; *U.S. Public*, pg. 868
ITW ITALIA S.P.A.—See Illinois Tool Works Inc.; *U.S. Public*, pg. 868
ITW KOREA INCORPORATED—See Illinois Tool Works Inc.; *U.S. Public*, pg. 868
ITW LIMITED—See Illinois Tool Works Inc.; *U.S. Public*, pg. 868
ITW LIMITED-BUILDEX EUROPE—See Illinois Tool Works Inc.; *U.S. Public*, pg. 868
ITW LINX—See Illinois Tool Works Inc.; *U.S. Public*, pg. 866
ITW MAGNAFLUX—See Illinois Tool Works Inc.; *U.S. Public*, pg. 866
ITW MAGNAFLUX LIMITED—See Illinois Tool Works Inc.; *U.S. Public*, pg. 866
ITW MAPLE ROLL LEAF—See Illinois Tool Works Inc.; *U.S. Public*, pg. 868
ITW MAPRI INDUSTRIA E COMERCIO LTDA.—See Illinois Tool Works Inc.; *U.S. Public*, pg. 868
ITW MERITEX SDN BHD—See Illinois Tool Works Inc.; *U.S. Public*, pg. 868
ITW MEYPACK GMBH—See Illinois Tool Works Inc.; *U.S. Public*, pg. 868
ITW MICRO-POISE DIVISION—See Illinois Tool Works Inc.; *U.S. Public*, pg. 865
ITW MIMA, INC.—See Illinois Tool Works Inc.; *U.S. Public*, pg. 866
ITW NEW ZEALAND, LTD.—See Illinois Tool Works Inc.; *U.S. Public*, pg. 868
ITW NEXUS—See Illinois Tool Works Inc.; *U.S. Public*, pg. 866
ITW NEXUS EUROPE—See Illinois Tool Works Inc.; *U.S. Public*, pg. 868
ITW NEXUS UK—See Illinois Tool Works Inc.; *U.S. Public*, pg. 868
ITW NIFCO, INC.—See Illinois Tool Works Inc.; *U.S. Public*, pg. 867
ITW NORWOOD MARKING SYSTEMS—See Illinois Tool Works Inc.; *U.S. Public*, pg. 866
ITW OBERFLACHENTECHNK GMBH—See Illinois Tool Works Inc.; *U.S. Public*, pg. 869
ITW PAKTRON—See Illinois Tool Works Inc.; *U.S. Public*, pg. 866
ITW PANEL SWITCHES AND SYSTEMS—See Illinois Tool Works Inc.; *U.S. Public*, pg. 866

ITW PASLODE—See Illinois Tool Works Inc.; *U.S. Public*, pg. 869
ITW PHILADELPHIA RESINS—See Illinois Tool Works Inc.; *U.S. Public*, pg. 867
ITW PLASTIGLIDE—See Illinois Tool Works Inc.; *U.S. Public*, pg. 867
ITW PLASTIGLIDE LTD. OF CANADA/ ITW FASTEX—See Illinois Tool Works Inc.; *U.S. Public*, pg. 869
ITW PRODUX—See Illinois Tool Works Inc.; *U.S. Public*, pg. 867
ITW PROFFITT & CO. LTD.—See Illinois Tool Works Inc.; *U.S. Public*, pg. 869
ITW RAMSET/RED HEAD—See Illinois Tool Works Inc.; *U.S. Public*, pg. 867
ITW RANSBURG ELECTROSTATIC SYSTEMS—See Illinois Tool Works Inc.; *U.S. Public*, pg. 867
ITW RED HEAD—See Illinois Tool Works Inc.; *U.S. Public*, pg. 869
ITW SCREEN PROCESS SPECIALIST, LTD.—See Illinois Tool Works Inc.; *U.S. Public*, pg. 867
ITW SHAKEPROOF/AUTOMOTIVE PRODUCTS—See Illinois Tool Works Inc.; *U.S. Public*, pg. 867
ITW SHAKEPROOF/INDUSTRIAL PRODUCTS—See Illinois Tool Works Inc.; *U.S. Public*, pg. 867
ITW SHAKEPROOF/SPECIALTY PRODUCTS—See Illinois Tool Works Inc.; *U.S. Public*, pg. 867
ITW SHIPPERS PAPER—See Illinois Tool Works Inc.; *U.S. Public*, pg. 867
ITW SIGNODE—See Illinois Tool Works Inc.; *U.S. Public*, pg. 867
ITW SIGNODE INDIA LIMITED—See Illinois Tool Works Inc.; *U.S. Public*, pg. 869
ITW SIGNODE SYSTEM GMBH—See Illinois Tool Works Inc.; *U.S. Public*, pg. 869
ITW SOUTHERN GAGE CO.—See Illinois Tool Works Inc.; *U.S. Public*, pg. 867
ITW SPIT—See Illinois Tool Works Inc.; *U.S. Public*, pg. 869
ITW SPIT FIXINGS—See Illinois Tool Works Inc.; *U.S. Public*, pg. 869
ITW SWITCHES—See Illinois Tool Works Inc.; *U.S. Public*, pg. 867
ITW SWITCHES-ASIA—See Illinois Tool Works Inc.; *U.S. Public*, pg. 868
ITW SWITCHES-EUROPE—See Illinois Tool Works Inc.; *U.S. Public*, pg. 869
ITW (THAILAND) CO. LTD.—See Illinois Tool Works Inc.; *U.S. Public*, pg. 869
ITW THIELEX PLASTICS CORP.—See Illinois Tool Works Inc.; *U.S. Public*, pg. 867
ITW WATERBURY BUCKLE—See Illinois Tool Works Inc.; *U.S. Public*, pg. 867
ITW WOODWORTH—See Illinois Tool Works Inc.; *U.S. Public*, pg. 867
I.V. ONE—See Bindley Western Industries, Inc.; *U.S. Public*, pg. 229
IV VERWALTUNGSGESELLSCHAFT GUR VERSICHERUNGEN M.B.H.—See Assicurazioni Generali S.p.A.; *Int'l*, pg. 89
IVAC FRANCE S.A.R.L.—See ALARIS Medical, Inc.; *U.S. Public*, pg. 35
IVAC SCANDANAVIA AB—See ALARIS Medical, Inc.; *U.S. Public*, pg. 35
IVHS TECHNOLOGIES INC.—See Eaton Corporation; *U.S. Public*, pg. 558
IVO CM SERVICES LTD.—See Imatran Voima Oy; *Int'l*, pg. 661
IVO EKO S.R.O.—See Imatran Voima Oy; *Int'l*, pg. 660
IVO ENERGI AB—See Imatran Voima Oy; *Int'l*, pg. 661
IVO ENERGIEANLAGEN GMBH—See Imatran Voima Oy; *Int'l*, pg. 661
IVO ENERGY LIMITED—See Imatran Voima Oy; *Int'l*, pg. 661
IVO GENERATION SERVICES LTD.—See Imatran Voima Oy; *Int'l*, pg. 660
IVO GENERATION SERVICES (UK) LTD.—See Imatran Voima Oy; *Int'l*, pg. 661
IVO INTERNATIONAL LTD.—See Imatran Voima Oy; *Int'l*, pg. 660
IVO POLSKA SP. Z.O.O.—See Imatran Voima Oy; *Int'l*, pg. 660
IVO SENDI PRIMA SDN BHD—See Imatran Voima Oy; *Int'l*, pg. 661
IVO SERVICE—See Imatran Voima Oy; *Int'l*, pg. 660
IVO SERVICE INDUSTRY—See Imatran Voima Oy; *Int'l*, pg. 660
IVO SERVICE, NORTH FINLAND—See Imatran Voima Oy; *Int'l*, pg. 660
IVO SERVICE SUBSTATIONS—See Imatran Voima Oy; *Int'l*, pg. 660
IVO SERVICE THERMAL POWER—See Imatran Voima Oy; *Int'l*, pg. 660
IVO TRANSMISSION SERVICES LTD.—See Imatran Voima Oy; *Int'l*, pg. 660
IVT GRAPHICS—See Baldwin Technology Company, Inc.; *U.S. Public*, pg. 170
IVTX—See Express Scripts, Inc.; *U.S. Public*, pg. 601
IWC INTERNATIONAL WATCH CO. AG—See Mannesmann A.G.; *Int'l*, pg. 839
IWC RESOURCES CORPORATION—See NIPSCO Industries, Inc.; *U.S. Public*, pg. 1185
IWC UHREN GMBH DEUTSCHLAND—See Mannesmann A.G.; *Int'l*, pg. 839
IWC SERVICES, INC.—See NIPSCO Industries, Inc.; *U.S. Public*, pg. 1185
IWG-ARDMORE—See Hicks, Muse, Tate & Furst Inc.; *U.S. Private*, pg. 526
IWI HOLDING LIMITED; *U.S. Public*, pg. 861
IWO A/S—See Electrolux, AB; *Int'l*, pg. 441
IXC COMMUNICATIONS, INC.; *U.S. Public*, pg. 556
IXL CABINETS—See Triangle Pacific Corporation; *U.S. Public*, pg. 1634
IAMS COMPANY; *U.S. Private*, pg. 556

IBARAGI SNOW BRAND MILK CO., LTD.—See Snow Brand Milk Products Co.; *Int'l*, pg. 1272
IBARAKI WORKS—See Hitachi Zosen Corporation; *Int'l*, pg. 623
IBER-SWISS CATERING, S.A.—See SEPI; *Int'l*, pg. 1225
IBERDROLA, S.A.; *Int'l*, pg. 657
IBERIA LINEAS AEREAS DE ESPANA, S.A.—See SEPI; *Int'l*, pg. 1224
IBERIA TECNOLOGIA, S.A.—See SEPI; *Int'l*, pg. 1225
IBERICA AGA S.A.—See AGA AB; *Int'l*, pg. 14
IBERICA DE CRISOLES S.A.—See Morgan Crucible Co. Plc; *Int'l*, pg. 894
IBERICA DE SUSPENSIONES, S.A.—See NHK Spring Co., Ltd.; *Int'l*, pg. 902
IBEROASISTENCIA ARGENTINA, S.A.—See Corporacion MAPFRE, Compania Internacional de Reaseguros, S.A.; *Int'l*, pg. 334
IBEROASISTENCIA PORTUGAL—See Corporacion MAPFRE, Compania Internacional de Reaseguros, S.A.; *Int'l*, pg. 334
IBEROASISTENCIA, S.A.—See Corporacion MAPFRE, Compania Internacional de Reaseguros, S.A.; *Int'l*, pg. 334
IBERPHONE ANDALUCIA, S.A.—See Caja de Madrid Group; *Int'l*, pg. 252
IBERPHONE CATALUNA, S.A.—See Caja de Madrid Group; *Int'l*, pg. 252
IBERPHONE LEVANTE, S.A.—See Caja de Madrid Group; *Int'l*, pg. 252
IBERPHONE PORTUGAL TELEMARKETING—See Caja de Madrid Group; *Int'l*, pg. 252
IBERPHONE, S.A.—See Caja de Madrid Group; *Int'l*, pg. 252
IBEX ENGINEERING CO. LTD.—See Tetra Laval Group; *Int'l*, pg. 1380
IBIDEN CO., LTD.—See Mitsui & Co., Ltd.; *Int'l*, pg. 878
IBSTOCK PLC; *Int'l*, pg. 658
I.C. THOMASSON ASS.—See I.C. Thomasson Associates, Inc.; *U.S. Private*, pg. 1083
ICAHN & CO., INC.; *U.S. Private*, pg. 556
ICART S.A.—See Carter-Wallace, Inc.; *U.S. Public*, pg. 310
ICATCHER—See Wyse Advertising; *U.S. Private*, pg. 1194
ICE CREAM SPECIALTIES, INC.—See Prairie Farms Dairy, Inc.; *U.S. Private*, pg. 879
ICEBERG PROPERTIES LIMITED—See Jardine Matheson Holdings Limited; *Int'l*, pg. 704
ICELAND FROZEN FOODS PLC.—See Iceland Group plc; *Int'l*, pg. 658
ICELAND GROUP PLC; *Int'l*, pg. 658
ICELAND SEAFOOD CORPORATION; *U.S. Private*, pg. 556
ICELANDAIR; *Int'l*, pg. 658
ICELANDAIR—See Icelandair; *Int'l*, pg. 658
ICELANDIC ALLOYS—See Elkem ASA; *Int'l*, pg. 448
ICHIKOH INDUSTRIES, LTD.—See Nissan Motor Co., Ltd.; *Int'l*, pg. 944
ICICLE SEAFOODS, INC.; *U.S. Private*, pg. 556
ICON HEALTH & FITNESS, INC.; *U.S. Private*, pg. 556
ICON INTERNATIONAL; *U.S. Private*, pg. 556
ICON INTERNATIONAL, INC.—See Sanyo Electric Co., Ltd.; *Int'l*, pg. 1191
ICONOVEX CORPORATION—See Innovex, Inc.; *U.S. Public*, pg. 880
ICOPAL AB—See Icopal a/s; *Int'l*, pg. 659
ICOPAL AG—See Icopal a/s; *Int'l*, pg. 659
ICOPAL A/S; *Int'l*, pg. 658
ICOPAL AS—See Icopal a/s; *Int'l*, pg. 659
ICOPAL ENTREPRENAD AB—See Icopal a/s; *Int'l*, pg. 659
ICOPAL HELSINKI OY—See Icopal a/s; *Int'l*, pg. 659
ICOPAL KOUVOLA OY—See Icopal a/s; *Int'l*, pg. 659
ICOPAL KUOPIO OY—See Icopal a/s; *Int'l*, pg. 659
ICOPAL OY—See Icopal a/s; *Int'l*, pg. 659
ICOPAL POLAND SP.Z.O.O.—See Icopal a/s; *Int'l*, pg. 659
ICOPAL TAGENTREPRISE SV SJAELAND A/S—See Icopal a/s; *Int'l*, pg. 658
ICOPAL TAMPERE OY—See Icopal a/s; *Int'l*, pg. 659
ICOPAL TURKU OY—See Icopal a/s; *Int'l*, pg. 659
ICOPAL-SIPLAST GMBH—See Icopal a/s; *Int'l*, pg. 659
ICORE INTERNATIONAL GMBH—See Smiths Industries plc; *Int'l*, pg. 1268
ICORE INTERNATIONAL INC.—See Smiths Industries plc; *Int'l*, pg. 1268
ICORE INTERNATIONAL LIMITED—See Smiths Industries plc; *Int'l*, pg. 1267
IDACORP, INC.—See Idaho Power Company; *U.S. Public*, pg. 862
IDAHO ENERGY RESOURCES CO.—See Idaho Power Company; *U.S. Public*, pg. 862
IDAHO FOREST INDUSTRY, INC.; *U.S. Private*, pg. 556
IDAHO INDEPENDENT TELEVISION, INC.—See Blade Communications, Inc.; *U.S. Private*, pg. 147
IDAHO POTATO OPERS.—See Diageo Plc; *Int'l*, pg. 411
IDAHO POWER COMPANY; *U.S. Public*, pg. 861
IDAHO POWER RESOURCES CORP.—See Idaho Power Company; *U.S. Public*, pg. 862
THE IDAHO STATESMAN—See Gannett Company, Inc.; *U.S. Public*, pg. 701
IDAHO SUPREME COMPANY; *U.S. Private*, pg. 557
IDAHO UTILITY PRODUCTS COMPANY—See Idaho Power Company; *U.S. Public*, pg. 862
IDAHOAN FOODS; *U.S. Private*, pg. 557
IDEA CORPORATION; *U.S. Private*, pg. 557
IDEA COURIER, INC.—See IDEA Corporation; *U.S. Private*, pg. 557
IDEA ENGINEERING & FABRICATING; *U.S. Private*, pg. 557
IDEA INTERNATIONAL DEVELOPMENT AND ENGINEERING ASSOCIATES LTD.—See Deutsche Babcock AG; *Int'l*, pg. 401
IDEA MAN, INC.; *U.S. Private*, pg. 557
IDEAL-ALAMBREC S.A.—See N.V. Bekaert S.A.; *Int'l*, pg. 185
IDEAL CEMENT COMPANY (B.C.) LTD.—See Holderbank Financiere Glaris Ltd.; *Int'l*, pg. 628

IDEAL CHEMICAL & SUPPLY COMPANY; *U.S. Private*, pg. 557
IDEAL CONCRETE—See Holderbank Financiere Glaris Ltd.; *Int'l*, pg. 628
IDEAL DIVISION—See Tomkins PLC; *Int'l*, pg. 1396
IDEAL DOMINICANA, S.A.—See Holderbank Financiere Glaris Ltd.; *Int'l*, pg. 628
IDEAL FORGING CORPORATION; *U.S. Private*, pg. 557
IDEAL FORM TEAM S.R.L.; *Int'l*, pg. 659
IDEAL HOMES HOLDINGS PLC—See Kvaerner a.s.a.; *Int'l*, pg. 773
IDEAL HOMES PTE., LIMITED—See Singapore Land Limited; *Int'l*, pg. 1253
IDEAL INDUSTRIES, INC.; *U.S. Private*, pg. 557
IDEAL/MRS. WEISS NOODLE CO.—See Hershey Foods Corporation; *U.S. Public*, pg. 812
IDEAL PARKING, INC.—See Allright Corporation; *U.S. Private*, pg. 44
IDEAL SCHOOL SUPPLY COMPANY—See Creative Publications; *U.S. Public*, pg. 288
IDEAL-STANDARD—See American Standard Inc.; *U.S. Public*, pg. 92
IDEAL TAPE-BELGIUM—See American Biltrite Inc.; *U.S. Public*, pg. 69
IDEAL TAPE COMPANY—See American Biltrite Inc.; *U.S. Public*, pg. 69
IDEAL WASA A/S—See Novartis AG; *Int'l*, pg. 982
IDEALEASE OF MEMPHIS—See Mid America International Trucks, Inc.; *U.S. Private*, pg. 743
IDEG S.C.—See Electrabel S.A.; *Int'l*, pg. 437
IDEMITSU KOSAN CO., LTD.; *Int'l*, pg. 659
IDENTICAM SYSTEMS LTD.—See IDenticard Systems, Inc.; *U.S. Private*, pg. 557
IDENTICARD SYSTEMS, INC.; *U.S. Private*, pg. 557
IDEON GROUP, INC.—See Cendant Corporation; *U.S. Public*, pg. 320
IDEX CORPORATION; *U.S. Public*, pg. 862
IDEX INVESTOR SERVICES, INC.—See AEGON N.V.; *Int'l*, pg. 27
IDEX MANAGEMENT, INC.—See AEGON N.V.; *Int'l*, pg. 27
IDMATICS INC.—See Thomson S.A.; *Int'l*, pg. 1384
IDMATICS S.A.—See Thomson S.A.; *Int'l*, pg. 1382
IEGA—See Electrabel S.A.; *Int'l*, pg. 437
IEI SERVICES, LLC—See Indiana Energy, Inc.; *U.S. Public*, pg. 875
IFASTGROUPE AND COMPANY, LIMITED PARTNERSHIP—See The Ivaco Group; *Int'l*, pg. 695
IFFLAND KAVANAGH WATERBURY, PLLC—See Edwards and Kelcey, Inc.; *U.S. Private*, pg. 364
IGAKU-SHOIN MYW LTD.—See Waverly, Inc.; *U.S. Public*, pg. 1748
IGEHÖ—See Electrabel S.A.; *Int'l*, pg. 437
IGELFORS PORTSYSTEM AB—See Cardo AB; *Int'l*, pg. 269
IGEMISA—See Heidemij N.V.; *Int'l*, pg. 608
IGETALLOY-KIRBY (PTY.), LTD.—See Sumitomo Electric Industries, Ltd.; *Int'l*, pg. 1313
IGGESUND AG—See Mo och Domsjo AB; *Int'l*, pg. 886
IGGESUND BENELUX B.V.—See Mo och Domsjo AB; *Int'l*, pg. 886
IGGESUND BENELUX N.V.—See Mo och Domsjo AB; *Int'l*, pg. 886
IGGESUND BOARD SALES LTD. (WALTHAM ABBEY)—See Mo och Domsjo AB; *Int'l*, pg. 886
IGGESUND CONVERTERS LTD.—See Mo och Domsjo AB; *Int'l*, pg. 886
IGGESUND PAPER & BOARD SERVICE B.V.—See Mo och Domsjo AB; *Int'l*, pg. 886
IGGESUND PAPERBOARD AB—See Mo och Domsjo AB; *Int'l*, pg. 886
IGGESUND PAPERBOARD FRANCE SA—See Mo och Domsjo AB; *Int'l*, pg. 886
IGGESUND PAPERBOARD INC.—See Mo och Domsjo AB; *Int'l*, pg. 886
IGGESUND PAPERBOARD NORDEN—See Mo och Domsjo AB; *Int'l*, pg. 886
IGGESUND PAPERBOARD (WORKINGTON) LTD.—See Mo och Domsjo AB; *Int'l*, pg. 886
IGGESUND SAWMILL—See Mo och Domsjo AB; *Int'l*, pg. 886
IGGESUND TIMBER AB—See Mo och Domsjo AB; *Int'l*, pg. 886
IGGESUND TIMBER AB SCANDINAVIA—See Mo och Domsjo AB; *Int'l*, pg. 886
IGGESUND TIMBER SALES LTD.—See Mo och Domsjo AB; *Int'l*, pg. 886
IGGESUND VERKAUFSGESELLSCHAFT G.M.B.H—See Mo och Domsjo AB; *Int'l*, pg. 886
IGGESUNDS BRUK—See Mo och Domsjo AB; *Int'l*, pg. 886
IGLO INDUSTRIAS DE GELADOS, LDA.—See Unilever Plc; *Int'l*, pg. 1437
IGLO-OLA B.V.—See Unilever Plc; *Int'l*, pg. 1437
IGLO-OLA N.V.—See Unilever Plc; *Int'l*, pg. 1437
IGLOO POOL—See Kvaerner a.s.a.; *Int'l*, pg. 766
IGLOO PRODUCTS CORPORATION—See Brunswick Corporation; *U.S. Public*, pg. 265
IGUAZU COMPANIA DE SEGUROS—See Zurich Insurance Company; *Int'l*, pg. 1531
IHOP CORP.; *U.S. Public*, pg. 862
IHOP REALTY CORP.—See IHOP Corp.; *U.S. Public*, pg. 862
IKEA HOLDINGS AB; *Int'l*, pg. 659
IKEA NORTH AMERICA, INC.—See Ikea Holdings AB; *Int'l*, pg. 660
IKEA SVENSKA AB—See Ikea Holdings AB; *Int'l*, pg. 660
IKEA SVENSKA FORSALJNINGS AB—See Ikea Holdings AB; *Int'l*, pg. 660
IKEDA BUSSAN CO., LTD.—See Nissan Motor Co., Ltd.; *Int'l*, pg. 944
IKEGAMI ELECTRONICS EUROPE—See Ikegami Tsushinki Co., Ltd.; *Int'l*, pg. 660
IKEGAMI ELECTRONICS UK—See Ikegami Tsushinki Co., Ltd.; *Int'l*, pg. 660

IKEGAMI ELECTRONICS (U.S.A.), INC.—See Ikegami Tsushinki Co., Ltd.; *Int'l*, pg. 660
IKEGAMI TSUSHINKI CO., LTD.; *Int'l*, pg. 660
IKEGAMI TSUSHINKI CO., OVERSEAS SALES DIV.—See Ikegami Tsushinki Co., Ltd.; *Int'l*, pg. 660
IKE'S—See Fleming Companies, Inc.; *U.S. Public*, pg. 653
IKON AG PRAZISIONSTECHNIK—See Assa Abloy AB; *Int'l*, pg. 18
IKON CAPITAL—See Ikon Office Solutions, Inc.; *U.S. Public*, pg. 863
IKON CULLY S.A.—See Assa Abloy AB; *Int'l*, pg. 18
IKON OFFICE SOLUTIONS—See Ikon Office Solutions, Inc.; *U.S. Public*, pg. 863
IKON OFFICE SOLUTIONS, INC.; *U.S. Public*, pg. 862
IKON OFFICE SYSTEMS—See Ikon Office Solutions, Inc.; *U.S. Public*, pg. 864
IKOS SYSTEMS, INC.; *U.S. Public*, pg. 864
IKOS SYSTEMS, INC.—See IKOS Systems, Inc.; *U.S. Public*, pg. 864
IKOS, U.K.—See IKOS Systems, Inc.; *U.S. Public*, pg. 864
IKSELAH CORPORATION—See Pubco Corporation; *U.S. Public*, pg. 1339
IL CARBONIO SPA—See Pechiney S.A.; *Int'l*, pg. 1030
IL CARBONIO SUD SPA—See Pechiney S.A.; *Int'l*, pg. 1030
IL FORNAIO AMERICA CORPORATION; *U.S. Public*, pg. 864
IL SEKRETESS—See IL Returpapper; *Int'l*, pg. 646
ILACO BV—See Heidemij N.V.; *Int'l*, pg. 606
ILACO SURINAME NV—See Heidemij N.V.; *Int'l*, pg. 606
ILCO ORION S.A.—See Unican Security Systems Ltd.; *Int'l*, pg. 1432
ILCO UNICAN AUSTRALIA (PTY.) LTD.—See Unican Security Systems Ltd.; *Int'l*, pg. 1432
ILCO UNICAN CORP., SAFELOCK DIVISION—See Unican Security Systems Ltd.; *Int'l*, pg. 1432
ILCO UNICAN CORP., SIMPLEX ACCESS CONTROLS DIVISION—See Unican Security Systems Ltd.; *Int'l*, pg. 1432
ILCO UNICAN CORP.—See Unican Security Systems Ltd.; *Int'l*, pg. 1432
ILCO UNICAN FRANCE S.A.—See Unican Security Systems Ltd.; *Int'l*, pg. 1432
ILCO UNICAN INC. (CAPITOL DIVISION)—See Unican Security Systems Ltd.; *Int'l*, pg. 1432
ILCO UNICAN INC. (DOMINION LOCK DIVISION)—See Unican Security Systems Ltd.; *Int'l*, pg. 1432
ILCO UNICAN INC. (ELECTRONIC ACCESS CONTROLS DIVISION)—See Unican Security Systems Ltd.; *Int'l*, pg. 1432
ILCO UNICAN MEXICO S.A. DE C.V.—See Unican Security Systems Ltd.; *Int'l*, pg. 1432
ILCO UNICAN (SA) (PTY) LTD.—See Unican Security Systems Ltd.; *Int'l*, pg. 1432
ILCO UNICAN (U.K.) LTD.—See Unican Security Systems Ltd.; *Int'l*, pg. 1432
ILFORD ANITEC SA—See International Paper Company; *U.S. Public*, pg. 906
ILFORD INC.—See International Paper Company; *U.S. Public*, pg. 904
ILFORD LIMITED—See International Paper Company; *U.S. Public*, pg. 905
ILFORD SA—See International Paper Company; *U.S. Public*, pg. 906
ILIGAN CEMENT CORPORATION—See Holderbank Financiere Glaris Ltd.; *Int'l*, pg. 629
ILIS/ILACO BV—See Heidemij N.V.; *Int'l*, pg. 606
ILLAWARRA NEWSPAPER HOLDINGS PTY. LIMITED—See John Fairfax Holdings Limited; *Int'l*, pg. 477
ILLINOIS-AMERICAN WATER CO.—See American Water Works Company, Inc.; *U.S. Public*, pg. 95
ILLINOIS AUTO CENTRAL DIV.—See Illinois Auto Electric Co.; *U.S. Private*, pg. 558
ILLINOIS AUTO ELECTRIC CO.; *U.S. Private*, pg. 557
ILLINOIS AUTO ELECTRIC MIDWEST ENGINE WAREHOUSE DIV.—See Illinois Auto Electric Co.; *U.S. Private*, pg. 558
ILLINOIS BANC ONE CORPORATION—See Banc One Corporation; *U.S. Public*, pg. 174
ILLINOIS BANC ONE INSURANCE SERVICES, INC.—See Banc One Corporation; *U.S. Public*, pg. 174
ILLINOIS BANC ONE LEASING CORP.—See Banc One Corporation; *U.S. Public*, pg. 174
ILLINOIS BANC ONE LIFE INSURANCE CO.—See Banc One Corporation; *U.S. Public*, pg. 174
ILLINOIS BANC ONE MORTGAGE CORPORATION—See Banc One Corporation; *U.S. Public*, pg. 174
ILLINOIS BANC ONE SERVICES, INC.—See Banc One Corporation; *U.S. Public*, pg. 174
ILLINOIS BANC ONE TITLE CO.—See Banc One Corporation; *U.S. Public*, pg. 174
ILLINOIS CEMENT CO.—See Centex Corporation; *U.S. Public*, pg. 322
ILLINOIS CENTRAL CORPORATION; *U.S. Public*, pg. 864
ILLINOIS FRUIT & PRODUCE CORP.—See JP Foodservice, Inc.; *U.S. Public*, pg. 918
ILLINOIS MENTOR, INC.—See Magellan Health Services, Inc.; *U.S. Public*, pg. 1036
ILLINOIS NATIONAL INSURANCE CO.—See American International Group, Inc.; *U.S. Public*, pg. 84
ILLINOIS POWER COMPANY—See Illinova Inc.; *U.S. Public*, pg. 869
ILLINOIS STAR-COURIER—See Lee Enterprises, Incorporated; *U.S. Public*, pg. 983
ILLINOIS TOOL WORKS INC.; *U.S. Public*, pg. 865
ILLINOIS UNION INSURANCE COMPANY—See Cigna Corp.; *U.S. Public*, pg. 365
ILLINOVA ENERGY PARTNERS, INC.—See Illinova Inc.; *U.S. Public*, pg. 870
ILLINOVA GENERATING CO.—See Illinova Inc.; *U.S. Public*, pg. 870
ILLINOVA INC.; *U.S. Public*, pg. 869
ILLUMS BOLIGHUS—See Royal Copenhagen A/S; *Int'l*, pg. 1134

ILLUSTRATED LONDON NEWS—See Sea Containers Ltd.; *Int'l*, pg. 1214
ILMOR ENGINEERING, LTD.—See General Motors Corporation; *U.S. Public*, pg. 724
ILSCO; *U.S. Private*, pg. 558
ILSE-BAYERNWERK ENERGIEANLAGEN GMBH—See Viag AG; *Int'l*, pg. 1464
ILVA—See IRI Istituto Ricostruzione Industriale; *Int'l*, pg. 654
ILVA BENELUX B.V.—See IRI Istituto Ricostruzione Industriale; *Int'l*, pg. 654
ILVA DEUTSCHLAND—See IRI Istituto Ricostruzione Industriale; *Int'l*, pg. 654
ILVA FINANCE—See IRI Istituto Ricostruzione Industriale; *Int'l*, pg. 654
ILVA FRANCE—See IRI Istituto Ricostruzione Industriale; *Int'l*, pg. 654
ILVA HELLAS S.A.—See IRI Istituto Ricostruzione Industriale; *Int'l*, pg. 654
ILVA TOKYO—See IRI Istituto Ricostruzione Industriale; *Int'l*, pg. 654
ILVA U.K.—See IRI Istituto Ricostruzione Industriale; *Int'l*, pg. 654
IMAGE ACQUISITION PRODUCTS DIVISION—See Eastman Kodak Company; *U.S. Public*, pg. 555
IMAGE BY DESIGN—See Dann Dee Display Fixtures; *U.S. Private*, pg. 310
IMAGE ENTERTAINMENT, INC.; *U.S. Public*, pg. 870
IMAGE (GLASSWARE) LIMITED—See Saint-Gobain; *Int'l*, pg. 1173
IMAGE REPROGRAPHICS—See Day & Zimmermann, Inc.; *U.S. Private*, pg. 317
IMAGE TECHNOLOGY CORPORATION—See Olin Corporation; *U.S. Public*, pg. 1219
IMAGERY & INFORMATION SYSTEMS—See Tracor, Inc.; *U.S. Public*, pg. 1627
THE IMAGINATION NETWORK—See America Online Incorporated; *U.S. Public*, pg. 66
IMAGINE EDUCATIONAL PRODUCTS, INC.—See Nobel Education Dynamics, Inc.; *U.S. Public*, pg. 1186
IMAGINE ENTERTAINMENT; *U.S. Private*, pg. 558
IMAGING PRODUCTS DIVISION—See International Paper Company; *U.S. Public*, pg. 902
IMAGING SERVICES—See Quebecor Inc.; *Int'l*, pg. 1076
IMAGING TECHNOLOGIES—See Wallace Computer Services, Inc.; *U.S. Public*, pg. 1735
IMAGING TECHNOLOGIES CORP.; *U.S. Public*, pg. 870
IMAGING TECHNOLOGIES SERVICES—See Wallace Computer Services, Inc.; *U.S. Public*, pg. 1735
IMAS S.A.—See Clouth Gummiwerke AG; *Int'l*, pg. 298
IMASCA S.A.—See B.A.T Industries P.L.C.; *Int'l*, pg. 112
IMASCO B.V.—See B.A.T Industries P.L.C.; *Int'l*, pg. 112
IMASCO B.V.-FRIBOURG BRANCH—See B.A.T Industries P.L.C.; *Int'l*, pg. 112
IMASCO FINANCE L.L.C.—See B.A.T Industries P.L.C.; *Int'l*, pg. 112
IMASCO HOLDINGS, INC.—See B.A.T Industries P.L.C.; *Int'l*, pg. 112
IMASCO LIMITED—See B.A.T Industries P.L.C.; *Int'l*, pg. 112
IMATION AUSTRALIA NEW ZEALAND PTY. LTD.—See Imation Corporation; *U.S. Public*, pg. 870
IMATION BEIJING BRANCH OFFICE—See Imation Corporation; *U.S. Public*, pg. 870
IMATION CORP. JAPAN—See Imation Corporation; *U.S. Public*, pg. 870
IMATION CORPORATION; *U.S. Public*, pg. 870
IMATION HONG KONG LTD.—See Imation Corporation; *U.S. Public*, pg. 870
IMATION INDIA REPRESENTATIVE OFFICE, BANGALORE—See Imation Corporation; *U.S. Public*, pg. 870
IMATION INDIA REPRESENTATIVE OFFICE, MUMBAI—See Imation Corporation; *U.S. Public*, pg. 870
IMATION KOREA—See Imation Corporation; *U.S. Public*, pg. 870
IMATION MALAYSIA REPRESENTATIVE OFFICE—See Imation Corporation; *U.S. Public*, pg. 870
IMATION NEW ZEALAND—See Imation Corporation; *U.S. Public*, pg. 870
IMATION PHILIPPINES REPRESENTATIVE OFFICE—See Imation Corporation; *U.S. Public*, pg. 870
IMATION SHAGHAI BRANCH OFFICE—See Imation Corporation; *U.S. Public*, pg. 870
IMATION SINGAPORE PTE. LTD.—See Imation Corporation; *U.S. Public*, pg. 870
IMATION TAIWAN LTD.—See Imation Corporation; *U.S. Public*, pg. 870
IMATION THAILAND REPRESENTATIVE OFFICE—See Imation Corporation; *U.S. Public*, pg. 870
IMATRA PAPERBOARDS—See Enso Oyj; *Int'l*, pg. 456
IMATRA POWER PLANT—See Imatran Voima Oy; *Int'l*, pg. 660
IMATRA STEEL OY AB—See Metra Corporation; *Int'l*, pg. 863
IMATRAN VOIMA OY; *Int'l*, pg. 660
IMAX CORPORATION; *U.S. Public*, pg. 661
IMBANK NOMINEES LIMITED—See Canadian Imperial Bank of Commerce; *Int'l*, pg. 257
IMBAU INDUSTRIELLES BAUEN GMBH—See Philipp Holzmann AG; *Int'l*, pg. 633
IMCO RECYCLING INC.; *U.S. Public*, pg. 870
IMCO RECYCLING INC.—See IMCO Recycling Inc.; *U.S. Public*, pg. 871
IMEA C.V.—See Electrabel S.A.; *Int'l*, pg. 437
IMEDIATE PHARMACEUTICAL SERVICES INC.—See Discount Drug Mart Inc.; *U.S. Private*, pg. 334
CURT GEORGI IMES, S.P.A.—See Universal Foods Corporation; *U.S. Public*, pg. 1696
IMETAL; *Int'l*, pg. 661
IMEWO—See Electrabel S.A.; *Int'l*, pg. 437
IMMERGUT MILCH GMBH—See Nutricia BV; *Int'l*, pg. 991
IMMINGHAM STORAGE CO. LTD.—See Simon Engineering plc; *Int'l*, pg. 1251

Company Index

IMMOBILIARE DICIANNOVE S.P.A.—See Assicurazioni Generali S.p.A.; *Int'l*, pg. 90
IMMOBILIARE MARAM S.R.L.—See Banco Ambrosiano Veneto S.p.A.; *Int'l*, pg. 138
IMMOBILIARE METANOPOLI S.P.A.—See ENI S.p.A.; *Int'l*, pg. 428
IMMOBILIARE ML S.R.L.—See Oerlikon-Buhrle Holding AG; *Int'l*, pg. 997
IMMOBILIARIA CONEK S.A.—See Caterpillar Inc.; *U.S. Public*, pg. 316
IMMOBILIARO SANDOZ S.P.A.—See Novartis AG; *Int'l*, pg. 982
N.V. IMMOBILIEN EN GRINDEXPLOITATLEMAATSCHAPPIJ—See Ballast Nedam NV; *Int'l*, pg. 135
IMMOBILIENGESELLSCHAFT—See Feldschlosschen Hurlimann Holding; *Int'l*, pg. 479
IMMOBILIENGESELLSCHAFT BETA VON BURKERSRODA KG—See Commerzbank AG; *Int'l*, pg. 309
IMMOBILIENGESELLSCHAFT DER FRANKFURTER SPARKASSE GMBH—See Frankfurter Sparkasse; *Int'l*, pg. 504
IMMOBILIENGESELLSCHAFT GAMMA VON BURKERSRODA KG—See Commerzbank AG; *Int'l*, pg. 309
IMMOBILIENGESELLSCHAFT OST BAUER & CO. KG—See Commerzbank AG; *Int'l*, pg. 310
IMMOBILIENGESELLSCHAFT OST HAEGLE SPOL. S.R.O.—See Commerzbank AG; *Int'l*, pg. 310
IMMOBILIENGESELLSCHAFT VON BURKERSRODA OBJEKT ZWEI KG—See Commerzbank AG; *Int'l*, pg. 309
AB IMMOBILIENVERWALTUNGS GMBH—See Bayerische Vereinsbank Group; *Int'l*, pg. 178
GS IMMOBILIENVERWALTUNGS GMBH—See Bayerische Vereinsbank Group; *Int'l*, pg. 178
IMMOBILIERE DE BEAUFAYS—See GIB Group; *Int'l*, pg. 533
IMMOBILIERE DE LA DISTRIBUTION—See Nestle S.A.; *Int'l*, pg. 919
S.A. IMMOBILIERE DE LA CHAUSSEE ROMAINE—See Schindler Holding S.p.A.; *Int'l*, pg. 1205
S.A. IMMOBILIERE DES 154/156 BD. DE LA GARE—See Assicurazioni Generali S.p.A.; *Int'l*, pg. 91
S.A. IMMOBILIERE DU CASINO—See Groupe Casino; *Int'l*, pg. 563
IMMOBILIERE SAINT DOMINIQUE—See Credit Nationale; *Int'l*, pg. 344
IMMOBILIERE TRACTEBEL S.A.—See Tractebel; *Int'l*, pg. 1415
IMMODISQUE—See Groupe Casino; *Int'l*, pg. 563
IMMOLEASE NV—See Almanij N.V.; *Int'l*, pg. 65
IMMTECH INTERNATIONAL, INC.—See Criticare Systems, Inc.; *U.S. Public*, pg. 459
IMMUNEX CORPORATION; *U.S. Public*, pg. 871
IMMUNEX MANUFACTURING CORPORATION—See Immunex Corporation; *U.S. Public*, pg. 871
IMMUNEX RESEARCH AND DEVELOPMENT CORPORATION—See Immunex Corporation; *U.S. Public*, pg. 871
IMMUNOBIOLOGY RESEARCH INSTITUTE—See Johnson & Johnson; *U.S. Public*, pg. 928
IMOCASCAIS GESTAO MOBILIARIA E IMMOBILIARIA—See Corporacion MAPFRE, Compania Internacional de Reaseguros, S.A.; *Int'l*, pg. 333
IMODIS—See GIB Group; *Int'l*, pg. 533
IMOLEASING—See Caixa Geral de Depositos; *Int'l*, pg. 250
IMPACT—See Philips Electronics N.V.; *Int'l*, pg. 1052
IMPACT COMMUNICATIONS GROUP—See True North Communications Inc.; *U.S. Public*, pg. 1641
IMPACT FURNITURE CO. INC.—See Bassett Furniture Industries, Incorporated; *U.S. Public*, pg. 193
IMPACT RECHERCHE—See Cossette Communication Marketing; *Int'l*, pg. 336
IMPACT/FCB—See FCB; *U.S. Private*, pg. 389
IMPAX TRADING A.S.—See Incentive AB; *Int'l*, pg. 669
IMPAXX, INC.; *U.S. Private*, pg. 558
IMPCO AIRSENSORS TECHNOLOGIES—See AirSensors, Inc.; *U.S. Public*, pg. 34
IMPELL CORPORATION U.K. LTD.—See ABB Asea Brown Boveri (Holding) Ltd.; *Int'l*, pg. 6
IMPELL-FRANCE S.A.R.L.—See ABB Asea Brown Boveri (Holding) Ltd.; *Int'l*, pg. 6
IMPERIA BROS., INC.; *U.S. Private*, pg. 558
IMPERIAL ADHESIVES & CHEMICALS, INC.—See NS Group, Inc.; *U.S. Public*, pg. 1147
IMPERIAL AUTO AUCTION—See Cox Enterprises, Inc.; *U.S. Private*, pg. 282
IMPERIAL BANCORP; *U.S. Public*, pg. 871
IMPERIAL BANK—See Imperial Bancorp; *U.S. Public*, pg. 871
IMPERIAL BANK REALTY COMPANY—See Imperial Bancorp; *U.S. Public*, pg. 872
IMPERIAL BONDWARE CORP.—See International Paper Company; *U.S. Public*, pg. 903
IMPERIAL BUSINESS CREDIT—See Imperial Credit Industries, Inc.; *U.S. Public*, pg. 872
IMPERIAL CASUALTY & INDEMNITY CO.—See Amoco Corporation; *U.S. Public*, pg. 103
IMPERIAL CHEMICAL INDUSTRIES PLC; *Int'l*, pg. 662
IMPERIAL COSMETICS—See CCL Industries, Inc.; *Int'l*, pg. 239
IMPERIAL CREDIT COMMERCIAL MORTGAGE INVESTMENT CORP.—See Imperial Credit Industries, Inc.; *U.S. Public*, pg. 872
IMPERIAL CREDIT INDUSTRIES, INC.; *U.S. Public*, pg. 872
IMPERIAL DIE CASTING—See RCM Industries; *U.S. Private*, pg. 903
THE IMPERIAL ELECTRIC COMPANY—See Jordan Industries, Inc.; *U.S. Private*, pg. 598
IMPERIAL EQUITIES—See Lone Star Equities Inc.; *U.S. Private*, pg. 674

IMPERIAL FUND MANAGERS—See Canadian Imperial Bank of Commerce; *Int'l*, pg. 257
IMPERIAL HOLLY CORPORATION; *U.S. Public*, pg. 872
IMPERIAL HOTELS; *U.S. Private*, pg. 558
IMPERIAL HOTELS AUSTRIA AG—See Creditanstalt-Bankverein; *Int'l*, pg. 347
IMPERIAL, INC.; *U.S. Private*, pg. 558
IMPERIAL INTERNATIONAL BANK—See Imperial Bancorp; *U.S. Public*, pg. 872
IMPERIAL INVESTMENTS LTD.—See Hanson PLC; *Int'l*, pg. 593
THE IMPERIAL LIFE ASSURANCE CO.—See Desjardins-Laurentian Financial Corporation; *Int'l*, pg. 396
IMPERIAL LITHO & DRYOGRAPHY, INC.; *U.S. Private*, pg. 558
IMPERIAL NURSERIES INC.—See General Cigar Holdings Inc; *U.S. Public*, pg. 707
IMPERIAL OIL LIMITED—See Exxon Corporation; *U.S. Public*, pg. 602
IMPERIAL POOLS, INC.; *U.S. Private*, pg. 558
IMPERIAL REAL ESTATE VENTURES—See Imperial Bancorp; *U.S. Public*, pg. 872
IMPERIAL SCHRADE CORP.; *U.S. Private*, pg. 559
IMPERIAL SKILLED CARE CENTER—See Horizon/CMS Healthcare Corporation; *U.S. Public*, pg. 838
IMPERIAL STAG LTD.—See Imperial Schrade Corp.; *U.S. Private*, pg. 559
IMPERIAL SWEETNER DISTRIBUTORS, INC.—See Imperial Holly Corporation; *U.S. Public*, pg. 872
IMPERIAL TOBACCO GROUP, LTD.; *Int'l*, pg. 666
IMPERIAL TOBACCO INTERNATIONAL LTD.—See Imperial Tobacco Group, Ltd.; *Int'l*, pg. 666
IMPERIAL TOBACCO LIMITED—See B.A.T Industries P.L.C.; *Int'l*, pg. 112
IMPERIAL TOBACCO LTD., CIGAR DIV.—See Imperial Tobacco Group, Ltd.; *Int'l*, pg. 666
IMPERIAL TOBACCO LTD., LIVERPOOL TRADING DIV.—See Imperial Tobacco Group, Ltd.; *Int'l*, pg. 666
IMPERIAL TOBACCO LTD., NORTHERN TRADING DIV.—See Imperial Tobacco Group, Ltd.; *Int'l*, pg. 666
IMPERIAL TOBACCO LTD., SOUTHERN TRADING DIV.—See Imperial Tobacco Group, Ltd.; *Int'l*, pg. 666
IMPERIAL TRUST CO.—See Imperial Bancorp; *U.S. Public*, pg. 872
IMPERIAL VENTURES, INC.—See Imperial Bancorp; *U.S. Public*, pg. 872
THE IMPEX GROUP LIMITED—See Goldman Financial Group; *U.S. Private*, pg. 461
IMPEX WALCHAR B.V.—See Illinois Tool Works Inc.; *U.S. Public*, pg. 869
IMPHY S.A.—See Usinor; *Int'l*, pg. 571
IMPO GLAZTILE—See The Siam Cement Public Company Limited; *Int'l*, pg. 1239
IMPO IMPORT PARFUMERIEN AG—See Coop Switzerland; *Int'l*, pg. 330
IMPOL SA—See ENI S.p.A.; *Int'l*, pg. 429
IMPORMOL INDUSTRIA PORTUGUESA DE MOLAS S.A.—See Fried. Krupp AG; *Int'l*, pg. 508
IMPORTATION DE PRODUCTS ALIMENTAIRES S.A.—See IRI Istituto Ricostruzione Industriale; *Int'l*, pg. 655
IMPRESIT S.P.A.—See Fiat Auto SpA; *Int'l*, pg. 481
IMPRESORA DONNECO INTERNACIONAL, S.A. DE C.V.—See R.R. Donnelley & Sons Company; *U.S. Public*, pg. 519
IMPRESSIONS ET TEINTURES DE TOURNON S.A.—See Liberty PLC; *Int'l*, pg. 807
IMPRIMERIE GAUTHIER-VILLARS—See C.E.P. Communication Group; *Int'l*, pg. 239
IMPRIMERIE HELIO CORBEIL—See Lagardere Groupe; *Int'l*, pg. 792
IMPRIMERIE QUEBECOR BARCLAY—See Quebecor Inc.; *Int'l*, pg. 1077
IMPRIMERIE QUEBECOR BROMONT—See Quebecor Inc.; *Int'l*, pg. 1077
IMPRIMERIE QUEBECOR CANADA—See Quebecor Inc.; *Int'l*, pg. 1077
IMPRIMERIE QUEBECOR GRAPHIQUE-COULEUR—See Quebecor Inc.; *Int'l*, pg. 1077
IMPRIMERIE QUEBECOR INC.—See Quebecor Inc.; *Int'l*, pg. 1077
IMPRIMERIE QUEBECOR JOLIETTE—See Quebecor Inc.; *Int'l*, pg. 1077
IMPRIMERIE QUEBECOR LASALLE—See Quebecor Inc.; *Int'l*, pg. 1077
IMPRIMERIE QUEBECOR LEBONFON—See Quebecor Inc.; *Int'l*, pg. 1077
IMPRIMERIE QUEBECOR L'ECLAIREUR—See Quebecor Inc.; *Int'l*, pg. 1077
IMPRIMERIE QUEBECOR MAGOG—See Quebecor Inc.; *Int'l*, pg. 1077
IMPRIMERIE QUEBECOR MONTREAL—See Quebecor Inc.; *Int'l*, pg. 1077
IMPRIMERIE QUEBECOR ST-JEAN—See Quebecor Inc.; *Int'l*, pg. 1077
IMPRIMERIE QUEBECOR ST-ROMUALD—See Quebecor Inc.; *Int'l*, pg. 1077
IMPRIMERIE WALLON—See Nestle S.A.; *Int'l*, pg. 919
IMPRINT NEWPAPERS—See Journal Register Company; *U.S. Public*, pg. 935
IMPROVED BLOW MOLDING EQUIPMENT COMPANY, INC.—See Goodman Equipment Corp.; *U.S. Private*, pg. 464
IMPULS ADVERTISING—See Impuls Advertising AG; *Int'l*, pg. 666
IMPULS ADVERTISING AG; *Int'l*, pg. 666
IMPULS DIRECT—See Impuls Advertising AG; *Int'l*, pg. 666
IMPULSE PRODUCTIONS, INC.—See Playboy Enterprises, Inc.; *U.S. Public*, pg. 1310
IMPULSORA DE BIENES INMUEBLES DE TOLUCA, S.A. DE C.V.—See Tablex, S.A. de C.V.; *Int'l*, pg. 1346
IMSAMET, INC.—See EnviroSource, Inc.; *U.S. Public*, pg. 587

IMTAC (INDUSTRIAL MGMT. TECHNOLOGY & CONTRACTING)—See Hewlett-Packard Company; *U.S. Public*, pg. 822
IMTECH-MAINTENANCE NV—See Internatio-Muller N.V.; *Int'l*, pg. 681
IMTECH PROJECTS NOORD-OOST BV—See Internatio-Muller N.V.; *Int'l*, pg. 681
IMTECH PROJECTS ZUIT B.V.—See Internatio-Muller N.V.; *Int'l*, pg. 681
IN FOCUS SERVICES, INC.—See In Focus Systems, Inc.; *U.S. Public*, pg. 873
IN FOCUS SYSTEMS, INC.; *U.S. Public*, pg. 873
IN-SINK-ERATOR—See Emerson Electric Co.; *U.S. Public*, pg. 573
IN-SITU RESEARCH AND ENGINEERING LTD.—See Scientific Software-Intercomp, Inc.; *U.S. Public*, pg. 1444
IN-STAT INCORPORATED—See Reed Elsevier plc; *Int'l*, pg. 1096
IN STENT ISRAEL—See Medtronic, Inc.; *U.S. Public*, pg. 1083
IN TESTA—See Testa International; *Int'l*, pg. 1377
IN TOWN HOTELS, INC.—See Forest City Enterprises, Inc.; *U.S. Public*, pg. 669
IN TOWN PARKING, INC.—See Forest City Enterprises, Inc.; *U.S. Public*, pg. 669
IN TOWN SHOPPING CENTER, INC.—See Forest City Enterprises, Inc.; *U.S. Public*, pg. 669
INACAN HOLDINGS LTD.—See Cigna Corp.; *U.S. Public*, pg. 366
INACAP - REASEGUROS, SOCIEDAD ANONIMA—See Cigna Corp.; *U.S. Public*, pg. 364
INACAP SOCIEDAD ANONIMA—See Cigna Corp.; *U.S. Public*, pg. 364
INACOM CORP.; *U.S. Public*, pg. 873
INAGUA GENERAL STORE, LTD.—See Morton International Inc.; *U.S. Public*, pg. 1135
INAGUA TRANSPORTS, INC.—See Morton International Inc.; *U.S. Public*, pg. 1135
INAMED B.V.—See Inamed Corporation; *U.S. Public*, pg. 874
INAMED B.V.B.A.—See Inamed Corporation; *U.S. Public*, pg. 874
INAMED CORPORATION; *U.S. Public*, pg. 873
INAMED DEVELOPMENT COMPANY—See Inamed Corporation; *U.S. Public*, pg. 873
INAMED GMBH—See Inamed Corporation; *U.S. Public*, pg. 874
INAMED LTD.—See Inamed Corporation; *U.S. Public*, pg. 874
INAMED S.R.L.—See Inamed Corporation; *U.S. Public*, pg. 874
INAMEX S.A.—See Cigna Corp.; *U.S. Public*, pg. 364
INAPRO, INC.—See Cigna Corp.; *U.S. Public*, pg. 366
INARCO LIMITED—See Armstrong World Industries, Inc.; *U.S. Public*, pg. 132
INATEL S.C.—See Electrabel S.A.; *Int'l*, pg. 437
INAVEN. C.A.—See Cigna Corp.; *U.S. Public*, pg. 363
INBAR COMPUTER TRAINING LTD.—See Onyx Technologies Ltd.; *Int'l*, pg. 1007
INCA INVESTIMENTI SPA ALFA ROMEO ALFASUD—See Fiat Auto SpA; *Int'l*, pg. 481
INCAB S.P.A.—See Julius Meinl AG; *Int'l*, pg. 856
INCEM S.A.—See Fried. Krupp AG; *Int'l*, pg. 512
INCENTIVE—See VNU Verenigde Nederlandse Uitgeversbedrijven B.V.; *Int'l*, pg. 1446
INCENTIVE AB; *Int'l*, pg. 666
INCENTIVE CREDIT AB—See Incentive AB; *Int'l*, pg. 670
INCENTIVE FINANCIAL SERVICES AB—See Incentive AB; *Int'l*, pg. 669
INCENTIVE GROUP INC.—See Incentive AB; *Int'l*, pg. 669
INCENTIVE INTERNATIONAL FINANCE—See Incentive AB; *Int'l*, pg. 669
INCHCAPE BDH—See Inchcape PLC; *Int'l*, pg. 672
INCHCAPE BELGIUM NV/SA—See Inchcape PLC; *Int'l*, pg. 672
INCHCAPE BERHAD—See Inchcape PLC; *Int'l*, pg. 672
INCHCAPE DODWELL K.K.—See Inchcape PLC; *Int'l*, pg. 672
INCHCAPE FAMILY INVESTMENT—See Inchcape PLC; *Int'l*, pg. 671
INCHCAPE GREECE S.A.—See Inchcape PLC; *Int'l*, pg. 672
INCHCAPE INSPECTION & TESTING SERVICES—See Inchcape PLC; *Int'l*, pg. 671
INCHCAPE MANAGEMENT SERVICES LTD.—See Inchcape PLC; *Int'l*, pg. 671
INCHCAPE MIDDLE EAST—See Inchcape PLC; *Int'l*, pg. 672
INCHCAPE MOTORS INTERNATIONAL—See Inchcape PLC; *Int'l*, pg. 672
INCHCAPE PACIFIC LTD.—See Inchcape PLC; *Int'l*, pg. 672
INCHCAPE PLC; *Int'l*, pg. 671
INCHCAPE PLC—See Inchcape PLC; *Int'l*, pg. 671
INCHCAPE SHIPPING SERVICES—See Inchcape PLC; *Int'l*, pg. 672
INCHCAPE TESTING SERVICES—See Inchcape PLC; *Int'l*, pg. 672
INCHCAPE THAILAND LTD.—See Inchcape PLC; *Int'l*, pg. 672
INCHCAPE TIMURAN BHD—See Inchcape PLC; *Int'l*, pg. 672
INCHCAPE (VIETNAM) LTD.—See Inchcape PLC; *Int'l*, pg. 672
INCHON IRON & STEEL CO., LTD.—See Hyundai Motor Company; *Int'l*, pg. 642
INCITEC LTD.—See Imperial Chemical Industries PLC; *Int'l*, pg. 665
INCO ALLOYS INTERNATIONAL, INC.—See Inco Limited; *Int'l*, pg. 672
INCO ALLOYS LIMITED—See Inco Limited; *Int'l*, pg. 672
INCO BRASIL PARTICIPACOES LTDA.—See Inco Limited; *Int'l*, pg. 673

INCO CHILE LTDA.—See Inco Limited; *Int'l*, pg. 673
INCO EUROPE LIMITED—See Inco Limited; *Int'l*, pg. 673
INCO LIMITED; *Int'l*, pg. 672
INCO LIMITED, JAPAN BRANCH—See Inco Limited; *Int'l*, pg. 672
INCO LIMITED, MANITOBA DIVISION—See Inco Limited; *Int'l*, pg. 672
INCO LIMITED, ONTARIO DIVISION—See Inco Limited; *Int'l*, pg. 672
INCO OCEANIE S.A.—See Inco Limited; *Int'l*, pg. 673
INCO PACIFIC SALES LIMITED—See Inco Limited; *Int'l*, pg. 673
INCO SPECIALTY POWDER PRODUCTS—See Inco Limited; *Int'l*, pg. 673
INCO UNITED STATES INC.—See Inco Limited; *Int'l*, pg. 672
INCOGNITO—See Havas Advertising; *Int'l*, pg. 601
INCOR, INC.—See Dale Industries Inc.; *U.S. Private*, pg. 308
INCOR OF ALABAMA—See Dale Industries Inc.; *U.S. Private*, pg. 309
INCOTEST—See Inco Limited; *Int'l*, pg. 673
INCOTHERM LIMITED—See Inco Limited; *Int'l*, pg. 673
INCSTAR B.V.—See Fiat Auto SpA; *Int'l*, pg. 483
INCSTAR CORPORATION—See Fiat Auto SpA; *Int'l*, pg. 483
INCSTAR LTD.—See Fiat Auto SpA; *Int'l*, pg. 483
THE INCTEC INC.—See Dai Nippon Printing Co., Ltd.; *Int'l*, pg. 363
INDECK ENERGY SERVICES, INC.—See Indeck Power Equipment Company; *U.S. Private*, pg. 559
INDECK POWER EQUIPMENT COMPANY; *U.S. Private*, pg. 559
INDECO, INC.—See Johnson Bros. Corporation; *U.S. Private*, pg. 591
INDEMNITY INSURANCE COMPANY OF NORTH AMERICA—See Cigna Corp.; *U.S. Public*, pg. 366
INDEPENDENCE CAPITAL MANAGEMENT, INC.—See The Penn Mutual Life Insurance Company; *U.S. Private*, pg. 849
THE INDEPENDENCE EXAMINER—See Shivers Trading & Operating Co.; *U.S. Private*, pg. 995
INDEPENDENCE HOLDING COMPANY—See Geneve Corporation; *U.S. Private*, pg. 446
INDEPENDENCE INVESTMENT ASSOCIATES, INC.—See John Hancock Mutual Life Insurance Company; *U.S. Private*, pg. 589
INDEPENDENCE SQUARE PROPERTIES—See The Penn Mutual Life Insurance Company; *U.S. Private*, pg. 849
INDEPENDENCE TELEVISION CO.—See Blade Communications, Inc.; *U.S. Private*, pg. 147
INDEPENDENCIA COMPANIA ARGENTINA DE SEGUROS, S.A.—See W.R. Berkley Corporation; *U.S. Public*, pg. 216
INDEPENDENT BANK—See Independent Bank Corporation; *U.S. Public*, pg. 874
INDEPENDENT BANK CORPORATION; *U.S. Public*, pg. 874
INDEPENDENT BANK-EAST MICHIGAN—See Independent Bank Corporation; *U.S. Public*, pg. 874
INDEPENDENT BANK-SOUTH MICHIGAN—See Independent Bank Corporation; *U.S. Public*, pg. 874
INDEPENDENT BANK-WEST MICHIGAN—See Independent Bank Corporation; *U.S. Public*, pg. 874
INDEPENDENT BANKSHARES, INC.; *U.S. Public*, pg. 874
INDEPENDENT CAN COMPANY; *U.S. Private*, pg. 559
INDEPENDENT CEMENT CORPORATION—See Holderbank Financiere Glaris Ltd.; *Int'l*, pg. 629
INDEPENDENT FINANCIAL PLANNERS CORP.—See Orion Capital Corporation; *U.S. Public*, pg. 1231
INDEPENDENT MAIL BV—See KPN Koninklyke PTT Nederland NV; *Int'l*, pg. 720
INDEPENDENT METALS; *U.S. Private*, pg. 559
INDEPENDENT NAIL COMPANY—See Maze Nails; *U.S. Private*, pg. 718
INDEPENDENT PUBLICATIONS, INC.; *U.S. Private*, pg. 559
INDEPENDENT PUBLISHING COMPANY—See Harte-Hanks Communications, Inc.; *U.S. Public*, pg. 794
INDEPENDENT RADIO FEATURES LIMITED—See Dow Jones & Company, Inc.; *U.S. Public*, pg. 525
THE INDEPENDENT RECORD—See Lee Enterprises, Incorporated; *U.S. Public*, pg. 983
INDEPENDENT TOOL & DIE—See Oberg Industries Corp.; *U.S. Private*, pg. 810
INDEPRO INGENIERIA LTDA.—See Outokumpu Oyj; *Int'l*, pg. 1017
INDESIT NEDERLAND N.V.—See Merloni Elettrodomestici S.P.A.; *Int'l*, pg. 860
INDI SERVICIOS C.I. LTDA.—See Cigna Corp.; *U.S. Public*, pg. 363
INDIA PHOTOGRAPHIC COMPANY LIMITED—See Eastman Kodak Company; *U.S. Public*, pg. 552
INDIA RESIDENT MISSION—See Asian Development Bank; *Int'l*, pg. 89
INDIAN ALUMINIUM CO. LTD.—See Alcan Aluminium Limited; *Int'l*, pg. 51
INDIAN CREEK NURSING CENTER—See Horizon/CMS Healthcare Corporation; *U.S. Public*, pg. 837
INDIAN HARBOR INSURANCE COMPANY—See NAC Re Corp.; *U.S. Public*, pg. 1144
INDIAN HEAD INDUSTRIES INC.; *U.S. Private*, pg. 559
INDIAN MEADOWS NURSING CENTER—See Horizon/CMS Healthcare Corporation; *U.S. Public*, pg. 837
INDIAN OIL BLENDING LIMITED—See Indian Oil Corporation Limited; *Int'l*, pg. 673
INDIAN OIL CORPORATION LIMITED; *Int'l*, pg. 673
INDIAN RIVER TRANSPORT CO.; *U.S. Private*, pg. 560
INDIAN ROCKS NATIONAL BANK—See F.N.B. Corporation; *U.S. Public*, pg. 608
INDIAN SHAVING PRODUCTS, LIMITED—See The Gillette Company; *U.S. Public*, pg. 745
INDIANA-AMERICAN WATER CO., INC.—See American Water Works Company, Inc.; *U.S. Public*, pg. 95

INDIANA BELL TELEPHONE COMPANY, INC.—See Ameritech Corporation; *U.S. Public*, pg. 98
INDIANA BROADCASTING CO. (WANE)—See AT&T Corporation; *U.S. Public*, pg. 11
INDIANA BROADCASTING CO. (WISH)—See AT&T Corporation; *U.S. Public*, pg. 11
INDIANA DIGITAL ACCESS—See Time Warner Inc.; *U.S. Public*, pg. 1610
INDIANA ENERGY, INC.; *U.S. Public*, pg. 874
INDIANA FINANCIAL INVESTORS, INC.—See R D I S Corporation; *U.S. Private*, pg. 903
INDIANA FINEBLANKING DIVISION—See Klockner-Werke AG; *Int'l*, pg. 737
INDIANA FRANKLIN REALTY, INC.—See American Electric Power Company, Inc.; *U.S. Public*, pg. 72
INDIANA GAS COMPANY, INC.—See Indiana Energy, Inc.; *U.S. Public*, pg. 874
INDIANA GLASS COMPANY—See Lancaster Colony Corporation; *U.S. Public*, pg. 976
INDIANA HARBOR BELT RAILROAD CO.—See Conrail, Inc.; *U.S. Public*, pg. 432
INDIANA HARDWOODS—See Kimball International, Inc.; *U.S. Public*, pg. 957
INDIANA HARDWOODS, CLOVERPORT MILL—See Kimball International, Inc.; *U.S. Public*, pg. 957
INDIANA INSURANCE COMPANY—See ING Groep N.V.; *Int'l*, pg. 648
INDIANA KENTUCKY ELECTRIC CORPORATION—See Ohio Valley Electric Corporation; *U.S. Public*, pg. 813
INDIANA LAWRENCE BANK—See First Financial Bancorp; *U.S. Public*, pg. 633
INDIANA MANUFACTURING FACILITY—See Monaco Coach Corporation; *U.S. Public*, pg. 1123
INDIANA MICHIGAN POWER COMPANY—See American Electric Power Company, Inc.; *U.S. Public*, pg. 72
INDIANA PICKLING & PROCESSING CORP.—See Preussag AG; *Int'l*, pg. 1070
INDIANA PLANT—See Oglebay Norton Company; *U.S. Public*, pg. 1214
INDIANA RECORDS MANAGERS; *U.S. Private*, pg. 560
INDIANA SEED CO., INC.—See Land O'Lakes, Inc.; *U.S. Private*, pg. 646
INDIANA TITLE INSURANCE COMPANY—See Ameriana Bancorp; *U.S. Public*, pg. 66
INDIANA TUBE CORP.—See Handy & Harman; *U.S. Public*, pg. 780
INDIANA TUBE DANMARK A/S—See Handy & Harman; *U.S. Public*, pg. 780
INDIANAPOLIS LIFE INSURANCE CO.; *U.S. Private*, pg. 560
INDIANAPOLIS NEWSPAPERS, INC.—See Central Newspapers, Inc.; *U.S. Public*, pg. 326
INDIANAPOLIS POWER & LIGHT COMPANY—See Ipalco Enterprises, Inc.; *U.S. Public*, pg. 913
INDIANAPOLIS WATER COMPANY—See NIPSCO Industries, Inc.; *U.S. Public*, pg. 1185
INDIANOLA PRIMARY CARE CLINIC, INC.—See Integrated Health Services, Inc.; *U.S. Public*, pg. 885
INDIGO DEVELOPMENT INC.—See Consolidated-Tomoka Land Co.; *U.S. Public*, pg. 437
INDIGO GROUP INC.—See Consolidated-Tomoka Land Co.; *U.S. Public*, pg. 437
INDIGO GROUP LTD.—See Consolidated-Tomoka Land Co.; *U.S. Public*, pg. 437
INDIMAC AGENCY, INC.—See INMC Mortgage Holdings, Inc.; *U.S. Public*, pg. 857
INDIMAC HOME IMPROVEMENT DIVISION—See INMC Mortgage Holdings, Inc.; *U.S. Public*, pg. 857
INDIMAC, INC.—See INMC Mortgage Holdings, Inc.; *U.S. Public*, pg. 857
INDIMAC MANUFACTURED HOUSING DIVISION—See INMC Mortgage Holdings, Inc.; *U.S. Public*, pg. 857
INDIMAC MORTGAGE OBLIGATIONS, II, INC.—See INMC Mortgage Holdings, Inc.; *U.S. Public*, pg. 856
INDIMAC MORTGAGE OBLIGATIONS, INC.—See INMC Mortgage Holdings, Inc.; *U.S. Public*, pg. 858
INDIMAC THIRD PARTY CONSTRUCTION LENDING DIVISION—See INMC Mortgage Holdings, Inc.; *U.S. Public*, pg. 857
INDISCO GMBH—See Sophus Berendsen A/S; *Int'l*, pg. 1286
INDISCO NEDERLAND BV—See Sophus Berendsen A/S; *Int'l*, pg. 1286
INDIVERS B.V.; *Int'l*, pg. 673
INDO BALZERS COATING LTD.—See Oerlikon-Buhrle Holding AG; *Int'l*, pg. 997
INDO NISSIN FOODS LTD.—See Nissin Food Products Co., Ltd.; *Int'l*, pg. 950
INDO-PACIFIC ENERGY LTD.—See Durum Energy Corp.; *Int'l*, pg. 422
INDO RAMA SYNTHETICS P.T.; *Int'l*, pg. 673
INDOCO, INC.—See Browning-Ferris Industries, Inc.; *U.S. Public*, pg. 264
P.T. INDOFOOD JAYA RAYA—See Nestle S.A.; *Int'l*, pg. 920
INDOMAG STEEL TECHNOLOGY PRIVATE LTD.—See Mannesmann A.G.; *Int'l*, pg. 837
P.T. INDOMOBIL SUZUKI INTERNATIONAL—See Suzuki Motor Corporation; *Int'l*, pg. 1323
P.T. INDONESIA DAI-ICHI KANGYO BANK—See The Dai-Ichi Kangyo Bank, Limited; *Int'l*, pg. 362
INDONESIA RESIDENT MISSION—See Asian Development Bank; *Int'l*, pg. 89
P.T. INDONESIA STEEL TUBE WORKS LTD.—See Nissho Iwai Corporation; *Int'l*, pg. 948
P.T. INDONESIA TORAY SYNTHETICS—See Mitsui & Co., Ltd.; *Int'l*, pg. 882
INDONESIA WACOAL CO., LTD.—See Wacoal Corporation; *Int'l*, pg. 1484
INDOSAT—See Oracle Corporation; *U.S. Public*, pg. 1228
INDOSUEZ CAPITAL EMERGING MARKETS—See Compagnie de Suez; *Int'l*, pg. 314
INDOSUEZ CAPITAL LTD.—See Compagnie de Suez; *Int'l*, pg. 314

INDOSUEZ CAPITAL SECURITIES (UK) LTD.—See Compagnie de Suez; *Int'l*, pg. 314
INDOSUEZ CAPITAL (US)—See Compagnie de Suez; *Int'l*, pg. 314
INDOSUEZ CARR FUTURES INC.—See Compagnie de Suez; *Int'l*, pg. 314
INDOSUEZ STRUCTURED FINANCE INTERNATIONAL—See Compagnie de Suez; *Int'l*, pg. 314
INDOSUEZ VENTURES—See Compagnie de Suez; *Int'l*, pg. 314
P.T. INDOTAISEI INDAH DEVELOPMENT—See Taisei Corporation; *Int'l*, pg. 1347
INDRA AB—See Nestle S.A.; *Int'l*, pg. 920
INDRAMAT GMBH—See Mannesmann A.G.; *Int'l*, pg. 838
INDUBOIS S.A.—See The East Asiatic Company Ltd. A/S; *Int'l*, pg. 431
INDUCTOHEAT PTY. LTD.—See Inductotherm Industries, Inc.; *U.S. Private*, pg. 560
INDUCTOTHERM CORP.—See Inductotherm Industries, Inc.; *U.S. Private*, pg. 560
INDUCTOTHERM INDUSTRIES, INC.; *U.S. Private*, pg. 560
INDUCTUS/INDUSTRIAL OPERATIONS—See AB Industrivarden; *Int'l*, pg. 678
INDUFOR (1975) N.V.—See The East Asiatic Company Ltd. A/S; *Int'l*, pg. 431
INDUGAS N.V.—See Praxair Inc.; *U.S. Public*, pg. 1320
INDUGEST S.A.R.L.—See Commerzbank AG; *Int'l*, pg. 312
INDUMAT GMBH & CO. KG—See Linde AG; *Int'l*, pg. 811
INDUMOB, S.A.—See Vallehermoso, S.A.; *Int'l*, pg. 1447
INDUPLAS SPA—See Smiths Industries plc; *Int'l*, pg. 1268
INDUPLAST—See ETEX; *Int'l*, pg. 430
INDUPLEX, INC.—See RGP Holding, Inc.; *U.S. Private*, pg. 904
INDUSQUIMA S.A.—See Henkel KGaA; *Int'l*, pg. 613
INDUSTAR B.V.—See Charter plc; *Int'l*, pg. 283
INDUSTICK GMBH—See Veba AG; *Int'l*, pg. 1458
INDUSTRA INC.—See American Eco Corporation; *Int'l*, pg. 74
INDUSTRA SERVICE CORP. - ALBERTA—See American Eco Corporation; *Int'l*, pg. 74
INDUSTRA SERVICE CORPORATION—See American Eco Corporation; *Int'l*, pg. 74
INDUSTRA THERMAL SERVICE CORPORATION—See American Eco Corporation; *Int'l*, pg. 74
INDUSTRI AB THULE—See Eldon AB; *Int'l*, pg. 436
INDUSTRIA AERONAUTICA NEIVA S.A.—See Embraer-Empresa Brasileira de Aeronautica S.A.; *Int'l*, pg. 452
INDUSTRIA CENTROAMERICANA DE SANITARIOS, S.A.—See American Standard Inc.; *U.S. Public*, pg. 92
INDUSTRIA CERAMICA CENTROAMERICANA, S.A.—See American Standard Inc.; *U.S. Public*, pg. 92
INDUSTRIA DE PNEUMATICOS FIRESTONE LTDA.—See Bridgestone Corporation; *Int'l*, pg. 215
INDUSTRIA DE PRODUCTOS ALIMENTICIOS CONFIANZA S.A.—See Nestle S.A.; *Int'l*, pg. 920
INDUSTRIA DE SUCOS BOLS LTDA.—See Koninklijke BolsWessanen nv; *Int'l*, pg. 752
INDUSTRIA E COMERCIO METALURGICA ATLAS S.A.—See S.A. Industrias Votorantim; *Int'l*, pg. 677
INDUSTRIA E COMERCIO VITRONAC LTDA.—See Carl-Zeiss-Stiftung; *Int'l*, pg. 1523
INDUSTRIA FOTOGRAFICA INTERAMERICANA S.A. DE C.V.—See Eastman Kodak Company; *U.S. Public*, pg. 554
INDUSTRIA FREIOS KNORR LTDA.—See Knorr-Bremse AG; *Int'l*, pg. 738
INDUSTRIA MAQUINAS E EQUIPAMENTOS ELECTRICOS LIMITADA—See ABB Asea Brown Boveri (Holding) Ltd.; *Int'l*, pg. 3
INDUSTRIA MEXICANA DE FOTOCOPIADORAS, S.A. DE C.V.—See Eastman Kodak Company; *U.S. Public*, pg. 554
INDUSTRIA NACIONAL DE CEMENTO S.A.—See Holderbank Financiere Glaris Ltd.; *Int'l*, pg. 630
INDUSTRIA NAVARRIA DEL ALUMINIO, S.A.—See Reynolds Metals Company; *U.S. Public*, pg. 1387
INDUSTRIA PANAMENA DE PAPEL, S.A.—See Georgia-Pacific Corporation; *U.S. Public*, pg. 739
INDUSTRIA QUIMICA DEL ISTMO, S.A. DE C.V.—See CYDSA S.A.; *Int'l*, pg. 246
INDUSTRIAL ACOUSTICS COMPANY GMBH—See Industrial Acoustics Company, Inc.; *U.S. Public*, pg. 875
INDUSTRIAL ACOUSTICS COMPANY, INC.; *U.S. Public*, pg. 875
INDUSTRIAL ACOUSTICS COMPANY, LTD.—See Industrial Acoustics Company, Inc.; *U.S. Public*, pg. 875
INDUSTRIAL ACOUSTICS COMPANY S.C. INC.—See Industrial Acoustics Company, Inc.; *U.S. Public*, pg. 875
INDUSTRIAL ADHESIVES LTD.—See Burmah Castrol plc; *Int'l*, pg. 234
INDUSTRIAL ALLOYS, INC.—See Industrial Wire Products Corporation; *U.S. Private*, pg. 561
INDUSTRIAL AMERICAS GROUP—See Aeroquip-Vickers, Inc.; *U.S. Public*, pg. 24
INDUSTRIAL & AUTOMOTIVE FASTENERS, INC.—See JPE, Inc.; *U.S. Public*, pg. 919
THE INDUSTRIAL AND COMMERCIAL BANK OF CHINA—See Swedbank; *Int'l*, pg. 1328
INDUSTRIAL & COMMERCIAL INTERNATIONAL LEASING CO., LTD.—See The Tokai Bank, Limited; *Int'l*, pg. 1391
INDUSTRIAL & OFFSHORE COMPUTER SERVICES (S) PTE. LTD.—See CSA Holdings Ltd.; *Int'l*, pg. 242
INDUSTRIAL AND TECHNICAL SUPPLIES (I.T.S.) JAMAICA, LTD.—See Hewlett-Packard Company; *U.S. Public*, pg. 822
INDUSTRIAL & TRANSPORTATION EQUIPMENT CO.—See American Grain & Related Industries; *U.S. Private*, pg. 55
INDUSTRIAL AUTOMATION DIVISION—See ABB Asea Brown Boveri (Holding) Ltd.; *Int'l*, pg. 4
INDUSTRIAL BANK OF FINLAND LTD.—See Merita Ltd.; *Int'l*, pg. 859

THE INDUSTRIAL BANK OF JAPAN (CANADA)—See The Industrial Bank of Japan, Limited; *Int'l*, pg. 676
THE INDUSTRIAL BANK OF JAPAN (KUALA LUMPUR)—See The Industrial Bank of Japan, Limited; *Int'l*, pg. 675
THE INDUSTRIAL BANK OF JAPAN, LIMITED (AKASAKA BRANCH)—See The Industrial Bank of Japan, Limited; *Int'l*, pg. 674
THE INDUSTRIAL BANK OF JAPAN, LIMITED (BAHRAIN)—See The Industrial Bank of Japan, Limited; *Int'l*, pg. 675
THE INDUSTRIAL BANK OF JAPAN, LIMITED (BANGKOK)—See The Industrial Bank of Japan, Limited; *Int'l*, pg. 675
THE INDUSTRIAL BANK OF JAPAN, LIMITED (BEIJING)—See The Industrial Bank of Japan, Limited; *Int'l*, pg. 675
THE INDUSTRIAL BANK OF JAPAN, LIMITED BERLIN—See The Industrial Bank of Japan, Limited; *Int'l*, pg. 675
THE INDUSTRIAL BANK OF JAPAN, LIMITED (CANADA)—See The Industrial Bank of Japan, Limited; *Int'l*, pg. 675
THE INDUSTRIAL BANK OF JAPAN, LIMITED (CHICAGO BRANCH)—See The Industrial Bank of Japan, Limited; *Int'l*, pg. 674
THE INDUSTRIAL BANK OF JAPAN, LIMITED (DALIAN)—See The Industrial Bank of Japan, Limited; *Int'l*, pg. 675
THE INDUSTRIAL BANK OF JAPAN, LIMITED (FRANKFURT)—See The Industrial Bank of Japan, Limited; *Int'l*, pg. 675
THE INDUSTRIAL BANK OF JAPAN, LIMITED (FUKUOKA BRANCH)—See The Industrial Bank of Japan, Limited; *Int'l*, pg. 674
THE INDUSTRIAL BANK OF JAPAN, LIMITED (FUKUSHIMA BRANCH)—See The Industrial Bank of Japan, Limited; *Int'l*, pg. 674
THE INDUSTRIAL BANK OF JAPAN, LIMITED (GUANGZHOU)—See The Industrial Bank of Japan, Limited; *Int'l*, pg. 675
THE INDUSTRIAL BANK OF JAPAN, LIMITED (HIROSHIMA BRANCH)—See The Industrial Bank of Japan, Limited; *Int'l*, pg. 674
THE INDUSTRIAL BANK OF JAPAN, LIMITED (HONG KONG BRANCH)—See The Industrial Bank of Japan, Limited; *Int'l*, pg. 675
THE INDUSTRIAL BANK OF JAPAN, LIMITED (HOUSTON)—See The Industrial Bank of Japan, Limited; *Int'l*, pg. 674
THE INDUSTRIAL BANK OF JAPAN, LIMITED (IKEBUKURO BRANCH)—See The Industrial Bank of Japan, Limited; *Int'l*, pg. 674
THE INDUSTRIAL BANK OF JAPAN, LIMITED (JAKARTA)—See The Industrial Bank of Japan, Limited; *Int'l*, pg. 675
THE INDUSTRIAL BANK OF JAPAN, LIMITED (KOBE BRANCH)—See The Industrial Bank of Japan, Limited; *Int'l*, pg. 674
THE INDUSTRIAL BANK OF JAPAN, LIMITED (KYOTO BRANCH)—See The Industrial Bank of Japan, Limited; *Int'l*, pg. 674
THE INDUSTRIAL BANK OF JAPAN, LIMITED (LONDON BRANCH)—See The Industrial Bank of Japan, Limited; *Int'l*, pg. 675
THE INDUSTRIAL BANK OF JAPAN, LIMITED (LOS ANGELES AGENCY)—See The Industrial Bank of Japan, Limited; *Int'l*, pg. 674
THE INDUSTRIAL BANK OF JAPAN, LIMITED (MACHIDA BRANCH)—See The Industrial Bank of Japan, Limited; *Int'l*, pg. 674
THE INDUSTRIAL BANK OF JAPAN, LIMITED (MADRID BRANCH)—See The Industrial Bank of Japan, Limited; *Int'l*, pg. 675
THE INDUSTRIAL BANK OF JAPAN, LIMITED (MEXICO)—See The Industrial Bank of Japan, Limited; *Int'l*, pg. 675
THE INDUSTRIAL BANK OF JAPAN, LIMITED (MILAN)—See The Industrial Bank of Japan, Limited; *Int'l*, pg. 675
THE INDUSTRIAL BANK OF JAPAN, LIMITED (NAGOYA BRANCH)—See The Industrial Bank of Japan, Limited; *Int'l*, pg. 674
THE INDUSTRIAL BANK OF JAPAN, LIMITED (NEW YORK BRANCH)—See The Industrial Bank of Japan, Limited; *Int'l*, pg. 674
THE INDUSTRIAL BANK OF JAPAN, LIMITED (NIHONBASHI BRANCH)—See The Industrial Bank of Japan, Limited; *Int'l*, pg. 674
THE INDUSTRIAL BANK OF JAPAN, LIMITED (NIIGATA BRANCH)—See The Industrial Bank of Japan, Limited; *Int'l*, pg. 674
THE INDUSTRIAL BANK OF JAPAN, LIMITED (OSAKA BRANCH)—See The Industrial Bank of Japan, Limited; *Int'l*, pg. 674
THE INDUSTRIAL BANK OF JAPAN, LIMITED (PANAMA)—See The Industrial Bank of Japan, Limited; *Int'l*, pg. 675
THE INDUSTRIAL BANK OF JAPAN, LIMITED (PARIS BRANCH)—See The Industrial Bank of Japan, Limited; *Int'l*, pg. 675
THE INDUSTRIAL BANK OF JAPAN, LIMITED (RIO DE JANEIRO)—See The Industrial Bank of Japan, Limited; *Int'l*, pg. 675
THE INDUSTRIAL BANK OF JAPAN, LIMITED (SAN FRANCISCO)—See The Industrial Bank of Japan, Limited; *Int'l*, pg. 674
THE INDUSTRIAL BANK OF JAPAN, LIMITED (SAO PAULO)—See The Industrial Bank of Japan, Limited; *Int'l*, pg. 675
THE INDUSTRIAL BANK OF JAPAN, LIMITED (SAPPORO BRANCH)—See The Industrial Bank of Japan, Limited; *Int'l*, pg. 674

THE INDUSTRIAL BANK OF JAPAN, LIMITED (SENDAI BRANCH)—See The Industrial Bank of Japan, Limited; *Int'l*, pg. 674
THE INDUSTRIAL BANK OF JAPAN, LIMITED (SEOUL)—See The Industrial Bank of Japan, Limited; *Int'l*, pg. 675
THE INDUSTRIAL BANK OF JAPAN, LIMITED (SHANGHAI)—See The Industrial Bank of Japan, Limited; *Int'l*, pg. 675
THE INDUSTRIAL BANK OF JAPAN, LIMITED (SHIBUYA BRANCH)—See The Industrial Bank of Japan, Limited; *Int'l*, pg. 674
THE INDUSTRIAL BANK OF JAPAN, LIMITED (SHINJUKU BRANCH)—See The Industrial Bank of Japan, Limited; *Int'l*, pg. 674
THE INDUSTRIAL BANK OF JAPAN, LIMITED (SHIZUOKA BRANCH)—See The Industrial Bank of Japan, Limited; *Int'l*, pg. 674
THE INDUSTRIAL BANK OF JAPAN, LIMITED (SINGAPORE BRANCH)—See The Industrial Bank of Japan, Limited; *Int'l*, pg. 675
THE INDUSTRIAL BANK OF JAPAN, LIMITED (SYDNEY)—See The Industrial Bank of Japan, Limited; *Int'l*, pg. 675
THE INDUSTRIAL BANK OF JAPAN, LIMITED (TAKAMATSU BRANCH)—See The Industrial Bank of Japan, Limited; *Int'l*, pg. 674
THE INDUSTRIAL BANK OF JAPAN, LIMITED; *Int'l*, pg. 674
THE INDUSTRIAL BANK OF JAPAN, LIMITED (TOKYO BRANCH)—See The Industrial Bank of Japan, Limited; *Int'l*, pg. 674
THE INDUSTRIAL BANK OF JAPAN, LIMITED (TORANOMON BRANCH)—See The Industrial Bank of Japan, Limited; *Int'l*, pg. 674
THE INDUSTRIAL BANK OF JAPAN, LIMITED (TOYAMA BRANCH)—See The Industrial Bank of Japan, Limited; *Int'l*, pg. 674
THE INDUSTRIAL BANK OF JAPAN, LIMITED (WASHINGTON)—See The Industrial Bank of Japan, Limited; *Int'l*, pg. 674
THE INDUSTRIAL BANK OF JAPAN, LIMITED (YOKOHAMA BRANCH)—See The Industrial Bank of Japan, Limited; *Int'l*, pg. 674
THE INDUSTRIAL BANK OF JAPAN LIMITED (ZURICH)—See The Industrial Bank of Japan, Limited; *Int'l*, pg. 675
THE INDUSTRIAL BANK OF JAPAN (LUXEMBOURG) S.A.—See The Industrial Bank of Japan, Limited; *Int'l*, pg. 676
THE INDUSTRIAL BANK OF JAPAN (SWITZERLAND) LIMITED—See The Industrial Bank of Japan, Limited; *Int'l*, pg. 676
THE INDUSTRIAL BANK OF JAPAN TRUST COMPANY—See The Industrial Bank of Japan, Limited; *Int'l*, pg. 675
THE INDUSTRIAL BANK OF JAPAN TRUST COMPANY (ATLANTA AGENCY)—See The Industrial Bank of Japan, Limited; *Int'l*, pg. 675
THE INDUSTRIAL BANK OF JAPAN TRUST COMPANY (NASSAU BRANCH)—See The Industrial Bank of Japan, Limited; *Int'l*, pg. 675
INDUSTRIAL BOOKSTORE—See Manufacturers' News, Inc.; *U.S. Private*, pg. 701
INDUSTRIAL BRUGER SA—See Akzo Nobel N.V.; *Int'l*, pg. 43
INDUSTRIAL BUILDING COMPONENTS LTD.—See Expamet International Plc; *Int'l*, pg. 467
INDUSTRIAL BURNER SYSTEMS—See Eclipse Inc.; *U.S. Private*, pg. 360
INDUSTRIAL CERAMICS, INC.; *U.S. Private*, pg. 560
INDUSTRIAL CHEMICAL & EQUIPMENT—See Hawkins Chemical, Inc.; *U.S. Public*, pg. 800
INDUSTRIAL CLINIC—See Vencor, Inc.; *U.S. Public*, pg. 1715
INDUSTRIAL COATINGS DIV.—See H.B. Fuller Company; *U.S. Public*, pg. 687
INDUSTRIAL COATINGS GROUP, INC.—See GCI Holdings Corporation; *U.S. Private*, pg. 434
INDUSTRIAL COMPONENTS-GRAVENHAGE B.V.—See Halliburton Company; *U.S. Public*, pg. 777
INDUSTRIAL COMPONENTS GROUP—See BTR plc; *Int'l*, pg. 127
INDUSTRIAL COMPUTER SOURCE, INC.—See Dynatech Corporation; *U.S. Public*, pg. 539
INDUSTRIAL CONSTRUCTION, INC.; *U.S. Private*, pg. 560
INDUSTRIAL CONTRACTING OF FAIRMONT, INC.—See Salem Group, Inc.; *U.S. Private*, pg. 961
INDUSTRIAL CONTROL GROUP—See Rockwell International Corporation; *U.S. Public*, pg. 1397
INDUSTRIAL CREDIT COMPANY LTD.—See Standard Chartered Bank PLC; *Int'l*, pg. 1297
S.A. INDUSTRIAL CURACAO COSTA RICA—See Ceteco N.V.; *Int'l*, pg. 280
INDUSTRIAL CUSTOM PRODUCTS L.L.C.—See E & A Industries, Inc.; *U.S. Private*, pg. 352
INDUSTRIAL DEPARTMENT (DEPIN)—See Petrobras - Petroleo Brasileiro S.A.; *Int'l*, pg. 1042
INDUSTRIAL DETERGENTS, LTD.—See Henkel KGaA; *Int'l*, pg. 612
INDUSTRIAL DIELECTRICS, INC.; *U.S. Private*, pg. 560
INDUSTRIAL DISTRIBUTION AND OEM, NORTH AMERICA—See Mark IV Industries Inc.; *U.S. Public*, pg. 1045
INDUSTRIAL DISTRIBUTION GROUP; *U.S. Public*, pg. 875
INDUSTRIAL ELECTRICAL PRODUCTS—See Thomas & Betts Corporation; *U.S. Public*, pg. 1598
INDUSTRIAL ELECTRONIC ENGINEERS, INC.; *U.S. Private*, pg. 561
INDUSTRIAL ELECTRONICS GROUP—See Raytheon Company; *U.S. Public*, pg. 1364
INDUSTRIAL ENERGY APPLICATIONS—See IES Industries Inc.; *U.S. Public*, pg. 855

INDUSTRIAL ENVIRONMENTAL PRODUCTS, INC.—See Oil-Dri Corporation of America; *U.S. Public*, pg. 1215
INDUSTRIAL EQUIPMENT NEWS—See Thomas Publishing Company; *U.S. Private*, pg. 1082
INDUSTRIAL EQUITY LIMITED; *Int'l*, pg. 676
INDUSTRIAL FASTENERS LTD.—See Haden Maclellan Holdings plc; *Int'l*, pg. 585
INDUSTRIAL FINANCE CORPORATION LIMITED—See The Bank of Nova Scotia; *Int'l*, pg. 156
THE INDUSTRIAL FINANCE CORPORATION OF THAILAND; *Int'l*, pg. 677
INDUSTRIAL FINANCE HOLDINGS LIMITED—See The Bank of Nova Scotia; *Int'l*, pg. 156
INDUSTRIAL GALVANIZERS CORPORATION PTY. LTD.—See Delta plc; *Int'l*, pg. 391
INDUSTRIAL GASES LTD.—See The BOC Group plc; *Int'l*, pg. 122
INDUSTRIAL INDEMNITY COMPANY—See Fremont General Corporation; *U.S. Public*, pg. 681
INDUSTRIAL INDEMNITY FINANCIAL CORPORATION—See Fremont General Corporation; *U.S. Public*, pg. 681
INDUSTRIAL INDEMNITY INSURANCE SERVICES, INC.—See Fremont General Corporation; *U.S. Public*, pg. 681
INDUSTRIAL INFORMATION HEADQUARTERS CO.—See Bearing Headquarters Co.; *U.S. Private*, pg. 127
INDUSTRIAL LATEX ADHESIVES LTD.—See The Dow Chemical Company; *U.S. Public*, pg. 523
INDUSTRIAL LATEX COMPOUNDS LTD.—See The Dow Chemical Company; *U.S. Public*, pg. 523
INDUSTRIAL LAUNDRY GROUP OF AMERCLEAN—See Dober Chemical Corp.; *U.S. Private*, pg. 337
INDUSTRIAL MAINTENANCE CORP.—See Ecolab Inc.; *U.S. Public*, pg. 562
INDUSTRIAL MAINTENANCE OVERFLOW CORPORATION; *U.S. Private*, pg. 561
INDUSTRIAL MATERIAL DISTRIBUTORS—See International Paper Company; *U.S. Public*, pg. 903
INDUSTRIAL METALS OF THE SOUTH; *U.S. Private*, pg. 561
INDUSTRIAL MINERA SA—See Svedala Industri AB; *Int'l*, pg. 1323
INDUSTRIAL PAPELERA MEXICANA S.A. DE C.V.—See Copamex Industrias S.A. de C.V.; *Int'l*, pg. 330
INDUSTRIAL PHARMACEUTICAL PRODUCTS DIVISION—See Royal Gist-Brocades N.V.; *Int'l*, pg. 1142
INDUSTRIAL PLASTICS COMPANY—See Alltrista Corporation; *U.S. Public*, pg. 56
INDUSTRIAL POWDER COATINGS, INC.—See Intermet Corporation; *U.S. Public*, pg. 894
INDUSTRIAL/PROCESS DIVISION—See Morrison Knudsen Corporation; *U.S. Public*, pg. 1134
INDUSTRIAL RESEARCH (SUPESQ)—See Petrobras - Petroleo Brasileiro S.A.; *Int'l*, pg. 1042
INDUSTRIAL RESINS (MALAYSIA) SDN. BHD.—See Tosoh Corporation; *Int'l*, pg. 1408
INDUSTRIAL RESINS (MALAYSIA) SDN. BHD.-JOHOR BAHARU PLANT—See Tosoh Corporation; *Int'l*, pg. 1408
INDUSTRIAL RESOURCES, INC.—See Salem Group, Inc.; *U.S. Private*, pg. 961
INDUSTRIAL RETAINING RING COMPANY—See TransTechnology Corporation; *U.S. Public*, pg. 1632
INDUSTRIAL RUBBER GOODS—See The Chardon Rubber Co.; *U.S. Private*, pg. 229
INDUSTRIAL RUBBER PRODUCTS COMPANY; *U.S. Private*, pg. 561
INDUSTRIAL SERVICES—See Det Norske Veritas; *Int'l*, pg. 396
INDUSTRIAL STEEL & WIRE COMPANY; *U.S. Private*, pg. 561
INDUSTRIAL TIRES INCORPORATED—See Cascade Corporation; *U.S. Public*, pg. 311
INDUSTRIAL TOWEL & UNIFORM; *U.S. Private*, pg. 561
INDUSTRIAL WASTE MANAGEMENT, INC.—See Perma-Fix Environmental Services, Inc.; *U.S. Public*, pg. 1279
INDUSTRIAL WATER TREATMENT CO.—See Air Liquide S.A.; *Int'l*, pg. 37
INDUSTRIAL WIRE PRODUCTS CORPORATION; *U.S. Private*, pg. 561
INDUSTRIAS ALIMENTICIAS CLUB S.A.—See Nestle S.A.; *Int'l*, pg. 920
INDUSTRIAS BACHOCO S.A. DE C.V.; *Int'l*, pg. 677
INDUSTRIAS BRASILEIRAS ARTIGOS REFRATARIOS S.A.—See S.A. Industrias Votorantim; *Int'l*, pg. 677
INDUSTRIAS CH, S.A. DE C.V.; *Int'l*, pg. 677
INDUSTRIAS CHILENAS DE ALAMBRE INCHALAM S.A.—See N.V. Bekaert S.A.; *Int'l*, pg. 185
INDUSTRIAS COUSIN FRERES—See Bertrand Faure; *Int'l*, pg. 193
INDUSTRIAS CYDSA BAYER, S.A. DE C.V.—See CYDSA S.A.; *Int'l*, pg. 246
INDUSTRIAS DE MAIZ Y ALIMENTOS S.A.—See Corn Products International, Inc.; *U.S. Public*, pg. 447
INDUSTRIAS DE TABLEROS Y DERIVADOS DE LA MADERA, S.A.—See International Paper Company; *U.S. Public*, pg. 905
INDUSTRIAS DE TELECOMMUNICACION S.A. (INTELSA)—See Telefonaktiebolaget LM Ericsson; *Int'l*, pg. 1368
INDUSTRIAS DEL LACADO, S.A. (INDULACSA)—See Reynolds Metals Company; *U.S. Public*, pg. 1387
INDUSTRIAS DEL MAIZ S.A.—See Corn Products International, Inc.; *U.S. Public*, pg. 447
INDUSTRIAS DEL UBIERNA, S.A.—See N.V. Bekaert S.A.; *Int'l*, pg. 184
INDUSTRIAS ELECTRICAS DE QUILMES—See Telefonaktiebolaget LM Ericsson; *Int'l*, pg. 1368
INDUSTRIAS FARMACEUTICAS FONTOURA WYETH S.A.—See American Home Products Corporation; *U.S. Public*, pg. 81
INDUSTRIAS GESSY LEVER LTDA.—See Unilever Plc; *Int'l*, pg. 1437
INDUSTRIAS GOMARIZ, S.A.—See Reynolds Metals Company; *U.S. Public*, pg. 1387

INDUSTRIAS KOLMEX, S.A.—See MacAndrews & Forbes Holdings Inc.; *U.S. Private*, pg. 690
INDUSTRIAS LA FAMOSA, INC.—See Borden, Inc.; *U.S. Private*, pg. 158
INDUSTRIAS LEVER PORTUGUESA, LDA.—See Unilever Plc; *Int'l*, pg. 1437
INDUSTRIAS LUBRIZOL S.A. DE C.V.—See The Lubrizol Corporation; *U.S. Public*, pg. 1017
INDUSTRIAS MERRIMAC INCORPORADA, S.A.—See Merrimac Industries, Inc.; *U.S. Private*, pg. 1098
INDUSTRIAS METALURGICAS LIEBAU S.A.—See FKI Plc; *Int'l*, pg. 473
INDUSTRIAS NACOBRE SA DE CV—See Grupo Carso S.A. de C.V.; *Int'l*, pg. 572
INDUSTRIAS OXFORD DE MERIDA, S.A. DE C.V.—See Oxford Industries, Inc.; *U.S. Public*, pg. 1239
INDUSTRIAS PACOCHA S.A. (UNILEVER)—See Unilever Plc; *Int'l*, pg. 1437
INDUSTRIAS PENOLES S.A. DE C.V.; *Int'l*, pg. 677
INDUSTRIAS PURINA, S.A. DE C.V.—See Ralston Purina Company; *U.S. Public*, pg. 1360
INDUSTRIAS PYROLAS, S.A.—See Dainippon Ink & Chemicals, Inc.; *Int'l*, pg. 371
INDUSTRIAS QUIMICAS ASOCIADAS, S.A.—See Royal Dutch/Shell Group of Companies; *Int'l*, pg. 1139
INDUSTRIAS QUIMICAS CARABOBO, C.A.—See Novartis AG; *Int'l*, pg. 982
INDUSTRIAS QUIMICAS DE NAVARRA, S.A.—See Novartis AG; *Int'l*, pg. 982
INDUSTRIAS QUIMICAS RESENDE S.A.—See Novartis AG; *Int'l*, pg. 983
INDUSTRIAS QUIRURGICAS DE LEVANTE, S.A.—See Biomet, Inc.; *U.S. Public*, pg. 232
INDUSTRIAS RESISTOL, S.A.—See Monsanto Company; *U.S. Public*, pg. 1125
INDUSTRIAS SOLA BASIC—See General Signal Corporation; *U.S. Public*, pg. 727
INDUSTRIAS TRANSFORMADORAS DEL CEMENTO ETERNIT S.A.—See Redland PLC; *Int'l*, pg. 1092
INDUSTRIAS TRATERH, S.A.—See Senior Engineering Group, plc.; *Int'l*, pg. 1222
INDUSTRIAS UNIVERSALES UNIONS DE MEXICO SA—See Superior Industries International, Inc.; *U.S. Public*, pg. 1539
INDUSTRIAS VENEZOLANAS VAN LEER, C.A.—See Royal Packaging Industries Van Leer B.V.; *Int'l*, pg. 1146
S.A. INDUSTRIAS VOTORANTIM; *Int'l*, pg. 677
INDUSTRIAS WYETH S.A.—See American Home Products Corporation; *U.S. Public*, pg. 81
INDUSTRIE-BETEILIGUNGS GESELLSCHAFTMBH—See BHF-BANK AG; *Int'l*, pg. 119
INDUSTRIE CAVI SUD-AZIENDA SOTIS—See Pirelli S.p.A.; *Int'l*, pg. 1058
INDUSTRIE DE FROID S.A.E.—See Nestle S.A.; *Int'l*, pg. 920
INDUSTRIE-EN HANDELSONDERNEMING BERNARD REIJN B.V.—See Gamma Holding N.V.; *Int'l*, pg. 540
INDUSTRIE HELLENIQUE DE DETERGENTS S.A. (E.V.A.)—See Unilever Plc; *Int'l*, pg. 1437
INDUSTRIE-IMMOBILIEN-VERWALTUNG GMBH—See Creditanstalt-Bankverein; *Int'l*, pg. 347
INDUSTRIE MAGNETI MARELLI S.R.L.—See Fiat Auto SpA; *Int'l*, pg. 482
INDUSTRIE-RING SACH-UND VERSICHERUNGS-VERMITTLUNGSGESELLSCHAFT MBH—See Saarbergwerke Aktiengesellschaft; *Int'l*, pg. 1166
INDUSTRIE STAMPI E STAMPAGGIO LAMIERE BERTO-LAMET-IMPES S.P.A.—See Fiat Auto SpA; *Int'l*, pg. 482
INDUSTRIE- UND FORST VERWALTUNG AG—See Creditanstalt-Bankverein; *Int'l*, pg. 347
INDUSTRIE-UND KRAFTWERKSROHRLEITUNGSBAU BITTERFELD GMBH—See Deutsche Babcock AG; *Int'l*, pg. 399
INDUSTRIE VERNICI ITALIANE S.R.L.—See Fiat Auto SpA; *Int'l*, pg. 482
INDUSTRIEBANK VON JAPAN (DEUTSCHLAND) AKTIENGESELLSCHAFT—See The Industrial Bank of Japan, Limited; *Int'l*, pg. 676
INDUSTRIEN CHIMIQUES MAGHREBINES COMPANY—See Kuwait Petroleum Corporation; *Int'l*, pg. 766
INDUSTRIES CASCADES INC.—See The Cascades Group; *Int'l*, pg. 273
INDUSTRIES MECANIQUES MAGHREBINES—See Isuzu Motors Limited; *Int'l*, pg. 693
INDUSTRIESCHUTZ ASSEKURANZ VERMITTLUNG GMBH—See Mannesmann A.G.; *Int'l*, pg. 836
INDUSTRIEWERK OBERURSEL GMBH—See Mannesmann A.G.; *Int'l*, pg. 839
INDUSTRIEWERK WEILMUNSTER GMBH—See Mannesmann A.G.; *Int'l*, pg. 839
INDUSTRIFILTER AB—See Trelleborg AB; *Int'l*, pg. 1422
INDUSTRIFORSIKRING A/S—See Norsk Hydro a.s; *Int'l*, pg. 960
INDUSTRIFORVALTNINGS AB KINNEVIK—See Korsnas AB; *Int'l*, pg. 759
INDUSTRIGRUPPEN JAS AB—See Telefonaktiebolaget LM Ericsson; *Int'l*, pg. 1364
A/S INDUSTRIHAERDERIET—See FLS Industries A/S; *Int'l*, pg. 476
INDUSTRIJA DELOVA AUTOMOBILA, KIKINDA—See General Motors Corporation; *U.S. Public*, pg. 724
INDUSTRISKOG AB—See Korsnas AB; *Int'l*, pg. 759
INDUSTRISKOG AB—See Mo och Domsjo AB; *Int'l*, pg. 886
AB INDUSTRIVARDEN; *Int'l*, pg. 678
INDUSTRIVENTILATION PRODUKT AB—See Skanska AB; *Int'l*, pg. 1260
INDUSTRIVENTILATION SVENSKA AB—See Skanska AB; *Int'l*, pg. 1261
INDUTINTA, S.A.—See Dainippon Ink & Chemicals, Inc.; *Int'l*, pg. 371
INDUTRADE AB—See AB Industrivarden; *Int'l*, pg. 678

INDY LIGHTING, INC.—See Juno Lighting, Inc.; *U.S. Public*, pg. 935
INEDECA S.A.—See Nestle S.A.; *Int'l*, pg. 920
INEMEX S.A. DE C.V.—See Eaton Corporation; *U.S. Public*, pg. 559
INERTIA DYNAMICS INC.—See Rockwell International Corporation; *U.S. Public*, pg. 1398
INEXCO OIL COMPANY—See Burlington Resources Inc.; *U.S. Public*, pg. 269
INFAR (INDIA) LTD.—See Akzo Nobel N.V.; *Int'l*, pg. 45
INFASCO DIVISION—See The Ivaco Group; *Int'l*, pg. 696
INFASCO NUT DIVISION—See The Ivaco Group; *Int'l*, pg. 696
INFATOOL—See The Ivaco Group; *Int'l*, pg. 696
INFINCOM—See Ikon Office Solutions, Inc.; *U.S. Public*, pg. 864
INFINET OPERATIONS—See Landmark Communications, Inc.; *U.S. Private*, pg. 649
INFINICOM; *U.S. Private*, pg. 561
INFINITY SYSTEMS, INC.—See Harman International Industries, Inc.; *U.S. Public*, pg. 787
INFO ENTERPRISES, INC.—See Motorola, Inc.; *U.S. Public*, pg. 1137
INFOBASE SERVICES—See Acxiom Corporation; *U.S. Public*, pg. 18
INFOCITY NRW INFORMATIONSDIENSTE GMBH & CO. KG—See Veba AG; *Int'l*, pg. 1461
INFOCOM TECHNOLOGIES, INC.—See Philippine Long Distance Telephone Company; *Int'l*, pg. 1051
INFOCORP—See Softbank Corporation; *Int'l*, pg. 1276
INFOINVEST, S.A.—See SEPI; *Int'l*, pg. 1225
INFOKOMPUTER—See International Data Group; *U.S. Private*, pg. 570
INFOLEASING SAF, S.A.—See SEPI; *Int'l*, pg. 1225
INFONET NEDERLAND BV—See KPN Koninklyke PTT Nederland NV; *Int'l*, pg. 720
INFO'PRODUCTS BELGIE NV—See N.V. Koninklijke KNP BT; *Int'l*, pg. 757
INFO'PRODUCTS BV—See N.V. Koninklijke KNP BT; *Int'l*, pg. 756
INFO'PRODUCTS HOLDING BV—See N.V. Koninklijke KNP BT; *Int'l*, pg. 756
INFO'PRODUCTS SERVICES BV—See N.V. Koninklijke KNP BT; *Int'l*, pg. 756
INFOR-TEAM—See Compagnie des Machines Bull; *Int'l*, pg. 318
INFORMATICA, NEGOCIOS Y TECNOLOGIA, S.A.—See Science Applications International Corp.; *U.S. Private*, pg. 976
P.T. INFORMATICS OASE—See The Kyoei Life Insurance Co., Ltd.; *Int'l*, pg. 777
INFORMATION ACCESS CO.—See The Thomson Corporation; *Int'l*, pg. 1600
INFORMATION & ENGINEERING TECHNOLOGY—See DynCorp; *U.S. Private*, pg. 351
INFORMATION BUILDERS; *U.S. Private*, pg. 561
INFORMATION DIMENSIONS—See Gores Technology Group; *U.S. Private*, pg. 465
INFORMATION ET TECHNOLOGIES—See C.E.P. Communication Group; *Int'l*, pg. 239
INFORMATION HANDLING SERVICES—See TBG Management S.A.M.; *Int'l*, pg. 1335
INFORMATION INTEGRATORS, INC.—See General Electric Company; *U.S. Public*, pg. 711
INFORMATION LEASING CORPORATION—See Provident Financial Group, Inc.; *U.S. Public*, pg. 1338
INFORMATION MANAGEMENT DIVISION—See Sterling Software, Inc.; *U.S. Public*, pg. 1516
INFORMATION PROCESSING PRODUCTS—See Fellowes Manufacturing Co.; *U.S. Private*, pg. 468
INFORMATION PRODUCTS, INC.—See Donnelly Corporation; *U.S. Public*, pg. 519
INFORMATION RESOURCES, INC.; *U.S. Public*, pg. 875
INFORMATION SERVICES DIVISION—See Keane, Inc.; *U.S. Public*, pg. 946
INFORMATION STORAGE DEVICES; *U.S. Public*, pg. 876
INFORMATION STORAGE PRODUCTS CENTER—See Mitsubishi Chemical Corporation; *Int'l*, pg. 871
INFORMATION SYSTEMS CO.—See Sony Corporation; *Int'l*, pg. 1281
INFORMATION SYSTEMS DIV.—See Avery Dennison Corporation; *U.S. Public*, pg. 152
INFORMATION SYSTEMS & NETWORK CORPORATION; *U.S. Private*, pg. 561
INFORMATION TECHNOLOGY DIVISION—See Sterling Software, Inc.; *U.S. Public*, pg. 1516
INFORMATION TECHNOLOGY (GETINF)—See Petrobras - Petroleo Brasileiro S.A.; *Int'l*, pg. 1041
INFORMATION TECHNOLOGY GROUP—See Northrop Grumman Corporation; *U.S. Public*, pg. 1199
INFORMATION TECHNOLOGY, INC.—See Fiserv, Inc.; *U.S. Public*, pg. 647
INFORMATION TECHNOLOGY (SOUTH AFRICA) PTY. LTD.—See Compagnie des Machines Bull; *Int'l*, pg. 315
INFORMATION TRANSMISSION SYSTEMS CORP.—See ADC Telecommunications, Inc.; *U.S. Public*, pg. 4
INFORMATION TRUST CORPORATION (PTY.) LTD.—See The Dun & Bradstreet Corporation; *U.S. Public*, pg. 537
INFORMATIQUE CONCORDE SISRO S.A.—See Assicurazioni Generali S.p.A.; *Int'l*, pg. 91
INFORMIX SOFTWARE; *U.S. Public*, pg. 876
INFOSEEK CORPORATON; *U.S. Public*, pg. 876
INFOSERVICIOS, S.A.—See Caja de Madrid Group; *Int'l*, pg. 251
INFOVEST, INC.; *U.S. Private*, pg. 562
INFOWORKS—See Omnicom Group Inc.; *U.S. Public*, pg. 1225
INFOWORLD PUBLISHING, INC.—See International Data Group; *U.S. Private*, pg. 569
INFRA DEL SUR, S.A. DE C.V.—See Air Products and Chemicals, Inc.; *U.S. Public*, pg. 32
INFRA READY PRODUCTS LTD.—See Saskatchewan Wheat Pool; *Int'l*, pg. 1195

INFRADEV INTERNATIONAL—See Caisse de depot et placement du Quebec; *Int'l*, pg. 249
INFRA-METALS CORP.—See Preussag AG; *Int'l*, pg. 1070
INFRARODTEKNIK AB—See Imatran Voima Oy; *Int'l*, pg. 661
INFRASTRUCTURE BUSINESS—See Black & Veatch; *U.S. Private*, pg. 146
INFRASTRUCTURE LEASING & FINANCIAL SERVICES LIMITED—See Orix Corporation; *Int'l*, pg. 1009
INFRESCO CORPORATION—See Computer Associates International, Inc.; *U.S. Public*, pg. 420
INFU-TECH—See Continental Health Affiliates, Inc.; *U.S. Public*, pg. 440
ING. BUREAU SONVICO AG—See Deutsche Babcock AG; *Int'l*, pg. 399
ING FA KJELL LIDSTROM AB—See Celsius AB; *Int'l*, pg. 277
ING. C. OLIVETTI & C.—See Olivetti SpA; *Int'l*, pg. 1002
ING-TECH. ENGINEERING CO.—See GESTRA GmbH; *Int'l*, pg. 550
INGALLS; *U.S. Private*, pg. 562
INGALLS MORANVILLE ADVERTISING—See DavisElen Advertising, Inc.; *U.S. Private*, pg. 316
INGALLS MORANVILLE ADVERTISING/SEATTLE—See DavisElen Advertising, Inc.; *U.S. Private*, pg. 316
INGALLS SHIPBUILDING—See Litton Industries, Inc.; *U.S. Public*, pg. 1003
INGASCI INC.—See Nippon Sanso Corporation; *Int'l*, pg. 939
INGECOL—See Novartis AG; *Int'l*, pg. 983
INGENIERA DE TELECOMUNICACIONES E INSTALACIONES S.A.—See Telefonaktiebolaget LM Ericsson; *Int'l*, pg. 1368
INGENIERIA Y GESTION DE REDES, S.A.—See Caja de Madrid Group; *Int'l*, pg. 252
INGENIEUR BERATUNGSGESELLSCHAFT ZUR RISIKOUND SCHADENSMINDERUNG M.B.H.—See Assicurazioni Generali S.p.A.; *Int'l*, pg. 89
INGENIEURBURO ANTRIEBSTECHNIK DRESDEN GMBH—See Deutsche Babcock AG; *Int'l*, pg. 400
INGENIEURSBUREAU GRABOWSKY & POORT BV—See Heidemij N.V.; *Int'l*, pg. 607
INGENIEURSBUREAU SCHIEBROEK-STRUIK BV—See Heidemij N.V.; *Int'l*, pg. 607
INGENIEURSBUREAU VAN DER MAST BV—See Heidemij N.V.; *Int'l*, pg. 607
INGENIEURSBUREAU VOOR SYSTEMEN EN OCTROOIEN SPANSTAAL B.V.—See Ballast Nedam NV; *Int'l*, pg. 134
A/S INGENIOR GRAN—See Dahl International AB; *Int'l*, pg. 359
INGENIORFIRMA SIGURD SORUM A.S.—See GESTRA GmbH; *Int'l*, pg. 550
INGERSOLL CM SYSTEMS INC.—See Ingersoll International Inc.; *U.S. Private*, pg. 562
INGERSOLL CUTTING TOOL CO.—See Ingersoll International Inc.; *U.S. Private*, pg. 562
INGERSOLL-DRESSER PUMP COMPANY—See Dresser Industries, Inc.; *U.S. Public*, pg. 529
INGERSOLL-DRESSER PUMP COMPANY—See Ingersoll-Rand Company; *U.S. Public*, pg. 877
INGERSOLL EQUIPMENT CO., INC.—See Rothenberger Group GmbH; *Int'l*, pg. 1129
INGERSOLL FASTENERS DIVISION—See The Ivaco Group; *Int'l*, pg. 696
INGERSOLL GMBH INC.—See Ingersoll International Inc.; *U.S. Private*, pg. 562
THE INGERSOLL GROUP—See Larkin Meeder & Schweidel; *U.S. Private*, pg. 651
INGERSOLL INTERNATIONAL INC.; *U.S. Private*, pg. 562
INGERSOLL MACHINE AND TOOL DIVISION—See The Ivaco Group; *Int'l*, pg. 695
INGERSOLL MASCHINEN UND WERKZEUGE GMBH—See Ingersoll International Inc.; *U.S. Private*, pg. 562
INGERSOLL MILLING MACHINE CO.—See Ingersoll International Inc.; *U.S. Private*, pg. 562
INGERSOLL MILLING MACHINES OVERSEAS LTD.—See Ingersoll International Inc.; *U.S. Private*, pg. 562
INGERSOLL-RAND AB—See Ingersoll-Rand Company; *U.S. Public*, pg. 878
INGERSOLL-RAND AIR CENTERS—See Ingersoll-Rand Company; *U.S. Public*, pg. 876
INGERSOLL-RAND (AUSTRALIA) PROPRIETARY LTD.—See Ingersoll-Rand Company; *U.S. Public*, pg. 878
INGERSOLL-RAND BENELUX S.A.—See Ingersoll-Rand Company; *U.S. Public*, pg. 878
INGERSOLL-RAND CANADA, INC.—See Ingersoll-Rand Company; *U.S. Public*, pg. 878
INGERSOLL-RAND CO. (IRELAND) LTD.—See Ingersoll-Rand Company; *U.S. Public*, pg. 878
INGERSOLL-RAND CO., LTD.—See Ingersoll-Rand Company; *U.S. Public*, pg. 878
INGERSOLL-RAND CO., SOUTH AFRICA (PROPRIETARY) LTD.—See Ingersoll-Rand Company; *U.S. Public*, pg. 878
INGERSOLL-RAND COMPANY; *U.S. Public*, pg. 876
INGERSOLL-RAND GMBH—See Ingersoll-Rand Company; *U.S. Public*, pg. 878
INGERSOLL-RAND HOLDINGS LTD.—See Ingersoll-Rand Company; *U.S. Public*, pg. 878
INGERSOLL-RAND (INDIA) PRIVATE LTD.—See Ingersoll-Rand Company; *U.S. Public*, pg. 878
INGERSOLL-RAND ITALIANA S.R.L.—See Ingersoll-Rand Company; *U.S. Public*, pg. 878
INGERSOLL-RAND (JAPAN) LTD.—See Ingersoll-Rand Company; *U.S. Public*, pg. 878
INGERSOLL-RAND PHILIPPINES, INC.—See Ingersoll-Rand Company; *U.S. Public*, pg. 878
INGERSOLL RAND - POWER TOOL DIV.—See Ingersoll-Rand Company; *U.S. Public*, pg. 877
INGERSOLL-RAND SALES CO., LTD.—See Ingersoll-Rand Company; *U.S. Public*, pg. 877
INGERSOLL-RAND SALES COMPANY LIMITED UK—See Ingersoll-Rand Company; *U.S. Public*, pg. 878

INGERSOLL RAND S.E. ASIA (PRIVATE) LIMITED—See Ingersoll-Rand Company; *U.S. Public*, pg. 878
INGERSOLL RAND TOOL & HOIST—See Ingersoll-Rand Company; *U.S. Public*, pg. 877
INGLES MARKETS, INCORPORATED; *U.S. Public*, pg. 878
INGLIS LIMITED—See Whirlpool Corporation; *U.S. Public*, pg. 1765
INGOLD ELECTRODES INC—See Novartis AG; *Int'l*, pg. 973
INGOLD FRANCE SARL—See Novartis AG; *Int'l*, pg. 983
INGOLD MESSTECHNIK AG—See Novartis AG; *Int'l*, pg. 972
INGOLD MESSTECHNIK GMBH—See Novartis AG; *Int'l*, pg. 983
INGRAM & BELL INC.—See MDS Inc.; *Int'l*, pg. 826
INGRAM BARGE COMPANY—See Ingram Industries Inc.; *U.S. Private*, pg. 563
INGRAM COAL COMPANY—See Ingram Industries Inc.; *U.S. Private*, pg. 563
INGRAM INDUSTRIES INC.; *U.S. Private*, pg. 562
INGRAM LIBRARY SERVICES, INC.—See Ingram Industries Inc.; *U.S. Private*, pg. 563
INGRAM MERCHANDISING SERVICE INC.—See Ingram Industries Inc.; *U.S. Private*, pg. 563
INGRAM MICRO INC.; *U.S. Public*, pg. 878
INGRAM PAPER COMPANY—See International Paper Company; *U.S. Public*, pg. 904
INGRAM PERIODICALS INC.—See Ingram Industries Inc.; *U.S. Private*, pg. 563
INGRAM PRODUCTION COMPANY—See Ingram Industries Inc.; *U.S. Private*, pg. 563
INGREDIANTS GROUP—See Goodman Fielder Limited; *Int'l*, pg. 555
INGRID DIVISION OF LAWNWARE—See Lawnware Products, Inc.; *U.S. Private*, pg. 654
INHA WORKS LTD.—See Fiskars Oy AB; *Int'l*, pg. 492
INIBERICA, S.A.—See Vallehermoso, S.A.; *Int'l*, pg. 1447
INISHTECH PLC—See James Crean PLC; *Int'l*, pg. 341
INITIAL TEXTILE SERVICE—See Sophus Berendsen A/S; *Int'l*, pg. 1285
INITIATIVE & FINANCE INVESTISSEMENT—See Credit National*e*; *Int'l*, pg. 344
INITIO, INC.; *U.S. Public*, pg. 879
INJECTION FOOTWEAR CORP.; *U.S. Private*, pg. 563
INJECTRON CORPORATION; *U.S. Private*, pg. 563
INKA PALETTEN GMBH; *Int'l*, pg. 678
INKEL USA CORPORATION; *U.S. Private*, pg. 563
INKEROINEN SAWMILL—See Enso Oyj; *Int'l*, pg. 456
INKOO POWER PLANT—See Imatran Voima Oy; *Int'l*, pg. 660
INKTEL MARKETING—See Avanti Press Inc.; *U.S. Private*, pg. 101
INLAN-INDUSTRIA DE COMPONENTES MECANICOS, S.A.—See General Motors Corporation; *U.S. Public*, pg. 723
INLAND ASSOCIATES; *U.S. Private*, pg. 563
INLAND CEMENT COMPANY—See Heidelberger Zement A.G.; *Int'l*, pg. 606
INLAND CONCRETE CONSTRUCTORS—See J.D. Diffenbaugh, Inc.; *U.S. Private*, pg. 332
INLAND CONTAINER-CONTAINER DIVISION—See Temple-Inland Inc.; *U.S. Public*, pg. 1575
INLAND CONTAINER-CONTAINERBOARD DIVISION—See Temple-Inland Inc.; *U.S. Public*, pg. 1575
INLAND CONTAINER CORPORATION—See Temple-Inland Inc.; *U.S. Public*, pg. 1575
INLAND DETROIT DIESEL ALLISON CO.; *U.S. Private*, pg. 564
INLAND DETROIT DIESEL-ALLISON—See Inland Detroit Diesel Allison Co.; *U.S. Private*, pg. 564
INLAND DIE CASTING—See RCM Industries; *U.S. Private*, pg. 903
INLAND EMPIRE DIVISION—See Albertson's, Inc.; *U.S. Public*, pg. 38
THE INLAND GROUP, INC.; *U.S. Private*, pg. 564
INLAND INTERNATIONAL, INC.—See Inland Steel Industries, Inc.; *U.S. Public*, pg. 879
INLAND MOTOR DIV.—See Kollmorgen Corporation; *U.S. Public*, pg. 965
INLAND NATIONAL INS. CO.—See American International Group, Inc.; *U.S. Public*, pg. 84
INLAND PACIFIC ENTERPRISES—See BC Gas Inc.; *Int'l*, pg. 114
INLAND PRINTING CO., INC.; *U.S. Private*, pg. 564
INLAND STEEL INDUSTRIES, INC.; *U.S. Public*, pg. 879
INLAND STEEL MINING CO—See Inland Steel Industries, Inc.; *U.S. Public*, pg. 879
INLAND STEEL PRODUCTS COMPANY—See Inland Steel Industries, Inc.; *U.S. Public*, pg. 879
INLAND SURGERY CENTER—See Healthsouth Corporation; *U.S. Public*, pg. 803
INLAND VALLEY REGIONAL MEDICAL CENTER—See Universal Health Services, Inc.; *U.S. Public*, pg. 1697
INMAN CONSTRUCTION CORPORATION; *U.S. Private*, pg. 564
INMAN MILLS; *U.S. Private*, pg. 564
PAUL INMAN ASSOCIATES INC.; *U.S. Private*, pg. 564
INMET MINING CORPORATION; *Int'l*, pg. 678
INMINSA SA—See Hesta Tex AG; *Int'l*, pg. 617
INMOBILIARIA CALVO-BARBARA—See Corporacion MAPFRE, Compania Internacional de Reaseguros, S.A.; *Int'l*, pg. 335
INMOBILIARIA CONDOMINIO PARQUE ZAPALLAR S.A.—See Corporacion MAPFRE, Compania Internacional de Reaseguros, S.A.; *Int'l*, pg. 335
INMOBILIARIA TECHNICA INDUSTRIAL, S.A.—See Baldwin Piano & Organ Company; *U.S. Public*, pg. 169
INMOBILIARIA WACKENHUT, S.A. DE C.V.—See The Wackenhut Corporation; *U.S. Public*, pg. 1731
INMONT INDUSTRIA QUIMICA LTDA.—See BASF AG; *Int'l*, pg. 108
INN AT HARRIS RANCH—See Harris Farms, Inc.; *U.S. Private*, pg. 506

INN MAID PRODUCTS—See Lancaster Colony Corporation; *U.S. Public*, pg. 977
INNCO MANAGEMENT CORP.—See Family Inns of America, Inc.; *U.S. Private*, pg. 392
INNER CERAMIC USA; *U.S. Private*, pg. 564
INNER CITY, INC.—See Polaroid Corporation; *U.S. Public*, pg. 1313
INNER SECRETS, INC.; *U.S. Private*, pg. 564
INNERVISION STUDIOS INC.—See Anheuser-Busch Companies, Inc.; *U.S. Public*, pg. 114
INNISBROOK/HILTON RESORT—See Starwood Capital Group LLC; *U.S. Private*, pg. 1036
INNISKILLIN WINES, INC.—See Vincor International; *Int'l*, pg. 1468
INNKRAFTWERKE GMBH—See Viag AG; *Int'l*, pg. 1464
INNO SA—See GIB Group; *Int'l*, pg. 533
INNOMEDICA—See Innovex, Inc.; *U.S. Public*, pg. 880
INNOSERV TECHNOLOGIES, INC.; *U.S. Public*, pg. 879
INNOSHIMA WORKS—See Hitachi Zosen Corporation; *Int'l*, pg. 623
INNOTECH AVIATION INDUSTRIES LTD.—See Air Canada; *Int'l*, pg. 36
INNOVATHERM GESELLSCHAFT ZUR INNOVATIVEN NUTZUNG VON BRENNSTOFFEN MBH—See Harpen AG; *Int'l*, pg. 597
THE INNOVATIVE COMPANY—See The Seibels Bruce Group, Inc.; *U.S. Public*, pg. 1454
INNOVATIVE DATA SERVICES INC.—See CDB Infotec Inc.; *U.S. Private*, pg. 193
INNOVATIVE HEALTH ALLIANCES—See Horizon/CMS Healthcare Corporation; *U.S. Public*, pg. 839
INNOVATIVE MEMBRANE SYSTEMS, INC.—See Praxair Inc.; *U.S. Public*, pg. 1320
INNOVATIVE PLASTICS CORPORATION; *U.S. Private*, pg. 565
INNOVATIVE SOUTH—See Innovative Plastics Corporation; *U.S. Private*, pg. 565
INNOVATIVE SPUTTERING TECHNOLOGY IST—See N.V. Bekaert S.A.; *Int'l*, pg. 183
INNOVATIVE STEAM TECHNOLOGIES—See Caterpillar Inc.; *U.S. Public*, pg. 316
INNOVATIVE VALVE TECHNOLOGY, INC.; *U.S. Public*, pg. 880
INNOVEX, INC.; *U.S. Public*, pg. 880
INNOVEX PRAIRIE WEST MANUFACTURING—See Innovex, Inc.; *U.S. Public*, pg. 880
INNOVEX PRECISION PRODUCTS—See Innovex, Inc.; *U.S. Public*, pg. 880
INNOVIR GMBH—See VIMRx Pharmaceuticals, Inc.; *U.S. Public*, pg. 1703
INNOVIR LABORATORIES, INC.—See VIMRx Pharmaceuticals, Inc.; *U.S. Public*, pg. 1702
INNOVIR (UK) LTD—See VIMRx Pharmaceuticals, Inc.; *U.S. Public*, pg. 1703
INNSE-HONG KONG—See IRI Istituto Ricostruzione Industriale; *Int'l*, pg. 655
INNSE-MOSCOW—See IRI Istituto Ricostruzione Industriale; *Int'l*, pg. 655
INNTREPRENEUR PUB COMPANY LIMITED—See The Nomura Securities Co., Ltd.; *Int'l*, pg. 956
INNWERK AG—See Viag AG; *Int'l*, pg. 1464
INORGANIC COLLOIDS BUSINESS—See PQ Corporation; *U.S. Private*, pg. 827
INOUE-NISSEI ENGINEERING PTE LTD.—See Superior Metal Printing Limited; *Int'l*, pg. 1322
INPAU, S.A.—See Caixa d'Estalvis de Catalunya; *Int'l*, pg. 250
INPEC ENGINEERING GMBH—See Panalpina Welttransport (Holding) AG; *Int'l*, pg. 1022
INPOWER INC.—See CSA Holdings Ltd.; *Int'l*, pg. 242
INPUT/OUTPUT, INC.; *U.S. Public*, pg. 880
INSECT CONTROL & RESEARCH CORP.—See McLaughlin Gormley King Company; *U.S. Private*, pg. 724
INSERRA SHOPRITE; *U.S. Private*, pg. 565
INSERT FRANCE—See EMAP Plc; *Int'l*, pg. 451
INSERVCO INSURANCE SERVICES, INC.—See Penn National Insurance; *U.S. Private*, pg. 850
INSIDE SPORTS, INC.—See Century Publishing Company; *U.S. Private*, pg. 226
INSIGHT ELECTRONICS INC.—See Veba AG; *Int'l*, pg. 1457
INSIGHT GRAPHIC SYSTEMS—See LSI Industries, Inc.; *U.S. Public*, pg. 971
INSIGHT HEALTH SERVICES CORP.; *U.S. Public*, pg. 880
INSIGNIA FINANCIAL GROUP, INC.; *U.S. Public*, pg. 881
INSIGNIA RESIDENTIAL GROUP—See Insignia Financial Group, Inc.; *U.S. Public*, pg. 881
INSIGNIA SYSTEMS, INC.; *U.S. Public*, pg. 881
INSILCO CORPORATION; *U.S. Public*, pg. 881
INSINOORITOIMISTO N. LIUKKONEN OY—See Imatran Voima Oy; *Int'l*, pg. 660
INSITUFORM CENTRAL, INC.—See Insituform Technologies, Inc.; *U.S. Public*, pg. 882
INSITUFORM DE PUERTO RICO, INC.—See Insituform Technologies, Inc.; *U.S. Public*, pg. 882
INSITUFORM EAST, INC.—See CERBCO, Inc.; *U.S. Public*, pg. 330
INSITUFORM MISSOURI, INC.—See Insituform Technologies, Inc.; *U.S. Public*, pg. 882
INSITUFORM NORTH, INC.—See Insituform Technologies, Inc.; *U.S. Public*, pg. 882
INSITUFORM PLAINS, INC.—See Insituform Technologies, Inc.; *U.S. Public*, pg. 882
INSITUFORM ROCKIES, INC.—See Insituform Technologies, Inc.; *U.S. Public*, pg. 882
INSITUFORM TECHNOLOGIES, INC.; *U.S. Public*, pg. 881
INSITUFORM TEXARK, INC.—See Insituform Technologies, Inc.; *U.S. Public*, pg. 882
INSO CHICAGO CORPORATION—See INSO Corporation; *U.S. Public*, pg. 882
INSO CORPORATION; *U.S. Public*, pg. 882
INSO CORPORATION, LTD.—See INSO Corporation; *U.S. Public*, pg. 882

INSO PROVIDENCE CORP.—See INSO Corporation; *U.S. Public*, pg. 882
INSOLAIR INDUSTRIES—See Apogee Enterprises, Inc.; *U.S. Public*, pg. 120
INSOLEQ SEMAFOUR—See M.C. Gill Corporation; *U.S. Private*, pg. 453
INSPECTORATE PLC; *Int'l*, pg. 679
INSPECTORATE (SUISSE) S.A.—See Inspectorate Plc; *Int'l*, pg. 679
INSPECTRUM BV—See Heidemij N.V.; *Int'l*, pg. 607
INSTA-FOAM PRODUCTS, INC.—See Flexible Products Company; *U.S. Private*, pg. 412
INSTA-PRO INTERNATIONAL, LTD.—See Triple F, Inc.; *U.S. Private*, pg. 1104
INSTALACIONES Y PROYECTOS DE TELECOMUNICACIONES, S.A.—See Vallehermoso, S.A.; *Int'l*, pg. 1447
INSTALLATIEGROEP VAN BUUREN-VAN SWAAY BV—See Internatio-Muller N.V.; *Int'l*, pg. 681
INSTALLATION PRODUCTS DIV.—See Armstrong World Industries, Inc.; *U.S. Public*, pg. 132
INSTANT S.R.L.—See Up-Right, Inc.; *U.S. Private*, pg. 1128
THE INSTANT WEB COMPANIES; *U.S. Private*, pg. 565
INSTEEL INDUSTRIES, INC.; *U.S. Public*, pg. 882
INSTEEL PANEL-MEX S.A. DE C.V.—See Insteel Industries, Inc.; *U.S. Public*, pg. 882
INSTEEL WIRE PRODUCTS—See Insteel Industries, Inc.; *U.S. Public*, pg. 882
INSTEIK AG—See Mannesmann A.G.; *Int'l*, pg. 839
INSTINET CORPORATION—See Reuters Holdings PLC; *Int'l*, pg. 1106
INSTITUT DE REESCOMPTE ET DE GARANTIE—See Bank Brussels Lambert; *Int'l*, pg. 147
THE INSTITUTE OF BIOPHARMACEUTICS LTD.—See Elan Corporation Plc; *Int'l*, pg. 436
INSTITUTE FOR HUMAN RESOURCES—See United HealthCare Corporation; *U.S. Public*, pg. 1678
INSTITUTE FOR MEDICAL SCIENCE—See Shionogi & Co., Ltd.; *Int'l*, pg. 1235
INSTITUTE FOR PROFESSIONAL DEVELOPMENT—See Apollo Group, Inc.; *U.S. Public*, pg. 120
INSTITUTE OF CERTIFIED BANKERS—See The American Bankers Association; *U.S. Private*, pg. 51
INSTITUTE FOR SCIENTIFIC INFORMATION—See The Thomson Corporation; *U.S. Public*, pg. 1600
INSTITUTION FOOD HOUSE, INC.—See Alex Lee, Inc.; *U.S. Private*, pg. 657
INSTITUTIONAL BROKERS ESTIMATE SYSTEM INC. (IBIS)—See Primark Corporation; *U.S. Public*, pg. 1325
INSTITUTIONAL EQUIPMENT & INTERIORS, INC.—See Piccadilly Cafeterias, Inc.; *U.S. Public*, pg. 1294
INSTITUTIONAL FINANCING SERVICES—See Tyler Corporation; *Int'l*, pg. 1652
INSTITUTIONAL INVESTOR, INC.—See The Walt Disney Company; *U.S. Public*, pg. 513
INSTITUTIONAL SERVICES, INC.—See Snyder Oil Corporation; *U.S. Public*, pg. 1482
INSTITUTIONAL TRUST & INVESTMENT SERVICES—See National City Corporation; *U.S. Public*, pg. 1154
INSTITUTO DE IDIOMAS COLOMBIA, S.A.—See Berlitz International, Inc.; *U.S. Public*, pg. 222
INSTITUTO PASTEUR DE LISBOA—See American Home Products Corporation; *U.S. Public*, pg. 81
INSTORE SATELLITE NETWORK/BUSINESS TV—See Data Broadcasting Corporation; *U.S. Public*, pg. 484
INSTRON ASIA, LTD.—See Instron Corporation; *U.S. Public*, pg. 882
INSTRON CANADA, INC.—See Instron Corporation; *U.S. Public*, pg. 883
INSTRON CORPORATION; *U.S. Public*, pg. 882
INSTRON EXPORT CORP.—See Instron Corporation; *U.S. Public*, pg. 882
INSTRON INTERNATIONAL LTD.—See Instron Corporation; *U.S. Public*, pg. 883
INSTRON JAPAN CO., LTD.—See Instron Corporation; *U.S. Public*, pg. 882
INSTRON LIMITED—See Instron Corporation; *U.S. Public*, pg. 883
INSTRON PTY. LTD.—See Instron Corporation; *U.S. Public*, pg. 883
INSTRON REALTY TRUST—See Instron Corporation; *U.S. Public*, pg. 883
INSTRON S.A.—See Instron Corporation; *U.S. Public*, pg. 883
INSTRON SCHENCK TESTING SYSTEMS LIMITED—See Instron Corporation; *U.S. Public*, pg. 883
INSTRUCTIONAL FAIR, INC.—See Creative Publications; *U.S. Private*, pg. 288
INSTRUMENT ASSOCIATES, INC.—See Salient 3 Communications, Inc.; *U.S. Public*, pg. 1430
INSTRUMENT MARKETING SERVICES, INC.—See SGS Societe Generale de Surveillance Holding S.A.; *Int'l*, pg. 1153
INSTRUMENT SPECIALTIES COMPANY; *U.S. Private*, pg. 565
INSTRUMENT SPECIALTIES EUROPE LTD.—See Instrument Specialties Company; *U.S. Private*, pg. 565
INSTRUMENT TRANSFORMER DIVISION—See ABB Asea Brown Boveri (Holding) Ltd.; *Int'l*, pg. 4
INSTRUMENTACION, LTDA.—See Hewlett-Packard Company; *U.S. Public*, pg. 822
INSTRUMENTARIUM IMAGING, INC.; *U.S. Private*, pg. 565
INSTRUMENTATION CONNECTORS DIV.—See Parker Hannifin Corporation; *U.S. Public*, pg. 1261
INSTRUMENTATION GROUP—See Parker Hannifin Corporation; *U.S. Public*, pg. 1261
INSTRUMENTATION MEDICALE & MAINTENANCE—See Hewlett-Packard Company; *U.S. Public*, pg. 822
INSTRUMENTATION VALVE DIVISION—See Parker Hannifin Corporation; *U.S. Public*, pg. 1261
INSTRUMENTOS BRISTOL S.A.—See FKI Plc; *Int'l*, pg. 473
INSULATE LLC—See Saint-Gobain; *Int'l*, pg. 1171
INSULATING MATERIALS, INC.; *U.S. Private*, pg. 565

INSUMOS FERROVIARIOS C.A.—See Dyckerhoff & Widmann AG; *Int'l*, pg. 425

INSURANCE ADMINISTRATION CENTER., INC.—See Poe & Brown, Inc.; *U.S. Public*, pg. 1312

INSURANCE AUTOMATION SYSTEMS—See USF&G Corporation; *U.S. Public*, pg. 1660

INSURANCE BROKERS & MANAGERS, INC.—See United Fire & Casualty Company; *U.S. Public*, pg. 1677

INSURANCE COMPANY OF AFRICA—See Cigna Corp.; *U.S. Public*, pg. 364

INSURANCE COMPANY OF GREATER NEW YORK—See Greater New York Mutual Insurance Company; *U.S. Private*, pg. 476

INSURANCE COMPANY OF NORTH AMERICA—See Cigna Corp.; *U.S. Public*, pg. 366

INSURANCE COMPANY OF NORTH AMERICA (U.K.) LIMITED—See Cigna Corp.; *U.S. Public*, pg. 363

INSURANCE COMPANY OF OHIO—See Meridian Insurance Group, Inc.; *U.S. Public*, pg. 1095

INSURANCE COMPANY OF THE STATE OF PENNSYLVANIA—See American International Group, Inc.; *U.S. Public*, pg. 84

INSURANCE CONFORMATION SERVICES—See The Progressive Corporation; *U.S. Public*, pg. 1334

THE INSURANCE CORP. OF NEW YORK—See Chartwell Re Corporation; *U.S. Public*, pg. 336

INSURANCE INTERMEDIARIES, INC.—See Nationwide Insurance Enterprise; *U.S. Private*, pg. 789

INSURANCE MANAGEMENT ASSOCIATES; *U.S. Private*, pg. 565

INSURANCE MANAGEMENT INCORPORATED—See Hilb, Rogal and Hamilton Company; *U.S. Public*, pg. 827

INSURANCE SYSTEMS NEDERLAND B.V.—See AEGON N.V.; *Int'l*, pg. 26

INSURATEX, LTD.—See Burlington Industries, Inc.; *U.S. Public*, pg. 268

INSURER PHYSICIAN SERVICES ORGANIZATION—See Highmark Inc.; *U.S. Private*, pg. 529

INTAIRDRIL LTD.—See Pool Energy Services Co.; *U.S. Public*, pg. 1316

INTAKE WATER CO.—See Tenneco Inc.; *U.S. Public*, pg. 1579

INTALCABLE USA INC.—See IRI Istituto Ricostruzione Industriale; *Int'l*, pg. 655

INTALCABLE-ARGENTINA—See IRI Istituto Ricostruzione Industriale; *Int'l*, pg. 655

INTALCABLE-CHINA—See IRI Istituto Ricostruzione Industriale; *Int'l*, pg. 655

INTALCABLE-INDIA—See IRI Istituto Ricostruzione Industriale; *Int'l*, pg. 655

INTALCABLE-SAUDI ARABIA—See IRI Istituto Ricostruzione Industriale; *Int'l*, pg. 655

INTALCABLE-SOMALIA—See IRI Istituto Ricostruzione Industriale; *Int'l*, pg. 655

INTALCABLE-UK—See IRI Istituto Ricostruzione Industriale; *Int'l*, pg. 656

INTALCO ALUMINUM CORP.—See Alumax Inc.; *U.S. Public*, pg. 60

INTEC—See AXA-UAP; *Int'l*, pg. 19

INTECH EDM AG—See Georg Fischer Ltd.; *Int'l*, pg. 491

INTECH EDM BV—See Georg Fischer Ltd.; *Int'l*, pg. 489

INTECH EDM GMBH—See Georg Fischer Ltd.; *Int'l*, pg. 489

INTECH EDM LTD.—See Georg Fischer Ltd.; *Int'l*, pg. 489

INTECH EDM SA—See Georg Fischer Ltd.; *Int'l*, pg. 489

INTECH INTERNATIONAL—See Georg Fischer Ltd.; *Int'l*, pg. 489

INTECH TECHNOLOGY CORPORATION—See Georg Fischer Ltd.; *Int'l*, pg. 490

INTECOM—See Lagardere Groupe; *Int'l*, pg. 794

INTEGON CASUALTY INSURANCE COMPANY—See General Motors Corporation; *U.S. Public*, pg. 720

INTEGON CORPORATION—See General Motors Corporation; *U.S. Public*, pg. 719

INTEGON GENERAL INSURANCE CORPORATION—See General Motors Corporation; *U.S. Public*, pg. 720

INTEGON INDEMNITY CORPORATION—See General Motors Corporation; *U.S. Public*, pg. 720

INTEGON NATIONAL INSURANCE CO.—See General Motors Corporation; *U.S. Public*, pg. 720

INTEGON PREFERRED INSURANCE COMPANY—See General Motors Corporation; *U.S. Public*, pg. 720

INTEGON SPECIALTY INSURANCE COMPANY—See General Motors Corporation; *U.S. Public*, pg. 720

INTEGRA RESORT MANAGEMENT, INC.—See The Hallwood Group Incorporated; *U.S. Public*, pg. 778

INTEGRA TECHNOLOGIES CORP.; *U.S. Private*, pg. 565

INTEGRAL CORP.—See Southwire Company; *U.S. Private*, pg. 1019

INTEGRAL HOME HEALTH CARE, INC.—See Integrated Health Services, Inc.; *U.S. Public*, pg. 885

INTEGRAL HYDRAULIK & CO.; *Int'l*, pg. 679

INTEGRAL MARKETING, INC.—See Integral Systems, Inc.; *U.S. Public*, pg. 883

INTEGRAL SYSTEMS, INC.—See CSA Holdings Ltd.; *Int'l*, pg. 242

INTEGRAL SYSTEMS, INC.; *U.S. Public*, pg. 883

INTEGRAL TECHNOLOGIE GMBH—See Integral Hydraulik & Co.; *Int'l*, pg. 679

INTEGRAMED AMERICA; *U.S. Public*, pg. 883

INTEGRATEC—See Equifax Inc.; *U.S. Public*, pg. 588

INTEGRATED BRANDS INC.; *U.S. Public*, pg. 883

INTEGRATED BUSINESS SERVICES—See Computer Sciences Corporation; *U.S. Public*, pg. 335

INTEGRATED BUSINESS SYSTEMS—See Effective Management Systems; *U.S. Public*, pg. 423

INTEGRATED CIRCUITS DIVISION—See Cadence Design Systems, Inc.; *U.S. Public*, pg. 290

INTEGRATED CIRCUITS MASTER CATALOG—See The Hearst Corporation; *U.S. Private*, pg. 516

INTEGRATED COMMUNICATIONS SERVICES, INC.—See Telephone and Data Systems, Inc.; *U.S. Public*, pg. 1570

INTEGRATED DEVICE TECHNOLOGY EUROPE, INC.—See Integrated Device Technology, Inc.; *U.S. Public*, pg. 884

INTEGRATED DEVICE TECHNOLOGY, INC.; *U.S. Public*, pg. 884

INTEGRATED DEVICE TECHNOLOGY, KK—See Integrated Device Technology, Inc.; *U.S. Public*, pg. 884

INTEGRATED DISTRIBUTIONS, INC.—See Arkansas Best Corporation; *U.S. Public*, pg. 131

INTEGRATED GRAIN & MILLING—See Zacky Farms, Inc.; *U.S. Private*, pg. 1203

INTEGRATED GRAPHIC SERVICES—See Wallace Computer Services, Inc.; *U.S. Public*, pg. 1736

INTEGRATED HEALTH CONCEPTS—See Longs Drug Stores Corporation; *U.S. Public*, pg. 1013

INTEGRATED HEALTH SERVICES, INC.; *U.S. Public*, pg. 884

INTEGRATED INFORMATION SERVICES INC.—See Pettibone Corporation; *U.S. Private*, pg. 860

INTEGRATED MARKETING GROUP; *U.S. Private*, pg. 566

INTEGRATED MARKETING SERVICES—See First Data Corporation; *U.S. Public*, pg. 631

INTEGRATED MATERIAL HANDLING COMPANY—See Tomkins PLC; *Int'l*, pg. 1397

INTEGRATED MEDIA—See Banta Corporation; *U.S. Public*, pg. 188

INTEGRATED METAL TECHNOLOGIES, INC.—See Herman Miller, Inc.; *U.S. Public*, pg. 1112

INTEGRATED NETWORK FOR COMPUTER ADMINISTRATION LTD.—See Franz Haniel & Cie, GmbH; *Int'l*, pg. 591

INTEGRATED PAYMENT SYSTEMS—See First Data Corporation; *U.S. Public*, pg. 631

INTEGRATED PERFORMANCE DECISIONS—See Analysis & Technology, Inc.; *U.S. Public*, pg. 110

INTEGRATED PHOTOMATRIX LTD.—See B. Elliott plc.; *Int'l*, pg. 448

INTEGRATED PRESS SYSTEMS—See Premier Mill Corp.; *U.S. Private*, pg. 881

INTEGRATED SYSTEMS—See Zero Corporation; *U.S. Public*, pg. 1791

INTEGRATED SYSTEMS ANALYSTS, INC.; *U.S. Private*, pg. 566

INTEGRATED SYSTEMS CONSULTATING GROUP—See Safeguard Scientifics, Inc.; *U.S. Public*, pg. 1425

INTEGRATED SYSTEMS, INC.; *U.S. Public*, pg. 885

INTEGRATED SYSTEMS, INC., LTD.—See Integrated Systems, Inc.; *U.S. Public*, pg. 886

INTEGRATED SYSTEMS, INC., S.A.—See Integrated Systems, Inc.; *U.S. Public*, pg. 886

INTEGRATED SYSTEMS OPERATIONS—See Xerox Corporation; *U.S. Public*, pg. 1784

INTEGRATED TECHNICAL SYSTEMS (ITS)—See Case Corporation; *U.S. Public*, pg. 311

INTEGRATED TECHNOLOGIES, Inc.—See Litton Industries, Inc.; *U.S. Public*, pg. 1004

INTEGRATED TERMINALS—See Gibraltar Steel Corp.; *U.S. Public*, pg. 703

INTEGRATED WASTE SERVICES, INC.; *U.S. Public*, pg. 886

INTEGRATION AND SYSTEMS PRODUCTS DIV.—See Eastman Kodak Company; *U.S. Public*, pg. 420

INTEGRIS DATA SERVICES FRANCE—See Compagnie des Machines Bull; *Int'l*, pg. 316

INTEGRIS DATA SERVICES INTERNATIONAL—See Compagnie des Machines Bull; *Int'l*, pg. 316

INTEGRIS LTD.—See Compagnie des Machines Bull; *Int'l*, pg. 318

INTEGRITY INCORPORATED; *U.S. Public*, pg. 886

INTEGRITY LIFE INSURANCE COMPANY—See National Mutual Holdings Limited; *Int'l*, pg. 908

INTEGRITY MUTUAL INSURANCE COMPANY; *U.S. Private*, pg. 566

INTEGROL—See Staveley Industries PLC; *Int'l*, pg. 1298

INTEL AUSTRALIA PTY. LTD.—See Intel Corporation; *U.S. Public*, pg. 887

INTEL CORPORATION; *U.S. Public*, pg. 886

INTEL CORPORATION ITALIA SPA—See Intel Corporation; *U.S. Public*, pg. 887

INTEL CORPORATION S.A.R.L.—See Intel Corporation; *U.S. Public*, pg. 887

INTEL CORPORATION U.K. LTD.—See Intel Corporation; *U.S. Public*, pg. 887

INTEL DATA AG—See Marcam Solutions, Inc.; *U.S. Public*, pg. 1043

INTEL DENMARK—See Intel Corporation; *U.S. Public*, pg. 887

INTEL EUROPE—See Intel Corporation; *U.S. Public*, pg. 887

INTEL FINLAND OY—See Intel Corporation; *U.S. Public*, pg. 887

INTEL GMBH—See Intel Corporation; *U.S. Public*, pg. 887

INTEL IBERIA S.A.—See Intel Corporation; *U.S. Public*, pg. 887

INTEL JAPAN—See Intel Corporation; *U.S. Public*, pg. 887

INTEL JAPAN K.K.—See Intel Corporation; *U.S. Public*, pg. 887

INTEL NORWAY—See Intel Corporation; *U.S. Public*, pg. 887

INTEL SEMICONDUCTOR ASIA LTD.—See Intel Corporation; *U.S. Public*, pg. 887

INTEL SEMICONDUCTOR B.V.—See Intel Corporation; *U.S. Public*, pg. 887

INTEL SEMICONDUCTOR GMBH—See Intel Corporation; *U.S. Public*, pg. 887

INTEL SEMICONDUCTOR LTD.—See Intel Corporation; *U.S. Public*, pg. 887

INTEL SEMICONDUTORES DO BRAZIL—See Intel Corporation; *U.S. Public*, pg. 887

INTEL SINGAPORE LTD.—See Intel Corporation; *U.S. Public*, pg. 887

INTEL SWEDEN—See Intel Corporation; *U.S. Public*, pg. 887

INTEL SWITZERLAND—See Intel Corporation; *U.S. Public*, pg. 887

INTEL TECHNOLOGY FAR EAST LTD.—See Intel Corporation; *U.S. Public*, pg. 887

INTELIDATA—See WorldCorp, Inc.; *Int'l*, pg. 1780

INTELLEDEX VISION PRODUCTS—See Electro Scientific Industries, Inc.; *U.S. Public*, pg. 568

INTELLICALL, INC.; *U.S. Public*, pg. 887

INTELLICORP INC.; *U.S. Public*, pg. 887

INTELLIGENCE, INFORMATION & AIRCRAFT INTEGRATION SYSTEMS—See Raytheon Company; *U.S. Public*, pg. 1364

INTELLIGENT CONTROLS INC.; *U.S. Private*, pg. 566

INTELLIGENT ELECTRONICS, INC.; *U.S. Public*, pg. 887

INTELLIGENT ENCLOSURES CORP.—See Intelligent Systems Corp.; *U.S. Public*, pg. 888

INTELLIGENT INSTRUMENTATION INC.—See Burr-Brown Corporation; *U.S. Public*, pg. 270

INTELLIGENT MEDIA VENTURES, INC.—See BellSouth Corporation; *U.S. Public*, pg. 208

INTELLIGENT SYSTEMS CORP.; *U.S. Public*, pg. 888

INTELLIGENT TECHNOLOGIES & SERVICES, INC.—See Fike Corporation; *U.S. Private*, pg. 404

INTELLIGRAPHICS INTERNATIONAL—See Analytical Surveys, Inc.; *U.S. Public*, pg. 110

INTELLIMEDIA COMMERCE, INC.—See American Software, Inc.; *U.S. Public*, pg. 91

INTELLISOURCE—See Safeguard Scientifics, Inc.; *U.S. Public*, pg. 1425

INTENSIVE HOME CARE NURSES, INC.—See Integrated Health Services, Inc.; *U.S. Public*, pg. 885

INTENSIVE HOME CARE SERVICES, INC.—See Integrated Health Services, Inc.; *U.S. Public*, pg. 885

INTEPLEX—See Bergen Brunswig Corporation; *U.S. Public*, pg. 215

INTER ALPHA—See Credit Commercial de France; *Int'l*, pg. 343

INTER-BETON S.A.—See Heidelberger Zement A.G.; *Int'l*, pg. 605

INTER-COMMERCIAL JAMAICA LTD.—See BASF AG; *Int'l*, pg. 108

INTER-COMMUNITY TELEPHONE COMPANY—See Lynch Corporation; *U.S. Public*, pg. 1022

INTER-CONTINENTAL AND FORUM HOTELS—See The Saison Group; *Int'l*, pg. 1178

INTER-CONTINENTAL HOTELS—See The Saison Group; *Int'l*, pg. 1178

INTER-CONTINENTAL HOTELS CORPORATION—See The Saison Group; *Int'l*, pg. 1178

INTER-GLOBAL INSURANCE AGENCY—See Torchmark Corporation; *U.S. Public*, pg. 1622

INTER-GLOBE SECURITY SERVICES LTD.—See Hanson PLC; *Int'l*, pg. 593

INTER ISLAND TELEPHONE CO., INC.—See PacifiCorp; *U.S. Public*, pg. 1252

INTER LEASING MOROCCO—See Banque Nationale de Paris; *Int'l*, pg. 163

PT INTER PACIFIC BANK—See Credit Commercial de France; *Int'l*, pg. 343

P.T. INTER-PACIFIC BANK—See The Sanwa Bank Limited; *Int'l*, pg. 1190

P.T. INTER-PACIFIC SECURITIES—See The Sanwa Bank Limited; *Int'l*, pg. 1190

INTER-PAK ELECTRONICS—See Litton Industries, Inc.; *U.S. Public*, pg. 1003

INTER PARFUMS-SELECTIVE INDUSTRIE—See Jean Philippe Fragrances, Inc.; *U.S. Public*, pg. 924

INTER REGIES CENTRE OUESR (I.R.C.O.)—See Lagardere Groupe; *Int'l*, pg. 792

INTER-SCAN AIRFREIGHT A/S—See Union-Transport Corporation; *U.S. Private*, pg. 1120

INTER-TEL DATACOMM, INC.—See Inter-Tel, Incorporated; *U.S. Public*, pg. 888

INTER-TEL EQUIPMENT UK, LTD.—See Inter-Tel, Incorporated; *U.S. Public*, pg. 888

INTER-TEL, INCORPORATED; *U.S. Public*, pg. 888

INTER-TEL, INCORPORATED-NEW JERSEY—See Inter-Tel, Incorporated; *U.S. Public*, pg. 888

INTER-TEL INTEGRATED SYSTEMS, INC.—See Inter-Tel, Incorporated; *U.S. Public*, pg. 888

INTER-TEL JAPAN, INC.—See Inter-Tel, Incorporated; *U.S. Public*, pg. 888

INTER-TEL LEASING, INC.—See Inter-Tel, Incorporated; *U.S. Public*, pg. 888

INTER-TEL MIDWEST, INC.—See Inter-Tel, Incorporated; *U.S. Public*, pg. 888

INTER-TEL NET SOLUTIONS—See Inter-Tel, Incorporated; *U.S. Public*, pg. 888

INTER-TEL TECHNOLOGIES, INC.—See Inter-Tel, Incorporated; *U.S. Public*, pg. 888

INTERA INFORMATION TECHNOLOGIES CORP.—See Trimac Corporation; *Int'l*, pg. 1424

INTERACT ACCESSORIES, INC.—See Recoton Corporation; *U.S. Public*, pg. 1369

INTERACTIVE DATA CORPORATION—See Pearson plc; *Int'l*, pg. 1025

INTERACTIVE DEUTSCH—See Deutsch, Inc.; *U.S. Private*, pg. 329

INTERACTIVE INSTRUCTIONAL SYSTEMS INC.—See Really Useful Holdings Limited; *Int'l*, pg. 1089

INTERACTIVE MARKET SYSTEMS, INC.—See VNU Verenigde Nederlandse Uitgeversbedrijven B.V.; *Int'l*, pg. 1447

INTERACTIVE MEDIA, INC.—See The Gazette Company; *U.S. Private*, pg. 442

INTERACTIVE SOLUTIONS—See Omnicom Group Inc.; *U.S. Public*, pg. 1224

INTERACTIVE TECHNOLOGIES, INC.; *U.S. Public*, pg. 888

INTERACTIVE TELECARD SERVICES, INC. (ITS); *U.S. Private*, pg. 566

INTERACTIVE VIDEO SYSTEMS LIMITED—See Really Useful Holdings Limited; *Int'l*, pg. 1089

Company Index

INTERADVIES (NNFD, REGIOBANK, NVB/VOLA)—See ING Groep N.V.; *Int'l*, pg. 647
INTERALLIANZ BANK ZURICH AG—See The Nippon Credit Bank, Ltd.; *Int'l*, pg. 933
INTERALPEN-HOTEL TYROL GMBH—See Liebherr-International AG; *Int'l*, pg. 808
INTERAMERICAN DEVELOPMENT BANK; *U.S. Private*, pg. 566
INTERAMERICAN FOODS CORPORATION—See Tablex, S.A. de C.V.; *Int'l*, pg. 1346
INTERAMERICAN ZINC—See IMCO Recycling Inc.; *U.S. Private*, pg. 871
INTERAMERICAN-STAR GROUP—See Zuercher Lagerhaus AG; *Int'l*, pg. 1529
INTERAPPIA PUBLICITA S.P.A.—See Koninklijke BolsWessanen nv; *Int'l*, pg. 751
INTERAVIA PUBLISHING GROUP—See The Thomson Corporation; *Int'l*, pg. 1601
INTERBAKE FOODS INC.—See George Weston Limited; *Int'l*, pg. 1495
INTERBANCA-BANCA PER FINANZIAMENTI A MEDIO E LUNGO TERMINE S.P.A.—See Banca di Roma; *Int'l*, pg. 136
INTERBATH-AUSTRALIA, PTY. LTD.—See Interbath, Inc.; *U.S. Private*, pg. 566
INTERBATH, INC.; *U.S. Private*, pg. 566
INTERBATH OF CANADA LTD.—See Interbath, Inc.; *U.S. Private*, pg. 566
INTERBETON B.V.—See Hollandsche Beton Groep NV; *Int'l*, pg. 630
INTER-BETON GMBH—See Heidelberger Zement A.G.; *Int'l*, pg. 606
INTERBIO INC.; *U.S. Private*, pg. 566
INTERBOLD—See International Business Machines Corporation; *U.S. Public*, pg. 897
INTERBOLD PACIFIC, LTD.—See Diebold, Incorporated; *U.S. Public*, pg. 506
INTERBRAND—See Omnicom Group Inc.; *U.S. Public*, pg. 1225
INTERBRAND SCHECHTER—See Omnicom Group Inc.; *U.S. Public*, pg. 1224
INTERBRANDS NV—See Koninklijke BolsWessanen nv; *Int'l*, pg. 752
INTERBREW ITALIA S.P.A.—See Interbrew S.A.; *Int'l*, pg. 679
INTERBREW NETHERLANDS—See Interbrew S.A.; *Int'l*, pg. 679
INTERBREW S.A.; *Int'l*, pg. 679
INTERBRUCKE GMBH-RÄM DEUTSCHLAND—See Koc Holding A.S.; *Int'l*, pg. 742
INTERCAI HOLDING BV—See KPN Koninklyke PTT Nederland NV; *Int'l*, pg. 720
INTERCAP GRAPHICS SYSTEMS—See Intergraph Corporation; *U.S. Public*, pg. 890
INTERCARE PRODUCTS LTD.—See Novartis AG; *Int'l*, pg. 983
INTERCARE TECHNOLOGIES, INC.—See Criticare Systems, Inc.; *U.S. Public*, pg. 459
INTERCASER S.A. DE SEGUROS Y REASEGUROS—See Skandia Insurance Company Limited; *Int'l*, pg. 1256
INTERCELL CO. LTD. PAPER SACK DIVISION—See UPM-Kymmene Corporation; *Int'l*, pg. 1429
INTERCERAMICA MANUFACTURING INC.—See Internacional de Ceramica S.A. de C.V.; *Int'l*, pg. 680
INTERCHANGE SOFTWARE DIVISION—See Sterling Commerce, Inc.; *U.S. Public*, pg. 1516
INTERCOM SYSTEMS, INC.—See TII Industries, Inc.; *U.S. Public*, pg. 1556
INTERCOMP (ICM)—See Kuhlman Corporation; *U.S. Public*, pg. 968
INTERCOMP RESORUCE DEVELOPMENT & ENGINEERING (CANADA) LTD.—See Scientific Software-Intercomp, Inc.; *U.S. Public*, pg. 1444
INTERCON GARMENTS INC.—See Sara Lee Corporation; *U.S. Public*, pg. 1434
INTERCON SECURITY LIMITED—See Jannock Limited; *Int'l*, pg. 699
INTERCONNECT PRODUCTS DIVISION—See Methode Electronics Inc.; *U.S. Public*, pg. 1101
INTERCONNECTION PRODUCTS—See Litton Industries, Inc.; *U.S. Public*, pg. 1005
INTERCONNECTIONS, INC.—See Emulex Corporation; *U.S. Public*, pg. 579
INTERCONNECTRON GMBH—See Smiths Industries plc; *Int'l*, pg. 1268
INTERCONSULT I FALKENBERG—See Svedala Industri AB; *Int'l*, pg. 1323
INTERCONSULT NORGE A/S—See Trelleborg AB; *Int'l*, pg. 1420
INTERCONTINENTAL APPAREL—See Hartmarx Corporation; *U.S. Public*, pg. 796
INTERCONTINENTAL BANK—See NationsBank Corporation; *U.S. Public*, pg. 1162
INTERCONTINENTAL BRANDED APPAREL—See Hartmarx Corporation; *U.S. Public*, pg. 796
INTERCONTINENTAL CORPORATION—See Eureko B.V.; *Int'l*, pg. 464
INTERCONTINENTAL FINANCE UNLTD.—See Kredietbank N.V.; *Int'l*, pg. 761
INTERCONTINENTAL MFG. CO.—See Datron Incorporated; *U.S. Private*, pg. 313
INTERCONTINENTAL QUIMICA, S.A. (INTERQUISA)—See Compania Espanola de Petroleos, S.A. (CEPSA); *Int'l*, pg. 323
INTERCONTROLE S.A.—See Technip; *Int'l*, pg. 1361
INTERCOOL ENERGY CORPORATION—See Intermagnetics General Corporation; *U.S. Public*, pg. 894
INTERCORD TONGESELLSCHAFT MBH—See EMI Group plc; *Int'l*, pg. 428
INTERCOSMETIC AB—See Wella Group; *Int'l*, pg. 1490
INTERCOSMETIC (GREAT BRITAIN) LTD.—See Wella Group; *Int'l*, pg. 1490
INTERCOSMETIC S.A.—See Wella Group; *Int'l*, pg. 1490

INTERCOSMETICS, INC.—See Wella Group; *Int'l*, pg. 1489
INTERCOUNTY NEWSPAPER—See Journal Register Company; *U.S. Public*, pg. 935
INTERCOUNTY TITLE CO. OF ILLINOIS; *U.S. Private*, pg. 567
INTERCRAFT COMPANY—See Newell Cc.; *U.S. Public*, pg. 1177
INTERCRAFT INDUSTRIES OF CANADA, LTD.—See Newell Co.; *U.S. Public*, pg. 1178
INTERDENTAL AB—See Axel Johnson AB; *Int'l*, pg. 708
INTERDIGITAL COMMUNICATIONS CORP.; *U.S. Public*, pg. 889
INTERDIGITAL PATENTS CORPORATION—See InterDigital Communications Corp.; *U.S. Public*, pg. 889
INTERDIGITAL TELECOM, INC.—See InterDigital Communications Corp.; *U.S. Public*, pg. 889
INTERDOCK—See Cardo AB; *Int'l*, pg. 269
INTEREALTY CORPORATION—See News Holdings Corp.; *U.S. Private*, pg. 797
INTERELEC S.C.—See Electrabel S.A.; *Int'l*, pg. 437
INTERELECTRICA ADMINISTRACAO E PARTICIPACOES LTDA.—See VARTA AG; *Int'l*, pg. 1452
INTERENERGIE S.C.—See Electrabel S.A.; *Int'l*, pg. 437
INTERENSCO N.V.—See Internatio-Muller N.V.; *Int'l*, pg. 682
INTEREST—See Electrabel S.A.; *Int'l*, pg. 437
INTERET CORPORATION; *U.S. Private*, pg. 567
INTERFAB—See National Restaurant Supply Company; *U.S. Private*, pg. 786
INTERFACE ELECTRONICS CORPORATION; *U.S. Private*, pg. 567
INTERFACE EUROPE B.V.—See Interface Inc.; *U.S. Public*, pg. 889
INTERFACE FLOORING SYSTEMS INC.—See Interface Inc.; *U.S. Public*, pg. 889
INTERFACE INC.; *U.S. Public*, pg. 889
INTERFACE RESEARCH CORPORATION—See Interface Inc.; *U.S. Public*, pg. 889
INTERFACE SYSTEMS, INC.; *U.S. Public*, pg. 889
INTERFACE SYSTEMS INTERNATIONAL—See Interface Systems, Inc.; *U.S. Public*, pg. 890
INTERFERON SCIENCES DEVELOPMENT CORP.—See GP Strategies Corporation; *U.S. Public*, pg. 694
INTERFERON SCIENCES, INC.—See GP Strategies Corporation; *U.S. Public*, pg. 694
INTERFORM CORPORATION—See Champion Industries; *U.S. Public*, pg. 333
INTERFREIGHT FORWARDERS UGANDA LIMITED—See Panalpina Welttransport (Holding) AG; *Int'l*, pg. 1022
INTERFREIGHT INVESTISSEMENTS RWANDA S.A.—See Panalpina Welttransport (Holding) AG; *Int'l*, pg. 1022
INTERFREIGHT INVESTMENTS LIMITED—See Panalpina Welttransport (Holding) AG; *Int'l*, pg. 1022
INTERFREIGHT (KENYA) LIMITED—See Panalpina Welttransport (Holding) AG; *Int'l*, pg. 1022
INTERFREIGHT TANZANIA LIMITED—See Panalpina Welttransport (Holding) AG; *Int'l*, pg. 1022
INTERGA S.C.—See Electrabel S.A.; *Int'l*, pg. 437
INTERGAS C.V.B.A.—See Electrabel S.A.; *Int'l*, pg. 437
INTERGEM—See Electrabel S.A.; *Int'l*, pg. 437
INTERGEN BEAUTY PRODUCTS—See Franz Haniel & Cie, GmbH; *Int'l*, pg. 591
INTERGEN CENTER FOR DIAGNOSTIC PRODUCTS—See Intergen Company; *U.S. Private*, pg. 567
INTERGEN COMPANY; *U.S. Private*, pg. 567
INTERGLOBE MONTREAL INC.—See G.T.C. Transcontinental Group Ltd.; *Int'l*, pg. 538
INTERGLOBE PRINTING INC.—See G.T.C. Transcontinental Group Ltd.; *Int'l*, pg. 538
INTERGRAPH—See Intergraph Corporation; *U.S. Public*, pg. 890
INTERGRAPH ASIA PACIFIC LIMITED—See Intergraph Corporation; *U.S. Public*, pg. 891
INTERGRAPH (BENELUX) B.V.—See Intergraph Corporation; *U.S. Public*, pg. 891
INTERGRAPH CAD/CAM (DENMARK) A/S—See Intergraph Corporation; *U.S. Public*, pg. 891
INTERGRAPH CANADA LTD.—See Intergraph Corporation; *U.S. Public*, pg. 891
INTERGRAPH CHINA, INC.—See Intergraph Corporation; *U.S. Public*, pg. 891
INTERGRAPH COMPUTER SERVICES INDUSTRY & TRADE—See Intergraph Corporation; *U.S. Public*, pg. 891
INTERGRAPH COMPUTER SERVICES INDUSTRY & TRADE, A.S.—See Intergraph Corporation; *U.S. Public*, pg. 891
INTERGRAPH COMPUTER SYSTEMS—See Intergraph Corporation; *U.S. Public*, pg. 891
INTERGRAPH CORP. (NZ) LIMITED—See Intergraph Corporation; *U.S. Public*, pg. 891
INTERGRAPH CORP. PTY. LTD.—See Intergraph Corporation; *U.S. Public*, pg. 891
INTERGRAPH CORPORATION; *U.S. Public*, pg. 890
INTERGRAPH CORPORATION—See Intergraph Corporation; *U.S. Public*, pg. 890
INTERGRAPH CORPORATION, ANA TECH DIV.—See Intergraph Corporation; *U.S. Public*, pg. 891
INTERGRAPH CORPORATION, OPTRONICS DIV.—See Intergraph Corporation; *U.S. Public*, pg. 891
INTERGRAPH CR—See Intergraph Corporation; *U.S. Public*, pg. 891
INTERGRAPH DE MEXICO S.A. DE C.V.—See Intergraph Corporation; *U.S. Public*, pg. 892
INTERGRAPH (DEUTSCHLAND) GMBH—See Intergraph Corporation; *U.S. Public*, pg. 892
INTERGRAPH ELECTRONICS—See Intergraph Corporation; *U.S. Public*, pg. 891
INTERGRAPH (ESPANA) S.A.—See Intergraph Corporation; *U.S. Public*, pg. 892
INTERGRAPH EUROPE (POLSKA)—See Intergraph Corporation; *U.S. Public*, pg. 892
INTERGRAPH (FINLAND) OY—See Intergraph Corporation; *U.S. Public*, pg. 892

INTERGRAPH FRANCE S.A.—See Intergraph Corporation; *U.S. Public*, pg. 892
INTERGRAPH GMB (AUSTRIA)—See Intergraph Corporation; *U.S. Public*, pg. 892
INTERGRAPH HELLAS S.A.—See Intergraph Corporation; *U.S. Public*, pg. 892
INTERGRAPH HONG KONG LIMITED—See Intergraph Corporation; *U.S. Public*, pg. 892
INTERGRAPH HUNGARY LTD.—See Intergraph Corporation; *U.S. Public*, pg. 892
INTERGRAPH (INDIA) PRIVATE LTD.—See Intergraph Corporation; *U.S. Public*, pg. 892
INTERGRAPH IRELAND LIMITED—See Intergraph Corporation; *U.S. Public*, pg. 892
INTERGRAPH ITALIA L.L.C.—See Intergraph Corporation; *U.S. Public*, pg. 892
INTERGRAPH KOREA, LTD.—See Intergraph Corporation; *U.S. Public*, pg. 892
INTERGRAPH NORGE A/S—See Intergraph Corporation; *U.S. Public*, pg. 892
INTERGRAPH PUBLIC SAFETY PTY., LTD.—See Intergraph Corporation; *U.S. Public*, pg. 892
INTERGRAPH SAUDI ARABIA LTD.—See Intergraph Corporation; *U.S. Public*, pg. 892
INTERGRAPH SERVICES B.V.—See Intergraph Corporation; *U.S. Public*, pg. 891
INTERGRAPH (SHENZHEN) COMPANY LTD.—See Intergraph Corporation; *U.S. Public*, pg. 892
INTERGRAPH (SWITZERLAND) AG—See Intergraph Corporation; *U.S. Public*, pg. 892
INTERGRAPH SYSTEMS (MALAYSIA) SDN BHD—See Intergraph Corporation; *U.S. Public*, pg. 892
INTERGRAPH TECHNICAL SERVICES MIDDLE EAST LIMITED—See Intergraph Corporation; *U.S. Public*, pg. 892
INTERGROUP HEALTH CORPORATION—See Foundation Health Systems, Inc.; *U.S. Public*, pg. 678
INTER-HEBDO—See Lagardere Groupe; *Int'l*, pg. 792
INTERIM—See Selas Corporation of America; *U.S. Public*, pg. 1455
INTERIM SERVICES (CANADA) LTD.—See Interim Services Inc.; *U.S. Public*, pg. 892
INTERIM SERVICES INC.; *U.S. Public*, pg. 892
INTERIOR FUELS COMPANY—See Tesoro Petroleum Corporation; *U.S. Public*, pg. 1582
INTERIOR SPACE INTERNATIONAL—See A. Epstein and Sons, Intl., Inc.; *U.S. Private*, pg. 379
INTERIORS—See VNU Verenigde Nederlandse Uitgeversbedrijven B.V.; *Int'l*, pg. 1446
INTERKAL, INC.—See Kotobuki Seating Co.; *Int'l*, pg. 759
INTERKOHLE BETEILIGUNGSGESELLSCHAFT MIT BESCHRANKTER HAFTUNG—See Veba AG; *Int'l*, pg. 1456
INTERKOSMETIK GES.M.B.H.—See Wella Group; *Int'l*, pg. 1490
THE INTERLAKE CORPORATION; *U.S. Public*, pg. 892
INTERLAKE MATERIAL HANDLING DIV—See The Interlake Corporation; *U.S. Public*, pg. 893
INTERLAKE PAPERS, INC.—See Consolidated Papers, Inc.; *U.S. Public*, pg. 436
INTERLAKEN CAPITAL AVIATION SERVICES, INC.—See W.R. Berkley Corporation; *U.S. Public*, pg. 216
INTERLAKEN CAPITAL, INC.; *U.S. Private*, pg. 567
INTERLEAF AUSTRALIA, PTY. LTD.—See Interleaf, Inc.; *U.S. Public*, pg. 893
INTERLEAF FRANCE, S.A.—See Interleaf, Inc.; *U.S. Public*, pg. 893
INTERLEAF GMBH—See Interleaf, Inc.; *U.S. Public*, pg. 893
INTERLEAF, INC.; *U.S. Public*, pg. 893
INTERLEAF JAPAN INC.—See Interleaf, Inc.; *U.S. Public*, pg. 893
INTERLEAF UK, LTD.—See Interleaf, Inc.; *U.S. Public*, pg. 893
INTERLEASE MANAGEMENT CORPORATION—See American International Group, Inc.; *U.S. Public*, pg. 85
INTERLEASE TRADING CORP.—See American International Group, Inc.; *U.S. Public*, pg. 85
INTERLOCK INDUSTRIES, INC.; *U.S. Private*, pg. 567
INTERLOK GMBH—See Rothenberger Group GmbH; *Int'l*, pg. 1128
INTERLUX S.C.—See Electrabel S.A.; *Int'l*, pg. 437
INTERMAGNETICS GENERAL CORPORATION; *U.S. Public*, pg. 893
INTERMAGNETICS GENERAL (EUROPE) LIMITED—See Intermagnetics General Corporation; *U.S. Public*, pg. 894
INTERMARINE S.P.A.—See Compart SpA; *Int'l*, pg. 324
INTERMARINE U.S.A. INC.—See Compart SpA; *Int'l*, pg. 324
INTERMARK CORP.—See H.M.G. Worldwide Corp.; *U.S. Public*, pg. 771
INTERMARK WORLD PRODUCTS, LTD.; *U.S. Private*, pg. 567
INTERMARKETS ADVERTISING; *Int'l*, pg. 680
INTERMARKETS ADVERTISING/LEBANON—See Intermarkets Advertising; *Int'l*, pg. 680
INTERMARKETS BAHRAIN—See Intermarkets Advertising; *Int'l*, pg. 680
INTERMARKETS EGYPT—See Intermarkets Advertising; *Int'l*, pg. 680
INTERMARKETS EUROPE ADVERTISING LTD.—See Intermarkets Advertising; *Int'l*, pg. 680
INTERMARKETS INTERNATIONAL—See TBWA Chiat/Day; *U.S. Private*, pg. 1062
INTERMARKETS JORDAN/JERUSALEM AD. AGENCY—See Intermarkets Advertising; *Int'l*, pg. 680
INTERMARKETS KUWAIT—See Intermarkets Advertising; *Int'l*, pg. 680
INTERMARKETS LEBANON—See TBWA Chiat/Day; *U.S. Private*, pg. 1062
INTERMARKETS PUBLIC RELATIONS (ME)—See Intermarkets Advertising; *Int'l*, pg. 680

INTERMARKETS SAUDI ARABIA—See Intermarkets Advertising; *Int'l*, pg. 680
INTERMARKETS U.A.E.—See Intermarkets Advertising; *Int'l*, pg. 680
INTERMARKETS UAE—See TBWA Chiat/Day; *U.S. Private*, pg. 1062
INTERMARKETS YEMEN/MASS—See Intermarkets Advertising; *Int'l*, pg. 680
INTERMAT—See Fiber Materials, Inc.; *U.S. Private*, pg. 402
INTERMATIC INC.; *U.S. Private*, pg. 567
INTERMEC GROUP—See Marcam Solutions, Inc.; *U.S. Public*, pg. 1043
INTERMEC MEDIA PRODUCTS—See UNOVA, Inc.; *U.S. Public*, pg. 1699
INTERMEC SOUTHWEST—See Litton Industries, Inc.; *U.S. Public*, pg. 1004
INTERMEC STRICHODE SYSTEME GMBH—See Litton Industries, Inc.; *U.S. Public*, pg. 1004
INTERMEC SYSTEMS CORP.—See Litton Industries, Inc.; *U.S. Public*, pg. 1005
INTERMEC TECHNOLOGIES CORPORATION—See UNOVA, Inc.; *U.S. Public*, pg. 1699
INTERMEC UK LTD.—See Litton Industries, Inc.; *U.S. Public*, pg. 1005
INTERMEDIA CAPITAL PARTNERS IV, L.P.—See Center Partners Management LLC; *U.S. Private*, pg. 222
INTERMEDIATE HOLDINGS, INC.—See Conseco Inc.; *U.S. Public*, pg. 433
INTERMEDICS INC.—See Sulzer Ltd.; *Int'l*, pg. 1307
INTERMEDICS JAPAN K.K.—See Sulzer Ltd.; *Int'l*, pg. 1307
INTERMEDICS ORTHOPEDICS, INC.—See Sulzer Ltd.; *Int'l*, pg. 1307
INTERMEDICS S.A.—See Sulzer Ltd.; *Int'l*, pg. 1307
INTERMET CORPORATION; *U.S. Public*, pg. 894
INTERMETRICS, INC.; *U.S. Private*, pg. 567
INTERMETRICS SECURITIES, INC.—See Intermetrics, Inc.; *U.S. Private*, pg. 568
INTERMODAL TRANSPORTATION SERVICES, INC.—See SGS Societe Generale de Surveillance Holding S.A.; *Int'l*, pg. 1153
INTERMOSANE—See Electrabel S.A.; *Int'l*, pg. 437
INTERMOSELLE—See Ciments Francais; *Int'l*, pg. 292
INTERMOSELLE S.A.R.L.—See Arbed S.A.; *Int'l*, pg. 80
INTERMOSELLE S.A.R.L.—See Dyckerhoff AG; *Int'l*, pg. 423
INTERMOTOR—See Standard Motor Products Inc.; *U.S. Public*, pg. 1503
INTERMOUNTAIN BANKSHARES OF COLORADO, INC.—See Banc One Corporation; *U.S. Public*, pg. 173
INTERMOUNTAIN FARMERS ASSOCIATION; *U.S. Private*, pg. 568
INTERMOUNTAIN GAS CO.—See Intermountain Industries, Inc.; *U.S. Private*, pg. 568
INTERMOUNTAIN HEALTH CARE INC.; *U.S. Private*, pg. 568
INTERMOUNTAIN INDUSTRIES, INC.; *U.S. Private*, pg. 568
INTERNACIONAL DE CERAMICA S.A. DE C.V.; *Int'l*, pg. 680
INTERNACO S.R.L.—See Hewlett-Packard Company; *U.S. Public*, pg. 822
INTERNAL MEDICINE GRAND VIEW, INC.—See Integrated Health Services, Inc.; *U.S. Public*, pg. 885
INTERNATIO HOUT B.V.—See Internatio-Muller N.V.; *Int'l*, pg. 682
INTERNATIO MINERALS & CHEMICALS—See Internatio-Muller N.V.; *Int'l*, pg. 682
INTERNATIO-MULLER N.V.; *Int'l*, pg. 680
INTERNATIO (PTY.) LTD.—See Internatio-Muller N.V.; *Int'l*, pg. 682
INTERNATIONAL AERO-SEA FORWARDERS, INC.—See International Aero-Sea Forwarders, Ltd.; *Int'l*, pg. 683
INTERNATIONAL AERO-SEA FORWARDERS, LTD.; *Int'l*, pg. 682
INTERNATIONAL AIRCRAFT SERVICES—See James Crean PLC; *Int'l*, pg. 340
INTERNATIONAL AIRLINE SUPPORT GROUP, INC.; *U.S. Public*, pg. 894
INTERNATIONAL ALUMINUM CORPORATION; *U.S. Public*, pg. 894
INTERNATIONAL APPAREL MARKETING CORP.—See Delta Woodside Industries, Inc.; *U.S. Public*, pg. 498
INTERNATIONAL AUTO CO., LTD.—See Isuzu Motors Limited; *Int'l*, pg. 693
INTERNATIONAL AUTOMATED ENERGY SYSTEMS, INC.—See Ceridian Corporation; *U.S. Public*, pg. 331
INTERNATIONAL AVIATION TERMINALS INC.—See Western Corporate Enterprises Inc.; *Int'l*, pg. 1494
INTERNATIONAL BAKING CO.—See Sara Lee Corporation; *U.S. Public*, pg. 1433
INTERNATIONAL BANCSHARES CORP; *U.S. Private*, pg. 568
INTERNATIONAL BANK OF SOUTHERN AFRICA SFOM LTD. (IBSA-SFOM)—See Bank Brussels Lambert; *Int'l*, pg. 149
INTERNATIONAL BANKING DIV.—See Imperial Bancorp; *U.S. Public*, pg. 872
INTERNATIONAL BENEFIT SERVICE CORPORATION—See Cigna Corp.; *U.S. Public*, pg. 362
INTERNATIONAL BILLING SERVICES—See USCS International, Inc.; *U.S. Public*, pg. 1659
INTERNATIONAL BIO-RESEARCH IBR FORSCHUNGS GMBH—See Genzyme Corporation; *U.S. Public*, pg. 733
INTERNATIONAL BRAKE INDUSTRIES, INC.—See MascoTech, Inc.; *U.S. Public*, pg. 1055
INTERNATIONAL BUSINESS ANALYSIS PROPRIETARY LIMITED—See Westpac Banking Corporation; *Int'l*, pg. 1496
INTERNATIONAL BUSINESS AND MERCANTILE REASSURANCE COMPANY—See Old Republic International Corporation; *U.S. Public*, pg. 1218

INTERNATIONAL BUSINESS DIVISION (TOYKO)—See The Daiwa Bank Limited; *Int'l*, pg. 373
INTERNATIONAL BUSINESS FORMS LIMITED—See International Paper Company; *U.S. Public*, pg. 905
OY INTERNATIONAL BUSINESS MACHINES AB—See International Business Machines Corporation; *U.S. Public*, pg. 898
INTERNATIONAL BUSINESS MACHINES A/S—See International Business Machines Corporation; *U.S. Public*, pg. 898
INTERNATIONAL BUSINESS MACHINES CORPORATION; *U.S. Public*, pg. 895
INTERNATIONAL BUSINESS MACHINES LIMITED—See International Business Machines Corporation; *U.S. Public*, pg. 898
INTERNATIONAL BUSINESS MACHINES OF BELGIUM S.A.—See International Business Machines Corporation; *U.S. Public*, pg. 898
INTERNATIONAL BUSINESS MACHINES, S.A.E.—See International Business Machines Corporation; *U.S. Public*, pg. 898
INTERNATIONAL BUSINESS SERVICES, INC.—See Comarco, Inc.; *U.S. Public*, pg. 406
INTERNATIONAL CALIFORNIA GLASS CORP.—See International Aluminum Corporation; *U.S. Public*, pg. 895
INTERNATIONAL CANCER SCREENING LABS—See GWC Health, Inc.; *U.S. Private*, pg. 436
INTERNATIONAL CAPITAL EQUIPMENT LIMITED; *Int'l*, pg. 683
INTERNATIONAL CAROLINA GLASS CORP.—See International Aluminum Corporation; *U.S. Public*, pg. 895
INTERNATIONAL CENTER FOR ENTREPRENEURIAL DEVELOPMENT; *U.S. Public*, pg. 568
INTERNATIONAL CHEMICAL COMPANY; *U.S. Private*, pg. 568
INTERNATIONAL CHEMICAL & COSMETIC CO. S.P.A.—See Unilever Plc; *Int'l*, pg. 1436
INTERNATIONAL CHEMPACK INC.—See The Dow Chemical Company; *U.S. Public*, pg. 523
INTERNATIONAL CIRCULATION DISTRIBUTORS—See The Hearst Corporation; *U.S. Private*, pg. 517
INTERNATIONAL COLD STORAGE CO., INC.; *U.S. Private*, pg. 568
INTERNATIONAL COLUMBIA RESOURCES CORPORATION—See Exxon Corporation; *U.S. Public*, pg. 602
INTERNATIONAL COMFORT PRODUCTS; *U.S. Public*, pg. 898
INTERNATIONAL COMFORT PRODUCTS CORP.—See International Comfort Products; *U.S. Public*, pg. 898
INTERNATIONAL COMMERCIAL BANK OF CATHAY—See The International Commercial Bank of China; *Int'l*, pg. 684
THE INTERNATIONAL COMMERCIAL BANK OF CHINA—See The International Commercial Bank of China; *Int'l*, pg. 683
THE INTERNATIONAL COMMERCIAL BANK OF CHINA; *Int'l*, pg. 683
THE INTERNATIONAL COMMERCIAL BANK OF CHINA—See The International Commercial Bank of China; *Int'l*, pg. 684
INTERNATIONAL COMMUNICATIONS (DENVER)—See Carat ICG; *U.S. Private*, pg. 208
INTERNATIONAL COMMUNICATIONS HOLDINGS, INC.—See PacifiCorp; *U.S. Public*, pg. 1252
INTERNATIONAL COMPONENTS CORPORATION; *U.S. Private*, pg. 569
INTERNATIONAL COMPONENTS TECHNOLOGY CORPORATION (CMD)—See The Furukawa Electric Co., Ltd.; *Int'l*, pg. 530
INTERNATIONAL COMPUTER SERVICES, INC.—See American International Group, Inc.; *U.S. Public*, pg. 84
INTERNATIONAL COMPUTERS (B) SDN.BHD—See Fujitsu Limited; *Int'l*, pg. 529
INTERNATIONAL COMPUTERS HONG KONG LIMITED—See Fujitsu Limited; *Int'l*, pg. 529
INTERNATIONAL COMPUTERS (MALAYSIA) SDN.BHD.—See Fujitsu Limited; *Int'l*, pg. 529
INTERNATIONAL COMPUTERS (NIGERIA) LIMITED—See Fujitsu Limited; *Int'l*, pg. 529
INTERNATIONAL COMPUTERS (SOUTH AFRICA) (PROPRIETARY) LIMITED—See Fujitsu Limited; *Int'l*, pg. 529
INTERNATIONAL CONSUMER & SERVICE SECTOR—See Kimberly-Clark Corporation; *U.S. Public*, pg. 958
INTERNATIONAL CONTAINER SYSTEMS—See Intertape Polymer Group Inc.; *Int'l*, pg. 685
INTERNATIONAL COPYING MACHINES—See Mannesmann A.G.; *Int'l*, pg. 836
INTERNATIONAL CORRESPONDENCE SCHOOLS (AUSTRALASIA) LIMITED—See Harcourt General, Inc.; *U.S. Public*, pg. 784
INTERNATIONAL CORRESPONDENCE SCHOOLS CANADIAN LTD.—See Harcourt General, Inc.; *U.S. Public*, pg. 784
INTERNATIONAL CORRESPONDENCE SCHOOLS, INC.—See Harcourt General, Inc.; *U.S. Public*, pg. 783
INTERNATIONAL CORRESPONDENCE SCHOOLS LTD.—See Harcourt General, Inc.; *U.S. Public*, pg. 784
INTERNATIONAL CORRESPONDENCE SCHOOLS (NEW ZEALAND) LIMITED—See Harcourt General, Inc.; *U.S. Public*, pg. 784
INTERNATIONAL CORRESPONDENCE SCHOOLS (OVERSEAS) LIMITED—See Harcourt General, Inc.; *U.S. Public*, pg. 784
INTERNATIONAL COSMETICS CO., LTD.; *Int'l*, pg. 684
INTERNATIONAL CREATIVE MANAGEMENT, INC.—See ICM Holdings Inc.; *U.S. Private*, pg. 554
INTERNATIONAL CREATIVE MANAGEMENT LTD.—See ICM Holdings Inc.; *U.S. Private*, pg. 554
INTERNATIONAL CUTLERY, LTD; *U.S. Private*, pg. 569

INTERNATIONAL DAIRY QUEEN, INC.—See Berkshire Hathaway Inc.; *U.S. Public*, pg. 220
INTERNATIONAL DATA CORP.—See International Data Group; *U.S. Public*, pg. 570
INTERNATIONAL DATA GROUP; *U.S. Private*, pg. 569
INTERNATIONAL DESSERT PARTNERS—See Corn Products International, Inc.; *U.S. Public*, pg. 447
INTERNATIONAL DESSERT PARTNERS—See General Mills, Inc.; *U.S. Public*, pg. 718
INTERNATIONAL DISPOSAL CORP. OF CALIFORNIA—See Browning-Ferris Industries, Inc.; *U.S. Public*, pg. 264
INTERNATIONAL DISPOSAL CORPORATION OF INDIANA—See Browning-Ferris Industries, Inc.; *U.S. Public*, pg. 264
INTERNATIONAL DISTILLERS AFRICA—See Diageo Plc; *Int'l*, pg. 410
INTERNATIONAL DISTILLERS & VINTNERS-EUROPE—See Diageo Plc; *Int'l*, pg. 409
INTERNATIONAL DISTILLERS & VINTNERS LTD.—See Diageo Plc; *Int'l*, pg. 409
INTERNATIONAL DISTILLERS CARIBBEAN—See Diageo Plc; *Int'l*, pg. 410
INTERNATIONAL DISTILLERS COLOMBIA—See Diageo Plc; *Int'l*, pg. 410
INTERNATIONAL DISTILLERS INDIA—See Diageo Plc; *Int'l*, pg. 410
INTERNATIONAL DISTILLERS JAPAN—See Diageo Plc; *Int'l*, pg. 410
INTERNATIONAL DISTILLERS NORTH ASIA—See Diageo Plc; *Int'l*, pg. 410
INTERNATIONAL DISTILLERS PHILIPPINES—See Diageo Plc; *Int'l*, pg. 410
INTERNATIONAL DISTILLERS SOUTH ASIA—See Diageo Plc; *Int'l*, pg. 410
INTERNATIONAL DIVERSE FOODS—See Levmark Capital Corporation; *U.S. Public*, pg. 663
INTERNATIONAL DIVISION—See The Broken Hill Proprietary Company Limited; *Int'l*, pg. 226
INTERNATIONAL DIVISION—See Gold Eagle Company; *U.S. Private*, pg. 459
INTERNATIONAL DIVISION—See Shiseido Company Ltd.; *Int'l*, pg. 1235
INTERNATIONAL DIV.—See Scholastic Corporation; *U.S. Public*, pg. 1440
INTERNATIONAL DIV.. AM INTERNATIONAL—See Multigraphics Inc.; *U.S. Public*, pg. 1141
INTERNATIONAL DIVISION (NARA)—See The Nanto Bank, Ltd.; *Int'l*, pg. 905
INTERNATIONAL ELCO, A.P.S.—See Kyocera Corporation; *Int'l*, pg. 775
INTERNATIONAL ELECTRONIC RESEARCH CORP.—See CTS Corporation; *U.S. Public*, pg. 286
INTERNATIONAL ENVELOPE COMPANY—See American Business Products, Inc.; *U.S. Public*, pg. 70
INTERNATIONAL ENVIRONMENTAL CORP.—See LSB Industries, Inc.; *U.S. Public*, pg. 970
INTERNATIONAL ENVIRONMENTAL EXPORT CORP.—See LSB Industries, Inc.; *U.S. Public*, pg. 970
INTERNATIONAL EQUIPMENT NEWS EUROPE NV—See Reed Elsevier plc; *Int'l*, pg. 1099
INTERNATIONAL EXPLORATION, INC.—See ERD Waste Corp.; *U.S. Public*, pg. 546
INTERNATIONAL EXTRUSION CORP.—See International Aluminum Corporation; *U.S. Public*, pg. 895
INTERNATIONAL EXTRUSION CORPORATION-TEXAS—See International Aluminum Corporation; *U.S. Public*, pg. 895
INTERNATIONAL FACTORS—See Bank Brussels Lambert; *Int'l*, pg. 147
INTERNATIONAL FACTORS LEASING PTE LTD.—See International Factors (Singapore) Ltd.; *Int'l*, pg. 684
INTERNATIONAL FACTORS LIMITED—See Lloyds TSB Group PLC; *Int'l*, pg. 813
INTERNATIONAL FACTORS NEDERLAND B.V.—See ABN-AMRO Holding N.V.; *Int'l*, pg. 9
INTERNATIONAL FACTORS (SINGAPORE) LTD.; *Int'l*, pg. 684
INTERNATIONAL FALLS POWER COMPANY—See Boise Cascade Corporation; *U.S. Public*, pg. 243
INTERNATIONAL FAMILY ENTERTAINMENT, INC.—See The News Corporation Limited; *Int'l*, pg. 927
INTERNATIONAL FIBERCOM; *U.S. Public*, pg. 898
INTERNATIONAL FIBRE SALES, S.A.—See The Mead Corporation; *U.S. Public*, pg. 1077
INTERNATIONAL FLAVORS & FRAGRANCES (CANADA) LTD.—See International Flavors & Fragrances, Inc.; *U.S. Public*, pg. 899
INTERNATIONAL FLAVORS & FRAGRANCES DE VENEZUELA C.A.—See International Flavors & Fragrances, Inc.; *U.S. Public*, pg. 899
INTERNATIONAL FLAVORS & FRAGRANCES (ESPANA) S.A.—See International Flavors & Fragrances, Inc.; *U.S. Public*, pg. 899
INTERNATIONAL FLAVORS & FRAGRANCES I.F.F. (DEUTSCHLAND) GMBH—See International Flavors & Fragrances, Inc.; *U.S. Public*, pg. 899
INTERNATIONAL FLAVORS & FRAGRANCES I.F.F. (NEDERLAND) B.V.—See International Flavors & Fragrances, Inc.; *U.S. Public*, pg. 899
INTERNATIONAL FLAVORS & FRAGRANCES I.F.F. (NORGE) A/S—See International Flavors & Fragrances, Inc.; *U.S. Public*, pg. 899
INTERNATIONAL FLAVORS & FRAGRANCES I.F.F. (PORTUGAL) LDA.—See International Flavors & Fragrances, Inc.; *U.S. Public*, pg. 899
INTERNATIONAL FLAVORS & FRAGRANCES I.F.F. (SWITZERLAND) A.G.—See International Flavors & Fragrances, Inc.; *U.S. Public*, pg. 899
INTERNATIONAL FLAVORS & FRAGRANCES, INC.; *U.S. Public*, pg. 898
INTERNATIONAL FLAVORS & FRAGRANCES (JAPAN) LTD.—See International Flavors & Fragrances, Inc.; *U.S. Public*, pg. 899

Company Index

INTERNATIONAL FLAVORS & FRAGRANCES (SINGAPORE) PTE. LTD.—See International Flavors & Fragrances, Inc.; *U.S. Public*, pg. 899
INTERNATIONAL FLAVORS & FRAGRANCES (THAILAND) LTD.—See International Flavors & Fragrances, Inc.; *U.S. Public*, pg. 899
INTERNATIONAL FOREST PRODUCTS—See Norske Skogindustrier A.S; *Int'l*, pg. 966
INTERNATIONAL FOREST SEED COMPANY—See Novartis AG; *Int'l*, pg. 973
INTERNATIONAL GAME TECHNOLOGY; *U.S. Public*, pg. 900
INTERNATIONAL GAS APPARATUS LIMITED—See Ruhrgas Aktiengesellschaft; *Int'l*, pg. 1149
INTERNATIONAL HERALD TRIBUNE S.A.—See The New York Times Company; *U.S. Public*, pg. 1176
INTERNATIONAL HOME FOODS INC.—See Hicks, Muse, Tate & Furst Inc.; *U.S. Private*, pg. 526
INTERNATIONAL HORTICULTURE PUBLICATIONS COMPANY—See Watt Publishing Co.; *U.S. Private*, pg. 1154
INTERNATIONAL HOUSE OF PANCAKES, INC.—See IHOP Corp.; *U.S. Public*, pg. 862
INTERNATIONAL IMAGING MATERIALS, INC.—See PAXAR Corporation; *U.S. Public*, pg. 1266
INTERNATIONAL INDEMNITY LTD.—See Merck & Co., Inc.; *U.S. Public*, pg. 1091
INTERNATIONAL IN-FLIGHT CATERING CO. LTD.—See Japan Airlines Company, Ltd.; *Int'l*, pg. 700
INTERNATIONAL INFRASTRUCTURE DIVISION—See Morrison Knudsen Corporation; *U.S. Public*, pg. 1134
INTERNATIONAL INSURANCE BROKERS LIMITED—See The Bank of Nova Scotia; *Int'l*, pg. 156
INTERNATIONAL INSURANCE UNDERWRITERS, INC.—See Berkshire Hathaway Inc.; *U.S. Public*, pg. 220
INTERNATIONAL INVESTMENT & UNDERWRITING LTD.; *Int'l*, pg. 684
INTERNATIONAL INVESTMENT MANAGEMENT GESELLSCHAFT S.A.—See Deutsche Bank AG; *Int'l*, pg. 405
INTERNATIONAL KENDIX TEXTILES B.V.—See Gamma Holding N.V.; *Int'l*, pg. 540
INTERNATIONAL LEARNING SYSTEMS (JAPAN) LTD.—See Berlitz International, Inc.; *U.S. Public*, pg. 222
INTERNATIONAL LEASE FINANCE CORPORATION—See American International Group, Inc.; *U.S. Public*, pg. 85
INTERNATIONAL LIFE INVESTORS INSURANCE COMPANY—See AEGON N.V.; *Int'l*, pg. 27
INTERNATIONAL LOGISTIC SYSTEMS S.R.L.—See Coeclerici Group; *Int'l*, pg. 303
INTERNATIONAL LOGISTICS LIMITED; *U.S. Private*, pg. 571
INTERNATIONAL LOTTERY & TOTALIZATOR SYSTEMS, INC.; *U.S. Public*, pg. 900
INTERNATIONAL MAIL HANDLING NV—See KPN Koninklyke PTT Nederland NV; *Int'l*, pg. 720
INTERNATIONAL MARINE CONSTRUCTION CO. S.A.K.—See Nissho Iwai Corporation; *Int'l*, pg. 948
INTERNATIONAL MARINE UNDERWRITERS OF NEW ENGLAND, INC.—See Xerox Corporation; *U.S. Public*, pg. 1784
INTERNATIONAL MARITIME SATELLITE ORGANISATION (INMARSAT)—See British Telecommunications plc; *Int'l*, pg. 222
INTERNATIONAL MARKETING & PROMOTIONS—See DMB&B Communications; *U.S. Private*, pg. 304
INTERNATIONAL MARKETING & PROMOTIONS BARCELONA—See DMB&B Communications; *U.S. Private*, pg. 304
INTERNATIONAL MARKETING & PROMOTIONS HELSINKI—See DMB&B Communications; *U.S. Private*, pg. 304
INTERNATIONAL MARKETING & PROMOTIONS LONDON—See DMB&B Communications; *U.S. Private*, pg. 304
INTERNATIONAL MARKETING & PROMOTIONS MADRID—See DMB&B Communications; *U.S. Private*, pg. 304
INTERNATIONAL MARKETING & PROMOTIONS—See DMB&B Communications; *U.S. Private*, pg. 304
INTERNATIONAL MATEX TANK TERMINALS, BAYONNE—See Koninklijke Van Ommeren NV; *Int'l*, pg. 758
INTERNATIONAL MEDIA—See True North Communications Inc.; *U.S. Public*, pg. 1641
INTERNATIONAL MEDIA CONCEPTS/DMB&B—See DMB&B Communications; *U.S. Private*, pg. 304
INTERNATIONAL MEDIA HOLDING BV—See Lagardere Groupe; *Int'l*, pg. 795
INTERNATIONAL MEDICAL SERVICES AND SUPPLIES, INC.—See Integrated Health Services, Inc.; *U.S. Public*, pg. 885
THE INTERNATIONAL METALS RECLAMATION COMPANY, INC.—See Inco Limited; *Int'l*, pg. 672
INTERNATIONAL MICROCIRCUITS, INC.; *U.S. Private*, pg. 571
INTERNATIONAL MICROWAVE CORPORATION; *U.S. Private*, pg. 571
INTERNATIONAL MOSKOW BANK—See Bayerische Vereinsbank Group; *Int'l*, pg. 181
INTERNATIONAL MULTIFOODS CORPORATION; *U.S. Public*, pg. 900
INTERNATIONAL MUREX TECHNOLOGIES CORPORATION; *Int'l*, pg. 684
INTERNATIONAL NICKEL FRANCE S.A.—See Inco Limited; *Int'l*, pg. 673
INTERNATIONAL NICKEL GBMH—See Inco Limited; *Int'l*, pg. 673
INTERNATIONAL NICKEL, INC.—See Inco Limited; *Int'l*, pg. 672
P.T. INTERNATIONAL NICKEL INDONESIA—See Sumitomo Metal Mining Co., Ltd.; *Int'l*, pg. 1316
P.T. INTERNATIONAL NICKEL INDONESIA—See Nissho Iwai Corporation; *Int'l*, pg. 947

INTERNATIONAL NICKEL SERVICES (U.K.) LIMITED—See Inco Limited; *Int'l*, pg. 673
INTERNATIONAL NUTRITION CO. APS—See The East Asiatic Company Ltd. A/S; *Int'l*, pg. 431
INTERNATIONAL PAINT CO., INC.—See Courtaulds plc; *Int'l*, pg. 338
INTERNATIONAL PAINT EASTERN DIV.—See Courtaulds plc; *Int'l*, pg. 339
INTERNATIONAL PAINT GULF DIV.—See Courtaulds plc; *Int'l*, pg. 339
INTERNATIONAL PAINT POWDER COATINGS DIV.—See Courtaulds plc; *Int'l*, pg. 339
INTERNATIONAL PAINT SOUTHWEST DIV.—See Courtaulds plc; *Int'l*, pg. 339
INTERNATIONAL PAINT WESTERN DIV.—See Courtaulds plc; *Int'l*, pg. 339
INTERNATIONAL PAINTS (CANADA) LTD.—See Courtaulds plc; *Int'l*, pg. 339
INTERNATIONAL PAPER (ASIA) LIMITED—See International Paper Company; *U.S. Public*, pg. 905
INTERNATIONAL PAPER CANADA, INC.—See International Paper Company; *U.S. Public*, pg. 905
INTERNATIONAL PAPER CO.—See International Paper Company; *U.S. Public*, pg. 902
INTERNATIONAL PAPER COMPANY; *U.S. Public*, pg. 901
INTERNATIONAL PAPER COMPANY (EUROPE) LIMITED—See International Paper Company; *U.S. Public*, pg. 905
INTERNATIONAL PAPER COMPANY (JAPAN) LTD.—See International Paper Company; *U.S. Public*, pg. 905
INTERNATIONAL PAPER COMPANY PTY. LIMITED—See International Paper Company; *U.S. Public*, pg. 905
INTERNATIONAL PAPER-DISTRIBUTION GROUP—See International Paper Company; *U.S. Public*, pg. 902
INTERNATIONAL PAPER (ESPANA), S.L.—See International Paper Company; *U.S. Public*, pg. 905
INTERNATIONAL PAPER (EUROPE) S.A.—See International Paper Company; *U.S. Public*, pg. 905
INTERNATIONAL PAPER ITALIA S.P.A.—See International Paper Company; *U.S. Public*, pg. 905
INTERNATIONAL PAPER KOREA LTD.—See International Paper Company; *U.S. Public*, pg. 906
INTERNATIONAL PAPER LABEL DIV.—See International Paper Company; *U.S. Public*, pg. 903
INTERNATIONAL PAPER REALTY CORP.—See International Paper Company; *U.S. Public*, pg. 904
INTERNATIONAL PAPER TAIWAN LTD.—See International Paper Company; *U.S. Public*, pg. 905
INTERNATIONAL PAPER USA LTD.—See International Paper Company; *U.S. Public*, pg. 906
INTERNATIONAL PETROLEUM CORPORATION—See International Recovery Corp.; *U.S. Public*, pg. 906
INTERNATIONAL PHARMACEUTICALS—See Alpharma Inc.; *U.S. Public*, pg. 58
INTERNATIONAL PIN—See Continental/Midland, Inc.; *U.S. Private*, pg. 269
INTERNATIONAL PIPE MACHINERY CORP.; *U.S. Private*, pg. 571
INTERNATIONAL PLASTICS COMPANY; *U.S. Private*, pg. 571
INTERNATIONAL POLAROID CORP.—See Polaroid Corporation; *U.S. Public*, pg. 1313
INTERNATIONAL POLYMER CORP.—See Courtaulds plc; *Int'l*, pg. 339
INTERNATIONAL POWER MACHINES CANADA LTD.—See BTR plc; *Int'l*, pg. 126
INTERNATIONAL POWER MACHINES CORPORATION—See BTR plc; *Int'l*, pg. 126
INTERNATIONAL POWER MACHINES GMBH—See BTR plc; *Int'l*, pg. 126
INTERNATIONAL PRESS DISTRIBUTORS LTD.—See Lagardere Groupe; *Int'l*, pg. 795
INTERNATIONAL PUBLIC RELATIONS CO. LTD.—See Shandwick International Plc; *Int'l*, pg. 1227
INTERNATIONAL PUBLIC RELATIONS (NZ) LTD.—See Shandwick International Plc; *Int'l*, pg. 1227
INTERNATIONAL PUBLIC RELATIONS, PTY. LTD.—See Shandwick International Plc; *Int'l*, pg. 1227
INTERNATIONAL PUBLIC RELATIONS, PTY LTD.—See Shandwick International Plc; *Int'l*, pg. 1227
INTERNATIONAL PUBLICATIONS HOLDING—See Lagardere Groupe; *Int'l*, pg. 795
THE INTERNATIONAL PUBLISHING GROUP—See Pearson plc; *Int'l*, pg. 1027
INTERNATIONAL QUAKER FOOD PRODUCTS—See The Quaker Oats Company; *U.S. Public*, pg. 1347
INTERNATIONAL RADIATOR SERVICES LTD.—See BTR plc; *Int'l*, pg. 126
INTERNATIONAL REAGENTS CORPORATION—See The Green Cross Corporation; *Int'l*, pg. 558
INTERNATIONAL RECOVERY CORP.; *U.S. Public*, pg. 906
INTERNATIONAL RECTIFIER COMPANY (GREAT BRITAIN) LTD.—See International Rectifier Corporation; *U.S. Public*, pg. 907
INTERNATIONAL RECTIFIER CORPORATION; *U.S. Public*, pg. 906
INTERNATIONAL RECTIFIER CORPORATION ITALIANA, S.P.A.—See International Rectifier Corporation; *U.S. Public*, pg. 907
INTERNATIONAL RECTIFIER CORPORATION ITALIANA, S.P.—See International Rectifier Corporation; *U.S. Public*, pg. 907
INTERNATIONAL RECTIFIER FAR EAST COMPANY, LTD.—See International Rectifier Corporation; *U.S. Public*, pg. 907
INTERNATIONAL RECTIFIER GMBH—See International Rectifier Corporation; *U.S. Public*, pg. 907
INTERNATIONAL RECTIFIER SOUTHEAST ASIA PTE. LTD.—See International Rectifier Corporation; *U.S. Public*, pg. 907
INTERNATIONAL REHABILITATION ASSOCIATES, INC.—See Cigna Corp.; *U.S. Public*, pg. 362
INTERNATIONAL RELOCATION INSURANCE SERVICES INC.—See Willis Corroon Group PLC; *Int'l*, pg. 1503

INTERNATIONAL RESEARCH & EVALUATION; *U.S. Private*, pg. 571
INTERNATIONAL RESISTIVE COMPANY INC.—See TT Group PLC; *Int'l*, pg. 1344
INTERNATIONAL RISK MANAGEMENT GROUP LTD.—See Swiss Reinsurance Company; *Int'l*, pg. 1333
INTERNATIONAL ROTEX, INC.—See Esselte AB; *Int'l*, pg. 460
INTERNATIONAL SAINT-GOBAIN—See Saint-Gobain; *Int'l*, pg. 1177
INTERNATIONAL SATELLITE SERVICES BV—See KPN Koninklyke PTT Nederland NV; *Int'l*, pg. 720
INTERNATIONAL SEA DRILLING LTD.—See Pool Energy Services Co.; *U.S. Public*, pg. 1316
INTERNATIONAL SEAWAY TRADING CORPORATION; *U.S. Private*, pg. 572
INTERNATIONAL SERVICES—See Medpartners Inc.; *U.S. Public*, pg. 1082
INTERNATIONAL SERVICES DEPARTMENT—See CVB Financial Corp.; *U.S. Public*, pg. 287
INTERNATIONAL SHIPHOLDING CORPORATION; *U.S. Public*, pg. 907
INTERNATIONAL SHOE MACHINE CORP.; *U.S. Private*, pg. 572
INTERNATIONAL SPECIALTY PRODUCTS, INC.—See ISP Holdings, Inc.; *U.S. Public*, pg. 858
INTERNATIONAL STEEL WOOL CORPORATION—See F.H. Bonn Company; *U.S. Private*, pg. 156
INTERNATIONAL SURPLUS ADJUSTING SERVICES—See Cigna Corp.; *U.S. Public*, pg. 366
INTERNATIONAL SYSTEMS & CONTROLS CORP.; *U.S. Private*, pg. 572
INTERNATIONAL TANK, INC.—See TSI Holdings, Inc.; *U.S. Private*, pg. 1066
INTERNATIONAL TECHNOLOGY CORPORATION; *U.S. Public*, pg. 907
INTERNATIONAL TELECOMMUNICATIONS SATELLITE ORGANIZATION (INTELSAT)—See British Telecommunications plc; *Int'l*, pg. 223
INTERNATIONAL THERAPEUTIC SERVICES, INC.—See Integrated Health Services, Inc.; *U.S. Public*, pg. 885
INTERNATIONAL THOMSON BUSINESS PUBLISHING—See The Thomson Corporation; *U.S. Public*, pg. 1601
INTERNATIONAL THOMSON PUBLISHING LIMITED—See The Thomson Corporation; *U.S. Public*, pg. 1600
INTERNATIONAL THOROUGHBRED BREEDERS, INC.; *U.S. Public*, pg. 908
INTERNATIONAL TOOL & SUPPLY, PLC; *Int'l*, pg. 684
INTERNATIONAL TOOL & SUPPLY COMPANY, INC.—See International Tool & Supply, PLC; *Int'l*, pg. 684
INTERNATIONAL TOTAL SERVICES; *U.S. Public*, pg. 908
INTERNATIONAL TRANSDUCER CORPORATION—See Channel Technologies, Inc.; *U.S. Private*, pg. 228
INTERNATIONAL TRAVEL ASSOCIATES CORP.—See ITA Group Inc.; *U.S. Private*, pg. 555
INTERNATIONAL TUBULAR PRODUCTS, INC.—See Acme Tube Inc.; *U.S. Private*, pg. 14
INTERNATIONAL TURBINE ENGINE CORPORATION (ITEC)—See AlliedSignal Inc.; *U.S. Public*, pg. 51
INTERNATIONAL TYPEFACE CORPORATION (iTC)—See Esselte AB; *Int'l*, pg. 460
INTERNATIONAL UNION LEASING CO., LTD.—See The Nomura Securities Co., Ltd.; *Int'l*, pg. 957
INTERNATIONAL VIDEO PRODUCTS PTE. LTD.—See Toshiba Corporation; *Int'l*, pg. 1405
INTERNATIONAL WATER LIMITED—See United Utilities plc; *Int'l*, pg. 1444
INTERNATIONAL WINDOW-ARIZONA, INC.—See International Aluminum Corporation; *U.S. Public*, pg. 895
INTERNATIONAL WINDOW CORP.—See International Aluminum Corporation; *U.S. Public*, pg. 895
INTERNATIONAL WINDOW-NORTHERN CALIFORNIA—See International Aluminum Corporation; *U.S. Public*, pg. 895
INTERNATIONAL WINE ACCESSORIES, INC.; *U.S. Private*, pg. 572
INTERNATIONAL WINE & SPIRITS LTD.—See UST Inc.; *U.S. Public*, pg. 1661
INTERNATIONAL WIRE GROUP INC.—See Hicks, Muse, Tate & Furst Inc.; *U.S. Private*, pg. 526
INTERNATIONAL WIRE LINE SERVICES, INC.—See Halliburton Company; *U.S. Public*, pg. 777
INTERNATIONAL WOMEN'S APPAREL GROUP—See Hartmarx Corporation; *U.S. Public*, pg. 796
INTERNATIONALE BANK FUR AUSSENHANDEL, A.G.—See CoreStates Financial Corp.; *U.S. Public*, pg. 447
INTERNATIONALE GAS APPARATEN B.V.—See Ruhrgas Aktiengesellschaft; *Int'l*, pg. 1149
INTERNATIONALE GAS APPARATUR A/S—See Ruhrgas Aktiengesellschaft; *Int'l*, pg. 1149
INTERNATIONALE LEASING GESELLSCHAFT—See Commerzbank AG; *Int'l*, pg. 312
INTERNATIONALE MAATSCHAPPIJ VOORHET BEHEER VAN GLASMAATSCHAPPIJEN BV—See Saint-Gobain; *Int'l*, pg. 1173
INTERNATIONALES IMMOBILIEN INSTITUT GMBH—See Bayerische Vereinsbank Group; *Int'l*, pg. 180
INTERNAZIONALE HOLDING FIAT SA—See Fiat Auto SpA; *Int'l*, pg. 483
INTERNCONTINENTAL LIFE CORP.—See Financial Industries Corp.; *U.S. Public*, pg. 622
INTERNET CAPITAL GROUP—See Safeguard Scientifics, Inc.; *U.S. Public*, pg. 1425
INTERNUT—See Snack America; *U.S. Private*, pg. 1010
INTEROP, INC.—See The Thomson Corporation; *U.S. Public*, pg. 1600
INTEROPTICS—See Sumitomo Heavy Industries, Ltd.; *Int'l*, pg. 1314
INTERORGANA CHEMIEHANDEL G.M.B.H.—See Internatio-Muller N.V.; *Int'l*, pg. 682
INTEROX AMERICA—See Solvay S.A.; *Int'l*, pg. 1278
INTEROX SOLVAY—See Solvay S.A.; *Int'l*, pg. 1278

INTERPACIFIC INVESTORS SERVICES; *U.S. Private*, pg. 572
INTERPAK TERMINALS, INC.—See Katoen Natie NV; *Int'l*, pg. 724
INTERPARTNERS BULGARIA—See Warwick Baker O'Neill; *U.S. Private*, pg. 1152
INTERPEX SERVICES PRIVATE LIMITED—See Singapore Land Limited; *Int'l*, pg. 1253
INTERPHARM BV—See Internatio-Muller N.V.; *Int'l*, pg. 681
INTERPHARM GROEP B.V.—See Internatio-Muller N.V.; *Int'l*, pg. 682
INTERPHASE CORPORATION; *U.S. Public*, pg. 908
INTERPLAN—See RNL Facilities Corporation; *U.S. Private*, pg. 905
INTERPLAS SA—See Smiths Industries plc; *Int'l*, pg. 1268
INTERPLAST UNIVERSAL INDUSTRIES, INC.; *U.S. Private*, pg. 572
INTERPLASTIC CORP.; *U.S. Private*, pg. 572
INTERPLAY OEM, INC.—See Interplay Productions, Inc.; *U.S. Private*, pg. 573
INTERPLAY PRODUCTIONS, INC.; *U.S. Private*, pg. 572
INTERPOINT—See Crane Co.; *U.S. Public*, pg. 457
INTERPOOL, INC.; *U.S. Public*, pg. 908
INTERPOST GROUP OF COMPANIES BV—See KPN Koninklyke PTT Nederland NV; *Int'l*, pg. 720
INTERPOST SYSTEMS CANADA LTD.—See KPN Koninklyke PTT Nederland NV; *Int'l*, pg. 720
INTERPOST SYSTEMS USA INC.—See KPN Koninklyke PTT Nederland NV; *Int'l*, pg. 720
INTERPOST THAILAND LTD.—See KPN Koninklyke PTT Nederland NV; *Int'l*, pg. 720
INTERPRESTIGE, S.A.—See Tabacalera, S.A.; *Int'l*, pg. 1345
INTERPRETATION OF STRATEGIC AREAS (GEIEST)—See Petrobras - Petroleo Brasileiro S.A.; *Int'l*, pg. 1041
INTERPROVINCIAL COOPERATIVE LIMITED (IPCO)—See Saskatchewan Wheat Pool; *Int'l*, pg. 1195
INTERPROVINCIAL PIPE LINE INC.—See IPL Energy Inc.; *Int'l*, pg. 652
INTERPROVINCIAL PIPE LINE (NW) LTD.—See IPL Energy Inc.; *Int'l*, pg. 652
THE INTERPUBLIC GROUP OF COMPANIES, INC.; *U.S. Public*, pg. 908
INTERRENT OY; *Int'l*, pg. 684
INTERSECURITIES, INC.—See AEGON N.V.; *Int'l*, pg. 27
INTERSERVICE GESELLSCHAFT FUR HUTTENWEKSANLAGEN MBH—See Mannesmann A.G.; *Int'l*, pg. 837
INTERSERVICIOS Y TECNOLOGIA S.A., BARCELONA—See Internatio-Muller N.V.; *Int'l*, pg. 681
INTERSPIRO INC.—See Spectra-Physics AB; *Int'l*, pg. 1289
INTERSTATE BAKERIES CORPORATION; *U.S. Public*, pg. 909
INTERSTATE BAKERIES CORPORATION-CENTRAL DIVISION—See Interstate Bakeries Corporation; *U.S. Public*, pg. 909
INTERSTATE BAKERIES CORPORATION-EASTERN DIVISION—See Interstate Bakeries Corporation; *U.S. Public*, pg. 909
INTERSTATE BAKERIES CORPORATION-WESTERN DIVISION—See Interstate Bakeries Corporation; *U.S. Public*, pg. 909
INTERSTATE BILLING SERVICE, INC.—See Regions Financial Corporation; *U.S. Public*, pg. 1373
INTERSTATE BRANDS CORPORATION—See Interstate Bakeries Corporation; *U.S. Public*, pg. 909
INTERSTATE BRICK COMPANY—See Pacific Coast Building Products Inc.; *U.S. Private*, pg. 830
INTERSTATE BROADCASTING COMPANY, INC.—See The New York Times Company; *U.S. Public*, pg. 1173
INTERSTATE COMMODITIES INC.; *U.S. Private*, pg. 573
INTERSTATE CONTAINER CORPORATION—See Interstate Resources, Inc.; *U.S. Private*, pg. 573
INTERSTATE CORE PACK—See Interstate Resources, Inc.; *U.S. Private*, pg. 573
INTERSTATE CORP.—See Interstate Bakeries Corporation; *U.S. Public*, pg. 909
INTERSTATE DISTRIBUTOR COMPANY; *U.S. Private*, pg. 573
INTERSTATE ELECTRONICS CORP.—See Figgie International Inc.; *U.S. Public*, pg. 622
INTERSTATE ENERGY CO.—See PP&L Resources; *U.S. Public*, pg. 1244
INTERSTATE ENGINEERING; *U.S. Private*, pg. 573
INTERSTATE GLASS CO. INC.—See Apogee Enterprises, Inc.; *U.S. Public*, pg. 120
INTERSTATE HIGHWAY SIGN—See Mark IV Industries Inc.; *U.S. Public*, pg. 1045
INTERSTATE JITNEY JUNGLE STORES, INC.—See Jitney-Jungle Stores of America, Inc.; *U.S. Public*, pg. 588
INTERSTATE/JOHNSON LANE CORPORATION—See Interstate/Johnson Lane, Inc.; *U.S. Public*, pg. 910
INTERSTATE/JOHNSON LANE, INC.; *U.S. Public*, pg. 909
INTERSTATE LAND CORP.—See Questar Corporation; *U.S. Public*, pg. 1352
INTERSTATE NATIONAL CORP.—See Allianz Aktiengesellschaft; *Int'l*, pg. 59
INTERSTATE PAPER CORPORATION—See Interstate Resources, Inc.; *U.S. Private*, pg. 573
INTERSTATE PAYCO SEED COMPANY; *U.S. Private*, pg. 573
INTERSTATE PHOTO SUPPLY CORP.—See AIC International, Inc.; *U.S. Private*, pg. 6
INTERSTATE POWER COMPANY; *U.S. Public*, pg. 910
INTERSTATE PRODUCERS LIVESTOCK ASSOCIATION; *U.S. Private*, pg. 573
INTERSTATE RAILROAD CO.—See Norfolk Southern Corporation; *U.S. Public*, pg. 1191
INTERSTATE REALTY INC. T/A SEA COLONY REALTY—See Carl M. Freeman Associates, Inc.; *U.S. Private*, pg. 426
INTERSTATE RESOURCES, INC.; *U.S. Private*, pg. 573

INTERSTATE STATIONS, INC.—See Colonial Oil Industries; *U.S. Private*, pg. 254
INTERSTATE STEEL CO. INC.—See Groupe Usinor; *Int'l*, pg. 572
INTERSTATE STEEL SUPPLY CO. OF MARYLAND—See Metals USA, Inc.; *U.S. Public*, pg. 1100
INTERSTATE STEEL SUPPLY CO. OF PITTSBURGH—See Metals USA, Inc.; *U.S. Public*, pg. 1100
INTERSTATE STEEL SUPPLY COMPANY—See Metals USA, Inc.; *U.S. Public*, pg. 1100
INTERSTATE VAN LINES, INC.; *U.S. Private*, pg. 573
INTERSTOFF AG—See Bayerische Vereinsbank Group; *Int'l*, pg. 181
INTERSYS, INC.—See Integral Systems, Inc.; *U.S. Public*, pg. 883
INTERTAN AUSTRALIA LTD.—See InterTAN Inc.; *U.S. Public*, pg. 910
INTERTAN CANADA LTD.—See InterTAN Inc.; *U.S. Public*, pg. 910
INTERTAN INC.; *U.S. Public*, pg. 910
INTERTAN U.K. LTD.—See InterTAN Inc.; *U.S. Public*, pg. 910
INTERTAPE POLYMER GROUP—See Intertape Polymer Group Inc.; *Int'l*, pg. 685
INTERTAPE POLYMER GROUP INC.; *Int'l*, pg. 684
INTERTEC LIMITED—See ICC Industries, Inc.; *U.S. Private*, pg. 554
INTERTEC PRESENTATIONS—See Primedia Inc.; *U.S. Public*, pg. 1328
INTERTEC PUBLISHING—See Primedia Inc.; *U.S. Public*, pg. 1327
THE INTERTECH GROUP INC.—See BBA Group plc; *Int'l*, pg. 113
INTERTEK—See North American Refractories Company; *U.S. Private*, pg. 803
INTERTEL, INC.—See Bell Atlantic Corporation; *U.S. Public*, pg. 203
INTERTEVE, N.V.—See Electrabel S.A.; *Int'l*, pg. 437
INTERTEXT GROUP, LTD.—See Harcourt General, Inc.; *U.S. Public*, pg. 784
INTERTRACE TECHNOLOGY, INC.—See Methode Electronics Inc.; *U.S. Public*, pg. 1101
INTERTRACTOR AMERICA CORPORATION—See Wirten GmbH; *Int'l*, pg. 1511
INTERTRACTOR ZWEIGNIEDERLASSUNG DER WIRTGEN GMBH—See Wirten GmbH; *Int'l*, pg. 1511
INTERTRADE INDUSTRIES; *U.S. Private*, pg. 573
INTERTRON—See Standex International Corporation; *U.S. Public*, pg. 1507
INTERTUFT S.A.R.L.—See Forbo Holding SA; *Int'l*, pg. 498
INTERTURBINE COMPRESSOR TECHNOLOGY PTE. LTD.—See United Technologies Corporation; *U.S. Public*, pg. 1690
INTERTURBINE DALLAS AIRFOIL—See United Technologies Corporation; *U.S. Public*, pg. 1690
INTERTURBINE DALLAS CASINGS—See United Technologies Corporation; *U.S. Public*, pg. 1690
INTERTURBINE GERMANY GMBH—See Indivers B.V.; *Int'l*, pg. 673
INTERTURBINE HOLLAND B.V.—See Indivers B.V.; *Int'l*, pg. 673
INTERTURBINE MOSCOW REP. OFFICE—See Indivers B.V.; *Int'l*, pg. 673
INTERTURBINE PATON B.V.—See Indivers B.V.; *Int'l*, pg. 673
INTERTURBINE SINGAPORE PTE. LTD.—See United Technologies Corporation; *U.S. Public*, pg. 1690
N.V. INTERTURBINE—See Indivers B.V.; *Int'l*, pg. 673
INTERUNFALL ALLGEMEINE RECHTSSCHUTZ-SCHADENABWICKLUNGS G.M.B.H.—See Assicurazioni Generali S.p.A.; *Int'l*, pg. 91
INTERUNFALL ALLGEMEINE VERSICHERUNGS AG—See Assicurazioni Generali S.p.A.; *Int'l*, pg. 91
INTERUNFALL LEASING—See Allianz Aktiengesellschaft; *Int'l*, pg. 61
INTERUNFALL VERSICHERING AG—See Assicurazioni Generali S.p.A.; *Int'l*, pg. 91
INTERURAN GMBH—See COGEMA - Compagnie Generale des Matieres Nucleaires; *Int'l*, pg. 305
INTERURANIUM AUSTRALIA PTY. LTD.—See COGEMA - Compagnie Generale des Matieres Nucleaires; *Int'l*, pg. 305
INTER-URBAN, INC.—See Urban Outfitters, Inc.; *U.S. Public*, pg. 1700
INTERVAL INTERNATIONAL INC.—See Cendant Corporation; *U.S. Public*, pg. 320
INTERVAM B.V.—See Hollandsche Beton Groep NV; *Int'l*, pg. 630
INTERVASCULAR GMBH—See Datascope Corp.; *U.S. Public*, pg. 488
INTERVASCULAR, INC.—See Datascope Corp.; *U.S. Public*, pg. 487
INTERVASCULAR, S.A.—See Datascope Corp.; *U.S. Public*, pg. 488
INTERVEN, S.A.—See Petroleos de Venezuela S.A.; *Int'l*, pg. 1045
INTERVEST-MORTGAGE INVESTMENT COMPANY—See Sterling Financial Corporation; *U.S. Public*, pg. 1516
INTERVET AMERICA, INC.—See Akzo Nobel N.V.; *Int'l*, pg. 48
INTERVET INTERNATIONAL BV—See Akzo Nobel N.V.; *Int'l*, pg. 44
INTERVET LABORATORIES—See Akzo Nobel N.V.; *Int'l*, pg. 45
INTERVET MEXICO SA DE CV—See Akzo Nobel N.V.; *Int'l*, pg. 45
INTERVET NEDERLAND BV—See Akzo Nobel N.V.; *Int'l*, pg. 44
INTERVET (U.K.) LTD.—See Akzo Nobel N.V.; *Int'l*, pg. 45
INTERVISUAL COMMUNICATIONS INC.—See R.R. Donnelley & Sons Company; *U.S. Public*, pg. 518
INTERVOICE, INC.; *U.S. Public*, pg. 910
INTERWOOD MARKETING GROUP; *Int'l*, pg. 685

INTERWORLD ENTERPRISES LTD.—See Hanson PLC; *Int'l*, pg. 594
INTERX RESEARCH CORP.—See Merck & Co., Inc.; *U.S. Public*, pg. 1091
INTESYS OF CALIFORNIA—See Intesys Technologies; *U.S. Private*, pg. 574
INTESYS TECHNOLOGIES; *U.S. Private*, pg. 574
INTEVEP, S.A.—See Petroleos de Venezuela S.A.; *Int'l*, pg. 1045
INTEX CORP.; *U.S. Public*, pg. 574
INTEX PLASTICS CORPORATION—See Intex Corp.; *U.S. Private*, pg. 574
INTIMATE BRANDS, INC.—See The Limited, Inc.; *U.S. Public*, pg. 995
INTIS BV—See KPN Koninklyke PTT Nederland NV; *Int'l*, pg. 720
INTIS ENTERPRISE BV—See KPN Koninklyke PTT Nederland NV; *Int'l*, pg. 720
INTIS RESEARCH & DEVELOPMENT VOF—See KPN Koninklyke PTT Nederland NV; *Int'l*, pg. 720
INTISYS, INC.—See Associated Process Controls; *U.S. Private*, pg. 93
INTOCHEM B.V.—See Internatio-Muller N.V.; *Int'l*, pg. 682
INTOCHIMICA MARKETING S.R.L.—See Internatio-Muller N.V.; *Int'l*, pg. 682
INTOOL ROTOR COMPANY; *U.S. Private*, pg. 574
INTRA-ACOUSTICS COMPANY, LTD.—See Industrial Acoustics Company, Inc.; *U.S. Public*, pg. 875
INTRACO ASIA SINGAPORE—See Novellus Systems, Inc.; *U.S. Public*, pg. 1205
INTRACORP, INC.—See Cigna Corp.; *U.S. Public*, pg. 362
INTRACORP PEER REVIEW ORGANIZATION, INC.—See Cigna Corp.; *U.S. Public*, pg. 362
INTRAFIN S.A.—See Bristol-Myers Squibb Company; *U.S. Public*, pg. 256
INTRAFIN SERVICES LTD.—See Bayerische Vereinsbank Group; *Int'l*, pg. 181
INTRAG—See Union Bank of Switzerland; *Int'l*, pg. 1440
INTRALOX A/S—See The Laitram Corporation; *U.S. Private*, pg. 643
INTRALOX, INC.—See The Laitram Corporation; *U.S. Private*, pg. 643
INTRALOX, INC. GMBH—See The Laitram Corporation; *U.S. Private*, pg. 643
INTRALOX ITALIA S.R.L.—See The Laitram Corporation; *U.S. Private*, pg. 643
INTRALOX LTD.—See The Laitram Corporation; *U.S. Private*, pg. 643
INTRAWEST CORPORATION; *Int'l*, pg. 685
INTRAX BV—See KPN Koninklyke PTT Nederland NV; *Int'l*, pg. 720
INTRENET, INC.; *U.S. Public*, pg. 910
INTREPID ENTERPRISES, INC.; *U.S. Private*, pg. 574
INTRO MARKETING LIMITED—See Meristem plc; *Int'l*, pg. 858
INTROPA BETEILIGUNGS GMBH—See Creditanstalt-Bankverein; *Int'l*, pg. 347
INTROTEK INTERNATIONAL—See Magnetrol International; *U.S. Private*, pg. 696
INTSEL SOUTHWEST—See Pechiney S.A.; *Int'l*, pg. 1029
INTUIT, INC.; *U.S. Public*, pg. 911
INVACARE CORPORATION; *U.S. Public*, pg. 911
INVACARE DEUTSCHLAND FAHRZEUGE KORPERBEHINDERTE—See Invacare Corporation; *U.S. Public*, pg. 911
INVACARE FRANCE—See Invacare Corporation; *U.S. Public*, pg. 911
INVACARE HEALTH CARE FURNISHINGS—See Invacare Corporation; *U.S. Public*, pg. 911
INVAMEX, S.A. DE C.V.—See Invacare Corporation; *U.S. Public*, pg. 911
INVENTIO AG—See Schindler Holding AG; *Int'l*, pg. 1204
INVENTORY MANAGEMENT CORP.—See GP Strategies Corporation; *U.S. Public*, pg. 694
INVER MILL—See Fort James Corporation; *U.S. Public*, pg. 672
INVERBAN GESTION, S.G.I.I.C., S.A.—See Caja de Madrid Group; *Int'l*, pg. 251
INVERBAN, S.V.B., S.A.—See Caja de Madrid Group; *Int'l*, pg. 251
INVERCARTERA, S.A.—See Caixa d'Estalvis de Catalunya; *Int'l*, pg. 251
INVERCON PAPERMILLS LTD.—See Fort James Corporation; *U.S. Public*, pg. 672
INVERNESS CORP.; *U.S. Private*, pg. 574
INVERNESS FRANCE—See Inverness Corp.; *U.S. Private*, pg. 574
INVERNESS UK LTD.—See Inverness Corp.; *U.S. Private*, pg. 574
INVERSION Y COMERCIALIZACION DE IMMUEBLES, S.A.—See Caja de Madrid Group; *Int'l*, pg. 251
INVERSIONES ARAUCARIA—See Corporacion MAPFRE, Compania Internacional de Reaseguros, S.A.; *Int'l*, pg. 335
INVERSIONES CAPITAL, S.A.—See Corporacion MAPFRE, Compania Internacional de Reaseguros, S.A.; *Int'l*, pg. 333
INVERSIONES CHASE MANHATTAN LIMITADA—See The Chase Manhattan Corporation; *U.S. Public*, pg. 341
INVERSIONES CONTINENTAL, S.A. DE C.V.—See Cigna Corp.; *U.S. Public*, pg. 363
INVERSIONES DE GUAYMAS S.A. DE C.V.; *Int'l*, pg. 685
INVERSIONES GENGIBRAL-REP. OFFICE OF PWT IN VENEZUELA—See Pechiney S.A.; *Int'l*, pg. 1030
INVERSIONES IBERICAS S.A.—See Corporacion MAPFRE, Compania Internacional de Reaseguros, S.A.; *Int'l*, pg. 335
INVERSIONES INA LIMITADA—See Cigna Corp.; *U.S. Public*, pg. 364
INVERSIONES INTERNACIONALES INCORPORADAS—See Banco Popular de Puerto Rico; *U.S. Public*, pg. 176
INVERSIONES ISICA, C.A.—See Jefferson Smurfit Group p.l.c.; *Int'l*, pg. 1271

INVERSIONES LA LIBERTAD, C.A.—See Cigna Corp.; *U.S. Public*, pg. 364
INVERSIONES MOORE CA (VENEZUELA)—See Moore Corporation (Holding) AG; *Int'l*, pg. 890
INVERSIONES NORTH (CHILE) LTDA.—See North Limited; *Int'l*, pg. 967
INVERSIONES ORTRAC C.A.—See Panalpina Welttransport (Holding) AG; *Int'l*, pg. 1022
INVERTRANS S.A. DE BOGOTA—See Panalpina Welttransport (Holding) AG; *Int'l*, pg. 1022
INVESCO CAPITAL MANAGEMENT—See Invesco Group Asset Management Ltd.; *Int'l*, pg. 685
INVESCO FUNDS GROUP—See Invesco Group Asset Management Ltd.; *Int'l*, pg. 685
INVESCO GROUP ASSET MANAGEMENT LTD.; *Int'l*, pg. 685
INVESCO INC.—See Invesco Group Asset Management Ltd.; *Int'l*, pg. 685
INVEST WEST FINANCIAL CORPORATION—See Pacifica Real Estate Group; *U.S. Private*, pg. 832
INVESTCO NV—See Almanij N.V.; *Int'l*, pg. 65
INVESTCORP INTERNATIONAL; *Int'l*, pg. 686
CIA. DE INVESTIGACION Y EXPLOTACIONES PETROLIFERAS, S.A. (CIEPSA)—See Compania Espanola de Petroleos, S.A. (CEPSA); *Int'l*, pg. 323
INVESTIGACIONES PIONEER S DE R.L. DE C.V.—See Pioneer Hi-Bred International, Inc.; *U.S. Public*, pg. 1299
INVESTIL - SOCIEDADE GESTORA FUNDOS INVESTIMENTO IMOBILIARIO, SA—See Caixa Geral de Depositos; *Int'l*, pg. 250
INVESTIR PUBLICATIONS—See LVMH Moet Hennessy Louis Vuitton; *Int'l*, pg. 780
INVESTIR TELECOM—See LVMH Moet Hennessy Louis Vuitton; *Int'l*, pg. 780
INVESTKREDIT HOLDING—See Creditanstalt-Bankverein; *Int'l*, pg. 347
INVESTMENT ADVISERS, INC.—See Lloyds TSB Group PLC; *Int'l*, pg. 813
INVESTMENT COUNSELORS OF MARYLAND, INC.—See United Asset Management Corporation; *U.S. Public*, pg. 1673
INVESTMENT ENGINEERING LTD.—See Delta plc; *Int'l*, pg. 391
INVESTMENT FUND BREDA B.V.—See Royal Begemann Group; *Int'l*, pg. 1133
INVESTMENT LEASING SERVICES, INC.—See Telco Capital Corporation; *U.S. Private*, pg. 1073
INVESTMENT MANAGEMENT & RESEARCH, INC.—See Raymond James Financial, Inc.; *U.S. Public*, pg. 923
INVESTMENT MANAGEMENT CO. CHILE SA—See HSBC Holdings plc; *Int'l*, pg. 583
INVESTMENT NETWORK, INC.—See St. Paul Bancorp, Inc.; *U.S. Public*, pg. 1428
INVESTMENT RESEARCH COMPANY—See United Asset Management Corporation; *U.S. Public*, pg. 1673
INVESTMENT SERVICES DEPARTMENT—See CVB Financial Corp.; *U.S. Public*, pg. 287
INVESTMENT TECHNOLOGY GROUP, INC.—See Jefferies Group, Inc.; *U.S. Public*, pg. 924
INVESTOR AB; *Int'l*, pg. 686
INVESTORS FIDELITY LIFE ASSURANCE CORP.—See Consumers Financial Corporation; *U.S. Public*, pg. 438
INVESTORS FIDUCIARY TRUST COMPANY—See Kansas City Southern Industries, Inc.; *U.S. Public*, pg. 944
INVESTORS FIDUCIARY TRUST COMPANY—See State Street Corporation; *U.S. Public*, pg. 1513
INVESTORS' FINANCE CORP.—See Citicorp; *U.S. Public*, pg. 379
INVESTORS HERITAGE LIFE INSURANCE CO.—See Kentucky Investors, Inc.; *U.S. Public*, pg. 952
INVESTORS INSURANCE COMPANY OF AMERICA—See Markel Corporation; *U.S. Public*, pg. 1046
INVESTORS INSURANCE CORP.—See Investors Insurance Group, Inc.; *U.S. Public*, pg. 912
INVESTORS INSURANCE GROUP, INC.; *U.S. Public*, pg. 911
INVESTORS MANAGEMENT CORP.; *U.S. Private*, pg. 574
INVESTORS MARKETING GROUP, INC.—See Investors Insurance Group, Inc.; *U.S. Public*, pg. 912
INVESTORS NATIONAL LIFE INSURANCE CO.—See The Seibels Bruce Group, Inc.; *U.S. Public*, pg. 1454
INVESTORS SERVICES GROUP—See First Data Corporation; *U.S. Public*, pg. 631
INVESTORS TRUST COMPANY—See National Penn Bancshares, Inc.; *U.S. Public*, pg. 1159
INVIARCO LTD.—See International Data Group; *U.S. Private*, pg. 570
INVINCIBLE OFFICE FURNITURE; *U.S. Private*, pg. 575
INVIRECHEM—See Pace International L.P.; *U.S. Private*, pg. 829
INVISTA CAPITAL MANAGEMENT INC.—See The Principal Financial Group; *U.S. Private*, pg. 885
INWOOD LABORATORIES, INC.—See Forest Laboratories, Inc.; *U.S. Public*, pg. 670
IOCHPE-MAXION ARGENTINA S.A.—See Iochpe-Maxion S.A.; *Int'l*, pg. 688
IOCHPE-MAXION OHIO, INC.—See Iochpe-Maxion S.A.; *Int'l*, pg. 688
IOCHPE-MAXION S.A.; *Int'l*, pg. 688
IOCHPE-MAXION S.A.—See Iochpe-Maxion S.A.; *Int'l*, pg. 688
IOFIL, S.A.—See Danone Group; *Int'l*, pg. 380
IOMEGA CORPORATION; *U.S. Public*, pg. 912
IOMEGA TAPE CO.—See Iomega Corporation; *U.S. Public*, pg. 912
ION IMPLANT SYSTEMS—See Varian Associates, Inc.; *U.S. Public*, pg. 1710
IONICS, INCORPORATED; *U.S. Public*, pg. 912
IONICS ITALBA S.P.A—See Ionics, Incorporated; *U.S. Public*, pg. 912
IONICS ULTRAPURE WATER CORPORATION—See Ionics, Incorporated; *U.S. Public*, pg. 912

IOT INTEGRIERTE OPTIK GMBH—See Carl-Zeiss-Stiftung; *Int'l*, pg. 1523
IOTA—See Lagardere Groupe; *Int'l*, pg. 792
IOWA-AMERICAN WATER CO.—See American Water Works Company, Inc.; *U.S. Public*, pg. 95
IOWA CELLULAR COMMUNICATIONS, INC.—See Motorola, Inc.; *U.S. Public*, pg. 1137
IOWA FARMER TODAY—See The Gazette Company; *U.S. Private*, pg. 442
IOWA FIDELITY LIFE INSURANCE CO.—See AEGON N.V.; *Int'l*, pg. 27
IOWA INDUSTRIES INC.—See Cooper Industries, Inc.; *U.S. Public*, pg. 442
IOWA MOLD TOOLING CO., INC.—See Intermet Corporation; *U.S. Public*, pg. 894
IOWA NORTHERN RAILROAD—See Iron Road Railways Inc.; *U.S. Private*, pg. 575
THE IOWA PACKING CO.; *U.S. Private*, pg. 575
IOWA PAINT MFG. COMPANY, INC.; *U.S. Private*, pg. 575
IOWA PORK INDUSTRIES, INC.—See American Foods Group, Inc.; *U.S. Private*, pg. 54
IOWA PRECISION INDUSTRIES—See Met-Coil Systems Corp.; *U.S. Public*, pg. 1100
IOWA SERVICE CENTER—See Pace Analytical Services; *U.S. Private*, pg. 829
IPALCO ENTERPRISES, INC.; *U.S. Public*, pg. 912
IPANEMA SHOE CORPORATION—See Sumitomo Corporation; *Int'l*, pg. 1312
G.I.E. IPEDEX INTERNATIONAL—See Technip; *Int'l*, pg. 1361
IPEK KAGIT SANAYI VE TICARET A.S.—See Fort James Corporation; *U.S. Public*, pg. 673
IPESA DE EL SALVADOR S.A.—See Hewlett-Packard Company; *Int'l*, pg. 822
IPESA DE GUATEMALA—See Hewlett-Packard Company; *U.S. Public*, pg. 822
IPEX—See The Ivaco Group; *Int'l*, pg. 695
IPRAGAZ A.S.—See SHV Holdings N.V.; *Int'l*, pg. 1155
IPSEN ABAR UK LIMITED—See Ruhrgas Aktiengesellschaft; *Int'l*, pg. 1149
IPSEN CERAMICS—See Ruhrgas Aktiengesellschaft; *Int'l*, pg. 1149
IPSEN INDUSTRIES INTERNATIONAL G.M.B.H.—See Ruhrgas Aktiengesellschaft; *Int'l*, pg. 1149
IPSEN INDUSTRIES NORDISKA AB—See Ruhrgas Aktiengesellschaft; *Int'l*, pg. 1149
IPSEN INTERNATIONAL, INC.—See Ruhrgas Aktiengesellschaft; *Int'l*, pg. 1149
IPTEST (HOLDINGS) LIMITED—See LTX Corporation; *U.S. Public*, pg. 972
IRAN HENKEL AG—See Henkel KGaA; *Int'l*, pg. 613
IRAN SCHINDLER LIFT MANUFACTURING COMPANY LTD.—See Schindler Holding AG; *Int'l*, pg. 1205
IRAN STEAM INDUSTRIES EQUIPMENT CO. LTD.—See GESTRA GmbH; *Int'l*, pg. 550
IRANIAN DIESEL ENGINEERING MANUFACTURING CO. (IDEM)—See Daimler-Benz Aktiengesellschaft; *Int'l*, pg. 368
IRANSEN ET SHELL—See Royal Dutch/Shell Group of Companies; *Int'l*, pg. 1136
IRCON GMBH—See Schneider S.A.; *Int'l*, pg. 1209
IRCON, LTD.—See Schneider S.A.; *Int'l*, pg. 1209
IRCON PYROMETERS, INC.—See Schneider S.A.; *Int'l*, pg. 1209
IRELAND ASSISTANCE LTD.—See Corporacion MAPFRE, Compania Internacional de Reaseguros, S.A.; *Int'l*, pg. 334
IRELAND COFFEE TEA, INC.—See Chock Full O' Nuts Corporation; *U.S. Public*, pg. 351
IRELAND GOURMET SHOP—See Chock Full O' Nuts Corporation; *U.S. Public*, pg. 351
IREX CORPORATION; *U.S. Public*, pg. 913
P.T. IRIAN MARINE PRODUCT DEVELOPMENT—See Nissho Iwai Corporation; *Int'l*, pg. 948
IRIANA S.R.L.—See Assicurazioni Generali S.p.A.; *Int'l*, pg. 90
IRIDIUM SERVICES DEUTSCHLAND GMBH—See Veba AG; *Int'l*, pg. 1461
IRIS GRAPHICS INC.—See IDB Holding Corporation; *Int'l*, pg. 644
IRISH BISCUITS; *Int'l*, pg. 688
IRISH BISCUITS EXPERTS LTD.—See Irish Biscuits; *Int'l*, pg. 688
IRISH BISCUITS LTD.—See Irish Biscuits; *Int'l*, pg. 688
IRISH BISCUITS (N.I.)—See Irish Biscuits; *Int'l*, pg. 688
IRISH BISCUITS SALES LTD.—See Irish Biscuits; *Int'l*, pg. 688
IRISH BISCUITS-W & R JACOB—See Danone Group; *Int'l*, pg. 381
IRISH BULK LIQUID STORAGE LTD.—See Simon Engineering plc; *Int'l*, pg. 1252
IRISH CEMENT LTD.—See CRH, plc; *Int'l*, pg. 242
THE IRISH CROWN CORK CO., LTD.—See Crown Cork & Seal Company, Inc.; *U.S. Public*, pg. 465
IRISH DISTILLERS LTD.—See Groupe Pernod Ricard; *Int'l*, pg. 567
IRISH DRIVER-HARRIS CO., LTD.—See Driver-Harris Company; *U.S. Public*, pg. 530
IRISH INTERCONTINENTAL BANK, LTD.—See Kredietbank N.V.; *Int'l*, pg. 761
IRISH LIFE FINANCE GROUP—See Kredietbank N.V.; *Int'l*, pg. 761
IRISH LIFE FINANCE LTD.—See Kredietbank N.V.; *Int'l*, pg. 761
IRISH LIFE HOMELOANS LTD.—See Kredietbank N.V.; *Int'l*, pg. 761
THE IRISH MIST LIQUEUR CO. LTD.—See Allied Domecq PLC; *Int'l*, pg. 63
IRISH SEWING LTD.—See Coats Viyella plc; *Int'l*, pg. 299
IRISH SHELL LTD.—See Royal Dutch/Shell Group of Companies; *Int'l*, pg. 1138
IRITECH—See IRI Istituto Ricostruzione Industriale; *Int'l*, pg. 654

IRITECNA—See IRI Istituto Ricostruzione Industriale; *Int'l*, pg. 654
IRITECNA-BEGIUM—See IRI Istituto Ricostruzione Industriale; *Int'l*, pg. 655
IRITECNA-MOSCOW—See IRI Istituto Ricostruzione Industriale; *Int'l*, pg. 655
IRKAFARM S.R.L.—See Pfizer Inc.; *U.S. Public*, pg. 1283
IRLANDUS CIRCUITS LIMITED—See DDL Electronics, Inc.; *U.S. Public*, pg. 473
IRON AGE CORPORATION—See Fenway Partners Inc.; *U.S. Private*, pg. 401
IRON AGE HOLDINGS CORPORATION—See Fenway Partners Inc.; *U.S. Private*, pg. 401
IRON-LIFT LLC—See Atlet AB; *Int'l*, pg. 97
IRON MOUNTAIN FORGE CORPORATION—See Rubbermaid Incorporated; *U.S. Public*, pg. 1411
IRON-ORE COMPANY OF CANADA—See North Limited; *Int'l*, pg. 967
IRON ROAD RAILWAYS INC.; *U.S. Private*, pg. 575
P.T. IRON WIRE WORKS INDONESIA—See Nissho Iwai Corporation; *Int'l*, pg. 948
IROQUOIS CAPITAL LIMITED—See Confederation Life Insurance Company; *Int'l*, pg. 326
IROQUOIS DIE & MFG. CO.; *U.S. Public*, pg. 575
IROQUOIS GAS TRANSMISSION SYSTEM—See Transcanada Pipelines Limited; *Int'l*, pg. 1417
IROQUOIS GAS TRANSMISSION SYSTEM—See Yankee Energy System, Inc.; *U.S. Public*, pg. 1787
IRRITOL SYSTEM—See The Toro Company; *U.S. Public*, pg. 1624
IRT ALAMBA INC.—See IRT Property Company; *U.S. Public*, pg. 858
IRT CAPITAL CORP.—See IRT Property Company; *U.S. Public*, pg. 858
IRVIN AEROSPACE CANADA LTD.—See Hunting Plc; *Int'l*, pg. 640
IRVIN AEROSPACE LTD.—See Hunting Plc; *Int'l*, pg. 640
IRVIN FALLSKARMS AB—See Hunting Plc; *Int'l*, pg. 640
IRVIN MANIFATTURE INDUSTRIALI S.P.A.—See Hunting Plc; *Int'l*, pg. 640
IRVINE APARTMENT COMMUNITIES INCORPORATED—See The Irvine Company; *U.S. Private*, pg. 575
THE IRVINE COMPANY; *U.S. Private*, pg. 575
IRVINE SCIENTIFIC SALES CO., LTD.—See Japan Energy Corporation; *Int'l*, pg. 702
IRVINE SENSORS CORPORATION; *U.S. Public*, pg. 913
IRVINE WORLD NEWS NEWSPAPER COMPANY—See The Irvine Company; *U.S. Private*, pg. 575
IRVING CONVENTION & VISITORS BUREAU; *U.S. Private*, pg. 575
IRVING TANNING CO.; *U.S. Private*, pg. 575
IRWIN SPORTS, INC.—See Irwin Toy Ltd.; *Int'l*, pg. 688
IRWIN TOY LTD.; *Int'l*, pg. 688
ISABELA SHOE CORP.—See Berkshire Hathaway Inc.; *U.S. Public*, pg. 217
ISABERG RAPID AB—See AB Industrivarden; *Int'l*, pg. 678
ISAR-SEINE IMMOBILIEN GMBH—See Bayerische Vereinsbank Group; *Int'l*, pg. 180
ISCAR BLADES LTD.—See IDB Holding Corporation; *Int'l*, pg. 644
ISCAR LTD.—See IDB Holding Corporation; *Int'l*, pg. 644
ISCHUA CREEK HOLDING COMPANY, INC.—See Motorola, Inc.; *U.S. Public*, pg. 1137
ISCO ENVIRONMENTAL DIVISION—See Isco, Inc.; *U.S. Public*, pg. 914
ISCO, INC.; *U.S. Public*, pg. 913
ISCO INSTRUMENTS (EUROPE) AG—See Isco, Inc.; *U.S. Public*, pg. 914
ISCO SEPARATION INSTRUMENTS DIVISION—See Isco, Inc.; *U.S. Public*, pg. 914
ISCOR; *Int'l*, pg. 688
ISCOSA INDUSTRIES & MAINTENANCE, LTD.—See Northrop Grumman Corporation; *U.S. Public*, pg. 1198
ISELI COMPANY—See Danaher Corporation; *U.S. Public*, pg. 481
ISEMOTO CONTRACTING CO. LTD.; *U.S. Private*, pg. 575
ISESAKI MFG. DIV.—See Fuji Heavy Industries, Ltd.; *Int'l*, pg. 522
ISFEL COMPANY, INC.; *U.S. Private*, pg. 576
ISHIHARA ARGENTINA S.A.—See Ishihara Sangyo Kaisha, Ltd.; *Int'l*, pg. 689
ISHIHARA CORPORATION (U.S.A.)—See Ishihara Sangyo Kaisha, Ltd.; *Int'l*, pg. 689
ISHIHARA SANGYO KAISHA, LTD.; *Int'l*, pg. 689
ISHIHARA TRADING CO., LTD.—See Ishihara Sangyo Kaisha, Ltd.; *Int'l*, pg. 689
ISHIKAWA SANKEN CO., LTD.—See Sanken Electric Co., Ltd.; *Int'l*, pg. 1188
ISHIKAWAJIMA EUROPE B.V.—See Ishikawajima-Harima Heavy Industries Co., Ltd.; *Int'l*, pg. 689
ISHIKAWAJIMA-HARIMA HEAVY INDUSTRIES CO., LTD.; *Int'l*, pg. 689
ISHINOMAKI MILL—See Nippon Paper Industries Company Limited; *Int'l*, pg. 938
ISIS DISTRIBUTED SYSTEMS, INC.—See Stratus Computer, Inc.; *U.S. Public*, pg. 1524
ISLAMBDA LTD.—See Siebe plc; *Int'l*, pg. 1242
THE ISLAMIC BANK OF BRUNEI BERHAD—See The Dai-Ichi Kangyo Bank, Limited; *Int'l*, pg. 362
ISLAND AGGREGATES LIMITED—See RMC Group p.l.c.; *Int'l*, pg. 1079
ISLAND AIR—See Aloha Airgroup, Inc.; *U.S. Private*, pg. 44
ISLAND ENTERTAINMENT GROUP, INC.—See Philips Electronics N.V.; *Int'l*, pg. 1052
ISLAND EXPRESS—See Caribe Express; *U.S. Private*, pg. 211
ISLAND LINCOLN-MERCURY; *U.S. Private*, pg. 576
ISLAND MUSIC, INC.—See Philips Electronics N.V.; *Int'l*, pg. 1052
ISLAND RESORT HOTEL CO., LTD.—See Siam City Bank Public Company Limited; *Int'l*, pg. 1239
ISLE OF MAN BANK LIMITED—See National Westminster Bank PLC; *Int'l*, pg. 910

ISLER'S REFUSE SERVICE, INC.—See Browning-Ferris Industries, Inc.; *U.S. Public*, pg. 264
ISMAC, INC.—See Komatsu Ltd.; *Int'l*, pg. 744
ISOLA WERKE AG—See Ruetgers A.G.; *Int'l*, pg. 1148
ISOLMAT—See Saint-Gobain; *Int'l*, pg. 1176
ISOLYSER COMPANY, INC.; *U.S. Public*, pg. 914
ISOMEDIX CORPORATION (CANADA)—See Steris Corporation; *U.S. Public*, pg. 1515
ISOMEDIX, INC.—See Steris Corporation; *U.S. Public*, pg. 1515
ISOMEDIX INVESTMENTS, INC.—See Steris Corporation; *U.S. Public*, pg. 1515
ISOMEDIX MANAGEMENT INC.—See Steris Corporation; *U.S. Public*, pg. 1515
ISOMEDIX OPERATIONS INC.—See Steris Corporation; *U.S. Public*, pg. 1515
ISOQUEST, INC.—See SRA International Inc.; *U.S. Private*, pg. 958
ISORA OY—See Neste Oy; *Int'l*, pg. 913
ISOTEC, INC.—See Nippon Sanso Corporation; *Int'l*, pg. 938
ISOTECH AG—See Novartis AG; *Int'l*, pg. 972
ISOTECH G.M.B.H.—See Novartis AG; *Int'l*, pg. 983
ISOTEX—See Saint-Gobain; *Int'l*, pg. 1176
ISOVEL INTERNATIONAL LTD.—See Haden Maclellan Holdings plc; *Int'l*, pg. 585
ISOVER AHLSTROM OY—See Saint-Gobain; *Int'l*, pg. 1176
ISOVER BV—See Saint-Gobain; *Int'l*, pg. 1176
ISOVER S.A.—See Saint-Gobain; *Int'l*, pg. 1176
ISOVER SA—See Saint-Gobain; *Int'l*, pg. 1176
ISOVER SAINT-GOBAIN—See Saint-Gobain; *Int'l*, pg. 1176
ISPO GMBH—See Dyckerhoff AG; *Int'l*, pg. 422
ISRAEL AIRCRAFT INDUSTRIES INTERNATIONAL INC.—See Israel Aircraft Industries Ltd.; *Int'l*, pg. 690
ISRAEL AIRCRAFT INDUSTRIES LTD.; *Int'l*, pg. 689
THE ISRAEL CIGARETTE CO. LTD.—See Dubek Ltd.; *Int'l*, pg. 421
ISRAEL DISCOUNT BANK LTD.—See IDB Holding Corporation; *Int'l*, pg. 645
ISRAEL DISCOUNT BANK OF NEW YORK—See IDB Holding Corporation; *Int'l*, pg. 645
ISRAEL DISTRIBUTOR—See Clarify Inc.; *U.S. Public*, pg. 382
ISRAEL EDIBLE PRODUCTS LTD.—See Bestfoods; *U.S. Public*, pg. 225
THE ISRAEL ELECTRIC CORPORATION LTD.; *Int'l*, pg. 690
THE ISRAEL LAND DEVELOPMENT CO., LTD.; *Int'l*, pg. 691
ISRAEL RESORT HOTELS—See The Israel Land Development Co., Ltd.; *Int'l*, pg. 691
THE ISRAEL TOBACCO CORP. (M.T.) LTD.—See Dubek Ltd.; *Int'l*, pg. 421
ISSELBURGER HUTTE GMBH—See Schuttersveld Holding N.V.; *Int'l*, pg. 1210
ISTA GMBH—See Veba AG; *Int'l*, pg. 1457
ISTITUTO BANCARIO SAN PAOLO DI TORINO S.P.A.; *Int'l*, pg. 691
ISTITUTO DELLE VITAMINE S.P.A.—See Roche Holding Ltd.; *Int'l*, pg. 1121
ISTITUTO MOBILIARE ITALIANO; *Int'l*, pg. 692
ISTROPOLITANA/DMB&B BRATISLAVA—See DMB&B Communications; *U.S. Private*, pg. 304
ISUZU ENGINE MANUFACTURING CO., (THAILAND) LTD.—See Isuzu Motors Limited; *Int'l*, pg. 693
ISUZU-GENERAL MOTORS AUSTRALIA LTD.—See Isuzu Motors Limited; *Int'l*, pg. 693
ISUZU-GENERAL MOTORS AUSTRALIA LTD.—See General Motors Corporation; *U.S. Public*, pg. 725
ISUZU MOTORS AMERICA INC.—See Isuzu Motors Limited; *Int'l*, pg. 692
ISUZU MOTORS CO., (THAILAND) LTD.—See Isuzu Motors Limited; *Int'l*, pg. 693
ISUZU MOTORS LIMITED; *Int'l*, pg. 692
ISUZU PILIPINAS CORPORATION—See Isuzu Motors Limited; *Int'l*, pg. 693
ISUZU TECHNICAL CENTER (THAILAND) CO., LTD.—See Isuzu Motors Limited; *Int'l*, pg. 693
ISUZU TRUCK (UK)—See Lex Service PLC; *Int'l*, pg. 807
ISVOR FIAT—See Fiat Auto SpA; *Int'l*, pg. 482
ISVOR S.P.A.—See Fiat Auto SpA; *Int'l*, pg. 482
ISYS SPOL SRO—See KPN Koninklyke PTT Nederland NV; *Int'l*, pg. 720
ITACARD S.P.A.—See Banco Ambrosiano Veneto S.p.A.; *Int'l*, pg. 138
ITAFINCO S.P.A.—See Banco Ambrosiano Veneto S.p.A.; *Int'l*, pg. 138
ITALACQUAE—See Danone Group; *Int'l*, pg. 381
ITALCOLOR, S.A.—See Borden, Inc.; *U.S. Private*, pg. 159
ITALFID ITALIANA FIDUCIARIA S.P.A.—See Banco Ambrosiano Veneto S.p.A.; *Int'l*, pg. 138
ITALGAS S.P.A.—See ENI S.p.A.; *Int'l*, pg. 428
ITALGEL S.P.A.—See Nestle S.A.; *Int'l*, pg. 920
ITALGESTRA S.R.L.—See GESTRA GmbH; *Int'l*, pg. 550
ITALIA ADVERTISING—See Italia/Gal Advertising; *U.S. Private*, pg. 576
ITALIA DI NAVIGAZIONE S.P.A.—See IRI Istituto Ricostruzione Industriale; *Int'l*, pg. 653
ITALIA/GAL ADVERTISING; *U.S. Private*, pg. 576
ITALIA S.P.A.—See Ionics, Incorporated; *U.S. Public*, pg. 912
ITALIAN AEROSPACE INDUSTRIES—See IRI Istituto Ricostruzione Industriale; *Int'l*, pg. 654
ITALIAN FOOD MANUFACTURERS, INC.; *U.S. Private*, pg. 576
ITALIAN LINE—See IRI Istituto Ricostruzione Industriale; *Int'l*, pg. 653
ITALIAN TOMATO LTD.—See Namco Ltd.; *Int'l*, pg. 905
S.P.A. ITALIANA LABORATORI BOUTY (ITALY)—See Carter-Wallace, Inc.; *U.S. Public*, pg. 310
ITALIANA LUCE S.R.L.—See IL International Inc.; *U.S. Public*, pg. 856
ITALIATOUR S.P.A.—See IRI Istituto Ricostruzione Industriale; *Int'l*, pg. 652

ITALIMPIANTI-ARGENTINA—See IRI Istituto Ricostruzione Industriale; *Int'l*, pg. 655
ITALIMPIANTI INTL.-AUSTRIA—See IRI Istituto Ricostruzione Industriale; *Int'l*, pg. 655
ITALIMPIANTI INTL.-BRAZIL—See IRI Istituto Ricostruzione Industriale; *Int'l*, pg. 655
ITALIMPIANTI INTL.-GERMANY—See IRI Istituto Ricostruzione Industriale; *Int'l*, pg. 655
ITALIMPIANTI INTL.-HONG KONG—See IRI Istituto Ricostruzione Industriale; *Int'l*, pg. 655
ITALIMPIANTI INTL.-IRAN—See IRI Istituto Ricostruzione Industriale; *Int'l*, pg. 655
ITALIMPIANTI INTL.-MONACO—See IRI Istituto Ricostruzione Industriale; *Int'l*, pg. 655
ITALIMPIANTI INTL.-UK—See IRI Istituto Ricostruzione Industriale; *Int'l*, pg. 655
ITALIMPIANTI INTL.-VENEZUALA—See IRI Istituto Ricostruzione Industriale; *Int'l*, pg. 655
ITALIMPIANTI INTL.-YEMEN—See IRI Istituto Ricostruzione Industriale; *Int'l*, pg. 655
ITALIMPIANTI OF AMERICA, INCORPORATED—See IRI Istituto Ricostruzione Industriale; *Int'l*, pg. 655
ITALIMPIANTI S.P.A.—See IRI Istituto Ricostruzione Industriale; *Int'l*, pg. 654
ITALMACERI—See Svenska Cellulosa Aktiebolaget (SCA); *Int'l*, pg. 1327
ITALPLAN SRL—See Alusuisse-Lonza Holding Ltd.; *Int'l*, pg. 68
ITALSAFETY SRL—See Williams Holdings Plc; *Int'l*, pg. 1500
ITALSTRADE-ALGERIA—See IRI Istituto Ricostruzione Industriale; *Int'l*, pg. 655
ITALSTRADE-IRAN—See IRI Istituto Ricostruzione Industriale; *Int'l*, pg. 655
ITALSTRADE-MOROCCO—See IRI Istituto Ricostruzione Industriale; *Int'l*, pg. 655
ITALSTRADE-PORTUGAL—See IRI Istituto Ricostruzione Industriale; *Int'l*, pg. 655
ITALSTRADE-SPAIN—See IRI Istituto Ricostruzione Industriale; *Int'l*, pg. 655
ITALTEL—See Telecom Italia S.p.A.; *Int'l*, pg. 1363
ITALTEST S.R.L.—See Breed Technologies, Inc.; *U.S. Public*, pg. 251
ITALTHAI CARBONE CY. LTD.—See Pechiney S.A.; *Int'l*, pg. 1030
ITALTRACTOR AMERICA INC.—See IRI Istituto Ricostruzione Industriale; *Int'l*, pg. 654
ITALTRACTOR - CEPRANO PLANT—See IRI Istituto Ricostruzione Industriale; *Int'l*, pg. 654
ITALTRACTOR ITM S.P.A.—See IRI Istituto Ricostruzione Industriale; *Int'l*, pg. 654
ITALY OBI SYSTEMZENTRALE SRL—See OBI Bau-und Heimwerkermaerkte GmbH & Co. KG; *Int'l*, pg. 993
ITAPEVA—See S.A. Industrias Votorantim; *Int'l*, pg. 677
ITAPSA, S.A. DE C.V.—See Echlin Inc.; *U.S. Public*, pg. 561
ITASERVICE S.P.A.—See Banco Ambrosiano Veneto S.p.A.; *Int'l*, pg. 138
ITEMS INTERNATIONAL/AIRWALK, INC.; *U.S. Private*, pg. 576
ITEQ, INC.; *U.S. Public*, pg. 914
ITHACA INDUSTRIES, INC.; *U.S. Private*, pg. 576
ITHACA JOURNAL—See Gannett Company, Inc.; *U.S. Public*, pg. 700
ITHACO INC.; *U.S. Private*, pg. 576
ITO CARIANI SAUSAGE CO.—See Itoham Foods Inc.; *Int'l*, pg. 695
ITO-YOKADO BANGKOK LIAISON OFFICE—See Ito-Yokado Co., Ltd.; *Int'l*, pg. 694
ITO-YOKADO CO., LTD.; *Int'l*, pg. 693
ITO-YOKADO TAIPEI LIAISON OFFICE—See Ito-Yokado Co., Ltd.; *Int'l*, pg. 694
ITOCHU BUILDING PRODUCTS CO., INC.—See Itochu Corporation; *Int'l*, pg. 694
ITOCHU CABLE T.V. ENG. CORP.—See Scientific-Atlanta, Inc.; *U.S. Public*, pg. 1443
ITOCHU CORPORATION; *Int'l*, pg. 694
ITOCHU COTTON, INC.—See Itochu Corporation; *Int'l*, pg. 694
ITOCHU DIGITAL PRODUCTS, INC.—See Itochu Corporation; *Int'l*, pg. 695
ITOCHU INTERNATIONAL INC.—See Itochu Corporation; *Int'l*, pg. 694
ITOH TEKKOSHO CO. LTD.—See Caterpillar Inc.; *U.S. Public*, pg. 317
ITOHAM FOODS (AUSTRALIA) PTY. LTD.—See Itoham Foods Inc.; *Int'l*, pg. 695
ITOHAM FOODS INC.; *Int'l*, pg. 695
ITRON INC.; *U.S. Public*, pg. 914
ITSEMAP AUSTRAL, S.A.—See Corporacion MAPFRE, Compania Internacional de Reaseguros, S.A.; *Int'l*, pg. 333
ITSEMAP DO BRASIL, LTDA.—See Corporacion MAPFRE, Compania Internacional de Reaseguros, S.A.; *Int'l*, pg. 333
ITSEMAP IBERICA, S.A.—See Corporacion MAPFRE, Compania Internacional de Reaseguros, S.A.; *Int'l*, pg. 332
ITSEMAP MEXICO, S.A. DE C.V.—See Corporacion MAPFRE, Compania Internacional de Reaseguros, S.A.; *Int'l*, pg. 333
ITSEMAP VENEZUELA C.A.—See Corporacion MAPFRE, Compania Internacional de Reaseguros, S.A.; *Int'l*, pg. 333
THE IVACO GROUP; *Int'l*, pg. 695
IVACO ROLLING MILLS LIMITED PARTNERSHIP—See The Ivaco Group; *Int'l*, pg. 695
IVACON B.V.—See Ballast Nedam NV; *Int'l*, pg. 134
IVANHOE—See Caisse de depot et placement du Quebec; *Int'l*, pg. 249
A/S IVARAN REDERI; *Int'l*, pg. 696
IVARAN SHIPPING A/S—See A/S Ivaran Rederi; *Int'l*, pg. 696
IVAX CORPORATION; *U.S. Public*, pg. 914

IVEC HANDELSONDERNEMING BV—See VNU Verenigde Nederlandse Uitgeversbedrijven B.V.; *Int'l*, pg. 1445
IVECO B.V.—See Fiat Auto SpA; *Int'l*, pg. 483
IVECO FIAT S.P.A.—See Fiat Auto SpA; *Int'l*, pg. 484
IVECO-FORD TRUCK LTD.—See Fiat Auto SpA; *Int'l*, pg. 484
IVECO FRANCE S.A.; *Int'l*, pg. 696
IVECO MAGIRUS A/G—See Fiat Auto SpA; *Int'l*, pg. 484
IVECO TRUCKS OF NORTH AMERICA INC.—See Fiat Auto SpA; *Int'l*, pg. 484
IVECO-UNIC S.A.—See Fiat Auto SpA; *Int'l*, pg. 484
IVEKA—See Electrabel S.A.; *Int'l*, pg. 437
IVERLEK—See Electrabel S.A.; *Int'l*, pg. 437
H.B. IVES—See Harrow Industries; *U.S. Private*, pg. 506
IVEX PACKAGING CORPORATION; *U.S. Public*, pg. 915
IVEX PACKAGING CORPORATION-AVENEL—See Ivex Packaging Corporation; *U.S. Public*, pg. 915
IVEX PACKAGING CORPORATION-BRIDGEVIEW—See Ivex Packaging Corporation; *U.S. Public*, pg. 915
IVEX PACKAGING CORPORATION-CANADIAN REGION—See Ivex Packaging Corporation; *U.S. Public*, pg. 915
IVEX PACKAGING CORPORATION-DETROIT—See Ivex Packaging Corporation; *U.S. Public*, pg. 915
IVEX PACKAGING CORPORATION-ENGINEERING GROUP—See Ivex Packaging Corporation; *U.S. Public*, pg. 915
IVEX PACKAGING CORPORATION-FLORAL AND NURSERY PRODUCTS—See Ivex Packaging Corporation; *U.S. Public*, pg. 915
IVEX PACKAGING CORPORATION-FOOD PACKAGING DIVISION—See Ivex Packaging Corporation; *U.S. Public*, pg. 915
IVEX PACKAGING CORPORATION-GRANT PARK—See Ivex Packaging Corporation; *U.S. Public*, pg. 915
IVEX PACKAGING CORPORATION-GROVE CITY—See Ivex Packaging Corporation; *U.S. Public*, pg. 915
IVEX PACKAGING CORPORATION-INDUSTRIAL PRODUCTS DIVISION—See Ivex Packaging Corporation; *U.S. Public*, pg. 915
IVEX PACKAGING CORPORATION-LONGUEUIL—See Ivex Packaging Corporation; *U.S. Public*, pg. 915
IVEX PACKAGING CORPORATION-MADISON—See Ivex Packaging Corporation; *U.S. Public*, pg. 915
IVEX PACKAGING CORPORATION-MANTENO—See Ivex Packaging Corporation; *U.S. Public*, pg. 915
IVEX PACKAGING CORPORATION-MILL DIVISION—See Ivex Packaging Corporation; *U.S. Public*, pg. 915
IVEX PACKAGING CORPORATION-PEORIA—See Ivex Packaging Corporation; *U.S. Public*, pg. 915
IVEX PACKAGING CORPORATION-POLYMERIZATION AND EXTRUSION DIVISION—See Ivex Packaging Corporation; *U.S. Public*, pg. 915
IVEX PACKAGING CORPORATION-TROY—See Ivex Packaging Corporation; *U.S. Public*, pg. 915
IVEX PACKAGING CORPORATION-VISALIA—See Ivex Packaging Corporation; *U.S. Public*, pg. 915
IVY—See Kellwood Company; *U.S. Public*, pg. 948
IVY HILL CORPORATION—See Time Warner Inc.; *U.S. Public*, pg. 1611
IWAKI-CORNING (MALAYSIA) SDN. BHD.—See Corning Incorporated; *U.S. Public*, pg. 449
IWAKUNI MILL—See Nippon Paper Industries Company Limited; *Int'l*, pg. 938
AB IWAN PAULSON—See Scancem AB; *Int'l*, pg. 1199
IWANOHARA VINEYARD CO., LTD.—See Suntory Ltd.; *Int'l*, pg. 1321
IWATE TOSHIBA ELECTRONICS CO., LTD.—See Toshiba Corporation; *Int'l*, pg. 1402
IWERKS ENTERTAINMENT; *U.S. Public*, pg. 915
IWERKS ENTERTAINMENT—See Iwerks Entertainment; *U.S. Public*, pg. 915
IZMIR BRANCH—See The Sakura Bank, Limited; *Int'l*, pg. 1180
IZOD—See Phillips-Van Heusen Corporation; *U.S. Public*, pg. 1292
IZUMI MOTOR INDUSTRIES INC.; *Int'l*, pg. 696

J

J AND O DIESEL—See Tri-State Mack Inc; *U.S. Private*, pg. 1101
J. HUNGERFORD SMITH COMPANY—See ConAgra, Inc.; *U.S. Public*, pg. 428
J & B PRODUCTS, INC.—See Federal Process Corp.; *U.S. Private*, pg. 399
J&B SCOTLAND—See Diageo Plc; *Int'l*, pg. 410
J & E DAVY HOLDINGS LIMITED—See Bank of Ireland; *Int'l*, pg. 152
J & F STEEL CORPORATION—See Arbed S.A.; *Int'l*, pg. 79
J&H MARSH & MCLENNAN, INC.—See Marsh & McLennan Companies, Inc.; *U.S. Public*, pg. 1049
J&H MARSH & MCLENNAN LTD.—See Marsh & McLennan Companies, Inc.; *U.S. Public*, pg. 1049
J&H MARSH & MCLENNAN MANAGEMENT SERVICES (BERMUDA) LTD.—See Marsh & McLennan Companies, Inc.; *U.S. Public*, pg. 1049
J & J CORRUGATED BOX—See Georgia-Pacific Corporation; *U.S. Public*, pg. 736
J&J DISTRIBUTION COMPANY—See The Jaydor Company; *U.S. Private*, pg. 584
J & J, INC.—See Hughes Supply, Inc.; *U.S. Public*, pg. 847
J & J REGISTER DIV.—See Tomkins PLC; *Int'l*, pg. 1397
J & J SNACK FOODS CORP.—See J & J Snack Foods Corporation; *U.S. Public*, pg. 916
J & J SNACK FOODS CORP./MIDWEST—See J & J Snack Foods Corporation; *U.S. Public*, pg. 916
J & J SNACK FOODS CORP. OF CALIFORNIA—See J & J Snack Foods Corporation; *U.S. Public*, pg. 916
J & J SNACK FOODS CORP. OF NEW JERSEY—See J & J Snack Foods Corporation; *U.S. Public*, pg. 916
J & J SNACK FOODS CORP. OF PENNSYLVANIA—See J & J Snack Foods Corporation; *U.S. Public*, pg. 916

J & J SNACK FOODS CORPORATION; *U.S. Public,* pg. 916
J & J SNACK FOODS INVESTMENT CORP.—See J & J Snack Foods Corporation; *U.S. Public,* pg. 916
J & J SNACK FOODS SALES CORP.—See J & J Snack Foods Corporation; *U.S. Public,* pg. 916
J & J SNACK FOODS TRANSPORT CORP.—See J & J Snack Foods Corporation; *U.S. Public,* pg. 916
J & L FIBER SERVICES, INC.—See Harnischfeger Industries, Inc.; *U.S. Public,* pg. 789
J & L METROLOGY COMPANY, INC.—See Goldman Financial Group; *U.S. Private,* pg. 461
J & L SPECIALTY PRODUCTS CORP.—See Groupe Usinor; *Int'l,* pg. 572
J & N WADE LIMITED—See James Crean PLC; *Int'l,* pg. 341
J. & P. COATS LIMITED—See Coats Viyella plc; *Int'l,* pg. 299
J & R FILM / MOVIOLA DIGITAL CO.; *U.S. Private,* pg. 576
J & R INTERFACING—See William Prym GmbH & Co. KG; *Int'l,* pg. 1499
J & R MUSIC WORLD; *U.S. Private,* pg. 576
J & S LEASING INC.—See National Commerce Bancorporation; *U.S. Public,* pg. 1155
J B LABS, INC.; *U.S. Private,* pg. 576
J. CREW GROUP, INC.—See Texas Pacific Group; *U.S. Private,* pg. 1078
J-M MANUFACTURING CO., INC.—See Formosa Plastics Corporation; *Int'l,* pg. 498
J-STAR INDUSTRIES, INC.; *U.S. Private,* pg. 576
J2, INC.—See Jordan Industries, Inc.; *U.S. Private,* pg. 598
OY JA-RO AB—See Outokumpu Oyj; *Int'l,* pg. 1018
JAE ELECTRONICS, INC.—See Japan Aviation Electronics Industry, Ltd.; *Int'l,* pg. 701
JAE ENGINEERING, LTD.—See Japan Aviation Electronics Industry, Ltd.; *Int'l,* pg. 701
JAE FOODS, LTD.—See Japan Aviation Electronics Industry, Ltd.; *Int'l,* pg. 701
JAE FUJI, LTD.—See Japan Aviation Electronics Industry, Ltd.; *Int'l,* pg. 701
JAE HIROSAKI, LTD.—See Japan Aviation Electronics Industry, Ltd.; *Int'l,* pg. 701
JAE OREGON, INC.—See Japan Aviation Electronics Industry, Ltd.; *Int'l,* pg. 701
JAE SERVICES, LTD.—See Japan Aviation Electronics Industry, Ltd.; *Int'l,* pg. 701
JAE SHINSHU, LTD.—See Japan Aviation Electronics Industry, Ltd.; *Int'l,* pg. 701
JAE TAIWAN, LTD.—See Japan Aviation Electronics Industry, Ltd.; *Int'l,* pg. 701
JAE YAMAGATA, LTD.—See Japan Aviation Electronics Industry, Ltd.; *Int'l,* pg. 701
JAFCO AMERICA VENTURES INC.—See The Nomura Securities Co., Ltd.; *Int'l,* pg. 955
JAH ENTERPRISES, INC.; *U.S. Private,* pg. 577
JAL INTERNATIONAL SERVICES—See Japan Airlines Company, Ltd.; *Int'l,* pg. 700
JB OXFORD HOLDINGS INC.; *U.S. Public,* pg. 916
JB/YOUNG & RUBICAM—See Young & Rubicam Inc.; *U.S. Private,* pg. 1200
JBA (HK) LTD.—See Sulcus Computer Corp.; *U.S. Public,* pg. 1527
JBB WORLDWIDE, INC.—See Fortune Brands, Inc.; *U.S. Public,* pg. 675
JBL CONSUMER—See Harman International Industries, Inc.; *U.S. Public,* pg. 787
JBL DIV.—See Parker Hannifin Corporation; *U.S. Public,* pg. 1262
JBL PROFESSIONAL—See Harman International Industries, Inc.; *U.S. Public,* pg. 787
J.B.N. FINANCE CORPORATION—See Lynch Corporation; *U.S. Public,* pg. 1021
J.B.N. TELEPHONE CO.—See Lynch Corporation; *U.S. Public,* pg. 1021
JBQ SPORT LLC; *U.S. Private,* pg. 577
JBS PRODUCTIONS HOLDING COMPANY, INC.—See The Walt Disney Company; *U.S. Public,* pg. 511
JC DISTRIBUTION LIMITED—See James Crean PLC; *Int'l,* pg. 340
JC PENNEY BUSINESS SERVICES—See JC Penney Company, Inc.; *U.S. Public,* pg. 917
JC PENNEY COMPANY, INC.; *U.S. Public,* pg. 916
JC PENNEY EUROPE, INC.—See JC Penney Company, Inc.; *U.S. Public,* pg. 917
JC PENNEY FINANCIAL SERVICES, INC.—See JC Penney Company, Inc.; *U.S. Public,* pg. 917
J.C. PENNEY LIFE INSURANCE COMPANY—See JC Penney Company, Inc.; *U.S. Public,* pg. 917
JC PENNEY NATIONAL BANK—See JC Penney Company, Inc.; *U.S. Public,* pg. 917
JC PENNEY PROPERTIES, INC.—See JC Penney Company, Inc.; *U.S. Public,* pg. 917
JC PENNEY PURCHASING CORP.—See JC Penney Company, Inc.; *U.S. Public,* pg. 917
JC PENNEY REINSURANCE COMPANY—See JC Penney Company, Inc.; *U.S. Public,* pg. 917
JCAIR, INC.—See The B.F. Goodrich Company; *U.S. Public,* pg. 751
JCB INTERNATIONAL CO., LTD.; *Int'l,* pg. 696
JCB INTERNATIONAL CREDIT CARD CO., LTD.-USA—See JCB International Co., Ltd.; *Int'l,* pg. 696
JCI DATA PROCESSING, INC.; *U.S. Private,* pg. 577
JCI LIMITED; *Int'l,* pg. 696
THE JCM GROUP—See Peck Jones Construction; *U.S. Private,* pg. 846
JCP REALTY, INC.—See JC Penney Company, Inc.; *U.S. Public,* pg. 917
JDAC—See TMP Worldwide, Inc.; *U.S. Private,* pg. 1065
JDS FITEL INC.—See The Furukawa Electric Co., Ltd.; *Int'l,* pg. 531
JE MERIT CONSTRUCTORS, INC.—See Jacobs Engineering Group Inc.; *U.S. Public,* pg. 921
JEOL ASIA PTE. LTD.—See JEOL, Ltd.; *Int'l,* pg. 697

JEOL (AUSTRALASIA) PTY. LTD.—See JEOL, Ltd.; *Int'l,* pg. 697
JEOL CANADA, INC.—See JEOL, Ltd.; *Int'l,* pg. 697
JEOL DE MEXICO S.A. DE C.V.—See JEOL, Ltd.; *Int'l,* pg. 697
JEOL (EUROPE)—See JEOL, Ltd.; *Int'l,* pg. 697
JEOL (ITALIA) S.P.A.—See JEOL, Ltd.; *Int'l,* pg. 697
JEOL KOREA LTD.—See JEOL, Ltd.; *Int'l,* pg. 697
JEOL, LTD.; *Int'l,* pg. 696
JEOL (SKANDINAVISKA) A.B.—See JEOL, Ltd.; *Int'l,* pg. 697
JEOL (U.K.) LTD.—See JEOL, Ltd.; *Int'l,* pg. 697
JEOL (U.S.A.), INC.—See JEOL, Ltd.; *Int'l,* pg. 697
J.F. JENS SOHNE WERKZEUGE-MASCHINEN GMBH—See Rothenberger Group GmbH; *Int'l,* pg. 1128
JFC INC.; *U.S. Private,* pg. 577
JFD DISTRIBUTION—See G.T.C. Transcontinental Group Ltd.; *Int'l,* pg. 539
JG INDUSTRIES, INC.; *U.S. Public,* pg. 917
JGC ARABIA LTD.—See JGC Corporation; *Int'l,* pg. 697
JGC CORPORATION; *Int'l,* pg. 697
JGC CORPORATION (UK) LTD.—See JGC Corporation; *Int'l,* pg. 697
JGC DORDTSE ENGINEERING B.V.—See JGC Corporation; *Int'l,* pg. 697
JGC ENGINEERS AUSTRALIA PTY. LTD.—See JGC Corporation; *Int'l,* pg. 697
JGC (MALAYSIA) SDN. BHD.—See JGC Corporation; *Int'l,* pg. 697
JGC NIGERIA LTD.—See JGC Corporation; *Int'l,* pg. 697
JGC SINGAPORE PTE. LTD.—See JGC Corporation; *Int'l,* pg. 697
JGC (U.S.A.), INC.—See JGC Corporation; *Int'l,* pg. 697
JHC HOLDING CORP.—See Zale Corporation; *U.S. Public,* pg. 1789
JHJ REALTY—See Millstein Industries; *U.S. Private,* pg. 749
J.I. SERVICES CORP.—See Hughes Supply, Inc.; *U.S. Public,* pg. 847
JIB GROUP PLC—See Jardine Matheson Holdings Limited; *Int'l,* pg. 705
JII/SALES PROMOTION ASSOCIATES, INC.—See Jordan Industries, Inc.; *U.S. Private,* pg. 598
JJC SPECIALIST CORP.—See Fleet Financial Group, Inc.; *U.S. Public,* pg. 650
JJI LIGHTING GROUP INC.—See Luxo A/S; *Int'l,* pg. 821
JJJ REALTY TRUST—See Action Equipment; *U.S. Private,* pg. 15
JK LASERS DEUTSCHLAND GMBH—See Sumitomo Heavy Industries, Ltd.; *Int'l,* pg. 1315
JKC JIDOSHA KIKI C., LTD.—See Knorr-Bremse AG; *Int'l,* pg. 738
JL MEDIA, INC.; *U.S. Private,* pg. 577
JL MEDIA, INC.—See JL Media, Inc.; *U.S. Private,* pg. 577
JL MEDIA INC.—See JL Media, Inc.; *U.S. Private,* pg. 577
JL PROPERTY HOLDINGS LTD.—See John Laing PLC; *Int'l,* pg. 796
JLG INDUSTRIES (AUSTRALIA) PTY. LIMITED—See JLG Industries, Inc.; *U.S. Public,* pg. 918
JLG INDUSTRIES (EUROPE)—See JLG Industries, Inc.; *U.S. Public,* pg. 918
JLG INDUSTRIES, INC.; *U.S. Public,* pg. 918
JLG INDUSTRIES (UNITED KINGDOM) LIMITED—See JLG Industries, Inc.; *U.S. Public,* pg. 918
JLH ADVERTISING, INC.—See BeautiControl Cosmetics, Inc.; *U.S. Public,* pg. 198
JLK AMERICA INC.—See Kennametal Inc.; *U.S. Public,* pg. 951
JLK DIRECT DISTRIBUTION INC.—See Kennametal Inc.; *U.S. Public,* pg. 951
JLN—See Jaclyn, Inc.; *U.S. Public,* pg. 920
JLW FINANCIAL MANAGEMENT SYSTEMS, INC.—See AEGON N.V.; *Int'l,* pg. 28
JM BYGGNADS OCH FASTIGHETS AB—See Skanska AB; *Int'l,* pg. 1260
JM COMPANY; *U.S. Private,* pg. 577
JM FAMILY ENTERPRISES, INC.; *U.S. Private,* pg. 577
J.M. PROCESS SYSTEMS INC.; *U.S. Private,* pg. 577
JM TELEVISION PRODUCTIONS—See Jazzercise; *U.S. Private,* pg. 584
JMB REALTY CORPORATION; *U.S. Private,* pg. 577
J.M.C./YOUNG & RUBICAM—See Young & Rubicam Inc.; *U.S. Private,* pg. 1200
JMCT/DIRECT—See Jordan, McGrath, Case & Taylor Inc.; *U.S. Private,* pg. 599
JMCT PUBLICIDAD—See Jordan, McGrath, Case & Taylor Inc.; *U.S. Private,* pg. 599
JMCTTOUCH—See Jordan, McGrath, Case & Taylor Inc.; *U.S. Private,* pg. 599
JMD DEVELOPMENT CORPORATION—See Science Applications International Corp.; *U.S. Private,* pg. 976
JMI-CANTON PHARMACEUTICALS, INC.—See Jones Medical Industries Inc.; *U.S. Public,* pg. 934
JMI-DANIELS PHARMACEUTICALS, INC.—See Jones Medical Industries Inc.; *U.S. Public,* pg. 934
JMI-PHOENIX LABORATORIES, INC.—See Jones Medical Industries Inc.; *U.S. Public,* pg. 934
J.M.P. BAKERY CO., INC.; *U.S. Private,* pg. 578
JMP NEWCOR HOLDINGS INC.—See Patra Ceramics Co., Ltd.; *Int'l,* pg. 1025
JMP NEWCOR INTERNATIONAL, INC.—See Patra Ceramics Co., Ltd.; *Int'l,* pg. 1025
JMS SPECIALTY FOODS, INC.—See J.M. Smucker Company; *U.S. Public,* pg. 1480
JNI INVESTMENTS N.V.—See Royal Begemann Group; *Int'l,* pg. 1133
JO DZ INT/IMPREGILO/ISTAKA KARYA—See Lyonnaise des Eaux S.A.; *Int'l,* pg. 823
JOEL (EUROPE) B.V.—See JEOL, Ltd.; *Int'l,* pg. 697
JOTSA, S.A. EMPRESSA CONSTRUCTOR—See Philipp Holzmann AG; *Int'l,* pg. 634
JP FOODSERVICE DISTRIBUTORS, INC.—See JP Foodservice, Inc.; *U.S. Public,* pg. 918
JP FOODSERVICE, INC.; *U.S. Public,* pg. 918

JP FOODSERVICE, INC.-ALLENTOWN—See JP Foodservice, Inc.; *U.S. Public,* pg. 918
JP FOODSERVICE, INC.-ALTOONA—See JP Foodservice, inc.; *U.S. Public,* pg. 918
JP FOODSERVICE, INC.-BALTIMORE—See JP Foodservice, Inc.; *U.S. Public,* pg. 918
JP FOODSERVICE, INC.-BOSTON—See JP Foodservice, Inc.; *U.S. Public,* pg. 918
JP FOODSERVICE, INC.-DES MOINES—See JP Foodservice, Inc.; *U.S. Public,* pg. 918
JP FOODSERVICE, INC.-FORT WAYNE—See JP Foodservice, Inc.; *U.S. Public,* pg. 918
JP FOODSERVICE, INC.-HARTFORD—See JP Foodservice, Inc.; *U.S. Public,* pg. 918
JP FOODSERVICE, INC.-MINNEAPOLIS—See JP Foodservice, Inc.; *U.S. Public,* pg. 918
JP FOODSERVICE, INC.-STREATOR—See JP Foodservice, Inc.; *U.S. Public,* pg. 918
JP INVESTMENT MANAGEMENT CO.—See Jefferson-Pilot Corporation; *U.S. Public,* pg. 925
JP MOREELS S.A.—See LVMH Moet Hennessy Louis Vuitton; *Int'l,* pg. 782
JPB GENERAL PLACERVILLE CORPORATION—See Boise Cascade Corporation; *U.S. Public,* pg. 243
JPE CANADA INC.—See JPE, Inc.; *U.S. Public,* pg. 919
JPE, INC.; *U.S. Public,* pg. 919
THE JPM COMPANY; *U.S. Public,* pg. 919
THE JPM COMPANY OF SOUTH CAROLINA, INC.—See The JPM Company; *U.S. Public,* pg. 919
JPM CORRETORA DE CAMBIO, TITULOS E VALORES MOBILIARIOS S.A.—See J.P. Morgan Co. Incorporated; *U.S. Public,* pg. 1130
JPM CORRETORA DE CAMBIO, TITULOS E VALORES MOBILIARIOS S.A. (RIO DE JANEIRO)—See J.P. Morgan Co. Incorporated; *U.S. Public,* pg. 1130
JPS AUTOMOTIVE L.P.—See Trace International Holdings, Inc.; *U.S. Private,* pg. 1095
JPS CONVERTER & INDUSTRIAL CORP.—See JPS Textile Group, Inc.; *U.S. Private,* pg. 578
JPS ELASTOMERICS CORP.—See JPS Textile Group, Inc.; *U.S. Private,* pg. 578
JPS TEXTILE GROUP, INC.; *U.S. Private,* pg. 578
J.R. TECHNICAL—See Arrow Pneumatics Co. Inc.; *U.S. Private,* pg. 85
JRC CANIDA, INC.; *U.S. Private,* pg. 578
JRN, INC.; *U.S. Private,* pg. 578
JS&A GROUP, INC.; *U.S. Private,* pg. 578
J S HEMKOPSKEDJAN AB—See Axel Johnson AB; *Int'l,* pg. 708
JS TELECOMMUNICATIONS S.A.—See Jeumont-Schneider Trenformeteurs; *Int'l,* pg. 706
JSB ELECTRICAL PLC—See Emess PLC; *Int'l,* pg. 453
JSB FINANCIAL; *U.S. Public,* pg. 919
JSI—See Jasper Seating Co., Inc.; *U.S. Private,* pg. 583
JT AMERICA INC.—See Japan Tobacco Inc.; *Int'l,* pg. 703
JT INTERNATIONAL CORP.—See Japan Tobacco Inc.; *Int'l,* pg. 703
JT INTERNATIONAL EUROPE LIMITED—See Japan Tobacco Inc.; *Int'l,* pg. 703
JT INTERNATIONAL (HK) LTD.—See Japan Tobacco Inc.; *Int'l,* pg. 703
JT INTERNATIONAL (SINGAPORE) PTE. LTD.—See Japan Tobacco Inc.; *Int'l,* pg. 703
JT INTERNATIONAL TAIWAN CORP.—See Japan Tobacco Inc.; *Int'l,* pg. 703
JT INTERNATIONAL U.S.A. INC.—See Japan Tobacco Inc.; *Int'l,* pg. 703
JT (UK) LTD.—See Japan Tobacco Inc.; *Int'l,* pg. 703
JTB AIR CARGO INC.—See Union-Transport Corporation; *U.S. Private,* pg. 1120
JTC ENVIRONMENTAL CONSULTANTS, INC.—See GP Strategies Corporation; *U.S. Public,* pg. 694
JTC LLC; *U.S. Private,* pg. 579
JTS CORPORATION; *U.S. Public,* pg. 919
JTUSA, INC.—See Nifco Inc.; *Int'l,* pg. 929
J.U.L. SEILAZ AG—See Henkel KGaA; *Int'l,* pg. 613
J.V. LAING-GTM EUROPE—See Lyonnaise des Eaux S.A.; *Int'l,* pg. 823
JVC MANUFACTURING COMPANY—See Matsushita Electric Industrial Co., Ltd.; *Int'l,* pg. 847
JVC PROFESSIONAL PRODUCTS COMPANY—See Matsushita Electric Industrial Co., Ltd.; *Int'l,* pg. 847
J.W. ALUMINUM COMPANY—See Walter Industries, Inc.; *U.S. Public,* pg. 1736
J.W. MESSNER, INC.—See J.W. Messner, Inc.; *U.S. Private,* pg. 734
J.W. WINDOW COMPONENTS, INC.—See Walter Industries, Inc.; *U.S. Public,* pg. 1736
JWG ASOCIADOS MEXICO—See JWG Associates. Inc.; *U.S. Private,* pg. 579
JWG ASSOCIATES, INC.; *U.S. Private,* pg. 579
JWG ASSOCIATES, INC.—See JWG Associates, Inc.; *U.S. Private,* pg. 579
JWK INTERNATIONAL CORP.; *U.S. Private,* pg. 579
JWT/ARK COMMUNICATIONS—See WPP Group plc; *Int'l,* pg. 1484
JA/MONT IRELAND LTD.—See Fort James Corporation; *U.S. Public,* pg. 673
JA/MONT N.V. - TECHNOLOGY OFFICE—See Fort James Corporation; *U.S. Public,* pg. 673
JABAWWAT, INC.—See Orion Capital Corporation; *U.S. Public,* pg. 1231
JABEL, INC.; *U.S. Private,* pg. 579
JABIL CIRCUIT, INC.; *U.S. Public,* pg. 919
JABIL CIRCUIT, INC./NORTH—See Jabil Circuit, Inc.; *U.S. Public,* pg. 920
JABIL CIRCUIT, INC./WEST—See Jabil Circuit, Inc.; *U.S. Public,* pg. 920
JABIL CIRCUIT, LTD.—See Jabil Circuit, Inc.; *U.S. Public,* pg. 920
JABIL CIRCUIT, SDN BHD—See Jabil Circuit, Inc.; *U.S. Public,* pg. 920
JAC PAC FOODS, LTD.; *U.S. Private,* pg. 579

JACARANDA WILEY LTD.—See John Wiley & Sons, Inc.; *U.S. Public*, pg. 1768

JACK DANIELS DISTILLERY—See Brown-Forman Corporation; *U.S. Public*, pg. 261

JACK LEVY ASSOCIATES, PUBLIC RELATIONS DEPT.—See Jack Levy Associates; *U.S. Private*, pg. 664

JACKHAMMER—See The Richards Group, Inc.; *U.S. Private*, pg. 929

JACKPOT CASINO, INC.—See Jackpot Enterprises, Inc.; *U.S. Public*, pg. 920

JACKPOT CITY, INC.—See Jackpot Enterprises, Inc.; *U.S. Public*, pg. 920

JACKPOT ENTERPRISES, INC.; *U.S. Public*, pg. 920

JACKPOT GAMING, INC.—See Jackpot Enterprises, Inc.; *U.S. Public*, pg. 920

JACKS BEAN COMPANY—See ConAgra, Inc.; *U.S. Public*, pg. 428

JACKS INTERNATIONAL LIMITED; *Int'l*, pg. 697

JACKSON & PERKINS—See Yamanouchi Pharmaceutical Co. Ltd.; *Int'l*, pg. 1518

JACKSON CORP.—See Lancaster Colony Corporation; *U.S. Public*, pg. 977

JACKSON FURNITURE INDUSTRIES; *U.S. Private*, pg. 579

GENE JACKSON FARMS—See A. Duda & Sons Inc.; *U.S. Private*, pg. 344

JACKSON HOLE SKI RESORT; *U.S. Private*, pg. 579

THE JACKSON-LEWIS COMPANY—See BFC Construction Corporation; *Int'l*, pg. 118

JACKSON MS STEEL DIVISION—See Birmingham Steel Corporation; *U.S. Public*, pg. 232

JACKSON MSC; *U.S. Private*, pg. 579

JACKSON NATIONAL LIFE INSURANCE COMPANY—See Prudential Corporation PLC; *Int'l*, pg. 1073

JACKSON PAPER COMPANY; *U.S. Private*, pg. 579

JACKSON SALES & STORAGE CO.—See National Presto Industries, Inc.; *U.S. Public*, pg. 1159

JACKSON SUN, INC.—See Gannett Company, Inc.; *U.S. Public*, pg. 701

JACKSONLEA—See Jason Incorporated; *U.S. Public*, pg. 924

JACKSONVILLE CRAWDADDY CORP.—See Specialty Restaurants Corporation; *U.S. Private*, pg. 1023

JACKSONVILLE PROPERTIES, INC.—See St. Joe Corp.; *U.S. Public*, pg. 1427

JACKSONVILLE WELDING SUPPLY, INC.—See Praxair Inc.; *U.S. Public*, pg. 1320

JACKY S.A.—See Nestle S.A.; *Int'l*, pg. 920

N.V. JACKY, S.A.—See Unilever Plc; *Int'l*, pg. 1437

JACLO INC.—See Durst Corporation; *U.S. Private*, pg. 349

JACLYN, INC.; *U.S. Public*, pg. 920

JACMAR BUILDERS INC.—See Jacmar Companies, Inc.; *U.S. Private*, pg. 580

JACMAR COMPANIES, INC.; *U.S. Private*, pg. 580

JACO ELECTRONICS—See Jaco Electronics, Inc.; *U.S. Public*, pg. 920

JACO ELECTRONICS, INC.; *U.S. Public*, pg. 920

JACO ELECTRONICS, INC.—See Jaco Electronics, Inc.; *U.S. Public*, pg. 920

JACO ELECTRONICS, INC.—See Jaco Electronics, Inc.; *U.S. Public*, pg. 920

JACO ELECTRONICS, INC.—See Jaco Electronics, Inc.; *U.S. Public*, pg. 921

JACOB SIGEL TRIAD—See Jacobs Engineering Group Inc.; *U.S. Public*, pg. 921

JACOBS APPLIED TECHNOLOGY, INC.—See Jacobs Engineering Group Inc.; *U.S. Public*, pg. 921

JACOBS ASSET MANAGEMENT—See United Asset Management Corporation; *U.S. Public*, pg. 1673

THE JACOB'S BAKERY LTD.—See Danone Group; *Int'l*, pg. 381

JACOBS BELGIQUE S.A.—See Philip Morris Companies Inc.; *U.S. Public*, pg. 1288

JACOBS BRAKE DIVISION—See Danaher Corporation; *U.S. Public*, pg. 481

JACOBS CHUCK MANUFACTURING—See Danaher Corporation; *U.S. Public*, pg. 481

JACOBS ENGINEERING GROUP INC.; *U.S. Public*, pg. 921

JACOBS INTERNATIONAL LIMITED, INC.—See Jacobs Engineering Group Inc.; *U.S. Public*, pg. 922

JAY JACOBS, INC.; *U.S. Public*, pg. 922

JACOBS KAFFEE GES.M.B.H.—See Philip Morris Companies Inc.; *U.S. Public*, pg. 1288

JACOBS MAINTENANCE, INC.—See Jacobs Engineering Group Inc.; *U.S. Public*, pg. 921

MYLON C. JACOBS SUPPLY CO.—See Sammons Enterprises, Inc.; *U.S. Private*, pg. 963

THE RICHARD E. JACOBS GROUP; *U.S. Private*, pg. 580

JACOBS SIRRINE ENGINEERS, INC.—See Jacobs Engineering Group Inc.; *U.S. Public*, pg. 921

JACOBS SUCHARD (AUSTRALIA) PTY. LTD.—See Philip Morris Companies Inc.; *U.S. Public*, pg. 1288

JACOBS SUCHARD BERLIN GMBH & CO. KG—See Philip Morris Companies Inc.; *U.S. Public*, pg. 1288

JACOBS SUCHARD ERZEUGNISSE GMBH & CO. KG—See Philip Morris Companies Inc.; *U.S. Public*, pg. 1289

JACOBS SUCHARD ESPANA S.A.—See Philip Morris Companies Inc.; *U.S. Public*, pg. 1288

JACOBS SUCHARD FINANZ AG—See Philip Morris Companies Inc.; *U.S. Public*, pg. 1288

JACOBS SUCHARD FRANCE S.A.—See Philip Morris Companies Inc.; *U.S. Public*, pg. 1289

JACOBS SUCHARD INTERNATIONAL MFG. GMBH & CO. KG—See Philip Morris Companies Inc.; *U.S. Public*, pg. 1289

JACOBS SUCHARD JAPAN CO., LTD.—See Philip Morris Companies Inc.; *U.S. Public*, pg. 1289

JACOBS SUCHARD KAFFE A/S—See Philip Morris Companies Inc.; *U.S. Public*, pg. 1289

JACOBS SUCHARD LTD.—See Philip Morris Companies Inc.; *U.S. Public*, pg. 1289

JACOBS SUCHARD MANAGEMENT & CONSULTING AG—See Philip Morris Companies Inc.; *U.S. Public*, pg. 1288

JACOBS SUCHARD PAVLIDES S.A.—See Philip Morris Companies Inc.; *U.S. Public*, pg. 1289

JACOBS SUCHARD SERVICE AG—See Philip Morris Companies Inc.; *U.S. Public*, pg. 1288

JACOBS SUCHARD SERVICE GMBH & CO. KG—See Philip Morris Companies Inc.; *U.S. Public*, pg. 1289

JACOBS SUCHARD TOBLER AG—See Philip Morris Companies Inc.; *U.S. Public*, pg. 1288

JACOBS VEHICLE EQUIPMENT COMPANY—See Danaher Corporation; *U.S. Public*, pg. 481

JAC JACOBSEN AB—See Luxo A/S; *Int'l*, pg. 821

JAC JACOBSEN ENTERPRISES, INC.—See Luxo A/S; *Int'l*, pg. 821

JACOBSEN MANUFACTURING, INC.; *U.S. Private*, pg. 580

JACOBSEN TEXTRON—See Textron Inc.; *U.S. Public*, pg. 1589

JACOBSON CREDIT CORPORATION—See Jacobson Stores Inc.; *U.S. Public*, pg. 922

K.F. JACOBSON CO.—See R.B. Pamplin Corp.; *U.S. Private*, pg. 836

JACOBSON STORES INC.; *U.S. Public*, pg. 922

JACOBSON STORES REALTY COMPANY—See Jacobson Stores Inc.; *U.S. Public*, pg. 922

JACOBY & MEYERS LAW OFFICES; *U.S. Private*, pg. 580

JACOR COMMUNICATIONS, INC.; *U.S. Public*, pg. 922

JACOR, INC.—See Jaymark, Inc.; *U.S. Private*, pg. 584

JACOR NETWORKS INC.—See Jaymark, Inc.; *U.S. Private*, pg. 584

JACQUES GEOSCIENCES, INC.—See Fugro Group Companies; *U.S. Private*, pg. 431

JACQUES MORET, INC.; *U.S. Private*, pg. 580

JACQUES ONONA & CO. LIMITED—See The Albert Fisher Group PLC; *Int'l*, pg. 491

JACQUET ORTHOPEDIE S.A.—See Pfizer Inc.; *U.S. Public*, pg. 1282

CHARLES JACQUIN ET CIE, INC.; *U.S. Private*, pg. 580

JACUZZI BROS., JACUZZI, INC.—See U.S. Industries, Inc.; *U.S. Public*, pg. 1684

JACUZZI CANADA—See U.S. Industries, Inc.; *U.S. Public*, pg. 1684

JACUZZI (CHILE) S.A.—See U.S. Industries, Inc.; *U.S. Public*, pg. 1684

JACUZZI DO BRASIL—See U.S. Industries, Inc.; *U.S. Public*, pg. 1684

JACUZZI EUROPE, S.P.A.—See U.S. Industries, Inc.; *U.S. Public*, pg. 1684

JACUZZI, INC.—See U.S. Industries, Inc.; *U.S. Public*, pg. 1684

JACUZZI UNIVERSAL, S.A.—See U.S. Industries, Inc.; *U.S. Public*, pg. 1684

JACUZZI WHIRLPOOL BATH INC.—See U.S. Industries, Inc.; *U.S. Public*, pg. 1684

JADE S.A.—See Martin Merkel GmbH & Co. KG; *Int'l*, pg. 859

JADE TECHNOLOGIES SINGAPORE PTE. LTD.—See U.S. Industries, Inc.; *U.S. Public*, pg. 1684

JAEGER BAKING CO.—See Specialty Foods Corporation; *U.S. Private*, pg. 1022

THE JAEGER COMPANY'S SHOPS LTD.—See Coats Viyella plc; *Int'l*, pg. 300

JAEGER HOLDINGS LIMITED—See Coats Viyella plc; *Int'l*, pg. 300

JAEGER-LE COULTRE; *Int'l*, pg. 697

JAEGER-LECOULTRE FRANCE SA—See Mannesmann A.G.; *Int'l*, pg. 839

JAEGER S.A.—See Fiat Auto SpA; *Int'l*, pg. 482

JAEGER SPORTSWEAR INC.—See Coats Viyella plc; *Int'l*, pg. 299

JAENEUNG EDUCATION CO., LTD.; *Int'l*, pg. 697

JAFCO INTERNATIONAL (ASIA) LIMITED—See The Nomura Securities Co., Ltd.; *Int'l*, pg. 955

JAFFREY FIRE PROTECTION CO.—See D.D. Bean & Sons Co.; *U.S. Private*, pg. 127

JAGENBERG AG—See Rheinmetall Group; *Int'l*, pg. 1108

FERD. JAGENBERG & SOHNE GMBH & CO. KG—See A. Ahlstrom Corporation; *Int'l*, pg. 35

JAGENBERG, INC.—See Rheinmetall Group; *Int'l*, pg. 1108

JAGENBERG PAPIER TECHNIK GMBH—See Rheinmetall Group; *Int'l*, pg. 1108

JAGUAR CANADA INC.—See Ford Motor Company; *U.S. Public*, pg. 667

JAGUAR CARS—See Ford Motor Company; *U.S. Public*, pg. 664

JAGUAR CARS FINANCE LIMITED—See National Westminster Bank PLC; *Int'l*, pg. 910

JAGUAR CARS LIMITED—See Ford Motor Company; *U.S. Public*, pg. 666

JAHN FOUNDRY CORP.—See Atchison Casting Corporation; *U.S. Public*, pg. 142

P.T. JAKARTA KYOEI MEDICAL CENTER—See The Kyoei Life Insurance Co., Ltd.; *Int'l*, pg. 777

JAKARTA OFFICE—See Mitsubishi Chemical Corporation; *Int'l*, pg. 871

JAKKS PACIFIC, INC.; *U.S. Public*, pg. 923

JAKOB TREFZ & SOHNE—See Veba AG; *Int'l*, pg. 1459

JAKOBSON SHIPYARD, INC—See Moran Transporation Company; *U.S. Private*, pg. 760

JAKSON-A CHF COMPANY—See Trace International Holdings, Inc.; *U.S. Private*, pg. 1094

JALAL-COSTAIN W.L.L.—See Costain Group PLC; *Int'l*, pg. 337

JALAN JENDERAL—See Toyota Motor Corporation; *Int'l*, pg. 1413

JALAN YOS SUDARSO—See Toyota Motor Corporation; *Int'l*, pg. 1413

A. JALANDER OY—See Kemira Oy; *Int'l*, pg. 727

JALLATTE S.A.—See ETEX; *Int'l*, pg. 430

JAMAICA FLOUR MILLS, LTD.—See Diageo Plc; *Int'l*, pg. 411

JAMAICA MATCH HOLDING LTD.—See D.D. Bean & Sons Co.; *U.S. Private*, pg. 127

JAMBI SHELL—See Royal Dutch/Shell Group of Companies; *Int'l*, pg. 1139

JAMECO INDUSTRIES, INC.—See Watts Industries, Inc.; *U.S. Public*, pg. 1746

JAMES & BLOOM LIMITED—See SLD Holdings Ltd.; *Int'l*, pg. 1160

JAMES BUILDING CORPORATION; *U.S. Private*, pg. 580

JAMES CHEVROLET INC.; *U.S. Private*, pg. 580

JAMES HARDIE ASIA—See James Hardie Industries Ltd.; *Int'l*, pg. 597

JAMES INDUSTRIES INC.; *U.S. Private*, pg. 580

JONATHAN JAMES LIMITED—See Taylor Woodrow plc; *Int'l*, pg. 1358

RAYMOND JAMES & ASSOCIATES, INC.—See Raymond James Financial, Inc.; *U.S. Public*, pg. 923

RAYMOND JAMES CAPITAL—See Raymond James Financial, Inc.; *U.S. Public*, pg. 923

RAYMOND JAMES FINANCIAL, INC.; *U.S. Public*, pg. 923

RAYMOND JAMES PARTNERS, INC.—See Raymond James Financial, Inc.; *U.S. Public*, pg. 923

RAYMOND JAMES REALTY ADVISORS, INC.—See Raymond James Financial, Inc.; *U.S. Public*, pg. 923

JAMES STEEL & TUBE COMPANY—See Avis Industrial Corporation; *U.S. Public*, pg. 102

T.L. JAMES & COMPANY; *U.S. Private*, pg. 580

T.L. JAMES & CO., INC.—See T.L. James & Company; *U.S. Private*, pg. 580

TOM JAMES COMPANY; *U.S. Private*, pg. 580

JAMES TRANSPORTATION—See Fort James Corporation; *U.S. Public*, pg. 672

JAMESTOWN METAL PRODUCTS, INC.—See Brittany Corporation; *U.S. Private*, pg. 169

JAMESTOWN PERFORATORS INC.—See Federal Signal Corporation; *U.S. Public*, pg. 617

JAMI, INC.; *U.S. Private*, pg. 581

JAMIESON FILM COMPANY, INC.—See Eastman Kodak Company; *U.S. Public*, pg. 551

JAMIN—See Koninklijke Ahold NV; *Int'l*, pg. 749

JAMINA RT.—See Redland PLC; *Int'l*, pg. 1092

JAMISON BEDDING, INC.; *U.S. Private*, pg. 581

JAMISON DOOR COMPANY; *U.S. Private*, pg. 581

JAMISON PLASTIC CORPORATION; *U.S. Private*, pg. 581

JAMONT N.V.—See Fort James Corporation; *U.S. Public*, pg. 672

JAN-CO., INC.; *U.S. Private*, pg. 581

AB JAN RALLING—See Skanska AB; *Int'l*, pg. 1261

JANE'S INFORMATION GROUP—See The Thomson Corporation; *U.S. Public*, pg. 1601

JANESVILLE PRODUCTS—See Jason Incorporated; *U.S. Public*, pg. 924

JANEWAY PROPERTIES, INC.—See Edison Parking Properties, LLC; *U.S. Private*, pg. 364

JANI KING FRANCHISING, INC.—See Jani King International, Inc.; *U.S. Private*, pg. 581

JANI KING, INC.—See Jani King International, Inc.; *U.S. Private*, pg. 581

JANI KING INTERNATIONAL, INC.; *U.S. Private*, pg. 581

JANI KING LEASING CORP.—See Jani King International, Inc.; *U.S. Private*, pg. 582

JANI KING OF DALLAS—See Jani King International, Inc.; *U.S. Private*, pg. 582

JANIK & ASSOCIATES, INC.; *U.S. Private*, pg. 582

JANIN—See Lyonnaise des Eaux S.A.; *Int'l*, pg. 823

JANLYNN CORPORATION; *U.S. Private*, pg. 582

JANNEY MONTGOMERY SCOTT INC.—See The Penn Mutual Life Insurance Company; *U.S. Private*, pg. 849

JANNOCK BRICK GROUP-HEAD OFFICE—See Jannock Limited; *Int'l*, pg. 698

JANNOCK IMAGING COMPANIES LIMITED—See Jannock Limited; *Int'l*, pg. 698

JANNOCK LIMITED; *Int'l*, pg. 698

JANNOCK STEEL FABRICATING COMPANY—See Jannock Limited; *Int'l*, pg. 698

JANNOCK STEEL FABRICATING, INC.—See Jannock Limited; *Int'l*, pg. 699

JANNOCK VINYL GROUP—See Jannock Limited; *Int'l*, pg. 699

JANOME SEWING MACHINE CO., LTD.; *Int'l*, pg. 699

JANSPORT—See VF Corporation; *U.S. Public*, pg. 1702

JANSSEN-CILAG—See Johnson & Johnson; *U.S. Public*, pg. 929

JANSSEN-CILAG AB—See Johnson & Johnson; *U.S. Public*, pg. 929

JANSSEN-CILAG A/S—See Johnson & Johnson; *U.S. Public*, pg. 929

JANSSEN CILAG BRAZIL—See Johnson & Johnson; *U.S. Public*, pg. 929

JANSSEN/CILAG B.V.—See Johnson & Johnson; *U.S. Public*, pg. 929

JANSSEN-CILAG FARMACEUTICI S.P.A.—See Johnson & Johnson; *U.S. Public*, pg. 929

JANSSEN/CILAG G.M.B.H.—See Johnson & Johnson; *U.S. Public*, pg. 929

JANSSEN CILAG GMBH—See Johnson & Johnson; *U.S. Public*, pg. 929

JANSSEN-CILAG K.K.—See Johnson & Johnson; *U.S. Public*, pg. 929

JANSSEN-CILAG LTD.—See Johnson & Johnson; *U.S. Public*, pg. 929

JANSSEN-CILAG PHARMACEUTICA AG—See Johnson & Johnson; *U.S. Public*, pg. 929

JANSSEN/CILAG PHARMACEUTICA GMBH—See Johnson & Johnson; *U.S. Public*, pg. 929

JANSSEN/CILAG (PTY) LIMITED—See Johnson & Johnson; *U.S. Public*, pg. 929

JANSSEN-CILAG PTY. LTD.—See Johnson & Johnson; *U.S. Public*, pg. 929

JANSSEN-CILAG S.A.—See Johnson & Johnson; *U.S. Public*, pg. 929

JANSSEN/CILAG S.A.C.I.—See Johnson & Johnson; *U.S. Public*, pg. 929

JANSSEN-CILAG S.P.A.—See Johnson & Johnson; *U.S. Public*, pg. 929
JANSSEN FARMACEUTICA, S.A. DE C.V.—See Johnson & Johnson; *U.S. Public*, pg. 929
J.P. JANSSEN B.V.—See Royal Nedlloyd Group N.V.; *Int'l*, pg. 1144
J.P. JANSSEN INTERNATIONAL FREIGHT FORWARDERS B.V.—See Royal Nedlloyd Group N.V.; *Int'l*, pg. 1144
J.P. JANSSEN N.V.—See Royal Nedlloyd Group N.V.; *Int'l*, pg. 1144
JANSSEN KOREA, LTD.—See Johnson & Johnson; *U.S. Public*, pg. 929
JANSSEN PHARMACEUTICA, INC.—See Johnson & Johnson; *U.S. Public*, pg. 928
JANSSEN PHARMACEUTICAL LIMITED—See Johnson & Johnson; *U.S. Public*, pg. 930
JANSSEN PHARMACEUTICAL LTD.—See Johnson & Johnson; *U.S. Public*, pg. 930
JANSSEN/ORTHO INC.—See Johnson & Johnson; *U.S. Public*, pg. 930
JANTZEN—See VF Corporation; *U.S. Public*, pg. 1702
JANUARY & ASSOCIATES, INC.—See Creative Alliance, Inc.; *U.S. Private*, pg. 287
JANUS CAPITAL CORPORATION—See Kansas City Southern Industries, Inc.; *U.S. Public*, pg. 944
JANUS ELEVATOR PRODUCTS INC.—See Halma p.l.c.; *Int'l*, pg. 590
JAPAN ACRYLIC CHEMICAL CO., LTD.—See Rohm and Haas Company; *U.S. Public*, pg. 1404
JAPAN AIRLINES—See Japan Airlines Company, Ltd.; *Int'l*, pg. 700
JAPAN AIRLINES AMERICAN REGION—See Japan Airlines Company, Ltd.; *Int'l*, pg. 700
JAPAN AIRLINES COMPANY, LTD.; *Int'l*, pg. 699
JAPAN AIRLINES COMPANY, LTD.—See Japan Airlines Company, Ltd.; *Int'l*, pg. 700
JAPAN AJAX MAGNETHERMIC CO. LTD.—See BBA Group plc; *Int'l*, pg. 113
JAPAN ALUMOWELD CO., LTD.—See Imetal; *Int'l*, pg. 662
JAPAN AREA—See CNF Transportation Inc.; *U.S. Public*, pg. 281
JAPAN ASSOCIATED FINANCE CO., LTD.—See The Nomura Securities Co., Ltd.; *Int'l*, pg. 955
JAPAN AVIATION ELECTRONICS INDUSTRY, LTD.; *Int'l*, pg. 700
THE JAPAN BOND RESEARCH INSTITUTE—See Nihon Keizai Shimbun, Inc.; *Int'l*, pg. 929
JAPAN BUSINESS SERVICES CO., LTD.—See Japan Securities Finance Co. Ltd.; *Int'l*, pg. 702
JAPAN CARGO CO., LTD.—See Skylark Co., Ltd.; *Int'l*, pg. 1262
JAPAN CBM CORPORATION—See Citizen Watch Company, Ltd.; *Int'l*, pg. 294
JAPAN COSMO SECURITIES (HONG KONG) LIMITED—See Cosmo Securities Co., Ltd.; *Int'l*, pg. 335
THE JAPAN DEVELOPMENT BANK; *Int'l*, pg. 701
THE JAPAN DEVELOPMENT BANK-LOS ANGELES REPRESENTATIVE OFFICE—See The Japan Development Bank; *Int'l*, pg. 701
THE JAPAN DEVELOPMENT BANK-WASHINGTON, D.C. REPRESENTATIVE OFFICE—See The Japan Development Bank; *Int'l*, pg. 702
JAPAN ELANCO COMPANY LIMITED (JELCO)—See Eli Lilly and Company; *U.S. Public*, pg. 994
JAPAN ELECTRONIC CONTROL SYSTEMS CO., LTD.—See Nissan Motor Co., Ltd.; *Int'l*, pg. 944
JAPAN ENCORE COMPUTER, INC.—See Encore Computer Corporation; *U.S. Public*, pg. 580
JAPAN ENERGY (AUSTRALIA) PTY. LTD.—See Japan Energy Corporation; *Int'l*, pg. 702
JAPAN ENERGY CORPORATION; *Int'l*, pg. 702
JAPAN ENERGY CORPORATION-BEIJING OFFICE—See Japan Energy Corporation; *Int'l*, pg. 702
JAPAN ENERGY (SINGAPORE) PTE., LTD.—See Japan Energy Corporation; *Int'l*, pg. 702
JAPAN ENERGY (U.K.) LTD.—See Japan Energy Corporation; *Int'l*, pg. 702
JAPAN ENERGY (U.S.A.), INC.—See Japan Energy Corporation; *Int'l*, pg. 702
JAPAN ENERGY USA INC.—See Japan Energy Corporation; *Int'l*, pg. 702
JAPAN ENERGY USA, INC.—See Japan Energy Corporation; *Int'l*, pg. 702
JAPAN FAWICK CO., LTD.—See Eaton Corporation; *U.S. Public*, pg. 559
JAPAN GAMMA ASSET MANAGEMENT LTD—See Credit Commercial de France; *Int'l*, pg. 343
K.K. JAPAN HELIUM CENTER—See The BOC Group plc; *Int'l*, pg. 122
JAPAN IMMUNORESEARCH LABORATORIES CO., LTD.—See Otsuka Pharmaceutical Co., Ltd.; *Int'l*, pg. 1013
JAPAN INFORMATION PROCESSING SERVICE CO. LTD.—See Japan Securities Finance Co. Ltd.; *Int'l*, pg. 702
JAPAN INTERNATIONAL ENTERPRISES, INC.—See Sony Corporation; *Int'l*, pg. 1282
JAPAN LUTRAVIL COMPANY—See Freudenberg & Company; *Int'l*, pg. 507
JAPAN MAINTENANCE CO., LTD.—See Mycal, Corp.; *Int'l*, pg. 898
JAPAN MARINE TECHNOLOGIES LTD.—See TI Group plc; *Int'l*, pg. 1339
JAPAN NUCLEAR FUEL CO., LTD.—See Toshiba Corporation; *Int'l*, pg. 1403
JAPAN OXYGEN, INC.—See Nippon Sanso Corporation; *Int'l*, pg. 938
JAPAN PHARMACIA & UPJOHN LIMITED—See Pharmacia & Upjohn, Inc.; *Int'l*, pg. 1049
JAPAN POLYCHEM CORP.—See Mitsubishi Chemical Corporation; *Int'l*, pg. 871
JAPAN POLYCHEM CORP.—See Tonen Corporation; *Int'l*, pg. 1399
JAPAN POWER FASTENING CO., LTD.—See NHK Spring Co., Ltd.; *Int'l*, pg. 901

THE JAPAN RAMTITE CO. LTD.—See ABB Asea Brown Boveri (Holding) Ltd.; *Int'l*, pg. 6
JAPAN SECURITIES AGENTS, LTD.—See Japan Securities Finance Co. Ltd.; *Int'l*, pg. 702
JAPAN SECURITIES FINANCE CO. LTD.; *Int'l*, pg. 702
JAPAN SERVO CO., LTD.—See Hitachi, Ltd.; *Int'l*, pg. 622
THE JAPAN STEEL WORKS, LTD.—See Mitsui & Co., Ltd.; *Int'l*, pg. 878
JAPAN STORAGE BATTERY CO., LTD.; *Int'l*, pg. 702
JAPAN SYSTEMS CORPORATION—See Toshiba Corporation; *Int'l*, pg. 1403
THE JAPAN TIMES, LTD.—See Nifco Inc.; *Int'l*, pg. 928
JAPAN TOBACCO INC.; *Int'l*, pg. 703
JAPAN TRAVEL BUREAU INTERNATIONAL, INC.; *U.S. Private*, pg. 582
JAPAN UNIVERSAL SECURITIES (HONG KONG) LIMITED—See Universal Securities Co., Ltd.; *Int'l*, pg. 1444
JAPAN VILENE COMPANY LTD.—See Freudenberg & Company; *Int'l*, pg. 507
JAPAN VISUAL-SOFT NETWORK CO.—See Hakuhodo Incorporated; *Int'l*, pg. 588
JAPAN WHISKER CO., LTD.—See Otsuka Pharmaceutical Co., Ltd.; *Int'l*, pg. 1013
JAPS-OLSON COMPANY; *U.S. Private*, pg. 582
JARAMIEL SOCIEDAD DE INVERSION MOBILIARIA S.A.—See Corporacion MAPFRE, Compania Internacional de Reaseguros, S.A.; *Int'l*, pg. 334
JARAN INC.; *U.S. Private*, pg. 582
JARCHEM INDUSTRIES, INC.; *U.S. Private*, pg. 582
JARCHEM SPECIALTY CHEMICAL DIVISION—See Jarchem Industries, Inc.; *U.S. Private*, pg. 583
JARDINAY MANUFACTURING—See Michael Anthony Jewelers, Inc.; *U.S. Public*, pg. 1103
JARDINE CREDIT INSURANCE LTD.—See Jardine Matheson Holdings Limited; *Int'l*, pg. 705
JARDINE DAVIES INC.—See Jardine Matheson Holdings Limited; *Int'l*, pg. 705
JARDINE FLEMING AUSTRALIA LIMITED—See Robert Fleming Holdings Ltd.; *Int'l*, pg. 494
JARDINE FLEMING BANK LIMITED—See Robert Fleming Holdings Ltd.; *Int'l*, pg. 494
JARDINE FLEMING EXCHANGE CAPITAL SECURITIES INC.—See Robert Fleming Holdings Ltd.; *Int'l*, pg. 494
JARDINE FLEMING HOLDINGS LTD—See Robert Fleming Holdings Ltd.; *Int'l*, pg. 494
JARDINE FLEMING INDIA SECURITIES PRIVATE LIMITED—See Robert Fleming Holdings Ltd.; *Int'l*, pg. 494
JARDINE FLEMING INTERNATIONAL SECURITIES LTD—See Robert Fleming Holdings Ltd.; *Int'l*, pg. 494
JARDINE FLEMING INTERNATIONAL SECURITIES LIMITED—See Robert Fleming Holdings Ltd.; *Int'l*, pg. 494
JARDINE FLEMING INVESTMENT ADVISERS (JAPAN) LIMITED—See Robert Fleming Holdings Ltd.; *Int'l*, pg. 494
JARDINE FLEMING INVESTMENT MANAGEMENT LIMITED—See Robert Fleming Holdings Ltd.; *Int'l*, pg. 494
JARDINE FLEMING LIMITED—See Robert Fleming Holdings Ltd.; *Int'l*, pg. 494
JARDINE FLEMING NEW ZEALAND LIMITED—See Robert Fleming Holdings Ltd.; *Int'l*, pg. 494
P T JARDINE FLEMING NUSANTARA—See Robert Fleming Holdings Ltd.; *Int'l*, pg. 494
JARDINE FLEMING ORD MINNETT PTY LIMITED—See Robert Fleming Holdings Ltd.; *Int'l*, pg. 494
JARDINE FLEMING PAKISTAN LIMITED—See Robert Fleming Holdings Ltd.; *Int'l*, pg. 494
JARDINE FLEMING SECURITIES LIMITED—See Robert Fleming Holdings Ltd.; *Int'l*, pg. 494
JARDINE FLEMING SECURITIES LTD.—See Robert Fleming Holdings Ltd.; *Int'l*, pg. 494
JARDINE FLEMING SECURITIES LTD. SERVICES—See Robert Fleming Holdings Ltd.; *Int'l*, pg. 494
JARDINE FLEMING TAIWAN INVESTMENT MANAGEMENT LIMITED—See Robert Fleming Holdings Ltd.; *Int'l*, pg. 494
JARDINE FLEMING TAIWAN SECURITIES LIMITED—See Robert Fleming Holdings Ltd.; *Int'l*, pg. 494
JARDINE FLEMING THANAKOM SECURITIES LIMITED—See Robert Fleming Holdings Ltd.; *Int'l*, pg. 494
P.T. JARDINE INSURANCE BROKERS INDONESIA—See Jardine Matheson Holdings Limited; *Int'l*, pg. 705
JARDINE INSURANCE BROKERS INTERNATIONAL LIMITED—See Jardine Matheson Holdings Limited; *Int'l*, pg. 705
JARDINE INSURANCE BROKERS LTD.—See Jardine Matheson Holdings Limited; *Int'l*, pg. 705
JARDINE INSURANCE SERVICES LIMITED—See Jardine Matheson Holdings Limited; *Int'l*, pg. 705
JARDINE (LLOYD'S UNDERWRITING AGENTS) LTD.—See Jardine Matheson Holdings Limited; *Int'l*, pg. 705
JARDINE MATHESON HOLDINGS LIMITED; *Int'l*, pg. 703
JARDINE MATHESON (THAILAND) LTD.—See Jardine Matheson Holdings Limited; *Int'l*, pg. 705
JARDINE PACIFIC LTD.—See Jardine Matheson Holdings Limited; *Int'l*, pg. 704
JARDINE RICHE MONDE LTD—See LVMH Moet Hennessy Louis Vuitton; *Int'l*, pg. 782
JARDINE STRATEGIC HOLDINGS LTD.—See Jardine Matheson Holdings Limited; *Int'l*, pg. 703
JARDINE WINES & SPIRITS K.K.—See LVMH Moet Hennessy Louis Vuitton; *Int'l*, pg. 782
JAREEN CO.—See Newell Co.; *U.S. Public*, pg. 1177
JARKE CORPORATION; *U.S. Private*, pg. 583
JARMAN SHOE CO.—See Genesco Inc.; *U.S. Public*, pg. 728
JARNIA AB—See Bergman & Beving AB; *Int'l*, pg. 188
JARVIS (EAST)—See Standex International Corporation; *U.S. Public*, pg. 1506
J. JARVIS & SONS P.L.C.—See Jarvis Plc; *Int'l*, pg. 705

JARVIS-PEMCO—See Standex International Corporation; *U.S. Public*, pg. 1506
JARVIS PLC; *Int'l*, pg. 705
JARVIS (WEST)—See Standex International Corporation; *U.S. Public*, pg. 1506
JASON INCORPORATED; *U.S. Public*, pg. 923
JASON INDUSTRIAL, INC.; *U.S. Private*, pg. 583
JASPER CORP.; *U.S. Private*, pg. 583
JASPER CORPORATION—See Kimball International, Inc.; *U.S. Public*, pg. 957
JASPER COUNTY FARM BUREAU CO-OP ASSOCIATION, INC.; *U.S. Private*, pg. 583
JASPER FURNITURE COMPANY—See Kimball International, Inc.; *U.S. Public*, pg. 957
JASPER LAMINATES—See Kimball International, Inc.; *U.S. Public*, pg. 957
JASPER NEWS-BOY—See The Hearst Corporation; *U.S. Private*, pg. 517
JASPER PLASTICS—See Kimball International, Inc.; *U.S. Public*, pg. 957
JASPER SEATING CO., INC.; *U.S. Private*, pg. 583
JASPER TEXTILE—See House of Ronnie, Inc.; *U.S. Private*, pg. 542
JATCO CORPORATION—See Nissan Motor Co., Ltd.; *Int'l*, pg. 944
JAUCH & HUEBENER—See AON Corporation; *U.S. Public*, pg. 118
JAUCH & HUEBENER KGAA—See AON Corporation; *U.S. Public*, pg. 118
JAUCH & HUEBENER—See AON Corporation; *U.S. Public*, pg. 118
JAUCH & HUEBENER SPOL. S.R.O.—See AON Corporation; *U.S. Public*, pg. 118
JAUCH & HUEBENER—See AON Corporation; *U.S. Public*, pg. 118
KARL JAUS GMBH—See Borden, Inc.; *U.S. Private*, pg. 159
JAVELIN SYSTEMS—See Pittway Corporation; *U.S. Public*, pg. 1306
JAVELIN/YOUNG & RUBICAM—See Young & Rubicam Inc.; *U.S. Private*, pg. 1199
JAX LTD.—See Volkswagen AG; *Int'l*, pg. 1475
JAY ADVERTISING CORP.-CHICAGO DIV.—See Jay Advertising, Inc.; *U.S. Private*, pg. 583
JAY ADVERTISING, INC.; *U.S. Private*, pg. 583
JAY ADVERTISING, INC.-TAMPA—See Jay Advertising, Inc.; *U.S. Private*, pg. 583
JAY-EL PRODUCTS, INC.—See Ducommun Incorporated; *U.S. Public*, pg. 534
JAY INCORPORATED-LOS ANGELES DIVISION—See Jay Advertising, Inc.; *U.S. Private*, pg. 583
JAY INCORPORATED-PHOENIX DIVISION—See Jay Advertising, Inc.; *U.S. Private*, pg. 583
JAY INSTRUMENT & SPECIALTY CO.; *U.S. Private*, pg. 583
P.T. JAYA FUJI LEASING PRATAMA—See The Fuji Bank, Limited; *Int'l*, pg. 521
P.T. JAYA MANDARIN AGUNG—See Jardine Matheson Holdings Limited; *Int'l*, pg. 704
P.T. JAYA OBAYASHI—See Obayashi Corporation; *Int'l*, pg. 996
C. JAYANT BROS. (OMAN) CO.—See BASF AG; *Int'l*, pg. 108
JAYCO INC.; *U.S. Private*, pg. 583
JAYDON INCORPORATED; *U.S. Private*, pg. 584
THE JAYDOR CORPORATION; *U.S. Private*, pg. 584
JAYHAWK PIPELINE, L.L.C.—See National Cooperative Refinery Association; *U.S. Private*, pg. 781
JAYMARK, INC.; *U.S. Private*, pg. 584
JAYS FOODS LLC; *U.S. Private*, pg. 584
J.M. JAYSON & CO., INC.; *U.S. Private*, pg. 584
JAZZERCISE, INC.; *U.S. Private*, pg. 584
THE JEAN COUTU (PJC) USA INC.—See The Jean Coutu Group (PJC) Inc.; *Int'l*, pg. 340
JEAN PHILIPPE FRAGRANCES, INC.; *U.S. Public*, pg. 924
JEAN-PIERRE GIRARDEAU SA—See Koninklijke BolsWessanen nv; *Int'l*, pg. 753
JEANS WEST, INC.—See Edison Brothers Stores, Inc.; *U.S. Public*, pg. 563
JEAVONS ENGINEERING, LTD.—See Ruhrgas Aktiengesellschaft; *Int'l*, pg. 1149
JEDDAH BEVERAGE CAN MAKING COMPANY LTD.—See Crown Cork & Seal Company, Inc.; *U.S. Public*, pg. 465
JEEP—See Chrysler Corporation; *U.S. Public*, pg. 353
JEEP CONSTRUCTION CO., LTD.—See Shimizu Corporation; *Int'l*, pg. 1233
JEEP/EAGLE DIVISION—See Chrysler Corporation; *U.S. Public*, pg. 353
JEEPERS! INC.—See Center Partners Management LLC; *U.S. Private*, pg. 222
JEFF WYLER BUICK, PONTIAC, INC.—See Jeff Wyler Dealer Group, Inc.; *U.S. Private*, pg. 1193
JEFF WYLER CHEVROLET, INC.—See Jeff Wyler Dealer Group, Inc.; *U.S. Private*, pg. 1193
JEFFCO LAND RECLAMATION, INC.—See Browning-Ferris Industries, Inc.; *U.S. Public*, pg. 264
JEFFERIES & COMPANY, INC.—See Jetferies Group, Inc.; *U.S. Public*, pg. 925
JEFFERIES GROUP, INC.; *U.S. Public*, pg. 924
JEFFERIES INTERNATIONAL LIMITED—See Jefferies Group, Inc.; *U.S. Public*, pg. 925
JEFFERIES (JAPAN) LIMITED TOKYO BRANCH—See Jefferies Group, Inc.; *U.S. Public*, pg. 925
JEFFERIES PACIFIC LIMITED—See Jefferies Group, Inc.; *U.S. Public*, pg. 925
JEFFERIES (SWITZERLAND) LTD.—See Jefferies Group, Inc.; *U.S. Public*, pg. 925
JEFFERS ELECTRONICS—See Vishay Intertechnology, Inc.; *U.S. Public*, pg. 1722
JEFFERSON ADAMS CORP.—See Volt Information Sciences, Inc.; *U.S. Public*, pg. 1724
JEFFERSON CHEVROLET CO.; *U.S. Private*, pg. 584
THE JEFFERSON DIVISION—See Chicago Rivet & Machine Company; *U.S. Public*, pg. 349

JEFFERSON INSURANCE COMPANY OF NEW YORK—See Allianz Aktiengesellschaft; *Int'l*, pg. 59

JEFFERSON MILLS, INC.; *U.S. Private*, pg. 584

JEFFERSON-PILOT COMMUNICATIONS—See Jefferson-Pilot Corporation; *U.S. Public*, pg. 925

JEFFERSON-PILOT CORPORATION; *U.S. Public*, pg. 925

JEFFERSON SQUARE, INC.—See Boise Cascade Corporation; *U.S. Public*, pg. 243

JEFFREY BUICK-NISSAN INC.; *U.S. Private*, pg. 585

JEFFREY STEEL PRODUCTS—See Metals USA, Inc.; *U.S. Public*, pg. 1100

L.O. JEFFS LTD.—See Geest PLC; *Int'l*, pg. 542

JEKEL VINEYARDS—See Brown-Forman Corporation; *U.S. Public*, pg. 261

THE JEL SERT CO.; *U.S. Private*, pg. 585

JELA SCHUH GMBH—See Freudenberg & Company; *Int'l*, pg. 506

JELD-WEN, INC.; *U.S. Private*, pg. 585

Y.F. JELENKO & CO.—See Heraeus Holding GmbH; *Int'l*, pg. 616

JELMAR COMPANY; *U.S. Private*, pg. 585

JELMOLI AG; *Int'l*, pg. 705

JELRUS INTERNATIONAL—See Air Techniques, Inc.; *U.S. Private*, pg. 28

JEN-COAT INC.—See American Business Products, Inc.; *U.S. Public*, pg. 70

JENAER GLASWERK GMBH—See Carl-Zeiss-Stiftung; *Int'l*, pg. 1523

JENA-OPTRONIK GMBH—See Daimler-Benz Aktiengesellschaft; *Int'l*, pg. 367

H.W. JENCKS, INC.—See Detroit Coil Company; *U.S. Private*, pg. 328

JENERIC/PENTRON CORP.—See Customedix Corporation; *U.S. Private*, pg. 298

JENESIS ADVERTISING—See Saatchi & Saatchi Advertising Worldwide; *U.S. Public*, pg. 1422

JENIFER SRL—See LVMH Moet Hennessy Louis Vuitton; *Int'l*, pg. 782

JENISYS ENGINEERED PRODUCTS—See Jannock Limited; *Int'l*, pg. 698

JENISYS ENGINEERED PRODUCTS, INC.—See Jannock Limited; *Int'l*, pg. 698

JENKINS & ASSOCIATES; *U.S. Private*, pg. 585

JENKINS SPIRITS CORP. LTD.; *U.S. Private*, pg. 585

JENKS (INMETCO)—See Independent Metals; *U.S. Private*, pg. 559

JENN-AIR—See Maytag Corporation; *U.S. Public*, pg. 1064

JENNIE-O FOODS, INC.—See Hormel Foods Corp.; *U.S. Public*, pg. 840

JENNIFER CONVERTIBLES, INC.; *U.S. Public*, pg. 926

JENNINGS & CHURELLA CONSTRUCTION COMPANY; *U.S. Private*, pg. 586

JENNINGS LAND COMPANY—See Danaher Corporation; *U.S. Public*, pg. 481

JENNY CRAIG, INC.; *U.S. Public*, pg. 926

C.G. JENSEN A/S—See Skanska AB; *Int'l*, pg. 1261

JENSEN DISTRIBUTION SERVICES—See Distribution America; *U.S. Private*, pg. 335

JENSEN INDUSTRIES—See Nortek, Inc.; *U.S. Public*, pg. 1193

IRVING F. JENSEN CO., INC.; *U.S. Private*, pg. 586

JEPPESEN AND CO. GMBH—See The Times Mirror Company; *U.S. Public*, pg. 1617

JEPPESEN SANDERSON—See The Times Mirror Company; *U.S. Public*, pg. 1616

JEPSON-MURRAY ADVERTISING; *U.S. Private*, pg. 586

JERDON PRODUCTS, INC.—See Windmere-Durable Holdings; *U.S. Public*, pg. 1771

JERELL, INC.; *U.S. Private*, pg. 586

THE ANDREW JERGENS COMPANY—See Kao Corporation; *Int'l*, pg. 717

JERGENS INC.; *U.S. Private*, pg. 586

JERNBERG INDUSTRIES, INC.; *U.S. Private*, pg. 586

JEROME-DUNCAN FORD; *U.S. Private*, pg. 586

JEROME FOODS INC.; *U.S. Private*, pg. 586

JERONIMO MARTINS; *Int'l*, pg. 705

JERR-DAN CORPORATION—See Durakon Industries, Inc.; *U.S. Public*, pg. 537

JERRY & KETCHUM—See Ketchum Communications Inc.; *U.S. Private*, pg. 616

JERSEY CENTRAL POWER & LIGHT CO.—See GPU, Inc.; *U.S. Public*, pg. 695

THE JERSEY TOBACCO DISTRIBUTORS LTD.—See the B.A.T Industries P.L.C.; *Int'l*, pg. 111

THE JERUSALEM CO. LTD.—See Dubek Ltd.; *Int'l*, pg. 421

JERUSALEM POST PUBLICATIONS LTD.—See Hollinger Inc.; *Int'l*, pg. 632

JESCO—See United Dominion Industries, Ltd.; *U.S. Public*, pg. 1676

JESCO COMPANY—See Al Johnson Construction Co.; *U.S. Private*, pg. 590

JESSE BRANCH COAL CO.—See Berwind Corporation; *U.S. Private*, pg. 139

JESSE R. DAWSON STATE JAIL—See Corrections Corporation of America; *U.S. Public*, pg. 450

JET AVION CORPORATION—See HEICO Corporation; *U.S. Public*, pg. 804

JET CHANDLER INTERNATIONAL—See Groupe Air France; *Int'l*, pg. 560

JET CHEF—See Groupe Air France; *Int'l*, pg. 560

JET DIE—See Barnes Group Inc.; *U.S. Public*, pg. 190

JET ELECTRONICS & TECHNOLOGY, INC.—See The B.F. Goodrich Company; *U.S. Public*, pg. 751

JET HOTEL—See Groupe Air France; *Int'l*, pg. 560

JET, INC.—See Jayco Inc.; *U.S. Private*, pg. 584

JET LOISIRS—See Groupe Air France; *Int'l*, pg. 560

JET SPRAY CORP.; *U.S. Private*, pg. 586

JET SPRAY INTERNATIONAL—See Jet Spray Corp.; *U.S. Private*, pg. 587

JET TOURS—See Groupe Air France; *Int'l*, pg. 560

JET TOURS CANADA—See Groupe Air France; *Int'l*, pg. 560

JET TOURS U.K.—See Groupe Air France; *Int'l*, pg. 560

JET VACATION—See Groupe Air France; *Int'l*, pg. 560

JETA POWER SYSTEMS, INC.—See Computer Products, Inc.; *U.S. Public*, pg. 422

JETBAG GMBH—See Eldon AB; *Int'l*, pg. 436

JETCOM—See PrimeSource Corporation; *U.S. Public*, pg. 1329

JETPHONE LIMITED—See British Telecommunications plc; *Int'l*, pg. 223

JETRO CASH & CARRY—See Jetro Holdings, Inc.; *U.S. Private*, pg. 587

JETRO HOLDINGS, INC.; *U.S. Private*, pg. 587

JETRONIC INDUSTRIES, INC.; *U.S. Public*, pg. 926

JETSET TRAVEL AND TECHNOLOGY HOLDINGS PTY. LTD.—See Air New Zealand Ltd.; *Int'l*, pg. 38

JETSTREAM AIRCRAFT LIMITED—See British Aerospace p.l.c.; *Int'l*, pg. 217

JETSTREAM SYSTEMS INC.—See Barry-Wehmiller Company; *U.S. Private*, pg. 118

JEUMONT-SCHNEIDER DE MEXICO—See Jeumont-Schneider Trenformeteurs; *Int'l*, pg. 706

JEUMONT-SCHNEIDER DO BRASIL—See Jeumont-Schneider Trenformeteurs; *Int'l*, pg. 706

JEUMONT-SCHNEIDER INDUSTRIAL SYSTEMS (JSIS)—See Jeumont-Schneider Trenformeteurs; *Int'l*, pg. 706

JEUMONT-SCHNEIDER OF AMERICA—See Jeumont-Schneider Trenformeteurs; *Int'l*, pg. 706

JEUMONT-SCHNEIDER QUEBEC INC.—See Jeumont-Schneider Trenformeteurs; *Int'l*, pg. 706

JEUMONT-SCHNEIDER TRENFORMETEURS; *Int'l*, pg. 706

JEVIC TRANSPORTATION; *U.S. Public*, pg. 927

JEWEL-OSCO—See American Stores Company; *U.S. Public*, pg. 93

JEWEL OSCO SOUTHWEST, INC.—See American Stores Company; *U.S. Public*, pg. 93

JEWEL RECOVERY, LP—See Zale Corporation; *U.S. Public*, pg. 1789

JEWELCOR COMPANIES; *U.S. Private*, pg. 587

JEWELCOR TRAVEL SERVICES, INC.—See Jewelcor Companies; *U.S. Private*, pg. 587

JEWELER'S FINANCIAL SERVICE, INC.—See Zale Corporation; *U.S. Public*, pg. 1789

JEWELERS MUTUAL INSURANCE COMPANY; *U.S. Private*, pg. 587

JEWELL BUILDING SYSTEMS; *U.S. Private*, pg. 587

JEWELMONT CORPORATION; *U.S. Private*, pg. 587

JEWETT INTERNATIONAL CORP.—See Ruslander & Sons, Inc.; *U.S. Private*, pg. 952

THE JEWETT REFRIGERATOR CO., INC.—See Ruslander & Sons, Inc.; *U.S. Private*, pg. 952

JEWO FERROUS B.V.—See Fried. Krupp AG; *Int'l*, pg. 514

JEWSON LTD.—See Meyer International PLC; *Int'l*, pg. 864

JEWSON PROPERTY HOLDINGS LTD.—See Meyer International PLC; *Int'l*, pg. 864

JIANGLING-ISUZU MOTORS Limited; *Int'l*, pg. 693—See Isuzu Motors Limited

JIANGSU CIBA AGROCHEMICALS CO., LTD.—See Novartis AG; *Int'l*, pg. 983

JIELDE S.A.—See Luxo A/S; *Int'l*, pg. 821

JIFFY LUBE INTERNATIONAL, INC.—See Pennzoil Company; *U.S. Public*, pg. 1272

JIFFY LUBE INTERNATIONAL OF MARYLAND, INC.—See Pennzoil Company; *U.S. Public*, pg. 1272

JIFFY PRODUCTS INTERNATIONAL LTD.; *Int'l*, pg. 706

JIFFY PRODUCTS OF AMERICA, INC.—See Jiffy Products International Ltd.; *Int'l*, pg. 706

JIL SANDERS COSMETICS G.M.B.H.—See SmithKline Beecham plc; *Int'l*, pg. 1265

JILLIAN'S ENTERTAINMENT CORPORATION; *U.S. Private*, pg. 587

THE JIM DANDY CO., INC.—See Nestle S.A.; *Int'l*, pg. 918

JIMEK—See Baldwin Technology Company, Inc.; *U.S. Public*, pg. 170

JIMENEZ/DMB&B—See DMB&B Communications; *U.S. Private*, pg. 304

JIMLAR CORPORATION; *U.S. Private*, pg. 587

JIMMY DEAN FOODS—See Sara Lee Corporation; *U.S. Public*, pg. 1433

JIMTEN—See ETEX; *Int'l*, pg. 430

JINBANG STEEL CO., LTD.—See Ssangyong Business Group; *Int'l*, pg. 1291

JINCO NONFERROUS METALS CO., LTD.—See Inco Limited; *Int'l*, pg. 673

JINWOONG HONG KONG LTD.—See Jinwoong Inc.; *Int'l*, pg. 707

JINWOONG INC.; *Int'l*, pg. 706

JINWOONG LANKA (PVT) LTD.—See Jinwoong Inc.; *Int'l*, pg. 707

JIP-PACK A.S.—See Royal Packaging Industries Van Leer B.V.; *Int'l*, pg. 1146

JIRVA AB—See Trelleborg AB; *Int'l*, pg. 1422

JISTRAL—See Jeumont-Schneider Trenformeteurs; *Int'l*, pg. 706

JITACHI ZOSEN SYSTEMS, INC.—See Effective Management Systems; *U.S. Public*, pg. 566

JITNEY-JUNGLE BAKERY, INC.—See Jitney-Jungle Stores of America, Inc.; *U.S. Private*, pg. 588

JITNEY-JUNGLE STORES OF AMERICA, INC.; *U.S. Private*, pg. 588

OY JIT-TRANS LTD—See Rautaruukki Oy; *Int'l*, pg. 1088

CURT G. JOA, INC.; *U.S. Private*, pg. 588

JOAN & DAVID HELPERN, INC.—See Joan & David Helpern, Inc.; *U.S. Private*, pg. 521

JOAN FABRICS CORP.; *U.S. Private*, pg. 588

JOANNE PLASTICS, INC.—See Burlington Basket Co.; *U.S. Private*, pg. 183

G. JOANNOU CYCLE CO. INC.; *U.S. Private*, pg. 588

JOBBER RETAILER—See VNU Verenigde Nederlandse Uitgeversbedrijven B.V.; *Int'l*, pg. 1446

JOBST GMBH—See Beiersdorf Group; *Int'l*, pg. 182

JOBU A/S—See Electrolux, AB; *Int'l*, pg. 443

JOCKEY INTERNATIONAL, INC.; *U.S. Private*, pg. 588

JOENSUU MILL—See UPM-Kymmene Corporation; *Int'l*, pg. 1429

JOENSUU POWER PLANT—See Imatran Voima Oy; *Int'l*, pg. 660

JOERN'S SUNRISE MEDICAL—See Sunrise Medical, Inc.; *U.S. Public*, pg. 1536

JOFCO INC.; *U.S. Private*, pg. 588

JOFFKO CAMEROON CORPORATION—See Joffko International; *U.S. Private*, pg. 589

JOFFKO INTERNATIONAL; *U.S. Private*, pg. 589

JOFFKO PHILIPPINES, INC.—See Joffko International; *U.S. Private*, pg. 589

AB JOH KOCK—See Scancem AB; *Int'l*, pg. 1199

JOHAN RONNING HF—See Telefonaktiebolaget LM Ericsson; *Int'l*, pg. 1368

JOHANN A. KRAUSE—See Thyssen AG; *Int'l*, pg. 1387

JOHANNA FOODS INC.; *U.S. Private*, pg. 589

JOHANSON MANUFACTURING CORPORATION; *U.S. Private*, pg. 589

C E JOHANSSON AB—See Spectra-Physics AB; *Int'l*, pg. 1289

C E JOHANSSON GMBH—See Spectra-Physics AB; *Int'l*, pg. 1290

C E JOHANSSON LTD.—See Spectra-Physics AB; *Int'l*, pg. 1290

B. JOHANSSONS PAPPERSFORADLING AB—See Electrolux, AB; *Int'l*, pg. 439

JOHN CRANE ARGENTINA—See TI Group plc; *Int'l*, pg. 1339

JOHN CRANE ASIA PACIFIC—See TI Group plc; *Int'l*, pg. 1339

JOHN CRANE CARIBE—See TI Group plc; *Int'l*, pg. 1339

JOHN CRANE CHILE—See TI Group plc; *Int'l*, pg. 1340

JOHN CRANE COLOMBIA—See TI Group plc; *Int'l*, pg. 1340

JOHN CRANE EAA—See TI Group plc; *Int'l*, pg. 1338

JOHN CRANE ENGINEERED SEALING SYSTEMS LTD.—See TI Group plc; *Int'l*, pg. 1339

JOHN CRANE FINLAND—See TI Group plc; *Int'l*, pg. 1339

JOHN CRANE FRANCE—See TI Group plc; *Int'l*, pg. 1339

JOHN CRANE HOLLAND B.V.—See TI Group plc; *Int'l*, pg. 1339

JOHN CRANE INC.—See TI Group plc; *Int'l*, pg. 1338

PT JOHN CRANE INDONESIA—See TI Group plc; *Int'l*, pg. 1339

JOHN CRANE INDUSTRIAL GASKETS—See TI Group plc; *Int'l*, pg. 1338

JOHN CRANE (JAPAN) INC.—See TI Group plc; *Int'l*, pg. 1339

JOHN CRANE LATIN AMERICA—See TI Group plc; *Int'l*, pg. 1339

JOHN CRANE MARINE-LIPS—See TI Group plc; *Int'l*, pg. 1339

JOHN CRANE MIDDLE EAST- CENTRAL REGION—See TI Group plc; *Int'l*, pg. 1339

JOHN CRANE MIDDLE EAST - WESTERN REGION—See TI Group plc; *Int'l*, pg. 1339

JOHN CRANE NORTH AMERICA—See TI Group plc; *Int'l*, pg. 1339

JOHN CRANE POLYMER DIVISION—See TI Group plc; *Int'l*, pg. 1338

JOHN CRANE POLYMER ENGINEERING—See TI Group plc; *Int'l*, pg. 1338

JOHN CRANE (PTY) LTD.—See TI Group plc; *Int'l*, pg. 1339

JOHN CRANE SIGMA A.S.—See TI Group plc; *Int'l*, pg. 1339

JOHN CRANE SVERIGE AB—See TI Group plc; *Int'l*, pg. 1339

JOHN CRANE (SWITZERLAND) AG—See TI Group plc; *Int'l*, pg. 1339

JOHN CRANE TIANJIN LTD.—See TI Group plc; *Int'l*, pg. 1339

JOHN CRANE TURKEY—See TI Group plc; *Int'l*, pg. 1339

JOHN CRANE VENEZUELA—See TI Group plc; *Int'l*, pg. 1340

JOHN CRANES MARINE INTERNATIONAL—See TI Group plc; *Int'l*, pg. 1339

JOHN DEERE LTD.—See Deere & Company; *U.S. Public*, pg. 493

JOHN DEERE OTTUMWA WORKS—See Deere & Company; *U.S. Public*, pg. 492

JOHN HANCOCK ADVISERS, INC.—See John Hancock Mutual Life Insurance Company; *U.S. Private*, pg. 589

JOHN HANCOCK ADVISERS INTERNATIONAL, LTD.—See John Hancock Mutual Life Insurance Company; *U.S. Private*, pg. 590

JOHN HANCOCK CAPITAL CORPORATION—See John Hancock Mutual Life Insurance Company; *U.S. Private*, pg. 590

JOHN HANCOCK CAPITAL GROWTH MANAGEMENT, INC.—See John Hancock Mutual Life Insurance Company; *U.S. Private*, pg. 590

JOHN HANCOCK INSURANCE COMPANY OF BERMUDA LTD.—See John Hancock Mutual Life Insurance Company; *U.S. Private*, pg. 590

JOHN HANCOCK INTL. SERVICES S.A.—See John Hancock Mutual Life Insurance Company; *U.S. Private*, pg. 590

JOHN HANCOCK LEASING CORPORATION—See John Hancock Mutual Life Insurance Company; *U.S. Private*, pg. 590

JOHN HANCOCK MUTUAL LIFE INSURANCE COMPANY; *U.S. Private*, pg. 589

JOHN HANCOCK SERVICOS INTERNACIONAIS S/C., LTDA.—See John Hancock Mutual Life Insurance Company; *U.S. Private*, pg. 590

JOHN HANCOCK SUBSIDIARIES, INC.—See John Hancock Mutual Life Insurance Company; *U.S. Private*, pg. 589

JOHN MENZIES PLC; *Int'l*, pg. 707

JOHN MENZIES RETAIL—See John Menzies plc; *Int'l*, pg. 707

JOHN MENZIES (UK) LIMITED—See John Menzies plc; *Int'l*, pg. 707

JOHN MENZIES WHOLESALE—See John Menzies plc;
Int'l, pg. 707
JOHN PLAYER & SONS IRELAND—See Hanson PLC; Int'l,
pg. 595
JOHN WILEY & SONS (ASIA) PTE. LTD.—See John Wiley
& Sons, Inc.; U.S. Public, pg. 1768
JOHNNY APPLESEED'S, INC.; U.S. Private, pg. 590
JOHNNY CARSON APPAREL, INC.—See Hartmarx
Corporation; U.S. Public, pg. 796
THE JOHNNY ROCKETS GROUP, INC—See Center
Partners Management LLC; U.S. Private, pg. 222
ANDY JOHNS FASHIONS, INC.—See Biscayne Apparel
Inc.; U.S. Public, pg. 233
ANDY JOHNS MACKINTOSH—See Biscayne Apparel Inc.;
U.S. Public, pg. 233
JOHNS MANVILLE CORPORATION; U.S. Public, pg. 927
A. JOHNSON & CO. A/S, OFFSHORE—See Axel Johnson
AB; Int'l, pg. 711
A. JOHNSON & CO. GMBH—See Axel Johnson AB; Int'l,
pg. 711
A. JOHNSON & CO. (INDIA) LTD.—See Axel Johnson AB;
Int'l, pg. 711
A. JOHNSON CORP (HK) LTD.—See Axel Johnson AB;
Int'l, pg. 711
JOHNSON ACOUSTICAL & SUPPLY CO.; U.S. Private,
pg. 590
AL JOHNSON CONSTRUCTION CO.; U.S. Private, pg. 590
JOHNSON & JOHNSON; U.S. Public, pg. 927
JOHNSON & JOHNSON AB—See Johnson & Johnson;
U.S. Public, pg. 930
JOHNSON & JOHNSON AG—See Johnson & Johnson;
U.S. Public, pg. 930
JOHNSON & JOHNSON ASIA PACIFIC—See Johnson &
Johnson; U.S. Public, pg. 930
JOHNSON & JOHNSON CENTRAL/EAST AFRICA—See
Johnson & Johnson; U.S. Public, pg. 930
JOHNSON & JOHNSON CONSUMER PRODUCTS—See
Johnson & Johnson; U.S. Public, pg. 928
JOHNSON & JOHNSON DE ARGENTINA, S.A.—See
Johnson & Johnson; U.S. Public, pg. 930
JOHNSON & JOHNSON DE CHILE S.A.—See Johnson &
Johnson; U.S. Public, pg. 930
JOHNSON & JOHNSON DE COLOMBIA S.A.—See
Johnson & Johnson; U.S. Public, pg. 930
JOHNSON & JOHNSON DE MEXICO SA DE CV—See
Johnson & Johnson; U.S. Public, pg. 930
JOHNSON & JOHNSON DE URUGUAY, S.A.—See
Johnson & Johnson; U.S. Public, pg. 930
JOHNSON & JOHNSON DE VENEZUELA, S.A.—See
Johnson & Johnson; U.S. Public, pg. 930
JOHNSON & JOHNSON DEL ECUADOR S.A.—See
Johnson & Johnson; U.S. Public, pg. 930
JOHNSON & JOHNSON DEVELOPMENT
CORPORATION—See Johnson & Johnson; U.S.
Public, pg. 928
JOHNSON & JOHNSON (EGYPT) S.A.E.—See Johnson &
Johnson; U.S. Public, pg. 930
JOHNSON & JOHNSON FINANCE CORPORATION—See
Johnson & Johnson; U.S. Public, pg. 928
JOHNSON & JOHNSON GABA B.V.—See Johnson &
Johnson; U.S. Public, pg. 930
JOHNSON & JOHNSON G.M.B.H.—See Johnson &
Johnson; U.S. Public, pg. 930
JOHNSON & JOHNSON HEALTH CARE SYSTEMS INC.—
See Johnson & Johnson; U.S. Public, pg. 928
JOHNSON & JOHNSON HELLAS S.A.—See Johnson &
Johnson; U.S. Public, pg. 930
JOHNSON & JOHNSON HEMISFERICA—See Johnson &
Johnson; U.S. Public, pg. 928
JOHNSON & JOHNSON INC.—See Johnson & Johnson;
U.S. Public, pg. 930
P.T. JOHNSON & JOHNSON INDONESIA—See Johnson &
Johnson; U.S. Public, pg. 930
JOHNSON & JOHNSON INTERNATIONAL—See Johnson
& Johnson; U.S. Public, pg. 930
JOHNSON & JOHNSON INTERNATIONAL (HONG
KONG)—See Johnson & Johnson; U.S. Public, pg. 930
JOHNSON & JOHNSON (IRELAND) LTD.—See Johnson &
Johnson; U.S. Public, pg. 930
JOHNSON & JOHNSON (JAMAICA) LIMITED—See
Johnson & Johnson; U.S. Public, pg. 930
JOHNSON & JOHNSON (KENYA) LTD.—See Johnson &
Johnson; U.S. Public, pg. 930
JOHNSON & JOHNSON KFT—See Johnson & Johnson;
U.S. Public, pg. 930
JOHNSON & JOHNSON K.K.—See Johnson & Johnson;
U.S. Public, pg. 930
JOHNSON & JOHNSON KOREA, LTD.—See Johnson &
Johnson; U.S. Public, pg. 930
JOHNSON & JOHNSON LIMITADA—See Johnson &
Johnson; U.S. Public, pg. 930
JOHNSON & JOHNSON LIMITED—See Johnson &
Johnson; U.S. Public, pg. 930
JOHNSON & JOHNSON LTDA.—See Johnson & Johnson;
U.S. Public, pg. 931
JOHNSON & JOHNSON MEDICAL B.V.—See Johnson &
Johnson; U.S. Public, pg. 931
JOHNSON & JOHNSON MEDICAL CARIBBEAN—See
Johnson & Johnson; U.S. Public, pg. 928
JOHNSON & JOHNSON MEDICAL GMBH—See Johnson
& Johnson; U.S. Public, pg. 931
JOHNSON & JOHNSON MEDICAL G.M.B.H.—See
Johnson & Johnson; U.S. Public, pg. 931
JOHNSON & JOHNSON MEDICAL HONG KONG—See
Johnson & Johnson; U.S. Public, pg. 931
JOHNSON & JOHNSON MEDICAL, INC.—See Johnson &
Johnson; U.S. Public, pg. 928
JOHNSON & JOHNSON MEDICAL K.K.—See Johnson &
Johnson; U.S. Public, pg. 931
JOHNSON & JOHNSON MEDICAL MFG., SDN. BHD.—See
Johnson & Johnson; U.S. Public, pg. 931
JOHNSON & JOHNSON MEDICAL (PHILIPPINES), INC.—
See Johnson & Johnson; U.S. Public, pg. 931

JOHNSON & JOHNSON MEDICAL PRODUCTS INC.—See
Johnson & Johnson; U.S. Public, pg. 931
JOHNSON & JOHNSON MEDICAL PTY. LTD.—See
Johnson & Johnson; U.S. Public, pg. 931
JOHNSON & JOHNSON MEDICAL THAILAND—See
Johnson & Johnson; U.S. Public, pg. 931
JOHNSON & JOHNSON MOROCCO S.A.—See Johnson &
Johnson; U.S. Public, pg. 931
JOHNSON & JOHNSON PACIFIC PTY. (NEW ZEALAND)
LTD.—See Johnson & Johnson; U.S. Public, pg. 931
JOHNSON & JOHNSON PAKISTAN (PRIVATE) LTD.—See
Johnson & Johnson; U.S. Public, pg. 931
JOHNSON & JOHNSON PANAMA S.A.—See Johnson &
Johnson; U.S. Public, pg. 931
JOHNSON & JOHNSON (PHILIPPINES) INC.—See
Johnson & Johnson; U.S. Public, pg. 931
JOHNSON & JOHNSON POLAND, SP.Z.O.O.—See
Johnson & Johnson; U.S. Public, pg. 931
JOHNSON & JOHNSON PRODUCTOS—See Johnson &
Johnson; U.S. Public, pg. 928
JOHNSON & JOHNSON PROFESSIONAL, INC.—See
Johnson & Johnson; U.S. Public, pg. 928
JOHNSON & JOHNSON PROFESSIONAL PRODUCTS
LTD.—See Johnson & Johnson; U.S. Public, pg. 931
JOHNSON & JOHNSON PROFESSIONAL PRODUCTS
(PTY) LTD.—See Johnson & Johnson; U.S. Public,
pg. 931
JOHNSON & JOHNSON S.A. CONSUMER—See Johnson
& Johnson; U.S. Public, pg. 931
JOHNSON & JOHNSON SDN. BHD.—See Johnson &
Johnson; U.S. Public, pg. 931
JOHNSON & JOHNSON S.P.A.—See Johnson & Johnson;
U.S. Public, pg. 931
JOHNSON & JOHNSON TAIWAN LTD.—See Johnson &
Johnson; U.S. Public, pg. 931
JOHNSON & JOHNSON (THAILAND) LTD.—See Johnson
& Johnson; U.S. Public, pg. 931
JOHNSON & JOHNSON WORLDWIDE ABSORBENT
PRODUCTS & MATERIALS RESEARCH—See
Johnson & Johnson; U.S. Public, pg. 928
JOHNSON & JOHNSON (ZAMBIA) LTD.—See Johnson &
Johnson; U.S. Public, pg. 931
JOHNSON & QUIN, INC.; U.S. Private, pg. 590
JOHNSON & TOWERS, INC.; U.S. Private, pg. 590
AXEL JOHNSON AB; Int'l, pg. 707
AXEL JOHNSON (ACOSE EQUIPAMENTOS) LDA—See
Axel Johnson AB; Int'l, pg. 711
AXEL JOHNSON (ACOSE EQUIPAMENTOS) LTD.—See
Axel Johnson AB; Int'l, pg. 711
AXEL JOHNSON & CO. (HELLAS) LTD.—See Axel
Johnson AB; Int'l, pg. 711
AXEL JOHNSON & CO. (INDIA) LTD.—See Axel Johnson
AB; Int'l, pg. 711
AXEL JOHNSON & CO. N.V. MARIN DIVISION—See Axel
Johnson AB; Int'l, pg. 711
AXEL JOHNSON & CO. (SEA) PTE. LTD.—See Axel
Johnson AB; Int'l, pg. 711
AXEL JOHNSON A/S—See Axel Johnson AB; Int'l, pg. 711
AXEL JOHNSON (CHINA) LTD.—See Axel Johnson AB;
Int'l, pg. 711
AXEL JOHNSON CORP. (AUSTRALIA) AB—See Axel
Johnson AB; Int'l, pg. 710
AXEL JOHNSON CORP. (HK) LTD.—See Axel Johnson
AB; Int'l, pg. 711
AXEL JOHNSON CORP. (TAIWAN) LTD—See Axel
Johnson AB; Int'l, pg. 711
AXEL JOHNSON DE MÉXICO SA DE CV—See Axel
Johnson AB; Int'l, pg. 711
AXEL JOHNSON DO BRASIL IND. E. COM. LTDA.—See
Axel Johnson AB; Int'l, pg. 711
AXEL JOHNSON FASTIGHETSFORVALTNING AB—See
Axel Johnson AB; Int'l, pg. 709
AXEL JOHNSON, INC.—See Axel Johnson AB; Int'l,
pg. 711
AXEL JOHNSON INTERNATIONAL AB—See Axel Johnson
AB; Int'l, pg. 709
AXEL JOHNSON LAB SYSTEM A/S—See Axel Johnson
AB; Int'l, pg. 711
AXEL JOHNSON LAB SYSTEMS A/S—See Axel Johnson
AB; Int'l, pg. 711
AXEL JOHNSON LTD.—See Axel Johnson AB; Int'l,
pg. 711
AXEL JOHNSON METALS, INC.—See Axel Johnson AB;
Int'l, pg. 709
AXEL JOHNSON MINERAIS & METAUX S.A.R.L.—See
Axel Johnson AB; Int'l, pg. 711
AXEL JOHNSON ORE & METALS GMBH—See Axel
Johnson AB; Int'l, pg. 711
AXEL JOHNSON ORE & METALS, INC.—See Axel
Johnson AB; Int'l, pg. 710
AXEL JOHNSON ORE & METALS LTD.—See Axel
Johnson AB; Int'l, pg. 711
AXEL JOHNSON OY—See Axel Johnson AB; Int'l, pg. 712
AXEL JOHNSON RESOURCES AB—See Axel Johnson
AB; Int'l, pg. 709
AXEL JOHNSON S.A.—See Axel Johnson AB; Int'l, pg. 712
AXEL JOHNSON (SEA) PTE. LTD.—See Axel Johnson AB;
Int'l, pg. 712
AXEL JOHNSON SERVICEHANDELSGRUPPEN AB—See
Axel Johnson AB; Int'l, pg. 709
AXEL JOHNSON STEEL AUSTRALIA PTY LTD—See Axel
Johnson AB; Int'l, pg. 712
AXEL JOHNSON STEEL INTERNATIONAL B.V.—See Axel
Johnson AB; Int'l, pg. 712
AXEL JOHNSON TEKNIK A/S—See Axel Johnson AB;
Int'l, pg. 712
JOHNSON BROS. CORPORATION; U.S. Private, pg. 590
JOHNSON BROTHERS WHOLESALE LIQUOR; U.S.
Private, pg. 591
JOHNSON COMPANY, LTD.—See S.C. Johnson & Son,
Inc.; U.S. Private, pg. 593
JOHNSON CONTROLS, INC.; U.S. Public, pg. 932
JOHNSON CONTROLS, INC.—See Johnson Controls, Inc.;
U.S. Public, pg. 932

JOHNSON CONTROLS, INC., BATTERY GROUP—See
Johnson Controls, Inc.; U.S. Public, pg. 932
JOHNSON CONTROLS, INC., CONTROLS GROUP—See
Johnson Controls, Inc.; U.S. Public, pg. 932
JOHNSON CONTROLS, INC. (ENGINEERED PLASTICS
DIV.)—See Johnson Controls, Inc.; U.S. Public, pg. 932
JOHNSON CONTROLS INTERNATIONAL, INC.—See
Johnson Controls, Inc.; U.S. Public, pg. 932
JOHNSON CONTROLS WORLD SERVICES INC.—See
Johnson Controls, Inc.; U.S. Public, pg. 932
THE JOHNSON CORPORATION; U.S. Private, pg. 591
JOHNSON COUNTY FARM BUREAU CO-OP; U.S. Private,
pg. 591
JOHNSON COUNTY TITLE COMPANY, INC.—See The
First American Financial Corporation; U.S. Public,
pg. 626
E.F. JOHNSON RADIO SYSTEMS—See Transcrypt
International; U.S. Public, pg. 1630
JOHNSON ELECTRIC HOLDINGS LIMITED; Int'l, pg. 712
JOHNSON FRY HOLDINGS PLC; Int'l, pg. 713
JOHNSON FRY PLC—See Johnson Fry Holdings PLC; Int'l,
pg. 713
G.E. JOHNSON CONSTRUCTION CO., INC.; U.S. Private,
pg. 591
JOHNSON GEAR—See Arrow Gear Company; U.S. Private,
pg. 85
JOHNSON INDUSTRIES—See Howe Furniture Corporation;
U.S. Private, pg. 543
THE JOHN JOHNSON CO.; U.S. Private, pg. 591
JOHNSON & JOHNSON/MERCK CONSUMER
PHARMACEUTICALS CO.—See Johnson & Johnson;
U.S. Public, pg. 929
JOHNSON & JOHNSON/MERCK CONSUMER
PHARMACEUTICALS CO.—See Merck & Co., Inc.;
U.S. Public, pg. 1091
JOHNSON LADDERS—See Greenbull Group; U.S. Private,
pg. 477
LEGRAND JOHNSON CONSTRUCTION CO.; U.S. Private,
pg. 591
JOHNSON-LOFT ENGINEERING, INC.—See Tetra Laval
Group; Int'l, pg. 1378
JOHNSON MATTHEY AB—See Johnson Matthey Public
Limited Company; Int'l, pg. 714
JOHNSON MATTHEY & BRANDENBERGER AG—See
Johnson Matthey Public Limited Company; Int'l,
pg. 714
JOHNSON MATTHEY & CO. GMBH—See Johnson
Matthey Public Limited Company; Int'l, pg. 714
JOHNSON MATTHEY CATALOG CO.—See Johnson
Matthey Public Limited Company; Int'l, pg. 713
JOHNSON MATTHEY INC.—See Johnson Matthey Public
Limited Company; Int'l, pg. 713
JOHNSON MATTHEY LIMITED—See Johnson Matthey
Public Limited Company; Int'l, pg. 714
JOHNSON MATTHEY NOBLE METALS BUSINESS UNIT—
See Johnson Matthey Public Limited Company; Int'l,
pg. 713
JOHNSON MATTHEY PHARMACEUTICALS MATERIALS—
See Johnson Matthey Public Limited Company; Int'l,
pg. 713
JOHNSON MATTHEY P.L.C.—See Johnson Matthey
Limited Company; Int'l, pg. 713
JOHNSON MATTHEY (PTY.) LIMITED—See Johnson
Matthey Public Limited Company; Int'l, pg. 714
JOHNSON MATTHEY PUBLIC LIMITED COMPANY; Int'l,
pg. 713
JOHNSON MATTHEY REFINING, INC.—See Johnson
Matthey Public Limited Company; Int'l, pg. 713
JOHNSON MATTHEY SA—See Johnson Matthey Public
Limited Company; Int'l, pg. 714
S.A. JOHNSON MATTHEY NV—See Johnson Matthey
Public Limited Company; Int'l, pg. 714
JOHNSON METALL AB—See Electrolux, AB; Int'l, pg. 439
JOHNSON MOVING & STORAGE—See Johnson Storage
Moving Co; U.S. Private, pg. 594
JOHNSON MOVING & STORAGE, BOULDER/
LONGMONT—See Johnson Storage Moving Co; U.S.
Private, pg. 594
JOHNSON NEDERLAND B.V.—See S.C. Johnson & Son,
Inc.; U.S. Private, pg. 593
JOHNSON NEWSPAPER CORPORATION; U.S. Private,
pg. 591
JOHNSON OUTBOARDS MARINE CORP.—See Greenway
Partners, L.P.; U.S. Private, pg. 478
JOHNSON PRODUCTS CO., INC.—See IVAX Corporation;
U.S. Public, pg. 915
JOHNSON PUBLISHING COMPANY, INC.; U.S. Private,
pg. 591
JOHNSON ROSS CORPORATION—See CMI Corporation;
U.S. Public, pg. 279
R.W. JOHNSON PHARMACEUTICAL RESEARCH
INSTITUTE—See Johnson & Johnson; U.S. Public,
pg. 928
S.C. JOHNSON—See S.C. Johnson & Son, Inc.; U.S.
Private, pg. 593
S.C. JOHNSON & SON COLOMBIANA S.A.—See S.C.
Johnson & Son, Inc.; U.S. Private, pg. 593
S.C. JOHNSON & SON DE ARGENTINA S.A.I.C.—See S.C.
Johnson & Son, Inc.; U.S. Private, pg. 593
S.C. JOHNSON & SON DE VENEZUELA, C.A.—See S.C.
Johnson & Son, Inc.; U.S. Private, pg. 593
S.C. JOHNSON & SON (HELLAS) E.P.E.—See S.C.
Johnson & Son, Inc.; U.S. Private, pg. 593
S.C. JOHNSON & SON, INC.; U.S. Private, pg. 592
P.T. S.C. JOHNSON & SON (INDONESIA) LTD.—See S.C.
Johnson & Son, Inc.; U.S. Private, pg. 593
S.C. JOHNSON & SON, LIMITED—See S.C. Johnson &
Son, Inc.; U.S. Private, pg. 593
S.C. JOHNSON & SON, LTD.—See S.C. Johnson & Son,
Inc.; U.S. Private, pg. 593
S.C. JOHNSON & SON OF SOUTH AFRICA (PTY.) LTD.—
See S.C. Johnson & Son, Inc.; U.S. Private, pg. 593
S.C. JOHNSON & SON PTE. LIMITED—See S.C. Johnson
& Son, Inc.; U.S. Private, pg. 593

Company Index

S.C. JOHNSON & SON PTY. LTD.—See S.C. Johnson & Son, Inc.; *U.S. Private*, pg. 593

S.C. JOHNSON & SON, S.A. DE C.V.—See S.C. Johnson & Son, Inc.; *U.S. Private*, pg. 593

S.C. JOHNSON & SON TAIWAN LTD.—See S.C. Johnson & Son, Inc.; *U.S. Private*, pg. 593

S.C. JOHNSON COMPANY LIMITED—See S.C. Johnson & Son, Inc.; *U.S. Private*, pg. 593

S.C. JOHNSON DE CENTROAMERICA S.A.—See S.C. Johnson & Son, Inc.; *U.S. Private*, pg. 593

S.C. JOHNSON, LTD.—See S.C. Johnson & Son, Inc.; *U.S. Private*, pg. 593

S.C. JOHNSON NEW ZEALAND LTD.—See S.C. Johnson & Son, Inc.; *U.S. Private*, pg. 593

JOHNSON-SAUNDERS S.A.—See Axel Johnson AB; *Int'l*, pg. 712

S.C. JOHNSON & SON INC.—See S.C. Johnson & Son, Inc.; *U.S. Private*, pg. 592

S.C. JOHNSON KIEV CORP.—See S.C. Johnson & Son, Inc.; *U.S. Private*, pg. 593

SHELBA D. JOHNSON TRUCKING; *U.S. Private*, pg. 594

JOHNSON STORAGE & MOVING, AURORA—See Johnson Storage Moving Co; *U.S. Private*, pg. 594

JOHNSON STORAGE & MOVING, CHEYENNE—See Johnson Storage Moving Co; *U.S. Private*, pg. 594

JOHNSON STORAGE & MOVING, CLEBURNE—See Johnson Storage Moving Co; *U.S. Private*, pg. 594

JOHNSON STORAGE & MOVING, COLORADO SPRINGS—See Johnson Storage Moving Co; *U.S. Private*, pg. 594

JOHNSON STORAGE & MOVING, ENGLEWOOD—See Johnson Storage Moving Co; *U.S. Private*, pg. 594

JOHNSON STORAGE & MOVING, SAN DIEGO—See Johnson Storage Moving Co; *U.S. Private*, pg. 594

JOHNSON STORAGE & MOVING, SANTA FE—See Johnson Storage Moving Co; *U.S. Private*, pg. 594

JOHNSON STORAGE MOVING CO; *U.S. Private*, pg. 594

JOHNSON SUPPLY & EQUIPMENT CORP.; *U.S. Private*, pg. 594

TOM JOHNSON INVESTMENT MANAGEMENT, INC.—See United Asset Management Corporation; *U.S. Public*, pg. 1673

JOHNSON VENTURE CAPITAL, INC.—See S.C. Johnson & Son, Inc.; *U.S. Private*, pg. 592

JOHNSON WAX—See S.C. Johnson & Son, Inc.; *U.S. Private*, pg. 593

JOHNSON WAX AG—See S.C. Johnson & Son, Inc.; *U.S. Private*, pg. 593

N.V. JOHNSON WAX BELGIUM S.A.—See S.C. Johnson & Son, Inc.; *U.S. Private*, pg. 593

JOHNSON WAX CONSUMER PRODUCTS—See S.C. Johnson & Son, Inc.; *U.S. Private*, pg. 593

JOHNSON WAX GMBH—See S.C. Johnson & Son, Inc.; *U.S. Private*, pg. 593

JOHNSON WAX INDUSTRIAL PRODUCTS (INNOCHEM)—See S.C. Johnson & Son, Inc.; *U.S. Private*, pg. 593

JOHNSON WAX NIGERIA LIMITED—See S.C. Johnson & Son, Inc.; *U.S. Private*, pg. 593

JOHNSON WAX RESEARCH AND DEVELOPMENT—See S.C. Johnson & Son, Inc.; *U.S. Private*, pg. 593

JOHNSON WAX S.P.A.—See S.C. Johnson & Son, Inc.; *U.S. Private*, pg. 593

W.B. JOHNSON PROPERTIES, LLC; *U.S. Private*, pg. 594

JOHNSON WORLDWIDE ASSOCIATES, INC.; *U.S. Public*, pg. 932

JOHNSON WORLDWIDE CANADA, INC.—See Johnson Worldwide Associates, Inc.; *U.S. Public*, pg. 933

JOHNSON YOKOGAWA CORPORATION—See Yokogawa Electric Corporation; *Int'l*, pg. 1521

JOHNSON PRESS—See Johnson Publishing Company, Inc.; *U.S. Private*, pg. 592

JOHNSON PRINTING CO.—See Johnson Publishing Company, Inc.; *U.S. Private*, pg. 592

GAY JOHNSON'S INC.; *U.S. Private*, pg. 595

JOHNSON'S WAX (EAST AFRICA) LTD.—See S.C. Johnson & Son, Inc.; *U.S. Private*, pg. 593

JOHNSON'S WAX ESPANOLA, S.A.—See S.C. Johnson & Son, Inc.; *U.S. Private*, pg. 593

JOHNSON'S WAX LTD.—See S.C. Johnson & Son, Inc.; *U.S. Private*, pg. 593

JOHNSONVILLE FOODS, INC.; *U.S. Private*, pg. 595

JOHNSONVILLE SAUSAGE, INC.—See Johnsonville Foods, Inc.; *U.S. Private*, pg. 595

JOHNSONWAX DEL ECUADOR S.A.—See S.C. Johnson & Son, Inc.; *U.S. Private*, pg. 593

JOHNSTON & MURPHY CO.—See Genesco Inc.; *U.S. Public*, pg. 728

JOHNSTON & MURPHY RETAIL/WHOLESALE STORES—See Genesco Inc.; *U.S. Public*, pg. 728

JOHNSTON COCA-COLA BOTTLING GROUP, INC.—See Coca-Cola Enterprises Inc.; *U.S. Public*, pg. 393

D.R. JOHNSTON GROUP PTY. LTD.—See ConAgra, Inc.; *U.S. Public*, pg. 429

FRED B. JOHNSTON COMPANY, INC.; *U.S. Private*, pg. 595

JOHNSTON INDUSTRIES COMPOSITE REINFORCEMENTS—See Johnston Industries, Inc.; *U.S. Public*, pg. 933

JOHNSTON INDUSTRIES, INC.; *U.S. Public*, pg. 933

JOHNSTON, LEMON & CO. INC.; *U.S. Private*, pg. 595

JOHNSTOWN AMERICA INDUSTRIES; *U.S. Public*, pg. 933

JOHNSTOWN CORPORATION; *U.S. Private*, pg. 595

JOHNSTOWN KNITTING MILL CO.; *U.S. Private*, pg. 595

JOHNSTOWN WIRE TECHNOLOGIES, INC.—See Dubin-Clark & Company; *U.S. Private*, pg. 344

JOHORE MINING & STEVEDORING CO.—See Alcan Aluminium Limited; *Int'l*, pg. 52

JOLIETTE DIVISION—See The Cascades Group; *Int'l*, pg. 273

JOMAC CANADA—See Jomac, Inc.; *U.S. Private*, pg. 595

JOMAC, INC.; *U.S. Private*, pg. 595

JONAKERPANNAN AB—See Redland PLC; *Int'l*, pg. 1092

JONAS & CO., LTD.—See Skylark Co., Ltd.; *Int'l*, pg. 1262

JONATHAN MANUFACTURING CORP.; *U.S. Private*, pg. 595

JONATHAN'S LANDING, INC.—See Aluminum Company of America; *U.S. Public*, pg. 61

JONES & JONES, INC.; *U.S. Private*, pg. 596

JONES APPAREL GROUP, INC.; *U.S. Public*, pg. 933

JONES APPAREL GROUP, INC. CANADA—See Jones Apparel Group, Inc.; *U.S. Public*, pg. 933

JONES & BABSON—See Assicurazioni Generali S.p.A.; *Int'l*, pg. 90

JONES BLAIR COMPANY; *U.S. Private*, pg. 596

JONES CAPITAL CORPORATION—See Philipp Holzmann AG; *Int'l*, pg. 633

JONES CAPITAL MARKETS, INC.—See Jones International, Ltd.; *U.S. Private*, pg. 597

JONES CHEMICALS, INC.; *U.S. Private*, pg. 596

JONES DAIRY FARM; *U.S. Private*, pg. 596

DAVID JONES LIMITED; *Int'l*, pg. 714

JONES, DAY, REAVIS & POGUE; *U.S. Private*, pg. 596

EDWARD JONES; *U.S. Private*, pg. 597

JONES ENVIRONMENTAL (IRELAND) LTD.—See United Utilities plc; *Int'l*, pg. 1444

ERNEST JONES (LONDON) LIMITED—See Signet Group plc; *Int'l*, pg. 1248

JONES FINANCIAL SERVICES—See Jones & Jones, Inc.; *U.S. Private*, pg. 596

FLETCHER JONES MANAGEMENT GROUP; *U.S. Private*, pg. 597

JONES GALACTIC RADIO—See Jones International, Ltd.; *U.S. Private*, pg. 597

HENRY JONES FOODS PTY, LTD.—See J.M. Smucker Company; *U.S. Public*, pg. 1480

JONES HOLDING CORPORATION—See Jones Apparel Group, Inc.; *U.S. Public*, pg. 933

JONES INTERACTIVE, INC.—See Jones International, Ltd.; *U.S. Private*, pg. 597

JONES INTERCABLE, INC.—See Jones International, Ltd.; *U.S. Private*, pg. 597

JONES INTERNATIONAL, LTD.; *U.S. Private*, pg. 597

JONES INTERNATIONAL LTD.—See Jones Apparel Group, Inc.; *U.S. Public*, pg. 933

JONES INTERNATIONAL SECURITIES, LTD.—See Jones International, Ltd.; *U.S. Private*, pg. 597

JONES INVESTMENT CO., INC.—See Jones Apparel Group, Inc.; *U.S. Public*, pg. 933

J.A. JONES, INC.—See Philipp Holzmann AG; *Int'l*, pg. 633

JAMES JONES COMPANY—See Tyco International Ltd.; *U.S. Public*, pg. 1650

JONES LUMBER—See Jeld-Wen, Inc.; *U.S. Private*, pg. 585

JONES MANAGEMENT SERVICES, INC.—See Philipp Holzmann AG; *Int'l*, pg. 633

JONES MEDICAL INDUSTRIES INC.; *U.S. Public*, pg. 933

JONES NEW YORK OUTERWEAR—See Amerex USA, Inc.; *U.S. Private*, pg. 49

JONES PROGRAMMING SERVICES, INC.—See Jones International, Ltd.; *U.S. Private*, pg. 597

JONES PROPERTIES, INC.—See Jones International, Ltd.; *U.S. Private*, pg. 597

QUINCY JONES ENTERTAINMENT—See Time Warner Inc.; *U.S. Public*, pg. 1611

R.A. JONES & CO. INC.; *U.S. Private*, pg. 597

JONES SPACELINK, LTD.—See Jones International, Ltd.; *U.S. Private*, pg. 597

THE JONES STORE CO.—See Mercantile Stores Company, Inc.; *U.S. Public*, pg. 1090

JONKOPINGS LANTMAN EK. FOR.; *Int'l*, pg. 714

JONSEREDS GODSSKYDD AB—See Electrolux, AB; *Int'l*, pg. 439

CARL JONSSON PAPIR A/S—See Metsa-Serla Corporation; *Int'l*, pg. 864

LARS JONSSON AB—See Nestle S.A.; *Int'l*, pg. 922

JORDACHE ENTERPRISES, INC.; *U.S. Private*, pg. 597

JORDACHE FRAGRANCES & COSMETICS—See Jean Philippe Fragrances, Inc.; *U.S. Public*, pg. 924

JORDAN A/S; *Int'l*, pg. 714

THE JORDAN CO.—See West Union Corporation; *U.S. Private*, pg. 1163

THE JORDAN COMPANY; *U.S. Private*, pg. 597

JORDAN INDUSTRIES, INC.; *U.S. Private*, pg. 598

JORDAN INVESTMENTS LIMITED: MIGRASHI HAKABLANIM LIMITED—See The Israel Electric Corporation Ltd.; *Int'l*, pg. 691

JORDAN, MCGRATH, CASE & TAYLOR INC.; *U.S. Private*, pg. 598

JORDAN MOTORS, INC.; *U.S. Private*, pg. 599

JORDAN TAMRAZ CARUSO ADVERTISING, INC.; *U.S. Private*, pg. 599

JORDAN'S FOODS-BANGOR DIVISION—See Jordan's Meats; *U.S. Private*, pg. 599

JORDAN'S FOODS-CARIBOU DIVISION—See Jordan's Meats; *U.S. Private*, pg. 599

JORDAN'S FOODS-COLCHESTER DIVISION—See Jordan's Meats; *U.S. Private*, pg. 599

JORDAN'S FOODS-WESTBROOK DIVISION—See Jordan's Meats; *U.S. Private*, pg. 599

JORDAN'S MEATS; *U.S. Private*, pg. 599

JORDON COMMERCIAL REFRIGERATOR CO.; *U.S. Private*, pg. 599

EARLE M. JORGENSEN COMPANY; *U.S. Private*, pg. 600

EARLE M. JORGENSEN COMPANY/BIRMINGHAM—See Earle M. Jorgensen Company; *U.S. Private*, pg. 600

EARLE M. JORGENSEN COMPANY/BOSTON—See Earle M. Jorgensen Company; *U.S. Private*, pg. 600

EARLE M. JORGENSEN COMPANY/CHARLOTTE—See Earle M. Jorgensen Company; *U.S. Private*, pg. 600

EARLE M. JORGENSEN COMPANY/CHICAGO—See Earle M. Jorgensen Company; *U.S. Private*, pg. 600

EARLE M. JORGENSEN COMPANY/CINCINNATI—See Earle M. Jorgensen Company; *U.S. Private*, pg. 600

EARLE M. JORGENSEN COMPANY/DALLAS—See Earle M. Jorgensen Company; *U.S. Private*, pg. 600

EARLE M. JORGENSEN COMPANY/DENVER—See Earle M. Jorgensen Company; *U.S. Private*, pg. 600

EARLE M. JORGENSEN COMPANY/HAYWARD—See Earle M. Jorgensen Company; *U.S. Private*, pg. 600

EARLE M. JORGENSEN COMPANY/INDIANAPOLIS—See Earle M. Jorgensen Company; *U.S. Private*, pg. 600

EARLE M. JORGENSEN COMPANY/KANSAS CITY—See Earle M. Jorgensen Company; *U.S. Private*, pg. 600

EARLE M. JORGENSEN COMPANY/LITTLE ROCK—See Earle M. Jorgensen Company; *U.S. Private*, pg. 600

EARLE M. JORGENSEN COMPANY/LOS ANGELES—See Earle M. Jorgensen Company; *U.S. Private*, pg. 600

EARLE M. JORGENSEN COMPANY/MEMPHIS—See Earle M. Jorgensen Company; *U.S. Private*, pg. 600

EARLE M. JORGENSEN COMPANY/MILWAUKEE—See Earle M. Jorgensen Company; *U.S. Private*, pg. 600

EARLE M. JORGENSEN COMPANY/MINNEAPOLIS—See Earle M. Jorgensen Company; *U.S. Private*, pg. 600

EARLE M. JORGENSEN COMPANY/ONTARIO—See Earle M. Jorgensen Company; *U.S. Private*, pg. 600

EARLE M. JORGENSEN COMPANY/PHILADELPHIA—See Earle M. Jorgensen Company; *U.S. Private*, pg. 600

EARLE M. JORGENSEN COMPANY/PORTLAND—See Earle M. Jorgensen Company; *U.S. Private*, pg. 600

EARLE M. JORGENSEN COMPANY/QUEBEC—See Earle M. Jorgensen Company; *U.S. Private*, pg. 600

EARLE M. JORGENSEN COMPANY/SEATTLE—See Earle M. Jorgensen Company; *U.S. Private*, pg. 600

EARLE M. JORGENSEN COMPANY/ST. LOUIS—See Earle M. Jorgensen Company; *U.S. Private*, pg. 600

EARLE M. JORGENSEN COMPANY/TULSA—See Earle M. Jorgensen Company; *U.S. Private*, pg. 600

EARLE M. JORGENSEN COMPANY/UNITED KINGDOM—See Earle M. Jorgensen Company; *U.S. Private*, pg. 600

EARLE M. JORGENSEN HONING CENTER/BLUE ISLAND—See Earle M. Jorgensen Company; *U.S. Private*, pg. 600

EARLE M. JORGENSEN HONING CENTER/TULSA—See Earle M. Jorgensen Company; *U.S. Private*, pg. 600

EARLE M. JORGENSEN-SPECIALTY TUBING DIV.—See Earle M. Jorgensen Company; *U.S. Private*, pg. 600

R. ANCKER JORGENSEN A/S—See Avery Dennison Corporation; *U.S. Public*, pg. 153

JOSAM COMPANY; *U.S. Private*, pg. 600

DAVID JOSEPH CO.; *U.S. Private*, pg. 601

THE DAVID J. JOSEPH COMPANY—See SHV Holdings N.V.; *Int'l*, pg. 1155

JOSEPH DAWSON AG—See Dawson International PLC; *Int'l*, pg. 386

JOSEPH, LITTLEJOHN & LEVY; *U.S. Private*, pg. 601

JOSEPHINE COSMETICS, INC.—See Rohto Pharmaceutical Co.; *Int'l*, pg. 1126

J. JOSEPHSON, INC.; *U.S. Private*, pg. 601

JOSLINS—See Mercantile Stores Company, Inc.; *U.S. Public*, pg. 1090

JOSLYN CANADA INC.—See Danaher Corporation; *U.S. Public*, pg. 482

JOSLYN CORPORATION—See Danaher Corporation; *U.S. Public*, pg. 481

JOSLYN ELECTRONIC SYSTEMS CORPORATION—See Danaher Corporation; *U.S. Public*, pg. 481

JOSLYN FOREIGN SALES CORPORATION—See Danaher Corporation; *U.S. Public*, pg. 481

JOSLYN JENNINGS CORPORATION—See Danaher Corporation; *U.S. Public*, pg. 481

JOSLYN MANUFACTURING CO.—See Danaher Corporation; *U.S. Public*, pg. 481

JOSLYN MANUFACTURING CO.-HARDWARE DIV.—See Danaher Corporation; *U.S. Public*, pg. 481

JOSLYN SIERRA CORPORATION—See Danaher Corporation; *U.S. Public*, pg. 482

JOSSEY-BASS, INC.—See National Amusements, Inc.; *U.S. Private*, pg. 778

JOSTENS; *U.S. Public*, pg. 934

THE JOSTENS FOUNDATION, INC.—See Jostens; *U.S. Public*, pg. 934

JOSTENS HOME LEARNING—See Jostens Learning Corporation; *U.S. Private*, pg. 601

JOSTENS LEARNING CORPORATION; *U.S. Private*, pg. 601

JOSTENS SPORTSWEAR—See Fruit of the Loom, Inc.; *U.S. Public*, pg. 686

JOTUL A.S.—See Aker Raj Asa; *Int'l*, pg. 42

A/S JOTUL INDUSTRIER—See Aker Raj Asa; *Int'l*, pg. 42

JOTUN ABU DHABI (L.L.C.)—See Jotun A/S; *Int'l*, pg. 715

JOTUN A/S; *Int'l*, pg. 714

JOTUN BOYA SAN. VE TICARET A.S.—See Jotun A/S; *Int'l*, pg. 715

JOTUN BRIGNOLA S.P.A.—See Jotun A/S; *Int'l*, pg. 715

JOTUN BULGARIA LTD.—See Jotun A/S; *Int'l*, pg. 715

JOTUN CATHODIC PROTECTION A/S—See Jotun A/S; *Int'l*, pg. 714

JOTUN-DANMARK A/S—See Jotun A/S; *Int'l*, pg. 714

JOTUN DANMARK A/S—See Jotun A/S; *Int'l*, pg. 714

JOTUN DECORATIVE COATINGS LTD.—See Jotun A/S; *Int'l*, pg. 715

JOTUN (DEUTSCHLAND) GMBH—See Jotun A/S; *Int'l*, pg. 715

JOTUN FRANCE S.A.—See Jotun A/S; *Int'l*, pg. 715

JOTUN HELLAS LTD.—See Jotun A/S; *Int'l*, pg. 715

JOTUN-HENRY CLARK LTD.—See Jotun A/S; *Int'l*, pg. 715

JOTUN ITALIA S.P.A.—See Jotun A/S; *Int'l*, pg. 715

JOTUN ITOC S.R.L.—See Jotun A/S; *Int'l*, pg. 716

JOTUN L.L.C.—See Jotun A/S; *Int'l*, pg. 716

JOTUN (MALAYSIA) SDN. BHD.—See Jotun A/S; *Int'l*, pg. 715

JOTUN MIDEX AB—See Jotun A/S; *Int'l*, pg. 715

JOTUN NEDERLAND B.V.—See Jotun A/S; *Int'l*, pg. 715

JOTUN NOF SINGAPORE PTE. LTD.—See Jotun A/S; *Int'l*, pg. 715

JOTUN OCEAN PAINT CO. LTD.—See Jotun A/S; *Int'l*, pg. 715

JOTUN POLISAN BOYA TIC A.S.—See Jotun A/S; *Int'l,* pg. 715
JOTUN POLYMER A/S—See Jotun A/S; *Int'l,* pg. 714
JOTUN POLYMER B.V.—See Jotun A/S; *Int'l,* pg. 714
JOTUN POLYMER FRANCE S.A.—See Jotun A/S; *Int'l,* pg. 714
JOTUN POLYMER HUNGARY KFT.—See Jotun A/S; *Int'l,* pg. 715
JOTUN POLYMER INC.—See Jotun A/S; *Int'l,* pg. 715
JOTUN POLYMER (UK) LTD.—See Jotun A/S; *Int'l,* pg. 714
JOTUN POWDER COATINGS PTY. LTD.-—See Jotun A/S; *Int'l,* pg. 715
JOTUN PROTECTIVE COATINGS B.V.—See Jotun A/S; *Int'l,* pg. 715
JOTUN S.A.E.—See Jotun A/S; *Int'l,* pg. 715
JOTUN SAUDIA CO. LTD.—See Jotun A/S; *Int'l,* pg. 716
OY JOTUN SCANPOL AB—See Jotun A/S; *Int'l,* pg. 715
JOTUN SPOLCHEMIE A.S.—See Jotun A/S; *Int'l,* pg. 715
JOTUN SVERIGE A.B.—See Jotun A/S; *Int'l,* pg. 715
JOTUN THAILAND LTD.—See Jotun A/S; *Int'l,* pg. 715
JOTUN-TINCO TINTAS MARITIMAS LDA.—See Jotun A/S; *Int'l,* pg. 716
JOTUN U.A.E. LTD.—See Jotun A/S; *Int'l,* pg. 716
JOUAN, INC.; *U.S. Private,* pg. 601
THE JOURNAL; *U.S. Private,* pg. 601
JOURNAL & COURIER—See Gannett Company, Inc.; *U.S. Public,* pg. 701
JOURNAL BROADCAST GROUP, INC.—See Journal Communications Inc.; *U.S. Private,* pg. 601
JOURNAL COMMUNICATIONS INC.; *U.S. Private,* pg. 601
JOURNAL OF COMMERCE, INC.—See Pearson plc; *Int'l,* pg. 1026
JOURNAL REGISTER COMPANY; *U.S. Public,* pg. 934
JOURNAL STAR LINCOLN—See Lee Enterprises, Incorporated; *U.S. Public,* pg. 983
THE JOURNAL TIMES—See Lee Enterprises, Incorporated; *U.S. Public,* pg. 983
JOVE PUBLICATIONS, INC.—See Pearson plc; *Int'l,* pg. 1027
JOWA AG—See Migros; *Int'l,* pg. 865
JOY CORPORATION—See Bristol-Myers Squibb Company; *U.S. Public,* pg. 256
JOY ENERGY SYSTEMS INC.—See Harnischfeger Industries, Inc.; *U.S. Public,* pg. 789
JOY ENVIRONMENTAL TECHNOLOGIES, INC.—See Harnischfeger Industries, Inc.; *U.S. Public,* pg. 789
JOY/GREEN FAN DIVISION—See Harnischfeger Industries, Inc.; *U.S. Public,* pg. 789
JOY MANUFACTURING COMPANY (AFRICA) (PTY) LTD. JOHANNESBURG PLANT—See Harnischfeger Industries, Inc.; *U.S. Public,* pg. 789
JOY MANUFACTURING COMPANY (PTY) LTD., SYDNEY PLANT—See Harnischfeger Industries, Inc.; *U.S. Public,* pg. 789
JOY MANUFACTURING COMPANY (UK) LTD., EAST KILBRIDE PLANT—See Harnischfeger Industries, Inc.; *U.S. Public,* pg. 789
JOY MINING MACHINERY—See Harnischfeger Industries, Inc.; *U.S. Public,* pg. 790
JOY SERVICE; *U.S. Private,* pg. 602
JOY TOY, CO.—See Strombecker Corporation; *U.S. Private,* pg. 1047
JOY WARENHANDELSGESELLSCHAFT—See Karstadt Aktiengesellschaft; *Int'l,* pg. 724
JOYAMA KAIHATSU LTD.—See Makita Corporation; *Int'l,* pg. 831
JOYCE INTERNATIONAL, INC.; *U.S. Private,* pg. 601
J.P. MORGAN & CO. INCORPORATED—See J.P. Morgan Co. Incorporated; *U.S. Public,* pg. 1130
J.P. MORGAN AUSTRALIA SECURITIES LIMITED—See J.P. Morgan Co. Incorporated; *U.S. Public,* pg. 1130
JUDD & DETWEILER, INC.—See Perry Graphic Communications, Inc.; *U.S. Private,* pg. 855
JUDD-OLIN (U.K.) LIMITED—See Olin Corporation; *U.S. Public,* pg. 1219
JUDD WIRE, INC.—See Sumitomo Electric Industries, Ltd.; *Int'l,* pg. 1313
JUDD'S, INC.—See Perry Graphic Communications, Inc.; *U.S. Private,* pg. 855
JUDD'S INCORPORATED—See Perry Graphic Communications, Inc.; *U.S. Private,* pg. 855
JUDEL PRODUCTS CORP.—See Tiffany & Co.; *U.S. Public,* pg. 1609
JUDSON-ATKINSON CANDIES, INC.; *U.S. Private,* pg. 602
JUGOBANKA BANKING GROUP; *Int'l,* pg. 716
JUGOS DEL VALLE DISTRIBUTION—See Jugos del Valle, S.A. de C.V.; *Int'l,* pg. 716
JUGOS DEL VALLE, S.A. DE C.V.; *Int'l,* pg. 716
JUICE WORKS DEVELOPMENT, INC.—See TCBY Enterprises, Inc.; *U.S. Public,* pg. 1554
JUJO PAPER GMBH—See Nippon Paper Industries Company Limited; *Int'l,* pg. 938
JUJO THERMAL OY—See Nippon Paper Industries Company Limited; *Int'l,* pg. 938
JUKI CORPORATION; *Int'l,* pg. 716
JUKI ELECTRONICS CORP.—See Juki Corporation; *Int'l,* pg. 716
JUKI (EUROPE) G.M.B.H.—See Juki Corporation; *Int'l,* pg. 717
JUKI (EUROPE) G.M.B.H.-PRAGUE OFFICE—See Juki Corporation; *Int'l,* pg. 717
JUKI (EUROPE) G.M.B.H.-U.K. OFFICE—See Juki Corporation; *Int'l,* pg. 717
JUKI (EUROPE) G.M.B.H.-WARSAW OFFICE—See Juki Corporation; *Int'l,* pg. 717
JUKI (HONG KONG) LTD.—See Juki Corporation; *Int'l,* pg. 717
JUKI (HONG KONG) LTD.-SINGAPORE BRANCH—See Juki Corporation; *Int'l,* pg. 717
JUKI LATIN AMERICA INC.—See Juki Corporation; *Int'l,* pg. 716
JUKI UNION SPECIAL, INC.—See Juki Corporation; *Int'l,* pg. 716

JUKI UNION SPECIAL INC.-ATLANTA OFFICE—See Juki Corporation; *Int'l,* pg. 716
JUKI UNION SPECIAL, INC.-CALIFORNIA OFFICE—See Juki Corporation; *Int'l,* pg. 716
JULIAN PRESS—See Advance Publications Inc.; *U.S. Private,* pg. 21
JULIANA CONSTRUCTORA GIJONESA, S.A.—See SEPI; *Int'l,* pg. 1223
JULIANA VINEYARDS—See Reunion Industries, Inc.; *U.S. Public,* pg. 1383
JULIUS BERGER NIGERIA PLC—See Bilfinger + Berger Bauaktiengesellschaft; *Int'l,* pg. 196
JULIUS KLEEMAN HANDEL MIT WERKZEUGEN UND MASCHINEN GMBH—See Rothenberger Group GmbH; *Int'l,* pg. 1128
JULIUS KLEEMAN WEKZEUGEN UND MASCHINEN GMBH—See Rothenberger Group GmbH; *Int'l,* pg. 1128
JULIUS MEINL STORES—See Julius Meinl AG; *Int'l,* pg. 856
JUMA AL MAJID—See Telefonaktiebolaget LM Ericsson; *Int'l,* pg. 1368
JUMBO SPORTS INC.; *U.S. Public,* pg. 935
JUMP—See BDDP Group; *Int'l,* pg. 116
JUMPING JACKS—See Munro & Company, Inc.; *U.S. Private,* pg. 767
GEBR. JUNG GMBH & CO. OHG—See Nestle S.A.; *Int'l,* pg. 920
JUNG GMBH—See Karstadt Aktiengesellschaft; *Int'l,* pg. 724
JUNG-PUMPEN GMBH—See Masco Corporation; *U.S. Public,* pg. 1054
JUNG PUMPEN VERWALTUNGS GMBH—See Masco Corporation; *U.S. Public,* pg. 1054
JUNIOR DISCOUNT SERVICE AG—See Fotolabo S.A.; *Int'l,* pg. 501
JUNIOR GALLERY LTD.; *U.S. Private,* pg. 602
JUNKER INC.—See Otto Junker GmbH Lammersdorf; *Int'l,* pg. 1014
JUNO, INC.—See The Cretex Companies; *U.S. Private,* pg. 290
JUNO INDUSTRIES, INC.—See Hughes Supply, Inc.; *U.S. Public,* pg. 847
JUNO LIGHTING, INC.; *U.S. Public,* pg. 935
JUNO LIGHTING LTD.—See Juno Lighting, Inc.; *U.S. Public,* pg. 935
JUNORS—See Russel Metals Inc.; *Int'l,* pg. 1150
JUPITER BEACH RESORT—See Noble House Hotels and Resorts; *U.S. Private,* pg. 800
JUPITER ENERGY CORP.—See Jupiter Industries, Inc.; *U.S. Private,* pg. 602
JUPITER INDUSTRIES, INC.; *U.S. Private,* pg. 602
JUPITER INTERNATIONAL GROUP PLC—See Commerzbank AG; *Int'l,* pg. 312
JUPITER TRANSPORTATION, INC.—See Mark VII, Inc.; *U.S. Public,* pg. 1046
JOHN R. JURGENSEN CO.—See Valley Asphalt Corporation; *U.S. Private,* pg. 1131
JURID N.V. (S.A.)—See AlliedSignal Inc.; *U.S. Public,* pg. 53
JURONG ENGINEERING LIMITED—See Ishikawajima-Harima Heavy Industries Co., Ltd.; *Int'l,* pg. 689
JUS-ROL LTD.—See Diageo Plc; *Int'l,* pg. 411
JUSCO CO., LTD.—See AEON Group; *Int'l,* pg. 28
JUSCO USA, INC.—See AEON Group; *Int'l,* pg. 28
JUST BORN, INC.; *U.S. Private,* pg. 602
JUST DATA—See Anixter International; *U.S. Public,* pg. 115
JUST FOR FEET, INC.; *U.S. Public,* pg. 935
JUST KID, INC.—See North Castle Partners Advertising, Inc.; *U.S. Private,* pg. 804
JUST RUBBER PLC.—See Scapa Group Plc; *Int'l,* pg. 1202
JUST TOYS—See RGA and East End Accessories; *U.S. Private,* pg. 903
JUSTERINI & BROOKS LTD.—See Diageo Plc; *Int'l,* pg. 409
JUSTIN BOOT COMPANY—See Justin Industries, Inc.; *U.S. Public,* pg. 937
JUSTIN INDUSTRIES, INC.; *U.S. Public,* pg. 936
JUSTISS OIL CO., INC.; *U.S. Private,* pg. 602
JUSTRITE MANUFACTURING COMPANY—See Federal Signal Corporation; *U.S. Public,* pg. 617
JUVELBAGERIERNA AB—See KF/Konsum Coop Group; *Int'l,* pg. 718
JUVENA (INTERNATIONAL) AG—See Beiersdorf Group; *Int'l,* pg. 183
JUVENA PRODUITS DE BEAUTE GMBH—See Beiersdorf Group; *Int'l,* pg. 182
JUVER INDUSTRIAL S.A. DE C.V.—See Maytag Corporation; *U.S. Public,* pg. 1065
JYVASKYLA MILLS—See UPM-Kymmene Corporation; *Int'l,* pg. 1429

K

K ADVERTISING—See Saatchi & Saatchi Advertising Worldwide; *U.S. Public,* pg. 1422
K&B MUNDELEIN INC.—See Kirkwood Industries, Inc.; *U.S. Private,* pg. 623
K & E TRYKFARVER—See BASF AG; *Int'l,* pg. 108
K & F INDUSTRIES INC.; *U.S. Private,* pg. 602
K & G OF WISCONSIN, INC.; *U.S. Private,* pg. 602
K & L FEEDS—See Empire Kosher Poultry, Inc.; *U.S. Private,* pg. 374
K & L MICROWAVE DIV.—See Dover Corporation; *U.S. Public,* pg. 521
K&M ASSOCIATES—See American Biltrite Inc.; *U.S. Public,* pg. 69
K AND M CO., LTD.—See Pasco Corporation; *Int'l,* pg. 1024
K & M ELECTRONICS, INC.—See Derlan Industries Limited; *Int'l,* pg. 395

K & M HAULIERS—See Franz Haniel & Cie, GmbH; *Int'l,* pg. 591
K & M PRODUCTS DIVISION—See Avery Dennison Corporation; *U.S. Public,* pg. 152
K & P LEYKAM AUSTRIA—See N.V. Koninklijke KNP BT; *Int'l,* pg. 757
K & R EXPRESS SYSTEMS INC.; *U.S. Private,* pg. 602
K-BIN INC.—See Shin-Etsu Chemical Co. ltd.; *Int'l,* pg. 1234
K-C ADVERTISING, INC.—See Kimberly-Clark Corporation; *U.S. Public,* pg. 959
K-C AVIATION, INC.—See Kimberly-Clark Corporation; *U.S. Public,* pg. 959
K-C DO BRASIL LTDA.—See Kimberly-Clark Corporation; *U.S. Public,* pg. 959
K-CASH & CARRY LTD.—See Kesko Ltd.; *Int'l,* pg. 732
K-G PACKAGING—See CCL Industries, Inc.; *Int'l,* pg. 238
K.G. SYSTEM CONSTRUCTION CO., LTD.—See Kumagai Gumi Co., Ltd.; *Int'l,* pg. 763
K-INSTITUUTI OY—See Kesko Ltd.; *Int'l,* pg. 732
K-LEA CO. LTD.—See Caterpillar Inc.; *U.S. Public,* pg. 317
"K" LINE (KAWASAKI KISEN KAISHA, LTD.); *Int'l,* pg. 717
K-LINKKI OY—See Kesko Ltd.; *Int'l,* pg. 732
K-LUOTTO OY—See Kesko Ltd.; *Int'l,* pg. 732
K-MAATALOUSYHTIOT OY—See Kesko Ltd.; *Int'l,* pg. 732
K N ENERGY, INC.; *U.S. Public,* pg. 937
K N FIELD SERVICES, INC.—See K N Energy, Inc.; *U.S. Public,* pg. 937
K N GAS GATHERING, INC.—See K N Energy, Inc.; *U.S. Public,* pg. 937
K N GAS MARKETING, INC.—See K N Energy, Inc.; *U.S. Public,* pg. 937
K N INTERSTATE GAS TRANSMISSION CO.—See K N Energy, Inc.; *U.S. Public,* pg. 937
K N SERVICES, INC.—See K N Energy, Inc.; *U.S. Public,* pg. 937
K-SWISS EUROPE LTD.—See K-Swiss Inc.; *U.S. Public,* pg. 937
K-SWISS INC.; *U.S. Public,* pg. 937
K-SWISS INTERNATIONAL LTD.—See K-Swiss Inc.; *U.S. Public,* pg. 937
K-T CORP.—See Triumph Group, Inc.; *U.S. Public,* pg. 1640
K-TEC ELECTRONICS—See Kent Electronics Corp.; *U.S. Public,* pg. 951
K-TEL (AUSTRALIA) PTY. LIMITED—See K-Tel International, Inc.; *U.S. Public,* pg. 938
K-TEL CONSUMER PRODUCTS, INC.—See K-Tel International, Inc.; *U.S. Public,* pg. 938
K-TEL DIRECT, INC.—See K-Tel International, Inc.; *U.S. Public,* pg. 938
K-TEL ENTERTAINMENT (CAN) INC.—See K-Tel International, Inc.; *U.S. Public,* pg. 938
K-TEL ENTERTAINMENT (U.K.) LTD.—See K-Tel International, Inc.; *U.S. Public,* pg. 938
K-TEL INTERNATIONAL FINLAND O.Y.—See K-Tel International, Inc.; *U.S. Public,* pg. 938
K-TEL INTERNATIONAL, INC.; *U.S. Public,* pg. 937
K-TEL INTERNATIONAL (USA) INC.—See K-Tel International, Inc.; *U.S. Public,* pg. 938
K-TEL IRELAND LTD.—See K-Tel International, Inc.; *U.S. Public,* pg. 938
K-III MEDIA GROUP—See Primedia Inc.; *U.S. Public,* pg. 1328
K-TRON AMERICA, INC.—See K-Tron International, Inc.; *U.S. Public,* pg. 938
K-TRON ASIA PACIFIC PTE—See K-Tron International, Inc.; *U.S. Public,* pg. 938
K-TRON ELECTRONICS—See K-Tron International, Inc.; *U.S. Public,* pg. 938
K-TRON FRANCE—See K-Tron International, Inc.; *U.S. Public,* pg. 938
K-TRON GERMANY-HASLER DIVISION—See K-Tron International, Inc.; *U.S. Public,* pg. 938
K-TRON GREAT BRITAIN, LTD.—See K-Tron International, Inc.; *U.S. Public,* pg. 938
K-TRON INSTITUTE—See K-Tron International, Inc.; *U.S. Public,* pg. 938
K-TRON INTERNATIONAL, INC.; *U.S. Public,* pg. 938
K-TRON SWITZERLAND-HASLER DIVISION—See K-Tron International, Inc.; *U.S. Public,* pg. 938
K-TRON SWITZERLAND-SODER DIVISION—See K-Tron International, Inc.; *U.S. Public,* pg. 938
K2 SKI-SPORT & MODE GMBH—See K2 Inc.; *U.S. Public,* pg. 940
K-VA-T; *U.S. Private,* pg. 603
K-YHTIOT OY—See Kesko Ltd.; *Int'l,* pg. 732
KABC-AM RADIO, INC.—See The Walt Disney Company; *U.S. Public,* pg. 512
KABC-TV—See The Walt Disney Company; *U.S. Public,* pg. 512
KAFI BV—See Heidemij N.V.; *Int'l,* pg. 607
KAIT-TV—See Liberty Corporation; *U.S. Public,* pg. 992
KAJA-FM—See Clear Channel Communications, Inc.; *U.S. Public,* pg. 384
KAKC-AM—See Clear Channel Communications, Inc.; *U.S. Public,* pg. 384
KAO CORPORATION; *Int'l,* pg. 717
KAPL, INC.—See Lockheed Martin Corporation; *U.S. Public,* pg. 1007
KARE-TV—See Gannett Company, Inc.; *U.S. Public,* pg. 702
KB ALLOYS, INC.—See Code, Hennessy & Simmons, Inc.; *U.S. Private,* pg. 249
KB BETEILIGUNGS- UND VERWATUNGS GMBH—See Creditanstalt-Bankverein; *Int'l,* pg. 347
KB FINANCE DUBLIN UNLTD—See Kredietbank N.V.; *Int'l,* pg. 761
KB FINANCIAL SERVICES (DUBLIN) UNLTD.—See Kredietbank N.V.; *Int'l,* pg. 761
KB FINANCIAL SERVICES (IRELAND) UNLTD.—See Kredietbank N.V.; *Int'l,* pg. 761

KBA-MOTTER CORP.—See Koenig & Bauer-Albert AG; *Int'l*, pg. 742
KBA-PLANETA AG—See Koenig & Bauer-Albert AG; *Int'l*, pg. 742
KBA-PLANETA NORTH AMERICA INC.—See Koenig & Bauer-Albert AG; *Int'l*, pg. 742
KBAK-TV—See Westwind Communications; *U.S. Private*, pg. 1170
KBC TRADING & PROCESSES—See ConAgra, Inc.; *U.S. Public*, pg. 428
KBC TRADING & PROCESSING—See ConAgra, Inc.; *U.S. Public*, pg. 428
KBHK TELEVISION, INC.—See Chris-Craft Industries, Inc.; *U.S. Public*, pg. 352
KBIM-TV—See Lee Enterprises, Incorporated; *U.S. Public*, pg. 984
KKBR/CONQUEST—See WPP Group plc; *Int'l*, pg. 1484
KBSG/KNDD-AM/FM—See Entertainment Communications; *U.S. Private*, pg. 378
KBXX-FM—See Clear Channel Communications, Inc.; *U.S. Public*, pg. 384
KCBA-TV—See The Ackerley Group; *U.S. Public*, pg. 16
KCBS-TV—See CBS Corporation; *U.S. Public*, pg. 275
KCCI TELEVISION, INC.—See Pulitzer Publishing Company; *U.S. Public*, pg. 1343
K.C.I. COATINGS, INC.—See Progress Paint Mfg. Co.; *U.S. Private*, pg. 890
KCI COMMUNICATIONS, INC—See National Information Corporation; *U.S. Private*, pg. 784
KCK CO., LTD.—See Mitsubishi Materials Corp.; *Int'l*, pg. 875
KCL CORPORATION; *U.S. Private*, pg. 603
KCOP TELEVISION—See Chris-Craft Industries, Inc.; *U.S. Public*, pg. 352
KCP HOLDING COMPANY—See Danielson Holding Corporation; *U.S. Public*, pg. 483
KCRG RADIO & TV STATIONS—See The Gazette Company; *U.S. Private*, pg. 442
KCS ENERGY INC.; *U.S. Public*, pg. 938
KCS ENERGY MARKETING, INC.—See KCS Energy Inc.; *U.S. Public*, pg. 939
KCS ENERGY RISK MANAGEMENT—See KCS Energy Inc.; *U.S. Public*, pg. 939
KCS ENERGY SERVICES, INC.—See KCS Energy Inc.; *U.S. Public*, pg. 939
KCS MICHIGAN RESOURCES, INC.—See KCS Energy Inc.; *U.S. Public*, pg. 939
KCS PIPELINE SYSTEMS, INC.—See KCS Energy Inc.; *U.S. Public*, pg. 939
KCS POWER MARKETING, INC.—See KCS Energy Inc.; *U.S. Public*, pg. 939
KCS RESOURCES, INC.—See KCS Energy Inc.; *U.S. Public*, pg. 939
KCS VILLANUEVA S.A. DE C.V.—See Banta Corporation; *U.S. Public*, pg. 188
K.C.S.A. HOLDINGS (PTY.) LTD.—See Kimberly-Clark Corporation; *Int'l*, pg. 959
KCTV—See Meredith Corporation; *U.S. Public*, pg. 1094
K-D LAMP COMPANY; *U.S. Private*, pg. 603
K-D MANITOU, INC.—See Manitou BF; *Int'l*, pg. 834
KDA/HEPY, P.C.—See Harley Ellington Design; *U.S. Private*, pg. 503
KDAF—See The News Corporation Limited; *Int'l*, pg. 926
KDAF (WB)—See Tribune Company; *U.S. Public*, pg. 1636
KDC FINANCIAL LIMITED PARTNERSHIP—See Komatsu Ltd.; *Int'l*, pg. 744
KDDK-FM—See Clear Channel Communications, Inc.; *U.S. Public*, pg. 384
KDFW—See The News Corporation Limited; *Int'l*, pg. 926
KDG HOUDEC SA—See Meggitt plc; *Int'l*, pg. 854
KDI PRECISION PRODUCTS, INC.; *U.S. Private*, pg. 603
KDJ-VMBH—See FAG Group; *Int'l*, pg. 468
KDKA-RADIO & KDKA-TV—See CBS Corporation; *U.S. Public*, pg. 275
KE-BURGMANN A/S—See Feodor Burgmann Dichtungswerke GmbH; *Int'l*, pg. 234
KE-BURGMANN SINGAPORE PTE. LTD.—See Feodor Burgmann Dichtungswerke GmbH; *Int'l*, pg. 234
KEBC-AM—See Clear Channel Communications, Inc.; *U.S. Public*, pg. 384
KEBE—See New Century Media; *U.S. Private*, pg. 792
KERO-TV—See The McGraw-Hill Companies; *U.S. Public*, pg. 1070
KETV—See Pulitzer Publishing Company; *U.S. Public*, pg. 1343
KEYI-FM—See Clear Channel Communications, Inc.; *U.S. Public*, pg. 384
KEZW-AM—See Tribune Company; *U.S. Public*, pg. 1636
KF FASTIGHETER AB—See KF/Konsum Coop Group; *Int'l*, pg. 718
KF INDUSTRIES—See Watts Industries, Inc.; *U.S. Public*, pg. 1746
KF/KONSUM COOP GROUP; *Int'l*, pg. 718
KF STORMARKNADER AB—See KF/Konsum Coop Group; *Int'l*, pg. 718
KFBK (AM) & KAER (FM) RADIO—See Chancellor Media Corporation; *U.S. Public*, pg. 335
K.F.C. (N.Z.) LTD.—See Tricon Global Restaurants, Inc.; *U.S. Public*, pg. 1637
KFI, INC.—See Cox Enterprises, Inc.; *U.S. Private*, pg. 282
KFON-AM—See Clear Channel Communications, Inc.; *U.S. Public*, pg. 384
KFOR-TV—See The New York Times Company; *U.S. Public*, pg. 1174
KFSM-TV—See The New York Times Company; *U.S. Public*, pg. 1174
KFSN-TV—See The Walt Disney Company; *U.S. Public*, pg. 512
KFW CANADA, INC.—See TI Group plc; *Int'l*, pg. 1338
KFW KREDITANSTALT FUR WIEDERAUFBAU; *Int'l*, pg. 718
KFWB RADIO—See CBS Corporation; *U.S. Public*, pg. 274
KFXX/KGON, INC.—See Entertainment Communications; *U.S. Private*, pg. 378

KG CONSTRUCTION—See Kumagai Gumi Co., Ltd.; *Int'l*, pg. 764
KG (HAWAII) CORPORATION—See Kumagai Gumi Co., Ltd.; *Int'l*, pg. 764
KG LAND CALIFORNIA CORPORATION—See Kumagai Gumi Co., Ltd.; *Int'l*, pg. 764
KG LAND NEW YORK CORPORATION—See Kumagai Gumi Co., Ltd.; *Int'l*, pg. 764
KG MARIS REISEN GMBH & CO—See Otto Versand GMBH & Co.); *Int'l*, pg. 1014
KGAN-TV—See Guy Gannett Communications; *U.S. Private*, pg. 439
KGE—See Western Resources, Inc.; *U.S. Public*, pg. 1759
KGET-TV—See The Ackerley Group; *U.S. Public*, pg. 16
KGL. BRAND A/S—See Skandia Insurance Company Limited; *Int'l*, pg. 1257
KGM KUGELFABRIK GEBAUER GMBH—See FAG Group; *Int'l*, pg. 468
KGMB-TV—See Lee Enterprises, Incorporated; *U.S. Public*, pg. 983
KGO-AM RADIO, INC.—See The Walt Disney Company; *U.S. Public*, pg. 512
KGO TELEVISION, INC.—See The Walt Disney Company; *U.S. Public*, pg. 512
KGTV—See The McGraw-Hill Companies; *U.S. Public*, pg. 1070
KGUN-TV—See Lee Enterprises, Incorporated; *U.S. Public*, pg. 983
KGV LAMBERT SMITH HAMPTON—See Lambert Smith Hampton; *Int'l*, pg. 797
KHD DEUTZ OF AMERICA CORPORATION—See Deutz AG; *Int'l*, pg. 408
KHD HUMBOLDT WEDAG AG—See Deutz AG; *Int'l*, pg. 408
KHEY-AM/FM—See Clear Channel Communications, Inc.; *U.S. Public*, pg. 384
KHFI-FM—See Clear Channel Communications, Inc.; *U.S. Public*, pg. 384
KHI (DALIAN) COMPUTER TECHNOLOGY CO., LTD.—See Kawasaki Heavy Industries, Ltd.; *Int'l*, pg. 726
KHI EUROPE FINANCE B.V.—See Kawasaki Heavy Industries, Ltd.; *Int'l*, pg. 726
KHKS-FM—See Chancellor Media Corporation; *U.S. Public*, pg. 335
KHON-TV—See USA Networks, Inc.; *U.S. Public*, pg. 1685
KHOU-TV INC.—See A.H. Belo Corporation; *U.S. Public*, pg. 209
KHOW-AM/FM—See Jacor Communications, Inc.; *U.S. Public*, pg. 922
KHR; *U.S. Private*, pg. 603
KHS KUNSTSTOFFMASCHINEN-HANDELS UND SERVICE GMBH—See Mannesmann A.G.; *Int'l*, pg. 836
KHT KOMMISSIONIER UND HANDHABUNGTECHNIK GMBH—See Mannesmann A.G.; *Int'l*, pg. 837
KHTV-TV—See Tribune Company; *U.S. Public*, pg. 1636
KHYS-FM—See Clear Channel Communications, Inc.; *U.S. Public*, pg. 384
KIC, LTD.—See Hanson PLC; *Int'l*, pg. 594
KIK CORPORATION HOLDINGS INC.—See Center Partners Management LLC; *U.S. Private*, pg. 222
KIKK AM/FM—See CBS Corporation; *U.S. Public*, pg. 274
KILT AM/FM RADIO—See CBS Corporation; *U.S. Public*, pg. 274
K.I.M COAL CO.—See Taylor Woodrow plc; *Int'l*, pg. 1359
KIMN AM & KYGO FM—See Jefferson-Pilot Corporation; *U.S. Public*, pg. 926
KITV—See The News Corporation Limited; *Int'l*, pg. 926
KJOJ-AM/FM—See Clear Channel Communications, Inc.; *U.S. Public*, pg. 384
K.J.P. LTD.—See Wolseley Plc.; *Int'l*, pg. 1512
KJR-AM—See New Century Media; *U.S. Public*, pg. 792
KJR-FM—See New Century Media; *U.S. Private*, pg. 792
KJRH—See The E.W. Scripps Company; *U.S. Public*, pg. 1448
KJYO-FM—See Clear Channel Communications, Inc.; *U.S. Public*, pg. 384
K.K. GEOTRONICS—See Spectra-Physics AB; *Int'l*, pg. 1290
KK-SERVICE GMBH—See Fried. Krupp AG; *Int'l*, pg. 515
KKB BANK KGAA—See Citicorp; *U.S. Public*, pg. 379
KKBC INTERNATIONAL LTD.—See Hyundai Motor Company; *Int'l*, pg. 642
KKBQ-AM-FM—See Chancellor Media Corporation; *U.S. Public*, pg. 335
KKHK—See Tribune Company; *U.S. Public*, pg. 1636
KKKK A/S—See Veba AG; *Int'l*, pg. 1459
KKLT-FM—See Pulitzer Publishing Company; *U.S. Public*, pg. 1344
KKND—See Clear Channel Communications, Inc.; *U.S. Public*, pg. 384
KKTV-TV—See The Ackerley Group; *U.S. Public*, pg. 16
KKW—See The Glen Dimplex Group; *Int'l*, pg. 554
KLA ACROTEC COMPANY, LTD.—See KLA Tencor Corporation; *U.S. Public*, pg. 939
KLA INSTRUMENTS FRANCE, S.A.—See KLA Tencor Corporation; *U.S. Public*, pg. 939
KLA INSTRUMENTS GMBH—See KLA Tencor Corporation; *U.S. Public*, pg. 939
KLA INSTRUMENTS ISRAEL—See KLA Tencor Corporation; *U.S. Public*, pg. 939
KLA INSTRUMENTS KOREA—See KLA Tencor Corporation; *U.S. Public*, pg. 939
KLA INSTRUMENTS LTD.—See KLA Tencor Corporation; *U.S. Public*, pg. 939
KLA INSTRUMENTS MALAYSIA—See KLA Tencor Corporation; *U.S. Public*, pg. 939
KLA INSTRUMENTS, S.—See KLA Tencor Corporation; *U.S. Public*, pg. 939
KLA INSTRUMENTS SINGAPORE, PTE LTD—See KLA Tencor Corporation; *U.S. Public*, pg. 939
KLA INSTRUMENTS TAIWAN—See KLA Tencor Corporation; *U.S. Public*, pg. 939
KLA JAPAN, LTD.—See KLA Tencor Corporation; *U.S. Public*, pg. 939

KLA TENCOR CORPORATION; *U.S. Public*, pg. 939
KLAS, INC.—See Landmark Communications, Inc.; *U.S. Private*, pg. 647
KLCC PICNIC FOOD COURT—See Scotts Holdings Limited; *Int'l*, pg. 1213
K.L.G. S.A.—See Fuchs Petrolub AG Oel + Chemie; *Int'l*, pg. 518
KLLM TRANSPORT SERVICES, INC.; *U.S. Public*, pg. 939
KLM AEROCARTO BV—See Heidemij N.V.; *Int'l*, pg. 607
KLM CITYHOPPER—See KLM Royal Dutch Airlines; *Int'l*, pg. 719
KLM/ERA HELICOPTERS—See KLM Royal Dutch Airlines; *Int'l*, pg. 719
KLM ROYAL DUTCH AIRLINES; *Int'l*, pg. 719
KLOS-FM RADIO, INC.—See The Walt Disney Company; *U.S. Public*, pg. 512
KLRT-TV—See Clear Channel Communications, Inc.; *U.S. Public*, pg. 384
KLT ENERGY SERVICES INC.—See Kansas City Power & Light Company; *U.S. Public*, pg. 943
KLT GAS, INC.—See Kansas City Power & Light Company; *U.S. Public*, pg. 943
KLT INC.—See Kansas City Power & Light Company; *U.S. Public*, pg. 943
KLT INVESTMENTS—See Kansas City Power & Light Company; *U.S. Public*, pg. 943
KLT POWER INC.—See Kansas City Power & Light Company; *U.S. Public*, pg. 943
KLT TELECOM INC.—See Kansas City Power & Light Company; *U.S. Public*, pg. 943
KM CONSTRUCTION CO.—See Kumagai Gumi Co., Ltd.; *Int'l*, pg. 764
KM DEVELOPMENT CORP.—See Zilber, Ltd.; *U.S. Private*, pg. 1206
KM-EUROPA METAL AKTIENGESELLSCHAFT; *Int'l*, pg. 719
KMA INSURANCE AGENCY, INC.—See Michigan Physicians Mutual Liability Inc.; *U.S. Private*, pg. 741
KMAZ—See Lee Enterprises, Incorporated; *U.S. Public*, pg. 983
KMBC DIVISION—See The Hearst Corporation; *U.S. Private*, pg. 516
KMBC-TV—See The Hearst Corporation; *U.S. Private*, pg. 516
KME ASIA PTE. LTD.—See KM-Europa Metal Aktiengesellschaft; *Int'l*, pg. 719
KME AUSTRIA VERTRIEBSGESELLSCHAFT M.B.H.—See KM-Europa Metal Aktiengesellschaft; *Int'l*, pg. 719
KME BELGIUM B.V.B.A.—See KM-Europa Metal Aktiengesellschaft; *Int'l*, pg. 719
KME DANMARK APS—See KM-Europa Metal Aktiengesellschaft; *Int'l*, pg. 719
KME EUROPA METAL PORTUGAL, LDA.—See KM-Europa Metal Aktiengesellschaft; *Int'l*, pg. 719
KME FRANCE S.A.R.L—See KM-Europa Metal Aktiengesellschaft; *Int'l*, pg. 719
KME HUNGARIA SZINESFEM KFT—See KM-Europa Metal Aktiengesellschaft; *Int'l*, pg. 719
KME IBERICA S.L.—See KM-Europa Metal Aktiengesellschaft; *Int'l*, pg. 719
KME IBERTUBOS S.A.—See KM-Europa Metal Aktiengesellschaft; *Int'l*, pg. 719
KME ITALIA S.R.L.—See KM-Europa Metal Aktiengesellschaft; *Int'l*, pg. 719
KME KABELMETAL AMERICA INC.—See KM-Europa Metal Aktiengesellschaft; *Int'l*, pg. 719
KME NEDERLAND BV—See KM-Europa Metal Aktiengesellschaft; *Int'l*, pg. 720
KME ROHSTOFF GMBH—See KM-Europa Metal Aktiengesellschaft; *Int'l*, pg. 719
KME SCHMOLE GMBH—See KM-Europa Metal Aktiengesellschaft; *Int'l*, pg. 719
KME (SUISSE) SA—See KM-Europa Metal Aktiengesellschaft; *Int'l*, pg. 720
KME UK LIMITED—See KM-Europa Metal Aktiengesellschaft; *Int'l*, pg. 720
KMGH-TV—See The McGraw-Hill Companies; *U.S. Public*, pg. 1070
KMIC INVESTMENT COMPANY—See Michigan Physicians Mutual Liability Inc.; *U.S. Private*, pg. 741
KMJQ-FM—See Clear Channel Communications, Inc.; *U.S. Public*, pg. 384
KMOD-FM—See Clear Channel Communications, Inc.; *U.S. Public*, pg. 384
KMOL TELEVISION, INC.—See Chris-Craft Industries, Inc.; *U.S. Public*, pg. 352
KMSP TELEVISION, INC.—See Chris-Craft Industries, Inc.; *U.S. Public*, pg. 352
KMTV-3—See Lee Enterprises, Incorporated; *U.S. Public*, pg. 983
KMVP-AM—See Pulitzer Publishing Company; *U.S. Public*, pg. 1344
KNC (KOREA NETWORK CORPORATION)—See KOHAP Group; *Int'l*, pg. 742
KNOGO CANADA—See Sentry Technology Corp.; *U.S. Public*, pg. 1458
KNP BELGIE NV—See N.V. Koninklijke KNP BT; *Int'l*, pg. 757
KNP BT NEDERLAND B.V.—See N.V. Koninklijke KNP BT; *Int'l*, pg. 756
KNP FINANCIERINGEN B.V.—See N.V. Koninklijke KNP BT; *Int'l*, pg. 756
KNP INTERNATIONAL B.V.—See N.V. Koninklijke KNP BT; *Int'l*, pg. 756
KNP LEYKAM B.V.—See N.V. Koninklijke KNP BT; *Int'l*, pg. 756
KNP MAASTRICHT B.V.—See N.V. Koninklijke KNP BT; *Int'l*, pg. 756
KNP OUD PAPIER B.V.—See N.V. Koninklijke KNP BT; *Int'l*, pg. 756
KNP PRESS PAPIER NV—See N.V. Koninklijke KNP BT; *Int'l*, pg. 757
KNP SECONDARY FIBRES B.V.—See N.V. Koninklijke KNP BT; *Int'l*, pg. 756

Company Index

KNRX-FM—See Clear Channel Communications, Inc.; U.S. Public, pg. 384

KNSD-TV—See General Electric Company; U.S. Public, pg. 712

KNSM GROUP B.V.—See Royal Nedlloyd Group N.V.; Int'l, pg. 1144

KNSM-KROONBURGH B.V.—See Royal Nedlloyd Group N.V.; Int'l, pg. 1144

KNXV-TV—See The E.W. Scripps Company; U.S. Public, pg. 1448

KO TRANSMISSION COMPANY—See Cinergy Corp.; U.S. Public, pg. 369

KOA-AM—See Jacor Communications, Inc.; U.S. Public, pg. 922

KOA HOLDINGS; U.S. Private, pg. 603

KOAS-FM—See Clear Channel Communications, Inc.; U.S. Public, pg. 384

KOAT-TV—See Pulitzer Publishing Company; U.S. Public, pg. 1344

KOB-TV, INC.—See Hubbard Broadcasting, Inc.; U.S. Private, pg. 544

KOIN-TV—See Lee Enterprises, Incorporated; U.S. Public, pg. 983

KOKI-TV—See Clear Channel Communications, Inc.; U.S. Public, pg. 384

KOLD-TV—See Raycom Media, Inc.; U.S. Private, pg. 912

KOP KOHLENSAURE-PRODUKTIONS-GESELLSCHAFT MBH—See Veba AG; Int'l, pg. 1461

KOSI-FM—See Tribune Company; U.S. Public, pg. 1636

KOTV INC.—See A.H. Belo Corporation; U.S. Public, pg. 209

KBA-MOTTER CORP.—See Publishers Equipment Corporation; U.S. Public, pg. 1341

KPEZ-FM—See Clear Channel Communications, Inc.; U.S. Public, pg. 384

KPHO-TV—See Meredith Corporation; U.S. Public, pg. 1094

KPI ELEVATORS, INC.—See Kone Corporation; Int'l, pg. 747

KPIX-TV—See CBS Corporation; U.S. Public, pg. 275

KPL—See Western Resources, Inc.; U.S. Public, pg. 1759

KPLC-TV—See Liberty Corporation; U.S. Public, pg. 992

KPMG LLP; U.S. Private, pg. 603

KPN KONINKLYKE PTT NEDERLAND NV; Int'l, pg. 720

KPNX—See Gannett Company, Inc.; U.S. Public, pg. 702

KPR—See Omnicom Group Inc.; U.S. Public, pg. 1224

KPRC-AM—See Clear Channel Communications, Inc.; U.S. Public, pg. 384

KPRC-TV—See The Washington Post Company; U.S. Public, pg. 1743

KPRR-FM—See Clear Channel Communications, Inc.; U.S. Public, pg. 384

KPTV TELEVISION, INC.—See Chris-Craft Industries, Inc.; U.S. Public, pg. 352

KQLL-AM/FM—See Clear Channel Communications, Inc.; U.S. Public, pg. 384

KQRS-AM/FM—See The Walt Disney Company; U.S. Public, pg. 512

KQRS HOLDING CORPORATION—See The Walt Disney Company; U.S. Public, pg. 512

KQRS, INC.—See The Walt Disney Company; U.S. Public, pg. 512

KQXT RADIO—See Clear Channel Communications, Inc.; U.S. Public, pg. 384

KRC (HEWITT) INC.—See Scapa Group Plc; Int'l, pg. 1202

KRC INC.—See Scapa Group Plc; Int'l, pg. 1202

KRC (NORTHERN) INC.—See Scapa Group Plc; Int'l, pg. 1202

KRC ROLLS (CANADA) INC.—See Scapa Group Plc; Int'l, pg. 1202

KRC (SOUTHERN) INC.—See Scapa Group Plc; Int'l, pg. 1202

KRFX-FM—See Jacor Communications, Inc.; U.S. Public, pg. 922

KRH ROLLS INC.—See Scapa Group Plc; Int'l, pg. 1202

KRIV—See The News Corporation Limited; Int'l, pg. 926

KRQE-TV—See Lee Enterprises, Incorporated; U.S. Public, pg. 984

KRT NEWS & INFORMATION SERVICES—See Knight-Ridder, Inc.; U.S. Public, pg. 965

K.S.—See CODELCO Chile (Corporacion Nacional Del Cobre De Chile); Int'l, pg. 303

KS KLIMA-SERVICE GMBH—See Hesta Tex AG; Int'l, pg. 617

KS OLYMPUS CO., LTD.—See Olympus Optical Co., Ltd.; Int'l, pg. 1004

KS WINSTON LTD.—See Metallgesellschaft AG; Int'l, pg. 861

KSA DICHTSYSTEME G.M.B.H & CO. KG—See Svedala Industri AB; Int'l, pg. 1323

KSAS-TV—See Clear Channel Communications, Inc.; U.S. Public, pg. 384

KSAT-TV—See The Washington Post Company; U.S. Public, pg. 1743

KSAX-TV—See Hubbard Broadcasting, Inc.; U.S. Public, pg. 544

KSB AJAX PUMPS PTY. LTD.—See KSB Aktiengesellschaft; Int'l, pg. 721

KSB AKTIENGESELLSCHAFT; Int'l, pg. 721

KSB-AMVI S.A.—See KSB Aktiengesellschaft; Int'l, pg. 721

KSB A/S, RODOVRE—See KSB Aktiengesellschaft; Int'l, pg. 721

N.V. KSB BELGIUM S.A.—See KSB Aktiengesellschaft; Int'l, pg. 721

KSB BOMBAS E VALVULAS S.A.—See KSB Aktiengesellschaft; Int'l, pg. 721

KSB BOMBAS HIDRAULICAS S.A.—See KSB Aktiengesellschaft; Int'l, pg. 721

KSB CERPADLA A ARMATURY—See KSB Aktiengesellschaft; Int'l, pg. 721

KSB CHILE S.A.—See KSB Aktiengesellschaft; Int'l, pg. 721

KSB COMPANIA SUDAMERICANA DE BOMBAS S.A.—See KSB Aktiengesellschaft; Int'l, pg. 721

KSB CONTROLADORA S.A. DE C.V.—See KSB Aktiengesellschaft; Int'l, pg. 721

KSB INC.—See KSB Aktiengesellschaft; Int'l, pg. 721

PT KSB INDONESIA—See KSB Aktiengesellschaft; Int'l, pg. 721

KSB ITALIA S.P.A.—See KSB Aktiengesellschaft; Int'l, pg. 721

KSB-JEBSEN (CHINA) LTD.—See KSB Aktiengesellschaft; Int'l, pg. 721

KSB KOREA LTD.—See KSB Aktiengesellschaft; Int'l, pg. 721

KSB LIMITED—See KSB Aktiengesellschaft; Int'l, pg. 721

KSB LTD.—See KSB Aktiengesellschaft; Int'l, pg. 721

KSB MEXICANA S.A. DE C.V.—See KSB Aktiengesellschaft; Int'l, pg. 721

KSB MORCK AB—See KSB Aktiengesellschaft; Int'l, pg. 721

KSB NEDERLANDER B.V.—See KSB Aktiengesellschaft; Int'l, pg. 721

KSB OSTERREICH GES.MBH—See KSB Aktiengesellschaft; Int'l, pg. 721

KSB POMPA—See KSB Aktiengesellschaft; Int'l, pg. 721

KSB PUMPS ARABIA LTD.—See KSB Aktiengesellschaft; Int'l, pg. 721

KSB PUMPS ASIA PACIFIC PTE. LTD.—See KSB Aktiengesellschaft; Int'l, pg. 721

KSB PUMPS CO. LTD.—See KSB Aktiengesellschaft; Int'l, pg. 721

KSB PUMPS CO. LTD., LAHORE—See KSB Aktiengesellschaft; Int'l, pg. 721

KSB PUMPS, INC.—See KSB Aktiengesellschaft; Int'l, pg. 721

KSB PUMPS LIMITED, PUNE (BOMBAY)—See KSB Aktiengesellschaft; Int'l, pg. 721

KSB PUMPS (S.A.) (PTY.) LTD.—See KSB Aktiengesellschaft; Int'l, pg. 721

KSB PUMPY + ARMATURY SPOL. SR.O.—See KSB Aktiengesellschaft; Int'l, pg. 721

KSB PUMPY I ARMATURA SP. ZO.O—See KSB Aktiengesellschaft; Int'l, pg. 721

KSB S.A.—See KSB Aktiengesellschaft; Int'l, pg. 721

KSB SERVICE GMBH—See KSB Aktiengesellschaft; Int'l, pg. 721

KSB SHANGHAI PUMP CO. LTD.—See KSB Aktiengesellschaft; Int'l, pg. 721

KSB SZIVATTYU ES ARMATURA KFT.—See KSB Aktiengesellschaft; Int'l, pg. 721

KSB TAIWAN LTD.—See KSB Aktiengesellschaft; Int'l, pg. 721

KSB TESMA AG—See KSB Aktiengesellschaft; Int'l, pg. 721

KSB VENEZOLANA C.A.—See KSB Aktiengesellschaft; Int'l, pg. 721

KSB ZURICH AG—See KSB Aktiengesellschaft; Int'l, pg. 721

KSBW, INC.—See FTSB Broadcasting; U.S. Private, pg. 389

KSDK, INC.—See Gannett Company, Inc.; U.S. Public, pg. 702

KSEV-AM—See Clear Channel Communications, Inc.; U.S. Public, pg. 384

KSFY-TV—See Raycom Media, Inc.; U.S. Private, pg. 912

KSHB-TV—See The E.W. Scripps Company; U.S. Public, pg. 1448

KSJL-TV—See Clear Channel Communications, Inc.; U.S. Public, pg. 384

KSL RADIO—See Deseret Management Corporation; U.S. Private, pg. 327

KSL-TV—See Deseret Management Corporation; U.S. Private, pg. 327

KSLA-TV—See Raycom Media, Inc.; U.S. Private, pg. 912

KSNC—See Lee Enterprises, Incorporated; U.S. Public, pg. 984

KSNT-TV—See Lee Enterprises, Incorporated; U.S. Public, pg. 983

KSNW-TV—See Lee Enterprises, Incorporated; U.S. Public, pg. 983

KSON AM & FM—See Jefferson-Pilot Corporation; U.S. Public, pg. 926

KSTP-AM, INC.—See Hubbard Broadcasting, Inc.; U.S. Private, pg. 544

KSTP-FM, INC.—See Hubbard Broadcasting, Inc.; U.S. Private, pg. 544

KSTP-TV—See Hubbard Broadcasting, Inc.; U.S. Private, pg. 544

KSWB-TV—See Tribune Company; U.S. Public, pg. 1636

KTAR-AM—See Pulitzer Publishing Company; U.S. Public, pg. 1344

KTBC—See The News Corporation Limited; Int'l, pg. 926

KTI; U.S. Public, pg. 939

KTI BELGIUM N.V.—See Mannesmann A.G.; Int'l, pg. 836

KTI FISH; U.S. Private, pg. 604

KTI GAS PROCESSORS LTD.—See Mannesmann A.G.; Int'l, pg. 837

KTI GROUP B.V.—See Mannesmann A.G.; Int'l, pg. 837

KTI, INC.; U.S. Public, pg. 939

KTKR-AM—See Clear Channel Communications, Inc.; U.S. Public, pg. 384

KTL TRUCK LINES—See Ameritruck Distribution Corporation; U.S. Private, pg. 66

KTLA, INC.—See Tribune Company; U.S. Public, pg. 1636

KTOK-AM—See Clear Channel Communications, Inc.; U.S. Public, pg. 384

KTRK TELEVISION, INC.—See The Walt Disney Company; U.S. Public, pg. 512

KTST-FM—See Clear Channel Communications, Inc.; U.S. Public, pg. 384

KTTU-TV—See Clear Channel Communications, Inc.; U.S. Public, pg. 384

KTTV—See The News Corporation Limited; Int'l, pg. 926

KTVE, INC., CHANNEL 10—See Gray Communications Systems, Inc.; U.S. Public, pg. 759

KTVI-TV, INC.—See The News Corporation Limited; Int'l, pg. 926

KTVU INC.—See Cox Enterprises, Inc.; U.S. Private, pg. 282

KTVX TELEVISION, INC.—See Chris-Craft Industries, Inc.; U.S. Public, pg. 352

K2 BIKE—See K2 Inc.; U.S. Public, pg. 940

K2 CORPORATION—See K2 Inc.; U.S. Public, pg. 940

K2 INC.; U.S. Public, pg. 940

KTXL CHANNEL 40—See Tribune Company; U.S. Public, pg. 1636

KU CAPITAL CORPORATION—See KU Energy; U.S. Public, pg. 940

KU ENERGY; U.S. Public, pg. 940

KUSA-TV—See Gannett Company, Inc.; U.S. Public, pg. 702

KUTP TELEVISION, INC.—See Chris-Craft Industries, Inc.; U.S. Public, pg. 352

KV PHARMACEUTICAL COMPANY; U.S. Public, pg. 941

KVB—See Air & Water Technologies Corporation; U.S. Public, pg. 26

KVH KREDITVERWALTUNGSGESELLSCHAFT HAMBURG MBH—See Commerzbank AG; Int'l, pg. 310

KVK (USA) INC.—See Dainippon Ink & Chemicals, Inc.; Int'l, pg. 370

KVOS TELEVISION CORP.—See The Ackerley Group; U.S. Public, pg. 16

KVP SYSTEMS, INC.—See Summa Industries; U.S. Public, pg. 1527

KVUE-TV, INC.—See Gannett Company, Inc.; U.S. Public, pg. 702

KVVU BROADCASTING CORPORATION—See Meredith Corporation; U.S. Public, pg. 1094

K.W. POWER SOURCE—See BTR plc; Int'l, pg. 127

K.W. SALES—See Klockner-Moeller AG; Int'l, pg. 736

KWB CONTROLS LTD.—See Delta plc; Int'l, pg. 391

KWE-KINTETSU WORLD EXPRESS(S)PTE LTD.—See Kintetsu World Express, Inc.; Int'l, pg. 735

KWG KUNSTSTOFFWERK GESSMANN GMBH & CO.—See DSM N.V.; Int'l, pg. 355

KWGN INC.—See Tribune Company; U.S. Public, pg. 1636

KWWL-TV—See Raycom Media, Inc.; U.S. Private, pg. 912

KXAN—See AT&T Corporation; U.S. Public, pg. 11

KXAS-TV—See AT&T Corporation; U.S. Public, pg. 11

KXTV INC.—See A.H. Belo Corporation; U.S. Public, pg. 209

KXXY-FM—See Clear Channel Communications, Inc.; U.S. Public, pg. 384

KYB CORPORATION OF AMERICA—See Kayaba Industry Co., Ltd.; Int'l, pg. 727

KYB INDUSTRIES INC.—See Kayaba Industry Co., Ltd.; Int'l, pg. 727

KYGO AM & FM/KWMX AM & FM—See Jefferson-Pilot Corporation; U.S. Public, pg. 926

KYW TV—See CBS Corporation; U.S. Public, pg. 275

KA-TEE-KA AG—See Philip Morris Companies Inc.; U.S. Public, pg. 1288

KAAGRO B.V.—See Nutricia BV; Int'l, pg. 991

KAALUNDS PRODUKTION A/S—See Henkel KGaA; Int'l, pg. 613

KAANAPALI WATER CORPORATION—See JMB Realty Corporation; U.S. Private, pg. 578

N.V. KAARDENFABRIEK "NEDERLAND"—See Carclo Engineering Group plc; Int'l, pg. 268

KABELSCHLEPP AMERICA INC.—See Kabelschlepp GmbH; Int'l, pg. 721

KABELSCHLEPP GMBH; Int'l, pg. 721

KABELWERKE REINSHAGEN GMBH—See General Motors Corporation; U.S. Public, pg. 723

KABI PHARMACIA & UPJOHN AG—See Pharmacia & Upjohn, Inc.; U.S. Public, pg. 1049

KABI PHARMACIA & UPJOHN FAR EAST—See Pharmacia & Upjohn, Inc.; U.S. Public, pg. 1049

KABI PHARMACIA & UPJOHN IRELAND LTD.—See Pharmacia & Upjohn, Inc.; U.S. Public, pg. 1049

KABI PHARMACIA & UPJOHN S.A.—See Pharmacia & Upjohn, Inc.; U.S. Public, pg. 1049

KABLE NEWS COMPANY—See AMREP Corporation; U.S. Public, pg. 105

KABUSHIKI KAISHA TMK—See Makita Corporation; Int'l, pg. 831

KABUTO DECOM INC.; Int'l, pg. 721

KABUTO INTERNATIONAL PHOENIX INC.—See Kabuto Decom Inc.; Int'l, pg. 721

KADABELL GMBH & CO. KG—See Wella Group; Int'l, pg. 1489

KADEE DELFT BV—See Esselte AB; Int'l, pg. 461

P.T. KADI INTERNATIONAL—See Kumagai Gumi Co., Ltd.; Int'l, pg. 764

THE KAEMPFER COMPANY, INVESTMENT BUILDERS; U.S. Private, pg. 604

KAEPA INC.; U.S. Private, pg. 604

AB KAFFEBONANS ROSTERI—See Nestle S.A.; Int'l, pg. 920

KAGA TOSHIBA ELECTRONICS COMPANY—See Toshiba Corporation; Int'l, pg. 1403

KAGAN LOWN—See Penobscot Shoe Company; U.S. Public, pg. 1273

MAX KAHAN INC.; U.S. Private, pg. 604

THE KAHLER HOTEL—See Sunstone Hotel Investors, Inc.; U.S. Public, pg. 1537

KAHLER INN & SUITES—See Sunstone Hotel Investors, Inc.; U.S. Public, pg. 1537

KAHLER PARK HOTEL—See Sunstone Hotel Investors, Inc.; U.S. Public, pg. 1537

KAHLER PLAZA HOTEL—See Sunstone Hotel Investors, Inc.; U.S. Public, pg. 1537

ALBERT KAHN ASSOCIATES, INC.; U.S. Private, pg. 604

THE ALBERT KAHN COLLABORATIVE, INC.—See Albert Kahn Associates, Inc.; U.S. Private, pg. 604

M.B. KAHN CONSTRUCTION CO., INC.; U.S. Private, pg. 604

KAHULUI TRUCKING & STORAGE, INC.—See Alexander & Baldwin, Inc.; U.S. Public, pg. 39

KAIBAB INDUSTRIES; *U.S. Private*, pg. 605
KAIBAB METALS, INC.—See Kaibab Industries; *U.S. Private*, pg. 605
KAISER AEROSPACE & ELECTRONICS CORP.; *U.S. Private*, pg. 605
KAISER ALUMINUM & CHEMICAL CORPORATION—See Maxxam Inc.; *U.S. Public*, pg. 1062
KAISER ALUMINUM & CHEMICAL OF CANADA LIMITED—See Maxxam Inc.; *U.S. Public*, pg. 1062
KAISER ALUMINUM CORPORATION—See Maxxam Inc.; *U.S. Public*, pg. 1062
KAISER CEMENT CORPORATION—See Hanson PLC; *Int'l*, pg. 593
KAISER EAGLE MOUNTAIN, INC.—See Kaiser Ventures, Inc.; *U.S. Public*, pg. 941
KAISER ELECTRO OPTICS—See Kaiser Aerospace & Electronics Corp.; *U.S. Private*, pg. 605
KAISER ELECTRONICS—See Kaiser Aerospace & Electronics Corp.; *U.S. Private*, pg. 605
KAISER INTERNATIONAL SERVICES CORP.—See Hanson PLC; *Int'l*, pg. 593
KAISER JAMAICA BAUXITE CO.—See Maxxam Inc.; *U.S. Public*, pg. 1062
KAISER PACIFIC PROPERTIES CORP.—See Hanson PLC; *Int'l*, pg. 593
KAISER PERMANENTE; *U.S. Private*, pg. 605
KAISER PERMANENTE, CALIFORNIA DIVISION—See Kaiser Permanente; *U.S. Private*, pg. 605
KAISER PERMANENTE, CENTRAL EAST DIVISION—See Kaiser Permanente; *U.S. Private*, pg. 605
KAISER PERMANENTE, HAWAII DIVISION—See Kaiser Permanente; *U.S. Private*, pg. 605
KAISER PERMANENTE, NORTHEAST DIVISION—See Kaiser Permanente; *U.S. Private*, pg. 605
KAISER PERMANENTE, NORTHWEST DIVISION—See Kaiser Permanente; *U.S. Private*, pg. 605
KAISER PERMANENTE, ROCKY MOUNTAIN DIVISION—See Kaiser Permanente; *U.S. Private*, pg. 605
KAISER PERMANENTE, SOUTHEAST DIVISION—See Kaiser Permanente; *U.S. Private*, pg. 605
KAISER PERMANENTE, SOUTHWEST DIVISION—See Kaiser Permanente; *U.S. Private*, pg. 605
KAISER RECYCLING CORP.—See Kaiser Ventures, Inc.; *U.S. Public*, pg. 941
KAISER STEEL CORPORATION—See Kaiser Ventures, Inc.; *U.S. Public*, pg. 941
KAISER STEEL LAND DEVELOPMENT, INC.—See Kaiser Ventures, Inc.; *U.S. Public*, pg. 941
KAISER VENTURES, INC.; *U.S. Public*, pg. 941
KAISER WASTE TREATMENT, INC.—See Kaiser Ventures, Inc.; *U.S. Public*, pg. 941
KAISER WHOLESALE, INC.; *U.S. Private*, pg. 605
KAISER'S KAFFEE-GESCHAEFT AG—See Tengelmann Warenhandelsgesellschaft; *Int'l*, pg. 1375
KAIZUKA SANYO INDUSTRIES CO., LTD.—See Sanyo Electric Co., Ltd.; *Int'l*, pg. 1191
AB KAJ MANDORF—See AB Industrivarden; *Int'l*, pg. 678
KAJIMA CORPORATION; *Int'l*, pg. 721
KAJIMA DEVELOPMENT CORP.—See Kajima Corporation; *Int'l*, pg. 722
KAJIMA ENGINEERING AND CONSTRUCTION INC.—See Kajima Corporation; *Int'l*, pg. 722
KAJIMA INTERNATIONAL, INC.—See Kajima Corporation; *Int'l*, pg. 722
KAJIMA U.S.A., INC.—See Kajima Corporation; *Int'l*, pg. 722
KAL GRAFX—See The Excellence Group; *U.S. Private*, pg. 387
KAL GRAFX IMAGING—See The Excellence Group; *U.S. Private*, pg. 387
KAL KAN FOODS, INC.—See Mars, Incorporated; *U.S. Private*, pg. 707
KALAG LAGERHAUS-UND SPEDITIONS GES. MBH—See The Peninsular and Oriental Steam Navigation Company; *Int'l*, pg. 1033
KALAMAZOO HOLDINGS, INC.; *U.S. Private*, pg. 606
KALAMAZOO SCRAP & PROCESSING—See Sturgis Iron & Metal Company, Inc.; *U.S. Private*, pg. 1048
KALAS MANUFACTURING, INC.; *U.S. Private*, pg. 606
KALDNES HEAVY LIFT TRUCKS—See Norsk Vekst ASA; *Int'l*, pg. 965
KALDNES HEAVY LIFT TRUCKS A/S—See Norsk Vekst ASA; *Int'l*, pg. 965
KALDNES INDUSTRI A/S—See Norsk Vekst ASA; *Int'l*, pg. 965
KALDNES MILJOTEKNOLOGI A/S—See Norsk Vekst ASA; *Int'l*, pg. 965
KALI-CHEMIE AKTIENGESELLSCHAFT—See Solvay S.A.; *Int'l*, pg. 1278
KALI-CHEMIE IBERIA, S.A.—See Solvay S.A.; *Int'l*, pg. 1279
KALI-CHEMIE PHARMA GESELLSCHAFT MBH—See Solvay S.A.; *Int'l*, pg. 1279
KALI-CHEMIE PHARMA GMBH—See Solvay S.A.; *Int'l*, pg. 1278
KALI-DUPHAR K.K.—See Solvay S.A.; *Int'l*, pg. 1279
KALI-IMPORTEN A/S—See BASF AG; *Int'l*, pg. 108
KALI UND SALZ BETEILIGUNGS AG—See BASF AG; *Int'l*, pg. 104
KALI UND SALZ CONSULTING GMBH—See BASF AG; *Int'l*, pg. 104
KALI UND SALZ GMBH—See BASF AG; *Int'l*, pg. 104
KALI UND SALZ POLSKA SP.Z.O.O.—See BASF AG; *Int'l*, pg. 108
KALIFARMA S.A.—See Solvay S.A.; *Int'l*, pg. 1279
KALIN ENTERPRISES, INC.; *U.S. Private*, pg. 606
KALIN FINANCIAL DIVISION—See Kalin Enterprises, Inc.; *U.S. Private*, pg. 606
KALITTA FLYING SERVICE—See American International Airways; *U.S. Private*, pg. 57
KALIUM CHEMICALS, LTD.—See IMC Global; *U.S. Public*, pg. 856
KALKZANDSTEENFABRIEK HOOGDONK B.V.—See Scancem AB; *Int'l*, pg. 1199

KALKZANDSTEENFABRIEK RIJSBERGEN B.V.—See Scancem AB; *Int'l*, pg. 1199
KALLISTA, INC.—See Kohler Company; *U.S. Private*, pg. 630
KALMAR INC.—See Trelleborg AB; *Int'l*, pg. 1421
KALMAR INDUSTRIES AB—See Trelleborg AB; *Int'l*, pg. 1420
KALMAR KOCKUM A/S—See Trelleborg AB; *Int'l*, pg. 1421
KALMAR KOCKUM FRANCE SA—See Trelleborg AB; *Int'l*, pg. 1421
KALMAR KOCKUM GMBH—See Trelleborg AB; *Int'l*, pg. 1421
KALMAR KOCKUM LTD.—See Trelleborg AB; *Int'l*, pg. 1421
KALMAR LAGAB AB—See Trelleborg AB; *Int'l*, pg. 1421
OY KALMAR LMV—See Trelleborg AB; *Int'l*, pg. 1421
KALMAR LMV AB—See Trelleborg AB; *Int'l*, pg. 1421
KALMAR LMV A/S—See Trelleborg AB; *Int'l*, pg. 1421
KALMAR LMV EAST ASIA PTE. LTD.—See Trelleborg AB; *Int'l*, pg. 1421
KALMAR NOHAB AB—See Trelleborg AB; *Int'l*, pg. 1421
KALMAR VERKSTAD AB—See Trelleborg AB; *Int'l*, pg. 1421
KALMBACH PUBLISHING CO.; *U.S. Private*, pg. 606
KALSEC, INC.—See Kalamazoo Holdings, Inc.; *U.S. Private*, pg. 606
KALSO S.A.—See UPM-Kymmene Corporation; *Int'l*, pg. 1428
KALSO-TEOLLISUUS OY—See UPM-Kymmene Corporation; *Int'l*, pg. 1428
KALYANI SHARP INDIA LIMITED—See Sharp Corporation; *Int'l*, pg. 1229
KAMAN AEROSPACE CORP.—See Kaman Corporation; *U.S. Public*, pg. 942
KAMAN AEROSPACE CORPORATION-GILMAN PLANT—See Kaman Corporation; *U.S. Public*, pg. 942
KAMAN AEROSPACE CORPORATION-MOOSUP PLANT—See Kaman Corporation; *U.S. Public*, pg. 942
KAMAN CORPORATION; *U.S. Public*, pg. 942
KAMAN DIVERSIFIED TECHNOLOGIES CORP.—See Kaman Corporation; *U.S. Public*, pg. 942
KAMAN ELECTROMAGNETICS CORP.—See Kaman Corporation; *U.S. Public*, pg. 942
KAMAN INDUSTRIAL TECHNOLOGIES CORP.—See Kaman Corporation; *U.S. Public*, pg. 942
KAMAN INSTRUMENTATION CORP.—See Kaman Corporation; *U.S. Public*, pg. 942
KAMAN MUSIC CORP.—See Kaman Corporation; *U.S. Public*, pg. 942
KAMAN MUSIC INTERNATIONAL—See Kaman Corporation; *U.S. Public*, pg. 942
KAMAN SCIENCES CORP.—See Kaman Corporation; *U.S. Public*, pg. 942
KAMATICS CORP.—See Kaman Corporation; *U.S. Public*, pg. 942
KAMAX-G.B. DUPONT L.P.; *U.S. Private*, pg. 606
KAMELEON BEHEER IV—See Royal Begemann Group; *Int'l*, pg. 1133
M. KAMENSTEIN, INC.; *U.S. Private*, pg. 606
KAMEWA AB—See Vickers PLC; *Int'l*, pg. 1468
KAMFAB AB—See Kvaerner a.s.a.; *Int'l*, pg. 771
KAMI SA—See LVMH Moet Hennessy Louis Vuitton; *Int'l*, pg. 781
KAMIK—See Genfoot Inc.; *Int'l*, pg. 549
H. R. KAMINSKY & SONS, INC.; *U.S. Private*, pg. 606
KAMINSOS OBNOVA KAMINU SPOL. S R.O.—See Redland PLC; *Int'l*, pg. 1092
THE KAMLOOPS DAILY NEWS—See Hollinger Inc.; *Int'l*, pg. 631
KAMMER VANNES—See Flowserve Corporation; *U.S. Public*, pg. 658
KAMMER VANNES S.A.R.L.—See Flowserve Corporation; *U.S. Public*, pg. 659
KAMMER VENTILE GMBH—See Flowserve Corporation; *U.S. Public*, pg. 659
KAMMERER GMBH—See A. Ahlstrom Corporation; *Int'l*, pg. 35
MAX KAMMERER GMBH—See Mannesmann A.G.; *Int'l*, pg. 839
KAMPGROUNDS OF AMERICA (CANADA) LTD.—See KOA Holdings; *U.S. Private*, pg. 603
KAMRO CHAMPION LIGHTING PRODUCTS INC.—See Kaufel Group Ltd.; *Int'l*, pg. 725
KAMRO LIGHTING PRODUCTS LTD.—See Kaufel Group Ltd.; *Int'l*, pg. 725
KAMTECH INC.—See A. Ahlstrom Corporation; *Int'l*, pg. 34
KAMYN INDUSTRIES (TANZANIA) LTD.—See Nissho Iwai Corporation; *Int'l*, pg. 948
KAMYR AB—See Kvaerner a.s.a.; *Int'l*, pg. 771
KAMYR CANADA INC.—See A. Ahlstrom Corporation; *Int'l*, pg. 35
KAMYR CHILE S A C EL—See Kvaerner a.s.a.; *Int'l*, pg. 771
KAMYR CONSTRUCTION—See A. Ahlstrom Corporation; *Int'l*, pg. 35
KAMYR DO BRASIL TECNICA DE CELULOSE LTDA.—See Kvaerner a.s.a.; *Int'l*, pg. 771
KAMYR ENGINEERING AB—See Kvaerner a.s.a.; *Int'l*, pg. 771
KAMYR ENTERPRISES INC.—See A. Ahlstrom Corporation; *Int'l*, pg. 35
KAMYR HOLDING AG—See Kvaerner a.s.a.; *Int'l*, pg. 770
KAMYR KK—See Kvaerner a.s.a.; *Int'l*, pg. 771
KAMYR OY—See Kvaerner a.s.a.; *Int'l*, pg. 771
KAMYR PTY LTD.—See Kvaerner a.s.a.; *Int'l*, pg. 771
KAMYR S.A.—See Kvaerner a.s.a.; *Int'l*, pg. 771
KANAFLEX DO BRASIL INDUSTRIA DE PLASTICOS LTDA.—See Nissho Iwai Corporation; *Int'l*, pg. 948
KANAGAWA CATERPILLAR MITSUBISHI CONSTRUCTION EQUIPMENT SALES, LTD.—See Caterpillar Inc.; *U.S. Public*, pg. 317
KANAGAWA TOYOTA MOTOR SALES CO., LTD.—See Toyota Motor Corporation; *Int'l*, pg. 1412

KANAGAWA WORKS—See Hitachi Zosen Corporation; *Int'l*, pg. 623
KANAL-MULLER-GRUPPE—See Harpen AG; *Int'l*, pg. 597
KANCOR FLAVOURS AND EXTRACTS LIMITED—See McCormick & Company, Incorporated; *U.S. Public*, pg. 1067
KANDELININ SEURAAJAT OY—See Outokumpu Oyj; *Int'l*, pg. 1018
AS KANDUR—See Kone Corporation; *Int'l*, pg. 748
KANE-MILLER CORP.; *U.S. Private*, pg. 607
SAM KANE BEEF PROCESSORS, INC.; *U.S. Private*, pg. 607
KANEB PIPE LINE CO.—See Kaneb Services, Inc.; *U.S. Public*, pg. 942
KANEB PIPE LINE PARTNERS, L.P.—See Kaneb Services, Inc.; *U.S. Public*, pg. 942
KANEB SERVICES, INC.; *U.S. Public*, pg. 942
KANEBO BELL TOUCH CO., LTD.—See Kanebo, Ltd.; *Int'l*, pg. 722
KANEBO C FEST MOII, LTD.—See Kanebo, Ltd.; *Int'l*, pg. 722
KANEBO COSMETICS—See Kanebo, Ltd.; *Int'l*, pg. 722
KANEBO COSMETICS OF HAWAII, INC.—See Kanebo, Ltd.; *Int'l*, pg. 722
KANEBO COSMETTE CO., LTD.—See Kanebo, Ltd.; *Int'l*, pg. 722
KANEBO COSMILLION, LTD.—See Kanebo, Ltd.; *Int'l*, pg. 722
KANEBO ELECTRONICS CO., LTD.—See Kanebo, Ltd.; *Int'l*, pg. 722
KANEBO ELEGANCE FAMILY, LTD.—See Kanebo, Ltd.; *Int'l*, pg. 722
KANEBO FOODS CO., LTD.—See Kanebo, Ltd.; *Int'l*, pg. 722
KANEBO GOSHEN SPINNING CORPORATION, LTD.—See Kanebo, Ltd.; *Int'l*, pg. 722
KANEBO HOME PRODUCTS CO., LTD.—See Kanebo, Ltd.; *Int'l*, pg. 722
KANEBO IIYAMA, LTD.—See Kanebo, Ltd.; *Int'l*, pg. 722
KANEBO KIKUCHI ELECTRONICS—See Kanebo, Ltd.; *Int'l*, pg. 722
KANEBO KUJI, LTD.—See Kanebo, Ltd.; *Int'l*, pg. 722
KANEBO, LTD.; *Int'l*, pg. 722
P.T. KANEBO-NISSHO IWAI-SAHABAT TEXTILE INDUSTRIES—See Nissho Iwai Corporation; *Int'l*, pg. 948
KANEBO PHARMACEUTICALS CO., LTD.—See Kanebo, Ltd.; *Int'l*, pg. 722
KANEBO SILK ELEGANCE, LTD.—See Kanebo, Ltd.; *Int'l*, pg. 722
KANEBO SOAP MANUFACTURING CO., LTD.—See Kanebo, Ltd.; *Int'l*, pg. 722
KANEBO SPINNING CORPORATION—See Kanebo, Ltd.; *Int'l*, pg. 722
KANEBO STOCKING, LTD.—See Kanebo, Ltd.; *Int'l*, pg. 722
KANEBO SYNTHETICS CO., LTD.—See Kanebo, Ltd.; *Int'l*, pg. 722
KANEBO TEXTILES CO., LTD.—See Kanebo, Ltd.; *Int'l*, pg. 722
KANEGASAKI PLANT—See Shionogi & Co., Ltd.; *Int'l*, pg. 1235
KANELK TRANSMISSION CO. LTD.—See Transalta Corporation; *Int'l*, pg. 1416
KANEMATSU CORPORATION; *Int'l*, pg. 722
KANEMATSU CORPORATION—See Kanematsu Corporation; *Int'l*, pg. 722
KANG NAM CHEMICAL CO., LTD.—See Dainippon Ink & Chemicals, Inc.; *Int'l*, pg. 372
P.T. KANGAR CONSOLIDATED INDUSTRIES—See BTR plc; *Int'l*, pg. 129
KANKAANPAA WORKS—See Rautaruukki Oy; *Int'l*, pg. 1088
KANKAKEE, IL STEEL DIVISION—See Birmingham Steel Corporation; *U.S. Public*, pg. 232
KANNAPOLIS REST HOME, INC.—See Vencor, Inc.; *U.S. Public*, pg. 1714
THE KANOO GROUP COMMERCIAL DIVISION ABU DHABI—See BASF AG; *Int'l*, pg. 108
KANOWNA BELLE GOLD MINES—See North Limited; *Int'l*, pg. 967
KANSA CORPORATION—See Baldwin Technology Company, Inc.; *U.S. Public*, pg. 170
KANSAI CATERPILLAR MITSUBISHI CONSTRUCTION EQUIPMENT SALES, LTD.—See Caterpillar Inc.; *U.S. Public*, pg. 317
KANSAI CENTRAL KITCHEN—See Skylark Co., Ltd.; *Int'l*, pg. 1262
KANSAI CITIZEN CORPORATION—See Citizen Watch Company, Ltd.; *Int'l*, pg. 294
THE KANSAI ELECTRIC POWER CO., INC.; *Int'l*, pg. 722
THE KANSAI ELECTRIC POWER CO. - NEW YORK OFFICE—See The Kansai Electric Power Co., Inc.; *Int'l*, pg. 723
THE KANSAI ELECTRIC POWER CO. - PARIS OFFICE—See The Kansai Electric Power Co., Inc.; *Int'l*, pg. 723
THE KANSAI ELECTRIC POWER CO. - WASHINGTON OFFICE—See The Kansai Electric Power Co., Inc.; *Int'l*, pg. 723
KANSAI PAINT (AMERICA), INC.—See Kansai Paint Co., Ltd.; *Int'l*, pg. 723
KANSAI PAINT CO., LTD.; *Int'l*, pg. 723
KANSAI PAINT EUROPE LIMITED—See Kansai Paint Co., Ltd.; *Int'l*, pg. 723
KANSAI PAINT H.K., LTD.—See Kansai Paint Co., Ltd.; *Int'l*, pg. 723
KANSAI PAINT JAKARTA OFFICE—See Kansai Paint Co., Ltd.; *Int'l*, pg. 723
KANSAI PAINTS (SINGAPORE) PTE. LTD.—See Kansai Paint Co., Ltd.; *Int'l*, pg. 723
KANSAS CITY AUTO AUCTION—See Cox Enterprises, Inc.; *U.S. Private*, pg. 282

KANSAS CITY CHIEFS FOOTBALL CLUB, INC.; *U.S. Private*, pg. 607
KANSAS CITY FIRE AND MARINE INSURANCE CO.—See Loews Corporation; *U.S. Public*, pg. 1011
KANSAS CITY LABORATORY—See Pace Analytical Services; *U.S. Private*, pg. 829
KANSAS CITY LIFE INSURANCE CO.; *U.S. Public*, pg. 942
KANSAS CITY POWER & LIGHT COMPANY; *U.S. Public*, pg. 943
KANSAS CITY RECYCLING CENTER—See Republic Group Incorporated; *U.S. Public*, pg. 1378
KANSAS CITY ROYALS RADIO NETWORK—See Shivers Trading & Operating Co.; *U.S. Private*, pg. 995
KANSAS CITY SOUTHERN INDUSTRIES, INC.; *U.S. Public*, pg. 943
THE KANSAS CITY SOUTHERN RAILWAY CO.—See Kansas City Southern Industries, Inc.; *U.S. Public*, pg. 944
THE KANSAS CITY STAR COMPANY—See Knight-Ridder, Inc.; *U.S. Public*, pg. 964
KANSAS CITY TERMINAL RAILWAY CO.—See Union Pacific Corporation; *U.S. Public*, pg. 1668
KANSAS FIRE & CASUALTY CO.—See Berkshire Hathaway Inc.; *U.S. Public*, pg. 221
KANSAS GAS SERVICE—See ONEOK Inc.; *U.S. Public*, pg. 1226
KANSAS GAS SUPPLY—See NGC Corporation; *U.S. Public*, pg. 1146
KANSAS INFORMATION NETWORK—See Shivers Trading & Operating Co.; *U.S. Private*, pg. 995
KANSAS PUBLIC SERVICE—See UtiliCorp United Inc.; *U.S. Public*, pg. 1701
KANSEI CORP.—See Nissan Motor Co., Ltd.; *Int'l*, pg. 944
KANTEL COMMUNICATIONS, INC.—See Peoples Telephone Company, Inc.; *U.S. Public*, pg. 1275
KANTERBRAU S.A.—See Danone Group; *Int'l*, pg. 381
KANTHAL AB; *Int'l*, pg. 723
KANTHAL AUSTRALIA PTY. LIMITED—See Kanthal AB; *Int'l*, pg. 724
KANTHAL BESIKATAS—See Kanthal AB; *Int'l*, pg. 723
KANTHAL BRAZIL LTDA.—See Kanthal AB; *Int'l*, pg. 724
KANTHAL BULGARIA—See Kanthal AB; *Int'l*, pg. 723
THE KANTHAL CORPORATION—See Kanthal AB; *Int'l*, pg. 723
KANTHAL ELECTROHEAT (HK) LTD.—See Kanthal AB; *Int'l*, pg. 724
KANTHAL ELECTROHEAT (SEA) PTE. LTD.—See Kanthal AB; *Int'l*, pg. 724
KANTHAL GMBH—See Kanthal AB; *Int'l*, pg. 724
KANTHAL INDIA LTD.—See Kanthal AB; *Int'l*, pg. 724
KANTHAL KK—See Kanthal AB; *Int'l*, pg. 724
KANTHAL KOREA LTD.—See Kanthal AB; *Int'l*, pg. 724
KANTHAL LTD.—See Kanthal AB; *Int'l*, pg. 724
KANTHAL NORDEN AB—See Kanthal AB; *Int'l*, pg. 723
KANTHAL PRAGUE—See Kanthal AB; *Int'l*, pg. 723
KANTHAL SPAIN S.A.—See Kanthal AB; *Int'l*, pg. 724
KANTHAL TRADING AUSTRALASIA LTD.—See Kanthal AB; *Int'l*, pg. 724
KANTHAL WARSAW—See Kanthal AB; *Int'l*, pg. 723
KANTO AUTO WORKS, LTD.—See Toyota Motor Corporation; *Int'l*, pg. 1412
KANTO MALTING CO., LTD.—See Suntory Ltd.; *Int'l*, pg. 1321
KANZAKI SPECIALTY PAPERS INC.—See Oji Paper Co., Ltd.; *Int'l*, pg. 998
KANZAKIGAWA LABORATORIES—See Shionogi & Co., Ltd.; *Int'l*, pg. 1235
KAOHSI CORPORATION—See Shimizu Corporation; *Int'l*, pg. 1233
KAOHSIUNG MONOMER CO LTD—See Imperial Chemical Industries PLC; *Int'l*, pg. 665
KAOHSIUNG REFINERY—See Chinese Petroleum Corporation; *Int'l*, pg. 286
KAOLIN-UND TONWERKE SEILITZ-LOTHAIN GMBH—See Watts Blake Bearne & Co. Plc; *Int'l*, pg. 1488
KAPA GMBH LEICHTSOFFTECHNIK—See Alusuisse-Lonza Holding Ltd.; *Int'l*, pg. 68
KAPALUA LAND CO., LTD.—See Maui Land & Pineapple Co., Inc.; *U.S. Public*, pg. 1060
KAPLAN EDUCATIONAL CENTERS LTD.—See The Washington Post Company; *U.S. Public*, pg. 1743
KAPLAN ELECTRONICS; *U.S. Private*, pg. 607
P.T. KAPO KIMIA KENCANA(CIBA DISTRIBUTOR)—See Novartis AG; *Int'l*, pg. 983
KAPPA B.V.—See N.V. Koninklijke KNP BT; *Int'l*, pg. 756
KAPPA ESKABOARD B.V.—See N.V. Koninklijke KNP BT; *Int'l*, pg. 756
KAPPA GOLFKARTON B.V.—See N.V. Koninklijke KNP BT; *Int'l*, pg. 756
KAPPA KARTON VERTRIEBS GMBH—See N.V. Koninklijke KNP BT; *Int'l*, pg. 757
KAPPA SCHOLTEN B.V.—See N.V. Koninklijke KNP BT; *Int'l*, pg. 756
KAPPAHL AB—See KF/Konsum Coop Group; *Int'l*, pg. 718
KAPPLER EUROPE, LTD.—See Kappler Safety Group, Inc.; *U.S. Private*, pg. 607
KAPPLER SAFETY GROUP, INC.; *U.S. Private*, pg. 607
KAPPLER USA—See Kappler Safety Group, Inc.; *U.S. Private*, pg. 607
KARA FOODS—See Northern Foods plc; *Int'l*, pg. 968
KARAHM COMPANY LIMITED—See Morgan Crucible Co. Plc; *Int'l*, pg. 891
KARAIR OY—See FinnAir Oy; *Int'l*, pg. 485
KARAKAS, VANSICKLE, OUELLETTE ADVERTISING & PUBLIC RELATIONS; *U.S. Private*, pg. 607
KARAKAS, VANSICKLE, OUELLETTE ADVERTISING & PUBLIC RELATIONS—See Karakas, VanSickle, Ouellette Advertising & Public Relations; *U.S. Private*, pg. 607
KARAMURSEL MILL—See Fort James Corporation; *U.S. Public*, pg. 673
KARAS TRUCKING CO., INC.—See Browning-Ferris Industries, Inc.; *U.S. Public*, pg. 264

KARASTAN—See Mohawk Industries, Inc.; *U.S. Public*, pg. 1121
KARASTAN BIGELOW COMMERCIAL—See Mohawk Industries, Inc.; *U.S. Public*, pg. 1121
KARBON GRAFIT SANAYI A.S.—See Morgan Crucible Co. Plc; *Int'l*, pg. 891
CARL KARCHER ENTERPRISES, INC.—See CKE Restaurants Inc.; *U.S. Public*, pg. 278
KARCHMER IRON & METAL COMPANY—See Commercial Metals Company; *U.S. Public*, pg. 413
KARELIA PROCUREMENT AREA—See Enso Oyj; *Int'l*, pg. 455
KARELIA TOBACCO COMPANY INC.; *Int'l*, pg. 724
THE KARGES FURNITURE COMPANY INC.; *U.S. Private*, pg. 607
KA-RI-FIX TRANSPORTBAND-TECHNIK GMBH—See Continental AG; *Int'l*, pg. 327
OY KARL BEUS AB—See Berner Ltd.; *Int'l*, pg. 189
KARL GEORG BAHNTECHNIK G.M.B.H.—See Varlen Corporation; *Int'l*, pg. 1711
KARL-LUTZ AMMANN, REPRESENTANTE DEL COMMERZBANK AG—See Commerzbank AG; *Int'l*, pg. 312
KARL VIEH GMBH—See PMC, Inc.; *U.S. Private*, pg. 827
KARLSHAMNS AB—See KF/Konsum Coop Group; *Int'l*, pg. 718
KARLSKRONAVARVET AB—See Celsius AB; *Int'l*, pg. 277
AB H. KARLSTROM—See Axel Johnson AB; *Int'l*, pg. 709
KARMELKORN SHOPPES—See Berkshire Hathaway Inc.; *U.S. Public*, pg. 220
KARNAK CORPORATION; *U.S. Private*, pg. 607
KARNEVAL COSMETIC CO., LTD.—See Wella Group; *Int'l*, pg. 1490
KARNU HOLDING LTD.—See ABB Asea Brown Boveri (Holding) Ltd.; *Int'l*, pg. 8
KAROSSERIEWERK PORSCHE GMBH—See Porsche AG; *Int'l*, pg. 1063
AB KAROSSERITILLBEHOR—See Axel Johnson AB; *Int'l*, pg. 709
L. KARP & SONS, INC.; *U.S. Private*, pg. 607
KARP'S BAKERY SUPPLY; *U.S. Private*, pg. 608
KARRENA GMBH—See Deutsche Babcock AG; *Int'l*, pg. 398
KARSDORFER ZEMENT BETEILIGUNGS GMBH—See Lafarge S.A.; *Int'l*, pg. 789
KARSKAR ENERGI—See Korsnas AB; *Int'l*, pg. 759
KARSTADT AKTIENGESELLSCHAFT; *Int'l*, pg. 724
KARSTADT HEIDELOH GMBH—See Karstadt Aktiengesellschaft; *Int'l*, pg. 724
KARSTADT UNTERSTUTZUNGSFONDS GMBH—See Karstadt Aktiengesellschaft; *Int'l*, pg. 724
KARSTADT VERSICHERUNGS-VERMITTLUNG GMBH—See Karstadt Aktiengesellschaft; *Int'l*, pg. 724
KARSTEN ENGINEERING CORP.—See Karsten Manufacturing Corporation; *U.S. Private*, pg. 608
KARSTEN MANUFACTURING CORPORATION; *U.S. Private*, pg. 608
KARTONFABRIEK "DE EENDRACHT" N.V.—See BPB Industries PLC; *Int'l*, pg. 123
KARTS INTERNATIONAL INC.; *U.S. Public*, pg. 944
KARWOSKI & COURAGE—See Martin/Williams Advertising Inc.; *U.S. Private*, pg. 710
P.T. KARYA YANSANTARA CAKTI—See Charter plc; *Int'l*, pg. 283
KASAI PAINT CO., LTD.—See Kansai Paint Co., Ltd.; *Int'l*, pg. 723
M.W. KASCH COMPANY; *U.S. Private*, pg. 608
KASCO CORPORATION—See Bairnco Corporation; *U.S. Public*, pg. 165
KASDORF S.A.—See Nutricia BV; *Int'l*, pg. 991
KASEI VERBATIM CORPORATION—See Eastman Kodak Company; *U.S. Public*, pg. 552
KASET INTERNATIONAL—See The Times Mirror Company; *U.S. Public*, pg. 1617
KASH N KARRY FOOD STORES, INC.—See Etablissements Delhaize Freres Et Cie "Le Lion" S.A.; *Int'l*, pg. 463
KASHIMA FACTORY—See Tokuyama Corporation; *Int'l*, pg. 1394
KASHIMA SANKEN CO., LTD.—See Sanken Electric Co., Ltd.; *Int'l*, pg. 1188
KASLE OF CANADA LTD—See Kasle Steel Corporation; *U.S. Private*, pg. 608
KASLE STEEL CORPORATION; *U.S. Private*, pg. 608
KASPAR WIRE WORKS, INC.; *U.S. Private*, pg. 608
KASPER MACHINE COMPANY; *U.S. Private*, pg. 608
KASS HOMES LIMITED—See British Building & Engineering Appliances Plc; *Int'l*, pg. 219
KASSBOHRER NORTH AMERICA—See Daimler-Benz Aktiengesellschaft; *Int'l*, pg. 368
KASSEM DARWISH FAKHROO & SONS—See Telefonaktiebolaget LM Ericsson; *Int'l*, pg. 1368
KASSER/LAIRD DISTILLING CO.—See Laird & Company; *U.S. Private*, pg. 643
KASSON & KELLER—See Keymark Corporation; *U.S. Private*, pg. 618
KASTLE SYSTEMS LLC; *U.S. Private*, pg. 608
KASUMI CO., LTD.; *Int'l*, pg. 724
KATALYSATORENWERKE HULS GMBH—See Veba AG; *Int'l*, pg. 1454
KATHABAR INCORPORATED; *U.S. Private*, pg. 609
KATHABAR SYSTEMS EUROPE, ZOETERMEER—See Internatio-Muller N.V.; *Int'l*, pg. 681
KATHARINE GIBBS SCHOOL, INC.—See Career Education Corporation; *U.S. Public*, pg. 209
KATIN—See K2 Inc.; *U.S. Public*, pg. 940
OY KATIONI AB—See Raisio Group; *Int'l*, pg. 1085
KATIVO CHEMICAL INDUSTRIES, S.A.—See H.B. Fuller Company; *U.S. Public*, pg. 687
KATIVO DE GUATEMALA, S.A.—See H.B. Fuller Company; *U.S. Public*, pg. 687
KATIVO DE HONDURAS, S.A.—See H.B. Fuller Company; *U.S. Public*, pg. 687

KATIVO DE PANAMA S.A.—See H.B. Fuller Company; *U.S. Public*, pg. 687
KATIVO EL SALVADOR, S.A.—See H.B. Fuller Company; *U.S. Public*, pg. 687
KATIVO NICARAGUA, S.A.—See H.B. Fuller Company; *U.S. Public*, pg. 687
KATO CRANES—See Svedala Industri AB; *Int'l*, pg. 1325
KATO CRANES (UK) LTD.—See Trelleborg AB; *Int'l*, pg. 1420
KATO ENGINEERING DIV.—See Rockwell International Corporation; *U.S. Public*, pg. 1398
KATO KRANER NORGE A/S—See Trelleborg AB; *Int'l*, pg. 1420
KATOEN NATIE NV; *Int'l*, pg. 724
PT KATSUSHIRO INDONESIA—See Komatsu Ltd.; *Int'l*, pg. 745
KATSUSHIRO ROME CORPORATION—See Komatsu Ltd.; *Int'l*, pg. 744
KATV, LLC—See Perpetual Corporation; *U.S. Private*, pg. 854
KATY INDUSTRIES, INC.; *U.S. Public*, pg. 944
KATZ AMERICAN TELEVISION—See Chancellor Media Corporation; *U.S. Public*, pg. 335
KATZ CONTINENTAL TELEVISION—See Chancellor Media Corporation; *U.S. Public*, pg. 335
KATZ DIMENSIONS—See Chancellor Media Corporation; *U.S. Public*, pg. 335
KATZ HISPANIC MEDIA—See Chancellor Media Corporation; *U.S. Public*, pg. 335
KATZ MEDIA GROUP, INC.—See Chancellor Media Corporation; *U.S. Public*, pg. 335
KATZ MILLENNIUM—See Chancellor Media Corporation; *U.S. Public*, pg. 335
KATZ NATIONAL TELEVISION—See Chancellor Media Corporation; *U.S. Public*, pg. 335
KATZ RADIO—See Chancellor Media Corporation; *U.S. Public*, pg. 335
KA'U AGRIBUSINESS CO., INC.—See Buyco, Inc.; *U.S. Private*, pg. 190
KAUAI COMMERCIAL COMPANY, INC.—See Alexander & Baldwin, Inc.; *U.S. Public*, pg. 39
KAUAI ELECTRIC DIV.—See Citizens Utilities Company; *U.S. Public*, pg. 380
KAUAI SUGAR STORAGE CO.—See JMB Realty Corporation; *U.S. Private*, pg. 578
KARL KAUERMAN NASSAUISCHE SPARKASSE; *Int'l*, pg. 724
KAUFEL AMERICA INC.—See Kaufel Group Ltd.; *Int'l*, pg. 725
KAUFEL GROUP LTD.; *Int'l*, pg. 724
KAUFEL INTERNATIONAL INC.—See Kaufel Group Ltd.; *Int'l*, pg. 725
KAUFFMAN PRODUCTS, INC.; *U.S. Private*, pg. 609
KAUFMAN AND BROAD-ANTELOPE VALLEY REGIONAL OFFICE—See Kaufman and Broad Home Corporation; *U.S. Public*, pg. 945
KAUFMAN AND BROAD CENTRAL VALLEY DIV.—See Kaufman and Broad Home Corporation; *U.S. Public*, pg. 945
KAUFMAN AND BROAD COASTAL—See Kaufman and Broad Home Corporation; *U.S. Public*, pg. 945
KAUFMAN AND BROAD COLORADO DIVISION—See Kaufman and Broad Home Corporation; *U.S. Public*, pg. 945
KAUFMAN AND BROAD DEVELOPPEMENT—See Kaufman and Broad Home Corporation; *U.S. Public*, pg. 945
KAUFMAN AND BROAD, FRANCE—See Kaufman and Broad Home Corporation; *U.S. Public*, pg. 945
KAUFMAN AND BROAD HOME CORPORATION; *U.S. Public*, pg. 944
KAUFMAN AND BROAD INLAND EMPIRE—See Kaufman and Broad Home Corporation; *U.S. Public*, pg. 945
KAUFMAN AND BROAD MAISONS INDIVIDUELLES—See Kaufman and Broad Home Corporation; *U.S. Public*, pg. 945
KAUFMAN AND BROAD-MONTEREY BAY, INC.—See Kaufman and Broad Home Corporation; *U.S. Public*, pg. 945
KAUFMAN AND BROAD MORTGAGE CO.—See Kaufman and Broad Home Corporation; *U.S. Public*, pg. 945
KAUFMAN AND BROAD MULTI-HOUSING GROUP—See Kaufman and Broad Home Corporation; *U.S. Public*, pg. 945
KAUFMAN AND BROAD NEW MEXICO DIVISION—See Kaufman and Broad Home Corporation; *U.S. Public*, pg. 945
KAUFMAN AND BROAD OF ARIZONA, INC.—See Kaufman and Broad Home Corporation; *U.S. Public*, pg. 945
KAUFMAN AND BROAD OF NEVADA, INC.—See Kaufman and Broad Home Corporation; *U.S. Public*, pg. 945
KAUFMAN AND BROAD OF NORTHERN CALIFORNIA, INC.—See Kaufman and Broad Home Corporation; *U.S. Public*, pg. 945
KAUFMAN AND BROAD OF SAN DIEGO, INC.—See Kaufman and Broad Home Corporation; *U.S. Public*, pg. 945
KAUFMAN AND BROAD OF TEXAS, LTD.—See Kaufman and Broad Home Corporation; *U.S. Public*, pg. 945
KAUFMAN AND BROAD RENOVATIONS—See Kaufman and Broad Home Corporation; *U.S. Public*, pg. 945
KAUFMAN AND BROAD-SOUTH BAY INC.—See Kaufman and Broad Home Corporation; *U.S. Public*, pg. 945
KAUFMAN AND BROAD UTAH DIVISION—See Kaufman and Broad Home Corporation; *U.S. Public*, pg. 945
KAUFMAN FOOTWEAR; *Int'l*, pg. 725
H.W. KAUFMAN FINANCIAL GROUP, INC.; *U.S. Private*, pg. 609
KAUFMAN Y BROAD DE MEXICO SA DE CV—See Kaufman and Broad Home Corporation; *U.S. Public*, pg. 945
KAUFMANN'S—See The May Department Stores Company; *U.S. Public*, pg. 1063

KAUFRING AG—See Commerzbank AG; *Int'l*, pg. 310
KAUKAS NEDERLAND B.V.—See UPM-Kymmene Corporation; *Int'l*, pg. 1429
KAUKAS OY—See UPM-Kymmene Corporation; *Int'l*, pg. 1428
KAUKAS PULP MILL—See UPM-Kymmene Corporation; *Int'l*, pg. 1428
KAUKAS SAWN GOODS INDUSTRY—See UPM-Kymmene Corporation; *Int'l*, pg. 1428
KAULT & BUX COMMUTATOR GMBH-DORSTETTEN—See Kirkwood Industries, Inc.; *U.S. Private*, pg. 623
KAULT & BUX COMMUTATOR GMBH-HERRENBERG—See Kirkwood Industries, Inc.; *U.S. Private*, pg. 623
KAUTEX WERKE REINOLD HAGEN AG—See Commerzbank AG; *Int'l*, pg. 310
KAUTSCHUK-GESELLSCHAFT GMBH—See Metallgesellschaft AG; *Int'l*, pg. 862
KAVERNEN BAU- UND BETRIEBS-GESELLSCHAFT MBH—See Preussag AG; *Int'l*, pg. 1069
KAW PIPELINE CO.—See Texaco Inc.; *U.S. Public*, pg. 1584
KAWAGUCHI DISTRIBUTION CENTER—See Gunze Sangyo, Inc.; *Int'l*, pg. 578
KAWAGUCHI TRAVEL SERVICES, INC.—See Washington Mutual Inc.; *U.S. Public*, pg. 1742
KAWAGUCHIKO COUNTRY CLUB CO., LTD.—See Matsuya Company Ltd.; *Int'l*, pg. 848
KAWAGUCHIKO SEIMITSU CO., LTD.—See Citizen Watch Company; *Int'l*, pg. 294
KAWAI AMERICA CORPORATION—See Kawai Musical Instruments Mfg. Co., Ltd.; *Int'l*, pg. 725
KAWAI AMERICA MFG. INC.—See Kawai Musical Instruments Mfg. Co., Ltd.; *Int'l*, pg. 725
KAWAI MUSICAL INSTRUMENTS MFG. CO., LTD.; *Int'l*, pg. 725
KAWAMATA SEIKI CO., LTD.—See Toshiba Corporation; *Int'l*, pg. 1403
KAWASAKI DO BRAZIL INDUSTRIA E COMERCIO LTDA.—See Kawasaki Heavy Industries, Ltd.; *Int'l*, pg. 726
KAWASAKI HEAVY INDUSTRIES (EUROPE) B.V.—See Kawasaki Heavy Industries, Ltd.; *Int'l*, pg. 726
KAWASAKI HEAVY INDUSTRIES GMBH—See Kawasaki Heavy Industries, Ltd.; *Int'l*, pg. 726
KAWASAKI HEAVY INDUSTRIES (H.K.) LTD.—See Kawasaki Heavy Industries, Ltd.; *Int'l*, pg. 726
KAWASAKI HEAVY INDUSTRIES, LTD.; *Int'l*, pg. 725
KAWASAKI HEAVY INDUSTRIES, LTD. (TOKYO)—See Kawasaki Heavy Industries, Ltd.; *Int'l*, pg. 725
KAWASAKI HEAVY INDUSTRIES (SINGAPORE) PTE. LTD.—See Kawasaki Heavy Industries, Ltd.; *Int'l*, pg. 726
KAWASAKI HEAVY INDUSTRIES (UK) LTD.—See Kawasaki Heavy Industries, Ltd.; *Int'l*, pg. 726
KAWASAKI HEAVY INDUSTRIES (U.S.A.), INC.—See Kawasaki Heavy Industries, Ltd.; *Int'l*, pg. 725
KAWASAKI KISEN KAISHA, LTD.; *Int'l*, pg. 726
KAWASAKI KIZAI CORPORATION—See Toshiba Corporation; *Int'l*, pg. 1403
KAWASAKI LOADERS MANUFACTURING CORP. (U.S.A.)—See Kawasaki Heavy Industries, Ltd.; *Int'l*, pg. 725
KAWASAKI MOTOREN GMBH—See Kawasaki Heavy Industries, Ltd.; *Int'l*, pg. 726
KAWASAKI MOTORS CORP., U.S.A.—See Kawasaki Heavy Industries, Ltd.; *Int'l*, pg. 725
KAWASAKI MOTORS MANUFACTURING CORP., U.S.A.—See Kawasaki Heavy Industries, Ltd.; *Int'l*, pg. 725
KAWASAKI MOTORS NETHERLANDS N.V.—See Kawasaki Heavy Industries, Ltd.; *Int'l*, pg. 726
KAWASAKI MOTORS N.V.—See Kawasaki Heavy Industries, Ltd.; *Int'l*, pg. 726
KAWASAKI MOTORS PTY. LTD.—See Kawasaki Heavy Industries, Ltd.; *Int'l*, pg. 726
KAWASAKI MOTORS (UK) LTD.—See Kawasaki Heavy Industries, Ltd.; *Int'l*, pg. 726
KAWASAKI PRECISION MACHINERY (UK) LTD.—See Kawasaki Heavy Industries, Ltd.; *Int'l*, pg. 726
KAWASAKI RAIL CAR, INC.—See Kawasaki Heavy Industries, Ltd.; *Int'l*, pg. 725
KAWASAKI ROBOTICS (U.S.A.), INC.—See Kawasaki Heavy Industries, Ltd.; *Int'l*, pg. 725
KAWASAKI STEEL AMERICA—See Kawasaki Steel Corporation; *Int'l*, pg. 726
KAWASAKI STEEL CO.—See Kawasaki Steel Corporation; *Int'l*, pg. 726
KAWASAKI STEEL CORPORATION; *Int'l*, pg. 726
KAWASAKI TERMINAL—See GATX Corporation; *U.S. Public*, pg. 693
KAWASAKI TOKUYAMA READY MIXED CONCRETE CO., LTD.—See Tokuyama Corporation; *Int'l*, pg. 1393
KAWASAKI WORKS—See Asahi Chemical Industry Co., Ltd.; *Int'l*, pg. 84
KAWASHO CORPORATION; *Int'l*, pg. 726
KAWNEER COMPANY—See Alumax Inc.; *U.S. Public*, pg. 60
KAY-BEE TOY & HOBBY SHOPS, INC.—See Consolidated Stores Corp.; *U.S. Public*, pg. 437
THE KAY COMPANY, INC.; *U.S. Private*, pg. 610
KAY HIAN PRIVATE LTD.—See HSBC Holdings plc; *Int'l*, pg. 583
KAY HOME PRODUCTS, INC.—See Park-Ohio Industries, Inc.; *U.S. Public*, pg. 1258
KAY RAY SENSALL INC.—See Emerson Electric Co.; *U.S. Public*, pg. 574
W. H. KAY COMPANY—See Eclipse Inc.; *U.S. Private*, pg. 360
KAYABA ARVIN S.A.—See Kayaba Industry Co., Ltd.; *Int'l*, pg. 727
KAYABA EUROPE GMBH—See Kayaba Industry Co., Ltd.; *Int'l*, pg. 727
P.T. KAYABA INDONESIA—See Kayaba Industry Co., Ltd.; *Int'l*, pg. 727
KAYABA INDUSTRY CO., LTD.; *Int'l*, pg. 727

KAYABA (MALAYSIA) SDN. BHD.—See Kayaba Industry Co., Ltd.; *Int'l*, pg. 727
KAYAKU-NOURY K.K.—See Akzo Nobel N.V.; *Int'l*, pg. 47
KAYDON CORPORATION; *U.S. Public*, pg. 945
KAYDON CORPORATION, BEARINGS DIVISION—See Kaydon Corporation; *U.S. Public*, pg. 946
KAYDON CORPORATION, FILTRATION DIVISION—See Kaydon Corporation; *U.S. Public*, pg. 946
KAYDON RING & SEAL, INC.—See Kaydon Corporation; *U.S. Public*, pg. 946
KAYDON S.A. DE C.V.—See Kaydon Corporation; *U.S. Public*, pg. 946
E. & E. KAYE LIMITED; *Int'l*, pg. 727
KAYE INSTRUMENTS, INC.—See Bowthorpe plc; *Int'l*, pg. 208
KAYEM FOODS, INC.; *U.S. Private*, pg. 610
KAYENESS, INC.—See Berwind Corporation; *U.S. Private*, pg. 138
KAYEX CORP.—See General Signal Corporation; *U.S. Public*, pg. 727
KAYNAR/K-FAST/APS—See KTI; *U.S. Public*, pg. 940
KAYSER-ROTH CORPORATION, INC.—See Grupo Synkro, S.A. de C.V.; *Int'l*, pg. 576
KAYSERSBERG S.A.—See Fort James Corporation; *U.S. Public*, pg. 673
KAYWOODIE—See S.M. Frank & Co., Inc.; *U.S. Private*, pg. 424
KAZ, INC.; *U.S. Private*, pg. 610
KE-MASTER—See Sunroc Corporation; *U.S. Private*, pg. 1053
KE-ZAN SECURITIES SDN BHD—See Kim Eng Holdings Limited; *Int'l*, pg. 733
KEANE CANADA, INC.—See Keane, Inc.; *U.S. Public*, pg. 946
KEANE FEDERAL SYSTEMS—See Keane, Inc.; *U.S. Public*, pg. 946
KEANE, INC.; *U.S. Public*, pg. 946
KEARFOTT GUIDANCE & NAVIGATION CORP.—See Astronautics Corporation of America; *U.S. Private*, pg. 93
KEARNEY COMPANY—See Cooper Industries, Inc.; *U.S. Public*, pg. 444
KEARNEY-NATIONAL CANADA LTD.—See The Dyson-Kissner-Moran Corporation; *U.S. Private*, pg. 351
KEARNEY-NATIONAL, INC.—See The Dyson-Kissner-Moran Corporation; *U.S. Private*, pg. 351
KEARSARGE TELEPHONE CO.—See Telephone and Data Systems, Inc.; *U.S. Public*, pg. 1571
KEATING BUILDING CORP.; *U.S. Private*, pg. 610
DANIEL J. KEATING CO.; *U.S. Private*, pg. 610
KEATING MATERIALS—See P.J. Keating Company; *U.S. Private*, pg. 611
P.J. KEATING COMPANY; *U.S. Private*, pg. 610
KEBE ERSATZTEILE GMBH—See Charter plc; *Int'l*, pg. 283
KECA DE CENTROAMERICA S.A.—See Enso Oyj; *Int'l*, pg. 458
KECK INSTRUMENTS, INC.—See CILCORP Inc.; *U.S. Public*, pg. 367
KECO INDUSTRY, INC.; *U.S. Private*, pg. 946
KEDAH SATO SDN. BHD.—See Sato Kogyo Co., Ltd.; *Int'l*, pg. 1197
THE KEDS CORPORATION—See The Stride Rite Corporation; *U.S. Public*, pg. 1525
KEE CUTTERS—See Masco Corporation; *U.S. Public*, pg. 1054
KEE SERVICES—See Masco Corporation; *U.S. Public*, pg. 1054
KEEBLER CO./CINCINNATI BAKERY—See Flowers Industries, Inc.; *U.S. Public*, pg. 657
KEEBLER CO./DENVER BAKERY—See Flowers Industries, Inc.; *U.S. Public*, pg. 657
KEEBLER CO./GRAND RAPIDS BAKERY—See Flowers Industries, Inc.; *U.S. Public*, pg. 657
KEEBLER CO./MACON BAKERY—See Flowers Industries, Inc.; *U.S. Public*, pg. 657
KEEBLER COMPANY—See Flowers Industries, Inc.; *U.S. Public*, pg. 657
KEEBLER CONE CO.—See Flowers Industries, Inc.; *U.S. Public*, pg. 657
KEELER BRASS COMPANY—See FKI Plc; *Int'l*, pg. 473
KEELER INSTRUMENTS INC.—See Halma p.l.c.; *Int'l*, pg. 590
KEELER LIMITED—See Halma p.l.c.; *Int'l*, pg. 589
KEELER MOTOR CAR COMPANY, INC.; *U.S. Private*, pg. 611
KEEN COMPRESSED GAS CO.; *U.S. Private*, pg. 611
KEEN WELDING DIVISION—See Keen Compressed Gas Co.; *U.S. Private*, pg. 611
KEENE DISTRIBUTORS—See Koninklijke BolsWessanen nv; *Int'l*, pg. 752
KEENELAND ASSOC., INC.; *U.S. Private*, pg. 611
KEENERS, INC.; *U.S. Private*, pg. 611
KEENEY MANUFACTURING CO.; *U.S. Private*, pg. 611
KEEPRITE INC—See International Comfort Products; *U.S. Public*, pg. 898
F. D. KEES POWER EQUIPMENT—See Yazoo Power Equipment, LLC; *U.S. Private*, pg. 1195
ROBERT KEESHAN ASSOCIATES, INC.—See ICM Holdings Inc.; *U.S. Private*, pg. 554
KEFICO CORPORATION—See Hyundai Motor Company; *Int'l*, pg. 642
KEG RESTAURANTS U.S., INC.—See Whitbread PLC; *Int'l*, pg. 1499
KEIL CHEMICAL DIV.—See Ferro Corporation; *U.S. Public*, pg. 619
KEILER & COMPANY; *U.S. Private*, pg. 611
BEN E. KEITH COMPANY; *U.S. Private*, pg. 611
BEN E. KEITH CO. OF OKLAHOMA—See Ben E. Keith Company; *U.S. Private*, pg. 611
GEO. E. KEITH COMPANY; *U.S. Private*, pg. 611
KEITH HIGHLANDERS SHOES—See Geo. E. Keith Company; *U.S. Private*, pg. 612

KEITHLEY FOREIGN SALES CORP.—See Keithley Instruments, Inc.; *U.S. Public*, pg. 947
KEITHLEY INSTRUMENTS B.V.—See Keithley Instruments, Inc.; *U.S. Public*, pg. 947
KEITHLEY INSTRUMENTS CHINA—See Keithley Instruments, Inc.; *U.S. Public*, pg. 947
KEITHLEY INSTRUMENTS GMBH—See Keithley Instruments, Inc.; *U.S. Public*, pg. 947
KEITHLEY INSTRUMENTS, INC.; *U.S. Public*, pg. 946
KEITHLEY INSTRUMENTS, INC.—See Keithley Instruments, Inc.; *U.S. Public*, pg. 946
KEITHLEY INSTRUMENTS INC.-RADIATION MEASUREMENTS DIV.—See Keithley Instruments, Inc.; *U.S. Public*, pg. 946
KEITHLEY INSTRUMENTS INDIA—See Keithley Instruments, Inc.; *U.S. Public*, pg. 947
KEITHLEY INSTRUMENTS LTD.—See Keithley Instruments, Inc.; *U.S. Public*, pg. 947
KEITHLEY INSTRUMENTS, S.A.—See Keithley Instruments, Inc.; *U.S. Public*, pg. 947
KEITHLEY INSTRUMENTS S.A.R.L.—See Keithley Instruments, Inc.; *U.S. Public*, pg. 947
KEITHLEY INSTRUMENTS SRL—See Keithley Instruments, Inc.; *U.S. Public*, pg. 947
KEITHLEY INTERNATIONAL INVESTMENT CORP.—See Keithley Instruments, Inc.; *U.S. Public*, pg. 947
KEIZER B.V. (WASPIK)—See McCain Foods Limited; *Int'l*, pg. 850
KEKAHA SUGAR COMPANY, LIMITED—See JMB Realty Corporation; *U.S. Private*, pg. 578
KELCO DIV.—See Monsanto Company; *U.S. Public*, pg. 1125
KELCO INTERNATIONAL LTD.—See Merck & Co., Inc.; *U.S. Public*, pg. 1091
KELIM TOTO CO., LTD.—See Toto Ltd.; *Int'l*, pg. 1410
KELKO QUAKER CHEMICAL, S.A.—See Quaker Chemical Corporation; *U.S. Public*, pg. 1346
KELLEMS DIV.—See Hubbell Incorporated; *U.S. Public*, pg. 844
KELLER & GANNON—See Lester B. Knight & Associates, Inc.; *U.S. Private*, pg. 626
KELLER BUILDING PRODUCTS OF CHARLOTTE, INC.; *U.S. Private*, pg. 612
KELLER CONSTRUCTION COMPANY LTD.; *U.S. Private*, pg. 612
KELLER CRESCENT CO.; *U.S. Private*, pg. 612
KELLER-DORIAN GRAVEURS, DIV. OF ROEHLEN INDUSTRIES/EUROPE—See Standex International Corporation; *U.S. Public*, pg. 1507
KELLER GRADUATE SCHOOL OF MANAGEMENT—See DeVry Institutes; *U.S. Public*, pg. 504
J.J. KELLER & ASSOCIATES, INC.; *U.S. Private*, pg. 612
KELLER KITCHEN CABINETS; *U.S. Private*, pg. 612
KELLER LADDERS INC.—See U.S. Industries, Inc.; *U.S. Public*, pg. 1684
THE KELLER MANUFACTURING CO., INC.; *U.S. Private*, pg. 612
KELLERMEYER CO.; *U.S. Private*, pg. 612
KELLEY ADVERTISING INC.—See Grey Advertising Inc.; *U.S. Public*, pg. 765
KELLEY ATLANTIC, LTD.—See Kelley Company, Inc.; *U.S. Private*, pg. 613
KELLEY AUTOMOTIVE GROUP; *U.S. Private*, pg. 612
KELLEY BEAN CO., INC.; *U.S. Private*, pg. 612
KELLEY BEMANNINGSLOSNINGER—See Kelly Services, Inc.; *U.S. Public*, pg. 949
KELLEY COMPANY, INC.; *U.S. Private*, pg. 612
KELLEY ELECTRIC COMPANY—See The Gilbert Companies, Inc.; *U.S. Private*, pg. 453
KELLOGG (AUST.) PROPRIETARY LTD.—See Kellogg Company; *U.S. Public*, pg. 947
KELLOGG BRASIL & CIA—See Kellogg Company; *U.S. Public*, pg. 947
KELLOGG CANADA INC.—See Kellogg Company; *U.S. Public*, pg. 947
KELLOGG COMPANY; *U.S. Public*, pg. 947
KELLOGG COMPANY ARGENTINA S.A.C.I.F.—See Kellogg Company; *U.S. Public*, pg. 947
KELLOGG COMPANY OF GREAT BRITAIN LTD.—See Kellogg Company; *U.S. Public*, pg. 947
KELLOGG COMPANY OF SOUTH AFRICA (PROPRIETARY) LIMITED—See Kellogg Company; *U.S. Public*, pg. 947
KELLOGG CONVENIENCE FOOD PLANT—See Kellogg Company; *U.S. Public*, pg. 947
KELLOGG DE CENTRO AMERICA S.A.—See Kellogg Company; *U.S. Public*, pg. 947
KELLOGG DE COLOMBIA S.A.—See Kellogg Company; *U.S. Public*, pg. 947
KELLOGG DE MEXICO S.A. DE C.V.—See Kellogg Company; *U.S. Public*, pg. 948
KELLOGG (DEUTSCHLAND) GESELLSCHAFT MIT BESCHRANKTER HARTUNG (GMBH)—See Kellogg Company; *U.S. Public*, pg. 948
KELLOGG ESPANA, S.A.—See Kellogg Company; *U.S. Public*, pg. 948
KELLOGG (JAPAN) K.K.—See Kellogg Company; *U.S. Public*, pg. 948
THE M.W. KELLOGG COMPANY—See Dresser Industries, Inc.; *U.S. Public*, pg. 528
M.W. KELLOGG LIMITED—See Dresser Industries, Inc.; *U.S. Public*, pg. 528
KELLOGG NORTH AMERICA DIVISION—See Kellogg Company; *U.S. Public*, pg. 947
KELLOGG SALES COMPANY—See Kellogg Company; *U.S. Public*, pg. 947
KELLOGG USA CONVENIENCE FOODS DIVISION—See Kellogg Company; *U.S. Public*, pg. 947
KELLOGG USA INC.—See Kellogg Company; *U.S. Public*, pg. 947
KELLOGG'S PRODUITS ALIMENTAIRES, S.A.—See Kellogg Company; *U.S. Public*, pg. 948
KELLWOOD ASIA LIMITED—See Kellwood Company; *U.S. Public*, pg. 948

Company Index

KELLWOOD COMPANY; *U.S. Public*, pg. 948
KELLWOOD LINGERIE/ACTIVE GROUP—See Kellwood Company; *U.S. Public*, pg. 948
KELLWOOD SPORTSWEAR—See Kellwood Company; *U.S. Public*, pg. 948
KELLY ASSISTED LIVING SERVICES, INC.—See Kelly Services, Inc.; *U.S. Public*, pg. 949
KELLY BRANDS DIVISION—See The Goodyear Tire & Rubber Company; *U.S. Public*, pg. 753
KELLY DE MEXICO—See Kelly Services, Inc.; *U.S. Public*, pg. 949
KELLY DOUGLAS & COMPANY LIMITED—See George Weston Limited; *Int'l*, pg. 1495
KELLY DOUGLASS WESTFAIR FOODS LTD.—See George Weston Limited; *Int'l*, pg. 1495
KELLY MARKETING—See Kelly Services, Inc.; *U.S. Public*, pg. 949
KELLY-MOORE PAINT COMPANY, INC.; *U.S. Private*, pg. 613
KELLY PAPER COMPANY—See N.V. Koninklijke KNP BT; *Int'l*, pg. 757
KELLY PROFESSIONAL SERVICES, INC.—See Kelly Services, Inc.; *U.S. Public*, pg. 949
KELLY PROPERTIES, INC.—See Kelly Services, Inc.; *U.S. Public*, pg. 949
KELLY, SCOTT AND MADISON, INC.; *U.S. Private*, pg. 613
KELLY SERVICES—See Kelly Services, Inc.; *U.S. Public*, pg. 949
KELLY SERVICES (AUSTRALIA), LTD.—See Kelly Services, Inc.; *U.S. Public*, pg. 949
KELLY SERVICES CANADA, LTD.—See Kelly Services, Inc.; *U.S. Public*, pg. 949
KELLY SERVICES, INC.; *U.S. Public*, pg. 949
KELLY SERVICES (LTD.)—See Kelly Services, Inc.; *U.S. Public*, pg. 949
KELLY SERVICES (UK) LTD.—See Kelly Services, Inc.; *U.S. Public*, pg. 949
THE KELLY-SPRINGFIELD TIRE COMPANY—See The Goodyear Tire & Rubber Company; *U.S. Public*, pg. 753
KELLY TECHNICAL—See Kelly Services, Inc.; *U.S. Public*, pg. 949
KELLY TEMPORARY SERVICES, LTD.—See Kelly Services, Inc.; *U.S. Public*, pg. 949
KELLY TEMPORARY SERVICES, LTD.-IRELAND—See Kelly Services, Inc.; *U.S. Public*, pg. 949
KELLY UITZENDBURO—See Kelly Services, Inc.; *U.S. Public*, pg. 949
KELLY (UK) SERVICES LTD.—See Kelly Services, Inc.; *U.S. Public*, pg. 949
KELLY VIKARER—See Kelly Services, Inc.; *U.S. Public*, pg. 949
KELLY WEEDON SHUTE PARTNERSHIP; *Int'l*, pg. 727
KELSAR, S.A.—See American Home Products Corporation; *U.S. Public*, pg. 81
KELSEY BAY DIV.—See MacMillan Bloedel Limited; *Int'l*, pg. 828
KELSEY CONSTRUCTION, INC.; *U.S. Private*, pg. 613
KELSEY DEVELOPMENT—See Kelsey Construction, Inc.; *U.S. Private*, pg. 613
KELSO-BURNETT COMPANY; *U.S. Private*, pg. 613
KELSO-BURNETT ROLLING MEADOWS BRANCH—See Kelso-Burnett Company; *U.S. Private*, pg. 613
KELSO-BURNETT ZION BRANCH—See Kelso-Burnett Company; *U.S. Private*, pg. 613
KELSO OIL COMPANY; *U.S. Private*, pg. 613
KELTATIM PUBLISHING COMPANY; *U.S. Private*, pg. 613
A/S KELVIN HUGHES—See Smiths Industries plc; *Int'l*, pg. 1268
KELVIN HUGHES LIMITED—See Smiths Industries plc; *Int'l*, pg. 1267
KELVIN HUGHES LIMITED-CHARTS & MARITIME SUPPLIES—See Smiths Industries plc; *Int'l*, pg. 1267
KELVIN HUGHES OBSERVATOR B.V.—See Smiths Industries plc; *Int'l*, pg. 1268
KELVIN HUGHES (SINGAPORE) PTE. LIMITED—See Smiths Industries plc; *Int'l*, pg. 1268
KELVINATOR APPLIANCES—See Electrolux, AB; *Int'l*, pg. 440
KEM KREST CORP.—See Accra Pac Group; *U.S. Private*, pg. 11
KEMCOM SDN BHD—See Sophus Berendsen A/S; *Int'l*, pg. 1286
KEMET CORPORATION; *U.S. Public*, pg. 949
KEMET DE MEXICO DE S.A. DE C.V.—See Kemet Corporation; *U.S. Public*, pg. 949
KEMET ELECTRONICS ASIA LTD.—See Kemet Corporation; *U.S. Public*, pg. 949
KEMET ELECTRONICS CORPORATION—See Kemet Corporation; *U.S. Public*, pg. 949
KEMET ELECTRONICS SA—See Kemet Corporation; *U.S. Public*, pg. 949
KEMETYL AB—See Orkla A.S.A.; *Int'l*, pg. 1011
AS KEMI VESI—See Enso Oyj; *Int'l*, pg. 456
KEMIJARVEN SELLU OY—See Enso Oyj; *Int'l*, pg. 456
KEMIPOL LTD.—See Kemira Oy; *Int'l*, pg. 729
KEMIRA AGRO OY—See Kemira Oy; *Int'l*, pg. 727
KEMIRA AGRO PERNIS B.V.—See Kemira Oy; *Int'l*, pg. 729
KEMIRA AGRO ROZENBURG B.V.—See Kemira Oy; *Int'l*, pg. 729
KEMIRA AGRO SERVICES S.A.—See Kemira Oy; *Int'l*, pg. 728
KEMIRA AGRO U.K. LTD.—See Kemira Oy; *Int'l*, pg. 728
KEMIRA CHEMICALS INC.—See Kemira Oy; *Int'l*, pg. 729
KEMIRA CHEMICALS OY—See Kemira Oy; *Int'l*, pg. 728
KEMIRA CHEMIDET GMBH—See Kemira Oy; *Int'l*, pg. 729
KEMIRA CHIMIE S.A.—See Kemira Oy; *Int'l*, pg. 728
KEMIRA COATINGS—See Kemira Oy; *Int'l*, pg. 729
KEMIRA COATINGS LTD.—See Kemira Oy; *Int'l*, pg. 729
KEMIRA COLOR B.V.—See Kemira Oy; *Int'l*, pg. 729
KEMIRA COLOR EUROPE B.V.—See Kemira Oy; *Int'l*, pg. 729

KEMIRA COLOR N.V.—See Kemira Oy; *Int'l*, pg. 729
KEMIRA DANMARK A/S—See Kemira Oy; *Int'l*, pg. 728
KEMIRA DEUTSCHLAND GMBH—See Kemira Oy; *Int'l*, pg. 728
KEMIRA ENGINEERING OY—See Kemira Oy; *Int'l*, pg. 728
KEMIRA FIBRES OY—See Kemira Oy; *Int'l*, pg. 728
KEMIRA HOLDING B.V.—See Kemira Oy; *Int'l*, pg. 729
KEMIRA HOLDINGS INC.—See Kemira Oy; *Int'l*, pg. 729
KEMIRA IBERICA S.A.—See Kemira Oy; *Int'l*, pg. 728
KEMIRA INCE LTD.—See Kemira Oy; *Int'l*, pg. 728
KEMIRA INCORPORATED—See Kemira Oy; *Int'l*, pg. 729
KEMIRA INTERNATIONAL FINANCE B.V.—See Kemira Oy; *Int'l*, pg. 729
KEMIRA INTERNATIONAL SERVICES S.A.—See Kemira Oy; *Int'l*, pg. 729
KEMIRA IRELAND LTD.—See Kemira Oy; *Int'l*, pg. 729
KEMIRA KATALYSAFOREN GMBH—See Kemira Oy; *Int'l*, pg. 729
KEMIRA KEMI AB—See Kemira Oy; *Int'l*, pg. 728
KEMIRA KEMI (UK) LTD.—See Kemira Oy; *Int'l*, pg. 728
KEMIRA KERESKEDELMI KFT—See Kemira Oy; *Int'l*, pg. 729
KEMIRA LTD.—See Kemira Oy; *Int'l*, pg. 728
KEMIRA METALKAT OY—See Kemira Oy; *Int'l*, pg. 729
KEMIRA MILJO A/S—See Kemira Oy; *Int'l*, pg. 728
KEMIRA N.I. LIMITED—See Kemira Oy; *Int'l*, pg. 728
KEMIRA OY; *Int'l*, pg. 727
KEMIRA OY—See Kemira Oy; *Int'l*, pg. 729
KEMIRA PAPER CHEMICALS CANADA, INC.—See Kemira Oy; *Int'l*, pg. 728
KEMIRA PAPER CHEMICALS, INC.—See Kemira Oy; *Int'l*, pg. 729
KEMIRA PAPIERCHEMIKALIEN—See Kemira Oy; *Int'l*, pg. 728
KEMIRA PEROXIDES B.V.—See Kemira Oy; *Int'l*, pg. 728
KEMIRA PIGMENTS B.V.—See Kemira Oy; *Int'l*, pg. 729
KEMIRA PIGMENTS OY—See Kemira Oy; *Int'l*, pg. 729
KEMIRA PIGMENTS S.A.—See Kemira Oy; *Int'l*, pg. 729
KEMIRA POLYMERS—See Kemira Oy; *Int'l*, pg. 729
KEMIRA S.A./N.V.—See Kemira Oy; *Int'l*, pg. 728
KEMIRA SAFETY LTD.—See Kemira Oy; *Int'l*, pg. 729
KEMIRA SAFETY OY—See Kemira Oy; *Int'l*, pg. 729
KEMIRA SERVICES HOLLAND B.V.—See Kemira Oy; *Int'l*, pg. 729
KEMIRA SVENSKA AB—See Kemira Oy; *Int'l*, pg. 729
KEMIRA THAI CO. LTD.—See Kemira Oy; *Int'l*, pg. 728
KEMIRA-UBE LTD.—See Kemira Oy; *Int'l*, pg. 728
KEMIRA WATER TREATMENT, INC.—See Kemira Oy; *Int'l*, pg. 728
KEMKLEN INDUSTRIAL SUPPL. LTD.—See Axel Johnson AB; *Int'l*, pg. 712
KEMLITE COMPANY—See Crane Co.; *U.S. Public*, pg. 457
KEMMONS WILSON, INC.; *U.S. Private*, pg. 613
LOUIS KEMP SEAFOOD CO.—See Tyson Foods, Inc.; *U.S. Public*, pg. 1652
KEMPER INSURANCE COMPANIES; *U.S. Private*, pg. 614
KEMPER INVESTORS LIFE INSURANCE COMPANY—See Zurich Insurance Company; *Int'l*, pg. 1530
KEMPER NATIONAL SERVICES—See Kemper Insurance Companies; *U.S. Private*, pg. 614
KEMPER REINSURANCE CO.—See Kemper Insurance Companies; *U.S. Private*, pg. 614
THOMAS KEMPER LAGER—See Pyramid Breweries, Inc.; *U.S. Public*, pg. 1345
THOMAS KEMPER SODA COMPANY—See Pyramid Breweries, Inc.; *U.S. Public*, pg. 1345
KEMPS FOODS, INC.—See Koninklijke BolsWessanen nv; *Int'l*, pg. 752
KEMRHONE S.A.R.L.—See Kemira Oy; *Int'l*, pg. 728
KEMRON ENVIRONMENTAL SERVICES, INC.; *U.S. Private*, pg. 614
KEMWATER A/S—See Kemira Oy; *Int'l*, pg. 728
KEMWATER B.V.—See Kemira Oy; *Int'l*, pg. 728
KEN-MAC METALS, INC.—See Thyssen AG; *Int'l*, pg. 1388
KEN TOOL—See Summit Tool Company; *U.S. Private*, pg. 1050
KENAI LNG CORPORATION—See Phillips Petroleum Company; *U.S. Public*, pg. 1291
KENAN TRANSPORT COMPANY; *U.S. Public*, pg. 949
KENANA SUGAR CO., LTD.—See Nissho Iwai Corporation; *Int'l*, pg. 948
KENCO—See Williams Controls, Inc.; *U.S. Public*, pg. 1769
KENDALE INDUSTRIES, INC.; *U.S. Private*, pg. 614
THE KENDALL-BETHAM DIVISION—See Tyco International Ltd.; *U.S. Public*, pg. 1647
THE KENDALL COMPANY—See Tyco International Ltd.; *U.S. Public*, pg. 1647
KENDALL DE VENEZUELA, C.A.—See Tyco International Ltd.; *U.S. Public*, pg. 1648
KENDALL REGIONAL MEDICAL CENTER—See Columbia/HCA Healthcare Corporation; *U.S. Public*, pg. 405
KENDALL THERAPY CENTER, LTD.—See Columbia/HCA Healthcare Corporation; *U.S. Public*, pg. 405
KENDALL YANTAI MEDICAL PRODUCTS CO. LTD.—See Tyco International Ltd.; *U.S. Public*, pg. 1648
KENDO—See Havas Advertising; *Int'l*, pg. 601
KENDRICK BAY MINING CO.—See Standard Metals Corporation; *U.S. Public*, pg. 1502
KENESAW LEASING INC.—See National Commerce Bancorporation; *U.S. Public*, pg. 1155
KENETECH CORP.; *U.S. Public*, pg. 950
KENEX CORPORATION—See Kenwood Corporation; *Int'l*, pg. 730
KENG HUA PAPER PRODUCTS CO., INC.; *Int'l*, pg. 729
KENHAR CORPORATION—See Cascade Corporation; *U.S. Public*, pg. 311
KENLAKE FOODS—See The Kroger Co.; *U.S. Public*, pg. 967
KENNAMETAL AUSTRALIA PTY. LTD.—See Kennametal Inc.; *U.S. Public*, pg. 951
KENNAMETAL CA. ME. S., S.P.A.—See Kennametal Inc.; *U.S. Public*, pg. 951
KENNAMETAL (CHINA) LIMITED—See Kennametal Inc.; *U.S. Public*, pg. 951

KENNAMETAL GTS GMBH KOREA BRANCH—See Kennametal Inc.; *U.S. Public*, pg. 951
KENNAMETAL HARDPOINT (TAIWAN) INC.—See Kennametal Inc.; *U.S. Public*, pg. 951
KENNAMETAL HERTEL AG—See Kennametal Inc.; *U.S. Public*, pg. 951
KENNAMETAL HERTEL BELGIUM, S.A.—See Kennametal Inc.; *U.S. Public*, pg. 951
KENNAMETAL HERTEL FRANCE, S.A.—See Kennametal Inc.; *U.S. Public*, pg. 951
KENNAMETAL HERTEL GMBH—See Kennametal Inc.; *U.S. Public*, pg. 951
KENNAMETAL HERTEL JAPAN LTD.—See Kennametal Inc.; *U.S. Public*, pg. 951
KENNAMETAL HERTEL LIMITED—See Kennametal Inc.; *U.S. Public*, pg. 951
KENNAMETAL HERTEL NEDERLAND, B.V.—See Kennametal Inc.; *U.S. Public*, pg. 951
KENNAMETAL HERTEL (SINGAPORE) PTE. LTD.—See Kennametal Inc.; *U.S. Public*, pg. 951
KENNAMETAL HERTEL S.P.A.—See Kennametal Inc.; *U.S. Public*, pg. 951
KENNAMETAL INC.; *U.S. Public*, pg. 950
KENNAMETAL, LTD.—See Kennametal Inc.; *U.S. Public*, pg. 951
KENNAMETAL METALWORKING SYSTEMS DIV.—See Kennametal Inc.; *U.S. Public*, pg. 950
KENNECOTT ENERGY AND COAL COMPANY—See Rio Tinto PLC; *Int'l*, pg. 1119
KENNECOTT HOLDINGS CORPORATION—See Rio Tinto PLC; *Int'l*, pg. 1119
KENNECOTT UTAH COPPER CORPORATION—See Rio Tinto PLC; *Int'l*, pg. 1119
KENNEDY & MITCHELL, INC.—See Harken Energy Corporation; *U.S. Public*, pg. 785
KENNEDY EQUIPMENT CO., INC.—See Kennedy Tank & Manufacturing Co., Inc.; *U.S. Private*, pg. 614
KENNEDY MANUFACTURING COMPANY; *U.S. Private*, pg. 614
KENNEDY SPACE CENTER OPERATIONS—See Thiokol Corporation; *U.S. Public*, pg. 1597
KENNEDY TANK & MANUFACTURING CO., INC.; *U.S. Private*, pg. 614
KENNEDY VALVE—See McWane, Inc.; *U.S. Private*, pg. 725
KENNEDY VAN SAUN CORP.—See Svedala Industri AB; *Int'l*, pg. 1326
KENNEDY-WILSON, INC.; *U.S. Public*, pg. 951
KENNELL & COMPANY INSURANCE MANAGERS, INC.—See Skandia Insurance Company Limited; *Int'l*, pg. 1257
KENNER PARKER (AUSTRALIA) LTD.—See Hasbro, Inc.; *U.S. Public*, pg. 797
KENNER PARKER EUROPE—See Hasbro, Inc.; *U.S. Public*, pg. 797
KENNER PARKER (H.K.) LTD.—See Hasbro, Inc.; *U.S. Public*, pg. 797
KENNER PARKER (N.Z.) LTD.—See Hasbro, Inc.; *U.S. Public*, pg. 798
KENNER PARKER TOYS—See Hasbro, Inc.; *U.S. Public*, pg. 798
KENNER PARKER TOYS INTERNATIONAL—See Hasbro, Inc.; *U.S. Public*, pg. 798
KENNER PRODUCTS (CANADA) LIMITED—See Hasbro, Inc.; *U.S. Public*, pg. 798
KENNETH COLE PRODUCTIONS; *U.S. Public*, pg. 951
KENNEY MANUFACTURING COMPANY; *U.S. Private*, pg. 615
KENNINGTON LTD., INC.; *U.S. Private*, pg. 615
J.J. KENNY CO., INC.—See The McGraw-Hill Companies; *U.S. Public*, pg. 1070
KENRAL INC.—See Pharmacia & Upjohn, Inc.; *Int'l*, pg. 1049
KENSINGTON & EASTERN RAILROAD—See Illinois Central Corporation; *U.S. Public*, pg. 865
KENT & SPIEGEL DIRECT; *U.S. Private*, pg. 615
KENT COAL MINING—See Rochester & Pittsburgh Coal Company; *U.S. Public*, pg. 1395
THE KENT COMPANY—See Electrolux, AB; *Int'l*, pg. 440
KENT DATACOMM CORP.—See Kent Electronics Corp.; *U.S. Public*, pg. 951
KENT ELECTRONICS CORP.; *U.S. Public*, pg. 951
KENT FEEDS INC.—See Varied Investments, Inc.; *U.S. Private*, pg. 1134
KENT INDUSTRIAL MEASUREMENTS LIMITED—See ABB Asea Brown Boveri (Holding) Ltd.; *Int'l*, pg. 2
KENT INDUSTRIES—See Premier Farnell plc; *Int'l*, pg. 1068
KENT INSTRUMENTS PTY. LTD.—See ABB Asea Brown Boveri (Holding) Ltd.; *Int'l*, pg. 2
KENT INSTRUMENTS SOUTH AFRICA PTY. LTD.—See ABB Asea Brown Boveri (Holding) Ltd.; *Int'l*, pg. 3
KENT INTROL LTD.—See ABB Asea Brown Boveri (Holding) Ltd.; *Int'l*, pg. 7
KENT LANDSBERG—See Amcor Limited; *Int'l*, pg. 72
THE KENT MANUFACTURING CO.; *U.S. Private*, pg. 615
KENT METERS, INC.—See ABB Asea Brown Boveri (Holding) Ltd.; *Int'l*, pg. 4
KENT METERS LTD.—See ABB Asea Brown Boveri (Holding) Ltd.; *Int'l*, pg. 2
KENT METERS S.A. (PTY.) LTD.—See ABB Asea Brown Boveri (Holding) Ltd.; *Int'l*, pg. 3
KENT PAPER CO., INC.—See American Pad and Paper Company; *U.S. Public*, pg. 89
KENT PLANT—See Stoneridge, Inc.; *U.S. Public*, pg. 1044
KENT PROCESS CONTROL LTD.—See ABB Asea Brown Boveri (Holding) Ltd.; *Int'l*, pg. 2
KENT SUSSEX TIRE SERVICE—See Service Tire Truck Centers, Inc.; *U.S. Private*, pg. 987
ABB KENT TAYLOR INC.—See ABB Asea Brown Boveri (Holding) Ltd.; *Int'l*, pg. 3
KENT-TIEGHI S.P.A.—See ABB Asea Brown Boveri (Holding) Ltd.; *Int'l*, pg. 3
KENTILE OPERTING CO.; *U.S. Private*, pg. 615

MASTER INDEX TO COMPANY NAMES KEWANEE

Company Index

KENTING NEDDRILL V.O.F.—See Royal Nedlloyd Group N.V.; *Int'l*, pg. 1144
KENTON GRAIN CO.—See Tom Wade Co.; *U.S. Private*, pg. 1145
T.J. KENTON & COMPANY—See Eastman Kodak Company; *U.S. Public*, pg. 552
KENTROX INDUSTRIES, INC.—See ADC Telecommunications, Inc.; *U.S. Public*, pg. 4
KENTSHIPS—See Tate & Lyle PLC; *Int'l*, pg. 1356
KENTUCKY-AMERICAN WATER CO.—See American Water Works Company, Inc.; *U.S. Public*, pg. 95
KENTUCKY BERWIND LAND COMPANY—See Berwind Corporation; *U.S. Private*, pg. 138
KENTUCKY FRIED CHICKEN (ADELAIDE) PTY. LTD.—See Tricon Global Restaurants, Inc.; *U.S. Public*, pg. 1637
KENTUCKY FRIED CHICKEN CORPORATION (KFC)—See Tricon Global Restaurants, Inc.; *U.S. Public*, pg. 1636
KENTUCKY FRIED CHICKEN, ESPANA S.A.—See Tricon Global Restaurants, Inc.; *U.S. Public*, pg. 1637
KENTUCKY FRIED CHICKEN (GREAT BRITAIN) LTD.—See Tricon Global Restaurants, Inc.; *U.S. Public*, pg. 1637
KENTUCKY FRIED CHICKEN JAPAN LTD.—See Tricon Global Restaurants, Inc.; *U.S. Public*, pg. 1637
KENTUCKY FRIED CHICKEN NETHERLANDS B.V.—See Tricon Global Restaurants, Inc.; *U.S. Public*, pg. 1637
KENTUCKY HYDROCARBON DIVISION—See Equitable Resources, Inc.; *U.S. Public*, pg. 589
KENTUCKY INDIANA LUMBER CO. INC.; *U.S. Private*, pg. 615
KENTUCKY INSURANCE CO.—See The Seibels Bruce Group, Inc.; *U.S. Public*, pg. 1454
KENTUCKY INVESTORS, INC.; *U.S. Public*, pg. 951
KENTUCKY MANUFACTURING CO.; *U.S. Private*, pg. 615
KENTUCKY MEDICAL INSURANCE COMPANY, HOSPITAL DIVISION—See Michigan Physicians Mutual Liability Inc.; *U.S. Private*, pg. 741
KENTUCKY MEDICAL INSURANCE COMPANY (KMIC)—See Michigan Physicians Mutual Liability Inc.; *U.S. Private*, pg. 741
THE KENTUCKY POST—See The E.W. Scripps Company; *U.S. Public*, pg. 1447
KENTUCKY POWER CO.—See American Electric Power Company, Inc.; *U.S. Public*, pg. 72
KENTUCKY STANDARD—See Landmark Communications, Inc.; *U.S. Private*, pg. 648
KENTUCKY-TENNESSEE CLAY CO.—See Hecla Mining Company; *U.S. Public*, pg. 804
KENTUCKY UTILITIES COMPANY—See KU Energy; *U.S. Public*, pg. 941
KENTUCKY WEST VIRGINIA GAS CO.—See Equitable Resources, Inc.; *U.S. Public*, pg. 590
KENWAL PRODUCTS CORP.; *U.S. Private*, pg. 615
KENWOOD AGENCY CORPORATION—See Kenwood Corporation; *Int'l*, pg. 730
KENWOOD AMERICAS CORPORATION—See Kenwood Corporation; *Int'l*, pg. 730
KENWOOD & LEE ELECTRONICS, LTD.—See Kenwood Corporation; *Int'l*, pg. 730
KENWOOD APPLIANCES PLC; *Int'l*, pg. 730
KENWOOD A/S—See Kenwood Appliances Plc; *Int'l*, pg. 730
KENWOOD BUSINESS CORPORATION—See Kenwood Corporation; *Int'l*, pg. 730
KENWOOD CORE CORPORATION—See Kenwood Corporation; *Int'l*, pg. 730
KENWOOD CORPORATION; *Int'l*, pg. 730
KENWOOD DEVICES CORPORATION—See Kenwood Corporation; *Int'l*, pg. 730
KENWOOD ELECTRONICS AUSTRALIA PTY. LTD.—See Kenwood Corporation; *Int'l*, pg. 730
KENWOOD ELECTRONICS BENELUX N.V.—See Kenwood Corporation; *Int'l*, pg. 730
KENWOOD ELECTRONICS BRASIL LTDA.—See Kenwood Corporation; *Int'l*, pg. 730
KENWOOD ELECTRONICS CANADA INC.—See Kenwood Corporation; *Int'l*, pg. 730
KENWOOD ELECTRONICS DEUTSCHLAND GMBH—See Kenwood Corporation; *Int'l*, pg. 731
KENWOOD ELECTRONICS EUROPE B.V.—See Kenwood Corporation; *Int'l*, pg. 731
KENWOOD ELECTRONICS (H.K.) LTD.—See Kenwood Corporation; *Int'l*, pg. 731
KENWOOD ELECTRONICS ITALIA S.P.A.—See Kenwood Corporation; *Int'l*, pg. 731
KENWOOD ELECTRONICS LATIN AMERICA S.A.—See Kenwood Corporation; *Int'l*, pg. 731
KENWOOD ELECTRONICS (MALAYSIA) SDN. BHD.—See Kenwood Corporation; *Int'l*, pg. 731
KENWOOD ELECTRONICS (MEXICO) S.A. DE C.V.—See Kenwood Corporation; *Int'l*, pg. 731
KENWOOD ELECTRONICS NEDERLAND B.V.—See Kenwood Corporation; *Int'l*, pg. 731
KENWOOD ELECTRONICS SINGAPORE PTE. LTD.—See Kenwood Corporation; *Int'l*, pg. 731
KENWOOD ENGINEERING CORPORATION—See Kenwood Corporation; *Int'l*, pg. 730
KENWOOD IBERICA S.A.—See Kenwood Corporation; *Int'l*, pg. 731
KENWOOD KOMAGANE CORPORATION—See Kenwood Corporation; *Int'l*, pg. 730
KENWOOD LINEAR S.P.A.—See Kenwood Corporation; *Int'l*, pg. 731
KENWOOD MANUFACTURING GMBH—See Kenwood Appliances Plc; *Int'l*, pg. 730
KENWOOD NAGANO CORPORATION—See Kenwood Corporation; *Int'l*, pg. 730
KENWOOD PARTS CENTER CORPORATION—See Kenwood Corporation; *Int'l*, pg. 730
KENWOOD PERSONNEL CORPORATION—See Kenwood Corporation; *Int'l*, pg. 730
KENWOOD PRECISION CORPORATION—See Kenwood Corporation; *Int'l*, pg. 730
KENWOOD (S.A.) (PTY.) LTD.—See Kenwood Appliances Plc; *Int'l*, pg. 730
KENWOOD SAITAMA CORPORATION—See Kenwood Corporation; *Int'l*, pg. 730
KENWOOD SERVICE CORPORATION—See Kenwood Corporation; *Int'l*, pg. 730
KENWOOD SERVICE CORPORATION-HAWAII BRANCH—See Kenwood Corporation; *Int'l*, pg. 730
KENWOOD SERVICE CORPORATION-NEW JERSEY BRANCH—See Kenwood Corporation; *Int'l*, pg. 730
KENWOOD SERVICE CORPORATION-PUERTO RICO BRANCH—See Kenwood Corporation; *Int'l*, pg. 730
KENWOOD USA—See Kenwood Corporation; *Int'l*, pg. 730
KENWOOD YAMAGATA CORPORATION—See Kenwood Corporation; *Int'l*, pg. 730
KENWORTH OF INDIANAPOLIS INC.; *U.S. Private*, pg. 615
KENWORTH MEXICANA, S.A. DE C.V.—See Paccar Inc.; *U.S. Public*, pg. 1246
KENWORTH TRUCK COMPANY—See Paccar Inc.; *U.S. Public*, pg. 1246
KENYA PETROLEUM REFINERIES—See Royal Dutch/Shell Group of Companies; *Int'l*, pg. 1136
KENYA SHELL LTD.—See Royal Dutch/Shell Group of Companies; *Int'l*, pg. 1136
KENYA-SWISS CHEMICAL CO. LTD.—See Novartis AG; *Int'l*, pg. 983
KENYON INDUSTRIES, INC.—See The Hallwood Group Incorporated; *U.S. Public*, pg. 778
KENYON MARINE, INC.—See Vector Industries, Ltd.; *Int'l*, pg. 1462
KENYON OIL COMPANY, INC.—See Warren Equities Inc.; *U.S. Private*, pg. 1151
KENZO—See LVMH Moet Hennessy Louis Vuitton; *Int'l*, pg. 781
KENZO PARIS K.K—See LVMH Moet Hennessy Louis Vuitton; *Int'l*, pg. 782
KEOMA SRL—See Masco Corporation; *U.S. Public*, pg. 1054
KEPA KAUFHAUS GMBH—See Karstadt Aktiengesellschaft; *Int'l*, pg. 724
KEPCO BEIJING OFFICE—See Korea Electric Power Corporation (KEPCO); *Int'l*, pg. 758
KEPCO - NEW YORK OFFICE—See Korea Electric Power Corporation (KEPCO); *Int'l*, pg. 758
KEPCO PARIS OFFICE—See Korea Electric Power Corporation (KEPCO); *Int'l*, pg. 758
KEPCO PHILIPPINES CORPORATION—See Korea Electric Power Corporation (KEPCO); *Int'l*, pg. 758
KEPCO RESOURCES AMERICA—See Korea Electric Power Corporation (KEPCO); *Int'l*, pg. 758
KEPCO RESOURCES AUSTRALIA—See Korea Electric Power Corporation (KEPCO); *Int'l*, pg. 758
KEPCO TOKYO OFFICE—See Korea Electric Power Corporation (KEPCO); *Int'l*, pg. 758
KEPCO TORONTO OFFICE—See Korea Electric Power Corporation (KEPCO); *Int'l*, pg. 758
KEPCO VANCOUVER OFFICE—See Korea Electric Power Corporation (KEPCO); *Int'l*, pg. 758
KEPEC CHEMISCHE FABRIK GMBH—See Henkel KGaA; *Int'l*, pg. 610
KEPEC RESOURCES LIMITED—See Empire Company Limited; *Int'l*, pg. 454
KEPNER-TREGOE, INC.—See USF&G Corporation; *U.S. Public*, pg. 1659
KEPPEL CORPORATION LIMITED; *Int'l*, pg. 731
KEPPEL FELS BALTECH LTD.—See Keppel Corporation Limited; *Int'l*, pg. 731
KEPPEL FELS CHINA LTD.—See Keppel Corporation Limited; *Int'l*, pg. 731
KEPPEL FELS ENERGY INCORPORATED—See Keppel Corporation Limited; *Int'l*, pg. 731
KEPPEL MARINE AGENCIES INC.—See Keppel Corporation Limited; *Int'l*, pg. 731
KEPPEL PRINCE ENGINEERING ENGINEERING PTY LTD.—See Keppel Corporation Limited; *Int'l*, pg. 731
KEPPEL (UK) LTD.—See Keppel Corporation Limited; *Int'l*, pg. 731
KEPPEL-FELS LTD.—See Keppel Corporation Limited; *Int'l*, pg. 731
KER MONOLITHICS—See Lafarge S.A.; *Int'l*, pg. 789
KERAGLASS—See Saint-Gobain; *Int'l*, pg. 1172
KERAMIK-ROHR VERTRIEBS-UND BERATUNGS GMBH—See Hepworth Plc; *Int'l*, pg. 615
KERANA OY—See Icopal a/s; *Int'l*, pg. 659
KERI—See Kao Corporation; *Int'l*, pg. 718
THE KERITE COMPANY—See Hubbell Incorporated; *U.S. Public*, pg. 844
KERLANE—See Saint-Gobain; *Int'l*, pg. 1176
KERMI GMBH—See Preussag AG; *Int'l*, pg. 1069
KERN COUNTY LAND CO.—See Tenneco Inc.; *U.S. Public*, pg. 1578
KERN INDUSTRIES; *U.S. Private*, pg. 616
KERN LIVESTOCK SUPPLEMENT CO., INC.—See Altair Corporation; *U.S. Private*, pg. 46
KERN RIVER CORPORATION—See Tenneco Inc.; *U.S. Public*, pg. 1578
KERN RIVER GAS SUPPLY CORPORATION—See Tenneco Inc.; *U.S. Public*, pg. 1579
KERN RIVER GAS TRANSMISSION—See The Williams Companies, Inc.; *U.S. Public*, pg. 1769
KERN RIVER SERVICE CORPORATION—See Tenneco Inc.; *U.S. Public*, pg. 1578
KERNITE—See NCH Corporation; *U.S. Public*, pg. 1145
KERNKRAFTWERK BROKDORF GMBH—See Veba AG; *Int'l*, pg. 1456
KERNKRAFTWERK BRUNSBUETTEL GMBH—See Veba AG; *Int'l*, pg. 1457
KERNKRAFTWERK KRUMMEL GMBH—See Veba AG; *Int'l*, pg. 1456
KERNKRAFTWERK STADE GMBH—See Veba AG; *Int'l*, pg. 1456
KERNKRAFTWERK UNTERWESER GMBH—See Veba AG; *Int'l*, pg. 1456
KERNKRAFTWERK WURGASSEN-KWW—See Veba AG; *Int'l*, pg. 1456
KERN'S BAKERIES, INCORPORATED—See The Earthgrains Company; *U.S. Public*, pg. 547
KERNVILLE DOMESTIC WATER COMPANY—See Dominguez Services Corporation; *U.S. Public*, pg. 516
KEROSEAN LIMITED—See Saint-Gobain; *Int'l*, pg. 1173
KERR GROUP, INC.; *U.S. Public*, pg. 952
KERR-MCGEE CHEMICAL CORP.—See Kerr-McGee Corporation; *U.S. Public*, pg. 952
KERR-MCGEE CHINA PETROLEUM LTD.—See Kerr-McGee Corporation; *U.S. Public*, pg. 952
KERR-MCGEE COAL CORP.—See Kerr-McGee Corporation; *U.S. Public*, pg. 952
KERR-MCGEE CORPORATION; *U.S. Public*, pg. 952
KERR-MCGEE OIL (U.K.) PLC—See Kerr-McGee Corporation; *U.S. Public*, pg. 952
KERR-MCGEE PETROLEUM EXPLORATION & PRODUCTION DIVISION—See Kerr-McGee Corporation; *U.S. Public*, pg. 952
KERRY GROUP PLC; *Int'l*, pg. 731
KERRY INGREDIENTS—See Kerry Group PLC; *Int'l*, pg. 732
KERRY INGREDIENTS, BROXBURN—See Kerry Group PLC; *Int'l*, pg. 732
KERRY INGREDIENTS UK LTD.—See Kerry Group PLC; *Int'l*, pg. 732
KERRY KELLY THOMPSON—See Earle Palmer Brown; *U.S. Private*, pg. 174
KERRY ULTRASONICS LIMITED—See Halma p.l.c.; *Int'l*, pg. 589
KERVICK ENTERPRISES, INC.; *U.S. Private*, pg. 616
PT KES SINAR MAS SECURITIES—See Kim Eng Holdings Limited; *Int'l*, pg. 733
KESHER ZAFON LTD.—See Motorola, Inc.; *U.S. Public*, pg. 1139
KESKO - AGRICULTURAL & BUILDERS' SUPPLIES DIV.—See Kesko Ltd.; *Int'l*, pg. 732
KESKO CENTRAL WAREHOUSE ONE—See Kesko Ltd.; *Int'l*, pg. 732
KESKO CENTRAL WAREHOUSE TWO—See Kesko Ltd.; *Int'l*, pg. 732
KESKO EXPORT LTD.—See Kesko Ltd.; *Int'l*, pg. 732
KESKO LTD.; *Int'l*, pg. 732
KESKO - TRAINING & EXPERIMENTAL FARM—See Kesko Ltd.; *Int'l*, pg. 732
KESKOMETALLI OY—See Kesko Ltd.; *Int'l*, pg. 732
KESOIL OY—See Neste Oy; *Int'l*, pg. 913
KESPED LTD.—See Kesko Ltd.; *Int'l*, pg. 732
KESSER—See Bouygues; *Int'l*, pg. 206
H. KESSLER & COMPANY; *U.S. Private*, pg. 616
KESTER SOLDER—See Litton Industries, Inc.; *U.S. Public*, pg. 1004
KESTER SOLDER CO.—See Litton Industries, Inc.; *U.S. Public*, pg. 1003
KESTER SOLDER CO. OF CANADA LTD.—See Litton Industries, Inc.; *U.S. Public*, pg. 1004
KESTERSON FOOD COMPANY, INC.; *U.S. Private*, pg. 616
KETCHIKAN PULP CO.—See Louisiana Pacific Corporation; *U.S. Public*, pg. 1015
KETCHUM ADVERTISING FRANCE—See Ketchum Communications Inc.; *U.S. Private*, pg. 617
KETCHUM ADVERTISING GMBH—See Ketchum Communications Inc.; *U.S. Private*, pg. 617
KETCHUM ADVERTISING/PITTSBURGH—See Ketchum Communications Inc.; *U.S. Private*, pg. 616
KETCHUM ADVERTISING/SAN FRANCISCO—See Ketchum Communications Inc.; *U.S. Private*, pg. 616
KETCHUM COMMUNICATIONS INC.; *U.S. Private*, pg. 616
KETCHUM DIRECTORY ADVERTISING/KANSAS CITY—See Ketchum Communications Inc.; *U.S. Private*, pg. 616
KETCHUM DIRECTORY ADVERTISING/NEW YORK—See Ketchum Communications Inc.; *U.S. Private*, pg. 616
KETCHUM, INC.; *U.S. Private*, pg. 617
KETCHUM PUBLIC RELATIONS—See Ketchum Communications Inc.; *U.S. Private*, pg. 617
KETCHUM PUBLIC RELATIONS, GMBH—See Ketchum Communications Inc.; *U.S. Private*, pg. 617
KETCHUM PUBLIC RELATIONS/PARIS—See Ketchum Communications Inc.; *U.S. Private*, pg. 617
KETCHUM PUBLIC RELATIONS, SRL—See Ketchum Communications Inc.; *U.S. Private*, pg. 617
KETCHUM PUBLIC RELATIONS WORLDWIDE—See Ketchum Communications Inc.; *U.S. Private*, pg. 617
KETEMA DIVISION—See Senior Engineering Group, plc.; *Int'l*, pg. 1222
KETEMA, INC.—See KTM Holdings Corp.; *U.S. Private*, pg. 604
KETER PLASTIC LTD.; *Int'l*, pg. 732
KETER (UK) LTD—See Keter Plastic Ltd.; *Int'l*, pg. 732
KETTLE FALLS LIMESTONE COMPANY—See Boise Cascade Corporation; *U.S. Public*, pg. 243
KETTLE RESTAURANTS; *U.S. Private*, pg. 617
KETTLE RIVER GOLD MINE, ECHO BAY MINERALS—See Echo Bay Mines Ltd.; *U.S. Public*, pg. 562
KETTLER BROTHERS, INC.; *U.S. Private*, pg. 617
KEUKENSTEL B.V.—See Vorwerk & Co.; *Int'l*, pg. 1481
KEUM KANG DEVELOPMENT INDUSTRIAL CO., LTD.—See Hyundai Motor Company; *Int'l*, pg. 642
KEVALAND CORP.—See Holderbank Financiere Glaris Ltd.; *Int'l*, pg. 628
KEVALAND TEXAS CORP.—See Holderbank Financiere Glaris Ltd.; *Int'l*, pg. 628
KEVCO, INC.; *U.S. Public*, pg. 952
KEVEX INSTRUMENTS—See Thermo Electron Corporation; *U.S. Public*, pg. 1594
KEVEX X-RAY—See Thermo Electron Corporation; *U.S. Public*, pg. 1594
KEVLIN CORPORATION; *U.S. Public*, pg. 953
KEWANEE BOILER MANUFACTURING COMPANY, INC.—See Burnham; *U.S. Public*, pg. 270

Company Index

KEWAUNEE ENGINEERING CORP.—See Marine Travelift, Inc.; *U.S. Private*, pg. 703
KEWAUNEE SCIENTIFIC CORPORATION; *U.S. Public*, pg. 953
KEX PRODUCTS, INC.—See Berwind Corporation; *U.S. Private*, pg. 138
KEXIM ASIA LIMITED—See The Export-Import Bank of Korea; *Int'l*, pg. 468
KEY BANK LIFE INSURANCE, LTD.—See Keycorp; *U.S. Public*, pg. 954
KEY BANK OF ALASKA—See Keycorp; *U.S. Public*, pg. 954
KEY BANK OF COLORADO—See Keycorp; *U.S. Public*, pg. 954
KEY BANK OF IDAHO—See Keycorp; *U.S. Public*, pg. 954
KEY BANK OF MAINE—See Keycorp; *U.S. Public*, pg. 954
KEY BANK OF NEW YORK—See Keycorp; *U.S. Public*, pg. 954
KEY BANK OF OREGON—See Keycorp; *U.S. Public*, pg. 954
KEY BANK OF UTAH—See Keycorp; *U.S. Public*, pg. 954
KEY BANK OF VERMONT—See Keycorp; *U.S. Public*, pg. 954
KEY BANK OF WASHINGTON—See Keycorp; *U.S. Public*, pg. 954
KEY BANK USA N.A.—See Keycorp; *U.S. Public*, pg. 954
KEY CADILLAC, INC.; *U.S. Private*, pg. 617
KEY CLEARING CORP.—See Keycorp; *U.S. Public*, pg. 955
KEY COMMUNICATIONS, INC.—See de la Cruz & Associates; *U.S. Private*, pg. 318
KEY COMMUNITY DEVELOPMENT CORPORATION—See Keycorp; *U.S. Public*, pg. 954
KEY CONTAINER CORPORATION; *U.S. Private*, pg. 617
KEY ENERGY GROUP INC.; *U.S. Public*, pg. 953
KEY EQUITY CAPITAL CORP.—See Keycorp; *U.S. Public*, pg. 955
KEY FOOD STORES CO-OPERATIVE, INC.; *U.S. Private*, pg. 617
KEY HANDLING SYSTEMS, INC.; *U.S. Private*, pg. 618
KEY INDUSTRIES, INC.; *U.S. Private*, pg. 618
KEY INVESTMENTS, INC.—See Keycorp; *U.S. Public*, pg. 954
KEY MORTGAGE SERVICES, INC.—See Keycorp; *U.S. Public*, pg. 954
KEY PERFURACOES MARITIMAS LIMITADA—See Kuwait Petroleum Corporation; *Int'l*, pg. 765
KEY PHARMACEUTICALS—See Schering-Plough Corporation; *U.S. Public*, pg. 1438
KEY PLASTICS FRANCE SA—See Key Plastics, Inc.; *U.S. Private*, pg. 618
KEY PLASTICS, INC.; *U.S. Private*, pg. 618
KEY PLASTICS UK—See Key Plastics, Inc.; *U.S. Private*, pg. 618
KEY PRODUCTION COMPANY, INC.; *U.S. Public*, pg. 953
KEY PRODUCTS—See Genesee Metal Stampings, Inc.; *U.S. Private*, pg. 446
KEY RADIO LIMITED—See Rogers Communications, Inc.; *Int'l*, pg. 1124
KEY RISK MANAGEMENT SERVICES, INC.—See W.R. Berkley Corporation; *U.S. Public*, pg. 216
KEY SERVICES CORPORATION—See Keycorp; *U.S. Public*, pg. 954
KEY TRONIC CORPORATION; *U.S. Public*, pg. 953
KEY TRUST COMPANY—See Keycorp; *U.S. Public*, pg. 954
KEY TRUST COMPANY OF ALASKA—See Keycorp; *U.S. Public*, pg. 954
KEY TRUST COMPANY OF FLORIDA, NATIONAL ASSOCIATION—See Keycorp; *U.S. Public*, pg. 954
KEY TRUST COMPANY OF INDIANA, NATIONAL ASSOCIATION—See Keycorp; *U.S. Public*, pg. 955
KEY TRUST COMPANY OF MAINE—See Keycorp; *U.S. Public*, pg. 954
KEY TRUST COMPANY OF OHIO, NATIONAL ASSOCIATION—See Keycorp; *U.S. Public*, pg. 955
KEY TRUST COMPANY OF THE NORTHWEST—See Keycorp; *U.S. Public*, pg. 954
KEY TRUST COMPANY OF THE WEST—See Keycorp; *U.S. Public*, pg. 954
KEYCORP; *U.S. Public*, pg. 954
KEYCORP LEASING LTD.—See Keycorp; *U.S. Public*, pg. 954
KEYCORP SHAREHOLDER SERVICES, INC.—See Keycorp; *U.S. Public*, pg. 955
KEYDRIL NIGERIA LIMITED—See Kuwait Petroleum Corporation; *Int'l*, pg. 765
KEYES ASSET MANAGEMET—See The Keyes Company Realtors; *U.S. Private*, pg. 618
THE KEYES COMPANY REALTORS; *U.S. Private*, pg. 618
KEYES INVESTMENTS—See The Keyes Company Realtors; *U.S. Private*, pg. 618
KEYES ITALIANA S.P.A.—See Royal Packaging Industries Van Leer B.V.; *Int'l*, pg. 1146
KEYES MARTIN; *U.S. Private*, pg. 618
KEYES MOTORS, INC.; *U.S. Private*, pg. 618
KEYES NATIONAL REFERRAL—See The Keyes Company Realtors; *U.S. Private*, pg. 618
KEYES NORWAY A/S—See Royal Packaging Industries Van Leer B.V.; *Int'l*, pg. 1146
KEYMARK CORPORATION; *U.S. Private*, pg. 618
KEYMED IRELAND LTD.—See Olympus Optical Co., Ltd.; *Int'l*, pg. 1005
KEYMED (MEDICAL & INDUSTRIAL EQUIPMENT) LTD.—See Olympus Optical Co., Ltd.; *Int'l*, pg. 1005
KEYNOTER PUBLISHING COMPANY, INC.—See Knight-Ridder, Inc.; *U.S. Public*, pg. 964
KEYPORT LIFE INSURANCE COMPANY—See Liberty Mutual Insurance Co.; *U.S. Private*, pg. 618
KEYSOR CENTURY CORPORATION; *U.S. Private*, pg. 618
KEYSPAN ENERGY MANAGEMENT INC.—See Brooklyn Union; *U.S. Public*, pg. 259
KEYSPAN ENERGY SERVICES INC.—See Brooklyn Union; *U.S. Public*, pg. 259

KEYSTONE & CHILDS, INC.—See Rock of Ages Corporation; *U.S. Public*, pg. 1396
KEYSTONE AUTOMOTIVE INDUSTRIES, INC.; *U.S. Public*, pg. 955
KEYSTONE AUTOMOTIVE INDUSTRIES, INC.-TIJUANA—See Keystone Automotive Industries, Inc.; *U.S. Public*, pg. 955
KEYSTONE BANK—See Keystone Financial Inc.; *U.S. Public*, pg. 956
KEYSTONE BREWERS, INC.; *U.S. Private*, pg. 618
KEYSTONE BROKERAGE, INC.—See Keystone Financial Inc.; *U.S. Public*, pg. 956
KEYSTONE BRUSH & CONTACT CO.—See Kirkwood Industries, Inc.; *U.S. Private*, pg. 623
KEYSTONE (CANADA) LTD.—See Tyco International Ltd.; *U.S. Public*, pg. 1650
KEYSTONE CEMENT CO.—See Giant Cement Holding Inc.; *U.S. Public*, pg. 741
KEYSTONE CENTER—See Universal Health Services, Inc.; *U.S. Public*, pg. 1697
KEYSTONE COAL MINING CORP.—See Rochester & Pittsburgh Coal Company; *U.S. Public*, pg. 1395
KEYSTONE CONSOLIDATED INDUSTRIES, INC.; *U.S. Public*, pg. 955
KEYSTONE DO BRASIL LTDA.—See Tyco International Ltd.; *U.S. Public*, pg. 1650
KEYSTONE FASTENERS—See Keystone Consolidated Industries, Inc.; *U.S. Public*, pg. 956
KEYSTONE FINANCIAL INC.; *U.S. Public*, pg. 956
KEYSTONE FINANCIAL SERVICE GROUP, INC.—See Keystone Financial Inc.; *U.S. Public*, pg. 956
KEYSTONE FOODS CORPORATION; *U.S. Private*, pg. 619
KEYSTONE G.M.B.H.—See Tyco International Ltd.; *U.S. Public*, pg. 1650
KEYSTONE GROUP INC.—See Security Group Inc.; *U.S. Private*, pg. 981
KEYSTONE HEALTH PLAN WEST, INC.—See Highmark Inc.; *U.S. Public*, pg. 529
KEYSTONE HERITAGE GROUP, INC.—See Fulton Financial Corp.; *U.S. Public*, pg. 687
KEYSTONE INDUSTRIES, INC.—See Varlen Corporation; *U.S. Public*, pg. 1711
KEYSTONE INTERNATIONAL HOLDINGS CORP.—See Tyco International Ltd.; *U.S. Public*, pg. 1650
KEYSTONE INTERNATIONAL, INC.—See Tyco International Ltd.; *U.S. Public*, pg. 1650
KEYSTONE LINES—See US 1 Industries Inc.; *U.S. Public*, pg. 1687
KEYSTONE MORIN, INC.—See Tyco International Ltd.; *U.S. Public*, pg. 1650
KEYSTONE PACIFIC PTY. LTD.—See Tyco International Ltd.; *U.S. Public*, pg. 1650
KEYSTONE PIPELINE SERVICES, INC.—See Pennsylvania Enterprises Inc.; *U.S. Public*, pg. 1271
KEYSTONE POWDERED METAL COMPANY; *U.S. Private*, pg. 619
KEYSTONE RAILWAY EQUIPMENT COMPANY—See Varlen Corporation; *U.S. Public*, pg. 1711
KEYSTONE SOUTHEAST ASIA PTY. LTD.—See Tyco International Ltd.; *U.S. Public*, pg. 1650
KEYSTONE STEEL & WIRE CO.—See Keystone Consolidated Industries, Inc.; *U.S. Public*, pg. 955
KEYSTONE THERMOMETRICS CORPORATION—See Bowthorpe plc; *Int'l*, pg. 208
KEYSTONE VALVE (CHINA) LTD.—See Tyco International Ltd.; *U.S. Public*, pg. 1650
KEYSTONE VALVE (EUROPA) B.V.—See Tyco International Ltd.; *U.S. Public*, pg. 1650
KEYSTONE VALVE (INDIA) PVT. LTD.—See Tyco International Ltd.; *U.S. Public*, pg. 1650
KEYSTONE VALVE (KOREA) LTD.—See Tyco International Ltd.; *U.S. Public*, pg. 1650
KEYSTONE VALVE (U.K.) LTD.—See Tyco International Ltd.; *U.S. Public*, pg. 1650
KEYSTONE VALVES AND CONTROLS, INC.—See Tyco International Ltd.; *U.S. Public*, pg. 1650
KEYSTONE VALVTRON, INC.—See Tyco International Ltd.; *U.S. Public*, pg. 1650
KEYSTONE VANESSA S.R.L.—See Tyco International Ltd.; *U.S. Public*, pg. 1650
KEYTEK INSTRUMENT CORPORATION—See Thermo Electron Corporation; *U.S. Public*, pg. 1592
KEYWELL CORPORATION; *U.S. Private*, pg. 619
KEZAR FALLS DIVISION—See Consumers Water Company; *U.S. Public*, pg. 438
KGALAGADI SOAP INDUSTRIES(PTY) LTD.—See H.J. Heinz Company; *U.S. Public*, pg. 806
KHIMLINE PUMPS LIMITED—See Sulzer Ltd.; *Int'l*, pg. 1305
KHONG GUAN FLOUR MILLING LIMITED; *Int'l*, pg. 732
KI PACIFIC ASSET MANAGEMENT—See United Asset Management Corporation; *U.S. Public*, pg. 1674
KIA MOTORS AMERICA, INC.—See KIA Motors Corp.; *Int'l*, pg. 733
KIA MOTORS CORP.; *Int'l*, pg. 732
KIBO COMPRESSOR CORP.—See Burk Royalty Co.; *U.S. Private*, pg. 183
KIBUN CO. LTD.; *Int'l*, pg. 733
KID THINK INC.—See Griffin Bacal Inc.; *U.S. Private*, pg. 480
KIDDE CONSUMER DURABLES CORP.—See Hanson PLC; *Int'l*, pg. 594
KIDDE-DEUGRA GMBH—See Williams Holdings Plc; *Int'l*, pg. 1500
KIDDE DEXAERO S.A.—See Williams Holdings Plc; *Int'l*, pg. 1500
KIDDE-FENWAL, INC.—See Williams Holdings Plc; *Int'l*, pg. 1500
KIDDE FIRE PROTECTION LTD.—See Williams Holdings Plc; *Int'l*, pg. 1499
KIDDE FRANCE—See Hanson PLC; *Int'l*, pg. 594
KIDDE-GRAVINER AUSTRALIA PTY. LIMITED—See Williams Holdings Plc; *Int'l*, pg. 1500

KIDDE-GRAVINER LTD.—See Williams Holdings Plc; *Int'l*, pg. 1500
KIDDE-GRAVINER MOSCOW—See Williams Holdings Plc; *Int'l*, pg. 1500
KIDDE INTERNATIONAL ITALY—See Williams Holdings Plc; *Int'l*, pg. 1500
KIDDE INTERNATIONAL PROTECTION SYSTEMS PRE. LTD.—See Williams Holdings Plc; *Int'l*, pg. 1500
KIDDE SYSTEMS, INC.—See Publicker Industries, Inc.; *U.S. Public*, pg. 1341
KIDDE TECHNOLOGIES INC.—See Williams Holdings Plc; *Int'l*, pg. 1500
KIDDE TECHNOLOGIES, INC.—See Williams Holdings Plc; *Int'l*, pg. 1500
KIDDE TECHNOLOGIES INC. (WALTER KIDDE AEROSPACE)—See Williams Holdings Plc; *Int'l*, pg. 1500
KIDDE THORN FIRE PROTECTION LIMITED—See Williams Holdings Plc; *Int'l*, pg. 1500
THE WALTER KIDDE CO. LTD.—See Hanson PLC; *Int'l*, pg. 593
WALTER KIDDE DE MEXICO S.A.—See Hanson PLC; *Int'l*, pg. 594
WALTER KIDDE PORTABLE EQUIPMENT INC.—See Williams Holdings Plc; *Int'l*, pg. 1500
WALTER KIDDE S.A. INDUSTRIA E COMERCIO—See Hanson PLC; *Int'l*, pg. 594
KIDRON INC.; *U.S. Private*, pg. 619
KIDRON, INC.—See Transportation Technologies, Inc.; *U.S. Private*, pg. 1097
KIDS "R" US—See Toys "R" Us, Inc.; *U.S. Public*, pg. 1626
KIDSTON GOLD MINES LIMITED—See Placer Dome Inc.; *Int'l*, pg. 1060
KIEKENS B.V., AMSTERDAM—See Internatio-Muller N.V.; *Int'l*, pg. 681
KIEN—See Vendex International N.V.; *Int'l*, pg. 1462
KIENA GOLD MINES, LTD.—See Placer Dome Inc.; *Int'l*, pg. 1060
KIENZLE ARGO DE MEXICO SA DE CV—See Mannesmann A.G.; *Int'l*, pg. 839
DR. HERBERT KIENZLE UNTERSSTUZUNGSKASSE GMBH—See Mannesmann A.G.; *Int'l*, pg. 839
KIESERLING GMBH—See Deutsche Babcock AG; *Int'l*, pg. 399
EMIL KIESSLING & CIE. G.M.B.H.—See Wella Group; *Int'l*, pg. 1489
KIEWIT CONSTRUCTION GROUP, INC.—See Peter Kiewit Sons Inc.; *U.S. Private*, pg. 619
KIEWIT MINING GROUP, INC.—See Peter Kiewit Sons Inc.; *U.S. Private*, pg. 619
PETER KIEWIT SONS INC.; *U.S. Private*, pg. 619
KIFFER ET HAMAIDE—See Lafarge S.A.; *Int'l*, pg. 789
KIFUKI U.S.A. CO., INC.—See Q.P. Corporation; *Int'l*, pg. 1074
KIGGEN AFVALTECHNIEK—See Powell Duffryn PLC; *Int'l*, pg. 1066
KII SANGYO CO., LTD.—See Kanebo, Ltd.; *Int'l*, pg. 722
KIJKSHOP/BEST-SELLERS—See Vendex International N.V.; *Int'l*, pg. 1462
KIKKOMAN CORPORATION; *Int'l*, pg. 733
KIKKOMAN FOODS, INC.—See Kikkoman Corporation; *Int'l*, pg. 733
KIKKOMAN (S) PTE. LTD.—See Kikkoman Corporation; *Int'l*, pg. 733
KIKKOMAN TRADING EUROPE GMBH—See Kikkoman Corporation; *Int'l*, pg. 733
KILAUEA AGRONOMICS, INC.—See Buyco, Inc.; *U.S. Private*, pg. 190
KILBORN DO BRASIL LTDA.—See SNC-Lavalin Group Inc.; *Int'l*, pg. 1162
KILBORN INC. Y COMPANIA LIMITADA—See SNC-Lavalin Group Inc.; *Int'l*, pg. 1162
PT KILBORN PAKAR REKAYASA—See SNC-Lavalin Group Inc.; *Int'l*, pg. 1162
KILBORN PERU S.A.—See SNC-Lavalin Group Inc.; *Int'l*, pg. 1162
KILBORN SNC-LAVALIN—See SNC-Lavalin Group Inc.; *Int'l*, pg. 1162
KILBORN SNC-LAVALIN INC.—See SNC-Lavalin Group Inc.; *Int'l*, pg. 1162
KILBORN SNC-LAVALIN—See SNC-Lavalin Group Inc.; *Int'l*, pg. 1162
KILGORE FIRST NATIONAL BANK—See First Commercial Corporation; *U.S. Public*, pg. 630
KILGORE OPERATIONS—See Alliant Techsystems; *U.S. Public*, pg. 47
KILLARK ELECTRIC MANUFACTURING CO.—See Hubbell Incorporated; *U.S. Public*, pg. 844
KILLARNEY HOTELS LTD.—See Liebherr-International AG; *Int'l*, pg. 809
KILLEARN ADVISERS, INC.—See Killearn Properties, Inc.; *U.S. Public*, pg. 956
KILLEARN APARTMENT MANAGEMENT, INC.—See Killearn Properties, Inc.; *U.S. Public*, pg. 956
KILLEARN CONSTRUCTION, INC.—See Killearn Properties, Inc.; *U.S. Public*, pg. 956
KILLEARN PROPERTIES, INC.; *U.S. Public*, pg. 956
KILLEARN PROPERTIES OF GEORGIA—See Killearn Properties, Inc.; *U.S. Public*, pg. 956
KILLEARN REALTY, INC.—See Killearn Properties, Inc.; *U.S. Public*, pg. 956
KILLIN VOIMA OY—See Imatran Voima Oy; *Int'l*, pg. 661
KILLINGHOLME WHARFAGE CO. LTD.—See Simon Engineering plc; *Int'l*, pg. 1251
KILLINGTON LIMITED—See American Skiing Company; *U.S. Private*, pg. 61
KILLINGTON WOOD PRODUCTS, INC.—See Carris Financial Group; *U.S. Private*, pg. 215
KILMEADEN FOODS LIMITED—See Avonmore Waterford Group plc; *Int'l*, pg. 102
KILOHEAT LTD.—See Masco Corporation; *U.S. Public*, pg. 1055
KILOMETRAGE S.A.—See ING Groep N.V.; *Int'l*, pg. 650

KILOVAC CORPORATION—See Communications Instruments Inc.; *U.S. Private*, pg. 259
KILROY STRUCTURAL STEEL—See Triumph Group, Inc.; *U.S. Public*, pg. 1640
KIM ENG HOLDINGS LTD.; *Int'l*, pg. 733
KIM ENG SECURITIES (HONG KONG) LIMITED—See Kim Eng Holdings Limited; *Int'l*, pg. 733
KIM ENG SECURITIES (LONDON) LIMITED—See Kim Eng Holdings Limited; *Int'l*, pg. 733
KIM ENG SECURITIES PHILIPPINES INC.—See Kim Eng Holdings Limited; *Int'l*, pg. 733
KIM ENG SECURITIES (PRIVATE) LIMITED—See Kim Eng Holdings Limited; *Int'l*, pg. 733
KIM ENG SECURITIES USA INC.—See Kim Eng Holdings Limited; *Int'l*, pg. 733
KIMBALL ELECTRONICS GROUP—See Kimball International, Inc.; *U.S. Public*, pg. 957
KIMBALL FLIGHT OPERATIONS—See Kimball International, Inc.; *U.S. Public*, pg. 957
KIMBALL FURNITURE REPRODUCTIONS—See Kimball International, Inc.; *U.S. Public*, pg. 957
KIMBALL INTERNATIONAL, INC.; *U.S. Public*, pg. 956
L. ROBERT KIMBALL & ASSOCIATES; *U.S. Private*, pg. 619
KIMBALL LODGING GROUP—See Kimball International, Inc.; *U.S. Public*, pg. 957
KIMBALL OFFICE FURNITURE CO.—See Kimball International, Inc.; *U.S. Public*, pg. 957
KIMBALL OFFICE FURNITURE MANUFACTURING—See Kimball International, Inc.; *U.S. Public*, pg. 957
KIMBALL SYSTEMS BV—See Esselte AB; *Int'l*, pg. 461
KIMBALL U.K., INC.—See Kimball International, Inc.; *U.S. Public*, pg. 958
KIMBALL UPHOLSTERED PRODUCTS—See Kimball International, Inc.; *U.S. Public*, pg. 957
P.T. KIMBALLMAS SEJATI—See McCormick & Company, Incorporated; *Int'l*, pg. 1067
KIMBERLY-CLARK—See Kimberly-Clark Corporation; *U.S. Public*, pg. 959
KIMBERLY-CLARK AUSTRALIA PTY. LTD.—See Kimberly-Clark Corporation; *U.S. Public*, pg. 959
KIMBERLY-CLARK BENELUX OPERATIONS B.V.—See Kimberly-Clark Corporation; *U.S. Public*, pg. 959
KIMBERLY-CLARK COMPUTER SERVICES, INC.—See Kimberly-Clark Corporation; *U.S. Public*, pg. 959
KIMBERLY-CLARK CONSUMER PRODUCTS—See Kimberly-Clark Corporation; *U.S. Public*, pg. 959
KIMBERLY-CLARK CORPORATION; *U.S. Public*, pg. 958
KIMBERLY-CLARK DE CENTRO AMERICA S.A.—See Kimberly-Clark Corporation; *U.S. Public*, pg. 959
KIMBERLY-CLARK DE MEXICO, S.A. DE C.V.—See Kimberly-Clark Corporation; *U.S. Public*, pg. 960
KIMBERLY-CLARK DURAFAB, INC.—See Kimberly-Clark Corporation; *U.S. Public*, pg. 959
KIMBERLY-CLARK, EVERETT—See Kimberly-Clark Corporation; *U.S. Public*, pg. 958
KIMBERLY-CLARK FAR EAST PTE. LTD.—See Kimberly-Clark Corporation; *U.S. Public*, pg. 959
KIMBERLY-CLARK FRANCE S.A.R.L.—See Kimberly-Clark Corporation; *U.S. Public*, pg. 959
KIMBERLY-CLARK GMBH—See Kimberly-Clark Corporation; *U.S. Public*, pg. 959
KIMBERLY-CLARK HOME HEALTHCARE—See Kimberly-Clark Corporation; *U.S. Public*, pg. 959
KIMBERLY-CLARK HOSPITAL SERVICE PRODUCTS—See Kimberly-Clark Corporation; *U.S. Public*, pg. 959
KIMBERLY-CLARK INC.—See Kimberly-Clark Corporation; *U.S. Public*, pg. 959
KIMBERLY-CLARK INTEGRATED SERVICES CORP.—See Kimberly-Clark Corporation; *U.S. Public*, pg. 959
KIMBERLY-CLARK INTERNATIONAL, S.A.—See Kimberly-Clark Corporation; *U.S. Public*, pg. 959
KIMBERLY-CLARK INTERNATIONAL SERVICES CORP.—See Kimberly-Clark Corporation; *U.S. Public*, pg. 959
KIMBERLY-CLARK ITALIANA S.R.L.—See Kimberly-Clark Corporation; *U.S. Public*, pg. 959
KIMBERLY-CLARK LIMITED—See Kimberly-Clark Corporation; *U.S. Public*, pg. 959
KIMBERLY-CLARK MALAYSIA SENDIRIAN BERHAD—See Kimberly-Clark Corporation; *U.S. Public*, pg. 960
KIMBERLY-CLARK, MOBILE—See Kimberly-Clark Corporation; *U.S. Public*, pg. 958
KIMBERLY-CLARK, NOVA SCOTIA—See Kimberly-Clark Corporation; *U.S. Public*, pg. 959
KIMBERLY-CLARK PHILIPPINES INC.—See Kimberly-Clark Corporation; *U.S. Public*, pg. 959
KIMBERLY-CLARK PUERTO RICO, INC.—See Kimberly-Clark Corporation; *U.S. Public*, pg. 959
KIMBERLY-CLARK, QUEBEC—See Kimberly-Clark Corporation; *U.S. Public*, pg. 959
KIMBERLY-CLARK SALES CORPORATION—See Kimberly-Clark Corporation; *U.S. Public*, pg. 959
KIMBERLY-CLARK SOPALIN S.A.—See Kimberly-Clark Corporation; *U.S. Public*, pg. 959
KIMBERLY-CLARK TECHNICAL PRODUCTS, INC.—See Kimberly-Clark Corporation; *U.S. Public*, pg. 959
KIMBERLY-CLARK TECNOL—See Kimberly-Clark Corporation; *U.S. Public*, pg. 959
KIMBERLY-CLARK THAILAND LTD.—See Kimberly-Clark Corporation; *U.S. Public*, pg. 959
KIMBERLY-CLARK, WINSLOW—See Kimberly-Clark Corporation; *U.S. Public*, pg. 958
KIMBERLY MANOR NURSING AND CONVALESCENT HOME—See Vencor, Inc.; *U.S. Public*, pg. 1714
KIMBLE GLASS INC.—See Viag AG; *Int'l*, pg. 1464
KIMCO REALTY CORPORATION; *U.S. Public*, pg. 960
KIMFIBERS LTD.—See Kimberly-Clark Corporation; *U.S. Public*, pg. 959
KIMMEL MOTZ REFRIGERATION CORP.—See Toromont Industries Ltd.; *Int'l*, pg. 1400
KIMMINS CORP.; *U.S. Public*, pg. 960
KIMRAY, INC.; *U.S. Private*, pg. 620
P.T. KIMSARI PAPER-INDONESIA—See Kimberly-Clark Corporation; *U.S. Public*, pg. 959

KIMYATEKS DIS TICARET A.S.—See Henkel KGaA; *Int'l*, pg. 614
KINARK CORPORATION; *U.S. Public*, pg. 960
KINCAID FURNITURE CO., INC.—See La-Z-Boy Incorporated; *U.S. Public*, pg. 972
KINCHENG-TOKYO FINANCE CO., LTD.—See The Bank of Tokyo-Mitsubishi, Ltd.; *Int'l*, pg. 158
KINDEL FURNITURE COMPANY; *U.S. Private*, pg. 620
KINDERCARE LEARNING CENTERS, INC.; *U.S. Public*, pg. 961
KINDERGARD—See Mace Security International, Inc.; *U.S. Public*, pg. 1030
KINDLER VERLAG GMBH—See Georg von Holtzbrinck GmbH; *Int'l*, pg. 1478
KINDRED INDUSTRIES—See Emco Limited; *Int'l*, pg. 453
KINEMETRICS, INC.—See OYO Corporation; *Int'l*, pg. 1019
KINEPAK, INCORPORATED—See Imperial Chemical Industries PLC; *Int'l*, pg. 664
KINETCO—See Cummins Engine Company, Inc.; *U.S. Public*, pg. 468
KINETIC CONCEPTS, INC.; *U.S. Private*, pg. 620
KINETIC SYSTEMS TEST MANAGEMENT SYSTEMS GROUP—See KineticSystems Corporation; *U.S. Private*, pg. 620
KINETICA LIMITED—See Du Pont (E.I. Du Pont De Nemours & Co.); *U.S. Public*, pg. 533
KINETICS, INC., A HAWORTH CO.—See Haworth, Inc.; *U.S. Private*, pg. 512
KINETICS TECHNOLOGY INDIA LTD.—See Mannesmann A.G.; *Int'l*, pg. 837
KINETICS TECHNOLOGY INTERNATIONAL BV—See Mannesmann A.G.; *Int'l*, pg. 837
KINETICS TECHNOLOGY INTERNATIONAL GMBH—See Mannesmann A.G.; *Int'l*, pg. 836
KINETICS TECHNOLOGY INTERNATIONAL LTD.—See Mannesmann A.G.; *Int'l*, pg. 837
KINETICS TECHNOLOGY (SINGAPORE) PTE. LTD.—See Mannesmann A.G.; *Int'l*, pg. 837
KINETICSYSTEMS CORPORATION; *U.S. Private*, pg. 620
KING & PRINCE SEAFOOD CORPORATION; *U.S. Private*, pg. 620
KING ARTHUR INC.—See Shelby Williams Industries, Inc.; *U.S. Public*, pg. 1465
KING BEARING, INC.—See Applied Industrial Technologies; *U.S. Public*, pg. 122
KING CAR OTSUKA CO., LTD.—See Otsuka Pharmaceutical Co., Ltd.; *Int'l*, pg. 1014
KING COMPANY—See United Dominion Industries, Ltd.; *U.S. Public*, pg. 1676
KING COTTON FOODS—See Sara Lee Corporation; *U.S. Public*, pg. 1433
KING FEATURES LICENSING—See The Hearst Corporation; *U.S. Public*, pg. 515
KING FEATURES SYNDICATE DIVISION—See The Hearst Corporation; *U.S. Public*, pg. 518
KING FIFTH WHEEL CO.—See TI Group plc; *Int'l*, pg. 1337
KING FISHER, INC.—See Seaman Timber Company, Inc.; *U.S. Private*, pg. 979
KING FUELS, INC.; *U.S. Private*, pg. 620
GEO. W. KING LTD.—See Fried. Krupp AG; *Int'l*, pg. 507
KING GROUP, INC.; *U.S. Private*, pg. 620
KING INDUSTRIES, INC.; *U.S. Private*, pg. 620
KING KOIL LICENSING COMPANY INC.; *U.S. Private*, pg. 621
KING KULLEN GROCERY CO., INC.; *U.S. Private*, pg. 621
KING LOUIE INTERNATIONAL; *U.S. Private*, pg. 621
KING MILLING COMPANY; *U.S. Private*, pg. 621
THE KING OF PRUSSIA COURIER—See Journal Register Company; *U.S. Public*, pg. 935
KING OF THE ROAD—See Chief Industries, Inc.; *U.S. Private*, pg. 236
KING PACIFIC LTD.—See Compagnie des Machines Bull; *Int'l*, pg. 315
KING PACKAGING COMPANY, INC.—See Imperial Holly Corporation; *U.S. Public*, pg. 872
KING PRESS CORPORATION—See Publishers Equipment Corporation; *U.S. Public*, pg. 1341
KING SEELY THERMOS COMPANY—See Eaton Corporation; *U.S. Public*, pg. 558
W.H. KING DRUG CO.—See Bergen Brunswig Corporation; *U.S. Public*, pg. 214
KING WILKINSON LTD.—See Babcock International Group PLC; *Int'l*, pg. 131
KING WIRE INC.; *U.S. Private*, pg. 621
KING WORLD PRODUCTIONS—See King World Productions, Inc.; *U.S. Public*, pg. 961
KING WORLD PRODUCTIONS, INC.; *U.S. Public*, pg. 961
KINGCOME NAVIGATION COMPANY LTD.—See MacMillan Bloedel Limited; *Int'l*, pg. 828
KINGFISHER CO-OP ELEVATOR ASSOCIATION; *U.S. Private*, pg. 621
KINGFISHER PLC; *Int'l*, pg. 733
KINGS MOUNTAIN MANUFACTURING—See ABB Asea Brown Boveri (Holding) Ltd.; *Int'l*, pg. 3
KINGS SUPER MARKETS INC.—See Marks & Spencer PLC; *Int'l*, pg. 843
KINGS TOYOTA SUZUKI; *U.S. Private*, pg. 621
KINGSBURY ASSEMBLY MACHINE DIV.—See Kingsbury Corporation; *U.S. Private*, pg. 622
KINGSBURY CORPORATION; *U.S. Private*, pg. 621
KINGSBURY, INC.; *U.S. Private*, pg. 622
KINGSBURY MACHINING CENTER, DIV.—See Kingsbury Corporation; *U.S. Private*, pg. 622
KINGSBURY SERVICE CORP.—See Kingsbury Corporation; *U.S. Private*, pg. 622
KINGSBURY WORLD SALES—See Kingsbury Corporation; *U.S. Private*, pg. 622
KINGSDOWN, INC.; *U.S. Private*, pg. 622
KINGSEY COGENERATION REGD.—See The Cascades Group; *Int'l*, pg. 273
THE KINGSFORD PRODUCTS COMPANY—See The Clorox Company; *U.S. Public*, pg. 387
KINGSLEY MACHINE CO.—See Illinois Tool Works Inc.; *U.S. Public*, pg. 866

KINGSOFT GMBH—See Electronic Arts; *U.S. Public*, pg. 569
KINGSPORT POWER CO.—See American Electric Power Company, Inc.; *U.S. Public*, pg. 72
KINGSTON CABLE DISTRIBUTORS—See Driver-Harris Company; *U.S. Public*, pg. 530
KINGSTON INDEPENDENT VOICE—See Gannett Company, Inc.; *U.S. Public*, pg. 701
KINGSTON MARKETING CO.—See Topco Associates, Inc.; *U.S. Private*, pg. 1091
KINGSTON OIL SUPPLY CORP.—See Getty Petroleum Marketing Inc.; *U.S. Public*, pg. 741
KINGSTON TECHNOLOGY CORPORATION; *U.S. Private*, pg. 622
KINGSTON-WARREN CORPORATION—See Harvard Industries, Inc.; *U.S. Public*, pg. 796
KINGSTON WHIG-STANDARD—See Hollinger Inc.; *Int'l*, pg. 631
KINGSWOOD ADVERTISING, INC.; *U.S. Private*, pg. 622
KINGSWOOD INTERACTIVE—See Kingswood Advertising, Inc.; *U.S. Private*, pg. 622
KINKI CATERPILLAR MITSUBISHI CONSTRUCTION EQUIPMENT SALES, LTD.—See Caterpillar Inc.; *U.S. Public*, pg. 317
KINKI KOKOKUSHA, LTD.—See Daiko Advertising, Inc.; *Int'l*, pg. 366
KINKI TRANSPORTATION SERVICES CO., LTD.—See Suntory Ltd.; *Int'l*, pg. 1321
KINKO'S CORPORATION; *U.S. Private*, pg. 622
KINKO'S SERVICE CORP.—See Kinko's Corporation; *U.S. Private*, pg. 622
KINLEITH MILL—See International Paper Company; *U.S. Public*, pg. 905
KINNEY SHOE CORPORATION—See Woolworth Corporation; *U.S. Public*, pg. 1777
KINNEY SHOES (AUSTRALIA), LTD.—See Woolworth Corporation; *U.S. Public*, pg. 1778
KINNEY SYSTEM, INC.; *U.S. Private*, pg. 622
KINNEY VACUUM COMPANY—See Tuthill Corporation; *U.S. Private*, pg. 1110
KINPAK, INC.—See Ocean Bio-Chem Inc.; *U.S. Public*, pg. 1211
KINRAY INC.; *U.S. Private*, pg. 622
KINRO, INC.—See Drew Industries Incorporated; *U.S. Public*, pg. 529
KINROSS GOLD CORPORATION; *Int'l*, pg. 734
KINROSS GOLD CORPORATION—See Kinross Gold Corporation; *Int'l*, pg. 734
KINSEKI, LTD.—See Oki Electric Industry Company, Ltd.; *Int'l*, pg. 999
KINSTON DIE CUTTING CORP.—See Hampton Industries, Inc.; *U.S. Public*, pg. 779
KINTECH (U.K.) LTD.—See Mannesmann A.G.; *Int'l*, pg. 837
KINTETSU EURO TRANSPORT LTD.—See Kintetsu World Express, Inc.; *Int'l*, pg. 735
KINTETSU INTEGRATED AIR SERVICES SDN BHD—See Kintetsu World Express, Inc.; *Int'l*, pg. 735
KINTETSU INTERMODAL (TAIWAN), INC.—See Kintetsu World Express, Inc.; *Int'l*, pg. 735
KINTETSU INTERMODAL (U.S.A.), INC.—See Kintetsu World Express, Inc.; *Int'l*, pg. 735
KINTETSU WORLD EXPRESS (AUSTRALIA) PTY. LTD.—See Kintetsu World Express, Inc.; *Int'l*, pg. 735
KINTETSU WORLD EXPRESS (BENELUX) B.V.—See Kintetsu World Express, Inc.; *Int'l*, pg. 735
KINTETSU WORLD EXPRESS (DEUTSCHLAND) GMBH—See Kintetsu World Express, Inc.; *Int'l*, pg. 735
KINTETSU WORLD EXPRESS (FRANCE) S.A.—See Kintetsu World Express, Inc.; *Int'l*, pg. 735
KINTETSU WORLD EXPRESS (H.K.) LTD.—See Kintetsu World Express, Inc.; *Int'l*, pg. 735
KINTETSU WORLD EXPRESS, INC.; *Int'l*, pg. 734
KINTETSU WORLD EXPRESS INC.—See Kintetsu World Express, Inc.; *Int'l*, pg. 734
KINTETSU WORLD EXPRESS (TAIWAN), INC.—See Kintetsu World Express, Inc.; *Int'l*, pg. 735
KINTETSU WORLD EXPRESS (THAILAND) CO., LTD.—See Kintetsu World Express, Inc.; *Int'l*, pg. 735
KINTETSU WORLD EXPRESS (U.K.) LTD.—See Kintetsu World Express, Inc.; *Int'l*, pg. 735
KINTETSU WORLD EXPRESS (U.S.A.), INC.—See Kintetsu World Express, Inc.; *Int'l*, pg. 734
KINUGAWA RUBBER INDUSTRIAL CO., LTD.—See Nissan Motor Co., Ltd.; *Int'l*, pg. 944
KINUURA LABORATORY—See JGC Corporation; *Int'l*, pg. 697
THE KIPLINGER WASHINGTON EDITORS, INC.; *U.S. Private*, pg. 623
KIPP GROUP; *U.S. Private*, pg. 623
KIP'S OF OKLAHOMA, INC.—See Frisch's Restaurants, Inc.; *U.S. Public*, pg. 682
KIR ALIMENTOS, S.A. DE C.V.—See Sara Lee Corporation; *U.S. Public*, pg. 1434
KIRAKINIAN ENGINEERING AND TECHNICAL SUPPLIES CENTER—See GESTRA GmbH; *Int'l*, pg. 550
KIRBY BUILDING SYSTEMS, INC.—See Jannock Limited; *Int'l*, pg. 699
KIRBY COMPANY—See Berkshire Hathaway Inc.; *U.S. Public*, pg. 217
KIRBY CORPORATION; *U.S. Public*, pg. 961
KIRBY TANKSHIPS, INC.—See Kirby Corporation; *U.S. Public*, pg. 962
FRANZ KIRCHFELD GMBH & CO. KG—See MAN Aktiengesellschaft; *Int'l*, pg. 824
KIRCHIMIE LTEE.—See Pfizer Inc.; *U.S. Public*, pg. 1283
KIRIN AMGEN, INC.—See Amgen Inc.; *U.S. Public*, pg. 101
KIRIN BREWERY CO., LTD.; *Int'l*, pg. 735
KIRIN U.S.A. C/O NOMUSA & CO.—See Kirin Brewery Co., Ltd.; *Int'l*, pg. 736
KIRIN USA, INC.—See Kirin Brewery Co., Ltd.; *Int'l*, pg. 736
KIRIU MACHINE MFG. CO., LTD.—See Nissan Motor Co., Ltd.; *Int'l*, pg. 944
THE KIRK & BLUM MFG. CO.; *U.S. Private*, pg. 623

KIRK & MATZ LTD.; *U.S. Private*, pg. 623
KIRKLAND & ROSE LTD.—See CSM N.V.; *Int'l*, pg. 244
KIRKPATRICK PETTIS SMITH POLIAN, INC.—See Mutual of Omaha Insurance Company; *U.S. Private*, pg. 770
KIRKSTONE COMPANY LTD.—See Charming Shoppes, Inc.; *U.S. Public*, pg. 336
KIRKWOOD CARBON—See Kirkwood Industries, Inc.; *U.S. Private*, pg. 623
KIRKWOOD COMMUTATOR—See Kirkwood Industries, Inc.; *U.S. Private*, pg. 623
KIRKWOOD FOREIGN SALES CORP—See Kirkwood Industries, Inc.; *U.S. Private*, pg. 623
KIRKWOOD INDUSTRIES, INC.; *U.S. Private*, pg. 623
KIRLOSKAR CUMMINS LTD.—See Cummins Engine Company, Inc.; *U.S. Public*, pg. 469
KIRLOSKAR EBARA PUMPS LTD.—See Ebara Corporation; *Int'l*, pg. 432
KIRLOSKAR ELECTRODYNE LTD.—See Knurr AG; *Int'l*, pg. 739
KIRLOSKAR WARNER SWASEY LTD.—See Thyssen AG; *Int'l*, pg. 1389
KIRSCH—See Newell Co.; *U.S. Public*, pg. 1176
MORRIS KIRSCHMAN & COMPANY, INC.; *U.S. Private*, pg. 623
JOSEPH KIRSCHNER CO.—See Jordan's Meats; *U.S. Private*, pg. 599
KIRSHENBAUM, BOND & PARTNERS; *U.S. Private*, pg. 624
KIRSHENBAUM BOND & PARTNERS/WEST—See Kirshenbaum, Bond & Partners; *U.S. Private*, pg. 624
KIRST CONSTRUCTION CO., INC.—See CalMat Co.; *U.S. Public*, pg. 296
KIRYU INDUSTRY CO., LTD.—See Fuji Heavy Industries, Ltd.; *Int'l*, pg. 523
J.I. KISLAK AGENCY, INC.—See J.I. Kislak Inc.; *U.S. Private*, pg. 624
J.I. KISLAK INC.; *U.S. Private*, pg. 624
J.I. KISLAK MORTGAGE CORPORATION—See J.I. Kislak Inc.; *U.S. Private*, pg. 624
KISS FM—See EMAP Plc; *Int'l*, pg. 452
KISSIMMEE TOYOTA INC.; *U.S. Private*, pg. 624
KISSING WORKS—See Fried. Krupp AG; *Int'l*, pg. 516
A.C. KISSLING, INC.; *U.S. Private*, pg. 624
KIT MANUFACTURING COMPANY; *U.S. Public*, pg. 962
KITASHIBA ELECTRIC CO., LTD.—See Toshiba Corporation; *Int'l*, pg. 1403
KITCHELL CEM, INC.—See Kitchell Corporation; *U.S. Private*, pg. 624
KITCHELL CONTRACTORS, INC. OF ARIZONA—See Kitchell Corporation; *U.S. Private*, pg. 624
KITCHELL CORPORATION; *U.S. Private*, pg. 624
KITCHELL DEVELOPMENT COMPANY—See Kitchell Corporation; *U.S. Private*, pg. 624
THE KITCHEN COLLECTION INC.—See NACCO Industries, Inc.; *U.S. Public*, pg. 1149
KITCHEN FAIR—See Regal Ware, Inc.; *U.S. Private*, pg. 917
KITCHEN INVESTMENT GROUP; *U.S. Private*, pg. 624
KITCHEN KOMPACT, INC.; *U.S. Private*, pg. 624
KITCHENAID CO.—See Whirlpool Corporation; *U.S. Public*, pg. 1765
KITCHENER CENTER—See The Cascades Group; *Int'l*, pg. 273
JOHN R. KITCHENS INSURANCE, INC.—See Skandia Insurance Company Limited; *Int'l*, pg. 1257
KITCHENS OF SARA LEE-UNITED KINGDOM—See Sara Lee Corporation; *U.S. Public*, pg. 1434
KITCHENS OF THE OCEANS, INC.; *U.S. Private*, pg. 625
KITCONS INSULATION PRODUCTS (U.K.) LIMITED—See Owens Corning; *U.S. Public*, pg. 1237
KITSUKI TOSHIBA ELECTRONICS CORPORATION—See Toshiba Corporation; *Int'l*, pg. 1403
KITTILA WOOD OY—See Enso Oyj; *Int'l*, pg. 456
A/O KIVIJARVI OY—See Outokumpu Oyj; *Int'l*, pg. 1016
KIWI BRANDS—See Sara Lee Corporation; *U.S. Public*, pg. 1433
KIWI BRANDS PTY. LTD.—See Sara Lee Corporation; *U.S. Public*, pg. 1434
KIWI BRANDS SOUTH AFRICA—See Sara Lee Corporation; *U.S. Public*, pg. 1434
KIWI PACKAGING—See Amcor Limited; *Int'l*, pg. 72
KJELLBERGS SUCCESSORS A/S—See Axel Johnson AB; *Int'l*, pg. 712
KJELLBERGS SUCCESSORS B.V.—See Axel Johnson AB; *Int'l*, pg. 712
KJELLSTROM & LEE, INC.—See Gilbane Building Company; *U.S. Private*, pg. 453
KLAFS SAUNABAU GMBH & CO. KG MEDIZINISCHE TECHNIK; *Int'l*, pg. 736
KLARANLAGEN WINTER & CO. GMBH—See Mannesmann A.G.; *Int'l*, pg. 836
KLARK-TEKNIK PLC—See Mark IV Industries Inc.; *U.S. Public*, pg. 1045
KLAUS RADIO INC.; *U.S. Private*, pg. 625
KLAUSSNER CORPORATION; *U.S. Private*, pg. 625
KLAUSSNER FURNITURE INDUSTRY—See Klaussner Corporation; *U.S. Private*, pg. 625
KLAXON SIGNALS LIMITED—See Halma p.l.c.; *Int'l*, pg. 590
KLEBER INDUSTRIE GMBH—See Compagnie Generale des Etablissements Michelin; *Int'l*, pg. 322
KLEBER ITALIANA S.P.A.—See Compagnie Generale des Etablissements Michelin; *Int'l*, pg. 322
KLEBER PNEUMATIQUES SA—See Compagnie Generale des Etablissements Michelin; *Int'l*, pg. 322
KLEBER REIFEN UND TECHNISCHE GUMMIWAREN AG—See Compagnie Generale des Etablissements Michelin; *Int'l*, pg. 322
KLECO CORP.; *U.S. Private*, pg. 625
KLEER-VU—See Kleer-Vu Plastics, Inc.; *U.S. Public*, pg. 962
KLEER-VU PLASTICS, INC.; *U.S. Public*, pg. 962
KLEER-VU PLASTICS CORP.—See Kleer-Vu Plastics, Inc.; *U.S. Public*, pg. 962

KLEIN ASSOCIATES, INC.—See OYO Corporation; *Int'l*, pg. 1019
KLEIN BROTHERS LTD., SNACK & PACKAGED NUT DIV.—See ConAgra, Inc.; *U.S. Public*, pg. 428
KLEIN TOOLS INC.; *U.S. Private*, pg. 625
KLEINERT'S, INC.; *U.S. Public*, pg. 625
KLEINERT'S, INC., OF ALABAMA—See Kleinert s, Inc.; *U.S. Public*, pg. 625
KLEINERT'S INC. OF FLORIDA—See Kleinert's, Inc.; *U.S. Public*, pg. 625
KLEINSCHMIDT INC.; *U.S. Private*, pg. 625
KLEINSLEEP—See Sleepy's The Mattress Professionals; *U.S. Private*, pg. 1006
KLEINWORT BENSON ARGENTINA SA—See Dresdner Bank AG; *Int'l*, pg. 420
KLEINWORT BENSON CAPITAL MANAGEMENT INCORPORATED—See Dresdner Bank AG; *Int'l*, pg. 420
KLEINWORT BENSON (GUERNSEY) LIMITED—See Dresdner Bank AG; *Int'l*, pg. 420
KLEINWORT BENSON (JERSEY) LIMITED—See Dresdner Bank AG; *Int'l*, pg. 420
KLEINWORT BENSON LIMITED—See Dresdner Bank AG; *Int'l*, pg. 420
KLEINWORT BENSON LTD.—See Dresdner Bank AG; *Int'l*, pg. 420
KLEINWORT BENSON RESEARCH (ASIA) PTE. LIMITED—See Dresdner Bank AG; *Int'l*, pg. 420
KLEM EURO RSCG—See Havas Advertising; *Int'l*, pg. 603
KLEM SUPPLY, INC.—See Kevco, Inc.; *U.S. Public*, pg. 953
ING. G. KLEMM BOHRTECHNIK GMBH—See Ingersoll-Rand Company; *U.S. Public*, pg. 878
KLEMME GMBH & GO., K.G.—See Borden, Inc.; *U.S. Private*, pg. 160
KLEMTNER ADVERTISING INC.—See Saatchi & Saatchi Advertising Worldwide; *U.S. Public*, pg. 1422
KLICK—See Vendex International N.V.; *Int'l*, pg. 1462
KLIL INDUSTRIES LTD.—See IDB Holding Corporation; *Int'l*, pg. 644
THE KLINE FURNITURE CO.—See Reliable Stores, Inc.; *U.S. Private*, pg. 920
KLINE IRON & STEEL CO., INC.; *U.S. Private*, pg. 626
KLINGE PHARMA GMBH—See Fujisawa Pharmaceutical Co. Ltd.; *Int'l*, pg. 525
GEORGETTE KLINGER, INC.; *U.S. Private*, pg. 626
GEORGETTE KLINGER LABORATORIES—See Georgette Klinger, Inc.; *U.S. Private*, pg. 626
KLIPPAN ESPANA—See Electrolux, AB; *Int'l*, pg. 443
KLIPSCH, INC.; *U.S. Private*, pg. 626
KLOCKNER BARRIER FILMS—See Klockner-Werke AG; *Int'l*, pg. 737
KLOCKNER-BARTELT, INC.—See Klockner-Werke AG; *Int'l*, pg. 737
KLOCKNER-BORSCH TOOLING TECHNOLOGIES—See Klockner-Werke AG; *Int'l*, pg. 737
KLOCKNER CAPITAL CORP.—See Klockner-Werke AG; *Int'l*, pg. 737
KLOCKNER-DOWTY—See TI Group plc; *Int'l*, pg. 1338
KLOCKNER ER-WE-PA—See Klockner-Werke AG; *Int'l*, pg. 737
KLOCKNER-HOOPER PACKAGING MACHINERY—See Klockner-Werke AG; *Int'l*, pg. 737
KLOCKNER INA INDUSTRIAL INSTALLATIONS, INC.—See RWE AG; *Int'l*, pg. 1081
KLOCKNER MASCHINEN - UND ANGLAGENBAU GMBH—See Babcock International Group PLC; *Int'l*, pg. 131
KLOCKNER-MOELLER—See Klockner-Moeller GmbH; *Int'l*, pg. 736
KLOCKNER-MOELLER CORP.—See Klockner-Moeller GmbH; *Int'l*, pg. 736
KLOCKNER-MOELLER GMBH; *Int'l*, pg. 736
KLOCKNER-PENTAPLAST GMBH—See Klockner-Werke AG; *Int'l*, pg. 737
KLOCKNER PENTAPLAST OF AMERICA, INC.—See Klockner-Werke AG; *Int'l*, pg. 737
KLOCKNER-PENTAPLAST OF CANADA, INC.—See Klockner-Werke AG; *Int'l*, pg. 737
KLOCKNER STADLER HURTER, LTD.—See RWE AG; *Int'l*, pg. 1081
KLOCKNER-WERKE AG; *Int'l*, pg. 736
KLOCKNER-MOELLER CORP.—See Klockner-Moeller GmbH; *Int'l*, pg. 736
KLOECKNER & CO. AG; *Int'l*, pg. 737
KLOECKNER DURILIT GMBH—See Klockner-Werke AG; *Int'l*, pg. 737
KLOECKNER INDUSTRIE-ANLAGEN GMBH—See RWE AG; *Int'l*, pg. 1081
KLOECKNER IONON GMBH—See Klockner-Werke AG; *Int'l*, pg. 737
KLOECKNER IONON OF AMERICA, INC.—See Klockner-Werke AG; *Int'l*, pg. 737
KLOECKNER-PENTAPACK GMBH—See Klockner-Werke AG; *Int'l*, pg. 737
KLOECKNER PENTAPACK LTD.—See Klockner-Werke AG; *Int'l*, pg. 737
KLOECKNER PENTAPLAST LTD.—See Klockner-Werke AG; *Int'l*, pg. 737
KLOECKNER-WILHELMSBURGER GMBH—See Klockner-Werke AG; *Int'l*, pg. 737
KLOOF GOLD MINING COMPANY LIMITED; *Int'l*, pg. 738
KLOPMAN FABRICS DIV.—See Burlington Industries, Inc.; *U.S. Public*, pg. 268
KLOSTERMAN BAKING COMPANY, INC.; *U.S. Private*, pg. 626
KLOTH-SENKING METALLGIESSEREI GMBH—See Thyssen AG; *Int'l*, pg. 1387
KLUBER CHEMIE KG—See Freudenberg & Company; *Int'l*, pg. 505
KLUBER GMBH—See Freudenberg & Company; *Int'l*, pg. 506
KLUBER LUBRICATION AG (SWITZERLAND)—See Freudenberg & Company; *Int'l*, pg. 506

KLUBER LUBRICATION ARGENTINA S.A.—See Freudenberg & Company; *Int'l*, pg. 506
KLUBER LUBRICATION A.S.—See Freudenberg & Company; *Int'l*, pg. 506
KLUBER LUBRICATION AUSTRALIA PTY. LTD.—See Freudenberg & Company; *Int'l*, pg. 507
KLUBER LUBRICATION AUSTRIA GES.M.B.H.—See Freudenberg & Company; *Int'l*, pg. 506
KLUBER LUBRICATION BENELUX S.A.—See Freudenberg & Company; *Int'l*, pg. 506
KLUBER LUBRICATION FRANCE S.A.—See Freudenberg & Company; *Int'l*, pg. 506
KLUBER LUBRICATION GMBH IBERICA S. EN C.—See Freudenberg & Company; *Int'l*, pg. 506
KLUBER LUBRICATION GREAT BRITAIN LTD.—See Freudenberg & Company; *Int'l*, pg. 506
KLUBER LUBRICATION (HONG KONG, CHINA) LTD.—See Freudenberg & Company; *Int'l*, pg. 506
KLUBER LUBRICATION IBERICA S.A.—See Freudenberg & Company; *Int'l*, pg. 506
KLUBER LUBRICATION ITALIA S.R.L.—See Freudenberg & Company; *Int'l*, pg. 506
KLUBER LUBRICATION (KOREA) LTD.—See Freudenberg & Company; *Int'l*, pg. 506
KLUBER LUBRICATION LUBRIFICANTES ESPECIAIS LTDA.—See Freudenberg & Company; *Int'l*, pg. 506
KLUBER LUBRICATION MEXICANA S.A. DE C.V.—See Freudenberg & Company; *Int'l*, pg. 507
KLUBER LUBRICATION MUNCHEN KG—See Freudenberg & Company; *Int'l*, pg. 505
KLUBER LUBRICATION N. AMERICA INC.—See Freudenberg & Company; *Int'l*, pg. 505
KLUBER LUBRICATION (PTY.) LTD.—See Freudenberg & Company; *Int'l*, pg. 506
KLUBER LUBRICATION SKANDINAVIEN A.S.—See Freudenberg & Company; *Int'l*, pg. 506
KLUBER LUBRICATION YAGLAMA URUNLERI SANAYI VE TICARET A.S.—See Freudenberg & Company; *Int'l*, pg. 506
KLUNGESS ELECTRONIC SUPPLY—See Cable Constructors, Inc.; *U.S. Private*, pg. 197
KLUWER ACADEMIC PUBLISHERS—See Wolters Kluwer N.V.; *Int'l*, pg. 1513
KLUWER LAW INTERNATIONAL—See Wolters Kluwer N.V.; *Int'l*, pg. 1512
KMART (CANADA) LTD.—See Kmart Corporation; *U.S. Public*, pg. 963
KMART CORPORATION; *U.S. Public*, pg. 963
KMART FAR EAST LTD.—See Kmart Corporation; *U.S. Public*, pg. 963
LOUIS KMITO & SON, INC.—See Browning-Ferris Industries, Inc.; *U.S. Public*, pg. 264
KNAPE & VOGT CANADA INC.—See Knape & Vogt Mfg. Co.; *U.S. Public*, pg. 963
KNAPE & VOGT MFG. CO.; *U.S. Public*, pg. 963
THE KNAPE GROUP—See Larkin Meeder & Schweidel; *U.S. Private*, pg. 651
THE KNAPHEIDE MFG. CO.; *U.S. Private*, pg. 626
KNAPP SHOES INC.—See Fenway Partners Inc.; *U.S. Private*, pg. 401
KNAPP SHOES-WHOLESALE DIVISION—See Fenway Partners Inc.; *U.S. Private*, pg. 401
KNAR GOLD & SILVER EXCHANGE; *U.S. Private*, pg. 626
E.W. KNAUSS & SON, INC.; *U.S. Private*, pg. 626
KNECHTEL WHOLESALE GROCERS—See The Oshawa Group Limited; *Int'l*, pg. 1012
KNIFE RIVER COAL MINING COMPANY—See MDU Resources Group, Inc.; *U.S. Public*, pg. 1025
KNIGHT ARCHITECTS ENGINEERS PLANNERS, INC.—See Lester B. Knight & Associates, Inc.; *U.S. Private*, pg. 626
KNIGHT EQUIPMENT INTERNATIONAL INC.—See IDEX Corporation; *U.S. Public*, pg. 862
LESTER B. KNIGHT & ASSOCIATES, INC.; *U.S. Private*, pg. 626
LESTER B. KNIGHT FACILITIES MANAGEMENT, INC.—See Lester B. Knight & Associates, Inc.; *U.S. Private*, pg. 627
THE KNIGHT PUBLISHING CO.—See Knight-Ridder, Inc.; *U.S. Public*, pg. 964
KNIGHT-RIDDER, INC.; *U.S. Public*, pg. 963
KNIGHT WENDLING AG—See Lester B. Knight & Associates, Inc.; *U.S. Private*, pg. 626
KNIGHT WENDLING LTD.—See Lester B. Knight & Associates, Inc.; *U.S. Private*, pg. 627
KNIGHTS FRANCHISE SYSTEMS, INC.—See Cendant Corporation; *U.S. Public*, pg. 321
KNIK CONSTRUCTION CO., INC.—See Lynden Incorporated; *U.S. Private*, pg. 683
KNOGO CARIBE, INC.—See Sentry Technology Corp.; *U.S. Public*, pg. 1458
KNOGO REGIONAL OFFICE-CHICAGO—See Sentry Technology Corp.; *U.S. Public*, pg. 1458
KNOLL AG—See BASF AG; *Int'l*, pg. 104
KNOLL AG WERK UETERSEN—See BASF AG; *Int'l*, pg. 104
KNOLL ALMAN ILAC VE ECZA TIC. LTD. STI.—See BASF AG; *Int'l*, pg. 108
KNOLL BEIJING—See BASF AG; *Int'l*, pg. 108
KNOLL BELGIUM S.A./N.V.—See BASF AG; *Int'l*, pg. 108
KNOLL-BIORESEARCH S.A.—See BASF AG; *Int'l*, pg. 108
KNOLL CENTROAMERICANA S.A.—See BASF AG; *Int'l*, pg. 108
KNOLL COLOMBIANA S.A.—See BASF AG; *Int'l*, pg. 108
KNOLL DEUTSCHLAND GMBH—See BASF AG; *Int'l*, pg. 104
KNOLL FARMACEUTICI S.P.A.—See BASF AG; *Int'l*, pg. 108
KNOLL FARMACEUTICI S.P.A—See BASF AG; *Int'l*, pg. 108
KNOLL GRAND RAPIDS—See Knoll, Inc.; *U.S. Private*, pg. 627
KNOLL, INC.; *U.S. Private*, pg. 627

KNOLL INTERNATIONAL—See Knoll, Inc.; *U.S. Private*, pg. 627
KNOLL INTL., INC.—See Knoll, Inc.; *U.S. Private*, pg. 627
KNOLL INTERNATIONAL ITALIA S.P.A.—See Knoll, Inc.; *U.S. Private*, pg. 627
KNOLL JAPAN K.K.—See BASF AG; *Int'l*, pg. 108
KNOLL LUSITANA, LDA.—See BASF AG; *Int'l*, pg. 109
KNOLL PHARMA—See BASF AG; *Int'l*, pg. 109
KNOLL PHARMACEUTICAL COMPANY—See BASF AG; *Int'l*, pg. 105
KNOLL PHARMACEUTICALS SOUTH AFRICA (PTY.) LTD.—See BASF AG; *Int'l*, pg. 109
KNOLL PHARMACEUTICALS TAIWAN—See BASF AG; *Int'l*, pg. 109
KNOLL S.A. PRODUTOS QUIMICOS E FARMACEUTICOS—See BASF AG; *Int'l*, pg. 109
KNOLL SCIENTIFIC OFFICE—See BASF AG; *Int'l*, pg. 109
KNOLL SPOL. S.R.O.—See BASF AG; *Int'l*, pg. 109
KNOLLPHARMA INC.—See BASF AG; *Int'l*, pg. 109
KNOLLS ASSOCIATES LIMITED PARTNERSHIP—See Cigna Corp.; *U.S. Public*, pg. 359
KNOLLWOOD ASSOCIATES LIMITED PARTNERSHIP—See Cigna Corp.; *U.S. Public*, pg. 359
KNOLLWOOD HALL—See Vencor, Inc.; *U.S. Public*, pg. 1714
KNOMARK, INC.; *U.S. Private*, pg. 627
ALFRED A. KNOPF, INC.—See Advance Publications Inc.; *U.S. Private*, pg. 21
KNORR ALIMENTARIA, S.A.—See Bestfoods; *U.S. Public*, pg. 224
KNORR-AUTOBRZDY S.R.O.—See Knorr-Bremse AG; *Int'l*, pg. 738
KNORR-BRAKE AUSTRIALIA PTY. LIMITED—See Knorr-Bremse AG; *Int'l*, pg. 738
KNORR BRAKE CORPORATION—See Knorr-Bremse AG; *Int'l*, pg. 738
KNORR BRAKE HOLDING CORP.—See Knorr-Bremse AG; *Int'l*, pg. 738
KNORR-BRAKE LTD.—See Knorr-Bremse AG; *Int'l*, pg. 738
KNORR BRAKE TRUCK SYSTEMS COMPANY—See Knorr-Bremse AG; *Int'l*, pg. 738
KNORR-BREMSE AG; *Int'l*, pg. 738
KNORR-BREMSE BENELUX B.V.B.A.—See Knorr-Bremse AG; *Int'l*, pg. 738
KNORR-BREMSE BERLIN—See Knorr-Bremse AG; *Int'l*, pg. 738
KNORR-BREMSE ELECTRONIC GMBH—See Knorr-Bremse AG; *Int'l*, pg. 738
KNORR-BREMSE GES.M.B.H.—See Knorr-Bremse AG; *Int'l*, pg. 738
KNORR-BREMSE RAIL SYSTEMS FAR EAST LTD.—See Knorr-Bremse AG; *Int'l*, pg. 739
KNORR-BREMSE RAIL SYSTEMS INDIA PVT. LTD.—See Knorr-Bremse AG; *Int'l*, pg. 738
KNORR-BREMSE RAIL SYSTEMS KOREA LTD.—See Knorr-Bremse AG; *Int'l*, pg. 738
KNORR-BREMSE S.A. (PTY.) LTD.—See Knorr-Bremse AG; *Int'l*, pg. 738
KNORR-BREMSE SISTEMI PER AUTOVEICOLI COMMERCIALI S.P.A.—See Knorr-Bremse AG; *Int'l*, pg. 738
KNORR-BREMSE SYSTEM FOR TUNGA FORDON AB—See Knorr-Bremse AG; *Int'l*, pg. 738
KNORR-BREMSE SYSTEME FUR NUTZFAHRZEUGE GMBH—See Knorr-Bremse AG; *Int'l*, pg. 738
KNORR-BREMSE SYSTEME FUR SCHIENENFAHRZEUGE GMBH—See Knorr-Bremse AG; *Int'l*, pg. 738
KNORR-BREMSE SYSTEMS FOR COMMERCIAL VEHICLES LTD.—See Knorr-Bremse AG; *Int'l*, pg. 738
KNORR-BREMSE UNGARN GMBH—See Knorr-Bremse AG; *Int'l*, pg. 738
KNORR-BREMSE VASUTI JARMU RENDSZEREK HUNGARIA KFT.—See Knorr-Bremse AG; *Int'l*, pg. 739
C.H. KNORR NAHRUNGSMITTELFABRIK, GES. MB H.—See Bestfoods; *U.S. Public*, pg. 225
KNORR-DAHL FREINAGE S.A.—See Knorr-Bremse AG; *Int'l*, pg. 738
P.T. KNORR INDONESIA—See Bestfoods; *U.S. Public*, pg. 224
KNORR-NAHRMITTEL AKTIENGESELLSCHAFT—See Bestfoods; *U.S. Public*, pg. 225
KNORR PORTUGUESA-PRODUTOS ALIMENTARES S.A.—See Bestfoods; *U.S. Public*, pg. 225
KNORRBRAKES LTD.—See Knorr-Bremse AG; *Int'l*, pg. 738
KNOTT'S BERRY FARM; *U.S. Private*, pg. 627
KNOTTSBERRY FAIR—See Cedar Fair, L.P.; *U.S. Public*, pg. 319
KNOUSE FOODS INC.; *U.S. Private*, pg. 627
KNOWLEDGE SYSTEMS INTERNATIONAL—See Oracle Corporation; *U.S. Public*, pg. 1228
KNOWLEDGE TREE INC.; *U.S. Private*, pg. 627
KNOWLES ELECTRONICS, INC.; *U.S. Private*, pg. 627
KNOWSLEY SK LTD.—See Internatio-Muller N.V.; *Int'l*, pg. 681
KNOX ALLRIGHT, INC.—See Allright Corporation; *U.S. Private*, pg. 43
KNOX OIL OF TEXAS INC.; *U.S. Private*, pg. 627
KNOX PORCELAIN CORP.—See Carpenter Technology Corporation; *U.S. Public*, pg. 308
KNOXVILLE NEWS-SENTINEL COMPANY—See The E.W. Scripps Company; *U.S. Public*, pg. 1448
KNOXVILLE UTILITIES BOARD; *U.S. Private*, pg. 627
KNUDSEN & SONS, INC.—See J.M. Smucker Company; *U.S. Public*, pg. 1480
KNURLET TOOL CO.—See Kasper Machine Company; *U.S. Private*, pg. 608
KNURR AG; *Int'l*, pg. 739
KNURR AG—See Knurr AG; *Int'l*, pg. 739
KNURR-ERCOTEC GMBH—See Knurr AG; *Int'l*, pg. 739
KNURR-HEINZINGER ELECTRONIC GMBH—See Knurr AG; *Int'l*, pg. 739
KNURR-INTERPLAST GMBH—See Knurr AG; *Int'l*, pg. 739

KNURR-LOMMATEC BETELILGUNGS-U. VERW GMBH—See Knurr AG; *Int'l*, pg. 739
KNURR-LOMMATEC GMBH & CO. KG—See Knurr AG; *Int'l*, pg. 739
KNURR NEDERLAND B.V.—See Knurr AG; *Int'l*, pg. 739
KNURR-NORGE AS—See Knurr AG; *Int'l*, pg. 739
KNURR NV BELGIE—See Knurr AG; *Int'l*, pg. 739
KNURR S.A.R.L.—See Knurr AG; *Int'l*, pg. 739
KNURR-SPECTRA (S.E.A.) PTE. LTD.—See Knurr AG; *Int'l*, pg. 739
KNURR SVERIGE AB—See Knurr AG; *Int'l*, pg. 739
KNURR-TAUNUS GMBH—See Knurr AG; *Int'l*, pg. 739
KNURR (UK) LTD.—See Knurr AG; *Int'l*, pg. 739
KNURR USA EAST—See Knurr AG; *Int'l*, pg. 739
KNURR USA, INC.—See Knurr AG; *Int'l*, pg. 739
KNUTSON CONSTRUCTION CO.; *U.S. Private*, pg. 627
KO-REC-TYPE—See Barouh Eaton Allen Corporation; *U.S. Private*, pg. 117
KOBAYASHI-BLOCK CO. LTD.—See Block Drug Company, Inc.; *U.S. Public*, pg. 237
KOBAYASHI PHARMACEUTICAL CO., LTD.; *Int'l*, pg. 740
KOBE ALUMINA ASSOCIATES (AUSTRALIA) PTY. LTD.—See Kobe Steel, Ltd.; *Int'l*, pg. 741
KOBE ALUMINA ASSOCIATES (AUSTRALIA) PTY. LTD.—See Nissho Iwai Corporation; *Int'l*, pg. 946
KOBE DEVELOPMENT CORP.—See Kobe Steel, Ltd.; *Int'l*, pg. 740
KOBE INTERNATIONAL (S) CO., PTE. LTD.—See Kobe Steel, Ltd.; *Int'l*, pg. 741
KOBE-MIDREX RESEARCH—See Kobe Steel, Ltd.; *Int'l*, pg. 740
KOBE STEEL ASIA PTE LTD—See Kobe Steel, Ltd.; *Int'l*, pg. 741
KOBE STEEL AUSTRALIA PTY. LTD.—See Kobe Steel, *Int'l*, pg. 741
KOBE STEEL EUROPE, LTD.—See Kobe Steel, Ltd.; *Int'l*, pg. 741
KOBE STEEL INTERNATIONAL (USA) INC.—See Kobe Steel, Ltd.; *Int'l*, pg. 740
KOBE STEEL, LTD.; *Int'l*, pg. 740
KOBE STEEL, LTD.—See Kobe Steel, Ltd.; *Int'l*, pg. 740
KOBE STEEL, LTD. (BEIJING)—See Kobe Steel, Ltd.; *Int'l*, pg. 741
KOBE STEEL, LTD. (DUSSELDORF)—See Kobe Steel, Ltd.; *Int'l*, pg. 741
KOBE STEEL, LTD. (MELBOURNE)—See Kobe Steel, Ltd.; *Int'l*, pg. 741
KOBE STEEL, LTD. (MOSCOW)—See Kobe Steel, Ltd.; *Int'l*, pg. 741
KOBE STEEL U.S.A. INC. (NEW YORK)—See Kobe Steel, Ltd.; *Int'l*, pg. 740
KOBE STEEL USA INC. (LOS ANGELES)—See Kobe Steel, Ltd.; *Int'l*, pg. 740
KOBE STEEL USA INC.—See Kobe Steel, Ltd.; *Int'l*, pg. 740
KOBE TERMINAL—See GATX Corporation; *U.S. Public*, pg. 693
KOBE WELDING (SINGAPORE) PTE. LTD.—See Kobe Steel, Ltd.; *Int'l*, pg. 741
KOBELCO AMERICA INC.—See Kobe Steel, Ltd.; *Int'l*, pg. 740
KOBELCO MIDDLE EAST (E.C.)—See Kobe Steel, Ltd.; *Int'l*, pg. 741
KOBELCO STEWART BOLLING INC.—See Kobe Steel, Ltd.; *Int'l*, pg. 740
KOBELCO STEWART BOLLING, INC.—See Kobe Steel, Ltd.; *Int'l*, pg. 740
KOBRA INTERNATIONAL LTD; *U.S. Private*, pg. 628
KOC HOLDING A.S.; *Int'l*, pg. 741
KOCBANK A.S.—See Koc Holding A.S.; *Int'l*, pg. 741
KOCH CONTAINER—See Buckeye Corrugated Inc.; *U.S. Private*, pg. 177
KOCH ENGINEERING CO., INC.—See Koch Industries, Incorporated; *U.S. Private*, pg. 628
KOCH ENGINEERING COMPANY, INC.—See Koch Industries, Incorporated; *U.S. Private*, pg. 628
KARL KOCH ERECTING CO. INC.—See Skanska AB; *Int'l*, pg. 1261
GEORGE KOCH SONS, INC.; *U.S. Private*, pg. 628
KOCH INDUSTRIES, INCORPORATED; *U.S. Private*, pg. 628
KOCH MATERIALS DIVISION—See Koch Industries, Incorporated; *U.S. Private*, pg. 628
KOCH MEMBRANE SYSTEMS—See Koch Industries, Incorporated; *U.S. Private*, pg. 628
KOCH MINERALS—See Koch Industries, Incorporated; *U.S. Private*, pg. 628
KOCH NITROGEN DIVISION—See Koch Industries, Incorporated; *U.S. Private*, pg. 628
KOCH OIL COMPANY—See Koch Industries, Incorporated; *U.S. Private*, pg. 628
KOCH OTTO H. YORK CO., INC.—See Koch Industries, Incorporated; *U.S. Private*, pg. 628
KOCH SUPPLIES INC.; *U.S. Private*, pg. 628
KOCKUMS AB—See Celsius AB; *Int'l*, pg. 277
KOCKUMS CANCAR CORP.—See BTR plc; *Int'l*, pg. 124
KOCKUMS COMPUTER SYSTEMS AB—See Celsius AB; *Int'l*, pg. 277
KOCKUMS COMPUTER SYSTEMS A/S—See Celsius AB; *Int'l*, pg. 277
KOCKUMS COMPUTER SYSTEMS GMBH—See Celsius AB; *Int'l*, pg. 278
KOCKUMS COMPUTER SYSTEMS K.K.—See Celsius AB; *Int'l*, pg. 278
KOCKUMS COMPUTER SYSTEMS (UK) LTD.—See Celsius AB; *Int'l*, pg. 278
KOCKUMS ENGINEERING AB—See Celsius AB; *Int'l*, pg. 277
KOCKUMS HOLDINGS AB—See Celsius AB; *Int'l*, pg. 277
KOCKUMS INDUSTRIER AB—See Celsius AB; *Int'l*, pg. 277
KOCKUMS PACIFIC PTY LTD.—See Celsius AB; *Int'l*, pg. 277

KOCKUMS SE ASIA PTE LTD.—See Celsius AB; *Int'l*, pg. 277
KOCKUMS SUBMARINE SYSTEMS AB—See Celsius AB; *Int'l*, pg. 277
KOCKUMS VERKSTADER AB—See Celsius AB; *Int'l*, pg. 277
KOCOLENE OIL CORP.; *U.S. Private*, pg. 629
KODAK AB—See Eastman Kodak Company; *U.S. Public*, pg. 552
KODAK AG—See Eastman Kodak Company; *U.S. Public*, pg. 552
KODAK AG-BERLIN—See Eastman Kodak Company; *U.S. Public*, pg. 552
KODAK AG-ESSEN—See Eastman Kodak Company; *U.S. Public*, pg. 552
KODAK AG-FRANKFURT—See Eastman Kodak Company; *U.S. Public*, pg. 552
KODAK AG-HAMBURG—See Eastman Kodak Company; *U.S. Public*, pg. 552
KODAK AG-HANOVER—See Eastman Kodak Company; *U.S. Public*, pg. 552
KODAK AG-KOLN—See Eastman Kodak Company; *U.S. Public*, pg. 552
KODAK AG-MANNHEIM—See Eastman Kodak Company; *U.S. Public*, pg. 552
KODAK AG-MUHLHAUSEN—See Eastman Kodak Company; *U.S. Public*, pg. 552
KODAK AG-MUNICH—See Eastman Kodak Company; *U.S. Public*, pg. 552
KODAK AG-OSTFILDERN—See Eastman Kodak Company; *U.S. Public*, pg. 552
KODAK AG-STUTTGART—See Eastman Kodak Company; *U.S. Public*, pg. 552
KODAK AMERICA, LTDA.—See Eastman Kodak Company; *U.S. Public*, pg. 554
KODAK & H-COLOR A/S—See Eastman Kodak Company; *U.S. Public*, pg. 552
KODAK ARGENTINA S.A.I.C.—See Eastman Kodak Company; *U.S. Public*, pg. 552
KODAK A/S—See Eastman Kodak Company; *U.S. Public*, pg. 552
KODAK (AUSTRALASIA) PTY. LTD.—See Eastman Kodak Company; *U.S. Public*, pg. 552
KODAK BERKELEY RESEARCH—See Eastman Kodak Company; *U.S. Public*, pg. 555
KODAK BIO-PRODUCTS DIVISION—See Eastman Kodak Company; *U.S. Public*, pg. 551
KODAK BIOSCIENCE / EMERGING BUSINESS DIVISION—See Eastman Kodak Company; *U.S. Public*, pg. 552
KODAK BRASILEIRA C.I.L.—See Eastman Kodak Company; *U.S. Public*, pg. 552
KODAK BUSINESS IMAGING SYSTEMS DIVISION—See Eastman Kodak Company; *U.S. Public*, pg. 555
KODAK BUSINESS INFORMATION SERVICES K.K. (KBISKK)—See Eastman Kodak Company; *U.S. Public*, pg. 551
KODAK CANADA INC.—See Eastman Kodak Company; *U.S. Public*, pg. 553
KODAK CARIBBEAN LIMITED—See Eastman Kodak Company; *U.S. Public*, pg. 551
KODAK CHILENA S.A.F.—See Eastman Kodak Company; *U.S. Public*, pg. 553
KODAK (CHINA) LIMITED—See Eastman Kodak Company; *U.S. Public*, pg. 553
KODAK CINESITE—See Eastman Kodak Company; *U.S. Public*, pg. 555
KODAK CLINICAL PRODUCTS DIVISION—See Eastman Kodak Company; *U.S. Public*, pg. 551
KODAK COLUMBIANA, LTD.—See Eastman Kodak Company; *U.S. Public*, pg. 553
KODAK COMMERCIAL & INFORMATION SYSTEMS MARKETING—See Eastman Kodak Company; *U.S. Public*, pg. 551
KODAK DO AMAZONAS INDUSTRIA E COMERCIO LTDA.—See Eastman Kodak Company; *U.S. Public*, pg. 553
KODAK DOMINICANA—See Eastman Kodak Company; *U.S. Public*, pg. 553
KODAK (EGYPT) S.A.—See Eastman Kodak Company; *U.S. Public*, pg. 553
KODAK ELECTRONIC PRINTING SYSTEMS—See Eastman Kodak Company; *U.S. Public*, pg. 555
KODAK (EXPORT SALES) LIMITED—See Eastman Kodak Company; *U.S. Public*, pg. 553
KODAK (FAR EAST) LIMITED—See Eastman Kodak Company; *U.S. Public*, pg. 553
KODAK FAR EAST PURCHASING CO. INC.—See Eastman Kodak Company; *U.S. Public*, pg. 552
KODAK FEDERAL SYSTEMS DIVISION—See Eastman Kodak Company; *U.S. Public*, pg. 555
KODAK FOTOSERVICE GESELLSCHAFT M.B.H.—See Eastman Kodak Company; *U.S. Public*, pg. 553
KODAK GESSELLSCHAFT M.B.H.—See Eastman Kodak Company; *U.S. Public*, pg. 553
KODAK GRAPHICS IMAGING SYSTEMS DIVISION—See Eastman Kodak Company; *U.S. Public*, pg. 551
KODAK HALIFAX—See Eastman Kodak Company; *U.S. Public*, pg. 553
KODAK HEALTH SCIENCES DIVISION—See Eastman Kodak Company; *U.S. Public*, pg. 551
KODAK IMAGICA K.K. (KI)—See Eastman Kodak Company; *U.S. Public*, pg. 555
K.K. KODAK INFORMATION SYSTEMS (KKKIS)—See Eastman Kodak Company; *U.S. Public*, pg. 552
KODAK IRELAND LIMITED—See Eastman Kodak Company; *U.S. Public*, pg. 553
KODAK ISRAEL—See Eastman Kodak Company; *U.S. Public*, pg. 553
KODAK JAPAN INDUSTRIES LTD.—See Eastman Kodak Company; *U.S. Public*, pg. 552
KODAK JAPAN LTD.-TECHNICAL CENTER—See Eastman Kodak Company; *U.S. Public*, pg. 552

KODAK (KENYA) LIMITED—See Eastman Kodak Company; *U.S. Public,* pg. 553
KODAK KFT. HUNGARY—See Eastman Kodak Company; *U.S. Public,* pg. 553
KODAK KOREA LTD.—See Eastman Kodak Company; *U.S. Public,* pg. 555
KODAK LIMITED—See Eastman Kodak Company; *U.S. Public,* pg. 553
KODAK LIMITED-CHEMICAL DIVISION—See Eastman Kodak Company; *U.S. Public,* pg. 553
KODAK LIMITED-MARKETING EDUCATION CENTER—See Eastman Kodak Company; *U.S. Public,* pg. 553
KODAK LIMITED-MIDLAND BUSINESS CENTRE—See Eastman Kodak Company; *U.S. Public,* pg. 553
KODAK LIMITED-SOUTHERN BUSINESS CENTRE—See Eastman Kodak Company; *U.S. Public,* pg. 553
KODAK LIMITED-WESTERN BUSINESS CENTRE—See Eastman Kodak Company; *U.S. Public,* pg. 553
KODAK (MALAYSIA) SENDIRIAN BERHAD—See Eastman Kodak Company; *U.S. Public,* pg. 554
KODAK MASS MEMORY DIVISION—See Eastman Kodak Company; *U.S. Public,* pg. 555
KODAK MEXICANA SA DE C.V.—See Eastman Kodak Company; *U.S. Public,* pg. 554
KODAK MOTION PICTURE & AUDIOVISUAL PRODUCTS DIVISION—See Eastman Kodak Company; *U.S. Public,* pg. 555
KODAK (NEAR EAST) INC.—See Eastman Kodak Company; *U.S. Public,* pg. 554
KODAK NEDERLAND B.V.—See Eastman Kodak Company; *U.S. Public,* pg. 554
KODAK NEW ZEALAND LTD.—See Eastman Kodak Company; *U.S. Public,* pg. 554
KODAK NORGE A/S—See Eastman Kodak Company; *U.S. Public,* pg. 554
KODAK OY—See Eastman Kodak Company; *U.S. Public,* pg. 554
KODAK PAKISTAN LTD.—See Eastman Kodak Company; *U.S. Public,* pg. 554
KODAK PANAMA LIMITED—See Eastman Kodak Company; *U.S. Public,* pg. 554
KODAK-PATHE—See Eastman Kodak Company; *U.S. Public,* pg. 554
KODAK PATHE S.A.—See Eastman Kodak Company; *U.S. Public,* pg. 554
KODAK PHILIPPINES LTD.—See Eastman Kodak Company; *U.S. Public,* pg. 554
KODAK PORTUGUESA, LTD.—See Eastman Kodak Company; *U.S. Public,* pg. 554
KODAK PRINTER PRODUCTS DIV.—See Eastman Kodak Company; *U.S. Public,* pg. 555
KODAK PROCESSING LABORATORIES—See Eastman Kodak Company; *U.S. Public,* pg. 551
KODAK PROFESSIONAL PHOTOGRAPHY DIVISION—See Eastman Kodak Company; *U.S. Public,* pg. 555
KODAK RAHOLA, INC.—See Eastman Kodak Company; *U.S. Public,* pg. 551
KODAK S.A.—See Eastman Kodak Company; *U.S. Public,* pg. 554
N.V. KODAK S.A.—See Eastman Kodak Company; *U.S. Public,* pg. 554
KODAK (SINGAPORE) PTE. LIMITED—See Eastman Kodak Company; *U.S. Public,* pg. 554
KODAK SOFTWARE SYSTEMS DIVISION—See Eastman Kodak Company; *U.S. Public,* pg. 555
KODAK S.P.A.—See Eastman Kodak Company; *U.S. Public,* pg. 554
KODAK TAIWAN LIMITED—See Eastman Kodak Company; *U.S. Public,* pg. 555
KODAK TAIWAN LIMITED, CHEMICAL DEPT.—See Eastman Kodak Company; *U.S. Public,* pg. 555
KODAK (THAILAND) LTD.—See Eastman Kodak Company; *U.S. Public,* pg. 555
KODAK URUGUAYA, LTD.—See Eastman Kodak Company; *U.S. Public,* pg. 555
KODAK VENEZUELA, S.A.—See Eastman Kodak Company; *U.S. Public,* pg. 555
KODAK (ZIMBABWE) LTD.—See Eastman Kodak Company; *U.S. Public,* pg. 555
KODANSHA AMERICA, INC.—See Kodansha Ltd.; *Int'l,* pg. 742
KODANSHA INTERNATIONAL LTD—See Kodansha Ltd.; *Int'l,* pg. 742
KODANSHA LTD.; *Int'l,* pg. 742
KODANSHA SCIENTIFIC LTD.—See Kodansha Ltd.; *Int'l,* pg. 742
KOEHLER MANUFACTURING COMPANY—See The Marmon Group, Inc.; *U.S. Private,* pg. 706
KOEI CHEMICAL COMPANY, LTD.—See Sumitomo Chemical Company, Ltd.; *Int'l,* pg. 1311
KOENIG & BAUER-ALBERT—See Publishers Equipment Corporation; *U.S. Public,* pg. 1341
KOENIG & BAUER-ALBERT AG; *Int'l,* pg. 742
KOFFIE HAG NV—See Philip Morris Companies Inc.; *U.S. Public,* pg. 1289
KOFISA ITALIA S.R.L.—See Koc Holding A.S.; *Int'l,* pg. 742
KOFISA TRADING COMPANY—See Koc Holding A.S.; *Int'l,* pg. 742
KOFISA TRADING COMPANY S.A.—See Koc Holding A.S.; *Int'l,* pg. 742
KOFISA TRADING ESPANA S.L.—See Koc Holding A.S.; *Int'l,* pg. 742
KOFLACH SPORT GMBH—See Amer Group Ltd.; *Int'l,* pg. 73
KOFU BELL FOODS, LTD.—See Kanebo, Ltd.; *Int'l,* pg. 722
KOGER EQUITY INC.; *U.S. Public,* pg. 965
KOH-I-NOOR, INC.; *U.S. Private,* pg. 629
KOH WAH FASHION LTD.—See Takashimaya Company, Limited; *Int'l,* pg. 1350
KOHALA JOINT VENTURE—See Hudson General Corporation; *U.S. Public,* pg. 845

KOHAP CHEMICAL CORPORATION—See KOHAP Group; *Int'l,* pg. 742
KOHAP ENG. & CONST. CO., LTD.—See KOHAP Group; *Int'l,* pg. 742
KOHAP ENGINEERING PLASTICS LTD.—See KOHAP Group; *Int'l,* pg. 742
KOHAP FINE CHEMICAL LTD.—See KOHAP Group; *Int'l,* pg. 742
KOHAP GROUP; *Int'l,* pg. 742
KOHAP INC.—See KOHAP Group; *Int'l,* pg. 742
KOHAP-NEW YORK LIFE INSURANCE LTD.—See KOHAP Group; *Int'l,* pg. 742
KOHAP PETROCHEMICAL CORPORATION—See KOHAP Group; *Int'l,* pg. 742
KOHAP TEXTILE CO., LTD.—See KOHAP Group; *Int'l,* pg. 742
KOHL & MADDEN PRINTING INK CORP. DIV.—See Dainippon Ink & Chemicals, Inc.; *Int'l,* pg. 370
KOHLBECHER & CO. GMBH—See Saarbergwerke Aktiengesellschaft; *Int'l,* pg. 1166
KOHLBERG & COMPANY, LLC; *U.S. Private,* pg. 629
KOHLBERG KRAVIS ROBERTS & CO.; *U.S. Private,* pg. 629
KOHLE-KONTOR-SAAR GMBH—See Saarbergwerke Aktiengesellschaft; *Int'l,* pg. 1167
KOHLENSAUREWERK DEUTSCHLAND GMBH—See Solvay S.A.; *Int'l,* pg. 1278
KOHLEOL-ANLAGE BOTTROP GMBH—See Veba AG; *Int'l,* pg. 1461
KOHLER AUSTRALIA—See Kohler Company; *U.S. Private,* pg. 631
KOHLER COMPANY; *U.S. Private,* pg. 630
KOHLER CONSTRUCTION COMPANY, INC.—See Dycom Industries, Inc.; *U.S. Public,* pg. 538
KOHLER DE MEXICO, S.A. DE C.V.—See Kohler Company; *U.S. Private,* pg. 631
KOHLER INTERCONSULT AB—See Trelleborg AB; *Int'l,* pg. 1420
KOHLER INTERCONSULT GMBH—See Trelleborg AB; *Int'l,* pg. 1420
KOHLER JAPAN K.K.—See Kohler Company; *U.S. Private,* pg. 631
KOHLER LTD.—See Kohler Company; *U.S. Private,* pg. 631
KOHL'S CORPORATION; *U.S. Public,* pg. 965
KOHL'S FOOD STORES—See Tengelmann Warenhandelsgesellschaft; *Int'l,* pg. 1375
KOHLSWA JERNVERK AB—See Electrolux, AB; *Int'l,* pg. 439
KOIPE S.A.—See Compart SpA; *Int'l,* pg. 324
KOITO MANUFACTURING CO.; *Int'l,* pg. 743
KOITO MANUFACTURING CO.-BRUSSELS OFFICE—See Koito Manufacturing Co.; *Int'l,* pg. 743
KOITO MANUFACTURING CO.-FUJIKAWA PLANT—See Koito Manufacturing Co.; *Int'l,* pg. 743
KOITO MANUFACTURING CO.-FUJIKAWA TOOLING PLANT—See Koito Manufacturing Co.; *Int'l,* pg. 743
KOITO MANUFACTURING CO.-HAIBARA PLANT—See Koito Manufacturing Co.; *Int'l,* pg. 743
KOITO MANUFACTURING CO.-KIKKAWA PLANT—See Koito Manufacturing Co.; *Int'l,* pg. 743
KOITO MANUFACTURING CO.-SAGARA PLANT—See Koito Manufacturing Co.; *Int'l,* pg. 743
KOITO MANUFACTURING CO.-SEATTLE OFFICE—See Koito Manufacturing Co.; *Int'l,* pg. 743
KOITO MANUFACTURING CO.-SHIZUOKA PLANT—See Koito Manufacturing Co.; *Int'l,* pg. 743
KOKEN MFG. CO. INC.—See Takara Belmont Co., Ltd.; *Int'l,* pg. 1347
KOKKOLA POWER PLANT—See Imatran Voima Oy; *Int'l,* pg. 660
KOKOMO GAS & FUEL COMPANY—See NIPSCO Industries, Inc.; *U.S. Public,* pg. 1185
KOKOMO GRAIN CO., INC.; *U.S. Private,* pg. 631
KOKOMO SANITARY POTTERY CORP.—See Gerber Plumbing Fixtures Corporation; *U.S. Private,* pg. 449
KOKOSING CONSTRUCTION COMPANY, INC.; *U.S. Private,* pg. 631
KOKOSING MATERIALS, INC.—See Kokosing Construction Company, Inc.; *U.S. Private,* pg. 631
KOKUSAI ELECTRIC CO., LTD.; *Int'l,* pg. 743
KOKUSAI ELECTRIC CO., LTD. AMERICA—See Kokusai Electric Co., Ltd.; *Int'l,* pg. 743
KOLANA S.A.—See American Home Products Corporation; *U.S. Public,* pg. 81
HERMANN KOLB MACHINERY AG—See Rothenberger Group GmbH; *Int'l,* pg. 1128
KOLD DRAFT—See Uniflow Manufacturing Co.; *U.S. Private,* pg. 1117
KOLL CENTER IRVINE NO. 2 PARTNERSHIP—See Cigna Corp.; *U.S. Public,* pg. 361
KOLL CO.; *U.S. Private,* pg. 631
KOLL-TUSTIN BUSINESS CENTER—See Cigna Corp.; *U.S. Public,* pg. 361
KOLLER ENTERPRISES, INC.; *U.S. Private,* pg. 631
KOLLMAN DIV.—See Emerson Electric Co.; *U.S. Public,* pg. 575
KOLLMORGAN ARTUS—See Kollmorgen Corporation; *U.S. Public,* pg. 966
KOLLMORGEN CORPORATION; *U.S. Public,* pg. 965
KOLLMORGEN HIGHTECH LTD.—See Kollmorgen Corporation; *U.S. Public,* pg. 966
KOLLMORGEN INTERNATIONAL LOGISTICS—See Kollmorgen Corporation; *U.S. Public,* pg. 966
KOLLMORGEN SMG—See Kollmorgen Corporation; *U.S. Public,* pg. 965
KOLLMORGEN TANDON INDIA—See Kollmorgen Corporation; *U.S. Public,* pg. 966
KOLLMORGEN VIRTUAL MOTION GROUP—See Kollmorgen Corporation; *U.S. Public,* pg. 965
KOLMAR (AUST.) PTY LTD.—See CCL Industries, Inc.; *Int'l,* pg. 239
KOLMAR DE MEXICO, S.A.—See CCL Industries, Inc.; *Int'l,* pg. 239

KOLMAR LABORATORIES—See CCL Industries, Inc.; *Int'l,* pg. 239
KOLMAR LABORATORIES, INC.—See CCL Industries, Inc.; *Int'l,* pg. 239
OY KOLMOSTELEVISIO AB—See MTV Finland; *Int'l,* pg. 828
KOLON-MET LIFE INSURANCE COMPANY LIMITED—See Metropolitan Life Insurance Co.; *U.S. Private,* pg. 738
KOLTEK OY—See Tetra Laval Group; *Int'l,* pg. 1379
KOLTEX, INC.—See Tetra Laval Group; *Int'l,* pg. 1378
KOLYNOS SAIC—See American Home Products Corporation; *U.S. Public,* pg. 81
KOMAG INCORPORATED—See Asahi Glass Co., Ltd.; *Int'l,* pg. 84
KOMAG, INCORPORATED; *U.S. Public,* pg. 966
KOMAG MATERIAL TECHNOLOGY INC.—See Komag, Incorporated; *U.S. Public,* pg. 966
CHARLES KOMAR & SONS, INC.; *U.S. Private,* pg. 631
P.T. KOMARITIM—See Stolt-Nielsen S.A.; *Int'l,* pg. 1302
KOMATSU AMERICA CORP.—See Komatsu Ltd.; *Int'l,* pg. 744
KOMATSU AMERICA INDUSTRIES CORP.—See Komatsu Ltd.; *Int'l,* pg. 744
KOMATSU AMERICA INTERNATIONAL COMPANY—See Komatsu Ltd.; *Int'l,* pg. 744
KOMATSU ASIA & PACIFIC PTE. LTD.—See Komatsu Ltd.; *Int'l,* pg. 744
KOMATSU CHANGLIN CONSTRUCTION MACHINERY CORP.—See Komatsu Ltd.; *Int'l,* pg. 745
KOMATSU CHANGLIN FOUNDRY CORPORATION—See Komatsu Ltd.; *Int'l,* pg. 745
KOMATSU DO BRASIL LTDA.—See Komatsu Ltd.; *Int'l,* pg. 744
KOMATSU ESPANA S.A.—See Komatsu Ltd.; *Int'l,* pg. 744
KOMATSU EUROPE INTERNATIONAL N.V.—See Komatsu Ltd.; *Int'l,* pg. 744
KOMATSU FRANCE S.A.—See Komatsu Ltd.; *Int'l,* pg. 744
KOMATSU HANOMAG AG—See Komatsu Ltd.; *Int'l,* pg. 744
KOMATSU HUANAN LTD.—See Komatsu Ltd.; *Int'l,* pg. 744
P.T. KOMATSU INDONESIA TBK—See Komatsu Ltd.; *Int'l,* pg. 744
KOMATSU LTD.; *Int'l,* pg. 743
KOMATSU MEXICANA S.A. DE C.V.—See Komatsu Ltd.; *Int'l,* pg. 744
KOMATSU SAIGON CO., LTD.—See Komatsu Ltd.; *Int'l,* pg. 744
KOMATSU (SHANGHAI) LTD.—See Komatsu Ltd.; *Int'l,* pg. 744
KOMATSU SHANTUI CONSTRUCTION MACHINERY CO., LTD.—See Komatsu Ltd.; *Int'l,* pg. 744
KOMATSU UK, LTD.—See Komatsu Ltd.; *Int'l,* pg. 744
KOMATSUGAWA KOKI CO., LTD.—See Nissho Iwai Corporation; *Int'l,* pg. 946
KOMATSUSHIMA MILL—See Nippon Paper Industries Company Limited; *Int'l,* pg. 938
KOMBI, LTD.; *U.S. Private,* pg. 631
KOMFORT CORPORATION—See Thor Industries, Inc.; *U.S. Public,* pg. 1602
KOMLINE-SANDERSON ENGINEERING CORP.; *U.S. Private,* pg. 631
KOMMUNALCONSULT GESELLSCHAFT FUR DIE BERATUNG DE OFFENTLICHEN HAND MBH—See Bankgesellschaft Berlin; *Int'l,* pg. 160
KOMORI AMERICA CORPORATION—See Komori Corporation; *Int'l,* pg. 745
KOMORI BENELUX B.V.—See Komori Corporation; *Int'l,* pg. 745
KOMORI CANADA LTD.—See Komori Corporation; *Int'l,* pg. 745
KOMORI-CHAMBON S.A.—See Komori Corporation; *Int'l,* pg. 745
KOMORI CORPORATION; *Int'l,* pg. 745
KOMORI CURRENCY TECHNOLOGY U.K. LIMITED—See Komori Corporation; *Int'l,* pg. 745
KOMORI DEUTSCHLAND GMBH—See Komori Corporation; *Int'l,* pg. 745
KOMORI ELECTRONICS CO., LTD.—See Komori Corporation; *Int'l,* pg. 745
KOMORI FRANCE S.A.—See Komori Corporation; *Int'l,* pg. 745
KOMORI INTERNATIONAL (EUROPE) B.V.—See Komori Corporation; *Int'l,* pg. 745
KOMORI INTERNATIONAL FINANCE B.V.—See Komori Corporation; *Int'l,* pg. 745
KOMORI ITALIA S.R.L.—See Komori Corporation; *Int'l,* pg. 745
KOMORI MACHINERY CO., LTD.—See Komori Corporation; *Int'l,* pg. 745
KOMORI PRECISION CO., LTD.—See Komori Corporation; *Int'l,* pg. 745
KOMORI PRECISION YAMAGATA CO., LTD.—See Komori Corporation; *Int'l,* pg. 745
KOMORI REALTY CO., LTD.—See Komori Corporation; *Int'l,* pg. 745
KOMORI SWEDEN AB—See Komori Corporation; *Int'l,* pg. 745
KOMORI U.K. LIMITED—See Komori Corporation; *Int'l,* pg. 745
KOMORI WEST INCORPORATED—See Komori Corporation; *Int'l,* pg. 745
KOMPASS INTERNATIONAL NEUENSCHWANDER SA; *Int'l,* pg. 745
KOMPLETT-BUROVERMIETUNGS GMBH—See Creditanstalt-Bankverein; *Int'l,* pg. 347
KOMPUTER WISMAN SDN. BHD.—See Hewlett-Packard Company; *U.S. Public,* pg. 822
KOMTEK—See Kervick Enterprises, Inc.; *U.S. Private,* pg. 616
KONA CORPORATION—See Berwind Corporation; *U.S. Private,* pg. 138
KONAMI ASIA (SINGAPORE) PTE. LTD.—See Konami Co. Ltd.; *Int'l,* pg. 746

KONAMI CO. LTD.; *Int'l*, pg. 745
KONAMI COMPUTER ENTERTAINMENT CHICAGO INC.—See Konami Co. Ltd.; *Int'l*, pg. 746
KONAMI COMPUTER ENTERTAINMENT JAPAN CO., LTD.—See Konami Co. Ltd.; *Int'l*, pg. 745
KONAMI COMPUTER ENTERTAINMENT NAGOYA CO., LTD.—See Konami Co. Ltd.; *Int'l*, pg. 745
KONAMI COMPUTER ENTERTAINMENT OSAKA CO., LTD.—See Konami Co. Ltd.; *Int'l*, pg. 745
KONAMI COMPUTER ENTERTAINMENT ROPPONGI CO., LTD.—See Konami Co. Ltd.; *Int'l*, pg. 745
KONAMI COMPUTER ENTERTAINMENT SAPPORO CO., LTD.—See Konami Co. Ltd.; *Int'l*, pg. 745
KONAMI COMPUTER ENTERTAINMENT TOKYO CO., LTD.—See Konami Co. Ltd.; *Int'l*, pg. 745
KONAMI COMPUTER GAMES AOYAMA CO., LTD.—See Konami Co. Ltd.; *Int'l*, pg. 746
KONAMI CORPORATION OF AMERICA INC.—See Konami Co. Ltd.; *Int'l*, pg. 746
KONAMI (DEUTSCHLAND) GMBH—See Konami Co. Ltd.; *Int'l*, pg. 746
KONAMI FINANCE CO., LTD.—See Konami Co. Ltd.; *Int'l*, pg. 746
KONAMI (HONG KONG) LTD.—See Konami Co. Ltd.; *Int'l*, pg. 746
KONAMI (KOREA) CO., LTD.—See Konami Co. Ltd.; *Int'l*, pg. 746
KONAMI KOSAN CO., LTD.—See Konami Co. Ltd.; *Int'l*, pg. 746
KONAMI MUSIC ENTERTAINMENT CO., LTD.—See Konami Co. Ltd.; *Int'l*, pg. 746
KONAMI OF AMERICA INC.—See Konami Co. Ltd.; *Int'l*, pg. 746
KONAMI PARLOR ENTERTAINMENT CO., LTD.—See Konami Co. Ltd.; *Int'l*, pg. 746
KONAMI SERVICE CO., LTD.—See Konami Co. Ltd.; *Int'l*, pg. 746
KONAMI (SINGAPORE) PTE. LTD.—See Konami Co. Ltd.; *Int'l*, pg. 746
KONAMI (UK) LTD.—See Konami Co. Ltd.; *Int'l*, pg. 746
KONATEC NASSBAGGERTECHNIK GMBH—See Heidemij N.V.; *Int'l*, pg. 608
KONCOR INDUSTRIES DIV.—See The Timken Company; *U.S. Public*, pg. 1617
KONE A/S—See Kone Corporation; *Int'l*, pg. 747
KONE ASANSOR SANAYI VE TICARET A.S.—See Kone Corporation; *Int'l*, pg. 747
KONE ASCENSORES C.A.—See Kone Corporation; *Int'l*, pg. 747
KONE ASCENSORES S.A.—See Kone Corporation; *Int'l*, pg. 747
KONE ASCENSORI S.P.A.—See Kone Corporation; *Int'l*, pg. 747
KONE AUFZUG GMBH—See Kone Corporation; *Int'l*, pg. 747
KONE AUFZUGWERKE—See Kone Corporation; *Int'l*, pg. 747
KONE BELGIUM S.A.—See Kone Corporation; *Int'l*, pg. 747
KONE CORPORATE OFFICE—See Kone Corporation; *Int'l*, pg. 746
KONE CORPORATION; *Int'l*, pg. 746
KONE ELEVADORES LTDA.—See Kone Corporation; *Int'l*, pg. 747
KONE ELEVADORES, S.A.—See Kone Corporation; *Int'l*, pg. 747
KONE ELEVATOR A/S—See Kone Corporation; *Int'l*, pg. 747
KONE ELEVATOR GMBH—See Kone Corporation; *Int'l*, pg. 748
KONE ELEVATOR (H.K.) LTD.—See Kone Corporation; *Int'l*, pg. 747
KONE ELEVATOR INDIA LTD.—See Kone Corporation; *Int'l*, pg. 747
KONE ELEVATOR (M) SDN. BHD.—See Kone Corporation; *Int'l*, pg. 747
KONE ELEVATOR PTE. LTD.—See Kone Corporation; *Int'l*, pg. 747
KONE ELEVATORS—See Kone Corporation; *Int'l*, pg. 747
KONE ELEVATORS ASIA PACIFIC—See Kone Corporation; *Int'l*, pg. 747
KONE ELEVATORS (AUSTRALIA) PTY. LTD.—See Kone Corporation; *Int'l*, pg. 747
KONE ELEVATORS, BU 1—See Kone Corporation; *Int'l*, pg. 747
KONE ELEVATORS, BU 2—See Kone Corporation; *Int'l*, pg. 746
KONE ELEVATORS C&N PRODUCTS CORPORATION—See Kone Corporation; *Int'l*, pg. 747
KONE ELEVATORS EXPORT—See Kone Corporation; *Int'l*, pg. 746
KONE ELEVATORS FINLAND—See Kone Corporation; *Int'l*, pg. 746
KONE ELEVATORS LTD.—See Kone Corporation; *Int'l*, pg. 747
KONE ELEVATORS NORTH AMERICA—See Kone Corporation; *Int'l*, pg. 746
KONE ELEVATORS OVERSEAS S.R.L.—See Kone Corporation; *Int'l*, pg. 746
KONE ELEVATORS POLAND SP.ZO.O.—See Kone Corporation; *Int'l*, pg. 747
KONE ELEVATORS (SHENZHEN) CO. LTD.—See Kone Corporation; *Int'l*, pg. 747
KONE FINANCE CORPORATION—See Kone Corporation; *Int'l*, pg. 746
KONE GARANT AUFZUG GMBH—See Kone Corporation; *Int'l*, pg. 747
KONE HISSAR AB—See Kone Corporation; *Int'l*, pg. 747
PT. KONE INDO ELEVATOR—See Kone Corporation; *Int'l*, pg. 747
KONE INTERNATIONAL S.A.—See Kone Corporation; *Int'l*, pg. 748
KONE ITALIA S.P.A.—See Kone Corporation; *Int'l*, pg. 747
KONE JAPAN CO. LTD.—See Kone Corporation; *Int'l*, pg. 747

KONE LIFTI LATVIJA OY—See Kone Corporation; *Int'l*, pg. 747
KONE LIFTS A.S.—See Kone Corporation; *Int'l*, pg. 747
KONE LIFTS LTD.—See Kone Corporation; *Int'l*, pg. 747
KONE LIFTS S.R.O.—See Kone Corporation; *Int'l*, pg. 747
ZAO KONE LIFTS ST. PETERSBURG—See Kone Corporation; *Int'l*, pg. 748
KONE LUXEMBOURG S.A.R.L.—See Kone Corporation; *Int'l*, pg. 747
KONE M-LIFT RT.—See Kone Corporation; *Int'l*, pg. 747
KONE MIDDLE EAST GIBCA LTD.—See Kone Corporation; *Int'l*, pg. 747
KONE REPRESENTATIVE OFFICE—See Kone Corporation; *Int'l*, pg. 747
KONE RULLTRAPPOR A.B.—See Kone Corporation; *Int'l*, pg. 748
KONE SANDER AUFZUG GMBH—See Kone Corporation; *Int'l*, pg. 748
KONE SOWITSCH AG—See Kone Corporation; *Int'l*, pg. 748
KONE STARLIFT B.V.—See Kone Corporation; *Int'l*, pg. 748
KONE WOOD CENTRAL EUROPE—See AGIV Group; *Int'l*, pg. 14
KONE WOOD LTD.—See AGIV Group; *Int'l*, pg. 14
KONE WOOD OY—See AGIV Group; *Int'l*, pg. 14
KONEPORTAAT OY—See Kone Corporation; *Int'l*, pg. 746
KONETA RUBBER CO. DIV.—See Lancaster Colony Corporation; *U.S. Public*, pg. 976
KONEZO, DIV. OF AKZO BELGIE N.V.—See Akzo Nobel N.V.; *Int'l*, pg. 44
KONICA ATHENS OFFICE—See Konica Corporation; *Int'l*, pg. 749
KONICA AUSTRALIA PTY.—See Konica Corporation; *Int'l*, pg. 749
KONICA BEIJING OFFICE—See Konica Corporation; *Int'l*, pg. 749
KONICA BUREAUTIQUE S.A.—See Konica Corporation; *Int'l*, pg. 749
KONICA BUSINESS MACHINES BELGIUM S.A./N.V.—See Konica Corporation; *Int'l*, pg. 749
KONICA BUSINESS MACHINES CANADA, LTD.—See Konica Corporation; *Int'l*, pg. 749
KONICA BUSINESS MACHINES DEUTSCHLAND GMBH—See Konica Corporation; *Int'l*, pg. 749
KONICA BUSINESS MACHINES EUROPE GMBH—See Konica Corporation; *Int'l*, pg. 749
KONICA BUSINESS MACHINES ITALIA—See Konica Corporation; *Int'l*, pg. 749
KONICA BUSINESS MACHINES (UK) LTD.—See Konica Corporation; *Int'l*, pg. 749
KONICA BUSINESS MACHINES USA, INC.—See Konica Corporation; *Int'l*, pg. 749
KONICA CANADA INC.—See Konica Corporation; *Int'l*, pg. 749
KONICA CORPORATION; *Int'l*, pg. 748
KONICA EUROPE GMBH—See Konica Corporation; *Int'l*, pg. 749
KONICA FRANCE S.A.—See Konica Corporation; *Int'l*, pg. 749
KONICA GESELLSCHAFT MBH—See Konica Corporation; *Int'l*, pg. 749
KONICA HEADQUARTERS NORTH AMERICA, INC.—See Konica Corporation; *Int'l*, pg. 748
KONICA HONG KONG LTD.—See Konica Corporation; *Int'l*, pg. 749
KONICA KOBE INDUSTRIAL CENTER—See Konica Corporation; *Int'l*, pg. 748
KONICA MANUFACTURING USA, INC.—See Konica Corporation; *Int'l*, pg. 749
KONICA MEDICAL CORPORATION—See Konica Corporation; *Int'l*, pg. 749
KONICA NEDERLAND B.V.—See Konica Corporation; *Int'l*, pg. 749
KONICA ODAWARA INDUSTRIAL CENTER—See Konica Corporation; *Int'l*, pg. 748
KONICA PHOTO SERVICE U.S.A., INC.—See Konica Corporation; *Int'l*, pg. 749
KONICA SINGAPORE PTE. LTD.—See Konica Corporation; *Int'l*, pg. 749
KONICA SUPPLIES MANUFACTURING U.S.A., INC.—See Konica Corporation; *Int'l*, pg. 749
KONICA TECHNOLOGY, INC.—See Konica Corporation; *Int'l*, pg. 748
KONICA (THAILAND) CO., LTD.—See Konica Corporation; *Int'l*, pg. 749
KONICA TOKYO INDUSTRIAL CENTER HACHIOJI—See Konica Corporation; *Int'l*, pg. 748
KONICA TOKYO INDUSTRIAL CENTER HINO—See Konica Corporation; *Int'l*, pg. 748
KONICA UK LTD.—See Konica Corporation; *Int'l*, pg. 749
THE OTTO KONIGSLOW MFG. CO.—See Triumph Group, Inc.; *U.S. Public*, pg. 1640
KONIGSWARTER & EBELL CHEMISCHE FABRIK GMBH—See VARTA AG; *Int'l*, pg. 1452
KONIJN BAGGERTECHNIEK BV—See Heidemij N.V.; *Int'l*, pg. 607
KONINKLIJKE AHOLD NV; *Int'l*, pg. 749
N.V. KONINKLIJKE BIJENKORF BEHEER KBB; *Int'l*, pg. 750
KONINKLIJKE BOLSWESSANEN NV; *Int'l*, pg. 750
KONINKLIJKE BRINK/MOLYN B.V.—See Akzo Nobel N.V.; *Int'l*, pg. 42
KONINKLIJKE BUNGE B.V.; *Int'l*, pg. 753
KONINKLIJKE DE RUYTER BV—See CSM N.V.; *Int'l*, pg. 244
KONINKLIJKE EDUARD VAN LEER B.V.—See Norske Skogindustrier A.S; *Int'l*, pg. 966
KONINKLIJKE GAZELLE BV—See Derby International Corporation S.A.; *Int'l*, pg. 394
KONINKLIJKE HOOGOVENS N.V.; *Int'l*, pg. 753
N.V. KONINKLIJKE KNP BT; *Int'l*, pg. 756
KONINKLIJKE MAATSCHAPPIJ DE BETUWE B.V.—See Unilever Plc; *Int'l*, pg. 1437

KONINKLIJKE PBNA BV—See Reed Elsevier plc; *Int'l*, pg. 1100
KONINKLIJKE TALENS BV—See Akzo Nobel N.V.; *Int'l*, pg. 42
KONINKLIJKE VAN OMMEREN NV; *Int'l*, pg. 758
KONINKLIJKE ZAADTEELT EN ZAADHANDEL SLUIS EN GROOT B.V.—See Novartis AG; *Int'l*, pg. 983
KONMAR—See Vendex International N.V.; *Int'l*, pg. 1463
P.T. KONSULTAN AKTUARIA KYOEINDO—See The Kyoei Life Insurance Co., Ltd.; *Int'l*, pg. 777
KONSUM VEREIN ZURICH AG—See Coop Switzerland; *Int'l*, pg. 330
KONTASET KFT.—See Knurr AG; *Int'l*, pg. 740
KONTES GLASS COMPANY—See Viag AG; *Int'l*, pg. 1464
KONTITE, U.K., LTD.—See Handy & Harman; *U.S. Public*, pg. 780
KONTO D.O.O.—See Borland International, Inc.; *U.S. Public*, pg. 246
KONTRON MESSTECHNIK GMBH—See Bayerische Motoren Werke Aktiengesellschaft; *Int'l*, pg. 177
KONTUUR-LEO BURNETT/ESTONIA—See Leo Burnett Company, Inc.; *U.S. Private*, pg. 184
KONUS-KESSEL GESELLSCHAFT FUR WARMETECHNIK MBH—See Deutsche Babcock AG; *Int'l*, pg. 399
OY KONWELL AB—See GESTRA GmbH; *Int'l*, pg. 550
KOO KOO ROO, INC.; *U.S. Public*, pg. 966
KOOB & PARTNER/THE CORPORATE COMPANY—See BDDP Group; *Int'l*, pg. 117
KOOKMIN LEASING CO., LTD.—See The Sakura Bank, Limited; *Int'l*, pg. 1180
KOOL SEAL, INC.; *U.S. Private*, pg. 632
KOOMAF-AALTEN B.V.—See British Steel Plc; *Int'l*, pg. 222
JIM KOONS MANAGEMENT; *U.S. Private*, pg. 632
KOP-COAT—See RPM, Inc.; *U.S. Public*, pg. 1357
KOPELE BEHEEN B.V.—See Royal Begemann Group; *Int'l*, pg. 1133
KOPEX INTERNATIONAL LIMITED—See Smiths Industries plc; *Int'l*, pg. 1267
PERRY H. KOPLIK & SONS; *U.S. Private*, pg. 632
KOPO AB—See Tamrock Corp.; *Int'l*, pg. 1353
KOPP ELECTRONICS LTD.—See Avnet, Inc.; *U.S. Public*, pg. 155
KOPPEL STEEL-BAYTOWN—See NS Group, Inc.; *U.S. Public*, pg. 1147
KOPPEL STEEL CORP.—See NS Group, Inc.; *U.S. Public*, pg. 1147
KORAG COMPANY, LTD.—See Monsanto Company; *U.S. Public*, pg. 1126
KORALLE VERLAG GMBH—See Axel Springer Verlag AG; *Int'l*, pg. 102
KORATRADE MTMC LTD.—See Koc Holding A.S.; *Int'l*, pg. 742
F. KORBEL BROS. INC.; *U.S. Private*, pg. 632
J. KORBER & COMPANY; *U.S. Private*, pg. 632
KOREA & PHARMACIA UPJOHN LIMITED—See Pharmacia & Upjohn, Inc.; *Int'l*, pg. 1049
KOREA BORDEN CHUSIK HOESA—See Borden, Inc.; *U.S. Private*, pg. 159
KOREA BUNDY CORPORATION—See TI Group plc; *Int'l*, pg. 1341
KOREA DEVELOPMENT LEASING CORPORATION—See Orix Corporation; *Int'l*, pg. 1010
KOREA DEVELOPMENT LEASING CORPORATION—See The Sanwa Bank Limited; *Int'l*, pg. 1190
KOREA ELECTRIC POWER CORPORATION (KEPCO); *Int'l*, pg. 758
KOREA ELECTRONICS INC.—See Shizuki Electric Corporation; *Int'l*, pg. 1236
KOREA FA SYSTEMS CO., LTD.—See Fuji Electric Co., Ltd.; *Int'l*, pg. 522
KOREA GREEN PHARM. CO. LTD.—See The Green Cross Corporation; *Int'l*, pg. 558
KOREA HEAVY INDUSTRIES & CONSTRUCTION CO., LTD.; *Int'l*, pg. 758
KOREA HIGH POLYMER COMPANY LIMITED—See Air Products and Chemicals, Inc.; *U.S. Public*, pg. 32
KOREA HIGH PRECISION CO., LTD.—See NSK Ltd.; *Int'l*, pg. 903
KOREA INDUSTRIAL GASES LTD.—See Air Products and Chemicals, Inc.; *U.S. Public*, pg. 32
THE KOREA INDUSTRIAL LEASING CO., LTD.—See The Nippon Credit Bank, Ltd.; *Int'l*, pg. 933
KOREA INTERNATIONAL MERCHANT BANK—See Commerzbank AG; *Int'l*, pg. 312
KOREA INVESTMENT & FINANCE CORP.—See CoreStates Financial Corp.; *U.S. Public*, pg. 447
KOREA-JAPAN FINANCE COMPANY LIMTED (KJF)—See The Long-Term Credit Bank of Japan, Limited; *Int'l*, pg. 816
KOREA JOHNSON CO., LTD.—See S.C. Johnson & Son, Inc.; *U.S. Private*, pg. 593
KOREA MAKRO COMPANY LTD.—See SHV Holdings N.V.; *Int'l*, pg. 1155
KOREA MASTER BUILDERS CO. LTD.—See Viag AG; *Int'l*, pg. 1465
KOREA NIPPON SANSO ENGINEERING CO., LTD.—See Nippon Sanso Corporation; *Int'l*, pg. 939
KOREA ORIX LEASE AND FINANCE LIMITED—See Orix Corporation; *Int'l*, pg. 1009
KOREA OTSUKA PHARMACEUTICAL CO., LTD.—See Otsuka Pharmaceutical Co., Ltd.; *Int'l*, pg. 1014
KOREA SANKEN CO., LTD.—See Sanken Electric Co., Ltd.; *Int'l*, pg. 1188
KOREA SANYO ELECTRIC CO., LTD.—See Sanyo Electric Co., Ltd.; *Int'l*, pg. 1192
KOREA SINTERED METAL CO., LTD.—See Sumitomo Electric Industries, Ltd.; *Int'l*, pg. 1313
KOREA TDK CO. LTD.—See TDK Corporation; *Int'l*, pg. 1336
KOREA TOKYO ELECTRONIC CO., LTD.—See Sanyo Electric Co., Ltd.; *Int'l*, pg. 1192
KOREA TOKYO SILICON CO., LTD.—See Sanyo Electric Co., Ltd.; *Int'l*, pg. 1192

KOREA TRANSFORMER CO. LTD.—See Tabuchi Electric Co., Ltd.; *Int'l*, pg. 1346
KOREA T.T. CO., LTD.—See Sanyo Electric Co., Ltd.; *Int'l*, pg. 1192
KOREA YAMANOUCHI PHARMACEUTICAL CO., LTD.—See Yamanouchi Pharmaceutical Co. Ltd.; *Int'l*, pg. 1519
KOREAN AIRLINES CO., LTD.; *Int'l*, pg. 758
KOREAN AMERICAN MUSICAL INSTRUMENT CORPORATION—See Baldwin Piano & Organ Company; *U.S. Public*, pg. 169
KORET OF CALIFORNIA, INC.; *U.S. Private*, pg. 632
KORET PIERRE CARDIN; *U.S. Private*, pg. 632
KOREY, KAY & PARTNERS; *U.S. Private*, pg. 632
KORF-TRANSPORT-FRANCE S.A.R.L—See Korf-Transport-GmbH; *Int'l*, pg. 759
KORF-TRANSPORT-GMBH; *Int'l*, pg. 758
KORF TRANSPORT GMBH—See Korf-Transport-GmbH; *Int'l*, pg. 758
KORF-TRANSPORT GMBH—See Korf-Transport-GmbH; *Int'l*, pg. 759
KORLOY INC.—See Sumitomo Electric Industries. Ltd.; *Int'l*, pg. 1313
KORMAN SERVICES, L.P.; *U.S. Private*, pg. 632
KORN/FERRY INTERNATIONAL; *U.S. Private*, pg. 632
KORN-OG FODERSTOF KOMPAGNIET (KFK) A/S—See Norsk Hydro a.s; *Int'l*, pg. 964
KORN/FERRY INTERNATIONAL—See Korn/Ferry International; *U.S. Private*, pg. 633
KORN/FERRY INTERNATIONAL - HIGH TECHNOLOGY RESEARCH CENTER—See Korn/Ferry International; *U.S. Private*, pg. 633
KORN/FERRY ORGANIZATIONAL CONSULTING—See Korn/Ferry International; *U.S. Private*, pg. 633
KORPIVAARA OY—See Amer Group Ltd.; *Int'l*, pg. 72
KORRY ELECTRONICS CO.—See Esterline Technologies Corporation; *U.S. Public*, pg. 594
KORSNAS AB; *Int'l*, pg. 759
KORSNAS FRANCE S.A.—See Korsnas AB; *Int'l*, pg. 759
KORSNAS GMBH—See Korsnas AB; *Int'l*, pg. 759
KORSNAS SAGVERKS AB—See Korsnas AB; *Int'l*, pg. 759
KORSNAS SALES LTD.—See Korsnas AB; *Int'l*, pg. 759
KORTMAN INTRADAL—See Sara Lee Corporation; *U.S. Public*, pg. 1434
KORYEO INDUSTRIAL DEVELOPMENT CO., LTD.—See Hyundai Motor Company; *Int'l*, pg. 642
KOSHIN CATERPILLAR MITSUBISHI CONSTRUCTION EQUIPMENT SALES, LTD.—See Caterpillar Inc.; *U.S. Public*, pg. 317
KOSHIN-KNORR LTD.—See Knorr-Bremse AG; *Int'l*, pg. 738
KOSMOBEL AG HANDELSAKTIENGESELLSCHAFT FUR KOSMETIK UND FRISEURBEDARF—See Wella Group; *Int'l*, pg. 1490
KOSMOS CEMENT COMPANY—See Lone Star Industries, Inc.; *U.S. Public*, pg. 1012
KOSS CLASSICS LTD.—See Koss Corporation; *U.S. Public*, pg. 966
KOSS CORPORATION; *U.S. Public*, pg. 966
KOSS EUROPE—See Koss Corporation; *U.S. Public*, pg. 966
KOSS LTD.—See Koss Corporation; *U.S. Public*, pg. 966
KOSSACK CHEMIE GMBH—See Henkel KGaA; *Int'l*, pg. 610
KOSTLIN' NAHRUNGSMITTEL EIN- UND AUSFUHRHANDEL GES.M.B.H.—See Julius Meinl AG; *Int'l*, pg. 856
KOSTRITZER SCHWARZBIERBRAUEREI GMBH & CO.—See Bitburger Brauerei Th. Simon GmbH; *Int'l*, pg. 197
KOSUGI SANGYO CO., LTD.; *Int'l*, pg. 759
KOTKA MILLS—See Enso Oyj; *Int'l*, pg. 457
KOTOBUKI CORPORATION - INTERNATIONAL DIVISION—See Kotobuki Seating Co.; *Int'l*, pg. 759
KOTOBUKI SEATING CO.; *Int'l*, pg. 759
KOUDIJS-WOUDA VOEDERS B.V.—See Goodman Fielder Limited; *Int'l*, pg. 555
KOVA FERTILIZER INC.; *U.S. Private*, pg. 634
GEORGE KOVACS LIGHTING, INC.; *U.S. Private*, pg. 634
KOVEL KRESSER & PARTNERS; *U.S. Private*, pg. 634
KOVEL KRESSER & PARTNERS/OAKLAND OFFICE—See Kovel Kresser & Partners; *U.S. Private*, pg. 634
KOWALSKI SAUSAGE CO., INC.; *U.S. Private*, pg. 634
KOYL COMMERCIAL REAL ESTATE SERVICES LTD.—See Royal LePage Limited; *Int'l*, pg. 1143
KOYO CORPORATION OF USA—See Koyo Seiko Company, Ltd.; *Int'l*, pg. 760
KOYO CORPORATION OF USA, MANUFACTURING DIVISION—See Koyo Seiko Company, Ltd.; *Int'l*, pg. 760
KOYO CORPORATION OF USA, SALES DIVISION—See Koyo Seiko Company, Ltd.; *Int'l*, pg. 760
KOYO INTERNATIONAL INC. OF AMERICA—See Koyo Seiko Company, Ltd.; *Int'l*, pg. 760
KOYO LINDBERG LTD.—See General Signal Corporation; *U.S. Public*, pg. 727
KOYO-MATTISON—See Mattison Technologies, Inc.; *U.S. Private*, pg. 715
KOYO SEIKO COMPANY, LTD.; *Int'l*, pg. 760
KRACO ENTERPRISES, INC.; *U.S. Private*, pg. 634
KRAFCOR UNLIMITED—See Specialty Industries, Inc.; *U.S. Private*, pg. 1022
KRAFFT, S.A.—See Compania Espanola de Petroleos, S.A. (CEPSA); *Int'l*, pg. 323
KRAFT CANADA INC.—See Philip Morris Companies Inc.; *U.S. Public*, pg. 1288
KRAFT FOOD INGREDIENTS CORP.—See Philip Morris Companies Inc.; *U.S. Public*, pg. 1288
KRAFT FOODS A/S—See Philip Morris Companies Inc.; *U.S. Public*, pg. 1290
KRAFT FOODS ASIA/PACIFIC, INC.—See Philip Morris Companies Inc.; *U.S. Public*, pg. 1288
KRAFT FOODS INC.—See Philip Morris Companies Inc.; *U.S. Public*, pg. 1290

KRAFT FOODS, INC.—See Philip Morris Companies Inc.; *U.S. Public*, pg. 1287
KRAFT FOODS INC.—See Philip Morris Companies Inc.; *U.S. Public*, pg. 1288
KRAFT FOODS INTERNATIONAL—See Philip Morris Companies Inc.; *U.S. Public*, pg. 1288
KRAFT FOODS LTD., YEAST EXTRACT PLANT—See Philip Morris Companies Inc.; *U.S. Public*, pg. 1290
KRAFT HARDWARE, INC., *U.S. Private*, pg. 634
KRAFT HOLDINGS LIMITED—See Philip Morris Companies Inc.; *U.S. Public*, pg. 1290
KRAFT JACOBS SUCHARD—See Philip Morris Companies Inc.; *U.S. Public*, pg. 1290
KRAFT JACOBS SUCHARD AG—See Philip Morris Companies Inc.; *U.S. Public*, pg. 1288
KRAFT LIMITED-KRAFT LIMITEE—See Philip Morris Companies Inc.; *U.S. Public*, pg. 1290
KRAFT VERSICHERUNGS-AG—See Allianz Aktiengesellschaft; *Int'l*, pg. 58
WARD KRAFT, INC.; *U.S. Private*, pg. 634
KRAFTMAID CABINETRY, INC.—See Masco Corporation; *U.S. Public*, pg. 1053
KRAFTMAID TRUCKING, INC.—See Masco Corporation; *U.S. Public*, pg. 1053
KRAFTVERKEHR BAYERN GMBH—See Heidelberger Zement A.G.; *Int'l*, pg. 606
KRAFTWERK AEGINA AG (AEGINA)—See Alusuisse-Lonza Holding Ltd.; *Int'l*, pg. 67
KRAFTWERK BUER BETRIEBSGESELLSCHAFT MBH—See Veba AG; *Int'l*, pg. 1460
KRAFTWERK BUER GBR—See Veba AG; *Int'l*, pg. 1460
KRAFTWERK EV3 1/S—See Veba AG; *Int'l*, pg. 1457
KRAFTWERK KASSEL GMBH—See Veba AG; *Int'l*, pg. 1456
KRAFTWERK LOTSCHEN AG-(LOTSCHEN)—See Alusuisse-Lonza Holding Ltd.; *Int'l*, pg. 67
KRAFTWERK MEHRUM GMBH—See Veba AG; *Int'l*, pg. 1456
KRAFTWERK RECKINGEN AG—See Alusuisse-Lonza Holding Ltd.; *Int'l*, pg. 67
KRAFTWERK SCHKOPAU GMBH—See Veba AG; *Int'l*, pg. 1460
KRAFTWERKE GOUGRA AG-(GOUDRA)—See Alusuisse-Lonza Holding Ltd.; *Int'l*, pg. 67
KRAFTWERKE MATTMARK AG—See Alusuisse-Lonza Holding Ltd.; *Int'l*, pg. 67
KRAFTWERKS- UND NETZGESELLSCHAFT MBH-KNG—See Veba AG; *Int'l*, pg. 1457
KRAGIE/NEWELL; *U.S. Private*, pg. 634
KRAGIE/NEWELL—See Kragie/Newell; *U.S. Private*, pg. 635
KRAMER CAPITAL CONSULTANTS, INC.—See Danielson Holding Corporation; *U.S. Public*, pg. 483
KRAMER INTERNATIONAL, INC.—See Atchison Casting Corporation; *U.S. Public*, pg. 142
KRAMES COMMUNICATIONS—See The Times Mirror Company; *U.S. Public*, pg. 1616
KRANLYFT—See Svedala Industri AB; *Int'l*, pg. 1323
AB KRANLYFT—See Trelleborg AB; *Int'l*, pg. 1420
KRANTOR CORPORATION; *U.S. Public*, pg. 966
KRANTZ AMERICA, INC.—See Deutsche Babcock AG; *Int'l*, pg. 401
H. KRANTZ TEXTILMASCHINEN GMBH—See Deutsche Babcock AG; *Int'l*, pg. 399
H. KRANTZ-TKT GMBH—See Deutsche Babcock AG; *Int'l*, pg. 399
P.T. KRIKRAS/BASF DEPARTMENT—See BASF AG; *Int'l*, pg. 109
KRASDALE FOODS INC.; *U.S. Private*, pg. 635
KRATON FABRICATORS—See Engineered Products, Inc.; *U.S. Private*, pg. 376
KRATOS GROUP PLC/KRATOS ANALYTICAL LTD.—See Shimadzu Corporation; *Int'l*, pg. 1232
KRAUS-ANDERSON CONSTRUCTION COMPANY—See Kraus-Anderson Incorporated; *U.S. Private*, pg. 635
KRAUS-ANDERSON INCORPORATED; *U.S. Private*, pg. 635
KRAUS-ANDERSON, INCORPORATED—See Kraus-Anderson Incorporated; *U.S. Private*, pg. 635
KRAUS-ANDERSON INSURANCE—See Kraus-Anderson Incorporated; *U.S. Private*, pg. 635
KRAUS-ANDERSON MORTGAGE COMPANY—See Kraus-Anderson Incorporated; *U.S. Private*, pg. 635
KRAUS-ANDERSON REALTY COMPANY—See Kraus-Anderson Incorporated; *U.S. Private*, pg. 635
CARL GUSTAV KRAUSE GMBH—See Fried. Krupp AG; *Int'l*, pg. 514
KRAUSE PLOW CORP.; *U.S. Private*, pg. 635
KRAUSE PUBLICATIONS, INC.; *U.S. Private*, pg. 635
KRAUSE'S FURNITURE INC.; *U.S. Public*, pg. 967
KRAUSE'S SOFA FACTORY—See Krause's Furniture Inc.; *U.S. Public*, pg. 967
KRAUSS-MAFFEI AG—See Mannesmann A.G.; *Int'l*, pg. 836
KRAUSS-MAFFEI (AIR DEFENCE) LTD.—See Mannesmann A.G.; *Int'l*, pg. 836
KRAUSS-MAFFEI ASIA PACIFIC PTE. LTD.—See Mannesmann A.G.; *Int'l*, pg. 836
KRAUSS-MAFFEI AUSTRIA GMBH—See Mannesmann A.G.; *Int'l*, pg. 836
KRAUSS-MAFFEI AUTOMATIONSTECHNIK GMBH—See Mannesmann A.G.; *Int'l*, pg. 836
KRAUSS-MAFFEI CHEMIOMECCANICA S.R.L.—See Mannesmann A.G.; *Int'l*, pg. 836
KRAUSS-MAFFEI CORP.—See Mannesmann A.G.; *Int'l*, pg. 836
KRAUSS-MAFFEI DIENSTLEISTUNG GMBH—See Mannesmann A.G.; *Int'l*, pg. 836
KRAUSS-MAFFEI FRANCE S.A.R.L.—See Mannesmann A.G.; *Int'l*, pg. 836
KRAUSS-MAFFEI GIBTECHNIK GMBH—See Mannesmann A.G.; *Int'l*, pg. 836
KRAUSS-MAFFEI HOLDINGS LTD.—See Mannesmann A.G.; *Int'l*, pg. 836

KRAUSS-MAFFEI KUNSTSOFFTECHNIK VERTRIEB & SERVICE NORD—See Mannesmann A.G.; *Int'l*, pg. 836
KRAUSS-MAFFEI KUNSTSOFFTECHNIK VERTRIEB & SERVICE SUD—See Mannesmann A.G.; pg. 836
KRAUSS-MAFFEI KUNSTSTOFFTECHNIK GMBH—See Mannesmann A.G.; *Int'l*, pg. 836
KRAUSS-MAFFEI KUNSTSOFFTECHNIK VERTRIEB & SERVICE SUD—See Mannesmann A.G.; *Int'l*, pg. 836
KRAUSS-MAFFEI (U.K.) LTD.—See Mannesmann A.G.; *Int'l*, pg. 836
KRAUSS-MAFFEI VERFAHRENSTECHNIK GMBH—See Mannesmann A.G.; *Int'l*, pg. 836
KRAUSS-MAFFEI VERKEHRSTECHNIK GMBH—See Mannesmann A.G.; *Int'l*, pg. 836
KRAUSS-MAFFEI VERSICHERUNGSDIENST GMBH—See Mannesmann A.G.; *Int'l*, pg. 836
KRAUSS-MAFFEI WEHRTECHNIK GMBH—See Mannesmann A.G.; *Int'l*, pg. 836
KRAUTKRAMER-BRANSON, INC.—See Emerson Electric Co.; *U.S. Public*, pg. 574
KRAUTKRAMER-FOERSTER JAPAN CO., LTD.—See Emerson Electric Co.; *U.S. Public*, pg. 577
KRAUTKRAMER G.M.B.H.—See Emerson Electric Co.; *U.S. Public*, pg. 577
KRAZY GLUE INC.—See Borden, Inc.; *U.S. Private*, pg. 158
KRE-LON, S.A.—See Velcro Industries N.V.; *Int'l*, pg. 1462
KREASINDO ADVERTISING & MARKETING CONSULTANTS—See Leo Burnett Company, Inc.; *U.S. Private*, pg. 184
KREDIETBANK ATLANTA BRANCH—See Kredietbank N.V.; *Int'l*, pg. 760
KREDIETBANK-BANKVEREIN AG—See Kredietbank N.V.; *Int'l*, pg. 761
KREDIETBANK DUBLIN BRANCH—See Kredietbank N.V.; *Int'l*, pg. 760
KREDIETBANK GRAND CAYMAN BRANCH—See Kredietbank N.V.; *Int'l*, pg. 760
KREDIETBANK HONG KONG BRANCH—See Kredietbank N.V.; *Int'l*, pg. 760
KREDIETBANK INTER-ALPHA REPRESENTATIVE OFFICE—See Kredietbank N.V.; *Int'l*, pg. 760
KREDIETBANK INTERNATIONAL FINANCE N.V.—See Kredietbank N.V.; *Int'l*, pg. 761
KREDIETBANK LONDON BRANCH—See Kredietbank N.V.; *Int'l*, pg. 760
KREDIETBANK MANCHESTER BRANCH—See Kredietbank N.V.; *Int'l*, pg. 760
KREDIETBANK (NEDERLAND) N.V.—See Kredietbank N.V.; *Int'l*, pg. 761
KREDIETBANK NEW YORK BRANCH—See Kredietbank N.V.; *Int'l*, pg. 760
KREDIETBANK NORTH AMERICAN FINANCE CORP.—See Kredietbank N.V.; *Int'l*, pg. 760
KREDIETBANK NV—See Almanij N.V.; *Int'l*, pg. 65
KREDIETBANK N.V.; *Int'l*, pg. 760
KREDIETBANK OFICINA DE REPRESENTACION—See Kredietbank N.V.; *Int'l*, pg. 760
KREDIETBANK REPRESENTATIVE OFFICE (ANKARA)—See Kredietbank N.V.; *Int'l*, pg. 760
KREDIETBANK REPRESENTATIVE OFFICE (BANGKOK)—See Kredietbank N.V.; *Int'l*, pg. 760
KREDIETBANK REPRESENTATIVE OFFICE (BUDAPEST)—See Kredietbank N.V.; *Int'l*, pg. 760
KREDIETBANK REPRESENTATIVE OFFICE (MILAN)—See Kredietbank N.V.; *Int'l*, pg. 760
KREDIETBANK REPRESENTATIVE OFFICE (MOSCOW)—See Kredietbank N.V.; *Int'l*, pg. 760
KREDIETBANK REPRESENTATIVE OFFICE (PRAGUE)—See Kredietbank N.V.; *Int'l*, pg. 760
KREDIETBANK REPRESENTATIVE OFFICE (WARSAW)—See Kredietbank N.V.; *Int'l*, pg. 760
KREDIETBANK S.A. FRANCE—See Kredietbank N.V.; *Int'l*, pg. 760
KREDIETBANK S.A. FRANCE AGENCE DE LILLE—See Kredietbank N.V.; *Int'l*, pg. 760
KREDIETBANK S.A. FRANCE AGENCE DE PARIS—See Kredietbank N.V.; *Int'l*, pg. 760
KREDIETBANK SA LUXEMBOURGEOISE—See Almanij N.V.; *Int'l*, pg. 65
KREDIETBANK S.A. LUXEMBOURGEOISE—See Kredietbank N.V.; *Int'l*, pg. 761
KREDIETBANK SHANGHAI BRANCH—See Kredietbank N.V.; *Int'l*, pg. 760
KREDIETBANK SINGAPORE BRANCH—See Kredietbank N.V.; *Int'l*, pg. 760
KREDIETBANK (SUISSE) S.A.—See Kredietbank N.V.; *Int'l*, pg. 761
KREDIETBANK TAIPEI BRANCH—See Kredietbank N.V.; *Int'l*, pg. 760
KREDIETCORP SA—See Almanij N.V.; *Int'l*, pg. 65
KREDIETFINANCE CORPORATION LTD.—See Kredietbank N.V.; *Int'l*, pg. 761
KREDIETFINANCE (U.K.) LTD—See Kredietbank N.V.; *Int'l*, pg. 761
KREDIETRUST SA—See Almanij N.V.; *Int'l*, pg. 65
KREDIETWAARBORG NV—See Almanij N.V.; *Int'l*, pg. 65
KREFIMA NV—See Almanij N.V.; *Int'l*, pg. 65
KREHER STEEL CO., INC.; *U.S. Private*, pg. 635
KREMS-CHEMI GMBH—See Bayer AG; *Int'l*, pg. 175
KREONITE, INC.; *U.S. Private*, pg. 635
KREPE-KRAFT, INC.—See Astronics Corporation; *U.S. Public*, pg. 142
KRESSON VIEW CENTER—See Genesis Health Ventures, Inc.; *U.S. Public*, pg. 729
LEONARD KREUSCH GMBH & CO.—See Leonard Kreusch, Inc.; *U.S. Private*, pg. 635
LEONARD KREUSCH, INC.; *U.S. Private*, pg. 635
KREYMBORG—See Vendex International N.V.; *Int'l*, pg. 1462
PAUL J. KREZ COMPANY; *U.S. Private*, pg. 635
KRIER FOODS, INC.; *U.S. Private*, pg. 636
KRIPS REPRO B.V.—See Reed Elsevier plc; *Int'l*, pg. 1100

KROEHLER FURNITURE MANUFACTURING COMPANY, INC.—See Schottenstein Stores Corporation; *U.S. Private,* pg. 972
KROFAM INC.: *U.S. Private,* pg. 636
THE KROGER CO.: *U.S. Public,* pg. 967
KROLL FAHRZEUGBAU GMBH—See Rothenberger Group GmbH; *Int'l,* pg. 1128
KROLL FAHRZEUGBAU UMWELTTECHNIK GMBH—See Rothenberger Group GmbH; *Int'l,* pg. 1128
KROLL FAHRZEUGBAU-UMWELTTECHNIK GMBH—See Rothenberger Group GmbH; *Int'l,* pg. 1128
KROMOS B.V.—See Ruhrgas Aktiengesellschaft; *Int'l,* pg. 1149
G. KROMSCHRODER AKTIENGESELLSCHAFT—See Ruhrgas Aktiengesellschaft; *Int'l,* pg. 1148
KROMSCHRODER (U.K.) LTD.—See Ruhrgas Aktiengesellschaft; *Int'l,* pg. 1149
KRONA MARIN AB—See Celsius AB; *Int'l,* pg. 277
KRONE CASTING CORP.; *U.S. Private,* pg. 636
KRONENBOURG—See Danone Group; *Int'l,* pg. 381
KRONOS CANADA INC.—See Contran Corporation; *U.S. Private,* pg. 271
KRONOS CHEMIE GMBH—See Contran Corporation; *U.S. Private,* pg. 271
KRONOS EUROPE, INC.—See Contran Corporation; *U.S. Private,* pg. 271
KRONOS, INC.—See Contran Corporation; *U.S. Private,* pg. 270
KRONOS INCORPORATED; *U.S. Public,* pg. 967
KRONOS INTERNATIONAL, INC.—See Contran Corporation; *U.S. Private,* pg. 271
KRONOS NORGE A/S—See Contran Corporation; *U.S. Private,* pg. 271
KRONOS SA/NV—See Contran Corporation; *U.S. Private,* pg. 271
KRONOS TITAN A/S—See Contran Corporation; *U.S. Private,* pg. 271
KRONOS TITAN GMBH—See Contran Corporation; *U.S. Private,* pg. 271
KRONOS (UK) LTD.—See Contran Corporation; *U.S. Private,* pg. 271
KRONOS WORLDWIDE SERVICES SA/NV—See Contran Corporation; *U.S. Private,* pg. 271
KROPP FORGE CO.—See TIC United Corporation; *U.S. Private,* pg. 1064
KROY INC.—See Pubco Corporation; *U.S. Public,* pg. 1339
H. KRUEGER MASCHINENFABRIK GMBH—See Cardo AB; *Int'l,* pg. 269
KRUG INTERNATIONAL CORP.; *U.S. Public,* pg. 967
KRUG INTERNATIONAL TECHNOLOGY/SCIENTIFIC SERVICES, INC.—See Krug International Corp.; *U.S. Public,* pg. 968
KRUG LIFE SCIENCES INC.—See Krug International Corp.; *U.S. Public,* pg. 968
KRUGER INC.; *Int'l,* pg. 761
KRUGER RECYCLING, INC.-HACKENSACK—See Kruger Inc.; *Int'l,* pg. 762
KRUGER SALES LIMITED—See Kruger Inc.; *Int'l,* pg. 762
KRUGER TISSUE (CONSUMER) LIMITED—See Kruger Inc.; *Int'l,* pg. 762
KRUGER TISSUE (INDUSTRIAL) LIMITED—See Kruger Inc.; *Int'l,* pg. 762
KRUGER URBAN FOREST PRODUCTS, INC.—See Kruger Inc.; *Int'l,* pg. 761
WOLFGANG KRUGER VERLAG GMBH—See Georg von Holtzbrinck GmbH; *Int'l,* pg. 1478
KRUNG THAI IBJ LEASING CO.—See The Industrial Bank of Japan, Limited; *Int'l,* pg. 676
KRUPP ANLAGENBAU GMBH—See Fried. Krupp AG; *Int'l,* pg. 511
KRUPP BINNENSCHIFFAHRT GMBH—See Fried. Krupp AG; *Int'l,* pg. 515
KRUPP BRUNINGHAUS GMBH—See Fried. Krupp AG; *Int'l,* pg. 508
KRUPP CANADA INC.—See Fried. Krupp AG; *Int'l,* pg. 511
KRUPP CORPOPLAST MASCHINENBAU GMBH—See Fried. Krupp AG; *Int'l,* pg. 510
KRUPP DRUCKEREIBETRIEBE GMBH—See Fried. Krupp AG; *Int'l,* pg. 513
KRUPP EDELSTAHLPROFILE GMBH—See Fried. Krupp AG; *Int'l,* pg. 512
KRUPP ENERGIEHANDEL GMBH—See Fried. Krupp AG; *Int'l,* pg. 513
KRUPP ENGINEERING (AUSTRALIA) (PTY.) LTD.—See Fried. Krupp AG; *Int'l,* pg. 511
KRUPP ENTWICKLUNGSZENTRUM GMBH—See Fried. Krupp AG; *Int'l,* pg. 512
KRUPP FORDERTECHNIK GMBH—See Fried. Krupp AG; *Int'l,* pg. 511
KRUPP GERLACH COMPANY—See Fried. Krupp AG; *Int'l,* pg. 508
KRUPP GFT GESELLSCHAFT FUR ANLAGEN-, BAU- UND GLEISTECHNIK MBH—See Fried. Krupp AG; *Int'l,* pg. 513
KRUPP GRUAS HIDRAULICAS, S.A. ARANJUEZ—See Fried. Krupp AG; *Int'l,* pg. 510
KRUPP HAZEMAG S.A.—See Fried. Krupp AG; *Int'l,* pg. 511
KRUPP HISPANIA S.A.—See Fried. Krupp AG; *Int'l,* pg. 510
KRUPP HOESCH ACCIAI S.R.L.—See Fried. Krupp AG; *Int'l,* pg. 515
KRUPP HOESCH ACIERS S.A.R.L.—See Fried. Krupp AG; *Int'l,* pg. 515
KRUPP HOESCH AUTOMOTIVE GMBH—See Fried. Krupp AG; *Int'l,* pg. 507
KRUPP HOESCH BASEL AG—See Fried. Krupp AG; *Int'l,* pg. 515
KRUPP HOESCH BERUFSBILDUNG GMBH—See Fried. Krupp AG; *Int'l,* pg. 512
KRUPP HOESCH COILEX GMBH—See Fried. Krupp AG; *Int'l,* pg. 512
KRUPP HOESCH DIENSTLEISTUNGEN GMBH—See Fried. Krupp AG; *Int'l,* pg. 512

KRUPP HOESCH EXPORT—See Fried. Krupp AG; *Int'l,* pg. 515
KRUPP HOESCH IMMOBILIEN GMBH—See Fried. Krupp AG; *Int'l,* pg. 512
KRUPP HOESCH INFORMATIONSVERARBEITUNG GMBH—See Fried. Krupp AG; *Int'l,* pg. 512
KRUPP HOESCH INTERNATIONAL GMBH—See Fried. Krupp AG; *Int'l,* pg. 513
KRUPP HOESCH MASCHINENBAU GMBH—See Fried. Krupp AG; *Int'l,* pg. 509
KRUPP HOESCH METALLHANDEL GMBH—See Fried. Krupp AG; *Int'l,* pg. 513
KRUPP HOESCH ROHSTOFF UND RECYCLING GMBH—See Fried. Krupp AG; *Int'l,* pg. 513
KRUPP HOESCH STAAL N.V.—See Fried. Krupp AG; *Int'l,* pg. 515
KRUPP HOESCH STAHL AB—See Fried. Krupp AG; *Int'l,* pg. 515
KRUPP HOESCH STAHL AG - BERLIN—See Fried. Krupp AG; *Int'l,* pg. 512
KRUPP HOESCH STAHL AG - BOCHUM—See Fried. Krupp AG; *Int'l,* pg. 513
KRUPP HOESCH STAHL AG - DORTMUND—See Fried. Krupp AG; *Int'l,* pg. 512
KRUPP HOESCH STAHL AG - DUSSELDORF—See Fried. Krupp AG; *Int'l,* pg. 513
KRUPP HOESCH STAHL AG - HANOVER—See Fried. Krupp AG; *Int'l,* pg. 512
KRUPP HOESCH STAHL AG - KREUZTAL—See Fried. Krupp AG; *Int'l,* pg. 513
KRUPP HOESCH STAHL AG - LEIPZIG—See Fried. Krupp AG; *Int'l,* pg. 512
KRUPP HOESCH STAHL AG - MANNHEIM—See Fried. Krupp AG; *Int'l,* pg. 512
KRUPP HOESCH STAHL AG - MUNICH—See Fried. Krupp AG; *Int'l,* pg. 512
KRUPP HOESCH STAHL AG - REMSCHEID—See Fried. Krupp AG; *Int'l,* pg. 512
KRUPP HOESCH STAHL AG - SIEGERLAND—See Fried. Krupp AG; *Int'l,* pg. 513
KRUPP HOESCH STAHL AG - STUTTGART—See Fried. Krupp AG; *Int'l,* pg. 515
KRUPP HOESCH STAHL APS—See Fried. Krupp AG; *Int'l,* pg. 515
KRUPP HOESCH STAHL UND METALL GMBH—See Fried. Krupp AG; *Int'l,* pg. 515
KRUPP HOESCH STAHLEXPORT GMBH—See Fried. Krupp AG; *Int'l,* pg. 515
KRUPP HOESCH STAHLHANDEL GMBH—See Fried. Krupp AG; *Int'l,* pg. 515
KRUPP HOESCH STAHLHANDEL RHEINLAND GMBH—See Fried. Krupp AG; *Int'l,* pg. 514
KRUPP HOESCH STAHLVERTRIEBS GMBH—See Fried. Krupp AG; *Int'l,* pg. 514
KRUPP HOESCH STEEL LTD.—See Fried. Krupp AG; *Int'l,* pg. 516
KRUPP HOESCH STEEL PRODUCTS INC.—See Fried. Krupp AG; *Int'l,* pg. 509
KRUPP HOESCH TECNA AG—See Fried. Krupp AG; *Int'l,* pg. 509
KRUPP HOESCH VERBARBEITUNG—See Fried. Krupp AG; *Int'l,* pg. 508
KRUPP IBERICA, S.A.—See Fried. Krupp AG; *Int'l,* pg. 510
KRUPP INDUSTRIES INDIA LTD.—See Fried. Krupp AG; *Int'l,* pg. 511
KRUPP INDUSTRIES LTD.—See Fried. Krupp AG; *Int'l,* pg. 510
KRUPP IRAN LTD.—See Fried. Krupp AG; *Int'l,* pg. 511
KRUPP KAUTEX MASCHINENBAU GMBH—See Fried. Krupp AG; *Int'l,* pg. 510
KRUPP KOPPERS GMBH—See Fried. Krupp AG; *Int'l,* pg. 511
KRUPP MACHINERY LTD.—See Fried. Krupp AG; *Int'l,* pg. 510
KRUPP MAK DIESEL INC.—See Fried. Krupp AG; *Int'l,* pg. 509
KRUPP MAK (LONDON) LTD.—See Fried. Krupp AG; *Int'l,* pg. 509
KRUPP MAK MASCHINENBAU GMBH—See Fried. Krupp AG; *Int'l,* pg. 509
KRUPP MAK SCANDINAVIA A/S—See Fried. Krupp AG; *Int'l,* pg. 510
KRUPP MASCHINENTECHNIK GMBH—See Fried. Krupp AG; *Int'l,* pg. 510
KRUPP MATERIALS HANDLING LTD.—See Fried. Krupp AG; *Int'l,* pg. 511
KRUPP MEDIZINTECHNIK GMBH—See Fried. Krupp AG; *Int'l,* pg. 510
KRUPP METALURGICA CAMPO LIMPO LTDA.—See Fried. Krupp AG; *Int'l,* pg. 508
KRUPP MINERALOLHANDEL GMBH—See Fried. Krupp AG; *Int'l,* pg. 513
KRUPP MOBILKRANE GMBH—See Fried. Krupp AG; *Int'l,* pg. 510
KRUPP MONTAGE- UND SERVICETECHNIK GMBH—See Fried. Krupp AG; *Int'l,* pg. 516
KRUPP NIROSTA GMBH—See Fried. Krupp AG; *Int'l,* pg. 513
KRUPP PLASTICS & RUBBER MACHINERY (CANADA), INC.—See Fried. Krupp AG; *Int'l,* pg. 510
KRUPP PLASTICS & RUBBER MACHINERY, FAR EAST—See Fried. Krupp AG; *Int'l,* pg. 510
KRUPP PLASTICS & RUBBER MACHINERY INC.—See Fried. Krupp AG; *Int'l,* pg. 510
KRUPP PLASTICS & RUBBER MACHINERY INC. (RUBBER DIVISION)—See Fried. Krupp AG; *Int'l,* pg. 510
KRUPP POLYSIUS AG—See Fried. Krupp AG; *Int'l,* pg. 512
KRUPP POLYSIUS ASIA PACIFIC (PTY.) LTD.—See Fried. Krupp AG; *Int'l,* pg. 512
KRUPP ROBINS, INC.—See Fried. Krupp AG; *Int'l,* pg. 511
KRUPP SCHEEPVAART B.V.—See Fried. Krupp AG; *Int'l,* pg. 515

KRUPP SEESCHIFFAHRT GMBH—See Fried. Krupp AG; *Int'l,* pg. 514
KRUPP SIGMA-STAHL GMBH—See Fried. Krupp AG; *Int'l,* pg. 513
KRUPP SOUTH AFRICA (PTY.) LTD.—See Fried. Krupp AG; *Int'l,* pg. 511
KRUPP STAHL AB—See Fried. Krupp AG; *Int'l,* pg. 516
KRUPP STAHL KALTFORM GMBH—See Fried. Krupp AG; *Int'l,* pg. 508
KRUPP STAHL WOHNUNGSBAU GMBH—See Fried. Krupp AG; *Int'l,* pg. 512
KRUPP STAHLBAU BERLIN GMBH & CO. KG—See Fried. Krupp AG; *Int'l,* pg. 508
KRUPP STEEL & ENGINEERING (NIGERIA) LTD.—See Fried. Krupp AG; *Int'l,* pg. 513
KRUPP TECHNIQUES INDUSTRIELLES S.A.—See Fried. Krupp AG; *Int'l,* pg. 510
KRUPP VDM GMBH—See Fried. Krupp AG; *Int'l,* pg. 509
KRUPP VDM GMBH - EVIDAL DIVISION—See Fried. Krupp AG; *Int'l,* pg. 509
KRUPP VDM GMBH - SEMI-FINISHED PRODUCTS & SYSTEMS DIVISION—See Fried. Krupp AG; *Int'l,* pg. 509
KRUPP VDM GMBH - TUBES & COMPONENTS DIVISION—See Fried. Krupp AG; *Int'l,* pg. 509
KRUPP WARMETECHNIK GMBH—See Fried. Krupp AG; *Int'l,* pg. 514
KRUPP WARMETECHNIK GMBH - BERLIN—See Fried. Krupp AG; *Int'l,* pg. 514
KRUPP WARMETECHNIK GMBH - BITTERFELD—See Fried. Krupp AG; *Int'l,* pg. 514
KRUPP WARMETECHNIK GMBH - BREMEN—See Fried. Krupp AG; *Int'l,* pg. 514
KRUPP WARMETECHNIK GMBH - COLOGNE—See Fried. Krupp AG; *Int'l,* pg. 514
KRUPP WARMETECHNIK GMBH - DITZINGEN—See Fried. Krupp AG; *Int'l,* pg. 514
KRUPP WARMETECHNIK GMBH - DORTMUND—See Fried. Krupp AG; *Int'l,* pg. 514
KRUPP WARMETECHNIK GMBH - DRESDEN—See Fried. Krupp AG; *Int'l,* pg. 515
KRUPP WARMETECHNIK GMBH - DUISBURG—See Fried. Krupp AG; *Int'l,* pg. 515
KRUPP WARMETECHNIK GMBH - ERFURT—See Fried. Krupp AG; *Int'l,* pg. 515
KRUPP WARMETECHNIK GMBH - ESSEN—See Fried. Krupp AG; *Int'l,* pg. 515
KRUPP WARMETECHNIK GMBH - FRANKFURT—See Fried. Krupp AG; *Int'l,* pg. 515
KRUPP WARMETECHNIK GMBH - FREIBURG—See Fried. Krupp AG; *Int'l,* pg. 515
KRUPP WARMETECHNIK GMBH - HAMBURG—See Fried. Krupp AG; *Int'l,* pg. 515
KRUPP WARMETECHNIK GMBH - HANNOVER—See Fried. Krupp AG; *Int'l,* pg. 515
KRUPP WARMETECHNIK GMBH - MUNICH—See Fried. Krupp AG; *Int'l,* pg. 515
KRUPP WARMETECHNIK GMBH - NUREMBURG—See Fried. Krupp AG; *Int'l,* pg. 515
KRUPP WIDIA FRANCE S.A.—See Fried. Krupp AG; *Int'l,* pg. 510
KRUPP WIDIA GMBH—See Fried. Krupp AG; *Int'l,* pg. 510
KRUPP WIDIA IBERICA—See Fried. Krupp AG; *Int'l,* pg. 510
KRUPP WIDIA JAPAN LTD.—See Fried. Krupp AG; *Int'l,* pg. 510
KRUPP WIDIA KOREA LTD.—See Fried. Krupp AG; *Int'l,* pg. 510
KRUPP WIDIA NEDERLAND B.V.—See Fried. Krupp AG; *Int'l,* pg. 510
KRUPP WIDIA S.E. ASIA (PTE.) LTD.—See Fried. Krupp AG; *Int'l,* pg. 510
KRUPP WIDIA S.P.A.—See Fried. Krupp AG; *Int'l,* pg. 510
KRUPP WIDIA U.K. LTD.—See Fried. Krupp AG; *Int'l,* pg. 510
KRUPP WIDIA VERTRIEBSGES. MBH—See Fried. Krupp AG; *Int'l,* pg. 512
KRUPP WILPUTTE CORP.—See Fried. Krupp AG; *Int'l,* pg. 512
KRUPS—See Moulinex S.A.; *Int'l,* pg. 896
KRUPS A/S—See Moulinex S.A.; *Int'l,* pg. 896
KRUPS B.V.—See Moulinex S.A.; *Int'l,* pg. 896
KRUPS GMBH & CO. KG—See Moulinex S.A.; *Int'l,* pg. 896
KRUPS LTD.—See Moulinex S.A.; *Int'l,* pg. 896
KRUPS NORTH AMERICA—See Moulinex S.A.; *Int'l,* pg. 896
KRUPS N.V.—See Moulinex S.A.; *Int'l,* pg. 896
KRUPS SALES LTD.—See Moulinex S.A.; *Int'l,* pg. 896
KRUPS S.P.A.—See Moulinex S.A.; *Int'l,* pg. 896
THE KRUSE COMPANY; *U.S. Private,* pg. 636
KRUSE INTERNATIONAL; *U.S. Private,* pg. 636
KRXY HOLDING CORPORATION—See The Walt Disney Company; *U.S. Public,* pg. 512
KRYSTAL COMPANY; *U.S. Private,* pg. 636
KRYTINA HRANICE SPOL. S R.O.—See Redland PLC; *Int'l,* pg. 1092
KRYTINA SLAPANICE A.S.—See Redland PLC; *Int'l,* pg. 1092
K-TRON GERMANY, SODER DIVISION—See K-Tron International, Inc.; *U.S. Public,* pg. 938
KTUL, LLC—See Perpetual Corporation; *U.S. Private,* pg. 854
KUAGGARN TEXTIL AG—See Akzo Nobel N.V.; *Int'l,* pg. 46
KUALA LUMPUR GLASS MANUFACTURERS CO. SDN. BHD.—See BTR plc; *Int'l,* pg. 129
KUALA LUMPUR GOLF & COUNTRY CLUB BERHAD—See Sime Darby Berhad; *Int'l,* pg. 1250
KUBOTA AGRI-MACHINERY PHILIPPINES, INC.—See Kubota Corp.; *Int'l,* pg. 763
KUBOTA AMERICA CORP.—See Kubota Corp.; *Int'l,* pg. 762

Company Index

KUBOTA BAUMASCHINEN GMBH—See Kubota Corp.; *Int'l*, pg. 763
KUBOTA BRASIL LTDA.—See Kubota Corp.; *Int'l*, pg. 763
KUBOTA CANADA LTD.—See Kubota Corp.; *Int'l*, pg. 763
KUBOTA CORP.; *Int'l*, pg. 762
KUBOTA CORP.-BANGKOK OFFICE—See Kubota Corp.; *Int'l*, pg. 762
KUBOTA CORP.-BEIJING OFFICE—See Kubota Corp.; *Int'l*, pg. 762
KUBOTA CORP.-CAIRO OFFICE—See Kubota Corp.; *Int'l*, pg. 762
KUBOTA CORP.-FRANKFURT OFFICE—See Kubota Corp.; *Int'l*, pg. 763
KUBOTA CORP.-JAKARTA OFFICE—See Kubota Corp.; *Int'l*, pg. 763
KUBOTA CORP.-LONDON OFFICE—See Kubota Corp.; *Int'l*, pg. 763
KUBOTA CORP.-LOS ANGELES OFFICE—See Kubota Corp.; *Int'l*, pg. 762
KUBOTA CORP.-NEW YORK OFFICE—See Kubota Corp.; *Int'l*, pg. 762
KUBOTA CORP.-SILICON VALLEY OFFICE—See Kubota Corp.; *Int'l*, pg. 762
KUBOTA CORP.-SINGAPORE OFFICE—See Kubota Corp.; *Int'l*, pg. 763
KUBOTA CORP.-TOKYO OFFICE—See Kubota Corp.; *Int'l*, pg. 762
KUBOTA CREDIT CORPORATION U.S.A.—See Kubota Corp.; *Int'l*, pg. 762
KUBOTA (DEUTSCHLAND) GMBH—See Kubota Corp.; *Int'l*, pg. 763
KUBOTA EUROPE S.A.—See Kubota Corp.; *Int'l*, pg. 763
KUBOTA FINANCE (UK) PLC—See Kubota Corp.; *Int'l*, pg. 763
KUBOTA FINANCE (U.S.A.), INC.—See Kubota Corp.; *Int'l*, pg. 762
KUBOTA GEORGE FISCHER LTD.—See Georg Fischer Ltd.; *Int'l*, pg. 490
P.T. KUBOTA INDONESIA—See Kubota Corp.; *Int'l*, pg. 763
KUBOTA MANUFACTURING OF AMERICA CORPORATION—See Kubota Corp.; *Int'l*, pg. 762
KUBOTA METAL CORPORATION (FAHRAMET DIVISION)—See Kubota Corp.; *Int'l*, pg. 763
KUBOTA SERVICIOS ESPANA S.A.—See Kubota Corp.; *Int'l*, pg. 763
KUBOTA SUPPLIES & ENGINEERING (ASIA) PTE. LTD.—See Kubota Corp.; *Int'l*, pg. 763
KUBOTA TRACTOR (AUSTRALIA) PTY. LTD.—See Kubota Corp.; *Int'l*, pg. 763
KUBOTA TRACTOR CORP.—See Kubota Corp.; *Int'l*, pg. 762
KUBOTA TRACTOR CORP. ENGINE DIVISION—See Kubota Corp.; *Int'l*, pg. 762
KUBOTA (U.K.) LIMITED—See Kubota Corp.; *Int'l*, pg. 763
KUCHENWELT HANDELS GMBH—See Vorwerk & Co.; *Int'l*, pg. 1480
KUCHENWELT SYSTEM GMBH—See Vorwerk & Co.; *Int'l*, pg. 1480
KUCHING STADIUM PROJECT OFFICE—See Nishimatsu Construction Co., Ltd.; *Int'l*, pg. 943
KUEHNE & NAGEL (AG & CO.)—See Kuehne & Nagel International AG; *Int'l*, pg. 763
KUEHNE & NAGEL GMBH—See Kuehne & Nagel International AG; *Int'l*, pg. 763
KUEHNE & NAGEL INC.—See Kuehne & Nagel International AG; *Int'l*, pg. 763
KUEHNE & NAGEL INTERNATIONAL AG; *Int'l*, pg. 763
KUEHNE & NAGEL INTERNATIONAL LTD.—See Kuehne & Nagel International AG; *Int'l*, pg. 763
KUEHNE & NAGEL N.V.—See Kuehne & Nagel International AG; *Int'l*, pg. 763
KUEHNE & NAGEL SPA—See Kuehne & Nagel International AG; *Int'l*, pg. 763
KUHLMAN CORPORATION; *U.S. Public*, pg. 968
KUHLMAN ELECTRIC CORPORATION—See Kuhlman Corporation; *U.S. Public*, pg. 968
KUHLMAN, INC.; *U.S. Public*, pg. 968
KUISE PLANT—See Shionogi & Co., Ltd.; *Int'l*, pg. 1235
KUKDONG SHELL OIL CO., LTD.—See Royal Dutch/Shell Group of Companies; *Int'l*, pg. 1140
KULICKE & SOFFA, AG—See Kulicke & Soffa Industries, Inc.; *U.S. Public*, pg. 969
KULICKE & SOFFA INDUSTRIES, INC.; *U.S. Public*, pg. 968
KULICKE & SOFFA (ISRAEL) LTD.—See Kulicke & Soffa Industries, Inc.; *U.S. Public*, pg. 969
KULICKE & SOFFA (JAPAN), LTD.—See Kulicke & Soffa Industries, Inc.; *U.S. Public*, pg. 969
KULICKE & SOFFA SINGAPORE, INC.—See Kulicke & Soffa Industries, Inc.; *U.S. Public*, pg. 969
KULICKE & SOFFA (ASIA), LTD.—See Kulicke & Soffa Industries, Inc.; *U.S. Public*, pg. 969
KULITE SEMICONDUCTOR PRODUCTS, INC.; *U.S. Private*, pg. 636
KULK & KRAMER KANTOORSYSTEMEN B.V.—See Ricoh Company, Ltd.; *Int'l*, pg. 1116
KULLING & PARTNER IDENTITY—See Young & Rubicam Inc.; *U.S. Private*, pg. 1199
KUM YANG OTSUKA CHEMICAL CO., LTD.—See Otsuka Pharmaceutical Co., Ltd.; *Int'l*, pg. 1014
KUMAGAI GUMI CO., LTD.; *Int'l*, pg. 763
KUMAGAI GUMI CO., LTD. HAWAII BRANCH—See Kumagai Gumi Co., Ltd.; *Int'l*, pg. 764
KUMAGAI INTERNATIONAL USA CORPORATION—See Kumagai Gumi Co., Ltd.; *Int'l*, pg. 764
KUMAGAI PROPERTIES INC.—See Kumagai Gumi Co., Ltd.; *Int'l*, pg. 764
KUMAGAYA PLANT—See Nikon Corporation; *Int'l*, pg. 931
KUNA CORPORATION—See Boise Cascade Corporation; *U.S. Public*, pg. 243
KUNER-EMPSON COMPANY—See Faribault Foods Inc.; *U.S. Private*, pg. 393
KUNGSFOTO AB—See Axel Johnson AB; *Int'l*, pg. 709

KUNHEIM CONSUMER PRODUCTS DIV.—See Fort James Corporation; *U.S. Public*, pg. 673
KUNSHAN HUADE METAL PACKAGING CONTAINER CO. LTD.—See Superior Metal Printing Limited; *Int'l*, pg. 1322
KUNZ & DIETFURT—See Oerlikon-Buhrle Holding AG; *Int'l*, pg. 998
KUNZ SPINNING MILLS LTD.—See Oerlikon-Buhrle Holding AG; *Int'l*, pg. 998
KUNZLER & COMPANY, INC.; *U.S. Private*, pg. 636
KUO HUA INC.—See Dentsu Inc.; *Int'l*, pg. 394
KUOPIO MILL—See UPM-Kymmene Corporation; *Int'l*, pg. 1429
KUOPION MATKATOIMISTO OY—See FinnAir Oy; *Int'l*, pg. 485
KUOZUI MOTORS, LTD.—See Toyota Motor Corporation; *Int'l*, pg. 1413
KUPFERMUHLE HOLZTECHNIK GMBH—See Deutsche Babcock AG; *Int'l*, pg. 399
KUPPER PARKER COMMUNICATIONS INC.; *U.S. Private*, pg. 637
KURAKI AMERICA CORP.—See Kuraki Company Ltd.; *Int'l*, pg. 764
KURAKI COMPANY LTD.; *Int'l*, pg. 764
KURARAY CO., LTD.; *Int'l*, pg. 764
KURDZIEL INDUSTRIES, INC.; *U.S. Private*, pg. 637
KURDZIEL IRON OF ROTHBURY, INC.—See Kurdziel Industries, Inc.; *U.S. Private*, pg. 637
KURDZIEL IRON OF WAUSEON, INC.—See Kurdziel Industries, Inc.; *U.S. Private*, pg. 637
KURE-NORTON CO., LTD.—See Saint-Gobain; *Int'l*, pg. 1174
KUREHA CHEMICALS (SINGAPORE) PTE. LTD.—See Rohm and Haas Company; *U.S. Public*, pg. 1404
KUROBANE NIKON CO., LTD.—See Nikon Corporation; *Int'l*, pg. 931
KURODA PRECISION INDUSTRIES LTD.; *Int'l*, pg. 764
KUROSAKI PLANT—See Mitsubishi Chemical Corporation; *Int'l*, pg. 871
KURSSENTERET BRATTEREIN—See Norsk Hydro a.s; *Int'l*, pg. 960
KURT MANUFACTURING CO. INC.; *U.S. Private*, pg. 637
KURTZ BROS., INC.; *U.S. Private*, pg. 637
KURZ-KASCH, INC.; *U.S. Private*, pg. 637
KURZ-KASCH, INC.—See Kurz-Kasch, Inc.; *U.S. Private*, pg. 637
KUSHIRO MILL—See Nippon Paper Industries Company Limited; *Int'l*, pg. 938
KUSS CORPORATION—See Cummins Engine Company, Inc.; *U.S. Public*, pg. 468
KUSTERS CORPORATION; *U.S. Private*, pg. 637
T.W. KUTTER, INC.—See Tetra Laval Group; *Int'l*, pg. 1378
KUUSANNIEMI PULP MILL—See UPM-Kymmene Corporation; *Int'l*, pg. 1428
KUWAIT AIRWAYS, CANADA—See Kuwait Airways Corp.; *Int'l*, pg. 764
KUWAIT AIRWAYS CORP.; *Int'l*, pg. 764
KUWAIT AVIATION FUELLING COMPANY K.S.C.—See Kuwait Petroleum Corporation; *Int'l*, pg. 765
KUWAIT AVIATION SERVICES CO.—See Kuwait Airways Corp.; *Int'l*, pg. 764
KUWAIT DRILLING CO.—See Kuwait Petroleum Corporation; *Int'l*, pg. 765
KUWAIT FOREIGN PETROLEUM EXPLORATION CO. KSC—See Kuwait Petroleum Corporation; *Int'l*, pg. 765
KUWAIT NATIONAL PETROLEUM COMPANY K.S.C.—See Kuwait Petroleum Corporation; *Int'l*, pg. 765
KUWAIT OIL COMPANY K.S.C.—See Kuwait Petroleum Corporation; *Int'l*, pg. 765
KUWAIT PETROLEUM CORPORATION; *Int'l*, pg. 764
KUWAIT PETROLEUM INTERNATIONAL (KPI)—See Kuwait Petroleum Corporation; *Int'l*, pg. 766
KUWAIT SHIPBUILDING & REPAIR YARD COMPANY K.S.C.—See Kuwait Petroleum Corporation; *Int'l*, pg. 765
KUWAIT SWEDISH CLEANING SERVICES CO. S.A.K.—See Electrolux, AB; *Int'l*, pg. 443
KUWANO ELECTRICAL INSTRUMENTS CO., LTD.—See Oki Electric Industry Company, Ltd.; *Int'l*, pg. 999
KVAERNER AM LTD.—See Kvaerner a.s.a.; *Int'l*, pg. 767
KVAERNER ARCTIC OFFSHORE A/S—See Kvaerner a.s.a.; *Int'l*, pg. 769
KVAERNER A.S—See Kvaerner a.s.a.; *Int'l*, pg. 766
KVAERNER A.S. FAST FERRIES—See Kvaerner a.s.a.; *Int'l*, pg. 766
KVAERNER A.S LONDON OFFICE—See Kvaerner a.s.a.; *Int'l*, pg. 766
KVAERNER A.S. REPRESENTATIVE OFFICE—See Kvaerner a.s.a.; *Int'l*, pg. 771
KVAERNER A.S.A.; *Int'l*, pg. 766
KVAERNER BOVING—See Kvaerner a.s.a.; *Int'l*, pg. 772
KVAERNER BOVING (ANZ) PTY LTD—See Kvaerner a.s.a.; *Int'l*, pg. 772
KVAERNER BOVING LIMITED—See Kvaerner a.s.a.; *Int'l*, pg. 772
KVAERNER BRASFAB LTDA—See Kvaerner a.s.a.; *Int'l*, pg. 767
KVAERNER BRUG (DEUTSCHLAND) GMBH—See Kvaerner a.s.a.; *Int'l*, pg. 771
KVAERNER BRUG (DEUTSCHLAND) GMBH AFTER SALES SERVICE—See Kvaerner a.s.a.; *Int'l*, pg. 771
KVAERNER CHILE S.A.—See Kvaerner a.s.a.; *Int'l*, pg. 767
KVAERNER COMPUTING & CONSULTANCY LTD.—See Kvaerner a.s.a.; *Int'l*, pg. 767
KVAERNER CONCRETE CONSTRUCTION A.S.—See Kvaerner a.s.a.; *Int'l*, pg. 766
KVAERNER DAVY—See Kvaerner a.s.a.; *Int'l*, pg. 774
KVAERNER DE MEXICO, S.A. DE C.V.—See Kvaerner a.s.a.; *Int'l*, pg. 767
KVAERNER DO BRASIL LTDA—See Kvaerner a.s.a.; *Int'l*, pg. 767
KVAERNER DORIS OFFSHORE CONCRETE A/S—See Kvaerner a.s.a.; *Int'l*, pg. 766

KVAERNER EARL AND WRIGHT, INC.—See Kvaerner a.s.a.; *Int'l*, pg. 771
KVAERNER EIENDOM A.S—See Kvaerner a.s.a.; *Int'l*, pg. 766
KVAERNER EIENDOM A.S, OSTFOLD FREDRIKSTAD DIVISION—See Kvaerner a.s.a.; *Int'l*, pg. 766
KVAERNER EIENDOM A.S, OSTFOLD MOSS DIVISION—See Kvaerner a.s.a.; *Int'l*, pg. 766
KVAERNER ENERGY, AGOTNES—See Kvaerner a.s.a.; *Int'l*, pg. 767
KVAERNER ENERGY A.S.—See Kvaerner a.s.a.; *Int'l*, pg. 767
KVAERNER ENERGY A.S. BUSINESS AREA HYDROPOWER—See Kvaerner a.s.a.; *Int'l*, pg. 767
KVAERNER ENERGY A.S. SOUTH EAST ASIA REPRESENTATIVE OFFICE—See Kvaerner a.s.a.; *Int'l*, pg. 767
KVAERNER ENERGY, DAMSGARD—See Kvaerner a.s.a.; *Int'l*, pg. 767
KVAERNER ENERGY DEVELOPMENT, INC.—See Kvaerner a.s.a.; *Int'l*, pg. 770
KVAERNER ENERGY, SORUMSAND—See Kvaerner a.s.a.; *Int'l*, pg. 767
KVAERNER ENERGY USA—See Kvaerner a.s.a.; *Int'l*, pg. 770
KVAERNER ENGINEERING A/S—See Kvaerner a.s.a.; *Int'l*, pg. 766
KVAERNER ENGINEERING, BERGEN—See Kvaerner a.s.a.; *Int'l*, pg. 766
KVAERNER ENGINEERING, MILJO—See Kvaerner a.s.a.; *Int'l*, pg. 766
KVAERNER ENGINEERING SDN BHD—See Kvaerner a.s.a.; *Int'l*, pg. 766
KVAERNER ENGINEERING, STAVANGER DIVISION—See Kvaerner a.s.a.; *Int'l*, pg. 766
KVAERNER ENGINEERING, TRONDHEIM—See Kvaerner a.s.a.; *Int'l*, pg. 766
KVAERNER ENGINEERING (UK) LTD.—See Kvaerner a.s.a.; *Int'l*, pg. 772
KVAERNER ENVIROPOWER AB—See Kvaerner a.s.a.; *Int'l*, pg. 767
KVAERNER ENVIROPOWER INC.—See Kvaerner a.s.a.; *Int'l*, pg. 770
KVAERNER ENVIROPOWER LTD.—See Kvaerner a.s.a.; *Int'l*, pg. 767
KVAERNER EUREKA, ALESUND DIVISION—See Kvaerner a.s.a.; *Int'l*, pg. 767
KVAERNER EUREKA A.S. DUBAI BRANCH OFFICE—See Kvaerner a.s.a.; *Int'l*, pg. 767
KVAERNER EUREKA A/S. TRANBY—See Kvaerner a.s.a.; *Int'l*, pg. 767
KVAERNER EUREKA, BRYNE DIVISION—See Kvaerner a.s.a.; *Int'l*, pg. 767
KVAERNER EUREKA ESPANOLA S A—See Kvaerner a.s.a.; *Int'l*, pg. 767
KVAERNER EUREKA ESPANOLA S.A.—See Kvaerner a.s.a.; *Int'l*, pg. 767
KVAERNER EUREKA GAEVLE AB—See Kvaerner a.s.a.; *Int'l*, pg. 767
KVAERNER EUREKA INC.—See Kvaerner a.s.a.; *Int'l*, pg. 770
KVAERNER EUREKA ISLANDI—See Kvaerner a.s.a.; *Int'l*, pg. 767
KVAERNER EUREKA, MOSS DIVISION—See Kvaerner a.s.a.; *Int'l*, pg. 767
KVAERNER EUREKA, TROMSO DIVISION—See Kvaerner a.s.a.; *Int'l*, pg. 767
KVAERNER FISH PROCESS, SEATTLE—See Kvaerner a.s.a.; *Int'l*, pg. 770
KVAERNER FISH PROCESS TECHNOLOGY A.S - KVAERNER KULDE—See Kvaerner a.s.a.; *Int'l*, pg. 768
KVAERNER FJELLSTRAND A/S—See Kvaerner a.s.a.; *Int'l*, pg. 768
KVAERNER FJELLSTRAND C/O FINANSHUSET—See Kvaerner a.s.a.; *Int'l*, pg. 768
KVAERNER FJELLSTRAND (S) PTE LTD.—See Kvaerner a.s.a.; *Int'l*, pg. 771
KVAERNER FJELLSTRAND (S) PTE LTD., HONG KONG REPRESENTATIVE OFFICE—See Kvaerner a.s.a.; *Int'l*, pg. 767
KVAERNER FJELLSTRAND SHIPPING A/S—See Kvaerner a.s.a.; *Int'l*, pg. 768
KVAERNER FLORO A.S.—See Kvaerner a.s.a.; *Int'l*, pg. 769
KVAERNER FLORO CONSULT A.S.—See Kvaerner a.s.a.; *Int'l*, pg. 769
KVAERNER FODEMA A.S.—See Kvaerner a.s.a.; *Int'l*, pg. 769
KVAERNER FSSL—See Kvaerner a.s.a.; *Int'l*, pg. 767
KVAERNER FSSL INC.—See Kvaerner a.s.a.; *Int'l*, pg. 770
KVAERNER FSSL LTD.—See Kvaerner a.s.a.; *Int'l*, pg. 767
KVAERNER GENERATOR AB—See Kvaerner a.s.a.; *Int'l*, pg. 767
KVAERNER GIBRALTAR LTD.—See Kvaerner a.s.a.; *Int'l*, pg. 772
KVAERNER GOTFAB AB—See Kvaerner a.s.a.; *Int'l*, pg. 767
KVAERNER GOVAN LTD.—See Kvaerner a.s.a.; *Int'l*, pg. 772
KVAERNER HAVTOR (UK) LIMITED—See Kvaerner a.s.a.; *Int'l*, pg. 771
KVAERNER HETLAND A.S—See Kvaerner a.s.a.; *Int'l*, pg. 769
KVAERNER H&G OFFSHORE LTD.—See Kvaerner a.s.a.; *Int'l*, pg. 771
KVAERNER H&G OFFSHORE LTD., ABERDEEN—See Kvaerner a.s.a.; *Int'l*, pg. 771
KVAERNER HILNOR A.S.—See Kvaerner a.s.a.; *Int'l*, pg. 769
KVAERNER HOLDING UK LTD.—See Kvaerner a.s.a.; *Int'l*, pg. 771

KVAERNER HONG KONG R O FOR KVAERNER SINGAPORE PTE LTD—See Kvaerner a.s.a.; *Int'l*, pg. 772

KVAERNER HUMBEROAK LTD.—See Kvaerner a.s.a.; *Int'l*, pg. 767

KVAERNER HYDRO POWER, BEIJING REPRESENTATIVE OFFICE—See Kvaerner a.s.a.; *Int'l*, pg. 767

KVAERNER HYDRO POWER, INC.—See Kvaerner a.s.a.; *Int'l*, pg. 770

KVAERNER HYDRO POWER, INC.-WEST COAST SALES DIVISION—See Kvaerner a.s.a.; *Int'l*, pg. 770

KVAERNER HYDROTECH A.S.—See Kvaerner a.s.a.; *Int'l*, pg. 769

KVAERNER HYMAC CORPORATION—See Kvaerner a.s.a.; *Int'l*, pg. 770

KVAERNER HYMAC INC.—See Kvaerner a.s.a.; *Int'l*, pg. 770

KVAERNER HYMAC, MOSCOW OFFICE—See Kvaerner a.s.a.; *Int'l*, pg. 770

KVAERNER INC.—See Kvaerner a.s.a.; *Int'l*, pg. 770

KVAERNER INCINERATION A/S—See Kvaerner a.s.a.; *Int'l*, pg. 769

KVAERNER INSTALLASJON, AGOTNES DIVISION—See Kvaerner a.s.a.; *Int'l*, pg. 769

KVAERNER INSTALLASJON A/S—See Kvaerner a.s.a.; *Int'l*, pg. 769

KVAERNER INSTALLASJON, BERGEN DIVISION—See Kvaerner a.s.a.; *Int'l*, pg. 769

KVAERNER INSTALLASJON, KRISTIANSUND DIVISION—See Kvaerner a.s.a.; *Int'l*, pg. 769

KVAERNER INSURANCE A/S—See Kvaerner a.s.a.; *Int'l*, pg. 769

KVAERNER INVEST A.S.—See Kvaerner a.s.a.; *Int'l*, pg. 769

KVAERNER-JOHN BROWN LTD.—See Kvaerner a.s.a.; *Int'l*, pg. 773

KVAERNER KAMFAB AB—See Kvaerner a.s.a.; *Int'l*, pg. 767

KVAERNER KIMEK A.S.—See Kvaerner a.s.a.; *Int'l*, pg. 770

KVAERNER KIMEK A.S., ARKHANGELSK OFFICE—See Kvaerner a.s.a.; *Int'l*, pg. 772

KVAERNER KIMEK A.S., MURMANSK OFFICE—See Kvaerner a.s.a.; *Int'l*, pg. 772

KVAERNER KINCAID LTD.—See Kvaerner a.s.a.; *Int'l*, pg. 772

KVAERNER KLEVEN A.S.—See Kvaerner a.s.a.; *Int'l*, pg. 769

KVAERNER KLEVEN FLORO A/S—See Kvaerner a.s.a.; *Int'l*, pg. 769

KVAERNER KLEVEN FORDE A/S—See Kvaerner a.s.a.; *Int'l*, pg. 769

KVAERNER KLEVEN LEIRVIK A/S—See Kvaerner a.s.a.; *Int'l*, pg. 769

KVAERNER KLEVEN ROVDE A/S—See Kvaerner a.s.a.; *Int'l*, pg. 769

KVAERNER KLEVEN ULSTEINVIK A/S—See Kvaerner a.s.a.; *Int'l*, pg. 769

KVAERNER KOREA LTD.—See Kvaerner a.s.a.; *Int'l*, pg. 767

KVAERNER MANDAL A/S—See Kvaerner a.s.a.; *Int'l*, pg. 769

KVAERNER MASA MARINE INC.—See Kvaerner a.s.a.; *Int'l*, pg. 770

KVAERNER MASA-YARDS INC., HELSINKI NEW SHIPYARD—See Kvaerner a.s.a.; *Int'l*, pg. 771

KVAERNER MASA-YARDS INC., MOSCOW—See Kvaerner a.s.a.; *Int'l*, pg. 771

KVAERNER MASA-YARDS INC., PIIKKIO WORKS—See Kvaerner a.s.a.; *Int'l*, pg. 771

KVAERNER MASA-YARDS INC., TURKU NEW SHIPYARD—See Kvaerner a.s.a.; *Int'l*, pg. 771

KVAERNER MESNA A/S—See Kvaerner a.s.a.; *Int'l*, pg. 769

KVAERNER MOSS, INC.—See Kvaerner a.s.a.; *Int'l*, pg. 770

KVAERNER MOSS STAL A.S—See Kvaerner a.s.a.; *Int'l*, pg. 769

KVAERNER MOSS TECHNOLOGY A.S.—See Kvaerner a.s.a.; *Int'l*, pg. 769

KVAERNER MOSS TECHNOLOGY A.S., MOSS DIVISION—See Kvaerner a.s.a.; *Int'l*, pg. 769

KVAERNER NATIONAL DIVISION OF KVAERNER SINGAPORE PTE. LTD.—See Kvaerner a.s.a.; *Int'l*, pg. 768

KVAERNER NATIONAL INC.—See Kvaerner a.s.a.; *Int'l*, pg. 770

KVAERNER NATIONAL, INC. CANADIAN DIVISION—See Kvaerner a.s.a.; *Int'l*, pg. 768

KVAERNER NATIONAL LTD.—See Kvaerner a.s.a.; *Int'l*, pg. 768

KVAERNER OIL & GAS SERVICES—See Kvaerner a.s.a.; *Int'l*, pg. 768

KVAERNER PALADON LTD.—See Kvaerner a.s.a.; *Int'l*, pg. 768

KVAERNER PROCESS SYSTEMS A/S—See Kvaerner a.s.a.; *Int'l*, pg. 766

KVAERNER PROCESS SYSTEMS A.S.—See Kvaerner a.s.a.; *Int'l*, pg. 769

KVAERNER PROCESS SYSTEMS ASIA PACIFIC SDN BHD.—See Kvaerner a.s.a.; *Int'l*, pg. 768

KVAERNER PROCESS SYSTEMS INC.—See Kvaerner a.s.a.; *Int'l*, pg. 768

KVAERNER PROFESSIONAL SERVICES LIMITED—See Kvaerner a.s.a.; *Int'l*, pg. 768

KVAERNER PROFESSIONAL SERVICES LTD.—See Kvaerner a.s.a.; *Int'l*, pg. 767

KVAERNER PROSJEKT A.S.—See Kvaerner a.s.a.; *Int'l*, pg. 769

KVAERNER PULP EQUIPMENT AB—See Kvaerner a.s.a.; *Int'l*, pg. 768

KVAERNER PULP EQUIPMENT A.S.—See Kvaerner a.s.a.; *Int'l*, pg. 769

KVAERNER PULPING AG—See Kvaerner a.s.a.; *Int'l*, pg. 768

KVAERNER PULPING GES. MBH—See Kvaerner a.s.a.; *Int'l*, pg. 768

KVAERNER PULPING INC.—See Kvaerner a.s.a.; *Int'l*, pg. 770

KVAERNER PULPING KK—See Kvaerner a.s.a.; *Int'l*, pg. 768

KVAERNER PULPING LTD.—See Kvaerner a.s.a.; *Int'l*, pg. 768

KVAERNER PULPING LTDA.—See Kvaerner a.s.a.; *Int'l*, pg. 768

KVAERNER PULPING OY—See Kvaerner a.s.a.; *Int'l*, pg. 768

KVAERNER PULPING PTE. LTD.—See Kvaerner a.s.a.; *Int'l*, pg. 768

KVAERNER PULPING PTY LTD—See Kvaerner a.s.a.; *Int'l*, pg. 768

KVAERNER PULPING SA—See Kvaerner a.s.a.; *Int'l*, pg. 768

KVAERNER PULPING TECHNOLOGIES—See Kvaerner a.s.a.; *Int'l*, pg. 772

KVAERNER PULPING TECHNOLOGIES AB—See Kvaerner a.s.a.; *Int'l*, pg. 768

KVAERNER R J BROWN PTE. LTD.—See Kvaerner a.s.a.; *Int'l*, pg. 767

KVAERNER R J BROWN PTY LTD—See Kvaerner a.s.a.; *Int'l*, pg. 767

KVAERNER ROSENBERG A.S.—See Kvaerner a.s.a.; *Int'l*, pg. 769

KVAERNER ROSENBERG A.S. INTERNATIONAL DEVELOPMENTS—See Kvaerner a.s.a.; *Int'l*, pg. 770

KVAERNER ROSENBERG A/S KVAERNER EGERSUND—See Kvaerner a.s.a.; *Int'l*, pg. 769

KVAERNER ROSENBERG A/S ROSENBERG VERFT—See Kvaerner a.s.a.; *Int'l*, pg. 769

KVAERNER ROSENBERG NEWFOUNDLAND LTD.—See Kvaerner a.s.a.; *Int'l*, pg. 768

KVAERNER ROTTERDAM BV—See Kvaerner a.s.a.; *Int'l*, pg. 772

KVAERNER SHIPPING A.S.—See Kvaerner a.s.a.; *Int'l*, pg. 770

KVAERNER SHIPPING MANILA, REPRESENTATIVE OFFICE—See Kvaerner a.s.a.; *Int'l*, pg. 772

KVAERNER SHIPS EQUIPMENT AB—See Kvaerner a.s.a.; *Int'l*, pg. 768

KVAERNER SHIPS EQUIPMENT A.S.—See Kvaerner a.s.a.; *Int'l*, pg. 770

KVAERNER SHIPS EQUIPMENT A.S DUBAI BRANCH—See Kvaerner a.s.a.; *Int'l*, pg. 768

KVAERNER SHIPS EQUIPMENT A.S GIBRALTAR BRANCH—See Kvaerner a.s.a.; *Int'l*, pg. 768

KVAERNER SHIPS EQUIPMENT A.S, KVAERNER MOSS—See Kvaerner a.s.a.; *Int'l*, pg. 770

KVAERNER SHIPS EQUIPMENT A.S MARINE AUTOMATION—See Kvaerner a.s.a.; *Int'l*, pg. 770

KVAERNER SHIPS EQUIPMENT A.S TRANBY—See Kvaerner a.s.a.; *Int'l*, pg. 770

KVAERNER SHIPS EQUIPMENT B.V.—See Kvaerner a.s.a.; *Int'l*, pg. 768

KVAERNER SHIPS EQUIPMENT GMBH—See Kvaerner a.s.a.; *Int'l*, pg. 768

KVAERNER SHIPS EQUIPMENT GMBH AFTER SALES SERVICE—See Kvaerner a.s.a.; *Int'l*, pg. 768

KVAERNER SHIPS EQUIPMENT INC.—See Kvaerner a.s.a.; *Int'l*, pg. 770

KVAERNER SHIPS EQUIPMENT LTDA.—See Kvaerner a.s.a.; *Int'l*, pg. 768

KVAERNER SINGAPORE PTE LTD—See Kvaerner a.s.a.; *Int'l*, pg. 768

KVAERNER TAMTURBINE OY—See Kvaerner a.s.a.; *Int'l*, pg. 772

KVAERNER THUNE A/S—See Kvaerner a.s.a.; *Int'l*, pg. 769

KVAERNER TURBIN AB—See Kvaerner a.s.a.; *Int'l*, pg. 770

KVAERNER VENTURE A.S—See Kvaerner a.s.a.; *Int'l*, pg. 770

KVAERNER VENTURE INC.—See Kvaerner a.s.a.; *Int'l*, pg. 770

KVAERNER WARNOW WERFT GMBH—See Kvaerner a.s.a.; *Int'l*, pg. 772

KVAERNERKONSERNETS PENSJONSKASSE—See Kvaerner a.s.a.; *Int'l*, pg. 769

KVARN AB JUVEL—See KF/Konsum Coop Group; *Int'l*, pg. 718

KWAL-HOWELLS, INC.(DENVER)—See Williams Holdings Plc; *Int'l*, pg. 1501

KWANGYANG WORKS—See Pohang Iron & Steel Co., Ltd.; *Int'l*, pg. 1061

KWICKIE/FLASH FOODS, INC.—See Jones Company, Inc.; *U.S. Private*, pg. 596

KWIK SAVE GROUP PLC—See Jardine Matheson Holdings Limited; *Int'l*, pg. 704

KWIK TRIP INC.; *U.S. Private*, pg. 637

KWIKEE ILLUSTRATION SYSTEMS—See Multi-Ad Services, Incorporated; *U.S. Private*, pg. 766

KWIKSET CORPORATION—See The Black & Decker Corporation; *U.S. Public*, pg. 233

KWONG ON BANK, LIMITED—See The Fuji Bank, Limited; *Int'l*, pg. 521

KYANITE MINING CORPORATION; *U.S. Private*, pg. 638

KYBER COAL CO.—See Berwind Corporation; *U.S. Private*, pg. 138

KYMI PAPER MILL—See UPM-Kymmene Corporation; *Int'l*, pg. 1428

KYMI PAPER MILLS LTD.—See UPM-Kymmene Corporation; *Int'l*, pg. 1428

KYMMENE LOGISTICS OY—See UPM-Kymmene Corporation; *Int'l*, pg. 1428

KYMMENE USA—See UPM-Kymmene Corporation; *Int'l*, pg. 1430

KYMTRANS FRANCE—See UPM-Kymmene Corporation; *Int'l*, pg. 1430

N.V. KYMTRANS S.A.—See UPM-Kymmene Corporation; *Int'l*, pg. 1430

KYMTRANS UK—See UPM-Kymmene Corporation; *Int'l*, pg. 1430

KYOBO INFORMATION & COMMUNICATION CO., LTD.—See The Kyoei Life Insurance Co., Ltd.; *Int'l*, pg. 777

KYOCERA AMERICA, INC.—See Kyocera Corporation; *Int'l*, pg. 775

KYOCERA ASIA, LTD.—See Kyocera Corporation; *Int'l*, pg. 775

KYOCERA CANADA, INC.—See Kyocera Corporation; *Int'l*, pg. 775

KYOCERA CORPORATION; *Int'l*, pg. 775

KYOCERA ELECTRONICS EUROPE GMBH—See Kyocera Corporation; *Int'l*, pg. 776

KYOCERA ELECTRONICS, INC.—See Kyocera Corporation; *Int'l*, pg. 776

KYOCERA ELECTRONICS U.K., LTD.—See Kyocera Corporation; *Int'l*, pg. 776

KYOCERA EUROPE GMBH—See Kyocera Corporation; *Int'l*, pg. 776

KYOCERA (HONG KONG), LTD.—See Kyocera Corporation; *Int'l*, pg. 776

KYOCERA INDUSTRIAL CERAMICS CORP.—See Kyocera Corporation; *Int'l*, pg. 776

KYOCERA INTERNATIONAL, INC.—See Kyocera Corporation; *Int'l*, pg. 775

KYOCERA MEXICANA S.A. DE C.V.—See Kyocera Corporation; *Int'l*, pg. 776

KYODO ADVERTISING CO., LTD.; *Int'l*, pg. 776

KYODO ADVERTISING CO., LTD.—See Kyodo Advertising Co., Ltd.; *Int'l*, pg. 776

KYODO BUILDING CORPORATION—See Toshiba Corporation; *Int'l*, pg. 1403

KYODO MORTGAGE ACCEPTANCE CO., LTD.—See The Asahi Bank, Ltd.; *Int'l*, pg. 82

KYODO PRINTING CO. PTE., LTD.—See Dainippon Ink & Chemicals, Inc.; *Int'l*, pg. 372

KYODO TDI LIMITED COMPANY—See Olin Corporation; *U.S. Public*, pg. 1219

KYODOH HAISOH CO., LTD.—See Matsuya Company Ltd.; *Int'l*, pg. 848

THE KYOEI ANNUITY HOME CO., LTD.—See The Kyoei Life Insurance Co., Ltd.; *Int'l*, pg. 776

KYOEI DO BRASIL COMPANHIA DE SEGUROS—See The Kyoei Mutual Fire & Marine Insurance Company; *Int'l*, pg. 777

KYOEI DO BRASIL EMPREENDIMENTOS COMERCIAIS LTDA—See The Kyoei Life Insurance Co., Ltd.; *Int'l*, pg. 777

KYOEI DO BRASIL S/A-EMPREENDIMENTOS IMOBILIARIOS—See The Kyoei Life Insurance Co., Ltd.; *Int'l*, pg. 777

KYOEI FACOM S/A-CENTRO DE COMPUTACAO—See The Kyoei Life Insurance Co., Ltd.; *Int'l*, pg. 777

KYOEI FIRE & MARINE INSURANCE CO. (U.K.) LTD.—See The Kyoei Mutual Fire & Marine Insurance Company; *Int'l*, pg. 777

KYOEI FIRE & MARINE INVESTMENT (BAHAMA) LTD.—See The Kyoei Mutual Fire & Marine Insurance Company; *Int'l*, pg. 777

KYOEI FIRE & MARINE INVESTMENT (LUXEMBOURG, S.A.)—See The Kyoei Mutual Fire & Marine Insurance Company; *Int'l*, pg. 777

KYOEI KASAI BUSINESS SERVICE CO., LTD.—See The Kyoei Mutual Fire & Marine Insurance Company; *Int'l*, pg. 777

KYOEI KASAI CLAIMS RESEARCH CO., LTD.—See The Kyoei Mutual Fire & Marine Insurance Company; *Int'l*, pg. 777

KYOEI KASAI FINANCE CO., LTD.—See The Kyoei Mutual Fire & Marine Insurance Company; *Int'l*, pg. 777

KYOEI KASAI INVESTMENT MANAGEMENT CO., LTD.—See The Kyoei Mutual Fire & Marine Insurance Company; *Int'l*, pg. 777

KYOEI KASAI MARINE SERVICE CO., LTD.—See The Kyoei Mutual Fire & Marine Insurance Company; *Int'l*, pg. 777

KYOEI KASAI TRAINING CENTER MANAGEMENT CO., LTD.—See The Kyoei Mutual Fire & Marine Insurance Company; *Int'l*, pg. 777

KYOEI KASAI TRAINING SERVICE CO., LTD.—See The Kyoei Mutual Fire & Marine Insurance Company; *Int'l*, pg. 777

THE KYOEI LIFE AMERICA CO., LTD.—See The Kyoei Life Insurance Co., Ltd.; *Int'l*, pg. 776

THE KYOEI LIFE EUROPE CO., LTD.—See The Kyoei Life Insurance Co., Ltd.; *Int'l*, pg. 777

THE KYOEI LIFE INSURANCE CO., LTD.; *Int'l*, pg. 776

THE KYOEI LIFE INSURANCE CO., LTD.-LONDON OFFICE—See The Kyoei Life Insurance Co., Ltd.; *Int'l*, pg. 777

THE KYOEI LIFE INSURANCE CO., LTD.-NEW YORK OFFICE—See The Kyoei Life Insurance Co., Ltd.; *Int'l*, pg. 776

THE KYOEI LIFE INSURANCE CO., LTD.-PARIS OFFICE—See The Kyoei Life Insurance Co., Ltd.; *Int'l*, pg. 777

THE KYOEI LIFE INVESTMENT JERSEY CO., LTD.—See The Kyoei Life Insurance Co., Ltd.; *Int'l*, pg. 777

KYOEI LIFE INVESTMENT LUXEMBOURG S/A—See The Kyoei Life Insurance Co., Ltd.; *Int'l*, pg. 777

KYOEI LOAN MANAGEMENT SERVICE CO., LTD.—See The Kyoei Mutual Fire & Marine Insurance Company; *Int'l*, pg. 777

THE KYOEI MUTUAL FIRE & MARINE INSURANCE COMPANY; *Int'l*, pg. 777

KYOEI REAL ESTATE CO., LTD.—See The Kyoei Mutual Fire & Marine Insurance Company; *Int'l*, pg. 777

KYOEI S/A-CENTRO DE CHECK-UPS MEDICOS—See The Kyoei Life Insurance Co., Ltd.; *Int'l*, pg. 777

THE KYOEI-SEIMEI INVESTMENT CAYMAN CO., LTD.—See The Kyoei Life Insurance Co., Ltd.; *Int'l*, pg. 777

KYOKUTO PETROLEUM INDUSTRIES LTD.—See Mitsui & Co., Ltd.; *Int'l*, pg. 877

Company Index

KYOKUYO AMERICA CORP.—See Kyokuyo Co. Ltd.; *Int'l*, pg. 777
KYOKUYO CO. LTD.; *Int'l*, pg. 777
KYOTARU CO., LTD.; *Int'l*, pg. 777
KYOTARU RESTAURANT—See Kyotaru Co., Ltd.; *Int'l*, pg. 777
KYOTARU USA—See Kyotaru Co., Ltd.; *Int'l*, pg. 778
KYOTO MACHINERY CO. LTD.—See Tetra Laval Group; *Int'l*, pg. 1380
KYOTO WORKS—See Mitsubishi Motors Corporation; *Int'l*, pg. 875
KYOTO WORKS - SHIGA PLANT—See Mitsubishi Motors Corporation; *Int'l*, pg. 875
KYOWA ELECTRIC WIRE CO., LTD.—See The Furukawa Electric Co., Ltd.; *Int'l*, pg. 530
KYOWA HAKKO DO BRASIL LTDA.—See Kyowa Hakko Kogyo Company, Ltd.; *Int'l*, pg. 778
KYOWA HAKKO EUROPE GMBH—See Kyowa Hakko Kogyo Company, Ltd.; *Int'l*, pg. 778
KYOWA HAKKO (H.K.) CO., LTD.—See Kyowa Hakko Kogyo Company, Ltd.; *Int'l*, pg. 778
KYOWA HAKKO INDUSTRY (SINGAPORE) PTE. LTD.—See Kyowa Hakko Kogyo Company, Ltd.; *Int'l*, pg. 778
KYOWA HAKKO KOGYO COMPANY, LTD.; *Int'l*, pg. 778
KYOWA HAKKO (MALAYSIA) SDN BHD.—See Kyowa Hakko Kogyo Company, Ltd.; *Int'l*, pg. 778
KYOWA HAKKO (THAILAND) LTD.—See Kyowa Hakko Kogyo Company, Ltd.; *Int'l*, pg. 778
KYOWA HAKKO U.K. LTD.—See Kyowa Hakko Kogyo Company, Ltd.; *Int'l*, pg. 778
KYOWA HAKKO U.S.A., INC.—See Kyowa Hakko Kogyo Company, Ltd.; *Int'l*, pg. 778
KYOWA HAKKO-WEST COAST OFFICE—See Kyowa Hakko Kogyo Company, Ltd.; *Int'l*, pg. 778
KYOWA ITALIANA FARMACEUTICI S.R.L.—See Kyowa Hakko Kogyo Company, Ltd.; *Int'l*, pg. 778
KYOWA PHARMACEUTICAL INC.—See Kyowa Hakko Kogyo Company, Ltd.; *Int'l*, pg. 778
KYOWA TAKKEN KAIHATSU CO., LTD.—See Kumagai Gumi Co., Ltd.; *Int'l*, pg. 763
KYSOR COOLING SYSTEMS—See Kuhlman Corporation; *U.S. Public*, pg. 968
KYSOR/MEDALLION—See Kuhlman Corporation; *U.S. Public*, pg. 968
KYSOR/MICHIGAN FLEET—See Kuhlman Corporation; *U.S. Public*, pg. 968
KYSOR PANEL SYSTEMS—See Scotsman Industries, Inc.; *U.S. Public*, pg. 1445
KYSOR/WARREN—See Scotsman Industries, Inc.; *U.S. Public*, pg. 1445
KYSOR/WESTRAN—See Kuhlman Corporation; *U.S. Public*, pg. 968
KYTTA-WERK SAUTER GMBH—See American Home Products Corporation; *U.S. Public*, pg. 81
KYUSHU CENTRAL KITCHEN—See Skylark Co., Ltd.; *Int'l*, pg. 1262
KYUSHU CITIZEN CORPORATION—See Citizen Watch Company, Ltd.; *Int'l*, pg. 294
KYUSHU ELECTRIC POWER CO.—See Kyushu Electric Power Co., Inc.; *Int'l*, pg. 778
KYUSHU ELECTRIC POWER CO., INC.; *Int'l*, pg. 778
KYUSHU MATSUSHITA ELECTRIC CO. LTD.—See Matsushita Electric Industrial Co., Ltd.; *Int'l*, pg. 846
KYUSHU SHIZUKI CO., INC.—See Shizuki Electric Corporation; *Int'l*, pg. 1236
KYUSHU TOKUYAMA READY MIXED CONCRETE CO., LTD.—See Tokuyama Corporation; *Int'l*, pg. 1393

L

L & N METALLURGIACAL PRODUCTS CO.—See Heraeus Holding GmbH; *Int'l*, pg. 616
L SIMS PORTEX LIMITED—See Smiths Industries plc; *Int'l*, pg. 1267
THE L & B GROUP—See United Asset Management Corporation; *U.S. Public*, pg. 1673
L & D GROUP; *U.S. Private*, pg. 638
L & H DIE, INC.—See Secom General Corporation; *U.S. Public*, pg. 1453
L&J TECHNOLOGIES; *U.S. Private*, pg. 638
L & L ENVIRONMENTAL SERVICES—See L & L Oil Company, Inc.; *U.S. Private*, pg. 638
L & L/JIROCH DISTRIBUTING CO.—See Spartan Stores Inc.; *U.S. Private*, pg. 1021
L & L MAINTENANCE & REPAIR—See L & L Oil Company, Inc.; *U.S. Private*, pg. 638
L & L NURSERY SUPPLY, INC.; *U.S. Private*, pg. 638
L & L OIL COMPANY, INC.; *U.S. Private*, pg. 638
L & L PLANT SOIL DIVISION—See L & L Nursery Supply, Inc.; *U.S. Private*, pg. 638
L & M CORRUGATED CONTAINER CORP.—See Stone Container Corporation; *U.S. Public*, pg. 1521
L & N SINGAPORE, PTE., LTD.—See General Signal Corporation; *U.S. Public*, pg. 727
L&P ACQUISITION COMPANY-7—See Leggett & Platt, Incorporated; *U.S. Public*, pg. 986
L&P ALUMINUM SMELTING ACQUISITION COMPANY—See Leggett & Platt, Incorporated; *U.S. Public*, pg. 986
L&P AUTOMOTIVE EUROPE GMBH—See Leggett & Platt, Incorporated; *U.S. Public*, pg. 987
L&P AUTOMOTIVE HOLDINGS COMPANY—See Leggett & Platt, Incorporated; *U.S. Public*, pg. 986
L&P INTERNATIONAL HOLDINGS COMPANY—See Leggett & Platt, Incorporated; *U.S. Public*, pg. 986
L&P MEXICO, S.A. DE C.V.—See Leggett & Platt, Incorporated; *U.S. Public*, pg. 986
L&P PROPERTY MANAGEMENT COMPANY—See Leggett & Platt, Incorporated; *U.S. Public*, pg. 986
L&P TRANSPORTATION CO.—See Leggett & Platt, Incorporated; *U.S. Public*, pg. 986
L&P WESTERN SPRING CO.—See Leggett & Platt, Incorporated; *U.S. Public*, pg. 986
L&R MANUFACTURING CO.; *U.S. Private*, pg. 638

L & S BEARING CO.—See LSB Industries, Inc.; *U.S. Public*, pg. 970
L&S MACHINE COMPANY, INC.—See Axsys Technologies. Inc.; *U.S. Public*, pg. 157
L & W SUPPLY CORP.—See USG Corporation; *U.S. Public*, pg. 1660
L-TEC DEUTSCHLAND GMBH—See Charter plc; *Int'l*, pg. 283
L-TEC FRANCE SARL—See Charter plc; *Int'l*, pg. 283
L3 COMMUNICATIONS; *U.S. Private*, pg. 638
L3 COMMUNICATIONS—See L3 Communications; *U.S. Private*, pg. 638
L3 COMMUNICATIONS ADVANCED RECORDERS DIV.—See L3 Communications; *U.S. Private*, pg. 638
L3 COMMUNICATIONS CONIC DIV.—See L3 Communications; *U.S. Private*, pg. 638
L3 COMMUNICATIONS NARDA-MICROWAVE WEST DIV.—See L3 Communications; *U.S. Private*, pg. 638
L3 COMMUNICATIONS NARDA-MICROWAVE DIV.—See L3 Communications; *U.S. Private*, pg. 638
L3 COMMUNICATIONS RANDTRON SYSTEMS—See L3 Communications; *U.S. Private*, pg. 639
L3 COMMUNICATIONS TELEMETRY & INSTRUMENTATION DIV.—See L3 Communications; *U.S. Private*, pg. 639
L-ZOS OPTICS, LTD.; *U.S. Private*, pg. 639
L.A. GAUGE CO.—See Triumph Group, Inc.; *U.S. Public*, pg. 1640
L.A. GEAR CALIFORNIA, INC.—See L.A. Gear, Inc.; *U.S. Public*, pg. 969
L.A. GEAR, INC.; *U.S. Public*, pg. 969
L.A.B. EQUIPMENT—See Noonan Machine Co.; *U.S. Private*, pg. 801
L.A.D.V. (LABORATOIRES D'APPLICATIONS DERMATOLOGIQUES DE VICHY)—See L'Oreal S.A.; *Int'l*, pg. 818
LB&P ECOLOGISCH ADVIES BV—See Heidemij N.V.; *Int'l*, pg. 607
LB INDUSTRIES INC.; *U.S. Private*, pg. 639
LB RHEINLAND PFALZ FINANCE B.V.—See Landesbank Rheinland-Pfalz; *Int'l*, pg. 799
LBB BETEILIGUNGSGESELLSCHAFT MBH—See Bankgesellschaft Berlin; *Int'l*, pg. 160
LBB BETRIEBSSERVICE GMBH—See Bankgesellschaft Berlin; *Int'l*, pg. 160
LBB GRUNDSTUCKS-GESELLSCHAFTMBH DER LANDESBANK BERLIN—See Bankgesellschaft Berlin; *Int'l*, pg. 160
LBB IMMOBILIEN-UND BAUMANAGEMENT GESELLSCHAFT MBH—See Bankgesellschaft Berlin; *Int'l*, pg. 160
LBB KARTENSERVICE GMBH—See Bankgesellschaft Berlin; *Int'l*, pg. 160
LBB SERVICE GESELLSCHAFT MBH—See Bankgesellschaft Berlin; *Int'l*, pg. 160
LBE BEHEIZUNGSEINRICHTUNGEN GMBH—See Ruhrgas Aktiengesellschaft; *Int'l*, pg. 1149
LBI FINANCE (HONG KONG) LTD.—See Lloyds TSB Group PLC; *Int'l*, pg. 813
LBI LUFTBEHANDLING AB—See Skanska AB; *Int'l*, pg. 1261
LBS IMMOBILIEN GMBH—See Landesbank Hessen-Thuringen Girozentrale; *Int'l*, pg. 799
LBS IMMOBILIEN GMBH BERLIN—See Bankgesellschaft Berlin; *Int'l*, pg. 160
LCC HOLDING COMPANY—See The Mead Corporation; *U.S. Public*, pg. 1076
LCC S.A.—See Thomson S.A.; *Int'l*, pg. 1384
L.C.G. MALMBERG BV—See VNU Verenigde Nederlandse Uitgeversbedrijven B.V.; *Int'l*, pg. 1445
LCI INTERNATIONAL, INC.; *U.S. Public*, pg. 969
LCS INDUSTRIES, INC.; *U.S. Public*, pg. 970
LCS SERVICES, INC.—See USA Waste Services, Inc.; *U.S. Public*, pg. 1686
LCTI, INC.—See Comarco, Inc.; *U.S. Public*, pg. 406
L.D. TOLEDO CORP.—See Forest City Enterprises, Inc.; *U.S. Public*, pg. 669
LDB CORPORATION; *U.S. Private*, pg. 639
LDB FOOD SERVICES, INC.—See LDB Corporation; *U.S. Private*, pg. 639
LDDS WORLDCOM—See WorldCom, Inc.; *U.S. Public*, pg. 1779
LDDS/WORLDCOM COMMUNICATIONS—See WorldCom, Inc.; *U.S. Public*, pg. 1779
LDI AUTO PAINT—See LDI, Ltd.; *U.S. Private*, pg. 639
LDI, LTD.; *U.S. Private*, pg. 639
LEC, INC.—See Nifco Inc.; *Int'l*, pg. 929
LEC REFRIGERATION PLC—See Sime Darby Berhad; *Int'l*, pg. 1251
LEI EXTRAS, INC.—See Lowrance Electronics, Inc.; *U.S. Public*, pg. 1016
LEP INTERNATIONAL INC.—See International Logistics Limited; *U.S. Private*, pg. 571
LEP PROFIT INTERNATIONAL, INC.—See International Logistics Limited; *U.S. Private*, pg. 571
LF CORP.—See Lowe's Companies, Inc.; *U.S. Public*, pg. 1015
LFE INDUSTRIAL SYSTEMS CORPORATION—See Mark IV Industries Inc.; *U.S. Public*, pg. 1045
LFE INSTRUMENTS—See Danaher Corporation; *U.S. Public*, pg. 482
LFE TRAFFIC CONTROL—See Mark IV Industries Inc.; *U.S. Public*, pg. 1045
LG & E ENERGY CORP.; *U.S. Public*, pg. 970
LG & E ENERGY SYSTEMS INC.—See LG & E Energy Corp.; *U.S. Public*, pg. 970
LG&E NATURAL, INC.—See LG & E Energy Corp.; *U.S. Public*, pg. 970
LG & E POWER SYSTEMS INC.—See LG & E Energy Corp.; *U.S. Public*, pg. 970
LG GROUP; *Int'l*, pg. 778
LG GROUP INC.—See LG Group; *Int'l*, pg. 779
LG OWENS CORNING—See Owens Corning; *U.S. Public*, pg. 1237

LG SEEDS INC.—See Groupe Limagrain; *Int'l*, pg. 566
LGC COMMUNICATIONS LTD.—See EMAP Plc; *Int'l*, pg. 451
LGC MANAGEMENT; *U.S. Private*, pg. 639
LGM OMEGA, INC.—See Omega Environmental Inc.; *U.S. Public*, pg. 1222
LGS CONCORD CORP.—See Citizens Utilities Company; *U.S. Public*, pg. 380
LGS ENERGY CORP.—See Citizens Utilities Company; *U.S. Public*, pg. 380
LGS EXPLORATION, INC.—See Citizens Utilities Company; *U.S. Public*, pg. 380
LGS FINANCIAL SERVICES. INC.—See Citizens Utilities Company; *U.S. Public*, pg. 380
LGS PIPELINE, INC.—See Citizens Utilities Company; *U.S. Public*, pg. 380
LGS SECURITIES, INC.—See Citizens Utilities Company; *U.S. Public*, pg. 380
LGT ASSET MANAGEMENT AG—See Liechtenstein Global Trust Limited; *Int'l*, pg. 810
LGT ASSET MANAGEMENT AG RAPPRESENTANZA DI LUGANO—See Liechtenstein Global Trust Limited; *Int'l*, pg. 810
LGT ASSET MANAGEMENT GMBH—See Liechtenstein Global Trust Limited; *Int'l*, pg. 810
LGT ASSET MANAGEMENT, INC.—See Liechtenstein Global Trust Limited; *Int'l*, pg. 809
LGT ASSET MANAGEMENT LTD.—See Liechtenstein Global Trust Limited; *Int'l*, pg. 810
LGT ASSET MANAGEMENT PLC—See Liechtenstein Global Trust Limited; *Int'l*, pg. 810
LGT ASSET MANAGEMENT PLC LUXEMBOURG—See Liechtenstein Global Trust Limited; *Int'l*, pg. 809
LGT ASSET MANAGEMENT PLC SPAIN—See Liechtenstein Global Trust Limited; *Int'l*, pg. 809
LGT ASSET MANAGEMENT PTE.—See Liechtenstein Global Trust Limited; *Int'l*, pg. 809
LGT ASSET MANAGEMENT PTY. LTD.—See Liechtenstein Global Trust Limited; *Int'l*, pg. 809
LGT BANK IN LIECHTENSTEIN AG HONG KONG—See Liechtenstein Global Trust Limited; *Int'l*, pg. 810
LGT BANK IN LIECHTENSTEIN AKTIENGESELLSCHAFT—See Liechtenstein Global Trust Limited; *Int'l*, pg. 809
LGT BANK IN LIECHTENSTEIN (CAYMAN) LTD.—See Liechtenstein Global Trust Limited; *Int'l*, pg. 810
LGT BANK IN LIECHTENSTEIN (DEUTSCHLAND) GMBH—See Liechtenstein Global Trust Limited; *Int'l*, pg. 810
LGT BANK IN LIECHTENSTEIN VADUZ—See Liechtenstein Global Trust Limited; *Int'l*, pg. 810
LGT FINANCE IRELAND LTD—See Liechtenstein Global Trust Limited; *Int'l*, pg. 810
LGT FINANZ AKTIENGESELLSCHAFT—See Liechtenstein Global Trust Limited; *Int'l*, pg. 809
LGT INVEST KAPITALANLAGEGESELLSCHAFT MBH—See Liechtenstein Global Trust Limited; *Int'l*, pg. 810
LGT INVESTMENT MANAGEMENT (ASIA) LTD.—See Liechtenstein Global Trust Limited; *Int'l*, pg. 810
LGT REAL ESTATE ADVISORS—See Liechtenstein Global Trust Limited; *Int'l*, pg. 809
LGT SERVICES AG—See Liechtenstein Global Trust Limited; *Int'l*, pg. 810
LGT TREUHAND AKTIENGESELLSCHAFT—See Liechtenstein Global Trust Limited; *Int'l*, pg. 809
LGT TRUST MANAGEMENT LIMITED—See Liechtenstein Global Trust Limited; *Int'l*, pg. 809
LGT UNIT MANAGERS (AUSTRALIA) LTD.—See Liechtenstein Global Trust Limited; *Int'l*, pg. 809
LH, INC.—See Magellan Health Services, Inc.; *U.S. Public*, pg. 1036
LHI LEASING FUR HANDEL UND INDUSTRIE GMBH—See Bankgesellschaft Berlin; *Int'l*, pg. 160
LI SERVICE COMPANY—See Lukens Inc.; *U.S. Public*, pg. 1020
L.I.A. LEASINGGESELLSCHAFT FUR IMMOBILIEN UND ANLAGEGUTER MBH—See Commerzbank AG; *Int'l*, pg. 310
LIC CARE AB—See Getinge Industrier AB; *Int'l*, pg. 551
LIC CARE LTD.—See Getinge Industrier AB; *Int'l*, pg. 551
LIC CARE OY—See Getinge Industrier AB; *Int'l*, pg. 551
LIC CARE S.A.R.L.—See Getinge Industrier AB; *Int'l*, pg. 551
LIC DENTAL AB—See Getinge Industrier AB; *Int'l*, pg. 551
LIC HYGIEN AB—See Getinge Industrier AB; *Int'l*, pg. 551
LIC HYGIEN A/S—See Getinge Industrier AB; *Int'l*, pg. 551
LIC NORDENTA A/S—See Getinge Industrier AB; *Int'l*, pg. 551
LIC ORTOPEDI AB—See Getinge Industrier AB; *Int'l*, pg. 551
LIC REHAB CARE AB—See Getinge Industrier AB; *Int'l*, pg. 551
LIC REHAB CARE A/S—See Getinge Industrier AB; *Int'l*, pg. 551
LIEF INTERNATIONAL PTY. LTD.—See Sinochem International Petroleum Co. Ltd.; *Int'l*, pg. 1255
LINC ANTHEM INC.—See LINC Capital Group; *U.S. Public*, pg. 996
LINC EQUIPMENT SERVICES—See LINC Capital Group; *U.S. Public*, pg. 996
LINC FINANCE CORPORATIONS—See LINC Capital Group; *U.S. Public*, pg. 996
LINC FINANCIAL SERVICES, INC.—See LINC Capital Group; *U.S. Public*, pg. 996
LINC MANAGEMENT SERVICES—See LINC Capital Group; *U.S. Public*, pg. 996
LINC MEDICAL IMAGING—See LINC Capital Group; *U.S. Public*, pg. 996
LINC QUANTUM ANALYTICS—See LINC Capital Group; *U.S. Public*, pg. 996
LIT AMERICA INC.—See BankAmerica Corporation; *U.S. Public*, pg. 181
LK LIMITED—See TransTec Plc; *Int'l*, pg. 1418

LK PRODUCTS OY—See Oy Nokia Ab/Nokia Group; *Int'l*, pg. 952
LK TOOL USA, INC.—See TransTec Plc; *Int'l*, pg. 1418
LKI—See Leonard Kreusch, Inc.; *U.S. Private*, pg. 635
LKM GROUP A/S—See Tetra Laval Group; *Int'l*, pg. 1379
LKS DATEN-SERVICE A.G.—See Compagnie des Machines Bull; *Int'l*, pg. 318
LKS DATEN - SERVICE GMBH.—See Compagnie des Machines Bull; *Int'l*, pg. 317
LL&E ALGERIA, LTD.—See Burlington Resources Inc.; *U.S. Public*, pg. 269
LL&E AUSTRALIA (OFFSHORE) PTY. LIMITED—See Burlington Resources Inc., pg. 269
LL&E COLOMBIA, INC.—See Burlington Resources Inc.; *U.S. Public*, pg. 269
LL&E EUROPE-AFRICA-MIDDLE EAST, INC.—See Burlington Resources Inc.; *U.S. Public*, pg. 269
LL&E, INC.—See Burlington Resources Inc.; *U.S. Public*, pg. 269
LL&E INDONESIA, LTD.—See Burlington Resources Inc.; *U.S. Public*, pg. 269
LL&E (NETHERLANDS), INC.—See Burlington Resources Inc.; *U.S. Public*, pg. 269
LL&E NETHERLANDS PETROLEUM COMPANY—See Burlington Resources Inc.; *U.S. Public*, pg. 269
LL&E PETROLEUM MARKETING, INC.—See Royal Dutch/Shell Group of Companies; *Int'l*, pg. 1136
LL&E PETROLEUM RESOURCES MARKETING, L.P.—See Burlington Resources Inc.; *U.S. Public*, pg. 269
LL&E PIPELINE CORP.—See Burlington Resources Inc.; *U.S. Public*, pg. 269
LL&E PROPERTIES, INC.—See Burlington Resources Inc.; *U.S. Public*, pg. 269
LL&E TUNISIA, LTD.—See Burlington Resources Inc.; *U.S. Public*, pg. 269
LL&E (UK) INC.—See Burlington Resources Inc.; *U.S. Public*, pg. 269
LL&E YEMEN, LTD.—See Burlington Resources Inc.; *U.S. Public*, pg. 269
L.L. BEAN, INC.; *U.S. Private*, pg. 639
THE LL HOLDING COMPANY, INC.—See Bell Atlantic Corporation; *U.S. Public*, pg. 203
LLB LURGL LENTJES BABCOCK ENERGIETECHNIK GMBH—See Deutsche Babcock AG; *Int'l*, pg. 398
LLE—See Mark IV Industries Inc.; *U.S. Public*, pg. 1045
LM&S/ORLANDO—See Larkin Meeder & Schweidel; *U.S. Private*, pg. 651
OY LM ERICSSON AB—See Telefonaktiebolaget LM Ericsson; *Int'l*, pg. 1368
LM ERICSSON A/S—See Telefonaktiebolaget LM Ericsson; *Int'l*, pg. 1369
LM ERICSSON DATA SERVICES AB—See Telefonaktiebolaget LM Ericsson; *Int'l*, pg. 1364
LM ERICSSON FASTIGHETER AB—See Telefonaktiebolaget LM Ericsson; *Int'l*, pg. 1364
LM ERICSSON FINANS A/S—See Telefonaktiebolaget LM Ericsson; *Int'l*, pg. 1368
AB LM ERICSSON FINANS—See Telefonaktiebolaget LM Ericsson; *Int'l*, pg. 1364
LM ERICSSON HOLDINGS LTD.—See Telefonaktiebolaget LM Ericsson; *Int'l*, pg. 1368
LM ERICSSON I NYNASHAMN AB—See Telefonaktiebolaget LM Ericsson; *Int'l*, pg. 1364
LM ERICSSON INTERNATIONAL AB—See Telefonaktiebolaget LM Ericsson; *Int'l*, pg. 1368
LM ERICSSON INTERNATIONAL AB JAPAN—See Telefonaktiebolaget LM Ericsson; *Int'l*, pg. 1368
LM ERICSSON INTERNATIONAL AB LATVIA—See Telefonaktiebolaget LM Ericsson; *Int'l*, pg. 1369
LM ERICSSON INTERNATIONAL AB SINGAPORE—See Telefonaktiebolaget LM Ericsson; *Int'l*, pg. 1369
LM ERICSSON INTERNATIONAL AB SOUTH AFRICA—See Telefonaktiebolaget LM Ericsson; *Int'l*, pg. 1369
LM ERICSSON INTERNATIONAL AB VIETNAM—See Telefonaktiebolaget LM Ericsson; *Int'l*, pg. 1369
LM ERICSSON INTERNATIONAL A/S DENMARK—See Telefonaktiebolaget LM Ericsson; *Int'l*, pg. 1369
LM ERICSSON INTERNATIONAL A/S LITHUANIA—See Telefonaktiebolaget LM Ericsson; *Int'l*, pg. 1369
LM ERICSSON INTERNATIONAL (CROATIA) AB—See Telefonaktiebolaget LM Ericsson; *Int'l*, pg. 1369
LM ERICSSON LTD.—See Telefonaktiebolaget LM Ericsson; *Int'l*, pg. 1369
LM ERICSSON (NIGERIA) LTD.—See Telefonaktiebolaget LM Ericsson; *Int'l*, pg. 1369
LM ERICSSON PTY. LTD.—See Telefonaktiebolaget LM Ericsson; *Int'l*, pg. 1369
LMC ASSOCIATES LTD.—See Meyer International PLC; *Int'l*, pg. 864
LMG FINANCE LTD.—See Alusuisse-Lonza Holding Ltd.; *Int'l*, pg. 68
LMG FINANCIAL SERVICES—See Alusuisse-Lonza Holding Ltd.; *Int'l*, pg. 68
LMG (LIFESTYLE MARKETING GROUP)—See Saatchi & Saatchi Advertising Worldwide; *U.S. Public*, pg. 1422
LMH LES MANUFACTURES HORLOGERES SA—See Mannesmann A.G.; *Int'l*, pg. 839
LNG ENERGY, INC.—See Southwest Gas Corporation; *U.S. Public*, pg. 1493
L.N.G. PLANT—See Gaz Metropolitain & Company; *Int'l*, pg. 541
LNG PROJECT & CONSTRUCTION DIVISION—See Chinese Petroleum Corporation; *Int'l*, pg. 286
LNG STORAGE INC.—See Essex County Gas Company; *U.S. Public*, pg. 593
LNR COMMUNICATIONS; *U.S. Private*, pg. 639
LNW NETWORKS—See CD Products, Inc.; *U.S. Public*, pg. 276
LP ASSOCIATES—See Cigna Corp.; *U.S. Public*, pg. 365
LPA ASSOCIATES—See Cigna Corp.; *U.S. Public*, pg. 365
LPB ASSOCIATES—See Cigna Corp.; *U.S. Public*, pg. 365
L.P.B. INSTITUTO FARMACEUTICO S.P.A.—See Novartis AG; *Int'l*, pg. 983
LPC ASSOCIATES—See Cigna Corp.; *U.S. Public*, pg. 365

LPC INDUSTRIAS ALIMENTICIAS S.A.—See Danone Group; *Int'l*, pg. 380
LPD ASSOCIATES—See Cigna Corp.; *U.S. Public*, pg. 365
LPI CORPORATION—See HEICO Corporation; *U.S. Public*, pg. 804
LPS LABORATORIES INC.—See Morgan Crucible Co. Plc; *Int'l*, pg. 892
LPY ASSOCIATES—See Cigna Corp.; *U.S. Public*, pg. 365
LPZ ASSOCIATES—See Cigna Corp.; *U.S. Public*, pg. 365
LQ-CIGNA I—See Cigna Corp.; *U.S. Public*, pg. 361
LQ-CIGNA II—See Cigna Corp.; *U.S. Public*, pg. 361
LR MEDIENVERLAG GMBH—See Georg von Holtzbrinck GmbH; *Int'l*, pg. 1478
L.S. HOLDING COMPANY—See Cigna Corp.; *U.S. Public*, pg. 358
LSB CHEMICAL CORP.—See LSB Industries, Inc.; *U.S. Public*, pg. 970
LSB EUROPA LTD.—See LSB Industries, Inc.; *U.S. Public*, pg. 971
LSB INDUSTRIES, INC.; *U.S. Public*, pg. 970
LSG LUFTHANSA SERVICE HOLDING AG—See Deutsche Lufthansa AG; *Int'l*, pg. 407
LSI ATLANTA—See Schawk, Inc.; *U.S. Public*, pg. 1437
LSI INDUSTRIES, INC.; *U.S. Public*, pg. 971
LSI INDUSTRIES, INC.—See LSI Industries, Inc.; *U.S. Public*, pg. 971
LSI/KALA—See Schawk, Inc.; *U.S. Public*, pg. 1437
LSI LOGIC CORP.; *U.S. Public*, pg. 971
LSI LOGIC CORPORATION OF CANADA, INC.—See LSI Logic Corp.; *U.S. Public*, pg. 971
LSI LOGIC EUROPE PLC—See LSI Logic Corp.; *U.S. Public*, pg. 971
LSI LOGIC JAPAN SEMICONDUCTOR INC.—See LSI Logic Corp.; *U.S. Public*, pg. 971
LSI LOGIC K.K.—See LSI Logic Corp.; *U.S. Public*, pg. 971
LSJ SPORTSWEAR INC.—See Merchant Capital Group Ltd.; *U.S. Private*, pg. 732
LSP SPECIALTY PRODUCTS CO.—See NCH Corporation; *U.S. Public*, pg. 1145
LTB—See Linbeck Construction Corp; *U.S. Private*, pg. 668
LTB WARD CONSTRUCTORS, INC.—See Dunn Industries Inc.; *U.S. Private*, pg. 347
LTCB AND F&C INVESTMENT MANAGEMENT CO. LIMITED—See The Long-Term Credit Bank of Japan, Limited; *Int'l*, pg. 816
LTCB ASIA LIMTED—See The Long-Term Credit Bank of Japan, Limited; *Int'l*, pg. 816
LTCB ATLANTA—See The Long-Term Credit Bank of Japan, Limited; *Int'l*, pg. 816
LTCB AUSTRALIA LIMITED—See The Long-Term Credit Bank of Japan, Limited; *Int'l*, pg. 816
LTCB FUTURES (SINGAPORE) PTE. LTD.—See The Long-Term Credit Bank of Japan, Limited; *Int'l*, pg. 816
LTCB INTERNATIONAL LEASING CO., LTD.—See The Long-Term Credit Bank of Japan, Limited; *Int'l*, pg. 816
LTCB INTERNATIONAL LIMITED—See The Long-Term Credit Bank of Japan, Limited; *Int'l*, pg. 816
LTCB INVESTMENT MANAGEMENT CO., LTD.—See The Long-Term Credit Bank of Japan, Limited; *Int'l*, pg. 816
LTCB LATIN AMERICA, INC. (LLA)—See The Long-Term Credit Bank of Japan, Limited; *Int'l*, pg. 816
LTCB-MAS INVESTMENT MANAGEMENT, INC.—See The Long-Term Credit Bank of Japan, Limited; *Int'l*, pg. 816
LTCB MERCHANT BANK (SINGAPORE) LIMITED—See The Long-Term Credit Bank of Japan, Limited; *Int'l*, pg. 816
LTCB RESEARCH INSTITUTE, INC.—See The Long-Term Credit Bank of Japan, Limited; *Int'l*, pg. 816
LTCB SECURITIES CO., LTD.—See The Long-Term Credit Bank of Japan, Limited; *Int'l*, pg. 816
LTCB TRUST COMPANY—See The Long-Term Credit Bank of Japan, Limited; *Int'l*, pg. 816
LTCBR CONSULTING, INC.—See The Long-Term Credit Bank of Japan, Limited; *Int'l*, pg. 816
L3 COMMUNICATIONS HYCOR DIV.—See L3 Communications; *U.S. Private*, pg. 638
LTI, INC.—See Lynden Incorporated; *U.S. Private*, pg. 683
LTR INDUSTRIES—See Kimberly-Clark Corporation; *U.S. Public*, pg. 960
THE LTV CORPORATION; *U.S. Public*, pg. 971
LTV STEEL TUBULAR PRODUCTS—See The LTV Corporation; *U.S. Public*, pg. 972
LTX ASIA INTERNATIONAL, INC.—See LTX Corporation; *U.S. Public*, pg. 972
LTX CO., LTD.—See LTX Corporation; *U.S. Public*, pg. 972
LTX CORPORATION; *U.S. Public*, pg. 972
LTX (DEUTSCHLAND) GMBH—See LTX Corporation; *U.S. Public*, pg. 972
LTX (EUROPE) LIMITED—See LTX Corporation; *U.S. Public*, pg. 972
LTX FRANCE S.A.—See LTX Corporation; *U.S. Public*, pg. 972
LTX INTERNATIONAL, INC.—See LTX Corporation; *U.S. Public*, pg. 972
LTX (ITALIA) S.R.L.—See LTX Corporation; *U.S. Public*, pg. 972
LTX TEST SYSTEMS CORPORATION—See LTX Corporation; *U.S. Public*, pg. 972
LVE VERFAHRENSELEKTRONIK GMBH—See Ruhrgas Aktiengesellschaft; *Int'l*, pg. 1149
LVL ADVERTISING; *U.S. Public*, pg. 640
LVL INTERACTIVE—See LVL Advertising; *U.S. Private*, pg. 640
LVMH B.V.—See LVMH Moet Hennessy Louis Vuitton; *Int'l*, pg. 782
LVMH MOET HENNESSY LOUIS VUITTON; *Int'l*, pg. 779
LVMH MOET HENNESSY LOUIS VUITTON (JAPAN) KK—See LVMH Moet Hennessy Louis Vuitton; *Int'l*, pg. 782
GIE LVMH RECHERCHE—See LVMH Moet Hennessy Louis Vuitton; *Int'l*, pg. 781
LVT—See Eastman Kodak Company; *U.S. Public*, pg. 551
LWI HOLDINGS INC.—See Hanover Direct, Inc.; *U.S. Public*, pg. 782

LXE INC.—See Electromagnetic Sciences, Inc.; *U.S. Public*, pg. 569
LA AMISTAD RESIDENTIAL TREATMENT CENTER—See Universal Health Services, Inc.; *U.S. Public*, pg. 1697
LA BANDA DE AGUSTIN MEDINA S.A.; *Int'l*, pg. 783
LA BLANCHE PORTE S.C.S.—See Otto Versand (GmbH & Co.); *Int'l*, pg. 1015
LA BRASSERIE LABATT LIMITEE—See Interbrew S.A.; *Int'l*, pg. 679
LA CAIXA; *Int'l*, pg. 784
LA CEMENTO NACIONAL C.A.—See Holderbank Financiere Glaris Ltd.; *Int'l*, pg. 630
LA CENTRALE CONSULENZA S.P.A.—See Banco Ambrosiano Veneto S.p.A.; *Int'l*, pg. 138
LA CENTRALE FONDI S.P.A.—See Banco Ambrosiano Veneto S.p.A.; *Int'l*, pg. 138
LA CENTRALE FORMAZIONE S.R.L.—See Banco Ambrosiano Veneto S.p.A.; *Int'l*, pg. 138
LA CHAPE LIQUIDE—See Lafarge S.A.; *Int'l*, pg. 788
LA CHOYA UNIT—See Hecla Mining Company; *U.S. Public*, pg. 804
LA CIMENTERIE GUYANAISE—See Lafarge S.A.; *Int'l*, pg. 788
LA-CO INDUSTRIES MARKAL COMPANY; *U.S. Private*, pg. 640
LA COMPAGNIE FOUNDATION LIMITEE—See BFC Construction Corporation; *Int'l*, pg. 118
LA CONCORDE S.A.—See Assicurazioni Generali S.p.A.; *Int'l*, pg. 91
LA CORNUBIA—See McKechnie PLC; *Int'l*, pg. 852
LA CROSS—See Del Laboratories, Inc.; *U.S. Public*, pg. 494
LA CROSSE TRIBUNE—See Lee Enterprises, Incorporated; *U.S. Public*, pg. 983
LA CROUZILLE MINING DIVISION—See COGEMA - Compagnie Generale des Matieres Nucleaires; *Int'l*, pg. 305
LA DOMINICIA, S.A. DE C.V.—See Du Pont (E.I. Du Pont De Nemours & Co.); *U.S. Public*, pg. 533
LA ESTRELLA S.A. DE SEGUROS Y REASEGUROS—See Assicurazioni Generali S.p.A.; *Int'l*, pg. 91
LA FAMILIA—See Danone Group; *Int'l*, pg. 380
LA FEDERACION COMPANIA DE SEGUROS, C.A.—See The Chubb Corporation; *U.S. Public*, pg. 355
LA FEDERAL COMPANIA DE SEGUROS, S.A.—See The Chubb Corporation; *U.S. Public*, pg. 355
LA FEDERATION CONTINENTALE COMPAGNIE D'ASSURANCES—See Assicurazioni Generali S.p.A.; *Int'l*, pg. 91
LA FER BLANC—See Groupe Usinor; *Int'l*, pg. 571
LA FONCIERE DE LAVALLOIS S.A.—See Exor Group; *Int'l*, pg. 467
LA FONCIERE PARIXEL—See Groupe GAN; *Int'l*, pg. 565
LA FONDIARIA ASSICURAZIONI S.P.A.; *Int'l*, pg. 784
LA FRANCE CORPORATION; *U.S. Public*, pg. 640
LA FRANCO PENN LIFE COMPANIA DE SEGURES DE VIDA S.A.—See PennCorp Financial Group, Inc.; *U.S. Public*, pg. 1271
LA GARANTIE GENERALE MAROCAINE (G.G.M.)—See Zurich Insurance Company; *Int'l*, pg. 1531
LA GLORIA OIL & GAS CO.—See Crown Central Petroleum Corporation; *U.S. Public*, pg. 462
LA GRANGE FOUNDRY INC.—See Atchison Casting Corporation; *U.S. Public*, pg. 142
LA HACIENDA S.A. DE C.V.—See International Multifoods Corporation; *U.S. Public*, pg. 901
LA HAGUE PLANT—See COGEMA - Compagnie Generale des Matieres Nucleaires; *Int'l*, pg. 305
LA JOHNSON FRANCAISE S.A.—See S.C. Johnson & Son, Inc.; *U.S. Private*, pg. 593
LA LUTECE S.A.—See Assicurazioni Generali S.p.A.; *Int'l*, pg. 91
LA MARCHE MFG. CO.; *U.S. Private*, pg. 640
LA MECCANOPTICA LEONARDO S.P.A.—See Luxottica Group S.p.A.; *Int'l*, pg. 822
LA MERIDIONALE DES BOIS ET MATERIAUX; *Int'l*, pg. 784
LA MESA R V CENTER, INC.; *U.S. Private*, pg. 640
LA METAIRE CLINIC—See Magellan Health Services, Inc.; *U.S. Public*, pg. 1036
LA MEUSIENNE—See Groupe Usinor; *Int'l*, pg. 571
LA MODERNA DE OCCIDENTE, S.A. DE C.V.—See Tablex, S.A. de C.V.; *Int'l*, pg. 1346
LA NACION S.A.; *Int'l*, pg. 784
LA NACIONAL COMPANIA DE SEGUROS GENERALES S.A.—See Assicurazioni Generali S.p.A.; *Int'l*, pg. 91
LA NACIONAL COMPANIA INMOBILIARIA—See Assicurazioni Generali S.p.A.; *Int'l*, pg. 91
LA PALMA INTERCOMMUNITY HOSPITAL—See UniHealth; *U.S. Private*, pg. 1118
LA PETITE ACADEMY INC.; *U.S. Private*, pg. 640
LA PLATA MINE—See The Broken Hill Proprietary Company Limited; *Int'l*, pg. 224
LA POSITIVA, COMPANIA NACIONAL DE SEGUROS S.A.—See Cigna Corp.; *U.S. Public*, pg. 363
LA POSTE GROUP; *Int'l*, pg. 785
LA PREFERIDA, INC.; *U.S. Private*, pg. 640
LA PRENSA ASOCIADA, INC.— See The Associated Press; *U.S. Private*, pg. 92
LA PREVIDENTE S.P.A.—See La Fondiaria Assicurazioni S.p.A.; *Int'l*, pg. 784
LA QUINOLEINE ET SES DERIVES S.A.—See Novartis AG; *Int'l*, pg. 983
LA QUINTA INNS, INC.; *U.S. Public*, pg. 972
LA REINA, INC.; *U.S. Private*, pg. 640
LA REINE, LTD.—See Kanebo. Ltd.; *Int'l*, pg. 722
LA REPUBLIQUE—See Lagardere Groupe; *Int'l*, pg. 792
LA ROSA'S, INC.; *U.S. Private*, pg. 640
LA ROSE D'ANJOU—See GIB Group; *Int'l*, pg. 534
LA RUCHE MERIDIONALE—See Groupe Casino; *Int'l*, pg. 563
LA RUCHE PICARDE—See Auchan S.A.; *Int'l*, pg. 98

LA RURAL DEL PARAGUAY S.A. , PARAGUAYA DE SEGUROS—See The Tokio Marine & Fire Insurance Company, Ltd.; *Int'l*, pg. 1392
LA SALLE COUNTY FARM SUPPLY; *U.S. Private*, pg. 640
LA SALLE LABS DIV.—See Del Laboratories, Inc.; *U.S. Public*, pg. 494
LA SEDA DE BARCELONA—See Akzo Nobel N.V.; *Int'l*, pg. 46
LA SEDA DE BARCELONA S.A.—See Akzo Nobel N.V.; *Int'l*, pg. 46
LA SOCIETE STEPHANOISE DES EAUX—See Lyonnaise des Eaux S.A.; *Int'l*, pg. 824
LA SUISSE - ASSURANCES (FRANCE)—See The Swiss Life/Rentenanstalt Group; *Int'l*, pg. 1332
LA SUISSE - ASSURANCES-VIE (FRANCE)—See The Swiss Life/Rentenanstalt Group; *Int'l*, pg. 1332
LA TELEDYNAMIQUE S.A.—See FKI Plc; *Int'l*, pg. 474
LA TONDENA DISTILLERS, INC.; *Int'l*, pg. 785
LA TOURAINE COFFEE COMPANY—See Chock Full O' Nuts Corporation; *U.S. Public*, pg. 351
SA LA TOURELLE PLACE ST. FRANCOIS—See Oerlikon-Buhrle Holding AG; *Int'l*, pg. 996
LA UNION GREMIAL COMPANIA ARGENTINA DE SEGUROS S.A.—See W.R. Berkley Corporation; *U.S. Public*, pg. 216
LA VASCO NAVARRA S.A. DE SEGUROS Y REASEGUROS—See Assicurazioni Generali S.p.A.; *Int'l*, pg. 91
LA VENECIANA S.A.—See Saint-Gobain; *Int'l*, pg. 1173
LA VENEZIA ASSICURAZIONI S.P.A.—See Assicurazioni Generali S.p.A.; *Int'l*, pg. 90
LA VENEZOLANA DE VIDA COMPANIA ANONIMA DE SEGUROS—See Cigna Corp.; *U.S. Public*, pg. 363
LA VERRERIE MEDICALE SARL—See Carl-Zeiss-Stiftung; *Int'l*, pg. 1523
LA VICTORIA FOODS, INC.; *U.S. Private*, pg. 641
LA VIGNA—See Assicurazioni Generali S.p.A.; *Int'l*, pg. 90
LA VITTORIA RIASSICURAZIONI—See SCOR; *Int'l*, pg. 1152
LA-Z-BOY ARKANSAS—See La-Z-Boy Incorporated; *U.S. Public*, pg. 973
LA-Z-BOY CANADA LTD.—See La-Z-Boy Incorporated; *U.S. Public*, pg. 973
LA-Z-BOY EAST—See La-Z-Boy Incorporated; *U.S. Public*, pg. 973
LA-Z-BOY INCORPORATED; *U.S. Public*, pg. 972
LA-Z-BOY LELAND—See La-Z-Boy Incorporated; *U.S. Public*, pg. 973
LA-Z-BOY MIDWEST—See La-Z-Boy Incorporated; *U.S. Public*, pg. 973
LA-Z-BOY SOUTH—See La-Z-Boy Incorporated; *U.S. Public*, pg. 973
LA-Z-BOY TENNESSEE—See La-Z-Boy Incorporated; *U.S. Public*, pg. 973
LA-Z-BOY UTAH—See La-Z-Boy Incorporated; *U.S. Public*, pg. 973
LA-Z-BOY WEST—See La-Z-Boy Incorporated; *U.S. Public*, pg. 973
LAB CRAFTERS INC.—See Aero Data Metal Crafters; *U.S. Private*, pg. 24
LAB ONE—See Seafield Capital Corporation; *U.S. Public*, pg. 1449
LAB PRODUCTS, INC.; *U.S. Private*, pg. 641
LAB SAFETY SUPPLY INC.—See W.W. Grainger, Inc.; *U.S. Public*, pg. 758
LABARGE CLAYCO WIRELESS—See LaBarge, Inc.; *U.S. Public*, pg. 973
LABARGE ELECTRONICS—See LaBarge, Inc.; *U.S. Public*, pg. 973
LABARGE, INC.; *U.S. Public*, pg. 973
LABARGE MIRRORS, INC.—See Furnishings International, Inc.; *U.S. Private*, pg. 432
LABARGE PIPE & STEEL COMPANY; *U.S. Private*, pg. 641
LABATT BREWERIES BRITISH COLUMBIA—See Interbrew S.A.; *Int'l*, pg. 679
LABATT BREWERIES OF CANADA—See Interbrew S.A.; *Int'l*, pg. 679
LABATT BREWERIES OF CANADA - PRAIRIE REGION—See Interbrew S.A.; *Int'l*, pg. 679
LABATT BREWERIES OF NEWFOUNDLAND—See Interbrew S.A.; *Int'l*, pg. 679
LABATT BREWING COMPANY LIMITED—See Interbrew S.A.; *Int'l*, pg. 679
LABATT FOOD SERVICE; *U.S. Private*, pg. 641
LABATT U.S.A.—See Interbrew S.A.; *Int'l*, pg. 679
LABAUTO IBERICA—See Labinal SA; *Int'l*, pg. 785
LABAUTO, INC.—See Labinal SA; *Int'l*, pg. 785
LABAUTO LTD.—See Labinal SA; *Int'l*, pg. 785
LABEL-AIRE A/S—See Label-Aire Inc.; *U.S. Private*, pg. 641
LABEL-AIRE INC.; *U.S. Private*, pg. 641
LABEL ART, INC.—See National Fiberstock Corporation; *U.S. Private*, pg. 782
LABEL ART LIMITED—See James Crean PLC; *Int'l*, pg. 340
LABEL PRODUCTS & DESIGN DIVISION—See Journal Communications Inc.; *U.S. Private*, pg. 602
LABELLE JARDINIERE—See Au Bon Marche; *Int'l*, pg. 98
LABELON CORPORATION; *U.S. Private*, pg. 641
LABELON/NOESTING COMPANY, LLC—See Labelon Corporation; *U.S. Private*, pg. 641
LABERGE & LABERGE LTEE.—See Domtar Inc.; *Int'l*, pg. 416
LABETTE COR CONSERVATION CAMP—See Corrections Corporation of America; *U.S. Public*, pg. 450
LABINAL AERO & DEFENSE SYSTEMS, INC.—See Labinal SA; *Int'l*, pg. 786
LABINAL AERO & DEFENSE SYSTEMS, INC.-TECHNOFAN INC.—See Labinal SA; *Int'l*, pg. 786
LABINAL AERO & DEFENSE SYSTEMS LTD.—See Labinal SA; *Int'l*, pg. 786
LABINAL AERO PLANT—See Labinal SA; *Int'l*, pg. 786

LABINAL AERO SYSTEMS DIVISION—See Labinal SA; *Int'l*, pg. 786
LABINAL COMPONENTS & SYSTEMS GMBH—See Labinal SA; *Int'l*, pg. 786
LABINAL COMPONENTS & SYSTEMS INC.—See Labinal SA; *Int'l*, pg. 786
LABINAL ELECTRONICA DE REYNOSA, SA DE CV—See Labinal SA; *Int'l*, pg. 786
LABINAL ESPANA—See Labinal SA; *Int'l*, pg. 787
LABINAL KABUSHIKI KAISHA—See Labinal SA; *Int'l*, pg. 786
LABINAL SA; *Int'l*, pg. 785
LABLANC—See SNCF; *Int'l*, pg. 1164
LABO INDUSTRIE S.A.—See Fuchs Petrolub AG Oel + Chemie; *Int'l*, pg. 518
LABORA MANNHEIM GMBH FUR LABORTECHNIK—See Corange Limited; *Int'l*, pg. 331
LABORATOIRE ALLARD S.A.—See Bristol-Myers Squibb Company; *U.S. Public*, pg. 256
LABORATOIRE BERAL, S.A.—See Pfizer Inc.; *U.S. Public*, pg. 1283
LABORATOIRE CENTRAL DE RECHERCHES—See Thomson S.A.; *Int'l*, pg. 1382
LABORATOIRE DE RECHERCHE, EUROLYSINE—See Ajinomoto Company Inc.; *Int'l*, pg. 41
LABORATOIRE LACHARTRE S.A.—See The Procter & Gamble Company; *U.S. Public*, pg. 1331
LABORATOIRE PORTEX S.A.—See Smiths Industries plc; *Int'l*, pg. 1268
LABORATOIRE ROGER BELLON—See Rhone-Poulenc S.A.; *Int'l*, pg. 1109
LABORATOIRE WELLCOME GLAXO S.A.—See Glaxo Wellcome plc; *Int'l*, pg. 553
LABORATOIRES ALCON S.A.R.L.—See Nestle S.A.; *Int'l*, pg. 920
LABORATOIRES BRISTOL S.A.—See Bristol-Myers Squibb Company; *U.S. Public*, pg. 256
LABORATOIRES CHIBRET S.A.—See Merck & Co., Inc.; *U.S. Public*, pg. 1092
LABORATOIRES CIBA-GEIGY S.A.—See Novartis AG; *Int'l*, pg. 983
LABORATOIRES CORVITA S.A.R.L.—See Pfizer Inc.; *U.S. Public*, pg. 1282
LABORATOIRES DE THERAPEUTHIQUE MODERNE LTM S.A.—See Solvay S.A.; *Int'l*, pg. 1279
LABORATOIRES DES PRODUITS DENTAIRES ODONCIA S.A.—See Fried. Krupp AG; *Int'l*, pg. 510
LABORATOIRES DUPHAR S.A.—See Solvay S.A.; *Int'l*, pg. 1279
LABORATOIRES FAURE—See Novartis AG; *Int'l*, pg. 983
LABORATOIRES FISON SA—See Rhone-Poulenc S.A.; *Int'l*, pg. 1111
LABORATOIRES FUMOUZE S.A.—See Carter-Wallace, Inc.; *U.S. Public*, pg. 310
LABORATOIRES GARNIER PARIS—See L'Oreal S.A.; *Int'l*, pg. 818
LABORATOIRES KNOLL FRANCE—See BASF AG; *Int'l*, pg. 109
LABORATOIRES MERCK SHARP & DOHME S.A.—See Merck & Co., Inc.; *U.S. Public*, pg. 1092
LABORATOIRES NEOLAIT S.A.—See SmithKline Beecham plc; *Int'l*, pg. 1265
LABORATOIRES NICHOLAS (MAROC) S.A.—See Roche Holding Ltd.; *Int'l*, pg. 1121
LABORATOIRES PFIZER S.A.—See Pfizer Inc.; *U.S. Public*, pg. 1283
LABORATOIRES PHARMACIA & UPJOHN SARL—See Pharmacia & Upjohn, Inc.; *Int'l*, pg. 1049
LABORATOIRES POLYMEDIC, S.A.—See Merck & Co., Inc.; *U.S. Public*, pg. 1092
LABORATOIRES P.O.S. S.A.—See Nestle S.A.; *Int'l*, pg. 920
LABORATOIRES PROSALUD S.A.—See Merck & Co., Inc.; *U.S. Public*, pg. 1092
LABORATOIRES SANDOZ S.A.R.L.—See Novartis AG; *Int'l*, pg. 983
LABORATOIRES SAUTER S.A.—See Roche Holding Ltd.; *Int'l*, pg. 1120
LABORATOIRES SOBIO S.A.—See SmithKline Beecham plc; *Int'l*, pg. 1265
LABORATOIRES STAFFORD-MILLER S.A.R.L.—See Block Drug Company, Inc.; *U.S. Public*, pg. 237
LABORATOIRES SYNTHELABO FRANCE—See L'Oreal S.A.; *Int'l*, pg. 818
LABORATOIRES TAKEDA—See Takeda Chemical Industries, Ltd.; *Int'l*, pg. 1350
LABORATOIRES VALDOR S.A.—See Scholl Plc; *Int'l*, pg. 1209
LABORATOIRES WYETH FRANCE—See American Home Products Corporation; *U.S. Public*, pg. 81
LABORATOIRES ZYMA S.A.—See Novartis AG; *Int'l*, pg. 983
LABORATORIES ASTRA FRANCE—See Astra AB; *Int'l*, pg. 94
LABORATORIES GRIFFITH DE MEXICO, S.A. DE C.V.—See Griffith Laboratories Worldwide, Inc.; *U.S. Private*, pg. 482
LABORATORIES LEDERLE SA—See American Home Products Corporation; *U.S. Public*, pg. 81
LABORATORIES ROCHE NICHOLAS S.A.—See Roche Holding Ltd.; *Int'l*, pg. 1121
LABORATORIES WELLCOME S.A.—See Glaxo Wellcome plc; *Int'l*, pg. 553
LABORATORIO ASTRA ESPANA, S.A.—See Astra AB; *Int'l*, pg. 94
LABORATORIO NORMAL PRODUCTOS FARMACEUTICOS, LDA.—See Novartis AG; *Int'l*, pg. 983
LABORATORIO PADRO SA—See Novartis AG; *Int'l*, pg. 983
LABORATORIOS AMERICANOS S.A.—See American Home Products Corporation; *U.S. Public*, pg. 81
LABORATORIOS BRISTOL DE VENEZUELA, S.A.—See Bristol-Myers Squibb Company; *U.S. Public*, pg. 256

LABORATORIOS BRISTOL DEL ECUADOR S.A.—See Bristol-Myers Squibb Company; *U.S. Public*, pg. 256
LABORATORIOS GRIFFITH DE CENTRO AMERICA S.A.—See Griffith Laboratories Worldwide, Inc.; *U.S. Private*, pg. 481
LABORATORIOS INTERVET S.A.—See Akzo Nobel N.V.; *Int'l*, pg. 45
LABORATORIOS JULIAN DE MEXICO, S.A.—See SmithKline Beecham plc; *Int'l*, pg. 1265
LABORATORIOS KNOLL, S.A.—See BASF AG; *Int'l*, pg. 109
LABORATORIOS MIQUEL, S.A.—See Otsuka Pharmaceutical Co., Ltd.; *Int'l*, pg. 1014
LABORATORIOS PFIZER DE VENEZUELA S.A.—See Pfizer Inc.; *U.S. Public*, pg. 1282
LABORATORIOS PFIZER LDA.—See Pfizer Inc.; *U.S. Public*, pg. 1283
LABORATORIOS PFIZER LTD.—See Pfizer Inc.; *U.S. Public*, pg. 1284
LABORATORIOS PHARMACIA & UPJOHN, C.A.—See Pharmacia & Upjohn, Inc.; *Int'l*, pg. 1049
LABORATORIOS SUBSTANTIA, C.A.—See Warner-Lambert Company; *U.S. Public*, pg. 1739
LABORATORIOS WELLCOME DE PORTUGAL LDA—See Glaxo Wellcome plc; *Int'l*, pg. 553
LABORATORIOS WYETH INC.—See American Home Products Corporation; *U.S. Public*, pg. 81
LABORATORIOS WYETH-WHITEHALL LTD.—See American Home Products Corporation; *U.S. Public*, pg. 81
LABORATORY CORP. OF AMERICA HOLDINGS; *U.S. Public*, pg. 973
LABORATORY DIV.—See L'Oreal S.A.; *Int'l*, pg. 819
LABORATORY SUPPLY COMPANY—See Laboratory Supply Company, Inc.; *U.S. Private*, pg. 642
LABORATORY SUPPLY COMPANY, INC.; *U.S. Private*, pg. 641
LABORELEC S.C.—See Electrabel S.A.; *Int'l*, pg. 437
LABORTERAPICA-BRISTOL QUIMICA E FARMACEUTICA LTDA.—See Bristol-Myers Squibb Company; *U.S. Public*, pg. 256
LABOUCHERE N.V.—See AEGON N.V.; *Int'l*, pg. 26
LABSCO—See Laboratory Supply Company, Inc.; *U.S. Private*, pg. 642
LAC BEAUPORT OFFICE—See The Cascades Group; *Int'l*, pg. 274
LACASSAGNE—See SNCF; *Int'l*, pg. 1164
LACKMAN FOOD SERVICE; *U.S. Private*, pg. 642
LACEY MFG. CO.—See FAG Group; *Int'l*, pg. 468
LACHMAR—See Duke Energy Corporation; *U.S. Public*, pg. 535
LACLEDE - ALTON PLANT—See Laclede Steel Company; *U.S. Public*, pg. 974
LACLEDE CHAIN MANUFACTURING COMPANY—See Laclede Steel Company; *U.S. Public*, pg. 974
LACLEDE CHAIN MANUFACTURING PLANT—See Laclede Steel Company; *U.S. Public*, pg. 974
LACLEDE DEVELOPMENT CO.—See Laclede Gas Company; *U.S. Public*, pg. 974
LACLEDE ENERGY RESOURCES, INC.—See Laclede Gas Company; *U.S. Public*, pg. 974
LACLEDE GAS COMPANY; *U.S. Public*, pg. 973
LACLEDE GAS FAMILY SERVICES, INC.—See Laclede Gas Company; *U.S. Public*, pg. 974
LACLEDE INVESTMENT CORP.—See Laclede Gas Company; *U.S. Public*, pg. 974
LACLEDE - METRO-EAST PROCESSING—See Laclede Steel Company; *U.S. Public*, pg. 974
LACLEDE MID AMERICA INC.—See Laclede Steel Company; *U.S. Public*, pg. 974
LACLEDE PIPELINE CO.—See Laclede Gas Company; *U.S. Public*, pg. 974
LACLEDE STEEL COMPANY; *U.S. Public*, pg. 974
LACLEDE - VANDALIA BRANCH—See Laclede Steel Company; *U.S. Public*, pg. 974
LACLEDE VENTURE CO.—See Laclede Gas Company; *U.S. Public*, pg. 974
LACONA SA—See Oerlikon-Buhrle Holding AG; *Int'l*, pg. 997
LACOS LAND COMPANY—See Scope Industries; *U.S. Public*, pg. 1444
LACTOS PTY. LTD.—See Bongrain S.A.; *Int'l*, pg. 201
LADBROKE & CO. LTD.—See Ladbroke Group Plc; *Int'l*, pg. 787
LADBROKE CASINO (HOLDINGS) LIMITED—See Ladbroke Group Plc; *Int'l*, pg. 787
LADBROKE CITY & COUNTY LAND COMPANY LIMITED—See Ladbroke Group Plc; *Int'l*, pg. 787
LADBROKE GROUP PLC; *Int'l*, pg. 787
LADBROKE GROUP PROPERTIES LTD.—See Ladbroke Group Plc; *Int'l*, pg. 787
LADBROKE RACECOURSE MANAGEMENT LTD.—See Ladbroke Group Plc; *Int'l*, pg. 787
LADBROKE RACING CORPORATION—See Ladbroke Group Plc; *Int'l*, pg. 788
LADBROKE RACING LTD.—See Ladbroke Group Plc; *Int'l*, pg. 787
LADD FURNITURE, INC.; *U.S. Public*, pg. 974
LADD INTERNATIONAL—See Ladd Furniture, Inc.; *U.S. Public*, pg. 975
LADD TRANSPORTATION, INC.—See Ladd Furniture, Inc.; *U.S. Public*, pg. 974
LADECO S.A.—See Grupo Iberia; *Int'l*, pg. 575
LADENBURG, THALMANN GROUP INC.—See New Valley Corporation; *U.S. Public*, pg. 1173
LADENSO OY—See Enso Oyj; *Int'l*, pg. 456
LADIES' HOME JOURNAL—See Meredith Corporation; *U.S. Public*, pg. 1094
LADY BALTIMORE FOODS, INC.; *U.S. Public*, pg. 975
LADY BALTIMORE OF MISSOURI, INC.—See Lady Baltimore Foods, Inc.; *U.S. Public*, pg. 975
LADY CAKE-FEINE KUCHEN GMBH—See Sudzucker AG Mannheim/Ochsenfurt; *Int'l*, pg. 1305

LADY FOOTLOCKER—See Woolworth Corporation; *U.S. Public*, pg. 1777
LADY JANE COLLIERIES, INC.—See PP&L Resources; *U.S. Public*, pg. 1244
LADY MARLENE SALES CORP.; *U.S. Private*, pg. 642
LADY ROSE DIV.—See Masters, Inc.; *U.S. Private*, pg. 714
LADYBIRD BOOKS LTD.—See Pearson plc; *Int'l*, pg. 1025
LADYSAN—See W.A. Flick & Co. Pty. Limited; *Int'l*, pg. 496
LAESSER KLEBSTOFFE AG—See Henkel KGaA; *Int'l*, pg. 613
RAY LAETHEM PONTIAC-BUICK-GMC-TRUCK, INC.; *U.S. Private*, pg. 642
LAFARGE ALUMINATES—See Lafarge S.A.; *Int'l*, pg. 789
LAFARGE ALUMINATES CO. LTD.—See Lafarge S.A.; *Int'l*, pg. 790
LAFARGE ALUMINOSO DO BRAZIL—See Lafarge S.A.; *Int'l*, pg. 790
LAFARGE ALUMINOUS CEMENT CO. LTD.—See Lafarge S.A.; *Int'l*, pg. 790
LAFARGE CALCIUM ALUMINATE—See Lafarge S.A.; *Int'l*, pg. 791
LAFARGE CANADA INC.—See Lafarge S.A.; *Int'l*, pg. 789
LAFARGE CIMENTS—See Lafarge S.A.; *Int'l*, pg. 788
LAFARGE CONCRETE LTD.—See Lafarge S.A.; *Int'l*, pg. 789
LAFARGE CONCRETE PRODUCTS—See Lafarge S.A.; *Int'l*, pg. 789
LAFARGE CONSTRUCTION MATERIALS—See Lafarge S.A.; *Int'l*, pg. 788
LAFARGE CONSTRUCTION MATERIALS PACIFIC/WESTERN REGION—See Lafarge S.A.; *Int'l*, pg. 789
LAFARGE COPPEE RECHERCHE-GIE—See Lafarge S.A.; *Int'l*, pg. 789
LAFARGE CORPORATION—See Lafarge S.A.; *Int'l*, pg. 788
LAFARGE CORP. DAVENPORT—See Lafarge S.A.; *Int'l*, pg. 788
LAFARGE EASTERN MONOLITHIC REFRACTORIES—See Lafarge S.A.; *Int'l*, pg. 791
LAFARGE GIPS BETEILIGUNGS GMBH—See Lafarge S.A.; *Int'l*, pg. 791
LAFARGE GIPS BV—See Lafarge S.A.; *Int'l*, pg. 791
LAFARGE GIPS GMBH—See Lafarge S.A.; *Int'l*, pg. 791
LAFARGE MATERIALS—See Lafarge S.A.; *Int'l*, pg. 789
LAFARGE MATERIAUX DE SPECIALITES—See Lafarge S.A.; *Int'l*, pg. 789
LAFARGE NOUVEAUX MATERIAUX—See Lafarge S.A.; *Int'l*, pg. 789
LAFARGE PLASTERBOARD LTD.—See Lafarge S.A.; *Int'l*, pg. 791
LAFARGE PLATRE—See Lafarge S.A.; *Int'l*, pg. 789
LAFARGE PLATRESINTERNATIONAL—See Lafarge S.A.; *Int'l*, pg. 788
LAFARGE PLATREUROPE S.A.—See Lafarge S.A.; *Int'l*, pg. 788
LAFARGE PRESTIA—See Lafarge S.A.; *Int'l*, pg. 790
LAFARGE REFRACTAIRES MONOLITHIQUES—See Lafarge S.A.; *Int'l*, pg. 789
LAFARGE REFRACTAIRES MONOLITHIQUES BENELUX—See Lafarge S.A.; *Int'l*, pg. 791
LAFARGE REFRACTAIRES TRADING—See Lafarge S.A.; *Int'l*, pg. 791
LAFARGE REFRATTARI MONOLITICI ITALIA SRL—See Lafarge S.A.; *Int'l*, pg. 791
LAFARGE S.A.; *Int'l*, pg. 788
LAFARGE ZEMENT GMBH—See Lafarge S.A.; *Int'l*, pg. 791
LAFARGESSI SPA—See Lafarge S.A.; *Int'l*, pg. 789
LAFAYETTE AMERICAN BANK—See Hubco, Inc.; *U.S. Public*, pg. 845
LAFAYETTE INSURANCE COMPANY—See United Fire & Casualty Company; *U.S. Public*, pg. 1677
LAFAYETTE MANUFACTURING—See Kimball International, Inc.; *U.S. Public*, pg. 957
LAFAYETTE METAL SERVICE CORPORATION—See Itochu Corporation; *Int'l*, pg. 695
LAFAYETTE PRECAST—See Walters & Wolf; *U.S. Private*, pg. 1149
LAFAYETTE STEEL—See Olympic Steel Inc.; *U.S. Public*, pg. 1221
LAFEHR CHAN TECHNOLOGIES; *U.S. Private*, pg. 642
STEPHEN LAFRANCE HOLDINGS, INC.; *U.S. Private*, pg. 642
LAGARDERE GROUPE; *Int'l*, pg. 791
LAGARDERE GROUPE NORTH AMERICA—See Lagardere Groupe; *Int'l*, pg. 794
HENRIQUE LAGE REFINERY—See Petrobras - Petroleo Brasileiro S.A.; *Int'l*, pg. 1042
LAGEEN BOX & CAN FACTORY, LTD.—See Pechiney S.A.; *Int'l*, pg. 1029
LAGERA GESELLSCHAFT FUR LAGERUNG UND SPEDITION—See The Peninsular and Oriental Steam Navigation Company; *Int'l*, pg. 1033
LAGERA S.A.R.L.—See The Peninsular and Oriental Steam Navigation Company; *Int'l*, pg. 1034
LAGERCRANTZ ELEKTRONIK AB—See Bergman & Beving AB; *Int'l*, pg. 188
LAGERHAUS ZURICH-ALTSTETTEN AG—See Hesta Tex AG; *Int'l*, pg. 617
LAGERQUIST CORPORATION—See Dover Corporation; *U.S. Public*, pg. 521
LAGON—See Havas Advertising; *Int'l*, pg. 601
LAGOVEN, S.A.—See Petroleos de Venezuela S.A.; *Int'l*, pg. 1045
LAGRANGE MOLDED PRODUCTS, INC.—See Lancaster Colony Corporation; *U.S. Public*, pg. 976
LAGUARDIA LEARNING CENTER—See Berkshire Hathaway Inc.; *U.S. Public*, pg. 218
LAHAV DIVISION/MILITARY AIRCRAFT GROUP—See Israel Aircraft Industries Ltd.; *Int'l*, pg. 690
LAHTI MILLS—See UPM-Kymmene Corporation; *Int'l*, pg. 1429
LAIDLAW & FAIRGRIEVE LTD—See Dawson International PLC; *Int'l*, pg. 385

LAIDLAW BROTHERS—See Bertelsmann AG; *Int'l*, pg. 191
LAIDLAW CARRIERS INC.—See Contrans Corporation; *Int'l*, pg. 328
LAIDLAW CORPORATION; *U.S. Private*, pg. 642
LAIDLAW ENVIRONMENTAL SERVICES, INC.; *U.S. Public*, pg. 975
LAIDLAW INC.—See Canadian Pacific Limited; *Int'l*, pg. 259
LAIDLAW TRANSIT—See Canadian Pacific Limited; *Int'l*, pg. 259
LAIDLAW TRANSIT, INC—See Canadian Pacific Limited; *Int'l*, pg. 259
LAIDLAW TRANSIT LIMITED—See Canadian Pacific Limited; *Int'l*, pg. 259
LAIDLOW DREW LTD.—See Selas Corporation of America; *U.S. Public*, pg. 1455
LAIKI FACTORS LIMITED—See HSBC Holdings plc; *Int'l*, pg. 581
LAIKI INSURANCE CO. LIMITED—See HSBC Holdings plc; *Int'l*, pg. 581
LAIKI INVESTMENTS LIMITED—See HSBC Holdings plc; *Int'l*, pg. 581
LAING ABU DHABI—See John Laing PLC; *Int'l*, pg. 797
LAING CONSTRUCTION SERVICES—See John Laing PLC; *Int'l*, pg. 797
LAING EMIRATES—See John Laing PLC; *Int'l*, pg. 797
LAING HOMES LTD.—See John Laing PLC; *Int'l*, pg. 796
JOHN LAING CONSTRUCTION LTD.—See John Laing PLC; *Int'l*, pg. 796
JOHN LAING DEVELOPMENTS, LTD.—See John Laing PLC; *Int'l*, pg. 796
JOHN LAING INTERNATIONAL—See John Laing PLC; *Int'l*, pg. 796
JOHN LAING PLC; *Int'l*, pg. 796
JOHN LAING SERVICES LTD.—See John Laing PLC; *Int'l*, pg. 796
LAING MANAGEMENT LTD.—See John Laing PLC; *Int'l*, pg. 796
LAING OMAN LLC—See John Laing PLC; *Int'l*, pg. 797
LAING PROJECTS BV—See John Laing PLC; *Int'l*, pg. 797
LAING TECHNOLOGY GROUP LTD.—See John Laing PLC; *Int'l*, pg. 796
LAIRD & COMPANY; *U.S. Private*, pg. 642
LAIT MONT BLANC S.A.—See Nestle S.A.; *Int'l*, pg. 920
LAITERIE DE VILLECOMTAL—See Danone Group; *Int'l*, pg. 379
THE LAITRAM CORPORATION; *U.S. Private*, pg. 643
LAITRAM MACHINERY INC.—See The Laitram Corporation; *U.S. Private*, pg. 643
LAKATEX B.V.—See Blydenstein-Willink N.V.; *Int'l*, pg. 198
LAKE BUENA VISTA COMMUNITIES, INC.—See The Walt Disney Company; *U.S. Public*, pg. 513
LAKE BUSINESS PRODUCTS, INC.; *U.S. Private*, pg. 643
LAKE CATHERINE—See Munro & Company, Inc.; *U.S. Private*, pg. 767
THE LAKE CHARLES GROUP—See American Eco Corporation; *Int'l*, pg. 74
LAKE CITY CORRECTIONAL FACILITY—See Corrections Corporation of America; *U.S. Public*, pg. 450
LAKE CITY REPORTER, INC.—See The New York Times Company; *U.S. Public*, pg. 1175
LAKE COUNTY CABLEVISION—See The E.W. Scripps Company; *U.S. Public*, pg. 1448
LAKE COUNTY PRESS; *U.S. Private*, pg. 643
LAKE ERIE DOCK CO.—See Norfolk Southern Corporation; *U.S. Public*, pg. 1191
LAKE ERIE ELECTRIC, INC.; *U.S. Private*, pg. 643
LAKE ERIE SCREW CORPORATION—See Masco Corporation; *U.S. Public*, pg. 1054
LAKE ERIE STEEL COMPANY LTD.—See Stelco Inc.; *Int'l*, pg. 1299
LAKE EUSTIS CARE CENTER—See Horizon/CMS Healthcare Corporation; *U.S. Public*, pg. 837
LAKE HAVEN HEALTH CARE CENTER—See Vencor, Inc.; *U.S. Public*, pg. 1714
LAKE HERITAGE UTILITIES, INC.—See Citizens Utilities Company; *U.S. Public*, pg. 432
LAKE INVESTMENT CO.—See Tech-Sym Corporation; *U.S. Public*, pg. 1563
LAKE KEOWEE COUNTRY CLUB, INC.—See Saint-Gobain; *Int'l*, pg. 1171
LAKE LIVINGSTON TELEPHONE COMPANY—See Telephone and Data Systems, Inc.; *U.S. Public*, pg. 1571
LAKE PLACID GRANITE CO.—See Cold Spring Granite Company; *U.S. Private*, pg. 251
LAKE PLACID GROVES—See Consolidated-Tomoka Land Co.; *U.S. Public*, pg. 437
LAKE REGION MANUFACTURING CO., LTD.—See Lake Region Manufacturing, Inc.; *U.S. Private*, pg. 643
LAKE REGION MANUFACTURING, INC.; *U.S. Private*, pg. 643
LAKE REGION MEDICAL, INC.—See Lake Region Manufacturing, Inc.; *U.S. Private*, pg. 643
LAKE RIVER CORPORATION—See Kinark Corporation; *U.S. Public*, pg. 961
LAKE SHORE, INC.—See The Oldenburg Group Companies; *U.S. Private*, pg. 814
LAKE SHORE PRESS, INC.—See Playboy Enterprises, Inc.; *U.S. Public*, pg. 1310
LAKE STATES INSURANCE CO.—See Harleysville Group; *U.S. Public*, pg. 787
LAKE SUPERIOR PAPER INDUSTRIES—See Consolidated Papers, Inc.; *U.S. Public*, pg. 436
LAKE TAMARISK DEVELOPMENT CORPORATION—See Kaiser Ventures, Inc.; *U.S. Public*, pg. 941
LAKE WALES DAILY HIGHLANDER—See Shivers Trading & Operating Co.; *U.S. Private*, pg. 995
THE LAKEFRONT DOCK & RAILROAD TERMINAL CO.—See Conrail, Inc.; *U.S. Public*, pg. 432
LAKEHEAD PIPE LINE CO., INC.—See IPL Energy Inc.; *Int'l*, pg. 690
LAKELAND AUTO AUCTION—See Cox Enterprises, Inc.; *U.S. Private*, pg. 282

LAKELAND FINANCIAL CORPORATION; *U.S. Public*, pg. 975
LAKELAND FLIGHT ACADEMY—See Berkshire Hathaway Inc.; *U.S. Public*, pg. 218
LAKELAND INDUSTRIES, INC.; *U.S. Public*, pg. 975
LAKELAND LEDGER PUBLISHING CORPORATION—See The New York Times Company; *U.S. Public*, pg. 1175
LAKESHORE LANDING—See BRE Properties, Inc.; *U.S. Public*, pg. 163
LAKESIDE COAL COMPANY—See Alabama Electric Cooperative, Inc.; *U.S. Private*, pg. 30
LAKESIDE ENTERPRISES, INC.—See Barton Press, Inc.; *U.S. Private*, pg. 120
LAKESIDE FARM INDUSTRIES LTD.—See IBP, Inc.; *U.S. Public*, pg. 852
LAKESIDE FOODS, INC.; *U.S. Private*, pg. 643
LAKESIDE INDUSTRIES; *U.S. Private*, pg. 644
LAKESIDE INSURANCE AGENCY, INC.—See The Progressive Corporation; *U.S. Public*, pg. 1334
LAKESIDE PACKING CO.—See Lakeside Foods, Inc.; *U.S. Private*, pg. 644
LAKESIDE PROCESSORS—See Saskatchewan Wheat Pool; *Int'l*, pg. 1195
LAKESIDE TRADING ESTATE LTD.—See Pearson plc; *Int'l*, pg. 1025
LAKEVIEW MANOR—See Vencor, Inc.; *U.S. Public*, pg. 1714
LAKEVIEW RESORT & CONFERENCE CENTER—See Sunstone Hotel Investors, Inc.; *U.S. Public*, pg. 1537
LAKEWOOD ENGINEERING & MANUFACTURING; *U.S. Private*, pg. 644
LAKIN GENERAL CORPORATION; *U.S. Private*, pg. 644
LAKSHMI MACHINE WORKS LTD.—See Rieter Holdings; *Int'l*, pg. 1117
LAKSO DIV.—See Package Machinery Co.; *U.S. Private*, pg. 832
LALIQUE NORTH AMERICA—See Lalique S.A.; *Int'l*, pg. 797
LALIQUE S.A.; *Int'l*, pg. 797
L'ALLIANCE AFRICAINE—See Groupe GAN; *Int'l*, pg. 565
LALLY, MCFARLAND & PANTELLO—See Havas Advertising; *Int'l*, pg. 603
LALLY, MCFARLAND & PANTELLO ADVERTISING CANADA LTD.—See Havas Advertising; *Int'l*, pg. 603
LALLY, MCFARLAND & PANTELLO INC.—See Havas Advertising; *Int'l*, pg. 601
L'ALTRA—See Testa International; *Int'l*, pg. 1377
LAM LIGHTING SYSTEMS INC.—See Luxo A/S; *Int'l*, pg. 821
LAM RESEARCH CORPORATION; *U.S. Public*, pg. 975
TONY LAMA CO., INC.—See Justin Industries, Inc.; *U.S. Public*, pg. 937
LAMAR CARIBBEAN SALES DIV.—See Superior Surgical Mfg. Co., Inc.; *U.S. Public*, pg. 1539
LAMAR CORPORATION; *U.S. Private*, pg. 644
LAMAR ELECTRO-AIR—See Triumph Group, Inc.; *U.S. Public*, pg. 1640
LAMB AG—See Enterprises International Inc.; *U.S. Private*, pg. 378
LAMB ELECTRIC DIV.—See AMETEK, Inc.; *U.S. Public*, pg. 100
LAMB ENGINEERING & CONSTRUCTION CO.; *U.S. Private*, pg. 644
LAMB GRAYS HARBOR CO—See Enterprises International Inc.; *U.S. Private*, pg. 378
LAMB LEASING & LAMB BROTHERS GENERAL—See Lamb Engineering & Construction Co.; *U.S. Private*, pg. 644
ROBERT E. LAMB, INC.; *U.S. Private*, pg. 644
LAMB SCEPTRE LTD.—See Litton Industries, Inc.; *U.S. Public*, pg. 1004
LAMB TECHNICON—See Litton Industries, Inc.; *U.S. Public*, pg. 1004
LAMB TECHNICON—See UNOVA, Inc.; *U.S. Public*, pg. 1699
LAMB TECHNICON UK—See Litton Industries, Inc.; *U.S. Public*, pg. 1004
LAMB-WESTON—See ConAgra, Inc.; *U.S. Public*, pg. 427
LAMBACHER HITIAG LEINEN AG—See Creditanstalt-Bankverein; *Int'l*, pg. 347
LAMBDA ADVANCED ANALOG—See Siebe plc; *Int'l*, pg. 1241
LAMBDA ELECTRONICA DE MEXICO, S.A.—See Siebe plc; *Int'l*, pg. 1242
LAMBDA ELECTRONICS—See Siebe plc; *Int'l*, pg. 1241
LAMBDA ELECTRONICS GMBH—See Siebe plc; *Int'l*, pg. 1242
LAMBDA ELECTRONICS INC.—See Siebe plc; *Int'l*, pg. 1241
LAMBDA ELECTRONICS SRL—See Siebe plc; *Int'l*, pg. 1242
LAMBDA ELECTRONIQUE SA—See Siebe plc; *Int'l*, pg. 1242
LAMBDA GMBH—See Siebe plc; *Int'l*, pg. 1242
LAMBDA-KOREA K.K.—See Siebe plc; *Int'l*, pg. 1242
LAMBDA NOVATRONICS INC.—See Siebe plc; *Int'l*, pg. 1241
LAMBDA PHYSIK—See Coherent, Inc.; *U.S. Public*, pg. 395
LAMBDA PHYSIK GMBH—See Coherent, Inc.; *U.S. Public*, pg. 396
LAMBDA PHYSIK JAPAN CO., LTD.—See Coherent, Inc.; *U.S. Public*, pg. 396
LAMBENT TECHNOLOGIES INC.—See Petroferm Inc.; *U.S. Private*, pg. 858
LAMBERT-KAY DIV.—See Carter-Wallace, Inc.; *U.S. Public*, pg. 310
LAMBERT SMITH HAMPTON; *Int'l*, pg. 797
TONY LAMBERT COMPANY; *U.S. Private*, pg. 644
LAMBERTS HEALTHCARE LTD.—See Novo Nordisk A/S; *Int'l*, pg. 989
LAMBERT'S POINT BARGE COMPANY, INC.—See Norfolk Southern Corporation; *U.S. Public*, pg. 1190

Company Index

LAMBERT'S POINT DOCKS, INC.—See Norfolk Southern Corporation; *U.S. Public,* pg. 1190
LAMBERTS POINT STEVEDORE & TERMINALS CO.—See Jack Gray Transport, Inc.; *U.S. Private,* pg. 472
LAMBESIS; *U.S. Private,* pg. 644
LAMBESIS—See Lambesis; *U.S. Private,* pg. 644
LAMBETH COMMUTATORS LTD.—See Delta plc; *Int'l,* pg. 390
LAMBORGHINI GREAT BRITAIN LTD.—See Porsche AG; *Int'l,* pg. 1063
LAMCO J.V. OPERATING CO.—See Electrolux, AB; *Int'l,* pg. 443
LAMETAL DEL NORTE S.A.—See Royal Packaging Industries Van Leer B.V.; *Int'l,* pg. 1146
LAMIC NV—See Internatio-Muller N.V.; *Int'l,* pg. 682
LAMIFORMA S.A. DE C.V.—See Henkel KGaA; *Int'l,* pg. 614
LAMINA INC.—See Anchor Lamina Inc.; *Int'l,* pg. 75
LAMINADOS OVIEDO-CORDOBA S.A.—See KM-Europa Metal Aktiengesellschaft; *Int'l,* pg. 720
LAMINAIRE CORPORATION—See Thermo-Mizer Environmental Corp.; *U.S. Public,* pg. 1596
LAMINATING PAPERS LTD.—See Enso Oyj; *Int'l,* pg. 457
LAMINOIR DE DUDELANGE S.A.—See Arbed S.A.; *Int'l,* pg. 79
LAMINOIRS DE BRETAGNE—See Groupe Usinor; *Int'l,* pg. 571
L'AMMONIAC AGRICOLE—See Norsk Hydro a.s; *Int'l,* pg. 964
LAMONS METAL GASKET CO.—See Masco Corporation; *U.S. Public,* pg. 1054
LAMONT HOLDINGS PLC; *Int'l,* pg. 797
LAMONTS APPAREL, INC.; *U.S. Public,* pg. 975
LAMOSA S.A. DE C.V. (MEXICO)—See Ford Motor Company; *U.S. Public,* pg. 667
LAMP DEPOT LIMITED—See Catalina Lighting, Inc.; *U.S. Public,* pg. 314
LAMP POST FRANCHISE CORPORATION; *U.S. Private,* pg. 644
LAMPERT YARDS, INC.; *U.S. Private,* pg. 645
LAMPLIGHTER HOMES, INC.—See Champion Enterprises, Inc.; *U.S. Public,* pg. 333
LAMS—See Integrated Health Services, Inc.; *U.S. Public,* pg. 885
LAMSON AND GOODNOW MFG. CO.—See Rogers, Lunt & Bowlen Co.; *U.S. Private,* pg. 940
THE LAMSON & SESSIONS CO.; *U.S. Public,* pg. 976
THE LAMSON & SESSIONS CO.—See The Lamson & Sessions Co.; *U.S. Public,* pg. 976
LAMSON & SESSIONS LTD.—See The Lamson & Sessions Co.; *U.S. Public,* pg. 976
LAN-O-SHEEN, INC.; *U.S. Private,* pg. 645
LANAI CO., LTD.—See Castle & Cooke Inc.; *U.S. Public,* pg. 313
LANCASHIRE DAIRIES LTD.; *Int'l,* pg. 798
LANCASHIRE DAIRIES (OVERSEAS) PTE. LTD.—See Lancashire Dairies Ltd.; *Int'l,* pg. 798
LANCASTER CANADA INC.—See Joh. A. Benckiser GmbH; *Int'l,* pg. 186
LANCASTER COLONY AUTOMOTIVE GROUP—See Lancaster Colony Corporation; *U.S. Public,* pg. 977
LANCASTER COLONY CANADA, INC.—See Lancaster Colony Corporation; *U.S. Public,* pg. 977
LANCASTER COLONY COMMERCIAL PRODUCTS, INC.—See Lancaster Colony Corporation; *U.S. Public,* pg. 977
LANCASTER COLONY CORPORATION; *U.S. Public,* pg. 976
LANCASTER FOODS, INC.—See Guest Services, Inc.; *U.S. Private,* pg. 487
LANCASTER GLASS CORPORATION—See Lancaster Colony Corporation; *U.S. Public,* pg. 977
LANCASTER GROUP AG—See Joh. A. Benckiser GmbH; *Int'l,* pg. 186
LANCASTER GROUP B.V.—See Joh. A. Benckiser GmbH; *Int'l,* pg. 186
LANCASTER GROUP DEUTSCHLAND GMBH—See Joh. A. Benckiser GmbH; *Int'l,* pg. 186
LANCASTER GROUP DUTY-FREE GMBH—See Joh. A. Benckiser GmbH; *Int'l,* pg. 185
LANCASTER GROUP EXPORT GMBH—See Joh. A. Benckiser GmbH; *Int'l,* pg. 185
LANCASTER GROUP GES.M.B.H.—See Joh. A. Benckiser GmbH; *Int'l,* pg. 186
LANCASTER GROUP LTD.—See Joh. A. Benckiser GmbH; *Int'l,* pg. 186
S.A. LANCASTER GROUP N.V.—See Joh. A. Benckiser GmbH; *Int'l,* pg. 186
LANCASTER GROUP PTY. LTD.—See Joh. A. Benckiser GmbH; *Int'l,* pg. 186
LANCASTER GROUP S.A.—See Joh. A. Benckiser GmbH; *Int'l,* pg. 186
LANCASTER GROUP S.P.A.—See Joh. A. Benckiser GmbH; *Int'l,* pg. 186
LANCASTER GROUP WORLDWIDE—See Joh. A. Benckiser GmbH; *Int'l,* pg. 185
LANCASTER INC.—See MacAndrews & Forbes Holdings Inc.; *U.S. Private,* pg. 690
LANCASTER LEAF TOBACCO CO. OF PENNSYLVANIA—See Universal Corporation; *U.S. Public,* pg. 1695
LANCASTER MALLEABLE CASTINGS COMPANY; *U.S. Private,* pg. 645
THE LANCASTER NEWS—See Landmark Communications, Inc.; *U.S. Private,* pg. 648
LANCASTER PLANT-KELLOGG U.S.A.—See Kellogg Company; *U.S. Public,* pg. 947
LANCASTER PLC—See Jardine Matheson Holdings Limited; *Int'l,* pg. 705
LANCASTER S.A.M.—See Joh. A. Benckiser GmbH; *Int'l,* pg. 186
LANCE CAMPER MANUFACTURING CORPORATION; *U.S. Private,* pg. 645
LANCE, INC.; *U.S. Public,* pg. 977
LANCE INDUSTRIES; *U.S. Private,* pg. 645

LANCE INTERNATIONAL S.A.—See Ricoh Company, Ltd.; *Int'l,* pg. 1116
LANCER HOLLAND BV—See Getinge Industrier AB; *Int'l,* pg. 552
LANCER S.A.—See Getinge Industrier AB; *Int'l,* pg. 552
LANCER USA INC.—See Getinge Industrier AB; *Int'l,* pg. 551
LANCERS—See Diageo Plc; *Int'l,* pg. 411
THE LANCET LIMITED—See Reed Elsevier plc; *Int'l,* pg. 1100
LANCHEM SPA—See Lafarge S.A.; *Int'l,* pg. 791
LANCHILE AIRLINES; *U.S. Private,* pg. 645
LANCIA-BRAVO FOODS—See Borden, Inc.; *U.S. Private,* pg. 159
LANCOME INSTITUT & CIE—See L'Oreal S.A.; *Int'l,* pg. 818
LANCOME PARFUMS ET BEAUTE—See L'Oreal S.A.; *Int'l,* pg. 818
LAND INFRAROT GMBH—See Land Instruments International Ltd.; *Int'l,* pg. 798
LAND INSTRUMENTS INTERNATIONAL, INC.—See Land Instruments International Ltd.; *Int'l,* pg. 798
LAND INSTRUMENTS INTERNATIONAL LTD.; *Int'l,* pg. 798
LAND INSTRUMENTS SARL—See Land Instruments International Ltd.; *Int'l,* pg. 798
LAND INSTRUMENTS SRL—See Land Instruments International Ltd.; *Int'l,* pg. 798
LAND KK—See Land Instruments International Ltd.; *Int'l,* pg. 798
LAND MOBILE PRODUCTS SECTOR, MID ATLANTIC—See Motorola, Inc.; *U.S. Public,* pg. 1137
LAND N SEA, INC.; *U.S. Private,* pg. 645
LAND O' LAKES—See Land O'Lakes, Inc.; *U.S. Private,* pg. 646
LAND O'LAKES FINANCE CO.—See Land O'Lakes, Inc.; *U.S. Private,* pg. 646
LAND O'LAKES, INC.; *U.S. Private,* pg. 645
LAND O'LAKES, INC.—See Land O'Lakes, Inc.; *U.S. Private,* pg. 646
LAND-O-SUN DAIRIES, INC.; *U.S. Private,* pg. 646
LAND OF AHHS—See Clear Channel Communications, Inc.; *U.S. Public,* pg. 384
LAND PRIDE—See Great Plains Manufacturing, Inc.; *U.S. Private,* pg. 475
LAND ROVER NORTH AMERICA—See Bayerische Motoren Werke Aktiengesellschaft; *Int'l,* pg. 177
LAND SECURITIES PLC; *Int'l,* pg. 798
LAND SECURITIES PROPERTIES LIMITED—See Land Securities Plc; *Int'l,* pg. 798
LAND SPAN INC.—See Watkins Associated Industries Inc.; *U.S. Private,* pg. 1153
LAND TITLE INSURANCE CO. OF ST. LOUIS—See The First American Financial Corporation; *U.S. Public,* pg. 626
LAND WIN ELECTRONIC CORPORATION—See Molex Incorporated; *U.S. Public,* pg. 1123
LANDA, INC.; *U.S. Private,* pg. 646
LANDA MOTOR LINES—See Kansas City Southern Industries, Inc.; *U.S. Public,* pg. 944
LANDAU & HEYMAN INC.; *U.S. Private,* pg. 646
LANDAU BUILDING CO.; *U.S. Private,* pg. 646
LANDAUER, INC.; *U.S. Public,* pg. 977
LANDBRUK/AGRICULTURE—See Norsk Hydro a.s; *Int'l,* pg. 960
LANDEGRENS MEKANISKA VERKSTAD AB—See Trelleborg AB; *Int'l,* pg. 1419
LANDER CO., INC.; *U.S. Private,* pg. 647
LANDESBANK BERLIN - GIROZENTRALE—See Bankgesellschaft Berlin; *Int'l,* pg. 160
LANDESBANK HESSEN-THURINGEN-BERLIN—See Landesbank Hessen-Thuringen Girozentrale; *Int'l,* pg. 799
LANDESBANK HESSEN-THURINGEN GIROZENTRALE; *Int'l,* pg. 798
LANDESBANK RHEINLAND-PFALZ; *Int'l,* pg. 799
LANDESBANK RHEINLAND-PFALZ—See Landesbank Rheinland-Pfalz; *Int'l,* pg. 799
LANDESBANK RHEINLAND PFALZ INTERNATIONAL S.A.—See Landesbank Rheinland-Pfalz; *Int'l,* pg. 799
LANDESGASVERSORGUNG NIEDERSACHSEN AG—See Veba AG; *Int'l,* pg. 1456
LANDESGIROKASSE BANK; *Int'l,* pg. 799
LANDESGIROKASSE BANK—See Landesgirokasse Bank; *Int'l,* pg. 800
LANDESVERLAGS UND DRUCKGESELLSCHAFT MBH - MECKLENBURG & CO. KG—See Burda Holding GmbH & Co., KG; *Int'l,* pg. 233
LANDFILL, INC.—See Browning-Ferris Industries, Inc.; *U.S. Public,* pg. 264
LANDIS—See UNOVA, Inc.; *U.S. Public,* pg. 1699
LANDIS & GYR SYSTEMS, INC.—See Landis & Staefa AG; *Int'l,* pg. 800
LANDIS & STAEFA AB—See Landis & Staefa AG; *Int'l,* pg. 800
LANDIS & STAEFA AG; *Int'l,* pg. 800
LANDIS & STAEFA (ARGENTINA) S.A.L.Y.C.—See Landis & Staefa AG; *Int'l,* pg. 800
LANDIS & STAEFA (AUSTRALIA) PTY. LTD.—See Landis & Staefa AG; *Int'l,* pg. 800
LANDIS & STAEFA BC, S.A.—See Landis & Staefa AG; *Int'l,* pg. 800
LANDIS & STAEFA BUILDING CONTROL (FRANCE) S.A.R.L.—See Landis & Staefa AG; *Int'l,* pg. 800
LANDIS & STAEFA BUILDING CONTROL (ITALIA) S.P.A.—See Landis & Staefa AG; *Int'l,* pg. 800
LANDIS & STAEFA BUILDING CONTROL (U.K.) LTD.—See Landis & Staefa AG; *Int'l,* pg. 800
LANDIS & STAEFA CHINA CO. LTD.—See Landis & Staefa AG; *Int'l,* pg. 800
LANDIS & STAEFA COMMUNCIATION SA—See Landis & Staefa AG; *Int'l,* pg. 800
LANDIS & STAEFA COMMUNICATIONS (DEUTSCHLAND) GMBH—See Landis & Staefa AG; *Int'l,* pg. 800

LANDIS & STAEFA COMMUNICATIONS (HK) LTD.—See Landis & Staefa AG; *Int'l,* pg. 800
LANDIS & STAEFA COMMUNICATIONS (U.K.) LTD.—See Landis & Staefa AG; *Int'l,* pg. 800
LANDIS & STAEFA DANMARK A/S—See Landis & Staefa AG; *Int'l,* pg. 800
LANDIS & STAEFA (DEUTSCHLAND) GMBH—See Landis & Staefa AG; *Int'l,* pg. 800
LANDIS & STAEFA DEUTSCHLAND PRODUKTION GMBH—See Landis & Staefa AG; *Int'l,* pg. 800
LANDIS & STAEFA ENERGY MANAGEMENT AB—See Landis & Staefa AG; *Int'l,* pg. 800
LANDIS & STAEFA ENERGY MANAGEMENT (DEUTSCHLAND) GMBH—See Landis & Staefa AG; *Int'l,* pg. 800
LANDIS & STAEFA ENERGY MANAGEMENT (FRANCE) S.A.R.L.—See Landis & Staefa AG; *Int'l,* pg. 800
LANDIS & STAEFA ENERGY MANAGEMENT (U.K.) LTD.—See Landis & Staefa AG; *Int'l,* pg. 801
LANDIS & STAEFA ESPANOLA S.A.—See Landis & Staefa AG; *Int'l,* pg. 801
LANDIS & STAEFA EUROPE AG—See Landis & Staefa AG; *Int'l,* pg. 801
LANDIS & STAEFA HELLAS AE—See Landis & Staefa AG; *Int'l,* pg. 801
LANDIS & STAEFA HONG KONG CO. LTD.—See Landis & Staefa AG; *Int'l,* pg. 801
LANDIS & STAEFA IMMOBILIEN AG—See Landis & Staefa AG; *Int'l,* pg. 800
LANDIS & STAEFA, INC.—See Landis & Staefa AG; *Int'l,* pg. 800
LANDIS & STAEFA INC.—See Landis & Staefa AG; *Int'l,* pg. 800
LANDIS & STAEFA INTERSYSTEM CORP.—See Landis & Staefa AG; *Int'l,* pg. 801
LANDIS & STAEFA (ITALIA) S.P.A.—See Landis & Staefa AG; *Int'l,* pg. 801
LANDIS & STAEFA JAPAN CO., LTD.—See Landis & Staefa AG; *Int'l,* pg. 801
LANDIS & STAEFA KOREA CO., LTD.—See Landis & Staefa AG; *Int'l,* pg. 801
LANDIS & STAEFA LDA—See Landis & Staefa AG; *Int'l,* pg. 801
LANDIS & STAEFA LEIT- UND FERNWIRKTECHNIK GES.M.B.H—See Landis & Staefa AG; *Int'l,* pg. 801
LANDIS & STAEFA (MAGYARORSZAG) KFT.—See Landis & Staefa AG; *Int'l,* pg. 801
LANDIS & STAEFA MALETEKNIK A/S—See Landis & Staefa AG; *Int'l,* pg. 801
LANDIS & STAEFA MANAGEMENT AG—See Landis & Staefa AG; *Int'l,* pg. 800
LANDIS & STAEFA MANAGEMENT CORP.—See Landis & Staefa AG; *Int'l,* pg. 801
LANDIS & STAEFA (NEDERLAND) B.V.—See Landis & Staefa AG; *Int'l,* pg. 801
LANDIS & STAEFA (NORGE) A/S—See Landis & Staefa AG; *Int'l,* pg. 801
LANDIS & STAEFA (NZ) LTD.—See Landis & Staefa AG; *Int'l,* pg. 801
LANDIS & STAEFA (OSTERREICH) AG—See Landis & Staefa AG; *Int'l,* pg. 801
LANDIS & STAEFA (POLSKA) SP.Z.O.O.—See Landis & Staefa AG; *Int'l,* pg. 801
LANDIS & STAEFA PRAHA S.R.O.—See Landis & Staefa AG; *Int'l,* pg. 801
LANDIS & STAEFA SCHWEIZ AG—See Landis & Staefa AG; *Int'l,* pg. 801
LANDIS & STAEFA (SEA) PTE LTD—See Landis & Staefa AG; *Int'l,* pg. 801
LANDIS & STAEFA (SLOVENSKO) S.R.O.—See Landis & Staefa AG; *Int'l,* pg. 801
LANDIS & STAEFA SMART SARL—See Landis & Staefa AG; *Int'l,* pg. 801
LANDIS & STAEFA SMSTAR CO., LTD.—See Landis & Staefa AG; *Int'l,* pg. 801
LANDIS & STAEFA SUOMI OY—See Landis & Staefa AG; *Int'l,* pg. 801
LANDIS & STAEFA TECHNOLOGY INNOVATION INC.—See Landis & Staefa AG; *Int'l,* pg. 800
LANDIS & STAEFA S.A./N.V.—See Landis & Staefa AG; *Int'l,* pg. 801
LANDISC SYSTEMS—See Day & Zimmermann, Inc.; *U.S. Private,* pg. 317
LANDMARK COMMUNICATIONS, INC.; *U.S. Private,* pg. 647
LANDMARK COMMUNITY NEWSPAPERS, INC.—See Landmark Communications, Inc.; *U.S. Private,* pg. 648
LANDMARK CONSTRUCTION CORP.—See Zilber, Ltd.; *U.S. Private,* pg. 1206
LANDMARK GRAPHICS CORPORATION—See Halliburton Company; *U.S. Public,* pg. 776
LANDMARK SPECIALTY PUBLICATIONS, INC.—See Landmark Communications, Inc.; *U.S. Private,* pg. 649
LANDMARK SYSTEMS CORPORATION; *U.S. Private,* pg. 649
LANDMARK SYSTEMS INC.; *U.S. Private,* pg. 649
LANDMARK WEB PRINTING—See Landmark Communications, Inc.; *U.S. Private,* pg. 648
LANDOR CARTONS; *Int'l,* pg. 801
LANDRY'S SEAFOOD RESTAURANTS INC.; *U.S. Public,* pg. 977
LANDS' END DIRECT MERCHANTS UK LIMITED—See Lands' End, Inc.; *U.S. Public,* pg. 978
LANDS' END GMBH—See Lands' End, Inc.; *U.S. Public,* pg. 978
LANDS' END, INC.; *U.S. Public,* pg. 977
LANDS' END JAPAN, K.K.—See Lands' End, Inc.; *U.S. Public,* pg. 978
LANDS OF SIERRA—See Sierra Pacific Resources; *U.S. Public,* pg. 1470
LANDSAFE TITLE AGENCY, INC.—See Countrywide Home Loans Inc.; *U.S. Public,* pg. 453
LANDSTAR DEVELOPMENT COMPANY; *U.S. Private,* pg. 649

LANDSTAR EXPRESS AMERICA, INC.—See Landstar Holding; *U.S. Public,* pg. 978
LANDSTAR GEMINI, INC.—See Landstar Holding; *U.S. Public,* pg. 978
LANDSTAR HOLDING; *U.S. Public,* pg. 978
LANDSTAR INWAY, INC.—See Landstar Holding; *U.S. Public,* pg. 978
LANDSTAR ITCO, INC.—See Landstar Holding; *U.S. Public, pg. 978*
LANDSTAR LIGON, INC.—See Landstar Holding; *U.S. Public,* pg. 978
LANDSTAR LOGISTICS, INC.—See Landstar Holding; *U.S. Public,* pg. 978
LANDSTAR POOLE, INC.—See Landstar Holding; *U.S. Public,* pg. 978
LANDSTAR RANGER, INC.—See Landstar Holding; *U.S. Public,* pg. 978
LANDSTAR T.L.C., INC.—See Landstar Holding; *U.S. Public,* pg. 978
LANDSVIRKJUN - THE NATIONAL POWER CO.; *Int'l,* pg. 801
LANE BROADCASTING, INC.—See Lane Industries, Inc.; *U.S. Private,* pg. 650
LANE BRYANT—See The Limited, Inc.; *U.S. Public,* pg. 995
THE LANE COMPANY, INC.—See Furniture Brands International Inc.; *U.S. Public,* pg. 688
THE LANE CONSTRUCTION CORP.; *U.S. Private,* pg. 649
LANE GRAPHICS PRODUCTS DIV.—See General Binding Corporation; *U.S. Public,* pg. 707
LANE HOSPITALITY, INC.—See Lane Industries, Inc.; *U.S. Private,* pg. 650
LANE INDUSTRIES, INC.; *U.S. Private,* pg. 649
LANE LIMITED—See Rothmans UK Holdings Limited; *Int'l,* pg. 1129
LANE PRESS, INC.; *U.S. Private,* pg. 650
LANE SAFE DEPOSIT CO. LTD.—See The Peninsular and Oriental Steam Navigation Company; *Int'l,* pg. 1033
LANE SECURITY, INC.—See Lane Industries, Inc.; *U.S. Private,* pg. 650
LANE UPHOLSTERY—See Furniture Brands International Inc.; *U.S. Public,* pg. 688
LANECO, INC.—See SuperValu, Inc.; *U.S. Public,* pg. 1541
LANG APPARATEBAU GMBH—See Henkel KGaA; *Int'l,* pg. 610
GEORGES LANG CONTINU S.A.—See Moore Corporation Limited; *Int'l,* pg. 889
LANGASJONAS PAPER MILL—See Duni AB; *Int'l,* pg. 421
LANGE BALLAST CONTRACTORS LTD.—See Ballast Nedam NV; *Int'l,* pg. 135
LANGE INTERNATIONAL S.A.—See Rossignol S.A.; *Int'l,* pg. 1127
LANGE UHREN—See Mannesmann A.G.; *Int'l,* pg. 839
LANGENBERG KUPFER UND MESSINGWERKE GMBH—See Olin Corporation; *U.S. Public,* pg. 1219
C.J. LANGENFELDER & SON, INC.; *U.S. Private,* pg. 650
THE LANGER BIOMECHANICS GROUP, INC.; *U.S. Public,* pg. 978
LANGFANG NIPPON PAINT CO., LTD.—See Nippon Paint Company Ltd.; *Int'l,* pg. 937
LANGFORD INC.—See American Home Products Corporation; *U.S. Public,* pg. 81
LANGMOEN AS—See Norske Skogindustrier A.S; *Int'l,* pg. 965
LANGMOEN PARKETT—See Norske Skogindustrier A.S; *Int'l,* pg. 965
LANGMOEN TRE—See Norske Skogindustrier A.S; *Int'l,* pg. 965
LANGNESE-IGLO G.M.B.H.—See Unilever Plc; *Int'l,* pg. 1437
LANGS COLD STORAGE DIV.—See The Oshawa Group Limited; *Int'l,* pg. 1012
LANGSTON COMPANIES; *U.S. Private,* pg. 650
LANGUAGE INSTITUTE FOR ENGLISH (L.I.F.E.)—See Berlitz International, Inc.; *U.S. Public,* pg. 221
LANGWOOD (PREPARED VEGETABLES) LIMITED—See Avonmore Waterford Group plc; *Int'l,* pg. 102
LANHAM WASTE CONTROL, INC.—See Browning-Ferris Industries, Inc.; *U.S. Public,* pg. 264
LANIER CLOTHES—See Oxford Industries, Inc.; *U.S. Public,* pg. 1239
LANIER WORLDWIDE INC.—See Harris Corporation; *U.S. Public,* pg. 791
LANIER WORLDWIDE, INC.-EUROPEAN DIVISION—See Harris Corporation; *U.S. Public,* pg. 791
LANKA ORIX LEASING COMPANY LIMITED—See Orix Corporation; *Int'l,* pg. 1009
LANKEM CEYLON—See Royal Dutch/Shell Group of Companies; *Int'l,* pg. 1140
LANKFORD-SYSCO FOOD SERVICES, INC.—See Sysco Corporation; *U.S. Public,* pg. 1551
LANOGA CORPORATION; *U.S. Private,* pg. 650
LANSDOWN CONQUEST—See WPP Group plc; *Int'l,* pg. 1482
LANSDOWNE TECHNOLOGIES INC.—See Canadian Shipbuilding & Engineering Ltd.; *Int'l,* pg. 259
LANSI-SUOMEN VOIMA OY—See UPM-Kymmene Corporation; *Int'l,* pg. 1428
LANSING LINDE (BLACKWOOD) LTD.—See Linde AG; *Int'l,* pg. 810
LANSING LINDE LTD.—See Linde AG; *Int'l,* pg. 810
LANSING STATE JOURNAL—See Gannett Company, Inc.; *U.S. Public,* pg. 701
LANSI-SUOMEN KAYNNISSAPITO OY—See Imatran Voima Oy; *Int'l,* pg. 660
AUBREY G. LANSTON & CO. INC.—See The Industrial Bank of Japan, Limited; *Int'l,* pg. 675
LANTECH INC.; *U.S. Private,* pg. 650
LANTZSCH-ANDREAS ENTERPRISES, INC.; *U.S. Private,* pg. 650
LANVIN PARFUMS—See L'Oreal S.A.; *Int'l,* pg. 818
LANZ, INC.; *U.S. Private,* pg. 650
LAPA ALIMENTOS S/A—See Sadia Group; *Int'l,* pg. 1168

LAPAZ—See Northern States Power Company; *U.S. Public,* pg. 1195
LAPEYRE STAIR, INC.—See The Laitram Corporation; *U.S. Private,* pg. 643
LAPHAM-HICKEY STEEL CORP.; *U.S. Private,* pg. 651
LAPHAM HICKEY STEEL (WI)—See Lapham-Hickey Steel Corp.; *U.S. Private,* pg. 651
LAPHAM-HICKEY STEEL CORP.—See Lapham-Hickey Steel Corp.; *U.S. Private,* pg. 651
LAPMASTER INTERNATIONAL LTD.—See TI Group plc; *Int'l,* pg. 1338
LAPORTE ABSORBENTS (BAULKING) LIMITED—See Laporte plc; *Int'l,* pg. 802
LAPORTE ABSORBENTS EUROPE—See Laporte plc; *Int'l,* pg. 802
LAPORTE ABSORBENTS-HOLLAND—See Laporte plc; *Int'l,* pg. 803
LAPORTE ALPHAGARY LTD.—See Laporte plc; *Int'l,* pg. 802
LAPORTE AMERICA INC.—See Laporte plc; *Int'l,* pg. 802
LAPORTE CHEMICALS (MALAYSIA) SDN BHD—See Laporte plc; *Int'l,* pg. 803
LAPORTE ELECTRONICS—See Laporte plc; *Int'l,* pg. 802
LAPORTE ESD-GERMANY—See Laporte plc; *Int'l,* pg. 803
LAPORTE FLUORIDES—See Laporte plc; *Int'l,* pg. 802
LAPORTE HYGIENE—See Laporte plc; *Int'l,* pg. 802
LAPORTE INC.—See Laporte plc; *Int'l,* pg. 802
LAPORTE INDUSTRIES (SINGAPORE) PTE LIMITED—See Laporte plc; *Int'l,* pg. 803
LAPORTE KEMWOOD AB—See Laporte plc; *Int'l,* pg. 803
LAPORTE (MALAYSIA) SDN BHD—See Laporte plc; *Int'l,* pg. 803
LAPORTE MINERALS—See Laporte plc; *Int'l,* pg. 802
LAPORTE PLC; *Int'l,* pg. 801
LAPORTE (TAIWAN) LIMITED—See Laporte plc; *Int'l,* pg. 803
LAPORTE (THAILAND) LTD.—See Laporte plc; *Int'l,* pg. 803
LAPORTE WOOD PRESERVATION—See Laporte plc; *Int'l,* pg. 802
LAPP INSULATOR COMPANY—See Great American Management & Investment, Inc.; *U.S. Private,* pg. 473
LAPPEENRANTA MILLS—See UPM-Kymmene Corporation; *Int'l,* pg. 1429
LAPPEENRANTA PAPER MILL—See UPM-Kymmene Corporation; *Int'l,* pg. 1428
LAPPEENRANTI PLANT—See Scancem AB; *Int'l,* pg. 1198
LAPPIN ELECTRIC COMPANY—See Consolidated Electrical Distributors; *U.S. Private,* pg. 265
LAPPOHJA WORKS—See Rautaruukki Oy; *Int'l,* pg. 1088
LAPUAN METALLI OY—See Tamrock Corp.; *Int'l,* pg. 1353
LAQUE CENTER FOR CORROSION TECHNOLOGY, INC.—See Inco Limited; *Int'l,* pg. 672
LARAMIE TIRE DISTRIBUTORS INC.—See Sumitomo Corporation; *Int'l,* pg. 1312
LARCH-LAP LIMITED—See Newmond PLC; *Int'l,* pg. 925
LARCOM INSURANCE COMPANY, LTD.—See Pride International, Inc.; *U.S. Public,* pg. 1325
L'ARDENNE PREVOYANTE—See Groupe Bruxelles Lambert S.A.; *Int'l,* pg. 562
LAREDO BOOT CO.—See Genesco Inc.; *U.S. Public,* pg. 728
THE LAREDO COCA-COLA BOTTLING COMPANY, INC.—See Coca-Cola Enterprises, Inc.; *U.S. Public,* pg. 393
LAREDO MORNING TIMES—See The Hearst Corporation; *U.S. Private,* pg. 517
LAREDO PROCESSING CENTER—See Corrections Corporation of America; *U.S. Public,* pg. 450
LARGE SYSTEMS GROUP—See BTR plc; *Int'l,* pg. 126
LARICHE CHEVROLET-CADILLAC—See Lou LaRiche Chevrolet Inc.; *U.S. Private,* pg. 651
LOU LARICHE CHEVROLET INC.; *U.S. Private,* pg. 651
LARICHE TOYOTA-SUBARU—See Lou LaRiche Chevrolet Inc.; *U.S. Private,* pg. 651
LARIO ENTERPRISES, INC.—See Lario Oil & Gas Company; *U.S. Private,* pg. 651
LARIO OIL & GAS COMPANY; *U.S. Private,* pg. 651
LARIO OIL & GAS COMPANY—See Lario Oil & Gas Company; *U.S. Private,* pg. 651
LARK LUGGAGE COMPANY, INC.—See Samsonite Corporation; *U.S. Public,* pg. 1430
LARKEN INC.; *U.S. Private,* pg. 651
LARKIN MEEDER & SCHWEIDEL; *U.S. Private,* pg. 651
LARKIN, MEEDER & SCHWEIDEL-TULSA—See Larkin Meeder & Schweidel; *U.S. Private,* pg. 651
LARMES, INC.—See Pennsylvania Real Estate Investment Trust; *U.S. Public,* pg. 1272
LAROCHE AIR SYSTEMS INC.—See LaRoche Industries Inc.; *U.S. Private,* pg. 652
GUY LAROCHE SA—See Societe BIC S.A.; *Int'l,* pg. 1273
LAROCHE INDUSTRIES INC.; *U.S. Private,* pg. 651
EDICIONES LAROUSSE ARGENTINA SA—See C.E.P. Communication Group; *Int'l,* pg. 240
LAROUSSE-BELGIQUE—See C.E.P. Communication Group; *Int'l,* pg. 240
EDICIONES LAROUSSE COLOMBIANA LTDA.—See C.E.P. Communication Group; *Int'l,* pg. 240
EDITORIA LAROUSSE DO BRASIL—See C.E.P. Communication Group; *Int'l,* pg. 240
LIBRAIRIE LAROUSSE—See C.E.P. Communication Group; *Int'l,* pg. 239
EDICIONES LAROUSSE SA—See C.E.P. Communication Group; *Int'l,* pg. 240
LAROUSSE (SUISSE) SA—See C.E.P. Communication Group; *Int'l,* pg. 240
LARRYS, INC.; *U.S. Private,* pg. 652
LARRY'S INDUSTRIES, INC.—See Yogen Fruz Worldwide Inc.; *Int'l,* pg. 1520
LARSAN MANUFACTURING CO.—See Emerson Electric Co.; *U.S. Public,* pg. 575
LARSCOM INC.—See Axel Johnson AB; *Int'l,* pg. 710
LARSE CORPORATION—See Axel Johnson AB; *Int'l,* pg. 710
JACK LENOR LARSEN, INC.; *U.S. Private,* pg. 652

LARSEN-READFIELD TELEPHONE COMPANY—See Century Telephone Enterprises, Inc.; *U.S. Public,* pg. 330
AL LARSON BOAT SHOP, INC.; *U.S. Private,* pg. 652
LARSON BOATS—See Genmar Holdings, Inc.; *U.S. Private,* pg. 447
J.H. LARSON ELECTRICAL COMPANY; *U.S. Private,* pg. 652
LARSON MANUFACTURING COMPANY; *U.S. Private,* pg. 652
S LENNART LARSSON AB—See Axel Johnson AB; *Int'l,* pg. 709
LARSSON & SUNDQVIST PAPER AB—See Axel Johnson AB; *Int'l,* pg. 709
LARUE COUNTY HERALD NEWS—See Landmark Communications, Inc.; *U.S. Private,* pg. 648
LARWIN COMPANY; *U.S. Private,* pg. 652
LAS COLINAS INN & CONFERENCE CENTER—See Four Seasons Hotels Inc.; *Int'l,* pg. 502
LAS CRUCES NURSING CENTER—See Horizon/CMS Healthcare Corporation; *U.S. Public,* pg. 838
LAS FLORES NURSING CENTER—See Paragon Health Network, Inc.; *U.S. Private,* pg. 1257
LAS PALMA NURSING CENTER—See Vencor, Inc.; *U.S. Public,* pg. 1714
LAS VEGAS CONVALESCENT CENTER—See Vencor, Inc.; *U.S. Public,* pg. 1714
LAS VEGAS SPORTS CONSULTANTS—See Data Broadcasting Corporation; *U.S. Public,* pg. 484
LAS VEGAS SUN; *U.S. Private,* pg. 652
LASAG AG—See SMH Swiss Corporation for Micro Electronics & Watchmaking Indus. Ltd.; *Int'l,* pg. 1161
LASALLE ADVISORS LIMITED—See LaSalle Partners; *U.S. Public,* pg. 979
LASALLE BANK LAKE VIEW—See ABN-AMRO Holding N.V.; *Int'l,* pg. 10
LASALLE BANK MADISON—See ABN-AMRO Holding N.V.; *Int'l,* pg. 10
LASALLE BANK NORTHBROOK—See ABN-AMRO Holding N.V.; *Int'l,* pg. 10
LASALLE BANK NORTHBROOK/VERNON HILLS—See ABN-AMRO Holding N.V.; *Int'l,* pg. 10
LASALLE BANK OF LISLE—See ABN-AMRO Holding N.V.; *Int'l,* pg. 10
LASALLE BANK WESTMONT—See ABN-AMRO Holding N.V.; *Int'l,* pg. 10
LASALLE BRISTOL CORP.—See Heywood Williams Group PLC; *Int'l,* pg. 618
LASALLE CRAGIN BANK—See ABN-AMRO Holding N.V.; *Int'l,* pg. 10
LASALLE NATIONAL BANK—See ABN-AMRO Holding N.V.; *Int'l,* pg. 10
LASALLE NORTHWEST NATIONAL BANK—See ABN-AMRO Holding N.V.; *Int'l,* pg. 10
LASALLE PARTNERS; *U.S. Public,* pg. 978
LASALLE STEEL COMPANY—See Niagara Corporation; *U.S. Public,* pg. 1181
LASALLE-TALMAN BANK—See ABN-AMRO Holding N.V.; *Int'l,* pg. 11
LASBRA KAVICSBANYA KFT.—See Redland PLC; *Int'l,* pg. 1092
LASCO BATHWARE—See Tomkins PLC; *Int'l,* pg. 1397
LASCO FLUID DISTRIBUTION PRODUCTS—See Tomkins PLC; *Int'l,* pg. 1398
LASCO PANEL PRODUCTS—See Tomkins PLC; *Int'l,* pg. 1398
LASCOR S.P.A.—See SMH Swiss Corporation for Micro Electronics & Watchmaking Indus. Ltd.; *Int'l,* pg. 1161
LASER DIODE PRODUCTS—See Morgan Crucible Co. Plc; *Int'l,* pg. 892
LASER INDUSTRIES LTD.—See ESC Medical Systems Ltd.; *Int'l,* pg. 429
LASER OPTRONIC TECHNOLOGIES (PTY.) LTD.—See Mannesmann A.G.; *Int'l,* pg. 836
LASER POWER CORPORATION; *U.S. Public,* pg. 652
LASER SYSTEMS—See Litton Industries, Inc.; *U.S. Public,* pg. 1002
S.A. LASERFLASH—See Cockerill Sambre; *Int'l,* pg. 301
LASERMASTER EXPORT CORPORATION—See LaserMaster Technologies, Inc.; *U.S. Public,* pg. 979
LASERMASTER TECHNOLOGIES, INC.; *U.S. Public,* pg. 979
LASERSCOPE INC.—See Heraeus Holding GmbH; *Int'l,* pg. 616
LASERSCOPE SURGICAL SYSTEMS; *U.S. Public,* pg. 979
LASERSIGHT INC.; *U.S. Public,* pg. 979
LASGRUPPEN A.S.—See Assa Abloy AB; *Int'l,* pg. 18
LASKO METAL PRODUCTS, INC.; *U.S. Private,* pg. 652
LASMO AMERICA INC.—See LASMO plc; *Int'l,* pg. 804
LASMO COMPANIES INDONESIA—See LASMO plc; *Int'l,* pg. 804
LASMO GRAND MAGHREB LIMITED—See LASMO plc; *Int'l,* pg. 804
LASMO INTERNATIONAL LIMITED—See LASMO plc; *Int'l,* pg. 804
LASMO MINERARIA SPA—See LASMO plc; *Int'l,* pg. 804
LASMO NEDERLAND B.V.—See LASMO plc; *Int'l,* pg. 804
LASMO NORTH SEA PLC—See LASMO plc; *Int'l,* pg. 804
LASMO OIL (COLOMBIA) LIMITED—See LASMO plc; *Int'l,* pg. 804
LASMO OIL PAKISTAN LIMITED—See LASMO plc; *Int'l,* pg. 804
LASMO PLC; *Int'l,* pg. 803
LASMO RUNTU LTD.—See LASMO plc; *Int'l,* pg. 804
LASMO - SINGAPORE REPRESENTATIVE OFFICE—See LASMO plc; *Int'l,* pg. 804
LASON, INC.; *U.S. Public,* pg. 979
LASON, INC.—See Lason, Inc.; *U.S. Public,* pg. 979
LASTING PRODUCTS, INC.; *U.S. Private,* pg. 652
LAT KRABANG PUMPING FACILITIES PROJECT—See Nishimatsu Construction Co., Ltd.; *Int'l,* pg. 943
LATAS DE ALUMINIO REYNOLDS, INC.—See Reynolds Metals Company; *U.S. Public,* pg. 1386

Company Index

LATAS DIRECTORY OF CORPORATE AFFILIATIONS

LATAS DE ALUMINIO, S/A-LATASA—See Reynolds Metals Company; *U.S. Public*, pg. 1387
LATCO II INC.—See Lagardere Groupe; *Int'l*, pg. 794
LATCO, INC.—See Universal Corporation; *U.S. Public*, pg. 1695
LATENSTEIN ZETMEEL B.V.—See Koninklijke BolsWessanen nv; *Int'l*, pg. 752
THE LATHROP COMPANY—See The Turner Corporation; *U.S. Public*, pg. 1645
LATI INDUSTRIA TERMOPLASTICI S.P.A.; *Int'l*, pg. 804
LATIMER & BUCK, INC.—See Legg Mason, Inc.; *U.S. Public*, pg. 985
LATIN AMERICA AREA—See CNF Transportation Inc.; *U.S. Public*, pg. 281
LATIN AMERICA OPERATION—See Sterling Software, Inc.; *U.S. Public*, pg. 1516
LATIN AMERICAN GROUP—See Parker Hannifin Corporation; *U.S. Public*, pg. 1262
LATIN AMERICAN REPRESENTATIVE COMDISCO, INC.—See Comdisco, Inc.; *U.S. Public*, pg. 408
LATINA HOLDINGS, LTD.—See Cigna Corp.; *U.S. Public*, pg. 363
LATITUDE—See The Richards Group, Inc.; *U.S. Private*, pg. 929
LATROBE BREWING CO.—See Interbrew S.A.; *Int'l*, pg. 680
LATROBE SPECIAL PRODUCTS DIV.—See The Timken Company; *U.S. Public*, pg. 1617
LATROBE STEEL COMPANY—See The Timken Company; *U.S. Public*, pg. 1617
LATSHAW ENTERPRISES, INC.; *U.S. Public*, pg. 979
LATTICE SEMICONDUCTOR CORPORATION; *U.S. Public*, *pg. 979*
LATVIAN TRAFFIC SERVICE—See Neste Oy; *Int'l*, pg. 914
LATVIJAS LIFTS-SCHINDLER—See Schindler Holding AG; *Int'l*, pg. 1205
LAU DIV.—See Tomkins PLC; *Int'l*, pg. 1398
LAU GMBH & CO.—See Spar Handels AG; *Int'l*, pg. 1288
LAUBECK CORPORATION/CROSS; *U.S. Private*, pg. 652
LAUBECK CORPORATION, LAUBENSTEIN DIVISION—See Laubeck Corporation/Cross; *U.S. Private*, pg. 653
LAUDERDALE COMPUTER AB—See Encore Computer Corporation; *U.S. Public*, pg. 580
LAUDERDALE-MIAMI AUTO AUCTION INC.—See Tyco International Ltd.; *U.S. Public*, pg. 1649
LAUGHLIN/CONSTABLE, INC.; *U.S. Private*, pg. 653
LAUGHLIN ENVIRONMENTAL, INC.—See Republic Industries, Inc.; *U.S. Public*, pg. 1379
THE HOMER LAUGHLIN CHINA COMPANY; *U.S. Private*, pg. 653
LAUGHTON & SONS, LTD.; *Int'l*, pg. 804
LAUNDRYMART, INC.—See Center Partners Management LLC; *U.S. Private*, pg. 222
LAURA ASHLEY (AUSTRALIA) PTY LTD.—See Laura Ashley Holdings Plc; *Int'l*, pg. 804
LAURA ASHLEY BV—See Laura Ashley Holdings Plc; *Int'l*, pg. 804
LAURA ASHLEY CER COUNTRIES BV—See Laura Ashley Holdings Plc; *Int'l*, pg. 804
LAURA ASHLEY DISTRIBUTION BV—See Laura Ashley Holdings Plc; *Int'l*, pg. 804
LAURA ASHLEY ESPANA SA—See Laura Ashley Holdings Plc; *Int'l*, pg. 804
LAURA ASHLEY GMBH—See Laura Ashley Holdings Plc; *Int'l*, pg. 804
LAURA ASHLEY HOLDINGS PLC; *Int'l*, pg. 804
LAURA ASHLEY INVESTMENTS BV—See Laura Ashley Holdings Plc; *Int'l*, pg. 804
LAURA ASHLEY LTD.—See Laura Ashley Holdings Plc; *Int'l*, pg. 804
LAURA ASHLEY NV—See Laura Ashley Holdings Plc; *Int'l*, pg. 804
LAURA ASHLEY SA—See Laura Ashley Holdings Plc; *Int'l*, pg. 804
LAURA ASHLEY SHOPS LTD.—See Laura Ashley Holdings Plc; *Int'l*, pg. 804
LAURA ASHLEY SRL—See Laura Ashley Holdings Plc; *Int'l*, pg. 804
LAURA ASHLEY TRADING BV—See Laura Ashley Holdings Plc; *Int'l*, pg. 804
LAURA ASHLEY (USA) INC.—See Laura Ashley Holdings Plc; *Int'l*, pg. 804
LAURA METAAL B.V.—See Koninklijke Hoogovens N.V.; *Int'l*, pg. 754
LAURA SECORD, INC.—See Nestle S.A.; *Int'l*, pg. 920
LAUREL BANK—See BT Financial Corporation; *U.S. Public*, *pg. 164*
LAUREL CAPITAL ADVISORS—See Mellon Bank Corporation; *U.S. Public*, pg. 1085
LAUREL COMMUNITY DEVELOPMENT CORPORATION—See BT Financial Corporation; *U.S. Public*, pg. 164
LAUREL PIPE LINE COMPANY, L.P.—See Buckeye Partners, L.P.; *U.S. Public*, pg. 267
LAUREL STEEL—See Harris Steel Group Inc.; *Int'l*, pg. 598
LAUREL TRUST COMPANY—See BT Financial Corporation; *U.S. Public*, pg. 164
R.G. LAURENCE CO., INC.—See Watts Industries, Inc.; *U.S. Public*, pg. 1747
LAURENTIAN BANK OF CANADA—See Desjardins-Laurentian Financial Corporation; *Int'l*, pg. 396
LAURENTIAN FINANCIAL SERVICES—See Desjardins-Laurentian Financial Corporation; *Int'l*, pg. 396
THE LAURENTIAN GROUP CORPORATION—See Desjardins-Laurentian Financial Corporation; *Int'l*, pg. 396
LAURENTIAN TRUST OF CANADA—See Desjardins-Laurentian Financial Corporation; *Int'l*, pg. 396
LAURENTIEN CABLE TV INC.—See CFCF Inc.; *Int'l*, pg. 241
LAURIAT INC.—See CMI Holding Corp.; *U.S. Private*, pg. 195
LAUSITZER BRAUNKOHLE AKTIENGESELLSCHAFT (LAUBAG)—See Veba AG; *Int'l*, pg. 1457
LAUSITZER RUNDSCHAU VERLAG UND DRUCKEREI GMBH—See Georg von Holtzbrinck GmbH; *Int'l*, pg. 1478
LAUSON ENGINE DIV.—See Tecumseh Products Company; *U.S. Public*, pg. 1566
P.T. LAUTAN OTSUKA CHEMICAL—See Otsuka Pharmaceutical Co., Ltd.; *Int'l*, pg. 1014
LAUX COMMUNICATIONS, INC.—See COMSAT Corporation; *U.S. Public*, pg. 424
LAVA WORLD INTERNATIONAL/HAGGERTY ENTERPRISES, INC.; *U.S. Private*, pg. 653
LAVACA REALTY CO.—See Southern Union Company; *U.S. Public*, pg. 1491
LAVELLE COMPANY; *U.S. Private*, pg. 653
LAVELLE INDUSTRIES INC.; *U.S. Private*, pg. 653
LAVINGTON PLANER DIVISION—See Tolko Industries Ltd.; *Int'l*, pg. 1395
LAVORO & SICURTA—See Allianz Aktiengesellschaft; *Int'l*, *pg. 61*
LAVORO BANK A.G.—See Banca Nazionale del Lavoro Sj.A.; *Int'l*, pg. 137
LAW COMPANIES GROUP—See Law Engineering, Inc.; *U.S. Private*, pg. 653
THE LAW COMPANY, INC.; *U.S. Private*, pg. 653
LAW ENGINEERING, INC.; *U.S. Private*, pg. 653
LAWLER'S, INC.—See Sunstone Hotel Investors, Inc.; *U.S. Public*, pg. 1537
LAWN-BOY INC.—See The Toro Company; *U.S. Public*, pg. 1624
N.V. LAWN COMFORT S.A.—See DSM N.V.; *Int'l*, pg. 355
LAWN DOCTOR INC.; *U.S. Private*, pg. 653
LAWNWARE PRODUCTS, INC.; *U.S. Private*, pg. 653
C.J. LAWRENCE, MORGAN GRENFELL INC.—See Deutsche Bank AG; *Int'l*, pg. 405
LAWRENCE & COMPANY—See White Rock Distilleries Inc.; *U.S. Private*, pg. 1173
CYRUS J. LAWRENCE (UK) LIMITED—See Deutsche Bank AG; *Int'l*, pg. 405
LAWRENCE DIVISION—See Aetrium Inc.; *U.S. Public*, pg. 27
THE F.D. LAWRENCE ELECTRIC CO.; *U.S. Private*, pg. 654
LAWRENCE METAL PRODUCTS, INC.; *U.S. Private*, pg. 654
LAWRENCE PAPER COMPANY; *U.S. Private*, pg. 654
LAWRENCE PRODUCTION CENTER—See Hallmark Cards, Inc.; *U.S. Private*, pg. 496
LAWRENCE PUMPS, INC.; *U.S. Private*, pg. 654
LAWRENCE SAVINGS BANK; *U.S. Public*, pg. 980
LAWRENCE SAVINGS BANK—See Lawrence Savings Bank; *U.S. Public*, pg. 980
LAWRENCE TECHNOLOGY—See Camco International Inc.; *U.S. Public*, pg. 298
LAWRENCEBURG GAS CO.—See Cinergy Corp.; *U.S. Public*, pg. 369
ALEX LAWRIE FACTORS LTD.—See Lloyds TSB Group PLC; *Int'l*, pg. 813
LAWRY'S FOODS, INC.—See Unilever Plc; *Int'l*, pg. 1435
LAWRY'S RESTAURANTS, INC.; *U.S. Private*, pg. 654
LAWSON MARDON BAK GRAYURE BASKILI KARTON SANAYI VE TICARET AS—See Alusuisse-Lonza Holding Ltd.; *Int'l*, pg. 68
LAWSON MARDON BOXAL FRANCE S.A.—See Alusuisse-Lonza Holding Ltd.; *Int'l*, pg. 68
LAWSON MARDON BOXAL NEDERLAND B.V.—See Alusuisse-Lonza Holding Ltd.; *Int'l*, pg. 68
LAWSON MARDON BOXAL SALES GMBH—See Alusuisse-Lonza Holding Ltd.; *Int'l*, pg. 68
LAWSON MARDON BOXAL SUISSE SA—See Alusuisse-Lonza Holding Ltd.; *Int'l*, pg. 67
LAWSON MARDON BRABANT BV—See Alusuisse-Lonza Holding Ltd.; *Int'l*, pg. 68
LAWSON MARDON BRISTOL LTD.—See Alusuisse-Lonza Holding Ltd.; *Int'l*, pg. 68
LAWSON MARDON CARTON LTD.—See Alusuisse-Lonza Holding Ltd.; *Int'l*, pg. 68
LAWSON MARDON CERLIVE S.A.—See Alusuisse-Lonza Holding Ltd.; *Int'l*, pg. 68
LAWSON MARDON CHARMETTES S.A.—See Alusuisse-Lonza Holding Ltd.; *Int'l*, pg. 68
LAWSON MARDON FLEXIBLE PACKAGING, INC.—See Alusuisse-Lonza Holding Ltd.; *Int'l*, pg. 67
LAWSON MARDON GROUP INTERNATIONAL LTD.—See Alusuisse-Lonza Holding Ltd.; *Int'l*, pg. 68
LAWSON MARDON HANSE-DRUCK GMBH—See Alusuisse-Lonza Holding Ltd.; *Int'l*, pg. 68
LAWSON MARDON MORIN S.A.—See Alusuisse-Lonza Holding Ltd.; *Int'l*, pg. 68
LAWSON MARDON NEHER AG—See Alusuisse-Lonza Holding Ltd.; *Int'l*, pg. 67
LAWSON MARDON PACKAGING GESELLSCHAFT FUR BETEILIGUNGEN MBH—See Alusuisse-Lonza Holding Ltd.; *Int'l*, pg. 68
LAWSON MARDON PACKAGING INC.—See Alusuisse-Lonza Holding Ltd.; *Int'l*, pg. 68
LAWSON MARDON PACKAGING LTD.—See Alusuisse-Lonza Holding Ltd.; *Int'l*, pg. 69
LAWSON MARDON PACKAGING S.A.—See Alusuisse-Lonza Holding Ltd.; *Int'l*, pg. 69
LAWSON MARDON PACKAGING SERVICES AG—See Alusuisse-Lonza Holding Ltd.; *Int'l*, pg. 67
LAWSON MARDON PACKAGING UK LTD.—See Alusuisse-Lonza Holding Ltd.; *Int'l*, pg. 69
LAWSON MARDON PHARMAFLEX LTD.—See Alusuisse-Lonza Holding Ltd.; *Int'l*, pg. 69
LAWSON MARDON PICOPAC BV—See Alusuisse-Lonza Holding Ltd.; *Int'l*, pg. 69
LAWSON MARDON PICOPAC GMBH—See Alusuisse-Lonza Holding Ltd.; *Int'l*, pg. 69
LAWSON MARDON PRE-PRESS LTD.—See Alusuisse-Lonza Holding Ltd.; *Int'l*, pg. 69
LAWSON MARDON ROTOPACK GMBH—See Alusuisse-Lonza Holding Ltd.; *Int'l*, pg. 69
LAWSON MARDON SELEPRINT SRL—See Alusuisse-Lonza Holding Ltd.; *Int'l*, pg. 69
LAWSON MARDON SINGEN GMBH—See Alusuisse-Lonza Holding Ltd.; *Int'l*, pg. 69
LAWSON MARDON STAR LTD.—See Alusuisse-Lonza Holding Ltd.; *Int'l*, pg. 69
LAWSON MARDON SUNER SA—See Alusuisse-Lonza Holding Ltd.; *Int'l*, pg. 69
LAWSON MARDON SUPERIOR PACKAGING—See Alusuisse-Lonza Holding Ltd.; *Int'l*, pg. 69
LAWSON MARDON SUTTON LTD.—See Alusuisse-Lonza Holding Ltd.; *Int'l*, pg. 69
LAWSON MARDON THYNE LTD—See Alusuisse-Lonza Holding Ltd.; *Int'l*, pg. 69
LAWSON MARDON TRENTESAUX SA—See Alusuisse-Lonza Holding Ltd.; *Int'l*, pg. 69
LAWSON MARGO PACKAGING CORP.—See Alusuisse-Lonza Holding Ltd.; *Int'l*, pg. 69
LAWSON MECHANICAL CONTRACTORS; *U.S. Private*, pg. 654
P. LAWSON TRAVEL, LTD.—See Carlson Companies, Inc.; *U.S. Private*, pg. 212
LAWSON PRODUCTS DE MEXICO, S.A.—See Lawson Products, Inc.; *U.S. Public*, pg. 980
LAWSON PRODUCTS, INC.; *U.S. Public*, pg. 980
LAWSON PRODUCTS, INC.—See Lawson Products, Inc.; *U.S. Public*, pg. 980
LAWSON PRODUCTS INC. (ONTARIO)—See Lawson Products, Inc.; *U.S. Public*, pg. 980
LAWSON PRODUCTS LTD.—See Lawson Products, Inc.; *U.S. Public*, pg. 980
LAWSON SOFTWARE; *U.S. Private*, pg. 654
LAWTER INTERNATIONAL, INC.; *U.S. Public*, pg. 980
LAWTER INTL. APS—See Lawter International, Inc.; *U.S. Public*, pg. 981
LAWTER INTL. B.V.—See Lawter International, Inc.; *U.S. Public*, pg. 981
LAWTER INTL. (CANADA) INC.—See Lawter International, Inc.; *U.S. Public*, pg. 981
LAWTER INTL., GMBH—See Lawter International, Inc.; *U.S. Public*, pg. 981
LAWTER INTL., LTD.—See Lawter International, Inc.; *U.S. Public*, pg. 981
LAWTER INTL. N.V.—See Lawter International, Inc.; *U.S. Public*, pg. 981
LAWTER INTL. PRODUCTS PTE. LTD.—See Lawter International, Inc.; *U.S. Public*, pg. 981
LAWTER INTL. (PROPRIETARY) LTD.—See Lawter International, Inc.; *U.S. Public*, pg. 981
LAWTER INTL. S.A.—See Lawter International, Inc.; *U.S. Public*, pg. 981
LAWTER INTL. SARL—See Lawter International, Inc.; *U.S. Public*, pg. 981
LAWTER INTL. SRL—See Lawter International, Inc.; *U.S. Public*, pg. 981
LAWTONS DRUG STORES LIMITED—See Empire Company Limited; *Int'l*, pg. 454
LAWYERS COOPERATIVE PUBLISHING CO.—See The Thomson Corporation; *U.S. Public*, pg. 1602
LAWYERS TITLE INSURANCE CORPORATION; *U.S. Public*, pg. 981
LAYEZEE BEDS—See Silentnight Holdings Plc; *Int'l*, pg. 1249
LAYMAN CANDY COMPANY, INC.; *U.S. Private*, pg. 655
LAYNE CHRISTENSON CO.; *U.S. Public*, pg. 981
LAYNE-WESTERN CO., INC.—See Layne Christenson Co.; *U.S. Public*, pg. 981
LAY'S FINE FOODS; *U.S. Private*, pg. 655
LAYTON HOMES CORP.—See Skyline Corporation; *U.S. Public*, pg. 1476
LAZARD BROTHERS & CO. LTD.—See Pearson plc; *Int'l*, pg. 1026
LAZARD FRERES & CO.—See Pearson plc; *Int'l*, pg. 1027
LAZARD FRERES ET CIE—See Pearson plc; *Int'l*, pg. 1027
LAZARE KAPLAN BELGIUM N.V.—See Lazare Kaplan Intl., Inc.; *U.S. Public*, pg. 981
LAZARE KAPLAN INTL., INC.; *U.S. Public*, pg. 981
LAZARE KAPLAN (SIERRA LEONE) LTD.—See Lazare Kaplan Intl., Inc.; *U.S. Public*, pg. 981
LAZERDATA—See BTR plc; *Int'l*, pg. 127
LAZY DAYS R V CENTER, INC.; *U.S. Private*, pg. 655
D. LAZZARONI & C. S.P.A.; *Int'l*, pg. 804
LE CARBONE (GREAT BRITAIN) LTD.—See Pechiney S.A.; *Int'l*, pg. 1030
LE CARBONE K.K.—See Pechiney S.A.; *Int'l*, pg. 1030
LE CARBONE LORRAINE—See Pechiney S.A.; *Int'l*, pg. 1028
LE CARBONE-LORRAINE AUSTRALIA PTY. LTD.—See Pechiney S.A.; *Int'l*, pg. 1030
LE CARBONE-LORRAINE INDUSTRIA Y COMERCIO LTD.—See Pechiney S.A.; *Int'l*, pg. 1030
LE CARBONE-LORRAINE (NEDERLAND) B.V.—See Pechiney S.A.; *Int'l*, pg. 1030
LE CARBONE-LORRIANE S.A.I.C.—See Pechiney S.A.; *Int'l*, pg. 1030
LE CARBONE S.A.—See Pechiney S.A.; *Int'l*, pg. 1030
LE CARBONE (SOUTH AFRICA) PTY. LTD.—See Pechiney S.A.; *Int'l*, pg. 1031
LE CHEQUE REPAS—See Sodexho S.A.; *Int'l*, pg. 1274
LE CLOS DE LA PELLERIE—See LVMH Moet Hennessy Louis Vuitton; *Int'l*, pg. 781
LE CONCORDE—See Loews Corporation; *U.S. Public*, pg. 1011
LE GROUPE COMMERCE—See ING Groep N.V.; *Int'l*, pg. 650
LE GROUPE DARTY—See Kingfisher plc; *Int'l*, pg. 734
LE LIVRE DE PARIS—See Lagardere Groupe; *Int'l*, pg. 792
LE MAGNESIUM INDUSTRIEL—See Pechiney S.A.; *Int'l*, pg. 1028
LE NICKEL INC.—See Imetal; *Int'l*, pg. 661
LE NOUVEAU MERIDIONAL—See Lagardere Groupe; *Int'l*, *pg. 792*

LE NOUVEL ELDORADO—See Havas Advertising; Int'l, pg. 600

LE PACTOLE—See GIB Group; Int'l, pg. 534

LE PEEP'S GRILL INC.; U.S. Private, pg. 655

LE PROVENCAL—See Lagardere Groupe; Int'l, pg. 792

LE SHUTTLE HOLIDAYS LIMITED—See The Eurotunnel Group; Int'l, pg. 466

LE SOLEIL S.A.—See Henkel KGaA; Int'l, pg. 613

LE TOURNEAU, INC.—See Rowan Companies, Inc.; pg. 1410

LE VITRAGE DU MIDI—See Saint-Gobain; Int'l, pg. 1172

LEA & PERRINS, INC.—See Danone Group; Int'l, pg. 380

LEA INDUSTRIES—See Ladd Furniture, Inc.; U.S. Public, pg. 974

LEA LUMBER & PLYWOOD LLC; U.S. Private, pg. 655

LEA REFINING COMPANY—See Holly Corporation; U.S. Public, pg. 830

LEACH & GARNER COMPANY; U.S. Private, pg. 655

LEACH INTERNATIONAL; U.S. Private, pg. 655

LEADER INSTRUMENTS CORPORATION; U.S. Private, pg. 655

LEADER NATIONAL INSURANCE COMPANY—See American Financial Group; U.S. Public, pg. 75

LEADTEC SYSTEMS, INC.—See Willcox & Gibbs, Inc.; U.S. Private, pg. 1177

LEAF BALTICS—See Huhtamaki Oy; Int'l, pg. 638

LEAF CHINA—See Huhtamaki Oy; Int'l, pg. 638

LEAF-CHRONICLE CO.—See Gannett Company, Inc.; U.S. Public, pg. 699

LEAF FINLAND—See Huhtamaki Oy; Int'l, pg. 638

LEAF GERMANY—See Huhtamaki Oy; Int'l, pg. 638

LEAF GROUP B.V.—See Huhtamaki Oy; Int'l, pg. 638

LEAF HOLLAND B.V.—See Huhtamaki Oy; Int'l, pg. 638

LEAF IBERIA S.A.—See Huhtamaki Oy; Int'l, pg. 638

LEAF IRELAND LTD.—See Huhtamaki Oy; Int'l, pg. 638

LEAF NORWAY A/S—See Huhtamaki Oy; Int'l, pg. 638

LEAF POLAND SP.Z.O.O—See Huhtamaki Oy; Int'l, pg. 638

LEAF RIVER CORP.—See Georgia-Pacific Corporation; U.S. Public, pg. 736

LEAF RIVER FOREST PRODUCTS, INC.—See Georgia-Pacific Corporation; U.S. Public, pg. 736

LEAF RUSSIA—See Huhtamaki Oy; Int'l, pg. 638

LEAF SWEDEN—See Huhtamaki Oy; Int'l, pg. 638

LEAF SWITZERLAND—See Huhtamaki Oy; Int'l, pg. 638

LEAF UNITED KINGDOM LTD.—See Huhtamaki Oy; Int'l, pg. 638

LEAFCO TRADING GMBH—See Standard Commercial Corporation; U.S. Public, pg. 1502

LEAGUE GENERAL INSURANCE COMPANY—See CUNA Mutual Insurance Society; U.S. Public, pg. 296

THE RICHARD LEAHY CORPORATION—See Lincoln National Corporation; U.S. Public, pg. 997

THE LEAP PARTNERSHIP; U.S. Private, pg. 655

THE LEAP PARTNERSHIP—See The Leap Partnership; U.S. Private, pg. 655

LEAR ASTRONICS CORP.—See The General Electric Company, p.l.c.; Int'l, pg. 544

LEAR CORPORATION; U.S. Public, pg. 981

LEAR CORPORATION—See Lear Corporation; U.S. Public, pg. 982

LEAR CORPORATION ITALIA S.P.A.—See Lear Corporation; U.S. Public, pg. 982

LEAR SIEGLER DIVERSIFIED HOLDINGS CORP.; U.S. Private, pg. 655

THE LEARNING CO., INC.; U.S. Public, pg. 982

LEARNING INTERNATIONAL—See The Times Mirror Company; U.S. Public, pg. 1617

LEARONAL AG—See LeaRonal, Inc.; U.S. Public, pg. 982

LEARONAL FRANCE—See LeaRonal, Inc.; U.S. Public, pg. 982

LEARONAL GMBH—See LeaRonal, Inc.; U.S. Public, pg. 982

LEARONAL, INC.; U.S. Public, pg. 982

LEARONAL JAPAN INC.—See LeaRonal, Inc.; U.S. Public, pg. 982

LEARONAL KOREA—See LeaRonal, Inc.; U.S. Public, pg. 982

LEARONAL S.E. ASIA LTD.—See LeaRonal, Inc.; U.S. Public, pg. 982

LEARONAL (S.E. ASIA) LTD. TAIWAN BRANCH—See LeaRonal, Inc.; U.S. Public, pg. 982

LEARONAL (SEASIA) LTD., REPRESENTATIVE OFFICE—See LeaRonal, Inc.; U.S. Public, pg. 982

LEARONAL SINGAPORE PTE. LTD.—See LeaRonal, Inc.; U.S. Public, pg. 982

LEARONAL UK LTD.—See LeaRonal, Inc.; U.S. Public, pg. 982

LEASE-ELEC, INC.—See Green Mountain Power Corporation; U.S. Public, pg. 761

LEASE INVESTMENT CORPORATION—See LINC Capital Group; U.S. Public, pg. 996

LEASECARD AUTO GROUP—See Trans Leasing International Inc.; U.S. Public, pg. 1628

LEASED HOTELS LIMITED—See Granada Group PLC; Int'l, pg. 556

LEASING ANDINO S.A.—See Orix Corporation; Int'l, pg. 1009

LEASING CATALUNYA, ESTABLECIMIENTO FINANCIERO DE CREDITO S.A.—See Caixa d'Estalvis de Catalunya; Int'l, pg. 250

LEASING SERVICES CORP.—See Novar Electronics; U.S. Private, pg. 808

LEASING SOLUTIONS, INC.; U.S. Public, pg. 982

LEASING SOLUTIONS INTERNATIONAL, LTD.—See Leasing Solutions, Inc.; U.S. Public, pg. 983

LEASING SOLUTIONS RECEIVABLES, INC.—See Leasing Solutions, Inc.; U.S. Public, pg. 983

LEASOBJEKT GMBH—See Commerzbank AG; Int'l, pg. 310

LEATHER CENTER, INC.; U.S. Private, pg. 656

LEATHER WAREHOUSE, INC.; U.S. Private, pg. 656

LEATHERS BEST; U.S. Private, pg. 656

LEAVENWORTH DETENTION CENTER—See Corrections Corporation of America; U.S. Public, pg. 450

LEAVENWORTH PRODUCTION CENTER—See Hallmark Cards, Inc.; U.S. Private, pg. 496

LEAVER MUSHROOMS CO. LIMITED—See ConAgra, Inc.; U.S. Public, pg. 428

THE LEBANON ENTERPRISE—See Landmark Communications, Inc.; U.S. Private, pg. 648

LEBANON EXPRESS—See Lee Enterprises, Incorporated; U.S. Public, pg. 983

LEBANON SEABOARD CORPORATION; U.S. Private, pg. 656

LEBANON VALLEY FARMERS BANK—See Fulton Financial Corp.; U.S. Public, pg. 688

LEBHAR-FRIEDMAN, INC.; U.S. Private, pg. 656

LEBLANC CASE CO.—See G. Leblanc Corporation; U.S. Private, pg. 657

LEBLANC COMMUNICATIONS, INC.; U.S. Private, pg. 656

G. LEBLANC CORPORATION; U.S. Private, pg. 656

G. LEBLANC S.A.—See G. Leblanc Corporation; U.S. Private, pg. 657

LEBUS MANUFACTURING CO.—See FKI Plc; Int'l, pg. 473

LECA DEUTSCHLAND GMBH—See Scancem AB; Int'l, pg. 1200

LECA PORTUGAL ARGILAS EXPANDIDAS S.D.A.—See Scancem AB; Int'l, pg. 1200

LECH-ELEKTRIZITATSWERKE AG; Int'l, pg. 805

LECHERA DEL SUR S.A.—See Nestle S.A.; Int'l, pg. 920

LECHTERS, INC.; U.S. Public, pg. 983

L'ECLAIRAGE TECHNIQUE S.A.—See Emess PLC; Int'l, pg. 453

LECLERC; Int'l, pg. 805

LECO INC.—See Giant Food Inc.; U.S. Public, pg. 741

LECOTEX—See Bertrand Faure; Int'l, pg. 193

LECTORIUM PUBLICATIONS—See Scholastic Corporation; U.S. Public, pg. 1440

LECTRO PRODUCTS, INC.—See BTR plc; Int'l, pg. 126

LECTRODRYER DIV., AJAX MAGNETHERMIC CORP.—See BBA Group plc; Int'l, pg. 113

LEDERLE (JAPAN) LTD.—See American Home Products Corporation; U.S. Public, pg. 81

LEDERWERKE GERHARDUS BETEILIGUNGSGESELLSCHAFT MBH—See Freudenberg & Company; Int'l, pg. 507

LEDGER DISPATCH—See Knight-Ridder, Inc.; U.S. Public, pg. 964

LEDU GMBH—See Luxo A/S; Int'l, pg. 821

LEDU INTERNATIONAL AB—See Luxo A/S; Int'l, pg. 821

LEDU LTD.—See Luxo A/S; Int'l, pg. 821

A.L. LEE CORP.—See Salem Group, Inc.; U.S. Private, pg. 961

ALEX LEE, INC.; U.S. Private, pg. 657

LEE & STEEL INC.—See Dagbladet Boersen A/S; Int'l, pg. 359

LEE COMPANY; U.S. Private, pg. 657

LEE COMPANY S.A.—See Lee Company; U.S. Private, pg. 657

LEE CONSTRUCTION CO.—See National Engineering & Contracting Co.; U.S. Private, pg. 782

LEE CONSUMER PRODUCTS—See Lee Pharmaceuticals; U.S. Public, pg. 984

LEE DENTAL & ORTHODONTICS DIV.—See Lee Pharmaceuticals; U.S. Public, pg. 984

LEE ENTERPRISES, INCORPORATED; U.S. Public, pg. 983

LEE EUROPE N.V.—See VF Corporation; U.S. Public, pg. 1702

LEE GROCERY COMPANY; U.S. Private, pg. 657

HENRY LEE COMPANY; U.S. Private, pg. 657

LEE HYDRAULISCHE MINIATURKOMPONENTEN—See Lee Company; U.S. Private, pg. 657

LEE INDUSTRIES—See Fleet Engineers, Inc.; U.S. Private, pg. 410

LEE-MOORE OIL CO., INC.; U.S. Private, pg. 657

LEE MYLES ASSOCIATES CORPORATION; U.S. Private, pg. 658

LEE NATIONAL CORPORATION; U.S. Private, pg. 658

LEE PHARMACEUTICALS; U.S. Public, pg. 984

LEE PRODUCTS LTD.—See Lee Company; U.S. Private, pg. 657

LEE RANCH COAL COMPANY—See Hanson PLC; Int'l, pg. 594

LEE, ROBINSON & STEINE, INC.—See First American Corporation; U.S. Public, pg. 624

LEE-ROWAN COMPANY—See Newell Co.; U.S. Public, pg. 1177

LEE SPRING COMPANY—See The Unimax Corporation; U.S. Private, pg. 1118

LEE SPRING CO., LTD.—See The Unimax Corporation; U.S. Private, pg. 1118

LEE SRI—See Lee Company; U.S. Private, pg. 657

LEE STEEL STRIP LIMITED—See Carclo Engineering Group plc; Int'l, pg. 268

LEE STEEL WIRE LIMITED—See Carclo Engineering Group plc; Int'l, pg. 268

THOMAS H. LEE CO.; U.S. Private, pg. 658

LEE VALLEY DEVELOPMENTS—See British Aerospace p.l.c.; Int'l, pg. 218

LEECH HOMES LIMITED—See Hanson PLC; Int'l, pg. 593

LEEDS—See National Westminster Bank PLC; Int'l, pg. 910

LEEDS & NORTHRUP LTD.—See General Signal Corporation; U.S. Public, pg. 727

LEEDSHILL-HERKENHOFF, INC.—See Arctic Slope Regional Corporation; U.S. Private, pg. 80

LEEMA CHEMICALS & COSMETICS PVT. LTD.—See Pfizer Inc.; U.S. Public, pg. 1282

LEEMILTS PETROLEUM, INC.—See Getty Petroleum Marketing Inc.; U.S. Public, pg. 741

LEERDAMS VERVOERS CENTRUM BV—See KPN Koninklyke PTT Nederland NV; Int'l, pg. 720

LEES CARPETS—See Burlington Industries, Inc.; U.S. Public, pg. 268

LEE'S FAMOUS RECIPE RESTAURANT—See R.T.M. Winners; U.S. Private, pg. 906

LEESONA—See Kvaerner a.s.a.; Int'l, pg. 774

LEESONA CORP.—See Kvaerner a.s.a.; Int'l, pg. 774

LEFEBURE, AREA NORTH—See De La Rue plc; Int'l, pg. 387

LEFEBURE, AREA WEST—See De La Rue plc; Int'l, pg. 387

LEFEBURE CORP.—See De La Rue plc; Int'l, pg. 387

LEFEBURE ELECTRONIC ASSEMBLY—See De La Rue plc; Int'l, pg. 387

LEFEBURE MANUFACTURING CORPORATION—See De La Rue plc; Int'l, pg. 387

LEFEBURE, SOUTH—See De La Rue plc; Int'l, pg. 387

LEFERSA ALIMENTOS S.A.—See Royal Gist-Brocades N.V.; Int'l, pg. 1143

LEFF & WOLF SPORTSWEAR, INC.—See Carole Wren, Inc.; U.S. Private, pg. 1192

CARLOS R. LEFFLER INC.; U.S. Private, pg. 658

LEFRAK ORGANIZATION INC.; U.S. Private, pg. 658

AL PAUL LEFTON CO., INC.; U.S. Private, pg. 658

LEGACY AUDIO INC.—See Allen Organ Company; U.S. Public, pg. 45

LEGACY MARKETING GROUP; U.S. Private, pg. 658

LEGACY STORAGE SYSTEMS CORP.; Int'l, pg. 805

LEGACY STORAGE SYSTEMS CORP.—See Legacy Storage Systems Corp.; Int'l, pg. 805

LEGAL COMMUNICATIONS CORPORATION—See The Walt Disney Company; U.S. Public, pg. 513

LEGAL & GENERAL AMERICA, INC.—See Legal & General Group PLC; Int'l, pg. 805

LEGAL & GENERAL ASSURANCE HOLDINGS (AUSTRALIA) LIMITED—See Legal & General Group PLC; Int'l, pg. 805

LEGAL & GENERAL ASSURANCE SOCIETY LIMITED—See Legal & General Group PLC; Int'l, pg. 805

LEGAL & GENERAL FINANCE PLC—See Legal & General Group PLC; Int'l, pg. 805

LEGAL & GENERAL FINANCIAL SERVICES LIMITED—See Legal & General Group PLC; Int'l, pg. 805

LEGAL & GENERAL GROUP PLC; Int'l, pg. 805

LEGAL & GENERAL HOLDINGS (FRANCE) S.A.—See Legal & General Group PLC; Int'l, pg. 805

LEGAL & GENERAL INVESTMENT MANAGEMENT (HOLDINGS) LIMITED—See Legal & General Group PLC; Int'l, pg. 805

LEGAL & GENERAL MORTGAGE SERVICES LIMITED—See Legal & General Group PLC; Int'l, pg. 805

LEGATO SYSTEMS, INC.; U.S. Public, pg. 984

LEGEND CAPITAL GROUP, L.P.—See Castle-Harlan, Inc.; U.S. Private, pg. 219

A.C. LEGG PACKING COMPANY, INC.; U.S. Private, pg. 658

LEGG MASON CAPITAL MANAGEMENT INC.—See Legg Mason, Inc.; U.S. Public, pg. 985

LEGG MASON, INC.; U.S. Public, pg. 984

LEGG MASON WOOD WALKER, INCORPORATED—See Legg Mason, Inc.; U.S. Public, pg. 985

LEGGETT & PLATT FOREIGN SALES CORPORATION—See Leggett & Platt, Incorporated; U.S. Public, pg. 986

LEGGETT & PLATT, INCORPORATED; U.S. Public, pg. 985

LEGGETT AND PLATT INTERNATIONAL CORPORATION—See Leggett & Platt, Incorporated; U.S. Public, pg. 986

LEGGETT & PLATT INTERNATIONAL DEVELOPMENT CO.—See Leggett & Platt, Incorporated; U.S. Public, pg. 986

LEGGETT WIRE COMPANY—See Leggett & Platt, Incorporated; U.S. Public, pg. 986

L'EGGS PRODUCTS, INC.—See Sara Lee Corporation; U.S. Public, pg. 1434

LEGI-SLATE INC.—See The Washington Post Company; U.S. Public, pg. 1743

LEGI-TECH—See McClatchy Newspapers Inc.; U.S. Public, pg. 1066

LEGION AG—See Lagardere Groupe; Int'l, pg. 795

LEGION & RUSCONI SRL—See Lagardere Groupe; Int'l, pg. 795

LEGION INTERNATIONAL SA—See Lagardere Groupe; Int'l, pg. 792

LEGION LTD.—See Lagardere Groupe; Int'l, pg. 795

LEGION PAPER CORPORATION—See Gould Paper Corporation; U.S. Private, pg. 467

LEGION TELECALL PTY LTD.—See Lagardere Groupe; Int'l, pg. 796

LEGION TELEKOMMUNIKATION GMBH—See Lagardere Groupe; Int'l, pg. 796

LEGION UK LTD.—See Lagardere Groupe; Int'l, pg. 796

LEGO AG—See Lego System A/S; Int'l, pg. 805

LEGO OVERSEAS A/S—See Lego System A/S; Int'l, pg. 805

LEGO S.P.A.—See Lego System A/S; Int'l, pg. 805

LEGO SYSTEM A/S; Int'l, pg. 805

LEGO SYSTEMS, INC.—See Lego System A/S; Int'l, pg. 805

S.A. LEGRAIN—See Cockerill Sambre; Int'l, pg. 301

LEGRAND; Int'l, pg. 805

LEGWEAR HOLDINGS, INC.—See Grupo Synkro, S.A. de C.V.; Int'l, pg. 576

LEHIGH ASPHALT, PAVING & CONSTRUCTION—See Barletta Materials & Construction; U.S. Private, pg. 116

LEHIGH PORTLAND CEMENT COMPANY—See Heidelberger Zement A.G.; Int'l, pg. 605

LEHIGH PRESS CADILLAC—See The Lehigh Press, Inc.; U.S. Private, pg. 659

LEHIGH PRESS-CARROLLTON—See The Lehigh Press, Inc.; U.S. Private, pg. 659

LEHIGH PRESS COLORTRONICS—See The Lehigh Press, Inc.; U.S. Private, pg. 659

THE LEHIGH PRESS, INC.; U.S. Private, pg. 658

LEHIGH PRESS LITHOGRAPHERS—See The Lehigh Press, Inc.; U.S. Private, pg. 659

LEHIGH PRESS-PUERTO RICO—See The Lehigh Press, Inc.; U.S. Private, pg. 659

LEHIGH SAFETY SHOE CO.—See U.S. Industries, Inc.; U.S. Public, pg. 1684
LEHIGH SECURITIES CORPORATION—See Summit Bancorp; U.S. Public, pg. 1528
LEHIGH UTILITIES INC.—See Minnesota Power; U.S. Public, pg. 1116
GEO. H. LEHLEITNER & CO., INC.; U.S. Private, pg. 659
LEHMAN ASSOCIATES, INC.—See United States Realty & Investment Co.; U.S. Private, pg. 1125
LEHMAN BROTHERS—See Lehman Brothers Holdings Inc.; U.S. Public, pg. 987
LEHMAN BROTHERS HOLDINGS INC.; U.S. Public, pg. 987
LEHMAN BROTHERS, INC.—See Lehman Brothers Holdings Inc.; U.S. Public, pg. 987
LEHMAN BROTHERS INTERNATIONAL LIMITED—See Lehman Brothers Holdings Inc.; U.S. Public, pg. 987
LEHMAN COMMERCIAL PAPER INC.—See Lehman Brothers Holdings Inc.; U.S. Public, pg. 987
LEHNKERING MONTAN TRANSPORT AG—See Metallgesellschaft AG; Int'l, pg. 862
LEHNKERING MONTAN TRANSPORT AG—See Preussag AG; Int'l, pg. 1069
LEHRER MCGOVERN BOVIS INC.—See The Peninsular and Oriental Steam Navigation Company; Int'l, pg. 1035
LEIBINGER S.A.R.L.—See Pfizer Inc.; U.S. Public, pg. 1282
AS LEIBUR—See Cultor Ltd.; Int'l, pg. 349
LEICA A.G.; Int'l, pg. 806
LEICA—See Leica A.G.; Int'l, pg. 806
LEIGHTON ASIA—See Hochtief AG; Int'l, pg. 624
LEIGHTON HOLDINGS LIMITED—See Hochtief AG; Int'l, pg. 624
JACOB LEINENKUGEL BREWING CO.—See Philip Morris Companies Inc.; U.S. Public, pg. 1289
LEINER-DAVIS INTERNATIONAL LIMITED—See Goodman Fielder Limited; Int'l, pg. 555
LEINER HEALTH PRODUCTS, INC.; U.S. Private, pg. 659
LEIRAS OY—See Huhtamaki Oy; Int'l, pg. 639
LEISEGANG MEDICAL, INC.—See Galileo Corp.; U.S. Public, pg. 698
LEISI AG NAHRUNGSMITTELFABRIK—See Nestle S.A.; Int'l, pg. 916
LEISURE ARTS, INC.—See Time Warner Inc.; U.S. Public, pg. 1613
LEISURE COLONY MANAGEMENT CORP.—See Lennar Corporation; U.S. Public, pg. 988
LEISURE LIFE, INC.—See Ajay Sports Inc.; U.S. Public, pg. 34
LEISURE RESORTS MANAGEMENT—See Barratt Developments Plc; Int'l, pg. 168
LEISURE SPORT LIMITED—See RMC Group p.l.c.; Int'l, pg. 1080
LEISURE TECHNOLOGY, INC.; U.S. Private, pg. 659
LEISURE TECHNOLOGY, NEW JERSEY DIV.—See Leisure Technology, Inc.; U.S. Private, pg. 659
LEISURE TIME INDUSTRIES—See Laporte plc; Int'l, pg. 802
LEITCHFIELD DIV.—See Emerson Electric Co.; U.S. Public, pg. 575
THE LEITH AGENCY—See Warwick Baker O'Neill; U.S. Private, pg. 1152
LEITZ MESSTECHNIK GMBH—See Brown & Sharpe Manufacturing Company; U.S. Public, pg. 260
LEKTURAMA, GOLDINA—See Vendex International N.V.; Int'l, pg. 1463
LEMKEN TRI-AG LIMITED—See Thrige-Titan Group; Int'l, pg. 1387
LEMO GMBH—See Lemo SA; Int'l, pg. 806
LEMO JAPAN—See Lemo SA; Int'l, pg. 806
LEMO SA; Int'l, pg. 806
LEMO U.K.—See Lemo SA; Int'l, pg. 806
LEMO U.S.A. INC.—See Lemo SA; Int'l, pg. 806
LEMONS WASTE SYSTEMS INC.—See Allied Waste Industries; U.S. Public, pg. 49
THE LEMOORE ADVANCE—See Pulitzer Publishing Company; U.S. Public, pg. 1343
LEMUSIMUN, S.A. DE C.V./Y&R—See Young & Rubicam Inc.; U.S. Private, pg. 1200
LEN S.A.—See Henkel KGaA; Int'l, pg. 613
LENAPE FORGE, INC.; U.S. Private, pg. 659
LENC-SMITH INC.—See WMS Industries Inc.; U.S. Public, pg. 1727
LEND LEASE CORPORATION LIMITED; Int'l, pg. 806
LENDER'S BAGEL BAKERY—See Philip Morris Companies Inc.; U.S. Public, pg. 1288
LENDER'S SINGLE INTEREST—See RLI Corp.; U.S. Public, pg. 1356
LENNAR COMMERCIAL PROPERTIES, INC.—See Lennar Corporation; U.S. Public, pg. 988
LENNAR CORPORATION; U.S. Public, pg. 987
LENNAR FINANCIAL SERVICES, INC.—See Lennar Corporation; U.S. Public, pg. 988
LENNAR HOMES OF ARIZONA, INC.—See Lennar Corporation; U.S. Public, pg. 988
LENNAR HOMES INC.—See Lennar Corporation; U.S. Public, pg. 988
LENNAR MANAGEMENT CORP.—See Lennar Corporation; U.S. Public, pg. 988
LENNAR REALTY, INC.—See Lennar Corporation; U.S. Public, pg. 988
LENNOX GLOBAL LTD.—See Lennox International Inc.; U.S. Private, pg. 659
LENNOX INDUSTRIES (CANADA) LTD.—See Lennox International Inc.; U.S. Private, pg. 660
LENNOX INDUSTRIES INC.—See Lennox International Inc.; U.S. Private, pg. 659
LENNOX INTERNATIONAL INC.; U.S. Private, pg. 659
LENOTRE—See Accor S.A.; Int'l, pg. 20
LENOX BRANDS—See Brown-Forman Corporation; U.S. Public, pg. 261
LENOX COLLECTIONS—See Brown-Forman Corporation; U.S. Public, pg. 261

LENOX, INCORPORATED—See Brown-Forman Corporation; U.S. Public, pg. 261
LENOX PRODUCTS GROUP—See Brown-Forman Corporation; U.S. Public, pg. 261
LENOX RETAIL—See Brown-Forman Corporation; U.S. Public, pg. 261
LENSCLEAN, INC.—See H.L. Bouton Company Inc.; U.S. Private, pg. 162
LENSCRAFTERS—See Luxottica Group S.p.A.; Int'l, pg. 822
LENTJES AG—See Metallgesellschaft AG; Int'l, pg. 861
LENTON FOODS—See Northern Foods plc; Int'l, pg. 968
LEO SATELLITE SERVICES, INC.—See Motorola, Inc.; U.S. Public, pg. 1137
LEOBERSDORFER MASCHINENFABUK AG—See Deutsche Babcock AG; Int'l, pg. 399
LEON-FERENBACH INC.; U.S. Private, pg. 660
LEON PLASTICS, INC.—See U.S. Industries, Inc.; U.S. Public, pg. 1684
LEONARD & HARRAL PACKING CO.; U.S. Private, pg. 660
CHARLES LEONARD, INC.; U.S. Private, pg. 660
HAROLD LEONARD & COMPANY, INC.; U.S. Private, pg. 660
LEONARD LIFTS LTD.—See Kone Corporation; Int'l, pg. 748
LEONARD WHOLESALE, INC.; U.S. Private, pg. 660
LEONBERGER BAUSPARKASSE AG—See Commerzbank AG; Int'l, pg. 310
LEONBERGER IMMOBILIEN GMBH—See Commerzbank AG; Int'l, pg. 310
LEONE FOOD SERVICE CORP.—See Clayton, Dubilier & Rice, Inc; U.S. Private, pg. 244
LEONG JIN CORPORATION PTE. LTD.—See Fried. Krupp AG; Int'l, pg. 516
LEOPACK B.V.—See Royal Packaging Industries Van Leer B.V.; Int'l, pg. 1146
LEOREITSMA B.V.—See Royal Packaging Industries Van Leer B.V.; Int'l, pg. 1146
LEOTECH B.V.—See Royal Packaging Industries Van Leer B.V.; Int'l, pg. 1146
LEPAGE BAKERY, INC.; U.S. Private, pg. 660
LEPAGE'S, INC.—See The Jordan Company; U.S. Private, pg. 598
LEPAGE'S LIMITED—See Henkel KGaA; Int'l, pg. 613
LEPEL CORPORATION—See Inductotherm Industries, Inc.; U.S. Private, pg. 560
LEPRINO FOODS; U.S. Private, pg. 660
LEQUEUX S.A.—See Getinge Industrier AB; Int'l, pg. 552
L'EQUITE S.A.—See Assicurazioni Generali S.p.A.; Int'l, pg. 91
LERNER NEW YORK—See The Limited, Inc.; U.S. Public, pg. 995
LES BOIS DE LA BALTIQUE SA—See Mo och Domsjo AB; Int'l, pg. 886
LES BOIS DE LA BALTIQUE SA (ROCHEFORT)—See Mo och Domsjo AB; Int'l, pg. 886
LES CABLES DE LYON—See Alcatel Alsthom Compagnie Generale D'Electricite; Int'l, pg. 56
LES CIMENTS DE L'ORIENTAL (CIOR)—See Holderbank Financiere Glaris Ltd.; Int'l, pg. 620
LES ECHOS SA—See Pearson plc; Int'l, pg. 1027
LES EDITIONS CEC INC.—See Lagardere Groupe; Int'l, pg. 794
LES EDITIONS CEC INC.—See Quebecor Inc.; Int'l, pg. 1078
LES EDITIONS DU FEU VERT—See G.T.C. Transcontinental Group Ltd.; Int'l, pg. 539
LES EDITIONS TEXTUEL—See BDDP Group; Int'l, pg. 116
LES EDITIONS TRANSCONTINENTAL INC.—See G.T.C. Transcontinental Group Ltd.; Int'l, pg. 539
LES EDITIONS TRANSCRIPT PUBLISHING—See G.T.C. Transcontinental Group Ltd.; Int'l, pg. 539
LES GRAINES CAILLARD S.A.—See Novartis AG; Int'l, pg. 983
LES GRANDS HOTELS ASSOCIES S.A.—See Granada Group PLC; Int'l, pg. 556
LES HEBDOS TRANSCONTINENTAL—See G.T.C. Transcontinental Group Ltd.; Int'l, pg. 539
LES JARDINS DE BENOUVILLE—See LVMH Moet Hennessy Louis Vuitton; Int'l, pg. 781
LES JARDINS DE FLINS—See LVMH Moet Hennessy Louis Vuitton; Int'l, pg. 781
LES LABORATOIRES BEECHAM S.A.—See SmithKline Beecham plc; Int'l, pg. 1455
LES MESSAGERIES DE LA MAURICIE—See G.T.C. Transcontinental Group Ltd.; Int'l, pg. 539
LES MESSAGERIES DE PRESSE INTERNATIONALE—See Lagardere Groupe; Int'l, pg. 796
LES MESSAGERIES PUBLI-NORD—See G.T.C. Transcontinental Group Ltd.; Int'l, pg. 539
LES MESSAGERIES PUBLI-TECH—See G.T.C. Transcontinental Group Ltd.; Int'l, pg. 539
LES MINES CASA BERARDI—See TVX Gold Inc.; Int'l, pg. 1345
LES PAPIERS GRAPHIQUES ROLLAND—See The Cascades Group; Int'l, pg. 274
LES PAYS BAS DE 1845 SA—See ING Groep N.V.; Int'l, pg. 650
LES PRESSES DE LA CITE—See Alcatel Alsthom Compagnie Generale D'Electricite; Int'l, pg. 53
LES PRESSES DE LA CITE—See C.E.P. Communication Group; Int'l, pg. 240
LES PRODUITS DUVERNAY LTEE—See Saint-Gobain; Int'l, pg. 1177
LES PRODUITS SILICEUX AND CONSTRUCTIONS THERMIQUES EUROPEENNES—See Hepworth Plc; Int'l, pg. 615
LES PUBLICATIONS CCH/FM LTEE—See Wolters Kluwer N.V.; Int'l, pg. 1513
LES PUBLICATIONS MDN INC.—See Quebecor Inc.; Int'l, pg. 1076
LES TECHNIQUES D'INTERIEUR—See Saint-Gobain; Int'l, pg. 1176

LES VINS ANDRES DU QUEBEC LTEE.—See Andres Wines Ltd.; Int'l, pg. 76
LESCHUPLAST KUNSTSTOFF-FABRIK GMBH—See Dyckerhoff AG; Int'l, pg. 422
LESCO, INC.; U.S. Public, pg. 989
LESHNER MILLS. INC.; U.S. Private, pg. 660
LESLIE BUILDING PRODUCTS, INC.; U.S. Public, pg. 989
LESLIE CONTROLS, INC.—See Watts Industries, Inc.; U.S. Public, pg. 1746
LESLIE COUNTY TELEPHONE COMPANY, INC.—See Telephone and Data Systems, Inc.; U.S. Public, pg. 1571
THE LESLIE FAY COMPANIES, INC.; U.S. Public, pg. 989
LESLIE FAY DRESS—See The Leslie Fay Companies, Inc.; U.S. Public, pg. 989
LESLIE FAY SPORTSWEAR—See The Leslie Fay Companies, Inc.; U.S. Public, pg. 989
LESLIE FAY II—See The Leslie Fay Companies, Inc.; U.S. Public, pg. 989
LESLIE - LOCKE, INC.—See Leslie Building Products, Inc.; U.S. Public, pg. 989
LESLIE METAL ARTS CO., INC.; U.S. Private, pg. 660
LESLIE-MICHIGAN—See International Paper Company; U.S. Public, pg. 903
LESLIE PAPER—See International Paper Company; U.S. Public, pg. 903
LESLIE PLACE—See Paragon Health Network, Inc.; U.S. Public, pg. 1257
LESON CHEVROLET COMPANY, INC.; U.S. Private, pg. 660
L'ESPRIT D'EQUIPE—See Compagnie des Machines Bull; Int'l, pg. 316
LESTER BUILDINGS DIVISION—See Butler Manufacturing Company; U.S. Public, pg. 271
J.L. LESTER & SON, INC.; U.S. Private, pg. 660
KENNETH O. LESTER, INC.—See Performance Food Group Company; U.S. Public, pg. 1278
LETICA CORPORATION; U.S. Private, pg. 661
L'ETOILE COMMERCIALE—See Corporacion MAPFRE, Compania Internacional de Reaseguros, S.A.; Int'l, pg. 335
LETRASET AG—See Esselte AB; Int'l, pg. 461
LETRASET AS—See Esselte AB; Int'l, pg. 461
LETRASET ASHFORD—See Esselte AB; Int'l, pg. 461
LETRASET AUSTRALIA PTY. LTD.—See Esselte AB; Int'l, pg. 461
SA LETRASET BELGIUM NV—See Esselte AB; Int'l, pg. 461
LETRASET CANADA LTD.—See Esselte AB; Int'l, pg. 461
LETRASET DEUTSCHLAND GMBH—See Esselte AB; Int'l, pg. 461
LETRASET EXPORT—See Esselte AB; Int'l, pg. 461
LETRASET ITALIA SRL—See Esselte AB; Int'l, pg. 462
LETRASET JAPAN LTD.—See Esselte AB; Int'l, pg. 462
LETRASET NEDERLAND BV—See Esselte AB; Int'l, pg. 462
LETRASET NEW ZEALAND LTD.—See Esselte AB; Int'l, pg. 462
LETRASET NIELSEN & BAINBRIDGE—See Esselte AB; Int'l, pg. 460
LETRASET UK—See Esselte AB; Int'l, pg. 462
LETTS INDUSTRIES, INC.; U.S. Private, pg. 661
LETTS INDUSTRIES, PIONEER DIV.—See Letts Industries, Inc.; U.S. Private, pg. 661
LETTUCE ENTERTAIN YOU ENTERPRISES, INC.; U.S. Private, pg. 661
LEU & GYGAX AG—See DSM N.V.; Int'l, pg. 356
LEUCADIA FINANCIAL CORPORATION—See Leucadia National Corporation; U.S. Public, pg. 990
LEUCADIA INC. MANUFACTURING DIVISION—See Leucadia National Corporation; U.S. Public, pg. 990
LEUCADIA NATIONAL CORPORATION; U.S. Public, pg. 989
LEUMI LE-ISRAEL (LATIN AMERICA)—See Bank Leumi le-Israel B.M.; Int'l, pg. 150
LEUPOLD & STEVENS, INC.; U.S. Private, pg. 662
LEVAILLANT SA—See Koninklijke BolsWessanen nv; Int'l, pg. 753
LEVCON, INC.—See Manufacturers Consolidation Service, Inc.; U.S. Private, pg. 700
LEVEL EXPORT SALES CORP.; U.S. Private, pg. 662
LEVEL FIVE RESEARCH INC.—See Information Builders; U.S. Private, pg. 561
LEVENSON & HILL, INC.; U.S. Private, pg. 662
NV LEVENSVERZEKERING MIJ. EERSTE HOLLANDSCHE—See Assicurazioni Generali S.p.A.; Int'l, pg. 91
LEVER—See Unilever Plc; Int'l, pg. 1435
LEVER & KITCHEN PTY. LTD.—See Unilever Plc; Int'l, pg. 1437
LEVER BROTHERS BANGLADESH LTD.—See Unilever Plc; Int'l, pg. 1437
LEVER BROTHERS (CEYLON) LTD.—See Unilever Plc; Int'l, pg. 1437
LEVER BROTHERS CO.—See Unilever Plc; Int'l, pg. 1435
LEVER BROTHERS HOUSEHOLD PRODUCTS DIV.—See Unilever Plc; Int'l, pg. 1436
LEVER BROTHERS INDUSTRIAL DIVISION—See Unilever Plc; Int'l, pg. 1436
LEVER BROTHERS (IRELAND) LTD.—See Unilever Plc; Int'l, pg. 1437
LEVER BROTHERS LTD.—See Unilever Plc; Int'l, pg. 1434
LEVER BROTHERS (MALAWI) LTD.—See Unilever Plc; Int'l, pg. 1437
LEVER BROTHERS (MALAYSIA) SDN. BHD.—See Unilever Plc; Int'l, pg. 1437
LEVER BROTHERS (NEW ZEALAND) LTD.—See Unilever Plc; Int'l, pg. 1437
LEVER BROTHERS PAKISTAN LTD.—See Unilever Plc; Int'l, pg. 1437
LEVER BROTHERS (PRIVATE) LTD.—See Unilever Plc; Int'l, pg. 1437
LEVER BROTHERS (PTY.) LTD.—See Unilever Plc; Int'l, pg. 1437

LEVER BROTHERS SINGAPORE SDN. BHD.—See Unilever Plc; *Int'l*, pg. 1437
LEVER BROTHERS (THAILAND) LTD.—See Unilever Plc; *Int'l*, pg. 1437
LEVER BROTHERS WEST INDIES LTD.—See Unilever Plc; *Int'l*, pg. 1437
LEVER CHILE S.A.—See Unilever Plc; *Int'l*, pg. 1437
LEVER IBERICA S.A.—See Unilever Plc; *Int'l*, pg. 1437
LEVER INDUSTRIAL B.V.—See Unilever Plc; *Int'l*, pg. 1437
LEVER N.V.—See Unilever Plc; *Int'l*, pg. 1438
LEVER POND'S LIMITED—See Unilever Plc; *Int'l*, pg. 1438
LEVER S.A.—See Unilever Plc; *Int'l*, pg. 1438
LEVER SOLOMONS LTD.—See Unilever Plc; *Int'l*, pg. 1438
LEVER SUNLIGHT LTD.—See Unilever Plc; *Int'l*, pg. 1438
LEVER SUNLIGHT G.M.B.H.—See Unilever Plc; *Int'l*, pg. 1438
LEVER Y ASOCIADOS SACIF—See Unilever Plc; *Int'l*, pg. 1438
LEVERINDUS AB—See Unilever Plc; *Int'l*, pg. 1438
OY LEVERINDUS AB—See Unilever Plc; *Int'l*, pg. 1438
LEVERTON GROUP LTD.—See Unilever Plc; *Int'l*, pg. 1434
LEVESQUE, BEAUBIEN AND COMPANY INC.—See National Bank of Canada; *Int'l*, pg. 907
J. PAUL LEVESQUE & SONS INC—See EdperBrascan Corporation; *Int'l*, pg. 434
LEVI STRAUSS & CO.; *U.S. Private*, pg. 662
LEVIMEX DE BAJA CALIFORNIA S.A. DE C.V.—See Leviton Mfg. Co., Inc.; *U.S. Private*, pg. 663
DAVID LEVIN CO.—See Sturgis Iron & Metal Company, Inc.; *U.S. Private*, pg. 1048
LARRY LEVINE—See S. Rothchild & Co., Inc.; *U.S. Private*, pg. 947
LEVI'S BRAND—See Levi Strauss & Co.; *U.S. Private*, pg. 663
LEVIS B.V.—See Akzo Nobel N.V.; *Int'l*, pg. 42
S.A. LEVIS—See Akzo Nobel N.V.; *Int'l*, pg. 43
LEVIS SAPT. SA—See Akzo Nobel N.V.; *Int'l*, pg. 43
ERIK LEVISON A/S—See The East Asiatic Company Ltd. A/S; *Int'l*, pg. 431
LEVITON—See Leviton Mfg. Co., Inc.; *U.S. Private*, pg. 663
LEVITON MFG. CO., INC.; *U.S. Private*, pg. 663
LEVITON TELECOM—See Leviton Mfg. Co., Inc.; *U.S. Private*, pg. 663
LEVITT CORPORATION—See Starrett HRH; *U.S. Private*, pg. 1035
LEVITZ FURNITURE CORPORATION—See Levitz Furniture Incorporated; *U.S. Public*, pg. 990
LEVITZ FURNITURE INCORPORATED; *U.S. Public*, pg. 990
LEVLAD, INC.; *U.S. Private*, pg. 663
LEVMARK CAPITAL CORPORATION; *U.S. Private*, pg. 663
LEVOLOR—See Newell Co.; *U.S. Public*, pg. 1177
LEVOLOR HOME FASHIONS—See Newell Co.; *U.S. Public*, pg. 1177
LEVONIAN BROTHERS INC.; *U.S. Private*, pg. 663
LEVTECH, INC.—See Orthofix International N.V.; *Int'l*, pg. 1011
A. LEVY & J. ZENTNER CO.; *U.S. Private*, pg. 663
THE CHAS. LEVY COMPANY; *U.S. Private*, pg. 664
CHARLES LEVY TRANSPORTATION CO.—See The Chas. Levy Company; *U.S. Private*, pg. 664
EDWARD C. LEVY CO.; *U.S. Private*, pg. 664
LEVY HOME ENTERTAINMENT—See The Chas. Levy Company; *U.S. Private*, pg. 664
JACK LEVY ASSOCIATES; *U.S. Private*, pg. 664
JACOB LEVY & BROS., INC.; *U.S. Private*, pg. 664
NORMAN LEVY ASSOCIATES, INC.; *U.S. Private*, pg. 664
NORMAN LEVY ASSOCIATES OVERSEAS—See Norman Levy Associates, Inc.; *U.S. Private*, pg. 664
THE LEVY ORGANIZATION; *U.S. Private*, pg. 664
LEVY REAL ESTATE PARTNERS—See The Levy Organization; *U.S. Private*, pg. 664
LEVY RESTAURANTS—See The Levy Organization; *U.S. Private*, pg. 664
LEVY SECURITY CORP.; *U.S. Private*, pg. 664
LEVY UNITED NEWS—See The Chas. Levy Company; *U.S. Private*, pg. 664
LEWIS & NORWOOD, GENERAL AGENTS, INC.—See Cigna Corp.; *U.S. Public*, pg. 366
LEWIS & SAUNDERS INC—See TI Group plc; *Int'l*, pg. 1337
LEWIS & TOWERS LIMITED—See TT Group PLC; *Int'l*, pg. 1344
LEWIS BROS. BAKERIES—See Lewis Brothers Bakeries, Inc.; *U.S. Private*, pg. 665
LEWIS BROS. BAKERIES (MO)—See Lewis Brothers Bakeries, Inc.; *U.S. Private*, pg. 665
LEWIS BROS. BAKERIES (TN)—See Lewis Brothers Bakeries, Inc.; *U.S. Private*, pg. 665
LEWIS BROTHERS BAKERIES, INC.; *U.S. Private*, pg. 665
LEWIS BUILDING CO., INC.—See Lewis Homes Management Corp.; *U.S. Private*, pg. 665
CHARLES S. LEWIS & CO., INC.—See Weir Group PLC; *Int'l*, pg. 1489
LEWIS CONSTRUCTION CO., INC.—See Lewis Homes Management Corp.; *U.S. Private*, pg. 665
LEWIS DEVELOPMENT CO.—See Lewis Homes Management Corp.; *U.S. Private*, pg. 665
LEWIS DRUG DISTRIBUTION CENTER—See Lewis Drug, Inc.; *U.S. Private*, pg. 665
LEWIS DRUG EASTGATE—See Lewis Drug, Inc.; *U.S. Private*, pg. 665
LEWIS DRUG HURON—See Lewis Drug, Inc.; *U.S. Private*, pg. 665
LEWIS DRUG, INC.; *U.S. Private*, pg. 665
LEWIS DRUG MANKATO—See Lewis Drug, Inc.; *U.S. Private*, pg. 665
LEWIS DRUG SOUTHEAST—See Lewis Drug, Inc.; *U.S. Private*, pg. 665
LEWIS DRUG SOUTHGATE—See Lewis Drug, Inc.; *U.S. Private*, pg. 665
LEWIS DRUG WESTGATE—See Lewis Drug, Inc.; *U.S. Private*, pg. 665

LEWIS DRUGS SOUTHWEST—See Lewis Drug, Inc.; *U.S. Private*, pg. 665
LEWIS ENGINEERING COMPANY—See Coltec Holdings Inc; *U.S. Public*, pg. 402
LEWIS GACE BOZELL HEALTHCARE WORLDWIDE—See True North Diversified Companies; *U.S. Public*, pg. 1642
LEWIS HOMES MANAGEMENT CORP.; *U.S. Private*, pg. 665
LEWIS HOMES OF CALIFORNIA—See Lewis Homes Management Corp.; *U.S. Private*, pg. 665
LEWIS HOMES OF NEVADA—See Lewis Homes Management Corp.; *U.S. Private*, pg. 665
LEWIS PROPERTIES—See Lewis Homes Management Corp.; *U.S. Private*, pg. 665
RICHARD LEWIS PAPER CORPORATION—See Gould Paper Corporation; *U.S. Private*, pg. 467
LEWIS VINCENNES, INC.—See Lewis Brothers Bakeries, Inc.; *U.S. Private*, pg. 665
LEWISON COMPANY LTD.—See Enso Oyj; *Int'l*, pg. 458
LEWMAR MARINE AB—See Vector Industries, Ltd.; *Int'l*, pg. 1462
LEWMAR MARINE HOLDINGS LTD.—See Vector Industries, Ltd.; *Int'l*, pg. 1461
LEWMAR MARINE MARKETING—See Vector Industries, Ltd.; *Int'l*, pg. 1461
LEWMAR MARINE S.A.R.L.—See Vector Industries, Ltd.; *Int'l*, pg. 1462
LEWMAR MID-EUROPE BV—See Vector Industries, Ltd.; *Int'l*, pg. 1462
LEWTAN INDUSTRIES CORP.; *U.S. Private*, pg. 666
LEX AUTOCENTRES—See Lex Service PLC; *Int'l*, pg. 807
LEX AUTOSALES—See Lex Service PLC; *Int'l*, pg. 807
LEX BODYCENTRES—See Lex Service PLC; *Int'l*, pg. 807
LEX COMMERCIALS—See Lex Service PLC; *Int'l*, pg. 807
LEX ELECTRONICS—See Arrow Electronics, Inc.; *U.S. Public*, pg. 134
LEX GROUP—See Alcatel Alsthom Compagnie Generale D'Electricite; *Int'l*, pg. 53
LEX HARVEY—See Lex Service PLC; *Int'l*, pg. 807
LEX KOMATSU FORKLIFT (UK)—See Lex Service PLC; *Int'l*, pg. 807
LEX MANUTENTION—See Lex Service PLC; *Int'l*, pg. 807
LEX RETAIL GROUP—See Lex Service PLC; *Int'l*, pg. 807
LEX SERVICE PLC; *Int'l*, pg. 806
LEX TRANSFLEET—See Lex Service PLC; *Int'l*, pg. 807
LEX VEHICLE LEASING—See Lex Service PLC; *Int'l*, pg. 807
LEX VEHICLE LEASING LIMITED—See National Westminster Bank PLC; *Int'l*, pg. 910
LEXALITE INTERNATIONAL CORPORATION—See Summa Industries; *U.S. Public*, pg. 1527
LEXAM EXPLORATIONS INC—See CSA Management Inc.; *Int'l*, pg. 243
LEXCO PETROLEUM—See Banc One Corporation; *U.S. Public*, pg. 174
LEXFORD RESIDENTIAL TRUST; *U.S. Public*, pg. 991
LEXICON PUBLICATIONS, INC.—See Lagardere Groupe; *Int'l*, pg. 794
LEXINGTON CO-OP OIL CO.; *U.S. Private*, pg. 666
LEXINGTON DIVISION—See Champion Industries; *U.S. Public*, pg. 333
LEXINGTON FURNITURE INDUSTRIES—See Furnishings International, Inc.; *U.S. Private*, pg. 432
LEXINGTON INSURANCE CO.—See American International Group, Inc.; *U.S. Public*, pg. 84
LEXINGTON PLANT—See Cooper Industries, Inc.; *U.S. Public*, pg. 444
LEXINGTON PRECISION CORPORATION; *U.S. Public*, pg. 991
LEXINGTON PRIMARY CARE, INC.—See Integrated Health Services, Inc.; *U.S. Public*, pg. 885
LEXIS DOCUMENT SERVICES—See Reed Elsevier plc; *Int'l*, pg. 1096
LEXIS LAW PUBLISHING—See Reed Elsevier plc; *Int'l*, pg. 1096
LEXIS-NEXIS—See Reed Elsevier plc; *Int'l*, pg. 1096
LEXMARK AUSTRALIA—See Lexmark International Group, Inc.; *U.S. Public*, pg. 991
LEXMARK CANADA INC.—See Lexmark International Group, Inc.; *U.S. Public*, pg. 991
LEXMARK FRANCE—See Lexmark International Group, Inc.; *U.S. Public*, pg. 991
LEXMARK INTERNATIONAL GROUP, INC.; *U.S. Public*, pg. 991
THE LEYLAND & BIRMINGHAM RUBBER GROUP—See BTR plc; *Int'l*, pg. 125
LEYLAND DAF LTD.—See Paccar Inc.; *U.S. Public*, pg. 1247
LHOMME S.A.—See Sonoco Products Company; *U.S. Public*, pg. 1487
LIANG COURT HOLDINGS LTD.; *Int'l*, pg. 807
LIANHUA AJINOMOTO CO., LTD.—See Ajinomoto Company Inc.; *Int'l*, pg. 41
LIAONING LIAO BIAN ADVANCED FASHION GARMENTS CO., LTD.—See Gunze Sangyo, Inc.; *Int'l*, pg. 579
LIAONING LIEBHERR DIESEL ENGINE CO. LTD.—See Liebherr-International AG; *Int'l*, pg. 807
LIAONING LIEBHERR HYDRAULIC EXCAVATOR CO. LTD.—See Liebherr-International AG; *Int'l*, pg. 807
LIAONING LIEBHERR WHEEL LOADER CO. LTD.—See Liebherr-International AG; *Int'l*, pg. 807
LIB INDUSTRIE BETEILIGUNG GMBH—See Carl-Zeiss-Stiftung; *Int'l*, pg. 1523
LIBAMEDI S.A.—See American Home Products Corporation; *U.S. Public*, pg. 81
LIBBEY OWENS FORD CO.—See Pilkington Plc; *Int'l*, pg. 1056
LIBERIA ARTE Y CULTURA, S.A.—See Corporacion MAPFRE, Compania Internacional de Reaseguros, S.A.; *Int'l*, pg. 334
LIBERIA CEMENT CORP.—See Scancem AB; *Int'l*, pg. 1201

LIBERIA MFG. CO.—See Decorator Industries, Inc.; *U.S. Public*, pg. 491
LIBERIA TELECOMMUNICATIONS CORPORATION—See Telefonaktiebolaget LM Ericsson; *Int'l*, pg. 1369
LIBERTY BANCORP, INC.—See Banc One Corporation; *U.S. Public*, pg. 174
LIBERTY BANK—See The Sanwa Bank Limited; *Int'l*, pg. 1189
LIBERTY BANK & TRUST OF OKLAHOAMA CITY—See Banc One Corporation; *U.S. Public*, pg. 174
LIBERTY BANK & TRUST COMPANY OF OKLAHOMA CITY—See Banc One Corporation; *U.S. Public*, pg. 174
LIBERTY BANK & TRUST COMPANY OF TULSA—See Banc One Corporation; *U.S. Public*, pg. 174
LIBERTY BANKING SERVICE—See Jack Henry & Associates, Inc.; *U.S. Public*, pg. 809
LIBERTY CABLE, INC.—See TCI Communications, Inc.; *U.S. Public*, pg. 1555
LIBERTY CORPORATION; *U.S. Public*, pg. 991
LIBERTY COUNTY JAIL/JUVENILE CENTER—See Corrections Corporation of America; *U.S. Public*, pg. 450
LIBERTY DAIRY—See Dean Foods Company; *U.S. Public*, pg. 490
LIBERTY DISTRIBUTION CENTER—See Hallmark Cards, Inc.; *U.S. Private*, pg. 496
LIBERTY DISTRIBUTORS INC.—See Liberty Mutual Insurance Co.; *U.S. Private*, pg. 666
LIBERTY FABRICS, INC.—See Courtaulds Textiles Plc; *Int'l*, pg. 340
LIBERTY FABRICS-GORDONSVILLE DIVISION—See Courtaulds Textiles Plc; *Int'l*, pg. 340
LIBERTY FINANCIAL COMPANIES—See Liberty Mutual Insurance Co.; *U.S. Private*, pg. 666
LIBERTY FINANCIAL SERVICES—See Banc One Corporation; *U.S. Public*, pg. 174
LIBERTY HOLDINGS, INC.—See TCI Communications, Inc.; *U.S. Public*, pg. 1555
LIBERTY HOME HEALTH CARE, INC.—See Integrated Health Services, Inc.; *U.S. Public*, pg. 885
LIBERTY HOMES, INC.; *U.S. Public*, pg. 992
LIBERTY HOUSE, INC.—See JMB Realty Corporation; *U.S. Private*, pg. 578
LIBERTY INSURANCE CORPORATION—See Liberty Mutual Insurance Co.; *U.S. Private*, pg. 666
LIBERTY INVESTMENT GROUP, INC.—See Liberty Corporation; *U.S. Public*, pg. 992
LIBERTY INVESTMENT SERVICES, INC.—See Banc One Corporation; *U.S. Public*, pg. 173
LIBERTY LIFE ASSURANCE COMPANY OF BOSTON—See Liberty Mutual Insurance Co.; *U.S. Private*, pg. 666
LIBERTY LIFE INSURANCE COMPANY—See Liberty Corporation; *U.S. Public*, pg. 992
LIBERTY MANAGEMENT SERVICES, INC.—See Torchmark Corporation; *U.S. Public*, pg. 1622
LIBERTY MEDIA CORPORATION—See TCI Communications, Inc.; *U.S. Public*, pg. 1555
LIBERTY MEDICAL SUPPLY, INC.—See PolyMedica Industries, Inc.; *U.S. Public*, pg. 1315
LIBERTY MEXICANA S.A. DE C.V.—See Aisin Seiki Co. Ltd.; *Int'l*, pg. 39
LIBERTY MORTGAGE CO.—See Banc One Corporation; *U.S. Public*, pg. 174
LIBERTY MUTUAL FIRE INSURANCE CO.—See Liberty Mutual Insurance Co.; *U.S. Private*, pg. 666
LIBERTY MUTUAL INSURANCE CO.; *U.S. Private*, pg. 666
LIBERTY NATIONAL AUTO CLUB, INC.—See Torchmark Corporation; *U.S. Public*, pg. 1623
LIBERTY NATIONAL BANK AND TRUST COMPANY OF INDIANA—See Banc One Corporation; *U.S. Public*, pg. 173
LIBERTY NATIONAL BANK AND TRUST COMPANY OF CENTRAL KENTUCKY—See Banc One Corporation; *U.S. Public*, pg. 173
LIBERTY NATIONAL BANK OF NORTHERN KENTUCKY—See Banc One Corporation; *U.S. Public*, pg. 173
LIBERTY NATIONAL BANK OF OWENSBORO—See Banc One Corporation; *U.S. Public*, pg. 173
LIBERTY NATIONAL BANK OF SHELBYVILLE—See Banc One Corporation; *U.S. Public*, pg. 173
LIBERTY NATIONAL BANK OF WESTERN KENTUCKY—See Banc One Corporation; *U.S. Public*, pg. 173
LIBERTY NATIONAL FIRE INSURANCE CO.—See Torchmark Corporation; *U.S. Public*, pg. 1623
LIBERTY NATIONAL GROUPCARE, INC.—See Torchmark Corporation; *U.S. Public*, pg. 1623
LIBERTY NATIONAL INSURANCE CORP.—See Torchmark Corporation; *U.S. Public*, pg. 1623
LIBERTY NATIONAL LIFE INSURANCE CO.—See Torchmark Corporation; *U.S. Public*, pg. 1622
LIBERTY NORTHWEST INSURANCE CORP.—See Liberty Mutual Insurance Co.; *U.S. Private*, pg. 666
LIBERTY OF LONDON PRINTS LIMITED—See Liberty PLC; *Int'l*, pg. 807
LIBERTY PAPER & BAG CO.—See Bunzl PLC; *Int'l*, pg. 233
LIBERTY-PENN DIV.—See Courtaulds Textiles Plc; *Int'l*, pg. 340
LIBERTY PLC; *Int'l*, pg. 807
LIBERTY PRECISION INDUSTRIES; *U.S. Private*, pg. 666
LIBERTY PROGRAM INVESTMENTS, INC.—See TCI Communications, Inc.; *U.S. Public*, pg. 1555
LIBERTY PROGRAMMING CORPORATION—See TCI Communications, Inc.; *U.S. Public*, pg. 1555
LIBERTY PROPERTY MANAGEMENT CO.—See Banc One Corporation; *U.S. Public*, pg. 174
LIBERTY REAL ESTATE CO.—See Banc One Corporation; *U.S. Public*, pg. 175
LIBERTY RETAIL LIMITED—See Liberty PLC; *Int'l*, pg. 807
LIBERTY SPORTS, INC.—See TCI Communications, Inc.; *U.S. Public*, pg. 1555
LIBERTY SYSTEMS—See AmeriSource Health Corp.; *U.S. Public*, pg. 97

LIBERTYVILLE LINCOLN-MERCURY SALES, INC.; *U.S. Private*, pg. 666
LIBMAR FOUR, INC.—See The Chase Manhattan Corporation; *U.S. Public*, pg. 341
LIBMAR SIX, INC.—See The Chase Manhattan Corporation; *U.S. Public*, pg. 341
LIBRAIRIE ARTHEME FAYARD—See Lagardere Groupe; *Int'l*, pg. 792
LIBRAIRIE DES CHAMPS-ELYSEES—See Lagardere Groupe; *Int'l*, pg. 792
LIBRAIRIE GENERALE FRANCAISE—See Lagardere Groupe; *Int'l*, pg. 792
LIBRERIA INTERNAZIONALE—See Arnoldo Mondadori Editore S.p.A.; *Int'l*, pg. 888
LICAN MEDICAL PRODUCTS LTD.—See Circon Corporation; *U.S. Public*, pg. 374
LICENSING WORKS!—See Griffin Bacal Inc.; *U.S. Private*, pg. 480
LICOM, INC.—See V-Band Corporation; *U.S. Public*, pg. 1702
AB LIDINGO VERKSTADER—See Tetra Laval Group; *Int'l*, pg. 1377
LIDKOPING MACHINE TOOLS AB—See AB SKF; *Int'l*, pg. 1157
LIDYE CHEMICAL CO., LTD.—See Dainippon Ink & Chemicals, Inc.; *Int'l*, pg. 372
LIEBERT CORPORATION—See Emerson Electric Co.; *U.S. Public*, pg. 573
LIEBERT CORPORATION AUSTRALIA PTY. LTD.—See Emerson Electric Co.; *U.S. Public*, pg. 577
LIEBERT FAR EAST LTD.—See Emerson Electric Co.; *U.S. Public*, pg. 577
LIEBERT G.M.B.H.—See Emerson Electric Co.; *U.S. Public*, pg. 577
LIEBERT HONG KONG—See Emerson Electric Co.; *U.S. Public*, pg. 577
LIEBERT INTERNATIONAL B.V.—See Emerson Electric Co.; *U.S. Public*, pg. 577
LIEBERT LTD.—See Emerson Electric Co.; *U.S. Public*, pg. 577
LIEBERT MALAYSIA SDN. BHD.—See Emerson Electric Co.; *U.S. Public*, pg. 577
LIEBHERR-AEROSPACE LINDENBERG GMBH—See Liebherr-International AG; *Int'l*, pg. 808
LIEBHERR-AEROSPACE TOULOUSE S.A.—See Liebherr-International AG; *Int'l*, pg. 808
LIEBHERR-AFRICA (PTY.) LTD.—See Liebherr-International AG; *Int'l*, pg. 808
LIEBHERR-AMERICA INC.—See Liebherr-International AG; *Int'l*, pg. 808
LIEBHERR-AUSTRALIA PTY. LTD.—See Liebherr-International AG; *Int'l*, pg. 808
LIEBHERR-AUSTRIA-HOLDING GMBH—See Liebherr-International AG; *Int'l*, pg. 808
LIEBHERR-BAUMASCHINEN AG—See Liebherr-International AG; *Int'l*, pg. 808
LIEBHERR BRASIL LTDA.—See Liebherr-International AG; *Int'l*, pg. 808
LIEBHERR-CANADA LTD.—See Liebherr-International AG; *Int'l*, pg. 808
LIEBHERR CONTAINER CRANES LTD.—See Liebherr-International AG; *Int'l*, pg. 809
LIEBHERR-EXPORT AG—See Liebherr-International AG; *Int'l*, pg. 808
LIEBHERR-FRANCE S.A.—See Liebherr-International AG; *Int'l*, pg. 808
LIEBHERR-GREAT BRITAIN LTD.—See Liebherr-International AG; *Int'l*, pg. 808
LIEBHERR-GUTSVERWALTUNG GMBH—See Liebherr-International AG; *Int'l*, pg. 808
LIEBHERR-HAUSGERATE GMBH—See Liebherr-International AG; *Int'l*, pg. 808
LIEBHERR (HKG) LIMITED—See Liebherr-International AG; *Int'l*, pg. 809
LIEBHERR-HOLDING GMBH—See Liebherr-International AG; *Int'l*, pg. 808
LIEBHERR-HYDRAULIKBAGGER GMBH—See Liebherr-International AG; *Int'l*, pg. 808
LIEBHERR IBERICA, S.A.—See Liebherr-International AG; *Int'l*, pg. 808
PT LIEBHERR INDONESIA PERKASA—See Liebherr-International AG; *Int'l*, pg. 808
LIEBHERR INDUSTRIAS METALICAS, S.A.—See Liebherr-International AG; *Int'l*, pg. 808
LIEBHERR-INDUSTRIEANLAGEN AG—See Liebherr-International AG; *Int'l*, pg. 808
LIEBHERR-INTERNATIONAL AG; *Int'l*, pg. 807
LIEBHERR-INTERTRADING AG—See Liebherr-International AG; *Int'l*, pg. 808
LIEBHERR-INVESTMENT AG—See Liebherr-International AG; *Int'l*, pg. 807
LIEBHERR (IRELAND) HOLDING LTD.—See Liebherr-International AG; *Int'l*, pg. 808
LIEBHERR ITALIA S.P.A.—See Liebherr-International AG; *Int'l*, pg. 809
LIEBHERR JAPAN CO. LTD.—See Liebherr-International AG; *Int'l*, pg. 809
LIEBHERR MACHINES BULLE S.A.—See Liebherr-International AG; *Int'l*, pg. 808
LIEBHERR-MIETPARTNER GMBH—See Liebherr-International AG; *Int'l*, pg. 808
LIEBHERR MINING TRUCK, INC.—See Liebherr-International AG; *Int'l*, pg. 808
LIEBHERR-MISCHTECHNIK GMBH—See Liebherr-International AG; *Int'l*, pg. 808
LIEBHERR-NEDERLAND B.V.—See Liebherr-International AG; *Int'l*, pg. 809
LIEBHERR-SERVICE AG—See Liebherr-International AG; *Int'l*, pg. 808
LIEBHERR-SINGAPORE PTE. LTD.—See Liebherr-International AG; *Int'l*, pg. 809
LIEBHERR-SWISSHOLDING AG—See Liebherr-International AG; *Int'l*, pg. 808

LIEBHERR-THAILAND CO., LTD.—See Liebherr-International AG; *Int'l*, pg. 809
LIEBHERR-VERKEHRSTECHNIK GMBH—See Liebherr-International AG; *Int'l*, pg. 808
LIEBHERR-VERZAHNTECHNIK GMBH—See Liebherr-International AG; *Int'l*, pg. 808
LIEBHERR-WERK BIBERACH GMBH—See Liebherr-International AG; *Int'l*, pg. 808
LIEBHERR-WERK BISCHOFSHOFEN GMBH—See Liebherr-International AG; *Int'l*, pg. 808
LIEBHERR-WERK EHINGEN GMBH—See Liebherr-International AG; *Int'l*, pg. 808
LIEBHERR-WERK LIENZ GMBH—See Liebherr-International AG; *Int'l*, pg. 808
LIEBHERR-WERK NENZING GMBH—See Liebherr-International AG; *Int'l*, pg. 808
LIEBHERR-WERK TELFS GMBH—See Liebherr-International AG; *Int'l*, pg. 808
LIEBHERR-WOHNUNGBAU GMBH—See Liebherr-International AG; *Int'l*, pg. 808
LIEBIG BENELUX NV—See Danone Group; *Int'l*, pg. 380
LIEBIG MAILLE AMORA—See Danone Group; *Int'l*, pg. 380
LIECHTENSTEIN GLOBAL TRUST LIMITED; *Int'l*, pg. 809
LIEFERBETON AG—See RMC Group p.l.c.; *Int'l*, pg. 1081
LIEGENSCHAFT HAINSTRASSE GBR—See Commerzbank AG; *Int'l*, pg. 310
LIELAHTI CTMP MILL—See Metsa-Serla Corporation; *Int'l*, pg. 863
OY LIESIMYYNTI-SPISFORSALJNING AB—See Electrolux, AB; *Int'l*, pg. 441
LIFE DIVISION—See Anglo American Corporation of South Africa Limited; *Int'l*, pg. 77
LIFE EQUIPMENT REBUILDERS—See Budco Group Inc.; *U.S. Private*, pg. 178
LIFE EXTENSION INSTITUTE—See U.M. Holding Limited; *U.S. Private*, pg. 1114
LIFE INSURANCE COMPANY OF NORTH AMERICA—See Cigna Corp.; *U.S. Public*, pg. 362
LIFE INSURANCE COMPANY OF GEORGIA—See ING Groep N.V.; *Int'l*, pg. 648
THE LIFE INSURANCE CO. OF VIRGINIA—See General Electric Company; *U.S. Public*, pg. 712
LIFE INVESTORS INSURANCE CO.—See AEGON N.V.; *Int'l*, pg. 28
LIFE-LIKE PRODUCTS, INC.; *U.S. Private*, pg. 666
LIFE MAGAZINE—See Time Warner Inc.; *U.S. Public*, pg. 1613
LIFE SCIENCE LABORATORIES LTD.—See Thermo Electron Corporation; *U.S. Public*, pg. 1594
LIFE SCIENCES INTERNATIONAL—See Day & Zimmermann, Inc.; *U.S. Private*, pg. 317
LIFE SCIENCES INTERNATIONAL (EUROPE) LIMITED—See Thermo Electron Corporation; *U.S. Public*, pg. 1594
LIFE SCIENCES INTERNATIONAL PLC—See Thermo Electron Corporation; *U.S. Public*, pg. 1594
LIFE SCIENCES-MEISSNER & WURST—See Day & Zimmermann, Inc.; *U.S. Private*, pg. 317
LIFE TECHNOLOGIES A.G.—See The Dexter Corporation; *U.S. Public*, pg. 505
LIFE TECHNOLOGIES A/S—See The Dexter Corporation; *U.S. Public*, pg. 505
LIFE TECHNOLOGIES B.V.—See The Dexter Corporation; *U.S. Public*, pg. 505
LIFE TECHNOLOGIES (EUROPE) LTD.—See The Dexter Corporation; *U.S. Public*, pg. 505
LIFE TECHNOLOGIES GMBH—See The Dexter Corporation; *U.S. Public*, pg. 505
LIFE TECHNOLOGIES, INC.—See The Dexter Corporation; *U.S. Public*, pg. 504
LIFE TECHNOLOGIES INVESTMENT HOLDINGS, INC.—See The Dexter Corporation; *U.S. Public*, pg. 505
N.V. LIFE TECHNOLOGIES SA—See The Dexter Corporation; *U.S. Public*, pg. 505
LIFE TECHNOLOGIES SARL—See The Dexter Corporation; *U.S. Public*, pg. 505
LIFE UNIFORM & SHOE SHOPS—See Angelica Corporation; *U.S. Public*, pg. 113
LIFELINE SYSTEMS, INC.; *U.S. Public*, pg. 992
LIFEROCA—See SNCF; *Int'l*, pg. 1164
LIFESAVERS COMPANY—See RJR Nabisco Holdings Corp.; *U.S. Public*, pg. 1355
LIFESAVERS PLANT—See Hershey Foods Corporation; *U.S. Public*, pg. 812
LIFESCAN CANADA LTD.—See Johnson & Johnson; *U.S. Public*, pg. 931
LIFESCAN, INC.—See Johnson & Johnson; *U.S. Public*, pg. 928
LIFESTYLE BRANDS, INC.—See Playboy Enterprises, Inc.; *U.S. Public*, pg. 1310
LIFESTYLE CONTRACT FURNISHINGS, INC.—See Furnishings International, Inc.; *U.S. Private*, pg. 431
LIFESTYLE FURNISHINGS INTERNATIONAL, LTD.—See Furnishings International, Inc.; *U.S. Private*, pg. 431
LIFETIME ADVISERS INC.—See Sun Life Assurance Company of Canada; *Int'l*, pg. 1319
LIFETIME ASSURANCE CO. LIMITED—See Bank of Ireland; *Int'l*, pg. 152
LIFETIME DOORS INC.; *U.S. Private*, pg. 666
LIFETIME HOAN CORP.; *U.S. Public*, pg. 992
LIFETIME PRODUCTS INC.; *U.S. Private*, pg. 667
LIFETIME TELEVISION/ABC—See The Walt Disney Company; *U.S. Public*, pg. 512
LIFETIME TELEVISION/ABC—See The Hearst Corporation; *U.S. Private*, pg. 516
LIFETOUCH NATIONAL SCHOOL STUDIOS INC.—See Lifetouch, Portrait Studios; *U.S. Private*, pg. 667
LIFETOUCH, PORTRAIT STUDIOS; *U.S. Private*, pg. 667
LIFETOUCH PORTRAIT STUDIOS INC.—See Lifetouch, Portrait Studios; *U.S. Private*, pg. 667
LIFETOUCH PUBLISHING INC.—See Lifetouch, Portrait Studios; *U.S. Private*, pg. 667
LIFETOUCH SENIOR PORTRAITS INC.—See Lifetouch, Portrait Studios; *U.S. Private*, pg. 667

LIFETOUCH VIDEO CREATIONS, INC.—See Lifetouch, Portrait Studios; *U.S. Private*, pg. 667
LIFT-ALL CO., INC.; *U.S. Private*, pg. 667
LIFT TECH INTERNATIONAL—See Columbus McKinnon Corp.; *U.S. Public*, pg. 406
LIFT TRUCK DISTRIBUTION—See Lex Service PLC; *Int'l*, pg. 807
LIGGETT GROUP INC.—See Brooke Group Ltd.; *U.S. Public*, pg. 259
LIGGETT-STASHOWER, INC.; *U.S. Private*, pg. 667
LIGGETT-STASHOWER PUBLIC RELATIONS—See Liggett-Stashower, Inc.; *U.S. Private*, pg. 667
LIGHT HELICOPTER TURBINE ENGINE COMPANY (LHTEC)—See AlliedSignal Inc.; *U.S. Public*, pg. 51
LIGHT SIGNATURES, INC.—See Equifax Inc.; *U.S. Public*, pg. 588
LIGHT VALVE TECHNOLOGY—See Eastman Kodak Company; *U.S. Public*, pg. 551
LIGHTALARMS ELECTRONICS CORPORATION—See Kaufel Group Ltd.; *Int'l*, pg. 725
LIGHTCRAFT—See Millstein Industries; *U.S. Private*, pg. 749
LIGHTING CORPORATION OF AMERICA—See U.S. Industries, Inc.; *U.S. Public*, pg. 1684
LIGHTNIN BELGIUM, S.A.—See General Signal Corporation; *U.S. Public*, pg. 727
LIGHTNIN FRANCE S.A.—See General Signal Corporation; *U.S. Public*, pg. 727
LIGHTNIN MIXERS—See General Signal Corporation; *U.S. Public*, pg. 726
LIGHTNIN MIXERS LIMITED—See General Signal Corporation; *U.S. Public*, pg. 727
LIGHTNIN MIXERS PTY. LTD.—See General Signal Corporation; *U.S. Public*, pg. 727
LIGHTNING OPTICAL CORPORATION—See II-VI Incorporated; *U.S. Public*, pg. 1647
LIGHTOLIER—See The Genlyte Group Incorporated; *U.S. Public*, pg. 730
LIGHTOLIER DIVISION—See The Genlyte Group Incorporated; *U.S. Public*, pg. 730
LIGHTS OF AMERICA, INC.; *U.S. Private*, pg. 667
LIGNAC & LEVISON BV—See N.V. Koninklijke KNP BT; *Int'l*, pg. 756
LIGNIN PRODUCTS—See Georgia-Pacific Corporation; *U.S. Public*, pg. 737
THE LIHUE PLANTATION COMPANY, LIMITED—See JMB Realty Corporation; *U.S. Private*, pg. 578
LIL'CHAMP/FOOD STORES INC.—See The Pantry, Inc.; *U.S. Private*, pg. 837
LILJENDALS BRUK A.B.—See Illinois Tool Works Inc.; *U.S. Public*, pg. 869
LILLI ANN CORPORATION—See Jaran Inc.; *U.S. Private*, pg. 582
LILLIE RUBIN FASHIONS INC.; *U.S. Private*, pg. 667
THE CHAS. H. LILLY CO.; *U.S. Private*, pg. 667
LILLY DEUTSCHLAND G.M.B.H.—See Eli Lilly and Company; *U.S. Public*, pg. 992
ELI LILLY AND COMPANY; *U.S. Public*, pg. 992
ELI LILLY ARGENTINA, S.A.—See Eli Lilly and Company; *U.S. Public*, pg. 993
ELI LILLY ASIA, INC.—See Eli Lilly and Company; *U.S. Public*, pg. 993
ELI LILLY BENELUX, S.A.—See Eli Lilly and Company; *U.S. Public*, pg. 993
ELI LILLY GROUP LIMITED—See Eli Lilly and Company; *U.S. Public*, pg. 994
ELI LILLY INTERNATIONAL CORPORATION—See Eli Lilly and Company; *U.S. Public*, pg. 993
ELI LILLY JAPAN K.K.—See Eli Lilly and Company; *U.S. Public*, pg. 994
ELI LILLY S.A.—See Eli Lilly and Company; *U.S. Public*, pg. 994
ELI LILLY (S.A.) (PROPRIETARY) LIMITED—See Eli Lilly and Company; *U.S. Public*, pg. 994
ELI LILLY Y COMPANIA DE MEXICO, S.A. DE C.V.—See Eli Lilly and Company; *U.S. Public*, pg. 994
ELI LILLY Y COMPANIA DE VENEZUELA, S.A.—See Eli Lilly and Company; *U.S. Public*, pg. 994
LILLY-FARMA PRODUTOS FARMACEUTICOS, LDA.—See Eli Lilly and Company; *U.S. Public*, pg. 994
LILLY FRANCE S.A.—See Eli Lilly and Company; *U.S. Public*, pg. 994
LILLY INDUSTRIES (FAR EAST), LTD.—See Lilly Industries, Inc.; *U.S. Public*, pg. 995
LILLY INDUSTRIES, INC.; *U.S. Public*, pg. 994
LILLY INDUSTRIES, INC.—See Lilly Industries, Inc.; *U.S. Public*, pg. 994
LILLY INDUSTRIES LIMITED—See Eli Lilly and Company; *U.S. Public*, pg. 994
LILLY INDUSTRIES (MALAYSIA) SND. BHD.—See Lilly Industries, Inc.; *U.S. Public*, pg. 995
LILLY RESEARCH CENTRE LIMITED—See Eli Lilly and Company; *U.S. Public*, pg. 994
LILLY RESEARCH LABORATORIES—See Eli Lilly and Company; *U.S. Public*, pg. 993
LILLY, S.A.—See Eli Lilly and Company; *U.S. Public*, pg. 994
LILLYWHITES LTD.—See Jeronimo Martins; *Int'l*, pg. 706
LILY TRANSPORTATION CORP.; *U.S. Private*, pg. 667
LILYETTE BRASSIERE CO.—See Maidenform Worldwide; *U.S. Private*, pg. 697
LIMA COMMUNICATIONS CORP.—See Blade Communications, Inc.; *U.S. Private*, pg. 147
LIMA LIMITED DIVIDEND CORP.—See Forest City Enterprises, Inc.; *U.S. Public*, pg. 669
LIMAGRAIN GENETICS CORP.—See Groupe Limagrain; *Int'l*, pg. 566
LIMBACH CO.—See Compagnie Generale Des Eaux; *Int'l*, pg. 322
LIMBACH CONSTRUCTORS, INC.—See Compagnie Generale Des Eaux; *Int'l*, pg. 322
LIMBACH HOLDINGS, INC.—See Compagnie Generale Des Eaux; *Int'l*, pg. 321

LIMBURGSE VINYL MAATSCHAPPIJ NV—See DSM N.V.; Int'l, pg. 355

LIMITED DISTRIBUTION SERVICES—See The Limited, Inc.; U.S. Public, pg. 995

THE LIMITED, INC.; U.S. Public, pg. 995

LIMITED REAL ESTATE—See The Limited, Inc.; U.S. Public, pg. 995

LIMITED STORE PLANNING—See The Limited, Inc.; U.S. Public, pg. 995

LIMITED STORES—See The Limited, Inc.; U.S. Public, pg. 996

LIMITED, TOO—See The Limited, Inc.; U.S. Public, pg. 996

LIMMATDRUCK AG—See Migros; Int'l, pg. 865

LIMOGES PLANT—See COGEMA - Compagnie Generale des Matieres Nucleaires; Int'l, pg. 305

LIMOUX OFFICE—See La Meridionale des Bois et Materiaux; Int'l, pg. 599

LIMOX CHEMIE B.V.—See Harrisons & Crosfield plc; Int'l, pg. 599

LIN CELLULAR GROUP—See AT&T Corporation; U.S. Public, pg. 11

LIN CENTRAL BROADCASTING CORPORATION (WOTV)—See AT&T Corporation; U.S. Public, pg. 11

LIN & ROE COMPANY—See Burns & Roe Enterprises, Inc.; U.S. Private, pg. 187

LINA BENEFIT PAYMENTS, INC.—See Cigna Corp.; U.S. Public, pg. 362

LINATEX A/S—See AB Industrivarden; Int'l, pg. 678

LINATEX AUSTRALIA PTY. LTD.—See Harrisons & Crosfield plc; Int'l, pg. 599

LINATEX CANADA INC.—See Harrisons & Crosfield plc; Int'l, pg. 599

LINATEX CORPORATION OF AMERICA—See Harrisons & Crosfield plc; Int'l, pg. 599

LINATEX LIMITED—See Harrisons & Crosfield plc; Int'l, pg. 598

LINBECK CONSTRUCTION CORP; U.S. Private, pg. 667

LINC CAPITAL GROUP; U.S. Public, pg. 996

THE LINC CORP.—See Compagnie Generale Des Eaux; Int'l, pg. 322

LINCAM PROPERTIES, INC.—See Lincoln National Corporation; U.S. Public, pg. 997

LINCARE HOLDINGS INC.; U.S. Public, pg. 996

LINCOLN AMERICAN LIFE INSURANCE CO.—See Conseco, Inc.; U.S. Public, pg. 433

LINCOLN ASSURANCE LIMITED—See Lincoln National Corporation; U.S. Public, pg. 998

LINCOLN AUTOMOTIVE—See Pentair, Inc.; U.S. Public, pg. 1273

LINCOLN BIG THREE, INC.—See Air Liquide S.A.; Int'l, pg. 37

LINCOLN CANADA LIMITED—See Pentair, Inc.; U.S. Public, pg. 1274

LINCOLN COURIER—See The Copley Press, Inc.; U.S. Private, pg. 275

THE LINCOLN ELECTRIC CO. (FRANCE) S.A.—See The Lincoln Electric Company; U.S. Public, pg. 996

THE LINCOLN ELECTRIC COMPANY; U.S. Public, pg. 996

THE LINCOLN ELECTRIC COMPANY (ASIA PACIFIC) PTE. LTD.—See The Lincoln Electric Company; U.S. Public, pg. 996

THE LINCOLN ELECTRIC CO. AUSTRALIA PTY. LTD.—See The Lincoln Electric Company; U.S. Public, pg. 996

THE LINCOLN ELECTRIC CO. OF CANADA LTD.—See The Lincoln Electric Company; U.S. Public, pg. 997

LINCOLN ELECTRIC DO BRASIL—See The Lincoln Electric Company; U.S. Public, pg. 997

LINCOLN ELECTRIC ITALIA SRL—See The Lincoln Electric Company; U.S. Public, pg. 997

LINCOLN ELECTRIC MEXICANA S.A. DE C.V.—See The Lincoln Electric Company; U.S. Public, pg. 997

LINCOLN ELECTRIC SYSTEMS; U.S. Private, pg. 668

LINCOLN ELECTRIC (U.K. LTD.)—See The Lincoln Electric Company; U.S. Public, pg. 997

LINCOLN FINANCIAL ADVISORS—See Lincoln National Corporation; U.S. Public, pg. 998

LINCOLN FINANCIAL GROUP, INC.—See Lincoln National Corporation; U.S. Public, pg. 997

LINCOLN FOODSERVICE PRODUCTS, INC.—See Berisford plc; Int'l, pg. 188

LINCOLN GMBH—See Pentair, Inc.; U.S. Public, pg. 1274

LINCOLN GRAPHICS—See Schawk, Inc.; U.S. Public, pg. 1437

LINCOLN GRAPHICS INC.—See Devon Group, Inc.; U.S. Public, pg. 503

LINCOLN HOLDINGS, INC.—See Fiserv, Inc.; U.S. Public, pg. 647

LINCOLN INDUSTRIAL—See Pentair, Inc.; U.S. Public, pg. 1273

LINCOLN INDUSTRIES; U.S. Private, pg. 668

LINCOLN INDUSTRIES, INC.—See Zoeller Co.; U.S. Private, pg. 1207

LINCOLN INVESTMENT MANAGEMENT INC.—See Lincoln National Corporation; U.S. Public, pg. 998

LINCOLN KD S.A.—See The Lincoln Electric Company; U.S. Public, pg. 997

LINCOLN MARKETING, INC.—See Synovus Financial Corp.; U.S. Public, pg. 1550

LINCOLN-MERCURY DIVISION—See Ford Motor Company; U.S. Public, pg. 662

LINCOLN NATIONAL ADMINISTRATIVE SERVICES CORP.—See Lincoln National Corporation; U.S. Public, pg. 998

LINCOLN NATIONAL (CHINA) INC.—See Lincoln National Corporation; U.S. Public, pg. 998

LINCOLN NATIONAL CORPORATION; U.S. Public, pg. 997

LINCOLN NATIONAL HEALTH & CASUALTY INSURANCE CO.—See Lincoln National Corporation; U.S. Public, pg. 998

LINCOLN NATIONAL INCOME FUND, INC.—See Lincoln National Corporation; U.S. Public, pg. 998

LINCOLN NATIONAL INTERMEDIARIES, INC.—See Lincoln National Corporation; U.S. Public, pg. 998

THE LINCOLN NATIONAL LIFE INSURANCE CO.—See Lincoln National Corporation; U.S. Public, pg. 998

LINCOLN NATIONAL MANAGEMENT SERVICES, INC.—See Lincoln National Corporation; U.S. Public, pg. 998

LINCOLN NATIONAL REALTY CORPORATION—See Lincoln National Corporation; U.S. Public, pg. 998

LINCOLN NATIONAL REINSURANCE COMPANY (BARBADOS) LIMITED—See Lincoln National Corporation; U.S. Public, pg. 998

LINCOLN NATIONAL REINSURANCE COMPANY (BERMUDA) LIMITED—See Lincoln National Corporation; U.S. Public, pg. 998

LINCOLN NATIONAL RISK MANAGEMENT, INC.—See Lincoln National Corporation; U.S. Public, pg. 998

LINCOLN NATIONAL STRUCTURED SETTLEMENT, INC.—See Lincoln National Corporation; U.S. Public, pg. 998

LINCOLN NATIONAL (UK) PLC—See Lincoln National Corporation; U.S. Public, pg. 998

LINCOLN NEWS MESSENGER—See Brehm Communications, Inc.; U.S. Private, pg. 167

LINCOLN NORWELD AS—See The Lincoln Electric Company; U.S. Public, pg. 997

LINCOLN NURSING CENTER, INC.—See Vencor, Inc.; U.S. Public, pg. 1714

LINCOLN PRODUCTS—See Wolseley Plc; Int'l, pg. 1512

LINCOLN PROPERTY COMPANY; U.S. Private, pg. 668

LINCOLN PROPERTY CO., NORTHERN CALIFORNIA—See Lincoln Property Company; U.S. Private, pg. 668

LINCOLN PROVISION, INC.; U.S. Private, pg. 668

LINCOLN SMITWELD BELGIUM NV—See The Lincoln Electric Company; U.S. Public, pg. 997

LINCOLN SMITWELD BV—See The Lincoln Electric Company; U.S. Public, pg. 997

LINCOLN SMITWELD GMBH—See The Lincoln Electric Company; U.S. Public, pg. 997

LINCOLN SNACKS COMPANY—See Noel Group, Inc.; U.S. Public, pg. 1187

LINCOLN SVETSHUSET AB—See The Lincoln Electric Company; U.S. Public, pg. 997

LINCS SURFACING CONTRACTORS LIMITED—See RMC Group p.l.c.; Int'l, pg. 1079

LINDAL CEDAR HOMES, INC.; U.S. Public, pg. 998

LINDALE MFG. INC.—See Greenwood Mills, Inc.; U.S. Private, pg. 479

LINDBERG, A GENERAL SIGNAL COMPANY—See General Signal Corporation; U.S. Public, pg. 727

LINDBERG CORPORATION; U.S. Public, pg. 999

LINDBERG HEAT TREATING CO.—See Lindberg Corporation; U.S. Public, pg. 999

LINDBERG HEAT TREATING COMPANY, BATSON DIV.—See Lindberg Corporation; U.S. Public, pg. 999

LINDE AG; See Linde AG; Int'l, pg. 810

LINDE AG WERKSGRUPPE GUELDNER ASCHAFFENBURG—See Linde AG; Int'l, pg. 810

LINDE AG WERKSGRUPPE KALTE- U. EINRICHTUNGSTECHNIK—See Linde AG; Int'l, pg. 810

LINDE AG WERKSGRUPPE TECHNISCHE GASE—See Linde AG; Int'l, pg. 810

LINDE AG WERKSGRUPPE TVT—See Linde AG; Int'l, pg. 811

LINDE (AUSTRALIA) PTY. LTD.—See Linde AG; Int'l, pg. 811

LINDE CARRETILLAS E HIDRAULICA S.A.—See Linde AG; Int'l, pg. 810

LINDE CHLADICI TECHNIKA SPOL. S.R.O.—See Linde AG; Int'l, pg. 810

LINDE-CONFRIO, S.A.—See Linde AG; Int'l, pg. 810

LINDE CRYOGENICS LTD.—See Linde AG; Int'l, pg. 810

LINDE FODERTECHNIK GMBH—See Linde AG; Int'l, pg. 810

LINDE FRIGERA SPOL. S.R.O.—See Linde AG; Int'l, pg. 810

LINDE FROID ET CLIMATISATION S.A.R.L.—See Linde AG; Int'l, pg. 810

LINDE GAS GMBH & CO. KG—See Linde AG; Int'l, pg. 811

LINDE GAS ITALIA S.R.L.—See Linde AG; Int'l, pg. 811

LINDE GAS PTY. LTD.—See Linde AG; Int'l, pg. 811

LINDE GAS U.K. LTD.—See Linde AG; Int'l, pg. 811

LINDE GAS UNGARN AG—See Linde AG; Int'l, pg. 811

LINDE GAZ INDUSTRIELS S.A.R.L.—See Linde AG; Int'l, pg. 811

LINDE GAZ POLSKA SPOLKA Z.O.O.—See Linde AG; Int'l, pg. 811

LINDE GULDNER ITALIANA S.P.A.—See Linde AG; Int'l, pg. 811

LINDE HEIMOX GMBH—See Linde AG; Int'l, pg. 811

LINDE HELLAS E.P.E.—See Linde AG; Int'l, pg. 811

LINDE HOLDING AG—See Linde AG; Int'l, pg. 811

LINDE HOLDING LTD.—See Linde AG; Int'l, pg. 811

LINDE HYDRAULICS CORPORATION—See Linde AG; Int'l, pg. 810

LINDE HYDRAULICS LTD.—See Linde AG; Int'l, pg. 810

LINDE KALTETECHNIK AG—See Linde AG; Int'l, pg. 810

LINDE KALTETECHNIK GES.M.B.H.—See Linde AG; Int'l, pg. 810

LINDE KALTETECHNIK HUNGARIA GMBH—See Linde AG; Int'l, pg. 810

LINDE-KCA-DRESDEN G.M.B.H—See Linde AG; Int'l, pg. 811

LINDE KRYOTECHNIK AG—See Linde AG; Int'l, pg. 811

LINDE K.T. ITALIANA S.P.A.—See Linde AG; Int'l, pg. 810

LINDE K.T. NORGE A/S—See Linde AG; Int'l, pg. 810

LINDE KYLTEKNIK SVERGIE AB—See Linde AG; Int'l, pg. 810

LINDE LANSING FODERTECHNIK AG—See Linde AG; Int'l, pg. 810

LINDE MATERIALS HANDLING PTY. LTD.—See Linde AG; Int'l, pg. 810

LINDE REFRIGERATION LTD.—See Linde AG; Int'l, pg. 811

LINDE REFRIGERATION SYSTEMS LTD.—See Linde AG; Int'l, pg. 811

LINDE SOGAS, LDA—See Linde AG; Int'l, pg. 811

LINDE TECHNOPLYN A.S.—See Linde AG; Int'l, pg. 811

LINDE-XIAMEN FORKLIFT TRUCK CORPORATION LTD.—See Linde AG; Int'l, pg. 810

LINDENMEYR BOOK PUBLISHING—See Central National-Gottesman Inc.; U.S. Private, pg. 224

LINDENMEYR CENTRAL—See Central National-Gottesman Inc.; U.S. Private, pg. 224

LINDENMEYR MUNROE—See Central National-Gottesman Inc.; U.S. Private, pg. 224

LINDENMEYR PAPER—See Central National-Gottesman Inc.; U.S. Private, pg. 224

LINDENMEYR PAPER COMPANY—See Central National-Gottesman Inc.; U.S. Private, pg. 224

LINDER & ASSOCIATES, INC.; U.S. Private, pg. 668

LINDSAY MANUFACTURING COMPANY; U.S. Public, pg. 999

LINDSAY MANUFACTURING INC.; U.S. Private, pg. 668

LINDSAY TRANSPORTATION INC.—See Lindsay Manufacturing Company; U.S. Public, pg. 1000

LINDSEY OIL REFINERY—See Petrofina S.A.; Int'l, pg. 1043

LINDUSTRIES LTD.—See Hanson PLC; Int'l, pg. 593

LINE EQUIPMENT SALES CO., INC.—See Utilities Construction Co., Inc. Of South Carolina; U.S. Private, pg. 1130

LINE INFORMATICA S.P.A.—See Compagnie des Machines Bull; Int'l, pg. 318

LINE SOFTECO S.R.L.—See Compagnie des Machines Bull; Int'l, pg. 318

LINEAR CORPORATION—See Nortek, Inc.; U.S. Public, pg. 1193

LINEAR DIVISION—See LTX Corporation; U.S. Public, pg. 972

LINEAR DYNAMICS INC.; U.S. Private, pg. 668

LINEAR SWITCH CORPORATION—See Allen Organ Company; U.S. Public, pg. 45

LINEAR TECHNOLOGY CORP.; U.S. Public, pg. 1000

LINENS 'N THINGS, INC.; U.S. Private, pg. 668

LINFINITY MICROELECTRONICS INC.—See SymmetriCom, Inc.; U.S. Public, pg. 1547

LING ELECTRONICS INC.—See Mechanical Technology Inc.; U.S. Public, pg. 1077

LING ELECTRONICS LTD.—See Mechanical Technology Inc.; U.S. Public, pg. 1077

LINHAS CORRENTE LTDA.—See Coats Viyella plc; Int'l, pg. 301

OY LINING AB—See AB Industrivarden; Int'l, pg. 678

LINJEBYGG AS—See Imatran Voima Oy; Int'l, pg. 660

LINK HOUSE ADVERTISING PERIODICALS LTD.—See United News & Media plc; Int'l, pg. 1443

LINK-MILES LIMITED—See Thomson S.A.; Int'l, pg. 1385

O.P. LINK HANDLE COMPANY; U.S. Private, pg. 668

LINK RESOURCES—See International Data Group; U.S. Private, pg. 570

LINK TECH, INC.—See ILC Industries, Inc.; U.S. Private, pg. 555

LINK-VTC, INC.—See Frontier Corporation; U.S. Public, pg. 684

LINKOUS CONSTRUCTION COMPANY, INC.; U.S. Private, pg. 668

LINKUSA CORPORATION—See Frontier Corporation; U.S. Public, pg. 684

LINN PRODUCTS, INC.; U.S. Private, pg. 669

B.V. LINNENWEVERIJEN V/H V DIJK EN ZONEN—See Gamma Holding N.V.; Int'l, pg. 540

LINOTYPE FRANCE SA—See N.V. Koninklijke KNP BT; Int'l, pg. 757

LINOTYPE-HELL COMPANY—See Heidelberger Druckmaschinen A.G.; Int'l, pg. 604

LINPAC MOULDINGS LIMITED; Int'l, pg. 811

LINREAD NORTH BRIDGE—See McKechnie PLC; Int'l, pg. 852

LINSCO/PRIVATE LEDGER BROKERAGE SERVICE—See Ameriana Bancorp; U.S. Public, pg. 66

LINSCO REINSURANCE COMPANY—See Lincoln National Corporation; U.S. Public, pg. 998

LINSELL ADVERTISING ASSOCIATES—See Saatchi & Saatchi Advertising Worldwide; U.S. Public, pg. 1422

LINTAPHARM AG—See DSM N.V.; Int'l, pg. 356

LINTAS:HAKUHODO AUSTRALIA PTY. LTD.—See Hakuhodo Incorporated; Int'l, pg. 588

LINTON AND HIRST LIMITED—See TT Group PLC; Int'l, pg. 1344

LINVATEC CORP.—See Conmed Corporation; U.S. Public, pg. 431

LINZ KIMYA TICARET LTD. SIRKETI—See DSM N.V.; Int'l, pg. 356

LINZER PRODUCTS CORP.; U.S. Private, pg. 669

LION—See Mercantile Stores Company, Inc.; U.S. Public, pg. 1090

LION AKZO CO. K.K.—See Akzo Nobel N.V.; Int'l, pg. 47

LION BRAND YARN CO.; U.S. Private, pg. 669

THE LION BREWERY, INC.; U.S. Public, pg. 1000

LION BROTHERS COMPANY, INC.; U.S. Private, pg. 669

LION FERRY AB—See Stena Line AB; Int'l, pg. 1300

LION FERRY A/S—See Stena Line AB; Int'l, pg. 1300

LION HENKEL CORPORATION—See Henkel KGaA; Int'l, pg. 614

LION HENKEL (HONGKONG) LTD.—See Henkel KGaA; Int'l, pg. 614

LION HENKEL TAIWAN LTD.—See Henkel KGaA; Int'l, pg. 614

LION INTERNATIONAL MANAGEMENT LIMITED—See HSBC Holdings plc; Int'l, pg. 580

THE LION MATCH COMPANY LIMITED—See South African Breweries, Ltd.; Int'l, pg. 1287

LION STEEL EQUIPMENT LTD.—See Firth-Rixson Plc; Int'l, pg. 488

LIONEL LLC; U.S. Private, pg. 669

LIPE LIMITED—See Echlin Inc.; *U.S. Public*, pg. 561
LIPHA CHEMICALS S.A.; *Int'l*, pg. 812
LIPHA PHARMACEUTICALS—See Lipha Chemicals S.A.; *Int'l*, pg. 812
LIPHA PHARMACEUTICALS, INC.—See Lipha Chemicals S.A.; *Int'l*, pg. 812
LIPHATECH, INC.—See Lipha Chemicals S.A.; *Int'l*, pg. 812
MARK LIPMAN DIV.—See Guardsmark, Inc.; *U.S. Private*, pg. 486
LIPOMA B.V.—See Unilever Plc; *Int'l*, pg. 1438
THE LIPOSOME COMPANY, INC.; *U.S. Public*, pg. 1000
THE LIPOSOME MANUFACTURING COMPANY, INC.—See The Liposome Company, Inc.; *U.S. Public*, pg. 1000
LIPPERT ABRASIVES INC.—See Fuchs Petrolub AG Oel + Chemie; *Int'l*, pg. 518
LIPPERT COMPONENTS, INC.—See Drew Industries Incorporated; *U.S. Public*, pg. 529
HEINRICH LIPPERT GMBH—See Fuchs Petrolub AG Oel + Chemie; *Int'l*, pg. 518
LIPPERT ITALIANA S.R.L.—See Fuchs Petrolub AG Oel + Chemie; *Int'l*, pg. 518
LIPPERT-PELISSIER S.A.—See Fuchs Petrolub AG Oel + Chemie; *Int'l*, pg. 518
LIPPERT S.A.—See Fuchs Petrolub AG Oel + Chemie; *Int'l*, pg. 518
J.B. LIPPINCOTT COMPANY—See Wolters Kluwer N.V.; *Int'l*, pg. 1513
LIPPINCOTT & MARGULIES, INC.—See Marsh & McLennan Companies, Inc.; *U.S. Public*, pg. 1048
LIPPINCOTT-RAVEN PUBLISHING—See Wolters Kluwer N.V.; *Int'l*, pg. 1513
LIPS ASIA PTE LTD.—See Lips United B.V.; *Int'l*, pg. 812
LIPS B.V.—See Lips United B.V.; *Int'l*, pg. 812
LIPS PROPELLER INC.—See Lips United B.V.; *Int'l*, pg. 812
LIPS PROPELLERS, INC.—See Lips United B.V.; *Int'l*, pg. 812
LIPS PROPELLERS WEST/COAST OPERATIONS—See Lips United B.V.; *Int'l*, pg. 812
LIPS UNITED B.V.; *Int'l*, pg. 812
LIPS USA INC.—See Lips United B.V.; *Int'l*, pg. 812
LIPSCHUTZ BROTHERS INC—See BAA plc; *Int'l*, pg. 103
LIPTON PAKISTAN LTD.—See Unilever Plc; *Int'l*, pg. 1438
LIPTON (SA) (PTY.) LTD.—See Unilever Plc; *Int'l*, pg. 1438
LIPTON TEA COMPANY LTD.—See Unilever Plc; *Int'l*, pg. 1434
THOMAS J. LIPTON COMPANY—See Unilever Plc; *Int'l*, pg. 1435
LIQUI-BOX ACQUISITION CORPORATION—See Liqui-Box Corporation; *U.S. Public*, pg. 1000
LIQUI-BOX CORP.—See Liqui-Box Corporation; *U.S. Public*, pg. 1000
LIQUI-BOX CORPORATION; *U.S. Public*, pg. 1000
LIQUI-DRI FOODS, INC.—See The Quaker Oats Company; *U.S. Public*, pg. 1348
LIQUID AIR CORPORATION, PACKAGE GASES DIV.—See Air Liquide S.A.; *Int'l*, pg. 37
LIQUID COATINGS & DISPERSIONS DIVISION—See Ferro Corporation; *U.S. Public*, pg. 619
LIQUID COLORANT OPERATION—See Morton International Inc.; *U.S. Public*, pg. 1134
LIQUID CONTROLS LLC; *U.S. Private*, pg. 669
LIQUID ENERGY CORPORATION—See Mitchell Energy & Development Corp.; *U.S. Public*, pg. 1117
LIQUID GAS EQUIPMENT LTD.—See Weir Group PLC; *Int'l*, pg. 1489
LIQUID MOLDING SYSTEMS, INC.—See AptarGroup, Inc.; *U.S. Public*, pg. 125
LIQUID PAPER CORP.—See The Gillette Company; *U.S. Public*, pg. 744
LIQUID TRANSPORTERS, INC.—See Trimac Corporation; *Int'l*, pg. 1424
THE LIQUIDATING COMPANY, INC.—See Cigna Corp.; *U.S. Public*, pg. 360
LIQUIED MOLKING RESINS B.V.—See Hercules Incorporated; *U.S. Public*, pg. 811
LIQUIGAS SPA—See SHV Holdings N.V.; *Int'l*, pg. 1155
LISA MOTOR LINES, INC.—See Frozen Food Express Industries, Inc.; *U.S. Public*, pg. 685
LISLE CORPORETUM OFFICES—See R.R. Donnelley & Sons Company; *U.S. Public*, pg. 518
LIST INDUSTRIES, INC.; *U.S. Private*, pg. 669
LISTA AG—See Lista Holding AG; *Int'l*, pg. 812
LISTA ARNEGG—See Lista Holding AG; *Int'l*, pg. 812
LISTA BETRIEBS- UND LAGEREINRICHTUNGEN GES.M.B.H.—See Lista Holding AG; *Int'l*, pg. 812
LISTA BUROEINRICHTUNGEN GES.M.B.H.—See Lista Holding AG; *Int'l*, pg. 812
LISTA DEGERSHEIM AG—See Lista Holding AG; *Int'l*, pg. 812
LISTA FRANCE S.A.—See Lista Holding AG; *Int'l*, pg. 812
LISTA HOLDING AG; *Int'l*, pg. 812
LISTA INTERNATIONAL CORPORATION—See Lista Holding AG; *Int'l*, pg. 812
LISTA ITALIA S.R.L.—See Lista Holding AG; *Int'l*, pg. 812
LISTA SISTEMAS DE ALMACENAJE, S.A.—See Lista Holding AG; *Int'l*, pg. 812
LISTA UK LTD.—See Lista Holding AG; *Int'l*, pg. 812
LISTER-PETTER INC.—See BTR plc; *Int'l*, pg. 127
LISTER-PETTER LTD.—See BTR plc; *Int'l*, pg. 125
L'ITALICA—See Allianz Aktiengesellschaft; *Int'l*, pg. 61
L'ITALICA - DIVAL VITA—See Allianz Aktiengesellschaft; *Int'l*, pg. 61
LITCHFIELD FINANCIAL CORPORATION; *U.S. Public*, pg. 1001
LITCHFIELD FINANCIAL CORPORATION—See Litchfield Financial Corporation; *U.S. Public*, pg. 1001
LITCHFIELD PRECISION COMPONENTS—See Innovex, Inc.; *U.S. Public*, pg. 880
LITECONTROL CORPORATION; *U.S. Private*, pg. 669
LITEF (GMBH)—See Litton Industries, Inc.; *U.S. Public*, pg. 1004
LITEF (LITTON TECHNISCHE WERKE)—See Litton Industries, Inc.; *U.S. Public*, pg. 1004
LITESPEC, INC.—See Sumitomo Electric Industries, Ltd.; *Int'l*, pg. 1313
LITEX A/S—See FMC Corporation; *U.S. Public*, pg. 607
LITFINN SERVICE—See Neste Oy; *Int'l*, pg. 914
LITHION, INC.—See Ener-Tek International Corporation; *U.S. Private*, pg. 376
LITHO ACME—See G.T.C. Transcontinental Group Ltd.; *Int'l*, pg. 538
LITHO ACME QUEBEC—See G.T.C. Transcontinental Group Ltd.; *Int'l*, pg. 538
LITHO COLORPLATE—See Schawk, Inc.; *U.S. Public*, pg. 1437
LITHO-KROME COMPANY—See Hallmark Cards, Inc.; *U.S. Private*, pg. 496
LITHOGRAPH PRINTING COMPANY, INC.—See Master Graphic, Inc.; *U.S. Private*, pg. 713
LITHOGRAPHIX, INC.; *U.S. Private*, pg. 670
LITHONIA LIGHTING CO.—See National Service Industries, Inc.; *U.S. Public*, pg. 1160
LITHOTRIPTERS, INC.—See Prime Medical Services, Inc.; *U.S. Public*, pg. 1327
LITHOTYPE COMPANY, INC.; *U.S. Private*, pg. 670
LITKOR LITTON KOREA LTD.—See Litton Industries, Inc.; *U.S. Public*, pg. 1004
LITTELFUSE AG—See Littelfuse, Inc.; *U.S. Public*, pg. 1001
LITTELFUSE B.V.—See Littelfuse, Inc.; *U.S. Public*, pg. 1001
LITTELFUSE DO BRASIL—See Littelfuse, Inc.; *U.S. Public*, pg. 1001
LITTELFUSE FAREAST, PTE LTD.—See Littelfuse, Inc.; *U.S. Public*, pg. 1001
LITTELFUSE HK LTD.—See Littelfuse, Inc.; *U.S. Public*, pg. 1001
LITTELFUSE, INC.; *U.S. Public*, pg. 1001
LITTELFUSE KK—See Littelfuse, Inc.; *U.S. Public*, pg. 1001
LITTELFUSE LTD.—See Littelfuse, Inc.; *U.S. Public*, pg. 1001
LITTELFUSE S.A. DE C.V.—See Littelfuse, Inc.; *U.S. Public*, pg. 1001
LITTELFUSE TRIAD, INC.—See Littelfuse, Inc.; *U.S. Public*, pg. 1001
LITTELL—See MetalTech International PLC; *Int'l*, pg. 862
LITTERMAID—See Windmere-Durable Holdings; *U.S. Public*, pg. 1771
LITTFIN LUMBER COMPANY; *U.S. Private*, pg. 670
LITTLE AMERICA HOTELS—See Sinclair Oil Corp.; *U.S. Private*, pg. 1003
LITTLE AMERICA REFINING, INC.—See Sinclair Oil Corp.; *U.S. Private*, pg. 1003
ARTHUR D. LITTLE ASIA PACIFIC INC.—See Arthur D. Little, Inc.; *U.S. Private*, pg. 670
ARTHUR D. LITTLE DE ARGENTINA S.A.—See Arthur D. Little, Inc.; *U.S. Private*, pg. 670
ARTHUR D. LITTLE DE COLUMBIA, LTDA.—See Arthur D. Little, Inc.; *U.S. Private*, pg. 670
ARTHUR D. LITTLE DE VENEZUELA, C.A.—See Arthur D. Little, Inc.; *U.S. Private*, pg. 670
ARTHUR D. LITTLE ENTERPRISES, INC.—See Arthur D. Little, Inc.; *U.S. Private*, pg. 670
ARTHUR D. LITTLE FAR EAST, INC.—See Arthur D. Little, Inc.; *U.S. Private*, pg. 670
ARTHUR D. LITTLE, INC.; *U.S. Private*, pg. 670
ARTHUR D. LITTLE, INC—See Arthur D. Little, Inc.; *U.S. Private*, pg. 670
ARTHUR D. LITTLE, INC.—See Arthur D. Little, Inc.; *U.S. Private*, pg. 670
ARTHUR D. LITTLE INTERNATIONAL GMBH—See Arthur D. Little, Inc.; *U.S. Private*, pg. 670
ARTHUR D. LITTLE INTERNATIONAL, INC.—See Arthur D. Little, Inc.; *U.S. Private*, pg. 670
ARTHUR D. LITTLE INTERNATIONAL, INC—See Arthur D. Little, Inc.; *U.S. Private*, pg. 671
ARTHUR D. LITTLE INTERNATIONAL, INC.—See Arthur D. Little, Inc.; *U.S. Private*, pg. 671
ARTHUR D. LITTLE (JAPAN), INC.—See Arthur D. Little, Inc.; *U.S. Private*, pg. 671
ARTHUR D. LITTLE KOREA, INC.—See Arthur D. Little, Inc.; *U.S. Private*, pg. 671
ARTHUR D. LITTLE (MALAYSIA) SDN BHD—See Arthur D. Little, Inc.; *U.S. Private*, pg. 671
ARTHUR D. LITTLE MEXICANA, S.A. DE C.V.—See Arthur D. Little, Inc.; *U.S. Private*, pg. 671
ARTHUR D. LITTLE OF CANADA LTD.—See Arthur D. Little, Inc.; *U.S. Private*, pg. 671
ARTHUR D. LITTLE SCHOOL OF MANAGEMENT—See Arthur D. Little, Inc.; *U.S. Private*, pg. 670
ARTHUR D. LITTLE/TMBK PARTNERS—See Arthur D. Little, Inc.; *U.S. Private*, pg. 671
LITTLE BEAR ORGANIC FOODS, INC.—See The Hain Food Group Inc.; *U.S. Public*, pg. 774
LITTLE, BROWN & CO.—See Time Warner Inc.; *U.S. Public*, pg. 1612
LITTLE BROWN & CO. (CANADA) LTD.—See Time Warner Inc.; *U.S. Public*, pg. 1615
LITTLE CAESAR ENTERPRISES, INC.; *U.S. Private*, pg. 671
LITTLE FALLS COLOR PRINT—See Sullivan Paper Company; *U.S. Private*, pg. 1050
LITTLE GIANT PUMP COMPANY—See Tecumseh Products Company; *U.S. Public*, pg. 1566
LITTLE LADY FOODS, INC.; *U.S. Private*, pg. 671
LITTLE NICKEL WANT ADS—See Lee Enterprises, Incorporated; *U.S. Public*, pg. 983
LITTLE SIMON—See National Amusements, Inc.; *U.S. Private*, pg. 777
LITTLE SWITZERLAND, INC.; *U.S. Public*, pg. 1001
LITTLE TIKES (CANADA) INC.—See Rubbermaid Incorporated; *U.S. Public*, pg. 1411
THE LITTLE TIKES COMPANY—See Rubbermaid Incorporated; *U.S. Public*, pg. 1411
THE LITTLE TIKES COMPANY (IRELAND), LIMITED—See Rubbermaid Incorporated; *U.S. Public*, pg. 1411
LITTLEFIELD, ADAMS & COMPANY; *U.S. Public*, pg. 1001
LITTLEFIELD FEED YARD—See Friona Industries, L.P.; *U.S. Private*, pg. 429
LITTLEFORD DAY INC.; *U.S. Private*, pg. 671
LITTLETON COIN CO., INC.; *U.S. Private*, pg. 671
LITTON APPLIED TECHNOLOGY—See Litton Industries, Inc.; *U.S. Public*, pg. 1003
LITTON AVIONICS SYSTEMS—See Litton Industries, Inc.; *U.S. Public*, pg. 1005
LITTON BUSINESS SYSTEMS HOLLAND B.V.—See Litton Industries, Inc.; *U.S. Public*, pg. 1004
LITTON CLIFTON PRECISION SOUTH—See Litton Industries, Inc.; *U.S. Public*, pg. 1003
LITTON COMPONENTS PRIVATE LTD.—See Litton Industries, Inc.; *U.S. Public*, pg. 1004
LITTON COMPUTER SERVICES DIV.—See Litton Industries, Inc.; *U.S. Public*, pg. 1002
LITTON COMPUTER SERVICES-WESTERN REGIONAL DATA CENTER—See Litton Industries, Inc.; *U.S. Public*, pg. 1002
LITTON INDUSTRIES, INC.; *U.S. Public*, pg. 1002
LITTON INSTRUMENTS & LIFE SUPPORT—See Litton Industries, Inc.; *U.S. Public*, pg. 1003
LITTON INTERNATIONAL S.A.—See Litton Industries, Inc.; *U.S. Public*, pg. 1004
LITTON ITALIA S.P.A.—See Litton Industries, Inc.; *U.S. Public*, pg. 1004
LITTON MARINE SYSTEMS—See Litton Industries, Inc.; *U.S. Public*, pg. 1003
LITTON POLY-SCIENTIFIC—See Litton Industries, Inc.; *U.S. Public*, pg. 1003
LITTON PRECISION GEAR DIV.—See Litton Industries, Inc.; *U.S. Public*, pg. 1003
LITTON PRECISION PRODUCTS INTERNATIONAL—See Litton Industries, Inc.; *U.S. Public*, pg. 1004
LITTON SAUDI ARABIA—See Litton Industries, Inc.; *U.S. Public*, pg. 1004
LITTON SAUDI ARABIA LTD.—See Litton Industries, Inc.; *U.S. Public*, pg. 1004
LITTON SERVOTECHNIK—See Litton Industries, Inc.; *U.S. Public*, pg. 1004
LITTON SOLID STATE—See Litton Industries, Inc.; *U.S. Public*, pg. 1003
LITTON SYSTEMS CANADA LTD.—See Litton Industries, Inc.; *U.S. Public*, pg. 1005
LITTON SYSTEMS CANADA LTD. (NOVA SCOTIA)—See Litton Industries, Inc.; *U.S. Public*, pg. 1005
LITTON SYSTEMS, INC. ADVANCED CIRCUITRY DIV.—See Litton Industries, Inc.; *U.S. Public*, pg. 1003
LITTON UK LTD.—See Litton Industries, Inc.; *U.S. Public*, pg. 1005
LITTON-WESTREX COMPANY, JAPAN—See Litton Industries, Inc.; *U.S. Public*, pg. 1005
LITTON WORLD TRADE CORPORATION—See Litton Industries, Inc.; *U.S. Public*, pg. 1005
LITTORALE OENOLOGIE S.A.—See Royal Gist-Brocades N.V.; *Int'l*, pg. 1143
LIUSKI INTERNATIONAL ATLANTA, INC.—See Liuski International, Inc.; *U.S. Public*, pg. 1005
LIUSKI INTERNATIONAL CALIFORNIA, INC.—See Liuski International, Inc.; *U.S. Public*, pg. 1005
LIUSKI INTERNATIONAL ILLINOIS, INC.—See Liuski International, Inc.; *U.S. Public*, pg. 1005
LIUSKI INTERNATIONAL, INC.; *U.S. Public*, pg. 1005
LIUSKI INTERNATIONAL MARYLAND, INC.—See Liuski International, Inc.; *U.S. Public*, pg. 1005
LIUSKI INTERNATIONAL MIAMI, INC.—See Liuski International, Inc.; *U.S. Public*, pg. 1005
LIUSKI INTERNATIONAL TORONTO, INC.—See Liuski International, Inc.; *U.S. Public*, pg. 1005
LIV-A-SNAPS, INC.—See Nestle S.A.; *Int'l*, pg. 917
LIVE ENTERTAINMENT INC.; *U.S. Private*, pg. 671
LIVE FILM & MEDIAWORKS—See LIVE Entertainment Inc.; *U.S. Private*, pg. 671
LIVERGOOD GRAIN CO.—See Tate & Lyle PLC; *Int'l*, pg. 1357
LIVERIGHT PUBLISHING CORP.—See W.W. Norton & Company, Inc.; *U.S. Private*, pg. 807
LIVERNOIS ENGINEERING COMPANY; *U.S. Private*, pg. 672
LIVERNOIS VEHICLE CO.—See Livernois Engineering Company; *U.S. Private*, pg. 672
LIVERPOOL AIRPORT PUBLIC LIMITED COMPANY—See British Aerospace p.l.c.; *Int'l*, pg. 217
LIVERPOOL COATED STONE—See RMC Group p.l.c.; *Int'l*, pg. 1079
LIVERPOOL SHOE CO. LTD.—See Pentland Group PLC; *Int'l*, pg. 1035
LIVESTOCK FEEDS PLC—See Pfizer Inc.; *U.S. Public*, pg. 1282
LIVEWIRE: TODAY'S FAMILIES ONLINE—See Griffin Bacal Inc.; *U.S. Private*, pg. 480
LIVING CENTERS OF AMERICA—See Paragon Health Network, Inc.; *U.S. Public*, pg. 1257
LIVING COLOR DIV.—See Genovese Drug Stores, Inc.; *U.S. Public*, pg. 730
LIVING EARTH TECHNOLOGY CO.—See Republic Industries, Inc.; *U.S. Public*, pg. 1379
LIVINGSTON CONVALESCENT CENTER NO. 434—See Vencor, Inc.; *U.S. Public*, pg. 1714
LIVINGSTON INTERNATIONAL FREIGHT—See Circle International Group, Inc.; *U.S. Public*, pg. 373
LIVINGSTON INTERNATIONAL FREIGHT BELGIUM—See Circle International Group, Inc.; *U.S. Public*, pg. 373
LIVINGSTON S.A.—See Brammer plc; *Int'l*, pg. 212
LIVINGSTON SERVICES GMBH—See Brammer plc; *Int'l*, pg. 212
LIVINGSTON UK LIMITED—See Brammer plc; *Int'l*, pg. 212
LIVINGSTON U.K. LIMITED—See Brammer plc; *Int'l*, pg. 212
LIVINGSTON UK LTD.—See Brammer plc; *Int'l*, pg. 212

LIVONIA-RUBBER & PLASTICS DIV.—See Newcor, Inc.; *U.S. Public*, pg. 1176
LIVORNO MARINE CONTAINERS S.R.L.—See Sea Containers Ltd.; *Int'l*, pg. 1214
LIVSFORSIKRINGS-AKTIESELSKABET UTRECHT—See Fortis; *Int'l*, pg. 499
LIXTON SPEZIALREINIGER GMBH—See Henkel KGaA; *Int'l*, pg. 610
LIZ & CO.—See Liz Claiborne, Inc.; *U.S. Public*, pg. 1006
LIZ CLAIBORNE COLLECTION DIVISION—See Liz Claiborne, Inc.; *U.S. Public*, pg. 1006
LIZ CLAIBORNE COSMETICS, INC.—See Liz Claiborne, Inc.; *U.S. Public*, pg. 1006
LIZ CLAIBORNE DRESS DIVISION—See Liz Claiborne, Inc.; *U.S. Public*, pg. 1006
LIZ CLAIBORNE, INC.; *U.S. Public*, pg. 1005
LIZ CLAIBORNE OUTLET DIVISION—See Liz Claiborne, Inc.; *U.S. Public*, pg. 1006
LIZ CLAIBORNE RETAIL DIVISION—See Liz Claiborne, Inc.; *U.S. Public*, pg. 1006
LIZ CLAIBORNE SHOE DIVISION—See Liz Claiborne, Inc.; *U.S. Public*, pg. 1006
LIZ CLAIBORNE SUIT DIVISION—See Liz Claiborne, Inc.; *U.S. Public*, pg. 1006
LIZSPORT DIVISION—See Liz Claiborne, Inc.; *U.S. Public*, pg. 1006
LIZWEAR DIVISION—See Liz Claiborne, Inc.; *U.S. Public*, pg. 1006
AB LJUNGBY STALGJUTERI—See Trelleborg AB; *Int'l*, pg. 1419
LJUNGBY STALGJUTERI LJUNGBY—See Svedala Industri AB; *Int'l*, pg. 1323
LLOYD ADRATICO ESPANA—See Allianz Aktiengesellschaft; *Int'l*, pg. 60
LLOYD ADRIATICO S.P.A.—See Allianz Aktiengesellschaft; *Int'l*, pg. 60
LLOYD CONTROLS, INC.; *U.S. Private*, pg. 672
LLOYD ELECTRIC APPARATUS CO.—See Lloyd Controls, Inc.; *U.S. Private*, pg. 672
LLOYD-IMMOBILIEN G.M.B.H.—See Assicurazioni Generali S.p.A.; *Int'l*, pg. 89
LLOYD INSTRUMENTS LTD.—See AMETEK, Inc.; *U.S. Public*, pg. 100
LLOYD PROPERTIES; *U.S. Private*, pg. 672
LLOYD 1885—See Allianz Aktiengesellschaft; *Int'l*, pg. 61
LLOYDAIRE/ELJER INC.—See Zurn Industries, Inc.; *U.S. Public*, pg. 1795
LLOYDMINSTER POOL—See Saskatchewan Wheat Pool; *Int'l*, pg. 1195
LLOYDS ABBEY LIFE PLC—See Lloyds TSB Group PLC; *Int'l*, pg. 813
LLOYDS ASSOCIATED AIR LEASING LTD.—See Lloyds TSB Group PLC; *Int'l*, pg. 813
LLOYDS BANK (AMERICAS) LTD.—See Lloyds TSB Group PLC; *Int'l*, pg. 813
LLOYDS BANK (BELGIUM) S.A.—See Lloyds TSB Group PLC; *Int'l*, pg. 813
LLOYDS BANK COMMERCIAL PROPERTIES LTD.—See Lloyds TSB Group PLC; *Int'l*, pg. 813
LLOYDS BANK EXPORT FINANCE LTD.—See Lloyds TSB Group PLC; *Int'l*, pg. 813
LLOYDS BANK FINANCE (ISLE OF MAN) LTD.—See Lloyds TSB Group PLC; *Int'l*, pg. 813
LLOYDS BANK INSURANCE SERVICES LTD.—See Lloyds TSB Group PLC; *Int'l*, pg. 813
LLOYDS BANK INTERNATIONAL LTD.—See Lloyds TSB Group PLC; *Int'l*, pg. 813
LLOYDS BANK (JERSEY) LTD.—See Lloyds TSB Group PLC; *Int'l*, pg. 813
LLOYDS BANK NZA LIMITED—See Lloyds TSB Group PLC; *Int'l*, pg. 813
LLOYDS BANK SA—See Lloyds TSB Group PLC; *Int'l*, pg. 813
LLOYDS BANK TRUST COMPANY (CHANNEL ISLANDS) LIMITED—See Lloyds TSB Group PLC; *Int'l*, pg. 813
LLOYDS BANK UNIT TRUST MANAGERS LTD.—See Lloyds TSB Group PLC; *Int'l*, pg. 813
LLOYDS BANK UK MANAGEMENT LTD.-CORP. BANKING & TREASURY—See Lloyds TSB Group PLC; *Int'l*, pg. 813
LLOYDS BOWMAKER FINANCE LTD.—See Lloyds TSB Group PLC; *Int'l*, pg. 813
LLOYDS DEVELOPMENT CAPITAL LTD.—See Lloyds TSB Group PLC; *Int'l*, pg. 813
LLOYDS EQUIPMENT LEASING LTD.—See Lloyds TSB Group PLC; *Int'l*, pg. 813
LLOYDS EUROFINANCE NV—See Lloyds TSB Group PLC; *Int'l*, pg. 813
LLOYDS INDUSTRIAL LEASING LTD.—See Lloyds TSB Group PLC; *Int'l*, pg. 813
LLOYDS INTERNATIONAL BANKING—See Lloyds TSB Group PLC; *Int'l*, pg. 813
LLOYDS INTERNATIONAL LTD.—See Lloyds TSB Group PLC; *Int'l*, pg. 813
LLOYDS LEASING LTD.—See Lloyds TSB Group PLC; *Int'l*, pg. 813
LLOYDS MERCHANT BANK LTD.—See Lloyds TSB Group PLC; *Int'l*, pg. 813
LLOYDS PRIVATE BANKING & FINANCIAL SERVICES—See Lloyds TSB Group PLC; *Int'l*, pg. 813
LLOYDS TSB GROUP PLC; *Int'l*, pg. 812
LMP IMPIANTI SRI—See Owens Corning; *U.S. Public*, pg. 1237
LM/YOUNG & RUBICAM—See Young & Rubicam Inc.; *U.S. Private*, pg. 1199
LOAN AMERICA FINANCIAL CORP.—See NationsBank Corporation; *U.S. Public*, pg. 1162
THE LOAN STORE, INC.—See Horizon Bancorp; *U.S. Private*, pg. 539
LOANWORKS—See INMC Mortgage Holdings, Inc.; *U.S. Public*, pg. 858
LOBLAW COMPANIES LIMITED—See George Weston Limited; *Int'l*, pg. 1495

LOBLAW INTERNATIONAL MERCHANTS—See George Weston Limited; *Int'l*, pg. 1495
LOBLAW SUPERMARKETS INC.—See George Weston Limited; *Int'l*, pg. 1495
LOC MANUTENTION—See Manitou BF; *Int'l*, pg. 834
LOCABEL S.A.—See Bank Brussels Lambert; *Int'l*, pg. 147
LOCAPOR - COMPANHIA PORTUGUESA LOCACAO FINANCEIRA MOBILIARIA, SA—See Caixa Geral de Depositos; *Int'l*, pg. 250
LOCATEL—See Alcatel Alsthom Compagnie Generale D'Electricite; *Int'l*, pg. 54
LOCAZIONI FINANZIARIE S.P.A.—See Banco Ambrosiano Veneto S.p.A.; *Int'l*, pg. 138
LOCKFORMER COMPANY—See Met-Coil Systems Corp.; *U.S. Public*, pg. 1100
LOCKHART CADILLAC INC.; *U.S. Private*, pg. 672
LOCKHART CADILLAC SOUTH—See Lockhart Cadillac Inc.; *U.S. Private*, pg. 672
LOCKHEED ADVANCED DEVELOPMENT COMPANY—See Lockheed Martin Corporation; *U.S. Public*, pg. 1007
LOCKHEED AEROMOD CENTER, INC.—See Lockheed Martin Corporation; *U.S. Public*, pg. 1007
LOCKHEED AERONAUTICAL SYSTEMS COMPANY—See Lockheed Martin Corporation; *U.S. Public*, pg. 1007
LOCKHEED AIRCRAFT (ASIA) LTD.—See Lockheed Martin Corporation; *U.S. Public*, pg. 1009
LOCKHEED AUSTIN DIVISION—See Lockheed Martin Corporation; *U.S. Public*, pg. 1008
LOCKHEED CANADA—See Lockheed Martin Corporation; *U.S. Public*, pg. 1009
LOCKHEED CORPORATION (INTERNATIONAL) S.A.—See Lockheed Martin Corporation; *U.S. Public*, pg. 1009
LOCKHEED ENGINEERING & SCIENCES CO., INC.—See Lockheed Martin Corporation; *U.S. Public*, pg. 1009
LOCKHEED ENVIRONMENTAL SYSTEMS & TECHNOLOGIES COMPANY—See Lockheed Martin Corporation; *U.S. Public*, pg. 1009
LOCKHEED FINANCE CORPORATION—See Lockheed Martin Corporation; *U.S. Public*, pg. 1008
LOCKHEED FORT WORTH COMPANY—See Lockheed Martin Corporation; *U.S. Public*, pg. 1007
LOCKHEED INFORMATION MANAGEMENT SERVICES CO.—See Lockheed Martin Corporation; *U.S. Public*, pg. 1009
LOCKHEED INTERNATIONAL GMBH—See Lockheed Martin Corporation; *U.S. Public*, pg. 1009
LOCKHEED-LATIN AMERICA—See Lockheed Martin Corporation; *U.S. Public*, pg. 1008
LOCKHEED MARTIN ADVANCED PROJECTS—See Lockheed Martin Corporation; *U.S. Public*, pg. 1008
LOCKHEED MARTIN AERONUTRONIC—See Lockheed Martin Corporation; *U.S. Public*, pg. 1008
LOCKHEED MARTIN AEROSTRUCTURE—See Lockheed Martin Corporation; *U.S. Public*, pg. 1006
LOCKHEED MARTIN AIR TRAFFIC MANAGEMENT—See Lockheed Martin Corporation; *U.S. Public*, pg. 1009
LOCKHEED MARTIN COMMAND & CONTROL SYSTEMS—See Lockheed Martin Corporation; *U.S. Public*, pg. 1008
LOCKHEED MARTIN CORPORATION; *U.S. Public*, pg. 1006
LOCKHEED MARTIN DEFENSE SYSTEMS—See Lockheed Martin Corporation; *U.S. Public*, pg. 1008
LOCKHEED MARTIN EDS-CANADA—See Lockheed Martin Corporation; *U.S. Public*, pg. 1008
LOCKHEED MARTIN ELECTRO-OPTICAL SYSTEMS—See Lockheed Martin Corporation; *U.S. Public*, pg. 1008
LOCKHEED MARTIN ELECTRONICS GROUP—See Lockheed Martin Corporation; *U.S. Public*, pg. 1006
LOCKHEED MARTIN-FAIRCHILD—See Lockheed Martin Corporation; *U.S. Public*, pg. 1008
LOCKHEED MARTIN FAIRCHILD IMAGING SENSORS—See Lockheed Martin Corporation; *U.S. Public*, pg. 1008
LOCKHEED MARTIN FAIRCHILD SYSTEMS—See Lockheed Martin Corporation; *U.S. Public*, pg. 1008
LOCKHEED MARTIN FEDERAL SYSTEMS-GAITHERSBURG—See Lockheed Martin Corporation; *U.S. Public*, pg. 1008
LOCKHEED MARTIN FEDERAL SYSTEMS-OWEGO—See Lockheed Martin Corporation; *U.S. Public*, pg. 1008
LOCKHEED MARTIN INFARED IMAGING SYSTEMS—See Lockheed Martin Corporation; *U.S. Public*, pg. 1008
LOCKHEED MARTIN INFORMATION DISPLAY SYSTEMS—See Lockheed Martin Corporation; *U.S. Public*, pg. 1008
LOCKHEED MARTIN LIBRASCOPE—See Lockheed Martin Corporation; *U.S. Public*, pg. 1008
LOCKHEED MARTIN MICROWAVE-FSI—See Lockheed Martin Corporation; *U.S. Public*, pg. 1008
LOCKHEED MARTIN MISSILES & SPACE—See Lockheed Martin Corporation; *U.S. Public*, pg. 1008
LOCKHEED MARTIN SKUNK WORKS—See Lockheed Martin Corporation; *U.S. Public*, pg. 1007
LOCKHEED MARTIN SOLARTRON SYSTEMS—See Lockheed Martin Corporation; *U.S. Public*, pg. 1009
LOCKHEED MARTIN SPACE INFORMATION SYSTEMS—See Lockheed Martin Corporation; *U.S. Public*, pg. 1009
LOCKHEED MARTIN SPACE & RANGE SYSTEMS—See Lockheed Martin Corporation; *U.S. Public*, pg. 1009
LOCKHEED MARTIN TACTICAL DEFENSE SYSTEMS—See Lockheed Martin Corporation; *U.S. Public*, pg. 1009
LOCKHEED MARTIN TACTICAL DEFENSE SYSTEMS (AKRON)—See Lockheed Martin Corporation; *U.S. Public*, pg. 1009
LOCKHEED MARTIN TACTICAL DEFENSE SYSTEMS (ARIZONA)—See Lockheed Martin Corporation; *U.S. Public*, pg. 1009
LOCKHEED MARTIN TACTICAL DEFENSE SYSTEMS-EAGAN—See Lockheed Martin Corporation; *U.S. Public*, pg. 1009

LOCKHEED MARTIN TRAINING & TECHNICAL SERVICES—See Lockheed Martin Corporation; *U.S. Public*, pg. 1009
LOCKHEED MARTIN WESTERN DEVELOPMENT LABS—See Lockheed Martin Corporation; *U.S. Public*, pg. 1009
LOCKHEED-MARTIN W.I.C.—See Lockheed Martin Corporation; *U.S. Public*, pg. 1007
LOCKHEED MIDDLE EAST SERVICES—See Lockheed Martin Corporation; *U.S. Public*, pg. 1010
LOCKHEED SPACE OPERATIONS CO.—See Lockheed Martin Corporation; *U.S. Public*, pg. 1009
LOCKHEED SUPPORT SYSTEMS, INC.—See Lockheed Martin Corporation; *U.S. Public*, pg. 1009
LOCKHEED TECHNICAL OPERATIONS COMPANY—See Lockheed Martin Corporation; *U.S. Public*, pg. 1009
LOCKLEY MANUFACTURING DIVISION—See The Entwistle Company; *U.S. Private*, pg. 378
LOCKNETICS SECURITY ENGINEERING—See Harrow Industries; *U.S. Private*, pg. 507
LOCKPORT UNION SUN & JOURNAL—See Media General, Inc.; *U.S. Public*, pg. 1078
LOCKSMITH PUBLISHING CORP.—See Unican Security Systems Ltd.; *Int'l*, pg. 1432
LOCKWOOD ANDREWS & NEWNAM, INC.—See Leo A. Daly Company; *U.S. Private*, pg. 309
LOCKWOOD GREENE ENGINEERS, INC.—See Philipp Holzmann AG; *Int'l*, pg. 633
LOCKWOOD GREENE TECHNOLOGIES—See Philipp Holzmann AG; *Int'l*, pg. 633
LOCKWOOD KESSLER & BARTLETT, INC.—See Continental Can Co.; *U.S. Public*, pg. 440
LOCTITE ARGENTINA—See Henkel KGaA; *Int'l*, pg. 611
LOCTITE ASIA LTD.—See Henkel KGaA; *Int'l*, pg. 611
LOCTITE (AUSTRALIA) PTY. LTD.—See Henkel KGaA; *Int'l*, pg. 611
LOCTITE BELGIUM N.V.—See Henkel KGaA; *Int'l*, pg. 611
LOCTITE BRASIL LTDA.—See Henkel KGaA; *Int'l*, pg. 611
LOCTITE CANADA INC.—See Henkel KGaA; *Int'l*, pg. 611
LOCTITE CO. DE MEXICO, S.A. DE C.V.—See Henkel KGaA; *Int'l*, pg. 611
LOCTITE CORP. CHILE LTDA.—See Henkel KGaA; *Int'l*, pg. 611
LOCTITE CORP. NORTH AMERICAN GROUP—See Henkel KGaA; *Int'l*, pg. 611
LOCTITE CORPORATION—See Henkel KGaA; *Int'l*, pg. 611
LOCTITE DE COLOMBIA S.A.—See Henkel KGaA; *Int'l*, pg. 611
LOCTITE DE VENEZUELA, C.A.—See Henkel KGaA; *Int'l*, pg. 611
LOCTITE DEUTSCHLAND G.M.B.H.—See Henkel KGaA; *Int'l*, pg. 611
LOCTITE ESPANA, S.A.—See Henkel KGaA; *Int'l*, pg. 611
LOCTITE EUROPA GESELLSCHAFT MBH—See Henkel KGaA; *Int'l*, pg. 611
LOCTITE (IRELAND) LTD.—See Henkel KGaA; *Int'l*, pg. 611
LOCTITE ITALIA S.P.A.—See Henkel KGaA; *Int'l*, pg. 611
LOCTITE (JAPAN) CORP.—See Henkel KGaA; *Int'l*, pg. 611
LOCTITE LUMINESCENT EUROPE—See Henkel KGaA; *Int'l*, pg. 611
LOCTITE PUERTO RICO, INC.—See Henkel KGaA; *Int'l*, pg. 611
LOCTITE (UK) LTD.—See Henkel KGaA; *Int'l*, pg. 611
LOCUS DEVELOPMENT LABORATORY—See Platinum Technology, Inc.; *U.S. Public*, pg. 1309
LOCUS, INC.—See Kaman Corporation; *U.S. Public*, pg. 942
LOCUST STREET SECURITIES, INC.—See ING Groep N.V.; *Int'l*, pg. 647
LOD CIGARETTES LTD.—See Dubek Ltd.; *Int'l*, pg. 421
LODAL, INC.; *U.S. Private*, pg. 672
LODERS & NUCOLINE LTD.—See Unilever Plc; *Int'l*, pg. 1434
LODESTAR ENERGY INC.; *U.S. Private*, pg. 672
LODGE IGNITION LIMITED—See Smiths Industries plc; *Int'l*, pg. 1267
LODGE PROPERTIES, INC. (LODGE AT VAIL)—See Sea Containers Ltd.; *Int'l*, pg. 1213
LODGISTIX, INC.—See Sulcus Computer Corp.; *U.S. Public*, pg. 1527
LOEB INC.—See Provigo Inc.; *Int'l*, pg. 1073
LOEBER MOTORS, INC.; *U.S. Private*, pg. 672
LOEBER MOTORS, INC.—See Loeber Motors, Inc.; *U.S. Private*, pg. 672
K. LOEGAGER A/S—See Martin Merkel GmbH & Co. KG; *Int'l*, pg. 859
LOEHMANN'S, INC.; *U.S. Public*, pg. 1010
LOEWA WARENHANDEL GES.MBH—See Tengelmann Warenhandelsgesellschaft; *Int'l*, pg. 1375
LOEWE AUSTRALIA PTY LTD—See LVMH Moet Hennessy Louis Vuitton; *Int'l*, pg. 782
LOEWE FASHION PTE LTD—See LVMH Moet Hennessy Louis Vuitton; *Int'l*, pg. 782
LOEWE FASHION SDN. EHD—See LVMH Moet Hennessy Louis Vuitton; *Int'l*, pg. 782
LOEWE FASHIONS INCORPORATED—See LVMH Moet Hennessy Louis Vuitton; *Int'l*, pg. 781
LOEWE FRANCE—See LVMH Moet Hennessy Louis Vuitton; *Int'l*, pg. 781
LOEWE GUAM, INC.—See LVMH Moet Hennessy Louis Vuitton; *Int'l*, pg. 781
LOEWE HAWAII INC.—See LVMH Moet Hennessy Louis Vuitton; *Int'l*, pg. 781
LOEWE HERMANOS (U.K.) LTD—See LVMH Moet Hennessy Louis Vuitton; *Int'l*, pg. 782
LOEWE HONG KONG LTD—See LVMH Moet Hennessy Louis Vuitton; *Int'l*, pg. 782
LOEWE INTERNATIONAL—See LVMH Moet Hennessy Louis Vuitton; *Int'l*, pg. 781
LOEWE ITALIA S.R.L.—See LVMH Moet Hennessy Louis Vuitton; *Int'l*, pg. 782

LOEWE JAPAN K.K.—See LVMH Moet Hennessy Louis Vuitton; *Int'l*, pg. 782
LOEWE SAIPAN INC.—See LVMH Moet Hennessy Louis Vuitton; *Int'l*, pg. 781
LOEWE TAIWAN LTD—See LVMH Moet Hennessy Louis Vuitton; *Int'l*, pg. 782
THE LOEWEN GROUP, INC.; *Int'l*, pg. 814
LOEWEN GROUP INTERNATIONAL, INC.—See The Loewen Group, Inc.; *Int'l*, pg. 814
LOEWS CORPORATION; *U.S. Public*, pg. 1010
LOEWS HOTELS—See Loews Corporation; *U.S. Public*, pg. 1011
LOEWS MONTE CARLO—See Loews Corporation; *U.S. Public*, pg. 1011
LOEWS NEW YORK—See Loews Corporation; *U.S. Public*, pg. 1011
LOEWS THEATRE MANAGEMENT CORP.—See Sony Corporation; *Int'l*, pg. 1282
LOFFLAND BROTHERS DE VENEZUELA, C.A.—See Nabors Industries, Inc.; *U.S. Public*, pg. 1149
LOFTS SEED, INC.—See AgriBioTech, Inc.; *U.S. Public*, pg. 29
LOGA ATHLETIC/HEADWEAR INC.—See Tultex Corporation; *U.S. Public*, pg. 1644
LOGADATA DUE S.P.A.—See Compagnie des Machines Bull; *Int'l*, pg. 318
LOGAN & KANAWHA COAL CO.; *U.S. Private*, pg. 672
LOGAN CORPORATION; *U.S. Private*, pg. 672
LOGAN MANUFACTURING—See Standard Manufacturing Co., Inc.; *U.S. Private*, pg. 1032
LOGETRONICS CORPORATION—See AFP Imaging Corporation; *U.S. Public*, pg. 6
LOGGHE STAMPING COMPANY; *U.S. Private*, pg. 672
LOGIC ASSOCIATES, INC.; *U.S. Private*, pg. 673
LOGICA B.V.—See Logica Plc; *Int'l*, pg. 814
LOGICA INC.—See Logica Plc; *Int'l*, pg. 814
LOGICA, INC.—See Logica Plc; *Int'l*, pg. 814
LOGICA INC.—See Logica Plc; *Int'l*, pg. 814
LOGICA INFORMATIK AG—See Logica Plc; *Int'l*, pg. 814
LOGICA INFORMATIQUE SA—See Logica Plc; *Int'l*, pg. 814
LOGICA LIMITED—See Logica Plc; *Int'l*, pg. 814
LOGICA (MALAYSIA) SDN. BHD.—See Logica Plc; *Int'l*, pg. 814
LOGICA NEW ZEALAND LIMITED—See Logica Plc; *Int'l*, pg. 815
LOGICA PLC; *Int'l*, pg. 814
LOGICA PTE LTD—See Logica Plc; *Int'l*, pg. 815
LOGICA SA/NV—See Logica Plc; *Int'l*, pg. 815
LOGICA S.R.O.—See Logica Plc; *Int'l*, pg. 815
LOGICA UK LTD.—See Logica Plc; *Int'l*, pg. 814
LOGICAL OPERATIONS—See Softbank Corporation; *Int'l*, pg. 1276
LOGICASIEL SPA—See Logica Plc; *Int'l*, pg. 815
LOGICOM CO., LTD.—See NHK Spring Co., Ltd.; *Int'l*, pg. 901
LOGICON EAGLE TECHNOLOGY, INC.—See Northrop Grumman Corporation; *U.S. Public*, pg. 1199
LOGICON GEODYNAMIC—See Northrop Grumman Corporation; *U.S. Public*, pg. 1199
LOGICON GEODYNAMICS CENTRAL DIVISION—See Northrop Grumman Corporation; *U.S. Public*, pg. 1199
LOGICON GEODYNAMICS EASTERN DIVISION—See Northrop Grumman Corporation; *U.S. Public*, pg. 1199
LOGICON GEODYNAMICS SERVICES CORPORATION—See Northrop Grumman Corporation; *U.S. Public*, pg. 1199
LOGICON GEODYNAMICS WESTERN DIVISION—See Northrop Grumman Corporation; *U.S. Public*, pg. 1199
LOGICON, INC.—See Northrop Grumman Corporation; *U.S. Public*, pg. 1198
LOGICON R & D ASSOCIATES—See Northrop Grumman Corporation; *U.S. Public*, pg. 1199
LOGICON SYSCON CORPORATION—See Northrop Grumman Corporation; *U.S. Public*, pg. 1199
LOGICON TECHNICAL SERVICES INC.—See Northrop Grumman Corporation; *U.S. Public*, pg. 1199
LOGILITY, INC.—See American Software, Inc.; *U.S. Public*, pg. 91
LOGION B.V.—See Royal Nedlloyd Group N.V.; *Int'l*, pg. 1144
LOGISTIC SERVICES DIVISION—See Royal Nedlloyd Group N.V.; *Int'l*, pg. 1144
COMP. LOGISTICA COMBUSTIVEIS, S.A.—See Petrogal, s.a.; *Int'l*, pg. 1045
LOGISTICS SECTOR—See Kimberly-Clark Corporation; *U.S. Public*, pg. 958
LOGISTICS WORLDWIDE—See CNF Transportation Inc.; *U.S. Public*, pg. 281
LOGISTIX; *U.S. Private*, pg. 673
LOGITECH INC.—See Logitech International SA; *Int'l*, pg. 815
LOGITECH INTERNATIONAL SA; *Int'l*, pg. 815
LOGITECH LTD.—See Radiometer A/S; *Int'l*, pg. 1084
LOGO OF THE AMERICAS—See Essilor International Compagnie Generale d'Optique; *Int'l*, pg. 462
LOGO 7, INC.—See Tultex Corporation; *U.S. Public*, pg. 1644
LOGOVAZ SYSTEMS—See Oracle Corporation; *U.S. Public*, pg. 1228
LOGWARE GESELLSCHAFT FUR ENTWICKLUNG UND FERTIGUNG ELEKTRONISCHER GERATE MBH—See Veba AG; *Int'l*, pg. 1459
LOHER AG—See Deutsche Babcock AG; *Int'l*, pg. 400
LOHER BENELUX B.V.—See Deutsche Babcock AG; *Int'l*, pg. 401
LOHER DRIVE SYSTEMS, INC.—See Deutsche Babcock AG; *Int'l*, pg. 400
LOHJA ABETONI OY AB—See Scancem AB; *Int'l*, pg. 1199
LOHJA RUDUS OY AG—See Scancem AB; *Int'l*, pg. 1200
LOHMANN & COMPANY GMBH—See Standard Commercial Corporation; *U.S. Public*, pg. 1502

LOHMANN & STOLTERFOHT GMBH—See Mannesmann A.G.; *Int'l*, pg. 838
LOHR & BROMKAMP GMBH—See GKN plc; *Int'l*, pg. 536
LOI FOURS INDUSTRIELS S.A.—See Ruhrgas Aktiengesellschaft; *Int'l*, pg. 1149
LOI, INC.—See Ruhrgas Aktiengesellschaft; *Int'l*, pg. 1149
LOIS/EJL—See Lois/USA Inc.; *U.S. Public*, pg. 1011
LOIS/EJL ADVERTISING/CHICAGO—See Lois/USA Inc.; *U.S. Public*, pg. 1011
LOIS/EJL CHICAGO—See Lois/USA Inc.; *U.S. Public*, pg. 1011
LOIS/EJL DETROIT—See Lois/USA Inc.; *U.S. Public*, pg. 1011
LOIS/EJL DIRECT—See Lois/USA Inc.; *U.S. Public*, pg. 1011
LOIS/EJL LOS ANGELES—See Lois/USA Inc.; *U.S. Public*, pg. 1011
LOIS/EJL NEW YORK—See Lois/USA Inc.; *U.S. Public*, pg. 1011
LOIS/USA INC.; *U.S. Public*, pg. 1011
LOIS/EJL LOS ANGELES; *U.S. Private*, pg. 673
LOISELET INTERNATIONAL S.A.—See Groupe Strafor Facom; *Int'l*, pg. 570
LOJACK CORPORATION; *U.S. Public*, pg. 1012
LOMAK OPERATING COMPANY—See Lomak Petroleum Inc.; *U.S. Public*, pg. 1012
LOMAK PETROLEUM INC.; *U.S. Public*, pg. 1012
LOMAK PRODUCTION COMPANY—See Lomak Petroleum Inc.; *U.S. Public*, pg. 1012
LOMAR DISTRIBUTING—See Hy-Vee Food Stores Incorporated; *U.S. Private*, pg. 551
LOMBARD AND ULSTER BANKING LIMITED—See National Westminster Bank PLC; *Int'l*, pg. 911
LOMBARD AND ULSTER LIMITED—See National Westminster Bank PLC; *Int'l*, pg. 911
LOMBARD ARCHITECTURAL PRECAST PROD. CO—See Lombard Company; *U.S. Private*, pg. 673
LOMBARD BANK LIMITED—See National Westminster Bank PLC; *Int'l*, pg. 910
LOMBARD COMPANY; *U.S. Private*, pg. 673
LOMBARD LINCOLN-MERCURY & LEASING, INC.; *U.S. Private*, pg. 673
LOMBARD NATWEST COMMERCIAL SERVICES LIMITED—See National Westminster Bank PLC; *Int'l*, pg. 910
LOMBARD NORTH CENTRAL PLC—See National Westminster Bank PLC; *Int'l*, pg. 910
LOMBARD TRICITY FINANCE LIMITED—See National Westminster Bank PLC; *Int'l*, pg. 910
LOMBARDI HOLDINGS INC.; *U.S. Private*, pg. 673
LOMITA GASOLINE COMPANY—See Tidelands Oil Production Co.; *U.S. Private*, pg. 1085
LOMPEL-BAUTENSCHUTZ GMBH & CO. KG—See Philipp Holzmann AG; *Int'l*, pg. 633
THE LONDON AGENCY, INC.—See Xerox Corporation; *U.S. Public*, pg. 1784
LONDON & EDINBURGH INSURANCE GROUP LIMITED—See The Hartford Financial Services Group Inc.; *U.S. Public*, pg. 795
LONDON & LEEDS (USA) CORPORATION—See Ladbroke Group Plc; *Int'l*, pg. 788
LONDON & SCANDINAVIAN METALLURGICAL CO. LIMITED—See Metallurg; *U.S. Private*, pg. 735
LONDON AND SOUTHERN GLASS DISTRIBUTERS LIMITED—See Saint-Gobain; *Int'l*, pg. 1173
LONDON ARCHITECTURAL GLASS LTD.—See Saint-Gobain; *Int'l*, pg. 1173
LONDON BREWERY—See Interbrew S.A.; *Int'l*, pg. 679
LONDON BRICK COMPANY LTD.—See Hanson PLC; *Int'l*, pg. 593
LONDON BUREAU LTD.—See The New York Times Company; *U.S. Public*, pg. 1176
LONDON-CANADA INSURANCE COMPANY—See The Hartford Financial Services Group Inc.; *U.S. Public*, pg. 795
LONDON CENTER—See The Cascades Group; *Int'l*, pg. 273
LONDON CITY & INTERNATIONAL LIMITED—See Lonrho plc; *Int'l*, pg. 817
LONDON CITY & WESTCLIFF PROPERTIES—See Lonrho plc; *Int'l*, pg. 817
LONDON FOG INDUSTRIES, INC.; *U.S. Private*, pg. 673
THE LONDON FREE PRESS—See Sun Media Corporation; *Int'l*, pg. 1320
LONDON HOUSE—See GIB Group; *Int'l*, pg. 534
LONDON HOUSE—See The McGraw-Hill Companies; *U.S. Public*, pg. 1070
LONDON INDUSTRIES, INC.—See Worthington Industries, Inc.; *U.S. Public*, pg. 1780
LONDON INTERNATIONAL GROUP PLC; *Int'l*, pg. 815
LONDON INTERNATIONAL, U.S. HOLDINGS INC.—See London International Group plc; *Int'l*, pg. 815
LONDON LABORATORIES GMBH—See Lilly Industries, Inc.; *U.S. Public*, pg. 995
LONDON LIFE—See Australian Mutual Provident; *Int'l*, pg. 100
LONDON LIFE INSURANCE GROUP—See EdperBrascan Corporation; *Int'l*, pg. 435
LONDON LITHO ALUMINUM CO., INC.; *U.S. Private*, pg. 673
LOUIS LONDON ADVERTISING & SALES PROMOTION; *U.S. Private*, pg. 674
LOUIS LONDON ADVERTISING & SALES PROMOTION—See Louis London Advertising & Sales Promotion; *U.S. Private*, pg. 674
LOUIS LONDON DALLAS—See Louis London Advertising & Sales Promotion; *U.S. Private*, pg. 674
LONDON RECORDS—See Philips Electronics N.V.; *Int'l*, pg. 1052
LONE STAR CONTAINER SALES CORP.—See Lone Star Corrugated Container Corporation; *U.S. Private*, pg. 674
LONE STAR CORRUGATED CONTAINER CORPORATION; *U.S. Private*, pg. 674

LONE STAR ENERGY CO.—See Texas Utilities Company; *U.S. Public*, pg. 1587
LONE STAR EQUITIES INC.; *U.S. Private*, pg. 674
LONE STAR GAS CO.—See Texas Utilities Company; *U.S. Public*, pg. 1587
LONE STAR INDUSTRIES, INC.; *U.S. Public*, pg. 1012
LONE STAR PIPELINE COMPANY—See Texas Utilities Company; *U.S. Public*, pg. 1587
LONE STAR PRODUCE ACQUISITION CORP.—See Fresh America Corp.; *U.S. Public*, pg. 682
LONE STAR STEEL COMPANY—See Lone Star Technologies, Inc.; *U.S. Public*, pg. 1012
LONE STAR TECHNOLOGIES, INC.; *U.S. Public*, pg. 1012
THE LONG & FOSTER COMPANIES, INC.; *U.S. Private*, pg. 674
THE LONG & FOSTER REAL ESTATE, INC.—See The Long & Foster Companies, Inc.; *U.S. Private*, pg. 674
LONG AUTOMOTIVE, INC.-DALLAS AFTERMARKET DIV.—See Long Manufacturing, Ltd.; *Int'l*, pg. 815
LONG BEACH COMMUNITY HOSPITAL—See UniHealth; *U.S. Public*, pg. 1118
LONG BEACH LEARNING CENTER—See Berkshire Hathaway Inc.; *U.S. Public*, pg. 218
LONG BEACH PRESS-TELEGRAM—See MediaNews Group Inc.; *U.S. Private*, pg. 727
THE LONG COMPANY; *U.S. Private*, pg. 674
LONG COOLING SYSTEMS INC.—See Long Manufacturing, Ltd.; *Int'l*, pg. 815
LONG DE MEXICO—See Long Manufacturing, Ltd.; *Int'l*, pg. 815
LONG DISTANCE INTERNATIONAL—See Sprint Corporation; *U.S. Public*, pg. 1501
LONG EQUIPMENT CO.—See Long MFG. NC, Inc.; *U.S. Private*, pg. 675
LONG HAYMES CARR, INC.—See The Interpublic Group of Companies, Inc.; *U.S. Public*, pg. 909
HOWARD LONG INTERNATIONAL LTD.—See The Albert Fisher Group PLC; *Int'l*, pg. 491
LONG ISLAND BANCORP, INC.; *U.S. Public*, pg. 1013
LONG ISLAND COMMUNICATIONS CORP.—See Data General Corporation; *U.S. Public*, pg. 485
LONG ISLAND LIGHTING COMPANY; *U.S. Public*, pg. 1013
LONG ISLAND WATER CORPORATION; *U.S. Private*, pg. 674
LONG JOHN SILVER'S, INC.; *U.S. Private*, pg. 674
LONG MANUFACTURING—See Long Manufacturing, Ltd.; *Int'l*, pg. 815
LONG MANUFACTURING INC.—See Long Manufacturing, Ltd.; *Int'l*, pg. 815
LONG MANUFACTURING, LTD.; *Int'l*, pg. 815
LONG MANUFACTURING LTD.—See Long Manufacturing, Ltd.; *Int'l*, pg. 815
LONG MANUFACTURING LTD.-AFTERMARKET DIVISION—See Long Manufacturing, Ltd.; *Int'l*, pg. 815
LONG MFG. NC, INC.; *U.S. Private*, pg. 674
LONG MILE RUBBER COMPANY—See The Standard Products Company; *U.S. Public*, pg. 1504
LONG OIL COOLERS, INC.—See Long Manufacturing, Ltd.; *Int'l*, pg. 815
PHIL LONG FORD; *U.S. Private*, pg. 675
LONG PRAIRIE PACKING CO.—See Rosens Diversified, Inc.; *U.S. Private*, pg. 945
LONG PRODUCTS DIVISION—See The Broken Hill Proprietary Company Limited; *Int'l*, pg. 227
LONG REACH HOLDINGS INC.; *U.S. Private*, pg. 675
LONG REACH MANUFACTURING—See Long Reach Holdings Inc.; *U.S. Private*, pg. 675
LONG-TERM CREDIT BANK OF JAPAN - AMERICAS DIVISION—See The Long-Term Credit Bank of Japan, Limited; *Int'l*, pg. 816
LONG-TERM CREDIT BANK OF JAPAN (DEUTSCHLAND) AG—See The Long-Term Credit Bank of Japan, Limited; *Int'l*, pg. 816
LONG-TERM CREDIT BANK OF JAPAN FINANCE N.V.—See The Long-Term Credit Bank of Japan, Limited; *Int'l*, pg. 816
THE LONG-TERM CREDIT BANK OF JAPAN, LIMITED; *Int'l*, pg. 815
LONG-TERM CREDIT BANK OF JAPAN, LIMITED - CHICAGO—See The Long-Term Credit Bank of Japan, Limited; *Int'l*, pg. 816
LONG-TERM CREDIT BANK OF JAPAN, LIMITED - GRAND CAYMAN—See The Long-Term Credit Bank of Japan, Limited; *Int'l*, pg. 816
LONG-TERM CREDIT BANK OF JAPAN, LIMITED - NEW YORK—See The Long-Term Credit Bank of Japan, Limited; *Int'l*, pg. 816
LONG-TERM CREDIT BANK OF JAPAN, LTD. - LONDON BRANCH—See The Long-Term Credit Bank of Japan, Limited; *Int'l*, pg. 816
LONG-TERM CREDIT BANK OF JAPAN, LTD. - PARIS BRANCH—See The Long-Term Credit Bank of Japan, Limited; *Int'l*, pg. 816
LONG-TERM CREDIT BANK OF JAPAN (SCHWEIZ) AG—See The Long-Term Credit Bank of Japan, Limited; *Int'l*, pg. 816
LONGA VIDA S.A.—See Nestle S.A.; *Int'l*, pg. 920
THE LONGABERGER COMPANY; *U.S. Private*, pg. 675
LONGACRES PARK, INC.—See The Boeing Company; *U.S. Public*, pg. 242
LONGEVITY INTERNATIONAL, LTD.—See General Media International Inc.; *U.S. Public*, pg. 444
LONGFIBRE LTD.—See Longview Fibre Company; *U.S. Public*, pg. 1014
LONGLAC WOOD INDUSTRIES INC.—See Kruger Inc.; *Int'l*, pg. 761
LONGMAN BOTSWANA (PTY) LTD.—See Pearson plc; *Int'l*, pg. 1025
LONGMAN CHESHIRE PTY. LTD.—See Pearson plc; *Int'l*, pg. 1025
LONGMAN FRANCE SA—See Pearson plc; *Int'l*, pg. 1025
LONGMAN GROUP (OVERSEAS HOLDING) LIMITED—See Pearson plc; *Int'l*, pg. 1025

LONGMAN GROUP UK LTD.—See Pearson plc; Int'l, pg. 1025
LONGMAN GROUP USA INC.—See Pearson plc; Int'l, pg. 1026
LONGMAN ITALIA SRL—See Pearson plc; Int'l, pg. 1025
LONGMAN KENYA LTD.—See Pearson plc; Int'l, pg. 1027
LONGMAN LESOTHO (PTY) LTD.—See Pearson plc; Int'l, pg. 1025
LONGMAN MALAYSIA SDN. BHD.—See Pearson plc; Int'l, pg. 1025
LONGMAN NIGERIA LTD.—See Pearson plc; Int'l, pg. 1027
LONGMAN PAUL LTD.—See Pearson plc; Int'l, pg. 1025
LONGMAN PENGUIN JAPAN CO. LTD.—See Pearson plc; Int'l, pg. 1025
LONGMAN PENGUIN LIMITED—See Pearson plc; Int'l, pg. 1025
LONGMAN SINGAPORE PUBLISHERS (PTE.) LTD.—See Pearson plc; Int'l, pg. 1025
LONGMAN SWAZILAND (PTY) LTD.—See Pearson plc; Int'l, pg. 1026
LONGMAN ZIMBABWE (PTE) LTD.—See Pearson plc; Int'l, pg. 1026
LONGMONT FOODS—See ConAgra, Inc.; U.S. Public, pg. 426
LONGOMETAL—See Groupe Usinor; Int'l, pg. 571
LONGS DRUG STORES CORPORATION; U.S. Public, pg. 1013
LONG'S ELECTRONICS, INC.; U.S. Private, pg. 675
LONGVA GROUP; Int'l, pg. 817
LONGVIEW FIBRE COMPANY; U.S. Public, pg. 1013
LONGVIEW FIBRE CO. WESTERN CONTAINER DIVISION—See Longview Fibre Company; U.S. Public, pg. 1014
LONGVIEW NATIONAL BANK—See First Commercial Corporation; U.S. Public, pg. 630
LONGWALL INTERNATIONAL LIMITED—See Harnischfeger Industries, Inc.; U.S. Public, pg. 789
LONHRO EXPORTS LTD.—See Lonrho plc; Int'l, pg. 817
LONHRO FINANCE PLC—See Lonrho plc; Int'l, pg. 817
LONHRO (CIS) LTD.—See Lonrho plc; Int'l, pg. 817
LONRHO PLC; Int'l, pg. 817
LONHRO TEXTILES LTD.—See Lonrho plc; Int'l, pg. 817
LONSTROFF-BTR AG—See BTR plc; Int'l, pg. 130
LONZA AG—See Alusuisse-Lonza Holding Ltd.; Int'l, pg. 67
LONZA BENELUX B.V.—See Alusuisse-Lonza Holding Ltd.; Int'l, pg. 69
LONZA BIOTEC SRO—See Alusuisse-Lonza Holding Ltd.; Int'l, pg. 69
LONZA EUROPE BV—See Alusuisse-Lonza Holding Ltd.; Int'l, pg. 69
LONZA-FOLIEN GMBH—See Alusuisse-Lonza Holding Ltd.; Int'l, pg. 69
LONZA FRANCE SARL—See Alusuisse-Lonza Holding Ltd.; Int'l, pg. 69
LONZA GMBH—See Alusuisse-Lonza Holding Ltd.; Int'l, pg. 69
LONZA GUANGZHOU FIN CHEMICALS LTD.—See Alusuisse-Lonza Holding Ltd.; Int'l, pg. 69
LONZA HONGKONG LTD.—See Alusuisse-Lonza Holding Ltd.; Int'l, pg. 69
LONZA IBERICA S.A.—See Alusuisse-Lonza Holding Ltd.; Int'l, pg. 69
LONZA INC.—See Alusuisse-Lonza Holding Ltd.; Int'l, pg. 67
LONZA JAPAN LTD.—See Alusuisse-Lonza Holding Ltd.; Int'l, pg. 69
LONZA SPA—See Alusuisse-Lonza Holding Ltd.; Int'l, pg. 69
LONZA (UK) LTD.—See Alusuisse-Lonza Holding Ltd.; Int'l, pg. 67
LONZA-WERKE GMBH—See Alusuisse-Lonza Holding Ltd.; Int'l, pg. 67
LOOK—See Eastman Kodak Company; U.S. Public, pg. 553
LOOK-O-LOOK BV—See Van Melle N.V.; Int'l, pg. 1451
LOOKSMART, INC.—See The Reader's Digest Association, Inc.; U.S. Public, pg. 1367
LOOMIS BROTHERS, INC.; U.S. Private, pg. 675
LOOMIS-FARGO & CO.—See Borg-Warner Security Corporation; U.S. Public, pg. 245
JENNIFER LOOMIS & ASSOCIATES—See Payco American Corporation; U.S. Public, pg. 1267
LOOMIS, SAYLES & CO.—See Metropolitan Life Insurance Co.; U.S. Private, pg. 737
LOOS & CO., INC.; U.S. Private, pg. 675
LOOSE TUBE INC.—See Lucent Technologies Inc.; U.S. Public, pg. 1018
LOR AL PRODUCTS INC—See Ag-Chem Equipment Co., Inc.; U.S. Public, pg. 6
LOR-E-LEI—See Ark Restaurants Corp.; U.S. Public, pg. 130
LORAD CORPORATION—See Thermo Electron Corporation; U.S. Public, pg. 1595
THE LORAIN JOURNAL COMPANY-THE MORNING JOURNAL—See Journal Register Company; U.S. Public, pg. 935
LORAIN PRODUCTS—See RELTEC Corporation; U.S. Private, pg. 921
LORAL SPACE & COMMUNICATIONS; U.S. Public, pg. 1014
LORBER INDUSTRIES OF CALIFORNIA; U.S. Private, pg. 675
LORD ABBETT & CO.; U.S. Private, pg. 675
LORD ABBETT BOND-DEBENTURE FUND, INC.—See Lord Abbett & Co.; U.S. Private, pg. 675
LORD ABBETT DEVELOPING GROWTH FUND, INC.—See Lord Abbett & Co.; U.S. Private, pg. 675
LORD ABBETT GLOBAL FUND, INC.—See Lord Abbett & Co.; U.S. Private, pg. 675
LORD ABBETT SECURITIES TRUST—See Lord Abbett & Co.; U.S. Private, pg. 675
LORD ABBETT TAX-FREE INCOME FUND, INC.—See Lord Abbett & Co.; U.S. Private, pg. 675

LORD ABBETT U.S. GOVERNMENT SECURITIES FUND, INC.—See Lord Abbett & Co.; U.S. Private, pg. 675
LORD & TAYLOR—See The May Department Stores Company; U.S. Public, pg. 1064
LORD BIBB DIV.—See Masters, Inc.; U.S. Private, pg. 714
LORD CORPORATION; U.S. Private, pg. 675
LORD CORP. (EUROPE) LTD.—See Lord Corporation; U.S. Private, pg. 676
LORD CORP., INDUSTRIAL ADHESIVES & COATINGS DIV.—See Lord Corporation; U.S. Private, pg. 676
LORD FAR EAST, INC.—See Lord Corporation; U.S. Private, pg. 676
THE LORD GROUP—See Dentsu Young & Rubicam Partnerships; U.S. Private, pg. 325
LORD INDUSTRIAL LTDA.—See Lord Corporation; U.S. Private, pg. 676
LORD KOREA LTD.—See Lord Corporation; U.S. Private, pg. 676
LORD RESEARCH & DEVELOPMENT—See Lord Corporation; U.S. Private, pg. 676
LORD, SULLIVAN & YODER INC. MARKETING COMMUNICATIONS; U.S. Private, pg. 676
LORDCO (AUSTRALIA) PTY. LTD.—See ABB Asea Brown Boveri (Holding) Ltd.; Int'l, pg. 6
THE LORDSBURG MINING COMPANY—See The Goldfield Corporation; U.S. Public, pg. 750
L'OREAL BELGILUX SA—See L'Oreal S.A.; Int'l, pg. 819
L'OREAL JAPAN INC.—See L'Oreal S.A.; Int'l, pg. 819
L'OREAL PARFUMERIE—See L'Oreal S.A.; Int'l, pg. 819
L'OREAL PRODESCA S.A.—See L'Oreal S.A.; Int'l, pg. 819
L'OREAL S.A.; Int'l, pg. 818
L'OREAL TECHNIQUE PROFESSIONAL DIV.—See L'Oreal S.A.; Int'l, pg. 819
L'OREAL (UK) LIMITED—See L'Oreal S.A.; Int'l, pg. 819
LOREFCO, INC.—See Holly Corporation; U.S. Public, pg. 830
AB LORENTZEN & WETTRE—See Cardo AB; Int'l, pg. 271
OY LORENTZEN & WETTRE AB—See Cardo AB; Int'l, pg. 271
LORENTZEN & WETTRE A/S—See Cardo AB; Int'l, pg. 271
LORENTZEN & WETTRE CANADA INC.—See Cardo AB; Int'l, pg. 271
LORENTZEN & WETTRE GMBH—See Cardo AB; Int'l, pg. 271
LORENTZEN & WETTRE S.A.R.L.—See Cardo AB; Int'l, pg. 271
LORENTZEN & WETTRE USA, INC.—See Cardo AB; Int'l, pg. 271
LORENZ & LIHN OBST-EDEL-ERZEUGNISSE GMBH—See Eckes AG; Int'l, pg. 433
WALTER LORENZ SURGICAL, INC.—See Biomet, Inc.; U.S. Public, pg. 231
LOREX PHARMACEUTICALS LTD.—See L'Oreal S.A.; Int'l, pg. 818
LORFONTE—See Groupe Usinor; Int'l, pg. 571
LORILLARD TOBACCO COMPANY—See Loews Corporation; U.S. Public, pg. 1011
LORIMAR TELEVISION—See Time Warner Inc.; U.S. Public, pg. 1611
LORLEA ARCHITECTURAL SYSTEMS DIVISION—See Jannock Limited; Int'l, pg. 698
LORMINES (SOCIETE DES MINES DE SACILOR)—See Groupe Usinor; Int'l, pg. 571
LORNA PHARMA G.M.B.H.—See Bristol-Myers Squibb Company; U.S. Public, pg. 256
LORTEC POWER SYSTEMS, INC.—See BTR plc; Int'l, pg. 126
LORTEC POWER SYSTEMS NATL. SLS. OFFICE—See BTR plc; Int'l, pg. 126
LOS ALAMOS MONITOR—See Landmark Communications, Inc.; U.S. Private, pg. 648
LOS ALAMOS TECHNICAL ASSOCIATES, INC.; U.S. Private, pg. 676
LOS ANGELES BRANCH OFFICE—See Nippon Life Insurance Co.; Int'l, pg. 935
LOS ANGELES CELLULAR TELEPHONE CO.—See AT&T Corporation; U.S. Public, pg. 11
L.A. COMPUTER CENTER; U.S. Private, pg. 676
LOS ANGELES DEALERS AUTO AUCTIONS—See Cox Enterprises, Inc.; U.S. Private, pg. 282
THE LOS ANGELES DEPARTMENT OF WATER AND POWER (DWP); U.S. Private, pg. 676
LOS ANGELES DIE CASTING—See Atchison Casting Corporation; U.S. Public, pg. 142
LOS ANGELES DIVISION—See Time Warner Inc.; U.S. Public, pg. 1613
LOS ANGELES MAGAZINE, INC.—See The Walt Disney Company; U.S. Public, pg. 513
LOS ANGELES MFG. DIVISION—See R.R. Donnelley & Sons Company; U.S. Public, pg. 518
LOS ANGELES MARINE TERMINAL—See GATX Corporation; U.S. Public, pg. 692
LOS ANGELES SMOKING & CURING COMPANY—See Ocean Beauty Seafoods, Inc.; U.S. Private, pg. 810
LOS ANGELES TIMES—See The Times Mirror Company; U.S. Public, pg. 1616
LOS ANGELES TIMES SYNDICATE—See The Times Mirror Company; U.S. Public, pg. 1616
LOS ANGELES TIMES-WASHINGTON POST NEWS SERVICE, INC.—See The Washington Post Company; U.S. Public, pg. 1743
LOS ANGELES TURF CLUB, INC.—See Meditrust Corporation; U.S. Public, pg. 1081
LOS ANGELES UNION TERMINAL, INC.—See Union Pacific Corporation; U.S. Public, pg. 1668
LOSS MANAGEMENT SERVICES, INC.—See Avemco Corporation; U.S. Public, pg. 152
LOST ARROW CORPORATION; U.S. Private, pg. 676
LOSURDO FOODS, INC.; U.S. Private, pg. 676
LOT POLISH AIRLINES SA—See Polskie Linie Lotnicze LOT S.A.; Int'l, pg. 1062
LOTAS MINARD PATTON MCGIVER; U.S. Private, pg. 677
LOTEPRO CORPORATION—See Linde AG; Int'l, pg. 811

LOTHROP, LEE & SHEPARD BOOKS—See The Hearst Corporation; U.S. Private, pg. 515
LOT$ OFF CORPORATION; U.S. Public, pg. 1014
LOTTE CANON CO., LTD.—See Canon Inc.; Int'l, pg. 262
LOTTE COMPANY LTD.; Int'l, pg. 819
LOTTE ICE CREAM CORP. LTD.—See Lotte Company Ltd.; Int'l, pg. 819
LOTTE SHOPPING CO. LTD.—See Lotte Company Ltd.; Int'l, pg. 819
LOTTE U.S.A., INC.—See Lotte Company Ltd.; Int'l, pg. 819
LOTTO S.P.A.; Int'l, pg. 819
LOTTO SPORT U.S.A.—See Lotto S.p.A.; Int'l, pg. 819
LOTTO TRE S.P.A.—See Assicurazioni Generali S.p.A.; Int'l, pg. 90
LOTUS BUSINESS PRODUCTS DIV.—See International Business Machines Corporation; U.S. Public, pg. 896
LOTUS CARPET DIVISION—See Columbus Mills, Inc.; U.S. Private, pg. 257
LOTUS CARS LTD.—See Proton; Int'l, pg. 1071
LOTUS CARS USA, INC.—See Proton; Int'l, pg. 1071
LOTUS DEVELOPMENT B.V.—See International Business Machines Corporation; U.S. Public, pg. 896
LOTUS DEVELOPMENT CORPORATION—See International Business Machines Corporation; U.S. Public, pg. 896
LOTUS DEVELOPMENT GMBH—See International Business Machines Corporation; U.S. Public, pg. 896
LOTUS DEVELOPMENT JAPAN LIMITED—See International Business Machines Corporation; U.S. Public, pg. 896
LOTUS DEVELOPMENT LTD.—See International Business Machines Corporation; U.S. Public, pg. 896
LOTUS DEVELOPMENT, SA—See International Business Machines Corporation; U.S. Public, pg. 896
LOTUS DEVELOPMENT (U.K.) LIMITED—See International Business Machines Corporation; U.S. Public, pg. 896
LOTUS ENGINEERING—See Proton; Int'l, pg. 1071
LOTUS ENGINEERING & SCIENTIFIC PRODUCTS DIV.—See International Business Machines Corporation; U.S. Public, pg. 896
LOTUS INFORMATION CENTER GROUP—See International Business Machines Corporation; U.S. Public, pg. 896
LOTUS INFORMATION NETWORK CORPORATION—See International Business Machines Corporation; U.S. Public, pg. 896
LOTUS INFORMATION SERVICES DIV.—See International Business Machines Corporation; U.S. Public, pg. 896
LOTUS LOGISTICA S.R.L.—See Coeclerici Group; Int'l, pg. 303
LOTUS RESEARCH & DEVELOPMENT GROUP—See International Business Machines Corporation; U.S. Public, pg. 896
LOTUS WORD PROCESSING DIVISION—See International Business Machines Corporation; U.S. Public, pg. 896
LOU ANA FOODS, INC.—See Mitsui & Co., Ltd.; Int'l, pg. 879
LOUIS ALLIS COMPANY; U.S. Private, pg. 677
LOUIS DREYFUS NATURAL GAS CORP.—See Louis Dreyfus Corporation; U.S. Private, pg. 342
LOUIS GOLAY S.A.—See LVMH Moet Hennessy Louis Vuitton; Int'l, pg. 782
LOUIS VUITTON—See LVMH Moet Hennessy Louis Vuitton; Int'l, pg. 781
LOUIS VUITTON AUSTRALIA PTY LTD—See LVMH Moet Hennessy Louis Vuitton; Int'l, pg. 782
LOUIS VUITTON BELGIQUE—See LVMH Moet Hennessy Louis Vuitton; Int'l, pg. 782
LOUIS VUITTON CANADA INC.—See LVMH Moet Hennessy Louis Vuitton; Int'l, pg. 782
LOUIS VUITTON CHILE LTDA—See LVMH Moet Hennessy Louis Vuitton; Int'l, pg. 782
LOUIS VUITTON DANMARK A/S—See LVMH Moet Hennessy Louis Vuitton; Int'l, pg. 782
LOUIS VUITTON DEUTSCHLAND G.M.B.H.—See LVMH Moet Hennessy Louis Vuitton; Int'l, pg. 782
LOUIS VUITTON DISTRIBUICAO LTDA.—See LVMH Moet Hennessy Louis Vuitton; Int'l, pg. 782
LOUIS VUITTON ESPANA S.A.—See LVMH Moet Hennessy Louis Vuitton; Int'l, pg. 782
LOUIS VUITTON GUAM, INC.—See LVMH Moet Hennessy Louis Vuitton; Int'l, pg. 781
LOUIS VUITTON HAWAII—See LVMH Moet Hennessy Louis Vuitton; Int'l, pg. 781
LOUIS VUITTON HELLAS SCA—See LVMH Moet Hennessy Louis Vuitton; Int'l, pg. 782
LOUIS VUITTON HONG KONG LTD—See LVMH Moet Hennessy Louis Vuitton; Int'l, pg. 782
LOUIS VUITTON ITALIA S.P.A.—See LVMH Moet Hennessy Louis Vuitton; Int'l, pg. 782
LOUIS VUITTON JAPAN K.K.—See LVMH Moet Hennessy Louis Vuitton; Int'l, pg. 782
LOUIS VUITTON KOREA, LTD.—See LVMH Moet Hennessy Louis Vuitton; Int'l, pg. 782
LOUIS VUITTON MALAYSIA SDN BHD—See LVMH Moet Hennessy Louis Vuitton; Int'l, pg. 782
LOUIS VUITTON MALLETIER—See LVMH Moet Hennessy Louis Vuitton; Int'l, pg. 781
LOUIS VUITTON MEXICO SARL DE CV—See LVMH Moet Hennessy Louis Vuitton; Int'l, pg. 782
LOUIS VUITTON MONACO SA—See LVMH Moet Hennessy Louis Vuitton; Int'l, pg. 782
LOUIS VUITTON NEW ZEALAND—See LVMH Moet Hennessy Louis Vuitton; Int'l, pg. 783
LOUIS VUITTON NORTH AMERICA, INC.—See LVMH Moet Hennessy Louis Vuitton; Int'l, pg. 781
LOUIS VUITTON OSTERREICH GES.M.B.H.—See LVMH Moet Hennessy Louis Vuitton; Int'l, pg. 783
LOUIS VUITTON PACIFIC LTD—See LVMH Moet Hennessy Louis Vuitton; Int'l, pg. 783
LOUIS VUITTON PORTUGAL MALEIRO LIMITADA—See LVMH Moet Hennessy Louis Vuitton; Int'l, pg. 783

LOUIS
DIRECTORY OF CORPORATE AFFILIATIONS

Company Index

LOUIS VUITTON SAIPAN LTD—See LVMH Moet Hennessy Louis Vuitton; *Int'l*, pg. 781
LOUIS VUITTON (SINGAPORE) PTE LTD—See LVMH Moet Hennessy Louis Vuitton; *Int'l*, pg. 783
LOUIS VUITTON (SUISSE) S.A.—See LVMH Moet Hennessy Louis Vuitton; *Int'l*, pg. 783
LOUIS VUITTON TAIWAN LTD—See LVMH Moet Hennessy Louis Vuitton; *Int'l*, pg. 783
LOUIS VUITTON U.K. LTD—See LVMH Moet Hennessy Louis Vuitton; *Int'l*, pg. 783
LOUIS VUITTON US MANUFACTURING INC.—See LVMH Moet Hennessy Louis Vuitton; *Int'l*, pg. 781
THE LOUISIANA COCA-COLA BOTTLING COMPANY LIMITED—See Coca-Cola Enterprises Inc.; *U.S. Public*, pg. 393
LOUISIANA COMMUNITY BAR & GRILL—See Ark Restaurants Corp.; *U.S. Public*, pg. 130
LOUISIANA DOWNS—See The Edward J. DeBartolo Corporation; *U.S. Private*, pg. 319
LOUISIANA FARM BUREAU CASUALTY INSURANCE COMPANY—See Southern Farm Bureau Casualty Insurance Company; *U.S. Private*, pg. 1016
LOUISIANA GAMING MANAGEMENT, INC.; *U.S. Private*, pg. 677
LOUISIANA GAS SERVICE CO.—See Citizens Utilities Company; *U.S. Public*, pg. 380
LOUISIANA INDUSTRIES DIV.—See Texas Industries, Inc.; *U.S. Public*, pg. 1585
LOUISIANA INTRASTATE GAS CORPORATION—See Equitable Resources, Inc.; *U.S. Public*, pg. 590
THE LOUISIANA LAND AND EXPLORATION COMPANY—See Burlington Resources Inc.; *U.S. Public*, pg. 269
LOUISIANA NEVADA TRANSIT CO.—See Holderbank Financiere Glaris Ltd.; *Int'l*, pg. 628
LOUISIANA PACIFIC CORPORATION; *U.S. Public*, pg. 1015
LOUISIANA PACIFIC NORTHERN DIV.—See Louisiana Pacific Corporation; *U.S. Public*, pg. 1015
LOUISIANA PACIFIC WESTERN DIV.—See Louisiana Pacific Corporation; *U.S. Public*, pg. 1015
THE LOUISIANA PURCHASE—See AMREP Corporation; *U.S. Public*, pg. 105
LOUISIANA REFERENCE LABORATORY—See SmithKline Beecham plc; *Int'l*, pg. 1265
LOUISIANA UTILITIES SUPPLY COMPANY—See Clayton Group, Inc.; *U.S. Private*, pg. 245
LOUISVILLE AIRLINE LEARNING CENTER—See Berkshire Hathaway Inc.; *U.S. Public*, pg. 219
LOUISVILLE BEDDING COMPANY; *U.S. Private*, pg. 677
LOUISVILLE GAS AND ELECTRIC COMPANY—See LG & E Energy Corp.; *U.S. Public*, pg. 970
LOUISVILLE SCRAP MATERIAL CO., INC.; *U.S. Private*, pg. 677
LOUISVILLE SHOPPING CENTER, INC.—See The Rouse Company; *U.S. Public*, pg. 1407
LOUISVILLE TRANSPORTATION—See Interlock Industries, Inc.; *U.S. Private*, pg. 567
LOUMIDIS S.A.—See Nestle S.A.; *Int'l*, pg. 920
LOVDAHL MANUFACTURING—See Kurz-Kasch, Inc.; *U.S. Private*, pg. 637
LOVE CONTROLS CORPORATION—See Dwyer Instruments Inc.; *U.S. Private*, pg. 350
LOVE PACKAGING GROUP; *U.S. Private*, pg. 677
LOVEJOY INC.; *U.S. Private*, pg. 677
LOVEJOY MEDICAL, INC.—See Integrated Health Services, Inc.; *U.S. Public*, pg. 885
LOVELACE HEALTH SYSTEMS, INC.—See Cigna Corp.; *U.S. Public*, pg. 360
LOVENE DORR AB—See Stora Kopparbergs Bergslags AB; *Int'l*, pg. 1302
T.A. LOVING COMPANY; *U.S. Private*, pg. 677
LOVYTEX SDN. BHD.—See Tyco International Ltd.; *U.S. Public*, pg. 1648
LOW MOOR SECURITIES LTD.—See Allied Colloids Group Plc.; *Int'l*, pg. 62
LOWARA BELGIUM S.A.—See ITT Industries, Inc.; *U.S. Public*, pg. 861
LOWARA DENMARK—See ITT Industries, Inc.; *U.S. Public*, pg. 861
LOWARA FRANCE—See ITT Industries, Inc.; *U.S. Public*, pg. 861
LOWARA GMBH—See ITT Industries, Inc.; *U.S. Public*, pg. 861
LOWARA IRELAND LTD.—See ITT Industries, Inc.; *U.S. Public*, pg. 861
LOWARA NEDERLAND B.V.—See ITT Industries, Inc.; *U.S. Public*, pg. 861
LOWARA PORTUGAL—See ITT Industries, Inc.; *U.S. Public*, pg. 861
LOWARA S.P.A—See ITT Industries, Inc.; *U.S. Public*, pg. 861
LOWDEN & PARTNERS LIMITED—See RMC Group p.l.c.; *Int'l*, pg. 1079
LOWE ADAM—See The Lowe Group; *U.S. Private*, pg. 678
LOWE & PARTNERS—See The Lowe Group; *U.S. Private*, pg. 678
LOWE & PARTNERS GMBH—See The Lowe Group; *U.S. Private*, pg. 678
LOWE & PARTNERS/LIVE—See The Lowe Group; *U.S. Private*, pg. 678
LOWE & PARTNERS/SMS—See The Lowe Group; *U.S. Private*, pg. 678
LOWE & PARTNERS/SMS DE MEXICO—See The Lowe Group; *U.S. Private*, pg. 678
LOWE BRINDFORS—See The Lowe Group; *U.S. Private*, pg. 678
CARL A. LOWE INDUSTRIES, INC.—See Greenway Partners, L.P.; *U.S. Private*, pg. 478
LOWE DIRECT—See The Lowe Group; *U.S. Private*, pg. 678
THE LOWE GROUP; *U.S. Private*, pg. 677
LOWE HOWARD-SPINK—See The Lowe Group; *U.S. Private*, pg. 678
LOWE & JAEGERS GMBH—See Van Leeuwen Pipe and Tube Group B.V.; *Int'l*, pg. 1450
LOWE KUIPER & SCHOUTEN—See The Lowe Group; *U.S. Private*, pg. 678
LOWE LODUCCA & PARTNERS—See The Lowe Group; *U.S. Private*, pg. 678
LOWE MBAC—See The Lowe Group; *U.S. Private*, pg. 678
LOWE MCADAMS HEALTHCARE; *U.S. Private*, pg. 678
LOWE PAPER CO.—See Simkins Industries, Inc.; *U.S. Private*, pg. 1000
LOWE RZR—See The Lowe Group; *U.S. Private*, pg. 678
LOWE TROOST—See The Lowe Group; *U.S. Private*, pg. 678
LOWELL PACKING COMPANY; *U.S. Private*, pg. 679
LOWELL SHOE, INC.—See Berkshire Hathaway Inc.; *U.S. Public*, pg. 217
LOWENBRAU ZURICH AG—See Feldschlosschen Hurlimann Holding; *Int'l*, pg. 479
LOWER BUCKS CABLEVISION, INC.—See Time Warner Inc.; *U.S. Public*, pg. 1611
LOWE'S COMPANIES, INC.; *U.S. Public*, pg. 1015
LOWE'S FOOD STORES, INC.—See Alex Lee, Inc.; *U.S. Private*, pg. 657
LOWE'S HOME CENTERS, INC.—See Lowe's Companies, Inc.; *U.S. Public*, pg. 1015
LOWLANDS CORPORATE SERVICES COMPANY LTD.—See Generale de Banque S.A.; *Int'l*, pg. 548
LOWRANCE AUSTRALIA—See Lowrance Electronics, Inc.; *U.S. Public*, pg. 1016
LOWRANCE AVIONICS—See Lowrance Electronics, Inc.; *U.S. Public*, pg. 1016
LOWRANCE CANADA—See Lowrance Electronics, Inc.; *U.S. Public*, pg. 1016
LOWRANCE ELECTRONICS, INC.; *U.S. Public*, pg. 1015
LOWRY HILL INVESTMENT ADVISORS, INC.—See Norwest Corporation; *U.S. Public*, pg. 1201
LOXCREEN COMPANY; *U.S. Private*, pg. 679
LOY INSTRUMENT CO., INC.—See Eclipse Inc.; *U.S. Private*, pg. 360
LOZIER CORPORATION; *U.S. Private*, pg. 679
LUBECON SYSTEMS, INC.; *U.S. Private*, pg. 679
LUBER-FINER, EUROPE, N.V./S.A.—See UIS, Inc.; *U.S. Private*, pg. 1113
LUBER-FINER, INC.—See UIS, Inc.; *U.S. Private*, pg. 1113
LUBRASYSTEMS—See NCH Corporation; *U.S. Public*, pg. 1145
LUBRICANTES DEL SUR, S.A. (LUBRISUR)—See Compania Espanola de Petroleos, S.A. (CEPSA); *Int'l*, pg. 323
LUBRICANTES FUCHS DE MEXICO, S.A. DE C.V.—See Fuchs Petrolub AG Oel + Chemie; *Int'l*, pg. 519
LUBRICANTES Y TAMBORES DEL ECUADOR, C.A.—See Texaco Inc.; *U.S. Public*, pg. 1584
LUBRICATION CONSULTANTS, L.L.C.—See Mid-Kansas Co-op Association; *U.S. Private*, pg. 743
LUBRICATION ENGINEERS, INC.; *U.S. Private*, pg. 679
LUBRINER (LUBRICATES DEL NERVION, S.A.)—See Compania Espanola de Petroleos, S.A. (CEPSA); *Int'l*, pg. 323
LUBRIQUIP, INC.—See IDEX Corporation; *U.S. Public*, pg. 862
LUBRIZOL AG (SWITZERLAND)—See The Lubrizol Corporation; *U.S. Public*, pg. 1016
LUBRIZOL CANADA LTD.—See The Lubrizol Corporation; *U.S. Public*, pg. 1016
THE LUBRIZOL CORPORATION; *U.S. Public*, pg. 1016
LUBRIZOL DE CHILE, LTDA.—See The Lubrizol Corporation; *U.S. Public*, pg. 1016
LUBRIZOL DE MEXICO, S. DE R.L.—See The Lubrizol Corporation; *U.S. Public*, pg. 1016
LUBRIZOL DO BRASIL ADITIVOS LTDA—See The Lubrizol Corporation; *U.S. Public*, pg. 1016
LUBRIZOL ESPANOLA, S. A.—See The Lubrizol Corporation; *U.S. Public*, pg. 1016
LUBRIZOL FRANCE S.A.—See The Lubrizol Corporation; *U.S. Public*, pg. 1016
LUBRIZOL GESELLSCHAFT M.B.H.—See The Lubrizol Corporation; *U.S. Public*, pg. 1016
LUBRIZOL GMBH—See The Lubrizol Corporation; *U.S. Public*, pg. 1016
LUBRIZOL INDIA LIMITED—See The Lubrizol Corporation; *U.S. Public*, pg. 1017
LUBRIZOL INTERNATIONAL, INC.—See The Lubrizol Corporation; *U.S. Public*, pg. 1016
LUBRIZOL ITALIANA S.P.A.—See The Lubrizol Corporation; *U.S. Public*, pg. 1016
LUBRIZOL JAPAN LIMITED—See The Lubrizol Corporation; *U.S. Public*, pg. 1016
LUBRIZOL JAPAN LTD.—See The Lubrizol Corporation; *U.S. Public*, pg. 1016
LUBRIZOL LIMITED—See The Lubrizol Corporation; *U.S. Public*, pg. 1016
LUBRIZOL LTD.—See The Lubrizol Corporation; *U.S. Public*, pg. 1017
LUBRIZOL SCANDINAVIA AB—See The Lubrizol Corporation; *U.S. Public*, pg. 1017
LUBRIZOL SERVICIOS TECNICOS S. DE R.L.—See The Lubrizol Corporation; *U.S. Public*, pg. 1017
LUBRIZOL SOUTH AFRICA (PTY.) LIMITED—See The Lubrizol Corporation; *U.S. Public*, pg. 1017
LUBRIZOL SOUTHEAST ASIA (PTE.) LTD.—See The Lubrizol Corporation; *U.S. Public*, pg. 1017
LUBY'S CAFETERIAS, INC.; *U.S. Public*, pg. 1017
LUCAS AARDENBURG B.V.—See Unilever Plc; *Int'l*, pg. 1438
LUCAS AEROSPACE—See LucasVarity plc; *Int'l*, pg. 819
LUCAS AEROSPACE CARGO SYSTEMS—See LucasVarity plc; *Int'l*, pg. 820
LUCAS AEROSPACE CUSTOMER SUPPORT—See LucasVarity plc; *Int'l*, pg. 819
LUCAS AEROSPACE POWER TRANSMISSION—See LucasVarity plc; *Int'l*, pg. 820
LUCAS AFTERMARKET OPERATIONS—See LucasVarity plc; *Int'l*, pg. 819
LUCAS AIRCRAFT CARGO SYSTEMS—See LucasVarity plc; *Int'l*, pg. 820
LUCAS AUTOMOTIVE GMBH—See LucasVarity plc; *Int'l*, pg. 820
LUCAS AUTOMOTIVE SA, SPAIN—See LucasVarity plc; *Int'l*, pg. 820
LUCAS BODY SYSTEMS—See LucasVarity plc; *Int'l*, pg. 820
LUCAS BODY SYSTEMS - NORTH AMERICA—See LucasVarity plc; *Int'l*, pg. 820
LUCAS CONTROL SYSTEMS PRODUCTS—See LucasVarity plc; *Int'l*, pg. 820
LUCAS DIESEL KOREA LTD.—See LucasVarity plc; *Int'l*, pg. 820
LUCAS DIESEL SYSTEMS—See LucasVarity plc; *Int'l*, pg. 820
LUCAS ELECTRICAL AND ELECTRONIC SYSTEMS—See LucasVarity plc; *Int'l*, pg. 819
LUCAS FRANCE SA—See LucasVarity plc; *Int'l*, pg. 820
LUCAS GIRLING S.A.—See LucasVarity plc; *Int'l*, pg. 820
LUCAS INDIEL ARGENTINA S.A.—See LucasVarity plc; *Int'l*, pg. 820
LUCAS INDUSTRIES INC.—See LucasVarity plc; *Int'l*, pg. 820
LUCAS INGREDIENTS—See Dalgety Plc; *Int'l*, pg. 376
LUCAS LIGHT VEHICLE BRAKING SYSTEMS—See LucasVarity plc; *Int'l*, pg. 819
LUCAS MILHAUPT - EUROPE—See Handy & Harman; *U.S. Public*, pg. 780
LUCAS-MILHAUPT, INC.—See Handy & Harman; *U.S. Public*, pg. 780
LUCAS NOVASENSOR INC.—See LucasVarity plc; *Int'l*, pg. 820
JOHN D. LUCAS PRINTING COMPANY—See Collman Graphics, Inc.; *U.S. Private*, pg. 253
LUCAS SEI ELECTRONICS, LLC—See Sumitomo Electric Industries, Ltd.; *Int'l*, pg. 1313
LUCAS SEI WIRING SYSTEMS, LTD.—See Sumitomo Electric Industries, Ltd.; *Int'l*, pg. 1313
LUCAS SUMITOMO BRAKES INC.—See LucasVarity plc; *Int'l*, pg. 819
LUCAS SUMITOMO BRAKES INC.—See Sumitomo Electric Industries, Ltd.; *Int'l*, pg. 1313
LUCAS-TVS LTD.—See LucasVarity plc; *Int'l*, pg. 820
LUCASFILM LTD.; *U.S. Private*, pg. 679
LUCASVARITY INC.—See LucasVarity plc; *Int'l*, pg. 820
LUCASVARITY PLC; *Int'l*, pg. 819
LUCASVARITY PLC—See LucasVarity plc; *Int'l*, pg. 819
LUCEDALE INDUSTRIES—See Harcrest International, Ltd.; *U.S. Private*, pg. 501
LUCENT NETCARE MESSAGING SERVICES—See Lucent Technologies Inc.; *U.S. Public*, pg. 1018
LUCENT TECHNOLOGIES—See Lucent Technologies Inc.; *U.S. Public*, pg. 1017
LUCENT TECHNOLOGIES ADVANCED TECHNOLOGY SYSTEMS—See Lucent Technologies Inc.; *U.S. Public*, pg. 1017
LUCENT TECHNOLOGIES AMERICAS INC.—See Lucent Technologies Inc.; *U.S. Public*, pg. 1018
LUCENT TECHNOLOGIES ARGENTINA S.A.—See Lucent Technologies Inc.; *U.S. Public*, pg. 1018
LUCENT TECHNOLOGIES ASIA/PACIFIC INC.—See Lucent Technologies Inc.; *U.S. Public*, pg. 1018
LUCENT TECHNOLOGIES ASIA/PACIFIC LTD.—See Lucent Technologies Inc.; *U.S. Public*, pg. 1018
LUCENT TECHNOLOGIES AUSTRALIA PTY. LTD.—See Lucent Technologies Inc.; *U.S. Public*, pg. 1018
LUCENT TECHNOLOGIES AUSTRIA GES.M.B.H.—See Lucent Technologies Inc.; *U.S. Public*, pg. 1018
LUCENT TECHNOLOGIES BCS S.A.—See Lucent Technologies Inc.; *U.S. Public*, pg. 1019
LUCENT TECHNOLOGIES BELGIUM S.A./N.V.—See Lucent Technologies Inc.; *U.S. Public*, pg. 1018
LUCENT TECHNOLOGIES (BERMUDA) LTD.—See Lucent Technologies Inc.; *U.S. Public*, pg. 1019
LUCENT TECHNOLOGIES BRASIL LTDA.—See Lucent Technologies Inc.; *U.S. Public*, pg. 1018
LUCENT TECHNOLOGIES, BUSINESS COMMUNICATIONS SYSTEMS DIV.—See Lucent Technologies Inc.; *U.S. Public*, pg. 1017
LUCENT TECHNOLOGIES BUSINESS COMMUNICATIONS SYSTEMS & MICROELECTRONICS GMBH—See Lucent Technologies Inc.; *U.S. Public*, pg. 1019
LUCENT TECHNOLOGIES (CHINA) CO., LTD.—See Lucent Technologies Inc.; *U.S. Public*, pg. 1018
LUCENT TECHNOLOGIES CONSTRUCTION SERVICES INC.—See Lucent Technologies Inc.; *U.S. Public*, pg. 1018
LUCENT TECHNOLOGIES, CONSUMER PRODUCTS DIV.—See Lucent Technologies Inc.; *U.S. Public*, pg. 1017
LUCENT TECHNOLOGIES CONSUMER PRODUCTS MEXICO, S.A. DE C.V.—See Lucent Technologies Inc.; *U.S. Public*, pg. 1018
LUCENT TECHNOLOGIES CONSUMER PRODUCTS PTD. LTD.—See Lucent Technologies Inc.; *U.S. Public*, pg. 1018
LUCENT TECHNOLOGIES DE COSTA RICA S.A.—See Lucent Technologies Inc.; *U.S. Public*, pg. 1018
LUCENT TECHNOLOGIES DE GUATEMALA S.A.—See Lucent Technologies Inc.; *U.S. Public*, pg. 1018
LUCENT TECHNOLOGIES DE HONDURAS S.A.—See Lucent Technologies Inc.; *U.S. Public*, pg. 1018
LUCENT TECHNOLOGIES DE MEXICO S.A. DE C.V.—See Lucent Technologies Inc.; *U.S. Public*, pg. 1019
LUCENT TECHNOLOGIES DEL PERU S.A.—See Lucent Technologies Inc.; *U.S. Public*, pg. 1018
LUCENT TECHNOLOGIES EASTERN VENTURES INC.—See Lucent Technologies Inc.; *U.S. Public*, pg. 1018
LUCENT TECHNOLOGIES EL SALVADOR S.A. DE C.V.—See Lucent Technologies Inc.; *U.S. Public*, pg. 1018
LUCENT TECHNOLOGIES EMEA B.V.—See Lucent Technologies Inc.; *U.S. Public*, pg. 1018

MASTER INDEX TO COMPANY NAMES LUWA

Company Index

LUCENT TECHNOLOGIES ENGINEERING INC.—See Lucent Technologies Inc.; *U.S. Public*, pg. 1018
LUCENT TECHNOLOGIES ENGINEERING RESEARCH CENTER—See Lucent Technologies Inc.; *U.S. Public*, pg. 1018
LUCENT TECHNOLOGIES EURASIA LTD.—See Lucent Technologies Inc.; *U.S. Public*, pg. 1018
LUCENT TECHNOLOGIES FOREIGN SALES CORPORATION—See Lucent Technologies Inc.; *U.S. Public*, pg. 1019
LUCENT TECHNOLOGIES HOLDINGS DE MEXICO S.A. DE C.V.—See Lucent Technologies Inc.; *U.S. Public*, pg. 1019
LUCENT TECHNOLOGIES HOLDINGS INC.—See Lucent Technologies Inc.; *U.S. Public*, pg. 1018
LUCENT TECHNOLOGIES INC.; *U.S. Public*, pg. 1017
LUCENT TECHNOLOGIES INDIA PVT. LTD.—See Lucent Technologies Inc.; *U.S. Public*, pg. 1019
LUCENT TECHNOLOGIES INTERNATIONAL INC.—See Lucent Technologies Inc.; *U.S. Public*, pg. 1018
LUCENT TECHNOLOGIES MANAGEMENT SERVICES INC.—See Lucent Technologies Inc.; *U.S. Public*, pg. 1018
LUCENT TECHNOLOGIES MANUFACTURING OF ST. PETERSBURG—See Lucent Technologies Inc.; *U.S. Public*, pg. 1018
LUCENT TECHNOLOGIES MICROELECTRONICA S.A.—See Lucent Technologies Inc.; *U.S. Public*, pg. 1019
LUCENT TECHNOLOGIES, MICROELECTRONICS DIV.—See Lucent Technologies Inc.; *U.S. Public*, pg. 1017
LUCENT TECHNOLOGIES MICROELECTRONICS PTE. LTD.—See Lucent Technologies Inc.; *U.S. Public*, pg. 1019
LUCENT TECHNOLOGIES MIDDLE EAST W.L.L.—See Lucent Technologies Inc.; *U.S. Public*, pg. 1019
LUCENT TECHNOLOGIES MULTIMEDIA BRASIL S.A.—See Lucent Technologies Inc.; *U.S. Public*, pg. 1019
LUCENT TECHNOLOGIES NETWORK SYSTEMS BELGIUM S.A./N.V.—See Lucent Technologies Inc.; *U.S. Public*, pg. 1018
LUCENT TECHNOLOGIES, NETWORK SYSTEMS DIV.—See Lucent Technologies Inc.; *U.S. Public*, pg. 1017
LUCENT TECHNOLOGIES NETWORK SYSTEMS DO BRASIL S.A.—See Lucent Technologies Inc.; *U.S. Public*, pg. 1019
LUCENT TECHNOLOGIES NETWORK SYSTEMS ESPANA S.A.—See Lucent Technologies Inc.; *U.S. Public*, pg. 1018
LUCENT TECHNOLOGIES NETWORK SYSTEMS GMBH—See Lucent Technologies Inc.; *U.S. Public*, pg. 1018
P.T. LUCENT TECHNOLOGIES NETWORK SYSTEMS INDONESIA—See Lucent Technologies Inc.; *U.S. Public*, pg. 1019
LUCENT TECHNOLOGIES NICARAGUA S.A.—See Lucent Technologies Inc.; *U.S. Public*, pg. 1018
LUCENT TECHNOLOGIES (NZ) LIMITED—See Lucent Technologies Inc.; *U.S. Public*, pg. 1019
LUCENT TECHNOLOGIES OF SHANGHAI, LTD.—See Lucent Technologies Inc.; *U.S. Public*, pg. 1018
LUCENT TECHNOLOGIES OF TIANJIN CABLE CO. LTD.—See Lucent Technologies Inc.; *U.S. Public*, pg. 1018
LUCENT TECHNOLOGIES OPTO INC.—See Lucent Technologies Inc.; *U.S. Public*, pg. 1018
LUCENT TECHNOLOGIES POLAND S.A.—See Lucent Technologies Inc.; *U.S. Public*, pg. 1019
LUCENT TECHNOLOGIES PUERTO RICO INC.—See Lucent Technologies Inc.; *U.S. Public*, pg. 1018
LUCENT TECHNOLOGIES REALTY INC.—See Lucent Technologies Inc.; *U.S. Public*, pg. 1019
LUCENT TECHNOLOGIES SEMICONDUCTOR MARKETING, LTD.—See NEC Corporation; *Int'l*, pg. 900
LUCENT TECHNOLOGIES SEMICONDUCTOR MARKETING, LTD.—See Lucent Technologies Inc.; *U.S. Public*, pg. 1019
LUCENT TECHNOLOGIES (SHANGHAI) INTERNATIONAL ENTERPRISES, LTD.—See Lucent Technologies Inc.; *U.S. Public*, pg. 1018
LUCENT TECHNOLOGIES SINGAPORE PTE. LTD.—See Lucent Technologies Inc.; *U.S. Public*, pg. 1019
LUCENT TECHNOLOGIES SP. Z.O.O.—See Lucent Technologies Inc.; *U.S. Public*, pg. 1019
LUCENT TECHNOLOGIES S.R.O.—See Lucent Technologies Inc.; *U.S. Public*, pg. 1018
LUCENT TECHNOLOGIES SWITCHING SYSTEMS (INDIA) LTD.—See Lucent Technologies Inc.; *U.S. Public*, pg. 1019
LUCENT TECHNOLOGIES THAILAND INC.—See Lucent Technologies Inc.; *U.S. Public*, pg. 1019
LUCENT TECHNOLOGIES VENEZUELA S.A.—See Lucent Technologies Inc.; *U.S. Public*, pg. 1019
LUCENT TECHNOLOGIES WESTERN INVESTMENTS INC.—See Lucent Technologies Inc.; *U.S. Public*, pg. 1018
LUCENT TECHNOLOGIES WORLD SERVICES INC.—See Lucent Technologies Inc.; *U.S. Public*, pg. 1018
LUCERNE LAKES GOLF COLONY INC.—See Lennar Corporation; *U.S. Public*, pg. 988
LUCHT, INC.—See Northwestern Public Service; *U.S. Public*, pg. 1201
LUCIDOL YOSHITOMI LTD.—See Elf Aquitane; *Int'l*, pg. 446
LUCKY ADVANCED MATERIALS INC.—See LG Group; *Int'l*, pg. 779
LUCKY DEVELOPMENT CO. LTD.—See LG Group; *Int'l*, pg. 779
LUCKY FRIDAY UNIT—See Hecla Mining Company; *U.S. Public*, pg. 804
LUCKY-GOLDSTAR INTERNATIONAL (AMERICA)—See LG Group; *Int'l*, pg. 779
LUCKY GOLDSTAR INTERNATIONAL AMERICA, INC.—See LG Group; *Int'l*, pg. 779
LUCKY GOLDSTAR INTERNATIONAL CORP.—See LG Group; *Int'l*, pg. 779
LUCKY GOLDSTAR-HONEYWELL CO. LTD.—See Honeywell Inc.; *U.S. Public*, pg. 835
LUCKY INNS OF AMERICA, INC.—See Family Inns of America, Inc.; *U.S. Private*, pg. 393
LUCKY LTD.—See LG Group; *Int'l*, pg. 779
LUCKY STORES NORTHERN CALIFORNIA DIVISION—See American Stores Company; *U.S. Public*, pg. 93
LUCKY STORES SOUTHERN CALIFORNIA DIVISION—See American Stores Company; *U.S. Public*, pg. 93
LUCKY WINNER, INC.; *U.S. Private*, pg. 679
LUDEN'S INC.—See Hershey Foods Corporation; *U.S. Public*, pg. 812
LUDGATE COMMUNICATIONS—See Weber Public Relations Worldwide; *U.S. Private*, pg. 1157
LUDGATE COMMUNICATIONS, INC.—See Weber Public Relations Worldwide; *U.S. Private*, pg. 1157
LUDGATE GROUP LIMITED—See Weber Public Relations Worldwide; *U.S. Private*, pg. 1157
LUDINGTON NEWS CO. INC.; *U.S. Private*, pg. 679
LUDLOW COMPOSITES CORPORATION; *U.S. Private*, pg. 680
LUDLOW CORPORATION—See Tyco International Ltd.; *U.S. Public*, pg. 1651
LUDLOW LAMINATING & COATING DIV.—See Tyco International Ltd.; *U.S. Public*, pg. 1647
LUDLOW-SAYLOR INC.—See Powerscreen International Plc; *Int'l*, pg. 1066
LUDLOW TECHNICAL PRODUCTS DIV.—See Tyco International Ltd.; *U.S. Public*, pg. 1647
LUDLOW TELEPHONE CO.—See Telephone and Data Systems, Inc.; *U.S. Public*, pg. 1571
LUDLOW TEXTILES CO., INC.; *U.S. Private*, pg. 680
LUDOWICI CELADON—See Saint-Gobain; *Int'l*, pg. 1171
LUDOWICI ROOF TILE, INC.—See Saint-Gobain; *Int'l*, pg. 1171
LUDVIGSEN & HERMANN A/S—See Celsius AB; *Int'l*, pg. 278
LUDWIG INDUSTRIES—See Steinway Musical Instruments, Inc.; *U.S. Public*, pg. 1514
LUDWIG METROLOGIE, SA—See Brown & Sharpe Manufacturing Company; *U.S. Public*, pg. 260
LUFKIN—See Cooper Industries, Inc.; *U.S. Public*, pg. 444
LUFKIN INDUSTRIES, GEAR DIV.—See Lufkin Industries, Inc.; *U.S. Public*, pg. 1019
LUFKIN INDUSTRIES, INC.; *U.S. Public*, pg. 1019
LUFKIN INDUSTRIES, INC., BOUNDARY DIVISION—See Lufkin Industries, Inc.; *U.S. Public*, pg. 1019
LUFKIN MACHINE CO. LTD.—See Lufkin Industries, Inc.; *U.S. Public*, pg. 1019
LUFKIN MILL, CHAMPION INTERNATIONAL CORPORATION—See Champion International Corp.; *U.S. Public*, pg. 334
LUFKIN NATIONAL BANK—See First Commercial Corporation; *U.S. Public*, pg. 630
LUFT, MAACK & CO. GMBH—See Norske Skogindustrier A.S; *Int'l*, pg. 966
LUFTHANSA CARGO AG—See Deutsche Lufthansa AG; *Int'l*, pg. 407
LUFTHANSA CITYLINE GMBH—See Deutsche Lufthansa AG; *Int'l*, pg. 407
LUFTHANSA COMMERCIAL HOLDING GMBH—See Deutsche Lufthansa AG; *Int'l*, pg. 407
LUFTHANSA SYSTEMS GMBH—See Deutsche Lufthansa AG; *Int'l*, pg. 407
LUFTHANSA TECHNIK AG—See Deutsche Lufthansa AG; *Int'l*, pg. 407
LUGANELLA S.A.—See Nestle S.A.; *Int'l*, pg. 916
LUHN & PULVERMACHER—See Fried. Krupp AG; *Int'l*, pg. 508
LUHRS CORPORATION; *U.S. Private*, pg. 680
LUIGI FONTANA S.P.A.—See Saint-Gobain; *Int'l*, pg. 1173
LUIGI LUCARDI—See Vendex International N.V.; *Int'l*, pg. 1462
LUIJCKX BV CHOCOLADE—See Koninklijke BolsWessanen nv; *Int'l*, pg. 751
LUKCOR, S.A.—See McCormick & Company, Incorporated; *U.S. Public*, pg. 1067
LUKENHEIMER ENERGO VALVES INC.; *U.S. Private*, pg. 680
LUKENS INC.; *U.S. Public*, pg. 1019
LUKENS STEEL COMPANY—See Lukens Inc.; *U.S. Public*, pg. 1020
LUKER INC.—See Gold Kist, Inc.; *U.S. Private*, pg. 459
LUMACELL INC.—See Kaufel Group Ltd.; *Int'l*, pg. 725
LUMAS REALTY, INC.; *U.S. Private*, pg. 680
LUMBER GROUP INC.; *U.S. Private*, pg. 680
LUMBERMENS MERCHANDISING CORPORATION; *U.S. Private*, pg. 680
LUMBERMEN'S MUTUAL CASUALTY COMPANY—See Kemper Insurance Companies; *U.S. Private*, pg. 614
LUMBERTON PLANT—See Cooper Industries, Inc.; *U.S. Public*, pg. 443
LUMEC, INC.—See Thomas Industries Inc.; *U.S. Public*, pg. 1599
LUMENX COMPANY—See Alltrista Corporation; *U.S. Public*, pg. 56
LUMEX MEDICAL PRODUCTS—See Graham-Field Health Products, Inc.; *U.S. Public*, pg. 758
LUMIERE—See Young & Rubicam Inc.; *U.S. Private*, pg. 1199
LUMINATOR—See Mark IV Industries Inc.; *U.S. Public*, pg. 1045
LUMIPAPER LTD.—See Enso Oyj; *Int'l*, pg. 458
LUMIPAPER N.V.—See Enso Oyj; *Int'l*, pg. 458
LUMMI FISHERIES SUPPLY—See ConAgra, Inc.; *U.S. Public*, pg. 429
LUMMUS ALIREZA LTD. CO.—See ABB Asea Brown Boveri (Holding) Ltd.; *Int'l*, pg. 6
THE LUMMUS CO. LTD.—See ABB Asea Brown Boveri (Holding) Ltd.; *Int'l*, pg. 6
LUMMUS CO. VENEZUELA C.A.—See ABB Asea Brown Boveri (Holding) Ltd.; *Int'l*, pg. 6
LUMMUS-JAPAN CO. LTD.—See ABB Asea Brown Boveri (Holding) Ltd.; *Int'l*, pg. 6
LUMMUS NEDERLAND B.V.—See ABB Asea Brown Boveri (Holding) Ltd.; *Int'l*, pg. 6
LUMMUS OVERSEAS CORP.—See ABB Asea Brown Boveri (Holding) Ltd.; *Int'l*, pg. 6
LUMONICS CORP.—See Sumitomo Heavy Industries, Ltd.; *Int'l*, pg. 1315
LUMONICS INC.—See Sumitomo Heavy Industries, Ltd.; *Int'l*, pg. 1314
LUNA AB—See Bergman & Beving AB; *Int'l*, pg. 188
LUNAIRE ENVIRONMENTAL—See Tenney Environmental; *U.S. Private*, pg. 1077
LUNALITE, INC.—See The Toro Company; *U.S. Public*, pg. 1624
LUNCH GARDEN—See GIB Group; *Int'l*, pg. 533
LUNCHEON VOUCHERS LTD.—See Accor S.A.; *Int'l*, pg. 21
LUND ACQUISITION CORP.—See Lund International Holdings, Inc.; *U.S. Public*, pg. 1020
LUND BOATS—See Genmar Holdings, Inc.; *U.S. Private*, pg. 447
LUND FOOD HOLDINGS, INC.; *U.S. Private*, pg. 680
LUND INDUSTRIES INC.—See Lund International Holdings, Inc.; *U.S. Public*, pg. 1020
LUND INTERNATIONAL HOLDINGS, INC.; *U.S. Public*, pg. 1020
L E LUNDBERGFORETAGEN AB; *Int'l*, pg. 820
LUNDBERGS-GOTEBORG REGION—See L E Lundbergforetagen AB; *Int'l*, pg. 821
LUNDBERGS-MALARDALEN REGION—See L E Lundbergforetagen AB; *Int'l*, pg. 821
LUNDBERGS-MALMO REGION—See L E Lundbergforetagen AB; *Int'l*, pg. 821
LUNDBERGS-NORRKOPING & GOTALAND REGION—See L E Lundbergforetagen AB; *Int'l*, pg. 821
LUNDBERGS-STOCKHOLM REGION—See L E Lundbergforetagen AB; *Int'l*, pg. 821
LUNDBERGS-VARMLAND REGION—See L E Lundbergforetagen AB; *Int'l*, pg. 821
LUNDBY BRUK AS—See Norske Skogindustrier A.S; *Int'l*, pg. 965
LUNDIA DIV. OF MII, INC.; *U.S. Private*, pg. 680
LUND'S INC.—See Lund Food Holdings, Inc.; *U.S. Private*, pg. 680
LUNDY CONSTRUCTION CO., INC.; *U.S. Private*, pg. 681
LUNDY ENTERPRISES, INC.; *U.S. Private*, pg. 681
LUNDY PACKING CO.; *U.S. Private*, pg. 681
L'UNITE HERMETIQUE S.A.—See Tecumseh Products Company; *U.S. Public*, pg. 1566
LUNN POLY LTD.—See The Thomson Corporation; *U.S. Public*, pg. 1601
W. LUNNON & COMPANY LIMITED—See N.V. Koninklijke KNP BT; *Int'l*, pg. 757
LUNSTEAD, A HAWORTH CO.—See Haworth, Inc.; *U.S. Private*, pg. 512
LUNTZ CORPORATION; *U.S. Private*, pg. 681
LUPIENT AUTOMOTIVE GROUP—See Jim Lupient Enterprises; *U.S. Private*, pg. 681
JIM LUPIENT ENTERPRISES; *U.S. Private*, pg. 681
LUPOS GMBH—See ETEX; *Int'l*, pg. 430
LUPRA GRUNDSTUCKSGELLSCHAFT MBH—See Dyckerhoff & Widmann AG; *Int'l*, pg. 423
LURGAN FIBRE LTD—See Royal Packaging Industries Van Leer B.V.; *Int'l*, pg. 1146
LURGI AG—See Metallgesellschaft AG; *Int'l*, pg. 861
LURGI (AUSTRALIA) PTY. LTD.—See Metallgesellschaft AG; *Int'l*, pg. 861
LURGI CANADA LTD.—See Metallgesellschaft AG; *Int'l*, pg. 861
LURGI CORPORATION—See Metallgesellschaft AG; *Int'l*, pg. 861
LURGI ESPANOLA S.A.—See Metallgesellschaft AG; *Int'l*, pg. 861
L. LURIA & SON, INC.; *U.S. Public*, pg. 1020
L'USINAGE ELECTRIQUE SARL—See Georg Fischer Ltd.; *Int'l*, pg. 489
LUSK; *U.S. Private*, pg. 681
LUSKEYS WESTERN STORES, INC.; *U.S. Private*, pg. 681
LUSKIN'S, INC.; *U.S. Private*, pg. 681
LUSOCERAM-EMPREENDIMENTOS CERAMICOS, S.A.—See Redland PLC; *Int'l*, pg. 1092
LUSOFACTOR - SOCIEDADE DE FACTORING, SA—See Caixa Geral de Depositos; *Int'l*, pg. 251
LUSOSIDER ACOS PLANOS SA—See Koninklijke Hoogovens N.V.; *Int'l*, pg. 755
LUSOTECNA—See Technip; *Int'l*, pg. 1361
LUSOTEL INDUSTRIA HOTELEIRA LTDA.—See Granada Group PLC; *Int'l*, pg. 556
LUSTINE OLDSMOBILE & BUICK, INC.; *U.S. Private*, pg. 681
LUTECE—See Ark Restaurants Corp.; *U.S. Public*, pg. 130
LUTGENS & REIMERS GMBH—See Hapag-Lloyd AG; *Int'l*, pg. 596
LUTHERAN BROTHERHOOD; *U.S. Private*, pg. 681
LUTHERAN BROTHERHOOD FAMILY FOR MUTUAL FUNDS—See Lutheran Brotherhood; *U.S. Private*, pg. 682
LUTHERAN BROTHERHOOD FINANCIAL CORPORATION—See Lutheran Brotherhood; *U.S. Private*, pg. 682
LUTHERAN BROTHERHOOD FOUNDATION—See Lutheran Brotherhood; *U.S. Private*, pg. 682
LUTHERAN BROTHERHOOD REAL ESTATE PRODUCTS COMPANY—See Lutheran Brotherhood; *U.S. Private*, pg. 682
LUTHERAN BROTHERHOOD RESEARCH CORP.—See Lutheran Brotherhood; *U.S. Private*, pg. 682
LUTHERAN BROTHERHOOD SECURITIES CORP.—See Lutheran Brotherhood; *U.S. Private*, pg. 682
LUTHERAN BROTHERHOOD VARIABLE INSURANCE PRODUCTS COMPANY—See Lutheran Brotherhood; *U.S. Private*, pg. 682
LUWA AG—See Hesta Tex AG; *Int'l*, pg. 617
LUWA ANLAGENTECHNIK GMBH—See Hesta Tex AG; *Int'l*, pg. 617

LUWA

DIRECTORY OF CORPORATE AFFILIATIONS

Company Index

LUWA BAHNSON, INC.; *U.S. Private*, pg. 682
LUWA BISINGER TEXTILTECHNIK GMBH—See Hesta Tex AG; *Int'l*, pg. 617
LUWA BV—See Hesta Tex AG; *Int'l*, pg. 617
LUWA CLIMATECNICA SA—See Hesta Tex AG; *Int'l*, pg. 617
LUWA ENGINEERING (HK) LTD.—See Hesta Tex AG; *Int'l*, pg. 617
LUWA ENGINEERING (PTE.) LTD.—See Hesta Tex AG; *Int'l*, pg. 617
LUWA ESPANOLA SA—See Hesta Tex AG; *Int'l*, pg. 617
LUWA FAHRZEUGKLIMATECHNIK GMBH—See Hesta Tex AG; *Int'l*, pg. 617
LUWA FILTER AND SHELTER LTD.—See Hesta Tex AG; *Int'l*, pg. 617
LUWA FILTER CORP.—See Hesta Tex AG; *Int'l*, pg. 617
LUWA FILTERTECHNIK GMBH—See Hesta Tex AG; *Int'l*, pg. 617
LUWA FILTRES SARL—See Hesta Tex AG; *Int'l*, pg. 617
LUWA FILTRI SRL—See Hesta Tex AG; *Int'l*, pg. 617
LUWA GES.M.B.H.—See Hesta Tex AG; *Int'l*, pg. 617
LUWA GMBH—See Hesta Tex AG; *Int'l*, pg. 617
LUWA ITALIA S.R.L.—See Hesta Tex AG; *Int'l*, pg. 617
LUWA JAPAN LTD.—See Hesta Tex AG; *Int'l*, pg. 617
LUWA LTA LUFTTECHNISCHE ANLAGEN GMBH—See Hesta Tex AG; *Int'l*, pg. 617
LUWA LUFTTECHNISCHE ANLAGEN GMBH—See Hesta Tex AG; *Int'l*, pg. 617
LUWA SERVICE GMBH—See Hesta Tex AG; *Int'l*, pg. 617
LUWA (SOUTH AFRICA) (PTY) LTD.—See Hesta Tex AG; *Int'l*, pg. 617
LUWA (TAIWAN) LTD.—See Hesta Tex AG; *Int'l*, pg. 618
LUWA (UK) LTD.—See Hesta Tex AG; *Int'l*, pg. 618
THE LUX CO., INC.—See Coachmen Industries, Inc.; *U.S. Public*, pg. 388
LUX DE MOREZ—See Essilor International Compagnie Generale d'Optique; *Int'l*, pg. 462
LUX GMBH & CO. KG—See OBI Bau-und Heimwerkermaerkte GmbH & Co. KG; *Int'l*, pg. 993
LUX INTERNATIONAL S.A.—See OBI Bau-und Heimwerkermaerkte GmbH & Co. KG; *Int'l*, pg. 993
LUXFER—See Alcan Aluminium Limited; *Int'l*, pg. 51
LUXFER USA LTD.—See Alcan Aluminium Limited; *Int'l*, pg. 50
LUXLIFE—See Groupe GAN; *Int'l*, pg. 565
LUXO A/S; *Int'l*, pg. 821
LUXO ASIA-PACIFIC PTY. LTD.—See Luxo A/S; *Int'l*, pg. 821
LUXO AUSTRALIA PTY. LTD.—See Luxo A/S; *Int'l*, pg. 821
LUXO DANMARK A/S—See Luxo A/S; *Int'l*, pg. 821
LUXO ESPANOLA—See Luxo A/S; *Int'l*, pg. 821
LUXO-FRANCE—See Luxo A/S; *Int'l*, pg. 821
LUXO ITALIANA S.P.A.—See Luxo A/S; *Int'l*, pg. 821
LUXO LAMP CORPORATION—See Luxo A/S; *Int'l*, pg. 821
LUXO LAMPS LTD.—See Luxo A/S; *Int'l*, pg. 821
LUXO LEUCHTEN GMBH—See Luxo A/S; *Int'l*, pg. 821
LUXO LTD./SVERIGE INC.—See Luxo A/S; *Int'l*, pg. 822
LUXO U.K. LTD.—See Luxo A/S; *Int'l*, pg. 822
LUXOR—See EBSCO Industries, Inc.; *U.S. Private*, pg. 359
LUXOR HOTEL—See Circus Circus - Las Vegas; *U.S. Public*, pg. 375
LUXOTTICA AUSTRALIA PTY LTD.—See Luxottica Group S.p.A.; *Int'l*, pg. 822
LUXOTTICA BELGIUM N.V.—See Luxottica Group S.p.A.; *Int'l*, pg. 822
LUXOTTICA CANADA INC.—See Luxottica Group S.p.A.; *Int'l*, pg. 822
LUXOTTICA DO BRASIL LTDA.—See Luxottica Group S.p.A.; *Int'l*, pg. 822
LUXOTTICA FASHION BRILLEN GMBH—See Luxottica Group S.p.A.; *Int'l*, pg. 822
OY LUXOTTICA FINLAND AB—See Luxottica Group S.p.A.; *Int'l*, pg. 822
LUXOTTICA FRANCE S.A.R.L.—See Luxottica Group S.p.A.; *Int'l*, pg. 822
LUXOTTICA GROUP S.P.A.; *Int'l*, pg. 822
LUXOTTICA HELLAS AE—See Luxottica Group S.p.A.; *Int'l*, pg. 822
LUXOTTICA IBERICA S.A.—See Luxottica Group S.p.A.; *Int'l*, pg. 822
LUXOTTICA MEXICO SA DE C.V.—See Luxottica Group S.p.A.; *Int'l*, pg. 822
LUXOTTICA NEDERLAND B.V.—See Luxottica Group S.p.A.; *Int'l*, pg. 822
LUXOTTICA PORTUGAL S.A.—See Luxottica Group S.p.A.; *Int'l*, pg. 822
LUXOTTICA SWEDEN A.B.—See Luxottica Group S.p.A.; *Int'l*, pg. 822
LUXOTTICA (SWITZERLAND) A.G.—See Luxottica Group S.p.A.; *Int'l*, pg. 822
LUXOTTICA U.K. LTD.—See Luxottica Group S.p.A.; *Int'l*, pg. 822
LUXOTTICA VERTRIEBSGESELLSHAFT MBH—See Luxottica Group S.p.A.; *Int'l*, pg. 822
LUXTRONIC MASCHINEN GMBH—See OBI Bau-und Heimwerkermaerkte GmbH & Co. KG; *Int'l*, pg. 993
LUZZATTO & FIGLIO (FRANCE) S.A.—See Baker Hughes Incorporated; *U.S. Public*, pg. 166
LYALL ASSEMBLIES, INC.—See Group Dekko; *U.S. Private*, pg. 484
LYCOM A/S—See Lucent Technologies Inc.; *U.S. Public*, pg. 1019
LYDALL & FOULDS DIV.—See Lydall, Inc.; *U.S. Public*, pg. 1021
LYDALL AXOHM—See Lydall, Inc.; *U.S. Public*, pg. 1021
LYDALL COMPOSITE MATERIALS—See Lydall, Inc.; *U.S. Public*, pg. 1021
LYDALL EXPRESS, INC.—See Lydall, Inc.; *U.S. Public*, pg. 1021
LYDALL, INC.; *U.S. Public*, pg. 1020
LYDALL, INC.—See Lydall, Inc.; *U.S. Public*, pg. 1021
LYDALL INTERNATIONAL, INC.—See Lydall, Inc.; *U.S. Public*, pg. 1021
LYDALL MANNING-GREEN ISLAND OPERATION—See Lydall, Inc.; *U.S. Public*, pg. 1021
LYDALL MANNING-HATBORO OPERATION—See Lydall, Inc.; *U.S. Public*, pg. 1021
LYDALL SOUTHERN PRODUCTS—See Lydall, Inc.; *U.S. Public*, pg. 1021
LYDALL TRANSPORT, LTD.—See Lydall, Inc.; *U.S. Public*, pg. 1021
LYDALL WESTEX—See Lydall, Inc.; *U.S. Public*, pg. 1021
LYDEX A/S—See Tenneco Inc.; *U.S. Public*, pg. 1580
LYDIG OF SCANDINAVIA A/S—See Harman International Industries, Inc.; *U.S. Public*, pg. 787
LYELL HOLDINGS LIMITED—See Xerox Corporation; *U.S. Public*, pg. 1785
B.V. LYEMPF—See Koninklijke BolsWessanen nv; *Int'l*, pg. 752
LYEMPF/VAN HEEL B.V.—See Koninklijke BolsWessanen nv; *Int'l*, pg. 752
LYKE CORPORATION; *U.S. Private*, pg. 682
LYKES AGRICULTURE—See Lykes Brothers Inc.; *U.S. Private*, pg. 682
LYKES BROTHERS INC.; *U.S. Private*, pg. 682
LYKES ENERGY, INC.; *U.S. Private*, pg. 682
LYKES INSURANCE INC.—See Lykes Brothers Inc.; *U.S. Private*, pg. 682
LYKES MEAT GROUP—See Smithfield Foods, Inc.; *U.S. Public*, pg. 1479
LYKES PASCO INC.—See Lykes Brothers Inc.; *U.S. Private*, pg. 682
LYKES TRANSPORT INC.—See Lykes Brothers Inc.; *U.S. Private*, pg. 682
LYM-TECH SCIENTIFIC—See John R. Lyman Company; *U.S. Private*, pg. 683
LYMAN—See Senior Engineering Group, plc.; *Int'l*, pg. 1222
JOHN R. LYMAN COMPANY; *U.S. Private*, pg. 683
LYMAN LUMBER COMPANY; *U.S. Private*, pg. 683
LYMAN PRODUCTS CORPORATION; *U.S. Private*, pg. 683
LYNCH & MAYER, INC—See Lincoln National Corporation; *U.S. Public*, pg. 998
LYNCH CAPITAL CORPORATION—See Lynch Corporation; *U.S. Public*, pg. 1021
LYNCH CORPORATION; *U.S. Public*, pg. 1021
LYNCH ENTERTAINMENT CORPORATION—See Lynch Corporation; *U.S. Public*, pg. 1021
LYNCH ENTERTAINMENT CORPORATION II—See Lynch Corporation; *U.S. Public*, pg. 1021
LYNCH MACHINERY, INC.—See Lynch Corporation; *U.S. Public*, pg. 1022
LYNCH MANUFACTURING CORPORATION—See Lynch Corporation; *U.S. Public*, pg. 1022
LYNCH MULTIMEDIA CORPORATION—See Lynch Corporation; *U.S. Public*, pg. 1022
LYNCH TELECOMMUNICATIONS CORPORATION—See Lynch Corporation; *U.S. Public*, pg. 1022
LYNCH TELEPHONE CORPORATION—See Lynch Corporation; *U.S. Public*, pg. 1022
LYNCHBURG GRAPHICS SERVICE CENTER—See R.R. Donnelley & Sons Company; *U.S. Public*, pg. 518
LYNCHBURG SERVICE CENTER—See Carolina Steel Corporation; *U.S. Private*, pg. 214
LYNDEN AIR FREIGHT, INC.—See Lynden Incorporated; *U.S. Private*, pg. 683
LYNDEN FINANCIAL SERVICES, INC.—See Lynden Incorporated; *U.S. Private*, pg. 684
LYNDEN FORWARDING, INC.—See Lynden Incorporated; *U.S. Private*, pg. 684
LYNDEN INCORPORATED; *U.S. Private*, pg. 683
LYNDEN INCORPORATED—See Lynden Incorporated; *U.S. Private*, pg. 683
LYNDEN LOGISTICS, INC.—See Lynden Incorporated; *U.S. Private*, pg. 684
LYNDEN TRANSPORT, INC.—See Lynden Incorporated; *U.S. Private*, pg. 684
LYNDON PROPERTY INSURANCE COMPANY—See Frontier Insurance Group, Inc.; *U.S. Public*, pg. 685
ED J. LYNG COMPANY—See Trinidad/Benham Corp.; *U.S. Private*, pg. 1103
JAC. O. LYNGAAS & CO. A/S (CORNHILL)—See Allianz Aktiengesellschaft; *Int'l*, pg. 60
LYNN ARTHUR ASSOCIATES—See USCS International, Inc.; *U.S. Public*, pg. 1659
LYNTONE BELTS—See Gem-Dandy, Inc.; *U.S. Private*, pg. 442
LYNWOOD MANOR—See Horizon/CMS Healthcare Corporation; *U.S. Public*, pg. 837
LYNWOOD SCIENTIFIC DEVELOPMENTS LIMITED—See NAI Technologies, Inc.; *U.S. Public*, pg. 1144
LYNX GOLF, INC.; *U.S. Private*, pg. 684
LYON COUNTY CO-OP OIL CO.; *U.S. Private*, pg. 684
LYON METAL PRODUCTS, INC.—See L & D Group; *U.S. Private*, pg. 638
WILLIAM LYON COMPANY; *U.S. Private*, pg. 684
LYONAISE COMMUNICATIONS—See Lyonnaise des Eaux S.A.; *Int'l*, pg. 824
LYONDELL-CITGO REFINING COMPANY, LTD.—See Lyondell Petrochemical Company; *U.S. Public*, pg. 1022
LYONDELL LICENSING, INC.—See Lyondell Petrochemical Company; *U.S. Public*, pg. 1022
LYONDELL PETROCHEMICAL COMPANY; *U.S. Public*, pg. 1022
LYONNAISE DE BANQUE—See Groupe GAN; *Int'l*, pg. 565
LYONNAISE DES EAUX S.A.; *Int'l*, pg. 822
LYONS BISCUITS—See Hillsdown Holdings Plc; *Int'l*, pg. 619
LYONS LAVEY NICKEL SWIFT, INC.—See Omnicom Group Inc.; *U.S. Public*, pg. 1224
LYON'S RESTAURANTS, INC.; *U.S. Private*, pg. 684
LYONS SEAFOODS LIMITED; *Int'l*, pg. 824
LYSAKER REISEBYRA A.S.—See Kvaerner a.s.a.; *Int'l*, pg. 769
LYSAKER REISEBYRA, STAVANGER—See Kvaerner a.s.a.; *Int'l*, pg. 770
LYSSIA GMBH—See Solvay S.A.; *Int'l*, pg. 1278
LYTRON INCORPORATED; *U.S. Private*, pg. 684

M

M&T REAL ESTATE—See First Empire State Corporation; *U.S. Public*, pg. 631
M/A-COM EUROTECH—See AMP Incorporated; *U.S. Public*, pg. 8
M/A-COM GREENPAR CONNECTORS—See AMP Incorporated; *U.S. Public*, pg. 8
M/A-COM INC.—See AMP Incorporated; *U.S. Public*, pg. 8
M/A-COM, INC. COMPONENTS GROUP—See AMP Incorporated; *U.S. Public*, pg. 8
M/A-COM LIMITED—See AMP Incorporated; *U.S. Public*, pg. 8
THE M/A/R/C GROUP; *U.S. Public*, pg. 1022
M/A/R/C MARKETING AND RESEARCH COUNSELORS, INC.—See The M/A/R/C Group; *U.S. Public*, pg. 1023
M&A SOCIETA DI MERGERS & ACQUISITIONS S.P.A.—See Swiss Bank Corporation; *Int'l*, pg. 1330
M & C BROKERAGE SERVICES, INC.—See Cigna Corp.; *U.S. Public*, pg. 366
M & C SPECIALTIES COMPANY; *U.S. Private*, pg. 684
M & C SPECIALTIES (IRELAND) LIMITED—See M & C Specialties Company; *U.S. Private*, pg. 684
M & C REMCO TAPE PRODUCTS CO.—See M & C Specialties Company; *U.S. Private*, pg. 684
M & E MANUFACTURING CO.—See Plastek Group; *U.S. Private*, pg. 870
M & F VERMOGENS- UND GRUNDSTUCKSVERWALTUNG GMBH—See Bayerische Vereinsbank Group; *Int'l*, pg. 180
M & H DAIRY—See Fleming Companies, Inc.; *U.S. Public*, pg. 653
M & H FINANCIAL CORP.—See Fleming Companies, Inc.; *U.S. Public*, pg. 653
M&H RETAIL FOOD GROUP—See Fleming Companies, Inc.; *U.S. Public*, pg. 653
M & I BANK—See Marshall & Ilsley Corporation; *U.S. Public*, pg. 1050
M & I BANK FOX VALLEY—See Marshall & Ilsley Corporation; *U.S. Public*, pg. 1050
M & I BANK NORTHEAST—See Marshall & Ilsley Corporation; *U.S. Public*, pg. 1050
M & I BANK OF BELOIT—See Marshall & Ilsley Corporation; *U.S. Public*, pg. 1050
M & I BANK OF BURLINGTON—See Marshall & Ilsley Corporation; *U.S. Public*, pg. 1050
M & I BANK OF DELAVAN—See Marshall & Ilsley Corporation; *U.S. Public*, pg. 1050
M & I BANK OF EAGLE RIVER—See Marshall & Ilsley Corporation; *U.S. Public*, pg. 1050
M & I BANK OF JANESVILLE—See Marshall & Ilsley Corporation; *U.S. Public*, pg. 1050
M & I BANK OF LACROSSE—See Marshall & Ilsley Corporation; *U.S. Public*, pg. 1050
M & I BANK OF MAYVILLE—See Marshall & Ilsley Corporation; *U.S. Public*, pg. 1050
M & I BANK OF MENOMONEE FALLS—See Marshall & Ilsley Corporation; *U.S. Public*, pg. 1050
M & I BANK OF RACINE—See Marshall & Ilsley Corporation; *U.S. Public*, pg. 1050
M & I BANK OF SHAWANO, N.A.—See Marshall & Ilsley Corporation; *U.S. Public*, pg. 1050
M & I BANK SOUTH CENTRAL—See Marshall & Ilsley Corporation; *U.S. Public*, pg. 1050
M & I BANK SOUTHWEST—See Marshall & Ilsley Corporation; *U.S. Public*, pg. 1050
M & I BANK S.S.B.—See Marshall & Ilsley Corporation; *U.S. Public*, pg. 1050
M & I BROKERAGE SERVICES, INC.—See Marshall & Ilsley Corporation; *U.S. Public*, pg. 1050
M & I CAPITAL MARKETS GROUP, INC.—See Marshall & Ilsley Corporation; *U.S. Public*, pg. 1051
M & I CENTRAL BANK & TRUST—See Marshall & Ilsley Corporation; *U.S. Public*, pg. 1050
M & I CENTRAL STATE BANK—See Marshall & Ilsley Corporation; *U.S. Public*, pg. 1050
M & I CITIZENS AMERICAN BANK—See Marshall & Ilsley Corporation; *U.S. Public*, pg. 1050
M & I COMMUNITY STATE BANK—See Marshall & Ilsley Corporation; *U.S. Public*, pg. 1050
M & I DATA SERVICES, INC.—See Marshall & Ilsley Corporation; *U.S. Public*, pg. 1050
M & I FIRST AMERICAN BANK—See Marshall & Ilsley Corporation; *U.S. Public*, pg. 1050
M & I FIRST NATIONAL BANK—See Marshall & Ilsley Corporation; *U.S. Public*, pg. 1050
M & I FIRST NATIONAL LEASING CORP.—See Marshall & Ilsley Corporation; *U.S. Public*, pg. 1051
M & I INVESTMENT MANAGEMENT CORP.—See Marshall & Ilsley Corporation; *U.S. Public*, pg. 1051
M & I LAKE COUNTRY BANK—See Marshall & Ilsley Corporation; *U.S. Public*, pg. 1050
M & I MADISON BANK—See Marshall & Ilsley Corporation; *U.S. Public*, pg. 1050
M & I MARSHALL & ILSLEY BANK—See Marshall & Ilsley Corporation; *U.S. Public*, pg. 1050
M & I MARSHALL & ILSLEY TRUST COMPANY OF ARIZONA—See Marshall & Ilsley Corporation; *U.S. Public*, pg. 1051
M & I MERCHANTS BANK—See Marshall & Ilsley Corporation; *U.S. Public*, pg. 1050
M & I MID-STATE BANK—See Marshall & Ilsley Corporation; *U.S. Public*, pg. 1050
M & I MORTGAGE CORP.—See Marshall & Ilsley Corporation; *U.S. Public*, pg. 1051
M & I NORTHERN BANK—See Marshall & Ilsley Corporation; *U.S. Public*, pg. 1050

M & I THUNDERBIRD BANK—See Marshall & Ilsley Corporation; *U.S. Public*, pg. 1050
M & I VENTURES CORPORATION—See Marshall & Ilsley Corporation; *U.S. Public*, pg. 1051
M&M/MARS—See Mars, Incorporated; *U.S. Private*, pg. 707
M & M PRECISION SYSTEMS CORPORATION—See Danaher Corporation; *U.S. Public*, pg. 482
M & M RESTAURANT SUPPLY—See Keystone Foods Corporation; *U.S. Private*, pg. 619
M&N VALVE—See Van Leeuwen Pipe and Tube Group B.V.; *Int'l*, pg. 1449
M&S EXPORT (IRELAND) LIMITED—See Marks & Spencer PLC; *Int'l*, pg. 843
M&S MODE—See N.V. Koninklijke Bijenkorf Beheer KBB; *Int'l*, pg. 750
M & S SYSTEMS, INC.—See Nortek, Inc.; *U.S. Public*, pg. 1193
M & S TOILETRIES LTD.—See Franz Haniel & Cie, GmbH; *Int'l*, pg. 591
M&T CAPITAL CORPORATION—See First Empire State Corporation; *U.S. Public*, pg. 631
THE M&T COMPANY—See CDI Corp.; *U.S. Public*, pg. 277
M&T CREDIT CORPORATION—See First Empire State Corporation; *U.S. Public*, pg. 631
M&T FINANCIAL CORPORATION—See First Empire State Corporation; *U.S. Public*, pg. 631
M&T MORTGAGE CORP.—See First Empire State Corporation; *U.S. Public*, pg. 631
M & T PARTNERS; *U.S. Private*, pg. 684
M&T SECURITIES, INC.—See First Empire State Corporation; *U.S. Public*, pg. 631
M&W—See Alamo Group, Inc.; *U.S. Public*, pg. 35
M-B COMPANIES INC. OF WISCONSIN; *U.S. Private*, pg. 684
M-B PULP COMPANY—See The Mead Corporation; *U.S. Public*, pg. 1076
M-C POWER CORPORATION—See Ishikawajima-Harima Heavy Industries Co., Ltd.; *Int'l*, pg. 689
M/D TOTCO INSTRUMENTATION—See Varco International, Inc.; *U.S. Public*, pg. 1709
M4 DATA LTD.—See Storage Technology Corporation; *U.S. Public*, pg. 1523
M/G TRANSPORTATION SERVICES, INC.—See The Midland Company; *U.S. Public*, pg. 1111
M-I L.L.C.—See Halliburton Company; *U.S. Public*, pg. 776
M-I L.L.C.—See Smith International, Inc.; *U.S. Public*, pg. 1478
M-INFORMATICS AG—See Migros; *Int'l*, pg. 865
M K DIAMOND PRODUCTS, INC.; *U.S. Public*, pg. 684
M M M SALES, INC.; *U.S. Private*, pg. 685
M M SYSTEMS CORPORATION; *U.S. Private*, pg. 685
M1 KIT MFG. CO.—See Kit Manufacturing Company; *U.S. Public*, pg. 962
M/S FISCHBEIN PACKAGING (SINGAPORE) PTE. LTD.—See AXIA Incorporated; *U.S. Private*, pg. 103
M6—See Groupe Bruxelles Lambert S.A.; *Int'l*, pg. 561
M-SMM ELECTRONICS SDN. BHD.—See Sumitomo Metal Mining Co., Ltd.; *Int'l*, pg. 1316
M-TRON INDUSTRIES, INC.—See Lynch Corporation; *U.S. Public*, pg. 1022
M21 INDUSTRIES, INC.—See Devcon International Corp.; *U.S. Public*, pg. 502
M.A. HANNA COLOR—See M.A. Hanna Company; *U.S. Public*, pg. 781
M.A. HANNA RESIN DISTRIBUTION—See M.A. Hanna Company; *U.S. Public*, pg. 781
MAA COMMUNICATIONS BOZELL—See True North Diversified Companies; *U.S. Public*, pg. 1642
MAC AMERICA COMMUNICATIONS, INC.; *U.S. Private*, pg. 685
MAC BETON HELLAS S.A.—See Novartis AG; *Int'l*, pg. 983
MAC EQUIPMENT INC.; *U.S. Private*, pg. 685
MAC S.P.A. MODERN ADVANCED CONCRETE—See Novartis AG; *Int'l*, pg. 983
MADD AGENCY—See Young & Rubicam Inc.; *U.S. Private*, pg. 1200
M.A.I.—See Lagardere Groupe; *Int'l*, pg. 795
M.A.I.L. FINANZBERATUNG GMBH—See Creditanstalt-Bankverein; *Int'l*, pg. 347
MAN AKTIENGESELLSCHAFT; *Int'l*, pg. 824
MAN AUTOMOTIVE (AUSTRALIA) PTY. LTD.—See MAN Aktiengesellschaft; *Int'l*, pg. 825
MAN AUTOMOTIVE (SOUTH AFRICA) (PROPRIETARY) LTD.—See MAN Aktiengesellschaft; *Int'l*, pg. 825
MAN B & W DIESEL AG—See MAN Aktiengesellschaft; *Int'l*, pg. 824
MAN B & W DIESEL A/S—See MAN Aktiengesellschaft; *Int'l*, pg. 824
MAN B & W JAPAN LTD.—See MAN Aktiengesellschaft; *Int'l*, pg. 824
MAN B & W NORGE A/S—See MAN Aktiengesellschaft; *Int'l*, pg. 824
MAN CAPITAL CORPORATION—See MAN Aktiengesellschaft; *Int'l*, pg. 826
MAN DEZENTRALE ENERGIESYSTEME GMBH—See MAN Aktiengesellschaft; *Int'l*, pg. 825
MAN GHH AUSTRALIA PTY. LTD.—See MAN Aktiengesellschaft; *Int'l*, pg. 824
MAN GHH CORP.—See MAN Aktiengesellschaft; *Int'l*, pg. 824
MAN GHH FRANCE SOCIETE ANONYME—See MAN Aktiengesellschaft; *Int'l*, pg. 824
MAN GHH (GREAT BRITAIN) LTD.—See MAN Aktiengesellschaft; *Int'l*, pg. 824
MAN GHH (IRAN) SHERKATE SAHAMI KHASS—See MAN Aktiengesellschaft; *Int'l*, pg. 824
MAN GHH LOGISTICS GMBH—See MAN Aktiengesellschaft; *Int'l*, pg. 824
MAN GUTEHOFFNUNGSHUETTE AG—See MAN Aktiengesellschaft; *Int'l*, pg. 824
MAN KAMYON VE OTOBUES TICARET LTD. SIRKETI—See MAN Aktiengesellschaft; *Int'l*, pg. 825

MAN NUTZFAHRZEUGE AG—See MAN Aktiengesellschaft; *Int'l*, pg. 824
MAN NUTZFAHRZEUGE LEASING GMBH—See MAN Aktiengesellschaft; *Int'l*, pg. 824
MAN PLAMAG DRUCKMASCHINEN AG—See MAN Aktiengesellschaft; *Int'l*, pg. 825
MAN ROLAND DRUCKMASCHINEN AKTIENGESELLSCHAFT—See MAN Aktiengesellschaft; *Int'l*, pg. 825
MAN TAKRAF FORDERTECHNIK GMBH—See MAN Aktiengesellschaft; *Int'l*, pg. 824
MAN TECHNOLOGIE AG—See MAN Aktiengesellschaft; *Int'l*, pg. 825
MAN URANIT GRONAU GMBH—See MAN Aktiengesellschaft; *Int'l*, pg. 825
MAN VERWALTUNGS-GESELLSCHAFT MIT BESCHRAENKTER HAFTUNG—See MAN Aktiengesellschaft; *Int'l*, pg. 825
M.A.P. BUILDERS INC.—See Lennar Corporation; *U.S. Public*, pg. 988
MAR, INC.—See NationsBank Corporation; *U.S. Public*, pg. 1163
M.A.R.C.O.—See Eagle-Picher Industries, Inc.; *U.S. Private*, pg. 355
MAS DEUTSCHLAND GMBH—See Ruetgers A.G.; *Int'l*, pg. 1148
MB AMERICA, INC.—See Caradon Plc; *Int'l*, pg. 267
MB-CLARKE LTD.—See De La Rue plc; *Int'l*, pg. 386
MB ESPANA, S.A.—See Hasbro, Inc.; *U.S. Public*, pg. 798
MB FRANCE S.A.—See Hasbro, Inc.; *U.S. Public*, pg. 798
MB GENERAL PACKAGING DIV.—See Caradon Plc; *Int'l*, pg. 266
MB GROUP ENTERPRISES, INC.—See Caradon Plc; *Int'l*, pg. 267
M/B INTERACTIVE—See Mezzina/Brown Inc.; *U.S. Private*, pg. 740
MB INTERNATIONAL B.V.—See Hasbro, Inc.; *U.S. Public*, pg. 798
MB IRELAND—See Hasbro, Inc.; *U.S. Public*, pg. 798
MB ITALY S.R.L.—See Hasbro, Inc.; *U.S. Public*, pg. 798
MB MANUFACTURING—See The Cypress Companies; *U.S. Private*, pg. 300
MB PAPER—See MacMillan Bloedel Limited; *Int'l*, pg. 829
MB (SWITZERLAND) AG—See Hasbro, Inc.; *U.S. Public*, pg. 798
MBA-KONE AG—See Kone Corporation; *Int'l*, pg. 748
MBC AGENCY, INC.—See Mercantile Bankshares Corporation; *U.S. Public*, pg. 1089
MBC LEASING—See Mercantile Bankshares Corporation; *U.S. Public*, pg. 1089
MBC REALTY, INC.—See Mercantile Bankshares Corporation; *U.S. Public*, pg. 1089
MBI INC.; *U.S. Private*, pg. 685
MBIA ASSURANCE S.A.—See MBIA Inc.; *U.S. Public*, pg. 1023
MBIA INC.; *U.S. Public*, pg. 1023
MBIA MUNICIPAL INVESTORS SERVICE CORPORATION—See MBIA Inc.; *U.S. Public*, pg. 1023
MBK NIGERIA LTD.—See Mitsui & Co., Ltd.; *Int'l*, pg. 880
MBL LIFE ASSURANCE CORPORATION; *U.S. Private*, pg. 685
MBM; *U.S. Public*, pg. 685
M B M TECHNOLOGY LIMITED—See Morgan Crucible Co. Plc; *Int'l*, pg. 892
MBNA AMERICA BANK N.A.—See MBNA Corporation; *U.S. Public*, pg. 1023
MBNA CONSUMER SERVICES, INC.—See MBNA Corporation; *U.S. Public*, pg. 1023
MBNA CORPORATION; *U.S. Public*, pg. 1023
MBNA HALLMARK INFORMATION SYSTEMS—See MBNA Corporation; *U.S. Public*, pg. 1023
MBNA INSURANCE SERVICES—See MBNA Corporation; *U.S. Public*, pg. 1023
MBNA MARKETING SYSTEMS, INC.—See MBNA Corporation; *U.S. Public*, pg. 1023
MBS HOLDING, INC.; *U.S. Private*, pg. 685
MBT ARCHITECTURE; *U.S. Private*, pg. 686
MBT (AUSTRALIA) PTY. LTD.—See Viag AG; *Int'l*, pg. 1465
MBT AUSTRIA GESELLSCHAFT M.B.H.—See Viag AG; *Int'l*, pg. 1465
MBT DE VENEZUELA, C.A.—See Viag AG; *Int'l*, pg. 1465
MBT DIVISION/ELECTRONICS GROUP—See Israel Aircraft Industries Ltd.; *Int'l*, pg. 690
MBT ENVIRONMENTAL ENGINEERING LTD.—See Viag AG; *Int'l*, pg. 1465
MBT FINANCE INC.—See Viag AG; *Int'l*, pg. 1465
MBT FRANCE S.A.—See Viag AG; *Int'l*, pg. 1465
MBT HOLDING, LTD.—See Viag AG; *Int'l*, pg. 1465
MBT (MALAYSIA) SDN. BHD.—See Viag AG; *Int'l*, pg. 1465
MBT (NEW ZEALAND) LTD.—See Viag AG; *Int'l*, pg. 1465
MBT PORTUGAL LDA.—See Viag AG; *Int'l*, pg. 1465
MBT (SINGAPORE) PTE. LTD.—See Viag AG; *Int'l*, pg. 1465
MBT (SWITZERLAND) LTD.—See Viag AG; *Int'l*, pg. 1465
MBT (TAIWAN) CO. LTD.—See Viag AG; *Int'l*, pg. 1465
MC BITOR LIMITED—See Petroleos de Venezuela S.A.; *Int'l*, pg. 1046
MC MICRO COMPACT CAR AG—See Daimler-Benz Aktiengesellschaft; *Int'l*, pg. 368
M.C. SHEET METAL LTD.—See Rieter Holdings; *Int'l*, pg. 1117
MC II CORP.—See Westwood Corporation; *U.S. Public*, pg. 1763
MC2 ADAMS—See Lowe McAdams Healthcare; *U.S. Private*, pg. 679
MC2 CYBERSPACE—See SBC Advertising; *U.S. Private*, pg. 955
MC2 INC.—See Occidental Petroleum Corporation; *U.S. Public*, pg. 1210
MCA/UNIVERSAL MERCHANDISING—See The Seagram Company Ltd.; *Int'l*, pg. 1215

MCC BEHAVIORAL CARE, INC.—See Cigna Corp.; *U.S. Public*, pg. 362
MCC DIV.—See Mallinckrodt Inc.; *U.S. Public*, pg. 1039
MCC GROUP, L.L.C.; *U.S. Private*, pg. 686
MCC INDEPENDENT PRACTICE ASSOCIATION OF GREATER NEW YORK—See Cigna Corp.; *U.S. Public*, pg. 362
MCDR, INC.; *U.S. Private*, pg. 686
MCF CONTROLS INC.—See IMI Plc; *Int'l*, pg. 647
MCG GRAFICARBO DIVISION—See Morgan Crucible Co. Plc; *Int'l*, pg. 891
MCG MORGAN CARBON GRAPHITE SRL—See Morgan Crucible Co. Plc; *Int'l*, pg. 891
MCI ACCEPTANCE CORP.—See Consorcio G. Grupo Dina, S.A. de C.V.; *Int'l*, pg. 326
MCI BUSINESS MARKETS—See MCI Communications Corp.; *U.S. Public*, pg. 1024
MCI COMMUNICATIONS CORP.; *U.S. Public*, pg. 1023
MCI INTERNATIONAL INC.—See MCI Communications Corp.; *U.S. Public*, pg. 1024
MCI MASS MARKETS—See MCI Communications Corp.; *U.S. Public*, pg. 1024
MCI SOFTWARE DEVELOPMENT & INFORMATION TECHNOLOGY—See MCI Communications Corp.; *U.S. Public*, pg. 1024
MCI SYSTEMHOUSE—See MCI Communications Corp.; *U.S. Public*, pg. 1024
MCI TELECOMMUNICATIONS CORP.—See MCI Communications Corp.; *U.S. Public*, pg. 1024
MCIMETRO—See MCI Communications Corp.; *U.S. Public*, pg. 1024
MCL—See Saatchi & Saatchi Advertising Worldwide; *U.S. Public*, pg. 1422
MCL PILE DRIVING—See Agra Inc.; *Int'l*, pg. 30
MCM ELECTRONICS INC.—See Premier Farnell plc; *Int'l*, pg. 1068
MCM ENTERPRISES, INC.; *U.S. Private*, pg. 686
MCM PRODUCTS, INC.—See Fortune Brands, Inc.; *U.S. Public*, pg. 675
MCMC CORRUGATING MACHINERY CO. HOLLAND B.V.—See Mitsubishi Heavy Industries Ltd.; *Int'l*, pg. 874
MCN ENERGY GROUP, INC.; *U.S. Public*, pg. 1024
MCN INVESTMENT—See MCN Energy Group, Inc.; *U.S. Public*, pg. 1025
M.C.N. SAT HOLDING—See Lagardere Groupe; *Int'l*, pg. 792
M.C.N. SAT SERVICE—See Lagardere Groupe; *Int'l*, pg. 792
M.C.N. SAT US—See Lagardere Groupe; *Int'l*, pg. 792
MCO PROPERTIES INC.—See Maxxam Inc.; *U.S. Public*, pg. 1062
MCRB SERVICE BUREAU, INC.; *U.S. Private*, pg. 686
MCS BUSINESS SOLUTIONS, INC.—See Canon Inc.; *Int'l*, pg. 262
MCS, INC.—See Mestek, Inc.; *U.S. Public*, pg. 1099
MCT DAIRIES, INC.—See Land O'Lakes, Inc.; *U.S. Private*, pg. 646
MD BETRIEBSWOHNUNGEN GMBH—See Metsa-Serla Corporation; *Int'l*, pg. 864
MD BIOMEDICAL ENGINEERING PTE. LTD.—See Hewlett-Packard Company; *U.S. Public*, pg. 822
S.A. MD DIFFUSION SUD EST—See Cockerill Sambre; *Int'l*, pg. 302
MD FOODS; *Int'l*, pg. 826
MD FOODS CALTSOYIAS HELLAS S.A.—See MD Foods; *Int'l*, pg. 826
MD FOODS CANADA INC.—See MD Foods; *Int'l*, pg. 826
MD FOODS DEUTSCHLAND GMBH—See MD Foods; *Int'l*, pg. 826
MD FOODS ESPANA—See MD Foods; *Int'l*, pg. 826
MD FOODS INGRIEDIENTS AMBA—See MD Foods; *Int'l*, pg. 826
MD FOODS ITALIA S.R.L.—See MD Foods; *Int'l*, pg. 826
MD FOODS NORGE A/S—See MD Foods; *Int'l*, pg. 826
MD FOODS SVERIGE AB—See MD Foods; *Int'l*, pg. 826
MD FOODS USA INC.—See MD Foods; *Int'l*, pg. 826
MD HOLMEN AUSTRALIA & NEW ZEALAND PTY. LTD.—See Mo och Domsjo AB; *Int'l*, pg. 886
MD INDUSTRIES, INC.—See Chris-Craft Industries, Inc.; *U.S. Public*, pg. 352
MD PAPER G.M.B.H.—See Mo och Domsjo AB; *Int'l*, pg. 886
MD PAPIER GMBH—See Metsa-Serla Corporation; *Int'l*, pg. 864
MD PAPIER GMBH - PLATTLING MILL—See Metsa-Serla Corporation; *Int'l*, pg. 864
MD PNEUMATICS—See Tuthill Corporation; *U.S. Private*, pg. 1111
M/D TOTCO INSTRUMENTATION—See Varco International, Inc.; *U.S. Public*, pg. 1709
MDA PACIFIC—See Hesta Tex AG; *Int'l*, pg. 618
MDA SCIENTIFIC, INC.—See Hesta Tex AG; *Int'l*, pg. 618
M.D.C. HOLDINGS, INC.; *U.S. Public*, pg. 1025
MDF LA BAIE INC.—See Uniboard Canada Inc.; *Int'l*, pg. 1432
MDI—See Motorola, Inc.; *U.S. Public*, pg. 1139
MDI CARIBE LIMITED—See Motorola, Inc.; *U.S. Public*, pg. 1139
MDI MANAGEMENT INC.—See Alex Lee, Inc.; *U.S. Private*, pg. 657
MDI PUERTO RICO, INC.—See Motorola, Inc.; *U.S. Public*, pg. 1137
MDI SCANDINAVIA A/S—See Motorola, Inc.; *U.S. Public*, pg. 1139
MDI SYSTEMS, INC.—See Motorola, Inc.; *U.S. Public*, pg. 1137
MDIS GROUP PLC; *Int'l*, pg. 826
MDK CONSULTANTS—See BDDP Group; *Int'l*, pg. 117
MDK CONSULTANTS (MALAYSIA)—See BDDP Group; *Int'l*, pg. 117

MDL INFORMATION SYSTEMS AG—See Reed Elsevier plc; *Int'l*, pg. 1100
MDL INFORMATION SYSTEMS-EASTERN SALES—See Reed Elsevier plc; *Int'l*, pg. 1100
MDL INFORMATION SYSTEMS, INC.—See Reed Elsevier plc; *Int'l*, pg. 1100
MDL INFORMATION SYSTEMS-MIDWEST SALES—See Reed Elsevier plc; *Int'l*, pg. 1100
MDL INFORMATION SYSTEMS (UK) LIMITED—See Reed Elsevier plc; *Int'l*, pg. 1100
MDL INFORMATION SYSTEMS-WESTERN SALES—See Reed Elsevier plc; *Int'l*, pg. 1100
MDPA—See Entreprise Miniere et Chimique; *Int'l*, pg. 459
MDR S.A.—See Kingfisher plc; *Int'l*, pg. 734
MDS COMMUNICARE—See MDS Inc.; *Int'l*, pg. 827
MDS HEALTH VENTURES CAPITAL CORP.—See MDS Inc.; *Int'l*, pg. 827
MDS INC.; *Int'l*, pg. 827
MDS MANNESMANN DEMAG SACK GMBH—See Mannesmann A.G.; *Int'l*, pg. 837
MDU RESOURCES GROUP, INC.; *U.S. Public*, pg. 1025
MEBIN B.V.—See Heidelberger Zement A.G.; *Int'l*, pg. 605
MEC INTERNATIONAL PTE. LTD.—See Molex Incorporated; *U.S. Public*, pg. 1122
MEC UK LIMITED—See Mitsubishi Estate Co., Ltd.; *Int'l*, pg. 873
MEC USA, INC.—See Mitsubishi Estate Co., Ltd.; *Int'l*, pg. 873
MECAR S.A.—See Allied Research Corporation; *U.S. Public*, pg. 49
MEG; *U.S. Private*, pg. 686
MEM LTD. 500V—See Delta plc; *Int'l*, pg. 390
MEM LTD. 250 V—See Delta plc; *Int'l*, pg. 390
MEMC ELECTRONIC MATERIALS, INC.—See Veba AG; *Int'l*, pg. 1455
MEMC ELECTRONIC MATERIALS, S.P.A.—See Veba AG; *Int'l*, pg. 1456
MEPC AMERICAN PROPERTIES; *U.S. Private*, pg. 686
MET—See Lagardere Groupe; *Int'l*, pg. 792
MET COMMUTATION—See Lagardere Groupe; *Int'l*, pg. 792
MET S.A.—See Telefonaktiebolaget LM Ericsson; *Int'l*, pg. 1369
MEZ POWER INDUSTRIES PTE. LTD.—See Axel Johnson AB; *Int'l*, pg. 712
M.F. BANK RESTORATION CO.—See M.F. Bank & Company, Inc.; *U.S. Private*, pg. 114
MFA INCORPORATED; *U.S. Private*, pg. 686
MFA MISR FREIGHT AGENCIES S.A.R.L.—See Danzas Holding Ltd.; *Int'l*, pg. 383
MFA OIL COMPANY; *U.S. Private*, pg. 687
MFG TRAY CO.—See Molded Fiber Glass Companies; *U.S. Private*, pg. 756
MFG UNION CITY OPERATIONS—See Molded Fiber Glass Companies; *U.S. Private*, pg. 756
MFI FURNITURE CENTER PLC; *Int'l*, pg. 827
MFRI INC.; *U.S. Public*, pg. 1026
MFS INTELENET COMPANIES—See WorldCom, Inc.; *U.S. Public*, pg. 1779
MFS INTERNATIONAL, INC.—See WorldCom, Inc.; *U.S. Public*, pg. 1779
MFS NETWORK TECHNOLOGIES, INC.—See WorldCom, Inc.; *U.S. Public*, pg. 1779
MFS SERVICE CENTER INC.—See Sun Life Assurance Company of Canada; *Int'l*, pg. 1319
MFS TELECOM COMPANIES—See WorldCom, Inc.; *U.S. Public*, pg. 1779
MFS WORLDCOM, INC.—See WorldCom, Inc.; *U.S. Public*, pg. 1779
MG ELECTRIC POWER, INC.—See Metallgesellschaft AG; *Int'l*, pg. 862
MG LOAN COMPANY—See Leggett & Platt, Incorporated; *U.S. Public*, pg. 986
MG NATURAL GAS CORPORATION—See Metallgesellschaft AG; *Int'l*, pg. 862
MG PRODUCTS; *U.S. Public*, pg. 1026
MG REFINING & MARKETING, INC.—See Metallgesellschaft AG; *Int'l*, pg. 862
M.G. (SCANDANAVIA) AB—See Mentor Graphics Corporation; *U.S. Public*, pg. 1087
MGB MEDIZINISCHE GERATE GMBH BERLIN—See Carl-Zeiss-Stiftung; *Int'l*, pg. 1523
MGH MEDICAL, INC.—See Columbia/HCA Healthcare Corporation; *U.S. Public*, pg. 405
MGI PHARMA INC.; *U.S. Public*, pg. 1026
MGI PUMPS, INC.—See Tetra Laval Group; *Int'l*, pg. 1378
MGIC INVESTMENT CORPORATION; *U.S. Public*, pg. 1026
MGM BRAKES DIV.—See Indian Head Industries Inc.; *U.S. Private*, pg. 560
MGM ENTERTAINMENT COMPANY—See Time Warner Inc.; *U.S. Public*, pg. 1614
MGM GRAND AUSTRALIA PTY, LTD.—See MGM Grand, Inc.; *U.S. Public*, pg. 1027
MGM GRAND DEVELOPMENT, INC.—See MGM Grand, Inc.; *U.S. Public*, pg. 1027
MGM GRAND HOTEL, INC.—See MGM Grand, Inc.; *U.S. Public*, pg. 1027
MGM GRAND, INC.; *U.S. Public*, pg. 1026
MGM GRAND MERCHANDISING, INC.—See MGM Grand, Inc.; *U.S. Public*, pg. 1027
MGM/UA DISTRIBUTION CO.—See Metro-Goldwyn-Mayer Inc.; *U.S. Public*, pg. 1102
MGM/UA HOME ENTERTAINMENT, INC.—See Metro-Goldwyn-Mayer Inc.; *U.S. Public*, pg. 1102
MGM/UA LICENSING & MERCHANDISING—See Metro-Goldwyn-Mayer Inc.; *U.S. Public*, pg. 1102
MGM/UA MUSIC—See Metro-Goldwyn-Mayer Inc.; *U.S. Public*, pg. 1102
MGM/UA TELECOMMUNICATIONS GROUP—See Metro-Goldwyn-Mayer Inc.; *U.S. Public*, pg. 1102
MGR EQUIPMENT CORP.; *U.S. Private*, pg. 687
MGR PERFORMANCE MEDIA—See True North Communications Inc.; *U.S. Public*, pg. 1641

MGR SPORTS—See True North Communications Inc.; *U.S. Public*, pg. 1641
MGS ENERGY SERVICES, INC.—See Mobile Gas Service Corp.; *U.S. Public*, pg. 1120
MGS STORAGE SERVICES, INC.—See Mobile Gas Service Corp.; *U.S. Public*, pg. 1120
MGTC, INC.—See Western Gas Resources, Inc.; *U.S. Public*, pg. 1758
MH LEASING INTERNATIONAL—See The Chase Manhattan Corporation; *U.S. Public*, pg. 338
MHD BERZELIUS DUISBURG GMBH—See Metallgesellschaft AG; *Int'l*, pg. 862
MHE DEMAG PTE. LTD.—See Mannesmann A.G.; *Int'l*, pg. 838
MHI EQUIPMENT EUROPE B.V. (MEE)—See Mitsubishi Heavy Industries Ltd.; *Int'l*, pg. 874
MHI MACHINE TOOL U.S.A INC.—See Mitsubishi Heavy Industries Ltd.; *Int'l*, pg. 874
MHI-MAHAJAK AIR CONDITIONERS CO., LTD. (MACO)—See Mitsubishi Heavy Industries Ltd.; *Int'l*, pg. 874
MHI PARTNERS WERBEAGENTUR GMBH—See Saatchi & Saatchi Advertising Worldwide; *U.S. Public*, pg. 1422
MHI SOUTH EAST ASIA PTE LTD (MHIS)—See Mitsubishi Heavy Industries Ltd.; *Int'l*, pg. 874
MHI TECHNICAL SERVICES CORPORATION (MTS)—See Mitsubishi Heavy Industries Ltd.; *Int'l*, pg. 874
MHIA MACHINE TOOL DIVISION—See Mitsubishi Heavy Industries Ltd.; *Int'l*, pg. 874
MHM SERVICES INC.; *U.S. Public*, pg. 1027
MHT DIVISION—See Israel Aircraft Industries Ltd.; *Int'l*, pg. 690
MIC TECHNOLOGY CORPORATION—See Aeroflex Incorporated; *U.S. Public*, pg. 24
MIC-USA INC.—See Millicom International Cellular SA; *Int'l*, pg. 867
MID-FAG SA—See N.V. Koninklijke KNP BT; *Int'l*, pg. 757
MIE, INC.—See TRC Companies, Inc.; *U.S. Public*, pg. 1558
MIGC, INC.—See Western Gas Resources, Inc.; *U.S. Public*, pg. 1758
MIL (FAR EAST) LIMITED—See The Bank of Bermuda Limited; *Int'l*, pg. 151
MIL (UK) LIMITED—See The Bank of Bermuda Limited; *Int'l*, pg. 151
M.I.M. HOLDINGS LTD.; *Int'l*, pg. 827
MIM INDUSTRIES, INC.—See Brother Industries, Ltd.; *Int'l*, pg. 229
MIMLIC CORP.—See The Minnesota Mutual Life Insurance Company; *U.S. Private*, pg. 750
MIPA MULLER VERWALTUNGS GMBH—See Commerzbank AG; *Int'l*, pg. 310
MIPS TECHNOLOGIES, INC.—See Silicon Graphics, Inc.; *U.S. Public*, pg. 1473
MIS—See Geotek Communications; *U.S. Public*, pg. 740
MISR-AMERICA INTERNATIONAL BANK S.A.E.—See BankAmerica Corporation; *U.S. Public*, pg. 183
MISR DYWIDAG—See Dyckerhoff & Widmann AG; *Int'l*, pg. 425
MISR PIONEER SEED CO. S.A.E.—See Pioneer Hi-Bred International, Inc.; *U.S. Public*, pg. 1299
MJB RICE COMPANY—See Nestle S.A.; *Int'l*, pg. 917
MJN—See Staveley Industries PLC; *Int'l*, pg. 1299
MK CENTENNIAL—See Morrison Knudsen Corporation; *U.S. Public*, pg. 1134
MK GROUP—See Computer Associates International, Inc.; *U.S. Public*, pg. 420
MK-MAINOS OY—See Kesko Ltd.; *Int'l*, pg. 732
MKRD-LASER SERVICE—See M K Diamond Products, Inc.; *U.S. Private*, pg. 685
MKTS—See Sandvik AB; *Int'l*, pg. 1186
M.L.&S. WERBEAGENTUR GMBH; *Int'l*, pg. 827
ML CAMPBELL & FABULON—See The Sherwin-Williams Company; *U.S. Public*, pg. 1466
MLC LIMITED—See Lend Lease Corporation Limited; *Int'l*, pg. 806
MLIG, INC.—See AEGON N.V.; *Int'l*, pg. 27
MLM DIVISION/ELECTRONICS GROUP—See Israel Aircraft Industries Ltd.; *Int'l*, pg. 690
MLM FLORIDA YELLOW PAGES COMPANY, INC.—See Multi-Local Media Corporation; *U.S. Private*, pg. 767
MLP CANADA LIMITED—See Mitsubishi Heavy Industries Ltd.; *Int'l*, pg. 874
MLP FRANCE S.A.—See Mitsubishi Heavy Industries Ltd.; *Int'l*, pg. 874
MLP HONG KONG LTD. (MLPHK)—See Mitsubishi Heavy Industries Ltd.; *Int'l*, pg. 874
MLP UK LTD.—See Mitsubishi Heavy Industries Ltd.; *Int'l*, pg. 874
MLT VACATIONS, INC.—See Northwest Airlines Corp.; *U.S. Public*, pg. 1200
MLV MUNCHENER LEBEN VERMOGENSANLAGEUND VERMITTLUNGS G.M.B.H.—See Assicurazioni Generali S.p.A.; *Int'l*, pg. 89
MM INDUSTRA, INC.—See American Eco Corporation; *Int'l*, pg. 74
MMC CORP.; *U.S. Private*, pg. 687
MMC DANMARK A.S.—See Mitsubishi Motors Corporation; *Int'l*, pg. 876
MMC ELECTRONICS AMERICA INC.—See Mitsubishi Materials Corp.; *Int'l*, pg. 875
MMC-GTM BINA SAMA—See Lyonnaise des Eaux S.A.; *Int'l*, pg. 823
MMC NETWORKS, INC.; *U.S. Public*, pg. 1027
MMC SITTIPOL COMPANY—See Mitsubishi Motors Corporation; *Int'l*, pg. 876
MMG DIVISION—See Optical Coating Laboratory, Inc.; *U.S. Public*, pg. 1227
MMG NORTH AMERICA—See TT Group PLC; *Int'l*, pg. 1344
M.M.H. SA—See Accor S.A.; *Int'l*, pg. 22
M.M.H. SA—See GIB Group; *Int'l*, pg. 533
MMI COMPANIES, INC.; *U.S. Public*, pg. 1027
MMI GENERAL INSURANCE (N.Z.) LTD—See Allianz Aktiengesellschaft; *Int'l*, pg. 60

MMI INSURANCE GROUP—See Allianz Aktiengesellschaft; *Int'l*, pg. 60
MMI PRODUCTS, INC.; *U.S. Private*, pg. 687
MML INVESTORS SERVICES, INC.—See Massachusetts Mutual Life Insurance Co.; *U.S. Public*, pg. 712
MMLJ, INC.; *U.S. Private*, pg. 687
MMRA METALLURGIQUE ET MINIERE DE RODANGE-ATHUS S.A.—See Arbed S.A.; *Int'l*, pg. 80
MMRI INC.—See American Shared Hospital Services; *U.S. Public*, pg. 91
MNC FINANCIAL, INC.—See First Tennessee National Corporation; *U.S. Public*, pg. 639
MNC MORTGAGE CORPORATION—See First Tennessee National Corporation; *U.S. Public*, pg. 639
MND ENERGY CORPORATION—See Mitchell Energy & Development Corp.; *U.S. Public*, pg. 1117
MNP CORP.; *U.S. Private*, pg. 687
MNX CARRIERS, INC.—See Mark VII, Inc.; *U.S. Public*, pg. 1046
MNX TRANSPORT, INC.—See Mark VII, Inc.; *U.S. Public*, pg. 1046
MNX TRUCKING, INC.—See Mark VII, Inc.; *U.S. Public*, pg. 1046
MO AMORIQUE—See Saint-Gobain; *Int'l*, pg. 1172
MO ATLANTIQUE—See Saint-Gobain; *Int'l*, pg. 1172
MO CHARENTES-LIMOUSIN—See Saint-Gobain; *Int'l*, pg. 1172
MO NORMANDIE—See Saint-Gobain; *Int'l*, pg. 1172
MO PAYS-DE-LOIRE—See Saint-Gobain; *Int'l*, pg. 1172
MO SEMIVER-CLIMAVER—See Saint-Gobain; *Int'l*, pg. 1172
MOC BV—See KPN Koninklyke PTT Nederland NV; *Int'l*, pg. 720
MOS DIGITAL-ANALOG INTEGRATED CIRCUITS DIVISION—See Motorola, Inc.; *U.S. Public*, pg. 1137
M.O.V. OF LOUISIANA, INC.—See Bovaird Supply Co.; *U.S. Private*, pg. 162
M.P. 55—See Lagardere Groupe; *Int'l*, pg. 792
M.P. 98—See Lagardere Groupe; *Int'l*, pg. 792
MP PUMPS, INC.—See Tecumseh Products Company; *U.S. Public*, pg. 1566
MP 65—See Lagardere Groupe; *Int'l*, pg. 792
M.P. 13—See Lagardere Groupe; *Int'l*, pg. 792
MPB CORPORATION—See The Timken Company; *U.S. Public*, pg. 1617
MPB FOLIEN GESELLSCHAFT MBH—See Schmalbach-Lubeca AG; *Int'l*, pg. 1206
MPC CUMBERNAULD—See McKechnie PLC; *Int'l*, pg. 851
MPC EASLEY—See McKechnie PLC; *Int'l*, pg. 851
MPC MINNEAPOLIS—See McKechnie PLC; *Int'l*, pg. 851
MPC STAMFORD BRIDGE—See McKechnie PLC; *Int'l*, pg. 851
MPC STAPLES—See McKechnie PLC; *Int'l*, pg. 851
MPC WRAGBY—See McKechnie PLC; *Int'l*, pg. 851
MPD, INC.; *U.S. Private*, pg. 687
MPH & CMI—See MPD, Inc.; *U.S. Private*, pg. 687
MPH INDUSTRIES—See General Signal Corporation; *U.S. Public*, pg. 726
MPI INTERNATIONAL, INC.—See Klockner-Werke AG; *Int'l*, pg. 737
MPL POWERWARE SYSTEMS, LTD.—See BTR plc; *Int'l*, pg. 126
MPL PUMPS LTD—See Tetra Laval Group; *Int'l*, pg. 1380
MPM MEDIA—See G.T.C. Transcontinental Group Ltd.; *Int'l*, pg. 539
MPM MEDIA RIVE-SUD—See G.T.C. Transcontinental Group Ltd.; *Int'l*, pg. 539
MPS CORPORATION; *U.S. Public*, pg. 687
MPSI SYSTEMS INC.; *U.S. Public*, pg. 1027
MPSI SYSTEMS LTD.—See MPSI Systems Inc.; *U.S. Public*, pg. 1027
MPX SYSTEMS, INC.—See SCANA Corporation; *U.S. Public*, pg. 1436
MQF PTY. LTD.—See Nippon Meat Packers, Inc.; *Int'l*, pg. 936
MR SRL—See Sony Corporation; *Int'l*, pg. 1283
MRA, AN INTEGRATED MARKETING COMMUNICATIONS AGENCY; *U.S. Private*, pg. 687
MRB GROUP, INC.—See WPP Group plc; *Int'l*, pg. 1483
MRB-SCHUMAG (U.K.) LTD.—See Deutsche Babcock AG; *Int'l*, pg. 399
MRC BEARINGS—See AB SKF; *Int'l*, pg. 1157
MRCO—See ULLICO Inc.; *U.S. Private*, pg. 1116
MRI CORPORATION—See Schnitzer Steel Industries, Inc.; *U.S. Public*, pg. 1440
MRI LOS ANGELES—See Media Resources International; *U.S. Private*, pg. 727
MRI UK—See Media Resources International; *U.S. Private*, pg. 727
MRM PROPERTIES, INC.—See NationsBank Corporation; *U.S. Public*, pg. 1163
MRNI—See The Glen Dimplex Group; *Int'l*, pg. 554
MRP MIDWEST—See IBT, Inc.; *U.S. Private*, pg. 553
MRS. FIELDS' ORIGINAL COOKIES, INC.; *U.S. Private*, pg. 688
MRV COMMUNICATIONS, INC.; *U.S. Public*, pg. 1027
M/S. AMARAVATI INTERNATIONAL—See BASF AG; *Int'l*, pg. 109
M.S. CARRIERS, INC.; *U.S. Public*, pg. 1027
KG MS "EUROPA" DER BRESCHAG BREMER SCHIFFSVERCH. AG & CO. KG—See Hapag-Lloyd AG; *Int'l*, pg. 596
MSA (AFRICA) (PTY) LTD.—See Mine Safety Appliances Co.; *U.S. Public*, pg. 1114
MSA-AUER HUNGARIA—See Mine Safety Appliances Co.; *U.S. Public*, pg. 1114
MSA-AUER POLSKA—See Mine Safety Appliances Co.; *U.S. Public*, pg. 1114
MSA (AUSTRALIA) PTY. LTD.—See Mine Safety Appliances Co.; *U.S. Public*, pg. 1114
MSA BELGIUM NV—See Mine Safety Appliances Co.; *U.S. Public*, pg. 1114
MSA (BRITAIN) LIMITED—See Mine Safety Appliances Co.; *U.S. Public*, pg. 1114

MSA CANADA, INC.—See Mine Safety Appliances Co.; *U.S. Public*, pg. 1114

MSA DE CHILE LTDA.—See Mine Safety Appliances Co.; *U.S. Public*, pg. 1114

MSA DE FRANCE—See Mine Safety Appliances Co.; *U.S. Public*, pg. 1114

MSA DE MEXICO, S.A. DE C.V.—See Mine Safety Appliances Co.; *U.S. Public*, pg. 1114

MSA DEL PERU S.A.—See Mine Safety Appliances Co.; *U.S. Public*, pg. 1115

MSA DO BRASIL, LTDA.—See Mine Safety Appliances Co.; *U.S. Public*, pg. 1115

MSA ESPANOLA, S.A.—See Mine Safety Appliances Co.; *U.S. Public*, pg. 1115

MSA EUROPE—See Mine Safety Appliances Co.; *U.S. Public*, pg. 1115

MSA INDIA LIMITED—See Mine Safety Appliances Co.; *U.S. Public*, pg. 1115

MSA ITALIANA S.P.A.—See Mine Safety Appliances Co.; *U.S. Public*, pg. 1115

MSA JAPAN LTD.—See Mine Safety Appliances Co.; *U.S. Public*, pg. 1115

MSA MIDDLE EAST—See Mine Safety Appliances Co.; *U.S. Public*, pg. 1115

MSA NEDERLAND B.V.—See Mine Safety Appliances Co.; *U.S. Public*, pg. 1115

MSA S.E. ASIA PTE. LTD.—See Mine Safety Appliances Co.; *U.S. Public*, pg. 1115

MSA SWITZERLAND LTD.—See Mine Safety Appliances Co.; *U.S. Public*, pg. 1115

MSA ZIMBABWE (PVT.) LIMITED—See Mine Safety Appliances Co.; *U.S. Public*, pg. 1115

MSC ARIES—See The Macneal-Schwendler Corp.; *U.S. Public*, pg. 1031

MSC CORPORATION—See Analytical Surveys, Inc.; *U.S. Public*, pg. 110

MSC DEARBORN OFFICE—See The Macneal-Schwendler Corp.; *U.S. Public*, pg. 1031

MSC DENVER OFFICE—See The Macneal-Schwendler Corp.; *U.S. Public*, pg. 1031

MSC EASTERN ENGINEERING SERVICES OFFICE—See The Macneal-Schwendler Corp.; *U.S. Public*, pg. 1031

MSC EASTERN REGIONAL OFFICE—See The Macneal-Schwendler Corp.; *U.S. Public*, pg. 1031

MSC/EMAS DEVELOPMENT—See The Macneal-Schwendler Corp.; *U.S. Public*, pg. 1031

MSC ENGINEERING/ELECTROMAGNETICS APPLICATIONS DEPARTMENT—See The Macneal-Schwendler Corp.; *U.S. Public*, pg. 1031

MSC ILLINOIS OFFICE—See The Macneal-Schwendler Corp.; *U.S. Public*, pg. 1031

MSC INDIANA OFFICE—See The Macneal-Schwendler Corp.; *U.S. Public*, pg. 1031

MSC INDUSTRIAL SUPPLY CO.—See Sid Tool Co. Inc.; *U.S. Private*, pg. 998

MSC (ITALIA) S.R.L.—See The Macneal-Schwendler Corp.; *U.S. Public*, pg. 1032

MSC JAPAN LTD.—See The Macneal-Schwendler Corp.; *U.S. Public*, pg. 1032

M.S.C. LEBENSMITTEL GMBH—See CSM N.V.; *Int'l*, pg. 244

MSC LIVONIA OFFICE—See The Macneal-Schwendler Corp.; *U.S. Public*, pg. 1031

MSC LOWELL OFFICE—See The Macneal-Schwendler Corp.; *U.S. Public*, pg. 1031

MSC MENLO PARK OFFICE—See The Macneal-Schwendler Corp.; *U.S. Public*, pg. 1031

MSC MIDWEST REGIONAL OFFICE—See The Macneal-Schwendler Corp.; *U.S. Public*, pg. 1031

MSC MILWAUKEE OFFICE—See The Macneal-Schwendler Corp.; *U.S. Public*, pg. 1031

MSC NEW JERSEY TECHNICAL OFFICE—See The Macneal-Schwendler Corp.; *U.S. Public*, pg. 1031

MSC NORTHEAST OFFICE—See The Macneal-Schwendler Corp.; *U.S. Public*, pg. 1031

MSC ORANGE COUNTY OFFICE—See The Macneal-Schwendler Corp.; *U.S. Public*, pg. 1031

MSC PTE. LTD.—See Shimano Inc.; *Int'l*, pg. 1232

MSC ROCHESTER OFFICE—See The Macneal-Schwendler Corp.; *U.S. Public*, pg. 1031

MSC SEATTLE TECHNICAL OFFICE—See The Macneal-Schwendler Corp.; *U.S. Public*, pg. 1031

MSC SOUTHEAST OFFICE—See The Macneal-Schwendler Corp.; *U.S. Public*, pg. 1031

MSC SOUTHERN REGIONAL OFFICE—See The Macneal-Schwendler Corp.; *U.S. Public*, pg. 1031

MSC SOUTHWEST REGIONAL OFFICE—See The Macneal-Schwendler Corp.; *U.S. Public*, pg. 1031

MSC TRADENAMES—See Musicland Group Inc.; *U.S. Public*, pg. 1142

MSC WASHINGTON, D.C. OFFICE—See The Macneal-Schwendler Corp.; *U.S. Public*, pg. 1031

MSC WESTERN REGIONAL OFFICE—See The Macneal-Schwendler Corp.; *U.S. Public*, pg. 1031

MSD AGVET (EC OFFICE)—See Merck & Co., Inc.; *U.S. Public*, pg. 1092

MSD AGVET-LISBON—See Merck & Co., Inc.; *U.S. Public*, pg. 1092

MSD (JAPAN) CO. LTD.—See Merck & Co., Inc.; *U.S. Public*, pg. 1092

MSD (NORGE) A/S—See Merck & Co., Inc.; *U.S. Public*, pg. 1092

MSD SHARP & DOHME GMBH—See Merck & Co., Inc.; *U.S. Public*, pg. 1092

M.S.G. ELSOFFARY & SONS—See BASF AG; *Int'l*, pg. 109

MSG SA DIVISIE PLANTIN—See N.V. Koninklijke KNP BT; *Int'l*, pg. 757

MSI AUSTRALIA PTY. LTD.—See Symbol Technologies, Inc.; *U.S. Public*, pg. 1546

MSI DATA AUSTRIA—See Symbol Technologies, Inc.; *U.S. Public*, pg. 1546

MSI DATA GMBH—See Symbol Technologies, Inc.; *U.S. Public*, pg. 1546

MSI DATA INTERNATIONAL, EUROPEAN HDQTRS.—See Symbol Technologies, Inc.; *U.S. Public*, pg. 1546

MSI DATA ITALIA S.R.L.—See Symbol Technologies, Inc.; *U.S. Public*, pg. 1546

MSI DATA LIMITED, UNITED KINGDOM—See Symbol Technologies, Inc.; *U.S. Public*, pg. 1546

MSI ENGINEERING SOFTWARE LTD.—See The Macneal-Schwendler Corp.; *U.S. Public*, pg. 1032

MSI FRANCE S.A.R.L.—See Symbol Technologies, Inc.; *U.S. Public*, pg. 1546

MSI INSURANCE COMPANIES; *U.S. Private*, pg. 688

MSI SWITZERLAND—See Symbol Technologies, Inc.; *U.S. Public*, pg. 1546

MSP STEEL WORKS LTD.—See Nissho Iwai Corporation; *Int'l*, pg. 948

MSR—See Recreational Equipment, Inc.; *U.S. Private*, pg. 914

MSW-CHEMIE GMBH—See BASF AG; *Int'l*, pg. 104

MTA LONG ISLAND RAIL ROAD—See Metropolitan Transportation Authority; *U.S. Private*, pg. 739

MTBC BANK DEUTSCHLAND GMBH—See The Mitsubishi Trust and Banking Corporation; *Int'l*, pg. 877

MTBC, FINANCE—See The Mitsubishi Trust and Banking Corporation; *Int'l*, pg. 876

MTBC FINANCE (ARUBA) A.E.C.—See The Mitsubishi Trust and Banking Corporation; *Int'l*, pg. 877

MTBC IRELAND—See The Mitsubishi Trust and Banking Corporation; *Int'l*, pg. 877

MTBE MALAYSIA SDN. BHD—See Neste Oy; *Int'l*, pg. 914

M.T.C. INTERIORS B.V.—See Gamma Holding N.V.; *Int'l*, pg. 540

MTD PRODUCTS, INC.; *U.S. Private*, pg. 688

MTD PRODUCTS LIMITED—See MTD Products, Inc.; *U.S. Private*, pg. 688

MTE—See Jeumont-Schneider Trenformeteurs; *Int'l*, pg. 706

MTE-TURCK LTD.—See B. Elliott plc.; *Int'l*, pg. 449

MTEL INTERNATIONAL—See Mobile Telecommunications Technologies Corp.; *U.S. Public*, pg. 1120

MTEL INTERNATIONAL (TOKYO)—See Mobile Telecommunications Technologies Corp.; *U.S. Public*, pg. 1120

MTEL SPACE TECHNOLOGIES CORP.—See Mobile Telecommunications Technologies Corp.; *U.S. Public*, pg. 1120

M.T.F.—See LVMH Moet Hennessy Louis Vuitton; *Int'l*, pg. 781

MTI GMBH—See MTI Technology Corporation; *U.S. Public*, pg. 1028

MTI/THE IMAGE GROUP, INC.; *U.S. Private*, pg. 688

MTI IRELAND—See MTI Technology Corporation; *U.S. Public*, pg. 1028

MTI LEASING, LTD.—See Marine Travelift, Inc.; *U.S. Private*, pg. 703

MTI SYSTEMS CORP.—See Arrow Electronics, Inc.; *U.S. Public*, pg. 134

MTI SYSTEMS DIV.—See Arrow Electronics, Inc.; *U.S. Public*, pg. 135

MTI TECHNOLOGY CORPORATION; *U.S. Public*, pg. 1028

MTI VACATIONS, INC.; *U.S. Private*, pg. 688

MTL INC.; *U.S. Public*, pg. 1028

MTM ENTERPRISES, INC.—See The News Corporation Limited; *Int'l*, pg. 927

MTN MEDIZINTECHNIK NEUBRANDENBURG GMBH I.G.—See Incentive AB; *Int'l*, pg. 669

MTN - MINERALOEL-UND TANKLAGER GMBH—See Fuchs Petrolub AG Oel + Chemie; *Int'l*, pg. 517

MTPB - EAST COAST REGION—See Malaysia Tourism Promotion Board (MTPB); *Int'l*, pg. 833

MTPB - NORTHERN REGION—See Malaysia Tourism Promotion Board (MTPB); *Int'l*, pg. 833

MTPB - SABAH REGION—See Malaysia Tourism Promotion Board (MTPB); *Int'l*, pg. 833

MTPB - SARAWAK REGION—See Malaysia Tourism Promotion Board (MTPB); *Int'l*, pg. 833

MTPB - SOUTHERN REGION—See Malaysia Tourism Promotion Board (MTPB); *Int'l*, pg. 833

MTS, INC.; *U.S. Private*, pg. 688

MTS JAPAN LTD. (TOKYO)—See MTS Systems Corporation; *U.S. Public*, pg. 1029

MTS SYSTEMS CHINA LTD.—See MTS Systems Corporation; *U.S. Public*, pg. 1029

MTS SYSTEMS CORPORATION; *U.S. Public*, pg. 1028

MTS SYSTEMS GMBH—See MTS Systems Corporation; *U.S. Public*, pg. 1029

MTS SYSTEMS LTD. (UK)—See MTS Systems Corporation; *U.S. Public*, pg. 1029

MTS SYSTEMS NORDEN AB—See MTS Systems Corporation; *U.S. Public*, pg. 1029

MTT LTD.—See Tokuyama Corporation; *Int'l*, pg. 1393

MTTC, INC.—See Comarco, Inc.; *U.S. Public*, pg. 406

MTU MAINTENANCE GMBH—See Daimler-Benz Aktiengesellschaft; *Int'l*, pg. 367

MTU MOTOREN-UND TURBINEN-UNION FRIEDRICHSHAFEN GMBH—See Daimler-Benz Aktiengesellschaft; *Int'l*, pg. 367

MTU MOTOREN-UND TURBINEN-UNION LUDWIGSFELDE GMBH—See Daimler-Benz Aktiengesellschaft; *Int'l*, pg. 367

MTU MOTOREN-UND TURBINEN-UNION MUNCHEN GMBH—See Daimler-Benz Aktiengesellschaft; *Int'l*, pg. 367

MTU TURBOMECA ROLLS-ROYCE GMBH—See Daimler-Benz Aktiengesellschaft; *Int'l*, pg. 367

MTV ASIA—See National Amusements, Inc.; *U.S. Private*, pg. 779

MTV AUSTRALIA—See National Amusements, Inc.; *U.S. Private*, pg. 779

MTV BRASIL—See National Amusements, Inc.; *U.S. Private*, pg. 779

MTV EUROPE—See National Amusements, Inc.; *U.S. Private*, pg. 779

MTV FINLAND; *Int'l*, pg. 827

MTV JAPAN—See National Amusements, Inc.; *U.S. Private*, pg. 779

MTV: MUSIC TELEVISION—See National Amusements, Inc.; *U.S. Private*, pg. 779

MTV NETWORKS—See National Amusements, Inc.; *U.S. Private*, pg. 779

MTV-PALVELUKIINTEISTOT—See MTV Finland; *Int'l*, pg. 828

MVC MILTON KEYNES—See McKechnie PLC; *Int'l*, pg. 851

MVC PICKERING—See McKechnie PLC; *Int'l*, pg. 851

MVT MAGAZIN VERLAG GMBH & CO. KG—See Burda Holding GmbH & Co., KG; *Int'l*, pg. 233

MW MANUFACTURERS INC.—See Hanson PLC; *Int'l*, pg. 593

MW PETROLEUM CORP.—See Apache Corporation; *U.S. Public*, pg. 119

MWCA—See Hecla Mining Company; *U.S. Public*, pg. 804

MWJR. PETROLEUM CORP.—See Apache Corporation; *U.S. Public*, pg. 119

MWR TELECOM INC.—See McLeodUSA Incorporated; *U.S. Public*, pg. 1073

MWS—See Cooper Industries, Inc.; *U.S. Public*, pg. 443

MXL INDUSTRIES, INC.—See GP Strategies Corporation; *U.S. Public*, pg. 694

MYR GROUP INC.; *U.S. Public*, pg. 1029

MYU PLANNING AND OPERATIONS INC.—See Suntory Ltd.; *Int'l*, pg. 1321

MA'ARIV MODIIN PUBLISHING HOUSE LTD.—See The Israel Land Development Co., Ltd.; *Int'l*, pg. 691

MA'BEROT HAYARDEN LIMITED—See The Israel Electric Corporation Ltd.; *Int'l*, pg. 691

MAACO ENTERPRISES INC.; *U.S. Private*, pg. 689

MAADHYAM ADVERTISING PVT. LTD—See DMB&B Communications; *U.S. Private*, pg. 304

MAAG AGROCHEMICALS INC—See Novartis AG; *Int'l*, pg. 973

DR. R. MAAG AG—See Novartis AG; *Int'l*, pg. 972

MAAGH LEITUNGSBAU GMBH—See Bilfinger + Berger Bauaktiengesellschaft; *Int'l*, pg. 195

MAATSCHAPPIJ TOT FINANCIERING VAN BEDRIJFSPANDEN N.V.—See ABN-AMRO Holding N.V.; *Int'l*, pg. 9

MAATSCHAPPIJ TOT VERWAARDING VAN "DUCAAT" VERWARMINGS EN KOOKAPPARATEN—See Schmalbach-Lubeca AG; *Int'l*, pg. 1207

MAATSCHAPPIJ VAN BERKEL'S PATENT NV—See The General Electric Company, p.l.c.; *Int'l*, pg. 546

MABAMEX S.A.—See Mattel, Inc.; *U.S. Public*, pg. 1059

MABE—See GiB Group; *Int'l*, pg. 533

MABON B.V.—See Hollandsche Beton Groep NV; *Int'l*, pg. 630

MABUHAY PHILIPPINES SATELLITE CORP.—See Philippine Long Distance Telephone Company; *Int'l*, pg. 1051

MAC COSMETICS—See Estee Lauder Companies Inc.; *U.S. Public*, pg. 594

MAC FRUGAL'S BARGAINS CLOSE-OUTS INC.—See Consolidated Stores Corp.; *U.S. Public*, pg. 437

MAC-GRAY CORPORATION; *U.S. Public*, pg. 1029

MAC-IN/MACWORLD PORTUGAL—See International Data Group; *U.S. Private*, pg. 570

MAC PAPERS, INC.; *U.S. Private*, pg. 689

MACALLAN GLENLIVET—See The Highland Distilleries Company plc; *Int'l*, pg. 619

MACANDREWS & FORBES GROUP, INC.—See MacAndrews & Forbes Holdings Inc.; *U.S. Private*, pg. 689

MACANDREWS & FORBES HOLDINGS INC.; *U.S. Private*, pg. 689

MACBETH DIV.—See Kollmorgen Corporation; *U.S. Public*, pg. 965

MACCHINE E ACCESSORI PER L'INDUSTRIA GRAFICA MACCHINGRAF SPA—See N.V. Koninklijke KNP BT; *Int'l*, pg. 757

MACDERMID ASIA, LTD.—See MacDermid Incorporated; *U.S. Public*, pg. 1030

MACDERMID AUSTRALIA BRANCH—See MacDermid Incorporated; *U.S. Public*, pg. 1030

MACDERMID BENELUX B.V.—See MacDermid Incorporated; *U.S. Public*, pg. 1030

MACDERMID CHEMICALS INC.—See MacDermid Incorporated; *U.S. Public*, pg. 1030

MACDERMID ESPANOLA S.A.—See MacDermid Incorporated; *U.S. Public*, pg. 1030

MACDERMID FRANCE S.A.—See MacDermid Incorporated; *U.S. Public*, pg. 1030

MACDERMID G.B., LTD.—See MacDermid Incorporated; *U.S. Public*, pg. 1030

MACDERMID GMBH—See MacDermid Incorporated; *U.S. Public*, pg. 1030

MACDERMID INCORPORATED; *U.S. Public*, pg. 1029

MACDERMID ISRAEL LTD.—See MacDermid Incorporated; *U.S. Public*, pg. 1030

MACDERMID ITALIANA SRL—See MacDermid Incorporated; *U.S. Public*, pg. 1030

MACDERMID KOREA LTD.—See MacDermid Incorporated; *U.S. Public*, pg. 1030

MACDERMID NEW ZEALAND, LTD.—See MacDermid Incorporated; *U.S. Public*, pg. 1030

MACDERMID S.A. (PTY) LTD.—See MacDermid Incorporated; *U.S. Public*, pg. 1030

MACDERMID SINGAPORE PTE. LTD.—See MacDermid Incorporated; *U.S. Public*, pg. 1030

MACDERMID SUISSE S.A.—See MacDermid Incorporated; *U.S. Public*, pg. 1030

MACDERMID SYSTEMS, INC.—See MacDermid Incorporated; *U.S. Public*, pg. 1030

MACDERMID TAIWAN LTD.—See MacDermid Incorporated; *U.S. Public*, pg. 1030

MACDONALD & CO. (PUBLISHERS) LTD.—See Time Warner Inc.; *U.S. Public*, pg. 1615

MACDONALD COMMUNICATIONS; *U.S. Private*, pg. 691

MACDONALD DETTWILER & ASSOCIATES LTD.—See Orbital Sciences Corporation; *U.S. Public*, pg. 1229
E.F. MACDONALD MOTIVATION DIV.—See Carlson Companies, Inc.; *U.S. Private*, pg. 212
THE E.F. MACDONALD VERKAUFSFORDERUNG GMBH—See Carlson Companies, Inc.; *U.S. Private*, pg. 212
J.P. MACDOUGALL & CO. LIMITED—See Imperial Chemical Industries PLC; *Int'l*, pg. 663
MACDUFF UNDERWRITERS—See Poe & Brown, Inc.; *U.S. Public*, pg. 1312
MACE PRODUCTS—See Osmonics, Inc.; *U.S. Public*, pg. 1234
MACE SECURITY INTERNATIONAL, INC.; *U.S. Public*, pg. 1030
MACEDONIAN AIRLINES—See Olympic Airways, S.A.; *Int'l*, pg. 1004
THE MACERICH COMPANY; *U.S. Public*, pg. 1030
MACFARMS OF HAWAII, INC.—See Campbell Soup Company; *U.S. Public*, pg. 299
MACFISH LIMITED—See The Albert Fisher Group PLC; *Int'l*, pg. 491
MACGREGOR (AUS) PTY. LTD.—See Incentive AB; *Int'l*, pg. 670
MACGREGOR (BEL) LTD.—See Incentive AB; *Int'l*, pg. 670
MACGREGOR (BRA) LTDA—See Incentive AB; *Int'l*, pg. 670
MACGREGOR (CHN) LTD.—See Incentive AB; *Int'l*, pg. 670
MACGREGOR CONVER GMBH—See Incentive AB; *Int'l*, pg. 670
MACGREGOR CRANES AB—See Incentive AB; *Int'l*, pg. 670
MACGREGOR (DEU) GMBH—See Incentive AB; *Int'l*, pg. 670
MACGREGOR (DNK) A/S—See Incentive AB; *Int'l*, pg. 670
MACGREGOR (ESP) S.A.—See Incentive AB; *Int'l*, pg. 670
MACGREGOR (FRA) S.A.—See Incentive AB; *Int'l*, pg. 670
MACGREGOR (GBR) LTD.—See Incentive AB; *Int'l*, pg. 670
MACGREGOR GOLF AUSTRALIA PTY. LTD.—See Amer Group Ltd.; *Int'l*, pg. 73
MACGREGOR GOLF COMPANY—See Amer Group Ltd.; *Int'l*, pg. 72
MACGREGOR GOLF FRANCE S.A.—See Amer Group Ltd.; *Int'l*, pg. 73
MACGREGOR GOLF GMBH—See Amer Group Ltd.; *Int'l*, pg. 73
MACGREGOR GOLF HONG KONG LTD.—See Amer Group Ltd.; *Int'l*, pg. 73
MACGREGOR GOLF IRELAND, LTD.—See Amer Group Ltd.; *Int'l*, pg. 73
MACGREGOR GOLF (JAPAN) LTD.—See Amer Group Ltd.; *Int'l*, pg. 73
MACGREGOR GOLF (TAIWAN) LTD.—See Amer Group Ltd.; *Int'l*, pg. 73
MACGREGOR GOLF UK, LTD.—See Amer Group Ltd.; *Int'l*, pg. 73
MACGREGOR (GRC) E.P.E.—See Incentive AB; *Int'l*, pg. 670
MACGREGOR GROUP—See Incentive AB; *Int'l*, pg. 670
MACGREGOR HAGGLUNDS—See Incentive AB; *Int'l*, pg. 671
MACGREGOR (HKG), LTD.—See Incentive AB; *Int'l*, pg. 671
MACGREGOR (HRV) D O O—See Incentive AB; *Int'l*, pg. 671
MACGREGOR (ITA) S.P.A.—See Incentive AB; *Int'l*, pg. 671
MACGREGOR KAYABA LTD.—See Incentive AB; *Int'l*, pg. 671
MACGREGOR (KOR) LTD.—See Incentive AB; *Int'l*, pg. 671
MACGREGOR (NLD) B.V.—See Incentive AB; *Int'l*, pg. 671
MACGREGOR (NOR) A/S—See Incentive AB; *Int'l*, pg. 671
MACGREGOR PARK, INC.—See DPL Inc.; *U.S. Public*, pg. 473
MACGREGOR (POL) SP. Z.O.O.—See Incentive AB; *Int'l*, pg. 671
MACGREGOR (PRT) LDA.—See Incentive AB; *Int'l*, pg. 671
MACGREGOR (RUS) A/O—See Incentive AB; *Int'l*, pg. 671
MACGREGOR (SGP) PTE. LTD.—See Incentive AB; *Int'l*, pg. 671
MACGREGOR (SWE) AB—See Incentive AB; *Int'l*, pg. 670
MACGREGOR (UKR) A/O—See Incentive AB; *Int'l*, pg. 671
MACGREGOR (USA) INC.—See Incentive AB; *Int'l*, pg. 670
MACH 2 LIBRI S.P.A.—See Arnoldo Mondadori Editore S.p.A.; *Int'l*, pg. 888
GUS MACHADO ENTERPRISES; *U.S. Private*, pg. 691
MACHIN & EWIN PTY. LTD.—See Delta plc; *Int'l*, pg. 392
MACHINE FABRICATORS—See Brunel Holdings Plc; *Int'l*, pg. 231
THE MACHINE TOOL GROUP—See DeVlieg-Bullard Inc.; *U.S. Public*, pg. 503
B.V. MACHINEFABRIEK BREDA—See Royal Begemann Group; *Int'l*, pg. 1133
B.V. MACHINEFABRIEK SPAANS—See FKI Plc; *Int'l*, pg. 472
MACHINEFABRIEK WERKLUST B.V.—See Royal Begemann Group; *Int'l*, pg. 1133
MACHINENFABRIEK ROBERINE B.V.—See Deere & Company; *U.S. Public*, pg. 493
MACHINERY ACCEPTANCE CORPORATION—See Stewart & Stevenson Services, Inc.; *U.S. Public*, pg. 1517
MACHINERY EAST—See NCC AB; *Int'l*, pg. 899
MACHINERY MANUFACTURING—See Sonoco Products Company; *U.S. Public*, pg. 1486
MACHINERY NORTH—See NCC AB; *Int'l*, pg. 899
MACHINERY SALES & SUPPLY CO.—See LSB Industries, Inc.; *U.S. Public*, pg. 971
MACHINERY SOUTH—See NCC AB; *Int'l*, pg. 899
MACHINERY STOCKHOLM—See NCC AB; *Int'l*, pg. 899

MACHINERY WEST—See NCC AB; *Int'l*, pg. 899
MACHINING AND ASSEMBLY SYSTEMS—See UNOVA, Inc.; *U.S. Public*, pg. 1699
MACHINING ENTERPRISES INC.; *U.S. Private*, pg. 691
M.E. MACK VALVES PTY. LIMITED—See Senior Engineering Group, plc.; *Int'l*, pg. 1222
MACK MOLDING COMPANY INC.; *U.S. Private*, pg. 691
MACK PRINTING COMPANY; *U.S. Private*, pg. 691
MACK PRINTING GROUP (EPHRATA DIV.)—See Mack Printing Company; *U.S. Private*, pg. 692
MACK REMANUFACTURING CENTER—See Renault; *Int'l*, pg. 1102
MACK TRUCKS, INC.—See Renault; *Int'l*, pg. 1102
MACK VALVES-NSW—See Senior Engineering Group, plc.; *Int'l*, pg. 1223
MACKAY, INC.—See Bemis Company, Inc.; *U.S. Public*, pg. 210
MACKAY RADIO SYSTEMS INC.—See Thomson S.A.; *Int'l*, pg. 1384
MACKAY-SHIELDS FINANCIAL CORP.—See New York Life Insurance Company; *U.S. Private*, pg. 795
MACKENZIE FINANCIAL CORPORATION; *Int'l*, pg. 828
MACKIE DESIGNS, INC.; *U.S. Public*, pg. 1030
MACKINNON MACKENZIE & CO. OF PAKISTAN (PRIVATE) LTD.—See The Peninsular and Oriental Steam Navigation Company; *Int'l*, pg. 1035
MACKINTOSH OF NEW ENGLAND, CO.—See Biscayne Apparel Inc.; *U.S. Public*, pg. 233
MACKLANBURG-DUNCAN CO.; *U.S. Private*, pg. 692
MACLEAN ESNA—See Maclean-Fogg Co.; *U.S. Private*, pg. 692
MACLEAN-FOGG CO.; *U.S. Private*, pg. 692
MACLEAN HUNTER GMBH—See Rogers Communications, Inc.; *Int'l*, pg. 1123
MACLEAN HUNTER PUBLISHING LTD.—See Rogers Communications, Inc.; *Int'l*, pg. 1123
MACLEAN POWER SYSTEMS—See Maclean-Fogg Co.; *U.S. Private*, pg. 692
MACLIN-ZIMMER MCGILL TOBACCO COMPANY, INC.—See Universal Corporation; *U.S. Public*, pg. 1695
THE MACMANUS GROUP, INC.; *U.S. Private*, pg. 692
MACMILLAN BATHURST INC.—See Abitibi-Consolidated Inc.; *Int'l*, pg. 20
MACMILLAN BATHURST INC.—See MacMillan Bloedel Limited; *Int'l*, pg. 828
MACMILLAN BLOEDEL INC.—See MacMillan Bloedel Limited; *Int'l*, pg. 828
MACMILLAN BLOEDEL LIMITED; *Int'l*, pg. 828
MACMILLAN COMPUTER PUBLISHING USA—See National Amusements, Inc.; *U.S. Private*, pg. 777
MACMILLAN DIGITAL USA—See National Amusements, Inc.; *U.S. Private*, pg. 777
MACMILLAN GENERAL REFERENCE USA—See National Amusements, Inc.; *U.S. Private*, pg. 777
MACMILLAN LIBRARY REFERENCE USA—See National Amusements, Inc.; *U.S. Private*, pg. 777
MACMILLAN LTD.—See Georg von Holtzbrinck GmbH; *Int'l*, pg. 1479
MACMILLAN/MCGRAW-HILL SCHOOL PUBLISHING COMPANY—See The McGraw-Hill Companies; *U.S. Public*, pg. 1070
MACMILLAN PUBLISHING USA—See National Amusements, Inc.; *U.S. Private*, pg. 777
MACMILLAN REFERENCE USA—See National Amusements, Inc.; *U.S. Private*, pg. 777
MACNAMARA, STEWART & SAPERSTEIN; *U.S. Private*, pg. 692
MACNAUGHTON EINSON GRAPHICS; *U.S. Private*, pg. 692
THE MACNEAL-SCHWENDLER CO. B.V.—See The Macneal-Schwendler Corp.; *U.S. Public*, pg. 1032
THE MACNEAL-SCHWENDLER CO. LTD.—See The Macneal-Schwendler Corp.; *U.S. Public*, pg. 1032
THE MACNEAL-SCHWENDLER COMPANY LTD.—See The Macneal-Schwendler Corp.; *U.S. Public*, pg. 1032
THE MACNEAL-SCHWENDLER COMPANY, LTD.—See The Macneal-Schwendler Corp.; *U.S. Public*, pg. 1032
THE MACNEAL-SCHWENDLER CORP.; *U.S. Public*, pg. 1030
MACNEAL-SCHWENDLER CORP.—See The Macneal-Schwendler Corp.; *U.S. Public*, pg. 1031
MACNEAL-SCHWENDLER FRANCE—See The Macneal-Schwendler Corp.; *U.S. Public*, pg. 1032
MACNEAL-SCHWENDLER GMBH—See The Macneal-Schwendler Corp.; *U.S. Public*, pg. 1032
MACNEAL-SCHWENDLER IBERICA S.A.—See The Macneal-Schwendler Corp.; *U.S. Public*, pg. 1032
FRANK R. MACNEILL & SON, INC.—See Jardine Matheson Holdings Limited; *Int'l*, pg. 705
MACOMB PLANT—See Cooper Industries, Inc.; *U.S. Public*, pg. 443
MACON BLUE PRINT COMPANY—See Wallace Computer Services, Inc.; *U.S. Public*, pg. 1735
MACON PRIMARY CARE CLINIC, INC.—See Integrated Health Services, Inc.; *U.S. Public*, pg. 885
MACON RECYCLING, INC.—See Caraustar Industries, Inc.; *U.S. Public*, pg. 304
MACON TELEGRAPH PUBLISHING COMPANY—See Knight-Ridder, Inc.; *U.S. Public*, pg. 964
C.E. MACPHERSON—See Canadian Erectors Ltd.; *Int'l*, pg. 256
MACPHERSON MEISTERGRAM, INC.—See Willcox & Gibbs, Inc.; *U.S. Public*, pg. 1177
MACRISTY INDUSTRIES, INC.; *U.S. Private*, pg. 693
MACRO COMPUTER PRODUCTS INC.; *U.S. Private*, pg. 693
MACRO SOFT—See Macro Computer Products Inc.; *U.S. Private*, pg. 693
MACROMEDIA INCORPORATED; *U.S. Private*, pg. 693
MACROMEDIA LEASING—See Macromedia Incorporated; *U.S. Private*, pg. 693
MACROMERIC DIVISION—See Furon Company; *U.S. Public*, pg. 689
MACROTECH PLYSEAL, INC.; *U.S. Private*, pg. 693

MACSAVEER FINANCIAL SERVICES—See Heilig-Meyers Company; *U.S. Public*, pg. 805
MACSTEEL DIV.—See Quanex Corporation; *U.S. Public*, pg. 1349
MACTAC EUROPE S.A.—See Bemis Company, Inc.; *U.S. Public*, pg. 210
MACTAC MEXICO, S.A.—See Bemis Company, Inc.; *U.S. Public*, pg. 210
MACTAC MORGAN ADHESIVE COMPANY—See Bemis Company, Inc.; *U.S. Public*, pg. 210
MACTAC NORTH AMERICA—See Bemis Company, Inc.; *U.S. Public*, pg. 210
MACTAC SCRANTON FACILITY—See Bemis Company, Inc.; *U.S. Public*, pg. 210
MACTAVISH FURNITURE INDUSTRIES—See Aaron Rents, Inc.; *U.S. Public*, pg. 12
MACTAVISH FURNITURE INDUSTRIES, COOLIDGE FACTORY—See Aaron Rents, Inc.; *U.S. Public*, pg. 12
MACTAVISH FURNITURE INDUSTRIES, QUINCY OFFICE PLANT—See Aaron Rents, Inc.; *U.S. Public*, pg. 12
MACTAVISH MACHINE MANUFACTURING COMPANY; *U.S. Private*, pg. 693
MACTEC AB—See ITT Industries, Inc.; *U.S. Public*, pg. 860
MACUSER—See Softbank Corporation; *Int'l*, pg. 1276
MACWAREHOUSE—See Micro Warehouse, Inc.; *U.S. Public*, pg. 1104
MACWHYTE CO.—See Amsted Industries Incorporated; *U.S. Public*, pg. 68
MACWORLD—See International Data Group; *U.S. Private*, pg. 569
MACWORLD COMMUNICATIONS JAPAN, INC.—See International Data Group; *U.S. Private*, pg. 570
MACWORLD/PC WORLD KOREA/HI-TECH INFORMATION—See International Data Group; *U.S. Private*, pg. 570
MACY'S EAST—See Federated Department Stores, Inc.; *U.S. Public*, pg. 618
MACY'S WEST—See Federated Department Stores, Inc.; *U.S. Public*, pg. 618
THE MAD BUTCHER, INC.; *U.S. Private*, pg. 693
MAD MAGAZINE, E. C. CREATIONS, INC.—See Time Warner Inc.; *U.S. Public*, pg. 1614
MADDAK INC.—See Bel-Art Products; *U.S. Private*, pg. 130
MADDEN & LAYMAN LIMITED—See Bausch & Lomb Incorporated; *U.S. Public*, pg. 196
MADE SISTEMAS ELECTRICOS, S.A.—See SEPI; *Int'l*, pg. 1224
MADEIRA OFFSHORE—See Caixa Geral de Depositos; *Int'l*, pg. 250
MADEMOISELLE—See Advance Publications Inc.; *U.S. Private*, pg. 5
MADER CONSTRUCTION CORP; *U.S. Private*, pg. 693
MADERAS SECAS C.A. (MASECA)—See Baltek Corporation; *U.S. Public*, pg. 172
MADISON ACCEPTANCE CORPORATION—See Citation Insurance Group; *U.S. Public*, pg. 376
MADISON DAIRY PRODUCE COMPANY; *U.S. Private*, pg. 694
MADISON DMB&B ADVERTISING—See DMB&B Communications; *U.S. Private*, pg. 305
MADISON DMB&B ADVERTISING, PVT LTD.—See DMB&B Communications; *U.S. Private*, pg. 304
MADISON ELECTRIC CO.; *U.S. Private*, pg. 694
MADISON FURNITURE INDUSTRIES—See Shelby Williams Industries, Inc.; *U.S. Public*, pg. 1465
MADISON GAS AND ELECTRIC COMPANY; *U.S. Public*, pg. 1032
MADISON GRAHAM COLORGRAPHICS, INC.; *U.S. Private*, pg. 694
MADISON GROCERY CO., INC.; *U.S. Private*, pg. 694
MADISON, INC.—See John S. Frey Enterprises; *U.S. Private*, pg. 428
MADISON INDUSTRIES—See John S. Frey Enterprises; *U.S. Private*, pg. 428
MADISON INDUSTRIES INC. OF ARIZONA—See John S. Frey Enterprises; *U.S. Private*, pg. 428
MADISON INDUSTRIES INC. OF GEORGIA—See John S. Frey Enterprises; *U.S. Private*, pg. 428
MADISON NATIONAL LIFE INSURANCE CO., INC.—See Geneve Corporation; *U.S. Private*, pg. 448
MADISON NEWSPAPERS, INC.—See Lee Enterprises, Incorporated; *U.S. Public*, pg. 984
MADISON PAPER INDUSTRIES—See The New York Times Company; *U.S. Public*, pg. 1174
MADISON PLANT—See Cooper Industries, Inc.; *U.S. Public*, pg. 444
MADISON SQUARE GARDEN CENTER INC.—See Cablevision Systems Corporation; *U.S. Public*, pg. 288
MADISON SQUARE GARDEN CORPORATION—See Cablevision Systems Corporation; *U.S. Public*, pg. 288
MADISON SQUARE GARDEN NETWORK—See Cablevision Systems Corporation; *U.S. Public*, pg. 288
MADISON SYSTEMS LTD.—See Marcam Solutions, Inc.; *U.S. Public*, pg. 1043
MADLER PASSAGE LEIPZIG GRUNDSTUCK GMBH & CO KG—See Commerzbank AG; *Int'l*, pg. 310
MADRID HIPOTECARIA, S.C.H., S.A.—See Caja de Madrid Group; *Int'l*, pg. 251
MADRID LEASING CORPORATION, S.A.F., S.A.—See Caja de Madrid Group; *Int'l*, pg. 251
MADSHUS A/S—See K2 Inc.; *U.S. Public*, pg. 940
MAEBASHI CENTRAL KITCHEN—See Skylark Co., Ltd.; *Int'l*, pg. 1262
MAECHLER FRERES S.A.—See Veba AG; *Int'l*, pg. 1459
MAERZ OFENBAU AG—See RGP Holding Inc.; *U.S. Private*, pg. 904
MAERZ OFENBAU G.M.B.H.—See RGP Holding, Inc.; *U.S. Private*, pg. 904
MAES S.A.—See Etablissements Delhaize Freres Et Cie "Le Lion" S.A.; *Int'l*, pg. 463
MAES S.C.I.—See Etablissements Delhaize Freres Et Cie "Le Lion" S.A.; *Int'l*, pg. 463
CHAS. V. MAESCHER & CO., INC.—See Maescher Industries, Inc.; *U.S. Private*, pg. 694

MAESCHER CONSTRUCTION CO.—See Maescher Industries, Inc.; *U.S. Private*, pg. 694
MAESCHER INDUSTRIES, INC.; *U.S. Private*, pg. 694
MAESTRO PRODUCTS INC.—See International Aluminum Corporation; *U.S. Public*, pg. 895
MAF S.P.A.—See Valmet Corporation; *Int'l*, pg. 1449
MAFCO CONSOLIDATED GROUP INC.—See MacAndrews & Forbes Holdings Inc.; *U.S. Private*, pg. 690
MAFCO, INC.—See General Electric Company; *U.S. Public*, pg. 711
MAFCO WORLDWIDE CORP.—See MacAndrews & Forbes Holdings Inc.; *U.S. Private*, pg. 690
MAFINA B.V.—See Petrofina S.A.; *Int'l*, pg. 1044
MAG-E FURNACES PTE LTD.—See Eclipse Inc.; *U.S. Private*, pg. 361
MAG INNOVISION CO., INC.; *U.S. Private*, pg. 694
MAGAEL, INC.—See Madison Gas and Electric Company; *U.S. Public*, pg. 1033
MAGASIN LOUIS VUITTON, KUWAIT—See LVMH Moet Hennessy Louis Vuitton; *Int'l*, pg. 783
MAGAZINE GROUP—See Scholastic Corporation; *U.S. Public*, pg. 1440
MAGAZINE SERVICES INC.—See The Kiplinger Washington Editors, Inc.; *U.S. Private*, pg. 623
MAGAZINES MACLEAN HUNTER QUEBEC—See Rogers Communications, Inc.; *Int'l*, pg. 1123
MAGAZYN SZWEDZKIEGO BIURA TECHNICZNEGO—See Axel Johnson AB; *Int'l*, pg. 712
MAGAZZINI FRUTTA SALERNO S.R.L.—See Coeclerici Group; *Int'l*, pg. 303
SA MAGAZZINI GENERALI—See Coop Switzerland; *Int'l*, pg. 330
MAGCO LTD.—See FKI Plc; *Int'l*, pg. 473
MAGDEBURGER ARMATURENWERKE MAW AG—See Deutsche Babcock AG; *Int'l*, pg. 400
MAGDEL SERVICES PTE. LTD.—See KPN Koninklyke PTT Nederland NV; *Int'l*, pg. 720
MAGEC AVIATION LTD.—See The General Electric Company, p.l.c.; *Int'l*, pg. 544
MAGEDOMA B.V.—See Rohto Pharmaceutical Co.; *Int'l*, pg. 1126
THE MAGEE CARPET COMPANY; *U.S. Private*, pg. 694
MAGEE CO.—See Tandycrafts, Inc.; *U.S. Public*, pg. 1561
MAGELLAN AEROSPACE CORPORATION; *Int'l*, pg. 829
MAGELLAN COLONIAL INSTITUTE, INC.—See Magellan Health Services, Inc.; *U.S. Public*, pg. 1036
MAGELLAN CONTRACT SERVICES, INC.—See Magellan Health Services, Inc.; *U.S. Public*, pg. 1036
MAGELLAN FINANCIAL OFFICES—See Magellan Health Services, Inc.; *U.S. Public*, pg. 1036
MAGELLAN HEALTH SERVICES, INC.; *U.S. Public*, pg. 1033
MAGELLAN IMAGING, INC.—See Magellan Health Services, Inc.; *U.S. Public*, pg. 1036
MAGELLAN INTERNATIONAL TRADING; *U.S. Private*, pg. 694
MAGELLAN MEDICAL EXECUTIVE CORPORATION—See Magellan Health Services, Inc.; *U.S. Public*, pg. 1036
MAGELLAN MEDICAL INFORMATION SERVICES, INC.—See Magellan Health Services, Inc.; *U.S. Public*, pg. 1036
MAGELLAN MEDICAL INTERNATIONAL, INC.—See Magellan Health Services, Inc.; *U.S. Public*, pg. 1036
MAGELLAN MEDICAL MANAGEMENT COMPANY—See Magellan Health Services, Inc.; *U.S. Public*, pg. 1036
MAGELLAN MENTAL HEALTH OPTIONS, INC.—See Magellan Health Services, Inc.; *U.S. Public*, pg. 1036
MAGELLAN PETROLEUM CORPORATION; *U.S. Public*, pg. 1036
MAGELLAN PUBLIC NETWORK, INC.—See Magellan Health Services, Inc.; *U.S. Public*, pg. 1036
MAGELLAN PUBLIC SOLUTIONS, INC.—See Magellan Health Services, Inc.; *U.S. Public*, pg. 1036
MAGGI AG—See Nestle S.A.; *Int'l*, pg. 916
MAGGI GMBH—See Nestle S.A.; *Int'l*, pg. 920
MAGGIANO'S LITTLE ITALY—See Lettuce Entertain You Enterprises, Inc.; *U.S. Private*, pg. 661
MAGHERALIN CHEESE AND WHEY PRODUCTS—See Avonmore Waterford Group plc; *Int'l*, pg. 102
MAGHIELSE TOOL CORPORATION; *U.S. Private*, pg. 694
MAGIC AMERICAN CORPORATION; *U.S. Private*, pg. 695
MAGIC CIRCLE MANUFACTURING DIV.—See Acme Foundry, Inc.; *U.S. Private*, pg. 5
MAGIC VALLEY FOODS, INC.; *U.S. Private*, pg. 695
MAGIKITCH'N, INC.—See Maytag Corporation; *U.S. Public*, pg. 1065
MAGLA PRODUCTS; *U.S. Private*, pg. 695
MAGLIFICIO BELLIA S.P.A.—See Sara Lee Corporation; *U.S. Public*, pg. 1434
MAGLINE, INC.; *U.S. Private*, pg. 695
MAGMA METALS COMPANY—See The Broken Hill Proprietary Company Limited; *Int'l*, pg. 224
MAGMA-PINTO VALLEY MINING DIVISION—See The Broken Hill Proprietary Company Limited; *Int'l*, pg. 224
MAGMA-ROBINSON MINING DISTRICT—See The Broken Hill Proprietary Company Limited; *Int'l*, pg. 224
MAGMA-SAN MANUEL MINING DIVISION—See The Broken Hill Proprietary Company Limited; *Int'l*, pg. 224
MAGMA-SUPERIOR MINING DIVISION—See The Broken Hill Proprietary Company Limited; *Int'l*, pg. 224
MAGNA BANK—See Magna Group, Inc.; *U.S. Public*, pg. 1037
MAGNA DIVISION—See Emerson Electric Co.; *U.S. Public*, pg. 575
MAGNA GROUP, INC.; *U.S. Public*, pg. 1037
MAGNA INTERNATIONAL INC.; *Int'l*, pg. 829
MAGNA INTERNATIONAL OF AMERICA, INC.—See Magna International Inc.; *Int'l*, pg. 830
MAGNA LOMASON CORP.—See Magna International Inc.; *Int'l*, pg. 830
MAGNA MEDIA INC.—See Macromedia Incorporated; *U.S. Private*, pg. 693

MAGNA MORTGAGE—See Union Planters Corporation; *U.S. Public*, pg. 1669
MAGNACRAFT, STRUTHERS, DUNN, INC.; *U.S. Private*, pg. 695
MAGNAGRIP—See Bidwell Industrial Group, Inc.; *U.S. Private*, pg. 142
MAGNASYNC MOVIOLA CORPORATION—See J & R Film / Moviola Digital Co.; *U.S. Private*, pg. 576
MAGNAVIEW INC.—See Video Display Corporation; *U.S. Public*, pg. 1720
MAGNECO/METREL, INC.; *U.S. Private*, pg. 695
MAGNEDYNE DIV.—See Sierracin Corporation; *U.S. Private*, pg. 999
MAGNESIUM ELEKTRON—See Alcan Aluminium Limited; *Int'l*, pg. 51
MAGNET CONTROLS DIV.—See Axsys Technologies, Inc.; *U.S. Public*, pg. 157
MAGNET DEVELOPMENTS LIMITED—See TT Group PLC; *Int'l*, pg. 1344
MAGNET LTD.—See Berisford plc; *Int'l*, pg. 188
MAGNET PROPERTIES—See Alliance Management, Inc.; *U.S. Public*, pg. 38
MAGNET WORLD TRAVEL LTD.—See The General Electric Company, p.l.c.; *Int'l*, pg. 544
MAGNETEK, INC.; *U.S. Public*, pg. 1037
MAGNETEK LIGHTING PRODUCTS GROUP—See MagneTek, Inc.; *U.S. Public*, pg. 1037
MAGNETEK MOTORS & GENERATORS—See MagneTek, Inc.; *U.S. Public*, pg. 1037
MAGNETI MARELLI S.P.A.—See Fiat Auto SpA; *Int'l*, pg. 482
MAGNETI MARELLI U.S.A., INC.—See Fiat Auto SpA; *Int'l*, pg. 483
MAGNETIC AB—See Telefonaktiebolaget LM Ericsson; *Int'l*, pg. 1364
MAGNETIC ANALYSIS CORP.; *U.S. Private*, pg. 695
MAGNETIC METALS CORP.—See Inductotherm Industries, Inc.; *U.S. Private*, pg. 560
THE MAGNETIC NORTH CORPORATION—See Rogers Communications, Inc.; *Int'l*, pg. 1124
MAGNETIC TECHNOLOGIES CORPORATION—See SPS Technologies, Inc.; *U.S. Public*, pg. 1420
MAGNETIC TECHNOLOGIES EUROPE, LTD.—See SPS Technologies, Inc.; *U.S. Public*, pg. 1420
MAGNETICS—See Spang & Company; *U.S. Private*, pg. 1020
MAGNETICS DATA INC.; *U.S. Private*, pg. 695
MAGNETICS DATA, INC.—See Magnetics Data Inc.; *U.S. Private*, pg. 696
MAGNETICS INTERNATIONAL, INC.—See Inland Steel Industries, Inc.; *U.S. Public*, pg. 879
MAGNETOELASTIC DEVICES INC. (MDI)—See Methode Electronics Inc.; *U.S. Public*, pg. 1101
MAGNETROL INTERNATIONAL; *U.S. Private*, pg. 696
MAGNIFIN MAGNESIAPRODUKTE GMBH—See Alusuisse-Lonza Holding Ltd.; *Int'l*, pg. 69
MAGNOLIA CHEMICALS & SOLVENTS—See Preussag AG; *Int'l*, pg. 1071
MAGNOLIA DIVISION—See Sanderson Plumbing Products Inc.; *U.S. Public*, pg. 964
MAGNOLIA HI-FI, INC.; *U.S. Private*, pg. 696
MAGNOMIN-GENERAL MINING S.A.—See RGP Holding, Inc.; *U.S. Private*, pg. 904
MAGNUM DIAMOND—See Chiron Corporation; *U.S. Public*, pg. 350
MAGNUS METALS—See Farley, Inc.; *U.S. Private*, pg. 394
MAGNUS SOFTWARE CORPORATION—See New York Life Insurance Company; *U.S. Private*, pg. 795
MAGRUDER COLOR COMPANY, INC.; *U.S. Private*, pg. 696
MAGSTREAM CORPORATION—See Intermagnetics General Corporation; *U.S. Public*, pg. 894
MAGUIRE GROUP ARCHITECTS, INC.—See Maguire Group Inc.; *U.S. Private*, pg. 696
MAGUIRE GROUP INC.; *U.S. Private*, pg. 696
MAGUIRE OIL CO.; *U.S. Private*, pg. 696
MAGUIRE PARTNERS; *U.S. Private*, pg. 696
MAGVS, INC.; *U.S. Private*, pg. 696
MAHAJAK INTERNATIONAL ELECTRIC CO., LTD.—See Fuji Electric Co., Ltd.; *Int'l*, pg. 522
MAHANADI COALFIELDS LIMITED—See Coal India Limited; *Int'l*, pg. 298
MAHANOY & MAHANTONGO TELEPHONE COMPANY—See Telephone and Data Systems, Inc.; *U.S. Public*, pg. 1571
MAHARAM; *U.S. Private*, pg. 696
MAHCO, INC.—See Mason & Hanger Corporation, Inc.; *U.S. Private*, pg. 711
MAHER TERMINALS INC.; *U.S. Private*, pg. 697
MAHLO GMBH & CO. KG; *Int'l*, pg. 830
MAHONING LANDFILL, INC.—See American Waste Services, Inc.; *U.S. Public*, pg. 94
MAHOU S.A.—See Danone Group; *Int'l*, pg. 381
MAICES HIBRIDOS Y SEMILLAS SA—See Novartis AG; *Int'l*, pg. 983
MAIDENFORM WORLDWIDE; *U.S. Private*, pg. 697
MAIL BOXES ETC.—See U.S. Office Products Company; *U.S. Public*, pg. 1687
MAIL MEDIA COMPANIES—See The Stanley Works; *U.S. Public*, pg. 1509
MAIL ORDER BOOK SALES—See Meredith Corporation; *U.S. Public*, pg. 1094
MAIL PROCESSING SYSTEMS—See Bell & Howell Holdings; *U.S. Public*, pg. 201
MAIL-WELL, INC.; *U.S. Public*, pg. 1037
MAIL WELL SERVICES INC.—See Primedia Inc.; *U.S. Public*, pg. 1328
MAILPROFS UITZENDBUREAUX BV—See KPN Koninklyke PTT Nederland NV; *Int'l*, pg. 720
MAILTEK, INC.—See Synovus Financial Corp.; *U.S. Public*, pg. 1550
MAILWAY SDN. BHD.—See KPN Koninklyke PTT Nederland NV; *Int'l*, pg. 720

MAIN BROTHERS OIL COMPANY, INC.; *U.S. Private*, pg. 697
MAIN-DONAU (RHEIN-MAIN-DONAU) SPEDITIONS GMBH—See Panalpina Welttransport (Holding) AG; *Int'l*, pg. 1022
MAIN LIFE INSURANCE CO.—See The Midland Company; *U.S. Public*, pg. 1111
MAIN PLAZA CORPORATION—See Cullen/Frost Bankers, Inc.; *U.S. Public*, pg. 467
MAIN STREET SOUTH CORP.—See Aquarion Company; *U.S. Public*, pg. 126
MAINCO ELEVATOR SERVICES CO.—See ISS-International Service System A/S; *Int'l*, pg. 656
MAINE AND NEW BRUNSWICK ELECTRICAL POWER COMPANY, LTD.—See Maine Public Service Company; *U.S. Public*, pg. 1038
MAINE ASSOCIATES—See Cigna Corp.; *U.S. Public*, pg. 361
MAINE BONDING & CASUALTY COMPANY—See Zurich Insurance Company; *Int'l*, pg. 1530
MAINE BOTTLERS—See White Rock Distilleries Inc.; *U.S. Private*, pg. 1173
MAINE ELECTRIC POWER CO., INC.—See Central Maine Power Company; *U.S. Public*, pg. 325
MAINE POTATO GROWERS, INC.; *U.S. Private*, pg. 697
MAINE PUBLIC SERVICE COMPANY; *U.S. Public*, pg. 1038
MAINE/SYSCO, INC.—See Sysco Corporation; *U.S. Public*, pg. 1551
MAINE YANKEE—See Central Maine Power Company; *U.S. Public*, pg. 325
MAINE YANKEE ATOMIC POWER CO.—See Maine Public Service Company; *U.S. Public*, pg. 1038
MAINLAND INSURANCE CO.—See Harleysville Group; *U.S. Public*, pg. 787
MAINLINE INDUSTRIAL DISTRIBUTORS, INC.—See Applied Industrial Technologies; *U.S. Public*, pg. 123
MAINSHIP CORPORATION; *U.S. Private*, pg. 697
MAINSTREET BANKGROUP INCORPORATED; *U.S. Public*, pg. 1038
MAINSTREET TRUST COMPANY, N.A.—See MainStreet BankGroup Incorporated; *U.S. Public*, pg. 1039
MAINTECH—See Volt Information Sciences, Inc.; *U.S. Public*, pg. 1724
MAINTENANCE BUILDING & SIGNAGE—See Vaux Group Plc; *Int'l*, pg. 1454
MAINTENANCE, INC.—See Premier Farnell plc; *Int'l*, pg. 1068
MAINTENANCE SERVICES GROUP—See Namanco LLC; *U.S. Private*, pg. 773
MAISON BLANCHE, INC.—See Mercantile Stores Company, Inc.; *U.S. Public*, pg. 1090
MAISON DEUTZ WINERY—See Nestle S.A.; *Int'l*, pg. 917
MAISON LAZARD ET CIE—See Pearson plc; *Int'l*, pg. 1027
MAITLAND-SMITH U.S., INC.—See Furnishings International, Inc.; *U.S. Private*, pg. 432
MAIWALD BAUSTOFFE GMBH—See Veba AG; *Int'l*, pg. 1459
MAIZENA S.A.—See Corn Products International, Inc.; *U.S. Public*, pg. 447
MAIZENA, INC.—See Corn Products International, Inc.; *U.S. Public*, pg. 447
MAIZURU WORKS—See Hitachi Zosen Corporation; *Int'l*, pg. 623
MAJESTIC CARPET MILLS—See Shaw Industries, Inc.; *U.S. Public*, pg. 1464
MAJESTIC PINES CARE CENTER—See Meritcare, Inc.; *U.S. Private*, pg. 733
MAJOR AEROSPACE ACCOUNTS—See The Macneal-Schwendler Corp.; *U.S. Public*, pg. 1031
MAJOR AUTOMOTIVE GROUP; *U.S. Private*, pg. 697
MAJOR & CO. LTD.—See Burmah Castrol plc; *Int'l*, pg. 234
MAJOR FOODS LTD.—See Aramark Corp.; *U.S. Private*, pg. 79
MAJOR FURNACE AND ENGINEERING PTY., LTD.—See Selas Corporation of America; *U.S. Public*, pg. 1455
MAJOR GROUP INC.—See Acceptance Insurance Co., Inc.; *U.S. Public*, pg. 15
MAJOR MEDICAL SUPPLY, INC.—See Integrated Health Services, Inc.; *U.S. Public*, pg. 885
MAJOR PHARMACEUTICALS—See Great Lakes Wholesale Drugs; *U.S. Private*, pg. 475
MAJOR PHARMACEUTICALS CORP.—See Great Lakes Wholesale Drugs; *U.S. Private*, pg. 475
MAJOR SMITH INC.—See Bongrain S.A.; *Int'l*, pg. 201
MAJOR SYSCO FOOD SERVICES INC.—See Sysco Corporation; *U.S. Public*, pg. 1551
MAJOR VIDEO CONCEPTS, INC.—See LDI, Ltd.; *U.S. Private*, pg. 639
MAJORICA JEWELRY GROUP; *U.S. Private*, pg. 697
MAK MEDITERRANEE S.A.R.L.—See Fried. Krupp AG; *Int'l*, pg. 510
MAKER'S MARK DISTILLERY, INC.—See Allied Domecq PLC; *Int'l*, pg. 63
MAKHTESHIM CHEMICAL WORKS LTD.; *Int'l*, pg. 830
MAKHTESHIM-AGAN DEUTSCHLAND GMBH—See Makhteshim Chemical Works Ltd.; *Int'l*, pg. 830
MAKHTESHIM-AGAN INTERNATIONAL—See Makhteshim Chemical Works Ltd.; *Int'l*, pg. 831
MAKHTESHIM-AGAN ITALIA S.R.L.—See Makhteshim Chemical Works Ltd.; *Int'l*, pg. 831
MAKI CORPORATION; *U.S. Private*, pg. 697
MAKI HOME CENTER, INC.—See Maki Corporation; *U.S. Private*, pg. 698
MAKINO INC.—See Makino Milling Machine Co. Ltd.; *Int'l*, pg. 831
MAKINO MILLING MACHINE CO. LTD.; *Int'l*, pg. 831
MAKINO USA INC.—See Makino Milling Machine Co. Ltd.; *Int'l*, pg. 831
MAKITA (AUSTRALIA) PTY. LTD.—See Makita Corporation; *Int'l*, pg. 831
MAKITA (AUSTRALIA) PTY. LTD.-ADELAIDE—See Makita Corporation; *Int'l*, pg. 831

MAKITA (AUSTRALIA) PTY. LTD.-BRISBANE—See Makita Corporation; *Int'l*, pg. 831
MAKITA (AUSTRALIA) PTY. LTD.-CANBERRA—See Makita Corporation; *Int'l*, pg. 831
MAKITA (AUSTRALIA) PTY. LTD.-DARWIN—See Makita Corporation; *Int'l*, pg. 832
MAKITA (AUSTRALIA) PTY. LTD.-HOBART—See Makita Corporation; *Int'l*, pg. 832
MAKITA (AUSTRALIA) PTY. LTD.-MELBOURNE—See Makita Corporation; *Int'l*, pg. 832
MAKITA (AUSTRALIA) PTY. LTD.-NEWCASTLE—See Makita Corporation; *Int'l*, pg. 832
MAKITA (AUSTRALIA) PTY. LTD.-PERTH—See Makita Corporation; *Int'l*, pg. 832
MAKITA (AUSTRALIA) PTY. LTD.-SYDNEY—See Makita Corporation; *Int'l*, pg. 832
MAKITA BENELUX B.V.—See Makita Corporation; *Int'l*, pg. 832
MAKITA (CHINA) CO., LTD.—See Makita Corporation; *Int'l*, pg. 832
MAKITA CORPORATION; *Int'l*, pg. 831
MAKITA CORPORATION-NAGOYA BRANCH—See Makita Corporation; *Int'l*, pg. 831
MAKITA CORPORATION OF AMERICA—See Makita Corporation; *Int'l*, pg. 831
MAKITA CORPORATION-OSAKA BRANCH—See Makita Corporation; *Int'l*, pg. 831
MAKITA CORPORATION-TOKYO BRANCH—See Makita Corporation; *Int'l*, pg. 831
MAKITA DO BRASIL FERRAMENTAS ELETRICAS LTDA.—See Makita Corporation; *Int'l*, pg. 832
MAKITA FRANCE S.A.—See Makita Corporation; *Int'l*, pg. 832
MAKITA FRANCE S.A.-BORDEAUX—See Makita Corporation; *Int'l*, pg. 832
MAKITA FRANCE S.A.-LYON—See Makita Corporation; *Int'l*, pg. 832
MAKITA FRANCE S.A.-MARSEILLE—See Makita Corporation; *Int'l*, pg. 832
MAKITA FRANCE S.A.-NANCY—See Makita Corporation; *Int'l*, pg. 832
MAKITA FRANCE S.A.-NANTES—See Makita Corporation; *Int'l*, pg. 832
MAKITA FRANCE S.A.-NORD—See Makita Corporation; *Int'l*, pg. 832
MAKITA FRANCE S.A.-TOULOUSE—See Makita Corporation; *Int'l*, pg. 832
MAKITA GULF FZE—See Makita Corporation; *Int'l*, pg. 832
MAKITA ICHINOMIYA CORPORATION—See Makita Corporation; *Int'l*, pg. 831
MAKITA INTERNATIONAL EUROPE LTD.—See Makita Corporation; *Int'l*, pg. 832
MAKITA KFT.—See Makita Corporation; *Int'l*, pg. 832
MAKITA KOREA CO., LTD.—See Makita Corporation; *Int'l*, pg. 832
MAKITA MANUFACTURING EUROPE LTD.—See Makita Corporation; *Int'l*, pg. 832
MAKITA MEXICO, S.A. DE C.V.—See Makita Corporation; *Int'l*, pg. 832
MAKITA (NEW ZEALAND) LTD.—See Makita Corporation; *Int'l*, pg. 832
MAKITA (NEW ZEALAND) LTD.-CHRISTCHURCH—See Makita Corporation; *Int'l*, pg. 832
S.A. MAKITA N.V.—See Makita Corporation; *Int'l*, pg. 832
MAKITA POWER TOOLS (H.K.) LTD.—See Makita Corporation; *Int'l*, pg. 832
MAKITA, S.A.—See Makita Corporation; *Int'l*, pg. 832
MAKITA SINGAPORE PTE. LTD.—See Makita Corporation; *Int'l*, pg. 832
MAKITA SP. Z O.O.—See Makita Corporation; *Int'l*, pg. 832
MAKITA S.P.A.—See Makita Corporation; *Int'l*, pg. 832
MAKITA S.R.O.—See Makita Corporation; *Int'l*, pg. 832
MAKITA (TAIWAN) LTD.—See Makita Corporation; *Int'l*, pg. 832
MAKITA (U.K.) LTD.—See Makita Corporation; *Int'l*, pg. 832
MAKITA U.S.A. INC.-ATLANTA—See Makita Corporation; *Int'l*, pg. 831
MAKITA U.S.A. INC.-CHICAGO—See Makita Corporation; *Int'l*, pg. 831
MAKITA U.S.A. INC.-DENVER—See Makita Corporation; *Int'l*, pg. 831
MAKITA U.S.A. INC.-HOUSTON—See Makita Corporation; *Int'l*, pg. 831
MAKITA U.S.A. INC.-LOS ANGELES—See Makita Corporation; *Int'l*, pg. 831
MAKITA U.S.A. INC.-NEW JERSEY—See Makita Corporation; *Int'l*, pg. 831
MAKITA U.S.A. INC.-SAN FRANCISCO—See Makita Corporation; *Int'l*, pg. 831
MAKITA WERKZEUG GESELLSCHAFT M.B.H.—See Makita Corporation; *Int'l*, pg. 832
MAKITA WERKZEUG GMBH—See Makita Corporation; *Int'l*, pg. 832
MAKITA WERKZEUG GMBH-DENMARK OFFICE—See Makita Corporation; *Int'l*, pg. 832
MAKO COMPRESSORS, INC.—See Siebe plc; *Int'l*, pg. 1243
MAKO CONSTRUCTION CO.—See Henkels & McCoy, Inc.; *U.S. Private*, pg. 522
MAKOLIN ELECTRONICS SDW. BHD.—See Tatung Company; *Int'l*, pg. 1357
MAKOTO SANGOYO CO., LTD.—See Fuchs Petrolub AG Oel + Chemie; *Int'l*, pg. 519
MAKRO CR SPOL. S.R.O.—See SHV Holdings N.V.; *Int'l*, pg. 1155
MAKRO DE COLOMBIA S.A.—See SHV Holdings N.V.; *Int'l*, pg. 1155
MAKRO IN INDONESIA—See SHV Holdings N.V.; *Int'l*, pg. 1155
MAKRO INTERNATIONAL AG—See SHV Holdings N.V.; *Int'l*, pg. 1155
MAKRO N.V.—See SHV Holdings N.V.; *Int'l*, pg. 1155
MAL PACIFIC TECHNOLOGY SDN. BHD.—See Ssangyong Business Group; *Int'l*, pg. 1293

MALAGA COMERCIAL S.A.—See Nestle S.A.; *Int'l*, pg. 920
MALAKOFF INDUSTRIES—See Reynolds Metals Company; *U.S. Public*, pg. 1386
MALAMA PACIFIC CORP.—See Hawaiian Electric Industries, Inc.; *U.S. Public*, pg. 800
HERBERT MALARKEY ROOFING COMPANY; *U.S. Private*, pg. 698
MALAT (UNMANNED AIR VEHICLES) DIVISION/MILITARY AIRCRAFT GROUP—See Israel Aircraft Industries Ltd.; *Int'l*, pg. 690
MALAYAN CEMENT BERHAD—See Blue Circle Industries PLC; *Int'l*, pg. 198
MALAYAN FIBRE CONTAINERS SDN. BHD.—See BTR plc; *Int'l*, pg. 129
MALAYAN INSURANCE COMPANY, INC.—See Zurich Insurance Company; *Int'l*, pg. 1532
MALAYAN LAW JOURNAL—See Reed Elsevier plc; *Int'l*, pg. 1095
MALAYSIA COCOA MANUFACTURING, SDN. BHD.—See Nestle S.A.; *Int'l*, pg. 920
MALAYSIA LNG—See Royal Dutch/Shell Group of Companies; *Int'l*, pg. 1140
MALAYSIA PACKAGING INDUSTRY BERHAD—See Ajinomoto Company Inc.; *Int'l*, pg. 41
MALAYSIA TOURISM PROMOTION BOARD (MTPB); *Int'l*, pg. 832
MALAYSIAN ELECTRONICS MATERIALS SDN. BHD—See Sumitomo Metal Mining Co., Ltd.; *Int'l*, pg. 1316
MALAYSIAN OXYGEN BERHAD—See The BOC Group plc; *Int'l*, pg. 122
MALAYSIAN ROOFING INDUSTRIES SDN. BHD.—See BTR plc; *Int'l*, pg. 129
MALAYSIAN TOBACCO CO./B.A.T. INDUST.—See B.A.T Industries P.L.C.; *Int'l*, pg. 111
MALCO PRODUCTS, INC.; *U.S. Private*, pg. 698
MALDEN MILLS INDUSTRIES, INC.; *U.S. Private*, pg. 698
MALETTE INC.—See Tembec Inc.; *U.S. Private*, pg. 1375
MALETTE QUEBEC, INC.; *Int'l*, pg. 833
MALEV HUNGARIAN AIRLINES, PLC.; *Int'l*, pg. 833
MALHARIA INDUSTRIAL DO NORDESTE S.A.—See Solvay S.A.; *Int'l*, pg. 1279
MALIBU ENTERTAINMENT WORLDWIDE; *U.S. Public*, pg. 1039
MALICHA BRENNSTOFFHANDEL GMBH—See Veba AG; *Int'l*, pg. 1457
MALILINE LTD—See Union-Transport Corporation; *U.S. Private*, pg. 1120
MALL OF NEW HAMPSHIRE—See Cigna Corp.; *U.S. Public*, pg. 361
MALL OFFICE—See Pinnacle Bank; *U.S. Public*, pg. 1297
MALL ST. MATTHEWS CORPORATION—See The Rouse Company; *U.S. Public*, pg. 1408
MALLERY LUMBER CORP.; *U.S. Private*, pg. 698
MALLET & CO.; *U.S. Private*, pg. 698
MALLINCKRODT AUSTRALIA PTY. LTD.—See Mallinckrodt Inc.; *U.S. Public*, pg. 1040
MALLINCKRODT BAKER INC.—See Mallinckrodt Inc.; *U.S. Public*, pg. 1039
MALLINCKRODT CANADA, INC.—See Mallinckrodt Inc.; *U.S. Public*, pg. 1040
MALLINCKRODT CARIBE.—See Mallinckrodt Inc.; *U.S. Public*, pg. 1039
MALLINCKRODT INC.; *U.S. Public*, pg. 1039
MALLINCKRODT INC.—See Mallinckrodt Inc.; *U.S. Public*, pg. 1039
MALLINCKRODT MEDICAL—See Mallinckrodt Inc.; *U.S. Public*, pg. 1040
MALLORY, INC.; *U.S. Private*, pg. 698
MALLOY LITHOGRAPHING INC.; *U.S. Private*, pg. 698
MALONE ADVERTISING, INC.; *U.S. Private*, pg. 698
MALONE & HYDE, INC.-DRUG DISTRIBUTORS—See Fleming Companies, Inc.; *U.S. Public*, pg. 653
E.B. MALONE CORP.—See Bassett Furniture Industries, Incorporated; *U.S. Public*, pg. 193
MALOYA FREDESTEIN—See Fredestein Banden; *Int'l*, pg. 505
MALRITE COMMUNICATIONS GROUP, INC.; *U.S. Private*, pg. 698
MALROSIAN, INC.—See Cigna Corp.; *U.S. Public*, pg. 357
MALT-O-MEAL COMPANY; *U.S. Private*, pg. 699
MALTA DIV.-TOMKINS INDUSTRIES, INC.—See Tomkins PLC; *Int'l*, pg. 1398
MALVAUX S.A.—See UPM-Kymmene Corporation; *Int'l*, pg. 1429
MAMAN DIVISION—See Israel Aircraft Industries Ltd.; *Int'l*, pg. 690
MAMBOSOCK—See Gerry Sportswear Company; *U.S. Private*, pg. 449
MAMMA ILARDO'S COMPANY; *U.S. Private*, pg. 699
MAMMOET CANADA LTD.—See Royal Nedlloyd Group N.V.; *Int'l*, pg. 1144
MAMMOET FERRY TRANSPORT B.V.—See Royal Nedlloyd Group N.V.; *Int'l*, pg. 1144
MAMMOET-HANSA A.G.—See Royal Nedlloyd Group N.V.; *Int'l*, pg. 1144
MAMMOET STOOF B.V.—See Royal Nedlloyd Group N.V.; *Int'l*, pg. 1144
MAMMOET TRANSPORT B.V.—See Royal Nedlloyd Group N.V.; *Int'l*, pg. 1144
MAMMOET TRANSPORT DIV. B.V.—See Royal Nedlloyd Group N.V.; *Int'l*, pg. 1144
MAMMOTH, INC.—See Nortek, Inc.; *U.S. Public*, pg. 1193
MAN-GILL CHEMICAL COMPANY; *U.S. Private*, pg. 699
MAN NEN SHA AGENCY, INC.—See Man Nen Sha Inc.; *Int'l*, pg. 834
MAN NEN SHA INC.; *Int'l*, pg. 834
MAN NEN SHA, INC.—See Man Nen Sha Inc.; *Int'l*, pg. 834
MAN ROLAND, INC.—See MAN Aktiengesellschaft; *Int'l*, pg. 825
MANAC SOLUTIONS—See Platinum Equity Holdings, LLC; *U.S. Private*, pg. 872

MANAGED PROPERTIES, INC.—See St. Paul Bancorp, Inc.; *U.S. Public*, pg. 1428
MANAGEMENT DATA DATENVERABEITUNGS- UND UNTERNEHMENSBERATUNG GMBH—See Creditanstalt-Bankverein; *Int'l*, pg. 347
MANAGEMENT DATA SERVICE—See US ServIs; *U.S. Public*, pg. 1687
MANAGEMENT DYNAMICS; *U.S. Public*, pg. 1040
MANAGEMENT ENGINEERS GMBH—See Bourton Group; *U.S. Private*, pg. 162
MANAGEMENT INFORMATION SYSTEMS CO. LTD. (MIS)—See Hewlett-Packard Company; *U.S. Public*, pg. 822
MANAGEMENT INTERNATIONAL (DUBLIN) LIMITED—See The Bank of Bermuda Limited; *Int'l*, pg. 151
MANAGEMENT INTERNATIONAL (GUERNSEY) LIMITED—See The Bank of Bermuda Limited; *Int'l*, pg. 151
MANAGEMENT INTERNATIONAL (JERSEY) LTD.—See The Bank of Bermuda Limited; *Int'l*, pg. 151
MANAGEMENT INTERNATIONAL (LUXEMBOURG) S.A.—See The Bank of Bermuda Limited; *Int'l*, pg. 152
MANAGEMENT RECRUITERS INTERNATIONAL, INC.—See CDI Corp.; *U.S. Public*, pg. 277
MANAGER MAGAZIN VERLAGSGESELLSCHAFT MBH—See Bertelsmann AG; *Int'l*, pg. 190
MANAGING AUTOMATION—See Thomas Publishing Company; *U.S. Private*, pg. 1082
MANAGISTICS INCORPORATED—See BankAmerica Corporation; *U.S. Public*, pg. 181
MANAMERICA - TAIWAN BRANCH—See Manulife Financial (The Manufacturers Life Insurance Company); *Int'l*, pg. 841
MANASCHEWITZ WINE COMPANY—See Canandaigua Wine Company, Inc.; *U.S. Public*, pg. 300
MANATEE HOLDING COMPANY—See Saint-Gobain; *Int'l*, pg. 1176
MANATEE TOWING COMPANY—See The Coastal Corporation; *U.S. Public*, pg. 390
MANATRON, INC.; *U.S. Public*, pg. 1040
MANAUS REFINERY—See Petrobras - Petroleo Brasileiro S.A.; *Int'l*, pg. 1042
MANCHEM INC.—See Rhone-Poulenc S.A.; *Int'l*, pg. 1110
MANCHESTER—See National Westminster Bank PLC; *Int'l*, pg. 910
MANCHESTER EQUIPMENT CO.; *U.S. Private*, pg. 699
MANCHESTER GUARDIAN—See Guardian Media Group plc; *Int'l*, pg. 577
MANCHESTER MALL JOINT VENTURE—See Cigna Corp.; *U.S. Public*, pg. 361
MANCHESTER PLASTICS—See Collins & Aikman Corporation; *U.S. Public*, pg. 399
MANCHESTER PLASTICS CO., INC.—See Summa Industries; *U.S. Public*, pg. 1527
MANCHESTER TANK & EQUIPMENT COMPANY; *U.S. Private*, pg. 699
MANCHESTER TOOL COMPANY—See Federal Signal Corporation; *U.S. Public*, pg. 617
B.T. MANCINI CO., INC.; *U.S. Private*, pg. 699
MANDARIN AIRLINES—See China Airlines Ltd.; *Int'l*, pg. 284
MANDARIN MEADOWS, INC.—See Magellan Health Services, Inc.; *U.S. Public*, pg. 1036
MANDARIN ORIENTAL, HONG KONG LIMITED—See Jardine Matheson Holdings Limited; *Int'l*, pg. 704
MANDARIN ORIENTAL HOTEL GROUP LIMITED—See Jardine Matheson Holdings Limited; *Int'l*, pg. 704
MANDARIN ORIENTAL INTERNATIONAL LIMITED—See Jardine Matheson Holdings Limited; *Int'l*, pg. 704
MANDARIN ORIENTAL, SAN FRANCISCO—See Jardine Matheson Holdings Limited; *Int'l*, pg. 704
MANDELLI INDUSTRIE S.P.A.; *Int'l*, pg. 834
MANDO MARKETING LIMITED—See WPP Group plc; *Int'l*, pg. 1482
MANELCO SA—See Alusuisse-Lonza Holding Ltd.; *Int'l*, pg. 69
MANESS INDUSTRIES, INC.; *U.S. Private*, pg. 699
MANETTA HOME FASHIONS—See Pillowtex Corporation; *U.S. Public*, pg. 1296
MANETTI-FARROW INCORPORATED—See A.T. Cross Co.; *U.S. Public*, pg. 461
MANEUROP S.A.—See Danfoss A/S; *Int'l*, pg. 377
MANGANESE METAL CO. PTY. LTD.—See Delta plc; *Int'l*, pg. 392
THE MANGANO COMPANY, INC.—See Centex Corporation; *U.S. Public*, pg. 323
MANGUM MFG. CO. OF MISSOURI, INC.—See Allen Telecom, Inc.; *U.S. Public*, pg. 46
MANHATTAN ACCESSORIES DIV.—See Salant Corporation; *U.S. Public*, pg. 1429
MANHATTAN AND BRONX SURFACE TRANSIT OPERATING AUTHORITY—See Metropolitan Transportation Authority; *U.S. Private*, pg. 739
MANHATTAN BEACH—See Lagardere Groupe; *Int'l*, pg. 795
MANHATTAN BRASS & COPPER CO.; *U.S. Private*, pg. 699
MANHATTAN/CDT—See Cable Design Technologies Corporation; *U.S. Public*, pg. 287
MANHATTAN CONSTRUCTION COMPANY—See Rooney Brothers Company; *U.S. Private*, pg. 943
MANHATTAN FACTORY—See Salant Corporation; *U.S. Public*, pg. 1429
MANHATTAN INDUSTRIES INTL. DIV.—See Salant Corporation; *U.S. Public*, pg. 1429
MANHATTAN LIFE INSURANCE COMPANY—See The Union Central Life Insurance Co.; *U.S. Private*, pg. 1118
MANHATTAN NATIONAL LIFE INSURANCE COMPANY—See Conseco Inc.; *U.S. Public*, pg. 434
MANHATTAN PAKISTAN (PRIVATE) LIMITED—See Leo Burnett Company, Inc.; *U.S. Private*, pg. 186
MANHATTAN PARTNERS L.P.; *U.S. Private*, pg. 699

THE MANHATTAN SHIRT CO.—See Salant Corporation; U.S. Public, pg. 1429
MANHATTAN STORE INTERIORS, INC.; U.S. Private, pg. 699
MANHEIM AUCTIONS, INC.—See Cox Enterprises, Inc.; U.S. Private, pg. 282
MANHEIM'S GREATER ORLANDO AUTO AUCTION—See Cox Enterprises, Inc.; U.S. Private, pg. 282
MANHEIM'S OSHAWA DEALERS EXCHANGE—See Cox Enterprises, Inc.; U.S. Private, pg. 283
MANICOUAGAN POWER CO.—See Reynolds Metals Company; U.S. Public, pg. 1387
MANILA MANDARIN HOTEL INCORPORATED—See Jardine Matheson Holdings Limited; Int'l, pg. 704
THE B. MANISCHEWITZ COMPANY; U.S. Private, pg. 699
MANISCHEWITZ FOOD PRODUCTS CORP.—See The B. Manischewitz Company; U.S. Private, pg. 699
MANISTIQUE PAPERS, INC.—See Kruger Inc.; Int'l, pg. 762
MANITEC AG—See H.A. Schlatter AG; Int'l, pg. 1205
MANITEC CONSULTING AG—See H.A. Schlatter AG; Int'l, pg. 1205
MANITEX, INC.—See The Manitowoc Company, Inc.; U.S. Public, pg. 1041
MANITOBA HYDRO; Int'l, pg. 834
MANITOU BF; Int'l, pg. 834
MANITOU TOUS TERRAINS ET INDUSTRIELS—See Manitou BF; Int'l, pg. 834
THE MANITOWOC COMPANY, INC.; U.S. Public, pg. 1040
MANITOWOC DEBANKING TECHNOLOGY—See Heavy Machines, Inc.; U.S. Private, pg. 518
MANITOWOC ENGINEERING CO.—See The Manitowoc Company, Inc.; U.S. Public, pg. 1041
MANITOWOC EUROPE LTD.—See The Manitowoc Company, Inc.; U.S. Public, pg. 1041
MANITOWOC ICE, INC.—See The Manitowoc Company, Inc.; U.S. Public, pg. 1041
MANITOWOC INTERNATIONAL SALES CORP.—See The Manitowoc Company, Inc.; U.S. Public, pg. 1041
MANITOWOC RE-MANUFACTURING, INC.—See The Manitowoc Company, Inc.; U.S. Public, pg. 1041
MANITOWOC WESTERN COMPANY, INC.—See The Manitowoc Company, Inc.; U.S. Public, pg. 1041
MANKE LUMBER COMPANY, INC.; U.S. Private, pg. 699
MANN & HUMMEL FILTER TECHNOLOGY INC.—See Filterwerk Mann & Hummel GmbH; Int'l, pg. 484
MANN & HUMMEL HYDROMATION GMBH—See Filterwerk Mann & Hummel GmbH; Int'l, pg. 484
MANN & HUMMEL HYDROMATION N.V.—See Filterwerk Mann & Hummel GmbH; Int'l, pg. 484
MANN & HUMMEL KUNSTSTOFFTECHNIK GMBH & CO. KG—See Filterwerk Mann & Hummel GmbH; Int'l, pg. 484
MANN & HUMMEL PTE. LTD.—See Filterwerk Mann & Hummel GmbH; Int'l, pg. 484
MANN FILTR JIPAP S.R.O.—See Filterwerk Mann & Hummel GmbH; Int'l, pg. 484
MANN THEATRES—See Cinamerica Theatres, L.P.; U.S. Private, pg. 239
MANNA PRO CORPORATION; U.S. Private, pg. 700
MANNA PRO PARTNER L.P. (LIMITED PARTNERSHIP)—See Manna Pro Corporation; U.S. Private, pg. 700
GEOFFREY MANNERS AND CO., LTD.—See American Home Products Corporation; U.S. Public, pg. 81
MANNESMANN ADMINISTRADORA LTDA.—See Mannesmann A.G.; Int'l, pg. 839
MANNESMANN A.G.; Int'l, pg. 834
MANNESMANN AG & CO. OHG—See Mannesmann A.G.; Int'l, pg. 836
MANNESMANN ANLAGENBAU AG—See Mannesmann A.G.; Int'l, pg. 836
MANNESMANN ANLAGENBAU ARABIA LTD.—See Mannesmann A.G.; Int'l, pg. 837
MANNESMANN ANLAGENBAU BOHEMIA MORAVIA SRO—See Mannesmann A.G.; Int'l, pg. 837
MANNESMANN ANLAGENBAU HUNGARIA KFT.—See Mannesmann A.G.; Int'l, pg. 837
MANNESMANN ANLAGENBAU POLONIA SP. ZOO—See Mannesmann A.G.; Int'l, pg. 837
MANNESMANN COMERCIAL SA—See Mannesmann A.G.; Int'l, pg. 839
MANNESMANN DATENVERARBEITUNG GMBH—See Mannesmann A.G.; Int'l, pg. 837
MANNESMANN DEMAG AG—See Mannesmann A.G.; Int'l, pg. 837
MANNESMANN DEMAG CORPORATION—See Mannesmann A.G.; Int'l, pg. 837
MANNESMANN DEMAG FAHRZEUGKRANE GMBH—See Mannesmann A.G.; Int'l, pg. 837
MANNESMANN DEMAG FORDERTECHNIK AG—See Mannesmann A.G.; Int'l, pg. 837
MANNESMANN DEMAG FORDERTECHNIK KRANBAU LUISENTHAL GMBH—See Mannesmann A.G.; Int'l, pg. 837
MANNESMANN DEMAG HAMILTON LTD.—See Mannesmann A.G.; Int'l, pg. 837
MANNESMANN DEMAG KUNSTSTOFFTECHNIK—See Mannesmann A.G.; Int'l, pg. 837
MANNESMANN DEMAG LOGISTIC CONSULT GMBH—See Mannesmann A.G.; Int'l, pg. 837
MANNESMANN DEMAG LTD.—See Mannesmann A.G.; Int'l, pg. 837
MANNESMANN DEMAG LTDA.—See Mannesmann A.G.; Int'l, pg. 837
MANNESMANN DEMAG MATERIAL HANDLING LTD.—See Mannesmann A.G.; Int'l, pg. 837
MANNESMANN DEMAG MATERIALHANDTERING A/S—See Mannesmann A.G.; Int'l, pg. 837
MANNESMANN DEMAG MATERIALHANTERING AB—See Mannesmann A.G.; Int'l, pg. 837
MANNESMANN DEMAG MOVICARGA LTDA.—See Mannesmann A.G.; Int'l, pg. 837

MANNESMANN DEMAG PIC INJETORAS INDUSTRIA E COMERCIO LTDA.—See Mannesmann A.G.; Int'l, pg. 837
MANNESMANN DEMAG PLASTIC TECHNICAL SERVICES (PTY.) LTD.—See Mannesmann A.G.; Int'l, pg. 837
MANNESMANN DEMAG (PTY.) LTD.—See Mannesmann A.G.; Int'l, pg. 837
MANNESMANN DEMAG PTY. LTD.—See Mannesmann A.G.; Int'l, pg. 837
MANNESMANN DEMAG S.A.—See Mannesmann A.G.; Int'l, pg. 837
MANNESMANN DEMAG SA—See Mannesmann A.G.; Int'l, pg. 837
MANNESMANN DEMAG SPA—See Mannesmann A.G.; Int'l, pg. 837
MANNESMANN DEMAG WEAN COMPANY—See Mannesmann A.G.; Int'l, pg. 837
MANNESMANN EDELSTAHLROHR GMBH—See Mannesmann A.G.; Int'l, pg. 835
MANNESMANN ENGINEERS & CONTRACTORS LTD.—See Mannesmann A.G.; Int'l, pg. 837
MANNESMANN EUROKOM GMBH—See Mannesmann A.G.; Int'l, pg. 838
MANNESMANN FAHRZEUGTEILE GMBH—See Mannesmann A.G.; Int'l, pg. 835
MANNESMANN FI-EL FLORESTAL LTDA.—See Mannesmann A.G.; Int'l, pg. 839
MANNESMANN FINANZ AG—See Mannesmann A.G.; Int'l, pg. 840
MANNESMANN FINANZ-HOLDING SA—See Mannesmann A.G.; Int'l, pg. 840
MANNESMANN FRANCE SA—See Mannesmann A.G.; Int'l, pg. 840
MANNESMANN HANDEL AG—See Mannesmann A.G.; Int'l, pg. 838
MANNESMANN HANDEL GMBH—See Mannesmann A.G.; Int'l, pg. 838
MANNESMANN HANDEL (SEA) PTE. LTD.—See Mannesmann A.G.; Int'l, pg. 838
MANNESMANN HOESCH PRAZISROHR GMBH—See Fried. Krupp AG; Int'l, pg. 513
MANNESMANN HOLDING NEDERLAND BV—See Mannesmann A.G.; Int'l, pg. 840
MANNESMANN HOLDINGS U.K. LTD.—See Mannesmann A.G.; Int'l, pg. 840
S.A. MANNESMANN IMPORT-EXPORT SUPPLY NV—See Mannesmann A.G.; Int'l, pg. 840
MANNESMANN IMPORTACION Y EXPORTCATION SA—See Mannesmann A.G.; Int'l, pg. 838
MANNESMANN INDUSTRIES SA—See Mannesmann A.G.; Int'l, pg. 838
MANNESMANN ITALIANA SPA—See Mannesmann A.G.; Int'l, pg. 838
MANNESMANN KIENZLE AB—See Mannesmann A.G.; Int'l, pg. 839
MANNESMANN KIENZLE AUTOCOM LTD.—See Mannesmann A.G.; Int'l, pg. 839
MANNESMANN KIENZLE BETEILIGUNGS GMBH—See Mannesmann A.G.; Int'l, pg. 839
MANNESMANN KIENZLE EXPORT GMBH—See Mannesmann A.G.; Int'l, pg. 839
MANNESMANN KIENZLE INSTRUMENTS GMBH—See Mannesmann A.G.; Int'l, pg. 839
MANNESMANN KIENZLE SA—See Mannesmann A.G.; Int'l, pg. 839
MANNESMANN KRONPRINZ—See Mannesmann A.G.; Int'l, pg. 835
MANNESMANN KTI GMBH—See Mannesmann A.G.; Int'l, pg. 836
MANNESMANN LEICHTBAU GMBH—See Mannesmann A.G.; Int'l, pg. 838
MANNESMANN MARKTFORSCHUNG GMBH—See Mannesmann A.G.; Int'l, pg. 838
MANNESMANN MINERACAO LTDA.—See Mannesmann A.G.; Int'l, pg. 839
MANNESMANN MOBILFUNK GMBH—See Mannesmann A.G.; Int'l, pg. 838
MANNESMANN NEDERLAND BV—See Mannesmann A.G.; Int'l, pg. 838
MANNESMANN OILFIELD TUBULARS CORPORATION—See Mannesmann A.G.; Int'l, pg. 835
MANNESMANN PILOTENTWICKLUNGS GMBH—See Mannesmann A.G.; Int'l, pg. 838
MANNESMANN PIPE & STEEL CORP.—See Mannesmann A.G.; Int'l, pg. 838
MANNESMANN PTY. LTD.—See Mannesmann A.G.; Int'l, pg. 840
MANNESMANN REVISION GMBH—See Mannesmann A.G.; Int'l, pg. 838
MANNESMANN REXROTH GMBH—See Mannesmann A.G.; Int'l, pg. 838
MANNESMANN REXROTH GRUNDBESITZ GMBH—See Mannesmann A.G.; Int'l, pg. 838
MANNESMANN REXROTH PNEUMATIK GMBH—See Mannesmann A.G.; Int'l, pg. 838
MANNESMANN REXROTH SAIC—See Mannesmann A.G.; Int'l, pg. 839
MANNESMANN ROHREN UND STAHLHANDEL GMBH—See Mannesmann A.G.; Int'l, pg. 838
MANNESMANN SA—See Mannesmann A.G.; Int'l, pg. 839
MANNESMANN SCANGRAPHIC FRANCE SARL—See Mannesmann A.G.; Int'l, pg. 840
MANNESMANN SCANGRAPHIC GMBH—See Mannesmann A.G.; Int'l, pg. 839
MANNESMANN SEIFFERT GMBH—See Mannesmann A.G.; Int'l, pg. 836
MANNESMANN SEIFFERT INDUSTRIEANLAGEN GMBH—See Mannesmann A.G.; Int'l, pg. 836
MANNESMANN SEIFFERT SERVICE GMBH—See Mannesmann A.G.; Int'l, pg. 836
MANNESMANN STAHLFLASCHEN GMBH—See Mannesmann A.G.; Int'l, pg. 835
MANNESMANN STEEL & PIPE SDN.BHD.—See Mannesmann A.G.; Int'l, pg. 838

MANNESMANN SUMERBANK BORU ENDUSTRISI TAS—See Mannesmann A.G.; Int'l, pg. 835
MANNESMANN SUPPLIES & SERVICES LTD.—See Mannesmann A.G.; Int'l, pg. 838
MANNESMANN SVERIGE AB—See Mannesmann A.G.; Int'l, pg. 838
MANNESMANN TALLY GMBH—See Mannesmann A.G.; Int'l, pg. 839
MANNESMANN TALLY LTD.—See Mannesmann A.G.; Int'l, pg. 840
MANNESMANN TALLY SA—See Mannesmann A.G.; Int'l, pg. 840
MANNESMANN TALLY SRL—See Mannesmann A.G.; Int'l, pg. 840
MANNESMANN TRADING (FAR EAST) LTD.—See Mannesmann A.G.; Int'l, pg. 838
MANNESMANN TRADING PTY. LTD.—See Mannesmann A.G.; Int'l, pg. 838
MANNESMANN TRADING (PTY.) LTD.—See Mannesmann A.G.; Int'l, pg. 838
MANNESMANN VENEZOLANA S.A.—See Mannesmann A.G.; Int'l, pg. 838
MANNESMANN VERWALTUNG GMBH—See Mannesmann A.G.; Int'l, pg. 835
MANNESMANN WEBE GMBH—See Mannesmann A.G.; Int'l, pg. 839
MANNESMANNROHREN-WERKE AG—See Mannesmann A.G.; Int'l, pg. 835
MANNESMANNROHREN WERKE SACHSEN GMBH—See Mannesmann A.G.; Int'l, pg. 835
MANNEX (LONDON) LTD.—See Mannesmann A.G.; Int'l, pg. 838
MANNING & LEWIS ENGINEERING CO.; U.S. Private, pg. 700
MANNING EQUIPMENT, INC.; U.S. Private, pg. 700
MANNING LIGHT TRUCK EQUIPMENT—See Manning Equipment, Inc.; U.S. Private, pg. 700
MANNING TRUCK MODIFICATION—See Manning Equipment, Inc.; U.S. Private, pg. 700
MANNINGS RETAIL LIMITED—See Jardine Matheson Holdings Limited; Int'l, pg. 704
MANNINGTON CARPET—See Mannington Mills, Inc.; U.S. Private, pg. 700
MANNINGTON MILLS, INC.; U.S. Private, pg. 700
MANOIR INDUSTRIES—See Groupe Strafor Facom; Int'l, pg. 570
MANOPA MANUFACTURE NORMANDE DE PAPETERIE—See Herlitz PBS Aktiengesellschaft; Int'l, pg. 616
MANOR BAKERIES LIMITED—See Tomkins PLC; Int'l, pg. 1396
MANOR CARE, INC.; U.S. Public, pg. 1041
MANOR HEALTHCARE CORP.—See Manor Care, Inc.; U.S. Public, pg. 1041
MANOX LTD.—See Rhone-Poulenc S.A.; Int'l, pg. 1113
MANPOWER INC.; U.S. Public, pg. 1042
MANS-STEEL DIV.—See Hutchens Industries Inc.; U.S. Private, pg. 550
MANS-STEEL FOUNDRY—See Hutchens Industries Inc.; U.S. Private, pg. 550
MANSFIELD KNITWEAR LIMITED—See Coats Viyella plc; Int'l, pg. 300
MANSFIELD OIL COMPANY; U.S. Private, pg. 700
MANSION HOMES—See Cavalier Homes, Inc.; U.S. Public, pg. 318
MANSOUR GENERAL DYNAMICS LTD.—See General Dynamics Corporation; U.S. Public, pg. 709
E.L. MANSURE DIV.—See Trace International Holdings, Inc.; U.S. Private, pg. 1094
MANTECH CO., LTD.—See Abdulla Fouad Co. Ltd.; Int'l, pg. 502
MANTECH COMPUTER & EDUCATION AIDS—See Abdulla Fouad Co. Ltd.; Int'l, pg. 502
MANTEK—See NCH Corporation; U.S. Public, pg. 1145
MANTEQUERIAS ARIAS S. A.—See Bongrain S.A.; Int'l, pg. 201
MANTEX, S.A.C.A.; Int'l, pg. 840
MANTROSE BRADSHAW ZINSSER GROUP—See RPM, Inc.; U.S. Public, pg. 1358
MANUCAB LTD.—See Manulife Financial (The Manufacturers Life Insurance Company); Int'l, pg. 840
MANUFACTURAS GARGO—See Sonoco Products Company; U.S. Public, pg. 1487
MANUFACTURAS MALLORCA S.A.—See Sara Lee Corporation; U.S. Public, pg. 1434
MANUFACTURAS RODEX S.A.—See DSM N.V.; Int'l, pg. 355
MANUFACTURE FRANCAISE DES PNEUMATIQUES MICHELIN—See Compagnie Generale des Etablissements Michelin; Int'l, pg. 322
MANUFACTURE JAEGER-LECOULTRE SA—See Mannesmann A.G.; Int'l, pg. 839
MANUFACTURE LEVITON DU CANADA—See Leviton Mfg. Co., Inc.; U.S. Private, pg. 663
MANUFACTURE MAROCAINE D'ALUMINIUM—See Pechiney S.A.; Int'l, pg. 1031
MANUFACTURED HOME—See Sanderson Plumbing Products Inc.; U.S. Private, pg. 964
MANUFACTURED HOUSING DIV.—See Kit Manufacturing Company; U.S. Public, pg. 962
MANUFACTURERA THERMON DE MEXICO, S.A.—See Thermon Manufacturing Company; U.S. Private, pg. 1081
MANUFACTURERS & TRADERS TRUST COMPANY—See First Empire State Corporation; U.S. Public, pg. 631
MANUFACTURERS BANK—See The Sakura Bank, Limited; Int'l, pg. 1179
MANUFACTURERS CHEMICAL LP—See Synalloy Corporation; U.S. Public, pg. 1548
MANUFACTURERS CONSOLIDATION SERVICE, INC.; U.S. Private, pg. 700
MANUFACTURERS FOLDING CARTON, INC.—See Stone Container Corporation; U.S. Public, pg. 1521
MANUFACTURERS' JUNCTION RAILROAD COMPANY—See Broe Companies; U.S. Private, pg. 171

MANUFACTURERS' NEWS, INC.; *U.S. Private,* pg. 700
MANUFACTURERS PRODUCTS COMPANY; *U.S. Private,* pg. 701
MANUFACTURERS RAILWAY COMPANY—See Anheuser-Busch Companies, Inc.; *U.S. Public,* pg. 114
MANUFACTURERS' SERVICES LTD.; *U.S. Private,* pg. 701
MANUFACTURERS SOAP & CHEMICAL CO.—See Synalloy Corporation; *U.S. Public,* pg. 1548
MANUFACTURERS TECHNOLOGIES, INC.; *U.S. Private,* pg. 701
MANUFACTURING TECHNOLOGY LABORATORY—See Reynolds Metals Company; *U.S. Public,* pg. 1386
MANUGISTICS GROUP, INC.; *U.S. Public,* pg. 1042
MANUGISTICS INC.—See Manugistics Group, Inc.; *U.S. Public,* pg. 1042
MANULIFE BANK OF CANADA—See Manulife Financial (The Manufacturers Life Insurance Company); *Int'l,* pg. 840
MANULIFE BANK OF CANADA-REGIONAL LENDING UNIT—See Manulife Financial (The Manufacturers Life Insurance Company); *Int'l,* pg. 840
MANULIFE DATA SERVICES INC.—See Manulife Financial (The Manufacturers Life Insurance Company); *Int'l,* pg. 841
MANULIFE FINANCIAL—See Manulife Financial (The Manufacturers Life Insurance Company); *Int'l,* pg. 840
MANULIFE FINANCIAL - ANCHORAGE—See Manulife Financial (The Manufacturers Life Insurance Company); *Int'l,* pg. 840
MANULIFE FINANCIAL - BIRMINGHAM—See Manulife Financial (The Manufacturers Life Insurance Company); *Int'l,* pg. 840
MANULIFE FINANCIAL - FRESNO—See Manulife Financial (The Manufacturers Life Insurance Company); *Int'l,* pg. 840
MANULIFE FINANCIAL - LITTLE ROCK—See Manulife Financial (The Manufacturers Life Insurance Company); *Int'l,* pg. 840
MANULIFE FINANCIAL - LOS ANGELES—See Manulife Financial (The Manufacturers Life Insurance Company); *Int'l,* pg. 841
MANULIFE FINANCIAL - ORANGE COUNTY—See Manulife Financial (The Manufacturers Life Insurance Company); *Int'l,* pg. 841
MANULIFE FINANCIAL - PHOENIX—See Manulife Financial (The Manufacturers Life Insurance Company); *Int'l,* pg. 841
MANULIFE FINANCIAL - SACRAMENTO—See Manulife Financial (The Manufacturers Life Insurance Company); *Int'l,* pg. 841
MANULIFE FINANCIAL - SAN DIEGO—See Manulife Financial (The Manufacturers Life Insurance Company); *Int'l,* pg. 841
MANULIFE FINANCIAL - SAN FERNANDO VALLEY—See Manulife Financial (The Manufacturers Life Insurance Company); *Int'l,* pg. 841
MANULIFE FINANCIAL - SAN FRANCISCO—See Manulife Financial (The Manufacturers Life Insurance Company); *Int'l,* pg. 841
MANULIFE FINANCIAL - SAN MATEO—See Manulife Financial (The Manufacturers Life Insurance Company); *Int'l,* pg. 841
MANULIFE FINANCIAL (THE MANUFACTURERS LIFE INSURANCE COMPANY); *Int'l,* pg. 840
MANULIFE INTERNATIONAL INVESTMENT OFFICE—See Manulife Financial (The Manufacturers Life Insurance Company); *Int'l,* pg. 841
MANUS (GREAT BRITAIN) LTD.—See Tetra Laval Group; *Int'l,* pg. 1380
MANUS PRESSE GMBH—See Georg von Holtzbrinck GmbH; *Int'l,* pg. 1478
MANUS PRESSE GMBH GRAPHIK INTERNATIONAL GMBH—See Georg von Holtzbrinck GmbH; *Int'l,* pg. 1478
MANVILLE CANADA INC.—See Johns Manville Corporation; *U.S. Public,* pg. 927
MANVILLE DO BRASIL—See Johns Manville Corporation; *U.S. Public,* pg. 927
MANVILLE GREAT BRITAIN LTD. (BRISTOL)—See Johns Manville Corporation; *U.S. Public,* pg. 927
MANVILLE JAPAN LTD.—See Johns Manville Corporation; *U.S. Public,* pg. 927
MANVILLE MEXICANA S.A. DE C.V.—See Johns Manville Corporation; *U.S. Public,* pg. 927
MANVILLE SALES CORPORATION—See Johns Manville Corporation; *U.S. Public,* pg. 927
MANX TELECOM LIMITED—See British Telecommunications plc; *Int'l,* pg. 223
MAP HOLDING—See Corporacion MAPFRE, Compania Internacional de Reaseguros, S.A.; *Int'l,* pg. 333
MAP SECURITIES LTD.—See Corporacion MAPFRE, Compania Internacional de Reaseguros, S.A.; *Int'l,* pg. 335
MAPA—See Total S.A.; *Int'l,* pg. 1409
MAPA PIONEER CORPORATION—See Total S.A.; *Int'l,* pg. 1409
MAPCO COAL INC.—See Mapco Inc.; *U.S. Public,* pg. 1042
MAPCO INC.; *U.S. Public,* pg. 1042
MAPCO NATURAL GAS LIQUIDS INC.—See Mapco Inc.; *U.S. Public,* pg. 1042
MAPCO PETROLEUM INC.—See Mapco Inc.; *U.S. Public,* pg. 1042
MAPELLI BROTHERS COMPANY—See ConAgra, Inc.; *U.S. Public,* pg. 427
MAPFRE ACONCAGUA CIA. DE SEGUROS, S.A.—See Corporacion MAPFRE, Compania Internacional de Reaseguros, S.A.; *Int'l,* pg. 333
MAPFRE ARGENTINA S.A.—See Corporacion MAPFRE, Compania Internacional de Reaseguros, S.A.; *Int'l,* pg. 333

MAPFRE ASISTENCIA CIA. INTERNACIONAL DE SEGUROS Y REASEGUROS, S.A.—See Corporacion MAPFRE, Compania Internacional de Reaseguros, S.A.; *Int'l,* pg. 334
MAPFRE BALEAR, CIA. DE SEGUROS GENERALES Y DE REASEGUROS—See Corporacion MAPFRE, Compania Internacional de Reaseguros, S.A.; *Int'l,* pg. 333
MAPFRE CAUCION Y CREDITO CIA INTERNACIONAL DE SEGUROS Y REASEGUROS, S.A.—See Corporacion MAPFRE, Compania Internacional de Reaseguros, S.A.; *Int'l,* pg. 335
MAPFRE CHILE REASEGUROS, S.A.—See Corporacion MAPFRE, Compania Internacional de Reaseguros, S.A.; *Int'l,* pg. 334
MAPFRE CHILE SEGUROS, S.A.—See Corporacion MAPFRE, Compania Internacional de Reaseguros, S.A.; *Int'l,* pg. 333
MAPFRE CONSULTORES DE SEGUROS Y REASEGUROS, S.A.—See Corporacion MAPFRE, Compania Internacional de Reaseguros, S.A.; *Int'l,* pg. 333
MAPFRE CORPORATION OF FLORIDA—See Corporacion MAPFRE, Compania Internacional de Reaseguros, S.A.; *Int'l,* pg. 333
MAPFRE DO BRASIL CONSULTORIA E SERVICIOS, LTDA.—See Corporacion MAPFRE, Compania Internacional de Reaseguros, S.A.; *Int'l,* pg. 333
MAPFRE ECUADOR, S.A.—See Corporacion MAPFRE, Compania Internacional de Reaseguros, S.A.; *Int'l,* pg. 333
MAPFRE FACTORING E.F., S.A.—See Corporacion MAPFRE, Compania Internacional de Reaseguros, S.A.; *Int'l,* pg. 332
MAPFRE FINANZAS ENTIDAD DE FINANCIACION, S.A.—See Corporacion MAPFRE, Compania Internacional de Reaseguros, S.A.; *Int'l,* pg. 332
MAPFRE GUANARTEME CIA. DE SEGUROS GENERALES Y REASEGUROS DE CANARIAS, S.A.—See Corporacion MAPFRE, Compania Internacional de Reaseguros, S.A.; *Int'l,* pg. 333
MAPFRE HIPOTECARIA S.C.H., S.A.—See Corporacion MAPFRE, Compania Internacional de Reaseguros, S.A.; *Int'l,* pg. 332
MAPFRE INDUSTRIAL, S.A. DE SEGUROS—See Corporacion MAPFRE, Compania Internacional de Reaseguros, S.A.; *Int'l,* pg. 333
MAPFRE INMUEBLES, S.A.—See Corporacion MAPFRE, Compania Internacional de Reaseguros, S.A.; *Int'l,* pg. 334
MAPFRE INSURANCE COMPANY OF AMERICA, INC.—See Corporacion MAPFRE, Compania Internacional de Reaseguros, S.A.; *Int'l,* pg. 333
MAPFRE INTERNATIONAL S.A.—See Corporacion MAPFRE, Compania Internacional de Reaseguros, S.A.; *Int'l,* pg. 333
MAPFRE INVERSION S.V.—See Corporacion MAPFRE, Compania Internacional de Reaseguros, S.A.; *Int'l,* pg. 334
MAPFRE INVERSION 2, SOC. GESTORA DE INSTITUCIONES DE INVERSION COLECTIVA—See Corporacion MAPFRE, Compania Internacional de Reaseguros, S.A.; *Int'l,* pg. 334
MAPFRE LEASING S.A.—See Corporacion MAPFRE, Compania Internacional de Reaseguros, S.A.; *Int'l,* pg. 332
MAPFRE LONDON LTD.—See Corporacion MAPFRE, Compania Internacional de Reaseguros, S.A.; *Int'l,* pg. 335
MAPFRE PARAGUAY CIA DE SEGUROS, S.A.—See Corporacion MAPFRE, Compania Internacional de Reaseguros, S.A.; *Int'l,* pg. 333
MAPFRE PROGRESS, S.P.A.—See Corporacion MAPFRE, Compania Internacional de Reaseguros, S.A.; *Int'l,* pg. 333
MAPFRE RE CIA REASEGUROS, S.A.—See Corporacion MAPFRE, Compania Internacional de Reaseguros, S.A.; *Int'l,* pg. 334
MAPFRE RE MANAGEMENT SERVICES U.K. COMPANY LIMITED—See Corporacion MAPFRE, Compania Internacional de Reaseguros, S.A.; *Int'l,* pg. 335
MAPFRE SEGUROS GENERALES CIA. DE SEGUROS Y REASEGUROS, S.A.—See Corporacion MAPFRE, Compania Internacional de Reaseguros, S.A.; *Int'l,* pg. 332
MAPFRE SERVICIOS DE CAUCION, S.A.—See Corporacion MAPFRE, Compania Internacional de Reaseguros, S.A.; *Int'l,* pg. 335
MAPFRE SERVICIOS INFORMATICA, S.A.—See Corporacion MAPFRE, Compania Internacional de Reaseguros, S.A.; *Int'l,* pg. 333
MAPFRE SERVICIOS MARITIMOS, COMISARIADO Y LIQUIDACION DE AVERIAS—See Corporacion MAPFRE, Compania Internacional de Reaseguros, S.A.; *Int'l,* pg. 333
MAPFRE SOFT AMERICA, S.A.—See Corporacion MAPFRE, Compania Internacional de Reaseguros, S.A.; *Int'l,* pg. 335
MAPFRE SOFT ARGENTINA S.A.—See Corporacion MAPFRE, Compania Internacional de Reaseguros, S.A.; *Int'l,* pg. 335
MAPFRE SOFT, S.A.—See Corporacion MAPFRE, Compania Internacional de Reaseguros, S.A.; *Int'l,* pg. 335
MAPFRE VIDA PENSIONES ENTIDAD GESTORA DE FONDOS DE PENSIONES, S.A.—See Corporacion MAPFRE, Compania Internacional de Reaseguros, S.A.; *Int'l,* pg. 334
MAPFRE VIDA, S.A. DE SEGUROS Y REASEGUROS SOBRE LA VIDA HUMANA—See Corporacion MAPFRE, Compania Internacional de Reaseguros, S.A.; *Int'l,* pg. 334
MAPFRE VIDEO Y COMUNICAION, S.A.—See Corporacion MAPFRE, Compania Internacional de Reaseguros, S.A.; *Int'l,* pg. 334

MAPINFO CORP.; *U.S. Public,* pg. 1042
MAPLE LEAF FOODS INC.; *Int'l,* pg. 841
MAPLE LEAF MEATS—See Maple Leaf Foods Inc.; *Int'l,* pg. 841
MAPLEHURST FARMS, INC.—See Dean Foods Company; *U.S. Public,* pg. 490
MAPLUX REINSURANCE COMPANY LTD.—See Corporacion MAPFRE, Compania Internacional de Reaseguros, S.A.; *Int'l,* pg. 335
MAPPINS JEWELERS—See Peoples Jewellers Corporation; *Int'l,* pg. 1036
MAPTEL, S.A.—See Telefonica de Espana, S.A.; *Int'l,* pg. 1372
MAQUILADORA GENERAL DE MATAMOROS, S.A. DE C.V.—See Rohm and Haas Company; *U.S. Public,* pg. 1403
MAQUINARIA ARTES GRAFICAS HARTMANN SA—See N.V. Koninklijke KNP BT; *Int'l,* pg. 757
MAQUINAS Y HERRAMIENTAS BLACK & DECKER DE CHILE S.A.—See The Black & Decker Corporation; *U.S. Public,* pg. 234
MAR-HYDE CORPORATION—See RPM, Inc.; *U.S. Public,* pg. 1357
MAR-JAC POULTRY INC.; *U.S. Private,* pg. 701
MAR-MAC MANUFACTURING COMPANY, INC.; *U.S. Private,* pg. 701
MARADYNE CORPORATION—See Dreison International, Inc.; *U.S. Private,* pg. 342
MARAND D.O.O.—See Borland International, Inc.; *U.S. Public,* pg. 246
MARANTZ JAPAN INC.; *Int'l,* pg. 841
MARATHON ASHLAND PETROLEUM LLC—See Ashland, Inc.; *U.S. Public,* pg. 139
MARATHON ASHLAND PETROLEUM LLC—See USX Corporation; *U.S. Public,* pg. 1662
MARATHON ASHLAND PETROLEUM LLC RETAIN MARKETING—See USX Corporation; *U.S. Public,* pg. 1662
MARATHON ASHLAND PILE LINE LLC—See USX Corporation; *U.S. Public,* pg. 1662
MARATHON CHEESE CORP.; *U.S. Private,* pg. 701
MARATHON ELECTRIC, LIMA—See Regal-Beloit Corporation; *U.S. Public,* pg. 1371
MARATHON ELECTRIC MANUFACTURING CORP.—See Regal-Beloit Corporation; *U.S. Public,* pg. 1371
MARATHON EQUIPMENT COMPANY—See Dover Corporation; *U.S. Public,* pg. 521
MARATHON INTERNATIONAL PETROLEUM SUPPLY COMPANY—See USX Corporation; *U.S. Public,* pg. 1662
MARATHON MONITORS INCORPORATED—See Halma p.l.c.; *Int'l,* pg. 590
MARATHON OIL COMPANY—See USX Corporation; *U.S. Public,* pg. 1661
MARATHON SPECIAL PRODS.—See Regal-Beloit Corporation; *U.S. Public,* pg. 1371
MARAVEN, S.A.—See Petroleos de Venezuela S.A.; *Int'l,* pg. 1045
THE MARBLE COMPANY—See Blevins Inc.; *U.S. Private,* pg. 149
MARBLEHEAD ENERGY CORP.—See Eaton Vance Corp.; *U.S. Public,* pg. 559
MARBLEHEAD LIME CO.—See General Dynamics Corporation; *U.S. Public,* pg. 709
MARC; *U.S. Private,* pg. 701
MARC DIRECT—See MARC; *U.S. Private,* pg. 701
MARC PLAZA CORP.—See The Marcus Corporation; *U.S. Public,* pg. 1044
MARC PROMOTION—See MARC; *U.S. Private,* pg. 701
MARC PUBLIC RELATIONS—See MARC; *U.S. Private,* pg. 701
MARCAL PAPER MILLS, INC.; *U.S. Private,* pg. 701
MARCAM ARGENTINA S.A.—See Marcam Solutions, Inc.; *U.S. Public,* pg. 1043
MARCAM ASIA-PACIFIC PTE., LTD—See Marcam Solutions, Inc.; *U.S. Public,* pg. 1043
MARCAM AUSTRALIA PTY., LTD.—See Marcam Solutions, Inc.; *U.S. Public,* pg. 1043
MARCAM BELGIUM N.V.—See Marcam Solutions, Inc.; *U.S. Public,* pg. 1043
MARCAM CANADA—See Marcam Solutions, Inc.; *U.S. Public,* pg. 1043
MARCAM DO BRASIL—See Marcam Solutions, Inc.; *U.S. Public,* pg. 1043
MARCAM EUROPE, MIDDLE EAST & AFICA S.R.L.—See Marcam Solutions, Inc.; *U.S. Public,* pg. 1043
MARCAM EUROPEAN SUPPORT CENTRE, BV—See Marcam Solutions, Inc.; *U.S. Public,* pg. 1043
MARCAM FRANCE—See Marcam Solutions, Inc.; *U.S. Public,* pg. 1043
MARCAM GERMANY GMBH—See Marcam Solutions, Inc.; *U.S. Public,* pg. 1043
MARCAM NEDERLAND B.V.—See Marcam Solutions, Inc.; *U.S. Public,* pg. 1043
MARCAM SOLUTIONS, INC.; *U.S. Public,* pg. 1042
MARCAM SOUTHERN AFRICA—See Marcam Solutions, Inc.; *U.S. Public,* pg. 1043
MARCAM SPAIN—See Marcam Solutions, Inc.; *U.S. Public,* pg. 1043
MARCAM U.A.E.—See Marcam Solutions, Inc.; *U.S. Public,* pg. 1043
MARCARD STEIN & CO.—See Compagnie de Suez; *Int'l,* pg. 315
MARCEGAGLIA SPA; *Int'l,* pg. 841
MARCH CORREDURIA DE SEGUROS S.A.—See Banca March S.A.; *Int'l,* pg. 136
MARCH MANUFACTURING INC.; *U.S. Private,* pg. 702
MARCHON ESPANOLA S.A.—See Tenneco Inc.; *U.S. Public,* pg. 1580
MARCHON EYEWEAR; *U.S. Private,* pg. 702
MARCHON FRANCE S.A.—See Tenneco Inc.; *U.S. Public,* pg. 1580
MARCHON HELLAS LIMITED—See Tenneco Inc.; *U.S. Public,* pg. 1580

MASTER INDEX TO COMPANY NAMES MARKS

Company Index

MARCHON ITALIANA S.P.A.—See Tenneco Inc.; *U.S. Public*, pg. 1580
MARCHON TOYS, LTD.—See Empire of Carolina, Inc.; *U.S. Public*, pg. 579
MARCLIN WESTEEL DIVISION—See Jannock Limited; *Int'l*, *pg. 698*
MARCO COLOR LABS, INC.; *U.S. Private*, pg. 702
MARCO DEL PONT S.A.; *Int'l*, pg. 842
MARCO ISLAND EAGLE—See The New York Times Company; *U.S. Public*, pg. 1175
MARCO SALES CO.—See George Koch Sons, Inc.; *U.S. Private*, pg. 628
MARCO SEATTLE, INC.—See Marine Construction & Design Co.; *U.S. Private*, pg. 703
MARCON ELECTRONICS CO., LTD.—See Toshiba Corporation; *Int'l*, pg. 1403
MARCON SHIPPING/A.N. DERINGER—See A.N. Deringer, Inc.; *U.S. Private*, pg. 326
MARCONI AUTOMAZIONE S.P.A.—See The General Electric Company, p.l.c.; *Int'l*, pg. 546
MARCONI DEFENCE SYSTEMS LTD.—See The General Electric Company, p.l.c.; *Int'l*, pg. 544
MARCONI ELECTRONIC SYSTEMS LTD.—See The General Electric Company, p.l.c.; *Int'l*, pg. 544
MARCONI INSTRUMENTS LTD.—See The General Electric Company, p.l.c.; *Int'l*, pg. 544
MARCONI RADAR & CONTROL SYSTEMS LTD.—See The General Electric Company, p.l.c.; *Int'l*, pg. 544
MARCONI S.P.A.—See The General Electric Company, p.l.c.; *Int'l*, pg. 546
MARCONI SPACE SYSTEMS PARTICIPATIONS BV—See Lagardere Groupe; *Int'l*, pg. 796
MARCONI UNDERWATER SYSTEMS LTD.—See The General Electric Company, p.l.c.; *Int'l*, pg. 544
MARCOR DEVELOPMENT CO.—See Rio Hotel & Casino Inc.; *U.S. Public*, pg. 1390
MARCOR RESORT PROPERTIES, INC.—See Rio Hotel & Casino Inc.; *U.S. Public*, pg. 1390
MARCOULE PLANT—See COGEMA - Compagnie Generale des Matieres Nucleaires; *Int'l*, pg. 305
MARCUS BROTHERS TEXTILES, INC.; *U.S. Private*, pg. 702
MARCUS CABLE COMPANY, L.P.; *U.S. Private*, pg. 702
THE MARCUS CORPORATION; *U.S. Public*, pg. 1044
MARCUS HOTEL CORP.—See The Marcus Corporation; *U.S. Public*, pg. 1044
MARCUS RESTAURANTS INC.—See The Marcus Corporation; *U.S. Public*, pg. 1044
MARCUS SUMMERS STRUCTURAL GLAZING LTD.—See Saint-Gobain; *Int'l*, pg. 1173
MARCUS THEATRES CORP.—See The Marcus Corporation; *U.S. Public*, pg. 1044
MARCUSAN AB—See LVMH Moet Hennessy Louis Vuitton; *Int'l*, pg. 783
MARCY FITNESS PRODUCTS, INC.—See Escalade Sports; *U.S. Public*, pg. 591
MARDAKLEVS INDUSTRI AB—See ACTIVE BioTech AB; *Int'l*, pg. 23
MARDEC-YOKOHAMA FERTLIZER CORP. SDN. BHD.—See The Yokohama Rubber Co., Ltd.; *Int'l*, pg. 1521
MARDEV—See Reed Elsevier plc; *Int'l*, pg. 1094
MARDEV-AUSTRALIA—See Reed Elsevier plc; *Int'l*, pg. 1094
MARDEVCO CREDIT CORP.—See Standard Motor Products Inc.; *U.S. Public*, pg. 1503
MAREB TRADING & DEVELOPMENT CORPORATION—See Telefonaktiebolaget LM Ericsson; *Int'l*, pg. 1369
MARELLI AUTRONICA S.P.A.—See Fiat Auto SpA; *Int'l*, pg. 482
MARESI HUNGARIA KFT.—See Maresi Markenartikelvertrieb Aktiengesellschaft; *Int'l*, pg. 842
MARESI MARKENARTIKELVERTRIEB AKTIENGESELLSCHAFT; *Int'l*, pg. 842
MAREST—See Groupe Casino; *Int'l*, pg. 563
MARGA B.V.—See Unilever Plc; *Int'l*, pg. 1438
MARGARINBOLAGET AB—See Unilever Plc; *Int'l*, pg. 1439
MARGEOTES/FERTITTA & PARTNERS INC.; *U.S. Private*, *pg. 702*
MARGEOTES INTERACTIVE—See Margeotes/Fertitta & Partners Inc.; *U.S. Private*, pg. 702
MARGETTS FOODS LIMITED—See Kerry Group PLC; *Int'l*, *pg. 732*
MARGLEN INDUSTRIES; *U.S. Private*, pg. 702
MARGLEN YARN PLANT—See Marglen Industries; *U.S. Private*, pg. 702
MARIANA PROPERTIES, INC.—See Cigna Corp.; *U.S. Public*, pg. 365
MARIE BRIZARD WINES & SPIRITS USA; *U.S. Private*, pg. 702
MARIE CLAIRE—See The Hearst Corporation; *U.S. Private*, *pg. 518*
MARIE ELISABETH PRODUTOS ALIMENTARES S.A.—See H.J. Heinz Company; *U.S. Public*, pg. 807
MARIENPLATZ GROBGARAGE GMBH—See Bayerische Vereinsbank Group; *Int'l*, pg. 180
MARIETTA CANADA, INC.—See Marietta Corporation; *U.S. Private*, pg. 703
MARIETTA CORPORATION; *U.S. Private*, pg. 702
MARIETTA, INC.—See Marietta Corporation; *U.S. Private*, pg. 703
MARIFARMS, INC.—See Hanson PLC; *Int'l*, pg. 593
MARIGOLD FOODS, INC.—See Koninklijke BolsWessanen nv; *Int'l*, pg. 752
MARIGOLD GLOVE DIVISION—See London International Group plc; *Int'l*, pg. 815
MARIGOLD MINING COMPANY—See Rayrock Yellowknife Resources Inc.; *Int'l*, pg. 1089
MARINA BAY HOTEL PRIVATE LIMITED—See Jardine Matheson Holdings Limited; *Int'l*, pg. 704
MARINCO/AFI—See Valley Forge Corporation; *U.S. Public*, *pg. 1705*
MARINE AIR SYSTEMS, INC.—See Taylor Made Group, Inc.; *U.S. Private*, pg. 1071
MARINE & INDUSTRIAL ENGINES & SERVICE DIV.—See General Electric Company; *U.S. Public*, pg. 710
MARINE & INDUSTRIAL PRODUCTS DIV.—See Chrysler Corporation; *U.S. Public*, pg. 353
MARINE CONSTRUCTION & DESIGN CO.; *U.S. Private*, pg. 703
THE MARINE CONTAINER INSURANCE CO. LTD.—See Sea Containers Ltd.; *Int'l*, pg. 1213
MARINE DRILLING COMPANIES, INC.; *U.S. Public*, pg. 1044
MARINE EXHIBITION CORPORATION—See Wometco Enterprises, Inc.; *U.S. Private*, pg. 1186
MARINE HARVEST MCCONNELL—See Booker PLC; *Int'l*, pg. 202
MARINE INDUSTRIE S.N.C.—See Freudenberg & Company; *Int'l*, pg. 506
MARINE MIDLAND BUSINESS LOANS, INC.—See HSBC Holdings plc; *Int'l*, pg. 581
MARINE MIDLAND LEASING CORPORATION—See HSBC Holdings plc; *Int'l*, pg. 581
MARINE MIDLAND MORTGAGE (USA), INC.—See HSBC Holdings plc; *Int'l*, pg. 581
MARINE MIDLAND REALTY CREDIT CORPORATION—See HSBC Holdings plc; *Int'l*, pg. 581
MARINE MIDLAND SECURITIES, INC.—See HSBC Holdings plc; *Int'l*, pg. 581
MARINE PORT TERMINALS INC.—See Koninklijke Van Ommeren NV; *Int'l*, pg. 758
MARINE SAFETY ROTTERDAM B.V.—See Berkshire Hathaway Inc.; *U.S. Public*, pg. 219
MARINE SYSTEMS, INC.—See Kirby Corporation; *U.S. Public*, pg. 961
MARINE SYSTEMS, INC.-EAST COAST—See Kirby Corporation; *U.S. Public*, pg. 961
MARINE SYSTEMS, INC.-GULF COAST—See Kirby Corporation; *U.S. Public*, pg. 961
MARINE TRANSPORT LINES, INC.; *U.S. Private*, pg. 703
MARINE TRANSPORTATION—See Oglebay Norton Company; *U.S. Public*, pg. 1213
MARINE TRAVELIFT, INC.; *U.S. Private*, pg. 703
MARINE UNDERWRITING AGENCIES (NZ) LTD. (CORNHILL)—See Allianz Aktiengesellschaft; *Int'l*, pg. 60
MARINE WORLD AFRICA USA; *U.S. Private*, pg. 703
MARINELLO SCHOOLS OF BEAUTY—See Scope Industries; *U.S. Public*, pg. 1444
MARINER NEWSPAPERS, INC.—See Gannett Company, Inc.; *U.S. Public*, pg. 701
MARINESAFETY INTERNATIONAL—See Berkshire Hathaway Inc.; *U.S. Public*, pg. 218
MARINETTE MARINE CORPORATION; *U.S. Private*, pg. 703
MARINTES D.O.O. LTD.—See The Macneal-Schwendler Corp.; *U.S. Public*, pg. 1032
MARION MACHINE COMPANY DIVISION—See Superior Machine Company Of South Carolina, Inc.; *U.S. Private*, pg. 1055
MARION MANUFACTURING—See Dreison International, Inc.; *U.S. Private*, pg. 342
MARION 100, INC.—See Marsh Company; *U.S. Private*, pg. 708
MARISA CHRISTINA INC.; *U.S. Public*, pg. 1044
MARISO BULLE S.A.—See Liebherr-International AG; *Int'l*, pg. 808
OY MARITIM AB—See Orkla A.S.A.; *Int'l*, pg. 1011
MARITIMA SERVICES—See Internatio-Muller N.V.; *Int'l*, pg. 682
MARITIME BROADCASTING SYSTEM LTD.; *Int'l*, pg. 842
MARITIME GENERAL INSURANCE COMPANY LIMITED—See Cigna Corp.; *U.S. Public*, pg. 364
MARITIME LEISURE CORPORATION—See Accor S.A.; *Int'l*, pg. 21
MARITIME LIFE ASSURANCE CO.—See John Hancock Mutual Life Insurance Company; *U.S. Private*, pg. 590
MARITIME PROTECTION A/S—See Monsanto Company; *U.S. Public*, pg. 1125
MARITIME TELEGRAPH & TELEPHONE COMPANY, LTD.—See BCE Inc.; *Int'l*, pg. 116
MARITREND, INC.—See Vectura Group, Inc.; *U.S. Private*, pg. 1135
MARITZ CANADA INC.—See Maritz Inc.; *U.S. Private*, pg. 704
MARITZ DE MEXICO S.A. DE C.V.—See Maritz Inc.; *U.S. Private*, pg. 704
MARITZ ESPANA S.A. (SPAIN)—See Maritz Inc.; *U.S. Private*, pg. 704
MARITZ EUROPA LIMITED—See Maritz Inc.; *U.S. Private*, pg. 704
MARITZ GMBH (GERMANY)—See Maritz Inc.; *U.S. Private*, *pg. 704*
MARITZ INC.; *U.S. Private*, pg. 703
MARITZ LTD. (BRITAIN)—See Maritz Inc.; *U.S. Private*, pg. 704
MARITZ MARKETING RESEARCH, INC.—See Maritz Inc.; *U.S. Private*, pg. 704
MARITZ PERFORMANCE IMPROVEMENT COMPANY—See Maritz Inc.; *U.S. Private*, pg. 704
MARITZ TRAVEL CO.—See Maritz Inc.; *U.S. Private*, pg. 704
MARK ANDY, INC.—See Dover Corporation; *U.S. Public*, pg. 521
MARK ANTENNA PRODUCTS, INC.—See COMSAT Corporation; *U.S. Public*, pg. 424
MARK CHEVROLET INC.; *U.S. Private*, pg. 704
MARK FABRICKS, INC.; *U.S. Private*, pg. 704
MARK IV AUTOMOTIVE—See Mark IV Industries Inc.; *U.S. Public*, pg. 1045
MARK IV AUTOMOTIVE CANADA INC.—See Mark IV Industries Inc.; *U.S. Public*, pg. 1045
MARK IV INDUSTRIAL—See Mark IV Industries Inc.; *U.S. Public*, pg. 1045
MARK IV INDUSTRIES INC.; *U.S. Public*, pg. 1044
MARK IV INSTRUMENTS LTD.—See Danaher Corporation; *U.S. Public*, pg. 482
MARK IV IVHS—See Mark IV Industries Inc.; *U.S. Public*, pg. 1045
MARK LIGHTING FIXTURE CO., INC.; *U.S. Private*, pg. 704
MARK NET WORLD—See BVK/McDonald; *U.S. Private*, pg. 108
MARK I MOLDED PLASTICS, INC.—See Excel Industries, Inc.; *U.S. Public*, pg. 599
MARK I MOLDED PLASTICS OF TENNESSEE, INC.—See Excel Industries, Inc.; *U.S. Public*, pg. 599
MARK PRODUCTS—See Shaw Industries Ltd.; *Int'l*, pg. 1231
MARK RESOURCES INC.; *Int'l*, pg. 842
MARK RISK MANAGEMENT, INC.—See Mark VII, Inc.; *U.S. Public*, pg. 1046
MARK VII, INC.; *U.S. Public*, pg. 1046
MARK VII TRANSPORTATION COMPANY, INC.—See Mark VII, Inc.; *U.S. Public*, pg. 1046
MARK VII TRANSPORTATION SOLUTIONS, INC.—See Mark VII, Inc.; *U.S. Public*, pg. 1046
MARK S.R.L.—See Tetra Laval Group; *Int'l*, pg. 1378
MARK III INDUSTRIES; *U.S. Private*, pg. 704
MARKANTSTAHL GMBH—See Arbed S.A.; *Int'l*, pg. 79
K/S MARKEDET HAUGESUND—See Aker Raj Asa; *Int'l*, pg. 41
MARKEL AMERICAN INSURANCE CO.—See Markel Corporation; *U.S. Public*, pg. 1046
MARKEL CORPORATION; *U.S. Public*, pg. 1046
MARKEL INSURANCE CO.—See Markel Corporation; *U.S. Public*, pg. 1046
MARKEL INSURANCE COMPANY—See Markel Corporation; *U.S. Public*, pg. 1046
MARKEL SERVICE, INC.—See Markel Corporation; *U.S. Public*, pg. 1046
MARKEM CORPORATION; *U.S. Private*, pg. 704
MARKET ACCESS LIMITED—See Omnicom Group Inc.; *U.S. Public*, pg. 1225
MARKET DATA RETRIEVAL—See The Dun & Bradstreet Corporation; *U.S. Public*, pg. 536
MARKET DEVELOPMENT CO.—See Spartan Stores Inc.; *U.S. Private*, pg. 1021
MARKET DEVELOPMENT INC.—See Associated Food Stores Inc.; *U.S. Private*, pg. 90
MARKET DIRECT—See St. Ives plc; *Int'l*, pg. 1177
MARKET ENTRY OMEGA—See Omega Environmental Inc.; *U.S. Public*, pg. 1222
MARKET FACTS, INC.; *U.S. Public*, pg. 1046
MARKET FACTS, INC.—See Market Facts, Inc.; *U.S. Public*, pg. 1047
MARKET FACTS OF CANADA, LTD.—See Market Facts, Inc.; *U.S. Public*, pg. 1047
MARKET GROWTH RESOURCES, INC.—See True North Communications Inc.; *U.S. Public*, pg. 1641
MARKET INFORMATION CORPORATION (BMI)—See Data Broadcasting Corporation; *U.S. Public*, pg. 484
MARKET LINK—See TBWA Chiat/Day; *U.S. Private*, pg. 1062
MARKET PLACE PRINT, INC.—See MARC; *U.S. Private*, pg. 701
MARKET SWEDEN—See Trelleborg AB; *Int'l*, pg. 1422
MARKETDYNE INTERNATIONAL, INC.—See Cigna Corp.; *U.S. Public*, pg. 366
MARKETFORCE ADVERTISING PHILIPPINES INC.—See Dentsu Young & Rubicam Partnerships; *U.S. Private*, pg. 325
MARKETFORCE (UK) LIMITED—See IPC Magazines Limited; *Int'l*, pg. 651
MARKETING AND CUSTOMER OPERATIONS—See Xerox Corporation; *U.S. Public*, pg. 1784
MARKETING AND MERCHANDISING HOLDING—See GIB Group; *Int'l*, pg. 533
MARKETING & PROJECT DEVELOPMENT—See Zurn Industries, Inc.; *U.S. Public*, pg. 1794
MARKETING COMMUNICATIONS—See Harte-Hanks Communications, Inc.; *U.S. Public*, pg. 794
MARKETING COMPUTERS—See VNU Verenigde Nederlandse Uitgeversbedrijven B.V.; *Int'l*, pg. 1446
MARKETING CORP. OF AMERICA; *U.S. Private*, pg. 704
MARKETING DISPLAYS INTERNATIONAL; *U.S. Private*, pg. 705
MARKETING RESOURCES PLUS—See VNU Verenigde Nederlandse Uitgeversbedrijven B.V.; *Int'l*, pg. 1447
MARKETING SUPPORT, INCORPORATED; *U.S. Private*, pg. 705
THE MARKETPLACE CAFE—See Ark Restaurants Corp.; *U.S. Public*, pg. 130
MARKETPULSE—See Computer Corporation of America; *U.S. Private*, pg. 260
MARKETSOURCE CORPORATION; *U.S. Private*, pg. 705
MARKETSOURCE CORPORATION—See MarketSource Corporation; *U.S. Private*, pg. 705
MARKGRAAF—See Vendex International N.V.; *Int'l*, pg. 1463
MARKHAM VINEYARDS—See Mercian Corporation; *Int'l*, pg. 858
MARKHON INDUSTRIES, INC—See Kennedy Manufacturing Company; *U.S. Private*, pg. 614
MARKIN TUBING, INC.; *U.S. Private*, pg. 705
MARKISCHE ENERGIEVERSORGUNG AG—See Veba AG; *Int'l*, pg. 1456
MARKLIN AG—See Electrolux, AB; *Int'l*, pg. 443
MARKOM/LEO BURNETT A.S.—See Leo Burnett Company, Inc.; *U.S. Private*, pg. 186
MARKS & MORGAN JEWELERS INC; *U.S. Private*, pg. 705
S.A. MARKS AND SPENCER BELGIUM N.V.—See Marks & Spencer PLC; *Int'l*, pg. 843
MARKS & SPENCER CANADA INC.—See Marks & Spencer PLC; *Int'l*, pg. 843
MARKS & SPENCER EXPORT CORPORATION LIMITED—See Marks & Spencer PLC; *Int'l*, pg. 842
MARKS & SPENCER FINANCE INC.—See Marks & Spencer PLC; *Int'l*, pg. 843

MARKS & SPENCER FINANCE PLC—See Marks & Spencer PLC; *Int'l*, pg. 842
MARKS & SPENCER FINANCIAL SERVICES LIMITED—See Marks & Spencer PLC; *Int'l*, pg. 842
MARKS & SPENCER (FRANCE) S.A.—See Marks & Spencer PLC; *Int'l*, pg. 843
MARKS & SPENCER HOLDINGS CANADA INC.—See Marks & Spencer PLC; *Int'l*, pg. 843
MARKS & SPENCER (IRELAND) LIMITED—See Marks & Spencer PLC; *Int'l*, pg. 843
MARKS & SPENCER PLC; *Int'l*, pg. 842
MARKS & SPENCER PROPERTY DEVELOPMENTS LIMITED—See Marks & Spencer PLC; *Int'l*, pg. 842
MARKS & SPENCER PROPERTY HOLDINGS LIMITED—See Marks & Spencer PLC; *Int'l*, pg. 842
MARKS & SPENCER RETAIL FINANCIAL SERVICES HOLDINGS LIMITED—See Marks & Spencer PLC; *Int'l*, pg. 842
MARKS & SPENCER SERVICES INC.—See Marks & Spencer PLC; *Int'l*, pg. 843
MARKS & SPENCER UNIT TRUST MANAGEMENT LIMITED—See Marks & Spencer PLC; *Int'l*, pg. 843
MARKS & SPENCER US HOLDINGS INC.—See Marks & Spencer PLC; *Int'l*, pg. 843
MARKS TRANSFER & STORAGE—See The Fabri-Form Company; *U.S. Private*, pg. 390
MARLBOROUGH CAPITAL ADVISORS, INC.—See Metropolitan Life Insurance Co.; *U.S. Private*, pg. 737
MARLETTE HOMES, INC.—See Schult Homes Corporation; *U.S. Public*, pg. 1442
THE MARLEY COOLING TOWER CO.—See United Dominion Industries, Ltd.; *U.S. Public*, pg. 1676
MARLEY ELECTRIC HEATING COMPANY—See United Dominion Industries, Ltd.; *U.S. Public*, pg. 1676
MARLEY FLOORS (USA) INC.—See Marley PLC; *Int'l*, pg. 843
MARLEY MOULDINGS INC.—See Marley PLC; *Int'l*, pg. 843
MARLEY PLASTICS HOLDINGS (USA) INC.—See Marley PLC; *Int'l*, pg. 843
MARLEY PLC; *Int'l*, pg. 843
MARLEY PUMP—See United Dominion Industries, Ltd.; *U.S. Public*, pg. 1676
MARLEY ROOF TILES HOLDINGS (U.S.A.) INC.—See Marley PLC; *Int'l*, pg. 844
MARLEY (U.S.A.) HOLDING CORPORATION—See Marley PLC; *Int'l*, pg. 843
MARLI DE MEXICO S.A. DE C.V., MEXICO D.F.—See Henkel KGaA; *Int'l*, pg. 613
MARLIM FIELD DEVELOPMENT—See Petrobras - Petroleo Brasileiro S.A.; *Int'l*, pg. 1041
MARLIN DRILLING CO., INC.—See Tenneco Inc.; *U.S. Public*, pg. 1579
MARLIN LIGHTING LIMITED—See Emess PLC; *Int'l*, pg. 453
ED MARLING STORES, INC.; *U.S. Private*, pg. 705
MARLITE; *U.S. Private*, pg. 705
MARLOW FOODS LTD.—See Zeneca Group Plc; *Int'l*, pg. 1524
MARLOW INDUSTRIES; *U.S. Private*, pg. 705
MARLOW ROPES LIMITED—See EIP Group plc; *Int'l*, pg. 426
MARMAC CORPORATION; *U.S. Private*, pg. 705
THE MARMAX GROUP—See The TJX Companies, Inc.; *U.S. Public*, pg. 1557
MARMID LIFE INSURANCE COMPANY—See HSBC Holdings plc; *Int'l*, pg. 581
THE MARMON GROUP, INC.; *U.S. Private*, pg. 706
MARMORAN AG—See Heidelberger Zement A.G.; *Int'l*, pg. 606
SA MAROCAINE DES PEINTURES ASTRAL CELLUCO (SAMPAC)—See Akzo Nobel N.V.; *Int'l*, pg. 43
MAROONE AUTOMOTIVE GROUP—See Republic Industries, Inc.; *U.S. Public*, pg. 1379
MAROTTA SCIENTIFIC CONTROLS, INC.; *U.S. Private*, pg. 706
MARPAN ONE, INC.—See The Chase Manhattan Corporation; *U.S. Public*, pg. 341
MARPAN TWO, INC.—See The Chase Manhattan Corporation; *U.S. Public*, pg. 341
MARQINT MARCAS INTERNACIONALES SA—See Diageo Plc; *Int'l*, pg. 410
MARQUARDT & CO.—See Central Lewmar; *U.S. Private*, pg. 223
MARQUETTE BANCSHARES INC.; *U.S. Private*, pg. 706
MARQUETTE BANK ROCHESTER—See Marquette Bancshares Inc.; *U.S. Private*, pg. 706
MARQUETTE BENELUX N.V./S.A.—See Marquette Medical Systems, Inc.; *U.S. Public*, pg. 1047
MARQUETTE COPPERSMITHING CO., INC.; *U.S. Private*, pg. 706
MARQUETTE ELECTRONICS (G.B.) LTD.—See Marquette Medical Systems, Inc.; *U.S. Public*, pg. 1047
MARQUETTE ESPANA S.A.—See Marquette Medical Systems, Inc.; *U.S. Public*, pg. 1047
MARQUETTE ITALIA, SRL—See Marquette Medical Systems, Inc.; *U.S. Public*, pg. 1047
MARQUETTE MEDICAL SYSTEMS, INC.; *U.S. Public*, pg. 1047
MARQUETTE NATIONAL LIFE INSURANCE CO.—See Southwestern Financial Corporation; *U.S. Private*, pg. 1018
MARQUETTE SCANDINAVIA—See Marquette Medical Systems, Inc.; *U.S. Public*, pg. 1047
MARQUINARIAS INGERSOLL-RAND DE COLOMBIA S.A.—See Ingersoll-Rand Company; *U.S. Public*, pg. 877
MARQUIS INVESTMENTS—See First Commerce Corporation; *U.S. Public*, pg. 629
MARQUIS WHO'S WHO—See Reed Elsevier plc; *Int'l*, pg. 1096
MARRIOTT DISTRIBUTION SERVICES (MDS)—See Marriott International, Inc.; *U.S. Public*, pg. 1048

MARRIOTT HOTELS, RESORTS, AND SUITES—See Marriott International, Inc.; *U.S. Public*, pg. 1048
MARRIOTT INTERNATIONAL, INC.; *U.S. Public*, pg. 1047
MARRIOTT MANAGEMENT SERVICES (MMS)—See Marriott International, Inc.; *U.S. Public*, pg. 1048
MARRIOTT OWNERSHIP RESORTS—See Marriott International, Inc.; *U.S. Public*, pg. 1048
MARRIOTT SENIOR LIVING SERVICES—See Marriott International, Inc.; *U.S. Public*, pg. 1048
MARRYAT & SCOTT EGYPT-S.A.—See Kone Corporation; *Int'l*, pg. 748
MARS ADVERTISING CO.; *U.S. Public*, pg. 706
MARS AIRCRAFT SERVICES CO. OF NEW JERSEY—See AAR Corp.; *U.S. Public*, pg. 1
MARS BV—See Mars, Incorporated; *U.S. Private*, pg. 707
MARS CONFECTIONERY—See Mars, Incorporated; *U.S. Private*, pg. 707
MARS GRAPHICS, INC.—See Harte-Hanks Communications, Inc.; *U.S. Public*, pg. 793
MARS, INCORPORATED; *U.S. Private*, pg. 707
MARS-LOS ANGELES—See Mars Advertising Co.; *U.S. Private*, pg. 707
MARS PETFOODS (UNISABI)—See Mars, Incorporated; *U.S. Private*, pg. 707
MARS-PHILADELPHIA—See Mars Advertising Co.; *U.S. Private*, pg. 707
MARS PUBLIC RELATIONS GROUP—See Mars Advertising Co.; *U.S. Private*, pg. 707
MARS-SOUTH—See Mars Advertising Co.; *U.S. Private*, pg. 707
MARS SUPER MARKETS, INC.; *U.S. Private*, pg. 707
MARSA KRAFT JACOBS SUCHARD SABANCI GIDA SANAYI VE TICARET A.S.—See Sabanci Holding A.S.; *Int'l*, pg. 1168
MARSA KRAFT JACOBS SUCHARD SABANCI GIDA SANAYI VE TICARET A.S.—See Philip Morris Companies Inc.; *U.S. Public*, pg. 1290
MARSAM PHARMACEUTICALS—See Schein Pharmaceutical, Inc.; *U.S. Private*, pg. 969
EDWARD MARSDEN LIMITED—See Imperial Chemical Industries PLC; *Int'l*, pg. 663
F.A. MARSDEN LTD.—See Georgia-Pacific Corporation; *U.S. Public*, pg. 739
MARSE CARE INC.—See National Home Health Care Corp.; *U.S. Public*, pg. 1157
MARSH & MCLENNAN COMPANIES, INC.; *U.S. Public*, pg. 1048
MARSH BELLOFRAM CORP.; *U.S. Private*, pg. 707
MARSH COMPANY; *U.S. Private*, pg. 707
MARSH COMPANY M.C.S.A.—See Marsh Company; *U.S. Private*, pg. 708
MARSH FURNITURE COMPANY; *U.S. Private*, pg. 708
MARSH & MCLENNAN RISK CAPITAL CORP.—See Marsh & McLennan Companies, Inc.; *U.S. Public*, pg. 1049
MARSH PRODUCTS CO.—See Premarc Corporation; *U.S. Private*, pg. 881
MARSH SUPERMARKETS, INC.; *U.S. Public*, pg. 1049
MARSHALL & ILSLEY CORPORATION; *U.S. Public*, pg. 1049
MARSHALL & ILSLEY TRUST COMPANY—See Marshall & Ilsley Corporation; *U.S. Public*, pg. 1051
MARSHALL & ILSLEY TRUST COMPANY OF FLORIDA—See Marshall & Ilsley Corporation; *U.S. Public*, pg. 1051
MARSHALL FIELD—See Dayton Hudson Corporation; *U.S. Public*, pg. 489
MARSHALL FIELD'S—See B.A.T Industries P.L.C.; *Int'l*, pg. 111
MARSHALL INDUSTRIES; *U.S. Public*, pg. 1051
MARSHALL JACCOMA MITCHELL ADVERTISING; *U.S. Private*, pg. 708
MARSHALL LABS INC.—See Du Pont (E.I. Du Pont De Nemours & Co.); *U.S. Public*, pg. 531
MARSHALL PICKERING HOLDINGS, LTD.—See The News Corporation Limited; *Int'l*, pg. 927
THE R.J. MARSHALL CO.; *U.S. Private*, pg. 708
ETS. MARSHALL S.A.—See Morgan Crucible Co. Plc; *Int'l*, pg. 891
MARSHALL STEEL, INC.—See Steel of West Virginia, Inc.; *U.S. Public*, pg. 1513
MARSHALLAN INDUSTRIES—See Park-Ohio Industries, Inc.; *U.S. Public*, pg. 1259
MARSHALLS FINANCE LIMITED—See British Telecommunications plc; *Int'l*, pg. 222
MARSHALLS, INC.—See The TJX Companies, Inc.; *U.S. Public*, pg. 1557
MARSHFIELD CLINIC; *U.S. Private*, pg. 708
MARSHFIELD MARINER—See Gannett Company, Inc.; *U.S. Public*, pg. 701
MARSHLAND ENERGY, INC.—See Borden, Inc.; *U.S. Public*, pg. 158
MARSILING LTD.—See Gunze Sangyo, Inc.; *Int'l*, pg. 579
MARS-NORTH CAROLINA—See Mars Advertising Co.; *U.S. Private*, pg. 706
MARSON/CREATIVE FASTENER, INC.; *U.S. Private*, pg. 708
MARSTON RING DIV.—See Freedom Forge Corporation; *U.S. Private*, pg. 425
MARSULEX INC.—See Harrowston Corporation; *Int'l*, pg. 599
MART CORPORATION—See Damsmith Corp.; *U.S. Private*, pg. 309
MARTA COOPERATIVE OF AMERICA INC.; *U.S. Private*, pg. 708
MARTA TECHNOLOGIES, INC.—See Allen Telecom, Inc.; *U.S. Public*, pg. 46
MARTEL CATALA ET CIE—See Albany International Corp.; *U.S. Public*, pg. 37
MARTELL ET CIE. S.A.—See The Seagram Company Ltd.; *Int'l*, pg. 1217
MARTEN TRANSPORT, LTD.; *U.S. Public*, pg. 1052
JOHN MARTENSSON ELMATERIAL AB—See Telefonaktiebolaget LM Ericsson; *Int'l*, pg. 1363

MARTEX INVESTMENTS (PTY) LTD—See Barlow Ltd.; *Int'l*, pg. 167
MARTI ELECTRONICS—See Hoak Capital; *U.S. Private*, pg. 531
AC MARTIN PARTNERS; *U.S. Private*, pg. 708
THE MARTIN AGENCY—See The Lowe Group; *U.S. Private*, pg. 678
THE MARTIN AGENCY—See The Interpublic Group of Companies, Inc.; *U.S. Public*, pg. 909
MARTIN & BAYLEY INC.; *U.S. Private*, pg. 708
MARTIN & PAGENSTECHER ROHSTOFFBET RIEBE GMBH & CO. KG—See Watts Blake Bearne & Co. Plc; *Int'l*, pg. 1488
MARTIN BAND INSTRUMENT CO.—See G. Leblanc Corporation; *U.S. Private*, pg. 657
THE MARTIN-BROWER COMPANY—See Dalgety Plc; *Int'l*, pg. 376
MARTIN-BROWER OF CANADA, LTD.—See Dalgety Plc; *Int'l*, pg. 376
MARTIN COLOR-FI; *U.S. Public*, pg. 1052
D. J. MARTIN EQUIPMENT CO., INC.—See Eclipse Inc.; *U.S. Private*, pg. 360
MARTIN DOOR MFG., INC.; *U.S. Private*, pg. 708
MARTIN ELECTRONICS, INC.; *U.S. Private*, pg. 709
MARTIN EXPLORATION MANAGEMENT COMPANY; *U.S. Private*, pg. 709
MARTIN/F. WEBER COMPANY—See Martin Universal Design, Inc.; *U.S. Private*, pg. 710
MARTIN GAS—See Martin Industries, Inc. (AL); *U.S. Private*, pg. 709
MARTIN GAS CORPORATION; *U.S. Private*, pg. 709
MARTIN INDUSTRIES, INC. (AL); *U.S. Private*, pg. 709
J.B. MARTIN COMPANY; *U.S. Private*, pg. 709
JAMES MARTIN INSIGHT, INC.—See Harcourt General, Inc.; *U.S. Public*, pg. 784
MARTIN LAWRENCE LIMITED EDITIONS, INC.; *U.S. Private*, pg. 709
MARTIN LAWRENCE LIMITED EDITIONS OF CALIFORNIA, INC.—See Martin Lawrence Limited Editions, Inc.; *U.S. Private*, pg. 709
MARTIN LUTHER HOSPITAL ANAHEIM—See UniHealth; *U.S. Public*, pg. 1118
MARTIN MARIETTA AGGREGATES—See Lockheed Martin Corporation; *U.S. Public*, pg. 1007
MARTIN MARIETTA AIR TRAFFIC SYSTEMS—See Lockheed Martin Corporation; *U.S. Public*, pg. 1007
MARTIN MARIETTA ASSEMBLY SERVICES—See Lockheed Martin Corporation; *U.S. Public*, pg. 1007
MARTIN MARIETTA ASTRO SPACE—See Lockheed Martin Corporation; *U.S. Public*, pg. 1007
MARTIN MARIETTA ASTRONAUTICS—See Lockheed Martin Corporation; *U.S. Public*, pg. 1007
MARTIN MARIETTA AUTOMATIONS SYSTEMS—See Lockheed Martin Corporation; *U.S. Public*, pg. 1007
MARTIN MARIETTA CANADA LTD.—See Lockheed Martin Corporation; *U.S. Public*, pg. 1009
MARTIN MARIETTA CONTROL SYSTEMS—See Lockheed Martin Corporation; *U.S. Public*, pg. 1006
MARTIN MARIETTA ELECTRONICS & MISSILES—See Lockheed Martin Corporation; *U.S. Public*, pg. 1007
MARTIN MARIETTA ENERGY GROUP—See Lockheed Martin Corporation; *U.S. Public*, pg. 1007
MARTIN MARIETTA NATIONAL COMPUTER CENTER—See Lockheed Martin Corporation; *U.S. Public*, pg. 1007
MARTIN MARIETTA FIELD SERVICES—See Lockheed Martin Corporation; *U.S. Public*, pg. 1007
MARTIN MARIETTA FLEET COMBAT SYSTEM SERVICES—See Lockheed Martin Corporation; *U.S. Public*, pg. 1007
MARTIN MARIETTA GOVERNMENT ELECTRONIC SYSTEMS—See Lockheed Martin Corporation; *U.S. Public*, pg. 1007
MARTIN MARIETTA INFORMATION GROUP—See Lockheed Martin Corporation; *U.S. Public*, pg. 1007
MARTIN MARIETTA INFORMATION SYSTEMS—See Lockheed Martin Corporation; *U.S. Public*, pg. 1007
MARTIN MARIETTA INTERNATIONAL, INC.—See Lockheed Martin Corporation; *U.S. Public*, pg. 1009
MARTIN MARIETTA MAGNESIA SPECIALTIES, INC.—See Lockheed Martin Corporation; *U.S. Public*, pg. 1007
MARTIN MARIETTA MANAGEMENT & DATA SYSTEMS—See Lockheed Martin Corporation; *U.S. Public*, pg. 1007
MARTIN MARIETTA MANNED SPACE SYSTEMS—See Lockheed Martin Corporation; *U.S. Public*, pg. 1007
MARTIN MARIETTA MATERIALS, INC.—See Lockheed Martin Corporation; *U.S. Public*, pg. 1007
MARTIN MARIETTA OCEAN, RADAR & SENSOR SYSTEMS—See Lockheed Martin Corporation; *U.S. Public*, pg. 1007
MARTIN MARIETTA RANGE SERVICES—See Lockheed Martin Corporation; *U.S. Public*, pg. 1007
MARTIN MARIETTA REGIONAL MANUFACTURING OPERATION—See Lockheed Martin Corporation; *U.S. Public*, pg. 1007
MARTIN MARIETTA SERVICES GROUP—See Lockheed Martin Corporation; *U.S. Public*, pg. 1007
MARTIN MARIETTA SOFTWARE SERVICES—See Lockheed Martin Corporation; *U.S. Public*, pg. 1007
MARTIN MARIETTA SPACE & AERONAUTICS SERVICES—See Lockheed Martin Corporation; *U.S. Public*, pg. 1007
MARTIN MARIETTA SPACE GROUP—See Lockheed Martin Corporation; *U.S. Public*, pg. 1007
MARTIN MARIETTA SPECIALTY COMPONENTS, INC.—See Lockheed Martin Corporation; *U.S. Public*, pg. 1007
MARTIN MARIETTA STATEGIC SYSTEMS—See Lockheed Martin Corporation; *U.S. Public*, pg. 1007
MARTIN MARIETTA TECHNICAL SUPPORT SERVICES—See Lockheed Martin Corporation; *U.S. Public*, pg. 1007

MASTER INDEX TO COMPANY NAMES
MASTER
Company Index

MARTIN MARIETTA URANIUM ENRICHMENT OPERATIONS—See Lockheed Martin Corporation; *U.S. Public*, pg. 1007
MARTIN MATHYS, NV—See RPM, Inc.; *U.S. Public*, pg. 1358
MARTIN MERKEL INC.—See Martin Merkel GmbH & Co. KG; *Int'l*, pg. 859
MARTIN REELS, A DIVISION OF ZEBCO—See Brunswick Corporation; *U.S. Public*, pg. 265
MARTIN S.A.—See Bobst S.A.; *Int'l*, pg. 199
SHERRI MARTIN—See Dawn Joy Fashions, Inc.; *U.S. Private*, pg. 316
MARTIN SPROCKET & GEAR DE MEXICO, S.A. DE C.V.—See Martin Sprocket & Gear, Inc.; *U.S. Private*, pg. 709
MARTIN SPROCKET & GEAR, INC.; *U.S. Private*, pg. 709
MARTIN SPROCKET & GEAR, INC.—See Martin Sprocket & Gear, Inc.; *U.S. Private*, pg. 709
MARTIN UNIVERSAL DESIGN, INC.; *U.S. Private*, pg. 709
MARTIN/WILLIAMS ADVERTISING INC.; *U.S. Private*, pg. 710
MARTIN-YALE INDUSTRIES, INC.—See Escalade Sports; *U.S. Public*, pg. 591
MARTINAIR HOLLAND—See KLM Royal Dutch Airlines; *Int'l*, pg. 719
MARTINAIR HOLLAND—See Royal Nedlloyd Group N.V.; *Int'l*, pg. 1145
MARTINDALE-HUBBELL—See Reed Elsevier plc; *Int'l*, pg. 1096
MARTINIQUE HOLDINGS—See Christiana Companies, Inc.; *U.S. Public*, pg. 352
MARTINO'S BAKERY, INC.; *U.S. Private*, pg. 710
MARTIN'S FAMOUS PASTRY SHOPPES; *U.S. Private*, pg. 710
MARTIN'S FOODS OF SOUTH BURLINGTON, INC.—See Hannaford Bros. Co.; *U.S. Public*, pg. 782
MARTIN'S SNACK DIVISION—See Martin's Famous Pastry Shoppes; *U.S. Private*, pg. 710
MARTIN'S UNIFORMS DIV.—See Superior Surgical Mfg. Co., Inc.; *U.S. Public*, pg. 1539
MARTIN'S UNIFORMS DIV.- NEW ORLEANS—See Superior Surgical Mfg. Co., Inc.; *U.S. Public*, pg. 1539
MARTINSWERK GMBH FUR CHEMISCHE UND METALLURGISCHE PRODUKTION—See Alusuisse-Lonza Holding Ltd.; *Int'l*, pg. 69
MARUBENI AMERICA CORPORATION—See Marubeni Corporation; *Int'l*, pg. 844
MARUBENI AMERICA CORPORATION, DALLAS BRANCH—See Marubeni Corporation; *Int'l*, pg. 844
MARUBENI AMERICA CORPORATION, DETROIT BRANCH—See Marubeni Corporation; *Int'l*, pg. 844
MARUBENI AMERICA CORPORATION, PORTLAND BRANCH—See Marubeni Corporation; *Int'l*, pg. 845
MARUBENI AMERICA CORPORATION, SAN FRANCISCO BRANCH—See Marubeni Corporation; *Int'l*, pg. 845
MARUBENI AMERICAN CORPORATION, SEATTLE BRANCH—See Marubeni Corporation; *Int'l*, pg. 845
MARUBENI AUSTRALIA LTD.—See Marubeni Corporation; *Int'l*, pg. 845
MARUBENI CANADA LTD.—See Marubeni Corporation; *Int'l*, pg. 845
MARUBENI CITIZENS CINCOM INC.—See Marubeni Corporation; *Int'l*, pg. 845
MARUBENI CORPORATION; *Int'l*, pg. 844
MARUBENI DEUTSCHLAND GMBH—See Marubeni Corporation; *Int'l*, pg. 845
MARUBENI INTERNATIONAL ELECTRONICS CORP.—See Marubeni Corporation; *Int'l*, pg. 845
MARUBENI MEXICO S.A. DE C.V.—See Marubeni Corporation; *Int'l*, pg. 845
MARUBENI NEW ZEALAND LTD.—See Marubeni Corporation; *Int'l*, pg. 845
MARUBENI PLASMA TECHNIK CO. LTD.—See Sulzer Ltd.; *Int'l*, pg. 1307
MARUBENI SCANDINAVIA AB—See Marubeni Corporation; *Int'l*, pg. 845
MARUBENI U.K. PLC.—See Marubeni Corporation; *Int'l*, pg. 845
MARUCHAN INC.; *U.S. Private*, pg. 710
MARUHA CORPORATION; *Int'l*, pg. 845
MARUICHI AMERICAN CORP.—See Nissho Iwai Corporation; *Int'l*, pg. 947
MARUMOTO K.K. LTD.—See Radiometer A/S; *Int'l*, pg. 1084
MARUZEN ASIA PRIVATE LTD.—See Maruzen Company Limited; *Int'l*, pg. 846
MARUZEN BOOKMATES CO., LTD.—See Maruzen Company Limited; *Int'l*, pg. 846
MARUZEN COMPANY LIMITED; *Int'l*, pg. 845
MARUZEN INTERNATIONAL CO., LTD.—See Maruzen Company Limited; *Int'l*, pg. 846
MARUZEN NIHONBASHI SDN. BHD.—See Maruzen Company Limited; *Int'l*, pg. 846
MARUZEN SYSTEM SERVICE CO., LTD.—See Maruzen Company Limited; *Int'l*, pg. 846
MARVAL INDUSTRIES, INC.; *U.S. Private*, pg. 710
MARVEL ENTERTAINMENT GROUP; *U.S. Public*, pg. 1052
THE MARVEL GROUP, INC.—See Masco Corporation; *U.S. Public*, pg. 1053
MARVELLA INC.—See The Monet Group, Inc.; *U.S. Private*, pg. 757
MARVELO B.V.—See Koninklijke Ahold NV; *Int'l*, pg. 749
MARVIN DE MEXICO, S.A. DE C.V.—See Arvin Industries, Inc.; *U.S. Public*, pg. 137
MARVIN ENGINEERING COMPANY, INC.; *U.S. Private*, pg. 710
MARVIN LUMBER & CEDAR COMPANY; *U.S. Private*, pg. 710
MARWIL PRODUCTS COMPANY—See Arvin Industries, Inc.; *U.S. Public*, pg. 137
MARWITZ & HAUSER GMBH—See Carl-Zeiss-Stiftung; *Int'l*, pg. 1523
GILDA MARX INC.; *U.S. Private*, pg. 710
MARY ELLEN, INC.—See J.M. Smucker Company; *U.S. Public*, pg. 1480
MARY KAY CORPORATION; *U.S. Private*, pg. 710
MARY KAY COSMETICOS DE MEXICO PTY., S.A. DE C.V.—See Mary Kay Corporation; *U.S. Private*, pg. 711
MARY KAY COSMETICS CHILE S.A.—See Mary Kay Corporation; *U.S. Private*, pg. 711
MARY KAY COSMETICS CHINA—See Mary Kay Corporation; *U.S. Private*, pg. 711
MARY KAY COSMETICS, GMBH—See Mary Kay Corporation; *U.S. Private*, pg. 711
MARY KAY COSMETICS (JAPAN) K.K.—See Mary Kay Corporation; *U.S. Private*, pg. 711
MARY KAY COSMETICS LTD.—See Mary Kay Corporation; *U.S. Private*, pg. 711
MARY KAY COSMETICS PTY. LTD.—See Mary Kay Corporation; *U.S. Private*, pg. 711
MARY KAY COSMETICS, S.A.—See Mary Kay Corporation; *U.S. Private*, pg. 711
MARY KAY CZECH REPUBLIC S.R.O.—See Mary Kay Corporation; *U.S. Private*, pg. 711
MARY KAY, INC.—See Mary Kay Corporation; *U.S. Private*, pg. 711
MARYLAND-AMERICAN WATER CO.—See American Water Works Company, Inc.; *U.S. Public*, pg. 95
MARYLAND & PENNSYLVANIA RAILROAD—See Emons Transportation Group, Inc.; *U.S. Public*, pg. 579
MARYLAND & VIRGINIA MILK PRODUCERS COOPERATIVE ASSOCIATION, INC.; *U.S. Private*, pg. 711
MARYLAND CASUALTY CO.—See Zurich Insurance Company; *Int'l*, pg. 1530
MARYLAND COMMERCIAL INSURANCE GROUP—See Zurich Insurance Company; *Int'l*, pg. 1530
MARYLAND CONCESSION & VENDING COMPANY—See Giant Food Inc.; *U.S. Public*, pg. 741
MARYLAND INSURANCE COMPANY—See Zurich Insurance Company; *Int'l*, pg. 1530
MARYLAND LLOYDS—See Zurich Insurance Company; *Int'l*, pg. 1530
MARYLAND NETHERLANDS CREDIT INSURANCE COMPANY—See Zurich Insurance Company; *Int'l*, pg. 1530
MARYLAND PERSONAL INSURANCE GROUP—See Zurich Insurance Company; *Int'l*, pg. 1530
MARYLAND PLASTICS, INC.—See Lab Products, Inc.; *U.S. Private*, pg. 641
MARYLAND RIBBON COMPANY—See C.M. Offray & Son Inc.; *U.S. Private*, pg. 812
MARYLAND ROCK INDUSTRIES, INC.—See Florida Rock Industries, Inc.; *U.S. Public*, pg. 656
MARYLAND SPECIALTY WIRE, INC.—See Handy & Harman; *U.S. Public*, pg. 780
MARYLAND STONE INC.—See Florida Rock Industries, Inc.; *U.S. Public*, pg. 656
MARYLAND VENTURES, INC.—See Berkshire Hathaway Inc.; *U.S. Public*, pg. 220
THE MARYLEBONE OPTICAL CO. LTD.—See Dolland & Aitchison Ltd.; *Int'l*, pg. 414
T. MARZETTI COMPANY—See Lancaster Colony Corporation; *U.S. Public*, pg. 977
THE MASAN STEEL TUBE WORKS CO. LTD.—See Nissho Iwai Corporation; *Int'l*, pg. 948
MASASA MINES (PRIVATE) LIMITED—See Delta Gold N.L.; *Int'l*, pg. 389
MASBATE GOLD OPERATION—See Atlas Consolidated Mining & Development Corporation; *Int'l*, pg. 95
MASCHINENFABRIK ANDRITZ AG—See AGIV Group; *Int'l*, pg. 14
MASCHINENFABRIK ESSLINGEN AG—See Daimler-Benz Aktiengesellschaft; *Int'l*, pg. 368
MASCHINENFABRIK HENNECKE GMBH—See Bayer AG; *Int'l*, pg. 172
MASCHINENFABRIK HOERAUF—See Spindelfabrik Suessen; *Int'l*, pg. 1290
MASCHINENFABRIK KBA MODLING AG—See Koenig & Bauer-Albert AG; *Int'l*, pg. 742
MASCHINENFABRIK LORENZ GMBH—See Liebherr-International AG; *Int'l*, pg. 808
MASCHINENFABRIK RIETER AG—See Rieter Holdings; *Int'l*, pg. 1116
MASCHINENVERWERTUNGSGESELLSCHAFT MBH—See Schmalbach-Lubeca AG; *Int'l*, pg. 1206
MASCO BUILDING PRODUCTS CORP.—See Masco Corporation; *U.S. Public*, pg. 1053
MASCO CORPORATION; *U.S. Public*, pg. 1052
MASCO CORPORATION LIMITED—See Masco Corporation; *U.S. Public*, pg. 1054
MASCO, GMBH—See Masco Corporation; *U.S. Public*, pg. 1055
MASCOTECH COATINGS—See MascoTech, Inc.; *U.S. Public*, pg. 1055
MASCOTECH FORMING TECHNOLOGIES—See MascoTech, Inc.; *U.S. Public*, pg. 1055
MASCOTECH, INC.; *U.S. Public*, pg. 1055
MASCOTECH INDUSTRIAL COMPONENTS, INC.—See MascoTech, Inc.; *U.S. Public*, pg. 1055
MASCOTECH SINTERED COMPONENTS, INC.—See MascoTech, Inc.; *U.S. Public*, pg. 1055
MASCOTECH TUBULAR PRODUCTS, INC.—See MascoTech, Inc.; *U.S. Public*, pg. 1055
MASE WESTPAC AUSTRALIA LIMITED—See Westpac Banking Corporation; *Int'l*, pg. 1496
MASE WESTPAC HONG KONG LIMITED—See Westpac Banking Corporation; *Int'l*, pg. 1497
MASE WESTPAC LIMITED—See Westpac Banking Corporation; *Int'l*, pg. 1497
MASEK DISTRIBUTING INC.; *U.S. Private*, pg. 711
MASERATI AUTOMOBILES, INCORPORATED—See Fiat Auto SpA; *Int'l*, pg. 482
MASHBURN CONSTRUCTION COMPANY; *U.S. Private*, pg. 711
MASKIN AB RAPID—See AB Industrivarden; *Int'l*, pg. 678
MASKIN A/S ZETA—See Tetra Laval Group; *Int'l*, pg. 1380
MASKINAKTIEBOLAGET AXAB—See Axel Johnson AB; *Int'l*, pg. 709
MASLAND—See Lear Corporation; *U.S. Public*, pg. 981
MASLAND CARPETS, INC.—See The Dixie Group, Inc.; *U.S. Public*, pg. 514
MASON & HANGER—See Mason & Hanger Corporation, Inc.; *U.S. Private*, pg. 711
MASON & HANGER CORPORATION, INC.; *U.S. Private*, pg. 711
MASON & HANGER CORPORATION, INC.—See Mason & Hanger Corporation, Inc.; *U.S. Private*, pg. 711
MASON & HANGER ENGINEERING INC.—See Mason & Hanger Corporation, Inc.; *U.S. Private*, pg. 711
B.A. MASON—See Mason Shoe Mfg. Co.; *U.S. Private*, pg. 712
MASON CANDLELIGHT—See Standex International Corporation; *U.S. Public*, pg. 1506
MASON DISTRIBUTORS, INC.; *U.S. Private*, pg. 712
MASON ELECTRIC CO.—See Esterline Technologies Corporation; *U.S. Public*, pg. 594
MASON ELECTRIC COMPANY—See BTR plc; *Int'l*, pg. 127
MASON METALS CO.—See Standex International Corporation; *U.S. Public*, pg. 1506
MASON SHOE MFG. CO.; *U.S. Private*, pg. 712
MASONEILAN NORTH AMERICAN OPERATIONS—See Dresser Industries, Inc.; *U.S. Public*, pg. 528
MASONITE CORPORATION—See International Paper Company; *U.S. Public*, pg. 904
MASONITE DIVISION—See International Paper Company; *U.S. Public*, pg. 903
MASS MARKET DIVISION—See VF Corporation; *U.S. Public*, pg. 1702
MASS PUBLICIDAD—See Saatchi & Saatchi Advertising Worldwide; *U.S. Public*, pg. 1422
MASS PUBLICIDAD S.R.L.—See Leo Burnett Company, Inc.; *U.S. Private*, pg. 186
MASS PUBLISHING—See Waverly, Inc.; *U.S. Public*, pg. 1748
MASSACHUSETTS-AMERICAN WATER CO.—See American Water Works Company, Inc.; *U.S. Public*, pg. 95
MASSACHUSETTS BAY INSURANCE CO.—See Allmerica Financial Corporation; *U.S. Public*, pg. 54
MASSACHUSETTS CAPITAL RESOURCES COMPANY—See American Water Works Company, Inc.; *U.S. Public*, pg. 95
MASSACHUSETTS CARING FOR CHILDREN FOUNDATION, INC.—See Blue Cross and Blue Shield of Massachusetts; *U.S. Private*, pg. 151
MASSACHUSETTS CASUALTY INSURANCE COMPANY—See Sun Life Assurance Company of Canada; *Int'l*, pg. 1319
MASSACHUSETTS CONTAINER CORPORATION—See Connecticut Container Corporation; *U.S. Private*, pg. 263
MASSACHUSETTS ELECTRIC CO.—See New England Electric System; *U.S. Public*, pg. 1171
MASSACHUSETTS ENVELOPE CO.; *U.S. Private*, pg. 712
MASSACHUSETTS FINANCIAL SERVICES COMPANY (MFS)—See Sun Life Assurance Company of Canada; *Int'l*, pg. 1319
MASSACHUSETTS MENTOR, INC.—See Magellan Health Services, Inc.; *U.S. Public*, pg. 1036
MASSACHUSETTS MUTUAL LIFE INSURANCE CO.; *U.S. Private*, pg. 712
MASSACHUSETTS MUTUAL LIFE INSURANCE COMPANY—See Massachusetts Mutual Life Insurance Co.; *U.S. Private*, pg. 712
MASSACHUSETTS STEEL TREATING—See The Presmet Corp.; *U.S. Private*, pg. 882
MASSALIN PARTICULARES S.A.—See Reemtsma Cigarettenfabriken GmbH, Hamburg; *Int'l*, pg. 1101
A.T. MASSEY COAL COMPANY, INC.—See Fluor Corporation; *U.S. Public*, pg. 660
MASSEY CADILLAC, INC.—See Don Massey Cadillac Inc.; *U.S. Private*, pg. 713
MASSEY CHEVROLET GEO, INC.—See Don Massey Cadillac Inc.; *U.S. Private*, pg. 713
DON MASSEY BUICK-PONTIAC—See Don Massey Cadillac Inc.; *U.S. Private*, pg. 712
DON MASSEY CADILLAC INC.; *U.S. Private*, pg. 712
MASSEY'S—See Craddock-Terry Inc.; *U.S. Private*, pg. 284
MASSGLAS B.V.—See Asahi Glass Co., Ltd.; *Int'l*, pg. 85
MASSMAN CONSTRUCTION COMPANY; *U.S. Private*, pg. 713
MASSMUTUAL CORPORATE INVESTORS; *U.S. Public*, pg. 1055
MASSON-WILLIAMS & WILKINS—See Waverly, Inc.; *U.S. Public*, pg. 1748
MASSWEST INSURANCE COMPANY—See Credit Suisse Group; *Int'l*, pg. 345
MAST INDUSTRIES—See The Limited, Inc.; *U.S. Public*, pg. 996
MAST MICROWAVE DIVISION—See Kevlin Corporation; *U.S. Public*, pg. 953
P.T. MASTE DAYAA—See GESTRA GmbH; *Int'l*, pg. 550
MASTEC, INC.; *U.S. Public*, pg. 1055
MASTER APPLIANCE CORP.; *U.S. Private*, pg. 713
MASTER-BILT PRODUCTS—See Standex International Corporation; *U.S. Public*, pg. 1506
MASTER BUILDERS INC.—See Viag AG; *Int'l*, pg. 1465
MASTER BUILDERS MATERIALS LTD.—See Viag AG; *Int'l*, pg. 1465
MASTER BUILDERS N.V.—See Viag AG; *Int'l*, pg. 1465
MASTER BUILDERS SCANDINAVIA AB—See Viag AG; *Int'l*, pg. 1465
MASTER BUILDERS TECHNOLOGIES (HONG KONG) LTD.—See Viag AG; *Int'l*, pg. 1465
MASTER BUILDERS TECHNOLOGIES LTD.—See Viag AG; *Int'l*, pg. 1465
MASTER CRAFT CORP.—See Caradon Plc; *Int'l*, pg. 267
MASTER DATA CENTER—See National Amusements, Inc.; *U.S. Private*, pg. 778

MASTER DISTRIBUTORS—See Master International Corp.; U.S. Private, pg. 714
MASTER FLEET INC.—See Ace Doran Hauling & Rigging Company; U.S. Private, pg. 340
MASTER FOODS, Incorporated; U.S. Private, pg. 707
MASTER FOODS AB—See Mars, Incorporated; U.S. Private, pg. 707
MASTER FOODS AUSTRIA GMBH—See Mars, Incorporated; U.S. Private, pg. 707
MASTER FOODS NV—See Mars, Incorporated; U.S. Private, pg. 707
MASTER GRAPHIC, INC.; U.S. Private, pg. 713
MASTER-HALCO, INC.—See Itochu Corporation; Int'l, pg. 695
MASTER INDUSTRIES CORP.; U.S. Private, pg. 713
MASTER INTERNATIONAL CORP.; U.S. Private, pg. 713
MASTER LOCK COMPANY—See Fortune Brands, Inc.; U.S. Public, pg. 675
MASTER MOLD—See Plastek Group; U.S. Private, pg. 870
MASTER MOLDED PRODUCTS CORPORATION; U.S. Private, pg. 714
MASTER PRODUCTS MFG. CO.—See James Crean PLC; Int'l, pg. 340
MASTER SHIELD BUILDING PRODUCTS—See Jannock Limited; Int'l, pg. 698
MASTER TOOLS S.P.A.—See Sandvik AB; Int'l, pg. 1186
MASTER TROUSER/ MASTER APPAREL/ BOTANY 500 SLACKS LTD.—See Master Industries Corp.; U.S. Private, pg. 713
MASTERBILT FIXTURES, INC.—See Grocers Supply Co. Inc.; U.S. Private, pg. 483
MASTERBLEND, INC.—See Leggett & Platt, Incorporated; U.S. Public, pg. 986
MASTERBRAND INDUSTRIES, INC.—See Fortune Brands, Inc.; U.S. Public, pg. 675
MASTERCARD INTERNATIONAL-CIRRUS BRAND—See Mastercard International, Inc.; U.S. Private, pg. 714
MASTERCARD INTERNATIONAL, INC.; U.S. Private, pg. 714
MASTERCARE LIMITED—See Dixons Group plc; Int'l, pg. 414
MASTERCHEM INDUSTRIES—See Williams Holdings Plc; Int'l, pg. 1501
MASTERCRAFT BOAT COMPANY—See MacAndrews & Forbes Holdings Inc.; U.S. Private, pg. 689
MASTERCRAFT CORPORATION—See Genmar Holdings, Inc.; U.S. Private, pg. 447
MASTERCRAFT FURNITURE CORP.; U.S. Private, pg. 714
MASTERDRIVE MANAGEMENT LTD.—See Lonrho plc; Int'l, pg. 817
MASTERFOODS LTD.—See Mars, Incorporated; U.S. Private, pg. 707
MASTERFOODS OY—See Mars, Incorporated; U.S. Private, pg. 707
MASTERGEAR DIVISION—See Regal-Beloit Corporation; U.S. Public, pg. 1370
MASTERPAK, S.A. DE C.V.—See CYDSA S.A.; Int'l, pg. 246
MASTERS INC.; U.S. Private, pg. 714
MASTERS, INC.; U.S. Private, pg. 714
THE MASTER'S WORKSHOP CORPORATION—See Rogers Communications, Inc.; Int'l, pg. 1124
MASTERVIEW WINDOW COMPANY, INC.—See Publicker Industries Inc.; U.S. Public, pg. 1341
MASTICO INDUSTRIES, LTD.—See Rieter Holdings; Int'l, pg. 1117
MASTRAK SDN BHD—See Scancem AB; Int'l, pg. 1199
MASTSYSTEM AB—See Neste Oy; Int'l, pg. 914
MASURY PAINT—See The Valspar Corporation; U.S. Public, pg. 1707
MATA (HELICOPTERS) DIVISION/MILITARY AIRCRAFT GROUP—See Israel Aircraft Industries Ltd.; Int'l, pg. 690
MATAC CARGO LTD.—See Air Canada; Int'l, pg. 36
AB MATAKI—See Trelleborg AB; Int'l, pg. 1422
MATAKI HELTACKANDE TÄK—See Trelleborg AB; Int'l, pg. 1422
MATAURA PAPER MILL—See International Paper Company; U.S. Public, pg. 905
MATCHBOX COLLECTIBLES PTY. LTD.—See Mattel, Inc.; U.S. Public, pg. 1059
MATCHBOX SPIELWAREN GMBH—See Mattel, Inc.; U.S. Public, pg. 1059
MATCO TOOLS—See Danaher Corporation; U.S. Public, pg. 482
MATEC—See Lagardere Groupe; Int'l, pg. 792
MATEC APPLIED SCIENCES, INC.—See Matec Corporation; U.S. Public, pg. 1056
MATEC CORPORATION; U.S. Public, pg. 1056
MATEC INSTRUMENTS, INC.—See Matec Corporation; U.S. Public, pg. 1056
MATEL TECNOLOGIA DE TELEINFORMATICA S.A.—See Telefonaktiebolaget LM Ericsson; Int'l, pg. 1369
MATERIAL HANDLING EQUIPMENT CO.—See Modern Group Ltd.; U.S. Private, pg. 754
MATERIAL SCIENCES CORPORATION; U.S. Public, pg. 1056
MATERIAL SERVICE CORP—See General Dynamics Corporation; U.S. Public, pg. 709
MATERIAL SUPPLY (SESUP)—See Petrobras - Petroleo Brasileiro S.A.; Int'l, pg. 1042
MATERIAL TRANSPORT CO.—See Ash Grove Cement Company; U.S. Private, pg. 88
MATERIALES INDUSTRIALES S.A.—See RGP Holding, Inc.; U.S. Private, pg. 904
MATERIALES MOLDEABLES S.A. DE C.V.—See Borden, Inc.; U.S. Private, pg. 159
MATERIALS GROUP NORTH AMERICA—See Avery Dennison Corporation; U.S. Public, pg. 153
MATERIALS HANDLING DIVISION—See Oy Algol AB; Int'l, pg. 15
MATERIALS HANDLING EQUIPMENT—See Jervis B. Webb Company; U.S. Private, pg. 1156

MATERIALS RESEARCH CORPORATION—See Sony Corporation; Int'l, pg. 1283
MATERIALS RESEARCH FRANCE—See Sony Corporation; Int'l, pg. 1283
MATERIALS RESEARCH GMBH—See Sony Corporation; Int'l, pg. 1283
MATERIALS RESEARCH LTD.—See Sony Corporation; Int'l, pg. 1283
MATERIALS RESEARCH S.A.—See Sony Corporation; Int'l, pg. 1283
MATERIAUX DE CONSTRUCTION INTERNATIONAL—See Saint-Gobain; Int'l, pg. 1170
MATERIAUX ISOLANTS LILLOIS—See Saint-Gobain; Int'l, pg. 1176
MATERIAUX S.A.—See Dyckerhoff AG; Int'l, pg. 423
MATERIEL DIVISION—See The Boeing Company; U.S. Public, pg. 240
MATERNE-FRUIBOURG—See Hillsdown Holdings Plc; Int'l, pg. 619
MATH ASSOCIATES—See General Microwave Corporation; U.S. Public, pg. 717
MATHEMATICAL REVIEWS—See American Mathematical Society, Inc.; U.S. Private, pg. 59
MATHER & PLATT (IRELAND) LIMITED—See Tyco International Ltd.; U.S. Public, pg. 1650
MATHER & PLATT WORMALD S.A.—See Tyco International Ltd.; U.S. Public, pg. 1650
CURTIS MATHES CORPORATION—See Curtis Mathes Holding Corp.; U.S. Public, pg. 1057
CURTIS MATHES HOLDING CORP.; U.S. Public, pg. 1057
MATHESON GAS PRODUCTS CANADA, INC.—See Nippon Sanso Corporation; Int'l, pg. 938
MATHESON GAS PRODUCTS, INC.—See Nippon Sanso Corporation; Int'l, pg. 938
MATHESON GAS PRODUCTS KOREA, INC.—See Nippon Sanso Corporation; Int'l, pg. 938
MATHEWS & BOUCHER; U.S. Private, pg. 714
MATHEWS READYMIX, INC.—See Centex Corporation; U.S. Public, pg. 323
MATHIEU ARGENTINA—See Maison Mathieu, S.A.; Int'l, pg. 846
MATHIEU C.A.—See Maison Mathieu, S.A.; Int'l, pg. 846
MATHIEU CHILE—See Maison Mathieu, S.A.; Int'l, pg. 846
MATHIEU (CHINA)—See Maison Mathieu, S.A.; Int'l, pg. 846
MATHIEU COLOMBIA—See Maison Mathieu, S.A.; Int'l, pg. 846
MATHIEU ECUADOR—See Maison Mathieu, S.A.; Int'l, pg. 846
MAISON MATHIEU, S.A.; Int'l, pg. 846
MATHIEU PERU—See Maison Mathieu, S.A.; Int'l, pg. 846
MATHIEU S.A.—See Maison Mathieu, S.A.; Int'l, pg. 846
MATHIEU VENEZUELA—See Maison Mathieu, S.A.; Int'l, pg. 846
MATILDA BAY BREWING CO. LTD.—See Foster's Brewing Group Limited; Int'l, pg. 501
MATINCENDIE—See Williams Holdings Plc; Int'l, pg. 1501
MATIVAL—See Saint-Gobain; Int'l, pg. 1176
MATLACK (DE), INC.—See Matlack Systems, Inc.; U.S. Public, pg. 1057
MATLACK SYSTEMS, INC.; U.S. Public, pg. 1057
MATRA AEROSPACE INC.—See Lagardere Groupe; Int'l, pg. 795
MATRA AUTOMOBILE—See Lagardere Groupe; Int'l, pg. 792
MATRA CAP SYSTEMS—See Lagardere Groupe; Int'l, pg. 792
MATRA COMMUNICATION—See Lagardere Groupe; Int'l, pg. 793
MATRA COMMUNICATION DISTRIBUTION—See Lagardere Groupe; Int'l, pg. 793
MATRA COMMUNICATION MEDITERRANEE—See Lagardere Groupe; Int'l, pg. 793
MATRA COMMUNICATION NORD-EST—See Lagardere Groupe; Int'l, pg. 793
MATRA COMMUNICATION OUEST—See Lagardere Groupe; Int'l, pg. 793
MATRA COMMUNICATION PUBLIQUE—See Lagardere Groupe; Int'l, pg. 793
MATRA COMMUNICATION RHONE-ALPES—See Lagardere Groupe; Int'l, pg. 793
MATRA COMMUNICATION SUD-WEST—See Lagardere Groupe; Int'l, pg. 793
MATRA COMMUNICATION USA INC—See Lagardere Groupe; Int'l, pg. 795
MATRA COMMUNICATIONS GMBH—See Lagardere Groupe; Int'l, pg. 796
MATRA COMMUNICATIONS ST PA—See Lagardere Groupe; Int'l, pg. 796
MATRA DATAVISION BEN—See Lagardere Groupe; Int'l, pg. 796
MATRA DATAVISION GMBH—See Lagardere Groupe; Int'l, pg. 796
MATRA DATAVISION KK—See Lagardere Groupe; Int'l, pg. 796
MATRA DATAVISION LTD.—See Lagardere Groupe; Int'l, pg. 796
MATRA DATAVISION S.A.—See Lagardere Groupe; Int'l, pg. 793
MATRA DATAVISION S.P.A.—See Lagardere Groupe; Int'l, pg. 796
MATRA DATAVISION U.S.A.—See Lagardere Groupe; Int'l, pg. 795
MATRA DE COMUNICACIONES ESPANA—See Lagardere Groupe; Int'l, pg. 796
MATRA DEFENSE—See Lagardere Groupe; Int'l, pg. 793
MATRA DEFENSE-ESPACE—See Lagardere Groupe; Int'l, pg. 793
MATRA DESIGN SEMICONDUCTOR CORP.—See Lagardere Groupe; Int'l, pg. 795
MATRA ELECTRONIQUE—See Lagardere Groupe; Int'l, pg. 793
MATRA ESPACE HOLDING BV—See Lagardere Groupe; Int'l, pg. 796

MATRA ESPACE PARTICIPATIONS—See Lagardere Groupe; Int'l, pg. 793
MATRA HACHETTE GENERAL—See Lagardere Groupe; Int'l, pg. 793
MATRA HACHETTE MULTIMEDIA—See Lagardere Groupe; Int'l, pg. 793
MATRA HACHETTE MULTIMEDIA ON LINE—See Lagardere Groupe; Int'l, pg. 793
MATRA HACHETTE MULTIMEDIA VOYAGER—See Lagardere Groupe; Int'l, pg. 793
MATRA HARRIS SEMICONDUCTEURS S.A.—See Harris Corporation; U.S. Public, pg. 791
MATRA MARCONI SPACE—See The General Electric Company, p.l.c.; Int'l, pg. 545
MATRA MARCONI SPACE—See Lagardere Groupe; Int'l, pg. 793
MATRA MARCONI SPACE BV—See Lagardere Groupe; Int'l, pg. 796
MATRA MARCONI SPACE NV—See The General Electric Company, p.l.c.; Int'l, pg. 545
MATRA MARCONI SPACE UK HOLDINGS—See Lagardere Groupe; Int'l, pg. 796
MATRA MARCONI SPACE UK LTD.—See The General Electric Company, p.l.c.; Int'l, pg. 545
MATRA M.H.S.—See Lagardere Groupe; Int'l, pg. 793
MATRA MS2I—See Lagardere Groupe; Int'l, pg. 793
MATRA NOKIA RADIOMOBILES—See Lagardere Groupe; Int'l, pg. 793
MATRA NORTEL COMMUNICATION—See Lagardere Groupe; Int'l, pg. 793
MATRA PARTICIPATIONS—See Lagardere Groupe; Int'l, pg. 793
MATRA SYSTEME—See Lagardere Groupe; Int'l, pg. 793
MATRA TELECOMMUNICATIONS ILE-DE-FRANCE—See Lagardere Groupe; Int'l, pg. 793
MATRA TELECOMMUNICATIONS MEDITERRANEE—See Lagardere Groupe; Int'l, pg. 793
MATRA TELECOMMUNICATIONS NORD-EST—See Lagardere Groupe; Int'l, pg. 793
MATRA TELECOMMUNICATIONS OUEST-NORMANDIE—See Lagardere Groupe; Int'l, pg. 793
MATRA TELECOMMUNICATIONS PARIS-LOIRE—See Lagardere Groupe; Int'l, pg. 793
MATRA TELECOMMUNICATIONS RHONE-ALPES—See Lagardere Groupe; Int'l, pg. 793
MATRA TELECOMMUNICATIONS SUD-OUEST—See Lagardere Groupe; Int'l, pg. 793
MATRA TRANSFINEX—See Lagardere Groupe; Int'l, pg. 793
MATRA TRANSIT—See Lagardere Groupe; Int'l, pg. 795
MATRA TRANSPORT—See Lagardere Groupe; Int'l, pg. 793
MATRA TRANSPORT INTERNATIONAL—See Lagardere Groupe; Int'l, pg. 793
MATRA-WERKE GMBH—See Linde AG; Int'l, pg. 811
MATREL—See Lagardere Groupe; Int'l, pg. 793
MATRIA HEALTHCARE, INC.; U.S. Public, pg. 1057
MATRIX AVIATION, INC.—See Banner Aerospace, Inc.; U.S. Public, pg. 187
MATRIX BUILDING CO., INC.—See Maescher Industries, Inc.; U.S. Private, pg. 694
MATRIX ESSENTIALS, INC.—See Bristol-Myers Squibb Company; U.S. Public, pg. 254
MATRIX SCIENCE CORPORATION—See AMP Incorporated; U.S. Public, pg. 8
MATRIX SERVICE COMPANY; U.S. Public, pg. 1057
MATRIX TECHNOLOGIES, INC.; U.S. Private, pg. 714
MATRIX TECHNOLOGIES, INC.—See Matrix Technologies Inc.; U.S. Private, pg. 714
MATRIXONE, INC.—See Adra Systems, Inc.; U.S. Private, pg. 18
MATRIXX MARKETING INC.—See Cincinnati Bell Telephone; U.S. Public, pg. 368
MATRIXX PHONE MARKETING SERVICES, S.A.—See Cincinnati Bell Telephone; U.S. Public, pg. 368
MATSON INTERMODAL SYSTEM, INC.—See Alexander & Baldwin, Inc.; U.S. Public, pg. 40
MATSON NAVIGATION COMPANY, INC.—See Alexander & Baldwin, Inc.; U.S. Public, pg. 39
MATSON TERMINALS, INC.—See Alexander & Baldwin, Inc.; U.S. Public, pg. 40
MATSUBO COMPANY (AMERICA), INC.—See Ebara Corporation; Int'l, pg. 432
MATSUBO GMBH—See Ebara Corporation; Int'l, pg. 432
MATSUE ASASHI KOKOKUSHA, LTD.—See Daiko Advertising, Inc.; Int'l, pg. 366
MATSUSHITA ELECTRIC INDUSTRIAL CO., LTD.; Int'l, pg. 846
MATSUSHITA ELECTRIC WORKS, LTD.; Int'l, pg. 847
MATSUSHITA ELECTRIC WORKS, LTD.- TOKYO—See Matsushita Electric Works, Ltd.; Int'l, pg. 847
MATSUSHITA ELECTRIC WORKS RESEARCH & DEVELOPMENT LABORATORY INC.—See Matsushita Electric Works, Ltd.; Int'l, pg. 848
MATSUSHITA ELECTRONIC MATERIALS, INC.—See Matsushita Electric Works, Ltd.; Int'l, pg. 848
MATSUYA ASAKUSA—See Matsuya Company Ltd.; Int'l, pg. 848
MATSUYA COMPANY LTD.; Int'l, pg. 848
MATSUYA ENGINEERING SERVICE CO., LTD.—See Matsuya Company Ltd.; Int'l, pg. 848
MATSUYA FASHION SERVICE CO., LTD.—See Matsuya Company Ltd.; Int'l, pg. 848
MATSUYA GINZA—See Matsuya Company Ltd.; Int'l, pg. 848
MATSUYA SHOJI CO., LTD.—See Matsuya Company Ltd.; Int'l, pg. 848
MATSUYA TRAVEL SERVICE—See Matsuya Company Ltd.; Int'l, pg. 848
MATSUYAMA PLANT—See Mitsubishi Chemical Corporation; Int'l, pg. 871

MASTER INDEX TO COMPANY NAMES MCARDLE
Company Index

MATT CONSTRUCTION SERVICES, INC.—See Columbia National Group, Inc.; U.S. Private, pg. 256
THE F.X. MATT BREWING CO.; U.S. Private, pg. 714
MATTEL ASIA LTD.—See Mattel, Inc.; U.S. Public, pg. 1059
MATTEL B.V. (NETHERLANDS)—See Mattel, Inc.; U.S. Public, pg. 1059
MATTEL CANADA, INC.—See Mattel, Inc.; U.S. Public, pg. 1059
MATTEL CHILE S.A. (CHILE)—See Mattel, Inc.; U.S. Public, pg. 1059
MATTEL ESPANA, S.A.—See Mattel, Inc.; U.S. Public, pg. 1059
MATTEL FRANCE S.A.—See Mattel, Inc.; U.S. Public, pg. 1059
MATTEL FUNDING CORPORATION—See Mattel, Inc.; U.S. Public, pg. 1058
MATTEL G, INC.—See Mattel, Inc.; U.S. Public, pg. 1058
MATTEL GAMES/PUZZLES—See Mattel, Inc.; U.S. Public, pg. 1058
MATTEL GMBH—See Mattel, Inc.; U.S. Public, pg. 1059
MATTEL HOLDING, INC.—See Mattel, Inc.; U.S. Public, pg. 1058
MATTEL I., INC.—See Mattel, Inc.; U.S. Public, pg. 1058
MATTEL, INC.; U.S. Public, pg. 1057
MATTEL INTERNATIONAL LIMITED—See Mattel, Inc.; U.S. Public, pg. 1058
MATTEL (K.L.) SDN. BHD. (MAYLAYSIA)—See Mattel, Inc.; U.S. Public, pg. 1059
MATTEL (MALAYSIA) SDN. BHD.—See Mattel, Inc.; U.S. Public, pg. 1059
MATTEL OVERSEAS, INC.—See Mattel, Inc.; U.S. Public, pg. 1058
MATTEL POWER WHEELS—See Mattel, Inc.; U.S. Public, pg. 1058
MATTEL PTY. LTD.—See Mattel, Inc.; U.S. Public, pg. 1059
MATTEL REALTY CORPORATION—See Mattel, Inc.; U.S. Public, pg. 1058
MATTEL T COMPANY LTD.—See Mattel, Inc.; U.S. Public, pg. 1059
MATTEL TOYS (H.K.) LTD.—See Mattel, Inc.; U.S. Public, pg. 1059
MATTEL TOYS MEXICO—See Mattel, Inc.; U.S. Public, pg. 1058
MATTEL TOYS (NZ) LIMITED (NEW ZEALAND)—See Mattel, Inc.; U.S. Public, pg. 1059
MATTEL TOYS, S.R.L.—See Mattel, Inc.; U.S. Public, pg. 1059
MATTEL (UK) LTD.—See Mattel, Inc.; U.S. Public, pg. 1059
MATTER LEO BURNETT—See Leo Burnett Company, Inc.; U.S. Private, pg. 186
MATTERHORN BANK PROGRAMS, INC.—See Avemco Corporation; U.S. Public, pg. 152
MATTERN HATCHERY—See Empire Kosher Poultry, Inc.; U.S. Private, pg. 374
MATTESSONS WALLS LTD.—See Unilever Plc; Int'l, pg. 1434
MATTHES & WEBER GMBH—See Henkel KGaA; Int'l, pg. 610
MATTHEW CLARK BRANDS—See Matthew Clark Taunton, Ltd.; Int'l, pg. 848
MATTHEW CLARK TAUNTON, LTD.; Int'l, pg. 848
MATTHEW WARREN INC.—See Harbour Group Ltd.; U.S. Private, pg. 500
MATTHEWS CANADA LTD.—See Matthews International Corp.; U.S. Public, pg. 1060
MATTHEWS INTERNATIONAL CORP.; U.S. Public, pg. 1059
MATTHEWS INTL. CORP.-GRAPHIC SYSTEMS DIV.—See Matthews International Corp.; U.S. Public, pg. 1060
MATTHEWS INTERNATIONAL MARKING SYSTEMS DIV.—See Matthews International Corp.; U.S. Public, pg. 1059
MATTHEWS INTERNATIONAL MEMORIAL DIVISION—See Matthews International Corp.; U.S. Public, pg. 1059
MATTHEWS INTL. TRADING CORP.—See Matthews International Corp.; U.S. Public, pg. 1060
MATTHEWS PRIME SIRLOIN, INC.—See WSMP, Inc.; U.S. Public, pg. 1729
MATTHEWS STUDIO EQUIPMENT; U.S. Public, pg. 1060
MATTHEWS-MORSE SUPPLY—See Associated Industrial Supply, Inc.; U.S. Private, pg. 91
MATTHEY BEYRAND & CIE S.A.—See Johnson Matthey Public Limited Company; Int'l, pg. 714
MATTISON TECHNOLOGIES, INC.; U.S. Private, pg. 714
MATTOON MFG. DIVISION—See R.R. Donnelley & Sons Company; U.S. Public, pg. 518
MATTSON TECHNOLOGY, INC.; U.S. Public, pg. 1060
MATUA FINANCE LIMITED—See Foster's Brewing Group Limited; Int'l, pg. 500
MATZEN & TIMM SCHLAUCHWERK—See Smiths Industries plc; Int'l, pg. 1268
MAUERHOFER, LANZ & CO. AG—See Coop Switzerland; Int'l, pg. 330
MAUI CUP—See Letica Corporation; U.S. Private, pg. 661
MAUI DEVELOPMENT—See Royal Dutch/Shell Group of Companies; Int'l, pg. 1137
MAUI DIVERS OF HAWAII; U.S. Private, pg. 715
MAUI ELECTRIC CO., LTD.—See Hawaiian Electric Industries, Inc.; U.S. Public, pg. 800
MAUI FRESH EGGS—See Valley Isle Produce, V.I.P. Food Service; U.S. Private, pg. 1132
MAUI LAND & PINEAPPLE CO., INC.; U.S. Public, pg. 1060
MAUI PINEAPPLE CO., LTD.—See Maui Land & Pineapple Co., Inc.; U.S. Public, pg. 1060
MAUI VARIETIES, LTD.; U.S. Private, pg. 715
MAUL-BELSER GMBH; Int'l, pg. 849
MAUNA KEA AGRIBUSINESS CO., INC.—See Buyco, Inc.; U.S. Private, pg. 190
MAUNA LOA MACADAMIA NUT CORPORATION—See Buyco, Inc.; U.S. Private, pg. 190
MAUNA LOA MACADAMIA PARTNERS, L.P.; U.S. Public, pg. 1060
MAUNA LOA ORCHIDS, LTD.—See Flowers of Hawaii; U.S. Private, pg. 415
MAUNA LOA RESOURCES INC.—See Buyco, Inc.; U.S. Private, pg. 191
MAUNEY HOSIERY MILLS, INC.; U.S. Private, pg. 715
MAUREL & CALBERSON MONTPELLIER—See SNCF; Int'l, pg. 1164
MAUREXCO EXPORTERS—See Maurice Electric Supply Company; U.S. Private, pg. 715
MAUREY MANUFACTURING CORP.; U.S. Private, pg. 715
MAURICE ELECTRIC SUPPLY COMPANY; U.S. Private, pg. 715
MAURIN-OGDEN MANAGEMENT CORPORATION—See Maurin-Ogden Properties; U.S. Private, pg. 715
MAURIN-OGDEN PROPERTIES; U.S. Private, pg. 715
MAUS FRERES S.A.; Int'l, pg. 849
MAUSER WALDECK AG—See Rheinmetall Group; Int'l, pg. 1108
MAUTNER MARKHOF INTERNATIONAL GMBH—See Koninklijke BolsWessanen nv; Int'l, pg. 753
MAUTZ PAINT CO.; U.S. Private, pg. 715
MAVERICK TUBE CORPORATION; U.S. Public, pg. 1060
MAVERIK COUNTRY STORES, INC.; U.S. Private, pg. 715
MAVIBEL INTERNATIONAL N.V.—See Unilever Plc; Int'l, pg. 1438
MAVIBEL (MAATSCHAPPIJ VOOR INTERNATIONALE BELEGGINGEN) B.V.—See Unilever Plc; Int'l, pg. 1438
MAVILOR S.A.—See Fried. Krupp AG; Int'l, pg. 508
MAX & ERMA'S RESTAURANTS; U.S. Public, pg. 1060
MAX COCHIUS GMBH - NUREMBERG BRANCH—See Fried. Krupp AG; Int'l, pg. 514
MAX FACTOR K.K.—See The Procter & Gamble Company; U.S. Public, pg. 1331
MAX-GB LTD.—See Royal Gist-Brocades N.V.; Int'l, pg. 1143
MAXCIMATOR AB—See Telefonaktiebolaget LM Ericsson; Int'l, pg. 1364
MAXCO, INC.; U.S. Public, pg. 1061
MAXCOR MANUFACTURING, INC.; U.S. Private, pg. 716
MAXELL CORP. OF AMERICA—See Hitachi, Ltd.; Int'l, pg. 621
MAXELL DE MEXICO S.A. DE C.V.—See Hitachi, Ltd.; Int'l, pg. 621
MAXI-PAPIER MARKET GMBH—See Staples, Inc.; U.S. Public, pg. 1510
MAXICARE HEALTH PLANS, INC.; U.S. Public, pg. 1061
MAXIM INTEGRATED PRODUCTS, INC.; U.S. Public, pg. 1061
MARY MAXIM, INC.; U.S. Private, pg. 716
MARY MAXIM, LTD.—See Mary Maxim, Inc.; U.S. Private, pg. 716
THE MAXIMA CORPORATION; U.S. Private, pg. 716
MAXIMET—See Karsten Manufacturing Corporation; U.S. Private, pg. 608
MAXIM'S CATERERS LTD.—See Jardine Matheson Holdings Limited; Int'l, pg. 704
MAXINE OF HOLLYWOOD, INC.; U.S. Private, pg. 716
MAXION COMPONENTES ESTRUTURAS LTDA—See Iochpe-Maxion S.A.; Int'l, pg. 688
MAXION FUND E EQUIPMENTES FERROVIAMS LTDA—See Iochpe-Maxion S.A.; Int'l, pg. 688
MAXIS—See Electronic Arts; U.S. Public, pg. 569
MAXIS B.V.—See SHV Holdings N.V.; Int'l, pg. 1156
MAXITILE INC.—See Saint-Gobain; Int'l, pg. 1171
MAXITROL CO.; U.S. Private, pg. 716
MAXITROL COMPANY M.B.H.—See Maxitrol Co.; U.S. Private, pg. 716
MAXON ADVANCED VEHICLE SYSTEMS—See Maxon Industries, Inc.; U.S. Private, pg. 717
MAXON COMBUSTION SYSTEMS, LTD.—See Maxon Corporation; U.S. Private, pg. 717
MAXON COMPACTOR CORP.—See Maxon Industries, Inc.; U.S. Private, pg. 717
MAXON CORPORATION; U.S. Private, pg. 716
MAXON GMBH—See Maxon Corporation; U.S. Private, pg. 717
MAXON INDUSTRIES, INC.; U.S. Private, pg. 717
MAXON INDUSTRIES, S.A. DE C.V.—See Maxon Industries, Inc.; U.S. Private, pg. 717
MAXON INTERNATIONAL, INC.—See Maxon Industries, Inc.; U.S. Private, pg. 717
N.V. MAXON INTERNATIONAL S.A.—See Maxon Corporation; U.S. Private, pg. 717
MAXON REFUSE CHASSIS CORP.—See Maxon Industries, Inc.; U.S. Private, pg. 717
MAXON S.A.R.L.—See Maxon Corporation; U.S. Private, pg. 717
MAXOPTIX CORP.—See Kubota Corp.; Int'l, pg. 762
MAXPRO—See Ultrak Inc.; U.S. Public, pg. 1663
MAXPRO SYSTEMS—See Ultrak Inc.; U.S. Public, pg. 1663
MAXTECH, INC.—See Vertex Communications Corporation; U.S. Public, pg. 1718
MAXTOR CORPORATION—See Hyundai Motor Company; Int'l, pg. 641
MAXUM ENGINEERING ENTERPRISES LTD.—See Agra Inc.; Int'l, pg. 31
MAXUM HEALTH CORP.—See Insight Health Services Corp.; U.S. Public, pg. 881
MAXUS ENERGY CORPORATION—See Y.P.F., S.A.; Int'l, pg. 1515
MAXUS SOUTHEAST SUMATRA—See Y.P.F., S.A.; Int'l, pg. 1515
MAXWELL MACMILLAN PROFESSIONAL & BUSINESS REFERENCE PUBLISHING—See The Thomson Corporation; U.S. Public, pg. 1602
MAXWELL TECHNOLOGIES-FEDERAL DIVISION—See Maxwell Technologies, Inc.; U.S. Public, pg. 1062
MAXWELL TECHNOLOGIES, INC.; U.S. Public, pg. 1061
MAXWELL TECHNOLOGIES-INFORMATION SYSTEMS DIVISION—See Maxwell Technologies, Inc.; U.S. Public, pg. 1062
MAXXAM INC.; U.S. Public, pg. 1062
MAXXAM PROPERTY COMPANY—See Maxxam Inc.; U.S. Public, pg. 1062
MAXXIM MEDICAL, INC.; U.S. Public, pg. 1063
MAY & SPEH, INC.; U.S. Public, pg. 1063
THE MAY APPAREL GROUP, INC.; U.S. Private, pg. 717
MAY & BAKER NIGERIA LTD.—See Rhone-Poulenc S.A.; Int'l, pg. 1112
THE MAY DEPARTMENT STORES COMPANY; U.S. Public, pg. 1063
MAY DEPARTMENT STORES INTERNATIONAL, INC.—See The May Department Stores Company; U.S. Public, pg. 1064
MAY DESIGN & CONSTRUCTION CO.—See The May Department Stores Company; U.S. Public, pg. 1064
GEORGE S. MAY CANADA, LTD.—See George S. May International Company; U.S. Private, pg. 717
GEORGE S. MAY INTERNATIONAL COMPANY; U.S. Private, pg. 717
GEORGE S. MAY INTERNATIONAL, S.P.A.—See George S. May International Company; U.S. Private, pg. 717
MAY MERCHANDISING COMPANY—See The May Department Stores Company; U.S. Public, pg. 1064
MAY SUPPLY COMPANY, INC.—See WLR Foods, Inc.; U.S. Public, pg. 1727
MAYBELLINE, INC.—See L'Oreal S.A.; Int'l, pg. 819
MAYC S.A.—See Candy S.p.A.; Int'l, pg. 260
MAYER/BERKSHIRE CORPORATION; U.S. Private, pg. 717
MAYER MYERS PAPER COMPANY; U.S. Private, pg. 718
MAYER & SCHWEITZER, INC.—See The Charles Schwab Corporation; U.S. Public, pg. 1443
MAYFAIR MILLS, INC.; U.S. Private, pg. 718
MAYFAIR MOLDED PRODUCTS CORPORATION—See Wozniak Industries, Inc.; U.S. Private, pg. 1192
MAYFIELD BUILDING SUPPLY CO.—See MBS Holding, Inc.; U.S. Private, pg. 686
MAYFIELD DAIRY FARMS INC.—See Dean Foods Company; U.S. Public, pg. 490
F R MAYFIELD—See AMEC Plc; Int'l, pg. 16
MAYFIELD SWAIN/KELLER—See MBS Holding, Inc.; U.S. Private, pg. 686
MAYFIELD SWAIN ROCKWALL—See MBS Holding, Inc.; U.S. Private, pg. 686
MAYFLOWER TRANSIT, INC.—See UniGroup, Inc.; U.S. Private, pg. 1117
MAYFRAN INTERNATIONAL, INC.—See Tomkins PLC; Int'l, pg. 1397
MAYFRAN LIMBURG, B.V.—See Tomkins PLC; Int'l, pg. 1398
MAYNARD OIL CO.; U.S. Public, pg. 1064
MAYNARD STEEL CASTING COMPANY; U.S. Private, pg. 718
MAYO CENTER—See Genesis Health Ventures, Inc.; U.S. Public, pg. 729
A.T. MAYS (U.K.)—See Carlson Companies, Inc.; U.S. Private, pg. 212
MAYS CHEMICAL COMPANY; U.S. Private, pg. 718
MAYTAG AIRCRAFT CORP.—See Mercury Air Group Inc.; U.S. Public, pg. 1093
MAYTAG CLARENCE COMPONENT PARTS—See Maytag Corporation; U.S. Public, pg. 1064
MAYTAG CLEVELAND COOKING PRODUCTS—See Maytag Corporation; U.S. Public, pg. 1064
MAYTAG COMPANY—See Maytag Corporation; U.S. Public, pg. 1064
MAYTAG CORPORATION; U.S. Public, pg. 1064
MAYTAG CUSTOMER SERVICE—See Maytag Corporation; U.S. Public, pg. 1064
MAYTAG FINANCIAL SERVICES CORP.—See Maytag Corporation; U.S. Public, pg. 1065
MAYTAG GALESBURG REFRIGERATION PRODUCTS—See Maytag Corporation; U.S. Public, pg. 1064
MAYTAG/HERRIN LAUNDRY PRODUCTS—See Maytag Corporation; U.S. Public, pg. 1064
MAYTAG INTERNATIONAL, INC.—See Maytag Corporation; U.S. Public, pg. 1065
MAYTAG/JEFFERSON CITY COMPONENT PARTS—See Maytag Corporation; U.S. Public, pg. 1064
MAYTAG/JACKSON DISHWASHING PRODUCTS—See Maytag Corporation; U.S. Public, pg. 1064
MAYVILLE ENGINEERING CO., INC.; U.S. Private, pg. 718
MAYWOOD ACRES HEALTHCARE—See Vencor, Inc.; U.S. Public, pg. 1714
MAZDA CANADA, INC.—See Itochu Corporation; Int'l, pg. 695
P.T. MAZDA INDONESIA MANUFACTURING—See Mazda Motor Corporation; Int'l, pg. 849
MAZDA MOTOR CORPORATION; Int'l, pg. 849
MAZE NAILS; U.S. Private, pg. 718
MAZIDI TRADING COMPANY W.L.L.—See BASF AG; Int'l, pg. 109
MAZO LERCH COMPANY, INC.—See JP Foodservice, Inc.; U.S. Public, pg. 918
MAZZUCCHELLI 1849 S.P.A.; Int'l, pg. 849
MAZZUCCHELLI POLIMERI SRL; Int'l, pg. 850
MBNA INTERNATIONAL BANK LIMITED (MBNA INTERNATIONAL)—See MBNA Corporation; U.S. Public, pg. 1023
MCALEAR ASSOCIATES, INC.—See Willis Corroon Group PLC; Int'l, pg. 1508
MCALESTER NEWS-CAPITAL & DEMOCRAT—See Media General, Inc.; U.S. Public, pg. 1078
MCALESTER PUBLISHING CO.—See Media General, Inc.; U.S. Public, pg. 1078
MCALLEN MEDICAL CENTER—See Universal Health Services, Inc.; U.S. Public, pg. 1697
MCALLEN PIPE & SUPPLY DIV.—See United States Filter Corporation; U.S. Public, pg. 1682
MCALPIN'S—See Mercantile Stores Company, Inc.; U.S. Public, pg. 1090
MCANALLY ENTERPRISES, INC.; U.S. Private, pg. 718
MCARDLE PRINTING CO., INC.—See The Bureau of National Affairs, Inc.; U.S. Private, pg. 182

MCARTHUR DAIRY, INC.—See Dean Foods Company; *U.S. Public*, pg. 491
THE MCARTHUR SHIPPING & AGENCY COMPANY PTY. LTD.—See Brambles Industries Limited; *Int'l*, pg. 211
MCBEE SYSTEMS, INC.; *U.S. Private*, pg. 718
MCBRIDE AND ASSOCIATES, INC.; *U.S. Private*, pg. 719
MCCABE & COMPANY; *U.S. Private*, pg. 719
MCCAIN ALIMENTAIRE SA—See McCain Foods Limited; *Int'l*, pg. 850
MCCAIN ALIMENTARI (ITALIA) SRL—See McCain Foods Limited; *Int'l*, pg. 850
MCCAIN ARGENTINA SA—See McCain Foods Limited; *Int'l*, pg. 850
MCCAIN BINDERY SYSTEMS, INC.; *U.S. Private*, pg. 719
MCCAIN CITRUS INC.—See McCain Foods Limited; *Int'l*, pg. 850
MCCAIN-ELLIOS FOOD INC.—See McCain Foods Limited; *Int'l*, pg. 850
MCCAIN ESPANA S.A. (SPAIN)—See McCain Foods Limited; *Int'l*, pg. 850
MCCAIN FERTILIZERS LIMITED—See McCain Foods Limited; *Int'l*, pg. 850
MCCAIN FOODS (AUSTRALIA) PTY. LTD.—See McCain Foods Limited; *Int'l*, pg. 850
MCCAIN FOODS BELGIUM N.V. (BELGIUM)—See McCain Foods Limited; *Int'l*, pg. 850
MCCAIN FOODS (GB) LIMITED—See McCain Foods Limited; *Int'l*, pg. 850
MCCAIN FOODS HOLLAND B.V. (THE NETHERLANDS)—See McCain Foods Limited; *Int'l*, pg. 850
MCCAIN FOODS INC.—See McCain Foods Limited; *Int'l*, pg. 850
MCCAIN FOODS (JAPAN) LIMITED—See McCain Foods Limited; *Int'l*, pg. 850
MCCAIN FOODS LIMITED; *Int'l*, pg. 850
MCCAIN FOODS (NZ) LTD.—See McCain Foods Limited; *Int'l*, pg. 850
MCCAIN GMBH (GERMANY)—See McCain Foods Limited; *Int'l*, pg. 850
MCCAIN PRODUCE INC.—See McCain Foods Limited; *Int'l*, pg. 850
MCCAIN REFRIGERATED FOODS INC.—See McCain Foods Limited; *Int'l*, pg. 850
MCCAIN SUNNYLAND BELGIUM—See McCain Foods Limited; *Int'l*, pg. 850
MCCALL OIL & CHEMICAL CORP.; *U.S. Private*, pg. 719
MCCALL OIL REAL ESTATE CORPORATION—See McCall Oil & Chemical Corp.; *U.S. Private*, pg. 719
MCCALL PROPERTIES, INC.—See McCall Oil & Chemical Corp.; *U.S. Private*, pg. 719
STERLING MCCALL TOYOTA GROUP; *U.S. Private*, pg. 719
MCCALL WINERIES & DISTILLERS—See Suntory Ltd.; *Int'l*, pg. 1321
MCCALL'S MAGAZINE—See Bertelsmann AG; *Int'l*, pg. 190
MCCANDLESS SAN TOMAS NO. 1—See Cigna Corp.; *U.S. Public*, pg. 361
MCCANDLESS TOWERS, PHASE II—See Cigna Corp.; *U.S. Public*, pg. 365
MCCANN-ERICKSON WORLDWIDE—See The Interpublic Group of Companies, Inc.; *U.S. Public*, pg. 909
MCCARTHY BAILEY LIMITED—See N.G. Bailey & Co. Ltd.; *Int'l*, pg. 133
MCCARTHY BROTHERS CO.—See McCarthy Building Companies; *U.S. Private*, pg. 719
MCCARTHY BUILDING COMPANIES; *U.S. Private*, pg. 719
MCCARTY FOODS, INC.—See Tyson Foods, Inc.; *U.S. Public*, pg. 1652
MCCAULEY PROPELLER SYSTEMS—See Textron Inc.; *U.S. Public*, pg. 1589
MCCLAIN EASY PACK—See McClain Industries, Inc.; *U.S. Public*, pg. 1065
MCCLAIN INDUSTRIES, INC.; *U.S. Public*, pg. 1065
MCCLAIN OF GEORGIA, INC.—See McClain Industries, Inc.; *U.S. Public*, pg. 1065
MCCLATCHY NEWSPAPERS INC.; *U.S. Public*, pg. 1065
MCCLATCHY PRINTING SERVICE—See McClatchy Newspapers Inc.; *U.S. Public*, pg. 1066
B.H. MCCLEERY & CO. LTD.—See Lamont Holdings Plc; *Int'l*, pg. 797
MCCLELLAND & STEWART; *Int'l*, pg. 851
MCCLELLAND-SUHAIMI, LTD.—See Fugro Group Companies; *Int'l*, pg. 431
MCCLELLANVILLE TELEPHONE CO., INC.—See Telephone and Data Systems, Inc.; *U.S. Public*, pg. 1571
JESSICA MCCLINTOCK INC.; *U.S. Private*, pg. 719
THE MCCLOSKEY CORPORATION—See McWhorter Technologies, Inc.; *U.S. Public*, pg. 1074
THE MCCLURE GROUP; *U.S. Private*, pg. 719
THE MCCLURE GROUP—See The McClure Group; *U.S. Private*, pg. 720
THE MCCLURE GROUP/AMERICAN TELEDIRECT—See The McClure Group; *U.S. Private*, pg. 720
THE MCCLURE GROUP/AMERICAN TELEDIRECT—See The McClure Group; *U.S. Private*, pg. 720
MCCOLLS DAIRY—See Crystal Cream & Butter Company; *U.S. Private*, pg. 294
MCCOMBS AUTOMOTIVE; *U.S. Private*, pg. 720
MCCONNAUGHY STEIN SCHMIDT BROWN; *U.S. Private*, pg. 720
MCCONNELL AUTOMOTIVE; *U.S. Private*, pg. 720
MCCONNELL CABINETS, INC.; *U.S. Private*, pg. 720
MCCORD PAYEN—See T & N Plc; *Int'l*, pg. 1335
MCCORD PAYEN INC.—See T & N Plc; *Int'l*, pg. 1334
MCCORD WINN TEXTRON COMPANY—See Textron Inc.; *U.S. Public*, pg. 1590
OY MCCORMICK AB—See McCormick & Company, Incorporated; *U.S. Public*, pg. 1067
MCCORMICK & COMPANY, INCORPORATED; *U.S. Public*, pg. 1066

MCCORMICK CANADA, LTD.—See McCormick & Company, Incorporated; *U.S. Public*, pg. 1067
MCCORMICK DE CENTRO AMERICA, S.A.—See McCormick & Company, Incorporated; *U.S. Public*, pg. 1067
MCCORMICK DE MEXICO, S.A. DE C.V.—See McCormick & Company, Incorporated; *U.S. Public*, pg. 1067
MCCORMICK DE VENEZUELA, C.A.—See McCormick & Company, Incorporated; *U.S. Public*, pg. 1067
MCCORMICK DISTILLING CO.; *U.S. Private*, pg. 720
MCCORMICK FLAVOR DIVISION-U.S.A.—See McCormick & Company, Incorporated; *U.S. Public*, pg. 1066
MCCORMICK FOODS AUSTRALIA PTY. LTD.—See McCormick & Company, Incorporated; *U.S. Public*, pg. 1067
MCCORMICK GLENTHAM (PTY)—See McCormick & Company, Incorporated; *U.S. Public*, pg. 1067
MCCORMICK (GUANGZHOU) FOOD COMPANY, LTD.—See McCormick & Company, Incorporated; *U.S. Public*, pg. 1067
J.H. MCCORMICK, INC.; *U.S. Private*, pg. 720
P.T. MCCORMICK INDONESIA—See McCormick & Company, Incorporated; *U.S. Public*, pg. 1067
MCCORMICK INGREDIENTS—See McCormick & Company, Incorporated; *U.S. Public*, pg. 1066
MCCORMICK-LION LTD.—See McCormick & Company, Incorporated; *U.S. Public*, pg. 1067
MCCORMICK PAINT WORKS COMPANY; *U.S. Private*, pg. 720
MCCORMICK PESA, S.A. DE C.V.—See McCormick & Company, Incorporated; *U.S. Public*, pg. 1067
MCCORMICK-PHILIPPINES, INC.—See McCormick & Company, Incorporated; *U.S. Public*, pg. 1067
MCCORMICK S.A.—See McCormick & Company, Incorporated; *U.S. Public*, pg. 1067
MCCORMICK/SCHILLING—See McCormick & Company, Incorporated; *U.S. Public*, pg. 1066
MCCORMICK THAILAND, INC.—See McCormick & Company, Incorporated; *U.S. Public*, pg. 1067
MCCORMICK (UK) PLC.—See McCormick & Company, Incorporated; *U.S. Public*, pg. 1067
MCCORQUODALE COLORCARD, INC.—See Rexam PLC; *Int'l*, pg. 1106
MCCOURT LABEL CO.; *U.S. Private*, pg. 720
MCCOWAN MOBILE MIX—See Holderbank Financiere Glaris Ltd.; *Int'l*, pg. 629
MCCOY/COVE MINES—See Echo Bay Mines Ltd.; *U.S. Public*, pg. 562
MCCOY ELECTRONICS CO.—See Oak Industries Inc.; *U.S. Public*, pg. 1209
MCCOY GROUP INC.; *U.S. Private*, pg. 720
MCCOY'S BUILDING SUPPLY CENTERS; *U.S. Private*, pg. 720
MCCRACKEN—See International Pipe Machinery Corp.; *U.S. Private*, pg. 571
MCCROMETER INC.—See Danaher Corporation; *U.S. Public*, pg. 482
MCCRORY CONSTRUCTION CO., INC.; *U.S. Private*, pg. 720
MCCRORY CORPORATION; *U.S. Private*, pg. 720
MCCRORY STORES DIV.—See McCrory Corporation; *U.S. Private*, pg. 721
MCCULLOUGH, AN ATLAS WIRELINE SERVICES OPERATION—See Litton Industries, Inc.; *U.S. Public*, pg. 1004
J.V. MCDANIEL LIMITED—See James Crean PLC; *Int'l*, pg. 340
DAVID MCDAVID AUTO DEALERSHIP; *U.S. Private*, pg. 721
P.T. MCDERMOTT INDONESIA—See McDermott International, Inc.; *U.S. Public*, pg. 1068
MCDERMOTT INTERNATIONAL, INC.; *U.S. Public*, pg. 1067
MCDERMOTT SCOTLAND—See McDermott International, Inc.; *U.S. Public*, pg. 1068
MCDERMOTT SOUTHEAST ASIA PTY. LTD.—See McDermott International, Inc.; *U.S. Public*, pg. 1068
MCDONALD & COMPANY INVESTMENTS, INC.; *U.S. Public*, pg. 1068
A.Y. MCDONALD INDUSTRIES, INC.; *U.S. Private*, pg. 721
A.Y. MCDONALD MFG. CO.—See A.Y. McDonald Industries, Inc.; *U.S. Private*, pg. 721
A.Y. MCDONALD SUPPLY CO. INC.—See A.Y. McDonald Industries, Inc.; *U.S. Private*, pg. 721
MCDONALD EQUIPMENT CO.; *U.S. Private*, pg. 721
MCDONALD PRODUCTS COMPANY—See Smith McDonald Corp.; *U.S. Private*, pg. 1009
MCDONALD'S CORPORATION; *U.S. Public*, pg. 1068
MCDONALD'S DEUTSCHLAND GMBH—See McDonald's Corporation; *U.S. Public*, pg. 1069
MCDONALD'S FRANCE SA—See McDonald's Corporation; *U.S. Public*, pg. 1069
MCDONALD'S HAMBURGERS LIMITED—See McDonald's Corporation; *U.S. Public*, pg. 1069
MCDONALD'S INTL.—See McDonald's Corporation; *U.S. Public*, pg. 1069
MCDONALD'S ITALIA S.R.L.—See McDonald's Corporation; *U.S. Public*, pg. 1069
MCDONALD'S RESTAURANTS (HONG KONG) LTD.—See McDonald's Corporation; *U.S. Public*, pg. 1069
MCDONALD'S RESTAURANTS OF CANADA LTD.—See McDonald's Corporation; *U.S. Public*, pg. 1069
MCDONALD'S SISTEMAS DE ESPANA—See McDonald's Corporation; *U.S. Public*, pg. 1069
MCDONALD'S SYSTEM OF AUSTRALIA LTD.—See McDonald's Corporation; *U.S. Public*, pg. 1069
MCDONALD'S SYSTEM OF NEW ZEALAND LTD.—See McDonald's Corporation; *U.S. Public*, pg. 1069
MCDONALD'S U.S.A.—See McDonald's Corporation; *U.S. Public*, pg. 1069
MCDONNELL AIRCRAFT & MISSILE SYSTEMS DIV.—See The Boeing Company; *U.S. Public*, pg. 241
W. & C. MCDONNELL LTD.—See Unilever Plc; *Int'l*, pg. 1438

MCDOUGAL/LITTELL—See Houghton Mifflin Company; *U.S. Public*, pg. 841
MCDOUGALLS CATERING FOODS LIMITED—See Tomkins PLC; *Int'l*, pg. 1396
MCDOWELL MFG. CO. INC.—See The Cypress Companies; *U.S. Private*, pg. 300
MCDOWELL NEWS—See Media General, Inc.; *U.S. Public*, pg. 1078
MARGARET K. MCELDERRY BOOKS—See National Amusements, Inc.; *U.S. Private*, pg. 777
MCEWEN LUMBER COMPANY—See International Paper Company; *U.S. Public*, pg. 903
MCFARLING FOODS, INC.; *U.S. Private*, pg. 721
MCGAVIN FOODS LTD.—See Maple Leaf Foods Inc.; *Int'l*, pg. 850
MCGEAN-ROHCO, INC.; *U.S. Private*, pg. 721
WM. H. MCGEE & CO., INC.—See Orion Capital Corporation; *U.S. Public*, pg. 1231
MCGHAN LIMITED—See Inamed Corporation; *U.S. Public*, pg. 874
MCGHAN MEDICAL CORPORATION—See Inamed Corporation; *U.S. Public*, pg. 873
MCGILL MANUFACTURING COMPANY, INC.—See Emerson Electric Co.; *U.S. Public*, pg. 573
MCGLYNN BAKERIES INC.; *U.S. Private*, pg. 721
MCGRATH RENTCORP; *U.S. Public*, pg. 1069
MCGRAW GLASS DIV.—See Chrysler Corporation; *U.S. Public*, pg. 353
MCGRAW-HILL AVIATION WEEK GROUP—See The McGraw-Hill Companies; *U.S. Public*, pg. 1070
MCGRAW-HILL BOOK CO. AUSTRALIA PTY. LTD.—See The McGraw-Hill Companies; *U.S. Public*, pg. 1072
MCGRAW-HILL BOOK CO. (U.K.) LTD.—See The McGraw-Hill Companies; *U.S. Public*, pg. 1072
MCGRAW-HILL BROADCASTING CO., INC.—See The McGraw-Hill Companies; *U.S. Public*, pg. 1070
MCGRAW-HILL COLLEGE DIVISION—See The McGraw-Hill Companies; *U.S. Public*, pg. 1070
THE MCGRAW-HILL COMPANIES; *U.S. Public*, pg. 1069
MCGRAW-HILL COMPUTERS & COMMUNICATIONS INFORMATION GROUP—See The McGraw-Hill Companies; *U.S. Public*, pg. 1070
MCGRAW-HILL CONSTRUCTION INFORMATION GROUP—See The McGraw-Hill Companies; *U.S. Public*, pg. 1070
MCGRAW-HILL CONTINUING EDUCATION CENTER—See The McGraw-Hill Companies; *U.S. Public*, pg. 1070
MCGRAW-HILL FINANCIAL INFORMATION SERVICES GROUP—See The McGraw-Hill Companies; *U.S. Public*, pg. 1071
MCGRAW-HILL HEALTHCARE PUBLICATIONS GROUP—See The McGraw-Hill Companies; *U.S. Public*, pg. 1071
MCGRAW-HILL INFORMATION SYSTEMS CO. OF CANADA LTD.—See The McGraw-Hill Companies; *U.S. Public*, pg. 1072
MCGRAW HILL INTERAMERICANA DE ESPANA S.A.—See The McGraw-Hill Companies; *U.S. Public*, pg. 1072
MCGRAW-HILL/INTERAMERICANA DE MEXICO, S.A. DE CV—See The McGraw-Hill Companies; *U.S. Public*, pg. 1072
MCGRAW-HILL INTERAMERICANA DE PORTUGAL, LTDA—See The McGraw-Hill Companies; *U.S. Public*, pg. 1072
MCGRAW-HILL INTERNATIONAL PUBLICATIONS CO. LTD.—See The McGraw-Hill Companies; *U.S. Public*, pg. 1072
MCGRAW-HILL LIBRI ITALIA, S.R.L.—See The McGraw-Hill Companies; *U.S. Public*, pg. 1072
MCGRAW-HILL PROFESSIONAL PUBLISHING GROUP—See The McGraw-Hill Companies; *U.S. Public*, pg. 1070
MCGRAW-HILL PUBLICATIONS SERVICES GROUP—See The McGraw-Hill Companies; *U.S. Public*, pg. 1071
MCGRAW-HILL PUBLISHING CO.-JAPAN LTD.—See The McGraw-Hill Companies; *U.S. Public*, pg. 1072
MCGRAW-HILL RYERSON, LTD.—See The McGraw-Hill Companies; *U.S. Public*, pg. 1072
MCGRAW-HILL SECURITIES TRADING, INC.—See The McGraw-Hill Companies; *U.S. Public*, pg. 1071
MCGRAW/KOKOSING, INC.—See Kokosing Construction Company, Inc.; *U.S. Public*, pg. 631
MCGREGOR GOLF JAPAN LTD.—See Suntory Ltd.; *Int'l*, pg. 1321
MCGUFFEY'S RESTAURANTS, INC.; *U.S. Private*, pg. 721
THE MCGUIRE FURNITURE COMPANY—See Kohler Company; *U.S. Private*, pg. 630
MCGUIRE MANUFACTURING—See Bead Industries Inc.; *U.S. Private*, pg. 126
W.B. MCGUIRE CO.—See Overhead Door Corporation; *U.S. Private*, pg. 823
MCHAL CORPORATION—See Salem Group, Inc.; *U.S. Private*, pg. 961
JAMES MCHUGH CONSTRUCTION CO.; *U.S. Private*, pg. 721
MCHUGH SOFTWARE INTERNATIONAL—See Pinnacle Automation Inc.; *U.S. Private*, pg. 866
MCHUTCHINSON DIV.—See Novartis AG; *Int'l*, pg. 973
MCILHENNY COMPANY; *U.S. Private*, pg. 722
MCILHENNY RESOURCES—See McIlhenny Company; *U.S. Private*, pg. 722
J. GIBSON MCILVAIN CO.; *U.S. Private*, pg. 722
MCINERNEY INC.; *U.S. Private*, pg. 722
MCINERNEY-MILLER BROTHERS INC.; *U.S. Private*, pg. 722
MCINNES ROLLED RINGS—See McInnes Steel Company; *U.S. Private*, pg. 722
MCINNES STEEL COMPANY; *U.S. Private*, pg. 722
MCINTOSH LABORATORY INC.—See Clarion Co., Ltd.; *Int'l*, pg. 296
MCJUNKIN - APPALACHAIN—See McJunkin Corporation; *U.S. Private*, pg. 722
MCJUNKIN CORPORATION; *U.S. Private*, pg. 722
MCKEAN OLDSMOBILE COMPANY; *U.S. Private*, pg. 722
MCKECHNIE CONSUMER EXPORT—See McKechnie PLC; *Int'l*, pg. 851

MASTER INDEX TO COMPANY NAMES MECO

Company Index

MCKECHNIE CONSUMER PRODUCTS AUSTRALASIA—See McKechnie PLC; Int'l, pg. 851
MCKECHNIE DELTA HOLDINGS (PTY.) LTD.—See Delta plc; Int'l, pg. 392
MCKECHNIE INVESTMENTS—See McKechnie PLC; Int'l, pg. 852
MCKECHNIE METAL PRODUCTS—See McKechnie PLC; Int'l, pg. 852
MCKECHNIE METALS—See McKechnie PLC; Int'l, pg. 852
MCKECHNIE PACIFIC—See McKechnie PLC; Int'l, pg. 852
MCKECHNIE PACKAGING-PHILMONT—See McKechnie PLC; Int'l, pg. 851
MCKECHNIE PLC; Int'l, pg. 851
C.S. MCKEE & COMPANY, INC.—See United Asset Management Corporation; U.S. Public, pg. 1673
MCKEE COMPLEX—See Ultramar Diamond Shamrock Corporation; U.S. Public, pg. 1663
DAVY MCKEE CORPORATION, SAN FRANCISCO—See Kvaerner a.s.a.; Int'l, pg. 774
MCKEE DOOR, INC.—See American Buildings Co.; U.S. Public, pg. 69
MCKEE FOODS CORPORATION; U.S. Private, pg. 723
MCKELLAR COMPANIES; U.S. Private, pg. 723
MCKENZIE TANK LINES, INC.; U.S. Private, pg. 723
MCKENZIE TECHNOLOGY—See Kyocera Corporation; Int'l, pg. 776
MCKENZIE TOWABLES BY MONACO—See Monaco Coach Corporation; U.S. Public, pg. 1123
MCKENZIES OF VERMONT, INC.; U.S. Private, pg. 723
MCKESSON CORPORATION; U.S. Public, pg. 1072
MCKESSON CORPORATION—See McKesson Corporation; U.S. Public, pg. 1073
MCKESSON HEALTH SYSTEMS—See McKesson Corporation; U.S. Public, pg. 1073
MCKESSON HOME HEALTH CARE DIVISION—See McKesson Corporation; U.S. Public, pg. 1073
MCKESSON MEDICAL SUPPLY—See McKesson Corporation; U.S. Public, pg. 1073
MCKESSON U.S. HEALTH CARE—See McKesson Corporation; U.S. Public, pg. 1073
MCKESSON WATER PRODUCTS COMPANY—See McKesson Corporation; U.S. Public, pg. 1073
MCKIM ADVERTISING LTD.—See N.W. Ayer & Partners; U.S. Private, pg. 104
MCKIM COMMUNICATIONS LIMITED—See N.W. Ayer & Partners; U.S. Private, pg. 104
MCKINLEY MANOR—See Horizon/CMS Healthcare Corporation; U.S. Public, pg. 838
MCKINNEY & MCKINNEY ADVERTISING; U.S. Private, pg. 723
MCKINNEY & SILVER; U.S. Private, pg. 723
MCKINNEY PRODUCTS COMPANY—See Assa Abloy AB; Int'l, pg. 18
MCKINNON BRIDGE CO.; U.S. Private, pg. 723
MCKINSEY & COMPANY, INC.; U.S. Private, pg. 723
MCKISSICK PRODUCTS CO.—See FKI Plc; Int'l, pg. 473
MCKNIGHT MEDICAL COMMUNICATIONS—See The Thomson Corporation; U.S. Public, pg. 1600
MCLANE COMPANY, INC.—See Wal-Mart Stores, Inc.; U.S. Public, pg. 1733
MCLANE FOOD SERVICE—See Wal-Mart Stores, Inc.; U.S. Public, pg. 1733
MCLAREN/HART ENVIRONMENTAL ENGINEERING COMPANY—See Viag AG; Int'l, pg. 1465
MCLAUGHLIN GORMLEY KING COMPANY; U.S. Private, pg. 723
MCLAUGHLIN INDUSTRIAL DISTRIBUTORS, INC.; U.S. Private, pg. 724
MCLAUGHLIN MANUFACTURING COMPANY; U.S. Private, pg. 724
MCLAUGHLIN MANUFACTURING CO. OF S.C.—See McLaughlin Manufacturing Company; U.S. Private, pg. 724
MCLAUGHLIN MINE—See Homestake Mining Company; U.S. Public, pg. 833
MCLEAN—See Zero Corporation; U.S. Public, pg. 1791
MCLEAN BROTHERS—See Jannock Limited; Int'l, pg. 698
MCLEAN ENGINEERING—See Zero Corporation; U.S. Public, pg. 1791
MCLEAN EUROPE—See Zero Corporation; U.S. Public, pg. 1791
MCLEAN MCCARTHY LIMITED—See Deutsche Bank AG; Int'l, pg. 405
MCLEAN MIDWEST—See Zero Corporation; U.S. Public, pg. 1791
MCLEAN-THOMAS INC.; U.S. Private, pg. 724
MCLEODUSA INCORPORATED; U.S. Public, pg. 1073
MCMASTER CARR SUPPLY CO. INC.; U.S. Private, pg. 724
MCMULLEN/ARGUS PUBLISHERS—See Primedia Inc.; U.S. Public, pg. 1328
JOHN J. MCMULLEN ASSOCIATES—See Carpenter Technology Corporation; U.S. Public, pg. 308
MCMURREY PIPE LINE COMPANY—See Crown Central Petroleum Corporation; U.S. Public, pg. 462
MCNALLY INDUSTRIES, INC.; U.S. Private, pg. 724
MCNALLY MANUFACTURING—See Svedala Industri AB; Int'l, pg. 1326
MCNALLY PITTSBURG MFG. CORP.—See Svedala Industri AB; Int'l, pg. 1326
MCNALLY WELLMAN—See Svedala Industri AB; Int'l, pg. 1326
MCNAMARA PONTIAC ISUZU INC.; U.S. Private, pg. 724
MCNAUGHTON & GUNN, INC.; U.S. Private, pg. 724
MCNAUGHTON-MCKAY ELECTRIC CO.; U.S. Private, pg. 724
MCNEEL INTERNATIONAL CORP.; U.S. Private, pg. 724
MCNEIL AKRON REPIQUET—See McNeil & NRM., Inc.; U.S. Private, pg. 725
MCNEIL & NRM., INC.; U.S. Private, pg. 725
MCNEIL CONSUMER PRODUCTS COMPANY—See Johnson & Johnson; U.S. Public, pg. 928
MCNEIL (OHIO) CORPORATION—See Pentair, Inc.; U.S. Public, pg. 1273
MCNEIL SPECIALTY PRODUCTS COMPANY—See Johnson & Johnson; U.S. Public, pg. 928
MCNEILUS COMPANIES; U.S. Private, pg. 725
MCPAPER GMBH—See Herlitz PBS Aktiengesellschaft; Int'l, pg. 616
MCPHERSON STRUT COMPANY INC.—See Tenneco Inc.; U.S. Public, pg. 1578
MCPHERSON'S AMERICA, INC.—See McPherson's Limited; Int'l, pg. 852
MCPHERSON'S LIMITED; Int'l, pg. 852
MCQUAY INT'L—See AAF McQuay, Inc.; U.S. Private, pg. 3
MCQUAY INTERNATIONAL—See AAF McQuay, Inc.; U.S. Private, pg. 3
MCQUICK'S OILUBE, INC.—See Quaker State Corporation; U.S. Public, pg. 1348
MCRAE FINANCIAL AND LEASING DIV.—See McRae Industries, Inc.; U.S. Public, pg. 1073
MCRAE FOOTWEAR DIV.—See McRae Industries, Inc.; U.S. Public, pg. 1073
MCRAE GRAPHICS, INC.—See McRae Industries, Inc.; U.S. Public, pg. 1074
MCRAE INDUSTRIES, INC.; U.S. Public, pg. 1073
MCRAE'S, INC.—See Proffitt's, Inc.; U.S. Public, pg. 1333
MCSWAIN CARPETS INC.; U.S. Private, pg. 725
MCWANE CAST IRON PIPE CO.—See McWane, Inc.; U.S. Private, pg. 725
MCWANE, INC.; U.S. Private, pg. 725
MCWHORTER TECHNOLOGIES, INC.; U.S. Public, pg. 1074
MCWILLIAMS FORGE CO.; U.S. Private, pg. 725
MEAD COATED BOARD—See The Mead Corporation; U.S. Public, pg. 1074
MEAD COATED BOARD DIVISION—See The Mead Corporation; U.S. Public, pg. 1074
MEAD COATED BOARD EUROPE B.V.—See The Mead Corporation; U.S. Public, pg. 1076
MEAD COATED BOARD EUROPE KARTONVERTRIEBS-A.G.—See The Mead Corporation; U.S. Public, pg. 1076
MEAD COATED BOARD INTL., INC.—See The Mead Corporation; U.S. Public, pg. 1076
MEAD COATED BOARD (MALAYSIA) SDN. BHD.—See The Mead Corporation; U.S. Public, pg. 1076
MEAD COATED BOARD U.K. LIMITED—See The Mead Corporation; U.S. Public, pg. 1076
MEAD CONTAINERBOARD—See The Mead Corporation; U.S. Public, pg. 1074
THE MEAD CORPORATION; U.S. Public, pg. 1074
MEAD EMBALAGENS LTDA—See The Mead Corporation; U.S. Public, pg. 1076
MEAD-EMBALLAGE S.A.—See The Mead Corporation; U.S. Public, pg. 1076
MEAD EMPAQUES S.A. DE C.V.—See The Mead Corporation; U.S. Public, pg. 1076
MEAD EUROPE ENGINEERING, S.A.R.L.—See The Mead Corporation; U.S. Public, pg. 1076
MEAD EUROPEAN HOLDINGS, INC.—See The Mead Corporation; U.S. Public, pg. 1076
MEAD EXPORT, INC.—See The Mead Corporation; U.S. Public, pg. 1076
MEAD FOREIGN HOLDINGS, INC.—See The Mead Corporation; U.S. Public, pg. 1076
MEAD HOLDINGS B.V.—See The Mead Corporation; U.S. Public, pg. 1076
D.J. MEAD-HUBBS & HOWE—See Sofco-Mead, Inc.; U.S. Private, pg. 1012
MEAD INTERNATIONAL HOLDINGS, INC.—See The Mead Corporation; U.S. Public, pg. 1076
MEAD JOHNSON & CO.—See Bristol-Myers Squibb Company; U.S. Public, pg. 254
MEAD JOHNSON BENELUX S.A.—See Bristol-Myers Squibb Company; U.S. Public, pg. 256
MEAD JOHNSON DE MEXICO, S.A. DE C.V.—See Bristol-Myers Squibb Company; U.S. Public, pg. 256
MEAD JOHNSON DE VENEZUELA, S.A.—See Bristol-Myers Squibb Company; U.S. Public, pg. 256
MEAD JOHNSON ECUADOR, S.A.—See Bristol-Myers Squibb Company; U.S. Public, pg. 256
MEAD JOHNSON JAMAICA LTD.—See Bristol-Myers Squibb Company; U.S. Public, pg. 256
MEAD JOHNSON LABORATORIES—See Bristol-Myers Squibb Company; U.S. Public, pg. 254
MEAD JOHNSON NUTRITIONAL GROUP—See Bristol-Myers Squibb Company; U.S. Public, pg. 254
MEAD JOHNSON NUTRITIONALS—See Bristol-Myers Squibb Company; U.S. Public, pg. 255
MEAD JOHNSON PHILIPPINES, INC.—See Bristol-Myers Squibb Company; U.S. Public, pg. 256
MEAD JOHNSON S.A.—See Bristol-Myers Squibb Company; U.S. Public, pg. 256
MEAD KK—See The Mead Corporation; U.S. Public, pg. 1076
MEAD MANAGEMENT SERVICES S.A.—See The Mead Corporation; U.S. Public, pg. 1076
MEAD PACKAGING—See The Mead Corporation; U.S. Public, pg. 1074
MEAD PACKAGING (CANADA) LTD.—See The Mead Corporation; U.S. Public, pg. 1076
MEAD PACKAGING CHILE LIMITADA—See The Mead Corporation; U.S. Public, pg. 1076
MEAD PACKAGING EUROPE S.A.R.L.—See The Mead Corporation; U.S. Public, pg. 1076
MEAD PACKAGING INTERNATIONAL, INC.—See The Mead Corporation; U.S. Public, pg. 1076
MEAD PACKAGING KOREA, INC.—See The Mead Corporation; U.S. Public, pg. 1076
MEAD PACKAGING LTD.—See The Mead Corporation; U.S. Public, pg. 1077
MEAD PACKAGING POLAND SP.Z O.O.—See The Mead Corporation; U.S. Public, pg. 1076
MEAD PACKAGING PROPRIETARY LTD.—See The Mead Corporation; U.S. Public, pg. 1077
MEAD PACKBOARD B.V.—See The Mead Corporation; U.S. Public, pg. 1076
MEAD PANELBOARD, INC.—See The Mead Corporation; U.S. Public, pg. 1076
MEAD PUBLISHING PAPER—See The Mead Corporation; U.S. Public, pg. 1074
MEAD PULP SALES, INC.—See The Mead Corporation; U.S. Public, pg. 1074
MEAD REALTY CORP.—See Consolidated Papers, Inc.; U.S. Public, pg. 436
MEAD REASSURANCE S.A.—See The Mead Corporation; U.S. Public, pg. 1076
MEAD SCHOOL & OFFICE PRODUCTS—See The Mead Corporation; U.S. Public, pg. 1074
MEAD SISTEMAS EMBALAJE S.A.—See The Mead Corporation; U.S. Public, pg. 1077
MEAD SPECIALTY PAPER—See The Mead Corporation; U.S. Public, pg. 1074
MEAD TIMBER CO.—See The Mead Corporation; U.S. Public, pg. 1076
MEAD VERPACKUNG G.M.B.H.—See The Mead Corporation; U.S. Public, pg. 1077
MEAD VERPAKKING B.V.—See The Mead Corporation; U.S. Public, pg. 1076
MEADE GROUP, INC.; U.S. Private, pg. 725
MEADOW LEA FOODS LTD.—See Goodman Fielder Limited; Int'l, pg. 555
MEADOW STEEL PRODUCTS—See Hanson PLC; Int'l, pg. 593
MEADOWBROOK CO.—See T.L. Diamond Company; U.S. Private, pg. 331
MEADOWCRAFT, INC.; U.S. Private, pg. 725
MEADOWLARK, INC.—See Cyprus Amax Minerals Company; U.S. Public, pg. 471
MEADOWS RESOURCES, INC.—See Public Service Company of New Mexico; U.S. Public, pg. 1339
MEADOWVIEW CARE CENTER—See Horizon/CMS Healthcare Corporation; U.S. Public, pg. 838
MEADOX MEDICALS, INC.—See Boston Scientific Corp.; U.S. Public, pg. 247
MEADVILLE FORGING CO.; U.S. Private, pg. 726
DON MEALEY CHEVROLET INC.; U.S. Private, pg. 726
MEANS INDUSTRIES, INC.—See Varlen Corporation; U.S. Public, pg. 1711
MEARS TRANSPORTATION GROUP; U.S. Private, pg. 726
MEASUREAIM—See Pfizer Inc.; U.S. Public, pg. 1283
MEASUREMENT SCIENCE, INC.—See The PBS&J Corporation; U.S. Private, pg. 826
MEASUREMENT SYSTEMS, INC.—See Ultra Electronics Holdings plc; Int'l, pg. 1431
MEASUREMENTS GROUP, INC.—See Vishay Intertechnology, Inc.; U.S. Public, pg. 1722
MEASUREMENTS GROUP U.K. LTD.—See Vishay Intertechnology, Inc.; U.S. Public, pg. 1722
MEASURING SYSTEMS DIVISION—See Brown & Sharpe Manufacturing Company; U.S. Public, pg. 260
MEAUX—See Fort James Corporation; U.S. Public, pg. 673
MEBANE PACKAGING GROUP; U.S. Private, pg. 726
MEBANE PACKAGING GROUP.—See Mebane Packaging Group; U.S. Private, pg. 726
MEBANE PLANT—See Stoneridge, Inc.; U.S. Private, pg. 1044
MEC-TRACK S.R.L.—See Caterpillar Inc.; U.S. Public, pg. 317
MECA 2000—See Rhone-Poulenc S.A.; Int'l, pg. 1111
MECAKONE OY—See Tamrock Corp.; Int'l, pg. 1353
MECANARBED DOMMELDANGE S.A.R.L.—See Arbed S.A.; Int'l, pg. 80
MECANICA PESADA S.A.—See MAN Aktiengesellschaft; Int'l, pg. 824
MECASLIN STREET CORPORATION—See The Ivaco Group; Int'l, pg. 696
MECATOOL AG—See Georg Fischer Ltd.; Int'l, pg. 489
MECATOOL GMBH—See Georg Fischer Ltd.; Int'l, pg. 490
MECATOOL ITALIA SRL—See Georg Fischer Ltd.; Int'l, pg. 490
MECATOOL USA—See Georg Fischer Ltd.; Int'l, pg. 490
MECEL AB—See Investor AB; Int'l, pg. 686
MECHANICAL ENGINEERS & CONTRACTORS (MEC)—See GESTRA GmbH; Int'l, pg. 550
MECHANICAL HEAT & COLD, INC.—See Compagnie Generale Des Eaux; Int'l, pg. 322
MECHANICAL TECHNOLOGY INC.; U.S. Public, pg. 1077
MECHANICS TOOL DIV.—See The Stanley Works; U.S. Public, pg. 1509
MECHANISCHE WEBEREI UND ZWIRNEREI ROSENHAMMER GMBH—See The Procter & Gamble Company; U.S. Public, pg. 1333
MECMAN A/S—See Mannesmann A.G.; Int'l, pg. 839
MECMAN EGER KFT.—See Mannesmann A.G.; Int'l, pg. 839
MECMAN ENGINEERING AB—See Mannesmann A.G.; Int'l, pg. 839
MECMAN GILLBERG HYDRAULIC AB—See Mannesmann A.G.; Int'l, pg. 839
MECMAN GMBH—See Mannesmann A.G.; Int'l, pg. 838
MECMAN NEDERLANDE BV—See Mannesmann A.G.; Int'l, pg. 839
OY MECMAN—See Mannesmann A.G.; Int'l, pg. 839
MECMAN SVENSKA AB—See Mannesmann A.G.; Int'l, pg. 839
MECO CORPORATION; U.S. Private, pg. 726
MECO DEVELOPMENT LIMITED; Int'l, pg. 852
MECO ENGINEERING CO.—See Meco Development Limited; Int'l, pg. 852
MECO HOLDINGS CO. LTD.—See Meco Development Limited; Int'l, pg. 852
MECO METAL FINISHING USA INC.—See L. Possehl & Co. mbH; Int'l, pg. 1064
MECO S.A.—See SMH Swiss Corporation for Micro Electronics & Watchmaking Indus. Ltd.; Int'l, pg. 1160
MECO USA INC.—See L. Possehl & Co. mbH; Int'l, pg. 1064

Company Index

MECOMB SINGAPORE LIMITED—See Sime Darby Berhad; *Int'l*, pg. 1251
MECOR, INC.—See Meiji Seika Kaisha, Ltd.; *Int'l*, pg. 855
MECUP/PFAUTER-MAAG—See Hermann Pfauter GmbH & Co.; *Int'l*, pg. 617
MED-LAB SUPPLY COMPANY, INC.; *U.S. Private*, pg. 726
MED+CARE HEALTH SERVICES—See Dynacare, Inc.; *Int'l*, pg. 425
MED/WASTE, INC.; *U.S. Public*, pg. 1077
MEDA SIM BIPIEMME S.P.A.—See Banca Popolare di Milano; *Int'l*, pg. 137
MEDAES INCORPORATED—See Cravey, Green & Wahlen, Incorporated; *U.S. Private*, pg. 287
MEDAL DISTRIBUTING CO.—See Waxman Industries, Inc.; *U.S. Public*, pg. 1748
MEDASONICS, INC.—See Settsu Corporation; *Int'l*, pg. 1225
MEDATA AB—See Axel Johnson AB; *Int'l*, pg. 709
MEDATA CZECHOSLOVAKIA SPOL.S.R.O.—See Axel Johnson AB; *Int'l*, pg. 712
MEDATA CZECHOSLOVAKIA SPOL.SR.O.—See Axel Johnson AB; *Int'l*, pg. 712
MEDCO CONTAINMENT SERVICES, INC.—See Merck & Co., Inc.; *U.S. Public*, pg. 1091
MEDCREST DIV.—See Medline Industries, Inc.; *U.S. Private*, pg. 728
MEDECO SECURITY LOCKS, INC.—See Hillenbrand Industries, Inc.; *U.S. Public*, pg. 828
MEDELEC ESPANA S.A.—See Vickers PLC; *Int'l*, pg. 1467
MEDELEC LIMITED—See Vickers PLC; *Int'l*, pg. 1467
MEDELEC NORTHERN EUROPE—See Vickers PLC; *Int'l*, pg. 1467
MEDEQUIP—See Hewlett-Packard Company; *U.S. Public*, pg. 822
MEDEVA PHARMACEUTICALS—See Medeva PLC; *Int'l*, pg. 852
MEDEVA PLC; *Int'l*, pg. 852
MEDEX ASSISTANCE CORPORATION—See Avemco Corporation; *U.S. Public*, pg. 152
MEDEX INC.—See Furon Company; *U.S. Public*, pg. 689
MEDEX MEDICAL GMBH—See Furon Company; *U.S. Public*, pg. 689
MEDEX MEDICAL INC.—See Furon Company; *U.S. Public*, pg. 689
MEDEX MEDICAL S.A.R.L.—See Furon Company; *U.S. Public*, pg. 689
MEDI-LAB A/S—See Roche Holding Ltd.; *Int'l*, pg. 1121
MEDI-MAIL, INC.; *U.S. Private*, pg. 726
MEDI-VAC/AIRLIFE RESPIRATORY CARE—See Allegiance Healthcare Corp.; *U.S. Public*, pg. 44
MEDIA ARTS GROUP, INC.; *U.S. Public*, pg. 1077
THE MEDIA CENTRE; *Int'l*, pg. 852
MEDIA DATEN AG—See EMAP Plc; *Int'l*, pg. 451
MEDIA DATEN GMBH—See EMAP Plc; *Int'l*, pg. 451
MEDIA DIRECT PARTNERS, INCORPORATED—See Media Incorporated; *U.S. Private*, pg. 726
MEDIA DUPLICATION INTERNATIONAL; *Int'l*, pg. 852
MEDIA DUPLICATION INTERNATIONAL—See Media Duplication International; *Int'l*, pg. 853
MEDIA FAIR VERLAG GMBH—See EMAP Plc; *Int'l*, pg. 451
MEDIA FIRST INTERNATIONAL, INC.; *U.S. Private*, pg. 726
MEDIA GENERAL BROADCAST GROUP, INC.—See Media General, Inc.; *U.S. Public*, pg. 1078
MEDIA GENERAL BROADCASTING, INC. (WJWB-TV)—See Media General, Inc.; *U.S. Public*, pg. 1078
MEDIA GENERAL CABLE OF FAIRFAX COUNTY INC.—See Media General, Inc.; *U.S. Public*, pg. 1078
MEDIA GENERAL FINANCIAL SERVICES, INC.—See Media General, Inc.; *U.S. Public*, pg. 1078
MEDIA GENERAL, INC.; *U.S. Public*, pg. 1077
MEDIA HANDELSGESELLSCHAFT MBH—See Otto Versand (GmbH & Co.); *Int'l*, pg. 1015
MEDIA INCORPORATED; *U.S. Private*, pg. 726
MEDIA INFORMATIQUE SERVICE (M.I.S.)—See Lagardere Groupe; *Int'l*, pg. 793
MEDIA INTERNATIONAL DATA S.A.—See Rogers Communications, Inc.; *Int'l*, pg. 1124
THE MEDIA INVESTMENT GROUP; *U.S. Private*, pg. 726
MEDIA ITALIA—See Testa International; *Int'l*, pg. 1377
THE MEDIA & MARKETING GROUP—See RBT/Strum; *U.S. Private*, pg. 902
MEDIA MARKETING TECHNOLOGIES, INC.—See Ceridian Corporation; *U.S. Public*, pg. 331
MEDIA NETWORKS INC.—See Time Warner Inc.; *U.S. Public*, pg. 1612
MEDIA 100, INC.; *U.S. Public*, pg. 1079
MEDIA PA—See BDDP Group; *Int'l*, pg. 116
MEDIA PARTNERSHIP CORPORATION—See Western International Media Corporation; *U.S. Private*, pg. 1168
MEDIA PLAY, INC.—See Musicland Group Inc.; *U.S. Public*, pg. 1142
MEDIA-POLIS/EURO RSCG MEDIA—See Havas Advertising; *Int'l*, pg. 601
MEDIA PRINTING CORPORATION; *U.S. Private*, pg. 726
MEDIA RECOVERY, INC.; *U.S. Private*, pg. 726
MEDIA RECOVERY INC.-CALIFORNIA—See Media Recovery, Inc.; *U.S. Private*, pg. 727
MEDIA RECOVERY INC.-COLORADO—See Media Recovery, Inc.; *U.S. Private*, pg. 727
MEDIA RECOVERY INC.-CONNECTICUT—See Media Recovery, Inc.; *U.S. Private*, pg. 727
MEDIA RECOVERY INC.-DALLAS, TX—See Media Recovery, Inc.; *U.S. Private*, pg. 727
MEDIA RECOVERY INC.-GEORGIA—See Media Recovery, Inc.; *U.S. Private*, pg. 727
MEDIA RECOVERY INC.-HOUSTON, TX—See Media Recovery, Inc.; *U.S. Private*, pg. 727
MEDIA RECOVERY INC.-MASSACHUSETTS—See Media Recovery, Inc.; *U.S. Private*, pg. 727
MEDIA RECOVERY INC.-MISSOURI—See Media Recovery, Inc.; *U.S. Private*, pg. 727

MEDIA RECOVERY INC.-SAN ANTONIO, TX—See Media Recovery, Inc.; *U.S. Private*, pg. 727
MEDIA RECOVERY INC.-TEXAS—See Media Recovery, Inc.; *U.S. Private*, pg. 727
MEDIA RECOVERY INTL.—See Media Recovery, Inc.; *U.S. Private*, pg. 727
MEDIA RESOURCES INTERNATIONAL; *U.S. Private*, pg. 727
MEDIA SERVICES, INC.—See Time Warner Inc.; *U.S. Public*, pg. 1613
THE MEDIA SHOP LIMITED; *Int'l*, pg. 853
THE MEDIA SHOP (SCOTLAND)—See The Media Shop Limited; *Int'l*, pg. 853
MEDIA SUD—See Lagardere Groupe; *Int'l*, pg. 793
MEDIA THAT WORKS; *U.S. Private*, pg. 727
MEDIA THAT WORKS—See Media That Works; *U.S. Private*, pg. 727
MEDIA TRANSASIA PVT. LTD.—See International Data Group; *U.S. Private*, pg. 570
MEDIA TRANSIA THAILAND LTD.—See International Data Group; *U.S. Private*, pg. 570
MEDIA.U.S.A.—See Black Rogers Sullivan Goodnight, Inc.; *U.S. Private*, pg. 147
MEDIACION Y DIAGNOSTICOS, S.A.—See Caja de Madrid Group; *Int'l*, pg. 251
MEDIACOMM NATIONAL, INC.—See Clear Channel Communications, Inc.; *U.S. Public*, pg. 384
MEDIAFINA S.A.—See Tractebel; *Int'l*, pg. 1415
MEDIALINX INTERACTIVE INC.—See BCE Inc.; *Int'l*, pg. 115
MEDIANET BV—See VNU Verenigde Nederlandse Uitgeversbedrijven B.V.; *Int'l*, pg. 1445
MEDIANEWS GROUP, EASTERN OPERATIONS—See MediaNews Group Inc.; *U.S. Private*, pg. 727
MEDIANEWS GROUP INC.; *U.S. Private*, pg. 727
MEDIAONE—See U S West Inc.; *U.S. Public*, pg. 1688
MEDIAPOLIS; *Int'l*, pg. 853
MEDIAPOLIS FRANCE—See Young & Rubicam Inc.; *U.S. Private*, pg. 1199
MEDIASPOT, INC.; *U.S. Private*, pg. 727
MEDIATEX COMMUNICATIONS CORPORATION; *U.S. Private*, pg. 727
MEDIAVEST—See The MacManus Group, Inc.; *U.S. Private*, pg. 692
MEDIAWEEK—See VNU Verenigde Nederlandse Uitgeversbedrijven B.V.; *Int'l*, pg. 1446
MEDIBARNA, S.L.—See Caixa d'Estalvis de Catalunya; *Int'l*, pg. 250
MEDIC-AIRE MEDICAL EQUIPMENT, INC.—See Integrated Health Services, Inc.; *U.S. Public*, pg. 885
MEDIC COMPUTER SYSTEMS, INC.—See Misys PLC; *Int'l*, pg. 870
MEDICA BV—See Maxxim Medical, Inc.; *U.S. Public*, pg. 1063
MEDICA GMBH—See Carl-Zeiss-Stiftung; *Int'l*, pg. 1523
MEDICAL ACTION INDUSTRIES INC.; *U.S. Public*, pg. 1079
MEDICAL ADVANCES INC.—See Intermagnetics General Corporation; *U.S. Public*, pg. 894
MEDICAL ANALYSIS SYSTEMS INC.; *U.S. Private*, pg. 727
MEDICAL ASSURANCE, INC.; *U.S. Public*, pg. 1079
MEDICAL ASSURANCE OF WEST VIRGINIA—See Medical Assurance, Inc.; *U.S. Public*, pg. 1080
MEDICAL CENTER NURSING FACILITY—See Horizon/CMS Healthcare Corporation; *U.S. Public*, pg. 839
MEDICAL CENTER OF BATON ROUGE—See Columbia/HCA Healthcare Corporation; *U.S. Public*, pg. 405
MEDICAL DATA INTELLIGENCE AB—See Incentive AB; *Int'l*, pg. 667
MEDICAL DEVICE REGISTER—See The Thomson Corporation; *U.S. Public*, pg. 1600
MEDICAL DIVISION—See Toshiba Corporation; *Int'l*, pg. 1406
MEDICAL ECONOMICS COMPANY INC.—See The Thomson Corporation; *U.S. Public*, pg. 1601
MEDICAL EDUCATION AND RESEARCH FOUNDATION—See Benjamin Franklin Literary & Medical Society, Inc.; *U.S. Private*, pg. 133
MEDICAL ELECTRO-THERAPEUTICS, INC.—See Integrated Health Services, Inc.; *U.S. Public*, pg. 885
MEDICAL GRAPHICS CORP.; *U.S. Public*, pg. 1080
MEDICAL IMAGING SYSTEMS LIMITED—See Halma p.l.c.; *Int'l*, pg. 589
MEDICAL INNOVATIONS CORP.—See Ballard Medical Products; *U.S. Public*, pg. 171
MEDICAL LABORATORY AUTOMATION, INC.; *U.S. Private*, pg. 727
MEDICAL LATEX (DUA) SDN. BHD.—See Beiersdorf Group; *Int'l*, pg. 183
MEDICAL MANAGEMENT ASSOCIATES, INC.—See Horizon/CMS Healthcare Corporation; *U.S. Public*, pg. 839
MEDICAL MANAGER CORPORATION; *U.S. Public*, pg. 1080
MEDICAL MARKETING GROUP, INC.—See Merck & Co., Inc.; *U.S. Public*, pg. 1091
MEDICAL MEADOW GOLD DAIRIES, INC.—See Southern Foods Group; *U.S. Private*, pg. 1016
MEDICAL PARK DIAGNOSTIC CENTER—See Columbia/HCA Healthcare Corporation; *U.S. Public*, pg. 405
MEDICAL PRODUCTS TECHNOLOGY—See 3M; *U.S. Public*, pg. 1605
MEDICAL PROFESSIONAL LIABILITY AGENCY, LTD.—See Frontier Insurance Group, Inc.; *U.S. Public*, pg. 685
THE MEDICAL PROTECTIVE COMPANY; *U.S. Private*, pg. 728
MEDICAL RESOURCES INC.; *U.S. Public*, pg. 1080
MEDICAL RESOURCES INC.—See Medical Resources Inc.; *U.S. Public*, pg. 1080
MEDICAL RUBBER AB—See Perstorp AB; *Int'l*, pg. 1036
MEDICAL SUPPLIES DIVISION—See Abdulla Fouad Co. Ltd.; *Int'l*, pg. 502

MEDICAL-SURGICAL DIVISION—See 3M; *U.S. Public*, pg. 1605
MEDICAL SURGICAL SPECIALTIES, LTD.; *U.S. Private*, pg. 728
MEDICALODGES, INC.; *U.S. Private*, pg. 728
MEDICALODGES, INC.—See Medicalodges, Inc.; *U.S. Private*, pg. 728
MEDICANA NURSING CENTER—See Paragon Health Network, Inc.; *U.S. Public*, pg. 1257
MEDICARAIBE GUYANE—See Hewlett-Packard Company; *U.S. Public*, pg. 822
MEDICARE—See Hewlett-Packard Company; *U.S. Public*, pg. 822
MEDICAS YOMA—See Hewlett-Packard Company; *U.S. Public*, pg. 822
MEDICENTER, CORPUS CHRISTI—See Vencor, Inc.; *U.S. Public*, pg. 1714
MEDIC-ESCHMANN GMBH—See Smiths Industries plc; *Int'l*, pg. 1268
MEDICINE HAT NEWS—See Hollinger Inc.; *Int'l*, pg. 631
MEDICINE SHOPPE INTERNATIONAL, INC.—See Cardinal Health Inc.; *U.S. Public*, pg. 304
MEDICIS PHARMACEUTICAL CORP.; *U.S. Public*, pg. 1080
MEDICO, INC.—See S.M. Frank & Co., Inc.; *U.S. Private*, pg. 424
MEDICO INDUSTRIES, INC.; *U.S. Private*, pg. 728
MEDICOM CO., LTD.—See Roche Holding Ltd.; *Int'l*, pg. 1121
MEDICORE INC.; *U.S. Public*, pg. 1080
MEDICORNEA S.A.—See Nestle S.A.; *Int'l*, pg. 920
MEDICUS SYSTEMS CORPORATION; *U.S. Public*, pg. 1080
MEDIDORES BAILEY S.A.—See FKI Plc; *Int'l*, pg. 474
MEDIEVAL TIMES DINNER & TOURNAMENT, INC.; *U.S. Private*, pg. 728
MEDIMATICA GROEP BV—See KPN Koninklyke PTT Nederland NV; *Int'l*, pg. 720
MEDIMMUNE, INC.; *U.S. Public*, pg. 1081
MEDINA JOURNAL-REGISTER—See Media General, Inc.; *U.S. Public*, pg. 1079
MEDINA REGAL—See Regal Ware, Inc.; *U.S. Private*, pg. 917
MEDIPLANT N.V./S.A.—See Biomet, Inc.; *U.S. Public*, pg. 232
MEDIQ DIAGNOSTIC CENTERS—See MEDIQ Incorporated; *U.S. Public*, pg. 1081
MEDIQ INCORPORATED; *U.S. Public*, pg. 1081
MEDIQ MANAGEMENT SERVICES, INC.—See MEDIQ Incorporated; *U.S. Public*, pg. 1081
MEDIQ/PRN LIFE SUPPORT SERVICES, INC.—See MEDIQ Incorporated; *U.S. Public*, pg. 1081
MEDIQUIP SDN. BHD.—See Tyco International Ltd.; *U.S. Public*, pg. 1648
MEDITE CORPORATION—See SierraPine Limited; *U.S. Private*, pg. 999
MEDITERRANEA INIZIATIVE TURISTICHE ALBERGHIERE SPA—See Granada Group PLC; *Int'l*, pg. 556
MEDITERRANEAN FERTILIZER INDUSTRIES COMPANY—See Kuwait Petroleum Corporation; *Int'l*, pg. 766
MEDITERRANEAN STANDARD OIL CO.—See Exxon Corporation; *U.S. Public*, pg. 602
MEDITRUST CORPORATION; *U.S. Public*, pg. 1081
MEDIUM VOLTAGE EQUIPMENT—See ABB Asea Brown Boveri (Holding) Ltd.; *Int'l*, pg. 4
MEDIUM VOLTAGE OUTDOOR EQUIPMENT—See ABB Asea Brown Boveri (Holding) Ltd.; *Int'l*, pg. 4
MEDIVATORS, INC.—See Cantel Industries, Inc.; *U.S. Public*, pg. 301
MEDLINE INDUSTRIES, INC.; *U.S. Private*, pg. 728
MEDLOG GMBH—See Criticare Systems, Inc.; *U.S. Public*, pg. 459
MEDNET, MPC CORPORATION; *U.S. Public*, pg. 1082
MEDPARTNERS INC.; *U.S. Public*, pg. 1082
MEDRAD, INC.—See Schering AG; *Int'l*, pg. 1204
MEDSCREEN LIMITED—See PharmChem Laboratories, Inc.; *U.S. Public*, pg. 1286
MEDSTONE INTERNATIONAL, INC.; *U.S. Public*, pg. 1082
MEDTEC PRODUCTS PTY. LTD.—See Hewlett-Packard Company; *U.S. Public*, pg. 822
MEDTECH INC.; *U.S. Private*, pg. 728
MEDTRAC, INC.—See Willis Corroon Group PLC; *Int'l*, pg. 1504
MEDTRONIC ANEU RX—See Medtronic, Inc.; *U.S. Public*, pg. 1083
MEDTRONIC ASIA, LTD.—See Medtronic, Inc.; *U.S. Public*, pg. 1083
MEDTRONIC AUSTRALASIA PTY. LTD.—See Medtronic, Inc.; *U.S. Public*, pg. 1083
MEDTRONIC AVALON LABORATORIES, INC.—See Medtronic, Inc.; *U.S. Public*, pg. 1083
MEDTRONIC BELGIUM—See Medtronic, Inc.; *U.S. Public*, pg. 1083
MEDTRONIC BIO-MEDICUS—See Medtronic, Inc.; *U.S. Public*, pg. 1083
MEDTRONIC B.V.—See Medtronic, Inc.; *U.S. Public*, pg. 1083
MEDTRONIC CARBON IMPLANTS, INC.—See Medtronic, Inc.; *U.S. Public*, pg. 1083
MEDTRONIC CARDIOPULMONARY—See Medtronic, Inc.; *U.S. Public*, pg. 1083
MEDTRONIC DLP—See Medtronic, Inc.; *U.S. Public*, pg. 1083
MEDTRONIC EUROPE S.A./N.V.—See Medtronic, Inc.; *U.S. Public*, pg. 1083
MEDTRONIC FRANCE S.A.—See Medtronic, Inc.; *U.S. Public*, pg. 1083
MEDTRONIC GMBH—See Medtronic, Inc.; *U.S. Public*, pg. 1083
MEDTRONIC HEART VALVE DIVISION—See Medtronic, Inc.; *U.S. Public*, pg. 1083
MEDTRONIC HISPANIA S.A.—See Medtronic, Inc.; *U.S. Public*, pg. 1083

MEDTRONIC IN STENT, INC.—See Medtronic, Inc.; U.S. Public, pg. 1083
MEDTRONIC, INC.; U.S. Public, pg. 1082
MEDTRONIC INTERNATIONAL, LTD.—See Medtronic, Inc.; U.S. Public, pg. 1083
MEDTRONIC INTERVENTIONAL VASCULAR—See Medtronic, Inc.; U.S. Public, pg. 1083
MEDTRONIC ITALIA S.P.A.—See Medtronic, Inc.; U.S. Public, pg. 1084
MEDTRONIC JAPAN CO., LTD.—See Medtronic, Inc.; U.S. Public, pg. 1084
MEDTRONIC LATIN AMERICA, INC.—See Medtronic, Inc.; U.S. Public, pg. 1084
MEDTRONIC MED REL, INC.—See Medtronic, Inc.; U.S. Public, pg. 1083
MEDTRONIC MICRO-REL—See Medtronic, Inc.; U.S. Public, pg. 1083
MEDTRONIC MILACA, INC.—See Medtronic, Inc.; U.S. Public, pg. 1083
MEDTRONIC NEUROLOGICAL DIV.—See Medtronic, Inc.; U.S. Public, pg. 1083
MEDTRONIC OF CANADA—See Medtronic, Inc.; U.S. Public, pg. 1084
MEDTRONIC PROMEON—See Medtronic, Inc.; U.S. Public, pg. 1083
MEDTRONIC PUERTO RICO, INC.—See Medtronic, Inc.; U.S. Public, pg. 1083
MEDTRONIC, S. DE R.L. DE C.V.—See Medtronic, Inc.; U.S. Public, pg. 1084
MEDTRONIC (SCHWEIZ) AG—See Medtronic, Inc.; U.S. Public, pg. 1084
MEDTRONIC WORLD TRADE CORP.—See Medtronic, Inc.; U.S. Public, pg. 1084
MEDTRONICS INC.—See Medtronic, Inc.; U.S. Public, pg. 1083
MEDUSA AGGREGATE CO.—See Medusa Corporation; U.S. Public, pg. 1084
MEDUSA CORPORATION; U.S. Public, pg. 1084
MEDUSA MINERALS CO—See Medusa Corporation; U.S. Public, pg. 1084
MEDWIRE—See Sigmund Cohn Corp.; U.S. Private, pg. 250
MEENAN LI DIV.—See Meenan Oil Co. L.P.; U.S. Private, pg. 729
MEENAN OIL CO. L.P.; U.S. Private, pg. 729
MEENAN OIL/YOUNG SUPPLY CO.—See Meenan Oil Co. L.P.; U.S. Private, pg. 729
MEERANER DAMPFKEESELBAU GMBH—See Deutsche Babcock AG; Int'l, pg. 398
MEES & HOPE CORPORATE FINANCE LTD.—See ABN-AMRO Holding N.V.; Int'l, pg. 12
MEES & HOPE FINANZGESELLSCHAFT AG—See ABN-AMRO Holding N.V.; Int'l, pg. 12
MEES & HOPE INVESTMENT MANAGEMENT LTD.—See ABN-AMRO Holding N.V.; Int'l, pg. 12
MEES & HOPE SECURITIES HOLDINGS LTD.—See ABN-AMRO Holding N.V.; Int'l, pg. 12
MEES & HOPE SECURITIES LTD.—See ABN-AMRO Holding N.V.; Int'l, pg. 12
MEESCHAERT-ROUSSELLE—See AXA-UAP; Int'l, pg. 19
MEESTER WIJHE BV—See Koninklijke Ahold NV; Int'l, pg. 749
MEFIAG NEDERLAND B.V.—See Met-Pro Corporation; U.S. Public, pg. 1100
MEGA ADVERTISING, INC.—See Media General, Inc.; U.S. Public, pg. 1078
MEGABYTE LTD.—See Oracle Corporation; U.S. Public, pg. 1228
MEGADOOR AB—See Cardo AB; Int'l, pg. 269
MEGADOOR INC.—See Cardo AB; Int'l, pg. 269
MEGAHERTZ HOLDING LTD.—See 3Com Corporation; U.S. Public, pg. 1604
MEGAL FINANCE COMPANY LTD.—See Ruhrgas Aktiengesellschaft; Int'l, pg. 1149
MEGAL GMBH MITTEL-EUROPAISCHE-GASLEITUNGS-GESELLSCHAFT—See Ruhrgas Aktiengesellschaft; Int'l, pg. 1149
MEGAMARKETS, INC.—See Fleming Companies, Inc.; U.S. Public, pg. 653
MEGAPULSE, INC.; U.S. Private, pg. 729
MEGAS BEAUTY CARE, INC.; U.S. Private, pg. 729
MEGGIT MOBREY LTD.—See Meggitt plc; Int'l, pg. 853
MEGGITT AVIONICS—See Meggitt plc; Int'l, pg. 853
MEGGITT AVIONICS INC.—See Meggitt plc; Int'l, pg. 853
MEGGITT COMPOSITES—See Meggitt plc; Int'l, pg. 853
MEGGITT ELECTRONIC COMPONENTS LTD.—See Meggitt plc; Int'l, pg. 853
MEGGITT HOLDINGS PLC.—See BTR plc; Int'l, pg. 124
S.A. MEGGITT PETROLEUM SYSTEMS NV—See Meggitt plc; Int'l, pg. 854
MEGGITT PETROLEUM SYSTEMS (UK)—See Meggitt plc; Int'l, pg. 853
MEGGITT PLC; Int'l, pg. 853
MEGGITT USA INC.—See Meggitt plc; Int'l, pg. 853
MEGON A.S.—See Norsk Hydro a.s; Int'l, pg. 960
MEGTEC—See Sequa Corporation; U.S. Public, pg. 1459
MEHERRIN AGRICULTURE & CHEMICAL CO.; U.S. Private, pg. 729
MEHNERT UND VEECK GMBH—See Nippon Paint Company Ltd.; Int'l, pg. 937
MEI HOY SPORTS CO. LTD.—See Mizuno Corporation; Int'l, pg. 885
MEIER & FRANK—See The May Department Stores Company; U.S. Public, pg. 1064
MEIER METAL SERVICE CENTERS, INC.—See Metals USA, Inc.; U.S. Public, pg. 1100
MEIJER, INC.; U.S. Private, pg. 729
MEIJER WHOLESALE INC.—See Meijer, Inc.; U.S. Private, pg. 729
MEIJERIOSUUSKUNTA/MEJERIANDELSLAGET MILKA; Int'l, pg. 854
MEIJI BAKING CO., LTD.—See Meiji Seika Kaisha, Ltd.; Int'l, pg. 855

MEIJI CHEWING GUM CO., LTD.—See Meiji Seika Kaisha, Ltd.; Int'l, pg. 855
MEIJI ENGINEERING LTD—See Meiji Seika Kaisha, Ltd.; Int'l, pg. 855
MEIJI FROZEN DESSERT CORP.—See Meiji Seika Kaisha, Ltd.; Int'l, pg. 855
P.T. MEIJI INDONESIAN PHARMACEUTICAL INDUSTRIES—See Meiji Seika Kaisha, Ltd.; Int'l, pg. 856
MEIJI INFORMATION SYSTEM CENTER LTD.—See Meiji Seika Kaisha, Ltd.; Int'l, pg. 855
MEIJI JEWELRY—See Meiji Seika Kaisha, Ltd.; Int'l, pg. 855
MEIJI KAIHATSU CO., LTD.—See Meiji Seika Kaisha, Ltd.; Int'l, pg. 855
MEIJI LIFE INSURANCE COMPANY; Int'l, pg. 854
THE MEIJI LIFE INSURANCE COMPANY BEIJING OFFICE—See Meiji Life Insurance Company; Int'l, pg. 854
THE MEIJI LIFE INSURANCE COMPANY FRANKFURT OFFICE—See Meiji Life Insurance Company; Int'l, pg. 854
THE MEIJI LIFE INSURANCE COMPANY SAO PAULO OFFICE—See Meiji Life Insurance Company; Int'l, pg. 854
THE MEIJI LIFE INSURANCE COMPANY SEOUL OFFICE—See Meiji Life Insurance Company; Int'l, pg. 854
THE MEIJI LIFE INSURANCE COMPANY SYDNEY OFFICE—See Meiji Life Insurance Company; Int'l, pg. 854
THE MEIJI LIFE INSURANCE COMPANY TORONTO OFFICE—See Meiji Life Insurance Company; Int'l, pg. 854
MEIJI-MCVITIE, LTD.—See Meiji Seika Kaisha, Ltd.; Int'l, pg. 855
MEIJI MILK PRODUCTS CO., LTD.; Int'l, pg. 855
MEIJI MILK PRODUCTS CO., LTD., KANSAI BR.—See Meiji Milk Products Co., Ltd.; Int'l, pg. 855
MEIJI SANGYO CO., LTD.—See Meiji Seika Kaisha, Ltd.; Int'l, pg. 855
MEIJI SEIKA DO BRASIL LTDA.—See Meiji Seika Kaisha, Ltd.; Int'l, pg. 856
MEIJI SEIKA EUROPE B.V.—See Meiji Seika Kaisha, Ltd.; Int'l, pg. 856
MEIJI SEIKA KAISHA, LTD.; Int'l, pg. 855
MEIJI SEIKA KAISHA, LTD. - YORK OFFICE—See Meiji Seika Kaisha, Ltd.; Int'l, pg. 855
MEIJI SEIKA PHARMA INTERNATIONAL, LTD.—See Meiji Seika Kaisha, Ltd.; Int'l, pg. 855
MEIJI SEIKA (SINGAPORE) PTE. LTD.—See Meiji Seika Kaisha, Ltd.; Int'l, pg. 856
MEIJI SEIKA (U.S.A.) INC.—See Meiji Seika Kaisha, Ltd.; Int'l, pg. 855
MEIJI SHOKUHIN CO., LTD.—See Meiji Seika Kaisha, Ltd.; Int'l, pg. 855
MEIJI TRADING CORP.—See Meiji Seika Kaisha, Ltd.; Int'l, pg. 855
THE MEIJISEIMEI ASSET MANAGEMENT OF AMERICA, LTD.—See Meiji Life Insurance Company; Int'l, pg. 854
THE MEIJISEIMEI INSURANCE AGENCY OF NEW YORK, INC.—See Meiji Life Insurance Company; Int'l, pg. 854
THE MEIJISEIMEI INSURANCE SERVICES OF CALIFORNIA, INC.—See Meiji Life Insurance Company; Int'l, pg. 854
MEIJISEIMEI INTERNATIONAL FRANCE S.A.—See Meiji Life Insurance Company; Int'l, pg. 854
THE MEIJISEIMEI INTERNATIONAL HONG KONG, LTD.—See Meiji Life Insurance Company; Int'l, pg. 854
MEIJISEIMEI INTERNATIONAL, LONDON LTD.—See Meiji Life Insurance Company; Int'l, pg. 854
THE MEIJISEIMEI INVESTMENT SINGAPORE PTE. LTD.—See Meiji Life Insurance Company; Int'l, pg. 854
THE MEIJISEIMEI PROPERTY AUSTRALIA LTD.—See Meiji Life Insurance Company; Int'l, pg. 854
THE MEIJISEIMEI PROPERTY GERMANY GMBH—See Meiji Life Insurance Company; Int'l, pg. 855
THE MEIJISEIMEI PROPERTY U.K. LTD.—See Meiji Life Insurance Company; Int'l, pg. 854
THE MEIJISEIMEI REALTY OF AMERICA, INC.—See Meiji Life Insurance Company; Int'l, pg. 854
MEIKA KOSAN CO., LTD.—See Meiji Seika Kaisha, Ltd.; Int'l, pg. 855
MEIKLE MINE PROJECT—See Barrick Gold Corporation; Int'l, pg. 169
MEINA HOLDING AG—See Unilever Plc; Int'l, pg. 1438
MEINEKE DISCOUNT MUFFLER SHOPS, INC.—See GKN plc; Int'l, pg. 535
MEINL BANK AG—See Julius Meinl AG; Int'l, pg. 856
GIULIO MEINL S.P.A.—See Julius Meinl AG; Int'l, pg. 856
JULIUS MEINL AG; Int'l, pg. 856
JULIUS MEINL A.S.—See Julius Meinl AG; Int'l, pg. 856
JULIUS MEINL BALIARNE A.S.—See Julius Meinl AG; Int'l, pg. 856
JULIUS MEINL GMBH—See Julius Meinl AG; Int'l, pg. 856
JULIUS MEINL GOURMET GES.M.B.H.—See Julius Meinl AG; Int'l, pg. 856
JULIUS MEINL GROSSHANDELS-GES.M.B.H.—See Julius Meinl AG; Int'l, pg. 856
JULIUS MEINL IMMOBILIEN VERWALTUNGS-VERMIETUNGS-VNOL LEASING GES.M.B.H.—See Julius Meinl AG; Int'l, pg. 856
JULIUS MEINL NAHRUNGSMITTEL PRODUKTIONS GES.M.B.H.—See Julius Meinl AG; Int'l, pg. 856
SAMUEL MEISEL & COMPANY, INC.—See BAA plc; Int'l, pg. 103
MEISTERMARKEN-WERKE G.M.B.H., SPEZIALFABRIK BACK-UND GROSSKUCHENBEDARF—See Unilever Plc; Int'l, pg. 1438
MEITO WAREHOUSE CO., LTD.—See Meiji Seika Kaisha, Ltd.; Int'l, pg. 855
MEITSU INC.; Int'l, pg. 856
MEIWA TRADING CO.—See Mitsubishi Corporation; Int'l, pg. 871

MEJERIERNES MAELKEDISPONERINGSSELSKAB A.M.B.A—See MD Foods; Int'l, pg. 826
MEJERIERNES PRODUKTIONSSELSKAB A.M.B.A.—See MD Foods; Int'l, pg. 826
AB MEKANPRODUKTER—See Mannesmann·A.G.; Int'l, pg. 838
MEL FARR AUTOMOTIVE GROUP, INC.; U.S. Private, pg. 729
MELAMINE CHEMICALS, INC.—See ChemFirst Inc.; U.S. Public, pg. 344
MELARD MANUFACTURING CORPORATION; U.S. Private, pg. 729
MELBEN PRODUCTS INC.—See Berkshire Hathaway Inc.; U.S. Public, pg. 218
MELBOURNE BREWERY—See Foster's Brewing Group Limited; Int'l, pg. 501
MELBOURNE DIVISIONS SUPPORT OPERATIONS—See Harris Corporation; U.S. Public, pg. 791
MELBOURNE LABORATORIES—See The Broken Hill Proprietary Company Limited; Int'l, pg. 227
MELBOURNE PORT CORPORATION; Int'l, pg. 856
MELBURN TRUCK LINES—See Slater Industries Inc.; Int'l, pg. 1262
MELCOR CORPORATION—See Fedders Corp.; U.S. Public, pg. 615
MELDISCO—See Footstar Inc.; U.S. Public, pg. 661
MELDRUM & FEWSMITH COMMUNICATIONS INC.; U.S. Private, pg. 730
MELDRUM & FEWSMITH DIRECTORY MARKETING—See Meldrum & Fewsmith Communications Inc.; U.S. Private, pg. 730
MELDRUM & FEWSMITH INTERACTIVE—See Meldrum & Fewsmith Communications Inc.; U.S. Private, pg. 730
MELDRUM & FEWSMITH RETAIL SERVICES GROUP—See Meldrum & Fewsmith Communications Inc.; U.S. Private, pg. 730
MELE MANUFACTURING CO., INC.; U.S. Private, pg. 730
MELIA LTD.—See Raisio Group; Int'l, pg. 1085
MELISSA—See Danone Group; Int'l, pg. 380
MELITTA AB—See Melitta Unternehmensgruppe Bentz KG; Int'l, pg. 857
MELITTA A/S—See Melitta Unternehmensgruppe Bentz KG; Int'l, pg. 857
MELITTA BENTZ & CO—See Melitta Unternehmensgruppe Bentz KG; Int'l, pg. 857
MELITTA CANADA INC.—See Melitta Unternehmensgruppe Bentz KG; Int'l, pg. 857
MELITTA CATERING PTY. LTD.—See Melitta Unternehmensgruppe Bentz KG; Int'l, pg. 857
MELITTA DO BRASIL INDUSTRIA E COMERCIO LTDA.—See Melitta Unternehmensgruppe Bentz KG; Int'l, pg. 857
MELITTA FOODSERVICE CORP.—See Melitta Unternehmensgruppe Bentz KG; Int'l, pg. 857
MELITTA-GESELLSCHAFT MBH & CO KG—See Melitta Unternehmensgruppe Bentz KG; Int'l, pg. 857
MELITTA GMBH—See Melitta Unternehmensgruppe Bentz KG; Int'l, pg. 857
MELITTA HONG KONG LTD.—See Melitta Unternehmensgruppe Bentz KG; Int'l, pg. 857
MELITTA HOUSE OF COFFEE PTY. LTD.—See Melitta Unternehmensgruppe Bentz KG; Int'l, pg. 857
MELITTA IBERICA S.A.—See Melitta Unternehmensgruppe Bentz KG; Int'l, pg. 857
MELITTA KAFFEE GMBH & CO., KOMMANDIT GESELLSCHAFT—See Melitta Unternehmensgruppe Bentz KG; Int'l, pg. 857
MELITTA MARKETING (H.K.) LTD.—See Melitta Unternehmensgruppe Bentz KG; Int'l, pg. 857
MELITTA NEDERLAND B.V.—See Melitta Unternehmensgruppe Bentz KG; Int'l, pg. 857
MELITTA NORTH AMERICA, INC.—See Melitta Unternehmensgruppe Bentz KG; Int'l, pg. 857
MELITTA PACIFIC LTD.—See Melitta Unternehmensgruppe Bentz KG; Int'l, pg. 857
MELITTA SOCIETE DE DISTRIBUTION BENTZ & CIE—See Melitta Unternehmensgruppe Bentz KG; Int'l, pg. 857
MELITTA UNTERNEHMENSGRUPPE BENTZ KG; Int'l, pg. 856
MELITTA U.S.A., INC.—See Melitta Unternehmensgruppe Bentz KG; Int'l, pg. 857
MELKUNIE—See Campina Melkunie BV; Int'l, pg. 254
MELLANSVENSKA ELEKTRISKA AB—See Telefonaktiebolaget LM Ericsson; Int'l, pg. 1363
GEORGE MELLER LTD.—See Axel Johnson AB; Int'l, pg. 712
MELLING FORGING COMPANY—See Avis Industrial Corporation; U.S. Private, pg. 102
MELLOBUTTERCUP ICE CREAM INC.; U.S. Private, pg. 730
MELLON BANK CANADA—See Mellon Bank Corporation; U.S. Public, pg. 1086
MELLON BANK CORPORATION; U.S. Public, pg. 1084
MELLON BANK (DE) NATIONAL ASSOCIATION—See Mellon Bank Corporation; U.S. Public, pg. 1085
MELLON BANK (MD)—See Mellon Bank Corporation; U.S. Public, pg. 1085
MELLON BANK, N.A.—See Mellon Bank Corporation; U.S. Public, pg. 1085
MELLON BANK, N.A.-COMMONWEALTH REGION—See Mellon Bank Corporation; U.S. Public, pg. 1085
MELLON BOND ASSOCIATES CORP.—See Mellon Bank Corporation; U.S. Public, pg. 1085
MELLON CAPITAL MANAGEMENT CORPORATION (MFSC 1085
MELLON CORPORATION; U.S. Private, pg. 730
MELLON EQUITY ASSOCIATES CORP.—See Mellon Bank Corporation; U.S. Public, pg. 1085
MELLON EUROPE-LONDON—See Mellon Bank Corporation; U.S. Public, pg. 1086
MELLON FIRST BUSINESS BANK—See Mellon Bank Corporation; U.S. Public, pg. 1085

Company Index

MELLON FUND ADMINISTRATION LTD—See Mellon Bank Corporation; *U.S. Public,* pg. 1086
MELLON MORTGAGE COMPANY—See Mellon Bank Corporation; *U.S. Public,* pg. 1085
MELLON PSFS—See Mellon Bank Corporation; *U.S. Public, pg. 1085*
MELLON SECURITIES TRUST CO.—See Mellon Bank Corporation; *U.S. Public,* pg. 1086
R.J. MELLOR & CO. LTD.—See Fuchs Petrolub AG Oel + Chemie; *Int'l,* pg. 519
H.B. MELLOTT ESTATE, INC.; *U.S. Private,* pg. 730
MELLOY BROS. ENTERPRISES; *U.S. Private,* pg. 730
MELLOY BROTHERS INC.—See Melloy Bros. Enterprises; *U.S. Private,* pg. 730
MELNOR INC.—See O'Sullivan Corporation; *U.S. Public,* pg. 1234
MELODY FARMS—See Melody Foods, Inc.; *U.S. Private,* pg. 730
MELODY FOODS, INC.; *U.S. Private,* pg. 730
MELODY RADIO—See Hanson PLC; *Int'l,* pg. 593
MELOX—See COGEMA - Compagnie Generale des Matieres Nucleaires; *Int'l,* pg. 305
MELROE COMPANY—See Ingersoll-Rand Company; *U.S. Public,* pg. 877
MELROSE—See Kellwood Company; *U.S. Public,* pg. 948
MELRU CORPORATION—See Jones Apparel Group, Inc.; *U.S. Public,* pg. 933
MELVILLE ADVERTISING INC.—See Sbarro, Inc.; *U.S. Public,* pg. 1436
MEMBER SERVICE LIFE INSURANCE CO.—See Blue Cross and Blue Shield of Oklahoma; *U.S. Private,* pg. 152
MEMBERS LIFE INSURANCE COMPANY—See CUNA Mutual Insurance Society; *U.S. Private,* pg. 296
MEMBERS ONLY BY EUROPE CRAFT—See Aris Industries, Inc.; *U.S. Public,* pg. 129
MEMBRANA GMBH—See Akzo Nobel N.V.; *Int'l,* pg. 46
MEMCO LIMITED—See Halma p.l.c.; *Int'l,* pg. 589
MEMCOR TRUOHM—See Ohmite Manufacturing Company; *U.S. Private,* pg. 813
MEMEC PLC—See Veba AG; *Int'l,* pg. 1458
MEMOREX S.A. DE C.V.—See Memorex Telex N.V.; *Int'l,* pg. 858
MEMOREX TELEX—See Memorex Telex N.V.; *Int'l,* pg. 857
MEMOREX TELEX AG—See Memorex Telex N.V.; *Int'l,* pg. 857
MEMOREX TELEX CANADA INC.—See Memorex Telex N.V.; *Int'l,* pg. 857
MEMOREX TELEX COMPUTER PRODUCTS GESMBH—See Memorex Telex N.V.; *Int'l,* pg. 857
MEMOREX TELEX CORP.—See Memorex Telex N.V.; *Int'l,* pg. 857
MEMOREX TELEX DE VENEZUELA, C.A.—See Memorex Telex N.V.; *Int'l,* pg. 857
MEMOREX TELEX FRANCE S.A.—See Memorex Telex N.V.; *Int'l,* pg. 857
MEMOREX TELEX GMBH—See Memorex Telex N.V.; *Int'l,* pg. 857
MEMOREX TELEX (H.K.) LTD.—See Memorex Telex N.V.; *Int'l,* pg. 857
MEMOREX TELEX IRELAND, LTD.—See Memorex Telex N.V.; *Int'l,* pg. 857
MEMOREX TELEX ISRAEL, LTD.—See Memorex Telex N.V.; *Int'l,* pg. 857
MEMOREX TELEX ITALIA S.P.A.—See Memorex Telex N.V.; *Int'l,* pg. 857
MEMOREX TELEX JAPAN LTD.—See Memorex Telex N.V.; *Int'l,* pg. 857
MEMOREX TELEX NETHERLAND BV—See Memorex Telex N.V.; *Int'l,* pg. 857
MEMOREX TELEX N.V.; *Int'l,* pg. 857
MEMOREX TELEX P.R., INC.—See Memorex Telex N.V.; *Int'l,* pg. 857
MEMOREX TELEX PTE., LTD.—See Memorex Telex N.V.; *Int'l,* pg. 857
MEMOREX TELEX PTY. LTD.—See Memorex Telex N.V.; *Int'l,* pg. 858
MEMOREX TELEX, S.A.—See Memorex Telex N.V.; *Int'l,* pg. 858
MEMOREX TELEX TAIWAN LTD.—See Memorex Telex N.V.; *Int'l,* pg. 858
MEMOREX TELEX (U.K.) LTD.—See Memorex Telex N.V.; *Int'l,* pg. 858
MEMORY LANE CAKES LTD.—See Diageo Plc; *Int'l,* pg. 410
MEMPHIS & CHARLESTON RAILWAY CO.—See Norfolk Southern Corporation; *U.S. Public,* pg. 1191
MEMPHIS BEVERAGE PRODUCTION COMPANY, INC.—See Coca-Cola Enterprises Inc.; *U.S. Public,* pg. 393
MEMPHIS GROUP, INC.; *U.S. Private,* pg. 730
MEMPHIS LIGHT, GAS & WATER; *U.S. Private,* pg. 731
MEMPHIS PLANT-KELLOGG U.S.A.—See Kellogg Company; *U.S. Public,* pg. 947
MEMPHIS PUBLISHING CO.—See The E.W. Scripps Company; *U.S. Public,* pg. 1448
MEMPHIS TITLE COMPANY—See The First American Financial Corporation; *U.S. Public,* pg. 626
MENACREDIT—See Kingfisher plc; *Int'l,* pg. 734
MENALUX S.A.—See Electrolux, AB; *Int'l,* pg. 443
MENALVARO, S.A.—See Vallehermoso, S.A.; *Int'l,* pg. 1447
MENARD ELECTRIC COOPERATIVE; *U.S. Private,* pg. 731
MENARDI-CRISWELL—See Hosokawa Micron Corporation; *Int'l,* pg. 636
MENARDS, INC.; *U.S. Private,* pg. 731
MENASCO AEROSPACE LTD.—See Coltec Holdings Inc; *U.S. Public,* pg. 402
MENASCO AEROSYSTEMS DIVISION—See Coltec Holdings Inc; *U.S. Public,* pg. 402
MENASCO CALIFORNIA OPERATION—See Coltec Holdings Inc; *U.S. Public,* pg. 402

MENASCO OVERHAUL DIVISION—See Coltec Holdings Inc; *U.S. Public,* pg. 402
MENASCO CORPORATION; *U.S. Private,* pg. 731
MENASHA CORP., MURFIN DIVISION—See Menasha Corporation; *U.S. Private,* pg. 731
MENASHA CORP., ORBIS DIVISION—See Menasha Corporation; *U.S. Private,* pg. 731
MENASHA CORP., POLY HI SOLIDUR—See Menasha Corporation; *U.S. Private,* pg. 731
MENASHA CORP., TRAEX DIVISION—See Menasha Corporation; *U.S. Private,* pg. 731
MENASHA CORP., PRINTED SYSTEMS DIV.—See Menasha Corporation; *U.S. Private,* pg. 731
MENASHA DEVELOPMENT CORPORATION—See Menasha Corporation; *U.S. Private,* pg. 731
MENASHA FOREIGN SALES CORPORATION—See Menasha Corporation; *U.S. Private,* pg. 731
MENASHA TRANSPORT INC.—See Menasha Corporation; *U.S. Private,* pg. 731
MENDELSOHN/ZIEN ADVERTISING, INC.; *U.S. Private,* pg. 731
A.W. MENDENHALL CO., INC.; *U.S. Private,* pg. 731
MENDIK MANAGEMENT CO., INC.; *U.S. Private,* pg. 731
MENDOZA, DILLON & ASOCIADOS, INC.—See WPP Group plc; *Int'l,* pg. 1483
MENEBA MEEL B.V.—See Goodman Fielder Limited; *Int'l,* pg. 555
MENEBA N.V.—See Goodman Fielder Limited; *Int'l,* pg. 555
MENLEY & JAMES LABORATORIES, INC.; *U.S. Public,* pg. 1086
MENLO LOGISTICS—See CNF Transportation Inc.; *U.S. Public,* pg. 281
MENNEN MEDICAL INC.—See Mennen Medical Ltd.; *Int'l,* pg. 858
MENNEN MEDICAL LTD.; *Int'l,* pg. 858
MEN'S JOURNAL—See Wenner Media; *U.S. Private,* pg. 1162
MEN'S WEARHOUSE; *U.S. Public,* pg. 1086
THE MENSWEAR COMPANY—See Coats Viyella plc; *Int'l,* pg. 300
MENTHOLATUM CANADA LTD.—See Rohto Pharmaceutical Co.; *Int'l,* pg. 1126
MENTHOLATUM COMPANY—See Rohto Pharmaceutical Co.; *Int'l,* pg. 1126
MENTHOLATUM CO. (HONG KONG) LTD.—See Rohto Pharmaceutical Co.; *Int'l,* pg. 1126
MENTHOLATUM CO., LTD.—See Rohto Pharmaceutical Co.; *Int'l,* pg. 1126
MENTHOLATUM DE MEXICO—See Rohto Pharmaceutical Co.; *Int'l,* pg. 1126
MENTHOLATUM INTL. LTD.—See Rohto Pharmaceutical Co.; *Int'l,* pg. 1126
MENTHOLATUM NIGERIA LTD.—See Rohto Pharmaceutical Co.; *Int'l,* pg. 1126
MENTHOLATUM (OVERSEAS) LTD.—See Rohto Pharmaceutical Co.; *Int'l,* pg. 1126
MENTHOLATUM TAIWAN LTD.—See Rohto Pharmaceutical Co.; *Int'l,* pg. 1126
THE MENTHOLATUM (ZHONGSHAM) PHARMACEUTICALS CO., LTD.—See Rohto Pharmaceutical Co.; *Int'l,* pg. 1126
MENTOR CORPORATION; *U.S. Public,* pg. 1086
MENTOR GRAPHICS (AUSTRALIA) PTY. LTD.—See Mentor Graphics Corporation; *U.S. Public,* pg. 1087
MENTOR GRAPHICS (CANADA) LIMITED—See Mentor Graphics Corporation; *U.S. Public,* pg. 1087
MENTOR GRAPHICS CORPORATION; *U.S. Public,* pg. 1086
MENTOR GRAPHICS CORPORATION, ASIA PACIFIC HEADQUARTERS—See Mentor Graphics Corporation; *U.S. Public,* pg. 1087
MENTOR GRAPHICS (DEUTSCHLAND) GMBH—See Mentor Graphics Corporation; *U.S. Public,* pg. 1087
MENTOR GRAPHICS (FRANCE) SARL—See Mentor Graphics Corporation; *U.S. Public,* pg. 1087
MENTOR GRAPHICS ITALIA S.P.A.—See Mentor Graphics Corporation; *U.S. Public,* pg. 1087
MENTOR GRAPHICS JAPAN CO., LTD.—See Mentor Graphics Corporation; *U.S. Public,* pg. 1087
MENTOR GRAPHICS (KOREA)—See Mentor Graphics Corporation; *U.S. Public,* pg. 1087
MENTOR GRAPHICS (NETHERLANDS) N.V.—See Mentor Graphics Corporation; *U.S. Public,* pg. 1087
MENTOR GRAPHICS (SCHWEIZ) AG—See Mentor Graphics Corporation; *U.S. Public,* pg. 1087
MENTOR GRAPHICS (SINGAPORE) PTE. LTD.—See Mentor Graphics Corporation; *U.S. Public,* pg. 1087
MENTOR GRAPHICS (TAIWAN) LTD.—See Mentor Graphics Corporation; *U.S. Public,* pg. 1087
MENTOR GRAPHICS (UK) LTD.—See Mentor Graphics Corporation; *U.S. Public,* pg. 1087
MENTOR H/S, INC.—See Mentor Corporation; *U.S. Public,* pg. 1086
MENTOR INVESTMENT GROUP—See First Union Corporation; *U.S. Public,* pg. 640
MENTOR MEDICAL SYSTEMS, AUSTRALIA—See Mentor Corporation; *U.S. Public,* pg. 1086
MENTOR MEDICAL SYSTEMS, CANADA—See Mentor Corporation; *U.S. Public,* pg. 1086
MENTOR MEDICAL SYSTEMS, U.K.—See Mentor Corporation; *U.S. Public,* pg. 1086
MENTOR OPTHALMICS, INC.—See Mentor Corporation; *U.S. Public,* pg. 1086
MENTOR UROLOGY, INC.—See Mentor Corporation; *U.S. Public,* pg. 1086
MENU FOODS, INC.; *U.S. Private,* pg. 731
MEONIA INSURANCE BROKERS LIMITED—See The East Asiatic Company Ltd. A/S; *Int'l,* pg. 431
MEPHICO SAL—See Novartis AG; *Int'l,* pg. 983
MEPPS S.A.—See Sheldons' Inc.; *U.S. Public,* pg. 992
MERAKER NAERINGSPARK—See Elkem ASA; *Int'l,* pg. 448

P.T. MERAPI UTAMA PHARMA—See Otsuka Pharmaceutical Co., Ltd.; *Int'l,* pg. 1014
MERAT OPTICAL COMMUNICATIONS—See Osicom Technologies Inc.; *U.S. Public,* pg. 1233
MERCADO GAS SERVICES—See Southern Union Company; *U.S. Public,* pg. 1491
OY MERCANTILE AB GRAPHISCHE INDUSTRIE—See BASF AG; *Int'l,* pg. 109
MERCANTILE BANCORPORATION INC.; *U.S. Public,* pg. 1087
MERCANTILE BANK; *U.S. Private,* pg. 731
MERCANTILE BANK—See Mercantile Bancorporation Inc.; *U.S. Public,* pg. 1087
MERCANTILE BANK OF CHARITON—See Mercantile Bancorporation Inc.; *U.S. Public,* pg. 1088
MERCANTILE BANK OF IOWA—See Mercantile Bancorporation Inc.; *U.S. Public,* pg. 1087
MERCANTILE BANK OF ST. LOUIS N.A.—See Mercantile Bancorporation Inc.; *U.S. Public,* pg. 1087
MERCANTILE BANKSHARES CORPORATION; *U.S. Public,* pg. 1088
MERCANTILE BUSINESS CREDIT, INC.—See Mercantile Bancorporation Inc.; *U.S. Public,* pg. 1087
MERCANTILE CANADA FINANCE B.V.—See National Bank of Canada; *Int'l,* pg. 907
MERCANTILE CREDIT CORP.—See Mercantile Stores Company, Inc.; *U.S. Public,* pg. 1090
MERCANTILE INSURANCE SERVICES, INC.—See Mercantile Bancorporation Inc.; *U.S. Public,* pg. 1088
MERCANTILE INVESTMENT SERVICES, INC.—See Mercantile Bancorporation Inc.; *U.S. Public,* pg. 1087
MERCANTILE INVESTMENT & TRUST SERVICES—See Mercantile Bancorporation Inc.; *U.S. Public,* pg. 1088
MERCANTILE MORTGAGE CORP.—See Mercantile Bankshares Corporation; *U.S. Public,* pg. 1089
MERCANTILE MUTUAL HOLDINGS LIMITED—See ING Groep N.V.; *Int'l,* pg. 650
MERCANTILE-SAFE DEPOSIT & TRUST CO.—See Mercantile Bankshares Corporation; *U.S. Public,* pg. 1089
MERCANTILE STORES COMPANY, INC.; *U.S. Public,* pg. 1089
MERCANTILE TRUST COMPANY N.A.—See Mercantile Bancorporation Inc.; *U.S. Public,* pg. 1088
MERCEDES-BENZ ADVANCED DESIGN OF NORTH AMERICA, INC.—See Daimler-Benz Aktiengesellschaft; *Int'l,* pg. 368
MERCEDES-BENZ AG—See Daimler-Benz Aktiengesellschaft; *Int'l,* pg. 368
MERCEDES-BENZ ARGENTINA S.A.—See Daimler-Benz Aktiengesellschaft; *Int'l,* pg. 368
MERCEDES-BENZ (AUSTRALIA) PTY. LTD.—See Daimler-Benz Aktiengesellschaft; *Int'l,* pg. 368
MERCEDES-BENZ BELGIUM S.A./N.V.—See Daimler-Benz Aktiengesellschaft; *Int'l,* pg. 368
MERCEDES-BENZ CANADA INC.—See Daimler-Benz Aktiengesellschaft; *Int'l,* pg. 368
MERCEDES-BENZ CHARTERWAY GMBH—See Daimler-Benz Aktiengesellschaft; *Int'l,* pg. 369
MERCEDES-BENZ CREDIT CORP.—See Daimler-Benz Aktiengesellschaft; *Int'l,* pg. 368
MERCEDES-BENZ DANMARK AS—See Daimler-Benz Aktiengesellschaft; *Int'l,* pg. 368
MERCEDES-BENZ DO BRASIL S.A.—See Daimler-Benz Aktiengesellschaft; *Int'l,* pg. 368
MERCEDES-BENZ ESPANA, S.A.—See Daimler-Benz Aktiengesellschaft; *Int'l,* pg. 369
MERCEDES-BENZ FINANZ GMBH—See Daimler-Benz Aktiengesellschaft; *Int'l,* pg. 368
MERCEDES-BENZ FRANCE S.A.—See Daimler-Benz Aktiengesellschaft; *Int'l,* pg. 369
MERCEDES-BENZ HELLAS S.A.—See Daimler-Benz Aktiengesellschaft; *Int'l,* pg. 369
MERCEDES-BENZ ITALIA S.P.A.—See Daimler-Benz Aktiengesellschaft; *Int'l,* pg. 369
MERCEDES-BENZ JAPAN CO., LTD.—See Daimler-Benz Aktiengesellschaft; *Int'l,* pg. 369
MERCEDES-BENZ LEASING GMBH—See Daimler-Benz Aktiengesellschaft; *Int'l,* pg. 369
MERCEDES-BENZ MEXICO, S.A. DE C.V.—See Daimler-Benz Aktiengesellschaft; *Int'l,* pg. 369
MERCEDES-BENZ NEDERLAND B.V.—See Daimler-Benz Aktiengesellschaft; *Int'l,* pg. 369
MERCEDES-BENZ OF NORTH AMERICA, INC.—See Daimler-Benz Aktiengesellschaft; *Int'l,* pg. 368
MERCEDES-BENZ OF SOUTH AFRICA (PTY.) LTD.—See Daimler-Benz Aktiengesellschaft; *Int'l,* pg. 369
MERCEDES-BENZ OSTERREICH VERTRIEBSGESELLSCHAFT MBH—See Daimler-Benz Aktiengesellschaft; *Int'l,* pg. 369
MERCEDES-BENZ PORTUGAL-COMERCIO DE AUTOMOVEIS, S.A.—See Daimler-Benz Aktiengesellschaft; *Int'l,* pg. 369
MERCEDES-BENZ (SCHWEIZ) AG—See Daimler-Benz Aktiengesellschaft; *Int'l,* pg. 369
MERCEDES-BENZ TURK A.S.—See Daimler-Benz Aktiengesellschaft; *Int'l,* pg. 369
MERCEDES-BENZ (UNITED KINGDOM) LTD.—See Daimler-Benz Aktiengesellschaft; *Int'l,* pg. 369
MERCER COMPANY—See Columbia National Group, Inc.; *U.S. Private,* pg. 256
MERCER CONSULTING GROUP, INC.—See Marsh & McLennan Companies, Inc.; *U.S. Public,* pg. 1049
MERCER FORGE, INC.—See Galesi Group; *U.S. Private,* pg. 438
MERCER MANAGEMENT CONSULTING, INC.—See Marsh & McLennan Companies, Inc.; *U.S. Public,* pg. 1049
MERCER PRODUCTS CO.—See Laporte plc; *Int'l,* pg. 802
THOMAS MERCER CHRONOMETER LTD.—See Brown & Sharpe Manufacturing Company; *U.S. Public,* pg. 260
THOMAS MERCER LTD.—See Brown & Sharpe Manufacturing Company; *U.S. Public,* pg. 260
MERCER TRANSPORTATION CO.; *U.S. Private,* pg. 732

MASTER INDEX TO COMPANY NAMES MERKEL

Company Index

WILLIAM M. MERCER COMPANIES, INC.—See Marsh & McLennan Companies, Inc.; *U.S. Public*, pg. 1049
WILLIAM M. MERCER LIMITED—See Marsh & McLennan Companies, Inc.; *U.S. Public*, pg. 1049
MERCHANDISING CORP. OF AMERICA, INC.—See The Seagram Company Ltd.; *Int'l*, pg. 1216
MERCHANT BANK (GHANA) LIMITED—See Standard Bank Investment Corporation Limited; *Int'l*, pg. 1293
MERCHANT CAPITAL GROUP LTD.; *U.S. Private*, pg. 732
MERCHANT & PLANTERS BANK N.A. OF CAMDEN—See First United Bancshares, Inc.; *U.S. Public*, pg. 641
MERCHANTS DESPATCH TRANSP. CO.—See Conrail, Inc.; *U.S. Public*, pg. 432
MERCHANTS DISTRIBUTORS, INC.—See Alex Lee, Inc.; *U.S. Private*, pg. 657
MERCHANTS GROUP, INC.; *U.S. Public*, pg. 1090
MERCHANTS HOME DELIVERY SERVICE INC.—See NFC plc; *Int'l*, pg. 901
MERCHANTS HOUSE—See Cendant Corporation; *U.S. Public*, pg. 321
MERCHANTS INFORMATION SOLUTIONS, INC.—See Micros Systems Inc.; *U.S. Public*, pg. 1106
MERCHANTS INFORMATION SOLUTIONS, LTD.—See Micros Systems Inc.; *U.S. Public*, pg. 1106
MERCHANT'S INVESTMENT CENTER, INC.—See Deposit Guaranty Corp.; *U.S. Public*, pg. 501
MERCHANTS NATIONAL BANK—See Deposit Guaranty Corp.; *U.S. Public*, pg. 501
MERCHANTS NATIONAL BANK—See Old National Bancorp; *U.S. Public*, pg. 1217
MERCHANTS NISSAN—See Merchants Rent A Car, Inc.; *U.S. Private*, pg. 732
MERCHANTS PUBLISHING CO.; *U.S. Private*, pg. 732
MERCHANTS RENT A CAR, INC.; *U.S. Private*, pg. 732
MERCHANTS TRANSPORT OF HICKORY—See Alex Lee, Inc.; *U.S. Private*, pg. 657
MERCIA DIAGNOSTICS LIMITED—See Centocor, Inc.; *U.S. Public*, pg. 323
MERCIAN CORPORATION; *Int'l*, pg. 858
MERCK & CO., INC.; *U.S. Public*, pg. 1090
MERCK BALZERS AG—See Oerlikon-Buhrle Holding AG; *Int'l*, pg. 997
MERCK BALZERS LTD.—See Oerlikon-Buhrle Holding AG; *Int'l*, pg. 997
MERCK CONSUMER HEALTHCARE GROUP—See Merck & Co., Inc.; *U.S. Public*, pg. 1090
MERCK DANMARK A/S—See Merck & Co., Inc.; *U.S. Public*, pg. 1092
MERCK FINCK & CO.—See Barclays Bank PLC; *Int'l*, pg. 166
MERCK FROSST CANADA INC.—See Merck & Co., Inc.; *U.S. Public*, pg. 1092
MERCK HOLDINGS, INC.—See Merck & Co., Inc.; *U.S. Public*, pg. 1091
MERCK HUMAN HEALTH DIVISION—See Merck & Co., Inc.; *U.S. Public*, pg. 1090
MERCK KOREA, LTD.—See Merck & Co., Inc.; *U.S. Public*, *pg. 1092*
MERCK MANUFACTURING DIV.—See Merck & Co., Inc.; *U.S. Public*, pg. 1091
MERCK MEDCO MANAGED CARE—See Merck & Co., Inc.; *U.S. Public*, pg. 1091
MERCK MEDCO MANAGED CARE, LLC—See Merck & Co., Inc.; *U.S. Public*, pg. 1090
MERCK RESEARCH LABORATORIES—See Merck & Co., Inc.; *U.S. Public*, pg. 1091
MERCK SHARP & DOHME A.B.—See Merck & Co., Inc.; *U.S. Public*, pg. 1092
MERCK SHARP & DOHME (ARGENTINA), INC.—See Merck & Co., Inc.; *U.S. Public*, pg. 1091
MERCK SHARP & DOHME (ASIA) INC.—See Merck & Co., Inc.; *U.S. Public*, pg. 1092
MERCK SHARP & DOHME (AUST.) P/L—See Merck & Co., Inc.; *U.S. Public*, pg. 1092
MERCK SHARP & DOHME (AUSTRALIA) PTY. LTD.—See Merck & Co., Inc.; *U.S. Public*, pg. 1092
MERCK SHARP & DOHME B.V.—See Merck & Co., Inc.; *U.S. Public*, pg. 1092
MERCK SHARP & DOHME-CHIBRET A.G.—See Merck & Co., Inc.; *U.S. Public*, pg. 1092
MERCK SHARP & DOHME DE MEXICO S.A. DE C.V.—See Merck & Co., Inc.; *U.S. Public*, pg. 1092
MERCK SHARP & DOHME DE VENEZUELA C.A.—See Merck & Co., Inc.; *U.S. Public*, pg. 1092
MERCK SHARP & DOHME (EUROPE), INC.—See Merck & Co., Inc.; *U.S. Public*, pg. 1091
MERCK SHARP & DOHME GMBH—See Merck & Co., Inc.; *U.S. Public*, pg. 1092
MERCK SHARP & DOHME (GREECE) INC.—See Merck & Co., Inc.; *U.S. Public*, pg. 1091
MERCK SHARP & DOHME-HOLLAND—See Merck & Co., Inc.; *U.S. Public*, pg. 1092
MERCK SHARP & DOHME (I.A.) CORP.—See Merck & Co., Inc.; *U.S. Public*, pg. 1091
MERCK SHARP & DOHME INTL.—See Merck & Co., Inc.; *U.S. Public*, pg. 1092
MERCK SHARP & DOHME INTL. INC.—See Merck & Co., Inc.; *U.S. Public*, pg. 1092
MERCK SHARP & DOHME (IRELAND) LTD.—See Merck & Co., Inc.; *U.S. Public*, pg. 1092
MERCK SHARP & DOHME (ITALIA) SPA—See Merck & Co., Inc.; *U.S. Public*, pg. 1092
MERCK SHARP & DOHME, LIMITADA—See Merck & Co., Inc.; *U.S. Public*, pg. 1092
MERCK SHARP & DOHME LTD.—See Merck & Co., Inc.; *U.S. Public*, pg. 1092
MERCK SHARP & DOHME (NEW ZEALAND) LTD.—See Merck & Co., Inc.; *U.S. Public*, pg. 1092
MERCK SHARP & DOHME OF PAKISTAN LTD.—See Merck & Co., Inc.; *U.S. Public*, pg. 1092
MERCK SHARP & DOHME QUIMICA DE PUERTO RICO, INC.—See Merck & Co., Inc.; *U.S. Public*, pg. 1091
MERCK SHARP & DOHME SCIENTIFIC & MANAGEMENT CORP.—See Merck & Co., Inc.; *U.S. Public*, pg. 1091
MERCK SHARP & DOHME (SWEDEN) AB—See Merck & Co., Inc.; *U.S. Public*, pg. 1092
MERCK SHARP Y DOHME (ARGENTINA) INC.—See Merck & Co., Inc.; *U.S. Public*, pg. 1092
MERCK SHARP Y DOHME ESPANA S.A.—See Merck & Co., Inc.; *U.S. Public*, pg. 1092
MERCK VACCINE DIVISION—See Merck & Co., Inc.; *U.S. Public*, pg. 1091
MERCO/SAVORY INC.—See Berisford plc; *Int'l*, pg. 189
MERCOID DIV.—See Dwyer Instruments Inc.; *U.S. Private*, pg. 350
MERCON STEEL STRUCTURES B.V.; *Int'l*, pg. 858
MERCUR MINE—See Barrick Gold Corporation; *Int'l*, pg. 169
MERCURY ADJUSTMENT BUREAU, INC.—See First Central Financial Corporation; *U.S. Private*, pg. 406
MERCURY AIR CARGO—See Mercury Air Group Inc.; *U.S. Public*, pg. 1093
MERCURY AIR CENTER—See Mercury Air Group Inc.; *U.S. Public*, pg. 1093
MERCURY AIR GROUP INC.; *U.S. Public*, pg. 1092
MERCURY ASSET MANAGEMENT GROUP PLC—See Swiss Bank Corporation; *Int'l*, pg. 1331
MERCURY ASSET MANAGEMENT PLC—See Swiss Bank Corporation; *Int'l*, pg. 1331
MERCURY COMPUTER SYSTEMS, INC.; *U.S. Private*, pg. 732
MERCURY DISTRIBUTING CO., INC.; *U.S. Private*, pg. 732
MERCURY FINANCE CO.; *U.S. Public*, pg. 1093
MERCURY FUND MANAGERS LTD.—See Swiss Bank Corporation; *Int'l*, pg. 1331
MERCURY GENERAL CORPORATION; *U.S. Public*, pg. 1093
MERCURY INTERACTIVE CORP.; *U.S. Public*, pg. 1093
MERCURY MARINE—See Brunswick Corporation; *U.S. Public*, pg. 265
MERCURY PRINTING COMPANY, INC.—See Wallace Computer Services, Inc.; *U.S. Public*, pg. 1736
MERCURY REFUELING, INC.—See Mercury Air Group Inc.; *U.S. Public*, pg. 1093
MEREDITH CORPORATION; *U.S. Public*, pg. 1094
MEREDITH LIST MARKETING—See Meredith Corporation; *U.S. Public*, pg. 1094
MEREDITH PUBLISHING GROUP—See Meredith Corporation; *U.S. Public*, pg. 1094
MEREDITH PUBLISHING SERVICES—See Meredith Corporation; *U.S. Public*, pg. 1094
MEREDITH VIDEO PUBLISHING—See Meredith Corporation; *U.S. Public*, pg. 1094
MERET COMMUNICATIONS—See Osicom Technologies Inc.; *U.S. Public*, pg. 1233
MERIAL LTD.—See Merck & Co., Inc.; *U.S. Public*, pg. 1092
MERIAL SAS—See Rhone-Poulenc S.A.; *Int'l*, pg. 1114
MERIAM INSTRUMENT—See Berkshire Hathaway Inc.; *U.S. Public*, pg. 218
MERIAN GMBH, WOHNUNGSUNTERNEHMEN—See Landesbank Hessen-Thuringen Girozentrale; *Int'l*, pg. 799
MERIDELL ACHIEVEMENT CENTER—See Universal Health Services, Inc.; *U.S. Public*, pg. 1697
MERIDEN TELEPHONE CO., INC.—See Telephone and Data Systems, Inc.; *U.S. Public*, pg. 1571
MERIDES GRUNDBESITZ- UND BEBAUUNGSGESELLSCHAFT MBH—See Bayerische Vereinsbank Group; *Int'l*, pg. 180
MERIDIAN COMMUNICATIONS SYSTEMS DIV.—See Northern Telecom Limited; *Int'l*, pg. 970
MERIDIAN DIAGNOSTICS EUROPE S.R.L.—See Meridian Diagnostics, Inc.; *U.S. Public*, pg. 1095
MERIDIAN DIAGNOSTICS, INC.; *U.S. Public*, pg. 1094
MERIDIAN ENVIRONMENTAL SERVICES, INC.—See Meridian National Corporation; *U.S. Public*, pg. 1095
MERIDIAN HOTELS, INC.—See Granada Group PLC; *Int'l*, pg. 556
MERIDIAN INC.—See Herman Miller, Inc.; *U.S. Public*, pg. 1112
MERIDIAN INDUSTRIES, INC.; *U.S. Private*, pg. 732
MERIDIAN INSURANCE GROUP, INC.; *U.S. Public*, pg. 1095
MERIDIAN LAMPS DEVELOPMENT, INC.—See Catalina Lighting, Inc.; *U.S. Public*, pg. 314
MERIDIAN LAMPS, INC.—See Catalina Lighting, Inc.; *U.S. Public*, pg. 314
MERIDIAN MACHINE WORKS, INC.—See Enterprises International Inc.; *U.S. Private*, pg. 378
MERIDIAN MEDICAL TECHNOLOGY, INC.; *U.S. Public*, pg. 1095
MERIDIAN NATIONAL CORPORATION; *U.S. Public*, pg. 1095
MERIDIAN NEURO CARE—See Horizon/CMS Healthcare Corporation; *U.S. Public*, pg. 839
MERIDIAN OIL HOLDING INC.—See Burlington Resources Inc.; *U.S. Public*, pg. 269
THE MERIDIAN RESOURCE CORPORATION; *U.S. Public*, *pg. 1095*
MERIDIAN RETAIL, INC.—See Devon Group, Inc.; *U.S. Public*, pg. 503
MERIDIAN SECURITY INSURANCE COMPANY—See Meridian Insurance Group, Inc.; *U.S. Public*, pg. 1095
MERIDIAN SPORTS/WATER SPORTS GROUP—See MacAndrews & Forbes Holdings Inc.; *U.S. Private*, pg. 689
MERIDIAN TECHNOLOGY LEASING SERVICES; *U.S. Private*, pg. 732
MERIDIEN S.A.—See Granada Group PLC; *Int'l*, pg. 556
MERIDIONALE CAVI S.P.A.—See Pirelli S.p.A.; *Int'l*, pg. 1058
MERIDIONALE DE TRAVAUX—See Bouygues; *Int'l*, pg. 206
MERILLAT CORPORATION—See Masco Corporation; *U.S. Public*, pg. 1054
MERILLAT INDUSTRIES INC.—See Masco Corporation; *U.S. Public*, pg. 1053
MERILLAT TRANSPORTATION COMPANY—See Masco Corporation; *U.S. Public*, pg. 1054
P.T. MERINCORP SECURITIES INDONESIA—See The Sumitomo Bank, Limited; *Int'l*, pg. 1310
MERINOS; *Int'l*, pg. 858
MERI-PORI POWER PLANT—See Imatran Voima Oy; *Int'l*, pg. 660
MERISEL AUSTRALIA—See Merisel, Inc.; *U.S. Public*, pg. 1096
MERISEL AUSTRIA—See Merisel, Inc.; *U.S. Public*, pg. 1096
MERISEL CANADA—See Merisel, Inc.; *U.S. Public*, pg. 1096
MERISEL CAT, LTD.—See Merisel, Inc.; *U.S. Public*, pg. 1096
MERISEL EUROPE—See Merisel, Inc.; *U.S. Public*, pg. 1096
MERISEL FRANCE—See Merisel, Inc.; *U.S. Public*, pg. 1096
MERISEL GERMANY—See Merisel, Inc.; *U.S. Public*, pg. 1096
MERISEL, INC.; *U.S. Public*, pg. 1095
MERISEL LATIN AMERICA—See Merisel, Inc.; *U.S. Public*, pg. 1096
MERISEL MEXICO—See Merisel, Inc.; *U.S. Public*, pg. 1096
MERISEL SWITZERLAND—See Merisel, Inc.; *U.S. Public*, pg. 1096
MERISEL U.K.—See Merisel, Inc.; *U.S. Public*, pg. 1096
MERISTEM PLC; *Int'l*, pg. 858
MERIT BEHAVIORAL CARE CORP.—See Magellan Health Services, Inc.; *U.S. Public*, pg. 1036
MERIT DISTRIBUTION SERVICES, INC.—See Wal-Mart Stores, Inc.; *U.S. Public*, pg. 1733
MERIT LIFE INSURANCE CO.—See American General Corporation; *U.S. Public*, pg. 77
MERIT-MALTA METHODE LTD.—See Methode Electronics Inc.; *U.S. Public*, pg. 1101
MERIT MEDICAL SYSTEMS, INC.; *U.S. Public*, pg. 1096
MERIT STEEL COMPANY, INC.—See Leggett & Platt, Incorporated; *U.S. Public*, pg. 986
MERITA BANK LTD.—See Merita Ltd.; *Int'l*, pg. 858
MERITA BANK LTD., BEIJING REPRESENTATIVE OFFICE—See Merita Ltd.; *Int'l*, pg. 859
MERITA BANK LTD., FRANKFURT REPRESENTATIVE OFFICE—See Merita Ltd.; *Int'l*, pg. 859
MERITA BANK LTD., HONG KONG REPRESENTATIVE OFFICE—See Merita Ltd.; *Int'l*, pg. 859
MERITA BANK LTD. LONDON BRANCH—See Merita Ltd.; *Int'l*, pg. 859
MERITA BANK LTD. - MOSCOW REPRESENTATIVE OFFICE—See Merita Ltd.; *Int'l*, pg. 859
MERITA BANK LTD. NEW YORK BRANCH—See Merita Ltd.; *Int'l*, pg. 859
MERITA BANK LTD., PARIS REPRESENTATIVE OFFICE—See Merita Ltd.; *Int'l*, pg. 859
MERITA BANK LTD. - ST. PETERSBURG REPRESENTATIVE OFFICE—See Merita Ltd.; *Int'l*, pg. 859
MERITA BANK LTD. - STOCKHOLM BRANCH—See Merita Ltd.; *Int'l*, pg. 859
MERITA BANK LTD., TOKYO REPRESENTATIVE OFFICE—See Merita Ltd.; *Int'l*, pg. 859
MERITA BANK LTD., WARSAW REPRESENTATIVE OFFICE—See Merita Ltd.; *Int'l*, pg. 859
MERITA BANK LTD.-TALLINN BRANCH—See Merita Ltd.; *Int'l*, pg. 859
MERITA BANK LUXEMBOURG S.A.—See Merita Ltd.; *Int'l*, *pg. 859*
MERITA BREAD BAKERIES—See Interstate Bakeries Corporation; *U.S. Public*, pg. 909
MERITA CAPITAL LTD.—See Merita Ltd.; *Int'l*, pg. 859
MERITA CUSTOMER FINANCE LTD.—See Merita Ltd.; *Int'l*, pg. 859
MERITA FINANCE LTD.—See Merita Ltd.; *Int'l*, pg. 859
MERITA FUND MANAGEMENT LTD.—See Merita Ltd.; *Int'l*, pg. 859
MERITA LIFE ASSURANCE LTD.—See Merita Ltd.; *Int'l*, pg. 859
MERITA LTD.; *Int'l*, pg. 858
MERITA MERCHANT BANK SINGAPORE LTD.—See Merita Ltd.; *Int'l*, pg. 859
MERITA REAL ESTATE LTD.—See Merita Ltd.; *Int'l*, pg. 859
MERITA SECURITIES LTD.—See Merita Ltd.; *Int'l*, pg. 859
MERITCARE FOUNDATION—See MeritCare Health System; *U.S. Private*, pg. 733
MERITCARE HEALTH SYSTEM; *U.S. Private*, pg. 733
MERITCARE HOSPITAL—See MeritCare Health System; *U.S. Private*, pg. 733
MERITCARE, INC.; *U.S. Private*, pg. 733
MERITCARE MEDICAL GROUP—See MeritCare Health System; *U.S. Private*, pg. 733
MERITEX PLASTICS INDUSTRIES, INC.—See Illinois Tool Works Inc.; *U.S. Public*, pg. 867
MERITOR AUTOMOTIVE, INC.; *U.S. Public*, pg. 1096
MERITOR WABCO VEHICLE CONTROL SYSTEMS—See Meritor Automotive, Inc.; *U.S. Public*, pg. 1096
MERIX CORPORATION; *U.S. Public*, pg. 1096
MERKANTILE INOZEMNA—See Telefonaktiebolaget LM Ericsson; *Int'l*, pg. 1369
MERKEL KUNSTSTOFF GMBH—See Martin Merkel GmbH & Co. KG; *Int'l*, pg. 859
MARTIN MERKEL DANMARK A/S—See Martin Merkel GmbH & Co. KG; *Int'l*, pg. 859
MARTIN MERKEL FINLAND OY—See Martin Merkel GmbH & Co. KG; *Int'l*, pg. 859
MARTIN MERKEL FRANCE-SARL—See Martin Merkel GmbH & Co. KG; *Int'l*, pg. 860
MARTIN MERKEL GMBH & CO. KG; *Int'l*, pg. 859
MARTIN MERKEL-I.M.S.—See Martin Merkel GmbH & Co. KG; *Int'l*, pg. 860
MARTIN MERKEL IRELAND LTD.—See Martin Merkel GmbH & Co. KG; *Int'l*, pg. 860

MARTIN MERKEL ITALIA S.R.L.—See Martin Merkel GmbH & Co. KG; *Int'l*, pg. 860
MARTIN MERKEL SVENSKA AB—See Martin Merkel GmbH & Co. KG; *Int'l*, pg. 860
MARTIN MERKEL VERTRIEBSGESELLSCHAFT MBH—See Martin Merkel GmbH & Co. KG; *Int'l*, pg. 860
MERKLEY NEWMAN HARTY—See Omnicom Group Inc.; *U.S. Public*, pg. 1224
MERKURHOF GRUNDSTUCKS GMBH—See Bayerische Vereinsbank Group; *Int'l*, pg. 180
MERLE NORMAN COSMETICS; *U.S. Private*, pg. 733
MERLINO'S MACARONI—See Borden, Inc.; *U.S. Private*, pg. 158
MERLONI DOMESTIC APPLIANCES LTD—See Merloni Elettrodomestici S.P.A.; *Int'l*, pg. 860
MERLONI ELECTRODOMESTICOS LDA.—See Merloni Elettrodomestici S.P.A.; *Int'l*, pg. 860
MERLONI ELECTROMENAGERS S.A.—See Merloni Elettrodomestici S.P.A.; *Int'l*, pg. 860
MERLONI ELETTRODOMESTICI S.A.—See Merloni Elettrodomestici S.P.A.; *Int'l*, pg. 860
MERLONI ELETTRODOMESTICI S.P.A.; *Int'l*, pg. 860
MERLONI HAUSGERATE GMBH—See Merloni Elettrodomestici S.P.A.; *Int'l*, pg. 860
MERLONI HUISHOUDAPPARTEN B.V.—See Merloni Elettrodomestici S.P.A.; *Int'l*, pg. 860
MERONA INDUSTRIES, INC.—See Oxford Industries, Inc.; *U.S. Public*, pg. 1239
MERRELL/CHISHOLM—See Howard, Merrell & Partners, Inc.; *U.S. Private*, pg. 543
MERRIAM-WEBSTER, INC.—See Encyclopaedia Britannica, Inc.; *U.S. Private*, pg. 375
MERRILD KAFFE—See Sara Lee Corporation; *U.S. Public*, pg. 1434
MERRILL/BOSTON—See Merrill Corporation; *U.S. Public*, pg. 1097
MERRILL BURRUPS WORLDWIDE—See Merrill Corporation; *U.S. Public*, pg. 1097
MERRILL CORPORATION; *U.S. Public*, pg. 1097
MERRILL CORPORATION-MONTREAL—See Merrill Corporation; *U.S. Public*, pg. 1097
MERRILL CORPORATION-TORONTO—See Merrill Corporation; *U.S. Public*, pg. 1097
MERRILL CUSTOM COMMUNICATIONS—See Merrill Corporation; *U.S. Public*, pg. 1097
MERRILL LYNCH & CO., INC.; *U.S. Public*, pg. 1097
MERRILL LYNCH BANK & TRUST CO.—See Merrill Lynch & Co., Inc.; *U.S. Public*, pg. 1097
MERRILL LYNCH BUSINESS FINANCIAL SERVICES INC.—See Merrill Lynch & Co., Inc.; *U.S. Public*, pg. 1098
MERRILL LYNCH CANADA INC.—See Merrill Lynch & Co., Inc.; *U.S. Public*, pg. 1098
MERRILL LYNCH CAPITAL SERVICES, INC.—See Merrill Lynch & Co., Inc.; *U.S. Public*, pg. 1097
MERRILL LYNCH CREDIT CORPORATION—See Merrill Lynch & Co., Inc.; *U.S. Public*, pg. 1098
MERRILL LYNCH DERIVATIVE PRODUCTS, INC.—See Merrill Lynch & Co., Inc.; *U.S. Public*, pg. 1097
MERRILL LYNCH FIDUCIARY SERVICES, INC.—See Merrill Lynch & Co., Inc.; *U.S. Public*, pg. 1098
MERRILL LYNCH FUTURES INC.—See Merrill Lynch & Co., Inc.; *U.S. Public*, pg. 1098
MERRILL LYNCH GOVERNMENT SECURITIES, INC.—See Merrill Lynch & Co., Inc.; *U.S. Public*, pg. 1097
MERRILL LYNCH GROUP, INC.—See Merrill Lynch & Co., Inc.; *U.S. Public*, pg. 1097
MERRILL LYNCH, HUBBARD, INC.—See Merrill Lynch & Co., Inc.; *U.S. Public*, pg. 1098
MERRILL LYNCH INSURANCE GROUP, INC.—See Merrill Lynch & Co., Inc.; *U.S. Public*, pg. 1098
MERRILL LYNCH INTERNATIONAL BANK—See Merrill Lynch & Co., Inc.; *U.S. Public*, pg. 1097
MERRILL LYNCH INTERNATIONAL, INC.—See Merrill Lynch & Co., Inc.; *U.S. Public*, pg. 1098
MERRILL LYNCH INVESTMENT MANAGEMENT, INC.—See Merrill Lynch & Co., Inc.; *U.S. Public*, pg. 1098
MERRILL LYNCH INVESTMENT PARTNERS, INC.—See Merrill Lynch & Co., Inc.; *U.S. Public*, pg. 1098
MERRILL LYNCH LIFE AGENCY INC.—See Merrill Lynch & Co., Inc.; *U.S. Public*, pg. 1098
MERRILL LYNCH, PIERCE, FENNER & SMITH, INC.—See Merrill Lynch & Co., Inc.; *U.S. Public*, pg. 1098
MERRILL LYNCH SPECIALISTS INC.—See Merrill Lynch & Co., Inc.; *U.S. Public*, pg. 1098
MERRILL LYNCH TRUST COMPANY (NEW JERSEY)—See Merrill Lynch & Co., Inc.; *U.S. Public*, pg. 1098
MERRIMAC INDUSTRIES, INC.; *U.S. Public*, pg. 1098
MERRY LAND & INVESTMENT COMPANY, INC.; *U.S. Public*, pg. 1098
MERRYHILL COUNTRY SCHOOLS, INC.—See Nobel Education Dynamics, Inc.; *U.S. Public*, pg. 1186
MERRYMAID LIMITED—See Arnotts plc; *Int'l*, pg. 81
THE MERTEN COMPANY—See Champion Industries; *U.S. Public*, pg. 333
MERTIK MAXITROL GMBH & CO., KG—See Maxitrol Co.; *U.S. Private*, pg. 716
MERTON CONTAINERS—See BPB Industries PLC; *Int'l*, pg. 123
MERVYN'S CALIFORNIA—See Dayton Hudson Corporation; *U.S. Public*, pg. 489
MESA AIR GROUP; *U.S. Public*, pg. 1099
MESA AIRLINES, INC.—See Mesa Air Group; *U.S. Public*, pg. 1099
MESA AIRLINES PILOT DEVELOPMENT, INC.—See Mesa Air Group; *U.S. Public*, pg. 1099
MESA CAPITAL CORPORATION—See Pioneer Natural Resources Co.; *U.S. Public*, pg. 1300
MESA CITRUS GROWERS; *U.S. Private*, pg. 733
MESA ENVIRONMENTAL—See Pioneer Natural Resources Co.; *U.S. Public*, pg. 1300
MESA HOLDING LIMITED PARTNERSHIP (MHLP)—See Pioneer Natural Resources Co.; *U.S. Public*, pg. 1300
MESA LABORATORIES, INC.; *U.S. Public*, pg. 1099

MESA MIDCONTINENT LIMITED PARTNERSHIP (MMLP)—See Pioneer Natural Resources Co.; *U.S. Public*, pg. 1300
MESA OPERATING LIMITED PARTNERSHIP (MOLP)—See Pioneer Natural Resources Co.; *U.S. Public*, pg. 1300
MESABA AVIATION, INC.—See Mesaba Holdings, Inc.; *U.S. Public*, pg. 1099
MESABA-CLIFFS MINING CO.—See NKK Corporation; *Int'l*, pg. 903
MESABA HOLDINGS, INC.; *U.S. Public*, pg. 1099
P.T. MESIN ISUZU INDONESIA—See Isuzu Motors Limited; *Int'l*, pg. 693
P.T. MESIN ISUZU INDONESIA—See General Motors Corporation; *U.S. Public*, pg. 724
MESIROW FINANCIAL; *U.S. Private*, pg. 733
MESOTEX S.A.—See Forbo Holding SA; *Int'l*, pg. 497
MESSAGERIES DE L'OUTAOUAIS—See G.T.C. Transcontinental Group Ltd.; *Int'l*, pg. 539
MESSAGERIES SAGUENAY—See G.T.C. Transcontinental Group Ltd.; *Int'l*, pg. 539
MESSAGES & TEQUILA—See BDDP Group; *Int'l*, pg. 116
MESSER GRIESHEIM GMBH—See Hoechst Aktiengesellschaft; *Int'l*, pg. 626
FRANK MESSER & SONS CONSTRUCTION CO.; *U.S. Private*, pg. 734
A. MESSERLI AG—See Oce-van der Grinten N.V.; *Int'l*, pg. 995
MESSIDOR—See Groupe Casino; *Int'l*, pg. 563
MESSIER-BUGATTI S.A.—See SNECMA - Societe Nationale d'Etude et de Construction de Moteurs d'Aviation; *Int'l*, pg. 1165
MESSIER-DOWTY—See TI Group plc; *Int'l*, pg. 1340
MESSIER-DOWTY CUSTOMER SUPPORT CENTER-AMERICAS—See TI Group plc; *Int'l*, pg. 1340
MESSIER-DOWTY CUSTOMER SUPPORT CENTRE-ASIA PACIFIC—See TI Group plc; *Int'l*, pg. 1340
MESSIER-DOWTY CUSTOMER SUPPORT CENTRE-EUROPE—See TI Group plc; *Int'l*, pg. 1340
MESSIER-DOWTY ELECTRONICS—See TI Group plc; *Int'l*, pg. 1340
MESSIER-DOWTY INC., MONTREAL—See TI Group plc; *Int'l*, pg. 1340
MESSIER-DOWTY INC., TORONTO—See TI Group plc; *Int'l*, pg. 1340
MESSIER-DOWTY INTERNATIONAL—See TI Group plc; *Int'l*, pg. 1340
MESSIER-DOWTY INTERNATIONAL MARKETING—See TI Group plc; *Int'l*, pg. 1340
MESSIER-DOWTY LTD.—See TI Group plc; *Int'l*, pg. 1340
MESSIER-DOWTY SAS—See TI Group plc; *Int'l*, pg. 1340
MESSIER S.A.—See SNECMA - Societe Nationale d'Etude et de Construction de Moteurs d'Aviation; *Int'l*, pg. 1166
MESSIER SERVICES INC.—See SNECMA - Societe Nationale d'Etude et de Construction de Moteurs d'Aviation; *Int'l*, pg. 1165
J.W. MESSNER, INC.—See J.W. Messner, Inc.; *U.S. Private*, pg. 734
J.W. MESSNER, INC.; *U.S. Private*, pg. 734
J.W. MESSNER, INC.—See J.W. Messner, Inc.; *U.S. Private*, pg. 734
MESSNER VETERE BERGER MCNAMEE SCHMETTERER/EURO RSCG—See Havas Advertising; *Int'l*, pg. 602
MESSO-CHEMIETECHNIK GMBH—See Mannesmann A.G.; *Int'l*, pg. 836
MESTEK, INC.; *U.S. Public*, pg. 1099
MET-COIL LTD.—See Met-Coil Systems Corp.; *U.S. Public*, pg. 1100
MET-COIL SYSTEMS CORP.; *U.S. Public*, pg. 1099
MET-PRO CORPORATION; *U.S. Public*, pg. 1100
MET SOLUTIONS, LLC—See True North Diversified Companies; *U.S. Public*, pg. 1642
META FARM—See Triple F, Inc.; *U.S. Private*, pg. 1104
META OIL INC.—See Fisca Oil Co., Inc.; *U.S. Private*, pg. 408
META SERVICES INC.—See Ederer Inc.; *U.S. Private*, pg. 363
METAALFABRIEK DRENTHINA B.V.—See Schmalbach-Lubeca AG; *Int'l*, pg. 1207
METAALWARENFAVRIEK PIELKENROOD B.V.—See Schmalbach-Lubeca AG; *Int'l*, pg. 1207
METABO CORPORATION; *U.S. Private*, pg. 734
METAL & PIPELINE ENDURANCE LTD.—See AMEC Plc; *Int'l*, pg. 16
METAL CONTAINER CORPORATION—See Anheuser-Busch Companies, Inc.; *U.S. Public*, pg. 114
METAL FAB CORPORATION—See Flowserve Corporation; *U.S. Public*, pg. 658
METAL FORGE—See General Signal Corporation; *U.S. Public*, pg. 727
METAL IMPROVEMENT CO.—See Curtiss-Wright Corp.; *U.S. Public*, pg. 469
METAL LUBRICANTS CO.—See Fuchs Petrolub AG Oel + Chemie; *Int'l*, pg. 518
METAL MANUFACTURES LIMITED—See BICC plc; *Int'l*, pg. 120
METAL MASTERS FOODSERVICE EQUIPMENT; *U.S. Private*, pg. 734
METAL PORTUGUESA S.A.—See Ferro Corporation; *U.S. Public*, pg. 619
METAL RESOURCES, INC.—See IMCO Recycling Inc.; *U.S. Public*, pg. 871
METAL SALES MANUFACTURING CORPORATION—See Interlock Industries, Inc.; *U.S. Private*, pg. 567
METAL SEAL & PRODUCTS, INC.; *U.S. Private*, pg. 734
METAL TRADES, INC.; *U.S. Private*, pg. 734
METAL TREATING, INC.—See Thermo Electron Corporation; *U.S. Public*, pg. 1592
THE METAL WARE CORP.; *U.S. Private*, pg. 734
METALAC S.A. INDUSTRIA E COMERCIO—See SPS Technologies, Inc.; *U.S. Public*, pg. 1420
METALAGRAGRAFICA DE ARAGON S.A.—See Senior Engineering Group, plc.; *Int'l*, pg. 1222

METAILAIR-FILLIAT LIMITED—See Powell Duffryn PLC; *Int'l*, pg. 1065
METALAIR-FILLIAT SA—See Powell Duffryn PLC; *Int'l*, pg. 1065
METALAIR LIMITED—See Powell Duffryn PLC; *Int'l*, pg. 1065
METALART CORPORATION—See Nissho Iwai Corporation; *Int'l*, pg. 946
METALASTIK VIBRATION CONTROL SYSTEMS—See BTR plc; *Int'l*, pg. 126
METALCENTER, INC.—See Reliance Steel & Aluminum Co.; *U.S. Public*, pg. 1375
METALCHIMICA SRL—See Metallurg, Inc.; *U.S. Private*, pg. 735
METALESCAUT (SOCIETE METALLURGIQUE DE L'ESCAUT)—See Groupe Usinor; *Int'l*, pg. 571
METALEUROP S.A.—See Preussag AG; *Int'l*, pg. 1071
METALL MINING CORPORATION—See Metallgesellschaft AG; *Int'l*, pg. 862
METALL ROHSTOFFE THURINGEN GMBH—See Fried. Krupp AG; *Int'l*, pg. 513
METALLAUFBEREITUNG ZWICKAU GMBH—See Fried. Krupp AG; *Int'l*, pg. 513
METALLBANK CAPITAL CORPORATION—See Metallgesellschaft AG; *Int'l*, pg. 861
METALLBANK GMBH—See Metallgesellschaft AG; *Int'l*, pg. 861
METALLGESELLSCHAFT AG; *Int'l*, pg. 860
METALLGESELLSCHAFT CAPITAL CORP.—See Metallgesellschaft AG; *Int'l*, pg. 861
METALLGESELLSCHAFT CORP.—See Metallgesellschaft AG; *Int'l*, pg. 861
METALLGESELLSCHAFT EMERGING MARKETS, INC.—See Metallgesellschaft AG; *Int'l*, pg. 862
METALLGESELLSCHAFT INDUSTRIE AG—See Metallgesellschaft AG; *Int'l*, pg. 861
METALLGESELLSCHAFT LTD.—See Nissho Iwai Corporation; *Int'l*, pg. 948
METALLGESELLSCHAFT SERVICES GMBH—See Metallgesellschaft AG; *Int'l*, pg. 861
METALLGESELLSCHAFT TRADE SERVICES CO.—See Metallgesellschaft AG; *Int'l*, pg. 862
METALLGESELLSCHAFT TRADING CORP.—See Metallgesellschaft AG; *Int'l*, pg. 862
METALLIC BUILDING COMPANY—See NCI Building Systems, Inc.; *U.S. Public*, pg. 1146
METALLICA S.A.—See Alusuisse-Lonza Holding Ltd.; *Int'l*, pg. 67
METALLICA SA—See UMS Swiss Metalworks Holding Ltd; *Int'l*, pg. 1427
METALLISED FILMS & PAPER, LTD.—See Avery Dennison Corporation; *U.S. Public*, pg. 154
METALLOY CORPORATION; *U.S. Private*, pg. 735
METALLURG (CANADA) LIMITED—See Metallurg, Inc.; *U.S. Private*, pg. 735
METALLURG DO BRAZIL LTDA.—See Metallurg, Inc.; *U.S. Private*, pg. 735
METALLURG (FAR EAST) LIMITED—See Metallurg, Inc.; *U.S. Private*, pg. 735
METALLURG, INC.; *U.S. Private*, pg. 735
METALLURG MEXICO, S.A. DE C.V.—See Metallurg, Inc.; *U.S. Private*, pg. 735
METALLURGICA ADRIATICA S.P.A.—See N.V. Bekaert S.A.; *Int'l*, pg. 185
METALLURGICAL, INC.—See Thermo Electron Corporation; *U.S. Public*, pg. 1594
METALLURGICAL PRODUCTS CO.—See General Signal Corporation; *U.S. Public*, pg. 727
METALLURGY—See ABB Asea Brown Boveri (Holding) Ltd.; *Int'l*, pg. 4
METALLWERKE REFONDA AG—See Alusuisse-Lonza Holding Ltd.; *Int'l*, pg. 67
METALS, INC.—See Hughes Supply, Inc.; *U.S. Public*, pg. 847
METALS USA, INC.; *U.S. Public*, pg. 1100
METALSA, S.A. DE C.V.—See A.O. Smith Corporation; *U.S. Public*, pg. 1477
METALTECH INTERNATIONAL PLC; *Int'l*, pg. 862
METALTECH, INC.; *U.S. Private*, pg. 735
METALUX LIGHTING—See Cooper Industries, Inc.; *U.S. Public*, pg. 443
METALWEST LLC—See O'Neal Steel Inc.; *U.S. Private*, pg. 817
METAMORA FIXTURES PRODUCTION CENTER—See Hallmark Cards, Inc.; *U.S. Private*, pg. 496
METANETICS CORP.—See Telxon Corporation; *U.S. Public*, pg. 1573
METAPHASE TECHNOLOGY, INC.—See Structural Dynamics Research Corp.; *U.S. Public*, pg. 1525
METAPLAS IONON GMBH—See Deutsche Babcock AG; *Int'l*, pg. 400
METAPLAS IONON LOHNHARTEREI GMBH—See Deutsche Babcock AG; *Int'l*, pg. 400
METAPLAS OBERDLACHENVEREDELUNGSTECHNIK GMBH—See Deutsche Babcock AG; *Int'l*, pg. 400
METAPOINT PARTNERS; *U.S. Private*, pg. 735
METAUX SPECIAUX—See Pechiney S.A.; *Int'l*, pg. 1028
METAWA-TRAY B.V.—See Sulzer Ltd.; *Int'l*, pg. 1307
METAXA DISTILLERIES—See Diageo Plc; *Int'l*, pg. 410
METAXA GREECE—See Diageo Plc; *Int'l*, pg. 410
METCAL, INC.; *U.S. Private*, pg. 735
METCALF & EDDY COMPANIES INC.—See Air & Water Technologies Corporation; *U.S. Public*, pg. 29
METCLAD S.A.—See Park Electrochemical Corporation; *U.S. Public*, pg. 1258
METCO LTD.—See Sulzer Ltd.; *Int'l*, pg. 1307
METCO S.A.—See Sulzer Ltd.; *Int'l*, pg. 1307
METCRAFT, INC.—See Emco Limited; *Int'l*, pg. 453
METEOR AG—See ABB Asea Brown Boveri (Holding) Ltd.; *Int'l*, pg. 2
METEOR CONSTRUZIONI AERONAUTICHE ED ELETTRONICHE S.P.A.—See IRI Istituto Ricostruzione Industriale; *Int'l*, pg. 653

MASTER INDEX TO COMPANY NAMES MEYER

Company Index

METEOR-EXPERIMENTAL FACILITY—See IRI Istituto Ricostruzione Industriale; Int'l, pg. 653
METEOR-GORIZIA PLANT—See IRI Istituto Ricostruzione Industriale; Int'l, pg. 653
METER DEVICES CO—See E.J. Brooks Company; U.S. Private, pg. 172
METEX CORPORATION—See United Capital Corp.; U.S. Public, pg. 1674
METEX EXPORT CORP.—See United Capital Corp.; U.S. Public, pg. 1675
METFOILS AB—See Perstorp AB; Int'l, pg. 1039
METFORM DIVISION—See Rautaruukki Oy; Int'l, pg. 1088
METFORM, INC.—See Maclean-Fogg Co.; U.S. Private, pg. 692
METHA-METHANHANDEL GMBH—See Ruhrgas Aktiengesellschaft; Int'l, pg. 1149
METHANEX CORPORATION; Int'l, pg. 862
METHANEX FORTIER INC.—See Methanex Corporation; Int'l, pg. 862
METHANOL CHEMIE NEDERLAND VOF—See Akzo Nobel N.V.; Int'l, pg. 43
METHANOR VOF—See Akzo Nobel N.V.; Int'l, pg. 43
METHANOR VOF—See DSM N.V.; Int'l, pg. 354
METHODE DEVELOPMENT COMPANY—See Methode Electronics Inc.; U.S. Public, pg. 1101
METHODE ELECTRONICS EUROPE LIMITED—See Methode Electronics Inc.; U.S. Public, pg. 1101
METHODE ELECTRONICS FAREAST PTE. LTD.—See Methode Electronics Inc.; U.S. Public, pg. 1101
METHODE ELECTRONICS INC.; U.S. Public, pg. 1101
METHODE MIKON LIMITED—See Methode Electronics Inc.; U.S. Public, pg. 1101
METHODE NEW ENGLAND CO., INC.—See Methode Electronics Inc.; U.S. Public, pg. 1101
METHODE TECHNICAL COMPONENTS—See Methode Electronics Inc.; U.S. Public, pg. 1101
METHODES ET INFORMATIQUE—See Compagnie des Machines Bull; Int'l, pg. 316
METHODS AND SERVICES GROUP S.A.—See Compagnie des Machines Bull; Int'l, pg. 319
METHODS & SERVICES GROUP S.A.—See Compagnie des Machines Bull; Int'l, pg. 318
MENTHOLATUM PTY. LTD.—See Rohto Pharmaceutical Co.; Int'l, pg. 1126
METHVEN TAPMAKERS—See McKechnie PLC; Int'l, pg. 851
METIER MANAGEMENT SYSTEMS—See Lockheed Martin Corporation; U.S. Public, pg. 1010
METINOX STEEL LTD.—See Sandvik AB; Int'l, pg. 1186
METLIFE BEIJING REPRESENTATIVE OFFICE—See Metropolitan Life Insurance Co.; U.S. Private, pg. 738
METLIFE CAPITAL HOLDINGS, INC.—See Metropolitan Life Insurance Co.; U.S. Private, pg. 737
METLIFE SECURITIES, INC.—See Metropolitan Life Insurance Co.; U.S. Private, pg. 738
METLIFE SHANGHAI REPRESENTATIVE OFFICE—See Metropolitan Life Insurance Co.; U.S. Private, pg. 738
METO—See Esselte AB; Int'l, pg. 462
METO B.V.—See Esselte AB; Int'l, pg. 462
METO FAR EAST—See Esselte AB; Int'l, pg. 462
METO KIMBAL SYSTEMS B.V.—See Esselte AB; Int'l, pg. 462
METONE, INC.—See Pacific Scientific Company; U.S. Public, pg. 1250
METPAR CORP.; U.S. Private, pg. 735
METPELA OY—See Kemira Oy; Int'l, pg. 729
METRA COMMUTER RAIL—See Regional Transportation Authority (RTA); U.S. Private, pg. 919
METRA, COMMUTER RAIL SERVICE BOARD—See Regional Transportation Authority (RTA); U.S. Private, pg. 919
METRA CORPORATION; Int'l, pg. 862
METRAILLE—See SNCF; Int'l, pg. 1164
METRIC & MULTISTANDARD COMPONENTS; U.S. Private, pg. 736
METRIC CONSTRUCTORS, INC.—See Philipp Holzmann AG; Int'l, pg. 633
METRIC SYSTEMS CORP.—See Tech-Sym Corporation; U.S. Public, pg. 1563
METRICA SYSTEMS—See ADC Telecommunications, Inc.; U.S. Public, pg. 4
METRO AG; Int'l, pg. 863
METRO ATLANTA PROPERTIES—See Fischbach & Dougherty, Inc.; U.S. Private, pg. 408
METRO AUTO AUCTION OF KANSAS CITY, INC.—See Tyco International Ltd.; U.S. Public, pg. 1649
METRO/BASICS—See Richfood Holdings, Inc.; U.S. Public, pg. 1388
METRO BREWERY—See Interbrew S.A.; Int'l, pg. 679
METRO BRICK COMPANY PTY. LIMITED—See Bristile Clay Tiles, Ltd.; Int'l, pg. 216
METRO CELL, INC.—See The Rao Group Inc.; U.S. Private, pg. 910
METRO COLOR ROP BUY—See Metropolitan Sunday Newspapers, Inc.; U.S. Private, pg. 739
METRO DAVIDSON CO. DF—See Corrections Corporation of America; U.S. Public, pg. 450
METRO FM—See EMAP Plc; Int'l, pg. 452
METRO FOODS, INC.; U.S. Private, pg. 736
METRO FORD INC.; U.S. Private, pg. 736
METRO FORD SALES, INC.; U.S. Private, pg. 736
METRO-GOLDWYN-MAYER INC.; U.S. Public, pg. 1101
METRO-GOLDWYN-MAYER PICTURES, INC.—See Metro-Goldwyn-Mayer Inc.; U.S. Public, pg. 1102
METRO GROUP—See WPP Group plc; Int'l, pg. 1482
METRO INFORMATION SERVICES; U.S. Public, pg. 1102
METRO LABEL CORP.; U.S. Private, pg. 736
METRO MILWAUKEE AUTO AUCTION—See Cox Enterprises, Inc.; U.S. Private, pg. 282
METRO-NORTH COMMUTER RAILROAD COMPANY—See Metropolitan Transportation Authority; U.S. Private, pg. 739
METRO PARKING SYSTEMS—See Metropolitan Properties Systems; U.S. Private, pg. 739
METRO 25 TIRE CENTERS—See The Rao Group Inc.; U.S. Private, pg. 910
METROCALL, INC.; U.S. Public, pg. 1102
METROCOM TRUNKED RADIO COMMUNICATION SYSTEMS, INC.—See Motorola, Inc.; U.S. Public, pg. 1137
METROCONTROL AG—See Hesta Tex AG; Int'l, pg. 618
PT METRODATA ELECTRONICS—See Acer Incorporated; Int'l, pg. 22
METROLAND PRINTING & DISTRIBUTING—See Torstar Corporation; Int'l, pg. 1402
METROLINK COMMUNICATIONS CORPORATION—See Motorola, Inc.; U.S. Public, pg. 1137
METROLITHO—See G.T.C. Transcontinental Group Ltd.; Int'l, pg. 538
METROLOGIC INSTRUMENTS GMBH—See Metrologic Instruments, Inc.; U.S. Public, pg. 1102
METROLOGIC INSTRUMENTS, INC.; U.S. Public, pg. 1102
METROMAIL CORPORATION; U.S. Public, pg. 1102
METROMEDIA COMPANY; U.S. Private, pg. 736
METROMEDIA INTERNATIONAL GROUP, INC.; U.S. Public, pg. 1102
METROMEDIA INTERNATIONAL TELECOMMUNICATIONS, INC.—See Metromedia International Group, Inc.; U.S. Public, pg. 1103
METROMEDIA STEAKHOUSES, INC.—See Metromedia Company; U.S. Private, pg. 736
METRON STEEL—See Groupe Usinor; Int'l, pg. 572
METRON STEEL CORP.; U.S. Private, pg. 736
METROPLEX BEHAVIORAL HEALTHCARE SERVICES, INC.—See Magellan Health Services, Inc.; U.S. Public, pg. 1036
METROPOLE HOTELS (HOLDINGS) LTD.—See Lonrho plc; Int'l, pg. 817
METROPOLE LITHO INC.—See G.T.C. Transcontinental Group Ltd.; Int'l, pg. 538
METROPOLIS GENERAL PARTNERSHIP—See Cigna Corp.; U.S. Public, pg. 361
METROPOLITAN ASPHALT, INC.—See Peter A. Basile Sons Inc.; U.S. Private, pg. 121
METROPOLITAN CAFE—See Ark Restaurants Corp.; U.S. Public, pg. 130
METROPOLITAN COMMUNICATIONS LTD.—See Telefonaktiebolaget LM Ericsson; Int'l, pg. 1369
METROPOLITAN EDISON CO.—See GPU, Inc.; U.S. Public, pg. 695
METROPOLITAN FURNITURE CORPORATION—See Steelcase Inc.; U.S. Private, pg. 1038
METROPOLITAN HOME MAGAZINE—See Lagardere Groupe; Int'l, pg. 795
METROPOLITAN INSURANCE & ANNUITY CO.—See Metropolitan Life Insurance Co.; U.S. Private, pg. 737
METROPOLITAN INSURANCE & ANNUITY COMPANY, TAIWAN BRANCH—See Metropolitan Life Insurance Co.; U.S. Private, pg. 738
METROPOLITAN LIFE HOLDINGS, LTD.—See Metropolitan Life Insurance Co.; U.S. Private, pg. 737
METROPOLITAN LIFE INSURANCE CO.; U.S. Private, pg. 737
METROPOLITAN LIFE INSURANCE COMPANY OF CANADA—See Metropolitan Life Insurance Co.; U.S. Private, pg. 738
METROPOLITAN LIFE INSURANCE COMPANY OF HONG KONG, LTD.—See Metropolitan Life Insurance Co.; U.S. Private, pg. 738
METROPOLITAN LIFE SEGUROS DE VIDA, S.A.—See Metropolitan Life Insurance Co.; U.S. Private, pg. 738
METROPOLITAN MORTGAGE & SECURITIES CO., INC.; U.S. Private, pg. 738
METROPOLITAN PROPERTIES SYSTEMS; U.S. Private, pg. 739
METROPOLITAN PROPERTY & CASUALTY INSURANCE CO. (MET P&C)—See Metropolitan Life Insurance Co.; U.S. Private, pg. 737
THE METROPOLITAN SAVINGS BANK OF OHIO—See F.N.B. Corporation; U.S. Public, pg. 608
METROPOLITAN SUBURBAN BUS AUTHORITY—See Metropolitan Transportation Authority; U.S. Private, pg. 739
METROPOLITAN SUNDAY NEWSPAPERS, INC.; U.S. Private, pg. 739
METROPOLITAN TOWER LIFE INSURANCE CO.—See Metropolitan Life Insurance Co.; U.S. Private, pg. 737
METROPOLITAN TRANSPORTATION AUTHORITY; U.S. Private, pg. 739
METROPOLITAN WOMEN'S CORRECTIONAL FACILITY—See Corrections Corporation of America; U.S. Public, pg. 451
METROPOLITANA DE PRESTAMOS, INC.—See Banco Popular de Puerto Rico; U.S. Public, pg. 176
METROPOLITANA MILANESE S.P.A.; Int'l, pg. 863
METROSONICS INC.—See Bowthorpe plc; Int'l, pg. 208
METROSONICS LTD.—See Bowthorpe plc; Int'l, pg. 207
OY METSA-BOTNIA AB—See Metsa-Serla Corporation; Int'l, pg. 863
METSA-SELLU OY—See Metsa-Serla Corporation; Int'l, pg. 863
METSA-SERLA AB (KATRINEFORS MILL)—See Metsa-Serla Corporation; Int'l, pg. 864
METSA-SERLA AB (NYBOHOLM MILL)—See Metsa-Serla Corporation; Int'l, pg. 864
METSA-SERLA AB (PAULISTROM MILL)—See Metsa-Serla Corporation; Int'l, pg. 864
METSA-SERLA AG—See Metsa-Serla Corporation; Int'l, pg. 864
METSA-SERLA CORPORATION; Int'l, pg. 863
METSA-SERLA TISSUE A/S—See Metsa-Serla Corporation; Int'l, pg. 864
METSA-SERLA TISSUE GMBH—See Metsa-Serla Corporation; Int'l, pg. 864
METSA-SERLA TISSUE LTD.—See Metsa-Serla Corporation; Int'l, pg. 864
METSA-SERLA TISSUE S.A.R.L.—See Metsa-Serla Corporation; Int'l, pg. 864
METTLER-TOLEDO AB—See AEA Investors Inc.; U.S. Private, pg. 4
METTLER-TOLEDO AG—See AEA Investors Inc.; U.S. Private, pg. 4
METTLER-TOLEDO AG-ABT. ANALYTICAL INSTRUMENTS—See AEA Investors Inc.; U.S. Private, pg. 4
METTLER-TOLEDO AG -BEREICH PROCESS—See AEA Investors Inc.; U.S. Private, pg. 4
METTLER-TOLEDO (ALBSTADT) GMBH—See AEA Investors Inc.; U.S. Private, pg. 4
METTLER TOLEDO ANALYSE INDUSTRIELLE S.A.R.L.—See AEA Investors Inc.; U.S. Private, pg. 4
METTLER-TOLEDO A/S—See AEA Investors Inc.; U.S. Private, pg. 4
METTLER-TOLEDO B.V.—See AEA Investors Inc.; U.S. Private, pg. 4
METTLER-TOLEDO GESELLSCHAFT MBH—See AEA Investors Inc.; U.S. Private, pg. 4
METTLER-TOLEDO GMBH—See AEA Investors Inc.; U.S. Private, pg. 4
METTLER-TOLEDO, INC.—See AEA Investors Inc.; U.S. Private, pg. 4
METTLER-TOLEDO INC.—See AEA Investors Inc.; U.S. Private, pg. 4
METTLER-TOLEDO IND. E. COM. LTDA.—See AEA Investors Inc.; U.S. Private, pg. 4
METTLER TOLEDO INSTRUMENTS (SHANGHAI) LTD.—See AEA Investors Inc.; U.S. Private, pg. 4
METTLER-TOLEDO (KOLN) GMBH—See AEA Investors Inc.; U.S. Private, pg. 4
METTLER-TOLEDO LTD.—See AEA Investors Inc.; U.S. Private, pg. 4
METTLER-TOLEDO PAC RIM LIMITED-JAPAN BRANCH OFFICE—See AEA Investors Inc.; U.S. Private, pg. 4
METTLER-TOLEDO PROCESS ANALYTICAL, INC.—See AEA Investors Inc.; U.S. Private, pg. 4
METTLER-TOLEDO PROZESSANALYTIK GMBH—See AEA Investors Inc.; U.S. Private, pg. 4
METTLER-TOLEDO S.A.—See AEA Investors Inc.; U.S. Private, pg. 4
METTLER-TOLEDO S.A. DE C.V.—See AEA Investors Inc.; U.S. Private, pg. 4
N.V. METTLER-TOLEDO S.A.—See AEA Investors Inc.; U.S. Private, pg. 4
METTLER-TOLEDO SAE—See AEA Investors Inc.; U.S. Private, pg. 4
METTLER-TOLEDO (SCHWEIZ) AG—See AEA Investors Inc.; U.S. Private, pg. 4
METTLER-TOLEDO (SEA) PTE LTD—See AEA Investors Inc.; U.S. Private, pg. 4
METTLER-TOLEDO SP. Z.O.O.—See AEA Investors Inc.; U.S. Private, pg. 4
METTLER-TOLEDO SPA—See AEA Investors Inc.; U.S. Private, pg. 4
METTOWEE LUMBER & PLASTIC CO., INC.—See Telescope Casual Furniture, Inc.; U.S. Private, pg. 1074
METWEST MORTGAGE SERVICES, INC.—See Metropolitan Mortgage & Securities Co., Inc.; U.S. Private, pg. 738
METZ BAKING CO.—See Specialty Foods Corporation; U.S. Private, pg. 1022
METZ BAKING COMPANY—See Specialty Foods Corporation; U.S. Private, pg. 1022
METZ BAKING COMPANY - GARDNER DIV.—See Specialty Foods Corporation; U.S. Private, pg. 1022
METZ BAKING COMPANY (WI)—See Specialty Foods Corporation; U.S. Private, pg. 1022
METZELER ANTIVIBRATION SYSTEMS, LTD.—See BTR plc; Int'l, pg. 130
METZELER AUTOMOTIVE PROFILES GMBH—See BTR plc; Int'l, pg. 130
METZELER (UK) LTD.—See Pirelli S.p.A.; Int'l, pg. 1059
J.B. METZLER VERLAG—See Georg von Holtzbrinck GmbH; Int'l, pg. 1478
MEUCCI S.P.A.—See Telefonaktiebolaget LM Ericsson; Int'l, pg. 1369
MEUER GMBH—See Fried. Krupp AG; Int'l, pg. 513
MEULES DEPLANQUE—See Saint-Gobain; Int'l, pg. 1173
MEXALIT INDUSTRIAL SA DE CV—See Saint-Gobain; Int'l, pg. 1171
MEXALIT S.A.—See Saint-Gobain; Int'l, pg. 1171
MEXIA FABRICATORS, INC.—See COMSAT Corporation; U.S. Public, pg. 424
MEXICAN INDUSTRIES IN MICHIGAN; U.S. Private, pg. 739
MEXICANA AIRLINES—See Corporacion Internacional de Aviacion (CINTRA); Int'l, pg. 332
MEXICANA DE AVIACION S.A. DE C.V.—See Corporacion Internacional de Aviacion (CINTRA); Int'l, pg. 332
MEXICANA DE BIENE DE CAPITAL, S.A. C/O CAMPOS HERMANOS, S.A.—See ABB Asea Brown Boveri (Holding) Ltd.; Int'l, pg. 6
MEXICO ASISTENCIA, S.A.—See Corporacion MAPFRE, Compania Internacional de Reaseguros, S.A.; Int'l, pg. 334
MEXICO PLANT—See Cooper Industries, Inc.; U.S. Public, pg. 443
MEXICORO S.A. DE C.V.—See Barrick Gold Corporation; Int'l, pg. 169
MEYER BROADCASTING COMPANY; U.S. Private, pg. 739
CARL G. MEYER HANDEL GMBH—See Mannesmann A.G.; Int'l, pg. 838
MEYER FOREST PRODUCTS LTD—See Meyer International PLC; Int'l, pg. 864
FRED MEYER INCORPORATED; U.S. Public, pg. 1103
FRED MEYER STORES—See Fred Meyer Incorporated; U.S. Public, pg. 1103
MEYER INTERNATIONAL FINANCE & PROPERTY PLC—See Meyer International PLC; Int'l, pg. 864
MEYER INTERNATIONAL GROUP PENSION TRUST—See Meyer International PLC; Int'l, pg. 864

MEYER DIRECTORY OF CORPORATE AFFILIATIONS

Company Index

MEYER INTERNATIONAL OVERSEAS INVESTMENTS LTD.—See Meyer International PLC; *Int'l*, pg. 864
MEYER INTERNATIONAL PLC; *Int'l*, pg. 864
MEYER JEWELERS; *U.S. Private*, pg. 739
MEYER LAMINATES GEORGIA INC.—See Meyer International PLC; *Int'l*, pg. 864
MEYER LAMINATES, INC.—See Meyer International PLC; *Int'l*, pg. 864
MEYER WIRE & CABLE COMPANY—See Cole Hersee Company; *U.S. Private*, pg. 251
THE MEYERCORD COMPANY—See Illinois Tool Works Inc.; *U.S. Public*, pg. 867
MEYHALL CHEMICAL AG—See Rhone-Poulenc S.A.; *Int'l*, pg. 1113
MEYNADIER AG—See Viag AG; *Int'l*, pg. 1465
THE MEYNE COMPANY—See Bulley & Andrews Company; *U.S. Private*, pg. 180
MEZZINA/BROWN INC.; *U.S. Private*, pg. 739
MGM WORLDWIDE TELEVISION, GROUP.—See Metro-Goldwyn-Mayer Inc.; *U.S. Public*, pg. 1102
MI-JACK PRODUCTS, INC.; *U.S. Private*, pg. 740
MIAMI ELEVATOR—See Dover Corporation; *U.S. Public*, pg. 521
MIAMI HEART INSTITUTE-SOUTH—See Columbia/HCA Healthcare Corporation; *U.S. Public*, pg. 405
THE MIAMI HERALD—See Knight-Ridder, Inc.; *U.S. Public*, *pg. 964*
MIAMI LEARNING CENTER—See Berkshire Hathaway Inc.; *U.S. Public*, pg. 219
THE MIAMI MARGARINE CO.; *U.S. Private*, pg. 740
MIAMI MILL—See EdperBrascan Corporation; *Int'l*, pg. 434
MIAMI POWER CORP.—See Cinergy Corp.; *U.S. Public*, pg. 369
MIAMI SUBS CORPORATION; *U.S. Public*, pg. 1103
MIAMI SYSTEMS CORPORATION; *U.S. Private*, pg. 740
MIAMI VALLEY BROADCASTING CORPORATION—See Cox Enterprises, Inc.; *U.S. Private*, pg. 282
MIAMI VALLEY CTC, INC.—See DPL Inc.; *U.S. Public*, pg. 474
MIAMI VALLEY DEVELOPMENT CO.—See DPL Inc.; *U.S. Public*, pg. 474
MIAMI VALLEY INSURANCE CO.—See DPL Inc.; *U.S. Public*, pg. 474
THE MIAMI VALLEY INSURANCE CO.—See Starbanc Corporation; *U.S. Public*, pg. 1510
MIAMI VALLEY LEASING, INC.—See DPL Inc.; *U.S. Public*, *pg. 474*
MIAMI VALLEY LIGHTING, INC.—See DPL Inc.; *U.S. Public*, pg. 474
MIAMI VALLEY PUBLISHING COMPANY, INC.—See G.T.C. Transcontinental Group Ltd.; *Int'l*, pg. 539
MIAMI VALLEY RESOURCES, INC.—See DPL Inc.; *U.S. Public*, pg. 474
MIBELLE AG—See Migros; *Int'l*, pg. 865
MICAFIL AG—See ABB Asea Brown Boveri (Holding) Ltd.; *Int'l*, pg. 2
MICANOL, INC.—See Secom General Corporation; *U.S. Public*, pg. 1453
MICARNA AG—See Migros; *Int'l*, pg. 865
MICARNA S.A.—See Migros; *Int'l*, pg. 865
MICHAEL ANTHONY JEWELERS, INC.; *U.S. Public*, pg. 1103
MICHAEL BUSINESS MACHINES CORPORATION; *U.S. Private*, pg. 740
DAVID MICHAEL & CO. INC.; *U.S. Private*, pg. 740
MICHAEL & CO (MICO) TONTRAGER VERTIEBS-GESELLSCHAFT MBH—See Philips Electronics N.V.; *Int'l*, pg. 1052
MICHAEL FOODS, INC.; *U.S. Public*, pg. 1103
MICHAEL'S DEVELOPMENT COMPANY; *U.S. Private*, pg. 740
MICHAELS DEVELOPMENT GROUP, INC.; *U.S. Private*, pg. 740
J.R. MICHAELS, INC.—See Circle International Group, Inc.; *U.S. Public*, pg. 372
MICHAELS STORES, INC.; *U.S. Public*, pg. 1104
MICHCON—See MCN Energy Group, Inc.; *U.S. Public*, pg. 1025
MICHELIN AIRCRAFT TIRE CORPORATION—See Compagnie Generale des Etablissements Michelin; *Int'l*, pg. 322
MICHELIN AMERICAS SMALL TIRES (MAST)—See Compagnie Generale des Etablissements Michelin; *Int'l*, pg. 322
MICHELIN CORPORATION—See Compagnie Generale des Etablissements Michelin; *Int'l*, pg. 322
MICHELIN INDUSTRIA E COMERCIO S/A—See Compagnie Generale des Etablissements Michelin; *Int'l*, pg. 322
MICHELIN KOREA TIRE COMPANY LIMITED—See Compagnie Generale des Etablissements Michelin; *Int'l*, pg. 322
MICHELIN NORTH AMERICA—See Compagnie Generale des Etablissements Michelin; *Int'l*, pg. 322
MICHELIN NORTH AMERICA (CANADA) INC.—See Compagnie Generale des Etablissements Michelin; *Int'l*, pg. 322
MICHELIN REIFENWERKE KGAA—See Compagnie Generale des Etablissements Michelin; *Int'l*, pg. 322
MICHELIN SIAM CO., LTD.—See The Siam Cement Public Company Limited; *Int'l*, pg. 1238
MICHELIN TYRE P.L.C.—See Compagnie Generale des Etablissements Michelin; *Int'l*, pg. 322
MICHELL BEARINGS—See Vickers PLC; *Int'l*, pg. 1467
MICHELL NBD LIMITED—See First Chicago NBD Corporation; *U.S. Public*, pg. 628
MICHELS MELSUNGEN HAUSTECHNIK GMBH—See Ruhrgas Aktiengesellschaft; *Int'l*, pg. 1149
MICHIGAN-AMERICAN WATER COMPANY—See American Water Works Company, Inc.; *U.S. Public*, pg. 95
MICHIGAN BLUEBERRY GROWERS ASSN.; *U.S. Private*, pg. 740
MICHIGAN CAT; *U.S. Private*, pg. 740
MICHIGAN CA-TV COMPANY—See Cable Michigan, Inc.; *U.S. Public*, pg. 287
MICHIGAN GAS COMPANY—See Southeastern Michigan Gas Enterprises, Inc.; *U.S. Public*, pg. 1489
MICHIGAN GAS STORAGE CO.—See CMS Energy Corporation; *U.S. Public*, pg. 280
MICHIGAN GAS UTILITIES—See UtiliCorp United Inc.; *U.S. Public*, pg. 1701
MICHIGAN HOLDINGS, INC.—See Bank of Montreal; *Int'l*, pg. 155
MICHIGAN MILK PRODUCERS ASSOCIATION; *U.S. Private*, pg. 741
MICHIGAN NATIONAL BANK, N.A.—See National Australia Bank Limited; *Int'l*, pg. 906
MICHIGAN NATIONAL CORPORATION—See National Australia Bank Limited; *Int'l*, pg. 906
MICHIGAN PACKAGING COMPANY—See Greif Brothers Corporation; *U.S. Public*, pg. 763
MICHIGAN PHYSICIANS MUTUAL LIABILITY INC.; *U.S. Private*, pg. 741
MICHIGAN SPRING COMPANY—See Precision Products Corporation; *U.S. Private*, pg. 880
MICHIGAN SUGAR COMPANY—See Imperial Holly Corporation; *U.S. Public*, pg. 873
MICHIGAN TUBE CO.—See Hofmann Industries, Inc.; *U.S. Private*, pg. 533
MICHIGAN WHEEL CORPORATION; *U.S. Private*, pg. 741
MICKE REIBBELAG GMBH—See Ruetgers A.G.; *Int'l*, pg. 1148
MICKELBERRY COMMUNICATIONS, INC.; *U.S. Private*, pg. 741
MICKEY & COMPANY—See Donnkenny, Inc.; *U.S. Public*, pg. 519
MICO INC.; *U.S. Private*, pg. 741
MICO INSURANCE COMPANY—See Motorists Mutual Insurance Co.; *U.S. Private*, pg. 764
MICO WEST—See Mico Inc.; *U.S. Private*, pg. 742
MICOM COMMUNICATIONS CORP.—See Northern Telecom Limited; *Int'l*, pg. 969
MICRO CARD TECHNOLOGIES INC.—See Compagnie des Machines Bull; *Int'l*, pg. 316
MICRO CIRCUIT ENGINEERING LIMITED—See Smiths Industries plc; *Int'l*, pg. 1267
MICRO COMPONENT TECHNOLOGY INC.; *U.S. Public*, pg. 1104
MICRO-CONTROLE ITALIA SRL—See Newport Corporation; *U.S. Public*, pg. 1179
MICRO-CONTROLE S.A.—See Newport Corporation; *U.S. Public*, pg. 1179
MICRO ELECTRONICS, INC.; *U.S. Private*, pg. 742
MICRO MEASUREMENTS DIV.—See Vishay Intertechnology, Inc.; *U.S. Public*, pg. 1722
MICRO-MECH. INC.—See Gunze Sangyo, Inc.; *Int'l*, pg. 578
MICRO-MET L CORP.; *U.S. Private*, pg. 742
MICRO MOTION INC.—See Emerson Electric Co.; *U.S. Public*, pg. 574
MICRO NETWORKS CORP.—See Sawgrass Electronics Group Inc.; *U.S. Private*, pg. 969
MICRO NETWORKS OF AMERICA, INC.—See General Electric Company; *U.S. Public*, pg. 711
MICRO-PRECISION OPERATIONS—See Textron Inc.; *U.S. Public*, pg. 1589
MICRO PROCESSOR SYSTEMS, INC.—See Eaton Corporation; *U.S. Public*, pg. 558
MICRO PRODUCTS—See Sheldahl, Inc.; *U.S. Public*, pg. 1465
MICRO SLIDES DIV.—See Bayside Motion Group; *U.S. Private*, pg. 125
MICRO-SWISS LTD., ISRAEL—See Kulicke & Soffa Industries, Inc.; *U.S. Public*, pg. 969
MICRO-TEC SCHALR-UND VERBINDUNGSELEMENTE GMBH—See Williams Holdings Plc; *Int'l*, pg. 1500
MICRO-TUBE FABRICATORS INC.—See Handy & Harman; *U.S. Public*, pg. 780
MICRO USPD INC.—See Microsemi Corporation; *U.S. Public*, pg. 1107
MICRO VESICULAR SYSTEMS, INC.—See IGI, Inc.; *U.S. Public*, pg. 855
MICRO WAREHOUSE (AUSTRALIA) PTY LTD.—See Micro Warehouse, Inc.; *U.S. Public*, pg. 1104
MICRO WAREHOUSE CANADA LIMITED—See Micro Warehouse, Inc.; *U.S. Public*, pg. 1104
MICRO WAREHOUSE, DENMARK APS—See Micro Warehouse, Inc.; *U.S. Public*, pg. 1104
MICRO WAREHOUSE (DEUTSCHLAND) GMBH—See Micro Warehouse, Inc.; *U.S. Public*, pg. 1104
MICRO WAREHOUSE, FINLAND OY—See Micro Warehouse, Inc.; *U.S. Public*, pg. 1104
MICRO WAREHOUSE FRANCE SARL—See Micro Warehouse, Inc.; *U.S. Public*, pg. 1104
MICRO WAREHOUSE HOLDING B.V.—See Micro Warehouse, Inc.; *U.S. Public*, pg. 1104
MICRO WAREHOUSE, INC.; *U.S. Public*, pg. 1104
MICRO WAREHOUSE, INC. OF NEW JERSEY—See Micro Warehouse, Inc.; *U.S. Public*, pg. 1104
MICRO WAREHOUSE, JAPAN KK—See Micro Warehouse, Inc.; *U.S. Public*, pg. 1104
MICRO WAREHOUSE LIMITED—See Micro Warehouse, Inc.; *U.S. Public*, pg. 1104
MICRO WAREHOUSE, NORWAY AS—See Micro Warehouse, Inc.; *U.S. Public*, pg. 1104
MICRO WAREHOUSE, S.A.—See Micro Warehouse, Inc.; *U.S. Public*, pg. 1104
MICRO WAREHOUSE, SWEDEN AB—See Micro Warehouse, Inc.; *U.S. Public*, pg. 1104
MICROAGE ENTERPRISES, INC.—See MicroAge, Inc.; *U.S. Public*, pg. 1104
MICROAGE, INC.; *U.S. Public*, pg. 1104
MICROAGE INTERNATIONAL INC.—See MicroAge, Inc.; *U.S. Public*, pg. 1104
MICROAGE SOLUTIONS, INC. (MAS)—See MicroAge, Inc.; *U.S. Public*, pg. 1105
MICROASSEMBLY SYSTEMS—See CompuDyne Corporation; *U.S. Public*, pg. 419
MICROBAS AB—See Spectra-Physics AB; *Int'l*, pg. 1289
MICROBE MASTERS—See InterBio Inc.; *U.S. Private*, pg. 567
MICROBILT CORPORATION—See First Data Corporation; *U.S. Public*, pg. 631
MICROBIT COMPUTADORES—See Hewlett-Packard Company; *U.S. Public*, pg. 822
MICROCHIP TECHNOLOGY, INC.; *U.S. Public*, pg. 1105
MICROCOM—See COMPAQ Computer Corporation; *U.S. Public*, pg. 417
MICROCOMP MANAGEMENT LTD.—See Scientific Software-Intercomp, Inc.; *U.S. Public*, pg. 1444
MICROCOSMOS, S.A.—See International Data Group; *U.S. Private*, pg. 570
MICRODYNE CORPORATION; *U.S. Public*, pg. 1105
MICROELECTRONICS CENTER—See Toshiba Corporation; *Int'l*, pg. 1405
MICROFINE MINERALS LTD. MICA WORKS—See Veba AG; *Int'l*, pg. 1459
MICROFLECT COMPANY, INC.—See Valmont Industries, Inc.; *U.S. Public*, pg. 1707
MICROFUSION—See Pechiney S.A.; *Int'l*, pg. 1028
MICROLITE CORPORATION—See Pittway Corporation; *U.S. Public*, pg. 1306
MICROLITE S.A. (GROUP)—See VARTA AG; *Int'l*, pg. 1452
MICROLOG CORPORATION; *U.S. Public*, pg. 1105
MICROM LABORGERATE GMBH—See Carl-Zeiss-Stiftung; *Int'l*, pg. 1523
MICROMATIC OPERATIONS (SWANNANOA PLANT)—See Textron Inc.; *U.S. Public*, pg. 1590
MICROMATIC TEXTRON—See Textron Inc.; *U.S. Public*, pg. 1589
MICROMECHANICS (MALAYSIA) SDN. BHD.—See SMH Swiss Corporation for Micro Electronics & Watchmaking Indus. Ltd.; *Int'l*, pg. 1161
MICROMEDEX, INC.—See The Thomson Corporation; *U.S. Public*, pg. 1601
MICROMEDIA LIMITED—See Bell & Howell Holdings; *U.S. Public*, pg. 201
MICROMET INSTRUMENTS, INC.—See Geo-Centers, Inc.; *U.S. Private*, pg. 447
MICROMOLD SPA—See Saint-Gobain; *Int'l*, pg. 1174
MICROMOTORS GROSCHOPP IRELAND LTD.—See Groschopp & Co. GmbH EMW Elektromotoren-Feinbauwerk; *Int'l*, pg. 559
MICRON COMMUNICATIONS, INC.—See Micron Technology Inc.; *U.S. Public*, pg. 1105
MICRON CUSTOM MANUFACTURING SERVICES, INC.—See Micron Technology Inc.; *U.S. Public*, pg. 1105
MICRON ELECTRONICS, INC.—See Micron Technology Inc.; *U.S. Public*, pg. 1105
MICRON QUANTUM DEVICES, INC.—See Micron Technology Inc.; *U.S. Public*, pg. 1105
MICRON SEMICONDUCTOR ASIA PACIFIC INC.—See Micron Technology Inc.; *U.S. Public*, pg. 1105
MICRON SEMICONDUCTOR ASIA PACIFIC PTE. LTD.—See Micron Technology Inc.; *U.S. Public*, pg. 1105
MICRON SEMICONDUCTOR (DEUTSCLAND) GMBH—See Micron Technology Inc.; *U.S. Public*, pg. 1106
MICRON SEPARATIONS, INC.; *U.S. Private*, pg. 742
MICRON SYSTEMS INTEGRATION, INC.—See Micron Technology Inc.; *U.S. Public*, pg. 1105
MICRON TECHNOLOGY INC.; *U.S. Public*, pg. 1105
MICRON TECHNOLOGY JAPAN, K.K.—See Micron Technology Inc.; *U.S. Public*, pg. 1106
MICRONAV INTERNATIONAL INC.—See The General Electric Company, p.l.c.; *Int'l*, pg. 546
MICRONICS COMPUTERS, INC.; *U.S. Public*, pg. 1106
MICRONICS LTD.—See Hewlett-Packard Company; *U.S. Public*, pg. 822
MICRONICS TECHNOLOGY, INC.—See Spectra-Physics AB; *Int'l*, pg. 1289
MICRONIZED FOOD PRODUCTS—See Tate & Lyle PLC; *Int'l*, pg. 1356
MICRONYL-WEDCO S.A.—See ICO, Inc.; *U.S. Public*, pg. 854
MICROPARTS GESELLSCHAFT FUR MIKROSTRUKTURTECHNIK MBH—See Veba AG; *Int'l*, pg. 1455
MICROPHASE CORPORATION; *U.S. Private*, pg. 742
MICROPOLIS A.B.—See Micropolis Corporation; *U.S. Private*, pg. 742
MICROPOLIS CORPORATION; *U.S. Private*, pg. 742
MICROPOLIS GMBH—See Micropolis Corporation; *U.S. Private*, pg. 742
MICROPOLIS LIMITED—See Micropolis Corporation; *U.S. Private*, pg. 742
MICROPOLIS S.A.R.L.—See Micropolis Corporation; *U.S. Private*, pg. 743
MICROPOLIS S.R.L.—See Micropolis Corporation; *U.S. Private*, pg. 743
MICROPOLISH—See Laporte plc; *Int'l*, pg. 803
MICROPUMP CORPORATION—See IDEX Corporation; *U.S. Public*, pg. 862
MICROPURE MEDICAL, INC.; *U.S. Private*, pg. 743
MICROS-FIDELIO HISPANIA S.L.—See Micros Systems Inc.; *U.S. Public*, pg. 1106
MICROS FIDELIO MAURICE LTEE—See Micros Systems Inc.; *U.S. Public*, pg. 1106
MICROS-FIDELIO SOFTWARE DEUTSCHLAND GMBH—See Micros Systems Inc.; *U.S. Public*, pg. 1106
MICROS OF SOUTH FLORIDA, INC.—See Micros Systems Inc.; *U.S. Public*, pg. 1106
MICROS SYSTEMS AG (LTD.)—See Micros Systems Inc.; *U.S. Public*, pg. 1107
MICROS SYSTEMS DEUTSCHLAND, GMBH—See Micros Systems Inc.; *U.S. Public*, pg. 1107
MICROS SYSTEMS HISPANIA S.L.—See Micros Systems Inc.; *U.S. Public*, pg. 1107
MICROS SYSTEMS INC.; *U.S. Public*, pg. 1106

MICROS SYSTEMS, INC.—See Micros Systems Inc.; *U.S. Public*, pg. 1107
MICROS SYSTEMS, INC. & FIDELIO SOFTWARE GMBH—See Micros Systems Inc.; *U.S. Public*, pg. 1107
MICROS SYSTEMS LATINO AMERICA—See Micros Systems Inc.; *U.S. Public*, pg. 1107
MICROS SYSTEMS LATINO AMERICA Y CARIBE—See Micros Systems Inc.; *U.S. Public*, pg. 1107
MICROSCIENCE LIMITED—See Bio-Rad Laboratories, Inc.; *U.S. Public*, pg. 230
MICROSEMI CORPORATION; *U.S. Public*, pg. 1107
MICROSEMI (H.K.) LTD.—See Microsemi Corporation; *U.S. Public*, pg. 1107
MICROSEMI PPC, INC.—See Microsemi Corporation; *U.S. Public*, pg. 1107
MICROSEMI RF PRODUCTS, INC.—See Microsemi Corporation; *U.S. Public*, pg. 1107
MICROSEP INTERNATIONAL THAILAND, LTD.—See Atkinson; *U.S. Public*, pg. 143
MICROSI—See Shin-Etsu Chemical Co. ltd.; *Int'l*, pg. 1234
MICROSOFT AG—See Microsoft Corporation; *U.S. Public*, pg. 1108
MICROSOFT A.G.—See Microsoft Corporation; *U.S. Public*, pg. 1108
MICROSOFT AKTIEBOLAG—See Microsoft Corporation; *U.S. Public*, pg. 1108
MICROSOFT BILGISAYAR YAZILIM HIZMETIERI LIMITED SIRKETI—See Microsoft Corporation; *U.S. Public*, pg. 1108
MICROSOFT B.V.—See Microsoft Corporation; *U.S. Public*, pg. 1108
MICROSOFT CANADA CO.—See Microsoft Corporation; *U.S. Public*, pg. 1108
MICROSOFT CARIBBEAN INC.—See Microsoft Corporation; *U.S. Public*, pg. 1108
MICROSOFT CH—See Microsoft Corporation; *U.S. Public*, pg. 1108
MICROSOFT CHILE S.A.—See Microsoft Corporation; *U.S. Public*, pg. 1108
MICROSOFT COLOMBIA INC.—See Microsoft Corporation; *U.S. Public*, pg. 1108
MICROSOFT COMPANY LIMITED—See Microsoft Corporation; *U.S. Public*, pg. 1108
MICROSOFT CONSULTING SERVICES—See Microsoft Corporation; *U.S. Public*, pg. 1108
MICROSOFT CORPORATION; *U.S. Public*, pg. 1107
MICROSOFT CORPORATION-BEIJING—See Microsoft Corporation; *U.S. Public*, pg. 1108
MICROSOFT CORPORATION (DUBAI BRANCH)—See Microsoft Corporation; *U.S. Public*, pg. 1108
MICROSOFT CORPORATION (INDIA) PRIVATE LIMITED—See Microsoft Corporation; *U.S. Public*, pg. 1108
MICROSOFT CORPORATION MFG. & DISTR. CTR.—See Microsoft Corporation; *U.S. Public*, pg. 1108
MICROSOFT DANMARK APS—See Microsoft Corporation; *U.S. Public*, pg. 1108
MICROSOFT DE CENTROAMERICA S.A.—See Microsoft Corporation; *U.S. Public*, pg. 1108
MICROSOFT D.O.O. LJUBLJANA—See Microsoft Corporation; *U.S. Public*, pg. 1108
MICROSOFT EUROPE—See Microsoft Corporation; *U.S. Public*, pg. 1108
MICROSOFT FEDERAL SYSTEMS—See Microsoft Corporation; *U.S. Public*, pg. 1108
MICROSOFT FRANCE S.A.R.L.—See Microsoft Corporation; *U.S. Public*, pg. 1108
MICROSOFT GESELLSCHAFT M.B.H.—See Microsoft Corporation; *U.S. Public*, pg. 1108
MICROSOFT GMBH—See Microsoft Corporation; *U.S. Public*, pg. 1108
MICROSOFT HELLAS S.A.—See Microsoft Corporation; *U.S. Public*, pg. 1108
MICROSOFT IBERICA S.R.L.—See Microsoft Corporation; *U.S. Public*, pg. 1108
MICROSOFT INFORMATICA LTDA.—See Microsoft Corporation; *U.S. Public*, pg. 1108
MICROSOFT ISRAEL LTD.—See Microsoft Corporation; *U.S. Public*, pg. 1108
MICROSOFT KFT—See Microsoft Corporation; *U.S. Public*, pg. 1108
MICROSOFT LATIN AMERICA—See Microsoft Corporation; *U.S. Public*, pg. 1108
MICROSOFT (MALAYSIA) SDN. BHD.—See Microsoft Corporation; *U.S. Public*, pg. 1108
MICROSOFT MANUFACTURING B.V.—See Microsoft Corporation; *U.S. Public*, pg. 1108
MICROSOFT MAROC S.A.R.L.—See Microsoft Corporation; *U.S. Public*, pg. 1108
MICROSOFT MEXICO S.A. DE C.V.—See Microsoft Corporation; *U.S. Public*, pg. 1108
MICROSOFT NEW ZEALAND LIMITED—See Microsoft Corporation; *U.S. Public*, pg. 1108
MICROSOFT N.V.—See Microsoft Corporation; *U.S. Public*, pg. 1108
MICROSOFT OY—See Microsoft Corporation; *U.S. Public*, pg. 1108
MICROSOFT PHILIPPINES—See Microsoft Corporation; *U.S. Public*, pg. 1108
MICROSOFT PRESS—See Microsoft Corporation; *U.S. Public*, pg. 1107
MICROSOFT PTY. LTD.—See Microsoft Corporation; *U.S. Public*, pg. 1108
MICROSOFT PUERTO RICO, INC.—See Microsoft Corporation; *U.S. Public*, pg. 1108
MICROSOFT (S.A.) (PROPRIETARY) LTD.—See Microsoft Corporation; *U.S. Public*, pg. 1108
MICROSOFT SP Z.O.O.—See Microsoft Corporation; *U.S. Public*, pg. 1108
MICROSOFT S.P.A.—See Microsoft Corporation; *U.S. Public*, pg. 1108
MICROSOFT S.R.O.—See Microsoft Corporation; *U.S. Public*, pg. 1108

MICROSOFT TAIWAN CORPORATION—See Microsoft Corporation; *U.S. Public*, pg. 1108
MICROSOFT (THAILAND) LIMITED—See Microsoft Corporation; *U.S. Public*, pg. 1108
MICROSOFT UNIVERSITY—See Microsoft Corporation; *U.S. Public*, pg. 1108
MICROSOFT ZAO—See Microsoft Corporation; *U.S. Public*, pg. 1108
MICROSOURCE CORP.—See MicroAge, Inc.; *U.S. Public*, pg. 1105
MICROTEC DIVISION—See Mentor Graphics Corporation; *U.S. Public*, pg. 1086
MICROTEK MEDICAL, INC.—See Isolyser Company, Inc.; *U.S. Public*, pg. 914
MICROTEL INTERNATIONAL INC.; *U.S. Public*, pg. 1108
MICROTEMPS SYSTEMS & PROGRAMMING—See Technical Aid Corporation; *U.S. Private*, pg. 1072
MICROTOUCH SYSTEMS, INC.; *U.S. Public*, pg. 1108
MICROTURBO DIVISION—See Labinal SA; *Int'l*, pg. 786
MICROTURBO GMBH—See Labinal SA; *Int'l*, pg. 787
MICROTURBO, INC.—See Labinal SA; *Int'l*, pg. 787
MICROTURBO LTD.—See Labinal SA; *Int'l*, pg. 787
MICROVENA CORPORATION—See Phillips Plastics Corporation; *U.S. Private*, pg. 862
MICROWAVE DATA SYSTEMS, INC.—See California Microwave, Inc.; *U.S. Public*, pg. 293
MICROWAVE MEASUREMENT DIVISION—See Anritsu Corporation; *Int'l*, pg. 77
MICROWAVE RADIO COMMUNICATIONS—See California Microwave, Inc.; *U.S. Public*, pg. 294
MICROWAVE SIGNAL, INC.—See AMP Incorporated; *U.S. Public*, pg. 8
MID-AM BUILDING SUPPLY, INC.; *U.S. Private*, pg. 743
MID-AMERICA AUTO AUCTION—See Tyco International Ltd.; *U.S. Public*, pg. 1649
MID-AMERICA CAPITAL RESOURCES, INC.—See Ipalco Enterprises, Inc.; *U.S. Public*, pg. 913
MID-AMERICA CREDIT LIFE ASSURANCE CO.—See Banc One Corporation; *U.S. Public*, pg. 175
MID-AMERICA DAIRYMEN, INC.; *U.S. Private*, pg. 743
MID-AMERICA ENERGY RESOURCES—See Ipalco Enterprises, Inc.; *U.S. Public*, pg. 913
MID-AMERICA FEED YARD—See Feed Service Corp.; *U.S. Private*, pg. 399
MID-AMERICA FINANCIAL CORP.—See Commerce Bancshares, Inc.; *U.S. Public*, pg. 410
MID-AMERICA INSURANCE AGENCY, INC.—See Banc One Corporation; *U.S. Public*, pg. 175
MID-AMERICA INSURANCE CO.—See Harleysville Group; *U.S. Public*, pg. 787
MID AMERICA INTERNATIONAL TRUCKS, INC.; *U.S. Private*, pg. 743
MID-AMERICA LEASING CORP.—See Banc One Corporation; *U.S. Public*, pg. 175
MID AMERICA STEEL, INC.; *U.S. Private*, pg. 743
MID-AMERICA TELEPHONE, INC.—See Telephone and Data Systems, Inc.; *U.S. Public*, pg. 1571
MID AMERICAN ELEVATOR CO., INC.; *U.S. Private*, pg. 743
MID-AMERICAN FINANCIAL SERVICES COMPANY—See Amcore Financial, Inc.; *U.S. Public*, pg. 65
MID ATLANTIC CONSTRUCTION, INC.—See Rodgers Builders, Inc.; *U.S. Private*, pg. 939
MID-ATLANTIC CORRECT CRAFT, INC.—See Correct Craft, Inc.; *U.S. Private*, pg. 277
MID ATLANTIC MEDICAL SERVICES, INC.; *U.S. Public*, pg. 1109
MID-CENTRAL/SYSCO FOOD SERVICES, INC.—See Sysco Corporation; *U.S. Public*, pg. 1551
MID CONTINENT BOTTLERS, INC—See Beverage America, Inc.; *U.S. Private*, pg. 142
MID-CONTINENT LIFE INSURANCE COMPANY—See Florida Progress Corporation; *U.S. Public*, pg. 655
MID CONTINENT MARKET CENTER—See Western Resources, Inc.; *U.S. Public*, pg. 1759
MID-CONTINENT SCREW PRODUCTS CO.; *U.S. Private*, pg. 743
MID-CORP., INC.—See Forest City Enterprises, Inc.; *U.S. Public*, pg. 669
MID-KANSAS CO-OP ASSOCIATION; *U.S. Private*, pg. 743
MID PACIFIC AIR CORPORATION—See KOA Holdings; *U.S. Private*, pg. 603
MID PACKAGING GROUP, INC.—See Caraustar Industries, Inc.; *U.S. Public*, pg. 304
MID RES SERVICE DIV.—See MFRI Inc.; *U.S. Public*, pg. 1026
MID-SOUTH COMPREHENSIVE HOME HEALTH—See Hospital Staffing Services, Inc.; *U.S. Public*, pg. 841
MID-SOUTH MANUFACTURING CO.—See UIS, Inc.; *U.S. Private*, pg. 1113
MID-SOUTH MICROWAVE, INC.—See Kansas City Southern Industries, Inc.; *U.S. Public*, pg. 944
MID-SOUTH MILLING COMPANY, INC.; *U.S. Private*, pg. 744
MID SOUTH SALES; *U.S. Private*, pg. 744
MID-STATE BANK—See Keystone Financial Inc.; *U.S. Public*, pg. 956
MID-STATE HOMES, INC.—See Walter Industries, Inc.; *U.S. Public*, pg. 1736
MID STATE PRODUCTS CO.—See Osco Industries Inc.; *U.S. Private*, pg. 821
MID-STATE TELEPHONE CO.—See Telephone and Data Systems, Inc.; *U.S. Public*, pg. 1571
MID-STATE WIRE COMPANY—See MCM Enterprises, Inc.; *U.S. Public*, pg. 686
MID-STATES FORGING DIE & TOOL CO.—See Modern Drop Forge Co.; *U.S. Private*, pg. 754
MID-STATES MORTGAGE CORP.—See Seligman & Associates, Inc.; *U.S. Private*, pg. 982
MID-VALLEY OIL COMPANY, INC.—See Warren Equities Inc.; *U.S. Private*, pg. 1151
MID VALLEY TITLE & ESCROW CO.—See The First American Financial Corporation; *U.S. Public*, pg. 626

MID-WEST AUTOMATION SYSTEMS, INC.—See DT Industries Inc.; *U.S. Public*, pg. 475
MID-WEST CONVEYOR CO., INC.—See Tomkins PLC; *Int'l*, pg. 1398
MID WEST CORRECT CRAFT, INC.—See Correct Craft, Inc.; *U.S. Private*, pg. 277
MID-WESTERN—See Berlin Glove Company Ltd.; *U.S. Private*, pg. 136
MID-WESTERN OF ALABAMA DIVISION—See American Nursery Products, LLC; *U.S. Private*, pg. 60
MIDAMERICAN CAPITAL COMPANY—See MidAmerican Energy Holdings; *U.S. Public*, pg. 1109
MIDAMERICAN ENERGY HOLDINGS; *U.S. Public*, pg. 1109
MIDAS-INTERNATIONAL CORP.—See Whitman Corporation; *U.S. Public*, pg. 1766
MID-ATLANTIC REGION—See MCI Communications Corp.; *U.S. Public*, pg. 1024
MIDCO INTERNATIONAL INC.; *U.S. Private*, pg. 744
MIDCOAST AVIATION, INC.—See Sabreliner Corporation; *U.S. Private*, pg. 959
MIDCOAST ENERGY RESOURCES, INC.; *U.S. Public*, pg. 1109
MIDCOAST MARKETING COMPANY—See Midcoast Energy Resources, Inc.; *U.S. Public*, pg. 1109
MIDCOAST MORTGAGE CORPORATION; *U.S. Private*, pg. 744
MIDCON CABLES CO.—See Esterline Technologies Corporation; *U.S. Public*, pg. 594
MIDCON CORP.—See Occidental Petroleum Corporation; *U.S. Public*, pg. 1210
MIDCON GAS PRODUCTS CORP.—See Occidental Petroleum Corporation; *U.S. Public*, pg. 1210
MIDCON GAS SERVICES CORP.—See Occidental Petroleum Corporation; *U.S. Public*, pg. 1210
MIDCON TEXAS PIPELINE OPERATOR, INC.—See Occidental Petroleum Corporation; *U.S. Public*, pg. 1210
MIDDLE EAST BANK KENYA LTD.—See Generale de Banque S.A.; *Int'l*, pg. 548
MIDDLE EAST CAN MANUFACTURING COMPANY—See Crown Cork & Seal Company, Inc.; *U.S. Public*, pg. 465
MIDDLE EAST ELECTRONICS—See Hewlett-Packard Company; *U.S. Public*, pg. 822
MIDDLE EAST FINANCE CO. LTD.—See HSBC Holdings plc; *Int'l*, pg. 583
THE MIDDLEBY CORPORATION; *U.S. Public*, pg. 1109
MIDDLEBY JAPAN CORPORATION—See The Middleby Corporation; *U.S. Public*, pg. 1110
MIDDLEBY MARSHALL/CTX—See The Middleby Corporation; *U.S. Public*, pg. 1110
MIDDLEBY PHILIPPINES CORPORATION—See The Middleby Corporation; *U.S. Public*, pg. 1110
MIDDLESEX INSURANCE—See Sentry Insurance, A Mutual Company; *U.S. Private*, pg. 985
MIDDLESEX INSURANCE CO.—See Sentry Insurance, A Mutual Company; *U.S. Private*, pg. 985
THE MIDDLESEX NEWS—See Harte-Hanks Communications, Inc.; *U.S. Public*, pg. 794
MIDDLESEX WATER COMPANY; *U.S. Public*, pg. 1110
MIDDLETON AEROSPACE CORPORATION—See BTR plc; *Int'l*, pg. 124
MIDDLETON AEROSPACE CORPORATION—See Magellan Aerospace Corporation; *Int'l*, pg. 829
MIDDLETON TRANSPORTATION CO.—See Frozen Food Express Industries, Inc.; *U.S. Public*, pg. 685
MIDDLETOWN OXYGEN CO., INC.—See Air Products and Chemicals, Inc.; *U.S. Public*, pg. 31
THE MIDDLETOWN PRESS—See Journal Register Company; *U.S. Public*, pg. 935
MIDGARD DEUTSCHE SEEVERKEHRS-AG—See Veba AG; *Int'l*, pg. 1459
MIDIAL S.A.; *Int'l*, pg. 865
MIDIMAT—See Saint-Gobain; *Int'l*, pg. 1176
MIDLAND BANK INTERNATIONAL FINANCE CORPORATION LIMITED—See HSBC Holdings plc; *Int'l*, pg. 580
MIDLAND BANK PLC—See HSBC Holdings plc; *Int'l*, pg. 580
MIDLAND BANK TRUST COMPANY LIMITED—See HSBC Holdings plc; *Int'l*, pg. 580
MIDLAND BANK TRUST CORPORATION (CAYMAN) LIMITED—See HSBC Holdings plc; *Int'l*, pg. 583
MIDLAND BANK TRUSTEE (GUERNSEY) LIMITED—See HSBC Holdings plc; *Int'l*, pg. 580
MIDLAND BRAKE, INC.—See Echlin Inc.; *U.S. Public*, pg. 561
MIDLAND COATED STONE—See RMC Group p.l.c.; *Int'l*, pg. 1079
THE MIDLAND COMPANY; *U.S. Public*, pg. 1110
MIDLAND DAILY NEWS—See The Hearst Corporation; *U.S. Private*, pg. 517
MIDLAND ENTERPRISES INC.—See Eastern Enterprises; *U.S. Public*, pg. 549
MIDLAND FINANCE CO.—See Mercury Finance Co.; *U.S. Public*, pg. 1093
MIDLAND FORGE DIVISION—See Columbus McKinnon Corp.; *U.S. Public*, pg. 406
MIDLAND GROCERY OF MICHIGAN CO.—See Roundy's, Inc.; *U.S. Private*, pg. 948
MIDLAND GUARDIAN CO.—See The Midland Company; *U.S. Public*, pg. 1111
MIDLAND HOLDING PARTICIPACAO, ADMINISTRACAO E REPRESENTACOES LIMITADA—See HSBC Holdings plc; *Int'l*, pg. 580
MIDLAND INTERNATIONAL FINANCIAL SERVICES (IRELAND) LIMITED—See HSBC Holdings plc; *Int'l*, pg. 583
MIDLAND INTERNATIONAL TRADE SERVICES (FRANCE) S.A.—See HSBC Holdings plc; *Int'l*, pg. 583
MIDLAND INTERNATIONAL TRADE SERVICES (USA) CORPORATION—See HSBC Holdings plc; *Int'l*, pg. 581
MIDLAND LIFE INSURANCE CO.; *U.S. Private*, pg. 744

MIDLAND LIFE LIMITED—See HSBC Holdings plc; *Int'l*, pg. 580
MIDLAND NATIONAL LIFE INSURANCE CO.—See Sammons Enterprises, Inc.; *U.S. Private*, pg. 963
MIDLAND PAPER CO.; *U.S. Private*, pg. 744
MIDLAND PRODUCTION DISTRICT OFFICE—See Hunt Oil Company; *U.S. Private*, pg. 548
MIDLAND REPORTER-TELEGRAM—See The Hearst Corporation; *U.S. Private*, pg. 517
MIDLAND SEABOARD PRINTING INK, INC.—See Sumitomo Chemical Company, Ltd.; *Int'l*, pg. 1311
MIDLAND TITLE SECURITY, INC.—See The First American Financial Corporation; *U.S. Public*, pg. 626
MIDLAND TOOL AND DESIGN LIMITED—See TT Group PLC; *Int'l*, pg. 1344
MIDLAND UNIT TRUST MANAGEMENT LIMITED—See HSBC Holdings plc; *Int'l*, pg. 580
MIDLAND WALWYN CAPITAL CORPORATION—See Midland Walwyn Inc.; *Int'l*, pg. 865
MIDLAND WALWYN CAPITAL INC.—See Midland Walwyn Inc.; *Int'l*, pg. 865
MIDLAND WALWYN INC.; *Int'l*, pg. 865
MIDLAND WALWYN INSURANCE SERVICES LIMITED—See Midland Walwyn Inc.; *Int'l*, pg. 865
MIDLANTIC BANK, N.A.—See PNC Bank Corp.; *U.S. Public*, pg. 1242
MIDLANTIC COMMERCIAL CO., INC.—See PNC Bank Corp.; *U.S. Public*, pg. 1242
MIDORI EUROPE B.V.—See The Green Cross Corporation; *Int'l*, pg. 558
MIDREX CORP.—See Kobe Steel, Ltd.; *Int'l*, pg. 740
MIDSOUTH ICE CO.—See Spencer Companies Inc.; *U.S. Private*, pg. 1025
MIDSOUTH MACHINE & SERVICE COMPANY—See Vulcan Materials Company; *U.S. Public*, pg. 1726
MIDVALE PLAZA—See National Guardian Life Insurance Company; *U.S. Private*, pg. 784
MIDWAY FORD TRUCK CENTER INC.; *U.S. Private*, pg. 744
MIDWAY GAMES, INC.—See WMS Industries Inc.; *U.S. Public*, pg. 1727
MIDWAY HOME ENTERTAINMENT INC.—See WMS Industries Inc.; *U.S. Public*, pg. 1727
MIDWAY PRODUCTS CORPORATION; *U.S. Private*, pg. 744
MIDWESCO MECHANICAL ENERGY—See MFRI Inc.; *U.S. Public*, pg. 1026
MIDWEST AGRI-COMMODITIES—See American Crystal Sugar Company; *U.S. Private*, pg. 53
MIDWEST AGRI-COMMODITIES—See Southern Minnesota Beet Sugar Cooperative; *U.S. Private*, pg. 1016
MIDWEST AUTO PARTS DISTRIBUTORS, INC.; *U.S. Private*, pg. 744
MIDWEST BEAUTY L.P.—See Opal Concepts, Inc.; *U.S. Private*, pg. 818
MIDWEST BOTTLE GAS COMPANY—See Consolidated Midwest, Inc.; *U.S. Private*, pg. 266
MIDWEST CAPITAL GROUP—See MidAmerican Energy Holdings; *U.S. Public*, pg. 1109
MIDWEST CARBIDE CORPORATION—See Airgas, Inc.; *U.S. Public*, pg. 33
MIDWEST COAST TRANSPORT L.P.; *U.S. Private*, pg. 744
MIDWEST DENTAL—See Dentsply International Inc.; *U.S. Public*, pg. 499
MIDWEST DIVISION—See Albertson's, Inc.; *U.S. Public*, pg. 38
MIDWEST EMPLOYER'S CASUALTY COMPANY—See W.R. Berkley Corporation; *U.S. Public*, pg. 215
MIDWEST ENERGY RESOURCES CO.—See DTE Energy Company; *U.S. Public*, pg. 476
MIDWEST EXPRESS AIRLINES, INC.—See Midwest Express Holdings, Inc.; *U.S. Public*, pg. 1111
MIDWEST EXPRESS HOLDINGS, INC.; *U.S. Public*, pg. 1111
MIDWEST FASTENERS CORPORATION; *U.S. Private*, pg. 744
MIDWEST GRAIN PRODUCTS, INC.; *U.S. Public*, pg. 1111
MIDWEST INDUSTRIES, INC.; *U.S. Private*, pg. 744
MIDWEST LITHO ARTS—See World Color Press, Inc.; *U.S. Public*, pg. 1779
MIDWEST LIVING MAGAZINE—See Meredith Corporation; *U.S. Public*, pg. 1094
MIDWEST MANAGEMENT CO.—See Lennar Corporation; *U.S. Public*, pg. 988
MIDWEST MANAGEMENT (1987) LIMITED—See Agra Inc.; *Int'l*, pg. 31
MIDWEST MECHANICAL CONTRACTORS INC.—See MMC Corp.; *U.S. Private*, pg. 687
MIDWEST METALLURGICAL LAB.—See United Industrial Corporation; *U.S. Public*, pg. 1679
MIDWEST MEZZANINE FUND—See ABN-AMRO Holding N.V.; *Int'l*, pg. 10
MIDWEST MICA—See Kirkwood Industries, Inc.; *U.S. Private*, pg. 623
MIDWEST MUTUAL INSURANCE CO.—See Preferred Risk Mutual Insurance; *U.S. Private*, pg. 881
MIDWEST NATIONAL BANK OF MIDWEST CITY—See Banc One Corporation; *U.S. Public*, pg. 174
MIDWEST NATURAL FOODS—See Koninklijke BolsWessanen nv; *Int'l*, pg. 752
MIDWEST PETROLEUM CO.; *U.S. Private*, pg. 745
MIDWEST PIPELINE CONTRACTORS LTD.—See Agra Inc.; *Int'l*, pg. 31
MIDWEST POLY—See Custom Pak, Inc.; *U.S. Private*, pg. 298
MIDWEST PRODUCTS, INC.—See Huntco Inc.; *U.S. Public*, pg. 849
MIDWEST RUBBER—See Newcor, Inc.; *U.S. Public*, pg. 1176
MIDWEST RUBBER CO.—See American Industrial Partners; *U.S. Private*, pg. 56
MIDWEST SANITATION, INC.—See USA Waste Services, Inc.; *U.S. Public*, pg. 1686

MIDWEST STEEL BUILDING COMPANY—See NCI Building Systems, Inc.; *U.S. Public*, pg. 1146
MIDWEST TIRE & MUFFLER, INC.; *U.S. Private*, pg. 745
MIDWEST VISION CENTERS; *U.S. Private*, pg. 745
MIDWESTERN GAS MARKETING COMPANY—See Tenneco Inc.; *U.S. Private*, pg. 1579
MIDWESTERN GAS TRANSMISSION CO.—See El Paso Natural Gas Co.; *U.S. Public*, pg. 567
MIDWESTERN HOLDINGS, INC.—See Bank of Montreal; *Int'l*, pg. 155
MIE LIQUID CRYSTAL DISPLAY GROUP—See Sharp Corporation; *Int'l*, pg. 1228
MIELE & CIE, GMBH; *Int'l*, pg. 865
MIELE APPLIANCES, INC.—See Miele & Cie, GmbH; *Int'l*, pg. 865
MIESEL/SYSCO FOOD SERVICE CO.—See Sysco Corporation; *U.S. Public*, pg. 1551
MIFA AG—See Migros; *Int'l*, pg. 866
MIFROMA S.A.—See Migros; *Int'l*, pg. 866
MIGHTY DISTRIBUTING SYSTEM; *U.S. Private*, pg. 745
THE MIGHTY DUCKS OF ANAHEIM—See The Walt Disney Company; *U.S. Public*, pg. 513
MIGHTY EXIM CORPORATION—See The Macneal-Schwendler Corp.; *U.S. Public*, pg. 1032
MARILYN MIGLIN, L.P.; *U.S. Private*, pg. 745
MIGRASHI HAKABLANIM LIMITED—See The Israel Electric Corporation Ltd.; *Int'l*, pg. 691
MIGROL COOPERATIVE SOCIETY—See Migros; *Int'l*, pg. 866
MIGROS; *Int'l*, pg. 865
MIGROS BANK—See Migros; *Int'l*, pg. 866
MIGROS DISTRIBUTION CENTER NEUENDORF AG—See Migros; *Int'l*, pg. 866
MIGROS ENTERPRISES BIRSFELDEN AG—See Migros; *Int'l*, pg. 866
LEOPOLDO A. MIGUEZ DE MELLO R&D CENTER—See Petrobras - Petroleo Brasileiro S.A.; *Int'l*, pg. 1042
MIJAC ENTERPRISES, INC.—See Motorola, Inc.; *U.S. Public*, pg. 1137
MIKEN COMPANIES, INC.; *U.S. Private*, pg. 745
MIKE'S MART—See Silcorp Limited; *Int'l*, pg. 1249
MIKI HOLDING COMPANY—See Miki Pulley Co., Ltd.; *Int'l*, pg. 866
MIKI PULLEY CO., LTD.; *Int'l*, pg. 866
MIKIMOTO (AMERICA) CO. LTD.—See K. Mikimoto & Co., Ltd.; *Int'l*, pg. 866
K. MIKIMOTO & CO., LTD.; *Int'l*, pg. 866
MIKKELIN MATKATOIMISTO—See FinnAir Oy; *Int'l*, pg. 485
MIKOHN GAMING CORPORATION; *U.S. Public*, pg. 1111
AB MIKRO-VERKTYG—See Investor AB; *Int'l*, pg. 686
AB MIKROELEKTRONIK GMBH—See TT Group PLC; *Int'l*, pg. 1344
MIKROKEMIA OY—See Neste Oy; *Int'l*, pg. 913
MIKRON AG BIEL—See Mikron Holding AG; *Int'l*, pg. 866
MIKRON AG NIDAU—See Mikron Holding AG; *Int'l*, pg. 866
MIKRON BEIJING OFFICE—See Mikron Holding AG; *Int'l*, pg. 867
MIKRON (BIRMINGHAM) LTD.—See Mikron Holding AG; *Int'l*, pg. 867
MIKRON CORP. ANDERSON—See Mikron Holding AG; *Int'l*, pg. 866
MIKRON CORP. MONROE—See Mikron Holding AG; *Int'l*, pg. 866
MIKRON CORP. STRATFORD—See Mikron Holding AG; *Int'l*, pg. 867
MIKRON FRANCE SARL—See Mikron Holding AG; *Int'l*, pg. 867
MIKRON HANNOVER GMBH—See Mikron Holding AG; *Int'l*, pg. 867
MIKRON HOLDING AG; *Int'l*, pg. 866
MIKRON LTD. TOKYO—See Mikron Holding AG; *Int'l*, pg. 867
MIKRON MACHINE TOOL ASIA PTE LTD—See Mikron Holding AG; *Int'l*, pg. 867
MIKRON PAVIA S.R.L.—See Mikron Holding AG; *Int'l*, pg. 867
MIKRON ROTTWEIL GMBH—See Mikron Holding AG; *Int'l*, pg. 867
MIKRON SA AGNO—See Mikron Holding AG; *Int'l*, pg. 866
MIKRON SA BOUDRY—See Mikron Holding AG; *Int'l*, pg. 866
MIKRON SA MULHOUSE—See Mikron Holding AG; *Int'l*, pg. 867
MIKRON SNC NERVIANO—See Mikron Holding AG; *Int'l*, pg. 867
MIKRON SPA ZINGONIA—See Mikron Holding AG; *Int'l*, pg. 867
MIKRON S.R.L. LUINO—See Mikron Holding AG; *Int'l*, pg. 867
MIKRON SRL TREZZO SULL'ADDA—See Mikron Holding AG; *Int'l*, pg. 867
MIKRON U.K. LTD.—See Mikron Holding AG; *Int'l*, pg. 867
MIKRONWERK GMBH—See AB SKF; *Int'l*, pg. 1157
MIKROPRECISION INSTRUMENTS, INC.—See Newport Corporation; *U.S. Public*, pg. 1179
MIKROPUL ENVIRONMENTAL SYSTEMS DIV.—See Hosokawa Micron Corporation; *Int'l*, pg. 636
MIKUNI ADEC—See Mikuni Corporation; *Int'l*, pg. 867
MIKUNI AMERICAN CORPORATION—See Mikuni Corporation; *Int'l*, pg. 867
MIKUNI CORPORATION; *Int'l*, pg. 867
MIKUNI INDUSTRY CO., LTD.—See Oki Electric Industry Company, Ltd.; *Int'l*, pg. 999
MIKUNI SHOKO CORP.—See Mikuni Corporation; *Int'l*, pg. 867
MIL INTERMODAL—See Davie Industries Inc.; *Int'l*, pg. 385
MIL (JERSEY) LIMITED—See The Bank of Bermuda Limited; *Int'l*, pg. 151
MIL LTD.—See Namco Ltd.; *Int'l*, pg. 905
MIL SYSTEMS ENGINEERING—See Davie Industries Inc.; *Int'l*, pg. 385

MILAGE PLUS, INC.—See UAL Corporation; *U.S. Public*, pg. 1653
MILBANK INSURANCE CO.—See Royal & Sun Alliance Insurance Group plc; *Int'l*, pg. 1131
MILBURN NEW ZEALAND LTD.—See Holderbank Financiere Glaris Ltd.; *Int'l*, pg. 629
MILCARE, INC.—See Herman Miller, Inc.; *U.S. Public*, pg. 1112
MILCHEM CANADA LTD.—See Baker Hughes Incorporated; *U.S. Public*, pg. 167
MILCHEM FRANCE S.A.R.L.—See Baker Hughes Incorporated; *U.S. Public*, pg. 167
MILCOM COMMUNICATION & ELECTRONICS LTD.—See Motorola, Inc.; *U.S. Public*, pg. 1137
MILDARA BLASS WINES—See Foster's Brewing Group Limited; *Int'l*, pg. 501
MILE HIGH EQUIPMENT CO.—See Berisford plc; *Int'l*, pg. 189
MILEAGE PLUS HOLDINGS, INC.—See UAL Corporation; *U.S. Public*, pg. 1653
MILEAGE PLUS MARKETING, INC.—See UAL Corporation; *U.S. Public*, pg. 1653
MILEI GMBH—See Morinaga Milk Industry Co., Ltd.; *Int'l*, pg. 895
MILES KIMBALL COMPANY; *U.S. Private*, pg. 745
MILES LABORATORIES AUSTRALIA PTY. LTD.—See Bayer AG; *Int'l*, pg. 175
MILES SAND & GRAVEL COMPANY; *U.S. Private*, pg. 745
MILESTONE CONTRACTORS INC.; *U.S. Private*, pg. 745
MILFORD FABRICATING CO.—See Thyssen AG; *Int'l*, pg. 1388
MILFORD FASTENING SYSTEMS; *U.S. Private*, pg. 745
MILFORD OFFICE—See The Cascades Group; *Int'l*, pg. 274
MILGRAY/AUSTIN—See Bell Industries, Inc.; *U.S. Public*, pg. 206
MILGRAY/CALIFORNIA, INC.—See Bell Industries, Inc.; *U.S. Public*, pg. 206
MILGRAY/COLORADO, INC.—See Bell Industries, Inc.; *U.S. Public*, pg. 206
MILGRAY/CONNECTICUT, INC.—See Bell Industries, Inc.; *U.S. Public*, pg. 206
MILGRAY ELECTRONICS, INC.—See Bell Industries, Inc.; *U.S. Public*, pg. 205
MILGRAY ELECTRONICS/P.R., INC.—See Bell Industries, Inc.; *U.S. Public*, pg. 206
MILGRAY/HOUSTON, INC.—See Bell Industries, Inc.; *U.S. Public*, pg. 206
MILGRAY/HUNTSVILLE, INC.—See Bell Industries, Inc.; *U.S. Public*, pg. 206
MILGRAY/INDIANA, INC.—See Bell Industries, Inc.; *U.S. Public*, pg. 206
MILGRAY/MONTREAL—See Bell Industries, Inc.; *U.S. Public*, pg. 206
MILGRAY/NEW JERSEY—See Bell Industries, Inc.; *U.S. Public*, pg. 206
MILGRAY/NORTHERN CALIFORNIA—See Bell Industries, Inc.; *U.S. Public*, pg. 206
MILGRAY/ORANGE COUNTY, INC.—See Bell Industries, Inc.; *U.S. Public*, pg. 206
MILGRAY/OREGON, INC.—See Bell Industries, Inc.; *U.S. Public*, pg. 207
MILGRAY/RALEIGH, INC.—See Bell Industries, Inc.; *U.S. Public*, pg. 207
MILGRAY/SAN DIEGO, INC.—See Bell Industries, Inc.; *U.S. Public*, pg. 207
MILGRAY/TORONTO, INC.—See Bell Industries, Inc.; *U.S. Public*, pg. 207
MILGRAY/UPSTATE NEW YORK, INC.—See Bell Industries, Inc.; *U.S. Public*, pg. 207
MILGRAY/WESTERN CANADA—See Bell Industries, Inc.; *U.S. Public*, pg. 207
MILITAIR AVIATION LIMITED—See Bridport-Gundry p.l.c.; *Int'l*, pg. 215
MILITARY AIRCRAFT GROUP—See Israel Aircraft Industries Ltd.; *Int'l*, pg. 690
MILITARY AIRCRAFT SYSTEMS DIVISION—See Northrop Grumman Corporation; *U.S. Public*, pg. 1198
MILITARY AVIONICS DIVISION—See Honeywell Inc.; *U.S. Public*, pg. 834
MILITARY BOOK CLUB—See Bertelsmann AG; *Int'l*, pg. 191
MILK MARKETING INC.; *U.S. Private*, pg. 745
MILK PRODUCTS HOLDINGS (AUSTRALIA) PTY LTD—See New Zealand Dairy Board; *Int'l*, pg. 923
MILK PRODUCTS HOLDINGS (EUROPE) LTD.—See New Zealand Dairy Board; *Int'l*, pg. 923
MILK PRODUCTS HOLDINGS (LATIN AMERICA) LTD.—See New Zealand Dairy Board; *Int'l*, pg. 923
MILK PRODUCTS HOLDINGS (MIDDLE EAST) EC—See New Zealand Dairy Board; *Int'l*, pg. 923
MILK PRODUCTS HOLDINGS (NORTH AMERICA) INC.—See New Zealand Dairy Board; *Int'l*, pg. 923
MILK PRODUCTS HOLDINGS (SEA)—See New Zealand Dairy Board; *Int'l*, pg. 923
MILK SPECIALTIES COMPANY; *U.S. Private*, pg. 746
MILKCO, INC.—See Ingles Markets, Incorporated; *U.S. Public*, pg. 878
MILKPAK LTD.—See Nestle S.A.; *Int'l*, pg. 920
MILKY WAY, INC.—See Lynden Incorporated; *U.S. Private*, pg. 683
MILL & ABRASIVE SUPPLY, INC.—See Kennametal Inc.; *U.S. Public*, pg. 951
MILL & CONTRACTORS SUPPLY—See Associated Industrial Supply, Inc.; *U.S. Private*, pg. 91
MILL-LOG EQUIPMENT CO., INC.—See Twin Disc, Incorporated; *U.S. Public*, pg. 1646
MILL MAPLE PROPERTIES, INC.—See Washington Mutual Inc.; *U.S. Public*, pg. 1742
MILL PLAIN FOUR, INC.—See Washington Mutual Inc.; *U.S. Public*, pg. 1742
MILL PLAIN THREE, INC.—See Washington Mutual Inc.; *U.S. Public*, pg. 1742

MILL PLAIN TWO, INC.—See Washington Mutual Inc.; *U.S. Public*, pg. 1742
MILL-ROSE COMPANY; *U.S. Private*, pg. 746
MILLAR ELEVATOR INDUSTRIES, INC.—See Schindler Holding AG; *Int'l*, pg. 1205
MILLBANK ELECTRONICS GROUP LTD.—See American Trading and Production Corporation; *U.S. Private*, pg. 64
MILLBROOK BREAD BAKERIES—See Interstate Bakeries Corporation; *U.S. Public*, pg. 909
MILLENNIUM CHEMICALS INC.; *U.S. Public*, pg. 1111
MILLENNIUM INORGANIC CHEMICALS—See Hanson PLC; *Int'l*, pg. 593
MILLENNIUM INORGANIC CHEMICALS—See Millennium Chemicals Inc.; *U.S. Public*, pg. 1111
MILLENNIUM PETROCHEMICALS, INC.—See Hanson PLC; *Int'l*, pg. 594
MILLENNIUM PETROCHEMICALS INC.—See Millennium Chemicals Inc.; *U.S. Public*, pg. 1111
MILLENNIUM TECHNOLOGY SERVICES, INC.; *U.S. Private*, pg. 746
MILLER ACCOUNTING PUBLICATIONS, INC.—See Harcourt General, Inc.; *U.S. Public*, pg. 784
MILLER ADVERTISING AGENCY INC.; *U.S. Private*, pg. 746
MILLER ADVERTISING AGENCY INC.-CHICAGO—See Miller Advertising Agency Inc.; *U.S. Private*, pg. 746
MILLER & CO.; *U.S. Private*, pg. 746
MILLER & CO.—See Veba AG; *Int'l*, pg. 1458
MILLER & LONG CO. INC.; *U.S. Private*, pg. 746
MILLER & SMITH, INC.; *U.S. Private*, pg. 746
MILLER, ANDERSON & SHERRERD—See Morgan Stanley Dean Witter & Co.; *U.S. Public*, pg. 1132
MILLER AUTOMATION, INC. (MO)—See Illinois Tool Works Inc.; *U.S. Public*, pg. 867
MILLER AUTOMATION, INC. (OH)—See Illinois Tool Works Inc.; *U.S. Public*, pg. 867
MILLER BRANDS OF PHOENIX—See Philip Morris Companies Inc.; *U.S. Public*, pg. 1289
MILLER BREWING COMPANY—See Philip Morris Companies Inc.; *U.S. Public*, pg. 1289
MILLER BUILDING CORP.; *U.S. Private*, pg. 746
MILLER CHEMICAL & FERTILIZER CORP.—See Alco Industries, Inc.; *U.S. Private*, pg. 33
THE MILLER COMPANY; *U.S. Private*, pg. 746
MILLER COMPREHENSIVE CPA REVIEW, INC.—See Harcourt General, Inc.; *U.S. Public*, pg. 783
MILLER CURTAIN CO., INC.; *U.S. Private*, pg. 746
E.A. MILLER COMPANY—See ConAgra, Inc.; *U.S. Public*, pg. 428
ECK MILLER TRANSPORTATION CORPORATION—See Intrenet, Inc.; *U.S. Public*, pg. 911
MILLER ELECTRIC COMPANY; *U.S. Private*, pg. 747
MILLER ELECTRIC MANUFACTURING CO.—See Illinois Tool Works Inc.; *U.S. Public*, pg. 867
MILLER EUROPA S.P.A.—See Illinois Tool Works Inc.; *U.S. Public*, pg. 869
MILLER FINANCE CORP.—See Miller-St. Nazianz, Inc.; *U.S. Private*, pg. 748
MILLER FLUID POWER CORP.; *U.S. Private*, pg. 747
MILLER FREEMAN ASIA LTD—See United News & Media plc; *Int'l*, pg. 1443
MILLER FREEMAN INC.—See United News & Media plc; *Int'l*, pg. 1443
MILLER FREEMAN PLC—See United News & Media plc; *Int'l*, pg. 1443
MILLER FREEMAN PTE LTD—See United News & Media plc; *Int'l*, pg. 1443
MILLER-FRIEDMAN ADVERTISING—See Miller Advertising Agency Inc.; *U.S. Private*, pg. 746
THE MILLER GROUP LIMITED (TELFORD)—See Illinois Tool Works Inc.; *U.S. Public*, pg. 869
H.C. MILLER COMPANY; *U.S. Private*, pg. 747
H. MILLER & SONS, INC.—See Lennar Corporation; *U.S. Public*, pg. 989
HERMAN MILLER BV—See Herman Miller, Inc.; *U.S. Public*, pg. 1112
HERMAN MILLER DEUTSCHLAND INC.—See Herman Miller, Inc.; *U.S. Public*, pg. 1112
HERMAN MILLER ET CIE—See Herman Miller, Inc.; *U.S. Public*, pg. 1112
HERMAN MILLER, INC.; *U.S. Public*, pg. 1111
HERMAN MILLER JAPAN—See Herman Miller, Inc.; *U.S. Public*, pg. 1112
HERMAN MILLER, LTD.—See Herman Miller, Inc.; *U.S. Public*, pg. 1112
HOWARD MILLER; *U.S. Private*, pg. 747
MILLER INDUSTRIES, INC.; *U.S. Public*, pg. 1112
MILLER INTERMODAL LOGISTICS SERVICES INC.—See Dewey Corporation; *U.S. Private*, pg. 329
MILLER INTL. SCHALLPLATTEN G.M.B.H.—See The Seagram Company Ltd.; *Int'l*, pg. 1216
J.W. MILLER DIV.—See Bell Industries, Inc.; *U.S. Public*, pg. 205
MILLER/KADANOFF/HUBER DIRECT & INTERACTIVE; *U.S. Private*, pg. 747
LARRY H. MILLER GROUP; *U.S. Private*, pg. 747
MILLER MEESTER ADVERTISING; *U.S. Private*, pg. 747
MILLER-MITCHELL DIVISION & REA GROUP—See Miller Advertising Agency Inc.; *U.S. Private*, pg. 746
MILLER OIL CO., INC.; *U.S. Private*, pg. 747
MILLER PATTERSON ALDRED MITCHELL—See Warwick Baker O'Neill; *U.S. Private*, pg. 1152
MILLER PERSONNEL, INC.—See Miller Resources International, Inc.; *U.S. Private*, pg. 748
MILLER PRODUCTS COMPANY, INC.; *U.S. Private*, pg. 747
MILLER PUBLISHING CO.—See The Walt Disney Company; *U.S. Public*, pg. 513
MILLER RESOURCES INTERNATIONAL, INC.; *U.S. Private*, pg. 748
MILLER-ST. NAZIANZ, INC.; *U.S. Private*, pg. 748

MILLER SCIENTIFIC, INC.—See Miller Resources International, Inc.; *U.S. Private*, pg. 748
MILLER/SHANDWICK COMMUNICATIONS LTD.—See Shandwick International Plc; *Int'l*, pg. 1226
MILLER SHANDWICK TECHNOLOGIES—See Shandwick International Plc; *Int'l*, pg. 1227
MILLER TEMPORARIES, INC.—See Miller Resources International, Inc.; *U.S. Private*, pg. 748
MILLER THERMAL, INC.—See Illinois Tool Works Inc.; *U.S. Public*, pg. 867
MILLER TRANSPORTERS, INC.—See Dewey Corporation; *U.S. Private*, pg. 329
MILLERS CLASSIFIED INSURANCE COMPANY—See Millers Mutual Insurance Assn.; *U.S. Private*, pg. 748
MILLERS MUTUAL INSURANCE ASSN.; *U.S. Private*, pg. 748
MILLER'S PUBLICATIONS—See Reed Elsevier plc; *Int'l*, pg. 1093
THE MILLGARD CORP.; *U.S. Private*, pg. 748
MILLHAVEN COMPANY, INC.—See Shivers Trading & Operating Co.; *U.S. Private*, pg. 994
MILLHOUSE GROUP; *U.S. Private*, pg. 748
MILLICOM INTERNATIONAL CELLULAR SA; *Int'l*, pg. 867
MILLIKEN & COMPANY; *U.S. Private*, pg. 748
MILLINOCKET DIVISION—See Consumers Water Company; *U.S. Public*, pg. 438
MILLIPORE AG—See Millipore Corporation; *U.S. Public*, pg. 1113
MILLIPORE ANALYTICAL DIV.—See Millipore Corporation; *U.S. Public*, pg. 1112
MILLIPORE AS—See Millipore Corporation; *U.S. Public*, pg. 1113
MILLIPORE ASIA LIMITED—See Millipore Corporation; *U.S. Public*, pg. 1113
MILLIPORE B.V.—See Millipore Corporation; *U.S. Public*, pg. 1113
MILLIPORE CHINA, LTD.—See Millipore Corporation; *U.S. Public*, pg. 1113
MILLIPORE CIDRA, INC.—See Millipore Corporation; *U.S. Public*, pg. 1113
MILLIPORE CORPORATION; *U.S. Public*, pg. 1112
MILLIPORE GES.M.B.H.—See Millipore Corporation; *U.S. Public*, pg. 1113
MILLIPORE GMBH—See Millipore Corporation; *U.S. Public*, pg. 1113
MILLIPORE IBERICA S.A.—See Millipore Corporation; *U.S. Public*, pg. 1113
MILLIPORE INDUSTRIA E COMMERCIO LTDA.—See Millipore Corporation; *U.S. Public*, pg. 1113
MILLIPORE INTERTECH—See Millipore Corporation; *U.S. Public*, pg. 1113
MILLIPORE INTERTECH (V.I.), INC.—See Millipore Corporation; *U.S. Public*, pg. 1113
MILLIPORE IRELAND—See Millipore Corporation; *U.S. Public*, pg. 1113
MILLIPORE KOREA, LTD.—See Millipore Corporation; *U.S. Public*, pg. 1113
MILLIPORE LTD.—See Millipore Corporation; *U.S. Public*, pg. 1113
MILLIPORE OF NEW HAMPSHIRE, INC.—See Millipore Corporation; *U.S. Public*, pg. 1113
MILLIPORE OY—See Millipore Corporation; *U.S. Public*, pg. 1113
MILLIPORE PROCESS DIV.—See Millipore Corporation; *U.S. Public*, pg. 1112
MILLIPORE PTY. LTD.—See Millipore Corporation; *U.S. Public*, pg. 1113
MILLIPORE/PUERTO RICO—See Millipore Corporation; *U.S. Public*, pg. 1112
MILLIPORE S.A.—See Millipore Corporation; *U.S. Public*, pg. 1113
MILLIPORE S.A. DE C.V.—See Millipore Corporation; *U.S. Public*, pg. 1113
MILLIPORE S.A.-N.V.—See Millipore Corporation; *U.S. Public*, pg. 1113
MILLIPORE SCANDINAVIA AB—See Millipore Corporation; *U.S. Public*, pg. 1113
MILLIPORE S.P.A.—See Millipore Corporation; *U.S. Public*, pg. 1113
MILLIPORE TYLAN PRODUCTS—See Millipore Corporation; *U.S. Public*, pg. 1112
MILLIPORE (U.K.) LTD.—See Millipore Corporation; *U.S. Public*, pg. 1113
MILLS & CLEMENT INC.; *U.S. Private*, pg. 749
MILLS & BOON LTD.—See Torstar Corporation; *Int'l*, pg. 1402
THE MILLS CORPORATION; *U.S. Public*, pg. 749
MILLS & LUPTON SUPPLY CO.—See Hughes Supply, Inc.; *U.S. Public*, pg. 847
MILLS MANUFACTURING TECHNOLOGY—See Haden Maclellan Holdings plc; *Int'l*, pg. 585
OLAN MILLS, INC.; *U.S. Private*, pg. 749
OLAN MILLS INC. OF OHIO—See Olan Mills, Inc.; *U.S. Private*, pg. 749
OLAN MILLS INC. OF TEXAS—See Olan Mills, Inc.; *U.S. Private*, pg. 749
MILLS & PARTNERS—See Hicks, Muse, Tate & Furst Inc.; *U.S. Private*, pg. 526
W.G. MILLS, INC.; *U.S. Private*, pg. 749
MILLSPORT—See Omnicom Group Inc.; *U.S. Public*, pg. 1224
MILLSTEIN INDUSTRIES; *U.S. Private*, pg. 749
MILLSTONE COFFEE, INC.—See The Procter & Gamble Company; *U.S. Public*, pg. 1331
MILLTECH—See Tate & Lyle PLC; *Int'l*, pg. 1356
MILLTRONICS—See Russel Metals Inc.; *Int'l*, pg. 1150
MILLVILLE QUARRY INC.—See Bardon Group PLC; *Int'l*, pg. 166
MILLWARD BROWN INTERNATIONAL—See WPP Group plc; *Int'l*, pg. 1482
MILLWOOD PLANT—See Oglebay Norton Company; *U.S. Public*, pg. 1213

MILLWORKS INDUSTRIES, INC.—See Taisei Corporation; *Int'l*, pg. 1347
MILNE & CRAIGHEAD CUSTOMS BROKERS, INC.—See Consolidated Freightways Corp.; *U.S. Public*, pg. 435
MILNE FOOD PRODUCTS, INC.—See Ocean Spray Cranberries, Inc.; *U.S. Private*, pg. 811
MILNE FRUIT PRODUCTS—See Ocean Spray Cranberries, Inc.; *U.S. Private*, pg. 811
MILNE MODELS LIMITED—See Arnotts plc; *Int'l*, pg. 81
THE MILNOT COMPANY; *U.S. Private*, pg. 749
MILPRINT INC.—See Bemis Company, Inc.; *U.S. Public*, pg. 210
MONROE G. MILSTEIN, INC.—See Burlington Coat Factory Warehouse Corporation; *U.S. Public*, pg. 268
MILTON BRADLEY AUSTRALIA PTY. LTD.—See Hasbro, Inc.; *U.S. Public*, pg. 798
MILTON BRADLEY COMPANY—See Hasbro, Inc.; *U.S. Public*, pg. 797
MILTON BRADLEY GMBH—See Hasbro, Inc.; *U.S. Public*, pg. 798
MILTON BRADLEY (N.Z.) LTD.—See Hasbro, Inc.; *U.S. Public*, pg. 798
MILTON CAN CO., INC.; *U.S. Private*, pg. 749
MILTON INDUSTRIES, INC.; *U.S. Private*, pg. 749
MILTON INVESTMENTS, INC.—See Etablissements Delhaize Freres Et Cie "Le Lion" S.A.; *Int'l*, pg. 463
MILTON ROY (BELGIUM) N.V.—See Sundstrand Corporation; *U.S. Public*, pg. 1534
MILTON ROY COMPANY—See Sundstrand Corporation; *U.S. Public*, pg. 1534
MILTON ROY (JAPAN) LTD.—See Sundstrand Corporation; *U.S. Public*, pg. 1534
MILTOPE CORPORATION—See Miltope Group, Inc.; *U.S. Public*, pg. 1114
MILTOPE GROUP, INC.; *U.S. Public*, pg. 1114
MILUPA A.G.—See Nutricia BV; *Int'l*, pg. 991
MILUPA A/G—See Nutricia BV; *Int'l*, pg. 991
MILUPA COMPANY—See Nutricia BV; *Int'l*, pg. 991
MILUPA GMBH—See Nutricia BV; *Int'l*, pg. 991
MILUPA GMBH & CO KG—See Nutricia BV; *Int'l*, pg. 991
MILUPA HELLAS EPE—See Nutricia BV; *Int'l*, pg. 991
MILUPA KFT.—See Nutricia BV; *Int'l*, pg. 991
MILUPA LTD.—See Nutricia BV; *Int'l*, pg. 991
MILUPA PORTUGUESA L.D.A.—See Nutricia BV; *Int'l*, pg. 991
MILUPA PRODUCTORA S.A.—See Nutricia BV; *Int'l*, pg. 991
MILUPA S.A.—See Nutricia BV; *Int'l*, pg. 991
N.V. MILUPA S.A.—See Nutricia BV; *Int'l*, pg. 992
MILUPA S.A.—See Nutricia BV; *Int'l*, pg. 992
MILUPA S.A.—See Nutricia BV; *Int'l*, pg. 992
MILUZ SAICIF—See Akzo Nobel N.V.; *Int'l*, pg. 43
MILWAUKEE BUCKS, INC.; *U.S. Private*, pg. 749
MILWAUKEE CONTAINER DIV.—See Philip Morris Companies Inc.; *U.S. Public*, pg. 1289
MILWAUKEE CYLINDER DIVISION—See Applied Power Inc.; *U.S. Public*, pg. 124
MILWAUKEE ELECTRIC TOOL (CANADA) LTD.—See Assa Abloy AB; *Int'l*, pg. 18
MILWAUKEE ELECTRIC TOOL CORP.—See Atlas Copco AB; *Int'l*, pg. 96
MILWAUKEE GREY IRON—See JTC LLC; *U.S. Private*, pg. 579
MILWAUKEE GUARDIAN INSURANCE INC.—See Unitrin, Inc.; *U.S. Public*, pg. 1694
MILWAUKEE INSURANCE GROUP—See Unitrin, Inc.; *U.S. Public*, pg. 1694
MILWAUKEE JOURNAL SENTINEL—See Journal Communications Inc.; *U.S. Private*, pg. 601
MILWAUKEE LOCK COMPANY—See Fortune Brands, Inc.; *U.S. Public*, pg. 675
MILWAUKEE SAFEGUARD INSURANCE CO.—See Unitrin, Inc.; *U.S. Public*, pg. 1694
MILWAUKEE SEASONINGS, INC.—See Bestfoods; *U.S. Public*, pg. 224
MIMLIC ASSET MANAGEMENT COMPANY—See The Minnesota Mutual Life Insurance Company; *U.S. Private*, pg. 750
MINAREK CORP; *U.S. Private*, pg. 749
MINAS DA SERRA BERAL S.A.—See Nissho Iwai Corporation; *Int'l*, pg. 948
MINAS DE FIGAREDO, S.A.—See SEPI; *Int'l*, pg. 1224
MINAS DE GADOR S.A.—See Laporte plc; *Int'l*, pg. 803
MINAS DE TORRELAVEGA S.A.—See Solvay S.A.; *Int'l*, pg. 1279
MINASGAS S.A. DISTRIBUIDORA DE GAS COMBUSTIVEL—See SHV Holdings N.V.; *Int'l*, pg. 1155
MINATO BUILDING CO., LTD.—See Toshiba Corporation; *Int'l*, pg. 1403
MINCE MASTER; *U.S. Private*, pg. 749
MINCO IBERICA—See Svedala Industri AB; *Int'l*, pg. 1326
MINCO INTERNATIONAL AB—See Trelleborg AB; *Int'l*, pg. 1423
MINCO PRODUCTS, INC.; *U.S. Private*, pg. 749
A. MINDEL & SON, INC.—See Seton Company; *U.S. Private*, pg. 987
MINDSCAPE, INC.—See Pearson plc; *Int'l*, pg. 1026
MINDSCAPE INTERNATIONAL—See Pearson plc; *Int'l*, pg. 1026
MINDSCAPE INTERNATIONAL, PTY. LIMITED—See Pearson plc; *Int'l*, pg. 1027
MINDSCAPE INTERNATIONAL SOFTWAREVERTRIEB GMBH—See Pearson plc; *Int'l*, pg. 1027
MINE SAFETY APPLIANCES CO.; *U.S. Public*, pg. 1114
MINE SAFETY APPLIANCES CO.—See Mine Safety Appliances Co.; *U.S. Public*, pg. 1114
MINEBEA CO., LTD.; *Int'l*, pg. 867
MINEBEA CO., LTD. - HONG KONG BRANCH—See Minebea Co., Ltd.; *Int'l*, pg. 869

MINEBEA CO., LTD. - KUALA LUMPUR BRANCH—See Minebea Co., Ltd.; *Int'l*, pg. 869
MINEBEA CO., LTD. - SHANGHAI OFFICE—See Minebea Co., Ltd.; *Int'l*, pg. 869
MINEBEA CREDIT CO., LTD.—See Minebea Co., Ltd.; *Int'l*, pg. 868
MINEBEA ELECTRONICS & HI-TECH COMPONENTS (SHANGHAI) LTD.—See Minebea Co., Ltd.; *Int'l*, pg. 868
MINEBEA ELECTRONICS CO., LTD.—See Minebea Co., Ltd.; *Int'l*, pg. 868
MINEBEA ELECTRONICS MEXICO S.A. DE C.V.—See Minebea Co., Ltd.; *Int'l*, pg. 868
MINEBEA ELECTRONICS (UK) LTD.—See Minebea Co., Ltd.; *Int'l*, pg. 868
MINEBEA EUROPE FINANCE B.V.—See Minebea Co., Ltd.; *Int'l*, pg. 868
MINEBEA INVESTMENT (PTE) LTD.—See Minebea Co., Ltd.; *Int'l*, pg. 868
MINEBEA ONKYO CO., LTD.—See Minebea Co., Ltd.; *Int'l*, pg. 868
MINEBEA TECHNOLOGIES PTE. LTD.—See Minebea Co., Ltd.; *Int'l*, pg. 868
MINEBEA TECHNOLOGIES PTE. LTD. - MANILA BRANCH—See Minebea Co., Ltd.; *Int'l*, pg. 869
MINEBEA TECHNOLOGIES PTE. LTD. - TAIPEI OFFICE—See Minebea Co., Ltd.; *Int'l*, pg. 869
MINEBEA THAI LIMITED—See Minebea Co., Ltd.; *Int'l*, pg. 868
CIA. MINEIRA DE METAIS—See S.A. Industrias Votorantim; *Int'l*, pg. 869
MINELCO, INC.—See Carpenter Technology Corporation; *U.S. Public*, pg. 308
MINEMET AUSTRALIA PTY. LTD.—See Imetal; *Int'l*, pg. 661
MINEMET-FRANCE—See Imetal; *Int'l*, pg. 661
MINEMET HOLDING—See Imetal; *Int'l*, pg. 661
MINEMET ITALIA—See Imetal; *Int'l*, pg. 661
MINEMET JAPAN—See Imetal; *Int'l*, pg. 661
MINEMET RECHERCHE—See Imetal; *Int'l*, pg. 661
MINEMET S.A.—See Imetal; *Int'l*, pg. 661
MINEMET SA-SPAIN—See Imetal; *Int'l*, pg. 661
MINER ENTERPRISES INC.; *U.S. Private*, pg. 749
MINERA BHP DE CHILE INC.—See The Broken Hill Proprietary Company Limited; *Int'l*, pg. 224
MINERA COMINCO BOLIVIA LTDA.—See Cominco, Ltd.; *Int'l*, pg. 308
MINERA COMINCO RESOURCES CHILE LTDA.—See Cominco, Ltd.; *Int'l*, pg. 308
CIA. MINERA CONSTELACION S.A. DE C.V.—See Cominco, Ltd.; *Int'l*, pg. 308
MINERA DEL NORTE—See Altos Hornos de Mexico, S.A.; *Int'l*, pg. 66
MINERA ESCONDIDA LIMITADA—See The Broken Hill Proprietary Company Limited; *Int'l*, pg. 227
MINERA HECLA S.A. DE CV—See Hecla Mining Company; *U.S. Public*, pg. 804
MINERA HISPANIOLA, S.A.—See Canyon Resources Corporation; *U.S. Public*, pg. 302
MINERA HOMESTAKE CHILE, S.A.—See Homestake Mining Company; *U.S. Public*, pg. 833
MINERA OUTOKUMPU CHILE S.A.—See Outokumpu Oyj; *Int'l*, pg. 1016
MINERA RAYROCK INC. CHILE—See Rayrock Yellowknife Resources Inc.; *Int'l*, pg. 1089
MINERA SUNSHINE DEL PERU, S.A.—See Sunshine Mining And Refining Company; *U.S. Public*, pg. 1536
S.A. MINERACAO DE AMIANTO—See Saint-Gobain; *Int'l*, pg. 1171
MINERACAO MAREX LTDA.—See The Broken Hill Proprietary Company Limited; *Int'l*, pg. 224
MINERACAO RIO DO NORTE S.A.—See Alcan Aluminium Limited; *Int'l*, pg. 52
MINERACAO SERRAS DO SUL LTDA.—See Inco Limited; *Int'l*, pg. 673
MINERAL DEPOSITS PTY. LTD.—See The Broken Hill Proprietary Company Limited; *Int'l*, pg. 224
MINERAL HILL MINE—See TVX Gold Inc.; *Int'l*, pg. 1345
A/O MINERAL PROCESSING ENGINEERS—See Outokumpu Oyj; *Int'l*, pg. 1017
MINERAL RESEARCH & DEVELOPMENT CORP.—See Laporte plc; *Int'l*, pg. 802
MINERAL SAN SEBASTIAN S.A.—See Commerce Group Corp.; *U.S. Public*, pg. 410
MINERAL UND HEILQUELLEN AG, ADELBODEN—See Koninklijke BolsWessanen nv; *Int'l*, pg. 751
MINERAL WELLS CORRECTION FACILITY—See Corrections Corporation of America; *U.S. Public*, pg. 450
MINERALLAC CO.; *U.S. Private*, pg. 750
MINERALMAHLWERK WESTERWALD HORN GMBH & CO. KG—See Fried. Krupp AG; *Int'l*, pg. 514
MINERALS AND MINING GROUP—See Global Industrial Technologies; *U.S. Public*, pg. 748
THE MINERALS LABORATORY—See The Broken Hill Proprietary Company Limited; *Int'l*, pg. 224
MINERALS TECHNOLOGIES, INC.; *U.S. Public*, pg. 1115
MINERVA ASSICURAZIONI S.P.A.—See Zurich Insurance Company; *Int'l*, pg. 1531
MINERVA VITA ASSICURAZIONI S.P.A.—See Zurich Insurance Company; *Int'l*, pg. 1531
MINES ASSAY DIVISION—See Acklands Limited; *Int'l*, pg. 23
MINET, INC.—See AON Corporation; *U.S. Public*, pg. 118
JUAN MINETTI S.A.; *Int'l*, pg. 869
MING SURVEYORS, INC.—See Hoffman Corporation; *U.S. Private*, pg. 532
MINGO OXYGEN COMPANY—See WHX Corporation; *U.S. Public*, pg. 1726
MINI INSTRUMENTS LIMITED—See Morgan Crucible Co. Plc; *Int'l*, pg. 892
MINI MART, INC.—See The Kroger Co.; *U.S. Public*, pg. 967
ED MINIAT, INC.; *U.S. Private*, pg. 750

MINIATURE PRECISION COMPONENTS; *U.S. Private*, pg. 750
MINIDATA SERVICES, INC.—See Ceridian Corporation; *U.S. Public*, pg. 331
MINIGRIP ZIP-PAK—See Illinois Tool Works Inc.; *U.S. Public*, pg. 867
MINIMAX GMBH—See Preussag AG; *Int'l*, pg. 1069
MINING AND CONSTRUCTION DIVISION—See Kennametal Inc.; *U.S. Public*, pg. 950
MINING CONTROLS, INC.—See Elgin National Industries, Inc.; *U.S. Private*, pg. 370
MINING DEVELOPMENT CO.—See Asarco Incorporated; *U.S. Public*, pg. 138
MINING EQUIPMENT DIVISION—See Harnischfeger Industries, Inc.; *U.S. Public*, pg. 788
MINING GROUP—See Morrison Knudsen Corporation; *U.S. Public*, pg. 1134
MINING SERVICES CO. MINSERCO—See Electrolux, AB; *Int'l*, pg. 443
MINING SERVICES INTERNATIONAL—See Mining Services International, Inc.; *U.S. Public*, pg. 1115
MINING SERVICES INTERNATIONAL, INC.; *U.S. Public*, pg. 1115
MINIPACK SYSTEMS LIMITED—See McCormick & Company, Incorporated; *U.S. Public*, pg. 1067
MINIRUF GMBH—See Veba AG; *Int'l*, pg. 1461
MINISTERS LIFE INSURANCE CO—See The Minnesota Mutual Life Insurance Company; *U.S. Private*, pg. 750
MINISTERS LIFE RESOURCES—See The Minnesota Mutual Life Insurance Company; *U.S. Private*, pg. 750
MINITEL USA—See France Telecom; *Int'l*, pg. 504
MINN-DAK GROWERS, LTD.; *U.S. Private*, pg. 750
MINNEAPOLIS AUTO AUCTION—See Cox Enterprises, Inc.; *U.S. Private*, pg. 282
MINNEAPOLIS MILLING—See Archer Daniels Midland Company (ADM); *U.S. Public*, pg. 128
MINNEGASCO—See Houston Industries Incorporated; *U.S. Public*, pg. 843
MINNESOTA BREWING COMPANY; *U.S. Public*, pg. 1115
MINNESOTA, DAKOTA & WESTERN RAILWAY CO.—See Boise Cascade Corporation; *U.S. Public*, pg. 243
MINNESOTA-DAKOTA GENERATING CO.—See Otter Tail Power Company; *U.S. Public*, pg. 1235
MINNESOTA ELECTRIC SUPPLY COMPANY; *U.S. Private*, pg. 750
MINNESOTA FIRE & CASUALTY COMPANY—See Harleysville Group; *U.S. Public*, pg. 787
MINNESOTA LABORATORY—See Pace Analytical Services; *U.S. Private*, pg. 829
THE MINNESOTA MUTUAL LIFE INSURANCE COMPANY; *U.S. Private*, pg. 750
MINNESOTA NIGERIA LIMITED—See 3M; *U.S. Public*, pg. 1606
MINNESOTA PAPER, INCORPORATED—See Minnesota Power; *U.S. Public*, pg. 1116
MINNESOTA POWER; *U.S. Public*, pg. 1116
MINNESOTA RUBBER EUROPE S.A.—See Quadion Corporation; *U.S. Private*, pg. 898
MINNESOTA (3M) DE PORTUGAL, LDA.—See 3M; *U.S. Public*, pg. 1606
MINNESOTA TWINS BASEBALL CLUB; *U.S. Private*, pg. 750
MINNESOTA VALLEY ENGINEERING/CRYOGENIC ASSOCIATION; *U.S. Private*, pg. 751
MINNITI—See Lyonnaise des Eaux S.A.; *Int'l*, pg. 823
MINNKOTA POWER COOPERATIVE, INC.; *U.S. Private*, pg. 751
MINOLTA CO., LTD.; *Int'l*, pg. 869
L.J. MINOR CORPORATION—See Nestle S.A.; *Int'l*, pg. 917
P.W. MINOR & SON, INC.; *U.S. Private*, pg. 751
MINOR RUBBER CO., INC.; *U.S. Private*, pg. 751
MINORCO—See Anglo American Corporation of South Africa Limited; *Int'l*, pg. 77
MINOS EMI—See EMI Group plc; *Int'l*, pg. 427
MINOT BUILDERS SUPPLY ASSOCIATION; *U.S. Private*, pg. 751
MINOTERIE COOP RIVAZ—See Coop Switzerland; *Int'l*, pg. 330
MINSERCO, INC.—See Bucyrus International; *U.S. Public*, pg. 177
THE MINSTER MACHINE COMPANY; *U.S. Private*, pg. 751
MINSTER MACHINE COMPANY-BEAUFORT OPERATION—See The Minster Machine Company; *U.S. Private*, pg. 751
MINTECH, INC.—See Perma-Fix Environmental Services, Inc.; *U.S. Public*, pg. 1279
MINTECH, INC.-TULSA—See Perma-Fix Environmental Services, Inc.; *U.S. Public*, pg. 1279
MINTZ & HOKE INC.; *U.S. Private*, pg. 751
THE MINUTE MAID COMPANY—See The Coca-Cola Company; *U.S. Public*, pg. 392
MINUTEMAN INTERNATIONAL, INC.—See Hako-Werke GmbH & Co.; *Int'l*, pg. 587
MINUTEMAN PRESS INTERNATIONAL; *U.S. Private*, pg. 752
MINWAX COMPANY DIV.—See The Sherwin-Williams Company; *U.S. Public*, pg. 1466
MINYARD FOOD STORES, INC.; *U.S. Private*, pg. 752
MINYARD PROPERTIES, INC.—See Minyard Food Stores, Inc.; *U.S. Private*, pg. 752
MIRA LANZA S.P.A.—See Joh. A. Benckiser GmbH; *Int'l*, pg. 186
MIRABELL SALZBURGER CONFISERIE-UND BISQUIT-GES.M.B.H—See Philip Morris Companies Inc.; *U.S. Public*, pg. 1289
MIRABELLA—See Lagardere Groupe; *Int'l*, pg. 795
MIRACETI, S.A.—See Corporacion MAPFRE, Compania Internacional de Reaseguros, S.A.; *Int'l*, pg. 334
MIRACLE ADHESIVES—See The Sherwin-Williams Company; *U.S. Public*, pg. 1466
MIRACLE FEEDS INC.—See Furst-McNess Company; *U.S. Private*, pg. 432

MIRACLE FOODS CO., LTD.—See Nissin Food Products Co., Ltd.; *Int'l*, pg. 950
MIRACLE RECREATION EQUIPMENT COMPANY; *U.S. Private*, pg. 752
THE MIRAGE CASINO/HOTEL—See Mirage Resorts Incorporated; *U.S. Public*, pg. 1117
MIRAGE RESORTS INCORPORATED; *U.S. Public*, pg. 1116
MIRAMAS PLANT—See COGEMA - Compagnie Generale des Matieres Nucleaires; *Int'l*, pg. 305
MIRAMAX FILMS, INC.—See The Walt Disney Company; *U.S. Public*, pg. 514
MIRAMICHI PULP & PAPER INC.—See Repap Enterprises Inc.; *Int'l*, pg. 1104
MIRANO COMPANY LIMITED—See Bilfinger + Berger Bauaktiengesellschaft; *Int'l*, pg. 196
MIRARI JAPAN LTD.—See Luxottica Group S.p.A.; *Int'l*, pg. 822
MIRAVAL—See NextHealth Inc.; *U.S. Public*, pg. 1181
MIRCAL—See Imetal; *Int'l*, pg. 662
MIRCOR INC.—See Quebecor Inc.; *Int'l*, pg. 1075
MIROITERIE DU RHIN—See Saint-Gobain; *Int'l*, pg. 1172
MIROITERIES DE L'OUEST—See Saint-Gobain; *Int'l*, pg. 1172
MIROVOY GLOBAL PARTS B.V.—See Exor Group; *Int'l*, pg. 467
MIRRLEES BLACKSTONE (CANADA) LTD.—See BTR plc; *Int'l*, pg. 125
MIRRLEES BLACKSTONE (STOCKPORT) LTD.—See BTR plc; *Int'l*, pg. 125
MIRRO COMPANY—See Newell Co.; *U.S. Public*, pg. 1177
MIRROR GROUP PLC; *Int'l*, pg. 869
MIRTONE—See General Signal Corporation; *U.S. Public*, pg. 727
MISCO INDUSTRIES; *U.S. Private*, pg. 752
MISENER MARINE CONSTRUCTION; *U.S. Private*, pg. 752
MISHIMA OLYMPUS CO., LTD.—See Olympus Optical Co., Ltd.; *Int'l*, pg. 1004
MISIMA MINES PTY. LTD.—See Placer Dome Inc.; *Int'l*, pg. 1060
MISR INTERNATIONAL BANK S.A.E.—See The Sakura Bank, Limited; *Int'l*, pg. 1181
MISS ELAINE INC.; *U.S. Private*, pg. 752
MISS UNIVERSE, L.P.—See Trump Organization; *U.S. Private*, pg. 1108
MISSET—See Reed Elsevier plc; *Int'l*, pg. 1099
MISSILES & SPACE DIVISION—See The Boeing Company; *U.S. Public*, pg. 241
MISSION AMERICAN INSURANCE COMPANY—See Danielson Holding Corporation; *U.S. Public*, pg. 483
MISSION EXPLORATION CO.—See Asarco Incorporated; *U.S. Public*, pg. 138
THE MISSION GROUP—See Edison International; *U.S. Public*, pg. 564
MISSION HILLS RESTAURANT CORP.—See Specialty Restaurants Corporation; *U.S. Private*, pg. 1022
MISSION INDUSTRIES; *U.S. Private*, pg. 752
MISSION LAND COMPANY—See Edison International; *U.S. Public*, pg. 564
MISSION LINEN SUPPLY—See Mission Industries; *U.S. Private*, pg. 752
MISSION MANAGEMENT SYSTEMS—See Tracor, Inc.; *U.S. Public*, pg. 1627
MISSION SUPPLY CO.—See Yellow Corporation; *U.S. Public*, pg. 1788
MISSION VALLEY DEVELOPMENT CO.—See CalMat Co.; *U.S. Public*, pg. 295
MISSION VIEJO ASSOCIATES—See Cigna Corp.; *U.S. Public*, pg. 361
MISSION VIEJO COMPANY—See Philip Morris Companies Inc.; *U.S. Public*, pg. 1289
MISSION WEST PROPERTIES; *U.S. Public*, pg. 1117
MISSISSAUGA CENTER—See The Cascades Group; *Int'l*, pg. 273
MISSISSAUGA OFFICE—See The Cascades Group; *Int'l*, pg. 274
MISSISSIPPI AUTO AUCTION INC.—See Tyco International Ltd.; *U.S. Public*, pg. 1649
MISSISSIPPI CHEMICAL CORPORATION; *U.S. Public*, pg. 1117
MISSISSIPPI ENERGIES, INC.—See Mississippi Valley Gas Co.; *U.S. Private*, pg. 753
MISSISSIPPI FARM BUREAU CASUALTY INSURANCE COMPANY—See Southern Farm Bureau Casualty Insurance Company; *U.S. Private*, pg. 1016
MISSISSIPPI LIME CO.; *U.S. Private*, pg. 753
MISSISSIPPI MARKETING, INC.—See Callon Petroleum Company; *U.S. Public*, pg. 295
MISSISSIPPI PHOSPHATES CORP.—See Mississippi Chemical Corporation; *U.S. Public*, pg. 1117
MISSISSIPPI POTASH, INC.—See Mississippi Chemical Corporation; *U.S. Public*, pg. 1117
MISSISSIPPI POWER CO.—See Southern Company; *U.S. Public*, pg. 1490
MISSISSIPPI RIVER TRANSMISSION—See Houston Industries Incorporated; *U.S. Public*, pg. 843
MISSISSIPPI VALLEY ADVISORS INC.—See Mercantile Bancorporation Inc.; *U.S. Public*, pg. 1087
MISSISSIPPI VALLEY CORP.—See Illinois Central Corporation; *U.S. Public*, pg. 865
MISSISSIPPI VALLEY GAS CO.; *U.S. Private*, pg. 753
MISSISSIPPI VALLEY LIFE INSURANCE COMPANY—See Mercantile Bancorporation Inc.; *U.S. Public*, pg. 1087
THE MISSOULIAN—See Lee Enterprises, Incorporated; *U.S. Public*, pg. 984
MISSOURI-AMERICAN WATER CO.—See American Water Works Company, Inc.; *U.S. Public*, pg. 95
MISSOURI AUCTION SERVICES CORP.—See Cox Enterprises, Inc.; *U.S. Private*, pg. 282
MISSOURI GAS ENERGY—See Southern Union Company; *U.S. Public*, pg. 1491
MISSOURI MEDICAL INSURANCE COMPANY—See Medical Assurance, Inc.; *U.S. Public*, pg. 1080

MISSOURI-NEBRASKA EXPRESS, INC.—See Mark VII, Inc.; *U.S. Public*, pg. 1046

MISSOURI PORTLAND CEMENT HOLDING—See Lafarge S.A.; *Int'l*, pg. 788

MISSOURI PUBLIC SERVICE—See UtiliCorp United Inc.; *U.S. Public*, pg. 1701

MISSOURI RIVER MANOR—See Horizon/CMS Healthcare Corporation; *U.S. Public*, pg. 837

MISSOURI VALLEY STEEL CO.—See Owen Industries, Inc.; *U.S. Private*, pg. 824

MISTAL, INC.—See Tenneco Inc.; *U.S. Public*, pg. 1579

MISTER COOKIE FACE, INC.; *U.S. Private*, pg. 753

MISTER DONUT OF AMERICA, INC.—See Allied Domecq PLC; *Int'l*, pg. 63

MISTER TWISTER—See Sheldons' Inc.; *U.S. Private*, pg. 992

MISTIC BRANDS, INC.—See Triarc Companies, Inc.; *U.S. Public*, pg. 1635

MISTRAL TRAVAUX—See Bouygues; *Int'l*, pg. 206

MISTUKOSHI ITALIA S.P.A.—See Mitsukoshi, Ltd.; *Int'l*, pg. 884

MISTY HARBOR—See Amerex USA, Inc.; *U.S. Private*, pg. 49

MISYS PLC; *Int'l*, pg. 870

MITA COPYSTAR AMERICA INC.—See Mita Industrial Company, Ltd.; *Int'l*, pg. 870

MITA INDUSTRIAL COMPANY, LTD.; *Int'l*, pg. 870

MITCHEL-LINCOLN PACKAGING; *Int'l*, pg. 870

MITCHEL & SCOTT MACHINE CO., INC.; pg. 753

MITCHELL BEAZLEY—See Reed Elsevier plc; *Int'l*, pg. 1093

MITCHELL-BRADFORD INTERNATIONAL—See Hubbard Hall Inc.; *U.S. Private*, pg. 544

MITCHELL COACH MANUFACTURING; *U.S. Private*, pg. 753

MITCHELL CO.—See Stonecutter Mills Corp.; *U.S. Private*, pg. 1044

MITCHELL CORPORATION, CLARE DIV.—See Mitchell Corporation of Owosso; *U.S. Private*, pg. 753

MITCHELL CORPORATION OF OWOSSO; *U.S. Private*, pg. 753

MITCHELL COTTS CHEMICALS LIMITED—See Ascot Holdings Plc; *Int'l*, pg. 88

MITCHELL COTTS REMANUFACTURING LIMITED—See Ascot Holdings Plc; *Int'l*, pg. 88

MITCHELL ENERGY & DEVELOPMENT CORP.; *U.S. Public*, pg. 1117

MITCHELL HUTCHINS ASSET MANAGEMENT INC.—See PaineWebber Group Incorporated; *U.S. Public*, pg. 1253

MITCHELL HUTCHINS INSTITUTIONAL INVESTORS INC.—See PaineWebber Group Incorporated; *U.S. Public*, pg. 1253

MITCHELL INTERNATIONAL—See The Thomson Corporation; *U.S. Public*, pg. 1601

JOHN PAUL MITCHELL SYSTEMS; *U.S. Private*, pg. 753

MITCHELL SHACKLETON & CO. LTD.—See National Forge Company; *U.S. Private*, pg. 783

MITCHELL SPORTS SA—See Johnson Worldwide Associates, Inc.; *U.S. Public*, pg. 933

MITEK, INC.—See Rexam PLC; *Int'l*, pg. 1106

MITEK SYSTEMS, INC.; *U.S. Public*, pg. 1117

MITEK SYSTEMS, INC.—See Mitek Systems, Inc.; *U.S. Public*, pg. 1118

MITEL CORPORATION; *Int'l*, pg. 870

MITEL FAR EAST LTD.—See Mitel Corporation; *Int'l*, pg. 870

MITEL SEMICONDUCTOR—See Mitel Corporation; *Int'l*, pg. 870

MITEL SEMICONDUCTOR AB—See Mitel Corporation; *Int'l*, pg. 870

MITEL TELECOM LIMITED—See Mitel Corporation; *Int'l*, pg. 870

MITO NIKON K.K.—See Nikon Corporation; *Int'l*, pg. 931

MITO PLANT—See Nikon Corporation; *Int'l*, pg. 931

MITO S.P.A.—See Fiat Auto SpA; *Int'l*, pg. 482

MITRANS CORPORATION—See Mitsubishi Logistics Corp.; *Int'l*, pg. 1347

P.T. MITRAPERMATA INDAH—See Taisei Corporation; *Int'l*, pg. 1347

MITRE CORPORATION; *U.S. Private*, pg. 753

MITRE SPORTS (U.S.)—See Pentland Group PLC; *Int'l*, pg. 1036

MITREX AB—See Trelleborg AB; *Int'l*, pg. 1420

MITSIAM INTERNATIONAL, LTD.—See Mitsui & Co., Ltd.; *Int'l*, pg. 880

MITSUBISHI BRASILEIRA DE INDUSTRIA PESADA LTDA. (MBI)—See Mitsubishi Heavy Industries Ltd.; *Int'l*, pg. 874

MITSUBISHI-BURLINGTON CO.—See Burlington Industries, Inc.; *U.S. Public*, pg. 268

MITSUBISHI CABLE AMERICA, INC.—See Mitsubishi Cable Industries, Ltd.; *Int'l*, pg. 870

MITSUBISHI CABLE INDUSTRIES, LTD.; *Int'l*, pg. 870

MITSUBISHI CATERPILLAR FORKLIFT AMERICA INC. (MCFA)—See Caterpillar Inc.; *U.S. Public*, pg. 316

MITSUBISHI CATERPILLAR FORKLIFT AMERICA INC. (MCFA)—See Mitsubishi Heavy Industries Ltd.; *Int'l*, pg. 874

MITSUBISHI CATERPILLAR FORKLIFT ASIA PTE. LTD.—See Caterpillar Inc.; *U.S. Public*, pg. 316

MITSUBISHI CATERPILLAR FORKLIFT EUROPE B.V.—See Caterpillar Inc.; *U.S. Public*, pg. 316

MITSUBISHI CHEMICAL AMERICA, INC.—See Mitsubishi Chemical Corporation; *Int'l*, pg. 871

MITSUBISHI CHEMICAL BASF CO., LTD.—See BASF AG; *Int'l*, pg. 106

MITSUBISHI CHEMICAL CORPORATION; *Int'l*, pg. 870

MITSUBISHI CHEMICAL DO BRASIL LTDA.—See Mitsubishi Chemical Corporation; *Int'l*, pg. 871

MITSUBISHI CHEMICAL EUROPE GMBH—See Mitsubishi Chemical Corporation; *Int'l*, pg. 871

MITSUBISHI CHEMICAL MKV CO.—See Mitsubishi Chemical Corporation; *Int'l*, pg. 871

MITSUBISHI CHEMICAL (THAILAND) CO., LTD.—See Mitsubishi Chemical Corporation; *Int'l*, pg. 871

MITSUBISHI CHEMICAL (U.K.) PLC—See Mitsubishi Chemical Corporation; *Int'l*, pg. 871

MITSUBISHI CONSUMER ELECTRONICS AMERICA—See Mitsubishi Electric Corporation; *Int'l*, pg. 872

MITSUBISHI CORPORATION; *Int'l*, pg. 871

MITSUBISHI ELECTRIC AMERICA, INC.—See Mitsubishi Electric Corporation; *Int'l*, pg. 872

MITSUBISHI ELECTRIC CORPORATION; *Int'l*, pg. 872

MITSUBISHI ELECTRIC INDUSTRIAL CONTROL—See Mitsubishi Electric Corporation; *Int'l*, pg. 872

MITSUBISHI ELECTRIC MFG.—See Mitsubishi Electric Corporation; *Int'l*, pg. 872

MITSUBISHI ELECTRIC SALES AMERICA—See Mitsubishi Electric Corporation; *Int'l*, pg. 872

MITSUBISHI ELECTRIC (UK) LTD.—See Mitsubishi Electric Corporation; *Int'l*, pg. 873

MITSUBISHI ELECTRONICS AMERICA—See Mitsubishi Electric Corporation; *Int'l*, pg. 872

MITSUBISHI ESTATE CO., LTD.; *Int'l*, pg. 873

MITSUBISHI ESTATE CO., LTD.—See Mitsubishi Estate Co., Ltd.; *Int'l*, pg. 873

MITSUBISHI ESTATE CO., LTD.-OSAKA—See Mitsubishi Estate Co., Ltd.; *Int'l*, pg. 873

MITSUBISHI ESTATE NEW YORK, INC.—See Mitsubishi Estate Co., Ltd.; *Int'l*, pg. 873

MITSUBISHI FOODS (MC), INC.—See Mitsubishi Corporation; *Int'l*, pg. 871

MITSUBISHI FUSO TRUCK OF AMERICA, INC.—See Mitsubishi Motors Corporation; *Int'l*, pg. 875

MITSUBISHI HEAVY INDUSTRIES EUROPE LTD. (MHIE)—See Mitsubishi Heavy Industries Ltd.; *Int'l*, pg. 874

MITSUBISHI HEAVY INDUSTRIES, (HONG KONG) LTD.—See Mitsubishi Heavy Industries Ltd.; *Int'l*, pg. 874

MITSUBISHI HEAVY INDUSTRIES LTD.; *Int'l*, pg. 873

MITSUBISHI INTERNATIONAL CORPORATION—See Mitsubishi Corporation; *Int'l*, pg. 871

P.T. MITSUBISHI KRAMA YUDHA MOTORS & MANUFACTURING—See Mitsubishi Motors Corporation; *Int'l*, pg. 876

MITSUBISHI LOGISTICS CORP.; *Int'l*, pg. 874

MITSUBISHI MATERIALS—See Mitsubishi Materials Corp.; *Int'l*, pg. 875

MITSUBISHI MATERIALS CORP.; *Int'l*, pg. 874

MITSUBISHI MONSANTO CHEMICAL CO.—See Monsanto Company; *U.S. Public*, pg. 1125

MITSUBISHI MOTOR MARKETING RESEARCH EUROPE GMBH—See Mitsubishi Motors Corporation; *Int'l*, pg. 876

MITSUBISHI MOTOR SALES EUROPE B.V.—See Mitsubishi Motors Corporation; *Int'l*, pg. 876

MITSUBISHI MOTOR SALES OF AMERICA, INC.—See Mitsubishi Motors Corporation; *Int'l*, pg. 876

MITSUBISHI MOTOR SALES OF CARIBBEAN INC.—See Mitsubishi Motors Corporation; *Int'l*, pg. 876

MITSUBISHI MOTORS AMERICA, INC.—See Mitsubishi Motors Corporation; *Int'l*, pg. 876

MITSUBISHI MOTORS AUSTRALIA LTD.—See Mitsubishi Motors Corporation; *Int'l*, pg. 876

MITSUBISHI MOTORS CORPORATION; *Int'l*, pg. 875

MITSUBISHI MOTORS CREDIT OF AMERICA, INC.—See Mitsubishi Motors Corporation; *Int'l*, pg. 875

MITSUBISHI MOTORS CREDIT OF AMERICA INC.—See Mitsubishi Motors Corporation; *Int'l*, pg. 875

MITSUBISHI MOTORS DE PORTUGAL, S.A.—See Mitsubishi Motors Corporation; *Int'l*, pg. 876

MITSUBISHI MOTORS EUROPE B.V.—See Mitsubishi Motors Corporation; *Int'l*, pg. 876

MITSUBISHI MOTORS NEW ZEALAND LTD.—See Mitsubishi Motors Corporation; *Int'l*, pg. 876

MITSUBISHI MOTORS R&D EUROPE GMBH—See Mitsubishi Motors Corporation; *Int'l*, pg. 876

MITSUBISHI OIL AMERICA—See Mitsubishi Oil Co. Ltd.; *Int'l*, pg. 876

MITSUBISHI OIL CO. LTD.; *Int'l*, pg. 876

MITSUBISHI RAYON AMERICA, INC.—See Mitsubishi Rayon Co., Ltd.; *Int'l*, pg. 876

MITSUBISHI RAYON CO., LTD.; *Int'l*, pg. 876

MITSUBISHI RAYON CO., LTD.—See Mitsubishi Rayon Co., Ltd.; *Int'l*, pg. 876

MITSUBISHI REAL ESTATE SERVICES CO., LTD.—See Mitsubishi Estate Co., Ltd.; *Int'l*, pg. 873

MITSUBISHI SEMICONDUCTOR AMERICA—See Mitsubishi Electric Corporation; *Int'l*, pg. 872

MITSUBISHI SHINDOH CO., LTD.—See Mitsubishi Materials Corp.; *Int'l*, pg. 875

MITSUBISHI SILICON AMERICA—See Mitsubishi Materials Corp.; *Int'l*, pg. 875

MITSUBISHI SILICON AMERICA-EASTERN REGIONAL SALES OFFICE—See Mitsubishi Materials Corp.; *Int'l*, pg. 875

MITSUBISHI SILICON AMERICA-SOUTHWEST REGIONAL SALES OFFICE—See Mitsubishi Materials Corp.; *Int'l*, pg. 875

THE MITSUBISHI TRUST AND BANKING CORPORATION; *Int'l*, pg. 876

MITSUBISHI TRUST & BANKING CORPORATION (U.S.A.)—See The Mitsubishi Trust and Banking Corporation; *Int'l*, pg. 876

THE MITSUBISHI TRUST & BANKING CORPORATION—See The Mitsubishi Trust and Banking Corporation; *Int'l*, pg. 876

THE MITSUBISHI TRUST & BANKING CORPORATION—See The Mitsubishi Trust and Banking Corporation; *Int'l*, pg. 876

MITSUBISHI TRUST & BANKING CORPORATION (EUROPE) S.A.—See The Mitsubishi Trust and Banking Corporation; *Int'l*, pg. 877

MITSUBISHI TRUST AUSTRALIA LIMITED—See The Mitsubishi Trust and Banking Corporation; *Int'l*, pg. 877

MITSUBISHI TRUST FINANCE (ASIA) LIMITED—See The Mitsubishi Trust and Banking Corporation; *Int'l*, pg. 877

MITSUBISHI TRUST FINANCE (IRELAND) PLC—See The Mitsubishi Trust and Banking Corporation; *Int'l*, pg. 877

MITSUBISHI TRUST INTERNATIONAL LIMITED—See The Mitsubishi Trust and Banking Corporation; *Int'l*, pg. 877

MITSUBISHI YUKA—See Royal Dutch/Shell Group of Companies; *Int'l*, pg. 1139

MITSUI AIR & SEA SERVICE CO., LTD.—See Mitsui & Co., Ltd.; *Int'l*, pg. 878

MITSUI ALUMINIUM CO., LTD.—See Mitsui & Co., Ltd.; *Int'l*, pg. 878

MITSUI & CO.—See Mitsui & Co., Ltd.; *Int'l*, pg. 880

MITSUI & CO. (AUSTRALIA)—See Mitsui & Co., Ltd.; *Int'l*, pg. 880

MITSUI & CO. (AUSTRALIA) LTD.—See Mitsui & Co., Ltd.; *Int'l*, pg. 880

MITSUI & CO. (CAMEROUN) SARL—See Mitsui & Co., Ltd.; *Int'l*, pg. 880

MITSUI & CO. (CANADA) LTD.—See Mitsui & Co., Ltd.; *Int'l*, pg. 880

N.V. MITSUI & CO. EUROPE (BENELUX) S.A.—See Mitsui & Co., Ltd.; *Int'l*, pg. 880

MITSUI & CO. EUROPE (ESPANA)—See Mitsui & Co., Ltd.; *Int'l*, pg. 880

MITSUI & CO. EUROPE (ESPANA) S.A.—See Mitsui & Co., Ltd.; *Int'l*, pg. 880

MITSUI & CO. EUROPE (FINLAND) OY—See Mitsui & Co., Ltd.; *Int'l*, pg. 880

MITSUI & CO. EUROPE G.M.B.H.—See Mitsui & Co., Ltd.; *Int'l*, pg. 880

MITSUI & CO. EUROPE (ITALIA) S.P.A.—See Mitsui & Co., Ltd.; *Int'l*, pg. 880

MITSUI & CO. EUROPE LTD.—See Mitsui & Co., Ltd.; *Int'l*, pg. 880

MITSUI & CO. EUROPE (PORTUGAL) LDA.—See Mitsui & Co., Ltd.; *Int'l*, pg. 880

MITSUI & CO. EUROPE S.A.—See Mitsui & Co., Ltd.; *Int'l*, pg. 880

MITSUI & CO. EUROPE (SCANDINAVIA) AB—See Mitsui & Co., Ltd.; *Int'l*, pg. 880

MITSUI & CO., (HONG KONG) LTD.—See Mitsui & Co., Ltd.; *Int'l*, pg. 880

MITSUI & CO. INTERNATIONAL (EUROPE) B.V.—See Mitsui & Co., Ltd.; *Int'l*, pg. 880

MITSUI & CO., IRAN LTD.—See Mitsui & Co., Ltd.; *Int'l*, pg. 880

MITSUI & CO., LTD.; *Int'l*, pg. 877

MITSUI & CO., LTD. (AMSTERDAM BRANCH)—See Mitsui & Co., Ltd.; *Int'l*, pg. 882

MITSUI & CO., LTD.- MAPUTO LIASON REPRESENTATIVE—See Mitsui & Co., Ltd.; *Int'l*, pg. 882

MITSUI & CO., LTD. (SOFIA)—See Mitsui & Co., Ltd.; *Int'l*, pg. 882

MITSUI & CO. (MIDDLE EAST) E.C.—See Mitsui & Co., Ltd.; *Int'l*, pg. 882

MITSUI & CO. (N.Z.) LTD.—See Mitsui & Co., Ltd.; *Int'l*, pg. 882

MITSUI & CO., (PANAMA INTERNATIONAL) S.A.—See Mitsui & Co., Ltd.; *Int'l*, pg. 882

MITSUI & CO. (THAILAND) LTD.—See Mitsui & Co., Ltd.; *Int'l*, pg. 882

MITSUI & CO. (U.S.A.)—See Mitsui & Co., Ltd.; *Int'l*, pg. 879

MITSUI ARGENTINA S.A.—See Mitsui & Co., Ltd.; *Int'l*, pg. 882

MITSUI BASF DYES LTD.—See BASF AG; *Int'l*, pg. 109

MITSUI BRASILEIRA IMP. E EXP. LTDA.—See Mitsui & Co., Ltd.; *Int'l*, pg. 882

MITSUI CHILENA COMMERCIAL LTDA.—See Mitsui & Co., Ltd.; *Int'l*, pg. 882

MITSUI COKE CO., LTD.—See Mitsui & Co., Ltd.; *Int'l*, pg. 877

MITSUI CONCRETE INDUSTRIES CO., LTD.—See Mitsui & Co., Ltd.; *Int'l*, pg. 877

MITSUI CONSTRUCTION CO., LTD.—See Mitsui & Co., Ltd.; *Int'l*, pg. 877

MITSUI CONSULTANTS CO., LTD.—See Mitsui & Co., Ltd.; *Int'l*, pg. 877

MITSUI DE COLOMBIA S.A.—See Mitsui & Co., Ltd.; *Int'l*, pg. 882

MITSUI DE MEXICO, S.A. DE C.V.—See Mitsui & Co., Ltd.; *Int'l*, pg. 882

MITSUI DE VENEZUELA C.A.—See Mitsui & Co., Ltd.; *Int'l*, pg. 882

MITSUI DEL ECUADOR S.A.—See Mitsui & Co., Ltd.; *Int'l*, pg. 882

MITSUI DEL PERU S.A.—See Mitsui & Co., Ltd.; *Int'l*, pg. 882

MITSUI DO BRASIL TRADING S.A.—See Mitsui & Co., Ltd.; *Int'l*, pg. 882

MITSUI ENGINEERING & SHIPBUILDING CO., LTD.—See Mitsui & Co., Ltd.; *Int'l*, pg. 879

MITSUI FOODS EXPORT—See Mitsui & Co., Ltd.; *Int'l*, pg. 879

MITSUI FOODS, INC.—See Mitsui & Co., Ltd.; *Int'l*, pg. 879

MITSUI FOODS, INC., WESTERN DIV.—See Mitsui & Co., Ltd.; *Int'l*, pg. 879

MITSUI FUDOSAN CO., LTD.; *Int'l*, pg. 882

MITSUI FUDOSAN (USA), INC.—See Mitsui Fudosan Co., Ltd.; *Int'l*, pg. 882

MITSUI HARBOUR & URBAN CONSTRUCTION CO., LTD.—See Mitsui & Co., Ltd.; *Int'l*, pg. 877

MITSUI HOME CO., LTD.—See Mitsui & Co., Ltd.; *Int'l*, pg. 877

MITSUI IRON ORE DEVELOPMENT PTY. LTD.—See Mitsui & Co., Ltd.; *Int'l*, pg. 879

MITSUI KANKO DEVELOPMENT CO., LTD.—See Mitsui & Co., Ltd.; *Int'l*, pg. 878

MITSUI KNOWLEDGE INDUSTRY CO., LTD.—See Mitsui & Co., Ltd.; *Int'l*, pg. 878

MITSUI LEASING & DEVELOPMENT LTD.—See Mitsui & Co., Ltd.; *Int'l*, pg. 878

MITSUI LIQUEFIED GAS CO., LTD.—See Mitsui & Co., Ltd.; *Int'l*, pg. 877
MITSUI LUMBER CO., LTD.—See Mitsui & Co., Ltd.; *Int'l*, pg. 877
MITSUI MARINE & FIRE INSURANCE CO., LTD.—See Mitsui & Co., Ltd.; *Int'l*, pg. 878
MITSUI MATSUSHIMA CO., LTD.—See Mitsui & Co., Ltd.; *Int'l*, pg. 877
MITSUI MIIKE ENGINEERING CORPORATION—See Mitsui & Co., Ltd.; *Int'l*, pg. 878
MITSUI MIIKE MACHINERY CO., LTD.—See Mitsui & Co., Ltd.; *Int'l*, pg. 878
MITSUI MINING & SMELTING CO., LTD.—See Mitsui & Co., Ltd.; *Int'l*, pg. 878
MITSUI MINING CO., LTD.—See Mitsui & Co., Ltd.; *Int'l*, pg. 878
MITSUI MUTUAL LIFE INSURANCE COMPANY—See Mitsui & Co., Ltd.; *Int'l*, pg. 878
MITSUI NORIN CO., LTD.—See Mitsui & Co., Ltd.; *Int'l*, pg. 878
MITSUI OCEAN DEVELOPMENT & ENGINEERING CO., LTD.—See Mitsui & Co., Ltd.; *Int'l*, pg. 878
MITSUI OIL CO., LTD.—See Mitsui & Co., Ltd.; *Int'l*, pg. 877
MITSUI O.S.K. LINES, LTD.—See Mitsui & Co., Ltd.; *Int'l*, pg. 878
MITSUI PETROCHEMICAL INDUSTRIES, LTD.—See Mitsui & Co., Ltd.; *Int'l*, pg. 877
MITSUI PHARMACEUTICALS, INC.—See Mitsui & Co., Ltd.; *Int'l*, pg. 877
MITSUI PRECON CO., LTD.—See Mitsui & Co., Ltd.; *Int'l*, pg. 877
MITSUI REAL ESTATE DEVELOPMENT CO., LTD.—See Mitsui & Co., Ltd.; *Int'l*, pg. 878
MITSUI REAL ESTATE SALES CO., LTD.—See Mitsui Fudosan Co., Ltd.; *Int'l*, pg. 882
MITSUI ROAD CO., LTD.—See Mitsui & Co., Ltd.; *Int'l*, pg. 878
MITSUI SEIKI KOGYO CO., LTD.—See Mitsui & Co., Ltd.; *Int'l*, pg. 878
MITSUI SUGAR CO., LTD.—See Mitsui & Co., Ltd.; *Int'l*, pg. 878
MITSUI T & B FUTURES—See The Mitsui Trust and Banking Company, Limited; *Int'l*, pg. 883
MITSUI T & B OPTIONS INC.—See The Mitsui Trust and Banking Company, Limited; *Int'l*, pg. 883
MITSUI TOATSU CHEMICALS, INC.—See Mitsui & Co., Ltd.; *Int'l*, pg. 877
THE MITSUI TRUST AND BANKING COMPANY - CAYMAN—See The Mitsui Trust and Banking Company, Limited; *Int'l*, pg. 883
THE MITSUI TRUST AND BANKING COMPANY - CHICAGO—See The Mitsui Trust and Banking Company, Limited; *Int'l*, pg. 883
THE MITSUI TRUST AND BANKING COMPANY - HONG KONG—See The Mitsui Trust and Banking Company, Limited; *Int'l*, pg. 883
THE MITSUI TRUST AND BANKING COMPANY, LIMITED; *Int'l*, pg. 882
THE MITSUI TRUST AND BANKING COMPANY - LONDON—See The Mitsui Trust and Banking Company, Limited; *Int'l*, pg. 883
THE MITSUI TRUST AND BANKING COMPANY - LOS ANGELES—See The Mitsui Trust and Banking Company, Limited; *Int'l*, pg. 883
THE MITSUI TRUST AND BANKING COMPANY - NEW YORK—See The Mitsui Trust and Banking Company, Limited; *Int'l*, pg. 883
THE MITSUI TRUST AND BANKING COMPANY - SINGAPORE—See The Mitsui Trust and Banking Company, Limited; *Int'l*, pg. 883
MITSUI TRUST BANK (EUROPE) S.A.—See The Mitsui Trust and Banking Company, Limited; *Int'l*, pg. 883
MITSUI TRUST BANK (SWITZERLAND) LTD.—See The Mitsui Trust and Banking Company, Limited; *Int'l*, pg. 883
MITSUI TRUST BANK (U.S.A.)—See The Mitsui Trust and Banking Company, Limited; *Int'l*, pg. 883
MITSUI TRUST FINANCE (AUSTRALIA) LTD.—See The Mitsui Trust and Banking Company, Limited; *Int'l*, pg. 883
MITSUI TRUST FINANCE (HONG KONG) LTD.—See The Mitsui Trust and Banking Company, Limited; *Int'l*, pg. 883
MITSUI TRUST FUTURES (SINGAPORE) PTE. LTD.—See The Mitsui Trust and Banking Company, Limited; *Int'l*, pg. 883
MITSUI TRUST INTERNATIONAL LTD.—See The Mitsui Trust and Banking Company, Limited; *Int'l*, pg. 883
THE MITSUI WAREHOUSE CO., LTD.—See Mitsui & Co., Ltd.; *Int'l*, pg. 878
MITSUI WHARF CO., LTD.—See Mitsui & Co., Ltd.; *Int'l*, pg. 878
MITSUKAN & NAKANO VINEGAR COMPANY LTD.; *Int'l*, pg. 883
MITSUKOSHI DEUTSCHLAND GMBH—See Mitsukoshi, Ltd.; *Int'l*, pg. 884
MITSUKOSHI DEUTSCHLAND GMBH-BERLIN BRANCH—See Mitsukoshi, Ltd.; *Int'l*, pg. 884
MITSUKOSHI DEUTSCHLAND GMBH-FRANKFURT BRANCH—See Mitsukoshi, Ltd.; *Int'l*, pg. 884
MITSUKOSHI DEUTSCHLAND GMBH-MUNICH BRANCH—See Mitsukoshi, Ltd.; *Int'l*, pg. 884
MITSUKOSHI ENTERPRISES CO., LTD.—See Mitsukoshi, Ltd.; *Int'l*, pg. 884
MITSUKOSHI ENTERPRISES CO., LTD.-TSIM SHA TSUI BRANCH—See Mitsukoshi, Ltd.; *Int'l*, pg. 884
MITSUKOSHI ESPANA S.A.—See Mitsukoshi, Ltd.; *Int'l*, pg. 884
MITSUKOSHI ESPANA S.A.-BARCELONA BRANCH—See Mitsukoshi, Ltd.; *Int'l*, pg. 884
MITSUKOSHI ETOILE—See Mitsukoshi, Ltd.; *Int'l*, pg. 884
MITSUKOSHI FRANCE S.A.—See Mitsukoshi, Ltd.; *Int'l*, pg. 884

MITSUKOSHI (GUAM) INC.—See Mitsukoshi, Ltd.; *Int'l*, pg. 883
MITSUKOSHI, LTD.; *Int'l*, pg. 883
MITSUKOSHI LTD.-BANGKOK OFFICE—See Mitsukoshi, Ltd.; *Int'l*, pg. 884
MITSUKOSHI LTD.-BEIJING OFFICE—See Mitsukoshi, Ltd.; *Int'l*, pg. 884
MITSUKOSHI LTD.-EUROPE HEAD OFFICE—See Mitsukoshi, Ltd.; *Int'l*, pg. 884
MITSUKOSHI LTD.-MILAN OFFICE—See Mitsukoshi, Ltd.; *Int'l*, pg. 884
MITSUKOSHI LTD.-SEOUL OFFICE—See Mitsukoshi, Ltd.; *Int'l*, pg. 884
MITSUKOSHI (U.K.) LTD.—See Mitsukoshi, Ltd.; *Int'l*, pg. 884
MITSUKOSHI (U.S.A.) INC.—See Mitsukoshi, Ltd.; *Int'l*, pg. 883
MITSUKOSHI (U.S.A.) INC.-HAWAII BRANCH—See Mitsukoshi, Ltd.; *Int'l*, pg. 883
MITSUKOSHI (U.S.A.) INC.-ORLANDO BRANCH—See Mitsukoshi, Ltd.; *Int'l*, pg. 883
MITSUMI ELECTRIC CO., LTD.; *Int'l*, pg. 884
MITSUMI ELECTRONICS CORP.—See Mitsumi Electric Co., Ltd.; *Int'l*, pg. 884
MITTELRHEINISCHE ERDGASTRANSPORT GESELLSCHAFT MBH—See Ruhrgas Aktiengesellschaft; *Int'l*, pg. 1149
MITY-LITE, INC.; *U.S. Public*, pg. 1118
MITY NICE GRILL—See Lettuce Entertain You Enterprises, Inc.; *U.S. Private*, pg. 661
MIURA BOILER CO. LTD.—See Miura Co. Ltd.; *Int'l*, pg. 884
MIURA BOILER CO., LTD. (CANADA)—See Miura Co., Ltd.; *Int'l*, pg. 884
MIURA BOILER CO., LTD. (TAIWAN)—See Miura Co., Ltd.; *Int'l*, pg. 884
MIURA BOILER U.S.A., INC.—See Miura Co., Ltd.; *Int'l*, pg. 884
MIURA BOILER WEST, INC. (U.S.A.)—See Miura Co., Ltd.; *Int'l*, pg. 884
MIURA CO., LTD.; *Int'l*, pg. 884
MIURA INSTITUTE OF R & D CO., LTD.—See Miura Co., Ltd.; *Int'l*, pg. 884
MIURA KOKI CO., LTD.—See Miura Co., Ltd.; *Int'l*, pg. 884
MIURA SEIKI CO., LTD.—See Miura Co., Ltd.; *Int'l*, pg. 884
MIURA TECHNO CO., LTD.—See Miura Co., Ltd.; *Int'l*, pg. 884
MIURA VIDER CO., LTD.—See Miura Co., Ltd.; *Int'l*, pg. 884
MIX-A-MIX A/S—See Masco Corporation; *U.S. Public*, pg. 1054
MIXIT—See JC Penney Company, Inc.; *U.S. Public*, pg. 917
MIYAKOJIMA MILL—See Nippon Paper Industries Company Limited; *Int'l*, pg. 938
MIYANO MACHINERY, INC.; *U.S. Private*, pg. 754
MIYATA INDUSTRY CO., LTD.; *Int'l*, pg. 884
MIYAZAKI DAISHIN CANON CO., LTD.—See Canon Inc.; *Int'l*, pg. 261
MIYAZAKI OKI ELECTRIC CO., LTD.—See Oki Electric Industry Company, Ltd.; *Int'l*, pg. 999
MIYOTA CO., LTD.—See Citizen Watch Company, Ltd.; *Int'l*, pg. 294
MIZUNO CANADA LIMITED—See Mizuno Corporation; *Int'l*, pg. 885
MIZUNO CORPORATION; *Int'l*, pg. 884
MIZUNO CORPORATION NIEDERLASSUNG DEUTSCHLAND—See Mizuno Corporation; *Int'l*, pg. 885
MIZUNO CORPORATION OF AMERICA—See Mizuno Corporation; *Int'l*, pg. 885
MIZUNO CORPORATION OF HONG KONG LTD.—See Mizuno Corporation; *Int'l*, pg. 885
MIZUNO FINANCE NETHERLANDS B.V.—See Mizuno Corporation; *Int'l*, pg. 885
MIZUNO (FRANCE) S.A.R.L.—See Mizuno Corporation; *Int'l*, pg. 885
MIZUNO GOLF COMPANY—See Mizuno Corporation; *Int'l*, pg. 885
MIZUNO HANDY HARMAN, LTD.—See Handy & Harman; *U.S. Public*, pg. 780
MIZUNO MEXICO USA, INC.—See Mizuno Corporation; *Int'l*, pg. 885
MIZUNO (TAIWAN) CORPORATION—See Mizuno Corporation; *Int'l*, pg. 885
MIZUNO (UK) LTD.—See Mizuno Corporation; *Int'l*, pg. 885
MIZUNO USA, INC.—See Mizuno Corporation; *Int'l*, pg. 885
MIZUSAWA INDUSTRIAL CHEMICALS, LTD.—See Takeda Chemical Industries, Ltd.; *Int'l*, pg. 1350
MIZUSHIMA MOTOR VEHICLE WORKS—See Mitsubishi Motors Corporation; *Int'l*, pg. 875
MIZUSHIMA PLANT—See Mitsubishi Chemical Corporation; *Int'l*, pg. 871
MIZUSHIMA WORKS—See Asahi Chemical Industry Co., Ltd.; *Int'l*, pg. 84
MJOLNIR WHOLESALERS LTD.—See Norske Skogindustrier A.S; *Int'l*, pg. 966
MLP DRUCKMASCHINEN GMBH—See Mitsubishi Heavy Industries Ltd.; *Int'l*, pg. 874
MO-KA SHOE CORP.—See Wellco Enterprises, Inc.; *U.S. Public*, pg. 1752
MO OCH DOMSJO AB; *Int'l*, pg. 885
MOBEL UNGER GMBH—See Metro AG; *Int'l*, pg. 863
MOBIL AMI, S.A.—See Mobil Oil Corporation; *U.S. Public*, pg. 1119
MOBIL CHEMICAL CANADA, LTD.—See Mobil Oil Corporation; *U.S. Public*, pg. 1119
MOBIL DATA SERVICES, LTD.—See Mobil Oil Corporation; *U.S. Public*, pg. 1119
MOBIL ERDGAS-ERDOEL (GMBH)—See Mobil Oil Corporation; *U.S. Public*, pg. 1119
MOBIL EUROPE—See Mobil Oil Corporation; *U.S. Public*, pg. 1119
MOBIL EUROPE, LTD.—See Mobil Oil Corporation; *U.S. Public*, pg. 1119

MOBIL EXPLORATION NORWAY, INC.—See Mobil Oil Corporation; *U.S. Public*, pg. 1119
MOBIL HOLDINGS (EUROPE)—See Mobil Oil Corporation; *U.S. Public*, pg. 1119
MOBIL KABUSHIKI KAISHA—See Mobil Oil Corporation; *U.S. Public*, pg. 1119
MOBIL LAND DEVELOPMENT CORPORATION—See Mobil Oil Corporation; *U.S. Public*, pg. 1118
MOBIL MINING & MINERALS COMPANY—See Mobil Oil Corporation; *U.S. Public*, pg. 1118
MOBIL NORTH SEA LIMITED—See Mobil Oil Corporation; *U.S. Public*, pg. 1119
MOBIL OIL ABU DHABI INC.—See Mobil Oil Corporation; *U.S. Public*, pg. 1119
MOBIL OIL A.G.—See Mobil Oil Corporation; *U.S. Public*, pg. 1119
MOBIL OIL A/S NORGE—See Mobil Oil Corporation; *U.S. Public*, pg. 1119
MOBIL OIL AUSTRALIA LTD.—See Mobil Oil Corporation; *U.S. Public*, pg. 1119
MOBIL OIL AUSTRIA A.G.—See Mobil Oil Corporation; *U.S. Public*, pg. 1119
MOBIL OIL BARBADOS, LTD.—See Mobil Oil Corporation; *U.S. Public*, pg. 1119
MOBIL OIL B.V.—See Mobil Oil Corporation; *U.S. Public*, pg. 1119
MOBIL OIL CANADA, LTD.—See Mobil Oil Corporation; *U.S. Public*, pg. 1119
MOBIL OIL COMPANY, LTD.—See Mobil Oil Corporation; *U.S. Public*, pg. 1119
MOBIL OIL CORPORATION; *U.S. Public*, pg. 1118
MOBIL OIL CYPRUS—See Mobil Oil Corporation; *U.S. Public*, pg. 1119
MOBIL OIL DANMARK A/S—See Mobil Oil Corporation; *U.S. Public*, pg. 1119
MOBIL OIL DE MEXICO S.A.—See Mobil Oil Corporation; *U.S. Public*, pg. 1119
MOBIL OIL DEL PERU (COMPANIA COMMERCIAL) S.A.—See Mobil Oil Corporation; *U.S. Public*, pg. 1119
MOBIL OIL DO BRASIL (INDUSTRIA E COMMERCIO) LTDA.—See Mobil Oil Corporation; *U.S. Public*, pg. 1119
MOBIL OIL EGYPT (S.A.E.)—See Mobil Oil Corporation; *U.S. Public*, pg. 1119
MOBIL OIL ESPANA, S.A.—See Mobil Oil Corporation; *U.S. Public*, pg. 1119
MOBIL OIL FRANCAISE—See Mobil Oil Corporation; *U.S. Public*, pg. 1119
MOBIL OIL GHANA LTD.—See Mobil Oil Corporation; *U.S. Public*, pg. 1119
MOBIL OIL HELLAS A.E. PETROLEUM CO.—See Mobil Oil Corporation; *U.S. Public*, pg. 1119
MOBIL OIL HONG KONG LTD.—See Mobil Oil Corporation; *U.S. Public*, pg. 1119
MOBIL OIL ITALIANA SOCIETA PER AZIONI—See Mobil Oil Corporation; *U.S. Public*, pg. 1119
MOBIL OIL LIBERIA INCORPORATED—See Mobil Oil Corporation; *U.S. Public*, pg. 1119
MOBIL OIL MALAYSIA SENDIRIAN BERHAD—See Mobil Oil Corporation; *U.S. Public*, pg. 1119
MOBIL OIL MICRONESIA, INC.—See Mobil Oil Corporation; *U.S. Public*, pg. 1119
MOBIL OIL NEW ZEALAND LTD.—See Mobil Oil Corporation; *U.S. Public*, pg. 1119
MOBIL OIL NIGERIA LTD.—See Mobil Oil Corporation; *U.S. Public*, pg. 1119
MOBIL OIL OY A.B.—See Mobil Oil Corporation; *U.S. Public*, pg. 1119
MOBIL OIL PORTUGUESA LDA.—See Mobil Oil Corporation; *U.S. Public*, pg. 1119
MOBIL OIL SIERRA LEONE LIMITED—See Mobil Oil Corporation; *U.S. Public*, pg. 1119
MOBIL OIL SINGAPORE PTE. LTD.—See Mobil Oil Corporation; *U.S. Public*, pg. 1119
MOBIL OIL SUDAN LIMITED—See Mobil Oil Corporation; *U.S. Public*, pg. 1119
MOBIL OIL SWITZERLAND—See Mobil Oil Corporation; *U.S. Public*, pg. 1119
MOBIL OIL THAILAND LIMITED—See Mobil Oil Corporation; *U.S. Public*, pg. 1119
MOBIL OIL TURK AS—See Mobil Oil Corporation; *U.S. Public*, pg. 1119
MOBIL OIL ZAMBIA LIMITED—See Mobil Oil Corporation; *U.S. Public*, pg. 1119
MOBIL OIL ZIMBABWE (PRIVATE) LTD.—See Mobil Oil Corporation; *U.S. Public*, pg. 1119
MOBIL PHILIPPINES, INC.—See Mobil Oil Corporation; *U.S. Public*, pg. 1119
MOBIL PIPE LINE COMPANY—See Mobil Oil Corporation; *U.S. Public*, pg. 1118
MOBIL PRODUCING NIGERIA—See Mobil Oil Corporation; *U.S. Public*, pg. 1119
MOBIL RESEARCH AND DEVELOPMENT CORPORATION—See Mobil Oil Corporation; *U.S. Public*, pg. 1119
MOBIL SOLAR ENERGY CORPORATION—See Mobil Oil Corporation; *U.S. Public*, pg. 1119
MOBIL TOOL INTERNATIONAL—See Wassall Plc; *Int'l*, pg. 1486
MOBILE & BIRMINGHAM RAILROAD CO.—See Norfolk Southern Corporation; *U.S. Public*, pg. 1191
MOBILE COMMUNICATIONS CORPORATION OF AMERICA—See MobileComm; *U.S. Public*, pg. 1120
MOBILE COMMUNICATIONS OF FLORIDA, INC.—See Nextel Communications; *U.S. Public*, pg. 1180
MOBILE DATA INTERNATIONAL LIMITED—See Motorola, Inc.; *U.S. Public*, pg. 1139
MOBILE GAS SERVICE CORP.; *U.S. Public*, pg. 1120
MOBILE OIL AB SWEDEN—See Mobil Oil Corporation; *U.S. Public*, pg. 1119
MOBILE OIL INDONESIA, INC.—See Mobil Oil Corporation; *U.S. Public*, pg. 1119
MOBILE PRODUCING NETHERLANDS INCORPORATED—See Mobil Oil Corporation; *U.S. Public*, pg. 1119

MOBILE RADIO OF ILLINOIS, INC.—See Nextel Communications; *U.S. Public*, pg. 1180
MOBILE RADIO PLANNING CORP.—See Motorola, Inc.; *U.S. Public*, pg. 1139
MOBILE-TECH CORP.—See Collins Industries, Inc.; *U.S. Public*, pg. 400
MOBILE TECHNOLOGY INC.; *U.S. Private*, pg. 754
MOBILE TELECOMMUNICATIONS TECHNOLOGIES CORP.; *U.S. Public*, pg. 1120
MOBILECOMM; *U.S. Public*, pg. 1120
MOBILIER INTERNATIONAL—See Haworth, Inc.; *U.S. Private*, pg. 512
MOBIM—See Allianz Aktiengesellschaft; *Int'l*, pg. 61
JOSEF MOBIUS BAU-GESELLSCHAFT (GMBH & CO.)—See Philipp Holzmann AG; *Int'l*, pg. 633
MOBREY AB—See Meggitt plc; *Int'l*, pg. 854
MOBREY SA—See Meggitt plc; *Int'l*, pg. 854
MOBREY SA-NV—See Meggitt plc; *Int'l*, pg. 854
MOCENPLAZA DEVELOPMENT CORPORATION—See Blount International, Inc.; *U.S. Public*, pg. 239
MOCK RESOURCES, INC.—See Wickland Corporation; *U.S. Public*, pg. 1175
MOCK SEED COMPANY—See Seed Corporation of America; *U.S. Private*, pg. 981
MOCON FSC CORPORATION—See Modern Controls, Inc.; *U.S. Public*, pg. 1121
MOD-PAC CORP—See Astronics Corporation; *U.S. Public*, pg. 142
MODAR COMMUNICATIONS, INC.—See Motorola, Inc.; *U.S. Public*, pg. 1137
MODCOMP—See CSP Inc.; *U.S. Public*, pg. 283
MODEL DAIRY—See Suiza Foods Corporation; *U.S. Public*, pg. 1527
MODEL GLASS COMPANY; *U.S. Private*, pg. 754
HENRY MODELL & COMPANY, INC.; *U.S. Private*, pg. 754
MODELLKRAFTWERK VOELKLINGEN GMBH—See Saarbergwerke Aktiengesellschaft; *Int'l*, pg. 1167
MODEM MEDIA HONG KONG—See True North Communications Inc.; *U.S. Public*, pg. 1641
MODEM MEDIA NEW YORK—See True North Communications Inc.; *U.S. Public*, pg. 1641
MODEM MEDIA SAN FRANCISCO—See True North Communications Inc.; *U.S. Public*, pg. 1641
MODEM MEDIA U.K.—See True North Communications Inc.; *U.S. Public*, pg. 1641
MODERN AMERICAN LIFE INSURANCE COMPANY—See I.C.H. Corporation; *U.S. Public*, pg. 633
MODERN-BAU GMBH LEIPZIG—See Bilfinger + Berger Bauaktiengesellschaft; *Int'l*, pg. 195
MODERN BRIDE MAGAZINE—See Primedia Inc.; *U.S. Public*, pg. 1328
MODERN BUILDING CLEANING INC.—See Aramark Corp.; *U.S. Private*, pg. 79
MODERN CONCRETE SEPTIC TANK COMPANY; *U.S. Private*, pg. 754
MODERN CONTROLS, INC.; *U.S. Public*, pg. 1120
MODERN DROP FORGE CO.; *U.S. Private*, pg. 754
MODERN ELECTRONIC ESTABLISHMENT (M.E.E.)—See Hewlett-Packard Company; *U.S. Public*, pg. 822
MODERN ENGINEERING, INC.—See CDI Corp.; *U.S. Public*, pg. 277
MODERN EQUIPMENT CO., INC.—See Alco Industries, Inc.; *U.S. Private*, pg. 33
MODERN EQUIPMENT RENTALS INC.—See Modern Group Ltd.; *U.S. Private*, pg. 754
MODERN FORGE/TENNESSEE—See Modern Drop Forge Co.; *U.S. Private*, pg. 754
MODERN GROUP LTD.; *U.S. Private*, pg. 754
MODERN HAIRDRESSING SUPPLIES (PTY) LTD.—See Wella Group; *Int'l*, pg. 1490
MODERN HANDLING EQUIPMENT CO.—See Modern Group Ltd.; *U.S. Private*, pg. 755
MODERN HANDLING EQUIPMENT OF N.J., INC.—See Modern Group Ltd.; *U.S. Private*, pg. 755
MODERN HEALTHCARE—See Crain Communications, Inc.; *U.S. Private*, pg. 285
MODERN HILIFT EQUIPMENT CO.—See Modern Group Ltd.; *U.S. Private*, pg. 755
MODERN MEDICAL MODALITIES CORP.; *U.S. Public*, pg. 1121
MODERN MERCHANDISING, INC.—See Shaykin & Company; *U.S. Private*, pg. 990
MODERN PACKAGING INDUSTRIES PTE. LTD.—See United Pulp & Paper Company Limited; *Int'l*, pg. 1444
MODERN PLASTICS—See The McGraw-Hill Companies, Inc.; *U.S. Public*, pg. 1071
MODERN PROTOTYPE COMPANY—See CDI Corp.; *U.S. Public*, pg. 277
MODERN PUBLISHING—See Unisystems, Inc.; *U.S. Private*, pg. 1120
MODERN STRUCTURAL PLASTICS LTD.—See Electrolux, AB; *Int'l*, pg. 444
MODERN TECHNOLOGIES—See Modern Group Ltd.; *U.S. Private*, pg. 755
MODERN TIRE DEALER—See VNU Verenigde Nederlandse Uitgeversbedrijven B.V.; *Int'l*, pg. 1446
MODERN WELDING CO., INC.; *U.S. Private*, pg. 755
MODERN WOODMEN OF AMERICA; *U.S. Private*, pg. 755
MODERNBAU GMBH—See Bilfinger + Berger Bauaktiengesellschaft; *Int'l*, pg. 195
MODERNE MECANIQUE SARL—See Carl-Zeiss-Stiftung; *Int'l*, pg. 1523
MODERNFOLD, INC.; *U.S. Private*, pg. 755
THE MODESTO BEE—See McClatchy Newspapers Inc.; *U.S. Public*, pg. 1065
MODI OLIVETTI LTD.—See Olivetti SpA; *Int'l*, pg. 1003
MODINE MANUFACTURING COMPANY; *U.S. Public*, pg. 1121
MODINFORM—See Olivetti SpA; *Int'l*, pg. 1002
MODIPACK BV—See Novartis AG; *Int'l*, pg. 983
MODO DANMARK A/S—See Mo och Domsjo AB; *Int'l*, pg. 887
MODO DATA—See Mo och Domsjo AB; *Int'l*, pg. 886

MODO DISTRIBUTION LTD.—See Mo och Domsjo AB; *Int'l*, pg. 887
MODO IBERICA SA—See Mo och Domsjo AB; *Int'l*, pg. 887
MODO MERCHANTS AB—See Mo och Domsjo AB; *Int'l*, pg. 886
MODO MERCHANTS LTD.—See Mo och Domsjo AB; *Int'l*, pg. 886
MODO PAPER AB—See Mo och Domsjo AB; *Int'l*, pg. 886
MODO PAPER AG—See Mo och Domsjo AB; *Int'l*, pg. 887
MODO PAPER AIPAP—See Mo och Domsjo AB; *Int'l*, pg. 887
MODO PAPER ALICEL—See Mo och Domsjo AB; *Int'l*, pg. 887
MODO PAPER ALIZAY—See Mo och Domsjo AB; *Int'l*, pg. 887
MODO PAPER BENELUX BV—See Mo och Domsjo AB; *Int'l*, pg. 887
MODO PAPER COUPE SERVICE—See Mo och Domsjo AB; *Int'l*, pg. 887
MODO PAPER FRANCE—See Mo och Domsjo AB; *Int'l*, pg. 887
MODO PAPER ITALIA SRL—See Mo och Domsjo AB; *Int'l*, pg. 887
MODO PAPER LTD.—See Mo och Domsjo AB; *Int'l*, pg. 887
MODO PAPER PSM—See Mo och Domsjo AB; *Int'l*, pg. 887
MODO PAPIER BELGIUM—See Mo och Domsjo AB; *Int'l*, pg. 886
MODO RESEARCH & DEVELOPMENT—See Mo och Domsjo AB; *Int'l*, pg. 887
MODO SKOG AB—See Mo och Domsjo AB; *Int'l*, pg. 887
MODO SKOG AB - IGGESUND—See Mo och Domsjo AB; *Int'l*, pg. 887
MODO SKOG AB - LYCKSELE—See Mo och Domsjo AB; *Int'l*, pg. 887
MODO SKOG AB - NORRKOPING—See Mo och Domsjo AB; *Int'l*, pg. 887
MODO SKOG AB - ORNSKOLDSVIK—See Mo och Domsjo AB; *Int'l*, pg. 887
MODO SKOG AB - ROBERTSFORS—See Mo och Domsjo AB; *Int'l*, pg. 887
MODO SKOG AB - STRANGNAS—See Mo och Domsjo AB; *Int'l*, pg. 887
MODO VAN GELDER—See Mo och Domsjo AB; *Int'l*, pg. 886
MODOCELL FRANCE S.A.R.L.—See Mo och Domsjo AB; *Int'l*, pg. 887
MODOCELL ITALIA S.R.L.—See Mo och Domsjo AB; *Int'l*, pg. 887
MODOCELL LTD.—See Mo och Domsjo AB; *Int'l*, pg. 887
MODOLO TECNOLOGIE AVANZATE SRL—See Mannesmann A.G.; *Int'l*, pg. 835
MODTECH, INC.; *U.S. Public*, pg. 1121
MODULAR POWER SYSTEMS—See Transistor Devices, Inc.; *U.S. Private*, pg. 1097
MODULAR SAMCO CO., LTD.—See Siam City Bank Public Company Limited; *Int'l*, pg. 1239
MODULINE INDUSTRIES, INC.—See Champion Enterprises, Inc.; *U.S. Public*, pg. 333
MODULINE INTERNATIONAL, INC.—See Champion Enterprises, Inc.; *U.S. Public*, pg. 333
MODUWALL N.V.—See Arbed S.A.; *Int'l*, pg. 80
I.C. MOELLER A/S—See ABB Asea Brown Boveri (Holding) Ltd.; *Int'l*, pg. 3
MOELLER PRODUCTS CO., INC.; *U.S. Private*, pg. 755
MOEN INCORPORATED—See Fortune Brands, Inc.; *U.S. Public*, pg. 675
MOENUS AG—See Deutsche Babcock AG; *Int'l*, pg. 399
MOET & CHANDON (LONDON) LTD—See LVMH Moet Hennessy Louis Vuitton; *Int'l*, pg. 783
MOET & CHANDON (SUISSE) S.A.—See LVMH Moet Hennessy Louis Vuitton; *Int'l*, pg. 783
MOET-HENNESSY (ASIA) PTE LTD—See LVMH Moet Hennessy Louis Vuitton; *Int'l*, pg. 783
MOET HENNESSY DEUTSCHLAND G.M.B.H.—See LVMH Moet Hennessy Louis Vuitton; *Int'l*, pg. 781
GIE MOET HENNESSY DISTRIBUTION—See LVMH Moet Hennessy Louis Vuitton; *Int'l*, pg. 783
MOFFET, LARSON, & JOHNSON—See The Washington Post Company; *U.S. Public*, pg. 1743
MOGAS INDUSTRIES, INC.; *U.S. Private*, pg. 755
MOGEN DAVID WINE CORP.—See The Wine Group; *U.S. Private*, pg. 1183
MOHAWK/CDT—See Cable Design Technologies Corporation; *U.S. Public*, pg. 287
MOHAWK COMMERCIAL CARPET—See Mohawk Industries, Inc.; *U.S. Public*, pg. 1121
MOHAWK FINISHING PRODUCTS, INC.—See RPM, Inc.; *U.S. Public*, pg. 1357
MOHAWK FLUSH DOORS, INC.—See Premdor Inc.; *Int'l*, pg. 1067
MOHAWK FLUSH DOORS, INC.-COMMERICAL DOOR PLANT—See Premdor Inc.; *Int'l*, pg. 1067
MOHAWK FURNITURE, INC.—See Gem Industries Finance Corporation; *U.S. Private*, pg. 443
MOHAWK INDUSTRIES, INC.; *U.S. Public*, pg. 1121
MOHAWK LABORATORIES DIV.—See NCH Corporation; *U.S. Public*, pg. 1145
MOHAWK MARKETING—See Minolta Co., Ltd.; *Int'l*, pg. 869
MOHAWK MEDIA SUPPLIES PTY. LTD.—See Compagnie des Machines Bull; *Int'l*, pg. 315
MOHAWK PAPER MILLS, INC.; *U.S. Private*, pg. 755
MOHAWK PLASTICS, INC.; *U.S. Private*, pg. 755
MOHAWK PLASTICS, INC.—See Mohawk Plastics, Inc.; *U.S. Private*, pg. 755
MOHICAN MILLS DIVISION—See Fab Industries, Inc.; *U.S. Public*, pg. 603
MOIRS PLANT—See Hershey Foods Corporation; *U.S. Public*, pg. 812
MOJ MIKRO—See International Data Group; *U.S. Private*, pg. 570

MOJAVE PIPELINE COMPANY—See El Paso Natural Gas Co.; *U.S. Public*, pg. 567
MOJONNIER DE MEXICO, S DE R.L. DE C.V.—See SASIB SpA; *Int'l*, pg. 1194
MOJONNIER DO BRASIL INDUSTRIA E COMMERCIO DE EQUIPAMENTOS LTDA.—See SASIB SpA; *Int'l*, pg. 1194
MOKON—See Mark IV Industries Inc.; *U.S. Public*, pg. 1045
MOLD-TECH—See Standex International Corporation; *U.S. Public*, pg. 1506
MOLD-TECH PORTUGAL—See Standex International Corporation; *U.S. Public*, pg. 1507
MOLD-TECH S.A.—See Standex International Corporation; *U.S. Public*, pg. 1507
MOLD-TECH S.A.R.L.—See Standex International Corporation; *U.S. Public*, pg. 1507
MOLDED FIBER GLASS COMPANIES; *U.S. Private*, pg. 755
MOLDED FIBER GLASS/WEST—See Molded Fiber Glass Companies; *U.S. Private*, pg. 756
MOLDED FIBER/NORTH CAROLINA—See Molded Fiber Glass Companies; *U.S. Private*, pg. 756
MOLDING COMPOUNDS SPA—See Alusuisse-Lonza Holding Ltd.; *Int'l*, pg. 69
MOLECULAR PACKAGING SYSTEMS, INC.—See IGI, Inc.; *U.S. Public*, pg. 855
MOLETT MARKETING—See American Israeli Paper Mills Ltd.; *Int'l*, pg. 75
MOLEX—See Molex Incorporated; *U.S. Public*, pg. 1122
MOLEX ALIN INTERNATIONAL INCORPORATED—See Molex Incorporated; *U.S. Public*, pg. 1122
MOLEX (BENELUX) B.V.—See Molex Incorporated; *U.S. Public*, pg. 1122
MOLEX CARIBE—See Molex Incorporated; *U.S. Public*, pg. 1122
MOLEX CHINA—See Molex Incorporated; *U.S. Public*, pg. 1123
MOLEX DE MEXICO S.A. DE C.V.—See Molex Incorporated; *U.S. Public*, pg. 1122
MOLEX EASTERN EUROPE S.A.—See Molex Incorporated; *U.S. Public*, pg. 1122
MOLEX ELECTRICAL SYSTEMS INC.—See Molex Incorporated; *U.S. Public*, pg. 1122
MOLEX ELECTRONICS LTD.—See Molex Incorporated; *U.S. Public*, pg. 1122
MOLEX ELEKTRONIK GMBH—See Molex Incorporated; *U.S. Public*, pg. 1122
MOLEX ELETRONICA LTDA.—See Molex Incorporated; *U.S. Public*, pg. 1122
MOLEX ELETTRONICA S.R.L.—See Molex Incorporated; *U.S. Public*, pg. 1122
MOLEX FAR EAST MANAGEMENT LTD. (NORTH)—See Molex Incorporated; *U.S. Public*, pg. 1122
MOLEX FIBER OPTIC INC.—See Molex Incorporated; *U.S. Public*, pg. 1122
MOLEX FRANCE S.A.R.L.—See Molex Incorporated; *U.S. Public*, pg. 1122
MOLEX-G. KNUTSEN A/S—See Molex Incorporated; *U.S. Public*, pg. 1122
MOLEX-G. OSTERVIG A/S—See Molex Incorporated; *U.S. Public*, pg. 1122
MOLEX GMBH—See Molex Incorporated; *U.S. Public*, pg. 1122
MOLEX INCORPORATED; *U.S. Public*, pg. 1121
MOLEX INDIA LTD.—See Molex Incorporated; *U.S. Public*, pg. 1122
MOLEX INTERNATIONAL, INC.—See Molex Incorporated; *U.S. Public*, pg. 1122
MOLEX IRELAND LTD.—See Molex Incorporated; *U.S. Public*, pg. 1122
MOLEX ITALIA S.P.A.—See Molex Incorporated; *U.S. Public*, pg. 1122
MOLEX-JAPAN CO., LTD.—See Molex Incorporated; *U.S. Public*, pg. 1122
MOLEX KOREA CO., LTD.—See Molex Incorporated; *U.S. Public*, pg. 1122
MOLEX LTD.—See Molex Incorporated; *U.S. Public*, pg. 1122
MOLEX (MALAYSIA) SND. BHD.—See Molex Incorporated; *U.S. Public*, pg. 1122
MOLEX OVERSEAS INC. DBA MOLEX ESPANA—See Molex Incorporated; *U.S. Public*, pg. 1122
MOLEX S.A. DE C.V.—See Molex Incorporated; *U.S. Public*, pg. 1122
MOLEX SERVICES GMBH—See Molex Incorporated; *U.S. Public*, pg. 1122
MOLEX SINGAPORE PTE. LTD.—See Molex Incorporated; *U.S. Public*, pg. 1122
MOLEX SVENSKA A.B.—See Molex Incorporated; *U.S. Public*, pg. 1123
MOLEX TAIWAN LTD.—See Molex Incorporated; *U.S. Public*, pg. 1123
MOLEX (THAILAND) LTD.—See Molex Incorporated; *U.S. Public*, pg. 1123
MOLEX US INC.—See Molex Incorporated; *U.S. Public*, pg. 1122
MOLIN AUTO PARTS INC.; *U.S. Private*, pg. 756
MOLINAS DE PUERTO RICO—See ConAgra, Inc.; *U.S. Public*, pg. 426
MOLINE ACCESSORIES COMPANY—See Kone Corporation; *Int'l*, pg. 746
MOLINE ACCESSORIES CORPORATION—See Kone Corporation; *Int'l*, pg. 746
MOLINOS CARACAS MARACAIBO S.A.—See Diageo Plc; *Int'l*, pg. 411
MOLINOS DEL SUDESTE, S.A. DE C.V.—See Tablex, S.A. de C.V.; *Int'l*, pg. 1346
MOLINOS EL SALVADOR, S.A.—See Diageo Plc; *Int'l*, pg. 411
MOLINOS MODERNOS, S.A.—See Diageo Plc; *Int'l*, pg. 411
MOLINOS NACIONALES, C.A. (VENEZUELA)—See International Multifoods Corporation; *U.S. Public*, pg. 901

MOLLENBERG-BETZ INC.; *U.S. Private*, pg. 756
MOLLER REISEBURO—See Fried. Krupp AG; *Int'l*, pg. 515
MOLNLYCKE AB—See Svenska Cellulosa Aktiebolaget (SCA); *Int'l*, pg. 1326
MOLOKAI RANCH LTD.—See Brierley Investments Limited; *Int'l*, pg. 216
MOLON MOTOR & COIL CORP.; *U.S. Private*, pg. 756
MOLOVENCA—See Pechiney S.A.; *Int'l*, pg. 1031
MOLSON ALBERTA BREWERY LTD.—See The Molson Companies Limited; *Int'l*, pg. 887
MOLSON BREWERIES—See The Molson Companies Limited; *Int'l*, pg. 887
MOLSON BREWERIES U.S.A. INC.—See Philip Morris Companies Inc.; *U.S. Public*, pg. 1289
MOLSON BREWERY B.C. LTD.—See The Molson Companies Limited; *Int'l*, pg. 887
MOLSON BREWERY QUEBEC LIMITED—See The Molson Companies Limited; *Int'l*, pg. 887
THE MOLSON COMPANIES LIMITED, *Int'l*, pg. 887
MOLSON SASKATCHEWAN BREWERY LTD.—See The Molson Companies Limited; *Int'l*, pg. 887
MOLSON SPORTS AND ENTERTAINMENT—See The Molson Companies Limited; *Int'l*, pg. 887
MOLTEN METAL TECHNOLOGY, INC.; *U.S. Public*, pg. 1123
MOLTO AG—See Williams Holdings Plc; *Int'l*, pg. 1501
MOLTO GES.M.B.H.—See Williams Holdings Plc; *Int'l*, pg. 1501
MOLTO GMBH—See Williams Holdings Plc; *Int'l*, pg. 1501
MOLTRUP STEEL PRODUCTS COMPANY, *U.S. Private*, pg. 756
MOLY-COP CANADA—See Stelco Inc.; *Int'l*, pg. 1300
MOLYCORP, INC.—See Unocal Corporation; *U.S. Public*, pg. 1698
MOMENTUM—See PrimeSource Corporation; *U.S. Public*, pg. 1329
MOMENTUM INC.—See The Macneal-Schwendler Corp.; *U.S. Public*, pg. 1032
MOMO S.P.A.—See Breed Technologies, Inc.; *U.S. Public*, pg. 251
MON RIVER TOWING INC.—See The Guttman Group; *U.S. Private*, pg. 489
MONA—See Campina Melkunie BV; *Int'l*, pg. 254
MONA INDUSTRIES, INC.; *U.S. Private*, pg. 756
MONA SPOL. SR.O.—See VNU Verenigde Nederlandse Uitgeversbedrijven B.V.; *Int'l*, pg. 1445
MONACHIA GRUNDSTUCKS-AKTIENGESELLSCHAFT—See Hochtief AG; *Int'l*, pg. 623
MONACO COACH CORPORATION; *U.S. Public*, pg. 1123
MONACO COACH CORPORATION—See Monaco Coach Corporation; *U.S. Public*, pg. 1123
THE MONAHAN COMPANY; *U.S. Private*, pg. 756
MONARCH AVALON, INC.; *U.S. Public*, pg. 1123
MONARCH CEMENT CO.; *U.S. Public*, pg. 1123
THE MONARCH COMPANY, INC.; *U.S. Private*, pg. 756
MONARCH CONSTRUCTION COMPANY; *U.S. Private*, pg. 757
MONARCH CONSTRUCTION LTD.—See Taylor Woodrow plc; *Int'l*, pg. 1359
MONARCH CORTLAND DIV.—See The Monarch Machine Tool Company; *U.S. Public*, pg. 1124
MONARCH CROWN CORPORATION—See Bristol-Myers Squibb Company; *U.S. Public*, pg. 254
MONARCH DEVELOPMENT CORPORATION—See Taylor Woodrow plc; *Int'l*, pg. 1359
THE MONARCH GROUP—See Taylor Woodrow plc; *Int'l*, pg. 1359
MONARCH HOMES INC.—See George Wimpey PLC; *Int'l*, pg. 1510
MONARCH INDUSTRIES, INC.—See Avery Dennison Corporation; *U.S. Public*, pg. 153
MONARCH INSURANCE COMPANY—See Cigna Corp.; *U.S. Public*, pg. 363
MONARCH LUGGAGE CO. INC.; *U.S. Private*, pg. 757
THE MONARCH MACHINE TOOL COMPANY; *U.S. Public*, pg. 1123
MONARCH MARKING SYSTEMS—See PAXAR Corporation; *U.S. Public*, pg. 1266
MONARCH TILE, INC.—See Cravey, Green & Wahlen, Incorporated; *U.S. Private*, pg. 287
MONARCH WETKZENGMASCHINEN GMBH—See The Monarch Machine Tool Company; *U.S. Public*, pg. 1124
MONARK EGG CORPORATION—See Michael Foods, Inc.; *U.S. Public*, pg. 1104
MONAS FEED CV AB—See Raisio Group; *Int'l*, pg. 1085
MONAVAL FINANZ AG—See ABN-AMRO Holding N.V.; *Int'l*, pg. 12
ARNOLDO MONDADORI EDITORE S.P.A.; *Int'l*, pg. 887
MONDADORI DE AGOSTINI LIBRI S.P.A.—See Arnoldo Mondadori Editore S.p.A.; *Int'l*, pg. 888
MONDADORI FACTOR S.P.A.—See Arnoldo Mondadori Editore S.p.A.; *Int'l*, pg. 888
MONDADORI INFORMATICA S.P.A.—See Arnoldo Mondadori Editore S.p.A.; *Int'l*, pg. 888
MONDADORI LEASING S.P.A.—See Arnoldo Mondadori Editore S.p.A.; *Int'l*, pg. 888
MONDADORI PUBBLICITA S.P.A.—See Arnoldo Mondadori Editore S.p.A.; *Int'l*, pg. 888
MONDAWMIN CORPORATION—See The Rouse Company; *U.S. Public*, pg. 1407
MONDI FOODS BELGIUM NV—See The Albert Fisher Group PLC; *Int'l*, pg. 491
MONDIALCINE S.P.A.—See Bastogi-S.p.A.; *Int'l*, pg. 170
MONENCO AGRA TECHMASTER LTD.—See Agra Inc.; *Int'l*, pg. 31
MONENCO IRAN—See Agra Inc.; *Int'l*, pg. 31
MONENCO NIGERIA LIMITED—See Agra Inc.; *Int'l*, pg. 31
THE MONET GROUP, INC.; *U.S. Private*, pg. 757
MONET JEWELERS—See The Monet Group, Inc.; *U.S. Private*, pg. 757
MONEX DEPOSIT CO.; *U.S. Private*, pg. 757
MONEY—See Time Warner Inc.; *U.S. Public*, pg. 1613
MONEY MAGAZINE LIMITED—See The Reader's Digest Association, Inc.; *U.S. Public*, pg. 1368

MONEY MANAGEMENT SYSTEMS, INC.—See SunGard Data Systems Inc.; *U.S. Public*, pg. 1535
MONEY MARKET DIRECTORIES—See The McGraw-Hill Companies; *U.S. Public*, pg. 1071
MONEY POINT DIAMOND CO.; *U.S. Private*, pg. 757
THE MONEY STORE; *U.S. Public*, pg. 1124
MONFORT, INC.—See ConAgra, Inc.; *U.S. Public*, pg. 427
MONIBEL NV—See The Albert Fisher Group PLC; *Int'l*, pg. 491
MONICO ALLOYS, INC.; *U.S. Private*, pg. 757
MONIDATA VOF—See KPN Koninklyke PTT Nederland NV; *Int'l*, pg. 720
MONIER INC.—See Redland PLC; *Int'l*, pg. 1091
P.T. MONIER INDONESIA—See Redland PLC; *Int'l*, pg. 1091
THE MONITOR—See Freedom Communication Inc.; *U.S. Private*, pg. 425
MONITOR AEROSPACE CORPORATION; *U.S. Private*, pg. 757
MONITOR CAPITAL ADVISORS INC.—See New York Life Insurance Company; *U.S. Private*, pg. 795
MONITOR DYNAMICS INC.—See Ultrak Inc.; *U.S. Public*, pg. 1663
MONITOR LIABILITY MANAGERS, INC.—See W.R. Berkley Corporation; *U.S. Public*, pg. 215
MONITOR LIFE INSURANCE COMPANY OF NEW YORK—See Commercial Travelers Mutual Insurance Company; *U.S. Private*, pg. 258
MONITOR MAGAZINE—See International Data Group; *U.S. Private*, pg. 570
MONITOR PRODUCTS COMPANY INC.—See Bowthorpe plc; *Int'l*, pg. 208
MONITOR SURETY MANAGERS, INC.—See W.R. Berkley Corporation; *U.S. Public*, pg. 215
MONK BRIDGE DIVISION—See Inco Limited; *Int'l*, pg. 673
MONKEYHAUS DESIGN—See Hadeler Sullivan Ewing; *U.S. Private*, pg. 493
MONMER FOUNDRY LIMITED—See Delta plc; *Int'l*, pg. 390
MONMOUTH PHARMACEUTICAL, LTD.—See Roberts Pharmaceutical Corporation; *U.S. Public*, pg. 1394
MONNICH GMBH & CO. KG—See Sudzucker AG Mannheim/Ochsenfurt; *Int'l*, pg. 1305
MONNOYEUR SCA; *Int'l*, pg. 888
MONO POWER COMPANY—See Edison International; *U.S. Public*, pg. 564
MONO PUMPS LTD.—See Dresser Industries, Inc.; *U.S. Public*, pg. 529
MONOCHEM, INC.—See Borden, Inc.; *U.S. Private*, pg. 158
MONOFORT—See Saint-Gobain; *Int'l*, pg. 1177
MONOGRAM AEROSPACE FASTENERS, INC.—See Masco Corporation; *U.S. Public*, pg. 1054
MONOLITH ENTERPRISES, INC.—See W.R. Grace & Co.; *U.S. Public*, pg. 755
MONOMET LIMITED—See RMC Group p.l.c.; *Int'l*, pg. 1079
MONONGAHELA POWER CO.—See Allegheny Power System, Inc.; *U.S. Public*, pg. 42
MONOPOLY INTERNATIONAL S.A.—See Warwick Baker O'Neill; *U.S. Private*, pg. 1152
MONOPTEROS WERBEAGENTUR GMBH—See Dyckerhoff & Widmann AG; *Int'l*, pg. 423
MONORAIL, INC.—See Columbian Rope Company; *U.S. Private*, pg. 256
MONRO MUFFLER/BRAKE, INC.; *U.S. Public*, pg. 1124
MONROC, INC.; *U.S. Public*, pg. 1124
MONROE AUTO EQUIPMENT CO.—See Tenneco Inc.; *U.S. Public*, pg. 1577
MONROE AUTO PECAS S.A.—See Tenneco Inc.; *U.S. Public*, pg. 1580
MONROE CABLEVISION INC.—See Blade Communications, Inc.; *U.S. Private*, pg. 147
MONROE CITY DIVISION—See Leggett & Platt, Incorporated; *U.S. Public*, pg. 986
MONROE COUNTY TELEPHONE CO.—See Century Telephone Enterprises, Inc.; *U.S. Public*, pg. 330
MONROE FORGINGS INC.—See Firth-Rixson Plc; *Int'l*, pg. 488
MONROE HARDWARE CO.—See Distribution America; *U.S. Private*, pg. 335
MONROE LITHO INC.—See Wallace Computer Services, Inc.; *U.S. Public*, pg. 1736
MONROE PROPERTIES, INC.—See National Commerce Bancorporation; *U.S. Public*, pg. 1155
MONROE SYSTEMS FOR BUSINESS, INC.; *U.S. Private*, pg. 757
MONROVIA NURSERY CO.; *U.S. Private*, pg. 757
MONSANTO A/S—See Monsanto Company; *U.S. Public*, pg. 1125
MONSANTO B.V.—See Monsanto Company; *U.S. Public*, pg. 1125
MONSANTO CANADA, INC.—See Monsanto Company; *U.S. Public*, pg. 1125
MONSANTO CHEMICAL PRODUCTS HELLAS, E.P.E.—See Monsanto Company; *U.S. Public*, pg. 1125
MONSANTO CHEMICALS OF INDIA LIMITED—See Monsanto Company; *U.S. Public*, pg. 1125
MONSANTO COMMERCIAL, S.A. DE C.V.—See Monsanto Company; *U.S. Public*, pg. 1125
MONSANTO COMPANY; *U.S. Public*, pg. 1124
MONSANTO DE COSTA RICA, S.A.—See Monsanto Company; *U.S. Public*, pg. 1125
MONSANTO (DEUTSCHLAND) GMBH—See Monsanto Company; *U.S. Public*, pg. 1125
MONSANTO DO BRASIL LTDA. (MOBRA S.A.)—See Monsanto Company; *U.S. Public*, pg. 1125
MONSANTO ENVIRO-CHEM SYSTEMS, INC.—See Monsanto Company; *U.S. Public*, pg. 1125
MONSANTO ENVIRONMENTAL HEALTH REDEVELOPMENT CORP.—See Monsanto Company; *U.S. Public*, pg. 1125
MONSANTO ESPANA S.A.—See Monsanto Company; *U.S. Public*, pg. 1125

MONSANTO EUROPE S.A.—See Monsanto Company; *U.S. Public*, pg. 1125
MONSANTO EXPORT LIMITED—See Monsanto Company; *U.S. Public*, pg. 1125
MONSANTO FAR EAST LTD.—See Monsanto Company; *U.S. Public*, pg. 1125
MONSANTO FINANCE AG—See Monsanto Company; *U.S. Public*, pg. 1125
MONSANTO GMBH—See Monsanto Company; *U.S. Public*, pg. 1125
MONSANTO IRELAND LTD.—See Monsanto Company; *U.S. Public*, pg. 1125
MONSANTO ITALIANA S.P.A.—See Monsanto Company; *U.S. Public*, pg. 1125
MONSANTO JAPAN LTD.—See Monsanto Company; *U.S. Public*, pg. 1126
MONSANTO (MALAYSIA) SENDIRIAN BERHAD—See Monsanto Company; *U.S. Public*, pg. 1126
MONSANTO NEW ZEALAND, LTD.—See Monsanto Company; *U.S. Public*, pg. 1126
MONSANTO NORGE A/S—See Monsanto Company; *U.S. Public*, pg. 1126
MONSANTO OVERSEAS, S.A.—See Monsanto Company; *U.S. Public*, pg. 1126
MONSANTO OY—See Monsanto Company; *U.S. Public*, pg. 1126
MONSANTO PHILIPPINES INC.—See Monsanto Company; *U.S. Public*, pg. 1126
MONSANTO P.L.C.—See Monsanto Company; *U.S. Public*, pg. 1126
MONSANTO (SCANDINAVIA) AB—See Monsanto Company; *U.S. Public*, pg. 1126
MONSANTO SINGAPORE COMPANY (PTE.) LTD.—See Monsanto Company; *U.S. Public*, pg. 1126
MONSANTO SOUTH AFRICA (PTY.) LIMITED—See Monsanto Company; *U.S. Public*, pg. 1126
MONSANTO (SUISSE) S.A.—See Monsanto Company; *U.S. Public*, pg. 1126
MONSANTO THAILAND LTD.—See Monsanto Company; *U.S. Public*, pg. 1126
MONSANTO (VENEZUELA) C.A.—See Monsanto Company; *U.S. Public*, pg. 1126
MONSERCO LIMITED—See Nycomed Amersham plc; *Int'l*, pg. 993
MONSEY-BAKOR; *U.S. Private*, pg. 757
MONSON TRUCKING, INC.; *U.S. Private*, pg. 758
MONT BELVIEU LAND COMPANY—See Tenneco Inc.; *U.S. Public*, pg. 1578
MONT BELVIEU OPERATIONS—See Ultramar Diamond Shamrock Corporation; *U.S. Public*, pg. 1663
MONT TREMBLANT RESORT, INC.—See Intrawest Corporation; *Int'l*, pg. 685
F.G. MONTABERT; *U.S. Private*, pg. 758
MONTAGU MANAGEMENT SERVICES (JERSEY) LIMITED—See HSBC Holdings plc; *Int'l*, pg. 580
MONTAGU NOMINEES (JERSEY) LIMITED—See HSBC Holdings plc; *Int'l*, pg. 580
SAMUEL MONTAGU & CO. LIMITED—See HSBC Holdings plc; *Int'l*, pg. 580
MONTAGUE MOULDERS PTY. LTD.—See Q.U.F. Industries Ltd.; *Int'l*, pg. 1074
MONTAIR ANDERSEN B.V.—See Crown Andersen Inc.; *U.S. Public*, pg. 462
MONTAL (INSURANCE) LIMITED—See Monsanto Company; *U.S. Public*, pg. 1126
MONTAN-ENTSORGUNG GMBH & CO.—See Veba AG; *Int'l*, pg. 1457
MONTAN GESELLSCHAFT WARENHANDEL MBH—See BASF AG; *Int'l*, pg. 104
MONTANA BAUSYSTEME AG—See Koninklijke Hoogovens N.V.; *Int'l*, pg. 754
MONTANA-DAKOTA UTILITIES CO.—See MDU Resources Group, Inc.; *U.S. Public*, pg. 1025
MONTANA MINERALS DEVELOPMENT CORP.—See AMCOL International Corp.; *U.S. Public*, pg. 64
MONTANA PARTICIPACOES LIMITADA—See Montana Power Company; *U.S. Public*, pg. 1127
MONTANA POWER COMPANY; *U.S. Public*, pg. 1126
MONTANA REFINING CO.—See Holly Corporation; *U.S. Public*, pg. 830
THE MONTANA STANDARD—See Lee Enterprises, Incorporated; *U.S. Public*, pg. 984
MONTANA SUN, INC.—See Energy West Inc.; *U.S. Public*, pg. 581
MONTANA TUNNELS MINING, INC.—See Pegasus Gold Corporation; *U.S. Public*, pg. 1269
MONTAUK—See DQE Inc.; *U.S. Public*, pg. 474
MONTAUP ELECTRIC CO.—See Eastern Utilities Associates; *U.S. Public*, pg. 550
MONTE GENEROSO RAILWAY AG—See Migros; *Int'l*, pg. 866
MONTE VISTA CO-OP ASSOCIATION, INC.; *U.S. Private*, pg. 758
MONTEBELLO BRANDS INC.; *U.S. Private*, pg. 758
MONTEDISON S.P.A.—See Compart SpA; *Int'l*, pg. 324
MONTEITH TRAVEL SERVICES LTD—See George Wimpey PLC; *Int'l*, pg. 1510
MONTEK DIV.—See Raytheon Company; *U.S. Public*, pg. 1366
MONTELL POLYOLEFINS—See Royal Dutch/Shell Group of Companies; *Int'l*, pg. 1136
MONTEPOLIMERI BELGIO S.A.—See ENI S.p.A.; *Int'l*, pg. 429
MONTEREY CONSTRUCTION COMPANY—See Atkinson; *U.S. Public*, pg. 143
MONTEREY KELP CORP.—See Monsanto Company; *U.S. Public*, pg. 1126
MONTEREY MANAGEMENT B.V.—See Banque Generale du Luxembourg SA; *Int'l*, pg. 162
MONTEREY MECHANICAL COMPANY; *U.S. Private*, pg. 758
MONTEREY MUSHROOMS, INC.; *U.S. Private*, pg. 758
MONTEREY NURSING CENTER—See Paragon Health Network, Inc.; *U.S. Public*, pg. 1257

MONTEREY'S ACQUISITION CORP.—See Monterey's Acquisition Corporation; *U.S. Private*, pg. 758
MONTEREY'S ACQUISITION CORPORATION; *U.S. Private*, pg. 758
BOB MONTGOMERY CHEVROLET/HONDA; *U.S. Private*, pg. 758
MONTGOMERY & COLLINS, INC.—See Cigna Corp.; *U.S. Public*, pg. 366
MONTGOMERY ELEVATOR EXPORT CORPORATION—See Kone Corporation; *Int'l*, pg. 746
MONTGOMERY ELEVATOR INTERNATIONAL COMPANY—See Kone Corporation; *Int'l*, pg. 746
MONTGOMERY KONE ELEVATOR CO. LTD.—See Kone Corporation; *Int'l*, pg. 748
MONTGOMERY KONE INC.—See Kone Corporation; *Int'l*, pg. 746
MONTGOMERY ST. INCOME SECURITIES, INC.; *U.S. Public*, pg. 1127
MONTGOMERY SURGERY CENTER—See Healthsouth Corporation; *U.S. Private*, pg. 803
MONTGOMERY TANK LINES, INC.—See MTL Inc.; *U.S. Public*, pg. 1028
MONTGOMERY WARD & CO., INC.; *U.S. Public*, pg. 758
MONTGOMERY WARD DIRECT—See Fingerhut Corp.; *U.S. Public*, pg. 623
MONTGOMERY WATSON; *U.S. Private*, pg. 759
MONTI NV—See Esselte AB; *Int'l*, pg. 888
MONTICELLO BANK—See The Monticello Companies, Inc.; *U.S. Private*, pg. 759
THE MONTICELLO COMPANIES, INC.; *U.S. Private*, pg. 759
MONTICELLO DRUG CO.—See The Monticello Companies, Inc.; *U.S. Private*, pg. 759
MONTICELLO EXCHANGER & MANUFACTURING—See Bryan Steam Corporation; *U.S. Private*, pg. 176
MONTICELLO MANAGEMENT CO.; *U.S. Private*, pg. 759
MONTICELLO PLANT—See Belden Inc.; *U.S. Public*, pg. 201
MONTIVO KFT—See Imatran Voima Oy; *Int'l*, pg. 660
MONTOI MATTEL TOYS—See Mattel, Inc.; *U.S. Public*, pg. 1058
MONTOI S.A. DE C.V.—See Mattel, Inc.; *U.S. Public*, pg. 1059
MONTOUR BANK—See Omega Financial Corporation; *U.S. Public*, pg. 1222
MONTREAL FAST PRINT—See American Fast Print, Limited; *U.S. Private*, pg. 54
MONTREAL LEARNING CENTER—See Berkshire Hathaway Inc.; *U.S. Public*, pg. 219
MONTREAL OFFICE—See Fort James Corporation; *U.S. Public*, pg. 672
MONTREAL PORT CORPORATION—See Canada Ports Corporation; *Int'l*, pg. 255
MONTREAL TRUSTCO—See The Bank of Nova Scotia; *Int'l*, pg. 155
MONTREAL TRUSTCO-CORPORATE SERVICES DIV.—See The Bank of Nova Scotia; *Int'l*, pg. 155
MONTREAL TRUSTCO-FINANCIAL OPERATIONS & CONTROL DIV.—See The Bank of Nova Scotia; *Int'l*, pg. 155
MONTREAL TRUSTCO INVESTMENT MANAGEMENT SERVICES—See The Bank of Nova Scotia; *Int'l*, pg. 155
MONTREAL TRUSTCO-PERSONAL SERVICES DIVISION—See The Bank of Nova Scotia; *Int'l*, pg. 155
MONTRES MOVADO, S.A.—See Movado Group, Inc.; *U.S. Public*, pg. 1140
MONTROSE BAY HEALTH CARE CENTER—See Paragon Health Network, Inc.; *U.S. Private*, pg. 1257
MONTROSE/CDT—See Cable Design Technologies Corporation; *U.S. Public*, pg. 287
MONTROSSE CROSSING INC.—See Giant Food Inc.; *U.S. Public*, pg. 741
MONTRUSCO ASSOCIATES, INC.; *Int'l*, pg. 888
MONTRUSCO ASSOCIATES—See Montrusco Associates, Inc.; *Int'l*, pg. 888
MONUMENTAL GENERAL ADMINISTRATORS, INC.—See AEGON N.V.; *Int'l*, pg. 27
MONUMENTAL GENERAL CASUALTY COMPANY—See AEGON N.V.; *Int'l*, pg. 27
MONUMENTAL GENERAL INSURANCE COMPANY—See AEGON N.V.; *Int'l*, pg. 27
MONUMENTAL GENERAL INSURANCE GROUP, INC.—See AEGON N.V.; *Int'l*, pg. 27
MONUMENTAL GENERAL MASS MARKETING, INC.—See AEGON N.V.; *Int'l*, pg. 27
MONUMENTAL LIFE INSURANCE COMPANY—See AEGON N.V.; *Int'l*, pg. 27
MONUMENTAL MILLWORK, INC.; *U.S. Private*, pg. 759
MONY ADVISERS, INC.—See The Mutual Life Insurance Company of New York; *U.S. Private*, pg. 769
MONY BROKERAGE, INC.—See The Mutual Life Insurance Company of New York; *U.S. Private*, pg. 769
MONY CREDIT CORPORATION—See The Mutual Life Insurance Company of New York; *U.S. Private*, pg. 769
MONY FUNDING, INC.—See The Mutual Life Insurance Company of New York; *U.S. Private*, pg. 769
MONY LIFE INSURANCE CO. OF AMERICA—See The Mutual Life Insurance Company of New York; *U.S. Private*, pg. 769
MONY REALTY PARTNERS, INC.—See The Mutual Life Insurance Company of New York; *U.S. Private*, pg. 769
MONY SECURITIES CORP.—See The Mutual Life Insurance Company of New York; *U.S. Private*, pg. 769
MONY VENTURES, INC.—See The Mutual Life Insurance Company of New York; *U.S. Private*, pg. 769
MONZINO S.P.A.; *Int'l*, pg. 888
M.D. MOODY & SONS INC.; *U.S. Private*, pg. 759
MOODY'S AMERICA LATINA LTDA.—See The Dun & Bradstreet Corporation; *U.S. Public*, pg. 537
MOODY'S ASIA PACIFIC, LTD.—See The Dun & Bradstreet Corporation; *U.S. Public*, pg. 537
MOODY'S CANADA INC.—See The Dun & Bradstreet Corporation; *U.S. Public*, pg. 537

MOODY'S DEUTSCHLAND GMBH—See The Dun & Bradstreet Corporation; *U.S. Public*, pg. 537
MOODY'S FIS—See The Dun & Bradstreet Corporation; *U.S. Public*, pg. 536
MOODY'S FRANCE S.A.—See The Dun & Bradstreet Corporation; *U.S. Public*, pg. 537
MOODY'S INTERBANK CREDIT SERVICE LTD.—See The Dun & Bradstreet Corporation; *U.S. Public*, pg. 537
MOODY'S INVESTORS SERVICE ESPANA, S.A.—See The Dun & Bradstreet Corporation; *U.S. Public*, pg. 537
MOODY'S INVESTORS SERVICE, INC.—See The Dun & Bradstreet Corporation; *U.S. Public*, pg. 537
MOODY'S JAPAN KK—See The Dun & Bradstreet Corporation; *U.S. Public*, pg. 537
MOODY'S SINGAPORE PTE. LTD.—See The Dun & Bradstreet Corporation; *U.S. Public*, pg. 537
MOOG AIRCRAFT CONTROLS DIV.—See Moog Incorporated; *U.S. Public*, pg. 1127
MOOG AUSTRALIA PTY. LTD.—See Moog Incorporated; *U.S. Public*, pg. 1127
MOOG AUTOMOTIVE, INC.—See Cooper Industries, Inc.; *U.S. Public*, pg. 443
MOOG BUHL AUTOMATION—See Moog Incorporated; *U.S. Public*, pg. 1128
MOOG CONTROLS CORP.—See Moog Incorporated; *U.S. Public*, pg. 1128
MOOG CONTROLS (HONG KONG) LTD.—See Moog Incorporated; *U.S. Public*, pg. 1128
MOOG CONTROLS LTD.—See Moog Incorporated; *U.S. Public*, pg. 1128
MOOG DO BRASIL—See Moog Incorporated; *U.S. Public*, pg. 1128
MOOG ENGINE CONTROLS DIV.—See Moog Incorporated; *U.S. Public*, pg. 1127
MOOG GMBH—See Moog Incorporated; *U.S. Public*, pg. 1127
MOOG INCORPORATED; *U.S. Public*, pg. 1127
MOOG INDUSTRIAL CONTROLS CORP.—See Moog Incorporated; *U.S. Public*, pg. 1127
MOOG INTERNATIONAL GROUP—See Moog Incorporated; *U.S. Public*, pg. 1127
MOOG ITALIANA (SRL)—See Moog Incorporated; *U.S. Public*, pg. 1128
MOOG JAPAN LTD.—See Moog Incorporated; *U.S. Public*, pg. 1128
MOOG KOREA—See Moog Incorporated; *U.S. Public*, pg. 1128
MOOG LTD.—See Moog Incorporated; *U.S. Public*, pg. 1128
MOOG MOTION SYSTEMS DIV.—See Moog Incorporated; *U.S. Public*, pg. 1127
MOOG NORDEN AB—See Moog Incorporated; *U.S. Public*, pg. 1128
MOOG S.A.R.L.—See Moog Incorporated; *U.S. Public*, pg. 1128
MOOG SINGAPORE PTE LTD.—See Moog Incorporated; *U.S. Public*, pg. 1128
MOOG SPACE PRODUCTS DIV.—See Moog Incorporated; *U.S. Public*, pg. 1127
MOOG SPAIN—See Moog Incorporated; *U.S. Public*, pg. 1128
MOOG TORRANCE—See Moog Incorporated; *U.S. Public*, pg. 1127
MOON VALLEY COUNTRY CLUB—See Karsten Manufacturing Corporation; *U.S. Private*, pg. 608
MOONEY AIRCRAFT CORPORATION; *U.S. Private*, pg. 759
MOONEY CHEMICALS—See OM Group; *U.S. Public*, pg. 1208
MOORE & MUNGER MARKETING INC.—See Sasol Limited; *Int'l*, pg. 1197
MOORE & TABER GROUTING SERVICES—See Agra Inc.; *Int'l*, pg. 31
MOORE BELGIUM NV—See Moore Corporation Limited; *Int'l*, pg. 889
B.M. MOORE PRE-RELEASE CENTER—See Corrections Corporation of America; *U.S. Public*, pg. 450
MOORE BUSINESS EQUIPMENT DIV.—See Moore Corporation Limited; *Int'l*, pg. 890
MOORE BUSINESS FORMS & SYSTEMS DIV.—See Moore Corporation Limited; *Int'l*, pg. 890
MOORE BUSINESS FORMS & SYSTEMS LTD.—See Moore Corporation Limited; *Int'l*, pg. 889
MOORE BUSINESS FORMS CARIBEAN LTD.—See Moore Corporation Limited; *Int'l*, pg. 890
MOORE BUSINESS FORMS DE CENTRO AMERICA, S.A. DE C.V.—See Moore Corporation Limited; *Int'l*, pg. 889
MOORE BUSINESS FORMS DE MEXICO S.A. DE C.V.—See Moore Corporation Limited; *Int'l*, pg. 889
MOORE BUSINESS FORMS DE PUERTO RICO, S.A.—See Moore Corporation Limited; *Int'l*, pg. 889
MOORE BUSINESS FORMS (SCANDINAVIA) AB—See Moore Corporation Limited; *Int'l*, pg. 890
MOORE BUSINESS FORMS U.K. LTD.—See Moore Corporation Limited; *Int'l*, pg. 889
MOORE BUSINESS PRODUCTS & SERVICES DIVISIONS—See Moore Corporation Limited; *Int'l*, pg. 890
MOORE BUSINESS SYSTEMS AUSTRALIA LTD.—See Moore Corporation Limited; *Int'l*, pg. 889
MOORE BUSINESS SYSTEMS PTY. LTD.—See Moore Corporation Limited; *Int'l*, pg. 889
CHELSEA MOORE COMPANY—See The Western and Southern Life Insurance Company; *U.S. Private*, pg. 1164
MOORE COMPANY; *U.S. Private*, pg. 759
MOORE CONTROLS PVT. LIMITED—See Moore Products Co.; *U.S. Public*, pg. 1128
MOORE CORPORATION LIMITED; *Int'l*, pg. 888
MOORE DOCUMENT SOLUTIONS—See Moore Corporation Limited; *Int'l*, pg. 890
E.R. MOORE CO.; *U.S. Public*, pg. 759
MOORE ELECTRIC SUPPLY, INC.—See Hughes Supply, Inc.; *U.S. Public*, pg. 847

MOORE FORMULARIOS LIMITADA—See Moore Corporation Limited; *Int'l*, pg. 889
MOORE FRANCE SA—See Moore Corporation Limited; *Int'l*, pg. 889
MOORE GES.M.B.H.—See Moore Corporation Limited; *Int'l*, pg. 889
MOORE GROUP LTD.—See Masco Corporation; *U.S. Public*, pg. 1055
MOORE-HANDLEY, INC.; *U.S. Public*, pg. 1128
HAROLD MOORE & ASSOCIATES, INC.; *U.S. Private*, pg. 759
MOORE HOLDINGS CURACAO N.V.—See Moore Corporation Limited; *Int'l*, pg. 890
MOORE INTELLIGENT IMAGING SYSTEMS PTY. LTD.—See Moore Corporation Limited; *Int'l*, pg. 889
MOORE INTERNATIONAL B.V.—See Moore Corporation Limited; *Int'l*, pg. 889
MOORE INTERNATIONAL HOLDINGS N.V.—See Moore Corporation Limited; *Int'l*, pg. 890
MOORE INTERNATIONAL SA (PANAMA)—See Moore Corporation Limited; *Int'l*, pg. 890
MOORE-LITHOREX DIRECT MARKETING SERVICES N.V./S.A.—See Moore Corporation Limited; *Int'l*, pg. 889
MOORE LITHOREX DIRECT MARKETING SERVICES N.V. S.A.—See Moore Corporation Limited; *Int'l*, pg. 890
MOORE LITHOREX DIRECT MARKETING SERVICES SA—See Moore Corporation Limited; *Int'l*, pg. 890
MOORE MEDICAL CORP.; *U.S. Public*, pg. 1128
MOORE NEDERLAND B.V.—See Moore Corporation Limited; *Int'l*, pg. 890
MOORE-O-MATIC, INC.—See Nortek, Inc.; *U.S. Public*, pg. 1193
MOORE PARAGON AUSTRALIA LIMITED—See Moore Corporation Limited; *Int'l*, pg. 889
MOORE PARAGON (CARIBBEAN) LIMITED—See Moore Corporation Limited; *Int'l*, pg. 889
MOORE PARAGON CENTRAL AFRICA LIMITED—See Moore Corporation Limited; *Int'l*, pg. 890
MOORE PARAGON NORGE A/S—See Moore Corporation Limited; *Int'l*, pg. 889
MOORE PARAGON (SUISSE) S.A.—See Moore Corporation Limited; *Int'l*, pg. 890
MOORE PARAGON SVENSKA AB—See Moore Corporation Limited; *Int'l*, pg. 890
MOORE PARAGON U.K. LIMITED—See Moore Corporation Limited; *Int'l*, pg. 889
MOORE PORTUGUESA LIMITADA—See Moore Corporation Limited; *Int'l*, pg. 890
MOORE PRODUCTS CO.; *U.S. Public*, pg. 1128
MOORE PRODUCTS CO. (AUSTRALIA) PTY. LTD.—See Moore Products Co.; *U.S. Public*, pg. 1128
MOORE PRODUCTS CO. B.V.—See Moore Products Co.; *U.S. Public*, pg. 1129
MOORE PRODUCTS CO (CANADA), INC.—See Moore Products Co.; *U.S. Public*, pg. 1129
MOORE PRODUCTS CO. (FRANCE) SARL—See Moore Products Co.; *U.S. Public*, pg. 1129
MOORE PRODUCTS CO. (ITALIA) S.R.L.—See Moore Products Co.; *U.S. Public*, pg. 1129
MOORE PRODUCTS CO. (JAPAN) K.K.—See Moore Products Co.; *U.S. Public*, pg. 1129
MOORE PRODUCTS CO. (S) PTE. LTD.—See Moore Products Co.; *U.S. Public*, pg. 1129
MOORE PRODUCTS CO. (U.K.) LTD.—See Moore Products Co.; *U.S. Public*, pg. 1129
MOORE PRODUCTS DE MEXICO, S.A. DE C.V.—See Moore Products Co.; *U.S. Public*, pg. 1129
MOORE RESPONSE GRAPHICS—See Moore Corporation Limited; *Int'l*, pg. 890
REX MOORE ELECTRICAL CONTRACTORS & ENGINEERS; *U.S. Private*, pg. 759
MOORE SIGMA, S.P.A.—See Moore Corporation Limited; *Int'l*, pg. 890
MOORE SPECIAL TOOL AG—See The Producto Machine Co.; *U.S. Private*, pg. 889
MOORE TOOL COMPANY, INC.—See The Producto Machine Co.; *U.S. Private*, pg. 889
MOORE'S FOOD SERVICE PRODUCTS—See H.J. Heinz Company; *U.S. Public*, pg. 805
MOORE'S QUALITY SNACK FOODS, INC.—See Borden, Inc.; *U.S. Private*, pg. 158
MOORESVILLE TRIBUNE INC.—See Media General, Inc.; *U.S. Public*, pg. 1079
MOORLAND FOODS—See Hillsdown Holdings Plc; *Int'l*, pg. 619
MOORMAN'S INC.; *U.S. Public*, pg. 760
MOORSIDE DIVISION—See Inco Limited; *Int'l*, pg. 673
MOOSE JAW PLANT—See The Clorox Company; *U.S. Public*, pg. 387
MORAD YOUSUF BEHBEHANI—See Telefonaktiebolaget LM Ericsson; *Int'l*, pg. 1369
MORALCO LTD.—See Aluminum Company of America; *U.S. Public*, pg. 62
ART MORAN PONTIAC-GMC INC.; *U.S. Private*, pg. 760
MORAN BARGE CORPORATION—See Moran Transporation Company; *U.S. Private*, pg. 760
MORAN BULK CORPORATION—See Moran Transporation Company; *U.S. Private*, pg. 760
MORAN COMPANY—See American International Group, Inc.; *U.S. Public*, pg. 84
MORAN FOODS, INC./SAVE-A-LOT LTD.—See SuperValu, Inc.; *U.S. Public*, pg. 1541
MORAN INDUSTRIES, INC.; *U.S. Private*, pg. 760
MORAN INSURANCE COMPANY LIMITED—See Moran Transporation Company; *U.S. Private*, pg. 760
MORAN SERVICES CORPORATION—See Moran Transporation Company; *U.S. Private*, pg. 760
MORAN SHIPYARD CORPORATION—See Moran Transporation Company; *U.S. Private*, pg. 761
MORAN TOWING & TRANSPORTATION—See Moran Transporation Company; *U.S. Private*, pg. 761
MORAN TOWING CORPORATION—See Moran Transporation Company; *U.S. Private*, pg. 760

MORAN TOWING OF FLORIDA—See Moran Transporation Company; *U.S. Private*, pg. 761
MORAN TOWING OF DELAWARE, INC—See Moran Transporation Company; *U.S. Private*, pg. 760
MORAN TOWING OF MARYLAND—See Moran Transporation Company; *U.S. Private*, pg. 761
MORAN TOWING OF MIAMI—See Moran Transporation Company; *U.S. Private*, pg. 761
MORAN TOWING OF NEW HAMPSHIRE—See Moran Transporation Company; *U.S. Private*, pg. 761
MORAN TOWING OF PENNSYLVANIA—See Moran Transporation Company; *U.S. Private*, pg. 761
MORAN TOWING OF TEXAS CORPORATION—See Moran Transporation Company; *U.S. Private*, pg. 761
MORAN TOWING OF TEXAS, INC.—See Moran Transporation Company; *U.S. Private*, pg. 761
MORAN TOWING OF VIRGINIA—See Moran Transporation Company; *U.S. Private*, pg. 761
MORAN TRANSPORTATION COMPANY; *U.S. Private*, pg. 760
MORAY FIRTH MALTINGS—See Scottish & Newcastle plc; *Int'l*, pg. 1211
MORECO INC—See Modern Group Ltd.; *U.S. Private*, pg. 755
MORFECOR, C.A.—See Morton International Inc.; *U.S. Public*, pg. 1135
MORFLEX, INC.—See Reilly Industries, Inc.; *U.S. Private*, pg. 919
MORGAN ASSET MANAGEMENT, INC.—See Morgan Keegan, Inc.; *U.S. Public*, pg. 1131
MORGAN AUSTRIA GMBH—See Morgan Crucible Co. Plc; *Int'l*, pg. 891
MORGAN CHEMICAL PRODUCTS INC.—See Morgan Crucible Co. Plc; *Int'l*, pg. 892
MORGAN CONSTRUCTION CO.; *U.S. Private*, pg. 761
MORGAN COUNTY NEWS—See Landmark Communications, Inc.; *U.S. Private*, pg. 648
MORGAN CRUCIBLE CO. PLC; *Int'l*, pg. 890
MORGAN DISTRIBUTION—See Morgan Products Ltd.; *U.S. Public*, pg. 1132
MORGAN DRIVE AWAY, INC.—See Lynch Corporation; *U.S. Public*, pg. 1022
MORGAN EUROPE—See Morgan Construction Co.; *U.S. Private*, pg. 761
MORGAN FOOD SPECIALTY INC.—See Associated British Foods plc; *Int'l*, pg. 92
MORGAN FOODS, INC.; *U.S. Private*, pg. 761
MORGAN FUTURES CORP.—See J.P. Morgan Co. Incorporated; *U.S. Public*, pg. 1129
MORGAN GESTION S.A.—See J.P. Morgan Co. Incorporated; *U.S. Public*, pg. 1131
MORGAN GMBH—See Morgan Crucible Co. Plc; *Int'l*, pg. 891
MORGAN GRENFELL & CO. LIMITED—See Deutsche Bank AG; *Int'l*, pg. 405
MORGAN GRENFELL ASIA LIMITED (SINGAPORE)—See Deutsche Bank AG; *Int'l*, pg. 406
MORGAN GRENFELL ASSET MANAGEMENT LIMITED—See Deutsche Bank AG; *Int'l*, pg. 405
MORGAN GRENFELL AUSTRALIA LTD.—See Deutsche Bank AG; *Int'l*, pg. 406
MORGAN GRENFELL CAPITAL MANAGEMENT INCORPORATED—See Deutsche Bank AG; *Int'l*, pg. 405
MORGAN GRENFELL (CAYMAN) LIMITED—See Deutsche Bank AG; *Int'l*, pg. 406
MORGAN GRENFELL (COLOMBIA)—See Deutsche Bank AG; *Int'l*, pg. 405
MORGAN GRENFELL DEUTSCHLAND GMBH—See Deutsche Bank AG; *Int'l*, pg. 406
MORGAN GRENFELL (ECUADOR)—See Deutsche Bank AG; *Int'l*, pg. 405
MORGAN GRENFELL FRANCE S.A.—See Deutsche Bank AG; *Int'l*, pg. 406
MORGAN GRENFELL GROUP PLC—See Deutsche Bank AG; *Int'l*, pg. 405
MORGAN GRENFELL (GUERNSEY, C.I.) LIMITED—See Deutsche Bank AG; *Int'l*, pg. 406
MORGAN GRENFELL (HONG KONG) LIMITED—See Deutsche Bank AG; *Int'l*, pg. 406
MORGAN GRENFELL INTERNATIONAL ASSET MANAGEMENT CO. LTD. (TOKYO)—See Deutsche Bank AG; *Int'l*, pg. 406
MORGAN GRENFELL ITALIA S.P.A.—See Deutsche Bank AG; *Int'l*, pg. 406
MORGAN GRENFELL JAPAN LIMITED—See Deutsche Bank AG; *Int'l*, pg. 406
MORGAN GRENFELL (JERSEY, C.I.) LIMITED—See Deutsche Bank AG; *Int'l*, pg. 406
MORGAN GRENFELL (KENYA)—See Deutsche Bank AG; *Int'l*, pg. 405
MORGAN GRENFELL LAURIE LTD.—See Deutsche Bank AG; *Int'l*, pg. 405
MORGAN GRENFELL (MALAYSIA)—See Deutsche Bank AG; *Int'l*, pg. 405
MORGAN GRENFELL (SCOTLAND) LIMITED—See Deutsche Bank AG; *Int'l*, pg. 405
MORGAN GRENFELL (SOVIET UNION)—See Deutsche Bank AG; *Int'l*, pg. 406
MORGAN GRENFELL (SPAIN)—See Deutsche Bank AG; *Int'l*, pg. 406
MORGAN GRENFELL (SWEDEN)—See Deutsche Bank AG; *Int'l*, pg. 406
MORGAN GRENFELL (VENEZUELA)—See Deutsche Bank AG; *Int'l*, pg. 406
THE MORGAN GROUP, INC.—See Lynch Corporation; *U.S. Public*, pg. 1022
MORGAN GUARANTY INTERNATIONAL FINANCE CORPORATION—See J.P. Morgan Co. Incorporated; *U.S. Public*, pg. 1129
MORGAN GUARANTY TRUST COMPANY—See J.P. Morgan Co. Incorporated; *U.S. Public*, pg. 1129

MORGAN GUARANTY TRUST COMPANY OF NEW YORK—See J.P. Morgan Co. Incorporated; *U.S. Public*, pg. 1129
MORGAN-HAYES DIV.—See Weyco Group, Inc.; *U.S. Public*, pg. 1764
MORGAN HILL TIMES—See McClatchy Newspapers Inc.; *U.S. Public*, pg. 1065
MORGAN HOLDINGS CORP.—See J.P. Morgan Co. Incorporated; *U.S. Public*, pg. 1129
J.P. MORGAN & CO. INCORPORATED—See J.P. Morgan Co. Incorporated; *U.S. Public*, pg. 1129
J.P. MORGAN CALIFORNIA—See J.P. Morgan Co. Incorporated; *U.S. Public*, pg. 1129
J.P. MORGAN CAPITAL CORPORATION—See J.P. Morgan Co. Incorporated; *U.S. Public*, pg. 1129
J.P. MORGAN INVESTMENT MANAGEMENT INC.—See J.P. Morgan Co. Incorporated; *U.S. Public*, pg. 1129
J.P. MORGAN SECURITIES LTD.—See J.P. Morgan Co. Incorporated; *U.S. Public*, pg. 1131
J.E. MORGAN KNITTING MILLS INC.—See Dawson International PLC; *Int'l*, pg. 386
J.P. MORGAN & CIE S.A.—See J.P. Morgan Co. Incorporated; *U.S. Public*, pg. 1130
J.P. MORGAN & CO. INCORPORATED—See J.P. Morgan Co. Incorporated; *U.S. Public*, pg. 1129
J.P. MORGAN ARGENTINA SOCIEDAD DE BOLSA S.A.—See J.P. Morgan Co. Incorporated; *U.S. Public*, pg. 1130
J.P. MORGAN AUSTRALIA LIMITED—See J.P. Morgan Co. Incorporated; *U.S. Public*, pg. 1130
J.P. MORGAN AUSTRALIA LIMITED (SYDNEY)—See J.P. Morgan Co. Incorporated; *U.S. Public*, pg. 1130
J.P. MORGAN AUSTRALIA SECURITIES LIMITED—See J.P. Morgan Co. Incorporated; *U.S. Public*, pg. 1130
J.P. MORGAN BENELUX S.A.—See J.P. Morgan Co. Incorporated; *U.S. Public*, pg. 1130
J.P. MORGAN CALIFORNIA—See J.P. Morgan Co. Incorporated; *U.S. Public*, pg. 1129
J.P. MORGAN CANADA—See J.P. Morgan Co. Incorporated; *U.S. Public*, pg. 1130
J.P. MORGAN CAPITAL CORPORATION—See J.P. Morgan Co. Incorporated; *U.S. Public*, pg. 1129
J.P. MORGAN CASA DE BOLSA S.A. DE C.V.—See J.P. Morgan Co. Incorporated; *U.S. Public*, pg. 1130
J.P. MORGAN CHILE LTDA.—See J.P. Morgan Co. Incorporated; *U.S. Public*, pg. 1130
J.P. MORGAN CO. INCORPORATED; *U.S. Public*, pg. 1129
J.P. MORGAN DELAWARE—See J.P. Morgan Co. Incorporated; *U.S. Public*, pg. 1129
J.P. MORGAN ESPANA S.A.—See J.P. Morgan Co. Incorporated; *U.S. Public*, pg. 1130
J.P. MORGAN FLORIDA, FSB—See J.P. Morgan Co. Incorporated; *U.S. Public*, pg. 1129
J.P. MORGAN FONDI ITALIA S.P.A.—See J.P. Morgan Co. Incorporated; *U.S. Public*, pg. 1130
J.P. MORGAN FUTURES HONG KONG LTD.—See J.P. Morgan Co. Incorporated; *U.S. Public*, pg. 1130
J.P. MORGAN FUTURES INC.—See J.P. Morgan Co. Incorporated; *U.S. Public*, pg. 1129
J.P. MORGAN GMBH—See J.P. Morgan Co. Incorporated; *U.S. Public*, pg. 1130
J.P. MORGAN GRUPO FINANCIERO, S.A. DE C.V.—See J.P. Morgan Co. Incorporated; *U.S. Public*, pg. 1130
J.P. MORGAN HOLDING DEUTSCHLAND GMBH—See J.P. Morgan Co. Incorporated; *U.S. Public*, pg. 1131
J.P. MORGAN IBERICA S.L.—See J.P. Morgan Co. Incorporated; *U.S. Public*, pg. 1131
J.P. MORGAN INTERNATIONAL CAPITAL CORPORATION—See J.P. Morgan Co. Incorporated; *U.S. Public*, pg. 1131
J.P. MORGAN INTERNATIONAL LTD.—See J.P. Morgan Co. Incorporated; *U.S. Public*, pg. 1131
J.P. MORGAN INVESTIMENTOS E FINANCAS LTDA. (RIO DE JANEIRO)—See J.P. Morgan Co. Incorporated; *U.S. Public*, pg. 1131
J.P. MORGAN INVESTIMENTOS E FINANCES LTDA.—See J.P. Morgan Co. Incorporated; *U.S. Public*, pg. 1131
J.P. MORGAN INVESTMENT GMBH—See J.P. Morgan Co. Incorporated; *U.S. Public*, pg. 1131
J.P. MORGAN INVESTMENT MANAGEMENT AUSTRALIA LTD.—See J.P. Morgan Co. Incorporated; *U.S. Public*, pg. 1131
J.P. MORGAN INVESTMENT MANAGEMENT INC.—See J.P. Morgan Co. Incorporated; *U.S. Public*, pg. 1129
J.P. MORGAN NEDERLAND N.V.—See J.P. Morgan Co. Incorporated; *U.S. Public*, pg. 1131
J.P. MORGAN OVERSEAS CAPITAL CORPORATION—See J.P. Morgan Co. Incorporated; *U.S. Public*, pg. 1129
J.P. MORGAN POLSKA S.A.—See J.P. Morgan Co. Incorporated; *U.S. Public*, pg. 1131
J.P. MORGAN SECURITIES ASIA LTD.—See J.P. Morgan Co. Incorporated; *U.S. Public*, pg. 1131
J.P. MORGAN SECURITIES CANADA INC.—See J.P. Morgan Co. Incorporated; *U.S. Public*, pg. 1131
J.P. MORGAN SECURITIES HONG KONG LTD.—See J.P. Morgan Co. Incorporated; *U.S. Public*, pg. 1131
J.P. MORGAN SECURITIES INC.—See J.P. Morgan Co. Incorporated; *U.S. Public*, pg. 1129
J.P. MORGAN SECURITIES LTD.—See J.P. Morgan Co. Incorporated; *U.S. Public*, pg. 1131
J.P. MORGAN SERVICES INC.—See J.P. Morgan Co. Incorporated; *U.S. Public*, pg. 1129
J.P. MORGAN SOCIEDAD DE VALORES Y BOLSA, S.A.—See J.P. Morgan Co. Incorporated; *U.S. Public*, pg. 1131
J.P. MORGAN STERLING SECURITIES LTD.—See J.P. Morgan Co. Incorporated; *U.S. Public*, pg. 1131
J.P. MORGAN (SUISSE) S.A.—See J.P. Morgan Co. Incorporated; *U.S. Public*, pg. 1131
J.P. MORGAN (SWITZERLAND) LTD.—See J.P. Morgan Co. Incorporated; *U.S. Public*, pg. 1131

J.P. MORGAN TRUST BANK LTD.—See J.P. Morgan Co. Incorporated; *U.S. Public*, pg. 1131
J.P. MORGAN TRUST COMPANY OF DELAWARE—See J.P. Morgan Co. Incorporated; *U.S. Public*, pg. 1130
J.P. MORGAN VENEZUELA, S.A.—See J.P. Morgan Co. Incorporated; *U.S. Public*, pg. 1131
MORGAN KEEGAN & COMPANY, INC.—See Morgan Keegan, Inc.; *U.S. Public*, pg. 1131
MORGAN KEEGAN FUNDING CORP.—See Morgan Keegan, Inc.; *U.S. Public*, pg. 1131
MORGAN KEEGAN, INC.; *U.S. Public*, pg. 1131
MORGAN KEEGAN INSURANCE AGENCY OF LOUISIANA, INC.—See Morgan Keegan, Inc.; *U.S. Public*, pg. 1131
MORGAN KEEGAN MANAGED FUTURES, INC.—See Morgan Keegan, Inc.; *U.S. Public*, pg. 1131
MORGAN KEEGAN MORTGAGE COMPANY, INC.—See Morgan Keegan, Inc.; *U.S. Public*, pg. 1131
MORGAN LUMBER SALES CO.; *U.S. Private*, pg. 761
MORGAN MANUFACTURING—See Morgan Products Ltd.; *U.S. Public*, pg. 1132
MORGAN MARSHALL INDUSTRIES, INC.—See RHC/Spacemaster Corporation; *U.S. Public*, pg. 904
MORGAN MATERIALS HUNGARY LIMITED—See Morgan Crucible Co. Plc; *Int'l*, pg. 891
MORGAN MATERIALS TECHNOLOGY LIMITED—See Morgan Crucible Co. Plc; *Int'l*, pg. 894
MORGAN MATROC—See Morgan Crucible Co. Plc; *Int'l*, pg. 893
MORGAN MATROC INC.-EAST COAST SALES DIVISION—See Morgan Crucible Co. Plc; *Int'l*, pg. 893
MORGAN MATROC INC.-ELECTRO CERAMICS DIVISION—See Morgan Crucible Co. Plc; *Int'l*, pg. 893
MORGAN MATROC INC.-MIDWEST SALES DIVISION—See Morgan Crucible Co. Plc; *Int'l*, pg. 893
MORGAN MATROC INC.-WEST COAST SALES DIVISION—See Morgan Crucible Co. Plc; *Int'l*, pg. 893
MORGAN MATROC LIMITED—See Morgan Crucible Co. Plc; *Int'l*, pg. 893
MORGAN MATROC S.A.—See Morgan Crucible Co. Plc; *Int'l*, pg. 893
MORGAN MATROC SRL—See Morgan Crucible Co. Plc; *Int'l*, pg. 893
MORGAN PRODUCTS LTD.; *U.S. Public*, pg. 1132
MORGAN REFRACTORIES INC.—See Morgan Crucible Co. Plc; *Int'l*, pg. 893
S.A. MORGAN—See Morgan Crucible Co. Plc; *Int'l*, pg. 891
MORGAN STANLEY & CO. INCORPORATED—See Morgan Stanley Dean Witter & Co.; *U.S. Public*, pg. 1132
MORGAN STANLEY ASSET MANAGEMENT, INC.—See Morgan Stanley Dean Witter & Co.; *U.S. Public*, pg. 1132
MORGAN STANLEY BEIJING—See Morgan Stanley Dean Witter & Co.; *U.S. Public*, pg. 1133
MORGAN STANLEY BOMBAY—See Morgan Stanley Dean Witter & Co.; *U.S. Public*, pg. 1133
MORGAN STANLEY CANADA LTD.—See Morgan Stanley Dean Witter & Co.; *U.S. Public*, pg. 1133
MORGAN STANLEY CAPITAL GROUP INC.—See Morgan Stanley Dean Witter & Co.; *U.S. Public*, pg. 1132
MORGAN STANLEY CAPITAL I INC.—See Morgan Stanley Dean Witter & Co.; *U.S. Public*, pg. 1132
MORGAN STANLEY CAPITAL SERVICES INC.—See Morgan Stanley Dean Witter & Co.; *U.S. Public*, pg. 1132
MORGAN STANLEY CHICAGO—See Morgan Stanley Dean Witter & Co.; *U.S. Public*, pg. 1132
MORGAN STANLEY DEAN WITTER & CO.; *U.S. Public*, pg. 1132
MORGAN STANLEY FRANKFURT—See Morgan Stanley Dean Witter & Co.; *U.S. Public*, pg. 1133
MORGAN STANLEY GROUP INC.—See Morgan Stanley Dean Witter & Co.; *U.S. Public*, pg. 1132
MORGAN STANLEY HONG KONG—See Morgan Stanley Dean Witter & Co.; *U.S. Public*, pg. 1133
MORGAN STANLEY INTERNATIONAL—See Morgan Stanley Dean Witter & Co.; *U.S. Public*, pg. 1133
MORGAN STANLEY INTERNATIONAL INC.—See Morgan Stanley Dean Witter & Co.; *U.S. Public*, pg. 1132
MORGAN STANLEY JAPAN LTD.—See Morgan Stanley Dean Witter & Co.; *U.S. Public*, pg. 1133
MORGAN STANLEY JOHANNESBURG—See Morgan Stanley Dean Witter & Co.; *U.S. Public*, pg. 1133
THE MORGAN STANLEY LEVERAGED EQUITY FUND L.P.—See Cigna Corp.; *U.S. Public*, pg. 357
THE MORGAN STANLEY LEVERAGED MEZZANINE FUND L.P.—See Cigna Corp.; *U.S. Public*, pg. 357
THE MORGAN STANLEY LEVERAGED SENIOR DEBT FUND L.P.—See Cigna Corp.; *U.S. Public*, pg. 357
MORGAN STANLEY LOS ANGELES—See Morgan Stanley Dean Witter & Co.; *U.S. Public*, pg. 1132
MORGAN STANLEY LUXEMBOURG—See Morgan Stanley Dean Witter & Co.; *U.S. Public*, pg. 1133
MORGAN STANLEY MADRID—See Morgan Stanley Dean Witter & Co.; *U.S. Public*, pg. 1133
MORGAN STANLEY MELBOURNE—See Morgan Stanley Dean Witter & Co.; *U.S. Public*, pg. 1133
MORGAN STANLEY MENLO PARK—See Morgan Stanley Dean Witter & Co.; *U.S. Public*, pg. 1132
MORGAN STANLEY MILAN—See Morgan Stanley Dean Witter & Co.; *U.S. Public*, pg. 1133
MORGAN STANLEY MONTREAL—See Morgan Stanley Dean Witter & Co.; *U.S. Public*, pg. 1133
MORGAN STANLEY MOSCOW—See Morgan Stanley Dean Witter & Co.; *U.S. Public*, pg. 1133
MORGAN STANLEY PARIS—See Morgan Stanley Dean Witter & Co.; *U.S. Public*, pg. 1133
MORGAN STANLEY REALTY, INC.—See Morgan Stanley Dean Witter & Co.; *U.S. Public*, pg. 1132
MORGAN STANLEY SAN FRANCISCO—See Morgan Stanley Dean Witter & Co.; *U.S. Public*, pg. 1132
MORGAN STANLEY SEOUL—See Morgan Stanley Dean Witter & Co.; *U.S. Public*, pg. 1133

MORGAN STANLEY SHANGHAI—See Morgan Stanley Dean Witter & Co.; *U.S. Public*, pg. 1133
MORGAN STANLEY SINGAPORE—See Morgan Stanley Dean Witter & Co.; *U.S. Public*, pg. 1133
MORGAN STANLEY SYDNEY—See Morgan Stanley Dean Witter & Co.; *U.S. Public*, pg. 1133
MORGAN STANLEY TAIPEI—See Morgan Stanley Dean Witter & Co.; *U.S. Public*, pg. 1133
MORGAN STANLEY ZURICH—See Morgan Stanley Dean Witter & Co.; *U.S. Public*, pg. 1133
MORGAN TECHNICAL CERAMICS—See Morgan Crucible Co. Plc; *Int'l*, pg. 893
MORGAN TECHNICAL SERVICES, INC—See Morgan Construction Co.; *U.S. Private*, pg. 761
MORGAN THERMAL CERAMICS GMBH—See Morgan Crucible Co. Plc; *Int'l*, pg. 894
MORGAN THERMIC S.A.—See Morgan Crucible Co. Plc; *Int'l*, pg. 894
MORGAN TRAILER MANUFACTURING CO.; *U.S. Private*, pg. 761
MORGAN TRANS BUDAPEST KFT—See Morgan Crucible Co. Plc; *Int'l*, pg. 895
MORGAN TRANS LIMITED—See Morgan Crucible Co. Plc; *Int'l*, pg. 894
MORGAN TRUST COMPANY OF THE BAHAMAS LIMITED—See J.P. Morgan Co. Incorporated; *U.S. Public*, pg. 1131
MORGAN TRUST COMPANY OF THE CAYMAN ISLANDS LTD.—See J.P. Morgan Co. Incorporated; *U.S. Public*, pg. 1131
MORGANFIELD NATIONAL BANK—See Old National Bancorp; *U.S. Public*, pg. 1217
MORGANITE AG—See Morgan Crucible Co. Plc; *Int'l*, pg. 891
MORGANITE AUSTRALIA PTY. LIMITED—See Morgan Crucible Co. Plc; *Int'l*, pg. 895
MORGANITE CANADA CORPORATION—See Morgan Crucible Co. Plc; *Int'l*, pg. 895
MORGANITE CARBON DIVISION—See Morgan Crucible Co. Plc; *Int'l*, pg. 895
MORGANITE CARBON KABUSHIKI KAISHA—See Morgan Crucible Co. Plc; *Int'l*, pg. 892
MORGANITE CARBON NZ LTD—See Morgan Crucible Co. Plc; *Int'l*, pg. 895
MORGANITE CARBON OF SINGAPORE PTE. LIMITED—See Morgan Crucible Co. Plc; *Int'l*, pg. 892
MORGANITE CERAMIC FIBRES PTY. LIMITED—See Morgan Crucible Co. Plc; *Int'l*, pg. 894
MORGANITE CONSUMER PRODUCTS (MCP)—See Morgan Crucible Co. Plc; *Int'l*, pg. 895
MORGANITE DO BRASIL INDUSTRIAL LIMITADA REFRACTORIES DIVISION—See Morgan Crucible Co. Plc; *Int'l*, pg. 894
MORGANITE DO BRASIL INDUSTRIAL LIMITADA—See Morgan Crucible Co. Plc; *Int'l*, pg. 894
MORGANITE ELECTRICAL CARBON LIMITED—See Morgan Crucible Co. Plc; *Int'l*, pg. 891
MORGANITE ELECTRONIC INSTRUMENTS LIMITED—See Morgan Crucible Co. Plc; *Int'l*, pg. 891
MORGANITE ENVIRONMENTAL SERVICES INC.—See Morgan Crucible Co. Plc; *Int'l*, pg. 894
MORGANITE ESPANOLA SA—See Morgan Crucible Co. Plc; *Int'l*, pg. 892
MORGANITE GMBH—See Morgan Crucible Co. Plc; *Int'l*, pg. 892
MORGANITE HONG KONG COMPANY LIMITED—See Morgan Crucible Co. Plc; *Int'l*, pg. 892
MORGANITE INC.—See Morgan Crucible Co. Plc; *Int'l*, pg. 893
MORGANITE INDUSTRIAL CARBON (MIC)—See Morgan Crucible Co. Plc; *Int'l*, pg. 895
MORGANITE INTERNATIONAL LIMITED—See Morgan Crucible Co. Plc; *Int'l*, pg. 894
MORGANITE ISOLANTES TERMICOS LIMITADA—See Morgan Crucible Co. Plc; *Int'l*, pg. 895
MORGANITE ITALIANA S.R.L.—See Morgan Crucible Co. Plc; *Int'l*, pg. 892
MORGANITE LUXEMBOURG S.A.—See Morgan Crucible Co. Plc; *Int'l*, pg. 892
MORGANITE NORD S.R.L.—See Morgan Crucible Co. Plc; *Int'l*, pg. 892
MORGANITE NORTH AMERICA INC.—See Morgan Crucible Co. Plc; *Int'l*, pg. 894
MORGANITE REFRACTORY INDUSTRIES (MRI)—See Morgan Crucible Co. Plc; *Int'l*, pg. 895
MORGANITE SOUTH AFRICA (PTY) LIMITED—See Morgan Crucible Co. Plc; *Int'l*, pg. 895
MORGANITE SPECIAL CARBONS LIMITED—See Morgan Crucible Co. Plc; *Int'l*, pg. 891
MORGANITE SPECIAL CARBONS LIMITED-MATERIALS DIVISION—See Morgan Crucible Co. Plc; *Int'l*, pg. 891
MORGANITE TAIWAN LIMITED—See Morgan Crucible Co. Plc; *Int'l*, pg. 892
MORGANITE THERMAL CERAMICS LIMITED—See Morgan Crucible Co. Plc; *Int'l*, pg. 893
MORGANITE THERMAL CERAMICS TAIWAN LIMITED—See Morgan Crucible Co. Plc; *Int'l*, pg. 894
MORGANS—See Associated Industrial Supply, Inc.; *U.S. Private*, pg. 91
MORGAN'S FOODS, INC.; *U.S. Public*, pg. 1133
MORGAN'S FOODS OF MISSOURI, INC.—See Morgan's Foods, Inc.; *U.S. Public*, pg. 1133
MORGAN'S RESTAURANTS OF NEW JERSEY, INC.—See Morgan's Foods, Inc.; *U.S. Public*, pg. 1133
MORGAN'S RESTAURANTS OF OHIO, INC.—See Morgan's Foods, Inc.; *U.S. Public*, pg. 1133
MORGAN'S RESTAURANTS OF PA., INC.—See Morgan's Foods, Inc.; *U.S. Public*, pg. 1133
MORGAN'S WEIRTON FOODS, INC.—See Morgan's Foods, Inc.; *U.S. Public*, pg. 1133
MORGANTOWN NEWS-HERALD—See Media General, Inc.; *U.S. Public*, pg. 1079
MORGANTOWN MACHINE & HYDRAULICS, INC.—See Charter plc; *Int'l*, pg. 280

MORGANTOWN MACHINE ANDERSON MAVOR—See Charter plc; *Int'l*, pg. 281
MORGANTOWN PLASTICS COMPANY—See Masco Corporation; *U.S. Public*, pg. 1054
MORGARDSHAMMAR AB—See Danielli & C. Officine Meccaniche S.p.A.; *Int'l*, pg. 378
MORGARDSHAMMAR INC.—See Danielli & C. Officine Meccaniche S.p.A.; *Int'l*, pg. 378
MORGENPOST DRUCK & VERLAGSANSTALT GMBH & CO.—See Bertelsmann AG; *Int'l*, pg. 190
MORGUARD INVESTMENTS LIMITED, TORONTO—See Metropolitan Life Insurance Co.; *U.S. Private*, pg. 738
MORIMURA BADISCHE CO., LTD.—See BASF AG; *Int'l*, pg. 109
MORINAGA MILK INDUSTRY CO., LTD.; *Int'l*, pg. 895
MORINAGA MILK INDUSTRY CO., LTD.—See Morinaga Milk Industry Co., Ltd.; *Int'l*, pg. 895
MORINAGA NUTRITIONAL FOODS DEUTSCHLAND GMBH—See Morinaga Milk Industry Co., Ltd.; *Int'l*, pg. 895
MORINAGA NUTRITIONAL FOODS EUROPE S.A.—See Morinaga Milk Industry Co., Ltd.; *Int'l*, pg. 895
MORINAGA NUTRITIONAL FOODS, INC.—See Morinaga Milk Industry Co., Ltd.; *Int'l*, pg. 895
MORIOKA HAKUHODO INC.—See Hakuhodo Incorporated; *Int'l*, pg. 588
MORITZ CADILLAC-BMW INC.; *U.S. Private*, pg. 761
MORLEY BUILDERS; *U.S. Private*, pg. 761
MORLEY CONSTRUCTION CO., INC.—See Morley Builders; *U.S. Private*, pg. 762
MORLEY SHIRT COMPANY—See HC Holdings; *U.S. Private*, pg. 490
MORLITE—See Luxo A/S; *Int'l*, pg. 821
MORLYNN CERAMICS PTY LIMITED—See Morgan Crucible Co. Plc; *Int'l*, pg. 893
MORMAC MARINE TRANSPORT, INC.; *U.S. Private*, pg. 762
THE MORNING CALL—See The Times Mirror Company; *U.S. Public*, pg. 1616
MORNING STAR CEMENT LTD.—See Holderbank Financiere Glaris Ltd.; *Int'l*, pg. 629
THE MORNING STAR GROUP—See Suiza Foods Corporation; *U.S. Public*, pg. 1527
MOROCH & ASSOC., INC.; *U.S. Private*, pg. 762
MOROCH & ASSOCIATES, INC.—See Moroch & Assoc., Inc.; *U.S. Private*, pg. 762
MOROCH ASSOCIATES, INC.—See Moroch & Assoc., Inc.; *U.S. Private*, pg. 762
MORPHY RICHARDS APPLIANCES—See The Glen Dimplex Group; *Int'l*, pg. 554
MORPHY RICHARDS CONSUMER ELECTRONICS—See The Glen Dimplex Group; *Int'l*, pg. 554
JOHN MORRELL & CO.—See Smithfield Foods, Inc.; *U.S. Public*, pg. 1479
THE MORRILL PRESS—See Sonoco Products Company; *U.S. Public*, pg. 1486
MORRILTON SECURITY BANK, N.A.—See First Commercial Corporation; *U.S. Public*, pg. 630
MORRIS COMMUNICATIONS CORPORATION—See Shivers Trading & Operating Co.; *U.S. Private*, pg. 995
MORRIS COUPLING CO.; *U.S. Private*, pg. 762
JOSHUA MORRIS PUBLISHING, INC.—See The Reader's Digest Association, Inc.; *U.S. Public*, pg. 1367
MORRIS MERCHANTS, INC.—See Valley Resources, Inc.; *U.S. Public*, pg. 1706
MORRIS NEWSPAPER CORPORATION; *U.S. Private*, pg. 762
THE ROBERT E. MORRIS COMPANY; *U.S. Private*, pg. 762
MORRISON BERKSHIRE INC.—See Morrison Textile Machinery Co.; *U.S. Private*, pg. 762
MORRISON BOWMORE DISTILLERS, LTD.—See Suntory Ltd.; *Int'l*, pg. 1322
MORRISON HEALTH CARE INC.; *U.S. Public*, pg. 1133
MORRISON HOMES—See George Wimpey PLC; *Int'l*, pg. 1510
MORRISON, INC.; *U.S. Private*, pg. 762
MORRISON KNUDSEN CORP. ENGINEERING & CONSTRUCTION—See Morrison Knudsen Corporation; *U.S. Public*, pg. 1134
MORRISON KNUDSEN CORPORATION; *U.S. Public*, pg. 1133
MORRISON NUCLEAR, INC.—See Morrison Petroleums Ltd.; *Int'l*, pg. 895
MORRISON PETROLEUMS LTD.; *Int'l*, pg. 895
MORRISON RESTAURANTS, INC.; *U.S. Public*, pg. 1134
MORRISON TEXTILE MACHINERY CO.; *U.S. Private*, pg. 762
MORROW JUNIOR BOOKS—See The Hearst Corporation; *U.S. Private*, pg. 515
MORROW WEST BEACH; *U.S. Public*, pg. 1134
WILLIAM MORROW & CO., INC.—See The Hearst Corporation; *U.S. Private*, pg. 515
MORSE CONTROLS—See IMO Industries Inc.; *U.S. Public*, pg. 857
MORSE CONTROLS LTD.—See IMO Industries Inc.; *U.S. Public*, pg. 857
MORSE DIESEL INTERNATIONAL, INC.; *U.S. Private*, pg. 762
ED MORSE AUTOMOTIVE GROUP; *U.S. Private*, pg. 763
MORSE HARDWARE COMPANY; *U.S. Private*, pg. 763
MORSE SHOE, INC.—See J. Baker, Inc.; *U.S. Public*, pg. 168
MORSE SHOE LEASED DIV.—See J. Baker, Inc.; *U.S. Public*, pg. 168
MORSON THOMAS & SON LTD.—See Merck & Co., Inc.; *U.S. Public*, pg. 1092
M.A. MORTENSON COMPANY; *U.S. Private*, pg. 763
MORTGAGE & FINANCE BERHAD—See HSBC Holdings plc; *Int'l*, pg. 583
MORTGAGE GUARANTEE & TITLE CO.—See The First American Financial Corporation; *U.S. Public*, pg. 626

MORTGAGE GUARANTY INSURANCE CORPORATION—See MGIC Investment Corporation; *U.S. Public*, pg. 1026
THE MORTGAGE INSURANCE COMPANY OF CANADA—See CIGL Holdings Ltd.; *Int'l*, pg. 241
MORTGAGE SERVICE CORPORATION—See F.N.B. Corporation; *U.S. Public*, pg. 607
MORTON AUTOMOTIVE COATINGS—See Morton International Inc.; *U.S. Public*, pg. 1135
MORTON BAHAMAS LTD.—See Morton International Inc.; *U.S. Public*, pg. 1135
MORTON CHEMICAL DIV.—See Morton International Inc.; *U.S. Public*, pg. 1135
MORTON CHEMICAL POWDER COATINGS—See Morton International Inc.; *U.S. Public*, pg. 1135
MORTON FOREST PRODUCTS CO.—See WTD Industries, Inc.; *U.S. Public*, pg. 1730
MORTON INTERNATIONAL B.V.—See Morton International Inc.; *U.S. Public*, pg. 1135
MORTON INTERNATIONAL G.M.B.H.—See Morton International Inc.; *U.S. Public*, pg. 1135
MORTON INTERNATIONAL INC.; *U.S. Public*, pg. 1134
MORTON INTERNATIONAL K.K.—See Morton International Inc.; *U.S. Public*, pg. 1135
MORTON INTERNATIONAL LIMITED—See Morton International Inc.; *U.S. Public*, pg. 1135
MORTON INTERNATIONAL, LTD.—See Morton International Inc.; *U.S. Public*, pg. 1136
MORTON INTERNATIONAL S.A.—See Morton International Inc.; *U.S. Public*, pg. 1136
MORTON INTERNATIONAL S.P.A.—See Morton International Inc.; *U.S. Public*, pg. 1136
ROBERT MORTON AEROSPACE LIMITED—See SLD Holdings Ltd.; *Int'l*, pg. 1160
MORTON SALT—See Morton International Inc.; *U.S. Public*, pg. 1135
MORTON THIOKOL S.A. DE C.V.—See Morton International Inc.; *U.S. Public*, pg. 1136
N.V. MORTON THIOKOL S.A.—See Morton International Inc.; *U.S. Public*, pg. 1136
MORTON'S JEWELRY CO.—See Reliable Stores, Inc.; *U.S. Private*, pg. 921
MORTON'S OF CHICAGO, INC.—See Morton's Restaurant Group, Inc.; *U.S. Public*, pg. 1136
MORTON'S RESTAURANT GROUP, INC.; *U.S. Public*, pg. 1136
MORVAN PARIS—See SNCF; *Int'l*, pg. 1164
MORVEN PARTNERS LP; *U.S. Private*, pg. 763
MOSAIK VERLAG—See Bertelsmann AG; *Int'l*, pg. 190
MOSBY - WILLIAMS & WILKINS PTY. LTD.—See Waverly, Inc.; *U.S. Public*, pg. 1748
MOSBY-YEAR BOOK, INC.—See The Times Mirror Company; *U.S. Public*, pg. 1616
MOSCOM CORPORATION; *U.S. Public*, pg. 1136
MOSCOW PRINTING INK—See Dainippon Ink & Chemicals, Inc.; *Int'l*, pg. 371
MOSER-BAU GMBH—See Bilfinger + Berger Bauaktiengesellschaft; *Int'l*, pg. 195
MOSINEE CONVERTED PRODUCTS DIV.—See Wausau-Mosinee Paper Corporation; *U.S. Public*, pg. 1747
MOSINEE INDUSTRIAL FOREST DIVISION—See Wausau-Mosinee Paper Corporation; *U.S. Public*, pg. 1747
MOSINEE PAPER INTERNATIONAL, INC.—See Wausau-Mosinee Paper Corporation; *U.S. Public*, pg. 1747
MOSLER CANADA—See American Standard Inc.; *U.S. Public*, pg. 92
MOSLER COUNTER SYSTEMS DIV.—See Mosler Inc.; *U.S. Private*, pg. 763
MOSLER ELECTRONIC SYSTEMS DIV.—See Mosler Inc.; *U.S. Private*, pg. 763
MOSLER INC.; *U.S. Private*, pg. 763
MOSLER SA DE C.D.—See Mosler Inc.; *U.S. Private*, pg. 763
MOSS BROS GROUP PLC; *Int'l*, pg. 895
MOSS/DRAGOTI—See BDDP Group; *Int'l*, pg. 117
E. MOSS LIMITED—See Alliance UniChem PLC; *Int'l*, pg. 58
MOSS TELECOMMUNICATIONS SERVICES; *U.S. Private*, pg. 763
MOSSBERG INDUSTRIES, INC.; *U.S. Private*, pg. 763
O.F. MOSSBERG & SONS, INC.; *U.S. Private*, pg. 764
MOST CROWN INDUSTRIES LTD.—See Citizen Watch Company, Ltd.; *Int'l*, pg. 295
MOSTRUPS FORLAG A/S—See The Thomson Corporation; *U.S. Public*, pg. 1602
MOTALA HISSAR A.B.—See Kone Corporation; *Int'l*, pg. 748
MOTALA TANK—See Trelleborg AB; *Int'l*, pg. 1420
MOTAPRODUCTS AUTOMOTIVE LIMITED—See Echlin Inc.; *U.S. Public*, pg. 561
MOTCH CORPORATION—See Rothenberger Group GmbH; *Int'l*, pg. 1128
MOTEK ENGINEERING & MANUFACTURING COMPANY; *U.S. Private*, pg. 764
MOTEL 6 OPERATING L.P.—See Accor S.A.; *Int'l*, pg. 21
MOTEURS GLOBE C/O LABINAL—See Labinal SA; *Int'l*, pg. 787
MOTHER EARTH NEWS—See Sussex Publishers, Inc.; *U.S. Private*, pg. 1056
MOTHERCARE WORLD UK LTD.—See Storehouse PLC; *Int'l*, pg. 1304
MOTHERS BACK ISSUES, INC.—See Sussex Publishers, Inc.; *U.S. Private*, pg. 1056
MOTHER'S BOOKSHELF—See Sussex Publishers, Inc.; *U.S. Private*, pg. 1056
MOTIF, INC.—See In Focus Systems, Inc.; *U.S. Public*, pg. 873
MOTIF, INC.—See Motorola, Inc.; *U.S. Public*, pg. 1137
MOTION & CONTROL GROUP—See Parker Hannifin Corporation; *U.S. Public*, pg. 1261
MOTION & CONTROL SALES DIV.—See Parker Hannifin Corporation; *U.S. Public*, pg. 1261
MOTION CONTROL INDUSTRIES, INC.—See Carlisle Companies Incorporated; *U.S. Public*, pg. 305

Company Index

MOTION INDUSTRIES (CANADA), INC.—See Genuine Parts Company; *U.S. Public*, pg. 732
MOTION INDUSTRIES, INC.—See Genuine Parts Company; *U.S. Public*, pg. 732
MOTO, INC.; *U.S. Private*, pg. 764
MOTO PHOTO, INC.; *U.S. Public*, pg. 1136
MOTOMETER AG—See Robert Bosch GmbH; *Int'l*, pg. 204
MOTOR BOATING & SAILING—See The Hearst Corporation; *U.S. Private*, pg. 517
MOTOR COACH INDUSTRIES, INC.—See Consorcio G. Grupo Dina, S.A. de C.V.; *Int'l*, pg. 326
MOTOR COACH INDUSTRIES INTERNATIONAL, INC.—See Consorcio G. Grupo Dina, S.A. de C.V.; *Int'l*, pg. 326
MOTOR COACH INDUSTRIES LTD.—See Consorcio G. Grupo Dina, S.A. de C.V.; *Int'l*, pg. 326
MOTOR CRASH ESTIMATING GUIDE—See The Hearst Corporation; *U.S. Private*, pg. 516
MOTOR-FINANZ GMBH—See Bayerische Vereinsbank Group; *Int'l*, pg. 180
MOTOR GROUP—See Rockwell International Corporation; *U.S. Public*, pg. 1398
MOTOR HOME SERVICE FACILITY-DECATUR, INDIANA—See Fleetwood Enterprises, Inc.; *U.S. Public*, pg. 652
MOTOR HOME SERVICE FACILITY-RIVERSIDE, CALIFORNIA—See Fleetwood Enterprises, Inc.; *U.S. Public*, pg. 652
MOTOR INDUSTRIES CO. LTD.—See Robert Bosch GmbH; *Int'l*, pg. 206
MOTOR MAGAZINE—See The Hearst Corporation; *U.S. Private*, pg. 516
MOTOR MASTER PRODUCTS—See Zeller Corp.; *U.S. Private*, pg. 1204
MOTOR PUBLICATIONS—See The Hearst Corporation; *U.S. Private*, pg. 516
MOTOR WHEEL DE MEXICO—See Hayes Wheels International, Inc.; *U.S. Private*, pg. 513
MOTORCAR PARTS & ACCESSORIES; *U.S. Public*, pg. 1136
MOTORENWERK CHEMNITZ GMBH—See Volkswagen AG; *Int'l*, pg. 1474
MOTOREN-WERKE MANNHEIM AG—See Deutz AG; *Int'l*, pg. 408
MOTORES U. S. DE MEXICO, S.A.—See Emerson Electric Co.; *U.S. Public*, pg. 577
MOTOREX AG—See Fuchs Petrolub AG Oel + Chemie; *Int'l*, pg. 518
MOTORISTS LIFE INSURANCE COMPANY—See Motorists Mutual Insurance Co.; *U.S. Private*, pg. 764
MOTORISTS MUTUAL INSURANCE CO.; *U.S. Private*, pg. 764
THE MOTORLEASE CORP.; *U.S. Private*, pg. 764
MOTOROLA AB—See Motorola, Inc.; *U.S. Public*, pg. 1139
MOTOROLA AB COMMUNICATIONS GROUP—See Motorola, Inc.; *U.S. Public*, pg. 1139
MOTOROLA AB INFORMATION SYSTEMS GROUP—See Motorola, Inc.; *U.S. Public*, pg. 1139
MOTOROLA A.C., INC.—See Motorola, Inc.; *U.S. Public*, pg. 1137
MOTOROLA ACCEPTANCE CORPORATION—See Motorola, Inc.; *U.S. Public*, pg. 1137
MOTOROLA AIEG HOLDING, INC.—See Motorola, Inc.; *U.S. Public*, pg. 1137
MOTOROLA ARDIS—See Motorola, Inc.; *U.S. Public*, pg. 1137
MOTOROLA ARGENTINA, S.A.—See Motorola, Inc.; *U.S. Public*, pg. 1139
MOTOROLA A/S—See Motorola, Inc.; *U.S. Public*, pg. 1139
MOTOROLA ASIA LTD.—See Motorola, Inc.; *U.S. Public*, pg. 1139
MOTOROLA ASIA PACIFIC LIMITED—See Motorola, Inc.; *U.S. Public*, pg. 1139
MOTOROLA AUSTRALIA PTY., LTD.—See Motorola, Inc.; *U.S. Public*, pg. 1139
MOTOROLA AUTOMOTIVE & INDUSTRIAL ELECTRONICS GROUP—See Motorola, Inc.; *U.S. Public*, pg. 1137
MOTOROLA AUTOMOTIVE PRODUCTS INC.—See Motorola, Inc.; *U.S. Public*, pg. 1137
MOTOROLA B.V.—See Motorola, Inc.; *U.S. Public*, pg. 1139
MOTOROLA CANADA LTD./MOTOROLA CANADA LIMITEE—See Motorola, Inc.; *U.S. Public*, pg. 1139
MOTOROLA CARIBE PACIFICO LTD.—See Motorola, Inc.; *U.S. Public*, pg. 1137
MOTOROLA CELLULAR SERVICE, INC. (CALIFORNIA)—See Motorola, Inc.; *U.S. Public*, pg. 1138
MOTOROLA CELLULAR SERVICE, INC. (ILLINOIS)—See Motorola, Inc.; *U.S. Public*, pg. 1138
MOTOROLA CELLULAR SUBSCRIBER GROUP—See Motorola, Inc.; *U.S. Public*, pg. 1137
MOTOROLA CENTER COMPUTERSYSTEME GESMBH—See Motorola, Inc.; *U.S. Public*, pg. 1139
MOTOROLA CHILE S.A.—See Motorola, Inc.; *U.S. Public*, pg. 1139
MOTOROLA CHINA ELECTRONICS LTD.—See Motorola, Inc.; *U.S. Public*, pg. 1139
MOTOROLA CHINA HOLDING LIMITED—See Motorola, Inc.; *U.S. Public*, pg. 1139
MOTOROLA CHINA, INC.—See Motorola, Inc.; *U.S. Public*, pg. 1138
MOTOROLA CHINA INC.—See Motorola, Inc.; *U.S. Public*, pg. 1139
MOTOROLA COMMUNICATIONS & ELECTRONICS, INC.—See Motorola, Inc.; *U.S. Public*, pg. 1138
MOTOROLA COMMUNICATIONS INTERNATIONAL, INC.—See Motorola, Inc.; *U.S. Public*, pg. 1138
MOTOROLA COMMUNICATIONS ISRAEL LIMITED—See Motorola, Inc.; *U.S. Public*, pg. 1139
MOTOROLA COMMUNICATIONS SERVICES LIMITED—See Motorola, Inc.; *U.S. Public*, pg. 1139
MOTOROLA COMPUTER GROUP—See Motorola, Inc.; *U.S. Public*, pg. 1137

MOTOROLA COMPUTER SALES & SERVICES, INC.—See Motorola, Inc.; *U.S. Public*, pg. 1138
MOTOROLA CPSTG, SENSORS PRODUCTS DIVISION—See Motorola, Inc.; *U.S. Public*, pg. 1137
MOTOROLA CREDIT CORPORATION—See Motorola, Inc.; *U.S. Public*, pg. 1138
MOTOROLA CVD, INC.—See Motorola, Inc.; *U.S. Public*, pg. 1138
MOTOROLA DE CENTROAMERICA, S.A.—See Motorola, Inc.; *U.S. Public*, pg. 1139
MOTOROLA DE COMERCIALIZACION Y SERVICIOS S.A.—See Motorola, Inc.; *U.S. Public*, pg. 1139
MOTOROLA DE LOS ANDES Y EL CARIBE—See Motorola, Inc.; *U.S. Public*, pg. 1139
MOTOROLA DE PUERTO RICO, INC.—See Motorola, Inc.; *U.S. Public*, pg. 1138
MOTOROLA DO BRASIL LTDA.—See Motorola, Inc.; *U.S. Public*, pg. 1139
MOTOROLA ELECTRONIC GMBH—See Motorola, Inc.; *U.S. Public*, pg. 1139
MOTOROLA ELECTRONICA DE PUERTO RICO, INC.—See Motorola, Inc.; *U.S. Public*, pg. 1138
MOTOROLA ELECTRONICA DE VENEZUELA S.A.—See Motorola, Inc.; *U.S. Public*, pg. 1139
MOTOROLA ELECTRONICS AUSTRALIA PTY., LTD.—See Motorola, Inc.; *U.S. Public*, pg. 1139
MOTOROLA ELECTRONICS & COMMUNICATIONS, INC.—See Motorola, Inc.; *U.S. Public*, pg. 1139
MOTOROLA ELECTRONICS PTE., LTD.—See Motorola, Inc.; *U.S. Public*, pg. 1139
MOTOROLA ELECTRONICS PTE. LTD., COMPONENTS DIV.—See Motorola, Inc.; *U.S. Public*, pg. 1139
MOTOROLA ELECTRONICS SDN. BHD.—See Motorola, Inc.; *U.S. Public*, pg. 1139
MOTOROLA ELECTRONICS TAIWAN, LTD.—See Motorola, Inc.; *U.S. Public*, pg. 1139
MOTOROLA ELECTRONIQUE AUTOMOBILE—See Motorola, Inc.; *U.S. Public*, pg. 1139
MOTOROLA ENERGY PRODUCTS DIVISION—See Motorola, Inc.; *U.S. Public*, pg. 1137
MOTOROLA ENERGY SYSTEMS, INC.—See Motorola, Inc.; *U.S. Public*, pg. 1138
MOTOROLA ESPANA S.A.—See Motorola, Inc.; *U.S. Public*, pg. 1139
MOTOROLA FINANCE B.V.—See Motorola, Inc.; *U.S. Public*, pg. 1139
MOTOROLA FOREIGN SALES CORPORATION—See Motorola, Inc.; *U.S. Public*, pg. 1138
MOTOROLA GALVIN CENTER—See Motorola, Inc.; *U.S. Public*, pg. 1138
MOTOROLA GENERAL SYSTEMS GROUP—See Motorola, Inc.; *U.S. Public*, pg. 1137
MOTOROLA GES.M.B.H.—See Motorola, Inc.; *U.S. Public*, pg. 1139
MOTOROLA GOVERNMENT ELECTRONICS GROUP—See Motorola, Inc.; *U.S. Public*, pg. 1137
MOTOROLA, INC.; *U.S. Public*, pg. 1136
MOTOROLA, INC.—See Motorola, Inc.; *U.S. Public*, pg. 1138
MOTOROLA INDALA CORPORATION—See Motorola, Inc.; *U.S. Public*, pg. 1138
MOTOROLA INDIA ELECTRONICS PRIVATE LIMITED—See Motorola, Inc.; *U.S. Public*, pg. 1139
MOTOROLA INFORMATION SYSTEMS, INC.—See Motorola, Inc.; *U.S. Public*, pg. 1138
MOTOROLA INFORMATION SYSTEMS LIMITED—See Motorola, Inc.; *U.S. Public*, pg. 1139
MOTOROLA INTERNATIONAL CAPITAL CORP.—See Motorola, Inc.; *U.S. Public*, pg. 1138
MOTOROLA INTERNATIONAL DEVELOPMENT CORP.—See Motorola, Inc.; *U.S. Public*, pg. 1138
MOTOROLA INTERNATIONAL, INC.—See Motorola, Inc.; *U.S. Public*, pg. 1138
MOTOROLA INTERNATIONAL PAGING, INC.—See Motorola, Inc.; *U.S. Public*, pg. 1138
MOTOROLA INTERNATIONAL SALES, INC.—See Motorola, Inc.; *U.S. Public*, pg. 1138
MOTOROLA IRELAND LTD.—See Motorola, Inc.; *U.S. Public*, pg. 1139
MOTOROLA ISRAEL INFORMATION SYSTEMS LTD.—See Motorola, Inc.; *U.S. Public*, pg. 1139
MOTOROLA ISRAEL INVESTMENTS LIMITED—See Motorola, Inc.; *U.S. Public*, pg. 1139
MOTOROLA ISRAEL LTD.—See Motorola, Inc.; *U.S. Public*, pg. 1139
MOTOROLA ISRAEL SEMICONDUCTOR & SYSTEMS (SPS) LTD.—See Motorola, Inc.; *U.S. Public*, pg. 1139
MOTOROLA KOREA LTD.—See Motorola, Inc.; *U.S. Public*, pg. 1139
MOTOROLA LAND MOBILE PRODUCT SECTOR—See Motorola, Inc.; *U.S. Public*, pg. 1137
MOTOROLA LIGHTING INC.—See Motorola, Inc.; *U.S. Public*, pg. 1138
MOTOROLA LIMITED—See Motorola, Inc.; *U.S. Public*, pg. 1139
MOTOROLA LTD.—See Motorola, Inc.; *U.S. Public*, pg. 1140
MOTOROLA MALAYSIA SDN. BHD.—See Motorola, Inc.; *U.S. Public*, pg. 1140
MOTOROLA MANUFACTURING TECHNOLOGY DIVISION—See Motorola, Inc.; *U.S. Public*, pg. 1138
MOTOROLA MCTG—See Motorola, Inc.; *U.S. Public*, pg. 1138
MOTOROLA MESSAGING, INFORMATION & MEDIA INC.—See Motorola, Inc.; *U.S. Public*, pg. 1138
MOTOROLA MESSAGING SYSTEMS PRODUCT GROUP—See Motorola, Inc.; *U.S. Public*, pg. 1137
MOTOROLA MILITARY & AEROSPACE ELECTRONICS, INC.—See Motorola, Inc.; *U.S. Public*, pg. 1138
MOTOROLA MMTG—See Motorola, Inc.; *U.S. Public*, pg. 1137
MOTOROLA MOBILE COMMUNICATIONS—See Motorola, Inc.; *U.S. Public*, pg. 1140

MOTOROLA MOBILE DATA DIVISION—See Motorola, Inc.; *U.S. Public*, pg. 1138
MOTOROLA MULTIMEDIA GROUP—See Motorola, Inc.; *U.S. Public*, pg. 1137
MOTOROLA NEW ZEALAND LIMITED—See Motorola, Inc.; *U.S. Public*, pg. 1140
MOTOROLA NORTEL—See Motorola, Inc.; *U.S. Public*, pg. 1138
MOTOROLA NORTEL COMMUNICATION—See Motorola, Inc.; *U.S. Public*, pg. 1138
MOTOROLA NORTH AMERICAN PAGING SUBSCRIBER DIVISION—See Motorola, Inc.; *U.S. Public*, pg. 1137
MOTOROLA NORWAY A/S—See Motorola, Inc.; *U.S. Public*, pg. 1140
S.A. MOTOROLA, N.V.—See Motorola, Inc.; *U.S. Public*, pg. 1140
MOTOROLA PAGETEL, INC.—See Motorola, Inc.; *U.S. Public*, pg. 1138
MOTOROLA PAGING SUBSCRIBER GROUP—See Motorola, Inc.; *U.S. Public*, pg. 1137
MOTOROLA PAN AMERICAN WIRELESS INFRASTRUCTURE DIVISION—See Motorola, Inc.; *U.S. Public*, pg. 1137
MOTOROLA PCS, INC.—See Motorola, Inc.; *U.S. Public*, pg. 1138
MOTOROLA PHILIPPINES INC.—See Motorola, Inc.; *U.S. Public*, pg. 1140
MOTOROLA PORTUGAL COMUNICACOES, LDA.—See Motorola, Inc.; *U.S. Public*, pg. 1140
MOTOROLA PRIVATE LIMITED—See Motorola, Inc.; *U.S. Public*, pg. 1140
MOTOROLA RADIO NETWORK SOLUTIONS GROUP—See Motorola, Inc.; *U.S. Public*, pg. 1138
MOTOROLA RADIO PRODUCTS GROUP—See Motorola, Inc.; *U.S. Public*, pg. 1138
MOTOROLA RADIUS—See Motorola, Inc.; *U.S. Public*, pg. 1138
MOTOROLA RECOVERY SERVICE, INC.—See Motorola, Inc.; *U.S. Public*, pg. 1138
MOTOROLA RFID, INC.—See Motorola, Inc.; *U.S. Public*, pg. 1138
MOTOROLA S.A.—See Motorola, Inc.; *U.S. Public*, pg. 1140
MOTOROLA SATELLITE COMMUNICATIONS, INC.—See Motorola, Inc.; *U.S. Public*, pg. 1138
MOTOROLA SEMICONDUCTOR ISRAEL LTD.—See Motorola, Inc.; *U.S. Public*, pg. 1140
MOTOROLA SEMICONDUCTORS HONG KONG LTD.—See Motorola, Inc.; *U.S. Public*, pg. 1140
MOTOROLA SEMICONDUCTORS SDN. BHD.—See Motorola, Inc.; *U.S. Public*, pg. 1140
MOTOROLA SF, INC.—See Motorola, Inc.; *U.S. Public*, pg. 1138
MOTOROLA SINGAPORE PTE., LTD.—See Motorola, Inc.; *U.S. Public*, pg. 1140
MOTOROLA SINGAPORE PTE. LTD.—See Motorola, Inc.; *U.S. Public*, pg. 1140
MOTOROLA SMR, INC.—See Motorola, Inc.; *U.S. Public*, pg. 1138
MOTOROLA SOUTH-ISRAEL LIMITED—See Motorola, Inc.; *U.S. Public*, pg. 1140
MOTOROLA S.P.A.—See Motorola, Inc.; *U.S. Public*, pg. 1140
MOTOROLA S.R.O.—See Motorola, Inc.; *U.S. Public*, pg. 1140
MOTOROLA SUISSE S.A.—See Motorola, Inc.; *U.S. Public*, pg. 1140
MOTOROLA TELEPHONE CELLULAR COMMUNICATIONS LTD—See Motorola, Inc.; *U.S. Public*, pg. 1140
MOTOROLA (THAILAND) LIMITED—See Motorola, Inc.; *U.S. Public*, pg. 1140
MOTOROLA USA—See Motorola, Inc.; *U.S. Public*, pg. 1138
MOTOROLA WIRELESS DATA GROUP—See Motorola, Inc.; *U.S. Public*, pg. 1137
MOTOROLA WIRELESS SERVICE, INC.—See Motorola, Inc.; *U.S. Public*, pg. 1138
MOTORS TRADING CORPORATION—See General Motors Corporation; *U.S. Public*, pg. 721
MOTORWAYS (1980) LIMITED—See Russel Metals Inc.; *Int'l*, pg. 1150
MOTOWN RECORD COMPANY, J.P.—See Philips Electronics N.V.; *Int'l*, pg. 1052
MOTT'S CANADA DIVISION—See Cadbury Schweppes p.l.c.; *Int'l*, pg. 248
MOTT'S HOLDINGS, INC.; *U.S. Private*, pg. 764
MOTT'S INC.—See Cadbury Schweppes p.l.c.; *Int'l*, pg. 248
MOTTS SUPERMARKETS—See Mott's Holdings, Inc.; *U.S. Private*, pg. 764
MOULINEX—See Moulinex S.A.; *Int'l*, pg. 896
MOULINEX APPLIANCES, INC.—See Moulinex S.A.; *Int'l*, pg. 896
MOULINEX A/S, SCA—See Moulinex S.A.; *Int'l*, pg. 896
MOULINEX B.V.—See Moulinex S.A.; *Int'l*, pg. 896
MOULINEX CANADA LTD.—See Moulinex S.A.; *Int'l*, pg. 896
MOULINEX ESPANA S.A.—See Moulinex S.A.; *Int'l*, pg. 896
MOULINEX GMBH—See Moulinex S.A.; *Int'l*, pg. 896
MOULINEX HUNGARIA—See Moulinex S.A.; *Int'l*, pg. 896
MOULINEX ITALIA SRL—See Moulinex S.A.; *Int'l*, pg. 896
MOULINEX MIDDLE EAST—See Moulinex S.A.; *Int'l*, pg. 896
MOULINEX S.A.; *Int'l*, pg. 896
MOULINEX/SWAN LTD.—See Moulinex S.A.; *Int'l*, pg. 896
MOULTRIE CONTAINER DIV.—See Philip Morris Companies Inc.; *U.S. Public*, pg. 1289
MOUNT BACHELOR VILLAGE CORP.—See Brooks Resources Corporation; *U.S. Private*, pg. 172
THE MOUNT COOK GROUP LIMITED—See Air New Zealand Ltd.; *Int'l*, pg. 38
MT. EAGLE CORPORATION—See Brown-Forman Corporation; *U.S. Public*, pg. 261

MT. HAWLEY INSURANCE COMPANY—See RLI Corp.; U.S. Public, pg. 1356
MOUNT HOLLY WATER CO.—See E'Town Corporation; U.S. Public, pg. 540
MT. HOOD LIFE INSURANCE, INC.—See U.S. Bancorp; Int'l, pg. 1681
MOUNT ISA INTERNATIONAL PTY. LTD.—See M.I.M. Holdings Ltd.; Int'l, pg. 827
MOUNT JACKSON PRESS, INC.—See Perry Graphic Communications, Inc.; U.S. Private, pg. 855
MOUNT NELSON HOTEL LTD.—See Sea Containers Ltd.; Int'l, pg. 1214
MOUNT SNOW RESORT—See American Skiing Company; U.S. Public, pg. 61
MOUNT VERNON DEMOCRAT—See Landmark Communications, Inc.; U.S. Private, pg. 648
MOUNT VERNON DRYER FABRICS—See R.B. Pamplin Corp.; U.S. Private, pg. 835
MOUNT VERNON MILLS, INC.—See R.B. Pamplin Corp.; U.S. Private, pg. 835
MOUNT VERNON MILLS, INC., CLARKTON, NC—See R.B. Pamplin Corp.; U.S. Private, pg. 835
MOUNT VERNON MILLS, INC., CONSUMER PRODUCTS DIV. (MCCORMICK)—See R.B. Pamplin Corp.; U.S. Private, pg. 835
MOUNT VERNON MILLS, INC., LAFRANCE INDUSTRIES—See R.B. Pamplin Corp.; U.S. Private, pg. 835
MOUNT VERNON MILLS, INC., MOUNT VERNON FORMING FABRICS—See R.B. Pamplin Corp.; U.S. Private, pg. 835
MOUNT VERNON MILLS, INC., RIEGEL CONSUMER PRODUCTS DIV.—See R.B. Pamplin Corp.; U.S. Private, pg. 835
MOUNT VERNON MILLS, INC., RIEGEL TEXTILE DIV.—See R.B. Pamplin Corp.; U.S. Private, pg. 835
MOUNT VERNON MILLS, INC., RIEGEL TEXTILE DIV. (ALTO)—See R.B. Pamplin Corp.; U.S. Private, pg. 835
MOUNT VERNON MILLS, INC., RIEGEL TEXTILE DIV. (TRION)—See R.B. Pamplin Corp.; U.S. Private, pg. 835
MOUNT VERNON MILLS, INC., TALLASSEE, AL—See R.B. Pamplin Corp.; U.S. Private, pg. 835
MOUNT VERNON MILLS, INC., WILLIAMSTON—See R.B. Pamplin Corp.; U.S. Private, pg. 835
MOUNT VERNON MILLS, INC., WOODRUFF—See R.B. Pamplin Corp.; U.S. Private, pg. 835
MOUNT VERNON MILLS SALES CORP.—See R.B. Pamplin Corp.; U.S. Private, pg. 836
MOUNT VERNON MILLS, SMITH & WATERS, INC.—See R.B. Pamplin Corp.; U.S. Private, pg. 835
MOUNT VERNON NEON—See Everbrite, Inc.; U.S. Private, pg. 386
MOUNT VERNON PLASTICS COMPANY—See Reynolds Metals Company; U.S. Public, pg. 1386
MT. VERNON TELEPHONE CO.—See Telephone and Data Systems, Inc.; U.S. Public, pg. 1571
MOUNT VERNON TEXTILE GROUP—See R.B. Pamplin Corp.; U.S. Private, pg. 836
MOUNTAIN CEMENT COMPANY—See Centex Corporation; U.S. Public, pg. 323
MOUNTAIN CHAI—See Celestial Seasonings; U.S. Public, pg. 320
MOUNTAIN ENERGY, INC.—See Green Mountain Power Corporation; U.S. Public, pg. 761
MOUNTAIN FUEL SUPPLY COMPANY—See Questar Corporation; U.S. Public, pg. 1352
MOUNTAIN GAS REOURCES, INC.—See Western Gas Resources, Inc.; U.S. Public, pg. 1758
MOUNTAIN IRON & SUPPLY COMPANY; U.S. Private, pg. 764
MOUNTAIN OPERATIONS LAND DIVISION—See U.S. Home Corporation; U.S. Public, pg. 1683
MOUNTAIN OPTECH INC.—See Phillips Service Industries, Inc.; U.S. Private, pg. 662
MOUNTAIN STATE TELEPHONE CO.—See Citizens Utilities Company; U.S. Public, pg. 380
MOUNTAIN STATES AIRGAS—See Airgas, Inc.; U.S. Public, pg. 33
MOUNTAIN STATES CONSTRUCTORS, INC.; U.S. Private, pg. 764
MOUNTAIN STATES PIPE & SUPPLY COMPANY; U.S. Private, pg. 764
MOUNTAIN TOWERS HEALTHCARE—See Vencor, Inc.; U.S. Public, pg. 1714
MOUNTAIN VALLEY SPRING COMPANY—See Sammons Enterprises, Inc.; U.S. Private, pg. 963
MOUNTAIN VIEW HEALTHCARE—See Vencor, Inc.; U.S. Public, pg. 1714
MOUNTAIN VIEW PLACE—See Horizon/CMS Healthcare Corporation; U.S. Public, pg. 839
MOUNTAINEER GAS SERVICES, INC.—See Eastern American Energy Corporation; U.S. Private, pg. 357
MOUNTAINEER RESOURCES, INC.—See Salem Group, Inc.; U.S. Private, pg. 961
MOUNTAINGATE DATA SYSTEMS, INC.—See Lockheed Martin Corporation; U.S. Public, pg. 1008
MOUNTAINGATE ENGINEERING, INC.—See Nordson Corporation; U.S. Public, pg. 1188
MOVADO GROUP, INC.; U.S. Public, pg. 1140
MOVADO GROUP INC.—See Movado Group, Inc.; U.S. Public, pg. 1140
MOVADO WATCH COMPANY, S.A.—See Movado Group, Inc.; U.S. Public, pg. 1140
MOVEMENTS INTERNATIONAL MOVERS (NSW) PTY. LTD.—See Brambles Industries Limited; Int'l, pg. 211
MOVIE STAR FACTORY OUTLET STORES—See Movie Star, Inc.; U.S. Public, pg. 1141
MOVIE STAR, INC.; U.S. Public, pg. 1140
MOVIECAM-VOEST-ALPINE KINEMATOGRAPHISCHE GERATE GES.M.B.H.—See Voest-Alpine Stahl AG; Int'l, pg. 1470
MOVIFIL-MOVIMENTACAO INDUSTRIAL LDA.—See Mannesmann A.G.; Int'l, pg. 838

MOVILIDAD MODERNA, S.A. DE C.V.—See Carpenter Technology Corporation; U.S. Public, pg. 94
MOWE TEIGWARENWERK GMBH—See CSM N.V.; Int'l, pg. 244
ERIC MOWER AND ASSOCIATES—See Eric Mower and Associates, Inc.; U.S. Private, pg. 765
ERIC MOWER AND ASSOCIATES/BUFFALO, INC.—See Eric Mower and Associates, Inc.; U.S. Private, pg. 765
ERIC MOWER AND ASSOCIATES, INC.; U.S. Private, pg. 765
ERIC MOWER & ASSOCIATES—See Eric Mower and Associates, Inc.; U.S. Private, pg. 765
JOHN MOWLEM & COMPANY PLC; Int'l, pg. 896
MOX-MED, INC.—See Applied Power Inc.; U.S. Public, pg. 124
MOXNESS PRODUCTS, INC.—See Applied Power Inc.; U.S. Public, pg. 124
MOXY TRUCKS AS—See Komatsu Ltd.; Int'l, pg. 745
MOY INSULATION LTD.—See BPB Industries PLC; Int'l, pg. 123
MOYER PACKING COMPANY; U.S. Private, pg. 765
MOYGASHEL LTD.—See Lamont Holdings Plc; Int'l, pg. 798
MOYGASHEL USA INC.—See Lamont Holdings Plc; Int'l, pg. 798
MOZEL DEVELOPMENT CORP.; U.S. Private, pg. 765
MOZZARELLA'S RESTAURANTS—See Ruby Tuesday, Inc.; U.S. Public, pg. 1412
MR. APPLIANCE CORP.—See The Dwyer Group, Inc.; U.S. Public, pg. 538
MR. BRACKET—See MascoTech, Inc.; U.S. Public, pg. 1055
MR. CHRISTMAS INC.; U.S. Private, pg. 765
MR. CHRISTMAS LIMITED—See Mr. Christmas Inc.; U.S. Private, pg. 765
MR. ELECTRIC CORPORATION—See The Dwyer Group, Inc.; U.S. Public, pg. 538
MR. GASKET INC.—See Echlin Inc.; U.S. Public, pg. 560
MR. GATTI'S, INC.—See LDB Corporation; U.S. Private, pg. 639
MR. ROOTER CORPORATION—See The Dwyer Group, Inc.; U.S. Public, pg. 538
MR. WRIGHT'S AMAZING COFFEE FACTORY; U.S. Private, pg. 765
MRS. ALISON'S COOKIE COMPANY; U.S. Private, pg. 765
MRS. BAIRD'S BAKERIES, INC.; U.S. Private, pg. 765
MRS. CLARKS FOOD INC—See American Grain & Related Industries; U.S. Private, pg. 55
MRS. CUBBISON'S FOODS, INC.—See Interstate Bakeries Corporation; U.S. Public, pg. 909
MRS. GILES COUNTRY KITCHENS, INC.—See Bob Evans Farms, Inc.; U.S. Public, pg. 596
MRS. GRIMES FOODS—See Faribault Foods Inc.; U.S. Private, pg. 394
MRS. SMITH'S BAKERIES, INC.—See Flowers Industries, Inc.; U.S. Public, pg. 657
MRS. SMITH'S BAKERIES OF PENNSYLVANIA, INC.—See Flowers Industries, Inc.; U.S. Public, pg. 658
MRS. SMITH'S BAKERY OF PENNSYLVANIA—See Flowers Industries, Inc.; U.S. Public, pg. 658
MRS. WINNER'S CHICKEN & BISCUIT RESTAURANTS; U.S. Private, pg. 766
MSFT SOFTWARE PARA MICROCOMPUTADORES, LDA—See Microsoft Corporation; U.S. Public, pg. 1108
MUCH PHARMA—See American Home Products Corporation; U.S. Public, pg. 81
MUDD JEANS, INC.; U.S. Private, pg. 766
MUEBLAS ANDES—See Eastman Kodak Company; U.S. Public, pg. 553
MUEBLES FINO BUENO—See Good Companies; U.S. Private, pg. 463
MUELLER CO.—See Tyco International Ltd.; U.S. Public, pg. 1650
MUELLER INDUSTRIES, INC.; U.S. Public, pg. 1141
MUELLER INTERNATIONAL SALES CORP.—See Paul Mueller Company; U.S. Public, pg. 1141
PAUL MUELLER COMPANY; U.S. Public, pg. 1141
R.A. MUELLER, INC.; U.S. Private, pg. 766
MUELLER SPORTS MEDICINE, INC.; U.S. Private, pg. 766
MUELLER STEAM SPECIALTY—See United Dominion Industries, Ltd.; U.S. Public, pg. 1676
MUELLER'S MUEHLE GMBH; Int'l, pg. 896
MUELLES Y BALLESTAS HISPANO-ALEMANAS S.A.—See NHK Spring Co., Ltd.; Int'l, pg. 902
MUENCH-KREUZER CANDLE COMPANY; U.S. Private, pg. 766
MUENCHENER LEBENSVERSICHERUNG AG—See Allianz Aktiengesellschaft; Int'l, pg. 61
C.A. MUER CORP.; U.S. Private, pg. 766
THIERRY MUGLER PARFUMS—See Clarins; Int'l, pg. 295
MUGLER TRIUMVIRAT—See Clarins; Int'l, pg. 295
MUIDEN CHEMIE INTERNATIONAL BV—See British Aerospace p.l.c.; Int'l, pg. 217
MUKAISHIMA WORKS—See Hitachi Zosen Corporation; Int'l, pg. 623
MUKUSOL KUFFNER GMBH—See Dyckerhoff & Widmann AG; Int'l, pg. 423
MUL-T-LOCK GROUP—See IDB Holding Corporation; Int'l, pg. 644
MUL-T-LOCK LTD.—See IDB Holding Corporation; Int'l, pg. 644
MULACH STEEL CORPORATION; U.S. Private, pg. 766
MULAY PLASTICS INC.—See Dubin-Clark & Company; U.S. Private, pg. 344
MULBERRY METAL PRODUCTS, INC.; U.S. Private, pg. 766
MULBERRY STREET CASUALS LTD.—See Amerex USA, Inc.; U.S. Private, pg. 49
MULHERN BELTING, INC.; U.S. Private, pg. 766
MULLEN ADVERTISING, INC.; U.S. Private, pg. 766
MULLEN ADVERTISING, INC., PUBLIC RELATIONS DIV.—See Mullen Advertising, Inc.; U.S. Private, pg. 766

MULLEN ENVIRONMENTAL SERVICES, INC.—See American Waste Services, Inc.; U.S. Public, pg. 94
MULLEN TESTERS—See Standex International Corporation; U.S. Public, pg. 1506
MULLER DATA CORP.—See The Thomson Corporation; U.S. Public, pg. 1600
MULLER LINER AGENCIES N.V., ANTWERP—See Internatio-Muller N.V.; Int'l, pg. 682
RUDOLF MULLER & CO. G.M.B.H.—See Chr. Hansen Holding A/S; Int'l, pg. 289
MULLER-THOMSEN ANTWERPEN—See Internatio-Muller N.V.; Int'l, pg. 682
WM. H. MULLER & CO. BREMEN/HAMBURG—See Internatio-Muller N.V.; Int'l, pg. 682
WM. H. MULLER & CO. NEDERLAND B.V.—See Internatio-Muller N.V.; Int'l, pg. 682
MULLER ZELL GMBH—See Blydenstein-Willink N.V.; Int'l, pg. 204
ED MULLINAX FORD, INC.—See Republic Industries, Inc.; U.S. Public, pg. 1379
MULLVERWERTUNG BORSIGSTRASSE GMBH—See Veba AG; Int'l, pg. 1460
MULTANOVA AG—See Hesta Tex AG; Int'l, pg. 618
MULTANOVA FRANCE S.A.R.L.—See Hesta Tex AG; Int'l, pg. 618
MULTANOVA VERKEHRSUBERWACHUNGSYSTEME GMBH—See Hesta Tex AG; Int'l, pg. 618
MULTI-AD SERVICES, INCORPORATED; U.S. Private, pg. 766
MULTI-ARC INC.—See Saurer AG; Int'l, pg. 1198
MULTI-ARC (U.K.) LTD.—See Saurer AG; Int'l, pg. 1198
P.T. MULTI BINTANG INDONESIA—See Heineken N.V.; Int'l, pg. 608
MULTI-CLEAN INC.—See Hako-Werke GmbH & Co.; Int'l, pg. 587
MULTI-CREDIT CORPORATION OF THAILAND LTD.—See The Daiwa Bank Limited; Int'l, pg. 374
MULTI FINANS A/S—See Skandia Insurance Company International; Int'l, pg. 1257
MULTI LANGUAGE CENTER SRL—See Berlitz International, Inc.; U.S. Public, pg. 222
MULTI-LINE CANS, INC.—See Lykes Brothers Inc.; U.S. Private, pg. 682
MULTI-LOCAL MEDIA CORPORATION; U.S. Private, pg. 767
MULTI-PLEX, INC.—See Davis Industries Inc.; U.S. Private, pg. 315
P.T. MULTI RAGA AGUNG—See Nestle S.A.; Int'l, pg. 920
MULTIASS ASSICURAZIONI S.P.A.—See Skandia Insurance Company Limited; Int'l, pg. 1256
MULTIBANCO INTERNACIONAL DE INVESTIMENTOS S.A. SAO PAULO HEAD OFFICE—See BankAmerica Corporation; U.S. Public, pg. 183
THE MULTICARE COMPANIES, INC.—See Genesis Health Ventures, Inc.; U.S. Public, pg. 729
MULTICHIP TECHNOLOGY—See Cypress Semiconductor Corporation; U.S. Public, pg. 470
MULTICOM TBWA ADVERTISING B.V.—See TBWA Chiat/Day; U.S. Private, pg. 1062
MULTICOPY INTERNATIONAL B.V.—See Moore Corporation Limited; Int'l, pg. 890
P.T. MULTICOR BANK—See The Long-Term Credit Bank of Japan; Int'l, pg. 817
P.T. MULTICOR SECURITIES—See The Long-Term Credit Bank of Japan, Limited; Int'l, pg. 817
MULTIFOOD INTERNATIONAL—See Meiji Seika Kaisha, Ltd.; Int'l, pg. 855
MULTIFOODS SPECIALTY DISTRIBUTION INC.—See International Multifoods Corporation; U.S. Public, pg. 901
MULTIFORM, INC.—See Wurzburg, Inc.; U.S. Private, pg. 1193
MULTIGEN INC.—See Safeguard Scientifics, Inc.; U.S. Public, pg. 1425
MULTIGRAPHICS, INC.; U.S. Public, pg. 1141
MULTILIN—See General Electric Company; U.S. Public, pg. 713
MULTIMATIC CORPORATION; U.S. Private, pg. 767
MULTIMEDIA CABLEVISION, CO.—See Gannett Company, Inc.; U.S. Public, pg. 699
MULTIMEDIA NEWSPAPER COMPANY—See Gannett Company, Inc.; U.S. Public, pg. 699
MULTIMEDIA PUBLISHING OF NORTH CAROLINA, INC.—See Gannett Company, Inc.; U.S. Public, pg. 699
MULTIMEDIA PUBLISHING OF SOUTH CAROLINA, INC.—See Gannett Company, Inc.; U.S. Public, pg. 699
MULTIMEDIA RADIO, INC.—See Gannett Company, Inc.; U.S. Public, pg. 699
MULTIMEDIA SECURITY SERVICE—See Gannett Company, Inc.; U.S. Public, pg. 699
MULTINACIONAL ASEGURADORA S.A., DE SEGURYOS Y REASEGUROS—See Caixa d'Estalvis de Catalunya; Int'l, pg. 250
P.T. MULTINATIONAL FINANCE CORPORATION—See The Royal Bank of Scotland plc; Int'l, pg. 1133
MULTIPAK DE VENEZUELA C.A.—See Illinois Tool Works Inc.; U.S. Public, pg. 869
MULTIPART DISTRIBUTION—See Lex Service PLC; Int'l, pg. 807
MULTIPHARMA BV—See Novartis AG; Int'l, pg. 983
MULTIPLE ALLIED SERVICES, INC.; U.S. Private, pg. 767
MULTIPLE PAKFOLD FORMS—See Data Business Forms Limited; Int'l, pg. 384
MULTIPLE PARKING SERVICES, INC.—See Allright Corporation; U.S. Public, pg. 43
MULTIPLEX TECHNOLOGY, INC.—See Valley Forge Corporation; U.S. Public, pg. 1705
MULTIQUIP, INC.—See Itochu Corporation; U.S. Public, pg. 695
MULTISERV INTERNATIONAL LTD.—See Harsco Corporation; U.S. Public, pg. 793
MULTITEK—See Knurr AG; Int'l, pg. 740
MULTIVISION—See Groupe Bruxelles Lambert S.A.; Int'l, pg. 561

MULTIWALL PACKAGING LIMITED—See International Paper Company; *U.S. Public*, pg. 905
A/S MULVA GRAFISKE PRODUKTER—See American Greetings Corporation; *U.S. Public*, pg. 78
MUNCHENER LEBENSVERSICHERUNG AG—See Assicurazioni Generali S.p.A.; *Int'l*, pg. 89
MUNCHENER RUCKVERSICHERUNGS-GESELLSCHAFT; *Int'l*, pg. 897
MUNCIE NEWSPAPERS, INC.—See Central Newspapers, Inc.; *U.S. Public*, pg. 326
MUNCK AUTOMATION TECHNOLOGY; *U.S. Private*, pg. 767
MUNCK SOFTECH—See Munck Automation Technology; *U.S. Private*, pg. 767
MUNDINTER INTERCAMBIO UNDIAL DE COMMERCIO—See Hewlett-Packard Company; *U.S. Public*, pg. 822
MICHAEL J. MUNGO COMPANY, INC.; *U.S. Private*, pg. 767
MUNICH AMERICAN REINSURANCE CO. (MARC)—See Munchener Ruckversicherungs-Gesellschaft; *Int'l*, pg. 897
MUNICH AMERICAN REINSURANCE CO. (MARC LIFE)—See Munchener Ruckversicherungs-Gesellschaft; *Int'l*, pg. 897
MUNICH BRANCH—See Deutsche Babcock AG; *Int'l*, pg. 401
MUNICIPAL BOND INVESTORS ASSURANCE CORPORATION—See MBIA Inc.; *U.S. Public*, pg. 1023
MUNICIPAL BUSINESS UNIT—See ITT Industries, Inc.; *U.S. Public*, pg. 861
THE MUNICIPAL SAVINGS & LOAN CORPORATION—See National Bank of Canada; *Int'l*, pg. 907
MUNITIONS TECHNOLOGY DIVISION—See Day & Zimmermann, Inc.; *U.S. Private*, pg. 317
MUNKSGAARD INTERNATIONAL BOOKSELLERS & PUBLISHERS LTD.—See B.H. Blackwell Ltd.; *Int'l*, pg. 197
MUNKSJO AB—See Trelleborg AB; *Int'l*, pg. 1423
MUNKSJOE FORPACKNINGAR AB—See Trelleborg AB; *Int'l*, pg. 1423
MUNKSJOE HYGIEN AB—See Trelleborg AB; *Int'l*, pg. 1423
MUNRADTECH GENERATORS LIMITED—See TT Group PLC; *Int'l*, pg. 1344
MUNRO & COMPANY, INC.; *U.S. Private*, pg. 767
MUNROE, INC.; *U.S. Private*, pg. 767
MUNSKJOE PAPER AB—See Trelleborg AB; *Int'l*, pg. 1423
MUNTERS AG—See Incentive AB; *Int'l*, pg. 669
MUNTERS AIR TREATMENT EQUIPMENT CO. LTD.—See Incentive AB; *Int'l*, pg. 669
MUNTERS A/S—See Incentive AB; *Int'l*, pg. 669
MUNTERS BEIJING LTD.—See Incentive AB; *Int'l*, pg. 669
MUNTERS BRAZIL INDESTRIA COMERICO LTDA—See Incentive AB; *Int'l*, pg. 669
MUNTERS BV—See Incentive AB; *Int'l*, pg. 669
AB CARL MUNTERS—See Incentive AB; *Int'l*, pg. 669
CARL MUNTERS APS—See Incentive AB; *Int'l*, pg. 669
AB CARL MUNTERS (SEA)—See Incentive AB; *Int'l*, pg. 669
MUNTERS COMPONENT AB—See Incentive AB; *Int'l*, pg. 669
MUNTERS DE MEXICO SA DE CV—See Incentive AB; *Int'l*, pg. 669
MUNTERS DROOGTECHNIEK BV—See Incentive AB; *Int'l*, pg. 669
MUNTERS DRY AIR AB—See Incentive AB; *Int'l*, pg. 669
MUNTERS EUROFORM GMBH—See Incentive AB; *Int'l*, pg. 669
MUNTERS FUGTTEKNIK A/S—See Incentive AB; *Int'l*, pg. 669
MUNTERS GMBH—See Incentive AB; *Int'l*, pg. 669
MUNTERS (HK) PTE. LTD.—See Incentive AB; *Int'l*, pg. 669
MUNTERS INC.—See Incentive AB; *Int'l*, pg. 669
MUNTERS KFT—See Incentive AB; *Int'l*, pg. 669
MUNTERS KK—See Incentive AB; *Int'l*, pg. 669
MUNTERS LTD.—See Incentive AB; *Int'l*, pg. 669
MUNTERS MOISTURE CONTROL SERVICES—See Incentive AB; *Int'l*, pg. 669
MUNTERS NEDERLAND B.V.—See Incentive AB; *Int'l*, pg. 669
MUNTERS NV—See Incentive AB; *Int'l*, pg. 669
MUNTERS OY—See Incentive AB; *Int'l*, pg. 669
MUNTERS PTE LTD.—See Incentive AB; *Int'l*, pg. 669
MUNTERS PTY LTD.—See Incentive AB; *Int'l*, pg. 669
MUNTERS (PTY) LTD.—See Incentive AB; *Int'l*, pg. 669
MUNTERS S.A.—See Incentive AB; *Int'l*, pg. 669
MUNTERS SERVICES SA—See Incentive AB; *Int'l*, pg. 669
MUNTERS SPAIN SA—See Incentive AB; *Int'l*, pg. 669
MUNTERS SRL—See Incentive AB; *Int'l*, pg. 669
MUNTERS SVERIGE—See Incentive AB; *Int'l*, pg. 669
MUNTERS TECNAR (TECNOLOGIA AMBIENTAL)—See Incentive AB; *Int'l*, pg. 669
MUNTERS TORKTEKNIK AB—See Incentive AB; *Int'l*, pg. 669
MUNTERS TROCKNUNGS SERVICE GES MBH—See Incentive AB; *Int'l*, pg. 669
MUNTERS TROCKNUNGS SERVICE GMBH—See Incentive AB; *Int'l*, pg. 669
MUNTERS UK—See Incentive AB; *Int'l*, pg. 669
MURALO CO., INC.; *U.S. Private*, pg. 767
MURATA ELECTRONICS NORTH AMERICA, INC.—See Murata Manufacturing Co., Ltd.; *Int'l*, pg. 897
MURATA MACHINERY, LTD.; *Int'l*, pg. 897
MURATA MANUFACTURING CO., LTD.; *Int'l*, pg. 897
MURATA OF AMERICA, INC.—See Murata Machinery, Ltd.; *Int'l*, pg. 897
MURATECH AMERICA, INC.—See Murata Machinery, Ltd.; *Int'l*, pg. 897
MURCO PETROLEUM LTD.—See Murphy Oil Corporation; *U.S. Public*, pg. 1142
MURDOCH MAGAZINES—See The News Corporation Limited; *Int'l*, pg. 925
MURE S.A.—See Fried. Krupp AG; *Int'l*, pg. 508

MURO PHARMACEUTICAL, INC.; *U.S. Private*, pg. 767
MUROMACHI CHEMICALS CO., LTD.—See Kanebo, Ltd.; *Int'l*, pg. 722
MURPHEY FAVRE HOUSING MANAGERS, INC.—See Washington Mutual Inc.; *U.S. Public*, pg. 1742
MURPHEY FAVRE, INC.—See Washington Mutual Inc.; *U.S. Public*, pg. 1742
MURPHEY FAVRE PROPERTIES, INC.—See Washington Mutual Inc.; *U.S. Public*, pg. 1742
MURPHEY FAVRE SECURITIES SERVICES, INC.—See Washington Mutual Inc.; *U.S. Public*, pg. 1742
MURPHY BREWERY IRELAND LTD.—See Heineken N.V.; *Int'l*, pg. 608
MURPHY COMPANY; *U.S. Private*, pg. 768
MURPHY EASTERN OIL CO.—See Murphy Oil Corporation; *U.S. Public*, pg. 1142
MURPHY EXPLORATION & PRODUCTION CO.—See Murphy Oil Corporation; *U.S. Public*, pg. 1142
MURPHY FAMILY FARMS; *U.S. Private*, pg. 768
MURPHY INTERNATIONAL—See Murphy Company; *U.S. Private*, pg. 768
MURPHY OIL CO., LTD.—See Murphy Oil Corporation; *U.S. Public*, pg. 1142
MURPHY OIL CORPORATION; *U.S. Public*, pg. 1141
MURPHY OIL TRADING CO. (EASTERN)—See Murphy Oil Corporation; *U.S. Public*, pg. 1142
MURPHY OIL USA, INC.—See Murphy Oil Corporation; *U.S. Public*, pg. 1142
MURPHY PETROLEUM LTD.—See Murphy Oil Corporation; *U.S. Public*, pg. 1142
MURPHY-PHOENIX CO.—See Colgate-Palmolive Company; *U.S. Public*, pg. 397
MURPHY PLYWOOD—See Murphy Company; *U.S. Private*, pg. 768
MURPHY PROPERTIES, INC.—See Murphy Company; *U.S. Private*, pg. 768
MURPHY TIMBER—See Murphy Company; *U.S. Private*, pg. 768
MURRAY CANADA—See Tomkins PLC; *Int'l*, pg. 1397
MURRAY EXPORT SALES B. V.—See Tomkins PLC; *Int'l*, pg. 1397
MURRAY JOHNSTONE LIMITED—See United Asset Management Corporation; *U.S. Public*, pg. 1674
THE MURRAY OHIO MFG. CO.—See Tomkins PLC; *Int'l*, pg. 1397
MURRAY TUBE—See Senior Engineering Group, plc.; *Int'l*, pg. 1222
MURRAY TURBOMACHINERY CORPORATION—See Tuthill Corporation; *U.S. Private*, pg. 1110
MURRAY'S DISCOUNT AUTO STORES; *U.S. Private*, pg. 768
MURRY'S, INC.; *U.S. Private*, pg. 768
MUSASHINO-GEIGY CO. LTD.—See Novartis AG; *Int'l*, pg. 983
MUSC (PTY.) LTD.—See The Macneal-Schwendler Corp.; *U.S. Public*, pg. 1032
MUSCAT (OVERSEAS) AGRICULTURE CO. LLC.—See BASF AG; *Int'l*, pg. 109
MUSCATINE HOLDINGS, INC.—See Bandag, Incorporated; *U.S. Public*, pg. 177
MUSCATINE JOURNAL—See Lee Enterprises, Incorporated; *U.S. Public*, pg. 984
MUSEUM BOUTIQUE INTERCONTINENTAL, LTD.; *U.S. Private*, pg. 768
MUSHKO ELECTRONICS (PVT) LIMITED—See Hewlett-Packard Company; *U.S. Public*, pg. 822
MUSIC & MEDIA—See VNU Verenigde Nederlandse Uitgeversbedrijven B.V.; *Int'l*, pg. 1446
THE MUSIC AND VIDEO CLUB LIMITED—See Kingfisher plc; *Int'l*, pg. 733
MUSIC CITY NEWS—See Gannett Company, Inc.; *U.S. Public*, pg. 701
MUSIC SALES CORPORATION; *U.S. Private*, pg. 768
MUSICIAN MAGAZINE—See VNU Verenigde Nederlandse Uitgeversbedrijven B.V.; *Int'l*, pg. 1446
MUSICLAND GROUP INC.; *U.S. Public*, pg. 1142
THE MUSICLAND GROUP, INC.—See Musicland Group Inc.; *U.S. Public*, pg. 1142
MUSICLAND RETAIL, INC.—See Musicland Group Inc.; *U.S. Public*, pg. 1142
MUSINI, SOCIEDAD MUTUA DE SEGUROS Y REASEGUROS A PRIMA FIJA—See SEPI; *Int'l*, pg. 1225
MUSKA ELECTRIC COMPANY; *U.S. Private*, pg. 768
MUSKEGON CONSTRUCTION COMPANY—See Owen-Ames-Kimball Co.; *U.S. Private*, pg. 824
MUSKIN LEISURE PRODUCTS, INC.; *U.S. Private*, pg. 768
MUSTANG INDUSTRIAL EQUIPMENT CO.—See Mustang Tractor & Equip. Co.; *U.S. Private*, pg. 769
MUSTANG MANUFACTURING COMPANY, INC.—See Gehl Company; *U.S. Public*, pg. 704
MUSTANG PIPELINE COMPANY—See Eastman Kodak Company; *U.S. Public*, pg. 551
MUSTANG POWER SYSTEMS—See Mustang Tractor & Equip. Co.; *U.S. Private*, pg. 769
MUSTANG TELEPHONE CO.—See Century Telephone Enterprises, Inc.; *U.S. Public*, pg. 329
MUSTANG TRACTOR & EQUIP. CO.; *U.S. Private*, pg. 768
MUTOH AMERICA INC.—See Mutoh Industries Ltd.; *Int'l*, pg. 897
MUTOH BELGIUM N.V.—See Mutoh Industries Ltd.; *Int'l*, pg. 897
MUTOH EUROPE GMBH—See Mutoh Industries Ltd.; *Int'l*, pg. 897
MUTOH INDUSTRIES LTD.; *Int'l*, pg. 897
MUTUA ASSICURATRICE COTONI—See Allianz Aktiengesellschaft; *Int'l*, pg. 62
MUTUAL ASSURANCE, INC.—See Medical Assurance, Inc.; *U.S. Public*, pg. 1080
THE MUTUAL FUND CO., LTD.—See The Industrial Finance Corporation of Thailand; *Int'l*, pg. 677
THE MUTUAL LIFE INSURANCE COMPANY OF NEW YORK; *U.S. Private*, pg. 769

MUTUAL MANUFACTURING & SUPPLY CO.; *U.S. Private*, pg. 769
MUTUAL OF AMERICA LIFE INSURANCE COMPANY; *U.S. Private*, pg. 769
MUTUAL OF OMAHA INSURANCE COMPANY; *U.S. Private*, pg. 769
MUTUAL OF OMAHA INVESTOR SERVICES, INC.—See Mutual of Omaha Insurance Company; *U.S. Private*, pg. 770
MUTUAL SAVINGS & LOAN ASSOCIATION—See Berkshire Hathaway Inc.; *U.S. Public*, pg. 217
MUTUAL SERVICE CORPORATION—See Pacific Life Insurance Company; *U.S. Private*, pg. 831
MUTUAL SIGNAL CORPORATION OF MICHIGAN—See IXC Communications, Inc.; *U.S. Private*, pg. 556
MUTUAL TRADING CO., INC.; *U.S. Private*, pg. 770
MUTUAL TRAVEL, INC.—See Washington Mutual Inc.; *U.S. Public*, pg. 1742
MUTUAL WELDING CO., LTD.; *U.S. Private*, pg. 770
MUTUAMAR - SOCIETA DI ASSICURAZIONI E RIASSICURAZIONI PER AZIONI—See IRI Istituto Ricostruzione Industriale; *Int'l*, pg. 652
MUTUEEL SAINT-CHRISTOPHE—See AXA-UAP; *Int'l*, pg. 19
MUTUELLE DE L'EST—See AXA-UAP; *Int'l*, pg. 19
MUTUELLE DE MARSEILLE—See AXA-UAP; *Int'l*, pg. 19
MUTUELLE PHOCEENNE ASSURANCE—See AXA-UAP; *Int'l*, pg. 19
MUTUELLE SOLVAY S.C.S.—See Solvay S.A.; *Int'l*, pg. 1277
MUVA GREETINGS B.V.—See American Greetings Corporation; *U.S. Public*, pg. 78
MUVA GREETINGS S.A.—See American Greetings Corporation; *U.S. Public*, pg. 78
MUZAK LIMITED PARTNERSHIP—See Center Partners Management LLC; *U.S. Private*, pg. 222
MXNET, INC.—See The Sherwood Group, Inc.; *U.S. Public*, pg. 1467
MY OWN MEALS, INC.; *U.S. Private*, pg. 770
MYANMA SHELL B.V.—See Royal Dutch/Shell Group of Companies; *Int'l*, pg. 1140
MYANMAR COMPUTER SYSTEMS PTE. LTD.—See CSA Holdings Ltd.; *Int'l*, pg. 242
MYANMAR DAEWOO INTERNATIONAL LTD.—See Daewoo Corporation; *Int'l*, pg. 358
MYCAL, CORP.; *Int'l*, pg. 897
MYCOGEN CORPORATION; *U.S. Public*, pg. 1142
MYCOGEN CROP PROTECTION—See Mycogen Corporation; *U.S. Public*, pg. 1142
MYCOGEN SEEDS—See Mycogen Corporation; *U.S. Public*, pg. 1142
MYCOM, INC.—See Motorola, Inc.; *U.S. Public*, pg. 1138
C.C. MYERS, INC.; *U.S. Private*, pg. 770
F.E. MYERS—See Pentair, Inc.; *U.S. Public*, pg. 1273
F.E. MYERS (CANADA) LTD./LTEE.—See Pentair, Inc.; *U.S. Public*, pg. 1274
F.W. MYERS & CO., INC.; *U.S. Private*, pg. 770
F.W. MYERS & CO.—See F.W. Myers & Co., Inc.; *U.S. Private*, pg. 771
MYERS INDUSTRIES, INC.; *U.S. Public*, pg. 1143
MYERS INTERNATIONAL, INC.—See Myers Industries, Inc.; *U.S. Public*, pg. 1143
M. MYERS & SON PLC—See Avery Dennison Corporation; *U.S. Public*, pg. 154
MYERS TIRE SUPPLY COMPANY—See Myers Industries, Inc.; *U.S. Public*, pg. 1143
BEN MYERSON CANDY COMPANY, INC.; *U.S. Private*, pg. 771
MYKORA OY—See Kemira Oy; *Int'l*, pg. 728
MYKOTRONX—See Rainbow Technologies, Inc.; *U.S. Public*, pg. 1359
MYLAN LABORATORIES, INC.; *U.S. Public*, pg. 1143
MYLAN PHARMACEUTICALS INC.—See Mylan Laboratories, Inc.; *U.S. Public*, pg. 1143
MYLEX CORPORATION; *U.S. Public*, pg. 1143
MYO-TECH ELECTRONICS—See Bollinger Industries Inc.; *U.S. Public*, pg. 244
MYRESJO AB—See Skanska AB; *Int'l*, pg. 1260
MYRICK CONSTRUCTION INC.; *U.S. Private*, pg. 771
MYRON MANUFACTURING CORPORATION; *U.S. Private*, pg. 771
MYRTLE/MUELLER, A HAWORTH CO.—See Haworth, Inc.; *U.S. Private*, pg. 512
MYSTERY GUILD—See Bertelsmann AG; *Int'l*, pg. 191
MYSTIC COLOR LAB, INC.—See Fotolabo S.A.; *Int'l*, pg. 501
MYSTIC STAMP COMPANY—See Littleton Coin Co., Inc.; *U.S. Private*, pg. 671
MYTON LIMITED—See Taylor Woodrow plc; *Int'l*, pg. 1358
MYTTON'S LIMITED—See Bristile Clay Tiles, Ltd.; *Int'l*, pg. 216

N

N & C BOOST N.V.—See Riviana Foods Inc.; *U.S. Public*, pg. 1392
N & N INC.—See Royal Begemann Group; *Int'l*, pg. 1134
N&T CO., LTD.—See Namco Ltd.; *Int'l*, pg. 905
N BASE COMMUNICATIONS—See MRV Communications, Inc.; *U.S. Public*, pg. 1027
N BASE COMUNICATIONS—See MRV Communications, Inc.; *U.S. Public*, pg. 1027
N COR LTD.—See Corning Incorporated; *U.S. Public*, pg. 449
N-LYNX ANDREW—See Andrew Corporation; *U.S. Public*, pg. 112
N.V. OWENS-CORNING S.A.—See Owens Corning; *U.S. Public*, pg. 1237
NA INDUSTRIES, INC.—See Nippon Shokubai Co., Ltd.; *Int'l*, pg. 939
N.A. TRADING LTD.—See Movado Group, Inc.; *U.S. Public*, pg. 1140

NAAO MARKETING—See Ford Motor Company; *U.S. Public*, pg. 662

NAAO PRODUCTION PURCHASING—See Ford Motor Company; *U.S. Public*, pg. 662

NABCO LTD.—See Kobe Steel, Ltd.; *Int'l*, pg. 740

NAC INC.—See Bandag, Incorporated; *U.S. Public*, pg. 177

NAC RE CORP.; *U.S. Public*, pg. 1144

NAC REINSURANCE CORPORATION—See NAC Re Corp.; *U.S. Public*, pg. 1144

NAC REINSURANCE INTERNATIONAL LIMITED—See NAC Re Corp.; *U.S. Public*, pg. 1144

NACAL, INC.—See Norfolk Southern Corporation; *U.S. Public*, pg. 1191

NAF AB—See Trelleborg AB; *Int'l*, pg. 1422

NAI TECHNOLOGIES, INC.; *U.S. Public*, pg. 1144

NAIS PRODUCTS SALES OFFICE—See Matsushita Electric Works, Ltd.; *Int'l*, pg. 848

NAL/PENGUIN INC.—See Pearson plc; *Int'l*, pg. 1027

NAO, INC.; *U.S. Private*, pg. 771

NAP-TV—See Dentsu Inc.; *Int'l*, pg. 394

N.A.P. COMMERCIAL ELECTRONIC CORP.—See Philips Electronics N.V.; *Int'l*, pg. 1054

NAPP SYSTEMS—See Polyfibron Technologies Corp.; *U.S. Private*, pg. 875

NAPS AUSTRALIA—See Neste Oy; *Int'l*, pg. 913

NAPS FRANCE S.A.—See Neste Oy; *Int'l*, pg. 913

NAPS INTERNATIONAL—See Neste Oy; *Int'l*, pg. 913

NAPS SWEDEN AB—See Neste Oy; *Int'l*, pg. 913

NAPS UNITED KINGDOM—See Neste Oy; *Int'l*, pg. 913

NAT—See Technip; *Int'l*, pg. 1360

NAT CAPITAL CORP.—See Taisei Corporation; *Int'l*, pg. 1347

NATIO-VIE—See Banque Nationale de Paris; *Int'l*, pg. 163

NAVINTEC - NAVAL DE INVESTIGACION Y TECNOLOGIA, S.A.—See SEPI; *Int'l*, pg. 1223

NAW NUTZFAHRZEUGGESELLSCHAFT ARBON & WETZIKON AG—See Daimler-Benz Aktiengesellschaft; *Int'l*, pg. 369

NB COAL COMPANY LIMITED—See New Brunswick Power Corporation; *Int'l*, pg. 923

NBBJ; *U.S. Private*, pg. 771

NBC BANK, FSB (BELZONI)—See National Commerce Bancorporation; *U.S. Public*, pg. 1155

NBC BANK, FSB (KNOXVILLE)—See National Commerce Bancorporation; *U.S. Public*, pg. 1155

NBC CLEARING SERVICES INCORPORATED—See National Bank of Canada; *Int'l*, pg. 907

NBC EXPORT DEVELOPMENT CORPORATION INC.—See National Bank of Canada; *Int'l*, pg. 907

NBC HOLDINGS USA, INC.—See National Bank of Canada; *Int'l*, pg. 907

NBD BANK—See First Chicago NBD Corporation; *U.S. Public*, pg. 628

NBD BANK, CANADA—See First Chicago NBD Corporation; *U.S. Public*, pg. 628

NBD BANKING COMPANY—See First Chicago NBD Corporation; *U.S. Public*, pg. 628

NBD BROKERAGE SERVICES, INC.—See First Chicago NBD Corporation; *U.S. Public*, pg. 628

NBD COMMUNITY DEVELOPMENT CORPORATION—See First Chicago NBD Corporation; *U.S. Public*, pg. 628

NBD CREDIT INSURANCE AGENCY, INC.—See First Chicago NBD Corporation; *U.S. Public*, pg. 628

NBD EQUIPMENT FINANCE, INC.—See First Chicago NBD Corporation; *U.S. Public*, pg. 628

NBD FINANCIAL SERVICES OF MICHIGAN, INC.—See First Chicago NBD Corporation; *U.S. Public*, pg. 628

NBD INCORPORATED—See Harcourt General, Inc.; *U.S. Public*, pg. 783

NBD INSURANCE AGENCY, INC.—See First Chicago NBD Corporation; *U.S. Public*, pg. 628

NBD LEASING, INC.—See First Chicago NBD Corporation; *U.S. Public*, pg. 628

NBD LIFE INSURANCE COMPANY—See First Chicago NBD Corporation; *U.S. Public*, pg. 628

NBD MORTGAGE COMPANY—See First Chicago NBD Corporation; *U.S. Public*, pg. 628

NBD MORTGAGE CORPORATION—See First Chicago NBD Corporation; *U.S. Public*, pg. 628

NBD NEIGHBORHOOD REVITALIZATION CORP.—See First Chicago NBD Corporation; *U.S. Public*, pg. 628

NBD SECURITIES, INC.—See First Chicago NBD Corporation; *U.S. Public*, pg. 628

NBD TRUST COMPANY OF FLORIDA N.A.—See First Chicago NBD Corporation; *U.S. Public*, pg. 628

N.B.F. BOLLINGER INDUSTRIES—See Bollinger Industries Inc.; *U.S. Public*, pg. 243

N.B.M. CORP.; *U.S. Private*, pg. 771

NBS CARD SERVICES—See NBS Technologies, Inc.; *Int'l*, pg. 898

NBS CARD SERVICES, INC.—See NBS Technologies, Inc.; *Int'l*, pg. 898

NBS IMAGING SYSTEMS, INC.—See NBS Technologies, Inc.; *Int'l*, pg. 898

NBS IMPRINTER—See NBS Technologies, Inc.; *Int'l*, pg. 898

N.B.S. INC.—See NBS Technologies, Inc.; *Int'l*, pg. 898

NBS LIMITED-CARD SERVICES DIVISION—See NBS Technologies, Inc.; *Int'l*, pg. 898

NBS LIMITED-PERSONALIZATION SYSTEMS DIVISION—See NBS Technologies, Inc.; *Int'l*, pg. 898

NBS TECHNOLOGIES, INC.; *Int'l*, pg. 898

NBS TECHNOLOGIES INC.—See NBS Technologies, Inc.; *Int'l*, pg. 898

NBSC CORPORATION—See Synovus Financial Corp.; *U.S. Public*, pg. 1549

NBSC HOLDINGS INC.—See High Point Financial Corp.; *U.S. Public*, pg. 826

NBSC INVESTMENT CO.—See High Point Financial Corp.; *U.S. Public*, pg. 826

NBSC PROPERTIES INC.—See High Point Financial Corp.; *U.S. Public*, pg. 826

NBSC REAL ESTATE COMPANY INC.—See High Point Financial Corp.; *U.S. Public*, pg. 826

NBT BANCORP INC.; *U.S. Public*, pg. 1144

NC BUILDERS INC.—See Nason and Cullen Group Incorporated; *U.S. Private*, pg. 775

NC COMERCIAL EXPORTADORA LTDA.—See The Chase Manhattan Corporation; *U.S. Public*, pg. 339

N.C. PRODUCTS CORP.—See CRH, plc; *Int'l*, pg. 242

NCB PROPERTIES, INC.—See Keycorp; *U.S. Public*, pg. 955

NCC AB; *Int'l*, pg. 898

NCC BUILDING—See NCC AB; *Int'l*, pg. 898

NCC BUILDING - GOTEBORG—See NCC AB; *Int'l*, pg. 898

NCC BUILDING - HELSINGBORG—See NCC AB; *Int'l*, pg. 898

NCC BUILDING - JONKOPING—See NCC AB; *Int'l*, pg. 898

NCC BUILDING - KARLSTAD—See NCC AB; *Int'l*, pg. 898

NCC BUILDING - UMEA—See NCC AB; *Int'l*, pg. 898

NCC BUILDING - UPPSALA—See NCC AB; *Int'l*, pg. 899

NCC BUILDING - VAXJO—See NCC AB; *Int'l*, pg. 899

NCC CIVIL ENGINEERING—See NCC AB; *Int'l*, pg. 899

NCC ESKILSTUNA—See NCC AB; *Int'l*, pg. 899

NCC FINANS—See NCC AB; *Int'l*, pg. 899

NCC GOTEBURG—See NCC AB; *Int'l*, pg. 899

NCC HUS—See NCC AB; *Int'l*, pg. 899

NCC INDUSTRIES, INC.—See Maidenform Worldwide; *U.S. Private*, pg. 697

NCC INDUSTRY—See NCC AB; *Int'l*, pg. 899

NCC INVEST—See NCC AB; *Int'l*, pg. 899

NCC LINKOPING—See NCC AB; *Int'l*, pg. 899

NCC PREFAB AB—See NCC AB; *Int'l*, pg. 899

NCC PUBLISHING—See Newfoundland Capital Corporation Limited; *Int'l*, pg. 924

NCC REAL ESTATE—See NCC AB; *Int'l*, pg. 899

NCC SPECIALTY PUBLICATIONS—See Newfoundland Capital Corporation Limited; *Int'l*, pg. 924

NCC STORA PROJELET—See NCC AB; *Int'l*, pg. 899

NCC SUNDSVALL—See NCC AB; *Int'l*, pg. 899

NCC UDDEVALLA—See NCC AB; *Int'l*, pg. 899

NCC UMEA—See NCC AB; *Int'l*, pg. 899

NCC VAXJO—See NCC AB; *Int'l*, pg. 899

NCE GROUP—See EMAP Plc; *Int'l*, pg. 451

NCH CORPORATION; *U.S. Public*, pg. 1145

NCH CORPORATION KOREA—See NCH Corporation; *U.S. Public*, pg. 1145

NCI—See TI Group plc; *Int'l*, pg. 1338

NCI BUILDING SYSTEMS, INC.; *U.S. Public*, pg. 1145

NCR CORPORATION; *U.S. Public*, pg. 1146

NCR-JAPAN LTD.—See NCR Corporation; *U.S. Public*, pg. 1146

NCS ABACUS—See National Computer Systems; *U.S. Public*, pg. 1155

NCS CUSTOMER SUPPORT & SERVICES—See National Computer Systems; *U.S. Public*, pg. 1155

NCS DATA COLLECTION SYSTEMS—See National Computer Systems; *U.S. Public*, pg. 1155

NCS DOCUMENT OPERATIONS—See National Computer Systems; *U.S. Public*, pg. 1155

NCS EDUCATION SOFTWARE & SERVICES—See National Computer Systems; *U.S. Public*, pg. 1155

NCS INFORMATION SERVICES—See National Computer Systems; *U.S. Public*, pg. 1155

NCS INFORMATION TECHNOLOGY—See National Computer Systems; *U.S. Public*, pg. 1155

NCS INFORMATION TECHNOLOGY & FEDERAL SYSTEMS—See National Computer Systems; *U.S. Public*, pg. 1155

NCS INFORMATION TECHNOLOGY & MEASUREMENTS DIVISION—See National Computer Systems; *U.S. Public*, pg. 1155

NCS OPERATIONS CENTER—See National Computer Systems; *U.S. Public*, pg. 1155

NCS CHARLES W. OSWALD TECHNOLOGY CENTER—See National Computer Systems; *U.S. Public*, pg. 1155

NCS RECOGNITION PRODUCTS GROUP—See National Computer Systems; *U.S. Public*, pg. 1155

NCS REGIONAL RESOURCE CENTER—See National Computer Systems; *U.S. Public*, pg. 1155

NCS VENTURES, INC.—See Lucent Technologies Inc.; *U.S. Public*, pg. 1019

NCT HOLLAND B.V.—See Neste Oy; *Int'l*, pg. 914

NCT HONG KONG LTD.—See Neste Oy; *Int'l*, pg. 914

NCT MIDDLE EAST—See Neste Oy; *Int'l*, pg. 914

NCT NORDEN AB—See Neste Oy; *Int'l*, pg. 913

NCT SINGAPORE PTE. LTD.—See Neste Oy; *Int'l*, pg. 914

NCT U.S.A. INC.—See Neste Oy; *Int'l*, pg. 913

ND COMMUNICATIONS CO. LTD.—See Daiwa Securities Co. Ltd.; *Int'l*, pg. 375

NDC CO., LTD.—See Nissan Motor Co., Ltd.; *Int'l*, pg. 944

NDC MERCHANT BANK LTD.—See DBS Bank Ltd.; *Int'l*, pg. 351

NDC MERCHANT BANK NOMINEES PTE LTD—See DBS Bank Ltd.; *Int'l*, pg. 351

NDC TOKYO REPRESENTATIVE OFFICE—See National Data Corporation; *U.S. Public*, pg. 1156

NDS—See Nestle S.A.; *Int'l*, pg. 918

NDSI, INC.—See American Media, Inc.; *U.S. Public*, pg. 87

N.D.T. ENGINEERING INC.—See Shannon & Wilson, Inc.; *U.S. Private*, pg. 989

N.E. CHEMCAT—See Engelhard Corporation; *U.S. Public*, pg. 583

NE-PRODUCTS OY—See Oy Nokia Ab/Nokia Group; *Int'l*, pg. 952

NE TECHNOLOGY LTD.—See Saint-Gobain; *Int'l*, pg. 1174

NEA-LINDBERG A/S—See FLS Industries A/S; *Int'l*, pg. 475

NEB SHIPPING CO.—See Commerzbank AG; *Int'l*, pg. 312

NEBS BUSINESS FORMS LIMITED—See New England Business Service, Inc.; *U.S. Public*, pg. 1171

NEBS BUSINESS STATIONERY—See New England Business Service, Inc.; *U.S. Public*, pg. 1171

NEC AMERICA, INC.—See NEC Corporation; *Int'l*, pg. 900

NEC AUSTRALIA PTY. LTD.—See NEC Corporation; *Int'l*, pg. 901

NEC BUSINESS COMMUNICATION SYSTEMS (EAST), INC.—See NEC Corporation; *Int'l*, pg. 900

NEC BUSINESS COMMUNICATION SYSTEMS (WEST), INC.—See NEC Corporation; *Int'l*, pg. 900

NEC CORPORATION; *Int'l*, pg. 899

NEC DE MEXICO, S.A. DE C.V.—See NEC Corporation; *Int'l*, pg. 901

NEC DEUTSCHLAND GMBH—See NEC Corporation; *Int'l*, pg. 901

NEC ELECTRONICS (EUROPE) GMBH—See NEC Corporation; *Int'l*, pg. 901

NEC ELECTRONICS (FRANCE) S.A.—See NEC Corporation; *Int'l*, pg. 901

NEC ELECTRONICS (GERMANY) GMBH—See NEC Corporation; *Int'l*, pg. 901

NEC ELECTRONICS HONG KONG LIMITED—See NEC Corporation; *Int'l*, pg. 901

NEC ELECTRONICS INC.—See NEC Corporation; *Int'l*, pg. 900

NEC ELECTRONICS ITALIANA S.R.L.—See NEC Corporation; *Int'l*, pg. 901

NEC ELECTRONICS SINGAPORE PTE. LTD.—See NEC Corporation; *Int'l*, pg. 901

NEC ELECTRONICS TAIWAN LTD.—See NEC Corporation; *Int'l*, pg. 901

NEC EUROPE LTD.—See NEC Corporation; *Int'l*, pg. 900

NEC HOME ELECTRONICS (MALAYSIA) SDN. BHD.—See NEC Corporation; *Int'l*, pg. 900

NEC HONG KONG LIMITED—See NEC Corporation; *Int'l*, pg. 900

NEC INDUSTRIES, INC.—See NEC Corporation; *Int'l*, pg. 900

NEC INDUSTRIES NETHERLANDS B.V.—See NEC Corporation; *Int'l*, pg. 900

NEC INDUSTRIES (UK) PLC.—See NEC Corporation; *Int'l*, pg. 900

NEC RESEARCH INSTITUTE, INC.—See NEC Corporation; *Int'l*, pg. 900

NEC SEMICONDUCTORS IRELAND LIMITED—See NEC Corporation; *Int'l*, pg. 900

NEC SEMICONDUCTORS (MALAYSIA) SDN. BERHAD—See NEC Corporation; *Int'l*, pg. 900

NEC SEMICONDUCTORS SINGAPORE PTE. LTD.—See NEC Corporation; *Int'l*, pg. 900

NEC SEMICONDUCTORS (UK) LIMITED—See NEC Corporation; *Int'l*, pg. 900

NEC SINGAPORE PTE. LTD.—See NEC Corporation; *Int'l*, pg. 900

NEC SYSTEMS LABORATORY, INC.—See NEC Corporation; *Int'l*, pg. 900

NEC TAIWAN LTD.—See NEC Corporation; *Int'l*, pg. 900

NEC TECHNOLOGIES HONG KONG LIMITED—See NEC Corporation; *Int'l*, pg. 900

NEC TECHNOLOGIES, INC.—See NEC Corporation; *Int'l*, pg. 900

NEC TECHNOLOGIES PHILIPPINES, INC.—See NEC Corporation; *Int'l*, pg. 900

NEC TECHNOLOGIES (THAILAND) CO., LTD.—See NEC Corporation; *Int'l*, pg. 900

NEC TECHNOLOGIES (UK) LTD.—See NEC Corporation; *Int'l*, pg. 900

NEC (UK) LTD.—See NEC Corporation; *Int'l*, pg. 901

NEC USA, INC.—See NEC Corporation; *Int'l*, pg. 900

N E D CORP.; *U.S. Private*, pg. 771

NEDCO (NEWPORT EUROPEAN DISTRIBUTION CO.)—See Newport Corporation; *U.S. Public*, pg. 1179

NEES ENERGY, INC.—See New England Electric System; *U.S. Public*, pg. 1171

NEFA CORPORATION—See Prime Bancorp, Inc.; *U.S. Public*, pg. 1326

NEHO VERSAND G.M.B.H.—See The Seagram Company Ltd.; *Int'l*, pg. 1216

NEK/CDT—See Cable Design Technologies Corporation; *U.S. Public*, pg. 287

NEM NEDERLANDSCHE ELEKTROLASCH MAATSCHAPPIG B.V.—See Philipp Holzmann AG; *Int'l*, pg. 633

NEO INDUSTRIES—See Russel Metals Inc.; *Int'l*, pg. 1150

NER HOLDINGS, INC.—See Hargro Enterprises, Inc.; *U.S. Private*, pg. 502

NES HOLDINGS, INC.; *U.S. Private*, pg. 771

NES, INC.—See EFD Waste Corp.; *U.S. Public*, pg. 546

N.E.T. FEDERAL—See Network Equipment Technologies, Inc.; *U.S. Public*, pg. 1169

NETG APPLIED LEARNING GMBH—See Harcourt General, Inc.; *U.S. Public*, pg. 784

NETG HOLDING, INC.—See Harcourt General, Inc.; *U.S. Public*, pg. 784

NETG LIMITED—See Harcourt General, Inc.; *U.S. Public*, pg. 784

NEUMAG-NEUMUNSTERSCHE MASCHINEN-UND ANLAGENBAU GMBH—See Deutsche Babcock AG; *Int'l*, pg. 399

NFC INTERNATIONAL HOLDINGS (U.S.A.) INC.—See NFC plc; *Int'l*, pg. 901

NFC PLC; *Int'l*, pg. 901

NFE CO., LTD.—See Ferro Corporation; *U.S. Public*, pg. 620

N.F.I. FRANCE—See Newly Weds Foods Inc.; *U.S. Private*, pg. 797

N.F.I. FRANCE—See Tomkins PLC; *Int'l*, pg. 1396

NFO RESEARCH, INC.; *U.S. Public*, pg. 1146

NFPA RESEARCH FOUNDATION—See National Fire Protection Association; *U.S. Private*, pg. 783

NFT CO., LTD.—See Shimano Inc.; *Int'l*, pg. 1232

NFT DISTRIBUTION—See Northern Foods plc; *Int'l*, pg. 968

NFT ERICSSON COMMUNICATIONS ANS—See Telefonaktiebolaget LM Ericsson; *Int'l*, pg. 1369

NGC CORPORATION; *U.S. Public*, pg. 1146

NGE ENTERPRISES, INC.—See New York State Electric & Gas Corporation; *U.S. Public*, pg. 1173

NGL AMERICAN LIFE—See National Guardian Life Insurance Company; *U.S. Private*, pg. 784

NGL FINANCIAL SERVICES INC.—See National Guardian Life Insurance Company; *U.S. Private*, pg. 784
NGL HOLDINGS INC.—See National Guardian Life Insurance Company; *U.S. Private*, pg. 784
NGL INVESTMENT SERVICES INC.—See National Guardian Life Insurance Company; *U.S. Private*, pg. 784
NGO DEVELOPMENT CORPORATION—See National Gas & Oil Company; *U.S. Public*, pg. 1157
NGT NEUE GEBAUDETECHNIK GMBH—See Ruhrgas Aktiengesellschaft; *Int'l*, pg. 1149
NGTC—See Gaz Metropolitain & Company; *Int'l*, pg. 541
NHD HARDWARE—See ACO Inc.; *U.S. Private*, pg. 3
NHK-ASSOCIATED SPRING SUSPENSION COMPONENTS INC.—See NHK Spring Co., Ltd.; *Int'l*, pg. 902
NHK CIMEBRA INDUSTRIA DE MOLAS LTDA.—See NHK Spring Co., Ltd.; *Int'l*, pg. 902
NHK FASTENER DO BRASIL INDUSTRIA E COMERCIO LTDA.—See NHK Spring Co., Ltd.; *Int'l*, pg. 902
NHK GASKET SINGAPORE CO., (PTE) LTD.—See NHK Spring Co., Ltd.; *Int'l*, pg. 902
NHK GASKET SINGAPORE CO. (PTE.) LTD.—See Nissho Iwai Corporation; *Int'l*, pg. 948
NHK GASKET (THAILAND) CO., LTD.—See NHK Spring Co., Ltd.; *Int'l*, pg. 902
NHK INTERNATIONAL CORP.—See NHK Spring Co., Ltd.; *Int'l*, pg. 902
NHK MORSE CO., LTD.—See NHK Spring Co., Ltd.; *Int'l*, pg. 901
NHK PRECISION CO., LTD.—See NHK Spring Co., Ltd.; *Int'l*, pg. 901
NHK SALES CO., LTD—See NHK Spring Co., Ltd.; *Int'l*, pg. 902
NHK SPRING CO., LTD.; *Int'l*, pg. 901
NHK SPRING R&D CENTER INC.—See NHK Spring Co., Ltd.; *Int'l*, pg. 902
NHK SPRING (THAILAND) CO., LTD.—See NHK Spring Co., Ltd.; *Int'l*, pg. 902
NHK SPRING (THAILAND) CO., LTD.—See Nissho Iwai Corporation; *Int'l*, pg. 946
NHK STEEL CO., LTD.—See NHK Spring Co., Ltd.; *Int'l*, pg. 902
NHK TRANSPORT CO., LTD.—See NHK Spring Co., Ltd.; *Int'l*, pg. 902
NHT—See Recoton Corporation; *U.S. Public*, pg. 1369
NI INDUSTRIES, INC.—See Masco Corporation; *U.S. Public*, pg. 1054
NI STEEL PRODUCTS CO., LTD.—See Nissho Iwai Corporation; *Int'l*, pg. 946
NI TUBULARS, INC.—See Nissho Iwai Corporation; *Int'l*, pg. 947
NIB NORDDEUTSCHE INNOVATIONS- UND BETEILIGUNGSGESELLSCHAFT MBH—See Bayerische Vereinsbank Group; *Int'l*, pg. 180
NIC COMPONENTS CORP.—See Nu Horizons Electronics Corp.; *U.S. Public*, pg. 1205
NIC RESOURCES, INC.—See Nissho Iwai Corporation; *Int'l*, pg. 948
NIDEC—See Nippon Densan (NIDEC); *Int'l*, pg. 933
NIF INTERNATIONAL (ASIA) LIMITED—See Daiwa Securities Co. Ltd.; *Int'l*, pg. 375
NIF MANAGEMENT SINGAPORE PTE LTD—See Daiwa Securities Co. Ltd.; *Int'l*, pg. 375
NIFE AB—See Alcatel Alsthom Compagnie Generale D'Electricite; *Int'l*, pg. 52
NIFE ARGENTINA S.A.—See Alcatel Alsthom Compagnie Generale D'Electricite; *Int'l*, pg. 54
NIFE A/S—See Alcatel Alsthom Compagnie Generale D'Electricite; *Int'l*, pg. 54
NIFE AUSTRALIA PTY. LTD.—See Alcatel Alsthom Compagnie Generale D'Electricite; *Int'l*, pg. 54
NIFE BRASIL SISTEMAS ELETRICOS LTDA.—See Alcatel Alsthom Compagnie Generale D'Electricite; *Int'l*, pg. 54
NIFE B.V.—See Alcatel Alsthom Compagnie Generale D'Electricite; *Int'l*, pg. 53
NIFE CORPORATION—See Alcatel Alsthom Compagnie Gencrale D'Electricite; *Int'l*, pg. 54
NIFE ESPANA S.A.—See Alcatel Alsthom Compagnie Generale D'Electricite; *Int'l*, pg. 53
NIFE FRANCE S.A.—See Alcatel Alsthom Compagnie Generale D'Electricite; *Int'l*, pg. 53
NIFE GES.M.B.H.—See Alcatel Alsthom Compagnie Generale D'Electricite; *Int'l*, pg. 53
NIG SKANDIA PLC—See Skandia Insurance Company Limited; *Int'l*, pg. 1258
NIIB GROUP LIMITED—See Bank of Ireland; *Int'l*, pg. 152
NIK METAL CORP.—See Nissho Iwai Corporation; *Int'l*, pg. 946
NIM CO., LTD.—See Nissho Iwai Corporation; *Int'l*, pg. 948
NIPA HARDWICKE, INC.; *U.S. Private*, pg. 771
NJC ENGINEERING—See Eclipse Inc.; *U.S. Private*, pg. 361
NK LAWN & GARDEN—See Novartis AG; *Int'l*, pg. 974
NK AMERICA INC.—See NKK Corporation; *Int'l*, pg. 902
NKK CORPORATION; *Int'l*, pg. 902
NKK CORPORATION-AL-KHOBAR—See NKK Corporation; *Int'l*, pg. 903
NKK CORPORATION BEIJING OFFICE—See NKK Corporation; *Int'l*, pg. 903
NKK CORPORATION DE MEXICO S.A. DE C.V.—See NKK Corporation; *Int'l*, pg. 903
NKK CORPORATION-HONG KONG—See NKK Corporation; *Int'l*, pg. 903
NKK CORPORATION INC.—See NKK Corporation; *Int'l*, pg. 903
NKK CORPORATION-JAKARTA OFFICE—See NKK Corporation; *Int'l*, pg. 903
NKK CORPORATION-SHANGHAI OFFICE—See NKK Corporation; *Int'l*, pg. 903
NKK CORPORATION-SINGAPORE—See NKK Corporation; *Int'l*, pg. 903
NKK CORPORATION-TAIPEI—See NKK Corporation; *Int'l*, pg. 903

NKK CORPORATION-THAILAND—See NKK Corporation; *Int'l*, pg. 903
NKK CORPORATION-YANGON—See NKK Corporation; *Int'l*, pg. 903
NKK EUROPE LTD.-DUSSELDORF OFFICE—See NKK Corporation; *Int'l*, pg. 903
NKK EUROPE LTD.-LONDON OFFICE—See NKK Corporation; *Int'l*, pg. 903
NKK NETHERLANDS B.V.-ROTTERDAM OFFICE—See NKK Corporation; *Int'l*, pg. 903
NKK-TOYAMA WORKS—See NKK Corporation; *Int'l*, pg. 902
NKU INVESTMENT MANAGEMENT CO., LTD.—See The Norinchukin Bank; *Int'l*, pg. 958
NL INDUSTRIES DEUTSCHLAND, GMBH—See Contran Corporation; *U.S. Private*, pg. 271
NL INDUSTRIES, INC.—See Contran Corporation; *U.S. Private*, pg. 270
NL SPECIALTY CHEMICALS LTD.—See Contran Corporation; *U.S. Private*, pg. 271
NLI ASSET MANAGEMENT CORPORATION—See Nippon Life Insurance Co.; *Int'l*, pg. 935
NLI INSURANCE SERVICES (EUROPE) LIMITED—See Nippon Life Insurance Co.; *Int'l*, pg. 936
NLI PROPERTIES—See Nippon Life Insurance Co.; *Int'l*, pg. 935
NLI PROPERTIES CENTRAL, INC.—See Nippon Life Insurance Co.; *Int'l*, pg. 935
NLI PROPERTIES WEST, INC.—See Nippon Life Insurance Co.; *Int'l*, pg. 935
NLI RESEARCH INSTITUTE—See Nippon Life Insurance Co.; *Int'l*, pg. 935
NLLE. CORP. CONSTRUCTION CORP.—See Daewoo Corporation; *Int'l*, pg. 358
NM-BETEILIGUNGEN AG—See Mannesmann A.G.; *Int'l*, pg. 836
NM FUNDS MANAGEMENT (EUROPE) LTD. UNITED KINGDOM—See National Mutual Holdings Limited; *Int'l*, pg. 908
NM FUNDS MANAGEMENT (NORTH AMERICA) INC.—See National Mutual Holdings Limited; *Int'l*, pg. 908
NMB CORPORATION—See Minebea Co., Ltd.; *Int'l*, pg. 868
NMB ELECTRO PRECISION INC.—See Minebea Co., Ltd.; *Int'l*, pg. 868
NMB HELLER N.V.—See The Fuji Bank, Limited; *Int'l*, pg. 521
NMB ITALIA S.R.L.—See Minebea Co., Ltd.; *Int'l*, pg. 868
NMB KOREA CO., LTD.—See Minebea Co., Ltd.; *Int'l*, pg. 868
NMB MINEBEA GMBH—See Minebea Co., Ltd.; *Int'l*, pg. 868
NMB PRECISION INC.—See Minebea Co., Ltd.; *Int'l*, pg. 868
NMB PRECISION TOOL & DIE (PTE) LTD.—See Minebea Co., Ltd.; *Int'l*, pg. 868
NMB SINGAPORE LIMITED—See Minebea Co., Ltd.; *Int'l*, pg. 868
NMB THAI LIMITED—See Minebea Co., Ltd.; *Int'l*, pg. 868
NMB (U.K.) LIMITED—See Minebea Co., Ltd.; *Int'l*, pg. 868
NMB (USA) INC.—See Minebea Co., Ltd.; *Int'l*, pg. 868
NMI CORPORATION—See NEC Corporation; *Int'l*, pg. 900
NMP CORP.—See Westwood Corporation; *U.S. Public*, pg. 1763
N.M.P.P.—See Lagardere Groupe; *Int'l*, pg. 793
NMU MARKETING INFORMATION SERVICES—See VNU Verenigde Nederlandse Uitgeversbedrijven B.V.; *Int'l*, pg. 1446
NMV OPOCNO A.S.—See Nutricia BV; *Int'l*, pg. 992
NN BALL & ROLLER, INC.; *U.S. Public*, pg. 1146
NN FINANCIAL—See ING Groep N.V.; *Int'l*, pg. 650
N.N. INVESTMENT LIMITED—See The Nomura Securities Co., Ltd.; *Int'l*, pg. 957
NNC LTD.—See The General Electric Company, p.l.c.; *Int'l*, pg. 545
NNG ENERGY SYSTEMS, INC.—See Northwest Natural Gas Company; *U.S. Public*, pg. 1200
NNG FINANCIAL CORPORATION—See Northwest Natural Gas Company; *U.S. Public*, pg. 1200
N.O.A. AIRSCREW HOWDEN INC.—See Howden Group Plc; *Int'l*, pg. 636
NOF JOTUN CO. LTD.—See Jotun A/S; *Int'l*, pg. 716
NOF JOTUN (H.K.) LTD.—See Jotun A/S; *Int'l*, pg. 716
NOK CORP.—See Freudenberg & Company; *Int'l*, pg. 507
NOK-KLUBER CO. LTD.—See Freudenberg & Company; *Int'l*, pg. 507
NOK-MEGULASTIK CO. LTD.—See Freudenberg & Company; *Int'l*, pg. 507
NOKO-NOKIA REPRESENTATIVE OFFICE—See Oy Nokia Ab/Nokia Group; *Int'l*, pg. 953
NOPI GMBH—See Beiersdorf Group; *Int'l*, pg. 182
NORDX/CDT—See Cable Design Technologies Corporation; *U.S. Public*, pg. 287
NP AUTOMOTIVE COATINGS (EUROPE) LTD.—See Nippon Paint Company Ltd.; *Int'l*, pg. 937
NPA COATINGS INC.—See Nippon Paint Company Ltd.; *Int'l*, pg. 937
NPC INTERNATIONAL, INC.; *U.S. Public*, pg. 1146
NPDC-AS101, INC.—See GP Strategies Corporation; *U.S. Public*, pg. 694
NPI—See Framatome SA; *Int'l*, pg. 503
NPR OF AMERICA INC.—See Nippon Piston Ring Co., Ltd.; *Int'l*, pg. 938
NPS ENERGY SERVICES, INC.—See Day & Zimmerman, Inc.; *U.S. Private*, pg. 317
NRC INC.—See Bayer AG; *Int'l*, pg. 173
NRCTSC—See Nichols Research Corporation; *U.S. Public*, pg. 1182
NRD—See Mark IV Industries Inc.; *U.S. Public*, pg. 1045
NRG BELGIUM S.A.—See Ricoh Company, Ltd.; *Int'l*, pg. 1116
NRG BENELUX B.V.—See Ricoh Company, Ltd.; *Int'l*, pg. 1116

NRG COMUNICACIONES S.A.—See Ricoh Company, Ltd.; *Int'l*, pg. 1116
NRG DEL CARIBE SA—See Ricoh Company, Ltd.; *Int'l*, pg. 1116
NRG DISTRIBUTION CORPORATION—See Ricoh Company, Ltd.; *Int'l*, pg. 1115
NRG ENERGY, INC.—See Northern States Power Company; *U.S. Public*, pg. 1195
NRG ENERGY MINING COMPANY—See Telco Capital Corporation; *U.S. Private*, pg. 1073
NRG FRANCE S.A.—See Ricoh Company, Ltd.; *Int'l*, pg. 1116
NRG GROUP, INC.—See Northern States Power Company; *U.S. Public*, pg. 1195
NRG GROUP LIMITED—See Ricoh Company, Ltd.; *Int'l*, pg. 1114
NRG INCORPORATED—See Telco Capital Corporation; *U.S. Private*, pg. 1073
NRG INTERNATIONAL LTD. (BERMUDA)—See Ricoh Company, Ltd.; *Int'l*, pg. 1116
NRG ITALIA S.P.A.—See Ricoh Company, Ltd.; *Int'l*, pg. 1116
NRG LATIN AMERICA S.A.—See Ricoh Company, Ltd.; *Int'l*, pg. 1116
NRG MANAGEMENT—See Sulcus Computer Corp.; *U.S. Public*, pg. 1527
NRG MEXICO S.A. DE C.V.—See Ricoh Company, Ltd.; *Int'l*, pg. 1116
NRG NUFUEL CO.—See Telco Capital Corporation; *U.S. Private*, pg. 1073
NRG OFFICE SYSTEMS GMBH—See Ricoh Company, Ltd.; *Int'l*, pg. 1116
NRG RESOURCE RECOVERY, INC.—See Northern States Power Company; *U.S. Public*, pg. 1195
NRG SERVICES SA—See Ricoh Company, Ltd.; *Int'l*, pg. 1116
NRG SOUTH AMERICA S.A.—See Ricoh Company, Ltd.; *Int'l*, pg. 1116
NRG TECHNOLOGY, INC.—See Telco Capital Corporation; *U.S. Public*, pg. 1073
NRG THERMAL CORPORATION—See Northern States Power Company; *U.S. Public*, pg. 1195
NRI IBERICA, S.A.—See Crane Co.; *U.S. Public*, pg. 457
NRI SCHOOLS—See The McGraw-Hill Companies; *U.S. Public*, pg. 1071
NRL FINANCIAL CORP.—See TSI Holdings, Inc.; *U.S. Private*, pg. 1066
NRV, INC.—See Alto Dairy Cooperative; *U.S. Private*, pg. 47
NS FIBER OPTICS, INC.—See Norfolk Southern Corporation; *U.S. Public*, pg. 1190
NS FINANCE, INC.—See Nippon Steel Corporation; *Int'l*, pg. 940
NS FINANCE III, INC.—See Nippon Steel Corporation; *Int'l*, pg. 940
NS GROUP, INC.; *U.S. Public*, pg. 1147
NS HOLDINGS NV—See Rabobank Nederland; *Int'l*, pg. 1082
NS INVEST, INC.—See Nippon Steel Corporation; *Int'l*, pg. 940
NS INVEST II, INC.—See Nippon Steel Corporation; *Int'l*, pg. 940
NS KOMATSU PTY., LTD.—See Komatsu Ltd.; *Int'l*, pg. 745
NS KOTE, INC.—See Nippon Steel Corporation; *Int'l*, pg. 940
NS MANAGEMENT CORP.—See The Rouse Company; *U.S. Public*, pg. 1409
NS PIPE TECHNOLOGY—See Nippon Steel Corporation; *Int'l*, pg. 940
NS SALES INC.—See Nippon Steel Corporation; *Int'l*, pg. 940
NS TEK—See Nippon Steel Corporation; *Int'l*, pg. 940
NS THERMO (MALAYSIA) SDN. BHD.—See Nippon Sanso Corporation; *Int'l*, pg. 938
NS TRANSPORTATION BROKERAGE CORPORATION—See Norfolk Southern Corporation; *U.S. Public*, pg. 1190
NSC CORPORATION—See OHM Corporation; *U.S. Public*, pg. 1208
NSC EUROPEAN OPERATIONS—See Storage Technology Corporation; *U.S. Public*, pg. 1522
NSI (NUSANTARA SYSTEMS INTERNATIONAL INC.)—See The Macneal-Schwendler Corp.; *U.S. Public*, pg. 1032
NSK-AKS PRECISION BALL EUROPE LTD.—See NSK Ltd.; *Int'l*, pg. 903
NSK-AUTOLIV, INC.—See Electrolux, AB; *Int'l*, pg. 439
NSK-AUTOLIV, INC.—See NSK Ltd.; *Int'l*, pg. 903
NSK BEARINGS EUROPE LTD.—See NSK Ltd.; *Int'l*, pg. 903
NSK BEARINGS (MALAYSIA) SDN. BHD.—See NSK Ltd.; *Int'l*, pg. 903
P.T. NSK BEARINGS MANUFACTURING (INDONESIA)—See NSK Ltd.; *Int'l*, pg. 903
NSK BEARINGS (THAILAND) CO., LTD.—See NSK Ltd.; *Int'l*, pg. 903
NSK CORPORATION—See NSK Ltd.; *Int'l*, pg. 903
NSK DO BRASIL INDUSTRIA E COMERCIO DE ROLAMENTOS LTDA.—See NSK Ltd.; *Int'l*, pg. 904
NSK LTD.; *Int'l*, pg. 903
NSK MICRO PRECISION (M) SDN. BHD.—See NSK Ltd.; *Int'l*, pg. 904
NSK-RHP AUSTRALIA PTY, LTD.—See NSK Ltd.; *Int'l*, pg. 904
NSK-RHP BEARINGS NEW ZEALAND LTD.—See NSK Ltd.; *Int'l*, pg. 904
NSK-RHP CANADA INC.—See NSK Ltd.; *Int'l*, pg. 904
NSK-RHP DEUTSCHLAND G.M.B.H.—See NSK Ltd.; *Int'l*, pg. 904
NSK-RHP EUROPE LIMITED—See NSK Ltd.; *Int'l*, pg. 904
NSK-RHP EUROPEAN TECHNOLOGY CO. LIMITED—See NSK Ltd.; *Int'l*, pg. 904
NSK-RHP FRANCE S.A.—See NSK Ltd.; *Int'l*, pg. 904

NSK-RHP IBERICA S.A.—See NSK Ltd.; *Int'l*, pg. 904
NSK-RHP ITALIA S.P.A.—See NSK Ltd.; *Int'l*, pg. 904
NSK-RHP NEDERLAND B.V.—See NSK Ltd.; *Int'l*, pg. 904
NSK-RHP UK LIMITED—See NSK Ltd.; *Int'l*, pg. 904
NSK RODAMIENTOS MEXICANA, S.A. DE C.V.—See NSK Ltd.; *Int'l*, pg. 904
NSK SINGAPORE (PRIVATE) LTD.—See NSK Ltd.; *Int'l*, pg. 904
NSO CO.—See Rhone-Poulenc S.A.; *Int'l*, pg. 1110
NSP-NORTH DEBATE REGION—See Northern States Power Company; *U.S. Public*, pg. 1195
NSP-NORTHWEST AREA—See Northern States Power Company; *U.S. Public*, pg. 1195
NSP-SIOUX FALLS REGION—See Northern States Power Company; *U.S. Public*, pg. 1195
NSP-SOUTHEAST REGION—See Northern States Power Company; *U.S. Public*, pg. 1195
NSSP MALAYSIA SDN. BHD.—See Nature's Sunshine Products, Inc.; *U.S. Public*, pg. 1166
NT DOR-OMATIC; *U.S. Private*, pg. 771
NT MERIDIAN S.A.—See Northern Telecom Limited; *Int'l*, pg. 970
NTC/CONTEMPORARY PUBLISHING GROUP—See Tribune Company; *U.S. Public*, pg. 1635
NTC GROUP; *U.S. Private*, pg. 772
NTG NETZWERK UND TELEMATIC GMBH I.L.—See Compagnie des Machines Bull; *Int'l*, pg. 317
NTH CONSULTANTS, LTD.; *U.S. Private*, pg. 772
NTO—See Royal Nedlloyd Group N.V.; *Int'l*, pg. 1145
NTO TRANSPORT ORGANISATION GMBH—See Royal Nedlloyd Group N.V.; *Int'l*, pg. 1145
NTS—See First Data Corporation; *U.S. Public*, pg. 631
NTS DETROIT—See National Technical Systems, Inc.; *U.S. Public*, pg. 1161
NTS DEVELOPMENT COMPANY; *U.S. Private*, pg. 772
NTS ENGINEERING—See National Technical Systems, Inc.; *U.S. Public*, pg. 1161
NTT AMERICA, INC.—See Nippon Telegraph and Telephone Company; *Int'l*, pg. 941
NUI CAPITAL CORP.—See NUI Corporation; *U.S. Public*, pg. 1148
NUI CORPORATION; *U.S. Public*, pg. 1147
NUI ENERGY BROKERS, INC.—See NUI Corporation; *U.S. Public*, pg. 1148
NUI ENERGY, INC.—See NUI Corporation; *U.S. Public*, pg. 1148
NUI ENVIRONMENTAL GROUP, INC.—See NUI Corporation; *U.S. Public*, pg. 1148
NUS DEUTSCHLAND GMBH—See National Utility Service, Inc.; *U.S. Private*, pg. 787
NUS INTERNATIONAL PTY. LTD.—See National Utility Service, Inc.; *U.S. Private*, pg. 787
NUS ITALIA, S.R.L.—See National Utility Service, Inc.; *U.S. Private*, pg. 787
NUS SCANDINAVIA AB—See National Utility Service, Inc.; *U.S. Private*, pg. 787
NV-MANNOR—See Nobles Mfg. Inc.; *U.S. Private*, pg. 800
NV SCHADEVERZEKERING MAATSCHAPPIJ N.V.—See Assicurazioni Generali S.p.A.; *Int'l*, pg. 92
N.V.A. SCHULMAN PLASTICS, S.A.—See A. Schulman, Inc.; *U.S. Public*, pg. 1441
NVF COMPANY; *U.S. Private*, pg. 772
NVF INDUSTRIES OF CANADA LTD.—See NVF Company; *U.S. Private*, pg. 772
NVG LEVENSVERZEKERINGMAATSCHAPPIJ NV—See AEGON N.V.; *Int'l*, pg. 26
NVG SCHADEVERZEKERINGMAATSCHAPPIJ NV—See AEGON N.V.; *Int'l*, pg. 26
NVG UITAARTVERZEKERINGMAATSCHAPPIJ NV—See AEGON N.V.; *Int'l*, pg. 26
NVR BUILDING PRODUCTS—See NVR, Inc.; *U.S. Public*, pg. 1148
NVR FINANCIAL SERVICES, INC.—See NVR, Inc.; *U.S. Public*, pg. 1148
NVR HOMES, INC.—See NVR, Inc.; *U.S. Public*, pg. 1148
NVR, INC.; *U.S. Public*, pg. 1148
NVR MORTGAGE—See NVR, Inc.; *U.S. Public*, pg. 1148
NVR SETTLEMENT SERVICES, INC.—See NVR, Inc.; *U.S. Public*, pg. 1148
NVS NORDISKA VARME SANA AB—See NCC AB; *Int'l*, pg. 899
NVS SALLAND VERZEKERINGEN N.V.—See Allianz Aktiengesellschaft; *Int'l*, pg. 61
NVW (USA) INC.—See Koninklijke Hoogovens N.V.; *Int'l*, pg. 754
NW MANAGEMENT CORP.—See The Rouse Company; *U.S. Public*, pg. 1409
NW TRANSPORT SERVICE, INC.; *U.S. Private*, pg. 772
NWL 806 MAIN, INC.—See National Western Life Insurance Company; *U.S. Public*, pg. 1161
NWL FINANCIAL, INC.—See National Western Life Insurance Company; *U.S. Public*, pg. 1161
NWL INVESTMENTS, INC.—See National Western Life Insurance Company; *U.S. Public*, pg. 1161
NWL PROPERTIES, INC.—See National Western Life Insurance Company; *U.S. Public*, pg. 1161
NWL SERVICES, INC.—See National Western Life Insurance Company; *U.S. Public*, pg. 1161
NWNL BENEFITS CORP.—See ReliaStar Financial Corp.; *U.S. Public*, pg. 1375
NWNL HEALTH MANAGEMENT CORP.—See ReliaStar Financial Corp.; *U.S. Public*, pg. 1375
NWNL MANAGEMENT CORP.—See ReliaStar Financial Corp.; *U.S. Public*, pg. 1375
NWQ INVESTMENT MANAGAEMENT COMPANY—See United Asset Management Corporation; *U.S. Public*, pg. 1673
NWS INC.; *U.S. Private*, pg. 772
NWW PROPERTIES LTD.—See United Utilities plc; *Int'l*, pg. 1444
NY*BO*E S.A.—See Nykredit; *Int'l*, pg. 993
NYCO MINERALS—See Canadian Pacific Limited; *Int'l*, pg. 259

NYK AGENCIES (M) SDN. BHD.—See Nippon Yusen K.K.; *Int'l*, pg. 941
NYK-BEIJING—See Nippon Yusen K.K.; *Int'l*, pg. 941
NYK-BOMBAY—See Nippon Yusen K.K.; *Int'l*, pg. 942
NYK-BUENOS AIRES—See Nippon Yusen K.K.; *Int'l*, pg. 941
NYK BULKSHIP (ASIA) PTE. LTD.—See Nippon Yusen K.K.; *Int'l*, pg. 941
NYK BULKSHIP-BRUSSELS—See Nippon Yusen K.K.; *Int'l*, pg. 941
NYK BULKSHIP-DETROIT—See Nippon Yusen K.K.; *Int'l*, pg. 941
NYK BULKSHIP (EUROPE) LTD.—See Nippon Yusen K.K.; *Int'l*, pg. 941
NYK BULKSHIP-LOS ANGELES—See Nippon Yusen K.K.; *Int'l*, pg. 941
NYK BULKSHIP-SEATTLE—See Nippon Yusen K.K.; *Int'l*, pg. 941
NYK BULKSHIP (USA) INC.—See Nippon Yusen K.K.; *Int'l*, pg. 941
NYK-DUBAI—See Nippon Yusen K.K.; *Int'l*, pg. 941
NYK-GUANGZHOU—See Nippon Yusen K.K.; *Int'l*, pg. 942
NYK-HO CHI MINH—See Nippon Yusen K.K.; *Int'l*, pg. 941
NYK INTERNATIONAL PLC—See Nippon Yusen K.K.; *Int'l*, pg. 941
NYK INTERNATIONAL (USA) INC.—See Nippon Yusen K.K.; *Int'l*, pg. 941
NYK-JAKARTA—See Nippon Yusen K.K.; *Int'l*, pg. 941
NYK-KAOHSIUNG—See Nippon Yusen K.K.; *Int'l*, pg. 941
NYK-KOBE BRANCH—See Nippon Yusen K.K.; *Int'l*, pg. 941
NYK-KYUSHU (HAKATA) BRANCH—See Nippon Yusen K.K.; *Int'l*, pg. 941
NYK-KYUSHU (MOJI) BRANCH—See Nippon Yusen K.K.; *Int'l*, pg. 941
NYK LINE-ADELAIDE—See Nippon Yusen K.K.; *Int'l*, pg. 941
NYK LINE (AUSTRALIA) PTY. LTD.—See Nippon Yusen K.K.; *Int'l*, pg. 941
NYK LINE BENELUX-ANTWERP—See Nippon Yusen K.K.; *Int'l*, pg. 942
NYK LINE (BENELUX) B.V.—See Nippon Yusen K.K.; *Int'l*, pg. 942
NYK LINE-BIRMINGHAM—See Nippon Yusen K.K.; *Int'l*, pg. 942
NYK LINE-BREMEN—See Nippon Yusen K.K.; *Int'l*, pg. 942
NYK LINE-BRISBANE—See Nippon Yusen K.K.; *Int'l*, pg. 941
NYK LINE (CANADA) INC.—See Nippon Yusen K.K.; *Int'l*, pg. 941
NYK LINE (DEUTSCHLAND)-DUSSELDORF—See Nippon Yusen K.K.; *Int'l*, pg. 942
NYK LINE (DEUTSCHLAND) GMBH—See Nippon Yusen K.K.; *Int'l*, pg. 942
NYK LINE-DUSSELDORF—See Nippon Yusen K.K.; *Int'l*, pg. 942
NYK LINE (EUROPE) LTD.—See Nippon Yusen K.K.; *Int'l*, pg. 942
NYK LINE-FRANKFURT—See Nippon Yusen K.K.; *Int'l*, pg. 942
NYK LINE-FREMANTLE—See Nippon Yusen K.K.; *Int'l*, pg. 941
NYK LINE-GLASGOW—See Nippon Yusen K.K.; *Int'l*, pg. 942
NYK LINE-HALIFAX—See Nippon Yusen K.K.; *Int'l*, pg. 942
NYK LINE-HAMBURG—See Nippon Yusen K.K.; *Int'l*, pg. 942
NYK LINE-HELSINGBORG—See Nippon Yusen K.K.; *Int'l*, pg. 942
NYK LINE (HONG KONG) LTD.—See Nippon Yusen K.K.; *Int'l*, pg. 942
NYK LINE-JEDDAH—See Nippon Yusen K.K.; *Int'l*, pg. 942
NYK LINE-JOHANNESBURG—See Nippon Yusen K.K.; *Int'l*, pg. 942
NYK LINE-LIVERPOOL—See Nippon Yusen K.K.; *Int'l*, pg. 942
NYK LINE-MELBOURNE—See Nippon Yusen K.K.; *Int'l*, pg. 941
NYK LINE-MILAN—See Nippon Yusen K.K.; *Int'l*, pg. 942
NYK LINE-MONTREAL—See Nippon Yusen K.K.; *Int'l*, pg. 942
NYK LINE-NEWCASTLE—See Nippon Yusen K.K.; *Int'l*, pg. 942
NYK LINE (NORTH AMERICA) INC.—See Nippon Yusen K.K.; *Int'l*, pg. 941
NYK LINE-PARIS—See Nippon Yusen K.K.; *Int'l*, pg. 942
NYK LINE (SINGAPORE) PTE. LTD.—See Nippon Yusen K.K.; *Int'l*, pg. 942
NYK LINE-SOUTHAMPTON—See Nippon Yusen K.K.; *Int'l*, pg. 942
NYK LINE-STOCKHOLM—See Nippon Yusen K.K.; *Int'l*, pg. 942
NYK LINE (SVERIGE) AB—See Nippon Yusen K.K.; *Int'l*, pg. 942
NYK-MANILA—See Nippon Yusen K.K.; *Int'l*, pg. 941
NYK-MEXICO CITY—See Nippon Yusen K.K.; *Int'l*, pg. 941
NYK-NAGOYA BRANCH—See Nippon Yusen K.K.; *Int'l*, pg. 941
NYK-NANJING—See Nippon Yusen K.K.; *Int'l*, pg. 942
NYK-NINGBO—See Nippon Yusen K.K.; *Int'l*, pg. 942
NYK-OSAKA BRANCH—See Nippon Yusen K.K.; *Int'l*, pg. 941
NYK-QINGDAO—See Nippon Yusen K.K.; *Int'l*, pg. 941
NYK-SAO PAULO—See Nippon Yusen K.K.; *Int'l*, pg. 942
NYK-SAPPORO BRANCH—See Nippon Yusen K.K.; *Int'l*, pg. 941
NYK-SEOUL—See Nippon Yusen K.K.; *Int'l*, pg. 941
NYK-SHANGHAI—See Nippon Yusen K.K.; *Int'l*, pg. 942
NYK SHIPPING-CHRISTCHURCH—See Nippon Yusen K.K.; *Int'l*, pg. 942
NYK SHIPPING (NZ) LTD.—See Nippon Yusen K.K.; *Int'l*, pg. 942
NYK SHIPPING SERVICE (THAILAND) CO., LTD.—See Nippon Yusen K.K.; *Int'l*, pg. 942

NYK SHIPPING-WELLINGTON—See Nippon Yusen K.K.; *Int'l*, pg. 942
NYK-TAIPEI—See Nippon Yusen K.K.; *Int'l*, pg. 941
NYK-TEHRAN—See Nippon Yusen K.K.; *Int'l*, pg. 941
NYK-YOKOHAMA BRANCH—See Nippon Yusen K.K.; *Int'l*, pg. 941
NYT BROADCAST HOLDINGS, INC.—See The New York Times Company; *U.S. Public*, pg. 1175
NYT CUSTOM PUBLISHING—See The New York Times Company; *U.S. Public*, pg. 1174
NYT EVENT/SPORTS MARKETING—See The New York Times Company; *U.S. Public*, pg. 1174
NYT SHARED SERVICES CENTER, INC.—See The New York Times Company; *U.S. Public*, pg. 1176
NYT VIDEO NEWS INTERNATIONAL—See The New York Times Company; *U.S. Public*, pg. 1174
NYT VIDEO PRODUCTIONS—See The New York Times Company; *U.S. Public*, pg. 1174
NYTRNG, INC.—See The New York Times Company; *U.S. Public*, pg. 1174
NZ ALUMINUM FRANCHISING—See International Paper Company; *U.S. Public*, pg. 905
NZ DEVELOPMENT CORPORATION—See New Mexico & Arizona Land Co.; *U.S. Public*, pg. 1172
NZ PROPERTIES, INC.—See New Mexico & Arizona Land Co.; *U.S. Public*, pg. 1172
NZU, INC.—See New Mexico & Arizona Land Co.; *U.S. Public*, pg. 1172
NA-CHURS PLANT FOOD COMPANY—See Trans Resources, Inc.; *U.S. Private*, pg. 1096
NAANTALI POWER PLANT—See Imatran Voima Oy; *Int'l*, pg. 660
NABALCO PTY. LTD.—See Alusuisse-Lonza Holding Ltd.; *Int'l*, pg. 69
NABANCO—See First Data Corporation; *U.S. Public*, pg. 631
NABHOLZ CONSTRUCTION CORP.; *U.S. Private*, pg. 772
NABI; *U.S. Public*, pg. 1148
NABISCO INC.—See RJR Nabisco Holdings Corp.; *U.S. Public*, pg. 1355
NABISCO INTERNATIONAL INCORPORATED—See RJR Nabisco Holdings Corp.; *U.S. Public*, pg. 1355
NABISCO MUSIC PUBLISHERS, INC.—See RJR Nabisco Holdings Corp.; *U.S. Public*, pg. 1355
NABISCO MUSIC VENTURES, INC.—See RJR Nabisco Holdings Corp.; *U.S. Public*, pg. 1355
NABOB FOODS LIMITED—See Philip Morris Companies Inc.; *U.S. Public*, pg. 1289
NABORS ALASKA DRILLING, INC.—See Nabors Industries, Inc.; *U.S. Public*, pg. 1148
NABORS ALASKA PETROLEUM SVCS.—See Nabors Industries, Inc.; *U.S. Public*, pg. 1148
NABORS DRILLING & ENERGY SERVICES UK, LTD.—See Nabors Industries, Inc.; *U.S. Public*, pg. 1149
NABORS DRILLING INTERNATIONAL LIMITED—See Nabors Industries, Inc.; *U.S. Public*, pg. 1148
NABORS DRILLING LIMITED—See Nabors Industries, Inc.; *U.S. Public*, pg. 1148
NABORS DRILLING USA, INC.—See Nabors Industries, Inc.; *U.S. Public*, pg. 1149
NABORS INDUSTRIES, INC.; *U.S. Public*, pg. 1148
NACAN PRODUCTS LTD.—See Unilever Plc; *Int'l*, pg. 1436
NACANCO FRANCE S.A.—See Pechiney S.A.; *Int'l*, pg. 1029
NACANCO GMBH & CO. KG—See Pechiney S.A.; *Int'l*, pg. 1029
NACANCO IRELAND LTD.—See Pechiney S.A.; *Int'l*, pg. 1029
NACANCO LTD.—See Pechiney S.A.; *Int'l*, pg. 1029
NACANCO PAKETLEME SANAYI A.S.—See Pechiney S.A.; *Int'l*, pg. 1029
NACANCO S.A.—See Pechiney S.A.; *Int'l*, pg. 1029
NACANCO S.P.A.—See Pechiney S.A.; *Int'l*, pg. 1029
NACCO INDUSTRIES, INC.; *U.S. Public*, pg. 1149
NACCO MATERIALS HANDLING GROUP, INC.—See NACCO Industries, Inc.; *U.S. Public*, pg. 1149
NACIONAL FINANCIERA; *Int'l*, pg. 904
NACIONAL FINANCIERA—See Nacional Financiera; *Int'l*, pg. 904
NACIONAL HISPANICA, S.A. DE SEGUROS Y REASEGUROS—See Assicurazioni Generali S.p.A.; *Int'l*, pg. 91
NACIONALGAS—See Tractebel; *Int'l*, pg. 1416
NACOLAH HOLDING CORP. INC.—See Sammons Enterprises, Inc.; *U.S. Private*, pg. 963
NACOMA PRODUCTS, INC.; *U.S. Private*, pg. 773
NADEL ARCHITECTS, INC.; *U.S. Private*, pg. 773
NADEL ARCHITECTS INC. & MARVIN FITCH—See Nadel Architects, Inc.; *U.S. Private*, pg. 773
NADEL ARCHITECTS, PC NEVADA—See Nadel Architects, Inc.; *U.S. Private*, pg. 773
JACK NADEL, INC.; *U.S. Private*, pg. 773
NADELLA U.K. LIMITED—See Ingersoll-Rand Company; *U.S. Public*, pg. 878
NADELLA WALZLAGER GMBH—See Ingersoll-Rand Company; *U.S. Public*, pg. 878
NADRO S.A. DE C.V.—See McKesson Corporation; *U.S. Public*, pg. 1073
NADY SYSTEMS, INC.; *U.S. Private*, pg. 773
NAEGELEN S.A.—See Emerson Electric Co.; *U.S. Public*, pg. 574
NAFCO NATIONAL FLOOR COMPANY—See Domco Inc.; *Int'l*, pg. 415
NAGAHAMA CANON, INC.—See Canon Inc.; *Int'l*, pg. 261
NAGANO OKI ELECTRIC CO., LTD.—See Oki Electric Industry Company, Ltd.; *Int'l*, pg. 999
NAGASCO, INC.—See Apache Corporation; *U.S. Public*, pg. 119
NAGASE-ALFA K. K.—See Tetra Laval Group; *Int'l*, pg. 1380
NAGASE-CIBA LTD.—See Novartis AG; *Int'l*, pg. 983
NAGASE-CIBA LIMITED-TATSUNO FACTORY—See Novartis AG; *Int'l*, pg. 983

Company Index

NAGASE-LANDAUER DIRECTORY OF CORPORATE AFFILIATIONS

NAGASE-LANDAUER, LTD.—See Landauer, Inc.; *U.S. Public*, pg. 977
NAGOYA BUS WORKS—See Mitsubishi Motors Corporation; *Int'l*, pg. 875
NAGOYA MITSUKOSHI, LTD.—See Mitsukoshi, Ltd.; *Int'l*, pg. 883
NAGOYA MOTOR VEHICLE WORKS—See Mitsubishi Motors Corporation; *Int'l*, pg. 875
NAGOYA MOTOR VEHICLE WORKS - OKAZAKI PLANT—See Mitsubishi Motors Corporation; *Int'l*, pg. 875
NAGOYA TOYOPET CO., LTD.—See Toyota Motor Corporation; *Int'l*, pg. 1412
NAHUELSAT S.A.—See Daimler-Benz Aktiengesellschaft; *Int'l*, pg. 367
NAIRN BODENBELAG GMBH—See Forbo Holding SA; *Int'l*, pg. 498
NAIRN FLOORS BENELUX S.A.—See Forbo Holding SA; *Int'l*, pg. 498
NAIRN SOL SA—See Forbo Holding SA; *Int'l*, pg. 498
NAKANO FOODS—See Mitsukan & Nakano Vinegar Company Ltd.; *Int'l*, pg. 883
NAKANO FOODS INC.—See Mitsukan & Nakano Vinegar Company Ltd.; *Int'l*, pg. 883
NAKANO METAL PRESS (SINGAPORE) PTE. LTD.—See Shimano Inc.; *Int'l*, pg. 1232
NAKANO VINEGAR CO., LTD.; *Int'l*, pg. 904
NAKORNTHON BANK PUBLIC COMPANY LIMITED; *Int'l*, pg. 904
NAKOSO MILL—See Nippon Paper Industries Company Limited; *Int'l*, pg. 938
NALCO ARGENTINA S.A.—See Nalco Chemical Company; *U.S. Public*, pg. 1150
NALCO AUSTRALIA—See Nalco Chemical Company; *U.S. Public*, pg. 1150
NALCO BRASIL LTDA.—See Nalco Chemical Company; *U.S. Public*, pg. 1150
NALCO CANADA INC.—See Nalco Chemical Company; *U.S. Public*, pg. 1150
NALCO CHEMICAL COMPANY; *U.S. Public*, pg. 1150
NALCO CHEMICAL CO. (PHILIPPINES), INC.—See Nalco Chemical Company; *U.S. Public*, pg. 1150
NALCO CHEMICAL CO. (THAILAND) LTD.—See Nalco Chemical Company; *U.S. Public*, pg. 1150
NALCO CHEMICAL (H.K.) LTD.—See Nalco Chemical Company; *U.S. Public*, pg. 1150
NALCO CHEMICAL PROCESS CHEMICALS DIVISION—See Nalco Chemical Company; *U.S. Public*, pg. 1150
NALCO CHEMICAL (SUZHOU) CO., LTD.—See Nalco Chemical Company; *U.S. Public*, pg. 1150
NALCO CHEMICAL WATER AND WASTE TREATMENT DIV.—See Nalco Chemical Company; *U.S. Public*, pg. 1150
NALCO CHEMICALS INDIA LIMITED—See Nalco Chemical Company; *U.S. Public*, pg. 1150
NALCO DE VENEZUELA, C.A.—See Nalco Chemical Company; *U.S. Public*, pg. 1150
NALCO ECUADOR S.A.—See Nalco Chemical Company; *U.S. Public*, pg. 1150
NALCO EUROPE—See Nalco Chemical Company; *U.S. Public*, pg. 1151
NALCO FUEL TECH—See Nalco Chemical Company; *U.S. Public*, pg. 1150
NALCO JAPAN CO., LTD.—See Nalco Chemical Company; *U.S. Public*, pg. 1151
NALCO KOREA CO., LTD.—See Nalco Chemical Company; *U.S. Public*, pg. 1151
NALCO PACIFIC—See Nalco Chemical Company; *U.S. Public*, pg. 1151
P.T. NALCO PERKASA—See Nalco Chemical Company; *U.S. Public*, pg. 1151
NALCO PRODUCTOS QUIMICOS DE CHILE S.A.—See Nalco Chemical Company; *U.S. Public*, pg. 1151
NALCO SAUDI CO. LTD.—See Nalco Chemical Company; *U.S. Public*, pg. 1151
NALCOMEX S.A. DE C.V.—See Nalco Chemical Company; *U.S. Public*, pg. 1151
NALLE PLASTICS INC.; *U.S. Private*, pg. 773
NALLEYS FINE FOODS—See Pro-Fac Cooperative, Inc.; *U.S. Private*, pg. 887
NAM KWONG PETROLEUM & CHEMICALS CO., LTD.—See Sinochem International Petroleum Co. Ltd.; *Int'l*, pg. 1255
NAMANCO LLC; *U.S. Private*, pg. 773
NAMASCOR B.V.—See Koninklijke Hoogovens N.V.; *Int'l*, pg. 754
NAMBA PRESS WORKS CO., LTD.; *Int'l*, pg. 904
NAMBOKUSHA INC.; *Int'l*, pg. 904
NAMCO-AMERICA, INC.—See Namco Ltd.; *Int'l*, pg. 905
NAMCO CONTROLS CORPORATION—See Danaher Corporation; *U.S. Public*, pg. 482
NAMCO CONTROLS GMBH—See Danaher Corporation; *U.S. Public*, pg. 482
NAMCO CYBERTAINMENT INC.—See Namco Ltd.; *Int'l*, pg. 905
NAMCO ENTERPRISES ASIA LTD.—See Namco Ltd.; *Int'l*, pg. 905
NAMCO EUROPE LTD.—See Namco Ltd.; *Int'l*, pg. 905
NAMCO-HOLDING, CORP.—See Namco Ltd.; *Int'l*, pg. 905
NAMCO HOMETEK, INC.—See Namco Ltd.; *Int'l*, pg. 905
NAMCO LTD.; *Int'l*, pg. 905
A/S NAMDALENS TRAESLIPERI—See Norske Skogindustrier A.S; *Int'l*, pg. 965
NAME SAVER COMPANY—See Home Juice Co.; *U.S. Private*, pg. 537
NAMEPLATE—See Fred B. Johnston Company, Inc.; *U.S. Private*, pg. 595
NAMES FOR DAMES, INC.; *U.S. Private*, pg. 773
NAMIC CARIBE, INC.—See Pfizer Inc.; *U.S. Public*, pg. 1284
NAMIC EIREANN B.V.—See Pfizer Inc.; *U.S. Public*, pg. 1284
NAMIC EIREANN LIMITED—See Pfizer Inc.; *U.S. Public*, pg. 1284
NAMIC INTERNATIONAL, INC.—See Pfizer Inc.; *U.S. Public*, pg. 1284
NAMIC WORLDWIDE B.V.—See Pfizer Inc.; *U.S. Public*, pg. 1284
NAMICO, INC.; *U.S. Private*, pg. 773
NAMKWANG ENGINEERING & CONSTRUCTION CO., LTD.—See Ssangyong Business Group; *Int'l*, pg. 1291
NAMSENBYGG—See Norske Skogindustrier A.S; *Int'l*, pg. 965
NAN SHAN LIFE INSURANCE COMPANY, LTD.—See American International Group, Inc.; *U.S. Public*, pg. 85
NAN WOVEN—See BBA Group plc; *Int'l*, pg. 113
NANA DEVELOPMENT CORPORATION—See Nana Regional Corporation, Inc.; *U.S. Private*, pg. 774
NANA REGIONAL CORPORATION, INC.; *U.S. Private*, pg. 774
NANBEI LTD.—See Dow Jones & Company, Inc.; *U.S. Public*, pg. 525
NANBU SEN-I KOGYO CO., LTD.—See Kosugi Sangyo Co., Ltd.; *Int'l*, pg. 759
NANCE'S FOOD PRODUCTS, INC.—See The Quaker Oats Company; *U.S. Public*, pg. 1347
NANGOKU NISSAY BUILDING CO., LTD.—See Nippon Life Insurance Co.; *Int'l*, pg. 935
NANISIVIK MINES LTD.—See Royal Dutch/Shell Group of Companies; *Int'l*, pg. 1138
NANJING ERICSSON COMMUNICATION COMPANY LTD.—See Telefonaktiebolaget LM Ericsson; *Int'l*, pg. 1369
NANJING GOULDS PUMPS LIMITED—See ITT Industries, Inc.; *U.S. Public*, pg. 861
NANJING OWENS CORNING XPS FOAM CO. LTD.—See Owens Corning; *U.S. Public*, pg. 1237
NANJING SHARP ELECTRONICS CO., LTD—See Sharp Corporation; *Int'l*, pg. 1229
NANJING TECHNOLOGY I/E CORP.—See China National Technical Import & Export Corporation (CNTIC); *Int'l*, pg. 285
NANJING TOTO CO., LTD.—See Toto Ltd.; *Int'l*, pg. 1410
NANOCOR, INC.—See AMCOL International Corp.; *U.S. Public*, pg. 64
NANOMETRICS INCORPORATED; *U.S. Public*, pg. 1151
NANOMETRICS JAPAN LTD.—See Nanometrics Incorporated; *U.S. Public*, pg. 1151
NANOMETRICS KOREA LTD.—See Nanometrics Incorporated; *U.S. Public*, pg. 1151
NANOQUEST DEFENCE PRODUCTS LIMITED—See British Aerospace p.l.c.; *Int'l*, pg. 218
NANTAHALA POWER AND LIGHT COMPANY—See Duke Energy Corporation; *U.S. Public*, pg. 534
NANTO BANK-HONG KONG REPRESENTATIVE OFFICE—See The Nanto Bank, Ltd.; *Int'l*, pg. 906
NANTO BANK-KYOTO BRANCH—See The Nanto Bank, Ltd.; *Int'l*, pg. 905
THE NANTO BANK, LTD.; *Int'l*, pg. 905
NANTO BANK-NEW YORK REPRESENTATIVE OFFICE—See The Nanto Bank, Ltd.; *Int'l*, pg. 906
NANTO BANK-OSAKA BRANCH—See The Nanto Bank, Ltd.; *Int'l*, pg. 905
NANTO BANK-TAKADA BRANCH—See The Nanto Bank, Ltd.; *Int'l*, pg. 905
NANTO BANK-TENRI BRANCH—See The Nanto Bank, Ltd.; *Int'l*, pg. 905
NANTO BANK-TOKYO BRANCH—See The Nanto Bank, Ltd.; *Int'l*, pg. 905
NANTO BUSINESS SERVICE CO., LTD.—See The Nanto Bank, Ltd.; *Int'l*, pg. 905
NANTO CARD SERVICES CO., LTD.—See The Nanto Bank, Ltd.; *Int'l*, pg. 905
NANTO COMPUTER SERVICE CO., LTD.—See The Nanto Bank, Ltd.; *Int'l*, pg. 905
NANTO CORPORATION—See The Nanto Bank, Ltd.; *Int'l*, pg. 905
NANTO CREDIT GUARANTEE CO., LTD.—See The Nanto Bank, Ltd.; *Int'l*, pg. 905
NANTO DC CARD CO., LTD.—See The Nanto Bank, Ltd.; *Int'l*, pg. 905
NANTO ESTATE CO., LTD.—See The Nanto Bank, Ltd.; *Int'l*, pg. 905
NANTO INVESTMENT MANAGEMENT CO., LTD.—See The Nanto Bank, Ltd.; *Int'l*, pg. 905
NANTO LEASE CO., LTD.—See The Nanto Bank, Ltd.; *Int'l*, pg. 906
NANTO STAFF SERVICE CO., LTD.—See The Nanto Bank, Ltd.; *Int'l*, pg. 906
NANTUCKET ELECTRIC COMPANY—See New England Electric System; *U.S. Public*, pg. 1171
NANTUCKET INDUSTRIES, INC.; *U.S. Public*, pg. 1151
NAOETSU PLANT—See Mitsubishi Chemical Corporation; *Int'l*, pg. 871
NAPA INC.—See Daiko Advertising, Inc.; *Int'l*, pg. 366
NAPA PIPE CORPORATION—See Oregon Steel Mills Inc.; *U.S. Public*, pg. 1230
NAPA VALLEY BANK—See Westamerica Bancorporation; *U.S. Public*, pg. 1756
THE NAPA VALLEY REGISTER—See Pulitzer Publishing Company; *U.S. Public*, pg. 1343
NAPCO EUROPE, LTD.—See Thermo Electron Corporation; *U.S. Public*, pg. 1596
NAPCO, INC.—See Thermo Electron Corporation; *U.S. Public*, pg. 1592
NAPCO INTERNATIONAL, INC.—See Venturian Corp.; *U.S. Public*, pg. 1716
NAPCO PLASTICS CO.—See Electrolux, AB; *Int'l*, pg. 440
NAPCO SECURITY SYSTEMS, INC.; *U.S. Public*, pg. 1151
THE NAPIER CO.; *U.S. Private*, pg. 774
NAPLES DAILY NEWS—See The E.W. Scripps Company; *U.S. Public*, pg. 1448
NAPLES FOODS, INC.—See WSMP, Inc.; *U.S. Public*, pg. 1729
NAPORANO IRON & METAL; *U.S. Private*, pg. 774
NAPP SYSTEMS INC—See Lee Enterprises, Incorporated; *U.S. Public*, pg. 984
NAPS KENYA—See Neste Oy; *Int'l*, pg. 913
NAPS NORWAY A/S—See Neste Oy; *Int'l*, pg. 913
NARA LIQUID CRYSTAL DISPLAY GROUP—See Sharp Corporation; *Int'l*, pg. 1228
NARASHINO SUNPEDEC CO., LTD.—See Nippon Life Insurance Co.; *Int'l*, pg. 935
NARCO MEDICAL SERVICES INC.—See Vickers PLC; *Int'l*, pg. 1468
NARITA GIKEN CO., LTD.—See Rohm Co., Ltd.; *Int'l*, pg. 1125
NARRAGANSETT CAPITAL INC.; *U.S. Private*, pg. 774
NARRAGANSETT ELECTRIC CO.—See New England Electric System; *U.S. Public*, pg. 1171
NARRAGANSETT ENERGY RESOURCES COMPANY—See New England Electric System; *U.S. Public*, pg. 1171
NARRAGANSETT TIMES—See Journal Register Company; *U.S. Public*, pg. 935
NARROW FABRIC INDUSTRIES, INC.; *U.S. Private*, pg. 774
NARSDORFER KLINKER GMBH—See Redland PLC; *Int'l*, pg. 1091
NARUMI CHINA CORPORATION; *Int'l*, pg. 906
NASAM INTERNATIONAL, INCORPORATED—See Banner Aerospace, Inc.; *U.S. Public*, pg. 187
NASCO—See Geneve Corporation; *U.S. Private*, pg. 446
NASCO INDUSTRIES INC.; *U.S. Private*, pg. 774
NASCO INTERNATIONAL, INC.—See Geneve Corporation; *U.S. Private*, pg. 446
NASCO MODESTO—See Geneve Corporation; *U.S. Private*, pg. 446
NASH DECAMP COMPANY—See Nash Finch Company; *U.S. Public*, pg. 1152
NASH FINCH CO.—See Nash Finch Company; *U.S. Public*, pg. 1152
NASH FINCH COMPANY; *U.S. Public*, pg. 1151
GUNTHER NASH MINING CONSTRUCTION—See J.S. Alberici Construction Co., Inc.; *U.S. Private*, pg. 32
NASHUA CORPORATION; *U.S. Public*, pg. 1152
NASHUA HOMES OF IDAHO INC.; *U.S. Private*, pg. 774
NASHUA PHOTO DELMONT LTD.—See Nashua Corporation; *U.S. Public*, pg. 1152
NASHUA PHOTO LIMITED—See Nashua Corporation; *U.S. Public*, pg. 1152
NASHVILLE AUTO AUCTION INC.—See Tyco International Ltd.; *U.S. Public*, pg. 1649
NASHVILLE BANK OF COMMERCE—See National Commerce Bancorporation; *U.S. Public*, pg. 1155
NASHVILLE MACHINE CO. INC.; *U.S. Private*, pg. 774
NASHVILLE STEEL CORP.; *U.S. Private*, pg. 775
NASHVILLE TEXTILE CORP.—See House of Ronnie, Inc.; *U.S. Private*, pg. 542
NASHVILLE WIRE PRODUCT CO.; *U.S. Private*, pg. 775
NASON AND CULLEN GROUP INCORPORATED; *U.S. Private*, pg. 775
NASON AND CULLEN INC.—See Nason and Cullen Group Incorporated; *U.S. Private*, pg. 775
NASSAU METALS CORPORATION—See Lucent Technologies Inc.; *U.S. Public*, pg. 1019
NASSAU TERMINALS—See Koninklijke Van Ommeren NV; *Int'l*, pg. 758
NASSAU/BAHAMAS TRANSATLANTIC BULK CARRIERS INC.—See Fried. Krupp AG; *Int'l*, pg. 514
NASSER TRADING & CONTRACTING—See Hewlett-Packard Company; *U.S. Public*, pg. 822
NASSHEUER LOI INDUSTRIEOFENANLAGEN GMBH—See Ruhrgas Aktiengesellschaft; *Int'l*, pg. 1149
NASTECH CORP.—See NSK Ltd.; *Int'l*, pg. 903
NASTECH EUROPE LTD.—See NSK Ltd.; *Int'l*, pg. 904
NASU NIKON CO., LTD.—See Nikon Corporation; *Int'l*, pg. 931
NATAL THREAD CO. (PTY) LTD.—See Coats Viyella plc; *Int'l*, pg. 299
NATALI—See The Israel Land Development Co., Ltd.; *Int'l*, pg. 691
NATALIE KNITTING MILLS—See Hampshire Group, Ltd.; *U.S. Public*, pg. 779
NATBANK, F.S.B.—See National Bank of Canada; *Int'l*, pg. 907
NATCAN FINANCE (ASIA) LIMITED—See National Bank of Canada; *Int'l*, pg. 907
NATCAN HOLDINGS INTERNATIONAL LIMITED—See National Bank of Canada; *Int'l*, pg. 907
NATCAN INSURANCE COMPANY LIMITED—See National Bank of Canada; *Int'l*, pg. 907
NATCAN INVESTMENT MANAGEMENT INC.—See National Bank of Canada; *Int'l*, pg. 907
NATCAN TRUST COMPANY—See National Bank of Canada; *Int'l*, pg. 907
NATCHIQ, INC.—See Arctic Slope Regional Corporation; *U.S. Private*, pg. 80
NATCITY INVESTMENTS, INC.—See National City Corporation; *U.S. Public*, pg. 1154
NATCO LIMITED PARTNERSHIP—See Ballast Nedam NV; *Int'l*, pg. 134
NATEXPORT—See National Bank of Canada; *Int'l*, pg. 907
FERNAND NATHAN—See C.E.P. Communication Group; *Int'l*, pg. 240
NATHAN'S FAMOUS INC.; *U.S. Public*, pg. 1152
NATIONAL ACCOUNT SYSTEMS, INC.—See Payco American Corporation; *U.S. Public*, pg. 1267
NATIONAL AEROSOL PRODUCTS CO.—See Imperial Chemical Industries PLC; *Int'l*, pg. 663
NATIONAL AIRMOTIVE CORPORATION; *U.S. Private*, pg. 775
NATIONAL AMERICAN CORPORATION—See U.S. Trails; *U.S. Public*, pg. 1688
NATIONAL AMERICAN INSURANCE COMPANY OF CALIFORNIA—See Danielson Holding Corporation; *U.S. Public*, pg. 483
NATIONAL AMUSEMENTS, INC.; *U.S. Private*, pg. 775
NATIONAL & PROVINCIAL BUILDING SOCIETY; *Int'l*, pg. 906
NATIONAL-ARNOLD MAGNETICS COMPANY—See SPS Technologies, Inc.; *U.S. Public*, pg. 1420

NATIONAL ASSET MANAGEMENT CORPORATION—See National City Corporation; *U.S. Public*, pg. 1154

NATIONAL ASSOCIATED DESIGN CO.—See Brierley Investments Limited; *Int'l*, pg. 215

THE NATIONAL ASSOCIATION FOR FEMALE EXECUTIVES, INC.—See MacDonald Communications; *U.S. Private*, pg. 691

NATIONAL ATTORNEYS' TITLE ASSURANCE FUND, INC.—See Attorneys' Title Insurance Fund; *U.S. Private*, pg. 98

NATIONAL AUSTRALIA ASSET MANAGEMENT—See National Australia Bank Limited; *Int'l*, pg. 906

NATIONAL AUSTRALIA BANK LIMITED; *Int'l*, pg. 906

NATIONAL AUSTRALIA BANK/GATX—See GATX Corporation; *U.S. Public*, pg. 691

NATIONAL AUSTRALIA FINANCIAL MANAGEMENT LTD.—See National Australia Bank Limited; *Int'l*, pg. 906

NATIONAL AUSTRALIA GROUP (UK) LIMITED—See National Australia Bank Limited; *Int'l*, pg. 906

NATIONAL AUSTRALIA LIFE—See National Australia Bank Limited; *Int'l*, pg. 906

NATIONAL AUSTRALIA TRUSTEES LTD.—See National Australia Bank Limited; *Int'l*, pg. 906

NATIONAL AUTO CREDIT INC.; *U.S. Public*, pg. 1152

NATIONAL AUTO DEALERS EXCHANGE—See Cox Enterprises, Inc.; *U.S. Private*, pg. 282

NATIONAL AUTO RESEARCH—See The Hearst Corporation; *U.S. Private*, pg. 516

NATIONAL BAKING—See Specialty Foods Corporation; *U.S. Public*, pg. 1022

NATIONAL BANCORP OF ALASKA, INC.; *U.S. Public*, pg. 1153

NATIONAL BANCORP, INC.—See Banco Popular de Puerto Rico; *U.S. Public*, pg. 176

NATIONAL BAND & TAG CO.; *U.S. Private*, pg. 780

NATIONAL BAND THREE LTD.—See Geotek Communications; *U.S. Public*, pg. 740

NATIONAL BANK FINANCIAL SERVICES INC.—See National Bank of Canada; *Int'l*, pg. 907

NATIONAL BANK INFORMATION CORPORATION INC.—See National Bank of Canada; *Int'l*, pg. 907

NATIONAL BANK LIFE INSURANCE COMPANY—See National Bank of Canada; *Int'l*, pg. 907

NATIONAL BANK OF ALASKA—See National Bancorp of Alaska, Inc.; *U.S. Public*, pg. 1153

THE NATIONAL BANK OF AMERICA—See UMB Financial Corporation; *U.S. Public*, pg. 1654

NATIONAL BANK OF ARIZONA—See Zions Bancorporation; *U.S. Public*, pg. 1793

NATIONAL BANK OF CANADA; *Int'l*, pg. 907

NATIONAL BANK OF CANADA (ASIA) LTD.—See National Bank of Canada; *Int'l*, pg. 907

NATIONAL BANK OF CANADA (INTERNATIONAL) LIMITED—See National Bank of Canada; *Int'l*, pg. 907

NATIONAL BANK OF COMMERCE—See First Commerce Bancshares, Inc.; *U.S. Public*, pg. 629

NATIONAL BANK OF COMMERCE—See National Commerce Bancorporation; *U.S. Public*, pg. 1155

THE NATIONAL BANK OF FREDERICKSBURG—See Mercantile Bankshares Corporation; *U.S. Public*, pg. 1089

NATIONAL BANK OF GREECE BRUSSELS BRANCH—See National Bank of Greece S.A.; *Int'l*, pg. 907

NATIONAL BANK OF GREECE CAIRO BRANCH—See National Bank of Greece S.A.; *Int'l*, pg. 907

NATIONAL BANK OF GREECE CANADA BRANCH—See National Bank of Greece S.A.; *Int'l*, pg. 907

NATIONAL BANK OF GREECE DUSSELDORF BRANCH—See National Bank of Greece S.A.; *Int'l*, pg. 907

NATIONAL BANK OF GREECE FRANKFURT BRANCH—See National Bank of Greece S.A.; *Int'l*, pg. 907

NATIONAL BANK OF GREECE MELBOURNE BRANCH—See National Bank of Greece S.A.; *Int'l*, pg. 907

NATIONAL BANK OF GREECE MOSCOW BRANCH—See National Bank of Greece S.A.; *Int'l*, pg. 907

NATIONAL BANK OF GREECE ROTTERDAM BRANCH—See National Bank of Greece S.A.; *Int'l*, pg. 907

NATIONAL BANK OF GREECE S.A.; *Int'l*, pg. 907

NATIONAL BANK OF GREECE SYDNEY BRANCH—See National Bank of Greece S.A.; *Int'l*, pg. 907

NATIONAL BANK OF HASTINGS—See First Financial Bancorp; *U.S. Public*, pg. 633

NATIONAL BANK OF MALAWI—See Standard Chartered Bank PLC; *Int'l*, pg. 1296

NATIONAL BANK OF NEW ZEALAND LTD.—See Lloyds TSB Group PLC; *Int'l*, pg. 814

NATIONAL BANK OF NEW ZEALAND SAVINGS BANK LTD.—See Lloyds TSB Group PLC; *Int'l*, pg. 814

NATIONAL BANK OF PAKISTAN; *Int'l*, pg. 907

NATIONAL BANK OF PAKISTAN—See National Bank of Pakistan; *Int'l*, pg. 908

NATIONAL BANK OF PAKISTAN-CAIRO—See National Bank of Pakistan; *Int'l*, pg. 908

NATIONAL BANK OF PAKISTAN-DHAKA—See National Bank of Pakistan; *Int'l*, pg. 908

NATIONAL BANK OF PAKISTAN-FRANKFURT—See National Bank of Pakistan; *Int'l*, pg. 908

NATIONAL BANK OF PAKISTAN-HONG KONG—See National Bank of Pakistan; *Int'l*, pg. 908

NATIONAL BANK OF PAKISTAN-KOWLOON—See National Bank of Pakistan; *Int'l*, pg. 908

NATIONAL BANK OF PAKISTAN-LONDON—See National Bank of Pakistan; *Int'l*, pg. 908

NATIONAL BANK OF PAKISTAN-MANAMA—See National Bank of Pakistan; *Int'l*, pg. 908

NATIONAL BANK OF PAKISTAN-OSAKA—See National Bank of Pakistan; *Int'l*, pg. 908

NATIONAL BANK OF PAKISTAN-PARIS—See National Bank of Pakistan; *Int'l*, pg. 908

NATIONAL BANK OF PAKISTAN-SEOUL—See National Bank of Pakistan; *Int'l*, pg. 908

NATIONAL BANK OF PAKISTAN-TOKYO—See National Bank of Pakistan; *Int'l*, pg. 908

NATIONAL BANK OF SOLOMON ISLANDS—See Pacific Century Financial Corporation; *U.S. Public*, pg. 1248

THE NATIONAL BANK OF SOUTH CAROLINA—See Synovus Financial Corp.; *U.S. Public*, pg. 1549

NATIONAL BANK OF SUMMERS—See Horizon Bancorp, Inc.; *U.S. Public*, pg. 836

THE NATIONAL BANK OF SUSSEX COUNTY—See High Point Financial Corp.; *U.S. Public*, pg. 826

NATIONAL BANK OF WALTON COUNTY—See Synovus Financial Corp.; *U.S. Public*, pg. 1549

NATIONAL BANK SECURITIES INC.—See National Bank of Canada; *Int'l*, pg. 907

NATIONAL BANNER COMPANY, INC.; *U.S. Private*, pg. 780

NATIONAL BASKETBALL ASSOCIATION; *U.S. Private*, pg. 780

NATIONAL BEARINGS LIMITED—See Wajax Limited; *Int'l*, pg. 1485

NATIONAL BEDDING CO.; *U.S. Private*, pg. 780

NATIONAL-BEN FRANKLIN INSURANCE CO. OF ILLINOIS—See Loews Corporation; *U.S. Public*, pg. 1011

NATIONAL BENEFIT LIFE INSURANCE CO.—See Travelers Group; *U.S. Public*, pg. 1633

NATIONAL BERYLLIA DIV.—See Tokuyama Corporation; *Int'l*, pg. 1394

NATIONAL BEVERAGE CORP.; *U.S. Public*, pg. 1153

NATIONAL BOOK COMPANY INC.—See W.W. Norton & Company, Inc.; *U.S. Private*, pg. 807

NATIONAL BOOK DISTRIBUTORS—See Handleman Company; *U.S. Public*, pg. 780

NATIONAL BRANDS, INC.; *U.S. Private*, pg. 780

NATIONAL BROADCAST UNIT—See True North Communications Inc.; *U.S. Public*, pg. 1641

NATIONAL BROADCASTING CO., INC.—See General Electric Company; *U.S. Public*, pg. 712

NATIONAL BULK CARRIERS, INC.; *U.S. Private*, pg. 780

NATIONAL BUSINESS EMPLOYMENT WEEKLY—See Dow Jones & Company, Inc.; *U.S. Public*, pg. 524

NATIONAL CABINET LOCK, INC.—See Contran Corporation; *U.S. Private*, pg. 270

NATIONAL CABLE—See Chancellor Media Corporation; *U.S. Public*, pg. 335

NATIONAL CAN IBERICA SA—See Pechiney S.A.; *Int'l*, pg. 1029

NATIONAL CAN ITALIANA SPA—See Pechiney S.A.; *Int'l*, pg. 1031

NATIONAL CAN PUERTO RICO INC.—See Pechiney S.A.; *Int'l*, pg. 1029

NATIONAL CANADA BUSINESS CORP.—See National Bank of Canada; *Int'l*, pg. 907

NATIONAL CANADA CORPORATION—See National Bank of Canada; *Int'l*, pg. 907

NATIONAL CANADA FINANCE CORPORATION—See National Bank of Canada; *Int'l*, pg. 907

NATIONAL CAR RENTAL SYSTEM, INC.—See Republic Industries, Inc.; *U.S. Public*, pg. 1379

NATIONAL CARD CONTROL, INC.—See Cendant Corporation; *U.S. Public*, pg. 321

NATIONAL CARRIERS, INC.—See Farmland Industries, Inc.; *U.S. Private*, pg. 396

NATIONAL CATTLEMEN'S BEEF ASSOCIATION; *U.S. Private*, pg. 780

NATIONAL CATTLEMEN'S BEEF ASSOCIATION—See National Cattlemen's Beef Association; *U.S. Private*, pg. 780

NATIONAL CHEMSEARCH—See NCH Corporation; *U.S. Public*, pg. 1145

NATIONAL CHEMSEARCH OF CANADA LTD.—See NCH Corporation; *U.S. Public*, pg. 1145

NATIONAL CHEMSEARCH (SWITZERLAND) AG—See NCH Corporation; *U.S. Public*, pg. 1145

NATIONAL CITY BANCORP; *U.S. Public*, pg. 1153

NATIONAL CITY BANK—See National City Corporation; *U.S. Public*, pg. 1154

NATIONAL CITY CAPITAL CORP.—See National City Corporation; *U.S. Public*, pg. 1154

NATIONAL CITY COMMERCIAL FINANCE, INC.—See National City Corporation; *U.S. Public*, pg. 1154

NATIONAL CITY COMMUNITY DEVELOPMENT CORP.—See National City Corporation; *U.S. Public*, pg. 1154

NATIONAL CITY CORPORATION; *U.S. Public*, pg. 1154

NATIONAL CITY LEASING CORPORATION—See National City Corporation; *U.S. Public*, pg. 1154

NATIONAL CITY MORTGAGE CO.—See National City Corporation; *U.S. Public*, pg. 1154

NATIONAL CITY PROCESSING, INC.—See National City Corporation; *U.S. Public*, pg. 1154

NATIONAL CITY TRUST COMPANY—See National City Corporation; *U.S. Public*, pg. 1154

NATIONAL CITY VENTURE CORP.—See National City Corporation; *U.S. Public*, pg. 1154

NATIONAL CLEANING PRODUCTS LTD.—See The Clorox Company; *U.S. Public*, pg. 387

NATIONAL COMMERCE BANCORPORATION; *U.S. Public*, pg. 1154

NATIONAL COMMERCE BANK SERVICES, INC.—See National Commerce Bancorporation; *U.S. Public*, pg. 1155

NATIONAL COMPUTER PRINT, INC.; *U.S. Private*, pg. 780

NATIONAL COMPUTER SUPPLIES—See Riccobon & Company, Inc.; *U.S. Private*, pg. 927

NATIONAL COMPUTER SYSTEMS; *U.S. Public*, pg. 1155

NATIONAL CONCRETE PRODUCTS COMPANY; *U.S. Private*, pg. 781

NATIONAL CONSOLIDATED; *Int'l*, pg. 908

NATIONAL CONTINENTAL INSURANCE CO.—See The Progressive Corporation; *U.S. Public*, pg. 1335

NATIONAL CONTROLS CORPORATION—See Cortec Group; *U.S. Private*, pg. 277

NATIONAL COOPERATIVE REFINERY ASSOCIATION; *U.S. Public*, pg. 781

NATIONAL CORSET SUPPLY HOUSE; *U.S. Private*, pg. 781

NATIONAL CRANE—See Hanson PLC; *Int'l*, pg. 593

NATIONAL DATA CENTER—See ING Groep N.V.; *Int'l*, pg. 648

NATIONAL DATA CORPORATION; *U.S. Public*, pg. 1155

NATIONAL DATA CORPORATION OF CANADA LTD.—See National Data Corporation; *U.S. Public*, pg. 1156

NATIONAL DEFENSE CORP.—See National Presto Industries, Inc.; *U.S. Public*, pg. 1159

NATIONAL DEHYDRATION COMPANY—See McCormick & Company, Incorporated; *U.S. Public*, pg. 1067

NATIONAL DEVELOPMENT CO., INC.—See Sunstates Corporation; *U.S. Private*, pg. 1536

NATIONAL DIECASTING MACHINERY—See Racine Federated, Inc.; *U.S. Private*, pg. 906

NATIONAL DISCOUNT BROKERS—See The Sherwood Group, Inc.; *U.S. Public*, pg. 1467

NATIONAL DISPOSAL SERVICE OF NEBRASKA, INC.—See Browning-Ferris Industries, Inc.; *U.S. Public*, pg. 264

NATIONAL DISTRIBUTING CO., INC.; *U.S. Private*, pg. 781

NATIONAL DISTRIBUTING CO., INC.—See National Distributing Co., Inc.; *U.S. Private*, pg. 781

NATIONAL DISTRIBUTORS—See National Distributing Co., Inc.; *U.S. Private*, pg. 781

NATIONAL DYNAMICS—See Sperry Owens, Inc.; *U.S. Private*, pg. 1025

NATIONAL ECONOMIC RESEARCH ASSOCIATES (NERA)—See Marsh & McLennan Companies, Inc.; *U.S. Public*, pg. 1049

NATIONAL EDUCATION CREDIT CORPORATION—See Harcourt General, Inc.; *U.S. Public*, pg. 784

NATIONAL EDUCATION PAYROLL CORP.—See Harcourt General, Inc.; *U.S. Public*, pg. 784

NATIONAL EDUCATION TRAINING GROUP—See Harcourt General, Inc.; *U.S. Public*, pg. 784

NATIONAL EDUCATIONAL INTERNATIONAL CORP.—See Harcourt General, Inc.; *U.S. Public*, pg. 784

NATIONAL ELECTRIC COIL; *U.S. Private*, pg. 782

NATIONAL ELECTRICAL CARBON A.B.—See Morgan Crucible Co. Plc; *Int'l*, pg. 892

NATIONAL ELECTRICAL CARBON B.V.—See Morgan Crucible Co. Plc; *Int'l*, pg. 892

NATIONAL ELECTRICAL CARBON CANADA—See Morgan Crucible Co. Plc; *Int'l*, pg. 892

NATIONAL ELECTRICAL CARBON CORPORATION—See Morgan Crucible Co. Plc; *Int'l*, pg. 891

NATIONAL ELECTRICAL CARBON GMBH—See Morgan Crucible Co. Plc; *Int'l*, pg. 892

NATIONAL ELECTRICAL MANUFACTURERS ASSOCIATION; *U.S. Private*, pg. 782

NATIONAL ELECTRONICS MANUFACTURING DIVISION—See Richardson Electronics, Ltd.; *U.S. Public*, pg. 1388

NATIONAL ELECTRONICS WARRANTY CORPORATION; *U.S. Private*, pg. 782

NATIONAL EMPLOYEE BENEFITS CORPORATION—See Cigna Corp.; *U.S. Public*, pg. 366

NATIONAL ENERDRILL—See KCS Energy Inc.; *U.S. Public*, pg. 939

NATIONAL ENERGY GROUP, INC.; *U.S. Public*, pg. 1156

NATIONAL ENERGY MANAGEMENT LLC—See Madison Gas and Electric Company; *U.S. Public*, pg. 1033

NATIONAL ENERGY PRODUCTION CORPORATION—See Zurn Industries, Inc.; *U.S. Public*, pg. 1795

NATIONAL ENGINEERING & CONTRACTING CO.; *U.S. Private*, pg. 782

NATIONAL FARMS INC.; *U.S. Private*, pg. 782

NATIONAL FEDERATION OF COMMUNITY DEVELOPMENT CREDIT UNIONS—See Credit Union National Association; *U.S. Private*, pg. 288

NATIONAL FIBERSTOCK CORPORATION; *U.S. Private*, pg. 782

NATIONAL FIDELITY LIFE INSURANCE CO.—See Conseco Inc.; *U.S. Public*, pg. 433

NATIONAL FINANCIAL INSURANCE COMPANY; *U.S. Private*, pg. 782

NATIONAL FIRE PROTECTION ASSOCIATION; *U.S. Private*, pg. 782

NATIONAL FLEET & LEASE—See Chrysler Corporation; *U.S. Public*, pg. 354

NATIONAL FOOD EXPRESS, INC.—See Thorn Apple Valley, Inc.; *U.S. Public*, pg. 1603

NATIONAL FOOD STORES, INC.; *U.S. Private*, pg. 783

NATIONAL FOODS INC.—See ConAgra, Inc.; *U.S. Public*, pg. 429

NATIONAL FOOTBALL LEAGUE PROPERTIES, INC.; *U.S. Private*, pg. 783

NATIONAL FORGE COMPANY; *U.S. Private*, pg. 783

NATIONAL FRAME COMPANY—See Leggett & Platt, Incorporated; *U.S. Public*, pg. 986

NATIONAL FROZEN FOODS CORP.; *U.S. Private*, pg. 783

NATIONAL FRUIT PRODUCT COMPANY; *U.S. Private*, pg. 783

NATIONAL FUEL GAS COMPANY; *U.S. Public*, pg. 1156

NATIONAL FUEL GAS DISTRIBUTION CORP.—See National Fuel Gas Company; *U.S. Public*, pg. 1156

NATIONAL FUEL GAS SUPPLY CORP.—See National Fuel Gas Company; *U.S. Public*, pg. 1156

NATIONAL FUEL RESOURCES—See National Fuel Gas Company; *U.S. Public*, pg. 1156

NATIONAL GAS & OIL COMPANY; *U.S. Public*, pg. 1156

NATIONAL GENERAL INSURANCE CO.—See General Motors Corporation; *U.S. Public*, pg. 721

NATIONAL GENERAL INSURANCE COMPANY—See General Motors Corporation; *U.S. Public*, pg. 720

NATIONAL-GENERAL SUPPLY, INC.—See Carl Weissman & Sons, Inc.; *U.S. Private*, pg. 1160

NATIONAL GEOGRAPHIC SOCIETY; *U.S. Private*, pg. 783

NATIONAL GRAPE CO-OP ASSOCIATION, INC.; *U.S. Private*, pg. 784

NATIONAL GROCERS CO. LTD.—See George Weston Limited; *Int'l*, pg. 1495

NATIONAL GROUP LIFE INSURANCE COMPANY—See Conseco Inc.; *U.S. Public*, pg. 433

Company Index

NATIONAL GROUP MARKETING CORP.—See Conseco Inc.; *U.S. Public*, pg. 433
NATIONAL GUARDIAN LIFE INSURANCE COMPANY; *U.S. Private*, pg. 784
NATIONAL GYPSUM COMPANY—See Lafarge S.A.; *Int'l*, pg. 790
NATIONAL HAND TOOLS—See The Stanley Works; *U.S. Public*, pg. 1509
NATIONAL HEALTH CARE AFFILIATES, INC.; *U.S. Private*, pg. 784
NATIONAL HEALTH ENHANCEMENT SYSTEMS, INC.; *U.S. Public*, pg. 1157
NATIONAL HEALTH PLANS—See Tenet Healthcare Corporation; *U.S. Public*, pg. 1577
NATIONAL HEALTH PRODUCTS; *U.S. Private*, pg. 784
NATIONAL HEALTH SERVICES, INC.—See Conseco Inc.; *U.S. Public*, pg. 433
NATIONAL HELIUM CORPORATION—See Duke Energy Corporation; *U.S. Public*, pg. 534
NATIONAL HOLDING INVESTMENT CO.—See National Presto Industries, Inc.; *U.S. Public*, pg. 1159
NATIONAL HOME HEALTH CARE CORP.; *U.S. Public*, pg. 1157
NATIONAL HOTEL CORP.—See Carlson Companies, Inc.; *U.S. Private*, pg. 212
NATIONAL INCOME REALTY TRUST; *U.S. Public*, pg. 1157
NATIONAL INDEMNITY CO.—See Berkshire Hathaway Inc.; *U.S. Public*, pg. 221
NATIONAL INDEMNITY COMPANY OF MID-AMERICA—See Berkshire Hathaway Inc.; *U.S. Public*, pg. 221
NATIONAL INDUSTRIAL GASES PTE. LTD.—See Nippon Sanso Corporation; *Int'l*, pg. 939
NATIONAL INDUSTRIES, INC.—See Thomas & Betts Corporation; *U.S. Public*, pg. 1598
NATIONAL INFORMATION CORPORATION; *U.S. Private*, pg. 784
NATIONAL INFORMATION SERVICES (NIS)—See Reed Elsevier plc; *Int'l*, pg. 1096
NATIONAL INFUSION SERVICES, INC.—See Bindley Western Industries, Inc.; *U.S. Public*, pg. 229
NATIONAL INSTITUTE OF BUSINESS MANAGEMENT, INC.—See National Information Corporation; *U.S. Private*, pg. 785
NATIONAL INSTRUMENTS CORP.; *U.S. Public*, pg. 1157
NATIONAL INSURANCE AGENCY, INC.—See American Bankers Insurance Group, Inc.; *U.S. Public*, pg. 67
NATIONAL INSURANCE GROUP; *U.S. Public*, pg. 1157
NATIONAL INTEGRATED SERVICES—See Sprint Corporation; *U.S. Public*, pg. 1500
NATIONAL IRISH BANK LIMITED—See National Australia Bank Limited; *Int'l*, pg. 906
NATIONAL ITALIA S.R.L.—See Morgan Crucible Co. Plc; *Int'l*, pg. 892
NATIONAL JOURNAL DAILY BRIEFINGS—See National Journal Group; *U.S. Private*, pg. 785
NATIONAL JOURNAL GROUP; *U.S. Private*, pg. 785
NATIONAL LABEL COMPANY; *U.S. Private*, pg. 785
NATIONAL LAMINATION CO.—See Tang Industries Inc.; *U.S. Private*, pg. 1068
THE NATIONAL LATEX PRODUCTS CO.; *U.S. Private*, pg. 785
NATIONAL LAW PUBLISHING CO.—See The Nomura Securities Co., Ltd.; *Int'l*, pg. 956
NATIONAL LEARNING SYSTEMS, INC.—See Harcourt General, Inc.; *U.S. Public*, pg. 783
NATIONAL LEISURE GROUP—See Cendant Corporation; *U.S. Public*, pg. 320
NATIONAL LIBERTY CORPORATION—See AEGON N.V.; *Int'l*, pg. 26
NATIONAL LIBERTY LIFE INSURANCE CO.—See AEGON N.V.; *Int'l*, pg. 27
NATIONAL LIFE INSURANCE COMPANY; *U.S. Private*, pg. 785
NATIONAL LIFE INVESTMENT MANAGEMENT CO., INC.—See National Life Insurance Company; *U.S. Private*, pg. 785
NATIONAL LINEN & UNIFORM SERVICE—See National Service Industries, Inc.; *U.S. Public*, pg. 1160
NATIONAL LOSS CONTROL SERVICE CORP.—See Kemper Insurance Companies; *U.S. Private*, pg. 614
NATIONAL LUMBER CO.; *U.S. Private*, pg. 785
NATIONAL MACHINERY; *U.S. Private*, pg. 785
THE NATIONAL MAGAZINE COMPANY LTD.—See The Hearst Corporation; *U.S. Private*, pg. 518
NATIONAL MANAGEMENT, INC.—See Georgia-Pacific Corporation; *U.S. Public*, pg. 736
NATIONAL MANUFACTURING CO.—See Pettibone Corporation; *U.S. Private*, pg. 860
NATIONAL MARINE, INC.—See Vectura Group, Inc.; *U.S. Private*, pg. 1135
NATIONAL MATERIAL LIMITED PARTNERSHIP—See Tang Industries Inc.; *U.S. Private*, pg. 1068
NATIONAL MEATS INC.—See Schneider Corp.; *Int'l*, pg. 1207
NATIONAL MEDIA CORPORATION; *U.S. Public*, pg. 1158
NATIONAL MEDICAL EQUIPMENT CENTERS, INC.—See Integrated Health Services, Inc.; *U.S. Public*, pg. 885
NATIONAL MEDICINE CENTER - GROVELAND, INC.—See Integrated Health Services, Inc.; *U.S. Public*, pg. 885
NATIONAL MENTOR HEALTHCARE, INC.—See Magellan Health Services, Inc.; *U.S. Public*, pg. 1036
NATIONAL MENTOR, INC—See Magellan Health Services, Inc.; *U.S. Public*, pg. 1036
NATIONAL METAL INDUSTRIES—See Standex International Corporation; *U.S. Public*, pg. 1506
NATIONAL MICRONETICS, INC.—See Tai-II Media Co.; *Int'l*, pg. 1347
NATIONAL MINE SERVICE COMPANY—See Charter plc; *Int'l*, pg. 281
NATIONAL MINE SERVICE COMPANY, ALABAMA DIV.—See Charter plc; *Int'l*, pg. 281
NATIONAL MINE SERVICE COMPANY, DISTRIBUTION DIV.—See Charter plc; *Int'l*, pg. 281

NATIONAL MINE SERVICE COMPANY, JENKINS DIV.—See Charter plc; *Int'l*, pg. 281
NATIONAL MINE SERVICE COMPANY, LOGAN DIV.—See Charter plc; *Int'l*, pg. 281
NATIONAL MINE SERVICE COMPANY, MADISONVILLE DIV.—See Charter plc; *Int'l*, pg. 281
NATIONAL MINE SERVICE COMPANY, MT. VERNON DIV.—See Charter plc; *Int'l*, pg. 281
NATIONAL MINE SERVICE COMPANY, PRICE DIV.—See Charter plc; *Int'l*, pg. 281
NATIONAL MINE SERVICE, INC.—See Charter plc; *Int'l*, pg. 280
NATIONAL MINES CORP.—See NKK Corporation; *Int'l*, pg. 903
NATIONAL MOBILE RADIO LIMITED—See Motorola, Inc.; *U.S. Public*, pg. 1140
NATIONAL MOUNT AIRY—See Bassett Furniture Industries, Incorporated; *U.S. Public*, pg. 193
NATIONAL MUTUAL ASIA LTD.—See National Mutual Holdings Limited; *Int'l*, pg. 909
NATIONAL MUTUAL BEIJING—See National Mutual Holdings Limited; *Int'l*, pg. 908
NATIONAL MUTUAL FUNDS MANAGEMENT (ASIA) HONG KONG—See National Mutual Holdings Limited; *Int'l*, pg. 909
NATIONAL MUTUAL FUNDS MANAGEMENT (GLOBAL) LTD.—See National Mutual Holdings Limited; *Int'l*, pg. 908
NATIONAL MUTUAL FUNDS MANAGEMENT (JAPAN) LIMITED—See National Mutual Holdings Limited; *Int'l*, pg. 909
NATIONAL MUTUAL FUNDS MANAGEMENT LTD.—See National Mutual Holdings Limited; *Int'l*, pg. 908
NATIONAL MUTUAL FUNDS MANAGEMENT NZ LIMITED—See National Mutual Holdings Limited; *Int'l*, pg. 909
NATIONAL MUTUAL HOLDINGS LIMITED; *Int'l*, pg. 908
THE NATIONAL MUTUAL LIFE ASSOCIATION OF AUSTRALIA LIMITED—See National Mutual Holdings Limited; *Int'l*, pg. 909
NATIONAL MUTUAL MACAO—See National Mutual Holdings Limited; *Int'l*, pg. 908
NATIONAL MUTUAL NEW SOUTH WALES—See National Mutual Holdings Limited; *Int'l*, pg. 908
NATIONAL MUTUAL NEW ZEALAND—See National Mutual Holdings Limited; *Int'l*, pg. 908
NATIONAL MUTUAL QUEENSLAND—See National Mutual Holdings Limited; *Int'l*, pg. 908
NATIONAL MUTUAL SOUTH AUSTRALIA—See National Mutual Holdings Limited; *Int'l*, pg. 908
NATIONAL MUTUAL TASMANIA—See National Mutual Holdings Limited; *Int'l*, pg. 908
NATIONAL MUTUAL VICTORIA—See National Mutual Holdings Limited; *Int'l*, pg. 908
NATIONAL MUTUAL WESTERN AUSTRALIA—See National Mutual Holdings Limited; *Int'l*, pg. 908
NATIONAL NUCLEAR CORPORATION—See Thermo Electron Corporation; *U.S. Public*, pg. 1594
NATIONAL OFFICE FURNITURE CO.—See Kimball International, Inc.; *U.S. Public*, pg. 957
NATIONAL OFFICE FURNITURE MANUFACTURING—See Kimball International, Inc.; *U.S. Public*, pg. 957
NATIONAL OIL & CHEMICAL MARKETING—See Royal Dutch/Shell Group of Companies; *Int'l*, pg. 1136
NATIONAL-OILWELL/DRECO—See National-Oilwell Inc.; *U.S. Public*, pg. 1158
NATIONAL-OILWELL/DRECO EASTERN EUROPE—See National-Oilwell Inc.; *U.S. Public*, pg. 1158
NATIONAL-OILWELL/DRECO EUROPE LTD—See National-Oilwell Inc.; *U.S. Public*, pg. 1158
NATIONAL-OILWELL/DRECO HOLDINGS, INC.—See National-Oilwell Inc.; *U.S. Public*, pg. 1158
NATIONAL-OILWELL/DRECO HOLDINGS LTD.—See National-Oilwell Inc.; *U.S. Public*, pg. 1158
NATIONAL-OILWELL/DRECO INC.—See National-Oilwell Inc.; *U.S. Public*, pg. 1158
NATIONAL-OILWELL/DRECO INDUSTRIAL—See National-Oilwell Inc.; *U.S. Public*, pg. 1158
NATIONAL-OILWELL/DRECO RIG TECHNOLOGY & CONSTRUCTION—See National-Oilwell Inc.; *U.S. Public*, pg. 1158
NATIONAL-OILWELL GRIFFITH DOWNHOLE PRODUCTS GMBH—See National-Oilwell Inc.; *U.S. Public*, pg. 1158
NATIONAL-OILWELL GRIFFITH OIL TOOL & TRUDRIL—See National-Oilwell Inc.; *U.S. Public*, pg. 1158
NATIONAL-OILWELL INC.; *U.S. Public*, pg. 1158
NATIONAL OLD LINE INSURANCE CO.—See AEGON N.V.; *Int'l*, pg. 27
NATIONAL ORGANIC CHEMICAL INDUSTRIES—See Royal Dutch/Shell Group of Companies; *Int'l*, pg. 1139
NATIONAL OXYGEN PTE. LTD.—See Nippon Sanso Corporation; *Int'l*, pg. 939
NATIONAL PARKS TRANSPORTATION, INC.—See SkyWest Inc.; *U.S. Public*, pg. 1476
NATIONAL PENN BANCSHARES, INC.; *U.S. Public*, pg. 1158
NATIONAL PENN BANK—See National Penn Bancshares, Inc.; *U.S. Public*, pg. 1159
NATIONAL PENN INVESTMENT COMPANY—See National Penn Bancshares, Inc.; *U.S. Public*, pg. 1159
NATIONAL PENN LIFE INSURANCE COMPANY—See National Penn Bancshares, Inc.; *U.S. Public*, pg. 1159
NATIONAL PHARMACIES, INC.—See Merck & Co., Inc.; *U.S. Public*, pg. 1091
NATIONAL PHARMPAK SERVICES, INC.—See Cardinal Health Inc.; *U.S. Public*, pg. 304
NATIONAL PIPE LINE CO.—See Park-Ohio Industries, Inc.; *U.S. Public*, pg. 1259
NATIONAL PLASTICS CORPORATION—See Perstorp AB; *Int'l*, pg. 1037
NATIONAL POSTERS, INC.—See National Print Group, Inc.; *U.S. Private*, pg. 786
NATIONAL PRECISION PRODUCTS—See Bisco Industries, Inc; *U.S. Private*, pg. 145

NATIONAL PRESTO INDUSTRIES, INC.; *U.S. Public*, pg. 1159
NATIONAL PRINT GROUP, INC.; *U.S. Private*, pg. 785
NATIONAL PROCUREMENT & LOGISTICS COMPANY—See American Stores Company; *U.S. Public*, pg. 93
NATIONAL PROGRAMS DIVISION—See Poe & Brown, Inc.; *U.S. Public*, pg. 1312
NATIONAL PROPANE CORP.—See Triarc Companies, Inc.; *U.S. Public*, pg. 1635
NATIONAL PUBLIC SERVICE INS. CO.—See American General Corporation; *U.S. Public*, pg. 77
NATIONAL PUBLISHING CO.—See Courier Corporation; *U.S. Public*, pg. 453
NATIONAL REAL ESTATE SERVICES, INC.; *Int'l*, pg. 909
NATIONAL REFINERY LIMITED; *Int'l*, pg. 909
NATIONAL REGISTER PUBLISHING—See Reed Elsevier plc; *Int'l*, pg. 1096
NATIONAL REINSURANCE COMPANY OF CANADA—See General American Life Insurance Co.; *U.S. Private*, pg. 443
NATIONAL REJECTORS, INC., G.M.B.H.—See Crane Co.; *U.S. Public*, pg. 456
NATIONAL REMOTE SENSING CENTRE LIMITED—See The General Electric Company, p.l.c.; *Int'l*, pg. 545
NATIONAL RESEARCH CORPORATION; *U.S. Public*, pg. 1159
NATIONAL RESTAURANT MANAGEMENT, INC.; *U.S. Private*, pg. 786
NATIONAL RESTAURANT SUPPLY COMPANY; *U.S. Private*, pg. 786
NATIONAL RESTORATION CONTRACTORS, INC.—See The Western Group; *U.S. Private*, pg. 1165
NATIONAL RETAIL HARDWARE ASSN.; *U.S. Private*, pg. 786
NATIONAL RIGGERS & ERECTORS—See Havens Steel Co.; *U.S. Private*, pg. 511
NATIONAL RIVET & MANUFACTURING COMPANY; *U.S. Private*, pg. 786
NATIONAL RURAL UTILITIES COOPERATIVE FINANCE CORPORATION; *U.S. Private*, pg. 786
NATIONAL R.V., INC.; *U.S. Public*, pg. 1159
NATIONAL SAFETY ASSOCIATES; *U.S. Private*, pg. 786
NATIONAL SCHOOL BUS SERVICE—See Scott's Restaurants Inc.; *Int'l*, pg. 1213
NATIONAL SEA PRODUCTS INCORPORATED—See National Sea Products Limited; *Int'l*, pg. 909
NATIONAL SEA PRODUCTS LIMITED; *Int'l*, pg. 909
NATIONAL SEATING CO.; *U.S. Public*, pg. 786
NATIONAL SECURITY CONTAINERS—See Centex Corporation; *U.S. Public*, pg. 323
NATIONAL SEMICONDUCTOR CORPORATION; *U.S. Public*, pg. 1159
NATIONAL SERVICE CENTER—See Telxon Corporation; *U.S. Public*, pg. 1573
NATIONAL SERVICE CLEANING CORPORATION—See OHM Corporation; *U.S. Public*, pg. 1208
NATIONAL SERVICE INDUSTRIES, INC.; *U.S. Public*, pg. 1160
NATIONAL SILICATES LTD.—See PQ Corporation; *U.S. Private*, pg. 827
NATIONAL SORGHUM BEER BREWERIES PTY. LTD. HIGHVELD DIVISION; *Int'l*, pg. 909
NATIONAL SPECIALTY SERVICES, INC.—See Cardinal Health Inc.; *U.S. Public*, pg. 304
NATIONAL SPINNING CO., INC.; *U.S. Private*, pg. 786
NATIONAL SPORTS GRILL—See American Restaurant Group, Inc.; *U.S. Private*, pg. 61
NATIONAL-STANDARD CO.; *U.S. Public*, pg. 1160
NATIONAL-STANDARD CO. CANADA—See National-Standard Co.; *U.S. Public*, pg. 1161
NATIONAL STANDARD INSURANCE COMPANY—See Zurich Insurance Company; *Int'l*, pg. 1530
NATIONAL STARCH AND CHEMICAL COMPANY—See Unilever Plc; *Int'l*, pg. 1435
NATIONAL STEEL & SHIPBUILDING COMPANY; *U.S. Private*, pg. 787
NATIONAL STEEL CORPORATION—See NKK Corporation; *Int'l*, pg. 902
NATIONAL STEEL CORP., GRANITE CITY DIVISION—See NKK Corporation; *Int'l*, pg. 902
NATIONAL STEEL CORP., GREAT LAKES DIVISION—See NKK Corporation; *Int'l*, pg. 903
NATIONAL STEEL CORP., MIDWEST DIVISION—See NKK Corporation; *Int'l*, pg. 903
THE NATIONAL SUPER SERVICE CO.; *U.S. Private*, pg. 787
NATIONAL SURETY CORPORATION—See Allianz Aktiengesellschaft; *Int'l*, pg. 59
NATIONAL SURFACE CLEANING, INC.—See OHM Corporation; *U.S. Public*, pg. 1208
NATIONAL SURFACE CLEANING-NEW JERSEY DIV.—See OHM Corporation; *U.S. Public*, pg. 1208
NATIONAL SURGERY CENTERS, INC.; *U.S. Public*, pg. 1161
NATIONAL SYSTEMS & RESEARCH CO.; *U.S. Private*, pg. 787
NATIONAL TECHNICAL SERVICES—See Strategic Distribution Inc.; *U.S. Public*, pg. 1523
NATIONAL TECHNICAL SYSTEMS, INC.; *U.S. Public*, pg. 1161
NATIONAL TELEGRAPH—See Independent Publications, Inc.; *U.S. Private*, pg. 559
NATIONAL THERMAL INSULATION—See Transco Inc.; *U.S. Private*, pg. 1096
NATIONAL TIRE & BATTERY—See Sears, Roebuck and Co.; *U.S. Public*, pg. 1452
NATIONAL TOBACCO CO. OF CANADA—See UST Inc.; *U.S. Public*, pg. 1661
NATIONAL TOOL & MANUFACTURING COMPANY; *U.S. Private*, pg. 787
NATIONAL TOWER TRUNKING SYSTEMS, INC.—See Motorola, Inc.; *U.S. Public*, pg. 1138
NATIONAL TRANSPORT SERVICES CO.—See Wakefern Food Corporation; *U.S. Private*, pg. 1146

NATIONAL TRAVELERS LIFE CO.; *U.S. Private*, pg. 787
NATIONAL TRIPLE R, INC.—See American Ecology Corporation; *U.S. Public*, pg. 71
NATIONAL TRUCK LEASING SYSTEM; *U.S. Private*, pg. 787
NATIONAL TRUST COMPANY—See National Trustco Inc.; *Int'l*, pg. 910
NATIONAL TRUSTCO INC.; *Int'l*, pg. 909
NATIONAL TWIST DRILL DIV.—See Regal-Beloit Corporation; *U.S. Public*, pg. 1370
NATIONAL TYRE SERVICE LTD.—See Continental AG; *Int'l*, pg. 328
NATIONAL UNIFORM SERVICE—See G&K Services, Inc.; *U.S. Public*, pg. 690
NATIONAL UNION ELECTRIC CORP.—See Electrolux, AB; *Int'l*, pg. 440
NATIONAL UNION FIRE INS. CO. OF PITTSBURGH, PA.—See American International Group, Inc.; *U.S. Public*, pg. 84
NATIONAL UTILITY SERVICE (CANADA) LTD.—See National Utility Service, Inc.; *U.S. Private*, pg. 787
NATIONAL UTILITY SERVICE, INC.; *U.S. Private*, pg. 787
NATIONAL UTILITY SERVICE LTD.—See National Utility Service, Inc.; *U.S. Private*, pg. 787
NATIONAL UTILITY SERVICE, S.A.—See National Utility Service, Inc.; *U.S. Private*, pg. 787
NATIONAL VAN LINES, INC.; *U.S. Private*, pg. 788
NATIONAL VENDORS—See Crane Co.; *U.S. Public*, pg. 457
NATIONAL VIDEO, INC.—See West Coast Entertainment Inc.; *U.S. Public*, pg. 1755
NATIONAL WASTE SERVICES INC.—See Allied Waste Industries; *U.S. Public*, pg. 49
NATIONAL WELDERS SUPPLY CO. INC.; *U.S. Private*, pg. 788
NATIONAL WESTERN LIFE INSURANCE COMPANY; *U.S. Public*, pg. 1161
NATIONAL WESTMINSTER BANK AG—See National Westminster Bank PLC; *Int'l*, pg. 911
NATIONAL WESTMINSTER BANK FINANCE (CI) LIMITED—See National Westminster Bank PLC; *Int'l*, pg. 911
NATIONAL WESTMINSTER BANK OF CANADA—See National Westminster Bank PLC; *Int'l*, pg. 911
NATIONAL WESTMINSTER BANK PLC; *Int'l*, pg. 910
NATIONAL WESTMINSTER BANK PLC—See National Westminster Bank PLC; *Int'l*, pg. 910
NATIONAL WESTMINSTER BANK S.A.—See National Westminster Bank PLC; *Int'l*, pg. 910
NATIONAL WESTMINSTER HOME LOANS LIMITED—See National Westminster Bank PLC; *Int'l*, pg. 910
NATIONAL WESTMINSTER INSURANCE SERVICES LIMITED—See National Westminster Bank PLC; *Int'l*, pg. 910
NATIONAL WESTMINSTER LIFE ASSURANCE LIMITED—See National Westminster Bank PLC; *Int'l*, pg. 910
NATIONAL WESTMINSTER UNIT TRUST MANAGERS LIMITED—See National Westminster Bank PLC; *Int'l*, pg. 910
NATIONAL WINE & SPIRITS CORP.; *U.S. Private*, pg. 788
NATIONAL WOOD PRODUCTS, CO.—See Saunders Brothers; *U.S. Private*, pg. 968
NATIONAL YARN CRAFTS—See National Spinning Co., Inc.; *U.S. Private*, pg. 787
NATIONAL YELLOW PAGES MONITOR (NYPM)—See NFO Research, Inc.; *U.S. Public*, pg. 1146
NATIONALE BANK VOOR MIDDELLANG KREDIET N.V.—See ABN-AMRO Holding N.V.; *Int'l*, pg. 9
N.V. NATIONALE BORG-MAATSCHAPPIJ—See ING Groep N.V.; *Int'l*, pg. 647
NATIONALE MAATSCHAPPIJ VOOR VLIEGTUIGFINANCIERING B.V.—See ABN-AMRO Holding N.V.; *Int'l*, pg. 9
NATIONALE-NEDERLANDEN—See ING Groep N.V.; *Int'l*, pg. 647
NATIONALE-NEDERLANDEN LIFE—See ING Groep N.V.; *Int'l*, pg. 651
NATIONALE-NEDERLANDEN SCHAADEVERZEKERING MAATSCHAPPIJ N.V.—See ING Groep N.V.; *Int'l*, pg. 647
NATIONALE-NEDERLANDEN SPAIN—See ING Groep N.V.; *Int'l*, pg. 651
NATIONALE-NEDERLANDEN ZIVOTNI POJIST'OVNA—See ING Groep N.V.; *Int'l*, pg. 651
NATIONALE-NEDERLANDEN ZORGVERZEKERING N.V.—See ING Groep N.V.; *Int'l*, pg. 647
NATIONALE TRUST MAATSCHAPPIJ (NEDERLANDSE ANTILLEN) N.V.—See ABN-AMRO Holding N.V.; *Int'l*, pg. 10
NATIONALE TRUST MAATSCHAPPIJ N.V.—See ABN-AMRO Holding N.V.; *Int'l*, pg. 9
NATION'S BUSINESS; *U.S. Private*, pg. 788
NATION'S CARE, INC.—See Orion Capital Corporation; *U.S. Public*, pg. 1231
NATIONS ENERGY CORPORATION—See UniSource Energy Corporation; *U.S. Public*, pg. 1670
NATIONSBANK CAPITAL MANAGEMENT CORPORATION—See NationsBank Corporation; *U.S. Public*, pg. 1163
NATIONSBANK COMMUNITY DEVELOPMENT CORP.—See NationsBank Corporation; *U.S. Public*, pg. 1163
NATIONSBANK CORPORATION; *U.S. Public*, pg. 1162
NATIONSBANK CREDIT CORPORATION—See NationsBank Corporation; *U.S. Public*, pg. 1163
NATIONSBANK EQUITY MORTGAGE CORPORATION—See NationsBank Corporation; *U.S. Public*, pg. 1163
NATIONSBANK FLORIDA—See NationsBank Corporation; *U.S. Public*, pg. 1162
NATIONSBANK FUNDING CORPORATION—See NationsBank Corporation; *U.S. Public*, pg. 1163
NATIONSBANK FUTURES CORP.—See NationsBank Corporation; *U.S. Public*, pg. 1165
NATIONSBANK FUTURES CORPORATION—See NationsBank Corporation; *U.S. Public*, pg. 1163

NATIONSBANK GEORGIA CORPORATION—See NationsBank Corporation; *U.S. Public*, pg. 1162
NATIONSBANK INSURANCE AGENCY, INC.—See NationsBank Corporation; *U.S. Public*, pg. 1163
NATIONSBANK INSURANCE INC.—See NationsBank Corporation; *U.S. Public*, pg. 1162
NATIONSBANK INTERNATIONAL—See NationsBank Corporation; *U.S. Public*, pg. 1165
NATIONSBANK INVESTMENT ADVISORS, INC.—See NationsBank Corporation; *U.S. Public*, pg. 1165
NATIONSBANK INVESTMENT CORPORATION—See NationsBank Corporation; *U.S. Public*, pg. 1163
NATIONSBANK (JAPAN)—See NationsBank Corporation; *U.S. Public*, pg. 1166
NATIONSBANK LEASE INVESTMENTS, INC.—See NationsBank Corporation; *U.S. Public*, pg. 1165
NATIONSBANK LEASING CORP.—See NationsBank Corporation; *U.S. Public*, pg. 1165
NATIONSBANK LEASING CORPORATION—See NationsBank Corporation; *U.S. Public*, pg. 1165
NATIONSBANK LIFE INSURANCE CO.—See NationsBank Corporation; *U.S. Public*, pg. 1164
NATIONSBANK MONTGOMERY SECURITIES LLC—See NationsBank Corporation; *U.S. Public*, pg. 1162
NATIONSBANK MORTGAGE CORPORATION—See NationsBank Corporation; *U.S. Public*, pg. 1165
NATIONSBANK MOUNTAIN GROVE—See NationsBank Corporation; *U.S. Public*, pg. 1164
NATIONSBANK OF ARKANSAS—See NationsBank Corporation; *U.S. Public*, pg. 1164
NATIONSBANK OF BATESVILLE—See NationsBank Corporation; *U.S. Public*, pg. 1164
NATIONSBANK OF BOONVILLE—See NationsBank Corporation; *U.S. Public*, pg. 1164
NATIONSBANK OF CAMDEN—See NationsBank Corporation; *U.S. Public*, pg. 1164
NATIONSBANK OF CASSVILLE—See NationsBank Corporation; *U.S. Public*, pg. 1164
NATIONSBANK OF CENTRAL IL—See NationsBank Corporation; *U.S. Public*, pg. 1164
NATIONSBANK OF CHARLESTON—See NationsBank Corporation; *U.S. Public*, pg. 1164
NATIONSBANK OF CONWAY—See NationsBank Corporation; *U.S. Public*, pg. 1164
NATIONSBANK OF FLORIDA CORPORATION—See NationsBank Corporation; *U.S. Public*, pg. 1162
NATIONSBANK OF FRANKLIN COUNTY—See NationsBank Corporation; *U.S. Public*, pg. 1164
NATIONSBANK OF HOT SPRINGS—See NationsBank Corporation; *U.S. Public*, pg. 1164
NATIONSBANK OF KANSAS CITY—See NationsBank Corporation; *U.S. Public*, pg. 1164
NATIONSBANK OF KENTUCKY—See NationsBank Corporation; *U.S. Public*, pg. 1163
NATIONSBANK OF LEBANON—See NationsBank Corporation; *U.S. Public*, pg. 1164
NATIONSBANK OF MARSHALL—See NationsBank Corporation; *U.S. Public*, pg. 1164
NATIONSBANK OF MOUNT VERNON—See NationsBank Corporation; *U.S. Public*, pg. 1164
NATIONSBANK OF NEVADA—See NationsBank Corporation; *U.S. Public*, pg. 1164
NATIONSBANK OF NEWARK—See NationsBank Corporation; *U.S. Public*, pg. 1164
NATIONSBANK OF NORTH CENTRAL ARKANSAS—See NationsBank Corporation; *U.S. Public*, pg. 1164
NATIONSBANK OF NORTHWEST ARKANSAS—See NationsBank Corporation; *U.S. Public*, pg. 1164
NATIONSBANK OF PINE BLUFF—See NationsBank Corporation; *U.S. Public*, pg. 1164
NATIONSBANK OF PULASKI COUNTY—See NationsBank Corporation; *U.S. Public*, pg. 1164
NATIONSBANK OF QUINCY—See NationsBank Corporation; *U.S. Public*, pg. 1164
NATIONSBANK OF RIVER VALLEY—See NationsBank Corporation; *U.S. Public*, pg. 1164
NATIONSBANK OF RUSSELLVILLE—See NationsBank Corporation; *U.S. Public*, pg. 1164
NATIONSBANK OF ST. LOUIS—See NationsBank Corporation; *U.S. Public*, pg. 1164
NATIONSBANK OF SOUTHERN MISSOURI—See NationsBank Corporation; *U.S. Public*, pg. 1164
NATIONSBANK OF SOUTHWEST MISSOURI—See NationsBank Corporation; *U.S. Public*, pg. 1164
NATIONSBANK OF TENNESSEE—See NationsBank Corporation; *U.S. Public*, pg. 1163
NATIONSBANK OF TEXAS—See NationsBank Corporation; *U.S. Public*, pg. 1164
NATIONSBANK OF TEXAS, N.A.—See NationsBank Corporation; *U.S. Public*, pg. 1163
NATIONSBANK OF TEXAS NATIONAL BANK PROPERTIES INC.—See NationsBank Corporation; *U.S. Public*, pg. 1163
NATIONSBANK OF TEXAS NATIONAL BANK SERVICES CORPORATION—See NationsBank Corporation; *U.S. Public*, pg. 1163
NATIONSBANK OF TEXAS NATIONAL INTERNATIONAL CO.—See NationsBank Corporation; *U.S. Public*, pg. 1163
NATIONSBANK OF TEXAS NATIONAL LEASING CORP.—See NationsBank Corporation; *U.S. Public*, pg. 1163
NATIONSBANK OF TEXAS NATIONAL LIFE INSURANCE CO.—See NationsBank Corporation; *U.S. Public*, pg. 1163
NATIONSBANK OF TEXAS NATIONAL MONEY ORDERS INC.—See NationsBank Corporation; *U.S. Public*, pg. 1163
NATIONSBANK OF TEXAS NATIONAL VENTURES GROUP INC.—See NationsBank Corporation; *U.S. Public*, pg. 1163
NATIONSBANK OF TROY—See NationsBank Corporation; *U.S. Public*, pg. 1165
NATIONSBANK OVERSEAS CORP.—See NationsBank Corporation; *U.S. Public*, pg. 1165

NATIONSBANK PLAZA CHARLOTTE, INC.—See NationsBank Corporation; *U.S. Public*, pg. 1165
NATIONSBANK PROPERTIES, INC.—See NationsBank Corporation; *U.S. Public*, pg. 1165
NATIONSBANK REALTY SERVICES CORP.—See NationsBank Corporation; *U.S. Public*, pg. 1164
NATIONSBANK RIVER VALLEY—See NationsBank Corporation; *U.S. Public*, pg. 1164
NATIONSBANK SECURITIES, INC.—See NationsBank Corporation; *U.S. Public*, pg. 1165
NATIONSBANK SERVICES CORPORATION—See NationsBank Corporation; *U.S. Public*, pg. 1164
NATIONSBANK SOUTH—See NationsBank Corporation; *U.S. Public*, pg. 1163
NATIONSBANK SOUTH CAROLINA CORPORATION—See NationsBank Corporation; *U.S. Public*, pg. 1163
NATIONSBANK SOUTH CAROLINA, N.A.—See NationsBank Corporation; *U.S. Public*, pg. 1163
NATIONSBANK SUNWEST, INC.—See NationsBank Corporation; *U.S. Public*, pg. 1165
NATIONSBANK TEXAS CORPORATION—See NationsBank Corporation; *U.S. Public*, pg. 1163
NATIONSBANK TRI-LAKES—See NationsBank Corporation; *U.S. Public*, pg. 1165
NATIONSBANK TRUST—See NationsBank Corporation; *U.S. Public*, pg. 1165
NATIONSBANK VIRGINIA—See NationsBank Corporation; *U.S. Public*, pg. 1163
NATIONSBANK WEST—See NationsBank Corporation; *U.S. Public*, pg. 1164
NATIONSCREDIT—See NationsBank Corporation; *U.S. Public*, pg. 1165
NATIONSCREDIT COMMERCIAL CORPORATION—See NationsBank Corporation; *U.S. Public*, pg. 1165
NATIONWIDE ACCEPTANCE—See Regal Ware, Inc.; *U.S. Private*, pg. 917
NATIONWIDE BEARINGS PTY. LTD.—See AB SKF; *Int'l*, pg. 1157
NATIONWIDE BEEF, INC.; *U.S. Private*, pg. 788
NATIONWIDE BUILDING SOCIETY; *Int'l*, pg. 912
NATIONWIDE COMMERCIAL CO.—See Amerco; *U.S. Private*, pg. 49
NATIONWIDE COMMUNICATIONS, INC.—See Nationwide Insurance Enterprise; *U.S. Private*, pg. 789
NATIONWIDE CONSUMER TESTING INSTITUTE, INC.—See SGS Societe Generale de Surveillance Holding S.A.; *Int'l*, pg. 1153
NATIONWIDE CREDIT—See First Data Corporation; *U.S. Public*, pg. 631
NATIONWIDE CREDIT INC.; *U.S. Private*, pg. 788
NATIONWIDE FREIGHT SERVICES, INC.—See AMCOL International Corp.; *U.S. Public*, pg. 64
NATIONWIDE GENERAL INSURANCE COMPANY—See Nationwide Insurance Enterprise; *U.S. Private*, pg. 789
NATIONWIDE HEALTH PROPERTIES INC.; *U.S. Public*, pg. 1166
NATIONWIDE HEALTH PROPERTIES INC., KANSAS—See Nationwide Health Properties Inc.; *U.S. Public*, pg. 1166
NATIONWIDE HMO, INC.—See Nationwide Insurance Enterprise; *U.S. Private*, pg. 789
NATIONWIDE HOMES, INC.; *U.S. Private*, pg. 788
NATIONWIDE INSURANCE ENTERPRISE; *U.S. Private*, pg. 788
NATIONWIDE LIFE—See Nationwide Building Society; *Int'l*, pg. 912
NATIONWIDE LIFE INSURANCE CO.—See Nationwide Insurance Enterprise; *U.S. Private*, pg. 789
NATIONWIDE MUTUAL INSURANCE CO.—See Nationwide Insurance Enterprise; *U.S. Private*, pg. 789
NATIONWIDE PAPERS—See Champion International Corp.; *U.S. Public*, pg. 334
NATIONWIDE PROPERTY & CASUALTY INSURANCE COMPANY—See Nationwide Insurance Enterprise; *U.S. Private*, pg. 789
NATIONWIDE REFRIGERATION SUPPLIES LIMITED—See Ascot Holdings Plc; *Int'l*, pg. 88
NATIONWIDE TRUST LTD.—See Nationwide Building Society; *Int'l*, pg. 912
NATIVE TEXTILES—See U.S. Industries, Inc.; *U.S. Public*, pg. 1684
NATKIN GROUP, INC.—See American International Group, Inc.; *U.S. Public*, pg. 84
THE NATKIN SERVICE CO.—See American International Group, Inc.; *U.S. Public*, pg. 84
P.T. NATRA RAYA—See Caterpillar Inc.; *U.S. Public*, pg. 317
NATREF—See Sasol Limited; *Int'l*, pg. 1197
NATREL INC.—See Agropur; *Int'l*, pg. 32
NATURAL FUELS CORPORATION—See New Century Energies, Inc.; *U.S. Public*, pg. 1170
NATURAL GAS DEVELOPMENT INC.—See Bay State Gas Company; *U.S. Public*, pg. 197
NATURAL GAS ODORIZING—See Occidental Petroleum Corporation; *U.S. Public*, pg. 1210
NATURAL GAS PIPELINE CO. AMERICA—See Occidental Petroleum Corporation; *U.S. Public*, pg. 1210
NATURAL STONE PRODUCTS LIMITED—See Tarmac plc; *Int'l*, pg. 1355
NATURALLE SPRINGS, INC.—See BCI Holding Corporation; *U.S. Private*, pg. 106
NATURALLY YOU—See Southeastern Medequip, Inc.; *U.S. Private*, pg. 1015
THE NATURE COMPANY—See Discovery Communications, Inc.; *U.S. Private*, pg. 334
NATURE MADE NUTRITIONAL PRODUCTS INC.—See Pharmavite Corp.; *U.S. Private*, pg. 860
NATURE'S BOUNTY INC.; *U.S. Public*, pg. 1166
NATURE'S RECIPE PET FOODS; *U.S. Private*, pg. 789
NATURE'S SUNSHINE DE COLOMBIA—See Nature's Sunshine Products, Inc.; *U.S. Public*, pg. 1166
NATURE'S SUNSHINE DE MEXICO—See Nature's Sunshine Products, Inc.; *U.S. Public*, pg. 1166

Company Index

NATURE'S SUNSHINE K.K. (JAPAN)—See Nature's Sunshine Products, Inc.; U.S. Public, pg. 1166
NATURE'S SUNSHINE PRODUCTS DE VENEZUELA—See Nature's Sunshine Products, Inc.; U.S. Public, pg. 1166
NATURE'S SUNSHINE PRODUCTS, INC.; U.S. Public, pg. 1166
NATURE'S SUNSHINE PRODUCTS OF CANADA, LTD.—See Nature's Sunshine Products, Inc.; U.S. Public, pg. 1167
NATURE'S SUNSHINE PRODUTOS NATURAIS LTDA.—See Nature's Sunshine Products, Inc.; U.S. Public, pg. 1167
NATURIN, S.A.—See Borden, Inc.; U.S. Private, pg. 159
NATURISTICS—See Del Laboratories, Inc.; U.S. Public, pg. 494
NATVEST, INC.—See Fiserv, Inc.; U.S. Public, pg. 647
NATWEST CAPITAL MARKETS AUSTRALIA LIMITED—See National Westminster Bank PLC; Int'l, pg. 911
NATWEST CAPITAL MARKETS LIMITED—See National Westminster Bank PLC; Int'l, pg. 910
NATWEST CORPORATE INVESTMENTS LIMITED—See National Westminster Bank PLC; Int'l, pg. 910
NATWEST EXPORT FINANCE LIMITED—See National Westminster Bank PLC; Int'l, pg. 910
NATWEST FINANCIAL PRODUCTS PLC—See National Westminster Bank PLC; Int'l, pg. 910
NATWEST FUTURES INC.—See National Westminster Bank PLC; Int'l, pg. 911
NATWEST FUTURES LIMITED—See National Westminster Bank PLC; Int'l, pg. 910
NATWEST GILTS LIMITED—See National Westminster Bank PLC; Int'l, pg. 910
NATWEST INTERNATIONAL TRUST CORPORATION (BAHAMAS) LIMITED—See National Westminster Bank PLC; Int'l, pg. 911
NATWEST INTERNATIONAL TRUST CORPORATION (CAYMAN) LIMITED—See National Westminster Bank PLC; Int'l, pg. 911
NATWEST INTERNATIONAL TRUST CORPORATION (EUROPE) LIMITED—See National Westminster Bank PLC; Int'l, pg. 911
NATWEST INTERNATIONAL TRUST CORPORATION (GUERNSEY) LIMITED—See National Westminster Bank PLC; Int'l, pg. 911
NATWEST INTERNATIONAL TRUST CORPORATION (ISLE OF MAN) LIMITED—See National Westminster Bank PLC; Int'l, pg. 911
NATWEST INTERNATIONAL TRUST CORPORATION (JERSEY) LIMITED—See National Westminster Bank PLC; Int'l, pg. 911
NATWEST INTERNATIONAL TRUST HOLDINGS LIMITED—See National Westminster Bank PLC; pg. 911
NATWEST INVESTMENT MANAGEMENT ASIA LIMITED—See National Westminster Bank PLC; Int'l, pg. 911
NATWEST INVESTMENT MANAGEMENT CHANNEL—See National Westminster Bank PLC; Int'l, pg. 910
NATWEST INVESTMENT MANAGEMENT JAPAN LIMITED—See National Westminster Bank PLC; Int'l, pg. 911
NATWEST INVESTMENT MANAGEMENT LIMITED—See National Westminster Bank PLC; Int'l, pg. 910
NATWEST MARKETS AUSTRALIA LIMITED—See National Westminster Bank PLC; Int'l, pg. 911
NATWEST MARKETS CORPORATE FINANCE LIMITED—See National Westminster Bank PLC; Int'l, pg. 910
NATWEST MARKETS GROUP INC.—See National Westminster Bank PLC; Int'l, pg. 911
NATWEST SECURITIES GMBH—See National Westminster Bank PLC; Int'l, pg. 911
NATWEST SECURITIES LIMITED—See National Westminster Bank PLC; Int'l, pg. 910
NATWEST SELLIER SA—See National Westminster Bank PLC; Int'l, pg. 911
NATWEST SPECIALIST FINANCE LIMITED—See National Westminster Bank PLC; Int'l, pg. 910
NATWEST STOCKBROKERS LIMITED—See National Westminster Bank PLC; Int'l, pg. 910
NATWEST U.K.—See National Westminster Bank PLC; Int'l, pg. 910
NATWEST VENTURES LIMITED—See National Westminster Bank PLC; Int'l, pg. 910
NATWEST WOOD MACKENZIE & CO LIMITED—See National Westminster Bank PLC; Int'l, pg. 911
NAUGATUCK GLASS COMPANY; U.S. Private, pg. 789
NAUTICA ENTERPRISES, INC.; U.S. Public, pg. 1167
NAUTICA FOOTWEAR—See Genesco Inc.; U.S. Public, pg. 728
NAUTICAL EXPRESS, LTD.—See Neptune Orient Lines Ltd.; Int'l, pg. 912
NAUTILUS INDUSTRIAL RELATION SERVICES INC.—See National Sea Products Limited; Int'l, pg. 909
NAUTILUS INSURANCE COMPANY—See W.R. Berkley Corporation; U.S. Public, pg. 216
NAUTILUS INTERNATIONAL—See Delta Woodside Industries, Inc.; U.S. Public, pg. 498
NAUTILUS VENTURES—See Royal Dutch/Shell Group of Companies; Int'l, pg. 1135
NAUTISK FORLAG A/S—See The A/S Norges Handels og Sjoefartstidende Group; Int'l, pg. 958
OY NAUTOR AB—See UPM-Kymmene Corporation; Int'l, pg. 1428
NAVAJO CORP.—See Holly Corporation; U.S. Public, pg. 830
NAVAJO HOLDINGS, INC.—See Holly Corporation; U.S. Public, pg. 830
NAVAJO PIPELINE CO.—See Holly Corporation; U.S. Public, pg. 830
NAVAJO REFINING CO.—See Holly Corporation; U.S. Public, pg. 830
NAVAJO WESTERN ASPHALT COMPANY—See Holly Corporation; U.S. Public, pg. 830
NAVAJO WESTERN LAND CO.—See Watkins Associated Industries Inc.; U.S. Private, pg. 1153

THE NAVAKIJ INSURANCE CO., LTD.—See Allianz Aktiengesellschaft; Int'l, pg. 61
NAVALE ASSICURAZIONI S.P.A.—See Assicurazioni Generali S.p.A.; Int'l, pg. 90
NAVAR BDDP—See BDDP Group; Int'l, pg. 117
NAVARRA DE COMPONENTES ELECTRONICOS SA (NACESA)—See Meggitt plc; Int'l, pg. 854
NAVCOM DEFENSE ELECTRONICS, INC.; U.S. Private, pg. 789
NAVCOM DEFENSE ELECTRONICS, INC.—See NavCom Defense Electronics, Inc.; U.S. Private, pg. 789
NAVIERA CASTELLANA, S.A.—See SEPI; Int'l, pg. 1223
NAVIGATION, GUIDANCE & CONTROL SYSTEMS—See Litton Industries, Inc.; U.S. Public, pg. 1002
NAVIGATOR AND GENERAL INSURANCE CO. LTD.—See B.A.T Industries P.L.C.; Int'l, pg. 110
NAVILLE—See Lagardere Groupe; Int'l, pg. 796
NAVILLUS INSURANCE LTD.—See Borden, Inc.; U.S. Private, pg. 159
NAVINCA, S.A.—See Vallehermoso, S.A.; Int'l, pg. 1447
NAVISTAR—See Lagardere Groupe; Int'l, pg. 793
NAVISTAR FINANCIAL CORPORATION—See Navistar International Corporation; U.S. Public, pg. 1167
NAVISTAR INTERNATIONAL—See Navistar International Corporation; U.S. Public, pg. 1167
NAVISTAR INTERNATIONAL CORPORATION; U.S. Public, pg. 1167
NAVISTAR INTERNATIONAL CORPORATION CANADA—See Navistar International Corporation; U.S. Public, pg. 1167
NAVISTAR INTERNATIONAL TRANSPORTATION CORP.—See Navistar International Corporation; U.S. Public, pg. 1167
NAVSTAR SYSTEMS LTD.—See SymmetriCom, Inc.; U.S. Public, pg. 1547
NAVSYMM—See SymmetriCom, Inc.; U.S. Public, pg. 1547
NAVTEC (A DIV. OF KENYON MARINE, INC.)—See Vector Industries, Ltd.; Int'l, pg. 1462
NAVTRANS CONTAINER LINES, INC.—See Norfolk Southern Corporation; U.S. Public, pg. 1192
NAVTRANS INTERNATIONAL FREIGHT FORWARDING, INC.—See Norfolk Southern Corporation; U.S. Public, pg. 1192
THE NAWALOHA INDUSTRY CO., LTD.—See The Siam Cement Public Company Limited; Int'l, pg. 1238
NAXOS UNION AG—See Rothenberger Group GmbH; Int'l, pg. 1128
NAYLOR PIPE COMPANY; U.S. Private, pg. 789
NAZ-DAR COMPANY—See Thrall Enterprises, Inc.; U.S. Private, pg. 1084
M.F. NEAL & CO.,INC.—See MacAndrews & Forbes Holdings Inc.; U.S. Private, pg. 689
NEAPCO, INC.—See UIS, Inc.; U.S. Private, pg. 1113
NEARBY EGGS, INC.—See Sun City Industries, Inc.; U.S. Public, pg. 1529
NEBAM NEDERLANDSE BEVRACHTING EN AGENTUUR MAATSCHAPPIJ—See Koninklijke Hoogovens N.V.; Int'l, pg. 754
NEBCO EVANS HOLDING CO.—See Holberg Industries, Inc.; U.S. Private, pg. 533
NEBRASKA BOOK CO., INC.; U.S. Private, pg. 789
NEBRASKA DAIRIES, INC.—See Nash Finch Company; U.S. Public, pg. 1152
NEBRASKA ENGINEERING CO.—See TIC United Corporation; U.S. Private, pg. 1064
NEBRASKA FURNITURE MART, INC.—See Berkshire Hathaway Inc.; U.S. Public, pg. 221
NEBRASKA PUBLIC POWER DISTRICT; U.S. Private, pg. 789
NECKAR-GETREIDE UND FUTTERMITTEL SPEDITIONS GESELLSCHAFT MBH—See The Peninsular and Oriental Steam Navigation Company; Int'l, pg. 1033
NECKERMANN VERSAND AG—See Karstadt Aktiengesellschaft; Int'l, pg. 724
NECKURA VERISCHERUNGS AG—See Nationwide Insurance Enterprise; U.S. Private, pg. 789
NEDDRILL HOLDING B.V.—See Royal Nedlloyd Group N.V.; Int'l, pg. 1144
NEDDRILL NEDERLAND B.V.—See Royal Nedlloyd Group N.V.; Int'l, pg. 1144
NEDERLANDS ALGEMEEN VERZEKERINGSKANTOOR B.V.—See Assicurazioni Generali S.p.A.; Int'l, pg. 91
NEDERLANDS STUDIECENTRUM—See Reed Elsevier plc; Int'l, pg. 1100
NEDERLANDSCHE KALI-IMPORT MAATSCHAPPIJ B.V. (N.K.I.M.)—See BASF AG; Int'l, pg. 109
NEDERLANDSCHE TRUST-MAATSCHAPPIJ B.V.—See ABN-AMRO Holding N.V.; Int'l, pg. 9
NEDERLANDSE AARDOLIE MAATSCHAPPIJ B.V.—See Exxon Corporation; U.S. Public, pg. 603
NEDERLANDSE AARDOLIE MAATSCHAPPIJ B.V.—See Royal Dutch/Shell Group of Companies; Int'l, pg. 1136
NEDERLANDSE GASUNIE N.V.—See Royal Dutch/Shell Group of Companies; Int'l, pg. 1135
N.V. NEDERLANDSE GASUNIE—See Exxon Corporation; U.S. Public, pg. 602
NEDERLANDSE HARDMETAAL FABRIEKEN B.V.—See Kennametal Inc.; U.S. Public, pg. 951
NEDERLANDSE IJZERGIETERIJ VULCANUS B.V.—See Schuttersveld Holding N.V.; Int'l, pg. 1210
NEDERLANDSE PERSDATABANK BV—See KPN Koninklyke PTT Nederland NV; Int'l, pg. 720
NEDERLANDSE UNILEVER BEDRIJVEN B.V.—See Unilever Plc; Int'l, pg. 1438
NEDERLANDSE VERZEKERINGS GROEP NV—See AEGON N.V.; Int'l, pg. 26
NEDERMAN A/S—See Charter plc; Int'l, pg. 283
NEDERMAN CANADA LTD.—See Charter plc; Int'l, pg. 283
NEDERMAN GES.M.B.H.—See Charter plc; Int'l, pg. 283
NEDERMAN GMBH—See Charter plc; Int'l, pg. 283
NEDERMAN IBERICA S.A.—See Charter plc; Int'l, pg. 283
NEDERMAN INC.—See Charter plc; Int'l, pg. 281
NEDERMAN LTD.—See Charter plc; Int'l, pg. 283
AB PH. NEDERMAN & CO.—See Charter plc; Int'l, pg. 281

NEDLLOYD (ARGENTINA) S.A.—See Royal Nedlloyd Group N.V.; Int'l, pg. 1145
NEDLLOYD AUSTRALIA PTY. LIMITED—See Royal Nedlloyd Group N.V.; Int'l, pg. 1145
NEDLLOYD BEDRIJFSGEBOUWEN C.V.—See Royal Nedlloyd Group N.V.; Int'l, pg. 1144
NEDLLOYD BEHEER B.V.—See Royal Nedlloyd Group N.V.; Int'l, pg. 1144
NEDLLOYD BULK B.V.—See Royal Nedlloyd Group N.V.; Int'l, pg. 1144
NEDLLOYD COMPUTER SERICES B.V.—See Royal Nedlloyd Group N.V.; Int'l, pg. 1144
NEDLLOYD DEUSTCHLAND HOLDING GMBH—See Royal Nedlloyd Group N.V.; Int'l, pg. 1145
NEDLLOYD DISTRIBUTION SYSTEMS—See Royal Nedlloyd Group N.V.; Int'l, pg. 1144
NEDLLOYD DISTRICENTERS B.V.—See Royal Nedlloyd Group N.V.; Int'l, pg. 1144
NEDLLOYD DISTRICENTERS GMBH—See Royal Nedlloyd Group N.V.; Int'l, pg. 1144
NEDLLOYD DISTRICENTERS INTERNATIONAL—See Royal Nedlloyd Group N.V.; Int'l, pg. 1144
NEDLLOYD DISTRICENTERS LTD.—See Royal Nedlloyd Group N.V.; Int'l, pg. 1144
NEDLLOYD DISTRICENTERS PTE. LTD.—See Royal Nedlloyd Group N.V.; Int'l, pg. 1144
NEDLLOYD DISTRICENTERS WESTPOORT B.V.—See Royal Nedlloyd Group N.V.; Int'l, pg. 1144
NEDLLOYD DO BRASIL NAVEGACAO LTDA.—See Royal Nedlloyd Group N.V.; Int'l, pg. 1145
NEDLLOYD (E.A.) LIMITED—See Royal Nedlloyd Group N.V.; Int'l, pg. 1144
NEDLLOYD ENERGY B.V.—See Royal Nedlloyd Group N.V.; Int'l, pg. 1144
NEDLLOYD FLEET SERVICES—See Royal Nedlloyd Group N.V.; Int'l, pg. 1145
NEDLLOYD FLOWMASTERS—See Royal Nedlloyd Group N.V.; Int'l, pg. 1145
NEDLLOYD GROUP HOLDINGS UK LTD.—See Royal Nedlloyd Group N.V.; Int'l, pg. 1145
NEDLLOYD (HK) LIMITED—See Royal Nedlloyd Group N.V.; Int'l, pg. 1145
NEDLLOYD HOLDING FRANCE S.A.—See Royal Nedlloyd Group N.V.; Int'l, pg. 1145
NEDLLOYD HOLDINGS (U.S.A.) INC.—See Royal Nedlloyd Group N.V.; Int'l, pg. 1145
NEDLLOYD LIJNEN B.V.—See Royal Nedlloyd Group N.V.; Int'l, pg. 1145
NEDLLOYD LINEAS AGENCIAS S.A.—See Royal Nedlloyd Group N.V.; Int'l, pg. 1145
NEDLLOYD LINES BELGIUM N.V.—See Royal Nedlloyd Group N.V.; Int'l, pg. 1145
NEDLLOYD LINES B.V.—See Royal Nedlloyd Group N.V.; Int'l, pg. 1145
NEDLLOYD LINES DEUTSCHLAND GMBH—See Royal Nedlloyd Group N.V.; Int'l, pg. 1145
NEDLLOYD LINES FRANCE S.A.—See Royal Nedlloyd Group N.V.; Int'l, pg. 1145
NEDLLOYD LINES K.K.—See Royal Nedlloyd Group N.V.; Int'l, pg. 1145
NEDLLOYD LINES NAVEGACAO S.A.—See Royal Nedlloyd Group N.V.; Int'l, pg. 1145
NEDLLOYD LINES NEDERLAND B.V.—See Royal Nedlloyd Group N.V.; Int'l, pg. 1145
NEDLLOYD LINES SA (PROPRIETARY) LIMITED—See Royal Nedlloyd Group N.V.; Int'l, pg. 1145
NEDLLOYD LINES (SWITZERLAND) A.G.—See Royal Nedlloyd Group N.V.; Int'l, pg. 1145
NEDLLOYD LINES U.K. LIMITED—See Royal Nedlloyd Group N.V.; Int'l, pg. 1145
NEDLLOYD LINES (U.S.A.) CORP.—See Royal Nedlloyd Group N.V.; Int'l, pg. 1145
NEDLLOYD (MALAYSIA) SDN BHD—See Royal Nedlloyd Group N.V.; Int'l, pg. 1145
NEDLLOYD (NEW ZEALAND) LIMITED—See Royal Nedlloyd Group N.V.; Int'l, pg. 1144
NEDLLOYD RIJN- EN BINNENVAART B.V.—See Royal Nedlloyd Group N.V.; Int'l, pg. 1144
NEDLLOYD ROAD CARGO A.E.—See Royal Nedlloyd Group N.V.; Int'l, pg. 1145
NEDLLOYD ROAD CARGO AG—See Royal Nedlloyd Group N.V.; Int'l, pg. 1145
NEDLLOYD ROAD CARGO B.V.—See Royal Nedlloyd Group N.V.; Int'l, pg. 1145
NEDLLOYD ROAD CARGO DIVISION—See Royal Nedlloyd Group N.V.; Int'l, pg. 1145
NEDLLOYD ROAD CARGO FTL—See Royal Nedlloyd Group N.V.; Int'l, pg. 1145
NEDLLOYD ROAD CARGO GMBH—See Royal Nedlloyd Group N.V.; Int'l, pg. 1145
NEDLLOYD ROAD CARGO INTERNATIONAL—See Royal Nedlloyd Group N.V.; Int'l, pg. 1145
NEDLLOYD ROAD CARGO LTD. STI.—See Royal Nedlloyd Group N.V.; Int'l, pg. 1145
NEDLLOYD ROAD CARGO N.V.—See Royal Nedlloyd Group N.V.; Int'l, pg. 1145
NEDLLOYD ROAD CARGO S.A.—See Royal Nedlloyd Group N.V.; Int'l, pg. 1145
NEDLLOYD ROAD CARGO SPA—See Royal Nedlloyd Group N.V.; Int'l, pg. 1145
NEDLLOYD ROAD CARGO TRANSITARIOS LDA.—See Royal Nedlloyd Group N.V.; Int'l, pg. 1145
NEDLLOYD ROQUE S.A.—See Royal Nedlloyd Group N.V.; Int'l, pg. 1145
NEDLLOYD SCHIFFMAKLER GMBH—See Royal Nedlloyd Group N.V.; Int'l, pg. 1144
NEDLLOYD (SINGAPORE) PTE. LTD.—See Royal Nedlloyd Group N.V.; Int'l, pg. 1145
NEDLLOYD UNITRANS GMBH—See Royal Nedlloyd Group N.V.; Int'l, pg. 1145
NEDLLOYD UNITRAS—See Royal Nedlloyd Group N.V.; Int'l, pg. 1145
NEDLLOYD VASTGOED BEHEER B.V.—See Royal Nedlloyd Group N.V.; Int'l, pg. 1145

K/S NEDRE ELVEHAVN TRONDHEIM—See Aker Raj Asa; *Int'l*, pg. 41
NEDSAFE—See Vendex International N.V.; *Int'l*, pg. 1463
NEDSHIP INTERNATIONAL.—See Rabobank Nederland; *Int'l*, pg. 1082
NEEB CORPORATION; *U.S. Private*, pg. 790
NEEF AG—See Sulzer Ltd.; *Int'l*, pg. 1306
NEEF ELEKTROTECHNIK GMBH & CO.—See Sulzer Ltd.; *Int'l*, pg. 1306
NEENAH FOUNDRY COMPANY; *U.S. Private*, pg. 790
NEENAH PAPER—See Kimberly-Clark Corporation; *U.S. Public*, pg. 958
NEER MANUFACTURING COMPANY INC.—See General Signal Corporation; *U.S. Public*, pg. 727
NEFF (UK) LIMITED; *Int'l*, pg. 912
NEFFSVILLE MUTUAL FIRE INSURANCE CO.—See Old Guard Insurance Group; *U.S. Public*, pg. 1216
NEGOCE PIERRE—See GIB Group; *Int'l*, pg. 534
NEHRING ELECTRICAL WORKS COMPANY—See Kuhlman Corporation; *U.S. Public*, pg. 968
NEILL-LAVIELLE SUPPLY CO.; *U.S. Private*, pg. 790
NEIMAN MARCUS CO.—See Harcourt General, Inc.; *U.S. Public*, pg. 785
THE NEIMAN-MARCUS GROUP, INC.—See Harcourt General, Inc.; *U.S. Public*, pg. 784
NEKOOSA PACKAGING COMPANY—See Georgia-Pacific Corporation; *U.S. Public*, pg. 736
NEKOOSA PACKAGING CORP.—See Georgia-Pacific Corporation; *U.S. Public*, pg. 736
NEKOTA RESOURCES INC.—See Northwestern Public Service; *U.S. Public*, pg. 1201
NELCO FRANCE—See Kirkwood Industries, Inc.; *U.S. Private*, pg. 623
NELCO INTERNATIONAL—See Park Electrochemical Corporation; *U.S. Public*, pg. 1258
NELCO PRODUCTS, INC.—See Park Electrochemical Corporation; *U.S. Public*, pg. 1258
NELCO PRODUCTS PTE. LTD.—See Park Electrochemical Corporation; *U.S. Public*, pg. 1258
NELCO S.A.—See Park Electrochemical Corporation; *U.S. Public*, pg. 1258
NELCO TECHNOLOGY, INC.—See Park Electrochemical Corporation; *U.S. Public*, pg. 1258
NELES-JAMESBURY CORP.—See UPM-Kymmene Corporation; *Int'l*, pg. 1428
NELLA OIL COMPANY; *U.S. Private*, pg. 790
NELLCOR DE MEXICO, S.A. DE C.V.—See Mallinckrodt Inc.; *U.S. Public*, pg. 1040
NELLCOR PURITAN BENNETT—See Mallinckrodt Inc.; *U.S. Public*, pg. 1040
NELLCOR PURITAN BENNETT BELGIUM N.V./S.A.—See Mallinckrodt Inc.; *U.S. Public*, pg. 1040
NELLCOR PURITAN BENNETT EUROPE B.V.—See Mallinckrodt Inc.; *U.S. Public*, pg. 1040
NELLCOR PURITAN BENNETT FINLAND OY—See Mallinckrodt Inc.; *U.S. Public*, pg. 1040
NELLCOR PURITAN BENNETT FRANCE S.A.R.L.—See Mallinckrodt Inc.; *U.S. Public*, pg. 1040
NELLCOR PURITAN BENNETT GMBH—See Mallinckrodt Inc.; *U.S. Public*, pg. 1040
NELLCOR PURITAN BENNETT HK LTD.—See Mallinckrodt Inc.; *U.S. Public*, pg. 1040
NELLCOR PURITAN BENNETT INCORPORATED—See Mallinckrodt Inc.; *U.S. Public*, pg. 1039
NELLCOR PURITAN-BENNETT INC. (IRELAND)—See Mallinckrodt Inc.; *U.S. Public*, pg. 1040
NELLCOR PURITAN BENNETT (UK) LIMITED—See Mallinckrodt Inc.; *U.S. Public*, pg. 1040
NELMOR CO., INC.—See Sterling, Inc.; *U.S. Private*, pg. 1041
NELSEN S.P.A.—See The Procter & Gamble Company; *U.S. Public*, pg. 1333
NELSEN STEEL & WIRE CO.; *U.S. Private*, pg. 790
ALLEN NELSON & SON.; *U.S. Private*, pg. 790
NELSON & SMALL INC.; *U.S. Private*, pg. 790
NELSON, BENSON & ZELLMER, INC.—See United Asset Management Corporation; *U.S. Public*, pg. 1673
NELSON CANADA—See The Thomson Corporation; *U.S. Public*, pg. 1601
L.R. NELSON CORPORATION; *U.S. Private*, pg. 790
MARSHALL W. NELSON & ASSOC.—See Eclipse Inc.; *U.S. Private*, pg. 360
NELSON PHOTO SUPPLIES; *U.S. Private*, pg. 791
NELSON PUBLICATIONS—See Primedia Inc.; *U.S. Public*, pg. 1328
NELSON-ROANOKE CORP.—See Distribution America; *U.S. Private*, pg. 335
THOMAS NELSON & SONS LTD.—See The Thomson Corporation; *U.S. Public*, pg. 1601
THOMAS NELSON AUSTRALIA—See The Thomson Corporation; *U.S. Public*, pg. 1601
THOMAS NELSON INC.; *U.S. Public*, pg. 1167
NELSON WESTERBERG—See Nelson Westerberg, Inc.; *U.S. Private*, pg. 1164
NELSON WESTERBERG ATLAS—See Nelson Westerberg, Inc.; *U.S. Private*, pg. 1164
NELSON WESTERBERG INTERNATIONAL INC.—See Nelson Westerberg, Inc.; *U.S. Private*, pg. 1164
NELSPRUIT BREWERY—See National Sorghum Beer Breweries Pty. Ltd. Highveld Division; *Int'l*, pg. 909
NEMA WARMETAUSCHER GMBH—See Deutsche Babcock AG; *Int'l*, pg. 399
NEMARC SHIPPING COMPANY C/O NESTE SHIPPING—See Kvaerner a.s.a.; *Int'l*, pg. 772
NEMATRON CORP.; *U.S. Private*, pg. 791
NEMEF B.V.—See The Black & Decker Corporation; *U.S. Public*, pg. 235
NEMIC-LAMBDA ISRAEL, LTD.—See Siebe plc; *Int'l*, pg. 1241
NEMIC-LAMBDA (ISRAEL) LTD.—See Siebe plc; *Int'l*, pg. 1242
NEMIC-LAMBDA (KANUTAN) SDN. BHD.—See Siebe plc; *Int'l*, pg. 1242
NEMIC-LAMBDA KK—See Siebe plc; *Int'l*, pg. 1242

NEMIC LAMBDA KK—See Siebe plc; *Int'l*, pg. 1242
NEMIC-LAMBDA (M) SDN. BHD.—See Siebe plc; *Int'l*, pg. 1242
NEMIC-LAMBDA PTE. LTD.—See Siebe plc; *Int'l*, pg. 1242
NEMSCHOFF CHAIRS, INC.; *U.S. Private*, pg. 791
NENPLAS EXTRUSIONS HOMELUX—See McKechnie PLC; *Int'l*, pg. 851
NENPLAS MOULDINGS—See McKechnie PLC; *Int'l*, pg. 851
NEO ABELLO S.P.A.—See Chr. Hansen Holding A/S; *Int'l*, pg. 289
NEOCOM PUBLICIDADE—See The Lowe Group; *U.S. Private*, pg. 678
THE NEOGARD CORPORATION—See Jones Blair Company; *U.S. Private*, pg. 596
NEOPAC A/S—See Metsa-Serla Corporation; *Int'l*, pg. 864
NEOPAC OY—See Metsa-Serla Corporation; *Int'l*, pg. 863
OY NEOREMEDIA AB—See Oy Algol AB; *Int'l*, pg. 15
NEORX CORPORATION; *U.S. Private*, pg. 791
NEOSID AUSTRALIA PTY. LIMITED—See TT Group PLC; *Int'l*, pg. 1344
NEOSID (CANADA) LIMITED—See TT Group PLC; *Int'l*, pg. 1344
NEOSID LIMITED—See TT Group PLC; *Int'l*, pg. 1344
NEOTECHA AG—See Tyco International Ltd.; *U.S. Public*, pg. 1651
NEOTERIC COSMETICS, INC.—See Scott's Liquid Gold-Inc.; *U.S. Public*, pg. 1447
NEPA—See C.E.P. Communication Group; *Int'l*, pg. 239
NEPAL GRINDLAYS BANK LIMITED—See Australia & New Zealand Banking Group Limited; *Int'l*, pg. 100
NEPAL RESIDENT MISSION—See Asian Development Bank; *Int'l*, pg. 89
NEPA-MASSACHUSETTS, INC.—See Magellan Health Services, Inc.; *U.S. Public*, pg. 1036
NEPA-NEW HAMPSHIRE, INC.—See Magellan Health Services, Inc.; *U.S. Public*, pg. 1036
NEPERA INC.—See Cambrex Corporation; *U.S. Public*, pg. 297
NEPROMA TEXTIEL SERVICE B.V.—See Sophus Berendsen A/S; *Int'l*, pg. 1285
NEPTUNE ORIENT LINES LTD.; *Int'l*, pg. 912
NEPTUNE TRUCKING, INC.—See Mark VII, Inc.; *U.S. Public*, pg. 1046
NERADT TOOL & STAMPING COMPANY—See Continental/Midland, Inc.; *U.S. Private*, pg. 269
NERISENA—See Compagnie des Machines Bull; *Int'l*, pg. 317
SOPHIE NERVAL S.A.—See Henkel KGaA; *Int'l*, pg. 612
THE NESBITT THOMSON CORPORATION LIMITED—See Bank of Montreal; *Int'l*, pg. 153
NESCO AMEICAN HARVEST INC.—See The Metal Ware Corp.; *U.S. Private*, pg. 735
NESCO, INC.; *U.S. Private*, pg. 791
NESCO LTD.—See Electrolux, AB; *Int'l*, pg. 443
NESKA SCHIFFAHRTS- UND SPEDITIONSKONTOR GMBH—See Harpen AG; *Int'l*, pg. 597
NESLAB INSTRUMENTS, INC.—See Thermo Electron Corporation; *U.S. Public*, pg. 1595
NESMA-COSTAIN PROCESS CO. LIMITED—See Costain Group PLC; *Int'l*, pg. 337
NESON LTD.—See Cultor Ltd.; *Int'l*, pg. 349
NESOTA CO.—See The Minnesota Mutual Life Insurance Company; *U.S. Private*, pg. 750
NESPRESSO S.A.—See Nestle S.A.; *Int'l*, pg. 916
NESS HOLDING CO.; *U.S. Private*, pg. 791
NESSEN LAMPS, INC.—See Luxo A/S; *Int'l*, pg. 821
NESSTRA (LIBERIA)—See BASF AG; *Int'l*, pg. 109
SA NETSTAL BELGIUM NV—See Mannesmann A.G.; *Int'l*, pg. 836
NESTAWAY—See AXIA Incorporated; *U.S. Private*, pg. 103
NESTE AIR—See Neste Oy; *Int'l*, pg. 913
NESTE ALFA OY—See Neste Oy; *Int'l*, pg. 914
NESTE ALGERIE S.A.R.L.—See Neste Oy; *Int'l*, pg. 914
NESTE ARABIA CO. LTD.—See Neste Oy; *Int'l*, pg. 914
NESTE AVIATION AND MARINE SALES—See Neste Oy; *Int'l*, pg. 913
NESTE CANADA INC.—See Neste Oy; *Int'l*, pg. 914
NESTE CELLPLAST AB—See Neste Oy; *Int'l*, pg. 914
NESTE CHEMICALS—See Neste Oy; *Int'l*, pg. 914
NESTE CHEMICALS BELGIUM N.V.—See Neste Oy; *Int'l*, pg. 914
NESTE CHEMICALS BENELUX HOLDING B.V.—See Neste Oy; *Int'l*, pg. 914
NESTE CHEMICALS GMBH—See Neste Oy; *Int'l*, pg. 914
NESTE CHEMICALS HANDELSGESELLSCHAFT MBH—See Neste Oy; *Int'l*, pg. 914
NESTE CHEMICALS HOLDING FRANCE S.A.—See Neste Oy; *Int'l*, pg. 914
NESTE CHEMICALS HOLDING INC.—See Neste Oy; *Int'l*, pg. 913
NESTE CHEMICALS IBERICA S.L.—See Neste Oy; *Int'l*, pg. 914
NESTE CHEMICALS ITALIA S.R.L.—See Neste Oy; *Int'l*, pg. 914
NESTE CHEMICALS (JAPAN) CO., LTD.—See Neste Oy; *Int'l*, pg. 914
NESTE CHEMICALS S.A.—See Neste Oy; *Int'l*, pg. 914
NESTE CHEMICALS SOUTH EAST ASIA LTD.—See Neste Oy; *Int'l*, pg. 914
NESTE CHEMICALS UK LTD.—See Neste Oy; *Int'l*, pg. 914
NESTE CHIMIE FRANCE S.N.C.—See Neste Oy; *Int'l*, pg. 914
NESTE COLOR COMPOUND S.A.—See Neste Oy; *Int'l*, pg. 914
NESTE CORPORATE HOLDING INC.—See Neste Oy; *Int'l*, pg. 913
NESTE CRUDE OIL, INC.—See Neste Oy; *Int'l*, pg. 914
NESTE EXPLORATION LTD.—See Neste Oy; *Int'l*, pg. 915
NESTE FINANCE B.V.—See Neste Oy; *Int'l*, pg. 915
NESTE GAS AB—See Neste Oy; *Int'l*, pg. 915
NESTE GAS LTD.—See Neste Oy; *Int'l*, pg. 915
NESTE INSURANCE LTD.—See Neste Oy; *Int'l*, pg. 915

NESTE KEMI DANMARK A/S—See Neste Oy; *Int'l*, pg. 915
NESTE KEMI FORSALJNINGS AB—See Neste Oy; *Int'l*, pg. 915
NESTE KIDE OY—See Neste Oy; *Int'l*, pg. 913
NESTE KJEMI A/S—See Neste Oy; *Int'l*, pg. 915
NESTE LIIKENNEPALVELU OY—See Neste Oy; *Int'l*, pg. 913
NESTE OEL GMBH—See Neste Oy; *Int'l*, pg. 915
NESTE OIL EESTI—See Neste Oy; *Int'l*, pg. 915
NESTE OIL LATVIA—See Neste Oy; *Int'l*, pg. 915
NESTE OIL LT—See Neste Oy; *Int'l*, pg. 915
NESTE OIL, MTBE—See Neste Oy; *Int'l*, pg. 914
NESTE OIL POLAND LTD.—See Neste Oy; *Int'l*, pg. 915
NESTE OIL SERVICES, INC.—See Neste Oy; *Int'l*, pg. 914
NESTE OXO AB—See Neste Oy; *Int'l*, pg. 915
NESTE OY; *Int'l*, pg. 912
NESTE OY, CHEMICALS—See Neste Oy; *Int'l*, pg. 915
NESTE OY CHEMICALS—See Neste Oy; *Int'l*, pg. 915
NESTE OY CHEMICALS - WARSAW—See Neste Oy; *Int'l*, pg. 915
NESTE OY, DUBAI—See Neste Oy; *Int'l*, pg. 915
NESTE OY, GAS LPG INTERNATIONAL—See Neste Oy; *Int'l*, pg. 915
NESTE OY INTERNATIONAL TRADING & SUPPLY—See Neste Oy; *Int'l*, pg. 915
NESTE OY, NAANTALI REFINERY—See Neste Oy; *Int'l*, pg. 914
NESTE OY, NATURAL GAS—See Neste Oy; *Int'l*, pg. 913
NESTE OY, PORVOO REFINERY—See Neste Oy; *Int'l*, pg. 914
NESTE OY, SHIPPING—See Neste Oy; *Int'l*, pg. 913
NESTE P.A.O. N.V.—See Neste Oy; *Int'l*, pg. 915
NESTE PETROLEUM A/S—See Neste Oy; *Int'l*, pg. 915
NESTE PETROLEUM, INC.—See Neste Oy; *Int'l*, pg. 914
NESTE PETROLEUM LTD.—See Neste Oy; *Int'l*, pg. 915
NESTE PETROLEUM (PRODUCTS), INC.—See Neste Oy; *Int'l*, pg. 914
NESTE PETROLEUM (SINGAPORE) PTE. LTD.—See Neste Oy; *Int'l*, pg. 915
NESTE POLYESTER INC.—See Neste Oy; *Int'l*, pg. 913
NESTE POLYESTER S.A.—See Neste Oy; *Int'l*, pg. 915
NESTE POLYMER COMPOUNDS AB—See Neste Oy; *Int'l*, pg. 915
NESTE PRODUCTION LIMITED SOVEREIGN OIL & GAS PLC—See Neste Oy; *Int'l*, pg. 915
NESTE QUIMICA COMERCIAL, S.A.—See Neste Oy; *Int'l*, pg. 915
NESTE REPRESENTATIVE OFFICE—See Neste Oy; *Int'l*, pg. 915
NESTE RESINAS S.A. DE C.V.—See Neste Oy; *Int'l*, pg. 915
NESTE RESINS B.V.—See Neste Oy; *Int'l*, pg. 915
NESTE RESINS CANADA—See Neste Oy; *Int'l*, pg. 915
NESTE RESINS CORPORATION—See Neste Oy; *Int'l*, pg. 913
NESTE RESINS OY—See Neste Oy; *Int'l*, pg. 913
NESTE ST. PETERSBURG—See Neste Oy; *Int'l*, pg. 915
NESTE SHANGAI OFFICE—See Neste Oy; *Int'l*, pg. 915
NESTE SHIPPING BENELUX, N.V.—See Neste Oy; *Int'l*, pg. 915
NESTE SHIPPING CANADA LTD.—See Neste Oy; *Int'l*, pg. 915
NESTE SINGAPORE HOLDINGS PTE. LTD.—See Neste Oy; *Int'l*, pg. 915
NESTE SVERIGE AB—See Neste Oy; *Int'l*, pg. 915
NESTE THERMISOL A/S—See Neste Oy; *Int'l*, pg. 915
NESTE (UK) LTD.—See Neste Oy; *Int'l*, pg. 915
NESTE YRITYSPALVELU OY—See Neste Oy; *Int'l*, pg. 913
NESTLE ARGENTINA S.A.—See Nestle S.A.; *Int'l*, pg. 920
P.T. NESTLE ASEAN (INDONESIA)—See Nestle S.A.; *Int'l*, pg. 920
NESTLE ASEAN (MALAYSIA)—See Nestle S.A.; *Int'l*, pg. 920
NESTLE ASEAN SINGAPORE (PTE) LTD.—See Nestle S.A.; *Int'l*, pg. 920
NESTLE ASEAN (THAILAND) LTD.—See Nestle S.A.; *Int'l*, pg. 920
NESTLE AUSTRALIA LTD.—See Nestle S.A.; *Int'l*, pg. 920
NESTLE BANGLADESH LTD.—See Nestle S.A.; *Int'l*, pg. 921
NESTLE BELGILUX S.A.—See Nestle S.A.; *Int'l*, pg. 921
NESTLE BEVERAGE COMPANY—See Nestle S.A.; *Int'l*, pg. 917
NESTLE CAMEROUN S.A.—See Nestle S.A.; *Int'l*, pg. 921
NESTLE CANADA INC.—See Nestle S.A.; *Int'l*, pg. 921
NESTLE CAPITAL CORPORATION—See Nestle S.A.; *Int'l*, pg. 916
NESTLE CARIBBEAN, INC.—See Nestle S.A.; *Int'l*, pg. 921
NESTLE CHILE S.A.—See Nestle S.A.; *Int'l*, pg. 921
NESTLE CHINA LTD.—See Nestle S.A.; *Int'l*, pg. 921
NESTLE CHOCOLATE & CONFECTION—See Nestle S.A.; *Int'l*, pg. 917
THE NESTLE COMPANY, NEW ZEALAND LTD.—See Nestle S.A.; *Int'l*, pg. 921
NESTLE CONFECTIONERY—See Nestle S.A.; *Int'l*, pg. 922
NESTLE CONFECTIONERY LTD.—See Nestle S.A.; *Int'l*, pg. 921
NESTLE DAIRY FARM LTD.—See Nestle S.A.; *Int'l*, pg. 921
NESTLE DAIRY SYSTEMS, LICENSING DIVISION—See Nestle S.A.; *Int'l*, pg. 918
NESTLE DAIRY SYSTEMS-PACKAGING/MACHINERY DIVISION—See Nestle S.A.; *Int'l*, pg. 918
NESTLE DANMARK A/S—See Nestle S.A.; *Int'l*, pg. 921
NESTLE DE COLOMBIA—See Nestle S.A.; *Int'l*, pg. 921
S.A. NESTLE DE PRODUCTOS ALIMENTICIOS—See Nestle S.A.; *Int'l*, pg. 921
NESTLE DEL URUGUAY S.A.—See Nestle S.A.; *Int'l*, pg. 921
NESTLE DEUTSCHLAND AG—See Nestle S.A.; *Int'l*, pg. 921
NESTLE DONGGUAN LTD.—See Nestle S.A.; *Int'l*, pg. 921

NESTLE DIRECTORY OF CORPORATE AFFILIATIONS

Company Index

NESTLE ECUADOR S.A.—See Nestle S.A.; *Int'l*, pg. 921
NESTLE ERZEUGNISSE GMBH—See Nestle S.A.; *Int'l*, pg. 921
NESTLE (FIJI) LTD.—See Nestle S.A.; *Int'l*, pg. 921
NESTLE-FINDUS OY—See Nestle S.A.; *Int'l*, pg. 921
NESTLE FOOD S.R.O.—See Nestle S.A.; *Int'l*, pg. 921
NESTLE FOODS KENYA LTD.—See Nestle S.A.; *Int'l*, pg. 921
NESTLE FOODS NIGERIA PLC—See Nestle S.A.; *Int'l*, pg. 921
NESTLE FOODSERVICE CANADA—See Nestle S.A.; *Int'l*, pg. 922
NESTLE FRANCE—See Nestle S.A.; *Int'l*, pg. 921
NESTLE FROZEN, REFRIGERATED, AND ICE CREAM COMPANIES—See Nestle S.A.; *Int'l*, pg. 918
NESTLE GHANA LTD.—See Nestle S.A.; *Int'l*, pg. 921
NESTLE HELLAS S.A.I.—See Nestle S.A.; *Int'l*, pg. 921
NESTLE HOLDINGS, INC.—See Nestle S.A.; *Int'l*, pg. 916
NESTLE HONDURENA S.A.—See Nestle S.A.; *Int'l*, pg. 921
NESTLE HUNGARIA KFT—See Nestle S.A.; *Int'l*, pg. 921
NESTLE ICE CREAM CO.—See Nestle S.A.; *Int'l*, pg. 918
NESTLE INDIA LTD.—See Nestle S.A.; *Int'l*, pg. 921
NESTLE INDUSTRIAL E COMMERCIAL LTDA.—See Nestle S.A.; *Int'l*, pg. 921
NESTLE (IRELAND) LTD.—See Nestle S.A.; *Int'l*, pg. 921
NESTLE ITALIANA S.P.A.—See Nestle S.A.; *Int'l*, pg. 921
NESTLE JAPAN LTD.—See Nestle S.A.; *Int'l*, pg. 921
NESTLE-JMP JAMAICA LTD.—See Nestle S.A.; *Int'l*, pg. 921
NESTLE KK—See Nestle S.A.; *Int'l*, pg. 921
NESTLE KOREA LTD.—See Nestle S.A.; *Int'l*, pg. 921
NESTLE LANKA LTD.—See Nestle S.A.; *Int'l*, pg. 921
NESTLE LYONS MAID—See Nestle S.A.; *Int'l*, pg. 918
NESTLE-MACKINTOSH K.K.—See Nestle S.A.; *Int'l*, pg. 921
NESTLE (MALAYSIA), SDN. BHD., NESMAL—See Nestle S.A.; *Int'l*, pg. 921
NESTLE MAROC S.A.—See Nestle S.A.; *Int'l*, pg. 921
NESTLE NEDERLAND B.V.—See Nestle S.A.; *Int'l*, pg. 921
NESTLE NEW ZEALAND LTD.—See Nestle S.A.; *Int'l*, pg. 921
A/S NESTLE NORGE—See Nestle S.A.; *Int'l*, pg. 921
NESTLE NOUVELLE-CALEDONIA S.A.—See Nestle S.A.; *Int'l*, pg. 921
NESTLE PANAMA S.A.—See Nestle S.A.; *Int'l*, pg. 921
NESTLE PERU S.A.—See Nestle S.A.; *Int'l*, pg. 921
NESTLE PHILIPPINES, INC.—See Nestle S.A.; *Int'l*, pg. 921
NESTLE (PNG) LTD.—See Nestle S.A.; *Int'l*, pg. 921
NESTLE PORTUGAL, S.A.—See Nestle S.A.; *Int'l*, pg. 921
NESTLE PRODUCTS (MAURITIUS) LTD.—See Nestle S.A.; *Int'l*, pg. 921
NESTLE PRODUCTS (THAILAND), INC.—See Nestle S.A.; *Int'l*, pg. 921
NESTLE PUERTO RICO, INC.—See Nestle S.A.; *Int'l*, pg. 917
NESTLE-ROWNTREE LTD.—See Nestle S.A.; *Int'l*, pg. 921
NESTLE S.A.; *Int'l*, pg. 915
NESTLE SENEGAL—See Nestle S.A.; *Int'l*, pg. 921
NESTLE SHUANGCHENG LTD.—See Nestle S.A.; *Int'l*, pg. 921
NESTLE SINGAPORE PTE. LTD.—See Nestle S.A.; *Int'l*, pg. 921
NESTLE SOURCES INTERNATIONAL S.A.—See Nestle S.A.; *Int'l*, pg. 921
NESTLE (SOUTH AFRICA) (PTE) LTD.—See Nestle S.A.; *Int'l*, pg. 921
NESTLE TAIWAN LTD.—See Nestle S.A.; *Int'l*, pg. 921
NESTLE (THAILAND) LTD.—See Nestle S.A.; *Int'l*, pg. 921
NESTLE TRINIDAD AND TOBAGO LTD.—See Nestle S.A.; *Int'l*, pg. 921
NESTLE TUNISIE—See Nestle S.A.; *Int'l*, pg. 921
NESTLE TURKIYE GIDA SANAYI A.S.—See Nestle S.A.; *Int'l*, pg. 921
NESTLE U.K. LTD.—See Nestle S.A.; *Int'l*, pg. 922
NESTLE USA—See Nestle S.A.; *Int'l*, pg. 916
NESTLE VENEZUELA S.A.—See Nestle S.A.; *Int'l*, pg. 922
NESTLE WORLD TRADE CORPORATION—See Nestle S.A.; *Int'l*, pg. 916
NESTLE ZIMBABWE (PVT) LTD.—See Nestle S.A.; *Int'l*, pg. 922
NESTOR GVG MBH—See Commerzbank AG; *Int'l*, pg. 309
NESTOR GVG MBH & CO. OBJEKT WIEMELHAUSEN KG—See Commerzbank AG; *Int'l*, pg. 309
NESTOR GVG MBH & CO. OBJEKT ERLANGEN KG—See Commerzbank AG; *Int'l*, pg. 309
NESTOR GVG MBH & CO. OBJEKT HAMME KG—See Commerzbank AG; *Int'l*, pg. 309
NESTOR GVG MBH & CO. OBJEKT ITTAE FRANKFURT KG—See Commerzbank AG; *Int'l*, pg. 309
NESTOR GVG MBH & CO. OBJEKT VILLINGEN-SCHWENNIGEN KG—See Commerzbank AG; *Int'l*, pg. 309
NESTRANS LOGISTIK GMBH—See Fried. Krupp AG; *Int'l*, pg. 515
NESTRANS SEEHAFENSPEDITION GMBH—See Fried. Krupp AG; *Int'l*, pg. 514
THE NET MARKET COMPANY—See Cendant Corporation; *U.S. Public*, pg. 321
NETAS-NORTHERN ELECTRIC TELEKOMUNIKASYON A.S.—See Northern Telecom Limited; *Int'l*, pg. 970
NETHAVEN—See Computer Associates International, Inc.; *U.S. Public*, pg. 420
NETHERLANDS CAR B.V.—See Mitsubishi Motors Corporation; *Int'l*, pg. 876
NETHERLANDS CARIBBEAN BANK CUBA—See ING Groep N.V.; *Int'l*, pg. 651
THE NETHERLANDS INSURANCE—See ING Groep N.V.; *Int'l*, pg. 651
THE NETHERLANDS LIFE INS CO—See ING Groep N.V.; *Int'l*, pg. 651
NETHERLANDS MANAGEMENT COMPANY BV—See Compagnie de Suez; *Int'l*, pg. 314
NETLAB A.G.—See Compagnie des Machines Bull; *Int'l*, pg. 317
NETOPIA, INC.; *U.S. Public*, pg. 1168
NETRIX, CORP.; *U.S. Private*, pg. 791
NETSCAPE COMMUNICATIONS CORP.; *U.S. Public*, pg. 1168
NETSTAL-FRANCE SA—See Mannesmann A.G.; *Int'l*, pg. 836
NETSTAL-MASCHINEN AG—See Mannesmann A.G.; *Int'l*, pg. 836
NETSTAL SINGAPORE PTE. LTD.—See Mannesmann A.G.; *Int'l*, pg. 836
NETSTAL SKANDINAVIEN A/S—See Mannesmann A.G.; *Int'l*, pg. 836
NETSTAL VERTRIEBS GMBH—See Mannesmann A.G.; *Int'l*, pg. 836
NETSTAL-MAQUINAS SA—See Mannesmann A.G.; *Int'l*, pg. 836
NETTENBOUW B.V., AMERSFOORT—See Internatio-Muller N.V.; *Int'l*, pg. 681
NETTINGSDORFER BETEILIGUNGS AG—See Jefferson Smurfit Group p.l.c.; *Int'l*, pg. 1271
NETTLEFOLDS LTD.—See Brunel Holdings Plc; *Int'l*, pg. 231
NETTO BOUWMARKT BEHEER B.V.—See Vorwerk & Co.; *Int'l*, pg. 1481
NETWAVE TECHNOLOGIES, INC.—See Technitrol, Inc.; *U.S. Public*, pg. 1564
NETWAY BV—See KPN Koninklyke PTT Nederland NV; *Int'l*, pg. 720
NETWIZ LTD.—See IIS Intelligent Information Systems Ltd.; *Int'l*, pg. 645
NETWORK ACQUISITION CORP.—See Network Long Distance, Inc.; *U.S. Public*, pg. 1169
NETWORK AIR MEDICAL SYSTEMS, INC.—See Conseco Inc.; *U.S. Public*, pg. 433
NETWORK ASSOCIATES, INC.; *U.S. Public*, pg. 1168
NETWORK BUSS DIVISION—See Methode Electronics Inc.; *U.S. Public*, pg. 1101
NETWORK COMPUTING DEVICES, INC.; *U.S. Public*, pg. 1168
NETWORK EPO, INC.—See Humana Inc.; *U.S. Public*, pg. 848
NETWORK EQUIPMENT TECHNOLOGIES, INC.; *U.S. Public*, pg. 1168
NETWORK LONG DISTANCE, INC.; *U.S. Public*, pg. 1169
NETWORK MARKETING LIMITED—See Hewlett-Packard Company; *U.S. Public*, pg. 822
THE NETWORK OF CITY BUSINESS JOURNALS, INC.—See Advance Publications Inc.; *U.S. Private*, pg. 19
NETWORK PERIPHERALS INC.; *U.S. Public*, pg. 1169
NETWORK POWER & LIGHT—See Mylex Corporation; *U.S. Public*, pg. 1144
NETWORK REAL ESTATE INC.; *U.S. Private*, pg. 791
NETWORK SERVICES COMPANY; *U.S. Private*, pg. 791
NETWORK SOLUTIONS, INC.—See Science Applications International Corp.; *U.S. Private*, pg. 976
NETWORK SUPPORT PRODUCTS—See Harris Corporation; *U.S. Public*, pg. 792
NETWORK SYSTEMS AB—See Storage Technology Corporation; *U.S. Public*, pg. 1522
NETWORK SYSTEMS CORPORATION—See Storage Technology Corporation; *U.S. Public*, pg. 1522
NETWORK SYSTEMS CREDIT CORP.—See Storage Technology Corporation; *U.S. Public*, pg. 1522
NETWORK SYSTEMS GMBH—See Storage Technology Corporation; *U.S. Public*, pg. 1523
NETWORK SYSTEMS INTEGRATION—See General Electric Company; *U.S. Public*, pg. 711
NETWORK SYSTEMS LIMITED—See Storage Technology Corporation; *U.S. Public*, pg. 1522
NETWORK SYSTEMS NEDERLAND B.V.—See Storage Technology Corporation; *U.S. Public*, pg. 1523
NETWORK SYSTEMS NORGE A/S—See Storage Technology Corporation; *U.S. Public*, pg. 1522
NETWORK VENTURES LONG DISTANCE MEXICO HOLDINGS, INC.—See Motorola, Inc.; *U.S. Public*, pg. 1138
NETWORK VENTURES I, INC.—See Motorola, Inc.; *U.S. Public*, pg. 1138
NETWORK VENTURES TELECOM MEXICO, INC.—See Motorola, Inc.; *U.S. Public*, pg. 1138
NETWORK VENTURES II, INC.—See Motorola, Inc.; *U.S. Public*, pg. 1138
NETWORK WORLD BRAZIL—See International Data Group; *U.S. Private*, pg. 570
NETWORK WORLD, INC.—See International Data Group; *U.S. Private*, pg. 569
NETWORKING PRODUCTS—See Microdyne Corporation; *U.S. Public*, pg. 1105
NETWORKMCI SERVICES—See MCI Communications Corp.; *U.S. Public*, pg. 1024
NETWORKS AND PERIPHERALS LTD.—See IIS Intelligent Information Systems Ltd.; *Int'l*, pg. 645
NETZSCH INCORPORATED; *U.S. Private*, pg. 792
NEUE BAUMWOLL SPINNEREI UND WEBEREI HOF AG—See Bayerische Vereinsbank Group; *Int'l*, pg. 180
NEUEBAUM WOLL-SPINNEREI UND WEBEREI HOF A.G.; *Int'l*, pg. 922
NEULAND WOHNUNGSGESELLSCHAFT MBH—See Volkswagen AG; *Int'l*, pg. 1474
NEUMA VERMOEGSVERWALTUNGS GMBH—See Commerzbank AG; *Int'l*, pg. 310
NEUMAG USA CORPORATION—See Deutsche Babcock AG; *Int'l*, pg. 399
NEUMAN DISTRIBUTORS, INC.; *U.S. Public*, pg. 1169
NEUMANN (USA)—See Sennheiser Electronic Corp.; *U.S. Private*, pg. 984
NEUMATICA HIDRAULICA S. DE RL DE CV—See Mannesmann A.G.; *Int'l*, pg. 839
NEUMATICOS GOODYEAR SA—See The Goodyear Tire & Rubber Company; *U.S. Public*, pg. 753
THE NEUMAYER COMPANY—See Outokumpu Oyj; *Int'l*, pg. 1016
NEUMAYER GMBH—See Outokumpu Oyj; *Int'l*, pg. 1017
NEUMEYER CR, SPOL. SR.O—See Koninklijke Hoogovens N.V.; *Int'l*, pg. 755
NEUMEYER FLIESSPRESSEN GMBH—See Koninklijke Hoogovens N.V.; *Int'l*, pg. 755
NEUPER BETON BAUSTOFFWERKE GMBH & CO. KG—See Heidelberger Zement A.G.; *Int'l*, pg. 606
NEUROGEN CORPORATION; *U.S. Public*, pg. 1169
NEUTRALIS GVG MBH—See Commerzbank AG; *Int'l*, pg. 309
NEUTROGENA CORPORATION—See Johnson & Johnson; *U.S. Public*, pg. 928
NEUTROGENA PROVENCE SARL—See Johnson & Johnson; *U.S. Public*, pg. 928
NEUWEG FERTIGUNG G.M.B.H.—See NSK Ltd.; *Int'l*, pg. 904
NEUWIESEN IMMOBILIEN AG—See Sulzer Ltd.; *Int'l*, pg. 1305
NEVADA BELL—See SBC Communications Inc.; *U.S. Public*, pg. 1416
NEVADA CEMENT CO.—See Centex Corporation; *U.S. Public*, pg. 323
NEVADA HOLDING CO.—See Viking Office Products; *U.S. Public*, pg. 1721
NEVADA LANDING—See Circus Circus - Las Vegas; *U.S. Public*, pg. 375
NEVADA NATIONAL BANCORPORATION—See BankAmerica Corporation; *U.S. Public*, pg. 181
NEVADA POWER COMPANY; *U.S. Public*, pg. 1169
NEVADA STATE BANK—See Zions Bancorporation; *U.S. Public*, pg. 1793
NEVAMAR DIVISION—See International Paper Company; *U.S. Public*, pg. 903
A/O NEVAMASH—See Caterpillar Inc.; *U.S. Public*, pg. 317
NEVCO HOUSEWARES, INC.—See Publicker Industries Inc.; *U.S. Public*, pg. 1341
NEVI DANMARK A/S—See Skandia Insurance Company Limited; *Int'l*, pg. 1257
NEVI FINANS A/S—See Skandia Insurance Company Limited; *Int'l*, pg. 1257
NEVINAR LTD.—See Clarins; *Int'l*, pg. 296
NEVITTS LIMITED—See HSBC Holdings plc; *Int'l*, pg. 583
NEW AGE INTIMATES INC.; *U.S. Private*, pg. 792
NEW ALBANY GAZETTE—See Landmark Communications, Inc.; *U.S. Private*, pg. 648
NEW AMERICA FINANCIAL, INC.—See FirstCity Financial Corporation; *U.S. Public*, pg. 644
NEW APPLE LINES, INC.; *U.S. Private*, pg. 792
THE NEW BAKERY COMPANY OF OHIO, INC.—See Wendy's International Inc.; *U.S. Public*, pg. 1754
NEW BALANCE ATHLETIC SHOE, INC.; *U.S. Private*, pg. 792
NEW BALANCE CANADA INC.—See New Balance Athletic Shoe, Inc.; *U.S. Private*, pg. 792
NEW BEDFORD PANORAMEX CORPORATION; *U.S. Private*, pg. 792
NEW BRITANNIA MINE—See TVX Gold Inc.; *Int'l*, pg. 1345
NEW BROOK PAPER—See Triangle Marketing Corp.; *U.S. Private*, pg. 1102
NEW BRUNSWICK POWER CORPORATION; *Int'l*, pg. 923
NEW BRUNSWICK SCIENTIFIC BENELUX B.V.—See New Brunswick Scientific Co., Inc.; *U.S. Public*, pg. 1170
NEW BRUNSWICK SCIENTIFIC CO., INC.; *U.S. Public*, pg. 1169
NEW BRUNSWICK SCIENTIFIC CO., INC.—See New Brunswick Scientific Co., Inc.; *U.S. Public*, pg. 1170
NEW BRUNSWICK SCIENTIFIC GMBH—See New Brunswick Scientific Co., Inc.; *U.S. Public*, pg. 1170
NEW BRUNSWICK SCIENTIFIC S.A.R.L.—See New Brunswick Scientific Co., Inc.; *U.S. Public*, pg. 1170
NEW BRUNSWICK SCIENTIFIC (UK) LTD.—See New Brunswick Scientific Co., Inc.; *U.S. Public*, pg. 1170
THE NEW BRUNSWICK TELEPHONE COMPANY, LIMITED (NBTEL)—See Bruncor, Inc.; *Int'l*, pg. 230
NEW BUSINESS—See The Rouse Company; *U.S. Public*, pg. 1407
NEW BUSINESS DEVELOPMENT—See The Broken Hill Proprietary Company Limited; *Int'l*, pg. 224
NEW CASTLE CHASSIS SYSTEMS DIV.—See Chrysler Corporation; *U.S. Public*, pg. 353
NEW CASTLE CORP.—See Circus Circus - Las Vegas; *U.S. Public*, pg. 375
NEW CASTLE INDUSTRIES, INC.—See Ampco-Pittsburgh Corporation; *U.S. Public*, pg. 104
NEW CASTLE REFRACTORY CO.—See Dixon Ticonderoga Company; *U.S. Public*, pg. 515
NEW CENTURY ENERGIES, INC.; *U.S. Public*, pg. 1170
NEW CENTURY MEDIA; *U.S. Private*, pg. 792
NEW CII COMPUTER, INC.—See Bell Atlantic Corporation; *U.S. Public*, pg. 203
NEW COLEMAN HOLDINGS INC.—See MacAndrews & Forbes Holdings Inc.; *U.S. Private*, pg. 690
NEW COMPUTER SERVICE CO., LTD. (NCS)—See Marcam Solutions, Inc.; *U.S. Public*, pg. 1043
NEW COOPERATIVE INC.; *U.S. Private*, pg. 792
NEW DELHI REPRESENTATIVE OFFICE—See The Fuji Bank, Limited; *Int'l*, pg. 520
S.A. NEW DENAEYER THERMAL INDUSTRIES N.D.T.I.—See Cockerill Sambre; *Int'l*, pg. 301
NEW DIMENSIONS IN EDUCATION—See Abrams & Co. Publishing Inc.; *U.S. Private*, pg. 10
NEW ELLIOTT CORPORATION—See Ebara Corporation; *Int'l*, pg. 432
THE NEW ENGLAND—See Metropolitan Life Insurance Co.; *U.S. Private*, pg. 737
NEW ENGLAND BUSINESS SERVICE, INC.; *U.S. Public*, pg. 1170
NEW ENGLAND CENTERLESS GRINDING—See Delta plc; *Int'l*, pg. 391
NEW ENGLAND COFFEE COMPANY; *U.S. Private*, pg. 792
NEW ENGLAND CONFECTIONERY CO.—See UIS, Inc.; *U.S. Private*, pg. 1113

MASTER INDEX TO COMPANY NAMES NEW

Company Index

NEW ENGLAND CONTROLS CORP.—See Applied Power Inc.; *U.S. Public*, pg. 124
NEW ENGLAND CORRECT CRAFT, INC.—See Correct Craft, Inc.; *U.S. Private*, pg. 277
NEW ENGLAND CRINC.—See Wellman, Inc.; *U.S. Public*, pg. 1753
NEW ENGLAND DAIRIES, INC.; *U.S. Private*, pg. 793
NEW ENGLAND ELECTRIC RESOURCES, INC.—See New England Electric System; *U.S. Public*, pg. 1171
NEW ENGLAND ELECTRIC SYSTEM; *U.S. Public*, pg. 1171
NEW ENGLAND ELECTRIC TRANSMISSION CORP.—See New England Electric System; *U.S. Public*, pg. 1171
NEW ENGLAND ENERGY, INC.—See New England Electric System; *U.S. Public*, pg. 1171
NEW ENGLAND FROZEN FOODS, INC.; *U.S. Private*, pg. 793
NEW ENGLAND HEALTH CARE—See National Home Health Care Corp.; *U.S. Public*, pg. 1157
NEW ENGLAND HYDRO FINANCE COMPANY, INC.—See New England Electric System; *U.S. Public*, pg. 1171
NEW ENGLAND HYDRO-TRANSMISSION CORPORATION—See New England Electric System; *U.S. Public*, pg. 1171
NEW ENGLAND HYDRO-TRANSMISSION ELECTRIC COMPANY, INC.—See New England Electric System; *U.S. Public*, pg. 1171
NEW ENGLAND INSURANCE COMPANY—See The Hartford Financial Services Group Inc.; *U.S. Public*, pg. 794
NEW ENGLAND INVESTMENT ASSOCIATES—See Metropolitan Life Insurance Co.; *U.S. Private*, pg. 737
NEW ENGLAND INVESTMENT COMPANIES, INC.—See Metropolitan Life Insurance Co.; *U.S. Private*, pg. 737
NEW ENGLAND LAMINATES CO., INC.—See Park Electrochemical Corporation; *U.S. Public*, pg. 1258
NEW ENGLAND LAMINATES (U.K.) LTD.—See Park Electrochemical Corporation; *U.S. Public*, pg. 1258
NEW ENGLAND LIFE INSURANCE CO—See Metropolitan Life Insurance Co.; *U.S. Private*, pg. 738
NEW ENGLAND LIFE MORTGAGE FUNDING CORP.—See Metropolitan Life Insurance Co.; *U.S. Private*, pg. 738
NEW ENGLAND MACHINERY, INC.; *U.S. Private*, pg. 793
NEW ENGLAND NEWSPAPER SUPPLY COMPANY, INC.; *U.S. Private*, pg. 793
NEW ENGLAND NEWSPAPERS, INC.-THE TIMES—See Journal Register Company; *U.S. Public*, pg. 935
NEW ENGLAND PENSION & ANNUITY CO.—See Metropolitan Life Insurance Co.; *U.S. Private*, pg. 738
NEW ENGLAND POWER CO.—See New England Electric System; *U.S. Public*, pg. 1171
NEW ENGLAND POWER SERVICE CO.—See New England Electric System; *U.S. Public*, pg. 1171
NEW ENGLAND REINSURANCE CORPORATION—See The Hartford Financial Services Group Inc.; *U.S. Public*, pg. 794
NEW ENGLAND RESEARCH, INC.—See McLaughlin Gormley King Company; *U.S. Private*, pg. 724
NEW ENGLAND SECURITIES CORP.—See Metropolitan Life Insurance Co.; *U.S. Private*, pg. 738
NEW ENGLAND STONE INDUSTRIES, INC.; *U.S. Private*, pg. 793
NEW ENGLAND TAP CORPORATION (NETCO)—See Cincinnati Milacron Inc.; *U.S. Public*, pg. 368
NEW ENGLAND TECHNOLOGY GROUP, INC.; *U.S. Private*, pg. 793
NEW ENGLAND TRUST COMPANY—See First of America Bank Corporation; *U.S. Public*, pg. 637
NEW ENGLAND WHOLESALE DRUG COMPANY—See Bindley Western Industries, Inc.; *U.S. Public*, pg. 229
NEW ERA CAP. CO.; *U.S. Private*, pg. 793
NEW FARM CROPS—See Novartis AG; *Int'l*, pg. 983
NEW FOOD INGREDIENTS, LTD.—See Newly Weds Foods Inc.; *U.S. Private*, pg. 797
NEW FORTIS CORP.—See Hovnanian Enterprises, Inc.; *U.S. Public*, pg. 843
NEW FRONTIERS—See Nouvelles Frontieres; *Int'l*, pg. 971
THE NEW GALVESTON COMPANY—See Cullen/Frost Bankers, Inc.; *U.S. Public*, pg. 467
NEW HAMPSHIRE BALL BEARINGS, INC.—See Minebea Co., Ltd.; *Int'l*, pg. 868
NEW HAMPSHIRE BALL BEARINGS, PRECISION PRODUCTS GROUP—See Minebea Co., Ltd.; *Int'l*, pg. 868
NEW HAMPSHIRE INSURANCE GROUP—See American International Group, Inc.; *U.S. Public*, pg. 84
NEW HAVEN MFG. CORP.; *U.S. Private*, pg. 793
NEW HAVEN REGISTER, INC.—See Journal Register Company; *U.S. Public*, pg. 935
NEW HAVEN SAVINGS BANK; *U.S. Private*, pg. 793
NEW HERMES INCORPORATED; *U.S. Private*, pg. 793
NEW HERMES, LTD.—See New Hermes Incorporated; *U.S. Private*, pg. 794
NEW HOLLAND LTD.—See Fiat Auto SpA; *Int'l*, pg. 484
THE NEW HOME SEWING MACHINE CO.—See Janome Sewing Machine Co., Ltd.; *Int'l*, pg. 699
NEW HOMEBUYER'S TITLE—See Washington Homes, Inc.; *U.S. Public*, pg. 1741
NEW HONG KONG TUNNEL CO., LTD.—See Kumagai Gumi Co., Ltd.; *Int'l*, pg. 764
NEW HORIZONS LLC; *U.S. Private*, pg. 794
NEW HUNTER ENGINEERING—See FKI Plc; *Int'l*, pg. 474
NEW INGENIA SA—See Mikron Holding AG; *Int'l*, pg. 866
NEW JERSEY-AMERICAN RESOURCES COMPANY—See American Water Works Company, Inc.; *U.S. Public*, pg. 95
NEW JERSEY-AMERICAN WATER CO.—See American Water Works Company, Inc.; *U.S. Public*, pg. 95
NEW JERSEY NATIONAL BANK—See CoreStates Financial Corp.; *U.S. Public*, pg. 447
NEW JERSEY NATURAL GAS CO.—See New Jersey Resources Corporation; *U.S. Public*, pg. 1172
NEW JERSEY RESOURCES CORPORATION; *U.S. Public*, pg. 1172
NEW JERSEY SIGN COMPANY INC.—See Edison Parking Properties, LLC; *U.S. Private*, pg. 364
NJ TRANSIT; *U.S. Private*, pg. 794
NEW JERSEY TRANSIT BUS OPERATIONS—See NJ Transit; *U.S. Private*, pg. 794
NEW JERSEY TRANSIT RAIL OPERATIONS—See NJ Transit; *U.S. Private*, pg. 794
NEW LINDEN PRICE RITE, INC.—See Foodarama Supermarkets, Inc.; *U.S. Public*, pg. 661
NEW LINE CINEMA CORPORATION—See Time Warner Inc.; *U.S. Public*, pg. 1614
NEW LINE DISTRIBUTION, INC.—See Time Warner Inc.; *U.S. Public*, pg. 1615
NEW LINE HOME VIDEO, INC.—See Time Warner Inc.; *U.S. Public*, pg. 1615
NEW LINE INTERNATIONAL RELEASING, INC.—See Time Warner Inc.; *U.S. Public*, pg. 1615
NEW LINE MARKETING, INC.—See Time Warner Inc.; *U.S. Public*, pg. 1615
NEW LINE PRODUCTIONS, INC.—See Time Warner Inc.; *U.S. Public*, pg. 1615
NEW LONDON TELEPHONE COMPANY—See Telephone and Data Systems, Inc.; *U.S. Public*, pg. 1571
THE NEW LONDON TRUST COMPANY—See Sun Life Assurance Company of Canada; *Int'l*, pg. 1319
NEW MARKET FOODS—See J. Sainsbury plc; *Int'l*, pg. 1170
NEW MATHER METALS INC.—See NHK Spring Co., Ltd.; *Int'l*, pg. 902
NEW MECH COMPANIES, INC.; *U.S. Private*, pg. 794
NEW MEDIA COMMUNICATION—See Harmonic Lightwaves; *U.S. Public*, pg. 788
NEW MEXICO-AMERICAN WATER CO.—See American Water Works Company, Inc.; *U.S. Public*, pg. 95
NEW MEXICO & ARIZONA LAND CO.; *U.S. Public*, pg. 1172
NEW MEXICO BROADCASTING CO.—See Lee Enterprises, Incorporated; *U.S. Public*, pg. 984
NEW MEXICO STAR TRIBUNE COMPANY—See The E.W. Scripps Company; *U.S. Public*, pg. 1448
NEW MEXICO UTILITIES, INC.—See Southwest Water Company; *U.S. Public*, pg. 1494
NEW MEXICO WOMENS CORRECTIONAL FACILITY—See Corrections Corporation of America; *U.S. Public*, pg. 450
NEW MOTOREST SA—See GIB Group; *Int'l*, pg. 533
NEW NORTH MEDIA INC.—See Bruncor, Inc.; *Int'l*, pg. 230
NEW NORTH MEDIA INC.—See Northern Telecom Limited; *Int'l*, pg. 969
NEW OJI PAPER CO., LTD.—See Oji Paper Co., Ltd.; *Int'l*, pg. 998
NEW ORLEANS LABORATORY—See Pace Analytical Services; *U.S. Private*, pg. 829
NEW ORLEANS RIVERWALK ASSOCIATES—See Cigna Corp.; *U.S. Public*, pg. 361
NEW ORLEANS WATERFRONT REST. CORP.—See Specialty Restaurants Corporation; *U.S. Private*, pg. 1023
NEW PIER OPERATING COMPANY, INC.—See Griffin Group, Inc.; *U.S. Private*, pg. 480
THE NEW PIPER AIRCRAFT, INC.; *U.S. Private*, pg. 794
NEW PLAN REALTY TRUST; *U.S. Public*, pg. 1172
NEW PLAN SECURITIES CORP.—See New Plan Realty Trust; *U.S. Public*, pg. 1173
NEW PROCESS GEAR DIV.—See Chrysler Corporation; *U.S. Public*, pg. 353
NEW PROGRESS—See TSI Holdings, Inc.; *U.S. Private*, pg. 1066
NEW PROVIDENCE CORP.—See Allendale Mutual Insurance Co.; *U.S. Private*, pg. 37
NEW SOUTH INSURANCE COMPANY—See General Motors Corporation; *U.S. Public*, pg. 720
NEW STANDARD CORPORATION; *U.S. Private*, pg. 794
NEW SYSTECH CORPORATION—See Lafarge S.A.; *Int'l*, pg. 788
NEW TAI MILK PRODUCTS CO. LTD.—See New Zealand Dairy Board; *Int'l*, pg. 923
NEW TECH COATINGS LTD.—See BTR plc; *Int'l*, pg. 124
NEW TENN COMPANY—See Tenneco Inc.; *U.S. Public*, pg. 1578
NEW UNITED MOTOR MANUFACTURING INC.—See Toyota Motor Corporation; *Int'l*, pg. 1413
NEW VALLEY CORPORATION; *U.S. Public*, pg. 1173
NEW VALLEY REALTY CORP.—See New Valley Corporation; *U.S. Public*, pg. 1173
NEW VANDEN BOORE S.A.—See Electrolux, AB; *Int'l*, pg. 441
NEW VENTURES DIVISION—See Blue Cross and Blue Shield of Massachusetts; *U.S. Private*, pg. 151
NEW VISION TELEVISION; *U.S. Private*, pg. 794
NEW WOMAN MAGAZINE—See Rodale Press, Inc.; *U.S. Private*, pg. 939
NEW WORLD DEVELOPMENT CO. LTD.; *Int'l*, pg. 923
NEW WORLD DEVELOPMENT CORP. LTD.—See CoreStates Financial Corp.; *U.S. Public*, pg. 447
NEW WORLD ENTERTAINMENT, INC.—See The News Corporation Limited; *Int'l*, pg. 926
NEW WORLD HOTELS (HOLDINGS) LTD.—See Marriott International, Inc.; *U.S. Public*, pg. 1048
NEW YORK AIR BRAKE CORPORATION—See Knorr-Bremse AG; *Int'l*, pg. 738
NEW YORK-AMERICAN WATER CO., INC.—See American Water Works Company, Inc.; *U.S. Public*, pg. 95
NEW YORK CARPET WORLD—See Shaw Industries, Inc.; *U.S. Public*, pg. 1464
NEW YORK CASUALTY INSURANCE CO.—See Harleysville Group; *U.S. Public*, pg. 787
NEW YORK CITY OFF-TRACK BETTING CORP.; *U.S. Private*, pg. 794
NEW YORK CITY TRANSIT AUTHORITY—See Metropolitan Transportation Authority; *U.S. Private*, pg. 739
NEW YORK ENVELOPE CORP; *U.S. Private*, pg. 794
NEW YORK FINANCIAL CORP.—See Shepaug Corporation; *U.S. Private*, pg. 993
NEW YORK FROZEN FOODS, INC.—See Lancaster Colony Corporation; *U.S. Public*, pg. 977
NEW YORK INSTITUTE OF FINANCE—See National Amusements, Inc.; *U.S. Private*, pg. 778
NEW YORK ISLANDERS HOCKEY CLUB; *U.S. Private*, pg. 794
NEW YORK KNICKERBOCKERS—See Cablevision Systems Corporation; *U.S. Public*, pg. 288
NEW YORK LANGUAGE CENTER—See Berlitz International, Inc.; *U.S. Public*, pg. 222
NEW YORK LAW JOURNAL—See The Nomura Securities Co., Ltd.; *Int'l*, pg. 956
NYLIFE ADMINISTRATION CORP.—See New York Life Insurance Company; *U.S. Private*, pg. 795
NEW YORK LIFE & HEALTH INSURANCE COMPANY—See New York Life Insurance Company; *U.S. Private*, pg. 795
NYLIFE CARE—See New York Life Insurance Company; *U.S. Private*, pg. 795
NYLIFE DEPOSITARY CORPORATION—See New York Life Insurance Company; *U.S. Private*, pg. 795
NYLIFE EQUITY INC.—See New York Life Insurance Company; *U.S. Private*, pg. 795
NYLIFE FUNDING INC.—See New York Life Insurance Company; *U.S. Private*, pg. 795
NYLIFE INC.—See New York Life Insurance Company; *U.S. Private*, pg. 795
NEW YORK LIFE INSURANCE AND ANNUITY CORPORATION—See New York Life Insurance Company; *U.S. Private*, pg. 795
NEW YORK LIFE INSURANCE COMPANY; *U.S. Private*, pg. 794
NYLIFE INSURANCE COMPANY OF ARIZONA—See New York Life Insurance Company; *U.S. Private*, pg. 795
NEW YORK LIFE INSURANCE WORLDWIDE LTD.—See New York Life Insurance Company; *U.S. Private*, pg. 795
NEW YORK LIFE INTERNATIONAL INVESTMENT—See New York Life Insurance Company; *U.S. Private*, pg. 795
NYLIFE REALTY INC.—See New York Life Insurance Company; *U.S. Private*, pg. 795
NYLIFE SECURITIES INC.—See New York Life Insurance Company; *U.S. Private*, pg. 795
NEW YORK LIFE (U.K.) LIMITED—See New York Life Insurance Company; *U.S. Private*, pg. 795
NEW YORK LIFE WORLDWIDE HOLDING, INC.—See New York Life Insurance Company; *U.S. Private*, pg. 795
NEW YORK MAGAZINE—See Primedia Inc.; *U.S. Public*, pg. 1328
THE NEW YORK OBSERVER—See Shepaug Corporation; *U.S. Private*, pg. 993
THE NEW YORK POST—See The News Corporation Limited; *Int'l*, pg. 927
NEW YORK RACING ASSOCIATION; *U.S. Private*, pg. 795
NEW YORK RANGERS HOCKEY CLUB—See Cablevision Systems Corporation; *U.S. Public*, pg. 288
NEW YORK REVENUE AUTOMATION—See Cubic Corporation; *U.S. Public*, pg. 466
NEW YORK STATE ELECTRIC & GAS CORPORATION; *U.S. Public*, pg. 1173
NEW YORK SWITCH CORPORATION—See The Chase Manhattan Corporation; *U.S. Public*, pg. 339
NEW YORK SYSTEMS EXCHANGE CORP.—See Syracuse Supply Company; *U.S. Private*, pg. 1060
THE NEW YORK TIMES—See The New York Times Company; *U.S. Public*, pg. 1174
THE NEW YORK TIMES BROADCASTING SERVICE, INC.—See The New York Times Company; *U.S. Public*, pg. 1173
THE NEW YORK TIMES COMPANY; *U.S. Public*, pg. 1173
THE NEW YORK TIMES COMPANY BROADCASTING GROUP—See The New York Times Company; *U.S. Public*, pg. 1173
NEW YORK TIMES COMPANY FOREST PRODUCTS GROUP—See The New York Times Company; *U.S. Public*, pg. 1174
THE NEW YORK TIMES COMPANY REGIONAL NEWSPAPER GROUP—See The New York Times Company; *U.S. Public*, pg. 1174
THE NEW YORK TIMES DISTRIBUTION CORP.—See The New York Times Company; *U.S. Public*, pg. 1176
THE NEW YORK TIMES ELECTRONIC MEDIA CO.—See The New York Times Company; *U.S. Public*, pg. 1176
THE NEW YORK TIMES INDEX—See The New York Times Company; *U.S. Public*, pg. 1174
THE NEW YORK TIMES INFORMATION SERVICES GROUP—See The New York Times Company; *U.S. Public*, pg. 1174
THE NEW YORK TIMES MAGAZINE COMPANY GROUP—See The New York Times Company; *U.S. Public*, pg. 1174
THE NEW YORK TIMES NEWS SERVICE—See The New York Times Company; *U.S. Public*, pg. 1174
NEW YORK TIMES NEWSPAPER GROUP—See The New York Times Company; *U.S. Public*, pg. 1174
THE NEW YORK TIMES SALES, INC.—See The New York Times Company; *U.S. Public*, pg. 1176
THE NEW YORK TIMES SYNDICATE—See The New York Times Company; *U.S. Public*, pg. 1174
THE NEW YORK TIMES SYNDICATION SALES CORPORATION—See The New York Times Company; *U.S. Public*, pg. 1174
NEW YORK TWIST DRILL DIV.—See Regal-Beloit Corporation; *U.S. Public*, pg. 1370
NEW YORK WATER SERVICE CORP.—See Shepaug Corporation; *U.S. Private*, pg. 993
NEW YORK WIRE CO.; *U.S. Private*, pg. 795
NEW YORKER BOILER CO., INC.—See Burnham; *U.S. Public*, pg. 270
THE NEW YORKER - CALIFORNIA—See The New Yorker Magazine; *U.S. Private*, pg. 796

THE NEW YORKER MAGAZINE; *U.S. Private*, pg. 795
NEW ZEALAND ALUMINIUM SMELTERS LTD.—See Comalco Limited; *Int'l*, pg. 307
NEW ZEALAND AMP LTD.—See AMP Incorporated; *U.S. Public*, pg. 9
NEW ZEALAND CONTROLS LTD.—See Siebe plc; *Int'l*, pg. 1244
NEW ZEALAND DAIRY BOARD; *Int'l*, pg. 923
NEW ZEALAND FIBRE GLASS—See International Paper Company; *U.S. Public*, pg. 904
NEW ZEALAND FOREST PRODUCTS LIMITED—See International Paper Company; *U.S. Public*, pg. 905
NEW ZEALAND GLASS MANUFACTURERS CO.—See BTR plc; *Int'l*, pg. 129
NEW ZEALAND LAMB CO., INC.; *U.S. Private*, pg. 796
NEW ZEALAND MILK PRODUCTS (CIS) AO—See New Zealand Dairy Board; *Int'l*, pg. 923
NEW ZEALAND MILK PRODUCTS (NORTH ASIA) LTD—See New Zealand Dairy Board; *Int'l*, pg. 923
NEW ZEALAND MILK PRODUCTS (PACIFIC) LTD.—See New Zealand Dairy Board; *Int'l*, pg. 923
NEW ZEALAND REFINING—See Royal Dutch/Shell Group of Companies; *Int'l*, pg. 1137
NEW ZEALAND STARCH—See Goodman Fielder Limited; *Int'l*, pg. 555
NEWAGE INDUSTRIES INC.; *U.S. Private*, pg. 796
NEWAGE INTERNATIONAL LTD.—See Cummins Engine Company, Inc.; *U.S. Public*, pg. 469
NEWARK ELECTRONICS CORPORATION—See Premier Farnell plc; *Int'l*, pg. 1068
THE NEWARK GROUP, INC.; *U.S. Private*, pg. 796
NEWARK INSURANCE CO.—See Royal & Sun Alliance Insurance Group plc; *Int'l*, pg. 1131
NEWARK MFG. DIVISION—See R.R. Donnelley & Sons Company; *U.S. Public*, pg. 518
NEWARK PAPERBOARD PRODUCTS MERCER DIV.—See The Newark Group, Inc.; *U.S. Private*, pg. 796
NEWAY ANCHORLOK INTERNATIONAL INC.; *U.S. Private*, pg. 796
NEWBERG PERINI—See Perini Corporation; *U.S. Public*, pg. 1278
NEWBOLD CORPORATION; *U.S. Private*, pg. 796
W.H. NEWBOLD—See Fahnestock Viner Holdings Inc.; *Int'l*, pg. 476
NEWBOLD'S ASSET MANAGEMENT INC.—See United Asset Management Corporation; *U.S. Public*, pg. 1673
NEWBRIDGE COMMUNICATIONS, INC.—See Bertelsmann AG; *Int'l*, pg. 191
NEWBRIDGE NETWORKS CORPORATION; *Int'l*, pg. 923
NEWBRIDGE NETWORKS CORPORATION—See Newbridge Networks Corporation; *Int'l*, pg. 924
NEWBRIDGE NETWORKS INC.—See Newbridge Networks Corporation; *Int'l*, pg. 924
NEWBRIDGE NETWORKS LIMITED—See Newbridge Networks Corporation; *Int'l*, pg. 924
NEWBRIDGE SECURITIES, INC.—See Citicorp; *U.S. Public*, pg. 378
NEWBURGH & SOUTH SHORE RAILROAD COMPANY—See Broe Companies; *U.S. Private*, pg. 171
NEWBURGH AUTO AUCTION—See Cox Enterprises, Inc.; *U.S. Private*, pg. 282
NEWBURY INSURANCE CO.—See Metropolitan Life Insurance Co.; *U.S. Private*, pg. 738
NEWCAP BROADCASTING—See Newfoundland Capital Corporation Limited; *Int'l*, pg. 924
NEWCARE HEALTH CORPORATION; *U.S. Public*, pg. 1176
THE NEWCASTLE BREWERIES, LTD.—See Scottish & Newcastle plc; *Int'l*, pg. 1211
NEWCASTLE COATED PAPER INC.—See Repap Enterprises Inc.; *Int'l*, pg. 1104
NEWCASTLE LABORATORIES—See The Broken Hill Proprietary Company Limited; *Int'l*, pg. 227
NEWCASTLE NEWSPAPERS PTY. LIMITED—See John Fairfax Holdings Limited; *Int'l*, pg. 477
NEWCASTLE STEELWORKS—See The Broken Hill Proprietary Company Limited; *Int'l*, pg. 227
NEWCASTLE WIRE MILL—See The Broken Hill Proprietary Company Limited; *Int'l*, pg. 226
NEWCOM, INC.—See Aura Systems, Inc.; *U.S. Public*, pg. 147
NEWCOM PUBLICATIONS INC.—See Lagardere Groupe; *Int'l*, pg. 795
D.W. NEWCOMER'S SONS, INC.; *U.S. Private*, pg. 796
NEWCOR BAY CITY DIVISION—See Newcor, Inc.; *U.S. Public*, pg. 1176
NEWCOR, INC.; *U.S. Public*, pg. 1176
NEWCOURT CREDIT GROUP INC.; *Int'l*, pg. 924
NEWCOURT FINANCIAL USA, INC.—See Newcourt Credit Group Inc.; *Int'l*, pg. 924
NEWELL BRIDGE & RAILWAY COMPANY—See The Homer Laughlin China Company; *U.S. Private*, pg. 653
NEWELL CO.; *U.S. Public*, pg. 1176
THE NEWELL COMPANY—See The Homer Laughlin China Company; *U.S. Private*, pg. 653
NEWELL INDUSTRIES CANADA, INC.—See Newell Co.; *U.S. Public*, pg. 1178
NEWELL OPERATING COMPANY—See Newell Co.; *U.S. Public*, pg. 1177
NEWELL PAPER CO. OF HATTIESBURG—See Jackson Paper Company; *U.S. Private*, pg. 579
NEWELL PAPER CO. OF MERIDIAN—See Jackson Paper Company; *U.S. Private*, pg. 579
NEWELL PUERTO RICO, LTD.—See Newell Co.; *U.S. Public*, pg. 1177
NEWELL WINDOW FURNISHINGS CO.—See Newell Co.; *U.S. Public*, pg. 1177
NEWEY & EYRE LTD.—See BTR plc; *Int'l*, pg. 125
NEWFOUNDLAND CAPITAL CORPORATION LIMITED; *Int'l*, pg. 924
NEWFOUNDLAND CONTAINERS LTD.—See The Cascades Group; *Int'l*, pg. 273
NEWFOUNDLAND GEOSCIENCES, LTD.—See Fugro Group Companies; *U.S. Private*, pg. 431

THE NEWHALL LAND AND FARMING COMPANY; *U.S. Public*, pg. 1178
NEWHALL REFINING CO.—See Lonrho plc; *Int'l*, pg. 818
NEWHAWK GOLD MINES LTD.—See Homestake Mining Company; *U.S. Public*, pg. 833
NEWHOUSE NEWSPAPERS METRO-SUBURBIA, INC.—See Advance Publications Inc.; *U.S. Private*, pg. 20
NEWLANDS COAL PTY. LTD.—See M.I.M. Holdings Ltd.; *Int'l*, pg. 827
NEWLY WEDS FOODS ASIA/PACIFIC—See Newly Weds Foods Inc.; *U.S. Private*, pg. 797
NEWLY WEDS FOODS INC.; *U.S. Private*, pg. 796
NEWMAN'S OWN, INC.; *U.S. Private*, pg. 797
NEWMANS OWN ORGANICS—See Newman's Own, Inc.; *U.S. Private*, pg. 797
NEWMARKET COMPANY—See The Jaydor Corporation; *U.S. Private*, pg. 584
NEWMAX CO., LTD.—See Tai-Il Media Co.; *Int'l*, pg. 1347
NEWMOND PLC; *Int'l*, pg. 924
NEWMONT EXPLORATION LTD.—See Newmont Mining Corporation; *U.S. Public*, pg. 1179
NEWMONT EXPLORATION OF CANADA—See Newmont Mining Corporation; *U.S. Public*, pg. 1179
NEWMONT GOLD COMPANY—See Newmont Mining Corporation; *U.S. Public*, pg. 1179
NEWMONT MINING CORPORATION; *U.S. Public*, pg. 1178
NEWPARK ENVIRONMENTAL SERVICES, INC.—See Newpark Resources, Inc.; *U.S. Public*, pg. 1179
NEWPARK RESOURCES, INC.; *U.S. Public*, pg. 1179
NEWPORT—See Metropolitan Life Insurance Co.; *U.S. Private*, pg. 738
NEWPORT AMERICA CORPORATION—See Providence Energy Corporation; *U.S. Public*, pg. 1337
NEWPORT B.V.—See Newport Corporation; *U.S. Public*, pg. 1179
NEWPORT CORPORATION; *U.S. Public*, pg. 1179
THE NEWPORT DAILY EXPRESS—See Pulitzer Publishing Company; *U.S. Public*, pg. 1343
NEWPORT ELECTRIC CORPORATION—See Eastern Utilities Associates; *U.S. Public*, pg. 550
NEWPORT ELECTRONICS B.V.—See OMEGA Engineering, Inc.; *U.S. Private*, pg. 816
NEWPORT ELECTRONICS GMBH—See OMEGA Engineering, Inc.; *U.S. Private*, pg. 816
NEWPORT ELECTRONICS, INC.—See OMEGA Engineering, Inc.; *U.S. Private*, pg. 816
NEWPORT ELECTRONICS LTD.—See OMEGA Engineering, Inc.; *U.S. Private*, pg. 816
NEWPORT ELECTRONIQUE, S.A.R.L.—See OMEGA Engineering, Inc.; *U.S. Private*, pg. 816
NEWPORT GMBH—See Newport Corporation; *U.S. Public*, pg. 1179
NEWPORT INSTRUMENTS AG—See Newport Corporation; *U.S. Public*, pg. 1179
NEWPORT INSTRUMENTS CANADA CORP.—See Newport Corporation; *U.S. Public*, pg. 1179
NEWPORT LANDING—See BRE Properties, Inc.; *U.S. Public*, pg. 163
NEWPORT LEARNING CENTER—See Berkshire Hathaway Inc.; *U.S. Public*, pg. 219
NEWPORT LTD.—See Newport Corporation; *U.S. Public*, pg. 1179
NEWPORT NEWS, INC.—See Spiegel, Inc.; *U.S. Public*, pg. 1499
NEWPORT NEWS INDUSTRIAL CORP.—See Newport News Shipbuilding, Inc.; *U.S. Public*, pg. 1180
NEWPORT NEWS INDUSTRIAL CORP. OF OHIO—See Newport News Shipbuilding, Inc.; *U.S. Public*, pg. 1180
NEWPORT NEWS OFFSHORE SYSTEMS CORP.—See Newport News Shipbuilding, Inc.; *U.S. Public*, pg. 1180
NEWPORT NEWS REACTOR SERVICES, INC.—See Newport News Shipbuilding, Inc.; *U.S. Public*, pg. 1180
NEWPORT NEWS SHIPBUILDING, INC.; *U.S. Public*, pg. 1179
NEWPORT NEWS TECHNICAL SERVICES, INC. (WISCONSIN)—See Newport News Shipbuilding, Inc.; *U.S. Public*, pg. 1180
NEWPORT-NEWS TIMES—See Lee Enterprises, Incorporated; *U.S. Public*, pg. 984
NEWPORT STEEL CORPORATION—See NS Group, Inc.; *U.S. Public*, pg. 1147
NEWPORT TIMBER—See Interstate Resources, Inc.; *U.S. Private*, pg. 573
NEWS AMERICA HOLDINGS INC.—See The News Corporation Limited; *Int'l*, pg. 925
NEWS AMERICA MARKETING—See The News Corporation Limited; *Int'l*, pg. 925
NEWS AMERICA PUBLISHING INC.—See The News Corporation Limited; *Int'l*, pg. 925
THE NEWS & OBSERVER—See McClatchy Newspapers Inc.; *U.S. Public*, pg. 1065
NEWS & RECORD—See Landmark Communications, Inc.; *U.S. Private*, pg. 649
THE NEWS AND REPORTER—See Landmark Communications, Inc.; *U.S. Private*, pg. 648
THE NEWS CORPORATION LIMITED; *Int'l*, pg. 925
THE NEWS-DEMOCRAT—See Landmark Communications, Inc.; *U.S. Private*, pg. 648
NEWS-ENTERPRISE—See Landmark Communications, Inc.; *U.S. Private*, pg. 648
NEWS HERALD—See Freedom Communication Inc.; *U.S. Private*, pg. 425
THE NEWS-HERALD (LAKE COUNTY)—See Journal Register Company; *U.S. Public*, pg. 935
NEWS HOLDINGS CORP.; *U.S. Private*, pg. 797
NEWS INTERNATIONAL PLC—See The News Corporation Limited; *Int'l*, pg. 927
THE NEWS-JOURNAL COMPANY—See Gannett Company, Inc.; *U.S. Public*, pg. 699
NEWS LIMITED OF AUSTRALIA—See The News Corporation Limited; *Int'l*, pg. 925
THE NEWS-PILOT—See The Copley Press, Inc.; *U.S. Private*, pg. 275

NEWS-PRESS & GAZETTE COMPANY; *U.S. Private*, pg. 797
NEWS-PRESS PUBLISHING CO.—See Gannett Company, Inc.; *U.S. Public*, pg. 701
NEWS PUBLISHING COMPANY—See Knight-Ridder, Inc.; *U.S. Public*, pg. 964
NEWS-STAR PUBLISHING COMPANY—See Gannett Company, Inc.; *U.S. Public*, pg. 700
THE NEWS-SUN—See The Copley Press, Inc.; *U.S. Private*, pg. 275
THE NEWS TRIBUNE—See McClatchy Newspapers Inc.; *U.S. Public*, pg. 1066
NEWSDAY—See The Times Mirror Company; *U.S. Public*, pg. 1616
NEWSEDGE—See NewsEdge Corporation; *U.S. Public*, pg. 1180
NEWSEDGE CANADA, INC.—See NewsEdge Corporation; *U.S. Public*, pg. 1180
NEWSEDGE CORP.—See NewsEdge Corporation; *U.S. Public*, pg. 1180
NEWSEDGE CORPORATION; *U.S. Public*, pg. 1180
NEWSEDGE CORPORATION—See NewsEdge Corporation; *U.S. Public*, pg. 1180
NEWSEDGE S.A.—See NewsEdge Corporation; *U.S. Public*, pg. 1180
NEWSPAPER ENTERPRISE ASSOC.—See The E.W. Scripps Company; *U.S. Public*, pg. 1448
NEWSPAPER ENTERPRISE ASSOCIATION—See The E.W. Scripps Company; *U.S. Public*, pg. 1448
NEWSPAPER SERVICES OF AMERICA, INC.—See The Interpublic Group of Companies, Inc.; *U.S. Public*, pg. 909
NEWSPAPERS FIRST—See Knight-Ridder, Inc.; *U.S. Public*, pg. 964
NEWSPRINT SOUTH; *U.S. Private*, pg. 797
NEWSQUEST MEDIA (CENTRAL)—See Newsquest Media Group; *Int'l*, pg. 927
NEWSQUEST MEDIA GROUP; *Int'l*, pg. 927
NEWSQUEST MEDIA (MANCHESTER)—See Newsquest Media Group; *Int'l*, pg. 927
NEWSWEEK INC.—See The Washington Post Company; *U.S. Public*, pg. 1743
NEWTEL COMMUNICATIONS—See BCE Inc.; *Int'l*, pg. 115
NEWTEL ENTERPRISES LIMITED—See BCE Inc.; *Int'l*, pg. 115
THE NEWTON KANSAN—See Shivers Trading & Operating Co.; *U.S. Private*, pg. 995
O.A. NEWTON & SON CO.; *U.S. Private*, pg. 797
NEWTON-SOUTHEASTERN MFG. DIV.—See R.R. Donnelley & Sons Company; *U.S. Public*, pg. 518
THE NEWTRON GROUP INC.; *U.S. Private*, pg. 797
NEXAIR—See nexAir, LLC; *U.S. Private*, pg. 797
NEXAIR, LLC; *U.S. Private*, pg. 797
NEXIS UK—See Reed Elsevier plc; *Int'l*, pg. 1096
NEXSTAR AUTOMATION, INC.—See Zygo Corporation; *U.S. Public*, pg. 1795
NEXSTAR PHARMACEUTICALS, INC.; *U.S. Public*, pg. 1180
NEXSTAR PHARMACEUTICALS, INC.—See Nexstar Pharmaceuticals, Inc.; *U.S. Public*, pg. 1180
NEXT DAY APPAREL—See The Leslie Fay Companies, Inc.; *U.S. Public*, pg. 989
NEXTEL COMMUNICATIONS; *U.S. Public*, pg. 1180
NEXTHEALTH INC.; *U.S. Public*, pg. 1181
NEXTLEVEL SYSTEMS (AUSTRALIA)—See General Instrument Corporation; *U.S. Public*, pg. 716
NEXTLEVEL SYSTEMS (BELGIUM)—See General Instrument Corporation; *U.S. Public*, pg. 716
NEXTLEVEL SYSTEMS (HONG KONG)—See General Instrument Corporation; *U.S. Public*, pg. 716
NEXTLEVEL SYSTEMS (JAPAN)—See General Instrument Corporation; *U.S. Public*, pg. 716
NEXTLINK COMMUNICATIONS INC.; *U.S. Public*, pg. 1181
NEXTRON—See Safeguard Scientifics, Inc.; *U.S. Public*, pg. 1424
NEXUS HEALTHCARE, INC.—See Cardinal Health Inc.; *U.S. Public*, pg. 304
NEXUS INTERNATIONAL INC.—See Caterpillar Inc.; *U.S. Public*, pg. 316
NEXUS PLASTICS, INC.; *U.S. Private*, pg. 797
NEY DENTAL INTERNATIONAL—See Degussa AG; *Int'l*, pg. 388
THE J.M. NEY COMPANY—See Andersen Group, Inc.; *U.S. Public*, pg. 111
NEY ULTRASONICS, INC.—See Andersen Group, Inc.; *U.S. Public*, pg. 111
AL NEYER, INC.; *U.S. Private*, pg. 797
NEYNABER CHEMIE GMBH—See Henkel KGaA; *Int'l*, pg. 610
NEYRPIC FRAMATOME MECANIQUE (NFM)—See Framatome SA; *Int'l*, pg. 503
NEZEL S.A.—See Solvay S.A.; *Int'l*, pg. 1279
NGEE ANN DEVELOPMENT PTE. LTD.—See Takashimaya Company, Limited; *Int'l*, pg. 1350
NHONG SHIM KELLOGG CO. LTD.—See Kellogg Company; *U.S. Public*, pg. 948
NI-TEX, INC.—See NIPSCO Industries, Inc.; *U.S. Public*, pg. 1185
NIACHLOR—See Olin Corporation; *U.S. Public*, pg. 1219
NIAGARA ASSET CORPORATION—See Keycorp; *U.S. Public*, pg. 955
NIAGARA BLOWER COMPANY; *U.S. Private*, pg. 798
NIAGARA COLD DRAWN CORP.—See Niagara Corporation; *U.S. Public*, pg. 1181
NIAGARA CORPORATION; *U.S. Public*, pg. 1181
NIAGARA CUTTER, INC.; *U.S. Private*, pg. 798
NIAGARA EXCHANGE CORPORATION—See Selective Insurance Group, Inc; *U.S. Public*, pg. 1455
NIAGARA FIRE INSURANCE CO.—See Loews Corporation; *U.S. Public*, pg. 1011
NIAGARA FRONTIER HOCKEY, L.P.; *U.S. Private*, pg. 798

NIAGARA FRONTIER TRANSIT & METRO SYSTEM—See Niagara Frontier Transportation Authority; *U.S. Private,* pg. 798
NIAGARA FRONTIER TRANSPORTATION AUTHORITY; *U.S. Private,* pg. 798
NIAGARA LANDFILL, INC.—See Browning-Ferris Industries, Inc.; *U.S. Public,* pg. 264
NIAGARA MOHAWK POWER CORPORATION; *U.S. Public,* pg. 1181
NIAGARA OF WISCONSIN—See Consolidated Papers, Inc.; *U.S. Public,* pg. 436
NIAGARA OF WISCONSIN PAPER CORP.—See Consolidated Papers, Inc.; *U.S. Public,* pg. 436
NIAGARA PORTFOLIO MANAGEMENT CORPORATION—See Keycorp; *U.S. Public,* pg. 955
NIAGARA RECYCLING, INC.—See Browning-Ferris Industries, Inc.; *U.S. Public,* pg. 264
NIAGARA STRUCTURAL STEEL—See Canadian Erectors Ltd.; *Int'l,* pg. 256
NIAGARA TRANSFORMER CORP.; *U.S. Private,* pg. 798
NIAGARASTEEL—See Canadian Erectors Ltd.; *Int'l,* pg. 256
NIANTIC NEWS—See Journal Register Company; *U.S. Public,* pg. 935
NIBCO, INC.; *U.S. Private,* pg. 798
NIBCO INC.—See NIBCO, Inc.; *U.S. Private,* pg. 798
NICA—See Groupe Casino; *Int'l,* pg. 563
NICE GARE—See GIB Group; *Int'l,* pg. 534
NICE-PAK PRODUCTS, INC.; *U.S. Private,* pg. 798
NICE SPECIALTY BEARINGS—See AB SKF; *Int'l,* pg. 1157
NICHES, INC.; *U.S. Public,* pg. 1181
NICHIFU AMERICA, INC.—See Nichifu Company Ltd.; *Int'l,* pg. 927
NICHIFU COMPANY LTD.; *Int'l,* pg. 927
NICHIMEN AMERICA, INC.—See Nichimen Corporation; *Int'l,* pg. 927
NICHIMEN AMERICA, INC., BOSTON OFFICE—See Nichimen Corporation; *Int'l,* pg. 928
NICHIMEN AMERICA, INC., CHICAGO BRANCH—See Nichimen Corporation; *Int'l,* pg. 928
NICHIMEN AMERICA, INC., DETROIT OFFICE—See Nichimen Corporation; *Int'l,* pg. 928
NICHIMEN AMERICA, INC., FRESNO OFFICE—See Nichimen Corporation; *Int'l,* pg. 928
NICHIMEN AMERICA, INC., HOUSTON BRANCH—See Nichimen Corporation; *Int'l,* pg. 928
NICHIMEN AMERICA, INC., LOS ANGELES BRANCH—See Nichimen Corporation; *Int'l,* pg. 928
NICHIMEN AMERICA, INC., SAN FRANCISCO BRANCH—See Nichimen Corporation; *Int'l,* pg. 928
NICHIMEN AMERICA, INC., SEATTLE BRANCH—See Nichimen Corporation; *Int'l,* pg. 928
NICHIMEN AMERICA, INC., WASHINGTON OFFICE—See Nichimen Corporation; *Int'l,* pg. 928
NICHIMEN AUSTRALIA LIMITED—See Nichimen Corporation; *Int'l,* pg. 928
NICHIMEN AUSTRALIA LTD.-MELBOURNE—See Nichimen Corporation; *Int'l,* pg. 928
NICHIMEN AUSTRALIA LTD.-PERTH—See Nichimen Corporation; *Int'l,* pg. 928
NICHIMEN CANADA INC.—See Nichimen Corporation; *Int'l,* pg. 928
NICHIMEN CANADA INC. VANCOUVER BRANCH—See Nichimen Corporation; *Int'l,* pg. 928
NICHIMEN CO., (HONG KONG) LTD.—See Nichimen Corporation; *Int'l,* pg. 928
NICHIMEN CORPORATION; *Int'l,* pg. 927
NICHIMEN DE MEXICO SA DE CV—See Nichimen Corporation; *Int'l,* pg. 928
NICHIMEN EUROPE PLC—See Nichimen Corporation; *Int'l,* pg. 928
NICHIMEN EUROPE PLC DUSSELDORF OFFICE—See Nichimen Corporation; *Int'l,* pg. 928
NICHIMEN ORIENT WEAR LTD.—See Nichimen Corporation; *Int'l,* pg. 928
NICHIREI CORPORATION; *Int'l,* pg. 928
NICHIREI FOODS—See Nichirei Corporation; *Int'l,* pg. 928
NICHIRO CORPORATION; *Int'l,* pg. 928
NICHIYU AUSTRALIA PTY.—See Atlet AB; *Int'l,* pg. 97
NICHIYU KOKI CO., LTD.—See Kumagai Gumi Co., Ltd.; *Int'l,* pg. 763
NICHOLAS, FAYETTE & GREENBRIER RR CO.—See Conrail, Inc.; *U.S. Public,* pg. 432
NICHOLAS LABORATORIES LTD.—See Roche Holding Ltd.; *Int'l,* pg. 1121
NICHOLAS PAPER, INC.; *U.S. Private,* pg. 798
NICHOLAS PRODUCTS PTY. LTD.—See Roche Holding Ltd.; *Int'l,* pg. 1121
NICHOLAS TURKEY BREEDING FARMS—See Booker PLC; *Int'l,* pg. 202
NICHOLS AIRCRAFT DIV.—See Parker Hannifin Corporation; *U.S. Public,* pg. 1262
NICHOLS ALUMINUM—See Quanex Corporation; *U.S. Public,* pg. 1350
AUSTIN NICHOLS & CO. INC.—See Groupe Pernod Ricard; *Int'l,* pg. 567
NICHOLS BERLIN—See Parker Hannifin Corporation; *U.S. Public,* pg. 1263
NICHOLS-HOMESHIELD—See Quanex Corporation; *U.S. Public,* pg. 1350
NICHOLS-HOMESHIELD CASTING—See Quanex Corporation; *U.S. Public,* pg. 1350
NICHOLS PORTLAND DIV.—See Parker Hannifin Corporation; *U.S. Public,* pg. 1260
NICHOLS RESEARCH CORPORATION; *U.S. Public,* pg. 1182
NICHOLS SELECT—See Nichols Research Corporation; *U.S. Public,* pg. 1182
NICHOLSON—See Cooper Industries, Inc.; *U.S. Public,* pg. 444
NICHOLSON FILE—See Cooper Industries, Inc.; *U.S. Public,* pg. 444
NICHOLSON LESLIE INTERNATIONAL LIMITED—See AON Corporation; *U.S. Public,* pg. 119

NICHOLSON STEAM TRAP—See Watts Industries, Inc.; *U.S. Public,* pg. 1747
NICKEL—See BDDP Group; *Int'l,* pg. 116
NICKEL ADS—See Lee Enterprises, Incorporated; *U.S. Public,* pg. 984
NICKEL NIK—See Lee Enterprises, Incorporated; *U.S. Public,* pg. 984
THE NICKEL PLATE IMPROVEMENT CO., INC.—See Norfolk Southern Corporation; *U.S. Public,* pg. 1190
NICKERSON LUMBER COMPANY; *U.S. Private,* pg. 798
NICKERSON SEEDS LTD.—See Royal Dutch/Shell Group of Companies; *Int'l,* pg. 1139
NICKERSON ZWAAN—See Royal Dutch/Shell Group of Companies; *Int'l,* pg. 1135
NICKLAUS GOLF COMPANY, L.C.; *U.S. Private,* pg. 799
ALFRED NICKLES BAKERY, INC.; *U.S. Private,* pg. 799
NICKLES BAKERY, INC.—See Alfred Nickles Bakery, Inc.; *U.S. Private,* pg. 799
NICKLES BAKERY OF INDIANA INC.—See Alfred Nickles Bakery, Inc.; *U.S. Private,* pg. 799
NICKLES BAKERY OF OHIO INC.—See Alfred Nickles Bakery, Inc.; *U.S. Private,* pg. 799
NICOLET ANALYTICAL—See Thermo Electron Corporation; *U.S. Public,* pg. 1593
NICOLET DIVISION—See International Paper Company; *U.S. Public,* pg. 903
NICOLET INSTRUMENT BENELUX—See Thermo Electron Corporation; *U.S. Public,* pg. 1594
NICOLET INSTRUMENT GMBH—See Thermo Electron Corporation; *U.S. Public,* pg. 1594
NICOLET INSTRUMENT S.A.R.L.—See Thermo Electron Corporation; *U.S. Public,* pg. 1594
NICOLET JAPAN CORP.-OSAKA—See Thermo Electron Corporation; *U.S. Public,* pg. 1594
NICOLET JAPAN CORP.-TOKYO—See Thermo Electron Corporation; *U.S. Public,* pg. 1594
NICOLET LIMITED—See Thermo Electron Corporation; *U.S. Public,* pg. 1594
NICOLET PAPER COMPANY—See International Paper Company; *U.S. Public,* pg. 903
NICOLET TEST & MEASUREMENT DIVISION—See Thermo Electron Corporation; *U.S. Public,* pg. 1593
NICOLITCH—See Vishay Intertechnology, Inc.; *U.S. Public,* pg. 1722
NICOLL—See ETEX; *Int'l,* pg. 430
NICOLL ASIA LTD—See ETEX; *Int'l,* pg. 430
NICOLL ETERPLAST—See ETEX; *Int'l,* pg. 430
NICOR ENERGY SERVICES COMPANY—See NICOR Inc.; *U.S. Public,* pg. 1182
NICOR ENERGY VENTURES COMPANY—See NICOR Inc.; *U.S. Public,* pg. 1182
NICOR GAS EXCHANGE COMPANY—See NICOR Inc.; *U.S. Public,* pg. 1182
NICOR HUB, INC.—See NICOR Inc.; *U.S. Public,* pg. 1182
NICOR INC.; *U.S. Public,* pg. 1182
NICOR NGV CORP.—See NICOR Inc.; *U.S. Public,* pg. 1183
NICOR TECHNOLOGIES—See NICOR Inc.; *U.S. Public,* pg. 1183
NICOTEC CO.—See Amada Co., Ltd.; *Int'l,* pg. 70
NICSAND, INC.; *U.S. Private,* pg. 799
NIDAR AS—See Orkla A.S.A.; *Int'l,* pg. 1011
NIDEC POWER GENERAL—See Nippon Densan (NIDEC); *Int'l,* pg. 933
NIECO CORPORATION; *U.S. Private,* pg. 799
NIEDERLASSUNG BAD KREUZNACH—See Bilfinger + Berger Bauaktiengesellschaft; *Int'l,* pg. 194
NIEDERLASSUNG BONN—See Bilfinger + Berger Bauaktiengesellschaft; *Int'l,* pg. 194
NIEDERLASSUNG BREMEN—See Bilfinger + Berger Bauaktiengesellschaft; *Int'l,* pg. 194
NIEDERLASSUNG CHEMNITZ—See Bilfinger + Berger Bauaktiengesellschaft; *Int'l,* pg. 194
NIEDERLASSUNG COTTBUS—See Bilfinger + Berger Bauaktiengesellschaft; *Int'l,* pg. 194
NIEDERLASSUNG DORTMUND—See Bilfinger + Berger Bauaktiengesellschaft; *Int'l,* pg. 195
NIEDERLASSUNG DUSSELDORF—See Bilfinger + Berger Bauaktiengesellschaft; *Int'l,* pg. 195
NIEDERLASSUNG ERFURT—See Bilfinger + Berger Bauaktiengesellschaft; *Int'l,* pg. 195
NIEDERLASSUNG FRANKFURT/ODER—See Bilfinger + Berger Bauaktiengesellschaft; *Int'l,* pg. 195
NIEDERLASSUNG FREIBURG—See Bilfinger + Berger Bauaktiengesellschaft; *Int'l,* pg. 195
NIEDERLASSUNG HALLE—See Bilfinger + Berger Bauaktiengesellschaft; *Int'l,* pg. 195
NIEDERLASSUNG HANOVER—See Bilfinger + Berger Bauaktiengesellschaft; *Int'l,* pg. 195
NIEDERLASSUNG HEILBRONN—See Bilfinger + Berger Bauaktiengesellschaft; *Int'l,* pg. 195
NIEDERLASSUNG JENA—See Bilfinger + Berger Bauaktiengesellschaft; *Int'l,* pg. 195
NIEDERLASSUNG KAISERSLAUTERN—See Bilfinger + Berger Bauaktiengesellschaft; *Int'l,* pg. 195
NIEDERLASSUNG KARLSRUHE—See Bilfinger + Berger Bauaktiengesellschaft; *Int'l,* pg. 195
NIEDERLASSUNG KASSEL—See Bilfinger + Berger Bauaktiengesellschaft; *Int'l,* pg. 195
NIEDERLASSUNG KIEL—See Bilfinger + Berger Bauaktiengesellschaft; *Int'l,* pg. 195
NIEDERLASSUNG KOBLENZ—See Bilfinger + Berger Bauaktiengesellschaft; *Int'l,* pg. 195
NIEDERLASSUNG LEIPZIG—See Bilfinger + Berger Bauaktiengesellschaft; *Int'l,* pg. 195
NIEDERLASSUNG LUXEMBOURG—See Frankfurter Sparkasse; *Int'l,* pg. 504
NIEDERLASSUNG MAGDEBURG—See Bilfinger + Berger Bauaktiengesellschaft; *Int'l,* pg. 195
NIEDERLASSUNG MAINZ—See Bilfinger + Berger Bauaktiengesellschaft; *Int'l,* pg. 195

NIEDERLASSUNG MANNHEIM—See Bilfinger + Berger Bauaktiengesellschaft; *Int'l,* pg. 195
NIEDERLASSUNG NURNBERG—See Bilfinger + Berger Bauaktiengesellschaft; *Int'l,* pg. 195
NIEDERLASSUNG PASSAU—See Bilfinger + Berger Bauaktiengesellschaft; *Int'l,* pg. 195
NIEDERLASSUNG POTSDAM—See Bilfinger + Berger Bauaktiengesellschaft; *Int'l,* pg. 195
NIEDERLASSUNG REGENSBURG—See Bilfinger + Berger Bauaktiengesellschaft; *Int'l,* pg. 195
NIEDERLASSUNG ROSTOCK—See Bilfinger + Berger Bauaktiengesellschaft; *Int'l,* pg. 195
NIEDERLASSUNG SCHWERIN—See Bilfinger + Berger Bauaktiengesellschaft; *Int'l,* pg. 195
NIEDERLASSUNG SPEZIALHOCHBAU—See Bilfinger + Berger Bauaktiengesellschaft; *Int'l,* pg. 195
NIEDERLASSUNG SPEZIALTIEFBAU MANNHEIM—See Bilfinger + Berger Bauaktiengesellschaft; *Int'l,* pg. 195
NIEDERLASSUNG SYSTEMBAU KERPEN—See Bilfinger + Berger Bauaktiengesellschaft; *Int'l,* pg. 195
NIEDERLASSUNG WIESBADEN—See Bilfinger + Berger Bauaktiengesellschaft; *Int'l,* pg. 195
NIEDERLASSUNG WURZBURG—See Bilfinger + Berger Bauaktiengesellschaft; *Int'l,* pg. 195
NIEDERMAYR PAPIERWARENFABRIK AG—See Heidelberger Zement A.G.; *Int'l,* pg. 606
NIEDERMEIER VERMOGENSVERWALTUNGSGESELLSCHAFT MBH—See Schmalbach-Lubeca AG; *Int'l,* pg. 1206
NIEDERSACHSEN VERSICHERUNGS-AG—See Hapag-Lloyd AG; *Int'l,* pg. 596
NIEDNER LIMITED—See Wajax Limited; *Int'l,* pg. 1485
NIELSEN—See Esselte AB; *Int'l,* pg. 460
A.C. NIELSEN; *U.S. Public,* pg. 1183
A.C. NIELSEN (ARGENTINA) S.A.—See A.C. Nielsen; *U.S. Public,* pg. 1183
A.C. NIELSEN COMPANY—See A.C. Nielsen; *U.S. Public,* pg. 1183
A.C. NIELSEN COMPANY AB—See A.C. Nielsen; *U.S. Public,* pg. 1183
A.C. NIELSEN CO. (BELGIUM) S.A.—See A.C. Nielsen; *U.S. Public,* pg. 1183
A.C. NIELSEN CO., GMBH—See A.C. Nielsen; *U.S. Public,* pg. 1183
A.C. NIELSEN CO., LTD.—See A.C. Nielsen; *U.S. Public,* pg. 1183
A.C. NIELSEN COMPANY (MINNEAPOLIS)—See A.C. Nielsen; *U.S. Public,* pg. 1183
A.C. NIELSEN COMPANY (NEW YORK)—See A.C. Nielsen; *U.S. Public,* pg. 1183
A.C. NIELSEN CO. OF CANADA, LTD.—See A.C. Nielsen; *U.S. Public,* pg. 1183
A.C. NIELSEN COMPANY OF KOREA—See A.C. Nielsen; *U.S. Public,* pg. 1183
A.C. NIELSEN COMPANY OF PORTUGAL—See A.C. Nielsen; *U.S. Public,* pg. 1183
A.C. NIELSEN COMPANY S.A.—See A.C. Nielsen; *U.S. Public,* pg. 1183
A.C. NIELSEN COMPANY-TAIWAN BRANCH—See A.C. Nielsen; *U.S. Public,* pg. 1183
A.C. NIELSEN DE COLOMBIA, S.A.—See A.C. Nielsen; *U.S. Public,* pg. 1183
A.C. NIELSEN HELLAS LTD.—See A.C. Nielsen; *U.S. Public,* pg. 1183
A.C. NIELSEN, LTDA.—See A.C. Nielsen; *U.S. Public,* pg. 1183
A.C. NIELSEN MANAGEMENT SERVICES S.A.—See A.C. Nielsen; *U.S. Public,* pg. 1183
A.C. NIELSEN (NEDERLAND) B.V.—See A.C. Nielsen; *U.S. Public,* pg. 1183
A.C. NIELSEN (N.Z.) LIMITED—See A.C. Nielsen; *U.S. Public,* pg. 1183
A.C. NIELSEN OF IRELAND, LTD.—See A.C. Nielsen; *U.S. Public,* pg. 1183
A.C. NIELSEN PTY., LTD.—See A.C. Nielsen; *U.S. Public,* pg. 1184
A.C. NIELSEN CO.—See A.C. Nielsen; *U.S. Public,* pg. 1183
A.C. NIELSEN CO., GMBH—See A.C. Nielsen; *U.S. Public,* pg. 1183
NIELSEN & BAINBRIDGE—See Esselte AB; *Int'l,* pg. 460
THE NIELSEN COMPANY; *U.S. Private,* pg. 799
NIELSEN DESIGN AB—See Esselte AB; *Int'l,* pg. 459
NIELSEN DESIGN GMBH—See Esselte AB; *Int'l,* pg. 462
NIELSEN DILLINGHAM BUILDERS, INC.—See Dillingham Construction Corporation; *U.S. Public,* pg. 333
NIELSEN LOGISTICS CO—See The Nielsen Company; *U.S. Private,* pg. 799
NIELSEN MARKETING RESEARCH A/S—See A.C. Nielsen; *U.S. Public,* pg. 1184
NIELSEN MEDIA RESEARCH—See Cognizant Corporation; *U.S. Public,* pg. 395
NIELSEN NORGE—See A.C. Nielsen; *U.S. Public,* pg. 1184
NIELSEN SARL—See Esselte AB; *Int'l,* pg. 462
NIELSEN/SESSIONS—See Zero Corporation; *U.S. Public,* pg. 1791
NIELSEN UK—See Esselte AB; *Int'l,* pg. 462
NIEMANN CHEMIE G.M.B.H.—See Safety-Kleen Corp.; *U.S. Public,* pg. 1426
NIEUW ROTTERDAM KNIGHT SCHIPPERS—See Groupe Bruxelles Lambert S.A.; *Int'l,* pg. 562
NIEUW WELGELGEN B.V.—See Assicurazioni Generali S.p.A.; *Int'l,* pg. 91
NIFAST CORPORATION—See Nissho Iwai Corporation; *Int'l,* pg. 947
NIFCO INC.; *Int'l,* pg. 928
NIFE FRANCE S.A.—See Alcatel Alsthom Compagnie Generale D'Electricite; *Int'l,* pg. 54
NIFE GMBH STROMVERSORGUNGSSYSTEME—See Alcatel Alsthom Compagnie Generale D'Electricite; *Int'l,* pg. 54
NIFE ITALIA S.P.A.—See Alcatel Alsthom Compagnie Generale D'Electricite; *Int'l,* pg. 54

NIFE POWER SYSTEMS LTD.—See Alcatel Alsthom Compagnie Generale D'Electricite; *Int'l*, pg. 53
NIFE POWER SYSTEMS PTE LTD.—See Alcatel Alsthom Compagnie Generale D'Electricite; *Int'l*, pg. 54
NIFE POWER SYSTEMS SDN. BHD.—See Alcatel Alsthom Compagnie Generale D'Electricite; *Int'l*, pg. 54
NIFE SILCON LTD.—See Alcatel Alsthom Compagnie Generale D'Electricite; *Int'l*, pg. 54
NIGBEL MERCHANT BANK (NIGERIA) LTD.—See Generale de Banque S.A.; *Int'l*, pg. 548
NIGER-AFRIQUE S.A.—See Gamma Holding N.V.; *Int'l*, pg. 540
NIGER FRANCE S.A.—See Gamma Holding N.V.; *Int'l*, pg. 540
NIGERIAN-AMERICAN MERCHANT BANK LTD.—See BankBoston Corporation; *U.S. Public*, pg. 185
NIGERIAN WIRE AND CABLE CO., LTD.—See Sumitomo Electric Industries, Ltd.; *Int'l*, pg. 1313
NIGERLEC CONTRACTORS LTD.—See Alcatel Alsthom Compagnie Generale D'Electricite; *Int'l*, pg. 53
NIGHTINGALE-CONANT CORP.; *U.S. Private*, pg. 799
NIGHTINGALE HOME HEALTH CARE, INC.—See Integrated Health Services, Inc.; *U.S. Public*, pg. 885
NIGU CHEMIE-BETEILIGUNGS GMBH—See Viag AG; *Int'l*, pg. 1465
NIHON BALZERS K.K.—See Oerlikon-Buhrle Holding AG; *Int'l*, pg. 997
NIHON BUILDING CO. LTD.—See Japan Securities Finance Co. Ltd.; *Int'l*, pg. 702
NIHON EXABYTE K.K.—See Exabyte Corporation; *U.S. Public*, pg. 597
NIHON FERRAS—See Pechiney S.A.; *Int'l*, pg. 1031
NIHON KEIZAI SHIMBUN AMERICA, INC.—See Nihon Keizai Shimbun, Inc.; *Int'l*, pg. 929
NIHON KEIZAI SHIMBUN EUROPE LTD.—See Nihon Keizai Shimbun, Inc.; *Int'l*, pg. 929
NIHON KEIZAI SHIMBUN EUROPE LTD.-FRANKFURT—See Nihon Keizai Shimbun, Inc.; *Int'l*, pg. 930
NIHON KEIZAI SHIMBUN EUROPE LTD.-PARIS—See Nihon Keizai Shimbun, Inc.; *Int'l*, pg. 930
NIHON KEIZAI SHIMBUN, INC.; *Int'l*, pg. 929
NIHON KEIZAI SHIMBUN SINGAPORE PTE. LTD.—See Nihon Keizai Shimbun, Inc.; *Int'l*, pg. 930
NIHON KENALL K.K.—See Tyco International Ltd.; *U.S. Public*, pg. 1648
NIHON KYOEI SECURITIES CO. LTD.—See Japan Securities Finance Co. Ltd.; *Int'l*, pg. 702
NIHON MEDI-PHYSICS COMPANY LIMITED—See Roche Holding Ltd.; *Int'l*, pg. 1121
NIHON MICROTEC RESEARCH—See Mentor Graphics Corporation; *U.S. Public*, pg. 1087
NIHON MILLIPORE LTD.-YONEZAWA—See Millipore Corporation; *U.S. Public*, pg. 1113
NIHON MRC CO. LTD.—See Sony Corporation; *Int'l*, pg. 1283
NIHON-PALL LTD.—See Pall Corporation; *U.S. Public*, pg. 1254
NIHON PHARMACEUTICAL CO., LTD.—See Takeda Chemical Industries, Ltd.; *Int'l*, pg. 1350
NIHON ROBINSON NUGENT K.K.—See Robinson Nugent, Inc.; *U.S. Public*, pg. 1395
NIHON SARA LEE—See Sara Lee Corporation; *U.S. Public*, pg. 1434
NIHON SCHERING K.K.—See Schering AG; *Int'l*, pg. 1204
NIHON SEIKO CO. LTD.—See Nissho Iwai Corporation; *Int'l*, pg. 947
NIHON SHOKUHIN KAKO CO., LTD.—See Corn Products International, Inc.; *U.S. Public*, pg. 447
NIHON SHORTWAVE BROADCASTING CO., LTD.—See Nihon Keizai Shimbun, Inc.; *Int'l*, pg. 929
NIHON SILICON GRAPHICS K.K.—See Silicon Graphics, Inc.; *U.S. Public*, pg. 1474
NIHON SUN MICROSYSTEMS K.K.—See Sun Microsystems, Inc.; *U.S. Public*, pg. 1531
NIHON TIMKEN K.K.—See The Timken Company; *U.S. Public*, pg. 1617
NIHON TOKUSHU NOYAKU SEIZO K.K.—See Bayer AG; *Int'l*, pg. 174
NIHON VEECO K.K.—See Veeco Instruments, Inc.; *U.S. Public*, pg. 1711
NIHON WANG K.K.—See Wang Laboratories, Inc.; *U.S. Public*, pg. 1737
NIIGATA CONVERTER CO., LTD.—See Twin Disc, Incorporated; *U.S. Public*, pg. 1646
NIIGATA SANYO ELECTRONIC CO., LTD.—See Sanyo Electric Co., Ltd.; *Int'l*, pg. 1191
NIIGATA TECHNIP CO., LTD.—See Technip; *Int'l*, pg. 1361
NIJECT—See Ingersoll-Rand Company; *U.S. Public*, pg. 877
NIJECT SERVICES COMPANY—See Praxair Inc.; *U.S. Public*, pg. 1320
NIJGH INTERPARTNERS—See Warwick Baker O'Neill; *U.S. Private*, pg. 1152
NIKE APPAREL—See Nike, Inc.; *U.S. Public*, pg. 1184
NIKE ASIA-PACIFIC—See Nike, Inc.; *U.S. Public*, pg. 1184
NIKE CANADA LTD.—See Nike, Inc.; *U.S. Public*, pg. 1184
NIKE EUROPEAN HEADQUARTERS—See Nike, Inc.; *U.S. Public*, pg. 1184
NIKE FOOTWEAR—See Nike, Inc.; *U.S. Public*, pg. 1184
NIKE FRANCE S.A.R.L.—See Nike, Inc.; *U.S. Public*, pg. 1184
NIKE GMBH—See Nike, Inc.; *U.S. Public*, pg. 1184
NIKE, INC.; *U.S. Public*, pg. 1184
NIKE INTERNATIONAL LTD.—See Nike, Inc.; *U.S. Public*, pg. 1184
NIKE LATIN AMERICAN HEADQUARTERS—See Nike, Inc.; *U.S. Public*, pg. 1184
NIKE (U.K.) LIMITED—See Nike, Inc.; *U.S. Public*, pg. 1184
THE NIKKAN KOGYO SHIMBUN-CHUGOKU—See The Nikkan Kogyo Shimbun, Ltd.; *Int'l*, pg. 930
THE NIKKAN KOGYO SHIMBUN; *Int'l*, pg. 930
THE NIKKAN KOGYO SHIMBUN-NAYGOYA—See The Nikkan Kogyo Shimbun, Ltd.; *Int'l*, pg. 930

THE NIKKAN KOGYO SHIMBUN-OSAKA—See The Nikkan Kogyo Shimbun, Ltd.; *Int'l*, pg. 930
THE NIKKAN KOGYO SHIMBUN-SEIBU—See The Nikkan Kogyo Shimbun, Ltd.; *Int'l*, pg. 930
THE NIKKAN KOGYO SHIMBUN-TOHOKU—See The Nikkan Kogyo Shimbun, Ltd.; *Int'l*, pg. 930
NIKKEI ADVERTISING CO.; *Int'l*, pg. 930
NIKKEI ADVERTISING CO.—See Nikkei Advertising Co.; *Int'l*, pg. 930
NIKKEI BUSINESS PUBLICATIONS INC.—See Nihon Keizai Shimbun, Inc.; *Int'l*, pg. 929
NIKKEI CUSTOM PUBLISHING SERVICES, INC.—See Nihon Keizai Shimbun, Inc.; *Int'l*, pg. 929
NIKKEI HOME PUBLISHING, INC.—See Nihon Keizai Shimbun, Inc.; *Int'l*, pg. 929
NIKKEI INTERNATIONAL LTD.—See Nihon Keizai Shimbun, Inc.; *Int'l*, pg. 929
NIKKEI MEDIA MARKETING, INC.—See Nihon Keizai Shimbun, Inc.; *Int'l*, pg. 929
NIKKEI NEWS BULLETIN, INC.—See Nihon Keizai Shimbun, Inc.; *Int'l*, pg. 929
NIKKEI NEWSPAPER MARKETING, INC.—See Nihon Keizai Shimbun, Inc.; *Int'l*, pg. 929
NIKKEI RESEARCH, INC.—See Nihon Keizai Shimbun, Inc.; *Int'l*, pg. 929
NIKKEI SCIENCE, INC.—See Nihon Keizai Shimbun, Inc.; *Int'l*, pg. 929
NIKKEI VISUAL IMAGES, INC.—See Nihon Keizai Shimbun, Inc.; *Int'l*, pg. 929
NIKKEL OG OLIVIN A/S—See Outokumpu Oyj; *Int'l*, pg. 1016
NIKKO BANK (DEUTSCHLAND) GMBH—See The Nikko Securities Co., Ltd.; *Int'l*, pg. 930
NIKKO BANK (LUXEMBOURG) S.A.—See The Nikko Securities Co., Ltd.; *Int'l*, pg. 930
NIKKO BANK (SWITZERLAND) LTD.—See The Nikko Securities Co., Ltd.; *Int'l*, pg. 930
THE NIKKO BANK (UK) PLC—See The Nikko Securities Co., Ltd.; *Int'l*, pg. 930
NIKKO DENKI SEISAKUSHO CO., LTD.—See Oki Electric Industry Company, Ltd.; *Int'l*, pg. 999
NIKKO ESPANA SOCIEDAD DE VALORES, S.A.—See The Nikko Securities Co., Ltd.; *Int'l*, pg. 930
NIKKO EUROPE PLC—See The Nikko Securities Co., Ltd.; *Int'l*, pg. 930
NIKKO EUROPE PLC.-AMSTERDAM BRANCH—See The Nikko Securities Co., Ltd.; *Int'l*, pg. 930
NIKKO FRANCE S.A.—See The Nikko Securities Co., Ltd.; *Int'l*, pg. 930
NIKKO GOULD FOIL (U.K.) LTD.—See Japan Energy Corporation; *Int'l*, pg. 702
NIKKO HOTELS INTERNATIONAL-USA—See Japan Airlines Company, Ltd.; *Int'l*, pg. 700
NIKKO INTERNATIONAL CAPITAL MANAGEMENT CO., LTD.—See The Nikko Securities Co., Ltd.; *Int'l*, pg. 930
NIKKO INTERNATIONAL CAPITAL MANAGEMENT (U.K.) LTD.—See The Nikko Securities Co., Ltd.; *Int'l*, pg. 930
NIKKO INVESTMENT BANKING (MIDDLE EAST) E.C.—See The Nikko Securities Co., Ltd.; *Int'l*, pg. 931
NIKKO ITALIA SOCIETA DI INTERMEDIAZIONE MOBILARE S.P.A.—See The Nikko Securities Co., Ltd.; *Int'l*, pg. 931
NIKKO LOGISTICS CORP.—See Japan Aviation Electronics Industry, Ltd.; *Int'l*, pg. 701
THE NIKKO MERCHANT BANK (SINGAPORE) LTD.—See The Nikko Securities Co., Ltd.; *Int'l*, pg. 931
NIKKO PETROLEUM (ASIA) PTE. LTD.—See Japan Energy Corporation; *Int'l*, pg. 702
THE NIKKO SECURITIES (AUSTRALIA) LTD.—See The Nikko Securities Co., Ltd.; *Int'l*, pg. 930
THE NIKKO SECURITIES CO., (ASIA) LIMITED—See The Nikko Securities Co., Ltd.; *Int'l*, pg. 931
NIKKO SECURITIES CO., CHICAGO—See The Nikko Securities Co., Ltd.; *Int'l*, pg. 930
THE NIKKO SECURITIES CO. INTERNATIONAL INC.—See The Nikko Securities Co., Ltd.; *Int'l*, pg. 930
NIKKO SECURITIES CO., LOS ANGELES—See The Nikko Securities Co., Ltd.; *Int'l*, pg. 930
THE NIKKO SECURITIES CO., LTD.; *Int'l*, pg. 930
P.T. NIKKO SECURITIES INDONESIA—See The Nikko Securities Co., Ltd.; *Int'l*, pg. 931
NIKO CO., LTD.—See Mitsukoshi, Ltd.; *Int'l*, pg. 883
NIKOLA TESLA—See Telefonaktiebolaget LM Ericsson; *Int'l*, pg. 1369
NIKON AG—See Nikon Corporation; *Int'l*, pg. 931
NIKON CANADA INC.—See Nikon Corporation; *Int'l*, pg. 931
NIKON CORPORATION; *Int'l*, pg. 931
NIKON EUROPE B.V.—See Nikon Corporation; *Int'l*, pg. 931
NIKON FRANCE S.A.—See Nikon Corporation; *Int'l*, pg. 931
NIKON GEOTECS CO., LTD.—See Nikon Corporation; *Int'l*, pg. 931
NIKON GMBH—See Nikon Corporation; *Int'l*, pg. 931
NIKON HONG KONG LTD.—See Nikon Corporation; *Int'l*, pg. 931
NIKON INC.—See Nikon Corporation; *Int'l*, pg. 931
NIKON INSTECH CO., LTD.—See Nikon Corporation; *Int'l*, pg. 931
NIKON INSTRUMENTS S.P.A.—See Nikon Corporation; *Int'l*, pg. 931
NIKON KFT.—See Nikon Corporation; *Int'l*, pg. 931
NIKON LIFE CO., LTD.—See Nikon Corporation; *Int'l*, pg. 931
NIKON LOGISTICS CORPORATION—See Nikon Corporation; *Int'l*, pg. 931
NIKON OPTICAL CANADA INC.—See Nikon Corporation; *Int'l*, pg. 931
NIKON OPTICAL U.K.—See Nikon Corporation; *Int'l*, pg. 931
NIKON PHOTO PRODUCTS INC.—See Nikon Corporation; *Int'l*, pg. 931

NIKON PRECISION EUROPE GMBH—See Nikon Corporation; *Int'l*, pg. 931
NIKON PRECISION INC.—See Nikon Corporation; *Int'l*, pg. 931
NIKON PRECISION KOREA LTD.—See Nikon Corporation; *Int'l*, pg. 931
NIKON SALES PROMOTION CO., LTD.—See Nikon Corporation; *Int'l*, pg. 931
NIKON S.R.O.—See Nikon Corporation; *Int'l*, pg. 931
NIKON SVENSKA AB—See Nikon Corporation; *Int'l*, pg. 932
NIKON TEC CORPORATION—See Nikon Corporation; *Int'l*, pg. 931
NIKON (THAILAND) CO., LTD.—See Nikon Corporation; *Int'l*, pg. 932
NIKON U.K. LTD.—See Nikon Corporation; *Int'l*, pg. 932
NILAX CO., LTD.—See Skylark Co., Ltd.; *Int'l*, pg. 1262
NILFISK A/S; *Int'l*, pg. 932
NILFISK DANMARK A/S—See Nilfisk A/S; *Int'l*, pg. 932
NILFISK-GERNI A/S—See Nilfisk A/S; *Int'l*, pg. 932
NILFISK OF AMERICA INC.—See Nilfisk A/S; *Int'l*, pg. 932
NILO HOLDING, S.A.—See Pfizer Inc.; *U.S. Public*, pg. 1283
NILS PUBLISHING COMPANY—See Wolters Kluwer N.V.; *Int'l*, pg. 1513
NIM-COR, INC.—See Haden Maclellan Holdings plc; *Int'l*, pg. 586
NIMTEC INC.—See Japan Energy Corporation; *Int'l*, pg. 702
NINGBO CNTIC UNITED IMPORT & EXPORT CO.—See China National Technical Import & Export Corporation (CNTIC); *Int'l*, pg. 285
NINE WEST GROUP, INC.; *U.S. Public*, pg. 1185
94TH AERO SQUADRON OF COLUMBUS, INC.—See Specialty Restaurants Corporation; *U.S. Private*, pg. 1023
94TH AERO SQUADRON OF MIAMI, INC.—See Specialty Restaurants Corporation; *U.S. Private*, pg. 1023
94TH AERO SQUADRON OF ORLANDO, INC.—See Specialty Restaurants Corporation; *U.S. Private*, pg. 1023
94TH AERO SQUADRON OF PALWAUKEE, INC.—See Specialty Restaurants Corporation; *U.S. Private*, pg. 1023
94TH AERO SQUADRON OF PINELLAS COUNTY, INC.—See Specialty Restaurants Corporation; *U.S. Private*, pg. 1023
94TH AERO SQUADRON OF SAN JOSE, INC.—See Specialty Restaurants Corporation; *U.S. Private*, pg. 1022
94TH AERO SQUADRON OF SARASOTA, INC.—See Specialty Restaurants Corporation; *U.S. Private*, pg. 1023
94TH AERO SQUADRON OF WEST PALM BEACH, INC.—See Specialty Restaurants Corporation; *U.S. Private*, pg. 1023
94TH AERO SQUADRON RESTAURANT, INC.—See Specialty Restaurants Corporation; *U.S. Private*, pg. 1023
94TH OF COLLEGE PARK, INC.—See Specialty Restaurants Corporation; *U.S. Private*, pg. 1023
94TH OF ST. LOUIS, INC.—See Specialty Restaurants Corporation; *U.S. Private*, pg. 1023
NINTEMAN CONSTRUCTION COMPANY, INC.—See Sundt Corp.; *U.S. Private*, pg. 1052
NINTENDO COMPANY, LTD.; *Int'l*, pg. 932
NINTENDO OF AMERICA—See Nintendo Company, Ltd.; *Int'l*, pg. 932
NINTENDO OF EUROPE GMBH—See Nintendo Company, Ltd.; *Int'l*, pg. 932
NIPPATSU AMEMITY CO., LTD.—See NHK Spring Co., Ltd.; *Int'l*, pg. 902
NIPPATSU SERVICE CO., LTD.—See NHK Spring Co., Ltd.; *Int'l*, pg. 902
THE NIPPERT COMPANY—See Outokumpu Oyj; *Int'l*, pg. 1016
NIPPERT-DAWSON LIMITED—See Outokumpu Oyj; *Int'l*, pg. 1017
NIPPLA KASEI CO., LTD.—See Nissho Iwai Corporation; *Int'l*, pg. 946
NIPPO CORPORATION; *Int'l*, pg. 932
NIPPO CORPORATION, EUROPE BRANCH—See Nippo Corporation; *Int'l*, pg. 932
NIPPO INC., KYUSHU BRANCH—See Nippo Corporation; *Int'l*, pg. 932
NIPPO INC., NAGOYA BRANCH—See Nippo Corporation; *Int'l*, pg. 932
NIPPO INC., OSAKA BRANCH—See Nippo Corporation; *Int'l*, pg. 932
NIPPO INC., SAPPORO BRANCH—See Nippo Corporation; *Int'l*, pg. 932
NIPPO MARKETING & ADVERTISING, INC.—See Nippo Corporation; *Int'l*, pg. 932
NIPPO PR CO., LTD.—See Nippo Corporation; *Int'l*, pg. 932
NIPPO SERVICE CO., LTD.—See Nippo Corporation; *Int'l*, pg. 932
NIPPON ALKYL PHENOL CO LTD.—See Novartis AG; *Int'l*, pg. 983
NIPPON AUTOMOTIVE BODY SYSTEMS CO., LTD.—See Rockwell International Corporation; *U.S. Public*, pg. 1399
NIPPON BECTON DICKINSON COMPANY LTD.—See Becton Dickinson & Company; *U.S. Public*, pg. 200
NIPPON BIO-RAD LABORATORIES K.K.—See Bio-Rad Laboratories, Inc.; *U.S. Public*, pg. 230
NIPPON BOC KK—See The BOC Group plc; *Int'l*, pg. 122
NIPPON BRUNSWICK CO., LTD.—See Mitsui & Co., Ltd.; *Int'l*, pg. 879
NIPPON BYK GULDEN CO., LTD.—See Altana AG; *Int'l*, pg. 66
NIPPON CENTOCOR, K.K.—See Centocor, Inc.; *U.S. Public*, pg. 323
NIPPON CHEMICAL HANDLING—See GATX Corporation; *U.S. Public*, pg. 693

NIPPON CREDIT AUSTRALIA LIMITED—See The Nippon Credit Bank, Ltd.; *Int'l*, pg. 933
NIPPON CREDIT BANK AG—See The Nippon Credit Bank, Ltd.; *Int'l*, pg. 933
THE NIPPON CREDIT BANK, LTD.; *Int'l*, pg. 932
NIPPON CREDIT BANK LTD.-BAHRAIN—See The Nippon Credit Bank, Ltd.; *Int'l*, pg. 933
NIPPON CREDIT BANK LTD.-BEIJING—See The Nippon Credit Bank, Ltd.; *Int'l*, pg. 933
NIPPON CREDIT BANK LTD.-FRANKFURT—See The Nippon Credit Bank, Ltd.; *Int'l*, pg. 933
NIPPON CREDIT BANK LTD.-GRAND CAYMAN—See The Nippon Credit Bank, Ltd.; *Int'l*, pg. 933
NIPPON CREDIT BANK LTD.-HONG KONG—See The Nippon Credit Bank, Ltd.; *Int'l*, pg. 933
NIPPON CREDIT BANK LTD.-PARIS—See The Nippon Credit Bank, Ltd.; *Int'l*, pg. 933
NIPPON CREDIT BANK LTD.-SAO PAULO—See The Nippon Credit Bank, Ltd.; *Int'l*, pg. 933
NIPPON CREDIT BANK LTD.-SEOUL—See The Nippon Credit Bank, Ltd.; *Int'l*, pg. 933
NIPPON CREDIT BANK LTD.-SINGAPORE—See The Nippon Credit Bank, Ltd.; *Int'l*, pg. 933
NIPPON CREDIT BANK LTD.-SYDNEY—See The Nippon Credit Bank, Ltd.; *Int'l*, pg. 933
NIPPON CREDIT INTERNATIONAL (HK) LIMITED—See The Nippon Credit Bank, Ltd.; *Int'l*, pg. 933
NIPPON CREDIT INTERNATIONAL LIMITED—See The Nippon Credit Bank, Ltd.; *Int'l*, pg. 933
NIPPON CREDIT (SCHWEIZ) AG—See The Nippon Credit Bank, Ltd.; *Int'l*, pg. 933
NIPPON CREDIT TRUST COMPANY—See The Nippon Credit Bank, Ltd.; *Int'l*, pg. 933
NIPPON CROWN HOUSE CO., LTD.—See Nissho Iwai Corporation; *Int'l*, pg. 946
NIPPON DENSAN (NIDEC); *Int'l*, pg. 933
NIPPON DIONEX K.K.—See Dionex Corporation; *U.S. Public*, pg. 510
NIPPON DOME STRUCTURES CO., LTD.—See Kumagai Gumi Co., Ltd.; *Int'l*, pg. 763
NIPPON DONALDSON LTD.—See Donaldson Company, Inc.; *U.S. Public*, pg. 517
NIPPON DPC CORP.—See Dainippon Ink & Chemicals, Inc.; *Int'l*, pg. 369
NIPPON DYNEEMA CO., LTD.—See DSM N.V.; *Int'l*, pg. 354
NIPPON ELECTRO RENT, LTD.—See Electro Rent Corporation; *U.S. Public*, pg. 568
NIPPON ESS-FOOD—See ESS-Food; *Int'l*, pg. 430
NIPPON EXPRESS (AUSTRALIA) PTY., LTD.—See Nippon Express Co., Ltd.; *Int'l*, pg. 934
NIPPON EXPRESS (BELGIUM) N.V./S.A.—See Nippon Express Co., Ltd.; *Int'l*, pg. 934
NIPPON EXPRESS CANADA, LTD.—See Nippon Express Co., Ltd.; *Int'l*, pg. 934
NIPPON EXPRESS CO., LTD.; *Int'l*, pg. 933
NIPPON EXPRESS (DEUTSCHLAND) GMBH—See Nippon Express Co., Ltd.; *Int'l*, pg. 934
NIPPON EXPRESS DO BRASIL TRANSPORTES INTERNACIONAIS LTDA.—See Nippon Express Co., Ltd.; *Int'l*, pg. 934
NIPPON EXPRESS FRANCE, S.A.—See Nippon Express Co., Ltd.; *Int'l*, pg. 934
NIPPON EXPRESS HAWAII INC.—See Nippon Express Co., Ltd.; *Int'l*, pg. 934
NIPPON EXPRESS (H.K.) CO., LTD.—See Nippon Express Co., Ltd.; *Int'l*, pg. 934
NIPPON EXPRESS (MALAYSIA) SDN. BHD.—See Nippon Express Co., Ltd.; *Int'l*, pg. 934
NIPPON EXPRESS (NEDERLAND) B.V.—See Nippon Express Co., Ltd.; *Int'l*, pg. 934
NIPPON EXPRESS (SINGAPORE) PTE., LTD.—See Nippon Express Co., Ltd.; *Int'l*, pg. 934
NIPPON EXPRESS TOURS (EUROPE) LTD.—See Nippon Express Co., Ltd.; *Int'l*, pg. 934
NIPPON EXPRESS TRAVEL U.S.A. INC.—See Nippon Express Co., Ltd.; *Int'l*, pg. 934
NIPPON EXPRESS (U.K.) LTD.—See Nippon Express Co., Ltd.; *Int'l*, pg. 934
NIPPON EXPRESS U.S.A. INC.—See Nippon Express Co., Ltd.; *Int'l*, pg. 934
NIPPON EXTERNA CORP.—See Freudenberg & Company; *Int'l*, pg. 507
NIPPON FISHER COMPANY, LTD.—See Monsanto Company; *U.S. Public*, pg. 1126
NIPPON FLOUR MILLS CO., LTD.—See Newly Weds Foods Inc.; *U.S. Private*, pg. 797
NIPPON GASKET CO., LTD.—See NHK Spring Co., Ltd.; *Int'l*, pg. 902
NIPPON GATX CO., LTD.—See GATX Corporation; *U.S. Public*, pg. 693
NIPPON GLAXO LTD.—See Glaxo Wellcome plc; *Int'l*, pg. 553
NIPPON HERR—See Salem Group, Inc.; *U.S. Private*, pg. 962
NIPPON HOMES CO., LTD.—See Takenaka Corporation; *Int'l*, pg. 1351
NIPPON INSURANCE SERVICE CO.—See Nippon Life Insurance Co.; *Int'l*, pg. 935
NIPPON INVESTMENT & FINANCE CO. LTD.—See Daiwa Securities Co. Ltd.; *Int'l*, pg. 366
NIPPON JARRELL-ASH COMPANY, LTD.—See Thermo Electron Corporation; *U.S. Public*, pg. 1596
NIPPON KAIJI KYOKAI; *Int'l*, pg. 934
NIPPON KAIJI KYOKAI—See Nippon Kaiji Kyokai; *Int'l*, pg. 934
NIPPON KAYAKU CO. LTD.; *Int'l*, pg. 934
NIPPON KAYAKU PHARMACEUTICAL DIV.—See Nippon Kayaku Co., Ltd.; *Int'l*, pg. 934
NIPPON KETJEN K.K.—See Akzo Nobel N.V.; *Int'l*, pg. 47
NIPPON KEYSTONE CORPORATION—See Tyco International Ltd.; *U.S. Public*, pg. 1650
NIPPON KOSHUHA STEEL CO., LTD.—See Kobe Steel, Ltd.; *Int'l*, pg. 740

NIPPON LEVER BV—See Unilever Plc; *Int'l*, pg. 1438
NIPPON LIFE - BEIJING REPRESENTATIVE OFFICE—See Nippon Life Insurance Co.; *Int'l*, pg. 936
NIPPON LIFE (DEUTSCHLAND) GMBH—See Nippon Life Insurance Co.; *Int'l*, pg. 936
NIPPON LIFE HEALTH CONSULTANT—See Nippon Life Insurance Co.; *Int'l*, pg. 935
NIPPON LIFE INSURANCE CO.; *Int'l*, pg. 934
NIPPON LIFE INSURANCE COMPANY OF AMERICA—See Nippon Life Insurance Co.; *Int'l*, pg. 935
NIPPON LIFE INSURANCE COMPANY OF THE PHILIPPINES, INC.—See Nippon Life Insurance Co.; *Int'l*, pg. 936
NIPPON LIFE INSURANCE FOUNDATION—See Nippon Life Insurance Co.; *Int'l*, pg. 935
NIPPON LIFE LIFESAVING SOCIETY (SAISEI-KAI)—See Nippon Life Insurance Co.; *Int'l*, pg. 935
NIPPON LIFE - SHANGHAI REPRESENTATIVE OFFICE—See Nippon Life Insurance Co.; *Int'l*, pg. 936
NIPPON LIFE - TAIPEI REPRESENTATIVE OFFICE—See Nippon Life Insurance Co.; *Int'l*, pg. 936
NIPPON LIGHT METAL CO. LTD.—See Alcan Aluminium Limited; *Int'l*, pg. 52
NIPPON LINCOLN ELECTRIC K.K.—See The Lincoln Electric Company; *U.S. Public*, pg. 997
NIPPON MACDERMID K.K.—See MacDermid Incorporated; *U.S. Public*, pg. 1030
NIPPON MAGPHANE COMPANY—See Rhone-Poulenc S.A.; *Int'l*, pg. 1109
NIPPON MEAT PACKERS AUSTRALIA PTY. LTD.—See Nippon Meat Packers, Inc.; *Int'l*, pg. 936
NIPPON MEAT PACKERS DO BRASIL EXP. E IMP. LTDA.—See Nippon Meat Packers, Inc.; *Int'l*, pg. 936
NIPPON MEAT PACKERS, INC.; *Int'l*, pg. 936
NIPPON MEAT PACKERS, INC. (CHILE) Y COMPANIA LIMITADA—See Nippon Meat Packers, Inc.; *Int'l*, pg. 936
NIPPON MEAT PACKERS, NEW ZEALAND LTD.—See Nippon Meat Packers, Inc.; *Int'l*, pg. 936
NIPPON MEAT PACKERS SINGAPORE PTE. LTD.—See Nippon Meat Packers, Inc.; *Int'l*, pg. 936
NIPPON MEAT PACKERS (TAIWAN), INC.—See Nippon Meat Packers, Inc.; *Int'l*, pg. 936
NIPPON MEAT PACKERS U.K. LTD.—See Nippon Meat Packers, Inc.; *Int'l*, pg. 936
NIPPON MONIER CO. LTD.—See Redland PLC; *Int'l*, pg. 1092
NIPPON MOTOROLA LTD.—See Motorola, Inc.; *U.S. Public*, pg. 1140
NIPPON MOTOROLA MICRO ELECTRONICS—See Motorola, Inc.; *U.S. Public*, pg. 1140
NIPPON NATIONAL SEIKAN CO., LTD.—See Pechiney S.A.; *Int'l*, pg. 1029
NIPPON NOVELLUS KK—See Novellus Systems, Inc.; *U.S. Public*, pg. 1204
NIPPON OIL (ASIA) PTE. LTD.—See Nippon Oil Company, Limited (NiSSEKI); *Int'l*, pg. 937
NIPPON OIL (AUSTRALIA) PTY. LIMITED—See Nippon Oil Company, Limited (NiSSEKI); *Int'l*, pg. 937
NIPPON OIL COMPANY, LIMITED (NiSSEKI); *Int'l*, pg. 936
NIPPON OIL EXPLORATION (MALAYSIA), LTD.—See Nippon Oil Company, Limited (NiSSEKI); *Int'l*, pg. 937
NIPPON OIL EXPLORATION U.K. LIMITED—See Nippon Oil Company, Limited (NiSSEKI); *Int'l*, pg. 937
NIPPON OIL EXPLORATION U.S.A. LIMITED—See Nippon Oil Company, Limited (NiSSEKI); *Int'l*, pg. 937
NIPPON OIL (U.K.) PUBLIC LIMITED COMPANY—See Nippon Oil Company, Limited (NiSSEKI); *Int'l*, pg. 937
NIPPON OIL (U.S.A.) LIMITED - DALLAS OFFICE—See Nippon Oil Company, Limited (NiSSEKI); *Int'l*, pg. 937
NIPPON OIL (U.S.A.) LIMITED - NEW YORK OFFICE—See Nippon Oil Company, Limited (NiSSEKI); *Int'l*, pg. 937
NIPPON OIL (U.S.A.) LIMITED - SAN FRANCISCO OFFICE—See Nippon Oil Company, Limited (NiSSEKI); *Int'l*, pg. 937
NIPPON PAINT (AMERICA) CORP.—See Nippon Paint Company Ltd.; *Int'l*, pg. 937
NIPPON PAINT (CHINA) CO., LTD.—See Nippon Paint Company Ltd.; *Int'l*, pg. 937
NIPPON PAINT (CHONGQING) CHEMICALS CO., LTD.—See Nippon Paint Company Ltd.; *Int'l*, pg. 937
NIPPON PAINT COMPANY LTD.; *Int'l*, pg. 936
NIPPON PAINT COMPANY LTD.-NEYAGAWA OFFICE—See Nippon Paint Company Ltd.; *Int'l*, pg. 937
NIPPON PAINT COMPANY LTD.-OSAKA—See Nippon Paint Company Ltd.; *Int'l*, pg. 937
NIPPON PAINT (EUROPE) LTD.—See Nippon Paint Company Ltd.; *Int'l*, pg. 937
NIPPON PAINT (GUANG DONG) CO., LTD.—See Nippon Paint Company Ltd.; *Int'l*, pg. 937
NIPPON PAINT (H.K.) CO., LTD.—See Nippon Paint Company Ltd.; *Int'l*, pg. 937
NIPPON PAINT (MALAYSIA) SDN. BHD.—See Nippon Paint Company Ltd.; *Int'l*, pg. 937
NIPPON PAINT (PHILIPPINES) INC.—See Nippon Paint Company Ltd.; *Int'l*, pg. 937
NIPPON PAINT RESEARCH INSTITUTE (AMERICA) INC.—See Nippon Paint Company Ltd.; *Int'l*, pg. 937
NIPPON PAINT (SINGAPORE) CO., PTE. LTD.—See Nippon Paint Company Ltd.; *Int'l*, pg. 937
NIPPON PAINT (SUZHOU) CO., LTD.—See Nippon Paint Company Ltd.; *Int'l*, pg. 937
NIPPON PAINT (THAILAND) CO., LTD.—See Nippon Paint Company Ltd.; *Int'l*, pg. 937
NIPPON PAINT (USA) INC.—See Nippon Paint Company Ltd.; *Int'l*, pg. 937
NIPPON PAINT (VIETNAM) CO., LTD.—See Superior Metal Products Inc.; *Int'l*, pg. 1322
NIPPON PAPER INDUSTRIES COMPANY LIMITED; *Int'l*, pg. 937
NIPPON PAPER INDUSTRIES COMPANY LIMITED SEATTLE OFFICE—See Nippon Paper Industries Company Limited; *Int'l*, pg. 938

NIPPON PAPER INDUSTRIES COMPANY LIMITED JAKARTA OFFICE—See Nippon Paper Industries Company Limited; *Int'l*, pg. 938
NIPPON PAPER INDUSTRIES COMPANY LIMITED VANCOUVER OFFICE—See Nippon Paper Industries Company Limited; *Int'l*, pg. 938
NIPPON PDA ENGINEERING K.K.—See The Macneal-Schwendler Corp.; *U.S. Public*, pg. 1031
NIPPON PHONOGRAM CO. LTD.—See Philips Electronics N.V.; *Int'l*, pg. 1052
NIPPON PISTON RING CO., LTD.; *Int'l*, pg. 938
NIPPON POLAROID K.K.—See Polaroid Corporation; *U.S. Public*, pg. 1314
NIPPON POLYPENCO LTD.—See DSM N.V.; *Int'l*, pg. 356
NIPPON QUAKER CHEMICAL, LTD.—See Quaker Chemical Corporation; *U.S. Public*, pg. 1346
NIPPON R-M CO., LTD.—See BASF AG; *Int'l*, pg. 109
NIPPON ROBALLO CO., LTD.—See Fried. Krupp AG; *Int'l*, pg. 509
NIPPON ROCHE K.K.—See Roche Holding Ltd.; *Int'l*, pg. 1121
NIPPON SANSO CORPORATION; *Int'l*, pg. 938
NIPPON SANSO EUROPE GMBH—See Nippon Sanso Corporation; *Int'l*, pg. 939
NIPPON SANSO TAIWAN, INC.—See Nippon Sanso Corporation; *Int'l*, pg. 939
NIPPON SANSO U.S.A., INC.—See Nippon Sanso Corporation; *Int'l*, pg. 938
NIPPON SELAS CO., LTD.—See Selas Corporation of America; *U.S. Public*, pg. 1455
NIPPON SHAFT CO., LTD.—See NHK Spring Co., Ltd.; *Int'l*, pg. 902
NIPPON SHINPAN CO., LTD.; *Int'l*, pg. 939
NIPPON SHIPPING CO.—See Nippon Express Co., Ltd.; *Int'l*, pg. 934
NIPPON SHOKUBAI CO., LTD.; *Int'l*, pg. 939
NIPPON SHOKUBAI GMBH—See Nippon Shokubai Co., Ltd.; *Int'l*, pg. 939
NIPPON SHOKUBAI-MATERIAL & FUNCTIONS RESEARCH LAB.—See Nippon Shokubai Co., Ltd.; *Int'l*, pg. 939
NIPPON SHOKUBAI-POLYMER RESEARCH LABORATORY—See Nippon Shokubai Co., Ltd.; *Int'l*, pg. 939
NIPPON SHOKUBAI-REPRESENTATIVE OFFICE—See Nippon Shokubai Co., Ltd.; *Int'l*, pg. 939
NIPPON SHOKUBAI-RESINS RESEARCH LABORATORY—See Nippon Shokubai Co., Ltd.; *Int'l*, pg. 939
NIPPON SHOKUBAI-SALES OFFICE—See Nippon Shokubai Co., Ltd.; *Int'l*, pg. 939
NIPPON SHOKUBAI-TSUKUBA RESEARCH LABORATORY—See Nippon Shokubai Co., Ltd.; *Int'l*, pg. 939
NIPPON SHOKUBAI-PROCESS DEVELOPMENT LABORATORY—See Nippon Shokubai Co., Ltd.; *Int'l*, pg. 939
NIPPON SILICA GLASS EUROPE LTD.—See Tosoh Corporation; *Int'l*, pg. 1408
NIPPON SILICA GLASS USA, INC.—See Tosoh Corporation; *Int'l*, pg. 1407
NIPPON SLEWING RING CO., LTD.—See Fried. Krupp AG; *Int'l*, pg. 509
NIPPON STEEL AUSTRALIA PTY., LIMITED—See Nippon Steel Corporation; *Int'l*, pg. 940
NIPPON STEEL CORPORATION; *Int'l*, pg. 939
NIPPON STEEL CORPORATION-BEIJING REP. OFFICE—See Nippon Steel Corporation; *Int'l*, pg. 940
NIPPON STEEL CORPORATION-EUROPEAN OFFICE—See Nippon Steel Corporation; *Int'l*, pg. 940
NIPPON STEEL CORPORATION-LONDON OFFICE—See Nippon Steel Corporation; *Int'l*, pg. 940
NIPPON STEEL CORPORATION-SINGAPORE REP. OFFICE—See Nippon Steel Corporation; *Int'l*, pg. 940
NIPPON STEEL-EMPREENDIMENTOS SIDERURGICOS LIMITADA—See Nippon Steel Corporation; *Int'l*, pg. 940
NIPPON STEEL SIDERURGIA LTDA.—See Nippon Steel Corporation; *Int'l*, pg. 940
NIPPON STEEL U.S.A., INC.—See Nippon Steel Corporation; *Int'l*, pg. 939
NIPPON SUISAN KAISHA, LTD.; *Int'l*, pg. 940
NIPPON SUISAN U.S.A.—See Nippon Suisan Kaisha, Ltd.; *Int'l*, pg. 940
NIPPON TELEGRAPH AND TELEPHONE CORPORATION; *Int'l*, pg. 940
NIPPON TRUCK CO., LTD.—See Nippon Express Co., Ltd.; *Int'l*, pg. 934
NIPPON TUNGSTEN CO., LTD.—See Toshiba Corporation; *Int'l*, pg. 1403
NIPPON TYPEWRITER CO., LTD.—See Canon Inc.; *Int'l*, pg. 261
NIPPON UNIVAC KAISHA, LTD.—See Mitsui & Co., Ltd.; *Int'l*, pg. 879
NIPPON VICKS K.K.—See The Procter & Gamble Company; *U.S. Public*, pg. 1331
NIPPON VISHAY K.K.—See Vishay Intertechnology, Inc.; *U.S. Public*, pg. 1722
NIPPON WELLCOME KK—See Glaxo Wellcome plc; *Int'l*, pg. 553
NIPPON YUSEN K.K.; *Int'l*, pg. 941
NIPPONDENSO (AUSTRALIA) PTY.—See Toyota Motor Corporation; *Int'l*, pg. 1414
NIPPONDENSO CO., LTD.—See Toyota Motor Corporation; *Int'l*, pg. 1412
NIPPONDENSO OF LOS ANGELES (CHICAGO)—See Toyota Motor Corporation; *Int'l*, pg. 1412
NIPSCO CAPITAL MARKETS, INC.—See NIPSCO Industries, Inc.; *U.S. Public*, pg. 1185
NIPSCO DEVELOPMENT COMPANY, INC.—See NIPSCO Industries, Inc.; *U.S. Public*, pg. 1185
NIPSCO ENERGY SERVICES, INC.—See NIPSCO Industries, Inc.; *U.S. Public*, pg. 1185

NIPSCO ENERGY TRADING CORPORATION, INC.—See NIPSCO Industries, Inc.; *U.S. Public*, pg. 1185
NIPSCO EXPLORATION CO., INC.—See NIPSCO Industries, Inc.; *U.S. Public*, pg. 1185
NIPSCO FUEL COMPANY, INC.—See NIPSCO Industries, Inc.; *U.S. Public*, pg. 1185
NIPSCO INDUSTRIES, INC.; *U.S. Public*, pg. 1185
NIPSEA CHEMICAL CO., LTD.—See Nippon Paint Company Ltd.; *Int'l*, pg. 937
NIPSEA PAINT RESEARCH PTE. LTD.—See Nippon Paint Company Ltd.; *Int'l*, pg. 937
NIPSON INTERNATIONAL—See Compagnie des Machines Bull; *Int'l*, pg. 316
NIPSON PRINTING SYSTEMS—See Compagnie des Machines Bull; *Int'l*, pg. 316
NIPSON PRINTING SYSTEMS GMBH—See Compagnie des Machines Bull; *Int'l*, pg. 316
NIPSON PRINTING SYSTEMS INC.—See Compagnie des Machines Bull; *Int'l*, pg. 316
NIPSON PRINTING SYSTEMS LTD.—See Compagnie des Machines Bull; *Int'l*, pg. 316
CIA. NIQUEL TOCANTINS—See S.A. Industrias Votorantim; *Int'l*, pg. 677
NIRA AUSTRALIA PTY. LTD.—See Telefonaktiebolaget LM Ericsson; *Int'l*, pg. 1369
N.V. NIRA COMMUNICATION SYSTEMS—See Telefonaktiebolaget LM Ericsson; *Int'l*, pg. 1369
NIRA DEUTSCHLAND ZWEIGNIEDERLASSUNG DER NIRA INTERNATIONAL B.V.—See Telefonaktiebolaget LM Ericsson; *Int'l*, pg. 1369
NIRA NEDERLAND B.V.—See Telefonaktiebolaget LM Ericsson; *Int'l*, pg. 1369
NIRA S.A.—See Telefonaktiebolaget LM Ericsson; *Int'l*, pg. 1369
NISCO STEEL SERVICES, INC.—See Nissho Iwai Corporation; *Int'l*, pg. 947
NISHI NIPPON ELECTRIC WIRE & CABLE CO., LTD.—See Mitsui & Co., Ltd.; *Int'l*, pg. 878
NISHIMATSU CONSTRUCTION CO., LTD.; *Int'l*, pg. 942
NISHIMATSU CONSTRUCTION CO., LTD.-HONG KONG BRANCH—See Nishimatsu Construction Co., Ltd.; *Int'l*, pg. 943
NISHIMATSU CONSTRUCTION CO., LTD.-LONDON OFFICE—See Nishimatsu Construction Co., Ltd.; *Int'l*, pg. 943
NISHIMATSU CONSTRUCTION CO., LTD.-SINGAPORE OFFICE—See Nishimatsu Construction Co., Ltd.; *Int'l*, pg. 943
NISHIMATSU CONSTRUCTION CO., LTD.-MALAYSIA OFFICE—See Nishimatsu Construction Co., Ltd.; *Int'l*, pg. 943
NISHIMATSU - CORPRO CONSTRUCTION (M) SDN. BHD.—See Nishimatsu Construction Co., Ltd.; *Int'l*, pg. 943
NISHIMATSU LUM CHANG JV PTE. LTD.—See Nishimatsu Construction Co., Ltd.; *Int'l*, pg. 943
NISHIMATSU (MALAYSIA) SDN. BHD.—See Nishimatsu Construction Co., Ltd.; *Int'l*, pg. 943
NISHISHIBA ELECTRIC CO., LTD.—See Toshiba Corporation; *Int'l*, pg. 1403
NISSAN ALTIA CO., LTD.—See Nissan Motor Co., Ltd.; *Int'l*, pg. 944
NISSAN BANK GMBH—See Nissan Motor Co., Ltd.; *Int'l*, pg. 945
NISSAN CANADA FINANCE, INC.—See Nissan Motor Co., Ltd.; *Int'l*, pg. 945
NISSAN CANADA INC.—See Nissan Motor Co., Ltd.; *Int'l*, pg. 945
NISSAN CAPITAL OF AMERICA, INC.—See Nissan Motor Co., Ltd.; *Int'l*, pg. 944
NISSAN CAR LEASING CO., LTD.—See Nissan Motor Co., Ltd.; *Int'l*, pg. 944
NISSAN CASTINGS AUSTRALIA PTY. LTD.—See Nissan Motor Co., Ltd.; *Int'l*, pg. 945
NISSAN CONSTRUCTION CO., LTD.—See Mycal, Corp.; *Int'l*, pg. 898
NISSAN CR CORPORATION—See Nissan Motor Co., Ltd.; *Int'l*, pg. 944
NISSAN CREDIT CORPORATION—See Nissan Motor Co., Ltd.; *Int'l*, pg. 944
NISSAN DATSUN HOLDINGS LTD.—See Nissan Motor Co., Ltd.; *Int'l*, pg. 945
NISSAN DESIGN EUROPE (NDE) GMBH—See Nissan Motor Co., Ltd.; *Int'l*, pg. 945
NISSAN DESIGN INTERNATIONAL, INC.—See Nissan Motor Co., Ltd.; *Int'l*, pg. 944
NISSAN DIESEL MOTOR CO., LTD.—See Nissan Motor Co., Ltd.; *Int'l*, pg. 944
NISSAN EUROPE N.V.—See Nissan Motor Co., Ltd.; *Int'l*, pg. 945
NISSAN EUROPEAN TECHNOLOGY CENTRE LTD.—See Nissan Motor Co., Ltd.; *Int'l*, pg. 945
NISSAN FERRO ORGANIC CHEMICAL CO. LTD.—See Ferro Corporation; *U.S. Public*, pg. 620
NISSAN FINANCE, B.V.—See Nissan Motor Co., Ltd.; *Int'l*, pg. 945
NISSAN FINANCE CORPORATION LTD.—See Nissan Motor Co., Ltd.; *Int'l*, pg. 945
NISSAN FINANCE OF AMERICA, INC.—See Nissan Motor Co., Ltd.; *Int'l*, pg. 944
NISSAN FINANCIACION, S.A.—See Nissan Motor Co., Ltd.; *Int'l*, pg. 945
NISSAN FINANZIARIA S.P.A.—See Nissan Motor Co., Ltd.; *Int'l*, pg. 945
NISSAN FORKLIFT CORPORATION, NORTH AMERICA—See Nissan Motor Co., Ltd.; *Int'l*, pg. 944
NISSAN FRANCE S.A.—See Nissan Motor Co., Ltd.; *Int'l*, pg. 945
NISSAN GRAPHIC ARTS CO., LTD.—See Nissan Motor Co., Ltd.; *Int'l*, pg. 944
NISSAN-INDUSTRIAL OXYGEN INCORPORATED SDN. BHD.—See Nippon Sanso Corporation; *Int'l*, pg. 939
NISSAN INTERNATIONAL FINANCE (EUROPE) LIMITED—See Nissan Motor Co., Ltd.; *Int'l*, pg. 945

NISSAN INTERNATIONAL FINANCE (NETHERLANDS) B.V.—See Nissan Motor Co., Ltd.; *Int'l*, pg. 945
NISSAN ITALIA S.P.A.—See Nissan Motor Co., Ltd.; *Int'l*, pg. 945
NISSAN KOEI CO., LTD.—See Nissan Motor Co., Ltd.; *Int'l*, pg. 944
NISSAN KOHKI CO., LTD.—See Nissan Motor Co., Ltd.; *Int'l*, pg. 944
NISSAN LEASING CO., LTD.—See Nissan Motor Co., Ltd.; *Int'l*, pg. 944
NISSAN MEXICANA, S.A. DE C.V.—See Nissan Motor Co., Ltd.; *Int'l*, pg. 945
NISSAN MOTOR ACCEPTANCE CORP.—See Nissan Motor Co., Ltd.; *Int'l*, pg. 945
NISSAN MOTOR CAR CARRIER CO., LTD.—See Nissan Motor Co., Ltd.; *Int'l*, pg. 944
NISSAN MOTOR CO. (AUSTRALIA) PTY. LTD.—See Nissan Motor Co., Ltd.; *Int'l*, pg. 945
NISSAN MOTOR CO., LTD.; *Int'l*, pg. 943
NISSAN MOTOR CORPORATION IN GUAM—See Nissan Motor Co., Ltd.; *Int'l*, pg. 945
NISSAN MOTOR CORPORATION IN HAWAII, LTD.—See Nissan Motor Co., Ltd.; *Int'l*, pg. 945
NISSAN MOTOR CORPORATION IN U.S.A.—See Nissan Motor Co., Ltd.; *Int'l*, pg. 945
NISSAN MOTOR DEL PERU S.A.—See Nissan Motor Co., Ltd.; *Int'l*, pg. 945
NISSAN MOTOR DEUTSCHLAND GMBH—See Nissan Motor Co., Ltd.; *Int'l*, pg. 945
NISSAN MOTOR (GB) LTD.—See Nissan Motor Co., Ltd.; *Int'l*, pg. 945
NISSAN MOTOR IBERICA S.A.—See Nissan Motor Co., Ltd.; *Int'l*, pg. 945
NISSAN MOTOR MANUFACTURING CO. (AUSTRALIA) LTD.—See Nissan Motor Co., Ltd.; *Int'l*, pg. 945
NISSAN MOTOR MFG. CORP., U.S.A.—See Nissan Motor Co., Ltd.; *Int'l*, pg. 945
NISSAN MOTOR MANUFACTURING (UK) LTD.—See Nissan Motor Co., Ltd.; *Int'l*, pg. 945
NISSAN MOTOR NEDERLAND B.V.—See Nissan Motor Co., Ltd.; *Int'l*, pg. 945
NISSAN MOTOR PARTS CENTRE (EUROPE) B.V.—See Nissan Motor Co., Ltd.; *Int'l*, pg. 945
NISSAN MOTOR SALES CO., LTD.—See Nissan Motor Co., Ltd.; *Int'l*, pg. 945
NISSAN MOTOR (SCHWEIZ) AG—See Nissan Motor Co., Ltd.; *Int'l*, pg. 945
NISSAN MOTORIST SERVICE CO., LTD.—See Nissan Motor Co., Ltd.; *Int'l*, pg. 944
NISSAN MUTUAL LIFE INSURANCE COMPANY; *Int'l*, pg. 945
NISSAN NORTH AMERICA, INC.—See Nissan Motor Co., Ltd.; *Int'l*, pg. 945
NISSAN PRINCE MOTOR SALES CO., LTD.—See Nissan Motor Co., Ltd.; *Int'l*, pg. 944
NISSAN REAL ESTATE CO., LTD.—See Nissan Motor Co., Ltd.; *Int'l*, pg. 944
NISSAN RESEARCH & DEVELOPMENT CORP.—See Nissan Motor Co., Ltd.; *Int'l*, pg. 945
NISSAN RIKUSO CO., LTD.—See Nissan Motor Co., Ltd.; *Int'l*, pg. 944
NISSAN SHATAI CO., LTD.—See Nissan Motor Co., Ltd.; *Int'l*, pg. 944
NISSAN SUNNY TOKYO MOTOR SALES CO., LTD.—See Nissan Motor Co., Ltd.; *Int'l*, pg. 944
NISSAN TEXSYS CO., LTD.—See Nissan Motor Co., Ltd.; *Int'l*, pg. 944
NISSAN TEXTILE MACHINERY CORP. IN U.S.A.—See Nissan Motor Co., Ltd.; *Int'l*, pg. 945
NISSAN TRADING CO., LTD.—See Nissan Motor Co., Ltd.; *Int'l*, pg. 944
NISSAN TRADING CORP., USA—See Nissan Motor Co., Ltd.; *Int'l*, pg. 945
NISSAN TRANSPORT CO., LTD.—See Nissan Motor Co., Ltd.; *Int'l*, pg. 944
NISSAY ASSET MANAGEMENT CORPORATION—See Nippon Life Insurance Co.; *Int'l*, pg. 935
NISSAY ATHLETICS CO., LTD.—See Nippon Life Insurance Co.; *Int'l*, pg. 935
NISSAY BUSINESS SERVICE CO., LTD.—See Nippon Life Insurance Co.; *Int'l*, pg. 935
NISSAY CAPITAL CO., LTD.—See Nippon Life Insurance Co.; *Int'l*, pg. 935
NISSAY CARD SERVICES CO., LTD.—See Nippon Life Insurance Co.; *Int'l*, pg. 935
NISSAY COMPUTER CO., LTD.—See Nippon Life Insurance Co.; *Int'l*, pg. 935
NISSAY CREDIT CO., LTD.—See Nippon Life Insurance Co.; *Int'l*, pg. 935
NISSAY CULTURE FOUNDATION—See Nippon Life Insurance Co.; *Int'l*, pg. 935
NISSAY GREEN FOUNDATION—See Nippon Life Insurance Co.; *Int'l*, pg. 935
NISSAY INVESTMENT CO., LTD.—See Nippon Life Insurance Co.; *Int'l*, pg. 935
NISSAY INVESTMENT TRUST MANAGEMENT CO., LTD.—See Nippon Life Insurance Co.; *Int'l*, pg. 935
NISSAY MANAGAMENT CO., LTD.—See Nippon Life Insurance Co.; *Int'l*, pg. 935
NISSAY MORTGAGE CO., LTD.—See Nippon Life Insurance Co.; *Int'l*, pg. 935
NISSAY NEW CREATION CO., LTD.—See Nippon Life Insurance Co.; *Int'l*, pg. 935
NISSAY OKINAWA KOGYO CO., LTD.—See Nippon Life Insurance Co.; *Int'l*, pg. 935
NISSAY SEIREI HEALTH & WELFARE FOUNDATION—See Nippon Life Insurance Co.; *Int'l*, pg. 935
NISSAY STADIUM CO., LTD.—See Nippon Life Insurance Co.; *Int'l*, pg. 935
NISSAY TRADING CO., LTD.—See Nippon Life Insurance Co.; *Int'l*, pg. 935
NISSEI LEASING CO., LTD.—See Nippon Life Insurance Co.; *Int'l*, pg. 935
NISSEI SANGYO CO., LTD.; *Int'l*, pg. 945

NISSEN TRAMPOLINE AG—See Hanson PLC; *Int'l*, pg. 595
NISSHIN BADISCHE CO., LTD.—See BASF AG; *Int'l*, pg. 109
NISSHIN FLOUR MILLING CO., LTD.; *Int'l*, pg. 946
NISSHIN STEEL CO., LTD.; *Int'l*, pg. 946
NISSHIN STEEL USA, INC.—See Nisshin Steel Co., Ltd.; *Int'l*, pg. 946
NISSHO ELECTRONICS CORP.—See Nissho Iwai Corporation; *Int'l*, pg. 946
NISSHO IWAI AEROSPACE (AMERICA) CORP.—See Nissho Iwai Corporation; *Int'l*, pg. 947
NISSHO IWAI AEROSPACE CORP.—See Nissho Iwai Corporation; *Int'l*, pg. 946
NISSHO IWAI APPAREL CO., LTD.—See Nissho Iwai Corporation; *Int'l*, pg. 946
NISSHO IWAI AUSTRALIA LTD.—See Nissho Iwai Corporation; *Int'l*, pg. 948
N.V. NISSHO IWAI (BENELUX) S.A.—See Nissho Iwai Corporation; *Int'l*, pg. 948
NISSHO IWAI BUILDING MATERIALS CORP.—See Nissho Iwai Corporation; *Int'l*, pg. 946
NISSHO IWAI CANADA LTD.—See Nissho Iwai Corporation; *Int'l*, pg. 948
NISSHO IWAI (CHILE) LTDA.—See Nissho Iwai Corporation; *Int'l*, pg. 948
NISSHO IWAI COAL DEVELOPMENT (CANADA) LTD.—See Nissho Iwai Corporation; *Int'l*, pg. 948
NISSHO IWAI CORPORATION; *Int'l*, pg. 946
NISSHO IWAI CORPORATION (IRAN) LTD.—See Nissho Iwai Corporation; *Int'l*, pg. 948
NISSHO IWAI DE COLUMBIA S.A.—See Nissho Iwai Corporation; *Int'l*, pg. 948
NISSHO IWAI DE VENEZUELA C.A.—See Nissho Iwai Corporation; *Int'l*, pg. 948
NISSHO IWAI DEL ECUADOR S.A.—See Nissho Iwai Corporation; *Int'l*, pg. 948
NISSHO IWAI DELICA CORP.—See Nissho Iwai Corporation; *Int'l*, pg. 946
NISSHO IWAI DEUTSCHLAND GMBH—See Nissho Iwai Corporation; *Int'l*, pg. 948
NISSHO IWAI DO BRASIL S.A.—See Nissho Iwai Corporation; *Int'l*, pg. 948
NISSHO IWAI EUROPE PLC—See Nissho Iwai Corporation; *Int'l*, pg. 948
NISSHO IWAI FIBER & YARN LTD.—See Nissho Iwai Corporation; *Int'l*, pg. 946
NISSHO IWAI FOODS CORP.—See Nissho Iwai Corporation; *Int'l*, pg. 946
NISSHO IWAI FRANCE S.A.—See Nissho Iwai Corporation; *Int'l*, pg. 948
NISSHO IWAI GAS CO., LTD.—See Nissho Iwai Corporation; *Int'l*, pg. 946
NISSHO IWAI GENERAL MERCHANDISE CORP.—See Nissho Iwai Corporation; *Int'l*, pg. 946
NISSHO IWAI HONG KONG CORPORATION LIMITED—See Nissho Iwai Corporation; *Int'l*, pg. 948
NISSHO IWAI IBERIA S.A.—See Nissho Iwai Corporation; *Int'l*, pg. 948
NISSHO IWAI INDUSTRIAL MACHINERY INC.—See Nissho Iwai Corporation; *Int'l*, pg. 946
NISSHO IWAI ITALIA S.P.A.—See Nissho Iwai Corporation; *Int'l*, pg. 948
NISSHO IWAI KOREA CORPORATION—See Nissho Iwai Corporation; *Int'l*, pg. 948
NISSHO IWAI MIDDLE EAST E.C.—See Nissho Iwai Corporation; *Int'l*, pg. 948
NISSHO IWAI NEW ZEALAND LIMITED—See Nissho Iwai Corporation; *Int'l*, pg. 948
NISSHO IWAI (NIGERIA) LTD.—See Nissho Iwai Corporation; *Int'l*, pg. 948
NISSHO IWAI NONFERROUS METALS CORP.—See Nissho Iwai Corporation; *Int'l*, pg. 947
NISSHO IWAI PANAMA INTERNATIONAL S.A.—See Nissho Iwai Corporation; *Int'l*, pg. 948
NISSHO IWAI PETROLEUM CORP.—See Nissho Iwai Corporation; *Int'l*, pg. 947
NISSHO IWAI POLYMERS & PRODUCTS CORP.—See Nissho Iwai Corporation; *Int'l*, pg. 947
NISSHO IWAI REAL ESTATE CORP.—See Nissho Iwai Corporation; *Int'l*, pg. 947
NISSHO IWAI (SHANGHAI) CORPORATION—See Nissho Iwai Corporation; *Int'l*, pg. 948
NISSHO IWAI STEEL LEASING CO. LTD.—See Nissho Iwai Corporation; *Int'l*, pg. 947
NISSHO IWAI TEXTILE CO., LTD.—See Nissho Iwai Corporation; *Int'l*, pg. 947
NISSHO IWAI (THAILAND) LIMITED PARTNERSHIP—See Nissho Iwai Corporation; *Int'l*, pg. 948
NISSHO PROPANE SEKIYU CORP.—See Nissho Iwai Corporation; *Int'l*, pg. 946
NISSHOKU SCHENECTADY CHEMICALS, INC.—See Schenectady International, Inc.; *U.S. Private*, pg. 970
NISSIN-AJINOMOTO ALIMENTOS LTDA.—See Nissin Food Products Co., Ltd.; *Int'l*, pg. 950
NISSIN COFCO FOODS CO., LTD.—See Nissin Food Products Co., Ltd.; *Int'l*, pg. 950
NISSIN FOOD PRODUCTS CO., LTD.; *Int'l*, pg. 949
NISSIN FOODS B.V.—See Nissin Food Products Co., Ltd.; *Int'l*, pg. 950
NISSIN FOODS (CANADA) INC.—See Nissin Food Products Co., Ltd.; *Int'l*, pg. 950
NISSIN FOODS CO., LTD—See Nissin Food Products Co., Ltd.; *Int'l*, pg. 950
NISSIN FOODS GMBH—See Nissin Food Products Co., Ltd.; *Int'l*, pg. 950
NISSIN FOODS (S) PTE. LTD.—See Nissin Food Products Co., Ltd.; *Int'l*, pg. 950
NISSIN FOODS (THAILAND) CO., LTD.—See Nissin Food Products Co., Ltd.; *Int'l*, pg. 950
NISSIN FOODS (U.S.A.) CALIFORNIA PLANT—See Nissin Food Products Co., Ltd.; *Int'l*, pg. 949
NISSIN FOODS (U.S.A.) CO., INC.—See Nissin Food Products Co., Ltd.; *Int'l*, pg. 949

NISSIN FOODS (U.S.A.) CO. LTD.—See Nissin Food Products Co., Ltd.; *Int'l*, pg. 949
NISSIN FOODS (U.S.A.) EASTERN DIVISION—See Nissin Food Products Co., Ltd.; *Int'l*, pg. 949
NISSIN FOODS (U.S.A.) PLANT—See Nissin Food Products Co., Ltd.; *Int'l*, pg. 950
NISSIN INTERNATIONAL CORP.—See Nissin Food Products Co., Ltd.; *Int'l*, pg. 950
NISSIN MOLECULAR BIOLOGY INSTITUTE, INC.—See Nissin Food Products Co., Ltd.; *Int'l*, pg. 950
P.T. NISSINMAS—See Nissin Food Products Co., Ltd.; *Int'l*, pg. 950
NISSIN-UNIVERSAL ROBINA CORPORATION—See Nissin Food Products Co., Ltd.; *Int'l*, pg. 950
NISSO MASTER BUILDERS CO. LTD.—See Viag AG; *Int'l*, pg. 1466
NITCHES (FAR EAST) LTD.—See Niches, Inc.; *U.S. Public*, pg. 1182
NITEC (EUROPE) B.V.—See Nissin Food Products Co., Ltd.; *Int'l*, pg. 950
NITEC (H.K.), LTD.—See Nissin Food Products Co., Ltd.; *Int'l*, pg. 950
NITEC (SOUTH ASIA) PTE. LTD.—See Nissin Food Products Co., Ltd.; *Int'l*, pg. 950
NITEC (U.S.A.), INC.—See Nissin Food Products Co., Ltd.; *Int'l*, pg. 950
NITODAN A/S—See Nilfisk A/S; *Int'l*, pg. 932
NITRAM ENERGY INC.; *U.S. Private*, pg. 799
NITRO STEEL DIV.—See Quanex Corporation; *U.S. Public*, pg. 1349
NITROMITE FERTILIZER—See Ultramar Diamond Shamrock Corporation; *U.S. Public*, pg. 1663
CIA. NITROQUIMICA BRASILEIRA—See S.A. Industrias Votorantim; *Int'l*, pg. 677
NITROUS OXIDE CORP. (DONORA)—See Airgas, Inc.; *U.S. Public*, pg. 33
NITTA-APITRON CO., LTD.—See American Precision Industries Inc.; *U.S. Public*, pg. 90
NITTAN VALVE COMPANY LTD.—See Eaton Corporation; *U.S. Public*, pg. 559
NITTANY INVESTMENT CO.—See Omega Financial Corporation; *U.S. Public*, pg. 1222
NITTANY PRINTING & PUBLISHING CO.—See Knight-Ridder, Inc.; *U.S. Public*, pg. 964
NITTETSU ITALIANA S.P.A.—See Nippon Steel Corporation; *int'l*, pg. 940
NITTETSU SHOJI AMERICA, INC.—See Nippon Steel Corporation; *Int'l*, pg. 939
NITTETSU SHOJI CO., LTD.—See Nippon Steel Corporation; *Int'l*, pg. 939
NITTO CO., LTD.—See Meiji Seika Kaisha, Ltd.; *Int'l*, pg. 855
NITTO DENKO AMERICA, INC.—See Nitto Denko Corporation; *Int'l*, pg. 950
NITTO DENKO (AUSTRALIA) PTY. LTD.—See Nitto Denko Corporation; *Int'l*, pg. 950
NITTO DENKO CORPORATION; *Int'l*, pg. 950
NITTO DENKO (MALAYSIA) SDN. BHD.—See Nitto Denko Corporation; *Int'l*, pg. 950
NITTO DENKO MATERIALS (MALAYSIA) SDN. BHD.—See Nitto Denko Corporation; *Int'l*, pg. 950
NITTO DENKO (SHAGHAI PU DONG NEW AREA) CO., LTD.—See Nitto Denko Corporation; *Int'l*, pg. 950
NITTO DENKO (TAIWAN) CORPORATION—See Nitto Denko Corporation; *Int'l*, pg. 950
NITTO DENKO (THAILAND) CO., LTD.—See Nitto Denko Corporation; *Int'l*, pg. 950
NITTO FORMOSA CO., LTD.—See Nitto Denko Corporation; *Int'l*, pg. 951
NITTO ITALIA S.R.L.—See Nitto Denko Corporation; *Int'l*, pg. 951
NITTO U.K. LIMITED—See Nitto Denko Corporation; *Int'l*, pg. 951
NITTOBO NORPLEX OAK CO., LTD. (NNO)—See AlliedSignal Inc.; *U.S. Public*, pg. 53
NITTSU KIKO UNYU CO., LTD.—See Nippon Express Co., Ltd.; *Int'l*, pg. 934
NITTSU REAL ESTATE CO., LTD.—See Nippon Express Co., Ltd.; *Int'l*, pg. 934
NITTSU SHOJI CO., LTD.—See Nippon Express Co., Ltd.; *Int'l*, pg. 934
NIVAROX-FAR S.A.—See SMH Swiss Corporation for Micro Electronics & Watchmaking Indus. Ltd.; *Int'l*, pg. 1161
NIVEA-KAO CO. LTD.—See Beiersdorf Group; *Int'l*, pg. 183
NIVEL PUBLICIDAD—See FCB; *U.S. Private*, pg. 389
NIVELLES—See TI Group plc; *Int'l*, pg. 1342
NIXDORFF KREIN INDUSTRIES INC.; *U.S. Private*, pg. 799
NJR ENERGY SERVICES CORPORATION—See New Jersey Resources Corporation; *U.S. Public*, pg. 1172
NO FRILLS (DIY) LIMITED—See RMC Group p.l.c.; *Int'l*, pg. 1080
NO SABE FALLAR S.A.—See Societe BIC S.A.; *Int'l*, pg. 1273
NO-SAG FOAM PRODUCTS COMPANY—See Leggett & Platt, Incorporated; *U.S. Public*, pg. 986
NOAMAN ENGINEERING CO.—See GESTRA GmbH; *Int'l*, pg. 550
NOB HILL GENERAL STORE, INC.; *U.S. Private*, pg. 799
NOBART, INC.—See Devon Group, Inc.; *U.S. Public*, pg. 503
NOBART, INC.; *U.S. Private*, pg. 800
NOBEL BIOCARE; *Int'l*, pg. 951
NOBEL CONSUMER GOODS AB—See Akzo Nobel N.V.; *Int'l*, pg. 48
NOBEL EDUCATION DYNAMICS, INC.; *U.S. Public*, pg. 1185
NOBEL ELECTRONIQUE S.A.R.L.—See Spectra-Physics AB; *Int'l*, pg. 1290
NOBEL ELEKTRONIIKKA OY AB—See Spectra-Physics AB; *Int'l*, pg. 1290
NOBEL ELEKTRONIK AB—See Spectra-Physics AB; *Int'l*, pg. 1289

NOBEL ELEKTRONIKK A/S—See Spectra-Physics AB; *Int'l*, pg. 1290
NOBEL INSURANCE AGENCY—See Nobel Insurance Limited; *Int'l*, pg. 951
NOBEL INSURANCE GROUP—See Nobel Insurance Limited; *Int'l*, pg. 951
NOBEL INSURANCE LIMITED; *Int'l*, pg. 951
NOBEL LLOYDS INSURANCE COMPANY—See Nobel Insurance Limited; *Int'l*, pg. 951
NOBEL PLANT—See GSW Inc.; *Int'l*, pg. 538
AB NOBEL PLAST—See Akzo Nobel N.V.; *Int'l*, pg. 48
NOBEL/SYSCO FOOD SERVICES CO.-ALBEQUERQUE—See Sysco Corporation; *U.S. Public*, pg. 1551
NOBEL/SYSCO FOOD SERVICES COMPANY-DENVER—See Sysco Corporation; *U.S. Public*, pg. 1551
NOBEL SYSTEMS LTD.—See Spectra-Physics AB; *Int'l*, pg. 1290
NOBEL'S EXPLOSIVES COMPANY LIMITED—See Imperial Chemical Industries PLC; *Int'l*, pg. 663
NOBEMA S.A.—See Tractebel; *Int'l*, pg. 1415
NOBILES-LEES S.A. DE C.V.—See Burlington Industries, Inc.; *U.S. Public*, pg. 268
NOBILITY HOMES, INC.; *U.S. Public*, pg. 1186
NOBIS SOCIETE DES BANQUES PRIVEES—See BHF-BANK AG; *Int'l*, pg. 119
NOBIS SOCIETE DES BANQUES PRIVEES—See IKB Deutsche Industriebank AG; *Int'l*, pg. 646
NOBLE AFFILIATES, INC.; *U.S. Public*, pg. 1186
NOBLE & ASSOCIATES; *U.S. Private*, pg. 800
NOBLE & ASSOCIATES/CHICAGO—See Noble & Associates; *U.S. Private*, pg. 800
NOBLE & ASSOCIATES PROMOTION GROUP—See Noble & Associates; *U.S. Private*, pg. 800
NOBLE & ASSOCIATES PUBLIC RELATIONS—See Noble & Associates; *U.S. Private*, pg. 800
NOBLE DRILLING (CANADA) LTD.—See Noble Drilling Corporation; *U.S. Public*, pg. 1187
NOBLE DRILLING CORPORATION; *U.S. Public*, pg. 1186
NOBLE DRILLING INTERNATIONAL, INC.—See Noble Drilling Corporation; *U.S. Public*, pg. 1186
NOBLE DRILLING (NIGERIA) LTD.—See Noble Drilling Corporation; *U.S. Public*, pg. 1187
NOBLE DRILLING SERVICES INC.—See Noble Drilling Corporation; *U.S. Public*, pg. 1186
NOBLE DRILLING (U.K.) LTD.—See Noble Drilling Corporation; *U.S. Public*, pg. 1187
NOBLE DRILLING (U.S.) INC.—See Noble Drilling Corporation; *U.S. Public*, pg. 1186
NOBLE DRILLING (WEST AFRICA) LTD.—See Noble Drilling Corporation; *U.S. Public*, pg. 1187
NOBLE GAS MARKETING, INC.—See Noble Affiliates, Inc.; *U.S. Public*, pg. 1186
NOBLE HOUSE HOTELS AND RESORTS; *U.S. Private*, pg. 800
NOBLE INTERNATIONAL LTD.; *U.S. Public*, pg. 1187
NOBLE-NATIONAL JOINT VENTURE—See Noble Drilling Corporation; *U.S. Public*, pg. 1186
NOBLE NEDDRILL—See Noble Drilling Corporation; *U.S. Public*, pg. 1187
NOBLE OFFSHORE CORPORATION—See Noble Drilling Corporation; *U.S. Public*, pg. 1186
NOBLE ROMAN'S INC.; *U.S. Public*, pg. 1187
NOBLE TRADING, INC.—See Noble Affiliates, Inc.; *U.S. Public*, pg. 1186
NOBLES MFG. INC.; *U.S. Private*, pg. 800
NOBLEX ARGENTINA S.A.C. E I.; *Int'l*, pg. 951
NOBLEZA-PICCARDO SAICF—See B.A.T Industries P.L.C.; *Int'l*, pg. 111
NOBODY BEATS THE WIZ; *U.S. Private*, pg. 800
NOCONA BOOT CO.—See Justin Industries, Inc.; *U.S. Public*, pg. 937
NODAK ELECTRIC CO-OP; *U.S. Private*, pg. 800
NODAK MUTUAL INSURANCE COMPANY; *U.S. Private*, pg. 800
NODECO (HIBERNIA PROJECT)—See Lyonnaise des Eaux S.A.; *Int'l*, pg. 823
NODECO, LTD.—See Weatherford Enterra Incorporated; *U.S. Public*, pg. 1750
NODEST A/S—See Jotun A/S; *Int'l*, pg. 715
NOEL CANNING CORPORATION; *U.S. Private*, pg. 800
NOEL GROUP, INC.; *U.S. Public*, pg. 1187
NOEL OF JAMAICA LTD.—See Fruit of the Loom, Inc.; *U.S. Public*, pg. 686
NOEL JOANNA, INC.—See Crown Crafts, Inc.; *U.S. Public*, pg. 465
NOEL OLSON GROUP; *U.S. Private*, pg. 800
NOELL GMBH—See Preussag AG; *Int'l*, pg. 1069
NOELL INC.—See Preussag AG; *Int'l*, pg. 1070
NOESIS/THE CORPORATE COMPANY—See BDDP Group; *Int'l*, pg. 117
NOFSINGER, INC.—See Burns & McDonnell Engineers-Architects-Consultants; *U.S. Private*, pg. 187
NOGATA TOSHIBA ELECTRONICS CO.—See Toshiba Corporation; *Int'l*, pg. 1403
NOISE DAIRY SYSTEMS, LP—See Code, Hennessy & Simmons, Inc.; *U.S. Private*, pg. 249
NOISE & VIBRATION SYSTEMS—See Ultra Electronics Holdings plc; *Int'l*, pg. 1431
NOK EG & G OPTOELECTRONICS CORPORATION—See EG & G, Inc.; *U.S. Public*, pg. 544
OY NOKIA AB/NOKIA GROUP; *Int'l*, pg. 951
NOKIA AUDIO & ELECTRONICS AB—See Oy Nokia Ab/Nokia Group; *Int'l*, pg. 954
NOKIA AUDIO ELECTRONICS GMBH—See Oy Nokia Ab/Nokia Group; *Int'l*, pg. 954
NOKIA CELLULAR SYSTEMS—See Oy Nokia Ab/Nokia Group; *Int'l*, pg. 953
NOKIA CELLULAR SYSTEMS BASE STATIONS—See Oy Nokia Ab/Nokia Group; *Int'l*, pg. 953
NOKIA CELLULAR SYSTEMS MOBILE SWITCHING—See Oy Nokia Ab/Nokia Group; *Int'l*, pg. 953
NOKIA CELLULAR SYSTEMS PMR TERMINALS—See Oy Nokia Ab/Nokia Group; *Int'l*, pg. 953

NOKIA CELLULAR SYSTEMS PRIVATE MOBILE RADIO (PMR)—See Oy Nokia Ab/Nokia Group; *Int'l*, pg. 953
NOKIA (DEUTSCHLAND) GMBH—See Oy Nokia Ab/Nokia Group; *Int'l*, pg. 954
NOKIA DISPLAY PRODUCTS—See Oy Nokia ·Ab/Nokia Group; *Int'l*, pg. 951
NOKIA DISPLAY PRODUCTS INC.—See Oy Nokia Ab/Nokia Group; *Int'l*, pg. 951
NOKIA DISPLAY PRODUCTS OY—See Oy Nokia Ab/Nokia Group; *Int'l*, pg. 951
NOKIA FINANCE INTERNATIONAL B.V.—See Oy Nokia Ab/Nokia Group; *Int'l*, pg. 954
NOKIA FINANCE INTERNATIONAL B.V., GENEVA BRANCH—See Oy Nokia Ab/Nokia Group; *Int'l*, pg. 954
NOKIA FRANCE S.A.—See Oy Nokia Ab/Nokia Group; *Int'l*, pg. 954
NOKIA GENERAL COMMUNICATIONS LTD.—See Oy Nokia Ab/Nokia Group; *Int'l*, pg. 954
NOKIA INC.—See Oy Nokia Ab/Nokia Group; *Int'l*, pg. 952
NOKIA INDUSTRIAL ELECTRONICS—See Oy Nokia Ab/Nokia Group; *Int'l*, pg. 951
NOKIA INVESTOR RELATIONS/USA—See Oy Nokia Ab/Nokia Group; *Int'l*, pg. 952
NOKIA JAPAN K.K. LTD.—See Oy Nokia Ab/Nokia Group; *Int'l*, pg. 954
NOKIA (MALAYSIA) SDN. BHD.—See Oy Nokia Ab/Nokia Group; *Int'l*, pg. 953
NOKIA MILL—See Fort James Corporation; *U.S. Public*, pg. 673
NOKIA MOBILE PHONES—See Oy Nokia Ab/Nokia Group; *Int'l*, pg. 951
NOKIA MOBILE PHONES AB—See Oy Nokia Ab/Nokia Group; *Int'l*, pg. 952
NOKIA MOBILE PHONES AUSTRALIA PTY. LTD.—See Oy Nokia Ab/Nokia Group; *Int'l*, pg. 952
NOKIA MOBILE PHONES (BENELUX) S.A.—See Oy Nokia Ab/Nokia Group; *Int'l*, pg. 952
NOKIA MOBILE PHONES CELLULAR DATA—See Oy Nokia Ab/Nokia Group; *Int'l*, pg. 952
NOKIA MOBILE PHONES FRANCE—See Oy Nokia Ab/Nokia Group; *Int'l*, pg. 952
NOKIA MOBILE PHONES GMBH—See Oy Nokia Ab/Nokia Group; *Int'l*, pg. 952
NOKIA MOBILE PHONES (GULF)—See Oy Nokia Ab/Nokia Group; *Int'l*, pg. 952
NOKIA MOBILE PHONES (H.K.) LTD.—See Oy Nokia Ab/Nokia Group; *Int'l*, pg. 952
NOKIA MOBILE PHONES INC.—See Oy Nokia Ab/Nokia Group; *Int'l*, pg. 952
NOKIA MOBILE PHONES, INC.—See Oy Nokia Ab/Nokia Group; *Int'l*, pg. 952
NOKIA MOBILE PHONES ITALIA S.R.L.—See Oy Nokia Ab/Nokia Group; *Int'l*, pg. 952
NOKIA MOBILE PHONES JAPAN K.K.—See Oy Nokia Ab/Nokia Group; *Int'l*, pg. 952
NOKIA MOBILE PHONES (KOREA) LTD.—See Oy Nokia Ab/Nokia Group; *Int'l*, pg. 952
NOKIA MOBILE PHONES MANUFACTURING (USA) LTD.—See Oy Nokia Ab/Nokia Group; *Int'l*, pg. 952
NOKIA MOBILE PHONES (MEXICO) S.A. DE C.V.—See Oy Nokia Ab/Nokia Group; *Int'l*, pg. 952
NOKIA MOBILE PHONES PRODUKTIONS GMBH—See Oy Nokia Ab/Nokia Group; *Int'l*, pg. 952
NOKIA MOBILE PHONES R & D—See Oy Nokia Ab/Nokia Group; *Int'l*, pg. 952
NOKIA MOBILE PHONES R & D CENTER—See Oy Nokia Ab/Nokia Group; *Int'l*, pg. 952
NOKIA MOBILE PHONES R&D CENTER, GERMANY—See Oy Nokia Ab/Nokia Group; *Int'l*, pg. 952
NOKIA MOBILE PHONES, S.E.A. PTE. LTD.—See Oy Nokia Ab/Nokia Group; *Int'l*, pg. 952
NOKIA MOBILE PHONES (SEA) PTE. LTD. (INDIA) LIASON OFFICE—See Oy Nokia Ab/Nokia Group; *Int'l*, pg. 952
NOKIA MOBILE PHONES (UK) LTD.—See Oy Nokia Ab/Nokia Group; *Int'l*, pg. 952
NOKIA MOBILE PHONES UK SALES LTD.—See Oy Nokia Ab/Nokia Group; *Int'l*, pg. 952
NOKIA MONITORS—See Oy Nokia Ab/Nokia Group; *Int'l*, pg. 951
NOKIA MULTIMEDIA NETWORK TERMINALS—See Oy Nokia Ab/Nokia Group; *Int'l*, pg. 952
NOKIA NETWORK AND ACCESS SYSTEMS—See Oy Nokia Ab/Nokia Group; *Int'l*, pg. 953
NOKIA PAGING—See Oy Nokia Ab/Nokia Group; *Int'l*, pg. 952
NOKIA PRODUCTS CORPORATION—See Oy Nokia Ab/Nokia Group; *Int'l*, pg. 952
NOKIA PRODUCTS LTD.—See Oy Nokia Ab/Nokia Group; *Int'l*, pg. 952
NOKIA SATELLITE SYSTEMS AB—See Oy Nokia Ab/Nokia Group; *Int'l*, pg. 954
NOKIA SHANGHAI REPRESENTATIVE OFFICE—See Oy Nokia Ab/Nokia Group; *Int'l*, pg. 953
NOKIA SOURCING, INC.—See Oy Nokia Ab/Nokia Group; *Int'l*, pg. 953
NOKIA SWITCHING SYSTEMS—See Oy Nokia Ab/Nokia Group; *Int'l*, pg. 954
NOKIA TELECOMMUNICATIONS—See Oy Nokia Ab/Nokia Group; *Int'l*, pg. 952
NOKIA TELECOMMUNICATIONS ACCESS SYSTEMS—See Oy Nokia Ab/Nokia Group; *Int'l*, pg. 953
NOKIA TELECOMMUNICATIONS AG—See Oy Nokia Ab/Nokia Group; *Int'l*, pg. 953
NOKIA TELECOMMUNICATIONS A/S—See Oy Nokia Ab/Nokia Group; *Int'l*, pg. 953
NOKIA TELECOMMUNICATIONS BELGIUM—See Oy Nokia Ab/Nokia Group; *Int'l*, pg. 953
NOKIA TELECOMMUNICATIONS GMBH—See Oy Nokia Ab/Nokia Group; *Int'l*, pg. 953
NOKIA TELECOMMUNICATIONS (H.K.) LTD.—See Oy Nokia Ab/Nokia Group; *Int'l*, pg. 953

NOKIA TELECOMMUNICATIONS INC.—See Oy Nokia Ab/Nokia Group; *Int'l*, pg. 953
NOKIA TELECOMMUNICATIONS ITALIA S.R.L.—See Oy Nokia Ab/Nokia Group; *Int'l*, pg. 953
NOKIA TELECOMMUNICATIONS ITALIA SRL—See Oy Nokia Ab/Nokia Group; *Int'l*, pg. 953
NOKIA TELECOMMUNICATIONS KFT—See Oy Nokia Ab/Nokia Group; *Int'l*, pg. 953
NOKIA TELECOMMUNICATIONS LTD.—See Oy Nokia Ab/Nokia Group; *Int'l*, pg. 953
NOKIA TELECOMMUNICATIONS LTD. TRANSMISSION SYSTEMS PRODUCT DEVELOPMENT—See Oy Nokia Ab/Nokia Group; *Int'l*, pg. 953
NOKIA TELECOMMUNICATIONS NZ LIMITED—See Oy Nokia Ab/Nokia Group; *Int'l*, pg. 953
NOKIA TELECOMMUNICATIONS PARKTOWN OFFICE SUITES—See Oy Nokia Ab/Nokia Group; *Int'l*, pg. 954
NOKIA TELECOMMUNICATIONS (PHILIPPINES) INC.—See Oy Nokia Ab/Nokia Group; *Int'l*, pg. 954
NOKIA TELECOMMUNICATIONS PTY. LTD.—See Oy Nokia Ab/Nokia Group; *Int'l*, pg. 954
NOKIA TELECOMMUNICATIONS (SINGAPORE) PTE. LTD.—See Oy Nokia Ab/Nokia Group; *Int'l*, pg. 954
NOKIA TELECOMMUNICATIONS SP.Z.O.O.—See Oy Nokia Ab/Nokia Group; *Int'l*, pg. 954
NOKIA TELECOMMUNICATIONS (THAILAND) LTD.—See Oy Nokia Ab/Nokia Group; *Int'l*, pg. 954
NOKIAN PAPERI OY—See Fort James Corporation; *U.S. Public*, pg. 673
NOKIAN TYRES—See Oy Nokia Ab/Nokia Group; *Int'l*, pg. 954
NOKSEL A.S.—See Oy Nokia Ab/Nokia Group; *Int'l*, pg. 954
NOLAND AIR CONDITIONING/REFRIGERATION DIV.—See Noland Company; *U.S. Public*, pg. 1187
NOLAND COMPANY; *U.S. Public*, pg. 1187
NOLAND ELECTRICAL DIV.—See Noland Company; *U.S. Public*, pg. 1187
NOLAND INDUSTRIAL DIV.—See Noland Company; *U.S. Public*, pg. 1187
NOLAND PLUMBING/HEATING DIV.—See Noland Company; *U.S. Public*, pg. 1187
NOLAND PROPERTIES, INC.—See Noland Company; *U.S. Public*, pg. 1188
J.S. NOLEN & ASSOCIATES—See Litton Industries, Inc.; *U.S. Public*, pg. 1004
NOLICA GVG MBH—See Commerzbank AG; *Int'l*, pg. 309
NOLL PRINTING CORPORATION—See Our Sunday Visitor, Inc.; *U.S. Private*, pg. 821
NOLTE MASTENFABRIEK—See Valmont Industries, Inc.; *U.S. Public*, pg. 1707
NOMA CORPORATION—See Noma Industries Limited; *Int'l*, pg. 955
NOMA (HONG KONG) LIMITED—See Noma Industries Limited; *Int'l*, pg. 955
NOMA INC.—See Noma Industries Limited; *Int'l*, pg. 955
NOMA INDUSTRIAL CORDS COMPANY—See Noma Industries Limited; *Int'l*, pg. 955
NOMA INDUSTRIES LIMITED; *Int'l*, pg. 954
NOMA-INTERNATIONAL, INC.—See Noma Industries Limited; *Int'l*, pg. 955
NOMA INTL. INC.—See Noma Industries Limited; *Int'l*, pg. 955
NOMA SHOWROOM—See Noma Industries Limited; *Int'l*, pg. 955
NOMA TOOLING ENTERPRISES—See Noma Industries Limited; *Int'l*, pg. 955
NOMACO, INC.; *U.S. Private*, pg. 801
NOMADIS S.A.—See Freudenberg & Company; *Int'l*, pg. 507
NOMAFA—See Albany International Corp.; *U.S. Public*, pg. 37
NOMECO EXPLORATION CANADA, INC.—See CMS Energy Corporation; *U.S. Public*, pg. 280
NOMON S.A. DE C.V.—See Fried. Krupp AG; *Int'l*, pg. 512
NOMURA ADVISORY COMPANY S.A.—See The Nomura Securities Co., Ltd.; *Int'l*, pg. 955
NOMURA ADVISORY SERVICES (MALAYSIA) SDN BHD—See The Nomura Securities Co., Ltd.; *Int'l*, pg. 956
NOMURA ASIA LTD.—See The Nomura Securities Co., Ltd.; *Int'l*, pg. 956
NOMURA ASSET CAPITAL CORPORATION—See The Nomura Securities Co., Ltd.; *Int'l*, pg. 956
NOMURA ASSET MANAGEMENT (ASIA) LIMITED—See The Nomura Securities Co., Ltd.; *Int'l*, pg. 955
NOMURA ASSET MANAGEMENT CO., LTD.—See The Nomura Securities Co., Ltd.; *Int'l*, pg. 955
NOMURA ASSET MANAGEMENT (INTERNATIONAL) LIMITED—See The Nomura Securities Co., Ltd.; *Int'l*, pg. 955
NOMURA ASSET MANAGEMENT (SINGAPORE) LIMITED—See The Nomura Securities Co., Ltd.; *Int'l*, pg. 955
NOMURA ASSET MANAGEMENT (U.S.A.) INC.—See The Nomura Securities Co., Ltd.; *Int'l*, pg. 955
NOMURA AUSTRALIA LIMITED—See The Nomura Securities Co., Ltd.; *Int'l*, pg. 956
NOMURA AUTOMATION MANAGEMENT INC.—See The Nomura Securities Co., Ltd.; *Int'l*, pg. 956
NOMURA BABCOCK & BROWN CO., LTD.—See The Nomura Securities Co., Ltd.; *Int'l*, pg. 955
NOMURA BANK (DEUTSCHLAND) GMBH—See The Nomura Securities Co., Ltd.; *Int'l*, pg. 956
NOMURA BANK INTERNATIONAL PLC—See The Nomura Securities Co., Ltd.; *Int'l*, pg. 956
NOMURA BANK (LUXEMBOURG) S.A.—See The Nomura Securities Co., Ltd.; *Int'l*, pg. 956
NOMURA BANK NEDERLAND N.V.—See The Nomura Securities Co., Ltd.; *Int'l*, pg. 957
NOMURA BANK (SWITZERLAND) LTD.—See The Nomura Securities Co., Ltd.; *Int'l*, pg. 957
NOMURA BOURSE S.A.—See The Nomura Securities Co., Ltd.; *Int'l*, pg. 957

NOMURA BUSINESS SERVICES CO., LTD.—See The Nomura Securities Co., Ltd.; *Int'l*, pg. 956
NOMURA CANADA INC.—See The Nomura Securities Co., Ltd.; *Int'l*, pg. 957
NOMURA CAPITAL SERVICES, INC.—See The Nomura Securities Co., Ltd.; *Int'l*, pg. 956
NOMURA CHINA INVESTMENT CO., LTD.—See The Nomura Securities Co., Ltd.; *Int'l*, pg. 955
NOMURA CITIC INTERNATIONAL ECONOMIC CONSULTANTS CO., LTD.—See The Nomura Securities Co., Ltd.; *Int'l*, pg. 957
NOMURA CORPORATE RESEARCH & ASSET MANAGEMENT INC.—See The Nomura Securities Co., Ltd.; *Int'l*, pg. 956
NOMURA ESPANA SOCIEDAD DE VALORES, S.A.—See The Nomura Securities Co., Ltd.; *Int'l*, pg. 957
NOMURA EUROPE PLC—See The Nomura Securities Co., Ltd.; *Int'l*, pg. 957
NOMURA FINANCE CO., LTD.—See The Nomura Securities Co., Ltd.; *Int'l*, pg. 955
NOMURA FINANCIAL ADVISORY CO., LTD.—See The Nomura Securities Co., Ltd.; *Int'l*, pg. 956
NOMURA FUTURES (HONG KONG) LIMITED—See The Nomura Securities Co., Ltd.; *Int'l*, pg. 957
NOMURA FUTURES (SINGAPORE) PTE. LTD.—See The Nomura Securities Co., Ltd.; *Int'l*, pg. 957
NOMURA HOLDING AMERICA, INC.—See The Nomura Securities Co., Ltd.; *Int'l*, pg. 956
NOMURA HUMAN RESOURCES DEVELOPMENT CO., LTD.—See The Nomura Securities Co., Ltd.; *Int'l*, pg. 955
P.T. NOMURA INDONESIA—See The Nomura Securities Co., Ltd.; *Int'l*, pg. 957
NOMURA INTERNATIONAL (HONG KONG) LIMITED—See The Nomura Securities Co., Ltd.; *Int'l*, pg. 957
NOMURA INTERNATIONAL PLC—See The Nomura Securities Co., Ltd.; *Int'l*, pg. 957
NOMURA INTERNATIONAL TRUST COMPANY—See The Nomura Securities Co., Ltd.; *Int'l*, pg. 957
NOMURA INVESTMENT BANK HUNGARY LTD.—See The Nomura Securities Co., Ltd.; *Int'l*, pg. 957
NOMURA INVESTMENT BANKING (MIDDLE EAST) E.C.—See The Nomura Securities Co., Ltd.; *Int'l*, pg. 957
NOMURA INVESTMENT MANAGEMENT CO., LTD. (NIMCO)—See The Nomura Securities Co., Ltd.; *Int'l*, pg. 955
NOMURA INVESTOR RELATIONS CO., LTD.—See The Nomura Securities Co., Ltd.; *Int'l*, pg. 956
NOMURA ITALIA S.P.A.—See The Nomura Securities Co., Ltd.; *Int'l*, pg. 957
NOMURA/JAFCO INVESTMENT (ASIA) LTD.—See The Nomura Securities Co., Ltd.; *Int'l*, pg. 957
NOMURA LAND & BUILDING CO. LTD.—See The Nomura Securities Co., Ltd.; *Int'l*, pg. 956
NOMURA MORTGAGE CAPITAL CORPORATION—See The Nomura Securities Co., Ltd.; *Int'l*, pg. 956
NOMURA MORTGAGE FUND MANAGEMENT CORPORATION—See The Nomura Securities Co., Ltd.; *Int'l*, pg. 956
NOMURA OPTION INTERNATIONAL PLC—See The Nomura Securities Co., Ltd.; *Int'l*, pg. 957
NOMURA REAL ESTATE DEVELOPMENT CO., LTD.—See The Nomura Securities Co., Ltd.; *Int'l*, pg. 956
NOMURA REALTY ADVISORS INC.—See The Nomura Securities Co., Ltd.; *Int'l*, pg. 956
NOMURA RESEARCH INSTITUTE AMERICA, INC.—See The Nomura Securities Co., Ltd.; *Int'l*, pg. 956
NOMURA RESEARCH INSTITUTE, LTD.—See The Nomura Securities Co., Ltd.; *Int'l*, pg. 956
NOMURA SATELLITE COMMUNICATIONS CO., LTD.—See The Nomura Securities Co., Ltd.; *Int'l*, pg. 956
THE NOMURA SECURITIES CO., LTD.; *Int'l*, pg. 955
NOMURA SECURITIES HONG KONG LIMITED—See The Nomura Securities Co., Ltd.; *Int'l*, pg. 957
NOMURA SECURITIES INTERNATIONAL, INC.—See The Nomura Securities Co., Ltd.; *Int'l*, pg. 956
NOMURA SECURITIES INVESTMENT ADVISORY CO., LTD.—See The Nomura Securities Co., Ltd.; *Int'l*, pg. 957
NOMURA SECURITIES SINGAPORE PTE. LTD.—See The Nomura Securities Co., Ltd.; *Int'l*, pg. 957
NOMURA SINGAPORE LIMITED—See The Nomura Securities Co., Ltd.; *Int'l*, pg. 957
NOMURA SYSTEM SERVICES CO., LTD.—See The Nomura Securities Co., Ltd.; *Int'l*, pg. 956
NOMURA SYSTEMS KANSAI CO., LTD.—See The Nomura Securities Co., Ltd.; *Int'l*, pg. 956
NOMURA TOURIST BUREAU, INC.—See The Nomura Securities Co., Ltd.; *Int'l*, pg. 956
THE NOMURA TRUST AND BANKING CO., LTD.—See The Nomura Securities Co., Ltd.; *Int'l*, pg. 956
NOMURA TRUST (CAYMAN) LIMITED—See The Nomura Securities Co., Ltd.; *Int'l*, pg. 957
NOMURA WASSERSTEIN PERELLA CO., LTD.—See The Nomura Securities Co., Ltd.; *Int'l*, pg. 956
NON FERROUS INTERNATIONAL CORP.—See Mitsubishi Corporation; *Int'l*, pg. 872
NONIUS BV—See Delft Instruments N.V.; *Int'l*, pg. 389
NOODLE KIDOODLE INC.; *U.S. Public*, pg. 1188
NOONAN MACHINE CO.; *U.S. Private*, pg. 801
NOONDAY PRESS—See Georg von Holtzbrinck GmbH; *Int'l*, pg. 1479
NOORDERVLIET & WINNINGHOFF/LEO BURNETT B.V.—See Leo Burnett Company, Inc.; *U.S. Private*, pg. 186
NOORD-EUROPESE HOUTIMPORT BV—See Mo och Domsjo AB; *Int'l*, pg. 886
NOORDGASTRANSPORT BV—See DSM N.V.; *Int'l*, pg. 354
NOORDZEE VEERDIENSTEN B.V.—See Royal Nedlloyd Group N.V.; *Int'l*, pg. 1145
NOOTER CONSTRUCTION CO.—See Nooter Corporation; *U.S. Private*, pg. 801
NOOTER CONSULTING SERVICES, INC.—See Nooter Corporation; *U.S. Private*, pg. 801

NOOTER CORPORATION; *U.S. Private*, pg. 801
NOOTER/ERIKSEN, INC.—See Nooter Corporation; *U.S. Private*, pg. 801
NOOTER FABRICATORS, INC.—See Nooter Corporation; *U.S. Private*, pg. 801
NOPCO COLOMBIANA S.A.—See Henkel KGaA; *Int'l*, pg. 614
NOPCO INDUSTRIAL S.A. DE C.V.—See Henkel KGaA; *Int'l*, pg. 614
NOPCO ITALIANA SPA—See Henkel KGaA; *Int'l*, pg. 612
NOPCO TRADING CORP.—See Henkel KGaA; *Int'l*, pg. 613
NOPRI—See GIB Group; *Int'l*, pg. 533
NOPRI SA—See GIB Group; *Int'l*, pg. 533
NOPTEK—See Neste Oy; *Int'l*, pg. 913
NOPTOR OY—See Neste Oy; *Int'l*, pg. 913
NOR-CAL BEVERAGE CO., INC.; *U.S. Private*, pg. 801
NOR HOLZ VERKAUFSGESELLSCHAFT—See Norske Skogindustrier A.S.; *Int'l*, pg. 966
NORA GVG MBH—See Commerzbank AG; *Int'l*, pg. 309
NORA GVG MBH & CO. OBJEKT DUESSELDORF KG—See Commerzbank AG; *Int'l*, pg. 309
NORA GVG MBH & CO. OBJEKT KOBLENZ KG—See Commerzbank AG; *Int'l*, pg. 309
NORA GVG MBH & CO. OBJEKT LAMPERTHEIM KG—See Commerzbank AG; *Int'l*, pg. 309
NORA GVG MBH & CO. OBJEKTE PLON UND PREETZ KG—See Commerzbank AG; *Int'l*, pg. 309
NORA TRANSMISSION—See Equitable Resources, Inc.; *U.S. Public*, pg. 590
NORAK A/S LE CARBONE-LORRAINE—See Pechiney S.A.; *Int'l*, pg. 1031
NORALU AG—See Norsk Hydro a.s; *Int'l*, pg. 964
NORAM ENERGY CORP.—See Houston Industries Incorporated; *U.S. Public*, pg. 843
NORAM FIELD SERVICES CORP.—See Houston Industries Incorporated; *U.S. Public*, pg. 843
NORAM FORWARDING, INC.—See Norfolk Southern Corporation; *U.S. Public*, pg. 1192
NORAM GAS TRANSMISSION—See Houston Industries Incorporated; *U.S. Public*, pg. 843
NORAMCO, INC.—See Johnson & Johnson; *U.S. Public*, pg. 929
NORAN INSTRUMENTS, INC.—See Thermo Electron Corporation; *U.S. Public*, pg. 1593
NORAND MOBILE SYSTEMS DIV.—See UNOVA, Inc.; *U.S. Public*, pg. 1699
NORANDA ALUMINIUM—See EdperBrascan Corporation; *Int'l*, pg. 434
NORANDA FOREST INC.—See EdperBrascan Corporation; *Int'l*, pg. 434
NORANDA INC.—See EdperBrascan Corporation; *Int'l*, pg. 433
NORANDA MINERALS—See EdperBrascan Corporation; *Int'l*, pg. 434
NORANDAL U.S.A.—See EdperBrascan Corporation; *Int'l*, pg. 434
NORANDEX VINYL PRODUCTS CO.—See Owens Corning; *U.S. Public*, pg. 1237
NORANPAC—See The Cascades Group; *Int'l*, pg. 273
NORBEST, INC.; *U.S. Private*, pg. 801
NORBETONG A/S—See Scancem AB; *Int'l*, pg. 1199
NORBURY CONSTRUCTION CO.—See The Rouse Company; *U.S. Public*, pg. 1409
NORCABLE A/S—See Norsk Hydro a.s; *Int'l*, pg. 960
NORCAL WASTE SYSTEMS; *U.S. Public*, pg. 1188
NORCAM CONSTRUCTION COMPANY—See Ritter Bros., Inc.; *U.S. Private*, pg. 801
NORCEM A.S.—See Scancem AB; *Int'l*, pg. 1199
NORCEM BETONG A/S—See Aker Raj Asa; *Int'l*, pg. 42
NORCEM INDUSTRIER—See Aker Raj Asa; *Int'l*, pg. 42
NORCEN ENERGY RESOURCES LIMITED—See EdperBrascan Corporation; *Int'l*, pg. 434
NORCHEM DISTRIBUIDORA DE TITULOS E VALORES MOBILIARIOS S.A.—See The Chase Manhattan Corporation; *U.S. Public*, pg. 339
NORCO WINDOWS, INC.—See TJ International, Inc.; *U.S. Public*, pg. 1556
NORCOLD—See The Dyson-Kissner-Moran Corporation; *U.S. Private*, pg. 352
NORCONN PROPERTIES, INC.—See Yankee Energy System, Inc.; *U.S. Public*, pg. 1787
NORCOSTCO, INC.; *U.S. Private*, pg. 801
NORCRAFT COMPANIES, INC.; *U.S. Private*, pg. 801
NORD FRANCE S.A.—See Philipp Holzmann AG; *Int'l*, pg. 634
NORD HELIOSERVICE SA—See Alusuisse-Lonza Holding Ltd.; *Int'l*, pg. 69
NORD/LB—See Norddeutsche Landesbank (NORD/LB); *Int'l*, pg. 957
NORD/LB - AMSTERDAM—See Norddeutsche Landesbank (NORD/LB); *Int'l*, pg. 958
NORD/LB - BUDAPEST—See Norddeutsche Landesbank (NORD/LB); *Int'l*, pg. 958
NORD/LB LANDESBANK FUR MECKLENBURG-VORPOMMERN—See Norddeutsche Landesbank (NORD/LB); *Int'l*, pg. 958
NORD/LB LONDON—See Norddeutsche Landesbank (NORD/LB); *Int'l*, pg. 958
NORD/LB MITTELDEUTSCHE LANDESBANK—See Norddeutsche Landesbank (NORD/LB); *Int'l*, pg. 958
NORD/LB NEW YORK—See Norddeutsche Landesbank (NORD/LB); *Int'l*, pg. 958
NORD/LB NORDDEUTSCHE SECURITIES—See Norddeutsche Landesbank (NORD/LB); *Int'l*, pg. 958
NORD/LB - PARIS—See Norddeutsche Landesbank (NORD/LB); *Int'l*, pg. 958
NORD/LB - PRAGUE—See Norddeutsche Landesbank (NORD/LB); *Int'l*, pg. 958
NORD/LB SINGAPORE—See Norddeutsche Landesbank (NORD/LB); *Int'l*, pg. 958
NORD/LB - WARSAW—See Norddeutsche Landesbank (NORD/LB); *Int'l*, pg. 958

Company Index

NORD-OSTSEE SCHIFFAHRT-UND TRANSPORT GMBH—See Stora Kopparbergs Bergslags AB; *Int'l*, pg. 1303
NORD PACIFIC LIMITED—See Nord Resources Corporation; *U.S. Public*, pg. 1188
NORD PHOTO ENGINEERING, INC.—See Photo Control Corporation; *U.S. Public*, pg. 1292
NORD RAIL—See Groupe Air France; *Int'l*, pg. 560
NORD RESOURCES CORPORATION; *U.S. Public*, pg. 1188
NORD RUTILE CORP.—See Nord Resources Corporation; *U.S. Public*, pg. 1188
NORD-WEST OELLEITUNG GMBH—See Veba AG; *Int'l*, pg. 1461
NORDBANKEN AB; *Int'l*, pg. 957
NORDBERG GROUP—See UPM-Kymmene Corporation; *Int'l*, pg. 1428
NORDBERG-READ, INC.—See UPM-Kymmene Corporation; *Int'l*, pg. 1428
NORDBRAND NORDHAUSEN—See Eckes AG; *Int'l*, pg. 433
NORDCEMENT AG—See Holderbank Financiere Glaris Ltd.; *Int'l*, pg. 628
NORDCO, INC.—See Oak Industries Inc.; *U.S. Public*, pg. 1209
NORDDEUTSCHE AFFINERIE AG—See Metallgesellschaft AG; *Int'l*, pg. 861
NORDDEUTSCHE GESELLSCHAFT ZUR BERATUNG UND DURCHFUEHRUNG VON ENTSORGUNGSAUFGABEN BEI KERNKRAFTWERKEN MBH—See Veba AG; *Int'l*, pg. 1456
NORDDEUTSCHE HYPOTHEKEN UND WECHSELBANK AG—See Dresdner Bank AG; *Int'l*, pg. 418
NORDDEUTSCHE IMMOBILIEN- UND VERWALTUNGS GMBH—See Commerzbank AG; *Int'l*, pg. 310
NORDDEUTSCHE LANDESBANK (NORD/LB); *Int'l*, pg. 957
NORDDEUTSCHE SALINEN GMBH—See Akzo Nobel N.V.; *Int'l*, pg. 44
NORDEN BANKING GROUP—See Swedbank; *Int'l*, pg. 1328
NORDENFJELSKE TREFOREDLING—See Norske Skogindustrier A.S; *Int'l*, pg. 965
NORDENHAMER TRANSPORTBOTEN GMBH & CO. KG—See Dyckerhoff AG; *Int'l*, pg. 422
AB NORDENTA—See Axel Johnson AB; *Int'l*, pg. 709
NORDESCLOR S.A.—See Olin Corporation; *U.S. Public*, pg. 1219
CIA. NORDESTINA DE PAPEL (CONPEL)—See S.A. Industrias Votorantim; *Int'l*, pg. 1189
NORDEUROPA FORSIKRINGSAKTIESELSKABET A/S—See Allianz Aktiengesellschaft; *Int'l*, pg. 62
NORDFOIL ODENSE FLEXIBLE A.P.S.—See Electrolux, AB; *Int'l*, pg. 441
NORDFOR TRAINING & CONSULTATION AB—See Electrolux, AB; *Int'l*, pg. 439
NORDIA S.A.—See Duni AB; *Int'l*, pg. 421
NORDIC BAUMASCHINENHANDEL GMBH—See Axel Johnson AB; *Int'l*, pg. 712
NORDIC BULL NET—See Compagnie des Machines Bull; *Int'l*, pg. 318
NORDIC BUSINESS MANAGEMENT SYSTEMS AB—See American Management Systems, Inc.; *U.S. Public*, pg. 87
NORDIC ELECTRONIC SYSTEMS A/S—See Telefonaktiebolaget LM Ericsson; *Int'l*, pg. 1369
NORDIC FIBRES AG—See Enso Oyj; *Int'l*, pg. 458
NORDIC FORESTRY EQUIPMENT AB—See Electrolux, AB; *Int'l*, pg. 439
NORDIC-HOTEL OY—See FinnAir Oy; *Int'l*, pg. 485
NORDIC POWER INVEST AB—See Vattenfall AB; *Int'l*, pg. 1453
NORDIC POWER INVEST-SOUTH EAST ASIA OFFICE—See Vattenfall AB; *Int'l*, pg. 1453
NORDIC SERVICE CENTER AB—See British Steel Plc; *Int'l*, pg. 221
NORDIC SERVICE CENTRE—See Swedbank; *Int'l*, pg. 1328
NORDIC SYNTHESIS AB—See Cambrex Corporation; *U.S. Public*, pg. 297
NORDIC SYNTHESIS GMBH—See Cambrex Corporation; *U.S. Public*, pg. 297
NORDIC SYNTHESIS, INC.—See Cambrex Corporation; *U.S. Public*, pg. 297
NORDIC SYNTHESIS LIMITED—See Cambrex Corporation; *U.S. Public*, pg. 297
NORDIC SYSTEMS, LTD.—See Flambeau Corporation; *U.S. Private*, pg. 410
NORDIC WARE—See Northland Aluminum Products, Inc.; *U.S. Private*, pg. 806
NORDIC WARE DIRECT, INC.—See Northland Aluminum Products, Inc.; *U.S. Private*, pg. 806
NORDICA S.R.L.—See A. Ahlstrom Corporation; *Int'l*, pg. 35
NORDICTRACK, INC.—See CML Group, Inc.; *U.S. Public*, pg. 279
NORDINVEST NORDDEUTSCHE INVESTMENT GMBH—See Bayerische Vereinsbank Group; *Int'l*, pg. 180
NORDION INTERNATIONAL INC.—See MDS Inc.; *Int'l*, pg. 827
NORDISK ALUMINIUM A.S.—See Norsk Hydro a.s; *Int'l*, pg. 964
NORDISK AVIATION PRODUCTS A.S.—See Norsk Hydro a.s; *Int'l*, pg. 964
NORDISK AVIATION PRODUCTS ASIA LTD.—See Norsk Hydro a.s; *Int'l*, pg. 964
NORDISK AVIATION PRODUCTS, INC.—See Norsk Hydro a.s; *Int'l*, pg. 961
NORDISK AVIATION PRODUCTS LTD.—See Norsk Hydro a.s; *Int'l*, pg. 964
NORDISK AVIATION PRODUCTS PTE. LTD.—See Norsk Hydro a.s; *Int'l*, pg. 964
NORDISK BYGGE KEMI A/S—See Viag AG; *Int'l*, pg. 1466

NORDISK CASE A/S—See Tenneco Inc.; *U.S. Public*, pg. 1580
NORDISK ELEKTRA AB—See Axel Johnson AB; *Int'l*, pg. 709
NORDISK ELEKTRONICS A/S—See Axel Johnson AB; *Int'l*, pg. 712
NORDISK ELEKTRONIK AB—See Axel Johnson AB; *Int'l*, pg. 709
NORDISK FACTORING A/S—See The Fuji Bank, Limited; *Int'l*, pg. 521
NORDISK FERAL A/S—See Norsk Hydro a.s; *Int'l*, pg. 960
NORDISK KELLOGGS A/S—See Kellogg Company; *U.S. Public*, pg. 948
NORDISK MELASSE A/S—See Tate & Lyle PLC; *Int'l*, pg. 1357
NORDISK MIKROSYSTEM APS—See Axel Johnson AB; *Int'l*, pg. 712
NORDISK SIMPLEX A/S—See Rautaruukki Oy; *Int'l*, pg. 1088
NORDISKA BALZERS AB—See Oerlikon-Buhrle Holding AG; *Int'l*, pg. 998
NORDISKA KOMPANIET (NK) AB—See NCC AB; *Int'l*, pg. 899
NORDISKAFILT AB—See Albany International Corp.; *U.S. Public*, pg. 37
NORDISKAFILT A/S—See Albany International Corp.; *U.S. Public*, pg. 37
NORDISKAFILT GMBH—See Albany International Corp.; *U.S. Public*, pg. 37
NORDKLIMA LUFT-UND WARMETECHNIK GMBH—See Senior Engineering Group, plc.; *Int'l*, pg. 1222
NORDLAND PAPIER AG—See UPM-Kymmene Corporation; *Int'l*, pg. 1430
NORDLYS SA—See Dominion Textile Inc.; *Int'l*, pg. 415
NORDMENDE GMBH—See Thomson S.A.; *Int'l*, pg. 1384
NORDSEA GAS TECHNOLOGY LTD.—See Selas Corporation of America; *U.S. Public*, pg. 1455
NORDSEE DEUTSCHE HOCHSEEFISCHEREI G.M.B.H.—See Unilever Plc; *Int'l*, pg. 1438
NORDSEE GES. M.B.H.—See Unilever Plc; *Int'l*, pg. 1438
NORDSON ANDINA LIMITADA—See Nordson Corporation; *U.S. Public*, pg. 1189
NORDSON APPLICATION EQUIPMENT, INC.—See Nordson Corporation; *U.S. Public*, pg. 1189
NORDSON AUSTRALIA PTY. LIMITED.—See Nordson Corporation; *U.S. Public*, pg. 1189
NORDSON AUSTRALIA PTY., LTD.—See Nordson Corporation; *U.S. Public*, pg. 1189
NORDSON BELGIUM N.V.—See Nordson Corporation; *U.S. Public*, pg. 1189
NORDSON CANADA LTD.—See Nordson Corporation; *U.S. Public*, pg. 1189
NORDSON CHINA CO., LTD.—See Nordson Corporation; *U.S. Public*, pg. 1189
NORDSON CORPORATION; *U.S. Public*, pg. 1188
NORDSON CS, SPOL.S.R.O.—See Nordson Corporation; *U.S. Public*, pg. 1189
NORDSON DANMARK A/S—See Nordson Corporation; *U.S. Public*, pg. 1189
NORDSON DE MEXICO, S.A. DE C.V.—See Nordson Corporation; *U.S. Public*, pg. 1189
NORDSON DEUTSCHLAND GMBH—See Nordson Corporation; *U.S. Public*, pg. 1189
NORDSON DO BRASIL INDUSTRIA E COMERCIO LTDA.—See Nordson Corporation; *U.S. Public*, pg. 1189
NORDSON ENGINEERING GMBH—See Nordson Corporation; *U.S. Public*, pg. 1189
NORDSON EUROPEAN DISTRIBUTION B.V.—See Nordson Corporation; *U.S. Public*, pg. 1189
NORDSON FINLAND OY—See Nordson Corporation; *U.S. Public*, pg. 1189
NORDSON FRANCE, S.A.—See Nordson Corporation; *U.S. Public*, pg. 1189
NORDSON GMBH (AUSTRIA)—See Nordson Corporation; *U.S. Public*, pg. 1189
NORDSON IBERICA S.A.—See Nordson Corporation; *U.S. Public*, pg. 1189
NORDSON INTERNATIONAL DE VENEZUELA, C.A.—See Nordson Corporation; *U.S. Public*, pg. 1189
NORDSON ITALIA SPA—See Nordson Corporation; *U.S. Public*, pg. 1189
NORDSON K.K.—See Nordson Corporation; *U.S. Public*, pg. 1189
NORDSON (MALAYSIA) SDN. BHD.—See Nordson Corporation; *U.S. Public*, pg. 1189
NORDSON NEDERLAND B.V.—See Nordson Corporation; *U.S. Public*, pg. 1189
NORDSON NORGE A/S—See Nordson Corporation; *U.S. Public*, pg. 1189
NORDSON NORTH AMERICAN DIV.—See Nordson Corporation; *U.S. Public*, pg. 1188
NORDSON PACIFIC SOUTH DIV.—See Nordson Corporation; *U.S. Public*, pg. 1188
NORDSON POLSKA SP.Z.O.O.—See Nordson Corporation; *U.S. Public*, pg. 1189
NORDSON PORTUGAL EQUIPAMENTO INDUSTRIAL, LDA.—See Nordson Corporation; *U.S. Public*, pg. 1189
NORDSON SANG SAN ENGINEERING CO.—See Nordson Corporation; *U.S. Public*, pg. 1190
NORDSON SCHWEIZ AG—See Nordson Corporation; *U.S. Public*, pg. 1189
NORDSON S.E. ASIA (PTE.), LTD.—See Nordson Corporation; *U.S. Public*, pg. 1189
NORDSON SVERIGE AB—See Nordson Corporation; *U.S. Public*, pg. 1189
NORDSON U.K., LTD.—See Nordson Corporation; *U.S. Public*, pg. 1189
NORDSON WALCOM B.V.—See Nordson Corporation; *U.S. Public*, pg. 1189
NORDSTEN—See Thrige-Titan Group; *Int'l*, pg. 1386
NORDSTROM CREDIT, INC.—See Nordstrom, Inc.; *U.S. Public*, pg. 1190

NORDSTROM DISTRIBUTION, INC.—See Nordstrom, Inc.; *U.S. Public*, pg. 1190
NORDSTROM, INC.; *U.S. Public*, pg. 1190
NORDYNE INC.—See Nortek, Inc.; *U.S. Public*, pg. 1193
NORECO S.A.—See Assicurazioni Generali S.p.A.; *Int'l*, pg. 91
NOREL PAPER CORPORATION—See Unisource Worldwide, Inc.; *U.S. Public*, pg. 1671
NORELCO CONSUMER PRODUCTS COMPANY—See Philips Electronics N.V.; *Int'l*, pg. 1054
NORELEM S.A.—See Applied Power Inc.; *U.S. Public*, pg. 125
NORELL PERFUMES, INC.—See MacAndrews & Forbes Holdings Inc.; *U.S. Private*, pg. 690
NORENCO CORP.—See Northern States Power Company; *U.S. Public*, pg. 1195
NORFI EXHAUST EXTRACTION SYSTEMS GMBH—See Charter plc; *Int'l*, pg. 283
NORFOLIER A/S & CO.—See Icopal a/s; *Int'l*, pg. 659
NORFOLK AND PORTSMOUTH BELT LINE R.R. CO.—See Norfolk Southern Corporation; *U.S. Public*, pg. 1191
NORFOLK AND WESTERN RAILWAY COMPANY—See Norfolk Southern Corporation; *U.S. Public*, pg. 1191
NORFOLK SHIPBUILDING & DRYDOCK CORPORATION; *U.S. Private*, pg. 802
NORFOLK SOUTHERN CORPORATION; *U.S. Public*, pg. 1190
NORFOLK SOUTHERN INDUSTRIAL DEVELOPMENT CORP.—See Norfolk Southern Corporation; *U.S. Public*, pg. 1190
NORFOLK SOUTHERN PROPERTIES, INC.—See Norfolk Southern Corporation; *U.S. Public*, pg. 1190
NORFOLK SOUTHERN RAILWAY COMPANY—See Norfolk Southern Corporation; *U.S. Public*, pg. 1191
NORFOODS, INC.; *U.S. Private*, pg. 802
THE A/S NORGES HANDELS OG SJOEFARTSTIDENDE GROUP; *Int'l*, pg. 958
NORGREN CO.—See IMI Plc; *Int'l*, pg. 647
NORGREN/DETROIT—See IMI Plc; *Int'l*, pg. 647
NORGREN/LOS ANGELES—See IMI Plc; *Int'l*, pg. 647
NORGRO A.S.—See Orkla A.S.A.; *Int'l*, pg. 1011
NORGYPS BV—See Lafarge S.A.; *Int'l*, pg. 791
THE NORINCHUKIN BANK; *Int'l*, pg. 958
NORINCHUKIN INTERNATIONAL PLC—See The Norinchukin Bank; *Int'l*, pg. 958
NORINCHUKIN INVESTMENT TRUST MANAGEMENT CO., LTD.—See The Norinchukin Bank; *Int'l*, pg. 958
NORINCHUKIN SECURITIES CO., LTD.—See The Norinchukin Bank; *Int'l*, pg. 958
THE NORINCHUKIN TRUST & BANKING CO., LTD.—See The Norinchukin Bank; *Int'l*, pg. 958
NORIT BELGIUM S.A.—See NORIT N.V.; *Int'l*, pg. 958
NORIT CO. LTD.—See NORIT N.V.; *Int'l*, pg. 958
NORIT DEUTSCHLAND—See NORIT N.V.; *Int'l*, pg. 958
NORIT FRANCE—See NORIT N.V.; *Int'l*, pg. 958
NORIT ITALIA S.P.A.—See NORIT N.V.; *Int'l*, pg. 958
NORIT N.V.; *Int'l*, pg. 958
NORIT SINGAPORE PGE LTD.—See NORIT N.V.; *Int'l*, pg. 958
NORIT (UK) LTD.—See NORIT N.V.; *Int'l*, pg. 958
NORITAKE CO., INC.—See Noritake Co., Limited; *Int'l*, pg. 959
NORITAKE CO., INC.-ABRASIVE DIVISION—See Noritake Co., Limited; *Int'l*, pg. 959
NORITAKE CO., INC.-ELECTRONICS DIVISION—See Noritake Co., Limited; *Int'l*, pg. 959
NORITAKE CO., INC.-TABLE TOP DIVISION—See Noritake Co., Limited; *Int'l*, pg. 959
NORITAKE CO., LIMITED; *Int'l*, pg. 958
NORLATEX OY—See Neste Oy; *Int'l*, pg. 913
NORLEASE, INC.—See Northern Trust Corporation; *U.S. Public*, pg. 1196
NORLEN LIFE INSURANCE COMPANY—See First Tennessee National Corporation; *U.S. Public*, pg. 639
A/S NORLETT—See Electrolux, AB; *Int'l*, pg. 443
NORLIGHT TELECOMMUNICATIONS INC.—See Journal Communications Inc.; *U.S. Private*, pg. 601
NORMA METALLBAU GMBH—See Fried. Krupp AG; *Int'l*, pg. 509
NORMACO LTD.—See Axel Johnson AB; *Int'l*, pg. 712
NORMALAIR-GARRETT LTD.—See AlliedSignal Inc.; *U.S. Public*, pg. 54
NORMALAIR-GARRETT MFG. AUSTRALIA—See AlliedSignal Inc.; *U.S. Public*, pg. 53
NORMAN ENTERPRISES, INC.—See Photo Control Corporation; *U.S. Public*, pg. 1292
NORMANDALE PROPERTIES—See Opus South Corporation; *U.S. Private*, pg. 818
NORMANDEAU ASSOCIATES, INC.—See Thermo Electron Corporation; *U.S. Public*, pg. 1594
NORMANDEAU ENGINEERS INC.—See Thermo Electron Corporation; *U.S. Public*, pg. 1593
NORMARK CORPORATION; *U.S. Private*, pg. 802
NOROESTE CHEMICAL S.A. ARRENDAMENTO MERCANTIL NORCHEM—See The Chase Manhattan Corporation; *U.S. Public*, pg. 341
NORPAC—See Bouygues; *Int'l*, pg. 206
NORPAC FOODS, INC.; *U.S. Private*, pg. 802
NORPAC SERVICES, INC.—See Norpac Foods, Inc.; *U.S. Private*, pg. 802
NORPIPE OIL A/S—See Petrofina S.A.; *Int'l*, pg. 1043
NORPLAST-LAMAF B.V.—See Schuttersveld Holding N.V.; *Int'l*, pg. 1210
NORRELL CORPORATION; *U.S. Public*, pg. 1192
NORRIS—See Dover Corporation; *U.S. Public*, pg. 521
NORRIS CYLINDER COMPANY—See Masco Corporation; *U.S. Public*, pg. 1054
JAY NORRIS CANADA INC.—See Russel Metals Inc.; *Int'l*, pg. 1150
NORRIS SCREEN & MFG., INC.—See Elgin National Industries, Inc.; *U.S. Private*, pg. 370
NORRISEAL CONTROLS—See Dover Corporation; *U.S. Public*, pg. 521

NORRKOPING AXTRADE AB—See Axel Johnson AB; *Int'l*, pg. 709
NORRKOPINGS SAND AB—See Scancem AB; *Int'l*, pg. 1200
NORSE CROWN (M) SDN. BHD.—See Tiedemanns - Joh.H.Andresen ANS; *Int'l*, pg. 1390
NORSE CROWN SEAFOOD A/S—See Tiedemanns - Joh.H.Andresen ANS; *Int'l*, pg. 1390
NORSE DAIRY SYSTEMS; *U.S. Private*, pg. 802
NORSEA GAS A/S—See Petrofina S.A.; *Int'l*, pg. 1043
NORSEA PIPELINE LTD.—See Petrofina S.A.; *Int'l*, pg. 1044
NORSHIPCO INDUSTRIAL ENTERPRISES—See Norfolk Shipbuilding & Drydock Corporation; *U.S. Private*, pg. 802
NORSK ALCOA A/S—See Aluminum Company of America; *U.S. Public*, pg. 62
NORSK BLIKKVALSEVERK A/S—See Koninklijke Hoogovens N.V.; *Int'l*, pg. 754
NORSK EXOLON A/S—See Exolon-Esk Company; *U.S. Public*, pg. 600
NORSK FORKONSERVERING (NOFO)—See Norsk Hydro a.s; *Int'l*, pg. 960
NORSK HYDRO A.S; *Int'l*, pg. 959
NORSK HYDRO A/S BREVIK PACKAGING DEPT.—See Norsk Hydro a.s; *Int'l*, pg. 960
NORSK HYDRO A/S-DEVELOPMENT & COMMERCIALIZATION—See Norsk Hydro a.s; *Int'l*, pg. 960
NORSK HYDRO A.S. HUNGARY—See Norsk Hydro a.s; *Int'l*, pg. 964
NORSK HYDRO A.S. MIDDLE EAST REPR.—See Norsk Hydro a.s; *Int'l*, pg. 964
NORSK HYDRO A.S. PETROCHEMICALS DIVISION—See Norsk Hydro a.s; *Int'l*, pg. 964
NORSK HYDRO A.S. POLAND—See Norsk Hydro a.s; *Int'l*, pg. 964
NORSK HYDRO A.S. ROMANIA—See Norsk Hydro a.s; *Int'l*, pg. 964
NORSK HYDRO CANADA, INC.—See Norsk Hydro a.s; *Int'l*, pg. 964
NORSK HYDRO COMERCIO E INDUSTRIA LTDA.—See Norsk Hydro a.s; *Int'l*, pg. 964
NORSK HYDRO DANMARK A.S—See Norsk Hydro a.s; *Int'l*, pg. 964
NORSK HYDRO DEUTSCHLAND GMBH—See Norsk Hydro a.s; *Int'l*, pg. 964
NORSK HYDRO ESPANA S.A.—See Norsk Hydro a.s; *Int'l*, pg. 964
NORSK HYDRO EXPLORATION EGYPT A.S—See Norsk Hydro a.s; *Int'l*, pg. 964
NORSK HYDRO (FAR EAST) LTD.—See Norsk Hydro a.s; *Int'l*, pg. 964
NORSK HYDRO GUATEMALA, S.A.—See Norsk Hydro a.s; *Int'l*, pg. 964
NORSK HYDRO HANDELSSELSKAP A/S—See Norsk Hydro a.s; *Int'l*, pg. 964
NORSK HYDRO MAGNESIUM-GESELLSCHAFT MBH—See Norsk Hydro a.s; *Int'l*, pg. 964
NORSK HYDRO MALAYSIA SDN BHD—See Norsk Hydro a.s; *Int'l*, pg. 964
NORSK HYDRO MOSCOW—See Norsk Hydro a.s; *Int'l*, pg. 964
NORSK HYDRO NAMIBIA A.S—See Norsk Hydro a.s; *Int'l*, pg. 964
NORSK HYDRO OLIE A.S—See Norsk Hydro a.s; *Int'l*, pg. 964
NORSK HYDRO OLJE AB—See Norsk Hydro a.s; *Int'l*, pg. 964
NORSK HYDRO PHILIPPINES INC.—See Norsk Hydro a.s; *Int'l*, pg. 964
NORSK HYDRO SVERIGE AB—See Norsk Hydro a.s; *Int'l*, pg. 964
NORSK HYDRO UDFORSKNING—See Norsk Hydro a.s; *Int'l*, pg. 964
NORSK HYDRO (U.K.) LTD.—See Norsk Hydro a.s; *Int'l*, pg. 964
NORSK HYDRO USA INC.—See Norsk Hydro a.s; *Int'l*, pg. 961
NORSK HYDRO VENEZUELA C.A.—See Norsk Hydro a.s; *Int'l*, pg. 964
NORSK HYDRO ZIMBABWE PRIVATE LTD.,—See Norsk Hydro a.s; *Int'l*, pg. 964
NORSK KRAFTREVISJON A/S—See Norsk Hydro a.s; *Int'l*, pg. 960
A.S. NORSK LECA—See Scancem AB; *Int'l*, pg. 1200
NORSK MAGNESIUM MARKET DEVELOPMENT CENTER—See Norsk Hydro a.s; *Int'l*, pg. 961
NORSK MICHELIN GUMMI A/S—See Compagnie Generale des Etablissements Michelin; *Int'l*, pg. 322
NORSK REHAB AS—See Sunrise Medical, Inc.; *U.S. Public*, pg. 1536
NORSK SCHERING A/S—See Schering-Plough Corporation; *U.S. Public*, pg. 1439
NORSK TEXACO A/S—See Texaco Inc.; *U.S. Public*, pg. 1584
NORSK VEKST ASA; *Int'l*, pg. 965
NORSK VIRKE NORSKE SKOGINDUSTRIER BA FIBRE—See Norske Skogindustrier A.S; *Int'l*, pg. 966
NORSKE FINA A/S—See Petrofina S.A.; *Int'l*, pg. 1043
A/S NORSKE SHELL—See Royal Dutch/Shell Group of Companies; *Int'l*, pg. 1139
NORSKE SKOG AB—See Norske Skogindustrier A.S; *Int'l*, pg. 965
N.V. NORSKE SKOG BELGIUM S.A.—See Norske Skogindustrier A.S; *Int'l*, pg. 966
NORSKE SKOG (CYPRUS) LTD.—See Norske Skogindustrier A.S; *Int'l*, pg. 966
NORSKE SKOG DANMARK A.S.—See Norske Skogindustrier A.S; *Int'l*, pg. 966
NORSKE SKOG DEUTSCHLAND GMBH—See Norske Skogindustrier A.S; *Int'l*, pg. 966
NORSKE SKOG FRANCE SARL—See Norske Skogindustrier A.S; *Int'l*, pg. 966

NORSKE SKOG HOLLAND B.V.—See Norske Skogindustrier A.S; *Int'l*, pg. 966
NORSKE SKOG (IRELAND) LIMITED—See Norske Skogindustrier A.S; *Int'l*, pg. 966
NORSKE SKOG ITALIA SRL—See Norske Skogindustrier A.S; *Int'l*, pg. 966
NORSKE SKOG (JAPAN) LTD.—See Norske Skogindustrier A.S; *Int'l*, pg. 966
NORSKE SKOG PORTUGAL, LDA—See Norske Skogindustrier A.S; *Int'l*, pg. 966
NORSKE SKOG PRESSPAIER GMBH—See Norske Skogindustrier A.S; *Int'l*, pg. 966
NORSKE SKOG SALES AS—See Norske Skogindustrier A.S; *Int'l*, pg. 965
NORSKE SKOG (SCHWEIZ) AG—See Norske Skogindustrier A.S; *Int'l*, pg. 966
NORSKE SKOG TRADING FAR EAST PTE. LTD.—See Norske Skogindustrier A.S; *Int'l*, pg. 966
NORSKE SKOG (UK) LTD.—See Norske Skogindustrier A.S; *Int'l*, pg. 967
NORSKE SKOGINDUSTRIER A.S.; *Int'l*, pg. 965
NORSKE SKOGINDUSTRIER A.S.—See Norske Skogindustrier A.S; *Int'l*, pg. 965
NORSKE SKOGINDUSTRIER A.S-PAPER—See Norske Skogindustrier A.S; *Int'l*, pg. 965
NORSKE SKOGINDUSTRIER BUSINESS AREA BUILDING MATERIALS—See Norske Skogindustrier A.S; *Int'l*, pg. 965
NORSOHAAS, S.A.—See Rohm and Haas Company; *U.S. Public*, pg. 1403
NORSTAN CANADA INC.—See Norstan, Inc.; *U.S. Public*, pg. 1192
NORSTAN COMMUNICATIONS, INC.—See Norstan, Inc.; *U.S. Public*, pg. 1192
NORSTAN FINANCIAL SERVICES, INC.—See Norstan, Inc.; *U.S. Public*, pg. 1192
NORSTAN, INC.; *U.S. Public*, pg. 1192
NORSTEEL LIMITED—See Canadian Erectors Ltd.; *Int'l*, pg. 256
NORSTONE A.S.—See Scancem AB; *Int'l*, pg. 1199
NORSULFID A/S—See Outokumpu Oyj; *Int'l*, pg. 1016
NORTA TIMBER B.V.—See Enso Oyj; *Int'l*, pg. 458
NORTEC AB—See Axel Johnson AB; *Int'l*, pg. 709
NORTEC ELECTRONICS AB—See Axel Johnson AB; *Int'l*, pg. 709
NORTEC ELECTRONICS A/S—See Axel Johnson AB; *Int'l*, pg. 712
OY NORTEC ELECTRONICS FINLAND AB—See Axel Johnson AB; *Int'l*, pg. 712
NORTECH SA—See Siebe plc; *Int'l*, pg. 1242
NORTEK, INC.; *U.S. Public*, pg. 1192
NORTEL—See Northern Telecom Limited; *Int'l*, pg. 970
NORTEL AUSTRALIA PTY. LIMITED—See Northern Telecom Limited; *Int'l*, pg. 970
NORTEL CALA INC.—See Northern Telecom Limited; *Int'l*, pg. 969
NORTEL COMMUNICATIONS—See Northern Telecom Limited; *Int'l*, pg. 969
NORTEL COMMUNICATIONS—See SBC Communications Inc.; *U.S. Public*, pg. 1416
NORTEL DASA NETWORK SYSTEMS GMBH & CO. KG—See Northern Telecom Limited; *Int'l*, pg. 970
NORTEL FRANCE S.A.—See Lagardere Groupe; *Int'l*, pg. 793
NORTEL LIMITED—See Northern Telecom Limited; *Int'l*, pg. 970
NORTEL MATRA CELLULAR SCA—See Northern Telecom Limited; *Int'l*, pg. 970
NORTEL POST & TELECOMMUNICATIONS TECHNICAL INS.—See Northern Telecom Limited; *Int'l*, pg. 970
NORTEL PROPERTIES LIMITED—See Northern Telecom Limited; *Int'l*, pg. 970
NORTEL TECHNOLOGY LIMITED—See Northern Telecom Limited; *Int'l*, pg. 970
NORTELCO AB—See Axel Johnson AB; *Int'l*, pg. 709
NORTEN PIPELINE CO.—See Southern Union Company; *U.S. Public*, pg. 1491
NORTH AMERICA SYNDICATE, INC.—See The Hearst Corporation; *U.S. Private*, pg. 515
NORTH AMERICAN ACCEPTANCE CORPORATION—See Washington Mutual Inc.; *U.S. Public*, pg. 1742
NORTH AMERICAN CAPACITOR CO.; *U.S. Private*, pg. 803
THE NORTH AMERICAN COAL CORPORATION—See NACCO Industries, Inc.; *U.S. Public*, pg. 1149
NORTH AMERICAN COAL ROYALTY COMPANY—See NACCO Industries, Inc.; *U.S. Public*, pg. 1149
NORTH AMERICAN COMPANY; *U.S. Private*, pg. 803
NORTH AMERICAN DISTRIBUTION SYSTEMS, INC.—See Norfolk Southern Corporation; *U.S. Public*, pg. 1192
NORTH AMERICAN ENCLOSURES, INC.; *U.S. Private*, pg. 803
NORTH AMERICAN ENERGY CONSERVATION, INC.—See York Research Corporation; *U.S. Public*, pg. 1789
NORTH AMERICAN ENERGY SERVICES CO., INC.—See Montana Power Company; *U.S. Public*, pg. 1127
NORTH AMERICAN FINANCIAL CORP.—See Carlson Companies, Inc.; *U.S. Private*, pg. 212
NORTH AMERICAN FORWARDING, INC.—See Norfolk Southern Corporation; *U.S. Public*, pg. 1192
NORTH AMERICAN GALVANIZING—See Kinark Corporation; *U.S. Public*, pg. 961
NORTH AMERICAN GRAIN DIV.—See Continental Grain Company; *U.S. Private*, pg. 268
NORTH AMERICAN LIGHTING, INC.—See Koito Manufacturing Co.; *Int'l*, pg. 743
THE NORTH AMERICAN MANUFACTURING CO.; *U.S. Private*, pg. 803
NORTH AMERICAN METALS CORP.—See Wheaton River Minerals Ltd.; *Int'l*, pg. 1498
NORTH AMERICAN METALS DISTRIBUTION GROUP—See Rio Algom Limited; *Int'l*, pg. 1118
NORTH AMERICAN MOVING & STORAGE, INC.—See Norfolk Southern Corporation; *U.S. Public*, pg. 1192

NORTH AMERICAN OUTDOOR GROUP, INC.—See Cendant Corporation; *U.S. Public*, pg. 321
NORTH AMERICAN PASSENGER CAR PLATFORMS—See General Motors Corporation; *U.S. Public*, pg. 719
NORTH AMERICAN PRODUCTS CORP.; *U.S. Private*, pg. 803
NORTH AMERICAN PROFESSIONAL PRODUCTS—See CCL Industries, Inc.; *Int'l*, pg. 238
NORTH AMERICAN PUBLISHING COMPANY; *U.S. Private*, pg. 803
NORTH AMERICAN PULP & PAPER SECTOR—See Kimberly-Clark Corporation; *U.S. Public*, pg. 958
NORTH AMERICAN RECREATION PRODUCTS COMPANY—See MacAndrews & Forbes Holdings Inc.; *U.S. Private*, pg. 691
NORTH AMERICAN REFRACTORIES COMPANY; *U.S. Private*, pg. 803
NORTH AMERICAN REPRESENTATIVE OFFICE (NARO)—See Asian Development Bank; *Int'l*, pg. 89
NORTH AMERICAN RESOURCES CO.—See Montana Power Company; *U.S. Public*, pg. 1127
NORTH AMERICAN ROOFING SYSTEMS, INC.; *U.S. Private*, pg. 803
NORTH AMERICAN ROOFING SYSTEMS, INC.—See North American Roofing Systems, Inc.; *U.S. Private*, pg. 803
NORTH AMERICAN ROYALTIES, INC.; *U.S. Private*, pg. 803
NORTH AMERICAN SALT COMPANY—See Harris Chemical Group, Inc.; *U.S. Private*, pg. 505
NORTH AMERICAN SPECIALTY INSURANCE COMPANY—See Swiss Reinsurance Company; *Int'l*, pg. 1332
NORTH AMERICAN STEEL MANAGEMENT CORP.—See Preussag AG; *Int'l*, pg. 1070
NORTH AMERICAN TRAILING CO.—See Great Lakes Dredge & Dock Co.; *U.S. Private*, pg. 474
NORTH AMERICAN TRANSFORMER, INC.—See Rockwell International Corporation; *U.S. Public*, pg. 1398
NORTH AMERICAN TRANSPORT INSURANCE CO.—See Norfolk Southern Corporation; *U.S. Public*, pg. 1192
NORTH AMERICAN UNDERWEAR COMPANY, INC.—See Fruit of the Loom, Inc.; *U.S. Public*, pg. 686
NORTH AMERICAN VAN LINES CANADA LTD.—See Norfolk Southern Corporation; *U.S. Public*, pg. 1192
NORTH AMERICAN VAN LINES, INC.—See Norfolk Southern Corporation; *U.S. Public*, pg. 1191
NORTH AMERICAN VAN LINES LTD.—See Norfolk Southern Corporation; *U.S. Public*, pg. 1192
NORTH AMERICAN VAN LINES OF TEXAS, INC.—See Norfolk Southern Corporation; *U.S. Public*, pg. 1192
NORTH & JUDD; *U.S. Private*, pg. 804
NORTH & SOUTH RAILWAYS LIMITED—See Wisconsin Central Transportation Corporation; *U.S. Public*, pg. 1772
NORTH ARKANSAS WHOLESALE CO., INC.—See Wal-Mart Stores, Inc.; *U.S. Public*, pg. 1733
NORTH ATLANTIC ENERGY CORP.—See Northeast Utilities; *U.S. Public*, pg. 1195
NORTH ATLANTIC ENERGY SERVICE CORP.—See Northeast Utilities; *U.S. Public*, pg. 1195
NORTH ATTLEBORO GAS COMPANY—See Providence Energy Corporation; *U.S. Public*, pg. 1337
NORTH BROS. CO.—See Performance Contracting Group; *U.S. Private*, pg. 853
NORTH CANADIAN MARKETING—See EdperBrascan Corporation; *Int'l*, pg. 434
NORTH CANADIAN POWER—See EdperBrascan Corporation; *Int'l*, pg. 434
NORTH CAROLINA EQUIPMENT CO.; *U.S. Private*, pg. 804
NORTH CAROLINA FOAM INDUSTRIES, INC.—See Barnhardt Manufacturing Co.; *U.S. Private*, pg. 117
NORTH CAROLINA GAS SERVICE—See NUI Corporation; *U.S. Public*, pg. 1148
THE NORTH CAROLINA MIDLAND RAILROAD CO.—See Norfolk Southern Corporation; *U.S. Public*, pg. 1191
NORTH CAROLINA MUTUAL LIFE INSURANCE CO.; *U.S. Private*, pg. 804
NORTH CAROLINA MUTUAL WHOLESALE DRUG CO.; *U.S. Private*, pg. 804
NORTH CAROLINA NATURAL GAS CORPORATION; *U.S. Public*, pg. 1194
NORTH CASTLE DESIGN—See North Castle Partners Advertising, Inc.; *U.S. Private*, pg. 804
NORTH CASTLE DIRECT—See North Castle Partners Advertising, Inc.; *U.S. Private*, pg. 804
NORTH CASTLE PARTNERS ADVERTISING—See North Castle Partners Advertising, Inc.; *U.S. Private*, pg. 804
NORTH CASTLE PARTNERS ADVERTISING, INC.; *U.S. Private*, pg. 804
NORTH CASTLE PUBLIC RELATIONS—See North Castle Partners Advertising, Inc.; *U.S. Private*, pg. 804
NORTH CENTRAL AMPI, INC.; *U.S. Private*, pg. 804
NORTH CENTRAL CRANE & EXCAVATOR SALES CORP.—See The Manitowoc Company, Inc.; *U.S. Public*, pg. 1041
NORTH CENTRAL DIVISION—See Pameco Corp.; *U.S. Public*, pg. 1255
NORTH CENTRAL LIFE INSURANCE COMPANY—See Financial Life Companies, Inc.; *U.S. Private*, pg. 404
NORTH CENTRAL MARKETING DIV.—See CUNA Mutual Insurance Society; *U.S. Private*, pg. 296
NORTH CENTRAL TEXAS INDEPENDANT PRACTICE ASSOCIATION, P.A.—See Cigna Corp.; *U.S. Public*, pg. 360
NORTH CHINA INTERNATIONAL LEASING CO. LTD.—See Standard Chartered Bank PLC; *Int'l*, pg. 1297
NORTH COAL, INC.—See Axel Johnson AB; *Int'l*, pg. 709
NORTH COAST BEHAVIORAL RESEARCH GROUP—See Wyse Advertising; *U.S. Private*, pg. 1194
NORTH COAST DIVISION—See Fuchs Petrolub AG Oel + Chemie; *Int'l*, pg. 518

NORTH COAST ELECTRIC COMPANY; *U.S. Private,* pg. 804

NORTH COAST INVESTMENT CORPORATION—See Cigna Corp.; *U.S. Public,* pg. 361

NORTH COAST MORTGAGE, INC.—See The Rottlund Company, Inc.; *U.S. Public,* pg. 1406

NORTH DAKOTA MILL & ELEVATOR ASSOCIATION; *U.S. Private,* pg. 804

NORTH DEKALB CABLE T.V. COMPANY—See The E.W. Scripps Company; *U.S. Public,* pg. 1448

NORTH DENVER HILL CORP.—See Specialty Restaurants Corporation; *U.S. Private,* pg. 1023

THE NORTH DOWN BRICK COMPANY LIMITED—See RMC Group p.l.c.; *Int'l,* pg. 1079

NORTH ELECTRIC SUPPLY, INC.; *U.S. Private,* pg. 805

NORTH EXPLORATION (EASTERN REGION)—See North Limited; *Int'l,* pg. 967

NORTH EXPLORATION (WESTERN REGION)—See North Limited; *Int'l,* pg. 967

NORTH FLORIDA PAIN INSTITUTE, INC.—See Integrated Health Services, Inc.; *U.S. Public,* pg. 885

NORTH FOREST EUCALYPT RESEARCH CENTER—See North Limited; *Int'l,* pg. 967

NORTH FOREST PRODUCTS—See North Limited; *Int'l,* pg. 967

NORTH FOREST PRODUCTS TAMAR—See North Limited; *Int'l,* pg. 967

NORTH FOREST PRODUCTS TRIABUNNA—See North Limited; *Int'l,* pg. 967

NORTH FORESTS BURNIE—See North Limited; *Int'l,* pg. 967

NORTH FORK BANCORPORATION, INC.; *U.S. Public,* pg. 1194

NORTH FORK BANK—See North Fork Bancorporation, Inc.; *U.S. Public,* pg. 1194

NORTH GROUP REALTY—See Banknorth Group Inc.; *U.S. Public,* pg. 187

NORTH KANTO CATERPILLAR MITSUBISHI CONSTRUCTION EQUIPMENT SALES, LTD.—See Caterpillar Inc.; *U.S. Public,* pg. 317

NORTH KILLINGHOLME CARGO TERMINAL—See Simon Engineering plc; *Int'l,* pg. 1251

NORTH LAS VEGAS CARE CENTER—See Horizon/CMS Healthcare Corporation; *U.S. Public,* pg. 837

NORTH LIMITED; *Int'l,* pg. 967

NORTH MIAMI BEACH SURGICAL CENTER—See Columbia/HCA Healthcare Corporation; *U.S. Public,* pg. 405

NORTH MINING—See North Limited; *Int'l,* pg. 967

NORTH MINING INC.—See North Limited; *Int'l,* pg. 967

NORTH MISSISSIPPI NATURAL GAS CORPORATION—See Atrion Corporation; *U.S. Public,* pg. 146

NORTH PACIFIC INSURANCE COMPANY—See General Accident Fire and Life Assurance Corporation p.l.c.; *Int'l,* pg. 543

NORTH PACIFIC LUMBER COMPANY; *U.S. Private,* pg. 805

NORTH PACIFIC PAPER CORPORATION (NORPAC)—See Nippon Paper Industries Company Limited; *Int'l,* pg. 938

NORTH PARK LINCOLN MERCURY INC.; *U.S. Private,* pg. 805

NORTH PINE PRODUCTS—See North Limited; *Int'l,* pg. 967

NORTH PLAZA STATE BANK—See UMB Financial Corporation; *U.S. Public,* pg. 1654

NORTH POINT PRESS—See Georg von Holtzbrinck GmbH; *Int'l,* pg. 1479

NORTH POWDER LUMBER CO.—See WTD Industries, Inc.; *U.S. Public,* pg. 1730

THE NORTH RIVER INSURANCE COMPANY—See Xerox Corporation; *U.S. Private,* pg. 1784

NORTH SAFETY PRODUCTS—See Siebe plc; *Int'l,* pg. 1243

NORTH SAFETY PRODUCTS, HAND PROTECTION DIVISION—See Siebe plc; *Int'l,* pg. 1243

NORTH SAFETY PRODUCTS, HEALTH CARE DIVISION—See Siebe plc; *Int'l,* pg. 1243

NORTH SAFETY PRODUCTS, SAFETY EQUIPMENT DIVISION—See Siebe plc; *Int'l,* pg. 1243

NORTH SAFETY PRODUCTS SIEBE NORTH CANADA LTD.—See Siebe plc; *Int'l,* pg. 1243

NORTH SEA FERRIES LTD.—See The Peninsular and Oriental Steam Navigation Company; *Int'l,* pg. 1035

NORTH SHORE GAS CO.—See Peoples Energy Corporation; *U.S. Public,* pg. 1275

NORTH SHORE MOVERS; *U.S. Private,* pg. 805

NORTH SPECIALTY PRODUCTS—See Siebe plc; *Int'l,* pg. 1243

NORTH STAR BHP STEEL LLC—See The Broken Hill Proprietary Company Limited; *Int'l,* pg. 226

NORTH STAR MALL, INC.—See The Rouse Company; *U.S. Public,* pg. 1409

NORTH STAR/NORWAY—See Journal Communications Inc.; *U.S. Private,* pg. 602

NORTH STAR PRINT GROUP INC.—See Journal Communications Inc.; *U.S. Private,* pg. 601

NORTH STAR STEEL CO.—See Cargill; *U.S. Private,* pg. 210

NORTH STAR TITLE—See TCF Financial Corp.; *U.S. Public,* pg. 1554

NORTH TEXAS CEMENT COMPANY—See Ash Grove Cement Company; *U.S. Private,* pg. 88

NORTH WEST AGGREGATES LIMITED—See RMC Group p.l.c.; *Int'l,* pg. 1079

NORTH WEST RADIO—See EMAP Plc; *Int'l,* pg. 452

NORTH WEST SHELF DEVELOPMENT—See Royal Dutch/Shell Group of Companies; *Int'l,* pg. 1137

NORTH WEST WATER AUSTRALIA PTY. LTD.—See United Utilities plc; *Int'l,* pg. 1444

NORTH WEST WATER INDONESIA—See United Utilities plc; *Int'l,* pg. 1444

NORTH WEST WATER LIMITED—See United Utilities plc; *Int'l,* pg. 1444

NORTH WEST WATER (MALAYSIA) LTD.—See United Utilities plc; *Int'l,* pg. 1444

NORTH WEST WATER (MEXICO)—See United Utilities plc; *Int'l,* pg. 1444

NORTH WEST WATER (THAILAND)—See United Utilities plc; *Int'l,* pg. 1444

NORTH WESTERN SHIPPING AND TOWAGE COMPANY PTY. LTD.—See Brambles Industries Limited; *Int'l,* pg. 211

NORTH WHITFORDS ESTATES PTY. LTD.—See Taylor Woodrow plc; *Int'l,* pg. 1359

NORTHEAST ENERGY MANAGEMENT—See Eastern Utilities Associates; *U.S. Public,* pg. 549

NORTHEAST ENVIRONMENTAL SERVICES, INC.—See ERD Waste Corp.; *U.S. Public,* pg. 546

NORTHEAST MARKETING DIV.—See CUNA Mutual Insurance Society; *U.S. Private,* pg. 296

NORTHEAST MARKETING-CLEVELAND BUSINESS CENTER—See Fleet Financial Group, Inc.; *U.S. Public,* pg. 649

NORTHEAST NUCLEAR ENERGY CO.—See Northeast Utilities; *U.S. Public,* pg. 1195

NORTHEAST OHIO CORRECTIONAL FACILITY—See Corrections Corporation of America; *U.S. Public,* pg. 451

NORTHEAST PROPERTIES, INC.—See Eaton Vance Corp.; *U.S. Public,* pg. 559

NORTHEAST PUBLISHING, INC.-THE HERALD NEWS—See Journal Register Company; *U.S. Public,* pg. 935

NORTHEAST REGION—See MCI Communications Corp.; *U.S. Public,* pg. 1024

NORTHEAST TEXAS FARMERS CO-OP; *U.S. Private,* pg. 805

NORTHEAST UTILITIES; *U.S. Public,* pg. 1194

NORTHEASTERN DIV.-OLD SAYBROOK—See R.R. Donnelley & Sons Company; *U.S. Public,* pg. 518

NORTHEASTERN GRAPHIC SUPPLY, INC.; *U.S. Private,* pg. 805

NORTHERN AGGREGATES LIMITED—See RMC Group p.l.c.; *Int'l,* pg. 1079

NORTHERN BANK LIMITED—See National Australia Bank Limited; *Int'l,* pg. 906

NORTHERN CABLE HOLDINGS LTD.—See CFCF Inc.; *Int'l,* pg. 241

NORTHERN CALIFORNIA LABORATORY—See Pace Analytical Services; *U.S. Private,* pg. 829

NORTHERN CALIFORNIA REGION—See Hanson PLC; *Int'l,* pg. 593

NORTHERN CAPITAL MANAGEMENT, INC.—See United Asset Management Corporation; *U.S. Public,* pg. 1673

NORTHERN CENTRAL BANK—See Keystone Financial Inc.; *U.S. Public,* pg. 956

NORTHERN COALFIELDS LIMITED—See Coal India Limited; *Int'l,* pg. 299

NORTHERN COMPUTERS INC.—See American Trading and Production Corporation; *U.S. Private,* pg. 64

NORTHERN CROSS, LTD.—See Barancorp; *U.S. Private,* pg. 115

THE NORTHERN DAILY NEWS—See Hollinger Inc.; *Int'l,* pg. 631

NORTHERN DAIRIES—See Northern Foods plc; *Int'l,* pg. 968

NORTHERN DAIRIES LTD.—See Northern Foods plc; *Int'l,* pg. 968

NORTHERN DISTRIBUTING CO.—See Seaway Food Town, Inc.; *U.S. Public,* pg. 1453

NORTHERN DIVISION—See Consumers Water Company; *U.S. Public,* pg. 438

NORTHERN ENERGY—See Essex County Gas Company; *U.S. Public,* pg. 593

NORTHERN ENGINEERING CORP.—See Crane Manufacturing; *U.S. Private,* pg. 286

NORTHERN FOODS PLC; *Int'l,* pg. 967

NORTHERN FUTURES CORPORATION—See Northern Trust Corporation; *U.S. Public,* pg. 1196

NORTHERN GAS COMPANY—See K N Energy, Inc.; *U.S. Public,* pg. 937

NORTHERN ILLINOIS GAS COMPANY—See NICOR Inc.; *U.S. Public,* pg. 1183

NORTHERN INDIANA PUBLIC SERVICE COMPANY—See NIPSCO Industries, Inc.; *U.S. Public,* pg. 1185

NORTHERN INSURANCE COMPANY OF NEW YORK—See Zurich Insurance Company; *Int'l,* pg. 1530

NORTHERN IRELAND CARPETS LTD.—See Lamont Holdings Plc; *Int'l,* pg. 797

NORTHERN IRELAND LIMITED—See Northern Telecom Limited; *Int'l,* pg. 970

NORTHERN IRELAND TRAILERS—See The Peninsular and Oriental Steam Navigation Company; *Int'l,* pg. 1033

NORTHERN ISLES—See Kellwood Company; *U.S. Public,* pg. 948

NORTHERN LABS, INC.; *U.S. Private,* pg. 805

NORTHERN LIFE INSURANCE COMPANY—See ReliaStar Financial Corp.; *U.S. Public,* pg. 1375

NORTHERN MICHIGAN VENEERS, INC.; *U.S. Private,* pg. 805

NORTHERN MINNESOTA UTILITIES—See UtiliCorp United Inc.; *U.S. Public,* pg. 1701

NORTHERN NATURAL GAS CO.—See Enron Corp.; *U.S. Public,* pg. 584

NORTHERN NAVIGATION INTERNATIONAL INC.; *U.S. Private,* pg. 805

NORTHERN PETROLEUM—See Bradford Oil Company, Inc.; *U.S. Private,* pg. 164

NORTHERN PIGMENT—See Russel Metals Inc.; *Int'l,* pg. 1150

NORTHERN PIPELINE CONSTRUCTION CO.—See Southwest Gas Corporation; *U.S. Public,* pg. 1493

NORTHERN PLAINS NATURAL GAS CO.—See Enron Corp.; *U.S. Public,* pg. 584

NORTHERN PLAINS STEEL CO.—See Owen Industries, Inc.; *U.S. Private,* pg. 824

NORTHERN RESEARCH & ENGINEERING CORP.—See Ingersoll-Rand Company; *U.S. Public,* pg. 877

NORTHERN ROCK ASSET MANAGEMENT LIMITED—See Northern Rock PLC; *Int'l,* pg. 968

NORTHERN ROCK FINANCIAL SERVICES LIMITED—See Northern Rock PLC; *Int'l,* pg. 968

NORTHERN ROCK HOMES LIMITED—See Northern Rock PLC; *Int'l,* pg. 968

NORTHERN ROCK PLC; *Int'l,* pg. 968

NORTHERN ROCK UNIT TRUST LIMITED—See Northern Rock PLC; *Int'l,* pg. 968

NORTHERN SC PAPER CORPORATION—See The New York Times Company; *U.S. Public,* pg. 1174

NORTHERN STAR INSURANCE COMPANY LTD.—See Assicurazioni Generali S.p.A.; *Int'l,* pg. 90

NORTHERN STATES POWER COMPANY; *U.S. Public,* pg. 1195

NORTHERN STORAGE AND TRANSPORTATION PROJECT AND CONSTRUCTION DIV.—See Chinese Petroleum Corporation; *Int'l,* pg. 286

NORTHERN TELECOM—See Northern Telecom Limited; *Int'l,* pg. 969

NORTHERN TELECOM (ASIA) LIMITED—See Northern Telecom Limited; *Int'l,* pg. 970

NORTHERN TELECOM CANADA LIMITED—See Northern Telecom Limited; *Int'l,* pg. 969

NORTHERN TELECOM DE COLOMBIA S.A.—See Northern Telecom Limited; *Int'l,* pg. 970

NORTHERN TELECOM DE MEXICO, S.A. DE C.V.—See Northern Telecom Limited; *Int'l,* pg. 970

NORTHERN TELECOM DO BRASIL INDUSTRIA E COMERCIO LTDA.—See Northern Telecom Limited; *Int'l,* pg. 970

NORTHERN TELECOM FINANCE CORPORATION—See Northern Telecom Limited; *Int'l,* pg. 969

NORTHERN TELECOM INC.—See Northern Telecom Limited; *Int'l,* pg. 970

NORTHERN TELECOM INDUSTRIES SDN. BHD.—See Northern Telecom Limited; *Int'l,* pg. 970

NORTHERN TELECOM INTERNATIONAL FINANCE B.V.—See Northern Telecom Limited; *Int'l,* pg. 970

NORTHERN TELECOM (IRELAND) LIMITED—See Northern Telecom Limited; *Int'l,* pg. 970

NORTHERN TELECOM JAPAN INC.—See Northern Telecom Limited; *Int'l,* pg. 970

NORTHERN TELECOM LIMITED; *Int'l,* pg. 968

NORTHERN TELECOM (LUXEMBOURG) S.A.—See Northern Telecom Limited; *Int'l,* pg. 970

NORTHERN TELECOM S.A.—See Northern Telecom Limited; *Int'l,* pg. 970

NORTHERN TELECOM SWITCHING NETWORKS—See Northern Telecom Limited; *Int'l,* pg. 970

NORTHERN TELEPHONE LIMITED—See BCE Inc.; *Int'l,* pg. 115

NORTHERN TREE SERVICE, INC.—See ESELCO, Inc.; *U.S. Public,* pg. 592

NORTHERN TRUST BANK OF ARIZONA, N.A.—See Northern Trust Corporation; *U.S. Public,* pg. 1196

NORTHERN TRUST BANK OF FLORIDA, N.A.—See Northern Trust Corporation; *U.S. Public,* pg. 1196

NORTHERN TRUST CAYMAN INTERNATIONAL, LTD.—See Northern Trust Corporation; *U.S. Public,* pg. 1197

THE NORTHERN TRUST COMPANY—See Northern Trust Corporation; *U.S. Public,* pg. 1197

NORTHERN TRUST CORPORATION; *U.S. Public,* pg. 1195

THE NORTHERN TRUST INTERNATIONAL BANKING CORPORATION—See Northern Trust Corporation; *U.S. Public,* pg. 1197

NORTHERN TRUST SECURITIES, INC.—See Northern Trust Corporation; *U.S. Public,* pg. 1196

NORTHERN TUBE—See Charterhouse Group International, Inc.; *U.S. Private,* pg. 230

NORTHERN UTILITIES, INC.—See Bay State Gas Company; *U.S. Public,* pg. 197

NORTHERN VERMONT RAILROAD—See Iron Road Railways Inc.; *U.S. Private,* pg. 575

NORTHFIELD EAST OPERATION—See Sheldahl, Inc.; *U.S. Public,* pg. 1465

NORTHFIELD FOODS—See Land O'Lakes, Inc.; *U.S. Private,* pg. 646

NORTHFIELD LABORATORIES PTY LTD.—See Nutricia BV; *Int'l,* pg. 992

NORTHFIELD METAL PRODUCTS LTD.—See Leggett & Platt, Incorporated; *U.S. Public,* pg. 987

NORTHFIELD TELEPHONE CO.—See Telephone and Data Systems, Inc.; *U.S. Public,* pg. 1571

NORTHFIELD WEST OPERATION—See Sheldahl, Inc.; *U.S. Public,* pg. 1465

NORTHLAND ALUMINUM PRODUCTS, INC.; *U.S. Private,* pg. 805

NORTHLAND CRANBERRIES, INC.; *U.S. Public,* pg. 1197

NORTHLAND ELECTRIC SUPPLY COMPANY; *U.S. Private,* pg. 806

NORTHLAND EVERGREENS, INC.—See American Nursery Products, LLC; *U.S. Private,* pg. 60

NORTHLAND FURNITURE CO., LLC—See The Apogee Companies, Inc.; *U.S. Private,* pg. 77

NORTHLAND PUBLISHING CO.—See Justin Industries, Inc.; *U.S. Public,* pg. 937

NORTHLAND SPORTS INC.—See Sportsman Supply; *U.S. Private,* pg. 1026

NORTHLAND UTILITIES (B.C.) LIMITED—See ATCO Group Co.; *Int'l,* pg. 95

NORTHLAND UTILITIES ENTERPRISES LTD.—See ATCO Group Co.; *Int'l,* pg. 95

NORTHLAND UTILITIES (NWT) LIMITED—See ATCO Group Co.; *Int'l,* pg. 95

NORTHLICH STOLLEY LAWARRE; *U.S. Private,* pg. 806

NORTHLICH STOLLEY LAWARRE PUBLIC RELATIONS—See Northlich Stolley LaWarre; *U.S. Private,* pg. 806

NORTHLINE COUPLING SYSTEMS LTD.—See Delta plc; *Int'l,* pg. 391

NORTHMAR DISTRIBUTORS—See Silcorp Limited; *Int'l*, pg. 1249
NORTHPARKES MINES—See North Limited; *Int'l*, pg. 967
NORTHPRINT B.V.—See Reed Elsevier plc; *Int'l*, pg. 1100
NORTHRIDGE HOSPITAL-ROSCOE BLVD. CAMPUS—See UniHealth; *U.S. Private*, pg. 1118
NORTHRIDGE HOSPITAL-SHERMAN WAY CAMPUS—See UniHealth; *U.S. Private*, pg. 1118
NORTHRIDGE INDUSTRIES, INC.—See Hyatt Corporation; *U.S. Private*, pg. 551
NORTHRIDGE SURGERY CENTER—See Vencor, Inc.; *U.S. Public*, pg. 1715
NORTHROCK RESOURCES LTD.; *Int'l*, pg. 970
NORTHROP GRUMMAN ALLIED INDUSTRIES, INC.—See Northrop Grumman Corporation; *U.S. Public*, pg. 1198
NORTHROP GRUMMAN CORPORATION; *U.S. Public*, pg. 1197
NORTHROP GRUMMAN INTERNATIONAL, INC.—See Northrop Grumman Corporation; *U.S. Public*, pg. 1198
NORTHRUP KING CO.—See Novartis AG; *Int'l*, pg. 974
NORTHRUP KING PTY. LTD.—See Novartis AG; *Int'l*, pg. 983
NORTHRUP KING SEEDS LTD.—See Novartis AG; *Int'l*, pg. 983
NORTHRUP KING SEMENCES S.A.—See Novartis AG; *Int'l*, pg. 983
NORTHRUP KING SEMENTI S.P.A.—See Novartis AG; *Int'l*, pg. 983
NORTHRUP KING SEMILLAS S.A.—See Novartis AG; *Int'l*, pg. 983
NORTHRUP KING Y COMPANIA, S.A. DE C.V.—See Novartis AG; *Int'l*, pg. 983
NORTHSIDE BLUEPRINT & SUPPLY COMPANY—See Wallace Computer Services, Inc.; *U.S. Public*, pg. 1735
NORTHSIDE INSURANCE COMPANY LTD.—See Otto Versand (GmbH & Co.); *Int'l*, pg. 1015
NORTHSTAR AUTO AUCTION INC.—See Tyco International Ltd.; *U.S. Public*, pg. 1649
NORTHSTAR INVESTMENT MANAGEMENT CORPORATION—See ReliaStar Financial Corp.; *U.S. Public*, pg. 1375
NORTHSTAR LIFE INS. COMPANY—See The Minnesota Mutual Life Insurance Company; *U.S. Private*, pg. 750
THE NORTHUMBERLAND CONCRETE COMPANY LIMITED—See Tarmac plc; *Int'l*, pg. 1355
NORTHUMBERLAND GROUP LTD.—See Banque Generale du Luxembourg SA; *Int'l*, pg. 162
NORTHVILLE INDUSTRIES CORP.; *U.S. Private*, pg. 806
NORTHWAY MOTORCAR CORPORATION; *U.S. Private*, pg. 806
NORTHWEST AEROSPACE TRAINING CORPORATION—See Northwest Airlines Corp.; *U.S. Public*, pg. 1200
NORTHWEST AIRCRAFT INC.—See Northwest Airlines Corp.; *U.S. Public*, pg. 1200
NORTHWEST AIRLINES CORP.; *U.S. Public*, pg. 1199
NORTHWEST AIRLINES, INC.—See Northwest Airlines Corp.; *U.S. Public*, pg. 1200
NORTHWEST ALLOYS, INC.—See Aluminum Company of America; *U.S. Public*, pg. 61
NORTHWEST DIETETIC SUPPLY, INC.—See Koninklijke BolsWessanen nv; *Int'l*, pg. 752
NORTHWEST FABRICS & CRAFTS—See Hancock Fabrics, Inc.; *U.S. Public*, pg. 779
NORTHWEST FENCE PRODUCTS CO.—See Carl Weissman & Sons, Inc.; *U.S. Private*, pg. 1160
NORTHWEST FLORIDA DAILY NEWS—See Freedom Communication Inc.; *U.S. Private*, pg. 425
NORTHWEST INDUSTRIES, INC.—See Triumph Group, Inc.; *U.S. Public*, pg. 1640
NORTHWEST MALL, INC.—See The Rouse Company; *U.S. Public*, pg. 1409
NORTHWEST MARKETING DIV.—See CUNA Mutual Insurance Society; *U.S. Private*, pg. 296
NORTHWEST NATURAL GAS COMPANY; *U.S. Public*, pg. 1200
NORTHWEST PACIFIC INDEMNITY CO.—See The Chubb Corporation; *U.S. Public*, pg. 355
NORTHWEST PARKING SERVICES INC.—See Allright Corporation; *U.S. Private*, pg. 43
NORTHWEST PARS, INC.—See Northwest Airlines Corp.; *U.S. Public*, pg. 1200
NORTHWEST PIPE FITTINGS, INC.; *U.S. Private*, pg. 806
NORTHWEST PIPELINE CORP.—See The Williams Companies, Inc.; *U.S. Public*, pg. 1769
NORTHWEST TERRITORIAL AIRWAYS LTD.—See Air Canada; *Int'l*, pg. 36
NORTHWEST TOBACCO & CANDY CO.; *U.S. Private*, pg. 806
NORTHWESTEL INC.—See BCE Inc.; *Int'l*, pg. 115
NORTHWESTERN ENERGY CORP.—See Northwestern Public Service; *U.S. Public*, pg. 1201
NORTHWESTERN ENGINEERING CO.; *U.S. Private*, pg. 806
NORTHWESTERN FLAVORS INC.—See Wm. Wrigley Jr. Company; *U.S. Public*, pg. 1781
NORTHWESTERN GOLF COMPANY; *U.S. Private*, pg. 806
NORTHWESTERN GROWTH CORP.—See Northwestern Public Service; *U.S. Public*, pg. 1201
NORTHWESTERN INDUSTRIAL PIPING; *U.S. Private*, pg. 806
NORTHWESTERN MEATS INC.; *U.S. Private*, pg. 807
NORTHWESTERN MUTUAL LIFE INSURANCE CO.; *U.S. Private*, pg. 807
NORTHWESTERN NATIONAL LIFE INSURANCE CO.—See ReliaStar Financial Corp.; *U.S. Public*, pg. 1375
NORTHWESTERN NETWORKS, INC.—See Northwestern Public Service; *U.S. Public*, pg. 1201
NORTHWESTERN PACIFIC RAILROAD CO.—See Union Pacific Corporation; *U.S. Public*, pg. 1668
NORTHWESTERN PUBLIC SERVICE; *U.S. Public*, pg. 1200
NORTHWESTERN RESOURCES COMPANY—See Montana Power Company; *U.S. Public*, pg. 1127

NORTHWESTERN STATES PORTLAND CEMENT—See Holderbank Financiere Glaris Ltd.; *Int'l*, pg. 628
NORTHWESTERN STEEL & WIRE CO.; *U.S. Public*, pg. 1201
NORTHWESTERN STEEL & WIRE COMPANY-KENTUCKY, A DELAWARE CORP.—See Northwestern Steel & Wire Co.; *U.S. Public*, pg. 1201
NORTHWESTERN SYSTEMS, INC.—See Northwestern Public Service; *U.S. Public*, pg. 1201
NORTHWESTERN TELEPHONE SYSTEMS, INC.—See PacifiCorp; *U.S. Public*, pg. 1252
NORTHWESTERN UTILITIES LIMITED—See ATCO Group Co.; *Int'l*, pg. 95
NORTHWOOD FOREST INDUSTRIES, LTD.—See The Mead Corporation; *U.S. Public*, pg. 1076
NORTHWOOD PULP & TIMBER LTD.—See The Mead Corporation; *U.S. Public*, pg. 1076
NORTON ABRASIVES—See Saint-Gobain; *Int'l*, pg. 1174
NORTON ABRASIVES LIMITED—See Saint-Gobain; *Int'l*, pg. 1174
NORTON ADVANCED CERAMICS LIMITED—See Saint-Gobain; *Int'l*, pg. 1174
NORTON ADVANCED CERAMICS OF CANADA INC.—See Saint-Gobain; *Int'l*, pg. 1174
NORTON ADVANCED MATERIALS GMBH—See Saint-Gobain; *Int'l*, pg. 1175
NORTON-ALCOA PROPPANTS—See Saint-Gobain; *Int'l*, pg. 1174
NORTON A/S—See Saint-Gobain; *Int'l*, pg. 1174
NORTON BETEILIGUNGS GMBH—See Saint-Gobain; *Int'l*, pg. 1175
NORTON B.V.—See Saint-Gobain; *Int'l*, pg. 1175
NORTON CANADA INC.—See Saint-Gobain; *Int'l*, pg. 1175
NORTON CAPITAL INC. (CANADA)—See Saint-Gobain; *Int'l*, pg. 1175
NORTON CHEMICAL PROCESS PRODUCTS CORPORATION—See Saint-Gobain; *Int'l*, pg. 1173
NORTON CHEMICAL PROCESS PRODUCTS (EUROPE) LIMITED—See Saint-Gobain; *Int'l*, pg. 1175
NORTON CHILE S.A.—See Saint-Gobain; *Int'l*, pg. 1175
NORTON CO. LTD.—See Saint-Gobain; *Int'l*, pg. 1175
NORTON COMPANY—See Saint-Gobain; *Int'l*, pg. 1173
NORTON COMPANY DE MEXICO SA DE CV—See Saint-Gobain; *Int'l*, pg. 1175
NORTON COMPANY UK LIMITED—See Saint-Gobain; *Int'l*, pg. 1175
NORTON CONSTRUCTION PRODUCTS—See Saint-Gobain; *Int'l*, pg. 1177
NORTON DESMARQUEST FINE CERAMICS—See Saint-Gobain; *Int'l*, pg. 1175
NORTON DO NORDESTE S.A. INDUSTRIA E COMERCIO—See Saint-Gobain; *Int'l*, pg. 1175
NORTON EAST ASIA, INC.—See Saint-Gobain; *Int'l*, pg. 1175
NORTON FLUORPLAST NEDERLAND BV—See Saint-Gobain; *Int'l*, pg. 1175
NORTON FOREIGN AFFILIATES HOLDING CORPORATION—See Saint-Gobain; *Int'l*, pg. 1174
NORTON (FSC) B.V.—See Saint-Gobain; *Int'l*, pg. 1175
NORTON GMBH—See Saint-Gobain; *Int'l*, pg. 1175
NORTON GMBH OBJEKT SCHIEFBAHN—See Saint-Gobain; *Int'l*, pg. 1175
NORTON HEALTHCARE LIMITED—See IVAX Corporation; *U.S. Public*, pg. 915
NORTON HOCHTEMPERATURKERAMIK GMBH—See Saint-Gobain; *Int'l*, pg. 1175
NORTON IBERICA—See Saint-Gobain; *Int'l*, pg. 1175
NORTON INDUSTRIE PRODUKTE GMBH—See Saint-Gobain; *Int'l*, pg. 1175
NORTON INDUSTRIEPRODUKTE GMBH—See Saint-Gobain; *Int'l*, pg. 1175
NORTON INSURANCE LIMITED—See Saint-Gobain; *Int'l*, pg. 1175
NORTON INTERNATIONAL INC.—See Saint-Gobain; *Int'l*, pg. 1174
J.R. NORTON COMPANY; *U.S. Private*, pg. 807
NORTON KABUSHIKI KAISHA—See Saint-Gobain; *Int'l*, pg. 1175
NORTON KK—See Saint-Gobain; *Int'l*, pg. 1175
NORTON MATERIAUX AVANCES S.A.R.L.—See Saint-Gobain; *Int'l*, pg. 1175
NORTON MINERIOS LTDA.—See Saint-Gobain; *Int'l*, pg. 1175
NORTON (NEW ZEALAND) LIMITED—See Saint-Gobain; *Int'l*, pg. 1175
NORTON NEW ZEALAND (OPERAT) LTD.—See Saint-Gobain; *Int'l*, pg. 1175
NORTON NV PERFORMANCE PLASTICS—See Saint-Gobain; *Int'l*, pg. 1175
NORTON PAMPUS GMBH—See Saint-Gobain; *Int'l*, pg. 1175
NORTON PAMPUS LIMITED—See Saint-Gobain; *Int'l*, pg. 1175
NORTON PERFORMANCE PLASTIC CO. LTD.—See Saint-Gobain; *Int'l*, pg. 1175
NORTON PERFORMANCE PLASTICS—See Saint-Gobain; *Int'l*, pg. 1174
NORTON PERFORMANCE PLASTICS CO.—See Saint-Gobain; *Int'l*, pg. 1176
NORTON PERFORMANCE PLASTICS (SHANGHAI)—See Saint-Gobain; *Int'l*, pg. 1175
NORTON PIKE DIVISION—See Saint-Gobain; *Int'l*, pg. 1176
NORTON PLC—See Saint-Gobain; *Int'l*, pg. 1175
NORTON PROCESS SERVICES INC.—See Saint-Gobain; *Int'l*, pg. 1176
NORTON PROPPANTS INC.—See Saint-Gobain; *Int'l*, pg. 1176
NORTON PTE. LTD.—See Saint-Gobain; *Int'l*, pg. 1175
NORTON PTY. LTD.—See Saint-Gobain; *Int'l*, pg. 1175
NORTON S.A.—See Saint-Gobain; *Int'l*, pg. 1175
NORTON S.A. INDUSTRIA E COMERCIO—See Saint-Gobain; *Int'l*, pg. 1175
NORTON S.A./N.V.—See Saint-Gobain; *Int'l*, pg. 1175

NORTON SCANDINAVIA AB—See Saint-Gobain; *Int'l*, pg. 1175
NORTON SCHLEIFMITTEL GMBH—See Saint-Gobain; *Int'l*, pg. 1175
NORTON S.P.A.—See Saint-Gobain; *Int'l*, pg. 1175
NORTON UK PENSIONS LIMITED—See Saint-Gobain; *Int'l*, pg. 1175
W.W. NORTON & COMPANY, INC.; *U.S. Private*, pg. 807
NORTONMAS SDN. BHD.—See Saint-Gobain; *Int'l*, pg. 1175
NORTRANS SPEDITIONGESELLSCHAFT MBH—See UPM-Kymmene Corporation; *Int'l*, pg. 1430
NORVAL, INC.—See Scancem AB; *Int'l*, pg. 1201
NORVISTA—See FinnAir Oy; *Int'l*, pg. 486
NORVISTA B.V.—See FinnAir Oy; *Int'l*, pg. 486
NORVISTA LTD.—See FinnAir Oy; *Int'l*, pg. 486
NORVISTA REISEN GMBH—See FinnAir Oy; *Int'l*, pg. 486
NORVISTA S.R.L.—See FinnAir Oy; *Int'l*, pg. 486
NORVISTA TRAVEL AB—See FinnAir Oy; *Int'l*, pg. 486
NORVISTA—See FinnAir Oy; *Int'l*, pg. 486
NORWALK CO., INC.; *U.S. Private*, pg. 807
NORWALK FURNITURE CORPORATION; *U.S. Private*, pg. 807
NORWALK FURNITURE CORPORATION OF TENNESSEE—See Norwalk Furniture Corporation; *U.S. Private*, pg. 808
NORWALK POWDERED METALS, INC.; *U.S. Private*, pg. 808
NORWEGIAN CONTRACTORS A/S—See Aker Raj Asa; *Int'l*, pg. 42
NORWEGIAN CRUISE LINE; *U.S. Private*, pg. 808
NORWEGIAN UNDERWATER TECHNOLOGY CENTER A.S.-NUTEC—See Statoil; *Int'l*, pg. 1298
NORWELL MARINER—See Gannett Company, Inc.; *U.S. Public*, pg. 701
NORWESCO A/S—See A. Ahlstrom Corporation; *Int'l*, pg. 33
NORWESCO, INC.; *U.S. Private*, pg. 808
NORWEST AGRICULTURAL CREDIT, INC.—See Norwest Corporation; *U.S. Public*, pg. 1201
NORWEST ASIA LIMITED—See Norwest Corporation; *U.S. Public*, pg. 1203
NORWEST AUDIT SERVICES, INC.—See Norwest Corporation; *U.S. Public*, pg. 1201
NORWEST BANK ARIZONA, N.A.—See Norwest Corporation; *U.S. Public*, pg. 1202
NORWEST BANK COLORADO N.A.—See Norwest Corporation; *U.S. Public*, pg. 1202
NORWEST BANK EL PASO, N.A.—See Norwest Corporation; *U.S. Public*, pg. 1201
NORWEST BANK FARIBAULT, N.A.—See Norwest Corporation; *U.S. Public*, pg. 1202
NORWEST BANK ILLINOIS, N.A.—See Norwest Corporation; *U.S. Public*, pg. 1202
NORWEST BANK INDIANA, N.A.—See Norwest Corporation; *U.S. Public*, pg. 1202
NORWEST BANK INTERNATIONAL—See Norwest Corporation; *U.S. Public*, pg. 1202
NORWEST BANK IOWA, N.A.—See Norwest Corporation; *U.S. Public*, pg. 1202
NORWEST BANK MINNESOTA N.A.—See Norwest Corporation; *U.S. Public*, pg. 1202
NORWEST BANK MINNESOTA SOUTH, N.A.—See Norwest Corporation; *U.S. Public*, pg. 1202
NORWEST BANK MONTANA, N.A.—See Norwest Corporation; *U.S. Public*, pg. 1202
NORWEST BANK NEBRASKA, N.A.—See Norwest Corporation; *U.S. Public*, pg. 1202
NORWEST BANK NEVADA, N.A.—See Norwest Corporation; *U.S. Public*, pg. 1202
NORWEST BANK NEW MEXICO, N.A.—See Norwest Corporation; *U.S. Public*, pg. 1202
NORWEST BANK NORTH DAKOTA, N.A.—See Norwest Corporation; *U.S. Public*, pg. 1202
NORWEST BANK OF WISCONSIN—See Norwest Corporation; *U.S. Public*, pg. 1202
NORWEST BANK OHIO, N.A.—See Norwest Corporation; *U.S. Public*, pg. 1202
NORWEST BANK RED WING, N.A.—See Norwest Corporation; *U.S. Public*, pg. 1202
NORWEST BANK SOUTH DAKOTA, N.A.—See Norwest Corporation; *U.S. Public*, pg. 1203
NORWEST BANK TEXAS, N.A.—See Norwest Corporation; *U.S. Public*, pg. 1203
NORWEST BANK WYOMING, N.A.—See Norwest Corporation; *U.S. Public*, pg. 1202
NORWEST BUSINESS CREDIT, INC.—See Norwest Corporation; *U.S. Public*, pg. 1202
NORWEST CORPORATION; *U.S. Public*, pg. 1201
NORWEST DIVISION—See R.R. Donnelley & Sons Company; *U.S. Public*, pg. 518
NORWEST EQUIPMENT FINANCE, INC.—See Norwest Corporation; *U.S. Public*, pg. 1202
NORWEST FINANCIAL BUSINESS CREDIT, INC.—See Norwest Corporation; *U.S. Public*, pg. 1202
NORWEST FINANCIAL COAST, INC.—See Norwest Corporation; *U.S. Public*, pg. 1202
NORWEST FINANCIAL, INC.—See Norwest Corporation; *U.S. Public*, pg. 1202
NORWEST FINANCIAL LEASING, INC.—See Norwest Corporation; *U.S. Public*, pg. 1202
NORWEST INSURANCE, INC.—See Norwest Corporation; *U.S. Public*, pg. 1202
NORWEST INVESTMENT SERVICES, INC.—See Norwest Corporation; *U.S. Public*, pg. 1202
NORWEST MORTGAGE, INC.—See Norwest Corporation; *U.S. Public*, pg. 1202
NORWEST PROPERTIES, INC.—See Norwest Corporation; *U.S. Public*, pg. 1202
NORWEST SERVICES, INC.—See Norwest Corporation; *U.S. Public*, pg. 1202
NORWEST VENTURE CAPITAL MANAGEMENT, INC.—See Norwest Corporation; *U.S. Public*, pg. 1202
NORWICH FINANCIAL CORP.; *U.S. Public*, pg. 1203

NORWICH PARK MINE—See The Broken Hill Proprietary Company Limited; *Int'l*, pg. 223

THE NORWICH SAVINGS SOCIETY—See Norwich Financial Corp.; *U.S. Public*, pg. 1203

NORWICH UNION LIFE INSURANCE; *Int'l*, pg. 970

NORWOOD INDUSTRIES, INC.—See Seton Company; *U.S. Private*, pg. 987

NOSCO GVG MBH—See Commerzbank AG; *Int'l*, pg. 309

NOSCO GVG MBH & CO. OBJEKT ALZEY KG—See Commerzbank AG; *Int'l*, pg. 309

NOTARIA GVG MBH—See Commerzbank AG; *Int'l*, pg. 310

NOTEMAT LEAU HELLIX S.A.—See Deutsche Babcock AG; *Int'l*, pg. 399

NOTEWORTHY INDUSTRIES INC.; *U.S. Private*, pg. 808

NOTIFIER AUSTRALIA—See Pittway Corporation; *U.S. Public*, pg. 1307

NOTIFIER (BENELUX) S.A.—See Pittway Corporation; *U.S. Public*, pg. 1307

NOTIFIER CANADA—See Pittway Corporation; *U.S. Public*, pg. 1306

NOTIFIER DEUTSCHLAND GMBH—See Pittway Corporation; *U.S. Public*, pg. 1307

NOTIFIER ENGINEERED SYSTEMS COMPANY, INC. (NESCO)—See Pittway Corporation; *U.S. Public*, pg. 1306

NOTIFIER ESPANA S.A.—See Pittway Corporation; *U.S. Public*, pg. 1307

NOTIFIER FAR EAST—See Pittway Corporation; *U.S. Public*, pg. 1306

NOTIFIER ITALIA S.R.L.—See Pittway Corporation; *U.S. Public*, pg. 1307

NOTIFIER LTD.—See Pittway Corporation; *U.S. Public*, pg. 1307

NOTIFIER MIDDLE EAST—See Pittway Corporation; *U.S. Public*, pg. 1307

NOTIFIER NETWORK TECHNOLOGIES COMPANY—See Pittway Corporation; *U.S. Public*, pg. 1306

A. NOTTERMANN & CIE GMBH—See Rhone-Poulenc S.A.; *Int'l*, pg. 1112

NOTTINGHAM COATED STONE—See RMC Group p.l.c.; *Int'l*, pg. 1079

NOURYPHARMA NEDERLAND B.V.—See Akzo Nobel N.V.; *Int'l*, pg. 44

NOUVELER—See Hydro-Quebec; *Int'l*, pg. 640

NOUVELLE LEMANIA S.A.; *Int'l*, pg. 971

NOUVELLE SOCIETE VICTORIA—See Club Mediterranee SA; *Int'l*, pg. 298

NOUVELLE VAGUE—See BDDP Group; *Int'l*, pg. 116

NOUVELLES EDITIONS MARABOUT—See Lagardere Groupe; *Int'l*, pg. 796

NOUVELLES FRONTIERES; *Int'l*, pg. 971

NOUVELLES MESSAGERIES DE LA PRESSE PARISIENNE—See Lagardere Groupe; *Int'l*, pg. 793

NOVA CHEMICALS (CANADA) LTD./NOVA CHIMIE (CANADA) LTEE—See Nova Corporation; *Int'l*, pg. 971

NOVA CHEMICALS, INC.—See Nova Corporation; *Int'l*, pg. 971

NOVA CHEMICALS LTD.—See Nova Corporation; *Int'l*, pg. 971

NOVA CIMANGOLA S.A.R.L.—See Scancem AB; *Int'l*, pg. 1201

NOVA CORPORATION; *Int'l*, pg. 971

NOVA ELECTRIC MFG. CO.—See Illinois Tool Works Inc.; *U.S. Public*, pg. 866

NOVA GAS INTERNATIONAL LTD.—See Nova Corporation; *Int'l*, pg. 971

NOVA GAS TRANSMISSION LTD.—See Nova Corporation; *Int'l*, pg. 971

NOVA PLAST S.A. DE C.V.—See Sun Coast Industries, Inc; *U.S. Public*, pg. 1530

NOVA PROMOTION GROUP INC.—See Dentsu Inc.; *Int'l*, pg. 393

NOVA SCOTIA POWER INC.; *Int'l*, pg. 971

NOVA TRADING—See Thyssen AG; *Int'l*, pg. 1389

NOVACARE EMPLOYEE SERVICES, INC.—See NovaCare Inc.; *U.S. Public*, pg. 1203

NOVACARE INC.; *U.S. Public*, pg. 1203

NOVACOTE INTERNATIONAL—See Zeneca Group Plc; *Int'l*, pg. 1525

NOVALIM-NESTLE—See Nestle S.A.; *Int'l*, pg. 922

NOVAMET SPECIALTY PRODUCTS—See Inco Limited; *Int'l*, pg. 672

NOVAMETRIX MEDICAL SYSTEMS INC.; *U.S. Public*, pg. 1203

NOVAQUIM S.A. DE C.V.—See Crompton & Knowles Corporation; *U.S. Public*, pg. 460

NOVAR CONTROLS CORP.—See Novar Electronics; *U.S. Private*, pg. 808

NOVAR ELECTRONICS; *U.S. Private*, pg. 808

NOVARA VITA—See Eureko B.V.; *Int'l*, pg. 464

NOVARTIS—See Novartis AG; *Int'l*, pg. 972

NOVARTIS AG; *Int'l*, pg. 971

NOVARTIS AG, FI 3.4—See Novartis AG; *Int'l*, pg. 972

NOVARTIS NUTRITION CORPORATION—See Novartis AG; *Int'l*, pg. 974

NOVARTIS-PHARMA GMBH—See Novartis AG; *Int'l*, pg. 984

NOVARTIS PHARMACEUTICALS—See Novartis AG; *Int'l*, pg. 973

NOVARTIS SEEDS, INC.—See Novartis AG; *Int'l*, pg. 974

OY NOVATOOL AB—See AB Industrivarden; *Int'l*, pg. 678

NOVAVAX INC.—See IGI, Inc.; *U.S. Public*, pg. 855

NOVEL BIOMEDICAL—See Colorado MEDtech, Inc.; *U.S. Public*, pg. 401

NOVELAIR-SIFRAG AG—See Sulzer Ltd.; *Int'l*, pg. 1306

NOVELL ARGENTINA—See Novell, Inc.; *U.S. Public*, pg. 1204

NOVELL AUSTRALIA—See Novell, Inc.; *U.S. Public*, pg. 1204

NOVELL AUSTRIA—See Novell, Inc.; *U.S. Public*, pg. 1204

NOVELL BELGIUM—See Novell, Inc.; *U.S. Public*, pg. 1204

NOVELL BRAZIL—See Novell, Inc.; *U.S. Public*, pg. 1204

NOVELL CANADA—See Novell, Inc.; *U.S. Public*, pg. 1204

NOVELL CHILE—See Novell, Inc.; *U.S. Public*, pg. 1204

NOVELL CHINA—See Novell, Inc.; *U.S. Public*, pg. 1204

NOVELL COLOMBIA—See Novell, Inc.; *U.S. Public*, pg. 1204

NOVELL CZECH REPUBLIC—See Novell, Inc.; *U.S. Public*, pg. 1204

NOVELL DANMARK—See Novell, Inc.; *U.S. Public*, pg. 1204

NOVELL FINLAND—See Novell, Inc.; *U.S. Public*, pg. 1204

NOVELL FRANCE—See Novell, Inc.; *U.S. Public*, pg. 1204

NOVELL GERMANY—See Novell, Inc.; *U.S. Public*, pg. 1204

NOVELL HONG KONG—See Novell, Inc.; *U.S. Public*, pg. 1204

NOVELL HUNGARY—See Novell, Inc.; *U.S. Public*, pg. 1204

NOVELL, INC.; *U.S. Public*, pg. 1203

NOVELL INDIA—See Novell, Inc.; *U.S. Public*, pg. 1204

NOVELL ITALY—See Novell, Inc.; *U.S. Public*, pg. 1204

NOVELL JAPAN LTD.—See Novell, Inc.; *U.S. Public*, pg. 1204

NOVELL KOREA—See Novell, Inc.; *U.S. Public*, pg. 1204

NOVELL MALAYSIA—See Novell, Inc.; *U.S. Public*, pg. 1204

NOVELL MEXICO—See Novell, Inc.; *U.S. Public*, pg. 1204

NOVELL MIDDLE EAST—See Novell, Inc.; *U.S. Public*, pg. 1204

NOVELL NETHERLANDS—See Novell, Inc.; *U.S. Public*, pg. 1204

NOVELL NORWAY—See Novell, Inc.; *U.S. Public*, pg. 1204

NOVELL POLAND—See Novell, Inc.; *U.S. Public*, pg. 1204

NOVELL PORTUGAL—See Novell, Inc.; *U.S. Public*, pg. 1204

NOVELL RUSSIA—See Novell, Inc.; *U.S. Public*, pg. 1204

NOVELL SINGAPORE—See Novell, Inc.; *U.S. Public*, pg. 1204

NOVELL SOUTH AFRICA—See Novell, Inc.; *U.S. Public*, pg. 1204

NOVELL SPAIN—See Novell, Inc.; *U.S. Public*, pg. 1204

NOVELL SWEDEN—See Novell, Inc.; *U.S. Public*, pg. 1204

NOVELL SWITZERLAND—See Novell, Inc.; *U.S. Public*, pg. 1204

NOVELL TAIWAN—See Novell, Inc.; *U.S. Public*, pg. 1204

NOVELL UNITED KINGDOM—See Novell, Inc.; *U.S. Public*, pg. 1204

NOVELL VENEZUELA—See Novell, Inc.; *U.S. Public*, pg. 1204

NOVELLUS SINGAPORE PTE LTD.—See Novellus Systems, Inc.; *U.S. Public*, pg. 1204

NOVELLUS SYSTEMS, B.V.—See Novellus Systems, Inc.; *U.S. Public*, pg. 1204

NOVELLUS SYSTEMS, INC.; *U.S. Public*, pg. 1204

NOVELLUS SYSTEMS KOREA—See Novellus Systems, Inc.; *U.S. Public*, pg. 1204

NOVELLUS SYSTEMS, LTD.—See Novellus Systems, Inc.; *U.S. Public*, pg. 1204

NOVELLUS SYSTEMS SHANGHAI—See Novellus Systems, Inc.; *U.S. Public*, pg. 1205

NOVELLUS SYSTEMS TAIWAN—See Novellus Systems, Inc.; *U.S. Public*, pg. 1205

NOVERCO—See Gaz de France; *Int'l*, pg. 541

NOVERGAZ—See Gaz de France; *Int'l*, pg. 541

NOVEX TOOL DIV.—See Federal Screw Works; *U.S. Public*, pg. 616

NOVIA LIVSMEDELSINDUSTRIER AB—See Unilever Plc; *Int'l*, pg. 1438

NOVILLE; *U.S. Private*, pg. 808

NOVILON LTD.—See Forbo Holding SA; *Int'l*, pg. 498

NOVO NORDISK—See Novo Nordisk A/S; *Int'l*, pg. 987

NOVO NORDISK A/S; *Int'l*, pg. 987

NOVO NORDISK A/S—See Novo Nordisk A/S; *Int'l*, pg. 987

NOVO NORDISK A/S (TIANJIN) BIOTECHNOLOGY CO. LTD.—See Novo Nordisk A/S; *Int'l*, pg. 988

NOVO NORDISK BIOCHEM, INC.—See Novo Nordisk A/S; *Int'l*, pg. 987

NOVO NORDISK BIOCHEMICALS KK—See Novo Nordisk A/S; *Int'l*, pg. 989

NOVO NORDISK BIOINDUSTRIAL DO BRASIL LTDA.—See Novo Nordisk A/S; *Int'l*, pg. 988

NOVO NORDISK BIOINDUSTRIAL, KOREA—See Novo Nordisk A/S; *Int'l*, pg. 989

NOVO NORDISK BIOINDUSTRIAL PTY LTD.—See Novo Nordisk A/S; *Int'l*, pg. 989

NOVO NORDISK BIOINDUSTRIALE SRL—See Novo Nordisk A/S; *Int'l*, pg. 989

NOVO NORDISK BIOINDUSTRIALS, INC.—See Novo Nordisk A/S; *Int'l*, pg. 989

NOVO NORDISK BIOINDUSTRIE SA, EUROPE—See Novo Nordisk A/S; *Int'l*, pg. 989

NOVO NORDISK BIOINDUSTRIES UK LTD.—See Novo Nordisk A/S; *Int'l*, pg. 989

NOVO NORDISK BIOTECH, INC.—See Novo Nordisk A/S; *Int'l*, pg. 987

NOVO NORDISK BIOTECHNOLOGIE GMBH—See Novo Nordisk A/S; *Int'l*, pg. 988

NOVO NORDISK CANADA, INC.—See Novo Nordisk A/S; *Int'l*, pg. 988

NOVO NORDISK (CHINA) BIOTECHNOLOGY CO. LTD.—See Novo Nordisk A/S; *Int'l*, pg. 988

NOVO NORDISK COMERCIO DE PRODUTOS FARMACEUTICOS, LDA—See Novo Nordisk A/S; *Int'l*, pg. 988

NOVO NORDISK DE MEXICO S.A. DE C.V.—See Novo Nordisk A/S; *Int'l*, pg. 989

NOVO NORDISK ENGINEERING A/S—See Novo Nordisk A/S; *Int'l*, pg. 987

NOVO NORDISK ENTOTECH, INC.—See Novo Nordisk A/S; *Int'l*, pg. 987

NOVO NORDISK FARMA B.V.—See Novo Nordisk A/S; *Int'l*, pg. 988

NOVO NORDISK FARMACEUTICA DO BRASIL LTDA.—See Novo Nordisk A/S; *Int'l*, pg. 988

NOVO NORDISK FARMACEUTICI SRL—See Novo Nordisk A/S; *Int'l*, pg. 988

NOVO NORDISK FARMAKA DANMARK A/S—See Novo Nordisk A/S; *Int'l*, pg. 987

NOVO NORDISK FERMENT LTD.—See Novo Nordisk A/S; *Int'l*, pg. 989

NOVO NORDISK HELLAS LTD.—See Novo Nordisk A/S; *Int'l*, pg. 988

NOVO NORDISK (INDIA) PVT LTD—See Novo Nordisk A/S; *Int'l*, pg. 988

NOVO NORDISK MAROC—See Novo Nordisk A/S; *Int'l*, pg. 988

NOVO NORDISK OF NORTH AMERICA, INC.—See Novo Nordisk A/S; *Int'l*, pg. 987

NOVO NORDISK PHARMA GESELLSCHAFT MBH—See Novo Nordisk A/S; *Int'l*, pg. 988

NOVO NORDISK PHARMA GMBH—See Novo Nordisk A/S; *Int'l*, pg. 988

NOVO NORDISK PHARMA KOREA LIMITED—See Novo Nordisk A/S; *Int'l*, pg. 988

S.A. NOVO NORDISK PHARMA NV—See Novo Nordisk A/S; *Int'l*, pg. 988

NOVO NORDISK PHARMA (TAIWAN) LTD.—See Novo Nordisk A/S; *Int'l*, pg. 988

NOVO NORDISK PHARMACEUTICALS, INC.—See Novo Nordisk A/S; *Int'l*, pg. 987

NOVO NORDISK PHARMACEUTICALS INDUSTRIES, INC.—See Novo Nordisk A/S; *Int'l*, pg. 987

NOVO NORDISK PHARMACEUTICALS LTD.—See Novo Nordisk A/S; *Int'l*, pg. 988

NOVO NORDISK PHARMACEUTICALS PTY. LTD.—See Novo Nordisk A/S; *Int'l*, pg. 988

NOVO NORDISK PHARMACEUTIQUE S.A.—See Novo Nordisk A/S; *Int'l*, pg. 988

NOVO NORDISK (PTY) LTD.—See Novo Nordisk A/S; *Int'l*, pg. 988

NOVO NORDISK SHENYANG BIOCHEMICAL PROCESSIN CO. LTD.—See Novo Nordisk A/S; *Int'l*, pg. 989

NOVO PRODUCTS—See MascoTech, Inc.; *U.S. Public*, pg. 1055

NOVOFERM ESPANA S.A.—See Fried. Krupp AG; *Int'l*, pg. 509

NOVOFERM FRANCE S.A.—See Fried. Krupp AG; *Int'l*, pg. 509

NOVOFERM GMBH—See Fried. Krupp AG; *Int'l*, pg. 509

NOVOFERM NEDERLAND B.V.—See Fried. Krupp AG; *Int'l*, pg. 509

NOVOFERM POLSKA GMBH—See Fried. Krupp AG; *Int'l*, pg. 509

NOVOTEL GOTEBORG AB—See Accor S.A.; *Int'l*, pg. 21

NOVOTEL HELLENIC—See Accor S.A.; *Int'l*, pg. 21

NOVOTEL INTERNATIONAL—See Accor S.A.; *Int'l*, pg. 21

NOVOTEL NEDERLAND BV—See Accor S.A.; *Int'l*, pg. 21

NOVOTEL UK LTD.—See Accor S.A.; *Int'l*, pg. 21

NOVOTRUCK—See Caterpillar Inc.; *U.S. Public*, pg. 317

AB NOVUM—See AB Industrivarden; *Int'l*, pg. 678

NOVUS FINANCIAL CORPORATION—See Morgan Stanley Dean Witter & Co.; *U.S. Public*, pg. 1132

NOVUS SERVICES, INC.—See Morgan Stanley Dean Witter & Co.; *U.S. Public*, pg. 1132

NOW HEAR THIS (NHT)—See Recoton Corporation; *U.S. Public*, pg. 1369

P.T. NOWL KNITTING INDONESIA—See Takashimaya Company, Limited; *Int'l*, pg. 1350

NOWSCO INC.—See Nowsco Well Service Ltd.; *Int'l*, pg. 990

NOWSCO PIPELINE SERVICES INC.—See Nowsco Well Service Ltd.; *Int'l*, pg. 990

NOWSCO WELL SERVICE GMBH—See Nowsco Well Service Ltd.; *Int'l*, pg. 990

NOWSCO WELL SERVICE INC.—See Nowsco Well Service Ltd.; *Int'l*, pg. 990

NOWSCO WELL SERVICE LTD.-ARGENTINA—See Nowsco Well Service Ltd.; *Int'l*, pg. 990

NOWSCO WELL SERVICE LTD.-ASIA & PACIFIC—See Nowsco Well Service Ltd.; *Int'l*, pg. 990

NOWSCO WELL SERVICE LTD.-EUROPE, AFRICA, MIDDLE EAST—See Nowsco Well Service Ltd.; *Int'l*, pg. 990

NOWSCO WELL SERVICE LTD.-UNITED STATES—See Nowsco Well Service Ltd.; *Int'l*, pg. 990

NOWSCO WELL SERVICE LTD.—See BJ Services Company; *U.S. Public*, pg. 161

NOWSCO WELL SERVICE LTD.; *Int'l*, pg. 989

NOXELL CORPORATION—See The Procter & Gamble Company; *U.S. Public*, pg. 1330

NOZAKI AMERICA, INC.—See Nozaki & Company Ltd.; *Int'l*, pg. 990

NOZAKI AMERICA, INC., SEATTLE BRANCH—See Nozaki & Company Ltd.; *Int'l*, pg. 990

NOZAKI & COMPANY LTD.; *Int'l*, pg. 990

NOZAL S.A.—See Groupe Usinor; *Int'l*, pg. 570

NU HORIZONS ELECTRONICS CORP.; *U.S. Public*, pg. 1205

NU HORIZONS INTERNATIONAL CORP.—See Nu Horizons Electronics Corp.; *U.S. Public*, pg. 1205

NU HORIZONS/MERIT ELECTRONICS CORP.—See Nu Horizons/Electronics Corp.; *U.S. Public*, pg. 1205

NU-KOTE INTERNATIONAL; *U.S. Public*, pg. 1205

NU SKIN INTERNATIONAL; *U.S. Private*, pg. 808

NU VISIONS MANUFACTURING CORP.—See Nu Horizons Electronics Corp.; *U.S. Public*, pg. 1205

NU-WAY ENERGY (N.Z.) LTD.—See Eclipse Inc.; *U.S. Private*, pg. 361

NUANCE COMMUNICATIONS—See SRI International; *U.S. Private*, pg. 958

NUARC COMPANY, INC.; *U.S. Private*, pg. 808

NUBURN CAPITAL; *Int'l*, pg. 990

NUCLEAR AND ADVANCED TECHNOLOGY DIVISION—See CBS Corporation; *U.S. Public*, pg. 273

NUCLEAR ENERGY SERVICES, INC.—See American Financial Group; *U.S. Public*, pg. 75

NUCLEAR MAGNETIC RESONANCE INSTRUMENTS—See Varian Associates, Inc.; *U.S. Public*, pg. 1710

NUCLEAR RESEARCH CENTER—See JGC Corporation; *Int'l*, pg. 697
NUCLEAR UPGRADE—See American Foundry Group, Inc.; *U.S. Private*, pg. 55
NUCLEO PUBLICIDAD—See Leo Burnett Company, Inc.; *U.S. Private*, pg. 186
NUCLEST—See Petrobras - Petroleo Brasileiro S.A.; *Int'l*, pg. 1042
NUCLETRON BV—See Delft Instruments N.V.; *Int'l*, pg. 389
NUCLETRON CORPORATION—See Delft Instruments N.V.; *Int'l*, pg. 389
NUCLETRON FAR EAST (HK) LTD.—See Delft Instruments N.V.; *Int'l*, pg. 389
NUCLETRON PTY LIMITED—See Delft Instruments N.V.; *Int'l*, pg. 389
NUCLETRON S.A.—See Delft Instruments N.V.; *Int'l*, pg. 389
NUCLETRON SARL—See Delft Instruments N.V.; *Int'l*, pg. 389
NUCLETRON UK LTD.—See Delft Instruments N.V.; *Int'l*, pg. 389
NUCLETUDES—See Aerospatiale; *Int'l*, pg. 29
NUCLITAL SRL—See Delft Instruments N.V.; *Int'l*, pg. 389
NUCOR BEARING PRODUCTS, INC.—See Nucor Corporation; *U.S. Public*, pg. 1206
NUCOR BUILDING SYSTEMS—See Nucor Corporation; *U.S. Public*, pg. 1205
NUCOR COLD FINISH-NEBRASKA—See Nucor Corporation; *U.S. Public*, pg. 1205
NUCOR COLD FINISH-SOUTH CAROLINA—See Nucor Corporation; *U.S. Public*, pg. 1205
NUCOR COLD FINISH-UTAH—See Nucor Corporation; *U.S. Public*, pg. 1205
NUCOR CORPORATION; *U.S. Public*, pg. 1205
NUCOR FASTENERS—See Nucor Corporation; *U.S. Public*, pg. 1205
NUCOR GRINDING BALLS—See Nucor Corporation; *U.S. Public*, pg. 1205
NUCOR IRON CARBIDE—See Nucor Corporation; *U.S. Public*, pg. 1206
NUCOR STEEL-ARKANSAS—See Nucor Corporation; *U.S. Public*, pg. 1205
NUCOR WIRE—See Nucor Corporation; *U.S. Public*, pg. 1205
NUCOR-YAMATO STEEL COMPANY—See Nucor Corporation; *U.S. Public*, pg. 1206
NUEAR ELECTRONICS—See Starkey Laboratories, Inc.; *U.S. Private*, pg. 1035
NUEVA VISION—See Eastman Kodak Company; *U.S. Public*, pg. 553
NUEVO CAMINO CONSTRUCTORS CO.—See Zurn Industries, Inc.; *U.S. Public*, pg. 1795
NUEVO ENERGY COMPANY; *U.S. Public*, pg. 1206
NUEVO FEDERAL S.A.; *Int'l*, pg. 990
NUGGET MOTORS—See Don Massey Cadillac Inc.; *U.S. Private*, pg. 713
THE NUGGET—See Hollinger Inc.; *Int'l*, pg. 631
NUHSE UND WERNER GUTTGES GMBH—See Mannesmann A.G.; *Int'l*, pg. 838
NUKEM GMBH—See RWE AG; *Int'l*, pg. 1081
NUKEM, INC.—See RWE AG; *Int'l*, pg. 1081
NULAID FOODS; *U.S. Private*, pg. 809
NUMAC ENERGY INC.; *Int'l*, pg. 990
NUMATEC INC.—See COGEMA - Compagnie Generale des Matieres Nucleaires; *Int'l*, pg. 305
NUMBER NINE VISUAL TECHNOLOGY; *U.S. Public*, pg. 1206
NUMEDAL BRUK—See Norske Skogindustrier A.S; *Int'l*, pg. 965
NUMERIA GVG MBH—See Commerzbank AG; *Int'l*, pg. 310
NUMERIA GVG MBH & CO. OBJEKT HUCKELHOVEN KG—See Commerzbank AG; *Int'l*, pg. 309
NUMERIA GVG MBH & CO. OBJEKT WALDKRAIBURG KG—See Commerzbank AG; *Int'l*, pg. 309
NUMETRIX GMBH—See Numetrix Ltd.; *Int'l*, pg. 990
NUMETRIX INC.—See Numetrix Ltd.; *Int'l*, pg. 990
NUMETRIX LTD.; *Int'l*, pg. 990
NUMETRIX S.A.—See Numetrix Ltd.; *Int'l*, pg. 990
NUNC A/S—See BTR plc; *Int'l*, pg. 130
NUNN-BUSH SHOE CO.—See Weyco Group, Inc.; *U.S. Public*, pg. 1763
NUOVA SIRMA—See Saint-Gobain; *Int'l*, pg. 1175
NUOVI TUBI BRINDISI SPA—See TI Group plc; *Int'l*, pg. 1341
NUOVO PIGNONE S.P.A.; *Int'l*, pg. 990
NUPAR—See Baldor Electric Company; *U.S. Public*, pg. 169
NUR HIER GMBH—See Borden, Inc.; *U.S. Private*, pg. 160
NUR TOURISTIC GMBH—See Karstadt Aktiengesellschaft; *Int'l*, pg. 724
NUREL S.A.—See Imperial Chemical Industries PLC; *Int'l*, pg. 665
NURI ENTERPRISE—See Crown Confectionery Co., Ltd.; *Int'l*, pg. 348
NURNBERGER HERCULES-WERKE GMBH—See Mannesmann A.G.; *Int'l*, pg. 835
NURNBERGER HYPOTHEKENBANK AG—See Bayerische Vereinsbank Group; *Int'l*, pg. 180
NURRE CAXTON—See Esselte AB; *Int'l*, pg. 460
NURSERYLAND GARDEN CENTERS—See General Host Corporation; *U.S. Public*, pg. 715
NURSES INC.—See Sophus Berendsen A/S; *Int'l*, pg. 1285
NUS-SOUTH AFRICA—See National Utility Service, Inc.; *U.S. Private*, pg. 787
NUSON INC.—See Koninklijke Hoogovens N.V.; *Int'l*, pg. 755
NUT TREE PECAN COMPANY, INC.—See Young Pecan Company (A Partnership); *U.S. Private*, pg. 1201
NUTMEG INSURANCE LIMITED—See Olin Corporation; *U.S. Public*, pg. 1219
NUTMEG MILLS INC.—See VF Corporation; *U.S. Public*, pg. 1702

NUTMEG PAVILION HEALTHCARE—See Vencor, Inc.; *U.S. Public*, pg. 1714
NUTONE CANADA INC.—See Williams Holdings Plc; *Int'l*, pg. 1499
NUTONE, INC.—See Williams Holdings Plc; *Int'l*, pg. 1499
NUTRACO S.A.—See Nutricia BV; *Int'l*, pg. 992
NUTRAMAX PRODUCTS, INC.; *U.S. Public*, pg. 1206
NUTRASWEET AG—See Ajinomoto Company Inc.; *Int'l*, pg. 41
THE NUTRASWEET COMPANY—See Monsanto Company; *U.S. Public*, pg. 1125
NUTRASWEET EUROPE—See Monsanto Company; *U.S. Public*, pg. 1126
NUTRASWEET INTERNATIONAL, LTD.—See Monsanto Company; *U.S. Public*, pg. 1125
THE NUTRASWEET KELCO COMPANY—See Monsanto Company; *U.S. Public*, pg. 1125
NUTREX AG—See Coop Switzerland; *Int'l*, pg. 330
NUTRI-QUEST, INC.—See Kyowa Hakko Kogyo Company, Ltd.; *Int'l*, pg. 778
NUTRI/SYSTEM INC.—See Pettibone Corporation; *U.S. Private*, pg. 859
NUTRI-TONIC INC.—See Del Laboratories, Inc.; *U.S. Public*, pg. 494
N.V. NUTRICIA AMERICAS—See Nutricia BV; *Int'l*, pg. 992
NUTRICIA A/S—See Nutricia BV; *Int'l*, pg. 992
NUTRICIA (ASIA-PACIFIC) LTD.—See Nutricia BV; *Int'l*, pg. 992
N.V. NUTRICIA BELGIE—See Nutricia BV; *Int'l*, pg. 992
NUTRICIA BV; *Int'l*, pg. 991
NUTRICIA CUJIK B.V.—See Nutricia BV; *Int'l*, pg. 991
NUTRICIA DANMARK A/S—See Nutricia BV; *Int'l*, pg. 992
NUTRICIA DEUTSCHLAND GMBH—See Nutricia BV; *Int'l*, pg. 992
NUTRICIA DIATETIK GMBH—See Nutricia BV; *Int'l*, pg. 992
NUTRICIA DIETARY PRODUCTS LTD.—See Nutricia BV; *Int'l*, pg. 992
NUTRICIA EXPORT B.V.—See Nutricia BV; *Int'l*, pg. 991
NUTRICIA FENNICA OY—See Nutricia BV; *Int'l*, pg. 992
NUTRICIA FINANCIAL SERVICES LTD.—See Nutricia BV; *Int'l*, pg. 992
NUTRICIA FRANCE S.A.—See Nutricia BV; *Int'l*, pg. 992
NUTRICIA GRUNDSTUCKSVERWALTUNG GMBH—See Nutricia BV; *Int'l*, pg. 992
NUTRICIA HELLAS S.A.—See Nutricia BV; *Int'l*, pg. 992
NUTRICIA HOLDINGS LTD.—See Nutricia BV; *Int'l*, pg. 992
NUTRICIA (HONG KONG) LTD.-TAIWAN BRANCH—See Nutricia BV; *Int'l*, pg. 992
NUTRICIA HUNGARY KFT—See Nutricia BV; *Int'l*, pg. 992
P.T. NUTRICIA INDONESIA SEJAHARTA—See Nutricia BV; *Int'l*, pg. 992
NUTRICIA INTERNATIONAL N.V.—See Nutricia BV; *Int'l*, pg. 991
NUTRICIA IRELAND LTD.—See Nutricia BV; *Int'l*, pg. 992
NUTRICIA KFT.—See Nutricia BV; *Int'l*, pg. 992
NUTRICIA LYEMPF B.V.—See Nutricia BV; *Int'l*, pg. 991
NUTRICIA MEDICAL DEVICES B.V.—See Nutricia BV; *Int'l*, pg. 991
NUTRICIA MLECNA A.S.—See Nutricia BV; *Int'l*, pg. 992
NUTRICIA NAHRUNGSMITTEL GMBH—See Nutricia BV; *Int'l*, pg. 992
NUTRICIA NATIONAAL B.V.—See Nutricia BV; *Int'l*, pg. 991
NUTRICIA NEDERLAND B.V.—See Nutricia BV; *Int'l*, pg. 991
NUTRICIA NEDERLANDER BEHEERMAATSCHAPPIJ B.V.—See Nutricia BV; *Int'l*, pg. 991
N.V. NUTRICIA—See Nutricia BV; *Int'l*, pg. 991
NUTRICIA NORDICA AB—See Nutricia BV; *Int'l*, pg. 991
NUTRICIA POLAND B.V.—See Nutricia BV; *Int'l*, pg. 991
NUTRICIA PORTUGAL L.D.A.—See Nutricia BV; *Int'l*, pg. 992
NUTRICIA S.A.—See Nutricia BV; *Int'l*, pg. 992
NUTRICIA S.P.A.—See Nutricia BV; *Int'l*, pg. 992
NUTRILITE PRODUCTS, INC.—See Amway Corporation; *U.S. Private*, pg. 69
NUTRINOVA NUTRITION SPECIALTIES & FOOD INGREDIENTS GMBH—See Hoechst Aktiengesellschaft; *Int'l*, pg. 626
NUTRINSA, S.A.—See Borden, Inc.; *U.S. Private*, pg. 160
NUTRITEC K.K.—See Roche Holding Ltd.; *Int'l*, pg. 1121
NUTRITION ET SANTE S.A.—See Novartis AG; *Int'l*, pg. 983
NUTRITIONAL PRODUCTS (THAILAND) LTD.—See Nestle S.A.; *Int'l*, pg. 922
NUTRIUS DAIRY FEED SUPPLEMENTS DIV.—See Bioproducts, Inc.; *U.S. Private*, pg. 145
EDMUND NUTTALL LTD.—See Hollandsche Beton Groep NV; *Int'l*, pg. 630
NUTTALL GEAR CORPORATION; *U.S. Private*, pg. 809
NUTTER ENGINEERING—See Harsco Corporation; *U.S. Public*, pg. 793
THE JOHN NUVEEN COMPANY—See The St. Paul Companies, Inc.; *U.S. Public*, pg. 1429
NUVOTRON—See Trans Leasing International Inc.; *U.S. Public*, pg. 1628
NU-WAY LTD.—See Wolseley Plc.; *Int'l*, pg. 1512
NUYENS LIQUOR IMPORTING, INC.—See White Rock Distilleries Inc.; *U.S. Private*, pg. 1173
NVIEW CORPORATION; *U.S. Public*, pg. 1206
NWE BRUNSWICK SCIENTIFIC CO., INC.—See New Brunswick Scientific Co., Inc.; *U.S. Public*, pg. 1170
NXTREND TECHNOLOGY, INC.; *U.S. Private*, pg. 809
NY-GLASS PLASTICS, INC.—See Summa Industries; *U.S. Public*, pg. 1527
NYACOL PRODUCTS, INC.—See PQ Corporation; *U.S. Private*, pg. 827
NYBORG ENGINEERING LTD.—See Electrolux, AB; *Int'l*, pg. 444
NYBORG PLAST INTERNATIONAL A/S—See FLS Industries A/S; *Int'l*, pg. 476
NYBORG VAS KERIMASKINER A/S—See Electrolux, AB; *Int'l*, pg. 441

NYBRO SMIDE—See Trelleborg AB; *Int'l*, pg. 1421
NYCOMED AMERSHAM—See Nycomed Amersham plc; *Int'l*, pg. 993
NYCOMED AMERSHAM PLC; *Int'l*, pg. 992
NYCOMED IMAGING AS—See Nycomed Amersham plc; *Int'l*, pg. 993
NYCOMED PHARMA AS—See Nycomed Amersham plc; *Int'l*, pg. 993
NYFFELER CORTI AG—See Koninklijke Hoogovens N.V.; *Int'l*, pg. 755
NYKREDIT; *Int'l*, pg. 993
NYKREDIT BANK A/S—See Nykredit; *Int'l*, pg. 993
NYLON CORPORATION OF AMERICA, INC.—See Fiat Auto SpA; *Int'l*, pg. 483
NYLON DE MEXICO, S.A.—See Du Pont (E.I. Du Pont De Nemours & Co.); *U.S. Public*, pg. 533
NYLONCRAFT—See Excel Industries, Inc.; *U.S. Public*, pg. 599
NYLTECH NORTH AMERICA INC.—See Fiat Auto SpA; *Int'l*, pg. 482
AB NYNAS PETROLEUM—See Neste Oy; *Int'l*, pg. 915
NYNAS PETROLEUM N.V.—See Neste Oy; *Int'l*, pg. 915
NYNEX NETWORK SYSTEMS COMPANY—See Bell Atlantic Corporation; *U.S. Public*, pg. 204
NYPRO SINGAPORE PTE. LTD.—See Mannesmann A.G.; *Int'l*, pg. 836
NYSTROM DIVISION OF HERFF JONES—See Herff Jones Inc.; *U.S. Private*, pg. 523
NYTRON INDUCTORS—See Vishay Intertechnology, Inc.; *U.S. Public*, pg. 1722

O

O.TEL.O COMMUNICATIONS GMBH CO.—See RWE AG; *Int'l*, pg. 1082
O&K ANTRIEBSTECHNIK GMBH, HATTINGEN WORKS—See Fried. Krupp AG; *Int'l*, pg. 516
O&K MINING GMBH, DORTMUND WORKS—See Fried. Krupp AG; *Int'l*, pg. 516
O&K ORENSTEIN & KOPPEL AKTIENGESELLSCHAFT—See Fried. Krupp AG; *Int'l*, pg. 516
O&K ROLLTREPPEN GMBH, HATTINGEN WORKS—See Fried. Krupp AG; *Int'l*, pg. 516
O&K ROLLTREPPEN GMBH, HATTINGEN WORKS—See Kone Corporation; *Int'l*, pg. 748
O & R DEVELOPMENT, INC.—See Orange and Rockland Utilities, Inc.; *U.S. Public*, pg. 1229
O&S CALIFORNIA, INC.—See Sumitomo Electric Industries, Ltd.; *Int'l*, pg. 1313
O&Y PROPERTIES CORPORATION; *Int'l*, pg. 993
O/B LEASING COMPANY—See Budco Group Inc.; *U.S. Private*, pg. 178
O-RING DIV.—See Parker Hannifin Corporation; *U.S. Public*, pg. 1262
O-SEAL DIV.—See Parker Hannifin Corporation; *U.S. Public*, pg. 1262
O-Z/GEDNEY CO.—See General Signal Corporation; *U.S. Public*, pg. 727
OAC INC.—See Nissho Iwai Corporation; *Int'l*, pg. 947
OAF & STEYR NUTZFAHRZEUGE OHG—See MAN Aktiengesellschaft; *Int'l*, pg. 825
OAG—See Reed Elsevier plc; *Int'l*, pg. 1097
OAG GRUPPE A.G.—See Wolseley Plc.; *Int'l*, pg. 1511
OAO ISTRA-NUTRICIA—See Nutricia BV; *Int'l*, pg. 992
OAO KOLA MINING—See Outokumpu Oyj; *Int'l*, pg. 1016
OAO KOMSOMOLETS—See Metsa-Serla Corporation; *Int'l*, pg. 864
OAO TECHNOLOGY SOLUTIONS, INC.—See Safeguard Scientifics, Inc.; *U.S. Public*, pg. 1425
OB HELLER A.S.—See The Fuji Bank, Limited; *Int'l*, pg. 521
OBI BAU-UND HEIMWERKERMAERKTE GMBH & CO. KG; *Int'l*, pg. 993
OBSI STORMARKNADEN AB—See KF/Konsum Coop Group; *Int'l*, pg. 718
OC AMERICA CONSTRUCTION, INC.—See Obayashi Corporation; *Int'l*, pg. 943
OC IMMOBILIENVERWALTUNGS GMBH—See Bayerische Vereinsbank Group; *Int'l*, pg. 178
OC ORGA CONSULT GMBH & CO. BAUBETREUUNGS KG—See Bayerische Vereinsbank Group; *Int'l*, pg. 179
OC REAL ESTATE MANAGEMENT, INC.—See Obayashi Corporation; *Int'l*, pg. 995
O.C.A. S.A.—See Tractebel; *Int'l*, pg. 1415
O.C.B.C. CENTRE EAST PROJECT—See Nishimatsu Construction Co., Ltd.; *Int'l*, pg. 943
OCE—See Oce-van der Grinten N.V.; *Int'l*, pg. 994
OCE-ASIA LTD.—See Oce-van der Grinten N.V.; *Int'l*, pg. 994
OCE-AUSTRALIA FINANCE PTY. LTD.—See Oce-van der Grinten N.V.; *Int'l*, pg. 994
OCE-AUSTRALIA LIMITED—See Oce-van der Grinten N.V.; *Int'l*, pg. 994
OCE-BELGIUM N.V./S.A.—See Oce-van der Grinten N.V.; *Int'l*, pg. 994
OCE-BRASIL COMERCIO E INDUSTRIA LTDA.—See Oce-van der Grinten N.V.; *Int'l*, pg. 994
OCE-CREDIT CORPORATION—See Oce-van der Grinten N.V.; *Int'l*, pg. 994
OCE-CZECH-REPUBLIC S.R.O.—See Oce-van der Grinten N.V.; *Int'l*, pg. 994
OCE-DANMARK AS—See Oce-van der Grinten N.V.; *Int'l*, pg. 994
OCE-DEUTSCHLAND GMBH—See Oce-van der Grinten N.V.; *Int'l*, pg. 994
OCE-DEUTSCHLAND LEASING GMBH—See Oce-van der Grinten N.V.; *Int'l*, pg. 994
OCE DIRECT EXPORT—See Oce-van der Grinten N.V.; *Int'l*, pg. 994
OCE-ESPANA S.A.—See Oce-van der Grinten N.V.; *Int'l*, pg. 994
OCE (FAR EAST) PTE. LTD.—See Oce-van der Grinten N.V.; *Int'l*, pg. 994

OCE-FRANCE FINANCEMENT S.A.—See Oce-van der Grinten N.V.; *Int'l*, pg. 994
OCE-FRANCE S.A.—See Oce-van der Grinten N.V.; *Int'l*, pg. 994
OCE GRAPHICS FRANCE S.A.—See Oce-van der Grinten N.V.; *Int'l*, pg. 994
OCE GRAPHICS SVENSKA AB—See Oce-van der Grinten N.V.; *Int'l*, pg. 994
OCE GRAPHICS (U.K.) LIMITED—See Oce-van der Grinten N.V.; *Int'l*, pg. 994
OCE HOLDING USA—See Oce-van der Grinten N.V.; *Int'l*, pg. 994
OCE (HONG KONG CHINA) LTD.—See Oce-van der Grinten N.V.; *Int'l*, pg. 994
OCE-HUNGARIA KFT.—See Oce-van der Grinten N.V.; *Int'l*, pg. 994
OCE-INTERSERVICES N.V./S.A.—See Oce-van der Grinten N.V.; *Int'l*, pg. 994
OCE-IRELAND LTD.—See Oce-van der Grinten N.V.; *Int'l*, pg. 994
OCE-ITALIA S.P.A.—See Oce-van der Grinten N.V.; *Int'l*, pg. 994
OCE-LIMA MAYER S.A.—See Oce-van der Grinten N.V.; *Int'l*, pg. 994
OCE-NEDERLAND B.V.—See Oce-van der Grinten N.V.; *Int'l*, pg. 994
OCE NEDERLANDSE VERKOOPMAATSCHAPPIJ B.V.—See Oce-van der Grinten N.V.; *Int'l*, pg. 994
OCE-NORGE A/S—See Oce-van der Grinten N.V.; *Int'l*, pg. 994
OCE OFFICE EQUIPMENT (BEIJING) CO. LTD.—See Oce-van der Grinten N.V.; *Int'l*, pg. 994
OCE OSTERREICH GES.M.B.H.—See Oce-van der Grinten N.V.; *Int'l*, pg. 995
OCE-POLAND LIMITED, SP. Z O.O.—See Oce-van der Grinten N.V.; *Int'l*, pg. 995
OCE-RENTING S.A.—See Oce-van der Grinten N.V.; *Int'l*, pg. 995
OCE (SINGAPORE) PTE. LTD.—See Oce-van der Grinten N.V.; *Int'l*, pg. 995
OCE SVENSKA AB—See Oce-van der Grinten N.V.; *Int'l*, pg. 995
OCE SYSTEMS (MALAYSIA) SDN. BHD.—See Oce-van der Grinten N.V.; *Int'l*, pg. 995
OCE (TAIWAN) LTD.—See Oce-van der Grinten N.V.; *Int'l*, pg. 995
OCE (THAILAND) LTD.—See Oce-van der Grinten N.V.; *Int'l*, pg. 995
OCE (U.K.) LIMITED—See Oce-van der Grinten N.V.; *Int'l*, pg. 995
OCE (U.K.) FINANCE LIMITED—See Oce-van der Grinten N.V.; *Int'l*, pg. 995
OCE (U.K.) PRINTING SYSTEMS LIMITED—See Oce-van der Grinten N.V.; *Int'l*, pg. 995
OCE-U.S.A.—See Oce-van der Grinten N.V.; *Int'l*, pg. 994
OCE USA, INC.—See Oce-van der Grinten N.V.; *Int'l*, pg. 994
OCE-VAN DER GRINTEN N.V.; *Int'l*, pg. 993
OCG HOLDINGS, INC.—See Olin Corporation; *U.S. Public*, pg. 1219
OCG MICROELECTRONIC MATERIALS AG—See Novartis AG; *Int'l*, pg. 973
OCG MICROELECTRONIC MATERIALS AG—See Olin Corporation; *U.S. Public*, pg. 1220
OCG MICROELECTRONIC MATERIALS GMBH—See Olin Corporation; *U.S. Public*, pg. 1219
OCG MICROELECTRONIC MATERIALS LIMITED—See Olin Corporation; *U.S. Public*, pg. 1220
OCG MICROELECTRONIC MATERIALS N.V.—See Olin Corporation; *U.S. Public*, pg. 1220
OCG MICROELECTRONIC MATERIALS S.A.—See Olin Corporation; *U.S. Public*, pg. 1220
OCG MICROELECTRONIC MATERIALS S.R.L.—See Olin Corporation; *U.S. Public*, pg. 1220
OCLI OPTICAL COATING LABORATORY GMBH—See Optical Coating Laboratory, Inc.; *U.S. Public*, pg. 1227
OCLI OPTICAL COATINGS ESPANA S.A.—See Optical Coating Laboratory, Inc.; *U.S. Public*, pg. 1227
OCLI OPTICAL COATINGS LTD.—See Optical Coating Laboratory, Inc.; *U.S. Public*, pg. 1227
ODL INCORPORATED; *U.S. Private*, pg. 809
ODS/HOOGOVENS HANDEL BV—See Koninklijke Hoogovens N.V.; *Int'l*, pg. 754
ODS NETWORKS, INC.; *U.S. Public*, pg. 1206
O/E AUTOMATION, INC.; *U.S. Private*, pg. 809
O.E., INC.—See Canon Inc.; *Int'l*, pg. 262
O.E. RUNGER GEBAUDEREINIGUNG GMBH—See Vorwerk & Co.; *Int'l*, pg. 1480
O.E. RUNGER KG—See Vorwerk & Co.; *Int'l*, pg. 1480
OEA AEROSPACE, INC.—See OEA, Inc.; *U.S. Public*, pg. 1207
OEA AUTOMOTIVE SAFETY PRODUCTS DIVISION—See OEA, Inc.; *U.S. Public*, pg. 1207
OEA, INC.; *U.S. Public*, pg. 1206
OEC MEDICAL SYSTEMS, INC.; *U.S. Public*, pg. 1207
OEL, LTD.—See Elcor Corporation; *U.S. Public*, pg. 568
OEM GROUP—See Harman International Industries, Inc.; *U.S. Public*, pg. 787
O/E/N INDIA LTD.—See Oak Industries Inc.; *U.S. Public*, pg. 1209
OES CAPITAL, INC.—See FirstEnergy Corp.; *U.S. Public*, pg. 645
OES FUEL, INCORPORATED—See FirstEnergy Corp.; *U.S. Public*, pg. 645
OFB BAUVERMITTLUNGS UND GEWERBEBAU GESELLSCHAFT MBH—See Landesbank Hessen-Thuringen Girozentrale; *Int'l*, pg. 799
OFB GRUNDSTUECKSVERWALTUNGS GMBH—See Landesbank Hessen-Thuringen Girozentrale; *Int'l*, pg. 799
OFC/DMB&B BUCHAREST—See DMB&B Communications; *U.S. Private*, pg. 305
CFI TECHNOLOGY, INC.—See Iwerks Entertainment; *U.S. Public*, pg. 915

OFMI-GARAMONT SA—See N.V. Koninklijke KNP BT; *Int'l*, pg. 757
OGE ENERGY CORP.; *U.S. Public*, pg. 1207
OHM CORPORATION; *U.S. Public*, pg. 1207
OHM ENVIRONMENTAL RESOURCES MANAGEMENT CORP.—See OHM Corporation; *U.S. Public*, pg. 1208
OHM INTERNATIONAL, INC.—See OHM Corporation; *U.S. Public*, pg. 1208
O.I. CORPORATION; *U.S. Public*, pg. 1208
OIP—See Reed Elsevier plc; *Int'l*, pg. 1097
OIP N.V.—See Delft Instruments N.V.; *Int'l*, pg. 389
O.J. PIPELINES CORP.—See Ocelot Energy Inc.; *Int'l*, pg. 996
OK BAZAARS (1929) LTD.—See South African Breweries, Ltd.; *Int'l*, pg. 1287
OK COOP AG—See Coop Switzerland; *Int'l*, pg. 330
O.K. PERSONNEL—See Kelly Services, Inc.; *U.S. Public*, pg. 949
OK TEDI MINING LIMITED—See The Broken Hill Proprietary Company Limited; *Int'l*, pg. 228
OKA TEPPICHWERKE GMBH.—See Vorwerk & Co.; *Int'l*, pg. 1480
OKB VERMOGENSVERWALTUNGS- UND BETEILIGUNGSGESELLSCHAFT M.B.H.—See Bayerische Vereinsbank Group; *Int'l*, pg. 181
O.L.F.—See Lagardere Groupe; *Int'l*, pg. 796
OLW-SNACKS AB—See Novartis AG; *Int'l*, pg. 983
OM GROUP; *U.S. Public*, pg. 1208
OMAI GOLD MINES LIMITED—See Cambior Inc.; *Int'l*, pg. 253
OMC ANDREWS—See Greenway Partners, L.P.; *U.S. Private*, pg. 478
OMC BURNSVILLE—See Greenway Partners, L.P.; *U.S. Private*, pg. 478
OMC CALHOUN—See Greenway Partners, L.P.; *U.S. Private*, pg. 478
OMC EL PASO—See Greenway Partners, L.P.; *U.S. Private*, pg. 478
OMC MARINE POWER PRODUCTS GROUP—See Greenway Partners, L.P.; *U.S. Private*, pg. 478
OMC MILWAUKEE—See Greenway Partners, L.P.; *U.S. Private*, pg. 478
OMC SPRUCE PINE—See Greenway Partners, L.P.; *U.S. Private*, pg. 478
OMG AMERICAS—See Hanson PLC; *Int'l*, pg. 594
OMI BULK MANAGEMENT CO.—See OMI Corp.; *U.S. Public*, pg. 1208
OMI CORP.; *U.S. Public*, pg. 1208
OMR TRANSPORTATION COMPANY—See Kirby Corporation; *U.S. Public*, pg. 962
OMV AG; *Int'l*, pg. 995
ONC COMPANY—See Sony Corporation; *Int'l*, pg. 1283
ONG SAYRE STORAGE CO.—See ONEOK Inc.; *U.S. Public*, pg. 1226
ONG TRANSMISSION COMPANY—See ONEOK Inc.; *U.S. Public*, pg. 1226
O.O.M. ONDERLINGE MOLESTVERZEKERING-MAATSCHAPPIJ U.A.—See AEGON N.V.; *Int'l*, pg. 26
O.O.M. ONDERLINGE VERZEKERING-MAATSCHAPPIJ U.A—See AEGON N.V.; *Int'l*, pg. 26
OPD LTD. HONG KONG—See Olivetti SpA; *Int'l*, pg. 1003
O.P.E.S.S.A.—See Y.P.F., S.A.; *Int'l*, pg. 1515
OPG INDUSTRIES; *U.S. Private*, pg. 809
OPIC (OVERSEAS PETROLEUM INVESTMENT GROUP)—See Chinese Petroleum Corporation; *Int'l*, pg. 286
OPT INDUSTRIES, INC.—See Torotel, Inc.; *U.S. Public*, pg. 1624
OPW FUELING COMPONENTS—See Dover Corporation; *U.S. Public*, pg. 521
O.R.E. SUBSIDIARY CORP.—See TrustCo Bank Corp., NY; *U.S. Public*, pg. 1643
ORM BERGOLD CHEMIE GMBH & CO.—See Safety-Kleen Corp.; *U.S. Public*, pg. 1426
O.S. ENGINES MFG. CO., LTD.—See Futaba Corporation; *Int'l*, pg. 531
O'S GOLD SEED CO.—See Pharmacia & Upjohn, Inc.; *Int'l*, pg. 1048
OSCA—See Great Lakes Chemical Corporation; *U.S. Public*, pg. 760
OSI—See Tang Industries Inc.; *U.S. Private*, pg. 1068
OSI SYSTEMS, INC.; *U.S. Public*, pg. 1208
OST-WEST ALLIANZ—See Allianz Aktiengesellschaft; *Int'l*, pg. 61
OST-WEST ALLIANZ (ST. PETERSBURG OFFICE)—See Allianz Aktiengesellschaft; *Int'l*, pg. 61
OSV PARTNERS—See United Asset Management Corporation; *U.S. Public*, pg. 1673
OTA GRUNDSTIUCKS UND BETEILIGUNGSVERWALTUNG GMBH—See Mannesmann A.G.; *Int'l*, pg. 839
OTD&C A/S (OFFSHORE TECHNOLOGY DEVELOPMENT & CONSULTING)—See The Macneal-Schwendler Corp.; *U.S. Public*, pg. 1032
OTOB CLEARING BANK AG—See Creditanstalt-Bankverein; *Int'l*, pg. 347
OTRASA—See Y.P.F., S.A.; *Int'l*, pg. 1515
OTSG, INC.—See Caterpillar Inc.; *U.S. Public*, pg. 316
OUB MANULIFE PTE. LTD.—See Manulife Financial (The Manufacturers Life Insurance Company); *Int'l*, pg. 841
OUP ESPANA—See Oxford University Press; *Int'l*, pg. 1019
OUP TRANSVAAL—See Oxford University Press; *Int'l*, pg. 1019
OWL AG LOGISTIK-SYSTEME—See Georg Fischer Ltd.; *Int'l*, pg. 490
OXO INTERNATIONAL—See General Housewares Corp.; *U.S. Public*, pg. 716
O-Z/GEDNEY, NELSON FIRESTOP PRODUCTS—See General Signal Corporation; *U.S. Public*, pg. 726
O.O.M. ONDERLINGE ZIEKTEKOSTENVERZEKERING-MAATSCHAPPIJ U.A.—See AEGON N.V.; *Int'l*, pg. 26
OACIS HEALTHCARE SYSTEMS, INC.; *U.S. Public*, pg. 1208
OAK DEDICATED LIMITED—See Chartwell Re Corporation; *U.S. Public*, pg. 337

OAK GRIGSBY—See Oak Industries Inc.; *U.S. Public*, pg. 1209
OAK GROVE PUBLICATIONS, INC.—See Shivers Trading & Operating Co.; *U.S. Private*, pg. 995
OAK HILL WEST, INC.—See Lennar Corporation; *U.S. Public*, pg. 988
OAK INDUSTRIES INC.; *U.S. Public*, pg. 1209
OAK LAWN IMAGING CENTER—See Medical Resources Inc.; *U.S. Public*, pg. 1080
THE OAK RIDGER—See Shivers Trading & Operating Co.; *U.S. Private*, pg. 995
OAK RUN UTILITIES—See Consumers Water Company; *U.S. Public*, pg. 438
OAKEY ABATTOIR PTY. LTD.—See Nippon Meat Packers, Inc.; *Int'l*, pg. 936
OAKEY HOLDINGS PTY. LTD.—See Nippon Meat Packers, Inc.; *Int'l*, pg. 936
OAKHURST DAIRY; *U.S. Private*, pg. 809
OAKITE CANADA, LTD.—See Metallgesellschaft AG; *Int'l*, pg. 861
OAKITE PRODUCTS, INC.—See Metallgesellschaft AG; *Int'l*, pg. 861
OAKLAND RAIDERS; *U.S. Private*, pg. 809
OAKLAND TOOL & MANUFACTURING COMPANY; *U.S. Private*, pg. 809
BRUCE OAKLEY, INC.; *U.S. Private*, pg. 809
OAKLEY YOUNG/4TH DIMENSION—See WPP Group plc; *Int'l*, pg. 1482
OAKMAN TELEPHONE COMPANY—See Telephone and Data Systems, Inc.; *U.S. Public*, pg. 1571
OAKREED FINANCIAL SERVICES LIMITED—See The Long-Term Credit Bank of Japan, Limited; *Int'l*, pg. 817
OAKS AT BAYMEADOW ASSOCIATES—See Cigna Corp.; *U.S. Public*, pg. 361
OAKS AT REGENCY ASSOCIATES—See Cigna Corp.; *U.S. Public*, pg. 361
OAKTREE—See Edison Brothers Stores, Inc.; *U.S. Public*, pg. 564
OAKWOOD ACCEPTANCE CORP.—See Oakwood Homes Corporation; *U.S. Public*, pg. 1209
OAKWOOD FINANCIAL CORPORATION—See Oakwood Homes Corporation; *U.S. Public*, pg. 1209
OAKWOOD FUNDING CORP.—See Oakwood Homes Corporation; *U.S. Public*, pg. 1209
OAKWOOD HOMES CORPORATION; *U.S. Public*, pg. 1209
OAKWOOD MOBILE HOMES, INC.—See Oakwood Homes Corporation; *U.S. Public*, pg. 1209
OAKY CREEK COAL PTY. LTD.—See M.I.M. Holdings Ltd.; *Int'l*, pg. 827
OAR BAR & GRILL—See Ark Restaurants Corp.; *U.S. Public*, pg. 130
OASIS-AMERON, LTD.—See Ameron International Corporation; *U.S. Public*, pg. 99
OASIS CORP.; *U.S. Private*, pg. 810
OASIS GROUP PLC—See Sybase, Inc.; *U.S. Public*, pg. 1544
OASIS OUTSOURCING, INC.—See The Wackenhut Corporation; *U.S. Public*, pg. 1731
OBALEX, A.S.—See Continental Can Co.; *U.S. Public*, pg. 440
OBAYASHI CORPORATION; *Int'l*, pg. 995
OBAYASHI CORPORATION-AMSTERDAM—See Obayashi Corporation; *Int'l*, pg. 995
OBAYASHI CORPORATION-BANGKOK—See Obayashi Corporation; *Int'l*, pg. 995
OBAYASHI CORPORATION-BEIJING—See Obayashi Corporation; *Int'l*, pg. 995
OBAYASHI CORPORATION-BERLIN—See Obayashi Corporation; *Int'l*, pg. 995
OBAYASHI CORPORATION-DALIAN—See Obayashi Corporation; *Int'l*, pg. 995
OBAYASHI CORPORATION-HANOI—See Obayashi Corporation; *Int'l*, pg. 995
OBAYASHI CORPORATION-HO CHI MINH—See Obayashi Corporation; *Int'l*, pg. 995
OBAYASHI CORPORATION-HONOLULU—See Obayashi Corporation; *Int'l*, pg. 995
OBAYASHI CORPORATION-JAKARTA—See Obayashi Corporation; *Int'l*, pg. 995
OBAYASHI CORPORATION-KUALA LUMPUR—See Obayashi Corporation; *Int'l*, pg. 995
OBAYASHI CORPORATION-LONDON—See Obayashi Corporation; *Int'l*, pg. 995
OBAYASHI CORPORATION-LOS ANGELES—See Obayashi Corporation; *Int'l*, pg. 995
OBAYASHI CORPORATION-MANILA—See Obayashi Corporation; *Int'l*, pg. 995
OBAYASHI CORPORATION-NEW YORK—See Obayashi Corporation; *Int'l*, pg. 995
OBAYASHI CORPORATION-PARIS—See Obayashi Corporation; *Int'l*, pg. 996
OBAYASHI CORPORATION-SAN FRANCISCO—See Obayashi Corporation; *Int'l*, pg. 995
OBAYASHI CORPORATION-SHANGHAI—See Obayashi Corporation; *Int'l*, pg. 996
OBAYASHI CORPORATION-SINGAPORE—See Obayashi Corporation; *Int'l*, pg. 996
OBAYASHI CORPORATION-SYDNEY—See Obayashi Corporation; *Int'l*, pg. 996
OBAYASHI FINANCE INTERNATIONAL (NETHERLANDS) B.V.—See Obayashi Corporation; *Int'l*, pg. 996
OBAYASHI HAWAII CORPORATION—See Obayashi Corporation; *Int'l*, pg. 996
OBAYASHI PHILIPPINES CORPORATION—See Obayashi Corporation; *Int'l*, pg. 996
OBAYASHI PROJECTBAU GMBH—See Obayashi Corporation; *Int'l*, pg. 996
OBAYASHI SINGAPORE PTE. LTD.—See Obayashi Corporation; *Int'l*, pg. 996
BENJAMIN OBDYKE, INC.; *U.S. Private*, pg. 810
OBEGI CHEMICALS S.A.L—See BASF AG; *Int'l*, pg. 109
OBERDORFER INDUSTRIES, INC.; *U.S. Private*, pg. 810

Company Index

OBERDORFER DIRECTORY OF CORPORATE AFFILIATIONS

F. OBERDORFER SIEBTECHNIK GMBH—See Scapa Group Plc; *Int'l*, pg. 1202
OBERDORFER SIEBTECHNIK GMBH—See Scapa Group Plc; *Int'l*, pg. 1202
OBERFLANCHENTECHNIK WAHL-CFR GMBH—See Fuchs Petrolub AG Oel + Chemie; *Int'l*, pg. 517
OBERG ARIZONA—See Oberg Industries Corp.; *U.S. Private*, pg. 810
OBERG CARBIDE PUNCH & DIE—See Oberg Industries Corp.; *U.S. Private*, pg. 810
OBERG INDUSTRIES CORP.; *U.S. Private*, pg. 810
OBERG MFG. CO.—See Oberg Industries Corp.; *U.S. Private*, pg. 810
OBERHAUSEN OFFICE—See Deutsche Babcock AG; *Int'l*, pg. 401
OBERLAND GLAS AG—See Saint-Gobain; *Int'l*, pg. 1171
OBERLANDER RECYCLING TECHNIK GMBH—See Fried. Krupp AG; *Int'l*, pg. 513
OBERRHEINISCHE MINERALOELWERKE GMBH—See Du Pont (E.I. Du Pont De Nemours & Co.); *U.S. Public*, pg. 533
OBI—See GIB Group; *Int'l*, pg. 534
OBION COMPANY, INC.—See Salant Corporation; *U.S. Public*, pg. 1429
OBJECT TECHNOLOGY GROUP—See SHL Systemhouse; *Int'l*, pg. 1154
OBJECT TECHNOLOGY GROUP - NORTHEAST REGION—See SHL Systemhouse; *Int'l*, pg. 1154
OBJECTIVE SYSTEMS INTEGRATORS, INC.; *U.S. Public*, pg. 1209
OBJECTORY AB—See Telefonaktiebolaget LM Ericsson; *Int'l*, pg. 1364
OBJEKTVERWALTUNGSGESELLSCHAFT DAMPFKRAFTWERK WET GBR—See Harpen AG; *Int'l*, pg. 597
THE O'BOISE CORPORATION; *U.S. Private*, pg. 810
S.A. OBOURG—See Holderbank Financiere Glaris Ltd.; *Int'l*, pg. 629
O'BRIEN INTERNATIONAL, INC.—See MacAndrews & Forbes Holdings Inc.; *U.S. Private*, pg. 689
O.H. O'BRIEN DIVISION—See Morgan Crucible Co. Plc; *Int'l*, pg. 895
ROY O'BRIEN INC.; *U.S. Private*, pg. 810
O'BRYAN BROTHERS INC.; *U.S. Private*, pg. 810
THE OBSERVER (SARNIA)—See Hollinger Inc.; *Int'l*, pg. 631
OCALA STAR-BANNER CORPORATION—See The New York Times Company; *U.S. Public*, pg. 1175
OCASCO BUDGET, INC.—See Ohio Casualty Corporation; *U.S. Public*, pg. 1214
OCCAM S.R.L.—See Compagnie des Machines Bull; *Int'l*, pg. 318
OCCIDENTAL CHEMICAL CORPORATION—See Occidental Petroleum Corporation; *U.S. Public*, pg. 1210
OCCIDENTAL EXPLORATION AND PRODUCTION COMPANY—See Occidental Petroleum Corporation; *U.S. Public*, pg. 1210
OCCIDENTAL INTERNATIONAL FINANCE N.V.—See Occidental Petroleum Corporation; *U.S. Public*, pg. 1210
OCCIDENTAL OIL & GAS CORPORATION—See Occidental Petroleum Corporation; *U.S. Public*, pg. 1210
OCCIDENTAL OVERSEAS FINANCE N.V.—See Occidental Petroleum Corporation; *U.S. Public*, pg. 1210
OCCIDENTAL PERUANA, INC.—See Occidental Petroleum Corporation; *U.S. Public*, pg. 1210
OCCIDENTAL PETROLEUM CORPORATION; *U.S. Public*, pg. 1210
OCCOQUAN LAND CORPORATION—See American Water Works Company, Inc.; *U.S. Public*, pg. 95
OCCUPATIONAL HEALTH ASSOCIATES-NORTH—See Vencor, Inc.; *U.S. Public*, pg. 1715
OCCUPATIONAL HEALTH SERVICES, INC.—See Foundation Health Systems, Inc.; *U.S. Public*, pg. 678
OCCUPATIONAL-URGENT CARE HEALTH SYSTEMS (OUCH)—See First Health Group Corp.; *U.S. Public*, pg. 635
OCEAN BEAUTY SEAFOODS, INC.; *U.S. Private*, pg. 810
OCEAN BIO-CHEM INC.; *U.S. Public*, pg. 1211
OCEAN CHEVROLET, INC.; *U.S. Private*, pg. 810
OCEAN MIST FARMS CORP.; *U.S. Private*, pg. 811
OCEAN PROPERTIES, LTD.; *U.S. Private*, pg. 811
OCEAN SHOWBOAT, INC.—See Showboat, Incorporated; *U.S. Public*, pg. 1469
OCEAN SPRAY CRANBERRIES, INC.; *U.S. Private*, pg. 811
OCEAN SPRAY INTERNATIONAL INC.—See Ocean Spray Cranberries, Inc.; *U.S. Private*, pg. 811
OCEAN SPRAY INTERNATIONAL SERVICES, INC.—See Ocean Spray Cranberries, Inc.; *U.S. Private*, pg. 811
OCEANA FOODS—See Cherry Central Cooperative; *U.S. Private*, pg. 234
OCEANEERING A/S—See Oceaneering International, Inc.; *U.S. Public*, pg. 1211
OCEANEERING AUSTRALIA PTY. LTD.—See Brambles Industries Limited; *Int'l*, pg. 211
OCEANEERING AUSTRALIA PTY. LTD.—See Oceaneering International, Inc.; *U.S. Public*, pg. 1211
OCEANEERING INTERNATIONAL, INC.; *U.S. Public*, pg. 1211
OCEANEERING INTERNATIONAL, INC.—See Oceaneering International, Inc.; *U.S. Public*, pg. 1211
OCEANEERING INTERNATIONAL SDN. BHD.—See Oceaneering International, Inc.; *U.S. Public*, pg. 1211
OCEANEERING INTERNATIONAL SERVICES, LTD.—See Oceaneering International, Inc.; *U.S. Public*, pg. 1211
OCEANEERING INTERVENTION ENGINEERING—See Oceaneering International, Inc.; *U.S. Public*, pg. 1211
OCEANEERING MULTIFLEX—See Oceaneering International, Inc.; *U.S. Public*, pg. 1211
OCEANEERING PRODUCTION SYSTEMS—See Oceaneering International, Inc.; *U.S. Public*, pg. 1211
OCEANEERING SPACE SYSTEMS—See Oceaneering International, Inc.; *U.S. Public*, pg. 1211
OCEANEERING TECHNOLOGIES—See Oceaneering International, Inc.; *U.S. Public*, pg. 1211
OCEANEX—See Newfoundland Capital Corporation Limited; *Int'l*, pg. 924
OCEANGRAIS—See Norsk Hydro a.s; *Int'l*, pg. 964
OCEANIC SHIPPING CO.—See Strachan Shipping Co.; *U.S. Private*, pg. 1046
OCEANS RACQUET CLUB, INC.—See The Chubb Corporation; *U.S. Public*, pg. 355
OCEL STYRIA A.S.—See Voest-Alpine Stahl AG; *Int'l*, pg. 1472
OCELOT ENERGY INC.; *Int'l*, pg. 996
OCELOT INTERNATIONAL LTD.—See Ocelot Energy Inc.; *Int'l*, pg. 996
OCELOT INTERNATIONAL TANZANIA LTD.—See Ocelot Energy Inc.; *Int'l*, pg. 996
OCELOT INTERNATIONAL U.K. LTD.—See Ocelot Energy Inc.; *Int'l*, pg. 996
OCENSA—See Transcanada Pipelines Limited; *Int'l*, pg. 1417
O'CHARLEY'S INC.; *U.S. Public*, pg. 1211
OCHOCO LUMBER COMPANY; *U.S. Private*, pg. 811
OCIDENTAL—See Eureko B.V.; *Int'l*, pg. 464
THE OCKLEY BRICK CO. LTD.—See Blue Circle Industries PLC; *Int'l*, pg. 197
OCLASSEN PHARMACEUTICALS—See Watson Pharmaceuticals, Inc.; *U.S. Public*, pg. 1746
OCONOMOWOC CANNING COMPANY—See Stokely USA, Inc.; *U.S. Public*, pg. 1519
OCTAGON PROCESS INC.; *U.S. Private*, pg. 811
OCTEL COMMUNICATIONS (ISRAEL) LTD.—See Lucent Technologies Inc.; *U.S. Public*, pg. 1018
OCTEL COMMUNICATIONS LTD.—See Lucent Technologies Inc.; *U.S. Public*, pg. 1018
OCTEL COMMUNICATIONS S.A.—See Lucent Technologies Inc.; *U.S. Public*, pg. 1018
OCTEL MESSAGING DIV.—See Lucent Technologies Inc.; *U.S. Public*, pg. 1018
OCTEL MESSAGING DIVISION—See Lucent Technologies Inc.; *U.S. Public*, pg. 1017
OCTOBER FILMS, INC.—See The Seagram Company Ltd.; *Int'l*, pg. 1216
OCYE S.A.—See Lyonnaise des Eaux S.A.; *Int'l*, pg. 823
ODAKYU ELECTRIC RAILWAY CO., LTD.; *Int'l*, pg. 996
ODAWARA PLANT—See Mitsubishi Chemical Corporation; *Int'l*, pg. 871
ODDA SMELTEVERK A/S—See The BOC Group plc; *Int'l*, pg. 122
ODDZON PRODUCTS, INC.—See Hasbro, Inc.; *U.S. Public*, pg. 797
ODELL STATE BANK—See Pontiac Bancorp, Inc.; *U.S. Public*, pg. 1316
ODEON CINEMAS LTD.—See The Rank Group PLC; *Int'l*, pg. 1086
ODER-SPREE ENERGIEVERSORGUNG AG—See Veba AG; *Int'l*, pg. 1456
ODESSA EXPLORATION, INC.—See Key Energy Group Inc.; *U.S. Public*, pg. 953
ODETICS INC.; *U.S. Public*, pg. 1212
THE ODOM CORPORATION; *U.S. Private*, pg. 811
O'DONNELL GRIFFIN (HONG KONG) LTD.—See Tyco International Ltd.; *U.S. Public*, pg. 1650
P.T. O'DONNELL GRIFFIN INDONESIA—See Tyco International Ltd.; *U.S. Public*, pg. 1651
O'DONNELL-USEN FISHERIES CORP.—See ConAgra, Inc.; *U.S. Public*, pg. 427
ODYSSEY REINSURANCE CORPORATION—See Skandia Insurance Company Limited; *Int'l*, pg. 1258
OECHSLE INTERNATIONAL ADVISORS L.P.—See Dresdner Bank AG; *Int'l*, pg. 418
OERLIKON AEROSPACE, INC.—See Oerlikon-Buhrle Holding AG; *Int'l*, pg. 998
OERLIKON-BUHRLE HOLDING AG; *Int'l*, pg. 996
OERLIKON BUHRLE IMMOBILIEN AG—See Oerlikon-Buhrle Holding AG; *Int'l*, pg. 998
OERLIKON BUHRLE USA, INC.—See Oerlikon-Buhrle Holding AG; *Int'l*, pg. 998
OERLIKON-CONTRAVES AG—See Oerlikon-Buhrle Holding AG; *Int'l*, pg. 998
OERLIKON-CONTRAVES PYROTEC AG—See Oerlikon-Buhrle Holding AG; *Int'l*, pg. 998
OERLIKON-CONTRAVES S.P.A.—See Oerlikon-Buhrle Holding AG; *Int'l*, pg. 998
OERLIKON-KNORR EISENBAHNTECHNIK AG—See Knorr-Bremse AG; *Int'l*, pg. 738
OERLIKON LOGISTICS LTD.—See Oerlikon-Buhrle Holding AG; *Int'l*, pg. 998
OERLIKON SINGAPORE PTE. LTD.—See Oerlikon-Buhrle Holding AG; *Int'l*, pg. 998
OESTERREICHISCH HERAKLITH, A.G.—See RGP Holding, Inc.; *U.S. Private*, pg. 904
OESTERREICHISCHE AUTOMOBILFABRIK—See MAN Aktiengesellschaft; *Int'l*, pg. 825
OEWA WASSER UND ABWASSER GMBH, POTSDAM—See Veba AG; *Int'l*, pg. 1460
OFA OY AB—See Gunnebo Industrier AB; *Int'l*, pg. 578
OFA-AKKUMULATOREN GES.M.B.H.—See VARTA AG; *Int'l*, pg. 1452
O'FALLON PROGRESS—See Knight-Ridder, Inc.; *U.S. Public*, pg. 964
OFFICE ANGELS LIMITED—See Olsten Corporation; *U.S. Public*, pg. 1221
OFFICE AUTOMATION CORP.—See Jeumont-Schneider Tranformeteurs; *Int'l*, pg. 706
OFFICE CONNECTION, INC.—See U.S. Office Products Company; *U.S. Public*, pg. 1687
OFFICE DEPOT INC.; *U.S. Public*, pg. 1212
OFFICE ELECTRONICS, INC.; *U.S. Private*, pg. 812
OFFICE EQUIPMENT COMPANY OF CHICAGO; *U.S. Private*, pg. 812
OFFICE LEASING—See IRI Istituto Ricostruzione Industriale; *Int'l*, pg. 652
OFFICE OF COMMUNICATIONS—See The Walt Disney Company; *U.S. Public*, pg. 511
OFFICE PAVILION DIVISION (SLS. & MKTG. DIV.)—See Herman Miller, Inc.; *U.S. Public*, pg. 1112
OFFICE PRODUCTS DIVISION—See FiberMark Inc.; *U.S. Public*, pg. 620
OFFICEMAX; *U.S. Public*, pg. 1212
OFFICEMAX DE MEXICO—See OfficeMax; *U.S. Public*, pg. 1212
OFFICETEAM—See Robert Half International Inc.; *U.S. Public*, pg. 775
OFFICINE A. MASERATI S.P.A.—See Fiat Auto SpA; *Int'l*, pg. 482
OFFICINE AERONAVALI VENEZIA S.P.A.—See IRI Istituto Ricostruzione Industriale; *Int'l*, pg. 653
OFFICINE ALFIERI MASERATI, SPA—See Chrysler Corporation; *U.S. Public*, pg. 354
R.D. OFFIT COMPANY; *U.S. Private*, pg. 812
C.M. OFFRAY & SON—See C.M. Offray & Son Inc.; *U.S. Private*, pg. 812
C.M. OFFRAY & SON INC.; *U.S. Private*, pg. 812
OFFSET PAPERBACK MFRS. (BPMC)—See Bertelsmann AG; *Int'l*, pg. 191
OFFSHORE EQUITIES, INC.—See The Chase Manhattan Corporation; *U.S. Public*, pg. 338
OFFSHORE LOGISTICS CARIBBEAN, S.A.—See Offshore Logistics, Inc.; *U.S. Public*, pg. 1213
OFFSHORE LOGISTICS FAR EAST (PTE) LTD.—See Offshore Logistics, Inc.; *U.S. Public*, pg. 1213
OFFSHORE LOGISTICS, INC.; *U.S. Public*, pg. 1212
OFFSHORE LOGISTICS INTERNATIONAL, INC.—See Offshore Logistics, Inc.; *U.S. Public*, pg. 1213
OFFSHORE LOGISTICS SERVICES, INC.—See Offshore Logistics, Inc.; *U.S. Public*, pg. 1213
OFFSHORE & OVERSEAS PETROLEUM EXPLORATION DIVISION—See Chinese Petroleum Corporation; *Int'l*, pg. 286
OFICINA TECNICA SAN LUIS—See Telefonaktiebolaget LM Ericsson; *Int'l*, pg. 1369
OFICINA TECNICA TIJUANA—See Telefonaktiebolaget LM Ericsson; *Int'l*, pg. 1369
OGALLALA ELECTRONICS—See SPS Technologies, Inc.; *U.S. Public*, pg. 1420
OGDEN AVIATION SERVICES—See Ogden Corporation; *U.S. Public*, pg. 1213
OGDEN CORPORATION; *U.S. Public*, pg. 1213
OGDEN ENERGY GROUP, INC.—See Ogden Corporation; *U.S. Public*, pg. 1213
OGDEN ENTERTAINMENT, INC.—See Ogden Corporation; *U.S. Public*, pg. 1213
OGDEN NEWSPAPERS, INC.; *U.S. Private*, pg. 812
OGDEN PUBLISHING—See Ogden Newspapers, Inc.; *U.S. Private*, pg. 812
THE OGDEN UNION RAILWAY AND DEPOT CO.—See Union Pacific Corporation; *U.S. Public*, pg. 1668
OGILVY & MATHER WORLDWIDE, INC.—See WPP Group plc; *Int'l*, pg. 1483
OGLEBAY NORTON COMPANY; *U.S. Public*, pg. 1213
OGLEBAY NORTON INDUSTRIAL SANDS, INC.—See Oglebay Norton Company; *U.S. Public*, pg. 1213
OGLEBAY NORTON REFRACTORIES & MINERALS, INC.—See Oglebay Norton Company; *U.S. Public*, pg. 1214
OGLETHORPE POWER CORP.; *U.S. Private*, pg. 812
OGOSE SANKEN CO., LTD.—See Sanken Electric Co., Ltd.; *Int'l*, pg. 1188
OH BOY CORPORATION; *U.S. Private*, pg. 812
OH!..POIVRIER!—See Sodexho S.A.; *Int'l*, pg. 1274
OHARA INC.—See Canon Inc.; *Int'l*, pg. 261
OHAUS CORPORATION—See Novartis AG; *Int'l*, pg. 974
OHI PLANT—See Nikon Corporation; *Int'l*, pg. 931
OHIO ALLOY STEELS CORPORATION—See The Timken Company; *U.S. Public*, pg. 1617
OHIO-AMERICAN WATER CO.—See American Water Works Company, Inc.; *U.S. Public*, pg. 95
THE OHIO ART COMPANY, INC.; *U.S. Public*, pg. 1214
OHIO AUTO AUCTION—See Cox Enterprises, Inc.; *U.S. Private*, pg. 283
THE OHIO BRASS CO.—See Hubbell Incorporated; *U.S. Public*, pg. 844
OHIO CASUALTY CORPORATION; *U.S. Public*, pg. 1214
OHIO CASUALTY INSURANCE CO.—See Ohio Casualty Corporation; *U.S. Public*, pg. 1214
THE OHIO CASUALTY INSURANCE GROUP—See Ohio Casualty Corporation; *U.S. Public*, pg. 1214
OHIO COUNTY BALEFILL, INC.—See Republic Industries, Inc.; *U.S. Public*, pg. 1379
OHIO CRANKSHAFT DIV.—See Park-Ohio Industries, Inc.; *U.S. Public*, pg. 1258
OHIO EBY BROWN—See Eby-Brown Co.; *U.S. Private*, pg. 359
OHIO EDISON COMPANY—See FirstEnergy Corp.; *U.S. Public*, pg. 645
OHIO EDISON CO.-SPRINGFIELD DIV.—See FirstEnergy Corp.; *U.S. Public*, pg. 645
OHIO EDISON CO. WESTERN DIV.—See FirstEnergy Corp.; *U.S. Public*, pg. 645
OHIO ENGINE POWER—See Ohio Machinery Co.; *U.S. Private*, pg. 813
OHIO GAS COMPANY; *U.S. Private*, pg. 812
OHIO GEAR/RICHMOND GEAR - LIBERTY DIV.—See Regal-Beloit Corporation; *U.S. Public*, pg. 1370
OHIO INDEMNITY COMPANY—See Bancinsurance Corp.; *U.S. Public*, pg. 175
OHIO LITHO INC.—See Prime Medical Services, Inc.; *U.S. Public*, pg. 1327
OHIO MACHINERY CO.; *U.S. Private*, pg. 812
THE OHIO MATTRESS COMPANY LICENSING & COMPONENTS GROUP—See Sealy Corporation; *U.S. Private*, pg. 979
OHIO MENTOR, INC.—See Magellan Health Services, Inc.; *U.S. Public*, pg. 1036
OHIO POWER COMPANY—See American Electric Power Company, Inc.; *U.S. Public*, pg. 72

THE OHIO RIVER COMPANY—See Eastern Enterprises; U.S. Public, pg. 549
OHIO ROD PRODUCTS COMPANY, INC.—See Elgin National Industries, Inc.; U.S. Private, pg. 370
OHIO SEALANTS INC.—See Laporte plc; Int'l, pg. 802
OHIO-SEALY MATTRESS MANUFACTURING CO.-FORT WORTH—See Sealy Corporation; U.S. Private, pg. 979
OHIO-SEALY MATTRESS MANUFACTURING CO.-HOUSTON—See Sealy Corporation; U.S. Private, pg. 979
OHIO STAR FORGE CO.—See Daido Steel Co., Ltd.; Int'l, pg. 364
OHIO STATE LIFE INSURANCE CO.—See B.A.T Industries P.L.C.; Int'l, pg. 110
OHIO TAR ASPHALT—See Central Allied Enterprises; U.S. Private, pg. 222
OHIO TRANSMISSION CORPORATION; U.S. Private, pg. 813
OHIO UTILITIES COMPANY—See Citizens Utilities Company; U.S. Public, pg. 380
OHIO VALLEY ALUMINUM COMPANY—See Interlock Industries, Inc.; U.S. Private, pg. 567
OHIO VALLEY ELECTRIC CORPORATION; U.S. Private, pg. 813
OHIO VALLEY PUBLISHING CO.—See Gannett Company, Inc.; U.S. Public, pg. 701
OHKURA PHARMACEUTICAL—See Meiji Milk Products Co., Ltd.; Int'l, pg. 855
OHKURA-ROSEMOUNT CO., LTD.—See Emerson Electric Co.; U.S. Public, pg. 577
OHMACHI OLYMPUS CO., LTD.—See Olympus Optical Co., Ltd.; Int'l, pg. 1004
OHMEDA—See The BOC Group plc; Int'l, pg. 121
OHMEDA BV—See The BOC Group plc; Int'l, pg. 122
OHMEDA CARIBE, INC.—See The BOC Group plc; Int'l, pg. 121
OHMEDA, INC.—See The BOC Group plc; Int'l, pg. 121
OHMEDA, LTD.—See The BOC Group plc; Int'l, pg. 121
OHMEDA MEDICAL ENGINEERING—See The BOC Group plc; Int'l, pg. 121
OHMEDA SA—See The BOC Group plc; Int'l, pg. 122
OHMITE MANUFACTURING COMPANY; U.S. Private, pg. 813
OHMIYA SONIC CITY CO., LTD.—See Nippon Life Insurance Co.; Int'l, pg. 935
OHSE FOODS INC.—See Farmland Industries, Inc.; U.S. Private, pg. 396
THE OHTSU TIRE & RUBBER CO., LTD.—See Sumitomo Rubber Industries Ltd.; Int'l, pg. 1317
OIL-DRI CORPORATION OF AMERICA; U.S. Public, pg. 1214
OIL-DRI PRODUCTION CO.—See Oil-Dri Corporation of America; U.S. Public, pg. 1215
OIL-DRI S.A.—See Oil-Dri Corporation of America; U.S. Public, pg. 1215
OIL-DRI TRANSPORTATION CO.—See Oil-Dri Corporation of America; U.S. Public, pg. 1215
OIL-DRI (U.K.) LTD.—See Oil-Dri Corporation of America; U.S. Public, pg. 1215
OIL DRILLING & EXPLORATION LIMITED—See Australian Oil & Gas Corporation Limited; Int'l, pg. 101
OIL DYNAMICS—See Franklin Electric Co., Inc.; U.S. Public, pg. 679
OIL MOP, INC.—See The Beacon Group; U.S. Private, pg. 126
OIL PATCH & INDUSTRIAL SERVICES, LTD.—See ABB Asea Brown Boveri (Holding) Ltd.; Int'l, pg. 6
OIL PURIFICATION SERVICES OF AMERICA, INC.—See Altair Corporation; U.S. Private, pg. 46
OIL SHALE PLANT—See Petrobras - Petroleo Brasileiro S.A.; Int'l, pg. 1042
OILDYNE—See Commercial Intertech Corp.; U.S. Public, pg. 411
OILDYNE ASG GROUP—See Commercial Intertech Corp.; U.S. Public, pg. 411
THE OILGEAR COMPANY; U.S. Public, pg. 1215
OILGEAR GMBH—See The Oilgear Company; U.S. Public, pg. 1215
OILGEAR MEXICANA S.A.—See The Oilgear Company; U.S. Public, pg. 1215
OILGEAR SRL—See The Oilgear Company; U.S. Public, pg. 1215
OILGEAR/TOWLER AUSTRALIA PTY. LTD.—See The Oilgear Company; U.S. Public, pg. 1215
OILGEAR TOWLER LTD.—See The Oilgear Company; U.S. Public, pg. 1215
OILGEAR TOWLER SA—See The Oilgear Company; U.S. Public, pg. 1215
OITA CANON INC.—See Canon Inc.; Int'l, pg. 261
OJAI MANOR—See Vencor, Inc.; U.S. Public, pg. 1714
OJI PAPER CO.; Int'l, pg. 998
OJI PAPER CO. LTD.—See Oji Paper Co., Ltd.; Int'l, pg. 998
OKABE COMPANY, INC.—See Okabe Company Limited; Int'l, pg. 999
OKABE COMPANY LIMITED; Int'l, pg. 999
OKAYA & CO. LTD.; Int'l, pg. 999
OKAYA OLYMPUS CO., LTD.—See Olympus Optical Co., Ltd.; Int'l, pg. 1004
OKAYA (U.S.A.), INC.—See Okaya & Co. Ltd.; Int'l, pg. 999
OKAYAMA SHIZUKI CO., INC.—See Shizuki Electric Corporation; Int'l, pg. 1236
OKAYAMA TAIHO PHARMACEUTICAL CO., LTD.—See Otsuka Pharmaceutical Co., Ltd.; Int'l, pg. 1013
OKAYAMAKEN SHOKUHIN CO., LTD.—See Meiji Seika Kaisha, Ltd.; Int'l, pg. 855
OKAZAKI GOLF CLUB KK—See Tekken Corporation; Int'l, pg. 1362
O'KEEFFE'S, INC.; U.S. Private, pg. 813
OKI—See Oki Electric Industry Company, Ltd.; Int'l, pg. 1000
OKI ADVANCED TECHNOLOGY DIVISION—See Oki Electric Industry Company, Ltd.; Int'l, pg. 1000

OKI AMERICA INC.—See Oki Electric Industry Company, Ltd.; Int'l, pg. 1000
OKI CERAMIC INDUSTRY CO., LTD.—See Oki Electric Industry Company, Ltd.; Int'l, pg. 999
OKI ELECTRIC CABLE CO., LTD.—See Oki Electric Industry Company, Ltd.; Int'l, pg. 999
OKI ELECTRIC EUROPE GMBH—See Oki Electric Industry Company, Ltd.; Int'l, pg. 1000
OKI ELECTRIC INDUSTRY CO., LTD.—See Oki Electric Industry Company, Ltd.; Int'l, pg. 999
OKI ELECTRIC INDUSTRY COMPANY, LTD.; Int'l, pg. 999
OKI ELECTRONICS (HONG KONG) LTD.—See Oki Electric Industry Company, Ltd.; Int'l, pg. 1000
OKI ELECTRONICS (HONG KONG) LTD.-SINGAPORE BRANCH—See Oki Electric Industry Company, Ltd.; Int'l, pg. 1000
OKI ELECTRONICS (HONG KONG) LTD.-TAIPEI BRANCH—See Oki Electric Industry Company, Ltd.; Int'l, pg. 1000
OKI ELECTRONICS (SINGAPORE) PTE LTD.—See Oki Electric Industry Company, Ltd.; Int'l, pg. 1000
OKI EUROPE LTD.—See Oki Electric Industry Company, Ltd.; Int'l, pg. 1000
OKI (FRANCE) SARL—See Oki Electric Industry Company, Ltd.; Int'l, pg. 1000
OKI SEMICONDUCTOR GROUP—See Oki Electric Industry Company, Ltd.; Int'l, pg. 1000
OKI SEMICONDUCTOR (UK) LTD.—See Oki Electric Industry Company, Ltd.; Int'l, pg. 1000
OKI SEMICONDUCTORES (PUERTO RICO) INC.—See Oki Electric Industry Company, Ltd.; Int'l, pg. 1000
OKI SYSTEMES (FRANCE) S.A.—See Oki Electric Industry Company, Ltd.; Int'l, pg. 1000
OKI SYSTEMS (DANMARK) A.S.—See Oki Electric Industry Company, Ltd.; Int'l, pg. 1000
OKI SYSTEMS (DEUTSCHLAND) GMBH—See Oki Electric Industry Company, Ltd.; Int'l, pg. 1000
OKI SYSTEMS (HOLLAND) B.V.—See Oki Electric Industry Company, Ltd.; Int'l, pg. 1000
OKI SYSTEMS (IBERICA) S.A.—See Oki Electric Industry Company, Ltd.; Int'l, pg. 1000
OKI SYSTEMS (IRELAND) LTD.—See Oki Electric Industry Company, Ltd.; Int'l, pg. 1000
OKI SYSTEMS (ITALIA) S.P.A.—See Oki Electric Industry Company, Ltd.; Int'l, pg. 1000
OKI SYSTEMS (NORWAY) A/S—See Oki Electric Industry Company, Ltd.; Int'l, pg. 1000
OKI SYSTEMS (SWEDEN) AB—See Oki Electric Industry Company, Ltd.; Int'l, pg. 1000
OKI SYSTEMS (UK) LTD.—See Oki Electric Industry Company, Ltd.; Int'l, pg. 999
OKI TELECOM GROUP—See Oki Electric Industry Company, Ltd.; Int'l, pg. 1000
OKI (THAILAND) CO., LTD.—See Oki Electric Industry Company, Ltd.; Int'l, pg. 1000
OKI (UK) LTD.—See Oki Electric Industry Company, Ltd.; Int'l, pg. 999
OKI UNISYS KAISHA, LTD.—See Oki Electric Industry Company, Ltd.; Int'l, pg. 999
OKIDATA GROUP—See Oki Electric Industry Company, Ltd.; Int'l, pg. 1000
OKINAWA SUNTORY LTD.—See Suntory Ltd.; Int'l, pg. 1321
OKLA HOMER SMITH FURNITURE CO.—See Century Products Co.; U.S. Private, pg. 226
OKLAHOMA COMMUNICATION SYSTEMS, INC.—See Telephone and Data Systems, Inc.; U.S. Public, pg. 1571
OKLAHOMA NATIONAL BANK OF DUNCAN—See First Commercial Corporation; U.S. Public, pg. 630
OKLAHOMA NATURAL GAS COMPANY—See ONEOK Inc.; U.S. Public, pg. 1226
OKLAHOMA PRESS PUBLISHING CO.—See Gannett Company, Inc.; U.S. Public, pg. 701
OKLAHOMA PUBLISHING COMPANY; U.S. Private, pg. 813
THE OKONITE COMPANY; U.S. Private, pg. 813
OKTAVIA GESELLSCHAFT FUR BEKLEIDUNG MBH—See Otto Versand (GmbH & Co.); Int'l, pg. 1015
OKUMA AMERICA CORPORATION—See Okuma Corporation; Int'l, pg. 1001
OKUMA CORPORATION; Int'l, pg. 1000
OKUMA EUROPE GMBH—See Okuma Corporation; Int'l, pg. 1001
OKUMURA METALS CO., LTD.—See The Furukawa Electric Co., Ltd.; Int'l, pg. 530
OKURA & CO.; Int'l, pg. 1001
OKURA & CO. (AMERICA) INC.—See Okura & Co.; Int'l, pg. 1001
OLAER GROUP—See Expamet International Plc; Int'l, pg. 467
OLAND BREWERIES LIMITED—See Interbrew S.A.; Int'l, pg. 575
OLANDER & BROPHY, INC.—See Hughes Supply, Inc.; U.S. Public, pg. 847
OLATHE DAILY NEWS—See Keltatim Publishing Company; U.S. Private, pg. 613
OLAY CO., INC.—See The Procter & Gamble Company; U.S. Public, pg. 1330
OLD AMERICA STORES; U.S. Public, pg. 1215
OLD AMERICAN INSURANCE CO.—See Kansas City Life Insurance Co.; U.S. Public, pg. 943
OLD BEN COAL CO.—See Zeigler Coal Holding Company; U.S. Public, pg. 1790
OLD DOMINION BOX CO., INC.; U.S. Private, pg. 814
OLD DOMINION FREIGHT LINE, INC.; U.S. Public, pg. 1216
OLD DOMINION LIFE INSURANCE CO.—See Shenandoah Life Insurance Company; U.S. Public, pg. 992
OLD DOMINION SYSTEMS OF MARYLAND—See Microlog Corporation; U.S. Public, pg. 1105
OLD DUTCH FOODS, INC.; U.S. Private, pg. 814
THE OLD EAST AFRICAN TRADING CO. LTD.—See The East Asiatic Company Ltd. A/S; Int'l, pg. 431

THE OLD EAST AFRICAN TRADING CO. (T) LTD.—See The East Asiatic Company Ltd. A/S; Int'l, pg. 431
OLD EAST GRAPHICS (KENYA) LIMITED—See The East Asiatic Company Ltd. A/S; Int'l, pg. 431
OLD EL PASO—See Diageo Plc; Int'l, pg. 408
OLD FASHION FOODS, INC.; U.S. Private, pg. 814
OLD-FIRST NATIONAL BANK IN BLUFFTON—See Fort Wayne National Corporation; U.S. Public, pg. 674
OLD FORT INSURANCE CO., LTD. (BERMUDA)—See Lincoln National Corporation; U.S. Public, pg. 998
OLD GUARD GROUP, INC.—See Old Guard Insurance Group; U.S. Public, pg. 1216
OLD GUARD INSURANCE GROUP; U.S. Public, pg. 1216
OLD GUARD MUTUAL FIRE INSURANCE CO.—See Old Guard Insurance Group; U.S. Public, pg. 1216
OLD GUARD MUTUAL INSURANCE CO.—See Old Guard Insurance Group; U.S. Public, pg. 1216
OLD HOME FOODS, INC.; U.S. Private, pg. 814
OLD KENT BANK—See Old Kent Financial Corporation; U.S. Public, pg. 1216
OLD KENT BANK-EAST—See Old Kent Financial Corporation; U.S. Public, pg. 1216
OLD KENT BANK-LANSING—See Old Kent Financial Corporation; U.S. Public, pg. 1216
OLD KENT BROKERAGE SERVICES, INC.—See Old Kent Financial Corporation; U.S. Public, pg. 1216
OLD KENT FINANCIAL CORPORATION; U.S. Public, pg. 1216
OLD KENT FINANCIAL LIFE INSURANCE COMPANY—See Old Kent Financial Corporation; U.S. Public, pg. 1217
OLD KENT MORTGAGE COMPANY—See Old Kent Financial Corporation; U.S. Public, pg. 1216
THE OLD LINE LIFE INSURANCE CO. OF AMERICA—See American General Corporation; U.S. Public, pg. 77
OLD MERCHANDISE COMPANY—See Spaghetti Warehouse, Inc.; U.S. Public, pg. 1495
OLD NATIONAL BANCORP; U.S. Public, pg. 1217
OLD NAVY STORES—See The Gap, Inc.; U.S. Public, pg. 703
OLD ORCHARD HOSPITAL, INC.—See Vencor, Inc.; U.S. Public, pg. 1714
THE OLD PHOENIX NATIONAL BANK OF MEDINA—See FirstMerit Corporation; U.S. Public, pg. 646
OLD RELIABLE CASUALTY CO.—See The Reliable Life Insurance Company; U.S. Public, pg. 1374
OLD REPUBLIC DEALER SERVICE CORPORATION—See Old Republic International Corporation; U.S. Public, pg. 1218
OLD REPUBLIC INSURANCE CO.—See Old Republic International Corporation; U.S. Public, pg. 1218
OLD REPUBLIC INTERNATIONAL CORPORATION; U.S. Public, pg. 1218
OLD REPUBLIC LIFE INSURANCE CO. OF NEW YORK—See Old Republic International Corporation; U.S. Public, pg. 1218
OLD SPAGHETTI FACTORY (CANADA) LTD.—See Spaghetti Warehouse, Inc.; U.S. Public, pg. 1495
OLD TG CORP.—See Motorola, Inc.; U.S. Public, pg. 1138
OLD TOWN CANOE—See Johnson Worldwide Associates, Inc.; U.S. Public, pg. 933
OLD WISCONSIN CHEESE CO., INC.—See Carl Buddig & Company; U.S. Private, pg. 178
OLD WISCONSIN SAUSAGE—See Carl Buddig & Company; U.S. Private, pg. 178
OLD WORLD AUTOMOTIVE PRODUCTS—See Old World Industries, Inc.; U.S. Private, pg. 814
OLD WORLD INDUSTRIES, INC.; U.S. Private, pg. 814
OLDCASTLE, INC.—See CRH, plc; Int'l, pg. 242
OLDE ENGLISH EQUINE INSURANCE AGENCY, INC.—See International Thoroughbred Breeders, Inc.; U.S. Public, pg. 908
OLDELFT B.V.—See Delft Instruments N.V.; Int'l, pg. 389
OLDELFT CORP. OF AMERICA—See Delft Instruments N.V.; Int'l, pg. 389
OLDELFT ELECTRONIC INSTRUMENTS SRL—See Delft Instruments N.V.; Int'l, pg. 389
OLDELFT GMBH MEDIZINGERATEVERTRIEB—See Delft Instruments N.V.; Int'l, pg. 389
OLDELFT INTERNATIONAL TRADING CY. N.V.—See Delft Instruments N.V.; Int'l, pg. 389
OLDELFT JAPAN LTD.—See Delft Instruments N.V.; Int'l, pg. 389
OLDELFT VESTIGING LEEUWARDEN—See Delft Instruments N.V.; Int'l, pg. 389
THE OLDENBURG GROUP COMPANIES; U.S. Private, pg. 814
OLDENBURGISCHE LANDESBANK AG—See Dresdner Bank AG; Int'l, pg. 418
OLDHAM CROMPTON BATTERIES LTD.—See BTR plc; Int'l, pg. 125
THE OLDHAM ERA—See Landmark Communications, Inc.; U.S. Private, pg. 648
OLDHAM FRANCE SA—See BTR plc; Int'l, pg. 125
L.L. OLDS SEED COMPANY; U.S. Private, pg. 814
OLDSMOBILE DIV. GENERAL MOTORS CORP.—See General Motors Corporation; U.S. Public, pg. 720
OLE-HUNGARIA KFT—See Oce-van der Grinten N.V.; Int'l, pg. 995
OLEAN ADVANCED PRODUCTS DIVISION—See Kyocera Corporation; Int'l, pg. 775
OLEANDRA GVG MBH & CO. OBJEKT NEPTUN KG—See Commerzbank AG; Int'l, pg. 310
OLEANDRA GVG MBH & CO. OBJEKT PLUTO KG—See Commerzbank AG; Int'l, pg. 310
OLEANDRA GVG MBH & CO. OBJEKT URANUS KG—See Commerzbank AG; Int'l, pg. 310
OLEANDRA GVG MBH & CO. OBJEKT JUPITER KG—See Commerzbank AG; Int'l, pg. 310
OLEANDRA GVG MBH & CO. OBJEKT VENUS KG—See Commerzbank AG; Int'l, pg. 310
OLEFINAS, S.A.—See McNeel International Corp.; U.S. Private, pg. 725

OLEFINES PTY LTD—See Imperial Chemical Industries PLC; *Int'l*, pg. 665
OLEN CORPORATION—See Kokosing Construction Company, Inc.; *U.S. Private*, pg. 631
OLETEX, INC.—See American Industrial Partners; *U.S. Private*, pg. 56
SYSCO FOOD SERVICES COMPANY—See Sysco Corporation; *U.S. Public*, pg. 1551
OLGA DIV.—See Warnaco Inc.; *U.S. Public*, pg. 1738
OLICOM AMERICAS - CANADA—See Olicom A/S; *Int'l*, pg. 1001
OLICOM AMERICAS - CENTRAL—See Clicom A/S; *Int'l*, pg. 1001
OLICOM AMERICAS - EAST—See Olicom A/S; *Int'l*, pg. 1001
OLICOM AMERICAS - LATIN AMERICA—See Olicom A/S; *Int'l*, pg. 1001
OLICOM AMERICAS - SOUTH—See Olicom A/S; *Int'l*, pg. 1001
OLICOM AMERICAS - WEST—See Olicom A/S; *Int'l*, pg. 1001
OLICOM A/S; *Int'l*, pg. 1001
OLICOM AUSTRIA—See Olicom A/S; *Int'l*, pg. 1001
OLICOM BENELUX—See Olicom A/S; *Int'l*, pg. 1001
OLICOM FRANCE—See Olicom A/S; *Int'l*, pg. 1001
OLICOM GMBH—See Olicom A/S; *Int'l*, pg. 1001
OLICOM INC.—See Olicom A/S; *Int'l*, pg. 1001
OLICOM, INC.—See Olicom A/S; *Int'l*, pg. 1001
OLICOM JAPAN—See Olicom A/S; *Int'l*, pg. 1001
OLICOM NORDIC—See Olicom A/S; *Int'l*, pg. 1001
OLICOM POLAND SP. Z.O.O.—See Olicom A/S; *Int'l*, pg. 1001
OLICOM SINGAPORE—See Olicom A/S; *Int'l*, pg. 1001
OLICOM SWEDEN—See Olicom A/S; *Int'l*, pg. 1001
OLICOM UK LIMITED—See Olicom A/S; *Int'l*, pg. 1001
OLIN-ASAHI INTERCONNECT TECHNOLOGIES—See Olin Corporation; *U.S. Public*, pg. 1219
OLIN AUSTRALIA LIMITED—See Olin Corporation; *U.S. Public*, pg. 1220
OLIN BRAZIL LTDA.—See Olin Corporation; *U.S. Public*, pg. 1220
OLIN CANADA INC.—See Olin Corporation; *U.S. Public*, pg. 1220
OLIN CHEMICALS, B.V.—See Olin Corporation; *U.S. Public*, pg. 1220
OLIN CORPORATION; *U.S. Public*, pg. 1218
OLIN CORPORATION N.Z. LIMITED—See Olin Corporation; *U.S. Public*, pg. 1220
OLIN ELECTRONIC MATERIALS, INC.—See Olin Corporation; *U.S. Public*, pg. 1218
N.V. OLIN EUROPE S.A.—See Olin Corporation; *U.S. Public*, pg. 1220
OLIN EXPORT TRADING CORPORATION—See Olin Corporation; *U.S. Public*, pg. 1219
OLIN FABRICATED METALS PRODUCTS, INC.—See Olin Corporation; *U.S. Public*, pg. 1219
OLIN FAR EAST, LIMITED—See Olin Corporation; *U.S. Public*, pg. 1219
OLIN GMBH—See Olin Corporation; *U.S. Public*, pg. 1220
N.V. OLIN HUNT SPECIALTY PRODUCTS—See Olin Corporation; *U.S. Public*, pg. 1220
OLIN HUNT SPECIALTY PRODUCTS S.R.L.—See Olin Corporation; *U.S. Public*, pg. 1220
OLIN HUNT SUB. I CORP.—See Olin Corporation; *U.S. Public*, pg. 1219
N.V. OLIN HUNT TRADING—See Olin Corporation; *U.S. Public*, pg. 1220
OLIN INDUSTRIAL (HONG KONG) LIMITED—See Olin Corporation; *U.S. Public*, pg. 1220
OLIN JAPAN, INC.—See Olin Corporation; *U.S. Public*, pg. 1220
OLIN MICROELECTRONIC MATERIALS, INC.—See Olin Corporation; *U.S. Public*, pg. 1219
OLIN PANTEX, INC.—See Olin Corporation; *U.S. Public*, pg. 1219
OLIN (PROPRIETARY) LIMITED—See Olin Corporation; *U.S. Public*, pg. 1220
OLIN PTE., LTD., SINGAPORE—See Olin Corporation; *U.S. Public*, pg. 1220
OLIN QUIMICA, S.A.—See Olin Corporation; *U.S. Public*, pg. 1220
OLIN QUIMICA, S.A. DE C.V.—See Olin Corporation; *U.S. Public*, pg. 1220
OLIN S.A.—See Olin Corporation; *U.S. Public*, pg. 1220
OLIN SPECIALTY METALS CORPORATION—See Olin Corporation; *U.S. Public*, pg. 1219
OLIN UK LTD.—See Olin Corporation; *U.S. Public*, pg. 1220
OLINDE HARDWARE & SUPPLY CO.; *U.S. Private*, pg. 814
OLIVE GARDEN ITALIAN RESTAURANTS—See Darden Restaurants, Inc.; *U.S. Public*, pg. 484
OLIVER OIL COMPANY, INC.; *U.S. Private*, pg. 815
OLIVER PRODUCTS COMPANY; *U.S. Private*, pg. 815
OLIVER RUBBER CO.—See The Standard Products Company; *U.S. Public*, pg. 1504
OLIVER RUBBER EUROPA LTD.—See The Standard Products Company; *U.S. Public*, pg. 1505
VICENTE PUIG OLIVER S.A.; *Int'l*, pg. 1001
OLIVETTI—See Olivetti SpA; *Int'l*, pg. 1002
OLIVETTI A/B—See Olivetti SpA; *Int'l*, pg. 1003
OLIVETTI ADVANCED TECHNOLOGY CENTER, INC.—See Olivetti SpA; *Int'l*, pg. 1002
OLIVETTI AFRICA PTY. LTD.—See Olivetti SpA; *Int'l*, pg. 1003
OLIVETTI ARGENTINA S.A.C. E I.—See Olivetti SpA; *Int'l*, pg. 1003
OLIVETTI A/S—See Olivetti SpA; *Int'l*, pg. 1003
OLIVETTI AUSTRALIA PTY. LTD.—See Olivetti SpA; *Int'l*, pg. 1003
OLIVETTI AUSTRIA G.M.B.H.—See Olivetti SpA; *Int'l*, pg. 1003
S.A. OLIVETTI BELGIUM N.V.—See Olivetti SpA; *Int'l*, pg. 1003
OLIVETTI CANADA LTD.—See Olivetti SpA; *Int'l*, pg. 1003

OLIVETTI-CANON INDUSTRIALE S.P.A.—See Canon Inc.; *Int'l*, pg. 262
OLIVETTI COLOMBIANA S.A.—See Olivetti SpA; *Int'l*, pg. 1003
OLIVETTI CORPORATION OF JAPAN—See Olivetti SpA; *Int'l*, pg. 1003
OLIVETTI DE CHILE S.A.—See Olivetti SpA; *Int'l*, pg. 1003
OLIVETTI DE PUERTO RICO INC.—See Olivetti SpA; *Int'l*, pg. 1002
OLIVETTI DE VENEZUELA C.A.—See Olivetti SpA; *Int'l*, pg. 1003
OLIVETTI DO BRASIL S.A.—See Olivetti SpA; *Int'l*, pg. 1003
OLIVETTI FRANCE S.A.—See Olivetti SpA; *Int'l*, pg. 1003
OLIVETTI GERMANY—See Olivetti SpA; *Int'l*, pg. 1003
OLIVETTI HELLAS S.A.—See Olivetti SpA; *Int'l*, pg. 1003
OLIVETTI HONG KONG LTD.—See Olivetti SpA; *Int'l*, pg. 1003
OLIVETTI INTERNATIONAL S.A.—See Olivetti SpA; *Int'l*, pg. 1003
OLIVETTI MALAYSIA SDN BHD—See Olivetti SpA; *Int'l*, pg. 1003
OLIVETTI MANAGEMENT OF AMERICA, INC.—See Olivetti SpA; *Int'l*, pg. 1002
OLIVETTI MEXICANA S.A.—See Olivetti SpA; *Int'l*, pg. 1003
OLIVETTI NEDERLAND B.V.—See Olivetti SpA; *Int'l*, pg. 1003
OLIVETTI NORTH AMERICA—See Olivetti SpA; *Int'l*, pg. 1002
OLIVETTI PERIPHERAL EQUIPMENT—See Olivetti SpA; *Int'l*, pg. 1002
OLIVETTI PERUANA S.A.—See Olivetti SpA; *Int'l*, pg. 1003
OLIVETTI PORTUGUESA S.A.—See Olivetti SpA; *Int'l*, pg. 1003
OLIVETTI RESEARCH LTD.—See Olivetti SpA; *Int'l*, pg. 1003
OLIVETTI RICERCA—See Olivetti SpA; *Int'l*, pg. 1002
OLIVETTI SANAY VE TICARET A.S.—See Olivetti SpA; *Int'l*, pg. 1003
OLIVETTI (SCHWEIZ) AG—See Olivetti SpA; *Int'l*, pg. 1003
OLIVETTI SINGAPORE PTE. LTD.—See Olivetti SpA; *Int'l*, pg. 1003
OLIVETTI SPA; *Int'l*, pg. 1002
OLIVETTI (SUOMI) OY—See Olivetti SpA; *Int'l*, pg. 1003
OLIVETTI SUPPLIES, INC.—See Olivetti SpA; *Int'l*, pg. 1002
OLIVETTI SYNTHESIS—See Olivetti SpA; *Int'l*, pg. 1002
OLIVETTI SYSTEMS & NETWORKS—See Olivetti SpA; *Int'l*, pg. 1002
OLIVETTI U.K. LTD.—See Olivetti SpA; *Int'l*, pg. 1003
OLIVIERI FOODS—See Maple Leaf Foods Inc.; *Int'l*, pg. 841
OLIVINE INDUSTRIES (PRIVATE) LIMITED—See H.J. Heinz Company; *U.S. Public*, pg. 807
OLLIER JACQUOT BOIS ET MATERIAUX—See La Meridionale des Bois et Materiaux; *Int'l*, pg. 784
OLOKELE SUGAR CO., LIMITED—See Buyco, Inc.; *U.S. Private*, pg. 191
OLPIDURR S.P.A.—See Durr AG; *Int'l*, pg. 422
JOHN M. OLSON COMPANY; *U.S. Private*, pg. 815
OLSON RUG COMPANY; *U.S. Private*, pg. 815
OLSONITE CORPORATION; *U.S. Private*, pg. 815
OLSTEN CORPORATION; *U.S. Public*, pg. 1220
OLSTEN FINANCIAL SERVICES—See Olsten Corporation; *U.S. Public*, pg. 1221
OLSTEN HEALTH SERVICES—See Olsten Corporation; *U.S. Public*, pg. 1221
OLSTEN STAFFING SERVICES—See Olsten Corporation; *U.S. Public*, pg. 1221
OLSTEN TECHNICAL SERVICES—See Olsten Corporation; *U.S. Public*, pg. 1221
OLSY NORTH AMERICA INC.—See Olivetti SpA; *Int'l*, pg. 1002
OLTECO—See Olivetti SpA; *Int'l*, pg. 1002
OLTMANS CONSTRUCTION COMPANY; *U.S. Private*, pg. 815
OLYMPIA INTERNATIONAL—See Olympic Steel Inc.; *U.S. Public*, pg. 1221
OLYMPIA PARK HOTEL—See Sunstone Hotel Investors, Inc.; *U.S. Public*, pg. 1537
OLYMPIA & YORK DEVELOPMENTS LTD.; *Int'l*, pg. 1004
THE OLYMPIAN—See Gannett Company, Inc.; *U.S. Public*, pg. 701
OLYMPIC AIRTOURS—See Olympic Airways, S.A.; *Int'l*, pg. 1004
OLYMPIC AIRWAYS, S.A.; *Int'l*, pg. 1004
OLYMPIC AVIATION—See Olympic Airways, S.A.; *Int'l*, pg. 1004
OLYMPIC CATERING—See Olympic Airways, S.A.; *Int'l*, pg. 1004
OLYMPIC CONTINENTAL RESOURCES, LLC—See Olympic Steel Inc.; *U.S. Public*, pg. 1221
OLYMPIC INDUSTRIES, INC.—See Forest City Enterprises, Inc.; *U.S. Public*, pg. 670
OLYMPIC LASER PROCESSING, LLC—See Olympic Steel Inc.; *U.S. Public*, pg. 1221
OLYMPIC LASER PROCESSING, LLC—See USX Corporation; *U.S. Public*, pg. 1661
OLYMPIC MANUFACTURING CO.—See Caldwell Manufacturing Company; *U.S. Private*, pg. 200
OLYMPIC MILL SERVICES—See Tube City Inc.; *U.S. Private*, pg. 1108
OLYMPIC PIPE LINE CO.—See Texaco Inc.; *U.S. Public*, pg. 1584
OLYMPIC STEEL INC.; *U.S. Public*, pg. 1221
OLYMPUS AMERICA INC.—See Olympus Optical Co., Ltd.; *Int'l*, pg. 1005
OLYMPUS ASIAN PACIFIC LIMITED—See Olympus Optical Co., Ltd.; *Int'l*, pg. 1005
OLYMPUS ASSET MANAGEMENT LTD.—See Olympus Optical Co., Ltd.; *Int'l*, pg. 1005
OLYMPUS DIAGNOSTICA GMBH—See Olympus Optical Co., Ltd.; *Int'l*, pg. 1005

OLYMPUS HONG KONG LTD.—See Olympus Optical Co., Ltd.; *Int'l*, pg. 1005
OLYMPUS JAPAN CO., LTD.—See Olympus Optical Co., Ltd.; *Int'l*, pg. 1004
OLYMPUS OPTICAL CO. (EUROPA) GMBH—See Olympus Optical Co., Ltd.; *Int'l*, pg. 1004
OLYMPUS OPTICAL CO., LTD.; *Int'l*, pg. 1004
OLYMPUS OPTICAL CO. (U.K.) LTD.—See Olympus Optical Co., Ltd.; *Int'l*, pg. 1005
OLYMPUS OPTO-ELECTRONICS CO., LTD.—See Olympus Optical Co., Ltd.; *Int'l*, pg. 1004
OLYMPUS (SHENZHEN) INDUSTRIAL LTD.—See Olympus Optical Co., Ltd.; *Int'l*, pg. 1005
OLYMPUS SINGAPORE PTE LTD.—See Olympus Optical Co., Ltd.; *Int'l*, pg. 1005
OLYMPUS SYSTEMS CORPORATION—See Olympus Optical Co., Ltd.; *Int'l*, pg. 1004
OLYMPUS (U.K.) LTD.—See Olympus Optical Co., Ltd.; *Int'l*, pg. 1005
OLYMPUS WINTER & IBE GMBH—See Olympus Optical Co., Ltd.; *Int'l*, pg. 1005
OMAHA AUTO AUCTION LTD.—See Tyco International Ltd.; *U.S. Public*, pg. 1649
OMAHA DIV.—See Curt Bullock Builders, Inc.; *U.S. Private*, pg. 180
OMAHA PLANT-KELLOGG USA—See Kellogg Company; *U.S. Public*, pg. 947
OMAHA PROPERTY AND CASUALTY INSURANCE CO.—See Mutual of Omaha Insurance Company; *U.S. Private*, pg. 770
OMAHA PUBLIC POWER DISTRICT; *U.S. Private*, pg. 815
OMAHA STEAKS; *U.S. Private*, pg. 815
OMAHA STEAKS-RETAIL STORES—See Omaha Steaks; *U.S. Private*, pg. 816
OMAHA VACCINE COMPANY—See KHR; *U.S. Private*, pg. 603
O'MALIA FOOD MARKETS INC.; *U.S. Private*, pg. 816
OMAN INTERNATIONAL DEVELOPMENT CO. (LLC)—See Taylor Woodrow plc; *Int'l*, pg. 1359
OMAN ORIX LEASING SAOG—See Orix Corporation; *Int'l*, pg. 1009
OMARK PROPERTIES, INC.—See Blount International, Inc.; *U.S. Public*, pg. 239
OMEGA BANK, N.A.—See Omega Financial Corporation; *U.S. Public*, pg. 1222
OMEGA ELECTRONICS SA—See SMH Swiss Corporation for Micro Electronics & Watchmaking Indus. Ltd.; *Int'l*, pg. 1161
OMEGA ENGINEERING, INC.; *U.S. Private*, pg. 816
OMEGA ENVIRONMENTAL INC.; *U.S. Public*, pg. 1221
OMEGA ENVIRONMENTAL INC.—See Omega Environmental Inc.; *U.S. Public*, pg. 1222
OMEGA ENVIRONMENTAL SERVICES—See Omega Environmental Inc.; *U.S. Public*, pg. 1222
OMEGA FINANCIAL CORPORATION; *U.S. Public*, pg. 1222
OMEGA PERFORMANCE GROUP; *U.S. Private*, pg. 816
OMEGA PERFORMANCE GROUP—See Omega Performance Group; *U.S. Private*, pg. 816
OMEGA PLASTICS—See Alpha Industries; *U.S. Private*, pg. 45
OMEGA RESEARCH INC.; *U.S. Private*, pg. 1222
OMEGA SA—See SMH Swiss Corporation for Micro Electronics & Watchmaking Indus. Ltd.; *Int'l*, pg. 1160
OMEGA SOUFRE, S.A.—See Solvay S.A.; *Int'l*, pg. 1279
OMEGA II INSURANCE, LIMITED—See Smith International, Inc.; *U.S. Public*, pg. 1478
OMEGA VERMONGENSVERWALTUNGS GMBH—See Commerzbank AG; *Int'l*, pg. 310
OMEGA VISION 2000 S.A.—See The Macneal-Schwendler Corp.; *U.S. Public*, pg. 1032
OMEGA WORLD TRAVEL, INC.; *U.S. Private*, pg. 816
OMICRON PROPRIETARY LTD.—See W.R. Grace & Co.; *U.S. Public*, pg. 756
OMNI BUSINESS SYSTEMS, INC.—See Ikon Office Solutions, Inc.; *U.S. Public*, pg. 864
OMNI CAPITAL PARTNERS, INC.—See Motorola, Inc.; *U.S. Public*, pg. 13
OMNI-FLOW, INC.—See Abbott Laboratories; *U.S. Public*, pg. 13
OMNI HOTELS—See TRT Holdings Inc.; *U.S. Private*, pg. 1065
OMNI INDUSTRY—See Global Turnkey Systems Inc.; *U.S. Private*, pg. 458
OMNI PRODUCTS, INC.; *U.S. Private*, pg. 816
OMNI PRODUCTS, INC.—See OMNI Products, Inc.; *U.S. Private*, pg. 816
OMNI PUBLICATIONS INTERNATIONAL LTD.—See General Media International Inc.; *U.S. Private*, pg. 444
OMNI SUPERSTORES—See The Yucaipa Companies; *U.S. Private*, pg. 1202
OMNIA GRUNDSTUCKS GMBH—See Bayerische Vereinsbank Group; *Int'l*, pg. 180
OMNIA GRUNDSTUCKS GMBH & CO. BETRIEBS KG—See Bayerische Vereinsbank Group; *Int'l*, pg. 180
OMNIA MINERIOS LTDA.—See Reynolds Metals Company; *U.S. Public*, pg. 1387
OMNIBUS BB TRANSPORTES, S.A.—See General Motors Corporation; *U.S. Public*, pg. 723
OMNICARE, INC.; *U.S. Public*, pg. 1223
OMNICARE PHARMACY SERVICES—See Omnicare, Inc.; *U.S. Public*, pg. 1223
S.A. OMNICHEM N.V. BALEN PLANT—See Ajinomoto Company Inc.; *Int'l*, pg. 41
S.A. OMNICHEM N.V.—See Ajinomoto Company Inc.; *Int'l*, pg. 41
S.A. OMNICHEM N.V., WETTEREN PLANT—See Ajinomoto Company Inc.; *Int'l*, pg. 41
S.A. OMNICHEM N.V., LOUVAIN-LA-NEUVE PLANT—See Ajinomoto Company Inc.; *Int'l*, pg. 41
OMNICOM GROUP INC.; *U.S. Public*, pg. 1223
OMNIFIT LTD.—See Halma p.l.c.; *Int'l*, pg. 589
OMNIFLIGHT HELICOPTERS, INC.—See Omniflight, Inc.; *U.S. Private*, pg. 817

OMNIFLIGHT, INC.; *U.S. Private*, pg. 816
OMNIPLASTIC—See Lafarge S.A.; *Int'l*, pg. 789
OMNIQUIP INTERNATIONAL, INC.—See Harbour Group Ltd.; *U.S. Private*, pg. 500
OMNIREL CORPORATION—See Zing Technologies, Inc.; *U.S. Public*, pg. 1792
OMNISOURCE CORPORATION; *U.S. Private*, pg. 817
OMNITECHNIC GMBH—See Henkel KGaA; *Int'l*, pg. 610
OMNITEL-SISTEMI RADIOCELLAI ITALIANI SPA—See Bell Atlantic Corporation; *U.S. Public*, pg. 204
OMNITRACS DIVISION—See QUALCOMM; *U.S. Public*, pg. 1349
OMNITRADE EST.—See Enso Oyj; *Int'l*, pg. 458
OMNITRAX INC.—See Broe Companies; *U.S. Private*, pg. 171
OMNIUM DE GESTION DES VALEURS INDUSTRIELLES ET COMMERCIALES (OGIC)—See Compagnie des Machines Bull; *Int'l*, pg. 316
OMNIUM GESTION FINANCIERE (OGF)—See Lyonnaise des Eaux S.A.; *Int'l*, pg. 824
OMNIVER NV—See Almanij N.V.; *Int'l*, pg. 65
OMRON ADVANCED SYSTEMS, INC.—See Omron Corporation; *Int'l*, pg. 1005
OMRON AUTOMOTIVE ELECTRONICS INC.—See Omron Corporation; *Int'l*, pg. 1005
OMRON AUTOMOTIVE ELECTRONICS KOREA CO., LTD.—See Omron Corporation; *Int'l*, pg. 1005
OMRON BUSINESS SYSTEMS MALAYSIA SDN. BHD.—See Omron Corporation; *Int'l*, pg. 1005
OMRON (CHINA) CO., LTD.—See Omron Corporation; *Int'l*, pg. 1005
OMRON COMPONENTS ELETRO ELETRONICOS DA AMAZONIA LTDA.—See Omron Corporation; *Int'l*, pg. 1005
OMRON CORPORATION; *Int'l*, pg. 1005
OMRON (DALLAN) CO., LTD.—See Omron Corporation; *Int'l*, pg. 1005
OMRON DUALTEC AUTOMOTIVE ELECTRONICS, INC.—See Omron Corporation; *Int'l*, pg. 1005
OMRON ELECTRONICS A.B.—See Omron Corporation; *Int'l*, pg. 1005
OMRON ELECTRONICS A/S—See Omron Corporation; *Int'l*, pg. 1005
OMRON ELECTRONICS INC.—See Omron Corporation; *Int'l*, pg. 1005
OMRON ELECTRONICS, KFT—See Omron Corporation; *Int'l*, pg. 1006
OMRON ELECTRONICS LDA.—See Omron Corporation; *Int'l*, pg. 1006
OMRON ELECTRONICS LTD.—See Omron Corporation; *Int'l*, pg. 1006
OMRON ELECTRONICS O.Y.—See Omron Corporation; *Int'l*, pg. 1006
OMRON ELECTRONICS PTY. LTD.—See Omron Corporation; *Int'l*, pg. 1006
OMRON ELECTRONICS SALES AND SERVICE (M) SDN. BHD.—See Omron Corporation; *Int'l*, pg. 1006
OMRON ELECTRONICS SPOL SRO—See Omron Corporation; *Int'l*, pg. 1006
OMRON ELECTRONICS SP.Z.O.O—See Omron Corporation; *Int'l*, pg. 1006
OMRON EUROPE B.V.—See Omron Corporation; *Int'l*, pg. 1006
OMRON HEALTHCARE GMBH—See Omron Corporation; *Int'l*, pg. 1006
OMRON HEALTHCARE, INC.—See Omron Corporation; *Int'l*, pg. 1006
OMRON HEALTHCARE LTD.—See Omron Corporation; *Int'l*, pg. 1006
OMRON KOREA CO., LTD.—See Omron Corporation; *Int'l*, pg. 1006
OMRON MALAYSIA SDN. BHD.—See Omron Corporation; *Int'l*, pg. 1006
OMRON MANAGEMENT CENTER OF AMERICA, INC.—See Omron Corporation; *Int'l*, pg. 1005
OMRON MANUFACTURING OF AMERICA, INC.—See Omron Corporation; *Int'l*, pg. 1006
OMRON MANUFACTURING OF GERMANY G.M.B.H.—See Omron Corporation; *Int'l*, pg. 1006
PT OMRON MANUFACTURING OF INDONESIA—See Omron Corporation; *Int'l*, pg. 1006
OMRON MANUFACTURING OF THE NETHERLANDS B.V.—See Omron Corporation; *Int'l*, pg. 1006
OMRON MEDIZINTECHNIK HANDELSGESELLSCHAFT MBH—See Omron Corporation; *Int'l*, pg. 1006
OMRON OFFICE AUTOMATION PRODUCTS, INC.—See Omron Corporation; *Int'l*, pg. 1005
OMRON RETAIL SYSTEMS FRANCE S.A.R.L.—See Omron Corporation; *Int'l*, pg. 1006
OMRON (SHANGHAI) CO., LTD.—See Omron Corporation; *Int'l*, pg. 1006
OMRON SHANGHAI COMPUTER CORPORATION—See Omron Corporation; *Int'l*, pg. 1006
OMRON SYSTEMS DEUTSCHLAND G.M.B.H.—See Omron Corporation; *Int'l*, pg. 1006
OMRON SYSTEMS MANAGEMENT G.M.B.H.—See Omron Corporation; *Int'l*, pg. 1006
OMRON SYSTEMS U.K. LTD.—See Omron Corporation; *Int'l*, pg. 1006
OMRON TELFORD LTD.—See Omron Corporation; *Int'l*, pg. 1006
OMSCO INDUSTRIES—See Shaw Industries Ltd.; *Int'l*, pg. 1231
OMSCO INDUSTRIES LIMITED—See Shaw Industries Ltd.; *Int'l*, pg. 1231
OMSTEAD FOODS LIMITED—See H.J. Heinz Company; *U.S. Public*, pg. 806
OMYA, INC.—See Pluess-Staufer AG; *Int'l*, pg. 1061
ON COMMAND VIDEO—See Ascent Entertainment Group, Inc.; *U.S. Public*, pg. 138
ON-COR FROZEN FOODS INC.; *U.S. Private*, pg. 817
ON CUE, INC.—See Musicland Group Inc.; *U.S. Public*, pg. 1142

ON-GUARD MINI-STORAGE INC.—See Cambridge Shopping Centres Limited; *Int'l*, pg. 253
ON TECHNOLOGY CORPORATION; *U.S. Public*, pg. 1225
ON TRACK—See Advance Publications Inc.; *U.S. Private*, pg. 19
ONAN CORPORATION—See Cummins Engine Company, Inc.; *U.S. Public*, pg. 468
ONAN POWER ELECTRONICS—See Cummins Engine Company, Inc.; *U.S. Public*, pg. 468
ONBANCORP, INC.—See First Empire State Corporation; *U.S. Public*, pg. 631
ONBANK—See First Empire State Corporation; *U.S. Public*, pg. 632
ONBANK & TRUST CO.—See First Empire State Corporation; *U.S. Public*, pg. 632
ONCE—See Corporacion MAPFRE, Compania Internacional de Reaseguros, S.A.; *Int'l*, pg. 334
ONCOLOGY SYSTEMS—See Varian Associates, Inc.; *U.S. Public*, pg. 1710
ONCOMEMBRANE, INC.—See Otsuka Pharmaceutical Co., Ltd.; *Int'l*, pg. 1013
ONDAL-FRANCE S.A.R.L.—See Wella Group; *Int'l*, pg. 1490
ONDAWEL (G.B.) LTD.—See Wella Group; *Int'l*, pg. 1490
ONDELLE S.A (PTY.) LTD.—See Wella Group; *Int'l*, pg. 1490
ONDINE DIV.—See Interbath; *U.S. Private*, pg. 566
ONDULADORES DEL NORTE S.A.—See Chloride Group PLC; *Int'l*, pg. 287
154-TESTA—See Testa International; *Int'l*, pg. 1377
154 TESTA—See Testa International; *Int'l*, pg. 1377
100 GOLD STREET LIMITED PARTNERSHIP—See Cigna Corp.; *U.S. Public*, pg. 359
ONE INVESTMENT AGENCY, INC.—See The Somerset Group, Inc.; *U.S. Public*, pg. 1484
ONE INVESTMENT CORPORATION—See The Somerset Group, Inc.; *U.S. Public*, pg. 1484
ONE MORE TIME INC.—See Baker Commodities, Inc.; *U.S. Private*, pg. 111
ONE MORTGAGE CORPORATION—See The Somerset Group, Inc.; *U.S. Public*, pg. 1484
104.6 RTL—See Groupe Bruxelles Lambert S.A.; *Int'l*, pg. 561
ONE PRICE CLOTHING STORES, INC.; *U.S. Public*, pg. 1225
ONE PROPERTY CORPORATION—See The Somerset Group, Inc.; *U.S. Public*, pg. 1484
177229 CANADA INC.—See The Ivaco Group; *Int'l*, pg. 696
ONE STOP MORTGAGE, INC.—See Aames Financial Corporation; *U.S. Public*, pg. 12
ONE STOP SUPPLY, INC.—See Hughes Supply, Inc.; *U.S. Public*, pg. 847
121 S.W. SALMON ST. CORP.—See Enron Corp.; *U.S. Public*, pg. 585
O'NEAL STEEL INC.; *U.S. Private*, pg. 817
ONEIDA CANADA LTD.—See Oneida Ltd.; *U.S. Public*, pg. 1226
ONEIDA FOODSERVICE DIVISION—See Oneida Ltd.; *U.S. Public*, pg. 1226
ONEIDA LTD.; *U.S. Public*, pg. 1225
ONEIDA MEXICANA, S.A.—See Oneida Ltd.; *U.S. Public*, pg. 1226
ONEIDA ROSTONE CORPORATION—See Reunion Industries, Inc.; *U.S. Public*, pg. 1383
ONEIDA SILVERSMITHS DIV.—See Oneida Ltd.; *U.S. Public*, pg. 1226
ONEIDA SILVERSMITHS LIMITED—See Oneida Ltd.; *U.S. Public*, pg. 1226
ONEIDA SILVERSMITHS, U.K.—See Oneida Ltd.; *U.S. Public*, pg. 1226
O'NEIL DATA SYSTEMS, INC.—See William O'Neil & Co., Inc.; *U.S. Private*, pg. 817
O'NEIL INDUSTRIES INC.; *U.S. Private*, pg. 817
W.E. O'NEIL CONSTRUCTION COMPANY—See O'Neil Industries Inc.; *U.S. Private*, pg. 817
W.E. O'NEIL CONSTRUCTION COMPANY OF ARIZONA—See O'Neil Industries Inc.; *U.S. Private*, pg. 817
WILLIAM O'NEIL & CO., INC.; *U.S. Private*, pg. 817
ONENA BOLSAS DE PAPEL, S.A.—See Continental Can Co.; *U.S. Public*, pg. 440
ONEOK GAS MARKETING—See ONEOK Inc.; *U.S. Public*, pg. 1226
ONEOK INC.; *U.S. Public*, pg. 1226
ONEOK LEASING CO.—See ONEOK Inc.; *U.S. Public*, pg. 1226
ONEOK PARKING CO.—See ONEOK Inc.; *U.S. Public*, pg. 1226
ONEOK PRODUCTS CO.—See ONEOK Inc.; *U.S. Public*, pg. 1226
ONEOK RESOURCES CO.—See ONEOK Inc.; *U.S. Public*, pg. 1226
ONEOK TECHNOLOGY CO.—See ONEOK Inc.; *U.S. Public*, pg. 1226
ONEX CORPORATION; *Int'l*, pg. 1006
ONEXA, S.A. DE C.V.—See Alfa, S.A. de C.V.; *Int'l*, pg. 56
ONGA PTY. LTD.—See WICOR, Inc.; *U.S. Public*, pg. 1767
ONKYO CORP.—See Toshiba Corporation; *Int'l*, pg. 1403
ONLINE ADVANCED SYSTEMS CORP.—See Hewlett-Packard Company; *U.S. Public*, pg. 822
ONLY DEALS, INC.—See Universal International, Inc.; *U.S. Public*, pg. 1697
ONO PLANT—See Amada Co., Ltd.; *Int'l*, pg. 70
ONODA NORTHWEST, INC.—See Chichibu Onoda Cement Corporation; *Int'l*, pg. 284
ONODA SINGAPORE PTE. LTD.—See Chichibu Onoda Cement Corporation; *Int'l*, pg. 284
ONONDAGA LITHO SUPPLY CO., INC.—See PrimeSource Corporation; *U.S. Public*, pg. 1329
ONROEREND GOED EXPLOITATIE MIJ. LEPAKA B.V.—See Assicurazioni Generali S.p.A.; *Int'l*, pg. 91
ONSLOW WHOLESALE, INC.—See AVA; *U.S. Private*, pg. 8
ONTARIO FOODS, INC.—See Genesee Corporation; *U.S. Public*, pg. 728

ONTARIO HYDRO; *Int'l*, pg. 1007
ONTARIO KNIFE CO.—See Servotronics, Inc.; *U.S. Public*, pg. 1462
ONTARIO LIMITED—See Confederation Life Insurance Company; *Int'l*, pg. 326
THE ONTARIO PRODUCE CO.—See The Oshawa Group Limited; *Int'l*, pg. 1012
ONTRAK SYSTEMS, INC.—See Lam Research Corporation; *U.S. Public*, pg. 975
ONYX INTERACTIVE MULTIMEDIA LTD.—See Onyx Technologies Ltd.; *Int'l*, pg. 1007
ONYX LATINOAMERICA—See Hewlett-Packard Company; *U.S. Public*, pg. 822
ONYX TECHNOLOGIES LTD.; *Int'l*, pg. 1007
OOMPHIES, INC.; *U.S. Private*, pg. 817
OOTONE R&D CENTER—See Advantest Corporation; *Int'l*, pg. 25
OPAL CONCEPTS, INC.; *U.S. Private*, pg. 817
OPELA LTD.—See Delta plc; *Int'l*, pg. 391
OPEN MARKET, INC.; *U.S. Public*, pg. 1226
OPEN SYSTEMS CONSULTING—See Effective Management Systems; *U.S. Private*, pg. 566
OPENCONNECT SYSTEMS, INC.—See Cigna Corp.; *U.S. Public*, pg. 361
OPERATIONS & MAINTENANCE DIVISION—See Morrison Knudsen Corporation; *U.S. Public*, pg. 1134
OPERATIONS MANAGEMENT DIVISION—See Sterling Software; *U.S. Public*, pg. 1516
OPERATIONS MANAGEMENT INTERNATIONAL, INC.—See CH2M Hill Companies, Ltd.; *U.S. Private*, pg. 195
OPERATIONS UNLIMITED, INC.—See St. Joe Corp.; *U.S. Public*, pg. 1427
OPICOIL HOUSTON, INC.—See Chinese Petroleum Corporation; *Int'l*, pg. 286
OPINAC ENERGY CORPORATION—See Niagara Mohawk Power Corporation; *U.S. Public*, pg. 1181
OPINION-TRIBUNE—See Landmark Communications, Inc.; *U.S. Private*, pg. 648
OPISEC, S.A. DE C.V.—See Tablex, S.A. de C.V.; *Int'l*, pg. 1346
OPP MICOLAS MILLS INC.—See Johnston Industries, Inc.; *U.S. Public*, pg. 933
OPPENHEIMER CAPITAL—See Canadian Imperial Bank of Commerce; *Int'l*, pg. 257
OPPENHEIMER FUNDS, INC.—See Massachusetts Mutual Life Insurance Co.; *U.S. Private*, pg. 712
OPPENHEIMERFUNDS DISTRIBUTOR, INC.; *U.S. Private*, pg. 818
OPTECH RESEARCH & ENGINEERING—See Quebecor Inc.; *Int'l*, pg. 1075
OPTECH S.A.R.L.—See Olympus Optical Co., Ltd.; *Int'l*, pg. 1005
OPTEK TECHNOLOGY, INC.; *U.S. Public*, pg. 1227
OPTIC GRAPHICS, INC.; *U.S. Private*, pg. 818
OPTIC POINT WARENHANDELS GESELLSCHAFT MBH—See Karstadt Aktiengesellschaft; *Int'l*, pg. 724
OPTICAL COATING LABORATORY EURL—See Optical Coating Laboratory, Inc.; *U.S. Public*, pg. 1227
OPTICAL COATING LABORATORY, INC.; *U.S. Public*, pg. 1227
THE OPTICAL CORPORATION—See Excel Technology, Inc.; *U.S. Public*, pg. 599
OPTICAL FIBRES—See Corning Incorporated; *U.S. Public*, pg. 449
OPTICAL NETWORKS PTY. LTD.—See Sumitomo Electric Industries, Ltd.; *Int'l*, pg. 1313
OPTICAL RADIATION CORPORATION—See BEC Group, Inc.; *U.S. Public*, pg. 160
OPTICAL WAVEGUIDES AUSTRALIA PTY,. LIMITED—See Corning Incorporated; *U.S. Public*, pg. 449
OPTICOS S.R.L.; *Int'l*, pg. 1007
OPTIGAL S.A.—See Migros; *Int'l*, pg. 866
OPTIGRAPHICS INC.—See Pinnacle Brands, Inc.; *U.S. Private*, pg. 866
OPTIM ELECTRONICS CORPORATION—See Bowthorpe plc; *Int'l*, pg. 208
OPTIMA DIRECT, INC.—See Omnicom Group Inc.; *U.S. Public*, pg. 1224
OPTIMA INDUSTRIAL S.A. DE C.V.—See Bausch & Lomb Incorporated; *U.S. Public*, pg. 196
OPTIMA SCHNEID UND LOSUNGSMITTEL GESELLSCHAFT MBH—See Fuchs Petrolub AG Oel + Chemie; *Int'l*, pg. 517
OPTIMAGE INTERACTIVE SERVICES CO.—See Philips Electronics N.V.; *Int'l*, pg. 1054
OPTIMAIL/DIRECKTWERBESERVICE GMBH—See The Reader's Digest Association, Inc.; *U.S. Public*, pg. 1368
OPTIMALGRUND BAUTRAGERGESELLSCHAFT MBH—See Dyckerhoff & Widmann AG; *Int'l*, pg. 423
OPTIMAXX INTERNATIONAL; *U.S. Private*, pg. 818
OPTIMEL SCHMELZGUSSTECHNIK GMBH & CO. KG—See Henkel KGaA; *Int'l*, pg. 610
OPTIMIX AS—See Scancem AB; *Int'l*, pg. 1200
OPTIMIZACION ADD—See Young & Rubicam Inc.; *U.S. Private*, pg. 1788
OPTIMOL OELWERKE GMBH—See Burmah Castrol plc; *Int'l*, pg. 236
THE OPTIMUM FINANCIAL CORPORATION LTD.—See EdperBrascan Corporation; *Int'l*, pg. 435
OPTIMUM—See Cossette Communication Marketing; *Int'l*, pg. 336
OPTIMUM PUBLIC RELATIONS (U.S.) INC.—See Cossette Communication Marketing; *Int'l*, pg. 336
OPTIMUM PUBLIC RELATIONS (VANCOUVER) INC.—See Cossette Communication Marketing; *Int'l*, pg. 336
OPTIO GVG MBH & CO. OBJEKT HANNOVER HANOMAGSTR. KG—See Commerzbank AG; *Int'l*, pg. 310
OPTION ONE—See Martin/Williams Advertising Inc.; *U.S. Private*, pg. 710
OPTIONS AND CHOICES, INC.—See UNUM Corporation; *U.S. Public*, pg. 1699
OPTIONS CLEARING CORP.—See The American Stock Exchange; *U.S. Private*, pg. 62

OPTIPAK SYSTEMS—See Royal Packaging Industries Van Leer B.V.; *Int'l*, pg. 1146
OPTIROC AB—See Scancem AB; *Int'l*, pg. 1200
OPTIROC AS—See Scancem AB; *Int'l*, pg. 1200
OPTIROC A.S.—See Scancem AB; *Int'l*, pg. 1200
OPTIROC ESTI AS—See Scancem AB; *Int'l*, pg. 1200
OPTIROC GROUP AB—See Scancem AB; *Int'l*, pg. 1200
OPTIROC GROUP SP.Z.O.O.—See Scancem AB; *Int'l*, pg. 1200
OPTIROC LTD.—See Scancem AB; *Int'l*, pg. 1200
OPTIROC OY AB—See Scancem AB; *Int'l*, pg. 1200
OPTISCHE WERKE G. RODENSTOCK; *Int'l*, pg. 1007
OPTIX AUSTRALIA LIMITED—See Sumitomo Electric Industries, Ltd.; *Int'l*, pg. 1313
OPTOELECTRONIC PRODUCTS DIVISION—See Methode Electronics Inc.; *U.S. Public*, pg. 1101
OPTON FEINTECHNIK GMBH—See Carl-Zeiss-Stiftung; *Int'l*, pg. 1523
OPTREX CORPORATION—See Asahi Glass Co., Ltd.; *Int'l*, pg. 84
OPTREX GLASS—See Asahi Glass Co., Ltd.; *Int'l*, pg. 84
OPTREX GLASS—See Mitsubishi Electric Corporation; *Int'l*, pg. 872
OPTRON INC.—See Canon Inc.; *Int'l*, pg. 261
OPTUS COMMUNICATIONS—See BellSouth Corporation; *U.S. Public*, pg. 209
OPUS CORP.; *U.S. Private*, pg. 818
OPUS SOUTH CONSTRUCTION CORPORATION—See Opus South Corporation; *U.S. Private*, pg. 818
OPUS SOUTH CORPORATION; *U.S. Private*, pg. 818
ORA-TECH SYSTEMS (PVT.) LTD.—See Oracle Corporation; *U.S. Public*, pg. 1228
ORACLE BELGIUM NV—See Oracle Corporation; *U.S. Public*, pg. 1228
ORACLE CORPORATION; *U.S. Public*, pg. 1227
ORACLE CORPORATION CANADA—See Oracle Corporation; *U.S. Public*, pg. 1228
ORACLE TAIWAN INC.—See Oracle Corporation; *U.S. Public*, pg. 1228
ORAG OSTERREICHISCHE REALITATEN AG—See Creditanstalt-Bankverein; *Int'l*, pg. 347
ORAL-B LABORATORIES—See The Gillette Company; *U.S. Public*, pg. 743
ORAL-B LABORATORIES GMBH—See The Gillette Company; *U.S. Public*, pg. 745
ORAL-B LABORATORIES, INC.—See The Gillette Company; *U.S. Public*, pg. 743
ORAL-B LABORATORIES INC.—See The Gillette Company; *U.S. Public*, pg. 745
ORAL-B LABORATORIES LIMITED—See The Gillette Company; *U.S. Public*, pg. 745
ORAL-B LABORATORIES PTY. LIMITED—See The Gillette Company; *U.S. Public*, pg. 745
ORAL-B LABORATORIES S.A. DE C.V.—See The Gillette Company; *U.S. Public*, pg. 745
ORANGE AND ROCKLAND UTILITIES, INC.; *U.S. Public*, pg. 1229
ORANGE-CO., INC.; *U.S. Public*, pg. 1229
ORANGE COUNTY CELLULAR TELEPHONE CORP.—See Vanguard Cellular Systems, Inc.; *U.S. Public*, pg. 1708
ORANGE COUNTY METAL WORKS—See Commercial Intertech Corp.; *U.S. Public*, pg. 411
THE ORANGE COUNTY REGISTER—See Freedom Communication Inc.; *U.S. Private*, pg. 425
ORANGE GROVE CO-OPERATIVE; *U.S. Private*, pg. 818
ORANGE HILL RESTAURANT CORP.—See Specialty Restaurants Corporation; *U.S. Private*, pg. 1022
ORANGE INFO 'PRODUCTS—See N.V. Koninklijke KNP BT; *Int'l*, pg. 757
ORANGE JULIUS CANADA, LTD.—See Berkshire Hathaway Inc.; *U.S. Public*, pg. 221
ORANGE JULIUS OF AMERICA—See Berkshire Hathaway Inc.; *U.S. Public*, pg. 220
ORANGE MOTOR COMPANY INC.; *U.S. Private*, pg. 818
ORANGEBURG INDUSTRIAL SUPPLY—See Associated Industrial Supply, Inc.; *U.S. Private*, pg. 91
ORANGEBURG TRUCKING, INC.—See Stone Container Corporation; *U.S. Public*, pg. 1521
ORANGINA FRANCE—See Groupe Pernod Ricard; *Int'l*, pg. 566
ORANGINA INTERNATIONAL—See Groupe Pernod Ricard; *Int'l*, pg. 567
ORASCOM—See Hewlett-Packard Company; *U.S. Public*, pg. 822
ORBEA ARGENTINA SOCIEDAD ANONIMA—See Imperial Chemical Industries PLC; *Int'l*, pg. 665
ORBEA 9 DE JULIO S.A.I.C.—See Imperial Chemical Industries PLC; *Int'l*, pg. 665
ORBEL CORPORATION; *U.S. Private*, pg. 819
ORBEX INC.—See Blount International, Inc.; *U.S. Public*, pg. 238
ORBIS INSURANCE AGENCIES LIMITED—See Cigna Corp.; *U.S. Public*, pg. 363
ORBIT SEMICONDUCTOR, INC.; *U.S. Private*, pg. 819
ORBIT VALVE INTERNATIONAL, INC.; *U.S. Private*, pg. 819
ORBITAL PARK LIMITED—See The Eurotunnel Group; *Int'l*, pg. 466
ORBITAL SCIENCES CORPORATION; *U.S. Public*, pg. 1229
ORBOTECH INC.—See Orbotech Ltd.; *Int'l*, pg. 1007
ORBOTECH LTD.; *Int'l*, pg. 1007
ORBOTECH PACIFIC LTD.—See Orbotech Ltd.; *Int'l*, pg. 1007
ORBOTECH S.A. EUROPE—See Orbotech Ltd.; *Int'l*, pg. 1007
ORCA BANK LTD.—See Union Bank of Switzerland; *Int'l*, pg. 1440
ORCAD INC.; *U.S. Public*, pg. 1230
ORCHARD FARM TELEPHONE COMPANY—See Telephone and Data Systems, Inc.; *U.S. Public*, pg. 1571
ORCHARD GLEN VENTURE—See Cigna Corp.; *U.S. Public*, pg. 361

ORCHARD PARADE HOLDINGS LIMITED; *Int'l*, pg. 1007
ORCHARD SUPPLY HARDWARE—See Sears, Roebuck and Co.; *U.S. Public*, pg. 1452
ORCHARD YARN & THREAD CO., INC.—See Lion Brand Yarn Co.; *U.S. Private*, pg. 669
ORCHEM (PTY) LTD. (PLANT)—See Crompton & Knowles Corporation; *U.S. Public*, pg. 460
THE ORCHID CENTER—See Sun Bulb Company, Inc.; *U.S. Private*, pg. 1050
ORCHIDIS S.A.—See Veba AG; *Int'l*, pg. 1461
ORCHIDS ETC.—See Yamanouchi Pharmaceutical Co. Ltd.; *Int'l*, pg. 1518
ORCHIDS PAPER PRODUCTS CO.; *U.S. Private*, pg. 819
ORCO BLOCK COMPANY; *U.S. Private*, pg. 819
ORD MINNETT GROUP—See Westpac Banking Corporation; *Int'l*, pg. 1496
ORD MINNETT GROUP LIMITED—See Westpac Banking Corporation; *Int'l*, pg. 1496
ORD O'CONNOR GRIEVE LIMITED—See Westpac Banking Corporation; *Int'l*, pg. 1497
ORDERS DISTRIBUTING CO.; *U.S. Private*, pg. 819
ORDO—See Haworth, Inc.; *U.S. Private*, pg. 512
THE ORE & CHEMICAL CORP.—See Metallgesellschaft AG; *Int'l*, pg. 862
ORE-IDA FOODS, INC.—See H.J. Heinz Company; *U.S. Public*, pg. 805
OREBRO KARTONGBRUCK AB—See Lafarge S.A.; *Int'l*, pg. 791
ORECK CORPORATION; *U.S. Private*, pg. 819
ORECK MANUFACTURING COMPANY—See Oreck Corporation; *U.S. Private*, pg. 819
OREG—See Danfoss A/S; *Int'l*, pg. 378
OREG DRAYTON ENERGIETECHNIK GMBH—See Siebe plc; *Int'l*, pg. 1242
OREG ONDAL REGELTECHNIK GMBH—See Wella Group; *Int'l*, pg. 1489
OREGON AUTOMOBILE INSURANCE COMPANY—See General Accident Fire and Life Assurance Corporation p.l.c.; *Int'l*, pg. 543
OREGON COAST FOODS—See Tillamook County Creamery Assn.; *U.S. Private*, pg. 1086
OREGON CULVERT CO., INC.—See Pitt-Des Moines, Inc.; *U.S. Public*, pg. 1305
OREGON FREEZE DRY, INC.; *U.S. Private*, pg. 819
OREGON METALLURGICAL CORPORATION—See Allegheny Teledyne Incorporated; *U.S. Public*, pg. 43
OREGON NATURAL GAS DEVELOPMENT CORP.—See Northwest Natural Gas Company; *U.S. Public*, pg. 1200
OREGON STEEL MILLS INC.; *U.S. Public*, pg. 1230
O'REILLY AUTOMOTIVE INC.; *U.S. Public*, pg. 1230
O'REILLY AVIATION—See O'Reilly Automotive Inc.; *U.S. Public*, pg. 1230
OREMCO INC.—See Koninklijke Hoogovens N.V.; *Int'l*, pg. 754
ORENDA AEROSPACE CORPORATION—See Magellan Aerospace Corporation; *Int'l*, pg. 829
ORENDA (CANADA)—See Hawker Siddeley Canada Inc.; *Int'l*, pg. 604
ORENT GRAPHICARTS, INC.—See Devon Group, Inc.; *U.S. Public*, pg. 503
OREO CORPORATION—See Keycorp; *U.S. Public*, pg. 955
ORESUNDSVARVET AB—See Celsius AB; *Int'l*, pg. 277
ORGA CARD SYSTEMS INC.—See Preussag AG; *Int'l*, pg. 1070
ORGA-SOFT ORGANISATION & SOFTWARE GMBH—See Compagnie des Machines Bull; *Int'l*, pg. 317
ORGANCHEMIE GES.M.B.H.—See BASF AG; *Int'l*, pg. 109
ORGANIC ONLINE—See Omnicom Group Inc.; *U.S. Public*, pg. 1224
ORGANISATION DE VENTE DES PRODUITS FASSON S.A.R.L.—See Avery Dennison Corporation; *U.S. Public*, pg. 154
ORGANIZACION ROBERTS S.A. DE C.V.—See Hartmarx Corporation; *U.S. Public*, pg. 796
ORGANIZACION SORIANA S.A. DE C.V.; *Int'l*, pg. 1008
ORGANIZATIONAL DYNAMICS INC.; *U.S. Private*, pg. 819
ORGANO SILICONES GROUP—See Witco Corporation; *U.S. Public*, pg. 1774
ORGANON ARGENTINA S.A.—See Akzo Nobel N.V.; *Int'l*, pg. 45
ORGANON (BANGLADESH) LTD.—See Akzo Nobel N.V.; *Int'l*, pg. 45
ORGANON BELGIE NV—See Akzo Nobel N.V.; *Int'l*, pg. 45
ORGANON CANADA LTD.—See Akzo Nobel N.V.; *Int'l*, pg. 45
LAB. ORGANON DO BRAZIL LTDA.—See Akzo Nobel N.V.; *Int'l*, pg. 45
ORGANON ESPANOLA SA—See Akzo Nobel N.V.; *Int'l*, pg. 45
ORGANON GMBH—See Akzo Nobel N.V.; *Int'l*, pg. 45
ORGANON INC.—See Akzo Nobel N.V.; *Int'l*, pg. 48
P.T. ORGANON INDONESIA—See Akzo Nobel N.V.; *Int'l*, pg. 45
ORGANON INTERNATIONAL B.V.—See Akzo Nobel N.V.; *Int'l*, pg. 44
ORGANON IRELAND LTD.—See Akzo Nobel N.V.; *Int'l*, pg. 45
ORGANON LABORATORIES LTD.—See Akzo Nobel N.V.; *Int'l*, pg. 45
ORGANON MEXICANA SA—See Akzo Nobel N.V.; *Int'l*, pg. 45
ORGANON NEDERLAND B.V.—See Akzo Nobel N.V.; *Int'l*, pg. 44
ORGANON PAKISTAN (PRIVATE) LIMITED—See Akzo Nobel N.V.; *Int'l*, pg. 45
ORGANON SA—See Akzo Nobel N.V.; *Int'l*, pg. 45
ORGANON TEKNIKA BV—See Akzo Nobel N.V.; *Int'l*, pg. 44
ORGANON TEKNIKA CORP.—See Akzo Nobel N.V.; *Int'l*, pg. 46
ORGANON TEKNIKA IRELAND LTD.—See Akzo Nobel N.V.; *Int'l*, pg. 45
ORGANON TEKNIKA MEDIZINSCHE PRODUKTE GMBH—See Akzo Nobel N.V.; *Int'l*, pg. 45

ORGANON TEKNIKA NEDERLAND BV—See Akzo Nobel N.V.; *Int'l*, pg. 44
ORGANON TEKNIKA NV—See Akzo Nobel N.V.; *Int'l*, pg. 45
ORGANON VENEZOLANA SA—See Akzo Nobel N.V.; *Int'l*, pg. 45
ORGILL INC.; *U.S. Private*, pg. 819
ORGULF TRANSPORT CO.—See Eastern Enterprises; *U.S. Public*, pg. 549
ORICOM; *Int'l*, pg. 1008
ORIEL INSTRUMENTS CORPORATION; *U.S. Private*, pg. 819
ORIENT-EXPRESS HOTELS INC.—See Sea Containers Ltd.; *Int'l*, pg. 1213
ORIENT LEAF TOBACCO CO., LTD.—See Universal Corporation; *U.S. Public*, pg. 1695
ORIENT LONGMAN LTD.—See Pearson plc; *Int'l*, pg. 1026
ORIENT MINING COMPANY—See Boise Cascade Corporation; *U.S. Public*, pg. 243
THE ORIENTAL HOTEL (THAILAND) PCL—See Jardine Matheson Holdings Limited; *Int'l*, pg. 704
ORIENTAL MOTOR CO., LTD.; *Int'l*, pg. 1008
ORIENTAL MOTOR U.S.A. CORP.—See Oriental Motor Co., Ltd.; *Int'l*, pg. 1008
ORIENTAL PROCESSORS & EXPORTERS OF KOREA, LTD.—See Universal Corporation; *U.S. Public*, pg. 1695
ORIENTAL TELECOMMUNICATION COMPANY LTD.—See Telefonaktiebolaget LM Ericsson; *Int'l*, pg. 1369
ORIENTED STRANDBOARD PLANT—See Georgia-Pacific Corporation; *U.S. Public*, pg. 737
ORIENTO INDUSTRIA E COMMERCIO—See Lafarge S.A.; *Int'l*, pg. 790
ORIGIN SYSTEMS, INC.—See Electronic Arts; *U.S. Public*, pg. 569
THE ORIGINAL CHILI BOWL, INC.—See Windsor Quality Food Co.; *U.S. Private*, pg. 1182
ORIOLE ENTERPRISES, INC.—See Oriole Homes Corp.; *U.S. Public*, pg. 1230
ORIOLE GOLF & TENNIS CLUB, INC.—See Oriole Homes Corp.; *U.S. Public*, pg. 1231
ORIOLE HOMES CORP.; *U.S. Public*, pg. 1230
ORIOLE HOMES CORP. OF MARYLAND—See Oriole Homes Corp.; *U.S. Public*, pg. 1231
ORIOLE INTERNATIONAL—See Oriole Homes Corp.; *U.S. Public*, pg. 1231
THE ORIOLES, INC.; *U.S. Private*, pg. 819
ORION CAPITAL COMPANIES, INC.—See Orion Capital Corporation; *U.S. Public*, pg. 1231
ORION CAPITAL CORPORATION; *U.S. Public*, pg. 1231
ORION EXPRESS, INC.—See Mark VII, Inc.; *U.S. Public*, pg. 1046
ORION INTL. SALES, INC.—See Thermo Electron Corporation; *U.S. Public*, pg. 1592
ORION NETWORK SYSTEMS INCORPORATED—See British Aerospace p.l.c.; *Int'l*, pg. 218
ORION PROPERTIES CORP.—See Orion Capital Corporation; *U.S. Public*, pg. 1231
ORION RESEARCH FAR EAST INC.—See Thermo Electron Corporation; *U.S. Public*, pg. 1592
ORION RESEARCH INC.—See Thermo Electron Corporation; *U.S. Public*, pg. 1592
ORION RESEARCH PUERTO RICO, INC.—See Thermo Electron Corporation; *U.S. Public*, pg. 1592
ORION SPA.—See Unican Security Systems Ltd.; *Int'l*, pg. 1432
ORIOR HOLDING S.A.; *Int'l*, pg. 1008
ORIX AIRCRAFT CORPORATION—See Orix Corporation; *Int'l*, pg. 1008
ORIX ALPHA CORPORATION—See Orix Corporation; *Int'l*, pg. 1008
ORIX ASIA LIMITED—See Orix Corporation; *Int'l*, pg. 1009
ORIX AUSTRALIA CORPORATION LIMITED—See Orix Corporation; *Int'l*, pg. 1008
ORIX AUTO FINANCE (INDIA) LIMITED—See Orix Corporation; *Int'l*, pg. 1009
ORIX AUTO LEASING ASIA LIMITED—See Orix Corporation; *Int'l*, pg. 1008
ORIX AUTO LEASING CORPORATION—See Orix Corporation; *Int'l*, pg. 1008
ORIX AVIATION SYSTEMS LIMITED—See Orix Corporation; *Int'l*, pg. 1008
ORIX BASEBALL CLUB—See Orix Corporation; *Int'l*, pg. 1008
ORIX CAPITAL CORPORATION—See Orix Corporation; *Int'l*, pg. 1009
ORIX CAR RENTALS PTE LTD.—See Orix Corporation; *Int'l*, pg. 1009
ORIX CAR RENTALS SDN. BHD.—See Orix Corporation; *Int'l*, pg. 1009
ORIX CLUB CORPORATION—See Orix Corporation; *Int'l*, pg. 1009
ORIX COMMERCIAL ALLIANCE CORPORATION—See Orix Corporation; *Int'l*, pg. 1009
ORIX COMMODITIES CORPORATION—See Orix Corporation; *Int'l*, pg. 1009
ORIX COMMODITIES SINGAPORE PTE LIMITED—See Orix Corporation; *Int'l*, pg. 1009
ORIX COMPUTER SYSTEMS CORPORATION—See Orix Corporation; *Int'l*, pg. 1008
ORIX CORPORATE FINANCE LIMITED—See Orix Corporation; *Int'l*, pg. 1009
ORIX CORPORATION; *Int'l*, pg. 1008
ORIX CREDIT CORPORATION—See Orix Corporation; *Int'l*, pg. 1008
ORIX ESTATE CORPORATION—See Orix Corporation; *Int'l*, pg. 1008
ORIX EUROPE LIMITED—See Orix Corporation; *Int'l*, pg. 1009
ORIX EUROPE LIMITED-PARIS LIAISON OFFICE—See Orix Corporation; *Int'l*, pg. 1009
ORIX HOTELS INTERNATIONAL PRIVATE LIMITED—See Orix Corporation; *Int'l*, pg. 1009
P.T. ORIX INDONESIA FINANCE—See Orix Corporation; *Int'l*, pg. 1009

ORIX INSURANCE SERVICES CORPORATION—See Orix Corporation; *Int'l*, pg. 1008
ORIX INTERIOR CORPORATION—See Orix Corporation; *Int'l*, pg. 1008
ORIX INVESTMENT AND MANAGEMENT PRIVATE LIMITED—See Orix Corporation; *Int'l*, pg. 1009
ORIX IRELAND LIMITED—See Orix Corporation; *Int'l*, pg. 1009
ORIX LEASING PAKISTAN LIMITED—See Orix Corporation; *Int'l*, pg. 1010
ORIX LEASING SINGAPORE LIMITED—See Orix Corporation; *Int'l*, pg. 1010
ORIX LIFE INSURANCE CORPORATION—See Orix Corporation; *Int'l*, pg. 1009
ORIX MARITIME CORPORATION—See Orix Corporation; *Int'l*, pg. 1009
ORIX NEW ZEALAND (NZ) LIMITED—See Orix Corporation; *Int'l*, pg. 1010
ORIX POLSKA S.A.—See Orix Corporation; *Int'l*, pg. 1010
ORIX REAL ESTATE EQUITIES, INC.—See Orix Corporation; *Int'l*, pg. 1009
ORIX RENT-A-CAR—See Orix Corporation; *Int'l*, pg. 1009
ORIX RENTEC CORPORATION—See Orix Corporation; *Int'l*, pg. 1009
ORIX RENTEC (MALAYSIA) SDN. BHD.—See Orix Corporation; *Int'l*, pg. 1010
ORIX RENTEC (SINGAPORE) PTE. LIMITED—See Orix Corporation; *Int'l*, pg. 1010
ORIX SECURITIES CO., LTD.—See Orix Corporation; *Int'l*, pg. 1009
ORIX TAIWAN CORPORATION—See Orix Corporation; *Int'l*, pg. 1010
ORIX USA CORPORATION-LOS ANGELES—See Orix Corporation; *Int'l*, pg. 1009
ORIX USA CORPORATION-NEW YORK—See Orix Corporation; *Int'l*, pg. 1009
ORIX USA CORPORATION-SAN FRANCISCO—See Orix Corporation; *Int'l*, pg. 1009
ORKIN EXTERMINATING CO., INC.—See Rollins, Inc.; *U.S. Public*, pg. 1404
ORKIN LAWN CARE—See Rollins, Inc.; *U.S. Public*, pg. 1405
ORKIN PLANTSCAPING—See Rollins, Inc.; *U.S. Public*, pg. 1405
ORKLA A.S.A.; *Int'l*, pg. 1010
K/S ORKLA EXOLON A/S & CO.—See Exolon-Esk Company; *U.S. Public*, pg. 600
ORKLA FINANS A.S—See Orkla A.S.A.; *Int'l*, pg. 1011
ORKLA FOODS AS—See Orkla A.S.A.; *Int'l*, pg. 1011
ORKLA MEDIA A.S—See Orkla A.S.A.; *Int'l*, pg. 1011
ORLANDI INC.—See Jefferson Smurfit Group p.l.c.; *Int'l*, pg. 1269
ORLANDO PAVING COMPANY—See Hubbard Construction Co.; *U.S. Private*, pg. 544
ORLANDO SENTINEL COMMUNICATIONS—See Tribune Company; *U.S. Public*, pg. 1636
ORLANDO WYNDHAM—See Groupe Pernod Ricard; *Int'l*, pg. 567
ORLANE; *Int'l*, pg. 1011
ORLANE INSTITUT DE BEAUTE—See Orlane; *Int'l*, pg. 1011
ORLEANS CORPORATION—See FPA Corporation; *U.S. Public*, pg. 608
ORLEANS FOOD CO.—See Borden, Inc.; *U.S. Private*, pg. 158
ORLEANS INTERNATIONAL, INC.; *U.S. Private*, pg. 820
ORLEANS LEASING CORPORATION—See CCI/Triad Corporation; *U.S. Private*, pg. 193
ORLEANS MATERIALS & EQUIPMENT CO., INC.; *U.S. Private*, pg. 820
ORLEY MEYER—See The Manitowoc Company, Inc.; *U.S. Public*, pg. 1041
ORLY AIR TRAITEUR—See Groupe Air France; *Int'l*, pg. 560
ORMANDY & STOLLERY ELECTRONIC COMPONENTS LIMITED—See Morgan Crucible Co. Plc; *Int'l*, pg. 892
ORMET CORPORATION; *U.S. Private*, pg. 820
ORMET PRIMARY ALUMINUM CORP—See Ormet Corporation; *U.S. Private*, pg. 820
ORNSKOLDSVIKS MEKANISKA VERKSTAD (OMV)—See British Steel Plc; *Int'l*, pg. 221
ORO GRANDE, INC.—See Forest City Enterprises, Inc.; *U.S. Public*, pg. 669
OROAMERICA, INC.; *U.S. Public*, pg. 1232
THE ORR FELT COMPANY; *U.S. Private*, pg. 820
ROBERT ORR-SYSCO FOOD SERVICES CO.—See Sysco Corporation; *U.S. Public*, pg. 1551
ORR SAFETY COMPANY; *U.S. Private*, pg. 820
ORR-SCHELEN-MAYERON & ASSOC., INC.—See Publicker Industries Inc.; *U.S. Public*, pg. 1341
ORSAN—See Lafarge S.A.; *Int'l*, pg. 791
ORSAN CORP.—See Lafarge S.A.; *Int'l*, pg. 791
ORSEM—See Lafarge S.A.; *Int'l*, pg. 790
ORSIM, S.A.—See Pfizer Inc.; *U.S. Public*, pg. 1284
ORTADOGU-KVK—See Dainippon Ink & Chemicals, Inc.; *Int'l*, pg. 371
ORTEL CORPORATION; *U.S. Public*, pg. 1232
PH. ORTH CO.—See CSM N.V.; *Int'l*, pg. 244
ORTHO BIOTECH INC.—See Johnson & Johnson; *U.S. Public*, pg. 929
ORTHO CLINICAL DIAGNOSTIC N.V.—See Johnson & Johnson; *U.S. Public*, pg. 931
ORTHO CLINICAL DIAGNOSTIC S.A.—See Johnson & Johnson; *U.S. Public*, pg. 931
ORTHO CLINICAL DIAGNOSTIC SYSTEMS INC.—See Johnson & Johnson; *U.S. Public*, pg. 929
ORTHO CLINICAL DIAGNOSTIC SYSTEMS K.K.—See Johnson & Johnson; *U.S. Public*, pg. 931
ORTHO CLINICAL DIAGNOSTIC SYSTEMS LIMITED—See Johnson & Johnson; *U.S. Public*, pg. 931
ORTHO CLINICAL DIAGNOSTIC SYSTEMS S.P.A.—See Johnson & Johnson; *U.S. Public*, pg. 931
ORTHO DIAGNOSTIC SYSTEMS G.M.B.H.—See Johnson & Johnson; *U.S. Public*, pg. 932

ORTHO-KINETICS, INC.; *U.S. Private*, pg. 820
ORTHOFIX INC.—See Orthofix International N.V.; *Int'l*, pg. 1011
ORTHOFIX INTERNATIONAL N.V.; *Int'l*, pg. 1011
ORTHOLOGIC CORPORATION; *U.S. Public*, pg. 1232
ORTHO-MCNEIL PHARMACEUTICAL CORPORATION—See Johnson & Johnson; *U.S. Public*, pg. 929
ORTHOPAEDIC REHABILITATION CENTER OF ATLANTA—See Vencor, Inc.; *U.S. Public*, pg. 1715
ORTHOPLANT GMBH—See Bristol-Myers Squibb Company; *U.S. Public*, pg. 256
ORTMAN FLUID POWER DIVISION—See Coltec Holdings Inc; *U.S. Public*, pg. 402
ORTMANN & HERBST GMBH—See Siebe plc; *Int'l*, pg. 1240
ORTRONICS, INC.—See LeGrand S.A.; *Int'l*, pg. 806
ORVAC SPA—See PAXAR Corporation; *U.S. Public*, pg. 1266
ORVAL KENT FOOD CO.; *U.S. Private*, pg. 820
THE ORVIS COMPANY, INC.; *U.S. Private*, pg. 820
ORWELL PLANT—See Stoneridge, Inc.; *U.S. Private*, pg. 1044
O'RYAN BOOKS—See Advance Publications Inc.; *U.S. Private*, pg. 21
ORYX ENERGY; *U.S. Public*, pg. 1232
OSAKA AGENCY OF NIPPON LIFE INSURANCE CO., LTD.—See Nippon Life Insurance Co.; *Int'l*, pg. 935
OSAKA BEVERAGE BOTTLING CO., LTD.—See Suntory Ltd.; *Int'l*, pg. 1321
OSAKA CHAIN & MACHINERY, LTD.—See Kobe Steel, Ltd.; *Int'l*, pg. 740
OSAKA DISTRIBUTION CENTER—See Gunze Sangyo, Inc.; *Int'l*, pg. 578
OSAKA GAS CO.—See Osaka Gas Co., Ltd.; *Int'l*, pg. 1011
OSAKA GAS CO.-ASIA REPRESENTATIVE OFFICE—See Osaka Gas Co., Ltd.; *Int'l*, pg. 1012
OSAKA GAS CO.-LONDON OFFICE—See Osaka Gas Co., Ltd.; *Int'l*, pg. 1012
OSAKA GAS CO.-LOS ANGELES—See Osaka Gas Co., Ltd.; *Int'l*, pg. 1012
OSAKA GAS CO., LTD.; *Int'l*, pg. 1011
OSAKA GAS CO.-NEW YORK—See Osaka Gas Co., Ltd.; *Int'l*, pg. 1012
OSAKA MILL—See Settsu Corporation; *Int'l*, pg. 1225
OSAKA TOYOPET CO., LTD.—See Toyota Motor Corporation; *Int'l*, pg. 1412
OSAKA TOYOTA CO., LTD.—See Toyota Motor Corporation; *Int'l*, pg. 1412
OSAKA XEROX CO., LTD.—See Suntory Ltd.; *Int'l*, pg. 1321
OSATO- AJINOMOTO ALIMENTOS S.A.—See Ajinomoto Company Inc.; *Int'l*, pg. 41
OSBORN MANUFACTURING—See Jason Incorporated; *U.S. Public*, pg. 924
OSBORNE/MCGRAW-HILL—See The McGraw-Hill Companies; *U.S. Public*, pg. 1071
OSBY ARMATUR AB—See Svedala Industri AB; *Int'l*, pg. 1323
OSBY ARMATUR AB—See Trelleborg AB; *Int'l*, pg. 1419
OSBY PARCA AB—See Trelleborg AB; *Int'l*, pg. 1422
OSBY TVATTUTRUSININGAR AB—See Electrolux, AB; *Int'l*, pg. 439
OSCAR FILM NV—See KPN Koninklyke PTT Nederland NV; *Int'l*, pg. 720
OSCAR MAYER FOODS CORP.—See Philip Morris Companies Inc.; *U.S. Public*, pg. 1288
BV OSCAR PRODUCTIONS—See KPN Koninklyke PTT Nederland NV; *Int'l*, pg. 720
OSCILLOQUARTZ SA—See SMH Swiss Corporation for Micro Electronics & Watchmaking Indus. Ltd.; *Int'l*, pg. 1161
OSCO DRUG—See American Stores Company; *U.S. Public*, pg. 93
OSCO INDUSTRIES INC.; *U.S. Private*, pg. 820
OSHAWA FOODS—See The Oshawa Group Limited; *Int'l*, pg. 1012
THE OSHAWA GROUP LIMITED; *Int'l*, pg. 1012
OSHKOSH B'GOSH HOSIERY CO.—See Heyman Corporation; *U.S. Private*, pg. 525
OSHKOSH B'GOSH, INC.; *U.S. Public*, pg. 1232
OSHKOSH TRUCK CORPORATION; *U.S. Public*, pg. 1233
OSHMAN'S SPORTING GOODS, INC.; *U.S. Public*, pg. 1233
OSICOM TECHNOLOGIES; *U.S. Public*, pg. 1233
OSICOM TECHNOLOGIES INC.—See Osicom Technologies Inc.; *U.S. Public*, pg. 1233
OSILLATEK CORPORATION—See Dover Corporation; *U.S. Public*, pg. 521
OSITEL SERVICES—See Compagnie des Machines Bull; *Int'l*, pg. 316
AS OSLO SPORVEIER; *Int'l*, pg. 1012
OSMAN TEXTILES—See Coats Viyella plc; *Int'l*, pg. 300
CARL OSMANN GMBH—See Internatio-Muller N.V.; *Int'l*, pg. 682
OSMONICS ASIA/PACIFIC, LTD.—See Osmonics, Inc.; *U.S. Public*, pg. 1234
OSMONICS, INC.; *U.S. Public*, pg. 1233
OSMOSE WOOD PRESERVING, INC.; *U.S. Private*, pg. 821
OSMOSE WOOD PRESERVING, INC.—See Osmose Wood Preserving, Inc.; *U.S. Private*, pg. 821
OSPREY—See Reed Elsevier plc; *Int'l*, pg. 1093
OSPREY PARK LTD.; *Int'l*, pg. 1012
OSRAM ARGENTINA S.A.C.I.—See Siemens AG; *Int'l*, pg. 1244
OSRAM DE MEXICO S.A. DE C.V.—See Siemens AG; *Int'l*, pg. 1244
OSRAM DO BRASIL COMPANHIA DE LAMPADAS ELETRICAS S.A.—See Siemens AG; *Int'l*, pg. 1244
OSRAM GMBH—See Siemens AG; *Int'l*, pg. 1244
OSRAM LTD.—See Siemens AG; *Int'l*, pg. 1244
OSRAM-MELCO LTD.—See Siemens AG; *Int'l*, pg. 1244
OSRAM S.A.—See Siemens AG; *Int'l*, pg. 1244

OSRAM SOCIETA RIUNITE OSRAM-EDISON-CLERICI S.P.A.—See Siemens AG; *Int'l*, pg. 1244
OSRAM SYLVANIA INC.—See Siemens AG; *Int'l*, pg. 1245
OSTBY & BARTON CO.—See Everett Charles Technologies; *U.S. Private*, pg. 386
A.J. OSTER CARIBE, INC.—See Olin Corporation; *U.S. Public*, pg. 1526
A.J. OSTER COMPANY—See Olin Corporation; *U.S. Public*, pg. 1219
A.J. OSTER FOILS, INC.—See Olin Corporation; *U.S. Public*, pg. 1219
A.J. OSTER WEST, INC.—See Olin Corporation; *U.S. Public*, pg. 1219
OSTER ALLOYS—See Cookson Group plc; *Int'l*, pg. 329
OSTER DE VENEZUELA S.A.—See Sunbeam Corporation; *U.S. Public*, pg. 1533
OSTERDALSBRUKET AS—See Norske Skogindustrier A.S; *Int'l*, pg. 965
OSTERMANN PETERSEN BROS. LTD.—See Scandinavian Airlines System (SAS); *Int'l*, pg. 1202
OSTERMAN'S INC.—See Signet Group plc; *Int'l*, pg. 1248
THE OSTERNECK CO. INC.; *U.S. Private*, pg. 821
OSTERREICHISCHE FERNMELDETECHNISCHE ENTWICKLUNGS- UND FORDERUNGS- GES.MBH—See Austrian Postal & Telegraph Administration; *Int'l*, pg. 101
OSTERREICHISCHE HOTEL- UND FREMDENVERKEHRS GMBH—See Creditanstalt-Bankverein; *Int'l*, pg. 347
OSTERREICHISCHE INDUSTRIEHOLDING AG; *Int'l*, pg. 1012
OSTERREICHISCHE INVESTITIONSKREDIT AG—See Creditanstalt-Bankverein; *Int'l*, pg. 347
OSTERREICHISCHE INVESTMENT GMBH—See Creditanstalt-Bankverein; *Int'l*, pg. 347
OSTERREICHISCHE KONTROLLBANK AG—See Creditanstalt-Bankverein; *Int'l*, pg. 347
OSTERREICHISCHE NESTLE GMBH—See Nestle S.A.; *Int'l*, pg. 922
OSTERREICHISCHE POSTSPARKASSE AG; *Int'l*, pg. 1012
OSTERREICHISCHE ROHRBAU GMBH—See Mannesmann A.G.; *Int'l*, pg. 837
OSTERREICHISCHE UNILEVER GES. M.B.H.—See Unilever Plc; *Int'l*, pg. 1438
OSTERREICHISCHEN BUNDESBAHNEN GMBH; *Int'l*, pg. 1012
OSTJYLLANDS ASFALTFABRIK I/S—See Icopal a/s; *Int'l*, pg. 659
BOB OSTROW CO.—See American Financial Group; *U.S. Public*, pg. 75
OSTROW TEXTILE CO., INC.; *U.S. Private*, pg. 821
O'SULLIVAN CORPORATION; *U.S. Public*, pg. 1234
O'SULLIVAN INDUSTRIES HOLDINGS; *U.S. Public*, pg. 1234
O'SULLIVAN PLASTICS CORP.—See O'Sullivan Corporation; *U.S. Public*, pg. 1234
OSVAL WERKZEUGE-MASCHINEN HANDELSGESELLSCHAFT MBH—See Rothenberger Group GmbH; *Int'l*, pg. 1128
OSWALD ARRIGO LIMITED—See Enso Oyj; *Int'l*, pg. 458
OTACO SEATING CO., LTD.—See American Seating Company; *U.S. Private*, pg. 61
OTARI CORPORATION—See Otari, Inc.; *Int'l*, pg. 1013
OTARI, INC.; *Int'l*, pg. 1013
OTIS CANADA INC.—See United Technologies Corporation; *U.S. Public*, pg. 1691
OTIS ELEVATOR COMPANY—See United Technologies Corporation; *U.S. Public*, pg. 1690
OTIS ELEVATOR CO. PTY. LTD.—See United Technologies Corporation; *U.S. Public*, pg. 1691
OTIS ELEVATOR PLC—See United Technologies Corporation; *U.S. Public*, pg. 1691
OTIS ENGINEERING INTERNATIONAL—See Halliburton Company; *U.S. Public*, pg. 777
OTIS GMBH—See United Technologies Corporation; *U.S. Public*, pg. 1690
OTIS HISS INC—See United Technologies Corporation; *U.S. Public*, pg. 1691
OTIS INTERNATIONAL, LTD.—See Halliburton Company; *U.S. Public*, pg. 776
LEN OTIS LIFT—See United Technologies Corporation; *U.S. Public*, pg. 1691
OTIS MERLA SYSTEMS—See Halliburton Company; *U.S. Public*, pg. 776
OTIS NIGERIA, LTD.—See Halliburton Company; *U.S. Public*, pg. 777
OTIS SPECIALTY PAPERS—See Rexam PLC; *Int'l*, pg. 1107
OTO-SONIC, INC.—See Beltone Electronics Corporation; *U.S. Private*, pg. 132
OTRESA—See Lafarge S.A.; *Int'l*, pg. 789
OTSUKA AMERICA, INC.—See Otsuka Pharmaceutical Co., Ltd.; *Int'l*, pg. 1013
OTSUKA AMERICA PHARMACEUTICAL, INC.—See Otsuka Pharmaceutical Co., Ltd.; *Int'l*, pg. 1013
OTSUKA BEVERAGE CO., LTD.—See Otsuka Pharmaceutical Co., Ltd.; *Int'l*, pg. 1013
OTSUKA CHEMICAL CO., LTD.—See Otsuka Pharmaceutical Co., Ltd.; *Int'l*, pg. 1013
OTSUKA ELECTRONICS CO., LTD.—See Otsuka Pharmaceutical Co., Ltd.; *Int'l*, pg. 1013
OTSUKA ELECTRONICS (U.S.A.) INC.—See Otsuka Pharmaceutical Co., Ltd.; *Int'l*, pg. 1013
OTSUKA FOODS CO., LTD.—See Otsuka Pharmaceutical Co., Ltd.; *Int'l*, pg. 1013
P.T. OTSUKA INDONESIA—See Otsuka Pharmaceutical Co., Ltd.; *Int'l*, pg. 1014
P.T. OTSUKA JAYA INDAH—See Otsuka Pharmaceutical Co., Ltd.; *Int'l*, pg. 1014
M.E. OTSUKA CO., LTD.—See Otsuka Pharmaceutical Co., Ltd.; *Int'l*, pg. 1014

Company Index

OTSUKA OHMI CERAMICS CO., LTD.—See Otsuka Pharmaceutical Co., Ltd.; *Int'l*, pg. 1013
OTSUKA PACKAGING INDUSTRIES LTD.—See Otsuka Pharmaceutical Co., Ltd.; *Int'l*, pg. 1013
OTSUKA PAKISTAN LTD.—See Otsuka Pharmaceutical Co., Ltd.; *Int'l*, pg. 1014
OTSUKA PHARMACEUTICAL AUSTRALIA PTY. LTD.—See Otsuka Pharmaceutical Co., Ltd.; *Int'l*, pg. 1014
OTSUKA PHARMACEUTICAL CO., LTD.; *Int'l*, pg. 1013
OTSUKA SCIENCE CO., LTD.—See Otsuka Pharmaceutical Co., Ltd.; *Int'l*, pg. 1013
OTSUKA TECHNO CO., LTD.—See Otsuka Pharmaceutical Co., Ltd.; *Int'l*, pg. 1013
OTSUKA TOKYO ASSAY LABORATORIES INC.—See Otsuka Pharmaceutical Co., Ltd.; *Int'l*, pg. 1013
OTT FOOD PRODUCTS; *U.S. Private*, pg. 821
OTTAVIO RICCADONNA S.P.A.—See Koninklijke BolsWessanen nv; *Int'l*, pg. 751
OTTAWA CENTER—See The Cascades Group; *Int'l*, pg. 273
THE OTTAWA CITIZEN—See Hollinger Inc.; *Int'l*, pg. 631
OTTAWA RIVER STEEL CO.—See Meridian National Corporation; *U.S. Public*, pg. 1095
THE OTTAWA SUN—See Sun Media Corporation; *Int'l*, pg. 1320
OTTAWAY NEWSPAPERS, INC.—See Dow Jones & Company, Inc.; *U.S. Public*, pg. 525
OTTER TAIL POWER COMPANY; *U.S. Public*, pg. 1234
OTTERMILL SWITCHGEAR LTD.—See Northrop Grumman Corporation; *U.S. Public*, pg. 1198
OTTO-BURLINGTONS MAIL ORDER PVT. LTD.—See Otto Versand (GmbH & Co.); *Int'l*, pg. 1015
OTTO B.V.—See Otto Versand (GmbH & Co.); *Int'l*, pg. 1015
OTTO ECKHOLD GMBH + CO. KG GLAS UND GEBAUDEREINIGUNG—See Vorwerk & Co.; *Int'l*, pg. 1480
OTTO ECKHOLD VERWALTUNGSGESELLSCHAFT MBH—See Vorwerk & Co.; *Int'l*, pg. 1480
OTTO HAENSEL EQUIPAMENTOS INDSTRIAIS LTDA.—See Klockner-Werke AG; *Int'l*, pg. 737
OTTO JUNKER GMBH LAMMERSDORF; *Int'l*, pg. 1014
OTTO KATALOGUSARUHAZ KFT—See Otto Versand (GmbH & Co.); *Int'l*, pg. 1015
OTTO SP. Z O.O.—See Otto Versand (GmbH & Co.); *Int'l*, pg. 1014
OTTO SUMISHO INC.—See Otto Versand (GmbH & Co.); *Int'l*, pg. 1015
OTTO-SUMISHO INC.—See Otto Versand (GmbH & Co.); *Int'l*, pg. 1015
OTTO-VERSAND GMBH—See Otto Versand (GmbH & Co.); *Int'l*, pg. 1015
OTTO VERSAND (GMBH & CO.); *Int'l*, pg. 1014
OTTO-VERSAND INTERNATIONAL GMBH—See Otto Versand (GmbH & Co.); *Int'l*, pg. 1015
OTTO WILD AG—See Hesta Tex AG; *Int'l*, pg. 617
OTTUMWA COURIER—See Lee Enterprises, Incorporated; *U.S. Public*, pg. 984
OUIMET CORP.; *U.S. Public*, pg. 672
OULAINEN WORKS—See Rautaruukki Oy; *Int'l*, pg. 1088
OULUJOKI POWER PLANTS—See Imatran Voima Oy; *Int'l*, pg. 660
OULUN KUMITEHDAS OY—See Valmet Corporation; *Int'l*, pg. 1449
OUR DESIGN CORPORATION—See Suntory Ltd.; *Int'l*, pg. 1321
OUR SUNDAY VISITOR, INC.; *U.S. Private*, pg. 821
OURISMAN CHEVROLET; *U.S. Private*, pg. 821
BUTCH OUSTALET FORD SAAB, INC.; *U.S. Private*, pg. 821
OUTBACK STEAKHOUSE INC.; *U.S. Public*, pg. 1235
OUTBOARD MARINE ASIA LTD.—See Greenway Partners, L.P.; *U.S. Private*, pg. 478
OUTBOARD MARINE CORPORATION—See Greenway Partners, L.P.; *U.S. Private*, pg. 478
OUTBOARD MARINE CORPORATION AUSTRALIA PTY. LTD.—See Greenway Partners, L.P.; *U.S. Private*, pg. 478
OUTBOARD MARINE CORP. OF CANADA LTD.—See Greenway Partners, L.P.; *U.S. Private*, pg. 478
OUTBOARD MARINE DE MEXICO S.A. DE C.V.—See Greenway Partners, L.P.; *U.S. Private*, pg. 479
OUTBOARD MARINE MOTORS DE AMAZONIA LTD.—See Greenway Partners, L.P.; *U.S. Private*, pg. 479
OUTDOOR COMMUNICATIONS, INC.; *U.S. Private*, pg. 822
THE OUTDOOR FOOTWEAR COMPANY—See The Timberland Company; *U.S. Public*, pg. 1609
OUTDOOR LIFE—See The Times Mirror Company; *U.S. Public*, pg. 1617
OUTDOOR SERVICES—See Western International Media Corporation; *U.S. Private*, pg. 1166
OUTDOOR SYSTEMS, INC.; *U.S. Public*, pg. 1235
OUTDOOR SYSTEMS, INC.—See Outdoor Systems, Inc.; *U.S. Public*, pg. 1235
OUTDOOR SYSTEMS, INC.-NEW YORK—See Outdoor Systems, Inc.; *U.S. Public*, pg. 1235
OUTDOOR TECHNOLOGIES - CANADA—See Outdoor Technologies Group; *U.S. Private*, pg. 822
OUTDOOR TECHNOLOGIES GROUP; *U.S. Private*, pg. 822
OUTDOOR TECHNOLOGIES WISCONSIN—See Outdoor Technologies Group; *U.S. Private*, pg. 822
OUTDOOR VENTURE CORP.; *U.S. Private*, pg. 822
OUTER DRIVE MANUFACTURING TECHNICAL CENTER—See Chrysler Corporation; *U.S. Public*, pg. 353

OUTLANDER—See The Leslie Fay Companies, Inc.; *U.S. Public*, pg. 989
OUTLET SQUARE OF ATLANTA, INC.—See The Rouse Company; *U.S. Public*, pg. 1408
THE OUTLOOK—See The Copley Press, Inc.; *U.S. Private*, pg. 275
OUTLOOK EYEWEAR COMPANY—See Bausch & Lomb Incorporated; *U.S. Public*, pg. 195
OUTLOOK FOODS, INC.—See Outlook Group Corporation; *U.S. Public*, pg. 1235
OUTLOOK GRAPHICS—See Outlook Group Corporation; *U.S. Public*, pg. 1235
OUTLOOK GROUP CORPORATION; *U.S. Public*, pg. 1235
OUTLOOK, INCORPORATED—See The Kiplinger Washington Editors, Inc.; *U.S. Private*, pg. 623
OUTLOOK LABEL SYSTEMS, INC.—See Outlook Group Corporation; *U.S. Public*, pg. 1235
OUTLOOK PACKAGING, INC.—See Outlook Group Corporation; *U.S. Public*, pg. 1236
OUTOKUMPU AMERICAN BRASS CO.—See Outokumpu Oyj; *Int'l*, pg. 1016
OUTOKUMPU BASE METALS OY—See Outokumpu Oyj; *Int'l*, pg. 1016
OUTOKUMPU BENELUX B.V.—See Outokumpu Oyj; *Int'l*, pg. 1015
OUTOKUMPU CASTFORM OY—See Outokumpu Oyj; *Int'l*, pg. 1017
OUTOKUMPU CENTRO SERVIZI S.P.A.—See Outokumpu Oyj; *Int'l*, pg. 1015
OUTOKUMPU CHINA OY—See Outokumpu Oyj; *Int'l*, pg. 1015
OUTOKUMPU CHINA OY (HONG KONG BRANCH OFFICE)—See Outokumpu Oyj; *Int'l*, pg. 1015
OUTOKUMPU CHROME OY—See Outokumpu Oyj; *Int'l*, pg. 1018
OUTOKUMPU CHROME OY, KEMI MINE—See Outokumpu Oyj; *Int'l*, pg. 1018
OUTOKUMPU COPPER BRASS ROD AB—See Outokumpu Oyj; *Int'l*, pg. 1017
OUTOKUMPU COPPER B.V.—See Outokumpu Oyj; *Int'l*, pg. 1017
OUTOKUMPU COPPER DRAWN PRODUCTS INC.—See Outokumpu Oyj; *Int'l*, pg. 1016
OUTOKUMPU COPPER FRANKLIN, INC.—See Outokumpu Oyj; *Int'l*, pg. 1016
OUTOKUMPU COPPER INC.—See Outokumpu Oyj; *Int'l*, pg. 1016
OUTOKUMPU COPPER KENOSHA, INC.—See Outokumpu Oyj; *Int'l*, pg. 1017
OUTOKUMPU COPPER LTD.—See Outokumpu Oyj; *Int'l*, pg. 1017
OUTOKUMPU COPPER PARTNER AB—See Outokumpu Oyj; *Int'l*, pg. 1017
OUTOKUMPU COPPER PRODUCTS (MALAYSIA) SDN. BHD.—See Outokumpu Oyj; *Int'l*, pg. 1017
OUTOKUMPU COPPER PRODUCTS OY—See Outokumpu Oyj; *Int'l*, pg. 1016
OUTOKUMPU COPPER RESOURCES B.V.—See Outokumpu Oyj; *Int'l*, pg. 1016
OUTOKUMPU COPPER STRIP AB—See Outokumpu Oyj; *Int'l*, pg. 1017
OUTOKUMPU COPPER STRIP B.V.—See Outokumpu Oyj; *Int'l*, pg. 1017
OUTOKUMPU COPPER TUBE (ZHONGSHAN) LTD.—See Outokumpu Oyj; *Int'l*, pg. 1017
OUTOKUMPU COPPER TUBES AB—See Outokumpu Oyj; *Int'l*, pg. 1017
OUTOKUMPU COPPER TUBES S.A.—See Outokumpu Oyj; *Int'l*, pg. 1017
OUTOKUMPU COPPER (U.S.A.) INC.—See Outokumpu Oyj; *Int'l*, pg. 1015
OUTOKUMPU DANMARK A/S—See Outokumpu Oyj; *Int'l*, pg. 1015
OUTOKUMPU DEUTSCHLAND GMBH—See Outokumpu Oyj; *Int'l*, pg. 1015
OUTOKUMPU ENGINEERING CONTRACTORS OY—See Outokumpu Oyj; *Int'l*, pg. 1017
OUTOKUMPU ENGINEERING SERVICES OY—See Outokumpu Oyj; *Int'l*, pg. 1017
OUTOKUMPU ESPANA, S.A.—See Outokumpu Oyj; *Int'l*, pg. 1015
OUTOKUMPU ESPANA S.A.—See Outokumpu Oyj; *Int'l*, pg. 1015
OUTOKUMPU FINANCIAL SERVICES AB—See Outokumpu Oyj; *Int'l*, pg. 1015
OUTOKUMPU FRANCE S.A.—See Outokumpu Oyj; *Int'l*, pg. 1015
OUTOKUMPU HARJAVALTA METALS OY—See Outokumpu Oyj; *Int'l*, pg. 1015
OUTOKUMPU ISTANBUL DIS TICARET LIMITED SIRKETI—See Outokumpu Oyj; *Int'l*, pg. 1015
OUTOKUMPU ITALIA S.R.L.—See Outokumpu Oyj; *Int'l*, pg. 1015
OUTOKUMPU JAPAN K.K.—See Outokumpu Oyj; *Int'l*, pg. 1015
OUTOKUMPU METALS (USA) INC.—See Outokumpu Oyj; *Int'l*, pg. 1015
OUTOKUMPU MEXICANA S.A. DE C.V.—See Outokumpu Oyj; *Int'l*, pg. 1017
OUTOKUMPU MINERA ESPANOLA S.A.—See Outokumpu Oyj; *Int'l*, pg. 1016
OUTOKUMPU MINES LTD.—See Outokumpu Oyj; *Int'l*, pg. 1016
OUTOKUMPU MINING AUSTRALIA PTY. LTD.—See Outokumpu Oyj; *Int'l*, pg. 1016
OUTOKUMPU MINING OY—See Outokumpu Oyj; *Int'l*, pg. 1016
OUTOKUMPU MINTEC AUSTRALIA PTY. LTD.—See Outokumpu Oyj; *Int'l*, pg. 1017
OUTOKUMPU MINTEC CANADA LTD.—See Outokumpu Oyj; *Int'l*, pg. 1017
OUTOKUMPU MINTEC OY—See Outokumpu Oyj; *Int'l*, pg. 1017

OUTOKUMPU MINTEC SOUTH AFRICA (PTY) LTD.—See Outokumpu Oyj; *Int'l*, pg. 1017
OUTOKUMPU MINTEC U.S.A., INC.—See Outokumpu Oyj; *Int'l*, pg. 1017
OUTOKUMPU NORGE A/S—See Outokumpu Oyj; *Int'l*, pg. 1016
OUTOKUMPU OYJ; *Int'l*, pg. 1015
OUTOKUMPU OYJ—See Outokumpu Oyj; *Int'l*, pg. 1015
OUTOKUMPU PLATING OY—See Outokumpu Oyj; *Int'l*, pg. 1016
OUTOKUMPU POLAND SP.ZO.O.—See Outokumpu Oyj; *Int'l*, pg. 1016
OUTOKUMPU POLARIT OY—See Outokumpu Oyj; *Int'l*, pg. 1018
OUTOKUMPU PORICOPPER OY—See Outokumpu Oyj; *Int'l*, pg. 1016
OUTOKUMPU (PORTUGAL) LTDA.—See Outokumpu Oyj; *Int'l*, pg. 1016
OUTOKUMPU RAWMET S.A.—See Outokumpu Oyj; *Int'l*, pg. 1017
OUTOKUMPU RAWMET (SWITZERLAND) LTD.—See Outokumpu Oyj; *Int'l*, pg. 1016
OUTOKUMPU RAWMET (U.K.) LTD.—See Outokumpu Oyj; *Int'l*, pg. 1017
OUTOKUMPU RESEARCH OY—See Outokumpu Oyj; *Int'l*, pg. 1015
OUTOKUMPU ROSSISJA OY—See Outokumpu Oyj; *Int'l*, pg. 1015
OUTOKUMPU (S.E.A.) PTE LTD.—See Outokumpu Oyj; *Int'l*, pg. 1016
OUTOKUMPU STAL & METALL AB—See Outokumpu Oyj; *Int'l*, pg. 1016
OUTOKUMPU STEEL OY—See Outokumpu Oyj; *Int'l*, pg. 1018
OUTOKUMPU STEEL PROCESSING B.V.—See Outokumpu Oyj; *Int'l*, pg. 1018
OUTOKUMPU SUPERCONDUCTORS OY—See Outokumpu Oyj; *Int'l*, pg. 1017
OUTOKUMPU TECHNOLOGY OY—See Outokumpu Oyj; *Int'l*, pg. 1017
OUTOKUMPU TECNICA-CHILE LTDA.—See Outokumpu Oyj; *Int'l*, pg. 1017
OUTOKUMPU TECNICA PERU S.A.—See Outokumpu Oyj; *Int'l*, pg. 1016
OUTOKUMPU (THAILAND) CO., LTD.—See Outokumpu Oyj; *Int'l*, pg. 1016
OUTOKUMPU (U.K.) LTD.—See Outokumpu Oyj; *Int'l*, pg. 1016
OUTOKUMPU WENMEC AB—See Outokumpu Oyj; *Int'l*, pg. 1017
OUTOKUMPU WENMEC, INC.—See Outokumpu Oyj; *Int'l*, pg. 1017
OUTOKUMPU WENMEC OY—See Outokumpu Oyj; *Int'l*, pg. 1017
OUTOKUMPU WTT AB—See Outokumpu Oyj; *Int'l*, pg. 1016
OUTOKUMPU ZINC COMMERCIAL B.V.—See Outokumpu Oyj; *Int'l*, pg. 1016
OUTOKUMPU ZINC OY—See Outokumpu Oyj; *Int'l*, pg. 1016
OUTPATIENT SURGERY CENTER OF CORAL SPRINGS—See Columbia/HCA Healthcare Corporation; *U.S. Public*, pg. 405
OUTPUT TECHNOLOGIES SRI GROUP, INC.—See Kansas City Southern Industries, Inc.; *U.S. Public*, pg. 817
GEORGE OUTRAM & COMPANY LTD.—See Lonrho plc; *Int'l*, pg. 817
OUTSOURCE INTERNATIONAL; *U.S. Public*, pg. 1236
OVAKO ACIER S.A.—See AB SKF; *Int'l*, pg. 1157
OVAKO AJAX, INC.—See AB SKF; *Int'l*, pg. 1157
OVAKO ARVIKA AB—See AB SKF; *Int'l*, pg. 1157
OVAKO COUPLINGS AB—See AB SKF; *Int'l*, pg. 1157
OVAKO LA FOULERIE S.A.—See AB SKF; *Int'l*, pg. 1157
OVAKO STAHL GMBH—See AB SKF; *Int'l*, pg. 1157
OVAKO STEEL AB—See AB SKF; *Int'l*, pg. 1157
OVAKO STEEL LTD.—See AB SKF; *Int'l*, pg. 1157
OVALSTRAPPING INC.—See Enterprises International Inc.; *U.S. Private*, pg. 378
OVALTINE (WEST AFRICA) LTD.—See Novartis AG; *Int'l*, pg. 983
OVATION INSTRUMENTS—See Kaman Corporation; *U.S. Public*, pg. 942
OVERHEAD CONVEYOR CO.; *U.S. Private*, pg. 822
OVERHEAD DOOR CORPORATION; *U.S. Private*, pg. 822
OVERHILL FARMS, INC.—See Polyphase Corporation; *U.S. Public*, pg. 1315
JULIUS OVERHOFF RUCKKUHLTECHNIK GES. M.B.H.—See Deutsche Babcock AG; *Int'l*, pg. 400
OVERHOLTZER CHURCH FURNITURE, INC.; *U.S. Private*, pg. 823
OVERLAND ENERGY, INC.—See Yellow Corporation; *U.S. Public*, pg. 1788
THE OVERLAND NATIONAL BANK—See First Commerce Bancshares, Inc.; *U.S. Public*, pg. 629
OVERLAND PARK STATE BANK & TRUST—See UMB Financial Corporation; *U.S. Public*, pg. 1654
OVERLAND TRANSPORTATION SYSTEM, INC.—See Vitran Corporation Inc.; *Int'l*, pg. 1469
OVERLY MANUFACTURING CO.; *U.S. Private*, pg. 823
OVERNITE TRANSPORTATION CO.—See Union Pacific Corporation; *U.S. Public*, pg. 1668
OVERPELT-PLASCOBEL, INC.—See Union Miniere; *Int'l*, pg. 1442
OVERSEA COURIER SERVICE CO., LTD.—See Nihon Keizai Shimbun, Inc.; *Int'l*, pg. 969
OVERSEAS ASSETS HOLDINGS INC.—See BankAmerica Corporation; *U.S. Public*, pg. 181
OVERSEAS CAPITAL CORPORATION—See Nasco Industries Inc.; *U.S. Public*, pg. 774
OVERSEAS COMMODEX CORP.—See Tiedemanns - Joh.H.Andresen ANS; *Int'l*, pg. 1390
OVERSEAS MILITARY SALES CORPORATION; *U.S. Private*, pg. 823

OVERSEAS SERVICE CORPORATION; *U.S. Private*, pg. 823

OVERSEAS SHIPHOLDING GROUP, INC.; *U.S. Public*, pg. 1236

OVERSLAGBEDRIJF DE IJBUNKER BV—See Akzo Nobel N.V.; *Int'l*, pg. 43

OVERSPECHT, B.V.—See Hershey Foods Corporation; *U.S. Public*, pg. 812

OVERSTREET PAVING COMPANY, pg. 823

OVERTON GEAR & TOOL CORP.; *U.S. Private*, pg. 823

OVERTON MOORE & ASSOCIATES; *U.S. Private*, pg. 823

AB OVERUMS BRUK—See Electrolux, AB; *Int'l*, pg. 439

AB OVERUMS FONSTERFABRIK—See Electrolux, AB; *Int'l*, pg. 439

OVITA NUTRICIA SP. Z O.O.—See Nutricia BV; *Int'l*, pg. 992

OVITA NUTRICIA WEGROW SP. Z O.O.—See Nutricia BV; *Int'l*, pg. 992

OVONIC BATTERY COMPANY, INC.—See Energy Conversion Devices, Inc.; *U.S. Public*, pg. 581

OWAT ASSURANTIE N.V.—See Royal Nedlloyd Group N.V.; *Int'l*, pg. 1145

OWATONNA CANNING COMPANY—See Chiquita Brands International, Inc.; *U.S. Public*, pg. 349

OWEN-AMES-KIMBALL CO.; *U.S. Private*, pg. 823

OWEN-AMES-KIMBALL ENGINEERING, INC.—See Owen-Ames-Kimball Co.; *U.S. Private*, pg. 824

OWEN HEALTH CARE, INC.—See Cardinal Health Inc.; *U.S. Private*, pg. 304

OWEN INDUSTRIES, INC.; *U.S. Private*, pg. 824

OWEN PACIFIC; *U.S. Private*, pg. 824

OWENS & MINOR, INC.; *U.S. Public*, pg. 1236

OWENS-BROCKWAY GLASS CONTAINERS—See Owens-Illinois, Inc.; *U.S. Public*, pg. 1238

OWENS-BROCKWAY PLASTIC CONTAINERS—See Owens-Illinois, Inc.; *U.S. Public*, pg. 1238

OWENS-BROCKWAY PRESCRIPTION PRODUCTS—See Owens-Illinois, Inc.; *U.S. Public*, pg. 1238

OWENS CORNING; *U.S. Public*, pg. 1236

OWENS CORNING ANDERCOL TUBERIAS—See Owens Corning; *U.S. Public*, pg. 1237

OWENS CORNING BUILDING MATERIALS ESPANA SA—See Owens Corning; *U.S. Public*, pg. 1237

OWENS-CORNING BUILDING PRODUCTS UK LTD.—See Owens Corning; *U.S. Public*, pg. 1237

OWENS-CORNING CANADA—See Owens Corning; *U.S. Public*, pg. 1237

OWENS-CORNING CANOS S.A.—See Owens Corning; *U.S. Public*, pg. 1237

OWENS-CORNING CHANGCHUN GUAN DAO COMPANY LTD.—See Owens Corning; *U.S. Public*, pg. 1237

OWENS-CORNING ETERNIT ROHRE GMBH—See Owens Corning; *U.S. Public*, pg. 1237

OWENS-CORNING FIBERGLAS A.S. LIMITADA—See Owens Corning; *U.S. Public*, pg. 1237

OWENS-CORNING FIBERGLAS DEUTSCHLAND G.M.B.H.—See Owens Corning; *U.S. Public*, pg. 1237

OWENS-CORNING FIBERGLAS FRANCE S.A.—See Owens Corning; *U.S. Public*, pg. 1237

OWENS-CORNING FIBERGLAS NORWAY AS—See Owens Corning; *U.S. Public*, pg. 1237

OWENS-CORNING FIBERGLAS S.A.—See Owens Corning; *U.S. Public*, pg. 1237

OWENS-CORNING FIBERGLAS (U.K.) LTD.—See Owens Corning; *U.S. Public*, pg. 1237

OWENS CORNING/FOAMULAR—See Owens Corning; *U.S. Public*, pg. 1237

OWENS-CORNING (GUANGZHOU) FIBERGLAS CO. LTD.—See Owens Corning; *U.S. Public*, pg. 1237

OWENS-CORNING (INDIA) LIMITED—See Owens Corning; *U.S. Public*, pg. 1237

OWENS-CORNING (JAPAN) LTD.—See Owens Corning; *U.S. Public*, pg. 1237

OWENS-CORNING ONTARIO HOLDINGS INC.—See Owens Corning; *U.S. Public*, pg. 1237

OWENS-CORNING PIPE (AFRICA) PVT. LTD.—See Owens Corning; *U.S. Public*, pg. 1237

OWENS CORNING PIPE BOTSWANA (PROPRIETARY) LTD.—See Owens Corning; *U.S. Public*, pg. 1238

OWENS CORNING POLYFOAM UK LIMITED—See Owens Corning; *U.S. Public*, pg. 1238

OWENS CORNING POLYPAN, SPA—See Owens Corning; *U.S. Public*, pg. 1237

OWENS-CORNING (SHANGHAI) FIBERGLAS CO., LTD.—See Owens Corning; *U.S. Public*, pg. 1237

OWENS-CORNING (SINGAPORE) PTE LTD.—See Owens Corning; *U.S. Public*, pg. 1237

OWENS CORNING SOUTH AFRICA PTY LTD.—See Owens Corning; *U.S. Public*, pg. 1238

OWENS-CORNING TUBS, S.A.—See Owens Corning; *U.S. Public*, pg. 1238

OWENS-CORNING VEIL NETHERLANDS B.V.—See Owens Corning; *U.S. Public*, pg. 1237

OWENS-CORNING YAPI MERKEZI BORU SANAYI VE TICARET A.S.—See Owens Corning; *U.S. Public*, pg. 1238

OWENS COUNTRY SAUSAGE, INC.—See Bob Evans Farms, Inc.; *U.S. Public*, pg. 596

OWENS-ILLINOIS CLOSURE INC.—See Owens-Illinois, Inc.; *U.S. Public*, pg. 1238

OWENS-ILLINOIS, INC.; *U.S. Public*, pg. 1238

R.S. OWENS; *U.S. Public*, pg. 824

OWENSBORO GRAIN CO., INC.; *U.S. Private*, pg. 824

OWENS-CORNING FIBERGLAS (G.B.) LTD.—See Owens Corning; *U.S. Public*, pg. 1237

OWENS-CORNING VEIL U.K. LIMITED—See Owens Corning; *U.S. Public*, pg. 1237

OWNED TELEVISION STATIONS—See Blair Television; *U.S. Private*, pg. 148

OWNER DRIVER MANAGEMENT (PTY) LTD.—See Transnet Ltd.; *Int'l*, pg. 1417

OWNERS INSURANCE CO.—See Auto-Owners Insurance; *U.S. Private*, pg. 100

OWOSSO CORPORATION; *U.S. Public*, pg. 1238

OWSLEY & SONS, INC.; *U.S. Private*, pg. 824

OXARC INC.; *U.S. Private*, pg. 825

OXBOW CORPORATION; *U.S. Private*, pg. 825

OXFORD APPAREL, INC.—See Oxford Industries, Inc.; *U.S. Public*, pg. 1239

OXFORD AUTOMOTIVE, INC.; *U.S. Private*, pg. 825

OXFORD COLLECTION—See Oxford Industries, Inc.; *U.S. Public*, pg. 1239

THE OXFORD COLLECTION LTD.—See Liberty PLC; *Int'l*, pg. 807

OXFORD DE COLON, S.A.—See Oxford Industries, Inc.; *U.S. Public*, pg. 1239

OXFORD HEALTH CENTERS—See Oxford Health Plans Inc.; *U.S. Public*, pg. 1239

OXFORD HEALTH INSURANCE, INC.—See Oxford Health Plans Inc.; *U.S. Public*, pg. 1239

OXFORD HEALTH PLANS (FL), INC.—See Oxford Health Plans Inc.; *U.S. Public*, pg. 1239

OXFORD HEALTH PLANS (IL), INC.—See Oxford Health Plans Inc.; *U.S. Public*, pg. 1239

OXFORD HEALTH PLANS INC.; *U.S. Public*, pg. 1238

OXFORD HOIST COMPANY LTD—See Sunrise Medical, Inc.; *U.S. Public*, pg. 1536

OXFORD INDUSTRIES, INC.; *U.S. Public*, pg. 1239

OXFORD INSTRUMENTS—See Oxford Instruments plc; *Int'l*, pg. 1018

OXFORD INSTRUMENTS-ACCELERATOR TECHNOLOGY GROUP—See Oxford Instruments plc; *Int'l*, pg. 1018

OXFORD INSTRUMENTS-INDUSTRIAL ANALYSIS GROUP—See Oxford Instruments plc; *Int'l*, pg. 1018

OXFORD INSTRUMENTS-MEDICAL SYSTEMS—See Oxford Instruments plc; *Int'l*, pg. 1018

OXFORD INSTRUMENTS-MEDICAL SYSTEMS DIV.—See Oxford Instruments plc; *Int'l*, pg. 1018

OXFORD INSTRUMENTS-MICROANALYSIS GROUP—See Oxford Instruments plc; *Int'l*, pg. 1018

OXFORD INSTRUMENTS-NMR INSTRUMENTS—See Oxford Instruments plc; *Int'l*, pg. 1018

OXFORD INSTRUMENTS-NUCLEAR MEASUREMENTS GROUP—See Oxford Instruments plc; *Int'l*, pg. 1018

OXFORD INSTRUMENTS-PLASMA TECHNOLOGY—See Oxford Instruments plc; *Int'l*, pg. 1018

OXFORD INSTRUMENTS PLC; *Int'l*, pg. 1018

OXFORD INSTRUMENTS-RESEARCH INSTRUMENTS—See Oxford Instruments plc; *Int'l*, pg. 1018

OXFORD INSTRUMENTS-SUPERCONDUCTING TECHNOLOGY—See Oxford Instruments plc; *Int'l*, pg. 1018

OXFORD INSTRUMENTS-X-RAY TECHNOLOGY GROUP—See Oxford Instruments plc; *Int'l*, pg. 1018

OXFORD INTERNATIONAL, INC.—See Oxford Industries, Inc.; *U.S. Public*, pg. 1239

OXFORD LIFE INSURANCE CO.—See Amerco; *U.S. Private*, pg. 49

OXFORD MAGNET TECHNOLOGY LIMITED—See Oxford Instruments plc; *Int'l*, pg. 1018

OXFORD MEN'S WEAR DIVISION—See Oxford Industries, Inc.; *U.S. Public*, pg. 1239

OXFORD OF LUVERNE, INC.—See Oxford Industries, Inc.; *U.S. Public*, pg. 1239

OXFORD PRODUCTS INTERNATIONAL LTD.—See Oxford Industries, Inc.; *U.S. Public*, pg. 1239

OXFORD REALTY FINANCIAL GROUP; *U.S. Private*, pg. 825

OXFORD SEPARATES—See Oxford Industries, Inc.; *U.S. Public*, pg. 1239

OXFORD SHIRTS—See Oxford Industries, Inc.; *U.S. Public*, pg. 1239

OXFORD SLACKS DIVISION—See Oxford Industries, Inc.; *U.S. Public*, pg. 1239

OXFORD UNIVERSITY (INDIA)—See Oxford University Press; *Int'l*, pg. 1019

OXFORD UNIVERSITY PRESS; *Int'l*, pg. 1018

OXFORD UNIVERSITY PRESS—See Oxford University Press; *Int'l*, pg. 1019

OXFORD UNIVERSITY PRESS, AUSTRALIA—See Oxford University Press; *Int'l*, pg. 1019

OXFORD UNIVERSITY PRESS CANADA—See Oxford University Press; *Int'l*, pg. 1019

OXFORD UNIVERSITY PRESS (DAR ES SALAAM)—See Oxford University Press; *Int'l*, pg. 1019

OXFORD UNIVERSITY PRESS (HONG KONG)—See Oxford University Press; *Int'l*, pg. 1019

OXFORD UNIVERSITY PRESS IN MADRAS—See Oxford University Press; *Int'l*, pg. 1019

OXFORD UNIVERSITY PRESS, INC.—See Oxford University Press; *Int'l*, pg. 1019

OXFORD UNIVERSITY PRESS (KENYA)—See Oxford University Press; *Int'l*, pg. 1019

OXFORD UNIVERSITY PRESS K.K.—See Oxford University Press; *Int'l*, pg. 1019

OXFORD UNIVERSITY PRESS OF BOMBAY—See Oxford University Press; *Int'l*, pg. 1019

OXFORD UNIVERSITY PRESS OF CALCUTTA—See Oxford University Press; *Int'l*, pg. 1019

OXFORD UNIVERSITY PRESS OF NEW DELHI—See Oxford University Press; *Int'l*, pg. 1019

OXFORD UNIVERSITY PRESS PTE. LTD.—See Oxford University Press; *Int'l*, pg. 1019

OXFORD UNIVERSITY PRESS (SOUTH AFRICA)—See Oxford University Press; *Int'l*, pg. 1019

OXIGENIO DO BRASIL S.A., CONSOLIDEE—See Air Liquide S.A.; *Int'l*, pg. 37

OXMOOR HOUSE, INC.—See Time Warner Inc.; *U.S. Public*, pg. 1613

S.A. OXYFLASH—See Cockerill Sambre; *Int'l*, pg. 301

OXYGEN THERAPY ASSOCIATES—See Integrated Health Services, Inc.; *U.S. Public*, pg. 885

OY TALENTUM AB—See International Data Group; *U.S. Private*, pg. 570

OYANG ESI, INC.—See Electro Scientific Industries, Inc.; *U.S. Public*, pg. 569

OYO CORPORATION; *Int'l*, pg. 1019

OYO CORPORATION U.S.A.—See OYO Corporation; *Int'l*, pg. 1019

OYO GEOSCIENCES CORPORATION—See OYO Corporation; *Int'l*, pg. 1019

OYO GEOSPACE CANADA, INC.—See OYO Corporation; *Int'l*, pg. 1019

OYSA ISKENDERUN CIMENTO SANAYI VE TICARET A.S.—See Sabanci Holding A.S.; *Int'l*, pg. 1168

OYSA NIDGE CIMENTO SANAYI VE TICARET A.S.—See Sabanci Holding A.S.; *Int'l*, pg. 1168

OZARK AUTOMOTIVE DISTRIBUTORS, INC.—See O'Reilly Automotive, Inc.; *U.S. Public*, pg. 1230

OZARK GAS PIPELINE CORPORATION—See NGC Corporation; *U.S. Public*, pg. 1146

OZARK MOTOR LINES; *U.S. Private*, pg. 825

OZARKA/OASIS WATER CO.—See Nestle S.A.; *Int'l*, pg. 919

OZEKI CORPORATION; *Int'l*, pg. 1019

OZEKI SAKE (U.S.A.) INC.—See Ozeki Corporation; *Int'l*, pg. 1019

OZEMAIL LIMITED; *Int'l*, pg. 1019

OZONE INDUSTRIES INC.—See BBA Group plc; *Int'l*, pg. 113

OZONE RESEARCH & EQUIPMENT CORP.—See Osmonics, Inc.; *U.S. Public*, pg. 1234

P

P/A INDUSTRIES, INC.; *U.S. Private*, pg. 825

P AND B STOCKGLASS—See Saint-Gobain; *Int'l*, pg. 1173

P & C FOOD MARKETS, INC.—See The Penn Traffic Company; *U.S. Public*, pg. 1270

P & E, INC.; *U.S. Private*, pg. 825

P & F INDUSTRIES, INC.; *U.S. Public*, pg. 1239

P AND G SPECIALTY INSURANCE SERVICES—See EQE International; *U.S. Private*, pg. 354

P&H TRANSPORTATION—See Bradford Oil Company, Inc.; *U.S. Private*, pg. 164

P & M MANUFACTURING—See NCH Corporation; *U.S. Public*, pg. 1145

P&O ASIA—See The Peninsular and Oriental Steam Navigation Company; *Int'l*, pg. 1035

P&O AUSTRALIA LTD.—See The Peninsular and Oriental Steam Navigation Company; *Int'l*, pg. 1035

P&O BULK CARRIERS LTD. (BERMUDA)—See The Peninsular and Oriental Steam Navigation Company; *Int'l*, pg. 1033

P&O BULK SHIPPING LTD.—See The Peninsular and Oriental Steam Navigation Company; *Int'l*, pg. 1033

P & O CENTRO SERVIZI S.P.A.—See Electrolux, AB; *Int'l*, pg. 442

P&O CRUISES LIMITED—See The Peninsular and Oriental Steam Navigation Company; *Int'l*, pg. 1033

P&O EUROPEAN FERRIES LTD.—See The Peninsular and Oriental Steam Navigation Company; *Int'l*, pg. 1033

P&O EUROPEAN TRANSPORT SERVICES LTD.—See The Peninsular and Oriental Steam Navigation Company; *Int'l*, pg. 1033

P&O HARBOURS LTD.—See The Peninsular and Oriental Steam Navigation Company; *Int'l*, pg. 1034

P&O LINES LTD.—See The Peninsular and Oriental Steam Navigation Company; *Int'l*, pg. 1034

P&O (NEW ZEALAND) LTD.—See The Peninsular and Oriental Steam Navigation Company; *Int'l*, pg. 1035

P&O PROPERTIES INTERNATIONAL—See The Peninsular and Oriental Steam Navigation Company; *Int'l*, pg. 1034

P&O PROPERTY DEVELOPMENTS LTD.—See The Peninsular and Oriental Steam Navigation Company; *Int'l*, pg. 1034

P&O PROPERTY HOLDINGS LTD.—See The Peninsular and Oriental Steam Navigation Company; *Int'l*, pg. 1034

P&O ROADTANKS LIMITED—See The Peninsular and Oriental Steam Navigation Company; *Int'l*, pg. 1034

P&O ROADWAYS LTD.—See The Peninsular and Oriental Steam Navigation Company; *Int'l*, pg. 1034

P&O SCOTTISH FERRIES LTD.—See The Peninsular and Oriental Steam Navigation Company; *Int'l*, pg. 1034

P&O SHOPPING CENTRES LTD.—See The Peninsular and Oriental Steam Navigation Company; *Int'l*, pg. 1034

P&O VENDING—See The Peninsular and Oriental Steam Navigation Company; *Int'l*, pg. 1034

P&S AUSTRALIA PTY LTD.—See Scapa Group Plc; *Int'l*, pg. 1202

P&S FILTRATION GMBH—See Scapa Group Plc; *Int'l*, pg. 1203

P&S FILTRATION INC.—See Scapa Group Plc; *Int'l*, pg. 1202

P&S FILTRATION LTD.—See Scapa Group Plc; *Int'l*, pg. 1202

P&S FILTRATION S.A. (PTY) LTD.—See Scapa Group Plc; *Int'l*, pg. 1203

P&S TEXTILES LTD.—See Scapa Group Plc; *Int'l*, pg. 1202

P/M BEARING DIV.—See Keystone Powdered Metal Company; *U.S. Private*, pg. 619

P/M STRUCTURAL PARTS DIV.—See Keystone Powdered Metal Company; *U.S. Private*, pg. 619

P.T. PRAXAIR INDONESIA—See Praxair Inc.; *U.S. Public*, pg. 1320

P-T TEMPLET COMPANY—See NCH Corporation; *U.S. Public*, pg. 1145

PA SUN LIFE INSURANCE COMPANY—See Sun Bancorp, Inc.; *U.S. Public*, pg. 1529

PAB SA—See Bertrand Faure; *Int'l*, pg. 193

S.A. P.A.G.E. MUNICIPAL—See Cockerill Sambre; *Int'l*, pg. 301

PAGSA—See Lagardere Groupe; *Int'l*, pg. 796

PAK PACIFIC CORP. PTY. LTD.—See BTR plc; *Int'l*, pg. 129

PAK PACIFIC (SOUTH EAST ASIA) PTE. LTD.—See BTR plc; *Int'l*, pg. 129

PAL-VDO INSTRUMENTS SRO—See Mannesmann A.G.; *Int'l*, pg. 839
P.A.M. TRANSPORT, INC.; *U.S. Private*, pg. 825
PAV (SOCIETE INDUSTRIELE DE PRE A VAROIS)—See Groupe Usinor; *Int'l*, pg. 570
P.A.Y.S.E.N., S.A. DE C.V.—See BASF AG; *Int'l*, pg. 109
P.B. & S. CHEMICAL CO.—See Veba AG; *Int'l*, pg. 1458
PB - KBB INC.—See Preussag AG; *Int'l*, pg. 1069
PB LEASING LTD.—See Pitney Bowes Inc.; *U.S. Public*, pg. 1304
PBD, INC.; *U.S. Private*, pg. 825
PBG PREUSSAG BUNDELFUNK GMBH—See Geotek Communications; *U.S. Public*, pg. 740
THE PBS&J CORPORATION; *U.S. Private*, pg. 825
PBZ PRIVATBANK ZURICH—See Union Bank of Switzerland; *Int'l*, pg. 1440
PC COMPUTING—See Softbank Corporation; *Int'l*, pg. 1276
PC CONNECTION, INC.; *U.S. Private*, pg. 826
P.C. DROP FORGINGS DIVISION—See The Ivaco Group; *Int'l*, pg. 695
P.C. HENDERSON (ESPANOLA) S.A.—See Hepworth Plc; *Int'l*, pg. 615
P.C. HENDERSON (FRANCE) S.A.—See Hepworth Plc; *Int'l*, pg. 615
PC INVESTMENT COMPANY—See The Progressive Corporation; *U.S. Public*, pg. 1335
PC MAGAZINE—See Softbank Corporation; *Int'l*, pg. 1276
PC QUOTE, INC.; *U.S. Public*, pg. 1240
PC SERVICE SOURCE, INC.; *U.S. Public*, pg. 1240
PC STATION S.R.L.—See Compagnie des Machines Bull; *Int'l*, pg. 318
PC WEEK—See Softbank Corporation; *Int'l*, pg. 1276
P.C. WIAUX—See Union Miniere; *Int'l*, pg. 1442
PC WORLD—See International Data Group; *U.S. Private*, pg. 569
PC WORLD EAST AFRICA—See International Data Group; *U.S. Private*, pg. 570
PC WORLD PAKISTAN/MICRO PUBLICATIONS—See International Data Group; *U.S. Private*, pg. 570
PC WORLD PANAMA/EDICOMOUTO, S.A.—See International Data Group; *U.S. Private*, pg. 570
PC WORLD VIETNAM—See International Data Group; *U.S. Private*, pg. 570
PCA INTERNATIONAL, INC.; *U.S. Public*, pg. 1240
PCA LIFE REINSURANCE—See Physician Corporation of America; *U.S. Public*, pg. 1293
PCA SOLUTIONS—See Physician Corporation of America; *U.S. Public*, pg. 1293
PCA WEST INC.—See Tenneco Inc.; *U.S. Public*, pg. 1578
PCC AIRFOILS, INC.—See Precision Castparts Corp.; *U.S. Public*, pg. 1320
PCC ENERGY INC.—See Cigna Corp.; *U.S. Public*, pg. 358
PCC EXPORTS, INC.—See Precision Castparts Corp.; *U.S. Public*, pg. 1320
PCC FLOW TECHNOLOGIES, INC.—See Precision Castparts Corp.; *U.S. Public*, pg. 1320
PCC SPECIALTY PRODUCTS, INC.—See Precision Castparts Corp.; *U.S. Public*, pg. 1321
PCC TECHNICAL INDUSTRIES, INC.—See American Financial Group; *U.S. Public*, pg. 75
PCGP, INC.—See Cigna Corp.; *U.S. Public*, pg. 361
PCI; *U.S. Private*, pg. 826
PCI AUGSBURG GMBH—See Viag AG; *Int'l*, pg. 1464
PCI INVESTMENTS INC.—See Ashley International & Paschen; *U.S. Private*, pg. 89
PCI PROPERTIES (ONE) (PTY.)—See Mannesmann A.G.; *Int'l*, pg. 835
PCI PROPERTIES (THREE) (PTY.) LTD.—See Mannesmann A.G.; *Int'l*, pg. 835
PCI PROPERTIES (TWO) (PTY.) LTD.—See Mannesmann A.G.; *Int'l*, pg. 835
PCI TANDEM DIV.—See Standard Pacific Corp.; *U.S. Public*, pg. 1504
PCL—See Pechiney S.A.; *Int'l*, pg. 1031
PCL-BRAUN-SIMONS LTD.—See Kuwait Petroleum Corporation; *Int'l*, pg. 765
PCL COURIER HOLDINGS INC.—See Air Canada; *Int'l*, pg. 36
PCL-REP. OFFICE OF PECHINEY HANDELSGESELLSCHAFT IN HUNGARY—See Pechiney S.A.; *Int'l*, pg. 1031
PCM BELGIUM—See DSM N.V.; *Int'l*, pg. 356
PCM CONSTRUCTION, INC.—See Henkels & McCoy, Inc.; *U.S. Private*, pg. 522
PCM-EWP—See DSM N.V.; *Int'l*, pg. 356
PCM FRANCE SA—See DSM N.V.; *Int'l*, pg. 356
PCS HEALTH SYSTEMS, INC.—See Eli Lilly and Company; *U.S. Public*, pg. 993
PCS NITROGEN—See Potash Corporation of Saskatchewan Inc.; *Int'l*, pg. 1064
PCS NITROGEN-TRINIDAD—See Potash Corporation of Saskatchewan Inc.; *Int'l*, pg. 1064
PCS PHOSPHATE - AURORA—See Potash Corporation of Saskatchewan Inc.; *Int'l*, pg. 1064
PCS PHOSPHATE - RALEIGH—See Potash Corporation of Saskatchewan Inc.; *Int'l*, pg. 1064
PCS PHOSPHATE - WHITE SPRINGS—See Potash Corporation of Saskatchewan Inc.; *Int'l*, pg. 1065
PCS POTASH - ALLAN—See Potash Corporation of Saskatchewan Inc.; *Int'l*, pg. 1064
PCS POTASH - CORY—See Potash Corporation of Saskatchewan Inc.; *Int'l*, pg. 1064
PCS POTASH - ESTERHAZY—See Potash Corporation of Saskatchewan Inc.; *Int'l*, pg. 1064
PCS POTASH - MOAB—See Potash Corporation of Saskatchewan Inc.; *Int'l*, pg. 1064
PCS POTASH - NEW BRUNSWICK—See Potash Corporation of Saskatchewan Inc.; *Int'l*, pg. 1064
PCS POTASH - PATIENCE LAKE—See Potash Corporation of Saskatchewan Inc.; *Int'l*, pg. 1064
PCT BV—See KPN Koninklyke PTT Nederland NV; *Int'l*, pg. 720

PD TERMINALS (PTY) LIMITED—See Powell Duffryn PLC; *Int'l*, pg. 1065
PDA INTERNATIONAL/JAPAN—See The Macneal-Schwendler Corp.; *Int'l*, pg. 1031
PDA INTERNATIONAL/UNITED KINGDOM—See The Macneal-Schwendler Corp.; *Int'l*, pg. 1031
PDC SECURITIES, INC.—See Petroleum Development Corporation; *U.S. Public*, pg. 1280
PDI (PRODUCTION.DESIGN.INTERACTIVE)—See Black Rogers Sullivan Goodnight, Inc.; *U.S. Private*, pg. 147
PDL, INC.—See Presidential Realty Corporation; *U.S. Public*, pg. 1323
PDM BRIDGE—See Pitt-Des Moines, Inc.; *U.S. Public*, pg. 1305
PDM BRIDGE CORP.—See Pitt-Des Moines, Inc.; *U.S. Public*, pg. 1304
PDM INTERNATIONAL LTD.—See Pitt-Des Moines, Inc.; *U.S. Public*, pg. 1304
PDM LATIN AMERICA LTD.—See Pitt-Des Moines, Inc.; *U.S. Public*, pg. 1304
PDM LTD.—See Meyer International PLC; *Int'l*, pg. 864
PDM STEEL SERVICE CENTER-CEDAR RAPIDS—See Pitt-Des Moines, Inc.; *U.S. Public*, pg. 1305
PDM STROCAL, INC.—See Pitt-Des Moines, Inc.; *U.S. Public*, pg. 1305
PDS AGENCY, INC.—See Proffitt's, Inc.; *U.S. Public*, pg. 1334
PDS HANDLING CV—See KPN Koninklyke PTT Nederland NV; pg. 720
PDTL TRADING CO., LTD.—See Sumitomo Electric Industries, Ltd.; *Int'l*, pg. 1313
PDV AMERICA CORP.—See Petroleos de Venezuela S.A.; *Int'l*, pg. 1045
PDV MARINA, S.A.—See Petroleos de Venezuela S.A.; *Int'l*, pg. 1045
PDVSA SERVICES B.V.—See Petroleos de Venezuela S.A.; *Int'l*, pg. 1046
PDVSA SERVICES, INC.—See Petroleos de Venezuela S.A.; *Int'l*, pg. 1045
PE BIOSYSTEMS—See The Perkin-Elmer Corporation; *U.S. Public*, pg. 1279
P.E./DEL MAR, INC.—See Watsco, Inc.; *U.S. Public*, pg. 1746
PE MOLECULAR INFORMATICS—See The Perkin-Elmer Corporation; *U.S. Public*, pg. 1279
PEC EL PASO—See Plastic Engineered Components Inc.; *U.S. Private*, pg. 871
PEC ISRAEL ECONOMIC CORPORATION—See IDB Holding Corporation; *Int'l*, pg. 644
PEC LOS ANGELES—See Plastic Engineered Components Inc.; *U.S. Private*, pg. 871
PEC MICHIGAN—See Plastic Engineered Components Inc.; *U.S. Private*, pg. 871
PEC MID WEST TECHNICAL CENTER—See Plastic Engineered Components Inc.; *U.S. Private*, pg. 871
PEC MOARK—See Plastic Engineered Components Inc.; *U.S. Private*, pg. 871
PEC WISCONSIN—See Plastic Engineered Components Inc.; *U.S. Private*, pg. 871
PEI N.V.—See PepsiCo, Inc.; *U.S. Public*, pg. 1277
PEM INTL. LTD.—See Penn Engineering & Manufacturing Corp.; *U.S. Public*, pg. 1270
PENCO-TENNESSEE—See Willis Corroon Group PLC; *Int'l*, pg. 1508
THE PFH GROUP—See N.V. Koninklijke Bijenkorf Beheer KBB; *Int'l*, pg. 750
PFS INVESTMENTS INC.—See Travelers Group; *U.S. Public*, pg. 1633
PFU LIMITED—See Fujitsu Limited; *Int'l*, pg. 526
PG&E CORPORATION; *U.S. Public*, pg. 1240
P.G. BELL DIV.—See Jannock Limited; *Int'l*, pg. 698
PG ENERGY, INC.—See Pennsylvania Enterprises Inc.; *U.S. Public*, pg. 1271
PG ENERGY SERVICES—See Pennsylvania Enterprises Inc.; *U.S. Public*, pg. 1272
P.G. GROUP—See Etablissements Delhaize Freres Et Cie "Le Lion" S.A.; *Int'l*, pg. 463
PG PUBLISHING CO.—See Blade Communications, Inc.; *U.S. Private*, pg. 147
PG TECHNOLOGY, LTD.—See COMSAT Corporation; *U.S. Public*, pg. 424
PG VINYL WINDOWS/PG PROGLASS CONSTRUCTION; *U.S. Private*, pg. 826
PGA MOTORS—See Lex Service PLC; *Int'l*, pg. 807
PG&E ENERGY SERVICES—See PG&E Corporation; *U.S. Public*, pg. 1241
PG&E ENERGY TRADING—See PG&E Corporation; *U.S. Public*, pg. 1241
PG&E GAS TRANSMISSION—See PG&E Corporation; *U.S. Public*, pg. 1241
PGF INTERNATIONAL PTY. LIMITED—See Haw Par Brothers International Limited; *Int'l*, pg. 604
PGF NEW ZEALAND LIMITED—See Haw Par Brothers International Limited; *Int'l*, pg. 604
PGH BRICKS PTY. LTD.—See BTR plc; *Int'l*, pg. 128
PGH EUREKA CERAMICS—See BTR plc; *Int'l*, pg. 128
PGL INDUSTRIES, INC.—See Staff Builders Inc.; *U.S. Public*, pg. 1501
PH HOLDING—See The Pantry, Inc.; *U.S. Private*, pg. 837
PHB DIE CASTING; *U.S. Private*, pg. 826
PHB MACHINING DIVISION—See PHB Die Casting; *U.S. Private*, pg. 826
PHB PLASTIC & RUBBER MOLDING DIVISION—See PHB Die Casting; *U.S. Private*, pg. 826
PHB TOOL & DIE—See PHB Die Casting; *U.S. Private*, pg. 826
PHC HOLDINGS, INC.—See Pacific Holding Corporation; *U.S. Public*, pg. 831
PHH CORPORATION—See Cendant Corporation; *U.S. Public*, pg. 321
PHH DEUTSCHLAND, INC.—See Cendant Corporation; *U.S. Public*, pg. 321
PHH FINANCIAL SERVICES, INC.—See Cendant Corporation; *U.S. Public*, pg. 321

PHH FRANCE ARVAL SERVICE LEASE—See Cendant Corporation; *U.S. Public*, pg. 321
PHH ITALY ARVAL SERVICE LEASE ITALIA SPA—See Cendant Corporation; *U.S. Public*, pg. 321
PHH MEXICAN CORPORATION—See Cendant Corporation; *U.S. Public*, pg. 321
PHH MORTGAGE SERVICES CORPORATION—See Cendant Corporation; *U.S. Public*, pg. 321
PHH TORONTO—See Cendant Corporation; *U.S. Public*, pg. 321
P.H.I. ENGINEERING LTD.—See Deutsche Babcock AG; *Int'l*, pg. 398
PHI MARKETING SERVICES—See Pioneer Hi-Bred International, Inc.; *U.S. Public*, pg. 1299
PHP HEALTHCARE CORPORATION; *U.S. Public*, pg. 1241
P.I. ACCEPTANCES (PTY.) LTD.—See Assicurazioni Generali S.p.A.; *Int'l*, pg. 91
P.I.B.F. AYUTTHAYA BRANCH—See The Sumitomo Bank, Limited; *Int'l*, pg. 1310
P.I.B.F. CHON BURI BRANCH—See The Sumitomo Bank, Limited; *Int'l*, pg. 1310
PIC REALTY CANADA LTD.—See The Prudential Insurance Company of America; *U.S. Private*, pg. 893
PKF/JONGEKRIJG HOLDING B.V.—See N.V. Koninklijke KNP BT; *Int'l*, pg. 756
PKF/STEUN B.V.—See N.V. Koninklijke KNP BT; *Int'l*, pg. 756
PKL HOLDING GMBH—See SIG Schweizersiche Industrie-Gesellschaft Holding AG; *Int'l*, pg. 1156
PKL HUNGARIA KFT—See SIG Schweizersiche Industrie-Gesellschaft Holding AG; *Int'l*, pg. 1156
PKL VERPACKUNGSSYSTEME GMBH; *Int'l*, pg. 1020
PKL VERPACKUNGSSYSTEME GMBH—See SIG Schweizersiche Industrie-Gesellschaft Holding AG; *Int'l*, pg. 1156
PKL VERPACKUNGSSYTEME SAALFELDEN GMBH—See SIG Schweizersiche Industrie-Gesellschaft Holding AG; *Int'l*, pg. 1156
PLD NORDIC AB—See Bergman & Beving AB; *Int'l*, pg. 188
PLE SYSTEMS GESELLSCHAFT FUR ENTWICKLUNG UND VERTRIEB VON SOFT- UND HARDWARE-SYSTEMEN NBH—See Ruhrgas Aktiengesellschaft; *Int'l*, pg. 1149
PLECON PIPELINE ENGINEERING CONSULTING GMBH—See Ruhrgas Aktiengesellschaft; *Int'l*, pg. 1149
PLEDOC GESELLSCHAFT FUR DOKUMENTATIONSERSTELLUNG UND PFLEGE MBH—See Ruhrgas Aktiengesellschaft; *Int'l*, pg. 1149
PLM FINANCIAL SERVICES, INC.—See PLM International, Inc.; *U.S. Public*, pg. 1241
PLM INTERNATIONAL, INC.; *U.S. Public*, pg. 1241
PLM RAILCAR MANAGEMENT SERVICES, INC.—See PLM International, Inc.; *U.S. Public*, pg. 1241
PLM TRAILER LEASING—See PLM International, Inc.; *U.S. Public*, pg. 1241
PLP PRODUTOS PARA LINHAS PROFORMADOS LTDA.—See Preformed Line Products; *U.S. Public*, pg. 1321
PLUM—See Willis Corroon Group PLC; *Int'l*, pg. 1504
PM FOODS INC.—See Petroleum Marketers, Inc.; *U.S. Private*, pg. 859
PM GROUP LIFE INSURANCE COMPANY—See Pacific Life Insurance Company; *U.S. Private*, pg. 831
PM HOLDINGS, INC.—See Phoenix Home Life Mutual Insurance Company; *U.S. Private*, pg. 863
PM PROPERTIES INC.—See Petroleum Marketers, Inc.; *U.S. Private*, pg. 859
PM REALTY ADVISORS INC.—See Pacific Life Insurance Company; *U.S. Private*, pg. 831
PM SERVICES LTD.—See The General Electric Company, p.l.c.; *Int'l*, pg. 545
PM TERMINALS, INC.—See Petroleum Marketers, Inc.; *U.S. Private*, pg. 859
PM TRANSPORT, INC.—See Petroleum Marketers, Inc.; *U.S. Private*, pg. 859
PMA REINSURANCE CORPORATION—See Pennsylvania Manufacturers Corp.; *U.S. Public*, pg. 1272
PMB ELEKTRONIK PRODUKTION GMBH—See Mannesmann A.G.; *Int'l*, pg. 836
PMB ENTERPRISES WEST, INC.—See Pancho's Mexican Buffet, Inc.; *U.S. Public*, pg. 1255
PMC CAPITAL INC.; *U.S. Public*, pg. 1242
PMC EASTERN EUROPE LTD—See Corporacion MAPFRE, Compania Internacional de Reaseguros, S.A.; *Int'l*, pg. 334
PMC, INC.; *U.S. Private*, pg. 827
PMC, INC.—See Polaroid Corporation; *U.S. Public*, pg. 1313
PMC INDUSTRIES, INC.; *U.S. Private*, pg. 827
PMC PERSONAL MANAGEMENT CONSULT GMBH—See Commerzbank AG; *Int'l*, pg. 310
PMC SIERRA, INC.—See Sierra Semiconductor; *U.S. Public*, pg. 1470
P.M.D.—See Package Machinery Co.; *U.S. Private*, pg. 832
PMI—See Todd & Sargent, Inc.; *U.S. Private*, pg. 1089
PMI MOTION TECHNOLOGIES—See Kollmorgen Corporation; *U.S. Public*, pg. 965
PMI MOTION TECHNOLOGIES DIV.—See Kollmorgen Corporation; *U.S. Public*, pg. 965
PML SECURITIES CO.—See Provident Mutual Life Insurance Co.; *U.S. Private*, pg. 892
PMM, INC.—See Columbia/HCA Healthcare Corporation; *U.S. Public*, pg. 405
PMP FERMENTATION PRODUCTS, INC.—See Fujisawa Pharmaceutical Co. Ltd.; *Int'l*, pg. 525
PMR CORPORATION; *U.S. Public*, pg. 1242
PMSI LTD.—See Policy Management Systems Corporation; *U.S. Public*, pg. 1314
PMSVW/YOUNG & RUBICAM B.V.—See Young & Rubicam Inc.; *U.S. Private*, pg. 1199
PMT OF THE SOUTHWEST, INC.—See Union Pacific Corporation; *U.S. Public*, pg. 1668

PMT PRAZISIONS-MEBTECHNIK GMBH—See FAG Group; *Int'l*, pg. 468
P.N.B., S.A.—See 3Com Corporation; *U.S. Public*, pg. 1604
PNC BANCORP INC.—See PNC Bank Corp.; *U.S. Public*, pg. 1243
PNC BANK—See PNC Bank Corp.; *U.S. Public*, pg. 1242
PNC BANK CORP.; *U.S. Public*, pg. 1242
PNC BANK, DELAWARE—See PNC Bank Corp.; *U.S. Public*, pg. 1243
PNC BANK MORTGAGE CENTER—See PNC Bank Corp.; *U.S. Public*, pg. 1243
PNC BANK, N.A.—See PNC Bank Corp.; *U.S. Public*, pg. 1243
PNC BANK NEW ENGLAND—See PNC Bank Corp.; *U.S. Public*, pg. 1243
PNC BANK, SOUTH CENTRAL—See PNC Bank Corp.; *U.S. Public*, pg. 1243
PNC CAPITAL CORP.—See PNC Bank Corp.; *U.S. Public*, pg. 1243
PNC COMMERCIAL CORPORATION—See PNC Bank Corp.; *U.S. Public*, pg. 1243
PNC COMMUNITY DEVELOPMENT CORP.—See PNC Bank Corp.; *U.S. Public*, pg. 1243
PNC CORP.—See PNC Bank Corp.; *U.S. Public*, pg. 1243
PNC DISCOUNT BROKERAGE—See PNC Bank Corp.; *U.S. Public*, pg. 1242
PNC ESOP FUNDING CORPORATION—See PNC Bank Corp.; *U.S. Public*, pg. 1243
PNC FINANCIAL SERVICES, INC.—See PNC Bank Corp.; *U.S. Public*, pg. 1243
PNC FLORIDA, INC.—See PNC Bank Corp.; *U.S. Public*, pg. 1243
PNC FUNDING CORP.—See PNC Bank Corp.; *U.S. Public*, pg. 1243
PNC INTERNATIONAL BANK—See PNC Bank Corp.; *U.S. Public*, pg. 1243
PNC INTERNATIONAL FINANCE, N.V.—See PNC Bank Corp.; *U.S. Public*, pg. 1243
PNC LEASING CORP.—See PNC Bank Corp.; *U.S. Public*, pg. 1243
PNC LIFE INSURANCE COMPANY—See PNC Bank Corp.; *U.S. Public*, pg. 1243
PNC MORTGAGE CORPORATION OF AMERICA—See PNC Bank Corp.; *U.S. Public*, pg. 1243
PNC NATIONAL BANK—See PNC Bank Corp.; *U.S. Public*, pg. 1243
PNC NATIONAL INVESTMENT CORPORATION—See PNC Bank Corp.; *U.S. Public*, pg. 1243
PNC-NJ N.A.—See PNC Bank Corp.; *U.S. Public*, pg. 1243
PNC REALTY CORPORATION—See PNC Bank Corp.; *U.S. Public*, pg. 1243
PNC REALTY HOLDING CORPORATION—See PNC Bank Corp.; *U.S. Public*, pg. 1244
PNC SECURITIES CORP.—See PNC Bank Corp.; *U.S. Public*, pg. 1243
PNC TRUST COMPANY OF FLORIDA, N.A.—See PNC Bank Corp.; *U.S. Public*, pg. 1244
PNC VENTURE CORPORATION—See PNC Bank Corp.; *U.S. Public*, pg. 1244
PNMR SECURITIES—See SAFECO Corporation; *U.S. Public*, pg. 1423
PNY TECHNOLOGIES, INC.; *U.S. Private*, pg. 827
PP&L RESOURCES; *U.S. Public*, pg. 1244
P.T. P.P. TAISEI INDONESIA CONSTRUCTION—See Taisei Corporation; *Int'l*, pg. 1347
PPA DESIGN LTD.—See BDDP Group; *Int'l*, pg. 118
PPC, INC.—See Thomas Nelson Inc.; *U.S. Public*, pg. 1168
PPD PHARMACO, INC.—See Pharmaceutical Product Development, Inc.; *U.S. Public*, pg. 1285
PPD PHARMACO INTL.—See Pharmaceutical Product Development, Inc.; *U.S. Public*, pg. 1285
PPF INTERNATIONAL LIMITED—See Unilever Plc; *Int'l*, pg. 1434
PPF INTL. LTD., FOOD INDUSTRIES DIV.—See Unilever Plc; *Int'l*, pg. 1434
PPG INC.; *U.S. Private*, pg. 827
PPG INDUSTRIES, INC.; *U.S. Public*, pg. 1245
PPIC UK LTD.—See KPN Koninklyke PTT Nederland NV; *Int'l*, pg. 720
PPM AMERICA INC.—See Prudential Corporation PLC; *Int'l*, pg. 1073
PPM VENTURES LTD.—See Prudential Corporation PLC; *Int'l*, pg. 1073
PPP BEAUMONT PLC—See PPP hc; *Int'l*, pg. 1020
PPP HC; *Int'l*, pg. 1020
PPP LIFETIME PLC—See PPP hc; *Int'l*, pg. 1020
PPT VISION, INC.; *U.S. Public*, pg. 1245
PPV VENTURE PRODUCTIONS—See Time Warner Inc.; *U.S. Public*, pg. 1610
PQ AUSTRALIA PTY., LTD.—See PQ Corporation; *U.S. Private*, pg. 827
PQ CORPORATION; *U.S. Private*, pg. 827
PQI INC.—See Pfizer Inc.; *U.S. Public*, pg. 1283
THE PR CENTRE LIMITED—See Shandwick International Plc; *Int'l*, pg. 1226
PR EUROPE—See Groupe Pernod Ricard; *Int'l*, pg. 566
P.R. NEWSWIRE ASSOCIATION INC.—See United News & Media plc; *Int'l*, pg. 1443
P.R. SOLO CUP, INC.—See Solo Cup Company; *U.S. Private*, pg. 1013
PRC ENVIRONMENTAL MANAGEMENT, INC.—See Tetra Tech, Inc.; *U.S. Public*, pg. 1582
PRC, INC.—See Litton Industries, Inc.; *U.S. Public*, pg. 1003
PRC (UK) LTD.—See Courtaulds plc; *Int'l*, pg. 339
PRESUR - PRERREDUCIDOS INTEGRADOS DEL SUROESTE DE ESPANA, S.A.—See SEPI; *Int'l*, pg. 1224
PRGR USA CORPORATION—See The Yokohama Rubber Co., Ltd.; *Int'l*, pg. 1521
PROCHEM MIXING EQUIPMENT LTD.—See Robbins & Myers, Inc.; *U.S. Public*, pg. 1393
PRS, INC.—See CPAC, Inc.; *U.S. Public*, pg. 282

P.S. COLORADO CREDIT CORP.—See New Century Energies, Inc.; *U.S. Public*, pg. 1170
PS GROUP HOLDINGS; *U.S. Public*, pg. 1245
PS INSURANCE CO.—See Public Storage, Inc.; *U.S. Public*, pg. 1341
P.S. INTERNATIONAL INC.; *U.S. Private*, pg. 827
PS...PLUS SIZES, PLUS SAVINGS—See Catherines Stores Corporation; *U.S. Public*, pg. 318
PS PROMOTIONS, INC.; *U.S. Private*, pg. 828
PS TRADING—See PS Group Holdings; *U.S. Public*, pg. 1245
PSA AIRLINES, INC.—See US Airways Group, Inc.; *U.S. Public*, pg. 1680
PSA INTERNATIONAL S.A.—See PSA Peugeot Citroen; *Int'l*, pg. 1021
PSA PEUGEOT CITROEN; *Int'l*, pg. 1020
PSB CO.—See White Castle System, Inc.; *U.S. Private*, pg. 1172
PSC BAR CODE LTD.—See PSC Inc.; *U.S. Public*, pg. 1246
PSC INC.; *U.S. Public*, pg. 1245
PSC SERVICES GROUP, INC.—See Philadelphia Suburban Corporation; *U.S. Public*, pg. 1287
PSD HOLDINGS BHD.—See Sime Darby Berhad; *Int'l*, pg. 1250
PSDI; *U.S. Private*, pg. 828
PSEG CAPITAL CORPORATION—See Public Service Enterprise Group Incorporated; *U.S. Public*, pg. 1340
PSG PILLO-PAK MAATSCHAPPIJ BV—See N.V. Koninklijke KNP BT; *Int'l*, pg. 756
PSI DATA SYSTEMS LTD.—See Compagnie des Machines Bull; *Int'l*, pg. 316
P.S.I. DIVISION—See Package Machinery Co.; *U.S. Private*, pg. 832
PSI HEALTH CARE, INC.—See Integrated Health Services, Inc.; *U.S. Public*, pg. 885
PSI INTERNATIONAL—See Storage Technology Corporation; *U.S. Public*, pg. 1522
PSI POWER RESOURCE DEVELOPMENT, INC.—See Cinergy Corp.; *U.S. Public*, pg. 369
PSI-PROCESS SYSTEMS INTERNATIONAL, INC.—See Chart Industries, Inc.; *U.S. Public*, pg. 336
PSICOR, INC.—See Baxter International Inc.; *U.S. Public*, pg. 196
PSK TECH, INC.—See Nippon Sanso Corporation; *Int'l*, pg. 939
PSM INTERNATIONAL—See McKechnie PLC; *Int'l*, pg. 852
PSNC BLUE RIDGE CORP.—See Public Service Company of North Carolina, Inc.; *U.S. Public*, pg. 1340
PSNC CARDINAL PIPELINE COMPANY—See Public Service Company of North Carolina, Inc.; *U.S. Public*, pg. 1340
PSR; *U.S. Private*, pg. 828
P.S.R. INVESTMENTS, INC.—See New Century Energies, Inc.; *U.S. Public*, pg. 1170
PSS—See Physician Sales and Services Inc.; *U.S. Public*, pg. 1294
PST VANS, INC.; *U.S. Public*, pg. 1246
PTA CORPORATION; *U.S. Private*, pg. 828
PTC CORRECTIONS—See Peoples Telephone Company, Inc.; *U.S. Public*, pg. 1275
PTC PARTNERS—See Pechiney S.A.; *Int'l*, pg. 1029
PTC SERVICES—See Peoples Telephone Company, Inc.; *U.S. Public*, pg. 1275
PTC THERMISTOR DIV.—See Bowthorpe plc; *Int'l*, pg. 208
PTDBS SECURITIES INDONESIA—See DBS Bank Ltd.; *Int'l*, pg. 351
PTG PLASMA-OBERFLACHENTECHNIK GMBH—See Deutsche Babcock AG; *Int'l*, pg. 400
PTH TRADING (PTY.) LTD.—See FAG Group; *Int'l*, pg. 469
PTI TECHNOLGIES, INC.—See ESCO Electronics Corporation; *U.S. Public*, pg. 546
PTK LIMITED—See Mitsui & Co., Ltd.; *Int'l*, pg. 878
PTP AERIAL PLATFORMS LTD.—See Sophus Berendsen A/S; *Int'l*, pg. 184
PTR-PRECISION TECHNOLOGIES, INC.—See Integral Hydraulik & Co.; *Int'l*, pg. 679
PTS ELECTRONICS CORPORATION; *U.S. Private*, pg. 828
PTT AUTOLEASE BV—See KPN Koninklyke PTT Nederland NV; *Int'l*, pg. 720
PTT CONTEST BV—See KPN Koninklyke PTT Nederland NV; *Int'l*, pg. 720
PTT FINANS BV—See KPN Koninklyke PTT Nederland NV; *Int'l*, pg. 720
PTT NETHERLANDS (UK) LTD.—See KPN Koninklyke PTT Nederland NV; *Int'l*, pg. 720
PTT POST BEHEER BV—See KPN Koninklyke PTT Nederland NV; *Int'l*, pg. 720
PTT POST BV—See KPN Koninklyke PTT Nederland NV; *Int'l*, pg. 720
PTT POST CARIBBEAN NV—See KPN Koninklyke PTT Nederland NV; *Int'l*, pg. 720
PTT POST LOGISTIEK MAARSSEN BV—See KPN Koninklyke PTT Nederland NV; *Int'l*, pg. 720
PTT POST LOGISTIEK NIJMEGEN BV—See KPN Koninklyke PTT Nederland NV; *Int'l*, pg. 720
PTT TELECOM BV—See KPN Koninklyke PTT Nederland NV; *Int'l*, pg. 720
PTT TELECOM CARRIBEAN NV—See KPN Koninklyke PTT Nederland NV; *Int'l*, pg. 720
PTT TELECOM NETHERLANDS (DEUTSCHLAND) GMBH—See KPN Koninklyke PTT Nederland NV; *Int'l*, pg. 720
PTT TELECOM NETHERLANDS (ITALY) SRL—See KPN Koninklyke PTT Nederland NV; *Int'l*, pg. 720
PTT TELECOM NETHERLANDS (UK) INC.—See KPN Koninklyke PTT Nederland NV; *Int'l*, pg. 720
PTT VASTGOED BV—See KPN Koninklyke PTT Nederland NV; *Int'l*, pg. 721
PU, S.A.—See Freudenberg & Company; *Int'l*, pg. 506
PUCARSA - PUERTO DE CARBONERAS, S.A.—See SEPI; *Int'l*, pg. 1224
PVB MEDIZINTECHNIK GMBH—See Smiths Industries plc; *Int'l*, pg. 1268

PVC COMPOUNDERS—See Group Dekko; *U.S. Private*, pg. 484
PVD BESCHICHTUNGSSERVICE GMBH—See Anchor Lamina Inc.; *Int'l*, pg. 75
PVS CHEMICALS, INC.; *U.S. Private*, pg. 828
PVS-NOLWOOD CHEMICALS, INC.—See PVS Chemicals, Inc.; *U.S. Private*, pg. 828
PVS TECHNOLOGIES, INC.—See PVS Chemicals, Inc.; *U.S. Private*, pg. 949
PWA ROLLAND DECOR INC.—See The Cascades Group; *Int'l*, pg. 274
PWH ANLAGEN + SYSTEME GMBH—See Fried. Krupp AG; *Int'l*, pg. 511
PWS-KENT PUBLISHING CO.—See The Thomson Corporation; *U.S. Public*, pg. 1600
PYA/MONARCH, INC.—See Sara Lee Corporation; *U.S. Public*, pg. 1433
P.Y.C.A.S.A.-LA COCINERA—See Danone Group; *Int'l*, pg. 380
PAASIVAARA OY—See Unilever Plc; *Int'l*, pg. 1438
PABCO METALS CORPORATION—See A.J. Gerrard and Company; *U.S. Private*, pg. 449
PABELLON DE OPERADORES EUROPEOS DE TELECOMUNICACIONES, S.A. (P.O.E.T.)—See Telefonica de Espana, S.A.; *Int'l*, pg. 1372
PABLO FERRANDO S.A.C.E.L.—See Hewlett-Packard Company; *U.S. Public*, pg. 822
P.T. PABRIK ARAYA INDONESIA—See Nissho Iwai Corporation; *Int'l*, pg. 949
PABST BREWING CO./MILWAUKEE—See S & P Company; *U.S. Private*, pg. 954
PABST BREWING CO./TUMWATER—See S & P Company; *U.S. Private*, pg. 954
PABTEX, INC.—See Kansas City Southern Industries, Inc.; *U.S. Public*, pg. 944
PAC-FAB, INC./EAST—See Essef Corporation; *U.S. Public*, pg. 593
PAC MANUFACTURING & DISTRIBUTING CO.—See Precision Tune Autocare Inc.; *U.S. Public*, pg. 1321
PAC PAPER INC.; *U.S. Private*, pg. 828
PAC RIM HOLDING CORPORATION; *U.S. Public*, pg. 1246
PACAERO—See Banner Aerospace, Inc.; *U.S. Public*, pg. 187
PACCAR AUTOMOTIVE INC.—See Paccar Inc.; *U.S. Public*, pg. 1247
PACCAR FINANCIAL CORP.—See Paccar Inc.; *U.S. Public*, pg. 1247
PACCAR FINANCIAL LIMITED—See Paccar Inc.; *U.S. Public*, pg. 1247
PACCAR FINANCIAL PTY, LTD.—See Paccar Inc.; *U.S. Public*, pg. 1247
PACCAR INC.; *U.S. Public*, pg. 1246
PACCAR INTERNATIONAL—See Paccar Inc.; *U.S. Public*, pg. 1246
PACCAR LEASING CORPORATION—See Paccar Inc.; *U.S. Public*, pg. 1247
PACCAR PARTS—See Paccar Inc.; *U.S. Public*, pg. 1246
PACCAR SALES NORTH AMERICA, INC.—See Paccar Inc.; *U.S. Public*, pg. 1247
PACCAR TECHNICAL CENTER—See Paccar Inc.; *U.S. Public*, pg. 1246
PACCAR WINCH DIVISION—See Paccar Inc.; *U.S. Public*, pg. 1246
PACCOM LEASING CORPORATION—See PacifiCorp; *U.S. Public*, pg. 1252
PACE—See Regional Transportation Authority (RTA); *U.S. Private*, pg. 919
PACE ADVERTISING—See WPP Group plc; *Int'l*, pg. 1483
PACE ANALYTICAL SERVICES; *U.S. Private*, pg. 829
THE PACE COLLECTION; *U.S. Private*, pg. 829
THE PACE CONSULTANTS, INC.—See Jacobs Engineering Group Inc.; *U.S. Public*, pg. 921
PACE DAIRY FOODS—See The Kroger Co.; *U.S. Public*, pg. 967
PACE DIE CAST PRODUCTS, INC.—See Leggett & Platt, Incorporated; *U.S. Public*, pg. 986
PACE INDUSTRIES, INC.—See Leggett & Platt, Incorporated; *U.S. Public*, pg. 986
PACE INDUSTRIES INC.—See Leggett & Platt, Incorporated; *U.S. Public*, pg. 986
PACE INDUSTRIES OF MEXICO, L.L.C.—See Emerson Electric Co.; *U.S. Public*, pg. 578
PACE INDUSTRIES PUGET DIVISION, INC.—See Leggett & Platt, Incorporated; *U.S. Public*, pg. 986
PACE INTERNATIONAL L.P.; *U.S. Private*, pg. 829
PACE MECHANICAL SERVICES, INC.—See EMCOR Group, Inc.; *U.S. Public*, pg. 572
PACE OIL CO., INC.; *U.S. Private*, pg. 829
PACE POWER CONSTRUCTORS, INC.—See Deutsche Babcock AG; *Int'l*, pg. 401
PACE PRESS, INC.; *U.S. Private*, pg. 829
PACE RESOURCES, INC.; *U.S. Private*, pg. 829
PACER INDUSTRIES, INC.—See Echlin Inc.; *U.S. Public*, pg. 560
PACER INFOTEC INC.; *U.S. Public*, pg. 830
PACESETTER CORPORATION; *U.S. Private*, pg. 830
PACESETTER INC.—See St. Jude Medical, Inc.; *U.S. Public*, pg. 1428
PACESETTER PRODUCTS INC.—See Fab Industries, Inc.; *U.S. Public*, pg. 603
PACESETTER STEEL SERVICE, INC.; *U.S. Private*, pg. 830
PACHMAYR LTD.—See Lyman Products Corporation; *U.S. Private*, pg. 683
PACHON S.A. MINERA—See Cambior Inc.; *Int'l*, pg. 253
PACIFIC AMERICAN INCOME SHARES, INC.; *U.S. Public*, pg. 1247
PACIFIC ANCHOR CHEMICAL CORPORATION—See Air Products and Chemicals, Inc.; *U.S. Public*, pg. 31
PACIFIC AUTOMOTIVE CO-OPERATION, INC.—See Toyota Motor Corporation; *Int'l*, pg. 1413
PACIFIC BEAUTY CARE PTE. LTD.—See Wella Group; *Int'l*, pg. 1490

PACIFIC DIRECTORY OF CORPORATE AFFILIATIONS

Company Index

PACIFIC BELL—See SBC Communications Inc.; *U.S. Public*, pg. 1416
PACIFIC BRANDS—See Pacific Dunlop Limited; *Int'l*, pg. 1021
PACIFIC CAPITAL BANCORP; *U.S. Public*, pg. 1247
PACIFIC CENTURY BANK—See Pacific Century Financial Corporation; *U.S. Public*, pg. 1248
PACIFIC CENTURY FINANCIAL CORPORATION; *U.S. Public*, pg. 1248
PACIFIC-CHARTER MEDICAL, INC.—See Magellan Health Services, Inc.; *U.S. Public*, pg. 1036
PACIFIC CLAY PRODUCTS—See Pacific Holding Corporation; *U.S. Private*, pg. 831
PACIFIC COAST BUILDING PRODUCTS INC.; *U.S. Private*, pg. 830
PACIFIC COAST LAMINATING—See J.E. Higgins Lumber Co.; *U.S. Private*, pg. 528
PACIFIC COAST PRODUCERS; *U.S. Private*, pg. 830
PACIFIC COILCOATERS LIMITED—See Fletcher Challenge Limited; *Int'l*, pg. 495
PACIFIC COMBINING CORP.—See Health-Chem Corporation; *U.S. Public*, pg. 802
PACIFIC COMMERCIAL BANK LIMITED—See Pacific Century Financial Corporation; *U.S. Public*, pg. 1248
PACIFIC COMMUNICATION SCIENCES, INC.—See Cirrus Logic, Inc.; *U.S. Public*, pg. 375
PACIFIC CREST CAPITAL, INC.; *U.S. Public*, pg. 1248
PACIFIC DISTRIBUTION—See Pacific Dunlop Limited; *Int'l*, *pg. 1021*
PACIFIC DIVERSIFIED CAPITAL COMPANY—See Enova Corp; *U.S. Public*, pg. 584
PACIFIC DUNLOP CABLES GROUP—See Pacific Dunlop Limited; *Int'l*, pg. 1021
PACIFIC DUNLOP LIMITED; *Int'l*, pg. 1021
PACIFIC ELECTRICORD CO.—See Leviton Mfg. Co., Inc.; *U.S. Private*, pg. 663
PACIFIC ELECTRO-DYNAMICS, INC.—See Olin Corporation; *U.S. Public*, pg. 1219
PACIFIC ELEVATORS LIMITED—See Saskatchewan Wheat Pool; *Int'l*, pg. 1195
PACIFIC EMPLOYERS INSURANCE COMPANY—See Cigna Corp.; *U.S. Public*, pg. 365
PACIFIC ENERGY CONSERVATION SERVICES, INC.—See Hawaiian Electric Industries, Inc.; *U.S. Public*, pg. 800
PACIFIC ENGINE DEVELOPMENT & CONSULTING, INC. (PEDC)—See Mitsubishi Heavy Industries Ltd.; *Int'l*, pg. 873
PACIFIC ENGINEERING CO., LTD.—See Pasco Corporation; *Int'l*, pg. 1024
PACIFIC ENTERPRISES; *U.S. Public*, pg. 1249
PACIFIC ENTERPRISES INTERNATIONAL—See Pacific Enterprises; *U.S. Public*, pg. 1249
PACIFIC ENTERPRISES LEASING CO.—See Pacific Enterprises; *U.S. Public*, pg. 1249
PACIFIC FILM LABORATORIES—See Eastman Kodak Company; *U.S. Public*, pg. 552
PACIFIC FIRE HOSE PTY LTD.—See Williams Holdings Plc; *Int'l*, pg. 1500
PACIFIC FOODS, INC.; *U.S. Private*, pg. 831
PACIFIC FORGE, INC.—See Avis Industrial Corporation; *U.S. Private*, pg. 102
PACIFIC FUEL TRADING CORPORATION—See Japan Airlines Company, Ltd.; *Int'l*, pg. 700
PACIFIC GAS & ELECTRIC COMPANY—See PG&E Corporation; *U.S. Public*, pg. 1241
PACIFIC GATEWAY PROPERTIES; *U.S. Public*, pg. 1250
PACIFIC GENERATION COMPANY—See PacifiCorp; *U.S. Public*, pg. 1252
PACIFIC GOLF CO., LTD.—See Pasco Corporation; *Int'l*, pg. 1024
PACIFIC GUARDIAN LIFE INSURANCE—See Meiji Life Insurance Company; *Int'l*, pg. 854
PACIFIC HANDY CUTTER, INC.; *U.S. Private*, pg. 831
PACIFIC HARDWOODS-SOUTH BEND CO.—See WTD Industries, Inc.; *U.S. Public*, pg. 1730
PACIFIC HEATER CORPORATION—See Watlow Electric Manufacturing Company; *U.S. Private*, pg. 1153
PACIFIC HIDE & FUR DEPOT; *U.S. Private*, pg. 831
PACIFIC HOLDING CORPORATION; *U.S. Private*, pg. 831
PACIFIC HOME FURNISHINGS—See Shelby Williams Industries, Inc.; *U.S. Public*, pg. 1465
PACIFIC HOTELS, INC.—See Promus Hotel Corporation; *U.S. Public*, pg. 1335
PACIFIC INDEMNITY CO.—See The Chubb Corporation; *U.S. Public*, pg. 355
PACIFIC INSURANCE CO.—See Loews Corporation; *U.S. Public*, pg. 1011
PACIFIC INTERNATIONAL BROKERS, LTD.—See Willis Corroon Group PLC; *Int'l*, pg. 1504
PACIFIC INTERSTATE COMPANY—See Pacific Enterprises; *U.S. Public*, pg. 1249
PACIFIC INTERSTATE MOJAVE COMPANY—See Pacific Enterprises; *U.S. Public*, pg. 1249
PACIFIC INTERSTATE OFFSHORE COMPANY—See Pacific Enterprises; *U.S. Public*, pg. 1249
PACIFIC INTERSTATE TRANSMISSION COMPANY—See Pacific Enterprises; *U.S. Public*, pg. 1249
PACIFIC LEASING CORPORATION—See The Long-Term Credit Bank of Japan, Limited; *Int'l*, pg. 817
PACIFIC LIBRARY TOWER—See Pacific Enterprises; *U.S. Public*, pg. 1249
PACIFIC LIFE INSURANCE COMPANY; *U.S. Private*, pg. 831
PACIFIC LIGHTING GAS DEVELOPMENT CO.—See Pacific Enterprises; *U.S. Public*, pg. 1249
PACIFIC LIGHTING REAL ESTATE GROUP—See Pacific Enterprises; *U.S. Public*, pg. 1249
PACIFIC LUMBER & SHIPPING CO.; *U.S. Private*, pg. 832
THE PACIFIC LUMBER COMPANY—See Maxxam Inc.; *U.S. Public*, pg. 1062
PACIFIC MARINE BATTERIES PTY. LTD.—See VARTA AG; *Int'l*, pg. 1452
PACIFIC MEDIA, INC.—See Gannett Company, Inc.; *U.S. Public*, pg. 702
PACIFIC METAL COMPANY; *U.S. Private*, pg. 832
PACIFIC MEZZANINE INVESTORS—See Pacific Life Insurance Company; *U.S. Private*, pg. 831
PACIFIC MINERALS, INC.—See PacifiCorp; *U.S. Public*, pg. 1252
PACIFIC MOTOR TRANSPORT CO.—See Union Pacific Corporation; *U.S. Public*, pg. 1668
PACIFIC MOTOR TRUCKING CO.—See Union Pacific Corporation; *U.S. Public*, pg. 1668
PACIFIC MUTUAL DISTRIBUTORS—See Pacific Life Insurance Company; *U.S. Private*, pg. 831
PACIFIC NORTHERN GAS LTD.—See Westcoast Energy Inc.; *Int'l*, pg. 1492
PACIFIC NORTHERN INC.; *U.S. Private*, pg. 832
PACIFIC NUCLEAR TRANSPORT LIMITED (PNTL)—See COGEMA - Compagnie Generale des Matieres Nucleaires; *Int'l*, pg. 305
PACIFIC NUCLEAR TRANSPORT LTD.—See Nissho Iwai Corporation; *Int'l*, pg. 949
PACIFIC OFFSHORE PIPELINE COMPANY—See Pacific Enterprises; *U.S. Public*, pg. 1249
PACIFIC ONE BANK—See First Hawaiian, Inc.; *U.S. Public*, *pg. 635*
PACIFIC ONE DEALER CENTER, INC.—See First Hawaiian, Inc.; *U.S. Public*, pg. 635
PACIFIC OPTICAL DIVISION—See Recon/Optical, Inc.; *U.S. Private*, pg. 914
PACIFIC PAINTS PTY LTD.—See Imperial Chemical Industries PLC; *Int'l*, pg. 665
THE PACIFIC PLAN, INC.—See Citicorp; *U.S. Public*, pg. 377
PACIFIC PLASTICS (THAILAND) LTD.—See The Siam Cement Public Company Limited; *Int'l*, pg. 1238
PACIFIC POWER & LIGHT COMPANY—See PacifiCorp; *U.S. Public*, pg. 1251
PACIFIC PRESS LTD.—See Hollinger Inc.; *Int'l*, pg. 631
PACIFIC PRIDE BAKERIES—See Grupo Industrial Bimbo S.A. de C.V.; *Int'l*, pg. 575
PACIFIC PROTEIN—See Cultor Ltd.; *Int'l*, pg. 350
PACIFIC REGION—See MCI Communications Corp.; *U.S. Public*, pg. 1024
PACIFIC RESORT CO., LTD.—See Pasco Corporation; *Int'l*, *pg. 1024*
THE PACIFIC RIM ASSURANCE COMPANY—See Pac Rim Holding Corporation; *U.S. Public*, pg. 1246
PACIFIC SCIENTIFIC COMPANY; *U.S. Public*, pg. 1250
PACIFIC SEEDS PTY LTD.—See Zeneca Group Plc; *Int'l*, pg. 1525
PACIFIC SEEDS (THAI)—See Zeneca Group Plc; *Int'l*, pg. 1525
PACIFIC SOFTWOODS CO.—See WTD Industries, Inc.; *U.S. Public*, pg. 1730
PACIFIC SQUARE CORPORATION—See Northwest Natural Gas Company; *U.S. Public*, pg. 1200
PACIFIC STEEL CASTING CO.; *U.S. Private*, pg. 832
PACIFIC STEEL LTD.—See Fletcher Challenge Limited; *Int'l*, pg. 495
PACIFIC SYNTHETIC FUEL COMPANY—See Pacific Enterprises; *U.S. Public*, pg. 1249
PACIFIC TECHNOLOGY PRIVATE LTD.—See Ssangyong Business Group; *Int'l*, pg. 1292
PACIFIC TELECOM CABLE, INC.—See Cable and Wireless plc; *Int'l*, pg. 247
PACIFIC TELECOM CELLULAR, INC.—See PacifiCorp; *U.S. Public*, pg. 1252
PACIFIC TELECOM, INC.—See Century Telephone Enterprises, Inc.; *U.S. Public*, pg. 330
PACIFIC TELESIS GROUP—See SBC Communications Inc.; *U.S. Public*, pg. 1415
PACIFIC TITLE/MIRAGE—See Safeguard Scientifics, Inc.; *U.S. Public*, pg. 1425
PACIFIC TRAIL INC.—See London Fog Industries, Inc.; *U.S. Private*, pg. 673
PACIFIC TRI-VIEW CORPORATION—See Leucadia National Corporation; *U.S. Public*, pg. 990
PACIFIC UNION ASSURANCE COMPANY—See American International Group, Inc.; *U.S. Public*, pg. 84
PACIFIC VALVES—See Crane Co.; *U.S. Public*, pg. 457
PACIFIC WESTEEL—See Jannock Limited; *Int'l*, pg. 698
PACIFIC WESTERN RESOURCES CO.—See Pacific Enterprises; *U.S. Public*, pg. 1249
PACIFIC WINE CO.—See Paterno Imports Limited; *U.S. Private*, pg. 843
PACIFICA HOTEL COMPANY—See Pacifica Real Estate Group; *U.S. Private*, pg. 832
PACIFICA REAL ESTATE GROUP; *U.S. Private*, pg. 832
PACIFICA SERVICES, INC.; *U.S. Private*, pg. 832
PACIFICARE BEHAVIORAL HEALTH—See PacifiCare Health Systems, Inc.; *U.S. Public*, pg. 1251
PACIFICARE DENTAL & VISION—See PacifiCare Health Systems, Inc.; *U.S. Public*, pg. 1251
PACIFICARE HEALTH SYSTEMS—See PacifiCare Health Systems, Inc.; *U.S. Public*, pg. 1251
PACIFICARE HEALTH SYSTEMS, INC.; *U.S. Public*, pg. 1250
PACIFICARE LIFE ASSURANCE—See PacifiCare Health Systems, Inc.; *U.S. Public*, pg. 1251
PACIFICARE LIFE & HEALTH INSURANCE CO.—See PacifiCare Health Systems, Inc.; *U.S. Public*, pg. 1251
PACIFICARE OF ARIZONA—See PacifiCare Health Systems, Inc.; *U.S. Public*, pg. 1251
PACIFICARE OF CALIFORNIA—See UniHealth; *U.S. Private*, pg. 1118
PACIFICARE OF COLORADO—See PacifiCare Health Systems, Inc.; *U.S. Public*, pg. 1251
PACIFICARE OF GUAM—See PacifiCare Health Systems, Inc.; *U.S. Public*, pg. 1251
PACIFICARE OF NEVADA—See PacifiCare Health Systems, Inc.; *U.S. Public*, pg. 1251
PACIFICARE OF OHIO—See PacifiCare Health Systems, Inc.; *U.S. Public*, pg. 1251
PACIFICARE OF UTAH—See PacifiCare Health Systems, Inc.; *U.S. Public*, pg. 1251
PACIFICO AUTO GROUP; *U.S. Private*, pg. 832
PACIFICOMP PTE. LTD.—See CSA Holdings Ltd.; *Int'l*, pg. 242
PACIFICORP; *U.S. Public*, pg. 1251
PACIFICORP AVIATION (HOLDINGS), INC.—See PacifiCorp; *U.S. Public*, pg. 1252
PACIFICORP CREDIT, INC.—See PacifiCorp; *U.S. Public*, pg. 1252
PACIFICORP FINANCIAL SERVICES, INC.—See PacifiCorp; *U.S. Public*, pg. 1252
PACIFICORP GROUP HOLDINGS COMPANY—See PacifiCorp; *U.S. Public*, pg. 1251
PACIFICORP TRANS, INC.—See PacifiCorp; *U.S. Public*, pg. 1252
PACING BUSINESS UNIT—See Medtronic, Inc.; *U.S. Public*, pg. 1083
PACK-O-MED MEDICAL SUPPLY SYSTEMS B.V.—See Nutricia BV; *Int'l*, pg. 991
PACKAGE MACHINERY CO.; *U.S. Private*, pg. 832
PACKAGE PRODUCTS SPECIALTY—See Sonoco Products Company; *U.S. Public*, pg. 1486
PACKAGE PRODUCTS SPECIALTY-LABELS DIV.—See Sonoco Products Company; *U.S. Public*, pg. 1486
PACKAGE PRODUCTS SPECIALTY-PAPERBOARD DIV.—See Sonoco Products Company; *U.S. Public*, pg. 1486
PACKAGE SERVICE COMPANY, LLC.; *U.S. Private*, pg. 833
PACKAGED PRODUCTS DIVISION—See The Wornick Company; *U.S. Private*, pg. 1191
PACKAGING BUSINESS—See Fort James Corporation; *U.S. Public*, pg. 671
PACKAGING & CONTAINER MANUFACTURERS LTD.—See DSM N.V.; *Int'l*, pg. 356
PACKAGING DIVISION—See The Broken Hill Proprietary Company Limited; *Int'l*, pg. 226
PACKAGING HOUSE NZFP LIMITED—See International Paper Company; *U.S. Public*, pg. 905
PACKAGING RESOURCES, INCORPORATED; *U.S. Private*, pg. 833
PACKAGING SYSTEMS DIVISION—See 3M; *U.S. Public*, pg. 1605
PACKARD BELL NEC; *U.S. Private*, pg. 833
PACKARD BIOSCIENCE—See Packard BioScience Company; *U.S. Private*, pg. 833
PACKARD BIOSCIENCE COMPANY; *U.S. Private*, pg. 833
PACKARD CTA PTY. LTD.—See General Motors Corporation; *U.S. Public*, pg. 723
PACKARD ELECTRIC BURGENLAND GES.M.B.H.—See General Motors Corporation; *U.S. Public*, pg. 723
PACKARD ELECTRIC EUROPA GES.M.B.H.—See General Motors Corporation; *U.S. Public*, pg. 723
PACKARD ELECTRIC VAS KFT—See General Motors Corporation; *U.S. Public*, pg. 723
PACKARD ELEKTRIK SISTEMLERI LIMITED SIRKETI—See General Motors Corporation; *U.S. Public*, pg. 723
PACKARD HUGHES INTERCONNECT—See General Motors Corporation; *U.S. Public*, pg. 719
PACKARD INSTRUMENT CO., INC.—See Packard BioScience Company; *U.S. Private*, pg. 833
PACKER SECURITY PATROL, INC.—See Thorn Apple Valley, Inc.; *U.S. Public*, pg. 1603
PACKERLAND PACKING CO.; *U.S. Private*, pg. 833
PACKINOX—See Framatome SA; *Int'l*, pg. 503
PACKRITE PACKAGING, INC.—See Caraustar Industries, Inc.; *U.S. Public*, pg. 304
PACKWOOD LIMITED—See Avonmore Waterford Group plc; *Int'l*, pg. 102
PACLINE (M) SDN. BHD.—See GESTRA GmbH; *Int'l*, pg. 550
PACO PHARMACEUTICAL SERVICES, INC.—See The West Company, Incorporated; *U.S. Public*, pg. 1755
PACO RABANNE COMPAR—See Antonio Puig SA; *Int'l*, pg. 1073
PACO RABANNE PARFUMS—See Antonio Puig SA; *Int'l*, pg. 1073
PACOR, INC.; *U.S. Private*, pg. 833
PACORD—See SPD Technologies; *U.S. Private*, pg. 957
PACTEM SYSTEMS, INC.—See Insituform Technologies, Inc.; *U.S. Public*, pg. 882
PACWEST CENTER—See Mitsubishi Estate Co., Ltd.; *Int'l*, pg. 873
PADDOCK POOL CONSTRUCTION CO., INC.; *U.S. Private*, pg. 833
PADDOCK PUBLICATIONS, INC.; *U.S. Private*, pg. 833
PADILLA SPEER BEARDSLEY INC.; *U.S. Private*, pg. 833
LOUIS PADNOS IRON & METAL CO.; *U.S. Private*, pg. 834
PADNOS-SUMMIT—See Louis Padnos Iron & Metal Co.; *U.S. Private*, pg. 834
PAGE HOLDINGS, INC.; *U.S. Private*, pg. 834
THE R.W. PAGE CORP.—See Knight-Ridder, Inc.; *U.S. Public*, pg. 964
PAGES DRUGS—See Randalls Food Markets, Inc.; *U.S. Private*, pg. 909
PAGING NETWORK, INC.; *U.S. Public*, pg. 1252
PAGO FABRICS, INC.—See Itochu Corporation; *Int'l*, pg. 695
PAGODA—See Brown Group, Inc.; *U.S. Public*, pg. 262
PAGOLUX BAUSYSTEME GMBH—See Ruetgers A.G.; *Int'l*, pg. 1148
PAIBOON WATANA CO., LTD.—See Takeda Chemical Industries, Ltd.; *Int'l*, pg. 1350
PAID PRESCRIPTIONS, INC.—See Merck & Co., Inc.; *U.S. Public*, pg. 1091
PAIGE PUBLICATIONS—See Black Entertainment Television Holdings Inc.; *U.S. Public*, pg. 235
PAIN JACQUET S.A.; *Int'l*, pg. 1021
PAIN JACQUET S.A.—See Pain Jacquet S.A.; *Int'l*, pg. 1021
PAINE CORP. N.V.—See PepsiCo, Inc.; *U.S. Public*, pg. 1277
PAINE FURNITURE CO.; *U.S. Private*, pg. 834

PAINE SUPPLY OF JACKSON, INC.—See Hughes Supply, Inc.; *U.S. Public,* pg. 847
PAINES & BYRNE, LIMITED—See Yamanouchi Pharmaceutical Co. Ltd.; *Int'l,* pg. 1519
PAINEWEBBER CAPITAL INC.—See PaineWebber Group Incorporated; *U.S. Public,* pg. 1252
PAINEWEBBER GROUP INCORPORATED; *U.S. Public,* pg. 1252
PAINEWEBBER INCORPORATED—See PaineWebber Group Incorporated; *U.S. Public,* pg. 1252
PAINEWEBBER INTERNATIONAL INC.—See PaineWebber Group Incorporated; *U.S. Public,* pg. 1253
PAINEWEBBER PROPERTIES INCORPORATED—See PaineWebber Group Incorporated; *U.S. Public,* pg. 1253
PAINT APPLICATION DIVISION—See ABB Asea Brown Boveri (Holding) Ltd.; *Int'l,* pg. 4
PAINT MARKETING COMPANY (M) SDN. BHD.—See Nippon Paint Company Ltd.; *Int'l,* pg. 937
PAIRGAIN TECHNOLOGIES INC.; *U.S. Public,* pg. 1253
PAISANO PUBLICATIONS, INC.; *U.S. Private,* pg. 834
PAIUTE PIPELINE CO.—See Southwest Gas Corporation; *U.S. Public,* pg. 1493
PAJIAS MILANI, S.A.—See Diageo Plc; *Int'l,* pg. 411
PAK-SAK INDUSTRIES, INC.—See Maxco, Inc.; *U.S. Public,* pg. 1061
PAK-SHER CO.—See T C Manufacturing Company, Inc.; *U.S. Private,* pg. 1062
PAKCO INDUSTRIAL CERAMICS, INC.—See Saint-Gobain; *Int'l,* pg. 1174
PAKENSO BALTICA SIA—See Enso Oyj; *Int'l,* pg. 458
PAKENSO EESTI AS—See Enso Oyj; *Int'l,* pg. 458
PAKENSO OY—See Enso Oyj; *Int'l,* pg. 456
PAKFOLD BUSINESS FORMS—See Data Business Forms Limited; *Int'l,* pg. 384
PAKHOED USA INC.—See Royal Pakhoed NV; *Int'l,* pg. 1147
PAKISTAN BURMAH SHELL—See Royal Dutch/Shell Group of Companies; *Int'l,* pg. 1140
PAKISTAN GUM & CHEMICALS LTD.—See Rhone-Poulenc S.A.; *Int'l,* pg. 1113
PAKISTAN GUM INDUSTRIES LIMITED—See Hercules Incorporated; *U.S. Public,* pg. 811
PAKISTAN INTERNATIONAL AIRLINES CORPORATION; *Int'l,* pg. 1021
PAKISTAN MOBILE COMMUNICATIONS (PVT.) LTD.—See Motorola, Inc.; *U.S. Public,* pg. 1140
PAKISTAN REFINERY—See Royal Dutch/Shell Group of Companies; *Int'l,* pg. 1140
PAKISTAN RESIDENT MISSION—See Asian Development Bank; *Int'l,* pg. 89
PAKISTAN TOBACCO CO. LTD.—See B.A.T Industries P.L.C.; *Int'l,* pg. 111
THE PAKS CORP.—See International Flavors & Fragrances, Inc.; *U.S. Public,* pg. 899
PAKTANK INTERNATIONAL B.V.—See Royal Pakhoed NV; *Int'l,* pg. 1147
PAKTRONICS CONTROLS, INC.—See Maxitrol Co.; *U.S. Private,* pg. 716
PALA GROUP, INC.; *U.S. Private,* pg. 834
PALA INTERSTATE—See Pala Group, Inc.; *U.S. Private,* pg. 834
PALABORA MINING CO. LTD.—See Rio Tinto PLC; *Int'l,* pg. 1119
PALACE THEATER LONDON LIMITED—See Really Useful Holdings Limited; *Int'l,* pg. 1089
PALAIS ROYAL—See Stage Stores, Inc.; *U.S. Public,* pg. 1029
PALATINIT SUSSUNGSMITTEL GMBH—See Sudzucker AG Mannheim/Ochsenfurt; *Int'l,* pg. 1305
THE PALATKA DAILY NEWS, INC.—See The New York Times Company; *U.S. Public,* pg. 1175
PALCO A.E.—See Hesta Tex AG; *Int'l,* pg. 618
PALCO MFG.—See Hagie Manufacturing Co.; *U.S. Private,* pg. 493
PALESTINE CONSTRUCTION COMPANY LIMITED—See The Israel Electric Corporation Ltd.; *Int'l,* pg. 691
PALETHORPES—See Northern Foods plc; *Int'l,* pg. 968
PALINTEST LIMITED—See Halma p.l.c.; *Int'l,* pg. 589
PALISADES ENERGY SERVICES—See Orange and Rockland Utilities, Inc.; *U.S. Public,* pg. 1229
PALISADES MEDIA GROUP, INC.; *U.S. Private,* pg. 834
PALL AERO POWER—See Pall Corporation; *U.S. Public,* pg. 1253
PALL AEROSPACE—See Pall Corporation; *U.S. Public,* pg. 1253
PALL ASIA—See Pall Corporation; *U.S. Public,* pg. 1254
PALL AUSTRALIA—See Pall Corporation; *U.S. Public,* pg. 1254
PALL AUSTRIA FILTER GMBH—See Pall Corporation; *U.S. Public,* pg. 1254
PALL BIOMEDICAL FRANCE—See Pall Corporation; *U.S. Public,* pg. 1254
PALL BIOMEDICAL PRODUCTS CORP.—See Pall Corporation; *U.S. Public,* pg. 1254
PALL BIOMEDICAL PUERTO RICO—See Pall Corporation; *U.S. Public,* pg. 1254
PALL BIOMEDIZIN GMBH—See Pall Corporation; *U.S. Public,* pg. 1254
PALL (CANADA) LTD.—See Pall Corporation; *U.S. Public,* pg. 1254
PALL CORPORATION; *U.S. Public,* pg. 1253
PALL DEUTSCHLAND GMBH—See Pall Corporation; *U.S. Public,* pg. 1254
PALL EAST HILLS MANUFACTURING CORP.—See Pall Corporation; *U.S. Public,* pg. 1254
PALL EUROPE LTD.—See Pall Corporation; *U.S. Public,* pg. 1254
PALL EXPANA S.A.—See Pall Corporation; *U.S. Public,* pg. 1254
PALL FILTER (BEIJING) CO., LTD.—See Pall Corporation; *U.S. Public,* pg. 1254
PALL FILTRATIONSTECHNIK GMBH—See Pall Corporation; *U.S. Public,* pg. 1254

PALL FLUID FILTRATION PTE. LTD.—See Pall Corporation; *U.S. Public,* pg. 1254
PALL FRANCE S.A.—See Pall Corporation; *U.S. Public,* pg. 1254
PALL ILFRACOMBE LTD.—See Pall Corporation; *U.S. Public,* pg. 1254
PALL INDUSTRIAL DO BRAZIL LTDA.—See Pall Corporation; *U.S. Public,* pg. 1254
PALL INDUSTRIAL HYDRAULICS CORP.—See Pall Corporation; *U.S. Public,* pg. 1254
PALL INDUSTRIAL HYDRAULICS LTD.—See Pall Corporation; *U.S. Public,* pg. 1254
PALL INDUSTRIE-HYDRAULIK GMBH—See Pall Corporation; *U.S. Public,* pg. 1254
PALL ITALIA S.R.L.—See Pall Corporation; *U.S. Public,* pg. 1254
PALL KOREA LIMITED—See Pall Corporation; *U.S. Public,* pg. 1254
PALL MALL SUPPORT SERVICES LIMITED—See The Davis Service Group Plc; *Int'l,* pg. 385
PALL POLAND LTD.—See Pall Corporation; *U.S. Public,* pg. 1254
PALL PROCESS FILTRATION COMPANY—See Pall Corporation; *U.S. Public,* pg. 1254
PALL PROCESS FILTRATION LTD.—See Pall Corporation; *U.S. Public,* pg. 1254
PALL PUERTO RICO, INC.—See Pall Corporation; *U.S. Public,* pg. 1254
PALL RAI, INC.—See Pall Corporation; *U.S. Public,* pg. 1254
PALL SAFETY ATMOSPHERES, INC.—See Pall Corporation; *U.S. Public,* pg. 1254
PALL (SCHWEIZ) AG—See Pall Corporation; *U.S. Public,* pg. 1254
PALL TRINCOR CORPORATION—See Pall Corporation; *U.S. Public,* pg. 1254
PALL TRINITY MICRO CORP.—See Pall Corporation; *U.S. Public,* pg. 1254
PALL ULTRAFINE FILTRATION COMPANY—See Pall Corporation; *U.S. Public,* pg. 1254
PALLADIN FINANCIAL, INC.—See TCC Industries; *U.S. Public,* pg. 1554
PALLADIUM PUBLISHING CORP.—See Gannett Company, Inc.; *U.S. Public,* pg. 701
PALLAS VERSICHERUNG AG—See Bayer AG; *Int'l,* pg. 172
PALLFLEX, INC.—See Pall Corporation; *U.S. Public,* pg. 1254
PALM BEACH BEAUTY PRODUCTS CO.; *U.S. Private,* pg. 834
PALM COURTT BANGKOK—See Scotts Holdings Limited; *Int'l,* pg. 1212
PALM COURTT SINGAPORE—See Scotts Holdings Limited; *Int'l,* pg. 1212
PALM ELECTRONICS MANUFACTURING CORP.—See All American Semiconductor, Inc.; *U.S. Public,* pg. 42
PALM HARBOR HOMES, INC.; *U.S. Public,* pg. 1254
PALM POOL PRODUCTS—See Hughes Supply, Inc.; *U.S. Public,* pg. 847
PALMAVEN, S.A.—See Petroleos de Venezuela S.A.; *Int'l,* pg. 1045
PALMER-AMERICAN NATIONAL BANK—See Old National Bancorp; *U.S. Public,* pg. 1217
ARNOLD PALMER CADILLAC INC.—See Don Massey Cadillac Inc.; *U.S. Private,* pg. 713
PALMER ELECTRIC CO.; *U.S. Private,* pg. 834
PALMER ENVIRONMENTAL LIMITED—See Halma p.l.c.; *Int'l,* pg. 589
PALMER HOUSE HEALTHCARE—See Vencor, Inc.; *U.S. Public,* pg. 1714
PALMER INTERNATIONAL, INC.; *U.S. Private,* pg. 834
PALMER INTERNATIONAL, INC.—See Palmer International, Inc.; *U.S. Private,* pg. 835
PALMER JARVIS ADVERTISING—See Palmer Jarvis Communications; *Int'l,* pg. 1022
PALMER JARVIS COMMUNICATIONS; *Int'l,* pg. 1022
PALMER MANUFACTURING COMPANY; *U.S. Private,* pg. 835
PALMER MOVING & STORAGE CO.; *U.S. Private,* pg. 835
PALMER PLAZA, LIMITED—See Cigna Corp.; *U.S. Public,* pg. 361
R.J. PALMER, INC.; *U.S. Private,* pg. 835
R.M. PALMER COMPANY; *U.S. Private,* pg. 835
PALMER REFRIGERATION LTD.—See Whitman Corporation; *U.S. Public,* pg. 1766
PALMER TUBE—See Australian National Industries Limited; *Int'l,* pg. 101
PALMER WATER CO.—See Horsehead Industries, Inc.; *U.S. Private,* pg. 540
PALMETTO SPINNING CORP.—See Martin Color-Fi; *U.S. Public,* pg. 1052
THE PALNUT COMPANY—See TransTechnology Corporation; *U.S. Public,* pg. 1632
PALO ALTO RESEARCH CENTER—See Xerox Corporation; *U.S. Public,* pg. 1784
PALOMA INDUSTRIES LIMITED; *Int'l,* pg. 1022
PALOMA PRODUCTION CO. INC.—See Pearce Industries Inc.; *U.S. Private,* pg. 845
PALOMAR MEDICAL TECHNOLOGIES; *U.S. Public,* pg. 1255
PALOMAR SYSTEMS, INC.—See Electro Scientific Industries, Inc.; *U.S. Public,* pg. 569
PALOMAR TRANSIT MIX CO.—See CalMat Co.; *U.S. Public,* pg. 296
PALTIER INC.—See L & D Group; *U.S. Private,* pg. 638
PALUPE-COMERCIO, PARTICIPACAO E SERVICOS LTDA.—See The Chase Manhattan Corporation; *U.S. Public,* pg. 341
PAM GAS B.V.—See SHV Holdings N.V.; *Int'l,* pg. 1155
PAMARCO TECHNOLOGIES, INC.; *U.S. Private,* pg. 835
PAMCO—See Stewart & Stevenson Services, Inc.; *U.S. Public,* pg. 1517
PAMCO DIVISION—See Toromont Industries Ltd.; *Int'l,* pg. 1400

PAMCO ESPANA SOCIEDAD ANONIMA DE SEGUROS—See The Prudential Insurance Company of America; *U.S. Private,* pg. 893
PAMCO PRINTED TAPE & LABEL COMPANY, INC.—See Jordan Industries, Inc.; *U.S. Private,* pg. 598
PAMECO CORP.; *U.S. Public,* pg. 1255
PAMEX OF TEXAS, INC.—See Pancho's Mexican Buffet, Inc.; *U.S. Public,* pg. 1255
PAMIDA HOLDINGS CORPORATION; *U.S. Public,* pg. 1255
PAMIDA, INC.—See Pamida Holdings Corporation; *U.S. Public,* pg. 1255
PAMIDA TRANSPORTATION CO.—See Pamida Holdings Corporation; *U.S. Public,* pg. 1255
PAMILO OY—See Imatran Voima Oy; *Int'l,* pg. 661
PAMOL (NIGERIA) LTD.—See Unilever Plc; *Int'l,* pg. 1438
PAMOL PLANTATIONS SDN. BHD.—See Unilever Plc; *Int'l,* pg. 1438
PAMOUR MINE—See Royal Oak Mines Inc.; *U.S. Public,* pg. 1411
PAMPAM WARENHANDEL GES.M.B.H.—See Julius Meinl AG; *Int'l,* pg. 856
THE PAMPERED CHEF, LTD.; *U.S. Private,* pg. 835
R.B. PAMPLIN CORP.; *U.S. Private,* pg. 835
PAMPUS VERMOGENSVERWALFUNGS GMBH & CO. KG.—See Saint-Gobain; *Int'l,* pg. 1175
PAN-ACC TRANSIT SYSTEMS INC.—See Kaufel Group Ltd.; *Int'l,* pg. 725
PAN-ALBERTA GAS LTD.—See Nova Corporation; *Int'l,* pg. 971
PAN-ALBERTA RESOURCES LTD.—See Alberta Energy Company, Ltd.; *Int'l,* pg. 49
PAN AMERICAN CORPORATION—See Corporacion MAPFRE, Compania Internacional de Reaseguros, S.A.; *Int'l,* pg. 333
PAN AMERICAN DIVISION—See Parker Hannifin Corporation; *U.S. Public,* pg. 1262
PAN AMERICAN FINANCE CORPORATION—See Corporacion MAPFRE, Compania Internacional de Reaseguros, S.A.; *Int'l,* pg. 333
PAN AMERICAN INSURANCE COMPANY—See Corporacion MAPFRE, Compania Internacional de Reaseguros, S.A.; *Int'l,* pg. 333
PAN-AMERICAN LIFE INSURANCE COMPANY; *U.S. Private,* pg. 836
PAN-AMERICAN SEED CO.—See Ball Horticultural Company; *U.S. Private,* pg. 112
PAN ARABIAN INSURANCE COMPANY LIMITED—See Cigna Corp.; *U.S. Public,* pg. 364
PAN EUROPEAN PUBLISHING CO.—See Reed Elsevier plc; *Int'l,* pg. 1099
PAN KOREA INSURANCE CO.—See LG Group; *Int'l,* pg. 779
PAN-LITSERVICE AO—See Panalpina Welttransport (Holding) AG; *Int'l,* pg. 1022
PAN-MALAYAN INSURANCE CORPORATION—See The Tokio Marine & Fire Insurance Company, Ltd.; *Int'l,* pg. 1392
PAN MALAYSIA CEMENT WORKS (SINGAPORE) PTE. LTD.—See Blue Circle Industries PLC; *Int'l,* pg. 198
PAN-MARINE INTERNATIONAL, INC.—See Tidewater Inc.; *U.S. Public,* pg. 1608
PAN OCEAN ENERGY COMPANY—See USX Corporation; *U.S. Public,* pg. 1662
PAN PACIFIC FOREST INDUSTRIES (N.Z.) LIMITED—See Nippon Paper Industries Company Limited; *Int'l,* pg. 938
PANACO, INC.; *U.S. Public,* pg. 1255
PANAGORA ASSET MANAGMENT, INC.—See Lehman Brothers Holdings Inc.; *U.S. Public,* pg. 987
PANAL SHOPFRONT SYSTEMS LIMITED—See Saint-Gobain; *Int'l,* pg. 1173
PANALARM PRODUCTS, AMETEK, INC.—See AMETEK, Inc.; *U.S. Public,* pg. 100
PANALPINA AB—See Panalpina Welttransport (Holding) AG; *Int'l,* pg. 1022
PANALPINA AKTIENGESELLSCHAFT WIEN—See Panalpina Welttransport (Holding) AG; *Int'l,* pg. 1022
PANALPINA C.A.—See Panalpina Welttransport (Holding) AG; *Int'l,* pg. 1022
PANALPINA CHILE TRANSPORTES MUNDIALES LTDA.—See Panalpina Welttransport (Holding) AG; *Int'l,* pg. 1023
PANALPINA CHINA LIMITED—See Panalpina Welttransport (Holding) AG; *Int'l,* pg. 1023
PANALPINA EAST AFRICA LIMITED—See Panalpina Welttransport (Holding) AG; *Int'l,* pg. 1023
PANALPINA FRANCE TRANSPORTS INTERNATIONAUX S.A.—See Panalpina Welttransport (Holding) AG; *Int'l,* pg. 1023
PANALPINA (GHANA) LIMITED—See Panalpina Welttransport (Holding) AG; *Int'l,* pg. 1023
PANALPINA GMBH—See Panalpina Welttransport (Holding) AG; *Int'l,* pg. 1023
PANALPINA GULF LLC—See Panalpina Welttransport (Holding) AG; *Int'l,* pg. 1023
PANALPINA IMMOBILIEN VERWALTUNGS GMBH—See Panalpina Welttransport (Holding) AG; *Int'l,* pg. 1023
PANALPINA, INC.—See Panalpina Welttransport (Holding) AG; *Int'l,* pg. 1022
PANALPINA INC.—See Panalpina Welttransport (Holding) AG; *Int'l,* pg. 1022
PANALPINA KENYA LIMITED—See Panalpina Welttransport (Holding) AG; *Int'l,* pg. 1023
PANALPINA KOREA LTD.—See Panalpina Welttransport (Holding) AG; *Int'l,* pg. 1023
PANALPINA LAGERHAUS-IMMOBILIEN GMBH—See Panalpina Welttransport (Holding) AG; *Int'l,* pg. 1023
PANALPINA LTD.—See Panalpina Welttransport (Holding) AG; *Int'l,* pg. 1022
PANALPINA MANAGEMENT AG—See Panalpina Welttransport (Holding) AG; *Int'l,* pg. 1022
PT PANALPINA NUSAJAYA TRANSPORT—See Panalpina Welttransport (Holding) AG; *Int'l,* pg. 1023

PANALPINA S.A.—See Panalpina Welttransport (Holding) AG; *Int'l*, pg. 1023
PANALPINA S.A.R.L.—See Panalpina Welttransport (Holding) AG; *Int'l*, pg. 1023
PANALPINA S.P.A. TRANSPORTI INTERNAZIONALI—See Panalpina Welttransport (Holding) AG; *Int'l*, pg. 1023
PANALPINA TAIWAN LTD.—See Panalpina Welttransport (Holding) AG; *Int'l*, pg. 1023
PANALPINA TRANSPORTES MUNDIAIS LDA.—See Panalpina Welttransport (Holding) AG; *Int'l*, pg. 1023
PANALPINA TRANSPORTES MUNDIALES C.A.—See Panalpina Welttransport (Holding) AG; *Int'l*, pg. 1023
PANALPINA TRANSPORTES MUNDIALES S.A.—See Panalpina Welttransport (Holding) AG; *Int'l*, pg. 1023
PANALPINA TRANSPORTS MONDIAUX CONGO S.A.R.L.—See Panalpina Welttransport (Holding) AG; *Int'l*, pg. 1023
PANALPINA TRANSPORTS MONDIAUX GABON S.A.—See Panalpina Welttransport (Holding) AG; *Int'l*, pg. 1023
PANALPINA WELLTRANSPORT (DEUTSCHLAND) GMBH—See Panalpina Welttransport (Holding) AG; *Int'l*, pg. 1023
PANALPINA WELLTRANSPORT GMBH—See Panalpina Welttransport (Holding) AG; *Int'l*, pg. 1023
PANALPINA WELLTRANSPORT (HOLDING) AG; *Int'l*, pg. 1022
PANALPINA WORLD TRANSPORT AO—See Panalpina Welttransport (Holding) AG; *Int'l*, pg. 1023
PANALPINA WORLD TRANSPORT B.V.—See Panalpina Welttransport (Holding) AG; *Int'l*, pg. 1023
PANALPINA WORLD TRANSPORT (EASTERN) LTD.—See Panalpina Welttransport (Holding) AG; *Int'l*, pg. 1023
PANALPINA WORLD TRANSPORT (JAPAN) LTD.—See Panalpina Welttransport (Holding) AG; *Int'l*, pg. 1023
PANALPINA WORLD TRANSPORT LIMITED—See Panalpina Welttransport (Holding) AG; *Int'l*, pg. 1023
PANALPINA WORLD TRANSPORT LTD.—See Panalpina Welttransport (Holding) AG; *Int'l*, pg. 1023
PANALPINA WORLD TRANSPORT (NIGERIA) LIMITED—See Panalpina Welttransport (Holding) AG; *Int'l*, pg. 1023
PANALPINA WORLD TRANSPORT N.V.—See Panalpina Welttransport (Holding) AG; *Int'l*, pg. 1023
PANALPINA WORLD TRANSPORT (PTY) LIMITED—See Panalpina Welttransport (Holding) AG; *Int'l*, pg. 1023
PANALPINA WORLD TRANSPORT (SINGAPORE) PTE. LTD.—See Panalpina Welttransport (Holding) AG; *Int'l*, pg. 1023
PANALPINA WORLD TRANSPORT (THAILAND) LIMITED—See Panalpina Welttransport (Holding) AG; *Int'l*, pg. 1023
PANALQUITA, PANALPINA TRANSPORTES MUNDIALES ECUADOR S.A.—See Panalpina Welttransport (Holding) AG; *Int'l*, pg. 1023
PANAMA CITY COCA-COLA BOTTLING CO.—See Coca-Cola Bottling Co. Consolidated; *U.S. Public*, pg. 392
PANASIAN MARKETING SERVICES (PVT) LIMITED—See Telefonaktiebolaget LM Ericsson; *Int'l*, pg. 1369
PANASONIC CONSUMER ELECTRIC CO.—See Matsushita Electric Industrial Co., Ltd.; *Int'l*, pg. 847
P.T. PANATA TAMA INTER INSTALASI INDONESIA—See Internatio-Muller N.V.; *Int'l*, pg. 681
PANAVIA AIRCRAFT GMBH—See British Aerospace p.l.c.; *Int'l*, pg. 218
PANAVIA AIRCRAFT GMBH—See IRI Istituto Ricostruzione Industriale; *Int'l*, pg. 653
PANCANADIAN PETROLEUM LIMITED—See Canadian Pacific Limited; *Int'l*, pg. 259
PANCHO'S MEXICAN BUFFET, INC.; *U.S. Public*, pg. 1255
PANDEL.—See Interface Inc.; *U.S. Public*, pg. 889
PANDORO LTD.—See The Peninsular and Oriental Steam Navigation Company; *Int'l*, pg. 1034
PANDROL INTERNATIONAL LIMITED—See Charter plc; *Int'l*, pg. 280
PANDROL JACKSON, INC.—See Charter plc; *Int'l*, pg. 280
PANDUIT AUST. PTY. LTD.—See Panduit Corp.; *U.S. Private*, pg. 836
PANDUIT CANADA LTD.—See Panduit Corp.; *U.S. Private*, pg. 836
PANDUIT CORP.; *U.S. Private*, pg. 836
PANDUIT CORP. JAPAN BRANCH—See Panduit Corp.; *U.S. Private*, pg. 836
PANDUIT GMBH—See Panduit Corp.; *U.S. Private*, pg. 836
PANDUIT INTERNATIONAL CORP.-TAIWAN BRANCH—See Panduit Corp.; *U.S. Private*, pg. 836
PANDUIT KOREA LTD.—See Panduit Corp.; *U.S. Private*, pg. 836
PANDUIT LIMITED—See Panduit Corp.; *U.S. Private*, pg. 836
PANDUIT MEXICO S. EN N.C.—See Panduit Corp.; *U.S. Private*, pg. 836
PANDUIT NEDERLAND—See Panduit Corp.; *U.S. Private*, pg. 836
PANDUIT S.N.C.—See Panduit Corp.; *U.S. Private*, pg. 836
PANDUIT S.A.S.—See Panduit Corp.; *U.S. Private*, pg. 836
PANDUIT SINGAPORE PTE. LTD.—See Panduit Corp.; *U.S. Private*, pg. 836
PANEL CONCEPTS, L.P.—See Standard Pacific Corp.; *U.S. Public*, pg. 1504
PANEL PRINTS, INC.; *U.S. Private*, pg. 836
PANEL PROCESSING, INC.; *U.S. Private*, pg. 836
PANEL PUBLISHERS, INC.—See Wolters Kluwer N.V.; *Int'l*, pg. 1513
PANEUROLIFE—See Compagnie UAP; *Int'l*, pg. 323
PANEUROLIFE—See Groupe Bruxelles Lambert S.A.; *Int'l*, pg. 562
PANGBURN CANDY COMPANY; *U.S. Private*, pg. 836
PANHANDLE PIPE & SUPPLY CO., INC.—See Hughes Supply, Inc.; *U.S. Public*, pg. 847
PANKAKOSKI BOARDS OY LTD.—See Enso Oyj; *Int'l*, pg. 456
CHARLES PANKOW BUILDERS, LTD.; *U.S. Private*, pg. 836

PANLABS INTERNATIONAL OPERATIONS—See MDS Inc.; *Int'l*, pg. 827
PANMURE GORDON BANKERS LTD.—See NationsBank Corporation; *U.S. Public*, pg. 1166
PANNAWONICA MINE—See North Limited; *Int'l*, pg. 967
PANNEAUX MALETTE-OSB INC.—See Malette Quebec, Inc.; *Int'l*, pg. 833
PANNEAUX VICPLY INC.—See Uniboard Canada Inc.; *Int'l*, pg. 1432
C.W. PANNEVIS ZAADTEELT EN ZAADHANDEL B.V.—See Novartis AG; *Int'l*, pg. 975
PANNEVIS ZAADTEELT EN ZAADHANDEL N.V.—See Novartis AG; *Int'l*, pg. 983
PANNIER CORPORATION; *U.S. Private*, pg. 837
PANOFINA AG—See Coop Switzerland; *Int'l*, pg. 330
PANOPA REISEBURO GMBH—See Fried. Krupp AG; *Int'l*, pg. 515
PANOPA VERKEHRS-GMBH—See Fried. Krupp AG; *Int'l*, pg. 514
PANORAMA APARTMENTS (EDMONTON) LIMITED—See Sun Life Assurance Company of Canada; *Int'l*, pg. 1319
PANTAINER AG—See Panalpina Welttransport (Holding) AG; *Int'l*, pg. 1022
PANTECH CONSTRUCTION CO.; *U.S. Private*, pg. 837
THE PANTENE CO.—See The Procter & Gamble Company; *U.S. Public*, pg. 1330
PANTENE GMBH—See The Procter & Gamble Company; *U.S. Public*, pg. 1331
PANTHEON BOOKS, INC.—See Advance Publications Inc.; *U.S. Private*, pg. 21
THE PANTHER CAR CO., LTD.—See Ssangyong Business Group; *Int'l*, pg. 1292
PANTRANS TRANSITARIOS S.A.—See Panalpina Welttransport (Holding) AG; *Int'l*, pg. 1023
THE PANTRY, INC.; *U.S. Public*, pg. 837
PANZALIM.—See Danone Group; *Int'l*, pg. 381
PANZALIM.—See Groupe Saint Louis; *Int'l*, pg. 568
PAOLI, INC.; *U.S. Private*, pg. 837
PAPA GINO'S INC.; *U.S. Private*, pg. 837
PAPA JOHN'S INTERNATIONAL INC.; *U.S. Public*, pg. 1255
P. PAPAS & CO. O.E. TRADING COMPANY—See BASF AG; *Int'l*, pg. 109
PAPEL DE IMPRENSA, S.A.—See Fletcher Challenge Limited; *Int'l*, pg. 495
PAPELERA DE CHIHUAHUA S.A. DE C.V.—See Copamex Industrias S.A. de C.V.; *Int'l*, pg. 330
PAPELES BIO BIO S.A.—See Fletcher Challenge Limited; *Int'l*, pg. 495
PAPELES CORRUGADOS, S.A. DE C.V.—See Tablex, S.A. de C.V.; *Int'l*, pg. 1346
PAPELES NACIONALES S.A.—See Kruger Inc.; *Int'l*, pg. 762
PAPER AGENCIES (AUST.) PTY. LTD.—See Enso Oyj; *Int'l*, pg. 458
PAPER AGENTS LTD.—See Norske Skogindustrier A.S.; *Int'l*, pg. 966
PAPER CALMENSON & CO.; *U.S. Private*, pg. 837
S.A. PAPER CHEMICALS (PROPRIETARY), LIMITED—See Tenneco Inc.; *U.S. Public*, pg. 1580
PAPER CORPORATION OF UNITED STATES—See Unisource Worldwide, Inc.; *U.S. Public*, pg. 1671
PAPER ENTERPRISES, INC.; *U.S. Private*, pg. 837
THE PAPER FACTORY OF WISCONSIN, INC.—See Gibson Greetings, Inc.; *U.S. Public*, pg. 742
PAPER-FIN S.P.A.—See A. Ahlstrom Corporation; *Int'l*, pg. 35
THE PAPER HOUSE/SOUTHERN PAPER—See Gould Paper Corporation; *U.S. Private*, pg. 467
THE PAPER MAGIC GROUP, INC.—See CSS Industries, Inc.; *U.S. Public*, pg. 284
PAPER PRODUCTS MARKETING—See Amcor Limited; *Int'l*, pg. 72
PAPER RECYCLING, INC.—See Caraustar Industries, Inc.; *U.S. Public*, pg. 304
PAPER RECYCLING INTERNATIONAL—See Stone Container Corporation; *U.S. Public*, pg. 1522
PAPER SACKS LTD.—See Korsnas AB; *Int'l*, pg. 759
PAPER STOCK DEALERS, INC.—See Sonoco Products Company; *U.S. Public*, pg. 1486
PAPERBOARD INDUSTRIES CORPORATION—See The Cascades Group; *Int'l*, pg. 273
PAPERDIRECT, INC.—See Deluxe Corporation; *U.S. Public*, pg. 498
PAPERFLOW SERVICES LIMTED—See Severn Trent Plc; *Int'l*, pg. 1226
PAPERION CHIMIE S.A.—See Raisio Group; *Int'l*, pg. 1086
PAPERMAKING MACHINERY & SYSTEMS—See Harnischfeger Industries, Inc.; *U.S. Public*, pg. 789
PAPETERIES DE MALAUCENE S.A.—See Kimberly-Clark Corporation; *U.S. Public*, pg. 959
PAPETERIES DE MAUDIT S.A.—See Kimberly-Clark Corporation; *U.S. Public*, pg. 959
PAPETERIES DE MONT SAINT GUIBERT SA—See N.V. Koninklijke KNP BT; *Int'l*, pg. 757
PAPETERIES DE MONTEVRAIN SA—See Groupe Saint Louis; *Int'l*, pg. 567
PAPETERIES LIBERT BV—See N.V. Koninklijke KNP BT; *Int'l*, pg. 756
PAPETERIES R. SOUSTRE & FILS S.A.—See Enso Oyj; *Int'l*, pg. 458
PAPETTI HYGRADE EGG PRODUCTS—See Michael Foods, Inc.; *U.S. Public*, pg. 1104
PAPIER KINGSEY-FALLS DIV.—See The Cascades Group; *Int'l*, pg. 273
PAPIER MALETTE—See Malette Quebec, Inc.; *Int'l*, pg. 833
PAPIERFABRIK ALBBRUCK GMBH—See Metsa-Serla Corporation; *Int'l*, pg. 864
PAPIERFABRIK MELITTA-WERK BENTZ KG—See Melitta Unternehmensgruppe Bentz KG; *Int'l*, pg. 857

BV PAPIERGROOTHANDEL V/H RIEM & HONIG—See N.V. Koninklijke KNP BT; *Int'l*, pg. 756
PAPIERSACKFABRIK JUNEMANN GMBH—See Korsnas AB; *Int'l*, pg. 759
PAPUA-NEW GUINEA DIVISION—See Goodman Fielder Limited; *Int'l*, pg. 556
PAPYRUS OY—See The East Asiatic Company Ltd. A/S; *Int'l*, pg. 431
PAR ENTERPRISES, INC.; *U.S. Private*, pg. 838
PAR FOUR DEVELOPMENT CORP.—See Lennar Corporation; *U.S. Public*, pg. 988
PAR GOVERNMENT SYSTEMS CORPORATION—See PAR Technology Corporation; *U.S. Public*, pg. 1256
PAR INDUSTRIES, INC.; *U.S. Private*, pg. 838
PAR MICROSYSTEMS CORPORATION—See PAR Technology Corporation; *U.S. Public*, pg. 1256
PAR ONE DEVELOPMENT CORP.—See Lennar Corporation; *U.S. Public*, pg. 988
PAR TECHNOLOGY CORPORATION; *U.S. Public*, pg. 1256
PAR TWO DEVELOPMENT CORP.—See Lennar Corporation; *U.S. Public*, pg. 988
PAR VISION SYSTEMS CORPORATION—See PAR Technology Corporation; *U.S. Public*, pg. 1256
PARA SYSTEMS INC.—See Components Corporation Of America; *U.S. Private*, pg. 260
PARABEAM INDUSTRIE-EN HANDELSONDERNEMING B.V.—See Gamma Holding N.V.; *Int'l*, pg. 540
PARACHUTE, INC.—See Clarity Coverdale Fury Advertising; *U.S. Private*, pg. 242
PARACORE COMPANY; *U.S. Private*, pg. 838
PARADATA FINANCIAL SYSTEMS.—See World Acceptance Corporation; *U.S. Public*, pg. 1778
PARADE PUBLICATIONS INC.—See Advance Publications Inc.; *U.S. Private*, pg. 20
PARADIGM COMMUNICATIONS; *U.S. Private*, pg. 838
PARADIGM LEARNING—See Paradigm Communications; *U.S. Private*, pg. 838
PARADIGM NATIONAL YELLOW PAGES GROUP—See Paradigm Communications; *U.S. Private*, pg. 838
PARADIGM TECHNOLOGY, INC.; *U.S. Public*, pg. 1256
PARADIS—See Groupe Casino; *Int'l*, pg. 563
PARADISE, INC.; *U.S. Public*, pg. 1256
PARADISE STREAM, INC.—See Starwood Hotels & Resorts; *U.S. Public*, pg. 1512
PARADISE VALLEY WATER CO.—See American Water Works Company, Inc.; *U.S. Public*, pg. 95
PARADYNE; *U.S. Private*, pg. 838
PARAFAX—See Paradigm Communications; *U.S. Private*, pg. 838
PARAFLUID MINERALOLGESELLSCHAFT MBH—See Fuchs Petrolub AG Oel + Chemie; *Int'l*, pg. 517
PARAGERM FRANCE S.A.—See Henkel KGaA; *Int'l*, pg. 612
PARAGON—See Essef Corporation; *U.S. Public*, pg. 593
PARAGON COMMUNICATIONS SDN. BHD. (KUALA LUMPUR)—See Dentsu Young & Rubicam Partnerships; *U.S. Private*, pg. 325
PARAGON COMMUNICATIONS (UK) LTD.—See Shandwick International Plc; *Int'l*, pg. 1226
PARAGON ELECTRIC CO., INC.—See Siebe plc; *Int'l*, pg. 1243
PARAGON HEALTH NETWORK, INC.; *U.S. Public*, pg. 1256
PARAGON INC.—See Windmere-Durable Holdings; *U.S. Public*, pg. 1771
PARAGON LIFE INSURANCE CO.—See General American Life Insurance Co.; *U.S. Private*, pg. 443
PARAGON PAINT & VARNISH CORP.; *U.S. Private*, pg. 838
PARAGON PLASTICS, INC.—See Caraustar Industries, Inc.; *U.S. Public*, pg. 304
PARAGON REINSURANCE RISK MANAGEMENT SERVICES, INC.—See E.W. Blanch Holdings, Inc.; *U.S. Public*, pg. 236
PARAGON RESOURCES, INC.—See Public Service Company of New Mexico; *U.S. Public*, pg. 1339
PARAGUS—See Lettuce Entertain You Enterprises, Inc.; *U.S. Private*, pg. 661
PARALLAX GRAPHICS, INC.—See Dynatech Corporation; *U.S. Public*, pg. 539
PARAMETRIC TECHNOLOGY CORPORATION; *U.S. Public*, pg. 1257
PARAMETRIC TECHNOLOGY CORPORATION—See Parametric Technology Corporation; *U.S. Public*, pg. 1257
PARAMOUNT BRITISH PICTURES LTD.—See National Amusements, Inc.; *U.S. Private*, pg. 777
PARAMOUNT CANADA'S WONDERLAND—See National Amusements, Inc.; *U.S. Private*, pg. 776
PARAMOUNT CAROWINDS—See National Amusements, Inc.; *U.S. Private*, pg. 776
PARAMOUNT CITRUS ASSOCIATION—See Roll International Corporation; *U.S. Private*, pg. 941
PARAMOUNT DEVELOPMENT ASSOCS., INC.—See Perini Corporation; *U.S. Public*, pg. 1278
PARAMOUNT FARMING COMPANY—See Roll International Corporation; *U.S. Private*, pg. 941
PARAMOUNT FITNESS CORP.; *U.S. Private*, pg. 838
PARAMOUNT NATURAL GAS COMPANY—See Petroleum Development Corporation; *U.S. Public*, pg. 1280
PARAMOUNT PARKS—See National Amusements, Inc.; *U.S. Private*, pg. 776
PARAMOUNT PETROLEUM CORP.; *U.S. Private*, pg. 838
PARAMOUNT PICTURES (AUSTRALIA) PTY. LTD.—See National Amusements, Inc.; *U.S. Private*, pg. 777
PARAMOUNT PICTURES CORPORATION—See National Amusements, Inc.; *U.S. Private*, pg. 776
PARAMOUNT PICTURES INTERNATIONAL—See National Amusements, Inc.; *U.S. Private*, pg. 777
PARAMOUNT PRODUCTIONS, INC.—See National Amusements, Inc.; *U.S. Private*, pg. 777
PARAMOUNT TECHNICAL PRODUCTS, INC.—See RPM, Inc.; *U.S. Public*, pg. 1357

MASTER INDEX TO COMPANY NAMES PARKLABREA

Company Index

PARAMOUNT TELEVISION INTERNATIONAL SERVICES LTD.—See National Amusements, Inc.; *U.S. Private*, pg. 777
PARAMOUNT TELEVISION LTD.—See National Amusements, Inc.; *U.S. Private*, pg. 777
PARAMOUNT TRANSMISSION CORP.—See Petroleum Development Corporation; *U.S. Public*, pg. 1281
PARAMOUNT TUBE—See Precision Products Corporation; *U.S. Private*, pg. 880
PARAMUS PARK, INC.—See The Rouse Company; *U.S. Public*, pg. 1408
PARAMUS PARK SHOPPING CENTER LIMITED PARTNERSHIP—See Cigna Corp.; *U.S. Public*, pg. 365
PARANATAL CARE OF AMERICA, INC.; *U.S. Private*, pg. 839
PARAVANT COMPUTER SYSTEMS, INC.; *U.S. Public*, pg. 1257
PARBEL INC.—See L'Oreal S.A.; *Int'l*, pg. 818
PARCELFORCE—See The Post Office; *Int'l*, pg. 1064
PARCO N. V.—See PepsiCo, Inc.; *U.S. Public*, pg. 1277
PARCO CO. LTD.—See The Saison Group; *Int'l*, pg. 1178
PARCOM VENTURES B.V.—See ING Groep N.V.; *Int'l*, pg. 647
PARCWOOD-SACRAMENTO JOINT VENTURE—See Cigna Corp.; *U.S. Public*, pg. 362
PARDEE CONSTRUCTION COMPANY—See Weyerhaeuser Company; *U.S. Public*, pg. 1764
P.T. PARDIC JAYA CHEMICALS—See Nissho Iwai Corporation; *Int'l*, pg. 949
PARDIOR KOZMETIK TIC. VE SAN A.S.—See LVMH Moet Hennessy Louis Vuitton; *Int'l*, pg. 783
PARDUE VIA IPM—See Telefonaktiebolaget LM Ericsson; *Int'l*, pg. 1369
PARDUX ANLAGESELLSCHAFT—See Assicurazioni Generali S.p.A.; *Int'l*, pg. 92
PARECO G.I.E.—See Bongrain S.A.; *Int'l*, pg. 201
PARENCO B.V.—See Haindl Papier GmbH; *Int'l*, pg. 586
PARENTING MAGAZINE PARTNERS—See Time Warner Inc.; *U.S. Public*, pg. 1614
PARENTS MAGAZINE—See Bertelsmann AG; *Int'l*, pg. 191
PARETAN GAROCHE—See Lafarge S.A.; *Int'l*, pg. 789
PAREX (CDZ)—See Lafarge S.A.; *Int'l*, pg. 789
PAREX, INC.—See Lafarge S.A.; *Int'l*, pg. 789
PAREXEL GMBH—See PAREXEL International Corporation; *U.S. Public*, pg. 1258
PAREXEL INTERNATIONAL—See PAREXEL International Corporation; *U.S. Public*, pg. 1258
PAREXEL INTERNATIONAL CORPORATION; *U.S. Public*, pg. 1257
PAREXEL INTERNATIONAL LIMITED—See PAREXEL International Corporation; *U.S. Public*, pg. 1258
PARFICOM—See Groupe Air France; *Int'l*, pg. 560
PARFINANCE S.A.—See Groupe Bruxelles Lambert S.A.; *Int'l*, pg. 562
PARFUMS ET BEAUTE FRANCE & CIE.—See L'Oreal S.A.; *Int'l*, pg. 818
PARFUMS CACHREL & CIE—See L'Oreal S.A.; *Int'l*, pg. 818
PARFUMS CHRISTIAN DIOR—See LVMH Moet Hennessy Louis Vuitton; *Int'l*, pg. 781
PARFUMS CHRISTIAN DIOR AG—See LVMH Moet Hennessy Louis Vuitton; *Int'l*, pg. 783
PARFUMS CHRISTIAN DIOR BV—See LVMH Moet Hennessy Louis Vuitton; *Int'l*, pg. 783
PARFUMS CHRISTIAN DIOR CANADA—See LVMH Moet Hennessy Louis Vuitton; *Int'l*, pg. 783
PARFUMS CHRISTIAN DIOR DE MEXICO S.A. DE C.V.—See LVMH Moet Hennessy Louis Vuitton; *Int'l*, pg. 783
PARFUMS CHRISTIAN DIOR DE PANAMA S.A.—See LVMH Moet Hennessy Louis Vuitton; *Int'l*, pg. 783
PARFUMS CHRISTIAN DIOR G.M.B.H.—See LVMH Moet Hennessy Louis Vuitton; *Int'l*, pg. 783
PARFUMS CHRISTIAN DIOR HONG KONG CO. LTD.—See LVMH Moet Hennessy Louis Vuitton; *Int'l*, pg. 783
PARFUMS CHRISTIAN DIOR (IRELAND) LTD—See LVMH Moet Hennessy Louis Vuitton; *Int'l*, pg. 783
PARFUMS CHRISTIAN DIOR JAPAN KK—See LVMH Moet Hennessy Louis Vuitton; *Int'l*, pg. 783
PARFUMS CHRISTIAN DIOR KOREA CO. LTD.—See LVMH Moet Hennessy Louis Vuitton; *Int'l*, pg. 783
PARFUMS CHRISTIAN DIOR (MALAYSIA) SDN BHD—See LVMH Moet Hennessy Louis Vuitton; *Int'l*, pg. 783
PARFUMS CHRISTIAN DIOR SAB—See LVMH Moet Hennessy Louis Vuitton; *Int'l*, pg. 783
PARFUMS CHRISTIAN DIOR (SINGAPORE) PTE LTD—See LVMH Moet Hennessy Louis Vuitton; *Int'l*, pg. 783
PARFUMS CHRISTIAN DIOR S.P.A.—See LVMH Moet Hennessy Louis Vuitton; *Int'l*, pg. 783
PARFUMS CHRISTIAN DIOR (U.K.) LTD—See LVMH Moet Hennessy Louis Vuitton; *Int'l*, pg. 783
PARFUMS DE COEUR LTD.; *U.S. Private*, pg. 839
PARFUMS GIVENCHY CANADA LTD—See LVMH Moet Hennessy Louis Vuitton; *Int'l*, pg. 783
PARFUMS GIVENCHY G.M.B.H.—See LVMH Moet Hennessy Louis Vuitton; *Int'l*, pg. 783
PARFUMS GIVENCHY INC.—See LVMH Moet Hennessy Louis Vuitton; *Int'l*, pg. 781
PARFUMS GIVENCHY ITALIA S.R.L.—See LVMH Moet Hennessy Louis Vuitton; *Int'l*, pg. 783
PARFUMS GIVENCHY K.K.—See LVMH Moet Hennessy Louis Vuitton; *Int'l*, pg. 783
PARFUMS GIVENCHY LTD—See LVMH Moet Hennessy Louis Vuitton; *Int'l*, pg. 783
PARFUMS GIVENCHY S.A.—See LVMH Moet Hennessy Louis Vuitton; *Int'l*, pg. 781
PARFUMS GIVENCHY W.H.D. INC.—See LVMH Moet Hennessy Louis Vuitton; *Int'l*, pg. 781
PARFUMS INTERNATIONAL LTD.—See Unilever Plc; *Int'l*, pg. 1435
PARFUMS RALPH LAUREN—See L'Oreal S.A.; *Int'l*, pg. 818
PARFUMS ROCHAS S.A.—See Wella Group; *Int'l*, pg. 1490
PARFUMS SCHIAPARELLI DIV.—See Del Laboratories, Inc.; *U.S. Public*, pg. 494
PARFUMS VAN CLEEF & ARPELS—See Elf Aquitane; *Int'l*, pg. 445
PARGAS PLANT—See Scancem AB; *Int'l*, pg. 1198
PARGO'S RESTAURANTS—See Shoney's, Inc.; *U.S. Public*, pg. 1467
PARI MUTUEL URBAIN; *Int'l*, pg. 1023
PARIBAS ASSET MANAGEMENT JAPAN LTD.—See Compagnie Financiere de Paribas; *Int'l*, pg. 321
PARIBAS ASSET MANAGEMENT S.A.—See Compagnie Financiere de Paribas; *Int'l*, pg. 321
PARIBAS BANK OF CANADA—See Compagnie Financiere de Paribas; *Int'l*, pg. 321
PARIBAS DO BRAZIL—See Compagnie Financiere de Paribas; *Int'l*, pg. 321
PARIBAS FINANZIARIA SPA—See Compagnie Financiere de Paribas; *Int'l*, pg. 321
PARIBAS NORTH AMERICA—See Compagnie Financiere de Paribas; *Int'l*, pg. 319
PARIBAS SUISSE (BAHAMAS) LTD.—See Compagnie Financiere de Paribas; *Int'l*, pg. 321
PARIS ACCESSORIES; *U.S. Private*, pg. 839
PARIS FOODS CORP.; *U.S. Private*, pg. 839
PARIS LEARNING CENTER—See Berkshire Hathaway Inc.; *U.S. Public*, pg. 219
PARIS PRESENTS; *U.S. Private*, pg. 839
PARIS SECURITIES—See Paris Foods Corp.; *U.S. Private*, pg. 839
PARISH WATER COMPANY, INC.—See Baton Rouge Water Works Company; *U.S. Private*, pg. 123
FRANCESCO PARISI G.M.B.H.—See Francesco Parisi S.p.A.; *Int'l*, pg. 504
FRANCESCO PARISI S.P.A.—See Francesco Parisi S.p.A.; *Int'l*, pg. 504
PARISI INC./ROYAL STORE FIXTURE; *U.S. Private*, pg. 839
PARISIAN BAKERIES—See Interstate Bakeries Corporation; *U.S. Public*, pg. 909
PARISIAN, INC.—See Proffitt's, Inc.; *U.S. Public*, pg. 1333
PARK ADVERTISING & DIRECT MARKETING—See FCB; *U.S. Private*, pg. 389
PARK AIR ELECTRONICS LTD.—See Northrop Grumman Corporation; *U.S. Public*, pg. 1198
THE PARK AT DASHPOINT—See BRE Properties, Inc.; *U.S. Public*, pg. 163
PARK AVENUE VILLA—See Horizon/CMS Healthcare Corporation; *U.S. Public*, pg. 838
PARK CAKES LTD.—See Northern Foods plc; *Int'l*, pg. 968
THE PARK CIRCLE MOTOR CO.; *U.S. Private*, pg. 839
PARK CONSTRUCTION COMPANY; *U.S. Private*, pg. 839
PARK CORP.; *U.S. Private*, pg. 839
PARK DIALYS AB—See Incentive AB; *Int'l*, pg. 667
PARK DISTRIBUTORS, INC.; *U.S. Private*, pg. 839
PARK DROP FORGE DIV.—See Park-Ohio Industries, Inc.; *U.S. Public*, pg. 1258
PARK ELECTROCHEMICAL CORPORATION; *U.S. Public*, pg. 1258
PARK FAST OF MARYLAND—See Edison Parking Properties, LLC; *U.S. Private*, pg. 364
PARK FOODS L.P.; *U.S. Private*, pg. 839
GEORGE W. PARK SEED CO., INC.; *U.S. Private*, pg. 839
PARK LANE TOBACCO COMPANY LTD.—See Reemtsma Cigarettenfabriken GmbH, Hamburg; *Int'l*, pg. 1101
PARK MANOR NURSING & CONVALESCENT HOME—See Vencor, Inc.; *U.S. Public*, pg. 1714
PARK MANUFACTURING, INC.; *U.S. Private*, pg. 840
PARK MOTOR SALES COMPANY; *U.S. Private*, pg. 840
PARK-OHIO INDUSTRIES, INC.; *U.S. Public*, pg. 1258
PARK PLACE MOTORCARS, LTD.; *U.S. Private*, pg. 840
PARKDALE MILLS; *U.S. Private*, pg. 840
PARKE-DAVIS—See Warner-Lambert Company; *U.S. Public*, pg. 1739
PARKE-DAVIS & COMPANY, LIMITED—See Warner-Lambert Company; *U.S. Public*, pg. 1739
PARKE DAVIS COMPANY, INC.—See Warner-Lambert Company; *U.S. Public*, pg. 1739
PARKE-DAVIS/ELAN LTD.—See Elan Corporation Plc; *Int'l*, pg. 436
PARKE-DAVIS GROUP—See Warner-Lambert Company; *U.S. Public*, pg. 1739
PARKE-DAVIS PTY. LTD.—See Warner-Lambert Company; *U.S. Public*, pg. 1739
PARKE-DAVIS S.A.—See Warner-Lambert Company; *U.S. Public*, pg. 1739
PARKE-DAVIS S.P.A.—See Warner-Lambert Company; *U.S.* Public, pg. 1739
PARKER AMCHEM S.A. DE C.V.—See Henkel KGaA; *Int'l*, pg. 614
PARKER & AMCHEM—See Henkel KGaA; *Int'l*, pg. 612
PARKER AUTOMOTIVE DE MEXICO SA DE CV—See Parker Hannifin Corporation; *U.S. Public*, pg. 1263
PARKER BATH COMPANY LTD.—See Sunrise Medical, Inc.; *U.S. Public*, pg. 1536
PARKER BERTEA AEROSPACE—See Parker Hannifin Corporation; *U.S. Public*, pg. 1262
PARKER BROTHERS—See Hasbro, Inc.; *U.S. Public*, pg. 797
PARKER CHEMICAL COMPANY PTE. LTD.—See Henkel KGaA; *Int'l*, pg. 613
PARKER CHEMICAL CORP. LTD.—See Henkel KGaA; *Int'l*, pg. 613
PARKER DRILLING COMPANY; *U.S. Public*, pg. 1259
PARKER DRILLING COMPANY INTERNATIONAL LIMITED—See Parker Drilling Company; *U.S. Public*, pg. 1259
PARKER ELECTROMECHANICAL-DIGIPLAN DIVISION—See Parker Hannifin Corporation; *U.S. Public*, pg. 1263
PARKER ENZED NEW ZEALAND PTY. LTD.—See Parker Hannifin Corporation; *U.S. Public*, pg. 1261
PARKER ERMETO GMBH—See Parker Hannifin Corporation; *U.S. Public*, pg. 1261
PARKER FLUID CONNECTORS DE MEXICO—See Parker Hannifin Corporation; *U.S. Public*, pg. 1261
PARKER FLUID VERBINDUNGSTELLE GMBH—See Parker Hannifin Corporation; *U.S. Public*, pg. 1260
PARKER HANNIFIN—See Parker Hannifin Corporation; *U.S. Public*, pg. 1260
PARKER HANNIFIN AFRICA PTY LTD.—See Parker Hannifin Corporation; *U.S. Public*, pg. 1263
PARKER HANNIFIN ARGENTINA SAIC—See Parker Hannifin Corporation; *U.S. Public*, pg. 1263
PARKER HANNIFIN A/S—See Parker Hannifin Corporation; *U.S. Public*, pg. 1263
PARKER HANNIFIN ASIA PACIFIC CO., LTD.—See Parker Hannifin Corporation; *U.S. Public*, pg. 1263
PARKER HANNIFIN (AUSTRALIA) (PTY.) LTD.—See Parker Hannifin Corporation; *U.S. Public*, pg. 1263
PARKER HANNIFIN B.V.—See Parker Hannifin Corporation; *U.S. Public*, pg. 1263
PARKER HANNIFIN CORPORATION; *U.S. Public*, pg. 1259
PARKER HANNIFIN CORPORATION—See Parker Hannifin Corporation; *U.S. Public*, pg. 1263
PARKER HANNIFIN DANMARK A/S—See Parker Hannifin Corporation; *U.S. Public*, pg. 1263
PARKER HANNIFIN DE VENEZUELA, S.A.—See Parker Hannifin Corporation; *U.S. Public*, pg. 1263
PARKER HANNIFIN DO BRAZIL INDUSTRIA COMERCIO LTDA.—See Parker Hannifin Corporation; *U.S. Public*, pg. 1263
PARKER HANNIFIN ESPANA S.A.—See Parker Hannifin Corporation; *U.S. Public*, pg. 1263
PARKER HANNIFIN GMBH—See Parker Hannifin Corporation; *U.S. Public*, pg. 1260
PARKER HANNIFIN GMBH, O-RING DIV. EUROPE—See Parker Hannifin Corporation; *U.S. Public*, pg. 1263
PARKER HANNIFIN GMBH/PRADIFA PACKING DIVISION—See Parker Hannifin Corporation; *U.S. Public*, pg. 1262
PARKER HANNIFIN HONG KONG LTD.—See Parker Hannifin Corporation; *U.S. Public*, pg. 1263
PARKER HANNIFIN HONG KONG LTD., FLUID HANDLING HEADQUARTERS—See Parker Hannifin Corporation; *U.S. Public*, pg. 1263
PARKER HANNIFIN HOOGEZAND B.V.—See Parker Hannifin Corporation; *U.S. Public*, pg. 1263
PARKER HANNIFIN INDUSTRIA E COMERCIO LTDA.—See Parker Hannifin Corporation; *U.S. Public*, pg. 1260
PARKER HANNIFIN INSTRUMENTATION DIVISION—See Parker Hannifin Corporation; *U.S. Public*, pg. 1263
PARKER HANNIFIN JAPAN LTD.—See Parker Hannifin Corporation; *U.S. Public*, pg. 1263
PARKER HANNIFIN MALAYSIA—See Parker Hannifin Corporation; *U.S. Public*, pg. 1263
PARKER HANNIFIN N.M.F. GMBH—See Parker Hannifin Corporation; *U.S. Public*, pg. 1261
PARKER HANNIFIN (NZ) LIMITED—See Parker Hannifin Corporation; *U.S. Public*, pg. 1261
PARKER HANNIFIN OY (FINLAND)—See Parker Hannifin Corporation; *U.S. Public*, pg. 1263
PARKER HANNIFIN PLC, BARBADOS WAY—See Parker Hannifin Corporation; *U.S. Public*, pg. 1263
PARKER HANNIFIN RAK—See Parker Hannifin Corporation; *U.S. Public*, pg. 1261
PARKER HANNIFIN RAK S.A.—See Parker Hannifin Corporation; *U.S. Public*, pg. 1261
PARKER HANNIFIN S.A.—See Parker Hannifin Corporation; *U.S. Public*, pg. 1261
PARKER HANNIFIN SA NV—See Parker Hannifin Corporation; *U.S. Public*, pg. 1263
PARKER HANNIFIN SINGAPORE PTE. LTD.—See Parker Hannifin Corporation; *U.S. Public*, pg. 1263
PARKER HANNIFIN SP. Z.O.O.—See Parker Hannifin Corporation; *U.S. Public*, pg. 1263
PARKER HANNIFIN SPA—See Parker Hannifin Corporation; *U.S. Public*, pg. 1263
PARKER HANNIFIN (SWEDEN) AB—See Parker Hannifin Corporation; *U.S. Public*, pg. 1263
PARKER HANNIFIN SWEDEN AB—See Parker Hannifin Corporation; *U.S. Public*, pg. 1264
PARKER HANNIFIN TAIWAN CO. LTD.—See Parker Hannifin Corporation; *U.S. Public*, pg. 1264
PARKER HANNIFIN (U.K.) LTD. INSTRUMENTATION PRODUCTS DIV.—See Parker Hannifin Corporation; *U.S. Public*, pg. 1264
PARKER KALON—See The Black & Decker Corporation; *U.S. Public*, pg. 233
PARKER KINETIC DESIGNS—See Parker Drilling Company; *U.S. Public*, pg. 1259
PARKER PAINT MANUFACTURING CO. INC.—See Williams Holdings Plc; *Int'l*, pg. 1501
PARKER PEN (AUSTRALIA) PTY. LTD.—See The Gillette Company; *U.S. Public*, pg. 745
PARKER PEN CANADA LIMITED—See The Gillette Company; *U.S. Public*, pg. 745
PARKER PEN JAPAN K.K.—See The Gillette Company; *U.S. Public*, pg. 745
PARKER PEN PLC—See The Gillette Company; *U.S. Public*, pg. 745
PARKER PNEUMATIC—See Parker Hannifin Corporation; *U.S. Public*, pg. 1264
PARKER PNEUMATIC AB—See Parker Hannifin Corporation; *U.S. Public*, pg. 1264
PARKER SEAL DE BAJA, S.A. DE C.V.—See Parker Hannifin Corporation; *U.S. Public*, pg. 1262
PARKER SEAL DE MEXICO SA—See Parker Hannifin Corporation; *U.S. Public*, pg. 1262
PARKER SEALS SPA—See Parker Hannifin Corporation; *U.S. Public*, pg. 1264
PARKER SWEEPER COMPANY—See Hako-Werke GmbH & Co.; *Int'l*, pg. 587
PARKER TECHNOLOGY, INC.—See Parker Drilling Company; *U.S. Public*, pg. 1259
PARKER/ZENITH—See Parker Hannifin Corporation; *U.S. Public*, pg. 1264
PARKERSBURG DIVISION—See Champion Industries; *U.S.* Public, pg. 333
PARKLABREA FINANCE CORP.—See Forest City Enterprises, Inc.; *U.S. Public*, pg. 669

PARKLANE INSURANCE CO.—See Ford Motor Company; *U.S. Public*, pg. 664
PARKS CORPORATION; *U.S. Private*, pg. 840
PARKS LLC; *U.S. Private*, pg. 840
PARKS OMEGA, INC.—See Omega Environmental Inc.; *U.S. Public*, pg. 1222
PARKS PRODUCTS, INC.; *U.S. Private*, pg. 840
PARKSON CORPORATION—See Axel Johnson AB; *Int'l*, pg. 710
PARKSON CORPORATOR—See Axel Johnson AB; *Int'l*, pg. 711
PARKVIEW ACRES—See Vencor, Inc.; *U.S. Public*, pg. 1714
PARKWAY HOLDINGS LIMITED; *Int'l*, pg. 1023
PARKWAY PAVILION HEALTHCARE—See Vencor, Inc.; *U.S. Public*, pg. 1714
PARKWOOD PLACE—See Horizon/CMS Healthcare Corporation; *U.S. Public*, pg. 839
PARKWORLD HOLIDAYS LTD.—See The Rank Group PLC; *Int'l*, pg. 1086
PARLEX CORPORATION; *U.S. Public*, pg. 1264
PARLEX LAMINATED CABLE—See Parlex Corporation; *U.S. Public*, pg. 1264
PARLIAMENT COMPANY; *U.S. Private*, pg. 840
PARLUX FRAGRANCES INC.; *U.S. Public*, pg. 1264
PARLUX, LTD.—See Parlux Fragrances Inc.; *U.S. Public*, pg. 1264
PARMALAT CANADA LTD.—See Parmalat S.p.A.; *Int'l*, pg. 1023
PARMALAT S.P.A.; *Int'l*, pg. 1023
PARMALAT USA CORPORATION—See Parmalat S.p.A.; *Int'l*, pg. 1023
PARMALAT WHITE KNIGHT—See Parmalat S.p.A.; *Int'l*, pg. 1023
THE PARMAN CORPORATION; *U.S. Private*, pg. 840
PARMAN LUBRICANTS—See The Parman Corporation; *U.S. Private*, pg. 840
PARMART STORES—See The Parman Corporation; *U.S. Private*, pg. 840
PARMATECH CORPORATION—See Carpenter Technology Corporation; *U.S. Public*, pg. 307
PARMELEE TRANSPORTATION CO.—See Stamford Capital; *U.S. Private*, pg. 1030
P.J. PARMITER & SONS LTD.—See Wolseley Plc.; *Int'l*, pg. 1512
PARRISH TIRE COMPANY, INC.; *U.S. Private*, pg. 840
PARS HANDEL AG—See Schindler Holding AG; *Int'l*, pg. 1204
PARSEC—See Budco Group Inc.; *U.S. Private*, pg. 178
PARSEC/DOTSON, INC.—See Budco Group Inc.; *U.S. Private*, pg. 178
PARSONS & WHITTEMORE, INC.; *U.S. Private*, pg. 840
PARSONS BRINCKERHOFF CONSTRUCTION SERVICES, INC.—See Parsons Brinckerhoff Inc.; *U.S. Private*, pg. 841
PARSONS BRINCKERHOFF ENERGY SERVICES INC.—See Parsons Brinckerhoff Inc.; *U.S. Private*, pg. 841
PARSONS BRINCKERHOFF INC.; *U.S. Private*, pg. 841
PARSONS BRINCKERHOFF INTERNATIONAL, PTE. LTD.—See Parsons Brinckerhoff Inc.; *U.S. Private*, pg. 841
PARSONS BRINCKERHOFF LTD.—See Parsons Brinckerhoff Inc.; *U.S. Private*, pg. 841
PARSONS BRINCKERHOFF QUADE & DOUGLAS, INC.—See Parsons Brinckerhoff Inc.; *U.S. Private*, pg. 841
PARSONS CHAIN COMPANY LTD—See FKI Plc; *Int'l*, pg. 473
PARSONS CHAIN EUROPE SA—See FKI Plc; *Int'l*, pg. 473
PARSONS CONSTRUCTION SERVICES, INC.—See Parsons Corporation; *U.S. Private*, pg. 842
PARSONS CONSTRUCTORS INC.—See Parsons Corporation; *U.S. Private*, pg. 842
PARSONS CORPORATION; *U.S. Private*, pg. 841
PARSONS DEVELOPMENT COMPANY—See Parsons Corporation; *U.S. Private*, pg. 842
PARSONS ENGINEERING SCIENCE, INC.—See Parsons Corporation; *U.S. Private*, pg. 842
PARSONS INFRASTRUCTURE & TECHNOLOGY GROUP INC.—See Parsons Corporation; *U.S. Private*, pg. 842
PARSONS INTERNATIONAL LTD.—See Parsons Corporation; *U.S. Private*, pg. 842
PARSONS OVERSEAS CO. CHILE LIMITADA—See Parsons Corporation; *U.S. Private*, pg. 842
PARSONS PAPER DIV. OF NVF CO.—See NVF Company; *U.S. Private*, pg. 772
PARSONS PRECISION PRODUCTS, INC.—See Jordan Industries, Inc.; *U.S. Private*, pg. 598
PARSONS PROCESS GROUP INC.—See Parsons Corporation; *U.S. Private*, pg. 842
PARSONS WATER RESOURCES, INC.—See Parsons Corporation; *U.S. Private*, pg. 842
PARTECH COMMUNICATIONS GROUP, INC.—See Tropic Communications Inc.; *U.S. Public*, pg. 1641
PARTEK CORPORATION; *Int'l*, pg. 1024
PARTEK OPERATION—See Parker Hannifin Corporation; *U.S. Public*, pg. 1262
PARTEL RESEARCH CORP.—See AEGON N.V.; *Int'l*, pg. 27
PARTENAVIA - CASORIA PLANT—See IRI Istituto Ricostruzione Industriale; *Int'l*, pg. 653
PARTENAVIA CONSTRUZIONI AERONAUTICHE—See IRI Istituto Ricostruzione Industriale; *Int'l*, pg. 653
PARTES DE TELEVISION DE REYNOSA S.A. DE C.V.—See Zenith Electronics Corp.; *U.S. Public*, pg. 1790
PARTHENON INSURANCE CO.—See Columbia/HCA Healthcare Corporation; *U.S. Public*, pg. 405
PARTICIPATE MAATSCHAPPIJ TRANSHOL B.V.—See Assicurazioni Generali S.p.A.; *Int'l*, pg. 92
PARTICIPATIE MAATSCHAPPIJ GRAAFSCHAP HOLLAND N.V.—See Assicurazioni Generali S.p.A.; *Int'l*, pg. 92
PARTICLE DYNAMICS, INC.—See KV Pharmaceutical Company; *U.S. Public*, pg. 941
PARTITA LTD.—See Merita Ltd.; *Int'l*, pg. 859

PARTLOW CORPORATION—See Danaher Corporation; *U.S. Public*, pg. 482
PARTNER IMMOBILIENDIENST GMBH—See Commerzbank AG; *Int'l*, pg. 310
PARTNER INDUSTRIAL PRODUCTS INC.—See Electrolux, AB; *Int'l*, pg. 440
PARTNER RELATIONS, EUROPE—See The Macneal-Schwendler Corp.; *U.S. Public*, pg. 1032
PARTNERRE LTD.; *Int'l*, pg. 1024
PARTNERS & SHEVACK DESIGN—See Partners & Shevack, Inc.; *U.S. Private*, pg. 842
PARTNERS & SHEVACK DIRECT—See Partners & Shevack, Inc.; *U.S. Private*, pg. 842
PARTNERS & SHEVACK, INC.; *U.S. Private*, pg. 842
PARTNERS & SHEVACK PUBLIC RELATIONS—See Partners & Shevack, Inc.; *U.S. Private*, pg. 842
PARTNERSHIP PACIFIC LIMITED—See Westpac Banking Corporation; *Int'l*, pg. 1496
PARTREDERIET NEMO A/S—See Neste Oy; *Int'l*, pg. 915
PARTRIDGE MEATS, INC.—See American Financial Group; *U.S. Public*, pg. 75
PARTS COMPANY OF AMERICA—See W.W. Grainger, Inc.; *U.S. Public*, pg. 758
PARTY PAC DIV.—See Gilster Mary Lee Corp.; *U.S. Private*, pg. 455
PARTYLITE GIFTS, INC.—See Blyth Industries; *U.S. Public*, pg. 239
PARVILAND GERANCE—See Credit Nationale; *Int'l*, pg. 344
PASCO-CERTEZA COMPUTER MAPPING CORPORATION—See Pasco Corporation; *Int'l*, pg. 1024
PASCO COMPUTER-MAPPING CENTER CO., LTD.—See Pasco Corporation; *Int'l*, pg. 1024
PASCO CORPORATION; *Int'l*, pg. 1024
PASCO CORP. OF AMERICA—See Shikishima Baking Co., Ltd.; *Int'l*, pg. 1231
PASCO DEVELOPMENT NEW ZEALAND LTD.—See Pasco Corporation; *Int'l*, pg. 1024
PASCO ENGINEERING CO., LTD.—See Pasco Corporation; *Int'l*, pg. 1024
PASCO ENGINEERING LIMITED—See Tarmac plc; *Int'l*, pg. 1355
PASCO ESTATE CO., LTD.—See Pasco Corporation; *Int'l*, pg. 1024
PASCO INTERNATIONAL INC.—See Pasco Corporation; *Int'l*, pg. 1024
PASCO RESTRUCTURING CO., LTD.—See Pasco Corporation; *Int'l*, pg. 1024
PASCO RETAIL CO., LTD.—See Pasco Corporation; *Int'l*, pg. 1024
PASCO ROAD TECHNOLOGY CENTER CO., LTD.—See Pasco Corporation; *Int'l*, pg. 1024
PASCO U.S.A., INC.—See Pasco Corporation; *Int'l*, pg. 1024
PASCOE BUILDING SYSTEMS, INC.; *U.S. Private*, pg. 842
PASCOL ENGINEERING—See Canadian Shipbuilding & Engineering Ltd.; *Int'l*, pg. 259
PASCON LTD.—See BTR plc; *Int'l*, pg. 124
PASLODE—See Illinois Tool Works Inc.; *U.S. Public*, pg. 867
PASOLDS LIMITED—See Coats Viyella plc; *Int'l*, pg. 300
PASOTEX CORPORATION; *U.S. Private*, pg. 842
ALBERTO PASQUALINI REFINERY—See Petrobras - Petroleo Brasileiro S.A.; *Int'l*, pg. 1042
PASS & SEYMOUR/LEGRAND—See LeGrand S.A.; *Int'l*, pg. 806
PASSAT LAUNDRY SYSTEMS; *U.S. Private*, pg. 842
PASSAVANT-WERKE AG—See Bilfinger + Berger Bauaktiengesellschaft; *Int'l*, pg. 195
PASSENGER CAR ENGINEERING CENTER—See Mitsubishi Motors Corporation; *Int'l*, pg. 875
PASSENGER RAILROAD INSURANCE LTD.—See Amtrak-National Railroad Passenger Corp.; *U.S. Private*, pg. 69
PASSIFLORE SA—See LVMH Moet Hennessy Louis Vuitton; *Int'l*, pg. 783
PASSITALIA—See LVMH Moet Hennessy Louis Vuitton; *Int'l*, pg. 783
PASSLUNCH-SODEXHO SRL—See Sodexho S.A.; *Int'l*, pg. 1275
GABRIEL PASSOS REFINERY—See Petrobras - Petroleo Brasileiro S.A.; *Int'l*, pg. 1042
PASSPORT BOOKS—See Tribune Company; *U.S. Public*, pg. 1636
PASSPORT TRAVEL, INC.; *U.S. Private*, pg. 842
PASTA CENTRAL—See Blimpie International, Inc.; *U.S. Public*, pg. 236
PASTA & CHEESE, INC.—See Nestle S.A.; *Int'l*, pg. 918
PASTA FOODS LIMITED—See Tomkins PLC; *Int'l*, pg. 1396
PASTA GALA SA—See Coop Switzerland; *Int'l*, pg. 330
THE PASTENE COMPANIES LTD.; *U.S. Private*, pg. 842
PASTEUR MERIEUX SERUMS ET VACCINS—See Rhone-Poulenc S.A.; *Int'l*, pg. 1109
PATAGONIA—See Lost Arrow Corporation; *U.S. Private*, pg. 677
PATCH COMMUNICATIONS; *U.S. Private*, pg. 842
PATCH RUBBER COMPANY—See Myers Industries, Inc.; *U.S. Public*, pg. 1143
PATCO L.P.—See Continental/Midland, Inc.; *U.S. Private*, pg. 269
PATCRAFT COMMERCIAL CARPET—See Queen Carpet Corporation; *U.S. Private*, pg. 900
PATENT CONSTRUCTION SYSTEMS—See Harsco Corporation; *U.S. Public*, pg. 793
PATERNO IMPORTS LIMITED; *U.S. Private*, pg. 843
PATERSON STAMP WORKS—See American Marking Systems; *U.S. Private*, pg. 59
PATERSON ZOCHONIS PLC; *Int'l*, pg. 1024
PATEX CHEMIE GMBH—See Hercules Incorporated; *U.S. Public*, pg. 811
PATHE; *Int'l*, pg. 1024
PATHE MARCONI EMI SA—See EMI Group plc; *Int'l*, pg. 427

PATHETEK—See Eastman Kodak Company; *U.S. Public*, pg. 551
PATHFINDER MINES CORPORATION—See COGEMA - Compagnie Generale des Matieres Nucleaires; *Int'l*, pg. 305
PATHMARK STORES INCORPORATED; *U.S. Private*, pg. 843
PATHOLOGY ASSOCIATES INTERNATIONAL CORPORATION—See Science Applications International Corp.; *U.S. Public*, pg. 976
PATHWAY BELLOWS, INC.—See Dover Corporation; *U.S. Public*, pg. 521
PATIENCE REALTY CORPORATION—See Providence Energy Corporation; *U.S. Public*, pg. 1337
PATIENT CARE COMMUNICATIONS, INC.—See The Thomson Corporation; *U.S. Public*, pg. 1601
PATIENT CARE, INC.—See Chemed Corporation; *U.S. Public*, pg. 344
PATIENT'S CHOICE, INC.—See Cigna Corp.; *U.S. Public*, pg. 360
PATINA OIL & GAS CORP.; *U.S. Public*, pg. 1264
PATONS & BALDWINS LIMITED—See Coats Viyella plc; *Int'l*, pg. 300
M.A. PATOUT & SON; *U.S. Private*, pg. 843
PATRA CERAMICS CO., LTD.; *Int'l*, pg. 1024
PATRIA VERSICHERUNG AKTIENGESELLSCHAFT—See Zurich Insurance Company; *Int'l*, pg. 1531
PATRICIAN ASSOCIATES, INC.—See The Principal Financial Group; *U.S. Private*, pg. 885
C.H. PATRICK & CO.—See The B.F. Goodrich Company; *U.S. Public*, pg. 751
PATRICK INDUSTRIES INC.; *U.S. Public*, pg. 1264
PATRICK METALS—See Patrick Industries Inc.; *U.S. Public*, pg. 1265
PATRIOT AMERICAN HOSPITALITY, INC.; *U.S. Public*, pg. 1265
PATRIOT AMERICAN HOSPITALITY OPERATING COMPANY—See Patriot American Hospitality, Inc.; *U.S. Public*, pg. 1265
PATRIOT GENERAL INSURANCE CO.—See Sentry Insurance, A Mutual Company; *U.S. Private*, pg. 985
PATSON'S PRESS; *U.S. Private*, pg. 843
PATSY'S, INC.; *U.S. Private*, pg. 843
PATTEN-BEERS CONSTRUCTORS—See Skanska AB; *Int'l*, pg. 1261
PATTERSON DENTAL CANADA INC.—See Patterson Dental Company; *U.S. Public*, pg. 1265
PATTERSON DENTAL COMPANY; *U.S. Public*, pg. 1265
PATTERSON DENTAL SUPPLY, INC.—See Patterson Dental Company; *U.S. Public*, pg. 1265
PATTERSON DRILLING CO.—See Patterson Energy, Inc.; *U.S. Public*, pg. 1265
PATTERSON ENERGY, INC.; *U.S. Public*, pg. 1265
PATTERSON-KELLEY COMPANY—See Harsco Corporation; *U.S. Public*, pg. 793
PATTERSON FROZEN FOODS, INC.; *U.S. Private*, pg. 843
PATTERSON LABORATORIES, INC.; *U.S. Private*, pg. 843
PATTERSON PUMP COMPANY—See The Gorman-Rupp Company; *U.S. Public*, pg. 754
PATTERSON SERVICES, INC.—See RPC Incorporated; *U.S. Public*, pg. 1356
PATTERSON TRUCK LINE, INC.—See RPC Incorporated; *U.S. Public*, pg. 1356
PATTON—See Sonoco Products Company; *U.S. Public*, pg. 1486
PATTON MANAGEMENT, INC.; *U.S. Private*, pg. 843
THE PATY COMPANY; *U.S. Private*, pg. 844
WALTER PATZ OHG—See Veba AG; *Int'l*, pg. 1459
PAUL & VINCENT LTD.—See Unilever Plc; *Int'l*, pg. 1438
THE PAUL REVERE CORPORATION—See Provident Companies, Inc.; *U.S. Public*, pg. 1338
PAUL REVERE INVESTMENT MANAGEMENT COMPANY INC. (PRIMCO)—See Provident Companies, Inc.; *U.S. Public*, pg. 1338
THE PAUL REVERE VARIABLE ANNUITY LIFE INSURANCE CO.—See Provident Companies, Inc.; *U.S. Public*, pg. 1338
PAUL-SON GAMING CORPORATION; *U.S. Public*, pg. 1265
PAUL STUART, INC.; *U.S. Private*, pg. 844
PAULA FINANCIAL; *U.S. Public*, pg. 1266
PAULINIA REFINERY—See Petrobras - Petroleo Brasileiro S.A.; *Int'l*, pg. 1042
PAULISTA CONTAINERS MARITIMOS LTDA.—See Sea Containers Ltd.; *Int'l*, pg. 1214
PAULS MALT LIMITED—See Harrisons & Crosfield plc; *Int'l*, pg. 598
PAULS PLC—See Harrisons & Crosfield plc; *Int'l*, pg. 598
PAULSBORO TERMINAL—See GATX Corporation; *U.S. Public*, pg. 692
PAULSTRA CRC CORPORATION—See Total S.A.; *Int'l*, pg. 1410
PAUMIER COMPANY INC.—See The Cypress Companies; *U.S. Private*, pg. 300
PAURUINIERRE GORDON & CO. LTD.—See Westdeutsche Landesbank Girozentrale; *Int'l*, pg. 1493
PAVAILLER EQUIPEMENT S.A.—See Financiere Equipment S.A.; *Int'l*, pg. 485
PAVAILLER U.S.A. INC.—See Financiere Equipment S.A.; *Int'l*, pg. 485
PAVEY ENVELOPE & TAG CORP.—See Mail-Well Inc.; *U.S. Public*, pg. 1038
THE PAVILION VENTURE—See Cigna Corp.; *U.S. Public*, pg. 365
PAVILIONS—See Safeway Inc.; *U.S. Public*, pg. 1426
PAVIMENTOS CERAMICOS S.A.—See Lafarge S.A.; *Int'l*, pg. 790
PAWLING CORPORATION; *U.S. Private*, pg. 844
PAWLING SAVINGS BANK—See Progressive Bank, Inc.; *U.S. Public*, pg. 1334
PAWTUCKET FASTENERS INC.; *U.S. Private*, pg. 844
PAX COMPANY—See Zipp Industries; *U.S. Private*, pg. 1207
PAX WORLD FUND FAMILY; *U.S. Public*, pg. 1266

PAXAR APPAREL IDENTIFICATION SYSTEMS—See PAXAR Corporation; *U.S. Public*, pg. 1266
PAXAR BENELUX BVBA—See PAXAR Corporation; *U.S. Public*, pg. 1266
PAXAR CANADA—See PAXAR Corporation; *U.S. Public*, pg. 1266
PAXAR CORPORATION; *U.S. Public*, pg. 1266
PAXAR DE MEXICO, S.A. DE C.V.—See PAXAR Corporation; *U.S. Public*, pg. 1266
PAXAR DEUTSCHLAND GMBH—See PAXAR Corporation; *U.S. Public*, pg. 1266
PAXAR EUROPE LTD.—See PAXAR Corporation; *U.S. Public*, pg. 1267
PAXAR FAR EAST LIMITED—See PAXAR Corporation; *U.S. Public*, pg. 1267
PAXAR GRAPHICS—See PAXAR Corporation; *U.S. Public*, pg. 1266
PAXAR IBERIA, S.A.—See PAXAR Corporation; *U.S. Public*, pg. 1267
PAXAR ITALIA S.R.L.—See PAXAR Corporation; *U.S. Public*, pg. 1267
PAXAR POLSKA SP.ZO.O.—See PAXAR Corporation; *U.S. Public*, pg. 1267
PAXAR PRINTED LABELS—See PAXAR Corporation; *U.S. Public*, pg. 1266
PAXAR WOVEN LABELS—See PAXAR Corporation; *U.S. Public*, pg. 1266
PAXTON—See McKechnie PLC; *Int'l*, pg. 851
PAXTON & VIERLING—See Owen Industries, Inc.; *U.S. Private*, pg. 824
PAXTON BEAUTIFUL WOODS—See Jeld-Wen, Inc.; *U.S. Private*, pg. 585
FRANK PAXTON COMPANY—See Jeld-Wen, Inc.; *U.S. Private*, pg. 585
FRANK PAXTON LUMBER COMPANY—See Jeld-Wen, Inc.; *U.S. Private*, pg. 585
PAY LESS SUPER MARKETS, INC., *U.S. Private*, pg. 844
PAYCHEX, INC.; *U.S. Public*, pg. 1267
PAYCO AMERICAN CORPORATION; *U.S. Public*, pg. 1267
PAYCO-GENERAL AMERICAN CREDITS, INC.—See Payco American Corporation; *U.S. Public*, pg. 1267
PAYLESS CAR RENTAL SYSTEM, INC.; *U.S. Private*, pg. 844
PAYLESS CASHWAYS, INC.; *U.S. Public*, pg. 1267
PAYLESS SHOESOURCE, INC.; *U.S. Public*, pg. 1268
THE PAYNE INVESTMENT COMPANY—See Brittany Corporation; *U.S. Private*, pg. 169
PAYNE & KELLER COMPANY, INC.—See Jacobs Engineering Group Inc.; *U.S. Public*, pg. 921
PAYNE STRACEY LTD. (DIRECT MARKETING)—See Warwick Baker O'Neill; *U.S. Private*, pg. 1152
PAYOT NAVILLE DISTRIBUTION—See Lagardere Groupe; *Int'l*, pg. 796
PAYOT SA—See Lagardere Groupe; *Int'l*, pg. 796
PAYSON BRONCO, INC.—See Payson Casters, Inc.; *U.S. Private*, pg. 844
PAYSON CASTERS, INC.; *U.S. Private*, pg. 844
PAYSON GEORGIA, INC.—See Payson Casters, Inc.; *U.S. Private*, pg. 844
PAYSON TEXAS, INC.—See Payson Casters, Inc.; *U.S. Private*, pg. 844
PEABODY COAL CO.—See Hanson PLC; *Int'l*, pg. 594
PEABODY COALSALES COMPANY—See Hanson PLC; *Int'l*, pg. 594
PEABODY CORPORATION USA—See Powell Duffryn PLC; *Int'l*, pg. 1066
PEABODY DEVELOPMENT COMPANY—See Hanson PLC; *Int'l*, pg. 594
PEABODY ENGINEERING CANADA LTD.—See Powell Duffryn PLC; *Int'l*, pg. 1066
PEABODY ENGINEERING CORP.—See Powell Duffryn PLC; *Int'l*, pg. 1065
PEABODY HOLDING COMPANY, INC.—See Hanson PLC; *Int'l*, pg. 594
PEABODY OFFICE FURNITURE CORPORATION; *U.S. Private*, pg. 844
PEABODY RESOURCES LIMITED—See Hanson PLC; *Int'l*, pg. 594
PEABODY TECTANK, INC.—See A.O. Smith Corporation; *U.S. Public*, pg. 1477
PEABODY WESTERN COAL COMPANY—See Hanson PLC; *Int'l*, pg. 594
PEACE INDUSTRIES INC.; *U.S. Private*, pg. 845
PEACE RIVER ELECTRIC COOPERATIVE, INC.; *U.S. Private*, pg. 845
PEACE RIVER TRANSMISSION CO., LTD.—See BC Gas Inc.; *Int'l*, pg. 114
PEACHFORD PROFESSIONAL NETWORK, INC.—See Magellan Health Services, Inc.; *U.S. Public*, pg. 1036
PEACHTREE NATIONAL—See Synovus Financial Corp.; *U.S. Public*, pg. 1549
PEACHTREE WYNFREY ASSOCIATES—See Cigna Corp.; *U.S. Public*, pg. 362
PEACOCK INC.—See Weir Group PLC; *Int'l*, pg. 1489
PEAK DOWNS MINE—See The Broken Hill Proprietary Company Limited; *Int'l*, pg. 223
PEAK HILL MINE—See North Limited; *Int'l*, pg. 967
PEAK OILFIELD SERVICES COMPANY—See Nabors Industries, Inc.; *U.S. Public*, pg. 1149
PEAK TECHNOLOGIES-EUROPE—See Moore Corporation Limited; *Int'l*, pg. 890
PEAK TECHNOLOGIES GROUP, INC.—See Moore Corporation Limited; *Int'l*, pg. 890
PEAKE ENERGY, INC.—See Texas Pacific Group; *U.S. Private*, pg. 1078
PEAKE PRINTERS, INC.; *U.S. Private*, pg. 845
PEARCE EQUIPMENT LEASING—See Pearce Industries Inc.; *U.S. Private*, pg. 845
PEARCE INDUSTRIES INC.; *U.S. Private*, pg. 845
PEARCE INTERNATIONAL INC.—See Pearce Industries Inc.; *U.S. Private*, pg. 845
PEARL CONTAINER CO.—See S & P Company; *U.S. Private*, pg. 954

PEARL DRUM CENTER—See Gibson Musical Instruments, Inc.; *U.S. Private*, pg. 452
PEARL GROUP PLC—See Australian Mutual Provident; *Int'l*, pg. 100
PEARL-PRESSMAN-LIBERTY COMMUNICATIONS GROUP; *U.S. Private*, pg. 845
PEARLE INC.—See Cole National Corporation; *U.S. Public*, pg. 396
PEARLE VISION EXPRESS—See Cole National Corporation; *U.S. Public*, pg. 397
PEARLE VISION, INC.—See Cole National Corporation; *U.S. Public*, pg. 397
PEARLSTINE DISTRIBUTORS INC.; *U.S. Private*, pg. 845
PEARSALLS SUTURES—See Bridport-Gundry p.l.c.; *Int'l*, pg. 215
CLYDE PEARSON DIV.—See Furniture Brands International Inc.; *U.S. Public*, pg. 688
PEARSON, INC.—See Pearson plc; *Int'l*, pg. 1026
PEARSON KK—See Pearson plc; *Int'l*, pg. 1027
PEARSON LONGMAN INC.—See Pearson plc; *Int'l*, pg. 1026
PEARSON NEW ENTERTAINMENT EUROPE—See Pearson plc; *Int'l*, pg. 1026
PEARSON PLC; *Int'l*, pg. 1025
PEARSON PROFESSIONAL LIMITED—See Pearson plc; *Int'l*, pg. 1026
PEARSON TELEVISION LTD.—See Pearson plc; *Int'l*, pg. 1026
PEASE INDUSTRIES, INC.; *U.S. Private*, pg. 845
PEAUDOUCE S.A. BABY PRODUCTS—See Svenska Cellulosa Aktiebolaget (SCA); *Int'l*, pg. 1326
PEAVEY ELECTRONICS CORP.; *U.S. Private*, pg. 845
PEAVEY ELECTRONICS LTD—See Peavey Electronics Corp.; *U.S. Private*, pg. 846
PEC ORGANIC CO., LTD.—See Pasco Corporation; *Int'l*, pg. 1024
PEC RIO GRANDE VALLEY—See Plastic Engineered Components Inc.; *U.S. Private*, pg. 871
PECHINEY AIM KOREA BRANCH—See Pechiney S.A.; *Int'l*, pg. 1031
PECHINEY AIM-REP. OFFICE IN ALGERIA—See Pechiney S.A.; *Int'l*, pg. 1031
PECHINEY AIM-REP. OFFICE IN TURKEY—See Pechiney S.A.; *Int'l*, pg. 1031
PECHINEY ALUMINIUM PRESSWORK GMBH—See Pechiney S.A.; *Int'l*, pg. 1031
PECHINEY ASIA PACIFIQUE SERVICES—See Pechiney S.A.; *Int'l*, pg. 1031
PECHINEY BAKER—See Pechiney S.A.; *Int'l*, pg. 1031
PECHINEY BALE—See Pechiney S.A.; *Int'l*, pg. 1031
PECHINEY BATIMENT—See Pechiney S.A.; *Int'l*, pg. 1028
PECHINEY BELGIUM S.A.—See Pechiney S.A.; *Int'l*, pg. 1031
PECHINEY BRAZIL LTDA.—See Pechiney S.A.; *Int'l*, pg. 1031
PECHINEY CEBAL PACKAGING LTD.—See Pechiney S.A.; *Int'l*, pg. 1031
PECHINEY CELOGRAF—See Pechiney S.A.; *Int'l*, pg. 1031
PECHINEY CORK & SEAL OF CALIFORNIA—See Pechiney S.A.; *Int'l*, pg. 1029
PECHINEY CORPORATION-AUSTRALIAN BRANCH—See Pechiney S.A.; *Int'l*, pg. 1031
PECHINEY CSFR-REP. OFFICE OF PECHINEY HANDELSGESELLSCHAFT & BRANDEIS IN CZECHOSLOVAKIA—See Pechiney S.A.; *Int'l*, pg. 1031
PECHINEY DENMARK—See Pechiney S.A.; *Int'l*, pg. 1031
PECHINEY DEUTSCHLAND GMBH—See Pechiney S.A.; *Int'l*, pg. 1031
PECHINEY ELECTROMETALLURGIE—See Pechiney S.A.; *Int'l*, pg. 1028
PECHINEY EMBALLAGE ALIMENTAIRE—See Pechiney S.A.; *Int'l*, pg. 1028
PECHINEY ENVASSE IBERICA S.A.—See Pechiney S.A.; *Int'l*, pg. 1031
PECHINEY ESPANA—See Pechiney S.A.; *Int'l*, pg. 1031
PECHINEY FAR EAST LTD.—See Pechiney S.A.; *Int'l*, pg. 1031
PECHINEY FOOD PACKAGING BENELUX—See Pechiney S.A.; *Int'l*, pg. 1031
PECHINEY FOOD PACKAGING JAPAN—See Pechiney S.A.; *Int'l*, pg. 1031
PECHINEY HANDELSGESELLSCHAFT MBH—See Pechiney S.A.; *Int'l*, pg. 1031
PECHINEY ITALIA SPA—See Pechiney S.A.; *Int'l*, pg. 1031
PECHINEY JAPAN—See Pechiney S.A.; *Int'l*, pg. 1031
PECHINEY LEBENSMITTELVERPACKUNGEN—See Pechiney S.A.; *Int'l*, pg. 1031
PECHINEY MEXICANA S.A. DE C.V.—See Pechiney S.A.; *Int'l*, pg. 1031
PECHINEY MOSCOW—See Pechiney S.A.; *Int'l*, pg. 1031
PECHINEY MOYEN-ORIENT—See Pechiney S.A.; *Int'l*, pg. 1031
PECHINEY NEDERLAND NV—See Pechiney S.A.; *Int'l*, pg. 1031
PECHINEY NORGE A/S-REP. OFFICE OF PECHINEY SVERIGE IN NORWAY—See Pechiney S.A.; *Int'l*, pg. 1031
PECHINEY PACKAGING ALIMENIARE—See Pechiney S.A.; *Int'l*, pg. 1031
PECHINEY PACKAGING FOOD & GENERAL LINES, LTD.—See Pechiney S.A.; *Int'l*, pg. 1031
PECHINEY PHILIPPINES INC.—See Pechiney S.A.; *Int'l*, pg. 1031
PECHINEY PORTUGAL LDA.—See Pechiney S.A.; *Int'l*, pg. 1031
PECHINEY RHENALU—See Pechiney S.A.; *Int'l*, pg. 1028
PECHINEY S.A.; *Int'l*, pg. 1027
PECHINEY SINGAPORE—See Pechiney S.A.; *Int'l*, pg. 1031
PECHINEY SINGAPORE PTE. LTD.—See Pechiney S.A.; *Int'l*, pg. 1031
PECHINEY STROJOBAL—See Pechiney S.A.; *Int'l*, pg. 1031

PECHINEY SUOMI-REP. OFFICE OF PECHINEY DENMARK IN FINLAND—See Pechiney S.A.; *Int'l*, pg. 1031
PECHINEY SVERIGE—See Pechiney S.A.; *Int'l*, pg. 1031
PECHINEY TAIWAN INC.—See Pechiney S.A.; *Int'l*, pg. 1031
PECHINEY TRADING COMPANY (PTC)—See Pechiney S.A.; *Int'l*, pg. 1031
PECHINEY UK LTD.—See Pechiney S.A.; *Int'l*, pg. 1031
PECHINEY VERKOOP B.V.—See Pechiney S.A.; *Int'l*, pg. 1031
PECHINEY WORLD TRADE (CANADA) INC.—See Pechiney S.A.; *Int'l*, pg. 1031
PECHINEY WORLD TRADE (HELLAS) S.A.—See Pechiney S.A.; *Int'l*, pg. 1031
PECHINEY WORLD TRADE S.A.—See Pechiney S.A.; *Int'l*, pg. 1028
PECK JONES CONSTRUCTION; *U.S. Private*, pg. 846
PECK ROAD FORD TRUCK SALES; *U.S. Private*, pg. 846
PECK SPRING COMPANY; *U.S. Private*, pg. 846
PECKHAM INDUSTRIES, INC.; *U.S. Private*, pg. 846
PECO ENERGY COMPANY; *U.S. Public*, pg. 1268
PECO ENERGY POWER CO.—See PECO Energy Company; *U.S. Public*, pg. 1268
PECO MFG. CO., INC.; *U.S. Private*, pg. 846
PECO SUIKERWERKEN B.V.—See Van Melle N.V.; *Int'l*, pg. 1451
PECOS VALLEY CARE CENTER—See Horizon/CMS Healthcare Corporation; *U.S. Public*, pg. 838
PEDERSHAAB LTD.—See FLS Industries A/S; *Int'l*, pg. 475
PEDERSHAAB MASCHINENFABRIK GMBH—See FLS Industries A/S; *Int'l*, pg. 475
PEDIGREE SEED CO.—See Novartis AG; *Int'l*, pg. 974
PEDONE & PARTNERS ADV., INC.; *U.S. Private*, pg. 846
PEDUS AVIATION—See Pedus Services, Inc.; *U.S. Private*, pg. 846
PEDUS BUILDING SERVICES—See Pedus Services, Inc.; *U.S. Private*, pg. 846
PEDUS FOOD SERVICES—See Pedus Services, Inc.; *U.S. Private*, pg. 846
PEDUS OFFICE SERVICES—See Pedus Services, Inc.; *U.S. Private*, pg. 846
PEDUS SECURITY SERVICES—See Pedus Services, Inc.; *U.S. Private*, pg. 846
PEDUS SERVICES, INC.; *U.S. Private*, pg. 846
PEEBLES, INC.; *U.S. Private*, pg. 846
PEELERS RUG COMPANY, INC.; *U.S. Private*, pg. 846
PEENEMUNDE PLANUNGS UND PROJEKT AG—See Harpen AG; *Int'l*, pg. 597
PEERLESS AIRE CORPORATION—See Masco Corporation; *U.S. Public*, pg. 1053
PEERLESS CARPET CORPORATION; *Int'l*, pg. 1032
PEERLESS CHAIN COMPANY—See Peerless Industrial Group, Inc.; *U.S. Public*, pg. 1268
PEERLESS CONFECTION COMPANY; *U.S. Private*, pg. 847
PEERLESS DISTRIBUTING CO.; *U.S. Private*, pg. 847
PEERLESS FAUCET CORPORATION—See Masco Corporation; *U.S. Public*, pg. 1053
PEERLESS IMPORTERS, INC.; *U.S. Private*, pg. 847
PEERLESS INDUSTRIAL GROUP, INC.; *U.S. Public*, pg. 1268
PEERLESS INSURANCE COMPANY—See ING Groep N.V.; *Int'l*, pg. 648
PEERLESS LIGHTING CORP.; *U.S. Private*, pg. 847
PEERLESS MFG. CO.; *U.S. Public*, pg. 1268
PEERLESS PAINT & VARNISH CORP.—See Paragon Paint & Varnish Corp.; *U.S. Private*, pg. 838
PEERLESS POTTERY, INC.; *U.S. Private*, pg. 847
PEERLESS PUMP—See TBG Management S.A.M.; *Int'l*, pg. 1335
PEERLESS TUBE COMPANY; *U.S. Public*, pg. 1269
PEERLESS TUBE CO. OF PUERTO RICO, INC.—See Peerless Tube Company; *U.S. Public*, pg. 1269
PEERLESS TYRE CO.; *U.S. Private*, pg. 847
PEERLESS UMBRELLA CO., INC.; *U.S. Private*, pg. 847
PEERS & CO.—See The Long-Term Credit Bank of Japan, Limited; *Int'l*, pg. 816
PEFIPRESA S.A.—See Preussag AG; *Int'l*, pg. 1071
PEGASUS BUCH-UND ZERTSCHRIFTEN GMBH—See The Reader's Digest Association, Inc.; *U.S. Public*, pg. 1368
PEGASUS ENGINEERING LTD.—See Jacobs Engineering Group Inc.; *U.S. Public*, pg. 922
PEGASUS GOLD CORPORATION; *U.S. Public*, pg. 1269
PEGASUS INTERNATIONAL CORPORATION—See Straube Regional Center LLC; *U.S. Private*, pg. 1046
PEGASUS INVESTMENT, INC.—See The Reader's Digest Association, Inc.; *U.S. Public*, pg. 1367
PEGASUS MINERA DE CHILE LTDA.—See Pegasus Gold Corporation; *U.S. Public*, pg. 1269
PEGASUS SALES, INC.—See The Reader's Digest Association, Inc.; *U.S. Public*, pg. 1367
PEGG HAINDL LTD.—See Haindl Papier GmbH; *Int'l*, pg. 586
PEGGY SAGE COSMETICOS LTDA.—See Unilever Plc; *Int'l*, pg. 1436
PEGLER HATTERSLEY AUSTRALIA PTY. LTD.—See GESTRA GmbH; *Int'l*, pg. 550
PEGLER HATTERSLEY NZ—See GESTRA GmbH; *Int'l*, pg. 550
PEGLER-HATTERSLEY PLC—See Tomkins PLC; *Int'l*, pg. 1395
PEGLER-SYSCO FOOD SERVICES CO.—See Sysco Corporation; *U.S. Public*, pg. 1550
PEIGNAGE DE LA TOSSEE—See Standard Commercial Corporation; *U.S. Public*, pg. 790
PEINTURES ET VERNIS DE LA MEDITERRANEE—See Lafarge S.A.; *Int'l*, pg. 790
PEINTURES PRODUITS PLASDOX—See Lafarge S.A.; *Int'l*, pg. 790
PEIRCE-PHELPS, INC.; *U.S. Private*, pg. 847
PEIRONE PRODUCE COMPANY—See URM Stores, Inc.; *U.S. Private*, pg. 1114

DAVID L. PEISTER CO., INC.; *U.S. Private*, pg. 848
PELAGO MARKETING CORP. SDN. BHD.—See Wella Group; *Int'l*, pg. 1490
PELICAN PRODUCTS; *U.S. Private*, pg. 848
PELICULAS PLASTICAS, S.A. DE C.V.—See Tablex, S.A. de C.V.; *Int'l*, pg. 1346
PELL, RUDMAN & COMPANY—See United Asset Management Corporation; *U.S. Public*, pg. 1673
PELLA CORPORATION; *U.S. Private*, pg. 848
PELLA TRAVEL INC.—See ITA Group Inc.; *U.S. Private*, pg. 555
PELLA WINDOW & DOOR COMPANY—See J.E. Higgins Lumber Co.; *U.S. Private*, pg. 528
PELLER WINES OF CALIFORNIA—See Andres Wines Ltd.; *Int'l*, pg. 76
PELLISSON—See LVMH Moet Hennessy Louis Vuitton; *Int'l*, pg. 781
PELLOS MILLS—See UPM-Kymmene Corporation; *Int'l*, pg. 1429
PELMAC THAI LIMITED—See Minebea Co., Ltd.; *Int'l*, pg. 868
PELMEC INDUSTRIES (PTE.) LIMITED—See Minebea Co., Ltd.; *Int'l*, pg. 868
GEORGE PELTIER & ASSOCS.—See Klockner-Moeller GmbH; *Int'l*, pg. 736
PEMBINA PIPELINE CORPORATION; *Int'l*, pg. 1032
PEMBROKE MARINER—See Garrett Company, Inc.; *U.S. Public*, pg. 701
PEMCO DIE CASTING CORPORATION; *U.S. Private*, pg. 848
PEMEX—See Petroleos Mexicanos; *Int'l*, pg. 1046
PEMEX EXPLORACION Y PRODUCCION—See Petroleos Mexicanos; *Int'l*, pg. 1046
PEMEX GAS Y PETROQUIMICA BASICA—See Petroleos Mexicanos; *Int'l*, pg. 1046
PEMEX PETROQUIMICA—See Petroleos Mexicanos; *Int'l*, pg. 1046
PEMEX REFINACION—See Petroleos Mexicanos; *Int'l*, pg. 1046
PEMKO MANUFACTURING COMPANY; *U.S. Private*, pg. 848
PEMPENA CONSULT SDN. BHD.—See Malaysia Tourism Promotion Board (MTPB); *Int'l*, pg. 833
PEN-TAB INDUSTRIES, INC.; *U.S. Private*, pg. 848
PENAFLOR S.A.; *Int'l*, pg. 1032
PENAJANS DMB&B TICARET—See DMB&B Communications; *U.S. Private*, pg. 305
PENARROYA ESPANA—See Imetal; *Int'l*, pg. 662
PENARROYA METAL EUROPE—See Imetal; *Int'l*, pg. 662
PENBERTHY DIV.—See Axel Johnson AB; *Int'l*, pg. 711
PENBERTHY LUMBER COMPANY; *U.S. Private*, pg. 848
PENCO—See Willis Corroon Group PLC; *Int'l*, pg. 1504
PENCO-ALAMBAMA—See Willis Corroon Group PLC; *Int'l*, pg. 1508
PENCO-ARIZONA—See Willis Corroon Group PLC; *Int'l*, pg. 1508
PENCO-FLORIDA—See Willis Corroon Group PLC; *Int'l*, pg. 1508
PENCO-GEORGIA—See Willis Corroon Group PLC; *Int'l*, pg. 1508
PENCO-HAWAII—See Willis Corroon Group PLC; *Int'l*, pg. 1508
PENCO-ILLINOIS—See Willis Corroon Group PLC; *Int'l*, pg. 1508
PENCO-INDIANA—See Willis Corroon Group PLC; *Int'l*, pg. 1508
PENCO-KANSAS—See Willis Corroon Group PLC; *Int'l*, pg. 1508
PENCO-KENTUCKY—See Willis Corroon Group PLC; *Int'l*, pg. 1508
PENCO-LOUISIANA—See Willis Corroon Group PLC; *Int'l*, pg. 1508
PENCO-MICHIGAN—See Willis Corroon Group PLC; *Int'l*, pg. 1508
PENCO-MISSISSIPPI—See Willis Corroon Group PLC; *Int'l*, pg. 1508
PENCO-MISSOURI—See Willis Corroon Group PLC; *Int'l*, pg. 1508
PENCO-NEBRASKA—See Willis Corroon Group PLC; *Int'l*, pg. 1508
PENCO-NEVADA—See Willis Corroon Group PLC; *Int'l*, pg. 1508
PENCO-NEW ENGLAND STATES—See Willis Corroon Group PLC; *Int'l*, pg. 1508
PENCO-NEW MEXICO—See Willis Corroon Group PLC; *Int'l*, pg. 1508
PENCO-NEW YORK—See Willis Corroon Group PLC; *Int'l*, pg. 1508
PENCO-NORTH CAROLINA—See Willis Corroon Group PLC; *Int'l*, pg. 1508
PENCO-OHIO—See Willis Corroon Group PLC; *Int'l*, pg. 1508
PENCO-OKLAHOMA—See Willis Corroon Group PLC; *Int'l*, pg. 1508
PENCO-PENNSYLVANIA—See Willis Corroon Group PLC; *Int'l*, pg. 1508
PENCO PROCESS ENGINEERING CO. W.L.L.—See GESTRA GmbH; *Int'l*, pg. 550
PENCO PRODUCTS; *U.S. Private*, pg. 848
PENCO-TEXAS—See Willis Corroon Group PLC; *Int'l*, pg. 1508
PENCO-UTAH—See Willis Corroon Group PLC; *Int'l*, pg. 1508
PENCO-VIRGINIA—See Willis Corroon Group PLC; *Int'l*, pg. 1508
PENCO-WASHINGTON—See Willis Corroon Group PLC; *Int'l*, pg. 1508
PENCO WEST—See Willis Corroon Group PLC; *Int'l*, pg. 1504
PENCO-WISCONSIN—See Willis Corroon Group PLC; *Int'l*, pg. 1508
PENCO-WYOMING—See Willis Corroon Group PLC; *Int'l*, pg. 1508
PENDA CORPORATION; *U.S. Private*, pg. 848

PENDIA PENSION FUND SERVICES—See The Swiss Life/ Rentenanstalt Group; *Int'l*, pg. 1332
PENDLETON WOOLEN MILLS, INC.; *U.S. Private*, pg. 848
PENDULUM—See Journal Register Company; *U.S. Public*, pg. 935
PENERBIT FAJAR BAKTI SDN BHD—See Oxford University Press; *Int'l*, pg. 1019
PENFABRIC SDN. BERHAD—See Toray Industries, Inc.; *Int'l*, pg. 1400
PENFORD CORP.; *U.S. Public*, pg. 1269
PENFORD FOOD INGREDIENTS COMPANY—See Penford Corp.; *U.S. Public*, pg. 1269
PENFORD PRODUCTS CO.—See Penford Corp.; *U.S. Public*, pg. 1269
PENGUIN AIR CONDITIONING CORP.—See EMCOR Group, Inc.; *U.S. Public*, pg. 572
PENGUIN HUIS B.V.—See Jotun A/S; *Int'l*, pg. 715
PENGUIN INDUSTRIES, INC.; *U.S. Private*, pg. 849
THE PENGUIN PUBLISHING CO. LTD.—See Pearson plc; *Int'l*, pg. 1026
PENGUIN PUTNAM INC.—See Pearson plc; *Int'l*, pg. 1027
PENGUIN'S INDUSTRIES—See Bongrain S.A.; *Int'l*, pg. 201
PENHALL DIAMOND PRODUCTS COMPANY—See Saint-Gobain; *Int'l*, pg. 1176
PENHALL INTERNATIONAL; *U.S. Private*, pg. 849
S.B. PENICK DEL ECUADOR, S.A.—See Corn Products International, Inc.; *U.S. Public*, pg. 447
PENINSULA BANK—See Mercantile Bankshares Corporation; *U.S. Public*, pg. 1089
PENINSULA EXCESS INSURANCE BROKERS, INC.—See Orion Capital Corporation; *U.S. Public*, pg. 1231
THE PENINSULAR AND ORIENTAL STEAM NAVIGATION COMPANY; *Int'l*, pg. 1032
PENINSULAR AVIATION SERVICES—See Royal Dutch/ Shell Group of Companies; *Int'l*, pg. 1141
PENN CENTRAL COMMUNICATIONS CORP.—See Conrail, Inc.; *U.S. Public*, pg. 432
PENN CENTRAL NATIONAL BANK—See Omega Financial Corporation; *U.S. Public*, pg. 1222
PENN CENTRAL REAL ESTATE GROUP—See American Financial Group; *U.S. Public*, pg. 75
PENN CMO CORPORATION—See The Penn Mutual Life Insurance Company; *U.S. Private*, pg. 850
THE PENN COMPANIES; *U.S. Private*, pg. 849
PENN-DANIELS, INC.—See ShopKo Stores, Inc.; *U.S. Public*, pg. 1467
PENN ENGINEERING & MANUFACTURING CORP.; *U.S. Public*, pg. 1269
PENN ERIE DIV.—See Plastek Group; *U.S. Private*, pg. 870
PENN FASHIONS, INC.—See Burlington Coat Factory Warehouse Corporation; *U.S. Public*, pg. 268
H.O. PENN MACHINERY CO. INC.; *U.S. Private*, pg. 849
PENN INSURANCE & ANNUITY CO.—See The Penn Mutual Life Insurance Company; *U.S. Private*, pg. 850
PENN LOCOMOTIVE GEAR—See Charter plc; *Int'l*, pg. 281
PENN MACHINE COMPANY—See Charter plc; *Int'l*, pg. 281
THE PENN MUTUAL LIFE INSURANCE COMPANY; *U.S. Private*, pg. 849
PENN NATIONAL GAMING, INC.; *U.S. Public*, pg. 1270
PENN NATIONAL INSURANCE; *U.S. Private*, pg. 850
PENN-OHIO LIFE INSURANCE COMPANY—See F.N.B. Corporation; *U.S. Public*, pg. 607
PENN RACQUET SPORTS—See GenCorp Inc.; *U.S. Public*, pg. 706
PENN SECURITY BANK AND TRUST CO.; *U.S. Public*, pg. 1270
THE PENN TRAFFIC COMPANY; *U.S. Public*, pg. 1270
PENN VIRGINIA COAL COMPANY—See Penn Virginia Corporation; *U.S. Public*, pg. 1271
PENN VIRGINIA CORPORATION; *U.S. Public*, pg. 1271
PENN VIRGINIA EQUITIES CORP.—See Penn Virginia Corporation; *U.S. Public*, pg. 1271
PENN VIRGINIA OIL & GAS COMPANY—See Penn Virginia Corporation; *U.S. Public*, pg. 1271
PENNCORP FINANCIAL GROUP, INC.; *U.S. Public*, pg. 1271
PENNCORP FINANCIAL, INC.—See PennCorp Financial Group, Inc.; *U.S. Public*, pg. 1271
PENNINE FOODS—See Northern Foods plc; *Int'l*, pg. 968
PENNINSULAR MEAT COMPANY, INC.; *U.S. Private*, pg. 850
PENNLAND INSURANCE CO.—See Harleysville Group; *Plc*, *U.S. Public*, pg. 787
PENNOCK; *U.S. Private*, pg. 850
PENNPOWER INC.—See Tamrock Corp.; *Int'l*, pg. 1353
THE PENNS LANDING MARINA CORPORATION—See Bell Atlantic Corporation; *U.S. Public*, pg. 203
PENNSYLVANIA-AMERICAN WATER CO.—See American Water Works Company, Inc.; *U.S. Public*, pg. 95
PENNSYLVANIA CELLULAR TELEPHONE CORP.—See Vanguard Cellular Systems, Inc.; *U.S. Public*, pg. 1708
PENNSYLVANIA COAL RESOURCES CORP.—See PP&L Resources; *U.S. Public*, pg. 1244
PENNSYLVANIA CRUSHER CORP.; *U.S. Private*, pg. 850
PENNSYLVANIA ELECTRIC COMPANY—See GPU, Inc.; *U.S. Public*, pg. 695
PENNSYLVANIA ENTERPRISES INC.; *U.S. Public*, pg. 1271
PENNSYLVANIA GENERAL INSURANCE COMPANY—See General Accident Fire and Life Assurance Corporation p.l.c.; *Int'l*, pg. 543
PENNSYLVANIA GENERAL INSURANCE COMPANY OF NEW YORK—See General Accident Fire and Life Assurance Corporation p.l.c.; *Int'l*, pg. 543
PENNSYLVANIA GRANITE CORP.—See Rock of Ages Corporation; *U.S. Public*, pg. 1396
PENNSYLVANIA HOUSE CASEGOODS—See Ladd Furniture, Inc.; *U.S. Public*, pg. 975
PENNSYLVANIA MANUFACTURERS CORP.; *U.S. Public*, pg. 1272

PENNSYLVANIA MINES CORP.—See PP&L Resources; *U.S. Public*, pg. 1244
PENNSYLVANIA NATIONAL BANK—See Keystone Financial Inc.; *U.S. Public*, pg. 956
PENNSYLVANIA PARKING, INC.—See Allright Corporation; *U.S. Private*, pg. 43
PENNSYLVANIA POWER CO.—See FirstEnergy Corp.; *U.S. Public*, pg. 645
PENNSYLVANIA REAL ESTATE INVESTMENT TRUST; *U.S. Public*, pg. 1272
PENNSYLVANIA STEEL FOUNDRY & MACHINE COMPANY—See Atchison Casting Corporation; *U.S. Public*, pg. 142
PENNWAY EXPRESS, INC.—See The Penn Traffic Company; *U.S. Public*, pg. 1271
PENNY & GILES AEROSPACE INC.—See Bowthorpe plc; *Int'l*, pg. 208
PENNY & GILES AEROSPACE LTD.—See Bowthorpe plc; *Int'l*, pg. 207
PENNY & GILES DRIVES TECHNOLOGY INC.—See Bowthorpe plc; *Int'l*, pg. 208
PENNY & GILES GMBH—See Bowthorpe plc; *Int'l*, pg. 209
PENNY & GILES POSITION SENSORS LTD.—See Bowthorpe plc; *Int'l*, pg. 207
PENNY & GILES STUDIO EQUIPMENT LTD.—See Bowthorpe plc; *Int'l*, pg. 207
PENNY & GILES COMPUTER PRODUCTS—See Bowthorpe plc; *Int'l*, pg. 207
PENNY & GILES CONTROLS INC.—See Bowthorpe plc; *Int'l*, pg. 208
PENNY & GILES DRIVES TECHNOLOGY LTD.—See Bowthorpe plc; *Int'l*, pg. 207
PENNY & GILES ELECTRONIC COMPONENTS LTD.—See Bowthorpe plc; *Int'l*, pg. 207
PENNY & GILES INC.—See Bowthorpe plc; *Int'l*, pg. 208
PENNY PLATE, INC.; *U.S. Private*, pg. 850
PENNY SAVER—See The Gazette Company; *U.S. Private*, pg. 442
PENNYPOWER SHOPPING NEWS, INC.—See Harte-Hanks Communications, Inc.; *U.S. Public*, pg. 794
PENNYSAVER—See Harte-Hanks Communications, Inc.; *U.S. Public*, pg. 794
PENNZOIL COMPANY; *U.S. Public*, pg. 1272
PENNZOIL EXPLORATION & PRODUCTION CO.—See Pennzoil Company; *U.S. Public*, pg. 1272
PENNZOIL PRODUCTS CO.—See Pennzoil Company; *U.S. Public*, pg. 1272
PENNZOIL SULPHUR CO.—See Pennzoil Company; *U.S. Public*, pg. 1273
PENOBSCOT FROZEN FOODS, INC.; *U.S. Private*, pg. 850
PENOBSCOT HYDRO COMPANY, INC.—See Bangor Hydro-Electric Company; *U.S. Public*, pg. 178
PENOBSCOT SHOE COMPANY; *U.S. Public*, pg. 1273
PENRECO—See Pennzoil Company; *U.S. Public*, pg. 1273
PENRIGHT!—See Telxon Corporation; *U.S. Public*, pg. 1573
PENSACOLA MILL, CHAMPION INTERNATIONAL CORPORATION—See Champion International Corp.; *U.S. Public*, pg. 334
PENSACOLA NEWS-JOURNAL, INC.—See Gannett Company, Inc.; *U.S. Public*, pg. 701
PENSIOEN ESC—See The Swiss Life/Rentenanstalt Group; *Int'l*, pg. 1332
NV PENSIOENVERZEKERINGSMAATSCHAPPIJ—See DSM N.V.; *Int'l*, pg. 354
PENSION SOLUTIONS, INC.—See MSI Insurance Companies; *U.S. Private*, pg. 688
PENSIONS & INVESTMENTS—See Crain Communications, Inc.; *U.S. Private*, pg. 285
PENSKE CORPORATION; *U.S. Private*, pg. 850
PENSKE LOGISTICS—See Penske Corporation; *U.S. Private*, pg. 851
PENSKE PERFORMANCE, INC.—See Penske Corporation; *U.S. Private*, pg. 850
PENSKE TRUCK LEASING COMPANY LP—See Penske Corporation; *U.S. Private*, pg. 850
PEN-STOCK, INC.—See Avnet, Inc.; *U.S. Public*, pg. 155
PENT ASSEMBLIES, INC.—See Group Dekko; *U.S. Private*, pg. 484
PENT HOLDING AG—See Coop Switzerland; *Int'l*, pg. 330
PENT PLASTICS, INC.—See Group Dekko; *U.S. Private*, pg. 484
PENT PRODUCTS, INC.—See Group Dekko; *U.S. Private*, pg. 484
PENTAGON CHEMICALS LIMITED—See Ascot Holdings Plc; *Int'l*, pg. 88
PENTAIR, INC.; *U.S. Public*, pg. 1273
PENTAL INSURANCE CO., LTD.—See Tidewater Inc.; *U.S. Public*, pg. 1608
PENTASTAR AVIATION, INC.—See Chrysler Corporation; *U.S. Public*, pg. 354
PENTASTAR TRANSPORTATION CORP.—See Chrysler Corporation; *U.S. Public*, pg. 354
PENTAX CANADA INC.—See Asahi Optical Co., Ltd.; *Int'l*, pg. 85
PENTAX CANADA-VANCOUVER—See Asahi Optical Co., Ltd.; *Int'l*, pg. 85
PENTAX CORPORATION—See Asahi Optical Co., Ltd.; *Int'l*, pg. 85
PENTAX PRECISION INSTRUMENT CORP.—See Asahi Optical Co., Ltd.; *Int'l*, pg. 85
PENTAX TECHNOLOGIES CORP.—See Asahi Optical Co., Ltd.; *Int'l*, pg. 85
PENTAX U.K. LTD.—See Asahi Optical Co., Ltd.; *Int'l*, pg. 85
PENTAX VISION INC.—See Asahi Optical Co., Ltd.; *Int'l*, pg. 85
PENTECH INTERNATIONAL, INC.; *U.S. Public*, pg. 1274
PENTEK CORPORATION—See The Dyson-Kissner-Moran Corporation; *U.S. Private*, pg. 352
PENTEL CO., LTD.; *Int'l*, pg. 1035
PENTEL OF AMERICA, LTD.—See Pentel Co., Ltd.; *Int'l*, pg. 1035

PENTEX AUSTRALIA PTY. LTD.—See Novartis AG; *Int'l*, pg. 983
PENTLAND GROUP PLC; *Int'l*, pg. 1035
PENTLAND SHIPPING SERVICES, LTD.—See Pentland Group PLC; *Int'l*, pg. 1035
PENTON PUBLISHING, INC.—See Pittway Corporation; *U.S. Public*, pg. 1306
PENTZER CORPORATION—See The Washington Water Power Company; *U.S. Public*, pg. 1744
PENWEST PHARM. CO.—See Penford Corp.; *U.S. Public*, pg. 1269
PENYORK PROPERTIES—See Caisse de depot et placement du Quebec; *Int'l*, pg. 249
PEOPLE—See Time Warner Inc.; *U.S. Public*, pg. 1613
PEOPLE AND COMPUTERS—See International Data Group; *U.S. Public*, pg. 570
PEOPLE CO., LTD.—See Mycal, Corp.; *Int'l*, pg. 898
PEOPLEMARK, INC.—See Guardsmark, Inc.; *U.S. Private*, pg. 486
PEOPLES—See Marks & Spencer PLC; *Int'l*, pg. 843
PEOPLES ABSTRACT CO.—See The First American Financial Corporation; *U.S. Public*, pg. 626
PEOPLES & UNION BANK—See First Tennessee National Corporation; *U.S. Public*, pg. 639
PEOPLES BANK—See First Tennessee National Corporation; *U.S. Public*, pg. 639
PEOPLE'S BANK; *U.S. Public*, pg. 1274
PEOPLES BANK & TRUST COMPANY—See First Financial Bancorp; *U.S. Public*, pg. 633
PEOPLE'S BANK & TRUST CO.—See Old National Bancorp; *U.S. Public*, pg. 1217
THE PEOPLES BANK OF MARYLAND—See Mercantile Bankshares Corporation; *U.S. Public*, pg. 1089
THE PEOPLES BANKING COMPANY—See Rurban Financial Corp.; *U.S. Public*, pg. 1413
PEOPLE'S CHOICE TV CORP.; *U.S. Public*, pg. 1274
PEOPLE'S CHOICE-TV CORP.—See People's Choice TV Corp.; *U.S. Public*, pg. 1274
PEOPLE'S CHOICE-TV CORP. OF PHOENIX, INC.—See People's Choice TV Corp.; *U.S. Public*, pg. 1274
PEOPLE'S CHOICE-TV CORP. PREFERRED ENTERTAINMENT, INC.—See People's Choice TV Corp.; *U.S. Public*, pg. 1274
PEOPLE'S CHOICE-TV OF HOUSTON, INC.—See People's Choice TV Corp.; *U.S. Public*, pg. 1274
PEOPLE'S CHOICE TV OF ST. LOUIS, INC.—See People's Choice TV Corp.; *U.S. Public*, pg. 1274
PEOPLE'S CHOICE TV OF TUCSON, INC.—See People's Choice TV Corp.; *U.S. Public*, pg. 1274
PEOPLES COMMUNICATIONS SYSTEM—See Peoples Electric Contractor, Inc.; *U.S. Private*, pg. 851
PEOPLES DISTRICT ENERGY CORPORATION—See Peoples Energy Corporation; *U.S. Public*, pg. 1275
PEOPLES ELECTRIC CONTRACTOR, INC.; *U.S. Private*, pg. 851
PEOPLES ENERGY CORPORATION; *U.S. Public*, pg. 1274
PEOPLES ENERGY SERVICES CORPORATION—See Peoples Energy Corporation; *U.S. Public*, pg. 1275
PEOPLES FEDERAL SAVINGS & LOAN ASSOCIATION—See First Financial Holdings, Inc.; *U.S. Public*, pg. 634
PEOPLES FEDERAL SAVINGS BANK—See FirstMerit Corporation; *U.S. Public*, pg. 647
THE PEOPLES GAS LIGHT & COKE CO.—See Peoples Energy Corporation; *U.S. Public*, pg. 1275
PEOPLES GAS SYSTEM, INC.—See TECO Energy, Inc.; *U.S. Public*, pg. 1565
PEOPLES HERITAGE FINANCIAL GROUP, INC.; *U.S. Public*, pg. 1275
PEOPLES HERITAGE SAVINGS BANK—See Peoples Heritage Financial Group, Inc.; *U.S. Public*, pg. 1275
PEOPLES JEWELLERS CORPORATION; *Int'l*, pg. 1036
PEOPLES NATIONAL BANK—See Old National Bancorp; *U.S. Public*, pg. 1217
PEOPLES NATIONAL BANK OF CENTRAL PENNSYLVANIA—See Omega Financial Corporation; *U.S. Public*, pg. 1222
THE PEOPLES NATURAL GAS CO.—See Consolidated Natural Gas Company; *U.S. Public*, pg. 435
PEOPLES NGV CORP.—See Peoples Energy Corporation; *U.S. Public*, pg. 1275
PEOPLES SAVINGS BANK OF ASHTABULA—See FirstMerit Corporation; *U.S. Public*, pg. 647
PEOPLE'S SECURITIES INCORPORATED—See People's Bank; *U.S. Public*, pg. 1274
PEOPLES SECURITY FINANCE COMPANY, INC.—See CNB Bancshares, Inc.; *U.S. Public*, pg. 280
PEOPLES SECURITY INSURANCE COMPANY—See AEGON N.V.; *Int'l*, pg. 27
PEOPLE'S SECURITY LIFE INSURANCE—See AEGON N.V.; *Int'l*, pg. 27
PEOPLES TELEPHONE COMPANY, INC.; *U.S. Public*, pg. 1275
PEOPLESOFT, INC.; *U.S. Public*, pg. 1276
PEORIA & PEKIN UNION RAILWAY CO.—See Conrail, Inc.; *U.S. Public*, pg. 432
PEORIA JOURNAL STAR, INC.—See The Copley Press, Inc.; *U.S. Private*, pg. 275
PEORIA MEDICAL RESEARCH CORPORATION—See Caterpillar Inc.; *U.S. Public*, pg. 316
THE PEP BOYS-MANNY, MOE & JACK; *U.S. Public*, pg. 1276
PEPCOM INDUSTRIES, INC.—See Suntory Ltd.; *Int'l*, pg. 1321
PEPCON SYSTEMS, INC.—See American Pacific Corporation; *U.S. Public*, pg. 88
PEPINIERES ET ROSERAIES GEROGES DELBARD—See LVMH Moet Hennessy Louis Vuitton; *Int'l*, pg. 781
THE PEPPER COMPANIES, INC.; *U.S. Private*, pg. 851
PEPPER CONSTRUCTION CO.—See The Pepper Companies, Inc.; *U.S. Private*, pg. 851
PEPPER CONSTRUCTION COMPANY—See The Pepper Companies, Inc.; *U.S. Private*, pg. 851
PEPPER CONSTRUCTION OF INDIANA, INC. LLC—See The Pepper Companies, Inc.; *U.S. Private*, pg. 851

PEPPER ENVIRONMENTAL TECHNOLOGIES, INC.—See The Pepper Companies, Inc.; *U.S. Private*, pg. 851
PEPPER, HAMILTON & SCHEETZ; *U.S. Private*, pg. 851
HARRY PEPPER & ASSOCIATES; *U.S. Private*, pg. 851
PEPPER-LAWSON—See The Pepper Companies, Inc.; *U.S. Private*, pg. 851
PEPPER-LAWSON CONSTRUCTION, INC.—See The Pepper Companies, Inc.; *U.S. Private*, pg. 851
PEPPERIDGE FARM, INCORPORATED—See Campbell Soup Company; *U.S. Public*, pg. 299
PEPPERONI GRILL—See Eateries, Inc.; *U.S. Public*, pg. 555
PEPSI-COLA ALBANY BOTTLING CO., INC.; *U.S. Private*, pg. 852
PEPSI-COLA ARGENTINA, S.A.C.I.—See PepsiCo, Inc.; *U.S. Public*, pg. 1276
PEPSI-COLA (BERMUDA) LIMITED—See PepsiCo, Inc.; *U.S. Public*, pg. 1276
PEPSI-COLA BOTTLING CO.; *U.S. Public*, pg. 1276
PEPSI-COLA BOTTLING COMPANY OF CHARLOTTE INC.; *U.S. Private*, pg. 852
PEPSI-COLA BOTTLING CO. OF LONG ISLAND CITY—See Pepsi-Cola Bottling Co.; *U.S. Public*, pg. 1276
PEPSI-COLA BOTTLING COMPANY OF RICHMOND, INC.—See PepsiCo, Inc.; *U.S. Public*, pg. 1277
PEPSI-COLA CANADA, LTD.—See PepsiCo, Inc.; *U.S. Public*, pg. 1277
PEPSI-COLA CENTRAL—See PepsiCo, Inc.; *U.S. Public*, pg. 1277
PEPSI-COLA CHILE CONSULTORES LTDA.—See PepsiCo, Inc.; *U.S. Public*, pg. 1277
PEPSI-COLA COMPANY—See PepsiCo, Inc.; *U.S. Public*, pg. 1277
PEPSI-COLA DE ESPANA, S.A.—See PepsiCo, Inc.; *U.S. Public*, pg. 1277
PEPSI-COLA DE FRANCE, S.A.R.L.—See PepsiCo, Inc.; *U.S. Public*, pg. 1277
PEPSI-COLA FAR EAST TRADE DEVELOPMENT CO., INC.—See PepsiCo, Inc.; *U.S. Public*, pg. 1277
PEPSI-COLA GENERAL BOTTLERS, INC.—See PepsiCo, Inc.; *U.S. Public*, pg. 1277
PEPSI-COLA GENERAL BOTTLERS, INC.—See Whitman Corporation; *U.S. Public*, pg. 1766
PEPSI-COLA GMBH—See PepsiCo, Inc.; *U.S. Public*, pg. 1277
PEPSI-COLA INTERNATIONAL LIMITED—See PepsiCo, Inc.; *U.S. Public*, pg. 1277
PEPSI-COLA MANUFACTURING (IRELAND)—See PepsiCo, Inc.; *U.S. Public*, pg. 1277
PEPSI-COLA N.V.—See PepsiCo, Inc.; *U.S. Public*, pg. 1277
PEPSI-COLA SOUTH—See PepsiCo, Inc.; *U.S. Public*, pg. 1277
PEPSI-COLA WEST—See PepsiCo, Inc.; *U.S. Public*, pg. 1277
PEPSI FOODS PRIVATE LTD.—See PepsiCo, Inc.; *U.S. Public*, pg. 1277
PEPSI-GEMEX SA DE CV; *Int'l*, pg. 1036
PEPSI INTERNATIONAL BOTTLERS—See Leucadia National Corporation; *U.S. Public*, pg. 990
PEPSI INTERNATIONAL BOTTLERS—See PepsiCo, Inc.; *U.S. Public*, pg. 1278
PEPSICO. AUSTRALIA PTY. LTD.—See PepsiCo, Inc.; *U.S. Public*, pg. 1277
PEPSICO. CAPITAL CORPORATION, N.V.—See PepsiCo, Inc.; *U.S. Public*, pg. 1277
PEPSICO DE MEXICO, S.A. DE C.V.—See PepsiCo, Inc.; *U.S. Public*, pg. 1277
PEPSICO FINANCE (ANTILLES A) NV—See PepsiCo, Inc.; *U.S. Public*, pg. 1277
PEPSICO FOODS & BEVERAGES INTERNATIONAL—See PepsiCo, Inc.; *U.S. Public*, pg. 1277
PEPSICO. HOLDINGS LTD. (UK)—See PepsiCo, Inc.; *U.S. Public*, pg. 1277
PEPSICO, INC.; *U.S. Public*, pg. 1276
PEPSICO WINES & SPIRITS INTERNATIONAL—See PepsiCo, Inc.; *U.S. Public*, pg. 1277
PEPSICO WORLD TRADING COMPANY (UK) LTD.—See PepsiCo, Inc.; *U.S. Public*, pg. 1277
PEQUIVEN, S.A.—See Petroleos de Venezuela S.A.; *Int'l*, pg. 1045
PEQUOD ASSOCIATES—See Equitable Resources, Inc.; *U.S. Public*, pg. 590
PER PAK (BROOK)—See Jefferson Smurfit Group p.l.c.; *Int'l*, pg. 1270
PER TRANSPORT S.P.A—See Union-Transport Corporation; *U.S. Private*, pg. 1120
PERAK HANJUNG SINIEN SDN. BHD.—See Korea Heavy Industries & Construction Co., Ltd.; *Int'l*, pg. 758
PERCHEM LTD.—See Akzo Nobel N.V.; *Int'l*, pg. 47
PERCHEM SA—See Akzo Nobel N.V.; *Int'l*, pg. 47
PERCHERON PROPERTIES—See Vaux Group Plc; *Int'l*, pg. 1454
PERDUE FARMS, INC.—See Perdue Farms Incorporated; *U.S. Private*, pg. 852
PERDUE FARMS INCORPORATED; *U.S. Private*, pg. 852
PERDUE TRANSPORTATION INC.—See Perdue Farms Incorporated; *U.S. Private*, pg. 852
PEREGRINE CAPITAL MANAGEMENT, INC.—See Norwest Corporation; *U.S. Public*, pg. 1202
PEREGRINE INCORPORATED; *U.S. Private*, pg. 852
PEREL OY—See Knurr AG; *Int'l*, pg. 740
N.V. PEREXMA—See VNU Verenigde Nederlandse Uitgeversbedrijven B.V.; *Int'l*, pg. 1447
RICARDO PEREZ ASOCIADOS; *Int'l*, pg. 1036
PEREZ TRADING CO. INC.; *U.S. Private*, pg. 852
PERFECSEAL COMPANY—See Bemis Company, Inc.; *U.S. Public*, pg. 210
PERFECSEAL, INC.—See Bemis Company, Inc.; *U.S. Public*, pg. 210
PERFECT CIRCLE PRODUCTS DIV.—See Dana Corporation; *U.S. Public*, pg. 479
PERFECT EQUIPMENT CORP.—See Berwind Corporation; *U.S. Private*, pg. 138

PERFECT FIT INDUSTRIES, INC.; *U.S. Private*, pg. 852
PERFECT PEARL COMPANY, INC.; *U.S. Private*, pg. 852
PERFECT PIZZA LTD.—See Scott's Restaurants Inc.; *Int'l*, pg. 1213
PERFECTION AUTOMOTIVE PRODUCTS CORPORATION—See Tenneco Inc.; *U.S. Public*, pg. 1577
PERFECTION BAKERIES INC.; *U.S. Private*, pg. 852
PERFECTION CORPORATION—See Ruhrgas Aktiengesellschaft; *Int'l*, pg. 1149
PERFECTION-SCHWANK INC.; *U.S. Private*, pg. 853
PERFORACIONES MARITIMAS PROTEXA S.A. DE C.V.—See Grupo Protexa S.A. de C.V.; *Int'l*, pg. 576
PERFORMA ENTERTAINMENT REAL ESTATE, INC.; *U.S. Private*, pg. 853
PERFORMANCE AUTOMOTIVE NETWORK; *U.S. Private*, pg. 853
PERFORMANCE BUILDING SYSTEM—See RK Mechanical, Inc.; *U.S. Private*, pg. 905
PERFORMANCE CHEVROLET & GEO; *U.S. Private*, pg. 853
PERFORMANCE CONTRACTING GROUP; *U.S. Private*, pg. 853
PERFORMANCE CONTRACTORS INC.; *U.S. Private*, pg. 853
PERFORMANCE ELASTOMERS DIVISION—See Furon Company; *U.S. Public*, pg. 689
PERFORMANCE FOOD GROUP COMPANY; *U.S. Public*, pg. 1278
PERFORMANCE MEDICAL GROUP; *U.S. Private*, pg. 853
PERFORMANCE POLYMERS B.V.—See Burmah Castrol plc; *Int'l*, pg. 236
PERFORMANCE PRODUCTS DIVISION—See Springs Industries, Inc.; *U.S. Public*, pg. 1500
PERFUMES CHRISTIAN DIOR DE MEXICO S.A. DE C.V.—See LVMH Moet Hennessy Louis Vuitton; *Int'l*, pg. 783
PERGAMENT HOME CENTERS, INC.; *U.S. Private*, pg. 853
PERIMETER CENTER, INC.—See The Rouse Company; *U.S. Public*, pg. 1408
PERIMETER MALL, INC.—See The Rouse Company; *U.S. Public*, pg. 1408
PERIMETER MALL MANAGEMENT CORP.—See The Rouse Company; *U.S. Public*, pg. 1408
PERIMISTOIMISTO CONTANT OY—See Merita Ltd.; *Int'l*, pg. 859
PERINI BUILDING CO., INC. U.S. HEAVY DIVISION—See Perini Corporation; *U.S. Public*, pg. 1278
PERINI CORPORATION; *U.S. Public*, pg. 1278
PERINI LAND AND DEVELOPMENT CO.—See Perini Corporation; *U.S. Public*, pg. 1278
PERINI MANAGEMENT SERVICES, INC.—See Perini Corporation; *U.S. Public*, pg. 1278
PERINI-METROPOLITAN NEW YORK DIV.—See Perini Corporation; *U.S. Public*, pg. 1278
PERIODICAL PUBLISHERS' SERVICE BUREAU, INC.—See The Hearst Corporation; *U.S. Private*, pg. 503
PERIPHERIE & NETZWERKE GMBH—See IIS Intelligent Information Systems Ltd.; *U.S. Public*, pg. 645
PERIPHONICS CORP.; *U.S. Public*, pg. 1278
PERIPHONICS CORPORATION—See Periphonics Corp.; *U.S. Public*, pg. 1279
PERIPHONICS S.A. DE C.V.—See Periphonics Corp.; *U.S. Public*, pg. 1279
PERIPHONICS UPS LTD.—See Periphonics Corp.; *U.S. Public*, pg. 1279
PERIPHONICS VOICE PROCESSING SYSTEMS LTD.—See Periphonics Corp.; *U.S. Public*, pg. 1279
PERISCOPE MARKETING COMMUNICATIONS; *U.S. Private*, pg. 853
PERISHABLE DISTRIBUTORS OF IA—See Hy-Vee Food Stores Incorporated; *U.S. Private*, pg. 551
PERITACIONES TECNICAS DE SEGUROS, S.A.—See Assicurazioni Generali S.p.A.; *Int'l*, pg. 92
P.T. PERJAHL LEASING INDONESIA—See The Sakura Bank, Limited; *Int'l*, pg. 1181
PERKASIE INDUSTRIES CORPORATION; *U.S. Private*, pg. 854
THE PERKIN-ELMER CORPORATION; *U.S. Public*, pg. 1279
PERKIN-ELMER LTD.—See The Perkin-Elmer Corporation; *U.S. Public*, pg. 1279
PERKIN ELMER PHYSICAL ELECTRONICS DIV.—See The Perkin-Elmer Corporation; *U.S. Public*, pg. 1279
PERKINS CORPORATION—See Sharp Corporation; *Int'l*, pg. 1229
PERKINS FAMILY RESTAURANTS—See The Restaurant Company; *U.S. Private*, pg. 925
PERKINS-GOODWIN CO. INC.—See Haindl Papier GmbH; *Int'l*, pg. 586
PERKINS INDUSTRIES, INC.—See Borden, Inc.; *U.S. Private*, pg. 158
PERKINS PAPERS—See The Cascades Group; *Int'l*, pg. 273
PERKINSVILLE TELEPHONE CO., INC.—See Telephone and Data Systems, Inc.; *U.S. Public*, pg. 1571
PERLAV-EUROCLEAN—See Temco Service Industries; *U.S. Public*, pg. 1574
PERLMOOSER ZEMENTWERKE AG—See Lafarge S.A.; *Int'l*, pg. 791
PERLMUTER PRINTING COMPANY—See St. Ives plc; *Int'l*, pg. 1177
PERMA-FIX ENVIRONMENTAL SERVICES, INC.; *U.S. Public*, pg. 1279
PERMA-FIX TREATMENT SERVICES, INC.—See Perma-Fix Environmental Services, Inc.; *U.S. Public*, pg. 1280
PERMA-FLEX (CANADA) INC.—See Scapa Group Plc; *Int'l*, pg. 1203
PERMA-FLEX ROLLERS, INC.—See Scapa Group Plc; *Int'l*, pg. 1202
PERMA-FLEX (SOUTHERN) INC.—See Scapa Group Plc; *Int'l*, pg. 1202
PERMA GLAS-MESH, INC.—See Saint-Gobain; *Int'l*, pg. 1171

Company Index

PERMA GLASS-MESH INC.—See Saint-Gobain; *Int'l,* pg. 1177
PERMA PURE INC.—See Halma p.l.c.; *Int'l,* pg. 590
PERMA-PIPE DIV.—See MFRI Inc.; *U.S. Public,* pg. 1026
PERMABOND INTERNATIONAL—See Unilever Plc; *Int'l,* pg. 1435
PERMACEL—See Nitto Denko Corporation; *Int'l,* pg. 950
PERMACEL TAPE—See Avery Dennison Corporation; *U.S. Public,* pg. 153
PERMACRETE PRODUCTS CORPORATION—See CSR Limited; *Int'l,* pg. 245
PERMA-FIX OF KANSAS CITY—See Perma-Fix Environmental Services, Inc.; *U.S. Public,* pg. 1280
PERMALI LTD.—See BTR plc; *Int'l,* pg. 126
PERMANENT GENERAL COMPANIES—See Ingram Industries Inc.; *U.S. Private,* pg. 563
PERMANENT LAFARGE—See Lafarge S.A.; *Int'l,* pg. 791
PERMANOVA LASERSYSTEM AB—See Spectra-Physics AB; *Int'l,* pg. 1290
PERMARK INTERNATIONAL (PTY) LTD.; *Int'l,* pg. 1036
PERMATECH, INC.—See Aluminum Company of America; *U.S. Public,* pg. 61
PERMEA CHINA, LTD.—See Air Products and Chemicals, Inc.; *U.S. Public,* pg. 32
PERMEA, INC.—See Air Products and Chemicals, Inc.; *U.S. Public,* pg. 31
PERMIPIPE TITANIUM A/S (PTI)—See USX Corporation; *U.S. Public,* pg. 1662
PERMOGLAZE PAINTS, LTD.—See Akzo Nobel N.V.; *Int'l,* pg. 47
PERNOD—See Groupe Pernod Ricard; *Int'l,* pg. 566
PERNOVO—See Perstorp AB; *Int'l,* pg. 1036
PERNOVO, PERSTORP NEW BUSINESS DEVELOPMENT INC.—See Perstorp AB; *Int'l,* pg. 1037
PEROT SYSTEMS CORPORATION *U.S. Private,* pg. 854
PEROXIDES ARGENTINOS SA—See Akzo Nobel N.V.; *Int'l,* pg. 47
PEROXIDOS DO BRAZIL—See Solvay S.A.; *Int'l,* pg. 1279
PEROXIDOS ORGANICOS, S.A.—See FMC Corporation; *U.S. Public,* pg. 607
PERPETUAL CORPORATION; *U.S. Private,* pg. 854
PERPETUAL MACHINE—See Textile Rubber & Chemical Company; *U.S. Private,* pg. 1079
PERQ RESEARCH CORPORATION—See VNU Verenigde Nederlandse Uitgeversbedrijven B.V.; *Int'l,* pg. 1447
PERRETTI—See Ark Restaurants Corp.; *U.S. Public,* pg. 130
PERRI SAUSAGE, INC.—See Johnsonville Foods, Inc.; *U.S. Private,* pg. 595
G.I.E. PERRIER-EXPORT—See Nestle S.A.; *Int'l,* pg. 919
THE PERRIER GROUP OF AMERICA—See Nestle S.A.; *Int'l,* pg. 919
PERRIER GROUP OF CANADA LTD.—See Nestle S.A.; *Int'l,* pg. 919
THE PERRIER GROUP OF CANADA LTD.—See Nestle S.A.; *Int'l,* pg. 922
PERRIER JAPON K.K.—See Nestle S.A.; *Int'l,* pg. 922
PERRIER UK LTD.—See Nestle S.A.; *Int'l,* pg. 919
L. PERRIGO COMPANY; *U.S. Public,* pg. 1280
PERRIGO OF TENNESSEE—See L. Perrigo Company; *U.S. Public,* pg. 1280
PERRIN GMBH—See Zimmermann & Jansen GmbH; *Int'l,* pg. 1528
PERRY & DERRICK CO.; *U.S. Private,* pg. 854
PERRY BROTHERS, INC.; *U.S. Private,* pg. 854
PERRY COUNTY NEWS—See Landmark Communications, Inc.; *U.S. Private,* pg. 648
PERRY ELLIS—See Salant Corporation; *U.S. Public,* pg. 1429
PERRY ENGINEERING COMPANY, INC.; *U.S. Private,* pg. 854
PERRY EQUIPMENT CORPORATION; *U.S. Private,* pg. 855
PERRY EQUIPMENT LTD.—See Perry Equipment Corporation; *U.S. Private,* pg. 855
PERRY FAMILY PRACTICE, INC.—See Integrated Health Services, Inc.; *U.S. Public,* pg. 885
G. PERRY & SONS LTD.—See Weir Group PLC; *Int'l,* pg. 1489
PERRY GRAPHIC COMMUNICATIONS, INC.; *U.S. Private,* pg. 855
HOWARD E. PERRY & CO. LTD.—See Arbed S.A.; *Int'l,* pg. 79
PERRY MACHINERY CORPORATION; *U.S. Private,* pg. 855
PERRY MACHINERY CZECH S.R.O.—See Perry Machinery Corporation; *U.S. Private,* pg. 855
PERRY MACHINERY POLAND—See Perry Machinery Corporation; *U.S. Private,* pg. 855
PERRY MFG. CO.—See Page Holdings, Inc.; *U.S. Private,* pg. 834
PERRY SPORT—See Vendex International N.V.; *Int'l,* pg. 1462
PERRY'S ICE CREAM CO., INC.; *U.S. Private,* pg. 855
PERRYTON EQUITY; *U.S. Private,* pg. 855
PERSEPTIVE BIOSYSTEMS, INC.—See The Perkin-Elmer Corporation; *U.S. Public,* pg. 1279
PERSEVERANCE MILLS LTD.—See Scapa Group Plc; *Int'l,* pg. 1202
PERSINGERS, INC.; *U.S. Private,* pg 855
PERSIS CORPORATION; *U.S. Private,* pg. 855
PERSOFT, INC.; *U.S. Private,* pg. 856
PERSOL S.P.A.—See Luxottica Group S.p.A.; *Int'l,* pg. 822
PERSONAL CARE SECTOR—See Kimberly-Clark Corporation; *U.S. Public,* pg. 958
PERSONAL FINANCE CO.—See The Minnesota Mutual Life Insurance Company; *U.S. Private,* pg. 750
PERSONAL FINANCE CORP.—See Bancorp South Inc.; *U.S. Public,* pg. 176
PERSONAL PERFORMANCE CONSULTANTS—See Magellan Health Services, Inc.; *U.S. Public,* pg. 1036
PERSONAL PERFORMANCE CONSULTANTS UK LIMITED (PPC)—See Willis Corroon Group PLC; *Int'l,* pg. 1502

PERSONAL PRODUCTS CO.—See Johnson & Johnson; *U.S. Public,* pg. 929
PERSTORP AB; *Int'l,* pg. 1036
PERSTORP AB DECORATIVE LAMINATE FURNITURE—See Perstorp AB; *Int'l,* pg. 1038
PERSTORP AB DECORATIVE LAMINATE NORTHERN EUROPE—See Perstorp AB; *Int'l,* pg. 1038
PERSTORP AB FLOORING LAMINATE—See Perstorp AB; *Int'l,* pg. 1038
PERSTORP ANALYTICAL—See Perstorp AB; *Int'l,* pg. 1039
PERSTORP ANALYTICAL AB-DISTRIBUTION HQ—See Perstorp AB; *Int'l,* pg. 1039
PERSTORP ANALYTICAL ANADIS—See Perstorp AB; *Int'l,* pg. 1039
PERSTORP ANALYTICAL B.V.—See Perstorp AB; *Int'l,* pg. 1039
PERSTORP ANALYTICAL GMBH—See Perstorp AB; *Int'l,* pg. 1039
PERSTORP ANALYTICAL INC.—See Perstorp AB; *Int'l,* pg. 1039
PERSTORP ANALYTICAL INC. DIVISION ALPKEM—See Perstorp AB; *Int'l,* pg. 1039
PERSTORP ANALYTICAL INC. DIVISION NIRSYSTEMS—See Perstorp AB; *Int'l,* pg. 1039
PERSTORP ANALYTICAL LTD.—See Perstorp AB; *Int'l,* pg. 1039
PERSTORP ANALYTICAL LUMAC B.V.—See Perstorp AB; *Int'l,* pg. 1039
PERSTORP ANALYTICAL LUMAC LTD.—See Perstorp AB; *Int'l,* pg. 1039
PERSTORP ANALYTICAL NIRSYSTEMS-EUROPEAN LIASON OFFICE—See Perstorp AB; *Int'l,* pg. 1039
PERSTORP ANALYTICAL S.A.—See Perstorp AB; *Int'l,* pg. 1040
PERSTORP ANALYTICAL TECATOR AB—See Perstorp AB; *Int'l,* pg. 1039
PERSTORP & HEINRICH PUZELIK GES.M.B.H.-DIV. CHEMETIC—See Perstorp AB; *Int'l,* pg. 1037
PERSTORP & HEINRICH PUZELIK GES.M.B.H-DIV. PLASTIC—See Perstorp AB; *Int'l,* pg. 1037
PERSTORP & HEINRICH PUZELIK GES.M.B.H.-INFORMATIONS -UND SERVICEBURO—See Perstorp AB; *Int'l,* pg. 1037
PERSTORP A/S DECORATIVE LAMINATE—See Perstorp AB; *Int'l,* pg. 1038
PERSTORP ASIA-PACIFIC LTD. CONCRETE ADMIXTURES—See Perstorp AB; *Int'l,* pg. 1037
PERSTORP ASIA-PACIFIC LTD.-DIV. SPECIALTY CHEMICALS—See Perstorp AB; *Int'l,* pg. 1038
PERSTORP ASIA-PACIFIC PTE. LTD.-DIV. CHEMITEC—See Perstorp AB; *Int'l,* pg. 1037
PERSTORP ASIA-PACIFIC PTE. LTD. DIV. FLOORING—See Perstorp AB; *Int'l,* pg. 1039
PERSTORP ASIA-PACIFIC PTE LTD.—See Perstorp AB; *Int'l,* pg. 1039
PERSTORP BAUCHEMIE—See Perstorp AB; *Int'l,* pg. 1037
PT PERSTORP BUMI RAYA-FACTORY MELAMINE WARE—See Perstorp AB; *Int'l,* pg. 1037
PT PERSTORP BUMI RAYA-FACTORY MOULDING COMPOUNDS—See Perstorp AB; *Int'l,* pg. 1037
PT PERSTORP BUMI RAYA—See Perstorp AB; *Int'l,* pg. 1037
PERSTORP BYGGKEMI-PELPLAST—See Perstorp AB; *Int'l,* pg. 1036
PERSTORP CHEMITEC—See Perstorp AB; *Int'l,* pg. 1037
PERSTORP CHEMITEC A/S—See Perstorp AB; *Int'l,* pg. 1037
PERSTORP COMPONENTS—See Perstorp AB; *Int'l,* pg. 1040
PERSTORP COMPONENTS EUROPE—See Perstorp AB; *Int'l,* pg. 1040
PERSTORP COMPONENTS INC.-MARSHALL—See Perstorp AB; *Int'l,* pg. 1040
PERSTORP COMPONENTS INC.-SPRINGFIELD—See Perstorp AB; *Int'l,* pg. 1040
PERSTORP COMPONENTS S.A.—See Perstorp AB; *Int'l,* pg. 1040
PERSTORP COMPONENTS S.A. DE C.V.—See Perstorp AB; *Int'l,* pg. 1040
PERSTORP COMPOUNDS INC.—See Perstorp AB; *Int'l,* pg. 1037
PERSTORP CONSTRUCTION CHEMICALS—See Perstorp AB; *Int'l,* pg. 1036
PERSTORP DO BRASIL INDUSTRIA E COMERCIO LTDA.-DIV. CHEMITEC—See Perstorp AB; *Int'l,* pg. 1037
PERSTORP DO BRASIL INDUSTRIA E COMERCIO LTDA-DECORATIVE LAMINATE DIV.—See Perstorp AB; *Int'l,* pg. 1038
PERSTORP DO BRASIL-TECHNICAL LAMINATE DIVISION—See Perstorp AB; *Int'l,* pg. 1040
PERSTORP EESTI AS—See Perstorp AB; *Int'l,* pg. 1037
PERSTORP ELEMENTE GMBH—See Perstorp AB; *Int'l,* pg. 1038
PERSTORP ENERGIE AB—See Perstorp AB; *Int'l,* pg. 1039
PERSTORP EVANPLAS S.A.—See Perstorp AB; *Int'l,* pg. 1039
PERSTORP FERGUSON LTD. INDUSTRIAL FLOORING—See Perstorp AB; *Int'l,* pg. 1039
PERSTORP FERGUSON LTD.-POLYOLS SALES—See Perstorp AB; *Int'l,* pg. 1038
PERSTORP FERGUSON LTD.-CHEMITEC & COMPOUNDS—See Perstorp AB; *Int'l,* pg. 1037
PERSTORP FLOORING—See Perstorp AB; *Int'l,* pg. 1039
PERSTORP FLOORING AB—See Perstorp AB; *Int'l,* pg. 1039
PERSTORP FLOORING BV—See Perstorp AB; *Int'l,* pg. 1039
PERSTORP FLOORING GMBH—See Perstorp AB; *Int'l,* pg. 1039
PERSTORP FLOORING IBERIA—See Perstorp AB; *Int'l,* pg. 1039

PERSTORP FLOORING INC.—See Perstorp AB; *Int'l,* pg. 1039
PERSTORP FLOORING NV—See Perstorp AB; *Int'l,* pg. 1039
PERSTORP FLOORING (UK) LTD.—See Perstorp AB; *Int'l,* pg. 1039
PERSTORP FORM—See Perstorp AB; *Int'l,* pg. 1037
PERSTORP FORM LTD.—See Perstorp AB; *Int'l,* pg. 1038
PERSTORP FORM OY—See Perstorp AB; *Int'l,* pg. 1038
PERSTORP FORMOX—See Perstorp AB; *Int'l,* pg. 1038
PERSTORP FRANCE—See Perstorp AB; *Int'l,* pg. 1040
PERSTORP GMBH—See Perstorp AB; *Int'l,* pg. 1040
PERSTORP GMBH DECORATIVE LAMINATE—See Perstorp AB; *Int'l,* pg. 1038
PERSTORP GMBH-SBU FURNITURE (UNIDUR)—See Perstorp AB; *Int'l,* pg. 1038
PERSTORP GMBH VERKAUFSBURO CHEMITEC—See Perstorp AB; *Int'l,* pg. 1037
PERSTORP GMBH VERKAUFSBURO COMPOUNDS—See Perstorp AB; *Int'l,* pg. 1037
PERSTORP GULV A/S—See Perstorp AB; *Int'l,* pg. 1039
PERSTORP IKI OY DECORATIVE LAMINATE—See Perstorp AB; *Int'l,* pg. 1038
PERSTORP INC.—See Perstorp AB; *Int'l,* pg. 1039
PERSTORP LATTIAT—See Perstorp AB; *Int'l,* pg. 1039
PERSTORP LTD.—See Perstorp AB; *Int'l,* pg. 1040
PERSTORP LTDA.—See Perstorp AB; *Int'l,* pg. 1037
PERSTORP-MAH SING SDN BHD.—See Perstorp AB; *Int'l,* pg. 1038
PERSTORP NEDERLAND B.V.—See Perstorp AB; *Int'l,* pg. 1038
PERSTORP NEDERLAND B.V. DECORATIVE LAMINATE—See Perstorp AB; *Int'l,* pg. 1038
PERSTORP NORKUN KUNSTOFFVERARBEITUNG GMBH—See Perstorp AB; *Int'l,* pg. 1038
PERSTORP PHARMA AB—See Perstorp AB; *Int'l,* pg. 1036
PERSTORP PHARMA GMBH—See Perstorp AB; *Int'l,* pg. 1037
PERSTORP PHARMA LTD. WOUND CARE DIVISION—See Perstorp AB; *Int'l,* pg. 1037
PERSTORP PLASTIC SYSTEMS—See Perstorp AB; *Int'l,* pg. 1038
PERSTORP POLYOLS—See Perstorp AB; *Int'l,* pg. 1038
PERSTORP POLYOLS INC.—See Perstorp AB; *Int'l,* pg. 1038
PERSTORP PRESSMASSOR—See Perstorp AB; *Int'l,* pg. 1037
PERSTORP RAILITE S.A. DECORATIVE LAMINATE—See Perstorp AB; *Int'l,* pg. 1038
PERSTORP REGENO—See Perstorp AB; *Int'l,* pg. 1039
PERSTORP RESINS—See Perstorp AB; *Int'l,* pg. 1037
PERSTORP S.A. CONCRETE ADMIXTURES—See Perstorp AB; *Int'l,* pg. 1037
PERSTORP S.A. DECORATIVE LAMINATE—See Perstorp AB; *Int'l,* pg. 1038
PERSTORP S.A.-DIV. BAKELITE—See Perstorp AB; *Int'l,* pg. 1037
PERSTORP S.A.-DIV. CHEMITEC—See Perstorp AB; *Int'l,* pg. 1037
PERSTORP S.A.-DIV. COMPONENTS FRANCE—See Perstorp AB; *Int'l,* pg. 1040
PERSTORP S.A.-DIV. PERSTORP STAMP—See Perstorp AB; *Int'l,* pg. 1038
PERSTORP S.A. FLOORING DIVISION—See Perstorp AB; *Int'l,* pg. 1039
PERSTORP SPA-DIV. COMPOUNDS—See Perstorp AB; *Int'l,* pg. 1037
PERSTORP SPA-POLYOLS DIV.—See Perstorp AB; *Int'l,* pg. 1038
PERSTORP SPECIALTY CHEMICALS—See Perstorp AB; *Int'l,* pg. 1038
PERSTORP SP.Z O.O.—See Perstorp AB; *Int'l,* pg. 1038
PERSTORP SP.Z O.O. DECORATIVE LAMINATE—See Perstorp AB; *Int'l,* pg. 1038
PERSTORP SP.Z O.O. INDUSTRIAL FLOORING—See Perstorp AB; *Int'l,* pg. 1037
PERSTORP STAMP—See Perstorp AB; *Int'l,* pg. 1038
PERSTORP SURFACE MATERIALS—See Perstorp AB; *Int'l,* pg. 1038
PERSTORP TREASURY AB—See Perstorp AB; *Int'l,* pg. 1039
PERSTORP UNIDUR BEIJING OFFICE—See Perstorp AB; *Int'l,* pg. 1038
PERSTORP UNIDUR, INC.—See Perstorp AB; *Int'l,* pg. 1038
PERSTORP UNIDUR LTD.—See Perstorp AB; *Int'l,* pg. 1039
PERSTORP VERTRIEBS AG—See Perstorp AB; *Int'l,* pg. 1039
PERSTORP WARERITE LTD.—See Perstorp AB; *Int'l,* pg. 1039
PERSTORP XYTEC, INC.—See Perstorp AB; *Int'l,* pg. 1037
PERSTRUP BETON INDUSTRI A/S—See Scancem AB; *Int'l,* pg. 1199
P.T. PERTÄFENIKKI ENGINEERING—See JGC Corporation; *Int'l,* pg. 697
PERTH BREWERY—See Foster's Brewing Group Limited; *Int'l,* pg. 501
PERTH LINEN SERVICE—See Brambles Industries Limited; *Int'l,* pg. 211
PERTUY—See Bouygues; *Int'l,* pg. 206
PERUANA DE SEGURIDAD Y VIGILANCIA, S.A. (PESEVISA)—See The Wackenhut Corporation; *U.S. Public,* pg. 1731
PERUGINA BRANDS OF AMERICA—See Nestle S.A.; *Int'l,* pg. 917
PERVASIVE SOFTWARE INC.; *U.S. Public,* pg. 1280
THE PERVO PAINT COMPANY; *U.S. Private,* pg. 856
PERWAKILAN BUREAU TECHNIQUE RHONE-POULENC—See Rhone-Poulenc S.A.; *Int'l,* pg. 1112
PERWANAL/D'ARCY MASIUS BENTON & BOWLES—See DMB&B Communications; *U.S. Private,* pg. 305
PERWIRA ERICSSON SDN. BHD.—See Telefonaktiebolaget LM Ericsson; *Int'l,* pg. 1369

PERWIRA HABIB BANK MALAYSIA BERHAD—See Habib Bank Ltd.; *Int'l*, pg. 585
PESAG AKTIENGESELLSCHAFT—See Veba AG; *Int'l*, pg. 1456
PESAKA JARDINE FLEMING SDN. BHD.—See Robert Fleming Holdings Ltd.; *Int'l*, pg. 494
PEST ELIMINATION—See Ecolab Inc.; *U.S. Public*, pg. 562
PET AG INC.—See Milk Specialties Company; *U.S. Private*, pg. 746
PET LIFE FOODS, INC.; *U.S. Private*, pg. 856
PET RESINS-EUROPE—See Wellman, Inc.; *U.S. Public*, pg. 1753
PETALS; *U.S. Private*, pg. 856
PETCARE PLUS, INC.; *U.S. Private*, pg. 856
PETER BROTHERHOOD LTD.—See Thermo Electron Corporation; *U.S. Public*, pg. 1596
PETER GRAY CORPORATION—See Westwood Corporation; *U.S. Public*, pg. 1763
PETER LUMBER COMPANY; *U.S. Private*, pg. 856
PETER PAK COMPANY—See Paper Enterprises, Inc.; *U.S. Private*, pg. 838
PETER PAN BUS LINES, INC.; *U.S. Private*, pg. 856
PETER PAN SEAFOODS, INC.—See Nichiro Corporation; *Int'l*, pg. 928
PETER PAUL—See Hershey Foods Corporation; *U.S. Public*, pg. 812
PETER PIPER, INC.—See The Bank of Tokyo-Mitsubishi, Ltd.; *Int'l*, pg. 157
PETERBILT MOTORS CO.—See Paccar Inc.; *U.S. Public*, pg. 1247
PETERBILT OF CANADA—See Paccar Inc.; *U.S. Public*, pg. 1247
PETERBOROUGH PORT HOPE READY MIX—See Holderbank Financiere Glaris Ltd.; *Int'l*, pg. 629
PETERBOROUGH QUARRIES LIMITED—See Bardon Group PLC; *Int'l*, pg. 166
PETERS & BROWNES FOODS LTD.; *Int'l*, pg. 1040
PETERS CONSTRUCTION CORP.; *U.S. Private*, pg. 856
J.M. PETERS CO.—See Capital Pacific Holdings; *U.S. Public*, pg. 302
PETERS MACHINERY CO.—See Katy Industries, Inc.; *U.S. Public*, pg. 944
PETERS MASCHINENFABRIK GMBH—See Bobst S.A; *Int'l*, pg. 199
PETERS-REVINGTON CORP.—See Chromcraft Revington, Inc.; *U.S. Public*, pg. 352
PETER'S SAVOURY PRODUCTS—See Diageo Plc; *Int'l*, pg. 410
PETERS STUBS LTD.—See Ascot Holdings Plc; *Int'l*, pg. 88
PETERSBURG LONG DISTANCE INC.; *Int'l*, pg. 1040
PETERSEN ALUMINUM CORPORATION; *U.S. Private*, pg. 856
PETERSEN GRAPHICS GROUP; *U.S. Private*, pg. 856
PETERSEN PUBLISHING COMPANY, L.L.C.; *U.S. Private*, pg. 856
PETERSON AMERICAN CORP.; *U.S. Private*, pg. 857
PETERSON BUILDERS, INC.; *U.S. Private*, pg. 857
PETERSON BUILDERS, INC.-INGLESIDE DIV.—See Peterson Builders, Inc.; *U.S. Private*, pg. 857
PETERSON FARMS; *U.S. Private*, pg. 857
THE PETERSON GROUP—See True North Diversified Companies; *U.S. Public*, pg. 1642
HARRY S. PETERSON CO., INC.—See Viag AG; *Int'l*, pg. 1465
PETERSON MOTOR COMPANY; *U.S. Private*, pg. 857
PETERSON SPRING-CIMA PLANT—See Peterson American Corp.; *U.S. Private*, pg. 857
PETERSON SPRING-COMMONWEALTH PLANT—See Peterson American Corp.; *U.S. Private*, pg. 857
PETERSON SPRING-GEORGIA PLANT—See Peterson American Corp.; *U.S. Private*, pg. 857
PETERSON SPRING-GREENVILLE PLANT—See Peterson American Corp.; *U.S. Private*, pg. 857
PETERSON SPRING-KINGSVILLE PLANT—See Peterson American Corp.; *U.S. Private*, pg. 857
PETERSON SPRING-MADISON HEIGHTS PLANT—See Peterson American Corp.; *U.S. Private*, pg. 857
PETERSON SPRING-MAUMEE PLANT—See Peterson American Corp.; *U.S. Private*, pg. 857
PETERSON SPRING-PACKAGING & DISTRIBUTION—See Peterson American Corp.; *U.S. Private*, pg. 857
PETERSON SPRING-THREE RIVERS PLANT—See Peterson American Corp.; *U.S. Private*, pg. 857
PETERSON SPRING-WINDSOR PLANT—See Peterson American Corp.; *U.S. Private*, pg. 857
PETERSON TRACTOR COMPANY; *U.S. Private*, pg. 858
PETERSON'S GUIDES, INC.; *U.S. Private*, pg. 858
PETE'S BREWING COMPANY; *U.S. Public*, pg. 1280
PETITE SOPHISTICATE—See Casual Corner Group, Inc.; *U.S. Private*, pg. 219
PETITE SOPHISTICATE OUTLET—See Casual Corner Group, Inc.; *U.S. Private*, pg. 219
PETOSEED CO.—See W. Atlee Burpee Co.; *U.S. Private*, pg. 188
PETRECO BAKER HUGHES COMPANY—See Baker Hughes Incorporated; *U.S. Public*, pg. 166
PETRESA INTERNATIONAL N.V.—See Compania Espanola de Petroleos, S.A. (CEPSA); *Int'l*, pg. 323
PETRICCA INDUSTRIES, INC.; *U.S. Private*, pg. 858
S.A. PETRIDES & SON LIMITED—See Telefonaktiebolaget LM Ericsson; *Int'l*, pg. 1369
PETRIE RETAIL, INC.; *U.S. Private*, pg. 858
PETRO-CANADA; *Int'l*, pg. 1041
PETRO CHEM DEVELOPMENT COMPANY; *U.S. Private*, pg. 858
P.T. PETRO CORP.—See Getty Petroleum Marketing Inc.; *U.S. Public*, pg. 741
PETRO-DIAMOND, INC.—See Mitsubishi Corporation; *Int'l*, pg. 872
PETRO-HUNT CORPORATION; *U.S. Private*, pg. 858
PETRO STAR INC.—See Arctic Slope Regional Corporation; *U.S. Private*, pg. 80

PETRO VIETNAM TOWERS—See Keppel Corporation Limited; *Int'l*, pg. 731
PETROBRAS AMERICA INC.—See Petrobras - Petroleo Brasileiro S.A.; *Int'l*, pg. 1042
PETROBRAS ARGENTINA—See Petrobras - Petroleo Brasileiro S.A.; *Int'l*, pg. 1042
PETROBRAS INTERNACIONAL S.A. (BRASPETRO)—See Petrobras - Petroleo Brasileiro S.A.; *Int'l*, pg. 1042
PETROBRAS - PETROLEO BRASILEIRO S.A.; *Int'l*, pg. 1041
PETROBRAS QUIMICA S.A. - PETROQUISA—See Petrobras - Petroleo Brasileiro S.A.; *Int'l*, pg. 1042
PETROCARBON DEVELOPMENTS INC.—See Costain Group PLC; *Int'l*, pg. 337
PETROCHEMICAL INDUSTRIES COMPANY K.S.C.—See Kuwait Petroleum Corporation; *Int'l*, pg. 765
PETROCOQUE S.A.—See Alcan Aluminium Limited; *Int'l*, pg. 52
PETROCORP—See Cigna Corp.; *U.S. Public*, pg. 358
PETROCORP EXPLORATION LIMITED—See Fletcher Challenge Limited; *Int'l*, pg. 495
PETROCORP INCORPORATED—See Cigna Corp.; *U.S. Public*, pg. 358
PETROCORP MANAGEMENT, INC.—See Cigna Corp.; *U.S. Public*, pg. 358
PETROCORP PRIVATE DRILLING LIMITED PARTNERSHIP 1983-1—See Cigna Corp.; *U.S. Public*, pg. 358
PETROCORP RESERVE ACQUISITION FUND, LTD. 1—See Cigna Corp.; *U.S. Public*, pg. 358
PETRODATA S.A.—See Halliburton Company; *U.S. Public*, pg. 777
PETRODYNE PRODUCTS—See The Oilgear Company; *U.S. Public*, pg. 1215
PETROFERM INC.; *U.S. Private*, pg. 858
PETROFIELDS EXPLORATION & DEVELOPMENT CO., INC.—See Benguet Corporation; *Int'l*, pg. 187
PETROFINA DELAWARE, INCORPORATED—See Petrofina S.A.; *Int'l*, pg. 1044
PETROFINA INTERNATIONAL GROUP S.A.—See Petrofina S.A.; *Int'l*, pg. 1044
PETROFINA JAPAN OFFICE—See Petrofina S.A.; *Int'l*, pg. 1044
PETROFINA S.A.; *Int'l*, pg. 1043
PETROGAL ESPANOLA, S.A.—See Petrogal, s.a.; *Int'l*, pg. 1045
PETROGAL, S.A.; *Int'l*, pg. 1044
PETROKJEMI/PETROCHEMICALS—See Norsk Hydro a.s; *Int'l*, pg. 960
PETROLCHEMIE UND KRAFTSTOFFE AG SCHWEDT—See Veba AG; *Int'l*, pg. 1461
PETROLEOS DE CANARIAS, S.A. (PETROCAN)—See Compania Espanola de Petroleos, S.A. (CEPSA); *Int'l*, pg. 323
PETROLEOS DE VENEZUELA S.A.; *Int'l*, pg. 1045
PETROLEOS DE VENEZUELA UK, S.A.—See Petroleos de Venezuela S.A.; *Int'l*, pg. 1046
PETROLEOS DEL SUR, S.A. (PETROSUR)—See Compania Espanola de Petroleos, S.A. (CEPSA); *Int'l*, pg. 323
PETROLEOS MEXICANOS; *Int'l*, pg. 1046
PETROLEOS TRANSANDINOS YPF S.A.—See Y.P.F. S.A.; *Int'l*, pg. 1515
PETROLEUM AND FACILITIES ENGINEERING LTD.—See Scientific Software-Intercomp, Inc.; *U.S. Public*, pg. 1444
PETROLEUM & RESOURCES CORP.; *U.S. Public*, pg. 1280
PETROLEUM AUTHORITY OF THAILAND; *Int'l*, pg. 1046
PETROLEUM CATALYSTS—See Engelhard Corporation; *U.S. Public*, pg. 582
PETROLEUM DEVELOPMENT CORPORATION; *U.S. Public*, pg. 1280
PETROLEUM DEVELOPMENT OMAN LLC—See Royal Dutch/Shell Group of Companies; *Int'l*, pg. 1141
PETROLEUM DRILLING SERVICES COLUMBIA PTY., LTD.—See Halliburton Company; *U.S. Public*, pg. 777
PETROLEUM FUEL & TERMINAL—See Apex Oil Company, Inc.; *U.S. Private*, pg. 77
PETROLEUM HEAT & POWER CO.; *U.S. Public*, pg. 1281
PETROLEUM HELICOPTERS, INC.; *U.S. Public*, pg. 1281
PETROLEUM INC.; *U.S. Private*, pg. 858
PETROLEUM MARKETERS, INC.; *U.S. Private*, pg. 859
PETROLEUM PRODUCTS CORP.; *U.S. Private*, pg. 859
PETROLEUM REFINERIES (AUSTRALIA) PTY., LTD.—See Mobil Oil Corporation; *U.S. Public*, pg. 1120
PETROLEUM SPECIALTIES GROUP—See Witco Corporation; *U.S. Public*, pg. 1774
PETROLEUM SUPPLY COMPANY—See Pride International, Inc.; *U.S. Public*, pg. 1325
PETROLEUM SYSTEMS STRATIGRAPHY (GESIP)—See Petrobras - Petroleo Brasileiro S.A.; *Int'l*, pg. 1041
PETROLEUM TRADERS CORPORATION; *U.S. Private*, pg. 859
PETROLEUM TRANSPORTATION CORPORATION—See Moran Transporation Company; *U.S. Private*, pg. 761
PETROLEUM WORLD—See Cleveland Capital Holdings; *U.S. Private*, pg. 246
PETROLI HUNGARY KFT—See ENI S.p.A.; *Int'l*, pg. 428
PETROLIAM NASIONAL BERHAD (PETRONAS); *Int'l*, pg. 1046
PETROLITE DE MEXICO S.A. DE C.V.—See Baker Hughes Incorporated; *U.S. Public*, pg. 166
PETROLITE FRANCE S.A.—See Baker Hughes Incorporated; *U.S. Public*, pg. 166
PETROLITE GMBH—See Baker Hughes Incorporated; *U.S. Public*, pg. 166
PETROLITE HANDELSGESELLSCHAFT M.B.H.—See Baker Hughes Incorporated; *U.S. Public*, pg. 166
PETROLITE IBERICA, S.A.—See Baker Hughes Incorporated; *U.S. Public*, pg. 166
P.T. PETROLITE INDONESIA PRATAMA—See Baker Hughes Incorporated; *U.S. Public*, pg. 166

PETROLITE ITALIANA S.P.A.—See Baker Hughes Incorporated; *U.S. Public*, pg. 166
PETROLITE LIMITED—See Baker Hughes Incorporated; *U.S. Public*, pg. 166
PETROLITE (MALAYSIA) SDN. BHD.—See Baker Hughes Incorporated; *U.S. Public*, pg. 166
PETROLITE NEDERLAND B.V.—See Baker Hughes Incorporated; *U.S. Public*, pg. 166
PETROLITE NORGE A/S—See Baker Hughes Incorporated; *U.S. Public*, pg. 166
PETROLITE PACIFIC PTE. LTD.—See Baker Hughes Incorporated; *U.S. Public*, pg. 166
PETROLITE SAUDI ARABIA LTD.—See Baker Hughes Incorporated; *U.S. Public*, pg. 166
PETROLITE SURAMERICANA, S.A.—See Baker Hughes Incorporated; *U.S. Public*, pg. 166
PETROMALI-SHELL—See Royal Dutch/Shell Group of Companies; *Int'l*, pg. 1136
PETRON CORPORATION—See Wechco, Inc.; *U.S. Private*, pg. 1158
PETRON, INC.; *U.S. Private*, pg. 859
PETRONOR—See Repsol S.A.; *Int'l*, pg. 1104
PETROQUIMICA ESPANOLA, S.A. (PETRESA)—See Compania Espanola de Petroleos, S.A. (CEPSA); *Int'l*, pg. 323
PETROS PETROPOULOS SA—See Atlet AB; *Int'l*, pg. 97
PETROSUL INTERNATIONAL LTD.; *Int'l*, pg. 1046
PETRUS S.A.—See Temco Service Industries; *U.S. Public*, pg. 1574
PETS-N-SUCH INC.; *U.S. Private*, pg. 859
PET'S PLACE—See Vendex International N.V.; *Int'l*, pg. 1463
PETSMART, INC.; *U.S. Public*, pg. 1281
PETTIBONE CORPORATION; *U.S. Private*, pg. 859
PETTIBONE MICHIGAN DIV.—See Pettibone Corporation; *U.S. Private*, pg. 860
PETTIBONE TIFFIN PARTS—See Pettibone Corporation; *U.S. Private*, pg. 860
PETTY COMPANY, INC.; *U.S. Private*, pg. 860
PETULA ASSOCIATES, LTD.—See The Principal Financial Group; *U.S. Private*, pg. 885
PETWA CANADA LTD.—See ABB Asea Brown Boveri (Holding) Ltd.; *Int'l*, pg. 6
PEUGEOT AUTOMOBILE NIGERIA LTD.—See PSA Peugeot Citroen; *Int'l*, pg. 1021
PEUGEOT-CITROEN MOTEURS (PCM)—See PSA Peugeot Citroen; *Int'l*, pg. 1021
PEUGEOT MOTOR CO. PLC—See PSA Peugeot Citroen; *Int'l*, pg. 1021
PEUGEOT MOTORS OF AMERICA INC.—See PSA Peugeot Citroen; *Int'l*, pg. 1020
PEUGEOT S.A.—See PSA Peugeot Citroen; *Int'l*, pg. 1020
PEUGEOT TALBOT ESPANA—See PSA Peugeot Citroen; *Int'l*, pg. 1021
HEINZ PEUKERT GMBH—See Freudenberg & Company; *Int'l*, pg. 506
PEVELY DAIRY COMPANY—See Prairie Farms Dairy, Inc.; *U.S. Private*, pg. 879
PEYMA CHR. HANSEN'S A.S.—See Chr. Hansen Holding A/S; *Int'l*, pg. 289
DAVID PEYSER SPORTSWEAR INC.; *U.S. Private*, pg. 860
PEYTON MEATS—See American Financial Group; *U.S. Public*, pg. 75
PEZZIOL B.V.—See Koninklijke BolsWessanen nv; *Int'l*, pg. 751
PFAFF AMERICAN SALES CORP.—See G.M. Pfaff Aktiengesellschaft; *Int'l*, pg. 1046
G.M. PFAFF AKTIENGESELLSCHAFT; *Int'l*, pg. 1046
PFAFF-PEGASUS OF U.S.A.—See G.M. Pfaff Aktiengesellschaft; *Int'l*, pg. 1046
THE PFALTZGRAFF CO.; *U.S. Private*, pg. 860
THE PFALTZGRAFF CO.—See The Pfaltzgraff Co.; *U.S. Private*, pg. 860
PFAUDLER, INC.—See Robbins & Myers, Inc.; *U.S. Public*, pg. 1393
PFAUTER ASIA LEYBOLD MACHINERY CO. LTD.—See Hermann Pfauter GmbH & Co.; *Int'l*, pg. 617
PFAUTER FRANCE S.A.R.L.—See Hermann Pfauter GmbH & Co.; *Int'l*, pg. 617
PFAUTER GMT SERVICE CENTER—See Hermann Pfauter GmbH & Co.; *Int'l*, pg. 617
PFAUTER ITALIA SPA—See Hermann Pfauter GmbH & Co.; *Int'l*, pg. 617
PFAUTER KOREA—See Hermann Pfauter GmbH & Co.; *Int'l*, pg. 617
PFAUTER-MAAG CUTTING TOOLS—See Hermann Pfauter GmbH & Co.; *Int'l*, pg. 617
PFAUTER SCHWEIZ—See Hermann Pfauter GmbH & Co.; *Int'l*, pg. 617
PFEIFFER FOODS, INC.—See Lancaster Colony Corporation; *U.S. Public*, pg. 977
PFEIFFER OF AMERICA, INC.—See AptarGroup, Inc.; *U.S. Public*, pg. 125
PFERD/AUGUST RUEGGEBERG; *Int'l*, pg. 1046
PFERD, INC.—See Pferd/August Rueggeberg; *Int'l*, pg. 1046
PFERSEE CHEMIE GMBH—See Novartis AG; *Int'l*, pg. 983
PFICONPROD PTY. LTD.—See Pfizer Inc.; *U.S. Public*, pg. 1282
PFISTER CORPORATION—See The Marcus Corporation; *U.S. Public*, pg. 1044
PFIZER AB—See Pfizer Inc.; *U.S. Public*, pg. 1283
PFIZER AG—See Pfizer Inc.; *U.S. Public*, pg. 1283
PFIZER ANIMAL HEALTH B.V.—See Pfizer Inc.; *U.S. Public*, pg. 1283
PFIZER ANIMAL HEALTH S.A.—See Pfizer Inc.; *U.S. Public*, pg. 1283
PFIZER A.S.—See Pfizer Inc.; *U.S. Public*, pg. 1282
PFIZER A/S—See Pfizer Inc.; *U.S. Public*, pg. 1283
PFIZER BIOQUIMICOS S.A.—See Pfizer Inc.; *U.S. Public*, pg. 1282
PFIZER B.V.—See Pfizer Inc.; *U.S. Public*, pg. 1283
PFIZER C.A.—See Pfizer Inc.; *U.S. Public*, pg. 1282

PFIZER CANADA, INC.—See Pfizer Inc.; *U.S. Public,* pg. 1283
PFIZER CHEMICAL CORP. LTD.—See Pfizer Inc.; *U.S. Public,* pg. 1282
PFIZER CORPORATION—See Pfizer Inc.; *U.S. Public,* pg. 1282
PFIZER CORPORATION AUSTRIA G.M.B.H.—See Pfizer Inc.; *U.S. Public,* pg. 1283
PFIZER EGYPT S.A.E.—See Pfizer Inc.; *U.S. Public,* pg. 1282
PFIZER ENTERPRISES—See Pfizer Inc.; *U.S. Public,* pg. 1282
PFIZER EUROPEAN SERVICE CENTER N.V.—See Pfizer Inc.; *U.S. Public,* pg. 1283
PFIZER G.M.B.H.—See Pfizer Inc.; *U.S. Public,* pg. 1283
PFIZER GROUP LIMITED—See Pfizer Inc.; *U.S. Public,* pg. 1283
PFIZER H.C.P. CORPORATION—See Pfizer Inc.; *U.S. Public,* pg. 1282
PFIZER HEALTH SOLUTIONS INC.—See Pfizer Inc.; *U.S. Public,* pg. 1282
PFIZER HEALTHCARE LTD.—See Pfizer Inc.; *U.S. Public,* pg. 1283
PFIZER HELLAS, A.E.—See Pfizer Inc.; *U.S. Public,* pg. 1282
PFIZER HOLDING MEXICO, S. DE R.L. DE C.V.—See Pfizer Inc.; *U.S. Public,* pg. 1283
PFIZER HOLDING UND VERWALTUNGS G.M.B.H.—See Pfizer Inc.; *U.S. Public,* pg. 1283
PFIZER HOLDINGS IRELAND—See Pfizer Inc.; *U.S. Public,* pg. 1283
PFIZER HOSPITAL PRODUCTS A.B.—See Pfizer Inc.; *U.S. Public,* pg. 1284
PFIZER HOSPITAL PRODUCTS (BELGIUM) N.V.—See Pfizer Inc.; *U.S. Public,* pg. 1284
PFIZER HOSPITAL PRODUCTS, LTD.—See Pfizer Inc.; *U.S. Public,* pg. 1283
PFIZER HOSPITAL PRODUCTS (NETHERLANDS) B.V.—See Pfizer Inc.; *U.S. Public,* pg. 1284
PFIZER ILACLARI, A.S.—See Pfizer Inc.; *U.S. Public,* pg. 1282
PFIZER INC.; *U.S. Public,* pg. 1281
P.T. PFIZER INDONESIA—See Pfizer Inc.; *U.S. Public,* pg. 1282
PFIZER INTERNATIONAL BANK EUROPE—See Pfizer Inc.; *U.S. Public,* pg. 1283
PFIZER INTERNATIONAL CORPORATION—See Pfizer Inc.; *U.S. Public,* pg. 1282
PFIZER INTERNATIONAL PROPERTIES, LLC—See Pfizer Inc.; *U.S. Public,* pg. 1284
PFIZER (IRELAND) LIMITED—See Pfizer Inc.; *U.S. Public,* pg. 1283
PFIZER ITALIANA S.P.A.—See Pfizer Inc.; *U.S. Public,* pg. 1283
PFIZER KOREA LIMITED—See Pfizer Inc.; *U.S. Public,* pg. 1282
PFIZER LABORATORIES LIMITED—See Pfizer Inc.; *U.S. Public,* pg. 1282
PFIZER LABORATORIES LTD.—See Pfizer Inc.; *U.S. Public,* pg. 1282
PFIZER LABORATORIES (PROPRIETARY) LIMITED—See Pfizer Inc.; *U.S. Public,* pg. 1282
PFIZER LIMITED—See Pfizer Inc.; *U.S. Public,* pg. 1282
PFIZER (MALAYSIA) SENDIRIAN BERHAD—See Pfizer Inc.; *U.S. Public,* pg. 1282
PFIZER MED-INFORM BERATUNGS G.M.B.H.—See Pfizer Inc.; *U.S. Public,* pg. 1283
PFIZER MEDICAL SYSTEMS, INC.—See Pfizer Inc.; *U.S. Public,* pg. 1284
PFIZER OVERSEAS INC.—See Pfizer Inc.; *U.S. Public,* pg. 1282
PFIZER OY—See Pfizer Inc.; *U.S. Public,* pg. 1283
PFIZER PENSION TRUSTEES (IRELAND) LIMITED—See Pfizer Inc.; *U.S. Public,* pg. 1283
PFIZER PHARM ALGERIE (PPA)—See Pfizer Inc.; *U.S. Public,* pg. 1283
PFIZER PHARMACEUTICAL TRADING LIMITED LIABILITY COMPANY—See Pfizer Inc.; *U.S. Public,* pg. 1283
PFIZER PHARMACEUTICALS INC.—See Pfizer Inc.; *U.S. Public,* pg. 1283
PFIZER PHARMACEUTICALS LTD.—See Pfizer Inc.; *U.S. Public,* pg. 1282
PFIZER PHARMACEUTICALS PRODUCTION CORPORATION—See Pfizer Inc.; *U.S. Public,* pg. 1282
PFIZER PHARMACEUTICS ISRAEL LTD.—See Pfizer Inc.; *U.S. Public,* pg. 1283
PFIZER PIGMENTS INC.—See Pfizer Inc.; *U.S. Public,* pg. 1284
PFIZER PRIVATE LIMITED—See Pfizer Inc.; *U.S. Public,* pg. 1282
PFIZER PRODUCTS CORPORATION—See Pfizer Inc.; *U.S. Public,* pg. 1284
PFIZER PRODUCTS PLC—See Pfizer Inc.; *U.S. Public,* pg. 1282
PFIZER PTY. LTD.—See Pfizer Inc.; *U.S. Public,* pg. 1282
PFIZER RESEARCH & DEVELOPMENT COMPANY—See Pfizer Inc.; *U.S. Public,* pg. 1283
PFIZER RINGASKIDDY PRODUCTION COMPANY—See Pfizer Inc.; *U.S. Public,* pg. 1283
PFIZER S.A.—See Pfizer Inc.; *U.S. Public,* pg. 1282
PFIZER S.A. DE C.V.—See Pfizer Inc.; *U.S. Public,* pg. 1282
PFIZER S.A.C.I.—See Pfizer Inc.; *U.S. Public,* pg. 1282
PFIZER SERVICE COMPANY IRELAND—See Pfizer Inc.; *U.S. Public,* pg. 1283
PFIZER SERVICIOS DE MEXICO, S.A. DE C.V.—See Pfizer Inc.; *U.S. Public,* pg. 1283
PFIZER S.G.P.S. LDA.—See Pfizer Inc.; *U.S. Public,* pg. 1283
PFIZER SHOJI CO. LTD.—See Pfizer Inc.; *U.S. Public,* pg. 1283
PFIZER SPECIALTIES LIMITED—See Pfizer Inc.; *U.S. Public,* pg. 1284
PFIZER S.R.O.—See Pfizer Inc.; *U.S. Public,* pg. 1284

PFIZER TRADING CORP.—See Pfizer Inc.; *U.S. Public,* pg. 1284
PFIZER ZONA FRANCA S.A.—See Pfizer Inc.; *U.S. Public,* pg. 1282
PFLEIDERER AG; *Int'l,* pg. 1046
PFLEIDERER INDUSTRIE GMBH WIRUS-WERKE GUETERSLOH—See Pfleiderer AG; *Int'l,* pg. 1047
PFRIMMER NUTRICIA GMBH & CO. KG—See Nutricia BV; *Int'l,* pg. 992
PHALO/CDT—See Cable Design Technologies Corporation; *U.S. Public,* pg. 287
PHAR-MOR, INC.; *U.S. Public,* pg. 1284
PHARM-ALLERGAN GMBH—See Allergan, Inc.; *U.S. Public,* pg. 46
PHARMA-METALL GMBH—See The West Company, Incorporated; *U.S. Public,* pg. 1755
PHARMA-TAP S.A. DE C.V.—See The West Company, Incorporated; *U.S. Public,* pg. 1756
PHARMA-WALDHOF GMBH—See Corange Limited; *Int'l,* pg. 331
PHARMACEUTICAL BASICS, INC.—See Akzo Nobel N.V.; *Int'l,* pg. 48
PHARMACEUTICAL FORMULATIONS, INC.; *U.S. Public,* pg. 1284
PHARMACEUTICAL MARKETING SERVICES INC.; *U.S. Public,* pg. 1284
PHARMACEUTICAL PRODUCT DEVELOPMENT, INC.; *U.S. Public,* pg. 1285
PHARMACEUTICAL RESOURCES; *U.S. Public,* pg. 1285
PHARMACEUTICAL, SALON & FOOD PRODUCTS DIVISION—See Shiseido Company Ltd.; *Int'l,* pg. 1236
PHARMACEUTICAL SERVICES—See Medpartners Inc.; *U.S. Public,* pg. 1082
PHARMACEUTICALS AND DIAGNOSTICS COMPANY—See Mitsubishi Chemical Corporation; *Int'l,* pg. 871
PHARMACEUTICALS DIVISION—See 3M; *U.S. Public,* pg. 1605
PHARMACIA & UPJOHN—See Pharmacia & Upjohn, Inc.; *Int'l,* pg. 1048
OY PHARMACIA & UPJOHN AB—See Pharmacia & Upjohn, Inc.; *Int'l,* pg. 1049
PHARMACIA & UPJOHN AB—See Pharmacia & Upjohn, Inc.; *Int'l,* pg. 1049
PHARMACIA & UPJOHN AS—See Pharmacia & Upjohn, Inc.; *Int'l,* pg. 1049
PHARMACIA & UPJOHN A/S—See Pharmacia & Upjohn, Inc.; *Int'l,* pg. 1049
PHARMACIA & UPJOHN (AUSTRALIA) PTY. LTD.—See Pharmacia & Upjohn, Inc.; *Int'l,* pg. 1050
PHARMACIA & UPJOHN BIOSCIENCE CENTER—See Pharmacia & Upjohn, Inc.; *Int'l,* pg. 1047
PHARMACIA & UPJOHN BIOSENSOR AB—See Pharmacia & Upjohn, Inc.; *Int'l,* pg. 1047
PHARMACIA & UPJOHN BIOSYSTEMS AB—See Pharmacia & Upjohn, Inc.; *Int'l,* pg. 1047
PHARMACIA & UPJOHN BIOTECH—See Pharmacia & Upjohn, Inc.; *Int'l,* pg. 1047
PHARMACIA & UPJOHN BIOTECH AB—See Pharmacia & Upjohn, Inc.; *Int'l,* pg. 1047
PHARMACIA & UPJOHN BIOTECH AG—See Pharmacia & Upjohn, Inc.; *Int'l,* pg. 1047
PHARMACIA & UPJOHN BIOTECH AO—See Pharmacia & Upjohn, Inc.; *Int'l,* pg. 1047
PHARMACIA & UPJOHN BIOTECH AS—See Pharmacia & Upjohn, Inc.; *Int'l,* pg. 1047
PHARMACIA & UPJOHN BIOTECH ASEAN SUPPORT CENTRE—See Pharmacia & Upjohn, Inc.; *Int'l,* pg. 1047
PHARMACIA & UPJOHN BIOTECH BENELUX—See Pharmacia & Upjohn, Inc.; *Int'l,* pg. 1047
PHARMACIA & UPJOHN BIOTECH (CHINA) LTD.—See Pharmacia & Upjohn, Inc.; *Int'l,* pg. 1047
PHARMACIA & UPJOHN BIOTECH DO BRASIL LTDA.—See Pharmacia & Upjohn, Inc.; *Int'l,* pg. 1047
PHARMACIA & UPJOHN BIOTECH EUROPE—See Pharmacia & Upjohn, Inc.; *Int'l,* pg. 1047
PHARMACIA & UPJOHN BIOTECH FAR EAST LTD.—See Pharmacia & Upjohn, Inc.; *Int'l,* pg. 1047
PHARMACIA & UPJOHN BIOTECH GMBH—See Pharmacia & Upjohn, Inc.; *Int'l,* pg. 1047
PHARMACIA & UPJOHN BIOTECH INC.—See Pharmacia & Upjohn, Inc.; *Int'l,* pg. 1047
PHARMACIA & UPJOHN BIOTECH K.K.—See Pharmacia & Upjohn, Inc.; *Int'l,* pg. 1048
PHARMACIA & UPJOHN BIOTECH NORDEN—See Pharmacia & Upjohn, Inc.; *Int'l,* pg. 1047
PHARMACIA & UPJOHN BIOTECH S.A.—See Pharmacia & Upjohn, Inc.; *Int'l,* pg. 1047
PHARMACIA & UPJOHN BIOTECH S.P.A.—See Pharmacia & Upjohn, Inc.; *Int'l,* pg. 1047
PHARMACIA & UPJOHN CENTRAL AMERICAN MANAGEMENT COMPANY—See Pharmacia & Upjohn, Inc.; *Int'l,* pg. 1048
PHARMACIA & UPJOHN COMPANIA LIMITADA—See Pharmacia & Upjohn, Inc.; *Int'l,* pg. 1049
PHARMACIA & UPJOHN COMPANY HONG KONG BRANCH—See Pharmacia & Upjohn, Inc.; *Int'l,* pg. 1049
PHARMACIA & UPJOHN COMPANY LIMITED—See Pharmacia & Upjohn, Inc.; *Int'l,* pg. 1049
PHARMACIA & UPJOHN COMPANY OF CANADA—See Pharmacia & Upjohn, Inc.; *Int'l,* pg. 1049
PHARMACIA & UPJOHN COMPANY S.A.—See Pharmacia & Upjohn, Inc.; *Int'l,* pg. 1049
PHARMACIA & UPJOHN CONSUMER PHARMA—See Pharmacia & Upjohn, Inc.; *Int'l,* pg. 1048
PHARMACIA & UPJOHN COORDINATION CENTER N.V.—See Pharmacia & Upjohn, Inc.; *Int'l,* pg. 1049
PHARMACIA & UPJOHN CORPORATE SERVICES—See Pharmacia & Upjohn, Inc.; *Int'l,* pg. 1049
PHARMACIA & UPJOHN DATA AB—See Pharmacia & Upjohn, Inc.; *Int'l,* pg. 1048
PHARMACIA & UPJOHN DELTEC, INC.—See Pharmacia & Upjohn, Inc.; *Int'l,* pg. 1049

PHARMACIA & UPJOHN DIAGNOSTICS, INC.—See Pharmacia & Upjohn, Inc.; *Int'l,* pg. 1048
PHARMACIA & UPJOHN DONG-IL CO, LTD.—See Pharmacia & Upjohn, Inc.; *Int'l,* pg. 1048
PHARMACIA & UPJOHN EUROCENTRE—See Pharmacia & Upjohn, Inc.; *Int'l,* pg. 1050
PHARMACIA & UPJOHN EXPORT AG—See Pharmacia & Upjohn, Inc.; *Int'l,* pg. 1049
PHARMACIA & UPJOHN FARMOQUIMICA, LDA.—See Pharmacia & Upjohn, Inc.; *Int'l,* pg. 1049
PHARMACIA & UPJOHN FARMOQUIMICA, S.A.—See Pharmacia & Upjohn, Inc.; *Int'l,* pg. 1049
PHARMACIA & UPJOHN GES.M.B.H.—See Pharmacia & Upjohn, Inc.; *Int'l,* pg. 1049
PHARMACIA & UPJOHN GMBH—See Pharmacia & Upjohn, Inc.; *Int'l,* pg. 1049
PHARMACIA & UPJOHN GROUP—See Pharmacia & Upjohn, Inc.; *Int'l,* pg. 1049
PHARMACIA & UPJOHN (HELLAS) S.A.—See Pharmacia & Upjohn, Inc.; *Int'l,* pg. 1050
PHARMACIA & UPJOHN HOLDING NEDERLAND BV—See Pharmacia & Upjohn, Inc.; *Int'l,* pg. 1050
PHARMACIA & UPJOHN HOSPITAL CARE—See Pharmacia & Upjohn, Inc.; *Int'l,* pg. 1048
PHARMACIA & UPJOHN, INC.; *Int'l,* pg. 1047
PHARMACIA & UPJOHN, INC.—See Pharmacia & Upjohn, Inc.; *Int'l,* pg. 1049
PHARMACIA & UPJOHN INC.—See Pharmacia & Upjohn, Inc.; *Int'l,* pg. 1050
P.T. PHARMACIA & UPJOHN INDONESIA—See Pharmacia & Upjohn, Inc.; *Int'l,* pg. 1049
PHARMACIA & UPJOHN INTER-AMERICAN CORP.—See Pharmacia & Upjohn, Inc.; *Int'l,* pg. 1048
PHARMACIA & UPJOHN INTER-AMERICAN CORPORATION-NEW ZEALAND—See Pharmacia & Upjohn, Inc.; *Int'l,* pg. 1048
PHARMACIA & UPJOHN INTER-AMERICAN CORPORATION-PERU—See Pharmacia & Upjohn, Inc.; *Int'l,* pg. 1048
PHARMACIA & UPJOHN INTER-AMERICAN CORPORATION-GREECE—See Pharmacia & Upjohn, Inc.; *Int'l,* pg. 1048
PHARMACIA & UPJOHN INTERNATIONAL NV—See Pharmacia & Upjohn, Inc.; *Int'l,* pg. 1050
PHARMACIA & UPJOHN INTL. INC.—See Pharmacia & Upjohn, Inc.; *Int'l,* pg. 1048
PHARMACIA & UPJOHN KOGE CHEMICALS A/S—See Pharmacia & Upjohn, Inc.; *Int'l,* pg. 1048
PHARMACIA & UPJOHN LABORATORIES LIMITED—See Pharmacia & Upjohn, Inc.; *Int'l,* pg. 1049
PHARMACIA & UPJOHN LABORATORIOS S.A.—See Pharmacia & Upjohn, Inc.; *Int'l,* pg. 1048
PHARMACIA & UPJOHN LIMITED—See Pharmacia & Upjohn, Inc.; *Int'l,* pg. 1049
PHARMACIA & UPJOHN LKB BIOCHROM LTD.—See Pharmacia & Upjohn, Inc.; *Int'l,* pg. 1048
PHARMACIA & UPJOHN LKB INSTRUMENT GMBH—See Pharmacia & Upjohn, Inc.; *Int'l,* pg. 1048
PHARMACIA & UPJOHN LTD.—See Pharmacia & Upjohn, Inc.; *Int'l,* pg. 1050
PHARMACIA & UPJOHN MANAGEMENT CENTRE AB—See Pharmacia & Upjohn, Inc.; *Int'l,* pg. 1048
PHARMACIA & UPJOHN MANUFACTURING CO.—See Pharmacia & Upjohn, Inc.; *Int'l,* pg. 1048
PHARMACIA & UPJOHN NEDERLAND B.V.—See Pharmacia & Upjohn, Inc.; *Int'l,* pg. 1050
PHARMACIA & UPJOHN NEW ZEALAND—See Pharmacia & Upjohn, Inc.; *Int'l,* pg. 1050
PHARMACIA & UPJOHN ONCOLOGY IMMUNOLOGY—See Pharmacia & Upjohn, Inc.; *Int'l,* pg. 1050
PHARMACIA & UPJOHN OPHTHALMICS—See Pharmacia & Upjohn, Inc.; *Int'l,* pg. 1048
PHARMACIA & UPJOHN PEPTIDE HORMONES—See Pharmacia & Upjohn, Inc.; *Int'l,* pg. 1048
PHARMACIA & UPJOHN PHARMACEUTICAL DIV.—See Pharmacia & Upjohn, Inc.; *Int'l,* pg. 1048
PHARMACIA & UPJOHN PLASMA PRODUCTS—See Pharmacia & Upjohn, Inc.; *Int'l,* pg. 1048
PHARMACIA & UPJOHN (PROPRIETARY) LIMITED—See Pharmacia & Upjohn, Inc.; *Int'l,* pg. 1049
PHARMACIA & UPJOHN PTY. LIMITED—See Pharmacia & Upjohn, Inc.; *Int'l,* pg. 1049
PHARMACIA & UPJOHN RISK MANAGEMENT SERVICE AB—See Pharmacia & Upjohn, Inc.; *Int'l,* pg. 1048
PHARMACIA & UPJOHN S.A.—See Pharmacia & Upjohn, Inc.; *Int'l,* pg. 1050
PHARMACIA & UPJOHN S.A. DE C.V.—See Pharmacia & Upjohn, Inc.; *Int'l,* pg. 1050
N.V. PHARMACIA & UPJOHN S.A.—See Pharmacia & Upjohn, Inc.; *Int'l,* pg. 1049
PHARMACIA & UPJOHN S.A.N.V.—See Pharmacia & Upjohn, Inc.; *Int'l,* pg. 1050
PHARMACIA & UPJOHN S.P.A.—See Pharmacia & Upjohn, Inc.; *Int'l,* pg. 1049
PHARMACIA & UPJOHN SVERIGE AB—See Pharmacia & Upjohn, Inc.; *Int'l,* pg. 1048
PHARMACIA & UPJOHN THERAPEUTICS—See Pharmacia & Upjohn, Inc.; *Int'l,* pg. 1048
PHARMACIA & UPJOHN TREASURY SERVICES AB—See Pharmacia & Upjohn, Inc.; *Int'l,* pg. 1048
PHARMACIA & UPJOHN U.S. INC.—See Pharmacia & Upjohn, Inc.; *Int'l,* pg. 1049
PHARMACISTS PUBLIC RELATIONS BUREAU—See Cullman Ventures, Inc.; *U.S. Private,* pg. 295
PHARMACO GMBH—See Pharmaceutical Product Development, Inc.; *U.S. Public,* pg. 1285
PHARMACO INTERNATIONAL HOLDINGS, INC.—See Pharmaceutical Product Development, Inc.; *U.S. Public,* pg. 1285
PHARMACO INTL. LTD.—See Pharmaceutical Product Development, Inc.; *U.S. Public,* pg. 1285
PHARMACO INTL. SP.—See Pharmaceutical Product Development, Inc.; *U.S. Public,* pg. 1285

PHARMACO PTY LTD—See Pharmaceutical Product Development, Inc.; *U.S. Public,* pg. 1285
PHARMAKINETICS LABORATORIES, INC.; *U.S. Public,* pg. 1285
PHARMAPLUS DRUGMARTS LIMITED—See The Oshawa Group Limited; *Int'l,* pg. 1012
PHARMAVITE CORP.; *U.S. Private,* pg. 860
PHARMAVITE CORPORATION—See Otsuka Pharmaceutical Co., Ltd.; *Int'l,* pg. 1013
PHARMAX LTD.—See Forest Laboratories, Inc.; *U.S. Public,* pg. 670
PHARMCHEM LABORATORIES, INC.; *U.S. Public,* pg. 1285
PHARMERICA, INC.; *U.S. Public,* pg. 1286
PHARMERICA-REGIONAL OFFICE—See PharMerica, Inc.; *U.S. Public,* pg. 1286
PHARMETRIX CORPORATION—See Recordati Industria Chimica e Farmaceutica S.p.A.; *Int'l,* pg. 1090
PHARMHOUSE, INC.; *U.S. Public,* pg. 1286
PHARMOSOL CORPORATION—See Elf Aquitaine; *Int'l,* pg. 446
PHAROS DE COSTA RICA S.A.—See Spectra-Physics AB; *Int'l,* pg. 1290
PHAROS HOLDINGS GMBH—See Spectra-Physics AB; *Int'l,* pg. 1290
PHAROS HOLDINGS, INC.—See Spectra-Physics AB; *Int'l,* pg. 1289
AB PHAROS MARINE—See Spectra-Physics AB; *Int'l,* pg. 1289
AB PHAROS MARINE PTE. LTD.—See Spectra-Physics AB; *Int'l,* pg. 1290
AB PHAROS MARINE LTD.—See Spectra-Physics AB; *Int'l,* pg. 1290
PHASE COMPONENTS LTD.—See American Technical Ceramics Corp.; *U.S. Public,* pg. 93
PHASE LINEAR—See Recoton Corporation; *U.S. Public,* pg. 1369
PHASE3 SYSTEMS INC.—See SunGard Data Systems Inc.; *U.S. Public,* pg. 1535
PHELPS DODGE & ALCOA FIOS E CABOS ELECTRICOS S.A.—See Phelps Dodge Corporation; *U.S. Public,* pg. 1286
PHELPS DODGE COPPER PRODUCTS COMPANY—See Phelps Dodge Corporation; *U.S. Public,* pg. 1287
PHELPS DODGE CORPORATION; *U.S. Public,* pg. 1286
PHELPS DODGE EXPLORATION CORPORATION—See Phelps Dodge Corporation; *U.S. Public,* pg. 1287
PHELPS DODGE HIDALGO—See Phelps Dodge Corporation; *U.S. Public,* pg. 1287
PHELPS DODGE INDUSTRIES—See Phelps Dodge Corporation; *U.S. Public,* pg. 1286
PHELPS DODGE INTL. CORP.—See Phelps Dodge Corporation; *U.S. Public,* pg. 1286
PHELPS DODGE MAGNET WIRE CO.—See Phelps Dodge Corporation; *U.S. Public,* pg. 1286
PHELPS DODGE MINING COMPANY—See Phelps Dodge Corporation; *U.S. Public,* pg. 1286
PHELPS DODGE MORENCI INC.—See Phelps Dodge Corporation; *U.S. Public,* pg. 1287
PHELPS DODGE REFINING CORP.—See Phelps Dodge Corporation; *U.S. Public,* pg. 1287
PHELPS DODGE SALES COMPANY—See Phelps Dodge Corporation; *U.S. Public,* pg. 1287
PHELPS DODGE THAILAND LTD.—See Sumitomo Electric Industries, Ltd.; *Int'l,* pg. 1313
PHELPS DODGE TYRONE—See Phelps Dodge Corporation; *U.S. Public,* pg. 1287
PHELPS TOINTON INC.; *U.S. Private,* pg. 860
PHELPS TOINTON MILLWORK—See Phelps Tointon Inc.; *U.S. Private,* pg. 861
PHENIX ALUMINIUM S.A.—See Koninklijke Hoogovens N.V.; *Int'l,* pg. 755
PHENIX CITY NURSING HOME—See Paragon Health Network, Inc.; *U.S. Public,* pg. 1257
PHENOLCHEMIE GMBH—See Veba AG; *Int'l,* pg. 1454
PHIBRO DIVISION OF SALOMON INC.—See Travelers Group; *U.S. Public,* pg. 1633
PHILADELPHIA AMERICAN LIFE INSURANCE COMPANY—See I.C.H. Corporation; *U.S. Public,* pg. 853
THE PHILADELPHIA BOURSE, INC.; *U.S. Private,* pg. 861
PHILADELPHIA CARPET DIV.—See Shaw Industries, Inc.; *U.S. Public,* pg. 1464
PHILADELPHIA COCA-COLA BOTTLING CO.; *U.S. Private,* pg. 861
PHILADELPHIA DAILY NEWS—See Knight-Ridder, Inc.; *U.S. Public,* pg. 964
PHILADELPHIA DRILLING COMPANY—See Cigna Corp.; *U.S. Public,* pg. 358
PHILADELPHIA EAGLE DRILLING CORPORATION—See Cigna Corp.; *U.S. Public,* pg. 358
PHILADELPHIA FALCON DRILLING CORPORATION—See Cigna Corp.; *U.S. Public,* pg. 358
THE PHILADELPHIA INQUIRER—See Knight-Ridder, Inc.; *U.S. Public,* pg. 964
PHILADELPHIA INTERNATIONAL INVESTMENT CORP.—See CoreStates Financial Corp.; *U.S. Public,* pg. 447
PHILADELPHIA INVESTMENT CORPORATION OF DELAWARE—See Cigna Corp.; *U.S. Public,* pg. 357
PHILADELPHIA JEFFERSON CORPORATION—See Cigna Corp.; *U.S. Public,* pg. 365
PHILADELPHIA LOCAL TELEGRAPH COMPANY—See New Valley Corporation; *U.S. Public,* pg. 1173
PHILADELPHIA NATIONAL LIMITED—See CoreStates Financial Corp.; *U.S. Public,* pg. 447
PHILADELPHIA NEWSPAPERS, INC.—See Knight-Ridder, Inc.; *U.S. Public,* pg. 964
PHILADELPHIA RESERVE SUPPLY COMPANY; *U.S. Private,* pg. 861
PHILADELPHIA SIGN COMPANY; *U.S. Private,* pg. 861
PHILADELPHIA SUBURBAN CORPORATION; *U.S. Public,* pg. 1287

PHILADELPHIA SUBURBAN WATER COMPANY—See Philadelphia Suburban Corporation; *U.S. Public,* pg. 1287
PHILADELPHIA TERMINAL—See GATX Corporation; *U.S. Public,* pg. 692
PHILAM LIFE HOLDING CO.—See American International Group, Inc.; *U.S. Public,* pg. 85
PHILCO FINANCE CORPORATION—See Ford Motor Company; *U.S. Public,* pg. 663
PHILDAS LTD.—See Haden Maclellan Holdings plc; *Int'l,* pg. 585
PHILIP ENVIRONMENTAL/DELSAN—See Philip Services Corp.; *Int'l,* pg. 1050
GEORGE PHILIP LIMITED—See Reed Elsevier plc; *Int'l,* pg. 1093
PHILIP INDUSTRIAL SERVICES GROUP—See Philip Services Corp.; *Int'l,* pg. 1050
PHILIP LASER MAGNETIC STORAGE—See Philips Electronics N.V.; *Int'l,* pg. 1054
PHILIP METALS INC.—See Philip Services Corp.; *Int'l,* pg. 1050
PHILIP METALS/STEINER-LIFF—See Philip Services Corp.; *Int'l,* pg. 1050
PHILIP MORRIS (AUSTRALIA) LIMITED—See Philip Morris Companies Inc.; *U.S. Public,* pg. 1290
PHILIP MORRIS CAPITAL CORPORATION—See Philip Morris Companies Inc.; *U.S. Public,* pg. 1289
PHILIP MORRIS COMPANIES INC.; *U.S. Public,* pg. 1287
PHILIP MORRIS EEC—See Philip Morris Companies Inc.; *U.S. Public,* pg. 1290
PHILIP MORRIS EFTA, (EASTERN EUROPE, MIDDLE EAST & AFRICA)—See Philip Morris Companies Inc.; *U.S. Public,* pg. 1290
PHILIP MORRIS ESPANA, S.A.—See Tabacalera, S.A.; *Int'l,* pg. 1346
PHILIP MORRIS GMBH—See Philip Morris Companies Inc.; *U.S. Public,* pg. 1290
PHILIP MORRIS INTERNATIONAL INC.—See Philip Morris Companies Inc.; *U.S. Public,* pg. 1289
PHILIP MORRIS K.K.—See Philip Morris Companies Inc.; *U.S. Public,* pg. 1290
PHILIP MORRIS MANAGEMENT CORP.—See Philip Morris Companies Inc.; *U.S. Public,* pg. 1289
PHILIP MORRIS SABANCI PAZALARMA VE SATIS A.S.—See Sabanci Holding A.S.; *Int'l,* pg. 1168
PHILIP MORRIS SABANCI PAZALARMA VE SATIS A.S.—See Philip Morris Companies Inc.; *U.S. Public,* pg. 1290
PHILIP MORRIS U.S.A.—See Philip Morris Companies Inc.; *U.S. Public,* pg. 1289
PHILIP MORRIS U.S.A., CABARRUS MFG. CENTER—See Philip Morris Companies Inc.; *U.S. Public,* pg. 1290
PHILIP SERVICES CORP.; *Int'l,* pg. 1050
PHILIPP BROTHERS CHEMICALS, INC.; *U.S. Private,* pg. 861
PHILIPP HOLZMANN USA, INC.—See Philipp Holzmann AG; *Int'l,* pg. 633
PHILIPP NIEDERMEIER METALLWARENFABRIK GMBH & CO. KG—See Schmalbach-Lubeca AG; *Int'l,* pg. 1206
PHILIPPINE AIRLINES, INC.; *Int'l,* pg. 1050
THE PHILIPPINE AMERICAN ACCIDENT INSURANCE CO., INC.—See American International Group, Inc.; *U.S. Public,* pg. 85
THE PHILIPPINE AMERICAN MANAGEMENT & FINANCING CO., INC.—See American International Group, Inc.; *U.S. Public,* pg. 85
PHILIPPINE AUTOMOTIVE MANUFACTURING CORPORATION—See Mitsubishi Motors Corporation; *Int'l,* pg. 876
PHILIPPINE COCOA ESTATES CORPORATION—See Benguet Corporation; *Int'l,* pg. 187
PHILIPPINE GEOTHERMAL INCORPORATED—See Unocal Corporation; *U.S. Public,* pg. 1698
PHILIPPINE LONG DISTANCE TELEPHONE COMPANY; *Int'l,* pg. 1051
PHILIPPINE REFINING COMPANY INC.—See Unilever Plc; *Int'l,* pg. 1438
PHILIPPINE SUNSYSTEMS PRODUCTS, INC.—See Sun Microsystems, Inc.; *U.S. Public,* pg. 1531
PHILIPPINE WACOAL CORP.—See Wacoal Corporation; *Int'l,* pg. 1484
THE PHILIPPINES AMERICAN ASSURANCE CO., INC.—See American International Group, Inc.; *U.S. Public,* pg. 85
PHILIPPINES DAIRY PRODUCTS CORP.—See New Zealand Dairy Board; *Int'l,* pg. 923
PHILIPPINES EXPLOSIVES CORPORATION—See Imperial Chemical Industries PLC; *Int'l,* pg. 665
PHILIPS & DUPONT OPTICAL COMPANY—See Philips Electronics N.V.; *Int'l,* pg. 1055
PHILIPS COMMUNICATION SYSTEMS B.V.—See Philips Electronics N.V.; *Int'l,* pg. 1051
PHILIPS COMMUNICATIONS & PROCESSING SERVICES B.V.—See Philips Electronics N.V.; *Int'l,* pg. 1051
PHILIPS COMPONENTS—See Philips Electronics N.V.; *Int'l,* pg. 1054
PHILIPS COMPONENTS B.V.—See Philips Electronics N.V.; *Int'l,* pg. 1051
PHILIPS CONSUMER ELECTRONICS—See Philips Electronics N.V.; *Int'l,* pg. 1054
PHILIPS CONSUMER ELECTRONICS INTERNATIONAL B.V.—See Philips Electronics N.V.; *Int'l,* pg. 1051
PHILIPS DOMESTIC APPLIANCES AND PERSONAL CARE B.V.—See Philips Electronics N.V.; *Int'l,* pg. 1051
PHILIPS ELECTRONICS NORTH AMERICA CORPORATION—See Philips Electronics N.V.; *Int'l,* pg. 1053
PHILIPS ELECTRONICS N.V.; *Int'l,* pg. 1051
PHILIPS INDUSTRIAL ELECTRONICS INTERNATIONAL B.V.—See Philips Electronics N.V.; *Int'l,* pg. 1051
PHILIPS INTERNATIONAL B.V.—See Philips Electronics N.V.; *Int'l,* pg. 1051
PHILIPS LIGHTING B.V.—See Philips Electronics N.V.; *Int'l,* pg. 1051

PHILIPS MACHINEFABRIEKEN B.V.—See Philips Electronics N.V.; *Int'l,* pg. 1051
PHILIPS MEDICAL SYSTEMS INTERNATIONAL B.V.—See Philips Electronics N.V.; *Int'l,* pg. 1051
PHILIPS MEDICAL SYSTEMS NORTH AMERICA COMPANY—See Philips Electronics N.V.; *Int'l,* pg. 1055
PHILIPS PMF INTERNATIONAL B.V.—See Philips Electronics N.V.; *Int'l,* pg. 1051
PHILIPS SEMICONDUCTORS B.V.—See Philips Electronics N.V.; *Int'l,* pg. 1051
PHILIPSSONS GRAV & SCHAKT AB—See Telefonaktiebolaget LM Ericsson; *Int'l,* pg. 1364
THE PHILLIES-A LIMITED PARTNERSHIP; *U.S. Private,* pg. 861
PHILLIES CIGAR COMPANY—See Havatampa, Inc.; *U.S. Private,* pg. 510
PHILLIPS ALASKA NATURAL GAS CORPORATION—See Phillips Petroleum Company; *U.S. Public,* pg. 1291
PHILLIPS & JACOBS/NORTH—See PrimeSource Corporation; *U.S. Public,* pg. 1329
PHILLIPS & TEMRO INDUSTRIES INC.—See Thyssen AG; *Int'l,* pg. 1388
PHILLIPS COAL COMPANY—See Phillips Petroleum Company; *U.S. Public,* pg. 1291
PHILLIPS COMMUNICATIONS, INC.—See Phillips Petroleum Company; *U.S. Public,* pg. 1291
PHILLIPS DRISCOPIPE, INC.—See Phillips Petroleum Company; *U.S. Public,* pg. 1291
PHILLIPS FINE ART AUCTIONEERS; *U.S. Private,* pg. 861
PHILLIPS GAS COMPANY—See Phillips Petroleum Company; *U.S. Public,* pg. 1291
PHILLIPS GAS SUPPLY CORPORATION—See Phillips Petroleum Company; *U.S. Public,* pg. 1291
PHILLIPS HENDERSON WARD LIMITED—See HSBC Holdings plc; *Int'l,* pg. 583
PHILLIPS INVESTMENT COMPANY—See Phillips Petroleum Company; *U.S. Public,* pg. 1291
J.R. PHILLIPS & CO., LTD.—See Whitbread PLC; *Int'l,* pg. 1499
PHILLIPS PETROLEUM COMPANY; *U.S. Public,* pg. 1290
PHILLIPS PETROLEUM INTERNATIONAL CORPORATION—See Phillips Petroleum Company; *U.S. Public,* pg. 1291
PHILLIPS PETROLEUM INTERNATIONAL INVESTMENT COMPANY—See Phillips Petroleum Company; *U.S. Public,* pg. 1291
PHILLIPS PETROLEUM SINGAPORE CHEMICALS PTE. LTD.—See Phillips Petroleum Company; *U.S. Public,* pg. 1291
PHILLIPS PIPE LINE COMPANY—See Phillips Petroleum Company; *U.S. Public,* pg. 1291
PHILLIPS PLASTICS CORPORATION; *U.S. Private,* pg. 862
PHILLIPS PUBLISHING INTERNATIONAL, INC.; *U.S. Private,* pg. 862
PHILLIPS SERVICE INDUSTRIES, INC.; *U.S. Private,* pg. 862
T.W. PHILLIPS GAS AND OIL CO.; *U.S. Private,* pg. 862
PHILLIPS-VAN HEUSEN CORPORATION; *U.S. Public,* pg. 1291
PHILLIPS-FITEL INC.—See The Furukawa Electric Co., Ltd.; *Int'l,* pg. 531
PHILMAC PTY LIMITED—See Glynwed International PLC; *Int'l,* pg. 555
PHILNET ERICSSON INC.—See Telefonaktiebolaget LM Ericsson; *Int'l,* pg. 1369
PHILOMATH FOREST PRODUCTS CO.—See WTD Industries, Inc.; *U.S. Public,* pg. 1730
PHILSA PHILIP MORRIS SABANCI SIGARA VE TUTUNCULUK A.S.—See Sabanci Holding A.S.; *Int'l,* pg. 1168
PHILSA PHILIP MORRIS SABANCI SIGARA VE TUTUNCULUK A.S.—See Philip Morris Companies Inc.; *U.S. Public,* pg. 1290
PHILWAY PRODUCTS, INC.; *U.S. Private,* pg. 862
PHIPPS & BIRD—See McKesson Corporation; *U.S. Public,* pg. 1073
GERALD H. PHIPPS, INC.; *U.S. Private,* pg. 862
PHIPPS PRESS, INC.—See Jannock Limited; *Int'l,* pg. 699
PHOENIX AMERICAN AFFILIATES, INC.—See Phoenix American Incorporated; *U.S. Private,* pg. 862
PHOENIX AMERICAN INCORPORATED; *U.S. Private,* pg. 862
PHOENIX AMERICAN LIFE INS. CO.—See Phoenix Home Life Mutual Insurance Company; *U.S. Private,* pg. 863
PHOENIX ASSURANCE OF NEW YORK, INC.—See Royal & Sun Alliance Insurance Group plc; *Int'l,* pg. 1130
PHOENIX CABLE INCORPORATED—See Phoenix American Incorporated; *U.S. Private,* pg. 862
PHOENIX CHEMICAL COMPANY—See IMC Global; *U.S. Public,* pg. 856
PHOENIX CONCRETE CUTTING—See Penhall International; *U.S. Private,* pg. 849
PHOENIX DEVELOPMENT CO., INC.—See Central Hudson Gas & Electric Corporation; *U.S. Public,* pg. 325
PHOENIX FIBER LINK INC.—See Phoenix American Incorporated; *U.S. Private,* pg. 863
PHOENIX FILMS & VIDEO—See The Phoenix Learning Group, Inc.; *U.S. Private,* pg. 863
PHOENIX FOUNDERS, INC—See Phoenix Home Life Mutual Insurance Company; *U.S. Private,* pg. 863
PHOENIX FUEL COMPANY, INC.; *U.S. Private,* pg. 863
PHOENIX GROWTH CAPITAL CORP.—See Phoenix American Incorporated; *U.S. Private,* pg. 863
PHOENIX HOME LIFE MUTUAL INSURANCE COMPANY; *U.S. Private,* pg. 863
PHOENIX INDUSTRIES—See Trinidad/Benham Corp.; *U.S. Private,* pg. 1103
PHOENIX INVESTMENT COUNSEL INC.—See Phoenix Home Life Mutual Insurance Company; *U.S. Private,* pg. 863
PHOENIX LAND COMPANY—See Zeigler Coal Holding Company; *U.S. Public,* pg. 1790

THE PHOENIX LEARNING GROUP, INC.; *U.S. Private,* pg. 863
PHOENIX LEARNING RESOURCES—See The Phoenix Learning Group, Inc.; *U.S. Private,* pg. 863
PHOENIX LEASING INCORPORATED—See Phoenix American Incorporated; *U.S. Private,* pg. 863
PHOENIX MAGAZINE—See MAC America Communications; *U.S. Private,* pg. 685
PHOENIX MANUFACTURING, INC.—See Continental Materials Corporation; *U.S. Public,* pg. 441
PHOENIX MEDICAL TECHNOLOGY, INC.; *U.S. Public,* pg. 1292
PHOENIX METALLICS, INC.—See John S. Frey Enterprises; *U.S. Private,* pg. 428
PHOENIX NEWSPAPERS, INC.—See Central Newspapers, Inc.; *U.S. Public,* pg. 326
PHOENIX OIL COMPANY (UK) LIMITED—See Fuchs Petrolub AG Oel + Chemie; *Int'l,* pg. 519
THE PHOENIX RESOURCE COMPANIES, INC.—See Apache Corporation; *U.S. Public,* pg. 119
PHOENIX SECURITIES, INC.—See Phoenix American Incorporated; *U.S. Private,* pg. 863
PHOENIX SECURITIES LIMITED—See Deutsche Bank AG; *Int'l,* pg. 405
PHOENIX STEEL TUBE—See Senior Engineering Group, plc.; *Int'l,* pg. 1221
PHOENIX SYSTEMS EXCHANGE, INC.—See Phoenix American Incorporated; *U.S. Private,* pg. 863
PHOENIX TECHNOLOGIES K.K.—See Phoenix Technologies Ltd.; *U.S. Public,* pg. 1292
PHOENIX TECHNOLOGIES LTD.; *U.S. Public,* pg. 1292
PHOENIX TECHNOLOGIES LTD.—See Phoenix Technologies Ltd.; *U.S. Public,* pg. 1292
PHOENIX TECHNOLOGIES (TAIWAN) LTD.—See Phoenix Technologies Ltd.; *U.S. Public,* pg. 1292
PHOENIXVILLE NEWSPAPERS, INC.—See Journal Register Company; *U.S. Public,* pg. 935
PHONETICS, INC.; *U.S. Private,* pg. 864
PHONOGRAM INTERNATIONAL B.V.—See Philips Electronics N.V.; *Int'l,* pg. 1052
PHONOGRAM LTD.—See Philips Electronics N.V.; *Int'l,* pg. 1053
PHOSPHATES DIVISION, ALBRIGHT & WILSON LIMITED—See Albright & Wilson plc; *Int'l,* pg. 49
PHOTO CONTROL CORPORATION; *U.S. Public,* pg. 1292
PHOTO DESIGN—See VNU Verenigde Nederlandse Uitgeversbedrijven B.V.; *Int'l,* pg. 1446
PHOTO DISTRICT NEWS—See VNU Verenigde Nederlandse Uitgeversbedrijven B.V.; *Int'l,* pg. 1446
PHOTO-ME INTERNATIONAL PLC; *Int'l,* pg. 1055
PHOTO MECHANICAL SERVICES INC.—See Proto Systems of Atlanta; *U.S. Private,* pg. 891
PHOTO MECHANIX INC.—See Proto Systems of Atlanta; *U.S. Private,* pg. 891
PHOTOCENTRON INC.—See Essilor International Compagnie Generale d'Optique; *Int'l,* pg. 462
PHOTOGENIC MACHINE COMPANY, INC.; *U.S. Private,* pg. 864
PHOTOLASTIC DIVISION—See Vishay Intertechnology, Inc.; *U.S. Public,* pg. 1722
PHOTOMATRIX CORPORATION; *U.S. Public,* pg. 1292
PHOTON KINETICS, INC.—See Relm Wireless Corp.; *U.S. Public,* pg. 1376
PHOTON SYSTEMS LTD.—See Tech-Sym Corporation; *U.S. Public,* pg. 1563
PHOTOPLAS LTD.—See Red Spot Paint & Varnish Co.; *U.S. Private,* pg. 915
PHOTOSUR GEOMAT INTERNATIONAL INC.—See SNC-Lavalin Group Inc.; *Int'l,* pg. 1162
PHOTOTYPE COLOR GRAPHICS, INC.; *U.S. Private,* pg. 864
PHOTRONICS, INC.; *U.S. Public,* pg. 1293
PHYCOR, INC.; *U.S. Public,* pg. 1293
PHYSICAL THERAPY CENTER—See Columbia/HCA Healthcare Corporation; *U.S. Public,* pg. 405
THE PHYSICIAN AND SPORTSMEDICINE—See The McGraw-Hill Companies; *U.S. Public,* pg. 1071
PHYSICIAN COMPUTER NETWORK, INC.; *U.S. Public,* pg. 1293
PHYSICIAN CORPORATION OF AMERICA; *U.S. Public,* pg. 1293
PHYSICIAN PARTNERS OF NEW ENGLAND, INC.—See Blue Cross and Blue Shield of Massachusetts; *U.S. Private,* pg. 151
PHYSICIAN PRACTICE MANAGEMENT—See Medpartners Inc.; *U.S. Public,* pg. 1082
PHYSICIAN SALES AND SERVICES INC.; *U.S. Public,* pg. 1293
PHYSICIAN SALES & SERVICES INC.—See Physician Sales and Services Inc.; *U.S. Public,* pg. 1294
PHYSICIAN'S FORMULARY SERVICES, INC.—See Integrated Health Services, Inc.; *U.S. Public,* pg. 885
PHYSICIANS HOSPITAL FOR EXTENDED CARE—See Horizon/CMS Healthcare Corporation; *U.S. Public,* pg. 837
PHYSICIANS INSURANCE COMPANY OF INDIANA—See Medical Assurance, Inc.; *U.S. Public,* pg. 1080
PHYSICIANS MUTUAL INSURANCE CO.; *U.S. Private,* pg. 864
PHYSICIANS WEIGHT LOSS CENTERS, INC.; *U.S. Private,* pg. 864
PHYSICS INTERNATIONAL CO.—See Olin Corporation; *U.S. Public,* pg. 1219
PHYSIO-CONTROL CORPORATION; *U.S. Public,* pg. 1294
PHYSIO-CONTROL S.A.R.L.—See Physio-Control Corporation; *U.S. Public,* pg. 1294
PHYSIOTHERAPY ASSOCIATES, INC.—See Stryker Corporation; *U.S. Public,* pg. 1526
PHYXIS CORPORATION—See Cardinal Health Inc.; *U.S. Public,* pg. 305
PI LIMITED—See Commerzbank AG; *Int'l,* pg. 312
PIASA MOTOR FUELS INC.; *U.S. Private,* pg. 864
PIASA OIL TRANSPORT INC.—See Piasa Motor Fuels Inc.; *U.S. Private,* pg. 864

PIAT PERE & FILS—See Diageo Plc; *Int'l,* pg. 410
PIBIVIESSE SPA (PBVS)—See Watts Industries, Inc.; *U.S. Public,* pg. 1747
PIBOON CONCRETE CO., LTD.—See Siam City Bank Public Company Limited; *Int'l,* pg. 1239
PIC DESIGN; *U.S. Private,* pg. 864
PIC'N PAY STORES, INC.; *U.S. Private,* pg. 864
PIC N'PAY SUPERMARKETS, INC.; *U.S. Private,* pg. 864
PALOMA PICASSO & CIE—See L'Oreal S.A.; *Int'l,* pg. 818
PICCADILLY ADVERTISING AGENCY, INC.—See Commerce Clearing House Corp.; *U.S. Public,* pg. 410
PICCADILLY CAFETERIAS, INC.; *U.S. Public,* pg. 1294
PICCADILLY RADIO—See EMAP Plc; *Int'l,* pg. 452
PICCADILLY RESTAURANTS, INC.—See Piccadilly Cafeterias, Inc.; *U.S. Public,* pg. 1294
PICK O' SEA FISHERIES, LTD.—See Clearwater Fine Foods Inc.; *Int'l,* pg. 297
PICK QUICK FOODS; *U.S. Private,* pg. 864
PICK QUICK PAPERS, INC.—See Central Lewmar; *U.S. Private,* pg. 223
PICKANDS MATHER & CO. INTERNATIONAL—See Cleveland-Cliffs Inc; *U.S. Public,* pg. 386
PICKER INTERNATIONAL CANADA INC.—See The General Electric Company, p.l.c.; *Int'l,* pg. 545
PICKER INTERNATIONAL GMBH—See The General Electric Company, p.l.c.; *Int'l,* pg. 545
PICKER INTERNATIONAL, INC.—See The General Electric Company, p.l.c.; *Int'l,* pg. 545
PICKERING INC.; *U.S. Private,* pg. 864
PICK'S COVE MARINA—See Pickering Inc.; *U.S. Private,* pg. 864
PICO BELLO WARENHANDELS GESELLSCHAFT MBH—See Karstadt Aktiengesellschaft; *Int'l,* pg. 724
PICO DESIGN, INC.—See Motorola, Inc.; *U.S. Public,* pg. 1138
PICO MACOM INC.—See Pico Products, Inc.; *U.S. Public,* pg. 1294
PICO-MATIC INC.—See Ohmite Manufacturing Company; *U.S. Private,* pg. 813
PICO PRODUCTS, INC.; *U.S. Public,* pg. 1294
THE PICTORIAL GAZETTE—See Journal Register Company; *U.S. Public,* pg. 935
PICTURETEL; *U.S. Public,* pg. 1294
PICTURETEL AG—See PictureTel; *U.S. Public,* pg. 1295
PICTURETEL CORPORATION-WORLD HEADQUARTERS—See PictureTel; *U.S. Public,* pg. 1295
PICTURETEL GMBH—See PictureTel; *U.S. Public,* pg. 1295
PICTURETEL INTERNATIONAL CORP.-ASIA PACIFIC/AMERICAS HEADQUARTERS—See PictureTel; *U.S. Public,* pg. 1295
PICTURETEL INTERNATIONAL CORPORATION-EUROPE/MIDDLE EAST/AFRICA—See PictureTel; *U.S. Public,* pg. 1295
PICTURETEL JAPAN KK—See PictureTel; *U.S. Public,* pg. 1295
PIE PIPER PRODUCTS, LTD.—See Vienna Sausage Mfg. Co.; *U.S. Private,* pg. 1140
PIEBURG AG—See Rheinmetall Group; *Int'l,* pg. 1108
PIEDMONT AIRLINES, INC.—See US Airways Group, Inc.; *U.S. Public,* pg. 1680
PIEDMONT AUTO EXCHANGE—See Republic Automotive Parts, Inc.; *U.S. Public,* pg. 1377
PIEDMONT ENERGY COMPANY—See Piedmont Natural Gas Co., Inc.; *U.S. Public,* pg. 1295
PIEDMONT INTERSTATE PIPELINE COMPANY—See Piedmont Natural Gas Co., Inc.; *U.S. Public,* pg. 1295
PIEDMONT INTRASTATE PIPELINE COMPANY—See Piedmont Natural Gas Co., Inc.; *U.S. Public,* pg. 1295
PIEDMONT MECHANICAL, INC.; *U.S. Private,* pg. 865
PIEDMONT METAL PRODUCTS, INC.—See Williams Industries, Inc.; *U.S. Public,* pg. 1770
PIEDMONT MINERALS—See Thiele Kaolin Co.; *U.S. Private,* pg. 1081
PIEDMONT MINERALS DIVISION—See Resco Products, Inc.; *U.S. Private,* pg. 924
PIEDMONT NATURAL GAS CO., INC.; *U.S. Public,* pg. 1295
PIEDMONT NURSING CENTER, INC.—See Vencor, Inc.; *U.S. Public,* pg. 1714
PIEDMONT OLSEN HENSLEY, INC.—See Heidemij N.V.; *Int'l,* pg. 607
PIEDMONT PUBLISHING CO., INC.—See Media General, Inc.; *U.S. Public,* pg. 1079
PIEDMONT TRUST BANK—See MainStreet BankGroup Incorporated; *U.S. Public,* pg. 1039
PIER CLUB, INC.—See Oriole Homes Corp.; *U.S. Public,* pg. 1231
PIER 1 IMPORTS CANADA—See Pier 1 Imports, Inc.; *U.S. Public,* pg. 1295
PIER 1 IMPORTS, INC.; *U.S. Public,* pg. 1295
PIERCE & STEVENS CORP.—See Sovereign Specialty Chemical, Inc.; *U.S. Private,* pg. 1019
PIERCE CHEMICAL COMPANY—See Perstorp AB; *Int'l,* pg. 1037
THE PIERCE CO., INC.—See Avis Industrial Corporation; *U.S. Private,* pg. 102
PIERCE COUNTY HERALD—See McClatchy Newspapers Inc.; *U.S. Public,* pg. 1066
PIERCE MANUFACTURING, INC.—See Oshkosh Truck Corporation; *U.S. Public,* pg. 1233
PIERCE NATIONAL LIFE INSURANCE CO.—See Liberty Corporation; *U.S. Public,* pg. 992
PIERCING PAGODA, INC.; *U.S. Public,* pg. 1296
THE PIERRE—See Four Seasons Hotels Inc.; *Int'l,* pg. 502
PIERRE CARDIN FORMAL WEAR—See West Mill Clothes, Inc.; *U.S. Private,* pg. 1163
PIERRE CARDIN KNITS—See Donnkenny, Inc.; *U.S. Public,* pg. 520
PIERRE FABRE—See Pierre Fabre S.A.; *Int'l,* pg. 1056
PIERRE FABRE S.A.; *Int'l,* pg. 1056
PIERRE ROBERT AB—See Unilever Plc; *Int'l,* pg. 1438
PIERRELATTE PLANT—See COGEMA - Compagnie Generale des Matieres Nucleaires; *Int'l,* pg. 305

PIERRE-LOTI—See Accor S.A.; *Int'l,* pg. 21
PIERS—See Pearson plc; *Int'l,* pg. 1026
PIERSON, HELDRING & PIERSON (CURACAO) N.V.—See ABN-AMRO Holding N.V.; *Int'l,* pg. 9
PIERSON, HELDRING & PIERSON N.V.—See ABN-AMRO Holding N.V.; *Int'l,* pg. 9
PIES, INC.—See Flowers Industries, Inc.; *U.S. Public,* pg. 658
PIETERMAN GLAS B.V.—See Carl-Zeiss-Stiftung; *Int'l,* pg. 1523
JOS. J. PIETRAFESA CO.; *U.S. Private,* pg. 865
PIETRO COSTA & C SRL—See Alusuisse-Lonza Holding Ltd.; *Int'l,* pg. 69
PIEZO CRYSTAL CO.; *U.S. Private,* pg. 865
PIG IMPROVEMENT GROUP LTD.—See Dalgety Plc; *Int'l,* pg. 376
PIGGING PRODUCTS—See T.D. Williamson, Inc.; *U.S. Private,* pg. 1180
PIGGLY WIGGLY CO.—See Fleming Companies, Inc.; *U.S. Public,* pg. 653
PIGGLY WIGGLY NORTHLAND CORP.—See Nash Finch Company; *U.S. Public,* pg. 1152
PIGGYBACK SERVICES, INC.—See Budco Group Inc.; *U.S. Private,* pg. 178
PIGMENTS & ADDITIVES—See Engelhard Corporation; *U.S. Public,* pg. 582
PIGNONE ENGINEERING LTD.—See Nuovo Pignone S.p.a.; *Int'l,* pg. 991
PIGNONE ESPANOLA S.A.—See Nuovo Pignone S.p.a.; *Int'l,* pg. 991
PIGNONE FRANCE S.A.R.L.—See Nuovo Pignone S.p.a.; *Int'l,* pg. 991
PIGNONE INC.—See Nuovo Pignone S.p.a.; *Int'l,* pg. 991
FREDERIC PIGUET S.A.—See SMH Swiss Corporation for Micro Electronics & Watchmaking Indus. Ltd.; *Int'l,* pg. 1160
PIHER BENELUX INTERNATIONAL BV—See Meggitt plc; *Int'l,* pg. 854
PIHER INTERNATIONAL CORPORATION—See Meggitt plc; *Int'l,* pg. 853
PIHER INTERNATIONAL GMBH—See Meggitt plc; *Int'l,* pg. 854
PIHER INTERNATIONAL LTD.—See Meggitt plc; *Int'l,* pg. 853
PIHER INTERNATIONAL SA—See Meggitt plc; *Int'l,* pg. 854
NV PIJPLEIDING ANTWERPEN-LIMBURG-LUIK—See DSM N.V.; *Int'l,* pg. 356
PIKE COUNTY LIGHT & POWER CO.—See Orange and Rockland Utilities, Inc.; *U.S. Public,* pg. 1229
PIKE & FISCHER—See The Bureau of National Affairs, Inc.; *U.S. Private,* pg. 182
PIKE INDUSTRIES INC.—See CRH, plc; *Int'l,* pg. 242
PIKNIK PRODUCTS COMPANY, INC.; *U.S. Private,* pg. 865
PILATUS BRITTEN-NORMAN LTD.—See Oerlikon-Buhrle Holding AG; *Int'l,* pg. 998
PILATUS FLUGZEUGWERKE AG—See Oerlikon-Buhrle Holding AG; *Int'l,* pg. 998
PILGRAM BAXTER & ASSOCIATES—See United Asset Management Corporation; *U.S. Public,* pg. 1673
PILGRIM'S PRIDE CORPORATION; *U.S. Public,* pg. 1296
PILIPINAS KAO INC.—See Kao Corporation; *Int'l,* pg. 718
PILIPINAS MAKRO INC.—See SHV Holdings N.V.; *Int'l,* pg. 1156
PILIPINAS SHELL PETROLEUM CORPORATION—See Royal Dutch/Shell Group of Companies; *Int'l,* pg. 1140
PILKINGTON AUSTRALASIA LIMITED—See Pilkington Plc; *Int'l,* pg. 1057
PILKINGTON (AUSTRALIA) OPERATIONS LIMITED—See Pilkington Plc; *Int'l,* pg. 1057
PILKINGTON BARNES HIND (PBH)—See Bain Capital; *U.S. Private,* pg. 111
PILKINGTON LAHDEN LASITEHDAS OY—See Pilkington Plc; *Int'l,* pg. 1056
PILKINGTON LAMINO OY—See Pilkington Plc; *Int'l,* pg. 1057
PILKINGTON (NEW ZEALAND) LIMITED—See Pilkington Plc; *Int'l,* pg. 1057
PILKINGTON PLC; *Int'l,* pg. 1056
PILKINGTON VIDROS LTDA—See Pilkington Plc; *Int'l,* pg. 1057
PILKINGTON'S TILES LTD.—See BTR plc; *Int'l,* pg. 124
PILLAR BUILDING PRODUCTS LTD.—See Caradon Plc; *Int'l,* pg. 267
PILLAR ELECTRICAL PLC—See Caradon Plc; *Int'l,* pg. 267
PILLAR ENGINEERING LTD.—See Caradon Plc; *Int'l,* pg. 267
PILLING WECK—See Teleflex Incorporated; *U.S. Public,* pg. 1569
PILLIOD FURNITURE—See Ladd Furniture, Inc.; *U.S. Public,* pg. 974
PILLOWTEX CORPORATION; *U.S. Public,* pg. 1296
PILLSBURY BAKERIES AND FOODSERVICE, INC.—See Diageo Plc; *Int'l,* pg. 411
PILLSBURY CANADA LTD.—See Diageo Plc; *Int'l,* pg. 411
PILLSBURY CO.—See Diageo Plc; *Int'l,* pg. 411
THE PILLSBURY COMPANY—See Diageo Plc; *Int'l,* pg. 411
PILLSBURY GRAIN EXPORT, INC.—See Diageo Plc; *Int'l,* pg. 411
PILMICO—See Diageo Plc; *Int'l,* pg. 411
PILOT AIR FREIGHT CORP.; *U.S. Private,* pg. 865
PILOT CORPORATION; *U.S. Public,* pg. 865
THE PILOT CORPORATION; *Int'l,* pg. 1057
THE PILOT CORPORATION OF AMERICA—See The Pilot Corporation; *Int'l,* pg. 1057
THE PILOT PEN CORP. OF AMERICA—See The Pilot Corporation; *Int'l,* pg. 1057
PILOT RECEIVABLES CORPORATION—See Pilot Corporation; *U.S. Private,* pg. 865
PILOT RESEARCH CORP.—See Alba-Waldensian, Inc.; *U.S. Public,* pg. 36

PILOT SOFTWARE—See Platinum Equity Holdings, LLC; *U.S. Private*, pg. 872
P.T. PIMAIMAS CITRA—See Mallinckrodt Inc.; *U.S. Public*, pg. 1040
PIMALCO INC.—See Aluminum Company of America; *U.S. Public*, pg. 61
PIMCO ADVISORS; *U.S. Public*, pg. 1296
PIMCO ADVISORS L.P.—See Pacific Life Insurance Company; *U.S. Private*, pg. 832
PINACO—See PNC Bank Corp.; *U.S. Public*, pg. 1244
PINAULT PRINTEMPS; *Int'l*, pg. 1057
PINAULT PRINTEMPS—See Pinault Printemps; *Int'l*, pg. 1057
PINCUS BROS., INC.; *U.S. Private*, pg. 865
PINE BEND LANDFILL, INC.—See Browning-Ferris Industries, Inc.; *U.S. Public*, pg. 264
PINE STATE BEVERAGE—See Pine State Trading Company; *U.S. Private*, pg. 865
PINE STATE TRADING COMPANY; *U.S. Private*, pg. 865
PINE STATE VENDING—See Pine State Trading Company; *U.S. Private*, pg. 865
PINE TOWERS CONVALESCENT HOSPITAL—See Vencor, Inc.; *U.S. Public*, pg. 1714
PINE TREE CASTINGS DIV.—See Sturm, Ruger & Co., Inc.; *U.S. Public*, pg. 1526
PINELANDS, INC.—See Chris-Craft Industries, Inc.; *U.S. Public*, pg. 352
PINELANDS WATER & WASTEWATER CO.—See Middlesex Water Company; *U.S. Public*, pg. 1110
PINELLAS CRABCOOKER, INC.—See Specialty Restaurants Corporation; *U.S. Private*, pg. 1023
PINELLAS FARMHOUSE, INC.—See Specialty Restaurants Corporation; *U.S. Private*, pg. 1023
PINEVILLE HEALTH CARE CENTER, INC.—See Vencor, Inc.; *U.S. Public*, pg. 1714
PINEWOOD STUDIOS LIMITED—See The Rank Group PLC; *Int'l*, pg. 1086
PINKERTON & LAWS INC.; *U.S. Private*, pg. 865
PINKERTON'S INC.; *U.S. Public*, pg. 1296
PINKHAM LUMBER—See Bowater Incorporated; *U.S. Public*, pg. 248
PINNACLE AUTOMATION INC.; *U.S. Private*, pg. 866
PINNACLE BANK; *U.S. Public*, pg. 1297
PINNACLE BANK—See Pinnacle Financial Services Inc.; *U.S. Public*, pg. 1297
PINNACLE BRANDS, INC.; *U.S. Private*, pg. 866
PINNACLE COATING & CONVERTING, INC.; *U.S. Private*, pg. 866
PINNACLE DATA CORPORATION—See National Insurance Group; *U.S. Public*, pg. 1158
PINNACLE EXPLORATION, INC.—See Coeur D'Alene Mines Corporation; *U.S. Public*, pg. 394
PINNACLE FINANCIAL SERVICES INC.; *U.S. Public*, pg. 1297
PINNACLE GAS TREATING, INC.—See Western Gas Resources, Inc.; *U.S. Public*, pg. 1758
PINNACLE MEDIA—See Wyse Advertising; *U.S. Private*, pg. 1194
PINNACLE SYSTEMS, INC.; *U.S. Public*, pg. 1297
PINNACLE TRADING CARD CO.—See Pinnacle Brands, Inc.; *U.S. Private*, pg. 866
PINNACLE WEST CAPITAL CORPORATION; *U.S. Public*, pg. 1297
PINSON MINE—See Barrick Gold Corporation; *Int'l*, pg. 169
PINSON MINING COMPANY—See Homestake Mining Company; *U.S. Public*, pg. 833
PINTACASA—See Corporacion Grupo Quimico, S.A.C.A.; *Int'l*, pg. 332
PIOLE—See Groupe Strafor Facom; *Int'l*, pg. 570
PIONEER AGRICULTURA LTDA.—See Pioneer Hi-Bred International, Inc.; *U.S. Private*, pg. 1299
PIONEER ALUMINUM, INC.; *U.S. Private*, pg. 866
PIONEER AMERICAN HOLDING COMPANY; *U.S. Public*, pg. 1298
PIONEER AMERICAN INSURANCE COMPANY—See PennCorp Financial Group, Inc.; *U.S. Public*, pg. 1271
PIONEER ARGENTINA, S.A.—See Pioneer Hi-Bred International, Inc.; *U.S. Public*, pg. 1299
PIONEER ASSOCIATES INC.—See The Pioneer Group, Inc.; *U.S. Public*, pg. 1298
PIONEER BIOGENE, PVT. LTD.—See Pioneer Hi-Bred International, Inc.; *U.S. Public*, pg. 1299
PIONEER CAPITAL CORPORATION—See The Pioneer Group, Inc.; *U.S. Public*, pg. 1298
PIONEER CLAIM MANAGEMENT, INC.—See Frontier Insurance Group, Inc.; *U.S. Public*, pg. 685
PIONEER CONCRETE OF AMERICA—See Pioneer International Ltd.; *Int'l*, pg. 1058
PIONEER CONCRETE OF TEXAS, INC.—See Pioneer International Ltd.; *Int'l*, pg. 1058
PIONEER DIRECT CORPORATION—See Conseco Inc.; *U.S. Public*, pg. 433
PIONEER/ECLIPSE CORP.—See Amano Corporation; *Int'l*, pg. 71
PIONEER ELECTRONIC CORPORATION; *Int'l*, pg. 1057
PIONEER ELECTRONIC (EUROPE) NV—See Pioneer Electronic Corporation; *Int'l*, pg. 1058
PIONEER ELECTRONICS ASIA CENTRE PTE. LTD.—See Pioneer Electronic Corporation; *Int'l*, pg. 1058
PIONEER ELECTRONICS MANUFACTURING NV—See Pioneer Electronic Corporation; *Int'l*, pg. 1058
PIONEER ELECTRONICS (USA) INC.—See Pioneer Electronic Corporation; *Int'l*, pg. 1058
PIONEER EXPRESS INC.—See Vitran Corporation Inc.; *Int'l*, pg. 1469
PIONEER FINANCE CORP.—See Santa Fe Gaming Corporation; *U.S. Public*, pg. 1432
PIONEER FIRST POLISH TRUST—See The Pioneer Group, Inc.; *U.S. Public*, pg. 1298
PIONEER FLOUR MILLS; *U.S. Private*, pg. 866
PIONEER FOODS, INC.; *U.S. Private*, pg. 866
G.I.E. PIONEER FRANCE—See Pioneer Hi-Bred International, Inc.; *U.S. Public*, pg. 1299

PIONEER FRANCE MAIS S.A.—See Pioneer Hi-Bred International, Inc.; *U.S. Public*, pg. 1299
PIONEER FUNDS DISTRIBUTOR, INC.—See The Pioneer Group, Inc.; *U.S. Public*, pg. 1298
PIONEER FUNDS MARKETING GMBH—See The Pioneer Group, Inc.; *U.S. Public*, pg. 1298
PIONEER GOLDFIELDS LIMITED—See The Pioneer Group, Inc.; *U.S. Public*, pg. 1298
THE PIONEER GROUP, INC.; *U.S. Public*, pg. 1298
PIONEER HI-BRED AUSTRALIA PTY. LTD.—See Pioneer Hi-Bred International, Inc.; *U.S. Public*, pg. 1298
PIONEER HI-BRED INTERNATIONAL, INC.; *U.S. Public*, pg. 1298
PIONEER HI-BRED ITALIA S.P.A.—See Pioneer Hi-Bred International, Inc.; *U.S. Public*, pg. 1299
PIONEER HI-BRED JAPAN CO. LTD.—See Pioneer Hi-Bred International, Inc.; *U.S. Public*, pg. 1299
PIONEER HI-BRED LIMITED—See Pioneer Hi-Bred International, Inc.; *U.S. Public*, pg. 1299
PIONEER HI-BRED (THAILAND) CO. LTD.—See Pioneer Hi-Bred International, Inc.; *U.S. Public*, pg. 1299
P.T. PIONEER HIBRIDA INDONESIA—See Pioneer Hi-Bred International, Inc.; *U.S. Public*, pg. 1299
PIONEER HOTEL INC.—See Santa Fe Gaming Corporation; *U.S. Public*, pg. 1432
PIONEER INTERNATIONAL CORPORATION—See The Pioneer Group, Inc.; *U.S. Public*, pg. 1298
PIONEER INTERNATIONAL LTD.; *Int'l*, pg. 1058
PIONEER INTERNATIONAL OPERATIONS DIVISION—See Pioneer Hi-Bred International, Inc.; *U.S. Public*, pg. 1299
PIONEER INVESTMENTS CORPORATION—See The Pioneer Group, Inc.; *U.S. Public*, pg. 1298
PIONEER INVESTMENTS POLAND LTD—See The Pioneer Group, Inc.; *U.S. Public*, pg. 1298
PIONEER LIFE INSURANCE CO. OF ILLINOIS—See Conseco Inc.; *U.S. Public*, pg. 434
PIONEER MANAGEMENT (IRELAND) LIMITED—See The Pioneer Group, Inc.; *U.S. Public*, pg. 1298
PIONEER MEDICAL SERVICES, INC.—See Integrated Health Services, Inc.; *U.S. Public*, pg. 885
PIONEER METALS & TECHNOLOGY, INC.—See The Pioneer Group, Inc.; *U.S. Public*, pg. 1298
PIONEER MILL COMPANY, LTD.—See JMB Realty Corporation; *U.S. Private*, pg. 578
PIONEER MUTUAL LIFE INSURANCE COMPANY; *U.S. Private*, pg. 866
PIONEER NATURAL RESOURCES CO.; *U.S. Public*, pg. 866
PIONEER NEW MEDIA TECHNOLOGIES; *U.S. Private*, pg. 866
PIONEER NEWS—See Landmark Communications, Inc.; *U.S. Private*, pg. 648
PIONEER OIL COMPANY INC.; *U.S. Private*, pg. 866
PIONEER OVERSEAS CORPORATION (THAILAND), LTD.—See Pioneer Hi-Bred International, Inc.; *U.S. Public*, pg. 1299
PIONEER OVERSEAS, GES.MBH.—See Pioneer Hi-Bred International, Inc.; *U.S. Public*, pg. 1299
PIONEER PAPER CORPORATION; *U.S. Private*, pg. 867
PIONEER PLANS CORPORATION—See The Pioneer Group, Inc.; *U.S. Public*, pg. 1298
PIONEER PLASTERBOARD PTY LTD.—See Lafarge S.A.; *Int'l*, pg. 791
PIONEER PLASTICS CORPORATION; *U.S. Private*, pg. 867
PIONEER POLAND U.K. L.P.—See Commerzbank AG; *Int'l*, pg. 312
PIONEER PRESS NEWSPAPERS INC.—See Hollinger Inc.; *Int'l*, pg. 632
PIONEER SAATEN AG—See Pioneer Hi-Bred International, Inc.; *U.S. Public*, pg. 1299
PIONEER SAATEN, GMBH—See Pioneer Hi-Bred International, Inc.; *U.S. Public*, pg. 1299
PIONEER SBIC CORP.—See The Pioneer Group, Inc.; *U.S. Public*, pg. 1298
PIONEER SECURITY LIFE INS. CO.—See PennCorp Financial Group, Inc.; *U.S. Public*, pg. 1271
PIONEER SEMENTES LTDA.—See Pioneer Hi-Bred International, Inc.; *U.S. Public*, pg. 1299
PIONEER SNACKS—See Melody Foods, Inc.; *U.S. Public*, pg. 730
PIONEER STANDARD CANADA INC.—See Pioneer-Standard Electronics, Inc.; *U.S. Public*, pg. 1300
PIONEER-STANDARD ELECTRONICS, INC.; *U.S. Public*, pg. 1300
PIONEER STANDARD OF MARYLAND, INC.—See Pioneer-Standard Electronics, Inc.; *U.S. Public*, pg. 1300
PIONEER STEEL & TUBE—See Russel Metals Inc.; *Int'l*, pg. 1150
PIONEER TOHUMCULUK A.S.—See Pioneer Hi-Bred International, Inc.; *U.S. Public*, pg. 1299
PIONEER TOOL & MOLD, INC.—See Plastek Group; *U.S. Private*, pg. 870
PIONEERING MANAGEMENT CORPORATION—See The Pioneer Group, Inc.; *U.S. Public*, pg. 1298
PIONEERING SERVICES CORPORATION—See The Pioneer Group, Inc.; *U.S. Public*, pg. 1298
PIP PRINTING—See Franchise Services, Inc.; *U.S. Public*, pg. 423
PIPE FABRICATING & SUPPLY COMPANY; *U.S. Private*, pg. 867
PIPE REPAIRS.—See Team, Inc.; *U.S. Public*, pg. 1562
PIPECO SERVICES; *U.S. Private*, pg. 867
PIPELINE ENGINEERING GESELLSCHAFT FUR PLANUNG, BAU- UND BETRIEBSUBERWACHUNG VON FERNLEITUNGEN MBH—See Ruhrgas Aktiengesellschaft; *Int'l*, pg. 1148
PIPELINE INDUCTION HEAT LIMITED—See Weatherford Enterra Incorporated; *U.S. Public*, pg. 1750
PIPELINE SUD-EUROPEEN—See Royal Dutch/Shell Group of Companies; *Int'l*, pg. 1138

THE PIPELINES OF PUERTO RICO, INC.—See Texaco Inc.; *U.S. Public*, pg. 1584
PIPER CAPITAL MANAGEMENT, INCORPORATED—See Piper Jaffray Companies, Inc.; *U.S. Public*, pg. 1303
PIPER IMPACT, INC.—See Quanex Corporation; *U.S. Public*, pg. 1349
PIPER INDEMNITY LTD.—See Occidental Petroleum Corporation; *U.S. Public*, pg. 1210
PIPER, JAFFRAY & HOPWOOD INCORPORATED, LONDON—See Piper Jaffray Companies, Inc.; *U.S. Public*, pg. 1303
PIPER JAFFRAY COMPANIES, INC.; *U.S. Public*, pg. 1300
PIPER JAFFRAY INC.—See Piper Jaffray Companies, Inc.; *U.S. Public*, pg. 1302
PIPER JAFFRAY, INC.—See Piper Jaffray Companies, Inc.; *U.S. Public*, pg. 1303
PIPER JAFFRAY INC.—See Piper Jaffray Companies, Inc.; *U.S. Public*, pg. 1303
PIPER JAFFRAY VENTURES INC.—See Piper Jaffray Companies, Inc.; *U.S. Public*, pg. 1303
PIPER TRUST COMPANY—See Piper Jaffray Companies, Inc.; *U.S. Public*, pg. 1303
PIPETRONIX INC.—See Preussag AG; *Int'l*, pg. 1070
PIPETRONIX LTD.—See Preussag AG; *Int'l*, pg. 1071
PIPING RESOURCES—See Bovaird Supply Co.; *U.S. Private*, pg. 162
PIQUNIQ MANAGEMENT CORP.—See Arctic Slope Regional Corporation; *U.S. Private*, pg. 80
PIRELLA GOTTSCHE LOWE—See The Lowe Group; *U.S. Private*, pg. 678
PIRELLA NASTRI TECNICI S.P.A.—See Pirelli S.p.A.; *Int'l*, pg. 1058
PIRELLI ARGENTINA DE MANDATOS S.A.—See Pirelli S.p.A.; *Int'l*, pg. 1059
PIRELLI ARMSTRONG EXTRUDED PRODUCTS DIVISION—See Pirelli S.p.A.; *Int'l*, pg. 1058
PIRELLI ARMSTRONG MIDWEST DIVISION—See Pirelli S.p.A.; *Int'l*, pg. 1058
PIRELLI ARMSTRONG PACIFIC COAST DIVISION—See Pirelli S.p.A.; *Int'l*, pg. 1058
PIRELLI ARMSTRONG SOUTHEAST DIVISION—See Pirelli S.p.A.; *Int'l*, pg. 1058
PIRELLI ARMSTRONG TIRE CORPORATION—See Pirelli S.p.A.; *Int'l*, pg. 1058
PIRELLI ATG VERTRIEBSGESELLSCHAFT M.B.H.—See Pirelli S.p.A.; *Int'l*, pg. 1059
PIRELLI BEDDING BENELUX S.A.—See Pirelli S.p.A.; *Int'l*, pg. 1059
PIRELLI CABLE CORPORATION—See Pirelli S.p.A.; *Int'l*, pg. 1059
PIRELLI CABLE, FIBER OPTIC DIV.—See Pirelli S.p.A.; *Int'l*, pg. 1059
PIRELLI CABLE, POWER CABLE DIV.—See Pirelli S.p.A.; *Int'l*, pg. 1059
PIRELLI CABLE, POWER DIV. SERVICE CENTER—See Pirelli S.p.A.; *Int'l*, pg. 1059
PIRELLI CABLES AUSTRALIA LIMITED—See Pirelli S.p.A.; *Int'l*, pg. 1059
PIRELLI CABLES SAIC—See Pirelli S.p.A.; *Int'l*, pg. 1059
PIRELLI CAVI S.P.A.—See Pirelli S.p.A.; *Int'l*, pg. 1058
PIRELLI CAVI S.P.A., DIVISIONE ITALIA - AZIENDA ACCESSORI CAVI—See Pirelli S.p.A.; *Int'l*, pg. 1058
PIRELLI CAVI S.P.A., DIVISIONE ITALIA - AZIENDA CAVI SPECIALI—See Pirelli S.p.A.; *Int'l*, pg. 1058
PIRELLI CONSTRUCTION COMPANY LTD.—See Pirelli S.p.A.; *Int'l*, pg. 1059
PIRELLI COORDINAMENTO PNEUMATICI S.P.A.—See Pirelli S.p.A.; *Int'l*, pg. 1058
PIRELLI DEUTSCHLAND A.G.—See Pirelli S.p.A.; *Int'l*, pg. 1059
PIRELLI ENFIELD SUPERTENSION CABLES LTD.—See Pirelli S.p.A.; *Int'l*, pg. 1059
PIRELLI FOCOM LTD.—See Pirelli S.p.A.; *Int'l*, pg. 1059
PIRELLI FRANCE S.A.—See Pirelli S.p.A.; *Int'l*, pg. 1059
PIRELLI GESELLSCHAFT M.B.H.—See Pirelli S.p.A.; *Int'l*, pg. 1059
PIRELLI INDUSTRIAL HOSES S.A.—See Pirelli S.p.A.; *Int'l*, pg. 1059
PIRELLI INFORMATICA S.P.A.—See Pirelli S.p.A.; *Int'l*, pg. 1058
PIRELLI JACOBSON, INC.—See Pirelli S.p.A.; *Int'l*, pg. 1059
PIRELLI JEROME INC.—See Pirelli S.p.A.; *Int'l*, pg. 1059
PIRELLI METZELER MOTOVELO S.R.L.—See Pirelli S.p.A.; *Int'l*, pg. 1059
PIRELLI NEUMSTICOS—See Pirelli S.p.A.; *Int'l*, pg. 1059
PIRELLI PLC—See Pirelli S.p.A.; *Int'l*, pg. 1058
PIRELLI REIFENWERKE GMBH—See Pirelli S.p.A.; *Int'l*, pg. 1059
PIRELLI S.A. COMPANHIA INDUSTRIAL BRASILEIRA—See Pirelli S.p.A.; *Int'l*, pg. 1059
PIRELLI S.A.C.I.C.—See Pirelli S.p.A.; *Int'l*, pg. 1059
PIRELLI SAPSA S.P.A.—See Pirelli S.p.A.; *Int'l*, pg. 1058
PIRELLI SCANDINAVIA AB—See Pirelli S.p.A.; *Int'l*, pg. 1059
PIRELLI SERVOCAVI S.P.A.—See Pirelli S.p.A.; *Int'l*, pg. 1058
PIRELLI SISTEMI ANTIVIBRANTI S.P.A.—See Pirelli S.p.A.; *Int'l*, pg. 1058
PIRELLI S.P.A.; *Int'l*, pg. 1058
PIRELLI TIRE INC.—See Pirelli S.p.A.; *Int'l*, pg. 1059
PIRELLI TRANSMISSIONS INDUSTRIELLES—See Pirelli S.p.A.; *Int'l*, pg. 1059
PIRELLI TRI-STATE INC.—See Pirelli S.p.A.; *Int'l*, pg. 1059
PIRELLI TYRES AUSTRALIA PTY. LTD.—See Pirelli S.p.A.; *Int'l*, pg. 1059
PIRELLI TYRES BENELUX S.A.—See Pirelli S.p.A.; *Int'l*, pg. 1059
PIRELLI UK PLC—See Pirelli S.p.A.; *Int'l*, pg. 1059
PIRELLI U.K. TYRES LIMITED—See Pirelli S.p.A.; *Int'l*, pg. 1059
PIRELLI VERTRIEBS G.M.B.H.—See Pirelli S.p.A.; *Int'l*, pg. 1059
MALCOLM PIRNIE, INC.; *U.S. Private*, pg. 867

Company Index

PITCO FRIALATOR INC.—See Maytag Corporation; *U.S. Public*, pg. 1065
PITCO MASTERMATIC INC.—See Heat & Control, Inc.; *U.S. Private*, pg. 518
PITKIN COUNTY BANK & TRUST COMPANY—See Zions Bancorporation; *U.S. Public*, pg. 1793
PITKIN GUIDES—See Reed Elsevier plc; *Int'l*, pg. 1094
HAROLD M. PITMAN CO., INC.; *U.S. Private*, pg. 867
PITMAN PUBLISHING LTD.—See Pearson plc; *Int'l*, pg. 1025
PITNEY BOWES BUSINESS SUPPLIES & SERVICES—See Pitney Bowes Inc.; *U.S. Public*, pg. 1303
PITNEY BOWES BUSINESS SYSTEMS-INTERNATIONAL—See Pitney Bowes Inc.; *U.S. Public*, pg. 1303
PITNEY BOWES BUSINESS SYSTEMS-U.S.—See Pitney Bowes Inc.; *U.S. Public*, pg. 1303
PITNEY BOWES CREDIT CORPORATION—See Pitney Bowes Inc.; *U.S. Public*, pg. 1303
PITNEY BOWES DEUTSCHLAND G.M.B.H.—See Pitney Bowes Inc.; *U.S. Public*, pg. 1303
PITNEY BOWES DIRECT—See Pitney Bowes Inc.; *U.S. Public*, pg. 1304
PITNEY BOWES FINANCIAL SERVICES—See Pitney Bowes Inc.; *U.S. Public*, pg. 1303
PITNEY BOWES FRANCE SOCIETE ANONYME (S.A.)—See Pitney Bowes Inc.; *U.S. Public*, pg. 1304
PITNEY BOWES GES.B.H.—See Pitney Bowes Inc.; *U.S. Public*, pg. 1304
PITNEY BOWES INC.; *U.S. Public*, pg. 1303
PITNEY BOWES JAPAN—See Pitney Bowes Inc.; *U.S. Public*, pg. 1304
PITNEY BOWES LTD.—See Pitney Bowes Inc.; *U.S. Public*, pg. 1304
PITNEY BOWES MANAGEMENT SERVICES—See Pitney Bowes Inc.; *U.S. Public*, pg. 1304
PITNEY BOWES OF CANADA LTD.—See Pitney Bowes Inc.; *U.S. Public*, pg. 1304
PITNEY BOWES OF CANADA LTD.-LEASING DIV.—See Pitney Bowes Inc.; *U.S. Public*, pg. 1304
PITNEY BOWES OY—See Pitney Bowes Inc.; *U.S. Public*, pg. 1304
PITNEY BOWES REAL ESTATE FINANCING CORPORATION—See Pitney Bowes Inc.; *U.S. Public*, pg. 1303
PITNEY BOWES SOFTWARE SYSTEMS—See Pitney Bowes Inc.; *U.S. Public*, pg. 1304
PITNEY BOWES SVENSKA AKTIEBOLAG—See Pitney Bowes Inc.; *U.S. Public*, pg. 1304
PITNEY BOWES (SWITZERLAND) AG—See Pitney Bowes Inc.; *U.S. Public*, pg. 1304
PITT-DES MOINES, INC.; *U.S. Public*, pg. 1304
PITTLER BENEVOLENT FUND GMBH—See Rothenberger Group GmbH; *Int'l*, pg. 1128
PITTLER GMBH—See Rothenberger Group GmbH; *Int'l*, pg. 1128
PITTLER INVENTION GMBH—See Rothenberger Group GmbH; *Int'l*, pg. 1128
PITTLER MAQUINAS LTDA.—See Rothenberger Group GmbH; *Int'l*, pg. 1128
PITTLER MASCHINENFABRIK AG—See Rothenberger Group GmbH; *Int'l*, pg. 1128
PITTLER-TORNOS GMBH—See Rothenberger Group GmbH; *Int'l*, pg. 1128
PITTLER TRAINING GMBH—See Rothenberger Group GmbH; *Int'l*, pg. 1128
PITTLER (U.K.) LTD.—See Rothenberger Group GmbH; *Int'l*, pg. 1128
THE PITTMAN COMPANY—See Penn Engineering & Manufacturing Corp.; *U.S. Public*, pg. 1270
PITTRA—See Atalanta Corporation; *U.S. Private*, pg. 94
THE PITTSBURG & MIDWAY COAL MINING CO.—See Chevron Corporation; *U.S. Public*, pg. 348
PITTSBURGH MORNING SUN—See Shivers Trading & Operating Co.; *U.S. Private*, pg. 995
PITTSBURGH ASSOCIATES; *U.S. Private*, pg. 867
PITTSBURGH BREWING COMPANY—See Keystone Brewers, Inc.; *U.S. Private*, pg. 619
PITTSBURGH-CANFIELD CORP.—See WHX Corporation; *U.S. Public*, pg. 1726
PITTSBURGH, CHARTIERS & YOUGHIOGHENY RAILWAY CO.—See Conrail, Inc.; *U.S. Public*, pg. 432
PITTSBURGH CORNING CORPORATION—See Corning Incorporated; *U.S. Public*, pg. 449
PITTSBURGH CORNING EUROPE, N.V.—See Corning Incorporated; *U.S. Public*, pg. 449
PITTSBURGH GEAR COMPANY—See Brad Foote Gear Works, Inc.; *U.S. Private*, pg. 417
PITTSBURGH PIRATES—See Pittsburgh Associates; *U.S. Private*, pg. 867
PITTSBURGH STADIUM CONCESSIONS, INC.—See Aramark Corp.; *U.S. Private*, pg. 79
PITTSBURGH TUBE CO.; *U.S. Private*, pg. 867
PITTSBURGH TUBE CO.-MONROE DIV.—See Pittsburgh Tube Co.; *U.S. Private*, pg. 868
THE PITTSTON COMPANY; *U.S. Public*, pg. 1305
PITTSTON MINERALS GROUP, INC.—See The Pittston Company; *U.S. Public*, pg. 1305
PITTWAY CORPORATION; *U.S. Public*, pg. 1305
PITTWAY CORP. OF CANADA—See Pittway Corporation; *U.S. Public*, pg. 1307
PITTWAY REAL ESTATE—See Pittway Corporation; *U.S. Public*, pg. 1306
PITTWAY SYSTEMS TECHNOLOGY GRP.—See Pittway Corporation; *U.S. Public*, pg. 1306
PITTWAY TECNOLOGICA S.P.A.—See Pittway Corporation; *U.S. Public*, pg. 1307
PIXAR ANIMATION STUDIOS; *U.S. Public*, pg. 1307
THE PIZZA FACTORY—See Northern Foods plc; *Int'l*, pg. 968
PIZZA HAVEN INC.; *U.S. Private*, pg. 868
PIZZA HUT—See Whitbread PLC; *Int'l*, pg. 1499
PIZZA HUT DIVISION—See NPC International, Inc.; *U.S. Public*, pg. 1147

PIZZA HUT, INC.—See Tricon Global Restaurants, Inc.; *U.S. Public*, pg. 1636
PIZZA HUT PROPERTIES PTY. LTD.—See Tricon Global Restaurants, Inc.; *U.S. Public*, pg. 1637
PIZZA HUT (UK) LTD.—See Whitbread PLC; *Int'l*, pg. 1499
PIZZA HUT (UK) LTD.—See Tricon Global Restaurants, Inc.; *U.S. Public*, pg. 1637
PIZZA HUT (USSR)—See Tricon Global Restaurants, Inc.; *U.S. Public*, pg. 1637
PIZZA INN, INC.; *U.S. Public*, pg. 1307
PIZZAGALLI CONSTRUCTION CO.; *U.S. Private*, pg. 868
PLACER DOME INC.; *Int'l*, pg. 1060
PLACER DOME LATIN AMERICA—See Placer Dome Inc.; *Int'l*, pg. 1060
PLACER DOME NORTH AMERICA—See Placer Dome Inc.; *Int'l*, pg. 1060
PLACER PACIFIC LIMITED—See Placer Dome Inc.; *Int'l*, pg. 1060
PLACOPLATRE S.A.—See BPB Industries PLC; *Int'l*, pg. 123
PLADA S.P.A.—See H.J. Heinz Company; *U.S. Public*, pg. 807
PLAID CLOTHING COMPANY—See Hartmarx Corporation; *U.S. Public*, pg. 796
PLAID ENTERPRISES INC.—See The Dyson-Kissner-Moran Corporation; *U.S. Private*, pg. 352
PLAID PANTRIES, INC.; *U.S. Private*, pg. 868
PLAIN STREET PROPERTIES, INC.—See Hannaford Bros. Co.; *U.S. Public*, pg. 782
PLAINS CO-OP OIL MILL; *U.S. Private*, pg. 868
PLAINS COTTON CO-OP ASSOCIATION; *U.S. Private*, pg. 868
PLAINS ELECTRIC GENERATION TRANSMISSION CO-OP, INC.; *U.S. Private*, pg. 868
PLAINS ILLINOIS, INC.—See Plains Resources Inc.; *U.S. Public*, pg. 1308
PLAINS MARKETING & TRANSPORTATION—See Plains Resources Inc.; *U.S. Public*, pg. 1308
PLAINS PETROLEUM COMPANY—See Barrett Resources Corporation; *U.S. Public*, pg. 191
PLAINS PETROLEUM OPERATING CO.—See Barrett Resources Corporation; *U.S. Public*, pg. 191
PLAINS RESOURCES INC.; *U.S. Public*, pg. 1307
PLAINVIEW DAILY HERALD—See The Hearst Corporation; *U.S. Private*, pg. 517
PLAINVILLE STOCK COMPANY, INC.; *U.S. Private*, pg. 868
PLAMEX, S.A. DE C.V.—See Plantronics Inc.; *U.S. Public*, pg. 1308
PLAN INTERNATIONAL USA, INC.; *U.S. Private*, pg. 869
PLAN OBJECT GMBH—See De La Rue plc; *Int'l*, pg. 388
PLAND STAINLESS LTD.—See Lonrho plc; *Int'l*, pg. 817
PLANES MOVING & STORAGE COMPANY OF COLUMBUS—See Planes Moving And Storage, Inc.; *U.S. Private*, pg. 869
PLANES MOVING AND STORAGE, INC.; *U.S. Private*, pg. 869
PLANES MOVING & STORAGE OF DAYTON, INC.—See Planes Moving And Storage, Inc.; *U.S. Private*, pg. 869
PLANES MOVING & STORAGE OF INDIANAPOLIS, INC.—See Planes Moving And Storage, Inc.; *U.S. Private*, pg. 869
PLANET EARTH PRODUCTS—See K2 Inc.; *U.S. Public*, pg. 940
PLANET MUSIC—See Borders Group, Inc.; *U.S. Public*, pg. 245
PLANET PRODUCTS CORP.; *U.S. Private*, pg. 869
PLANNING CORPORATION OF AMERICA—See Raymond James Financial, Inc.; *U.S. Public*, pg. 923
PLANNING SYSTEMS INC.; *U.S. Private*, pg. 869
PLANO CORPORATION; *U.S. Private*, pg. 869
PLANOX B.V.—See Gamma Holding N.V.; *Int'l*, pg. 540
PLANT ALDERSBACH—See Knorr-Bremse AG; *Int'l*, pg. 738
PLANT & TOOLS LTD.—See Wolseley Plc; *Int'l*, pg. 1512
PLANT BENNECKENSTEIN—See Knorr-Bremse AG; *Int'l*, pg. 738
PLANT CITY STEEL CO.—See Harsco Corporation; *U.S. Public*, pg. 793
PLANT CONSTRUCTION PLC—See Haden Maclellan Holdings plc; *Int'l*, pg. 585
PLANT DESIGN & MANAGEMENT CORP.—See EEI Corporation; *Int'l*, pg. 426
PLANT ENGINEERING CONSULTANTS—See TB Wood's Corporation; *U.S. Public*, pg. 1562
PLANT MAINTENANCE, INC.—See Snelling Personnel Services; *U.S. Private*, pg. 1011
PLANT MAINTENANCE SERVICE CORPORATION; *U.S. Private*, pg. 869
PLANTA KODAK—See Eastman Kodak Company; *U.S. Public*, pg. 554
PLANTACIONES MESOPOTAMICAS—See Corporacion MAPFRE, Compania Internacional de Reaseguros, S.A.; *Int'l*, pg. 333
PLANTATION FOODS INC.; *U.S. Private*, pg. 869
PLANTATION PIPE LINE CO.—See Chevron Corporation; *U.S. Public*, pg. 348
PLANTATIONS LEVER AU ZAIRE S.A.R.L.—See Unilever Plc; *Int'l*, pg. 1438
PLANTATIONS PAMOL DU CAMEROON LTD.—See Unilever Plc; *Int'l*, pg. 1438
PLANTERS BANK—See First Tennessee National Corporation; *U.S. Public*, pg. 639
PLANTERS COMPANY—See RJR Nabisco Holdings Corp.; *U.S. Public*, pg. 1355
PLANTRONICS ACOUSTICS ITALIA S.R.L.—See Plantronics Inc.; *U.S. Public*, pg. 1308
PLANTRONICS A.G.—See Plantronics Inc.; *U.S. Public*, pg. 1308
PLANTRONICS B.V.—See Plantronics Inc.; *U.S. Public*, pg. 1308
PLANTRONICS CANADA LIMITED—See Plantronics Inc.; *U.S. Public*, pg. 1308

PLANTRONICS FRANCE S.A.R.L.—See Plantronics Inc.; *U.S. Public*, pg. 1308
PLANTRONICS GMBH—See Plantronics Inc.; *U.S. Public*, pg. 1308
PLANTRONICS HONG KONG—See Plantronics Inc.; *U.S. Public*, pg. 1308
PLANTRONICS INC.; *U.S. Public*, pg. 1308
PLANTRONICS INTERNATIONAL DO BRASIL LTDA—See Plantronics Inc.; *U.S. Public*, pg. 1308
PLANTRONICS K.K.—See Plantronics Inc.; *U.S. Public*, pg. 1308
PLANTRONICS LTD.—See Plantronics Inc.; *U.S. Public*, pg. 1308
PLANTRONICS NORDIC—See Plantronics Inc.; *U.S. Public*, pg. 1308
PLANTRONICS SINGAPORE—See Plantronics Inc.; *U.S. Public*, pg. 1308
PLANTS, SITES & PARKS—See VNU Verenigde Nederlandse Uitgeversbedrijven B.V.; *Int'l*, pg. 1446
PLAS-TECHS, INC.—See Badger Paper Mills, Inc.; *U.S. Public*, pg. 165
PLASANIT HAUSTECHNIK—See Mannesmann A.G.; *Int'l*, pg. 838
PLASANIT SARL—See Mannesmann A.G.; *Int'l*, pg. 838
PLASBOARD PLASTICS LIMITED—See James Cream PLC; *Int'l*, pg. 341
PLASCAL CORPORATION; *U.S. Private*, pg. 870
PLASCOAT SYSTEMS LIMITED—See BTR plc; *Int'l*, pg. 129
PLASCON (PTY) LTD.—See Barlow Ltd.; *Int'l*, pg. 167
PLASDOX—See Lafarge S.A.; *Int'l*, pg. 789
PLASKOLITE INC.; *U.S. Public*, pg. 870
PLASKON ELECTRONIC MATERIALS, LTD.—See Rohm and Haas Company; *U.S. Public*, pg. 1404
PLASMA ENERGY CORPORATION—See ChemFirst Inc.; *U.S. Public*, pg. 344
PLASMA TECHNIK COATING SYSTEMS S.E.A. PTE LTD.—See Sulzer Ltd.; *Int'l*, pg. 1307
PLASMA TECHNOLOGY, INC.; *U.S. Private*, pg. 870
PLASMA-THERM, INC.; *U.S. Public*, pg. 1308
PLASMAR LTD.—See Scapa Group Plc; *Int'l*, pg. 1202
PLASMA-TECHNIK LTD.—See Sulzer Ltd.; *Int'l*, pg. 1308
PLASMA-TECHNIK S.A.—See Sulzer Ltd.; *Int'l*, pg. 1308
PLASRO PLASTICS LIMITED—See Carclo Engineering Group plc; *Int'l*, pg. 268
PLASTAG CORPORATION; *U.S. Private*, pg. 870
PLASTECH CORPORATION; *U.S. Private*, pg. 870
PLASTEK GROUP; *U.S. Private*, pg. 870
PLASTEK INDUSTRIES, INC.—See Plastek Group; *U.S. Private*, pg. 870
PLASTEX EXTRUDERS, INC., USA—See Enterprises International Inc.; *U.S. Private*, pg. 378
PLASTI-KOTE COMPANY INC.; *U.S. Private*, pg. 870
PLASTI-LINE COLUMBIA, INC.—See Plasti-Line, Inc.; *U.S. Public*, pg. 1309
PLASTI-LINE, INC.; *U.S. Public*, pg. 1308
PLASTI-LINE WEST—See Plasti-Line, Inc.; *U.S. Public*, pg. 1309
PLASTIC CONTAINERS, INC.—See Continental Can Co.; *U.S. Public*, pg. 440
PLASTIC ENGINEERED COMPONENTS INC.; *U.S. Public*, pg. 870
PLASTIC ENGINEERING CO. INC.; *U.S. Private*, pg. 871
PLASTIC FORM INC.—See MascoTech, Inc.; *U.S. Public*, pg. 1055
PLASTIC MOLDINGS CORP.; *U.S. Private*, pg. 871
PLASTIC PACKAGING COMPANY—See Alltrista Corporation; *U.S. Public*, pg. 57
PLASTIC PACKAGING, INC.; *U.S. Private*, pg. 871
PLASTIC PADDING A/S—See Henkel KGaA; *Int'l*, pg. 611
PLASTIC PARTS, INC.—See Myers Industries, Inc.; *U.S. Public*, pg. 1143
PLASTIC REEL CORP. OF AMERICA; *U.S. Private*, pg. 871
PLASTIC SUPPLIERS, INC.; *U.S. Private*, pg. 871
PLASTIC TRIM, INC.—See JPE, Inc.; *U.S. Public*, pg. 919
PLASTICHANGE INTERNATIONAL—See The Cascades Group; *Int'l*, pg. 273
PLASTICOS BEST SA—See Saint-Gobain; *Int'l*, pg. 1171
PLASTICOS DE MANTENIMIENTO SA DE CV—See DSM N.V.; *Int'l*, pg. 356
PLASTICOS EXTRUIDOS, S.A.—See FMC Corporation; *U.S. Public*, pg. 607
PLASTICOS MARATON, S.A.—See Mattel, Inc.; *U.S. Public*, pg. 1059
PLASTICOS PLAVINIL S.A.—See Solvay S.A.; *Int'l*, pg. 1279
PLASTICOS REX. S.A. DE C.V.—See CYDSA S.A.; *Int'l*, pg. 246
PLASTICRETE BLOCK & SUPPLY CORP.; *U.S. Private*, pg. 871
PLASTICS COLOR CORP.—See PMC, Inc.; *U.S. Private*, pg. 827
PLASTICS, INC.—See Newell Co.; *U.S. Public*, pg. 1167
PLASTICS MANUFACTURING COMPANY—See Sun Coast Industries, Inc.; *U.S. Public*, pg. 1530
PLASTICS NEWS—See Crain Communications, Inc.; *U.S. Private*, pg. 285
PLASTICS RESEARCH & DEVELOPMENT CO.—See EBSCO Industries, Inc.; *U.S. Private*, pg. 359
PLASTICS TECHNOLOGY—See VNU Verenigde Nederlandse Uitgeversbedrijven B.V.; *Int'l*, pg. 1446
PLASTIGAGE CORPORATION; *U.S. Private*, pg. 871
PLASTILON—See Neste Oy; *Int'l*, pg. 915
PLASTILON FRANCE S.A.—See Neste Oy; *Int'l*, pg. 915
PLASTILON OY—See Neste Oy; *Int'l*, pg. 913
PLASTIMO S.A.—See Johnson Worldwide Associates, Inc.; *U.S. Public*, pg. 933
PLASTIPAK PACKAGING INC.; *U.S. Private*, pg. 872
PLASTIQUES CASCADES INC.—See The Cascades Group; *Int'l*, pg. 273
S.A. PLASTIQUES DEVELOPPEMENT—See Cockerill Sambre; *Int'l*, pg. 302

PLASTOFILM INDUSTRIES, INC.—See Ivex Packaging Corporation; *U.S. Public*, pg. 915
PLASTOMER CORP.; *U.S. Private*, pg. 872
PLASTOMER PRODUCTS DIV.—See Coltec Holdings Inc; *U.S. Public*, pg. 402
PLASTOOLS LTD.—See Delta plc; *Int'l*, pg. 391
PLASTROM S.A.—See Henkel KGaA; *Int'l*, pg. 612
PLASTRON—See Action Technology Company; *U.S. Private*, pg. 15
PLASTRON DALTON—See Action Technology Company; *U.S. Private*, pg. 15
PLAST-TEKNIK CURVER AB—See DSM N.V.; *Int'l*, pg. 356
PLAST-TEKNIK CURVER AS—See DSM N.V.; *Int'l*, pg. 356
PLAST-TEKNIK CURVER OY—See DSM N.V.; *Int'l*, pg. 356
PLATE GLASS & SHUTTERPRUFE INDUSTRIES LIMITED—See South African Breweries, Ltd.; *Int'l*, pg. 1287
PLATEAU ELECTRIC CONSTRUCTION INC.—See Amelco Corporation; *U.S. Public*, pg. 65
C. PLATH—See Litton Industries, Inc.; *U.S. Public*, pg. 1005
C. PLATH NORTH AMERICAN DIV.—See Litton Industries, Inc.; *U.S. Public*, pg. 1002
PLATINUM EQUITY HOLDINGS, LLC; *U.S. Private*, pg. 872
PLATINUM SOLUTIONS—See Platinum Technology, Inc.; *U.S. Public*, pg. 1309
PLATINUM TECHNOLOGY, INC.; *U.S. Public*, pg. 1309
PLATLUNA AB—See Trelleborg AB; *Int'l*, pg. 1422
PLAVINA & CIE S.N.C.—See Solvay S.A.; *Int'l*, pg. 1277
PLAVINA BENELUX B.V.—See Solvay S.A.; *Int'l*, pg. 1279
PLAVIS VERMIETUNGSGESELLSCHAFT MBH—See Commerzbank AG; *Int'l*, pg. 310
PLAXICON COMPANY—See Vorwerk & Co.; *Int'l*, pg. 1481
PLAY BY PLAY TOYS & NOVELTIES, INC.; *U.S. Public*, pg. 1309
PLAY SYSTEMS—See Stainless Incorporated; *U.S. Private*, pg. 1029
PLAYA DE MADRID, S.A.—See Telefonica de Espana, S.A.; *Int'l*, pg. 1371
PLAYBOY CLUBS INTERNATIONAL, INC.—See Playboy Enterprises, Inc.; *U.S. Public*, pg. 1310
PLAYBOY ENTERPRISES, INC.; *U.S. Public*, pg. 1309
PLAYBOY ENTERTAINMENT GROUP, INC.—See Playboy Enterprises, Inc.; *U.S. Public*, pg. 1310
PLAYBOY FRANCHISINGS INC.—See Playboy Enterprises, Inc.; *U.S. Public*, pg. 1310
PLAYBOY MODELS, INC.—See Playboy Enterprises, Inc.; *U.S. Public*, pg. 1310
PLAYBOY PREFERRED, INC.—See Playboy Enterprises, Inc.; *U.S. Public*, pg. 1310
PLAYBOY PRODUCTS & SERVICES INTERNATIONAL, B.V.—See Playboy Enterprises, Inc.; *U.S. Public*, pg. 1310
PLAYBOY SHOWS, INC.—See Playboy Enterprises, Inc.; *U.S. Public*, pg. 1310
PLAYBOY VIDEO ENTERPRISES, INC.—See Playboy Enterprises, Inc.; *U.S. Public*, pg. 1310
PLAYERS INTERNATIONAL, INC.; *U.S. Public*, pg. 1310
PLAYERS LAKE CHARLES, INC.—See Players International, Inc.; *U.S. Public*, pg. 1310
PLAYFIELD INDUSTRIES INC.—See TecSyn International, Inc.; *Int'l*, pg. 1362
PLAYHOUSE SQUARE INVESTMENTS, INC.—See Forest City Enterprises, Inc.; *U.S. Public*, pg. 669
PLAYMATES HOLDINGS LTD.; *Int'l*, pg. 1060
PLAYMATES TOYS INC.—See Playmates Holdings Ltd.; *Int'l*, pg. 1060
PLAYSKOOL, INC.—See Hasbro, Inc.; *U.S. Public*, pg. 797
PLAYTEX APPAREL CANADA, LTD.—See Sara Lee Corporation; *U.S. Public*, pg. 1433
PLAYTEX APPAREL, INC.—See Sara Lee Corporation; *U.S. Public*, pg. 1433
PLAYTEX BEAUTY CARE, INC.—See Playtex Products Inc.; *U.S. Public*, pg. 1311
PLAYTEX EUROPE—See Sara Lee Corporation; *U.S. Public*, pg. 1434
PLAYTEX INVESTMENT CORP.—See Playtex Products Inc.; *U.S. Public*, pg. 1311
PLAYTEX MARKETING CORPORATION—See Playtex Products Inc.; *U.S. Public*, pg. 1311
PLAYTEX PRODUCTS CORP.—See Playtex Products Inc.; *U.S. Public*, pg. 1311
PLAYTEX PRODUCTS INC.; *U.S. Public*, pg. 1310
PLAYTEX SOUTH AFRICA—See Sara Lee Corporation; *U.S. Public*, pg. 1434
PLAZA CREATE; *Int'l*, pg. 1060
PLAZA RESOURCES COMPANY—See Berkshire Hathaway Inc.; *U.S. Public*, pg. 220
PLAZA Y JANES S.A.—See Bertelsmann AG; *Int'l*, pg. 192
PLEASANT COMPANY; *U.S. Private*, pg. 872
PLEASANTVILLE MUSIC PUBLISHING, INC.—See The Reader's Digest Association, Inc.; *U.S. Public*, pg. 1367
PLEJ'S LINEN SUPERMARKET—See Ostrow Textile Co., Inc.; *U.S. Private*, pg. 821
PLENUM INTERNATIONAL SALES CORPORATION—See Plenum Publishing Corporation; *U.S. Public*, pg. 1311
PLENUM PUBLISHING COMPANY, LTD.—See Plenum Publishing Corporation; *U.S. Public*, pg. 1311
PLENUM PUBLISHING CORPORATION; *U.S. Public*, pg. 1311
PLENUM PUBLISHING CORPORATION—See Plenum Publishing Corporation; *U.S. Public*, pg. 1311
PLENUM PUBLISHING DISTRIBUTION—See Plenum Publishing Corporation; *U.S. Public*, pg. 1311
PLENUM PUBLISHING FACILITIES—See Plenum Publishing Corporation; *U.S. Public*, pg. 1311
PLETTAC AG; *Int'l*, pg. 1061
PLETTAC DISTRIBUTION SPOLKA ZO.O—See Plettac AG; *Int'l*, pg. 1061
PLETTAC ELECTRONIC SECURITY GMBH—See Plettac AG; *Int'l*, pg. 1061
PLETTAC ITALY S.R.L.—See Plettac AG; *Int'l*, pg. 1061
PLETTAC-PLANA GMBH—See Plettac AG; *Int'l*, pg. 1061

PLETTAC-REM SPOLKA ZO.O.—See Plettac AG; *Int'l*, pg. 1061
PLETTAC UMFORMTECHNIK GMBH & CO. KG—See Plettac AG; *Int'l*, pg. 1061
PLEWS/EDELMANN—See Tomkins PLC; *Int'l*, pg. 1396
PLEXCO/SPIROLITE—See Chevron Corporation; *U.S. Public*, pg. 348
PLEYADE PENINSULAR CORREDURIA DE SEGUROS, S.A.—See Telefonica de Espana, S.A.; *Int'l*, pg. 1371
PLIBRICO CO.; *U.S. Private*, pg. 872
PLIGAS—See Electrabel S.A.; *Int'l*, pg. 437
PLIX PACKAGING LIMITED—See International Paper Company; *U.S. Public*, pg. 904
PLOOF TRUCK LINES, INC.; *U.S. Private*, pg. 872
PLOUGH (UK) LTD.—See Schering-Plough Corporation; *U.S. Public*, pg. 1439
PLOUGH U.S.A.—See Schering-Plough Corporation; *U.S. Public*, pg. 1438
PLOVER BLFC BRANCH—See W.A. Roosevelt Co.; *U.S. Private*, pg. 943
PLOYCHROME GMBH—See Dainippon Ink & Chemicals, Inc.; *Int'l*, pg. 370
PLUESS-STAUFER AG; *Int'l*, pg. 1061
PLUESS-STAUFER (CALIFORNIA), INC.—See Pluess-Staufer AG; *Int'l*, pg. 1061
PLUESS-STAUFER INDUSTRIES, INC.—See Pluess-Staufer AG; *Int'l*, pg. 1061
PLUM BUILDING SYSTEMS, INC.—See Great Plains Companies, Inc.; *U.S. Private*, pg. 88
PLUM CREEK MANUFACTURING—See Plum Creek Timber Co., L.P.; *U.S. Public*, pg. 1311
PLUM CREEK TIMBER CO., L.P.; *U.S. Public*, pg. 1311
PLUMBERS QUALITY TOOL MANUFACTURING CO., INC.—See Masco Corporation; *U.S. Public*, pg. 1053
PLUMBING SPECIALTIES & SUPPLIES, INC.—See Wolseley Inc.; *Int'l*, pg. 1512
PLUMBMASTER INC.—See NCH Corporation; *U.S. Public*, pg. 1145
PLUMLEY COMPANIES—See Dana Corporation; *U.S. Public*, pg. 480
PLUMROSE LATINOAMERICANA C.A.—See The East Asiatic Company Ltd. A/S; *Int'l*, pg. 431
PLUNKETT-WEBSTER, INC.; *U.S. Private*, pg. 872
PLUNT ACROW LTD.—See Ashtead Group PLC; *Int'l*, pg. 88
PLURITEL DE COMUNICACAIONES, S.A.—See Caja de Madrid; *Int'l*, pg. 251
PLUS ALLGEMEINE—See Groupe GAN; *Int'l*, pg. 565
PLUS GROSSIST AB—See Axel Johnson AB; *Int'l*, pg. 709
PLUS LEBEN—See Groupe GAN; *Int'l*, pg. 565
PLUS LOGIC—See Xilinx, Inc.; *U.S. Public*, pg. 78
PLUS MARK, INC.—See American Greetings Corporation; *U.S. Public*, pg. 78
PLUS PACK A/S HAUSTRUP EKCO—See Alusuisse-Lonza Holding Ltd.; *Int'l*, pg. 69
PLUS ULTRA, COMPANIA ARGENTINA DE SEGUROS S.A.—See Allianz Aktiengesellschaft; *Int'l*, pg. 62
PLUSPOINT—See N.V. Koninklijke Bijenkorf Beheer KBB; *Int'l*, pg. 750
PLY-GEM MANUFACTURING—See Nortek, Inc.; *U.S. Public*, pg. 1193
PLYMKRAFT INC.—See Columbian Rope Company; *U.S. Private*, pg. 256
PLYMOUTH CREAMERIES, INC.; *U.S. Private*, pg. 872
PLYMOUTH INDUSTRIES, INC.; *U.S. Private*, pg. 873
PLYMOUTH INSURANCE COMPANY LTD.—See Magellan Health Services, Inc.; *U.S. Public*, pg. 1036
PLYMOUTH MEETING MALL, INC.—See The Rouse Company; *U.S. Public*, pg. 1407
PLYMOUTH RUBBER COMPANY, INC.; *U.S. Public*, pg. 1311
PLYMOUTH TUBE COMPANY; *U.S. Private*, pg. 873
PLYWOOD PLASTICS INC.; *U.S. Private*, pg. 873
PNEU-HYDRO PRODUCTS, INC.—See Thermo Electron Corporation; *U.S. Public*, pg. 1593
PNEU UNIROYAL ENGLEBERT S.A.—See Continental AG; *Int'l*, pg. 327
PNEUMAFIL CORPORATION; *U.S. Private*, pg. 873
PNEUMATIC DIV.—See Parker Hannifin Corporation; *U.S. Public*, pg. 1259
PNEUMATIC DIVISION; INDUSTRIA E COMERCIO LTDA.—See Parker Hannifin Corporation; *U.S. Public*, pg. 1264
PNEUMATIC PRODUCTS CORP.—See United Dominion Industries, Ltd.; *U.S. Public*, pg. 1676
PNEUMATIC SCALE-AKRON—See Barry-Wehmiller Company; *U.S. Private*, pg. 118
PNEUMATIC SCALE CORPORATION—See Barry-Wehmiller Company; *U.S. Private*, pg. 118
PNEUMATIC SCALE EUROPE—See Barry-Wehmiller Company; *U.S. Private*, pg. 118
PNEUS PIRELLI S.A.—See Pirelli S.p.A.; *Int'l*, pg. 1059
PNEUTRONICS DIV.—See Parker Hannifin Corporation; *U.S. Public*, pg. 1262
POAP-AD—See Dainippon Ink & Chemicals, Inc.; *Int'l*, pg. 371
POCAHONTAS DEVELOPMENT CORPORATION—See Norfolk Southern Corporation; *U.S. Public*, pg. 1192
POCAHONTAS FOODS, USA—See Performance Food Group Company; *U.S. Public*, pg. 1278
POCAHONTAS LAND CORPORATION—See Norfolk Southern Corporation; *U.S. Public*, pg. 1192
POCHENTONG AIRPORT CONSTRUCTION JV—See Lyonnaise des Eaux S.A.; *Int'l*, pg. 823
POCKET BOOKS—See National Amusements, Inc.; *U.S. Private*, pg. 777
POCLAIN DO BRASIL S.A.—See Tenneco Inc.; *U.S. Public*, pg. 1580
POCLAIN HISPANA S.A.—See Tenneco Inc.; *U.S. Public*, pg. 1580
POCO GRAPHITE, INCORPORATED—See Unocal Corporation; *U.S. Public*, pg. 1698
POCO PETROLEUMS LTD.; *Int'l*, pg. 1061

POCONO FABRICATORS—See Harsco Corporation; *U.S. Public*, pg. 793
POCONO KNITS, INC.—See Jack Young Associates; *U.S. Private*, pg. 1201
POCONO PALACE, INC.—See Starwood Hotels & Resorts; *U.S. Public*, pg. 1512
POE & BROWN, INC.; *U.S. Public*, pg. 1312
POE & BROWN OF ARIZONA—See Poe & Brown, Inc.; *U.S. Public*, pg. 1312
POE & BROWN OF CALIFORNIA—See Poe & Brown, Inc.; *U.S. Public*, pg. 1312
POE & BROWN OF FLORIDA—See Poe & Brown, Inc.; *U.S. Public*, pg. 1312
POE & BROWN OF NEVADA—See Poe & Brown, Inc.; *U.S. Public*, pg. 1312
POE & BROWN OF NEW JERSEY—See Poe & Brown, Inc.; *U.S. Public*, pg. 1312
POE & BROWN OF PENNSYLVANIA—See Poe & Brown, Inc.; *U.S. Public*, pg. 1312
POE SUPPLY—See Associated Industrial Supply, Inc.; *U.S. Private*, pg. 91
POGGENPOHL MOBELWERKE GMBH—See Skanska AB; *Int'l*, pg. 1261
POGO PRODUCING COMPANY; *U.S. Public*, pg. 1312
POGO PRODUCING COMPANY, INTERNATIONAL DIVISION—See Pogo Producing Company; *U.S. Public*, pg. 1313
POHANG IRON & STEEL CO., LTD.; *Int'l*, pg. 1061
POHANG IRON & STEEL CO., LTD.—See Pohang Iron & Steel Co., Ltd.; *Int'l*, pg. 1062
POHANG IRON & STEEL CO., LTD.-SEOUL—See Pohang Iron & Steel Co., Ltd.; *Int'l*, pg. 1061
POHANG STEEL AMERICA PTY., LTD (POSAM)—See Pohang Iron & Steel Co., Ltd.; *Int'l*, pg. 1062
POHANG STEEL AUSTRALIA PTY, LTD (POSA)—See Pohang Iron & Steel Co., Ltd.; *Int'l*, pg. 1062
POHANG STEEL CANADA LTD.(POSCAN)—See Pohang Iron & Steel Co., Ltd.; *Int'l*, pg. 1062
POHANG WORKS—See Pohang Iron & Steel Co., Ltd.; *Int'l*, pg. 1062
POHL GMBH—See Freudenberg & Company; *Int'l*, pg. 506
POHL GMBH & CO. KG—See Freudenberg & Company; *Int'l*, pg. 505
POHLSCHRODER GMBH & CO. KG—See Steelcase Inc.; *U.S. Private*, pg. 1038
POINT BREEZE REFINERY—See Sun Company, Inc.; *U.S. Public*, pg. 1530
POINT MARINE, INC.—See Tidewater Inc.; *U.S. Public*, pg. 1608
POINT PLEASANT REGISTER CO.—See Gannett Company, Inc.; *U.S. Public*, pg. 701
POINTE BUILDERS—See Pointe Group Ltd.; *U.S. Private*, pg. 873
POINTE GROUP LTD.; *U.S. Private*, pg. 873
POIRIER S.A.—See Invacare Corporation; *U.S. Public*, pg. 911
POL BALTIC INTERNATIONAL PTE. LTD.—See Hapag-Lloyd AG; *Int'l*, pg. 596
POL GULF INTERNATIONAL PTE. LTD.—See Hapag-Lloyd AG; *Int'l*, pg. 596
POL KRUSZ S.A.—See Scancem AB; *Int'l*, pg. 1200
POLAND OBI CENTRALA SYSTEMOWA—See OBI Bau-und Heimwerkermaerkte GmbH & Co. KG; *Int'l*, pg. 993
POLAND SPRING CORPORATION—See Nestle S.A.; *Int'l*, pg. 919
POLAR BEVERAGES; *U.S. Private*, pg. 873
POLAR MATERIAL INC.—See Alusuisse-Lonza Holding Ltd.; *Int'l*, pg. 68
POLAR SEALS APS; PTFE-PACKING MFG. OPERATION—See Parker Hannifin Corporation; *U.S. Public*, pg. 1262
POLAR WARE COMPANY; *U.S. Private*, pg. 873
POLARCUP (AUSTRALIA) LTD.—See Huhtamaki Oy; *Int'l*, pg. 638
POLARCUP BENELUX B.V.—See Huhtamaki Oy; *Int'l*, pg. 638
POLARCUP FINLAND—See Huhtamaki Oy; *Int'l*, pg. 638
POLARCUP FRANCE S.A.—See Huhtamaki Oy; *Int'l*, pg. 638
POLARCUP GERMANY—See Huhtamaki Oy; *Int'l*, pg. 638
POLARCUP GROUP HEADQUARTERS—See Huhtamaki Oy; *Int'l*, pg. 638
POLARCUP NORWAY—See Huhtamaki Oy; *Int'l*, pg. 638
POLARCUP (N.Z.) LIMITED—See Huhtamaki Oy; *Int'l*, pg. 638
POLARCUP POLAND SP. Z.O.O.—See Huhtamaki Oy; *Int'l*, pg. 638
POLARCUP PORTUGAL—See Huhtamaki Oy; *Int'l*, pg. 639
POLARCUP RUSSIA—See Huhtamaki Oy; *Int'l*, pg. 638
POLARCUP S.A.—See Huhtamaki Oy; *Int'l*, pg. 638
POLARCUP SINGAPORE PTE. LTD.—See Huhtamaki Oy; *Int'l*, pg. 639
POLARCUP S.R.L.—See Huhtamaki Oy; *Int'l*, pg. 639
POLARCUP SWEDEN—See Huhtamaki Oy; *Int'l*, pg. 639
POLARCUP UNITED KINGDOM LTD.—See Huhtamaki Oy; *Int'l*, pg. 638
POLARIS INDUSTRIES, INC.; *U.S. Public*, pg. 1313
POLARIS PACKAGING INC.—See Sonoco Products Company; *U.S. Public*, pg. 1486
POLARIS POOL SYSTEMS, INC.; *U.S. Private*, pg. 873
OY POLARKESTI AB—See Sodexho S.A.; *Int'l*, pg. 1274
POLAROID AB—See Polaroid Corporation; *U.S. Public*, pg. 1314
POLAROID AG—See Polaroid Corporation; *U.S. Public*, pg. 1314
POLAROID A.S.—See Polaroid Corporation; *U.S. Public*, pg. 1314
POLAROID ASIA PACIFIC LIMITED—See Polaroid Corporation; *U.S. Public*, pg. 1313
POLAROID AUSTRALIA PTY. LTD.—See Polaroid Corporation; *U.S. Public*, pg. 1314
POLAROID (BELGIUM) NV—See Polaroid Corporation; *U.S. Public*, pg. 1314
POLAROID CANADA INC.—See Polaroid Corporation; *U.S. Public*, pg. 1314

POLAROID CARIBBEAN CORP.—See Polaroid Corporation; U.S. Public, pg. 1313
POLAROID COPY SERVICES—See Polaroid Corporation; U.S. Public, pg. 1313
POLAROID CORPORATION; U.S. Public, pg. 1313
POLAROID CORP.- CAMERA DIVISION—See Polaroid Corporation; U.S. Public, pg. 1313
POLAROID CORPORATION OF JAPAN (OSAKA)—See Polaroid Corporation; U.S. Public, pg. 1314
POLAROID DE MEXICO S.A. DE C.V.—See Polaroid Corporation; U.S. Public, pg. 1314
POLAROID DO BRAZIL LTDA.—See Polaroid Corporation; U.S. Public, pg. 1314
POLAROID (ESPANA) S.A.—See Polaroid Corporation; U.S. Public, pg. 1314
POLAROID (EUROPA) B.V.—See Polaroid Corporation; U.S. Public, pg. 1314
POLAROID FAR EAST LTD.—See Polaroid Corporation; U.S. Public, pg. 1314
POLAROID FOUNDATION—See Polaroid Corporation; U.S. Public, pg. 1314
POLAROID (FRANCE) S.A.—See Polaroid Corporation; U.S. Public, pg. 1314
POLAROID GES.M.B.H.—See Polaroid Corporation; U.S. Public, pg. 1314
POLAROID GMBH—See Polaroid Corporation; U.S. Public, pg. 1314
POLAROID ITALIA S.A.R.L.—See Polaroid Corporation; U.S. Public, pg. 1314
POLAROID MAG MEDIA—See Polaroid Corporation; U.S. Public, pg. 1314
POLAROID NEDERLAND B.V.—See Polaroid Corporation; U.S. Public, pg. 1314
POLAROID (NORGE) A/S—See Polaroid Corporation; U.S. Public, pg. 1314
POLAROID SINGAPORE (PTE) LTD.—See Polaroid Corporation; U.S. Public, pg. 1314
POLAROID (UK) LTD.—See Polaroid Corporation; U.S. Public, pg. 1314
POLAROID (U.K.) LTD.-THE VALE—See Polaroid Corporation; U.S. Public, pg. 1314
POLAROIL S.A.—See Fuchs Petrolub AG Oel + Chemie; Int'l, pg. 519
POLAROME INTERNATIONAL; U.S. Private, pg. 874
P.T. POLEKAO INDONESIA CHEMICALS—See Kao Corporation; Int'l, pg. 718
POLESE COMPANY—See Semiconductor Packaging Materials Co., Inc.; U.S. Public, pg. 1456
POLESTAR LABS, INC.; U.S. Private, pg. 874
POLFLOAT SAINT-GOBAIN—See Saint-Gobain; Int'l, pg. 1173
POLHEMUS INC.—See Kaiser Aerospace & Electronics Corp.; U.S. Private, pg. 605
POLI-TWINE CANADA (BELLEVILLE)—See TecSyn International, Inc.; Int'l, pg. 1361
POLI-TWINE CANADA (CALGARY)—See TecSyn International, Inc.; Int'l, pg. 1362
POLI-TWINE SOUTHERN INC.—See TecSyn International, Inc.; Int'l, pg. 1362
POLI-TWINE WESTERN INC.—See TecSyn International, Inc.; Int'l, pg. 1362
POLIALDEN-PETROQUIMICA S.A.—See Nissho Iwai Corporation; Int'l, pg. 949
POLICY MANAGEMENT SYSTEMS AUSTRALIA PTY. LTD.—See Policy Management Systems Corporation; U.S. Public, pg. 1315
POLICY MANAGEMENT SYSTEMS CANADA, LTD.—See Policy Management Systems Corporation; U.S. Public, pg. 1315
POLICY MANAGEMENT SYSTEMS CORPORATION; U.S. Public, pg. 1314
POLICY MANAGEMENT SYSTEMS EUROPE, LTD.—See Policy Management Systems Corporation; U.S. Public, pg. 1315
POLICY MANAGEMENT SYSTEMS INFORMATION AND ADMINISTRATION SERVICES, INC.—See Policy Management Systems Corporation; U.S. Public, pg. 1315
POLICY MANAGEMENT SYSTEMS INTERNATIONAL, LTD.—See Policy Management Systems Corporation; U.S. Public, pg. 1314
POLICY MANAGEMENT SYSTEMS LIFE, INC.—See Policy Management Systems Corporation; U.S. Public, pg. 1314
POLICYD, S.A. DE C.V.—See CYDSA S.A.; Int'l, pg. 246
POLIESA FRANCE S.A.R.L.—See Schmalbach-Lubeca AG; Int'l, pg. 1207
POLIET—See Saint-Gobain; Int'l, pg. 1177
POLIFIN LIMITED—See Sasol Limited; Int'l, pg. 1197
POLIFOAM PLASTIC PROCESSING CO., LTD.—See The Furukawa Electric Co., Ltd.; Int'l, pg. 531
POLIGONO DE ACTIVIDADES LOGISTICAS, PAL -COSLADA, S.A.—See Caja de Madrid Group; Int'l, pg. 252
POLIOLES, S.A. DE C.V.—See BASF AG; Int'l, pg. 109
POLISISTEM S.R.L.—See Durr AG; Int'l, pg. 422
POLITA GEBAUDEREINIGUNG GES.M.B.H—See Vorwerk & Co.; Int'l, pg. 1481
POLITUBOS S.A.—See Siebe plc; Int'l, pg. 1244
POLIVE/TRICOSTERIL—See Fort James Corporation; U.S. Public, pg. 673
POLK AUDIO, INC.; U.S. Public, pg. 1315
POLK AUTOMOTIVE DATA SERVICES DIV.—See R.L. Polk & Co.; U.S. Private, pg. 874
POLK CITY PHARMACY, INC.—See Integrated Health Services, Inc.; U.S. Public, pg. 885
R.L. POLK & CO.; U.S. Private, pg. 874
POLKA DOT DAIRY/TOM THUMB FOOD MARKETS—See Polka Dot Dairy/Tom Thumb, Inc.; U.S. Private, pg. 874
POLKA DOT DAIRY/TOM THUMB, INC.; U.S. Private, pg. 874
POLLACK CORPORATION; U.S. Private, pg. 874

MAYER POLLACK STEEL CORPORATION—See The Pollock Corp.; U.S. Private, pg. 874
POLLAK-ACTUATION—See Stoneridge, Inc.; U.S. Private, pg. 1045
POLLAK DIVISION—See Stoneridge, Inc.; U.S. Private, pg. 1045
POLLAK-SWITCHING—See Stoneridge, Inc.; U.S. Private, pg. 1045
POLLENEX—See The Rival Company; U.S. Public, pg. 1391
POLLIO DAIRY PRODUCTS—See Philip Morris Companies Inc.; U.S. Public, pg. 1288
POLLIO DAIRY PRODUCTS COMPANY—See Philip Morris Companies Inc.; U.S. Public, pg. 1288
POLLO TROPICAL, INC.; U.S. Public, pg. 1315
THE POLLOCK CORP.; U.S. Private, pg. 874
POLLUX BV—See N.V. Koninklijke KNP BT; Int'l, pg. 756
POLO INDUSTRIA E COMERCIO LTDA.—See Hercules Incorporated; U.S. Public, pg. 811
POLO/RALPH LAUREN—See Polo/Ralph Lauren Corporation; U.S. Private, pg. 875
POLO/RALPH LAUREN CORPORATION; U.S. Private, pg. 874
POLSKIE LINIE LOTNICZE LOT S.A.; Int'l, pg. 1062
POLSKIE TOWORZYSTWO PRYWATYACYJNE KLEINWORT BENSON—See Dresdner Bank AG; Int'l, pg. 420
POLY-BOND INC.—See Dominion Textile Inc.; Int'l, pg. 415
POLY COATING PLANT—See Georgia-Pacific Corporation; U.S. Public, pg. 737
POLY-CRAFT SYSTEMS—See Binks Sames Corporation; U.S. Public, pg. 229
POLY HI SOLIDUR, INC.—See Menasha Corporation; U.S. Private, pg. 731
POLY PAK AMERICA, INC.; U.S. Private, pg. 875
POLY-SEAL CORPORATION; U.S. Private, pg. 875
POLY-SCIENTIFIC DIV.—See Litton Industries, Inc.; U.S. Public, pg. 1003
POLYCELL PRODUCTS LIMITED—See Williams Holdings Plc; Int'l, pg. 1501
POLYCELL RAWPLUG IRELAND LIMITED—See Newmond PLC; Int'l, pg. 925
POLYCHEM CORPORATION—See Brittany Corporation; U.S. Private, pg. 169
POLYCHROME (AUSTRALIA) PTY. LTD.—See Dainippon Ink & Chemicals, Inc.; Int'l, pg. 370
POLYCHROME CORP. (CANADA) CO., LTD.—See Dainippon Ink & Chemicals, Inc.; Int'l, pg. 370
POLYCHROME CORP. DIV.—See Dainippon Ink & Chemicals, Inc.; Int'l, pg. 370
POLYCHROME FRANCE S.A.—See Dainippon Ink & Chemicals, Inc.; Int'l, pg. 370
POLYCOAT SYSTEMS, INC.; U.S. Private, pg. 875
POLYCOLD SYSTEMS INTERNATIONAL, INC.—See Intermagnetics General Corporation; U.S. Public, pg. 894
POLYDACH-DACHSYSTEME GMBH—See Cockerill Sambre; Int'l, pg. 302
POLYDEX PHARMACEUTICALS LIMITED; Int'l, pg. 1062
POLYDEX PHARMACEUTICALS LIMITED—See Polydex Pharmaceuticals Limited; Int'l, pg. 1063
POLYDOR B.V.—See Philips Electronics N.V.; Int'l, pg. 1052
POLYENKA SA—See Akzo Nobel N.V.; Int'l, pg. 46
POLYFIBRON TECHNOLOGIES CORP.; U.S. Private, pg. 875
POLYFILLA SA—See Williams Holdings Plc; Int'l, pg. 1501
POLYFLEX BUSINESS UNIT—See Parker Hannifin Corporation; U.S. Public, pg. 1260
POLYFLEX DIVISION—See Parker Hannifin Corporation; U.S. Public, pg. 1264
POLYFLEX FRANCE S.A.—See Parker Hannifin Corporation; U.S. Public, pg. 1261
POLYFLON COMPANY—See Crane Co.; U.S. Public, pg. 457
POLYFLUORO PRIVATE LIMITED—See Saint-Gobain; Int'l, pg. 1175
A/S POLYGON—See Incentive AB; Int'l, pg. 669
POLYGRAM DIRECT MARKETING AND TRADING—See Philips Electronics N.V.; Int'l, pg. 1053
POLYGRAM N.V.—See Philips Electronics N.V.; Int'l, pg. 1051
POLYKEN TECHNOLOGIES—See Tyco International Ltd.; U.S. Public, pg. 1647
POLYLOOM CORP. OF AMERICA; U.S. Private, pg. 875
POLYMASK CORPORATION—See Sealed Air Corporation; U.S. Public, pg. 1451
POLYMEDICA HEALTHCARE, INC.—See PolyMedica Industries, Inc.; U.S. Public, pg. 1315
POLYMEDICA INDUSTRIES, INC.; U.S. Public, pg. 1315
POLYMEDICA INDUSTRIES UK, LTD.—See PolyMedica Industries, Inc.; U.S. Public, pg. 1315
POLYMEDICA PHARMACEUTICALS (U.S.A.), INC.—See PolyMedica Industries, Inc.; U.S. Public, pg. 1315
POLYMEDICA WOUND CARE COMPANY—See PolyMedica Industries, Inc.; U.S. Public, pg. 1315
POLYMER CHEMICALS ADDITIVES GROUP—See Witco Corporation; U.S. Public, pg. 1774
POLYMER CHEMICALS GROUP—See Witco Corporation; U.S. Public, pg. 1774
POLYMER COMPOSITES INC.—See Hoechst Aktiengesellschaft; Int'l, pg. 624
THE POLYMER CORPORATION—See DSM N.V.; Int'l, pg. 355
POLYMER PLASTICS CORPORATION; U.S. Private, pg. 875
POLYMER TECHNOLOGIES—See Maclean-Fogg Co.; U.S. Private, pg. 692
POLYMER TECHNOLOGY CORPORATION—See Bausch & Lomb Incorporated; U.S. Public, pg. 195
POLYMET CORP.; U.S. Private, pg. 875
POLYMETRON SIEGER S.R.L.—See Hesta Tex AG; Int'l, pg. 618

POLYNESIENNE DES EAUX—See Lyonnaise des Eaux S.A.; Int'l, pg. 824
POLYPENCO B.V.—See DSM N.V.; Int'l, pg. 354
POLYPENCO CANADA LTD.—See DSM N.V.; Int'l, pg. 354
POLYPENCO G.M.B.H.—See DSM N.V.; Int'l, pg. 354
POLYPENCO GMBH—See DSM N.V.; Int'l, pg. 354
POLYPENCO KOREA CO. LTD.—See DSM N.V.; Int'l, pg. 354
POLYPENCO LTD.—See DSM N.V.; Int'l, pg. 354
POLYPENCO NV—See DSM N.V.; Int'l, pg. 354
POLYPENCO (PTY) LTD.—See DSM N.V.; Int'l, pg. 354
POLYPENCO S.R.L.—See DSM N.V.; Int'l, pg. 354
POLYPHASE CORPORATION; U.S. Public, pg. 1315
POLYPHASE INSTRUMENTS CO.—See Polyphase Corporation; U.S. Public, pg. 1315
POLYPHASER CORPORATION—See Smiths Industries plc; Int'l, pg. 1268
POLYPURE RHONE-POULENC—See Rhone-Poulenc S.A.; Int'l, pg. 1110
POLYSAR—See Bayer AG; Int'l, pg. 174
POLYSAR RUBBER CORPORATION—See Bayer AG; Int'l, pg. 175
POLYSIUS CORP.—See Fried. Krupp AG; Int'l, pg. 512
POLYSIUS DIVISION OF KRUPP SOUTH AFRICA PTY. LTD.—See Fried. Krupp AG; Int'l, pg. 512
POLYSIUS LTD.—See Fried. Krupp AG; Int'l, pg. 512
POLYSIUS PROJETOS IND. LTDA.—See Fried. Krupp AG; Int'l, pg. 512
POLYSIUS S.A.—See Fried. Krupp AG; Int'l, pg. 512
POLYSTAR CO. LTD.—See Philips Electronics N.V.; Int'l, pg. 1053
POLYTECH NETTING INDUSTRIES—See TecSyn International, Inc.; Int'l, pg. 1362
POLYTUIL FRANCE S.A.—See Cockerill Sambre; Int'l, pg. 302
S.A. POLYTUIL—See Cockerill Sambre; Int'l, pg. 301
POLYTUIL S.A.—See International Paper Company; U.S. Public, pg. 903
POLYURETAN-ELEMENT-TECHNIK PURET GMBH—See Dyckerhoff & Widmann AG; Int'l, pg. 423
POLYURETHANE ENGINEERING CO., LTD.—See BASF AG; Int'l, pg. 109
POLYVINYL FILMS, INC.; U.S. Private, pg. 875
POLYVISION CORP.; U.S. Public, pg. 1315
A. POMERANTZ & COMPANY; U.S. Private, pg. 875
POMEROY COMPUTER RESOURCES; U.S. Public, pg. 1315
POMMERY DISTRIBUTION S.A.—See LVMH Moet Hennessy Louis Vuitton; Int'l, pg. 783
POMOSIN GMBH—See Hercules Incorporated; U.S. Public, pg. 811
POMPEIIAN, INC.; U.S. Private, pg. 875
PONCE REGIONAL INSTITUTIONS—See Corrections Corporation of America; U.S. Public, pg. 451
PONCE SALT INDUSTRIES CORP.—See Morton International Inc.; U.S. Public, pg. 1135
PONCEBANK, F.S.B.; U.S. Public, pg. 1316
PONDERAS HOLDINGS INC.—See Amerco; U.S. Private, pg. 49
PONDEROSA STEAKHOUSE—See Metromedia Company; U.S. Private, pg. 736
POND'S ARGENTINA S.A.I.C.—See Unilever Plc; Int'l, pg. 1436
POND'S DO BRASIL PRODUTOS DE BELEZA LTDA.—See Unilever Plc; Int'l, pg. 1436
POND'S G.M.B.H.—See Unilever Plc; Int'l, pg. 1436
PONS—See Thomson S.A.; Int'l, pg. 1382
PONT-A-MOUSSON SA—See Saint-Gobain; Int'l, pg. 1176
PONT PACKAGING B.V.—See TT Group PLC; Int'l, pg. 1345
PONTIAC BANCORP, INC.; U.S. Public, pg. 1316
PONTIAC DIVISION—See R.R. Donnelley & Sons Company; U.S. Public, pg. 518
PONTIAC-GMC DIVISION—See General Motors Corporation; U.S. Public, pg. 720
PONTIAC-GMC TRUCK DIVISION—See General Motors Corporation; U.S. Public, pg. 720
PONTIN'S LIMITED—See Scottish & Newcastle plc; Int'l, pg. 1211
PONTMEYER NV—See Meyer International PLC; Int'l, pg. 864
PONY EXPRESS DELIVERY SERVICES, INC—See Borg-Warner Security Corporation; U.S. Public, pg. 245
PONY INTERNATIONAL INC.—See Pentland Group PLC; Int'l, pg. 1036
PONY SPORTS UK LTD.—See Pentland Group PLC; Int'l, pg. 1036
PONY U.S.A.—See Pentland Group PLC; Int'l, pg. 1036
POOL ARABIA, LTD.—See Pool Energy Services Co.; U.S. Public, pg. 1316
POOL ARCTIC ALASKA—See Pool Energy Services Co.; U.S. Public, pg. 1316
POOL CALIFORNIA ENERGY SERVICES, INC.—See Pool Energy Services Co.; U.S. Public, pg. 1316
POOL COMPANY—See Pool Energy Services Co.; U.S. Public, pg. 1316
POOL COMPANY (TEXAS), INC.—See Pool Energy Services Co.; U.S. Public, pg. 1316
POOL ENERGY SERVICES CO.; U.S. Public, pg. 1316
POOL INSURANCE—See Saskatchewan Wheat Pool; Int'l, pg. 1195
POOL INTERNATIONAL ARGENTINA S.A.—See Pool Energy Services Co.; U.S. Public, pg. 1316
POOLE LIGHTING LIMITED—See Emess PLC; Int'l, pg. 453
POOLE WOOD EQUIPMENT LTD.—See Brunel Holdings Plc; Int'l, pg. 231
POPCORN COMMUNICATIONS—See Cineplex Odeon Corporation; Int'l, pg. 293
THE POPCORN FACTORY—See Foster & Gallagher, Inc.; U.S. Public, pg. 421
POPE & TALBOT, INC.; U.S. Public, pg. 1316
POPE & TALBOT LTD.—See Pope & Talbot, Inc.; U.S. Public, pg. 1317

MASTER INDEX TO COMPANY NAMES POTASH

Company Index

POPE RESOURCES; *U.S. Public*, pg. 1317
POPE TECHNOLOGIES LTD.—See FAG Group; *Int'l*, pg. 469
POPLAR BLUFF COMPANIES—See Allied Waste Industries; *U.S. Public*, pg. 49
POPPE TYSON—See True North Diversified Companies; *U.S. Public*, pg. 1642
POPULAR BANK COMPUTERS LIMITED—See HSBC Holdings plc; *Int'l*, pg. 581
POPULAR BUSINESS TRUST—See Banco Popular de Puerto Rico; *U.S. Public*, pg. 176
POPULAR CLUB PLAN—See Texas Pacific Group; *U.S. Private*, pg. 1078
POPULAR CONSUMER SERVICES, INC.—See Banco Popular de Puerto Rico; *U.S. Public*, pg. 176
POPULAR FINANCE, INC.—See Banco Popular de Puerto Rico; *U.S. Public*, pg. 176
POPULAR HOME MORTGAGE, INC.—See Banco Popular de Puerto Rico; *U.S. Public*, pg. 176
POPULAR LEASING AND RENTAL, INC.—See Banco Popular de Puerto Rico; *U.S. Public*, pg. 176
POPULAR LEASING & RENTAL, INC.—See Banco Popular de Puerto Rico; *U.S. Public*, pg. 176
POPULAR MECHANICS—See The Hearst Corporation; *U.S. Private*, pg. 517
POPULAR SCIENCE—See The Times Mirror Company; *U.S. Public*, pg. 1617
POPULAR SECURITIES, INC.—See Banco Popular de Puerto Rico; *U.S. Public*, pg. 176
PORCELAIN METALS CORP.; *U.S. Private*, pg. 876
PORCELAIN PRODUCTS—See Carpenter Technology Corporation; *U.S. Public*, pg. 308
PORCELANITE, INC.—See Grupo Carso S.A. de C.V.; *Int'l*, pg. 573
PORCELANITE SA DE CV—See Grupo Carso S.A. de C.V.; *Int'l*, pg. 572
POREX CORP.—See Synetic, Inc.; *U.S. Public*, pg. 1548
POREX TECHNOLOGIES CORP. OF GEORGIA—See Synetic, Inc.; *U.S. Public*, pg. 1548
PORGERA JOINT VENTURE—See Placer Dome Inc.; *Int'l*, pg. 1060
PORK FARMS/BOWYERS—See Northern Foods plc; *Int'l*, pg. 968
PORKKALA SUGAR REFINERY—See Cultor Ltd.; *Int'l*, pg. 349
PORNON ET CIE, S.A.R.L.—See Watts Blake Bearne & Co. Plc; *Int'l*, pg. 1488
PORNPAT CHEMICALS CO., LTD.—See Tokuyama Corporation; *Int'l*, pg. 1394
PORRITTS & SPENCER (ASIA) LTD.—See Scapa Group Plc; *Int'l*, pg. 1203
PORRITTS & SPENCER CANADA, INC.—See Scapa Group Plc; *Int'l*, pg. 1203
PORRITTS & SPENCER INC.—See Scapa Group Plc; *Int'l*, pg. 1202
PORRITTS & SPENCER LTD.—See Scapa Group Plc; *Int'l*, pg. 1202
PORRITTS & SPENCER (WESTERN), INC.—See Scapa Group Plc; *Int'l*, pg. 1202
PORSCHE AG; *Int'l*, pg. 1063
PORSCHE CARS AUSTRALIA (DISTRIBUTION) PTY. LTD.—See Porsche AG; *Int'l*, pg. 1063
PORSCHE CARS AUSTRALIA (FINANCE) PTY. LTD.—See Porsche AG; *Int'l*, pg. 1063
PORSCHE CARS AUSTRALIA PTY. LTD.—See Porsche AG; *Int'l*, pg. 1063
PORSCHE CARS GREAT BRITAIN LTD.—See Porsche AG; *Int'l*, pg. 1063
PORSCHE CARS NORTH AMERICA, INC.—See Porsche AG; *Int'l*, pg. 1063
PORSCHE CLASSIC GMBH—See Porsche AG; *Int'l*, pg. 1063
PORSCHE CONSULTING GMBH—See Porsche AG; *Int'l*, pg. 1063
PORSCHE CREDIT CORPORATION, INC.—See Porsche AG; *Int'l*, pg. 1063
PORSCHE-DELTA ENGINEERING CO.—See Porsche AG; *Int'l*, pg. 1063
PORSCHE ENGINEERING JAPAN CO.. LTD.—See Porsche AG; *Int'l*, pg. 1063
PORSCHE ENTERPRISES INC.—See Porsche AG; *Int'l*, pg. 1063
PORSCHE ESPANA S.A.—See Porsche AG; *Int'l*, pg. 1063
PORSCHE FINANCIAL MANAGEMENT SERVICES LTD.—See Porsche AG; *Int'l*, pg. 1063
PORSCHE INTERNATIONAL FINANCING LTD.—See Porsche AG; *Int'l*, pg. 1063
PORSCHE INTERNATIONAL INSURANCE LTD.—See Porsche AG; *Int'l*, pg. 1063
PORSCHE ITALIA S.P.A PADOVA—See Porsche AG; *Int'l*, pg. 1063
PORSCHE LEASING GMBH—See Porsche AG; *Int'l*, pg. 1063
PORSCHE MOTORSPORTS NORTH AMERICA, INC.—See Porsche AG; *Int'l*, pg. 1063
PORSCHE ZENTRUM HOPPEGARTEN GMBH—See Porsche AG; *Int'l*, pg. 1063
PORT CHATHAM PACKING COMPANY—See Icicle Seafoods, Inc.; *U.S. Private*, pg. 556
PORT CITY ELECTRICAL SUPPLY, INC.—See Hughes Supply, Inc.; *U.S. Public*, pg. 847
PORT CITY PRESS, INC.—See Perry Graphic Communications, Inc.; *U.S. Private*, pg. 855
PORT COLBOURNE—See Canada Ports Corporation; *Int'l*, pg. 255
PORT CURTIS MOULDERS PTY. LTD.—See Q.U.F. Industries Ltd.; *Int'l*, pg. 1074
PORT HOPE EVENING GUIDE—See Hollinger Inc.; *Int'l*, pg. 631
PORT KEMBLA COAL TERMINAL LTD.—See The Broken Hill Proprietary Company Limited; *Int'l*, pg. 226
PORT KEMBLA LABORATORIES—See The Broken Hill Proprietary Company Limited; *Int'l*, pg. 227
PORT KEMBLA STEELWORKS—See The Broken Hill Proprietary Company Limited; *Int'l*, pg. 227
PORT LAWRENCE TITLE & TRUST CO.—See The First American Financial Corporation; *U.S. Public*, pg. 626
PORT MORESBY BHP PAPUA NEW GUINEA—See The Broken Hill Proprietary Company Limited; *Int'l*, pg. 228
PORT OF BELLEDUNE—See Canada Ports Corporation; *Int'l*, pg. 255
PORT OF CHURCHILL—See Canada Ports Corporation; *Int'l*, pg. 255
PORT OF HOUSTON AUTHORITY; *U.S. Private*, pg. 876
PORT OF OAKLAND; *U.S. Private*, pg. 876
PORT OF PORTLAND; *U.S. Private*, pg. 876
PORT OF PRESCOTT—See Canada Ports Corporation; *Int'l*, pg. 255
PORT OF QUEBEC CORPORATION—See Canada Ports Corporation; *Int'l*, pg. 255
PORT OF SEPT-ILES—See Canada Ports Corporation; *Int'l*, pg. 255
PORT OF TIANJIN COMMERCIAL BONDED WAREHOUSING & SERVICE CO. LTD.—See Royal Nedlloyd Group N.V.; *Int'l*, pg. 1144
PORT OF TROIS RIVIERES—See Canada Ports Corporation; *Int'l*, pg. 255
PORT SAGUENAY/BAIE DES HA! HA!—See Canada Ports Corporation; *Int'l*, pg. 255
PORT TOWNSEND PAPER CORPORATION—See Haindl Papier GmbH; *Int'l*, pg. 586
PORT WARATAH COAL SERVICES PTY. LTD.—See Nissho Iwai Corporation; *Int'l*, pg. 949
PORT WELLER DRY DOCKS—See Canadian Shipbuilding & Engineering Ltd.; *Int'l*, pg. 259
PORTA HOLDINGS INC.—See Melitta Unternehmensgruppe Bentz KG; *Int'l*, pg. 857
PORTA SYSTEMS CORP.; *U.S. Public*, pg. 1317
PORTA SYSTEMS LIMITED—See Porta Systems Corp.; *U.S. Public*, pg. 1317
PORTA SYSTEMS S.A. DE C.V.—See Porta Systems Corp.; *U.S. Public*, pg. 1317
PORTABLE CELLULAR COMMUNICATIONS—See Peoples Telephone Company, Inc.; *U.S. Public*, pg. 1276
PORTAGE DEVELOPMENT, INC.—See Forest City Enterprises, Inc.; *U.S. Public*, pg. 669
PORTAGE TOOL COMPANY—See Tempel Steel Company; *U.S. Private*, pg. 1075
PORTAL AIRD PUBLICATIONS PTY. LTD.—See Devon Group, Inc.; *U.S. Public*, pg. 503
PORTAL PUBLICATIONS, LTD.—See Devon Group, Inc.; *U.S. Public*, pg. 503
PORTAL PUBLICATIONS LTD.—See Devon Group, Inc.; *U.S. Public*, pg. 503
PORTALS (BATHFORD) LTD.—See De La Rue plc; *Int'l*, pg. 386
PORTALS CONFEDERATION CORPORATION—See Confederation Life Insurance Company; *Int'l*, pg. 326
PORTALS LTD.—See De La Rue plc; *Int'l*, pg. 386
PORTALS PACKAGING TAPES—See De La Rue plc; *Int'l*, pg. 386
PORTCEMEN S.A.—See Lafarge S.A.; *Int'l*, pg. 790
PORTEC, INC.; *U.S. Public*, pg. 1317
PORTEC LTD.—See Portec, Inc.; *U.S. Public*, pg. 1318
PORTEC (U.K.) LTD.—See Portec, Inc.; *U.S. Public*, pg. 1318
PORTER-CABLE CORPORATION—See Pentair, Inc.; *U.S. Public*, pg. 1274
PORTER NOVELLI INTERNATIONAL—See Omnicom Group Inc.; *U.S. Public*, pg. 1224
P.L. PORTER CO.; *U.S. Private*, pg. 876
THE PORTFOLIO GROUP, INC.—See The Chase Manhattan Corporation; *U.S. Public*, pg. 338
PORTFOLIO INMOBILIARIO, S.A.—See Caja de Madrid Group; *Int'l*, pg. 251
PORTFOLIO INTERIORS BY J.C. PENNEY—See JC Penney Company, Inc.; *U.S. Public*, pg. 917
PORTGAS—See Gaz de France; *Int'l*, pg. 541
PORTH PLASTIC CO.—See Bunzl PLC; *Int'l*, pg. 233
PORTI AND OUTDOOR ADVERTISING LTD.—See Dentsu Inc.; *Int'l*, pg. 394
PORTLAND AUTO AUCTION—See Cox Enterprises, Inc.; *U.S. Private*, pg. 283
PORTLAND CHAIN MFG. CO.—See Webster Industries Inc.; *U.S. Private*, pg. 1158
PORTLAND FOOD PRODUCTS COMPANY; *U.S. Private*, pg. 876
PORTLAND GENERAL ELECTRIC CO.—See Enron Corp.; *U.S. Public*, pg. 584
PORTLAND GENERAL HOLDINGS, INC.—See Enron Corp.; *U.S. Public*, pg. 585
PORTLAND HOLIDAYS LTD.—See The Thomson Corporation; *U.S. Public*, pg. 1602
PORTLAND HOUSE—See Advance Publications Inc.; *U.S. Private*, pg. 21
THE PORTLAND NEWSPAPERS—See Guy Gannett Communications; *U.S. Private*, pg. 439
PORTLAND PLANT—See Stoneridge, Inc.; *U.S. Private*, pg. 1044
PORTLAND TERMINAL RAILROAD CO.—See Union Pacific Corporation; *U.S. Public*, pg. 1668
PORTLAND TRACTION CO.—See Union Pacific Corporation; *U.S. Public*, pg. 1668
C. PORTMANN—See Commerzbank AG; *Int'l*, pg. 310
PORTOCEL-TERMINAL ESPECIALIZADO DE BARRA DO RIACHO—See Aracruz Celulose S.A.; *Int'l*, pg. 78
THE PORTRUSH COLUMNAR BASALT COMPANY LIMITED—See RMC Group p.l.c.; *Int'l*, pg. 1079
PORTS O'CALL RESTAURANT CORP.—See Specialty Restaurants Corporation; *U.S. Private*, pg. 1022
PORTSMOUTH NAVIGATION CORPORATION—See Moran Transportation Company; *U.S. Private*, pg. 761
PORTSMOUTH SAVINGS BANK—See CFX Bank; *U.S. Public*, pg. 278
PORTUGAL PREVIDENTE COMPANHIA DE SEGUROS (RAS)—See Allianz Aktiengesellschaft; *Int'l*, pg. 61
PORTUGUESE RAILWAYS (CP); *Int'l*, pg. 1063
PORTUMBRIA, S.A.—See Vallehermoso, S.A.; *Int'l*, pg. 1447
POSADAS USA INC.—See Grupo Posadas S.A. de C.V.; *Int'l*, pg. 576
POSAM NEW YORK OFFICE—See Pohang Iron & Steel Co., Ltd.; *Int'l*, pg. 1062
POSAM WASHINGTON OFFICE—See Pohang Iron & Steel Co., Ltd.; *Int'l*, pg. 1062
POSCO ASIA CO., LTD. (POA)—See Pohang Iron & Steel Co., Ltd.; *Int'l*, pg. 1062
POSCO BEIJING OFFICE—See Pohang Iron & Steel Co., Ltd.; *Int'l*, pg. 1062
POSCO HANOI OFFICE—See Pohang Iron & Steel Co., Ltd.; *Int'l*, pg. 1062
POSCO HONG KONG OFFICE—See Pohang Iron & Steel Co., Ltd.; *Int'l*, pg. 1062
POSCO INTERNATIONAL OSAKA (PIO)—See Pohang Iron & Steel Co., Ltd.; *Int'l*, pg. 1062
POSCO RESEARCH CENTER EUROPE—See Pohang Iron & Steel Co., Ltd.; *Int'l*, pg. 1062
POSCO SHANGHAI OFFICE—See Pohang Iron & Steel Co., Ltd.; *Int'l*, pg. 1062
POSCO TOKYO OFFICE—See Pohang Iron & Steel Co., Ltd.; *Int'l*, pg. 1062
POSCO TOKYO RESEARCH LAB—See Pohang Iron & Steel Co., Ltd.; *Int'l*, pg. 1062
POSCO YANGON OFFICE—See Pohang Iron & Steel Co., Ltd.; *Int'l*, pg. 1062
POSEC HANOI OFFICE—See Pohang Iron & Steel Co., Ltd.; *Int'l*, pg. 1062
POSEC HOCHIMINH OFFICE—See Pohang Iron & Steel Co., Ltd.; *Int'l*, pg. 1062
POSEC SHANGHAI OFFICE—See Pohang Iron & Steel Co., Ltd.; *Int'l*, pg. 1062
POSITECH CORPORATION—See Columbus McKinnon Corp.; *U.S. Public*, pg. 406
POSITRONIC INDUSTRIES, INC.; *U.S. Private*, pg. 876
POSMETAL—See Pohang Iron & Steel Co., Ltd.; *Int'l*, pg. 1062
POSNICK & KOLKER, INC.; *U.S. Private*, pg. 876
POSSEHL ELECTRONIC NEDERLAND BV—See L. Possehl & Co. mbH; *Int'l*, pg. 1064
L. POSSEHL & CO. MBH; *Int'l*, pg. 1063
POSSEHL SUMIKO ELECTRONICS SINGAPORE PTE. LTD.—See Sumitomo Metal Mining Co., Ltd.; *Int'l*, pg. 1316
POSSO S.A.; *Int'l*, pg. 1064
POST ACUTE DIVISION—See Paragon Health Network, Inc.; *U.S. Public*, pg. 1256
POST BUCKLEY INTERNATIONAL INC.—See The PBS&J Corporation; *U.S. Private*, pg. 826
POST BUCKLEY SCHUH & JERNIGAN—See The PBS&J Corporation; *U.S. Private*, pg. 826
POST GLOVER RESISTORS INC.—See Halma p.l.c.; *Int'l*, pg. 590
POST-NEWSWEEK CABLE DIVISION—See The Washington Post Company; *U.S. Public*, pg. 1743
POST-NEWSWEEK STATIONS, INC.—See The Washington Post Company; *U.S. Public*, pg. 1743
THE POST OFFICE; *Int'l*, pg. 1064
POST OFFICE BANK LIMITED—See Australia & New Zealand Banking Group Limited; *Int'l*, pg. 100
POST OFFICE BUILDING CO.—See Forest City Enterprises, Inc.; *U.S. Public*, pg. 669
POST OFFICE COUNTERS—See The Post Office; *Int'l*, pg. 1064
POST TELECOM AUSTRIA BETEILIGUNGS GMBH—See Austrian Postal & Telegraph Administration; *Int'l*, pg. 101
POST-TRIBUNE—See Hollinger Inc.; *Int'l*, pg. 632
POSTAL COMMEMORATIVE SOCIETY COLLECTION—See MBI Inc.; *U.S. Private*, pg. 685
POSTAL SYSTEMS INC.—See Bell & Howell Holdings; *U.S. Public*, pg. 201
POSTALMARKET; *Int'l*, pg. 1064
POSTBANK FUNDS TRANSFER OPERATIONS—See ING Groep N.V.; *Int'l*, pg. 647
POSTBANK INSURANCE—See ING Groep N.V.; *Int'l*, pg. 647
POSTBANK LEASE—See ING Groep N.V.; *Int'l*, pg. 647
POSTBANK RETAIL BANKING—See ING Groep N.V.; *Int'l*, pg. 647
POSTERLOID CORPORATION—See PolyVision Corp.; *U.S. Public*, pg. 1315
POSTGRADUATE MEDICINE—See The McGraw-Hill Companies; *U.S. Public*, pg. 1071
POSTIPANKKI LTD.; *Int'l*, pg. 1064
POSTRADE BANHKOK OFFICE—See Pohang Iron & Steel Co., Ltd.; *Int'l*, pg. 1062
POSTRADE HANOI OFFICE—See Pohang Iron & Steel Co., Ltd.; *Int'l*, pg. 1062
POSTRADE JAKARTA OFFICE—See Pohang Iron & Steel Co., Ltd.; *Int'l*, pg. 1062
POSTRADE LA OFFICE—See Pohang Iron & Steel Co., Ltd.; *Int'l*, pg. 1062
POSTRADE MOSCOW OFFICE—See Pohang Iron & Steel Co., Ltd.; *Int'l*, pg. 1062
POSTRADE RIO OFFICE—See Pohang Iron & Steel Co., Ltd.; *Int'l*, pg. 1062
POSVINA CO., LTD.—See Pohang Iron & Steel Co., Ltd.; *Int'l*, pg. 1062
POTAMKIN COMPANY; *U.S. Private*, pg. 876
POTAMKIN MANHATTAN—See Potamkin Company; *U.S. Private*, pg. 876
POTAMKIN TOYOTA, INC.—See Potamkin Company; *U.S. Private*, pg. 877
POTASAS DE LLOBREGAT, S.A.—See SEPI; *Int'l*, pg. 1225
POTASH COMPANY OF CANADA LTD. (POTACAN)—See BASF AG; *Int'l*, pg. 109
POTASH CORPORATION OF SASKATCHEWAN INC.; *Int'l*, pg. 1064

POTENTIA HEALTHCARE COMMUNICATIONS PARTNERS—See Omnicom Group Inc.; U.S. Public, pg. 1224
POTENTIOMETER DIV.—See Litton Industries, Inc.; U.S. Public, pg. 1003
POTHONIER SINGAPORE PTE LTD.—See Singapore Land Limited; Int'l, pg. 1253
POTLATCH CORPORATION; U.S. Public, pg. 1318
POTLATCH TELEPHONE COMPANY—See Telephone and Data Systems, Inc.; U.S. Public, pg. 1571
POTO PI, S.A.—See Vallehermoso, S.A.; Int'l, pg. 1447
POTOMAC CAPITAL INVESTMENT CORPORATION—See Potomac Electric Power Company; U.S. Public, pg. 1319
POTOMAC DIGITAL, INC./SCOTT DATA—See General Electric Company; U.S. Public, pg. 711
THE POTOMAC EDISON CO.—See Allegheny Power System, Inc.; U.S. Public, pg. 42
POTOMAC ELECTRIC POWER COMPANY; U.S. Public, pg. 1318
POTOMAC GRAPHIC INDUSTRIES, INC.—See Jannock Limited; Int'l, pg. 699
POTOMAC INSURANCE CO. OF ILLINOIS—See General Accident Fire and Life Assurance Corporation p.l.c.; Int'l, pg. 543
POTOMAC VALLEY BANK—See Mercantile Bankshares Corporation; U.S. Public, pg. 1089
POTPOURRI (HARTE-HANKS NORTHERN CALIFORNIA CDM, INC.)—See Harte-Hanks Communications, Inc.; U.S. Public, pg. 794
CLARKSON N. POTTER, INC.—See Advance Publications Inc.; U.S. Private, pg. 21
POTTER-SHACKELFORD CONSTRUCTION CO.; U.S. Private, pg. 877
POTTER WARBURG ASSET MANAGEMENT—See Swiss Bank Corporation; Int'l, pg. 1331
POTTER WARBURG ASSET MANAGEMENT LTD.—See Swiss Bank Corporation; Int'l, pg. 1331
POTTER WARBURG PTY. LTD.—See Swiss Bank Corporation; Int'l, pg. 1331
POTTERS INDUSTRIES, INC.—See PQ Corporation; U.S. Private, pg. 827
POTTERTON MYSON—See Blue Circle Industries PLC; Int'l, pg. 197
THE POTTERY BARN EAST, INC.—See Williams-Sonoma, Inc.; U.S. Public, pg. 1770
POUGHKEEPSIE FINANCIAL CORP.; U.S. Public, pg. 1319
POUGHKEEPSIE NEWSPAPERS—See Gannett Company, Inc.; U.S. Public, pg. 700
POULTER COMMUNICATIONS PLC; Int'l, pg. 1065
POULTRY GROUP—See Goodman Fielder Limited; Int'l, pg. 555
POUNDER EMULSIONS, LTD.—See Husky Oil Ltd.; Int'l, pg. 640
POW CON—See Illinois Tool Works Inc.; U.S. Public, pg. 867
POWDER RIVER COAL COMPANY—See Hanson PLC; Int'l, pg. 594
POWDERTECH CORPORATION—See Mitsui & Co., Ltd.; Int'l, pg. 878
POWELL DUFFRYN (FINANCE) LIMITED—See Powell Duffryn PLC; Int'l, pg. 1066
POWELL DUFFRYN INTERNATIONAL FUELS LTD.—See Powell Duffryn PLC; Int'l, pg. 1065
POWELL DUFFRYN PLC; Int'l, pg. 1065
POWELL DUFFRYN SHIPPING LTD.—See Powell Duffryn PLC; Int'l, pg. 1065
POWELL DUFFRYN STANDARD LIMITED—See Powell Duffryn PLC; Int'l, pg. 1065
POWELL DUFFRYN STORAGE LIMITED—See Powell Duffryn PLC; Int'l, pg. 1065
POWELL DUFFRYN TOOLS LIMITED—See Powell Duffryn PLC; Int'l, pg. 1066
POWELL ELECTRICAL MFG. CO.—See Powell Industries, Inc.; U.S. Public, pg. 1319
POWELL ELECTRONICS INC.; U.S. Private, pg. 877
POWELL EQUIPMENT LTD.; Int'l, pg. 1066
POWELL ESCO COMPANY—See Powell Industries, Inc.; U.S. Public, pg. 1319
POWELL INDUSTRIES, INC.; U.S. Public, pg. 1319
L. POWELL CO., INC.; U.S. Private, pg. 877
THE WM. POWELL COMPANY; U.S. Private, pg. 877
POWELL'S PEST CONTROL PTY. LTD.—See Sophus Berendsen A/S; Int'l, pg. 1286
POWER—See The McGraw-Hill Companies; U.S. Public, pg. 1071
POWER AND COMPRESSION GROUP—See Toromont Industries Ltd.; Int'l, pg. 1400
POWER & MOTORYACHT MAGAZINE—See Primedia Inc.; U.S. Public, pg. 1328
POWER & TELEPHONE SUPPLY COMPANY; U.S. Private, pg. 877
POWER BUSINESS—See Black & Veatch; U.S. Private, pg. 146
POWER CON—See Klockner-Moeller GmbH; Int'l, pg. 736
POWER CONTRACTING & ENGINEERING CORP.; U.S. Private, pg. 877
POWER CONVERSION—See American Power Conversion Corporation; U.S. Public, pg. 90
POWER CONVERSION—See Computer Products, Inc.; U.S. Public, pg. 422
POWER CONVERSION ASIA-PACIFIC—See Computer Products, Inc.; U.S. Public, pg. 422
POWER CONVERSION EUROPE—See Computer Products, Inc.; U.S. Public, pg. 422
POWER CONVERSION, INC.—See BTR plc; Int'l, pg. 127
POWER CONVERSION NORTH AMERICA—See Computer Products, Inc.; U.S. Public, pg. 422
POWER CONVERSION-NORTH AMERICA WEST—See Computer Products, Inc.; U.S. Public, pg. 422
POWER DESIGNS, INC.; U.S. Private, pg. 878
POWER DEVELOPMENT—See Bowthorpe plc; Int'l, pg. 207

POWER DEVELOPMENT COMPANY—See Tractebel; Int'l, pg. 1415
POWER DIVISION—See Morrison Knudsen Corporation; U.S. Public, pg. 1134
POWER ENGINEERING LTD.—See Tamrock Corp.; Int'l, pg. 1353
POWER EQUIPMENT CO.—See Eclipse Inc.; U.S. Private, pg. 360
POWER EQUIPMENT SUPPLY COMPANY—See Cinergy Corp.; U.S. Public, pg. 369
POWER FUELS, INC.—See Bell Atlantic Corporation; U.S. Public, pg. 203
POWER GEAR—See Applied Power Inc.; U.S. Public, pg. 124
POWER HOUSE TECHNOLOGIES, INC.; U.S. Public, pg. 1319
POWER INDUSRIES LTD.—See Powers Fastening, Inc.; U.S. Private, pg. 878
J.D. POWER AND ASSOCIATES; U.S. Private, pg. 878
THE POWER LINE—See Publishers Clearing House; U.S. Private, pg. 893
POWER MANAGEMENT ASSOCIATES, INC.—See GP Strategies Corporation; U.S. Public, pg. 695
POWER MARKETS DEVELOPMENT COMPANY—See PP&L Resources; U.S. Public, pg. 1244
POWER-ONE, INC.; U.S. Private, pg. 878
POWER-PACKER EUROPA B.V.—See Applied Power Inc.; U.S. Public, pg. 125
POWER-PACKER FRANCE—See Applied Power Inc.; U.S. Public, pg. 125
POWER-PACKER U.S.—See Applied Power Inc.; U.S. Public, pg. 124
POWER PIPING COMPANY—See MYR Group Inc.; U.S. Public, pg. 1029
POWER PLASTICS INC.—See Tiffany Extruders, Inc.; U.S. Private, pg. 1086
POWER PROCESS PIPING, INC.; U.S. Private, pg. 878
POWER PRODUCT GROUP—See BTR plc; Int'l, pg. 126
POWER PURCHASING, INC.—See Chemical Leaman Corporation; U.S. Private, pg. 233
POWER SHRED DIVISION—See Fellowes Manufacturing Co.; U.S. Private, pg. 400
POWER SOURCES, INC.—See ChemFirst Inc.; U.S. Public, pg. 344
POWER SOUTH—See Alabama Electric Cooperative, Inc.; U.S. Private, pg. 30
POWER SPECTRUM TECHNOLOGY LTD.—See Geotek Communications; U.S. Public, pg. 740
POWER SYSTEMS GROUP—See Jetronic Industries, Inc.; U.S. Private, pg. 927
POWER SYSTEMS INC.—See Minebea Co., Ltd.; Int'l, pg. 868
POWER TEAM DIVISION—See SPX Corporation; U.S. Public, pg. 1421
POWER TRANSFORMER DIVISION—See ABB Asea Brown Boveri (Holding) Ltd.; Int'l, pg. 4
POWER TRANSFORMERS & COMPONENTS—See ABB Asea Brown Boveri (Holding) Ltd.; Int'l, pg. 4
POWER TRANSMISSION INDUSTRIES DO BRASIL S.A.—See Sundstrand Corporation; U.S. Public, pg. 1534
THE POWERBASE MARKETING GROUP—See Larkin Meeder & Schweidel; U.S. Private, pg. 651
POWERCONTRACTING S.A.—See Tractebel; Int'l, pg. 1415
POWERCOR AUSTRALIA LIMITED—See PacifiCorp; U.S. Public, pg. 1252
POWER-DYNE—See Bidwell Industrial Group, Inc.; U.S. Private, pg. 142
POWERED BY MOTOROLA—See Motorola, Inc.; U.S. Public, pg. 1137
POWEREX INC.—See Mitsubishi Electric Corporation; Int'l, pg. 873
POWERFIN S.A.—See Tractebel; Int'l, pg. 1415
POWERFIN UK—See Tractebel; Int'l, pg. 1415
POWERFLEX—See Senior Engineering Group, plc.; Int'l, pg. 1221
POWERHOUSE SYSTEMS, INC.—See Canon Inc.; Int'l, pg. 261
POWERINE OIL COMPANY—See Castle Energy Corporation; U.S. Public, pg. 314
POWERLINES CENTRAL AFRICA (PVT.)—See ABB Asea Brown Boveri (Holding) Ltd.; Int'l, pg. 3
POWERLINES LTD.—See ABB Asea Brown Boveri (Holding) Ltd.; Int'l, pg. 3
POWERMATIC—See DeVlieg-Bullard Inc.; U.S. Public, pg. 502
POWERPLAN SYSTEMS LTD—See Wolseley Plc.; Int'l, pg. 1512
POWERS CONSTRUCTION CO., INC.; U.S. Private, pg. 878
POWERS FASTENING, INC.; U.S. Private, pg. 878
POWERS PROCESS CONTROLS—See Crane Co.; U.S. Public, pg. 457
POWERSCREEN INTERNATIONAL PLC; Int'l, pg. 1066
POWERSERV LIMITED—See Borland International, Inc.; U.S. Public, pg. 246
POWERTECH—See Klockner-Moeller GmbH; Int'l, pg. 736
POWERTV, INC.—See Scientific-Atlanta, Inc.; U.S. Public, pg. 1443
POWLIFT TRUCKS & SYSTEMS—See Powell Equipment Ltd.; Int'l, pg. 1066
POZUELO, S.A.—See Riviana Foods Inc.; U.S. Public, pg. 1392
ARTHUR A. POZZI CO., INC.; U.S. Private, pg. 878
POZZOLITH BUSSAN CO. LTD.—See Novartis AG; Int'l, pg. 983
PRAB, INC.; U.S. Public, pg. 1319
PRACHT SPEDITION & LOGISTIK GMBH—See Hapag-Lloyd AG; Int'l, pg. 596
PRACON—See Reed Elsevier plc; Int'l, pg. 1100
PRACTICAL PERIPHERALS—See Hayes Corporation; U.S. Public, pg. 801

PRACTICE DEVELOPMENT INSTITUTE—See Friedman, Eisenstein, Raemer and Schwartz, LLP; U.S. Private, pg. 428
PRACTICE PATTERNS SCIENCE—See Express Scripts, Inc.; U.S. Public, pg. 601
PRACTITIONERS PUBLISHING CO.—See The Thomson Corporation; U.S. Public, pg. 1601
PRAEMIX WIRKSTOFF GMBH—See Corange Limited; Int'l, pg. 331
PRAGER HANDELSBANK AG—See Raiffeisen Zentralbank Osterreich; Int'l, pg. 1085
PRAGMA/DMB&B—See DMB&B Communications; U.S. Private, pg. 305
PRAGMATON—See Omnicom Group Inc.; U.S. Public, pg. 1224
PRAGOPLETTAC S.R.O.—See Plettac AG; Int'l, pg. 1061
PRAGUE OFFICE—See TVX Gold Inc.; Int'l, pg. 1345
PRAIRIE COMMUNICATIONS, INC.—See Aliant Communications; U.S. Public, pg. 41
PRAIRIE FARMS DAIRY, INC.; U.S. Private, pg. 878
PRAIRIE FARMS DAIRY SUPPLY CORP.—See Prairie Farms Dairy, Inc.; U.S. Private, pg. 879
PRAIRIE MALT LIMITED—See Saskatchewan Wheat Pool; Int'l, pg. 1195
PRAIRIELANDS ENERGY MARKETING, INC.—See MDU Resources Group, Inc.; U.S. Public, pg. 1025
PRAKIT/FCB—See FCB; U.S. Private, pg. 389
PRAKLA-SEISMOS AG—See Schlumberger Limited; U.S. Public, pg. 1439
PRAKOLL, S.A.—See H.B. Fuller Company; U.S. Public, pg. 687
PRAKTIKER BAU- UND HEIMWERKEMARKT AG—See Metro AG; Int'l, pg. 863
PRAP JAPAN, INC.—See Ketchum Communications Inc.; U.S. Private, pg. 617
PRAT DE ALLO MILL—See Fort James Corporation; U.S. Public, pg. 673
ETS. PRATE S.A.—See Fuchs Petrolub AG Oel + Chemie; Int'l, pg. 518
PRATT & LAMBERT PAINTS—See The Sherwin-Williams Company; U.S. Public, pg. 1466
PRATT & LAMBERT SPECIALTY PRODUCTS—See The Sherwin-Williams Company; U.S. Public, pg. 1466
PRATT & LAMBERT UNITED, INC.—See The Sherwin-Williams Company; U.S. Public, pg. 1466
PRATT & WHITNEY—See Moore Products Co.; U.S. Public, pg. 1128
PRATT & WHITNEY CANADA INC.—See United Technologies Corporation; U.S. Public, pg. 1690
PRATT & WHITNEY—See United Technologies Corporation; U.S. Public, pg. 1690
PRATT CASINO CORPORATION—See Greate Bay Casino Corporation; U.S. Public, pg. 761
HENRY PRATT CO.—See Tyco International Ltd.; U.S. Public, pg. 1651
PRATT INDUSTRIES; Int'l, pg. 1066
PRATT INDUSTRIES USA—See Pratt Industries; Int'l, pg. 1066
PRATT-READ CORPORATION; U.S. Private, pg. 879
PRATTEN CONSTRUCTION—See British Building & Engineering Appliances Plc; Int'l, pg. 219
PRATTVILLE MFG., INC.—See Echlin Inc.; U.S. Public, pg. 561
PRATTVILLE PROGRESS—See Gannett Company, Inc.; U.S. Public, pg. 699
PRAWEMA BERUFSAUSBILDUNG GMBH—See Rothenberger Group GmbH; Int'l, pg. 1128
PRAWEMA MACHINE TOOLS GMBH—See Rothenberger Group GmbH; Int'l, pg. 1128
PRAXAIR ARGENTINA S.A.—See Praxair Inc.; U.S. Public, pg. 1320
PRAXAIR ASIA, INC.—See Praxair Inc.; U.S. Public, pg. 1320
PRAXAIR B.V.—See Praxair Inc.; U.S. Public, pg. 1320
PRAXAIR ESPANIA S.A.—See Praxair Inc.; U.S. Public, pg. 1320
PRAXAIR GMBH—See Praxair Inc.; U.S. Public, pg. 1320
PRAXAIR IBERICA S.A.—See Praxair Inc.; U.S. Public, pg. 1320
PRAXAIR INC.; U.S. Public, pg. 1319
PRAXAIR K.K.—See Praxair Inc.; U.S. Public, pg. 1320
PRAXAIR KOREA—See Praxair Inc.; U.S. Public, pg. 1320
PRAXAIR N.V.—See Praxair Inc.; U.S. Public, pg. 1320
PRAXAIR PUERTO RICO, INC.—See Praxair Inc.; U.S. Public, pg. 1320
PRAXAIR S.A.—See Praxair Inc.; U.S. Public, pg. 1320
PRAXAIR SURFACE TECHNOLOGIES, INC.—See Praxair Inc.; U.S. Public, pg. 1320
PRAXIS DOE-HET-ZELF CENTER B.V.—See N.V. Koninklijke Bijenkorf Beheer KBB; Int'l, pg. 750
PRAYON DE PAUW N.V.—See Carclo Engineering Group plc; Int'l, pg. 268
PRE FINISH METALS (EG) INC.—See Bethlehem Steel Corporation; U.S. Public, pg. 226
PRE FINISH METALS (EG) INC.—See Inland Steel Industries, Inc.; U.S. Public, pg. 879
PRE FINISH METALS INCORPORATED—See Material Sciences Corporation; U.S. Public, pg. 1056
PRE-MIX CONCRETE CO.—See H.G. Fenton Material Company; U.S. Private, pg. 400
PRE-PAID LEGAL SERVICES, INC.; U.S. Public, pg. 1320
PRE-STAR LTD.—See Fried. Krupp AG; Int'l, pg. 507
PREBETONG IBIZA S.A.—See Lafarge S.A.; Int'l, pg. 790
PREBOUND PERIODICALS, INC.—See The American Companies; U.S. Private, pg. 52
PRECIOUS METALS MANAGEMENT—See Engelhard Corporation; U.S. Public, pg. 582
PRECIPITAIR POLLUTION CONTROL—See Cendant Corporation; U.S. Public, pg. 320
PRECIPTECH, INC.—See BHA Group Holdings Inc.; U.S. Public, pg. 161
PRECISION—See Jami, Inc.; U.S. Private, pg. 581

PRECISION ARC CO.—See Smith Industries, Inc.; *U.S. Private*, pg. 1008
PRECISION ASBESTOS ABATEMENT COMPANY—See Hoffman Corporation; *U.S. Private*, pg. 532
PRECISION CARBIDE TOOL COMPANY, INC.; *U.S. Private*, pg. 879
PRECISION CASTPARTS CORP.; *U.S. Public*, pg. 1320
PRECISION CLEAN PIPING, INC.—See McJunkin Corporation; *U.S. Private*, pg. 722
PRECISION CONSTRUCTION COMPANY—See Hoffman Corporation; *U.S. Private*, pg. 532
PRECISION CONTROLS DIVISION—See COMSAT Corporation; *U.S. Public*, pg. 424
PRECISION DIE & ENGINEERING, INC.—See Premark International, Inc.; *U.S. Public*, pg. 1322
PRECISION DISC CORP.—See North American Products Corp.; *U.S. Private*, pg. 803
PRECISION DRAWN TUBE—See Senior Engineering Group, plc.; *Int'l*, pg. 1222
PRECISION DRILLING CORPORATION; *Int'l*, pg. 1066
PRECISION DYNAMICS CORPORATION; *U.S. Private*, pg. 879
PRECISION DYNAMICS INTERNATIONAL INC.—See Precision Dynamics Corporation; *U.S. Private*, pg. 879
PRECISION ELECTRONIQUE—See Hewlett-Packard Company; *U.S. Public*, pg. 822
PRECISION EXTRUSIONS; *U.S. Private*, pg. 879
PRECISION FASTENERS LTD.—See SPS Technologies, Inc.; *U.S. Public*, pg. 1420
PRECISION FIBERGLASS—See Maclean-Fogg Co.; *U.S. Private*, pg. 692
PRECISION FOODS, INC.—See Varied Investments, Inc.; *U.S. Private*, pg. 1134
PRECISION FORMING FACILITY—See GKN plc; *Int'l*, pg. 535
PRECISION INDUSTRIES; *U.S. Private*, pg. 879
PRECISION INDUSTRIES DIVISION—See Leggett & Platt, Incorporated; *U.S. Public*, pg. 986
PRECISION INTERCONNECT—See AMP Incorporated; *U.S. Public*, pg. 8
PRECISION LAMP, INC.—See ILC Technology, Inc.; *U.S. Public*, pg. 856
PRECISION METALCRAFT—See Bell Industries, Inc.; *U.S. Public*, pg. 205
PRECISION MOTORS - DEUTSCHE MINEBEA GMBH—See Minebea Co., Ltd.; *Int'l*, pg. 869
PRECISION MOULDS, INC.—See Mattel, Inc.; *U.S. Public*, pg. 1059
PRECISION OFFICE INDUSTRIES—See International Paper Company; *U.S. Public*, pg. 904
PRECISION PARTS CORP.; *U.S. Private*, pg. 879
PRECISION PLASTICS INC.; *U.S. Private*, pg. 879
PRECISION POWER DIV.—See AEI Holding Co., Inc.; *U.S. Private*, pg. 5
PRECISION POWER, INC.—See United Illuminating Company; *U.S. Public*, pg. 1678
PRECISION PRINTING & PACKAGING—See Anheuser-Busch Companies, Inc.; *U.S. Public*, pg. 115
PRECISION PRODUCTS CORPORATION; *U.S. Private*, pg. 879
PRECISION PRODUCTS DIVISION—See NSK Ltd.; *Int'l*, pg. 903
PRECISION RESOURCE CALIFORNIA DIV.—See Precision Resource Inc.; *U.S. Private*, pg. 880
PRECISION RESOURCE CANADIAN DIV.—See Precision Resource Inc.; *U.S. Private*, pg. 880
PRECISION RESOURCE FLORIDA DIV.—See Precision Resource Inc.; *U.S. Private*, pg. 880
PRECISION RESOURCE INC.; *U.S. Private*, pg. 880
PRECISION RESOURCE-KENTUCKY DIV.—See Precision Resource Inc.; *U.S. Private*, pg. 880
PRECISION ROLL GRINDERS, INC.; *U.S. Private*, pg. 880
PRECISION RUBBER SEALINGS S.R.L.—See Freudenberg & Company; *Int'l*, pg. 506
PRECISION S.A.—See Siebe plc; *Int'l*, pg. 1244
PRECISION SCIENTIFIC INC.—See Jouan, Inc.; *U.S. Private*, pg. 601
PRECISION SOLAR CONTROLS—See Stabler Companies, Inc.; *U.S. Private*, pg. 1028
PRECISION SPECIALTY METALS, INC.—See Dubin-Clark & Company; *U.S. Private*, pg. 344
PRECISION STANDARD, INC.; *U.S. Public*, pg. 1321
PRECISION STEEL WAREHOUSE, INC.—See Berkshire Hathaway Inc.; *U.S. Public*, pg. 217
PRECISION SYSTEMS, INC.; *U.S. Public*, pg. 1321
PRECISION TECH SERVICES (PVT.) LTD.—See Hewlett-Packard Company; *U.S. Public*, pg. 822
PRECISION TECHNOLOGY—See ARC International Corporation; *Int'l*, pg. 17
PRECISION TUBE FORMERS—See HMI Industries; *U.S. Public*, pg. 771
PRECISION TUNE AUTOCARE INC.; *U.S. Public*, pg. 1321
PRECISION TWIST DRILL CO.—See Sandvik AB; *Int'l*, pg. 1185
PRECISION UNIVERSAL JOINT CO.—See Cooper Industries, Inc.; *U.S. Public*, pg. 443
PRECISION VALVE CORPORATION; *U.S. Private*, pg. 880
PRECISIONAIRE, INC.—See Flanders Corp.; *U.S. Public*, pg. 648
PRECISMECA-MONTAN GESELLSCHAFT FUR FORDERTECHNIK MBH—See Deutsche Babcock AG; *Int'l*, pg. 399
PRECISMECA S.A.—See Deutsche Babcock AG; *Int'l*, pg. 399
PRECON AB—See Scancem AB; *Int'l*, pg. 1199
PRECON HUS AB—See Scancem AB; *Int'l*, pg. 1199
PRECON TEKNIK AB—See Scancem AB; *Int'l*, pg. 1199
PRECON VA SYSTEM AB—See Scancem AB; *Int'l*, pg. 1199
PRECONAL—See Falkema AB; *Int'l*, pg. 477
PRECOR, INC.—See Premark International, Inc.; *U.S. Public*, pg. 1322
PREDELIVERY SERVICE CORPORATION—See Ford Motor Company; *U.S. Public*, pg. 664

PREDICASTS—See The Thomson Corporation; *U.S. Public*, pg. 1600
PREDIL-PERTUSOLA—See Imetal; *Int'l*, pg. 662
PREDSTAVEITLSTVO FIRMY "ENSO"—See Enso Oyj; *Int'l*, pg. 458
PREDSTAVITELSTVO "ENSO"—See Enso Oyj; *Int'l*, pg. 458
PREEM PETROLEUM AB; *Int'l*, pg. 1066
PREFA LYSA NAD LABEM A.S.—See Dyckerhoff & Widmann AG; *Int'l*, pg. 425
PREFERRED ABSTAINERS INSURANCE COMPAN—See Preferred Risk Mutual Insurance; *U.S. Private*, pg. 880
PREFERRED AMERICA INSURANCE COMPANY—See Preferred Risk Mutual Insurance; *U.S. Private*, pg. 880
PREFERRED DIRECT—See Eureko B.V.; *Int'l*, pg. 464
PREFERRED HEALTH NETWORK—See Foundation Health Systems, Inc.; *U.S. Public*, pg. 678
PREFERRED INSTRUMENTS—See Preferred Utilities Manufacturing Corp.; *U.S. Private*, pg. 881
PREFERRED/KAHLER ASSOCIATES—See Sunstone Hotel Investors, Inc.; *U.S. Public*, pg. 1537
PREFERRED MILLWORK, INC.—See Marmac Corporation; *U.S. Private*, pg. 706
PREFERRED PRODUCTS, INC.—See SuperValu, Inc.; *U.S. Public*, pg. 1541
PREFERRED PROPERTIES—See Tucson Realty & Trust Co.; *U.S. Private*, pg. 1109
PREFERRED PUBLIC STORAGE CO.—See Certified Grocers of California; *U.S. Public*, pg. 227
PREFERRED RISK INSURANCE COMPANY—See Corporacion MAPFRE, Compania Internacional de Reaseguros, S.A.; *Int'l*, pg. 333
PREFERRED RISK LIFE INSURANCE CO.—See Preferred Risk Mutual Insurance; *U.S. Private*, pg. 880
PREFERRED RISK LLOYD'S INSURANCE COMPANY—See Preferred Risk Mutual Insurance; *U.S. Private*, pg. 880
PREFERRED RISK MUTUAL INSURANCE; *U.S. Private*, pg. 880
PREFERRED SURETY CORPORATION—See SunTrust Banks, Inc.; *U.S. Public*, pg. 1538
PREFERRED UTILITIES MANUFACTURING CORP.; *U.S. Private*, pg. 881
PREFORMADOS DE MEXICO SA—See Preformed Line Products; *U.S. Public*, pg. 1321
PREFORMED LINE PRODUCTS; *U.S. Public*, pg. 1321
PREFORMED LINE PRODUCTS CANADA—See Preformed Line Products; *U.S. Public*, pg. 1321
PREFORMED LINE PRODUCTS(GREAT BRITAIN) LTD.—See Preformed Line Products; *U.S. Public*, pg. 1321
PREMARC CORPORATION; *U.S. Private*, pg. 881
PREMARK FOOD EQUIPMENT GROUP BELGIUM, N.V.—See Premark International, Inc.; *U.S. Public*, pg. 1323
PREMARK INTERNATIONAL, INC.; *U.S. Public*, pg. 1321
PREMDOR ENTRY SYSTEMS—See Premdor Inc.; *Int'l*, pg. 1067
PREMDOR INC.; *Int'l*, pg. 1066
PREMDOR, INC.—See Premdor Inc.; *Int'l*, pg. 1067
PREMDOR INC.-ATLANTIC DIVISION—See Premdor Inc.; *Int'l*, pg. 1067
PREMDOR INC.-DOOR DISTRIBUTION—See Premdor Inc.; *Int'l*, pg. 1067
PREMDOR INC.-FLUSH DOOR PLANT—See Premdor Inc.; *Int'l*, pg. 1067
PREMDOR INC.-LOUVRE DOOR—See Premdor Inc.; *Int'l*, pg. 1067
PREMDOR INC.-MOULDINGS DISTRIBUTION—See Premdor Inc.; *Int'l*, pg. 1067
PREMDOR INC.-QUEBEC DIVISION—See Premdor Inc.; *Int'l*, pg. 1067
PREMDOR MOULDINGS INC.—See Premdor Inc.; *Int'l*, pg. 1067
PREMDOR U.S. HOLDINGS, INC.—See Premdor Inc.; *Int'l*, pg. 1067
PREMDOR WOOD PRODUCTS—See Premdor Inc.; *Int'l*, pg. 1067
PREMETALCO INC.—See Preussag AG; *Int'l*, pg. 1071
PREMIER AUTOWARE—See Premier Farnell plc; *Int'l*, pg. 1068
PREMIER BANK N.A.—See Banc One Corporation; *U.S. Public*, pg. 173
PREMIER BANKING—See Bank of Ireland; *Int'l*, pg. 152
PREMIER BRANDS, INC.—See Premier CDN Enterprises Ltd.; *Int'l*, pg. 1068
PREMIER BUILDING GROUP—See AAF Industries Plc; *Int'l*, pg. 1
PREMIER CDN ENTERPRISES LTD.; *Int'l*, pg. 1067
PREMIER CHEMICAL CO., LTD.—See Crompton & Knowles Corporation; *U.S. Public*, pg. 460
PREMIER CHEMICAL PLANT—See Crompton & Knowles Corporation; *U.S. Public*, pg. 460
PREMIER COATINGS, INC.—See Wattyl; *Int'l*, pg. 1488
PREMIER CRUISES—See Cruise Holdings Ltd.; *U.S. Private*, pg. 293
PREMIER DAIRIES (WEXFORD) LIMITED—See Avonmore Waterford Group plc; *Int'l*, pg. 102
PREMIER DENTAL PRODUCTS COMPANY; *U.S. Private*, pg. 881
PREMIER DRYWALL TOOL COMPANY—See Kelly-Moore Paint Company, Inc.; *U.S. Private*, pg. 613
PREMIER EDIBLE OILS CORP.—See Mitsubishi Corporation; *Int'l*, pg. 872
PREMIER ENERGY CORPORATION—See Premier Farnell plc; *Int'l*, pg. 1068
PREMIER FARNELL—See Premier Farnell plc; *Int'l*, pg. 1068
PREMIER FARNELL PLC; *Int'l*, pg. 1068
PREMIER FASTENER—See Premier Farnell plc; *Int'l*, pg. 1068
PREMIER FASTENER LTD.—See Premier Farnell plc; *Int'l*, pg. 1068
PREMIER FOREIGN SALES CORPORATION, INC.—See Premier Farnell plc; *Int'l*, pg. 1068

PREMIER, INC.—See Lander Co., Inc.; *U.S. Private*, pg. 647
PREMIER INDUSTRIAL BELGIUM S.A.—See Premier Farnell plc; *Int'l*, pg. 1068
PREMIER INDUSTRIAL CORPORATION (INDIANA)—See Premier Farnell plc; *Int'l*, pg. 1068
PREMIER INDUSTRIAL FRANCE S.A.R.L.—See Premier Farnell plc; *Int'l*, pg. 1068
PREMIER INDUSTRIAL HOLLAND B.V.—See Premier Farnell plc; *Int'l*, pg. 1068
PREMIER INDUSTRIAL (U.K.) LTD.—See Premier Farnell plc; *Int'l*, pg. 1068
PREMIER INDUSTRIES, INC.; *U.S. Private*, pg. 881
PREMIER INSURANCE COMPANY—See Fremont General Corporation; *U.S. Public*, pg. 681
PREMIER INVESTMENT ADVISORS, L.C.—See Banc One Corporation; *U.S. Public*, pg. 173
PREMIER METAL PRODUCTS—See Premier Metal Products Co.; *U.S. Private*, pg. 881
PREMIER METAL PRODUCTS CO.; *U.S. Private*, pg. 881
PREMIER MILL CORP.; *U.S. Private*, pg. 881
PREMIER PARKS INC.; *U.S. Public*, pg. 1323
PREMIER POLYMERS, INC.—See Dainippon Ink & Chemicals, Inc.; *Int'l*, pg. 323
PREMIER POWER LTD.—See BG Plc; *Int'l*, pg. 119
PREMIER PRECISION LTD.—See Citizen Watch Company, Ltd.; *Int'l*, pg. 295
PREMIER REFRACTORIES (CANADA) LTD.—See The Alpine Group, Inc.; *U.S. Public*, pg. 58
PREMIER REFRACTORIES INTERNATIONAL INC.—See The Alpine Group, Inc.; *U.S. Public*, pg. 58
PREMIER SALONS INTERNATIONAL; *U.S. Private*, pg. 881
PREMIER SECURITIES CORPORATION—See Banc One Corporation; *U.S. Public*, pg. 173
PREMIER TECH LTEE—See Premier CDN Enterprises Ltd.; *Int'l*, pg. 1068
PREMIER TROPIC STAFFING, INC.—See Columbia/HCA Healthcare Corporation; *U.S. Public*, pg. 405
PREMIERCO SERVICE CORP.—See Premier Farnell plc; *Int'l*, pg. 1068
PREMISYS COMMUNICATIONS, INC.; *U.S. Public*, pg. 1323
PREMISYS COMMUNICATIONS LTD.—See Premisys Communications, Inc.; *U.S. Public*, pg. 1323
PREMISYS COMMUNICATIONS PTE LTD.—See Premisys Communications, Inc.; *U.S. Public*, pg. 1323
PREMIUM ADVANCE COMPANY—See Robert F. Driver Co., Inc.; *U.S. Private*, pg. 343
PREMIUM BUDGET PLAN, INC.—See The Seibels Bruce Group, Inc.; *U.S. Public*, pg. 1453
PREMIUM POLYMERS INC.—See Flexible Products Company; *U.S. Private*, pg. 412
PREMIUM PRODUCTS DIVISION—See MacAndrews & Forbes Holdings Inc.; *U.S. Private*, pg. 690
PREMIUM RECOVERY SERVICES INTERNATIONAL, INC.—See Cigna Corp.; *U.S. Public*, pg. 366
PREMIUM SERVICE CORP.—See The Seibels Bruce Group, Inc.; *U.S. Public*, pg. 1454
PREMIUM TANK LINE INC.—See Dewey Corporation; *U.S. Private*, pg. 329
PREMIUMS INTL. LTD.—See Carlson Companies, Inc.; *U.S. Private*, pg. 212
PREMIUMWEAR, INC.; *U.S. Public*, pg. 1323
PRENATAL B.V.—See N.V. Koninklijke Bijenkorf Beheer KBB; *Int'l*, pg. 750
PRENATAL, S.A.; *Int'l*, pg. 1068
PRENTICE HALL BUSINESS PUBLISHING—See National Amusements, Inc.; *U.S. Private*, pg. 778
PRENTICE HALL CANADA, INC.—See National Amusements, Inc.; *U.S. Private*, pg. 778
PRENTICE HALL EDUCATION, CAREER & TECHNOLOGY—See National Amusements, Inc.; *U.S. Private*, pg. 778
PRENTICE HALL ENGINEERING, SCIENCE & MATH—See National Amusements, Inc.; *U.S. Private*, pg. 778
PRENTICE-HALL HISPANOAMERICANA, S.A.—See National Amusements, Inc.; *U.S. Private*, pg. 778
PRENTICE HALL HUMANITIES & SOCIAL SCIENCES—See National Amusements, Inc.; *U.S. Private*, pg. 778
PRENTICE HALL OF AUSTRALIA PTY., LTD.—See National Amusements, Inc.; *U.S. Private*, pg. 778
PRENTICE-HALL OF INDIA PRIVATE LTD.—See National Amusements, Inc.; *U.S. Private*, pg. 778
PRENTICE HALL REGENTS/ESL—See National Amusements, Inc.; *U.S. Private*, pg. 778
PRENTICE HALL REGENTS JAPAN, INC.—See National Amusements, Inc.; *U.S. Private*, pg. 778
PRENTICE HALL SCHOOL—See National Amusements, Inc.; *U.S. Private*, pg. 778
PRENTISS INCORPORATED; *U.S. Private*, pg. 882
PREP - STAT/SPECTRUM; *U.S. Private*, pg. 882
PREPLATE LIMITED—See Campbells/Bewley Group; *Int'l*, pg. 254
PREPLINK—See Great Lakes Lithograph Co.; *U.S. Private*, pg. 475
PREPRESS SOLUTIONS, INC.; *U.S. Private*, pg. 882
PRESCO INTERNATIONAL B.V.—See Koninklijke BolsWessanen nv; *Int'l*, pg. 752
PRESCOLITE MOLDCAST LIGHTING COMPANY—See U.S. Industries, Inc.; *U.S. Public*, pg. 1684
THE PRESCOTT & NORTHWESTERN RAILROAD CO.—See Potlatch Corporation; *U.S. Public*, pg. 1318
GEORGE W. PRESCOTT PUBLISHING CO.; *U.S. Private*, pg. 882
PRESCRIPTION SOLUTIONS—See PacifiCare Health Systems, Inc.; *U.S. Public*, pg. 1251
PRESERVATIVE PAINT COMPANY—See Kelly-Moore Paint Company, Inc.; *U.S. Private*, pg. 613
PRESICARRE CORP.—See Carrefour; *Int'l*, pg. 273
PRESIDENT BAKING-AUGUSTA—See President Enterprises Corp.; *Int'l*, pg. 1069
PRESIDENT BAKING-BISHOP DIV—See President Enterprises Corp.; *Int'l*, pg. 1069

PRESIDENT BAKING-CHARLOTTE—See President Enterprises Corp.; *Int'l,* pg. 1069
PRESIDENT BAKING COMPANY—See President Enterprises Corp.; *Int'l,* pg. 1069
PRESIDENT BAKING INC.—See President Enterprises Corp.; *Int'l,* pg. 1069
PRESIDENT BAKING-LITTLE ROCK—See President Enterprises Corp.; *Int'l,* pg. 1069
PRESIDENT BAKING-LOUISVILLE—See President Enterprises Corp.; *Int'l,* pg. 1069
PRESIDENT BAKING-MARIETTA—See President Enterprises Corp.; *Int'l,* pg. 1069
PRESIDENT BAKING-PLANTATION—See President Enterprises Corp.; *Int'l,* pg. 1069
PRESIDENT CASINOS, INC.; *U.S. Public,* pg. 1323
PRESIDENT ENTERPRISES CORP.; *Int'l,* pg. 1068
PRESIDENT FOODS CO., LTD.—See President Enterprises Corp.; *Int'l,* pg. 1069
PRESIDENT FRITO-LAY CORP.—See President Enterprises Corp.; *Int'l,* pg. 1069
PRESIDENT HOMES—See Scherer Bros. Lumber Company; *U.S. Private,* pg. 970
PRESIDENT INC.—See Time Warner Inc.; *U.S. Public,* pg. 1615
PRESIDENTE BERNARDES REFINERY—See Petrobras - Petroleo Brasileiro S.A.; *Int'l,* pg 1042
PRESIDENTE GETULIO VARGAS REFINERY—See Petrobras - Petroleo Brasileiro S.A.; *Int'l,* pg. 1042
PRESIDENTIAL CONTINENTAL GARDENS CORP.—See Presidential Realty Corporation; *U.S. Public,* pg. 1323
PRESIDENTIAL LIFE CORPORATION; *U.S. Public,* pg. 1323
PRESIDENTIAL REALTY CORPORATION; *U.S. Public,* pg. 1323
PRESIDENTIAL REALTY OF IOWA, INC.—See Presidential Realty Corporation; *U.S. Public,* pg. 1324
PRESIDIO EXPLORATION, INC.—See Tom Brown, Inc.; *U.S. Public,* pg. 262
PRESLEY-HOME MAC FINANCE CO., INC.—See Pacific Enterprises; *U.S. Private,* pg. 1249
PRESLEY RAC FINANCE CO.; INC.—See Pacific Enterprises; *U.S. Private,* pg. 1249
THE PRESMET CORP.; *U.S. Private,* pg. 882
PRESQUE ISLE INSURANCE DIV.—See W.R. Berkley Corporation; *U.S. Public,* pg. 215
PRESRAY CORP.—See Pawling Corporation; *U.S. Private,* pg. 844
PRESS & SUN-BULLETIN—See Gannett Company, Inc.; *U.S. Public,* pg. 700
PRESS-CITIZEN COMPANY, INC.—See Gannett Company, Inc.; *U.S. Public,* pg. 701
PRESS COMMUNICATIONS, LLC; *U.S. Private,* pg. 882
PRESS CONSTRUCTION LTD., UTILITIES DIV.—See AMEC Plc; *Int'l,* pg. 16
THE PRESS DEMOCRAT—See The New York Times Company; *U.S. Public,* pg. 1175
PRESS ENTERPRISE COMPANY—See A.H. Belo Corporation; *U.S. Public,* pg. 209
PRESS OFFSHORE LTD.—See AMEC Plc; *Int'l,* pg. 16
PRESS-SHOP ALG.—See Lagardere Groupe; *Int'l,* pg. 796
PRESS- UND STANZWERK AG—See Fried. Krupp AG; *Int'l,* pg. 508
WILLIAM PRESS ENGINEERING SERVICES (NZ) LTD.— See AMEC Plc; *Int'l,* pg. 16
PRESSED STEEL TANK CO., INC.; *U.S. Private,* pg. 882
PRESSMAN TOY CORP.; *U.S. Private,* pg. 882
PRESSMAN TOY CORP.—See Pressman Toy Corp.; *U.S. Private,* pg. 882
PRESSPART MANUFACTURING LTD.—See BTR plc; *Int'l,* pg. 124
PRESSTECH CONTROLS GMBH—See Harnischfeger Industries, Inc.; *U.S. Public,* pg. 790
PRESSTECH CONTROLS INC.—See Harnischfeger Industries, Inc.; *U.S. Public,* pg. 790
PRESSTECH CONTROLS LIMITED—See Harnischfeger Industries, Inc.; *U.S. Public,* pg. 789
PRESSTECH CONTROLS LTD.—See Harnischfeger Industries, Inc.; *U.S. Public,* pg. 790
PRESSTECH CONTROLS SA—See Harnischfeger Industries, Inc.; *U.S. Public,* pg. 790
PRESSTECH CONTROLS SRL—See Harnischfeger Industries, Inc.; *U.S. Public,* pg. 790
PRESSTEK, INC.; *U.S. Public,* pg. 1324
PRESSURE PAK CONTAINER, INC.—See The Cypress Group LLC; *U.S. Private,* pg. 300
PRESSURE PRODUCTS INDUSTRIES—See Superior Group, Inc.; *U.S. Private,* pg. 1055
PRESSURE SYSTEMS, INC.—See The Roxboro Group PLC; *Int'l,* pg. 1130
PRESSURE SYSTEMS, INC.; *U.S. Private,* pg. 882
PRESTACIONES MEXICANAS—See Sodexho S.A.; *Int'l,* pg. 1275
PRESTACIONES VENEZOLANAS—See Sodexho S.A.; *Int'l,* pg. 1275
PRESTEC—See Cooper Industries, Inc.; *U.S. Public,* pg. 444
PRESTIA THAILANDE—See Lafarge S.A.; *Int'l,* pg. 791
PRESTIGE AB (SCANDINAVIAN MUSIC CLUB)—See Philips Electronics N.V.; *Int'l,* pg. 1053
PRESTIGE ET COLLECTIONS INTER. & CIE.—See L'Oreal S.A.; *Int'l,* pg. 818
PRESTIGE FORD; *U.S. Private,* pg. 882
PRESTIGE FRAGRANCE & COSMETICS, INC.—See MacAndrews & Forbes Holdings Inc.; *U.S. Private,* pg. 690
PRESTIGE FRAGRANCES, LTD.—See MacAndrews & Forbes Holdings Inc.; *U.S. Private,* pg. 690
PRESTIGE PERFUMES LTD.—See MacAndrews & Forbes Holdings Inc.; *U.S. Private,* pg. 690
PRESTIGE STAMPING, INC.; *U.S. Private,* pg. 882
PRESTIGE STATIONS INC.—See Atlantic Richfield Company; *U.S. Public,* pg. 144
PRESTO ENGINEERS CUTTING TOOLS LTD.—See Kennametal Inc.; *U.S. Public,* pg. 951

PRESTO EXPORT LTD.—See National Presto Industries, Inc.; *U.S. Public,* pg. 1159
PRESTO FOOD PRODUCTS, INC.—See Suiza Foods Corporation; *U.S. Public,* pg. 1527
PRESTO FOOD STORES, INC.; *U.S. Private,* pg. 882
PRESTO MANUFACTURING COMPANY—See National Presto Industries, Inc.; *U.S. Public,* pg. 1159
PRESTO PRODUCTS MANUFACTURING CO.—See National Presto Industries, Inc.; *U.S. Public,* pg. 1159
PRESTON COATED STONE—See RMC Group p.l.c.; *Int'l,* pg. 1079
PRESTON PROPERTIES OF ARIZONA, INC.—See Washington Mutual Inc.; *U.S. Public,* pg. 1742
PRESTON PROPERTIES OF CALIFORNIA, INC.—See Washington Mutual Inc.; *U.S. Public,* pg. 1742
PRESTON PROPERTIES TEXAS, INC.—See Washington Mutual Inc.; *U.S. Public,* pg. 1742
PRESTON PROPERTY MANAGEMENT COMPANY—See Washington Mutual Inc.; *U.S. Public,* pg. 1742
PRESTON RIDGE FINANCIAL SERVICES CORPORATION—See Washington Mutual Inc.; *U.S. Public,* pg. 1742
PRESTON TRUCKING COMPANY, INC.—See Yellow Corporation; *U.S. Public,* pg. 1788
PRESTONE PRODUCTS CORPORATION—See AlliedSignal Inc.; *U.S. Public,* pg. 51
PRETABAIL-SICOMI—See Total S.A.; *Int'l,* pg. 1409
PRETEC PRECISIE TECHNIEK B.V.—See Bell & Howell Holdings; *U.S. Public,* pg. 201
PRETORIA PORTLAND CEMENT CO. LTD.—See Barlow Ltd.; *Int'l,* pg. 167
PRETTY NEAT PRODUCTS—See Newell Co.; *U.S. Public,* pg. 1177
PRETTY POLLY LIMITED—See Sara Lee Corporation; *U.S. Public,* pg. 1434
PRETZEL TIME INC.—See Mrs. Fields' Original Cookies, Inc.; *U.S. Private,* pg. 688
PREUSSAG AG; *Int'l,* pg. 1069
PREUSSAG ANLAGENBAU GMBH—See Preussag AG; *Int'l,* pg. 1069
PREUSSAG ANTHRAZIT GMBH—See Preussag AG; *Int'l,* pg. 1069
PREUSSAG ENERGIE GMBH—See Preussag AG; *Int'l,* pg. 1069
PREUSSAG HANDEL GMBH—See Preussag AG; *Int'l,* pg. 1069
PREUSSAG IMMOBILIEN GMBH—See Preussag AG; *Int'l,* pg. 1070
PREUSSAG INTERNATIONAL STEEL CORP.—See Preussag AG; *Int'l,* pg. 1070
PREUSSAG NORTH AMERICA—See Preussag AG; *Int'l,* pg. 1070
PREUSSAG VERSICHERUNGSDIENST GMBH—See Preussag AG; *Int'l,* pg. 1070
PREUSSENELEKTRA AKTIENGESELLSCHAFT—See Veba AG; *Int'l,* pg. 1456
PREUSSENELEKTRA-KERNBRENNSTOFF GMBH—See Veba AG; *Int'l,* pg. 1457
PREUSSENELEKTRA SCANDINAVIA AB—See Veba AG; *Int'l,* pg. 1457
PREUSSENELEKTRA TELEKOM GMBH—See Veba AG; *Int'l,* pg. 1456
PREUSSENELEKTRA/VKR—See Veba AG; *Int'l,* pg. 1456
PREUSSENELEKTRA WINDKRAFT NIEDERSACHSEN GMBH—See Veba AG; *Int'l,* pg. 1456
PREUSSENELEKTRA WINDKRAFT SCHLESWIG-HOLSTEIN GMBH—See Veba AG; *Int'l,* pg. 1456
PREVAG PROVINZIALSACHSISCHE ENERGIEVERSORGUNGS-GMBH—See Veba AG; *Int'l,* pg. 1457
PREVICOMMERICO—See Allianz Aktiengesellschaft; *Int'l,* pg. 62
PREVINDUSTRIA—See Allianz Aktiengesellschaft; *Int'l,* pg. 62
PRIAB AB—See Axel Johnson AB; *Int'l,* pg. 709
PRIBAS—See Groupe Casino; *Int'l,* pg. 563
PRICE BROTHERS CO.; *U.S. Private,* pg. 883
PRICE CHOPPER OPERATING CO. IN VT., INC.—See Golub Corporation; *U.S. Private,* pg. 463
PRICE CHOPPER OPERATING CO., INC.—See Golub Corporation; *U.S. Private,* pg. 463
PRICE CHOPPER OPERATING CO. OF MASS., INC.—See Golub Corporation; *U.S. Private,* pg. 463
PRICE CHOPPER OPERATING CO. OF PA, INC.—See Golub Corporation; *U.S. Private,* pg. 463
PRICE COMMUNICATIONS CORPORATION; *U.S. Public,* pg. 1324
PRICE ENTERPRISES, INC.; *U.S. Public,* pg. 1324
PRICE/MCNABB, INC.; *U.S. Public,* pg. 883
PRICE/MCNABB, INC.—See Price/McNabb, Inc.; *U.S. Private,* pg. 883
PRICE PFISTER, INC.—See The Black & Decker Corporation; *U.S. Public,* pg. 234
PRICE RIVER COAL CO., INC.—See American Electric Power Company, Inc.; *U.S. Public,* pg. 72
PRICE STERN SLOAN INC.—See The Seagram Company Ltd.; *Int'l,* pg. 1215
T. ROWE PRICE ASSOCIATES, INC.; *U.S. Public,* pg. 1324
T. ROWE PRICE INVESTMENT SERVICES INC.—See T. Rowe Price Associates, Inc.; *U.S. Public,* pg. 1324
PRICE WATERHOUSE L.L.P. - U.S.; *U.S. Private,* pg. 883
PRICE WOODS, INC.—See Joe E. Woods, Inc.; *U.S. Private,* pg. 1187
PRICELLULAR CORPORATION; *U.S. Public,* pg. 1324
PRICE/PALMER WIRELESS CORP—See Price Communications Corporation; *U.S. Public,* pg. 1324
PRICE'S CREAMERIES—See Dean Foods Company; *U.S. Public,* pg. 491
PRICE'S PATENT CANDLE CO. LTD.—See Royal Dutch/ Shell Group of Companies; *Int'l,* pg. 1139
PRICESMART INC.; *U.S. Public,* pg. 1324
PRIDE HEALTH CARE, INC.; *U.S. Private,* pg. 883
PRIDE INTERNATIONAL, INC.; *U.S. Public,* pg. 1324

PRIDE INTERNATIONAL, LTD.—See Pride International, Inc.; *U.S. Public,* pg. 1325
PRIDE OFFSHORE, INC.—See Pride International, Inc.; *U.S. Public,* pg. 1325
PRIDE OIL CO., INC.—See Kelso Oil Company; *U.S. Private,* pg. 613
PRIDE PRODUCTS, INC.; *U.S. Private,* pg. 883
PRIDGEON & CLAY, INC.; *U.S. Private,* pg. 883
PRIESTLEY FOOTWEAR LTD.—See Pentland Group PLC; *Int'l,* pg. 1036
PRIESTLY INSURANCE CO. LTD.—See The BOC Group plc; *Int'l,* pg. 122
PRIFAST AB—See Axel Johnson AB; *Int'l,* pg. 709
PRIMA ENERGY CORPORATION; *U.S. Public,* pg. 1325
PRIMA INTERNATIONAL—See Imaging Technologies Corp.; *U.S. Public,* pg. 870
PRIMA NATURAL GAS MARKETING, INC.—See Prima Energy Corporation; *U.S. Public,* pg. 1325
PRIMA OIL AND GAS COMPANY—See Prima Energy Corporation; *U.S. Public,* pg. 1325
PRIMAC CORP.; *U.S. Private,* pg. 883
PRIMAGAS DUSSELDORF GMBH—See SHV Holdings N.V.; *Int'l,* pg. 1155
PRIMAGAS GMBH—See SHV Holdings N.V.; *Int'l,* pg. 1155
PRIMAGAZ BELGIUM N.V.—See SHV Holdings N.V.; *Int'l,* pg. 1155
PRIMAGAZ DANMARK A/S—See SHV Holdings N.V.; *Int'l,* pg. 1155
PRIMAGAZ GMBH—See SHV Holdings N.V.; *Int'l,* pg. 1155
PRIMAGAZ HUNGARIA RT.—See SHV Holdings N.V.; *Int'l,* pg. 1155
PRIMAGAZ NEDERLAND B.V.—See SHV Holdings N.V.; *Int'l,* pg. 1155
PRIMAPLYN S.R.O.—See SHV Holdings N.V.; *Int'l,* pg. 1155
PRIMARK CORPORATION; *U.S. Public,* pg. 1325
PRIMARK DECISION ECONOMICS, INC.—See Primark Corporation; *U.S. Public,* pg. 1325
PRIMARK INVESTMENT MANAGEMENT SERVICES, LIMITED—See Primark Corporation; *U.S. Public,* pg. 1326
PRIMARK STORAGE LEASING CORPORATION—See Primark Corporation; *U.S. Public,* pg. 1325
PRIMARK TOOL GROUP—See Emerson Electric Co.; *U.S. Public,* pg. 575
PRIMARY HOME HEALTH CARE, INC.—See Integrated Health Services, Inc.; *U.S. Public,* pg. 885
PRIMARY MEDICAL MANAGEMENT, INC.—See Columbia/ HCA Healthcare Corporation; *U.S. Public,* pg. 405
PRIMARY PULP & PAPER PLANT—See Georgia-Pacific Corporation; *U.S. Public,* pg. 736
PRIMARY STEEL, INC.—See Primac Corp.; *U.S. Private,* pg. 884
PRIMAVERA SYSTEMS, INC.; *U.S. Private,* pg. 884
PRIME ABSTRACT, INC.—See Prime Bancorp, Inc.; *U.S. Public,* pg. 1326
PRIME BANCORP, INC.; *U.S. Public,* pg. 1326
PRIME BANCSHARES INC.; *U.S. Public,* pg. 1326
PRIME BANK—See Prime Bancorp, Inc.; *U.S. Public,* pg. 1326
PRIME CARDIAC REHABILITATION SERVICES, INC.— See Prime Medical Services, Inc.; *U.S. Public,* pg. 1327
PRIME CAST, INC.—See Atchison Casting Corporation; *U.S. Public,* pg. 142
PRIME COMMUNICATIONS LTD.—See Shandwick International Plc; *Int'l,* pg. 1226
PRIME DIAGNOSTIC CORP. OF FLORIDA—See Prime Medical Services, Inc.; *U.S. Public,* pg. 1327
PRIME DIAGNOSTIC SERVICES, INC.—See Prime Medical Services, Inc.; *U.S. Public,* pg. 1327
PRIME FINANCIAL, INC.—See Prime Bancorp, Inc.; *U.S. Public,* pg. 1326
PRIME GROUP REALTY TRUST; *U.S. Public,* pg. 1326
PRIME HOSPITALITY CORP.; *U.S. Public,* pg. 1326
PRIME KIDNEY STONE TREATMENT, INC.—See Prime Medical Services, Inc.; *U.S. Public,* pg. 1327
PRIME LITHOTRIPSY SERVICES, INC.—See Prime Medical Services, Inc.; *U.S. Public,* pg. 1327
PRIME LITHOTRIPTER OPERATIONS, INC.—See Prime Medical Services, Inc.; *U.S. Public,* pg. 1327
PRIME MANAGEMENT, INC.—See Prime Medical Services, Inc.; *U.S. Public,* pg. 1327
PRIME MANUFACTURING COMPANY—See Varlen Corporation; *U.S. Public,* pg. 1711
PRIME MATRIX WIRELESS COMMUNICATIONS; *U.S. Private,* pg. 884
PRIME MEDICAL OPERATING, INC.—See Prime Medical Services, Inc.; *U.S. Public,* pg. 1327
PRIME MEDICAL SERVICES, INC.; *U.S. Public,* pg. 1327
PRIME OPERATING COMPANY—See PrimeEnergy Corporation; *U.S. Public,* pg. 1329
PRIME OPTION SERVICES—See Morgan Stanley Dean Witter & Co.; *U.S. Public,* pg. 1132
PRIME SIRLOIN, INC. (TENNESSEE)—See WSMP, Inc.; *U.S. Public,* pg. 1729
PRIME SOURCE INC.; *U.S. Private,* pg. 884
PRIME SYSTEMS GROUP—See PrimeSource Corporation; *U.S. Public,* pg. 1329
PRIME TANNING CO., INC.; *U.S. Private,* pg. 884
PRIME TANNING CORP—See Prime Tanning Co., Inc.; *U.S. Private,* pg. 884
PRIME TECHNOLOGY IMPORTS, LTD.—See Prime Technology, Inc.; *U.S. Private,* pg. 884
PRIME TECHNOLOGY, INC.; *U.S. Private,* pg. 884
PRIMECARE HEALTH PLAN, INC.—See United HealthCare Corporation; *U.S. Public,* pg. 1678
PRIMEDIA INC.; *U.S. Public,* pg. 1327
PRIMEDIA INC.—See Primedia Inc.; *U.S. Public,* pg. 1328
PRIMEDIA INFORMATIN GROUP—See Primedia Inc.; *U.S. Public,* pg. 1328
PRIMEDIA INFORMATION INC.—See Primedia Inc.; *U.S. Public,* pg. 1328
PRIMEDIA MAGAZINE CORPORATION—See Primedia Inc.; *U.S. Public,* pg. 1328

PRIMEDIA WORKPLACE LEARNING—See Primedia Inc.; U.S. Public, pg. 1328
PRIMEDICA—See Genzyme Corporation; U.S. Public, pg. 733
PRIMEENERGY CORPORATION; U.S. Public, pg. 1328
PRIMEENERGY MANAGEMENT CORPORATION—See PrimeEnergy Corporation; U.S. Public, pg. 1329
PRIMENET MARKETING SERVICES—See Journal Communications Inc.; U.S. Private, pg. 602
PRIMEPAK COMPANY; U.S. Private, pg. 884
PRIMERICA BANK—See Travelers Group; U.S. Public, pg. 1633
PRIMERICA FINANCIAL SERVICES—See Travelers Group; U.S. Public, pg. 1633
PRIMERICA LIFE INSURANCE COMPANY—See Travelers Group; U.S. Public, pg. 1633
PRIMES DE LUXE INC.—See Russel Metals Inc.; Int'l, pg. 1150
PRIMESOURCE CORPORATION; U.S. Public, pg. 1329
PRIMESOUTH, INC.—See SCANA Corporation; U.S. Public, pg. 1436
PRIMEVEST FINANCIAL SERVICES, INC.—See ReliaStar Financial Corp.; U.S. Public, pg. 1376
PRIMEX PLASTICS CORP.—See ICC Industries, Inc.; U.S. Private, pg. 553
PRIMEX TECHNOLOGIES, INC.; U.S. Public, pg. 1329
PRIMUS INC.; U.S. Private, pg. 884
THE PRINCE CO. OF MICHIGAN—See Borden, Inc.; U.S. Private, pg. 158
PRINCE CORPORATION—See Johnson Controls, Inc.; U.S. Public, pg. 932
PRINCE FOODS DIV.—See Borden, Inc.; U.S. Private, pg. 158
THE PRINCE GEORGE CITIZEN—See Hollinger Inc.; Int'l, pg. 631
PRINCE GOLF INTERNATIONAL—See Prince Sports Group Inc.; U.S. Private, pg. 884
PRINCE HOUSING DEVELOPMENT CORP.—See Tainan Spinning Co., Ltd.; Int'l, pg. 1347
PRINCE RUPERT GRAIN LTD.—See Saskatchewan Wheat Pool; Int'l, pg. 1195
PRINCE RUPERT PORT CORPORATION—See Canada Ports Corporation; Int'l, pg. 255
PRINCE SPORTS GROUP INC.; U.S. Private, pg. 884
PRINCESS CASINOS INC.—See Lonrho plc; Int'l, pg. 818
PRINCESS CRUISE LINES—See The Peninsular and Oriental Steam Navigation Company; Int'l, pg. 1035
PRINCESS HOTELS INTERNATIONAL INC.—See Lonrho plc; Int'l, pg. 818
PRINCESS HOUSE, INC.—See Colgate-Palmolive Company; U.S. Public, pg. 399
THE PRINCESS MARCELLA BORGHESE, INC.—See MacAndrews & Forbes Holdings Inc.; U.S. Private, pg. 690
PRINCESS SOFT TOYS; U.S. Private, pg. 884
PRINCETON BANK & TRUST COMPANY NATIONAL ASSOCIATION—See The Chase Manhattan Corporation; U.S. Public, pg. 338
PRINCETON GAMMA-TECH, INC.—See Outokumpu Oyj; Int'l, pg. 1015
PRINCETON GAMMA-TECH U.K. LTD.—See Outokumpu Oyj; Int'l, pg. 1016
PRINCETON LANGUAGE CENTER—See Berlitz International, Inc.; U.S. Public, pg. 222
PRINCETON UNIVERSITY PRESS; U.S. Private, pg. 885
PRINCEVILLE CANNING CO.—See Chiquita Brands International, Inc.; U.S. Public, pg. 349
PRINCEVILLE CORPORATION; U.S. Private, pg. 885
PRINCEVILLE CORPORATION—See Suntory Ltd.; Int'l, pg. 1321
PRINCEVILLE HOTEL CORPORATION—See Princeville Corporation; U.S. Private, pg. 885
PRINCEVILLE MANAGEMENT CORPORATION—See Princeville Corporation; U.S. Private, pg. 885
PRINCEVILLE REALTY CORPORATION—See Princeville Corporation; U.S. Private, pg. 885
PRINCEVILLE UTILITIES COMPANY, INC.—See Princeville Corporation; U.S. Private, pg. 885
PRINCIPAL BEHAVIORAL HEALTH CARE, INC.—See The Principal Financial Group; U.S. Private, pg. 885
PRINCIPAL COMMERCIAL ADVISORS, INC.—See The Principal Financial Group; U.S. Private, pg. 885
PRINCIPAL DEVELOPMENT ASSOCIATES, INC.—See The Principal Financial Group; U.S. Private, pg. 885
PRINCIPAL FINANCIAL ADVISORS, INC.—See The Principal Financial Group; U.S. Private, pg. 885
THE PRINCIPAL FINANCIAL GROUP; U.S. Private, pg. 885
PRINCIPAL FINANCIAL SECURITIES—See The Principal Financial Group; U.S. Private, pg. 885
PRINCIPAL HEALTH CARE, INC.—See The Principal Financial Group; U.S. Private, pg. 885
PRINCIPAL HEALTH CARE OF THE CAROLINAS, INC.—See The Principal Financial Group; U.S. Private, pg. 885
PRINCIPAL HEALTH CARE OF DELAWARE, INC.—See The Principal Financial Group; U.S. Private, pg. 885
PRINCIPAL HEALTH CARE OF FLORIDA, INC.—See The Principal Financial Group; U.S. Private, pg. 885
PRINCIPAL HEALTH CARE OF GEORGIA, INC.—See The Principal Financial Group; U.S. Private, pg. 885
PRINCIPAL HEALTH CARE OF ILLINOIS, INC.—See The Principal Financial Group; U.S. Private, pg. 885
PRINCIPAL HEALTH CARE OF INDIANA, INC.—See The Principal Financial Group; U.S. Private, pg. 885
PRINCIPAL HEALTH CARE OF IOWA, INC.—See The Principal Financial Group; U.S. Private, pg. 885
PRINCIPAL HEALTH CARE OF KANSAS CITY, INC.—See The Principal Financial Group; U.S. Private, pg. 885
PRINCIPAL HEALTH CARE OF LOUISIANA, INC.—See The Principal Financial Group; U.S. Private, pg. 885
PRINCIPAL HEALTH CARE OF THE MID-ATLANTIC, INC.—See The Principal Financial Group; U.S. Private, pg. 886

PRINCIPAL HEALTH CARE OF NEBRASKA, INC.—See The Principal Financial Group; U.S. Private, pg. 886
PRINCIPAL HEALTH CARE OF TEXAS, INC.—See The Principal Financial Group; U.S. Private, pg. 886
PRINCIPAL INSURANCE COMPANY (HONG KONG) LTD.—See The Principal Financial Group; U.S. Private, pg. 886
PRINCIPAL INTERNACIONAL, S.A. COMPANIA DE SEGUROS—See The Principal Financial Group; U.S. Private, pg. 886
PRINCIPAL INTERNATIONAL ARGENTINA, S.A.—See The Principal Financial Group; U.S. Private, pg. 886
PRINCIPAL INTERNATIONAL ASIA LIMITED—See The Principal Financial Group; U.S. Private, pg. 886
PRINCIPAL INTERNATIONAL CHINA—See The Principal Financial Group; U.S. Private, pg. 886
PRINCIPAL INTERNATIONAL ESPANA S.A. DE SEGUROS DE VIDA—See The Principal Financial Group; U.S. Private, pg. 886
PRINCIPAL INTERNATIONAL, INC.—See The Principal Financial Group; U.S. Private, pg. 886
PRINCIPAL INVESTMENT MANAGEMENT LTD.—See PPP hc; Int'l, pg. 1020
PRINCIPAL INVESTORS CORPORATION—See The Principal Financial Group; U.S. Private, pg. 886
PRINCIPAL MARKETING SERVICES, INC.—See The Principal Financial Group; U.S. Private, pg. 886
PRINCIPAL MARQUES INC.—See Harrowston Corporation; Int'l, pg. 599
PRINCIPAL MARQUES MEAT CO.—See Maple Leaf Foods Inc.; Int'l, pg. 841
PRINCIPAL MUTUAL LIFE INSURANCE CO.—See The Principal Financial Group; U.S. Private, pg. 886
PRINCIPAL PLAZA LEASEHOLDS LTD.—See Confederation Life Insurance Company; Int'l, pg. 326
PRINCIPAL PORTFOLIO SERVICES, INC.—See The Principal Financial Group; U.S. Private, pg. 886
PRINCIPAL RESIDENTIAL MORTGAGE, INC.—See The Principal Financial Group; U.S. Private, pg. 886
PRINCIPAL SPECTRUM ASSOCIATES, INC.—See The Principal Financial Group; U.S. Private, pg. 886
PRINCOR COMPANIA DE SEGUROS DE RETIRO S.A.—See The Principal Financial Group; U.S. Private, pg. 886
PRINCOR FINANCIAL SERVICES CORPORATION—See The Principal Financial Group; U.S. Private, pg. 886
PRINCOR MANAGEMENT CORPORATION—See The Principal Financial Group; U.S. Private, pg. 886
PRINGLE OF SCOTLAND—See Dawson International PLC; Int'l, pg. 386
PRINGLE OF SCOTLAND LTD—See Dawson International PLC; Int'l, pg. 385
PRINLIFE COMPANIA DE SEGUROS DE VIDA S.A.—See The Principal Financial Group; U.S. Private, pg. 886
PRINT NORTHWEST COMPANY, L.P.—See Quebecor Inc.; Int'l, pg. 1076
PRINT-O-STAT, INC.—See Pace Resources, Inc.; U.S. Private, pg. 830
PRINT-O-TAPE, INC.; U.S. Private, pg. 886
PRINTCO GROUP—See Big Flower Press Holdings, Inc.; U.S. Public, pg. 228
PRINTED CIRCUITRY DIV.—See NVF Company; U.S. Private, pg. 772
PRINTED CIRCUIT CORPORATION; U.S. Private, pg. 886
PRINTED MOTORS LTD.—See B. Elliott plc.; Int'l, pg. 448
PRINTEMPS GINZA S.A.—See The Daiei, Inc.; Int'l, pg. 364
PRINTER OPERATIONS-STORAGE TEK—See Storage Technology Corporation; U.S. Public, pg. 1523
PRINTER SYSTEMS CORPORATION—See Genicom Corporation; U.S. Public, pg. 729
PRINTING DEVELOPMENTS, INC.—See The General Chemical Group; U.S. Public, pg. 707
PRINTING HOUSE, INC.; U.S. Private, pg. 886
PRINTING SERVICE INCORPORATED—See Wallace Computer Services, Inc.; U.S. Public, pg. 1736
PRINTPACK INC.; U.S. Private, pg. 886
PRINTPAC-UEB CARTON GROUP—See International Paper Company; U.S. Public, pg. 905
PRINTPAC-UEB CASE GROUP—See International Paper Company; U.S. Public, pg. 905
PRINTRONIX, AG—See Printronix, Inc.; U.S. Public, pg. 1330
PRINTRONIX, INC.; U.S. Public, pg. 1329
PRINTWEST COMMUNICATIONS LTD.—See Saskatchewan Wheat Pool; Int'l, pg. 1195
PRINZ BRAU ITALIA S.P.A.—See Interbrew S.A.; Int'l, pg. 680
PRIOR DATA SCIENCES LTD.—See Spar Aerospace Limited; Int'l, pg. 1288
PRIOR GASKETS INC.—See The Cypress Companies; U.S. Private, pg. 300
PRIOR REMANUFACTURERS, INC.—See The Cypress Companies; U.S. Private, pg. 300
PRIORITY FINISHING CORP.; U.S. Private, pg. 887
PRIORITY FULFILLMENT SERVICES, INC.—See Daisytek International Corporation; U.S. Public, pg. 477
PRIORITY HEALTHCARE CORPORATION—See Bindley Western Industries, Inc.; U.S. Public, pg. 229
PRIORITY HEALTHCARE-W. COAST DIVISION—See Bindley Western Industries, Inc.; U.S. Public, pg. 229
PRIORY HOSPITALS GROUP—See Vencor, Inc.; U.S. Public, pg. 1716
PRIPPS RINGNES A.S.—See Orkla A.S.A.; Int'l, pg. 1011
PRISM COMMUNICATIONS LLC—See Bozell Retail; Int'l, pg. 209
PRISM COMMUNICATIONS LTEE—See Bozell Retail; Int'l, pg. 209
PRISM-DAE, INC.—See Analysis & Technology, Inc.; U.S. Public, pg. 110
PRISM INTEGRATED SANITATION MANAGEMENT, INC.—See S.C. Johnson & Son, Inc.; U.S. Private, pg. 592

PRISM INTERNATIONAL—See Omnicom Group Inc.; U.S. Public, pg. 1224
PRISM SYSTEMS INC.—See Northern Telecom Limited; Int'l, pg. 969
PRISMA PANAMA S.A.—See Dainippon Ink & Chemicals, Inc.; Int'l, pg. 371
PRISMA PRESSE & CIE—See Bertelsmann AG; Int'l, pg. 191
PRISMA VERLAG GMBH—See Bertelsmann AG; Int'l, pg. 190
PRISMA-VERLAG GMBH & CO. KG—See Bertelsmann AG; Int'l, pg. 190
PRITT PRODUKTIONSGESELLSCHAFT MBH—See Henkel KGaA; Int'l, pg. 610
THE PRIVATE BANK GROUP—See Credit Suisse Group; Int'l, pg. 345
PRIVATE BRANDS—See Harvest States Cooperatives; U.S. Public, pg. 508
P.T. PRIVATE DEVELOPMENT FINANCE COMPANY OF INDONESIA—See The Nippon Credit Bank, Ltd.; Int'l, pg. 933
PRIVATE ELECTRICITY COMPANY LTD.—See Veba AG; Int'l, pg. 1460
PRIVATE INVESTMENT CO. FOR ASIA S.A.—See Nissho Iwai Corporation; Int'l, pg. 949
PRIVATE LABEL DIVISION—See Gold Eagle Company; U.S. Private, pg. 459
PRIVATE PATIENTS PLAN LIMITED—See PPP hc; Int'l, pg. 1020
PRIZMA PHOTOGRAPHICS—See Wallace Computer Services, Inc.; U.S. Public, pg. 1735
PRO—See Comforce Corporation; U.S. Public, pg. 409
PRO-CUT PRODUCTS, INC.—See Saint-Gobain; Int'l, pg. 1171
PRO-CUTS, INC.—See Opal Concepts, Inc.; U.S. Private, pg. 818
PRO-FAC COOPERATIVE, INC.; U.S. Private, pg. 887
PRO FLEISCH BE- UND VERARBEITUNGS GES.M.B.H.—See Julius Meinl AG; Int'l, pg. 856
PRO GROUP, INC.; U.S. Private, pg. 887
PRO IMAGE—See Rentrak Corporation; U.S. Public, pg. 1377
PRO-IMMO VAGYONKEZELO ES SZOLGALTATO KFT.—See Assicurazioni Generali S.p.A.; Int'l, pg. 92
PRO-LINE BOATS—See Americamr Marine Holdings Inc.; U.S. Private, pg. 58
PRO-LINE CORPORATION; U.S. Private, pg. 887
PRO-LOG CORPORATION; U.S. Private, pg. 887
PRO/MARK—See Illinois Tool Works Inc.; U.S. Public, pg. 867
PRO MUSICA MUSIK-UND KUNSTVERSAND GMBH—See Philips Electronics N.V.; Int'l, pg. 1053
PRO-PASTRIES INC.—See H.J. Heinz Company; U.S. Public, pg. 806
PRO PORTION INDUSTRIES, INC.—See Yogen Fruz Worldwide Inc.; Int'l, pg. 1520
PRO-SELECT—See Northwestern Golf Company; U.S. Private, pg. 806
PRO SHOP (NORTHERN CALIFORNIA)—See ITT Industries, Inc.; U.S. Public, pg. 868
PRO-THERAPY OF AMERICA—See Horizon/CMS Healthcare Corporation; U.S. Public, pg. 839
PROBUGAS A.S.—See SHV Holdings N.V.; Int'l, pg. 1155
PROBUSINESS SERVICES, INC.; U.S. Public, pg. 1330
E.R. PROBYN EXPORT LTD.—See E.R. Probyn Ltd.; Int'l, pg. 1071
E.R. PROBYN LTD.; Int'l, pg. 1071
PROBYN LOG, LTD.—See E.R. Probyn Ltd.; Int'l, pg. 1071
PROCAL GMBH—See Freudenberg & Company; Int'l, pg. 506
PROCARE DIVISION—See Harnischfeger Industries, Inc.; U.S. Public, pg. 788
PROCARSA—See Industrias CH, S.A. de C.V.; Int'l, pg. 677
PROCERMEX INC.—See Anheuser-Busch Companies, Inc.; U.S. Public, pg. 115
PROCES-STYRING APS—See Perstorp AB; Int'l, pg. 1040
PROCESS ANALYTICAL SERVICES (HK) LTD.—See Mannesmann A.G.; Int'l, pg. 835
PROCESS ANALYTICAL SERVICES PTE. LTD.—See Mannesmann A.G.; Int'l, pg. 835
PROCESS ANALYTICS—See ABB Asea Brown Boveri (Holding) Ltd.; Int'l, pg. 6
PROCESS ANALYTICS BENELUX—See ABB Asea Brown Boveri (Holding) Ltd.; Int'l, pg. 6
PROCESS & ENERGY CONSULTANTS LTD.—See Texas Utilities Company; U.S. Public, pg. 1588
PROCESS & INDUSTRIAL DIVISION-S.E.—See Day & Zimmermann, Inc.; U.S. Private, pg. 317
PROCESS AUTOMATION—See Computer Products, Inc.; U.S. Public, pg. 422
PROCESS COLOR PLATE—See Schawk, Inc.; U.S. Public, pg. 1437
PROCESS CONTROL INSTRUMENTATION DIV.—See FKI Plc; Int'l, pg. 473
PROCESS EQUIPMENT—See Sony Corporation; Int'l, pg. 1283
PROCESS EQUIPMENT—See United Utilities plc; Int'l, pg. 1444
PROCESS INSTRUMENTATION—See United Utilities plc; Int'l, pg. 1444
PROCESS PLANT CONTRACTING DIV.—See FKI Plc; Int'l, pg. 472
PROCESS SYSTEMS INC.; U.S. Private, pg. 888
PROCESS SYSTEMS, INC. CONSTRUCTION CO.—See Process Systems Inc.; U.S. Private, pg. 888
PROCESSED MEATS/POULTRY—See ConAgra, Inc.; U.S. Public, pg. 426
PROCESSED PLASTIC COMPANY; U.S. Private, pg. 888
PROCESSED PRODUCTS DIVISION—See The Wornick Company; U.S. Private, pg. 1191
PROCESSED TIMBER PRODUCTS—See UPM-Kymmene Corporation; Int'l, pg. 1428
PROCHIBAT—See Lafarge S.A.; Int'l, pg. 790
PROCHIMAR S.A.—See Internatio-Muller N.V.; Int'l, pg. 682

PROCON PRODUCTS—See Standex International Corporation; *U.S. Private*, pg. 1506
PROCORDIA FOOD AB—See Orkla A.S.A.; *Int'l*, pg. 1011
PROCOTER, S.A.—See Vallehermoso, S.A.; *Int'l*, pg. 1447
PROCTER & GAMBLE AUSTRALIA—See The Procter & Gamble Company; *U.S. Public*, pg. 1332
PROCTER & GAMBLE AUSTRIA GMBH—See The Procter & Gamble Company; *U.S. Public*, pg. 1332
PROCTER & GAMBLE BENELUX S.A.—See The Procter & Gamble Company; *U.S. Public*, pg. 1332
PROCTER & GAMBLE COMMERCIAL CO.—See The Procter & Gamble Company; *U.S. Public*, pg. 1331
THE PROCTER & GAMBLE COMPANY; *U.S. Public*, pg. 1330
PROCTER & GAMBLE COSMETICS CO.—See The Procter & Gamble Company; *U.S. Public*, pg. 1330
PROCTER & GAMBLE DE VENEZUELA C.A.—See The Procter & Gamble Company; *U.S. Public*, pg. 1332
PROCTER & GAMBLE DISTR. CO.—See The Procter & Gamble Company; *U.S. Public*, pg. 1331
PROCTER & GAMBLE ESPANA S.A.—See The Procter & Gamble Company; *U.S. Public*, pg. 1332
PROCTER & GAMBLE FRANCE—See The Procter & Gamble Company; *U.S. Public*, pg. 1332
PROCTER & GAMBLE GMBH—See The Procter & Gamble Company; *U.S. Public*, pg. 1332
PROCTER & GAMBLE GREECE—See The Procter & Gamble Company; *U.S. Public*, pg. 1332
PROCTER & GAMBLE (H & B CARE) LTD.-MFG. DIV.—See The Procter & Gamble Company; *U.S. Public*, pg. 1332
PROCTER & GAMBLE HEALTH & BEAUTY CARE SCANDINAVIA—See The Procter & Gamble Company; *U.S. Public*, pg. 1332
PROCTER & GAMBLE (HEALTH & BEAUTY CARE) LIMITED—See The Procter & Gamble Company; *U.S. Public*, pg. 1332
PROCTER & GAMBLE HEALTH & BEAUTY CARE BELGIUM—See The Procter & Gamble Company; *U.S. Public*, pg. 1332
PROCTER & GAMBLE HEALTH & BEAUTY CARE GERMANY—See The Procter & Gamble Company; *U.S. Public*, pg. 1332
PROCTER & GAMBLE HEALTH & BEAUTY CARE SO. EUROPE—See The Procter & Gamble Company; *U.S. Public*, pg. 1332
PROCTER & GAMBLE INDIA—See The Procter & Gamble Company; *U.S. Public*, pg. 1332
PROCTER & GAMBLE ITALIA S.P.A.—See The Procter & Gamble Company; *U.S. Public*, pg. 1332
PROCTER & GAMBLE LAUNDRY CLEANING & PAPER PRODUCTS BENELUX—See The Procter & Gamble Company; *U.S. Public*, pg. 1332
PROCTER & GAMBLE LTD.—See The Procter & Gamble Company; *U.S. Public*, pg. 1332
PROCTER & GAMBLE (MALAYSIA)—See The Procter & Gamble Company; *U.S. Public*, pg. 1332
PROCTER & GAMBLE MFG. CO.—See The Procter & Gamble Company; *U.S. Public*, pg. 1331
PROCTER & GAMBLE OF PERU—See The Procter & Gamble Company; *U.S. Public*, pg. 1332
PROCTER & GAMBLE PHARMACEUTICALS, INC.—See The Procter & Gamble Company; *U.S. Public*, pg. 1331
PROCTER & GAMBLE PHILIPPINES INC.—See The Procter & Gamble Company; *U.S. Public*, pg. 1332
PROCTER & GAMBLE PORTUGAL—See The Procter & Gamble Company; *U.S. Public*, pg. 1332
PROCTER & GAMBLE PRODUCTIONS, INC.—See The Procter & Gamble Company; *U.S. Public*, pg. 1331
PROCTER & GAMBLE (SINGAPORE) PTE. LTD.—See The Procter & Gamble Company; *U.S. Public*, pg. 1332
PROCTOR SILEX CANADA, INC.—See NACCO Industries, Inc.; *U.S. Public*, pg. 1150
PROCTOR-SILEX, S.A. DE C.V.—See NACCO Industries, Inc.; *U.S. Public*, pg. 1150
PROCUREMENT AREA SOUTH OF FINLAND—See Enso Oyj; *Int'l*, pg. 455
PRODAIR, AIR PRODUCTS CANADA LTD.—See Air Products and Chemicals, Inc.; *U.S. Public*, pg. 32
PRODAIR CORPORATION—See Air Products and Chemicals, Inc.; *U.S. Public*, pg. 31
PRODAIR, S.A.—See Air Products and Chemicals, Inc.; *U.S. Public*, pg. 32
PRODALIM GIDA MAMULLERI IMALAT VE PAZARLAMA ANONIM SIRKETI—See Nestle S.A.; *Int'l*, pg. 922
PRODEMAR—See Norsk Hydro a.s; *Int'l*, pg. 964
PRODETIS B.V.—See Compagnie des Machines Bull; *Int'l*, pg. 317
PRODIGY INC.; *U.S. Public*, pg. 888
PRODORITE LTD.—See Ameron International Corporation; *U.S. Public*, pg. 99
PRODOTTI BAUMANN SPA—See Baumann Federn AG; *Int'l*, pg. 171
PRODUCCIONES AUTOMOTRICES , S.A. DE C.V.—See Echlin Inc.; *U.S. Public*, pg. 561
PRODUCERS CO-OP ASSOCIATION, INC.; *U.S. Private*, pg. 888
PRODUCERS GAS SALES, INC.—See National Gas & Oil Company; *U.S. Public*, pg. 1157
PRODUCERS LIVESTOCK; *U.S. Private*, pg. 888
PRODUCERS MASTERGUIDE—See VNU Verenigde Nederlandse Uitgeversbedrijven B.V.; *Int'l*, pg. 1446
PRODUCERS RICE MILL INC.; *U.S. Private*, pg. 888
THE PRODUCT DESIGN CENTER, INC.—See Dainippon Ink & Chemicals, Inc.; *Int'l*, pg. 370
PRODUCT DISTRIBUTION & DIRECTORY PUBLISHING—See Sprint Corporation; *U.S. Public*, pg. 1501
PRODUCT INFORMATION NETWORK—See Jones International, Inc.; *U.S. Private*, pg. 597
PRODUCT PLUS INTERNATIONAL—See Omnicom Group Inc.; *U.S. Public*, pg. 1225
PRODUCT SUPPORT DIVISION—See The Boeing Company; *U.S. Public*, pg. 241

PRODUCTA-TBWA—See TBWA Chiat/Day; *U.S. Private*, pg. 1062
PRODUCTION AG MEILEN—See Migros; *Int'l*, pg. 866
PRODUCTION MANAGEMENT COMPANIES, INC.; *U.S. Private*, pg. 888
PRODUCTION MANAGEMENT CORPORATION—See Production Management Companies, Inc.; *U.S. Private*, pg. 889
PRODUCTION MANAGEMENT INDUSTRIES, INC.—See Production Management Companies, Inc.; *U.S. Private*, pg. 889
PRODUCTION OIL TOOLS—See EVI, Inc.; *U.S. Public*, pg. 547
PRODUCTION OPERATORS INC.—See Camco International Inc.; *U.S. Public*, pg. 298
PRODUCTION OPERATORS, INC.—See Camco International Inc.; *U.S. Public*, pg. 298
PRODUCTION PAYMENTS, INC.—See IDC Services, Inc.; *U.S. Private*, pg. 554
PRODUCTION TOOL CORPORATION; *U.S. Private*, pg. 889
PRODUCTION TOOL SUPPLY CO.; *U.S. Private*, pg. 889
PRODUCTIVE BUSINESS INTERIORS—See Indiana Records Managers; *U.S. Private*, pg. 560
PRODUCTO DIEMAKERS SUPPLIES LTD.—See The Producto Machine Co.; *U.S. Private*, pg. 889
THE PRODUCTO MACHINE CO.; *U.S. Private*, pg. 889
THE PRODUCTO MACHINE COMPANY—See The Producto Machine Co.; *U.S. Private*, pg. 889
PRODUCTO MACHINE CO. RING DIVISION—See The Producto Machine Co.; *U.S. Private*, pg. 889
PRODUCTORA ANDINA DE ACIDOS Y DERIVADOS LTDA—See Tenneco Inc.; *U.S. Public*, pg. 1578
PRODUCTORA DE ALCOHOLES HIDRATADOS, C.A. (PRALCA)—See Olin Corporation; *U.S. Public*, pg. 1220
PRODUCTORA DE COSMETICOS S.A.—See Wella Group; *Int'l*, pg. 1490
PRODUCTORA DE PAPELES S.A. (PROPAL)—See International Paper Company; *U.S. Public*, pg. 906
PRODUCTORA INDUSTRIAL, S.A. DE C.V.—See Air Products and Chemicals, Inc.; *U.S. Public*, pg. 32
PRODUCTORES DE SEMILLAS S.A.—See Novartis AG; *Int'l*, pg. 983
PRODUCTOS AGROINDUSTRIALES DEL CARIBE S.A.—See Corn Products International, Inc.; *U.S. Public*, pg. 447
PRODUCTOS ALIMENTICIOS IMPERIAL, S.A.—See Diageo Plc; *Int'l*, pg. 411
PRODUCTOS ALIMENTICIOS, S.A.—See Borden, Inc.; *U.S. Private*, pg. 160
PRODUCTOS ALIMENTICIOS SAVORY S.A.I.C.—See Nestle S.A.; *Int'l*, pg. 922
PRODUCTOS ASFALTICOS, S.A. (PROAS)—See Compania Espanola de Petroleos, S.A. (CEPSA); *Int'l*, pg. 323
PRODUCTOS AVON DE GUATEMALA S.A.—See Avon Products, Inc.; *U.S. Public*, pg. 156
PRODUCTOS AVON, S.A.—See Avon Products, Inc.; *U.S. Public*, pg. 156
PRODUCTOS BORDEN, INC.—See Borden, Inc.; *U.S. Private*, pg. 158
PRODUCTOS BRASILIA S.A.—See Nestle S.A.; *Int'l*, pg. 922
PRODUCTOS CIBA S.A.—See Novartis AG; *Int'l*, pg. 983
PRODUCTOS COSMETICOS S.A.—See Wella Group; *Int'l*, pg. 1490
PRODUCTOS DE ACERO S.A. PRODINSA—See N.V. Bekaert S.A.; *Int'l*, pg. 185
PRODUCTOS DE CONCRETO S.A.—See Holderbank Financiere Glaris Ltd.; *Int'l*, pg. 629
PRODUCTOS DE MAIZ S.A.—See Corn Products International, Inc.; *U.S. Public*, pg. 447
PRODUCTOS DE MAIZ Y ALIMENTOS, S.A.—See Corn Products International, Inc.; *U.S. Public*, pg. 447
PRODUCTOS DEL PACIFICO S.A.—See Baltek Corporation; *U.S. Public*, pg. 172
PRODUCTOS DEL TROPICO C. POR A.—See Borden, Inc.; *U.S. Private*, pg. 160
PRODUCTOS EATON LIVIA S.A. ENGINE COMPONENTS OPERATIONS—See Eaton Corporation; *U.S. Public*, pg. 559
PRODUCTOS ELECTROLITICOS, S.A.—See Bayer AG; *Int'l*, pg. 175
PRODUCTOS ELECTRONICOS LAGUNA—See Thomson S.A.; *Int'l*, pg. 1383
PRODUCTOS FARMOQUIMICOS ROCHE LTDA.—See Roche Holding Ltd.; *Int'l*, pg. 1121
PRODUCTOS GERBER DE CENTROAMERICA, S.A.—See Novartis AG; *Int'l*, pg. 973
PRODUCTOS GERBER S.A. DE C.V.—See Novartis AG; *Int'l*, pg. 983
PRODUCTOS GILLETTE CHILE LIMITADA—See The Gillette Company; *U.S. Public*, pg. 745
PRODUCTOS INDUSTRIALES, C.A.—See Ford Motor Company; *U.S. Public*, pg. 666
PRODUCTOS INDUSTRIALES S.A. DE C.V.—See Durr AG; *Int'l*, pg. 422
PRODUCTOS MAESTROS—See James Crean PLC; *Int'l*, pg. 341
PRODUCTOS MODIFICADOS, S.A. DE C.V—See Corn Products International, Inc.; *U.S. Public*, pg. 448
PRODUCTOS NESTLE (COSTA RICA) S.A.—See Nestle S.A.; *Int'l*, pg. 922
PRODUCTOS NESTLE (EL SALVADOR) S.A.—See Nestle S.A.; *Int'l*, pg. 922
PRODUCTOS NESTLE (GUATEMALA) S.A.—See Nestle S.A.; *Int'l*, pg. 922
PRODUCTOS NESTLE (NICARAGUA) S.A.—See Nestle S.A.; *Int'l*, pg. 922
PRODUCTOS PARA ESCUELA Y OFICINA, S.A. DE C.V.—See The Mead Corporation; *U.S. Public*, pg. 1077
PRODUCTOS PEPSI CO., S.A.—See PepsiCo, Inc.; *U.S. Public*, pg. 1278

PRODUCTOS PIRELLI S.A.—See Pirelli S.p.A.; *Int'l*, pg. 1059
PRODUCTOS PIRELLI S.A.- GRUPO MOLTEX—See Pirelli S.p.A.; *Int'l*, pg. 1059
PRODUCTOS QUAKER, C.A.—See The Quaker Oats Company; *U.S. Public*, pg. 1348
PRODUCTOS QUAKER, S.A.—See The Quaker Oats Company; *U.S. Public*, pg. 1348
PRODUCTOS QUIMICOS CIBA-GEIGY LTDA.—See Novartis AG; *Int'l*, pg. 983
PRODUCTOS ROCHE INTERAMERICANA S.A.—See Roche Holding Ltd.; *Int'l*, pg. 1121
PRODUCTOS ROCHE PANAMA S.A.—See Roche Holding Ltd.; *Int'l*, pg. 1121
PRODUCTOS ROCHE QUIMICA FARMACEUTICA S.A.—See Roche Holding Ltd.; *Int'l*, pg. 1121
PRODUCTOS ROCHE S.A.—See Roche Holding Ltd.; *Int'l*, pg. 1121
PRODUCTOS ROCHE, S.A. DE C.V.—See Roche Holding Ltd.; *Int'l*, pg. 1121
PRODUCTOS ROCHE S.A. QUIMICA E INDUSTRIAL—See Roche Holding Ltd.; *Int'l*, pg. 1121
PRODUCTOS STAHL DE COLOMBIA SA—See Zeneca Group Plc; *Int'l*, pg. 1525
PRODUCTOS STAHL POLYVINYL CA—See Zeneca Group Plc; *Int'l*, pg. 1525
PRODUCTOS TUBULARES, S.A.—See SEPI; *Int'l*, pg. 1224
PRODUCTS—See Tracor, Inc.; *U.S. Public*, pg. 1627
PRODUCTS RESEARCH & CHEMICAL CORP. MANUFACTURING FACILITIES DIV.—See Courtaulds plc; *Int'l*, pg. 339
PRODUCTS RESEARCH & CHEMICAL CORP. RESEARCH LABORATORIES—See Courtaulds plc; *Int'l*, pg. 339
PRODUCTS RESEARCH & CHEMICAL CORP., SEMCO DIVISION—See Courtaulds plc; *Int'l*, pg. 339
PRODUIMICA, S.A.—See GATX Corporation; *U.S. Public*, pg. 693
PRODUITS ALIMENTAIRES ET DIETETIQUES (SIDPAD)—See Nestle S.A.; *Int'l*, pg. 922
PRODUITS CHIMIQUES DU NORD (PCN)—See Lafarge S.A.; *Int'l*, pg. 789
PRODUITS ET ENGRAIS CHIMIQUES DU RHIN S.A. (PEC-RHIN)—See BASF AG; *Int'l*, pg. 109
S.A. PRODUITS METALLURGIQUES DE CHAMPAGNE—See Cockerill Sambre; *Int'l*, pg. 302
PRODUITS ROCHE S.A.—See Roche Holding Ltd.; *Int'l*, pg. 1121
PRODUITS SANDOZ S.A.—See Novartis AG; *Int'l*, pg. 983
PRODUTEC HOUGHTON S.A.—See Houghton International Inc.; *U.S. Private*, pg. 541
PRODUTOS MEDICO HOSPITALARES ELSCINT LTDA.—See Elscint Ltd.; *Int'l*, pg. 450
PRODUTOS QUIMICAS ALBA S.A.—See Borden, Inc.; *U.S. Private*, pg. 160
PRODUTOS ROCHE QUIMICOS E FARMACEUTICOS S.A.—See Roche Holding Ltd.; *Int'l*, pg. 1121
PRODUTOS SANDOZ LDA.—See Novartis AG; *Int'l*, pg. 983
PROEQUITIES, INC.—See Protective Life Corporation; *U.S. Public*, pg. 1336
PROFARMACO NOBEL S.R.L.—See Cambrex Corporation; *U.S. Public*, pg. 297
PROFESCO CORPORATION—See John Hancock Mutual Life Insurance Company; *U.S. Private*, pg. 590
PROFESSIONAL APARTMENT MANAGEMENT, INC.; *U.S. Private*, pg. 889
PROFESSIONAL ASSISTANCE, INC.—See Bell Atlantic Corporation; *U.S. Public*, pg. 203
PROFESSIONAL AUTO WAREHOUSE—See Hahn Automotive Warehouse, Inc.; *U.S. Public*, pg. 774
PROFESSIONAL AVIATION ASSOCIATES, INC.—See Banner Aerospace, Inc.; *U.S. Public*, pg. 187
PROFESSIONAL BOOK GROUP—See The McGraw-Hill Companies; *U.S. Public*, pg. 1071
PROFESSIONAL DETAIL SERVICES, INC.—See Staff Builders Inc.; *U.S. Public*, pg. 1501
PROFESSIONAL ECONOMIC SERVICES, INC.—See John Hancock Mutual Life Insurance Company; *U.S. Private*, pg. 590
PROFESSIONAL/FIRST TRAVELCORP—See First Travelcorp Inc.; *U.S. Private*, pg. 408
PROFESSIONAL FOOD SYSTEMS—See ConAgra, Inc.; *U.S. Public*, pg. 427
PROFESSIONAL INDUSTRIAL SALES—See Hitachi, Ltd.; *Int'l*, pg. 622
PROFESSIONAL INFORMATION MANAGMENT—See Seligman & Associates, Inc.; *U.S. Private*, pg. 982
PROFESSIONAL LEARNING SYSTEMS—See Waverly, Inc.; *U.S. Public*, pg. 1748
PROFESSIONAL LIFE ASSURANCE CO. LTD.—See Skandia Insurance Company Limited; *Int'l*, pg. 1257
PROFESSIONAL LOSS CONTROL—See The Hartford Steam Boiler Inspection & Insurance Co.; *U.S. Public*, pg. 795
THE PROFESSIONAL PRODUCTS DIVISION—See Bristol-Myers Squibb Company; *U.S. Public*, pg. 254
PROFESSIONAL PUBLISHING LTD.—See The Thomson Corporation; *U.S. Public*, pg. 1601
PROFESSIONAL PUTTERS ASSOCIATION—See Putt Putt Golf Courses of America, Inc.; *U.S. Private*, pg. 896
PROFESSIONAL RECOVERIES, INC.—See Payco American Corporation; *U.S. Public*, pg. 1267
PROFFITT'S, INC.; *U.S. Public*, pg. 1333
PROFFITT'S INVESTMENT INC.—See Proffitt's, Inc.; *U.S. Public*, pg. 1334
PROFFITT'S OF TRI-CITIES, INC.—See Proffitt's, Inc.; *U.S. Public*, pg. 1334
PROFIDATA AG—See Georg Fischer Ltd.; *Int'l*, pg. 489
AB PROFILA—See Tetra Laval Group; *Int'l*, pg. 1377
PROFILARBED—See Arbed S.A.; *Int'l*, pg. 79
PROFIMEX, S.A. DE C.V.—See Enso Oyj; *Int'l*, pg. 458
PROFIT MANAGEMENT CORP.—See Family Inns of America, Inc.; *U.S. Private*, pg. 393

PROFORMANCE AWARDS INC.—See ITA Group Inc.; *U.S. Private*, pg. 555
PROGEST SPA (IMPELL/FIAT TTG J.V.)—See ABB Asea Brown Boveri (Holding) Ltd.; *Int'l*, pg. 6
PROGNOS AG—See Georg von Holtzbrinck GmbH; *Int'l*, pg. 1480
PROGOLD—See American Crystal Sugar Company; *U.S. Private*, pg. 53
THE PROGRAM EXCHANGE—See Saatchi & Saatchi Advertising Worldwide; *U.S. Public*, pg. 1422
PROGRAM LIGHTING LTD.—See SAS Holdings Limited; *Int'l*, pg. 1152
PROGRAM MANAGEMENT—See The Gillette Company; *U.S. Public*, pg. 744
PROGRAM WATER TECHNOLOGIES—See Sloan Valve Company; *U.S. Private*, pg. 1006
PROGRAMART CORPORATION; *U.S. Private*, pg. 890
PROGRAMART FRANCE INCORPORATED—See Programart Corporation; *U.S. Private*, pg. 890
PROGRAMMED COMPOSITES, INC.—See Pressure Systems, Inc.; *U.S. Private*, pg. 882
PROGRAMMES MARKETING ANNUAIRES (PMA)—See TMP Worldwide, Inc.; *U.S. Private*, pg. 1065
PROGRESS ADVERTISING—See FCA!BMZ; *Int'l*, pg. 470
PROGRESS CAPITAL HOLDINGS, INC.—See Florida Progress Corporation; *U.S. Public*, pg. 141
PROGRESS CASTING GROUP, INC.; *U.S. Private*, pg. 890
PROGRESS-ELEKTROGERATE MAUZ & PFEIFFER GMBH & CO.—See Electrolux, AB; *Int'l*, pg. 442
PROGRESS INTERNATIONAL LIMITED—See Astrex, Inc.; *U.S. Public*, pg. 141
PROGRESS LIGHTING—See U.S. Industries, Inc.; *U.S. Public*, pg. 1684
PROGRESS LIGHTING CANADA—See U.S. Industries, Inc.; *U.S. Public*, pg. 1684
PROGRESS PAINT MFG. CO.; *U.S. Private*, pg. 890
PROGRESS PRINTING COMPANY; *U.S. Private*, pg. 890
PROGRESS SOFTWARE CORPORATION; *U.S. Public*, pg. 1334
PROGRESS VERKAUF GMBH—See Electrolux, AB; *Int'l*, pg. 442
PROGRESS WEST CORPORATION; *U.S. Private*, pg. 890
PROGRESSIVE AMERICAN INSURANCE CO.—See The Progressive Corporation; *U.S. Public*, pg. 1334
PROGRESSIVE BANK, INC.; *U.S. Public*, pg. 1334
PROGRESSIVE BAYSIDE INSURANCE CO.—See The Progressive Corporation; *U.S. Public*, pg. 1334
PROGRESSIVE CASUALTY INSURANCE CO.—See The Progressive Corporation; *U.S. Public*, pg. 1334
THE PROGRESSIVE CORPORATION; *U.S. Public*, pg. 1334
PROGRESSIVE CORP., AGENCY GROUP—See The Progressive Corporation; *U.S. Public*, pg. 1334
PROGRESSIVE CORP., FINANCIAL SERVICES DIV.—See The Progressive Corporation; *U.S. Public*, pg. 1334
PROGRESSIVE COUNTY MUTUAL INSURANCE CO.—See The Progressive Corporation; *U.S. Public*, pg. 1335
PROGRESSIVE DISTRIBUTORS, INC.—See Hannaford Bros. Co.; *U.S. Public*, pg. 782
PROGRESSIVE DRIVER SERVICES, INC.; *U.S. Private*, pg. 890
PROGRESSIVE FARMER, INC.—See Time Warner Inc.; *U.S. Public*, pg. 1613
PROGRESSIVE FARMER INSURANCE SERVICE, INC.—See Time Warner Inc.; *U.S. Public*, pg. 1613
PROGRESSIVE FARMER NETWORK, INC.—See Time Warner Inc.; *U.S. Public*, pg. 1613
PROGRESSIVE GULF INSURANCE CO.—See The Progressive Corporation; *U.S. Public*, pg. 1334
PROGRESSIVE INSURANCE AGENCY, INC.—See The Progressive Corporation; *U.S. Public*, pg. 1335
PROGRESSIVE INVESTMENT COMPANY, INC.—See The Progressive Corporation; *U.S. Public*, pg. 1335
PROGRESSIVE MAX INSURANCE CO.—See The Progressive Corporation; *U.S. Public*, pg. 1335
PROGRESSIVE NORTHERN INSURANCE CO.—See The Progressive Corporation; *U.S. Public*, pg. 1335
PROGRESSIVE NORTHWESTERN INSURANCE CO.—See The Progressive Corporation; *U.S. Public*, pg. 1335
PROGRESSIVE PREFERRED INSURANCE CO.—See The Progressive Corporation; *U.S. Public*, pg. 1335
PROGRESSIVE PREMIUM BUDGET, INC.—See The Progressive Corporation; *U.S. Public*, pg. 1335
PROGRESSIVE RENT-A-CAR, INC.—See Wendy's International Inc.; *U.S. Public*, pg. 1754
PROGRESSIVE SOUTHEASTERN INSURANCE CO.—See The Progressive Corporation; *U.S. Public*, pg. 1335
PROGRESSIVE SPECIALTY INSURANCE CO.—See The Progressive Corporation; *U.S. Public*, pg. 1335
PROGRESSIVE TOOL & INDUSTRIES CO.; *U.S. Private*, pg. 890
PROJECTA B.V.—See Da-Lite Screen Company, Inc.; *U.S. Private*, pg. 306
B.V. PROJECTONTWIKKELINGSMAATSCHAPPIJ AMRO—See ABN-AMRO Holding N.V.; *Int'l*, pg. 9
PROJECTS UNLIMITED, INC.; *U.S. Private*, pg. 890
PROJEKTGESELLSCHAFT FÜR KREISLAUFWIRTSCHAFT PK MBH—See Viag AG; *Int'l*, pg. 1464
PROJIDATA A.G.—See Georg Fischer Ltd.; *Int'l*, pg. 489
PROK GROUP LIMITED—See Tamrock Corp.; *Int'l*, pg. 1353
PROK GROUP LTD.—See Tamrock Corp.; *Int'l*, pg. 1353
PROK INTERNATIONAL CANADA INC.—See Tamrock Corp.; *Int'l*, pg. 1353
PROK INTERNATIONAL USA INC.—See Tamrock Corp.; *Int'l*, pg. 1353
PROKIT ELECTRONICS COMPANY LTD.—See Compagnie des Machines Bull; *Int'l*, pg. 317
PROLANSA S.A.—See N.V. Bekaert S.A.; *Int'l*, pg. 185
PROLER INTERNATIONAL SERVICES, INC.—See Schnitzer Steel Industries, Inc.; *U.S. Public*, pg. 1440
PROLER INTERNATIONAL CORP.—See Schnitzer Steel Industries, Inc.; *U.S. Public*, pg. 1440

PROLER RECYCLING, INC.—See Schnitzer Steel Industries, Inc.; *U.S. Public*, pg. 1440
PROLERIDE TRANSPORT SYSTEMS, INC.—See Schnitzer Steel Industries, Inc.; *U.S. Public*, pg. 1440
PROLERIZED NEW ENGLAND CO.—See Schnitzer Steel Industries, Inc.; *U.S. Public*, pg. 1440
PROLERIZED SCHIABO-NEU CO.—See Schnitzer Steel Industries, Inc.; *U.S. Public*, pg. 1440
PROLIFIX—See Lafarge S.A.; *Int'l*, pg. 789
PROLIMPER S.A.—See Henkel KGaA; *Int'l*, pg. 612
PROLIQ, INC.—See KCS Energy Inc.; *U.S. Public*, pg. 939
PROLOGUE S.A.—See Compagnie des Machines Bull; *Int'l*, pg. 316
PROMAPF, S.A.—See Corporacion MAPFRE, Compania Internacional de Reaseguros, S.A.; *Int'l*, pg. 333
PROMARK—See Hewlett-Packard Company; *U.S. Public*, pg. 815
PROMATEL—See Jeumont-Schneider Trenformeteurs; *Int'l*, pg. 706
PROMETAL LUXEMBOURG S.A.—See GESTRA GmbH; *Int'l*, pg. 550
N.V. PROMETAL—See GESTRA GmbH; *Int'l*, pg. 550
PROMETAL S.A.—See GESTRA GmbH; *Int'l*, pg. 550
PROMETCOR INC.—See Ronson Corporation; *U.S. Public*, pg. 1405
PROMETHEE—See Jeumont-Schneider Trenformeteurs; *Int'l*, pg. 706
PROMETHEUS AG—See Electrolux, AB; *Int'l*, pg. 443
PROMINDUSTRIA - SOCIEDADE DE INVESTMENTS—See Caixa Geral de Depositos; *Int'l*, pg. 251
PROMO—See Testa International; *Int'l*, pg. 1377
PROMO INDUSTRIE GV S.A.—See Henkel KGaA; *Int'l*, pg. 613
PROMO MARKETING CANADA, INC.—See Carlson Companies, Inc.; *U.S. Private*, pg. 212
PROMOCIO DE CIUTAT VELLA—See Telefonica de Espana, S.A.; *Int'l*, pg. 1372
PROMODES SA; *Int'l*, pg. 1071
PROMOMAR S.L.—See Coeclerici Group; *Int'l*, pg. 304
PROMONTORY POINT APARTMENTS—See BRE Properties, Inc.; *U.S. Public*, pg. 163
PROMOPORT GUINEA S.A.—See Coeclerici Group; *Int'l*, pg. 304
PROMOPORT INTERNATIONAL S.R.L.—See Coeclerici Group; *Int'l*, pg. 303
PROMOPUB/DMB&B KUWAIT—See DMB&B Communications; *U.S. Private*, pg. 305
PROMOREF GMBH—See Saint-Gobain; *Int'l*, pg. 1175
PROMOREF SA—See Saint-Gobain; *Int'l*, pg. 1173
PROMOTION BLITZ INC.—See Cossette Communication Marketing; *Int'l*, pg. 336
PROMOTION ET SPECTACLES D'EUROPE 1—See Lagardere Groupe; *Int'l*, pg. 793
PROMOTION HOUSE—See Western International Media Corporation; *U.S. Private*, pg. 1166
THE PROMOTION IN MOTION COMPANIES; *U.S. Private*, pg. 890
PROMOTION INFORMATION MANAGEMENT (PIM)—See Landmark Communications, Inc.; *U.S. Private*, pg. 649
PROMOTION LEOPOLD S.A.—See Tractebel; *Int'l*, pg. 1416
PROMOTIONAL BROADCAST SERVICES—See Western International Media Corporation; *U.S. Private*, pg. 1166
PROMOTORA CAPITAL LTDA.—See Corporacion MAPFRE, Compania Internacional de Reaseguros, S.A.; *Int'l*, pg. 333
PROMOTORA CATALUNYA MEDITERRANEA, S.A.—See Caixa d'Estalvis de Catalunya; *Int'l*, pg. 250
PROMOTORA DE PARTES ELECTRICAS AUTOMOTRICES, S.A. DE C.V.—See General Motors Corporation; *U.S. Public*, pg. 724
PROMOTORA MAPFRE CARIBE CARIMA, S.A.—See Corporacion MAPFRE, Compania Internacional de Reaseguros, S.A.; *Int'l*, pg. 334
PROMSA—See Ciments Francais; *Int'l*, pg. 292
PROMUS HOTEL CORPORATION; *U.S. Public*, pg. 1335
PROMWESTORG AUSSENHANDEL GMBH—See Fried. Krupp AG; *Int'l*, pg. 514
PRONER COMATEL—See Siebe plc; *Int'l*, pg. 1242
PRONER COMATEL ESPAGNE—See Siebe plc; *Int'l*, pg. 1242
PRONER COMATEL GMBH—See Siebe plc; *Int'l*, pg. 1242
PRONER COMATEL SA—See Siebe plc; *Int'l*, pg. 1242
PRONER COMATEL USA INC.—See Siebe plc; *Int'l*, pg. 1241
PRONESTO—See Investor AB; *Int'l*, pg. 687
PRONEXUS, INC.—See Active Voice Corporation; *U.S. Public*, pg. 17
PRONOVA A/S—See Norsk Hydro a.s; *Int'l*, pg. 961
PRONOVA BIOCARE A.S.—See Norsk Hydro a.s; *Int'l*, pg. 961
PRONOVA BIOPOLYMER A.S.—See Norsk Hydro a.s; *Int'l*, pg. 961
PRONOVA BIOPOLYMER GMBH—See Norsk Hydro a.s; *Int'l*, pg. 961
PRONOVA BIOPOLYMER INC.—See Norsk Hydro a.s; *Int'l*, pg. 961
PRONOVA BIOPOLYMER KIMYEVI—See Norsk Hydro a.s; *Int'l*, pg. 964
PRONOVA BIOPOLYMER LTD.—See Norsk Hydro a.s; *Int'l*, pg. 964
PRONOVA BIOPOLYMERS A/S—See Norsk Hydro a.s; *Int'l*, pg. 961
PRONOVA OLEOCHEMICALS A.S.—See Norsk Hydro a.s; *Int'l*, pg. 961
PRONOVA POLYMER LTD.—See Norsk Hydro a.s; *Int'l*, pg. 961
PRONTO, INC.—See The Chase Manhattan Corporation; *U.S. Public*, pg. 338
PRONTOR-WERK ALFRED GAUTHIER GMBH—See Carl-Zeiss-Stiftung; *Int'l*, pg. 1523
PROOF POSITIVE/FARROWLYNE ASSOCIATES, INC.—See Devon Group, Inc.; *U.S. Public*, pg. 503

PROOST EN BRANDT NV—See N.V. Koninklijke KNP BT; *Int'l*, pg. 756
PROOST-VRG PAPER INTERNATIONAL—See N.V. Koninklijke KNP BT; *Int'l*, pg. 757
PROPACK PRODUKTE FUR HAUSHALT UND KORPERPFLEGE GMBH—See Joh. A. Benckiser GmbH; *Int'l*, pg. 185
PROPAK—See International Paper Company; *U.S. Public*, pg. 904
PROPAK SYSTEMS (CYPRUS) LIMITED—See Propak Systems Ltd.; *Int'l*, pg. 1071
PROPAK SYSTEMS INC.—See Propak Systems Ltd.; *Int'l*, pg. 1071
PROPAK SYSTEMS LTD.; *Int'l*, pg. 1071
PROPERTIES DIVISION—See Reynolds Metals Company; *U.S. Public*, pg. 1386
PROPERTY ASSET MANAGEMENT; *U.S. Private*, pg. 891
PROPERTY ASSET MANAGEMENT—See Property Asset Management; *U.S. Private*, pg. 891
PROPERTY CAPITAL TRUST; *U.S. Public*, pg. 1335
PROPERTY DEVELOPMENT ASSOCIATES—See Safeway Inc.; *U.S. Public*, pg. 1426
PROPERTY-OWNERS INSURANCE CO.—See Auto-Owners Insurance; *U.S. Private*, pg. 101
PROPERTY VENTURES, LTD.—See DQE Inc.; *U.S. Public*, pg. 474
PROPPER MANUFACTURING CO., INC.; *U.S. Private*, pg. 891
S.A. PROPRETE, ASSAINISSEMENT, GESTION DE L'ENVIRONNEMENT P.A.G.E.—See Cockerill Sambre; *Int'l*, pg. 301
PROPRIA BAUTRAGER UND VERWALTUNGSGESELLSCHAFT MBH—See Bilfinger + Berger Bauaktiengesellschaft; *Int'l*, pg. 195
PROPRIA S.R.L.—See Electrolux, AB; *Int'l*, pg. 442
PROPRIETORY PRODUCTS GROUP—See Esco Corporation; *U.S. Private*, pg. 383
PROPULSION SYSTEMS DIVISION—See The Boeing Company; *U.S. Public*, pg. 240
PROQUIMED S.A.—See UBE Industries Ltd.; *Int'l*, pg. 1427
PROQUIMO PRODS. QUIMS OPOT. LTDA.—See Akzo Nobel N.V.; *Int'l*, pg. 45
PROREMA AN-UND VERMIETUNGSGESELLSCHAFT MBH—See Dyckerhoff & Widmann AG; *Int'l*, pg. 423
PROSANA S.A.—See Royal Gist-Brocades N.V.; *Int'l*, pg. 1143
PROSEC FORSAKINGSAKTIEBOLAG—See Pharmacia & Upjohn, Inc.; *Int'l*, pg. 1048
PROSER—See Framatome SA; *Int'l*, pg. 503
PROSESS-STYRING A/S—See Perstorp AB; *Int'l*, pg. 1040
PROSOFT INTERNATIONAL CO., INC.—See Continental Materials Corporation; *U.S. Public*, pg. 441
PROSPECT FOUNDRY, INC.—See Atchison Casting Corporation; *U.S. Public*, pg. 142
PROSPECT MOTORS, INC.; *U.S. Private*, pg. 891
PROSPECTUS LTD.—See Merita Ltd.; *Int'l*, pg. 859
PROSTROLLO MOTOR COMPANY; *U.S. Private*, pg. 891
PROSTROLLO MOTOR SALES, INC.—See Prostrollo Motor Company; *U.S. Private*, pg. 891
PROTAC—See Thomson S.A.; *Int'l*, pg. 1382
PROTEC-FEU S.A.—See Preussag AG; *Int'l*, pg. 1071
PROTECTION MUTUAL INSURANCE CO.; *U.S. Private*, pg. 891
PROTECTION SERVICES—See Stabler Companies, Inc.; *U.S. Private*, pg. 1028
PROTECTION TECHNOLOGY—See Day & Zimmerman, Inc.; *U.S. Private*, pg. 317
PROTECTIVE BENEFITS COMMUNICATIONS—See Protective Life Corporation; *U.S. Public*, pg. 1336
PROTECTIVE CLOSURES CO., INC.—See Mark IV Industries, Inc.; *U.S. Public*, pg. 1045
PROTECTIVE INSURANCE COMPANY—See Baldwin & Lyons, Inc.; *U.S. Public*, pg. 169
PROTECTIVE LIFE CORPORATION; *U.S. Public*, pg. 1336
PROTECTIVE LIFE INSURANCE CO.—See Protective Life Corporation; *U.S. Public*, pg. 1336
THE PROTECTOR CORPORATION; *U.S. Private*, pg. 891
PROTEIN BLENDERS—See Ridley Canada Limited; *Int'l*, pg. 1116
PROTEK GMBH—See Sulzer Ltd.; *Int'l*, pg. 1307
PROTEK GROUP—See Sulzer Ltd.; *Int'l*, pg. 1307
PROTEK SYNTHES S.A.—See Sulzer Ltd.; *Int'l*, pg. 1307
PROTELLICES SOFTWARE DEVELOPMENT LABORATORY—See Platinum Technology, Inc.; *U.S. Public*, pg. 1309
PROTENDIDOS DYWIDAG LTDA.—See Dyckerhoff & Widmann AG; *Int'l*, pg. 425
PROTEON, INC.; *U.S. Public*, pg. 1336
PROTEXA INDUSTRIAS S.A. DE C.V.—See Grupo Protexa S.A. de C.V.; *Int'l*, pg. 576
PROTIM SOLIGNUM LTD.—See Burmah Castrol plc; *Int'l*, pg. 234
PROTIMETER, INC.—See Bowthorpe plc; *Int'l*, pg. 208
PROTIMETER PLC—See Bowthorpe plc; *Int'l*, pg. 207
PROTIMETER ZWEIGNIEDERLASSUNG DER BOWTHORPE GMBH—See Bowthorpe plc; *Int'l*, pg. 209
PROTO-POWER CORPORATION—See Kollmorgen Corporation; *U.S. Public*, pg. 965
PROTO SYSTEMS OF ATLANTA; *U.S. Private*, pg. 891
PROTOCALL VENTURES—See Geotek Communications; *U.S. Public*, pg. 740
PROTOCOL SYSTEMS, INC.; *U.S. Public*, pg. 1336
PROTON; *Int'l*, pg. 1071
PROTOSOFT DEVELOPMENT LABORATORY—See Platinum Technology, Inc.; *U.S. Public*, pg. 1309
PROTOTYP-WERKE GMBH—See Sandvik AB; *Int'l*, pg. 1186
THE PROVEN METHOD—See American Software, Inc.; *U.S. Public*, pg. 91
PROVENTUS AB; *Int'l*, pg. 1072

PROVESTCO, INC.—See Provident Mutual Life Insurance Co.; *U.S. Private*, pg. 892

PROVIDENCE AND WORCESTER RAILROAD COMPANY; *U.S. Public*, pg. 1336

PROVIDENCE ENERGY CORPORATION; *U.S. Public*, pg. 1337

PROVIDENCE ENERGY SERVICES—See Providence Energy Corporation; *U.S. Public*, pg. 1337

PROVIDENCE GAS CO.—See Providence Energy Corporation; *U.S. Public*, pg. 1337

PROVIDENCE JOURNAL BROADCASTING CORP.—See A.H. Belo Corporation; *U.S. Public*, pg. 209

PROVIDENCE JOURNAL-BULLETIN—See A.H. Belo Corporation; *U.S. Public*, pg. 209

PROVIDENCIA COMPANIA ARGENTINA DE SEGUROS S.A.—See Assicurazioni Generali S.p.A.; *Int'l*, pg. 92

PROVIDENCIA COMPANIA DE SEGURO DE RETIRO S.A.—See Assicurazioni Generali S.p.A.; *Int'l*, pg. 92

PROVIDENCIA OSZTRAK-MAGYAR BIZTOSITO RT.—See Assicurazioni Generali S.p.A.; *Int'l*, pg. 92

THE PROVIDENT BANK—See Provident Financial Group, Inc.; *U.S. Public*, pg. 1338

PROVIDENT BANK OF FLORIDA—See Provident Financial Group, Inc.; *U.S. Public*, pg. 1338

THE PROVIDENT BANK OF KENTUCKY—See Provident Financial Group, Inc.; *U.S. Public*, pg. 1338

PROVIDENT BANK OF MARYLAND—See Provident Bankshares Corporation; *U.S. Public*, pg. 1337

PROVIDENT BANKSHARES CORPORATION; *U.S. Public*, pg. 1337

PROVIDENT COMMERCIAL GROUP, INC.—See Provident Financial Group, Inc.; *U.S. Public*, pg. 1338

PROVIDENT COMPANIES, INC.; *U.S. Public*, pg. 1337

PROVIDENT CONSUMER FINANCIAL SERVICES—See Provident Financial Group, Inc.; *U.S. Public*, pg. 1338

PROVIDENT FINANCIAL GROUP, INC.; *U.S. Public*, pg. 1338

PROVIDENT INVESTMENT COUNSEL, INC.—See United Asset Management Corporation; *U.S. Public*, pg. 1674

PROVIDENT LIFE AND CASUALTY INSURANCE CO.—See Provident Companies, Inc.; *U.S. Public*, pg. 1338

PROVIDENT LIFE CAPITAL CO.—See Provident Companies, Inc.; *U.S. Public*, pg. 1338

PROVIDENT MUSIC DISTRIBUTION—See Zomba Recording Corp.; *Int'l*, pg. 1529

PROVIDENT MUSIC GROUP—See Zomba Recording Corp.; *Int'l*, pg. 1529

PROVIDENT MUTUAL LIFE & ANNUITY COMPANY OF AMERICA—See Provident Mutual Life Insurance Co.; *U.S. Private*, pg. 892

PROVIDENT MUTUAL LIFE INSURANCE CO.; *U.S. Private*, pg. 891

PROVIDENT NATIONAL ASSURANCE CO.—See Provident Companies, Inc.; *U.S. Public*, pg. 1338

PROVIDENT SECURITIES & INVESTMENT COMPANY—See Provident Financial Group, Inc.; *U.S. Public*, pg. 1338

PROVIDENTIA; *Int'l*, pg. 1072

PROVIDIAN AGENCY GROUP—See AEGON N.V.; *Int'l*, pg. 27

PROVIDIAN AUTO & HOME INSURANCE GROUP—See AEGON N.V.; *Int'l*, pg. 27

PROVIDIAN FINANCIAL CORPORATION; *U.S. Public*, pg. 1338

PROVIDIAN LIFE & HEALTH INSURANCE CO.—See AEGON N.V.; *Int'l*, pg. 27

PROVIDIAN PROPERTY & CASUALTY INSURANCE CO.—See AEGON N.V.; *Int'l*, pg. 27

PROVIFIN LTDA—See LVMH Moet Hennessy Louis Vuitton; *Int'l*, pg. 783

PROVIGO DISTRIBUTION—See Provigo Inc.; *Int'l*, pg. 1073

PROVIGO INC.; *Int'l*, pg. 1072

PROVIMI VEAL CORPORATION; *U.S. Private*, pg. 892

THE PROVINCE—See Hollinger Inc.; *Int'l*, pg. 631

PROVINZIALSAECHSISCHE ENERGIE-VERSORGUNGS GMBH—See Veba AG; *Int'l*, pg. 1457

PROVITAL—See LVMH Moet Hennessy Louis Vuitton; *Int'l*, pg. 781

PROVONA A/S—See Norsk Hydro a.s; *Int'l*, pg. 961

PROXIM, INC.; *U.S. Public*, pg. 1338

PROXIMA CORPORATION; *U.S. Public*, pg. 1339

PROXIMITY CONTROLS CORP.—See Dwyer Instruments Inc.; *U.S. Private*, pg. 350

PROYECTOS ENERGETICOS S.A.—See Transcanada Pipelines Limited; *Int'l*, pg. 1417

PROYECTOS Y CONSTRUCCIONES CATALUNYA, S.A.—See Caixa d'Estalvis de Catalunya; *Int'l*, pg. 250

PROYECTOS Y DESARROLLOS URBANISTICOS, S.A.—See Caja de Madrid Group; *Int'l*, pg. 252

PROYECTOS Y PROGRAMAS INMOBILIARIOS, S.A.—See Caja de Madrid Group; *Int'l*, pg. 251

PROYEPARSONS, C.A.—See Parsons Corporation; *U.S. Private*, pg. 842

PRUDENCE VIE, S.A.—See AMB Aachener und Muenchener Beteiligungs-AG; *Int'l*, pg. 16

PRUDENTIAL AGRICULTURAL CREDIT, INC.—See The Prudential Insurance Company of America; *U.S. Private*, pg. 892

PRUDENTIAL ASIA—See Prudential Corporation PLC; *Int'l*, pg. 1073

PRUDENTIAL ASIA CAPITAL LIMITED—See The Prudential Insurance Company of America; *U.S. Private*, pg. 893

PRUDENTIAL ASIA INVESTMENTS LIMITED—See The Prudential Insurance Company of America; *U.S. Private*, pg. 893

PRUDENTIAL ASSURANCE CO. LTD.—See Prudential Corporation PLC; *Int'l*, pg. 1073

PRUDENTIAL ASSURANCE CO.-NEW ZEALAND LTD.—See Prudential Corporation PLC; *Int'l*, pg. 1073

PRUDENTIAL CAPITAL & INVESTMENT SERVICES, INC.—See The Prudential Insurance Company of America; *U.S. Private*, pg. 892

PRUDENTIAL COMMERCIAL INSURANCE CO.—See The Prudential Insurance Company of America; *U.S. Private*, pg. 892

PRUDENTIAL CORPORATION ASIA LTD.—See Prudential Corporation PLC; *Int'l*, pg. 1073

PRUDENTIAL CORPORATION AUSTRALIA LTD.—See Prudential Corporation PLC; *Int'l*, pg. 1073

PRUDENTIAL CORPORATION PLC; *Int'l*, pg. 1073

PRUDENTIAL DEFINED CONTRIBUTION SERVICES—See The Prudential Insurance Company of America; *U.S. Private*, pg. 892

PRUDENTIAL FUND MANAGEMENT CANADA LTD.—See The Prudential Insurance Company of America; *U.S. Private*, pg. 893

PRUDENTIAL GENERAL INSURANCE CO.—See The Prudential Insurance Company of America; *U.S. Private*, pg. 892

THE PRUDENTIAL INSURANCE COMPANY OF AMERICA; *U.S. Private*, pg. 892

THE PRUDENTIAL INVESTMENT CORP.—See The Prudential Insurance Company of America; *U.S. Private*, pg. 892

THE PRUDENTIAL - JON DOUGLAS COMPANY—See The Prudential Insurance Company of America; *U.S. Private*, pg. 892

THE PRUDENTIAL LIFE INSURANCE COMPANY, LTD.—See The Prudential Insurance Company of America; *U.S. Private*, pg. 893

PRUDENTIAL METAL SUPPLY CORP.; *U.S. Private*, pg. 893

PRUDENTIAL OF AMERICA GENERAL INSURANCE CO. (CANADA)—See The Prudential Insurance Company of America; *U.S. Private*, pg. 893

PRUDENTIAL OVERSEAS FUNDING CORP. N.V.—See The Prudential Insurance Company of America; *U.S. Private*, pg. 893

PRUDENTIAL PORTFOLIO MANAGERS LIMITED—See Prudential Corporation PLC; *Int'l*, pg. 1073

PRUDENTIAL PROPERTY & CASUALTY INSURANCE COMPANY—See The Prudential Insurance Company of America; *U.S. Private*, pg. 892

PRUDENTIAL REAL ESTATE AFFILIATES INC.—See The Prudential Insurance Company of America; *U.S. Private*, pg. 892

THE PRUDENTIAL REALTY GROUP—See The Prudential Insurance Company of America; *U.S. Private*, pg. 892

PRUDENTIAL SECURITIES GROUP INC.—See The Prudential Insurance Company of America; *U.S. Private*, pg. 893

PRUDENTIAL SECURITIES INC.—See The Prudential Insurance Company of America; *U.S. Private*, pg. 892

PRUDENTIAL SERVICE CO.—See The Prudential Insurance Company of America; *U.S. Private*, pg. 893

PRUM-TURENWERK GMBH—See Hochtief AG; *Int'l*, pg. 623

PRUMYSLOVY PENZIJNI FOND, A.S.—See ING Groep N.V.; *Int'l*, pg. 651

PRUNUS S.P.A.—See Assicurazioni Generali S.p.A.; *Int'l*, pg. 90

PRUSERVICOS PARTICIPACOES, S.A., C/O PRUDENTIAL ATLANTIC COMPANHIA BRASILEIRA DE SEGUROS—See The Prudential Insurance Company of America; *U.S. Private*, pg. 893

PRYM-DRITZ CORPORATION—See William Prym GmbH & Co. KG; *Int'l*, pg. 1499

PRYON CORPORATION—See Protocol Systems, Inc.; *U.S. Public*, pg. 1336

PRYOR FOUNDRY, INC.—See Case Corporation; *U.S. Public*, pg. 312

PRZEDSTAWICIELSTWO KNOLL AG W POLSCE—See BASF AG; *Int'l*, pg. 109

PSI REPAIR SERVICES, INC.—See Phillips Service Industries, Inc.; *U.S. Private*, pg. 862

PSOMAS & ASSOCIATES; *U.S. Private*, pg. 893

PSOMAS ASSOCIATES—See Psomas & Associates; *U.S. Private*, pg. 893

PSYCARE—See Intelligent Systems Corp.; *U.S. Public*, pg. 888

THE PSYCHOLOGICAL CORP.—See Harcourt General, Inc.; *U.S. Public*, pg. 784

PSYCHOLOGY TODAY—See Sussex Publishers, Inc.; *U.S. Private*, pg. 1056

PT METLIFE SEJAHTERA—See Metropolitan Life Insurance Co.; *U.S. Private*, pg. 738

PT QUANTUM PERIPHERALS INDONESIA—See Quantum Corporation; *U.S. Public*, pg. 1350

P.T. SMITH TOOL INDONESIA—See Smith International, Inc.; *U.S. Public*, pg. 1478

PTI ENVIRONMENTAL—See The Failure Group, Inc.; *U.S. Public*, pg. 609

PUB/DATA, INC.—See Quebecor Inc.; *Int'l*, pg. 1076

PUBCO CORPORATION; *U.S. Public*, pg. 1339

PUBLI-HOME DISTRIBUTORS LTD.—See G.T.C. Transcontinental Group Ltd.; *Int'l*, pg. 539

PUBLIC EMPLOYEES BENEFIT SERVICES CORP.—See Nationwide Insurance Enterprise; *U.S. Private*, pg. 789

PUBLIC HEALTH SOFTWARE SYSTEMS—See Intelligent Systems Corp.; *U.S. Public*, pg. 888

PUBLIC OPINION—See Gannett Company, Inc.; *U.S. Public*, pg. 700

PUBLIC SERVICE COMPANY OF COLORADO—See New Century Energies, Inc.; *U.S. Public*, pg. 1170

PUBLIC SERVICE COMPANY OF NEW HAMPSHIRE—See Northeast Utilities; *U.S. Public*, pg. 1195

PUBLIC SERVICE COMPANY OF NEW MEXICO; *U.S. Public*, pg. 1339

PUBLIC SERVICE COMPANY OF NORTH CAROLINA, INC.; *U.S. Public*, pg. 1340

PUBLIC SERVICE COMPANY OF OKLAHOMA—See Central and South West Corporation; *U.S. Public*, pg. 324

PUBLIC SERVICE ELECTRIC & GAS CO.—See Public Service Enterprise Group Incorporated; *U.S. Public*, pg. 1340

PUBLIC SERVICE ENTERPRISE GROUP INCORPORATED; *U.S. Public*, pg. 1340

PUBLIC SERVICE RESOURCES CORPORATION—See Public Service Enterprise Group Incorporated; *U.S. Public*, pg. 1340

PUBLIC STORAGE COMMERCIAL PROPERTIES GROUP, INC.—See Public Storage, Inc.; *U.S. Public*, pg. 1341

PUBLIC STORAGE, INC.; *U.S. Public*, pg. 1340

PUBLIC UTILITY DISTRICT NO. 2 OF GRANT COUNTY; *U.S. Private*, pg. 893

PUBLIC WATER SUPPLY COMPANY—See Middlesex Water Company; *U.S. Public*, pg. 1110

PUBLICACIONES EN COMPUTACIÓN LTDA.—See International Data Group; *U.S. Private*, pg. 570

PUBLICATIONS ECONOMIQUES—See G.T.C. Transcontinental Group Ltd.; *Int'l*, pg. 539

PUBLICATIONS FRANCE MONDE—See Lagardere Groupe; *Int'l*, pg. 793

PUBLICATIONS GROUPE LOISIRS—See Lagardere Groupe; *Int'l*, pg. 793

PUBLICFACTORING S.P.A.—See Banco Ambrosiano Veneto S.p.A.; *Int'l*, pg. 138

PUBLICIAA CUADRA CHAMBERLAIN—See Leo Burnett Company, Inc.; *U.S. Private*, pg. 186

PUBLICIDAD CLAVE, S.A. DE C.V.—See Publicidad Ferrer y Asociados, S.A. de C.V.; *Int'l*, pg. 1073

PUBLICIDAD DIAZ, S.A. DE C.V.—See Leo Burnett Company, Inc.; *U.S. Private*, pg. 186

PUBLICIDAD FERRER DE OCCIDENTE, S.A. DE C.V.—See Publicidad Ferrer y Asociados, S.A. de C.V.; *Int'l*, pg. 1073

PUBLICIDAD FERRER Y ASOCIADOS, S.A. DE C.V.; *Int'l*, pg. 1073

PUBLICIS BCP DIRECT INC.—See BCP Group Ltd.; *Int'l*, pg. 116

PUBLICIS BCP MONTREAL INC.—See BCP Group Ltd.; *Int'l*, pg. 116

PUBLICIS BCP PROMOTION INC.—See BCP Group Ltd.; *Int'l*, pg. 116

PUBLICIS BCP TORONTO INC.—See BCP Group Ltd.; *Int'l*, pg. 116

PUBLICIS/BLOOM—See FCA!BMZ; *Int'l*, pg. 469

PUBLICIS/BLOOM INC.—See FCA!BMZ; *Int'l*, pg. 470

PUBLICIS PUBLIC RELATIONS—See FCA!BMZ; *Int'l*, pg. 470

PUBLICITARIA CUMBRE—See Saatchi & Saatchi Advertising Worldwide; *U.S. Public*, pg. 1422

PUBLICITAS C.A.—See Saatchi & Saatchi Advertising Worldwide; *U.S. Public*, pg. 1422

PUBLICITE MCKIM LTEE.—See N.W. Ayer & Partners; *U.S. Private*, pg. 104

PUBLICKER INDUSTRIES INC.; *U.S. Public*, pg. 1341

PUBLIFACTORING S.P.A.—See Banco Ambrosiano Veneto S.p.A.; *Int'l*, pg. 138

PUBLIK AG—See Impuls Advertising AG; *Int'l*, pg. 666

PUBLINTER/BDDP—See BDDP Group; *Int'l*, pg. 118

PUBLIPROX—See Lagardere Groupe; *Int'l*, pg. 793

PUBLISHER RESOURCES INC.—See Ingram Industries Inc.; *U.S. Private*, pg. 563

PUBLISHERS CLEARING HOUSE; *U.S. Private*, pg. 893

PUBLISHERS EQUIPMENT CORPORATION; *U.S. Public*, pg. 1341

PUBLISHERS WORLD TRADE CORPORATION—See Lagardere Groupe; *Int'l*, pg. 795

PUBLISPANA/BDDP—See BDDP Group; *Int'l*, pg. 118

PUBLIX SUPERMARKETS INC.; *U.S. Private*, pg. 893

PUCCI SULZER—See Testa International; *Int'l*, pg. 1377

PUEBLO INTERNATIONAL, INC.—See Pueblo Xtra International, Inc.; *U.S. Private*, pg. 894

PUEBLO INTERNATIONAL, INC.-P.R. DIV.—See Pueblo Xtra International, Inc.; *U.S. Private*, pg. 894

PUEBLO MALL LIMITED PARTNERSHIP—See Cigna Corp.; *U.S. Public*, pg. 362

PUEBLO XTRA INTERNATIONAL, INC.; *U.S. Private*, pg. 894

PUERTO RICAN AMERICAN INSURANCE COMPANY—See Corporacion MAPFRE, Compania Internacional de Reaseguros, S.A.; *Int'l*, pg. 333

PUERTO RICAN CEMENT CO., INC.; *U.S. Public*, pg. 1341

PUERTO RICAN INSURANCE AGENCY INC.—See Corporacion MAPFRE, Compania Internacional de Reaseguros, S.A.; *Int'l*, pg. 333

PUERTO RICO CONTAINER CO.—See Union Camp Corporation; *U.S. Public*, pg. 1666

PUERTO RICO SAFETY CORPORATION—See Eastco Industrial Safety Corp.; *U.S. Public*, pg. 548

PUERTO RICO SAFETY EQUIPMENT CORPORATION—See Eastco Industrial Safety Corp.; *U.S. Public*, pg. 548

PUERTO RICO TOURISM COMPANY; *U.S. Private*, pg. 894

PUGET ENERGY INC.—See Puget Sound Energy, Inc.; *U.S. Public*, pg. 1342

PUGET PLASTICS CORPORATION—See Arctic Slope Regional Corporation; *U.S. Private*, pg. 80

PUGET SOUND AUTO AUCTION, INC.—See Tyco International Ltd.; *U.S. Public*, pg. 1649

PUGET SOUND ENERGY CO.—See Puget Sound Energy, Inc.; *U.S. Public*, pg. 1342

PUGET SOUND ENERGY, INC.; *U.S. Public*, pg. 1342

PUGET WESTERN, INC.—See Puget Sound Energy, Inc.; *U.S. Public*, pg. 1342

PUGH MARINA—See Pugh Oil Company; *U.S. Private*, pg. 894

PUGH OIL COMPANY; *U.S. Private*, pg. 894

PUHOS-BOARD OY—See UPM-Kymmene Corporation; *Int'l*, pg. 1428

PUICOUYOUL—See SNCF; *Int'l*, pg. 1164

ANTONIO PUIG SA; *Int'l*, pg. 1073

PUJOL Y TARRAGO S.A.—See FKI Plc; *Int'l*, pg. 474

PULASKI FURNITURE CORPORATION; *U.S. Public*, pg. 1342

PULASKI RUBBER CO.—See R.C.A. Rubber Company; *U.S. Private*, pg. 902

PULCRA S.A.—See Henkel KGaA; *Int'l*, pg. 612

MASTER INDEX TO COMPANY NAMES
QUAIFE
Company Index

BRIAN PULFREY LTD.—See PAXAR Corporation; *U.S. Public*, pg. 1267
PULIMAT S.P.A.—See Electrolux, AB; *Int'l*, pg. 442
PULITZER PUBLISHING COMPANY; *U.S. Public*, pg. 1343
PULKKILA WORKS—See Rautaruukki Oy; *Int'l*, pg. 1088
PULLEN PUMPS DIVISION—See Cardo AB; *Int'l*, pg. 271
PULLIAM MOTOR COMPANY; *U.S. Private*, pg. 894
PULLMAN BELGIUM SA—See Accor S.A.; *Int'l*, pg. 21
PULLMAN/HOLT CORP.—See White Mop Wringer Company; *U.S. Private*, pg. 1173
PULLMAN HOTELS DEUTSCHLAND—See Accor S.A.; *Int'l*, pg. 21
PULLMAN INDUSTRIES, INC.; *U.S. Private*, pg. 894
PULLMAN INTERNATIONAL HOTEL—See Accor S.A.; *Int'l*, pg. 20
PULLMAN SUISSE SA—See Accor S.A.; *Int'l*, pg. 21
PULMO-DOSE, INC.—See Integrated Health Services, Inc.; *U.S. Public*, pg. 885
PULP ASIA LIMITED—See The Mead Corporation; *U.S. Public*, pg. 1076
PULP & PAPER DIVISION—See ABB Asea Brown Boveri (Holding) Ltd.; *Int'l*, pg. 4
PULSAFEEDER INC.—See IDEX Corporation; *U.S. Public*, pg. 862
PULSARR—See Advanced Machine Vision Corp.; *U.S. Public*, pg. 20
PULSE BANCORP, INC.; *U.S. Public*, pg. 1344
PULSE COMMUNICATIONS, INC.—See Hubbell Incorporated; *U.S. Public*, pg. 844
PULSE COMPONENTS LTD.-HONG KONG—See Technitrol, Inc.; *U.S. Public*, pg. 1564
PULSE ELECTRONICS, INC.—See Westinghouse Air Brake Company; *U.S. Public*, pg. 1761
PULSE ENGINEERING, INC.—See Technitrol, Inc.; *U.S. Public*, pg. 1564
PULSE ENGINEERING-IRELAND—See Technitrol, Inc.; *U.S. Public*, pg. 1564
PULSE ENGINEERING-PHILIPPINES—See Technitrol, Inc.; *U.S. Public*, pg. 1564
PULSE ENGINEERING-SINGAPORE—See Technitrol, Inc.; *U.S. Public*, pg. 1564
PULSE ENGINEERING-TAIWAN—See Technitrol, Inc.; *U.S.* Public, pg. 1564
PULSE MAGAZINE—See MTS, Inc.; *U.S. Private*, pg. 688
PULSE SAVINGS BANK—See Pulse Bancorp, Inc.; *U.S. Public*, pg. 1344
PULSE SCIENCES, INC.—See The Titan Corporation; *U.S. Public*, pg. 1618
PULTE CORPORATION; *U.S. Public*, pg. 1344
PULTE DIVERSIFIED COMPANIES, INC.—See Pulte Corporation; *U.S. Public*, pg. 1344
PULTE FINANCIAL COMPANIES, INC.—See Pulte Corporation; *U.S. Public*, pg. 1345
PULTE HOME CORPORATION—See Pulte Corporation; *U.S. Public*, pg. 1344
PULTE MORTGAGE CORPORATION—See Pulte Corporation; *U.S. Public*, pg. 1345
PUM INOX—See Cockerill Sambre; *Int'l*, pg. 301
PUMA AG RUDOLF DASSLER SPORT—See Proventus AB; *Int'l*, pg. 1072
PUMA AUSTRALIA PTY. LTD.—See Proventus AB; *Int'l*, pg. 1072
PUMA BENELUX B.V.—See Proventus AB; *Int'l*, pg. 1072
PUMA FRANCE S.A.—See Proventus AB; *Int'l*, pg. 1072
PUMA NORTH AMERICA—See Proventus AB; *Int'l*, pg. 1072
PUMA (SWITZERLAND) AG—See Proventus AB; *Int'l*, pg. 1072
PUMP AND SAVE, INC.—See Jitney-Jungle Stores of America, Inc.; *U.S. Private*, pg. 588
PUMP REPAIR CENTERS—See Ingersoll-Rand Company; *U.S. Public*, pg. 877
PUMPELLY OIL, INC.; *U.S. Private*, pg. 895
PUMPEX AB—See Cardo AB; *Int'l*, pg. 271
PUMPEX GMBH—See Cardo AB; *Int'l*, pg. 271
PUMPEX INC.—See Cardo AB; *Int'l*, pg. 270
PUMPEX S.A.R.L.—See Cardo AB; *Int'l*, pg. 271
PUNA PLANTATION HAWAII LTD.; *U.S. Private*, pg. 895
PUNA SUGAR CO., LTD.—See JMB Realty Corporation; *U.S. Private*, pg. 578
PUNCH PRESS PRODUCTS, INC.; *U.S. Private*, pg. 895
PUNCHCRAFT COMPANY—See Masco Corporation; *U.S. Public*, pg. 1054
PUNTO APARTE PUBLICIDAD, S.A.—See DMB&B Communications; *U.S. Private*, pg. 305
PURAC AMERICA, INC.—See CSM N.V.; *Int'l*, pg. 244
PURAC BIOCHEM (UK) LIMITED—See CSM N.V.; *Int'l*, pg. 244
PURAC BIOQUIMICA S.A.—See CSM N.V.; *Int'l*, pg. 244
PURAC FAR EAST—See CSM N.V.; *Int'l*, pg. 245
PURAC GROUP—See CSM N.V.; *Int'l*, pg. 244
PURAC SINTESES—See CSM N.V.; *Int'l*, pg. 245
PURCELL CO., INC.; *U.S. Private*, pg. 895
PURDEL, COOPERATIVE AGRO-ALIMENTAIRE; *Int'l*, pg. 1073
THE PURDY CORPORATION; *U.S. Private*, pg. 895
THE PURE CANE MOLASSES CO. (DURBAN) (PTY.) LTD.—See Tate & Lyle PLC; *Int'l*, pg. 1357
PURE CARBON COMPANY—See Morgan Crucible Co. Plc; *Int'l*, pg. 891
PURE PULSE TECHNOLOGIES, INC.—See Maxwell Technologies, Inc.; *U.S. Public*, pg. 1062
PURE SOLUTIONS—See Ionics, Incorporated; *U.S. Public*, pg. 912
PURFLUX FILTER GMBH—See Labinal SA; *Int'l*, pg. 786
PURINA ALIMENTOS LTDA.—See Ralston Purina Company; *U.S. Public*, pg. 1360
PURINA GROCERY PRODUCTS GROUP—See Ralston Purina Company; *U.S. Public*, pg. 1360
PURINA-HAGE LTD.—See Ralston Purina Company; *U.S. Public*, pg. 1360
PURINA ITALIA SPA—See Ralston Purina Company; *U.S. Public*, pg. 1360
PURINA KOREA INC.—See Ralston Purina Company; *U.S. Public*, pg. 1360
PURINA MILLS, INC.; *U.S. Private*, pg. 895
PURINA PROTEIN EUROPE S.A.—See Ralston Purina Company; *U.S. Public*, pg. 1360
PURITAN BAKERY, INC.; *U.S. Private*, pg. 895
PURITAN-BENNETT AERO SYSTEMS CO.—See Mallinckrodt Inc.; *U.S. Public*, pg. 1040
PURITAN-BENNETT AUSTRALIA PTY. LTD.—See Mallinckrodt Inc.; *U.S. Public*, pg. 1040
PURITAN-BENNETT CANADA (KIRKLAND)—See Mallinckrodt Inc.; *U.S. Public*, pg. 1040
PURITAN-BENNETT CANADA LTD.—See Mallinckrodt Inc.; *U.S. Public*, pg. 1040
PURITAN/CHURCHILL CHEMICAL COMPANY; *U.S. Private*, pg. 895
PURITAN MAID LTD.—See Brake Bros plc; *Int'l*, pg. 210
PURITAN OIL COMPANY, INC.—See Warren Equities Inc.; *U.S. Private*, pg. 1151
PURITY DAIRIES INC.; *U.S. Private*, pg. 895
PURITY PRODUCTS INC.; *U.S. Private*, pg. 896
PURITY WHOLESALE GROCERS; *U.S. Private*, pg. 896
PUROFLOW CORP.—See Puroflow Incorporated; *U.S. Public*, pg. 1345
PUROFLOW INCORPORATED; *U.S. Public*, pg. 1345
PUROLATOR—See Air Canada; *Int'l*, pg. 36
PUROLATOR PRODUCTS CO.—See Mark IV Industries Inc.; *U.S. Public*, pg. 1045
PURSELL INDUSTRIES; *U.S. Private*, pg. 896
LAT PURSER & ASSOCIATES; *U.S. Private*, pg. 896
PUSAN OFFICE—See Pohang Iron & Steel Co., Ltd.; *Int'l*, pg. 1062
PUSAN PRECISION INDUSTRIES, LTD.—See Brother Industries, Ltd.; *Int'l*, pg. 230
PUTMAN PUBLISHING CO.; *U.S. Private*, pg. 896
THE PUTNAM & GROSSET GROUP—See Pearson plc; *Int'l*, pg. 1027
THE PUTNAM BERKLEY GROUP, INC.—See Pearson plc; *Int'l*, pg. 1027
G.P. PUTNAM SONS—See The Seagram Company Ltd.; *Int'l*, pg. 1215
PUTNAM GRAPHIC INNOVATIONS, INC.—See National Fiberstock Corporation; *U.S. Private*, pg. 782
PUTNAM INVESTMENTS, INC.—See Marsh & McLennan Companies, Inc.; *U.S. Public*, pg. 1049
PUTNAM REINSURANCE CO.—See American International Group, Inc.; *U.S. Public*, pg. 84
PUTT PUTT GOLF COURSES OF AMERICA, INC.; *U.S. Private*, pg. 896
PUTZMEISTER, INC.; *U.S. Private*, pg. 896
PUUMERKKI OY—See Enso Oyj; *Int'l*, pg. 456
PVS TRANSPORTATION—See PVS Chemicals, Inc.; *U.S. Private*, pg. 828
PY-O-MY DIV.—See Gilster Mary Lee Corp.; *U.S. Private*, pg. 455
PYLE INC.—See Kohlberg Kravis Roberts & Co.; *U.S. Private*, pg. 629
PYLON MANUFACTURING CORP.—See MascoTech, Inc.; *U.S. Public*, pg. 1055
PYRAL S.A.—See BASF AG; *Int'l*, pg. 109
PYRAMID BREWERIES, INC.; *U.S. Public*, pg. 1345
THE PYRAMID COMPANIES; *U.S. Private*, pg. 896
PYRAMID HANDBAGS INC.; *U.S. Private*, pg. 896
THE PYRAMID LIFE INSURANCE CO.—See Unitrin, Inc.; *U.S. Public*, pg. 1694
PYRAMID MOULDINGS—See TBG Management S.A.M.; *Int'l*, pg. 1335
PYRAMID MOUNTAIN LUMBER; *U.S. Private*, pg. 896
PYRAMID SERVICES, INC.—See AON Corporation; *U.S. Public*, pg. 118
PYRAMID SOUTHERN MOULDINGS—See TBG Management S.A.M.; *Int'l*, pg. 1335
PYRION-CHEMIE GMBH—See Ruetgers A.G.; *Int'l*, pg. 1148
PYRO ENGINEERING DIVISION—See Resco Products, Inc.; *U.S. Private*, pg. 924
PYRO MINING CO.—See Costain Group PLC; *Int'l*, pg. 337
PYROFUSE—See Sigmund Cohn Corp.; *U.S. Private*, pg. 250
PYROIL CANADA LIMITED—See Noma Industries Limited; *Int'l*, pg. 955
PYROINDUSTRIE S.A.—See OEA, Inc.; *U.S. Public*, pg. 1207
PYROMET, INC.; *U.S. Private*, pg. 897
PYRON CORP.—See Zemex Corporation; *Int'l*, pg. 1524
PYRON METAL POWDERS, INC.—See Zemex Corporation; *Int'l*, pg. 1524

Q

Q & B FOODS, INC.—See Q.P. Corporation; *Int'l*, pg. 1074
Q-ARC LIMITED—See ILC Technology, Inc.; *U.S. Public*, pg. 856
Q-CHECK SYSTEMS—See Synergis Technologies Group; *U.S. Private*, pg. 1060
QA PRODUCTS, INC.—See CSM N.V.; *Int'l*, pg. 244
QAD.AB—See QAD Inc; *U.S. Public*, pg. 1345
QAD.ASIA-PACIFIC—See QAD Inc; *U.S. Public*, pg. 1345
QAD.AUSTRALIA PTY LTD—See QAD Inc; *U.S. Public*, pg. 1345
QAD.AUSTRALIA PTY LTD.—See QAD Inc; *U.S. Public*, pg. 1345
QAD.BRAZIL—See QAD Inc; *U.S. Public*, pg. 1345
QAD.CHINA—See QAD Inc; *U.S. Public*, pg. 1345
QAD.EUROPE B.V.—See QAD Inc; *U.S. Public*, pg. 1345
QAD.FRANCE EURL—See QAD Inc; *U.S. Public*, pg. 1345
QAD.GERMANY GMBH—See QAD Inc; *U.S. Public*, pg. 1345
QAD INC; *U.S. Public*, pg. 1345
QAD.INC.—See QAD Inc; *U.S. Public*, pg. 1345
QAD.JAPAN K.K.—See QAD Inc; *U.S. Public*, pg. 1345
QAD.MEXICO S.A. DE C.V.—See QAD Inc; *U.S. Public*, pg. 1345
QAD.UNITED KINGDOM LTD.—See QAD Inc; *U.S. Public*, pg. 1345
QAL GLADSTONE PLANT—See Maxxam Inc.; *U.S. Public*, pg. 1062
QC, INC.—See Land O'Lakes, Inc.; *U.S. Private*, pg. 646
QC OPTICS, INC.; *U.S. Public*, pg. 1345
QDI, INC.—See Arizona Wholesale Supply Company; *U.S. Private*, pg. 82
QEI, INC.; *U.S. Private*, pg. 897
QF, INC.—See Nippon Suisan Kaisha, Ltd.; *Int'l*, pg. 940
QIT-FER ET TITANE—See Rio Tinto PLC; *Int'l*, pg. 1119
QMS CANADA—See QMS, Inc.; *U.S. Public*, pg. 1346
QMS CIRCUITS, INC.—See QMS, Inc.; *U.S. Public*, pg. 1346
QMS, INC.; *U.S. Public*, pg. 1346
QMS INTERNATIONAL GMBH—See QMS, Inc.; *U.S. Public*, pg. 1346
QMS S.A.R.L.—See QMS, Inc.; *U.S. Public*, pg. 1346
Q.P. CORPORATION; *Int'l*, pg. 1074
QPI FINANCIAL SERVICES—See Quebecor Inc.; *Int'l*, pg. 1078
QSP DISTRIBUTION SERVICES, INC.—See The Reader's Digest Association, Inc.; *U.S. Public*, pg. 1367
QSP, INC.—See The Reader's Digest Association, Inc.; *U.S. Public*, pg. 1367
QST COMMUNICATIONS, INC.—See CILCORP Inc.; *U.S. Public*, pg. 367
QST ENERGY, INC.—See CILCORP Inc.; *U.S. Public*, pg. 367
QST ENTERPRISES INC.—See CILCORP Inc.; *U.S. Public*, pg. 367
QST ENVIRONMENTAL INC.—See CILCORP Inc.; *U.S. Public*, pg. 367
QST FAR EAST LIMITED—See QST Industries, Inc.; *U.S. Private*, pg. 897
QST INDUSTRIES, INC.; *U.S. Private*, pg. 897
QT OPTOELECTRONICS; *U.S. Private*, pg. 897
Q3 INDUSTRIES—See Q3 Stamped Metal; *U.S. Private*, pg. 897
Q3 STAMPED METAL; *U.S. Private*, pg. 897
Q.U.F. INDUSTRIES LTD.; *Int'l*, pg. 1074
Q.U.F. MILK MARKETING—See Q.U.F. Industries Ltd.; *Int'l*, pg. 1074
QVC, INC.—See Comcast Corporation; *U.S. Public*, pg. 407
QVC, INC.; *U.S. Private*, pg. 897
QVC, INC.—See TCI Communications, Inc.; *U.S. Public*, pg. 1555
Q.V.F. GLASTECHNIK GMBH—See Corning Incorporated; *U.S. Public*, pg. 449
QANBAR DYWIDAG PRECAST CONCRETE LTD.—See Dyckerhoff & Widmann AG; *Int'l*, pg. 425
QANBAR STEETLEY (SAUDI) LIMITED—See Redland PLC; *Int'l*, pg. 1092
QANTAS AIRWAYS LTD.; *Int'l*, pg. 1074
QANTAS FLIGHT CATERING—See Qantas Airways Ltd.; *Int'l*, pg. 1075
QANTAS HOLIDAYS—See Qantas Airways Ltd.; *Int'l*, pg. 1075
QANTAS INFORMATION TECHNOLOGY—See Qantas Airways Ltd.; *Int'l*, pg. 1075
QATAR DATAMATION SYSTEMS—See Hewlett-Packard Company; *U.S. Public*, pg. 823
QATAR DRILLING CO.—See Kuwait Petroleum Corporation; *Int'l*, pg. 765
QATAR FERTILISER CO. S.A.Q.—See Norsk Hydro a.s; *Int'l*, pg. 964
QATAR SHELL SERVICE—See Royal Dutch/Shell Group of Companies; *Int'l*, pg. 1141
QATAR STEEL CO. LTD.—See Kobe Steel, Ltd.; *Int'l*, pg. 741
QFC HOLDING COMPANY—See Quality Food Centers, Inc.; *U.S. Public*, pg. 1349
QINGDAO CIBA AGRO CO., LTD.—See Novartis AG; *Int'l*, pg. 983
QINGDAO DAEWOO STONE CO., LTD.—See Daewoo Corporation; *Int'l*, pg. 358
QINGDAO FLOAT GLASS CO., LTD.—See Taiwan Glass Industry Corp.; *Int'l*, pg. 1348
QINGDAO ROLLED GLASS CO., LTD.—See Taiwan Glass Industry Corp.; *Int'l*, pg. 1348
QINGDAO SSANGYONG APPAREL CO., LTD.—See Ssangyong Business Group; *Int'l*, pg. 1291
QINGLING MOTORS CO., LTD.—See Isuzu Motors Limited; *Int'l*, pg. 693
OY QTRONIC AB—See Axel Johnson AB; *Int'l*, pg. 712
QUACKENBUSH CO. INC.; *U.S. Private*, pg. 897
QUAD-CITY TIMES—See Lee Enterprises, Incorporated; *U.S. Public*, pg. 984
QUAD COUNTY PUBLISHING, INC.—See Knight-Ridder, Inc.; *U.S. Public*, pg. 964
QUAD/GRAPHICS, INC.; *U.S. Private*, pg. 897
QUAD SYSTEMS CORPORATION; *U.S. Private*, pg. 898
QUAD/WEST PRE-PRESS—See Quad/Graphics, Inc.; *U.S.* Private, pg. 898
QUADION CORPORATION; *U.S. Private*, pg. 898
QUADRA PACK—See Enso Oyj; *Int'l*, pg. 458
QUADRANGLE DEVELOPMENT CORPORATION; *U.S. Private*, pg. 898
QUADRANGLE MANAGEMENT COMPANY—See Quadrangle Development Corporation; *U.S. Private*, pg. 898
THE QUADRANT CORPORATION—See Weyerhaeuser Company; *U.S. Public*, pg. 1764
QUADRANT INTERNATIONAL PTY. LTD.—See Fujitsu Limited; *Int'l*, pg. 528
QUADRAS, INC.—See Wallace Computer Services, Inc.; *U.S. Public*, pg. 1736
QUADRASTAT CORP.—See Adams Rite Manufacturing Co.; *U.S. Private*, pg. 17
QUAESTOR INVESTMENT MANAGEMENT LTD.—See Yasuda Mutual Life Insurance Co.; *Int'l*, pg. 1520
QUAIFE PAPERS, LTD.—See Groupe Saint Louis; *Int'l*, pg. 567

QUAIL CREEK NURSING & RETIREMENT CENTER—See Horizon/CMS Healthcare Corporation; *U.S. Public,* pg. 839
QUAIL PIPING PRODUCTS, INC.—See Asahi/America, Inc.; *U.S. Public,* pg. 137
QUAKER ALLOY, INC.—See Atchison Casting Corporation; *U.S. Public,* pg. 142
QUAKER BRASIL, LTDA.—See The Quaker Oats Company; *U.S. Public,* pg. 1348
QUAKER CHEMICAL (AUSTRALASIA) PTY. LTD.—See Quaker Chemical Corporation; *U.S. Public,* pg. 1346
QUAKER CHEMICAL B.V.—See Quaker Chemical Corporation; *U.S. Public,* pg. 1346
QUAKER CHEMICAL CORPORATION; *U.S. Public,* pg. 1346
QUAKER CHEMICAL ENVIRONMENTAL PRODUCTS DIVISION—See Quaker Chemical Corporation; *U.S. Public,* pg. 1346
QUAKER CHEMICAL EUROPE B.V.—See Quaker Chemical Corporation; *U.S. Public,* pg. 1346
QUAKER CHEMICAL INDIA LTD.—See Quaker Chemical Corporation; *U.S. Public,* pg. 1346
QUAKER CHEMICAL INDUSTRIAL COMERCIO LTDA.—See Quaker Chemical Corporation; *U.S. Public,* pg. 1346
QUAKER CHEMICAL LIMITED—See Quaker Chemical Corporation; *U.S. Public,* pg. 1346
QUAKER CHEMICAL PARTICIPACOES LTDA—See Quaker Chemical Corporation; *U.S. Public,* pg. 1347
QUAKER CHEMICAL, S.A.—See Quaker Chemical Corporation; *U.S. Public,* pg. 1347
QUAKER CHEMICAL S.A.—See Quaker Chemical Corporation; *U.S. Public,* pg. 1347
QUAKER CHEMICAL SOUTH AFRICA (PTY.) LTD.—See Quaker Chemical Corporation; *U.S. Public,* pg. 1347
QUAKER-CHIARI & FORTI S.P.A.—See The Quaker Oats Company; *U.S. Public,* pg. 1348
QUAKER CITY MOTOR PARTS COMPANY; *U.S. Private,* pg. 898
QUAKER CITY STAMP CO.—See American Marking Systems; *U.S. Private,* pg. 59
QUAKER FABRIC CORPORATION; *U.S. Public,* pg. 1347
QUAKER INDUSTRIES—See Park-Ohio Industries, Inc.; *U.S. Public,* pg. 1259
QUAKER OATS B.V.—See The Quaker Oats Company; *U.S. Public,* pg. 1348
THE QUAKER OATS COMPANY; *U.S. Public,* pg. 1347
THE QUAKER OATS CO. OF CANADA LTD.—See The Quaker Oats Company; *U.S. Public,* pg. 1348
QUAKER OATS LIMITED—See The Quaker Oats Company; *U.S. Public,* pg. 1348
QUAKER STATE CORPORATION; *U.S. Public,* pg. 1348
QUAKER STATE INC.—See Quaker State Corporation; *U.S. Public,* pg. 1348
QUAKER STATE JAPAN CO., LTD.—See Quaker State Corporation; *U.S. Public,* pg. 1348
QUAKER STATE Q-LUBE, INC.—See Quaker State Corporation; *U.S. Public,* pg. 1348
QUAL-MED, INC.—See Foundation Health Systems, Inc.; *U.S. Public,* pg. 678
QUALA SYSTEMS, INC.—See Chemical Leaman Corporation; *U.S. Private,* pg. 233
QUALCOMM; *U.S. Public,* pg. 1348
QUALEX INC.—See Eastman Kodak Company; *U.S. Public,* pg. 551
QUALHEIM, INC.—See CTS Corporation; *U.S. Public,* pg. 286
QUALIDYNE SYSTEMS INC.—See Siebe plc; *Int'l,* pg. 1241
QUALITAS BATHROOMS LTD.—See Blue Circle Industries PLC; *Int'l,* pg. 197
QUALITROL CORP.—See Danaher Corporation; *U.S. Public,* pg. 482
QUALITY BAKERS (ASIA) PTE LTD.—See Goodman Fielder Limited; *Int'l,* pg. 555
QUALITY BAKERS AUSTRALIA LTD.—See Goodman Fielder Limited; *Int'l,* pg. 555
QUALITY BAKERS NEDERLAND B.V.—See Goodman Fielder Limited; *Int'l,* pg. 555
QUALITY BAKERS NEW ZEALAND LTD.—See Goodman Fielder Limited; *Int'l,* pg. 556
QUALITY BAKERS OF AMERICA COOPERATIVE, INC.; *U.S. Private,* pg. 898
THE QUALITY BAKERY CO., INC.—See Lancaster Colony Corporation; *U.S. Public,* pg. 977
QUALITY BEARING SERVICE OF KENTUCKY, INC.—See Varlen Corporation; *U.S. Public,* pg. 1711
QUALITY BEARING SERVICE OF MISSOURI, INC.—See Varlen Corporation; *U.S. Public,* pg. 1711
QUALITY BEARING SERVICE OF NEVADA, INC.—See Varlen Corporation; *U.S. Public,* pg. 1711
QUALITY CASTING COMPANY—See Michigan Wheel Corporation; *U.S. Private,* pg. 741
QUALITY CHEKD DAIRIES, INC.; *U.S. Private,* pg. 898
QUALITY CHEMICALS, INC.—See ChemFirst Inc.; *U.S. Public,* pg. 344
QUALITY COFFEE PRODUCTS LTD.—See Nestle S.A.; *Int'l,* pg. 922
QUALITY COIL PROCESSING—See Kasle Steel Corporation; *U.S. Private,* pg. 608
QUALITY COMPUTER FORMS, INC.—See Rotary Forms Press, Inc.; *U.S. Private,* pg. 947
QUALITY CONTROL CORPORATION; *U.S. Private,* pg. 898
QUALITY DINING INC.; *U.S. Public,* pg. 1349
QUALITY EDUCATION DATA (QED)—See Peterson's Guides, Inc.; *U.S. Private,* pg. 858
QUALITY FOOD CENTERS, INC.; *U.S. Public,* pg. 1349
QUALITY FOOD OILS, INC.—See Associated British Foods plc; *Int'l,* pg. 92
QUALITY FOODS INC.; *U.S. Private,* pg. 898
QUALITY HEAT TREATMENT—See Driver-Harris Company; *U.S. Public,* pg. 530

QUALITY HOME HEALTH CARE, INC.—See Integrated Health Services, Inc.; *U.S. Public,* pg. 885
QUALITY HOTEL CENTRAL—See Frisch's Restaurants, Inc.; *U.S. Public,* pg. 682
QUALITY HOTEL DOWNTOWN—See Taj International Hotels; *U.S. Private,* pg. 1067
QUALITY HOTEL RIVERVIEW—See Frisch's Restaurants, Inc.; *U.S. Public,* pg. 682
QUALITY INCENTIVE & TRAVEL—See Fleming Companies, Inc.; *U.S. Public,* pg. 653
QUALITY KING DISTRIBUTORS, INC.; *U.S. Private,* pg. 899
QUALITY LIGHTING, INC.—See Luxo A/S; *Int'l,* pg. 821
QUALITY MARKETS, INC.—See The Penn Traffic Company; *U.S. Public,* pg. 1270
QUALITY MEDICAL ADJUDICATION, INC.—See Health Management Systems, Inc.; *U.S. Public,* pg. 802
QUALITY METALS—See Sony Corporation; *Int'l,* pg. 1283
QUALITY MUSIC—See Quality Special Products; *Int'l,* pg. 1075
QUALITY NATURALLY FOODS; *U.S. Private,* pg. 899
QUALITY PACKAGING PRODUCTS, INC.; *U.S. Private,* pg. 899
QUALITY PARK PRODUCTS—See Mail-Well Inc.; *U.S. Public,* pg. 1038
QUALITY PETROLEUM CORP.; *U.S. Private,* pg. 899
QUALITY PONTIAC GMC BUICK; *U.S. Private,* pg. 899
QUALITY SERVICE PLAN, INC. CANADA—See The Reader's Digest Association, Inc.; *U.S. Public,* pg. 1368
QUALITY SERVICE TANK LINES, INC.—See Trimac Corporation; *Int'l,* pg. 1424
QUALITY SERVICES INTERNATIONAL, INC.—See Encore Marketing International, Inc.; *U.S. Public,* pg. 580
QUALITY SPECIAL PRODUCTS; *Int'l,* pg. 1075
QUALITY STAMP—See Fleming Companies, Inc.; *U.S. Public,* pg. 653
QUALITY STORES INC.; *U.S. Private,* pg. 899
QUALITY SYSTEMS INC.—See Tracor, Inc.; *U.S. Public,* pg. 1627
QUALITY TOYOTA; *U.S. Private,* pg. 899
QUALIVEST CAPITAL MANAGEMENT, INC.—See U.S. Bancorp; *U.S. Public,* pg. 1681
QUALTERS & SMITH—See Carclo Engineering Group plc; *Int'l,* pg. 268
QUANEX CORPORATION; *U.S. Public,* pg. 1349
QUANTA ADVERTISING CORPORATION—See Carrols Corporation; *U.S. Private,* pg. 216
QUANTA SECURSYSTEMS, INC.—See CompuDyne Corporation; *U.S. Public,* pg. 420
QUANTA SYSTEMS CORPORATION—See CompuDyne Corporation; *U.S. Public,* pg. 420
QUANTERRA ENVIRONMENTAL SERVICES; *U.S. Private,* pg. 899
QUANTIC INDUSTRIES, INC.; *U.S. Private,* pg. 899
QUANTIC INDUSTRIES, INC.—See Quantic Industries, Inc.; *U.S. Private,* pg. 899
QUANTRONIX, GMBH—See Excel Technology, Inc.; *U.S. Public,* pg. 599
QUANTUM—See Quantum Corporation; *U.S. Public,* pg. 1350
QUANTUM ASIA-PACIFIC PTE. LTD. LOGISTICS CENTER—See Quantum Corporation; *U.S. Public,* pg. 1350
QUANTUM ASIA-PACIFIC PTE. LTD.—See Quantum Corporation; *U.S. Public,* pg. 1350
QUANTUM COMPUTER SYSTEMS—See Quantum Corporation; *U.S. Public,* pg. 1350
QUANTUM CORPORATION; *U.S. Public,* pg. 1350
QUANTUM CORPORATION—See Quantum Corporation; *U.S. Public,* pg. 1350
QUANTUM CORPORATION AUSTRALIA BRANCH—See Quantum Corporation; *U.S. Public,* pg. 1350
QUANTUM CORPORATION TAIWAN BRANCH—See Quantum Corporation; *U.S. Public,* pg. 1350
QUANTUM FRANCE—See Quantum Corporation; *U.S. Public,* pg. 1350
QUANTUM GMBH—See Quantum Corporation; *U.S. Public,* pg. 1350
QUANTUM HONG KONG LTD.—See Quantum Corporation; *U.S. Public,* pg. 1350
QUANTUM HONG KONG LTD. PRC BRANCH—See Quantum Corporation; *U.S. Public,* pg. 1350
QUANTUM INSPECTION & TESTING LTD.—See CBS Corporation; *U.S. Public,* pg. 273
QUANTUM INTERNATIONAL LTD.—See National Media Corporation; *U.S. Public,* pg. 1158
QUANTUM INTL. DISC, INC.—See Quantum Corporation; *U.S. Public,* pg. 1350
QUANTUM JAPAN PROCUREMENT CENTER, INC.—See Quantum Corporation; *U.S. Public,* pg. 1350
QUANTUM KOREA—See Quantum Corporation; *U.S. Public,* pg. 1350
QUANTUM MEDIA INTERNATIONAL, INC.; *U.S. Private,* pg. 899
QUANTUM MEDIA INTERNATIONAL, INC.—See Quantum Media International, Inc.; *U.S. Private,* pg. 899
QUANTUM PERIPHERAL PRODUCTS (IRELAND) LTD.—See Quantum Corporation; *U.S. Public,* pg. 1350
QUANTUM PERIPHERAL PRODUCTS, LTD.—See Quantum Corporation; *U.S. Public,* pg. 1350
QUANTUM PERIPHERALS COLORADO—See Quantum Corporation; *U.S. Public,* pg. 1350
QUANTUM PERIPHERALS (EUROPE) SA—See Quantum Corporation; *U.S. Public,* pg. 1350
QUANTUM PERIPHERALS JAPAN CORPORATION—See Quantum Corporation; *U.S. Public,* pg. 1350
QUANTUM PERIPHERALS (MALAYSIA)—See Quantum Corporation; *U.S. Public,* pg. 1350
QUANTUM PLUS—See Omnicom Group Inc.; *U.S. Public,* pg. 1224
QUANTUM SPORT—See JbQ Sport LLC; *U.S. Private,* pg. 577
QUANTUM SPORT; *U.S. Private,* pg. 900

QUANTUM, USI DIVISION—See Quantum Corporation; *U.S. Public,* pg. 1350
QUARK INC.; *U.S. Private,* pg. 900
QUARTERDECK CORP.; *U.S. Public,* pg. 1350
QUARTERDECK INTERNATIONAL LIMITED—See Quarterdeck Corp.; *U.S. Public,* pg. 1351
QUARTERDECK OFFICE SYSTEMS AUSTRALIA PTY. LTD.—See Quarterdeck Corp.; *U.S. Public,* pg. 1351
QUARTERDECK OFFICE SYSTEMS CANADA, INC.—See Quarterdeck Corp.; *U.S. Public,* pg. 1351
QUARTERDECK OFFICE SYSTEMS GMBH—See Quarterdeck Corp.; *U.S. Public,* pg. 1351
QUARTERDECK OFFICE SYSTEMS S.A.R.L.—See Quarterdeck Corp.; *U.S. Public,* pg. 1351
QUARTERDECK OFFICE SYSTEMS UK LIMITED—See Quarterdeck Corp.; *U.S. Public,* pg. 1351
QUARTET MANUFACTURING CO.—See General Binding Corporation; *U.S. Public,* pg. 707
QUARTIER LEOPOLD REALTY S.A.—See Temco Service Industries; *U.S. Public,* pg. 1574
QUARTZ & SILICE—See Saint-Gobain; *Int'l,* pg. 1176
QUARZSANDWERK GESELLSCHAFT MBH—See Redland PLC; *Int'l,* pg. 1092
QUAVITAE, S.A.—See Caja de Madrid Group; *Int'l,* pg. 252
QUEBEC & MARITIMES DIV. ST. LAWRENCE CEMENT—See Holderbank Financiere Glaris Ltd.; *Int'l,* pg. 629
QUEBEC CARTIER MINING CO.—See DoFasco, Inc.; *Int'l,* pg. 414
QUEBEC SOUTHERN RAILROAD—See Iron Road Railways Inc.; *U.S. Public,* pg. 575
QUEBEC STREET INVESTMENTS, INC.—See Cigna Corp.; *U.S. Public,* pg. 361
QUEBEC-TELEPHONE—See GTE Corporation; *U.S. Public,* pg. 697
QUEBECOR COMMUNICATIONS, INC.—See Quebecor Inc.; *Int'l,* pg. 1076
QUEBECOR IMAGING (ALPHATEXT)—See Quebecor Inc.; *Int'l,* pg. 1077
QUEBECOR INC.; *Int'l,* pg. 1075
QUEBECOR INTEGRATED MEDIA—See Quebecor Inc.; *Int'l,* pg. 1076
QUEBECOR INTERACTIVE ELECTRONIC PUBLISHING GROUP—See Quebecor Inc.; *Int'l,* pg. 1076
QUEBECOR LIST SERVICES—See Quebecor Inc.; *Int'l,* pg. 1078
QUEBECOR LITHO PLUS—See Quebecor Inc.; *Int'l,* pg. 1076
QUEBECOR MERRILL CANADA INC.—See Quebecor Inc.; *Int'l,* pg. 1076
QUEBECOR MULTIMEDIA INC.—See Quebecor Inc.; *Int'l,* pg. 1076
QUEBECOR PHOTOLITHO—See Quebecor Inc.; *Int'l,* pg. 1077
QUEBECOR PRINTING ARLINGTON HEIGHTS—See Quebecor Inc.; *Int'l,* pg. 1076
QUEBECOR PRINTING ATGLEN INC.—See Quebecor Inc.; *Int'l,* pg. 1076
QUEBECOR PRINTING ATLANTIC SAINT JOHN—See Quebecor Inc.; *Int'l,* pg. 1077
QUEBECOR PRINTING BOOK PRESS INC.—See Quebecor Inc.; *Int'l,* pg. 1078
QUEBECOR PRINTING BUFFALO INC.—See Quebecor Inc.; *Int'l,* pg. 1078
QUEBECOR PRINTING CLARKSVILLE—See Quebecor Inc.; *Int'l,* pg. 1076
QUEBECOR PRINTING CONCORD—See Quebecor Inc.; *Int'l,* pg. 1077
QUEBECOR PRINTING CORPORATION—See Quebecor Inc.; *Int'l,* pg. 1078
QUEBECOR PRINTING DALLAS INC.—See Quebecor Inc.; *Int'l,* pg. 1076
QUEBECOR PRINTING DICKSON INC.—See Quebecor Inc.; *Int'l,* pg. 1076
QUEBECOR PRINTING EDMONTON—See Quebecor Inc.; *Int'l,* pg. 1077
QUEBECOR PRINTING EUSEY PRESS INC.—See Quebecor Inc.; *Int'l,* pg. 1078
QUEBECOR PRINTING FAIRFIELD INC.—See Quebecor Inc.; *Int'l,* pg. 1076
QUEBECOR PRINTING FEDERATED INC.—See Quebecor Inc.; *Int'l,* pg. 1078
QUEBECOR PRINTING GLEN BURNIE—See Quebecor Inc.; *Int'l,* pg. 1076
QUEBECOR PRINTING HAUGHTON—See Quebecor Inc.; *Int'l,* pg. 1077
QUEBECOR PRINTING HAWKINS—See Quebecor Inc.; *Int'l,* pg. 1076
QUEBECOR PRINTING HAZLETON INC.—See Quebecor Inc.; *Int'l,* pg. 1076
QUEBECOR PRINTING, INC.—See Quebecor Inc.; *Int'l,* pg. 1076
QUEBECOR PRINTING KINGSPORT INC.—See Quebecor Inc.; *Int'l,* pg. 1076
QUEBECOR PRINTING MARTINSBURG—See Quebecor Inc.; *Int'l,* pg. 1076
QUEBECOR PRINTING MEMPHIS INC.—See Quebecor Inc.; *Int'l,* pg. 1077
QUEBECOR PRINTING MIL INC.—See Quebecor Inc.; *Int'l,* pg. 1077
QUEBECOR PRINTING MODERN INC.—See Quebecor Inc.; *Int'l,* pg. 1078
QUEBECOR PRINTING MT. MORRIS INC.—See Quebecor Inc.; *Int'l,* pg. 1076
QUEBECOR PRINTING NASHVILLE—See Quebecor Inc.; *Int'l,* pg. 1076
QUEBECOR PRINTING ORLANDO—See Quebecor Inc.; *Int'l,* pg. 1076
QUEBECOR PRINTING PE&E—See Quebecor Inc.; *Int'l,* pg. 1077
QUEBECOR PRINTING PENDELL INC.—See Quebecor Inc.; *Int'l,* pg. 1077
QUEBECOR PRINTING PROVIDENCE INC.—See Quebecor Inc.; *Int'l,* pg. 1077

QUEBECOR PRINTING RICHMOND HILL—See Quebecor Inc.; *Int'l*, pg. 1077
QUEBECOR PRINTING RICHMOND INC.—See Quebecor Inc.; *Int'l*, pg. 1078
QUEBECOR PRINTING ST. PAUL INC.—See Quebecor Inc.; *Int'l*, pg. 1078
QUEBECOR PRINTING SAN JOSE INC.—See Quebecor Inc.; *Int'l*, pg. 1077
QUEBECOR PRINTING SEMLINE INC.—See Quebecor Inc.; *Int'l*, pg. 1077
QUEBECOR PRINTING SHERWOOD—See Quebecor Inc.; *Int'l*, pg. 1076
QUEBECOR PRINTING (USA) CORP.—See Quebecor Inc.; *Int'l*, pg. 1076
QUEBECOR PRINTING (USA) HOLDINGS INC.—See Quebecor Inc.; *Int'l*, pg. 1078
QUEBECOR PRINTING VANCOUVER—See Quebecor Inc.; *Int'l*, pg. 1077
QUEBEDEAUX PONTIAC, INC.; *U.S. Private*, pg. 900
QUEBRADA BLANCA—See Cominco, Ltd.; *Int'l*, pg. 308
QUEEN CARPET CORPORATION; *U.S. Private*, pg. 900
QUEEN CUTLERY CO.—See Servotronics, Inc.; *U.S. Public*, pg. 1462
QUEENS GROUP, INC.; *U.S. Private*, pg. 900
QUEENS GROUP KENTUCKY, INC.—See Queens Group, Inc.; *U.S. Private*, pg. 900
QUEENS GROUP NEW JERSEY, INC.—See Queens Group, Inc.; *U.S. Private*, pg. 900
QUEENS GROUP NORTH CAROLINA, INC.—See Queens Group, Inc.; *U.S. Private*, pg. 900
QUEENS PROPERTIES—See Philipp Holzmann AG; *Int'l*, pg. 633
QUEENSBORO STEEL CORPORATION—See Metals USA, Inc.; *U.S. Public*, pg. 1101
QUEENSLAND ALUMINA LIMITED—See Alcan Aluminium Limited; *Int'l*, pg. 52
QUEENSLAND ALUMINA LIMITED—See Maxxam Inc.; *U.S. Public*, pg. 1063
QUEENSLAND CEMENT LTD.—See Holderbank Financiere Glaris Ltd.; *Int'l*, pg. 629
QUEENSLAND GLASS MANUFACTURERS CO.—See BTR plc; *Int'l*, pg. 128
QUELLE GROUP; *Int'l*, pg. 1078
QUEMENEUR—See Bouygues; *Int'l*, pg. 206
QUEMETCO, INC.—See Quexco Incorporated; *U.S. Private*, pg. 900
QUEMETCO METALS LIMITED, INC.—See Quexco Incorporated; *U.S. Private*, pg. 900
QUEMETCO REALTY, INC.—See Quexco Incorporated; *U.S. Private*, pg. 900
QUENCHER DIV.—See Del Laboratories, Inc.; *U.S. Public*, pg. 494
QUERCY S.A.—See American Standard Inc.; *U.S. Public*, pg. 92
QUEST DIAGNOSTICS, INC.; *U.S. Public*, pg. 1351
QUEST FUTURES GROUP, INC.—See The Interpublic Group of Companies, Inc.; *U.S. Public*, pg. 909
QUEST INC.—See Unilever Plc; *Int'l*, pg. 1435
QUEST INTERNATIONAL—See Unilever Plc; *Int'l*, pg. 1438
QUEST INTERNATIONAL FLAVORS & FOODS INC.—See Unilever Plc; *Int'l*, pg. 1436
QUEST INTERNATIONAL FRAGRANCES INC.—See Unilever Plc; *Int'l*, pg. 1436
QUEST JAPAN INC.—See Jinwoong Inc.; *Int'l*, pg. 707
QUEST LEISURE PRODUCTS (AUST) PTY. LTD.—See Jinwoong Inc.; *Int'l*, pg. 707
QUEST MEDICAL, INC.; *U.S. Public*, pg. 1352
QUEST STAFFING—See Allegiant Physician Services; *U.S. Public*, pg. 45
QUEST TECHNOLOGIES, INC.; *U.S. Private*, pg. 900
QUESTAR CORPORATION; *U.S. Public*, pg. 1352
QUESTAR DEVELOPMENT CORPORATION—See Questar Corporation; *U.S. Public*, pg. 1352
QUESTAR INFOCOMM—See Questar Corporation; *U.S. Public*, pg. 1352
QUESTAR PIPELINE COMPANY—See Questar Corporation; *U.S. Public*, pg. 1352
QUESTRON DIV.—See The Seagram Company Ltd.; *Int'l*, pg. 1215
QUEXCO INCORPORATED; *U.S. Private*, pg. 900
QUICK CORP.—See Nihon Keizai Shimbun, Inc.; *Int'l*, pg. 929
QUICK INTERNATIONAL—See GIB Group; *Int'l*, pg. 533
QUICK INTERNATIONAL DEVELOPMENT—See GIB Group; *Int'l*, pg. 533
QUICK NIKKEI NEWS, INC.—See Nihon Keizai Shimbun, Inc.; *Int'l*, pg. 929
THE QUICK & REILLY GROUP INC.—See Fleet Financial Group, Inc.; *U.S. Public*, pg. 650
QUICK & REILLY, INC.—See Fleet Financial Group, Inc.; *U.S. Public*, pg. 650
QUICK RESTAURANTS SA—See GIB Group; *Int'l*, pg. 533
QUICK 10—See Investors Management Corp.; *U.S. Private*, pg. 575
QUICKLOGIC CORPORATION; *U.S. Private*, pg. 900
QUICKMIX CONCRETE COMPANY LIMITED—See RMC Group p.l.c.; *Int'l*, pg. 1080
QUIDEL CORPORATION; *U.S. Public*, pg. 1352
QUIGLEY CO., INC.—See Pfizer Inc.; *U.S. Public*, pg. 1284
QUIK N TASTY FOODS—See QuikTrip Corporation; *U.S. Private*, pg. 901
QUIK PARK INC.—See Quadrangle Development Corporation; *U.S. Private*, pg. 898
QUIK PRINT INC.—See Foster Management Co.; *U.S. Private*, pg. 421
QUIK STIK INTERNATIONAL LTD.—See Esselte AB; *Int'l*, pg. 462
QUIKRETE MATERIALS, INC.—See Ash Grove Cement Company; *U.S. Private*, pg. 88
THE QUIKSET ORGANIZATION—See For Better Living, Inc.; *U.S. Private*, pg. 417
QUIKSILVER, INC.; *U.S. Public*, pg. 1353
QUIKTRIP CORPORATION; *U.S. Private*, pg. 901
QUILL CORP.; *U.S. Private*, pg. 901

QUILL TRADE PAPERBACKS—See The Hearst Corporation; *U.S. Private*, pg. 515
QUILLET S.A.—See Lagardere Groupe; *Int'l*, pg. 793
QUILTER & CO. LTD.—See Credit Commercial de France; *Int'l*, pg. 343
QUIMI-KAO S.A. DE C.V.—See Kao Corporation; *Int'l*, pg. 718
QUIMICA BORDEN ECUATORIANA, S.A.—See Borden, Inc.; *U.S. Private*, pg. 160
QUIMICA DEL REY S.A. DE C.V.—See Industrias Penoles S.A. de C.V.; *Int'l*, pg. 677
QUIMICA DOMINICANA—See Royal Dutch/Shell Group of Companies; *Int'l*, pg. 1141
QUIMICA ESTEROIDAL SA DE CV—See Akzo Nobel N.V.; *Int'l*, pg. 45
QUIMICA FARMACEUTICA BAYER, S.A.—See Bayer AG; *Int'l*, pg. 175
QUIMICA FLESCH, S.A.—See Dainippon Ink & Chemicals, *Int'l*, pg. 371
QUIMICA FLUOR, S.A. DE C.V.—See Du Pont (E.I. Du Pont De Nemours & Co.); *U.S. Public*, pg. 533
QUIMICA HARTING S.A.—See Henkel KGaA; *Int'l*, pg. 614
QUIMICA HENKEL CENTROAMERICANA DE COSTA RICA S.A.—See Henkel KGaA; *Int'l*, pg. 613
QUIMICA HENKEL CENTROAMERICANA DE EL SALVADOR S.A.—See Henkel KGaA; *Int'l*, pg. 613
QUIMICA HENKEL CENTROAMERICANA DE HONDURAS S.A. DE C.V.—See Henkel KGaA; *Int'l*, pg. 613
QUIMICA HENKEL CENTROAMERICANA S.A.—See Henkel KGaA; *Int'l*, pg. 613
QUIMICA HENKEL S.A. DE C.V.—See Henkel KGaA; *Int'l*, pg. 613
QUIMICA HERCULES, S.A. DE C.V.—See Hercules Incorporated; *U.S. Public*, pg. 811
QUIMICA KNOLL DE MEXICO, S.A. DE C.V. BASF PHARMA—See BASF AG; *Int'l*, pg. 109
QUIMICA NALCO DE COLOMBIA, S.A.—See Nalco Chemical Company; *U.S. Public*, pg. 1151
QUIMICA NICARAGUENSE—See Royal Dutch/Shell Group of Companies; *Int'l*, pg. 1141
QUIMICA ORGANICA DE MEXICO, S.A. DE C.V.—See CYDSA S.A.; *Int'l*, pg. 246
QUIMICA PARKER S.A. DE C.V.—See Henkel KGaA; *Int'l*, pg. 614
QUIMICA S.A. DE C.V.—See Henkel KGaA; *Int'l*, pg. 614
QUIMICA S.C. JOHNSON & SON CHILENA S.A.C.I.—See S.C. Johnson & Son, Inc.; *U.S. Private*, pg. 593
QUIMICA SCHERING COLOMBIANA S. A.—See Schering AG; *Int'l*, pg. 1204
QUIMICA SOL S.A.—See Dainippon Ink & Chemicals, Inc.; *Int'l*, pg. 371
QUIMIFAR, LDA.—See Solvay S.A.; *Int'l*, pg. 1279
QUIMOBASICOS, S.A. DE C.V.—See CYDSA S.A.; *Int'l*, pg. 247
QUINCY COMPRESSOR DIVISION COLTEC INDUSTRIES—See Coltec Holdings Inc; *U.S. Public*, pg. 402
QUINCY DESIGN & MANUFACTURING—See Brunner Engineering & Manufacturing, Inc.; *U.S. Private*, pg. 176
QUINCY FAMILY STEAK HOUSE—See Advantica Restaurant Group, Inc.; *U.S. Public*, pg. 23
QUINCY INSURANCE AGENCY, INC.—See D & N Financial Corporation; *U.S. Public*, pg. 472
QUINCY MUTUAL FIRE INSURANCE COMPANY; *U.S. Private*, pg. 901
THE QUINCY STATE BANK—See Synovus Financial Corp.; *U.S. Public*, pg. 1549
QUINCY TELEPHONE COMPANY—See Telephone and Data Systems, Inc.; *U.S. Public*, pg. 1571
QUINLAN PRETZEL CO., INC.—See Borden, Inc.; *U.S. Private*, pg. 158
K.J. QUINN S. A.—See Novartis AG; *Int'l*, pg. 984
QUINN MACHINE & FOUNDRY—See International Pipe Machinery Corp.; *U.S. Private*, pg. 571
QUINN MCDONNELL PATTISON DMB&B DUBLIN—See DMB&B Communications; *U.S. Private*, pg. 305
THE QUINNEHTUK COMPANY—See Northeast Utilities; *U.S. Public*, pg. 1195
QUINNESEC MILL, CHAMPION INTERNATIONAL CORP.—See Champion International Corp.; *U.S. Public*, pg. 334
QUINTANA ENVIRONMENTAL SERVICES, INC.—See Quintana Petroleum Corp.; *U.S. Private*, pg. 901
QUINTANA PETROLEUM CORP.; *U.S. Private*, pg. 901
QUINTANA PETROLEUM SERVICES—See Quintana Petroleum Corp.; *U.S. Private*, pg. 901
QUINTON ELECTRO PHYSIOLOGY—See American Home Products Corporation; *U.S. Public*, pg. 82
QUINTON HAZELL PLC, BARCELONA—See Echlin Inc.; *U.S. Public*, pg. 561
QUINTON HAZELL PLC, BRUSSELS—See Echlin Inc.; *U.S. Public*, pg. 561
QUINTON INSTRUMENT COMPANY—See American Home Products Corporation; *U.S. Public*, pg. 80
QUINTRON SYSTEMS, INC.; *U.S. Private*, pg. 901
QUINTUS CORPORATION; *U.S. Private*, pg. 901
QUIPP, INC.; *U.S. Public*, pg. 1353
QUIPP SYSTEMS, INC.—See Quipp, Inc.; *U.S. Public*, pg. 1353
QUIVERA MINING COMPANY—See Rio Algom Limited; *Int'l*, pg. 1118
QUIXOTE CORPORATION; *U.S. Public*, pg. 1353
QUIXX CORPORATION—See New Century Energies, Inc.; *U.S. Public*, pg. 1170
QUIZEL INC.; *U.S. Private*, pg. 901
QUORIUM CAPITAL MANAGEMENT LTD.—See Westdeutsche Landesbank Girozentrale; *Int'l*, pg. 1493
QUORUM GRAPHIC DESIGN CONSULTANTS LTD.—See Shandwick International Plc; *Int'l*, pg. 1226
QUORUM HEALTH GROUP, INC.; *U.S. Public*, pg. 1353
QUORUM HEALTH RESOURCES, INC.—See Quorum Health Group, Inc.; *U.S. Public*, pg. 1354
QUORUM PUBLICIDAD—See Saatchi & Saatchi Advertising Worldwide; *U.S. Public*, pg. 1422

R

R & C INC.—See Reckitt & Colman plc; *Int'l*, pg. 1090
R&B FALCON CORPORATION; *U.S. Public*, pg. 1354
R&B, INC.; *U.S. Public*, pg. 1354
R & B MACHINE TOOL CO.; *U.S. Private*, pg. 901
R&D SYSTEMS EUROPE LTD.—See Techne Corporation; *U.S. Public*, pg. 1564
R&D SYSTEMS GMBH—See Techne Corporation; *U.S. Public*, pg. 1564
R&D SYSTEMS INC.—See Techne Corporation; *U.S. Public*, pg. 1564
R & G PLUMBING—See Hughes Supply, Inc.; *U.S. Public*, pg. 847
R&H AUSTRALIA PTY. LTD.—See Internatio-Muller N.V.; *Int'l*, pg. 681
R. & H. SYSTEMS B.V.—See Internatio-Muller N.V.; *Int'l*, pg. 680
R & J GARROWAY LIMITED—See Laporte plc; *Int'l*, pg. 802
R & L CARRIERS—See Gator Freightways, Inc.; *U.S. Private*, pg. 441
R&R ADVERTISING; *U.S. Private*, pg. 902
R&R ADVERTISING—See R&R Advertising; *U.S. Private*, pg. 902
R & R HOMES, INC.—See Forest City Enterprises, Inc.; *U.S. Public*, pg. 669
R & R MARKETING; *U.S. Private*, pg. 902
R & R PLASTICS—See Fulton Industries Inc.; *U.S. Public*, pg. 431
R&R TOBACCO LIMITED—See Rothmans UK Holdings Limited; *Int'l*, pg. 1128
R & R UNIFORMS—See Horace Small Apparel PLC; *Int'l*, pg. 635
R C FREIGHTWAY—See R.R. Donnelley & Sons Company; *U.S. Public*, pg. 518
R-CUBED COMPOSITES INC.—See Perstorp AB; *Int'l*, pg. 1037
R-4 KIT MFG. CO.—See Kit Manufacturing Company; *U.S. Public*, pg. 962
R/GA INTERACTIVE—See True North Communications Inc.; *U.S. Public*, pg. 1641
R-PARTNERS—See Vendex International N.V.; *Int'l*, pg. 1463
R-2 KIT MFG. CO.—See Kit Manufacturing Company; *U.S. Public*, pg. 962
R-V CHEMICALS LTD.—See The Procter & Gamble Company; *U.S. Public*, pg. 1332
R.A. BRAND & CO. LIMITED—See Enso Oyj; *Int'l*, pg. 458
R.A. BRIGGS & CO.—See Home Innovations, Inc.; *U.S. Private*, pg. 536
RA, INC.—See Pennsylvania Real Estate Investment Trust; *U.S. Public*, pg. 1272
R.A. INDUSTRIES, INC.; *U.S. Private*, pg. 902
R.A. SALES, INC.—See Republic Automotive Parts, Inc.; *U.S. Public*, pg. 1377
RAI CORPORATION CANADA—See IRI Istituto Ricostruzione Industriale; *Int'l*, pg. 655
R&R ADVERTISING—See R&R Advertising; *U.S. Public*, pg. 902
R.A.R.E. (PTY) LTD.—See Sulzer Ltd.; *Int'l*, pg. 1306
RATP VAL SERVICE (RVS)—See Lagardere Groupe; *Int'l*, pg. 793
RAV CONSTRUCTION COMPANY—See Jennings & Churella Construction Company; *U.S. Private*, pg. 586
RB&W CORPORATION—See Park-Ohio Industries, Inc.; *U.S. Public*, pg. 1259
RBB NV—See Redland PLC; *Int'l*, pg. 1092
RBC DOMINION SECURITIES LTD.—See Royal Bank of Canada; *Int'l*, pg. 1131
RBC FRANCE B.V.—See Royal Bank of Canada; *Int'l*, pg. 1131
RBC INSURANCE HOLDINGS INC.—See Royal Bank of Canada; *Int'l*, pg. 1131
RBC REALTY INC.—See Daniel Industries, Inc.; *U.S. Public*, pg. 483
RBH DISPERSIONS, INC.—See Dainippon Ink & Chemicals, Inc.; *Int'l*, pg. 370
RBS/PNCF INC.—See PNC Bank Corp.; *U.S. Public*, pg. 1244
RBT/STRUM; *U.S. Private*, pg. 902
RBX CORPORATION—See American Industrial Partners; *U.S. Private*, pg. 56
RC COMMUNICATIONS, INC.—See Omnicom Group Inc.; *U.S. Public*, pg. 1224
RCA RECORDS U.S.—See Bertelsmann AG; *Int'l*, pg. 192
R.C.A. RUBBER COMPANY; *U.S. Private*, pg. 902
RCB BAKING COMPANY; *U.S. Private*, pg. 1354
RCC/MOODY-TOTTRUP—See Reliance Group Holdings, Inc.; *U.S. Public*, pg. 1374
RCG INFORMATION SERVICES, CORPORATION—See Integrated Health Services, Inc.; *U.S. Public*, pg. 885
RCG INTERNATIONAL INC.—See Reliance Group Holdings, Inc.; *U.S. Public*, pg. 1374
RCG/VECTRON—See Reliance Group Holdings, Inc.; *U.S. Public*, pg. 1374
RCI RILEY CONSTRUCTION, INC.—See Deutsche Babcock AG; *Int'l*, pg. 401
RCI TRAVEL—See Cendant Corporation; *U.S. Public*, pg. 322
RCLJ CONSTRUCTION, INC.—See Republic Industries, Inc.; *U.S. Public*, pg. 1379
RCM CAPITAL MANAGEMENT—See Dresdner Bank AG; *Int'l*, pg. 418
RCM DESIGN—See S. Rothchild & Co., Inc.; *U.S. Private*, pg. 947
RCM INDUSTRIES; *U.S. Private*, pg. 902
RCN CORPORATION; *U.S. Public*, pg. 1354
RCN LONG DISTANCE—See RCN Corporation; *U.S. Public*, pg. 1354
RCR PUBLICATIONS—See Crain Communications, Inc.; *U.S. Private*, pg. 285
R.C.S. EDITORI S.P.A.; *Int'l*, pg. 1078

RD MANUFACTURING CORPORATION—See The Reader's Digest Association, Inc.; *U.S. Public,* pg. 1367
R.D. MEMBER SERVICES, INC.—See The Reader's Digest Association, Inc.; *U.S. Public,* pg. 1368
R.D. PROPERTIES, LTD.—See The Reader's Digest Association, Inc.; *U.S. Public,* pg. 1368
RD PUBLICATIONS, INC.—See The Reader's Digest Association, Inc.; *U.S. Public,* pg. 1367
RDC MARINE, INC.—See Rowan Companies, Inc.; *U.S. Public,* pg. 1410
R D I S CORPORATION; *U.S. Private,* pg. 903
RDM SPORTS GROUP; *U.S. Public,* pg. 1354
RDM TECHNOLOGY INVESTMENTS B.V.—See Royal Begemann Group; *Int'l,* pg. 1133
RE SERVICES, INC.—See Firstar Corporation; *U.S. Public,* pg. 643
RE WRIGHT ENVIRONMENTAL, INC.—See Science Applications International Corp.; *U.S. Private,* pg. 976
REC EQUIPMENT CORP.—See The Rados Companies; *U.S. Public,* pg. 907
REDA—See Camco International Inc.; *U.S. Public,* pg. 298
RENK AKTIENGESELLSCHAFT—See MAN Aktiengesellschaft; *Int'l,* pg. 825
RET CORP.—See Time Warner Inc.; *U.S. Public,* pg. 1615
RF MICROSYSTEMS—See Remec, Inc.; *U.S. Public,* pg. 1376
R.F. TECHNOLOGY, INC.—See Spectra-Physics AB; *Int'l,* pg. 1289
R.F.A. GROUP LTD.—See Brunel Holdings Plc; *Int'l,* pg. 231
RFA GROUP LIMITED—See British Building & Engineering Appliances Plc; *Int'l,* pg. 219
RFI SHIELDING LIMITED—See Siebe plc; *Int'l,* pg. 1241
RFI CORP.—See Del Global Technologies; *U.S. Public,* pg. 494
RFL ELECTRONICS, INC.; *U.S. Private,* pg. 903
R.F.R./ARIP—See Testa International; *Int'l,* pg. 1377
RFT S.P.A—See AB SKF; *Int'l,* pg. 1158
RGA AND EAST END ACCESSORIES; *U.S. Private,* pg. 903
RGA PRODUCTS INC.—See Rice Growers Association of California; *U.S. Private,* pg. 927
RGB STAINLESS LTD.—See Sandvik AB; *Int'l,* pg. 1186
RGP HOLDING, INC.; *U.S. Private,* pg. 903
RGV ROHOL-GEWINNUNGS UND VERARBEITUNGS GMBH—See Veba AG; *Int'l,* pg. 1461
RH COMMUNICATIONS (M) SDN BHD—See SAIT-RadioHolland Group S.A.; *Int'l,* pg. 1152
RHB CAPITAL BERHAD—See The Sakura Bank, Limited; *Int'l,* pg. 1180
RHC/SPACEMASTER CORPORATION; *U.S. Private,* pg. 904
RHG ARUBA—See SAIT-RadioHolland Group S.A.; *Int'l,* pg. 1152
RHG FISHING OFFICE HONG KONG—See SAIT-RadioHolland Group S.A.; *Int'l,* pg. 1152
RHG FORT LAUDERDALE—See SAIT-RadioHolland Group S.A.; *Int'l,* pg. 1151
RHG NORFOLK/RH DEFENSE SYSTEMS INC.—See SAIT-RadioHolland Group S.A.; *Int'l,* pg. 1151
RHG PANAMA CITY (FLORIDA)—See SAIT-RadioHolland Group S.A.; *Int'l,* pg. 1151
RHG PORTLAND—See SAIT-RadioHolland Group S.A.; *Int'l,* pg. 1151
RHG ST. MAARTEN—See SAIT-RadioHolland Group S.A.; *Int'l,* pg. 1152
RHG SEATTLE—See SAIT-RadioHolland Group S.A.; *Int'l,* pg. 1151
RHG YACHTING OFFICE HONG KONG—See SAIT-RadioHolland Group S.A.; *Int'l,* pg. 1152
RHI CONSULTING—See Robert Half International Inc.; *U.S. Public,* pg. 775
RHI MANAGEMENT RESOURCES—See Robert Half International Inc.; *U.S. Public,* pg. 775
RHM FOODS LIMITED—See Tomkins PLC; *Int'l,* pg. 1396
RHM INGREDIENT SUPPLIES LIMITED—See Tomkins PLC; *Int'l,* pg. 1396
RHM INGREDIENTS, LTD.—See Newly Weds Foods Inc.; *U.S. Private,* pg. 797
RHM TECHNOLOGY LTD.—See Tomkins PLC; *Int'l,* pg. 1396
RHP BEARINGS LIMITED—See NSK Ltd.; *Int'l,* pg. 904
RHP SOUTH AFRICA PTY LTD.—See NSK Ltd.; *Int'l,* pg. 904
R.I. DEVELOPMENT & EXPLORATION CO.—See Valley Resources, Inc.; *U.S. Public,* pg. 1706
RI HOLDINGS; *U.S. Private,* pg. 904
RIH GROUP (PTY) LIMITED—See Barlow Ltd.; *Int'l,* pg. 167
RIHT FINANCIAL CORPORATION—See BankBoston Corporation; *U.S. Public,* pg. 184
RIHT LIFE INSURANCE COMPANY—See BankBoston Corporation; *U.S. Public,* pg. 184
RII HOLDING, INC.—See The Rouse Company; *U.S. Public,* pg. 1407
RIL VIII RAIFFEISEN IMMOBILIEN LEASING GMBH & CO.—See Bayerische Vereinsbank Group; *Int'l,* pg. 181
RIM - RHEINMETALL IMMOBILIEN MANAGEMENT GMBH—See Rheinmetall Group; *Int'l,* pg. 1108
RIS - RHEINMETALL INFORMATIONSSYSTEME GMBH—See Rheinmetall Group; *Int'l,* pg. 1108
RIU INTERNATIONAL PAN AMERICAN OCEAN RESORT HOTEL; *U.S. Private,* pg. 904
RJ ASSOCIATES—See RisComp Industries, Inc.; *U.S. Private,* pg. 932
RJ CREDIT PARTNERS—See Raymond James Financial, Inc.; *U.S. Public,* pg. 923
RJ LEASING, INC.—See Raymond James Financial, Inc.; *U.S. Public,* pg. 923
RJ PROPERTIES, INC.—See Raymond James Financial, Inc.; *U.S. Public,* pg. 923
RJ REALTY, INC.—See Raymond James Financial, Inc.; *U.S. Public,* pg. 923

R.J. REYNOLDS TOBACCO ESPANA, S.A.E.—See RJR Nabisco Holdings Corp.; *U.S. Public,* pg. 1355
RJO ENTERPRISES, INC.; *U.S. Private,* pg. 904
RJR NABISCO HOLDINGS CORP.; *U.S. Public,* pg. 1354
RJR NABISCO, INC.—See RJR Nabisco Holdings Corp.; *U.S. Public,* pg. 1354
RJR TOBACCO COMPANY, INC.—See RJR Nabisco Holdings Corp.; *U.S. Public,* pg. 1355
RK MECHANICAL, INC.; *U.S. Private,* pg. 904
RKN RHEINKRAFTWERK NEUHAUSEN AG—See Alusuisse-Lonza Holding Ltd.; *Int'l,* pg. 67
RLC INDUSTRIES CO.; *U.S. Private,* pg. 905
RLI BOSTON—See RLI Corp.; *U.S. Public,* pg. 1356
RLI CLAIMS/P&C—See RLI Corp.; *U.S. Public,* pg. 1356
RLI CORP.; *U.S. Public,* pg. 1356
RLI/HAWAII PRODUCT LINES—See RLI Corp.; *U.S. Public,* pg. 1356
RLI PROFESSIONAL RISK—See RLI Corp.; *U.S. Public,* pg. 1356
RLI PROGRAM UNDERWRITERS—See RLI Corp.; *U.S. Public,* pg. 1356
RLI SPECIAL RISK—See RLI Corp.; *U.S. Public,* pg. 1356
RLI TRANSPORTATION—See RLI Corp.; *U.S. Public,* pg. 1356
R-M AUTOLACKE GMBH—See BASF AG; *Int'l,* pg. 104
RM INDUSTRIAL GROUP A/S—See FLS Industries A/S; *Int'l,* pg. 476
RM RAVARUMAKLARNA AB—See Axel Johnson AB; *Int'l,* pg. 709
R.M. SERVICES, INC.—See Yankee Energy System, Inc.; *U.S. Public,* pg. 1787
RMA - LAND DEVELOPMENT PRIVATE LTD.—See Singapore Land Limited; *Int'l,* pg. 1253
RMC CATHERWOOD (SCOTLAND) LIMITED—See RMC Group p.l.c.; *Int'l,* pg. 1079
RMC CATHERWOOD (SURFACING) LIMITED—See RMC Group p.l.c.; *Int'l,* pg. 1079
RMC CONCRETE FLOORS LIMITED—See RMC Group p.l.c.; *Int'l,* pg. 1080
RMC CONCRETE PRODUCTS LIMITED-CENTRAL—See RMC Group p.l.c.; *Int'l,* pg. 1080
RMC CONCRETE PRODUCTS LIMITED-EASTERN—See RMC Group p.l.c.; *Int'l,* pg. 1080
RMC CONCRETE PRODUCTS LIMITED-WESTERN—See RMC Group p.l.c.; *Int'l,* pg. 1080
RMC ENGINEERING & TRANSPORT—See RMC Group p.l.c.; *Int'l,* pg. 1080
RMC FRANCE S.A.—See RMC Group p.l.c.; *Int'l,* pg. 1081
RMC GROUP P.L.C.; *Int'l,* pg. 1078
RMC INDUSTRIAL MINERALS LIMITED—See RMC Group p.l.c.; *Int'l,* pg. 1080
RMC INDUSTRIES CORPORATION—See RMC Group p.l.c.; *Int'l,* pg. 1081
RMC MORTARS LIMITED—See RMC Group p.l.c.; *Int'l,* pg. 1080
RMC PANEL PRODUCTS LIMITED—See RMC Group p.l.c.; *Int'l,* pg. 1080
RMC QUARRIES (ULSTER) LIMITED—See RMC Group p.l.c.; *Int'l,* pg. 1079
RMC ROADSTONE LIMITED-MIDLANDS AND SOUTH EAST—See RMC Group p.l.c.; *Int'l,* pg. 1079
RMC ROADSTONE LIMITED-NORTHERN—See RMC Group p.l.c.; *Int'l,* pg. 1079
RMC SURFACING LIMITED-MIDLANDS AREA—See RMC Group p.l.c.; *Int'l,* pg. 1080
RMC SURFACING LIMITED-NORTH WEST AREA—See RMC Group p.l.c.; *Int'l,* pg. 1080
RMC SURFACING LIMITED-SOUTH WEST AREA—See RMC Group p.l.c.; *Int'l,* pg. 1080
RMI EDUCATIONAL SERVICES—See Robertson Marketing Inc.; *U.S. Private,* pg. 936
RMI TITANIUM COMPANY—See USX Corporation; *U.S. Public,* pg. 1662
RMP PROPERTIES LTD.; *Int'l,* pg. 1081
RMS INFORMATION SYSTEMS, INC.—See Safeguard Scientifics, Inc.; *U.S. Public,* pg. 1425
RMS TECHS, INC.; *U.S. Private,* pg. 905
RMT, INC.—See WPL Holdings, Inc.; *U.S. Public,* pg. 1728
RMT TECHNOLOGY—See Reynolds Machine Tool Corp.; *U.S. Private,* pg. 927
RN HOME CARE MEDICAL EQUIPMENT COMPANY, INC.—See Integrated Health Services, Inc.; *U.S. Public,* pg. 885
RNBNY BRANCH OFFICE-LONDON—See Republic New York Corporation; *U.S. Public,* pg. 1381
RNF MEDIA CORPORATION INC.; *U.S. Private,* pg. 905
RNL DESIGN—See RNL Facilities Corporation; *U.S. Private,* pg. 905
RNL FACILITIES CORPORATION; *U.S. Private,* pg. 905
RNL/INTERPLAN—See RNL Facilities Corporation; *U.S. Private,* pg. 905
ROB MONTAGEBEDRIF N.V.—See Deutsche Babcock AG; *Int'l,* pg. 400
ROL ROLAMENTOS PORTUGUESES S.A.—See FAG Group; *Int'l,* pg. 469
ROR ROCKWELL B.V.—See Rockwell International Corporation; *U.S. Public,* pg. 1399
ROR ROCKWELL ESPANA S.A.—See Rockwell International Corporation; *U.S. Public,* pg. 1399
ROR ROCKWELL (IRELAND) LIMITED—See Rockwell International Corporation; *U.S. Public,* pg. 1399
ROR ROCKWELL ITALIA S.R.L.—See Rockwell International Corporation; *U.S. Public,* pg. 1399
ROR ROCKWELL LIMITED—See Rockwell International Corporation; *U.S. Public,* pg. 1399
ROR ROCKWELL S.A.—See Rockwell International Corporation; *U.S. Public,* pg. 1399
ROWO-ROHR-UND KANALREINIGUNGSGERATE GMBH—See Rothenberger Group GmbH; *Int'l,* pg. 1128
RP ALPHA—See Rubin Postaer & Associates; *U.S. Private,* pg. 950
RP ALPHA/ATLANTA—See Rubin Postaer & Associates; *U.S. Private,* pg. 950
RP ALPHA/BOSTON—See Rubin Postaer & Associates; *U.S. Private,* pg. 950

RP ALPHA/CHICAGO—See Rubin Postaer & Associates; *U.S. Private,* pg. 950
RP ALPHA/DALLAS—See Rubin Postaer & Associates; *U.S. Private,* pg. 950
RP ALPHA/DENVER—See Rubin Postaer & Associates; *U.S. Private,* pg. 950
RP ALPHA/NEW JERSEY—See Rubin Postaer & Associates; *U.S. Private,* pg. 950
RP ALPHA/PORTLAND—See Rubin Postaer & Associates; *U.S. Private,* pg. 950
RP & C—See Conbraco Industries Inc.; *U.S. Private,* pg. 261
RP EUROPE B.V.—See N.V. Koninklijke KNP BT; *Int'l,* pg. 757
RPC INCORPORATED; *U.S. Public,* pg. 1356
RPM BELGIUM N.V.—See RPM, Inc.; *U.S. Public,* pg. 1357
RPM, INC.; *U.S. Public,* pg. 1356
RPM/RADAR-CDP EUROPE—See Dentsu Inc.; *Int'l,* pg. 394
RPR & ASSOCIATES, INC.; *U.S. Private,* pg. 905
RPR CORRESPONDANT CLEARING—See Dain Rauscher Corporation; *U.S. Public,* pg. 476
RPS INC.—See FDX Corporation; *U.S. Public,* pg. 604
R.R. LITHO, INC.—See Prime Medical Services, Inc.; *U.S. Public,* pg. 1327
RR-1 LIMITED PARTNERSHIP—See Caterpillar Inc.; *U.S. Public,* pg. 316
R.R.M. PRAGUE—See Lagardere Groupe; *Int'l,* pg. 796
RS ELECTRONICS; *U.S. Private,* pg. 905
RS ELECTRONICS—See RS Electronics; *U.S. Private,* pg. 905
RSG RHENANIA SCHIFFAHRTS-GESELLSCHAFT MIT BESCHRANKTER HAFTUNG—See The Peninsular and Oriental Steam Navigation Company; *Int'l,* pg. 1033
RSI—See Wakefern Food Corporation; *U.S. Private,* pg. 1146
RSI HOLDINGS INC.; *U.S. Public,* pg. 1358
RSI INTERNATIONAL, LTD.—See COMSAT Corporation; *U.S. Public,* pg. 424
RSR CORPORATION—See Quexco Incorporated; *U.S. Private,* pg. 900
RT REKLAMEBUREAU A/S; *Int'l,* pg. 1081
RTC ROSTFREI-TECHNIK-CENTER GMBH—See Outokumpu Oyj; *Int'l,* pg. 1018
RTCDIRECT—See WPP Group plc; *Int'l,* pg. 1483
RTE FAR EAST CORPORATION—See Cooper Industries, Inc.; *U.S. Public,* pg. 445
RTG FURNITURE CORP.; *U.S. Private,* pg. 905
R.T.I. CAMEROON DISTRIBUTION/SERVICES—See Hewlett-Packard Company; *U.S. Public,* pg. 823
RTI ELECTRONICS INC.—See Selas Corporation of America; *U.S. Public,* pg. 1455
RTI EXPORT, INC. (BARBADOS)—See Selas Corporation of America; *U.S. Public,* pg. 1455
R.T.I. INFOTECH—See Hewlett-Packard Company; *U.S. Public,* pg. 823
RTI LABORATORIES DIVISION—See Detrex Corporation; *U.S. Public,* pg. 502
R.T.I. SENEGAL SERVICES—See Hewlett-Packard Company; *U.S. Public,* pg. 823
RTKL ASSOCIATES INC.; *U.S. Private,* pg. 906
RTL—See Groupe Bruxelles Lambert S.A.; *Int'l,* pg. 561
RTL4—See Groupe Bruxelles Lambert S.A.; *Int'l,* pg. 561
RTL9—See Groupe Bruxelles Lambert S.A.; *Int'l,* pg. 561
RTL RADIO-DIE GROSSTEN OLDIES—See Groupe Bruxelles Lambert S.A.; *Int'l,* pg. 561
RTL RADIO LETZEBUERG—See Groupe Bruxelles Lambert S.A.; *Int'l,* pg. 561
RTL TELE LETZEBUERG—See Groupe Bruxelles Lambert S.A.; *Int'l,* pg. 561
RTL TELEVISION—See Groupe Bruxelles Lambert S.A.; *Int'l,* pg. 561
RTL TVI—See Groupe Bruxelles Lambert S.A.; *Int'l,* pg. 562
RTL 2—See Groupe Bruxelles Lambert S.A.; *Int'l,* pg. 561
R.T.M. WINNERS; *U.S. Private,* pg. 906
RTP—See Computer Products, Inc.; *U.S. Public,* pg. 422
RTS SYSTEMS—See Telex Communications, Inc.; *U.S. Private,* pg. 1074
THE RTZ CORPORATION PLC—See Rio Tinto PLC; *Int'l,* pg. 1118
RTZ-CRA JAPAN LIMITED—See Comalco Limited; *Int'l,* pg. 307
RTZ PILLAR LTD.—See Caradon Plc; *Int'l,* pg. 267
RUG-RHEINISCHE UMSCHLAG-GESELLSCHAFT MBH—See The Peninsular and Oriental Steam Navigation Company; *Int'l,* pg. 1033
RV CLIMA-TKT S.A.—See Deutsche Babcock AG; *Int'l,* pg. 400
RVS LEVENSVERZEKERING—See ING Groep N.V.; *Int'l,* pg. 647
RVS SCHADEVERZEKERING N.V.—See ING Groep N.V.; *Int'l,* pg. 647
RVS VERZEKERINGEN NV—See ING Groep N.V.; *Int'l,* pg. 651
RWE AG; *Int'l,* pg. 1081
RWE-DEA AG—See RWE AG; *Int'l,* pg. 1081
RWE ENERGIE AG—See RWE AG; *Int'l,* pg. 1081
RWE ENTSORGUNG AG—See RWE AG; *Int'l,* pg. 1081
RWE TELLIANCE AG—See RWE AG; *Int'l,* pg. 1081
RWM-ROHRWERKE MULDENSTEIN GMBH—See Arbed S.A.; *Int'l,* pg. 79
RX AMERICA—See American Stores Company; *U.S. Public,* pg. 93
RX INFORMATION CENTRE LTD.—See The Jean Coutu Group (PJC) Inc.; *Int'l,* pg. 340
R.X.D., INC.—See Relm Wireless Corp.; *U.S. Public,* pg. 1376
RZB BEIJING—See Raiffeisen Zentralbank Osterreich; *Int'l,* pg. 1084
RZB BOMBAY—See Raiffeisen Zentralbank Osterreich; *Int'l,* pg. 1084

RZB BUCHAREST—See Raiffeisen Zentralbank Osterreich; Int'l, pg. 1084
RZB HONG KONG—See Raiffeisen Zentralbank Osterreich; Int'l, pg. 1084
RZB KIEV—See Raiffeisen Zentralbank Osterreich; Int'l, pg. 1084
RZB LONDON—See Raiffeisen Zentralbank Osterreich; Int'l, pg. 1084
RZB MILAN—See Raiffeisen Zentralbank Osterreich; Int'l, pg. 1084
RZB MOSCOW—See Raiffeisen Zentralbank Osterreich; Int'l, pg. 1085
RZB NEW YORK—See Raiffeisen Zentralbank Osterreich; Int'l, pg. 1084
RZB PARIS—See Raiffeisen Zentralbank Osterreich; Int'l, pg. 1085
RZB SINGAPORE—See Raiffeisen Zentralbank Osterreich; Int'l, pg. 1085
RZB TEHRAN—See Raiffeisen Zentralbank Osterreich; Int'l, pg. 1085
RAAB KARCHER AG—See Veba AG; Int'l, pg. 1457
RAAB KARCHER AMBIENTE GMBH—See Veba AG; Int'l, pg. 1457
RAAB KARCHER AUSTRIA GMBH—See Veba AG; Int'l, pg. 1458
RAAB KARCHER BAUSTOFFE—See Veba AG; Int'l, pg. 1458
RAAB KARCHER BOUWSTOFFEN B.V.—See Veba AG; Int'l, pg. 1458
RAAB KARCHER ELEKTONIK GMBH—See Veba AG; Int'l, pg. 1457
RAAB KARCHER ENERGIESERVICE GMBH—See Veba AG; Int'l, pg. 1457
RAAB KARCHER FRANCE S.A.—See Veba AG; Int'l, pg. 1458
RAAB KARCHER HOLZ GMBH—See Veba AG; Int'l, pg. 1457
RAAB KARCHER NEDERLAND B.V.—See Veba AG; Int'l, pg. 1458
RAAB KARCHER SANITAR HEIZUNG FLIESEN GMBH—See Veba AG; Int'l, pg. 1457
RAAB KARCHER SICHERHEIT GMBH—See Veba AG; Int'l, pg. 1457
RAAB KARCHER TANKSTELLENTECHNIK GMBH, HAMBURG—See Veba AG; Int'l, pg. 1457
RAAB KARCHER (U.K.) PLC—See Veba AG; Int'l, pg. 1458
RAAB KARCHER WARMETECHNIK GMBH—See Veba AG; Int'l, pg. 1457
RAADGEVEND INGENIEURSBUREAU VOOR BOUWCONTROLE BV—See Heidemij N.V.; Int'l, pg. 607
RAADGEVENDE INGENIEURS JONGEN BV—See Heidemij N.V.; Int'l, pg. 607
RAAHE STEEL WORKS—See Rautaruukki Oy; Int'l, pg. 1088
RABBIT EARS BOOK & AUDIO—See National Amusements, Inc.; U.S. Private, pg. 777
RABEN & SJOGREN AB—See KF/Konsum Coop Group; Int'l, pg. 718
AUGUST RABENEICK GMBH—See Mannesmann A.G.; Int'l, pg. 835
E. RABINOWE & COMPANY, INC.—See GP Strategies Corporation; U.S. Public, pg. 694
P.T. RABO FINANCE INDONESIA—See Rabobank Nederland; Int'l, pg. 1082
RABOBANK BELGIE, ANTWERP BRANCH—See Rabobank Nederland; Int'l, pg. 1082
RABOBANK BELGIE, BRUSSELS OFFICE—See Rabobank Nederland; Int'l, pg. 1082
RABOBANK DEUTSCHLAND AG—See Rabobank Nederland; Int'l, pg. 1082
RABOBANK NEDERLAND; Int'l, pg. 1082
RABOBANK (SCHWIEZ) AG—See Rabobank Nederland; Int'l, pg. 1082
RABOBANK TRUST COMPANY—See Rabobank Nederland; Int'l, pg. 1082
RABOFIN ITALIA SPA—See Rabobank Nederland; Int'l, pg. 1082
RACAL AVIONICS, INC.—See Racal Electronics Plc; Int'l, pg. 1082
RACAL CANADA INC.—See Racal Electronics Plc; Int'l, pg. 1083
RACAL COMMUNICATIONS, INC.—See Racal Electronics Plc; Int'l, pg. 1083
THE RACAL CORPORATION—See Racal Electronics Plc; Int'l, pg. 1083
RACAL-DATACOM—See Racal Electronics Plc; Int'l, pg. 1083
RACAL-DATACOM LTD—See Racal Electronics Plc; Int'l, pg. 1082
RACAL ELECTRONICS PLC; Int'l, pg. 1082
RACAL FILTER TECHNOLOGIES, INC.—See Racal Electronics Plc; Int'l, pg. 1083
RACAL HEALTH & SAFETY, INC.—See Racal Electronics Plc; Int'l, pg. 1083
RACAL INSTRUMENTS, INC.—See Racal Electronics Plc; Int'l, pg. 1083
RACAL INSTRUMENTS LTD.—See Racal Electronics Plc; Int'l, pg. 1082
RACAL NCS INC.—See Racal Electronics Plc; Int'l, pg. 1083
RACAL PROTECTION CANADA—See Racal Electronics Plc; Int'l, pg. 1083
RACAL RADAR DEFENCE—See Racal Electronics Plc; Int'l, pg. 1083
RACAL RADIO LIMITED—See Racal Electronics Plc; Int'l, pg. 1082
RACAL RECORDERS INC.—See Racal Electronics Plc; Int'l, pg. 1083
RACELAND RAW SUGAR CORP.—See M.A. Patout & Son; U.S. Private, pg. 843
RACET COMPUTES LIMITED—See Kobe Steel, Ltd.; Int'l, pg. 740
RACETRAC PETROLEUM, INC.; U.S. Private, pg. 906

RACINE FEDERATED, INC.; U.S. Private, pg. 906
RACING COLLECTABLES CLUB OF AMERICA—See Action Performance Companies, Inc.; U.S. Public, pg. 17
A. RACKE GMBH; Int'l, pg. 1083
RACKE USA—See A. Racke GmbH; Int'l, pg. 1083
JOS. RACKL & CO. GMBH—See Fried. Krupp AG; Int'l, pg. 514
RACO, INC.—See Hubbell Incorporated; U.S. Public, pg. 845
RACO TRADING PHILS., INC.—See CODELCO Chile (Corporacion Nacional Del Cobre De Chile); Int'l, pg. 303
RACOR DIVISION—See Parker Hannifin Corporation; U.S. Public, pg. 1260
RAD (ROSE ABASCAL SA)—See Dentsu Inc.; Int'l, pg. 394
RADAR COMPANIES, INC.—See Harnischfeger Industries, Inc.; U.S. Public, pg. 789
RADAR N.V.—See Roche Holding Ltd.; Int'l, pg. 1121
RADAR SYSTEMS—See Raytheon Company; U.S. Public, pg. 1364
RADCLIFFE PAPER TUBES—See BPB Industries PLC; Int'l, pg. 134
RADCO SPORTSWEAR, INC.—See Farah Incorporated; U.S. Public, pg. 613
RADEMAKERS GIETERIJ B.V.—See Ballast Nedam NV; Int'l, pg. 134
RADEX INTERNATIONAL S.A.—See RGP Holding, Inc.; U.S. Private, pg. 904
RADIAN INTERNATIONAL LLC—See The Dow Chemical Company; U.S. Public, pg. 522
RADIANT COLOR NV—See RPM, Inc.; U.S. Public, pg. 1357
RADIANT LAMP—See Philips Electronics N.V.; Int'l, pg. 1055
RADIATOR SPECIALTY COMPANY; U.S. Private, pg. 906
RADICA USA LIMITED; U.S. Private, pg. 906
RADIO AIRE—See EMAP Plc; Int'l, pg. 452
RADIO-AUSTRIA AG—See Austrian Postal & Telegraph Administration; Int'l, pg. 101
RADIO CITY—See EMAP Plc; Int'l, pg. 452
RADIO CITY PRODUCTIONS—See Mitsubishi Estate Co., Ltd.; Int'l, pg. 873
RADIO CONNECTIONS—See EMAP Plc; Int'l, pg. 452
RADIO CONTACT—See Groupe Bruxelles Lambert S.A.; Int'l, pg. 561
RADIO DIRECT RESPONSE; U.S. Private, pg. 906
RADIO FRANCE; Int'l, pg. 1083
RADIO-HOLLAND AV SYSTEMS GROUP—See SAIT-RadioHolland Group S.A.; Int'l, pg. 1151
RADIO-HOLLAND DE VENEZUELA S.A.—See SAIT-RadioHolland Group S.A.; Int'l, pg. 1152
RADIO HOLLAND ELECTRONICS—See SAIT-RadioHolland Group S.A.; Int'l, pg. 1151
RADIO HOLLAND GROUP CARRIBBEAN—See SAIT-RadioHolland Group S.A.; Int'l, pg. 1152
RADIO HOLLAND GROUP-DEFENSE STAFF DIV.—See SAIT-RadioHolland Group S.A.; Int'l, pg. 1151
RADIO HOLLAND GROUP-FISHERY EQUIP.—See SAIT-RadioHolland Group S.A.; Int'l, pg. 1151
RADIO HOLLAND GROUP HEAD OFFICE-HOUSTON—See SAIT-RadioHolland Group S.A.; Int'l, pg. 1152
RADIO HOLLAND GROUP HONG KONG—See SAIT-RadioHolland Group S.A.; Int'l, pg. 1152
RADIO HOLLAND GROUP-SURVEY EQUIP.—See SAIT-RadioHolland Group S.A.; Int'l, pg. 1151
RADIO-HOLLAND SECURITY SYSTEMS—See SAIT-RadioHolland Group S.A.; Int'l, pg. 1151
RADIO INDIANAPOLIS, INC.—See The Pfaltzgraff Co.; U.S. Private, pg. 860
RADIO METROPLEX INC.—See The Pfaltzgraff Co.; U.S. Private, pg. 860
THE RADIO NETWORK—See Clear Channel Communications, Inc.; U.S. Public, pg. 386
RADIO ONE INC.; U.S. Private, pg. 906
RADIO ONE OF MARYLAND—See Radio One Inc.; U.S. Private, pg. 906
RADIO STATIONS WFLS FM & WYSK-AM-FM—See The Free Lance-Star Publishing Co.; U.S. Private, pg. 425
RADIO TV STEINER AG—See Coop Switzerland; Int'l, pg. 330
RADIOCOR TELERATE S.P.A.—See Dow Jones & Company, Inc.; U.S. Public, pg. 525
RADIOLOGIC SCIENCES, INC.—See Pfizer Inc.; U.S. Public, pg. 1284
RADIOMETER AMERICA INC.—See Radiometer A/S; Int'l, pg. 1083
RADIOMETER ANALYTICAL S.A.—See Radiometer A/S; Int'l, pg. 1084
RADIOMETER A/S; Int'l, pg. 1083
RADIOMETER DEUTSCHLAND GMBH—See Radiometer A/S; Int'l, pg. 1084
RADIOMETER ESPANA S.A.—See Radiometer A/S; Int'l, pg. 1084
RADIOMETER GMBH—See Radiometer A/S; Int'l, pg. 1084
RADIOMETER INTERNATIONAL A/S—See Radiometer A/S; Int'l, pg. 1084
RADIOMETER K.K.—See Radiometer A/S; Int'l, pg. 1084
RADIOMETER LTD.—See Radiometer A/S; Int'l, pg. 1084
RADIOMETER MEDICAL A/S—See Radiometer A/S; Int'l, pg. 1083
RADIOMETER NEDERLAND B.V.—See Radiometer A/S; Int'l, pg. 1084
RADIOMETER PACIFIC LTD.—See Radiometer A/S; Int'l, pg. 1084
RADIOMETER PACIFIC PTY. LTD.—See Radiometer A/S; Int'l, pg. 1084
RADIOMETER RSCH GMBH—See Radiometer A/S; Int'l, pg. 1084
RADIOMETER S.A.—See Radiometer A/S; Int'l, pg. 1084
RADIOMETER TRADING K.K.—See Radiometer A/S; Int'l, pg. 1084

RADIOMETER (UK) LTD.—See Radiometer A/S; Int'l, pg. 1084
RADIONICS, INC.—See Detection Systems, Inc.; U.S. Public, pg. 501
RADIORED UNO, S.A.—See Telefonica de Espana, S.A.; Int'l, pg. 1372
RADIOSHACK—See Tandy Corporation; U.S. Public, pg. 1560
RADIOSURGERY CENTERS, INC.—See Insight Health Services Corp.; U.S. Public, pg. 881
RADIOSYSTEM SWEDEN AB—See Telefonaktiebolaget LM Ericsson; Int'l, pg. 1364
RADISSON HOTEL CORPORATION—See Carlson Companies, Inc.; U.S. Private, pg. 212
RADISSON HOTELS INTERNATIONAL INC.—See Carlson Companies, Inc.; U.S. Private, pg. 212
RADISSON SUITE HOTEL—See Pacific Gateway Properties; U.S. Public, pg. 1250
RADIUS INC.; U.S. Public, pg. 1358
RADIX CORPORATION; U.S. Private, pg. 906
RADIX MICRO DEVICES, PLC—See Radix Corporation; U.S. Private, pg. 907
RADIX WIRE COMPANY; U.S. Private, pg. 907
RADO UHREN AG—See SMH Swiss Corporation for Micro Electronics & Watchmaking Indus. Ltd.; Int'l, pg. 1160
THE RADOS COMPANIES; U.S. Private, pg. 907
STEVE P. RADOS, INC.—See The Rados Companies; U.S. Private, pg. 907
RADSYSTEM GMBH—See Mannesmann A.G.; Int'l, pg. 835
RAE BETOON AS—See Scancem AB; Int'l, pg. 1201
RAE-PRINT PRINTING & PACKAGING—See McRae Industries, Inc.; U.S. Public, pg. 1074
RAECO—See Esselte AB; Int'l, pg. 462
RAFFAY INDUSTRIEPRODUKTE GMBH—See Volkswagen AG; Int'l, pg. 1474
ETS RAFFEL SARREBOURG S.A.—See Ascot Holdings Plc; Int'l, pg. 88
RAFFI & SWANSON, INC.; U.S. Private, pg. 907
RAFFINERIA DI ROMA SPA—See Petrofina S.A.; Int'l, pg. 1043
RAFFINERIE DE CRESSIER, S.A.—See Royal Dutch/Shell Group of Companies; Int'l, pg. 1139
RAFFINERIE DE MARSEILLE—See Generale Sucriere SNC; Int'l, pg. 549
RAFFINERIE DES ANTILLES—See Royal Dutch/Shell Group of Companies; Int'l, pg. 1141
RAFFINERING & MARKEDSFORING—See Norsk Hydro a.s; Int'l, pg. 961
RAFI GMBH & CO. ELEKTROTECHNISCHE SPEZIALFABRIK—See Fried. Krupp AG; Int'l, pg. 516
RAG SHOPS, INC.; U.S. Public, pg. 1358
RAGAL FEINBLECH-VERTRIEBS GMBH—See Rautaruukki Oy; Int'l, pg. 1088
BRAD RAGAN, INC.—See The Goodyear Tire & Rubber Company; U.S. Public, pg. 753
RAGAZZIS, INC.—See Investors Management Corp.; U.S. Private, pg. 575
C.B. RAGLAND COMPANY; U.S. Private, pg. 907
RAGLAND MANUFACTURING COMPANY INC.—See International Aluminum Corporation; U.S. Public, pg. 895
RAGNAR BENSON, INC.—See The Austin Company; U.S. Private, pg. 99
RAGNO HOLDING S.P.A.—See Hesta Tex AG; Int'l, pg. 618
RAGOLD, INC.—See Ragolds Susswaren GmbH & Co.; Int'l, pg. 1084
RAGOLDS SUSSWAREN GMBH & CO.; Int'l, pg. 1084
RAGU FOODS, INC.—See Unilever Plc; Int'l, pg. 1436
RAHBEK-FOOD LIMITED—See The Albert Fisher Group PLC; Int'l, pg. 491
RAHBEKFISK AS—See The Albert Fisher Group PLC; Int'l, pg. 491
RAHN INDUSTRIES—See TransPro, Inc.; U.S. Public, pg. 1632
RAHNS SPECIALTY METALS, INC.—See Groupe Usinor; Int'l, pg. 572
RAHWAY RIVER LAND CO.—See GATX Corporation; U.S. Public, pg. 692
RAI CORPORATION URUGUAY—See IRI Istituto Ricostruzione Industriale; Int'l, pg. 655
RAI CORPORATIONS—See IRI Istituto Ricostruzione Industriale; Int'l, pg. 655
RAI - RADIOTELEVISIONE ITALIANA S.P.A.—See IRI Istituto Ricostruzione Industriale; Int'l, pg. 655
RAIBOBANK DO BRASIL LTDA.—See Rabobank Nederland; Int'l, pg. 1082
RAIFFEISEN CENTROBANK S.A.—See Raiffeisen Zentralbank Osterreich; Int'l, pg. 1085
RAIFFEISEN ZENTRALBANK OSTERREICH; Int'l, pg. 1084
RAIFFEISENBANK A.S.—See Raiffeisen Zentralbank Osterreich; Int'l, pg. 1085
RAIFFEISENBANK AUSTRIA D.D.—See Raiffeisen Zentralbank Osterreich; Int'l, pg. 1085
RAIFFEISENBANK (BULGARIA) A.D.—See Raiffeisen Zentralbank Osterreich; Int'l, pg. 1085
RAIL BEARING SERVICE CORP.—See The Timken Company; U.S. Public, pg. 1617
RAIL EUROPE ESPANA—See SNCF; Int'l, pg. 1165
RAIL EUROPE INC.—See SNCF; Int'l, pg. 1165
RAIL PRODUCTS DIVISION—See AmeriSteel; U.S. Private, pg. 65
RAIL SYSTEMS, INC.—See Kirby Corporation; U.S. Public, pg. 961
RAILCO, INC.—See Broe Companies; U.S. Private, pg. 171
RAILROAD CONCRETE CROSSTIE CORP.—See St. Joe Company; U.S. Public, pg. 1427
RAILROAD FRICTION PRODUCTS AND OTHERS—See Westinghouse Air Brake Company; U.S. Public, pg. 1761
RAILROAD FRICTION PRODUCTS CORPORATION—See Cardo AB; Int'l, pg. 271

Company Index

RAILROAD

DIRECTORY OF CORPORATE AFFILIATIONS

RAILROAD INSURANCE BROKERS, INC.—See Cigna Corp.; *U.S. Public*, pg. 366
RAILROAD PASS CASINO—See Circus Circus - Las Vegas; *U.S. Public*, pg. 375
RAILROAD TRACK CONSTRUCTION CORP.—See St. Joe Corp.; *U.S. Public*, pg. 1427
RAILTECH SCHLATTER SYSTEMS, S.A.S.—See H.A. Schlatter AG; *Int'l*, pg. 1206
RAILTEK AUSTRALIA PTY. LTD.—See Fujitsu Limited; *Int'l, pg. 528*
RAILWAY EDUCATIONAL BUREAU—See Simmons-Boardman Publishing Corp.; *U.S. Private*, pg. 1000
RAIN AND HAIL INSURANCE SERVICES INC.—See Cigna Corp.; *U.S. Public*, pg. 365
RAIN BIRD SPRINKLERS MANUFACTURING CORP.; *U.S.* Private, pg. 907
RAINBOW ADVERTISING SALES CORPORATION (RASCO)—See Cablevision Systems Corporation; *U.S. Public*, pg. 288
RAINBOW APPAREL DISTRIBUTION CENTER; *U.S. Private*, pg. 907
RAINBOW CASINO—See Alliance Gaming Corporation; *U.S. Public*, pg. 47
RAINBOW CASINO VICKSBURG L.P.—See Alliance Gaming Corporation; *U.S. Public*, pg. 47
RAINBOW INTERNATIONAL CARPET DYEING & CLEANING CO.—See The Dwyer Group, Inc.; *U.S. Public*, pg. 538
RAINBOW PROGRAMMING HOLDINGS, INC.—See Cablevision Systems Corporation; *U.S. Public*, pg. 288
RAINBOW RENTALS, INC.; *U.S. Private*, pg. 907
RAINBOW TECHNOLOGIES—See Rainbow Technologies, Inc.; *U.S. Public*, pg. 1359
RAINBOW TECHNOLOGIES, GMBH—See Rainbow Technologies, Inc.; *U.S. Public*, pg. 1359
RAINBOW TECHNOLOGIES, INC.; *U.S. Public*, pg. 1359
RAINBOW TECHNOLOGIES, LTD.—See Rainbow Technologies, Inc.; *U.S. Public*, pg. 1359
RAINBOW VERSANDHANDELS-GESELLSCHAFR MBH—See Otto Versand (GmbH & Co.); *Int'l*, pg. 1015
RAINFAIR, INC.; *U.S. Private*, pg. 907
RAINOLDI, KERZNER & RADCLIFFE—See Omnicom Group Inc.; *U.S. Public*, pg. 1224
RAINSFORDS METAL PRODUCTS PTY. LIMITED—See Britax International plc; *Int'l*, pg. 217
RAINSOFT WATER TREATMENT SYSTEMS—See Aquion; *U.S. Private*, pg. 78
RAINY RIVER ENERGY CORPORATION—See Minnesota Power; *U.S. Public*, pg. 1116
RAISIO CATERING OY—See Raisio Group; *Int'l*, pg. 1085
RAISIO CHEMICALS CANADA INC.—See Raisio Group; *Int'l*, pg. 1086
RAISIO CHEMICALS LTD.—See Raisio Group; *Int'l*, pg. 1085
RAISIO ENGINEERING LTD.—See Raisio Group; *Int'l*, pg. 1085
RAISIO FEED LTD.—See Raisio Group; *Int'l*, pg. 1085
RAISIO FEED LTD—See Raisio Group; *Int'l*, pg. 1085
RAISIO FEED LTD.—See Raisio Group; *Int'l*, pg. 1085
RAISIO FRANCE S.A.—See Raisio Group; *Int'l*, pg. 1086
RAISIO GROUP; *Int'l*, pg. 1085
RAISIO GROUP PLC—See Raisio Group; *Int'l*, pg. 1085
RAISIO GROUP PLC-MARGARINE—See Raisio Group; *Int'l*, pg. 1085
RAISIO, INC.—See Raisio Group; *Int'l*, pg. 1086
RAISIO INC.—See Raisio Group; *Int'l*, pg. 1086
RAISIO NORDIC EESTI AS—See Raisio Group; *Int'l*, pg. 1085
RAISIO POLSKA FOODS SP. Z.O.O.—See Raisio Group; *Int'l*, pg. 1085
RAISIO PORTUGAL - PRODUTOS QUIMICOS LDA.—See Raisio Group; *Int'l*, pg. 1086
RAISIO SVENSKA AB—See Raisio Group; *Int'l*, pg. 1086
RAISION LATEKSI OY—See Raisio Group; *Int'l*, pg. 1085
OY RAISIONAL AB—See Raisio Group; *Int'l*, pg. 1085
RAISO BELGIUM N.V.—See Raisio Group; *Int'l*, pg. 1086
RAISO CHEMICALS ITALIA S.R.L.—See Raisio Group; *Int'l, pg. 1086*
RAKONA—See The Procter & Gamble Company; *U.S. Public*, pg. 1333
RAKYAT MERCHANT BANKERS BERHAD—See Raiffeisen Zentralbank Osterreich; *Int'l*, pg. 1085
RALCORP HOLDINGS INC.; *U.S. Public*, pg. 1359
RALEIGH ENTERPRISES, INC.; *U.S. Private*, pg. 907
RALEIGH INDUSTRIES LTD.—See Derby International Corporation S.A.; *Int'l*, pg. 394
RALEIGH INDUSTRIES OF CANADA LTD.—See Derby International Corporation S.A.; *Int'l*, pg. 394
RALEIGH NUTRITIONAL PRODUCTS LTD.—See Nestle S.A.; *Int'l*, pg. 922
RALEY'S & BEL AIR; *U.S. Private*, pg. 907
RALLYE SUPER—See Groupe Casino; *Int'l*, pg. 563
RALLY'S HAMBURGERS, INC.; *U.S. Public*, pg. 1359
RALPH LAUREN WOMENSWEAR CO., L.P.—See Polo/Ralph Lauren Corporation; *U.S. Private*, pg. 875
RALPHS GROCERY COMPANY—See The Yucaipa Companies; *U.S. Private*, pg. 1202
RALSTON FOODS, INC.—See Ralcorp Holdings Inc.; *U.S. Public*, pg. 1359
RALSTON PURINA CANADA INC.—See Ralston Purina Company; *U.S. Public*, pg. 1360
RALSTON PURINA COMPANY; *U.S. Public*, pg. 1359
RALSTON PURINA INTERNATIONAL—See Ralston Purina Company; *U.S. Public*, pg. 1360
RALSTON PURINA OVERSEAS FINANCE N.V.—See Ralston Purina Company; *U.S. Public*, pg. 1360
RAM & KOFISA PACIFIC—See Koc Holding A.S.; *Int'l*, pg. 742
RAM FRANCE—See Koc Holding A.S.; *Int'l*, pg. 742
RAM GOLF CORPORATION; *U.S. Private*, pg. 908
RAM GOLF UK—See RAM Golf Corporation; *U.S. Private*, pg. 908
RAM GRAPHICS, INC.; *U.S. Private*, pg. 908
RAM MOBILE DATA BELGIUM S.C.S.—See BellSouth Corporation; *U.S. Public*, pg. 208
RAM MOBILE DATA LIMITED—See BellSouth Corporation; *U.S. Public*, pg. 208
RAM MOBILE DATA (NETHERLANDS) B.V.—See BellSouth Corporation; *U.S. Public*, pg. 208
RAM MOBILE DATA NETWORK GMBH—See BellSouth Corporation; *U.S. Public*, pg. 208
RAM OPTICAL INSTRUMENTATION, INC.—See Newport Corporation; *U.S. Public*, pg. 1179
RAM REPRESENTATIVE OFFICE-ALGERIA—See Koc Holding A.S.; *Int'l*, pg. 741
RAM REPRESENTATIVE OFFICE-AZERBAIJAN—See Koc Holding A.S.; *Int'l*, pg. 741
RAM REPRESENTATIVE OFFICE-BULGARIA—See Koc Holding A.S.; *Int'l*, pg. 741
RAM REPRESENTATIVE OFFICE-EGYPT—See Koc Holding A.S.; *Int'l*, pg. 741
RAM REPRESENTATIVE OFFICE-KAZAKHSTAN—See Koc Holding A.S.; *Int'l*, pg. 741
RAM REPRESENTATIVE OFFICE-ROMANIA—See Koc Holding A.S.; *Int'l*, pg. 741
RAM REPRESENTATIVE OFFICE-RUSSIA—See Koc Holding A.S.; *Int'l*, pg. 742
RAM REPRESENTATIVE OFFICE-TURKMENISTAN—See Koc Holding A.S.; *Int'l*, pg. 742
RAM REPRESENTATIVE OFFICE-UKRAINE—See Koc Holding A.S.; *Int'l*, pg. 742
RAM REPRESENTATIVE OFFICE-UZBEKISTAN—See Koc Holding A.S.; *Int'l*, pg. 742
RAMA GROUP OF COMPANIES; *U.S. Private*, pg. 908
RAMADA EXPRESS—See Aztar Corporation; *U.S. Public*, pg. 158
RAMADA INTERNATIONAL HOTELS & RESORTS—See Marriott International, Inc.; *U.S. Public*, pg. 1048
RAMAPO FINANCIAL CORPORATION; *U.S. Public*, pg. 1360
RAMATECH LLC—See Horizon Enterprises Group LLC; *U.S. Private*, pg. 539
RAMCO MANUFACTURING COMPANY—See Reynolds Metals Company; *U.S. Public*, pg. 1386
RAMERICA—See Koc Holding A.S.; *Int'l*, pg. 741
RAMMER DEUTSCHLAND GMBH—See Tamrock Corp.; *Int'l*, pg. 1352
RAMMER FRANCE—See Tamrock Corp.; *Int'l*, pg. 1352
RAMMER INC.—See Tamrock Corp.; *Int'l*, pg. 1352
RAMMER NORGE A/S—See Tamrock Corp.; *Int'l*, pg. 1352
RAMMER OY—See Tamrock Corp.; *Int'l*, pg. 1352
RAMMER OY JAPAN OFFICE—See Tamrock Corp.; *Int'l*, pg. 1352
RAMMER SVENSKA AB—See Tamrock Corp.; *Int'l*, pg. 1352
RAMSAY-HAVENWYCK, INC.—See Ramsay Health Care, Inc.; *U.S. Public*, pg. 1361
RAMSAY HEALTH CARE, INC.; *U.S. Public*, pg. 1360
THE RAMSEY COMPANY—See The Butcher Company; *U.S. Private*, pg. 189
RAMSEY TECHNOLOGY, INC.—See Thermo Electron Corporation; *U.S. Public*, pg. 1592
RAMTA DIVISION/BEDEK AVIATION GROUP—See Israel Aircraft Industries Ltd.; *Int'l*, pg. 690
THE RAMTITE CO. (AUSTRALIA) PTY. LTD.—See ABB Asea Brown Boveri (Holding) Ltd.; *Int'l*, pg. 6
RANCARE INC.—See McKesson Corporation; *U.S. Public*, pg. 1073
RANCH-WAY FEED INC.; *U.S. Private*, pg. 908
RANCHERS COTTON OIL; *U.S. Private*, pg. 908
RANCHERS SUPPLY COMPANY, INC.; *U.S. Private*, pg. 908
RANCO AUTOMOTIVE DIV.—See Siebe plc; *Int'l*, pg. 1243
RANCO CONTROLS CANADA, LTD.—See Siebe plc; *Int'l*, pg. 1243
RANCO CONTROLS LTD.—See Siebe plc; *Int'l*, pg. 1243
RANCO DE MEXICO, S.A. DE C.V.—See Siebe plc; *Int'l*, pg. 1243
RANCO EUROPE PLYMOUTH UK—See Siebe plc; *Int'l*, pg. 1243
RANCO FRANCE, S.R.L.—See Siebe plc; *Int'l*, pg. 1243
RANCO INC.—See Siebe plc; *Int'l*, pg. 1243
RANCO ITALIAN CONTROLS—See Siebe plc; *Int'l*, pg. 1243
RANCO NORTH AMERICA—See Siebe plc; *Int'l*, pg. 1243
RAND; *U.S. Private*, pg. 908
RAND MCNALLY & COMPANY; *U.S. Private*, pg. 908
RANDA CORP.; *U.S. Private*, pg. 909
RANDALL COUNTY FEED YARD—See Friona Industries, L.P.; *U.S. Private*, pg. 429
RANDALL STORES, INC.; *U.S. Private*, pg. 909
RANDALL TEXTRON—See Textron Inc.; *U.S. Public*, pg. 1590
RANDALLS FOOD MARKETS, INC.; *U.S. Private*, pg. 909
RANDALLS WAREHOUSE CORPORATION—See Randalls Food Markets, Inc.; *U.S. Private*, pg. 909
RANDELL—See Dover Corporation; *U.S. Public*, pg. 520
RANDOLPH COMPUTER CORPORATION—See BankBoston Corporation; *U.S. Public*, pg. 184
RANDOLPH MARINER—See Gannett Company, Inc.; *U.S. Public*, pg. 701
WILLIAM A. RANDOLPH, INC.; *U.S. Private*, pg. 909
RANDOM HOUSE ADULT TRADE BOOKS—See Advance Publications Inc.; *U.S. Private*, pg. 21
RANDOM HOUSE, INC.—See Advance Publications Inc.; *U.S. Private*, pg. 20
RANDY INTERNATIONAL; *U.S. Private*, pg. 909
RANDY INTERNATIONAL—See Randy International; *U.S. Private*, pg. 909
RANGAIRE INC.—See Nortek, Inc.; *U.S. Public*, pg. 1193
RANGEN AQUACULTURE RESEARCH—See Rangen, Inc.; *U.S. Private*, pg. 909
RANGEN, INC.; *U.S. Private*, pg. 909
RANGER FOREST PRODUCTS LTD.—See Alberta Energy Company, Ltd.; *Int'l*, pg. 49
RANGER OIL COMPANY—See Ranger Oil Limited; *Int'l*, pg. 1086
RANGER OIL LIMITED; *Int'l*, pg. 1086
RANGSIT MACHINE & MATERIAL CENTER—See Nishimatsu Construction Co., Ltd.; *Int'l*, pg. 943
RANIR CORPORATION/DCP; *U.S. Private*, pg. 909
RANJIT CORPORATION; *U.S. Private*, pg. 909
RANK AMERICA, INC.—See The Rank Group PLC; *Int'l*, pg. 1087
RANK AMUSEMENTS LIMITED—See The Rank Group PLC; *Int'l*, pg. 1087
RANK BRIMAR LTD.—See The Rank Group PLC; *Int'l*, pg. 1087
RANK CINTEL LTD.—See The Rank Group PLC; *Int'l*, pg. 1087
RANK ENTERTAINMENT LIMITED—See The Rank Group PLC; *Int'l*, pg. 1087
RANK FILM LABORATORIES LIMITED—See The Rank Group PLC; *Int'l*, pg. 1087
THE RANK GROUP PLC; *Int'l*, pg. 1086
RANK HOLIDAYS & HOTELS LIMITED—See The Rank Group PLC; *Int'l*, pg. 1087
RANK HOVIS LIMITED—See Tomkins PLC; *Int'l*, pg. 1396
RANK INVESTMENTS LIMITED—See The Rank Group PLC; *Int'l*, pg. 1087
RANK LEISURE HOLDINGS PLC—See The Rank Group PLC; *Int'l*, pg. 1087
RANK LEISURE MACHINE SERVICES LTD.—See The Rank Group PLC; *Int'l*, pg. 1087
RANK ORLANDO, INC.—See The Rank Group PLC; *Int'l*, pg. 1087
RANK OVERSEAS HOLDING LIMITED—See The Rank Group PLC; *Int'l*, pg. 1087
RANK RX HOLDINGS LIMITED—See The Rank Group PLC; *Int'l*, pg. 1087
RANK TAYLOR HOBSON LIMITED—See The Rank Group PLC; *Int'l*, pg. 1087
RANK VIDEO SERVICES AMERICA INC.—See The Rank Group PLC; *Int'l*, pg. 1087
RANK VIDEO SERVICES LTD.—See The Rank Group PLC; *Int'l*, pg. 1087
RANK XEROX AG—See Xerox Corporation; *U.S. Public*, pg. 1785
RANK XEROX LIMITED—See The Rank Group PLC; *Int'l*, pg. 1087
RANK XEROX LIMITED—See Xerox Corporation; *U.S. Public*, pg. 1785
RANKS HOVIS MCDOUGALL LIMITED—See Tomkins PLC; *Int'l*, pg. 1395
AS RANNILA PROFIIL—See Rautaruukki Oy; *Int'l*, pg. 1088
RANNILA STEEL LATVIA SIA—See Rautaruukki Oy; *Int'l*, pg. 1088
RANNILA STEEL OY—See Rautaruukki Oy; *Int'l*, pg. 1088
RANNILA TALDOM A/O—See Rautaruukki Oy; *Int'l*, pg. 1088
RANSBURG INDUSTRIAL FINISHING—See Illinois Tool Works Inc.; *U.S. Public*, pg. 869
RANSCO INDUSTRIES, INC.—See Despatch Industries; *U.S. Private*, pg. 327
RANSOM & RANDOLPH DIVISION—See Dentsply International Inc.; *U.S. Public*, pg. 499
RANSOME ENGINE—See Giles & Ransome, Inc.; *U.S. Private*, pg. 453
RANSOME LIFT—See Giles & Ransome, Inc.; *U.S. Private, pg. 453*
RANSOME/TEMPIL—See Air Liquide S.A.; *Int'l*, pg. 37
RANSOMES-CUSHMAN-RYAN—See Ransomes Plc; *Int'l*, pg. 1088
RANSOMES INC.—See Ransomes Plc; *Int'l*, pg. 1088
RANSOMES PLC; *Int'l*, pg. 1087
RANTARUUKKI HOLDING AB—See Rautaruukki Oy; *Int'l*, pg. 1089
RANTEC MICROWAVE AND ELECTRONICS, INC.—See ESCO Electronics Corporation; *U.S. Public*, pg. 546
RANTOUL PRODUCTS TEXTRON INC.—See Textron Inc.; *U.S. Public*, pg. 1589
THE RAO GROUP INC.; *U.S. Private*, pg. 910
RAPID BUILDING SYSTEMS, INC.—See Dynamic Homes, Inc.; *U.S. Public*, pg. 539
RAPID CITY JOURNAL—See Lee Enterprises, Incorporated; *U.S. Public*, pg. 984
RAPID ENGINEERING INC.; *U.S. Private*, pg. 910
RAPID INDUSTRIAL PLASTICS COMPANY; *U.S. Private*, pg. 910
RAPID INDUSTRIES, INC.; *U.S. Private*, pg. 910
RAPID MOUNTING & FINISHING CO.; *U.S. Private*, pg. 910
RAPID POWER TECHNOLOGIES, INC.; *U.S. Private*, pg. 910
RAPID PRINT—See Bidwell Industrial Group, Inc.; *U.S. Private*, pg. 142
RAPID RAIL SYSTEMS—See Dover Corporation; *U.S. Public*, pg. 521
RAPIDES BANK & TRUST COMPANY OF ALEXANDRIA—See First Commerce Corporation; *U.S. Public*, pg. 630
RAPIDFORMS, INC.—See New England Business Service, Inc.; *U.S. Public*, pg. 1171
RAPIDPARTS INC.—See Caterpillar Inc.; *U.S. Public*, pg. 315
RAPISARDA INDUSTRIES SRL—See Caterpillar Inc.; *U.S. Public*, pg. 317
RAPISTAN DEMAG CORP.—See Mannesmann A.G.; *Int'l*, pg. 837
RAPISTAN DEMAG INDUSTRIA E COMERCIO LTDA.—See Mannesmann A.G.; *Int'l*, pg. 838
RAPISTAN DEMAG LTD.—See Mannesmann A.G.; *Int'l*, pg. 838
RAPISTAN DEMAG SA DE CV—See Mannesmann A.G.; *Int'l*, pg. 838
RAPP COLLINS WORLDWIDE—See Omnicom Group Inc.; *U.S. Public*, pg. 1224
RAPPOLD, HERMANN & CO. GMBH—See Viag AG; *Int'l*, pg. 1464

MASTER INDEX TO COMPANY NAMES READERS

Company Index

RAPPRESENTANZA GENERALE DELLA KRUPP MAK PER L'ITALIA—See Fried. Krupp AG; *Int'l*, pg. 510
MEL RAPTON HONDA; *U.S. Private*, pg. 911
RARITAN BANCORP INC.; *U.S. Public*, pg. 1361
RARITAN DISPLAY DIVISION—See R & R Marketing; *U.S. Private*, pg. 902
RASCHIG AG (FRANCE)—See PMC, Inc.; *U.S. Private*, pg. 827
RASCHIG CORP.—See PMC, Inc.; *U.S. Private*, pg. 827
RASCHIG GMBH—See PMC, Inc.; *U.S. Private*, pg. 827
RASCHIG (U.K.) LTD.—See PMC, Inc.; *U.S. Private*, pg. 827
RASFID—See Allianz Aktiengesellschaft; *Int'l*, pg. 62
RASSINI S.A. DE C.V.—See Corporacion Industrial Sanluis; *Int'l*, pg. 332
RASSINI-NHK TORSION BARS S.A. DE C.V.—See NHK Spring Co., Ltd.; *Int'l*, pg. 902
RAT UND TAT TECHNISCHER KUNDENDIENST GMBH—See Karstadt Aktiengesellschaft; *Int'l*, pg. 724
RATH BLACK HAWK—See American Financial Group; *U.S. Public*, pg. 75
RATHBONE, KING & SEELEY INSURANCE SERVICES—See H.W. Kaufman Financial Group, Inc.; *U.S. Private*, pg. 610
RATHBONE, KING & SEELEY INSURANCE SERVICES, INC.—See H.W. Kaufman Financial Group, Inc.; *U.S. Private*, pg. 610
RATHBONE PRECISION METALS—See Carpenter Technology Corporation; *U.S. Public*, pg. 307
JOHN G. RATHBORNE—See Royal Dutch/Shell Group of Companies; *Int'l*, pg. 1138
RATIER-FIGEAC—See Bertrand Faure; *Int'l*, pg. 192
RATIONAL SOFTWARE CORPORATION; *U.S. Public*, pg. 1361
RAUCH INDUSTRIES, INC.—See Syratech Corporation; *U.S. Private*, pg. 1061
RAUHALAHTI POWER PLANT—See Imatran Voima Oy; *Int'l*, pg. 660
RAULAND-BORG (CANADA) INC.—See Rauland-Borg Corporation; *U.S. Private*, pg. 911
RAULAND-BORG CORPORATION; *U.S. Private*, pg. 911
RAULAND-BORG CORPORATION OF FLORIDA—See Rauland-Borg Corporation; *U.S. Private*, pg. 911
RAUMA ECOPLANNING—See UPM-Kymmene Corporation; *Int'l*, pg. 1428
RAUMA LTD.—See UPM-Kymmene Corporation; *Int'l*, pg. 1428
RAUMA OFFSHORE CONTRACTING OY—See UPM-Kymmene Corporation; *Int'l*, pg. 1428
RAUMA USA, INC.—See UPM-Kymmene Corporation; *Int'l*, pg. 1428
RAUTARUUKKI ENGINEERING—See Rautaruukki Oy; *Int'l*, pg. 1089
RAUTARUUKKI INFORMATION SYSTEMS—See Rautaruukki Oy; *Int'l*, pg. 1089
RAUTARUUKKI OY; *Int'l*, pg. 1088
RAUTARUUKKI OY—See Rautaruukki Oy; *Int'l*, pg. 1088
RAUTARUUKKI POLSKA SP. Z.O.O.—See Rautaruukki Oy; *Int'l*, pg. 1088
RAUTARUUKKI STAHLSERVICE GMBH—See Rautaruukki Oy; *Int'l*, pg. 1089
RAUTARUUKKI STEEL—See Rautaruukki Oy; *Int'l*, pg. 1088
RAVAL LACE DIVISION—See Fab Industries, Inc.; *U.S. Public*, pg. 603
RAVALLI REPUBLIC—See Pulitzer Publishing Company; *U.S. Public*, pg. 1343
RAVARINO & FRESCHI, INC.—See Borden, Inc.; *U.S. Private*, pg. 158
RAVEN INDUSTRIES, INC.; *U.S. Public*, pg. 1361
RAVENNA ARSENAL, INC.—See Olin Corporation; *U.S. Public*, pg. 1219
RAVENSBERGER SCHMIERSTOFFVERTRIEB GMBH—See Fuchs Petrolub AG Oel + Chemie; *Int'l*, pg. 517
RAVENSEFT INDUSTRIAL ESTATES LIMITED—See Land Securities Plc; *Int'l*, pg. 798
RAVENSEFT PROPERTIES LIMITED—See Land Securities Plc; *Int'l*, pg. 798
RAVENSIDE INVESTMENTS LIMITED—See Land Securities Plc; *Int'l*, pg. 798
RAVENSWOOD ALUMINUM CORP.—See Century Aluminum Company; *U.S. Public*, pg. 328
RAVO INTERNATIONAL—See Federal Signal Corporation; *U.S. Public*, pg. 617
RAW MATERIALS LTD.—See CODELCO Chile (Corporacion Nacional Del Cobre De Chile); *Int'l*, pg. 303
RAWAL ENGRAVERS—See Standex International Corporation; *U.S. Public*, pg. 1506
RAWL S.A.—See Newmond PLC; *Int'l*, pg. 925
RAWLINGS CANADA—See Rawlings Sporting Goods Company; *U.S. Public*, pg. 1362
RAWLINGS COSTA RICA—See Rawlings Sporting Goods Company; *U.S. Public*, pg. 1362
RAWLINGS SPORTING GOODS COMPANY; *U.S. Public*, pg. 1361
THE RAWLPLUG COMPANY LIMITED—See Newmond PLC; *Int'l*, pg. 925
RAWMARSH FOODS—See Northern Foods plc; *Int'l*, pg. 968
RAWSON-KOENIG, INC.; *U.S. Public*, pg. 1362
RAX RESTAURANTS; *U.S. Private*, pg. 911
BILL RAY NISSAN, INC.; *U.S. Private*, pg. 911
RAY-CARROLL COUNTY GRAIN CO-OP; *U.S. Private*, pg. 911
RAY COMMUNICATIONS, INC.; *U.S. Private*, pg. 911
RAY SATELLITE NETWORK—See Ray Communications, Inc.; *U.S. Private*, pg. 911
RAY SPORTS NETWORK—See Ray Communications, Inc.; *U.S. Private*, pg. 911
RAYBESTOS AFTERMARKET PRODUCTS CO.—See Raytech Corporation; *U.S. Public*, pg. 1363
RAYBESTOS/BRAKE PARTS INC.—See Echlin Inc.; *U.S. Public*, pg. 560
RAYBESTOS INDUSTRIE-PRODUKTE GMBH—See Raytech Corporation; *U.S. Public*, pg. 1364
RAYBESTOS PRODUCTS CO.—See Raytech Corporation; *U.S. Public*, pg. 1363
RAYBESTOS REIBTECHNIK—See Raytech Corporation; *U.S. Public*, pg. 1364
RAYBRO ELECTRIC SUPPLIES—See Consolidated Electrical Distributors; *U.S. Private*, pg. 265
RAYCHEM AG—See Raychem Corporation; *U.S. Public*, pg. 1362
RAYCHEM AKTIEBOLAG—See Raychem Corporation; *U.S. Public*, pg. 1362
RAYCHEM A/S—See Raychem Corporation; *U.S. Public*, pg. 1362
RAYCHEM (AUSTRALIA) PTY. LIMITED—See Raychem Corporation; *U.S. Public*, pg. 1362
RAYCHEM CORPORATION; *U.S. Public*, pg. 1362
RAYCHEM DE VENEZUELA, CA—See Raychem Corporation; *U.S. Public*, pg. 1362
RAYCHEM EGYPT LTD.—See Raychem Corporation; *U.S. Public*, pg. 1362
RAYCHEM ELEKTRO YALITIM SISTEMLERI LIMITED SIRKETY—See Raychem Corporation; *U.S. Public*, pg. 1362
RAYCHEM GES.M.B.H.—See Raychem Corporation; *U.S. Public*, pg. 1362
RAYCHEM GMBH—See Raychem Corporation; *U.S. Public*, pg. 1362
RAYCHEM (H.K.) LTD.—See Raychem Corporation; *U.S. Public*, pg. 1362
RAYCHEM INDUSTRIAL Y COMERCIAL LIMITADA—See Raychem Corporation; *U.S. Public*, pg. 1362
RAYCHEM INTERNATIONAL CORPORATION—See Raychem Corporation; *U.S. Public*, pg. 1362
RAYCHEM INTERNATIONAL LTD.—See Raychem Corporation; *U.S. Public*, pg. 1362
RAYCHEM INTERNATIONAL MANUFACTURING CORP.—See Raychem Corporation; *U.S. Public*, pg. 1362
K.K. RAYCHEM—See Raychem Corporation; *U.S. Public*, pg. 1362
RAYCHEM KOREA LIMITED—See Raychem Corporation; *U.S. Public*, pg. 1362
RAYCHEM LTD.—See Raychem Corporation; *U.S. Public*, pg. 1362
RAYCHEM (NEDERLAND) BV—See Raychem Corporation; *U.S. Public*, pg. 1362
RAYCHEM NEW ZEALAND LIMITED—See Raychem Corporation; *U.S. Public*, pg. 1362
RAYCHEM OY—See Raychem Corporation; *U.S. Public*, pg. 1362
RAYCHEM (PORTUGAL) PRODUTOS QUIMICOS LDA.—See Raychem Corporation; *U.S. Public*, pg. 1363
RAYCHEM PRODUTOS IRRADIADOS LTDA—See Raychem Corporation; *U.S. Public*, pg. 1363
RAYCHEM RPG LIMITED—See Raychem Corporation; *U.S. Public*, pg. 1363
RAYCHEM SDN BERHAD—See Raychem Corporation; *U.S. Public*, pg. 1363
RAYCHEM SA—See Raychem Corporation; *U.S. Public*, pg. 1363
RAYCHEM S.A. INDUSTRIAL Y COMMERCIAL—See Raychem Corporation; *U.S. Public*, pg. 1363
RAYCHEM SAUDI ARABIA LIMITED—See Raychem Corporation; *U.S. Public*, pg. 1363
RAYCHEM-SHANGHAI CABLE ACCESSORIES LIMITED—See Raychem Corporation; *U.S. Public*, pg. 1363
RAYCHEM SINGAPORE PTE LTD—See Raychem Corporation; *U.S. Public*, pg. 1363
RAYCHEM S.P.A.—See Raychem Corporation; *U.S. Public*, pg. 1363
RAYCHEM TAIWAN LIMITED—See Raychem Corporation; *U.S. Public*, pg. 1363
RAYCHEM TECHNOLOGIAS, S.A. DE C.V.—See Raychem Corporation; *U.S. Public*, pg. 1363
RAYCHEM TECHNOLOGIES LIMITED—See Raychem Corporation; *U.S. Public*, pg. 1363
RAYCHEM THAI LIMITED—See Raychem Corporation; *U.S. Public*, pg. 1363
RAYCOM MEDIA, INC.; *U.S. Private*, pg. 911
RAYDEX/CDT—See Cable Design Technologies Corporation; *U.S. Public*, pg. 287
RAYLAN—See AMP Incorporated; *U.S. Public*, pg. 8
THE RAYMOND CORPORATION—See BT Industries AB; *Int'l*, pg. 123
RAYMOND ENGINEERING—See Kaman Corporation; *U.S. Public*, pg. 942
THE RAYMOND EXPORT CORPORATION—See BT Industries AB; *Int'l*, pg. 123
RAYMOND GRANITE CO.—See Cold Spring Granite Company; *U.S. Private*, pg. 251
RAYMOND INDUSTRIAL EQUIPMENT LTD.—See BT Industries AB; *Int'l*, pg. 123
RAYMOND LEASING CORPORATION—See BT Industries AB; *Int'l*, pg. 123
RAYMOND MERCHANDISE—See Barnes Group Inc.; *U.S. Public*, pg. 190
RAYMOND SALES CORPORATION—See BT Industries AB; *Int'l*, pg. 123
RAYMOND TRANSPORTATION CORPORATION—See BT Industries AB; *Int'l*, pg. 123
RAYMOUR AND FLANIGAN FURNITURE CO.; *U.S. Private*, pg. 912
J.H. RAYNER (MINCING LANE) LIMITED—See Berisford plc; *Int'l*, pg. 188
RAYNOR GARAGE DOORS; *U.S. Private*, pg. 912
RAYONIER FOREST RESOURCES—See Rayonier Inc.; *U.S. Public*, pg. 1363
RAYONIER INC.; *U.S. Public*, pg. 1363
RAYONIER NEW ZEALAND LIMITED—See Rayonier Inc.; *U.S. Public*, pg. 1363
RAYOVAC CORPORATION; *U.S. Private*, pg. 912
RAYOVAC LIMITED—See RAYOVAC Corporation; *U.S. Private*, pg. 912
RAYOVAC UK LIMITED—See RAYOVAC Corporation; *U.S. Private*, pg. 912
RAYOVAC/VIDOR LIMITED—See RAYOVAC Corporation; *U.S. Private*, pg. 912
RAYPAK CANADA, LTD.—See Paloma Industries Limited; *Int'l*, pg. 1022
RAYPAK, INC.—See Paloma Industries Limited; *Int'l*, pg. 1022
RAYROCK FINANCE COMPANY—See Rayrock Yellowknife Resources Inc.; *Int'l*, pg. 1089
RAYROCK MINES, INC.—See Rayrock Yellowknife Resources Inc.; *Int'l*, pg. 1089
RAYROCK YELLOWKNIFE RESOURCES INC.; *Int'l*, pg. 1089
RAYSIL GOWNS LTD.—See Coats Viyella plc; *Int'l*, pg. 300
RAYTECH CORPORATION; *U.S. Public*, pg. 1363
RAYTECH INDUSTRIES DIVISION—See Lyman Products Corporation; *U.S. Private*, pg. 683
RAYTEX FINISHING CO.—See Cone Mills Corporation; *U.S. Public*, pg. 430
RAYTHEON—See Raytheon Company; *U.S. Public*, pg. 1365
RAYTHEON AIRCRAFT COMPANY—See Raytheon Company; *U.S. Public*, pg. 1365
RAYTHEON APPLIANCES—See Raytheon Company; *U.S. Public*, pg. 1366
RAYTHEON CANADA LIMITED—See Raytheon Company; *U.S. Public*, pg. 1366
RAYTHEON COMPANY; *U.S. Public*, pg. 1364
RAYTHEON CORPORATE JETS, INC.—See Raytheon Company; *U.S. Public*, pg. 1366
RAYTHEON E-SYSTEMS—See Raytheon Company; *U.S. Public*, pg. 1365
RAYTHEON ELECTRONICS SYSTEMS—See Raytheon Company; *U.S. Public*, pg. 1364
RAYTHEON ENGINEERS & CONSTRUCTORS, INC.—See Raytheon Company; *U.S. Public*, pg. 1366
RAYTHEON ENGINEERS & CONSTRUCTORS INTERNATIONAL, INC.—See Raytheon Company; *U.S. Public*, pg. 1366
RAYTHEON ENGINEERS & CONSTRUCTORS INTERNATIONAL—See Raytheon Company; *U.S. Public*, pg. 1366
RAYTHEON ENVIRONMENTAL SERVICES COMPANY—See Raytheon Company; *U.S. Public*, pg. 1366
RAYTHEON INFRASTRUCTURE INCORPORATED—See Raytheon Company; *U.S. Public*, pg. 1366
RAYTHEON MARINE—See Raytheon Company; *U.S. Public*, pg. 1366
RAYTHEON MARINE SALES & SERVICES CO.—See Raytheon Company; *U.S. Public*, pg. 1366
RAYTHEON OPTICAL SYSTEMS—See Raytheon Company; *U.S. Public*, pg. 1364
RAYTHEON OPTICAL SYSTEMS, INCORPORATED—See Raytheon Company; *U.S. Public*, pg. 1364
RAYTHEON OVERSEAS LTD.—See Raytheon Company; *U.S. Public*, pg. 1366
RAYTHEON SERVICE CO.—See Raytheon Company; *U.S. Public*, pg. 1366
RAYTHEON SUPPORT SYSTEMS—See Raytheon Company; *U.S. Public*, pg. 1364
RAYTHEON SYSTEMS CO.—See Raytheon Company; *U.S. Public*, pg. 1364
RAYTHEON SYSTEMS COMPANY—See Raytheon Company; *U.S. Public*, pg. 1364
RAYTHEON SYSTEMS MISSISSIPPI—See Raytheon Company; *U.S. Public*, pg. 1365
RAYTHEON TI SYSTEMS—See Raytheon Company; *U.S. Public*, pg. 1365
RE CAS—See Multi-Ad Services, Incorporated; *U.S. Private*, pg. 766
RE/MAX INTERNATIONAL, INC.; *U.S. Private*, pg. 912
RE-MI FOODS INC.—See Borden, Inc.; *U.S. Private*, pg. 158
REA CONSTRUCTION CO.—See Philipp Holzmann AG; *Int'l*, pg. 633
REA MAGNET WIRE COMPANY, INC.; *U.S. Private*, pg. 913
REAC, INC.—See WPL Holdings, Inc.; *U.S. Public*, pg. 1728
REACT MAGAZINE—See Advance Publications Inc.; *U.S. Private*, pg. 20
REACTIVE METALS & ALLOYS CORPORATION (REMACOR); *U.S. Private*, pg. 913
REACTOR EXPERIMENTS, INC.—See Thermo Electron Corporation; *U.S. Public*, pg. 1594
READ-RITE CORPORATION; *U.S. Public*, pg. 1366
READ-RITE CORPORATION—See Read-Rite Corporation; *U.S. Public*, pg. 1367
READ-RITE INTERNATIONAL—See Read-Rite Corporation; *U.S. Public*, pg. 1367
READ-RITE (MALAYSIA)—See Read-Rite Corporation; *U.S. Public*, pg. 1367
READ-RITE (PHILIPPINES), INC.—See Read-Rite Corporation; *U.S. Public*, pg. 1367
READ-RITE SMI CORPORATION—See Read-Rite Corporation; *U.S. Public*, pg. 1367
READ-RITE SMI (THAILAND) CO. LTD.—See Read-Rite Corporation; *U.S. Public*, pg. 1367
READ-RITE (THAILAND) CO. LTD.—See Read-Rite Corporation; *U.S. Public*, pg. 1367
READER'S DIGEST AB—See The Reader's Digest Association, Inc.; *U.S. Public*, pg. 1368
READER'S DIGEST ASIA, LTD.—See The Reader's Digest Association, Inc.; *U.S. Public*, pg. 1368
THE READER'S DIGEST ASSOCIATION (CANADA) LTD.—See The Reader's Digest Association, Inc.; *U.S. Public*, pg. 1368
READER'S DIGEST ASSOCIATION FAR EAST LTD.—See The Reader's Digest Association, Inc.; *U.S. Public*, pg. 1368
THE READER'S DIGEST ASSOCIATION, INC.; *U.S. Public*, pg. 1367

THE READER'S DIGEST ASSOCIATION LIMITED—See The Reader's Digest Association, Inc.; *U.S. Public*, pg. 1368
THE READER'S DIGEST ASSOCIATION PTY. LIMITED—See The Reader's Digest Association, Inc.; *U.S. Public*, pg. 1368
THE READER'S DIGEST ASSOCIATION (RUSSIA) INCORPORATED—See The Reader's Digest Association, Inc.; *U.S. Public*, pg. 1367
READER'S DIGEST BRASIL LTDA.—See The Reader's Digest Association, Inc.; *U.S. Public*, pg. 1368
READER'S DIGEST COLOMBIA S.A.—See The Reader's Digest Association, Inc.; *U.S. Public*, pg. 1368
READER'S DIGEST ENTERTAINMENT, INC.—See The Reader's Digest Association, Inc.; *U.S. Public*, pg. 1367
READER'S DIGEST EUROPEAN SYSTEMS GROUP, LIMITED—See The Reader's Digest Association, Inc.; *U.S. Public*, pg. 1368
READER'S DIGEST (FAMILY INSURANCE SERVICES) LIMITED—See The Reader's Digest Association, Inc.; *U.S. Public*, pg. 1368
READER'S DIGEST GLOBAL ADVERTISING, LTD.—See The Reader's Digest Association, Inc.; *U.S. Public*, pg. 1368
READER'S DIGEST INVESTMENTS (PTY.) LIMITED—See The Reader's Digest Association, Inc.; *U.S. Public*, pg. 1368
READER'S DIGEST KFT—See The Reader's Digest Association, Inc.; *U.S. Public*, pg. 1368
READER'S DIGEST LATINOAMERICA S.A.—See The Reader's Digest Association, Inc.; *U.S. Public*, pg. 1367
READER'S DIGEST (MALAYSIA) SDN. BHD—See The Reader's Digest Association, Inc.; *U.S. Public*, pg. 1368
READER'S DIGEST MEXICO S.A. DE C.V.—See The Reader's Digest Association, Inc.; *U.S. Public*, pg. 1368
READER'S DIGEST NEW COUNTRY DEVELOPMENT LIMITED—See The Reader's Digest Association, Inc.; *U.S. Public*, pg. 1368
THE READER'S DIGEST N.V.—See The Reader's Digest Association, Inc.; *U.S. Public*, pg. 1368
READER'S DIGEST PERU—See The Reader's Digest Association, Inc.; *U.S. Public*, pg. 1367
READER'S DIGEST PRZEGLAD SP.Z.O.O.—See The Reader's Digest Association, Inc.; *U.S. Public*, pg. 1368
READER'S DIGEST PUBLICATIONS-US SALES DIV.—See The Reader's Digest Association, Inc.; *U.S. Public*, pg. 1367
N.V. READER'S DIGEST S.A.—See The Reader's Digest Association, Inc.; *U.S. Public*, pg. 1368
READER'S DIGEST SALES & SERVICES, INC.—See The Reader's Digest Association, Inc.; *U.S. Public*, pg. 1367
READER'S DIGEST SELECCIONES S.A.—See The Reader's Digest Association, Inc.; *U.S. Public*, pg. 1367
READER'S DIGEST SERVICES, INC.—See The Reader's Digest Association, Inc.; *U.S. Public*, pg. 1368
READER'S DIGEST SUB EIGHT—See The Reader's Digest Association, Inc.; *U.S. Public*, pg. 1367
READER'S DIGEST SUB SEVEN—See The Reader's Digest Association, Inc.; *U.S. Public*, pg. 1367
READER'S DIGEST SUB SIX, INC.—See The Reader's Digest Association, Inc.; *U.S. Public*, pg. 1367
READER'S DIGEST (THAILAND) LIMITED—See The Reader's Digest Association, Inc.; *U.S. Public*, pg. 1368
READER'S DIGEST WORLD SERVICES, S.A.—See The Reader's Digest Association, Inc.; *U.S. Public*, pg. 1368
READER'S DIGEST YOUNG FAMILIES, INC.—See The Reader's Digest Association, Inc.; *U.S. Public*, pg. 1367
READER'S UNION LIMITED—See The Reader's Digest Association, Inc.; *U.S. Public*, pg. 1368
READICRETE LIMITED—See RMC Group p.l.c.; *Int'l*, pg. 1080
READING & BATES CORPORATION—See R&B Falcon Corporation; *U.S. Public*, pg. 1354
READING ANTHRACITE CO.; *U.S. Private*, pg. 913
READING & BATES DEVELOPMENT CO.—See R&B Falcon Corporation; *U.S. Public*, pg. 1354
READING & BATES DRILLING CO.—See R&B Falcon Corporation; *U.S. Public*, pg. 1354
READING BODY WORKS, INC.; *U.S. Private*, pg. 913
READING EAGLE COMPANY; *U.S. Private*, pg. 913
READING ENTERTAINMENT INC.—See Craig Corporation; *U.S. Public*, pg. 456
READING PAPERBOARD CORPORATION—See Caraustar Industries, Inc.; *U.S. Public*, pg. 304
READING TUBE CORP.—See Cambridge-Lee Industries, Inc.; *U.S. Private*, pg. 202
READMORE PUBLICATIONS INC.—See B.H. Blackwell Ltd.; *Int'l*, pg. 197
READ-RITE CORPORATION—See Read-Rite Corporation; *U.S. Public*, pg. 1367
READY BAKE FOODS INC.—See George Weston Limited; *Int'l*, pg. 1495
READY-LITE MFG. LTD.—See Kaufel Group Ltd.; *Int'l*, pg. 725
READY METAL MANUFACTURING COMPANY; *U.S. Private*, pg. 913
READY MIXED CONCRETE (EAST MIDLANDS) LIMITED—See RMC Group p.l.c.; *Int'l*, pg. 1080
READY MIXED CONCRETE (EASTERN COUNTIES) LIMITED—See RMC Group p.l.c.; *Int'l*, pg. 1080
READY MIXED CONCRETE (LONDON) LIMITED—See RMC Group p.l.c.; *Int'l*, pg. 1080
READY MIXED CONCRETE (NORTH WEST) LIMITED—See RMC Group p.l.c.; *Int'l*, pg. 1080
READY MIXED CONCRETE (NORTHERN) LIMITED—See RMC Group p.l.c.; *Int'l*, pg. 1080
READY MIXED CONCRETE (SCOTLAND) LIMITED—See RMC Group p.l.c.; *Int'l*, pg. 1080
READY MIXED CONCRETE (SOUTH-COAST) LIMITED—See RMC Group p.l.c.; *Int'l*, pg. 1080
READY MIXED CONCRETE (SOUTH EAST) LIMITED—See RMC Group p.l.c.; *Int'l*, pg. 1080
READY MIXED CONCRETE (SOUTH-WEST) LIMITED—See RMC Group p.l.c.; *Int'l*, pg. 1080

READY MIXED CONCRETE (TRANSITE) LIMITED—See RMC Group p.l.c.; *Int'l*, pg. 1080
READY MIXED CONCRETE (ULSTER) LIMITED—See RMC Group p.l.c.; *Int'l*, pg. 1079
READY MIXED CONCRETE (WALES) LIMITED—See RMC Group p.l.c.; *Int'l*, pg. 1080
READY MIXED CONCRETE (WEST MIDLANDS) LIMITED—See RMC Group p.l.c.; *Int'l*, pg. 1080
READY MIXED CONCRETE (WESTERN) LIMITED—See RMC Group p.l.c.; *Int'l*, pg. 1080
READY MIXED CONCRETE (YORKSHIRE) LIMITED—See RMC Group p.l.c.; *Int'l*, pg. 1080
READYMIX AG FUR BETEILIGUNGEN—See RMC Group p.l.c.; *Int'l*, pg. 1081
READYMIX ASLAND S.A.—See Lafarge S.A.; *Int'l*, pg. 791
N.V. READYMIX BELGIUM S.A.—See RMC Group p.l.c.; *Int'l*, pg. 1081
READYMIX GULF LTD.—See Redland PLC; *Int'l*, pg. 1092
READYMIX INDUSTRIES (ISRAEL) LIMITED—See RMC Group p.l.c.; *Int'l*, pg. 1081
READYMIX MUSCAT LLC & PREMIX LLC—See Redland PLC; *Int'l*, pg. 1092
READYMIX MUSCAT LLC & PREMIX LLC—See Royal Dutch/Shell Group of Companies; *Int'l*, pg. 1136
READYMIX P.L.C.—See RMC Group p.l.c.; *Int'l*, pg. 1081
READYMIX QATAR WLL & THE QUATAR QUARRY CO. WLL—See Redland PLC; *Int'l*, pg. 1092
READYMIXED DRYPACK LIMITED—See RMC Group p.l.c.; *Int'l*, pg. 1080
REAFIN—See SCOR; *Int'l*, pg. 1152
REAGAN EQUIPMENT COMPANY, INC.; *U.S. Private*, pg. 913
REAL APPLICATIONS, LTD.—See El Camino Resources, Ltd.; *U.S. Private*, pg. 366
REAL BRICK PRODUCTS, INC.—See Jannock Limited; *Int'l*, pg. 699
REAL CITY CASINO—See Alliance Gaming Corporation; *U.S. Public*, pg. 47
REAL DE TENNIS S.A. DE C.V.—See Proventus AB; *Int'l*, pg. 1072
REAL DECISIONS CORP.—See Cognizant Corporation; *U.S. Public*, pg. 395
REAL ESTATE DELIVERY, INC.—See First Hawaiian, Inc.; *U.S. Public*, pg. 635
REAL HOLDING MANAGEMENT CORP.; *U.S. Private*, pg. 913
REAL SB-WARENHAUS GF-GMBH—See Metro AG; *Int'l*, pg. 863
REAL TIME SOLUTIONS—See Pinnacle Automation Inc.; *U.S. Private*, pg. 866
REAL WORLD; *U.S. Private*, pg. 913
REALCOLD STORAGE—See Spiegel Meats, Inc.; *U.S. Private*, pg. 1025
REALCONN, INC.—See Cigna Corp.; *U.S. Public*, pg. 365
THE REALLY USEFUL COMPANY, INC.—See Really Useful Holdings Limited; *Int'l*, pg. 1089
REALLY USEFUL HOLDINGS LIMITED; *Int'l*, pg. 1089
THE REALLY USEFUL PICTURE COMPANY—See Really Useful Holdings Limited; *Int'l*, pg. 1089
THE REALLY USEFUL THEATER COMPANY LIMITED—See Really Useful Holdings Limited; *Int'l*, pg. 1089
REALTY CO. OF PENNSYLVANIA—See PP&L Resources; *U.S. Public*, pg. 1244
REALTY MANAGEMENT SERVICES (PTE) LTD.—See Singapore Land Limited; *Int'l*, pg. 1253
REALTY ONE; *U.S. Private*, pg. 914
REAMES FOODS INC.—See Lancaster Colony Corporation; *U.S. Public*, pg. 977
REASEGURADORA HEMISFERICA, S.A.—See Corporacion MAPFRE, Compania Internacional de Reaseguros, S.A.; *Int'l*, pg. 335
REASSURANTIE MAATSCHAPPIJ NEDERLAND NV—See Swiss Reinsurance Company; *Int'l*, pg. 1333
WILLIAM REAY (BELFAST) LTD.—See Delta plc; *Int'l*, pg. 390
REBER-SCHINDLER HEIS A/S—See Schindler Holding AG; *Int'l*, pg. 1205
RECARO NORTH AMERICA, INC.; *U.S. Private*, pg. 914
RECEPTIONELLE—See Vendex International N.V.; *Int'l*, pg. 1463
RECHEM INTERNATIONAL LTD—See Shanks & McEwan Group Plc; *Int'l*, pg. 1228
RECHENZENTRUM WESER GMBH—See Volkswagen AG; *Int'l*, pg. 1474
RECHTSSCHUTZ UNION VERSICHERUNGS-AG—See Alte Leipziger Versicherung Aktiengesellschaft; *Int'l*, pg. 66
RECI INDUSTRI AB—See Scancem AB; *Int'l*, pg. 1200
RECICLAJES ENVALIC, C.A.—See Reynolds Metals Company; *U.S. Public*, pg. 1387
RECKITT & COLMAN CANADA INC.—See Reckitt & Colman plc; *Int'l*, pg. 1090
RECKITT & COLMAN INC.—See Reckitt & Colman plc; *Int'l*, pg. 1090
RECKITT & COLMAN INDUSTRIAL LTDA.—See Reckitt & Colman plc; *Int'l*, pg. 1090
RECKITT & COLMAN PHARMACEUTICALS—See Reckitt & Colman plc; *Int'l*, pg. 1090
RECKITT & COLMAN PLC; *Int'l*, pg. 1089
RECKITT & COLMAN PRODUCTS—See Reckitt & Colman plc; *Int'l*, pg. 1090
RECKITT & COLMAN PRODUCTS LTD.—See Reckitt & Colman plc; *Int'l*, pg. 1090
RECKITT & COLMAN PRODUCTS PTY. LTD.—See Reckitt & Colman plc; *Int'l*, pg. 1090
RECKITT & COLMAN S.A.—See Reckitt & Colman plc; *Int'l*, pg. 1090
RECKSON ASSOCIATES REALTY CORP.; *U.S. Public*, pg. 1368
RECLAIMERS, INC.—See Philip Services Corp.; *Int'l*, pg. 1050
RECLAMATION SYSTEMS, INC.—See Perma-Fix Environmental Services, Inc.; *U.S. Public*, pg. 1280
RECLAMIZER—See Steiner Corporation; *U.S. Private*, pg. 1039

RECO TRANSPORTATION INC.—See Vulcan Materials Company; *U.S. Public*, pg. 1726
RECOGNITA—See Caere Corporation; *U.S. Public*, pg. 291
RECOGNITION DIVISION—See Jostens; *U.S. Public*, pg. 934
RECOGNITION SYSTEMS INC.—See Harrow Industries; *U.S. Private*, pg. 507
RECOLETOS COMPANIA EDITORIAL SA—See Pearson plc; *Int'l*, pg. 1027
RECOLL MANAGEMENT CORP.—See Fleet Financial Group, Inc.; *U.S. Public*, pg. 650
RECOMP, INC.; *U.S. Private*, pg. 914
RECON—See Heidemij N.V.; *Int'l*, pg. 608
RECON CONSULTANTS, INC.—See FCA International Ltd.; *Int'l*, pg. 471
RECON/OPTICAL, INC.; *U.S. Private*, pg. 914
RECON SERVICES, INC.—See Computer Sales International Inc.; *U.S. Private*, pg. 260
THE RECORD—See Hollinger Inc.; *Int'l*, pg. 631
THE RECORD-JOURNAL PUBLISHING COMPANY; *U.S. Private*, pg. 914
RECORDATI CORPORATION—See Recordati Industria Chimica e Farmaceutica S.p.A.; *Int'l*, pg. 1090
RECORDATI-ELMU S.L.—See Recordati Industria Chimica e Farmaceutica S.p.A.; *Int'l*, pg. 1090
RECORDATI FARMA S.R.L.—See Recordati Industria Chimica e Farmaceutica S.p.A.; *Int'l*, pg. 1090
RECORDATI INDUSTRIA CHIMICA E FARMACEUTICA S.P.A.; *Int'l*, pg. 1090
RECORDATI PHARMACEUTICAL CHEMICALS DIVISION—See Recordati Industria Chimica e Farmaceutica S.p.A.; *Int'l*, pg. 1090
RECORDATI PHARMACEUTICAL CHEMICALS PRODUCTIONS—See Recordati Industria Chimica e Farmaceutica S.p.A.; *Int'l*, pg. 1090
RECOTON AUTO CORPORATION—See Recoton Corporation; *U.S. Public*, pg. 1369
RECOTON CANADA LTD.—See Recoton Corporation; *U.S. Public*, pg. 1369
RECOTON CORPORATION; *U.S. Public*, pg. 1369
RECOVERY INN OF MENLO PARK—See Vencor, Inc.; *U.S. Public*, pg. 1715
RECOVERY SERVICES INTERNATIONAL, INC.—See Cigna Corp.; *U.S. Public*, pg. 366
RECREATIONAL EQUIPMENT, INC.; *U.S. Private*, pg. 914
RECREATIONAL PRODUCTS DIV.—See Bell Industries, Inc.; *U.S. Public*, pg. 205
RECREATIONAL VEHICLE DIV.—See Kit Manufacturing Company; *U.S. Public*, pg. 962
RECTIFICADORES INTERNACIONALES, S.A.—See International Rectifier Corporation; *U.S. Public*, pg. 907
RECTOR CANADA LTD.—See ABB Asea Brown Boveri (Holding) Ltd.; *Int'l*, pg. 6
RECTOR-GRAY, LTD.—See ABB Asea Brown Boveri (Holding) Ltd.; *Int'l*, pg. 6
RECUPERATION CASCADES INC.—See The Cascades Group; *Int'l*, pg. 273
RECYCLING MAATSCHAPPIJ FENIKS B.V.—See Ballast Nedam NV; *Int'l*, pg. 134
RED APPLE COMPANIES; *U.S. Private*, pg. 914
RED APPLE, INC.; *U.S. Private*, pg. 915
RED BALL CORPORATION—See Atlas World Group, Inc.; *U.S. Private*, pg. 97
RED BALL FORWARDERS, INC.—See Atlas World Group, Inc.; *U.S. Private*, pg. 97
RED BALL LEASING, INC.—See Atlas World Group, Inc.; *U.S. Private*, pg. 97
RED BAND—See CSM N.V.; *Int'l*, pg. 244
N.V. RED BAND S.A.—See CSM N.V.; *Int'l*, pg. 245
RED BAND SERVICES N.V.—See CSM N.V.; *Int'l*, pg. 245
RED BAND SUSSWAREN VERTRIEBS GMBH—See CSM N.V.; *Int'l*, pg. 244
RED BAND VENCO—See CSM N.V.; *Int'l*, pg. 244
RED CALLIOPE & ASSOCIATES, INC.—See Crown Crafts, Inc.; *U.S. Public*, pg. 465
RED CARNATION GUMS LTD.—See The Peninsular and Oriental Steam Navigation Company; *Int'l*, pg. 1034
RED CIRCLE TRANSPORT CO.—See Eastern Enterprises; *U.S. Public*, pg. 549
RED DEVIL INC.; *U.S. Private*, pg. 915
RED DOG—See Cominco, Ltd.; *Int'l*, pg. 308
RED DRAGON RADIO—See EMAP Plc; *Int'l*, pg. 452
RED-E-CRETE, INC.—See Lonrho plc; *Int'l*, pg. 818
RED ELECTRICA DE ESPANA, S.A.—See SEPI; *Int'l*, pg. 1224
RED HAWK RANCH—See BRE Properties, Inc.; *U.S. Public*, pg. 163
RED HILL COAL CO.—See Kansas City Power & Light Company; *U.S. Public*, pg. 943
RED KAP INDUSTRIES—See VF Corporation; *U.S. Public*, pg. 1702
RED LAKE MINE—See CSA Management Inc.; *Int'l*, pg. 243
RED LINE HEALTHCARE CORP.—See Novartis AG; *Int'l*, pg. 974
RED LOBSTER USA—See Darden Restaurants, Inc.; *U.S. Public*, pg. 484
RED OAK EXPRESS—See Landmark Communications, Inc.; *U.S. Private*, pg. 648
RED RIVER SAND & GRAVEL COMPANY—See Texas Industries, Inc.; *U.S. Public*, pg. 1585
RED ROBIN INTERNATIONAL INC.—See Skylark Co., Ltd.; *Int'l*, pg. 1262
RED ROCKS CARE CENTER—See Horizon/CMS Healthcare Corporation; *U.S. Public*, pg. 838
RED ROOF INNS, INC.; *U.S. Public*, pg. 1369
RED ROSE RADIO—See EMAP Plc; *Int'l*, pg. 452
RED SEAL LABORATORIES LTD.—See Wella Group; *Int'l*, pg. 1490
RED SEAL QUALITY FOODS, INC.—See Borden, Inc.; *U.S. Private*, pg. 158
RED SKY INTERACTIVE—See Omnicom Group Inc.; *U.S. Public*, pg. 1224
RED SPOT PAINT & VARNISH CO.; *U.S. Private*, pg. 915

RED SPOT WESTLAND INC.—See Red Spot Paint & Varnish Co.; *U.S. Private*, pg. 915
RED STAR BIO PRODUCTS—See Universal Foods Corporation; *U.S. Public*, pg. 1695
RED STAR DE PUERTO RICO, S.A.—See Universal Foods Corporation; *U.S. Public*, pg. 1696
RED STAR YEAST & PRODUCTS DIV.—See Universal Foods Corporation; *U.S. Public*, pg. 1695
RED WING COMPANY—See Tomkins PLC; *Int'l*, pg. 1398
RED WING CO. INC.—See Tomkins PLC; *Int'l*, pg. 1398
RED WING PRODUCTS, INC.—See Ferguson International Holdings; *Int'l*, pg. 480
RED WING PUBLISHING COMPANY; *U.S. Private*, pg. 915
RED WING SHOE CO., INC.; *U.S. Private*, pg. 915
RED WING SHOE VASQUE DIV.—See Red Wing Shoe Co., Inc.; *U.S. Private*, pg. 915
RED WINGS INC.—See Tomkins PLC; *Int'l*, pg. 1398
REDBOOK—See The Hearst Corporation; *U.S. Private*, pg. 517
REDBURN TIRE COMPANY; *U.S. Private*, pg. 915
REDCO CORPORATION; *U.S. Private*, pg. 915
REDCO, INC.—See Jetronic Industries, Inc.; *U.S. Public*, pg. 926
WILLI REDDEMANN IMPORT-EXPORT GMBH—See N.V. Koninklijke KNP BT; *Int'l*, pg. 757
REDDING RECORD SEARCHLIGHT—See The E.W. Scripps Company; *U.S. Public*, pg. 1448
REDDIWIRE LIMITED—See N.V. Bekaert S.A.; *Int'l*, pg. 184
REDDY ICE—See Suiza Foods Corporation; *U.S. Public*, pg. 1527
REDELCOVER S.A.—See Etablissements Delhaize Freres Et Cie "Le Lion" S.A.; *Int'l*, pg. 463
REDGATE COMMUNICATIONS CORP.—See America Online Incorporated; *U.S. Public*, pg. 66
REDGO PROPERTIES, INC.—See Relm Wireless Corp.; *U.S. Public*, pg. 1376
REDHILL—See National Westminster Bank PLC; *Int'l*, pg. 910
REDI—See ETEX; *Int'l*, pg. 430
REDI-SERVE FOODS—See On-Cor Frozen Foods Inc.; *U.S. Private*, pg. 817
REDIFFUSION-DENTSU, YOUNG & RUBICAM (BANGALORE)—See Dentsu Young & Rubicam Partnerships; *U.S. Private*, pg. 326
REDIFFUSION-DENTSU, YOUNG & RUBICAM (CALCUTTA)—See Dentsu Young & Rubicam Partnerships; *U.S. Private*, pg. 326
REDIFFUSION-DENTSU, YOUNG & RUBICAM (MADRAS)—See Dentsu Young & Rubicam Partnerships; *U.S. Private*, pg. 326
REDIFFUSION-DENTSU, YOUNG & RUBICAM (MUMBAI)—See Dentsu Young & Rubicam Partnerships; *U.S. Private*, pg. 326
REDIFFUSION-DENTSU, YOUNG & RUBICAM (NEW DELHI)—See Dentsu Young & Rubicam Partnerships; *U.S. Private*, pg. 326
REDIFFUSION-DY&R PVT. LTD.—See Dentsu Young & Rubicam Partnerships; *U.S. Private*, pg. 326
REDLAND AGGREGATES LTD.—See Redland PLC; *Int'l*, pg. 1090
REDLAND AMERICA CORPORATION—See Redland PLC; *Int'l*, pg. 1091
REDLAND AUSTRALIA LTD.—See Redland PLC; *Int'l*, pg. 1092
REDLAND CAPITAL PLC—See Redland PLC; *Int'l*, pg. 1090
REDLAND CREDIT CORPORATION—See Redland PLC; *Int'l*, pg. 1091
REDLAND DAKPRODUKTEN B.V.—See Redland PLC; *Int'l*, pg. 1093
REDLAND (DEUTSCHLAND) GMBH—See Redland PLC; *Int'l*, pg. 1093
REDLAND DISTRIBUTION LIMITED—See Redland PLC; *Int'l*, pg. 1090
REDLAND FINANCE INC.—See Redland PLC; *Int'l*, pg. 1090
REDLAND FINANCE PLC—See Redland PLC; *Int'l*, pg. 1090
REDLAND FRANCE S.A.—See Redland PLC; *Int'l*, pg. 1093
REDLAND FUNDING CORPORATION—See Redland PLC; *Int'l*, pg. 1091
REDLAND FUNDING PLC—See Redland PLC; *Int'l*, pg. 1090
REDLAND GENSTAR STONE PRODUCTS COMPANY—See Redland PLC; *Int'l*, pg. 1091
REDLAND GLOBAL FUNDING PLC—See Redland PLC; *Int'l*, pg. 1090
REDLAND GRANULATS SA—See Redland PLC; *Int'l*, pg. 1093
REDLAND HOLDING BV—See Redland PLC; *Int'l*, pg. 1093
REDLAND IBERICA S.A.—See Redland PLC; *Int'l*, pg. 1093
REDLAND, INC.—See Redland PLC; *Int'l*, pg. 1091
REDLAND INTERNATIONAL FUNDING PLC—See Redland PLC; *Int'l*, pg. 1091
REDLAND KORAMIC BRICKS N.V.—See Redland PLC; *Int'l*, pg. 1093
REDLAND OHIO INC.—See Redland PLC; *Int'l*, pg. 1091
REDLAND OVERSEAS FUNDING PLC—See Redland PLC; *Int'l*, pg. 1091
REDLAND PLASTERBOARD HOLDINGS—See Lafarge S.A.; *Int'l*, pg. 789
REDLAND PLC; *Int'l*, pg. 1090
REDLAND PREFERRED STOCK PLC—See Redland PLC; *Int'l*, pg. 1091
REDLAND PROPERTIES LTD.—See Redland PLC; *Int'l*, pg. 1091
REDLAND QUARRIES INC.—See Redland PLC; *Int'l*, pg. 1093
REDLAND READYMIX LTD.—See Redland PLC; *Int'l*, pg. 1091

REDLAND ROOF TILES LTD.—See Redland PLC; *Int'l*, pg. 1091
REDLAND STERLING FUNDING PLC—See Redland PLC; *Int'l*, pg. 1091
REDLAND STONE PRODUCTS CO.—See Redland PLC; *Int'l*, pg. 1091
REDLAND TECHNOLOGIES LTD.—See Redland PLC; *Int'l*, pg. 1091
REDLAND TILE & BRICK—See Redland PLC; *Int'l*, pg. 1091
REDLAND UNIVERSAL FUNDING PLC—See Redland PLC; *Int'l*, pg. 1091
REDLAND U.S. FUNDING PLC—See Redland PLC; *Int'l*, pg. 1091
REDMOND PRODUCTS, INC.—See Bristol-Myers Squibb Company; *U.S. Public*, pg. 254
REDONDO'S INC.—See Nippon Meat Packers, Inc.; *Int'l*, pg. 936
REDOZE HOLDING N.V.—See Assicurazioni Generali S.p.A.; *Int'l*, pg. 92
REDPATH INDUSTRIES LTD.—See Tate & Lyle PLC; *Int'l*, pg. 1357
REDPOINT THERMALLOY LIMITED—See Bowthorpe plc; *Int'l*, pg. 207
REDRING ELECTRIC LTD.—See The General Electric Company, p.l.c.; *Int'l*, pg. 545
REDSTONE PROPERTIES, INC.—See National Life Insurance Company; *U.S. Private*, pg. 785
REDWOOD SYSTEMS—See Consolidated Freightways Corp.; *U.S. Public*, pg. 435
THE REDWOODS GROUP—See Front Royal, Inc.; *U.S. Private*, pg. 430
REEBOK INTERNATIONAL LTD.; *U.S. Public*, pg. 1369
REECE-CAMPBELL, INC.; *U.S. Private*, pg. 916
REED & BARTON CORPORATION; *U.S. Private*, pg. 916
REED ASIAN INFORMATION—See Reed Elsevier plc; *Int'l*, pg. 1094
REED & BARTON HOUSEWARES—See Reed & Barton Corporation; *U.S. Private*, pg. 916
REED & BARTON SILVERSMITHS—See Reed & Barton Corporation; *U.S. Private*, pg. 916
REED BOOKS—See Reed Elsevier plc; *Int'l*, pg. 1093
REED BOOKS AUSTRALIA—See Reed Elsevier plc; *Int'l*, pg. 1094
REED BROTHERS INC.—See Reed Grain & Bean Company; *U.S. Private*, pg. 916
REED BUSINESS INFORMATION—See Reed Elsevier plc; *Int'l*, pg. 1094
REED BUSINESS INFORMATION-CHINA—See Reed Elsevier plc; *Int'l*, pg. 1094
REED BUSINESS INFORMATION (USA)—See Reed Elsevier plc; *Int'l*, pg. 1094
REED BUSINESS INFORMATION-EAST GRINSTEAD—See Reed Elsevier plc; *Int'l*, pg. 1094
REED DATA SERVICES LIMITED—See Reed Elsevier plc; *Int'l*, pg. 1096
REED EDUCATIONAL AND PROFESSIONAL PUBLISHING—See Reed Elsevier plc; *Int'l*, pg. 1094
REED ELSEVIER BUSINESS INFORMATION—See Reed Elsevier plc; *Int'l*, pg. 1095
REED ELSEVIER BUSINESS INFORMATION-DES PLAINES—See Reed Elsevier plc; *Int'l*, pg. 1095
REED ELSEVIER BUSINESS INFORMATION-GREENSBORO—See Reed Elsevier plc; *Int'l*, pg. 1095
REED ELSEVIER BUSINESS INFORMATION-MORRIS PLAINS—See Reed Elsevier plc; *Int'l*, pg. 1095
REED ELSEVIER BUSINESS INFORMATION-NEW YORK—See Reed Elsevier plc; *Int'l*, pg. 1095
REED ELSEVIER INC.—See Reed Elsevier plc; *Int'l*, pg. 1095
REED ELSEVIER LEGAL DIVISION—See Reed Elsevier plc; *Int'l*, pg. 1095
REED ELSEVIER NEDERLAND BV—See Reed Elsevier plc; *Int'l*, pg. 1095
REED ELSEVIER PLC; *Int'l*, pg. 1093
REED ELSEVIER (SINGAPORE) PTE LIMITED—See Reed Elsevier plc; *Int'l*, pg. 1095
REED EXHIBITION COMPANIES—See Reed Elsevier plc; *Int'l*, pg. 1096
REED EXHIBITION COMPANIES-AUSTRALIA—See Reed Elsevier plc; *Int'l*, pg. 1097
REED EXHIBITION COMPANIES-INDONESIA—See Reed Elsevier plc; *Int'l*, pg. 1097
REED EXHIBITION COMPANIES-NORTH AMERICA—See Reed Elsevier plc; *Int'l*, pg. 1096
REED EXHIBITION COMPANIES-SOUTH ASIA/PACIFIC—See Reed Elsevier plc; *Int'l*, pg. 1097
REED EXPOSITIONS-FRANCE—See Reed Elsevier plc; *Int'l*, pg. 1097
GENE REED CHEVROLET—See Trace International Holdings, Inc.; *U.S. Private*, pg. 1095
REED GRAIN & BEAN COMPANY; *U.S. Private*, pg. 916
REED INTERNATIONAL P.L.C.—See Reed Elsevier plc; *Int'l*, pg. 1093
REED MIDEM ORGANISATION INC.—See Reed Elsevier plc; *Int'l*, pg. 1096
REED MIDEM ORGANISATION-UK—See Reed Elsevier plc; *Int'l*, pg. 1096
REED MINERALS—See Harsco Corporation; *U.S. Public*, pg. 793
REED MOTORS, INC.; *U.S. Private*, pg. 916
REED PLASTICS (MI)—See Novartis AG; *Int'l*, pg. 974
REED PLASTICS (TX)—See Novartis AG; *Int'l*, pg. 974
REED PUBLISHING (NZ) LTD.—See Reed Elsevier plc; *Int'l*, pg. 1094
REED STENHOUSE COMPANIES LTD.—See AON Corporation; *U.S. Public*, pg. 118
REED TECHNOLOGY AND INFORMATION SERVICES-GOVERNMENT SERVICES—See Reed Elsevier plc; *Int'l*, pg. 1096
REED TECHNOLOGY AND INFORMATION SERVICES INC.—See Reed Elsevier plc; *Int'l*, pg. 1096
REED TOOL COMPANY—See Camco International Inc.; *U.S. Public*, pg. 298

REED TRAVEL GROUP—See Reed Elsevier plc; *Int'l*, pg. 1097
REED TRAVEL GROUP-FRANCE—See Reed Elsevier plc; *Int'l*, pg. 1097
REED TRAVEL GROUP-GERMANY—See Reed Elsevier plc; *Int'l*, pg. 1097
REED TRAVEL GROUP-ITALY—See Reed Elsevier plc; *Int'l*, pg. 1097
REED TRAVEL PUBLISHING—See Reed Elsevier plc; *Int'l*, pg. 1097
REED TRAVEL PUBLISHING-ASIA/PACIFIC—See Reed Elsevier plc; *Int'l*, pg. 1097
REED TRAVEL PUBLISHING-AUSTRALIA—See Reed Elsevier plc; *Int'l*, pg. 1097
REED TRAVEL PUBLISHING-AUSTRALIA/SOUTH PACIFIC—See Reed Elsevier plc; *Int'l*, pg. 1097
REED TRAVEL PUBLISHING-DALLAS—See Reed Elsevier plc; *Int'l*, pg. 1097
REED TRAVEL PUBLISHING-HAWAII—See Reed Elsevier plc; *Int'l*, pg. 1097
REED TRAVEL PUBLISHING-HONG KONG—See Reed Elsevier plc; *Int'l*, pg. 1097
REED TRAVEL PUBLISHING-JAPAN—See Reed Elsevier plc; *Int'l*, pg. 1097
REED TRAVEL PUBLISHING-LOS ANGELES—See Reed Elsevier plc; *Int'l*, pg. 1097
REED TRAVEL PUBLISHING-MIAMI—See Reed Elsevier plc; *Int'l*, pg. 1097
REED TRAVEL PUBLISHING-OMAHA—See Reed Elsevier plc; *Int'l*, pg. 1097
REED TRAVEL PUBLISHING-SAN FRANCISCO—See Reed Elsevier plc; *Int'l*, pg. 1097
REED TRAVEL PUBLISHING-SWITZERLAND—See Reed Elsevier plc; *Int'l*, pg. 1097
REED TRAVEL PUBLISHING-UK—See Reed Elsevier plc; *Int'l*, pg. 1097
REED TRAVEL PUBLISHING-WASHINGTON D.C.—See Reed Elsevier plc; *Int'l*, pg. 1097
REEDCO, INC.—See Block Drug Company, Inc.; *U.S. Public*, pg. 237
REEDEX CORPORATION—See IMI Plc; *Int'l*, pg. 647
REED NATIONAL COMPANY—See Mestek, Inc.; *U.S. Public*, pg. 1099
REEDRILL INC.—See Svedala Industri AB; *Int'l*, pg. 1325
REEDS FINANCIAL SERVICES, INC.—See Reeds Jewelers, Inc.; *U.S. Public*, pg. 1370
REEDS JEWELERS, INC.; *U.S. Public*, pg. 1370
REEDS JEWELERS OF NORTH CAROLINA, INC.—See Reeds Jewelers, Inc.; *U.S. Public*, pg. 1370
REEDSPECTRUM—See Hoechst Aktiengesellschaft; *Int'l*, pg. 624
REEDY CREEK ENERGY SERVICES, INC.—See The Walt Disney Company; *U.S. Public*, pg. 514
REEL-TECH SINGAPORE PTE. LTD.—See Data I/O Corporation; *U.S. Public*, pg. 486
REEM SCIENTIFIC & ENERGY TECHNOLOGIES LLC—See BASF AG; *Int'l*, pg. 109
REEMAY INC.—See BBA Group plc; *Int'l*, pg. 113
REEMTSMA CHERKASSY TYUTYUNOVA FABRIKA—See Reemtsma Cigarettenfabriken GmbH, Hamburg; *Int'l*, pg. 1101
REEMTSMA CIGARETTEN AG—See Reemtsma Cigarettenfabriken GmbH, Hamburg; *Int'l*, pg. 1101
REEMTSMA CIGARETTENFABRIKEN GMBH, HAMBURG; *Int'l*, pg. 1100
REEMTSMA DEBRECENI DOHANYGYAR KFT—See Reemtsma Cigarettenfabriken GmbH, Hamburg; *Int'l*, pg. 1101
REEMTSMA DISTRIBUTION COMPANY ITALY S.R.L.—See Reemtsma Cigarettenfabriken GmbH, Hamburg; *Int'l*, pg. 1101
REEMTSMA ESPANA S.A.—See Reemtsma Cigarettenfabriken GmbH, Hamburg; *Int'l*, pg. 1101
H.F. & PH. F. REEMTSMA GMBH—See Reemtsma Cigarettenfabriken GmbH, Hamburg; *Int'l*, pg. 1101
REEMTSMA HELLAS S.A.—See Reemtsma Cigarettenfabriken GmbH, Hamburg; *Int'l*, pg. 1101
REEMTSMA HUNGARY KERESKEDELMI KFT.—See Reemtsma Cigarettenfabriken GmbH, Hamburg; *Int'l*, pg. 1101
REEMTSMA INTERNATIONAL CHINA LTD.—See Reemtsma Cigarettenfabriken GmbH, Hamburg; *Int'l*, pg. 1101
REEMTSMA INTERNATIONAL FAR EAST PTE. LTD.—See Reemtsma Cigarettenfabriken GmbH, Hamburg; *Int'l*, pg. 1101
REEMTSMA INTERNATIONAL GMBH - RUSSIA—See Reemtsma Cigarettenfabriken GmbH, Hamburg; *Int'l*, pg. 1101
REEMTSMA INTERNATIONAL PRAHA SPOL. S.R.O.—See Reemtsma Cigarettenfabriken GmbH, Hamburg; *Int'l*, pg. 1101
REEMTSMA JAPAN LTD.—See Reemtsma Cigarettenfabriken GmbH, Hamburg; *Int'l*, pg. 1101
REEMTSMA KIEW TYUTYUNOVA FABRIKA—See Reemtsma Cigarettenfabriken GmbH, Hamburg; *Int'l*, pg. 1101
REEMTSMA NEDERLAND B.V.—See Reemtsma Cigarettenfabriken GmbH, Hamburg; *Int'l*, pg. 1101
REEMTSMA UKRAINE—See Reemtsma Cigarettenfabriken GmbH, Hamburg; *Int'l*, pg. 1101
REESE ENTERPRISES, INC., *U.S. Private*, pg. 916
H.B. REESE CANDY CO.—See Hershey Foods Corporation; *U.S. Public*, pg. 812
REESE PRODUCTS, INC.—See Masco Corporation; *U.S. Public*, pg. 1054
REEVES BANK—See F.N.B. Corporation; *U.S. Public*, pg. 607
REEVES BROTHERS, INC.—See Hart Holding Company, Inc.; *U.S. Private*, pg. 507
REEVES BROTHERS, INC. (BISHOPVILLE DIV.)—See Hart Holding Company, Inc.; *U.S. Private*, pg. 507
REEVES BROTHERS, INC. (CHESNEE DIV.)—See Hart Holding Company, Inc.; *U.S. Private*, pg. 507

REEVES DIRECTORY OF CORPORATE AFFILIATIONS

Company Index

REEVES DIVISION—See Rockwell International Corporation; U.S. Public, pg. 1398
REEVES-HOFFMAN DIV.—See CTS Corporation; U.S. Public, pg. 286
REEVES INTERNATIONAL—See Hart Holding Company, Inc.; U.S. Private, pg. 507
REEVES RUBBER—See BTR plc; Int'l, pg. 127
REEVES SOUTHEASTERN CORPORATION; U.S. Private, pg. 916
REEVES S.P.A.—See Hart Holding Company, Inc.; U.S. Private, pg. 507
REFCO GROUP LTD.; U.S. Private, pg. 917
REFCO INC.—See Refco Group Ltd.; U.S. Private, pg. 917
REFERENCE PATHOLOGY LABORATORY, INC.—See Laboratory Corp. of America Holdings; U.S. Public, pg. 973
REFINACOES DE MILHO, BRASIL LTDA.—See Corn Products International, Inc.; U.S. Public, pg. 448
REFINED OIL PRODUCTS (PTY.) LTD.—See H.J. Heinz Company; U.S. Public, pg. 806
REFINED SUGARS, INC.—See Jannock Limited; Int'l, pg. 699
REFINERIA DE CAJAMARQUILLA—See Cominco, Ltd.; Int'l, pg. 308
REFINERIA DOMINICANA DE PETROLEO, S.A.—See Royal Dutch/Shell Group of Companies; Int'l, pg. 1141
REFINERIA ISLA (CURAZAO), S.A.—See Petroleos de Venezuela S.A.; Int'l, pg. 1046
REFINERIA PANAMA S.A.—See Texaco Inc.; U.S. Public, pg. 1584
REFINERIA PETROLERA ACAJUTLA, S.A.—See Royal Dutch/Shell Group of Companies; Int'l, pg. 1141
REFINERIA TEXACO DE HONDURAS, S.A.—See Texaco Inc.; U.S. Public, pg. 1584
REFINERIAS DE MAIZ S.A.I.C.F.—See Corn Products International, Inc.; U.S. Public, pg. 448
REFINING & MANUFACTURING RESEARCH CENTER—See Chinese Petroleum Corporation; Int'l, pg. 286
REFLECTIONS PARTNERS CORP.—See Cigna Corp.; U.S. Public, pg. 361
REFLECTONE TRAINING SYSTEMS, INC.—See British Aerospace p.l.c.; Int'l, pg. 218
REFLECTONE U.K. LTD.—See British Aerospace p.l.c.; Int'l, pg. 218
REFLEX-WELLMATE GMBH—See Essef Corporation; U.S. Public, pg. 593
REFORMA-DIANATA B.V.—See Novartis AG; Int'l, pg. 984
REFRACTARIOS MEXICANOS S.A. DE C.V. (REFMEX)—See Global Industrial Technologies; U.S. Public, pg. 748
REFRACTARIOS MULTIPLES S.A.—See Morgan Crucible Co. Plc; Int'l, pg. 894
REFRACTARIOS NACIONALES S.A.—See Morgan Crucible Co. Plc; Int'l, pg. 894
REFRACTARIOS NORTON, S.A.—See Saint-Gobain; Int'l, pg. 1175
REFRACTIVE CENTERS INTERNATIONAL—See Summit Technology, Inc.; U.S. Public, pg. 1529
REFRACTORIES CONSULTING & ENGINEERING GMBH—See RGP Holding, Inc.; U.S. Private, pg. 904
REFRACTORIOS CHILENOS S.A. (RECSA)—See Global Industrial Technologies; U.S. Public, pg. 748
REFRADIGE—See Saint-Gobain; Int'l, pg. 1176
REFRALOR—See Lafarge S.A.; Int'l, pg. 789
REFRATTARI ITALIA S.R.L.—See Morgan Crucible Co. Plc; Int'l, pg. 894
REFRIGERATION & AIR CONDITIONING DIV.—See Parker Hannifin Corporation; U.S. Public, pg. 1264
REFRIGERATION & COPPER PRODUCT DIVISION—See Parker Hannifin Corporation; U.S. Public, pg. 1259
REFRIGERATION DIV.—See Southcorp Holdings Ltd.; Int'l, pg. 1287
REFRIGERATION HUSSMANN LTEE.—See Whitman Corporation; U.S. Public, pg. 1766
REFRIGERATION SUPPLIES DISTRIBUTORS; U.S. Private, pg. 917
REFRIGIWEAR, INC.; U.S. Private, pg. 917
REGAL—See Amerex USA, Inc.; U.S. Private, pg. 49
REGAL-BELOIT CORPORATION; U.S. Public, pg. 1370
REGAL CINEMAS INC.; U.S. Public, pg. 1371
REGAL CUTTING TOOLS DIV.—See Regal-Beloit Corporation; U.S. Public, pg. 1370
REGAL DRUGS, INC.—See Foodarama Supermarkets, Inc.; U.S. Public, pg. 661
REGAL GREETINGS & GIFTS—See Russel Metals Inc.; Int'l, pg. 1150
REGAL JAPAN CO. LTD.—See Regal Ware, Inc.; U.S. Private, pg. 917
REGAL KOREA—See Regal Ware, Inc.; U.S. Private, pg. 917
REGAL MARINE INDUSTRIES INC.; U.S. Private, pg. 917
REGAL WARE, INC.; U.S. Private, pg. 917
REGAL WARE, INC.—See Regal Ware, Inc.; U.S. Private, pg. 917
REGALLITE PLASTIC CORP.—See O'Sullivan Corporation; U.S. Public, pg. 1234
REGAM MEDICAL SYSTEMS INTERNATIONAL AB—See AFP Imaging Corporation; U.S. Public, pg. 6
REGENCE BLUECROSS BLUESHIELD OF OREGON; U.S. Private, pg. 917
REGENCE LIFE & HEALTH INSURANCE CO.—See Regence BlueCross BlueShield of Oregon; U.S. Private, pg. 918
REGENCY—See McKechnie PLC; Int'l, pg. 851
REGENCY ASSOCIATES LIMITED PARTNERSHIP; U.S. Private, pg. 918
REGENCY CRUISES INC.; U.S. Private, pg. 918
REGENCY DODGE INC.; U.S. Private, pg. 918
REGENCY ENGRAVERS, INC.—See American Pad and Paper Company; U.S. Public, pg. 89
REGENCY FINANCE COMPANY—See F.N.B. Corporation; U.S. Public, pg. 607
REGENCY GROUP INC.; U.S. Private, pg. 918
REGENCY HOTEL—See Loews Corporation; U.S. Public, pg. 1011
REGENCY INSURANCE COMPANY—See Frontier Insurance Group, Inc.; U.S. Public, pg. 685
REGENCY LINCOLN MERCURY, INC.; U.S. Private, pg. 918
REGENCY MANAGEMENT SERVICE L.L.C.—See Regency Associates Limited Partnership; U.S. Private, pg. 918
REGENCY MARITIME CORP./REGSUN HOLDING CORP., LTD—See Regency Cruises Inc.; U.S. Private, pg. 918
REGENCY PROPERTY SERVICES L.L.C.—See Regency Associates Limited Partnership; U.S. Private, pg. 918
REGENCY SAVINGS BANK—See The First Bank of Oak Park; U.S. Private, pg. 406
REGENCY-SONNELL GREETINGS—See American Pad and Paper Company; U.S. Public, pg. 89
REGENCY THERMOGRAPHERS—See American Pad and Paper Company; U.S. Public, pg. 89
REGENCY THERMOGRAPHERS OF BUFFALO, INC.—See American Pad and Paper Company; U.S. Public, pg. 89
REGENCY THERMOGRAPHICS OF WASHINGTON, INC.—See American Pad and Paper Company; U.S. Public, pg. 89
REGENT INTERNATIONAL; U.S. Private, pg. 918
REGENT INTERNATIONAL INSURANCE COMPANY, LTD.—See Reliance Group Holdings, Inc.; U.S. Public, pg. 1374
REGENT MOTORS LIMITED—See Sime Darby Berhad; Int'l, pg. 1251
REGENT-SHEFFIELD LTD.—See McPherson's Limited; Int'l, pg. 852
REGIE S.A. (RECHERCHE, ETUDES, GESTION DES POUR L'INFORMATISATION DE L'ENTREPRISE—See Compagnie des Machines Bull; Int'l, pg. 316
REGINA FINANZ- U. VERSICHERUNGSVERMITTLUNG—See Commerzbank AG; Int'l, pg. 310
REGINA HAW PAR PRIVATE LIMITED—See Haw Par Brothers International Limited; Int'l, pg. 603
REGINA SEED PROCESSORS LTD.—See Saskatchewan Wheat Pool; Int'l, pg. 1195
REGION AUSTRALIA TAMCORP AUSTRALIA PTY. LIMITED—See Tamrock Corp.; Int'l, pg. 1353
REGION CIS—See Tamrock Corp.; Int'l, pg. 1352
REGION EUROPE TAMROCK EUROPE GMBH—See Tamrock Corp.; Int'l, pg. 1353
REGION FAR EAST—See Tamrock Corp.; Int'l, pg. 1353
REGION WESTERN HEMISPHERE TAMROCK EJC—See Tamrock Corp.; Int'l, pg. 1352
REGIONAL & LOCAL EXPRESS PARCELS DIVISION—See SNCF; Int'l, pg. 1163
REGIONAL AIRCRAFT SERVICES—See Mesa Air Group; U.S. Public, pg. 1099
REGIONAL DEVELOPMENT CORP.—See Family Inns of America, Inc.; U.S. Private, pg. 393
REGIONAL MALL DEVELOPMENT PARTNERS L.P.—See Cigna Corp.; U.S. Public, pg. 359
REGIONAL OFFICE SOUTH LATIN AMERICA—See ING Groep N.V.; Int'l, pg. 651
THE REGIONAL STANDARD—See Journal Register Company; U.S. Public, pg. 935
REGIONAL TRANSPORTATION AUTHORITY (RTA); U.S. Private, pg. 918
REGIONS BANK—See Regions Financial Corporation; U.S. Public, pg. 1371
REGIONS BANK/ATLANTA—See Regions Financial Corporation; U.S. Public, pg. 1371
REGIONS BANK/BANKS COUNTY—See Regions Financial Corporation; U.S. Public, pg. 1371
REGIONS BANK/BARROW COUNTY—See Regions Financial Corporation; U.S. Public, pg. 1371
REGIONS BANK/CARROLL COUNTY—See Regions Financial Corporation; U.S. Public, pg. 1372
REGIONS BANK-CEDARTOWN/ROCKMART—See Regions Financial Corporation; U.S. Public, pg. 1372
REGIONS BANK/CENTRAL LOUISIANA—See Regions Financial Corporation; U.S. Public, pg. 1372
REGIONS BANK/CITRUS COUNTY—See Regions Financial Corporation; U.S. Public, pg. 1372
REGIONS BANK/COLUMBUS—See Regions Financial Corporation; U.S. Public, pg. 1372
REGIONS BANK/DALTON/CARTERSVILLE/CHATTANOOGA—See Regions Financial Corporation; U.S. Public, pg. 1372
REGIONS BANK/DOUGLAS COUNTY—See Regions Financial Corporation; U.S. Public, pg. 1372
REGIONS BANK/ELBERT COUNTY—See Regions Financial Corporation; U.S. Public, pg. 1372
REGIONS BANK/FORSYTH COUNTY—See Regions Financial Corporation; U.S. Public, pg. 1372
REGIONS BANK/GILMER COUNTY—See Regions Financial Corporation; U.S. Public, pg. 1372
REGIONS BANK/HABERSHAM COUNTY—See Regions Financial Corporation; U.S. Public, pg. 1372
REGIONS BANK/HEARD COUNTY—See Regions Financial Corporation; U.S. Public, pg. 1372
REGIONS BANK/JACKSON COUNTY—See Regions Financial Corporation; U.S. Public, pg. 1372
REGIONS BANK/LEE COUNTY—See Regions Financial Corporation; U.S. Public, pg. 1372
REGIONS BANK/MARIANNA—See Regions Financial Corporation; U.S. Public, pg. 1372
REGIONS BANK/MIDDLE TENNESSEE—See Regions Financial Corporation; U.S. Public, pg. 1372
REGIONS BANK/NEW IBERIA—See Regions Financial Corporation; U.S. Public, pg. 1372
REGIONS BANK/NORTH LOUISIANA—See Regions Financial Corporation; U.S. Public, pg. 1372
REGIONS BANK/OKALOOSA/BAY COUNTY—See Regions Financial Corporation; U.S. Public, pg. 1372
REGIONS BANK/ORLANDO—See Regions Financial Corporation; U.S. Public, pg. 1372
REGIONS BANK/PAULDING COUNTY—See Regions Financial Corporation; U.S. Public, pg. 1372
REGIONS BANK/PICKENS COUNTY—See Regions Financial Corporation; U.S. Public, pg. 1372
REGIONS BANK/RAYBUN COUNTY—See Regions Financial Corporation; U.S. Public, pg. 1372
REGIONS BANK/ROCKDALE COUNTY—See Regions Financial Corporation; U.S. Public, pg. 1372
REGIONS BANK/ROME—See Regions Financial Corporation; U.S. Public, pg. 1372
REGIONS BANK/SANTA ROSA COUNTY—See Regions Financial Corporation; U.S. Public, pg. 1372
REGIONS BANK/SOUTHERN LOUISIANA—See Regions Financial Corporation; U.S. Public, pg. 1373
REGIONS BANK/STEPHENS COUNTY—See Regions Financial Corporation; U.S. Public, pg. 1373
REGIONS BANK/WALTON/HOLMES COUNTY—See Regions Financial Corporation; U.S. Public, pg. 1373
REGIONS BANK/WHITE COUNTY—See Regions Financial Corporation; U.S. Public, pg. 1373
REGIONS BANK/WINCHESTER—See Regions Financial Corporation; U.S. Public, pg. 1373
REGIONS FINANCIAL CORPORATION; U.S. Public, pg. 1371
REGIONS INVESTMENTS, INC.—See Regions Financial Corporation; U.S. Public, pg. 1371
REGIONS MORTGAGE, INC.—See Regions Financial Corporation; U.S. Public, pg. 1373
REGIS CORPORATION; U.S. Public, pg. 1373
THE REGISTER CITIZEN—See Journal Register Company; U.S. Public, pg. 935
REGISTRO DE PRESTACIONES INFORMATICAS, S.A.—See Caja de Madrid Group; Int'l, pg. 252
REGLAR SRL—See Alusuisse-Lonza Holding Ltd.; Int'l, pg. 69
REGMA—See Rhone-Poulenc S.A.; Int'l, pg. 1109
REHAB LEASING CORP.—See Prime Medical Services, Inc.; U.S. Public, pg. 1327
REHABCARE GROUP, INC.; U.S. Public, pg. 1373
REHABCARE OUTPATIENT SERVICES, INC.—See RehabCare Group, Inc.; U.S. Public, pg. 1373
REHABILITATION INSTITUTE OF OKLAHOMA—See Vencor, Inc.; U.S. Public, pg. 1714
REHABILITATION & NURSING CARE CENTER—See Meritcare, Inc.; U.S. Private, pg. 733
REHABILITATIVE BACK CENTER OF ATLANTA, INC.—See Vencor, Inc.; U.S. Public, pg. 1715
REHABILITATIVE HEALTH SERVICES, INC.—See Columbia/HCA Healthcare Corporation; U.S. Public, pg. 405
REHABWORKS INC.—See Horizon/CMS Healthcare Corporation; U.S. Public, pg. 839
REHRIG INTERNATIONAL—See Cravey, Green & Wahlen, Incorporated; U.S. Private, pg. 287
REHRIG PACIFIC COMPANY; U.S. Private, pg. 919
REICH & TANG—See Metropolitan Life Insurance Co.; U.S. Private, pg. 737
KARL M. REICH MASCHINENFABRIK GMBH; Int'l, pg. 1101
REICH SPEZIALMASCHINEN GMBH—See Karl M. Reich Maschinenfabrik GmbH; Int'l, pg. 1101
OTTO REICHELT GMBH—See SHV Holdings N.V.; Int'l, pg. 1156
REICHHOLD CHEMICALS DIV.—See Dainippon Ink & Chemicals, Inc.; Int'l, pg. 370
REICHHOLD CHEMICALS, INC.—See Dainippon Ink & Chemicals, Inc.; Int'l, pg. 370
REICHHOLD CHEMIE AG—See Dainippon Ink & Chemicals, Inc.; Int'l, pg. 370
REICHHOLD CHEMIE GMBH—See Dainippon Ink & Chemicals, Inc.; Int'l, pg. 370
REICHHOLD CHIMIE S.A.—See Dainippon Ink & Chemicals, Inc.; Int'l, pg. 370
REICHHOLD LIMITED—See Dainippon Ink & Chemicals, Inc.; Int'l, pg. 370
REICHHOLD LTD.—See Dainippon Ink & Chemicals, Inc.; Int'l, pg. 370
REICHHOLD QUIMICA DE MEXICO, S.A. DE C.V.—See Dainippon Ink & Chemicals, Inc.; Int'l, pg. 370
REICHS-KREDIT-GESELLSCHAFT MBH—See Viag AG; Int'l, pg. 1464
REICO, INC.; U.S. Private, pg. 919
REIDSVILLE CONTAINER DIV.—See Philip Morris Companies Inc.; U.S. Public, pg. 1289
REIFENHAUSER GMBH & CO. MASCHINENFABRIK; Int'l, pg. 1101
REIFENHAUSER IND. DE MAQUINAS LTDA.—See Reifenhauser GmbH & Co. Maschinenfabrik; Int'l, pg. 1101
REIFENHAUSER LTD.—See Reifenhauser GmbH & Co. Maschinenfabrik; Int'l, pg. 1101
REIFENHAUSER MASKINER A/S—See Reifenhauser GmbH & Co. Maschinenfabrik; Int'l, pg. 1101
BERNARD REIJN B.V.—See Gamma Holding N.V.; Int'l, pg. 540
REILLY INDUSTRIES, INC.; U.S. Private, pg. 919
REILY ELECTRICAL SUPPLY, INC.; U.S. Private, pg. 919
REILY FOODS & CO.—See William B. Reily & Co., Inc.; U.S. Private, pg. 919
REILY FOODS COMPANY—See William B. Reily & Co., Inc.; U.S. Private, pg. 919
WILLIAM B. REILY & CO., INC.; U.S. Private, pg. 919
REIN ELEKTRONIK GMBH—See Veba AG; Int'l, pg. 1457
REINALT-THOMAS CORP.; U.S. Private, pg. 919
REINER CHEMISCHE FABRIK GMBH—See Fuchs Petrolub AG Oel + Chemie; Int'l, pg. 517
REINFELDT & TRENSCHEL HANDEL GMBH—See Mannesmann A.G.; Int'l, pg. 838
ETS REINHARD RAFFEL GALVANISATION SARL—See Ascot Holdings Plc; Int'l, pg. 88
REINHARD RAFFEL METALLWARENFABRIK GMBH—See Ascot Holdings Plc; Int'l, pg. 88
REINHOLD INDUSTRIES INC.; U.S. Private, pg. 920
REINKE MANUFACTURING CO., INC.; U.S. Private, pg. 920

REINSHAGEN ITALIA SRL.—See General Motors Corporation; *U.S. Public*, pg. 723
REINSHAGEN TOURNAI S.A.—See General Motors Corporation; *U.S. Public*, pg. 723
REINSHAGEN U.K.—See General Motors Corporation; *U.S. Public*, pg. 723
REINSURANCE ALTERNATIVES—See Willis Corroon Group PLC; *Int'l*, pg. 1503
REINSURANCE ALTERNATIVES, INC.—See Willis Corroon Group PLC; *Int'l*, pg. 1503
REINSURANCE DERIVATIVES HOLDING AG—See Swiss Reinsurance Company; *Int'l*, pg. 1332
REINSURANCE FINANCE CONSULTANTS LIMITED—See Swiss Reinsurance Company; *Int'l*, pg. 1332
REINSURANCE GROUP OF AMERICA—See General American Life Insurance Co.; *U.S. Private*, pg. 443
REINTER BC—See Willis Corroon Group PLC; *Int'l*, pg. 1502
REINZ-DICHTUNGS-GMBH—See Dana Corporation; *U.S. Public*, pg. 480
REISBURO POPULARIS AG—See Coop Switzerland; *Int'l*, pg. 330
REISE-AS GMBH—See Fried. Krupp AG; *Int'l*, pg. 515
REISE-PALETTE GMBH—See Fried. Krupp AG; *Int'l*, pg. 515
REISE-UND VERKEHRS VERLAG GMBH—See Bertelsmann AG; *Int'l*, pg. 190
REISEBURO ATLANTIS-AKADEMISCHER REISEDIENST GMBH—See Hapag-Lloyd AG; *Int'l*, pg. 596
REISEBURO DR. TIGGES GMBH—See Fried. Krupp AG; *Int'l*, pg. 515
REISELAND GMBH—See Otto Versand (GmbH & Co.); *Int'l*, pg. 1015
OTTO REISEN GMBH—See Otto Versand (GmbH & Co.); *Int'l*, pg. 1015
REISESCHRAND GMBH—See Fried. Krupp AG; *Int'l*, pg. 515
REISMUHLE BRUNNEN AG—See Coop Switzerland; *Int'l*, pg. 330
REISREVUE AND MEDICAL JOURNALS—See Reed Elsevier plc; *Int'l*, pg. 1099
REISTERTOWN FEDERAL SAVINGS BANK—See Susquehanna Bancshares, Inc.; *U.S. Public*, pg. 1543
REITER DAIRY, INC.—See Dean Foods Company; *U.S. Public*, pg. 491
REITMAN DIVISION—See R & R Marketing; *U.S. Private*, pg. 902
REITMANS (CANADA) LIMITED; *Int'l*, pg. 1102
REITMANS INC.—See Reitmans (Canada) Limited; *Int'l*, pg. 1102
REITZ COAL COMPANY—See Berwind Corporation; *U.S. Private*, pg. 139
HANS REITZELS FORLAG A/S—See B.H. Blackwell Ltd.; *Int'l*, pg. 197
REJUVIA PROD. GROUP—See Del Laboratories, Inc.; *U.S. Public*, pg. 494
REKAM ENGINEERING GMBH—See Cockerill Sambre; *Int'l*, pg. 302
REKO B.V.—See DSM N.V.; *Int'l*, pg. 354
REKORD NUTRICIA S.R.O.—See Nutricia BV; *Int'l*, pg. 992
RELA, INC.—See Colorado MEDtech, Inc.; *U.S. Public*, pg. 401
RELCO—See Reliable Stores, Inc.; *U.S. Public*, pg. 920
RELECMAP, S.A.—See Corporacion MAPFRE, Compania Internacional de Reaseguros, S.A.; *Int'l*, pg. 333
RELEPLEX AS—See Schuttersveld Holding N.V.; *Int'l*, pg. 1210
RELIABILITY INCORPORATED; *U.S. Public*, pg. 1373
RELIABLE AUTOMATIC SPRINKLER CO., INC.; *U.S. Private*, pg. 920
RELIABLE/BETHEA POWER PRODUCTS INC.—See Maclean-Fogg Co.; *U.S. Private*, pg. 692
RELIABLE CASTINGS CORPORATION; *U.S. Private*, pg. 920
RELIABLE CHEVROLET; *U.S. Private*, pg. 920
RELIABLE KNITTING WORKS; *U.S. Private*, pg. 920
THE RELIABLE LIFE INSURANCE COMPANY; *U.S. Private*, pg. 1374
RELIABLE STORES, INC.; *U.S. Public*, pg. 920
RELIANCE CONSULTING GROUP—See Reliance Group Holdings, Inc.; *U.S. Public*, pg. 1374
RELIANCE DEVELOPMENT GROUP INC.—See Reliance Group Holdings, Inc.; *U.S. Public*, pg. 1374
RELIANCE ELECTRIC—See Rockwell International Corporation; *U.S. Public*, pg. 1397
RELIANCE ELECTRIC AG—See Rockwell International Corporation; *U.S. Public*, pg. 1400
RELIANCE ELECTRIC COMPANY—See Rockwell International Corporation; *U.S. Public*, pg. 1398
RELIANCE ELECTRIC S.A.—See Rockwell International Corporation; *U.S. Public*, pg. 1400
RELIANCE ELEVATOR COMPANY; *U.S. Private*, pg. 921
RELIANCE GROUP HOLDINGS, INC.; *U.S. Public*, pg. 1374
RELIANCE INSURANCE COMPANY—See Reliance Group Holdings, Inc.; *U.S. Public*, pg. 1374
RELIANCE LAND CO.—See CalMat Co.; *U.S. Public*, pg. 296
RELIANCE MEDICAL PRODUCTS, INC.; *U.S. Private*, pg. 921
RELIANCE MOTION CONTROL, INC.—See Rockwell International Corporation; *U.S. Public*, pg. 1398
RELIANCE NATIONAL (BARBADOS) INSURANCE, LTD.—See Reliance Group Holdings, Inc.; *U.S. Public*, pg. 1374
RELIANCE NATIONAL INSURANCE COMPANY—See Reliance Group Holdings, Inc.; *U.S. Public*, pg. 1374
RELIANCE NATIONAL INSURANCE COMPANY LTD—See Payco American Corporation; *U.S. Public*, pg. 1267
RELIANCE NATIONAL U.K. LIMITED—See Reliance Group Holdings, Inc.; *U.S. Public*, pg. 1374
RELIANCE REALTY, INC.—See The Chubb Corporation; *U.S. Public*, pg. 355

RELIANCE REINSURANCE CORP.—See Reliance Group Holdings, Inc.; *U.S. Public*, pg. 1374
RELIANCE STANDARD LIFE INSURANCE COMPANY—See Delphi Financial Group, Inc.; *U.S. Public*, pg. 496
RELIANCE STEEL & ALUMINUM CO.; *U.S. Public*, pg. 1375
RELIANCE STEEL FABRICATORS LIMITED—See Anchor Lamina Inc.; *Int'l*, pg. 75
RELIANCE SURETY CORP.—See Reliance Group Holdings, Inc.; *U.S. Public*, pg. 1374
RELIANCE TRANSPORT CO.—See CalMat Co.; *U.S. Public*, pg. 296
RELIASTAR EMPLOYER FINANCIAL SERVICES COMPANY—See ReliaStar Financial Corp.; *U.S. Public*, pg. 1376
RELIASTAR FINANCIAL CORP.; *U.S. Public*, pg. 1375
RELIASTAR FINANCIAL MARKETING CORP.—See ReliaStar Financial Corp.; *U.S. Public*, pg. 1376
RELIASTAR INVESTMENT RESEARCH, INC.—See ReliaStar Financial Corp.; *U.S. Public*, pg. 1376
RELIASTAR MORTGAGE COMPANY—See ReliaStar Financial Corp.; *U.S. Public*, pg. 1376
RELIEF PRINTING; *U.S. Private*, pg. 1375
RELM COMMUNICATIONS, INC.—See Relm Wireless Corp.; *U.S. Public*, pg. 1376
RELM DEMAND SIDE MANAGEMENT SYSTEMS—See Relm Wireless Corp.; *U.S. Public*, pg. 1376
RELM WIRELESS CORP.; *U.S. Public*, pg. 1376
RELOCATION CONSULTANTS—See Tribune Company; *U.S. Public*, pg. 1635
RELOCATION MANAGEMENT SYSTEMS, INC.—See Norfolk Southern Corporation; *U.S. Public*, pg. 1192
RELTEC CORPORATION; *U.S. Private*, pg. 921
RELTEC, INC.—See RELTEC Corporation; *U.S. Private*, pg. 921
RELTEC SERVICES—See RELTEC Corporation; *U.S. Private*, pg. 921
RELTEC SYSTEMS—See RELTEC Corporation; *U.S. Private*, pg. 921
RELTECH DEVELOPMENT LABORATORY—See Platinum Technology, Inc.; *U.S. Public*, pg. 1309
REMA BAKEWARE—See Newell Co.; *U.S. Public*, pg. 1177
REMBRANDT—See Recoton Corporation; *U.S. Public*, pg. 1369
REMBRANDT PHOTO SERVICES—See Center Partners Management LLC; *U.S. Private*, pg. 222
REMCO AMERICA, INC.—See Thorn plc; *Int'l*, pg. 1385
REMCO BABY—See JAKKS Pacific, Inc.; *U.S. Public*, pg. 923
REMCO TOYS—See JAKKS Pacific, Inc.; *U.S. Public*, pg. 923
REMCOR PRODUCTS CO.—See IMI Plc; *Int'l*, pg. 646
REMEC, INC.; *U.S. Public*, pg. 1376
REMEDYTEMP, INC.; *U.S. Public*, pg. 1376
THE REMEMBRANCE INSTITUTE—See Fortis; *Int'l*, pg. 499
REMINGTON ARMS COMPANY, INC.; *U.S. Private*, pg. 921
REMINGTON AUSTRALIA—See Remington Products Company, L.L.C.; *U.S. Private*, pg. 921
REMINGTON CONSUMER PRODUCTS, LTD.—See Remington Products Company, L.L.C.; *U.S. Private*, pg. 921
REMINGTON PRODUCTS (CANADA) INC.—See Remington Products Company, L.L.C.; *U.S. Private*, pg. 921
REMINGTON PRODUCTS COMPANY, L.L.C.; *U.S. Private*, pg. 921
REMINGTON PRODUCTS GMBH—See Remington Products Company, L.L.C.; *U.S. Private*, pg. 921
REMMELE ENGINEERING, INC.; *U.S. Private*, pg. 921
REMO GMBH RENOVIEREN UND MODERNISIEREN—See Bilfinger + Berger Bauaktiengesellschaft; *Int'l*, pg. 195
REMO PRECISION TOOLS LTD.—See FAG Group; *Int'l*, pg. 469
REMOTE SERVICES, INC.—See Dairy Mart Convenience Stores, Inc.; *U.S. Public*, pg. 477
REMOVAL, INC.—See Browning-Ferris Industries, Inc.; *U.S. Public*, pg. 264
REMSAN—See ABB Asea Brown Boveri (Holding) Ltd.; *Int'l*, pg. 6
REMSDAQ LIMITED—See DAQ Electronics Inc.; *U.S. Private*, pg. 300
REMTOX (CHEMICALS) LIMITED—See Laporte plc; *Int'l*, pg. 802
REMY AMERIQUE INC.—See Remy Cointreau; *Int'l*, pg. 1102
REMY COINTREAU; *Int'l*, pg. 1102
REN-VASK A/S—See Electrolux, AB; *Int'l*, pg. 441
RENA-WARE DISTRIBUTORS INC.; *U.S. Private*, pg. 922
RENA-WARE GMBH—See Rena-Ware Distributors Inc.; *U.S. Private*, pg. 922
RENAISSANCE—See Paragon Health Network, Inc.; *U.S. Public*, pg. 1257
RENAISSANCE CENTER VENTURE—See Ford Motor Company; *U.S. Public*, pg. 663
RENAISSANCE COSMETICS, INC.; *U.S. Public*, pg. 922
RENAISSANCE ENERGY LTD.; *Int'l*, pg. 1102
RENAISSANCE HOTEL GROUP N.V.—See Marriott International, Inc.; *U.S. Public*, pg. 1048
RENAISSANCE INTERNATIONAL HOTELS—See Marriott International, Inc.; *U.S. Public*, pg. 1048
RENAISSANCE PUBLISHING CO., INC.—See Bemrose Corporation; *Int'l*, pg. 185
RENATA AG—See SMH Swiss Corporation for Micro Electronics & Watchmaking Indus. Ltd.; *Int'l*, pg. 1160
RENATA SA—See SMH Swiss Corporation for Micro Electronics & Watchmaking Indus. Ltd.; *Int'l*, pg. 1161
RENAULT BISQUIT—See Groupe Pernod Ricard; *Int'l*, pg. 566
RENAULT; *Int'l*, pg. 1102
RENAULT USA—See Renault; *Int'l*, pg. 1102
RENAULT V.I.—See Renault; *Int'l*, pg. 1102

RENCO GROUP; *U.S. Private*, pg. 922
RENDFIELD LAND COMPANY, INC.—See Minnesota Power; *U.S. Public*, pg. 1116
RENDIC INTERNATIONAL—See Flint Ink Corp.; *U.S. Private*, pg. 413
RENDVA—See Eastern Utilities Associates; *U.S. Public*, pg. 549
RENEX CORP.; *U.S. Public*, pg. 1377
RENPRO CORP.; *U.S. Private*, pg. 922
DR. RENGER GMBH—See Morton International Inc.; *U.S. Public*, pg. 1135
RENISHAW A.G.—See Renishaw plc; *Int'l*, pg. 1103
RENISHAW GMBH—See Renishaw plc; *Int'l*, pg. 1103
RENISHAW (HONG KONG) LTD.—See Renishaw plc; *Int'l*, pg. 1103
RENISHAW IBERICA S.A.—See Renishaw plc; *Int'l*, pg. 1103
RENISHAW INC.—See Renishaw plc; *Int'l*, pg. 1103
RENISHAW INTERNATIONAL B.V.—See Renishaw plc; *Int'l*, pg. 1103
RENISHAW INVESTMENTS LIMITED—See Renishaw plc; *Int'l*, pg. 1103
RENISHAW (IRELAND) LIMITED—See Renishaw plc; *Int'l*, pg. 1103
RENISHAW K.K.—See Renishaw plc; *Int'l*, pg. 1103
RENISHAW LATINO AMERICANA LTD.—See Renishaw plc; *Int'l*, pg. 1103
RENISHAW PLC; *Int'l*, pg. 1103
RENISHAW PLC—See Renishaw plc; *Int'l*, pg. 1103
RENISHAW S.A.—See Renishaw plc; *Int'l*, pg. 1103
RENISHAW S.P.A.—See Renishaw plc; *Int'l*, pg. 1103
RENISHAW'S REPRESENTATIVE OFFICE—See Renishaw plc; *Int'l*, pg. 1103
RENISON GOLDFIELDS CONSOLIDATED LIMITED—See Hanson PLC; *Int'l*, pg. 595
RENNER GES.M.B.H.—See Julius Meinl AG; *Int'l*, pg. 856
RENNES—See TI Group plc; *Int'l*, pg. 1342
RENNIES GROUP LIMITED—See Anglo American Corporation of South Africa Limited; *Int'l*, pg. 76
RENNOC CORPORATION; *U.S. Private*, pg. 922
RENO CONVALESCENT CENTER—See Vencor, Inc.; *U.S. Public*, pg. 1714
RENO GAZETTE JOURNAL—See Gannett Company, Inc.; *U.S. Public*, pg. 701
RENO MFG. DIVISION—See R.R. Donnelley & Sons Company; *U.S. Public*, pg. 518
RENOAIR INC.; *U.S. Private*, pg. 922
RENOLD, INC.—See Renold PLC; *Int'l*, pg. 1104
RENOLD PLC; *Int'l*, pg. 1103
RENOSA - REMOLCADORES DEL NOROESTE, S.A.—See SEPI; *Int'l*, pg. 1223
RENOSOL CORP.; *U.S. Private*, pg. 922
GEORGES RENOULT S.A.—See Atlas Copco AB; *Int'l*, pg. 96
THE RENOVATOR'S SUPPLY, INC.; *U.S. Private*, pg. 923
RENOWN STEEL—See Slater Industries Inc.; *Int'l*, pg. 1262
RENT-A-CENTER, INC.—See Thorn plc; *Int'l*, pg. 1385
RENT ROLL, INC.—See Computer Language Research, Inc.; *U.S. Public*, pg. 421
RENT-WAY, INC.; *U.S. Public*, pg. 1377
RENTAL SANWA CO., LTD.—See Caterpillar Inc.; *U.S. Public*, pg. 317
RENTCO TRAILER CORPORATION—See Xtra Corporation; *U.S. Public*, pg. 1787
RENTENBACH CONSTRUCTORS INCORPORATED—See Rentenbach Engineering Company; *U.S. Private*, pg. 923
RENTENBACH ENGINEERING COMPANY; *U.S. Private*, pg. 923
A/S RENTOKIL—See Sophus Berendsen A/S; *Int'l*, pg. 1286
RENTOKIL BAHAMAS LTD.—See Sophus Berendsen A/S; *Int'l*, pg. 1286
RENTOKIL BARBADOS LTD.—See Sophus Berendsen A/S; *Int'l*, pg. 1286
RENTOKIL BV—See Sophus Berendsen A/S; *Int'l*, pg. 1286
BV RENTOKIL CHEMIE—See Sophus Berendsen A/S; *Int'l*, pg. 1286
RENTOKIL GMBH—See Sophus Berendsen A/S; *Int'l*, pg. 1286
RENTOKIL GUYANA LTD.—See Sophus Berendsen A/S; *Int'l*, pg. 1286
RENTOKIL HONG KONG LTD.—See Sophus Berendsen A/S; *Int'l*, pg. 1286
RENTOKIL INITIAL PLANT SERVICES (USA) INC.—See Sophus Berendsen A/S; *Int'l*, pg. 1285
RENTOKIL INITIAL PLC—See Sophus Berendsen A/S; *Int'l*, pg. 1285
RENTOKIL INITIAL USA—See Sophus Berendsen A/S; *Int'l*, pg. 1285
RENTOKIL INSURANCE LTD.—See Sophus Berendsen A/S; *Int'l*, pg. 1285
RENTOKIL JAMAICA LTD.—See Sophus Berendsen A/S; *Int'l*, pg. 1286
RENTOKIL JAPAN LTD—See Sophus Berendsen A/S; *Int'l*, pg. 1286
RENTOKIL LABORATORIES LTD.—See Sophus Berendsen A/S; *Int'l*, pg. 1285
RENTOKIL LTD.—See Sophus Berendsen A/S; *Int'l*, pg. 1285
RENTOKIL MARTINIQUE SARL—See Sophus Berendsen A/S; *Int'l*, pg. 1286
RENTOKIL PEST CONTROL LTD.—See Sophus Berendsen A/S; *Int'l*, pg. 1286
RENTOKIL (PORTUGAL) DESINFESTACOES LIMITADA—See Sophus Berendsen A/S; *Int'l*, pg. 1286
RENTOKIL (PTY.) LTD.—See Sophus Berendsen A/S; *Int'l*, pg. 1286
RENTOKIL SA—See Sophus Berendsen A/S; *Int'l*, pg. 1286
N.V. RENTOKIL SA—See Sophus Berendsen A/S; *Int'l*, pg. 1286

Company Index

RENTOKIL SINGAPORE PTE. LTD.—See Sophus Berendsen A/S; *Int'l*, pg. 1286
RENTOKIL (THAILAND) LTD—See Sophus Berendsen A/S; *Int'l*, pg. 1286
RENTRAK CORPORATION; *U.S. Public*, pg. 1377
RENTSCH LTD.—See Amcor Limited; *Int'l*, pg. 72
RENTWAY INC.—See Trimac Corporation; *Int'l*, pg. 1424
RENTWAY TRUCK LEASING—See Trimac Corporation; *Int'l*, pg. 1424
REOBIJN B.V.—See Schuttersveld Holding N.V.; *Int'l*, pg. 1210
REPAP ENTERPRISES INC.; *Int'l*, pg. 1104
REPAP INTERNATIONAL INC.—See Repap Enterprises Inc.; *Int'l*, pg. 1104
REPAP NEW BRUNSWICK INC.—See Repap Enterprises Inc.; *Int'l*, pg. 1104
REPEELACKI SAJTYRE—See Bongrain S.A.; *Int'l*, pg. 201
REPERGAL LDA.—See Fuchs Petrolub AG Oel + Chemie; *Int'l*, pg. 519
REPLACEMENT RENT-A-CAR—See National Auto Credit Inc.; *U.S. Public*, pg. 1153
REPLACEMENTS, LTD.; *U.S. Private*, pg. 923
REPLIGEN SANDOZ RESEARCH CORP.—See Novartis AG; *Int'l*, pg. 974
REPLOGLE GLOBES, INC.; *U.S. Private*, pg. 923
AB REPORTAGEBILD—See Aftonbladet AB; *Int'l*, pg. 29
THE REPORTER EQUITABLE PUBLISHING CO.—See Gannett Company, Inc.; *U.S. Public*, pg. 701
REPOXIT SA—See Forbo Holding SA; *Int'l*, pg. 497
REPP LTD. BIG AND TALL—See Edison Brothers Stores, Inc.; *U.S. Public*, pg. 564
REPRASENTANZ OMV AG—See DSM N.V.; *Int'l*, pg. 356
REPRES. OFF. INTERN. TRADE CENTER—See Olivetti SpA; *Int'l*, pg. 1004
REPRESENTACION DEL DEUTSCHE BANK AG (CARACAS)—See Deutsche Bank AG; *Int'l*, pg. 405
REPRESENTACION DEL DEUTSCHE BANK AG (SANTIAGO)—See Deutsche Bank AG; *Int'l*, pg. 405
REPRESENTACION DEUTSCH-SUDAMERIKANISCHE BANK AG Y DRESDNER BANK AG—See Dresdner Bank AG; *Int'l*, pg. 420
REPRESENTATION OF CIBA-GEIGY SERVICES LTD.—See Novartis AG; *Int'l*, pg. 984
REPROGRAPHICS IMAGING TECHNOLOGIES—See Wallace Computer Services, Inc.; *U.S. Public*, pg. 1736
REPSOL BUTANO S.A.—See Repsol S.A.; *Int'l*, pg. 1104
REPSOL CHEMIE DEUTSCHLAND—See Repsol S.A.; *Int'l*, pg. 1105
REPSOL COMERCIAL DE PRODUCTOS PETROLIFEROS, S.A.—See Repsol S.A.; *Int'l*, pg. 1104
REPSOL DERIVADOS—See Repsol S.A.; *Int'l*, pg. 1104
REPSOL DERIVADOS CARLESS REFINING & MKTG. LTD.—See Repsol S.A.; *Int'l*, pg. 1104
REPSOL DISTRIBUCION, S.A.—See Repsol S.A.; *Int'l*, pg. 1104
REPSOL EXPLORACION—See Repsol S.A.; *Int'l*, pg. 1104
REPSOL EXPLORACION ALGERIE, S.A.—See Repsol S.A.; *Int'l*, pg. 1105
REPSOL GAS NUEVO LAREDO—See Repsol S.A.; *Int'l*, pg. 1105
REPSOL INTL. FINANCE B.V.—See Repsol S.A.; *Int'l*, pg. 1104
REPSOL OIL INTERNATIONAL—See Repsol S.A.; *Int'l*, pg. 1105
REPSOL OIL INTERNATIONAL (ROIL)—See Repsol S.A.; *Int'l*, pg. 1105
REPSOL PETROLEO—See Repsol S.A.; *Int'l*, pg. 1104
REPSOL PETROLEUM LTD.—See Repsol S.A.; *Int'l*, pg. 1105
REPSOL PORTUGAL PETROLEO E DENVADOS LDA.—See Repsol S.A.; *Int'l*, pg. 1105
REPSOL QUIMICA—See Repsol S.A.; *Int'l*, pg. 1104
REPSOL S.A.; *Int'l*, pg. 1104
REPSOL S.A. DE C.V. MEXICO—See Repsol S.A.; *Int'l*, pg. 1105
REPSOL S.A., REPSOL QUIMICA—See Repsol S.A.; *Int'l*, pg. 1105
REPSOL (U.K.) LTD.—See Repsol S.A.; *Int'l*, pg. 1105
REPTRON ELECTRONICS, INC.; *U.S. Public*, pg. 1377
REPUBLIC ALLOYS, INC.; *U.S. Private*, pg. 923
REPUBLIC AMERICAN CORPORATION—See American Financial Group; *U.S. Public*, pg. 75
REPUBLIC AUTOMOTIVE-AEA DIVISION—See Republic Automotive Parts, Inc.; *U.S. Public*, pg. 1377
REPUBLIC AUTOMOTIVE PARTS, INC.; *U.S. Public*, pg. 1377
REPUBLIC AUTOMOTIVE PARTS SALES, INC.—See Republic Automotive Parts, Inc.; *U.S. Public*, pg. 1378
REPUBLIC BANK FOR SAVINGS—See Republic New York Corporation; *U.S. Public*, pg. 1380
REPUBLIC BEVERAGE CO.—See Block Distributing Company; *U.S. Private*, pg. 150
REPUBLIC BEVERAGE COMPANY—See Block Distributing Company; *U.S. Private*, pg. 149
REPUBLIC CHEMICAL COMPANY—See Harwick Standard Distribution Corporation; *U.S. Private*, pg. 509
REPUBLIC CONTAINER CORP.; *U.S. Private*, pg. 923
REPUBLIC CONTRACTING CORP.; *U.S. Private*, pg. 923
REPUBLIC DIE & TOOL COMPANY; *U.S. Private*, pg. 923
REPUBLIC DIVERSIFIED SERVICES, INC.—See Credit Suisse Group; *Int'l*, pg. 346
REPUBLIC ENGINEERED STEELS, INC.; *U.S. Public*, pg. 1378
REPUBLIC ENTERTAINMENT, INC.—See National Amusements, Inc.; *U.S. Private*, pg. 776
REPUBLIC ENVIRONMENTAL RECYCLING (NEW JERSEY), INC.—See Philip Services Corp.; *Int'l*, pg. 1050
REPUBLIC ENVIRONMENTAL SYSTEMS (CLEVELAND)—See Republic Industries, Inc.; *U.S. Public*, pg. 1380
REPUBLIC ENVIRONMENTAL SYSTEMS, INC.—See Philip Services Corp.; *Int'l*, pg. 1050
REPUBLIC ENVIRONMENTAL SYSTEMS LTD.—See Republic Industries, Inc.; *U.S. Public*, pg. 1380

REPUBLIC ENVIRONMENTAL SYSTEMS (PENNSYLVANIA), INC.—See Philip Services Corp.; *Int'l*, pg. 1050
REPUBLIC FACTORS CORP.—See Republic New York Corporation; *U.S. Public*, pg. 1380
REPUBLIC FASTENER PRODUCTS CORP.; *U.S. Private*, pg. 923
REPUBLIC FINANCIAL SERVICES, INC.—See Credit Suisse Group; *Int'l*, pg. 346
REPUBLIC FIRE & CASUALTY INSURANCE COMPANY—See Credit Suisse Group; *Int'l*, pg. 346
REPUBLIC FRANKLIN INSURANCE CO.—See Utica Mutual Insurance Company; *U.S. Private*, pg. 1130
REPUBLIC GROUP INCORPORATED; *U.S. Public*, pg. 1378
REPUBLIC GROUP NO. TWO—See Credit Suisse Group; *Int'l*, pg. 346
REPUBLIC HOSE MANUFACTURING CO.—See Trelleborg AB; *Int'l*, pg. 1423
REPUBLIC IMPERIAL AND EL CENTRO SANITATION SERVICE CO.—See Republic Industries, Inc.; *U.S. Public*, pg. 1379
REPUBLIC INDUSTRIES, INC.; *U.S. Public*, pg. 1378
REPUBLIC INSURANCE CO.—See Credit Suisse Group; *Int'l*, pg. 346
REPUBLIC INTERNATIONAL BANK OF NEW YORK—See Republic New York Corporation; *U.S. Public*, pg. 1380
REPUBLIC LLOYDS—See Credit Suisse Group; *Int'l*, pg. 346
REPUBLIC/MALOY LANDFILL & SANITATION—See Republic Industries, Inc.; *U.S. Public*, pg. 1379
REPUBLIC MASE AUSTRALIA LTD.—See Republic New York Corporation; *U.S. Public*, pg. 1380
REPUBLIC MASE HONG KONG LTD.—See Republic New York Corporation; *U.S. Public*, pg. 1380
REPUBLIC NATIONAL BANK OF MIAMI; *U.S. Private*, pg. 924
REPUBLIC NATIONAL BANK OF NEW YORK—See Republic New York Corporation; *U.S. Public*, pg. 1380
REPUBLIC NATIONAL BANK OF NEW YORK (CANADA)—See Republic New York Corporation; *U.S. Public*, pg. 1381
REPUBLIC NATIONAL BANK OF NEW YORK (CAYMAN) LIMITED—See Republic New York Corporation; *U.S. Public*, pg. 1381
REPUBLIC NATIONAL BANK OF NEW YORK (GIBRALTAR) LTD.—See Republic New York Corporation; *U.S. Public*, pg. 1381
REPUBLIC NATIONAL BANK OF NEW YORK (U.K.)—See Republic New York Corporation; *U.S. Public*, pg. 1381
REPUBLIC NATIONAL BANK OF NEW YORK (URUGUAY) S.A.—See Republic New York Corporation; *U.S. Public*, pg. 1381
REPUBLIC NEW YORK CORPORATION; *U.S. Public*, pg. 1380
REPUBLIC NEW YORK INVESTMENT CORP.—See Republic New York Corporation; *U.S. Public*, pg. 1380
REPUBLIC NEW YORK MORTGAGE CORPORATION—See Republic New York Corporation; *U.S. Public*, pg. 1381
REPUBLIC NEW YORK SECURITIES CORPORATION—See Republic New York Corporation; *U.S. Public*, pg. 1381
REPUBLIC NEW YORK TRUST COMPANY OF FLORIDA, NATIONAL ASSOCIATION—See Republic New York Corporation; *U.S. Public*, pg. 1381
REPUBLIC OVERSEAS BANKS HOLDING CORPORATION—See Republic New York Corporation; *U.S. Public*, pg. 1380
REPUBLIC PAPERBOARD CO.-COMMERCE CITY MILL—See Republic Group Incorporated; *U.S. Public*, pg. 1378
REPUBLIC POWDERED METALS, INC.—See RPM, Inc.; *U.S. Public*, pg. 1357
REPUBLIC SALES CO., INC.—See Lewis Homes Management Corp.; *U.S. Private*, pg. 665
REPUBLIC SECURITY BANK—See Republic Security Financial Corporation; *U.S. Public*, pg. 1382
REPUBLIC SECURITY FINANCIAL CORPORATION; *U.S. Public*, pg. 1381
REPUBLIC SERVICES CORPORATION—See Republic New York Corporation; *U.S. Public*, pg. 1381
REPUBLIC STORAGE SYSTEMS COMPANY INC.; *U.S. Private*, pg. 924
REPUBLIC TOBACCO CO. S.A.—See B.A.T Industries P.L.C.; *Int'l*, pg. 111
REPUBLIC UNDERWRITERS INSURANCE CO.—See Credit Suisse Group; *Int'l*, pg. 346
REPUBLIC-VANGUARD LIFE INSURANCE CO.—See Credit Suisse Group; *Int'l*, pg. 346
REPUBLIC VANGUARD (OF ARIZONA) INSURANCE CO.—See Credit Suisse Group; *Int'l*, pg. 346
REPUBLIC-VANGUARD REINSURANCE CO.—See Credit Suisse Group; *Int'l*, pg. 346
REPUBLIC WESTERN INSURANCE CO.—See Amerco; *U.S. Public*, pg. 49
REPUTATION MANAGEMENT—See HMS Partners; *U.S. Private*, pg. 492
REQUEST—See Musicland Group Inc.; *U.S. Public*, pg. 1142
RES-CARE INCORPORATED; *U.S. Public*, pg. 1382
RESART GMBH—See BASF AG; *Int'l*, pg. 104
RESCAL S.A.—See Inco Limited; *Int'l*, pg. 673
RESCO PRODUCTS, INC.; *U.S. Private*, pg. 924
RESCO PRODUCTS OF MISSOURI—See Resco Products, Inc.; *U.S. Private*, pg. 924
RESCO STEEL PRODUCTS CORP.—See Roanoke Electric Steel Corporation; *U.S. Public*, pg. 1392
RESCO UK—See Resco Products, Inc.; *U.S. Private*, pg. 924
RESDISPACE LTD.—See Sophus Berendsen A/S; *Int'l*, pg. 1285
RESEARCH CENTER, INC.—See United Illuminating Company; *U.S. Public*, pg. 1678

RESEARCH-COTTRELL—See Air & Water Technologies Corporation; *U.S. Public*, pg. 29
RESEARCH-COTTRELL (BELGIUM) S.A.—See Air & Water Technologies Corporation; *U.S. Public*, pg. 29
RESEARCH-COTTRELL (DEUTSCHLAND) G.M.B.H.—See Air & Water Technologies Corporation; *U.S. Public*, pg. 29
RESEARCH COTTRELL, EUROPE—See Air & Water Technologies Corporation; *U.S. Public*, pg. 29
RESEARCH-COTTRELL (FRANCE) S.A.—See Air & Water Technologies Corporation; *U.S. Public*, pg. 30
RESEARCH DATA CORP—See U.M. Holding Limited; *U.S. Private*, pg. 1114
RESEARCH ENVIRONMENTAL INDUSTRIES, INC.; *U.S. Private*, pg. 924
RESEARCH ENVIRONMENTAL MANAGEMENT, INC.—See Research Environmental Industries, Inc.; *U.S. Private*, pg. 924
THE RESEARCH GROUP—See Maritz Inc.; *U.S. Private*, pg. 704
RESEARCH, INCORPORATED; *U.S. Public*, pg. 1382
RESEARCH INDUSTRIES CORP.—See Baxter International Inc.; *U.S. Public*, pg. 196
RESEARCH INSTITUTE OF AMERICA—See The Thomson Corporation; *U.S. Public*, pg. 1602
THE RESEARCH INSTITUTE OF LIFE INSURANCE WELFARE—See Nippon Life Insurance Co.; *Int'l*, pg. 935
RESEARCH INTERNATIONAL—See WPP Group plc; *Int'l*, pg. 1482
RESEARCH OIL CO.—See Research Environmental Industries, Inc.; *U.S. Private*, pg. 924
RESEARCH PRODUCTS CORPORATION; *U.S. Private*, pg. 924
RESEARCH PUBLICATIONS, INC.—See The Thomson Corporation; *U.S. Public*, pg. 1600
RESEARCH SEEDS, INC.—See Land O'Lakes, Inc.; *U.S. Private*, pg. 646
RESEARCH TRIANGLE INSTITUTE; *U.S. Private*, pg. 924
RESEARCH TRUCKING COMPANY, INC.—See Research Environmental Industries, Inc.; *U.S. Private*, pg. 924
RESEAU DE TELEVISION QUATRE SAISONS INC.—See CFCF Inc.; *Int'l*, pg. 241
RESEAU PUBLI-MAISON—See G.T.C. Transcontinental Group Ltd.; *Int'l*, pg. 539
THE RESERVE GROUP; *U.S. Private*, pg. 924
RESERVES AND RESERVOIRS COORDINATION AND CONTROL (GECOR)—See Petrobras - Petroleo Brasileiro S.A.; *Int'l*, pg. 1041
RESERVOIR TECHNOLOGY AND SIMULATION (GETEC)—See Petrobras - Petroleo Brasileiro S.A.; *Int'l*, pg. 1042
RESIDENCE INN—See Marriott International, Inc.; *U.S. Public*, pg. 1048
THE RESIDENTIAL PRODUCTS GROUP—See Tomkins PLC; *Int'l*, pg. 1398
RESIDENTIAL SERVICE, INC.—See Browning-Ferris Industries, Inc.; *U.S. Public*, pg. 264
RESIDENTIAL SUPPORT SERVICES, INC.—See John Wieland Homes Inc.; *U.S. Private*, pg. 1175
RESIDIO GVG MBH—See Commerzbank AG; *Int'l*, pg. 310
THE RESIN EXCHANGE—See Spartech Corporation; *U.S. Public*, pg. 1496
RESIN FORMULATORS—See E.V. Roberts & Associates, Inc.; *U.S. Private*, pg. 935
RESINAS SINTETICAS, S.A. (RESISA)—See Compania Espanola de Petroleos, S.A. (CEPSA); *Int'l*, pg. 323
RESINMEC SPA—See Alusuisse-Lonza Holding Ltd.; *Int'l*, pg. 69
RESINS & ORGANICS DIVISION, ALBRIGHT & WILSON LIMITED—See Albright & Wilson plc; *Int'l*, pg. 49
RESINTER—See Accor S.A.; *Int'l*, pg. 20
RESISTANCE TECHNOLOGY GMBH—See Selas Corporation of America; *U.S. Public*, pg. 1455
RESISTANCE TECHNOLOGY INC.—See Selas Corporation of America; *U.S. Public*, pg. 1455
RESKA SPLINE PRODUCTS INC.—See Masco Corporation; *U.S. Public*, pg. 1054
RESOLUTE GROUP, INC.—See Berkshire Hathaway Inc.; *U.S. Public*, pg. 220
RESOLUTE MANAGEMENT CORP —See Berkshire Hathaway Inc.; *U.S. Public*, pg. 220
RESOLUTE MANAGEMENT CORPORATION—See Berkshire Hathaway Inc.; *U.S. Public*, pg. 220
RESOPAL GMBH—See Premark International, Inc.; *U.S. Public*, pg. 1322
RESORCOH INC.—See Niagara Blower Company; *U.S. Private*, pg. 798
RESORT CONDOMINIUMS INTERNATIONAL—See Cendant Corporation; *U.S. Public*, pg. 322
RESORT DEVELOPMENT DIVISION—See Tokyu Corporation; *Int'l*, pg. 1395
RESORT MARKETING INTERNATIONAL—See Santa Fe Gaming Corporation; *U.S. Public*, pg. 1432
RESORTES MECANICOS, S.A.—See Barnes Group Inc.; *U.S. Public*, pg. 190
RESORTES Y PRODUCTOS METALICOS-MEXICO CITY PLANT—See Peterson American Corp.; *U.S. Private*, pg. 857
RESORTES Y PRODUCTOS METALICOS-QUERETARO PLANT—See Peterson American Corp.; *U.S. Private*, pg. 857
RESORTS CASINO HOTEL—See Sun International Hotels Limited; *U.S. Public*, pg. 1531
RESORTS USA INC.—See The Rank Group PLC; *Int'l*, pg. 1087
RESOUND CORPORATION; *U.S. Public*, pg. 1382
RESOURCE AMERICA, INC.; *U.S. Public*, pg. 1382
RESOURCE, INC.—See International Business Machines Corporation; *U.S. Public*, pg. 896
RESOURCE MARKETING, INC.; *U.S. Private*, pg. 924
RESOURCE MARKETING, INC.—See Resource Marketing, Inc.; *U.S. Private*, pg. 924

RESOURCE MONITORS, INC.—See Providence Energy Corporation; *U.S. Public,* pg. 1337
RESOURCE MORTGAGE CAPITAL, INC.; *U.S. Public,* pg. 1382
RESOURCE NET INTERNATIONAL—See International Paper Company; *U.S. Public,* pg. 903
RESOURCE TRANSPORTATION SERVICES, INC.—See The GNI Group, Inc.; *U.S. Public,* pg. 694
RESOURCENET INTERNATIONAL—See International Paper Company; *U.S. Public,* pg. 903
RESOURCES INTERLINK LTD.—See Oracle Corporation; *U.S. Public,* pg. 1228
RESOURCES TRUST COMPANY—See SunAmerica Inc.; *U.S. Public,* pg. 1533
RESPATEX INTERNATIONAL LTD.—See Norske Skogindustrier A.S.; *Int'l,* pg. 967
RESPATEX VERTRIEB—See Norske Skogindustrier A.S.; *Int'l,* pg. 966
RESPIRATORY SUPPORT PRODUCTS INC.—See Smiths Industries plc; *Int'l,* pg. 1268
RESPIRONICS (HK), LTD.—See Respironics, Inc.; *U.S. Public,* pg. 1383
RESPIRONICS, INC.; *U.S. Public,* pg. 1383
RESPIRONICS, INC.—See Respironics, Inc.; *U.S. Public,* pg. 1383
RESPITECH HOME HEALTH CARE, INC.—See Integrated Health Services, Inc.; *U.S. Public,* pg. 885
RESPONSE ONCOLOGY, INC.—See Seafield Capital Corporation; *U.S. Public,* pg. 1449
RESPONSIVE HOME HEALTH CARE, INC.—See Integrated Health Services, Inc.; *U.S. Public,* pg. 885
RESTAURA, INC.—See Viad Corp; *U.S. Public,* pg. 1718
RESTAURA S.A.—See Sodexho S.A.; *Int'l,* pg. 1275
AB RESTAURANGFRYS—See Nestle S.A.; *Int'l,* pg. 920
RESTAURANT ASSOCIATES CATERING—See Restaurant Associates Corporation; *U.S. Private,* pg. 925
RESTAURANT ASSOCIATES CORPORATION; *U.S. Private,* pg. 924
RESTAURANT BUSINESS—See VNU Verenigde Nederlandse Uitgeversbedrijven B.V.; *Int'l,* pg. 1446
THE RESTAURANT COMPANY; *U.S. Private,* pg. 925
RESTAURANT DEVELOPERS CORP.; *U.S. Private,* pg. 925
RESTAURANT FINANCE CORPORATION—See Wendy's International Inc.; *U.S. Public,* pg. 1754
RESTAURANTS UNLIMITED; *U.S. Private,* pg. 925
RESTAURAP—See GIB Group; *Int'l,* pg. 534
RESTAURATION FRANCAISE—See Sodexho S.A.; *Int'l,* pg. 1275
RESTAUREL—See Sodexho S.A.; *Int'l,* pg. 1274
RESTEUROP—See Accor S.A.; *Int'l,* pg. 20
RESTHOTEL INTERNATIONAL—See Accor S.A.; *Int'l,* pg. 21
RESTIVA S.R.L.—See Pfizer Inc.; *U.S. Public,* pg. 1283
RESTONIC MATTRESS CORPORATION; *U.S. Private,* pg. 925
RESTOPLAN—See Vendex International N.V.; *Int'l,* pg. 1463
RESUMIX—See Ceridian Corporation; *U.S. Public,* pg. 331
RESURRECTION MINING CO.—See Newmont Mining Corporation; *U.S. Public,* pg. 1179
RETAIL BRANDS SA—See Cott Corporation; *Int'l,* pg. 338
RETAIL SALES, INC.—See The New York Times Company; *U.S. Public,* pg. 1175
RETAIL SERVICES—See Fleming Companies, Inc.; *U.S. Public,* pg. 316
RETAIL SOFT INTERNATIONAL (RSI)—See Compagnie des Machines Bull; *Int'l,* pg. 316
RETAIL SOLUTIONS—See EMAP Plc; *Int'l,* pg. 452
RETAIL STORES, INC.—See VSI Holdings, Inc.; *U.S. Public,* pg. 1703
RETAILER DEVELOPMENT—See Fleming Companies, Inc.; *U.S. Public,* pg. 653
RETAILNET B.V.—See N.V. Koninklijke Bijenkorf Beheer KBB; *Int'l,* pg. 750
RETCONN—See Semiconductor Packaging Materials Co., Inc.; *U.S. Public,* pg. 1456
RETI SA—See Akzo Nobel N.V.; *Int'l,* pg. 45
RETIREMENT ADVISORS, INC.—See The Hearst Corporation; *U.S. Private,* pg. 516
RETIREMENT COMMUNITY SPECIALISTS, INC.; *U.S. Private,* pg. 925
RETIREMENT LIVING PUBLISHING COMPANY, INC.—See The Reader's Digest Association, Inc.; *U.S. Public,* pg. 1367
RETIX UNITED KINGDOM—See Vertel; *U.S. Public,* pg. 1717
RETO 2000, S.A.—See Telefonica de Espana, S.A.; *Int'l,* pg. 1372
RETROSPETTIVA, INC.; *U.S. Public,* pg. 1383
RETZLAFF INCORPORATED; *U.S. Private,* pg. 925
REUBEN ORGANIZATION; *U.S. Private,* pg. 925
REULAND ELECTRIC COMPANY; *U.S. Private,* pg. 925
REUNERT LTD.; *Int'l,* pg. 1105
REUNION ENERGY COMPANY—See Reunion Industries, Inc.; *U.S. Public,* pg. 1383
REUNION INDUSTRIES, INC.; *U.S. Public,* pg. 1383
REUNION OPERATING COMPANY—See Reunion Industries, Inc.; *U.S. Public,* pg. 1383
REUNION RECORDS—See Zomba Recording Corp.; *Int'l,* pg. 1529
REUNIONNAIS DE PRODUITS PETROLIERS—See Royal Dutch/Shell Group of Companies; *Int'l,* pg. 1136
REUTER MANUFACTURING, INC.; *U.S. Public,* pg. 1383
REUTERS AG—See Reuters Holdings PLC; *Int'l,* pg. 1105
REUTERS AMERICA INC.—See Reuters Holdings PLC; *Int'l,* pg. 1106
REUTERS AUSTRALIA PTY. LTD.—See Reuters Holdings PLC; *Int'l,* pg. 1105
REUTERS ESPANA S.A.—See Reuters Holdings PLC; *Int'l,* pg. 1105
REUTERS HOLDINGS PLC; *Int'l,* pg. 1105
REUTERS HONG KONG LIMITED—See Reuters Holdings PLC; *Int'l,* pg. 1105

REUTERS ITALIA SPA—See Reuters Holdings PLC; *Int'l,* pg. 1105
REUTERS JAPAN KABUSHIKI KAISHA—See Reuters Holdings PLC; *Int'l,* pg. 1105
REUTERS LIMITED—See Reuters Holdings PLC; *Int'l,* pg. 1105
REUTERS SA—See Reuters Holdings PLC; *Int'l,* pg. 1105
REUTERS SERVICES SARL—See Reuters Holdings PLC; *Int'l,* pg. 1105
REUTERS SINGAPORE PTE LIMITED—See Reuters Holdings PLC; *Int'l,* pg. 1105
REUTERS SOUTH EAST ASIA LTD.—See Reuters Holdings PLC; *Int'l,* pg. 1106
REUTERS TELEVISION LIMITED—See Reuters Holdings PLC; *Int'l,* pg. 1105
REUVENI PRIDAN ADVERTISING AGENCY LTD.—See Leo Burnett Company, Inc.; *U.S. Private,* pg. 186
REV-A-SHELF; *U.S. Private,* pg. 925
REVCO SCIENTIFIC—See General Signal Corporation; *U.S. Public,* pg. 727
REVCOR; *U.S. Private,* pg. 925
REVELL AG—See Revell-Monogram Inc.; *U.S. Private,* pg. 926
REVELL-MONOGRAM INC.; *U.S. Private,* pg. 926
REVELSTOKE HOME CENTERS—See West Fraser Timber Co. Ltd.; *Int'l,* pg. 1490
REVENUE COLLECTION GROUP—See Cubic Corporation; *U.S. Public,* pg. 466
REVENUE COLLECTION GROUP WORLD HEADQUARTERS—See Cubic Corporation; *U.S. Public,* pg. 466
REVERE ELECTRIC SUPPLY CO.; *U.S. Private,* pg. 926
REVERE SMELTING & REFINING CORP.—See Quexco Incorporated; *U.S. Private,* pg. 901
REVERE TRANSDUCERS BV—See Harnischfeger Industries, Inc.; *U.S. Public,* pg. 790
REVERE TRANSDUCERS INC.—See Harnischfeger Industries, Inc.; *U.S. Public,* pg. 790
REVERE WARE CORPORATION—See Corning Incorporated; *U.S. Public,* pg. 448
REVERTEX-AMERICAS—See Dennis Chemical Co., Inc.; *U.S. Public,* pg. 1177
REVETEX—See Saint-Gobain; *Int'l,* pg. 1177
REVIEW CO.—See Foundation Health Systems, Inc.; *U.S. Public,* pg. 678
REVIEW PUBLISHING COMPANY LTD.—See Dow Jones & Company, Inc.; *U.S. Public,* pg. 525
REVIMA—See Groupe Air France; *Int'l,* pg. 560
REVLON INTERNATIONAL CORPORATION—See MacAndrews & Forbes Holdings Inc.; *U.S. Private,* pg. 690
REVLON MANUFACTURING FACILITIES—See MacAndrews & Forbes Holdings Inc.; *U.S. Private,* pg. 690
REVLON-REALISTIC PROFESSIONAL PRODUCTS, INC.—See MacAndrews & Forbes Holdings Inc.; *U.S. Private,* pg. 690
REVLON RESEARCH CENTER, INC.—See MacAndrews & Forbes Holdings Inc.; *U.S. Private,* pg. 690
REVLON SERVICE, INC.—See MacAndrews & Forbes Holdings Inc.; *U.S. Private,* pg. 690
REVLON S.P.A.—See MacAndrews & Forbes Holdings Inc.; *U.S. Private,* pg. 690
REVO, INC.—See Bausch & Lomb Incorporated; *U.S. Public,* pg. 195
REVOLUTION, INC.—See Valentine Radford, Inc.; *U.S. Private,* pg. 1131
REVOMAC—See The Ivaco Group; *Int'l,* pg. 696
CHARLES REVSON, INC.—See MacAndrews & Forbes Holdings Inc.; *U.S. Private,* pg. 690
REVUE AUSTRALIA PTY. LTD.—See The Seagram Company Ltd.; *Int'l,* pg. 1216
REWE-HANDELSGRUPPE; *Int'l,* pg. 1106
REWO CHEMICHE WERKE GMBH—See Witco Corporation; *U.S. Public,* pg. 1774
REX LUMBER COMPANY; *U.S. Private,* pg. 926
REX MARINE CENTER, INC.; *U.S. Private,* pg. 926
REX-ROTARY AG—See Ricoh Company, Ltd.; *Int'l,* pg. 1116
REX-ROTARY S.A.—See Ricoh Company, Ltd.; *Int'l,* pg. 1116
REX-ROTARY UK LIMITED—See Ricoh Company, Ltd.; *Int'l,* pg. 1114
REX STORES CORP.; *U.S. Public,* pg. 1384
REX SUPPLY COMPANY—See Production Tool Supply Co.; *U.S. Private,* pg. 889
REXAIR, INC.—See U.S. Industries, Inc.; *U.S. Public,* pg. 1684
REXALL INC. CONSUMER PRODUCTS DIV.—See Rexall Sundown Inc.; *U.S. Public,* pg. 1384
REXALL SUNDOWN INC.; *U.S. Public,* pg. 1384
REXAM CARTONS—See Rexam PLC; *Int'l,* pg. 1106
REXAM CLOSURES—See Rexam PLC; *Int'l,* pg. 1106
REXAM CONTAINERS—See Rexam PLC; *Int'l,* pg. 1107
REXAM CONTAINERS - US—See Rexam PLC; *Int'l,* pg. 1106
REXAM CUSTOM—See Rexam PLC; *Int'l,* pg. 1106
REXAM EXTRUSIONS—See Rexam PLC; *Int'l,* pg. 1106
REXAM FLEXIBLE PACKAGING—See Rexam PLC; *Int'l,* pg. 1106
REXAM GRAPHICS—See Rexam PLC; *Int'l,* pg. 1107
REXAM INC.—See Rexam PLC; *Int'l,* pg. 1106
REXAM MEDICAL PACKAGING, INC.—See Rexam PLC; *Int'l,* pg. 1106
REXAM MEDICAL PACKAGING LAKEVILLE—See Rexam PLC; *Int'l,* pg. 1106
REXAM MEDICAL PACKAGING LTD.—See Rexam PLC; *Int'l,* pg. 1106
REXAM MEDICAL PACKAGING SA—See Rexam PLC; *Int'l,* pg. 1106
REXAM MULOX—See Rexam PLC; *Int'l,* pg. 1106
REXAM MULOX USA—See Rexam PLC; *Int'l,* pg. 1106
REXAM PERFORMANCE PRODUCTS—See Rexam PLC; *Int'l,* pg. 1106

REXAM PLC; *Int'l,* pg. 1106
REXAM RELEASE—See Rexam PLC; *Int'l,* pg. 1107
REXAM RELEASE, INC.—See Rexam PLC; *Int'l,* pg. 1107
REXCAN CIRCUITS INC.—See Hokuriku Electric Industry Co., Ltd.; *Int'l,* pg. 628
REXEL BUSINESS MACHINES LTD.—See Fortune Brands, Inc.; *U.S. Public,* pg. 675
REXEL ENGINEERING LTD.—See Fortune Brands, Inc.; *U.S. Public,* pg. 675
REXEL, INC.—See Rexel, S.A.; *Int'l,* pg. 1107
REXEL LIMITED—See Fortune Brands, Inc.; *U.S. Public,* pg. 675
REXEL, S.A.; *Int'l,* pg. 1107
REXENE CORPORATION—See Huntsman Corporation; *U.S. Private,* pg. 549
REXHALL INDUSTRIES, INC.; *U.S. Public,* pg. 1384
REXNORD CORPORATION—See BTR plc; *Int'l,* pg. 127
REXROTH AG—See Mannesmann A.G.; *Int'l,* pg. 839
REXROTH A/S—See Mannesmann A.G.; *Int'l,* pg. 839
REXROTH AUTOMACAO LTDA—See Mannesmann A.G.; *Int'l,* pg. 839
REXROTH (CHINA) LTD.—See Mannesmann A.G., *Int'l,* pg. 839
REXROTH DANUVIA HAJTASTECHNIKAI KFT.—See Mannesmann A.G.; *Int'l,* pg. 839
G.L. REXROTH A/S—See Mannesmann A.G.; *Int'l,* pg. 838
G.L. REXROTH GMBH—See Mannesmann A.G.; *Int'l,* pg. 838
G.L. REXROTH LTD.—See Mannesmann A.G.; *Int'l,* pg. 838
G.L. REXROTH PRIVATE LTD.—See Mannesmann A.G.; *Int'l,* pg. 838
G.L. REXROTH SA—See Mannesmann A.G.; *Int'l,* pg. 838
G.L. REXROTH (SCOTLAND) LTD.—See Mannesmann A.G.; *Int'l,* pg. 838
REXROTH HIDROPAR AS—See Mannesmann A.G.; *Int'l,* pg. 839
REXROTH HYDRAULICS LTD.—See Mannesmann A.G.; *Int'l,* pg. 839
REXROTH HYDRAULICS PTY. LTD.—See Mannesmann A.G.; *Int'l,* pg. 839
REXROTH HYDRAULIKANLAGEN UND SERVICE GMBH—See Mannesmann A.G.; *Int'l,* pg. 838
REXROTH KABUSHIKI KAISHA—See Mannesmann A.G.; *Int'l,* pg. 839
AB REXROTH MECMAN—See Mannesmann A.G.; *Int'l,* pg. 838
REXROTH MEXICO SA DE CV—See Mannesmann A.G.; *Int'l,* pg. 839
REXROTH OY—See Mannesmann A.G.; *Int'l,* pg. 839
REXROTH PNEUMATIC SA—See Mannesmann A.G.; *Int'l,* pg. 839
REXROTH PNEUMATICS LTD.—See Mannesmann A.G.; *Int'l,* pg. 839
REXROTH PNEUMATIK AG—See Mannesmann A.G.; *Int'l,* pg. 839
REXROTH SA—See Mannesmann A.G.; *Int'l,* pg. 839
REXROTH SDN BHD—See Mannesmann A.G.; *Int'l,* pg. 839
REXROTH SEKI CO. LTD.—See Mannesmann A.G.; *Int'l,* pg. 839
REXROTH SIGMA SA—See Mannesmann A.G.; *Int'l,* pg. 839
REXROTH SPA—See Mannesmann A.G.; *Int'l,* pg. 839
REXROTH SP.ZOO—See Mannesmann A.G.; *Int'l,* pg. 839
REXROTH SRO—See Mannesmann A.G.; *Int'l,* pg. 839
REXROTH VERTRIEBS UND SERVICE GMBH—See Mannesmann A.G.; *Int'l,* pg. 839
REXWORKS INC.; *U.S. Private,* pg. 926
REXX ENVIRONMENTAL CORP.; *U.S. Public,* pg. 1384
REYCO-CANADA, INC.—See Reyco Industries, Inc.; *U.S. Private,* pg. 926
REYCO INDUSTRIES, INC.; *U.S. Private,* pg. 926
JOHN REYER COMPANY; *U.S. Private,* pg. 926
REYNA CAPITAL CORP.—See The Reynolds and Reynolds Company; *U.S. Public,* pg. 1385
REYNEN, BARDIS & WINN; *U.S. Private,* pg. 926
REYNOLDS ALUMINIUM FRANCE—See Reynolds Metals Company; *U.S. Public,* pg. 1387
REYNOLDS ALUMINIUM HOLLAND B.V.—See Reynolds Metals Company; *U.S. Public,* pg. 1387
REYNOLDS ALUMINUM DEUTSCHLAND, INC.—See Reynolds Metals Company; *U.S. Public,* pg. 1387
REYNOLDS ALUMINUM OF CANADA—See Reynolds Metals Company; *U.S. Public,* pg. 1387
REYNOLDS ALUMINUM RECYCLING CO.—See Reynolds Metals Company; *U.S. Public,* pg. 1386
REYNOLDS ALUMINUM RECYCLING COMPANY—See Reynolds Metals Company; *U.S. Public,* pg. 1386
REYNOLDS ALUMINUM SUPPLY CO. DIV.—See Reynolds Metals Company; *U.S. Public,* pg. 1386
REYNOLDS ALUMINUM SUPPLY COMPANY—See Reynolds Metals Company; *U.S. Public,* pg. 1386
REYNOLDS AND REYNOLDS-BUSINESS FORMS DIVISION—See The Reynolds and Reynolds Company; *U.S. Public,* pg. 1385
REYNOLDS AND REYNOLDS (CANADA) LTD.—See The Reynolds and Reynolds Company; *U.S. Public,* pg. 1385
THE REYNOLDS AND REYNOLDS COMPANY; *U.S. Public,* pg. 1384
REYNOLDS EXTRUSION COMPANY—See Reynolds Metals Company; *U.S. Public,* pg. 1387
F.T. REYNOLDS COMPANY; *U.S. Private,* pg. 926
REYNOLDS INTERNATIONAL, INC.—See Reynolds Metals Company; *U.S. Public,* pg. 1387
REYNOLDS MACHINE TOOL CORP.; *U.S. Private,* pg. 926
REYNOLDS METALS COMPANY; *U.S. Public,* pg. 1385
REYNOLDS METALS COMPANY-WESTON—See Reynolds Metals Company; *U.S. Public,* pg. 1387
REYNOLDS PHILIPPINE CORPORATION—See Reynolds Metals Company; *U.S. Public,* pg. 1387
R.J. REYNOLDS FINANCE S.A.—See RJR Nabisco Holdings Corp.; *U.S. Public,* pg. 1355

R.J. REYNOLDS, INC.—See RJR Nabisco Holdings Corp.; *U.S. Public*, pg. 1355
R.J. REYNOLDS OVERSEAS FINANCE CO. N.V.—See RJR Nabisco Holdings Corp.; *U.S. Public*, pg. 1355
R.J. REYNOLDS (PORTUGAL) LIMITADA—See RJR Nabisco Holdings Corp.; *U.S. Public*, pg. 1355
R.J. REYNOLDS SCANDINAVIA AB—See RJR Nabisco Holdings Corp.; *U.S. Public*, pg. 1355
R.J. REYNOLDS TOBACCO B.V.—See RJR Nabisco Holdings Corp.; *U.S. Public*, pg. 1355
R.J. REYNOLDS TOBACCO CO. (ASIA PACIFIC) LIMITED—See RJR Nabisco Holdings Corp.; *U.S. Public*, pg. 1355
R.J. REYNOLDS TOBACCO CO. GMBH—See RJR Nabisco Holdings Corp.; *U.S. Public*, pg. 1355
R.J. REYNOLDS TOBACCO CO. (HONG KONG) LTD.—See RJR Nabisco Holdings Corp.; *U.S. Public*, pg. 1355
R.J. REYNOLDS TOBACCO COMPANY—See RJR Nabisco Holdings Corp.; *U.S. Public*, pg. 1355
R.J. REYNOLDS TOBACCO COMPANY P.R.—See RJR Nabisco Holdings Corp.; *U.S. Public*, pg. 1355
R.J. REYNOLDS TOBACCO COMPANY SDN. BHD.—See RJR Nabisco Holdings Corp.; *U.S. Public*, pg. 1355
R.J. REYNOLDS TOBACCO (ENGLAND) LIMITED—See RJR Nabisco Holdings Corp.; *U.S. Public*, pg. 1355
R.J. REYNOLDS TOBACCO FRANCE, S.A.—See RJR Nabisco Holdings Corp.; *U.S. Public*, pg. 1356
R.J. REYNOLDS TOBACCO (HELLAS) A.E.B.E.—See RJR Nabisco Holdings Corp.; *U.S. Public*, pg. 1356
R.J. REYNOLDS TOBACCO INTERNATIONAL (MEXICO) INC.—See RJR Nabisco Holdings Corp.; *U.S. Public*, pg. 1355
R.J. REYNOLDS TOBACCO INTERNATIONAL S.A.—See RJR Nabisco Holdings Corp.; *U.S. Public*, pg. 1356
R.J. REYNOLDS TOBACCO ESPANA, S.L.—See Tabacalera, S.A.; *Int'l*, pg. 1346
R.J. REYNOLDS TOBACCO INTL., INC.—See RJR Nabisco Holdings Corp.; *U.S. Public*, pg. 1355
REYNOLDS SYSTEMS (N.I.) LIMITED—See Reynolds Metals Company; *U.S. Public*, pg. 1387
REYNOLDS TIRE & RUBBER—See Ganin Tire Co., Inc.; *U.S. Private*, pg. 439
REYNOLDS WHEELS S.P.A.—See Reynolds Metals Company; *U.S. Public*, pg. 1387
REYNOLDS YILGARN GOLD OPERATIONS LIMITED—See Reynolds Metals Company; *U.S. Public*, pg. 1387
REZSOLUTIONS, INC.—See Reed Elsevier plc; *Int'l*, pg. 1098
RHEA & KAISER MARKETING COMMUNICATIONS; *U.S. Private*, pg. 927
RHEEM AIR CONDITIONING DIV.—See Paloma Industries Limited; *Int'l*, pg. 1022
RHEEM CANADA, LTD.—See Paloma Industries Limited; *Int'l*, pg. 1022
RHEEM MANUFACTURING CO.—See Paloma Industries Limited; *Int'l*, pg. 1022
RHEEM WATER HEATER—See Paloma Industries Limited; *Int'l*, pg. 1022
RHEEM WATER HEATER-DIVISION HEADQUARTERS—See Paloma Industries Limited; *Int'l*, pg. 1022
RHEIN CHEMIE CORPORATION—See Bayer AG; *Int'l*, pg. 173
RHEIN-CHEMIE RHEINAU GMBH—See Bayer AG; *Int'l*, pg. 174
RHEIN-PHARMA ARZNEIMITTELWERK GMBH—See Zeneca Group Plc; *Int'l*, pg. 1525
RHEIN-WESER TRANSPORT- UND HANDELSGESELLSCHAFT MBH—See Fried. Krupp AG; *Int'l*, pg. 514
RHEINBRAUN AG—See RWE AG; *Int'l*, pg. 1081
RHEINHYP EUROPE PLC—See Commerzbank AG; *Int'l*, pg. 310
RHEINHYP FINANCE, N.V.—See Commerzbank AG; *Int'l*, pg. 310
RHEINHYP RHEINISCHE HYPOTHEKENBANK—See Commerzbank AG; *Int'l*, pg. 310
RHEINISCHE BAUSTOFFWERKE GMBH & CO. KG—See Hochtief AG; *Int'l*, pg. 623
RHEINISCHE CHAMOTTE UND DINAS GMBH—See Viag AG; *Int'l*, pg. 1464
RHEINISCHE KALKSTEINWERKE GMBH—See Thyssen AG; *Int'l*, pg. 1388
RHEINISCHE OLEFINWERKE GMBH—See BASF AG; *Int'l*, pg. 105
RHEINISCHE OLEFINWERKE GMBH—See Royal Dutch/Shell Group of Companies; *Int'l*, pg. 1137
RHEINISCHE PRESSHEFE - UND SPIRTWERKE GMBH—See Royal Gist-Brocades N.V.; *Int'l*, pg. 1143
RHEINISCHE ZINKGESELLSCHAFT GMBH—See Metallgesellschaft AG; *Int'l*, pg. 861
RHEINMETALL AG—See Rheinmetall Group; *Int'l*, pg. 1108
RHEINMETALL ELEKTRONIK AG—See Rheinmetall Group; *Int'l*, pg. 1108
RHEINMETALL GROUP; *Int'l*, pg. 1108
RHEINMETALL INDUSTRIE AG—See Rheinmetall Group; *Int'l*, pg. 1108
RHEINTAL WERKSTOFF-TECHNIK AG—See Oerlikon-Buhrle Holding AG; *Int'l*, pg. 998
RHENANE DE RAFFINAGE—See Royal Dutch/Shell Group of Companies; *Int'l*, pg. 1136
RHENANIA A.G.—See Coats Viyella plc; *Int'l*, pg. 299
RHENANIA ALLGEMEINE SPEDITIONS-GESELLSCHAFT MIT BESCHRANKTER HAFTUNG—See The Peninsular and Oriental Steam Navigation Company; *Int'l*, pg. 1033
RHENANIA COMMERCIAL DELEGATION—See The Peninsular and Oriental Steam Navigation Company; *Int'l*, pg. 1034
RHENANIA COMPAGNIE EUROPEENNE DE TRANSPORTS ET D'AFFRETEMENT S.A.R.L.—See The Peninsular and Oriental Steam Navigation Company; *Int'l*, pg. 1034

RHENANIA COMPAGNIE EUROPEENNE DE TRANSPORTS ET D'AFFRETEMENT—See The Peninsular and Oriental Steam Navigation Company; *Int'l*, pg. 1034
RHENANIA CONTAINER GMBH—See The Peninsular and Oriental Steam Navigation Company; *Int'l*, pg. 1033
RHENANIA-FRIEDRICH KRAUSS SPEDITIONS GES. MBH—See The Peninsular and Oriental Steam Navigation Company; *Int'l*, pg. 1033
RHENANIA INTERNATIONAL TRANSPORT SERVICES PTE. LTD.—See The Peninsular and Oriental Steam Navigation Company; *Int'l*, pg. 1034
RHENANIA INTERNATIONAL TRANSPORT SERVICES (H.K.) LIMITED—See The Peninsular and Oriental Steam Navigation Company; *Int'l*, pg. 1034
RHENANIA MUNCHENER LAGERHAUS-UND TRANSPORT-GES.MBH—See The Peninsular and Oriental Steam Navigation Company; *Int'l*, pg. 1033
RHENANIA-SAAR SPEDITIONS-GMBH—See The Peninsular and Oriental Steam Navigation Company; *Int'l*, pg. 1033
RHENANIA SCHIFFAHRTS-UND SPEDITIONS-GESELLSCHAFT MBH—See The Peninsular and Oriental Steam Navigation Company; *Int'l*, pg. 1033
RHENANIA TRADING CORP.—See Henkel KGaA; *Int'l*, pg. 613
RHENANIA TRANSPORT B.V.—See The Peninsular and Oriental Steam Navigation Company; *Int'l*, pg. 1034
RHENANIA TRANSPORT GMBH—See The Peninsular and Oriental Steam Navigation Company; *Int'l*, pg. 1033
RHENANIA UMSCHLAG UND LAGEREI GMBH—See The Peninsular and Oriental Steam Navigation Company; *Int'l*, pg. 1033
RHENANIA WORMSER LAGERHAUS-UND SPEDITIONS-AG—See The Peninsular and Oriental Steam Navigation Company; *Int'l*, pg. 1034
RHENO UMWELTTECHNIK AG—See H.A. Schlatter AG; *Int'l*, pg. 1205
RHENUM METALL LTD.—See Georg Fischer Ltd.; *Int'l*, pg. 491
RHENUS LAGER UND UMSCHLAG AG—See Veba AG; *Int'l*, pg. 1459
RHENUS NORDIC B.V.—See Elkem ASA; *Int'l*, pg. 447
RHENUS TRANSPORT INTERNATIONAL CORP.—See Veba AG; *Int'l*, pg. 1460
RHENUS-WEICHELT AG—See Veba AG; *Int'l*, pg. 1459
RHEOMETRIC SCIENTIFIC; *U.S. Public*, pg. 1387
RHEOMETRIC SCIENTIFIC FRANCE SARL—See Rheometric Scientific; *U.S. Public*, pg. 1387
RHEOMETRIC SCIENTIFIC, INC.—See Rheometric Scientific; *U.S. Public*, pg. 1387
RHEOMETRICS SCIENTIFIC FAR EAST LTD.—See Rheometric Scientific; *U.S. Public*, pg. 1387
RHEOX—See Contran Corporation; *U.S. Private*, pg. 270
RHIN ET MOSELLE ASSURANCES COMPAGNIE D'ASSURANCES SUR LA VIE SOCIETE ANONYME—See Allianz Aktiengesellschaft; *Int'l*, pg. 61
THE RHO COMPANY—See Comforce Corporation; *U.S. Public*, pg. 409
RHO SIGMA, INC.—See Watsco, Inc.; *U.S. Public*, pg. 1746
RHOADES DEVELOPMENT; *U.S. Private*, pg. 927
RHODANID CHEMIE GMBH—See Akzo Nobel N.V.; *Int'l*, pg. 47
CIE. RHODANIENNE DE DEVELOPPEMENT—See Lafarge S.A.; *Int'l*, pg. 788
RHODE ISLAND HOSPITAL TRUST NATIONAL BANK—See BankBoston Corporation; *U.S. Public*, pg. 184
RHODES, INC.—See Heilig-Meyers Company; *U.S. Public*, pg. 605
RHODES INTERNATIONAL—See Rhodes International, Inc.; *U.S. Private*, pg. 927
RHODES INTERNATIONAL, INC.; *U.S. Private*, pg. 927
M.H. RHODES, INC.; *U.S. Private*, pg. 927
RHODIA A.G.—See Rhone-Poulenc S.A.; *Int'l*, pg. 1112
RHODIA-MERIEUX CHILE—See Rhone-Poulenc S.A.; *Int'l*, pg. 1112
RHODIA NORDESTE—See Rhone-Poulenc S.A.; *Int'l*, pg. 1109
RHODIA S.A.—See Rhone-Poulenc S.A.; *Int'l*, pg. 1112
RHODIACO INDUSTRIES QUIMICAS LTDA.—See Amoco Corporation; *U.S. Public*, pg. 103
RHONE-POULENC—See Rhone-Poulenc S.A.; *Int'l*, pg. 1109
RHONE-POULENC AFRIQUE CENTRALE—See Rhone-Poulenc S.A.; *Int'l*, pg. 1112
RHONE-POULENC AGRICHEM S.A. (PTY) LTD—See Rhone-Poulenc S.A.; *Int'l*, pg. 1112
RHONE-POULENC, AGROCHEMICAL DIVISION—See Rhone-Poulenc S.A.; *Int'l*, pg. 1109
RHONE-POULENC AGROCHIMIE—See Rhone-Poulenc S.A.; *Int'l*, pg. 1109
RHONE-POULENC ALCOLAC—See Rhone-Poulenc S.A.; *Int'l*, pg. 1110
RHONE-POULENC ARGENTINA S.A.—See Rhone-Poulenc S.A.; *Int'l*, pg. 1112
RHONE-POULENC (ASIA)—See Rhone-Poulenc S.A.; *Int'l*, pg. 1111
RHONE-POULENC AUSTRALIA HOLDINGS PTY. LTD.—See Rhone-Poulenc S.A.; *Int'l*, pg. 1112
RHONE-POULENC BANGLADESH LTD.—See Rhone-Poulenc S.A.; *Int'l*, pg. 1112
RHONE POULENC - BASIC CHEMICAL DIVISION—See Rhone-Poulenc S.A.; *Int'l*, pg. 1112
RHONE-POULENC BASIC CHEMICALS CO.—See Rhone-Poulenc S.A.; *Int'l*, pg. 1110
RHONE-POULENC BELGIQUE S.A.—See Rhone-Poulenc S.A.; *Int'l*, pg. 1112
RHONE-POULENC BUCAREST—See Rhone-Poulenc S.A.; *Int'l*, pg. 1112
RHONE-POULENC CANADA, LTD.—See Rhone-Poulenc S.A.; *Int'l*, pg. 1112
RHONE-POULENC, CHEMICAL DIVISION—See Rhone-Poulenc S.A.; *Int'l*, pg. 1109

RHONE-POULENC CHEMICALS (INDIA)—See Rhone-Poulenc S.A.; *Int'l*, pg. 1112
RHONE-POULENC CHEMICALS LTD.—See Rhone-Poulenc S.A.; *Int'l*, pg. 1109
RHONE-POULENC CHEMICALS SA (PTY) LTD.—See Rhone-Poulenc S.A.; *Int'l*, pg. 1112
RHONE-POULENC CHEMICALS THAILAND (LTD.)—See Rhone-Poulenc S.A.; *Int'l*, pg. 1112
RHONE-POULENC CHINE—See Rhone-Poulenc S.A.; *Int'l*, pg. 1112
RHONE-POULENC COLOMBIA LTDA.—See Rhone-Poulenc S.A.; *Int'l*, pg. 1112
RHONE-POULENC DANMARK A/S—See Rhone-Poulenc S.A.; *Int'l*, pg. 1112
RHONE-POULENC DE MEXICO S.A. DE C.V.—See Rhone-Poulenc S.A.; *Int'l*, pg. 1112
RHONE-POULENC DE VENEZUELA—See Rhone-Poulenc S.A.; *Int'l*, pg. 1113
RHONE-POULENC DELEGATION GENERALE—See Rhone-Poulenc S.A.; *Int'l*, pg. 1113
RHONE-POULENC FIBRES—See Rhone-Poulenc S.A.; *Int'l*, pg. 1109
RHONE-POULENC FILMS—See Rhone-Poulenc S.A.; *Int'l*, pg. 1109
RHONE-POULENC HELLAS—See Rhone-Poulenc S.A.; *Int'l*, pg. 1113
RHONE-POULENC INC.—See Rhone-Poulenc S.A.; *Int'l*, pg. 1112
RHONE POULENC INC.—See Rhone-Poulenc S.A.; *Int'l*, pg. 1112
RHONE-POULENC INC., FILMS DIVISION—See Rhone-Poulenc S.A.; *Int'l*, pg. 1110
RHONE-POULENC INC., FINE INORGANIC CHEMICAL DIVISION—See Rhone-Poulenc S.A.; *Int'l*, pg. 1110
RHONE-POULENC ITALIA SPA—See Rhone-Poulenc S.A.; *Int'l*, pg. 1113
RHONE-POULENC JAPAN, LTD.—See Rhone-Poulenc S.A.; *Int'l*, pg. 1113
RHONE-POULENC KENYA LTD.—See Rhone-Poulenc S.A.; *Int'l*, pg. 1113
RHONE-POULENC KIMYEVI MADDELER LTD.—See Rhone-Poulenc S.A.; *Int'l*, pg. 1113
RHONE-POULENC MALAYSIA SDN, BHD—See Rhone-Poulenc S.A.; *Int'l*, pg. 1113
RHONE-POULENC MAROC—See Rhone-Poulenc S.A.; *Int'l*, pg. 1113
RHONE-POULENC MULTI-TECHNIQUES—See Rhone-Poulenc S.A.; *Int'l*, pg. 1109
RHONE-POULENC NEDERLAND B.V.—See Rhone-Poulenc S.A.; *Int'l*, pg. 1113
RHONE-POULENC NEW ZEALAND LTD.—See Rhone-Poulenc S.A.; *Int'l*, pg. 1113
RHONE-POULENC OY—See Rhone-Poulenc S.A.; *Int'l*, pg. 1113
RHONE-POULENC PAKISTAN (PVT.) LTD.—See Rhone-Poulenc S.A.; *Int'l*, pg. 1113
RHONE-POULENC PERFORMANCE RESINS & COATINGS—See Rhone-Poulenc S.A.; *Int'l*, pg. 1110
RHONE-POULENC PHILIPPINES INC.—See Rhone-Poulenc S.A.; *Int'l*, pg. 1113
RHONE-POULENC POLSKA—See Rhone-Poulenc S.A.; *Int'l*, pg. 1113
RHONE-POULENC RORER—See Rhone-Poulenc S.A.; *Int'l*, pg. 1111
RHONE-POULENC RORER A.E.B.E.—See Rhone-Poulenc S.A.; *Int'l*, pg. 1113
RHONE-POULENC RORER CANADA INC.-ETHICAL DIVISION—See Rhone-Poulenc S.A.; *Int'l*, pg. 1113
RHONE-POULENC RORER GMBH—See Rhone-Poulenc S.A.; *Int'l*, pg. 1113
RHONE-POULENC RORER LTD.—See Rhone-Poulenc S.A.; *Int'l*, pg. 1110
RHONE-POULENC RORER PHILIPPINES INC.—See Rhone-Poulenc S.A.; *Int'l*, pg. 1111
RHONE-POULENC RORER - U.S.—See Rhone-Poulenc S.A.; *Int'l*, pg. 1110
RHONE-POULENC S.A.; *Int'l*, pg. 1108
RHONE-POULENC S.A.—See Rhone-Poulenc S.A.; *Int'l*, pg. 1113
RHONE-POULENC SANTE—See Rhone-Poulenc S.A.; *Int'l*, pg. 1109
RHONE-POULENC SANTE C.I.—See Rhone-Poulenc S.A.; *Int'l*, pg. 1114
RHONE-POULENC SENEGAL-SSPT—See Rhone-Poulenc S.A.; *Int'l*, pg. 1114
RHONE-POULENC SINGAPORE PTE. LTD.—See Rhone-Poulenc S.A.; *Int'l*, pg. 1114
RHONE-POULENC SPECIALTY CHEMICALS—See Rhone-Poulenc S.A.; *Int'l*, pg. 1110
RHONE-POULENC SPECIALTY CHEMICALS DIV.—See Rhone-Poulenc S.A.; *Int'l*, pg. 1110
RHONE-POULENC SPECIALTY CHEMICALS DIVISION—See Rhone-Poulenc S.A.; *Int'l*, pg. 1110
RHONE-POULENC, SPECIALTY PLASTICS DIVISION—See Rhone-Poulenc S.A.; *Int'l*, pg. 1110
RHONE-POULENC SVERIGE AB—See Rhone-Poulenc S.A.; *Int'l*, pg. 1114
RHONE-POULENC SYSTEMES—See Rhone-Poulenc S.A.; *Int'l*, pg. 1109
RHONE-POULENC TAIWAN LTD.—See Rhone-Poulenc S.A.; *Int'l*, pg. 1114
RHONE-POULENC-TEXTILE—See Rhone-Poulenc S.A.; *Int'l*, pg. 1109
RHONE-POULENC VIETNAM—See Rhone-Poulenc S.A.; *Int'l*, pg. 1114
RHONE-POULENC VISCOSUISSE—See Rhone-Poulenc S.A.; *Int'l*, pg. 1114
RHONE-POULENC WALSH—See Rhone-Poulenc S.A.; *Int'l*, pg. 1109
RHONE POULENC - WATER TREATMENT CHEMICALS—See Rhone-Poulenc S.A.; *Int'l*, pg. 1109
RHONE-SILITEC—See Rhone-Poulenc S.A.; *Int'l*, pg. 1109
RHOVYL—See Rhone-Poulenc S.A.; *Int'l*, pg. 1109

MASTER INDEX TO COMPANY NAMES RIGBY

Company Index

RHOWAG RHONEWERKE AG—See Alusuisse-Lonza Holding Ltd.; *Int'l*, pg. 67
RHYTHM MOTOR PARTS MFG. CO., LTD.—See Nissan Motor Co., Ltd.; *Int'l*, pg. 944
RIADA & CO.—See ABN-AMRO Holding N.V.; *Int'l*, pg. 12
RIAU TIN MINING—See Royal Dutch/Shell Group of Companies; *Int'l*, pg. 1139
RIBBON NARROW FABRIC COMPANY; *U.S. Private*, pg. 927
RIBER; *Int'l*, pg. 1114
RIBNY OVERSEAS INVESTMENTS HOLDING CORPORTATION—See Republic New York Corporation; *U.S. Public*, pg. 1380
RICARD—See Groupe Pernod Ricard; *Int'l*, pg. 566
RICART FORD INC.; *U.S. Private*, pg. 927
RICCARDO RICCIARDI EDITORE S.P.A.—See Arnoldo Mondadori Editore S.p.A.; *Int'l*, pg. 888
RICCOBON & COMPANY, INC.; *U.S. Private*, pg. 927
RICE & SUGAR DIV.—See Connell Co.; *U.S. Private*, pg. 264
RICE-CARDEN CORP.—See Kansas City Southern Industries, Inc.; *U.S. Public*, pg. 944
RICE CORPORATION OF HAITI, S.A.—See Erly Industries, Inc.; *U.S. Public*, pg. 591
RICE FOOD MARKETS INC.; *U.S. Private*, pg. 927
GEORGE RICE & SONS—See World Color Press, Inc.; *U.S. Public*, pg. 1779
RICE GROWERS ASSOCIATION OF CALIFORNIA; *U.S. Private*, pg. 927
RICE, HALL, JAMES & ASSOCIATES—See United Asset Management Corporation; *U.S. Public*, pg. 1674
RICE LAKE WEIGHING SYSTEMS; *U.S. Private*, pg. 927
RICE PARK PROPERTIES—See Green Tree Financial Corporation; *U.S. Public*, pg. 763
RICE, SANGALIS, TOOLE & WILSON; *U.S. Private*, pg. 928
RICELAND FOODS, INC.; *U.S. Private*, pg. 928
RICERA INC.—See Ishihara Sangyo Kaisha, Ltd.; *Int'l*, pg. 689
JOHN RICH & SONS—See Woolrich, Inc.; *U.S. Private*, pg. 1188
RICH'S/LAZARUS/GOLDSMITH'S—See Federated Department Stores, Inc.; *U.S. Public*, pg. 618
RICH-MIX PRODUCTS—See Ritchie Corporation; *U.S. Private*, pg. 933
RICH PRODUCTS CORP.; *U.S. Private*, pg. 928
RICHARD DE BOO PUBLISHERS—See The Thomson Corporation; *U.S. Public*, pg. 1601
RICHARD HIRSCHMANN ELECTRONICA NEDERLAND B.V.—See Rheinmetall Group; *Int'l*, pg. 1108
J. RICHARD INDUSTRIES, L.P.—See Code, Hennessy & Simmons, Inc.; *U.S. Private*, pg. 249
P.C. RICHARD & SON; *U.S. Private*, pg. 928
RICHARD SHOPS HOLDINGS LTD.—See Sears plc; *Int'l*, pg. 1217
RICHARD SIMON AND SONS LIMITED—See Harnischfeger Industries, Inc.; *U.S. Public*, pg. 789
RICHARDS, BROCK, MILLER, MITCHELL & ASSOC. INC.—See The Richards Group, Inc.; *U.S. Private*, pg. 929
RICHARDS BROTHERS OF MOUNTAIN GROVE; *U.S. Private*, pg. 928
RICHARDS/GRAVELLE—See The Richards Group, Inc.; *U.S. Private*, pg. 929
RICHARDS/GRAVELLE PUBLIC RELATIONS—See The Richards Group, Inc.; *U.S. Private*, pg. 929
THE RICHARDS GROUP, INC.; *U.S. Private*, pg. 929
RICHARDS INDUSTRIES, INC.; *U.S. Private*, pg. 929
RICHARDS INDUSTRIES METALWORKING GROUP—See Richards Industries, Inc.; *U.S. Private*, pg. 929
RICHARDS INDUSTRIES VALVE GROUP—See Richards Industries, Inc.; *U.S. Private*, pg. 929
RICHARDS MICRO-TOOL, INC.—See Masco Corporation; *U.S. Public*, pg. 1054
S.P. RICHARDS CO.—See Genuine Parts Company; *U.S. Public*, pg. 732
RICHARDS (SHIPBUILDERS) LTD.—See Tate & Lyle PLC; *Int'l*, pg. 1356
RICHARDSON ELECTRONICS CANADA LTD.—See Richardson Electronics, Ltd.; *U.S. Public*, pg. 1388
RICHARDSON ELECTRONICS GMBH—See Richardson Electronics, Ltd.; *U.S. Public*, pg. 1388
RICHARDSON ELECTRONICS IBERICA S.A.—See Richardson Electronics, Ltd.; *U.S. Public*, pg. 1388
RICHARDSON ELECTRONICS ITALY, S.R.L.—See Richardson Electronics, Ltd.; *U.S. Public*, pg. 1388
RICHARDSON ELECTRONICS JAPAN CO., LTD.—See Richardson Electronics, Ltd.; *U.S. Public*, pg. 1388
RICHARDSON ELECTRONICS, LTD.; *U.S. Public*, pg. 1387
RICHARDSON ELECTRONICS SECURITY SYSTEMS DIVISION—See Richardson Electronics, Ltd.; *U.S. Public*, pg. 1388
RICHARDSON FOODS CORPORATION—See The Quaker Oats Company; *U.S. Public*, pg. 1347
RICHARDSON FRANC SNC—See Richardson Electronics, Ltd.; *U.S. Public*, pg. 1388
RICHARDSON INDUSTRIES, INC.; *U.S. Private*, pg. 929
RICHARDSON LUMBER CO.—See Richardson Industries, Inc.; *U.S. Private*, pg. 929
RICHARDSON-VICKS AB—See The Procter & Gamble Company; *U.S. Public*, pg. 1333
OY RICHARDSON-VICKS A.B.—See The Procter & Gamble Company; *U.S. Public*, pg. 1332
RICHARDSON-VICKS DO BRASIL QUIMICA E FARMACEUTICA LTDA.—See The Procter & Gamble Company; *U.S. Public*, pg. 1333
RICHARDSON-VICKS, INC.—See The Procter & Gamble Company; *U.S. Public*, pg. 1331
P.T. RICHARDSON-VICKS INDONESIA—See The Procter & Gamble Company; *U.S. Public*, pg. 1333
RICHARDSON-VICKS LTD.—See The Procter & Gamble Company; *U.S. Public*, pg. 1333
RICHARDSON-VICKS (OVERSEAS) FINANCE N.V.—See The Procter & Gamble Company; *U.S. Public*, pg. 1333
RICHARDSON-VICKS S.A.—See The Procter & Gamble Company; *U.S. Public*, pg. 1333
RICHARDSON-VICKS S.A. DE C.V.—See The Procter & Gamble Company; *U.S. Public*, pg. 1333
RICHARDSON'S FURNITURE EMPORIUM—See Richardson Industries, Inc.; *U.S. Private*, pg. 929
RICHARDTON MFG. CO.—See United Dominion Industries, Ltd.; *U.S. Public*, pg. 1676
RICHCO INC.; *U.S. Private*, pg. 929
RICHCO STRUCTURES—See Richardson Industries, Inc.; *U.S. Private*, pg. 929
RICHDALE DAIRY STORES, INC.—See Scangas Brothers Holdings, Inc.; *U.S. Private*, pg. 969
RICHE MONDE (BANGKOK) LTD—See LVMH Moet Hennessy Louis Vuitton; *Int'l*, pg. 783
RICHE MONDE LTD.—See LVMH Moet Hennessy Louis Vuitton; *Int'l*, pg. 783
RICHE MONDE PTE LTD—See LVMH Moet Hennessy Louis Vuitton; *Int'l*, pg. 783
RICHE MONDE SDN BHD, INC.—See LVMH Moet Hennessy Louis Vuitton; *Int'l*, pg. 783
RICHELL CORPORATION—See Rubbermaid Incorporated; *U.S. Public*, pg. 1411
RICHEY ELECTRONICS, INC.; *U.S. Public*, pg. 1388
RICHFIELD HOSPITALITY SERVICES; *U.S. Private*, pg. 929
RICHFOOD DAIRY—See Richfood Holdings, Inc.; *U.S. Public*, pg. 1389
RICHFOOD HOLDINGS, INC.; *U.S. Public*, pg. 1388
RICHFOOD, INC.—See Richfood Holdings, Inc.; *U.S. Public*, pg. 1389
RICHFOOD PENNSYLVANIA—See Richfood Holdings, Inc.; *U.S. Public*, pg. 1389
RICHHEIMER FOOD—See Wechsler Coffee Corp.; *U.S. Private*, pg. 1158
THE RICHMAN BROTHERS CO.—See Woolworth Corporation; *U.S. Public*, pg. 1777
S.D. RICHMAN SONS, INC.; *U.S. Private*, pg. 929
RICHMOND AMERICAN HOMES, INC.—See M.D.C. Holdings, Inc.; *U.S. Public*, pg. 1025
RICHMOND AMERICAN HOMES OF CALIFORNIA, INC.—See M.D.C. Holdings, Inc.; *U.S. Public*, pg. 1025
RICHMOND AMERICAN HOMES OF NEVADA, INC.—See M.D.C. Holdings, Inc.; *U.S. Public*, pg. 1025
RICHMOND AMERICAN HOMES OF VIRGINIA, INC.—See M.D.C. Holdings, Inc.; *U.S. Public*, pg. 1025
RICHMOND CONVERTERS, INC.—See Pirelli S.p.A.; *Int'l*, pg. 1059
RICHMOND DENTAL—See Barnhardt Manufacturing Co.; *U.S. Private*, pg. 117
RICHMOND FOUNDRY AND MANUFACTURING CO.—See Josam Company; *U.S. Private*, pg. 601
RICHMOND HOMES, INC. I—See M.D.C. Holdings, Inc.; *U.S. Public*, pg. 1025
RICHMOND HOUSE—See NAI Technologies, Inc.; *U.S. Public*, pg. 1144
RICHMOND INTERNATIONAL FOREST PRODUCTS, INC.—See Forest City Enterprises, Inc.; *U.S. Public*, pg. 669
RICHMOND LEASING—See Richmond Motor Company; *U.S. Private*, pg. 929
RICHMOND MOB, INC.—See Magellan Health Services, Inc.; *U.S. Public*, pg. 1036
RICHMOND MOTOR COMPANY; *U.S. Private*, pg. 929
RICHMOND NEWSPAPERS, INC.—See Media General, Inc.; *U.S. Public*, pg. 1079
RICHMOND PAPERBOARD CORPORATION—See Caraustar Industries, Inc.; *U.S. Public*, pg. 304
RICHMOND SCREW ANCHOR COMPANY—See Ripplewood Holdings L.L.C.; *U.S. Private*, pg. 932
RICHMOND TECHNOLOGY INC.; *U.S. Private*, pg. 929
RICHMOND TERMINAL—See GATX Corporation; *U.S. Public*, pg. 692
RICHTER & RATNER CONTRACTING CORPORATION; *U.S. Private*, pg. 930
RICHTER-SCHROEDER COMPANY, INC.—See Marshall & Ilsley Corporation; *U.S. Public*, pg. 1051
RICHTEX CORPORATION—See Jannock Limited; *Int'l*, pg. 699
RICHTON INTERNATIONAL CORPORATION; *U.S. Public*, pg. 1389
RICKMERS-LINIE BELGIUM N.V.—See Hapag-Lloyd AG; *Int'l*, pg. 596
RICKMERS-LINIE GMBH—See Hapag-Lloyd AG; *Int'l*, pg. 596
JOHN RICKSON PROPERTIES—See I.C. System, Inc.; *U.S. Private*, pg. 553
RICKY CONTACT LENS INC.—See Novartis AG; *Int'l*, pg. 984
RICO GESELLSCHAFT FUR MICROELECTRONIK MBH—See Rothenberger Group GmbH; *Int'l*, pg. 1129
RICO MOTOR COMPANY; *U.S. Private*, pg. 930
RICOH CALIFORNIA RESEARCH CENTER—See Ricoh Company, Ltd.; *Int'l*, pg. 1114
RICOH COMPANY, LTD.; *Int'l*, pg. 1114
RICOH CORPORATION—See Ricoh Company, Ltd.; *Int'l*, pg. 1114
RICOH DEUTSCHLAND GMBH—See Ricoh Company, Ltd.; *Int'l*, pg. 1116
RICOH DEVELOPMENT OF CALIFORNIA, INC.—See Ricoh Company, Ltd.; *Int'l*, pg. 1114
RICOH ELECTRONICS, INC.—See Ricoh Company, Ltd.; *Int'l*, pg. 1114
RICOH ESPANA, S.A.—See Ricoh Company, Ltd.; *Int'l*, pg. 1116
RICOH EUROPE B.V.—See Ricoh Company, Ltd.; *Int'l*, pg. 1116
RICOH FRANCE S.A.—See Ricoh Company, Ltd.; *Int'l*, pg. 1116
RICOH ITALIA S.P.A.—See Ricoh Company, Ltd.; *Int'l*, pg. 1116
RICOH UK LTD.—See Ricoh Company, Ltd.; *Int'l*, pg. 1116
RICON PTY LTD—See Knurr AG; *Int'l*, pg. 740
RIDDELL SPORTS, INC.; *U.S. Public*, pg. 1389
RIDDELL SPORTS, INC.—See Riddell Sports, Inc.; *U.S. Public*, pg. 1389
RIDDLEBERGER BROS.. INC.; *U.S. Private*, pg. 930
RIDG-U-RAK, INC.; *U.S. Private*, pg. 930
RIDGE TOOL (AUSTRALIA) PTY., LTD.—See Emerson Electric Co.; *U.S. Public*, pg. 577
RIDGE TOOL CO.—See Emerson Electric Co.; *U.S. Public*, pg. 574
RIDGE TOOL EM. ELEC. S.R.L.—See Emerson Electric Co.; *U.S. Public*, pg. 577
RIDGE TOOL EUROPE, S.A.—See Emerson Electric Co.; *U.S. Public*, pg. 577
RIDGE TOOL GMBH—See Emerson Electric Co.; *U.S. Public*, pg. 577
RIDGE TOOL, N.V.—See Emerson Electric Co.; *U.S. Public*, pg. 577
RIDGE VINEYARDS INC.—See Otsuka Pharmaceutical Co., Ltd.; *Int'l*, pg. 1013
RIDGECREST CARE CENTER—See Horizon/CMS Healthcare Corporation; *U.S. Public*, pg. 838
RIDGEDALE CENTER—See The Rouse Company; *U.S. Public*, pg. 1407
RIDGEVIEW, INC.; *U.S. Private*, pg. 930
RIDGEWAY CLOCK COMPANY—See Pulaski Furniture Corporation; *U.S. Public*, pg. 1343
RIDGEWAY INSURANCE CO. LTD.—See Kimberly-Clark Corporation; *U.S. Public*, pg. 960
RIDGEWOOD PROPERTIES, INC.; *U.S. Public*, pg. 1389
RIDGID FERRAMENTAS E MAGUINAS, LTDA.—See Emerson Electric Co.; *U.S. Public*, pg. 577
RIDGID VAERKTOJ A/S—See Emerson Electric Co.; *U.S. Public*, pg. 577
RIDG'S FINER FOODS—See Philip Morris Companies Inc.; *U.S. Public*, pg. 1288
RIDGWAY'S, INC.—See Wilco Reprographic, Inc.; *U.S. Private*, pg. 1176
RIDLEY CANADA LIMITED; *Int'l*, pg. 1116
RIEDEL-SMITH ENVIRONMENTAL SERVICES—See Smith Environmental Technologies Corp.; *U.S. Public*, pg. 1478
RIEDEL WASTE DISPOSAL SYSTEMS—See Smith Environmental Technologies Corp.; *U.S. Public*, pg. 1478
RIEDEL-DE HAEN AG—See Hoechst Aktiengesellschaft; *Int'l*, pg. 625
RIEKE CORPORATION—See Masco Corporation; *U.S. Public*, pg. 1054
RIEMEIER LUMBER COMPANY, INC.; *U.S. Private*, pg. 930
RIETER ASIA (HONG KONG) LTD.—See Rieter Holdings; *Int'l*, pg. 1117
RIETER ASIA (TAIWAN) LTD.—See Rieter Holdings; *Int'l*, pg. 1117
RIETER AUTOMATIK GMBH—See Rieter Holdings; *Int'l*, pg. 1117
RIETER AUTOMOTIVE BELGIUM N.V.—See Rieter Holdings; *Int'l*, pg. 1117
RIETER AUTOMOTIVE CARPETS LTD.—See Rieter Holdings; *Int'l*, pg. 1117
RIETER AUTOMOTIVE FRANCE S.A.—See Rieter Holdings; *Int'l*, pg. 1117
RIETER AUTOMOTIVE GERMANY GMBH—See Rieter Holdings; *Int'l*, pg. 1117
RIETER AUTOMOTIVE GREAT BRITAIN LTD.—See Rieter Holdings; *Int'l*, pg. 1117
RIETER AUTOMOTIVE HEATSHIELDS—See Rieter Holdings; *Int'l*, pg. 1116
RIETER AUTOMOTIVE ITALIANA S.P.A.—See Rieter Holdings; *Int'l*, pg. 1117
RIETER AUTOMOTIVE MANAGEMENT AG—See Rieter Holdings; *Int'l*, pg. 1116
RIETER AUTOMOTIVE NEDERLAND B.V.—See Rieter Holdings; *Int'l*, pg. 1117
RIETER AUTOMOTIVE NORTH AMERICA INC—See Rieter Holdings; *Int'l*, pg. 1117
RIETER AUTOMOTIVE POLYMERS S.A.—See Rieter Holdings; *Int'l*, pg. 1117
RIETER AUTOMOTIVE SYSTEMS S.P.A.—See Rieter Holdings; *Int'l*, pg. 1117
RIETER COMPONENTES PARA VEICULOS LDA.—See Rieter Holdings; *Int'l*, pg. 1117
RIETER DEUTSCHLAND GMBH & CO. OHG—See Rieter Holdings; *Int'l*, pg. 1117
RIETER ELLTEX A.S.—See Rieter Holdings; *Int'l*, pg. 1117
RIETER HOLDINGS; *Int'l*, pg. 1116
RIETER IMMOBILIEN AG—See Rieter Holdings; *Int'l*, pg. 1116
RIETER INDIA PVT. LTD.—See Rieter Holdings; *Int'l*, pg. 1117
RIETER INGOLSTADT SPINNERELMASCHINENBAU AG—See Rieter Holdings; *Int'l*, pg. 1117
RIETER ITALIANA S.R.L.—See Rieter Holdings; *Int'l*, pg. 1117
RIETER JINGWEI TEXTILE MACHINERY LTD.—See Rieter Holdings; *Int'l*, pg. 1117
RIETER MANAGEMENT AG—See Rieter Holdings; *Int'l*, pg. 1116
RIETER-SCRAGG LTD.—See Rieter Holdings; *Int'l*, pg. 1117
RIETER VERTRIEBS GMBH—See Rieter Holdings; *Int'l*, pg. 1117
RIETH-RILEY CONSTRUCTION CO. INC.; *U.S. Private*, pg. 930
RIG-A-LITE CO.—See Aztec Manufacturing Co.; *U.S. Public*, pg. 159
RIGBY EDUCATION—See Reed Elsevier plc; *Int'l*, pg. 1094
RIGBY HEINEMANN—See Reed Elsevier plc; *Int'l*, pg. 1095
RIGBY-MARYLAND (STAINLESS) LTD.—See Handy & Harman; *U.S. Public*, pg. 780
RIGBY METAL COMPONENTS LIMITED—See Morgan Crucible Co. Plc; *Int'l*, pg. 891
PERCY L. RIGBY & SONS LIMITED—See Avonmore Waterford Group plc; *Int'l*, pg. 102

RIGEL DIRECTORY OF CORPORATE AFFILIATIONS
Company Index

RIGEL ENERGY CORPORATION; *Int'l*, pg. 1117
RIGEL OIL & GAS LTD.—See Rigel Energy Corporation; *Int'l*, pg. 1117
RIGEL PETROLEUM, INC.—See Rigel Energy Corporation; *Int'l*, pg. 1117
RIGEL PETROLEUM (NI) LIMITED—See Rigel Energy Corporation; *Int'l*, pg. 1117
RIGEL PETROLEUM UK LIMITED—See Rigel Energy Corporation; *Int'l*, pg. 1117
RIGESA, LTDA.—See Westvaco Corporation; *U.S. Public*, pg. 1762
J. RIGGINGS—See Edison Brothers Stores, Inc.; *U.S. Public*, pg. 564
RIGGS A P BANK LIMITED—See Riggs National Corporation; *U.S. Public*, pg. 1390
RIGGS BANK N.A.—See Riggs National Corporation; *U.S. Public*, pg. 1390
RIGGS INDUSTRIES, INC.; *U.S. Private*, pg. 930
RIGGS INTERNATIONAL BANKING CORPORATION—See Riggs National Corporation; *U.S. Public*, pg. 1390
RIGGS INVESTMENT MANAGEMENT CORPORATION—See Riggs National Corporation; *U.S. Public*, pg. 1390
J.A. RIGGS TRACTOR CO.; *U.S. Private*, pg. 930
THE RIGGS NATIONAL BANK OF MARYLAND—See Riggs National Corporation; *U.S. Public*, pg. 1390
THE RIGGS NATIONAL BANK OF VIRGINIA—See Riggs National Corporation; *U.S. Public*, pg. 1390
RIGGS NATIONAL CORPORATION; *U.S. Public*, pg. 1389
RIGHT COMPUTER SYSTEMS—See Marcam Solutions, Inc.; *U.S. Public*, pg. 1043
RIGHT IDEAS INC.; *U.S. Private*, pg. 930
RIGHT MANAGEMENT CONSULTANTS, INC.; *U.S. Public*, *pg. 1390*
THE RIGHT SHOE ONLY, INC.—See Brown Group, Inc.; *U.S. Public*, pg. 262
RIGHT START, INC.; *U.S. Private*, pg. 930
RIGIPS AUSTRIA GMBH—See BPB Industries PLC; *Int'l*, pg. 123
RIGIPS GMBH—See BPB Industries PLC; *Int'l*, pg. 123
RIGO/BLACK LEAF—See Ringer Corporation; *U.S. Public*, pg. 1390
RIGS AND SPECIAL WELL SERVICES COORDINATION (GESEP)—See Petrobras - Petroleo Brasileiro S.A.; *Int'l*, pg. 1042
RIHM MOTOR COMPANY; *U.S. Private*, pg. 931
RIKA-HERCULES INC.—See Hercules Incorporated; *U.S. Public*, pg. 811
RIKEN ELECTRIC WIRE CO., LTD.—See The Furukawa Electric Co., Ltd.; *Int'l*, pg. 530
RIKER PRODUCTS, INC.—See The Cypress Companies; *U.S. Private*, pg. 300
RIKSKUPONGER—See Accor S.A.; *Int'l*, pg. 21
RILEY ADVERTISING (ABERDEEN) LTD.—See Riley Advertising Limited; *Int'l*, pg. 1117
RILEY ADVERTISING (BIRMINGHAM) LTD.—See Riley Advertising Limited; *Int'l*, pg. 1117
RILEY ADVERTISING (BRISTOL) LTD.—See Riley Advertising Limited; *Int'l*, pg. 1117
RILEY ADVERTISING (EDINBURGH) LTD.—See Riley Advertising Limited; *Int'l*, pg. 1117
RILEY ADVERTISING (LEEDS) LTD.—See Riley Advertising Limited; *Int'l*, pg. 1117
RILEY ADVERTISING LIMITED; *Int'l*, pg. 1117
RILEY ADVERTISING (LONDON) LTD.—See Riley Advertising Limited; *Int'l*, pg. 1117
RILEY ADVERTISING (MANCHESTER) LTD.—See Riley Advertising Limited; *Int'l*, pg. 1117
RILEY ADVERTISING (NORWICH) LTD.—See Riley Advertising Limited; *Int'l*, pg. 1117
RILEY ADVERTISING (NOTTINGHAM) LTD.—See Riley Advertising Limited; *Int'l*, pg. 1117
RILEY ADVERTISING (SCOTLAND) LTD.—See Riley Advertising Limited; *Int'l*, pg. 1117
RILEY CONSOLIDATED, INC.—See Deutsche Babcock AG; *Int'l*, pg. 401
RILEY CREEK LUMBER COMPANY; *U.S. Private*, pg. 931
RILEY NATURAL GAS—See Petroleum Development Corporation; *U.S. Public*, pg. 1281
RILEY STOKER CORPORATION—See Deutsche Babcock AG; *Int'l*, pg. 401
RILLFUNG COMPANY LTD.—See Sinochem International Petroleum Co. Ltd.; *Int'l*, pg. 1255
RIMA AB—See Cardo AB; *Int'l*, pg. 270
RIMI SVENSKA AB—See ICA Handlarnas AB; *Int'l*, pg. 643
RIMIR, S.A. DE C.V.—See General Motors Corporation; *U.S. Public*, pg. 723
RIMOLDI DA AMAZONIA IND. E COM. LTDA.—See Rimoldi Necchi S.R.L.; *Int'l*, pg. 1118
RIMOLDI ESPANOLA S.A.—See Rimoldi Necchi S.R.L.; *Int'l*, pg. 1118
RIMOLDI FRANCE S.A.—See Rimoldi Necchi S.R.L.; *Int'l*, pg. 1118
RIMOLDI (GREAT BRITAIN) LTD.—See Rimoldi Necchi S.R.L.; *Int'l*, pg. 1118
RIMOLDI NECCHI S.R.L.; *Int'l*, pg. 1117
RIMOLDI OF AMERICA INC.—See Rimoldi Necchi S.R.L.; *Int'l*, pg. 1118
RIMPLEX, S.A.—See Hewlett-Packard Company; *U.S. Public*, pg. 823
RINBROS, S.A.—See Sara Lee Corporation; *U.S. Public*, pg. 1434
RINCON SECURITIES, INC.—See Dominion Resources, Inc.; *U.S. Public*, pg. 516
HAL RINEY & PARTNERS, INC.; *U.S. Private*, pg. 931
RING AROUND PRODUCTS, INC.—See Occidental Petroleum Corporation; *U.S. Public*, pg. 1210
RING KING VISIBLES, INC.—See Esselte AB; *Int'l*, pg. 460
RING SCREW WORKS; *U.S. Private*, pg. 931
RING TECHNOLOGIES, INC.; *U.S. Private*, pg. 931
RINGDEX—See Lafarge S.A.; *Int'l*, pg. 790
RINGER CORPORATION; *U.S. Public*, pg. 1390
RINGIER AG; *Int'l*, pg. 1118
RINGIER AMERICA, JONESBORO DIVISION—See World Color Press, Inc.; *U.S. Public*, pg. 1778
RINGIER AMERICA, NEW BERLIN DIVISION—See World Color Press, Inc.; *U.S. Public*, pg. 1778
RINGLING BROS., BARNUM & BAILEY COMBINED SHOWS, INC.—See Feld Productions; *U.S. Private*, pg. 400
RINI-REGO SUPERMARKETS, INC.—See Giant Eagle, Inc.; *U.S. Private*, pg. 451
RINKE PONTIAC-GMC CO.; *U.S. Private*, pg. 931
RINKER MATERIALS CORP.—See CSR Limited; *Int'l*, pg. 246
RINN CORPORATION—See Dentsply International Inc.; *U.S. Public*, pg. 499
RINNAI AMERICA CORP.—See Rinnai Corp.; *Int'l*, pg. 1118
RINNAI CORP.; *Int'l*, pg. 1118
RINTEKNO OY—See Technip; *Int'l*, pg. 1361
RINTEKNO OY - SWEDEN—See Technip; *Int'l*, pg. 1361
RIO ALGOM EXPLORATION, INC.—See Rio Algom Limited; *Int'l*, pg. 1118
RIO ALGOM LIMITED; *Int'l*, pg. 1118
RIO ALGOM MINING CORP.—See Rio Algom Limited; *Int'l*, *pg. 1118*
RIO BRAVO ELECTRICOS, S.A. DE C.V.—See General Motors Corporation; *U.S. Public*, pg. 724
RIO-GETRANKEMARKT AG—See Feldschlosschen Hurlimann Holding; *Int'l*, pg. 479
RIO GRANDE LAND CO.—See Union Pacific Corporation; *U.S. Public*, pg. 1668
RIO HOTEL & CASINO INC.; *U.S. Public*, pg. 1390
RIO LINDA CHEMICAL CO., INC.—See Albright & Wilson plc; *Int'l*, pg. 49
RIO MINERALES—See Wheaton River Minerals Ltd.; *Int'l*, pg. 1498
RIO NORTE ESTE CO.—See CalMat Co.; *U.S. Public*, pg. 296
RIO PROPERTIES, INC.—See Rio Hotel & Casino Inc.; *U.S. Public*, pg. 1390
RIO RANCHO—See AMREP Corporation; *U.S. Public*, pg. 105
RIO TINTO PLC; *Int'l*, pg. 1118
RIO TINTO SOUTH AFRICA LTD.—See Rio Tinto PLC; *Int'l*, pg. 1119
RIO TINTO ZIMBABWE LIMITED—See Rio Tinto PLC; *Int'l*, *pg. 1119*
RIO-TUBA NICKEL MINING CORP.—See Nissho Iwai Corporation; *Int'l*, pg. 949
RIOQUIMA S.A.—See Novartis AG; *Int'l*, pg. 984
RIPLEY GRAPHICS—See American Greetings Corporation; *U.S. Public*, pg. 78
RIPON FOODS, INC.; *U.S. Private*, pg. 931
RIPPLEWOOD HOLDINGS L.L.C.; *U.S. Private*, pg. 931
RIS PAPER COMPANY; *U.S. Private*, pg. 932
RISC MICROPROCESSOR DIVISION—See Motorola, Inc.; *U.S. Public*, pg. 1137
RISCOMP INDUSTRIES, INC.; *U.S. Private*, pg. 932
RISDON CORPORATION—See Crown Cork & Seal Company, Inc.; *U.S. Public*, pg. 463
RISER FOODS, INC.—See Giant Eagle, Inc.; *U.S. Private*, pg. 450
RISERIA TAVERNE S.A.—See Migros; *Int'l*, pg. 866
RISEXO S.A.—See Freudenberg & Company; *Int'l*, pg. 507
RISH EQUIPMENT COMPANY; *U.S. Private*, pg. 932
RISHAUG MASKIN A/S—See Atlet AB; *Int'l*, pg. 97
RISING PAPER PRODUCTS PRIVATE LIMITED—See Sime Darby Berhad; *Int'l*, pg. 1251
RISING SUN—See Royal Dutch/Shell Group of Companies; *Int'l*, pg. 1139
RISK & INSURANCE SERVICES—See Eureko B.V.; *Int'l*, pg. 464
RISK MANAGEMENT ASSOCIATES INC.—See Insurance Management Associates; *U.S. Private*, pg. 565
RISK MANAGEMENT SOLUTIONS, INC.—See H M K Enterprises, Inc.; *U.S. Private*, pg. 489
RISK MANAGEMENT TECHNOLOGIES—See Fair, Isaac and Company, Inc.; *U.S. Public*, pg. 610
RISK PLANNERS, INC.—See SuperValu, Inc.; *U.S. Public*, pg. 1541
RISK SCIENCE INTERNATIONAL INC.—See AON Corporation; *U.S. Public*, pg. 117
RISK SCIENCES GROUP, INC.—See Crawford & Company; *U.S. Public*, pg. 458
RISPARMIO ASSICURAZIONI S.P.A.—See Assicurazioni Generali S.p.A.; *Int'l*, pg. 90
RISPARMIO VITA ASSICURAZIONI S.P.A.—See Assicurazioni Generali S.p.A.; *Int'l*, pg. 90
RISSER OIL CORP.; *U.S. Private*, pg. 932
RISSLER & MCMURRY COMPANY; *U.S. Private*, pg. 933
RISTANCE CORPORATION—See Echlin Inc.; *U.S. Public*, pg. 561
RITA-ANN DISTRIBUTORS—See AmeriSource Health Corp.; *U.S. Public*, pg. 97
RITASA FREIGHT SERVICES PTY. LTD.—See A.I. Ocean; *Int'l*, pg. 14
RITCHIE CORPORATION; *U.S. Private*, pg. 933
RITCHIE INDUSTRIES, INC.; *U.S. Private*, pg. 933
RITCHIE PAVING, INC.—See Ritchie Corporation; *U.S. Private*, pg. 933
RITCHIE SAND COMPANY, INC.—See Ritchie Corporation; *U.S. Private*, pg. 933
RITE AID CORPORATION; *U.S. Public*, pg. 1390
RITE-HITE CORPORATION; *U.S. Private*, pg. 933
RITE-HITE DIVISION—See Rite-Hite Corporation; *U.S. Private*, pg. 933
RITE-HITE DOOR DIVISION—See Rite-Hite Corporation; *U.S. Private*, pg. 933
RITE-HITE FROMMELT DIVISION—See Rite-Hite Corporation; *U.S. Private*, pg. 933
RITEWAY TRUCKING—See Quexco Incorporated; *U.S. Private*, pg. 900
RITTENHOUSE CARE CENTER—See Genesis Health Ventures, Inc.; *U.S. Public*, pg. 729
RITTENHOUSE INC.; *U.S. Private*, pg. 933
RITTENHOUSE PAPER CO.—See Rittenhouse Inc.; *U.S. Private*, pg. 933
RITTER BROS., INC.; *U.S. Private*, pg. 933
RITTER SYSCO FOOD SERVICE, INC.—See Sysco Corporation; *U.S. Public*, pg. 1550
RITZ-C.INDUSTRIA E COMERCIO SA—See Emerson Electric Co.; *U.S. Public*, pg. 577
THE RITZ-CARLTON—See Four Seasons Hotels Inc.; *Int'l*, pg. 502
THE RITZ-CARLTON HOTEL COMPANY LLC—See W.B. Johnson Properties, LLC; *U.S. Private*, pg. 594
RITZ CORPORATION—See MacAndrews & Forbes Holdings Inc.; *U.S. Private*, pg. 690
THE RITZ HOTEL (LONDON) LIMITED—See Kvaerner a.s.a.; *Int'l*, pg. 773
RIUNIONE ADRIATICA DI SICURTA—See Allianz Aktiengesellschaft; *Int'l*, pg. 61
RIUNIONE ADRIATICA DI SICURTA S.P.A.—See Allianz Aktiengesellschaft; *Int'l*, pg. 61
RIVA HYDROART S.P.A.—See J.M. Voith, GmbH; *Int'l*, pg. 1473
THE RIVAL COMPANY; *U.S. Public*, pg. 1391
ALFONZO RIVAS CO., C.A.—See Corn Products International, Inc.; *U.S. Public*, pg. 447
RIVAS & HERRERA C./YOUNG & RUBICAM—See Young & Rubicam Inc.; *U.S. Private*, pg. 1200
RIVER BEND CORP.—See CalMat Co.; *U.S. Public*, pg. 296
RIVER CITY REFUSE REMOVAL, INC.—See Browning-Ferris Industries, Inc.; *U.S. Public*, pg. 264
RIVER CREST HOSPITAL—See Universal Health Services, Inc.; *U.S. Public*, pg. 1697
RIVER OAKS BANCORPORATION—See Compass Bancshares, Inc.; *U.S. Public*, pg. 419
RIVER OAKS HOSPITAL—See Universal Health Services, Inc.; *U.S. Public*, pg. 1697
RIVER OAKS TRUST COMPANY—See Compass Bancshares, Inc.; *U.S. Public*, pg. 419
RIVER PARISHES HOSPITAL—See Universal Health Services, Inc.; *U.S. Public*, pg. 1697
RIVER RAISIN CABLEVISION INC.—See Cable Michigan, Inc.; *U.S. Public*, pg. 287
RIVER RANCH - LOS ANGELES—See The Albert Fisher Group PLC; *Int'l*, pg. 491
RIVER RANCH - NORTHEAST—See The Albert Fisher Group PLC; *Int'l*, pg. 491
RIVER RANCH NORTHEAST, INC.; *U.S. Private*, pg. 934
RIVER RANCH - ORLANDO—See The Albert Fisher Group PLC; *Int'l*, pg. 491
RIVER RANCH - SALINAS—See The Albert Fisher Group PLC; *Int'l*, pg. 491
RIVER RANCH - SOUTHWEST—See The Albert Fisher Group PLC; *Int'l*, pg. 491
RIVER RANCH SOUTHWEST, INC.; *U.S. Private*, pg. 934
RIVER TERRACE HEALTHCARE—See Vencor, Inc.; *U.S. Public*, pg. 1714
RIVER VISTA DEVELOPMENT CO.—See CalMat Co.; *U.S. Public*, pg. 296
RIVER WOOD INTERNATIONAL CORP.—See Johns Manville Corporation; *U.S. Public*, pg. 927
RIVER WOOD PRODUTOS FLORESTAIS LTDA.—See Johns Manville Corporation; *U.S. Public*, pg. 927
RIVERCHASE HOMES—See Cavalier Homes, Inc.; *U.S. Public*, pg. 319
RIVERDALE CHEMICAL CO.; *U.S. Private*, pg. 934
RIVERLAND NEWS—See Landmark Communications, Inc.; *U.S. Private*, pg. 648
RIVERSIDE BAKERY—See Northern Foods plc; *Int'l*, pg. 968
RIVERSIDE BOOK & BIBLE HOUSE, INC.—See Jordan Industries, Inc.; *U.S. Private*, pg. 598
RIVERSIDE CEMENT CO.—See Ssangyong Business Group; *Int'l*, pg. 1293
RIVERSIDE GROUP, INC.; *U.S. Public*, pg. 1391
RIVERSIDE MANUFACTURING CO.; *U.S. Private*, pg. 934
RIVERSIDE MILLWORK COMPANY, INC.; *U.S. Private*, pg. 934
RIVERSIDE MINE—See The Broken Hill Proprietary Company Limited; *Int'l*, pg. 224
RIVERSIDE PRODUCTS DIV.—See Everett Smith Group, Ltd.; *U.S. Private*, pg. 1008
THE RIVERSIDE PUBLISHING CO.—See Houghton Mifflin Company; *U.S. Public*, pg. 841
RIVERSIDE RESTAURANT—See Boury Enterprises; *U.S. Private*, pg. 162
RIVERSIDE TERRACE (OTTAWA) LIMITED—See Sun Life Assurance Company of Canada; *Int'l*, pg. 1319
RIVERTON TRUCKERS, INC.—See Gohmann Asphalt & Construction Inc.; *U.S. Private*, pg. 459
RIVERWALK—See The Rouse Company; *U.S. Public*, pg. 1408
RIVERWOOD INTERNATIONAL CORPORATION; *U.S. Public*, pg. 1391
RIVERWOODS—See Wolters Kluwer N.V.; *Int'l*, pg. 1513
RIVES CARLBERG; *U.S. Private*, pg. 934
THE RIVET GROUP L.L.C.; *U.S. Private*, pg. 934
RIVIANA FOODS INC.; *U.S. Public*, pg. 1392
RIVIANA INTERNATIONAL INC.—See Riviana Foods Inc.; *U.S. Public*, pg. 1392
RIVIERA LAND CORP.—See Lennar Corporation; *U.S. Public*, pg. 989
RIVOLI, INC.—See Magellan Health Services, Inc.; *U.S. Public*, pg. 1036
RIVUS LEASOBJEKT GMBH—See Commerzbank AG; *Int'l*, *pg. 310*
RIXIE PAPER PRODUCTS—See Sonoco Products Company; *U.S. Public*, pg. 1486
RIYAD INSURANCE COMPANY LTD.—See Cigna Corp.; *U.S. Public*, pg. 363
RIZAL COMMERCIAL BANKING CORPORATION—See The Sanwa Bank Limited; *Int'l*, pg. 1190
RIZZOLI INTERNATIONAL PUBLICATIONS, INC.—See R.C.S. Editori S.p.A.; *Int'l*, pg. 1078
RMI INSURANCE CO.—See Michigan Physicians Mutual Liability Inc.; *U.S. Private*, pg. 741

MASTER INDEX TO COMPANY NAMES ROCHESTER

Company Index

RO-SEARCH, INC.—See Wellco Enterprises, Inc.; *U.S. Public*, pg. 1752
ROAD AND TRACK—See Lagardere Groupe; *Int'l*, pg. 795
ROAD CHAMPS, INC.—See JAKKS Pacific, Inc.; *U.S. Public*, pg. 923
ROAD MACHINERY & SUPPLIES CO.; *U.S. Private*, pg. 934
ROAD MACHINERY COMPANY; *U.S. Private*, pg. 934
ROAD SYSTEMS, INC—See CNF Transportation Inc.; *U.S. Public*, pg. 281
ROAD TRANSPORT, WAREHOUSING & DISTRIBUTION DIVISION—See SNCF; *Int'l*, pg. 1163
ROADMASTER/BRUNSWICK—See Brunswick Corporation; *U.S. Public*, pg. 265
ROADRUNNER DISTRIBUTION SYSTEMS, INC.—See Intrenet, Inc.; *U.S. Public*, pg. 911
ROADRUNNER TRUCKING, INC.—See Intrenet, Inc.; *U.S. Public*, pg. 911
ROADSTONE SURFACE DRESSING LIMITED—See RMC Group p.l.c.; *Int'l*, pg. 1081
ROADTEC, INC.—See Astec Industries, Inc.; *U.S. Public*, pg. 141
ROADWAY EXPRESS, INC.; *U.S. Public*, pg. 1392
ROAN RESOURCES LTD—See Montana Power Company; *U.S. Public*, pg. 1127
ROANE COUNTY NEWS—See Landmark Communications, Inc.; *U.S. Private*, pg. 648
ROANOKE ELECTRIC STEEL CORPORATION; *U.S. Public*, pg. 1392
ROANOKE GAS COMPANY; *U.S. Public*, pg. 1392
ROANOKE RAPIDS MILL, CHAMPION INTERNATIONAL CORPORATION—See Champion International Corp.; *U.S. Public*, pg. 334
THE ROANOKE TIMES—See Landmark Communications, Inc.; *U.S. Private*, pg. 649
ROANOKE VALLEY PLANT—See LG & E Energy Corp.; *U.S. Public*, pg. 970
ROARING CREEK DIVISION—See Consumers Water Company; *U.S. Public*, pg. 439
ROB—See GIB Group; *Int'l*, pg. 533
ROBALLO ENGINEERING CO. LTD.—See Fried. Krupp AG; *Int'l*, pg. 509
ROBALLO-FRANCE S.A.R.L.—See Fried. Krupp AG; *Int'l*, pg. 509
ROBARB INC.—See Laporte plc; *Int'l*, pg. 802
ROBATOR AB—See Scancem AB; *Int'l*, pg. 1199
ROBBE RADIATOREN B.V.—See Caradon Plc; *Int'l*, pg. 267
ROBBINS & MYERS, INC.; *U.S. Public*, pg. 1393
ROBBINS AUTO PARTS, INC.; *U.S. Private*, pg. 934
ROBBINS, INC.; *U.S. Private*, pg. 934
ROBBINS MANUFACTURING COMPANY; *U.S. Private*, pg. 935
ROBBY LEN FASHIONS—See Apparel America, Inc.; *U.S. Public*, pg. 121
ROBE RIVER IRON ASSOCIATES—See North Limited; *Int'l*, pg. 967
ROBEIN S.A.—See Veba AG; *Int'l*, pg. 1459
ROBERDS, INC.; *U.S. Public*, pg. 1393
ROBERN, INC.—See Kohler Company; *U.S. Private*, pg. 630
ROBERT BOSCH D.O.O.—See Robert Bosch GmbH; *Int'l*, pg. 205
ROBERT BOSCH LTD.—See Robert Bosch GmbH; *Int'l*, pg. 205
ROBERT BOSCH SA—See Robert Bosch GmbH; *Int'l*, pg. 206
ROBERT BOSCH SPOL. S.R.O.—See Robert Bosch GmbH; *Int'l*, pg. 206
ROBERT JAMES SALES INC.; *U.S. Private*, pg. 935
ROBERT MONDAVI WINERY, INC.; *U.S. Public*, pg. 1393
ROBERTET FLAVORS—See Robertet S.A.; *Int'l*, pg. 1119
ROBERTET FRAGRANCE, INC.—See Robertet S.A.; *Int'l*, pg. 1119
ROBERTET, INC.—See Robertet S.A.; *Int'l*, pg. 1119
ROBERTET S.A.; *Int'l*, pg. 1119
ROBERTS & SCHAEFER CO.—See Elgin National Industries, Inc.; *U.S. Private*, pg. 371
ROBERTS & SCHAEFER COMPANY-SALT LAKE CITY—See Elgin National Industries, Inc.; *U.S. Private*, pg. 371
CHAS ROBERTS AIR CONDITIONING, INC.; *U.S. Private*, pg. 935
E.V. ROBERTS & ASSOCIATES, INC.; *U.S. Private*, pg. 935
ROBERTS EXPRESS, INC.—See FDX Corporation; *U.S. Public*, pg. 604
F.L. ROBERTS & CO. INC.; *U.S. Private*, pg. 935
ROBERTS FOODS, INC.; *U.S. Private*, pg. 935
J.H. ROBERTS INDUSTRIES INC.; *U.S. Private*, pg. 935
JAMES E. ROBERTS-OBAYASHI CORPORATION—See Obayashi Corporation; *Int'l*, pg. 995
JOHN ROBERTS COMPANY; *U.S. Private*, pg. 935
ROBERTS LABORATORIES, INC.—See Roberts Pharmaceutical Corporation; *U.S. Public*, pg. 1393
ROBERTS PHARMACEUTICAL CORPORATION; *U.S. Public*, pg. 1393
ROBERTS PHARMACEUTICAL OF CANADA—See Roberts Pharmaceutical Corporation; *U.S. Public*, pg. 1394
STANLEY ROBERTS, INC.; *U.S. Private*, pg. 936
ROBERTS SYSTEMS, INC.—See Derlan Industries Limited; *Int'l*, pg. 395
ROBERTS TRADING CORP.—See Canandaigua Wine Company, Inc.; *U.S. Public*, pg. 300
C.E.T. ROBERTSHAW—See Siebe plc; *Int'l*, pg. 1244
ROBERTSHAW CONTROLS CANADA INC.—See GESTRA GmbH; *Int'l*, pg. 550
ROBERTSHAW CONTROLS (CANADA) INC.—See Siebe plc; *Int'l*, pg. 1244
ROBERTSHAW CONTROLS COMPANY—See Siebe plc; *Int'l*, pg. 1243
ROBERTSHAW CONTROLS NEW ZEALAND—See Siebe plc; *Int'l*, pg. 1244
ROBERTSHAW DO BRASIL S.A.—See Siebe plc; *Int'l*, pg. 1244
ROBERTSHAW PYROTEC S.A.—See Siebe plc; *Int'l*, pg. 1244
ROBERTSHAW TENNESSEE—See Siebe plc; *Int'l*, pg. 1243
ROBERTSON & BAXTER LIMITED—See The Highland Distilleries Company plc; *Int'l*, pg. 619
ROBERTSON-CECO CORPORATION; *U.S. Public*, pg. 1394
ROBERTSON FACTORIES, INC.; *U.S. Private*, pg. 936
ROBERTSON MARKETING INC.; *U.S. Private*, pg. 936
ROBERTSON TOOLING LTD.—See B. Elliott plc.; *Int'l*, pg. 449
ROBERTSON, WILSON, JAMIL (M) SDN BHD.—See Haw Par Brothers International Limited; *Int'l*, pg. 604
ROBERTSONS AUTO BODY—See Robertson's Auto Salvage; *U.S. Private*, pg. 936
ROBERTSON'S AUTO SALVAGE; *U.S. Private*, pg. 936
THE ROBERVAL & SAGUENAY RAILWAY CO.—See Alcan Aluminium Limited; *Int'l*, pg. 50
ROBESON APPLIANCE, INC.; *U.S. Public*, pg. 1394
ROBESON APPLIANCES—See Robeson Appliance, Inc.; *U.S. Public*, pg. 1394
ROBESON SALES CORPORATION—See Robeson Appliance, Inc.; *U.S. Public*, pg. 1394
ROBESONIAN—See Media General, Inc.; *U.S. Public*, pg. 1078
ROBICON—See High Voltage Engineering Corporation; *U.S. Private*, pg. 528
ROBIN AMERICA, INC.—See Fuji Heavy Industries, Ltd.; *Int'l*, pg. 523
ROBIN HOOD MULTIFOODS INC.—See International Multifoods Corporation; *U.S. Public*, pg. 901
ROBINHOOD HOMES, INC.; *U.S. Private*, pg. 936
A.H. ROBINS FARMACEUTICA, S.A.—See American Home Products Corporation; *U.S. Public*, pg. 82
A.H. ROBINS INTERNATIONAL, S.A.—See American Home Products Corporation; *U.S. Public*, pg. 82
A.H. ROBINS (IRAN) COMPANY—See American Home Products Corporation; *U.S. Public*, pg. 82
ROBIN'S FOODS INC.—See Saskatchewan Wheat Pool; *Int'l*, pg. 1195
ROBINSON-BLACKMORE EXPRESS—See Newfoundland Capital Corporation Limited; *Int'l*, pg. 924
ROBINSON BUS SERVICE; *U.S. Private*, pg. 936
ROBINSON BUS SERVICE—See Robinson Bus Service; *U.S. Private*, pg. 936
C.H. ROBINSON CO.; *U.S. Public*, pg. 1394
ROBINSON COACHES—See Robinson Bus Service; *U.S. Private*, pg. 936
ROBINSON CONE—See Dover Industries Limited; *Int'l*, pg. 417
ROBINSON HELICOPTER COMPANY; *U.S. Private*, pg. 936
THE ROBINSON-HUMPHREY COMPANY, INC.—See Travelers Group; *U.S. Public*, pg. 1633
J.B. ROBINSON JEWELERS, INC.—See Signet Group plc; *Int'l*, pg. 1248
ROBINSON LUMBER & EXPORT COMPANY; *U.S. Private*, *pg. 936*
ROBINSON LUMBER COMPANY—See Robinson Lumber & Export Company; *U.S. Private*, pg. 936
ROBINSON MILLING SYSTEMS B.V.—See Brunel Holdings Plc; *Int'l*, pg. 231
ROBINSON NUGENT—See Robinson Nugent, Inc.; *U.S. Public*, pg. 1395
ROBINSON NUGENT-DALLAS, INC.—See Robinson Nugent, Inc.; *U.S. Public*, pg. 1395
ROBINSON NUGENT (EUROPE) B.V.—See Robinson Nugent, Inc.; *U.S. Public*, pg. 1395
ROBINSON-NUGENT GMBH—See Robinson Nugent, Inc.; *U.S. Public*, pg. 1395
ROBINSON NUGENT, INC.; *U.S. Public*, pg. 1394
ROBINSON NUGENT, INC.—See Robinson Nugent, Inc.; *U.S. Public*, pg. 1394
ROBINSON NUGENT, INC.-INDIANA—See Robinson Nugent, Inc.; *U.S. Public*, pg. 1395
ROBINSON-NUGENT LTD.—See Robinson Nugent, Inc.; *U.S. Public*, pg. 1395
ROBINSON NUGENT (MALAYSIA) SDN. BHD.—See Robinson Nugent, Inc.; *U.S. Public*, pg. 1395
ROBINSON NUGENT NORDIC—See Robinson Nugent, Inc.; *U.S. Public*, pg. 1395
ROBINSON-NUGENT S.A.—See Robinson Nugent, Inc.; *U.S. Public*, pg. 1395
ROBINSON NUGENT, SARL—See Robinson Nugent, Inc.; *U.S. Public*, pg. 1395
ROBINSON NUGENT (SCOTLAND) LIMITED—See Robinson Nugent, Inc.; *U.S. Public*, pg. 1395
ROBINSON NUGENT, S.P.A—See Robinson Nugent, Inc.; *U.S. Public*, pg. 1395
ROBINSON-RANSBOTTOM POTTERY COMPANY—See Brittany Corporation; *U.S. Private*, pg. 169
SWAYNE ROBINSON & COMPANY; *U.S. Private*, pg. 936
ROBINSON TERMINAL WAREHOUSE CORP.—See The Washington Post Company; *U.S. Public*, pg. 1743
THOMAS ROBINSON GROUP PLC—See Brunel Holdings Plc; *Int'l*, pg. 231
ROBINSONS-MAY—See The May Department Stores Company; *U.S. Public*, pg. 1064
ROBOT POMPEN B.V.—See Trelleborg AB; *Int'l*, pg. 1421
ROBOT RESEARCH, INC.—See Sensormatic Electronics Corporation; *U.S. Public*, pg. 1457
ROBOTIC VISION SYSTEMS, INC.; *U.S. Public*, pg. 1395
ROBRASA-ROLAMENTOS ESPECIAS ROTHE ERDE LTDA.—See Fried. Krupp AG; *Int'l*, pg. 509
ROBSON COMMUNITIES; *U.S. Private*, pg. 937
ROBUR—See Swedbank; *Int'l*, pg. 1328
ROBUR BUIZENFABRIEK B.V.—See Fried. Krupp AG; *Int'l*, *pg. 513*
ROCCO BUILDING SUPPLIES INC.—See Rocco Inc.; *U.S. Private*, pg. 937
ROCCO FARM FOODS, INC.—See Rocco Inc.; *U.S. Private*, pg. 937
ROCCO FARMS—See Rocco Inc.; *U.S. Private*, pg. 937
ROCCO FEEDS, INC.—See Rocco Inc.; *U.S. Private*, pg. 937
ROCCO INC.; *U.S. Private*, pg. 937
ROCCO QUALITY FOODS—See Rocco Inc.; *U.S. Private*, pg. 937
ROCCO QUALITY FOODS, INC.—See Rocco Inc.; *U.S. Private*, pg. 937
ROCCO REALTY INC.—See Rocco Inc.; *U.S. Private*, pg. 937
P. ROCH, LTD.—See Brown & Sharpe Manufacturing Company; *U.S. Public*, pg. 260
ROCHE AB—See Roche Holding Ltd.; *Int'l*, pg. 1121
ROCHE AG—See Roche Holding Ltd.; *Int'l*, pg. 1120
ROCHE A/S—See Roche Holding Ltd.; *Int'l*, pg. 1121
ROCHE BIOMEDICAL LABORATORIES—See Roche Holding Ltd.; *Int'l*, pg. 1120
ROCHE CONSTRUCTORS, INC.; *U.S. Private*, pg. 937
ROCHE CONSUMER HEALTH (WORLDWIDE) S.A.—See Roche Holding Ltd.; *Int'l*, pg. 1121
ROCHE DIAGNOSTIC SYSTEMS, INC.—See Roche Holding Ltd.; *Int'l*, pg. 1120
ROCHE ECUADOR S.A.—See Roche Holding Ltd.; *Int'l*, pg. 1121
ROCHE FARMACEUTICA QUIMICA LIMITADA—See Roche Holding Ltd.; *Int'l*, pg. 1121
ROCHE FINANZ AG—See Roche Holding Ltd.; *Int'l*, pg. 1120
ROCHE (HELLAS) S.A.—See Roche Holding Ltd.; *Int'l*, pg. 1121
ROCHE HOLDING LTD.; *Int'l*, pg. 1119
P.T. ROCHE INDONESIA—See Roche Holding Ltd.; *Int'l*, pg. 1121
ROCHE INTERNATIONAL LTD.—See Roche Holding Ltd.; *Int'l*, pg. 1121
ROCHE KIMYASAL URUNLER VE TEKNIK CIHAZLAR LTD.—See Roche Holding Ltd.; *Int'l*, pg. 1121
ROCHE KOREA COMPANY LTD.—See Roche Holding Ltd.; *Int'l*, pg. 1121
ROCHE MACAULAY & PARTNERS—See The Lowe Group; *U.S. Private*, pg. 678
ROCHE MALAYSIA SDN. BHD.—See Roche Holding Ltd.; *Int'l*, pg. 1121
ROCHE MEXICANA DE FARMACOS, S.A. DE C.V.—See Roche Holding Ltd.; *Int'l*, pg. 1121
ROCHE MEXICANA DE FARMACOS, S.A. DE C.V. EL SALTO (JALISCO)—See Roche Holding Ltd.; *Int'l*, pg. 1121
ROCHE MOLECULAR SYSTEMS, INC.—See Roche Holding Ltd.; *Int'l*, pg. 1120
ROCHE MOSCOW LTD.—See Roche Holding Ltd.; *Int'l*, pg. 1121
ROCHE MUSTAHZARLARI SANAYI LIMITED SIRKETI—See Roche Holding Ltd.; *Int'l*, pg. 1121
ROCHE NEDERLAND B.V.—See Roche Holding Ltd.; *Int'l*, pg. 1121
ROCHE NICHOLAS B.V.—See Roche Holding Ltd.; *Int'l*, pg. 1121
ROCHE NICHOLAS (DEUTSCHLAND) GMBH—See Roche Holding Ltd.; *Int'l*, pg. 1121
ROCHE NICHOLAS HEALTH PRODUCTS S.A.—See Roche Holding Ltd.; *Int'l*, pg. 1121
S.A. ROCHE NICHOLAS N.V.—See Roche Holding Ltd.; *Int'l*, pg. 1121
ROCHE (NIGERIA) LTD.—See Roche Holding Ltd.; *Int'l*, pg. 1121
ROCHE NORGE A/S—See Roche Holding Ltd.; *Int'l*, pg. 1121
ROCHE OY—See Roche Holding Ltd.; *Int'l*, pg. 1121
ROCHE PAKISTAN LTD.—See Roche Holding Ltd.; *Int'l*, pg. 1121
ROCHE PHARMA (SWITZERLAND) LTD.—See Roche Holding Ltd.; *Int'l*, pg. 1120
ROCHE PHARMACEUTICAL (IRELAND) LIMITED—See Roche Holding Ltd.; *Int'l*, pg. 1121
ROCHE PHARMACEUTICALS & CHEMICALS LTD.—See Roche Holding Ltd.; *Int'l*, pg. 1121
ROCHE (PHILIPPINES) INC.—See Roche Holding Ltd.; *Int'l*, pg. 1121
ROCHE POLSKA SP. Z O. O.—See Roche Holding Ltd.; *Int'l*, pg. 1121
ROCHE PRODUCTS INC.—See Roche Holding Ltd.; *Int'l*, pg. 1121
ROCHE PRODUCTS LTD.—See Roche Holding Ltd.; *Int'l*, pg. 1121
ROCHE PRODUCTS LTD. KOREA—See Roche Holding Ltd.; *Int'l*, pg. 1122
ROCHE PRODUCTS (NEW ZEALAND) LTD.—See Roche Holding Ltd.; *Int'l*, pg. 1122
ROCHE PRODUCTS (PROPRIETARY) LIMITED—See Roche Holding Ltd.; *Int'l*, pg. 1122
ROCHE PRODUCTS (PTY.) LTD.—See Roche Holding Ltd.; *Int'l*, pg. 1122
ROCHE PROFESSIONAL SERVICE CENTERS, INC.—See Roche Holding Ltd.; *Int'l*, pg. 1120
ROCHE REGISTRATION LIMITED—See Roche Holding Ltd.; *Int'l*, pg. 1122
N.V. ROCHE S.A.—See Roche Holding Ltd.; *Int'l*, pg. 1122
ROCHE SINGAPORE PTE. LTD.—See Roche Holding Ltd.; *Int'l*, pg. 1122
ROCHE SLOVAKIA SPOL.S.R.O.—See Roche Holding Ltd.; *Int'l*, pg. 1122
ROCHE S.P.A.—See Roche Holding Ltd.; *Int'l*, pg. 1122
ROCHE S.R.O.—See Roche Holding Ltd.; *Int'l*, pg. 1122
ROCHE THAILAND LTD.—See Roche Holding Ltd.; *Int'l*, pg. 1122
ROCHEFORT PLANT—See Fort James Corporation; *U.S. Public*, pg. 673
ROCHESTER & PITTSBURGH COAL COMPANY; *U.S. Public*, pg. 1395

Company Index

ROCHESTER & PITTSBURGH COAL COMPANY (CANADA) LTD.—See Rochester & Pittsburgh Coal Company; *U.S. Public*, pg. 1395
ROCHESTER COMMUNITY SAVINGS BANK—See Charter One Financial, Inc.; *U.S. Public*, pg. 336
ROCHESTER FUND MUNICIPALS; *U.S. Private*, pg. 937
ROCHESTER GAS AND ELECTRIC CORPORATION; *U.S. Public*, pg. 1395
ROCHESTER GAUGES INC. OF TEXAS—See Gas Equipment Company, Inc.; *U.S. Private*, pg. 440
ROCHESTER GEAR, INC.—See Newcor, Inc.; *U.S. Public*, pg. 1176
ROCHESTER MIDLAND CORPORATION; *U.S. Private*, pg. 937
ROCHESTER-MIDLAND ICL—See Rochester Midland Corporation; *U.S. Private*, pg. 937
ROCHESTER TELEPHONE CORP.—See Frontier Corporation; *U.S. Public*, pg. 684
ROCK BOTTOM RESTAURANTS; *U.S. Public*, pg. 1396
ROCK FALLS TECHNOLOGY—See Anixter International; *U.S. Public*, pg. 115
ROCK HILL HERALD—See McClatchy Newspapers Inc.; *U.S. Public*, pg. 1066
ROCK HILL MATERIALS COMPANY; *U.S. Private*, pg. 938
ROCK OF AGES ASIA CORP.—See Rock of Ages Corporation; *U.S. Public*, pg. 1396
ROCK OF AGES CANADA, INC.—See Rock of Ages Corporation; *U.S. Public*, pg. 1396
ROCK OF AGES CORPORATION; *U.S. Public*, pg. 1396
ROCK OF AGES MEMORIALS LLC—See Rock of Ages Corporation; *U.S. Public*, pg. 1396
ROCK-TENN CO.—See Rock-Tenn Company; *U.S. Public*, pg. 1397
ROCK-TENN COMPANY; *U.S. Public*, pg. 1396
ROCK-TENN CONVERTING CO.—See Rock-Tenn Company; *U.S. Public*, pg. 1397
ROCKBESTOS-SUPRENANT CABLE CORP.; *U.S. Private*, pg. 938
ROCKBOTTOM STORES, INC.; *U.S. Private*, pg. 938
THE ROCKDALE CITIZEN PUBLISHING COMPANY—See Gray Communications Systems, Inc.; *U.S. Public*, pg. 759
ROCKEFELLER CENTER DEVELOPMENT CORPORATION—See Mitsubishi Estate Co., Ltd.; *Int'l*, pg. 873
ROCKEFELLER CENTER MANAGEMENT CORPORATION—See Mitsubishi Estate Co., Ltd.; *Int'l*, pg. 873
ROCKEFELLER GROUP, INC.—See Mitsubishi Estate Co., Ltd.; *Int'l*, pg. 873
ROCKEFELLER GROUP TELECOMMUNICATIONS SERVICES, INC.—See Mitsubishi Estate Co., Ltd.; *Int'l*, pg. 873
ROCKET SUPPLY CORP.—See Hicks Oil-Hicks Gas, Inc.; *U.S. Private*, pg. 527
ROCKETT, BURKHEAD, LEWIS & WINSLOW; *U.S. Private*, pg. 938
ROCKFORD ACROMATIC PRODUCT CO.; *U.S. Private*, pg. 938
ROCKFORD INTERNATIONAL GROUP—See Rockford Products Corp.; *U.S. Private*, pg. 938
ROCKFORD MERCANTILE AGENCY—See Amcore Financial, Inc.; *U.S. Public*, pg. 65
ROCKFORD NEWSPAPERS, INC.—See Gannett Company, Inc.; *U.S. Public*, pg. 701
ROCKFORD PRODUCTS CORP.; *U.S. Private*, pg. 938
ROCKING HORSE DEVELOPMENT CORPORATION—See Nobel Education Dynamics, Inc.; *U.S. Public*, pg. 1186
ROCKING HORSE ONE—See Nobel Education Dynamics, Inc.; *U.S. Public*, pg. 1186
ROCKINGHAM-HAMLET CABLEVISION, INC.—See Time Warner Inc.; *U.S. Public*, pg. 1610
ROCKINGHAM-HAMLET, INC.—See Time Warner Inc.; *U.S. Public*, pg. 1610
ROCKINGHAM NURSING CENTER—See Vencor, Inc.; *U.S. Public*, pg. 1714
ROCKLAND ELECTRIC CO.—See Orange and Rockland Utilities, Inc.; *U.S. Public*, pg. 1229
ROCKLAND PIPELINE COMPANY—See Groupe Bruxelles Lambert S.A.; *Int'l*, pg. 562
ROCKLAND REACT-RITE, INC.—See Interface Inc.; *U.S. Public*, pg. 889
ROCKNEL FASTENER, INC.—See Textron Inc.; *U.S. Public*, pg. 1590
THE ROCKPORT COMPANY—See Reebok International Ltd.; *U.S. Public*, pg. 1370
ROCKTON ASSOCIATES, INCORPORATED—See Stone & Webster, Incorporated; *U.S. Public*, pg. 1519
ROCKTON TECHNICAL SERVICES CORPORATION—See Stone & Webster, Incorporated; *U.S. Public*, pg. 1519
ROCKVILLE CRUSHED STONE, INC.—See Bardon Group PLC; *Int'l*, pg. 166
ROCKVILLE FABRICS CORPORATION; *U.S. Private*, pg. 938
ROCKVILLE NATIONAL BANK—See Old National Bancorp; *U.S. Public*, pg. 1217
ROCKWARE GLASS LTD.—See BTR plc; *Int'l*, pg. 124
ROCKWARE GLASS LTD.-BAGLEYS FACTORY—See BTR plc; *Int'l*, pg. 124
ROCKWARE GLASS LTD.-HEADLANDS FACTORY—See BTR plc; *Int'l*, pg. 124
ROCKWARE GLASS LTD.-PORTLAND FACTORY—See BTR plc; *Int'l*, pg. 124
ROCKWARE GLASS LTD.-WHEATLEY FACTORY—See BTR plc; *Int'l*, pg. 124
ROCKWARE GLASS LTD.-WIGAN FACTORY—See BTR plc; *Int'l*, pg. 124
ROCKWARE GLASS LTD.-WORKSOP FACTORY—See BTR plc; *Int'l*, pg. 124
ROCKWARE GLASS RECLAMATION CENTRE—See BTR plc; *Int'l*, pg. 124
ROCKWARE GLASS TECHNICAL CENTRE—See BTR plc; *Int'l*, pg. 124
ROCKWARE GROUP PLC—See BTR plc; *Int'l*, pg. 124

ROCKWARE PLASTICS LTD.—See BTR plc; *Int'l*, pg. 124
ROCKWATER CO.—See Halliburton Company; *U.S. Public*, pg. 776
ROCKWELL ARGENTINA S.A.—See Rockwell International Corporation; *U.S. Public*, pg. 1399
ROCKWELL AUSTRALIA LIMITED—See Rockwell International Corporation; *U.S. Public*, pg. 1399
ROCKWELL AUTOMACAO, LDA.—See Rockwell International Corporation; *U.S. Public*, pg. 1399
ROCKWELL AUTOMATION—See Rockwell International Corporation; *U.S. Public*, pg. 1397
ROCKWELL AUTOMATION AB—See Rockwell International Corporation; *U.S. Public*, pg. 1399
ROCKWELL AUTOMATION A/S—See Rockwell International Corporation; *U.S. Public*, pg. 1399
ROCKWELL AUTOMATION ASIA PACIFIC LTD.—See Rockwell International Corporation; *U.S. Public*, pg. 1399
ROCKWELL AUTOMATION B.V.—See Rockwell International Corporation; *U.S. Public*, pg. 1399
ROCKWELL AUTOMATION DE MEXICO S.A. DE C.V.—See Rockwell International Corporation; *U.S. Public*, pg. 1399
ROCKWELL AUTOMATION DE VENEZUELA, C.A.—See Rockwell International Corporation; *U.S. Public*, pg. 1399
ROCKWELL AUTOMATION DODGE-CHILE—See Rockwell International Corporation; *U.S. Public*, pg. 1399
ROCKWELL AUTOMATION DRIVE SYSTEMS—See Rockwell International Corporation; *U.S. Public*, pg. 1397
ROCKWELL AUTOMATION EUROPEAN HEADQUARTERS S.A./N.V.—See Rockwell International Corporation; *U.S. Public*, pg. 1399
ROCKWELL AUTOMATION GESMBH—See Rockwell International Corporation; *U.S. Public*, pg. 1399
ROCKWELL AUTOMATION (HONG KONG) LIMITED—See Rockwell International Corporation; *U.S. Public*, pg. 1399
ROCKWELL AUTOMATION LIMITED—See Rockwell International Corporation; *U.S. Public*, pg. 1399
ROCKWELL AUTOMATION LIMITED ELECTRO-CRAFT—See Rockwell International Corporation; *U.S. Public*, pg. 1400
ROCKWELL AUTOMATION LTD. U.K. DRIVE SYSTEMS—See Rockwell International Corporation; *U.S. Public*, pg. 1400
ROCKWELL AUTOMATION (MALAYSIA) SDN. BHD.—See Rockwell International Corporation; *U.S. Public*, pg. 1400
ROCKWELL AUTOMATION (N.Z.) LTD.—See Rockwell International Corporation; *U.S. Public*, pg. 1400
ROCKWELL AUTOMATION (PROPRIETARY) LIMITED—See Rockwell International Corporation; *U.S. Public*, pg. 1400
ROCKWELL AUTOMATION S.A.—See Rockwell International Corporation; *U.S. Public*, pg. 1400
ROCKWELL AUTOMATION SOUTHEAST ASIA PTE. LTD.—See Rockwell International Corporation; *U.S. Public*, pg. 1400
ROCKWELL AUTOMATION S.R.O.—See Rockwell International Corporation; *U.S. Public*, pg. 1400
ROCKWELL AUTOMATION TAIWAN—See Rockwell International Corporation; *U.S. Public*, pg. 1400
ROCKWELL AUTOMATION TECATE S.A. DE C.V.—See Rockwell International Corporation; *U.S. Public*, pg. 1398
ROCKWELL AUTOMATION THAI CO., LTD.—See Rockwell International Corporation; *U.S. Public*, pg. 1400
ROCKWELL AUTOMOTIVE (U.K.) LTD.—See Rockwell International Corporation; *U.S. Public*, pg. 1400
ROCKWELL CLUTCH COMPANY—See Meritor Automotive, Inc.; *U.S. Public*, pg. 1096
ROCKWELL-COLLINS FRANCE, S.A.—See Rockwell International Corporation; *U.S. Public*, pg. 1400
ROCKWELL-COLLINS INTERNATIONAL, INC.—See Rockwell International Corporation; *U.S. Public*, pg. 1400
ROCKWELL-COLLINS (U.K.) LTD.—See Rockwell International Corporation; *U.S. Public*, pg. 1400
ROCKWELL CVC S.P.A.—See Rockwell International Corporation; *U.S. Public*, pg. 1400
ROCKWELL DO BRASIL LTDA.—See Rockwell International Corporation; *U.S. Public*, pg. 1400
ROCKWELL FRANCE—See Rockwell International Corporation; *U.S. Public*, pg. 1400
ROCKWELL FUMAGALLI, S.A. DE C.V. LIGHT VEHICLE SYSTEMS—See Rockwell International Corporation; *U.S. Public*, pg. 1400
ROCKWELL HEAVY VEHICLE SUSPENSION SYSTEMS COMPANY, INC.—See Meritor Automotive, Inc.; *U.S. Public*, pg. 1096
ROCKWELL INTERNATIONAL (ASIA PACIFIC) LIMITED—See Rockwell International Corporation; *U.S. Public*, pg. 1400
ROCKWELL INTERNATIONAL CORPORATION; *U.S. Public*, pg. 1397
ROCKWELL INTERNATIONAL GMBH—See Rockwell International Corporation; *U.S. Public*, pg. 1401
ROCKWELL INTERNATIONAL JAPAN CO., LTD.—See Rockwell International Corporation; *U.S. Public*, pg. 1401
ROCKWELL INTERNATIONAL KOREA LTD.—See Rockwell International Corporation; *U.S. Public*, pg. 1401
ROCKWELL INTERNATIONAL LIMITED—See Rockwell International Corporation; *U.S. Public*, pg. 1401
ROCKWELL INTERNATIONAL MANUFACTURING PTE. LTD.—See Rockwell International Corporation; *U.S. Public*, pg. 1401
ROCKWELL INTERNATIONAL OF CANADA—See Rockwell International Corporation; *U.S. Public*, pg. 1401

ROCKWELL INTERNATIONAL OF CANADA LTD.—See Rockwell International Corporation; *U.S. Public*, pg. 1401
ROCKWELL INTERNATIONAL OF CANADA SWITCHING SYSTEMS—See Rockwell International Corporation; *U.S. Public*, pg. 1401
ROCKWELL INTERNATIONAL OVERSEAS CORPORATION—See Rockwell International Corporation; *U.S. Public*, pg. 1401
ROCKWELL INTERNATIONAL S.A.—See Rockwell International Corporation; *U.S. Public*, pg. 1401
ROCKWELL INTERNATIONAL SUSPENSION SYSTEMS COMPANY—See Rockwell International Corporation; *U.S. Public*, pg. 1401
ROCKWELL INTERNATIONAL TAIWAN CO., LTD.—See Rockwell International Corporation; *U.S. Public*, pg. 1401
ROCKWELL INTERNATIONAL TAIWAN COMPANY, LTD.—See Rockwell International Corporation; *U.S. Public*, pg. 1401
ROCKWELL INTERNATIONALE DU CANADA AVIONICS & COMMUNICATIONS—See Rockwell International Corporation; *U.S. Public*, pg. 1400
ROCKWELL LIGHT VEHICLE SYSTEMS (AUSTRALIA) PTY. LIMITED—See Rockwell International Corporation; *U.S. Public*, pg. 1401
ROCKWELL LIGHT VEHICLE SYSTEMS AVELLINO S.R.L.—See Rockwell International Corporation; *U.S. Public*, pg. 1401
ROCKWELL LIGHT VEHICLE SYSTEMS-COMO S.P.A.—See Rockwell International Corporation; *U.S. Public*, pg. 1401
ROCKWELL LIGHT VEHICLE SYSTEMS-ESPANA, S.A.—See Rockwell International Corporation; *U.S. Public*, pg. 1401
ROCKWELL LIGHT VEHICLE SYSTEMS-FRANCE—See Rockwell International Corporation; *U.S. Public*, pg. 1401
ROCKWELL LIGHT VEHICLE SYSTEMS (U.K.) LTD. - ROOF SYSTEMS—See Rockwell International Corporation; *U.S. Public*, pg. 1401
ROCKWELL LVS - LIBEREC A.S.—See Rockwell International Corporation; *U.S. Public*, pg. 1401
ROCKWELL LVS ZHENJIANG CO., LTD. LIGHT VEHICLE SYSTEMS—See Rockwell International Corporation; *U.S. Public*, pg. 1401
ROCKWELL MEXICANA, S.A. DE C.V.—See Rockwell International Corporation; *U.S. Public*, pg. 1402
ROCKWELL OTOMASYON TICARET A.S.—See Rockwell International Corporation; *U.S. Public*, pg. 1402
ROCKWELL PLASTIC PRODUCTS—See BBA Group plc; *Int'l*, pg. 113
ROCKWELL PMC/BAKER PERKINS—See Siebe plc; *Int'l*, pg. 1240
ROCKWELL SALES & SUPPORT SERVICES—See Rockwell International Corporation; *U.S. Public*, pg. 1402
ROCKWELL SEMICONDUCTOR SYSTEMS—See Rockwell International Corporation; *U.S. Public*, pg. 1402
ROCKWELL SEMICONDUCTOR SYSTEMS LIMITED—See Rockwell International Corporation; *U.S. Public*, pg. 1402
ROCKWELL SEMICONDUCTOR SYSTEMS PLC—See Rockwell International Corporation; *U.S. Public*, pg. 1402
ROCKWELL SEMICONDUCTOR SYSTEMS S.A.R.L.—See Rockwell International Corporation; *U.S. Public*, pg. 1402
ROCKWELL STANDARD OF AUSTRALIA LTD.—See Rockwell International Corporation; *U.S. Public*, pg. 1402
ROCKWELL SVI S.A.—See Rockwell International Corporation; *U.S. Public*, pg. 1402
ROCKWELL SWITCHING SYSTEMS LIMITED—See Rockwell International Corporation; *U.S. Public*, pg. 1402
ROCKWELL SYSTEMS INTERNATIONAL, INC.—See Rockwell International Corporation; *U.S. Public*, pg. 1402
ROCKWELL-COLLINS INTERNATIONAL, INC.—See Rockwell International Corporation; *U.S. Public*, pg. 1400
ROCKWOOD TIMES—See Landmark Communications, Inc.; *U.S. Private*, pg. 648
ROCKY MOUNT INSTRUMENTS, INC.—See Allen Organ Company; *U.S. Public*, pg. 45
ROCKY MOUNTAIN BANKCARD SYSTEM, INC.—See U.S. Bancorp; *U.S. Public*, pg. 1680
ROCKY MOUNTAIN COMPANY; *U.S. Private*, pg. 938
ROCKY MOUNTAIN NATURAL GAS CO.—See K N Energy, Inc.; *U.S. Public*, pg. 937
ROCKY MOUNTAIN NEWS—See The E.W. Scripps Company; *U.S. Public*, pg. 1448
ROCKY MOUNTAIN PRESTRESS—See Phelps Tointon Inc.; *U.S. Private*, pg. 861
ROCKY MOUNTAIN WATER CO.—See Adolph Coors Company; *U.S. Public*, pg. 445
ROCKY POINT VILLAGE CORP.—See Specialty Restaurants Corporation; *U.S. Private*, pg. 1023
ROCKY RIVER REALTY COMPANY—See Northeast Utilities; *U.S. Public*, pg. 1195
ROCKY ROCOCO CORPORATION; *U.S. Private*, pg. 938
ROCKY SHOES & BOOTS, INC.; *U.S. Public*, pg. 1402
ROCOL DANMARK—See Morgan Crucible Co. Plc; *Int'l*, pg. 892
ROCOL GMBH—See Morgan Crucible Co. Plc; *Int'l*, pg. 892
ROCOL (HONG KONG) LIMITED—See Morgan Crucible Co. Plc; *Int'l*, pg. 892
ROCOL KOREA LIMITED—See Morgan Crucible Co. Plc; *Int'l*, pg. 892
ROCOL LIMITED—See Morgan Crucible Co. Plc; *Int'l*, pg. 892

MASTER INDEX TO COMPANY NAMES ROLL

Company Index

ROCOL MEXICANA S.A. DE C.V.—See Morgan Crucible Co. Plc; *Int'l*, pg. 893
ROCOL/MOLYBOND LABORATORIES DIVISION—See Morgan Crucible Co. Plc; *Int'l*, pg. 895
ROCOR TRANSPORTATION COMPANIES INC.; *U.S. Private*, pg. 938
ROD & BAR PRODUCTS DIVISION—See The Broken Hill Proprietary Company Limited; *Int'l*, pg. 227
RODALE PRESS, INC.; *U.S. Private*, pg. 939
RODAMIENTOS FAG—See FAG Group; *Int'l*, pg. 469
RODAMIENTOS FAG S.A. DE C.V.—See FAG Group; *Int'l*, pg. 469
RODAMIENTOS USA SA—See Brammer plc; *Int'l*, pg. 212
THE RODD GROUP—See Omnicom Group Inc.; *U.S. Public*, pg. 1224
RODEFELD CO., INC.; *U.S. Private*, pg. 939
RODEN CANADA INC.—See Optische Werke G. Rodenstock; *Int'l*, pg. 1007
RODENSTOCK PRECISION OPTICS, INC.—See Optische Werke G. Rodenstock; *Int'l*, pg. 1007
RODENSTOCK USA, INC.—See Optische Werke G. Rodenstock; *Int'l*, pg. 1007
RODEO DRIVE PROPERTIES, INC.—See Takashimaya Company, Limited; *Int'l*, pg. 1349
RODGARD CORPORATION—See Astronics Corporation; *U.S. Public*, pg. 142
RODGERS BUILDERS, INC.; *U.S. Private*, pg. 939
J.B. RODGERS MECHANICAL CONTRACTORS; *U.S. Private*, pg. 939
RODGERS WAREHOUSE AND TRANSPORT COMPANY—See The Jaydor Corporation; *U.S. Private*, pg. 584
RODIC CO., LTD.—See Roche Holding Ltd.; *Int'l*, pg. 1122
RODNEY METALS—See Allegheny Teledyne Incorporated; *U.S. Public*, pg. 43
ROE LEE CANADA INC.—See Raisio Group; *Int'l*, pg. 1086
ROE LEE PAPER CHEMICALS CO. LTD.—See Raisio Group; *Int'l*, pg. 1086
ROEDERSTEIN GMBH—See Vishay Intertechnology, Inc.; *U.S. Public*, pg. 1722
ROEDIGER ANLAGENBAU GMBH—See Bilfinger + Berger Bauaktiengesellschaft; *Int'l*, pg. 195
ROEHLEN ENGLAND—See Standex International Corporation; *U.S. Public*, pg. 1507
ROEHLEN ENGRAVING—See Standex International Corporation; *U.S. Public*, pg. 1506
ROEHLEN INDUSTRIES PTY. LTD. MOLD-TECH DIV.—See Standex International Corporation; *U.S. Public*, pg. 1507
ROEHLEN INDUSTRIES PTY. LTD. PROCON PUMP DIV.—See Standex International Corporation; *U.S. Public*, pg. 1507
ROEHLEN INDUSTRIES PTY. LTD. (SIDNEY DIVISION)—See Standex International Corporation; *U.S. Public*, pg. 1507
ROELL PRUEFSYSTEME GMBH—See Zwick/Roell Group; *Int'l*, pg. 1533
ROERIG A.B.—See Pfizer Inc.; *U.S. Public*, pg. 1282
ROERIG B.V.—See Pfizer Inc.; *U.S. Public*, pg. 1283
ROERIG FARMACEUTICI ITALIANA S.R.L.—See Pfizer Inc.; *U.S. Public*, pg. 1283
ROERIG S.A.—See Pfizer Inc.; *U.S. Public*, pg. 1284
ROESSING BRONZE CO.; *U.S. Private*, pg. 939
ROGERS & COWAN BRAND PLACEMENT—See Shandwick International Plc; *Int'l*, pg. 1226
ROGERS & COWAN, INC.—See Shandwick International Plc; *Int'l*, pg. 1227
ROGERS BRIDGE COMPANY, INC.—See Shepherd Construction Co., Inc.; *U.S. Private*, pg. 993
ROGERS BROTHERS SEED COMPANY—See Novartis AG; *Int'l*, pg. 974
ROGERS CABLE TV—See Rogers Communications, Inc.; *Int'l*, pg. 1122
ROGERS CABLE TV-ALBERTA LIMITED—See Rogers Communications, Inc.; *Int'l*, pg. 1122
ROGERS CABLE TV-BRAMPTON—See Rogers Communications, Inc.; *Int'l*, pg. 1122
ROGERS CABLE TV-BRANTFORD DIV.—See Rogers Communications, Inc.; *Int'l*, pg. 1122
ROGERS CABLE TV-CORNWALL—See Rogers Communications, Inc.; *Int'l*, pg. 1122
ROGERS CABLE TV-FRASER—See Rogers Communications, Inc.; *Int'l*, pg. 1122
ROGERS CABLE TV-HAMILTON—See Rogers Communications, Inc.; *Int'l*, pg. 1122
ROGERS CABLE TV-KITCHENER—See Rogers Communications, Inc.; *Int'l*, pg. 1122
ROGERS CABLE TV-LONDON—See Rogers Communications, Inc.; *Int'l*, pg. 1122
ROGERS CABLE TV-MISSISSAUGA DIV.—See Rogers Communications, Inc.; *Int'l*, pg. 1122
ROGERS CABLE TV-NEWMARKET DIV.—See Rogers Communications, Inc.; *Int'l*, pg. 1122
ROGERS CABLE TV-PINE RIDGE—See Rogers Communications, Inc.; *Int'l*, pg. 1122
ROGERS CABLE TV-SURREY—See Rogers Communications, Inc.; *Int'l*, pg. 1122
ROGERS CABLE TV-TORONTO DIV.—See Rogers Communications, Inc.; *Int'l*, pg. 1122
ROGERS CABLE TV-VANCOUVER—See Rogers Communications, Inc.; *Int'l*, pg. 1122
ROGERS CABLE TV-VICTORIA—See Rogers Communications, Inc.; *Int'l*, pg. 1122
ROGERS CANTEL MOBILE COMMUNICATIONS INC.—See Rogers Communications, Inc.; *Int'l*, pg. 1122
ROGERS CFAC-AM—See Rogers Communications, Inc.; *Int'l*, pg. 1123
ROGERS CFGP-AM—See Rogers Communications, Inc.; *Int'l*, pg. 1123
ROGERS CFTR-AM—See Rogers Communications, Inc.; *Int'l*, pg. 1123
ROGERS CHFI-FM—See Rogers Communications, Inc.; *Int'l*, pg. 1123
ROGERS CJVI-AM—See Rogers Communications, Inc.; *Int'l*, pg. 1123
ROGERS CKKS-FM—See Rogers Communications, Inc.; *Int'l*, pg. 1123
ROGERS CKWX-AM—See Rogers Communications, Inc.; *Int'l*, pg. 1123
ROGERS COMMUNICATIONS, INC.; *Int'l*, pg. 1122
ROGERS CORPORATION; *U.S. Public*, pg. 1402
ROGERS ENTERTAINMENT INC.—See Rogers Communications, Inc.; *Int'l*, pg. 1123
ROGERS FOODS—See Universal Foods Corporation; *U.S. Public*, pg. 1696
ROGERS GROUP INC.; *U.S. Private*, pg. 939
ROGERS INOAC CORPORATION—See Rogers Corporation; *U.S. Public*, pg. 1403
ROGERS JAPAN INC.—See Rogers Corporation; *U.S. Public*, pg. 1403
KENNY ROGERS ROASTERS; *U.S. Private*, pg. 939
ROGERS, LUNT & BOWLEN CO.; *U.S. Private*, pg. 939
ROGERS MARKETS INC.; *U.S. Private*, pg. 940
ROGERS N.K. SEED CO.—See Novartis AG; *Int'l*, pg. 974
ROGERS N.V.—See Rogers Corporation; *U.S. Public*, pg. 1403
ROGERS SUGAR—See B C Sugar Refinery, Ltd.; *Int'l*, pg. 103
T.H. ROGERS LUMBER CO.; *U.S. Private*, pg. 940
ROGERS TOOL WORKS, INC.—See Kennametal Inc.; *U.S. Public*, pg. 950
ROGERSON AIRCRAFT CONTROLS—See Rogerson Aircraft Corporation; *U.S. Private*, pg. 940
ROGERSON AIRCRAFT CORPORATION; *U.S. Private*, pg. 940
ROGERSON AIRCRAFT SYSTEMS—See Rogerson Aircraft Corporation; *U.S. Private*, pg. 940
ROGERSON ATS—See Rogerson Aircraft Corporation; *U.S. Private*, pg. 940
ROGERSON KRATOS—See Rogerson Aircraft Corporation; *U.S. Private*, pg. 940
ROGGE GLOBAL PLC—See United Asset Management Corporation; *U.S. Public*, pg. 1674
ROGNONI S.P.A.—See Freudenberg & Company; *Int'l*, pg. 506
ROHDE & SCHWARZ ENGINEERING & SALES GMBH—See Rohde & Schwarz GmbH & Co. KG; *Int'l*, pg. 1124
ROHDE & SCHWARZ GMBH—See Rohde & Schwarz GmbH & Co. KG; *Int'l*, pg. 1124
ROHDE & SCHWARZ GMBH & CO. KG; *Int'l*, pg. 1124
ROHDE & SCHWARZ, INC.—See Rohde & Schwarz GmbH & Co. KG; *Int'l*, pg. 1124
ROHDE & SCHWARZ MESSGERAETEBAU GMBH—See Rohde & Schwarz GmbH & Co. KG; *Int'l*, pg. 1124
ROHDE & SCHWARZ VERTRIEBS GMBH—See Rohde & Schwarz GmbH & Co. KG; *Int'l*, pg. 1124
ROHDE & SCHWARZ GMBH—See Rohde & Schwarz GmbH & Co. KG; *Int'l*, pg. 1124
C. ROHER INC.; *U.S. Private*, pg. 940
ROHM AMAGI CO., LTD.—See Rohm Co., Ltd.; *Int'l*, pg. 1125
ROHM & HAAS AUSTRALIA PTY. LTD.—See Rohm and Haas Company; *U.S. Public*, pg. 1404
ROHM & HAAS (AUSTRALIA) PTY. LTD.—See Rohm and Haas Company; *U.S. Public*, pg. 1404
ROHM & HAAS BRAZIL LTDA.—See Rohm and Haas Company; *U.S. Public*, pg. 1404
ROHM & HAAS CANADA INC.—See Rohm and Haas Company; *U.S. Public*, pg. 1404
ROHM AND HAAS CAPITAL CORPORATION—See Rohm and Haas Company; *U.S. Public*, pg. 1403
ROHM & HAAS CENTRO AMERICA S.A.—See Rohm and Haas Company; *U.S. Public*, pg. 1404
ROHM & HAAS COLOMBIA S.A.—See Rohm and Haas Company; *U.S. Public*, pg. 1404
ROHM AND HAAS COMPANY; *U.S. Public*, pg. 1403
ROHM & HAAS CO. RESEARCH LABS—See Rohm and Haas Company; *U.S. Public*, pg. 1403
ROHM AND HAAS CREDIT CORPORATION—See Rohm and Haas Company; *U.S. Public*, pg. 1403
ROHM & HAAS DEUTSCHLAND GMBH—See Rohm and Haas Company; *U.S. Public*, pg. 1404
ROHM AND HAAS EQUITY CORPORATION—See Rohm and Haas Company; *U.S. Public*, pg. 1403
ROHM & HAAS ESPANA, S.A.—See Rohm and Haas Company; *U.S. Public*, pg. 1404
ROHM & HAAS (FAR EAST) LTD.—See Rohm and Haas Company; *U.S. Public*, pg. 1404
ROHM & HAAS FRANCE S.A.—See Rohm and Haas Company; *U.S. Public*, pg. 1404
ROHM & HAAS HOLDINGS LTD.—See Rohm and Haas Company; *U.S. Public*, pg. 1404
ROHM & HAAS ILLINOIS INC.—See Rohm and Haas Company; *U.S. Public*, pg. 1403
ROHM & HAAS ITALIA, S.P.A.—See Rohm and Haas Company; *U.S. Public*, pg. 1404
ROHM & HAAS JAPAN K.K.—See Rohm and Haas Company; *U.S. Public*, pg. 1404
ROHM AND HAAS LATIN AMERICA, INC.—See Rohm and Haas Company; *U.S. Public*, pg. 1403
ROHM & HAAS MEXICO S.A. DE C.V.—See Rohm and Haas Company; *U.S. Public*, pg. 1404
ROHM & HAAS NEW ZEALAND LTD.—See Rohm and Haas Company; *U.S. Public*, pg. 1404
ROHM & HAAS NORDISKA AB—See Rohm and Haas Company; *U.S. Public*, pg. 1404
ROHM AND HAAS PERFORMANCE PLASTICS INC.—See Rohm and Haas Company; *U.S. Public*, pg. 1403
ROHM AND HAAS PHILADELPHIA INC.—See Rohm and Haas Company; *U.S. Public*, pg. 1403
ROHM & HAAS PHILIPPINES, INC.—See Rohm and Haas Company; *U.S. Public*, pg. 1404
ROHM & HAAS (SCOTLAND) LIMITED—See Rohm and Haas Company; *U.S. Public*, pg. 1404
ROHM & HAAS (SINGAPORE) PTE. LTD.—See Rohm and Haas Company; *U.S. Public*, pg. 1404
ROHM & HAAS TAIWAN, INC.—See Rohm and Haas Company; *U.S. Public*, pg. 1404
ROHM & HAAS (UK) LTD.—See Rohm and Haas Company; *U.S. Public*, pg. 1404
ROHM APOLLO ELECTRONICS (THAILAND) CO., LTD.—See Rohm Co., Ltd.; *Int'l*, pg. 1125
ROHM BRASILEIRA INDUSTRIA QUIMICA LTDA.—See Veba AG; *Int'l*, pg. 1456
ROHM CO., LTD.; *Int'l*, pg. 1124
ROHM CO., LTD. - TOKYO BRANCH—See Rohm Co., Ltd.; *Int'l*, pg. 1125
ROHM CORPORATION—See Rohm Co., Ltd.; *Int'l*, pg. 1125
ROHM ELECTRONICS ASIA PTE. LTD., INVESTMENT DIV.—See Rohm Co., Ltd.; *Int'l*, pg. 1125
ROHM ELECTRONICS BRASIL LTDA.—See Rohm Co., Ltd.; *Int'l*, pg. 1125
ROHM ELECTRONICS DALIAN CO., LTD.—See Rohm Co., Ltd.; *Int'l*, pg. 1125
ROHM ELECTRONICS, EASTERN SALES DIV.—See Rohm Co., Ltd.; *Int'l*, pg. 1125
ROHM ELECTRONICS (FRANCE) S.A.S.—See Rohm Co., Ltd.; *Int'l*, pg. 1125
ROHM ELECTRONICS GMBH—See Rohm Co., Ltd.; *Int'l*, pg. 1125
ROHM ELECTRONICS (H.K.) CO., LTD.—See Rohm Co., Ltd.; *Int'l*, pg. 1125
ROHM ELECTRONICS KOREA CORPORATION—See Rohm Co., Ltd.; *Int'l*, pg. 1125
ROHM ELECTRONICS (MALAYSIA) SDN. BHD.—See Rohm Co., Ltd.; *Int'l*, pg. 1125
ROHM ELECTRONICS NORTH-WEST SALES DIVISION—See Rohm Co., Ltd.; *Int'l*, pg. 1125
ROHM ELECTRONICS PHILIPPINES, INC.—See Rohm Co., Ltd.; *Int'l*, pg. 1125
ROHM ELECTRONICS (PHILIPPINES) SALES CORPORATION—See Rohm Co., Ltd.; *Int'l*, pg. 1125
ROHM ELECTRONICS SOUTH-WEST SALES DIVISION—See Rohm Co., Ltd.; *Int'l*, pg. 1125
ROHM ELECTRONICS TAIWAN CO., LTD.—See Rohm Co., Ltd.; *Int'l*, pg. 1125
ROHM ELECTRONICS (TIANJIN) CO., LTD.—See Rohm Co., Ltd.; *Int'l*, pg. 1125
ROHM ELECTRONICS (U.K.) LIMITED—See Rohm Co., Ltd.; *Int'l*, pg. 1125
ROHM FUJI CO., LTD.—See Rohm Co., Ltd.; *Int'l*, pg. 1125
ROHM FUKUOKA CO., LTD.—See Rohm Co., Ltd.; *Int'l*, pg. 1125
ROHM GMBH—See Veba AG; *Int'l*, pg. 1454
ROHM HOLDING GMBH—See Veba AG; *Int'l*, pg. 1454
ROHM KOREA CORPORATION—See Rohm Co., Ltd.; *Int'l*, pg. 1125
ROHM LOGISTEC CO., LTD.—See Rohm Co., Ltd.; *Int'l*, pg. 1125
ROHM LSI SYSTEMS INC.—See Rohm Co., Ltd.; *Int'l*, pg. 1125
ROHM MECHATECH CO., LTD.—See Rohm Co., Ltd.; *Int'l*, pg. 1125
ROHM MECHATECH PHILIPPINES, INC.—See Rohm Co., Ltd.; *Int'l*, pg. 1125
ROHM U.S.A., INC.—See Rohm Co., Ltd.; *Int'l*, pg. 1125
ROHM-WAKO (KELANTAN) SDN. BHD.—See Rohm Co., Ltd.; *Int'l*, pg. 1125
ROHM-WAKO (MALAYSIA) SDN. BHD.—See Rohm Co., Ltd.; *Int'l*, pg. 1126
ROHN INDUSTRIES, INC.; *U.S. Public*, pg. 1404
ROHOL-AUFSUCHUNGS—See Royal Dutch/Shell Group of Companies; *Int'l*, pg. 1138
ROHR AERO SERVICES, INC.—See The B.F. Goodrich Company; *U.S. Public*, pg. 751
ROHR AERO SERVICES-ASIA—See The B.F. Goodrich Company; *U.S. Public*, pg. 752
ROHR CREDIT CORPORATION—See The B.F. Goodrich Company; *U.S. Public*, pg. 751
ROHR EUROPE—See The B.F. Goodrich Company; *U.S. Public*, pg. 752
ROHR EUROPE-HAMBURG—See The B.F. Goodrich Company; *U.S. Public*, pg. 752
ROHR, INC.—See The B.F. Goodrich Company; *U.S. Public*, pg. 751
ROHR, INCORPORATED-HTA AEROSTRUCTURES, INC.—See The B.F. Goodrich Company; *U.S. Public*, pg. 751
ROHREN UND SANITAR GROBHANDEL GMBH—See Mannesmann A.G.; *Int'l*, pg. 838
ROHRENWERKE BOUS/SAAR GMBH—See Mannesmann A.G.; *Int'l*, pg. 835
ROHRER CORPORATION; *U.S. Private*, pg. 940
BOB ROHRMAN AUTO GROUP; *U.S. Private*, pg. 940
ROHTO PHARMACEUTICAL CO.; *Int'l*, pg. 1126
ROIBOX OY—See Honeywell Inc.; *U.S. Public*, pg. 834
ROINS HOLDINGS LIMITED—See Royal & Sun Alliance Insurance Group plc; *Int'l*, pg. 1131
ROKEACH FOOD DISTRIBUTING INC.; *U.S. Private*, pg. 940
ROKENJ LA COURONNE NV—See The Albert Fisher Group PLC; *Int'l*, pg. 491
ROKOP CORPORATION; *U.S. Private*, pg. 941
ROLAMENTOS FAG LTDA.—See FAG Group; *Int'l*, pg. 469
ROLAND MURTEN AG—See Novartis AG; *Int'l*, pg. 972
ROLANE FACTORY OUTLETS; *U.S. Private*, pg. 941
ROLERO OMEGA OPERATIONS—See Cooper Industries, Inc.; *U.S. Public*, pg. 443
ROLEX INDUSTRIES, INC.—See Rolex Watch Co. SA; *Int'l*, pg. 1126
ROLEX WATCH CO. SA; *Int'l*, pg. 1126
ROLEX WATCH U.S.A., INC.—See Rolex Watch Co. SA; *Int'l*, pg. 1126
ROLF BUTENSCHON GMBH—See Electrolux, AB; *Int'l*, pg. 442
ROLFS—See AR Accessories Group, Inc.; *U.S. Private*, pg. 7
ROLL COATER, INC.—See Arvin Industries, Inc.; *U.S. Public*, pg. 137
ROLL FORMING CORPORATION; *U.S. Private*, pg. 941

ROLL INTERNATIONAL CORPORATION; *U.S. Private*, pg. 941
ROLL-IT—See Knape & Vogt Mfg. Co.; *U.S. Public*, pg. 963
ROLL SOURCE, INC.—See Unisource Worldwide, Inc.; *U.S. Public*, pg. 1671
ROLLALONG LIMITED—See Hanson PLC; *Int'l*, pg. 593
ROLLAND INC.—See The Cascades Group; *Int'l*, pg. 273
ROLLAND INC., DISTRIBUTION DIVISION—See The Cascades Group; *Int'l*, pg. 273
ROLLAND INC., FINE PAPERS DIVISION—See The Cascades Group; *Int'l*, pg. 274
ROLLED ALLOYS/ATEK METALS DIVISION—See Rolled Alloys, Inc.; *U.S. Private*, pg. 941
ROLLED ALLOYS, INC.; *U.S. Private*, pg. 941
ROLLED ALLOYS LTD.—See Rolled Alloys, Inc.; *U.S. Private*, pg. 941
ROLLED STEEL PRODUCTS CORPORATION; *U.S. Private*, pg. 941
ROLLEPAAL B.V.—See Royal Dutch/Shell Group of Companies; *Int'l*, pg. 1136
ALBERT ROLLER GMBH & CO. KG; *Int'l*, pg. 1126
ROLLER DERBY SKATE CORP.; *U.S. Private*, pg. 941
ROLLERBLADE, INC.; *U.S. Private*, pg. 941
ROLLEX CORPORATION; *U.S. Private*, pg. 941
ROLLING MILL SUPPLIES & ENG. (PTY.) LTD.—See Selas Corporation of America; *U.S. Public*, pg. 1455
ROLLING STONE MAGAZINE—See Wenner Media; *U.S. Private*, pg. 1162
ROLLINS BURDICK HUNTER (CAYMAN) LIMITED—See AON Corporation; *U.S. Public*, pg. 119
ROLLINS BURDICK HUNTER CO. (BERMUDA) LTD.—See AON Corporation; *U.S. Public*, pg. 119
ROLLINS BURDICK HUNTER INTL. INC.—See AON Corporation; *U.S. Public*, pg. 119
ROLLINS CONTINENTAL INC.—See Rollins, Inc.; *U.S. Public*, pg. 1405
ROLLINS HUDIG HALL OF HAWAII, INC.—See AON Corporation; *U.S. Public*, pg. 117
ROLLINS, INC.; *U.S. Public*, pg. 1404
ROLLINS LOGISTICS INC.—See Rollins Truck Leasing Corp.; *U.S. Public*, pg. 1405
ROLLINS SUPPLY, INC.—See Rollins, Inc.; *U.S. Public*, pg. 1405
ROLLINS TRUCK LEASING CORP.; *U.S. Public*, pg. 1405
ROLLIX-DEFONTAINE S.A.—See Fried. Krupp AG; *Int'l*, pg. 509
ROLLMAN SUPPLY COMPANY—See First Mount Joy Corporation; *U.S. Private*, pg. 407
ROLLS-ROYCE & ASSOCIATES LIMITED—See FKI Plc; *Int'l*, pg. 472
ROLLS-ROYCE-COMMERCIAL AERO ENGINES LTD.—See Rolls-Royce plc; *Int'l*, pg. 1127
ROLLS-ROYCE INC.—See Rolls-Royce plc; *Int'l*, pg. 1127
ROLLS-ROYCE MILITARY AERO ENGINES LTD.—See Rolls-Royce plc; *Int'l*, pg. 1127
ROLLS-ROYCE MOTOR CARS LIMITED—See Vickers PLC; *Int'l*, pg. 1467
ROLLS-ROYCE PLC; *Int'l*, pg. 1126
ROLLS-ROYCE POWER ENGINEERING PLC—See Rolls-Royce plc; *Int'l*, pg. 1127
ROLLS-ROYCE INDUSTRIAL & MARINE GAS TURBINES LTD.—See Rolls-Royce plc; *Int'l*, pg. 1127
ROLLS-ROYCE INDUSTRIES CANADA LTD.—See Rolls-Royce plc; *Int'l*, pg. 1127
ROLM RESALE SYSTEMS—See Norstan, Inc.; *U.S. Public*, pg. 1192
ROLOCK, INC.; *U.S. Private*, pg. 942
ROLOCK OF CALIFORNIA—See Rolock, Inc.; *U.S. Private*, pg. 942
ROLTECH—See Esselte AB; *Int'l*, pg. 462
ROLTRA-MORSE S.P.A.—See IMO Industries Inc.; *U.S. Private*, pg. 857
ROMAC INDUSTRIES, INC.; *U.S. Private*, pg. 942
ROMACORP, INC.—See NPC International, Inc.; *U.S. Public*, pg. 1147
ROMAN ELECTRIC COMPANY, INC.; *U.S. Private*, pg. 942
ROMAN, INC.; *U.S. Private*, pg. 942
ROMAN MEAL COMPANY; *U.S. Private*, pg. 942
ROMANN & TANNENHOLZ ADVERTISING, INC.; *U.S. Private*, pg. 942
ROMANTIS GESELLSCHAFT FIR SATELLITENKOMMUNIKATION M.B.H.—See Daimler-Benz Aktiengesellschaft; *Int'l*, pg. 367
ROME CABLE CORPORATION; *U.S. Private*, pg. 942
ROME RESEARCH CORPORATION—See PAR Technology Corporation; *U.S. Public*, pg. 1256
ROME STRIP STEEL CO., INC.; *U.S. Private*, pg. 942
ROMEO RIM INC.—See The Cypress Companies; *U.S. Private*, pg. 300
ROMER-BRITAX AUTOGURTE GMBH—See Britax International plc; *Int'l*, pg. 217
ROMINGER REISEBUERO GMBH; *Int'l*, pg. 1127
ROMPER ROOM ENTERPRISES, INC.—See Hasbro, Inc.; *U.S. Public*, pg. 797
RONALDS PRINTING CALGARY—See Quebecor Inc.; *Int'l*, pg. 1077
RONCO COMMUNICATIONS & ELECTRONICS INC.; *U.S. Private*, pg. 943
RONCO, INVENTIONS. LLC; *U.S. Private*, pg. 943
RONDE CORP.—See Meiji Seika Kaisha, Ltd.; *Int'l*, pg. 855
RONEY & CO.; *U.S. Private*, pg. 943
RONEY OTMAN, INC.; *U.S. Private*, pg. 943
RONNINGEN-PETTER DIV.—See Dover Corporation; *U.S. Public*, pg. 521
RONSON AVIATION, INC.—See Ronson Corporation; *U.S. Public*, pg. 1405
RONSON CONSUMER PRODUCTS CORP.—See Ronson Corporation; *U.S. Public*, pg. 1405
RONSON CORPORATION; *U.S. Public*, pg. 1405
ROOF TILE MANUFACTURING CO.—See International Paper Company; *U.S. Public*, pg. 905
ROOFING WHOLESALE CO., INC.; *U.S. Private*, pg. 943
ROONEY BROTHERS COMPANY; *U.S. Private*, pg. 943

ROOSE & PARTNERS—See Testa International; *Int'l*, pg. 1377
ROOSEVELT PAPER CO.; *U.S. Private*, pg. 943
W.A. ROOSEVELT CO.; *U.S. Private*, pg. 943
THE ROOST, INC.—See The Rouse Company; *U.S. Public*, pg. 1409
A.I. ROOT COMPANY; *U.S. Private*, pg. 944
ROOT DRY GOODS COMPANY, INC.—See Mercantile Stores Company, Inc.; *U.S. Public*, pg. 1090
ROOTS DIVISION—See Dresser Industries, Inc.; *U.S. Public*, pg. 528
ROPAK ATLANTIC INC.—See Linpac Mouldings Limited; *Int'l*, pg. 811
ROPAK CENTRAL INC.—See Linpac Mouldings Limited; *Int'l*, pg. 811
ROPAK CORPORATION—See Linpac Mouldings Limited; *Int'l*, pg. 811
ROPAK MATERIALS HANDLING DIV.—See Linpac Mouldings Limited; *Int'l*, pg. 812
ROPAK NORTHWEST INC.—See Linpac Mouldings Limited; *Int'l*, pg. 812
ROPAK SOUTHWEST INC.—See Linpac Mouldings Limited; *Int'l*, pg. 812
ROPAK WEST—See Linpac Mouldings Limited; *Int'l*, pg. 812
ROPER BROS. LUMBER CO., INC.; *U.S. Private*, pg. 944
ROPER CORPORATION—See General Electric Company; *U.S. Public*, pg. 710
ROPER INDUSTRIES, INC.; *U.S. Public*, pg. 1405
ROPER STARCH WORLDWIDE; *U.S. Public*, pg. 944
ROPPE CORP.; *U.S. Private*, pg. 944
ROQUETTE AMERICA INC.; *U.S. Private*, pg. 944
RORER ARGENTINA S.A.—See Rhone-Poulenc S.A.; *Int'l*, pg. 1111
RORER AUSTRALIA PTY. LTD.—See Rhone-Poulenc S.A.; *Int'l*, pg. 1111
RORER B.V.—See Rhone-Poulenc S.A.; *Int'l*, pg. 1111
RORER (CARIBBEAN) CORP.—See Rhone-Poulenc S.A.; *Int'l*, pg. 1111
RORER DE CENTRO AMERICA (GUATEMALA) S.A.—See Rhone-Poulenc S.A.; *Int'l*, pg. 1111
RORER DE CENTRO AMERICA S.A. DE C.V.—See Rhone-Poulenc S.A.; *Int'l*, pg. 1111
RORER DE ECUADOR, S.A.—See Rhone-Poulenc S.A.; *Int'l*, pg. 1111
RORER DE MEXICO, S.A. DE C.V.—See Rhone-Poulenc S.A.; *Int'l*, pg. 1111
RORER DO BRASIL QUIMICA E. FARMACEUTICA LTDA.—See Rhone-Poulenc S.A.; *Int'l*, pg. 1111
RORER GMBH—See Rhone-Poulenc S.A.; *Int'l*, pg. 1111
RORER HEALTH CARE LTD.—See Rhone-Poulenc S.A.; *Int'l*, pg. 1112
RORER-INTER-AMERICAN CORP.—See Rhone-Poulenc S.A.; *Int'l*, pg. 1111
RORER IRELAND, LTD.—See Rhone-Poulenc S.A.; *Int'l*, pg. 1112
RORER JAPAN, INC.—See Rhone-Poulenc S.A.; *Int'l*, pg. 1112
S.A. RORER N.V.—See Rhone-Poulenc S.A.; *Int'l*, pg. 1112
RORER PANAMA S.A.—See Rhone-Poulenc S.A.; *Int'l*, pg. 1112
RORER PHARMACEUTICAL (SINGAPORE) PTE. LTD.—See Rhone-Poulenc S.A.; *Int'l*, pg. 1112
RORER PUERTO RICO INC.—See Rhone-Poulenc S.A.; *Int'l*, pg. 1111
RORER, S.A.—See Rhone-Poulenc S.A.; *Int'l*, pg. 1112
RORER S.P.A.—See Rhone-Poulenc S.A.; *Int'l*, pg. 1112
ROSAUERS SUPERMARKETS, INC.; *U.S. Private*, pg. 944
ROSCO LABORATORIES, INC.; *U.S. Private*, pg. 944
ROSCO MANUFACTURING CO.; *U.S. Private*, pg. 944
ROSE ACRE FARMS; *U.S. Private*, pg. 944
ROSE & LAFLAMME CO. LTD.—See Saskatchewan Wheat Pool; *Int'l*, pg. 1195
ROSE ART INDUSTRIES; *U.S. Private*, pg. 945
ROSE BEARINGS LTD.—See Minebea Co., Ltd.; *Int'l*, pg. 869
CLARE ROSE INC./CLARE ROSE OF NASSAU; *U.S. Private*, pg. 945
ROSE FUEL CORPORATION—See Bayside Fuel Oil Depot Corp.; *U.S. Private*, pg. 125
ROSE PACKING COMPANY; *U.S. Private*, pg. 945
ROSE PRINTING COMPANY, INC.; *U.S. Private*, pg. 945
THE ROSEBUD MINING COMPANY, L.L.C.—See Hecla Mining Company; *U.S. Public*, pg. 804
ROSEBURG FOREST PRODUCTS CO.—See RLC Industries Co.; *U.S. Private*, pg. 905
ROSEBURG RESOURCES CO.—See RLC Industries Co.; *U.S. Private*, pg. 905
ROSELLA LIPTON PTY. LTD.—See Unilever Plc; *Int'l*, pg. 1438
ROSELLE PAPER CO., INC.; *U.S. Private*, pg. 945
ROSEMOUNT AG—See Emerson Electric Co.; *U.S. Public*, pg. 577
ROSEMOUNT ANALYTICAL, INC.—See Emerson Electric Co.; *U.S. Public*, pg. 574
ROSEMOUNT ANALYTICAL, UNILOC DIV.—See Emerson Electric Co.; *U.S. Public*, pg. 574
ROSEMOUNT B.V.—See Emerson Electric Co.; *U.S. Public*, pg. 577
ROSEMOUNT ENGINEERING GMBH—See Emerson Electric Co.; *U.S. Public*, pg. 577
ROSEMOUNT HOLDING AG—See Emerson Electric Co.; *U.S. Public*, pg. 577
ROSEMOUNT INSTRUMENTS LTD.—See Emerson Electric Co.; *U.S. Public*, pg. 577
ROSEMOUNT LTD.—See Emerson Electric Co.; *U.S. Public*, pg. 577
ROSEMOUNT MEASUREMENT DIVISION—See Emerson Electric Co.; *U.S. Public*, pg. 574
ROSEMOUNT S.A.R.L.—See Emerson Electric Co.; *U.S. Public*, pg. 577
ROSEN ASSOCIATES MANAGEMENT CORP.; *U.S. Private*, pg. 945
ROSENBERGERS DAIRIES, INC.; *U.S. Private*, pg. 945

ROSENDIN ELECTRIC, INC.; *U.S. Private*, pg. 945
ROSENDORF/EVANS—See Evans, Inc.; *U.S. Public*, pg. 597
W. ROSENLEW LTD.—See UPM-Kymmene Corporation; *Int'l*, pg. 1428
ROSENS DIVERSIFIED, INC.; *U.S. Private*, pg. 945
ROSENS, INC.—See Rosens Diversified, Inc.; *U.S. Private*, pg. 945
ROSENSHEIN ASSOCIATES; *U.S. Private*, pg. 945
WILHELM ROSENSTEIN LTD.—See BASF AG; *Int'l*, pg. 109
ROSENTHAL AG; *Int'l*, pg. 1127
ROSENTHAL AUTOMOTIVE ORGANIZATION; *U.S. Private*, pg. 946
ROSENTHAL U.S.A. LIMITED—See Rosenthal AG; *Int'l*, pg. 1127
ROSE'S STORES, INC.; *U.S. Public*, pg. 1405
ROSEVILLE CHRYSLER PLYMOUTH JEEP INC.; *U.S. Private*, pg. 946
ROSEWOOD CORPORATION—See Caroline Hunt Trust Estate; *U.S. Private*, pg. 548
ROSEWOOD MANOR—See Horizon/CMS Healthcare Corporation; *U.S. Public*, pg. 838
ROSEWOOD PROPERTY COMPANY; *U.S. Private*, pg. 946
ROSH TELECOM LTD.—See IDB Holding Corporation; *Int'l*, pg. 644
ROSIERES S.A.—See Candy S.p.A.; *Int'l*, pg. 260
ROSINOX—See Candy S.p.A.; *Int'l*, pg. 260
ROSLER DRAHT AG—See N.V. Bekaert S.A.; *Int'l*, pg. 185
ROSPATCH JESSCO, INC.—See Ameriwood Industries International Inc.; *U.S. Private*, pg. 98
ROSS ALUMINUM FOUNDRIES—See Eagle-Picher Industries, Inc.; *U.S. Private*, pg. 355
ROSS & CATHERALL CERAMICS LIMITED—See Vickers PLC; *Int'l*, pg. 1467
ROSS & CATHERALL LIMITED—See Vickers PLC; *Int'l*, pg. 1467
ROSS & GLAS GMBH—See Fried. Krupp AG; *Int'l*, pg. 509
ROSS BICYCLES USA LTD.; *U.S. Private*, pg. 946
ROSS BREEDERS, INC.—See Hillsdown Holdings Plc; *Int'l*, pg. 619
ROSS DATA CANADA LTD.—See Ross Systems, Inc.; *U.S. Public*, pg. 1406
ROSS-ELLIS LTD.—See G.T.C. Transcontinental Group Ltd.; *Int'l*, pg. 538
ROSS-ELLIS PRINTING INC.—See G.T.C. Transcontinental Group Ltd.; *Int'l*, pg. 538
FRANK B. ROSS CO. INC.; *U.S. Private*, pg. 946
ROSS HILL CONTROLS—See IRI Istituto Ricostruzione Industriale; *Int'l*, pg. 653
ROSS ISOLIER- UND FASSADENBAU GMBH—See Fried. Krupp AG; *Int'l*, pg. 509
ROSS ISLAND SAND & GRAVEL CO., INC.—See R.B. Pamplin Corp.; *U.S. Private*, pg. 836
JACK ROSS MOTORS INC.; *U.S. Private*, pg. 946
ROSS-LOOS HEALTH PLAN OF CALIFORNIA—See Cigna Corp.; *U.S. Public*, pg. 359
ROSS LOOS HOSPITAL, INC.—See Cigna Corp.; *U.S. Public*, pg. 360
ROSS-MCNATT NAVAL ARCHITECTS—See Analysis & Technology, Inc.; *U.S. Public*, pg. 110
P.A. ROSS (FOOD BROKERS), LTD.—See Koninklijke BolsWessanen nv; *Int'l*, pg. 753
ROSS PRODUCTS—See Abbott Laboratories; *U.S. Public*, pg. 13
ROSS ROY COMMUNICATIONS CANADA, LIMITED—See Ross Roy Communications, Inc.; *U.S. Private*, pg. 946
ROSS ROY COMMUNICATIONS, INC.; *U.S. Private*, pg. 946
ROSS STORES, INC.; *U.S. Public*, pg. 1405
ROSS SYSTEMS EUROPE N.V.—See Ross Systems, Inc.; *U.S. Public*, pg. 1406
ROSS SYSTEMS FRANCE S.A.—See Ross Systems, Inc.; *U.S. Public*, pg. 1406
ROSS SYSTEMS GERMANY GMBH—See Ross Systems, Inc.; *U.S. Public*, pg. 1406
ROSS SYSTEMS IBERICA—See Ross Systems, Inc.; *U.S. Public*, pg. 1406
ROSS SYSTEMS, INC.; *U.S. Public*, pg. 1406
ROSS SYSTEMS NEDERLAND B.V.—See Ross Systems, Inc.; *U.S. Public*, pg. 1406
ROSS SYSTEMS S.L. IBERICA—See Ross Systems, Inc.; *U.S. Public*, pg. 1406
ROSS SYSTEMS (UK) LIMITED—See Ross Systems, Inc.; *U.S. Public*, pg. 1406
ROSS TECHNOLOGY CORP.; *U.S. Private*, pg. 946
ROSS TECHNOLOGY, INC.—See Fujitsu Limited; *Int'l*, pg. 526
ROSSER INTERNATIONAL, INC.; *U.S. Private*, pg. 946
ROSSIGNOL S.A.; *Int'l*, pg. 1127
ROSSIGNOL SC S.P.A.—See Rossignol S.A.; *Int'l*, pg. 1127
ROSSIGNOL SKI AG—See Rossignol S.A.; *Int'l*, pg. 1127
ROSSIGNOL SKI CO.—See Rossignol S.A.; *Int'l*, pg. 1127
ROSSIGNOL SKI DEUTSCHLAND GMBH—See Rossignol S.A.; *Int'l*, pg. 1127
ROSSING URANIUM—See Mining Services International, Inc.; *U.S. Public*, pg. 1115
ROSSING URANIUM LTD.—See Rio Tinto PLC; *Int'l*, pg. 1119
ROSWELL NURSING CENTER—See Horizon/CMS Healthcare Corporation; *U.S. Public*, pg. 838
ROTANIUM PRODUCTS—See Premier Farnell plc; *Int'l*, pg. 1068
ROTARY FORMS PRESS, INC.; *U.S. Private*, pg. 947
ROTARY LIFT—See Dover Corporation; *U.S. Public*, pg. 521
ROTARY MULTIFORMS, INC.; *U.S. Private*, pg. 947
ROTARY PAPER MANIFOLD CO.—See Bradner Central Company; *U.S. Private*, pg. 165
ROTATIONAL MOLDING, INC.—See Rotonics Manufacturing Inc.; *U.S. Public*, pg. 1406
ROTECH EMPLOYEE BENEFITS CORPORATION—See Integrated Health Services, Inc.; *U.S. Public*, pg. 885

ROTECH HOME MEDICAL CARE, INC.—See Integrated Health Services, Inc.; *U.S. Public*, pg. 885
ROTECH MEDICAL CORPORATION—See Integrated Health Services, Inc.; *U.S. Public*, pg. 884
ROTECH OXYGEN & MEDICAL EQUIPMENT, INC.—See Integrated Health Services, Inc.; *U.S. Public*, pg. 885
ROTECH/TEXAS, INC.—See Integrated Health Services, Inc.; *U.S. Public*, pg. 885
ROTEK INCORPORATED—See Fried. Krupp AG; *Int'l*, pg. 509
ROTEK INDUSTRIES (PTY) LTD.—See Eskom; *Int'l*, pg. 459
ROTELLE, INC.—See Richfood Holdings, Inc.; *U.S. Public*, pg. 1389
ROTEQ SERVICES SDN. BHD.—See Sulzer Ltd.; *Int'l*, pg. 1305
ROTEX CANADA INC.—See Esselte AB; *Int'l*, pg. 462
ROTH CORPORATION—See Trek Corporation; *U.S. Private*, pg. 1099
ROTH SA—See Expamet International Plc; *Int'l*, pg. 467
ROTHCHILD ASSET MANAGEMENT INC.—See Rothschild North America Inc.; *U.S. Private*, pg. 947
ROTHCHILD REALTY INC.—See Rothschild North America Inc.; *U.S. Private*, pg. 947
S. ROTHCHILD & CO., INC.; *U.S. Private*, pg. 947
ROTHCHILD'S LARRY L.—See S. Rothchild & Co., Inc.; *U.S. Private*, pg. 947
ROTHE ERDE IBERICA S.A.—See Fried. Krupp AG; *Int'l*, pg. 509
ROTHE ERDE-METALLURGICA ROSSI S.P.A.—See Fried. Krupp AG; *Int'l*, pg. 509
ROTHENBERGER AUSTRALIA PTY. LTD.—See Rothenberger Group GmbH; *Int'l*, pg. 1129
ROTHENBERGER BENELUX BVBA—See Rothenberger Group GmbH; *Int'l*, pg. 1129
ROTHENBERGER-EXACT A/S—Rothenberger Group GmbH; *Int'l*, pg. 1129
ROTHENBERGER FRANCE S.A.R.L.—See Rothenberger Group GmbH; *Int'l*, pg. 1129
ROTHENBERGER GROUP GMBH; *Int'l*, pg. 1127
ROTHENBERGER (HELLAS) S.A.—See Rothenberger Group GmbH; *Int'l*, pg. 1129
ROTHENBERGER HOLDING GES.M.B.H.—See Rothenberger Group GmbH; *Int'l*, pg. 1129
ROTHENBERGER (HUNGARY)—See Rothenberger Group GmbH; *Int'l*, pg. 1129
ROTHENBERGER (IRELAND) LTD.—See Rothenberger Group GmbH; *Int'l*, pg. 1129
ROTHENBERGER ITALIANA S.R.L.—See Rothenberger Group GmbH; *Int'l*, pg. 1129
ROTHENBERGER NEDERLAND B.V.—See Rothenberger Group GmbH; *Int'l*, pg. 1129
ROTHENBERGER OSTEUROPA GMBH—See Rothenberger Group GmbH; *Int'l*, pg. 1128
ROTHENBERGER PRODUCTIONS GMBH—See Rothenberger Group GmbH; *Int'l*, pg. 1128
ROTHENBERGER ROHRSANIERUNG GMBH—See Rothenberger Group GmbH; *Int'l*, pg. 1128
ROTHENBERGER (SCHWEIZ) AG—See Rothenberger Group GmbH; *Int'l*, pg. 1129
ROTHENBERGER TOOLS CANADA INC.—See Rothenberger Group GmbH; *Int'l*, pg. 1129
ROTHENBERGER TOOLS (FAR EAST) PTE LTD.—See Rothenberger Group GmbH; *Int'l*, pg. 1129
ROTHENBERGER (UK) LTD.—See Rothenberger Group GmbH; *Int'l*, pg. 1129
ROTHENBERGER UMWELTTECHNIK GMBH—See Rothenberger Group GmbH; *Int'l*, pg. 1128
ROTHENBERGER USA, INC.—See Rothenberger Group GmbH; *Int'l*, pg. 1129
ROTHENBERGER WERKZEUG-UND MASCHINENHANDELSGESELLSCHAFT M.B.H.—See Rothenberger Group GmbH; *Int'l*, pg. 1129
ROTHENBERGER WERKZEUGE AKTIENGESELLSCHAFT—See Rothenberger Group GmbH; *Int'l*, pg. 1128
ROTHENBERGER WERKZEUGE MASCHINEN GMBH—See Rothenberger Group GmbH; *Int'l*, pg. 1128
ROTHERT'S HOSPITAL EQUIPMENT, INC.—See Integrated Health Services, Inc.; *U.S. Public*, pg. 885
ROTHMANS BENSON & HEDGES INC.—See Rothmans UK Holdings Limited; *Int'l*, pg. 1130
ROTHMANS HOLDINGS LTD.—See Rothmans UK Holdings Limited; *Int'l*, pg. 1130
ROTHMANS INC.—See Rothmans UK Holdings Limited; *Int'l*, pg. 1129
ROTHMANS INDUSTRIES LTD.—See Rothmans UK Holdings Limited; *Int'l*, pg. 1130
ROTHMANS UK HOLDINGS LIMITED; *Int'l*, pg. 1129
ROTHMANS (UK) LTD.—See Rothmans UK Holdings Limited; *Int'l*, pg. 1130
ROTHSCHILD INC.—See Rothschild North America Inc.; *U.S. Private*, pg. 947
J. ROTHSCHILD ASSURANCE HOLDINGS—See St. James's Place Capital plc; *Int'l*, pg. 1178
J. ROTHSCHILD INVESTMENT MANAGEMENT LIMITED—See St. James's Place Capital plc; *Int'l*, pg. 1178
J. ROTHSCHILD WOLFENSOHN & CO.—See St. James's Place Capital plc; *Int'l*, pg. 1178
ROTHSCHILD NORTH AMERICA INC.; *U.S. Private*, pg. 947
ROTHSCHILD/PELL, RUDMAN & CO., INC.—See United Asset Management Corporation; *U.S. Public*, pg. 1674
ROTOFLOW CORPORATION—See Atlas Copco AB; *Int'l*, pg. 96
ROTOINK S.P.A.—See Dainippon Ink & Chemicals, Inc.; *Int'l*, pg. 371
ROTONICS MANUFACTURING INC.; *U.S. Public*, pg. 1406
ROTOPACK SAHRE GMBH—See Alusuisse-Lonza Holding Ltd.; *Int'l*, pg. 69
ROTOREX COMPANY, INC.—See Fedders Corp.; *U.S. Public*, pg. 615
ROTO-ROOTER—See Chemed Corporation; *U.S. Public*, pg. 344

ROTT-KELLER SUPPLY CO.; *U.S. Private*, pg. 947
ROTTA FARMACEUTICI, S.P.A.—See Rhone-Poulenc S.A.; *Int'l*, pg. 1112
ROTTERDAM INDUSTRIAL PARK—See Galesi Group; *U.S. Private*, pg. 437
N.V. ROTTERDAM RIJN PIJPLEIDING—See Veba AG; *Int'l*, pg. 1461
ROTTERDAM VENTURES INC.—See Galesi Group; *U.S. Private*, pg. 437
ROTTERDAM-RIJN PIJPLEIDING—See Royal Dutch/Shell Group of Companies; *Int'l*, pg. 1135
ROTTERDAMSE POLYOLEFINEN—See Royal Dutch/Shell Group of Companies; *Int'l*, pg. 1135
THE ROTTLUND COMPANY, INC.; *U.S. Public*, pg. 1406
ROTTLUND HOMES OF FLORIDA, INC.—See The Rottlund Company, Inc.; *U.S. Public*, pg. 1406
ROTTLUND HOMES OF INDIANA, INC.—See The Rottlund Company, Inc.; *U.S. Public*, pg. 1406
ROTTLUND HOMES OF IOWA, INC.—See The Rottlund Company, Inc.; *U.S. Public*, pg. 1406
ROTUNDA PLC—See Scapa Group Plc; *Int'l*, pg. 1202
ROUGE STEEL COMPANY; *U.S. Public*, pg. 1406
ROUGH BROTHERS, INC.; *U.S. Private*, pg. 947
ROULEMENT SERVICE S.A.—See Brammer; *Int'l*, pg. 212
ROUND MOUNTAIN GOLD CORPORATION—See Echo Bay Mines Ltd.; *U.S. Public*, pg. 562
ROUND MOUNTAIN GOLD CORPORATION—See Homestake Mining Company; *U.S. Public*, pg. 833
ROUNDTREE AUTOMOTIVE GROUP; *U.S. Private*, pg. 947
ROUNDY'S-COLUMBUS DIVISION—See Roundy's, Inc.; *U.S. Private*, pg. 948
ROUNDY'S GENERAL MERCHANDISE DIVISION—See Roundy's, Inc.; *U.S. Private*, pg. 948
ROUNDY'S, INC.; *U.S. Private*, pg. 948
ROUNDY'S, MILWAUKEE DIVISION—See Roundy's, Inc.; *U.S. Private*, pg. 948
ROUSE CENTRAL PARK SHOPPING CENTER, INC.—See The Rouse Company; *U.S. Public*, pg. 1409
ROUSE COMMERCE, INC.—See The Rouse Company; *U.S. Public*, pg. 1407
ROUSE COMMERCIAL DEVELOPMENT DIV.—See The Rouse Company; *U.S. Public*, pg. 1407
THE ROUSE COMPANY; *U.S. Public*, pg. 1407
THE ROUSE CO. FINANCIAL SERVICES, INC.—See The Rouse Company; *U.S. Public*, pg. 1407
ROUSE CONTROLLERS DIV.—See The Rouse Company; *U.S. Public*, pg. 1407
ROUSE MANAGEMENT, INC.—See The Rouse Company; *U.S. Public*, pg. 1409
ROUSE-MILWAUKEE GARAGE MAINTENANCE, INC.—See The Rouse Company; *U.S. Public*, pg. 1409
ROUSE-MILWAUKEE, INC.—See The Rouse Company; *U.S. Public*, pg. 1409
ROUSE PERSONNEL & ADMINISTRATIVE SERVICES DIV.—See The Rouse Company; *U.S. Public*, pg. 1407
ROUSE RESEARCH & SITE STRATEGY DIV.—See The Rouse Company; *U.S. Public*, pg. 1407
ROUSE SERVICE (CANADA) LIMITED—See The Rouse Company; *U.S. Public*, pg. 1409
ROUSE SI SHOPPING MANAGEMENT, INC.—See The Rouse Company; *U.S. Public*, pg. 1408
ROUSE THOMPSON & LLOYD LTD.—See Delta plc; *Int'l*, pg. 391
ROUSH INDUSTRIES INC.; *U.S. Private*, pg. 948
ROUSH PRODUCTS CO., INC.—See Diageo Plc; *Int'l*, pg. 411
ROUSSEL CORPORATION—See Hoechst Aktiengesellschaft; *Int'l*, pg. 625
ROUSSEL QUIMICA MEXICANA S.A. DE C.V.—See Hoechst Aktiengesellschaft; *Int'l*, pg. 625
ROUSSEL UCLAF S.A.—See Hoechst Aktiengesellschaft; *Int'l*, pg. 626
ROUTE 206 DEVELOPMENT CORP.—See High Point Financial Corp.; *U.S. Public*, pg. 826
J.H. ROUTH PACKING CO.; *U.S. Private*, pg. 948
ROUX COMBALUZIER SCHINDLER—See Schindler Holding AG; *Int'l*, pg. 1205
ROVAL S.A.R.L.—See Valmet Corporation; *Int'l*, pg. 1449
ROVER FINANCE HOLDING LIMITED—See National Westminster Bank PLC; *Int'l*, pg. 911
ROVER GROUP PLC—See Bayerische Motoren Werke Aktiengesellschaft; *Int'l*, pg. 178
ROVER GROUP LIMITED—See Bayerische Motoren Werke Aktiengesellschaft; *Int'l*, pg. 178
ROVIFARMA S.A.—See Pfizer Inc.; *U.S. Public*, pg. 1283
ROVIGYPT LTD.—See Roche Holding Ltd.; *Int'l*, pg. 1122
ROVIN ROTTERDAMSE VINYLUNIE VOF—See Akzo Nobel N.V.; *Int'l*, pg. 43
ROVITHAI LIMITED—See Roche Holding Ltd.; *Int'l*, pg. 1122
ROWAN COMPANIES, INC.; *U.S. Public*, pg. 1409
ROWAN DRILLING CO., INC.-ALASKA DIV.—See Rowan Companies, Inc.; *U.S. Public*, pg. 1410
ROWAN DRILLING (U.K.) LIMITED—See Rowan Companies, Inc.; *U.S. Public*, pg. 1410
D. ROWE & CO. LTD.—See Wolseley Plc.; *Int'l*, pg. 1512
ROWE & PITMAN LTD.—See Swiss Bank Corporation; *Int'l*, pg. 1331
ROWE & PITMAN MONEY BROKING LTD.—See Swiss Bank Corporation; *Int'l*, pg. 1331
THE ROWE CORPORATION; *U.S. Private*, pg. 948
ROWE FURNITURE CORP.; *U.S. Public*, pg. 1410
ROWE INDUSTRIES—See Carpenter Technology Corporation; *U.S. Public*, pg. 308
ROWE INTERNATIONAL, INC.—See RI Holdings; *U.S. Private*, pg. 904
ROWE PRICE-FLEMING INTERNATIONAL INC.—See Robert Fleming Holdings Ltd.; *Int'l*, pg. 493
ROWEN DRILLING & AVIATION B.V.—See Rowan Companies, Inc.; *U.S. Public*, pg. 1410
ROWENTA BELGIUM S.A.—See Groupe SEB; *Int'l*, pg. 569
ROWENTA ESPANA S.A.—See Groupe SEB; *Int'l*, pg. 569

ROWENTA FRANCE S.A.—See Groupe SEB; *Int'l*, pg. 569
ROWENTA ITALIA S.P.A.—See Groupe SEB; *Int'l*, pg. 569
ROWENTA NEDERLAND B.V.—See Groupe SEB; *Int'l*, pg. 569
ROWENTA U.K. LTD.—See Groupe SEB; *Int'l*, pg. 569
ROWENTA (USA), INC.—See Groupe SEB; *Int'l*, pg. 569
ROWENTA-VERTRIEBSGESELLSCHAFT MBH—See Groupe SEB; *Int'l*, pg. 569
ROWENTA WERKE—See Groupe SEB; *Int'l*, pg. 569
ROWLAND SERVICE CORPORATION—See Prime Bancorp, Inc.; *U.S. Public*, pg. 1326
ROWMAN & LITTLEFIELD PUBLISHERS, INC.—See University Press of America, Inc.; *U.S. Private*, pg. 1128
ROWOCO—See Wilton Industries, Inc.; *U.S. Private*, pg. 1182
ROWOHLT BERLIN VERLAG GMBH—See Georg von Holtzbrinck GmbH; *Int'l*, pg. 1478
ROWOHLT TASCHENBUCH VERLAG GMBH—See Georg von Holtzbrinck GmbH; *Int'l*, pg. 1478
ROWOHLT VERLAG GMBH—See Georg von Holtzbrinck GmbH; *Int'l*, pg. 1478
ROXANE LABORATORIES, INC.—See Boehringer Ingelheim GmbH; *Int'l*, pg. 199
ROXBORO ASSEMBLY FACILITY—See GKN plc; *Int'l*, pg. 535
THE ROXBORO GROUP PLC; *Int'l*, pg. 1130
ROXON AB—See Tamrock Corp.; *Int'l*, pg. 1353
ROXON COMPANIES OY—See Tamrock Corp.; *Int'l*, pg. 1353
ROXON KOMPONENTIT OY—See Tamrock Corp.; *Int'l*, pg. 1353
ROXON OY—See Tamrock Corp.; *Int'l*, pg. 1353
ROY ROGERS RESTAURANTS—See McDonald's Corporation; *U.S. Public*, pg. 1069
ROYAL ALLIANCE ASSOCIATES, INC.—See SunAmerica Inc.; *U.S. Public*, pg. 1533
ROYAL & SUN ALLIANCE INSURANCE GROUP—See Royal & Sun Alliance Insurance Group plc; *Int'l*, pg. 1130
ROYAL & SUN ALLIANCE INSURANCE GROUP PLC; *Int'l*, pg. 1130
ROYAL APPLIANCE MFG. CO.; *U.S. Public*, pg. 1410
ROYAL BANK ACTION DIRECT INC.—See Royal Bank of Canada; *Int'l*, pg. 1131
ROYAL BANK DEVELOPMENT CAPITAL LIMITED—See The Royal Bank of Scotland plc; *Int'l*, pg. 1132
ROYAL BANK EXPORT FINANCE CO. LTD. (REFCO)—See Royal Bank of Canada; *Int'l*, pg. 1131
ROYAL BANK INSURANCE CONSULTANTS LTD.—See The Royal Bank of Scotland plc; *Int'l*, pg. 1132
ROYAL BANK INSURANCE SERVICES LTD.—See The Royal Bank of Scotland plc; *Int'l*, pg. 1132
ROYAL BANK INVOICE FINANCE LIMITED—See The Royal Bank of Scotland plc; *Int'l*, pg. 1132
ROYAL BANK LEASING LTD.—See The Royal Bank of Scotland plc; *Int'l*, pg. 1132
ROYAL BANK OF CANADA; *Int'l*, pg. 1131
ROYAL BANK OF CANADA AG—See Royal Bank of Canada; *Int'l*, pg. 1131
ROYAL BANK OF CANADA (ASIA) LIMITED—See Royal Bank of Canada; *Int'l*, pg. 1131
ROYAL BANK OF CANADA (CHANNEL ISLANDS) LIMITED—See Royal Bank of Canada; *Int'l*, pg. 1131
ROYAL BANK OF CANADA FINANCIAL CORPORATION—See Royal Bank of Canada; *Int'l*, pg. 1132
THE ROYAL BANK OF SCOTLAND AG—See The Royal Bank of Scotland plc; *Int'l*, pg. 1133
THE ROYAL BANK OF SCOTLAND (GIBRALTAR) LIMITED—See The Royal Bank of Scotland plc; *Int'l*, pg. 1133
THE ROYAL BANK OF SCOTLAND (GUERNSEY) LIMITED—See The Royal Bank of Scotland plc; *Int'l*, pg. 1133
THE ROYAL BANK OF SCOTLAND (I.O.M.) LIMITED—See The Royal Bank of Scotland plc; *Int'l*, pg. 1133
THE ROYAL BANK OF SCOTLAND (JERSEY) LTD.—See The Royal Bank of Scotland plc; *Int'l*, pg. 1133
THE ROYAL BANK OF SCOTLAND (NASSAU) LIMITED—See The Royal Bank of Scotland plc; *Int'l*, pg. 1133
THE ROYAL BANK OF SCOTLAND PLC; *Int'l*, pg. 1132
THE ROYAL BANK OF SCOTLAND TRUST COMPANY (GUERNSEY) LIMITED—See The Royal Bank of Scotland plc; *Int'l*, pg. 1133
THE ROYAL BANK OF SCOTLAND TRUST COMPANY (JERSEY) LIMITED—See The Royal Bank of Scotland plc; *Int'l*, pg. 1133
ROYAL BEECH-NUT PTY LTD.—See Del Monte Royal Corporation; *Int'l*, pg. 388
ROYAL BEGEMANN GROUP; *Int'l*, pg. 1133
ROYAL CARIBBEAN CRUISES LTD.; *U.S. Public*, pg. 1410
ROYAL CHAMPIGNON—See Groupe Saint Louis; *Int'l*, pg. 567
THE ROYAL CHINA & PORCELAIN COMPANIES INC.; *U.S. Private*, pg. 948
ROYAL CONSUMER BUSINESS PRODUCTS—See Olivetti SpA; *Int'l*, pg. 1002
ROYAL COPENHAGEN & GEORG JENSEN PTY. LTD.—See Royal Copenhagen A/S; *Int'l*, pg. 1135
ROYAL COPENHAGEN ANTIQUES—See Royal Copenhagen A/S; *Int'l*, pg. 1134
ROYAL COPENHAGEN A/S; *Int'l*, pg. 1134
ROYAL COPENHAGEN GMBH—See Royal Copenhagen A/S; *Int'l*, pg. 1135
ROYAL COPENHAGEN HAWAII, INC.—See Royal Copenhagen A/S; *Int'l*, pg. 1135
ROYAL COPENHAGEN (HONG KONG) LTD.—See Royal Copenhagen A/S; *Int'l*, pg. 1135
ROYAL COPENHAGEN JAPAN LTD.—See Royal Copenhagen A/S; *Int'l*, pg. 1135
ROYAL COPENHAGEN LTD.—See Royal Copenhagen A/S; *Int'l*, pg. 1135

ROYAL COPENHAGEN NORGE A/S—See Royal
Copenhagen A/S; Int'l, pg. 1135
ROYAL COPENHAGEN PORCELAIN—See Royal
Copenhagen A/S; Int'l, pg. 1134
ROYAL COPENHAGEN PORCELAIN & GEORG JENSEN
SILVER—See Royal Copenhagen A/S; Int'l, pg. 1135
ROYAL COPENHAGEN PORCELAIN CORPORATION—
See Royal Copenhagen A/S; Int'l, pg. 1134
ROYAL COPENHAGEN RETAIL A/S—See Royal
Copenhagen A/S; Int'l, pg. 1134
ROYAL COPENHAGEN SINGAPORE PTE. LTD.—See
Royal Copenhagen A/S; Int'l, pg. 1135
ROYAL COPENHAGEN SVENSKA AB—See Royal
Copenhagen A/S; Int'l, pg. 1135
ROYAL COPENHAGEN (TAIWAN) LTD.—See Royal
Copenhagen A/S; Int'l, pg. 1135
ROYAL CROWN COMPANY, INC.—See Triarc Companies,
Inc.; U.S. Public, pg. 1635
ROYAL DEVELOPMENT CO., INC.—See Furniture Brands
International Inc.; U.S. Public, pg. 688
ROYAL DIVISION—See R & R Marketing; U.S. Private,
pg. 902
ROYAL DOULTON AUSTRALIA PTY. LIMITED—See Royal
Doulton Plc.; Int'l, pg. 1135
ROYAL DOULTON BENELUX BV—See Royal Doulton Plc.;
Int'l, pg. 1135
ROYAL DOULTON CANADA LIMITED—See Royal Doulton
Plc.; Int'l, pg. 1135
ROYAL DOULTON HONG KONG LIMITED—See Royal
Doulton Plc.; Int'l, pg. 1135
ROYAL DOULTON JAPAN KK—See Royal Doulton Plc.;
Int'l, pg. 1135
ROYAL DOULTON PLC.; Int'l, pg. 1135
ROYAL DOULTON (UK) LIMITED—See Royal Doulton Plc.;
Int'l, pg. 1135
ROYAL DOULTON USA INC.—See Royal Doulton Plc.;
Int'l, pg. 1135
ROYAL DUTCH/SHELL GROUP OF COMPANIES; Int'l,
pg. 1135
ROYAL FARMS INC.; U.S. Private, pg. 948
ROYAL FINANCIAL SERVICES INC.—See Royal & Sun
Alliance Insurance Group plc; Int'l, pg. 1131
ROYAL FOODS DISTRIBUTORS, INC.—See Fleming
Companies, Inc.; U.S. Public, pg. 653
ROYAL GIST-BROCADES N.V.; Int'l, pg. 1142
ROYAL GOLD—See Vendex International N.V.; Int'l,
pg. 1462
ROYAL GUEST, S.A.—See Caja de Madrid Group; Int'l,
pg. 252
ROYAL INDEMNITY CO.—See Royal & Sun Alliance
Insurance Group plc; Int'l, pg. 1131
ROYAL INSURANCE—See Royal & Sun Alliance Insurance
Group plc; Int'l, pg. 1130
ROYAL INSURANCE ATLANTIC REGIONAL CENTRE—
See Royal & Sun Alliance Insurance Group plc; Int'l,
pg. 1131
ROYAL INSURANCE COMPANY OF AMERICA—See Royal
& Sun Alliance Insurance Group plc; Int'l, pg. 1131
ROYAL INSURANCE COMPANY OF CANADA—See Royal
& Sun Alliance Insurance Group plc; Int'l, pg. 1131
ROYAL INSURANCE HAMILTON REGIONAL CENTRE—
See Royal & Sun Alliance Insurance Group plc; Int'l,
pg. 1131
ROYAL INSURANCE ONTARIO REGIONAL CENTRE—See
Royal & Sun Alliance Insurance Group plc; Int'l,
pg. 1131
ROYAL INSURANCE OTTAWA REGIONAL CENTRE—See
Royal & Sun Alliance Insurance Group plc; Int'l,
pg. 1131
ROYAL INSURANCE SERVICE CO. (GUERNSEY) LTD.—
See Royal & Sun Alliance Insurance Group plc; Int'l,
pg. 1130
ROYAL INSURANCE SERVICE CO. (ISLE OF MAN)
LTD.—See Royal & Sun Alliance Insurance Group plc;
Int'l, pg. 1130
ROYAL INSURANCE (UK) LTD.—See Royal & Sun Alliance
Insurance Group plc; Int'l, pg. 1130
ROYAL JEEP EAGLE CHRYSLER PLYMOUTH, INC.; U.S.
Private, pg. 948
ROYAL LEPAGE—See Royal LePage Limited; Int'l,
pg. 1143
ROYAL LEPAGE - BRITISH COLUMBIA OFFICE—See
Royal LePage Limited; Int'l, pg. 1143
ROYAL LEPAGE LIMITED; Int'l, pg. 1143
ROYAL LEPAGE - OTTAWA OFFICE—See Royal LePage
Limited; Int'l, pg. 1143
ROYAL LEPAGE - QUEBEC OFFICE—See Royal LePage
Limited; Int'l, pg. 1143
ROYAL LIFE HOLDINGS LIMITED—See Royal & Sun
Alliance Insurance Group plc; Int'l, pg. 1130
ROYAL LIFE INSURANCE COMPANY OF AMERICA—See
Royal & Sun Alliance Insurance Group plc; Int'l,
pg. 1131
ROYAL LIFE INSURANCE COMPANY OF CANADA—See
Royal & Sun Alliance Insurance Group plc; Int'l,
pg. 1130
ROYAL LIFE INSURANCE COMPANY OF NEW YORK—
See Royal & Sun Alliance Insurance Group plc; Int'l,
pg. 1131
ROYAL MAIL—See The Post Office; Int'l, pg. 1064
ROYAL MELROSE GRANITES—See Cold Spring Granite
Company; U.S. Private, pg. 251
ROYAL MUTUAL FUNDS INC.—See Royal Bank of
Canada; Int'l, pg. 1131
ROYAL NEDERLAND LEVENSVERZEKERING N.V.—See
AMB Aachener und Muenchener Beteiligungs-AG; Int'l,
pg. 16
ROYAL NEDERLAND SCHADEVERZEKERING—See AMB
Aachener und Muenchener Beteiligungs-AG; Int'l,
pg. 16
ROYAL NEDLLOYD GROUP N.V.; Int'l, pg. 1143
ROYAL OAK ENTERPRISES, INC.; U.S. Private, pg. 948
ROYAL OAK FORD INC.; U.S. Private, pg. 948
ROYAL OAK MINES INC.; U.S. Public, pg. 1410

ROYAL OLDSMOBILE MAZDA, INC.; U.S. Private, pg. 948
ROYAL OLYMPIC CRUISES; U.S. Public, pg. 1411
ROYAL ORDNANCE SPECIALTY METALS LTD.—See
British Aerospace plc; Int'l, pg. 217
ROYAL PACKAGING INDUSTRIES VAN LEER B.V.; Int'l,
pg. 1145
ROYAL PAKHOED NV; Int'l, pg. 1147
ROYAL PAPER BOX OF CALIFORNIA; U.S. Private,
pg. 949
ROYAL PLASTIC—See M.C. Gill Corporation; U.S. Private,
pg. 453
ROYAL PREMIUM BUDGET, INC.—See H.W. Kaufman
Financial Group, Inc.; U.S. Private, pg. 609
ROYAL RUBBER & MANUFACTURING CO.; U.S. Private,
pg. 949
ROYAL SCOTTISH ASSURANCE PLC—See The Royal
Bank of Scotland plc; Int'l, pg. 1132
ROYAL SKANDIA LIFE ASSURANCE LTD.—See Skandia
Insurance Company Limited; Int'l, pg. 1257
ROYAL TIME CITI CO., LTD.—See Citizen Watch
Company, Ltd.; Int'l, pg. 295
ROYAL TOTO METAL CO., LTD.—See Toto Ltd.; Int'l,
pg. 1410
ROYAL TOURIST, LTD.—See Sanyo Electric Co., Ltd.; Int'l,
pg. 1191
ROYAL WATERBEDS, LTD.; U.S. Private, pg. 949
ROYALE BELGE FINANCE—See Groupe Bruxelles
Lambert S.A.; Int'l, pg. 562
ROYALE BELGE RE—See Groupe Bruxelles Lambert S.A.;
Int'l, pg. 562
ROYALE BELGE S.A.—See Groupe Bruxelles Lambert
S.A.; Int'l, pg. 562
ROYALE COACH—See Monaco Coach Corporation; U.S.
Public, pg. 1123
ROYALE PAINT & BODY—See Regency Lincoln Mercury,
Inc.; U.S. Private, pg. 918
ROYALE UAP IARD—See Groupe Bruxelles Lambert S.A.;
Int'l, pg. 562
ROYALE UAP VIE—See Groupe Bruxelles Lambert S.A.;
Int'l, pg. 562
ROYCE LABORATORIES—See Watson Pharmaceuticals,
Inc.; U.S. Public, pg. 1746
ROYER INDUSTRIES, INC.—See Powerscreen
International Plc; Int'l, pg. 1066
LOUIS ROYER S.A.—See Suntory Ltd.; Int'l, pg. 1322
ROYER/MOGENSEN, INC.—See Powerscreen
International Plc; Int'l, pg. 1066
ROYLE SYSTEMS GROUP; U.S. Private, pg. 949
ROYNAT—See The Bank of Nova Scotia; Int'l, pg. 155
ROYNEAU—See SNCF; Int'l, pg. 1164
ROYSCOT FACTORS LIMITED—See The Royal Bank of
Scotland plc; Int'l, pg. 1132
ROYSCOT FINANCE GROUP PLC—See The Royal Bank
of Scotland plc; Int'l, pg. 1132
ROYSCOT FINANCIAL SERVICES—See The Royal Bank
of Scotland plc; Int'l, pg. 1132
ROYSCOT TRUST PLC—See The Royal Bank of Scotland
plc; Int'l, pg. 1132
ROYSTER-CLARK, INC.; U.S. Private, pg. 949
ROYSTON LABORATORIES—See Chase Corporation; U.S.
Public, pg. 337
ROYTEX, INC.; U.S. Private, pg. 949
ROZES LIMITADA—See LVMH Moet Hennessy Louis
Vuitton; Int'l, pg. 783
RUBATEX CORPORATION—See American Industrial
Partners; U.S. Private, pg. 56
RUBBER & PLASTICS NEWS—See Crain Communications,
Inc.; U.S. Private, pg. 285
RUBBER GROUP—See National-Standard Co.; U.S. Public,
pg. 1160
RUBBER MOLDING DIVISION—See Eagle-Picher
Industries, Inc.; U.S. Private, pg. 355
RUBBERHIDE COMPANY—See Trelleborg AB; Int'l,
pg. 1423
RUBBERMAID CANADA INC. CONSUMER PRODUCTS—
See Rubbermaid Incorporated; U.S. Public, pg. 1411
RUBBERMAID DE MEXICO—See Rubbermaid
Incorporated; U.S. Public, pg. 1411
RUBBERMAID HEALTHCARE PRODUCTS—See
Rubbermaid Incorporated; U.S. Public, pg. 1411
RUBBERMAID HOME PRODUCTS DIV.—See Rubbermaid
Incorporated; U.S. Public, pg. 1411
RUBBERMAID INCORPORATED; U.S. Public, pg. 1411
RUBBERMAID-STATESVILLE INC.—See Rubbermaid
Incorporated; U.S. Public, pg. 1411
RUBEROID AG—See Ruetgers A.G.; Int'l, pg. 1148
RUBICON INC.—See Crompton & Knowles Corporation;
U.S. Public, pg. 460
RUBIN EHRENTHAL & ASSOCIATES; U.S. Private,
pg. 949
M. RUBIN & SONS INC.; U.S. Private, pg. 949
RUBIN POSTAER & ASSOCIATES; U.S. Private, pg. 949
RUBIN POSTAER & ASSOCIATES—See Rubin Postaer &
Associates; U.S. Private, pg. 950
RUBINETTERIE MARIANI S.P.A.—See Masco Corporation;
U.S. Public, pg. 1055
RUBSON BENELUX S.A.—See Henkel KGaA; Int'l, pg. 614
RUBSON IBERICA S.A.—See Henkel KGaA; Int'l, pg. 612
RUBSON S.A.F.C.—See Henkel KGaA; Int'l, pg. 614
RUBSTEEL AB—See Royal Packaging Industries Van Leer
B.V.; Int'l, pg. 1146
RUBY TUESDAY, INC.; U.S. Public, pg. 1411
RUBY TUESDAY RESTAURANTS—See Ruby Tuesday,
Inc.; U.S. Public, pg. 1412
RUD, BLASS & CIE LTD. BANKERS—See Zurich
Insurance Company; Int'l, pg. 1529
RUDDICK CORPORATION; U.S. Public, pg. 1412
RUDDLES BREWERY LTD.—See Grolsch N.V.; Int'l,
pg. 559
RUDEL MACHINERY COMPANY, INC.; U.S. Private,
pg. 950
RUDOLPH AND SLETTEN, INC.; U.S. Private, pg. 950
RUDOLPH FOODS COMPANY; U.S. Private, pg. 950
RUDOLPH/LIBBE, INC.; U.S. Private, pg. 950

RUDOLPHE HALLER AG—See Panalpina Welttransport
(Holding) AG; Int'l, pg. 1022
RUDUS EESTI AS—See Scancem AB; Int'l, pg. 1201
RUEDAS DE ALUMINIO C.A. "RUALCA"—See Reynolds
Metals Company; U.S. Public, pg. 1387
GEORGES RUEDIN SA—See SMH Swiss Corporation for
Micro Electronics & Watchmaking Indus. Ltd.; Int'l,
pg. 1160
RUETGERS A.G.; Int'l, pg. 1147
RUETGERS-NEASE CORPORATION—See Ruetgers A.G.;
Int'l, pg. 1148
RUF AG—See Hesta Tex AG; Int'l, pg. 618
RUF DATENSYSTEME GMBH—See Hesta Tex AG; Int'l,
pg. 618
RUFAS RUTGERS FAHRZEUG-SYSTEME AG—See
Ruetgers A.G.; Int'l, pg. 1148
RUFFIN BUILDING SYSTEMS, INC.; U.S. Private, pg. 950
RUGBY FARMERS UNION ELEVATOR COMPANY; U.S.
Private, pg. 950
THE RUGBY GROUP, INC.—See Hoechst
Aktiengesellschaft; Int'l, pg. 625
RUGER INVESTMENT CASTINGS—See Sturm, Ruger &
Co., Inc.; U.S. Public, pg. 1526
RUGG MANUFACTURING COMPANY; U.S. Private,
pg. 950
RUHLE COMPANIES, INC.; U.S. Private, pg. 950
THE RUHLIN COMPANY; U.S. Private, pg. 951
RUHR OEL GMBH—See Veba AG; Int'l, pg. 1461
RUHR PULVERLACK G.M.B.H.—See Ferro Corporation;
U.S. Public, pg. 620
RUHR-SCHWEFELSAURE GMBH & CO. KG—See Veba
AG; Int'l, pg. 1461
RUHRGAS AG—See Ruhrgas Aktiengesellschaft; Int'l,
pg. 1149
RUHRGAS AKTIENGESELLSCHAFT; Int'l, pg. 1148
RUHRGAS ENERGIE BETEILIGUNGS-
AKTIENGESELLSCHAFT—See Ruhrgas
Aktiengesellschaft; Int'l, pg. 1149
RUHRGAS INDUSTRIE BETEILIGUNGSGESELLSCHAFT
MBH—See Ruhrgas Aktiengesellschaft; Int'l, pg. 1149
RUHRGAS UK EXPLORATION AND PRODUCTION
LIMITED—See Ruhrgas Aktiengesellschaft; Int'l,
pg. 1149
RUHRKOHLE-UMWELTTECHNIK GMBH (RUT)—See Veba
AG; Int'l, pg. 1460
RUHRPUMPEN GMBH—See Derlan Industries Limited;
Int'l, pg. 395
RUIDOSO CARE CENTER—See Horizon/CMS Healthcare
Corporation; U.S. Public, pg. 838
RUIZ FOOD PRODUCTS, INC.; U.S. Private, pg. 951
RUIZ NICOLI GROUP—See Havas Advertising; Int'l,
pg. 603
A/S RUKO—See Assa Abloy AB; Int'l, pg. 18
RUKO GMBH PRAZISIONSWERKZEUGE—See
Rothenberger Group GmbH; Int'l, pg. 1128
RULE CUTTING TOOLS, INC.—See Kennametal Inc.; U.S.
Public, pg. 951
RULE INDUSTRIES, INC.—See Kennametal Inc.; U.S.
Public, pg. 950
L.A. RUMBOLD LIMITED—See Britax International plc; Int'l,
pg. 216
RUMENCO—See Tate & Lyle PLC; Int'l, pg. 1356
RUMS OF PUERTO RICO; U.S. Private, pg. 951
RUMSEY ELECTRIC COMPANY; U.S. Private, pg. 951
RUNCORN TERMINAL—See GATX Corporation; U.S.
Public, pg. 693
RUNDEL PRODUCTS, INC.; U.S. Private, pg. 951
RUNNERS POINT WARENHANDELSGESELLSCHAFT
MBH—See Karstadt Aktiengesellschaft; Int'l, pg. 724
RUNNYMEDE DISPERSION LTD.—See Dainippon Ink &
Chemicals, Inc.; Int'l, pg. 371
RUNOTO BELGIUM—See ING Groep N.V.; Int'l, pg. 651
RUNWAY TWO FIVE CORPORATION—See Specialty
Restaurants Corporation; U.S. Private, pg. 1022
RUPP AUTOMOTIVE—See Republic Automotive Parts, Inc.;
U.S. Public, pg. 1378
RUPPKERAMIK GMBH—See Redland PLC; Int'l, pg. 1091
RUPPMAN MARKETING TECHNOLOGIES, INC.; U.S.
Private, pg. 951
RUPPMAN MARKETING TECHNOLOGIES, INC.—See
Ruppman Marketing Technologies, Inc.; U.S. Private,
pg. 952
RUPPMAN NATIONAL YELLOW PAGES SERVICE INC.—
See Ruppman Marketing Technologies, Inc.; U.S.
Private, pg. 952
RURAL ELECTRIC CO-OP; U.S. Private, pg. 952
RURAL METRO CORPORATION; U.S. Public, pg. 1412
RURBAN FINANCIAL CORP.; U.S. Public, pg. 1412
RURBAN LIFE INSURANCE COMPANY—See Rurban
Financial Corp.; U.S. Public, pg. 1413
RURBANC DATA SERVICES, INC.—See Rurban Financial
Corp.; U.S. Public, pg. 1413
RUSCH—See Teleflex Incorporated; U.S. Public, pg. 1569
RUSCON CORP.; U.S. Private, pg. 952
C.J. RUSH INC.—See Derlan Industries Limited; Int'l,
pg. 395
RUSH PRESS—See Continental Graphics Holdings, Inc.;
U.S. Private, pg. 268
RUSHTON MINING CO.—See PP&L Resources; U.S.
Public, pg. 1244
RUSKA INSTRUMENT CORPORATION; U.S. Private,
pg. 952
RUSKIN DIV.—See Tomkins PLC; Int'l, pg. 1398
RUSLANDER & SONS, INC.; U.S. Private, pg. 952
JOHN RUSLING LTD.—See Up-Right, Inc.; U.S. Private,
pg. 1128
RUSS REID CO.—See Russ Reid Company, Inc.; U.S.
Private, pg. 952
RUSS REID COMPANY, INC.; U.S. Private, pg. 952
RUSSEL METALS INC.; Int'l, pg. 1149
RUSSELL ASSOCIATES INC.—See Pall Corporation; U.S.
Public, pg. 1254
RUSSELL CASTINGS LTD.—See B. Elliott plc; Int'l,
pg. 449

RUSSELL CHEVROLET COMPANY; *U.S. Private*, pg. 952
RUSSELL CORPORATION; *U.S. Public*, pg. 1413
RUSSELL CORP. UK LIMITED—See Russell Corporation; *U.S. Public*, pg. 1413
RUSSELL DEVELOPMENT CORP.—See Russell Corporation; *U.S. Public*, pg. 1413
FRANK RUSSELL COMPANY; *U.S. Private*, pg. 952
FRANK RUSSELL SECURITIES, INC.—See Frank Russell Company; *U.S. Private*, pg. 952
FRANK RUSSELL TRUST CO.—See Frank Russell Company; *U.S. Private*, pg. 952
H.J. RUSSELL & CO.; *U.S. Private*, pg. 952
THE RUSSELL NATIONAL BANK—See Omega Financial Corporation; *U.S. Public*, pg. 1222
RUSSELL PETROLEUM CORPORATION; *U.S. Private*, pg. 953
RUSSELL PH LIMITED—See Thermo Electron Corporation; *U.S. Public*, pg. 1592
RUSSELL-STANLEY CORPORATION; *U.S. Private*, pg. 953
RUSSELL STATE BANK—See UMB Financial Corporation; *U.S. Public*, pg. 1654
RUSSELL STOVER CANDIES, INC.; *U.S. Private*, pg. 953
RUSSER FOODS—See Zemco Industries, Inc.; *U.S. Private*, pg. 1204
RUSSIAN RIVER BREWING COMPANY—See F. Korbel Bros. Inc.; *U.S. Private*, pg. 632
RUST CRAFT CANADA, INC.—See American Greetings Corporation; *U.S. Public*, pg. 78
RUST CRAFT GREETING CARDS (U.K.) LIMITED—See American Greetings Corporation; *U.S. Public*, pg. 78
RUST CRAFT INTERNATIONAL, S.A.—See American Greetings Corporation; *U.S. Public*, pg. 78
RUST ENGINEERING & CONSTRUCTION CO.—See Raytheon Company; *U.S. Public*, pg. 1366
RUST ENVIRONMENT AND INFRASTRUCTURE—See Raytheon Company; *U.S. Public*, pg. 1366
RUST ENVIRONMENT & INFRASTRUCTURE—See CBS Corporation; *U.S. Public*, pg. 273
RUST ENVIRONMENT & INFRASTRUCTURE, INC.—See Waste Management, Inc.; *U.S. Public*, pg. 1745
RUST FEDERAL SERVICES INC.—See Raytheon Company; *U.S. Public*, pg. 1366
RUST INTERNATIONAL INC.—See Raytheon Company; *U.S. Public*, pg. 1366
RUST LIMITED—See Raytheon Company; *U.S. Public*, pg. 1366
RUST-OLEUM CORPORATION—See RPM, Inc.; *U.S. Public*, pg. 1358
RUST-OLEUM NEDERLAND B.V.—See RPM, Inc.; *U.S. Public*, pg. 1358
RUST REMEDIAL—See Raytheon Company; *U.S. Public*, pg. 1366
RUTGERS KUREHA SOLVENTS GMBH—See Ruetgers A.G.; *Int'l*, pg. 1148
RUTGERS PAGID AG—See Ruetgers A.G.; *Int'l*, pg. 1148
RUTHERFORD WAREHOUSE CORP.—See Stonecutter Mills Corp.; *U.S. Private*, pg. 1044
RUTHIN INVESTMENTS LIMITED—See Jardine Matheson Holdings Limited; *Int'l*, pg. 704
RUTLAND PLASTIC TECHNOLOGIES, INC.—See Florida Capital Partners; *U.S. Private*, pg. 414
RUTT CUSTOM CABINETRY—See Harrow Industries; *U.S. Private*, pg. 507
RUTTER GROUP—See The Thomson Corporation; *U.S. Public*, pg. 1602
RYAN CONSTRUCTION COMPANY—See Ryan Construction Company of Minnesota, Inc.; *U.S. Private*, pg. 953
RYAN CONSTRUCTION COMPANY OF MINNESOTA—See Ryan Construction Company of Minnesota, Inc.; *U.S. Private*, pg. 953
RYAN CONSTRUCTION COMPANY OF MINNESOTA, INC.; *U.S. Private*, pg. 953
RYAN DROSSMAN & PARTNERS; *U.S. Private*, pg. 953
RYAN FOODS—See Dean Foods Company; *U.S. Public*, pg. 491
RYAN HERCO PRODUCTS CORP.; *U.S. Private*, pg. 953
RYAN INSURANCE GROUP, INC.—See AON Corporation; *U.S. Public*, pg. 118
RYAN OLDSMOBILE; *U.S. Private*, pg. 953
RYAN'S FAMILY STEAK HOUSES, INC.; *U.S. Public*, pg. 1413
RYCO-ALBERICI, LTD.—See J.S. Alberici Construction Co., Inc.; *U.S. Private*, pg. 32
RYDELLE LABORATORIES—See S.C. Johnson & Son, Inc.; *U.S. Private*, pg. 592
RYDER INTERNATIONAL—See Atrion Corporation; *U.S. Public*, pg. 146
RYDER SYSTEM, INC.; *U.S. Public*, pg. 1413
RYDS BATINDUSTRI AB—See Greenway Partners, L.P.; *U.S. Private*, pg. 479
RYERSON DE MEXICO—See Altos Hornos de Mexico, S.A.; *Int'l*, pg. 66
RYERSON DE MEXICO/MEXICO, D.F.—See Altos Hornos de Mexico, S.A.; *Int'l*, pg. 66
RYERSON DE MEXICO, MONCLOVA DIV.—See Altos Hornos de Mexico, S.A.; *Int'l*, pg. 66
RYERSON DE MEXICO/WEST DIVISION—See Altos Hornos de Mexico, S.A.; *Int'l*, pg. 66
JOSEPH T. RYERSON & SON, INC.—See Inland Steel Industries, Inc.; *U.S. Public*, pg. 879
RYERSON TULL—See Inland Steel Industries, Inc.; *U.S. Public*, pg. 879
RYKA INCORPORATED; *U.S. Public*, pg. 1414
RYKOFF-SEXTON, INC.—See JP Foodservice, Inc.; *U.S. Public*, pg. 918
THE RYLAND GROUP, INC.; *U.S. Public*, pg. 1414
RYLANDS WHITECROSS LTD.—See N.V. Bekaert S.A.; *Int'l*, pg. 185
RYMER FOODS INC.; *U.S. Public*, pg. 1414
RYMER INTERNATIONAL SEAFOOD INC.—See Rymer Foods Inc.; *U.S. Public*, pg. 1414

RYMER MEAT INC.—See Rymer Foods Inc.; *U.S. Public*, pg. 1414
RYNONE MANUFACTURING CORPORATION; *U.S. Private*, pg. 953
RYOBI AMERICA CORP.—See Ryobi Ltd.; *Int'l*, pg. 1151
RYOBI ELECTRIC TOOL MFG.—See Ryobi Ltd.; *Int'l*, pg. 1151
RYOBI LTD.; *Int'l*, pg. 1151
RYOBI MOTOR PRODUCTS—See Ryobi Ltd.; *Int'l*, pg. 1151
RYOBI NORTH AMERICA, INC.—See Ryobi Ltd.; *Int'l*, pg. 1151
RYON'S SADDLE & RANCH SUPPLY—See Luskeys Western Stores, Inc.; *U.S. Private*, pg. 681
RYSTAN COMPANY, INC.—See GWC Health, Inc.; *U.S. Private*, pg. 436
THE RYTEX COMPANY—See American Stationery Co., Inc.; *U.S. Private*, pg. 62
RYTHM WATCH CO., LTD.—See Citizen Watch Company, Ltd.; *Int'l*, pg. 294

S

S & A LESME CALLEBAUT—See Barry Callebaut N.V.; *Int'l*, pg. 252
S & G SEEDS B.V.—See Novartis AG; *Int'l*, pg. 984
S & G SEMENCES S.A.—See Novartis AG; *Int'l*, pg. 984
S & G SAMEN G.M.B.H.—See Novartis AG; *Int'l*, pg. 984
S & B ALTIM—See BTR plc; *Int'l*, pg. 129
S & C ELECTRIC CANADA LTD.—See S & C Electric Company; *U.S. Private*, pg. 954
S & C ELECTRIC COMPANY; *U.S. Private*, pg. 954
S & C MAINTENANCE CORP.—See Spatz Centers Inc.; *U.S. Private*, pg. 1021
S&C WILLIS CORROON CORREDURIA DE SEGUROS Y REASEGUROS S.A.—See Willis Corroon Group PLC; *Int'l*, pg. 1509
S&D COFFEE INC.; *U.S. Private*, pg. 954
S&G CONCRETE CO.—See Florida Rock Industries, Inc.; *U.S. Public*, pg. 656
S & G IMPLANTS GMBH—See Bristol-Myers Squibb Company; *U.S. Public*, pg. 256
S&H CITADEL, INC.—See Leucadia National Corporation; *U.S. Public*, pg. 990
S & J INDUSTRIES—See North American Products Corp.; *U.S. Private*, pg. 803
S & K FAMOUS BRANDS, INC.; *U.S. Public*, pg. 1414
S & M DEVELOPMENTS LIMITED—See Sun Life Assurance Company of Canada; *Int'l*, pg. 1319
S&N KATZ JEWELERS—See Reliable Stores, Inc.; *U.S. Private*, pg. 921
S & P COIL PRODUCTS LIMITED—See Halma p.l.c.; *Int'l*, pg. 590
S & P COMPANY; *U.S. Private*, pg. 954
S & P COMSTOCK—See The McGraw-Hill Companies; *U.S. Public*, pg. 1071
S & S CAFETERIAS—See Smith & Sons Foods, Inc.; *U.S. Private*, pg. 1007
S & S (DIHALL) COGENERATION, INC.—See Stewart & Stevenson Services, Inc.; *U.S. Public*, pg. 1517
S & S DIVERSIFIED FOOD SERVICE, INC.—See Smith & Sons Foods, Inc.; *U.S. Private*, pg. 1007
S&S DOMESTIC INTERNATIONAL SALES CORP.—See Stewart & Stevenson Services, Inc.; *U.S. Public*, pg. 1517
S&S ENERGY PRODUCTS—See General Electric Company; *U.S. Public*, pg. 711
S & S FOOD ADMINISTRATORS—See Smith & Sons Foods, Inc.; *U.S. Private*, pg. 1007
S & S GRAPHICS, INC.; *U.S. Private*, pg. 955
S&S-HARTWELL CO., INC.—See Axel Johnson AB; *Int'l*, pg. 710
S & W CONSTRUCTION SERVICES INC—See Shannon & Wilson, Inc.; *U.S. Private*, pg. 989
S & W ELEKTROMEDIZIN GMBH—See Vickers PLC; *Int'l*, pg. 1467
S & W MEDICO TEKNIK A/S—See Vickers PLC; *Int'l*, pg. 1468
S-B POWER TOOL COMPANY—See Robert Bosch GmbH; *Int'l*, pg. 205
S-BETEILIGUNGSGESELLSCHAFT HESSEN- THURINGEN MBH—See Landesbank Hessen-Thuringen Girozentrale; *Int'l*, pg. 799
S-E-BANKEN BOLAN AB—See Skandinaviska Enskilda Banken; *Int'l*, pg. 1259
S-E-BANKEN CUSTODY SERVICE—See Skandinaviska Enskilda Banken; *Int'l*, pg. 1259
S-E-BANKEN FORETAGSINVEST—See Skandinaviska Enskilda Banken; *Int'l*, pg. 1259
S-E-BANKEN FORSAKRING—See Skandinaviska Enskilda Banken; *Int'l*, pg. 1259
S-E-BANKEN LUXEMBOURG S.A.—See Skandinaviska Enskilda Banken; *Int'l*, pg. 1259
S-E-BANKEN LUXEMBOURG S.A., LONDON—See Skandinaviska Enskilda Banken; *Int'l*, pg. 1259
S-E-BANKEN LUXEMBOURG S.A., NICE—See Skandinaviska Enskilda Banken; *Int'l*, pg. 1259
S-E-BANKEN LUXEMBOURG S.A., SAN PEDRO—See Skandinaviska Enskilda Banken; *Int'l*, pg. 1259
SHL SYSTEMHOUSE - ASIA/PACIFIC—See SHL Systemhouse; *Int'l*, pg. 1154
SHL SYSTEMHOUSE - ATLANTIC REGION—See SHL Systemhouse; *Int'l*, pg. 1154
SHL SYSTEMHOUSE - CALGARY—See SHL Systemhouse; *Int'l*, pg. 1154
SHL SYSTEMHOUSE - REGINA—See SHL Systemhouse; *Int'l*, pg. 1154
SHL SYSTEMHOUSE - WESTERN REGION—See SHL Systemhouse; *Int'l*, pg. 1154
SHL SYSTEMHOUSE - WINNIPEG—See SHL Systemhouse; *Int'l*, pg. 1154
S INVEST AB—See Axel Johnson AB; *Int'l*, pg. 709

S.L. BUILDING INVESTMENTS PTE LIMITED—See Singapore Land Limited; *Int'l*, pg. 1253
S L C GRAPHICS, LP; *U.S. Private*, pg. 955
S.L. CIVIC INVESTMENTS PTE LIMITED—See Singapore Land Limited; *Int'l*, pg. 1253
S.L. DEVELOPMENT MANAGEMENT PTE LIMITED—See Singapore Land Limited; *Int'l*, pg. 1253
S.L. EARN INVESTMENTS PTE LIMITED—See Singapore Land Limited; *Int'l*, pg. 1253
S.L. HOME LOANS PTE LTD.—See Singapore Land Limited; *Int'l*, pg. 1253
S.L. MANAGEMENT SERVICES PTE LIMITED—See Singapore Land Limited; *Int'l*, pg. 1253
S.L. MARINA CENTRE DEVELOPMENT PRIVATE LIMITED—See Singapore Land Limited; *Int'l*, pg. 1253
S.L. PRIME DEVELOPMENT PTE LTD.—See Singapore Land Limited; *Int'l*, pg. 1253
S.L. PRIME SECURITIES PTE LTD.—See Singapore Land Limited; *Int'l*, pg. 1253
S.L. PROPERTIES LIMITED—See Singapore Land Limited; *Int'l*, pg. 1253
S.L. REALTY MANAGEMENT SERVICES (HK) LIMITED—See Singapore Land Limited; *Int'l*, pg. 1253
S.L. REALTY SERVICES PTE LIMITED—See Singapore Land Limited; *Int'l*, pg. 1253
SM5—See Thomson S.A.; *Int'l*, pg. 1382
S MOS SYSTEMS, INC.—See Seiko Epson Corporation; *Int'l*, pg. 1219
S-N BEDDING CO. INC.—See Silentnight Holdings Plc; *Int'l*, pg. 1249
S3 INCORPORATED; *U.S. Public*, pg. 1415
S.TWO SYSTEMS CORPORATION—See Stratus Computer, Inc.; *U.S. Public*, pg. 1524
S.TWO SYSTEMS, INC.—See Stratus Computer, Inc.; *U.S. Public*, pg. 1524
SA-SO COMPANY; *U.S. Private*, pg. 955
S.A. USA—See Ship Analytics, Inc.; *U.S. Private*, pg. 994
SAA INTERMARKETS—See Intermarkets Advertising; *Int'l*, pg. 680
SAB ELECTRONIC DEVICES LTD.—See Telefonaktiebolaget LM Ericsson; *Int'l*, pg. 1369
SAB IBERICA S.A.—See Cardo AB; *Int'l*, pg. 271
SAB INTERNATIONAL INC.—See South African Breweries, Ltd.; *Int'l*, pg. 1287
SAB NIFE OY—See Alcatel Alsthom Compagnie Generale D'Electricite; *Int'l*, pg. 54
SAB NIFE (SUISSE) S.A.—See Alcatel Alsthom Compagnie Generale D'Electricite; *Int'l*, pg. 54
SAB PROFIEL B.V.—See Koninklijke Hoogovens N.V.; *Int'l*, pg. 754
SAB-PROFIL GMBH—See Koninklijke Hoogovens N.V.; *Int'l*, pg. 754
SAB SISTEMI S.P.A.—See Cardo AB; *Int'l*, pg. 271
SAB WABCO AB—See Cardo AB; *Int'l*, pg. 271
SAB WABCO BENELUX—See Cardo AB; *Int'l*, pg. 271
SAB WABCO CS, S.R.O.—See Cardo AB; *Int'l*, pg. 271
SAB WABCO DO BRASIL SA—See Cardo AB; *Int'l*, pg. 271
SAB WABCO ENGINEERING S.R.L.—See Cardo AB; *Int'l*, pg. 271
SAB WABCO GMBH—See Cardo AB; *Int'l*, pg. 271
SAB WABCO HOLDINGS B.V.—See Cardo AB; *Int'l*, pg. 271
SAB WABCO LTD.—See Cardo AB; *Int'l*, pg. 271
SAB WABCO N.V.—See Cardo AB; *Int'l*, pg. 271
SAB WABCO S.A.—See Cardo AB; *Int'l*, pg. 271
SAB WABCO S.P.A.—See Cardo AB; *Int'l*, pg. 271
SABM, SOCIETE AFRICAINE DE BETON MANUFACTURE S.A.—See Dyckerhoff & Widmann AG; *Int'l*, pg. 425
SABO-MASCHINENFABRIK GMBH—See Deere & Company; *U.S. Public*, pg. 493
SACOC—See Amcor Limited; *Int'l*, pg. 72
SADE—See Compagnie Generale Des Eaux; *Int'l*, pg. 321
SAE ENGINEERING, INC.; *U.S. Private*, pg. 955
SAE (INDIA) LTD.—See ABB Asea Brown Boveri (Holding) Ltd.; *Int'l*, pg. 3
SAE-SOCIETA ANONIMA ELECTRIFICAZIONE S.P.A.—See ABB Asea Brown Boveri (Holding) Ltd.; *Int'l*, pg. 3
S.A.E. WANDER—See Novartis AG; *Int'l*, pg. 984
SAEL—See ISS-International Service System A/S; *Int'l*, pg. 657
SAFA—See Rhone-Poulenc S.A.; *Int'l*, pg. 1114
SAFT—See Alcatel Alsthom Compagnie Generale D'Electricite; *Int'l*, pg. 54
SAFT NIFE AB—See Alcatel Alsthom Compagnie Generale D'Electricite; *Int'l*, pg. 54
S.A.G.A.R.—See Accor S.A.; *Int'l*, pg. 21
S.A.G.E. SERENGI AZIENDA GRAFICA ED EDITORIALE S.P.A.—See Arnoldo Mondadori Editore S.p.A.; *Int'l*, pg. 888
SAGEM ALLUMAGE—See Societe d'Applications Generales d'Electricite et de Mechanique; *Int'l*, pg. 1273
SAGEM ELECTRONICS AND INDUSTRY DIVISION—See Societe d'Applications Generales d'Electricite et de Mechanique; *Int'l*, pg. 1273
SAGEM NAVIGATION AND DEFENSE DIVISION—See Societe d'Applications Generales d'Electricite et de Mechanique; *Int'l*, pg. 1273
SAGEM TERMINALS & TELECOMMUNICATIONS DIVISION—See Societe d'Applications Generales d'Electricite et de Mechanique; *Int'l*, pg. 1273
SAI DISTRIBUTORS—See Sound Advice, Inc.; *U.S. Public*, pg. 1488
SAI PTY LTD.—See Science Applications International Corp.; *U.S. Private*, pg. 976
SAIA AG—See Williams Holdings Plc; *Int'l*, pg. 1500
SAIA-BURGESS—See Williams Holdings Plc; *Int'l*, pg. 1500
SAIA-BURGESS ELECTRONICS GMBH—See Williams Holdings Plc; *Int'l*, pg. 1501
SAIA-BURGESS GES.MBH—See Williams Holdings Plc; *Int'l*, pg. 1501
SAIA-BURGESS GMBH—See Williams Holdings Plc; *Int'l*, pg. 1501

Company Index

SAIA-BURGESS SRL—See Williams Holdings Plc; *Int'l*, pg. 1501
SAIC—See Science Applications International Corp.; *U.S. Private*, pg. 976
SAIC COLOMBIA, LIMITADA—See Science Applications International Corp.; *U.S. Private*, pg. 976
SAIC COMMERCIAL ENTERPRISES, INC.—See Science Applications International Corp.; *U.S. Private*, pg. 976
SAIC COMSYSTEMS—See Science Applications International Corp.; *U.S. Private*, pg. 976
SAIC DE MEXICO, S.A. DE C.V.—See Science Applications International Corp.; *U.S. Private*, pg. 976
SAIC ENGINEERING, INC.—See Science Applications International Corp.; *U.S. Private*, pg. 976
SAIC IN NOVOSIBIRSK—See Science Applications International Corp.; *U.S. Private*, pg. 976
SAIC INDONESIA LIMITED—See Science Applications International Corp.; *U.S. Private*, pg. 976
SAIC-MIR/SAIC GLOBAL TECHNOLOGY—See Science Applications International Corp.; *U.S. Private*, pg. 976
SAIC TECHNOLOGY—See Science Applications International Corp.; *U.S. Private*, pg. 976
SAIC UK LIMITED—See Science Applications International Corp.; *U.S. Private*, pg. 976
SAIFA-KELLER S.A.—See Rieter Holdings; *Int'l*, pg. 1117
SAIM SOCIETE LES ADHESIFS ET INSONORISANTS MODERNES, SA—See Henkel KGaA; *Int'l*, pg. 614
SAIS—See Unilever Plc; *Int'l*, pg. 1438
SAIT-RADIOHOLLAND GROUP S.A.; *Int'l*, pg. 1151
SAM (SOCIETE DES ACIERIES DE MONTEREAU)—See Groupe Usinor; *Int'l*, pg. 571
SAMAB CIA. INDUSTRIA E COMERCIO DE PAPEL—See Enso Oyj; *Int'l*, pg. 458
SAMC ACIERES—See Groupe Usinor; *Int'l*, pg. 572
SAPA AG—See Electrolux, AB; *Int'l*, pg. 443
SAPA ALUMINIUM PROFILE GMBH—See Electrolux, AB; *Int'l*, pg. 442
SAPA A/S—See Electrolux, AB; *Int'l*, pg. 441
A/S SAPA—See Electrolux, AB; *Int'l*, pg. 443
SAPA LTD.—See Electrolux, AB; *Int'l*, pg. 444
SAR-SOCIETE D'APPLICATIONS ROUTIERES—See Lafarge S.A.; *Int'l*, pg. 789
SAR U.S.A. INCORPORATED—See AptarGroup, Inc.; *U.S. Public*, pg. 125
SAS—See ETEX; *Int'l*, pg. 430
SAS—See SAS Holdings Limited; *Int'l*, pg. 1152
SAS AIRLINE—See Scandinavian Airlines System (SAS); *Int'l*, pg. 1201
SAS CONSULTING SERVICES, INC.—See SAS Institute Inc.; *U.S. Private*, pg. 966
SAS FINANCIAL SERVICES—See Scandinavian Airlines System (SAS); *Int'l*, pg. 1201
SAS HOLDINGS LIMITED; *Int'l*, pg. 1152
SAS INSTITUTE AB—See SAS Institute Inc.; *U.S. Private*, pg. 966
SAS INSTITUTE A/S—See SAS Institute Inc.; *U.S. Private*, pg. 967
SAS INSTITUTE AUSTRALIA PTY. LTD.—See SAS Institute Inc.; *U.S. Private*, pg. 966
SAS INSTITUTE B.V.—See SAS Institute Inc.; *U.S. Private*, pg. 967
SAS INSTITUTE (CANADA) INC.—See SAS Institute Inc.; *U.S. Private*, pg. 967
SAS INSTITUTE GMBH—See SAS Institute Inc.; *U.S. Private*, pg. 967
SAS INSTITUTE JAPAN LTD.—See SAS Institute Inc.; *U.S. Private*, pg. 967
SAS INSTITUTE LTD.—See SAS Institute Inc.; *U.S. Private*, pg. 967
SAS INSTITUTE LTD. (PHILIPPINES)—See SAS Institute Inc.; *U.S. Private*, pg. 967
SAS INSTITUTE NV/SA—See SAS Institute Inc.; *U.S. Private*, pg. 967
SAS INSTITUTE (NZ) LTD.—See SAS Institute Inc.; *U.S. Private*, pg. 967
SAS INSTITUTE OY—See SAS Institute Inc.; *U.S. Private*, pg. 967
SAS INSTITUTE PTE. LTD.—See SAS Institute Inc.; *U.S. Private*, pg. 967
SAS INSTITUTE S.A.—See SAS Institute Inc.; *U.S. Private*, pg. 967
SAS INSTITUTE S.A. (GENEVE)—See SAS Institute Inc.; *U.S. Private*, pg. 967
SAS INSTITUTE S.A. (MADRID)—See SAS Institute Inc.; *U.S. Private*, pg. 967
SAS INSTITUTE SDN. BHD.—See SAS Institute Inc.; *U.S. Private*, pg. 967
SAS INSTITUTE S.R.L.—See SAS Institute Inc.; *U.S. Private*, pg. 967
SAS INTERNATIONAL—See SAS Holdings Limited; *Int'l*, pg. 1152
SAS INTERNATIONAL HOTELS A/S—See Scandinavian Airlines System (SAS); *Int'l*, pg. 1202
SAS MEDIAPARTNER AB—See Scandinavian Airlines System (SAS); *Int'l*, pg. 1202
SAS PARK ROYAL HOTEL—See Scandinavian Airlines System (SAS); *Int'l*, pg. 1202
SAS RUBBER COMPANY—See The Yokohama Rubber Co., Ltd.; *Int'l*, pg. 1521
SAS SERVICE PARTNER A/S—See Scandinavian Airlines System (SAS); *Int'l*, pg. 1202
SAS SOFTWARE KOREA LTD.—See SAS Institute Inc.; *U.S. Private*, pg. 967
SAS SOFTWARE, LTD.—See SAS Institute Inc.; *U.S. Private*, pg. 967
SAS SOFTWARE TAIWAN LTD.—See SAS Institute Inc.; *U.S. Private*, pg. 967
SAS TRADING—See Scandinavian Airlines System (SAS); *Int'l*, pg. 1202
S.A.S.A.-ASSICURAZIONI RIASSICURAZIONI SOCIETA PER AZIONI—See IRI Istituto Ricostruzione Industriale; *Int'l*, pg. 652
S.A.S.I. CORPORATION; *U.S. Private*, pg. 955

SASIB PACKAGING NORTH AMERICA—See SASIB SpA; *Int'l*, pg. 1194
SAT CHEMIE G.M.B.H.—See Veba AG; *Int'l*, pg. 1460
SATAS - SOCIETE POUR L'AFFRANCHISSEMENT ET LE TIMBRAGE AUTOMATIQUES—See Alcatel Alsthom Compagnie Generale D'Electricite; *Int'l*, pg. 54
SATS APRON SERVICES PTE., LTD.—See Temasek Holdings Pte. Ltd.; *Int'l*, pg. 1374
SATS PASSENGER SERVICES PTE. LTD.—See Temasek Holdings Pte. Ltd.; *Int'l*, pg. 1374
S.A.V. MOULINEX—See Moulinex S.A.; *Int'l*, pg. 896
S.B. MERCHANT BANK (SINGAPORE) LIMITED—See The Sumitomo Bank, Limited; *Int'l*, pg. 1309
SBC ADVERTISING; *U.S. Private*, pg. 955
SBC ARBITECH AB—See Swiss Bank Corporation; *Int'l*, pg. 1330
SBC-ASSET MANAGEMENT INC.—See SBC Communications Inc.; *U.S. Public*, pg. 1416
SBC AUSTRALIA LIMITED—See Swiss Bank Corporation; *Int'l*, pg. 1330
SBC BANQUE WARBURG—See Swiss Bank Corporation; *Int'l*, pg. 1331
SBC CABLECOMMS—See SBC Communications Inc.; *U.S. Public*, pg. 1416
SBC CAPITAL MARKETS INC.—See Swiss Bank Corporation; *Int'l*, pg. 1329
SBC COMMUNICATIONS INC.; *U.S. Public*, pg. 1415
SBC LTDA.—See Swiss Bank Corporation; *Int'l*, pg. 1330
SBC PORTFOLIO MANAGEMENT (CANADA) INC.—See Swiss Bank Corporation; *Int'l*, pg. 1332
SBC PORTFOLIO MANAGEMENT INTERNATIONAL, INC.—See Swiss Bank Corporation; *Int'l*, pg. 1329
SBC PORTFOLIO MANAGEMENT INTERNATIONAL LIMITED—See Swiss Bank Corporation; *Int'l*, pg. 1330
SBC PORTFOLIO MANAGEMENT INTERNATIONAL K.K.—See Swiss Bank Corporation; *Int'l*, pg. 1330
SBC PUBLIC RELATIONS—See SBC Advertising; *U.S. Private*, pg. 955
SBC SPECIALIZED MARKETING—See SBC Advertising; *U.S. Private*, pg. 955
SBC WARBURG & CO. LTD.—See Swiss Bank Corporation; *Int'l*, pg. 1331
SBC WARBURG ASSET MANAGEMENT LUXEMBOURG S.A.—See Swiss Bank Corporation; *Int'l*, pg. 1331
SBC WARBURG DILLON READ—See Swiss Bank Corporation; *Int'l*, pg. 1329
SBC WARBURG DILLON READ INC.—See Swiss Bank Corporation; *Int'l*, pg. 1329
SBC WARBURG ESPANA S.A.—See Swiss Bank Corporation; *Int'l*, pg. 1331
SBC WARBURG FUTURES & OPTIONS LTD.—See Swiss Bank Corporation; *Int'l*, pg. 1331
SBC WARBURG GROUP MANAGEMENT LTD.—See Swiss Bank Corporation; *Int'l*, pg. 1331
SBC WARBURG GROUP PLC—See Swiss Bank Corporation; *Int'l*, pg. 1330
SBC WARBURG ITALIA S.P.A.—See Swiss Bank Corporation; *Int'l*, pg. 1331
SBC WARBURG SECURITIES (FAR EAST) LTD.—See Swiss Bank Corporation; *Int'l*, pg. 1331
SBC WARBURG SECURITIES (JAPAN) INC.—See Swiss Bank Corporation; *Int'l*, pg. 1331
SBC WARBURG SECURITIES LTD.—See Swiss Bank Corporation; *Int'l*, pg. 1331
SBC WARBURG SECURITIES (SINGAPORE) PTE. LTD.—See Swiss Bank Corporation; *Int'l*, pg. 1331
SBCM LIMITED—See The Sumitomo Bank, Limited; *Int'l*, pg. 1310
SBCM LIMITED HONG KONG BRANCH—See The Sumitomo Bank, Limited; *Int'l*, pg. 1310
SBCS COMPANY LIMITED—See The Sakura Bank, Limited; *Int'l*, pg. 1181
SBE, INC.; *U.S. Public*, pg. 1416
SBG ENTERPRISE—See WPP Group plc; *Int'l*, pg. 1483
SBS ENTERPRISES INC.; *U.S. Private*, pg. 955
SBS ESPANAN S.A.—See Swiss Bank Corporation; *Int'l*, pg. 1331
SBS GESTION S.A.—See Swiss Bank Corporation; *Int'l*, pg. 1331
SBS HOLDINGS, INC.; *U.S. Public*, pg. 955
SBS IBERSUIZAS S.A.—See Swiss Bank Corporation; *Int'l*, pg. 1332
SBS PHARMACEUTICALS—See C.D. Smith Drug Company; *U.S. Private*, pg. 1007
SBS PRODUCTS, INC.—See SBS Holdings, Inc.; *U.S. Private*, pg. 955
SBS SIM S.P.A.—See Swiss Bank Corporation; *Int'l*, pg. 1331
SBS SOCIEDAD DE VALORES S.A.—See Swiss Bank Corporation; *Int'l*, pg. 1331
SBS VALEURS S.A.—See Swiss Bank Corporation; *Int'l*, pg. 1331
S.B.T.N.V.—See Unilever Plc; *Int'l*, pg. 1438
SBU DECORATIVE LAMINATE—See Perstorp AB; *Int'l*, pg. 1038
SBU FLOORING LAMINATE—See Perstorp AB; *Int'l*, pg. 1038
SBV VERMOGENSVERWALTUNGS-GESELLSCHAFT MBH—See Hapag-Lloyd AG; *Int'l*, pg. 596
S.C. CORPORATION OF MICRONESIA, LTD.—See Shimizu Corporation; *Int'l*, pg. 1233
S.C. FOOD SERVICES (CANADA) INC.—See Scott's Restaurants Inc.; *Int'l*, pg. 1213
SC POLYMERS INC.—See Sinochem International Petroleum Co. Ltd.; *Int'l*, pg. 1255
S.C. PROPERTIES (GUAM), INC.—See Shimizu Corporation; *Int'l*, pg. 1233
S.C. PROPERTIES (NZ) LTD.—See Shimizu Corporation; *Int'l*, pg. 1233
S.C. PROPERTIES (SAIPAN), INC.—See Shimizu Corporation; *Int'l*, pg. 1233
S.C. PROPERTIES (SINGAPORE) PTE. LTD.—See Shimizu Corporation; *Int'l*, pg. 1233

S.C. RECHERCHE ET DEVELOPPEMENT DU GROUPE COCKERILL SAMBRE R.D.C.S.—See Cockerill Sambre; *Int'l*, pg. 301
SC SUITES CORP.—See Shimizu Corporation; *Int'l*, pg. 1233
SCA PACKAGING—See Svenska Cellulosa Aktiebolaget (SCA); *Int'l*, pg. 1326
SCAC-FISONS SA—See Rhone-Poulenc S.A.; *Int'l*, pg. 1111
SCE CAPITAL COMPANY—See Edison International; *U.S. Public*, pg. 564
SCEM REINSURANCE S.A.—See Skanska AB; *Int'l*, pg. 1261
SCF FINANCE & SECURITIES CO., LTD.—See Siam City Bank Public Company Limited; *Int'l*, pg. 1239
SCI MANUFACTURING, INC.—See SCI Systems, Inc.; *U.S. Public*, pg. 1417
S.C.I. MATRA TOULOUSE—See Lagardere Groupe; *Int'l*, pg. 793
SCI OPERATIONS DIVISION—See Sasol Limited; *Int'l*, pg. 1196
S.C.I. STEEL MILL PTY. LTD.—See Smorgon A.R.C.; *Int'l*, pg. 1269
SCI SYSTEMS, INC.; *U.S. Public*, pg. 1416
SCI TECHNOLOGY, INC.—See SCI Systems, Inc.; *U.S. Public*, pg. 1417
SCI (THAILAND) LTD.—See SCI Systems, Inc.; *U.S. Public*, pg. 1417
SCI UK LTD.—See SCI Systems, Inc.; *U.S. Public*, pg. 1417
SCIEX—See MDS Inc.; *Int'l*, pg. 827
SCIEX, INC.—See MDS Inc.; *Int'l*, pg. 827
SCM—See Hanson PLC; *Int'l*, pg. 594
SCM CHEM COLORS & SILICA DIV.—See Hanson PLC; *Int'l*, pg. 594
SCM CHEMICALS - EUROPE—See Hanson PLC; *Int'l*, pg. 593
SCM GLIDCO ORGANIC—See Hanson PLC; *Int'l*, pg. 594
SCM METAL PRODUCTS INC.—See Hanson PLC; *Int'l*, pg. 594
SCM MICROSYSTEMS, INC.; *U.S. Public*, pg. 1417
SCM OPERATING TRAINING CO. LTD.—See Caterpillar Inc.; *U.S. Public*, pg. 317
SCM SPECIALTY CHEMICALS INC.—See Hanson PLC; *Int'l*, pg. 594
SCM SYSTEM SERVICE CO., LTD.—See Caterpillar Inc.; *U.S. Public*, pg. 317
SCOGAT S.A. (SOCIETE POUR LA CONSTRUCTION DU GAZODUC TRANST.)—See ENI S.p.A.; *Int'l*, pg. 429
SCOR; *Int'l*, pg. 1152
SCOR ASIA-PACIFIC PTE. LTD.—See SCOR; *Int'l*, pg. 1152
SCOR CANADA REINSURANCE COMPANY—See SCOR; *Int'l*, pg. 1152
SCOR DEUTSCHLAND—See SCOR; *Int'l*, pg. 1153
SCOR REASSURANCE—See SCOR; *Int'l*, pg. 1152
SCOR UK GROUP—See SCOR; *Int'l*, pg. 1153
SCOR U.S. CORPORATION—See SCOR; *Int'l*, pg. 1152
SCOR VIE—See SCOR; *Int'l*, pg. 1152
SCP DIRECT INC.—See Omnicom Group Inc.; *U.S. Public*, pg. 1224
SCP (MAUI 5), INC.—See Shimizu Corporation; *Int'l*, pg. 1233
SCP POOL CORPORATION—See Code, Hennessy & Simmons, Inc.; *U.S. Private*, pg. 249
SCP PRIVATE EQUITY PARTNERS—See Safeguard Scientifics, Inc.; *U.S. Public*, pg. 1424
SCPA—See Entreprise Miniere et Chimique; *Int'l*, pg. 459
SCR DIVISION—See Peerless Mfg. Co.; *U.S. Public*, pg. 1268
SCR, INC.; *U.S. Private*, pg. 955
SCS ENGINEERS; *U.S. Private*, pg. 955
SCS FIELD SERVICES, INC.—See SCS Engineers; *U.S. Private*, pg. 956
SCSG (SCS-GRUMMAN SYSTEMS PTE LTD.)—See The Macneal-Schwendler Corp.; *U.S. Public*, pg. 1032
SCSM (SCS COMPUTER SYSTEMS SDN.BHD.)—See The Macneal-Schwendler Corp.; *U.S. Public*, pg. 1032
SCT—See Systems & Computer Technology Corporation; *U.S. Public*, pg. 1552
SCT B INC.—See Saint-Gobain; *Int'l*, pg. 1176
SCT CO., LTD.—See The Siam Cement Public Company Limited; *Int'l*, pg. 1238
SCT GOVERNMENT SYSTEMS—See Systems & Computer Technology Corporation; *U.S. Public*, pg. 1552
SCT UTILITIES SYSTEMS, INC.—See Systems & Computer Technology Corporation; *U.S. Public*, pg. 1552
SCT YARNS, INC.; *U.S. Private*, pg. 956
S.D. INVESTMENTS PTY. LTD.—See Pfizer Inc.; *U.S. Public*, pg. 1282
S.D.D. S.R.L.—See Viag AG; *Int'l*, pg. 1466
SDI TECHNOLOGIES INC.; *U.S. Private*, pg. 956
SDIG—See Gaz de France; *Int'l*, pg. 541
SDL CONSTRUCTION—See McCarthy Building Companies; *U.S. Private*, pg. 719
SDP—See IRI Istituto Ricostruzione Industriale; *Int'l*, pg. 654
SDRC AG—See Structural Dynamics Research Corp.; *U.S. Public*, pg. 1525
SDRC BELGIUM N.V./S.A.—See Structural Dynamics Research Corp.; *U.S. Public*, pg. 1525
SDRC ENGINEERING SERVICES DIVISION, INC.—See Structural Dynamics Research Corp.; *U.S. Public*, pg. 1525
SDRC ESPANA, S.A.—See Structural Dynamics Research Corp.; *U.S. Public*, pg. 1525
SDRC FRANCE S.A.—See Structural Dynamics Research Corp.; *U.S. Public*, pg. 1525
SDRC ITALIA, SRL.—See Structural Dynamics Research Corp.; *U.S. Public*, pg. 1525
SDRC JAPAN K.K.—See Structural Dynamics Research Corp.; *U.S. Public*, pg. 1525

SDRC KOREA LIMITED—See Structural Dynamics Research Corp.; *U.S. Public*, pg. 1525
SDRC NEDERLAND B.V.—See Structural Dynamics Research Corp.; *U.S. Public*, pg. 1525
SDRC SINGAPORE PTE. LTD.—See Structural Dynamics Research Corp.; *U.S. Public*, pg. 1525
SDRC SOFTWARE & SERVICES GMBH—See Structural Dynamics Research Corp.; *U.S. Public*, pg. 1525
SDRC SVENSKA AB—See Structural Dynamics Research Corp.; *U.S. Public*, pg. 1525
SDRC U.K. LIMITED—See Structural Dynamics Research Corp.; *U.S. Public*, pg. 1525
SDS BIOTECH K.K.—See Novartis AG; *Int'l*, pg. 984
SDS (SAMSUNG DATA SYSTEMS CO. LTD.)—See The Macneal-Schwendler Corp.; *U.S. Public*, pg. 1032
S-E-BANKEN FASTIGHETER AB—See Skandinaviska Enskilda Banken; *Int'l*, pg. 1259
S-E-BANKEN FONDER AB—See Skandinaviska Enskilda Banken; *Int'l*, pg. 1259
S-E BANKEN KAPITALFORVALTNING—See Skandinaviska Enskilda Banken; *Int'l*, pg. 1259
SEA—See ETEX; *Int'l*, pg. 430
S.E.A. GLASS IND. PTE. LTD.—See Taiwan Glass Industry Corp.; *Int'l*, pg. 1348
SEA, INC.—See Datamarine International, Inc.; *U.S. Public*, pg. 487
SEAC LIMITED—See Halma p.l.c.; *Int'l*, pg. 590
S.E.A.V.T. SA—See Accor S.A.; *Int'l*, pg. 20
SEB ASIA—See Groupe SEB; *Int'l*, pg. 568
SEB DEVELOPPEMENT S.A.—See Groupe SEB; *Int'l*, pg. 568
SEB INTERNATIONALE—See Groupe SEB; *Int'l*, pg. 568
SEB JAPAN CO. LTD.—See Groupe SEB; *Int'l*, pg. 568
SEB S.A.—See Groupe SEB; *Int'l*, pg. 569
SEC (SOFT, EVENT & PROMOTION) PLANNING, INC.—See Hakuhodo Incorporated; *Int'l*, pg. 588
SECA (SOCIETE D'EXPLOITATION ET DE CONSTRUCTION AERONAUTIQUES)—See Aerospatiale; *Int'l*, pg. 29
SECO INDUSTRIES, INC.—See Serv-Tech, Inc.; *U.S. Public*, pg. 1460
SECON GMBH—See Incentive AB; *Int'l*, pg. 669
SEECO, INC.—See Southwestern Energy Company; *U.S. Public*, pg. 1494
SEEQ TECHNOLOGY INC.; *U.S. Public*, pg. 1417
SEFEA S.A.—See SMH Swiss Corporation for Micro Electronics & Watchmaking Indus. Ltd.; *Int'l*, pg. 1161
SEH AMERICA INC.—See Shin-Etsu Chemical Co. ltd.; *Int'l*, pg. 1234
SEI BENEFIT SERVICES CORPORATION—See SEI Investments; *U.S. Public*, pg. 1417
SEI CORPORATION—See SEI Investments; *U.S. Public*, pg. 1417
SEI FINANCIAL MANAGEMENT CORPORATION—See SEI Investments; *U.S. Public*, pg. 1417
SEI FINANCIAL SERVICES COMPANY—See SEI Investments; *U.S. Public*, pg. 1417
SEI HOLDING CORP.; *U.S. Private*, pg. 956
SEI INVESTMENTS; *U.S. Public*, pg. 1417
SEI NIGERIA LTD.—See Sumitomo Electric Industries, Ltd.; *Int'l*, pg. 1313
S.E.I. SERVIZI ELICOTTERISTICI ITALIANI S.P.A.—See Agusta S.P.A.; *Int'l*, pg. 32
S.E.L. MADURO & SONS (CURACAO) INC.—See Telefonaktiebolaget LM Ericsson; *Int'l*, pg. 1369
SEM LTD.—See Hewlett-Packard Company; *U.S. Public*, pg. 823
SEMA GROUP DIVISION—See Hewlett-Packard Company; *U.S. Public*, pg. 823
SEMCO ENERGY SERVICES, INC.—See Southeastern Michigan Gas Enterprises, Inc.; *U.S. Public*, pg. 1489
SEMIA, INC.—See Sumitomo Electric Industries, Ltd.; *Int'l*, pg. 1313
S.E.M.T. PIELSTICK S.A.—See Daimler-Benz Aktiengesellschaft; *Int'l*, pg. 367
S.E.P.—See Accor S.A.; *Int'l*, pg. 20
SEP INC.—See SNECMA - Societe Nationale d'Etude et de Construction de Moteurs d'Aviation; *Int'l*, pg. 1166
SERV TRAYVOU INTERVERROUILLAGE SA—See Halma p.l.c.; *Int'l*, pg. 590
SES EUROPE N.V./S.A.—See Zeneca Group Plc; *Int'l*, pg. 1525
S.E.S. FRANCE S.A.—See Zeneca Group Plc; *Int'l*, pg. 1526
SES IBERICA SA—See Zeneca Group Plc; *Int'l*, pg. 1526
SET ENGINEERING CO., LTD.—See Sanken Electric Co., Ltd.; *Int'l*, pg. 1188
SEVA—See Saint-Gobain; *Int'l*, pg. 1176
SF AIR FILTRATION AG—See BHA Group Holdings Inc.; *U.S. Public*, pg. 161
SF BROADCASTING COMPANIES—See USA Networks, Inc.; *U.S. Public*, pg. 1685
SF SERVICES; *U.S. Private*, pg. 956
SFA DATACOMM INC.—See SFA, Inc.; *U.S. Private*, pg. 956
SFA, INC.; *U.S. Private*, pg. 956
SFAM SOCIETE FRANCAISE D'AMPOULES MECANIQUES SARL—See Carl-Zeiss-Stiftung; *Int'l*, pg. 1523
SFIC—See Saint-Gobain; *Int'l*, pg. 1176
SFIC PROPERTIES, INC.—See Kuwait Petroleum Corporation; *Int'l*, pg. 765
SFM ENTERTAINMENT—See SFM Media Corporation; *U.S. Private*, pg. 957
SFM/LOS ANGELES—See SFM Media Corporation; *U.S. Private*, pg. 957
SFM MEDIA CORPORATION; *U.S. Private*, pg. 956
SFM POLITICAL ADVISORY—See SFM Media Corporation; *U.S. Private*, pg. 957
SFM RETAIL ADVISORY—See SFM Media Corporation; *U.S. Private*, pg. 957
SFM/SAN FRANCISCO—See SFM Media Corporation; *U.S. Private*, pg. 957
SFMRA—See Lagardere Groupe; *Int'l*, pg. 793

SFP CORPORATION—See Kerr Group, Inc.; *U.S. Public*, pg. 952
SFP SA—See Accor S.A.; *Int'l*, pg. 20
S.F.T. GONGRAND FRERES—See Union-Transport Corporation; *U.S. Private*, pg. 1120
S.F.T.C.—See SNCF; *Int'l*, pg. 1165
SFX BROADCASTING INCORPORATED; *U.S. Public*, pg. 1417
SFZ TRANSPORTATION INC.—See Berkshire Hathaway Inc.; *U.S. Public*, pg. 218
SGB CONSTRUCTION SERVICES, INC.—See John Mowlem & Company plc; *Int'l*, pg. 896
SGD GLASHUTTENWERKE GMBH—See Saint-Gobain; *Int'l*, pg. 1171
SGD GLASS INC.—See Saint-Gobain; *Int'l*, pg. 1171
SGD INTERNATIONAL CORP.; *U.S. Private*, pg. 957
SGI CANADA INSURANCE SERVICES LTD.—See Saskatchewan Government Insurance, SGI; *Int'l*, pg. 1195
S.G.I. GUARANTEE ACCEPTANCES (PTY.) LTD.—See Assicurazioni Generali S.p.A.; *Int'l*, pg. 92
SGI INTEGRATED GRAPHIC SYSTEMS—See LSI Industries, Inc.; *U.S. Public*, pg. 971
S.G.I. PROPERTIES (PTY.) LTD.—See Assicurazioni Generali S.p.A.; *Int'l*, pg. 92
S.G.N. SOCIETA GRAFICA NOVARESE S.P.A.—See Arnoldo Mondadori Editore S.p.A.; *Int'l*, pg. 888
SGS CONTROL SERVICES INC.—See SGS Societe Generale de Surveillance Holding S.A.; *Int'l*, pg. 1153
SGS GOVERNMENT PROGRAMS INC.—See SGS Societe Generale de Surveillance Holding S.A.; *Int'l*, pg. 1153
SGS INDUSTRIAL SERVICES—See SGS Societe Generale de Surveillance Holding S.A.; *Int'l*, pg. 1153
SGS INTERNATIONAL CERTIFICATION SERVICES, INC.—See SGS Societe Generale de Surveillance Holding S.A.; *Int'l*, pg. 1153
SGS NORTH AMERICA INC.—See SGS Societe Generale de Surveillance Holding S.A.; *Int'l*, pg. 1153
SGS - PERMANENT DELEGATION TO THE INTERNATIONAL FINANCIAL INSTITUTIONS—See SGS Societe Generale de Surveillance Holding S.A.; *Int'l*, pg. 1153
SGS SOCIÉTÉ GENERALE DE SURVEILLANCE HOLDING S.A.; *Int'l*, pg. 1153
SGS-THOMSON MICROELECTRONICS, INC.—See SGS Societe Generale de Surveillance Holding S.A.; *Int'l*, pg. 1153
SGS-THOMSON MICROELECTRONICS, INC.—See Thomson S.A.; *Int'l*, pg. 1384
SGS-THOMSON MICROELECTRONICS NETHERLANDS—See IRI Istituto Ricostruzione Industriale; *Int'l*, pg. 654
SGS (URUGUAY) LIMITADA—See SGS Societe Generale de Surveillance Holding S.A.; *Int'l*, pg. 1154
SGS U.S. TESTING COMPANY, INC.—See SGS Societe Generale de Surveillance Holding S.A.; *Int'l*, pg. 1153
SH-TRADE OY—See British Steel Plc; *Int'l*, pg. 222
SHK-SHIMIZU CO., LTD.—See Shimizu Corporation; *Int'l*, pg. 1233
SHL CLARION EDUCATION—See SHL Systemhouse; *Int'l*, pg. 1154
SHL COMPUTER INNOVATIONS—See SHL Systemhouse; *Int'l*, pg. 1154
SHL DIVISION/COMMERCIAL AIRCRAFT GROUP—See Israel Aircraft Industries Ltd.; *Int'l*, pg. 690
SHL INTERNATIONAL—See SHL Systemhouse; *Int'l*, pg. 1154
SHL LEARNING TECHNOLOGIES—See SHL Systemhouse; *Int'l*, pg. 1154
SHL SYSTEMHOUSE; *Int'l*, pg. 1154
SHL SYSTEMHOUSE ARGENTINA S.A.—See SHL Systemhouse; *Int'l*, pg. 1154
SHL SYSTEMHOUSE - CANADA/ASIA—See SHL Systemhouse; *Int'l*, pg. 1154
SHL SYSTEMHOUSE - CENTRAL CANADA REGION—See SHL Systemhouse; *Int'l*, pg. 1154
SHL SYSTEMHOUSE EUROPE LTD.—See SHL Systemhouse; *Int'l*, pg. 1154
SHL SYSTEMHOUSE - LATIN AMERICA OPERATIONS—See SHL Systemhouse; *Int'l*, pg. 1154
SHL SYSTEMHOUSE NEDERLAND B.V.—See SHL Systemhouse; *Int'l*, pg. 1154
SHL SYSTEMHOUSE - OTTAWA REGION—See SHL Systemhouse; *Int'l*, pg. 1154
SHL SYSTEMHOUSE - QUEBEC REGION—See SHL Systemhouse; *Int'l*, pg. 1154
SHL TECHNOLOGY SOLUTIONS—See SHL Systemhouse; *Int'l*, pg. 1154
SHL VISION SOLUTIONS—See SHL Systemhouse; *Int'l*, pg. 1154
SHSO—See Accor S.A.; *Int'l*, pg. 20
SHV ENERGY N.V.—See SHV Holdings N.V.; *Int'l*, pg. 1155
SHV HOLDINGS N.V.; *Int'l*, pg. 1154
SI/BAKER, INC.—See SI Handling Systems, Inc.; *U.S. Public*, pg. 1418
S.I. DE MEXICO S.A. DE C.V.—See Standex International Corporation; *U.S. Public*, pg. 1507
S.I. GRAND PONT NO 1—See Oerlikon-Buhrle Holding AG; *Int'l*, pg. 997
SI HANDLING SYSTEMS, INC.; *U.S. Public*, pg. 1418
S.I. NEDERLAND, B.V.—See Smith International, Inc.; *U.S. Public*, pg. 1478
S I PROPERTIES LIMITED—See Smiths Industries plc; *Int'l*, pg. 1267
SI SEALING PARTS SPA—See TI Group plc; *Int'l*, pg. 1338
SIA CO., LTD.—See Sankosha Advertising Agency, Ltd.; *Int'l*, pg. 1189
SIA LUSTGARDEN AB—See Electrolux, AB; *Int'l*, pg. 439
S.I.A.—See Bastogi-S.p.A.; *Int'l*, pg. 170
SIA (UK) LTD.—See Electrolux, AB; *Int'l*, pg. 444
S.I.A.M. MONTICCHIO SRL—See Koninklijke BolsWessanen nv; *Int'l*, pg. 753
SIAS - MPA—See Groupe Pernod Ricard; *Int'l*, pg. 566
S.I.C.A. S.P.A.—See Fiat Auto SpA; *Int'l*, pg. 481

SICO ASIA PTE LTD.—See Sico Incorporated; *U.S. Private*, pg. 997
SICO EUROPE LIMITED—See Sico Incorporated; *U.S. Private*, pg. 997
SICO SOUTH PACIFIC—See Sico Incorporated; *U.S. Private*, pg. 998
SICUP SNC—See Continental AG; *Int'l*, pg. 328
SIE SYSTEMS SPA—See Mannesmann A.G.; *Int'l*, pg. 835
S.I.E.F.—See LVMH Moet Hennessy Louis Vuitton; *Int'l*, pg. 781
SIELTE DATA NET S.P.A.—See Telefonaktiebolaget LM Ericsson; *Int'l*, pg. 1370
SIELTE ENGINEERING S.P.A.—See Telefonaktiebolaget LM Ericsson; *Int'l*, pg. 1370
SIELTE PADANA S.P.A.—See Telefonaktiebolaget LM Ericsson; *Int'l*, pg. 1370
SIG ASIA PTE. LTD.—See SIG Schweizersiche Industrie-Gesellschaft Holding AG; *Int'l*, pg. 1156
SIG BAUTECHNIK—See SIG Schweizersiche Industrie-Gesellschaft Holding AG; *Int'l*, pg. 1156
SIG EMBALLAGE FRANCE S.A.R.L.—See SIG Schweizersiche Industrie-Gesellschaft Holding AG; *Int'l*, pg. 1156
SIG HOLDING GMBH DEUTSCHLAND—See SIG Schweizersiche Industrie-Gesellschaft Holding AG; *Int'l*, pg. 1156
SIG HOLDING USA INC.—See SIG Schweizersiche Industrie-Gesellschaft Holding AG; *Int'l*, pg. 1156
SIG HOLDINGS (UK) LTD.—See SIG Schweizersiche Industrie-Gesellschaft Holding AG; *Int'l*, pg. 1156
SIG INDUSTRIA E COMERCIO LTDA.—See SIG Schweizersiche Industrie-Gesellschaft Holding AG; *Int'l*, pg. 1156
SIG PACKAGING TECHNOLOGY (UK) LTD.—See SIG Schweizersiche Industrie-Gesellschaft Holding AG; *Int'l*, pg. 1156
S.I.G., S.A. POLIG. IND. JUMAPI—See Knurr AG; *Int'l*, pg. 740
SIG POSITEC—See SIG Schweizersiche Industrie-Gesellschaft Holding AG; *Int'l*, pg. 1156
SIG SCHWEIZERISCHE INDUSTRIE-GESELLSCHAFT—See SIG Schweizersiche Industrie-Gesellschaft Holding AG; *Int'l*, pg. 1156
SIG SCHWEIZERSICHE INDUSTRIE-GESELLSCHAFT HOLDING AG; *Int'l*, pg. 1156
SIG VERPACKUNGSMASCHINEN GMBH—See SIG Schweizersiche Industrie-Gesellschaft Holding AG; *Int'l*, pg. 1156
SIGARMS INC.—See SIG Schweizersiche Industrie-Gesellschaft Holding AG; *Int'l*, pg. 1156
S.I.GA.T. S.P.A.—See ENI S.p.A.; *Int'l*, pg. 428
SIHI GMBH & CO. KG; *Int'l*, pg. 1156
SIHI INTERNATIONAL AG—See SIHI GmbH & Co. KG; *Int'l*, pg. 1156
SIHI PUMPS INC.—See SIHI GmbH & Co. KG; *Int'l*, pg. 1156
SIHI PUMPS LTD.—See SIHI GmbH & Co. KG; *Int'l*, pg. 1156
SIMCI S.A.—See Renishaw plc; *Int'l*, pg. 1103
SIMCO ERICSSON LTD.—See Telefonaktiebolaget LM Ericsson; *Int'l*, pg. 1370
SIP-SOCIETE IMMOBILIERE PROSPECTION—See Lafarge S.A.; *Int'l*, pg. 790
SPEC STE INTERNATIONALE DE PETROLE ET DE CHIMIE A R.L.—See Saarbergwerke Aktiengesellschaft; *Int'l*, pg. 1167
S.I.S.—See Groupe SEB; *Int'l*, pg. 569
SIS SICHERHEITS-SERVICE FUR INFORMATIONS-SYSTEME GMBH—See Compagnie des Machines Bull; *Int'l*, pg. 317
SISTO ARMATUREN S.A.—See KSB Aktiengesellschaft; *Int'l*, pg. 721
SITEL-SOCIETE INDUSTRIELLE ALGERIENNE DE TELECOMMUNICATIONS—See Telefonaktiebolaget LM Ericsson; *Int'l*, pg. 1370
SITQ IMMOBILIER—See Caisse de depot et placement du Quebec; *Int'l*, pg. 249
SJ ENERTRADE—See South Jersey Industries, Inc.; *U.S. Public*, pg. 1488
SJL OF KANSAS CORP.—See Lee Enterprises, Incorporated; *U.S. Public*, pg. 968
SJLP INC.—See St. Joseph Light & Power Co.; *U.S. Public*, pg. 1427
SJNB FINANCIAL CORP.; *U.S. Public*, pg. 1418
SJW CORP.; *U.S. Public*, pg. 1418
SK BV GRUNDSTUCKSENTWICKLUNGS GMBH & CO. KG—See Bayerische Vereinsbank Group; *Int'l*, pg. 178
SK BV GRUNDSTUCKSENTWICKLUNGS VERWALTUNG GMBH—See Bayerische Vereinsbank Group; *Int'l*, pg. 178
SK EMBALLAGE A/S—See FLS Industries A/S; *Int'l*, pg. 476
SK HAND TOOL CORP.—See Groupe Strafor Facom; *Int'l*, pg. 570
SKA STORKOKKEN—See Electrolux, AB; *Int'l*, pg. 441
SKBM N.V.—See Royal Begemann Group; *Int'l*, pg. 1134
SKE COUNTERTRADE GMBH—See Veba AG; *Int'l*, pg. 1458
AB SKF; *Int'l*, pg. 1156
OY SKF AB—See AB SKF; *Int'l*, pg. 1418
SKF ABIDJAN S.A.R.L.—See AB SKF; *Int'l*, pg. 1158
SKF ARGENTINA S.A.—See AB SKF; *Int'l*, pg. 1158
SKF AUSTRALIA PTY. LTD.—See AB SKF; *Int'l*, pg. 1158
SKF BEARING IND. (MALAYSIA) SDN. BHD.—See AB SKF; *Int'l*, pg. 1158
SKF BEARING MFRS. PTY. LTD.-—See AB SKF; *Int'l*, pg. 1158
SKF BEARING SERVICES TAIWAN LTD.—See AB SKF; *Int'l*, pg. 1158
SKF BEARINGS INDIA LTD.—See AB SKF; *Int'l*, pg. 1158
SKF BELGIUM S.A.—See AB SKF; *Int'l*, pg. 1158
SKF CANADA LTD.—See AB SKF; *Int'l*, pg. 1158
SKF CENTR. HANDLOWO-TECHN. SP. Z.O.O.—See AB SKF; *Int'l*, pg. 1158

SKF CHILENA S.A.I.C.—See AB SKF; *Int'l*, pg. 1158
SKF CHINA LTD.—See AB SKF; *Int'l*, pg. 1158
SKF COLOMBIA S.A.—See AB SKF; *Int'l*, pg. 1158
SKF CONDITION MONITORING INC.—See AB SKF; *Int'l*, pg. 1157
SKF DANMARK A/S—See AB SKF; *Int'l*, pg. 1158
SKF DATASERVICE AB—See AB SKF; *Int'l*, pg. 1157
SKF DE MEXICO, S.A. DE C.V.—See AB SKF; *Int'l*, pg. 1158
SKF DEL PERU S.A.—See AB SKF; *Int'l*, pg. 1158
SKF DO BRASIL LTDA.—See AB SKF; *Int'l*, pg. 1158
SKF ENGINEERING & RES. CENTRE B.V.—See AB SKF; *Int'l*, pg. 1158
SKF ENGINEERING PRODUCTS LIMITED—See AB SKF; *Int'l*, pg. 1158
SKF EQUIPEMENTS S.N.C.—See AB SKF; *Int'l*, pg. 1158
SKF ESPANOLA S.A.—See AB SKF; *Int'l*, pg. 1158
SKF EUROPEAN DISTRIBUTION CENTRE—See AB SKF; *Int'l*, pg. 1158
SKF EUROTRADE AB—See AB SKF; *Int'l*, pg. 1157
SKF FRANCE S.A.—See AB SKF; *Int'l*, pg. 1158
SKF GLEITLAGER GMBH—See AB SKF; *Int'l*, pg. 1158
SKF GMBH—See AB SKF; *Int'l*, pg. 1158
SKF (HANOI)—See AB SKF; *Int'l*, pg. 1158
SKF HELLAS S.A.—See AB SKF; *Int'l*, pg. 1158
SKF (HO CHI MINH CITY)—See AB SKF; *Int'l*, pg. 1158
SKF INDUSTRIE S.P.A.—See AB SKF; *Int'l*, pg. 1158
SKF INTERTRADE REP. OFFICE—See AB SKF; *Int'l*, pg. 1158
SKF INTERTRADE S.A.—See AB SKF; *Int'l*, pg. 1158
SKF INTERTRADE S.A. AMMAN—See AB SKF; *Int'l*, pg. 1158
SKF JAPAN LTD.—See AB SKF; *Int'l*, pg. 1159
SKF KENYA LTD.—See AB SKF; *Int'l*, pg. 1159
SKF KOGELLAGERINDUSTRIE B.V.—See AB SKF; *Int'l*, pg. 1159
SKF KOREA LTD.—See AB SKF; *Int'l*, pg. 1159
SKF LATINTRADE, INC.—See AB SKF; *Int'l*, pg. 1159
SKF LINEARSYSTEME GMBH—See AB SKF; *Int'l*, pg. 1159
SKF LOZISKA A.S.—See AB SKF; *Int'l*, pg. 1159
SKF MAINTENANCE PRODUCTS B.V.—See AB SKF; *Int'l*, pg. 1159
SKF MAKTRADE D.O.O.—See AB SKF; *Int'l*, pg. 1159
SKF MALAYSIA SDN. BHD.—See AB SKF; *Int'l*, pg. 1159
SKF MFG. SINGAPORE (PTE.) LTD.—See AB SKF; *Int'l*, pg. 1159
SKF MEKAN AB—See AB SKF; *Int'l*, pg. 1157
SKF MOSCOW—See AB SKF; *Int'l*, pg. 1159
SKF MULTITEC—See AB SKF; *Int'l*, pg. 1159
SKF MULTITEC AB—See AB SKF; *Int'l*, pg. 1157
SKF MULTITEC A/S—See AB SKF; *Int'l*, pg. 1159
SKF MULTITEC B.V.—See AB SKF; *Int'l*, pg. 1159
SKF NEDERLAND B.V.—See AB SKF; *Int'l*, pg. 1159
SKF NEW ZEALAND LTD.—See AB SKF; *Int'l*, pg. 1159
SKF NIGERIA LIMITED—See AB SKF; *Int'l*, pg. 1159
SKF NORGE A/S—See AB SKF; *Int'l*, pg. 1159
SKF NOVA AB—See AB SKF; *Int'l*, pg. 1157
SKF OSTERREICH AG—See AB SKF; *Int'l*, pg. 1159
SKF PANAMA REGION—See AB SKF; *Int'l*, pg. 1159
SKF PHILIPPINES INC.—See AB SKF; *Int'l*, pg. 1160
SKF PLAIN BEARINGS—See AB SKF; *Int'l*, pg. 1157
SKF PORTUGAL ROLAMENTOS, LDA.—See AB SKF; *Int'l*, pg. 1159
SKF PRODUCTOS INDUSTRIALES S.A.—See AB SKF; *Int'l*, pg. 1159
SKF REINSURANCE CO. LTD.—See AB SKF; *Int'l*, pg. 1157
SKF RIGA—See AB SKF; *Int'l*, pg. 1159
SKF (SCHWEIZ)—See AB SKF; *Int'l*, pg. 1159
SKF SERVICES D.O.O.—See AB SKF; *Int'l*, pg. 1159
SKF SINGAPORE—See AB SKF; *Int'l*, pg. 1159
SKF SLEWING BEARINGS (RKS S.A)—See AB SKF; *Int'l*, pg. 1159
SKF SOFIA—See AB SKF; *Int'l*, pg. 1159
SKF SOUTH AFRICA (PTY.) LTD.—See AB SKF; *Int'l*, pg. 1159
SKF SPECIALTY PRODUCTS—See AB SKF; *Int'l*, pg. 1157
SKF SPECIALTY PRODUCTS AB—See AB SKF; *Int'l*, pg. 1157
SKF SVED GOLYOSCSAPAGY RESZVENYTARSASAG—See AB SKF; *Int'l*, pg. 1159
SKF SVERIGE AB—See AB SKF; *Int'l*, pg. 1157
SKF TEXTILMASCHINEN-KOMPONENTEN GMBH—See AB SKF; *Int'l*, pg. 1159
SKF (THAILAND) LTD.—See AB SKF; *Int'l*, pg. 1159
SKF TOHMAC TRANSMISSION OY—See AB SKF; *Int'l*, pg. 1159
SKF TRANSMISSION AB—See AB SKF; *Int'l*, pg. 1157
SKF TREASURY CENTRE—See AB SKF; *Int'l*, pg. 1157
SKF TRGOVINA D.O.O.—See AB SKF; *Int'l*, pg. 1159
SKF TURK SANAYI VE TICARET—See AB SKF; *Int'l*, pg. 1159
SKF (U.K.) LTD.—See AB SKF; *Int'l*, pg. 1159
SKF USA INC.—See AB SKF; *Int'l*, pg. 1157
SKF URUGUAY S.A.—See AB SKF; *Int'l*, pg. 1159
SKF VEHICLE PARTS ASIA (PTE) LTD.—See AB SKF; *Int'l*, pg. 1159
SKF VENEZOLANA S.A.—See AB SKF; *Int'l*, pg. 1159
SKF (ZAMBIA) LTD.—See AB SKF; *Int'l*, pg. 1159
SKF (ZIMBABWE) (PVT.) LTD.—See AB SKF; *Int'l*, pg. 1160
SKI—See The Times Mirror Company; *U.S. Public*, pg. 1617
SKJ-YHTIOT OY—See Rautaruukki Oy; *Int'l*, pg. 1088
SKS TECHNIK SAURE UND KORROSIONSSCHUTZ GMBH—See Viag AG; *Int'l*, pg. 1465
SKW ALLOYS, INC.—See Viag AG; *Int'l*, pg. 1465
SKW BAUWERKSTOFFE PIESTERITZ GMBH—See Viag AG; *Int'l*, pg. 1465
SKW CANADA INC.—See Viag AG; *Int'l*, pg. 1466
SKW CHEMICALS CANADA INC.—See Viag AG; *Int'l*, pg. 1466
SKW CHEMICALS INC.—See Viag AG; *Int'l*, pg. 1465

SKW CHEMICALS UK LTD.—See Viag AG; *Int'l*, pg. 1466
SKW CHEMIE - TECHNIK GMBH—See Viag AG; *Int'l*, pg. 1465
SKW EAST ASIA LTD.—See Viag AG; *Int'l*, pg. 1466
SKW/ESKIMOS INC.—See Arctic Slope Regional Corporation; *U.S. Private*, pg. 80
SKW FRANCE S.A.—See Viag AG; *Int'l*, pg. 1466
SKW ITALIA S.R.L.—See Viag AG; *Int'l*, pg. 1466
SKW METALS & ALLOYS, INC.—See Viag AG; *Int'l*, pg. 1465
SKW METALS U.K. LTD., MOLYPRESS DIVISION—See Viag AG; *Int'l*, pg. 1465
SKW METALS U.K. LTD., MUREX DIVISION—See Viag AG; *Int'l*, pg. 1465
SKW NATURES INC.—See Viag AG; *Int'l*, pg. 1465
SKW STICKSTOFFWERKE PIESTERITZ GMBH—See Viag AG; *Int'l*, pg. 1464
SKW TROSTBERG AKTIENGESELLSCHAFT—See Viag AG; *Int'l*, pg. 1464
SL AUBURN, INC.—See Cooper Industries, Inc.; *U.S. Public*, pg. 443
S.L. DE GESTION MOBILIARIA—See Caja de Madrid Group; *Int'l*, pg. 252
SL INDUSTRIES, INC.; *U.S. Public*, pg. 1418
SL MONTEVIDEO TECHNOLOGY, INC.—See SL Industries, Inc.; *U.S. Public*, pg. 1419
S.L. PRIME PROPERTIES PTE. LTD.—See Singapore Land Limited; *Int'l*, pg. 1253
S.L. PRIME REALTY PTE. LTD.—See Singapore Land Limited; *Int'l*, pg. 1253
SL SURFACE TECHNOLOGY, INC.—See SL Industries, Inc.; *U.S. Public*, pg. 1419
SL WABER, INC.—See SL Industries, Inc.; *U.S. Public*, pg. 1419
SLAPIS—See Lafarge S.A.; *Int'l*, pg. 790
SLC S.A. INDUSTRIA E COMERCIO—See Deere & Company; *U.S. Public*, pg. 493
SLC TECHNOLOGIES—See Berwind Corporation; *U.S. Private*, pg. 138
SLD GENLITE LIMITED—See SLD Holdings Ltd.; *Int'l*, pg. 1160
SLD HOLDINGS LTD.; *Int'l*, pg. 1160
SLD PUMPS LIMITED—See SLD Holdings Ltd.; *Int'l*, pg. 1160
SLD SKIDHIRE LIMITED—See SLD Holdings Ltd.; *Int'l*, pg. 1160
SLE S.A.R.L.—See Mark IV Industries Inc.; *U.S. Public*, pg. 1045
SLG CHEMICALS, INC.—See Scott's Liquid Gold-Inc.; *U.S. Public*, pg. 1447
SLG PLASTICS, INC.—See Scott's Liquid Gold-Inc.; *U.S. Public*, pg. 1447
SLI INTERNATIONAL CORP.—See Smiths Industries plc; *Int'l*, pg. 1268
SLJ RETAIL LLC; *U.S. Private*, pg. 957
SLM ELECTRONICS—See St. Louis Music, Inc.; *U.S. Private*, pg. 961
SLM HOLDING CORP.; *U.S. Public*, pg. 1419
SLM IMMOBILIEN AG—See Sulzer Ltd.; *Int'l*, pg. 1305
SLPM—See Groupe Usinor; *Int'l*, pg. 571
SLW-VERSICHERUNGSDIENST GMBH—See Schmalbach-Lubeca AG; *Int'l*, pg. 1206
SM&R CAPITAL FUNDS INC.—See American National Insurance Company; *U.S. Public*, pg. 88
SM-CYCLO CHILE—See Sumitomo Heavy Industries, Ltd.; *Int'l*, pg. 1315
SM-CYCLO DE MEXICO, S.A. DE C.V.—See Sumitomo Heavy Industries, Ltd.; *Int'l*, pg. 1315
SM-CYCLO NEW ZEALAND—See Sumitomo Heavy Industries, Ltd.; *Int'l*, pg. 1315
SM-CYCLO OF AUSTRALIA PTY. LTD.—See Sumitomo Heavy Industries, Ltd.; *Int'l*, pg. 1315
SM-CYCLO OF CANADA, LTD.—See Sumitomo Heavy Industries, Ltd.; *Int'l*, pg. 1315
SM-CYCLO REDUTORES DO BRASIL LTDA.—See Sumitomo Heavy Industries, Ltd.; *Int'l*, pg. 1315
SM-CYCLO SOUTH AFRICA—See Sumitomo Heavy Industries, Ltd.; *Int'l*, pg. 1315
SMAC—See Thomson S.A.; *Int'l*, pg. 1382
SMC—See Quad/Graphics, Inc.; *U.S. Private*, pg. 898
SMC—See Standard Microsystems Corp.; *U.S. Public*, pg. 1503
SMC ENVIRONMENTAL SERVICES GROUP INC.—See Versar Inc.; *U.S. Public*, pg. 1717
SMC INTERNATIONAL, S.A.—See Versar Inc.; *U.S. Public*, pg. 1717
SMC INTERNATIONAL U.K. 7392—See Versar Inc.; *U.S. Public*, pg. 1717
SMC MCEVER INC.—See Versar Inc.; *U.S. Public*, pg. 1717
SMC MINING COMPANY—See Zeigler Coal Holding Company; *U.S. Public*, pg. 1790
SMC MORTGAGE CORP.—See Lennar Corporation; *U.S. Public*, pg. 989
SMC SOUTH—See Sommer Metalcraft Corporation; *U.S. Private*, pg. 1014
SMDA—See Danone Group; *Int'l*, pg. 381
SMDDMS, INC.—See The Reader's Digest Association, Inc.; *U.S. Public*, pg. 1368
SME INTERNATIONAL—See IRI Istituto Ricostruzione Industriale; *Int'l*, pg. 655
SME SOCIETA MERIDIONALE FINANZIARIA—See IRI Istituto Ricostruzione Industriale; *Int'l*, pg. 655
SMET—See TMP Worldwide, Inc.; *U.S. Private*, pg. 1065
SMH (ASIA) INC., TAIWAN—See SMH Swiss Corporation for Micro Electronics & Watchmaking Indus. Ltd.; *Int'l*, pg. 1161
SMH AUSTRALIA LTD.—See SMH Swiss Corporation for Micro Electronics & Watchmaking Indus. Ltd.; *Int'l*, pg. 1161
SMH AUTOMATION—See SMH Swiss Corporation for Micro Electronics & Watchmaking Indus. Ltd.; *Int'l*, pg. 1160

SMH AUTOMOBILE AG—See SMH Swiss Corporation for Micro Electronics & Watchmaking Indus. Ltd.; *Int'l*, pg. 1161
SMH BELGIUM SA—See SMH Swiss Corporation for Micro Electronics & Watchmaking Indus. Ltd.; *Int'l*, pg. 1161
SMH DO BRAZIL—See SMH Swiss Corporation for Micro Electronics & Watchmaking Indus. Ltd.; *Int'l*, pg. 1161
SMH ESPANA S.A.—See SMH Swiss Corporation for Micro Electronics & Watchmaking Indus. Ltd.; *Int'l*, pg. 1161
SMH FINANCE (LUXEMBOURG) SA—See SMH Swiss Corporation for Micro Electronics & Watchmaking Indus. Ltd.; *Int'l*, pg. 1161
SMH FRANCE S.A.—See SMH Swiss Corporation for Micro Electronics & Watchmaking Indus. Ltd.; *Int'l*, pg. 1161
SMH HONG KONG LTD.—See SMH Swiss Corporation for Micro Electronics & Watchmaking Indus. Ltd.; *Int'l*, pg. 1161
SMH IMMOBILIEN S.A.—See SMH Swiss Corporation for Micro Electronics & Watchmaking Indus. Ltd.; *Int'l*, pg. 1161
SMH ITALIA S.P.A.—See SMH Swiss Corporation for Micro Electronics & Watchmaking Indus. Ltd.; *Int'l*, pg. 1161
SMH JAPAN KK—See SMH Swiss Corporation for Micro Electronics & Watchmaking Indus. Ltd.; *Int'l*, pg. 1161
SMH (KOREA) LTD.—See SMH Swiss Corporation for Micro Electronics & Watchmaking Indus. Ltd.; *Int'l*, pg. 1161
SMH OSTERREICH VERTRIEBS GMBH—See SMH Swiss Corporation for Micro Electronics & Watchmaking Indus. Ltd.; *Int'l*, pg. 1161
SMH S.E.A. (S) PTE. LTD.—See SMH Swiss Corporation for Micro Electronics & Watchmaking Indus. Ltd.; *Int'l*, pg. 1161
SMH SWEDEN AB—See SMH Swiss Corporation for Micro Electronics & Watchmaking Indus. Ltd.; *Int'l*, pg. 1161
SMH SWISS CORPORATION FOR MICRO ELECTRONICS & WATCHMAKING INDUS. LTD.; *Int'l*, pg. 1160
SMH SWISS WATCHES & MICROELECTRONICS (CANADA) LTD.—See SMH Swiss Corporation for Micro Electronics & Watchmaking Indus. Ltd.; *Int'l*, pg. 1161
SMH TRADING SDN. BHD.—See SMH Swiss Corporation for Micro Electronics & Watchmaking Indus. Ltd.; *Int'l*, pg. 1161
SMH UHRON UND MIKROELEKTRONIK GMBH—See SMH Swiss Corporation for Micro Electronics & Watchmaking Indus. Ltd.; *Int'l*, pg. 1161
SMH (UK) LTD.—See SMH Swiss Corporation for Micro Electronics & Watchmaking Indus. Ltd.; *Int'l*, pg. 1161
SMH (U.S.) INC.—See SMH Swiss Corporation for Micro Electronics & Watchmaking Indus. Ltd.; *Int'l*, pg. 1161
SMI CO., LTD.—See Sanyo Electric Co., Ltd.; *Int'l*, pg. 1191
SMI JOIST COMPANY—See Commercial Metals Company; *U.S. Public*, pg. 413
SMI JOIST NEVADA—See Commercial Metals Company; *U.S. Public*, pg. 413
SMI JOIST SOUTH CAROLINA—See Commercial Metals Company; *U.S. Public*, pg. 412
SMI MISCELLANEOUS—See Commercial Metals Company; *U.S. Public*, pg. 412
SMI-OWEN STEEL COMPANY—See Commercial Metals Company; *U.S. Public*, pg. 413
SMI-OWEN SUPPLY COMPANY—See Commercial Metals Company; *U.S. Public*, pg. 412
SMI RAIL—See Commercial Metals Company; *U.S. Public*, pg. 413
SMI REBAR SOUTH CAROLINA—See Commercial Metals Company; *U.S. Public*, pg. 412
SMI SPECIALTIES—See Commercial Metals Company; *U.S. Public*, pg. 413
SMI STEEL, INC.—See Commercial Metals Company; *U.S. Public*, pg. 412
SMM GROUP—See Sumitomo Metal Mining Co., Ltd.; *Int'l*, pg. 1316
SMM SPINDEL AG—See AB SKF; *Int'l*, pg. 1160
SMN (SOCIETE METALLURGIQUE DE NORMANDIE)—See Groupe Usinor; *Int'l*, pg. 571
S.M.P.—See Lyonnaise des Eaux S.A.; *Int'l*, pg. 823
SMP II, L.P.—See Sunstone Hotel Investors, Inc.; *U.S. Public*, pg. 1537
SMR (SOCIETE METALLURGIQUE DE REVIGNY)—See Groupe Usinor; *Int'l*, pg. 571
SMS AKTIENGESELLSCHAFT—See MAN Aktiengesellschaft; *Int'l*, pg. 825
SMS BELGIUM—See Shared Medical Systems Corporation; *U.S. Public*, pg. 1463
SMS-BOSTON—See Shared Medical Systems Corporation; *U.S. Public*, pg. 1463
SMS-CHICAGO—See Shared Medical Systems Corporation; *U.S. Public*, pg. 1463
SMS CORP Y CIA S.R.C.—See Shared Medical Systems Corporation; *U.S. Public*, pg. 1463
SMS EUROPE—See Shared Medical Systems Corporation; *U.S. Public*, pg. 1463
SMS FRANCE—See Shared Medical Systems Corporation; *U.S. Public*, pg. 1463
SMS HUNGARY—See Shared Medical Systems Corporation; *U.S. Public*, pg. 1463
SMS INTERNATIONAL DIVISION—See Shared Medical Systems Corporation; *U.S. Public*, pg. 1463
SMS IRELAND UNLIMITED—See Shared Medical Systems Corporation; *U.S. Public*, pg. 1464
SMS ITALIA, S.R.L.—See Shared Medical Systems Corporation; *U.S. Public*, pg. 1464
SMS NEDERLAND B. V.—See Shared Medical Systems Corporation; *U.S. Public*, pg. 1464
SMS PHYSICIAN SERVICES DIVISION—See Shared Medical Systems Corporation; *U.S. Public*, pg. 1463
SMS PROPERTIES CORP.—See Shared Medical Systems Corporation; *U.S. Public*, pg. 1463
SMS SCHLOEMANN GMBH—See MAN Aktiengesellschaft; *Int'l*, pg. 826

SMS SCHLOEMANN-SIEMAG AG—See MAN Aktiengesellschaft; *Int'l*, pg. 826
SMS SERVICES CORP.—See Shared Medical Systems Corporation; *U.S. Public*, pg. 1463
SMS SYSTEMS MAINTENANCE INC.—See Shared Medical Systems Corporation; *U.S. Public*, pg. 1463
SMS TELECOM AB—See Celsius AB; *Int'l*, pg. 277
SMS UNITED KINGDOM, LTD.—See Shared Medical Systems Corporation; *U.S. Public*, pg. 1464
SMS-WASHINGTON, D.C.—See Shared Medical Systems Corporation; *U.S. Public*, pg. 1463
SMS ZWEIGNIEDERLASSUNG DER SMS CORP.—See Shared Medical Systems Corporation; *U.S. Public*, pg. 1464
SMT MACHINE COMPANY AB—See Trelleborg AB; *Int'l*, pg. 1421
SNAM INTERNATIONAL LTD.—See ENI S.p.A.; *Int'l*, pg. 429
SNC - AKER OFFSHORE INC. (AE)—See Aker Raj Asa; *Int'l*, pg. 42
SNC ALFA-LAVAL & CIE—See Tetra Laval Group; *Int'l*, pg. 1379
SNC GEC COMPOSANTS ET CIE—See The General Electric Company, p.l.c.; *Int'l*, pg. 546
SNC-LAVALIN—See SNC-Lavalin Group Inc.; *Int'l*, pg. 1162
SNC LAVALIN - BEIJING—See SNC-Lavalin Group Inc.; *Int'l*, pg. 1162
SNC-LAVALIN EUROPE—See SNC-Lavalin Group Inc.; *Int'l*, pg. 1162
SNC-LAVALIN EUROPE LTD.—See SNC-Lavalin Group Inc.; *Int'l*, pg. 1163
S.A. SNC-LAVALIN EUROPE N.V.—See SNC-Lavalin Group Inc.; *Int'l*, pg. 1163
SNC-LAVALIN GROUP INC.; *Int'l*, pg. 1161
SNC-LAVALIN INC.—See SNC-Lavalin Group Inc.; *Int'l*, pg. 1162
SNC LAVALIN - MOSCOW—See SNC-Lavalin Group Inc.; *Int'l*, pg. 1162
SNC-LAVALIN NIGERIA LTD.—See SNC-Lavalin Group Inc.; *Int'l*, pg. 1163
P.T. SNC-LAVALIN TPS—See SNC-Lavalin Group Inc.; *Int'l*, pg. 1163
SNCF; *Int'l*, pg. 1163
SNE ENTERPRISES, INC.—See Nortek, Inc.; *U.S. Public*, pg. 1193
SNECMA INC.—See SNECMA - Societe Nationale d'Etude et de Construction de Moteurs d'Aviation; *Int'l*, pg. 1166
SNECMA SERVICES INTERNATIONAL (SSI)—See SNECMA - Societe Nationale d'Etude et de Construction de Moteurs d'Aviation; *Int'l*, pg. 1166
SNECMA - SOCIETE NATIONALE D'ETUDE ET DE CONSTRUCTION DE MOTEURS D'AVIATION; *Int'l*, pg. 1165
SNET DIVERSIFIED GROUP, INC.—See Southern New England Telecommunications Corporation; *U.S. Public*, pg. 1491
SNET MATERIAUX—See Saint-Gobain; *Int'l*, pg. 1176
SNET MOBILECOM, INC.—See Southern New England Telecommunications Corporation; *U.S. Public*, pg. 1491
SNET MOBILITY, INC.—See Southern New England Telecommunications Corporation; *U.S. Public*, pg. 1491
SNET REAL ESTATE INC.—See Southern New England Telecommunications Corporation; *U.S. Public*, pg. 1491
SNET SYSTEMS INC.—See Southern New England Telecommunications Corporation; *U.S. Public*, pg. 1491
SNK AMERICA, INC.—See Shin Nippon Koki Co. Ltd.; *Int'l*, pg. 1234
SNLFT (SOCIETE NOUVELLE DES LAMINOIRS A FROID DE THIONVILLE)—See Groupe Usinor; *Int'l*, pg. 571
SNS INVESTMENT COMPANY—See Consolidated Products, Inc.; *U.S. Public*, pg. 436
SNT CALBERSON—See SNCF; *Int'l*, pg. 1164
SNT CALBERSON AGEN—See SNCF; *Int'l*, pg. 1164
SNT CALBERSON ARRAS—See SNCF; *Int'l*, pg. 1164
SNT CALBERSON AVIGNON—See SNCF; *Int'l*, pg. 1164
SNT NOYON—See SNCF; *Int'l*, pg. 1164
S.N.T.M. S.A.—See Tractebel; *Int'l*, pg. 1416
SNTR CALBERSON—See SNCF; *Int'l*, pg. 1164
SNTR CALBERSON DIJON—See SNCF; *Int'l*, pg. 1164
SNTR CALBERSON LA-ROCHE-SUR-YON—See SNCF; *Int'l*, pg. 1164
SNTR CALBERSON MARSEILLE—See SNCF; *Int'l*, pg. 1164
SNTR CALBERSON NANTES—See SNCF; *Int'l*, pg. 1164
SNTR CALBERSON NICE—See SNCF; *Int'l*, pg. 1164
SNTR CALBERSON NIEVRE—See SNCF; *Int'l*, pg. 1164
SNTR CALBERSON NIMES—See SNCF; *Int'l*, pg. 1164
SNTR CALBERSON ORLEANS—See SNCF; *Int'l*, pg. 1164
SNTR CALBERSON PARIS—See SNCF; *Int'l*, pg. 1164
SNTR CALBERSON ROANNE—See SNCF; *Int'l*, pg. 1164
SNTR CALBERSON ROUEN—See SNCF; *Int'l*, pg. 1164
SNTR CALBERSON ST. ETIENNE—See SNCF; *Int'l*, pg. 1164
SNTR CALBERSON TOULON—See SNCF; *Int'l*, pg. 1164
SNTR CALBERSON VALENCE—See SNCF; *Int'l*, pg. 1164
SO.GE.AM S.P.A.—See Nestle S.A.; *Int'l*, pg. 922
SO.GE.PLAST S.R.L.—See Nestle S.A.; *Int'l*, pg. 922
SO OVITEOLLISUUS OY—See Stora Kopparbergs Bergslags AB; *Int'l*, pg. 1302
SOCAP LTD ELF TRADING SA—See Elf Aquitane; *Int'l*, pg. 445
S.O.C.A.T.A.(SOCIETE DE CONSTRUCTION D'AVIONS DE TOURISMES ET D'AFFAIRES)—See Aerospatiale; *Int'l*, pg. 29
SOCO CALIFORNIA PROPERTIES, INC.—See Snyder Oil Corporation; *U.S. Public*, pg. 1482
SOCO CHEMICAL, INC.—See Veba AG; *Int'l*, pg. 1458
SOCO HOLDINGS INC.—See Snyder Oil Corporation; *U.S. Public*, pg. 1482
SOCO-LYNCH CORP.—See Veba AG; *Int'l*, pg. 1458
SOCO THOMASVILLE, INC.—See Snyder Oil Corporation; *U.S. Public*, pg. 1482

SOCO WATTENBERG CORPORATION—See Snyder Oil Corporation; *U.S. Public*, pg. 1482
SODAP-STE D'APPLICATION DES SYNTHESES TECHNIQUES—See Lafarge S.A.; *Int'l*, pg. 789
SODIAAL; *Int'l*, pg. 1166
SODIAN - SOCIEDAD PARA EL DESARROLLO INDUSTRIAL DE ANALUCIA, S.A.—See SEPI; *Int'l*, pg. 1225
SODIAR - SOCIEDAD PARA EL DESARROLLO INDUSTRIAL DE ARAGON, S.A.—See SEPI; *Int'l*, pg. 1225
SODICAL - SOCIEDAD PARA EL DESARROLLO INDUSTRIAL DE CASTILLA Y LEON, S.A.—See SEPI; *Int'l*, pg. 1225
SODICAMAN - SOCIEDAD PARA EL DESARROLLO INDUSTRIAL DE CASTILLA-LA MANCHA, S.A.—See SEPI; *Int'l*, pg. 1225
SODIEX - SOCIEDAD PARA EL DESARROLLO INDUSTRIAL DE EXTREMADURA, S.A.—See SEPI; *Int'l*, pg. 1225
SOFID—See ENI S.p.A.; *Int'l*, pg. 429
SOFITEC, SOCIETE FINANCIERE ET TECHNIQUE SA—See Philipp Holzmann AG; *Int'l*, pg. 634
SOFUNGE LTDA.—See Daimler-Benz Aktiengesellschaft; *Int'l*, pg. 369
SOR EUROPE, LTD.—See SOR Inc.; *U.S. Private*, pg. 957
SOR INC.; *U.S. Private*, pg. 957
SOS INTERNATIONAL—See Fluor Corporation; *U.S. Public*, pg. 660
S.O.S. NEWALL—See S.O.S. Newall Limited; *Int'l*, pg. 1166
S.O.S. NEWALL LIMITED; *Int'l*, pg. 1166
SOTELEC—See Lagardere Groupe; *Int'l*, pg. 793
SP AEROSPACE & VEHICLE SYSTEMS B.V.—See Liebherr-International AG; *Int'l*, pg. 809
SP-SNICKERIER AB—See Stora Kopparbergs Bergslags AB; *Int'l*, pg. 1302
SPA-ALUMINIUM LTD.—See Norsk Hydro a.s; *Int'l*, pg. 964
SPA/FCB—See FCB; *U.S. Public*, pg. 389
SPAFI—See Saint-Gobain; *Int'l*, pg. 1177
SPC COMPANY OF NEW YORK, INC.—See Shorewood Packaging Corporation; *U.S. Public*, pg. 1468
SPC COMPANY OF VIRGINIA, INC.—See Shorewood Packaging Corporation; *U.S. Public*, pg. 1468
SPC CORPORATION, LIMITED—See Shorewood Packaging Corporation; *U.S. Public*, pg. 1468
SPC INTERNATIONAL CORP.—See System Planning Corp.; *U.S. Private*, pg. 1061
S.P.C. TRANSPORT; *U.S. Private*, pg. 957
SPCI SOCIETE DE PRODUITS CHIMIQUES INDUSTRIELS SA—See Internatio-Muller N.V.; *Int'l*, pg. 682
SPD MAGNET WIRE CO.—See Sumitomo Electric Industries, Ltd.; *Int'l*, pg. 1313
SPD TECHNOLOGIES; *U.S. Private*, pg. 957
SPF INSURANCE AGENCY—See St. Paul Bancorp, Inc.; *U.S. Public*, pg. 1428
SPF PROMOTIO SIM SPA—See Crediop-Credito Per Le Imprese e le Opere Pubbliche SpA; *Int'l*, pg. 341
SPI PLC—See The Albert Fisher Group PLC; *Int'l*, pg. 491
SPI POLYOLS, INC.—See Harrowston Corporation; *Int'l*, pg. 599
SPICA S.P.A.—See Fiat Auto SpA; *Int'l*, pg. 481
SPR, INC.; *U.S. Public*, pg. 1419
S.P.R.B.—See GIB Group; *Int'l*, pg. 534
SPS—See AXA-UAP; *Int'l*, pg. 19
SPS INTERNATIONAL LTD.—See SPS Technologies, Inc.; *U.S. Public*, pg. 1420
SPS PAYMENT SYSTEMS, INC.—See Morgan Stanley Dean Witter & Co.; *U.S. Public*, pg. 1132
SPS TECHNOLOGIES, INC.; *U.S. Public*, pg. 1419
SPS TECHNOLOGIES LIMITED—See SPS Technologies, Inc.; *U.S. Public*, pg. 1420
SPS/UNBRAKO K.K.—See SPS Technologies, Inc.; *U.S. Public*, pg. 1420
SPSS INC.; *U.S. Public*, pg. 1420
S.P.T.E. S.A.—See Tractebel; *Int'l*, pg. 1415
SPX CORPORATION; *U.S. Public*, pg. 1420
SQA EUROPE, LTD.—See Rational Software Corporation; *U.S. Public*, pg. 1361
SQA, INC.—See Rational Software Corporation; *U.S. Public*, pg. 1361
SQL SOFTWARE DEVELOPMENT LABORATORY—See Platinum Technology, Inc.; *U.S. Public*, pg. 1309
SR INTERNATIONAL BUSINESS INSURANCE COMPANY LTD.—See Swiss Reinsurance Company; *Int'l*, pg. 1333
SR RISK MANAGEMENT SERVICES LTD.—See Swiss Reinsurance Company; *Int'l*, pg. 1333
SRA - ATLANTA—See SRA International Inc.; *U.S. Private*, pg. 958
SRA - BOSTON—See SRA International Inc.; *U.S. Private*, pg. 958
SRA - DAYTON—See SRA International Inc.; *U.S. Private*, pg. 958
SRA EUROPE, S.A.—See SRA International Inc.; *U.S. Private*, pg. 958
SRA - FAIRFAX—See SRA International Inc.; *U.S. Private*, pg. 958
SRA - FAIRVIEW HEIGHTS—See SRA International Inc.; *U.S. Private*, pg. 958
SRA - FALLS CHURCH—See SRA International Inc.; *U.S. Private*, pg. 958
SRA INTERNATIONAL INC.; *U.S. Private*, pg. 957
SRA MCGRAW HILL—See The McGraw-Hill Companies; *U.S. Public*, pg. 1070
SRA - NEW YORK—See SRA International Inc.; *U.S. Private*, pg. 958
SRA PACIFIC NORTHWEST OPERATIONS—See SRA International Inc.; *U.S. Private*, pg. 958
SRA - ROCKVILLE—See SRA International Inc.; *U.S. Private*, pg. 958
SRA - SAN ANTONIO—See SRA International Inc.; *U.S. Private*, pg. 958
SRC VISION—See Advanced Machine Vision Corp.; *U.S. Public*, pg. 20

SRDC, INC.—See Forest City Enterprises, Inc.; *U.S. Public*, pg. 670
SRDS; *U.S. Private*, pg. 958
SRI CONSULTING—See SRI International; *U.S. Private*, pg. 958
SRI DEVELOPMENT CORP.—See SRI International; *U.S. Private*, pg. 958
SRI INTERNATIONAL; *U.S. Private*, pg. 958
SRI-SOIL & ROCK INSTRUMENTATION—See GZA GeoEnvironmental Technologies, Inc.; *U.S. Public*, pg. 697
SRL OPERATIONS—See Veridian; *U.S. Private*, pg. 1136
SRS—See Carolina Power & Light Company; *U.S. Public*, pg. 307
SRS TECHNOLOGIES; *U.S. Private*, pg. 958
SS COILS LIMITED—See Ascot Holdings Plc; *Int'l*, pg. 88
SS SERVICE CORPORATION—See Washington Mutual Inc.; *U.S. Public*, pg. 1742
SSB ADVERTISING BRISBANE—See Dentsu Inc.; *Int'l*, pg. 394
SSB ADVERTISING MELBOURNE—See Dentsu Inc.; *Int'l*, pg. 394
SSB ADVERTISING SYDNEY—See Dentsu Inc.; *Int'l*, pg. 394
SSB LEEWAY CORP.—See Somerset Savings Bank; *U.S. Public*, pg. 1484
SSC RADEBEUL GMBH—See Fried. Krupp AG; *Int'l*, pg. 512
SSD&W INTEGRATED MARKETING COMMUNICATIONS; *U.S. Private*, pg. 958
SSE TELECOM, INC.; *U.S. Public*, pg. 1421
SSH SVENSK SERVICEHANDEL AB—See Axel Johnson AB; *Int'l*, pg. 709
SSI MEDICAL SYSTEMS, INC.—See Hillenbrand Industries, Inc.; *U.S. Public*, pg. 828
SSIG—See Compagnie des Machines Bull; *Int'l*, pg. 316
SSM COAL B.V.—See SHV Holdings N.V.; *Int'l*, pg. 1155
SSP PUMPS LTD.—See Tetra Laval Group; *Int'l*, pg. 1380
ST ENVIRONMENTAL SERVICES CORP. (II)—See Severn Trent Plc; *Int'l*, pg. 1226
ST LIEGENDCHAFTSVERWERTUNGS AG—See Creditanstalt-Bankverein; *Int'l*, pg. 347
ST MOBILE DATA PTE. LTD.—See BellSouth Corporation; *U.S. Public*, pg. 208
ST PIPING, INC.—See Serv-Tech, Inc.; *U.S. Public*, pg. 1460
S.T. RESEARCH; *U.S. Private*, pg. 958
STA (SISTEMAS DE TECNOLOGIA AVANZADA, S.A.)—See Digital Equipment Corporation; *U.S. Public*, pg. 508
STAC SOCIETE TECHNIQUE D'APPLICATION CHIMIQUE S.A.—See ENI S.p.A.; *Int'l*, pg. 429
STB—See Compagnie des Machines Bull; *Int'l*, pg. 318
STB CORPORATE DEVELOPMENT, INC.—See The Sumitomo Trust & Banking Co., Ltd.; *Int'l*, pg. 1317
STB-EUROPE—See STB Systems, Inc.; *U.S. Public*, pg. 1421
STB FINANCE CAYMAN LIMITED—See The Sumitomo Trust & Banking Co., Ltd.; *Int'l*, pg. 1318
STB FINANCIAL FUTURES (SINGAPORE) PTE LIMITED—See The Sumitomo Trust & Banking Co., Ltd.; *Int'l*, pg. 1318
STB SYSTEMS, INC.; *U.S. Public*, pg. 1421
STC INVESTMENTS LIMITED—See Fujitsu Limited; *Int'l*, pg. 528
STC (NORTHERN IRELAND) LIMITED—See Fujitsu Limited; *Int'l*, pg. 529
STC PROPERTIES LIMITED—See Fujitsu Limited; *Int'l*, pg. 528
STC TECHNOLOGY LIMITED—See Fujitsu Limited; *Int'l*, pg. 529
STECD—See Lyonnaise des Eaux S.A.; *Int'l*, pg. 823
STEN—See Lagardere Groupe; *Int'l*, pg. 793
STER—See SNC-Lavalin Group Inc.; *Int'l*, pg. 1163
STET-ARGENTINA—See IRI Istituto Ricostruzione Industriale; *Int'l*, pg. 656
STET-BELGIUM—See IRI Istituto Ricostruzione Industriale; *Int'l*, pg. 656
STI CONTROLS, L.P.—See Magnetrol International; *U.S. Private*, pg. 696
STI INTERNATIONAL LIMITED—See Meridian Medical Technology, Inc.; *U.S. Public*, pg. 1095
STI OPTRONICS—See Spectra-Physics AB; *Int'l*, pg. 1289
STILL GMBH—See Linde AG; *Int'l*, pg. 811
S.T.I.M.A. S.A.R.L.—See BASF AG; *Int'l*, pg. 109
STM WIRELESS, INC.; *U.S. Public*, pg. 1421
STP CONSUMER SERVICES—See First Brands Corporation; *U.S. Public*, pg. 627
STP CORPORATION—See First Brands Corporation; *U.S. Public*, pg. 627
STP PRODUCTS, INC.—See First Brands Corporation; *U.S. Public*, pg. 627
STR SHANGHAI OFFICE—See Springborn Testing & Research; *U.S. Private*, pg. 1027
STS BINASI ANKARA—See GESTRA GmbH; *Int'l*, pg. 550
STS CONSULTANTS, INC.; *U.S. Private*, pg. 959
STS, INC.—See Dycom Industries, Inc.; *U.S. Public*, pg. 538
STS SERVICES INC.—See CDI Corp.; *U.S. Public*, pg. 277
STS TESISAT ARMATUERLER PAZARLAMA A.S.—See GESTRA GmbH; *Int'l*, pg. 550
STV—See Svedala Industri AB; *Int'l*, pg. 1324
STV ARCHITECTS—See STV Group, Inc.; *U.S. Public*, pg. 1421
STV CONSTRUCTION SERVICES—See STV Group, Inc.; *U.S. Public*, pg. 1421
STV ENVIRONMENTAL—See STV Group, Inc.; *U.S. Public*, pg. 1421
STV GROUP, INC.; *U.S. Public*, pg. 1421
STV INCORPORATED—See STV Group, Inc.; *U.S. Public*, pg. 1421
STV INTERNATIONAL—See STV Group, Inc.; *U.S. Public*, pg. 1421
STV/SILVER & ZISKIND—See STV Group, Inc.; *U.S. Public*, pg. 1421

S.U. AUTOMOTIVE LIMITED—See Echlin Inc.; *U.S. Public,* pg. 561
SUAB SVENSK UNDERVATTENSELEKTRONIK AB—See Celsius AB; *Int'l,* pg. 277
SV-ACER CO. LTD.—See Acer Incorporated; *Int'l,* pg. 22
SV INFORMATION COMPUTER ENTERPRISE—See International Data Group; *U.S. Private,* pg. 570
SVC SHANGHAI VOITH PAPER MACHINERY LTD.—See J.M. Voith, GmbH; *Int'l,* pg. 1473
SVG LITHOGRAPHY SYSTEMS—See Silicon Valley Group, Inc.; *U.S. Public,* pg. 1474
SVG THERMCO SYSTEMS—See Silicon Valley Group, Inc.; *U.S. Public,* pg. 1474
SVG TRACK SYSTEMS—See Silicon Valley Group, Inc.; *U.S. Public,* pg. 1474
SVM OF TEXAS, INC.—See Service America Corporation; *U.S. Private,* pg. 986
S.W. AIRFREIGHT—See Circle International Group, Inc.; *U.S. Public,* pg. 373
S.W.B. & COMPANY—See Rokeach Food Distributing Inc.; *U.S. Private,* pg. 941
SWMIC, INC.—See The Sherwin-Williams Company; *U.S. Public,* pg. 1465
SWUMC (SOUTH WEST UNITED MACHINERY CORPORATION)—See The Macneal-Schwendler Corp.; *U.S. Public,* pg. 1032
S.A. FORGES DE ZEEBRUGGE—See Thomson S.A.; *Int'l,* pg. 1385
SAAB AB—See Investor AB; *Int'l,* pg. 686
SAAB AIRCRAFT DIVISION—See Investor AB; *Int'l,* pg. 686
SAAB AIRCRAFT INTERNATIONAL LTD.—See Investor AB; *Int'l,* pg. 687
SAAB AIRCRAFT OF AMERICA INC.—See Investor AB; *Int'l,* pg. 687
OY SAAB-AUTO AB—See Valmet Corporation; *Int'l,* pg. 1449
SAAB AUTOMATION AB—See Investor AB; *Int'l,* pg. 686
SAAB AUTOMATION LTD—See Investor AB; *Int'l,* pg. 686
SAAB AUTOMOBILE AB—See Investor AB; *Int'l,* pg. 687
SAAB AUTOMOBILE AB—See General Motors Corporation; *U.S. Public,* pg. 725
SAAB CARS USA, INC.—See Investor AB; *Int'l,* pg. 687
SAAB DANMARK A/S—See Investor AB; *Int'l,* pg. 687
SAAB DEUTSCHLAND GMBH—See Investor AB; *Int'l,* pg. 687
SAAB FRANCE S.A.—See Investor AB; *Int'l,* pg. 687
SAAB GREAT BRITAIN LTD.—See Investor AB; *Int'l,* pg. 687
SAAB INSTRUMENTS—See Investor AB; *Int'l,* pg. 686
SAAB MARINE ELECTRONICS AB—See Investor AB; *Int'l,* pg. 686
SAAB MISSILES AB—See Investor AB; *Int'l,* pg. 686
SAAB NORGE A/S—See Investor AB; *Int'l,* pg. 688
SAAB-SCANIA COMBITECH—See Investor AB; *Int'l,* pg. 686
SAAB-SCANIA FINANCE LTD—See Investor AB; *Int'l,* pg. 688
SAAB-SCANIA FINANCIAL SERVICES CORP—See Investor AB; *Int'l,* pg. 687
SAAB SPACE AB—See Investor AB; *Int'l,* pg. 687
SAAB SWEDEN AB—See Investor AB; *Int'l,* pg. 687
SAAB SYSTEMS, INC.—See Investor AB; *Int'l,* pg. 687
SAAB TECHTRADE AB—See Investor AB; *Int'l,* pg. 687
SAAB TRAINING SYSTEMS AB—See Investor AB; *Int'l,* pg. 687
SAAR FERNGAS AG—See Ruhrgas Aktiengesellschaft; *Int'l,* pg. 1148
SAAR-GUMMIWERK GMBH—See Saarbergwerke Aktiengesellschaft; *Int'l,* pg. 1167
SAARBACH—See Lagardere Groupe; *Int'l,* pg. 796
SAARBACH GMBH—See Lagardere Groupe; *Int'l,* pg. 796
SAARBERG BRENNSTOFFHANDEL GMBH—See Saarbergwerke Aktiengesellschaft; *Int'l,* pg. 1167
SAARBERG COAL AUSTRALIA PTY. LIMITED—See Saarbergwerke Aktiengesellschaft; *Int'l,* pg. 1167
SAARBERG-FERNWAERME GMBH—See Saarbergwerke Aktiengesellschaft; *Int'l,* pg. 1166
SAARBERG HANDEL GMBH—See Saarbergwerke Aktiengesellschaft; *Int'l,* pg. 1167
SAARBERG-HOELTER-LURGI GMBH—See Saarbergwerke Aktiengesellschaft; *Int'l,* pg. 1167
SAARBERG-HOELTER UMWELTTECHNIK GMBH—See Saarbergwerke Aktiengesellschaft; *Int'l,* pg. 1167
SAARBERG-INTERPLAN GESELLSCHAFT FUER ROHSTOFF-, ENERGIE-UND INGENIEURTECHNIK MBH—See Saarbergwerke Aktiengesellschaft; *Int'l,* pg. 1167
SAARBERGWERKE AKTIENGESELLSCHAFT; *Int'l,* pg. 1166
SAARBRUCKER ZEITUNG VERLAG UND DRUCKEREI GMBH—See Georg von Holtzbrinck GmbH; *Int'l,* pg. 1478
SAAR-INDUSTRIE, GMBH—See Ford Motor Company; *U.S. Public,* pg. 666
SAARLAENDISCHE KRAFTWERKSGESELLSCHAFT MBH—See Saarbergwerke Aktiengesellschaft; *Int'l,* pg. 1167
SAARLUX BETEILIGUNG—See Groupe Usinor; *Int'l,* pg. 572
SAARLUX GMBH—See Groupe Usinor; *Int'l,* pg. 572
SAATCHI & SAATCHI ADVERTISING WORLDWIDE; *U.S. Public,* pg. 1422
SAATCHI & SAATCHI KID CONNECTION—See Saatchi & Saatchi Advertising Worldwide; *U.S. Public,* pg. 1422
SAB WABCO AB—See Cardo AB; *Int'l,* pg. 271
SAB WABCO AB—See Cardo AB; *Int'l,* pg. 271
SAB WABCO DIMETAL EQUIPOS FERROVIARRIOS—See Cardo AB; *Int'l,* pg. 271
SAB WABCO GROUP SYSTEMS CENTRE—See Cardo AB; *Int'l,* pg. 271
SAB WABCO KP GMBH—See Cardo AB; *Int'l,* pg. 271
SAB WABCO PTY. LTD.—See Cardo AB; *Int'l,* pg. 271

SABA FASTIGHETS AB—See Carnegie Holding AB; *Int'l,* pg. 272
SABA FORETAGSHALSOVARD AB—See Axel Johnson AB; *Int'l,* pg. 709
SABA TRADING AB—See Axel Johnson AB; *Int'l,* pg. 709
SABAN ENTERTAINMENT; *U.S. Private,* pg. 959
SABANCI HOLDING A.S.; *Int'l,* pg. 1167
SABBETH INDUSTRIES LTD; *U.S. Private,* pg. 959
SABEL SERVEIS, S.A.—See Caixa d'Estalvis de Catalunya; *Int'l,* pg. 250
SABEMA MATERIAL AB—See Scancem AB; *Int'l,* pg. 1199
SABENA; *Int'l,* pg. 1168
SABENA INTERSERVICE CENTER LIMITED—See Sabena; *Int'l,* pg. 1168
S.A. SABFRAN, BRUNELLE & CIE—See Kemira Oy; *Int'l,* pg. 728
SABIEM ELEVATORS (PTY.) LTD.—See Kone Corporation; *Int'l,* pg. 748
SABIEM S.R.L.—See Kone Corporation; *Int'l,* pg. 748
SABIM—See Groupe Casino; *Int'l,* pg. 563
SABIN ROBBINS PAPER CO.; *U.S. Private,* pg. 959
THE SABINE MINING CO.—See NACCO Industries, Inc.; *U.S. Public,* pg. 1149
SABINE TRANSPORTATION COMPANY—See Kirby Corporation; *U.S. Public,* pg. 962
SABLE CARE CENTER—See Horizon/CMS Healthcare Corporation; *U.S. Public,* pg. 836
SABLIERE DU VENTOUX—See Nestle S.A.; *Int'l,* pg. 919
SABOMA—See GIB Group; *Int'l,* pg. 533
SABRE DECISION TECHNOLOGIES—See AMR Corporation; *U.S. Public,* pg. 10
THE SABRE GROUP HOLDINGS, INC.—See AMR Corporation; *U.S. Public,* pg. 10
SABRE SYSTEMS & SERVICE INC.—See Moore Corporation Limited; *Int'l,* pg. 890
SABRE TRAVEL INFORMATION NETWORK—See AMR Corporation; *U.S. Public,* pg. 10
SABRELINER CORPORATION; *U.S. Private,* pg. 959
SABRETECH, INC.—See Sabreliner Corporation; *U.S. Private,* pg. 959
SABRITAS S.A. DE C.V.—See PepsiCo, Inc.; *U.S. Public,* pg. 1278
SACEM—See Imetal; *Int'l,* pg. 662
SACHERIE DE PONT-AUDEMER S.N.C.—See Royal Packaging Industries Van Leer B.V.; *Int'l,* pg. 1146
SACHS AG—See Mannesmann A.G.; *Int'l,* pg. 839
SACHS ALLINQUANT SA—See Mannesmann A.G.; *Int'l,* pg. 835
SACHS AUTO SA—See Mannesmann A.G.; *Int'l,* pg. 835
SACHS AUTOMOTIVE COMPONENTS, INC.—See Mannesmann A.G.; *Int'l,* pg. 835
SACHS AUTOMOTIVE COMPONENTS LTD.—See Mannesmann A.G.; *Int'l,* pg. 835
SACHS AUTOMOTIVE CORP.-NORTH AMERICAN OEM OPERATIONS—See Mannesmann A.G.; *Int'l,* pg. 835
SACHS AUTOMOTIVE LTDA.—See Mannesmann A.G.; *Int'l,* pg. 835
SACHS BOGE ITALIA SPA—See Mannesmann A.G.; *Int'l,* pg. 835
SACHS BOGE OF AMERICA—See Mannesmann A.G.; *Int'l,* pg. 835
SACHS (FAR EAST) PTE. LTD.—See Mannesmann A.G.; *Int'l,* pg. 835
SACHS-GIEBEREI GMBH—See Mannesmann A.G.; *Int'l,* pg. 835
SACHS HOLDING COMPANY; *U.S. Private,* pg. 959
SACHS IBERICA SA—See Mannesmann A.G.; *Int'l,* pg. 835
SACHS INDUSTRIES SA—See Mannesmann A.G.; *Int'l,* pg. 835
SACHS MALAYSIA SDN.BHD.—See Mannesmann A.G.; *Int'l,* pg. 835
SACHS MÉXICO SA DE CV—See Mannesmann A.G.; *Int'l,* pg. 835
SACHS PROPERTIES—See Sachs Holding Company; *U.S. Private,* pg. 959
SACHS RIEDL GMBH—See Mannesmann A.G.; *Int'l,* pg. 835
SACHS SA (PTY.) LTD.—See Mannesmann A.G.; *Int'l,* pg. 835
SACHS TRNAVA SRO—See Mannesmann A.G.; *Int'l,* pg. 835
SACHSEN PAPIER EILENBURG GMBH—See Enso Oyj; *Int'l,* pg. 458
SACHSEN-SCHWERTRANSPORT GMBH—See Dyckerhoff & Widmann AG; *Int'l,* pg. 423
SACHSENMETALL HANDELGESELLSCHAFT INHABER MAX COCHIUS GMBH—See Fried. Krupp AG; *Int'l,* pg. 514
SACHSISCHE AUTOMOBILBAU GMBH—See Volkswagen AG; *Int'l,* pg. 1473
SACHSISCHE QUARZPORPHYRWERKE GMBH—See Philipp Holzmann AG; *Int'l,* pg. 632
SACHTLEBEN CHEMIE GMBH—See Metallgesellschaft AG; *Int'l,* pg. 861
SACIT, S.P.A.—See Emerson Electric Co.; *U.S. Public,* pg. 577
SACK INSTALACOES SIDERURGICAS LTDA.—See Mannesmann A.G.; *Int'l,* pg. 837
SACKNER PRODUCTS—See Jason Incorporated; *U.S. Public,* pg. 924
ANN SACKS TILE & STONE, INC.—See Kohler Company; *U.S. Private,* pg. 630
THE SACKS GROUP—See Rexel, S.A.; *Int'l,* pg. 1107
SACOM, INC.—See SFA, Inc.; *U.S. Private,* pg. 956
SACOR INC.—See Chiron Corporation; *U.S. Public,* pg. 350
SACOR MARITIMA, S.A.—See Petrogal, s.a.; *Int'l,* pg. 1045
THE SACRAMENTO BEE—See McClatchy Newspapers Inc.; *U.S. Public,* pg. 1066
SACRAMENTO BRANCH OFFICE—See U.S. Home Corporation; *U.S. Public,* pg. 1683
SACRAMENTO CABLE—See The E.W. Scripps Company; *U.S. Public,* pg. 1448
SACRAMENTO JAGUAR, INC.—See Von Housen Motors; *U.S. Private,* pg. 1143

SACRAMENTO KINGS; *U.S. Private,* pg. 959
SACRAMENTO MUNICIPAL UTILITY DISTRICT; *U.S. Private,* pg. 959
SADCO LTD.—See Joffko International; *U.S. Private,* pg. 589
SADDLE RIVER HOLDINGS CORP.—See Orange and Rockland Utilities, Inc.; *U.S. Public,* pg. 1229
SADDLEBACK ASSOCIATES—See Cigna Corp.; *U.S. Public,* pg. 362
SADDLEBAG LAKE RESORTS, INC.—See Alico, Inc.; *U.S. Public,* pg. 41
SADEF N.V.—See Voest-Alpine Stahl AG; *Int'l,* pg. 1472
SADEM—See Groupe Casino; *Int'l,* pg. 563
SADIA AGROAVICOLA S/A INDUSTRIA E COMERCIO—See Sadia Group; *Int'l,* pg. 1168
SADIA CONCORDIA S.A. INDUSTRIA E COMERCIO—See Sadia Group; *Int'l,* pg. 1168
SADIA GROUP; *Int'l,* pg. 1168
SADIA MATO GROSSO S/A—See Sadia Group; *Int'l,* pg. 1168
SADIA OESTE S.A. INDUSTRIA E COMERCIO—See Sadia Group; *Int'l,* pg. 1169
SADLER MATERIALS CORP.—See Florida Rock Industries, Inc.; *U.S. Public,* pg. 656
WILLIAM H. SADLIER, INC.; *U.S. Public,* pg. 1422
SADTLER RESEARCH LABORATORIES—See Bio-Rad Laboratories, Inc.; *U.S. Public,* pg. 230
SADUC—See Lyonnaise des Eaux S.A.; *Int'l,* pg. 823
SAEHAN MERCHANT BANKING CORPORATION—See The Industrial Bank of Japan, Limited; *Int'l,* pg. 676
SAEHAN MERCHANT BANKING CORPORATION—See The Long-Term Credit Bank of Japan, Limited; *Int'l,* pg. 817
SAEL DECORS—See Duni AB; *Int'l,* pg. 421
SAETRE AS—See Orkla A.S.A.; *Int'l,* pg. 1011
SAFA, LLC—See Sumitomo Electric Industries, Ltd.; *Int'l,* pg. 1313
SAFARE-CROUZET—See Thomson S.A.; *Int'l,* pg. 1382
SAFARI TOOL—See Pratt-Read Corporation; *U.S. Private,* pg. 879
SAFCO SELECT MARKETS DIVISION—See SAFECO Corporation; *U.S. Public,* pg. 1423
SAFCO TECHNOLOGIES, INC.—See Salient 3 Communications, Inc.; *U.S. Public,* pg. 1430
SAFE ALARM, INC.; *U.S. Private,* pg. 960
SAFE HARBOR WATER POWER CORP.—See Baltimore Gas and Electric Company; *U.S. Public,* pg. 172
SAFE HARBOR WATER POWER CORP.—See PP&L Resources; *U.S. Public,* pg. 1244
SAFE INSURANCE—See GIB Group; *Int'l,* pg. 533
SAFE PARTNERS AB—See Celsius AB; *Int'l,* pg. 277
SAFE REINSURANCE—See GIB Group; *Int'l,* pg. 534
SAFE S.A.—See Groupe Usinor; *Int'l,* pg. 571
SAFE SERVICE AB—See Celsius AB; *Int'l,* pg. 277
SAFE SERVICE LTD.—See Celsius AB; *Int'l,* pg. 277
SAFECARD SERVICES, INC.—See Cendant Corporation; *U.S. Public,* pg. 320
SAFECARE COMPANY—See SAFECO Corporation; *U.S. Public,* pg. 1423
SAFECO ADMINISTRATIVE SERVICES, INC.—See SAFECO Corporation; *U.S. Public,* pg. 1423
SAFECO ASSET MANAGEMENT COMPANY—See SAFECO Corporation; *U.S. Public,* pg. 1423
SAFECO CORPORATION; *U.S. Public,* pg. 1423
SAFECO CREDIT COMPANY, INC.—See SAFECO Corporation; *U.S. Public,* pg. 1423
SAFECO INSURANCE CO. OF AMERICA—See SAFECO Corporation; *U.S. Public,* pg. 1423
SAFECO INSURANCE CO. OF ILLINOIS—See SAFECO Corporation; *U.S. Public,* pg. 1423
SAFECO LIFE AND HEALTH INSURANCE COMPANIES—See SAFECO Corporation; *U.S. Public,* pg. 1423
SAFECO LLOYDS INSURANCE CO.—See SAFECO Corporation; *U.S. Public,* pg. 1423
SAFECO MUTUAL FUNDS—See SAFECO Corporation; *U.S. Public,* pg. 1423
SAFECO NATIONAL INSURANCE CO.—See SAFECO Corporation; *U.S. Public,* pg. 1423
SAFECO PROPERTIES, INC.—See SAFECO Corporation; *U.S. Public,* pg. 1423
SAFECO PROPERTY & CASUALTY INSURANCE COMPANIES—See SAFECO Corporation; *U.S. Public,* pg. 1423
SAFECO SECURITIES, INC.—See SAFECO Corporation; *U.S. Public,* pg. 1423
SAFECO SELECT INSURANCE SERVICES—See SAFECO Corporation; *U.S. Public,* pg. 1423
SAFECO SERVICES CO.—See SAFECO Corporation; *U.S. Public,* pg. 1423
SAFECO SURPLUS LINES INSURANCE CO.—See SAFECO Corporation; *U.S. Public,* pg. 1423
SAFECO TRUST COMPANY—See SAFECO Corporation; *U.S. Public,* pg. 1423
SAFEGUARD BUSINESS SYSTEMS, INC.; *U.S. Private,* pg. 960
SAFEGUARD BUSINESS SYSTEMS LIMITED—See Safeguard Business Systems, Inc.; *U.S. Private,* pg. 960
SAFEGUARD FINANCIAL CORP.—See Safeguard Business Systems, Inc.; *U.S. Private,* pg. 960
SAFEGUARD HEALTH ENTERPRISES, INC.; *U.S. Public,* pg. 1424
SAFEGUARD HEALTH PLANS, INC.—See Safeguard Health Enterprises, Inc.; *U.S. Public,* pg. 1424
SAFEGUARD INSURANCE CO.—See Royal & Sun Alliance Insurance Group plc; *Int'l,* pg. 1131
SAFEGUARD INTERNATIONAL GROUP—See Safeguard Scientifics, Inc.; *U.S. Public,* pg. 1424
SAFEGUARD SCIENTIFICS, INC.; *U.S. Public,* pg. 1424
SAFEGUARDS TECHNOLOGY, INC.—See Sophus Berendsen A/S; *Int'l,* pg. 1286
SAFE-HIT CORPORATION—See Quixote Corporation; *U.S. Public,* pg. 1353
SAFELITE AUTOGLASS; *U.S. Private,* pg. 960

SAFEMAL DRILLING SDN. BHD.—See Kuwait Petroleum Corporation; *Int'l*, pg. 765

SAFER, LTD.—See Ringer Corporation; *U.S. Public*, pg. 1390

SAFESKIN CORPORATION; *U.S. Public*, pg. 1425

SAFETRAN SYSTEMS CORPORATION—See BTR plc; *Int'l*, pg. 127

SAFETY AND FIRE TECHNOLOGY, INC.—See O'Keeffe's, Inc.; *U.S. Private*, pg. 813

SAFETY DISPOSAL SYSTEM, INC.—See Med/Waste, Inc.; *U.S. Public*, pg. 1077

SAFETY 1ST, INC.; *U.S. Public*, pg. 1425

SAFETY FUND NATIONAL BANK—See CFX Bank; *U.S. Public*, pg. 278

SAFETY-KLEEN CANADA, LTD.—See Safety-Kleen Corp.; *U.S. Public*, pg. 1426

SAFETY-KLEEN CORP.; *U.S. Public*, pg. 1425

SAFETY-KLEEN OIL RECOVERY CO.—See Safety-Kleen Corp.; *U.S. Public*, pg. 1426

SAFETY-KLEEN U.K., LTD.—See Safety-Kleen Corp.; *U.S. Public*, pg. 1426

SAFETY NATIONAL CASUALTY CORP.—See Delphi Financial Group, Inc.; *U.S. Public*, pg. 496

SAFETY NET, INC.—See Nextel Communications; *U.S. Public*, pg. 1181

SAFETY RAILWAY SERVICE—See Commercial Metals Company; *U.S. Public*, pg. 412

SAFETY RAILWAY SERVICE-TULSA—See Commercial Metals Company; *U.S. Public*, pg. 412

SAFETY STEEL SERVICE, INC.—See Commercial Metals Company; *U.S. Public*, pg. 412

SAFETY WEAR CORP.—See Eastco Industrial Safety Corp.; *U.S. Public*, pg. 548

SAFETYMASTER CORPORATION—See Strategic Distribution, Inc.; *U.S. Public*, pg. 1523

SAFEWAY INC.; *U.S. Public*, pg. 1426

SAFEWAY PLC; *Int'l*, pg. 1169

SAFEWAY PRODUCTS, INC.—See The B.F. Goodrich Company; *U.S. Public*, pg. 752

SAFEWAY STORES PLC—See Safeway PLC; *Int'l*, pg. 1169

SAFEWAY SUPPLY, INC.—See Safeway Inc.; *U.S. Public*, pg. 1426

SAFEWAY U.S. HOLDINGS, INC.—See Safeway Inc.; *U.S. Public*, pg. 1426

SAFIAL B.V.—See Unilever Plc; *Int'l*, pg. 1438

SAFIC ALCAN & CIE S.A.—See Metallgesellschaft AG; *Int'l*, pg. 862

SAFIRE PRIVATE LIMITED—See Cigna Corp.; *U.S. Public*, pg. 363

SAFT AMERICA INC.—See Alcatel Alsthom Compagnie Generale D'Electricite; *Int'l*, pg. 55

SAFT BATTERIES LTD.—See Alcatel Alsthom Compagnie Generale D'Electricite; *Int'l*, pg. 55

SAFTEYWEAR LIMITED—See Bridport-Gundry p.l.c.; *Int'l*, pg. 215

SAFWAY STEEL PRODUCTS INC.—See Thyssen AG; *Int'l*, pg. 1389

SAG HARBOR—See Kellwood Company; *U.S. Public*, pg. 948

SAGA COMMUNICATIONS—See DMB&B Communications; *U.S. Private*, pg. 305

SAGA PETROLEUM ASA; *Int'l*, pg. 1169

SAGA PETROLEUM ASA—See Saga Petroleum ASA; *Int'l*, pg. 1169

SAGA PETROLEUM ASA - LIBYA—See Saga Petroleum ASA; *Int'l*, pg. 1169

SAGA PETROLEUM FLORO—See Saga Petroleum ASA; *Int'l*, pg. 1169

SAGA PETROLEUM HARSTAD—See Saga Petroleum ASA; *Int'l*, pg. 1169

SAGA PETROLEUM INDONESIA AS—See Saga Petroleum ASA; *Int'l*, pg. 1169

SAGA PETROLEUM STAVANGER—See Saga Petroleum ASA; *Int'l*, pg. 1169

SAGA PETROLEUM UK LIMITED—See Saga Petroleum ASA; *Int'l*, pg. 1169

SAGAMI GS CO., LTD.—See Caterpillar Inc.; *U.S. Public*, pg. 317

SAGAMIHARA PLANT—See Nikon Corporation; *Int'l*, pg. 931

SAGAMORE INSURANCE COMPANY—See Baldwin & Lyons, Inc.; *U.S. Public*, pg. 169

SAGAR-RICHARDS LIMITED—See Ascot Holdings Plc; *Int'l*, pg. 88

SAGE ENERGY COMPANY; *U.S. Public*, pg. 1426

SAGE ENTERPRISES, INC.; *U.S. Private*, pg. 960

SAGEBRUSH SALES COMPANY—See Nortek, Inc.; *U.S. Public*, pg. 1193

SAGEM—See Societe d'Applications Generales d'Electricite et de Mecanique; *Int'l*, pg. 1273

SAGEM CORPORATION—See Societe d'Applications Generales d'Electricite et de Mecanique; *Int'l*, pg. 1273

SAGIT S.P.A.—See Unilever Plc; *Int'l*, pg. 1438

PT SAGITA DUMEZ—See Lyonnaise des Eaux S.A.; *Int'l*, pg. 823

SAHA WOODALL-DUCKHAM (PRIVATE) LIMITED—See FKI plc; *Int'l*, pg. 472

SAHAKOL CHASSIS CO., LTD.—See Siam City Bank Public Company Limited; *Int'l*, pg. 1239

SAHAPATHANAPIBUL PUBLIC COMPANY LIMITED; *Int'l*, pg. 1169

SAHARA ENTERPRISES INC.; *U.S. Private*, pg. 960

SAHARA ILLINOIS CORP.—See Santa Fe Gaming Corporation; *U.S. Public*, pg. 1432

SAHARA LAS VEGAS CORP.—See Santa Fe Gaming Corporation; *U.S. Public*, pg. 1432

SAHARA MISSISSIPPI MANAGEMENT COMPANY, INC.—See Santa Fe Gaming Corporation; *U.S. Public*, pg. 1432

SAHARA NEVADA CORP.—See Santa Fe Gaming Corporation; *U.S. Public*, pg. 1432

SAHARA PARKVILLE, INC.—See Santa Fe Gaming Corporation; *U.S. Public*, pg. 1432

SAHARA RESORTS—See Santa Fe Gaming Corporation; *U.S. Public*, pg. 1432

SAHKOLAHTEENMAKI OY—See ABB Asea Brown Boveri (Holding) Ltd.; *Int'l*, pg. 8

GEORG SAHM GMBH & CO. KG MASCHINENFABRIK; *Int'l*, pg. 1169

GEORG SAHM SINGAPORE PTE. LTD.—See Georg Sahm GmbH & Co. KG Maschinenfabrik; *Int'l*, pg. 1169

SAIA MOTOR FREIGHT LINES—See Yellow Corporation; *Int'l*, pg. 1788

SAIDEN CO., LTD.—See Sanken Electric Co., Ltd.; *Int'l*, pg. 1188

SAIHARA & CO., LTD.—See Suntory Ltd.; *Int'l*, pg. 1321

SAIL MAGAZINE—See Primedia Inc.; *U.S. Public*, pg. 1328

SAILING BUSINESS—See The New York Times Company; *U.S. Public*, pg. 1174

SAILING WORLD—See The New York Times Company; *U.S. Public*, pg. 1174

SAILTRON B.V.—See SAIT-RadioHolland Group S.A.; *Int'l*, pg. 1151

SAIMAA PROCUREMENT AREA—See Enso Oyj; *Int'l*, pg. 455

J. SAINSBURY PLC; *Int'l*, pg. 1169

ST. ALBANS SAND & GRAVEL CO. LIMITED—See RMC Group p.l.c.; *Int'l*, pg. 1079

ST. ANDREWS HOMES—See Vaux Group Plc; *Int'l*, pg. 1454

ST. ANNE CHEMICAL CO., LTD.—See Parsons & Whittemore, Inc.; *U.S. Private*, pg. 841

ST. ANNE INDUSTRIES LTD.—See Parsons & Whittemore, Inc.; *U.S. Private*, pg. 841

ST. ANNE - NACKAWIC PULP CO., LTD.—See Parsons & Whittemore, Inc.; *U.S. Private*, pg. 841

ST. ANNE PULP SALES CO. LTD.—See Parsons & Whittemore, Inc.; *U.S. Private*, pg. 841

SAINT AUGUSTINE FOODS, INC.—See WSMP, Inc.; *U.S. Public*, pg. 1729

SAINT BRICE S.A.—See Otto Versand (GmbH & Co.); *Int'l*, pg. 1015

THE ST. CATHARINES STANDARD—See Hollinger Inc.; *Int'l*, pg. 631

ST. CLAIR MANUFACTURING CO.—See Stockham Valves & Fittings, Inc.; *U.S. Private*, pg. 1044

ST. CLAIR PAINT AND WALLPAPER CORPORATION; *Int'l*, pg. 1170

ST. CLAIR PIPELINES—See Westcoast Energy Inc.; *Int'l*, pg. 1492

ST. CLAIRE PLASTICS CO.; *U.S. Private*, pg. 960

ST. CLEMENT VINEYARDS—See Sapporo Breweries Ltd.; *Int'l*, pg. 1193

ST. CLOUD DAILY TIMES, INC.—See Gannett Company, Inc.; *U.S. Public*, pg. 701

ST. CLOUD MINING CO.—See The Goldfield Corporation; *U.S. Public*, pg. 750

ST. CROIX PRESS, INC.; *U.S. Private*, pg. 960

ST. CROIX WATER POWER CO.—See Georgia-Pacific Corporation; *U.S. Public*, pg. 736

SAINT DOMINIQUE FINANCE—See Credit Nationale; *Int'l*, pg. 344

SAINT DOMINIQUE PARTICIPATIONS—See Credit Nationale; *Int'l*, pg. 344

STE. EUROPEENNE DE RESTAURATION—See Accor S.A.; *Int'l*, pg. 20

THE ST. GEORGE GROUP, INC.; *U.S. Private*, pg. 960

SAINT-GOBAIN; *Int'l*, pg. 1170

SAINT-GOBAIN ADVANCED MATERIALS CORPORATION—See Saint-Gobain; *Int'l*, pg. 1173

SAINT-GOBAIN & GLAC. SAINT-ROCH OHG—See Saint-Gobain; *Int'l*, pg. 1173

SAINT-GOBAIN CORPORATION—See Saint-Gobain; *Int'l*, pg. 1177

SAINT-GOBAIN DELAWARE CORPORATION—See Saint-Gobain; *Int'l*, pg. 1177

SAINT-GOBAIN DESJONQUERES—See Saint-Gobain; *Int'l*, pg. 1171

SAINT-GOBAIN EMBALLAGE—See Saint-Gobain; *Int'l*, pg. 1171

SAINT-GOBAIN FINANZIARIA SPA—See Saint-Gobain; *Int'l*, pg. 1171

SAINT-GOBAIN NEDERLAND—See Saint-Gobain; *Int'l*, pg. 1177

SAINT-GOBAIN PRODUITS INDUSTRIELS—See Saint-Gobain; *Int'l*, pg. 1172

SAINT-GOBAIN PROMOTION ET PARTICIPATIONS INTERNATIONALES—See Saint-Gobain; *Int'l*, pg. 1177

SAINT-GOBAIN VETRO ITALIA SPA—See Saint-Gobain; *Int'l*, pg. 1173

SAINT-GOBAIN VITRAGE—See Saint-Gobain; *Int'l*, pg. 1172

STE IMMOBILIERE AEROPORTUAIRE—See Groupe Air France; *Int'l*, pg. 560

ST. IVES PLC; *Int'l*, pg. 1177

ST. JAMES'S PLACE CAPITAL PLC.; *Int'l*, pg. 1177

ST. JEROME PAPER MILL—See The Cascades Group; *Int'l*, pg. 274

ST. JOE COMMUNICATIONS, INC.—See St. Joe Corp.; *U.S. Public*, pg. 1427

ST. JOE CONTAINER CO.—See St. Joe Corp.; *U.S. Public*, pg. 1427

ST. JOE CORP.; *U.S. Public*, pg. 1426

ST. JOE FOREST PRODUCTS COMPANY—See St. Joe Corp.; *U.S. Public*, pg. 1427

ST. JOE INDUSTRIES, INC.—See St. Joe Corp.; *U.S. Public*, pg. 1427

ST. JOE TELEPHONE & TELEGRAPH COMPANY—See St. Joe Corp.; *U.S. Public*, pg. 1427

ST. JOHANN LAGERHAUS & SCHIFFAHRTS-GESELLSCHAFT—See Coop Switzerland; *Int'l*, pg. 330

ST. JOHN KNITS; *U.S. Public*, pg. 960

SAINT JOHN PORT CORPORATION—See Canada Ports Corporation; *Int'l*, pg. 255

ST. JOHN'S PORT CORPORATION—See Canada Ports Corporation; *Int'l*, pg. 255

ST. JOSEPH LAND & DEVELOPMENT COMPANY—See St. Joe Corp.; *U.S. Public*, pg. 1427

ST. JOSEPH LIGHT & POWER CO.; *U.S. Public*, pg. 1427

ST. JUDE INTERNATIONAL SALES CORP.—See St. Jude Medical, Inc.; *U.S. Public*, pg. 1428

ST. JUDE MEDICAL EUROPE, INC.—See St. Jude Medical, Inc.; *U.S. Public*, pg. 1428

ST. JUDE MEDICAL, INC.; *U.S. Public*, pg. 1427

ST. JUDE MEDICAL LTD.—See St. Jude Medical, Inc.; *U.S. Public*, pg. 1428

ST. JUDE PUERTO RICO, INC.—See St. Jude Medical, Inc.; *U.S. Public*, pg. 1428

ST. JUST MILL—See Fort James Corporation; *U.S. Public*, pg. 673

ST. KATHARINE BY THE TOWER LIMITED—See Taylor Woodrow plc; *Int'l*, pg. 1358

THE ST. LAWRENCE & ADIRONDACK RAILWAY CO.—See Conrail, Inc.; *U.S. Public*, pg. 432

ST. LAWRENCE & ATLANTIC RAILROAD—See Emons Transportation Group, Inc.; *U.S. Public*, pg. 578

ST. LAWRENCE BRICK DIVISION—See Jannock Limited; *Int'l*, pg. 698

ST. LAWRENCE CEMENT INC.—See Holderbank Financiere Glaris Ltd.; *Int'l*, pg. 628

ST. LOUIS AIRLINE LEARNING CENTER—See Berkshire Hathaway Inc.; *U.S. Public*, pg. 219

ST. LOUIS AUTO AUCTION—See Cox Enterprises, Inc.; *U.S. Private*, pg. 283

ST. LOUIS BUSINESS JOURNAL CORP.—See Advance Publications Inc.; *U.S. Private*, pg. 20

ST. LOUIS COUNTIAN—See The Walt Disney Company; *U.S. Public*, pg. 513

ST. LOUIS DAILY RECORD—See The Walt Disney Company; *U.S. Public*, pg. 513

ST. LOUIS METALLIZING CO.—See Nooter Corporation; *U.S. Private*, pg. 801

ST. LOUIS MUSIC, INC.; *U.S. Private*, pg. 960

ST. LOUIS NATIONAL BASEBALL CLUB L.P.; *U.S. Private*, pg. 961

ST. LOUIS POST-DISPATCH—See Pulitzer Publishing Company; *U.S. Public*, pg. 1343

ST. LOUIS REFRIGERATOR CAR COMPANY—See Anheuser-Busch Companies, Inc.; *U.S. Public*, pg. 114

ST. LOUIS SABRELINER LEARNING CENTER—See Berkshire Hathaway Inc.; *U.S. Public*, pg. 219

ST. LOUIS SALES—See Fairfield Communities, Inc.; *U.S. Public*, pg. 611

ST. LOUIS SOUTHWESTERN RAILWAY CO.—See Union Pacific Corporation; *U.S. Public*, pg. 1318

ST. MARIES RIVER RAILROAD—See Potlatch Corporation; *U.S. Public*, pg. 1318

ST. MARTINS PRESS, INC.—See Georg von Holtzbrinck GmbH; *Int'l*, pg. 1479

ST. MARX BRANCH—See Raiffeisen Zentralbank Osterreich; *Int'l*, pg. 1084

SAINT MARYS RAILROAD—See Gilman Investment Company; *Int'l*, pg. 454

ST. MICHAEL FINANCE LIMITED—See Marks & Spencer PLC; *Int'l*, pg. 843

ST. MICHAELS BANK—See Mercantile Bankshares Corporation; *U.S. Public*, pg. 1089

ST. PAUL BANCORP, INC.; *U.S. Public*, pg. 1428

ST. PAUL BANK FOR COOPERATIVES—See Federal Farm Credit Banks Funding Corporation; *U.S. Private*, pg. 398

THE ST. PAUL COMPANIES, INC.; *U.S. Public*, pg. 1429

ST. PAUL FEDERAL BANK FOR SAVINGS—See St. Paul Bancorp, Inc.; *U.S. Public*, pg. 1428

ST. PAUL FINANCIAL DEVELOPMENT CORP.—See St. Paul Bancorp, Inc.; *U.S. Public*, pg. 1429

ST. PAUL FIRE AND MARINE INSURANCE CO.—See The St. Paul Companies, Inc.; *U.S. Public*, pg. 1429

ST. PAUL METALCRAFT, INC.; *U.S. Private*, pg. 961

SAINT PAUL PIONEER PRESS DIVISION—See Knight-Ridder, Inc.; *U.S. Public*, pg. 964

ST. PAUL SERVICE, INC.—See St. Paul Bancorp, Inc.; *U.S. Public*, pg. 1428

ST. PETE AUTO AUCTION—See Cox Enterprises, Inc.; *U.S. Private*, pg. 283

ST. PETERSBURG TIMES—See The Times Publishing Co.; *U.S. Private*, pg. 1088

STE. RESTAURANTS DES NOUVEAUX SITES—See Accor S.A.; *Int'l*, pg. 20

STE. URSULA WEINGUT UND WEINKELLEREI GMBH—See Nestle S.A.; *Int'l*, pg. 922

SAINT-GOBAIN VITRO ITALIA—See Saint-Gobain; *Int'l*, pg. 1173

SAIPEM INTERNATIONAL A.G.—See ENI S.p.A.; *Int'l*, pg. 429

SAIPEM S.P.A.—See ENI S.p.A.; *Int'l*, pg. 428

THE SAISON GROUP; *Int'l*, pg. 1178

SAITAMA TOYOPET CO., LTD.—See Toyota Motor Corporation; *Int'l*, pg. 1412

SAITAMA TOYOTA MOTOR SALES CO., LTD.—See Toyota Motor Corporation; *Int'l*, pg. 1412

SAIWA—See Danone Group; *Int'l*, pg. 381

SAKAI WORKS—See Hitachi Zosen Corporation; *Int'l*, pg. 623

SAKAIDE PLANT—See Mitsubishi Chemical Corporation; *Int'l*, pg. 871

SAKAKI OLYMPUS CO., LTD.—See Olympus Optical Co., Ltd.; *Int'l*, pg. 1004

SAKATA INX CORPORATION—See Sumitomo Chemical Company, Ltd.; *Int'l*, pg. 1311

SAKATA INX USA CORP.—See Sumitomo Chemical Company, Ltd.; *Int'l*, pg. 1311

SAKATA SEED AMERICA, INC.—See Sakata Seed Corporation; *Int'l*, pg. 1178

SAKATA SEED CORPORATION; *Int'l*, pg. 1178

SAKATA SEED DE MEXICO, S.A. DE C.V.—See Sakata Seed Corporation; *Int'l*, pg. 1178

SAKATA DIRECTORY OF CORPORATE AFFILIATIONS

Company Index

SAKATA SEED DO BRASIL LTDA.—See Sakata Seed Corporation; *Int'l*, pg. 1178
SAKATA SEED EUROPE B.V.—See Sakata Seed Corporation; *Int'l*, pg. 1178
SAKO OY—See Oy Nokia Ab/Nokia Group; *Int'l*, pg. 954
SAKRETE, INC.; *U.S. Private*, pg. 961
BOB SAKS JEEP-EAGLE—See Farmington Hills Holding Company; *U.S. Private*, pg. 395
BOB SAKS OLDSMOBILE INC.—See Farmington Hills Holding Company; *U.S. Private*, pg. 395
BOB SAKS TOYOTA—See Farmington Hills Holding Company; *U.S. Private*, pg. 395
SAKS FIFTH AVENUE; *U.S. Public*, pg. 1429
THE SAKURA BANK—See The Sakura Bank, Limited; *Int'l*, *pg. 1179*
THE SAKURA BANK - AYUDHYA BRANCH—See The Sakura Bank, Limited; *Int'l*, pg. 1179
THE SAKURA BANK - BANGKOK BRANCH—See The Sakura Bank, Limited; *Int'l*, pg. 1179
THE SAKURA BANK - BARCELONA BRANCH—See The Sakura Bank, Limited; *Int'l*, pg. 1179
THE SAKURA BANK - BEIJING REPRESENTATIVE OFFICE—See The Sakura Bank, Limited; *Int'l*, pg. 1179
THE SAKURA BANK - BRUSSELS BRANCH—See The Sakura Bank, Limited; *Int'l*, pg. 1179
THE SAKURA BANK (CANADA)—See The Sakura Bank, Limited; *Int'l*, pg. 1180
THE SAKURA BANK - CAYMAN BRANCH—See The Sakura Bank, Limited; *Int'l*, pg. 1179
THE SAKURA BANK - DALIAN REPRESENTATIVE OFFICE—See The Sakura Bank, Limited; *Int'l*, pg. 1179
SAKURA BANK - DETROIT REPRESENTATIVE OFFICE—See The Sakura Bank, Limited; *Int'l*, pg. 1179
SAKURA BANK (DEUTSCHLAND) GMBH—See The Sakura Bank, Limited; *Int'l*, pg. 1180
THE SAKURA BANK - DUSSELDORF BRANCH—See The Sakura Bank, Limited; *Int'l*, pg. 1179
THE SAKURA BANK - GUANGZHOU BRANCH—See The Sakura Bank, Limited; *Int'l*, pg. 1179
THE SAKURA BANK - HO CHI MINH CITY REPRESENTATIVE OFFICE—See The Sakura Bank, Limited; *Int'l*, pg. 1179
THE SAKURA BANK - HONG KONG BRANCH—See The Sakura Bank, Limited; *Int'l*, pg. 1179
SAKURA BANK HONG KONG TRUSTEE LIMITED—See The Sakura Bank, Limited; *Int'l*, pg. 1180
THE SAKURA BANK - JAKARTA REPRESENTATIVE OFFICE—See The Sakura Bank, Limited; *Int'l*, pg. 1179
THE SAKURA BANK - KUALA LUMPUR REPRESENTATIVE OFFICE—See The Sakura Bank, Limited; *Int'l*, pg. 1180
THE SAKURA BANK - LABUAN BRANCH—See The Sakura Bank, Limited; *Int'l*, pg. 1179
THE SAKURA BANK, LIMITED; *Int'l*, pg. 1178
THE SAKURA BANK (LUXEMBOURG) S.A.—See The Sakura Bank, Limited; *Int'l*, pg. 1180
THE SAKURA BANK - MADRID BRANCH—See The Sakura Bank, Limited; *Int'l*, pg. 1179
THE SAKURA BANK - MANILA REPRESENTATIVE OFFICE—See The Sakura Bank, Limited; *Int'l*, pg. 1180
THE SAKURA BANK - MELBOURNE REPRESENTATIVE OFFICE—See The Sakura Bank, Limited; *Int'l*, pg. 1180
THE SAKURA BANK - MEXICO REPRESENTATIVE OFFICE—See The Sakura Bank, Limited; *Int'l*, pg. 1180
THE SAKURA BANK - MILAN REPRESENTATIVE OFFICE—See The Sakura Bank, Limited; *Int'l*, pg. 1180
THE SAKURA BANK - MUMBAI BRANCH—See The Sakura Bank, Limited; *Int'l*, pg. 1179
THE SAKURA BANK - NEW DELHI BRANCH—See The Sakura Bank, Limited; *Int'l*, pg. 1179
SAKURA BANK - NEW YORK BRANCH—See The Sakura Bank, Limited; *Int'l*, pg. 1179
THE SAKURA BANK - PARIS BRANCH—See The Sakura Bank, Limited; *Int'l*, pg. 1179
THE SAKURA BANK - REPRESENTATIVE OFFICE FOR THE MIDDLE EAST—See The Sakura Bank, Limited; *Int'l*, pg. 1180
SAKURA BANK - SAN FRANCISCO AGENCY—See The Sakura Bank, Limited; *Int'l*, pg. 1179
THE SAKURA BANK - SAO PAULO REPRESENTATIVE OFFICE—See The Sakura Bank, Limited; *Int'l*, pg. 1180
SAKURA BANK (SCHWEIZ) AG—See The Sakura Bank, Limited; *Int'l*, pg. 1180
THE SAKURA BANK - SEOUL BRANCH—See The Sakura Bank, Limited; *Int'l*, pg. 1179
THE SAKURA BANK - SHANGHAI BRANCH—See The Sakura Bank, Limited; *Int'l*, pg. 1179
THE SAKURA BANK - SINGAPORE BRANCH—See The Sakura Bank, Limited; *Int'l*, pg. 1179
THE SAKURA BANK - SYDNEY REPRESENTATIVE OFFICE—See The Sakura Bank, Limited; *Int'l*, pg. 1180
THE SAKURA BANK - TAIPEI REPRESENTATIVE OFFICE—See The Sakura Bank, Limited; *Int'l*, pg. 1180
THE SAKURA BANK - TASHKENT REPRESENTATIVE OFFICE—See The Sakura Bank, Limited; *Int'l*, pg. 1180
THE SAKURA BANK - TIANJIN BRANCH—See The Sakura Bank, Limited; *Int'l*, pg. 1179
THE SAKURA BANK - YANGON REPRESENTATIVE OFFICE—See The Sakura Bank, Limited; *Int'l*, pg. 1180
SAKURA CAPITAL FUNDING (CAYMAN) LIMITED—See The Sakura Bank, Limited; *Int'l*, pg. 1180
SAKURA CAPITAL INDIA, LIMITED—See The Sakura Bank, Limited; *Int'l*, pg. 1180
SAKURA DELLSHER, INC.—See The Sakura Bank, Limited; *Int'l*, pg. 1179
SAKURA FINANCE ASIA LTD.—See The Sakura Bank, Limited; *Int'l*, pg. 1180
SAKURA FINANCE AUSTRALIA LIMITED—See The Sakura Bank, Limited; *Int'l*, pg. 1180
SAKURA FINANCE (CAYMAN) LIMITED—See The Sakura Bank, Limited; *Int'l*, pg. 1180
SAKURA FINANCE INTERNATIONAL LIMITED—See The Sakura Bank, Limited; *Int'l*, pg. 1180
SAKURA FINANCIAL FUTURES (SINGAPORE) PTE. LTD.—See The Sakura Bank, Limited; *Int'l*, pg. 1180
SAKURA FINANZ (DEUTSCHLAND) GMBH—See The Sakura Bank, Limited; *Int'l*, pg. 1180
SAKURA GLOBAL CAPITAL ASIA LIMITED—See The Sakura Bank, Limited; *Int'l*, pg. 1179
SAKURA GLOBAL CAPITAL, INC.—See The Sakura Bank, Limited; *Int'l*, pg. 1179
SAKURA GLOBAL CAPITAL LIMITED—See The Sakura Bank, Limited; *Int'l*, pg. 1179
SAKURA MERCHANT BANK (SINGAPORE) LTD.—See The Sakura Bank, Limited; *Int'l*, pg. 1180
SAKURA SECURITIES—See The Sakura Bank, Limited; *Int'l*, pg. 1179
SAKURA TRUST COMPANY—See The Sakura Bank, Limited; *Int'l*, pg. 1179
SAKURA TRUST INTERNAIONAL LIMITED—See The Sakura Bank, Limited; *Int'l*, pg. 1180
SALADMASTER; *U.S. Private*, pg. 961
SALADMASTER, INC.—See Regal Ware, Inc.; *U.S. Private*, *pg. 917*
SALANFE SA—See Alusuisse-Lonza Holding Ltd.; *Int'l*, pg. 67
SALANT CHILDRENS APPAREL GROUP—See Salant Corporation; *U.S. Public*, pg. 1429
SALANT CORPORATION; *U.S. Public*, pg. 1429
SALCOMP OY—See Oy Nokia Ab/Nokia Group; *Int'l*, pg. 951
SALEM ASSET MANAGEMENT CORP.—See Salem Group, Inc.; *U.S. Private*, pg. 961
SALEM AUTOMATION LIMITED—See Salem Group, Inc.; *U.S. Private*, pg. 962
SALEM CARPET MILLS, INC.—See Shaw Industries, Inc.; *U.S. Public*, pg. 1464
SALEM CARRIERS, INC.—See Salem National Corporation; *U.S. Private*, pg. 962
SALEM CORPORATION—See Salem Group, Inc.; *U.S. Private*, pg. 961
SALEM ELECTRIC COMPANY—See Salem Group, Inc.; *U.S. Private*, pg. 961
SALEM ENGINEERING CO., LTD.—See Salem Group, Inc.; *U.S. Private*, pg. 962
SALEM ERECTORS—See Salem Group, Inc.; *U.S. Private*, pg. 961
SALEM FOREIGN SALES CORP.—See Salem Group, Inc.; *U.S. Private*, pg. 961
SALEM FURNACE CO.—See Salem Group, Inc.; *U.S. Private*, pg. 961
SALEM GROUP, INC.; *U.S. Private*, pg. 961
SALEM INTERNATIONAL SERVICES INC.—See Salem Group, Inc.; *U.S. Private*, pg. 961
SALEM LEASING CORP.—See Salem National Corporation; *U.S. Private*, pg. 962
SALEM MALL, INC.—See The Rouse Company; *U.S. Public*, pg. 1408
SALEM MANUFACTURING FACILITY—See Mitsubishi Materials Corp.; *Int'l*, pg. 875
SALEM NATIONAL CORPORATION; *U.S. Private*, pg. 962
SALEM PRODUCTS—See The Oilgear Company; *U.S. Public*, pg. 1215
SALEM SPORTSWEAR—See Fruit of the Loom, Inc.; *U.S. Public*, pg. 686
SALEMHAVEN—See Vencor, Inc.; *U.S. Public*, pg. 1714
SALEN COAL AB—See Scancem AB; *Int'l*, pg. 1201
SALES AND MARKETING MANAGEMENT—See VNU Verenigde Nederlandse Uitgeversbedrijven B.V.; *Int'l*, pg. 1446
SALES DEL ISTMO, S.A. DE C.V.—See CYDSA S.A.; *Int'l*, pg. 247
SALES TECHNOLOGIES—See Cognizant Corporation; *U.S. Public*, pg. 395
SALFORD ELECTRICAL INSTRUMENTS LTD.—See The General Electric Company, p.l.c.; *Int'l*, pg. 545
SALICK HEALTH CARE, INC.—See Zeneca Group Plc; *Int'l*, pg. 1524
SALIENT 3 COMMUNICATIONS, INC.; *U.S. Public*, pg. 1429
SALINAS CALIFORNIAN—See Gannett Company, Inc.; *U.S. Public*, pg. 701
SALINAS CARE CENTER—See Meritcare, Inc.; *U.S. Private*, pg. 733
SALINE INVESTMENT CO.—See R & B Machine Tool Co.; *U.S. Private*, pg. 902
W.H. SALISBURY & COMPANY—See Siebe plc; *Int'l*, pg. 1244
THE SALISBURY WATER SUPPLY CO.—See American Water Works Company, Inc.; *U.S. Public*, pg. 95
SALLES/DMB&B PUBLICIDADE S.A.—See DMB&B Communications; *U.S. Private*, pg. 305
SALLY BEAUTY COMPANY, INC.—See Alberto-Culver Company; *U.S. Public*, pg. 38
SALLY HAIR & BEAUTY—See Alberto-Culver Company; *U.S. Public*, pg. 38
SALLY HANSEN—See Del Laboratories, Inc.; *U.S. Public*, pg. 494
SALLY LOU FASHIONS CORPORATION; *U.S. Private*, pg. 962
SALOMON-NORTH AMERICA INC.—See Salomon S.A.; *Int'l*, pg. 1181
SALOMON S.A.; *Int'l*, pg. 1181
SALOMON SMITH BARNEY HOLDINGS, INC.—See Travelers Group; *U.S. Public*, pg. 1633
SALOMON SPORTS LTD.—See Salomon S.A.; *Int'l*, pg. 1181
SALON DIVISION—See Wella Group; *Int'l*, pg. 1489
SALON & FITNESS SYSTEMS; *U.S. Private*, pg. 962
SALS INVESTORS PARTNERSHIP—See Colonial Commercial Corp.; *U.S. Public*, pg. 400
SALSBURY CHEMICALS, INC.—See Cambrex Corporation; *U.S. Public*, pg. 297
SALSBURY LABORATORIES, INC.—See Solvay S.A.; *Int'l*, pg. 1277
SALSI SA—See Lafarge S.A.; *Int'l*, pg. 790
SALT LAKE CITY AIRLINE LEARNING CENTER—See Berkshire Hathaway Inc.; *U.S. Public*, pg. 219
SALT LAKE CITY BUZZ—See Minnesota Twins Baseball Club; *U.S. Private*, pg. 751
SALT RIVER PROJECT AGRICULTURAL IMPROVEMENT AND POWER DISTRICT; *U.S. Private*, pg. 962
SALT WATER SPORTSMAN—See The Times Mirror Company; *U.S. Public*, pg. 1617
SALTON/MAXIM HOUSEWARES, INC.; *U.S. Public*, pg. 1430
SALTZBURGER KREDIT-UND WECHSEL-BANK AG—See Bayerische Hypotheken-und Wechsel-Bank Aktiengesellschaft; *Int'l*, pg. 176
SALZGITTER-LUMMUS G.M.B.H.—See ABB Asea Brown Boveri (Holding) Ltd.; *Int'l*, pg. 6
SALVADOR CAETANO I.M.V.T., S.A.R.L.—See Toyota Motor Corporation; *Int'l*, pg. 1413
SALVAT EDITORES ARGENTINA, SA—See Lagardere Groupe; *Int'l*, pg. 796
SALVAT EDITORES S.A.—See Lagardere Groupe; *Int'l*, pg. 796
SALVAT SA DE DISTRIBUCION—See Lagardere Groupe; *Int'l*, pg. 796
SALVATORPLATZ GRUNDSTUCKSGESELLSCHAFT MBH & CO. OHG SAARLAND—See Bayerische Vereinsbank Group; *Int'l*, pg. 180
SALVATORPLATZ-GRUNDSTUECKSGESELLSCHAFT MBH—See Bayerische Vereinsbank Group; *Int'l*, pg. 180
SALVIA—See Nestle S.A.; *Int'l*, pg. 922
SALVIS AG—See Brauerei Eichhof; *Int'l*, pg. 213
SALWASSER MANUFACTURING COMPANY, INC.; *U.S. Private*, pg. 963
SALZ LEATHERS, INC.; *U.S. Private*, pg. 963
SALZGEWINNUNGSGESELLSCHAFT WESTFALEN MBH—See Solvay S.A.; *Int'l*, pg. 1279
SALZGITTER GMBH—See Preussag AG; *Int'l*, pg. 1070
SALZGITTER OBERFLACHENTECHNIK GMBH—See Sulzer Ltd.; *Int'l*, pg. 1308
SAMAG—See Groupe Air France; *Int'l*, pg. 560
SAMARCO MINERACAO SA—See The Broken Hill Proprietary Company Limited; *Int'l*, pg. 224
SAMAS UNIVERSAL OFFICE SUPPLIES—See John Menzies plc; *Int'l*, pg. 707
SAMBOW PLASTICS CO., LTD.—See Nissho Iwai Corporation; *Int'l*, pg. 947
SAMCO SCIENTIFIC, INC.—See Corning Incorporated; *U.S. Public*, pg. 448
SAMCOR GLASS LIMITED—See Corning Incorporated; *U.S. Public*, pg. 449
SAMEDAN OIL CORPORATION—See Noble Affiliates, Inc.; *U.S. Public*, pg. 1186
SAMEDAN OIL OF CANADA, INC.—See Noble Affiliates, Inc.; *U.S. Public*, pg. 1186
SAMEIET AKER BRYGGE A/S—See Aker Raj Asa; *Int'l*, pg. 41
SAMES ELECTROSTATIC, INC.—See Binks Sames Corporation; *U.S. Public*, pg. 229
SAMES, S.A.—See Binks Sames Corporation; *U.S. Public*, pg. 230
SAMIN—See Saint-Gobain; *Int'l*, pg. 1171
SAMMLER KABINETT, INC.—See Time Warner Inc.; *U.S. Public*, pg. 1613
SAMMONS ENTERPRISES, INC.; *U.S. Private*, pg. 963
SAMNA GMBH—See International Business Machines Corporation; *U.S. Public*, pg. 896
SAMPLER PUBLICATIONS INC.; *U.S. Private*, pg. 963
SAMPO CORPORATION (TAIPEI)—See Sharp Corporation; *Int'l*, pg. 1229
SAMPO TECHNO CONSTRUCTION CO., LTD.—See Kumagai Gumi Co., Ltd.; *Int'l*, pg. 764
SAMPSON TYRRELL ENTERPRISE—See WPP Group plc; *Int'l*, pg. 1482
SAM'S CLUBS DIV.—See Wal-Mart Stores, Inc.; *U.S. Public*, pg. 1733
SAMSILL CORPORATION; *U.S. Private*, pg. 963
SAMSON APPAREL CORP.—See Hampton Industries, Inc.; *U.S. Public*, pg. 779
SAMSON INDEPENDENT, INC.—See Media General, Inc.; *U.S. Public*, pg. 1078
SAMSON MANUFACTURING CORP.—See Hampton Industries, Inc.; *U.S. Public*, pg. 779
SAMSONITE CORPORATION; *U.S. Public*, pg. 1430
SAMSONITE OF CANADA—See Samsonite Corporation; *U.S. Public*, pg. 1430
SAMSTEEL, INC.—See Ferro Union, Inc.; *U.S. Private*, pg. 402
SAMSUNG AEROSPACE INDUSTRIES, LTD.—See Samsung Group; *Int'l*, pg. 1181
SAMSUNG AMERICA APPAREL SHOWROOM—See Samsung Group; *Int'l*, pg. 1183
SAMSUNG ASIA HEADQUARTERS—See Samsung Group; *Int'l*, pg. 1183
SAMSUNG CHINA HEADQUARTERS—See Samsung Group; *Int'l*, pg. 1183
SAMSUNG-CORNING COMPANY LTD.—See Corning Incorporated; *U.S. Public*, pg. 449
SAMSUNG ELECTRON DEVICES CO., LTD.—See Samsung Group; *Int'l*, pg. 1181
SAMSUNG ELECTRONICS AMERICA, INC.—See Samsung Group; *Int'l*, pg. 1183
SAMSUNG ELECTRONICS CO., LTD.—See Samsung Group; *Int'l*, pg. 1181

SAMSUNG ELECTRONICS NORTH AMERICA INC.—See Samsung Group; *Int'l*, pg. 1183
SAMSUNG EUROPE HEADQUARTERS—See Samsung Group; *Int'l*, pg. 1183
SAMSUNG GROUP; *Int'l*, pg. 1181
SAMSUNG HEWLETT-PACKARD—See Hewlett-Packard Company; *U.S. Public*, pg. 823
SAMSUNG JAPAN CORPORATION—See Samsung Group; *Int'l*, pg. 1183
SAMSUNG LIFE INSURANCE CO. LTD.—See Samsung Group; *Int'l*, pg. 1183
SAMSUNG PACIFIC INTERNATIONAL, INC.—See Samsung Group; *Int'l*, pg. 1183
SAMSUNG PETROCHEMICAL CO. LTD.—See Amoco Corporation; *U.S. Public*, pg. 102
SAMSUNG SEMICONDUCTORS, INC.—See Samsung Group; *Int'l*, pg. 1183
SAMSUNG SHIPBUILDING & HEAVY INDUSTRIES CO. LTD.—See Samsung Group; *Int'l*, pg. 1183
SAMTEC INC.; *U.S. Private*, pg. 963
H. SAMUEL LIMITED—See Signet Group plc; *Int'l*, pg. 1248
SAMUEL SPECIALTY METALS; *U.S. Private*, pg. 964
SAMUEL SPECIALTY METALS INC.—See Samuel Specialty Metals; *U.S. Private*, pg. 964
ALLEN SAMUELS CHEVROLET GEO; *U.S. Private*, pg. 964
SAN ANGELO NATIONAL BANK—See First Financial Bankshares, Inc.; *U.S. Public*, pg. 633
SAN ANGELO STANDARD, INC.—See Harte-Hanks Communications, Inc.; *U.S. Public*, pg. 794
SAN ANTONIO AUTO AUCTION—See Cox Enterprises, Inc.; *U.S. Private*, pg. 283
SAN ANTONIO DIV.—See U.S. Home Corporation; *U.S. Public*, pg. 1683
SAN ANTONIO DIVISION—See Albertson's, Inc.; *U.S. Public*, pg. 38
SAN ANTONIO EXPRESS NEWS—See The Hearst Corporation; *U.S. Private*, pg. 517
SAN ANTONIO LEARNING CENTER—See Berkshire Hathaway Inc.; *U.S. Public*, pg. 219
SAN BERNARDO S.P.A.—See Nestle S.A.; *Int'l*, pg. 922
SAN CRISTOBAL MILL & PLANT—See Commerce Group Corp.; *U.S. Public*, pg. 410
SAN DIEGO AUTO AUCTION INC.—See Tyco International Ltd.; *U.S. Public*, pg. 1649
SAN DIEGO CHARGERS; *U.S. Private*, pg. 964
SAN DIEGO DIVISION—See Aetrium Inc.; *U.S. Public*, pg. 27
SAN DIEGO GAS & ELECTRIC COMPANY—See Enova Corp; *U.S. Public*, pg. 584
SAN DIEGO LEARNING CENTER—See Berkshire Hathaway Inc.; *U.S. Public*, pg. 219
SAN DIEGO UNION TRIBUNE—See The Copley Press, Inc.; *U.S. Private*, pg. 275
SAN DIEGO WILD ANIMAL PARK—See Zoological Society of San Diego; *U.S. Private*, pg. 1207
THE SAN FRANCISCO CO.; *U.S. Public*, pg. 1430
SAN FRANCISCO CONVALESCENT CENTER—See Vencor, Inc.; *U.S. Public*, pg. 1714
SAN FRANCISCO EXAMINER—See The Hearst Corporation; *U.S. Private*, pg. 518
SAN FRANCISCO FRENCH BREAD COMPANY—See Interstate Bakeries Corporation; *U.S. Public*, pg. 909
SAN FRANCISCO GIANTS BASEBALL CLUB; *U.S. Private*, pg. 964
SAN FRANCISCO INSURANCE COMPANY (U.K.) LTD.—See Allianz Aktiengesellschaft; *Int'l*, pg. 59
SAN FRANCISCO KNITWORKS—See Hampshire Group, Ltd.; *U.S. Public*, pg. 779
SAN FRANCISCO NEWSPAPER AGENCY—See Chronicle Publishing Co. Inc.; *U.S. Private*, pg. 239
SAN FRANCISCO REALTIES—See The Hearst Corporation; *U.S. Private*, pg. 518
SAN FRANCISCO REINSURANCE CO.—See Allianz Aktiengesellschaft; *Int'l*, pg. 59
SAN FU CHEMICAL CO., LTD.—See Air Products and Chemicals, Inc.; *U.S. Public*, pg. 32
SAN GABRIEL VALLEY MEDICAL CENTER—See UniHealth; *U.S. Private*, pg. 1118
SAN GIORGIO MACARONI—See Hershey Foods Corporation; *U.S. Public*, pg. 812
SAN GIORGIO SERVIZI DISTRIBUZIONE S.R.L.—See Assicurazioni Generali S.p.A.; *Int'l*, pg. 90
SAN-J INTL. INC.—See San-Jirushi; *Int'l*, pg. 1183
SAN JACINTO MANOR—See Horizon/CMS Healthcare Corporation; *U.S. Public*, pg. 839
SAN-JIRUSHI; *Int'l*, pg. 1183
SAN JOSE MERCURY NEWS—See Knight-Ridder, Inc.; *U.S. Public*, pg. 964
SAN JOSE NATIONAL BANK—See SJNB Financial Corp.; *U.S. Public*, pg. 1418
SAN JOSE WATER COMPANY—See SJW Corp.; *U.S. Public*, pg. 1418
SAN JUAN MANOR—See Horizon/CMS Healthcare Corporation; *U.S. Public*, pg. 838
SAN JUAN MINE—See The Broken Hill Proprietary Company Limited; *Int'l*, pg. 224
SAN JUVA, S.A.—See Vallehermoso, S.A.; *Int'l*, pg. 1447
SAN LUIS ESTATES, INC.—See Commerce Group Corp.; *U.S. Public*, pg. 410
SAN LUIS OBISPO TELEGRAM-TRIBUNE—See Knight-Ridder, Inc.; *U.S. Public*, pg. 964
SAN MIGUEL CORP.; *Int'l*, pg. 1183
SAN MIGUEL (HONG KONG)—See San Miguel Corp.; *Int'l*, pg. 1183
SAN NOPCO LTD.—See Henkel KGaA; *Int'l*, pg. 614
SAN RAMON CORPORATION—See Cigna Corp.; *U.S. Public*, pg. 361
SAN RAMON PARTNERS—See Cigna Corp.; *U.S. Public*, pg. 362
SAN SEBASTIAN GOLD MINES, INC.—See Commerce Group Corp.; *U.S. Public*, pg. 410

SAN TOMAS NO. 1 LIMITED PARTNERSHIP—See Cigna Corp.; *U.S. Public*, pg. 362
SANABO GESELLSCHAFT M.B.H.—See Novartis AG; *Int'l*, pg. 984
SANBORN HERMANOS—See Grupo Carso S.A. de C.V.; *Int'l*, pg. 573
SANCHEZ COMPUTER ASSOCIATES—See Safeguard Scientifics, Inc.; *U.S. Public*, pg. 1425
SANCHO S.A.—See Saatchi & Saatchi Advertising Worldwide; *U.S. Public*, pg. 1422
SANCO INC.—See Allied Waste Industries; *U.S. Public*, pg. 49
SANCOR COOPERATIVAS UNIDAS LIMITADAS; *Int'l*, pg. 1183
SAND & GRUS AB JEHANDER—See Scancem AB; *Int'l*, pg. 1200
H. SAND & CO., INC.—See Skanska AB; *Int'l*, pg. 1261
SAND TECHNOLOGY SYSTEMS; *Int'l*, pg. 1183
SAND-UND KIES-KONTOR GESELLSCHAFT MIT BESCHRANKTER HAFTUNG—See The Peninsular and Oriental Steam Navigation Company; *Int'l*, pg. 1034
SAND- UND KIESWERK STEINBACH GMBH & CO. KG—See Redland PLC; *Int'l*, pg. 1091
SANDE PAPER MILL A/S—See Norske Skogindustrier A.S.; *Int'l*, pg. 965
SANDEN CORPORATION; *Int'l*, pg. 1184
SANDEN INTERNATIONAL (EUROPE) LTD.—See Sanden Corporation; *Int'l*, pg. 1184
SANDEN INTERNATIONAL OCEANIA (AUSTRALIA) PTY. LTD.—See Sanden Corporation; *Int'l*, pg. 1184
SANDEN INTERNATIONAL (SINGAPORE) PTE. LTD.—See Sanden Corporation; *Int'l*, pg. 1184
SANDEN INTERNATIONAL TAIWAN CORPORATION—See Sanden Corporation; *Int'l*, pg. 1184
SANDEN INTERNATIONAL (U.S.A.), INC.—See Sanden Corporation; *Int'l*, pg. 1184
SANDEN MANUFACTURING EUROPE S.A.—See Sanden Corporation; *Int'l*, pg. 1184
WILHELM SANDER FERTIGUNG GMBH—See KM-Europa Metal Aktiengesellschaft; *Int'l*, pg. 719
SANDERS—See Entreprise Miniere et Chimique; *Int'l*, pg. 459
SANDERS, A LOCKHEED MARTIN COMPANY—See Lockheed Martin Corporation; *U.S. Public*, pg. 1008
SANDERS BEHANG B.V.—See Gamma Holding N.V.; *Int'l*, pg. 540
SANDERS TAPETEN GMBH—See Gamma Holding N.V.; *Int'l*, pg. 540
ARTHUR SANDERSON AND SONS LTD.—See Gamma Holding N.V.; *Int'l*, pg. 540
SANDERSON BROOKSTREET LIMITED—See Sanderson Technology Ltd.; *Int'l*, pg. 1184
SANDERSON CBT LIMITED—See Sanderson Technology Ltd.; *Int'l*, pg. 1184
SANDERSON CFL LIMITED—See Sanderson Technology Ltd.; *Int'l*, pg. 1184
SANDERSON COMPUTER SERVICES—See Sanderson Technology Ltd.; *Int'l*, pg. 1184
SANDERSON COMPUTERS HONG KONG LTD.—See Sanderson Technology Ltd.; *Int'l*, pg. 1185
SANDERSON COMPUTERS LIMITED—See Sanderson Technology Ltd.; *Int'l*, pg. 1184
SANDERSON COMPUTERS NEW ZEALAND LTD.—See Sanderson Technology Ltd.; *Int'l*, pg. 1185
SANDERSON COMPUTERS PTE. LTD.—See Sanderson Technology Ltd.; *Int'l*, pg. 1185
SANDERSON COMPUTERS PTY. LTD.—See Sanderson Technology Ltd.; *Int'l*, pg. 1185
SANDERSON COTSWOLD LIMITED—See Sanderson Technology Ltd.; *Int'l*, pg. 1184
SANDERSON FARMS, INC.; *U.S. Public*, pg. 1430
SANDERSON GA LIMITED—See Sanderson Technology Ltd.; *Int'l*, pg. 1184
SANDERSON INSIGHT LIMITED—See Sanderson Technology Ltd.; *Int'l*, pg. 1184
SANDERSON NI LIMITED—See Sanderson Technology Ltd.; *Int'l*, pg. 1184
SANDERSON PLUMBING PRODUCTS INC.; *U.S. Private*, pg. 964
SANDERSON PSS LIMITED—See Sanderson Technology Ltd.; *Int'l*, pg. 1184
SANDERSON TECHNOLOGY LTD.; *Int'l*, pg. 1184
SANDESTIN RESORT INC.—See Sime Darby Berhad; *Int'l*, pg. 1250
SANDHILLS INC.—See The Pantry, Inc.; *U.S. Private*, pg. 837
SANDIACRE SCREW LTD.—See Haden Maclellan Holdings plc; *Int'l*, pg. 585
L.M. SANDLER & SONS; *U.S. Private*, pg. 964
SANDOZ AB—See Novartis AG; *Int'l*, pg. 984
SANDOZ AG—See Novartis AG; *Int'l*, pg. 984
SANDOZ AGRICOLA S.A. DE C.V.—See Novartis AG; *Int'l*, pg. 984
SANDOZ AGRO CORPORATION—See Novartis AG; *Int'l*, pg. 974
SANDOZ AGRO, INC.—See Novartis AG; *Int'l*, pg. 974
SANDOZ AGRO LTD.—See Novartis AG; *Int'l*, pg. 972
SANDOZ AGRO S.A.—See Novartis AG; *Int'l*, pg. 984
SANDOZ AGRO S.A.E.—See Novartis AG; *Int'l*, pg. 984
SANDOZ AGRO S.P.A.—See Novartis AG; *Int'l*, pg. 984
SANDOZ ARGENTINA S.A.I.C.—See Novartis AG; *Int'l*, pg. 984
SANDOZ A/S—See Novartis AG; *Int'l*, pg. 984
SANDOZ AUSTRALIA PTY. LTD.—See Novartis AG; *Int'l*, pg. 984
P.T. SANDOZ-BIOCHEMIE FARMA INDONESIA—See Novartis AG; *Int'l*, pg. 984
SANDOZ BIOSCIENCES LTD.—See Novartis AG; *Int'l*, pg. 972
SANDOZ B.V.—See Novartis AG; *Int'l*, pg. 984
SANDOZ CANADA LTD.—See Novartis AG; *Int'l*, pg. 984
SANDOZ CAPITAL BVI LTD.—See Novartis AG; *Int'l*, pg. 984

SANDOZ CHEMICAL CORP., PURCHASING—See Novartis AG; *Int'l*, pg. 974
SANDOZ CHEMICAL CORPORATION—See Novartis AG; *Int'l*, pg. 974
SANDOZ CHEMICALS LTD.—See Novartis AG; *Int'l*, pg. 972
SANDOZ CHEMICALS PTE. LTD. SINGAPORE—See Novartis AG; *Int'l*, pg. 984
SANDOZ CHEMICALS (THAILAND) LTD.—See Novartis AG; *Int'l*, pg. 984
SANDOZ CHEMICALS (UK) LTD.—See Novartis AG; *Int'l*, pg. 984
SANDOZ CHIMICA S.P.A.—See Novartis AG; *Int'l*, pg. 984
SANDOZ CHIMIE S.A.—See Novartis AG; *Int'l*, pg. 984
SANDOZ CLINICAL & NUTRITION DIV.—See Novartis AG; *Int'l*, pg. 974
SANDOZ COLOMBIANA S.A.—See Novartis AG; *Int'l*, pg. 984
SANDOZ COLORQUIMICA LTDA.—See Novartis AG; *Int'l*, pg. 984
SANDOZ CONSUMER PHARMACEUTICAL—See Novartis AG; *Int'l*, pg. 974
SANDOZ CORPORATION—See Novartis AG; *Int'l*, pg. 974
SANDOZ CROP PROTECTION LTD.—See Novartis AG; *Int'l*, pg. 984
SANDOZ DE MEXICO S.A. DE C.V.—See Novartis AG; *Int'l*, pg. 984
SANDOZ DEUTSCHLAND G.M.B.H.—See Novartis AG; *Int'l*, pg. 984
SANDOZ DOMINICA, C. POR A.—See Novartis AG; *Int'l*, pg. 984
SANDOZ DONGKOOK LTD.—See Novartis AG; *Int'l*, pg. 984
SANDOZ ERNAHRUNG G.M.B.H.—See Novartis AG; *Int'l*, pg. 984
SANDOZ FARMACEUTICA LTDA.—See Novartis AG; *Int'l*, pg. 984
SANDOZ FINANCE N.V.—See Novartis AG; *Int'l*, pg. 984
SANDOZ FINANCE SERVICES LTD.—See Novartis AG; *Int'l*, pg. 984
SANDOZ FOOD SERVICE & INDUSTRIAL DIVISION—See Novartis AG; *Int'l*, pg. 974
SANDOZ FORSCHUNGSINSTITUT GESELLSCHAFT M.B.H.—See Novartis AG; *Int'l*, pg. 984
SANDOZ FORSCHUNGSINSTITUT HANDELSGESELLSCHAFT M.B.H.—See Novartis AG; *Int'l*, pg. 984
SANDOZ FRANCE S.A.—See Novartis AG; *Int'l*, pg. 984
SANDOZ (HELLAS) S.A.C.I.—See Novartis AG; *Int'l*, pg. 984
SANDOZ HISPANIA S.A.—See Novartis AG; *Int'l*, pg. 984
SANDOZ HOLDING LTD.—See Novartis AG; *Int'l*, pg. 972
SANDOZ HOLDING NETHERLANDS B.V.—See Novartis AG; *Int'l*, pg. 984
SANDOZ HOLDINGS GREAT BRITAIN LTD.—See Novartis AG; *Int'l*, pg. 984
SANDOZ HUNINGUE S.A.—See Novartis AG; *Int'l*, pg. 984
SANDOZ (INDIA) LTD.—See Novartis AG; *Int'l*, pg. 984
SANDOZ INDUSTRIAL CHEMICALS LTD.—See Novartis AG; *Int'l*, pg. 984
SANDOZ INTERNATIONAL LTD.—See Novartis AG; *Int'l*, pg. 972
SANDOZ INTERNATIONAL PARTICIPATIONS B.V.—See Novartis AG; *Int'l*, pg. 984
SANDOZ INVESTMENT N.V.—See Novartis AG; *Int'l*, pg. 984
SANDOZ JAPAN K.K.—See Novartis AG; *Int'l*, pg. 984
SANDOZ KIMYA SANAYII LTD. SIRKETI—See Novartis AG; *Int'l*, pg. 984
SANDOZ K.K.—See Novartis AG; *Int'l*, pg. 984
SANDOZ KOREA LTD.—See Novartis AG; *Int'l*, pg. 985
SANDOZ LATINOAMERICA S.A.—See Novartis AG; *Int'l*, pg. 985
SANDOZ LATINOAMERICANA (ECUADOR) S.A.—See Novartis AG; *Int'l*, pg. 985
SANDOZ LATINOAMERICANA (PANAMA) S.A.—See Novartis AG; *Int'l*, pg. 985
SANDOZ MANAGEMENT SERVICES—See Novartis AG; *Int'l*, pg. 985
SANDOZ-MAROC S.A.—See Novartis AG; *Int'l*, pg. 985
SANDOZ (NIGERIA) LTD.—See Novartis AG; *Int'l*, pg. 985
SANDOZ NUTRITION B.V.—See Novartis AG; *Int'l*, pg. 985
SANDOZ NUTRITION FINANCE LTD.—See Novartis AG; *Int'l*, pg. 985
SANDOZ NUTRITION LTD.—See Novartis AG; *Int'l*, pg. 972
SANDOZ NUTRITION S.A.—See Novartis AG; *Int'l*, pg. 985
N.V. SANDOZ NUTRITION S.A.—See Novartis AG; *Int'l*, pg. 985
SANDOZ NUTRITION TRADING LTD.—See Novartis AG; *Int'l*, pg. 972
SANDOZ OVERSEAS FINANCE LTD.—See Novartis AG; *Int'l*, pg. 985
SANDOZ OVERSEAS N.V.—See Novartis AG; *Int'l*, pg. 985
SANDOZ OY—See Novartis AG; *Int'l*, pg. 985
SANDOZ (PAKISTAN) LTD.—See Novartis AG; *Int'l*, pg. 985
SANDOZ PERU S.A.—See Novartis AG; *Int'l*, pg. 985
SANDOZ PHARMA A/S—See Novartis AG; *Int'l*, pg. 985
SANDOZ PHARMA B.V.—See Novartis AG; *Int'l*, pg. 985
SANDOZ PHARMA LTD.—See Novartis AG; *Int'l*, pg. 972
SANDOZ PHARMA S.A.E.—See Novartis AG; *Int'l*, pg. 985
SANDOZ PHARMA SERVICES LTD.—See Novartis AG; *Int'l*, pg. 972
SANDOZ PHARMACEUTICALS CORP.—See Novartis AG; *Int'l*, pg. 974
SANDOZ PHARMACEUTICALS LTD.—See Novartis AG; *Int'l*, pg. 985
SANDOZ PHARMACEUTICALS (UK) LTD.—See Novartis AG; *Int'l*, pg. 985
SANDOZ (PHILIPPINES) INC.—See Novartis AG; *Int'l*, pg. 985
SANDOZ PRODOTTI FARMACEUTICI S.P.A.—See Novartis AG; *Int'l*, pg. 985

SANDOZ DIRECTORY OF CORPORATE AFFILIATIONS

Company Index

SANDOZ PRODUCTOS QUIMICOS S.A.—See Novartis AG; *Int'l*, pg. 985
SANDOZ PRODUCTS (IRELAND) LTD.—See Novartis AG; *Int'l*, pg. 985
SANDOZ PRODUCTS LTD.—See Novartis AG; *Int'l*, pg. 985
SANDOZ PRODUCTS (MALAYSIA) SDN. BHD.—See Novartis AG; *Int'l*, pg. 985
SANDOZ PRODUCTS (PTY.) LTD.—See Novartis AG; *Int'l*, pg. 985
SANDOZ PRODUCTS (SWITZERLAND) LTD.—See Novartis AG; *Int'l*, pg. 972
SANDOZ PRODUKTE (SCHWEIZ) AG—See Novartis AG; *Int'l*, pg. 974
SANDOZ QUIMICA S.A.E.—See Novartis AG; *Int'l*, pg. 985
SANDOZ QUIMICA Y FARMACEUTICA S.A.—See Novartis AG; *Int'l*, pg. 985
SANDOZ QUIMICO FARMACETICA CUBANA S.A.—See Novartis AG; *Int'l*, pg. 985
SANDOZ QUIMICOS S.A. DE C.V.—See Novartis AG; *Int'l*, pg. 985
SANDOZ-QUINN PRODUCKTIE GMBH—See Novartis AG; *Int'l*, pg. 985
SANDOZ RESEARCH INSTITUTE—See Novartis AG; *Int'l*, pg. 974
SANDOZ RESEARCH INSTITUTE BERNE LTD.—See Novartis AG; *Int'l*, pg. 972
SANDOZ RINGASKIDDY LTD.—See Novartis AG; *Int'l*, pg. 985
SANDOZ S.A.—See Novartis AG; *Int'l*, pg. 985
SANDOZ SEEDS LTD.—See Novartis AG; *Int'l*, pg. 972
SANDOZ-SODYECO LTD.—See Novartis AG; *Int'l*, pg. 985
SANDOZ S.P.A.—See Novartis AG; *Int'l*, pg. 985
SANDOZ SVENSKA AB—See Novartis AG; *Int'l*, pg. 985
SANDOZ TECHNOLOGIES AND PROPRIETARY SUPPLIES LTD.—See Novartis AG; *Int'l*, pg. 985
SANDOZ TECHNOLOGY LTD.—See Novartis AG; *Int'l*, pg. 972
SANDOZ URUNLERI LTD.—See Novartis AG; *Int'l*, pg. 985
SANDOZ VENEZUELA S.A.—See Novartis AG; *Int'l*, pg. 985
SANDOZ VERWALTUNGS G.M.B.H.—See Novartis AG; *Int'l*, pg. 985
SANDOZ-WANDER PHARMA AG—See Novartis AG; *Int'l*, pg. 972
SANDOZ YAKUHIN K.K.—See Novartis AG; *Int'l*, pg. 985
SANDS INVESTMENTS, INC.; *U.S. Private*, pg. 964
SANDS MOTOR COMPANY, INC.; *U.S. Private*, pg. 964
THE SANDS REGENT; *U.S. Public*, pg. 1431
SANDUSKY INTERNATIONAL INC.; *U.S. Private*, pg. 964
SANDUSKY LIMITED—See Sandusky International Inc.; *U.S. Private*, pg. 965
SANDUSKY PLASTICS, INC.—See Envirodyne Industries, Inc.; *U.S. Public*, pg. 586
SANDVIK AB; *Int'l*, pg. 1185
SANDVIK ACIERS S.N.C.—See Sandvik AB; *Int'l*, pg. 1186
SANDVIK A/S—See Sandvik AB; *Int'l*, pg. 1186
SANDVIK ASIA LTD.—See Sandvik AB; *Int'l*, pg. 1187
SANDVIK AUSTRALIA PTY. LTD.—See Sandvik AB; *Int'l*, pg. 1187
SANDVIK BAHCO ARGENTINA S.A.C.EL.—See Sandvik AB; *Int'l*, pg. 1187
SANDVIK BAHCO NORDEN AB—See Sandvik AB; *Int'l*, pg. 1185
SANDVIK BAHCO NORDEN A/S—See Sandvik AB; *Int'l*, pg. 1186
AB SANDVIK BELTS—See Sandvik AB; *Int'l*, pg. 1185
SANDVIK BELZER GMBH—See Sandvik AB; *Int'l*, pg. 1186
SANDVIK BELZER PRODUKTION GMBH—See Sandvik AB; *Int'l*, pg. 1186
SANDVIK BENELUX—See Sandvik AB; *Int'l*, pg. 1186
SANDVIK BENELUX B.V.—See Sandvik AB; *Int'l*, pg. 1185
SANDVIK-BISOV—See Sandvik AB; *Int'l*, pg. 1186
SANDVIK-BULGARIA—See Sandvik AB; *Int'l*, pg. 1186
SANDVIK CANADA INC.—See Sandvik AB; *Int'l*, pg. 1188
SANDVIK CHILE S.A.—See Sandvik AB; *Int'l*, pg. 1187
SANDVIK CHINA LTD.—See Sandvik AB; *Int'l*, pg. 1187
SANDVIK CHOMUTOV—See Sandvik AB; *Int'l*, pg. 1186
SANDVIK COLOMBIA S.A.—See Sandvik AB; *Int'l*, pg. 1188
SANDVIK COROMANT—See Sandvik AB; *Int'l*, pg. 1186
AB SANDVIK COROMANT—See Sandvik AB; *Int'l*, pg. 1185
SANDVIK COROMANT COMPANY—See Sandvik AB; *Int'l*, pg. 1185
SANDVIK COROMANT SKANDINAVIEN AB—See Sandvik AB; *Int'l*, pg. 1185
SANDVIK COROMANT S.N.C.—See Sandvik AB; *Int'l*, pg. 1186
SANDVIK COROMANT U.K.—See Sandvik AB; *Int'l*, pg. 1186
SANDVIK CZECHOSLOVAKIA S.R.O.—See Sandvik AB; *Int'l*, pg. 1186
SANDVIK DE MEXICO S.A. DE C.V.—See Sandvik AB; *Int'l*, pg. 1188
SANDVIK DEL PERU S.A.—See Sandvik AB; *Int'l*, pg. 1188
SANDVIK DO BRASIL S.A.—See Sandvik AB; *Int'l*, pg. 1188
SANDVIK ESPANOLA S.A.—See Sandvik AB; *Int'l*, pg. 1186
SANDVIK GMBH—See Sandvik AB; *Int'l*, pg. 1186
AB SANDVIK HAND TOOLS—See Sandvik AB; *Int'l*, pg. 1185
SANDVIK HARD MATERIALS—See Sandvik AB; *Int'l*, pg. 1186
AB SANDVIK HARD MATERIALS—See Sandvik AB; *Int'l*, pg. 1185
SANDVIK HARD MATERIALS A/S—See Sandvik AB; *Int'l*, pg. 1186
SANDVIK HARD MATERIALS LTD.—See Sandvik AB; *Int'l*, *pg. 1186*
SANDVIK HARD MATERIALS NORDEN AB—See Sandvik AB; *Int'l*, pg. 1185
SANDVIK HARD MATERIALS PTY. LTD.—See Sandvik AB; *Int'l*, pg. 1187
SANDVIK HARD MATERIALS S.A.—See Sandvik AB; *Int'l*, pg. 1186
SANDVIK HONG KONG LTD.—See Sandvik AB; *Int'l*, pg. 1187
SANDVIK IN AUSTRIA GES.M.B.H.—See Sandvik AB; *Int'l*, *pg. 1186*
SANDVIK, INC.—See Sandvik AB; *Int'l*, pg. 1185
AB SANDVIK INFORMATION SYSTEMS—See Sandvik AB; *Int'l*, pg. 1185
SANDVIK INTERNATIONAL—See Sandvik AB; *Int'l*, pg. 1186
AB SANDVIK INTERNATIONAL—See Sandvik AB; *Int'l*, pg. 1186
SANDVIK IRELAND LIMITED—See Sandvik AB; *Int'l*, pg. 1186
SANDVIK ITALIA S.P.A.—See Sandvik AB; *Int'l*, pg. 1186
SANDVIK KENYA LTD.—See Sandvik AB; *Int'l*, pg. 1187
SANDVIK K.K.—See Sandvik AB; *Int'l*, pg. 1187
SANDVIK KOREA LTD.—See Sandvik AB; *Int'l*, pg. 1187
SANDVIK KOSTA GMBH—See Sandvik AB; *Int'l*, pg. 1186
SANDVIK LATIN AMERICA, INC.—See Sandvik AB; *Int'l*, pg. 1185
SANDVIK LTD.—See Sandvik AB; *Int'l*, pg. 1186
SANDVIK MAGYARORZAGON KFT—See Sandvik AB; *Int'l*, *pg. 1186*
SANDVIK MALAYSIA SDN. BHD.—See Sandvik AB; *Int'l*, pg. 1187
AB SANDVIK METAL SAWS—See Sandvik AB; *Int'l*, pg. 1185
SANDVIK/MILFORD CORPORATION—See Sandvik AB; *Int'l*, pg. 1185
SANDVIK NEW ZEALAND LTD.—See Sandvik AB; *Int'l*, pg. 1187
SANDVIK NORGE A/S—See Sandvik AB; *Int'l*, pg. 1186
SANDVIK OBERGUE-LIMAS E MECANICA LDA.—See Sandvik AB; *Int'l*, pg. 1186
SANDVIK OUTILLAGE S.N.C.—See Sandvik AB; *Int'l*, pg. 1186
SANDVIK PHILIPPINES, INC.—See Sandvik AB; *Int'l*, pg. 1187
SANDVIK POLSKA LTD.—See Sandvik AB; *Int'l*, pg. 1186
SANDVIK PORTUGUESA LDA.—See Sandvik AB; *Int'l*, pg. 1186
SANDVIK (PRIVATE) LTD.—See Sandvik AB; *Int'l*, pg. 1187
SANDVIK PROCESS SYSTEMS B.V.—See Sandvik AB; *Int'l*, pg. 1186
SANDVIK PROCESS SYSTEMS CANADA LTD.—See Sandvik AB; *Int'l*, pg. 1188
SANDVIK PROCESS SYSTEMS GES.M.B.H.—See Sandvik AB; *Int'l*, pg. 1187
SANDVIK PROCESS SYSTEMS GMBH—See Sandvik AB; *Int'l*, pg. 1187
SANDVIK PROCESS SYSTEMS, INC.—See Sandvik AB; *Int'l*, pg. 1185
SANDVIK PROCESS SYSTEMS LTD.—See Sandvik AB; *Int'l*, pg. 1187
SANDVIK PROCESS SYSTEMS S.A.—See Sandvik AB; *Int'l*, pg. 1187
SANDVIK PROCESS SYSTEMS S.P.A.—See Sandvik AB; *Int'l*, pg. 1187
SANDVIK (PTY.) LTD.—See Sandvik AB; *Int'l*, pg. 1187
SANDVIK ROCK TOOLS—See Sandvik AB; *Int'l*, pg. 1187
AB SANDVIK ROCK TOOLS—See Sandvik AB; *Int'l*, pg. 1185
SANDVIK ROCK TOOLS, INC.—See Sandvik AB; *Int'l*, pg. 1185
SANDVIK ROCK TOOLS LTD.—See Sandvik AB; *Int'l*, pg. 1187
SANDVIK ROCK TOOLS S.N.C.—See Sandvik AB; *Int'l*, pg. 1187
SANDVIK ROCK TOOLS SVENSKA FORSALJNINGS AB—See Sandvik AB; *Int'l*, pg. 1185
SANDVIK RUSSIA A/O—See Sandvik AB; *Int'l*, pg. 1187
SANDVIK S.A.—See Sandvik AB; *Int'l*, pg. 1187
SANDVIK S.A. BUREAU DE LIASION—See Sandvik AB; *Int'l*, pg. 1187
SANDVIK SAWS AND TOOLS—See Sandvik AB; *Int'l*, pg. 1187
AB SANDVIK SAWS & TOOLS—See Sandvik AB; *Int'l*, pg. 1185
SANDVIK SAWS AND TOOLS BENELUX B.V.—See Sandvik AB; *Int'l*, pg. 1187
SANDVIK SAWS AND TOOLS U.K.—See Sandvik AB; *Int'l*, *pg. 1187*
SANDVIK SAWS & TOOLS CO.—See Sandvik AB; *Int'l*, pg. 1185
SANDVIK (SCHWEIZ) AG—See Sandvik AB; *Int'l*, pg. 1187
AB SANDVIK SERVICE—See Sandvik AB; *Int'l*, pg. 1185
SANDVIK SLOVAKIA S.R.O.—See Sandvik AB; *Int'l*, pg. 1187
SANDVIK SORTING SYSTEMS—See Sandvik AB; *Int'l*, pg. 1186
SANDVIK SOUTH EAST ASIA LTD.—See Sandvik AB; *Int'l*, *pg. 1187*
SANDVIK STAL FORSALJININGS AB—See Sandvik AB; *Int'l*, pg. 1185
SANDVIK STEEL—See Sandvik AB; *Int'l*, pg. 1187
AB SANDVIK STEEL—See Sandvik AB; *Int'l*, pg. 1185
SANDVIK STEEL CANADA—See Sandvik AB; *Int'l*, pg. 1188
SANDVIK STEEL CO.—See Sandvik AB; *Int'l*, pg. 1185
SANDVIK STEEL U.K.—See Sandvik AB; *Int'l*, pg. 1187
SANDVIK TAIWAN LTD.—See Sandvik AB; *Int'l*, pg. 1187
SANDVIK TICARET LTD. AS—See Sandvik AB; *Int'l*, pg. 1187
SANDVIK TITAN PTY. LTD.—See Sandvik AB; *Int'l*, pg. 1187
SANDVIK TOBLER S.A.—See Sandvik AB; *Int'l*, pg. 1187
SANDVIK VENEZUELA C.A.—See Sandvik AB; *Int'l*, pg. 1188
SANDVIK-VILLARES WIRE INDUSTRIA E COMERICO LTDA.—See Sandvik AB; *Int'l*, pg. 1188
SANDVIK WINDSOR CORP.—See Sandvik AB; *Int'l*, pg. 1185
SANDVIK (ZAMBIA) LTD.—See Sandvik AB; *Int'l*, pg. 1187
SANDWELL INC.; *Int'l*, pg. 1188
SANDY BAY HOTEL LIMITED—See International Investment & Underwriting Ltd.; *Int'l*, pg. 684
SANDY POST—See Lee Enterprises, Incorporated; *U.S. Public*, pg. 984
SANEL AUTO PARTS CO.—See Automotive Supply Associates, Inc.; *U.S. Private*, pg. 101
SANELCO S.A.—See Sanyo Electric Co., Ltd.; *Int'l*, pg. 1192
AB SANERA—See Celsius AB; *Int'l*, pg. 277
JOHN B. SANFILIPPO & SON, INC.; *U.S. Public*, pg. 1431
SANFORD & HAWLEY, INC.; *U.S. Private*, pg. 965
SANFORD BEROC CORP.—See Newell Co.; *U.S. Public*, pg. 1178
SANFORD CORPORATION—See Newell Co.; *U.S. Public*, pg. 1178
SANGAM BOOKS LTD.—See Pearson plc; *Int'l*, pg. 1026
SANGAM COMMUNICATIONS CO., LTD.—See Grey Advertising Inc.; *U.S. Public*, pg. 765
SANGAMON INDUSTRIES; *U.S. Private*, pg. 965
SANGEMINI S.P.A.; *Int'l*, pg. 1188
SANGER ROCK AND SAND—See CalMat Co.; *U.S. Public*, *pg. 296*
SANGRE DE CRISTOS RANCHES INC.—See Forbes, Inc.; *U.S. Private*, pg. 418
AB SANI-MASKINER—See Cooper Industries, Inc.; *U.S. Public*, pg. 444
SANI-MATIC SYSTEMS—See DEC International, Inc.; *U.S. Private*, pg. 301
SANI-MIST, INC.; *U.S. Private*, pg. 965
SANI-TECH INC.—See Sybron International Corporation; *U.S. Public*, pg. 1545
SANI-TECH SOUTHEAST—See Sybron International Corporation; *U.S. Public*, pg. 1545
SANIFILL, INC.—See USA Waste Services, Inc.; *U.S. Public*, pg. 1686
SANI-MED—See Sanderson Plumbing Products Inc.; *U.S. Private*, pg. 964
SANIN LEARNING—See Cargill; *U.S. Private*, pg. 210
SANISERV MANUFACTURING CORP.; *U.S. Private*, pg. 965
SANISERV-KOREA—See SaniServ Manufacturing Corp.; *U.S. Private*, pg. 965
SANIT—See ETEX; *Int'l*, pg. 430
SANITARIA MEXICANA S.A. DE C.V.—See Henkel KGaA; *Int'l*, pg. 614
SANITARIOS DOMINICANOS, S.A.—See American Standard Inc.; *U.S. Public*, pg. 92
SANITARY-DASH MANUFACTURING CO., INC.—See Zurn Industries, Inc.; *U.S. Public*, pg. 1795
SANITARY WARES MFG. CORP.—See American Standard Inc.; *U.S. Public*, pg. 92
SANITEC LTD. OY—See Metra Corporation; *Int'l*, pg. 863
SANKEN-AIRPAX CO., LTD.—See Sanken Electric Co., Ltd.; *Int'l*, pg. 1188
SANKEN DENSETSU CO., LTD.—See Sanken Electric Co., Ltd.; *Int'l*, pg. 1188
SANKEN ELECTRIC CO., LTD.; *Int'l*, pg. 1188
SANKEN ELECTRIC EUROPE LIMITED—See Sanken Electric Co., Ltd.; *Int'l*, pg. 1188
SANKEN ELECTRIC HONG KONG CO., LTD.—See Sanken Electric Co., Ltd.; *Int'l*, pg. 1188
SANKEN ELECTRIC SINGAPORE PTE. LIMITED—See Sanken Electric Co., Ltd.; *Int'l*, pg. 1189
SANKEN ELECTRIC U.S.A. CORP.—See Sanken Electric Co., Ltd.; *Int'l*, pg. 1188
SANKEN KOSAN CO., LTD.—See Sanken Electric Co., Ltd.; *Int'l*, pg. 1188
SANKEN POWER SYSTEM—See Sanken Electric Co., Ltd.; *Int'l*, pg. 1189
SANKI ENGINEERING CO., LTD.—See Mitsui & Co., Ltd.; *Int'l*, pg. 877
SANKI KENSETSU CO., LTD.—See Tekken Corporation; *Int'l*, pg. 1362
SANKO PETERSON CORPORATION—See Peterson American Corp.; *U.S. Private*, pg. 857
SANKO-STEVENS CHEMICAL, INC.—See The Sherwin-Williams Company; *U.S. Public*, pg. 1466
SANKOSHA ADVERTISING AGENCY, LTD.; *Int'l*, pg. 1189
SANKOSHA ADVERTISING AGENCY, LTD.—See Sankosha Advertising Agency, Ltd.; *Int'l*, pg. 1189
SANKOSHA CORPORATION; *Int'l*, pg. 1189
SANKOSHA ENGINEERING SINGAPORE PTE. LTD.—See Sankosha Corporation; *Int'l*, pg. 1189
SANKOSHA U.S.A., INC.—See Sankosha Corporation; *Int'l*, *pg. 1189*
SANKYO COMPANY LIMITED; *Int'l*, pg. 1189
SANLAM CORPORATION—See Baltek Corporation; *U.S. Public*, pg. 172
SANMARK GROUP—See Movie Star, Inc.; *U.S. Public*, pg. 1141
SANMEX, S.A. DE C.V.—See Sanyo Electric Co., Ltd.; *Int'l*, *pg. 1192*
SANMINA CORPORATION; *U.S. Public*, pg. 1431
SANMINA CORPORATION-DURHAM PLANT—See Sanmina Corporation; *U.S. Public*, pg. 1431
SANMINA CORPORATION-MANCHESTER PLANT—See Sanmina Corporation; *U.S. Public*, pg. 1431
SANMINA CORPORATION-RICHARDSON PLANT—See Sanmina Corporation; *U.S. Public*, pg. 1431
SANMINA CORPORATION-SAN JOSE—See Sanmina Corporation; *U.S. Public*, pg. 1431
SANMINA IRELAND—See Sanmina Corporation; *U.S. Public*, pg. 1431
SANOFI—See Elf Aquitane; *Int'l*, pg. 446
SANOFI BEAUTE, INC.—See Elf Aquitane; *Int'l*, pg. 445
SANOFI CANADA—See Elf Aquitane; *Int'l*, pg. 445
SANOFI, DIAGNOSTIAS PASTEUR—See Elf Aquitane; *Int'l*, *pg. 446*

SANOFI-MEIJI PHARMACEUTICALS CO., LTD.—See Meiji Seika Kaisha, Ltd.; *Int'l*, pg. 855
SANOFI PHARMACEUTICALS INC.—See Elf Aquitane; *Int'l*, pg. 445
SANOFI PHARMACEUTICALS, INC.—See Elf Aquitane; *Int'l*, pg. 445
SANOFI RESEARCH CO. INC.—See Elf Aquitane; *Int'l*, pg. 445
SANOFI RESEARCH DIVISION—See Elf Aquitane; *Int'l*, pg. 445
SANOFI YAMANOUCHI INC.—See Yamanouchi Pharmaceutical Co., Ltd.; *Int'l*, pg. 1518
SANORANIA GMBH—See Pharmacia & Upjohn, Inc.; *Int'l*, pg. 1049
SANPAOLO-ISTANBUL REPRESENTATIVE OFFICE—See Istituto Bancario San Paolo Di Torino S.p.A.; *Int'l*, pg. 691
SANPAOLO-LOS ANGELES BRANCH—See Istituto Bancario San Paolo Di Torino S.p.A.; *Int'l*, pg. 691
SANPAOLO-MONACO BRANCH—See Istituto Bancario San Paolo Di Torino S.p.A.; *Int'l*, pg. 692
SANPAOLO-NEW YORK BRANCH—See Istituto Bancario San Paolo Di Torino S.p.A.; *Int'l*, pg. 691
SANS, S.A.—See Sara Lee Corporation; *U.S. Public*, pg. 1434
SANSHIN ELECTRIC CO., LTD.—See Sanken Electric Co., Ltd.; *Int'l*, pg. 1188
SANSHUI REDLAND BUILDING MATERIALS CO. LTD.—See Redland PLC; *Int'l*, pg. 1093
SANSONE AUTO MALL; *U.S. Private*, pg. 965
THE SANTA ANITA COMPANIES—See Meditrust Corporation; *U.S. Public*, pg. 1081
SANTA ANITA ENTERPRISES, INC.—See Meditrust Corporation; *U.S. Public*, pg. 1081
SANTA BARBARA EMPRESA NACIONAL DE INDUSTRIAS MILITARES, S.A.—See SEPI; *Int'l*, pg. 1224
SANTA BARBARA NEWS-PRESS—See The New York Times Company; *U.S. Public*, pg. 1175
SANTA BARBARA RESEARCH CENTER—See Raytheon Company; *U.S. Public*, pg. 1365
SANTA FE COFFEE COMPANY—See Santa Fe Gaming Corporation; *U.S. Public*, pg. 1432
SANTA FE DETENTION CENTER—See Corrections Corporation of America; *U.S. Public*, pg. 454
SANTA FE DRILLING CO.—See Kuwait Petroleum Corporation; *Int'l*, pg. 765
SANTA FE ENERGY RESOURCES, INC.; *U.S. Public*, pg. 1431
SANTA FE FOR ENGINEERING & PETROLEUM PROJECTS COMPANY K.S.C.—See Kuwait Petroleum Corporation; *Int'l*, pg. 765
SANTA FE GAMING CORPORATION; *U.S. Public*, pg. 1432
SANTA FE HOTEL INC.—See Santa Fe Gaming Corporation; *U.S. Public*, pg. 1432
SANTA FE INTERNATIONAL CORPORATION—See Kuwait Petroleum Corporation; *Int'l*, pg. 765
SANTA FE MINERALS INC.—See Kuwait Petroleum Corporation; *Int'l*, pg. 765
SANTA FE OFFSHORE CONSTRUCTION CO.—See Kuwait Petroleum Corporation; *Int'l*, pg. 765
SANTA FE SHAFT DRILLING CO.—See Kuwait Petroleum Corporation; *Int'l*, pg. 765
SANTA FE SPRINGS HOLDING COMPANY—See Hicks, Muse, Tate & Furst Inc.; *U.S. Private*, pg. 526
SANTA FE VALLEY, INC.—See Santa Fe Gaming Corporation; *U.S. Public*, pg. 1432
SANTA LUCIA CRISTAL SACIF—See Pilkington Plc; *Int'l*, pg. 1057
SANTA MARIA TIMES—See Pulitzer Publishing Company; *U.S. Public*, pg. 1343
SANTA MARINA—See Saint-Gobain; *Int'l*, pg. 1177
SANTA MONICA BANK—See Western Bancorp; *U.S. Public*, pg. 1757
SANTA MONICA FORD COMPANY; *U.S. Private*, pg. 965
SANTA MONICA PLACE—See The Rouse Company; *U.S. Public*, pg. 1408
SANTA PAULA HEALTHCARE—See Vencor, Inc.; *U.S. Public*, pg. 1714
SANTA ROSA STEEL FORMING, INC.; *U.S. Private*, pg. 965
SANTA VERONICA EMPR PARTICIPATIONES S/C LTDA—See Saint-Gobain; *Int'l*, pg. 1518
SANTANDER DE FACTORING—See Banco Santander; *Int'l*, pg. 143
SANTANDER DE LEASING—See Banco Santander; *Int'l*, pg. 143
SANTANDER DE PATRIMONIOS—See Banco Santander; *Int'l*, pg. 143
SANTANDER DE PENSIONES—See Banco Santander; *Int'l*, pg. 143
SANTANDER DIREKT BANK A.G.—See Banco Santander; *Int'l*, pg. 143
SANTANDER INVESTMENT ASIA LTD.—See Banco Santander; *Int'l*, pg. 144
SANTANDER INVESTMENT BANK—See Banco Santander; *Int'l*, pg. 143
SANTANDER INVESTMENT SPA—See Banco Santander; *Int'l*, pg. 144
SANTANDER MERCHANT, S.A.—See Banco Santander; *Int'l*, pg. 144
SANTANDER OVERSEAS BANK (PUERTO RICO)—See Banco Santander; *Int'l*, pg. 143
SANTEE DAIRIES—See Quality Food Centers, Inc.; *U.S. Public*, pg. 1349
SANTEE MANUFACTURING—See Global Motor Sport Group, Inc.; *U.S. Public*, pg. 748
SANTEE PRINT WORKS, INC.; *U.S. Private*, pg. 965
SANTINO—See Lagardere Groupe; *Int'l*, pg. 796
SANTIPA S.A.R.L.—See Novartis AG; *Int'l*, pg. 985
SANTO TOURS & TRAVEL, INC.—See Adventure Tours USA, Inc.; *U.S. Private*, pg. 23
SANTOS BASIN DEVELOPMENT—See Petrobras - Petroleo Brasileiro S.A.; *Int'l*, pg. 1041

SANTRADE LTD.—See Sandvik AB; *Int'l*, pg. 1187
SANTRAN INC.—See Sanderson Plumbing Products Inc.; *U.S. Private*, pg. 964
SANWA AUSTRALIA FINANCE LIMITED—See The Sanwa Bank Limited; *Int'l*, pg. 1190
SANWA AUSTRALIA LIMITED—See The Sanwa Bank Limited; *Int'l*, pg. 1190
SANWA BANK CALIFORNIA—See The Sanwa Bank Limited; *Int'l*, pg. 1189
SANWA BANK CANADA—See The Sanwa Bank Limited; *Int'l*, pg. 1190
SANWA BANK (DEUTSCHLAND) AG—See The Sanwa Bank Limited; *Int'l*, pg. 1190
THE SANWA BANK, LTD.; *Int'l*, pg. 1189
THE SANWA BANK, LIMITED-TOKYO HEADQUARTERS—See The Sanwa Bank Limited; *Int'l*, pg. 1189
SANWA BANK-NEW YORK—See The Sanwa Bank Limited; *Int'l*, pg. 1190
SANWA BANK (SCHWEIZ) AG—See The Sanwa Bank Limited; *Int'l*, pg. 1190
SANWA BANK TRUST COMPANY OF NEW YORK—See The Sanwa Bank Limited; *Int'l*, pg. 1190
P.T. SANWA-BRI FINANCE—See The Sanwa Bank Limited; *Int'l*, pg. 1190
SANWA BUSINESS CREDIT CORPORATION—See The Sanwa Bank Limited; *Int'l*, pg. 1189
SANWA BUSINESS CREDIT (UK) LIMITED—See The Sanwa Bank Limited; *Int'l*, pg. 1190
SANWA-DSP CREDIT LIMITED—See The Sanwa Bank Limited; *Int'l*, pg. 1190
SANWA FINANCIAL PRODUCTS CO., L.P.—See The Sanwa Bank Limited; *Int'l*, pg. 1189
SANWA FINANCIAL PRODUCTS CO., L.P. HONG KONG—See The Sanwa Bank Limited; *Int'l*, pg. 1190
SANWA FINANCIAL PRODUCTS (UK) CO. LTD.—See The Sanwa Bank Limited; *Int'l*, pg. 1190
SANWA FINANCIAL SERVICES LIMITED—See The Sanwa Bank Limited; *Int'l*, pg. 1190
SANWA FOODS, INC.—See Campbell Soup Company; *U.S. Public*, pg. 299
SANWA FUTURES L.L.C.—See The Sanwa Bank Limited; *Int'l*, pg. 1189
SANWA FUTURES (SINGAPORE) PTE LIMITED—See The Sanwa Bank Limited; *Int'l*, pg. 1190
SANWA GENERAL EQUIPMENT LEASING—See The Sanwa Bank Limited; *Int'l*, pg. 1189
SANWA HOUSING LOAN (HONG KONG) LIMITED—See The Sanwa Bank Limited; *Int'l*, pg. 1190
P.T. SANWA INDONESIA BANK—See The Sanwa Bank Limited; *Int'l*, pg. 1190
SANWA INTERNATIONAL FINANCE LIMITED—See The Sanwa Bank Limited; *Int'l*, pg. 1190
SANWA INTERNATIONAL (IRELAND) PLC—See The Sanwa Bank Limited; *Int'l*, pg. 1190
SANWA INTERNATIONAL PLC—See The Sanwa Bank Limited; *Int'l*, pg. 1190
SANWA LEASING CORP.—See The Sanwa Bank Limited; *Int'l*, pg. 1189
SANWA LEASING (DEUTSCHLAND) GMBH—See The Sanwa Bank Limited; *Int'l*, pg. 1190
SANWA SECURITIES (USA) CO., L.P.—See The Sanwa Bank Limited; *Int'l*, pg. 1189
SANWA SINGAPORE LIMITED—See The Sanwa Bank Limited; *Int'l*, pg. 1190
SANWELL CO., LTD.—See Yamanouchi Pharmaceutical Co. Ltd.; *Int'l*, pg. 1518
SANYO—See Sanyo Electric Co., Ltd.; *Int'l*, pg. 1191
SANYO AIRCONDITIONERS (SINGAPORE) PTE. LTD.—See Sanyo Electric Co., Ltd.; *Int'l*, pg. 1192
SANYO ARMCO (KENYA) LIMITED—See Sanyo Electric Co., Ltd.; *Int'l*, pg. 1194
SANYO AUSTRALIA PTY. LTD.—See Sanyo Electric Co., Ltd.; *Int'l*, pg. 1192
SANYO BUSINESS SYSTEMS (HONG KONG) LIMITED—See Sanyo Electric Co., Ltd.; *Int'l*, pg. 1192
SANYO CANADA INC.—See Sanyo Electric Co., Ltd.; *Int'l*, pg. 1192
SANYO CORP.—See Sanyo Electric Co., Ltd.; *Int'l*, pg. 1191
SANYO E & E CORPORATION—See Sanyo Electric Co., Ltd.; *Int'l*, pg. 1191
SANYO ELECTRIC CO., LTD.; *Int'l*, pg. 1190
SANYO ELECTRIC CREDIT CO. LTD.—See Sanyo Electric Co., Ltd.; *Int'l*, pg. 1191
SANYO ELECTRIC (HONG KONG) LIMITED—See Sanyo Electric Co., Ltd.; *Int'l*, pg. 1192
SANYO ELECTRIC (SHEKOU) LTD.—See Sanyo Electric Co., Ltd.; *Int'l*, pg. 1192
SANYO ELECTRIC (TAIWAN) CO., LTD.—See Sanyo Electric Co., Ltd.; *Int'l*, pg. 1192
SANYO ELECTRIC TRADING CO., LTD.—See Sanyo Electric Co., Ltd.; *Int'l*, pg. 1191
SANYO ELECTRONIC (TAICHUNG) CO., LTD.—See Sanyo Electric Co., Ltd.; *Int'l*, pg. 1192
SANYO ELECTRONICS (HONG KONG) LIMITED—See Sanyo Electric Co., Ltd.; *Int'l*, pg. 1192
SANYO ELECTRONICS (SINGAPORE) PTE. LTD.—See Sanyo Electric Co., Ltd.; *Int'l*, pg. 1192
SANYO ENERGY (U.S.A.) CORPORATION—See Sanyo Electric Co., Ltd.; *Int'l*, pg. 1191
SANYO ESPANA S.A.—See Sanyo Electric Co., Ltd.; *Int'l*, pg. 1192
SANYO E.T. CANADA INC.—See Sanyo Electric Co., Ltd.; *Int'l*, pg. 1192
SANYO (EUROPE) INTERNATIONAL AG—See Sanyo Electric Co., Ltd.; *Int'l*, pg. 1192
SANYO FISHER COMPANY—See Sanyo Electric Co., Ltd.; *Int'l*, pg. 1191
SANYO FISHER HOME APPLIANCE & CONSUMER PRODUCTS DIV.—See Sanyo Electric Co., Ltd.; *Int'l*, pg. 1191
SANYO FISHER SERVICE CORP.—See Sanyo Electric Co., Ltd.; *Int'l*, pg. 1191

SANYO FISHER VERTRIEBS GMBH—See Sanyo Electric Co., Ltd.; *Int'l*, pg. 1192
SANYO HOME TECH CO., LTD.—See Sanyo Electric Co., Ltd.; *Int'l*, pg. 1191
SANYO INDUSTRIES CANADA INC.—See Sanyo Electric Co., Ltd.; *Int'l*, pg. 1192
SANYO INDUSTRIES DEUTSCHLAND GMBH—See Sanyo Electric Co., Ltd.; *Int'l*, pg. 1192
P.T. SANYO INDUSTRIES INDONESIA—See Sanyo Electric Co., Ltd.; *Int'l*, pg. 1192
SANYO INDUSTRIES (MALAYSIA) BERHAD—See Sanyo Electric Co., Ltd.; *Int'l*, pg. 1192
SANYO INDUSTRIES (SINGAPORE) PRIVATE LIMITED—See Sanyo Electric Co., Ltd.; *Int'l*, pg. 1192
SANYO INDUSTRIES (U.K.) LIMITED—See Sanyo Electric Co., Ltd.; *Int'l*, pg. 1192
SANYO ITALIANA S.P.A.—See Sanyo Electric Co., Ltd.; *Int'l*, pg. 1192
SANYO LOGISTICS CORPORATION—See Sanyo Electric Co., Ltd.; *Int'l*, pg. 1191
SANYO MALAYSIA SDN. BHD—See Sanyo Electric Co., Ltd.; *Int'l*, pg. 1192
SANYO MARKETING CORPORATION—See Sanyo Electric Co., Ltd.; *Int'l*, pg. 1192
SANYO NORTH AMERICAN CORPORATION—See Sanyo Electric Co., Ltd.; *Int'l*, pg. 1191
SANYO OFFICE AUTOMATION—See Sanyo Electric Co., Ltd.; *Int'l*, pg. 1191
SANYO OFFICE MACHINES DIV.—See Sanyo Electric Co., Ltd.; *Int'l*, pg. 1191
SANYO (PHILIPPINES), INC.—See Sanyo Electric Co., Ltd.; *Int'l*, pg. 1192
SANYO SALES & SERVICE SDN. BHD.—See Sanyo Electric Co., Ltd.; *Int'l*, pg. 1192
SANYO SEMICONDUCTOR CORPORATION—See Sanyo Electric Co., Ltd.; *Int'l*, pg. 1191
SANYO SEMICONDUCTOR DISTRIBUTION (USA) CORPORATION—See Sanyo Electric Co., Ltd.; *Int'l*, pg. 1191
SANYO SEMICONDUCTOR (H.K.) CO., LTD.—See Sanyo Electric Co., Ltd.; *Int'l*, pg. 1192
SANYO SEMICONDUCTOR (SHEKOU) LTD.—See Sanyo Electric Co., Ltd.; *Int'l*, pg. 1192
SANYO (THAILAND) CO., LTD.—See Sanyo Electric Co., Ltd.; *Int'l*, pg. 1193
SANYO TOKUYAMA READY MIXED CONCRETE CO., LTD.—See Tokuyama Corporation; *Int'l*, pg. 1393
SANYO TOURIST SALES CO., LTD.—See Sanyo Electric Co., Ltd.; *Int'l*, pg. 1191
SANYO U.K. LIMITED—See Sanyo Electric Co., Ltd.; *Int'l*, pg. 1193
SANYO UNIVERSAL ELECTRIC PUBLIC CO., LTD.—See Sanyo Electric Co., Ltd.; *Int'l*, pg. 1192
SANYO VIDEO COMPONENTS (USA) CORPORATION—See Sanyo Electric Co., Ltd.; *Int'l*, pg. 1191
SANYO VLSI ENGINEERING CO., LTD.—See Sanyo Electric Co., Ltd.; *Int'l*, pg. 1191
SANYU CO., LTD.—See Yamanouchi Pharmaceutical Co. Ltd.; *Int'l*, pg. 1518
SAO LOURENCO—See Saint-Gobain; *Int'l*, pg. 1177
SAO MARCOS EMPREENDIMENTOS E PARTICIPACOES S.A.—See Assicurazioni Generali S.p.A.; *Int'l*, pg. 92
SAO PAULO ALPARGATAS S.A.; *Int'l*, pg. 1193
SAPAC CORP., LTD.—See Roche Holding Ltd.; *Int'l*, pg. 1122
SAPAL SA—See SIG Schweizersiche Industrie-Gesellschaft Holding AG; *Int'l*, pg. 1156
SAPHIR PRODUCE LIMITED—See The Albert Fisher Group PLC; *Int'l*, pg. 491
SAPIENS INTERNATIONAL—See Sapiens International Corporation N.V.; *Int'l*, pg. 1193
SAPIENS INTERNATIONAL CORPORATION N.V.; *Int'l*, pg. 1193
SAPIENS USA, INC.—See Sapiens International Corporation N.V.; *Int'l*, pg. 1193
SAPIO—See Air Products and Chemicals, Inc.; *U.S. Public*, pg. 32
SAPONIA B.V.—See Unilever Plc; *Int'l*, pg. 1438
SAPPI LIMITED; *Int'l*, pg. 1193
SAPPORO BREWERIES LTD.; *Int'l*, pg. 1193
SAPPORO U.S.A., INC., NEW YORK—See Sapporo Breweries Ltd.; *Int'l*, pg. 1193
SAPPORO U.S.A., INC., SAN FRANCISCO—See Sapporo Breweries Ltd.; *Int'l*, pg. 1194
SAPROMA S.A.—See Carlson Companies, Inc.; *U.S. Private*, pg. 212
SAPROPUR, S.A.R.L.—See ConAgra, Inc.; *U.S. Public*, pg. 429
SAPURA-NOKIA TELECOMMUNICATIONS SDN. BHD.—See Oy Nokia Ab/Nokia Group; *Int'l*, pg. 954
SARA LEE BAKERY—See Sara Lee Corporation; *U.S. Public*, pg. 1433
SARA LEE BAKERY WORLDWIDE—See Sara Lee Corporation; *U.S. Public*, pg. 1433
SARA LEE CORPORATION; *U.S. Public*, pg. 1432
SARA LEE CORP.-ASIA—See Sara Lee Corporation; *U.S. Public*, pg. 1434
SARA LEE/DE—See Sara Lee Corporation; *U.S. Public*, pg. 1434
SARA LEE/DE ASIA—See Sara Lee Corporation; *U.S. Public*, pg. 1435
SARA LEE DIRECT—See Sara Lee Corporation; *U.S. Public*, pg. 1434
SARA LEE HOLDINGS—See Sara Lee Corporation; *U.S. Public*, pg. 1435
SARA LEE HOSIERY—See Sara Lee Corporation; *U.S. Public*, pg. 1434
SARA LEE HOUSEHOLD & PERSONAL CARE-U.K.—See Sara Lee Corporation; *U.S. Public*, pg. 1435
SARA LEE INTIMATES—See Sara Lee Corporation; *U.S. Public*, pg. 1434
SARA LEE KNIT PRODUCTS—See Sara Lee Corporation; *U.S. Public*, pg. 1434

SARA LEE KNIT PRODUCTS-MEXICO—See Sara Lee Corporation; *U.S. Public*, pg. 1435
SARA LEE MEATS—See Sara Lee Corporation; *U.S. Public*, pg. 1434
SARA LEE PERSONAL PRODUCTS—See Sara Lee Corporation; *U.S. Public*, pg. 1434
SARA LEE PERSONAL PRODUCTS AUSTRALIA—See Sara Lee Corporation; *U.S. Public*, pg. 1435
SARA LEE PERSONAL PRODUCTS EUROPE—See Sara Lee Corporation; *U.S. Public*, pg. 1435
SARA LEE PROCESSED MEATS-EUROPE—See Sara Lee Corporation; *U.S. Public*, pg. 1435
SARA LEE SOCK COMPANY—See Sara Lee Corporation; *U.S. Public*, pg. 1434
SARAGEN JAPAN K.K.—See Adidas AG; *Int'l*, pg. 25
SARAIVA S/A LIVREIROS EDITORES—See Corporacion MAPFRE, Compania Internacional de Reaseguros, S.A.; *Int'l*, pg. 334
SARAJI MINE—See The Broken Hill Proprietary Company Limited; *Int'l*, pg. 223
SARASOTA HERALD-TRIBUNE COMPANY—See The New York Times Company; *U.S. Public*, pg. 1175
SARATOGA BRANDS, INC.; *U.S. Public*, pg. 1435
SARATOGA EQUINE SPORTS CENTER; *U.S. Private*, pg. 965
THE SARATOGA EQUIP. CORP.—See The Rouse Company; *U.S. Public*, pg. 1409
SARATOGA INDUSTRIES—See Espey Mfg. & Electronics Corp.; *U.S. Public*, pg. 592
SARATOGA PROCESSING COMPANY LTD.—See Westcoast Energy Inc.; *Int'l*, pg. 1492
THE SARATOGIAN—See Gannett Company, Inc.; *U.S. Public*, pg. 700
SARAWAK SHELL—See Royal Dutch/Shell Group of Companies; *Int'l*, pg. 1140
SARCA N.V.—See Linde AG; *Int'l*, pg. 811
SARCAL—See Imetal; *Int'l*, pg. 662
SARELEM—See Jeumont-Schneider Trenformeteurs; *Int'l*, pg. 706
SARGENT & GREENLEAF, INC.; *U.S. Public*, pg. 965
SARGENT AND GREENLEAF—See Security Group Inc.; *U.S. Private*, pg. 981
SARGENT & LUNDY; *U.S. Private*, pg. 965
SARGENT CONTROLS—See Dover Corporation; *U.S. Public*, pg. 521
SARGENT-FLETCHER INC.—See Cobham plc; *Int'l*, pg. 301
H.E. SARGENT, INC.; *U.S. Private*, pg. 966
SARGENT MANUFACTURING COMPANY—See Assa Abloy AB; *Int'l*, pg. 18
SARGENT METAL FABRICATING—See Todd & Sargent, Inc.; *U.S. Private*, pg. 1089
SARGENT-WELCH SCIENTIFIC COMPANY—See VWR Scientific Products; *U.S. Public*, pg. 1704
SARGENTO FOODS INC.; *U.S. Private*, pg. 966
SARGENTO FOODS INC.—See Sargento Foods Inc.; *U.S. Private*, pg. 966
SARGENTO FOODS INC. - CONSUMER PRODUCTS DIV.—See Sargento Foods Inc.; *U.S. Private*, pg. 966
SARGENTO FOODS INC.- FOOD SERVICE DIV.—See Sargento Foods Inc.; *U.S. Private*, pg. 966
C.G. SARGENTS SONS—See Aeroglide Corporation; *U.S. Private*, pg. 24
SARIC INTERNATIONAL—See Compagnie des Machines Bull; *Int'l*, pg. 316
SARIMMO—See GIB Group; *Int'l*, pg. 533
P.T. SARINITOKYU HOTEL CORP.—See Nissho Iwai Corporation; *Int'l*, pg. 949
SARK HAYAT SIGORTA T.A.S—See Allianz Aktiengesellschaft; *Int'l*, pg. 61
SARK SIGORTA T.A.S. (RAS)—See Allianz Aktiengesellschaft; *Int'l*, pg. 62
SARKES TARZIAN; *U.S. Private*, pg. 966
SARKU COMEX SDN. BHD.—See Stolt-Nielsen S.A.; *Int'l*, pg. 1302
SARMA—See AB SKF; *Int'l*, pg. 1158
SARMA-NOPRI GROUP—See GIB Group; *Int'l*, pg. 533
SARMA-SHOP—See GIB Group; *Int'l*, pg. 533
SARMAG—See GIB Group; *Int'l*, pg. 533
SARMIENTO RAPPAN INDUSTRIES; *Int'l*, pg. 1194
SARNOFF CORPORATION—See SRI International; *U.S. Private*, pg. 958
SAROPH HOLDINGS B.V.—See Spectra-Physics AB; *Int'l*, pg. 1290
SAROTTI GMBH—See Nestle S.A.; *Int'l*, pg. 922
SARRAGAN BENELUX S.A.—See Adidas AG; *Int'l*, pg. 25
SARRIO TISU S.A.—See Fort James Corporation; *U.S. Public*, pg. 673
SARTELL MILL, CHAMPION INTERNATIONAL CORP.—See Champion International Corp.; *U.S. Public*, pg. 334
SARTOGA NATIONAL BANK & TRUST COMPANY—See Arrow Financial Corporation; *U.S. Public*, pg. 135
SAS INSTITUTE INC.; *U.S. Private*, pg. 966
SASAL—See Bertrand Faure; *Int'l*, pg. 193
SASCO ELECTRIC—See Sasco Group; *U.S. Private*, pg. 967
SASCO GROUP; *U.S. Private*, pg. 967
SASCO/VALLEY ELECTRIC—See Sasco Group; *U.S. Private*, pg. 967
SASIB BAKERY HOLLAND N.V.—See SASIB SpA; *Int'l*, pg. 1194
SASIB BAKERY ITALIA S.P.A.—See SASIB SpA; *Int'l*, pg. 1194
SASIB BAKERY NORDIC A/S—See SASIB SpA; *Int'l*, pg. 1194
SASIB BAKERY NORTH AMERICA INC.—See SASIB SpA; *Int'l*, pg. 1194
SASIB BAKERY UK LTD.—See SASIB SpA; *Int'l*, pg. 1194
SASIB BEVERAGE & FOOD N.A., INC.—See SASIB SpA; *Int'l*, pg. 1194
SASIB BEVERAGE AUSTRALIA—See SASIB SpA; *Int'l*, pg. 1194
SASIB BEVERAGE DEUTSCHLAND GMBH—See SASIB SpA; *Int'l*, pg. 1195

SASIB BEVERAGE IBERICA S.A.—See SASIB SpA; *Int'l*, pg. 1195
SASIB BEVERAGE MEXICANA S.A.—See SASIB SpA; *Int'l*, pg. 1195
SASIB BEVERAGE M.S. S.P.A.—See SASIB SpA; *Int'l*, pg. 1194
SASIB BEVERAGE S.P.A.—See SASIB SpA; *Int'l*, pg. 1194
SASIB BEVERAGE UK LTD.—See SASIB SpA; *Int'l*, pg. 1195
SASIB CORPORATION OF AMERICA—See SASIB SpA; *Int'l*, pg. 1194
SASIB FOOD S.P.A.-FOOD PROCESSING DIVISION—See SASIB SpA; *Int'l*, pg. 1194
SASIB FOOD S.P.A.-PACKAGING DIVISION—See SASIB SpA; *Int'l*, pg. 1194
SASIB HELLAS SIGNALING SYSTEMS I.C.S.A.—See SASIB SpA; *Int'l*, pg. 1195
SASIB HONG KONG LTD.—See SASIB SpA; *Int'l*, pg. 1195
SASIB LABELING S.P.A.—See SASIB SpA; *Int'l*, pg. 1194
SASIB MACHINERY (CHINA) COMPANY LIMITED—See SASIB SpA; *Int'l*, pg. 1195
SASIB PACIFIC SDN BHD—See SASIB SpA; *Int'l*, pg. 1195
SASIB PACKAGING ITALIA S.R.L.—See SASIB SpA; *Int'l*, pg. 1194
SASIB PACKAGING ITALIA S.R.L.-WRAPPER DIVISION—See SASIB SpA; *Int'l*, pg. 1194
SASIB PACKAGING NORTH AMERICA—See SASIB SpA; *Int'l*, pg. 1194
SASIB PACKAGING NORTH AMERICA INC.-WRAPPER DIVISION—See SASIB SpA; *Int'l*, pg. 1194
SASIB RAILWAY ELECTRIFICATION S.P.A.—See SASIB SpA; *Int'l*, pg. 1194
SASIB RAILWAY IBERICA S.A.—See SASIB SpA; *Int'l*, pg. 1195
SASIB RAILWAY S.P.A.—See SASIB SpA; *Int'l*, pg. 1194
SASIB S/A—See SASIB SpA; *Int'l*, pg. 1195
SASIB SPA; *Int'l*, pg. 1194
SASIB S.P.A.-TOBACCO DIVISION—See SASIB SpA; *Int'l*, pg. 1194
SASIB SUPPORT SERVICE (SSS)—See SASIB SpA; *Int'l*, pg. 1195
SASIB-WEST—See SASIB SpA; *Int'l*, pg. 1194
SASKATCHEWAN GOVERNMENT INSURANCE, SGI; *Int'l*, pg. 1195
SASKATCHEWAN MINERAL DIV.—See CSA Management Inc.; *Int'l*, pg. 243
SASKATCHEWAN WHEAT POOL; *Int'l*, pg. 1195
SASKPOWER; *Int'l*, pg. 1195
SASKPOWER COMMERCIAL—See SaskPower; *Int'l*, pg. 1196
SASOL AKRYLO—See Sasol Limited; *Int'l*, pg. 1196
SASOL ALPHA OLEFINS—See Sasol Limited; *Int'l*, pg. 1196
SASOL AMMONIA—See Sasol Limited; *Int'l*, pg. 1196
SASOL CARBO-TAR—See Sasol Limited; *Int'l*, pg. 1196
SASOL CHEMICAL INDUSTRIES LTD.—See Sasol Limited; *Int'l*, pg. 1196
SASOL CHEMICALS EUROPE LIMITED—See Sasol Limited; *Int'l*, pg. 1196
SASOL CHEMICALS PACIFIC LIMITED—See Sasol Limited; *Int'l*, pg. 1196
SASOL ENGINEERING DIVISION—See Sasol Limited; *Int'l*, pg. 1197
SASOL FERTILIZERS—See Sasol Limited; *Int'l*, pg. 1196
SASOL FIBRES—See Sasol Limited; *Int'l*, pg. 1196
SASOL FUEL OIL—See Sasol Limited; *Int'l*, pg. 1197
SASOL GAS—See Sasol Limited; *Int'l*, pg. 1197
SASOL LIMITED; *Int'l*, pg. 1196
SASOL MINCHEM—See Sasol Limited; *Int'l*, pg. 1196
SASOL MINING—See Sasol Limited; *Int'l*, pg. 1197
SASOL MINING EXPLOSIVES (SMX)—See Sasol Limited; *Int'l*, pg. 1196
SASOL MINING (PTY.) LTD.—See Sasol Limited; *Int'l*, pg. 1197
SASOL OIL—See Sasol Limited; *Int'l*, pg. 1197
SASOL OIL (PTY) LTD.—See Sasol Limited; *Int'l*, pg. 1197
SASOL PETROLEUM INTERNATIONAL (PTY) LTD.—See Sasol Limited; *Int'l*, pg. 1197
SASOL PHENOLICS—See Sasol Limited; *Int'l*, pg. 1196
SASOL SOLVENTS—See Sasol Limited; *Int'l*, pg. 1196
SASOL SYNTHETIC FUELS (PTY.) LTD.—See Sasol Limited; *Int'l*, pg. 1197
SASOL SYNTHETIC (OPERATING DIVISION)—See Sasol Limited; *Int'l*, pg. 1197
SASOL TECHNOLOGY DIVISION—See Sasol Limited; *Int'l*, pg. 1197
SASOL TECHNOLOGY (PTY) LTD.—See Sasol Limited; *Int'l*, pg. 1197
SASOL THREE DIV.—See Sasol Limited; *Int'l*, pg. 1197
SASOL TWO DIV.—See Sasol Limited; *Int'l*, pg. 1197
SASOLCHEM—See Sasol Limited; *Int'l*, pg. 1196
SASSON LICENSING CORP.; *U.S. Private*, pg. 967
SATAM S.A.—See Maison Mathieu, S.A.; *Int'l*, pg. 846
SATCHWELL CONTROL SYSTEMS LTD.—See Siebe plc; *Int'l*, pg. 1241
SATCOM INTERNATIONAL—See British Aerospace p.l.c.; *Int'l*, pg. 218
SATCOM TECHNOLOGIES DIVISION—See COMSAT Corporation; *U.S. Public*, pg. 424
SATE-LITE MANUFACTURING COMPANY—See Jordan Industries, Inc.; *U.S. Private*, pg. 598
SATEC SYSTEMS INC.; *U.S. Private*, pg. 967
SATEL FERNSEH- UND FILMPRODUKTIONS GMBH—See Creditanstalt-Bankverein; *Int'l*, pg. 347
SATELLITE BUSINESS TELEVISION BV—See KPN Koninklyke PTT Nederland NV; *Int'l*, pg. 720
SATELLITE DATA BROADCAST NETWORKS, INC. (SATNET)—See The Associated Press; *U.S. Private*, pg. 92
SATELLITE DATA NETWORKS—See General Instrument Corporation; *U.S. Public*, pg. 716
SATELLITE NETWORKS DIVISION—See COMSAT Corporation; *U.S. Public*, pg. 424

SATELLITE PLANT JUATUBA—See TI Group plc; *Int'l*, pg. 1342
SATELLITE TECHNICAL MANAGEMENT—See SGS Societe Generale de Surveillance Holding S.A.; *Int'l*, pg. 1154
SATELLITE TECHNOLOGY GROUP—See Uniden Corporation; *Int'l*, pg. 1433
SATHERS INC.—See Favorite Brands International, Inc.; *U.S. Private*, pg. 397
SATO AMOY CONSTRUCTION (MALAYSIA) SDN. BHD.—See Sato Kogyo Co., Ltd.; *Int'l*, pg. 1197
SATO ENGINEERING CONSULTANTS, INC.—See Sato Kogyo Co., Ltd.; *Int'l*, pg. 1197
SATO KOGYO CO., LTD.; *Int'l*, pg. 1197
SATO KOGYO CO., LTD.-HANOI—See Sato Kogyo Co., Ltd.; *Int'l*, pg. 1197
SATO KOGYO CO., LTD.-BANGKOK—See Sato Kogyo Co., Ltd.; *Int'l*, pg. 1197
SATO KOGYO CO., LTD.-KUALA LUMPUR—See Sato Kogyo Co., Ltd.; *Int'l*, pg. 1197
SATO KOGYO CO., LTD.-PARIS—See Sato Kogyo Co., Ltd.; *Int'l*, pg. 1197
SATO KOGYO CO., LTD.-SINGAPORE—See Sato Kogyo Co., Ltd.; *Int'l*, pg. 1197
SATO KOGYO (M) SDN. BHD.—See Sato Kogyo Co., Ltd.; *Int'l*, pg. 1197
SATO KOGYO U.S.A. CORPORATION—See Sato Kogyo Co., Ltd.; *Int'l*, pg. 1197
SATO KOGYO U.S.A. CORPORATION - ATLANTA—See Sato Kogyo Co., Ltd.; *Int'l*, pg. 1197
SATO KOGYO U.S.A. CORPORATION - LOS ANGELES—See Sato Kogyo Co., Ltd.; *Int'l*, pg. 1197
PT. SATOMO INDOVYL POLYMER—See Tosoh Corporation; *Int'l*, pg. 1408
SATTCONTROL AB—See Tetra Laval Group; *Int'l*, pg. 1378
THE SATURDAY EVENING POST SOCIETY—See Benjamin Franklin Literary & Medical Society, Inc.; *U.S. Private*, pg. 133
SATURDAY NIGHT MAGAZINE LIMITED—See Hollinger Inc.; *Int'l*, pg. 631
THE SATURN CORPORATION—See General Motors Corporation; *U.S. Public*, pg. 721
SATURN OF FARMINGTON—See Don Massey Cadillac Inc.; *U.S. Private*, pg. 713
SATURN OF GREENWOOD—See Lockhart Cadillac Inc.; *U.S. Private*, pg. 672
SATURN OF INDIANAPOLIS—See Lockhart Cadillac Inc.; *U.S. Private*, pg. 672
SATURN OF OKEMOS—See Don Massey Cadillac Inc.; *U.S. Private*, pg. 713
SATURN OF PLYMOUTH—See Don Massey Cadillac Inc.; *U.S. Private*, pg. 713
SAU-SEA FOODS, INC.; *U.S. Private*, pg. 967
SAUDER MANUFACTURING CORPORATION; *U.S. Private*, pg. 967
SAUDER WOODWORKING CO.; *U.S. Private*, pg. 967
SAUDI AMERICAN BANK—See Citicorp; *U.S. Public*, pg. 379
SAUDI AMERICAN GENERAL ELECTRIC—See General Electric Company; *U.S. Public*, pg. 713
SAUDI ARABIA CONCRETE PRODUCTS LTD.—See Ameron International Corporation; *U.S. Public*, pg. 99
SAUDI ARABIAN BIOKAT LTD.—See Mannesmann A.G.; *Int'l*, pg. 837
SAUDI ARABIAN PARSONS LTD.—See Parsons Corporation; *U.S. Private*, pg. 842
SAUDI ARABIAN TEXACO INC.—See Texaco Inc.; *U.S. Public*, pg. 1583
THE SAUDI BRITISH BANK—See HSBC Holdings plc; *Int'l*, pg. 583
SAUDI BUILDING SYSTEMS, LTD.—See Butler Manufacturing Company; *U.S. Public*, pg. 271
SAUDI CRAWFORD DOORS FACTORY LTD.—See Cardo AB; *Int'l*, pg. 270
SAUDI ELECTRO-MECHANICAL CONSTRUCTION CO. (PETCON)—See Abdulla Fouad Co. Ltd.; *Int'l*, pg. 502
SAUDI ERICSSON COMMUNICATIONS CO. LTD.—See Telefonaktiebolaget LM Ericsson; *Int'l*, pg. 1369
SAUDI FACTORY FOR ELECTRICAL APPLIANCES COMPANY LTD.—See Mitsubishi Heavy Industries Ltd.; *Int'l*, pg. 874
SAUDI FOOD INDUSTRIES LTD. LIABILITY CO.—See Nestle S.A.; *Int'l*, pg. 922
SAUDI INDUSTRIAL RESINS LTD.—See Ashland, Inc.; *U.S. Public*, pg. 140
SAUDI LIEBHERR COMPANY LTD.—See Liebherr-International AG; *Int'l*, pg. 809
SAUDI NATIONAL INSURANCE COMPANY EC (SNIC)—See Zurich Insurance Company; *Int'l*, pg. 1532
SAUDI SNC-LAVALIN COMPANY LIMITED—See SNC-Lavalin Group Inc.; *Int'l*, pg. 1163
SAUDI-SWISS BANK—See Union Bank of Switzerland; *Int'l*, pg. 1440
SAUDI TKT AIR CONDITIONING COMPANY LTD.—See Deutsche Babcock AG; *Int'l*, pg. 400
SAUER HOLDINGS—See Sauer Industries, Inc.; *U.S. Private*, pg. 968
SAUER INDUSTRIES, INC.; *U.S. Private*, pg. 967
J.P. SAUER & SOHN GMBH—See SIG Schweizerische Industrie-Gesellschaft Holding AG; *Int'l*, pg. 1156
SAUER-SUNDSTRAND—See Sauer Sundstrand Gmbh & Co.; *Int'l*, pg. 1198
SAUER-SUNDSTRAND BENELUX BV—See Sauer Sundstrand Gmbh & Co.; *Int'l*, pg. 1198
SAUER-SUNDSTRAND BENELUX N.V.—See Sauer Sundstrand Gmbh & Co.; *Int'l*, pg. 1198
SAUER-SUNDSTRAND COMPANY—See Sauer Sundstrand Gmbh & Co.; *Int'l*, pg. 1198
SAUER-SUNDSTRAND CS—See Sauer Sundstrand Gmbh & Co.; *Int'l*, pg. 1198
SAUER SUNDSTRAND GMBH & CO.; *Int'l*, pg. 1198
SAUER-SUNDSTRAND HYDRAULIQUE S.A.—See Sauer Sundstrand Gmbh & Co.; *Int'l*, pg. 1198

SAUER-SUNDSTRAND IBERICA S.A.—See Sauer Sundstrand Gmbh & Co.; *Int'l,* pg. 1198
SAUER-SUNDSTRAND LTD.—See Sauer Sundstrand Gmbh & Co.; *Int'l,* pg. 1198
SAUER-SUNDSTRAND S.P.A.—See Sauer Sundstrand Gmbh & Co.; *Int'l,* pg. 1198
SAUER-SUNDSTRAND SVENSKA AB—See Sauer Sundstrand Gmbh & Co.; *Int'l,* pg. 1198
SAUGBRUG TRELAST A/S—See Norske Skogindustrier A.S; *Int'l,* pg. 966
SAUGBRUGSFORENINGEN AS—See Norske Skogindustrier A.S; *Int'l,* pg. 966
B.F. SAUL ADVISORY CO.—See Saul Centers Inc.; *U.S. Public,* pg. 1435
SAUL BROS. & COMPANY, INC.; *U.S. Private,* pg. 968
SAUL CENTERS INC.; *U.S. Public,* pg. 1435
SAULT STE. MARIE BRIDGE CO.—See Wisconsin Central Transportation Corporation; *U.S. Public,* pg. 1772
THE SAULT STAR LTD.—See Hollinger Inc.; *Int'l,* pg. 631
SAUNDERS BROTHERS; *U.S. Private,* pg. 968
SAUNDERS OIL COMPANY, INC.; *U.S. Private,* pg. 968
SAUNDERS REALTY CORPORATION—See Trans-Lux Corporation; *U.S. Public,* pg. 1629
SAUNDERS VALVE CO. LTD.—See Tetra Laval Group; *Int'l,* pg. 1379
SAUNDERS VALVE, INC.—See Tetra Laval Group; *Int'l,* pg. 1379
W.B. SAUNDERS COMPANY—See Harcourt General, Inc.; *U.S. Public,* pg. 784
SAUNIER DUVAL BELGIQUE S.A.—See Hepworth Plc; *Int'l,* pg. 615
SAUNIER DUVAL EAU CHAUDE CHAUFFAGE SA—See Hepworth Plc; *Int'l,* pg. 615
SAUNIER DUVAL ITALIA SRL—See Hepworth Plc; *Int'l,* pg. 615
SAUNIER DUVAL NEDERLAND BV—See Hepworth Plc; *Int'l,* pg. 615
K.G. SAUR—See Reed Elsevier plc; *Int'l,* pg. 1099
SAURER AG; *Int'l,* pg. 1198
SAV-ON—See American Stores Company; *U.S. Public,* pg. 93
SAV-ON, INC.—See Tandycrafts, Inc.; *U.S. Public,* pg. 1561
SAVA LEASING S.P.A.—See Fiat Auto SpA; *Int'l,* pg. 482
SAVACENTRE LIMITED—See J. Sainsbury plc; *Int'l,* pg. 1170
SAVAFACTORING S.P.A.—See Fiat Auto SpA; *Int'l,* pg. 482
SAVAFINBUS S.P.A.—See Fiat Auto SpA; *Int'l,* pg. 482
SAVAGE ARMS INC.; *U.S. Private,* pg. 968
SAVAGLIO TBWA & ASSOCIADOS S.A.—See TBWA Chiat/Day; *U.S. Private,* pg. 1063
SAVAL B.V., PRINSENBEEK—See Internatio-Muller N.V.; *Int'l,* pg. 681
SAVAL N.V.—See Internatio-Muller N.V.; *Int'l,* pg. 681
SAVANNAH BANK OF NIGERIA LTD.—See BankAmerica Corporation; *U.S. Public,* pg. 183
SAVANNAH CONVALESCENT CENTER—See Vencor, Inc.; *U.S. Public,* pg. 1714
SAVANNAH ELECTRIC & POWER CO.—See Southern Company; *U.S. Public,* pg. 1490
SAVANNAH FOODS & INDUSTRIES, INC.—See Imperial Holly Corporation; *U.S. Public,* pg. 872
SAVANNAH INVESTMENT COMPANY—See Imperial Holly Corporation; *U.S. Public,* pg. 873
SAVANNAH LEARNING CENTER—See Berkshire Hathaway Inc.; *U.S. Public,* pg. 219
SAVANT INSTRUMENTS INC.—See Thermo Electron Corporation; *U.S. Public,* pg. 1595
SAVARA PURFLUX SRL—See Labinal SA; *Int'l,* pg. 786
SAVE-A-LOT—See Houchens Industries Inc.; *U.S. Private,* pg. 541
SAVE-A-LOT, INC.—See SuperValu, Inc.; *U.S. Public,* pg. 1541
SAVE MART SUPERMARKETS; *U.S. Private,* pg. 968
SAVE & PROSPER GROUP LIMITED—See Robert Fleming Holdings Ltd.; *Int'l,* pg. 493
SAVIA S.A.—See Tesco PLC; *Int'l,* pg. 1376
SAVILLE TRACTORS (BELFAST) LTD.—See Lonrho plc; *Int'l,* pg. 817
SAVILLE TRACTORS LTD.—See Lonrho plc; *Int'l,* pg. 817
SAVILLES AUTO VILLAGE LTD.—See Lonrho plc; *Int'l,* pg. 817
SAVIM—See Manitou BF; *Int'l,* pg. 834
SAVIMA—See Groupe Casino; *Int'l,* pg. 563
SAVIN CANADA INC.—See Ricoh Company, Ltd.; *Int'l,* pg. 1116
SAVIN CORPORATION—See Ricoh Company, Ltd.; *Int'l,* pg. 1114
SAVIN CREDIT CORPORATION—See Ricoh Company, Ltd.; *Int'l,* pg. 1114
SAVIN OF TAMPA BAY—See Ricoh Company, Ltd.; *Int'l,* pg. 1114
SAVINGS OF AMERICA INC.—See H.F. Ahmanson & Co.; *U.S. Public,* pg. 29
SAVO PROCUREMENT AREA—See Enso Oyj; *Int'l,* pg. 455
THE SAVOGRAN COMPANY; *U.S. Private,* pg. 968
MIKE SAVOIE CHEVROLET INC.; *U.S. Private,* pg. 968
SAVOIE REFRACTAIRES—See Saint-Gobain; *Int'l,* pg. 1176
SAVON SELLU OY—See Metsa-Serla Corporation; *Int'l,* pg. 863
SAVONLINNA MILL—See UPM-Kymmene Corporation; *Int'l,* pg. 1429
SAVORY CO., LTD.—See Matsuya Company Ltd.; *Int'l,* pg. 848
SAVORY PAPER LTD—See N.V. Koninklijke KNP BT; *Int'l,* pg. 757
SAVOY DRAPERY DIV.—See Trace International Holdings, Inc.; *U.S. Private,* pg. 1094
SAVSJO FALGAR AB—See Trelleborg AB; *Int'l,* pg. 1422
SAW CONSTRUCTION CORPORATION—See Stone & Webster, Incorporated; *U.S. Public,* pg. 1519

SAW DRILLING, INC.—See Stone & Webster, Incorporated; *U.S. Public,* pg. 1519
SAWGRASS ELECTRONICS GROUP INC.; *U.S. Private,* pg. 968
SAWHILL TUBULAR DIV.—See Armco Inc.; *U.S. Public,* pg. 131
THE SAWTOOTH GROUP; *U.S. Private,* pg. 969
SAWYER RILEY COMPTON INC.; *U.S. Private,* pg. 969
SAX ARTS & CRAFTS, INC.—See U.S. Office Products Company; *U.S. Public,* pg. 1687
RON SAXON FORD, INC.; *U.S. Private,* pg. 969
SAXONIA BAUSTOFFE GMBH—See Veba AG; *Int'l,* pg. 1459
SAXONY DISTILLERS ET CIE, INC.—See Charles Jacquin et Cie, Inc.; *U.S. Private,* pg. 580
SAXTON—See Kuhlman Corporation; *U.S. Public,* pg. 968
SAYAMA PRECISION INDUSTRIES CO., LTD.—See Citizen Watch Company, Ltd.; *Int'l,* pg. 294
SAYANAL—See Reynolds Metals Company; *U.S. Public,* pg. 1387
CECIL SAYDAH COMPANY; *U.S. Private,* pg. 969
SAYERLACK INDUSTRIA VERNICI SPECIALI S.P.A.—See Hickson International Plc; *Int'l,* pg. 619
SAYLOR LANE CONVALESCENT HOSPITAL—See Vencor, Inc.; *U.S. Public,* pg. 1714
SAZTEC EUROPE LTD.—See Saztec International, Inc.; *U.S. Public,* pg. 1435
SAZTEC INTERNATIONAL, INC.; *U.S. Public,* pg. 1435
SBARRO, INC.; *U.S. Public,* pg. 1435
SCAB ELETTRONICA SYSTEMS SPA—See Williams Holdings Plc; *Int'l,* pg. 1500
SCABA AB—See Cardo AB; *Int'l,* pg. 270
SCABA PRODUCTION AB—See Cardo AB; *Int'l,* pg. 270
SCALAMANDRE, INC.; *U.S. Private,* pg. 969
SCALDIA-BUHRMANN NV—See N.V. Koninklijke KNP BT; *Int'l,* pg. 757
SCALED COMPOSITES, INC.—See Wyman-Gordon; *U.S. Public,* pg. 1782
SCALES TRANSPORT CORPORATION—See Ameritruck Distribution Corporation; *U.S. Public,* pg. 66
SCAMP AUTO—See Chrysler Corporation; *U.S. Public,* pg. 354
SCAN-AD GRUPPEN A/S; *Int'l,* pg. 1198
SCAN-AD HADERSLEV A/S—See Scan-Ad Gruppen A/S; *Int'l,* pg. 1198
SCAN-AD KOBENHAVN A/S—See Scan-Ad Gruppen A/S; *Int'l,* pg. 1198
SCAN-AD ODENSE A/S—See Scan-Ad Gruppen A/S; *Int'l,* pg. 1198
A/S SCAN-ATLAS HUSHOLDNINGSAPPARATER—See Electrolux, AB; *Int'l,* pg. 441
OY SCAN-AUTO AB—See Investor AB; *Int'l,* pg. 686
OY SCAN-AUTO AB—See Valmet Corporation; *Int'l,* pg. 1449
SCAN CARE A/S—See ISS-International Service System A/S; *Int'l,* pg. 656
SCAN CONTROL SERVICES—See Alcatel Alsthom Compagnie Generale D'Electricite; *Int'l,* pg. 53
SCAN GLOBE A/S—See Replogle Globes, Inc.; *U.S. Private,* pg. 923
SCAN GOBAIN GLASS A/S—See Saint-Gobain; *Int'l,* pg. 1173
SCAN-OPTICS (CANADA), LTD.—See Scan-Optics, Inc.; *U.S. Public,* pg. 1436
SCAN-OPTICS GMBH—See Scan-Optics, Inc.; *U.S. Public,* pg. 1436
SCAN-OPTICS, INC.; *U.S. Public,* pg. 1436
SCAN-OPTICS, LTD.—See Scan-Optics, Inc.; *U.S. Public,* pg. 1436
SCANA—See SCANA Corporation; *U.S. Public,* pg. 1436
SCANA CORPORATION; *U.S. Public,* pg. 1436
SCANA ENERGY MARKETING INC.—See SCANA Corporation; *U.S. Public,* pg. 1436
SCANA PETROLEUM RESOURCES, INC.—See SCANA Corporation; *U.S. Public,* pg. 1436
SCANA RESOURCES, INC.—See SCANA Corporation; *U.S. Public,* pg. 1436
SCANALYTICS—See CSP Inc.; *U.S. Public,* pg. 283
SCANBETON INDUSTRIE GMBH—See Scancem AB; *Int'l,* pg. 1200
SCANCABLES AB—See Telefonaktiebolaget LM Ericsson; *Int'l,* pg. 1363
SCANCEM AB; *Int'l,* pg. 1198
A/S SCANCEM CHEMICALS—See Scancem AB; *Int'l,* pg. 1199
SCANCEM FASTIGHETER AB—See Scancem AB; *Int'l,* pg. 1200
SCANCEM INDUSTRIES, INC.—See Scancem AB; *Int'l,* pg. 1201
SCANCEM INTERNATIONAL ANS—See Scancem AB; *Int'l,* pg. 1201
SCANCEM RESEARCH AB—See Scancem AB; *Int'l,* pg. 1200
SCANCEM SERVICE AB—See Scancem AB; *Int'l,* pg. 1200
SCANDATA S.A.—See BancTec, Inc.; *U.S. Public,* pg. 177
SCANDEX ALUMINIUM N.V.—See Electrolux, AB; *Int'l,* pg. 443
SCANDI-GLASS A/S—See Saint-Gobain; *Int'l,* pg. 1173
SCANDIA DOWN SHOPS LIMITED—See Hanover Direct, Inc.; *U.S. Public,* pg. 782
A/S SCANDIA KJEMISKE—See Jotun A/S; *Int'l,* pg. 715
SCANDIAFELT IT AB—See Scapa Group Plc; *Int'l,* pg. 1203
SCANDIFLOAT AB—See Saint-Gobain; *Int'l,* pg. 1173
SCANDINAVIA TELEPHONE CO.—See Telephone and Data Systems, Inc.; *U.S. Public,* pg. 1571
SCANDINAVIAN AIRLINES SYSTEM (SAS); *Int'l,* pg. 1201
SCANDINAVIAN BELLYLOADING CO. AB—See Teleflex Incorporated; *U.S. Public,* pg. 1570
SCANDINAVIAN HEART CENTER AB—See Incentive AB; *Int'l,* pg. 670
SCANDINAVIAN LEISURE GROUP A.B.—See Airtours Plc; *Int'l,* pg. 39

SCANDINAVISKA ENSKILDA BANKEN LONDON—See Skandinaviska Enskilda Banken; *Int'l,* pg. 1259
SCANDURA CANADA INC.—See BBA Group plc; *Int'l,* pg. 114
SCANDURA INC.—See BBA Group plc; *Int'l,* pg. 113
SCANDURA OHIO INC.—See BBA Group plc; *Int'l,* pg. 113
SCANDUST AB—See AB SKF; *Int'l,* pg. 1157
SCANFORMS, INC.—See Big Flower Press Holdings, Inc.; *U.S. Public,* pg. 228
SCANGAS BROTHERS HOLDINGS, INC.; *U.S. Private,* pg. 969
SCANGLAS A/S—See Saint-Gobain; *Int'l,* pg. 1173
SCANGLAS LTD.—See Owens Corning; *U.S. Public,* pg. 1237
SCANIA ARGENTINA S.A.—See Investor AB; *Int'l,* pg. 687
SCANIA AUSTRALIA PTY. LTD.—See Investor AB; *Int'l,* pg. 687
SCANIA BELGIUM SA-NV—See Investor AB; *Int'l,* pg. 687
SCANIA-BUSSAR AB—See Investor AB; *Int'l,* pg. 687
SCANIA DANMARK A/S—See Investor AB; *Int'l,* pg. 687
SCANIA DEUTSCHLAND GMBH—See Investor AB; *Int'l,* pg. 687
SCANIA DIVISION—See Investor AB; *Int'l,* pg. 687
SCANIA DO BRASIL LTDA—See Investor AB; *Int'l,* pg. 687
SCANIA FRANCE S.A.—See Investor AB; *Int'l,* pg. 687
SCANIA (GREAT BRITAIN) LTD.—See Investor AB; *Int'l,* pg. 687
SCANIA NEDERLAND B.V.—See Investor AB; *Int'l,* pg. 687
SCANIA OSTERREICH GES.M.B.H.—See Investor AB; *Int'l,* pg. 687
SCANIA USA INC.—See Investor AB; *Int'l,* pg. 687
SCANIA-VABIS DEL PERU S.A.—See Investor AB; *Int'l,* pg. 687
SCANLAB SDN. BHD.—See Tiedemanns - Joh.H.Andresen ANS; *Int'l,* pg. 1390
SCANLAND AGENCIES LTD.—See Norske Skogindustrier A.S; *Int'l,* pg. 967
SCANPOINT TECHNOLOGY A/S—See Cubic Corporation; *U.S. Public,* pg. 466
SCANSPED GROUP—See BTL AB; *Int'l,* pg. 123
SCANSTONE GROUP—See Scancem AB; *Int'l,* pg. 1199
SCANTRON CORPORATION—See John H. Harland Company; *U.S. Public,* pg. 786
SCANVEST OLIVETTI A/S—See Olivetti SpA; *Int'l,* pg. 1004
SCAPA CANADA, INC.—See Scapa Group Plc; *Int'l,* pg. 1203
SCAPA DE MEXICO S.A. DE C.V.—See Scapa Group Plc; *Int'l,* pg. 1203
SCAPA DRYER FABRICS, INC.—See Scapa Group Plc; *Int'l,* pg. 1202
SCAPA GROUP PLC; *Int'l,* pg. 1202
SCAPA ITALIA—See Accor S.A.; *Int'l,* pg. 21
SCAPA-KERN GMBH—See Scapa Group Plc; *Int'l,* pg. 1203
SCAPA-KERN WALZENSERVICE GMBH—See Scapa Group Plc; *Int'l,* pg. 1203
SCAPA MOULDINGS LTD.—See Scapa Group Plc; *Int'l,* pg. 1202
SCAPA SCANDIA AB—See Scapa Group Plc; *Int'l,* pg. 1203
SCAPA SCANDIA (ASIA) SDN. BHD.—See Scapa Group Plc; *Int'l,* pg. 1203
SCAPA SCANDIA (AUSTRALASIA) LTD.—See Scapa Group Plc; *Int'l,* pg. 1203
SCAPA SCANDIA (ESPANA) S.A.—See Scapa Group Plc; *Int'l,* pg. 1203
SCAPA SCANDIA LTD.—See Scapa Group Plc; *Int'l,* pg. 1202
SCAPA SCANDIA S.A. (PROPRIETARY) LTD.—See Scapa Group Plc; *Int'l,* pg. 1203
SCARBOROUGH CENTER—See The Cascades Group; *Int'l,* pg. 273
SCARBOROUGH RESEARCH CORPORATION—See VNU Verenigde Nederlandse Uitgeversbedrijven B.V.; *Int'l,* pg. 1447
SCARECROW PRESS, INC.—See Lagardere Groupe; *Int'l,* pg. 794
SCARFINI S.P.A.—See Telefonaktiebolaget LM Ericsson; *Int'l,* pg. 1369
SCAW METAL LTD.—See Anglo American Corporation of South Africa Limited; *Int'l,* pg. 76
SCENIC AIRLINES INC.—See SkyWest Inc.; *U.S. Public,* pg. 1476
SCEPTRE HOSPITALITY RESOURCES, INC.—See Richfield Hospitality Services; *U.S. Private,* pg. 929
SCEPTRE RESOURCES LIMITED; *Int'l,* pg. 1203
SCETA VOYAGEURS—See SNCF; *Int'l,* pg. 1165
SCHAAKE CORPORATION; *U.S. Private,* pg. 969
SCHAAP & CITROEN—See Vendex International N.V.; *Int'l,* pg. 1462
SCHABMULLER GMBH—See Thrige-Titan Group; *Int'l,* pg. 1387
SCHACHENMANN & CO. AG—See Sulzer Ltd.; *Int'l,* pg. 1306
N.V. SCHADEVERZELERING MIJ. DE NEDERLANDEN VAN 1870—See Assicurazioni Generali S.p.A.; *Int'l,* pg. 92
SCHAEDLER BROTHERS, INC.; *U.S. Private,* pg. 969
MIDO G. SCHAEREN & CO., SA—See SMH Swiss Corporation for Micro Electronics & Watchmaking Indus. Ltd.; *Int'l,* pg. 1161
SCHAFFER-POESCHEL VERLAG—See Georg von Holtzbrinck GmbH; *Int'l,* pg. 1478
SCHAFFNER-BEHREND AG—See GKN plc; *Int'l,* pg. 536
SCHAFFT FLEISCHWERKE G.M.B.H.—See Unilever Plc; *Int'l,* pg. 1438
SCHAL BOVIS INC.—See The Peninsular and Oriental Steam Navigation Company; *Int'l,* pg. 1033
SCHALTAG AG—See Rieter Holdings; *Int'l,* pg. 1116
SCHAUMAN B.V.—See UPM-Kymmene Corporation; *Int'l,* pg. 1429

Company Index

SCHAUMAN IBERICA S.A.—See UPM-Kymmene Corporation; *Int'l*, pg. 1429
SCHAUMAN PANELS LTD.—See UPM-Kymmene Corporation; *Int'l*, pg. 1429
SCHAUMAN S.A.—See UPM-Kymmene Corporation; *Int'l*, pg. 1429
SCHAUMAN (UK) LTD.—See UPM-Kymmene Corporation; *Int'l*, pg. 1429
WILH. SCHAUMAN GMBH—See UPM-Kymmene Corporation; *Int'l*, pg. 1429
SCHAUMAN WOOD AB—See UPM-Kymmene Corporation; *Int'l*, pg. 1429
SCHAUMAN WOOD OY—See UPM-Kymmene Corporation; *Int'l*, pg. 1428
SCHAUMAN WOOD OY-ISTANBUL OFFICE—See UPM-Kymmene Corporation; *Int'l*, pg. 1429
SCHAUMAN WOOD OY-REGIONAL OFFICE—See UPM-Kymmene Corporation; *Int'l*, pg. 1429
SCHAWK, INC.; *U.S. Public*, pg. 1437
SCHAWKGRAPHICS—See Schawk, Inc.; *U.S. Public*, pg. 1437
THE SCHEBLER CO.—See Egan Cos.; *U.S. Private*, pg. 366
DIETER SCHEEL GMBH—See Korf-Transport-GmbH; *Int'l*, pg. 759
EARL SCHEIB AUTOMOTIVE PAINT FINISHES, INC.—See Earl Scheib, Inc.; *U.S. Public*, pg. 1437
EARL SCHEIB, INC.; *U.S. Public*, pg. 1437
EARL SCHEIB REALTY CORP.—See Earl Scheib, Inc.; *U.S. Public*, pg. 1437
SCHEID STRASSENBAUGESELLSCHAFT MBH—See Philipp Holzmann AG; *Int'l*, pg. 633
HENRY SCHEIN, INC.; *U.S. Public*, pg. 1437
SCHEIN PHARMACEUTICAL, INC.; *U.S. Private*, pg. 969
SCHELDE CHEMIE BRUNSBUTTEL GMBH—See Bayer AG; *Int'l*, pg. 172
LEO SCHELLENS B.V.—See Gamma Holding N.V.; *Int'l*, pg. 540
SCHEMA S.P.A.—See Compagnie des Machines Bull; *Int'l*, pg. 318
SCHENECTADY AUSTRALIA PTY. LTD.—See Schenectady International, Inc.; *U.S. Private*, pg. 970
SCHENECTADY BRASIL LIMITADA—See Schenectady International, Inc.; *U.S. Private*, pg. 970
SCHENECTADY CANADA LTD.—See Schenectady International, Inc.; *U.S. Private*, pg. 970
SCHENECTADY EUROPE, LTD.—See Schenectady International, Inc.; *U.S. Private*, pg. 970
SCHENECTADY EUROPE, S.A.—See Schenectady International, Inc.; *U.S. Private*, pg. 970
SCHENECTADY INTERNATIONAL, INC.; *U.S. Private*, pg. 969
SCHENECTADY MEXICO, S.A.—See Schenectady International, Inc.; *U.S. Private*, pg. 970
SCHENECTADY PRATTELN, AG—See Schenectady International, Inc.; *U.S. Private*, pg. 970
SCHENECTADY PRATTELN A.G.—See Schenectady International, Inc.; *U.S. Private*, pg. 970
SCHENKER & CO. AG—See Veba AG; *Int'l*, pg. 1460
SCHENKER EUROCARGO AG—See Veba AG; *Int'l*, pg. 1459
SCHENKER INTERNATIONAL AG—See Veba AG; *Int'l*, pg. 1459
SCHENKER-RHENUS AG—See Veba AG; *Int'l*, pg. 1459
SCHENKERS INTERNATIONAL FORWARDERS, INC.—See Veba AG; *Int'l*, pg. 1459
SCHERAX ARZNEIMITTEL GMBH—See Schering AG; *Int'l*, pg. 1203
SCHERBAUER SPEDITION GMBH—See Royal Nedlloyd Group N.V.; *Int'l*, pg. 1145
SCHERER BROS. LUMBER COMPANY; *U.S. Private*, pg. 970
SCHERER DDS LTD.—See R.P. Scherer Corporation; *U.S. Public*, pg. 1438
SCHERER HEALTHCARE, INC.; *U.S. Public*, pg. 1437
R.P. SCHERER ARGENTINA S.A.I.C.—See R.P. Scherer Corporation; *U.S. Public*, pg. 1438
R.P. SCHERER CORPORATION; *U.S. Public*, pg. 1437
R.P. SCHERER DO BRASIL ENCAPSULACOES LTDA.—See R.P. Scherer Corporation; *U.S. Public*, pg. 1438
R.P. SCHERER EGYPT—See R.P. Scherer Corporation; *U.S. Public*, pg. 1438
R.P. SCHERER (EUROPE) AG—See R.P. Scherer Corporation; *U.S. Public*, pg. 1438
R.P. SCHERER GMBH—See R.P. Scherer Corporation; *U.S. Public*, pg. 1438
R.P. SCHERER GMBH-WERK STREHLA—See R.P. Scherer Corporation; *U.S. Public*, pg. 1438
R.P. SCHERER HOLDINGS PTY. LTD.—See R.P. Scherer Corporation; *U.S. Public*, pg. 1438
R.P. SCHERER K.K.—See R.P. Scherer Corporation; *U.S. Public*, pg. 1438
R.P. SCHERER KOREA LIMITED—See R.P. Scherer Corporation; *U.S. Public*, pg. 1438
R.P. SCHERER LIMITED—See R.P. Scherer Corporation; *U.S. Public*, pg. 1438
R.P. SCHERER NORTH AMERICA—See R.P. Scherer Corporation; *U.S. Public*, pg. 1438
R.P. SCHERER PRODUCTION S.A.—See R.P. Scherer Corporation; *U.S. Public*, pg. 1438
R.P. SCHERER S.A.—See R.P. Scherer Corporation; *U.S. Public*, pg. 1438
R.P. SCHERER S.P.A.—See R.P. Scherer Corporation; *U.S. Public*, pg. 1438
SCHERING AG; *Int'l*, pg. 1203
SCHERING AGRO B.V.—See Schering AG; *Int'l*, pg. 1203
SCHERING ALMAN ILAC VE ECZA TICARET LTD.—See Schering AG; *Int'l*, pg. 1204
SCHERING ARGENTINA S.A.I.C.—See Schering AG; *Int'l*, pg. 1204
SCHERING A/S—See Schering AG; *Int'l*, pg. 1204
SCHERING BERLIN INC.—See Schering AG; *Int'l*, pg. 1204
SCHERING CHEMICALS LTD.—See Schering AG; *Int'l*, pg. 1204

SCHERING DO BRASIL LTDA.—See Schering AG; *Int'l*, pg. 1204
SCHERING ESPANA S. A.—See Schering AG; *Int'l*, pg. 1204
SCHERING HOLDINGS LTD.—See Schering AG; *Int'l*, pg. 1204
P.T. SCHERING INDONESIA—See Schering AG; *Int'l*, pg. 1204
SCHERING KOREA LTD.—See Schering AG; *Int'l*, pg. 1204
SCHERING LABORATORIES—See Schering-Plough Corporation; *U.S. Public*, pg. 1438
SCHERING MEXICANA SA—See Schering AG; *Int'l*, pg. 1204
SCHERING NEDERLAND B.V.—See Schering AG; *Int'l*, pg. 1204
SCHERING-PLOUGH ANIMAL HEALTH—See Schering-Plough Corporation; *U.S. Public*, pg. 1438
SCHERING PLOUGH BRASIL—See Schering-Plough Corporation; *U.S. Public*, pg. 1439
SCHERING-PLOUGH CORPORATION; *U.S. Public*, pg. 1438
SCHERING-PLOUGH HEALTHCARE PRODUCTS—See Schering-Plough Corporation; *U.S. Public*, pg. 1438
SCHERING-PLOUGH HEALTHCARE PRODUCTS INC.—See Schering-Plough Corporation; *U.S. Public*, pg. 1438
SCHERING-PLOUGH HOLDINGS LTD.—See Schering-Plough Corporation; *U.S. Public*, pg. 1439
SCHERING-PLOUGH INTERNATIONAL—See Schering-Plough Corporation; *U.S. Public*, pg. 1438
SCHERING-PLOUGH PHARMACEUTICALS—See Schering-Plough Corporation; *U.S. Public*, pg. 1438
SCHERING-PLOUGH RESEARCH INSTITUTE—See Schering-Plough Corporation; *U.S. Public*, pg. 1438
SCHERING PTY. LTD.—See Schering AG; *Int'l*, pg. 1204
SCHERING S.A.—See Schering AG; *Int'l*, pg. 1204
N.V. SCHERING S.A./BELGIEN—See Schering AG; *Int'l*, pg. 1204
SCHERING (SCHWEIZ) AG—See Schering AG; *Int'l*, pg. 1204
SCHERING S.P.A.—See Schering AG; *Int'l*, pg. 1204
SCHERING WIEN GES.M.B.H.—See Schering AG; *Int'l*, pg. 1204
SCHERZ VERLAG GMBH—See Georg von Holtzbrinck GmbH; *Int'l*, pg. 1480
SCHEU & WIRTH AG—See Philipp Holzmann AG; *Int'l*, pg. 633
CV SCHEUER VERZEKERINGEN—See Koninklijke Hoogovens N.V.; *Int'l*, pg. 755
E. SCHEURICH PHARMWERK GMBH—See American Home Products Corporation; *U.S. Public*, pg. 82
OTTO SCHEURMANN BANK-KG—See Dresdner Bank AG; *Int'l*, pg. 418
HEINRICH SCHEVEN ANLAGEN- UND LEITUNGSBAU GMBH—See Bilfinger + Berger Bauaktiengesellschaft; *Int'l*, pg. 195
SCHIAPPARELLI; *Int'l*, pg. 1204
SCHIAPPARELLI BIOSYSTEMS INC.—See Schiapparelli; *Int'l*, pg. 1204
SCHIAVI S.P.A.—See Bobst S.A.; *Int'l*, pg. 199
SCHIAVONE CONSTRUCTION CO.; *U.S. Private*, pg. 970
SCHICK NEDERLAND B.V.—See Warner-Lambert Company; *U.S. Public*, pg. 1739
DR. RUDOLF SCHIEBER CHEMISCHE FABRIK GMBH & CO. KG—See Henkel KGaA; *Int'l*, pg. 610
SCHIEDEL GMBH & CO.—See Redland PLC; *Int'l*, pg. 1091
SCHIEDEL KAMINWERKE GMBH—See Redland PLC; *Int'l*, pg. 1092
SCHIEDEL KEMENYGYAR KFT.—See Redland PLC; *Int'l*, pg. 1092
SCHIEDEL PROIZVODNJA DIMNJAKA D.D.—See Redland PLC; *Int'l*, pg. 1092
SCHIEDEL S.A.R.L.—See Redland PLC; *Int'l*, pg. 1092
SCHIEDEL SPOL. S R.O.—See Redland PLC; *Int'l*, pg. 1092
SCHIEFFELIN & SOMERSET CO.—See Diageo Plc; *Int'l*, pg. 412
SCHIEFFELIN & SOMERSET CO.—See LVMH Moet Hennessy Louis Vuitton; *Int'l*, pg. 781
SCHIESS-AMERICA CORP.—See Metallgesellschaft AG; *Int'l*, pg. 860
SCHIESS-METALNA GMBH—See Metallgesellschaft AG; *Int'l*, pg. 860
SCHIESS MOWEG GMBH—See Metallgesellschaft AG; *Int'l*, pg. 860
SCHIESS (UK) LTD.—See Metallgesellschaft AG; *Int'l*, pg. 860
SCHIESSER AG—See Hesta Tex AG; *Int'l*, pg. 618
SCHIESSER EMINENCE HOLDING AG—See Hesta Tex AG; *Int'l*, pg. 618
SCHIESSER-HELLAS S.R.L.—See Hesta Tex AG; *Int'l*, pg. 618
SCHIESSER INTERNATIONAL A/S—See Hesta Tex AG; *Int'l*, pg. 618
SCHIESSER INTERNATIONAL BELGIE N.V.—See Hesta Tex AG; *Int'l*, pg. 618
SCHIESSER INTERNATIONAL GES.M.B.H.—See Hesta Tex AG; *Int'l*, pg. 618
SCHIESSER INTERNATIONAL (IRELAND) LTD.—See Hesta Tex AG; *Int'l*, pg. 618
SCHIESSER INTERNATIONAL NEDERLAND BV—See Hesta Tex AG; *Int'l*, pg. 618
SCHIESSER INTERNATIONAL S.A.R.L.—See Hesta Tex AG; *Int'l*, pg. 618
SCHIESSER INTERNATIONAL S.R.L.—See Hesta Tex AG; *Int'l*, pg. 618
SCHIESSER INVERSIONES CHILE LTDA.—See Hesta Tex AG; *Int'l*, pg. 618
SCHIESSER IRELAND (TRADING) LTD.—See Hesta Tex AG; *Int'l*, pg. 618
SCHIESSER-PALLAS S.R.L.—See Hesta Tex AG; *Int'l*, pg. 618

SCHIESSER + SCHERRER AG—See Hesta Tex AG; *Int'l*, pg. 618
SCHIESSER SACHSEN AG—See Hesta Tex AG; *Int'l*, pg. 618
SCHIFFSBETRIEBSGESELLSCHAFT BREMEN MBH—See Commerzbank AG; *Int'l*, pg. 310
SCHILLING COMPANIES, INC.; *U.S. Private*, pg. 970
SCHILLING MOTORS, INC.—See Schilling Companies, Inc.; *U.S. Private*, pg. 970
SCHILLING PLANT—See McCormick & Company, Incorporated; *U.S. Public*, pg. 1066
SCHILPEROORT BEHEER, B.V.—See Sulzer Ltd.; *Int'l*, pg. 1306
SCHINAC B.V.—See Schindler Holding AG; *Int'l*, pg. 1205
SCHINDLER—See Schindler Holding AG; *Int'l*, pg. 1205
SCHINDLER ASCENSORI E MOTORI S.A.—See Schindler Holding AG; *Int'l*, pg. 1204
SCHINDLER AUFZUGE AG—See Schindler Holding AG; *Int'l*, pg. 1205
SCHINDLER AUFZUGE GMBH—See Schindler Holding AG; *Int'l*, pg. 1205
SCHINDLER AUFZUGE UND FAHRTREPPEN AG—See Schindler Holding AG; *Int'l*, pg. 1205
SCHINDLER AUFZUGEFABRIK GMBH—See Schindler Holding AG; *Int'l*, pg. 1205
SCHINDLER CORPORATION OF PUERTO RICO—See Schindler Holding AG; *Int'l*, pg. 1205
SCHINDLER ELEVATOR CORPORATION—See Schindler Holding AG; *Int'l*, pg. 1205
SCHINDLER ELEVATOR K.K.—See Schindler Holding AG; *Int'l*, pg. 1205
SCHINDLER ELEVATORER A/S—See Schindler Holding AG; *Int'l*, pg. 1205
SCHINDLER-GANZ LIFT GMBH—See Schindler Holding AG; *Int'l*, pg. 1205
SCHINDLER HISSI OY—See Schindler Holding AG; *Int'l*, pg. 1205
SCHINDLER HOLDING AG; *Int'l*, pg. 1204
SCHINDLER IMMOBILIENTREUHAND UND-VERWALTUNGS AG—See Schindler Holding AG; *Int'l*, pg. 1204
SCHINDLER INFORMATIK AG—See Schindler Holding AG; *Int'l*, pg. 1205
SCHINDLER LIFTAS AG—See Schindler Holding AG; *Int'l*, pg. 1205
SCHINDLER LIFTEN B.V.—See Schindler Holding AG; *Int'l*, pg. 1205
SCHINDLER LIFTS AUSTRALIA PTY. LTD.—See Schindler Holding AG; *Int'l*, pg. 1205
SCHINDLER LIFTS (HONG KONG) LTD.—See Schindler Holding AG; *Int'l*, pg. 1205
SCHINDLER LIFTS (NAMIBIA) (PTY) LTD.—See Schindler Holding AG; *Int'l*, pg. 1205
SCHINDLER LIFTS NZ LTD.—See Schindler Holding AG; *Int'l*, pg. 1205
SCHINDLER LIFTS (PTY) LTD.—See Schindler Holding AG; *Int'l*, pg. 1205
SCHINDLER LIFTS (PVT) LTD.—See Schindler Holding AG; *Int'l*, pg. 1205
SCHINDLER LIFTS (S.A.) (PTY) LTD.—See Schindler Holding AG; *Int'l*, pg. 1205
SCHINDLER LIFTS (ZIMBABWE) (PVT) LTD.—See Schindler Holding AG; *Int'l*, pg. 1205
SCHINDLER LTD.—See Schindler Holding AG; *Int'l*, pg. 1205
SCHINDLER MANAGEMENT AG—See Schindler Holding AG; *Int'l*, pg. 1204
SCHINDLER MONACO—See Schindler Holding AG; *Int'l*, pg. 1205
SCHINDLER-MOSMONTASH-LIFT—See Schindler Holding AG; *Int'l*, pg. 1205
S.A. SCHINDLER N.V.—See Schindler Holding AG; *Int'l*, pg. 1205
SCHINDLER S.A.—See Schindler Holding AG; *Int'l*, pg. 1205
SCHINDLER S.A.R.L.—See Schindler Holding AG; *Int'l*, pg. 1205
SCHINDLER SCANDINAVIAN HOLDING AB—See Schindler Holding AG; *Int'l*, pg. 1205
SCHINDLER S.P.A.—See Schindler Holding AG; *Int'l*, pg. 1205
SCHINDLER TRADING AG—See Schindler Holding AG; *Int'l*, pg. 1205
SCHINDLER TURKELI ASANSOR SAN A.S.—See Schindler Holding AG; *Int'l*, pg. 1205
SCHINDLER WAGGON AG—See Schindler Holding AG; *Int'l*, pg. 1205
VICTOR O. SCHINNERER & CO., LTD.—See Marsh & McLennan Companies, Inc.; *U.S. Public*, pg. 1049
SCHIPHOL TELEMATICS BV—See KPN Koninklyke PTT Nederland NV; *Int'l*, pg. 720
SCHIPHOL TELEMATICS CV—See KPN Koninklyke PTT Nederland NV; *Int'l*, pg. 720
SCHIRMER BOOKS—See National Amusements, Inc.; *U.S. Private*, pg. 777
G. SCHIRMER, INC.—See Music Sales Corporation; *U.S. Private*, pg. 768
SCHIZOPHRENIA TREATMENT AND REHABILITATION, INC.—See Magellan Health Services, Inc.; *U.S. Public*, pg. 1036
SCHLAGE LOCK COMPANY—See Ingersoll-Rand Company; *U.S. Public*, pg. 876
SCHLATTER BENELUX B.V.—See H.A. Schlatter AG; *Int'l*, pg. 1206
SCHLATTER DO BRASIL—See H.A. Schlatter AG; *Int'l*, pg. 1206
SCHLATTER FRANCE S.A.R.L.—See H.A. Schlatter AG; *Int'l*, pg. 1206
SCHLATTER GMBH—See H.A. Schlatter AG; *Int'l*, pg. 1206
H.A. SCHLATTER AG; *Int'l*, pg. 1205
H.A. SCHLATTER, INC.—See H.A. Schlatter AG; *Int'l*, pg. 1206

SCHLATTER ITALIANA S.R.L.—See H.A. Schlatter AG; *Int'l*, pg. 1206
SCHLATTER LTD.—See H.A. Schlatter AG; *Int'l*, pg. 1206
SCHLEGEL BUILDING PRODUCTS DIV.—See BTR plc; *Int'l*, pg. 128
SCHLEGEL CAROLINA DIV.—See BTR plc; *Int'l*, pg. 128
SCHLEGEL CORPORATION—See BTR plc; *Int'l*, pg. 128
SCHLEGEL INDUSTRIAL PRODUCTS DIV.—See BTR plc; *Int'l*, pg. 128
SCHLEGEL LINING TECHNOLOGY, INC.—See BTR plc; *Int'l*, pg. 128
SCHLEGEL MARYLAND—See BTR plc; *Int'l*, pg. 128
SCHLEGEL NAAO—See BTR plc; *Int'l*, pg. 128
SCHLEGEL NORTH AMERICAN AUTOMOTIVE OPERATIONS—See BTR plc; *Int'l*, pg. 128
SCHLEGEL OKLAHOMA, INC.—See BTR plc; *Int'l*, pg. 128
SCHLEGEL RETROFIT CORPORATION—See BTR plc; *Int'l*, pg. 128
SCHLEGEL ROCHESTER DIV.—See BTR plc; *Int'l*, pg. 128
SCHLEGEL TENNESSEE, INC.—See BTR plc; *Int'l*, pg. 128
SCHLEGEL WEST UNITY INC.—See BTR plc; *Int'l*, pg. 128
SCHLEICHER & SCHUELL—See Schleicher & Schuell GmbH; *Int'l*, pg. 1206
SCHLEICHER & SCHUELL AG—See Schleicher & Schuell GmbH; *Int'l*, pg. 1206
SCHLEICHER & SCHUELL FRANCE SARL—See Schleicher & Schuell GmbH; *Int'l*, pg. 1206
SCHLEICHER & SCHUELL GMBH; *Int'l*, pg. 1206
SCHLEICHER & SCHUELL, INC.—See Schleicher & Schuell GmbH; *Int'l*, pg. 1206
SCHLEICHER & SCHUELL ITALIA SRL—See Schleicher & Schuell GmbH; *Int'l*, pg. 1206
SCHLEICHER & SCHUELL NEDERLAND BV—See Schleicher & Schuell GmbH; *Int'l*, pg. 1206
SCHLEICHER & SCHUELL N.V. S.A.—See Schleicher & Schuell GmbH; *Int'l*, pg. 1206
EMIL SCHLEMPER G.M.B.H.—See Acme United Corporation; *U.S. Public*, pg. 17
SCHLESWAG AKTIENGESELLSCHAFT—See Veba AG; *Int'l*, pg. 1456
I.H. SCHLEZINGER, INC.—See Worthington Industries, Inc.; *U.S. Public*, pg. 1780
GEORG SCHLITT WERKZEUGE UND WERKZEUGMASCHINEN GMBH—See Rothenberger Group GmbH; *Int'l*, pg. 1128
SCHLOSSER CASTING COMPANY—See Schlosser Forge Company; *U.S. Private*, pg. 970
SCHLOSSER FORGE COMPANY; *U.S. Private*, pg. 970
SCHLOTZSKY'S, INC.; *U.S. Public*, pg. 1439
SCHLUMBERGER ANTILLES N.V.—See Schlumberger Limited; *U.S. Public*, pg. 1439
SCHLUMBERGER B.V., NETHERLANDS—See Schlumberger Limited; *U.S. Public*, pg. 1439
SCHLUMBERGER CANADA LIMITED—See Schlumberger Limited; *U.S. Public*, pg. 1439
SCHLUMBERGER HOLDING GMBH—See Schlumberger Limited; *U.S. Public*, pg. 1439
SCHLUMBERGER HOLDINGS LIMITED—See Schlumberger Limited; *U.S. Public*, pg. 1439
SCHLUMBERGER INDUSTRIES—See Schlumberger Limited; *U.S. Public*, pg. 1439
SCHLUMBERGER INDUSTRIES, INC.—See Schlumberger Limited; *U.S. Public*, pg. 1439
SCHLUMBERGER LIMITED; *U.S. Public*, pg. 1439
SCHLUMBERGER LIMITED—See Schlumberger Limited; *U.S. Public*, pg. 1439
SCHLUMBERGER MALCO INC.—See N. Schlumberger & Cie; *Int'l*, pg. 1206
SCHLUMBERGER MALCO, INC.—See Schlumberger Limited; *U.S. Public*, pg. 1439
N. SCHLUMBERGER & CIE; *Int'l*, pg. 1206
N. SCHLUMBERGER & CO. (U.K.) LTD.—See N. Schlumberger & Cie; *Int'l*, pg. 1206
N. SCHLUMBERGER E C. ITALIA S.R.L.—See N. Schlumberger & Cie; *Int'l*, pg. 1206
N. SCHLUMBERGER (USA) INC.—See N. Schlumberger & Cie; *Int'l*, pg. 1206
SCHLUMBERGER OFFSHORE SERVICES LIMITED—See Schlumberger Limited; *U.S. Public*, pg. 1439
SCHLUMBERGER OILFIELD HOLDINGS—See Schlumberger Limited; *U.S. Public*, pg. 1439
SCHLUMBERGER OILFIELD SERVICES—See Schlumberger Limited; *U.S. Public*, pg. 1439
SCHLUMBERGER OVERSEAS, S.A.—See Schlumberger Limited; *U.S. Public*, pg. 1439
SCHLUMBERGER PLC—See Schlumberger Limited; *U.S. Public*, pg. 1439
SCHLUMBERGER SATELLITE—See Schlumberger Limited; *U.S. Public*, pg. 1439
SCHLUMBERGER SEISMIC HOLDINGS—See Schlumberger Limited; *U.S. Public*, pg. 1439
SCHLUMBERGER SURENCO, S.A.—See Schlumberger Limited; *U.S. Public*, pg. 1439
SCHLUMBERGER TECHNOLOGIES, INC.—See Schlumberger Limited; *U.S. Public*, pg. 1439
SCHLUMBERGER TECHNOLOGY CORPORATION—See Schlumberger Limited; *U.S. Public*, pg. 1439
SCHMALBACH-LUBECA AG; *Int'l*, pg. 1206
SCHMALBACH-LUBECA AUSTRIA GES.M.B.H.—See Schmalbach-Lubeca AG; *Int'l*, pg. 1207
SCHMALBACH-LUBECA STRALSUNDER METALLVERPACKUNGEN GMBH—See Schmalbach-Lubeca AG; *Int'l*, pg. 1207
SCHMALBACH-LUBECA UNTERSTUTZUNGSKASSE GMBH—See Schmalbach-Lubeca AG; *Int'l*, pg. 1207
SCHMIDT & CO. (HONG KONG) LTD.—See Hewlett-Packard Company; *U.S. Public*, pg. 823
SCHMIDT BAKING CO., INC.; *U.S. Private*, pg. 970
GEORGE T. SCHMIDT; *U.S. Private*, pg. 970
SCHMIDT & HAGEN GMBH & CO. KG—See Henkel KGaA; *Int'l*, pg. 610
THOMAS SCHMIDT DEMAG MATERIALEHANDTERING A/S—See Mannesmann A.G.; *Int'l*, pg. 838
SCHMIEDING ENTERPRISES INC.; *U.S. Private*, pg. 971

PAUL A. SCHMITT MUSIC COMPANY; *U.S. Private*, pg. 971
SCHMITT & WEITZ BAUSTOFFWERKE GMBH & CO. KG—See Heidelberger Zement A.G.; *Int'l*, pg. 606
SCHMITZ & APELT LOI INDUSTRIEOFENANLAGEN GMBH—See Ruhrgas Aktiengesellschaft; *Int'l*, pg. 1149
SCHNADIG CORPORATION; *U.S. Private*, pg. 971
SCHNEEKOPPE GMBH—See Eckes AG; *Int'l*, pg. 433
ALLAN SCHNEIDER ASSOCIATES; *U.S. Private*, pg. 971
SCHNEIDER AUTOMATION, INC.—See Schneider S.A.; *Int'l*, pg. 1208
SCHNEIDER COMMUNICATIONS—See Frontier Corporation; *U.S. Public*, pg. 684
SCHNEIDER CORP.; *Int'l*, pg. 1207
SCHNEIDER ELECTRIC S.A.—See Schneider S.A.; *Int'l*, pg. 1207
SCHNEIDER (EUROPE) AG—See Pfizer Inc.; *U.S. Public*, pg. 1283
SCHNEIDER FARMS DAIRY—See Schneider's Dairy, Inc.; *U.S. Private*, pg. 971
SCHNEIDER GROUP—See Schneider S.A.; *Int'l*, pg. 1208
SCHNEIDER JAPAN K.K.—See Pfizer Inc.; *U.S. Public*, pg. 1283
SCHNEIDER JEUMONT RAIL—See Jeumont-Schneider Trenformeteurs; *Int'l*, pg. 706
J.M. SCHNEIDER INC.—See Schneider Corp.; *Int'l*, pg. 1207
SCHNEIDER & KLEIN METALLWAREN GMBH & CO. KG—See Dyckerhoff AG; *Int'l*, pg. 423
SCHNEIDER MILLS, INC.; *U.S. Private*, pg. 971
SCHNEIDER/NAMIC—See Pfizer Inc.; *U.S. Public*, pg. 1284
SCHNEIDER NATIONAL, INC.; *U.S. Private*, pg. 971
SCHNEIDER S.A.; *Int'l*, pg. 1207
SCHNEIDER (USA) INC.—See Pfizer Inc.; *U.S. Public*, pg. 1284
SCHNEIDER'S DAIRY, INC.; *U.S. Private*, pg. 971
SCHNELLER, INC.; *U.S. Private*, pg. 971
SCHNIEBER FINE FOODS, INC.; *U.S. Private*, pg. 971
SCHNITZER STEEL INDUSTRIES, INC.; *U.S. Public*, pg. 1439
SCHNUCK MARKETS, INC.; *U.S. Private*, pg. 971
SCHNURPFEIL BOHR-GMBH—See Dyckerhoff & Widmann AG; *Int'l*, pg. 423
SCHOCKEN BOOKS—See Advance Publications Inc.; *U.S. Private*, pg. 21
SCHOELLER-BECKMANN NOOTER APPARATETECHNIK GMBH—See Nooter Corporation; *U.S. Private*, pg. 801
SELIX F. SCHOELLER LTD.; *Int'l*, pg. 1209
SCHOENECKERS, INC.; *U.S. Private*, pg. 972
SCHOENEMAN BROTHERS COMPANY; *U.S. Private*, pg. 972
SCHOEP'S ICE CREAM, INC.; *U.S. Private*, pg. 972
SCHOLASTIC BOOK FAIRS, INC.—See Scholastic Corporation; *U.S. Public*, pg. 1440
SCHOLASTIC BOOK FAIRS, LTD.—See Scholastic Corporation; *U.S. Public*, pg. 1440
SCHOLASTIC-CANADA, LTD.—See Scholastic Corporation; *U.S. Public*, pg. 1440
SCHOLASTIC CORPORATION; *U.S. Public*, pg. 1440
SCHOLASTIC INC.—See Scholastic Corporation; *U.S. Public*, pg. 1440
SCHOLASTIC INC. INFORMATION CENTER—See Scholastic Corporation; *U.S. Public*, pg. 1440
SCHOLASTIC INC. NATIONAL DISTRIBUTION CENTER—See Scholastic Corporation; *U.S. Public*, pg. 1440
SCHOLASTIC PRODUCTIONS INC.—See Scholastic Corporation; *U.S. Public*, pg. 1440
SCHOLASTIC PUBLICATIONS LTD.—See Scholastic Corporation; *U.S. Public*, pg. 1441
SCHOLL AG—See Scholl Plc; *Int'l*, pg. 1209
SCHOLL (ASIA) LIMITED—See Scholl Plc; *Int'l*, pg. 1209
SCHOLL BELGIQUE SA—See Scholl Plc; *Int'l*, pg. 1209
SCHOLL CONSUMER PRODUCTS LTD.—See Scholl Plc; *Int'l*, pg. 1209
SCHOLL DANMARK A/S—See Scholl Plc; *Int'l*, pg. 1209
SCHOLL DEUTCHLAND GMBH—See Scholl Plc; *Int'l*, pg. 1209
SCHOLL HELLAS SA—See Scholl Plc; *Int'l*, pg. 1209
SCHOLL INTERNATIONAL (ANZ) PTY. LTD.—See Scholl Plc; *Int'l*, pg. 1209
SCHOLL INTERNATIONAL (NZ) LTD.—See Scholl Plc; *Int'l*, pg. 1209
SCHOLL JAPAN LIMITED—See Scholl Plc; *Int'l*, pg. 1210
SCHOLL KFT—See Scholl Plc; *Int'l*, pg. 1210
SCHOLL (MALAYSIA) SDN BHD.—See Scholl Plc; *Int'l*, pg. 1210
SCHOLL (NORGE) A/S—See Scholl Plc; *Int'l*, pg. 1210
SCHOLL OESTERREICH GMBH—See Scholl Plc; *Int'l*, pg. 1210
SCHOLL PLC; *Int'l*, pg. 1209
SCHOLL (POLSKA) SP ZOO—See Scholl Plc; *Int'l*, pg. 1210
SCHOLL SA—See Scholl Plc; *Int'l*, pg. 1210
SCHOLL SPOL SRO—See Scholl Plc; *Int'l*, pg. 1210
SCHOLL S.R.O.—See Scholl Plc; *Int'l*, pg. 1210
SCHOLL (SVERIGE) SA—See Scholl Plc; *Int'l*, pg. 1210
SCHOLL (UK) LTD.—See Schering-Plough Corporation; *U.S. Public*, pg. 1439
SCHOLL U.S.A.—See Schering-Plough Corporation; *U.S. Public*, pg. 1438
SCHOLLER BETEILIGUNGS GMBH—See Bayerische Vereinsbank Group; *Int'l*, pg. 181
SCHOLLER DIENSTLEISTUNGS GMBH—See Bayerische Vereinsbank Group; *Int'l*, pg. 181
SCHOLLER HOLDING AG—See Bayerische Vereinsbank Group; *Int'l*, pg. 181
SCHOLLER LEASING GESELLSCHAFT MBH—See Bayerische Vereinsbank Group; *Int'l*, pg. 181
SCHOLLER LEASING GESELLSCHAFT MBH & CO. KG—See Bayerische Vereinsbank Group; *Int'l*, pg. 181
SCHOLLER LEBENSMITTEL GMBH & CO. KG—See Sudzucker AG Mannheim/Ochsenfurt; *Int'l*, pg. 1305

SCHOLLER MUNZHANDEL GMBH—See Bayerische Vereinsbank Group; *Int'l*, pg. 181
SCHOLLERBANK AG—See Bayerische Vereinsbank Group; *Int'l*, pg. 181
SCHOLLS INC.; *U.S. Private*, pg. 972
SCHOLZ & FRIENDS GMBH; *Int'l*, pg. 1210
SCHOOL ANNUAL PUBLISHING CO.—See Jordan Industries, Inc.; *U.S. Private*, pg. 598
SCHOOL APPAREL, INC.; *U.S. Private*, pg. 972
THE SCHOOL OF ACCOUNTANCY—See Harcourt General, Inc.; *U.S. Public*, pg. 784
SCHOOL PRODUCTS GROUP—See Jostens; *U.S. Public*, pg. 934
SCHOPPE & FRASER GMBH—See Mannesmann A.G.; *Int'l*, pg. 835
SCHOTT BROTHERS, INC.; *U.S. Private*, pg. 972
SCHOTT CORPORATION; *U.S. Private*, pg. 972
SCHOTT GLASS TECHNOLOGIES, INC.—See Carl-Zeiss-Stiftung; *Int'l*, pg. 1523
SCHOTT GLASWERKE—See Carl-Zeiss-Stiftung; *Int'l*, pg. 1523
SCHOTTENSTEIN STORES CORPORATION; *U.S. Private*, pg. 972
SCHOTT'S BAKERY, INC.—See Flowers Industries, Inc.; *U.S. Public*, pg. 658
SCHOTT-ZEISS ASSEKURANTZKONTOR GMBH—See Carl-Zeiss-Stiftung; *Int'l*, pg. 1523
SCHRACK-ERICSSON SPOL. S.R.O. CZECH REPUBLIC—See Telefonaktiebolaget LM Ericsson; *Int'l*, pg. 1369
SCHRACK-ERICSSON SP. Z.O.O.—See Telefonaktiebolaget LM Ericsson; *Int'l*, pg. 1369
SCHRACK ERICSSON SPOL. S.R.O. SLOVAKIA—See Telefonaktiebolaget LM Ericsson; *Int'l*, pg. 1369
SCHRACK TELECOM RT—See Telefonaktiebolaget LM Ericsson; *Int'l*, pg. 1369
SCHRADER BELLOWS DIVISION—See Parker Hannifin Corporation; *U.S. Public*, pg. 1261
SCHRADER BELLOWS GMBH—See Parker Hannifin Corporation; *U.S. Public*, pg. 1264
SCHRADER-BELLOWS PARKER S.A. DE C.V.—See Parker Hannifin Corporation; *U.S. Public*, pg. 1261
SCHREIBER FOODS, INC.; *U.S. Private*, pg. 972
SCHREIBER, YONLEY & ASSOCIATES—See Perma-Fix Environmental Services, Inc.; *U.S. Public*, pg. 1280
SCHREIER MALTING CO.; *U.S. Private*, pg. 972
SCHRODER & CO. INC.—See Schroders PLC; *Int'l*, pg. 1210
SCHRODERS PLC; *Int'l*, pg. 1210
SCHROEDEL SCHULBUCHVERLAG GMBH—See Georg von Holtzbrinck GmbH; *Int'l*, pg. 1478
SCHROFF—See Pentair, Inc.; *U.S. Public*, pg. 1274
SCHUBERT INDUSTRIES INC.; *U.S. Private*, pg. 973
SCHUBERT SEALS A/S—See The West Company, Incorporated; *U.S. Public*, pg. 1755
SCHUCK & SONS CONSTRUCTION CO.; *U.S. Private*, pg. 973
SCHUFF STEEL CO.; *U.S. Private*, pg. 973
SCHUHLE GMBH—See Veba AG; *Int'l*, pg. 1458
SCHULLER GMBH—See Johns Manville Corporation; *U.S. Public*, pg. 927
SCHULLER INTERNATIONAL, INC.—See Johns Manville Corporation; *U.S. Public*, pg. 927
A. SCHULMAN—See A. Schulman, Inc.; *U.S. Public*, pg. 1441
A. SCHULMAN AG—See A. Schulman, Inc.; *U.S. Public*, pg. 1441
A. SCHULMAN CANADA LTD.—See A. Schulman, Inc.; *U.S. Public*, pg. 1441
A. SCHULMAN DE MEXICO, S.A. DE C.V.—See A. Schulman, Inc.; *U.S. Public*, pg. 1441
A. SCHULMAN GMBH—See A. Schulman, Inc.; *U.S. Public*, pg. 1441
A. SCHULMAN, INC.; *U.S. Public*, pg. 1441
A. SCHULMAN, INC.—See A. Schulman, Inc.; *U.S. Public*, pg. 1441
A. SCHULMAN INC. LIMITED—See A. Schulman, Inc.; *U.S. Public*, pg. 1441
A. SCHULMAN PLASTICS S.A.—See A. Schulman, Inc.; *U.S. Public*, pg. 1442
A. SCHULMAN S.A.—See A. Schulman, Inc.; *U.S. Public*, pg. 1442
PAUL SCHULMAN CO.—See BDDP Group; *Int'l*, pg. 117
SCHULT HOMES CORPORATION; *U.S. Public*, pg. 1442
SCHULTE ROHREARBEITUNG GMBH—See Fried. Krupp AG; *Int'l*, pg. 513
SCHULTHEIS BRAUEREI GMBH & CO.—See Bitburger Brauerei Th. Simon GmbH; *Int'l*, pg. 197
SCHULTZ SAV-O STORES, INC.; *U.S. Public*, pg. 1442
SCHULTZ STEEL COMPANY; *U.S. Private*, pg. 973
SCHULVERLAG VIEWEG GMBH—See Bertelsmann AG; *Int'l*, pg. 190
SCHULZE & BURCH BISCUIT COMPANY; *U.S. Private*, pg. 973
SCHUMACHER-DUGAN CONSTRUCTION; *U.S. Private*, pg. 973
SCHUMACHER ELECTRIC CORPORATION; *U.S. Private*, pg. 973
F. SCHUMACHER & CO.; *U.S. Private*, pg. 973
SCHUMAG AG—See Deutsche Babcock AG; *Int'l*, pg. 399
SCHUMAG-KIESERLING MACHINERY, INC.—See Deutsche Babcock AG; *Int'l*, pg. 399
SCHUMAN CARRIAGE COMPANY—See Fuji Heavy Industries, Ltd.; *Int'l*, pg. 523
SCHUMANN SASOL GMBH & CO KG—See Sasol Limited; *Int'l*, pg. 1197
SCHUMANN SASOL INTERNATIONAL AG—See Sasol Limited; *Int'l*, pg. 1196
SCHUMANN SASOL (SOUTH AFRICA) PTY LTD.—See Sasol Limited; *Int'l*, pg. 1197
SCHUNK GMBH—See Commerzbank AG; *Int'l*, pg. 310
SCHURZ COMMUNICATIONS, INC.; *U.S. Private*, pg. 973
SCHUSTER & PARTNER—See Dentsu Inc.; *Int'l*, pg. 394
SCHUSTER & PARTNER; *Int'l*, pg. 1210

SCHUTTE & KOERTING DIVISION—See KTM Holdings Corp.; *U.S. Private*, pg. 604
SCHUTTE LUMBER COMPANY; *U.S. Private*, pg. 973
SCHUTTERSVELD HOLDING N.V.; *Int'l*, pg. 1210
CHARLES SCHWAB & CO. INC.—See The Charles Schwab Corporation; *U.S. Public*, pg. 1443
THE CHARLES SCHWAB CORPORATION; *U.S. Public*, pg. 1442
THE CHARLES SCHWAB TRUST COMPANY—See The Charles Schwab Corporation; *U.S. Public*, pg. 1443
SCHWAB CORP.; *U.S. Private*, pg. 974
SCHWAB HOLDINGS, INC.—See The Charles Schwab Corporation; *U.S. Public*, pg. 1443
LES SCHWAB TIRE CENTERS; *U.S. Private*, pg. 974
S. SCHWAB COMPANY; *U.S. Private*, pg. 974
SCHWAB VERSAND AKTIENGESELLSCHAFT—See Otto Versand (GmbH & Co.); *Int'l*, pg. 1015
SCHWAEBISCHE HUETTENWERKE GMBH—See MAN Aktiengesellschaft; *Int'l*, pg. 826
SCHWANK—See Perfection-Schwank Inc.; *U.S. Private*, pg. 853
SCHWAN'S SALES ENTERPRISES; *U.S. Private*, pg. 974
SCHWARTZ & BENJAMIN, INC.; *U.S. Private*, pg. 974
BEN SCHWARTZ MARKET, INC.; *U.S. Private*, pg. 974
JACK SCHWARTZ SHOES, INC.; *U.S. Private*, pg. 974
SCHWARZ EXTRUSIONSWERKZEUGE GMBH—See MAN Aktiengesellschaft; *Int'l*, pg. 825
SCHWARZ PAPER COMPANY; *U.S. Private*, pg. 974
SCHWARZ PHARMA AG; *Int'l*, pg. 1211
SCHWARZ PHARMA INC.—See Schwarz Pharma AG; *Int'l*, pg. 1211
SCHWARZ PHARMA MANUFACTURING, INC.—See Schwarz Pharma AG; *Int'l*, pg. 1211
HANS SCHWARZKOPF GMBH—See Henkel KGaA; *Int'l*, pg. 610
SCHWEGMANN GIANT SUPER MARKETS—See Kohlberg & Company, LLC; *U.S. Private*, pg. 629
SCHWEISSTECHNISCHES BILDUNGSZSNTRUM ZWICKAU GMBH—See Volkswagen AG; *Int'l*, pg. 1474
SCHWEIZER AIRCRAFT CORPORATION; *U.S. Private*, pg. 975
SCHWEIZER VERBAND DER RAIFFEISENBANKEN; *Int'l*, pg. 1211
SCHWEIZERISCHE BANKGESELLSCHAFT (DEUTSCHLAND) AG—See Union Bank of Switzerland; *Int'l*, pg. 1440
SCHWEIZERISCHE BUNDESBAHNEN - SBB AG; *Int'l*, pg. 1211
SCHWEIZERISCHE GENPSSENSCHAFT FUR GEMUSEBAU—See Coop Switzerland; *Int'l*, pg. 330
SCHWEIZERISCHE KASEUNION AG; *Int'l*, pg. 1211
SCHWEIZERISCHE RENTENANSTALT—See The Swiss Life/Rentenanstalt Group; *Int'l*, pg. 1332
SCHWEIZERISCHER BANKVEREIN—See Swiss Bank Corporation; *Int'l*, pg. 1329
SCHWEIZERISCHER BANKVEREIN AG—See Swiss Bank Corporation; *Int'l*, pg. 1330
SCHWEIZERISCHER BANKVEREIN (DEUTSCHLAND) AG—See Swiss Bank Corporation; *Int'l*, pg. 1331
SCHWEIZERISCHER BANKVEREIN REPRASENTANZ—See Swiss Bank Corporation; *Int'l*, pg. 1330
SCHWEPPES CANADA DIVISION—See Cadbury Schweppes p.l.c.; *Int'l*, pg. 248
SCHWEPPES EUROPE LIMITED—See Cadbury Schweppes p.l.c.; *Int'l*, pg. 248
SCHWEPPES FRANCE S.A.—See Cadbury Schweppes p.l.c.; *Int'l*, pg. 248
SCHWEPPES S.A.—See Cadbury Schweppes p.l.c.; *Int'l*, pg. 248
SCHWERMETALL HALBZEUGWERK GMBH & CO. KG—See Olin Corporation; *U.S. Public*, pg. 1220
SCHWING AMERICA INC.; *Int'l*, pg. 1211
SCHWING AMERICA, INC., SLUDGE PUMP DIV.—See Schwing Gmbh; *Int'l*, pg. 1211
SCHWING EQUIPAMENTOS INDUSTRIAIS LTDA.—See Schwing Gmbh; *Int'l*, pg. 1211
F.W. SCHWING GMBH—See Schwing Gmbh; *Int'l*, pg. 1211
SCHWING GMBH; *Int'l*, pg. 1211
SCHWINN CYCLING & FITNESS INC.—See Schwinn Holdings; *U.S. Private*, pg. 975
SCHWINN HOLDINGS; *U.S. Private*, pg. 975
SCHWITZER, INC.—See Kuhlman Corporation; *U.S. Public*, pg. 968
SCIAKY ELECTRIC WELDING MACHINES LTD.—See Sciaky S.A.; *Int'l*, pg. 1211
SCIAKY GMBH—See Sciaky S.A.; *Int'l*, pg. 1211
SCIAKY, INC.—See Phillips Service Industries, Inc.; *U.S. Private*, pg. 862
SCIAKY S.A.; *Int'l*, pg. 1211
SCIAM S.N.C.—See Freudenberg & Company; *Int'l*, pg. 506
F.J. SCIAME CONSTRUCTION CO. INC.; *U.S. Private*, pg. 975
SCICOM DATA SERVICES, LTD.; *U.S. Private*, pg. 975
SCIENCE & ENGINEERING ASSOCIATES; *U.S. Private*, pg. 975
SCIENCE AND ENGINEERING HUNTSVILLE OFFICE—See Thiokol Corporation; *U.S. Public*, pg. 1597
SCIENCE AND ENGINEERING LANCASTER OFFICE—See Thiokol Corporation; *U.S. Public*, pg. 1597
SCIENCE & TECHNOLOGY GROUP—See The McGraw-Hill Companies; *U.S. Public*, pg. 1071
SCIENCE APPLICATIONS INTERNATIONAL, BARBADOS—See Science Applications International Corp.; *U.S. Private*, pg. 976
SCIENCE APPLICATIONS INTERNATIONAL CORP.; *U.S. Private*, pg. 975
SCIENCE APPLICATIONS INTERNATIONAL, EUROPE S.A.—See Science Applications International Corp.; *U.S. Private*, pg. 976
SCIENCE CENTER—See Rockwell International Corporation; *U.S. Public*, pg. 1398

SCIENCE FICTION BOOK CLUB—See Bertelsmann AG; *Int'l*, pg. 191
SCIENCE MANAGEMENT CORPORATION—See Versar Inc.; *U.S. Public*, pg. 1717
SCIENTIFIC ADVANCES INC.—See Battelle Memorial Institute; *U.S. Public*, pg. 123
SCIENTIFIC AMERICAN, INC.—See Georg von Holtzbrinck GmbH; *Int'l*, pg. 1479
SCIENTIFIC AMERICAN MAGAZINE—See Georg von Holtzbrinck GmbH; *Int'l*, pg. 1479
SCIENTIFIC AMERICAN MEDICINE—See Georg von Holtzbrinck GmbH; *Int'l*, pg. 1479
SCIENTIFIC AND MEDICAL SUPPLIES CO.—See Hewlett-Packard Company; *U.S. Public*, pg. 823
SCIENTIFIC-ATLANTA CANADA, INC.—See Scientific-Atlanta, Inc.; *U.S. Public*, pg. 1443
SCIENTIFIC-ATLANTA CHILE Y COMPANIA LIMITADA—See Scientific-Atlanta, Inc.; *U.S. Public*, pg. 1443
SCIENTIFIC-ATLANTA (H.K.) LIMITED—See Scientific-Atlanta, Inc.; *U.S. Public*, pg. 1443
SCIENTIFIC-ATLANTA, INC.; *U.S. Public*, pg. 1443
SCIENTIFIC-ATLANTA, INC.—See Scientific-Atlanta, Inc.; *U.S. Public*, pg. 1443
SCIENTIFIC ATLANTIC LIMITED—See Scientific-Atlanta, Inc.; *U.S. Public*, pg. 1443
SCIENTIFIC CALCULATIONS, INC.—See Harris Corporation; *U.S. Public*, pg. 792
SCIENTIFIC COMMUNICATIONS, INC.—See Andrew Corporation; *U.S. Public*, pg. 112
SCIENTIFIC DESIGN CO., INC.—See Linde AG; *Int'l*, pg. 811
SCIENTIFIC DUST COLLECTORS—See Venturedyne, Ltd.; *U.S. Private*, pg. 1136
SCIENTIFIC HOSPITAL SUPPLIES HOLDINGS LTD.—See Nutricia BV; *Int'l*, pg. 992
SCIENTIFIC IMAGING SYSTEMS—See Eastman Kodak Company; *U.S. Public*, pg. 550
SCIENTIFIC MEASUREMENT SYSTEMS, INC.—See Thermo Electron Corporation; *U.S. Public*, pg. 1593
SCIENTIFIC PROTEIN LABORATORIES, INC.—See American Home Products Corporation; *U.S. Public*, pg. 80
SCIENTIFIC SOFTWARE-INTERCOMP, INC.; *U.S. Public*, pg. 1443
SCIENTIFIC SOFTWARE-INTERCOMP (U.K.) LIMITED—See Scientific Software-Intercomp, Inc.; *U.S. Public*, pg. 1444
SCIENTIFIC SYSTEMS DIVISION—See Sterling Software, Inc.; *U.S. Public*, pg. 1516
SCIERIE PARENT INC.—See Kruger Inc.; *Int'l*, pg. 761
SCINTILLA AG—See Robert Bosch GmbH; *Int'l*, pg. 206
SCIOM S.A.—See Henkel KGaA; *Int'l*, pg. 614
SCIOS INC.; *U.S. Public*, pg. 1444
SCITEC CORPORATION—See Andros Incorporated; *U.S. Private*, pg. 74
SCITEL TELEMATICS LTD.—See SASIB SpA; *Int'l*, pg. 1195
SCITEX AMERICA CORP.—See IDB Holding Corporation; *Int'l*, pg. 644
SCITEX CORPORATION LTD.—See IDB Holding Corporation; *Int'l*, pg. 644
SCITUATE MARINER—See Gannett Company, Inc.; *U.S. Public*, pg. 701
L.M. SCOFIELD COMPANY; *U.S. Private*, pg. 976
SCOOZI—See Lettuce Entertain You Enterprises, Inc.; *U.S. Private*, pg. 661
SCOPE BEAUTY ENT., INC.—See Scope Industries; *U.S. Public*, pg. 1444
SCOPE ENERGY RESOURCES, INC.—See Scope Industries; *U.S. Public*, pg. 1444
SCOPE INDUSTRIES; *U.S. Public*, pg. 1444
SCOPE KETCHUM COMMUNICATIONS LTD.—See Ketchum Communications Inc.; *U.S. Private*, pg. 617
SCOPE PRODUCTS, INC.—See Scope Industries; *U.S. Public*, pg. 1444
SCOPE PROPERTIES—See Scope Industries; *U.S. Public*, pg. 1444
SCOPUS TECHNOLOGY, INC.; *U.S. Public*, pg. 1444
THE SCORE BOARD, INC.; *U.S. Public*, pg. 1444
SCORI—See Lafarge S.A.; *Int'l*, pg. 788
SCORI HOLDING—See Ciments Francais; *Int'l*, pg. 292
SCORIA INCORPORATED—See Northern States Power Company; *U.S. Public*, pg. 1195
SCORPIO POWER SYSTEMS LIMITED—See TT Group PLC; *Int'l*, pg. 1344
SCOT LABORATORIES—See Berkshire Hathaway Inc.; *U.S. Public*, pg. 218
SCOTCH PREMIUM MEAT—See FMC Corporation; *U.S. Public*, pg. 607
SCOTCHBROOK COMMUNICATIONS LTD.—See Fleishman-Hillard Inc.; *U.S. Private*, pg. 411
SCOTCHMAN INDUSTRIES, INC.—See Krofam Inc.; *U.S. Private*, pg. 636
SCOTIA CAPITAL MARKETS—See The Bank of Nova Scotia; *Int'l*, pg. 156
SCOTIA DISCOUNT BROKERAGE INC.—See The Bank of Nova Scotia; *Int'l*, pg. 155
SCOTIA INDUSTRIAL PARK, INC.—See Galesi Group; *U.S. Private*, pg. 438
SCOTIA INSURANCE (BARBADOS) LIMITED—See The Bank of Nova Scotia; *Int'l*, pg. 156
SCOTIA INVESTMENT MANAGEMENT LTD.—See The Bank of Nova Scotia; *Int'l*, pg. 155
SCOTIA JAMAICA INSURANCE AGENCY LIMITED—See The Bank of Nova Scotia; *Int'l*, pg. 156
SCOTIA LIFE INSURANCE COMPANY—See The Bank of Nova Scotia; *Int'l*, pg. 156
SCOTIA PROPERTIES QUEBEC INC.—See The Bank of Nova Scotia; *Int'l*, pg. 156
SCOTIA REALTY BAHAMAS LIMITED—See The Bank of Nova Scotia; *Int'l*, pg. 156
SCOTIA REALTY LIMITED—See The Bank of Nova Scotia; *Int'l*, pg. 156

SCOTIA TRAWLER EQUIPMENT LIMITED—See National Sea Products Limited; *Int'l*, pg. 909
SCOTIABANK DE PUERTO RICO—See The Bank of Nova Scotia; *Int'l*, pg. 156
SCOTIABANK (IRELAND) LIMITED—See The Bank of Nova Scotia; *Int'l*, pg. 156
SCOTIABANK JAMAICA BUILDING SOCIETY—See The Bank of Nova Scotia; *Int'l*, pg. 156
SCOTIABANK JAMAICA TRUST AND MERCHANT BANK LIMITED—See The Bank of Nova Scotia; *Int'l*, pg. 156
SCOTIAMOCATTA—See The Bank of Nova Scotia; *Int'l*, pg. 156
SCOTIATRUST (ASIA) LIMITED—See The Bank of Nova Scotia; *Int'l*, pg. 156
SCOTOIL SERVICES LIMITED—See Imperial Chemical Industries PLC; *Int'l*, pg. 663
SCOTSMAN HOLDING INC.; *U.S. Private*, pg. 976
SCOTSMAN ICE SYSTEMS—See Scotsman Industries, Inc.; *U.S. Public*, pg. 1445
SCOTSMAN INDUSTRIES, INC.; *U.S. Public*, pg. 1444
SCOTT & STRINGFELLOW CAPITAL MANAGEMENT, INC.—See Scott & Stringfellow Financial, Inc.; *U.S. Public*, pg. 1445
SCOTT & STRINGFELLOW FINANCIAL, INC.; *U.S. Public*, pg. 1445
SCOTT & STRINGFELLOW, INC.—See Scott & Stringfellow Financial, Inc.; *U.S. Public*, pg. 1445
SCOTT AVIATION—See Figgie International Inc.; *U.S. Public*, pg. 622
SCOTT CONTINENTAL N.V.—See Kimberly-Clark Corporation; *U.S. Public*, pg. 960
SCOTT & ENGLISH LIMITED—See Haw Par Brothers International Limited; *Int'l*, pg. 603
SCOTT ENVIRONMENTAL TECHNOLOGY—See ERD Waste Corp.; *U.S. Public*, pg. 546
SCOTT FELDMUHLE—See Kimberly-Clark Corporation; *U.S. Public*, pg. 960
SCOTT FORSEMAN/ADDISON WESLEY—See The News Corporation Limited; *Int'l*, pg. 927
SCOTT IBERICA, S.A.—See Kimberly-Clark Corporation; *U.S. Public*, pg. 960
JAMES SCOTT MECHANICAL & ELECTRICAL SERVICES LTD.—See AMEC Plc; *Int'l*, pg. 16
SCOTT JEWELERS—See Reliable Stores, Inc.; *U.S. Private*, pg. 921
SCOTT LIMITED—See Kimberly-Clark Corporation; *U.S. Public*, pg. 960
SCOTT LUMBER COMPANY; *U.S. Private*, pg. 977
SCOTT MILLS—See Kleinert's, Inc.; *U.S. Public*, pg. 625
THE SCOTT MOTORS COMPANY—See Jordan Industries, Inc.; *U.S. Private*, pg. 598
SCOTT NATIONAL—See The Oshawa Group Limited; *Int'l*, pg. 1012
SCOTT PACKING & WAREHOUSING LIMITED (SCOTLAND)—See The Peninsular and Oriental Steam Navigation Company; *Int'l*, pg. 1034
SCOTT PAPER CO. DE COSTA RICA, S.A.—See Kimberly-Clark Corporation; *U.S. Public*, pg. 960
SCOTT PAPER LIMITED—See Kruger Inc.; *Int'l*, pg. 762
SCOTT PAPER (MALAYSIA) SDN. BHD.—See Kimberly-Clark Corporation; *U.S. Public*, pg. 960
SCOTT PAPER (SINGAPORE) PTE. LTD.—See Kimberly-Clark Corporation; *U.S. Public*, pg. 960
SCOTT PRINTING CORPORATION; *U.S. Private*, pg. 977
SCOTT RESOURCES—See American Educational Products; *U.S. Public*, pg. 71
ROBERT SCOTT/DAVID BROOKS—See Kellwood Company; *U.S. Public*, pg. 948
SCOTT S.N.C.—See Kimberly-Clark Corporation; *U.S. Public*, pg. 960
SCOTT S.P.A.—See Kimberly-Clark Corporation; *U.S. Public*, pg. 960
SCOTT SPECIALTY GASES; *U.S. Private*, pg. 977
SCOTT SPORTS GROUP; *U.S. Private*, pg. 977
SCOTT STERN ASSOCIATES LIMITED—See WPP Group plc; *Int'l*, pg. 1482
SCOTT & STRINGFELLOW, INC.—See Scott & Stringfellow Financial, Inc.; *U.S. Public*, pg. 1445
SCOTT TIMBER CO.—See RLC Industries Co.; *U.S. Private*, pg. 905
SCOTT TOBACCO—See Conwood Company L.P.; *U.S. Private*, pg. 272
SCOTT U.S.A.—See Scott Sports Group; *U.S. Private*, pg. 977
SCOTT WESTERN LTD.—See Getinge Industrier AB; *Int'l*, pg. 552
SCOTTI BROTHERS ENTERTAINMENT INDUSTRIES—See All American Communications, Inc.; *U.S. Public*, pg. 41
SCOTTISCH EQUITABLE—See AEGON N.V.; *Int'l*, pg. 28
SCOTTISH AGGREGATES LIMITED—See RMC Group p.l.c.; *Int'l*, pg. 1079
SCOTTISH AMICABLE PLC—See Prudential Corporation PLC; *Int'l*, pg. 1073
SCOTTISH & COURAGE BEER DIV.—See Scottish & Newcastle; *Int'l*, pg. 1212
SCOTTISH & COURAGE BEER PRODUCTION LIMITED—See Scottish & Newcastle plc; *Int'l*, pg. 1212
SCOTTISH & COURAGE BREWERIES (SALES) LIMITED—See Scottish & Newcastle plc; *Int'l*, pg. 1212
SCOTTISH & COURAGE BREWERIES (SERVICES) LIMITED—See Scottish & Newcastle plc; *Int'l*, pg. 1212
SCOTTISH & NEW CASTLE RETAIL—See Scottish & Newcastle plc; *Int'l*, pg. 1212
SCOTTISH & NEWCASTLE IMPORTERS CO.—See Scottish & Newcastle plc; *Int'l*, pg. 1212
SCOTTISH & NEWCASTLE PLC; *Int'l*, pg. 1211
SCOTTISH & UNIVERSAL NEWSPAPERS LIMITED—See Lonrho plc; *Int'l*, pg. 817
SCOTTISH BREWERS LIMITED—See Scottish & Newcastle plc; *Int'l*, pg. 1212
SCOTTISH COURAGE LIMITED—See Scottish & Newcastle plc; *Int'l*, pg. 1212
SCOTTISH ENTERPRISE; *Int'l*, pg. 1212

SCOTTISH WIDOWS' FUND & LIFE ASSURANCE SOCIETY; *Int'l*, pg. 1212
SCOTTPOLAR CORPORATION—See Toromont Industries Ltd.; *Int'l*, pg. 1400
SCOTTS CENTRE MANAGEMENT PTE LTD.—See Scotts Holdings Limited; *Int'l*, pg. 1213
THE SCOTTS COMPANY; *U.S. Public*, pg. 1446
SCOTTS DEVELOPMENT (SARACA) PTE. LTD.—See Scotts Holdings Limited; *Int'l*, pg. 1213
SCOTT'S FOOD SERVICES INC.—See Scott's Restaurants Inc.; *Int'l*, pg. 1213
SCOTT'S FOOD STORES INC.—See SuperValu, Inc.; *U.S. Public*, pg. 1541
SCOTTS HOLDINGS LIMITED; *Int'l*, pg. 1212
SCOTT'S HOTELS LIMITED—See Scott's Restaurants Inc.; *Int'l*, pg. 1213
SCOTT'S LIQUID GOLD-INC.; *U.S. Public*, pg. 1447
SCOTT'S MANAGEMENT SERVICES INC.—See Scott's Restaurants Inc.; *Int'l*, pg. 1213
SCOTTS MIRACLE-GRO PRODUCTS, INC.—See The Scotts Company; *U.S. Public*, pg. 1447
SCOTT'S RESTAURANTS INC.; *Int'l*, pg. 1213
SCOTTS SHOPPING CENTRE—See Scotts Holdings Limited; *Int'l*, pg. 1213
THE SCOTTSDALE EXECUTIVE CENTRE CORPORATION—See Cigna Corp.; *U.S. Public*, pg. 365
SCOTTSDALE INSURANCE COMPANY—See Nationwide Insurance Enterprise; *U.S. Private*, pg. 789
THE SCOULAR COMPANY; *U.S. Private*, pg. 977
SCOULAR PROPERTIES, INC.—See The Scoular Company; *U.S. Private*, pg. 977
SCOVILLE PRESS, INC.; *U.S. Private*, pg. 977
SCREEN ART—See Sonoco Products Company; *U.S. Public*, pg. 1486
SCREEN GRAPHICS—See Sonoco Products Company; *U.S. Public*, pg. 1486
SCREEN PRODUCTS AUSTRALIAN PTY LTD—See Flexible Products Company; *U.S. Private*, pg. 412
SCREW CONVEYOR CORP.; *U.S. Private*, pg. 977
SCRIBNER'S BOOKSTORES—See Barnes & Noble Inc.; *U.S. Public*, pg. 189
THE E.W. SCRIPPS COMPANY; *U.S. Public*, pg. 1447
SCRIPPS HOWARD BROADCASTING—See The E.W. Scripps Company; *U.S. Public*, pg. 1447
SCRIPPS HOWARD BROADCASTING CO.—See The E.W. Scripps Company; *U.S. Public*, pg. 1448
SCRIPPS HOWARD CABLE COMPANY—See The E.W. Scripps Company; *U.S. Public*, pg. 1448
SCRIPPS HOWARD CABLE CO. OF SACRAMENTO—See The E.W. Scripps Company; *U.S. Public*, pg. 1448
SCRIPPS HOWARD CABLE OF NORTHWEST GEORGIA—See The E.W. Scripps Company; *U.S. Public*, pg. 1448
SCRIPPS HOWARD CABLE T.V. COMPANY—See The E.W. Scripps Company; *U.S. Public*, pg. 1448
SCRIPPS HOWARD PRODUCTIONS—See The E.W. Scripps Company; *U.S. Public*, pg. 1448
JOHN P. SCRIPPS NEWSPAPERS—See The E.W. Scripps Company; *U.S. Public*, pg. 1448
SCRIPTO-TOKAI CORP.; *U.S. Private*, pg. 977
SCRUFARI CONSTRUCTION CO. INC.; *U.S. Private*, pg. 977
SCUBAPRO FRANCE S.A.—See Johnson Worldwide Associates, Inc.; *U.S. Public*, pg. 933
SCUDDER KEMPER INVESTMENTS, INC.—See Zurich Insurance Company; *Int'l*, pg. 1530
SEA CLIFF WATER COMPANY—See Aquarion Company; *U.S. Public*, pg. 126
SEA CONTAINERS AGENCIES INC.—See Sea Containers Ltd.; *Int'l*, pg. 1214
SEA CONTAINERS AMERICA INC.—See Sea Containers Ltd.; *Int'l*, pg. 1213
SEA CONTAINERS ASIA LTD.—See Sea Containers Ltd.; *Int'l*, pg. 1214
SEA CONTAINERS ASIA PTE. LTD.—See Sea Containers Ltd.; *Int'l*, pg. 1214
SEA CONTAINERS AUSTRALIA LTD.—See Sea Containers Ltd.; *Int'l*, pg. 1214
SEA CONTAINERS BRITISH ISLES LTD.—See Sea Containers Ltd.; *Int'l*, pg. 1214
SEA CONTAINERS CARIBBEAN INC.—See Sea Containers Ltd.; *Int'l*, pg. 1214
SEA CONTAINERS FRANCE S.A.—See Sea Containers Ltd.; *Int'l*, pg. 1214
SEA CONTAINERS GMBH—See Sea Containers Ltd.; *Int'l*, pg. 1214
SEA CONTAINERS HONG KONG LTD.—See Sea Containers Ltd.; *Int'l*, pg. 1214
SEA CONTAINERS ITALIA SRL—See Sea Containers Ltd.; *Int'l*, pg. 1214
SEA CONTAINERS LTD.; *Int'l*, pg. 1213
SEA CONTAINERS NORTH AMERICAN OPERATIONS & ACCOUNTING GROUP—See Sea Containers Ltd.; *Int'l*, pg. 1214
SEA CONTAINERS SERVICES LTD.—See Sea Containers Ltd.; *Int'l*, pg. 1214
SEA CONTAINERS U.S. GULF INC.—See Sea Containers Ltd.; *Int'l*, pg. 1214
SEA CONTAINERS WEST INC.—See Sea Containers Ltd.; *Int'l*, pg. 1214
SEA ISLAND BANK—See Synovus Financial Corp.; *U.S. Public*, pg. 1549
SEA ISLAND COMPANY; *U.S. Private*, pg. 977
SEA ISLAND PROPERTIES, INC.—See Sea Island Company; *U.S. Private*, pg. 978
SEA ISLAND SERVICES, INC.—See Sea Island Company; *U.S. Private*, pg. 978
SEA-LAND ORIENT LTD.—See CSX Corporation; *U.S. Public*, pg. 284
SEA-LAND SERVICE, INC.—See CSX Corporation; *U.S. Public*, pg. 284
SEA NYMPH INC.—See Greenway Partners, L.P.; *U.S. Private*, pg. 478

SEA OIL HOMCO LTD.—See The Peninsular and Oriental Steam Navigation Company; *Int'l*, pg. 1034
SEA RANCH PROPERTIES—See North American Company; *U.S. Private*, pg. 803
SEA RANGER PRODUCTS—See West Marine, Inc.; *U.S. Public*, pg. 1756
SEA RAY—See Brunswick Corporation; *U.S. Public*, pg. 266
SEA RIVER MARITIME, INC.—See Exxon Corporation; *U.S. Public*, pg. 601
SEA-3, INC., HOUSTON—See Transammonia Inc.; *U.S. Private*, pg. 1096
SEA WATCH INTERNATIONAL, LTD.—See Nichirei Corporation; *Int'l*, pg. 928
SEA WORLD OF CALIFORNIA—See Anheuser-Busch Companies, Inc.; *U.S. Public*, pg. 114
SEA WORLD OF FLORIDA—See Anheuser-Busch Companies, Inc.; *U.S. Public*, pg. 114
SEA WORLD OF OHIO—See Anheuser-Busch Companies, Inc.; *U.S. Public*, pg. 114
SEA WORLD OF TEXAS—See Anheuser-Busch Companies, Inc.; *U.S. Public*, pg. 114
SEABEAM INSTRUMENTS, INC.—See Channel Technologies, Inc.; *U.S. Private*, pg. 228
SEABOARD BARGE CORPORATION—See Moran Transporation Company; *U.S. Private*, pg. 761
SEABOARD CORPORATION; *U.S. Public*, pg. 1448
SEABOARD FLOUR CORPORATION—See Seaboard Corporation; *U.S. Public*, pg. 1449
SEABOARD INTERNATIONAL FOREST PRODUCTS, INC.—See Forest City Enterprises, Inc.; *U.S. Public*, pg. 669
SEABOARD LIFE—See Eureko B.V.; *Int'l*, pg. 464
SEABOARD LIFE (USA)—See Eureko B.V.; *Int'l*, pg. 464
SEABOARD UNDERWRITERS AGENCY, INC.—See Fremont General Corporation; *U.S. Public*, pg. 681
SEABOARD UNDERWRITERS, INC.—See Fremont General Corporation; *U.S. Public*, pg. 681
SEABREEZE PROPERTIES, INC.—See Oriole Homes Corp.; *U.S. Public*, pg. 1231
SEABROOK BROTHERS & SONS, INC.; *U.S. Private*, pg. 978
SEABROOK WALLCOVERINGS, INC.; *U.S. Private*, pg. 978
SEABURY & SMITH, INC.—See Marsh & McLennan Companies, Inc.; *U.S. Public*, pg. 1049
SEACO TEXAS PROPERTIES INC.—See Sea Containers Ltd.; *Int'l*, pg. 1213
SEACOR SMIT INC.; *U.S. Public*, pg. 1449
SEACORE LIMITED—See Agra Inc.; *Int'l*, pg. 31
SEADRIFT COKE, L.P.—See The Carbide/Graphite Group, Inc.; *U.S. Public*, pg. 304
SEADRIFT PIPELINE CORP.—See Union Carbide Corporation; *U.S. Public*, pg. 1667
SEAFARER BOAT CORPORATION—See Tidewater Inc.; *U.S. Public*, pg. 1608
SEAFIELD CAPITAL CORPORATION; *U.S. Public*, pg. 1449
SEAFIRST CORPORATION—See BankAmerica Corporation; *U.S. Public*, pg. 181
SEAFIRST INSURANCE CORPORATION—See BankAmerica Corporation; *U.S. Public*, pg. 181
SEAFOOD EUROPE—See EMAP Plc; *Int'l*, pg. 452
SEAFOOD IMPORTERS, INC.—See Hicks, Muse, Tate & Furst Inc.; *U.S. Private*, pg. 526
SEAFORTH MARITIME LIMITED—See Halliburton Company; *U.S. Public*, pg. 776
SEAGATE CONTROL DATA—See Seagate Technology Inc.; *U.S. Public*, pg. 1450
SEAGATE MAGNETICS—See Seagate Technology Inc.; *U.S. Public*, pg. 1450
SEAGATE RECORDING MEDIA—See Seagate Technology Inc.; *U.S. Public*, pg. 1450
SEAGATE SOFTWARE, INC.—See Seagate Technology Inc.; *U.S. Public*, pg. 1449
SEAGATE TAPE TECHNOLOGIES, INC.—See Seagate Technology Inc.; *U.S. Public*, pg. 1449
SEAGATE TECHNOLOGY CO. LTD.—See Seagate Technology Inc.; *U.S. Public*, pg. 1450
SEAGATE TECHNOLOGY EUROPE S.P.A.—See Seagate Technology Inc.; *U.S. Public*, pg. 1450
SEAGATE TECHNOLOGY FRANCE, S.A.R.L.—See Seagate Technology Inc.; *U.S. Public*, pg. 1450
SEAGATE TECHNOLOGY GMBH—See Seagate Technology Inc.; *U.S. Public*, pg. 1450
SEAGATE TECHNOLOGY HOLDINGS—See Seagate Technology Inc.; *U.S. Public*, pg. 1449
SEAGATE TECHNOLOGY (HONG KONG) LIMITED—See Seagate Technology Inc.; *U.S. Public*, pg. 1450
SEAGATE TECHNOLOGY INC.; *U.S. Public*, pg. 1449
SEAGATE TECHNOLOGY INTERNATIONAL—See Seagate Technology Inc.; *U.S. Public*, pg. 1450
SEAGATE TECHNOLOGY K.K.—See Seagate Technology Inc.; *U.S. Public*, pg. 1450
SEAGATE TECHNOLOGY KOREA, INC.—See Seagate Technology Inc.; *U.S. Public*, pg. 1450
SEAGATE TECHNOLOGY KOREA, INC.—See Seagate Technology Inc.; *U.S. Public*, pg. 1450
SEAGATE TECHNOLOGY MALAYSIA SDN. BHD.—See Seagate Technology Inc.; *U.S. Public*, pg. 1450
SEAGATE TECHNOLOGY SIMI VALLEY—See Seagate Technology Inc.; *U.S. Public*, pg. 1450
SEAGATE TECHNOLOGY SINGAPORE, LTD.—See Seagate Technology Inc.; *U.S. Public*, pg. 1450
SEAGATE TECHNOLOGY (SINGAPORE) PCB ASSEMBLY OPERATIONS—See Seagate Technology Inc.; *U.S. Public*, pg. 1450
SEAGATE TECHNOLOGY (SINGAPORE) PTE. LTD.—See Seagate Technology Inc.; *U.S. Public*, pg. 1450
SEAGATE TECHNOLOGY (U.K.), LIMITED—See Seagate Technology Inc.; *U.S. Public*, pg. 1450
SEAGRAM ASIA PACIFIC/GLOBAL DUTY FREE—See The Seagram Company Ltd.; *Int'l*, pg. 1217

SEAGRAM BEVERAGE CO.—See The Seagram Company Ltd.; *Int'l*, pg. 1217
THE SEAGRAM BEVERAGE GROUP—See The Seagram Company Ltd.; *Int'l*, pg. 1217
SEAGRAM CANADA—See The Seagram Company Ltd.; *Int'l*, pg. 1215
SEAGRAM CHATEAU & ESTATE WINES CO.—See The Seagram Company Ltd.; *Int'l*, pg. 1215
THE SEAGRAM CLASSICS WINE COMPANY—See The Seagram Company Ltd.; *Int'l*, pg. 1215
THE SEAGRAM COMPANY LTD.; *Int'l*, pg. 1214
SEAGRAM EUROPE AND AFRICA—See The Seagram Company Ltd.; *Int'l*, pg. 1217
SEAGRAM GLOBAL BRANDS—See The Seagram Company Ltd.; *Int'l*, pg. 1217
JOSEPH E. SEAGRAM & SONS, INC.—See The Seagram Company Ltd.; *Int'l*, pg. 1215
SEAGRAM LATIN AMERICA—See The Seagram Company Ltd.; *Int'l*, pg. 1217
THE SEAGRAM SPIRITS AND WINE GROUP—See The Seagram Company Ltd.; *Int'l*, pg. 1217
SEAGRAM'S CORP. RESEARCH AND DEVELOPMENT—See The Seagram Company Ltd.; *Int'l*, pg. 1217
SEAGULL ENERGY CORPORATION; *U.S. Public*, pg. 1450
SEAGULL ENERGY E & P, INC.—See Seagull Energy Corporation; *U.S. Public*, pg. 1450
SEAL GROUP—See Parker Hannifin Corporation; *U.S. Public*, pg. 1262
SEAL PRODUCTS INCORPORATED—See Hunt Corporation; *U.S. Public*, pg. 849
SEAL SANDS CHEMICALS LTD.—See Cambrex Corporation; *U.S. Public*, pg. 297
SEAL SANDS STORAGE LTD.—See Simon Engineering plc; *Int'l*, pg. 1251
SEALAND TECHNOLOGY—See Taylor Made Group, Inc.; *U.S. Public*, pg. 1071
SEALASKA CORPORATION; *U.S. Private*, pg. 978
SEALASKA TIMBER CORPORATION—See Sealaska Corporation; *U.S. Private*, pg. 978
SEALED AIR AUSTRALIA—See Sealed Air Corporation; *U.S. Public*, pg. 1451
SEALED AIR BRASIL LTDA.—See Sealed Air Corporation; *U.S. Public*, pg. 1451
SEALED AIR B.V.—See Sealed Air Corporation; *U.S. Public*, pg. 1451
SEALED AIR CAMBRIDGE—See Sealed Air Corporation; *U.S. Public*, pg. 1451
SEALED AIR CORPORATION; *U.S. Public*, pg. 1450
SEALED AIR ESPANA, S.A.—See Sealed Air Corporation; *U.S. Public*, pg. 1451
SEALED AIR (FAR EAST) LTD.—See Sealed Air Corporation; *U.S. Public*, pg. 1451
SEALED AIR FOOD PACKAGING DIVISION—See Sealed Air Corporation; *U.S. Public*, pg. 1451
SEALED AIR (FPD) LIMITED—See Sealed Air Corporation; *U.S. Public*, pg. 1451
SEALED AIR G.M.B.H.—See Sealed Air Corporation; *U.S. Public*, pg. 1451
SEALED AIR JAPAN LTD.—See Sealed Air Corporation; *U.S. Public*, pg. 1451
SEALED AIR KOREA LTD.—See Sealed Air Corporation; *U.S. Public*, pg. 1451
SEALED AIR LIMITED—See Sealed Air Corporation; *U.S. Public*, pg. 1451
SEALED AIR (MALAYSIA) SDN BHD—See Sealed Air Corporation; *U.S. Public*, pg. 1451
SEALED AIR (NEW ZEALAND) FOOD PACKAGING DIVISION—See Sealed Air Corporation; *U.S. Public*, pg. 1451
SEALED AIR (NEW ZEALAND) PACKAGING PRODUCTS DIVISION—See Sealed Air Corporation; *U.S. Public*, pg. 1451
SEALED AIR NORGE A S—See Sealed Air Corporation; *U.S. Public*, pg. 1451
SEALED AIR N.V.—See Sealed Air Corporation; *U.S. Public*, pg. 1451
SEALED AIR OF CANADA INC.—See Sealed Air Corporation; *U.S. Public*, pg. 1451
SEALED AIR OY—See Sealed Air Corporation; *U.S. Public*, pg. 1451
SEALED AIR PACKAGING PRODUCTS DIVISION—See Sealed Air Corporation; *U.S. Public*, pg. 1451
SEALED AIR PACKAGING (SHANGHAI) CO. LTD.—See Sealed Air Corporation; *U.S. Public*, pg. 1451
SEALED AIR PHILIPPINES, INC.—See Sealed Air Corporation; *U.S. Public*, pg. 1451
SEALED AIR POLSKA SP. Z.O.O.—See Sealed Air Corporation; *U.S. Public*, pg. 1451
SEALED AIR S.P.A.—See Sealed Air Corporation; *U.S. Public*, pg. 1451
SEALED AIR (S) PTE. LTD.—See Sealed Air Corporation; *U.S. Public*, pg. 1451
SEALED AIR (SINGAPORE) PTE. LTD.—See Sealed Air Corporation; *U.S. Public*, pg. 1451
SEALED AIR SVENSKA A.B.—See Sealed Air Corporation; *U.S. Public*, pg. 1451
SEALED AIR SYSTEMS—See Sealed Air Corporation; *U.S. Public*, pg. 1451
SEALED AIR (TAIWAN) LTD.—See Sealed Air Corporation; *U.S. Public*, pg. 1451
SEALED AIR (THAILAND) LTD.—See Sealed Air Corporation; *U.S. Public*, pg. 1451
SEALED-SWEET GROWERS, INC.; *U.S. Private*, pg. 978
SEALING DEVICES INC.; *U.S. Private*, pg. 978
SEALING EQUIPMENT PRODUCTS CO., INC.; *U.S. Private*, pg. 978
SEALRIGHT COMPANY, INC.; *U.S. Public*, pg. 1451
SEALRIGHT MFG. EAST, INC.—See Sealright Company, Inc.; *U.S. Public*, pg. 1452
SEALRIGHT MFG. WEST, INC.—See Sealright Company, Inc.; *U.S. Public*, pg. 1452
SEALS N.V./S.A.—See Furon Company; *U.S. Public*, pg. 689

SEALTRON, INC.—See HCC Industries; *U.S. Private*, pg. 490

SEALY CANADA, LTD.—See Sealy Corporation; *U.S. Private*, pg. 979

SEALY CORPORATION; *U.S. Private*, pg. 978

SEALY, INC.—See Sealy Corporation; *U.S. Private*, pg. 979

SEALY MATTRESS COMPANY—See Sealy Corporation; *U.S. Private*, pg. 979

SEALY MATTRESS COMPANY - CLARION—See Sealy Corporation; *U.S. Private*, pg. 979

SEALY MATTRESS COMPANY - DENVER—See Sealy Corporation; *U.S. Private*, pg. 979

SEALY MATTRESS COMPANY - LEXINGTON—See Sealy Corporation; *U.S. Private*, pg. 979

SEALY MATTRESS COMPANY OF ALBANY, INC.—See Sealy Corporation; *U.S. Private*, pg. 979

SEALY MATTRESS COMPANY OF ILLINOIS—See Sealy Corporation; *U.S. Private*, pg. 979

SEALY MATTRESS COMPANY OF KANSAS CITY, INC.—See Sealy Corporation; *U.S. Private*, pg. 979

SEALY MATTRESS COMPANY OF MEMPHIS—See Sealy Corporation; *U.S. Private*, pg. 979

SEALY MATTRESS COMPANY OF MICHIGAN, INC.—See Sealy Corporation; *U.S. Private*, pg. 979

SEALY MATTRESS COMPANY OF PUERTO RICO—See Sealy Corporation; *U.S. Private*, pg. 979

SEALY MATTRESS COMPANY - ORLANDO—See Sealy Corporation; *U.S. Private*, pg. 979

SEALY MATTRESS COMPANY - PHOENIX—See Sealy Corporation; *U.S. Private*, pg. 979

SEALY MATTRESS COMPANY - PORTLAND—See Sealy Corporation; *U.S. Private*, pg. 979

SEALY MATTRESS COMPANY - SOUTHGATE—See Sealy Corporation; *U.S. Private*, pg. 979

SEALY OF MARYLAND & VIRGINIA, INC.—See Sealy Corporation; *U.S. Private*, pg. 979

SEALY OF MINNESOTA, INC.—See Sealy Corporation; *U.S. Private*, pg. 979

SEALY-STEARNS & FOSTER BEDDING CO. - ATLANTA—See Sealy Corporation; *U.S. Private*, pg. 979

SEAMAN FURNITURE COMPANY, INC.; *U.S. Public*, pg. 1452

SEAMAN-PATRICK PAPER COMPANY; *U.S. Private*, pg. 979

SEAMAN TIMBER COMPANY, INC.; *U.S. Private*, pg. 979

SEAPORT MARKETPLACE, INC.—See The Rouse Company; *U.S. Public*, pg. 1408

SEAPORT MARKETPLACE THEATRE, INC.—See The Rouse Company; *U.S. Public*, pg. 1408

SEAPORT THEATRE MANAGEMENT CORPORATION—See The Rouse Company; *U.S. Public*, pg. 1408

SEAQUIST CLOSURES—See AptarGroup, Inc.; *U.S. Public*, pg. 125

SEAQUISTPERFECT DISPENSING—See AptarGroup, Inc.; *U.S. Public*, pg. 125

SEARCH ORGANIZATION OF SEGURIDAD, S.A.—See The Wackenhut Corporation; *U.S. Public*, pg. 1731

SEARLE & CO.—See Monsanto Company; *U.S. Public*, pg. 1125

SEARLE CANADA INC.—See Monsanto Company; *U.S. Public*, pg. 1126

SEARLE CHEMICALS, INC.—See Monsanto Company; *U.S. Public*, pg. 1125

SEARLE CIBA-GEIGY KOREA LTD.—See Novartis AG; *Int'l*, pg. 985

SEARLE (FRANCE)—See Ascot Holdings Plc; *Int'l*, pg. 88

G.D. SEARLE & COMPANY LIMITED—See Monsanto Company; *Int'l*, pg. 1126

SEARLE LABORATORIES—See Monsanto Company; *U.S. Public*, pg. 1125

SEARLE MANUFACTURING CO.—See Ascot Holdings Plc; *Int'l*, pg. 88

SEARLE S.R.L.; *Int'l*, pg. 1217

SEARS AUTO CENTERS—See Sears, Roebuck and Co.; *U.S. Public*, pg. 1452

SEARS CANADA, INC.—See Sears, Roebuck and Co.; *U.S. Public*, pg. 1452

SEARS DE MEXICO—See Grupo Carso S.A. de C.V.; *Int'l*, pg. 573

SEARS LOGISTICS SERVICES—See Sears, Roebuck and Co.; *U.S. Public*, pg. 1452

SEARS PLC; *Int'l*, pg. 1217

SEARS POINT RACEWAY—See Speedway Motorsports, Inc.; *U.S. Public*, pg. 1498

SEARS PORTRAIT STUDIOS—See CPI Corp.; *U.S. Public*, pg. 283

SEARS, ROEBUCK AND CO.; *U.S. Public*, pg. 1452

SEARS TIRE GROUP—See Sears, Roebuck and Co.; *U.S. Public*, pg. 1452

SEASIDE FINANCIAL CORPORATION—See FirstFed Financial Corp.; *U.S. Public*, pg. 646

SEASON-ALL INDUSTRIES, INC.—See Caradon Plc; *Int'l*, pg. 267

SEASONS CONGREGATE LIVING, INC.—See The Western and Southern Life Insurance Company; *U.S. Private*, pg. 1164

SEASONS MANAGEMENT COMPANY—See The Western and Southern Life Insurance Company; *U.S. Private*, pg. 1164

S.E.A.T.—See Danone Group; *Int'l*, pg. 381

SEAT DEUTSCHLAND GMBH—See Volkswagen AG; *Int'l*, pg. 1475

SEAT METAL COMPONENTS OF INDIA PVT. LTD.—See Bertrand Faure; *Int'l*, pg. 193

SEAT RICAMBI S.P.A.—See Volkswagen AG; *Int'l*, pg. 1474

SEAT, S.A.—See Volkswagen AG; *Int'l*, pg. 1475

KENNETH M. SEATON ENTERPRISES—See Family Inns of America, Inc.; *U.S. Private*, pg. 393

SEATRONICS COMPANY—See Thermo Electron Corporation; *U.S. Public*, pg. 1593

SEATS INCORPORATED—See Flambeau Corporation; *U.S. Private*, pg. 410

SEATTLE AIRLINE LEARNING CENTER—See Berkshire Hathaway Inc.; *U.S. Public*, pg. 219

THE SEATTLE BUSINESS JOURNAL, INC.—See Advance Publications Inc.; *U.S. Private*, pg. 20

SEATTLE CITY LIGHT; *U.S. Public*, pg. 979

SEATTLE-FIRST ASIA LTD.—See BankAmerica Corporation; *U.S. Public*, pg. 183

SEATTLE PACIFIC INDUSTRIES, INC.; *U.S. Private*, pg. 980

SEATTLE PACKAGING CORPORATION; *U.S. Private*, pg. 980

SEATTLE POST-INTELLIGENCER—See The Hearst Corporation; *U.S. Private*, pg. 517

SEATTLE TIMES COMPANY; *U.S. Private*, pg. 980

SEATTLE WA STEEL DIVISION—See Birmingham Steel Corporation; *U.S. Public*, pg. 232

SEAWAY FOOD TOWN, INC.; *U.S. Public*, pg. 1452

SEAWAY IMPORTING COMPANY—See Pamida Holdings Corporation; *U.S. Public*, pg. 1255

SEAWAY PROPERTIES, INC.—See Seaway Food Town, Inc.; *U.S. Public*, pg. 1453

SEAWAY SHOPPING CENTERS, INC.—See Charan Industries, Inc.; *U.S. Private*, pg. 229

SEAWAY TRANSPORTATION, INC.—See American Waste Services, Inc.; *U.S. Public*, pg. 94

SEAWAYS LEASING CO.—See Coeclerici Group; *Int'l*, pg. 304

SEAWHEEL LTD.—See Sophus Berendsen A/S; *Int'l*, pg. 1285

SEBA APROZ S.A.—See Migros; *Int'l*, pg. 866

SEBAGO, INC.; *U.S. Private*, pg. 980

SEBASTIAN COTTON & GRAIN CORP.; *U.S. Private*, pg. 980

SEBRING NEWS-SUN—See The New York Times Company; *U.S. Public*, pg. 1175

SECHRIST INDUSTRIES, INC.; *U.S. Private*, pg. 980

SECIL S.A.—See FLS Industries A/S; *Int'l*, pg. 476

SECO S.A.—See Kemira Oy; *Int'l*, pg. 729

SECO WARWICK CORPORATION; *U.S. Private*, pg. 980

SECOM CO., LTD.; *Int'l*, pg. 1217

SECOM GENERAL CORPORATION; *U.S. Public*, pg. 1453

SECOMERICA, INC.—See Secom Co., Ltd.; *Int'l*, pg. 1217

SECON PROPERTIES—See Cigna Corp.; *U.S. Public*, pg. 362

THE SECOND CUP—See Cara Operations Limited; *Int'l*, pg. 266

SECOND NATIONAL BANK OF BAY CITY—See Citizens Banking Corporation; *U.S. Public*, pg. 379

SECOROC INC.—See Atlas Copco AB; *Int'l*, pg. 96

SECRETLY YOURS INC.—See Inner Secrets, Inc.; *U.S. Private*, pg. 565

SECUNDO GVG MBH—See Commerzbank AG; *Int'l*, pg. 310

SECURA INSURANCE COMPANIES—See Migros; *Int'l*, pg. 866

SECURAIR LTD.—See Jardine Matheson Holdings Limited; *Int'l*, pg. 705

SECURALL, INC.—See Damsmith Corp.; *U.S. Private*, pg. 309

SECURE COMMUNICATIONS DIVISION—See General Kinetics Incorporated; *U.S. Public*, pg. 717

SECURESPACE INC.—See Cambridge Shopping Centres Limited; *Int'l*, pg. 253

SECUREWARE INTERNATIONAL PRIVAT LTD.—See Assa Abloy AB; *Int'l*, pg. 18

SECURIPLEX INC.—See SNC-Lavalin Group Inc.; *Int'l*, pg. 1162

SECURITAS CAPITAL PARTNERS I, L.P.—See Swiss Reinsurance Company; *Int'l*, pg. 1333

SECURITAS ISM—See Telefonaktiebolaget LM Ericsson; *Int'l*, pg. 1369

SECURITIES DATA COMPANY, INC.—See The Thomson Corporation; *U.S. Public*, pg. 1600

SECURITIES MANAGEMENT & RESEARCH—See American National Insurance Company; *U.S. Public*, pg. 88

SECURITIES ONE LIMITED—See Finance One Public Company Limited; *Int'l*, pg. 485

SECURITY AMERICAN FINANCIAL ENTERPRISES, INC.; *U.S. Private*, pg. 980

SECURITY BANK AND TRUST COMPANY—See Synovus Financial Corp.; *U.S. Public*, pg. 1549

THE SECURITY BANK, HARRISON—See First Commercial Corporation; *U.S. Public*, pg. 630

SECURITY BANK & TRUST CO.—See Old National Bancorp; *U.S. Public*, pg. 1217

SECURITY CAPITAL GROUP INCORPORATED; *U.S. Private*, pg. 980

SECURITY CAPITAL PACIFIC TRUST—See Security Capital Group Incorporated; *U.S. Private*, pg. 981

SECURITY CHIMNEYS INTERNATIONAL LTD.; *Int'l*, pg. 1217

SECURITY DYNAMICS TECHNOLOGIES; *U.S. Public*, pg. 1453

SECURITY EQUITY LIFE INSURANCE COMPANY—See General American Life Insurance Co.; *U.S. Private*, pg. 443

SECURITY GLASS GROUP PLC—See Saint-Gobain; *Int'l*, pg. 1173

SECURITY GROUP INC.; *U.S. Private*, pg. 981

SECURITY HOUSE—See Pittway Corporation; *U.S. Public*, pg. 1307

SECURITY INDUSTRIAL INSURANCE CO., INC.—See The Loewen Group, Inc.; *Int'l*, pg. 814

SECURITY INSURANCE CO. OF HARTFORD—See Orion Capital Corporation; *U.S. Public*, pg. 1231

SECURITY INSURANCE CO. (U.K.) LTD.—See Orion Capital Corporation; *U.S. Public*, pg. 1231

SECURITY LIFE INSURANCE COMPANY OF AMERICA—See Security American Financial Enterprises, Inc.; *U.S. Private*, pg. 980

SECURITY LIFE OF DENVER REINSURANCE COMPANY—See ING Groep N.V.; *Int'l*, pg. 648

SECURITY MUTUAL LIFE INSURANCE CO. OF NEW YORK; *U.S. Private*, pg. 981

SECURITY NATIONAL BANK & TRUST CO. OF NORMAN—See First Commercial Corporation; *U.S. Public*, pg. 630

SECURITY NATIONAL LIFE INSURANCE CO.—See Corporacion MAPFRE, Compania Internacional de Reaseguros, S.A.; *Int'l*, pg. 334

SECURITY PACIFIC ASIAN BANK, LTD.—See BankAmerica Corporation; *U.S. Public*, pg. 183

SECURITY PACIFIC BANK A.G.—See BankAmerica Corporation; *U.S. Public*, pg. 183

SECURITY PACIFIC BANK ALASKA, N.A.—See BankAmerica Corporation; *U.S. Public*, pg. 180

SECURITY PACIFIC BANK CANADA—See BankAmerica Corporation; *U.S. Public*, pg. 183

SECURITY PACIFIC BANK OREGON—See BankAmerica Corporation; *U.S. Public*, pg. 182

SECURITY PACIFIC EUROFINANCE, INC.—See BankAmerica Corporation; *U.S. Public*, pg. 183

SECURITY PACIFIC HOARE GOVETT (HOLDINGS) LIMITED—See BankAmerica Corporation; *U.S. Public*, pg. 183

SECURITY PACIFIC HOUSING SERVICES, INC.—See BankAmerica Corporation; *U.S. Public*, pg. 182

SECURITY PACIFIC INFORMATION SERVICES CORPORATION—See BankAmerica Corporation; *U.S. Public*, pg. 182

SECURITY PACIFIC INTERNATIONAL FINANCE, INC.—See BankAmerica Corporation; *U.S. Public*, pg. 182

SECURITY PACIFIC INVESTMENTS, INC.—See BankAmerica Corporation; *U.S. Public*, pg. 182

SECURITY PACIFIC LEASING CORPORATION—See BankAmerica Corporation; *U.S. Public*, pg. 182

SECURITY PACIFIC LIMITED—See BankAmerica Corporation; *U.S. Public*, pg. 183

SECURITY PACIFIC NATIONAL BANK, MANILA—See BankAmerica Corporation; *U.S. Public*, pg. 183

SECURITY PACIFIC NATIONAL BANK, SEOUL—See BankAmerica Corporation; *U.S. Public*, pg. 183

SECURITY PACIFIC NATIONAL BANK, SINGAPORE—See BankAmerica Corporation; *U.S. Public*, pg. 183

SECURITY PACIFIC NATIONAL BANK, TAIPEI—See BankAmerica Corporation; *U.S. Public*, pg. 183

SECURITY PACIFIC NATIONAL BANK, TOKYO—See BankAmerica Corporation; *U.S. Public*, pg. 183

SECURITY PACIFIC OREGON BANCORP—See BankAmerica Corporation; *U.S. Public*, pg. 182

SECURITY PACIFIC SERVICES CORPORATION—See BankAmerica Corporation; *U.S. Public*, pg. 182

SECURITY PACIFIC STATE BANK—See BankAmerica Corporation; *U.S. Public*, pg. 182

SECURITY PLASTICS CARIBE, INC.—See Security Plastics, Inc.; *U.S. Private*, pg. 981

SECURITY PLASTICS DE MEXICO—See Security Plastics, Inc.; *U.S. Private*, pg. 981

SECURITY PLASTICS, INC.; *U.S. Private*, pg. 981

SECURITY PLASTICS WEST, INC.—See Security Plastics, Inc.; *U.S. Private*, pg. 981

SECURITY REINSURANCE CO.—See Orion Capital Corporation; *U.S. Public*, pg. 1231

SECURITY STATE BANK—See UMB Financial Corporation; *U.S. Public*, pg. 1654

SECURITY WARRANTY ASSOCIATION OF FLORIDA—See Orion Capital Corporation; *U.S. Public*, pg. 1231

SECURITYLINK FROM AMERITECH—See Ameritech Corporation; *U.S. Public*, pg. 98

SEDCO FOREX HOLDINGS LIMITED—See Schlumberger Limited; *U.S. Public*, pg. 1439

SEDCO FOREX OFFSHORE INTERNATIONAL LIMITED—See Schlumberger Limited; *U.S. Public*, pg. 1439

SEDEC S.A.R.L.—See Unilever Plc; *Int'l*, pg. 1438

SEDGWICK CHARTERED LIMITED—See Standard Chartered Bank PLC; *Int'l*, pg. 1297

SEDGWICK CHARTERED PRIVATE LIMITED—See Standard Chartered Bank PLC; *Int'l*, pg. 1297

SEDGWICK GROUP PLC; *Int'l*, pg. 1217

SEDGWICK, INC.—See Sedgwick Group plc; *Int'l*, pg. 1218

SEDGWICK INSURANCE BROKERS (PTY) LIMITED—See Standard Chartered Bank PLC; *Int'l*, pg. 1297

SEDGWICK JAMES INSURANCE BROKERS (PRIVATE) LIMITED—See Standard Chartered Bank PLC; *Int'l*, pg. 1297

SEDGWICK LIMITED—See Sedgwick Group plc; *Int'l*, pg. 1218

SEDGWICK NOBLE LOWNDES—See Sedgwick Group plc; *Int'l*, pg. 1218

SEDGWICK NOBLE LOWNDES GROUP LIMITED—See Sedgwick Group plc; *Int'l*, pg. 1218

SEDGWICK NOBLE LOWNDES LIMITED—See Sedgwick Group plc; *Int'l*, pg. 1218

SEDGWICK OAKWOOD UNDERWRITING AGENTS LIMITED—See Sedgwick Group plc; *Int'l*, pg. 1218

SEDILEC S.C.—See Electrabel S.A.; *Int'l*, pg. 437

SEDIN-SCHIESS—See Metallgesellschaft AG; *Int'l*, pg. 860

SEDITEL S.C.—See Electrabel S.A.; *Int'l*, pg. 437

SEDNETH, SEA DRILLING NETHERLANDS BV—See Hollandsche Beton Groep NV; *Int'l*, pg. 630

SEDRI—See Accor S.A.; *Int'l*, pg. 20

SEDRO-WOOLLEY LUMBER CO.—See WTD Industries, Inc.; *U.S. Public*, pg. 1730

SEDWICK JOHNSON OY—See Axel Johnson AB; *Int'l*, pg. 712

SEE TECHNOLOGIES INC.—See SSE Telecom, Inc.; *U.S. Public*, pg. 1421

SEED CORPORATION OF AMERICA; *U.S. Private*, pg. 981

SEED RESTAURANT GROUP, INC.; *U.S. Private*, pg. 981

SEELOW KASEWERKE GMBH—See Koninklijke BolsWessanen nv; *Int'l*, pg. 753

SEELY EQUIPMENT & SUPPLY CO., INC.—See Modern Group Ltd.; *U.S. Private*, pg. 755

SEER TECHNOLOGIES, INC.; *U.S. Public*, pg. 1453

SEE'S CANDIES, INC.—See Berkshire Hathaway Inc.; *U.S. Public*, pg. 221

SEE'S CANDY SHOPS, INC.—See Berkshire Hathaway Inc.; *U.S. Public*, pg. 221
SEESSEL HOLDINGS, INC.; *U.S. Private*, pg. 981
SEFCAL S.A.—See Chr. Hansen Holding A/S; *Int'l*, pg. 289
SEFRANEZ—See Pechiney S.A.; *Int'l*, pg. 1028
SEGA ENTERPRISES LTD.; *Int'l*, pg. 1218
SEGA OF AMERICA INC.—See Sega Enterprises Ltd.; *Int'l*, pg. 1218
SEGAL SA—See Koninklijke Hoogovens N.V.; *Int'l*, pg. 756
SEGAL S.C.R.L.—See Arbed S.A.; *Int'l*, pg. 79
SEGAL, SOCIETE COOPERATIVE—See Koninklijke Hoogovens N.V.; *Int'l*, pg. 754
SEGERA—See Lagardere Groupe; *Int'l*, pg. 793
THE SEGERDAHL CORP.; *U.S. Private*, pg. 981
SEGURADORA ROMA, S.A.—See Corporacion MAPFRE, Compania Internacional de Reaseguros, S.A.; *Int'l*, pg. 334
SEGURCAJA, CORREDURIA DE SEGUROS, S.A.—See Caja de Madrid Group; *Int'l*, pg. 252
SEGURCAT, S.A.—See Caixa d'Estalvis de Catalunya; *Int'l*, pg. 250
SEGURIDAD MAPFRE, S.A.—See Corporacion MAPFRE, Compania Internacional de Reaseguros, S.A.; *Int'l*, pg. 333
SEGURIDAD MOVIL DEL ECUADOR, S.A.—See The Wackenhut Corporation; *U.S. Public*, pg. 1731
SEGUROS AZTECA, S.A.—See Cigna Corp.; *U.S. Public*, pg. 363
SEGUROS BANAMEX-AEGON, S.A. DE C.V.—See Grupo Financiero Banamex/Accival, S.A. de C.V.; *Int'l*, pg. 574
SEGUROS CARIBE, S.A.—See Corporacion MAPFRE, Compania Internacional de Reaseguros, S.A.; *Int'l*, pg. 333
SEGUROS CIGNA, S.A.—See Cigna Corp.; *U.S. Public*, pg. 363
SEGUROS DE VIDA Y PENSIONES ANTARES, S.A.—See Telefonica de Espana, S.A.; *Int'l*, pg. 1371
SEGUROS E PENSOES—See Eureko B.V.; *Int'l*, pg. 464
SEGUROS GENESIS, S.A.—See Metropolitan Life Insurance Co.; *U.S. Private*, pg. 738
SEGUROS MONTERREY, S.A.—See Aetna Inc.; *U.S. Public*, pg. 27
SEGUROS ORBITA S.A.—See Fortis; *Int'l*, pg. 499
SEGUROS SAINT PAUL DE VENEZUELA, C.A.—See Cigna Corp.; *U.S. Public*, pg. 363
SEGUROS TEPEYAC, S.A.—See Corporacion MAPFRE, Compania Internacional de Reaseguros, S.A.; *Int'l*, pg. 334
SEGUROS UNIVERSALES, S.A.—See Corporacion MAPFRE, Compania Internacional de Reaseguros, S.A.; *Int'l*, pg. 334
SEIBEL & STERN CORP.; *U.S. Private*, pg. 981
SEIBELS, BRUCE & CO.—See The Seibels Bruce Group, Inc.; *U.S. Public*, pg. 1454
THE SEIBELS BRUCE GROUP, INC.; *U.S. Public*, pg. 1453
SEIBERT-OXIDERMO, INC.—See Detrex Corporation; *U.S. Public*, pg. 502
SEIBU ALLSTATE LIFE INSURANCE CO., LTD.—See The Saison Group; *Int'l*, pg. 1178
SEIBU DEPARTMENT STORES, LTD.—See The Saison Group; *Int'l*, pg. 1178
SEIBU SEKIYO—See Royal Dutch/Shell Group of Companies; *Int'l*, pg. 1139
SEIBU TOKUYAMA READY MIXED CONCRETE CO., LTD.—See Tokuyama Corporation; *Int'l*, pg. 1393
GRAY SEIFART & CO.—See Legg Mason, Inc.; *U.S. Public*, pg. 985
SEIGLE'S HOME & BUILDING CENTERS; *U.S. Private*, pg. 981
SEIKA ELECTRIC CO., LTD.; *Int'l*, pg. 1218
SEIKO AUSTRALIA PTY. LTD.—See Seiko Corporation; *Int'l*, pg. 1218
SEIKO BUILDING MAINTENANCE SERVICE CO., LTD.—See Nippon Life Insurance Co.; *Int'l*, pg. 935
SEIKO CANADA INC.—See Seiko Corporation; *Int'l*, pg. 1218
SEIKO CORPORATION; *Int'l*, pg. 1218
SEIKO CORPORATION OF AMERICA—See Seiko Corporation; *Int'l*, pg. 1218
SEIKO DEUTSCHLAND GMBH—See Seiko Corporation; *Int'l*, pg. 1218
SEIKO EG & G CO. LTD.—See EG & G, Inc.; *U.S. Public*, pg. 544
SEIKO EPSON CORPORATION; *Int'l*, pg. 1219
SEIKO FRANCE S.A.—See Seiko Corporation; *Int'l*, pg. 1218
SEIKO HONG KONG LTD.—See Seiko Corporation; *Int'l*, pg. 1218
SEIKO INSTRUMENTS INC.; *Int'l*, pg. 1219
SEIKO TIME CORP.—See Seiko Corporation; *Int'l*, pg. 1218
SEIKO UK LIMITED—See Seiko Corporation; *Int'l*, pg. 1218
SEIMENS NIXDORF INFORMATIONSSYSTEM AB, SOLNA (STOCKHOLM)—See Siemens AG; *Int'l*, pg. 1247
SEIN MENDEZ LABORATORIES, INC.—See Forest Laboratories, Inc.; *U.S. Public*, pg. 670
SEITA, SOCIETE NATIONALE D'EXPLOITATION INDUSTRIELLE DES TABACS ET DES ALLUMETTES; *Int'l*, pg. 1219
SEITEL DATA CORP.—See Seitel, Inc.; *U.S. Public*, pg. 1454
SEITEL GAS & ENERGY CORP.—See Seitel, Inc.; *U.S. Public*, pg. 1454
SEITEL GEOPHYSICAL, INC. DBA EAGLE GEOPHYSICAL, INC.—See Seitel, Inc.; *U.S. Public*, pg. 1454
SEITEL, INC.; *U.S. Public*, pg. 1454
SEITEL INTERNATIONAL, INC.—See Seitel, Inc.; *U.S. Public*, pg. 1454
SEITEL OFFSHORE CORP.—See Seitel, Inc.; *U.S. Public*, pg. 1454
SEITZ ENZINGER NOLL—See Klockner-Werke AG; *Int'l*, pg. 737

SEITZ FOODS INC.—See Sara Lee Corporation; *U.S. Public*, pg. 1434
SEIWA KAIKAN CO., LTD.—See Nippon Life Insurance Co.; *Int'l*, pg. 935
SEIYO CORPORATION—See The Saison Group; *Int'l*, pg. 1178
SEIYO FOOD SYSTEMS, LTD.—See The Saison Group; *Int'l*, pg. 1178
SEIYO, LTD.—See The Saison Group; *Int'l*, pg. 1178
SEJONG - AMC CORP., LTD.—See Ruhrgas Aktiengesellschaft; *Int'l*, pg. 1149
SEKISUI CHEMICAL CO., LTD.; *Int'l*, pg. 1219
SEKISUI HOUSE, LTD.; *Int'l*, pg. 1219
SEKTIONSBYGGARNA AB—See Skanska AB; *Int'l*, pg. 1260
SEKUR S.p.A.—See Pirelli S.p.A.; *Int'l*, pg. 1058
SEKURIT SAINT-GOBAIN BENELUX—See Saint-Gobain; *Int'l*, pg. 1173
SEKURIT SAINT-GOBAIN DEUTSCHLAND BETEILIGUNGEN (SSGD) GMBH—See Saint-Gobain; *Int'l*, pg. 1173
SEKURIT SAINT-GOBAIN DEUTSCHLAND (SSGD) KG—See Saint-Gobain; *Int'l*, pg. 1173
SEKURIT SAINT-GOBAIN FRANCE (SSGF)—See Saint-Gobain; *Int'l*, pg. 1172
SEKURIT SAINT-GOBAIN ITALIA SRL—See Saint-Gobain; *Int'l*, pg. 1173
SEKURIT SAINT-GOBAIN MODÜLARTECHNIK GMBH—See Saint-Gobain; *Int'l*, pg. 1173
SEKURIT SAINT-GOBAIN NUTZFAHRZEUGGLAS KG—See Saint-Gobain; *Int'l*, pg. 1173
SEKURIT SAINT-GOBAIN SCANDINAVIA AB—See Saint-Gobain; *Int'l*, pg. 1173
SEKURIT SAINT-GOBAIN TORGAU GMBH—See Saint-Gobain; *Int'l*, pg. 1173
SEKURIT SAINT-GOBAIN VEHICULES INDUSTRIELS (SSGVI)—See Saint-Gobain; *Int'l*, pg. 1172
SELANDIA FINANCE AND INVESTMENT B.V.—See The East Asiatic Company Ltd. A/S; *Int'l*, pg. 431
SELANDIA INSURANCE COMPANY LIMITED—See The East Asiatic Company Ltd. A/S; *Int'l*, pg. 431
SELAS CORPORATION OF AMERICA; *U.S. Public*, pg. 1454
SELAS FLUID PROCESSING CORP.—See Linde AG; *Int'l*, pg. 811
SELAS ITALIANA, S.R.L.—See Selas Corporation of America; *U.S. Public*, pg. 1455
SELAS-KIRCHNER GMBH—See Linde AG; *Int'l*, pg. 811
SELAS S.A.—See Selas Corporation of America; *U.S. Public*, pg. 1455
SELAS WAERMETECHNIK GMBH—See Selas Corporation of America; *U.S. Public*, pg. 1455
SELECCIONES MERCANTILES, S.A. DE C.V.—See Bristol-Myers Squibb Company; *U.S. Public*, pg. 256
SELECCOES DO READER'S DIGEST (PORTUGAL) S.A.—See The Reader's Digest Association, Inc.; *U.S. Public*, pg. 1368
SELECT BEVERAGES, INC.; *U.S. Private*, pg. 982
SELECT CANFIELD—See Select Beverages, Inc.; *U.S. Private*, pg. 982
SELECT COMMUNICATIONS, GMBH, HAMBURG—See Select Communications, L.P.; *U.S. Private*, pg. 982
SELECT COMMUNICATIONS, GMBH, KOBLENZ—See Select Communications, L.P.; *U.S. Private*, pg. 982
SELECT COMMUNICATIONS, L.P.; *U.S. Private*, pg. 982
SELECT COMMUNICATIONS, PARIS—See Select Communications, L.P.; *U.S. Private*, pg. 982
SELECT GAUGES—See Brown & Sharpe Manufacturing Company; *U.S. Public*, pg. 260
SELECT HOME HEALTH CARE, INC.—See Integrated Health Services, Inc.; *U.S. Public*, pg. 885
SELECT PRESSE—See Lagardere Groupe; *Int'l*, pg. 793
SELECT RESTAURANTS, INC.; *U.S. Private*, pg. 982
SELECT ROBINSON INC.—See The Cascades Group; *Int'l*, pg. 274
SELECT SIRES, INC.; *U.S. Private*, pg. 982
SELECTION DU READER'S DIGEST S.A.—See The Reader's Digest Association, Inc.; *U.S. Public*, pg. 1368
SELECTION LIGHTING INC.—See Kaufel Group Ltd.; *Int'l*, pg. 725
SELECTIVE BEAUTY INTERNATIONAL DIV.—See L'Oreal S.A.; *Int'l*, pg. 819
SELECTIVE INSURANCE GROUP, INC; *U.S. Public*, pg. 1455
SELECTIVE TECHNICAL ADMINISTRATIVE SERVICES, INC.—See Selective Insurance Group, Inc; *U.S. Public*, pg. 1456
SELECTO-FLASH, INC.; *U.S. Private*, pg. 982
SELECTONE, INC.; *U.S. Private*, pg. 982
SELECTPACK BV—See Koninklijke BolsWessanen nv; *Int'l*, pg. 751
SELECTPACK SA—See Koninklijke BolsWessanen nv; *Int'l*, pg. 753
SELECTREHAB—See Horizon/CMS Healthcare Corporation; *U.S. Public*, pg. 839
SELEKTVRACHT B.V.—See Royal Nedlloyd Group N.V.; *Int'l*, pg. 1145
SELEZIONE DAL READER'S DIGEST S.P.A.—See The Reader's Digest Association, Inc.; *U.S. Public*, pg. 1368
SELF—See Advance Publications Inc.; *U.S. Private*, pg. 20
SELF AUTO—See Castorama Dubois Investissements S.C.A.; *Int'l*, pg. 276
SELF-INSURANCE ADMINISTRATORS, INC.—See Atlantic American Corporation; *U.S. Public*, pg. 144
SELF-INSURERS' MANAGEMENT CORPORATION—See Cigna Corp.; *U.S. Public*, pg. 366
SELF-INSURERS SERVICE, INC.—See AON Corporation; *U.S. Public*, pg. 117
SELFIX, INC.—See Home Products International, Inc.; *U.S. Public*, pg. 832
SELIG CHEMICAL INDUSTRIES—See National Service Industries, Inc.; *U.S. Public*, pg. 1160
SELIGMAN & ASSOCIATES, INC.; *U.S. Private*, pg. 982

SELIGMAN & ASSOCS. OF MICHIGAN—See Seligman & Associates, Inc.; *U.S. Private*, pg. 982
SELIGMAN FINANCIAL SERVICES, INC.—See J. & W. Seligman & Co.; *U.S. Private*, pg. 982
SELIGMAN HENDERSON CO.—See Henderson Administration Group PLC; *Int'l*, pg. 609
SELIGMAN HENDERSON CO.—See J. & W. Seligman & Co.; *U.S. Private*, pg. 982
J. & W. SELIGMAN & CO.; *U.S. Private*, pg. 982
SELKIRK CANADA LTD.—See Zurn Industries, Inc.; *U.S. Public*, pg. 1795
SELKIRK EUROPE—See Zurn Industries, Inc.; *U.S. Public*, pg. 1795
SELKIRK HVAC—See Zurn Industries, Inc.; *U.S. Public*, pg. 1795
SELKIRK (HVAC) EUROPE—See Zurn Industries, Inc.; *U.S. Public*, pg. 1795
SELKIRK METALBESTOS—See Zurn Industries, Inc.; *U.S. Public*, pg. 1794
SELKIRK METALBESTOS N.A.—See Zurn Industries, Inc.; *U.S. Public*, pg. 1794
SELLEN CONSTRUCTION COMPANY; *U.S. Private*, pg. 982
SELLERS & JOSEPHSON—See Shelby Williams Industries, Inc.; *U.S. Public*, pg. 1465
BOB SELLERS PONTIAC GMC TRUCK INC.; *U.S. Private*, pg. 983
SELLERS CLEANING SYSTEMS—See Crane Co.; *U.S. Public*, pg. 457
DEAN SELLERS FORD INC.; *U.S. Private*, pg. 983
SELLERSBURG STONE COMPANY, INC.—See Gohmann Asphalt & Construction Inc.; *U.S. Private*, pg. 459
SELLES MEDICAL LIMITED—See Alliance UniChem PLC; *Int'l*, pg. 58
SELLEYS CHEMICAL CO NZ LTD—See Imperial Chemical Industries PLC; *Int'l*, pg. 665
SELLEYS CHEMICAL CO PTY LIMITED—See Imperial Chemical Industries PLC; *Int'l*, pg. 665
SELLSTROM MANUFACTURING CO.; *U.S. Private*, pg. 983
SELMABIPIEMME LEASING SPA—See Banca Popolare di Milano; *Int'l*, pg. 137
THE SELMER CO., INC.—See Steinway Musical Instruments, Inc.; *U.S. Public*, pg. 1514
SELOVER BUICK, INC.; *U.S. Private*, pg. 983
SELTEC SELECTIVE TECHNOLOGY INC.—See Zexel Corporation; *Int'l*, pg. 1528
SELTEL, INC.—See Chancellor Media Corporation; *U.S. Public*, pg. 335
SELTRA—See Lex Service PLC; *Int'l*, pg. 807
WILLIAM R. SELWOOD LTD.—See BTR plc; *Int'l*, pg. 124
DIPL.-ING SELZER AUFZUGE GMBH—See Kone Corporation; *Int'l*, pg. 747
SEMAC INDUSTRIES INC.; *U.S. Private*, pg. 983
SEMAFOR A/S—See Telefonaktiebolaget LM Ericsson; *Int'l*, pg. 1369
SEMBAWANG MARITIME LIMITED; *Int'l*, pg. 1219
SEMBLEX CORPORATION; *U.S. Private*, pg. 983
SEMCO INDUSTRIES INC.; *U.S. Private*, pg. 983
SEMCON ELECTRONICS PVT. LTD.—See Microsemi Corporation; *U.S. Public*, pg. 1107
P.T. SEMEN ANDALAS INDONESIA—See Lafarge S.A.; *Int'l*, pg. 791
SEMENTI DOTTO S.P.A.—See Assicurazioni Generali S.p.A.; *Int'l*, pg. 90
SEMI-GAS SYSTEMS, INC.—See Nippon Sanso Corporation; *Int'l*, pg. 938
SEMI-TECH CORP.—See Semi-Tech Corporation; *Int'l*, pg. 1220
SEMI-TECH CORPORATION; *Int'l*, pg. 1220
SEMI-TECH (GLOBAL) CO.—See Semi-Tech Corporation; *Int'l*, pg. 1220
SEMICON ASSOCIATES—See Ceradyne, Inc; *U.S. Public*, pg. 330
SEMICONDUCTOR ELECTRONICS LTD.—See International Rectifier Corporation; *U.S. Public*, pg. 907
SEMICONDUCTOR EQUIPMENT GROUP—See Watkins-Johnson Company; *U.S. Public*, pg. 1745
SEMICONDUCTOR MINIATURE PRODUCTS (M) SDN. BHD.—See Motorola, Inc.; *U.S. Public*, pg. 1140
SEMICONDUCTOR PACKAGING MATERIALS CO., INC.; *U.S. Public*, pg. 1456
SEMIKRON INC.—See Semikron International, GmbH & Co. KG; *Int'l*, pg. 1220
SEMIKRON INTERNATIONAL, GMBH & CO. KG; *Int'l*, pg. 1220
SEMILAB AG—See Laporte plc; *Int'l*, pg. 803
SEMILLAS MERIEL—See Pioneer Hi-Bred International, Inc.; *U.S. Public*, pg. 1299
SEMILLAS PIONEER CHILE LTDA.—See Pioneer Hi-Bred International, Inc.; *U.S. Public*, pg. 1299
SEMILLAS PIONEER, S.A.—See Pioneer Hi-Bred International, Inc.; *U.S. Public*, pg. 1299
SEMITEC, INC.—See Kulicke & Soffa Industries, Inc.; *U.S. Public*, pg. 969
SEMITOOL, INC.; *U.S. Public*, pg. 1456
SEMP TOSHIBA AMAZONAS S.A.—See Toshiba Corporation; *Int'l*, pg. 1406
SEMPELL VALVES PVT. LTD.—See Deutsche Babcock AG; *Int'l*, pg. 401
SEMPERIT AG HOLDING—See Creditanstalt-Bankverein; *Int'l*, pg. 347
SEMPERIT REIFEN AG—See Continental AG; *Int'l*, pg. 328
SEMPRA ENERGY TRADING—See Pacific Enterprises; *U.S. Public*, pg. 1249
SEMTECH CORPORATION; *U.S. Public*, pg. 1456
SEMTECH CORPUS CHRISTI—See Semtech Corporation; *U.S. Public*, pg. 1456
SEMTECH CORPUS CHRISTI S.A. DE C.V.—See Semtech Corporation; *U.S. Public*, pg. 1456
SEMTECH LTD.—See Semtech Corporation; *U.S. Public*, pg. 1456
SEMTECH NORTHEAST REGION—See Semtech Corporation; *U.S. Public*, pg. 1456

SENALIZACION Y ACCESORIOS DEL AUTOMOVIL YORKA, S.A.—See General Motors Corporation; *U.S. Public*, pg. 724

SENATOBIA DIVISION—See R.R. Donnelley & Sons Company; *U.S. Public*, pg. 518

SENATOBIA FAMILY PRACTICE, INC.—See Integrated Health Services; *U.S. Public*, pg. 885

SENATOR FORD; *U.S. Private*, pg. 983

SENCO PRODUCTS, INC.—See SENCORP; *U.S. Private*, pg. 984

SENCORE, INC.; *U.S. Private*, pg. 983

SENCORP; *U.S. Private*, pg. 983

SENDAI NIKON K.K.—See Nikon Corporation; *Int'l*, pg. 931

SENECA FALLS TECHNOLOGY GROUP; *U.S. Private*, pg. 984

SENECA FLIGHT OPER.—See Seneca Foods Corporation; *U.S. Public*, pg. 1456

SENECA FOODS CORPORATION; *U.S. Public*, pg. 1456

SENECA RESOURCES CORP.—See National Fuel Gas Company; *U.S. Public*, pg. 1156

SENECA WIRE & MANUFACTURING CO.; *U.S. Private*, pg. 984

SENERCOMM INC.—See Sulcus Computer Corp.; *U.S. Public*, pg. 1527

SENETICS—See The West Company, Incorporated; *U.S. Public*, pg. 1755

SENIOR AUSTRALIA LIMITED—See Senior Engineering Group, plc.; *Int'l*, pg. 1222

SENIOR BIGWOOD LIMITED—See Senior Engineering Group, plc.; *Int'l*, pg. 1220

SENIOR CHRISTCHURCH LIMITED—See Senior Engineering Group, plc.; *Int'l*, pg. 1223

SENIOR COLMAN LIMITED—See Senior Engineering Group, plc.; *Int'l*, pg. 1220

SENIOR CONFLOW—See Senior Engineering Group, plc.; *Int'l*, pg. 1222

SENIOR CONFLOW INC.—See Senior Engineering Group, plc.; *Int'l*, pg. 1222

SENIOR CONSTRUCTION SERVICES LIMITED—See Senior Engineering Group, plc.; *Int'l*, pg. 1220

SENIOR CONTROL ENGINEERING LIMITED—See Senior Engineering Group, plc.; *Int'l*, pg. 1220

SENIOR DAVIS DERBY—See Senior Engineering Group, plc.; *Int'l*, pg. 1220

SENIOR ENGINEERING—See Senior Engineering Group, plc.; *Int'l*, pg. 1222

SENIOR ENGINEERING CO.-BERLIN—See Senior Engineering Group, plc.; *Int'l*, pg. 1222

SENIOR ENGINEERING CO.-CENTRAL REGION—See Senior Engineering Group, plc.; *Int'l*, pg. 1222

SENIOR ENGINEERING CO.-EASTERN REGION—See Senior Engineering Group, plc.; *Int'l*, pg. 1222

SENIOR ENGINEERING CO.-ECONOMISER DIV.—See Senior Engineering Group, plc.; *Int'l*, pg. 1222

SENIOR ENGINEERING CO.-JOPLIN—See Senior Engineering Group, plc.; *Int'l*, pg. 1222

SENIOR ENGINEERING CO.-MILWAUKEE—See Senior Engineering Group, plc.; *Int'l*, pg. 1222

SENIOR ENGINEERING COMPANY-USA—See Senior Engineering Group, plc.; *Int'l*, pg. 1222

SENIOR ENGINEERING GROUP, PLC.; *Int'l*, pg. 1220

SENIOR ENGINEERING PRODUCTS BUSINESS AREA—See Senior Engineering Group, plc.; *Int'l*, pg. 1220

SENIOR ENGINEERING (PTY) LIMITED-SOUTH AFRICA—See Senior Engineering Group, plc.; *Int'l*, pg. 1223

SENIOR ENGINEERING SERVICES CO. (HEAD OFFICE)—See Senior Engineering Group, plc.; *Int'l*, pg. 1222

SENIOR ENGINEERING TIFT GMBH—See Senior Engineering Group, plc.; *Int'l*, pg. 1223

SENIOR ENTEX—See Senior Engineering Group, plc.; *Int'l*, pg. 1220

SENIOR FLEXONICS—See Senior Engineering Group, plc.; *Int'l*, pg. 1223

SENIOR FLEXONICS AUSTRALIA—See Senior Engineering Group, plc.; *Int'l*, pg. 1223

SENIOR FLEXONICS INC.—See Senior Engineering Group, plc.; *Int'l*, pg. 1222

SENIOR FLEXONICS LTD.—See Senior Engineering Group, plc.; *Int'l*, pg. 1221

SENIOR FOSTER WHEELER CONSTRUCTION DIVISION—See Senior Engineering Group, plc.; *Int'l*, pg. 1221

SENIOR FOSTER WHEELER INDUSTRIAL BOILER DIVISION—See Senior Engineering Group, plc.; *Int'l*, pg. 1221

SENIOR FOSTER WHEELER POWER DIVISION—See Senior Engineering Group, plc.; *Int'l*, pg. 1221

SENIOR GREEN ECONOMISER DIVISION—See Senior Engineering Group, plc.; *Int'l*, pg. 1221

SENIOR HARGREAVES LIMITED—See Senior Engineering Group, plc.; *Int'l*, pg. 1221

SENIOR HEAT TREATMENT-ALDRIDGE—See Senior Engineering Group, plc.; *Int'l*, pg. 1221

SENIOR HEAT TREATMENT-BLACKBURN—See Senior Engineering Group, plc.; *Int'l*, pg. 1221

SENIOR HEAT TREATMENT LIMITED—See Senior Engineering Group, plc.; *Int'l*, pg. 1221

SENIOR HEAT TREATMENT-LUTON—See Senior Engineering Group, plc.; *Int'l*, pg. 1221

SENIOR HEAT TREATMENT-NEWPORT—See Senior Engineering Group, plc.; *Int'l*, pg. 1221

SENIOR HEAT TREATMENT-PUDSEY—See Senior Engineering Group, plc.; *Int'l*, pg. 1221

SENIOR HEAT TREATMENT-TIPTON—See Senior Engineering Group, plc.; *Int'l*, pg. 1221

SENIOR HEAT TREATMENT-WATFORD—See Senior Engineering Group, plc.; *Int'l*, pg. 1221

SENIOR HEAT TREATMENT-WEST BROMWICH—See Senior Engineering Group, plc.; *Int'l*, pg. 1221

SENIOR LUKE MATERIALS HANDLING DIVISION—See Senior Engineering Group, plc.; *Int'l*, pg. 1029

SENIOR MARKETS DIVISION—See Blue Cross and Blue Shield of Massachusetts; *U.S. Private*, pg. 151

SENIOR MODUCEL LIMITED—See Senior Engineering Group, plc.; *Int'l*, pg. 1221

SENIOR NEW ZEALAND LIMITED—See Senior Engineering Group, plc.; *Int'l*, pg. 1223

SENIOR PHOENIX RFS LIMITED—See Senior Engineering Group, plc.; *Int'l*, pg. 1221

SENIOR PUBLICATIONS HOLDINGS, INC.—See G.T.C. Transcontinental Group Ltd.; *Int'l*, pg. 539

SENIOR PUBLICIDAD S.R.L.—See DMB&B Communications; *Int'l*, pg. 305

SENIOR SERVICE TOBACCO LTD.—See Gallaher Limited; *Int'l*, pg. 539

SENIOR SPECTRUM—See McClatchy Newspapers Inc.; *U.S. Public*, pg. 1066

SENIOR THERMAL ENGINEERING LIMITED—See Senior Engineering Group, plc.; *Int'l*, pg. 1221

SENIOR TIFT AUSTRALIA PTY LIMITED—See Senior Engineering Group, plc.; *Int'l*, pg. 1223

SENIOR TIFT B.V.—See Senior Engineering Group, plc.; *Int'l*, pg. 1223

SENIOR TIFT, INC.—See Senior Engineering Group, plc.; *Int'l*, pg. 1222

SENIOR TIFT LIMITED—See Senior Engineering Group, plc.; *Int'l*, pg. 1221

SENIOR TIFT-PROSPECT—See Senior Engineering Group, plc.; *Int'l*, pg. 1223

SENIOR TIFT PTE. LTD.—See Senior Engineering Group, plc.; *Int'l*, pg. 1223

SENIOR TIFT-QUEENSLAND—See Senior Engineering Group, plc.; *Int'l*, pg. 1223

SENIOR TIFT-VICTORIA—See Senior Engineering Group, plc.; *Int'l*, pg. 1223

SENIOR TIFT-WESTERN AUSTRALIA—See Senior Engineering Group, plc.; *Int'l*, pg. 1223

SENIOR TUBE LIMITED—See Senior Engineering Group, plc.; *Int'l*, pg. 1221

SENIOR WELLINGTON LIMITED—See Senior Engineering Group, plc.; *Int'l*, pg. 1223

SENLSYS—See BTR plc; *Int'l*, pg. 127

SENMATEL—See Jeumont-Schneider Trenformeteurs; *Int'l*, pg. 706

SENNA NOHRUNPSMITTEL GMBH—See Maresi Markenartikelvertrieb Aktiengesellschaft; *Int'l*, pg. 842

SENNHEISER ELECTRONIC CORP.; *U.S. Private*, pg. 984

SENSALL, DIV. OF ROSEMOUNT, INC.—See Emerson Electric Co.; *U.S. Public*, pg. 574

SENSENICH PROPELLER MANUFACTURING CO., INC.—See The Philadelphia Bourse, Inc.; *U.S. Private*, pg. 861

SENSENICH WOOD PROPELLER CO., INC.—See The Philadelphia Bourse, Inc.; *U.S. Private*, pg. 861

SENSODEC OY—See Valmet Corporation; *Int'l*, pg. 1449

SENSOR SYSTEMS DIVISION—See Axsys Technologies, Inc.; *U.S. Public*, pg. 158

SENSORE NEDERLAND B.V.—See Halliburton Company; *U.S. Public*, pg. 777

SENSORE S.A.—See Halliburton Company; *U.S. Public*, pg. 777

SENSORMATIC AB (SWEDEN)—See Sensormatic Electronics Corporation; *U.S. Public*, pg. 1457

SENSORMATIC AG—See Sensormatic Electronics Corporation; *U.S. Public*, pg. 1457

SENSORMATIC A/S—See Sensormatic Electronics Corporation; *U.S. Public*, pg. 1457

SENSORMATIC A/S (DENMARK)—See Sensormatic Electronics Corporation; *U.S. Public*, pg. 1457

SENSORMATIC ASIA/PACIFIC—See Sensormatic Electronics Corporation; *U.S. Public*, pg. 1457

SENSORMATIC AUSTRALIA PTY LIMITED—See Sensormatic Electronics Corporation; *U.S. Public*, pg. 1457

SENSORMATIC (BELGIUM) S.A.—See Sensormatic Electronics Corporation; *U.S. Public*, pg. 1457

SENSORMATIC B.V.—See Sensormatic Electronics Corporation; *U.S. Public*, pg. 1457

SENSORMATIC CAMERA LTD.—See Sensormatic Electronics Corporation; *U.S. Public*, pg. 1457

SENSORMATIC DEL CARIBE—See Sensormatic Electronics Corporation; *U.S. Public*, pg. 1457

SENSORMATIC DO BRAZIL ELECTRONICA LTDA.—See Sensormatic Electronics Corporation; *U.S. Public*, pg. 1457

SENSORMATIC E.C., S.A.—See Sensormatic Electronics Corporation; *U.S. Public*, pg. 1457

SENSORMATIC E.C., S.R.L.—See Sensormatic Electronics Corporation; *U.S. Public*, pg. 1457

SENSORMATIC ELECTRONICS CORPORATION; *U.S. Public*, pg. 1457

SENSORMATIC ELECTRONICS CORP. DE PUERTO RICO—See Sensormatic Electronics Corporation; *U.S. Public*, pg. 1457

SENSORMATIC (FRANCE) S.A.—See Sensormatic Electronics Corporation; *U.S. Public*, pg. 1457

SENSORMATIC GES.M.B.H—See Sensormatic Electronics Corporation; *U.S. Public*, pg. 1457

SENSORMATIC HONG KONG LIMITED—See Sensormatic Electronics Corporation; *U.S. Public*, pg. 1458

SENSORMATIC KFI—See Sensormatic Electronics Corporation; *U.S. Public*, pg. 1458

SENSORMATIC LDA.—See Sensormatic Electronics Corporation; *U.S. Public*, pg. 1458

SENSORMATIC LIMITED—See Sensormatic Electronics Corporation; *U.S. Public*, pg. 1458

SENSORMATIC NEW ZEALAND LTD.—See Sensormatic Electronics Corporation; *U.S. Public*, pg. 1458

SENSORMATIC OY—See Sensormatic Electronics Corporation; *U.S. Public*, pg. 1458

SENSORMATIC S.A. DE C.V.—See Sensormatic Electronics Corporation; *U.S. Public*, pg. 1458

SENSORS DIVISION—See MTS Systems Corporation; *U.S. Public*, pg. 1029

SENSORS & ELECTRONIC SYSTEMS—See Raytheon Company; *U.S. Public*, pg. 1365

SENSORS, INC.; *U.S. Private*, pg. 984

SENSORY SYSTEMS LTD.—See Telesensory Corporation; *U.S. Private*, pg. 1074

SENSTAR CAPITAL CORPORATION—See SENCORP; *U.S. Private*, pg. 984

SENSYCON CORPORATION—See Mannesmann A.G.; *Int'l*, pg. 835

SENSYCON GESELLSCHAFT FUR INDUSTRIELLE SENSORSYSTEME UND PROZEBLEITTECHNIK MBH—See Mannesmann A.G.; *Int'l*, pg. 835

SENSYCON SENSORTECHNIK GMBH—See Mannesmann A.G.; *Int'l*, pg. 835

SENSYM INC.—See BTR plc; *Int'l*, pg. 127

SENTINEL ADMINISTRATIVE SERVICE CORPORATION—See National Life Insurance Company; *U.S. Private*, pg. 785

SENTINEL ADVISORS, INC.—See National Life Insurance Company; *U.S. Private*, pg. 785

SENTINEL CONSUMER PRODUCTS, INC.; *U.S. Private*, pg. 984

SENTINEL-NEWS—See Landmark Communications, Inc.; *U.S. Private*, pg. 648

SENTINEL SELF-STORAGE CORPORATION—See Cambridge Shopping Centres Limited; *Int'l*, pg. 253

SENTINEL TECHNOLOGIES INC.; *U.S. Private*, pg. 984

SENTROL CONTROLS GROUP—See Berwind Corporation; *U.S. Private*, pg. 139

SENTRY DRUGS, INC.—See Fleming Companies, Inc.; *U.S. Public*, pg. 653

SENTRY GROUP; *U.S. Private*, pg. 984

SENTRY INSURANCE, A MUTUAL COMPANY; *U.S. Private*, pg. 984

SENTRY MARKETS, INC.—See Fleming Companies, Inc.; *U.S. Public*, pg. 653

SENTRY POLYMERS, INC.—See RPM, Inc.; *U.S. Public*, pg. 1357

SENTRY RADIO—See Chancellor Media Corporation; *U.S. Public*, pg. 335

SENTRY TECHNOLOGY CORP.; *U.S. Public*, pg. 1458

SENTRY TECHNOLOGY GROUP—See Safeguard Scientifics, Inc.; *U.S. Public*, pg. 1425

SEO ACHAT D'ESPACE—See BDDP Group; *Int'l*, pg. 116

SEOUL DMB&B, INC.—See DMB&B Communications; *U.S. Private*, pg. 305

SEOUL DMB&B, INC.; *Int'l*, pg. 1223

SEOUL FINANCE CORPORATION—See KOHAP Group; *Int'l*, pg. 743

SEOUL LIAISON OFFICE—See COGEMA - Compagnie Generale des Matieres Nucleaires; *Int'l*, pg. 305

SEOUL OFFICE—See Gunze Sangyo, Inc.; *Int'l*, pg. 578

SEOUL-HEINZ LTD.—See H.J. Heinz Company; *U.S. Public*, pg. 807

SEP CONGO S.A.R.L.—See Petrofina S.A.; *Int'l*, pg. 1044

SEPAM—See Williams Holdings Plc; *Int'l*, pg. 1501

SEPARATION & RECOVERY SYSTEMS—See American Eco Corporation; *Int'l*, pg. 74

SEPARATION MATERIALS DIVISION—See Mitsubishi Chemical Corporation; *Int'l*, pg. 871

SEPARATION TECHNOLOGIES, INC.—See Cummins Engine Company, Inc.; *U.S. Public*, pg. 468

SEPECAT SA—See British Aerospace p.l.c.; *Int'l*, pg. 218

SEPELCOM—See Reed Elsevier plc; *Int'l*, pg. 1097

SEPHI—See Accor S.A.; *Int'l*, pg. 20

SEPI; *Int'l*, pg. 1223

SEPIC—See C.E.P. Communication Group; *Int'l*, pg. 239

SEPPALA—See OY Stockmann AB; *Int'l*, pg. 1301

SEPROB—See Bouygues; *Int'l*, pg. 207

SEPTIMA SA—See EMAP Plc; *Int'l*, pg. 451

SEQUA CAN MACHINERY—See Sequa Corporation; *U.S. Public*, pg. 1458

SEQUA CHEMICALS, INC.—See Sequa Corporation; *U.S. Public*, pg. 1459

SEQUA CORPORATION; *U.S. Public*, pg. 1458

SEQUATCHIE HANDLE WORKS, INC.—See O.P. Link Handle Company; *U.S. Private*, pg. 669

SEQUENT COMPUTER SYSTEMS (AUSTRALIA)—See Sequent Computer Systems, Inc.; *U.S. Public*, pg. 1459

SEQUENT COMPUTER SYSTEMS (AUSTRALIA) PTY. LTD.—See Sequent Computer Systems, Inc.; *U.S. Public*, pg. 1459

SEQUENT COMPUTER SYSTEMS, B.V.—See Sequent Computer Systems, Inc.; *U.S. Public*, pg. 1459

SEQUENT COMPUTER SYSTEMS (CANADA) LTD.—See Sequent Computer Systems, Inc.; *U.S. Public*, pg. 1459

SEQUENT COMPUTER SYSTEMS (FRANCE) S.A.—See Sequent Computer Systems, Inc.; *U.S. Public*, pg. 1459

SEQUENT COMPUTER SYSTEMS GMBH—See Sequent Computer Systems, Inc.; *U.S. Public*, pg. 1459

SEQUENT COMPUTER SYSTEMS (HONG KONG) LTD.—See Sequent Computer Systems, Inc.; *U.S. Public*, pg. 1460

SEQUENT COMPUTER SYSTEMS, INC.; *U.S. Public*, pg. 1459

SEQUENT COMPUTER SYSTEMS (NEW ZEALAND)—See Sequent Computer Systems, Inc.; *U.S. Public*, pg. 1460

SEQUENT COMPUTER SYSTEMS (NEW ZEALAND) LTD.—See Sequent Computer Systems, Inc.; *U.S. Public*, pg. 1460

SEQUENT COMPUTER SYSTEMS (SCOTLAND)—See Sequent Computer Systems, Inc.; *U.S. Public*, pg. 1460

SEQUENT COMPUTER SYSTEMS (SINGAPORE)—See Sequent Computer Systems, Inc.; *U.S. Public*, pg. 1460

SEQUENT COMPUTER SYSTEMS, S.R.O.—See Sequent Computer Systems, Inc.; *U.S. Public*, pg. 1460

SEQUENT COMPUTER SYSTEMS (UNITED KINGDOM)—See Sequent Computer Systems, Inc.; *U.S. Public*, pg. 1460

SEQUENT COMPUTERS JAPAN, LTD.—See Sequent Computer Systems, Inc.; *U.S. Public*, pg. 1460

SEQUENT EUROPE LTD.—See Sequent Computer Systems, Inc.; *U.S. Public*, pg. 1460

SEQUENT GMBH—See Sequent Computer Systems, Inc.; *U.S. Public*, pg. 1460

SEQUENTIA INC.; *U.S. Private*, pg. 985

Company Index

SEQUOIA—See Ark Restaurants Corp.; *U.S. Public*, pg. 130
SEQUOIA (NY)—See Ark Restaurants Corp.; *U.S. Public*, pg. 130
SEQUOIA-PACIFIC SYSTEMS CORP.—See Jefferson Smurfit Group p.l.c.; *Int'l*, pg. 1270
SEGURIDAD TECNICA, S.A.—See The Wackenhut Corporation; *U.S. Public*, pg. 1731
SEQUUS PHARMACEUTICALS; *U.S. Public*, pg. 1460
SERADYN, INC.—See Mitsubishi Chemical Corporation; *Int'l*, pg. 871
SERAPE—See Accor S.A.; *Int'l*, pg. 20
SERASEA BV—See Heidemij N.V.; *Int'l*, pg. 607
SERAT—See Aerospatiale; *Int'l*, pg. 29
SERATRONICS, INC.—See Fresenius AG; *Int'l*, pg. 505
SERCA—See Groupe Casino; *Int'l*, pg. 563
SERCA FOOD SERVICE-FITZSIMMONS DIV.—See The Oshawa Group Limited; *Int'l*, pg. 1012
SERCA FOOD SERVICE-HICKESON DIV.—See The Oshawa Group Limited; *Int'l*, pg. 1012
SERCA FOOD SERVICES, INC.—See The Oshawa Group Limited; *Int'l*, pg. 1012
SERCK AUDCO VALVES—See BTR plc; *Int'l*, pg. 125
SERCK CONTROLS LIMITED—See Clayhithe P.L.C.; *Int'l*, pg. 297
SERCK HEAT TRANSFER—See BTR plc; *Int'l*, pg. 125
SERCO COMPANY—See United Dominion Industries, Ltd.; *U.S. Public*, pg. 1676
SERES—See Compagnie des Machines Bull; *Int'l*, pg. 316
SERESE (SERVICE DE RESTAURATION DU SUD EST)—See Groupe Air France; *Int'l*, pg. 560
SERETRAM—See Diageo Plc; *Int'l*, pg. 411
SERFILCO, LTD.; *U.S. Private*, pg. 985
SERGAZ S.A. (SOCIETE DE SERVICE DU GAZODUC TRANST.)—See ENI S.p.A.; *Int'l*, pg. 429
SERGEANT'S PET PRODUCTS COMPANY—See ConAgra, Inc.; *U.S. Public*, pg. 427
SERICOL AG—See Burmah Castrol plc; *Int'l*, pg. 236
SERICOL GMBH—See Burmah Castrol plc; *Int'l*, pg. 236
SERICOL INC.—See Burmah Castrol plc; *Int'l*, pg. 235
SERICOL INTERNATIONAL LTD.—See Burmah Castrol plc; *Int'l*, pg. 235
SERICOL SA—See Burmah Castrol plc; *Int'l*, pg. 235
SERIE CLUB—See Groupe Bruxelles Lambert S.A.; *Int'l*, pg. 562
SERIGRAPH, INC.; *U.S. Private*, pg. 985
SERINFOR—See Hewlett-Packard Company; *U.S. Public*, pg. 823
SERINO COYNE INC.; *U.S. Private*, pg. 985
SERINO COYNE PUBLIC RELATIONS—See Serino Coyne Inc.; *U.S. Private*, pg. 985
SERLA OY—See Metsa-Serla Corporation; *Int'l*, pg. 863
SERMATECH CANADA—See Teleflex Incorporated; *U.S. Public*, pg. 1570
SERMATECH INTERNATIONAL, INC.—See Teleflex Incorporated; *U.S. Public*, pg. 1569
SERMATECH KLOCK—See Teleflex Incorporated; *U.S. Public*, pg. 1570
SERMATECH MAINE—See Teleflex Incorporated; *U.S. Public*, pg. 1570
SERMATECH MIDDLE ATLANTIC—See Teleflex Incorporated; *U.S. Public*, pg. 1570
SERMATECH SOUTHEAST—See Teleflex Incorporated; *U.S. Public*, pg. 1570
SERMATECH SOUTHWEST—See Teleflex Incorporated; *U.S. Public*, pg. 1570
SERMATECH (U.K.) LIMITED—See Teleflex Incorporated; *U.S. Public*, pg. 1570
SERMATECH WEST, AIRFOIL MANAGEMENT CO.—See Teleflex Incorporated; *U.S. Public*, pg. 1570
SERMETO—See Valmont Industries, Inc.; *U.S. Public*, pg. 1707
P.T. SERNIWA STEEL WORKS—See Nissho Iwai Corporation; *Int'l*, pg. 949
SEROLOGICALS CORPORATION; *U.S. Public*, pg. 1460
SERPO AS—See Scancem AB; *Int'l*, pg. 1200
SERPO FRANCE S.A.—See Scancem AB; *Int'l*, pg. 1200
SERPO ONENA S.A.—See Scancem AB; *Int'l*, pg. 1200
SERS—See Pechiney S.A.; *Int'l*, pg. 1028
SERTA, INC.—See Serta Mattress Company; *U.S. Private*, pg. 985
SERTA MATTRESS COMPANY; *U.S. Private*, pg. 985
SERTECH LABORATORIES, INC./SSI—See Microsemi Corporation; *U.S. Public*, pg. 1107
SERV-AIR, INC.—See Raytheon Company; *U.S. Public*, pg. 1366
SERV-TECH EUROPE—See Serv-Tech, Inc.; *U.S. Public*, pg. 1460
SERV-TECH, INC.; *U.S. Public*, pg. 1460
SERVAAS, INC.; *U.S. Private*, pg. 986
SERVAIR CHANNEL—See Groupe Air France; *Int'l*, pg. 560
SERVAIR ESPAGNE—See Groupe Air France; *Int'l*, pg. 560
SERVCO CALIFORNIA INC.—See Servco Pacific Inc.; *U.S. Private*, pg. 986
SERVCO INSURANCE AGENCY, INC.—See Servco Pacific Inc.; *U.S. Private*, pg. 986
SERVCO INVESTMENT CORP.—See Servco Pacific Inc.; *U.S. Private*, pg. 986
SERVCO PACIFIC INC.; *U.S. Private*, pg. 986
SERVERA R & S AB—See Axel Johnson AB; *Int'l*, pg. 709
SERVICAT, S.A.—See Caixa d'Estalvis de Catalunya; *Int'l*, pg. 250
SERVICE AMERICA CORPORATION; *U.S. Private*, pg. 986
SERVICE AMERICA CORPORATION OF WISCONSIN—See Service America Corporation; *U.S. Private*, pg. 986
SERVICE AMERICA OF TEXAS INC.—See Service America Corporation; *U.S. Private*, pg. 986
SERVICE AMERICA SYSTEMS, INC.—See Chemed Corporation; *U.S. Public*, pg. 344
SERVICE & INDUSTRIAL SECTOR—See Kimberly-Clark Corporation; *U.S. Public*, pg. 958

SERVICE & SUPPLY CO. OF WEST AFRICA—See ABB Asea Brown Boveri (Holding) Ltd.; *Int'l*, pg. 6
SERVICE ASSETS CORP.—See Bromar Inc.; *U.S. Private*, pg. 171
SERVICE CENTRAL DE PROPRIETE INDUSTRIELLE—See Thomson S.A.; *Int'l*, pg. 1382
SERVICE CENTRALE VOOR KOELTECHNIEK B.V.—See Internatio-Muller N.V.; *Int'l*, pg. 681
SERVICE CORPORATION INTERNATIONAL; *U.S. Public*, pg. 1460
SERVICE GENERAL—See H.W. Kaufman Financial Group, Inc.; *U.S. Private*, pg. 609
SERVICE GENERAL EAST—See H.W. Kaufman Financial Group, Inc.; *U.S. Private*, pg. 609
SERVICE GENERAL SOUTH—See H.W. Kaufman Financial Group, Inc.; *U.S. Private*, pg. 609
SERVICE GENERAL SOUTHEAST—See H.W. Kaufman Financial Group, Inc.; *U.S. Private*, pg. 609
SERVICE GENETIQUES S.A.R.L.—See Pioneer Hi-Bred International, Inc.; *U.S. Public*, pg. 1299
SERVICE INVESTMENTS—See GIB Group; *Int'l*, pg. 534
SERVICE MERCHANDISE COMPANY, INC.; *U.S. Public*, pg. 1461
SERVICE MOTOR CO.—See Service Motor Company; *U.S. Private*, pg. 986
SERVICE MOTOR COMPANY; *U.S. Private*, pg. 986
SERVICE PACKING COMPANY-UNITED FOOD GROUP; *U.S. Private*, pg. 986
SERVICE PARTS OPERATIONS—See General Motors Corporation; *U.S. Public*, pg. 720
SERVICE PRODUCTS BUILDINGS, INC.—See The Turner Corporation; *U.S. Public*, pg. 1645
SERVICE SOLUTION—See SPX Corporation; *U.S. Public*, pg. 1421
SERVICE STEEL DIVISION—See Van Pelt Corporation; *U.S. Private*, pg. 1133
SERVICE SUPPLY CO. INC. OF INDIANA; *U.S. Private*, pg. 987
SERVICE SUPPLY CORPORATION—See Stephenson Equipment, Inc.; *U.S. Private*, pg. 1040
SERVICE TELEPHONE CO., INC.—See Telephone and Data Systems, Inc.; *U.S. Public*, pg. 1572
SERVICE TIRE TRUCK CENTERS, LTD.; *U.S. Private*, pg. 987
SERVICE UNIFORMS DIV.—See Superior Surgical Mfg. Co., Inc.; *U.S. Public*, pg. 1539
SERVICE WEB OFFSET CORPORATION; *U.S. Private*, pg. 987
SERVICECARE, INC.—See SCANA Corporation; *U.S. Public*, pg. 1436
SERVICELINE—See CVB Financial Corp.; *U.S. Public*, pg. 287
SERVICEMASTER AG—See The ServiceMaster Company; *U.S. Public*, pg. 1462
SERVICEMASTER BUSINESS & INDUSTRY GROUP—See The ServiceMaster Company; *U.S. Public*, pg. 1462
THE SERVICEMASTER COMPANY; *U.S. Public*, pg. 1461
SERVICEMASTER CONSUMER SERVICES COMPANY—See The ServiceMaster Company; *U.S. Public*, pg. 1461
SERVICEMASTER DIVERSIFIED HEALTH SERVICES, INC.—See The ServiceMaster Company; *U.S. Public*, pg. 1462
SERVICEMASTER ENERGY MANAGEMENT—See The ServiceMaster Company; *U.S. Public*, pg. 1462
SERVICEMASTER FOOD MANAGEMENT SERVICES—See The ServiceMaster Company; *U.S. Public*, pg. 1462
SERVICEMASTER HEALTHCARE MANAGEMENT SERVICES, INC.—See The ServiceMaster Company; *U.S. Public*, pg. 1462
SERVICEMASTER HOME HEALTH CARE SERVICES INC.—See The ServiceMaster Company; *U.S. Public*, pg. 1462
SERVICEMASTER INTERNATIONAL—See The ServiceMaster Company; *U.S. Public*, pg. 1462
SERVICEMASTER LTD.—See The ServiceMaster Company; *U.S. Public*, pg. 1462
SERVICEMASTER MANAGEMENT SERVICES CORPORATION—See The ServiceMaster Company; *U.S. Public*, pg. 1462
SERVICEMASTER MANUFACTURING SERVICES—See The ServiceMaster Company; *U.S. Public*, pg. 1462
SERVICEMASTER OF CANADA LTD.—See The ServiceMaster Company; *U.S. Public*, pg. 1462
SERVICEMASTER RESIDENTIAL/COMMERCIAL SERVICES CO.—See The ServiceMaster Company; *U.S. Public*, pg. 1461
SERVICENTER USA—See Northwestern Public Service; *U.S. Public*, pg. 1201
SERVICEPLAN GMBH; *Int'l*, pg. 1225
SERVICES CONSELIS DOWELL—See Schlumberger Limited; *U.S. Public*, pg. 1439
SERVICES DIVISION—See California Microwave, Inc.; *U.S. Public*, pg. 293
SERVICES ET SYSTEMES LOGISTIQUE INTERNATIONAL (SSLI)—See Compagnie des Machines Bull; *Int'l*, pg. 316
SERVICES GROUP OF AMERICA; *U.S. Private*, pg. 987
SERVICES PETROLIERS SCHLUMBERGER S.A., FRANCE—See Schlumberger Limited; *U.S. Public*, pg. 1439
SERVICES SECURIVOL INC.—See The Jean Coutu Group (PJC) Inc.; *Int'l*, pg. 340
SERVICIO DE VENTA AUTOMATICA, S.A. (S.V.A.)—See Tabacalera, S.A.; *Int'l*, pg. 1345
SERVICIOS AVANZADOS DE METODOS Y SISTEMAS, S.A. (SAMS)—See Hewlett-Packard Company; *U.S. Public*, pg. 823
SERVICIOS CORPORATIVOS, S.A.—See Corporacion MAPFRE, Compania Internacional de Reaseguros, S.A.; *Int'l*, pg. 333
SERVICIOS EMPRESARIALES SEREMCA CA—See Accor S.A.; *Int'l*, pg. 21

SERVICIOS ESPECIALES DE VENTAS AUTOMOTRICES, S.A. DE C.V.—See Volkswagen AG; *Int'l*, pg. 1475
SERVICIOS EXPECIALES DE EDICION—See International Data Group; *U.S. Private*, pg. 570
SERVICIOS FINANCIEROS MAPFRE—See Corporacion MAPFRE, Compania Internacional de Reaseguros, S.A.; *Int'l*, pg. 334
SERVICIOS LOGISTICOS INTEGRADOS S.A.—See Union-Transport Corporation; *U.S. Private*, pg. 1120
SERVICIOS SANITARIOS SA—See Sophus Berendsen A/S; *Int'l*, pg. 1286
SERVICIOS TELEDISTRIBUCION, S.A. (ST-HILO)—See Telefonica de Espana, S.A.; *Int'l*, pg. 1371
SERVICIOS TICKET SA—See Accor S.A.; *Int'l*, pg. 21
SERVICIOS WESTINGHOUSE DE MEXICO, S.A. DE C.V.—See CBS Corporation; *U.S. Public*, pg. 273
SERVICIOS Y SUMINISTROS, S.A.—See Assicurazioni Generali S.p.A.; *Int'l*, pg. 92
SERVICO, INC.; *U.S. Public*, pg. 1462
SERVIPHARM LTD.—See Novartis AG; *Int'l*, pg. 972
SERVIRAIL—See Groupe Air France; *Int'l*, pg. 560
SERVIRED YPF S.A.—See Y.P.F., S.A.; *Int'l*, pg. 1515
SERVITEX, INC.—See National Distributing Co., Inc.; *U.S. Private*, pg. 781
SERVITEX LINEN—See National Distributing Co., Inc.; *U.S. Private*, pg. 782
SERVIZI TECNICI SWISS RE S.R.L.—See Swiss Reinsurance Company; *Int'l*, pg. 1333
SERVO COMPONENTS—See Litton Industries, Inc.; *U.S. Public*, pg. 1003
SERVO CORPORATION OF AMERICA; *U.S. Private*, pg. 987
SERVO DELDEN B.V.—See Veba AG; *Int'l*, pg. 1456
SERVOCORP (TRITON INDONESIA)—See Triton Energy Limited; *U.S. Public*, pg. 1640
SERVOMATION DUCHESS, INC.—See Service America Corporation; *U.S. Private*, pg. 986
SERVOMATION FOOD SERVICE OF ONTARIO LIMITED—See Service America Corporation; *U.S. Private*, pg. 986
SERVONSITE INTERNATIONAL BV—See KPN Koninklyke PTT Nederland NV; *Int'l*, pg. 720
SERVOTRONICS, INC.; *U.S. Public*, pg. 1462
SERVOTRONIX LTD.—See Kollmorgen Corporation; *U.S. Public*, pg. 966
SERVTECH LIMITED—See Caterpillar Inc.; *U.S. Public*, pg. 316
SESAME PLACE—See Anheuser-Busch Companies, Inc.; *U.S. Public*, pg. 114
SESTO—See OY Stockmann AB; *Int'l*, pg. 1301
SETAL INSTALACOES INDUSTRIAIS S.A.—See ABB Asea Brown Boveri (Holding) Ltd.; *Int'l*, pg. 6
SETAO—See Bouygues; *Int'l*, pg. 207
SETCO; *U.S. Private*, pg. 987
SETCO, INC.—See McCormick & Company, Incorporated; *U.S. Public*, pg. 1066
SETEMER, S.P.A.—See Telefonaktiebolaget LM Ericsson; *Int'l*, pg. 1369
SETON COMPANY; *U.S. Public*, pg. 987
SETPOINT INC.—See Alcatel Alsthom Compagnie Generale D'Electricite; *Int'l*, pg. 53
SETTAS S.A.—See Inco Limited; *Int'l*, pg. 673
SETTEF SPA—See Laporte plc; *Int'l*, pg. 803
SETTLER INTERNATIONAL S.A.—See Assicurazioni Generali S.p.A.; *Int'l*, pg. 92
SETTSU CORPORATION; *Int'l*, pg. 1225
SETTSU PLANT—See Shionogi & Co., Ltd.; *Int'l*, pg. 1235
SETTSU USA—See Settsu Corporation; *Int'l*, pg. 1225
SETZER FOREST PRODUCTS; *U.S. Private*, pg. 987
SETZER FOREST PRODUCTS-OROVILLE PLANT—See Setzer Forest Products; *U.S. Private*, pg. 988
SEVCON, INC.—See Tech/Ops Sevcon, Inc.; *U.S. Public*, pg. 1563
SEVCON LIMITED—See Tech/Ops Sevcon, Inc.; *U.S. Public*, pg. 1563
SEVCON SA—See Tech/Ops Sevcon, Inc.; *U.S. Public*, pg. 1563
SEVEN-ELEVEN JAPAN CO., LTD.—See Ito-Yokado Co., Ltd.; *Int'l*, pg. 693
7-ELEVEN STORES—See Ito-Yokado Co., Ltd.; *Int'l*, pg. 693
SEVEN OAKS CARE CENTER—See Horizon/CMS Healthcare Corporation; *U.S. Public*, pg. 839
SEVEN SEAS LIMITED—See Hanson PLC; *Int'l*, pg. 593
777 PROGRAM—See The Boeing Company; *U.S. Public*, pg. 240
SEVEN STARS, INC.—See WSMP, Inc.; *U.S. Public*, pg. 1729
737/757 PROGRAMS—See The Boeing Company; *U.S. Public*, pg. 240
SEVEN-UP BOTTLING CO. OF ST. LOUIS—See Beverage America, Inc.; *U.S. Private*, pg. 142
SEVEN-UP CONCESSIONS S.A.—See PepsiCo, Inc.; *U.S. Public*, pg. 1278
SEVEN-UP EUROPE—See PepsiCo, Inc.; *U.S. Public*, pg. 1278
SEVEN-UP IRELAND LTD.—See PepsiCo, Inc.; *U.S. Public*, pg. 1278
SEVEN-UP NEDERLANDS N.V.—See PepsiCo, Inc.; *U.S. Public*, pg. 1278
7-UP OF CORPUS CHRISTI—See Grant-Lydick Beverage Co.; *U.S. Private*, pg. 470
7-UP OF LAGRANGE, TX—See Grant-Lydick Beverage Co.; *U.S. Private*, pg. 470
7-UP OF VICTORIA—See Grant-Lydick Beverage Co.; *U.S. Private*, pg. 470
SEVEN-UP PHILIPPINES, INC.—See PepsiCo, Inc.; *U.S. Public*, pg. 1278
7-UP/RC OF AUSTIN—See Grant-Lydick Beverage Co.; *U.S. Private*, pg. 470
7-UP/RC OF HARLINGEN—See Grant-Lydick Beverage Co.; *U.S. Private*, pg. 470
SEVENSON ENVIRONMENTAL, LTD.—See Sevenson Environmental Services, Inc.; *U.S. Public*, pg. 1463

SEVENSON ENVIRONMENTAL SERVICES, INC.; *U.S. Public*, pg. 1462
SEVENSON INDUSTRIAL SERVICES, INC.—See Sevenson Environmental Services, Inc.; *U.S. Public*, pg. 1463
SEVENTEEN MAGAZINE—See Primedia Inc.; *U.S. Public*, pg. 1328
THE 1792 COMPANY—See Cigna Corp.; *U.S. Public*, pg. 365
SEVENTH STREET CORP.—See Flanigan's Enterprises, Inc.; *U.S. Public*, pg. 648
SEVERN FURNACES LIMITED—See Instron Corporation; *U.S. Public*, pg. 883
SEVERN TRENT (DEL) INC.—See Severn Trent Plc; *Int'l*, pg. 1226
SEVERN TRENT LABORATORIES LIMITED—See Severn Trent Plc; *Int'l*, pg. 1226
SEVERN TRENT OVERSEAS HOLDINGS LIMITED—See Severn Trent Plc; *Int'l*, pg. 1226
SEVERN TRENT PLC; *Int'l*, pg. 1225
SEVERN TRENT PROPERTY LIMITED—See Severn Trent Plc; *Int'l*, pg. 1226
SEVERN TRENT SYSTEMS LIMITED—See Severn Trent Plc; *Int'l*, pg. 1226
SEVERN TRENT TECHNOLOGY LIMITED—See Severn Trent Plc; *Int'l*, pg. 1226
SEVERN TRENT WATER INTERNATIONAL LIMITED—See Severn Trent Plc; *Int'l*, pg. 1226
SEVERN TRENT WATER INTERNATIONAL (OVERSEAS HOLDINGS) LIMITED—See Severn Trent Plc; *Int'l*, pg. 1226
SEVERN TRENT WATER LTD.—See Severn Trent Plc; *Int'l*, pg. 1225
SEVIERVILLE FACILITY, WAGNER LIGHTING DIVISION—See Cooper Industries, Inc.; *U.S. Public*, pg. 442
SEWARD INC.; *U.S. Public*, pg. 988
SEWELL VILLAGE CADILLAC CO.; *U.S. Private*, pg. 988
SEWELLS INTERNATIONAL LTD.—See EMAP Plc; *Int'l*, pg. 451
J.A. SEXAUER, INC.—See The Dyson-Kissner-Moran Corporation; *U.S. Private*, pg. 352
SEXTANT AVIONIQUE—See Aerospatiale; *Int'l*, pg. 29
SEXTANT AVIONIQUE—See Thomson S.A.; *Int'l*, pg. 1382
SEXTANT AVIONIQUE ITALIA S.P.A.—See Thomson S.A.; *Int'l*, pg. 1385
SEXTON CAN CO., INC.; *U.S. Private*, pg. 988
SEYCHELLES INTERNATIONAL MERCANTILE BANKING CORPORATION LIMITED—See Standard Chartered Bank PLC; *Int'l*, pg. 1296
SEYFERT FOODS, INC.; *U.S. Private*, pg. 988
SEYMOUR DISTRIBUTION LTD.—See Lagardere Groupe; *Int'l*, pg. 796
SEYMOUR HOUSEWARES—See Home Products International, Inc.; *U.S. Public*, pg. 832
SEYMOUR INTERNATIONAL—See EMAP Plc; *Int'l*, pg. 452
SEYMOUR MANUFACTURING COMPANY; *U.S. Private*, pg. 988
SEYMOUR OF SYCAMORE, INC.; *U.S. Private*, pg. 988
SFERNICE, S.A.—See Vishay Intertechnology, Inc.; *U.S. Public*, pg. 1722
SHADE FOODS, INC.—See Norfoods, Inc.; *U.S. Private*, pg. 802
SHADE PASTA, INC.—See Norfoods, Inc.; *U.S. Private*, pg. 802
SHADE/ALLIED, INC.—See American Pad and Paper Company; *U.S. Public*, pg. 89
SHADFORTHS LIMITED—See HSBC Holdings plc; *Int'l*, pg. 583
SHADOW BROADCAST SERVICES—See Westwood One, Inc.; *U.S. Public*, pg. 1763
SHADOWOOD GOLF INC.—See Kocolene Oil Corp.; *U.S. Private*, pg. 629
SHADY BROOK FARMS—See Rocco Inc.; *U.S. Private*, pg. 937
SHADY MAPLE FARMS LTD.—See H.J. Heinz Company; *U.S. Public*, pg. 806
SHAER SHOE CORPORATION; *U.S. Private*, pg. 988
SHAFER; *U.S. Private*, pg. 988
SHAFER—See Shafer; *U.S. Private*, pg. 988
SHAFER COMMERCIAL SEATING INC.; *U.S. Private*, pg. 988
SHAIN/SHOPBILT—See John Boos & Company; *U.S. Private*, pg. 156
SHAKER ADVERTISING AGENCY; *U.S. Private*, pg. 988
SHAKER ADVERTISING AGENCY—See Shaker Advertising Agency; *U.S. Private*, pg. 296
SHAKERTOWN 1992, INC.—See The Clark Group; *Int'l*, pg. 296
SHAKESPEARE (AUSTRALIA) PTY. LTD.—See K2 Inc.; *U.S. Public*, pg. 940
SHAKESPEARE COMPANY UNITED KINGDOM—See K2 Inc.; *U.S. Public*, pg. 940
SHAKESPEARE COMPOSITES & ELECTRONICS—See K2 Inc.; *U.S. Public*, pg. 940
SHAKESPEARE FISHING TACKLE—See K2 Inc.; *U.S. Public*, pg. 940
SHAKESPEARE HENGELSPORT B.V.—See K2 Inc.; *U.S. Public*, pg. 940
SHAKESPEARE (HONG KONG) LTD.—See K2 Inc.; *U.S. Public*, pg. 940
SHAKESPEARE MONOFILAMENT—See K2 Inc.; *U.S. Public*, pg. 940
SHAKESPEARE MONOFILAMENT U.K. LTD.—See K2 Inc.; *U.S. Public*, pg. 940
SHAKEY'S INCORPORATED; *U.S. Private*, pg. 989
SHAKLEE (ASIA) INC., TAIWAN BRANCH—See Yamanouchi Pharmaceutical Co. Ltd.; *Int'l*, pg. 1518
SHAKLEE CANADA INC.—See Yamanouchi Pharmaceutical Co. Ltd.; *Int'l*, pg. 1518
SHAKLEE CORPORATION—See Yamanouchi Pharmaceutical Co. Ltd.; *Int'l*, pg. 1518
SHAKLEE JAPAN K.K.—See Yamanouchi Pharmaceutical Co. Ltd.; *Int'l*, pg. 1518

SHAKLEE MEXICO, S.A. DE C.V.—See Yamanouchi Pharmaceutical Co. Ltd.; *Int'l*, pg. 1518
SHAKLEE PHILIPPINES, INC.—See Yamanouchi Pharmaceutical Co. Ltd.; *Int'l*, pg. 1518
SHAKLEE PRODUCTS (MALAYSIA) SDN. BHD.—See Yamanouchi Pharmaceutical Co. Ltd.; *Int'l*, pg. 1519
SHAKLEE U.S.—See Yamanouchi Pharmaceutical Co. Ltd.; *Int'l*, pg. 1518
MARK SHALE; *U.S. Private*, pg. 989
MARK SHALE DIRECT—See Mark Shale; *U.S. Private*, pg. 989
SHALLOWFORD PROVIDERS, INC.—See Magellan Health Services, Inc.; *U.S. Public*, pg. 1036
SHALMOR AVNON AMICHAY—See TBWA Chiat/Day; *U.S. Private*, pg. 1063
SHAMROCK AGGREGATES, INC.—See Ash Grove Cement Company; *U.S. Private*, pg. 989
SHAMROCK FOODS COMPANY; *U.S. Private*, pg. 989
SHAMROCK (GREAT BRITAIN) LTD.—See Bausch & Lomb Incorporated; *U.S. Public*, pg. 196
SHAMROCK HOLDINGS, INC.; *U.S. Private*, pg. 989
SHAMROCK HOLDINGS OF CALIFORNIA, INC.—See Shamrock Holdings, Inc.; *U.S. Private*, pg. 989
SHAND MINING INC.—See Charter plc; *Int'l*, pg. 281
SHAND, MORAHAN & CO., INC.—See Markel Corporation; *U.S. Public*, pg. 1046
SHANDON LIPSHAW INC.—See Thermo Electron Corporation; *U.S. Public*, pg. 1595
SHANDONG NISSIN FOODS CO., LTD.—See Nissin Food Products Co., Ltd.; *Int'l*, pg. 950
SHANDONG ZIBO KINHUA-CHEMFERM INDUSTRIAL PHARM. LTD.—See Royal Gist-Brocades N.V.; *Int'l*, pg. 1143
SHANDWICK AMERICAS—See Shandwick International Plc; *Int'l*, pg. 1226
SHANDWICK ASIA PACIFIC—See Shandwick International Plc; *Int'l*, pg. 1227
SHANDWICK BARCELONA—See Shandwick International Plc; *Int'l*, pg. 1227
SHANDWICK CHINA—See Shandwick International Plc; *Int'l*, pg. 1227
SHANDWICK COMMUNICATIONS LTD.—See Shandwick International Plc; *Int'l*, pg. 1226
SHANDWICK CONSULTANTS LTD.—See Shandwick International Plc; *Int'l*, pg. 1227
SHANDWICK CORPORATE COMMUNICATIONS S.P.A.—See Shandwick International Plc; *Int'l*, pg. 1227
SHANDWICK DETROIT—See Shandwick International Plc; *Int'l*, pg. 1227
SHANDWICK DEUTSCHLAND GMBH—See Shandwick International Plc; *Int'l*, pg. 1227
SHANDWICK EUROPE HOLDING CO. GMBH—See Shandwick International Plc; *Int'l*, pg. 1227
SHANDWICK FRANCE—See Shandwick International Plc; *Int'l*, pg. 1227
SHANDWICK HONG KONG LTD.—See Shandwick International Plc; *Int'l*, pg. 1227
SHANDWICK INTERACTIVE LTD.—See Shandwick International Plc; *Int'l*, pg. 1227
SHANDWICK INTERNATIONAL PLC; *Int'l*, pg. 1226
SHANDWICK INTERNATIONAL PLC—See Shandwick International Plc; *Int'l*, pg. 1226
SHANDWICK LUTZ BOHME PUBLIC RELATIONS GMBH—See Shandwick International Plc; *Int'l*, pg. 1227
SHANDWICK MADRID—See Shandwick International Plc; *Int'l*, pg. 1227
SHANDWICK MARKETING COMMUNICATION SRL—See Shandwick International Plc; *Int'l*, pg. 1227
SHANDWICK MINNEAPOLIS—See Shandwick International Plc; *Int'l*, pg. 1227
SHANDWICK NORTH LTD.—See Shandwick International Plc; *Int'l*, pg. 1226
SHANDWICK NORTHERN IRELAND LTD.—See Shandwick International Plc; *Int'l*, pg. 1226
SHANDWICK/PRESKO LTD.—See Shandwick International Plc; *Int'l*, pg. 1227
SHANDWICK PTE LTD.—See Shandwick International Plc; *Int'l*, pg. 1227
SHANDWICK PUBLIC RELATIONS LTD.—See Shandwick International Plc; *Int'l*, pg. 1226
SHANDWICK ROME SRL—See Shandwick International Plc; *Int'l*, pg. 1228
SHANDWICK S.A. INFOPUBLIC N.V.—See Shandwick International Plc; *Int'l*, pg. 1228
SHANDWICK SCOTLAND LTD.—See Shandwick International Plc; *Int'l*, pg. 1226
SHANDWICK SDN. BHD.—See Shandwick International Plc; *Int'l*, pg. 1228
SHANDWICK SPAIN—See Shandwick International Plc; *Int'l*, pg. 1228
SHANDWICK UNITED KINGDOM—See Shandwick International Plc; *Int'l*, pg. 1226
SHANDWICK USA—See Shandwick International Plc; *Int'l*, pg. 1227
SHANDWICK VAN DE MEEBERG PR—See Shandwick International Plc; *Int'l*, pg. 1227
THE SHANE GROUP INC.; *U.S. Private*, pg. 989
SHANE HANDBAGS—See Jaclyn, Inc.; *U.S. Public*, pg. 920
SHANE UNIFORMS—See Superior Surgical Mfg. Co., Inc.; *U.S. Public*, pg. 1539
SHANGHAI AGMET ELECTRO-SCIENCE LABORATORY, LTD—See Electro-Science Laboratories, Inc.; *U.S. Private*, pg. 369
SHANGHAI BAO TAI LONG CONCRETE PRODUCTS CO., LTD.—See Ssangyong Business Group; *Int'l*, pg. 1293
SHANGHAI BI BA BATTERIES CO. LTD.—See GP Batteries International Ltd.; *Int'l*, pg. 537
SHANGHAI CHUGAI PHARMACEUTICAL CO., LTD.—See Chugai Pharmaceutical Co., Ltd.; *Int'l*, pg. 291
SHANGHAI CIBA GAO-QIAO CHEMICAL COMPANY LTD.—See Novartis AG; *Int'l*, pg. 985
SHANGHAI CIBA GAO-QIAO CHEMICAL COMPANY LTD.-PUDONG SITE OFFICE—See Novartis AG; *Int'l*, pg. 985

SHANGHAI CIBA-GEIGY ANIMAL HEALTH LIMITED—See Novartis AG; *Int'l*, pg. 985
SHANGHAI CIBA VISION CONTACT LENSES CO., LTD.—See Novartis AG; *Int'l*, pg. 985
SHANGHAI CORNING ENGINEERING CORPORATION—See Corning Incorporated; *U.S. Public*, pg. 449
SHANGHAI CROWN PACKAGING COMPANY LTD.—See Crown Cork & Seal Company, Inc.; *U.S. Public*, pg. 465
SHANGHAI DONNELLY FU HUA WINDOW SYSTEMS COMPANY, LTD.—See Donnelly Corporation; *U.S. Public*, pg. 519
SHANGHAI EBARA ENGINEERING AND SERVICES CO., LTD.—See Ebara Corporation; *Int'l*, pg. 432
SHANGHAI GENERAL BISCUITS FOODS CO. LTD.—See Danone Group; *Int'l*, pg. 381
SHANGHAI HENKEL CHEMICALS LTD.—See Henkel KGaA; *Int'l*, pg. 614
SHANGHAI HENKEL OLEOCHEMICALS LTD.—See Henkel KGaA; *Int'l*, pg. 614
SHANGHAI HENKEL-TEROSON ADHESIVES AND COATINGS LTD.—See Henkel KGaA; *Int'l*, pg. 614
SHANGHAI HUANGHE DHA PHARMACEUTICAL CO., LTD.—See Haw Par Brothers International Limited; *Int'l*, pg. 603
SHANGHAI HUILI KANSAI PAINT CO., LTD.—See Kansai Paint Co., Ltd.; *Int'l*, pg. 723
SHANGHAI INDUSTRIAL CONSULTANTS; *Int'l*, pg. 1228
SHANGHAI INTERNATIONAL FINANCE COMPANY LIMITED—See The Sanwa Bank Limited; *Int'l*, pg. 1190
SHANGHAI INTERNATIONAL REALTY CO., LTD.—See Daiwa House Industry Co., Ltd.; *Int'l*, pg. 374
SHANGHAI JINJIANG BATTERY CO. LTD.—See GP Batteries International Ltd.; *Int'l*, pg. 537
SHANGHAI JOHNSON & JOHNSON LTD.—See Johnson & Johnson; *U.S. Public*, pg. 932
SHANGHAI JSD ELECTRONICS CO., LTD.—See Oy Nokia Ab/Nokia Group; *Int'l*, pg. 954
SHANGHAI KENWOOD ELECTRONICS CO., LTD.—See Kenwood Corporation; *Int'l*, pg. 731
SHANGHAI LIEBHERR MACHINERY EQUIPMENT CO., LTD.—See Liebherr-International AG; *Int'l*, pg. 809
SHANGHAI LONG FENG FOOD ADDITIVES CO., LTD.—See Dainippon Ink & Chemicals, Inc.; *Int'l*, pg. 372
SHANGHAI LUCENT TECHNOLOGIES TRANSMISSION EQUIPMENT CO., LTD.—See Lucent Technologies Inc.; *U.S. Public*, pg. 1018
SHANGHAI MASTER BUILDERS CO., LTD.—See Novartis AG; *Int'l*, pg. 985
SHANGHAI MCCORMICK SEASONING & FOODSTUFFS COMPANY, LIMITED—See McCormick & Company, Incorporated; *U.S. Public*, pg. 1067
SHANGHAI MIURA BOILER CO. LTD. (CHINA)—See Miura Co., Ltd.; *Int'l*, pg. 884
SHANGHAI MIZUNO CORPORATION LTD.—See Mizuno Corporation; *Int'l*, pg. 885
SHANGHAI MORGAN CARBON COMPANY LIMITED—See Morgan Crucible Co.; *Int'l*, pg. 892
SHANGHAI NISSIN NOODLES FOODS CO., LTD.—See Nissin Food Products Co., Ltd.; *Int'l*, pg. 950
SHANGHAI NORTEL SEMICONDUCTOR CORPORATION—See Northern Telecom Limited; *Int'l*, pg. 970
SHANGHAI OFFICE—See Gunze Sangyo, Inc.; *Int'l*, pg. 578
SHANGHAI OMRON AUTOMATION SYSTEM CO., LTD.—See Omron Corporation; *Int'l*, pg. 1006
SHANGHAI OMRON CONTROL COMPONENTS CO., LTD.—See Omron Corporation; *Int'l*, pg. 1006
SHANGHAI PULONG CONCRETE PRODUCTS CO., LTD.—See Ssangyong Business Group; *Int'l*, pg. 1293
SHANGHAI ROCHE PHARMACEUTICALS LIMITED—See Roche Holding Ltd.; *Int'l*, pg. 1122
SHANGHAI SHARED DATA NETWORK CO.—See IPC Corporation Ltd.; *Int'l*, pg. 651
SHANGHAI SHARP ELECTRONICS CO., INC—See Sharp Corporation; *Int'l*, pg. 1229
SHANGHAI SHOWA PLASTICS CO. LTD.—See Showpla Asia Limited; *Int'l*, pg. 1237
SHANGHAI SMPIC BROTHER INDUSTRIES, LTD.—See Brother Industries, Ltd.; *Int'l*, pg. 230
SHANGHAI SPS BIAO WU FASTENER CO. LTD.—See SPS Technologies, Inc.; *U.S. Public*, pg. 1420
SHANGHAI TEKTRONIX ELECTRONIC INSTRUMENT CO. LTD.—See Tektronix, Inc.; *U.S. Public*, pg. 1567
SHANGHAI-VOLKSWAGEN AUTOMOTIVE COMPANY LTD.—See Volkswagen AG; *Int'l*, pg. 1475
SHANGHAI YADIE FASHION CO., LTD.—See Wacoal Corporation; *Int'l*, pg. 1494
SHANGHAI YIN TONG TRUST CO., LTD.—See Orix Corporation; *Int'l*, pg. 1010
SHANKS & MCEWAN GROUP PLC; *Int'l*, pg. 1228
SHANKS & MCEWAN (NORTHERN) LTD—See Shanks & McEwan Group Plc; *Int'l*, pg. 1228
SHANKS & MCEWAN (SOUTHERN WASTE SERVICES) LTD—See Shanks & McEwan Group Plc; *Int'l*, pg. 1228
SHANNOCK QUEBEC AUDIO AND VIDEO INC.—See TSC Shannock Corporation; *Int'l*, pg. 1343
SHANNON DIVISION—See Tecumseh Products Company; *U.S. Public*, pg. 1566
THE SHANNON GROUP—See The Manitowoc Company, Inc.; *U.S. Public*, pg. 1041
SHANNON PROPERTIES—See Dana Corporation; *U.S. Public*, pg. 480
SHANNON TRADING CO., LTD.—See Tokuyama Corporation; *Int'l*, pg. 1393
SHANNON TURBINE TECHNOLOGIES LTD.—See Sulzer Ltd.; *Int'l*, pg. 1308
SHANNON & WILSON, INC.; *U.S. Private*, pg. 989
SHANNON & WILSON INTL.—See Shannon & Wilson, Inc.; *U.S. Private*, pg. 989
SHANON CO., LTD.—See Tokuyama Corporation; *Int'l*, pg. 1393

SHANTON MEIJI PHARMACEUTICALS CO., LTD.—See Meiji Seika Kaisha, Ltd.; *Int'l*, pg. 856

SHANTOU HENKEL CONSUMER ADHESIVES & BUILDING CHEMICALS CO. LTD.—See Henkel KGaA; *Int'l*, pg. 614

SHANXI JAPAN ENERGY LUBRICANTS CO., LTD.—See Japan Energy Corporation; *Int'l*, pg. 702

SHAOXING REDLAND BUILDING MATERIALS CO., INC.—See Redland PLC; *Int'l*, pg. 1093

SHAP CONCRETE PRODUCTS LIMITED—See RMC Group p.l.c.; *Int'l*, pg. 1080

SHAPCO, INC.; *U.S. Private*, pg. 989

SHAPE INC.; *U.S. Private*, pg. 990

SHAPE SOUTH, INC.—See Shape Inc.; *U.S. Private*, pg. 990

SHAPELL INDUSTRIES, INC.; *U.S. Private*, pg. 990

SHARE TECHNOLOGIES - FAIRCHILD—See Tel-Save Holdings, Inc.; *U.S. Public*, pg. 1568

SHARED MEDICAL SYSTEMS CORPORATION; *U.S. Public*, pg. 1463

SHARED SERVICES DIVISION—See Black & Veatch; *U.S. Private*, pg. 146

SHARIKAT AL ASMIDA AL MUTTAHIDA LTD. (UNIFERT)—See BASF AG; *Int'l*, pg. 109

SHARON CONCEPTS; *U.S. Private*, pg. 990

SHARON SEZ, INC.—See Burlington Coat Factory Warehouse Corporation; *U.S. Public*, pg. 268

SHARON TUBE COMPANY; *U.S. Private*, pg. 990

SHARONVILLE HOTEL CORPORATION—See Saul Centers Inc.; *U.S. Public*, pg. 1435

SHARP CORPORATION; *Int'l*, pg. 1228

SHARP CORPORATION OF AUSTRALIA PTY. LTD.—See Sharp Corporation; *Int'l*, pg. 1229

SHARP CORPORATION OF NEW ZEALAND LTD.—See Sharp Corporation; *Int'l*, pg. 1229

SHARP CORPORATION (TAIWAN)—See Sharp Corporation; *Int'l*, pg. 1229

SHARP DIGITAL INFORMATION PRODUCTS, INC.—See Sharp Corporation; *Int'l*, pg. 1229

SHARP DO BRASIL S.A. INDUSTRIA DE EQUIPAMENTOS ELECTRONICOS—See Sharp Corporation; *Int'l*, pg. 1229

SHARP ELECTRONIC COMPONENTS (TAIWAN) CORPORATION—See Sharp Corporation; *Int'l*, pg. 1229

SHARP ELECTRONICA ESPANA S.A. (BARCELONA)—See Sharp Corporation; *Int'l*, pg. 1229

SHARP ELECTRONICS BENELUX B.V.—See Sharp Corporation; *Int'l*, pg. 1230

SHARP ELECTRONICS CORPORATION—See Sharp Corporation; *Int'l*, pg. 1228

SHARP ELECTRONICS (EUROPE)—See Sharp Corporation; *Int'l*, pg. 1230

SHARP ELECTRONICS (EUROPE) GMBH—See Sharp Corporation; *Int'l*, pg. 1230

SHARP ELECTRONICS FRANCE S.A.—See Sharp Corporation; *Int'l*, pg. 1230

SHARP ELECTRONICS GMBH—See Sharp Corporation; *Int'l*, pg. 1230

SHARP ELECTRONICS (ITALIA) S.P.A.—See Sharp Corporation; *Int'l*, pg. 1230

SHARP ELECTRONICS (MALAYSIA) SDN. BHD.—See Sharp Corporation; *Int'l*, pg. 1230

SHARP ELECTRONICS OF CANADA—See Sharp Corporation; *Int'l*, pg. 1230

SHARP ELECTRONICS OF CANADA LTD.—See Sharp Corporation; *Int'l*, pg. 1230

SHARP ELECTRONICS (SCHWEIZ) AG—See Sharp Corporation; *Int'l*, pg. 1230

SHARP ELECTRONICS (SINGAPORE) PTE. LTD.—See Sharp Corporation; *Int'l*, pg. 1230

SHARP ELECTRONICS (SVENSKA) AB—See Sharp Corporation; *Int'l*, pg. 1230

SHARP ELECTRONICS (TAIWAN) CO., LTD.—See Sharp Corporation; *Int'l*, pg. 1230

SHARP ELECTRONICS (THAILAND) INC.—See Sharp Corporation; *Int'l*, pg. 1230

SHARP ELECTRONICS (U.K.)—See Sharp Corporation; *Int'l*, pg. 1230

SHARP ELECTRONICS (U.K.) LTD.—See Sharp Corporation; *Int'l*, pg. 1230

SHARP ENERGY, INC.—See Chesapeake Utilities Corporation; *U.S. Public*, pg. 347

SHARP FINANCE NETHERLAND B.V. (AMSTERDAM)—See Sharp Corporation; *Int'l*, pg. 1230

SHARP FLAT DISPLAY MANUFACTURING COMPANY—See Sharp Corporation; *Int'l*, pg. 1229

SHARP INTERNATIONAL FINANCE (U.K.) PLC.—See Sharp Corporation; *Int'l*, pg. 1230

SHARP KOREA CORPORATION (INCHON)—See Sharp Corporation; *Int'l*, pg. 1230

SHARP LABORATORIES OF AMERICA, INC.—See Sharp Corporation; *Int'l*, pg. 1229

SHARP LABORATORIES OF EUROPE, LTD.—See Sharp Corporation; *Int'l*, pg. 1230

SHARP MANUFACTURING COMPANY OF U.K.—See Sharp Corporation; *Int'l*, pg. 1230

SHARP MANUFACTURING CORPORATION (M) SDN. BHD.—See Sharp Corporation; *Int'l*, pg. 1230

SHARP MANUFACTURING FRANCE S.A.—See Sharp Corporation; *Int'l*, pg. 1230

SHARP MICROELECTRONICS TECHNOLOGY, INC.—See Sharp Corporation; *Int'l*, pg. 1229

SHARP OFFICE EQUIPMENTS (CHANGSU) CO., LTD.—See Sharp Corporation; *Int'l*, pg. 1230

SHARP OIL COMPANY; *U.S. Private*, pg. 990

SHARP (PHILIPPINES) CORPORATION—See Sharp Corporation; *Int'l*, pg. 1230

SHARP PRECISION MANUFACTURING (U.K.) LTD.—See Sharp Corporation; *Int'l*, pg. 1230

SHARP-ROXY APPLIANCES CORP. (M) SDN. BHD.—See Sharp Corporation; *Int'l*, pg. 1230

SHARP-ROXY CORPORATION (M) SDN. BHD.—See Sharp Corporation; *Int'l*, pg. 1230

SHARP-ROXY ELECTRONICS CORPORATION (M) SDN. BHD.—See Sharp Corporation; *Int'l*, pg. 1230

SHARP-ROXY (HONG KONG) LTD.—See Sharp Corporation; *Int'l*, pg. 1230

SHARP-ROXY SALES & SERVICE COMPANY (M) SDN. BHD.—See Sharp Corporation; *Int'l*, pg. 1230

SHARP-ROXY SALES (SINGAPORE) PTE. LTD.—See Sharp Corporation; *Int'l*, pg. 1230

P.T. SHARP SEMICONDUCTOR INDONESIA—See Sharp Corporation; *Int'l*, pg. 1230

SHARP TECHNOLOGY (TAIWAN) CORPORATION—See Sharp Corporation; *Int'l*, pg. 1230

SHARP THEBNAKORN CO., LTD. (BANGKOK)—See Sharp Corporation; *Int'l*, pg. 1230

SHARP THEBNAKORN MANUFACTURING (THAILAND)—See Sharp Corporation; *Int'l*, pg. 1230

P.T. SHARP YASNOTA ANTARNUSA—See Sharp Corporation; *Int'l*, pg. 1230

P.T. SHARP YASONTA INDONESIA—See Sharp Corporation; *Int'l*, pg. 1230

SHARPE DRY GOODS CO., INC.; *U.S. Private*, pg. 990

THE SHARPER IMAGE; *U.S. Public*, pg. 1464

SHARPGAS, INC.—See Chesapeake Utilities Corporation; *U.S. Public*, pg. 347

SHARPLAN LASERS (EUROPE) LTD.—See ESC Medical Systems Ltd.; *Int'l*, pg. 429

SHARPLAN LASERS GMBH—See ESC Medical Systems Ltd.; *Int'l*, pg. 429

SHARPLAN LASERS, INC.—See ESC Medical Systems Ltd.; *Int'l*, pg. 429

SHARPS PIXLEY INC.—See Deutsche Bank AG; *Int'l*, pg. 403

J.A. SHARWOOD & COMPANY LIMITED—See Tomkins PLC; *Int'l*, pg. 1396

SHASTA BEVERAGES, INC.—See National Beverage Corp.; *U.S. Public*, pg. 990

SHASTA INDUSTRIES—See Coachmen Industries, Inc.; *U.S. Public*, pg. 386

SHATO HOLDINGS LTD.; *Int'l*, pg. 1230

BENJAMIN F. SHAW CO.—See Blount International, Inc.; *U.S. Public*, pg. 239

SHAW COMMUNITY SUPERMARKET—See Giant Food Inc.; *U.S. Public*, pg. 741

SHAW CREATIONS, INC.; *U.S. Private*, pg. 990

SHAW DATA SERVICES—See SunGard Data Systems Inc.; *U.S. Public*, pg. 1534

SHAW INDUSTRIES, INC.; *U.S. Public*, pg. 1464

SHAW INDUSTRIES LTD.; *Int'l*, pg. 1231

SHAW INTERNATIONAL LIMITED—See Shaw Industries Ltd.; *Int'l*, pg. 1231

JOHN SHAW (N.Z.) LIMITED—See Carclo Engineering Group plc; *Int'l*, pg. 268

SHAW-PERKINS INC.—See Reactive Metals & Alloys Corporation (REMACOR); *U.S. Private*, pg. 913

SHAW PIPE PROTECTION—See Shaw Industries Ltd.; *Int'l*, pg. 1231

SHAW PIPE PROTECTION PTY. LTD.—See Shaw Industries Ltd.; *Int'l*, pg. 1231

SHAW PIPELINE SERVICES, INC.—See Shaw Industries Ltd.; *Int'l*, pg. 1231

SHAW PIPELINE SERVICES LTD.—See Shaw Industries Ltd.; *Int'l*, pg. 1231

SHAWFLEX INC.—See Shaw Industries Ltd.; *Int'l*, pg. 1231

SHAWNEE NEWS-STAR—See Shivers Trading & Operating Co.; *U.S. Private*, pg. 995

SHAWNEE PRESS, INC.—See Music Sales Corporation; *U.S. Private*, pg. 768

SHAW'S CRAB HOUSE/CHICAGO—See Lettuce Entertain You Enterprises, Inc.; *U.S. Private*, pg. 661

SHAW'S DEERFIELD—See Lettuce Entertain You Enterprises, Inc.; *U.S. Private*, pg. 661

SHAW'S SUPERMARKETS, INC.—See J. Sainsbury plc; *Int'l*, pg. 1170

SHAWVER PRICE, INC.—See Havens Steel Co.; *U.S. Private*, pg. 511

SHAYKIN & COMPANY; *U.S. Private*, pg. 990

SHCHERBINKA OTIS LIFT—See United Technologies Corporation; *U.S. Public*, pg. 1691

SHEA COMMUNICATIONS CO.; *U.S. Private*, pg. 990

SHEA HOMES; *U.S. Private*, pg. 990

SHEA HOMES ARIZONA—See Shea Homes; *U.S. Private*, pg. 991

SHEA HOMES NORTHERN CALIFORNIA—See Shea Homes; *U.S. Private*, pg. 991

SHEA HOMES SAN DIEGO—See Shea Homes; *U.S. Private*, pg. 991

SHEA HOMES SOUTHERN CALIFORNIA—See Shea Homes; *U.S. Private*, pg. 991

SHEA HOMES-COLORADO—See Shea Homes; *U.S. Private*, pg. 991

SHEAFFER INC.—See Gefinor S.A. Luxembourg; *Int'l*, pg. 542

SHEAFFER PEN CROWNMARK—See Gefinor S.A. Luxembourg; *Int'l*, pg. 542

SHEALY ELECTRICAL WHOLESALERS; *U.S. Private*, pg. 991

SHEARINGS LIMITED—See The Rank Group PLC; *Int'l*, pg. 1087

SHEARMAN CORPORATION; *U.S. Private*, pg. 991

JOHN G. SHEDD AQUARIUM; *U.S. Private*, pg. 991

SHEER PRIDE LTD.—See Lonrho plc; *Int'l*, pg. 817

SHEET & COIL PRODUCTS DIVISION—See The Broken Hill Proprietary Company Limited; *Int'l*, pg. 227

SHEET & COIL PRODUCTS NEW SOUTH WALES—See The Broken Hill Proprietary Company Limited; *Int'l*, pg. 227

SHEET & COIL PRODUCTS VICTORIA—See The Broken Hill Proprietary Company Limited; *Int'l*, pg. 227

SHEETZ, INC.; *U.S. Private*, pg. 991

SHEF S.A.—See Electrabel S.A.; *Int'l*, pg. 437

SHEFCO, INC.—See Torchmark Corporation; *U.S. Public*, pg. 1622

SHEFCUT TOOL & ENGINEERING LTD.—See Cogsdill Tool Products, Inc.; *U.S. Private*, pg. 250

SHEFFIELD COATED STONE—See RMC Group p.l.c.; *Int'l*, pg. 1079

SHEFFIELD HARDWARE COMPANY—See Distribution America; *U.S. Private*, pg. 335

SHEFFIELD INSURANCE CO.—See Torchmark Corporation; *U.S. Public*, pg. 1622

SHEFFIELD INSURANCE CORPORATION—See Torchmark Corporation; *U.S. Public*, pg. 1623

SHEFFIELD SILVER CO.—See Reed & Barton Corporation; *U.S. Private*, pg. 916

SHEFFIELD STEEL CORPORATION-JOLIET; *U.S. Private*, pg. 991

JOHN SHELBOURNE & CO. LTD.—See Costain Group PLC; *Int'l*, pg. 337

THE SHELBURNE CORPORATION; *U.S. Private*, pg. 991

SHELBURNE HUSKY DIV.—See The Shelburne Corporation; *U.S. Private*, pg. 991

SHELBY COUNTY TRAINING CENTER—See Corrections Corporation of America; *U.S. Public*, pg. 451

SHELBY GROUP INTERNATIONAL, INC.; *U.S. Private*, pg. 991

THE SHELBY INSURANCE COMPANIES—See Vesta Insurance Group, Inc.; *U.S. Public*, pg. 1718

SHELBY STEEL PROCESSING CO.—See McClain Industries, Inc.; *U.S. Public*, pg. 1065

SHELBY WILLIAMS INDUSTRIES, INC.; *U.S. Public*, pg. 1464

SHELBY WILLIAMS TEXTILES—See Shelby Williams Industries, Inc.; *U.S. Public*, pg. 1465

SHELBY YARN COMPANY; *U.S. Private*, pg. 991

SHELDAHL, INC.; *U.S. Public*, pg. 1465

SHELDAHL INTL., INC.—See Sheldahl, Inc.; *U.S. Public*, pg. 1465

SHELDON GOOD & COMPANY AUCTIONS—See Sheldon Good & Co.; *U.S. Private*, pg. 464

SHELDON GOOD & COMPANY AUCTIONS NE—See Sheldon Good & Co.; *U.S. Private*, pg. 464

H.A. SHELDON, INC.—See Tandy Brands Accessories, Inc.; *U.S. Public*, pg. 1560

SHELDON MILL, CHAMPION INTERNATIONAL CORPORATION—See Champion International Corp.; *U.S. Public*, pg. 334

SHELDONS' INC.; *U.S. Private*, pg. 992

OY SHELL AB—See Royal Dutch/Shell Group of Companies; *Int'l*, pg. 1138

SHELL AEROCENTRE—See Royal Dutch/Shell Group of Companies; *Int'l*, pg. 1138

SHELL & INTERAG KFT.—See Royal Dutch/Shell Group of Companies; *Int'l*, pg. 1138

SHELL ANTILLES—See Royal Dutch/Shell Group of Companies; *Int'l*, pg. 1141

SHELL ANTILLES & GUIANAS LTD.—See Royal Dutch/Shell Group of Companies; *Int'l*, pg. 1141

SHELL ARGENTINA DE PETROLEO—See Royal Dutch/Shell Group of Companies; *Int'l*, pg. 1141

SHELL AUSTRALIA LTD.—See Royal Dutch/Shell Group of Companies; *Int'l*, pg. 1137

SHELL AUSTRIA AG—See Royal Dutch/Shell Group of Companies; *Int'l*, pg. 1138

SHELL AVIATION GUINEA—See Royal Dutch/Shell Group of Companies; *Int'l*, pg. 1136

SHELL AVIATION SERVICE—See Royal Dutch/Shell Group of Companies; *Int'l*, pg. 1139

SHELL BAHAMAS LTD.—See Royal Dutch/Shell Group of Companies; *Int'l*, pg. 1141

SHELL BELIZE—See Royal Dutch/Shell Group of Companies; *Int'l*, pg. 1141

SHELL BERMUDA—See Royal Dutch/Shell Group of Companies; *Int'l*, pg. 1141

SHELL BP & TODD—See Royal Dutch/Shell Group of Companies; *Int'l*, pg. 1137

SHELL BRASIL SA—See Royal Dutch/Shell Group of Companies; *Int'l*, pg. 1141

SHELL BRASIL SA (PETROLEO)—See Royal Dutch/Shell Group of Companies; *Int'l*, pg. 1141

SHELL CANADA LTD.—See Royal Dutch/Shell Group of Companies; *Int'l*, pg. 1138

SHELL CANADA PRODUCTS LTD.—See Royal Dutch/Shell Group of Companies; *Int'l*, pg. 1138

SHELL CHEMICAL (AUSTRALIA)—See Royal Dutch/Shell Group of Companies; *Int'l*, pg. 1137

SHELL CHEMICAL CO.—See Royal Dutch/Shell Group of Companies; *Int'l*, pg. 1136

SHELL CHEMICAL CO. (PHILIPPINES) INC.—See Royal Dutch/Shell Group of Companies; *Int'l*, pg. 1140

SHELL CHEMICAL DISTRIBUTING CO. LTD.—See Royal Dutch/Shell Group of Companies; *Int'l*, pg. 1140

SHELL CHEMICAL MOZAMBIQUE (PTY.) LTD.—See Royal Dutch/Shell Group of Companies; *Int'l*, pg. 1136

SHELL CHEMICALS & SERVICES (EAST CARIBBEAN) LTD.—See Royal Dutch/Shell Group of Companies; *Int'l*, pg. 1141

SHELL CHEMICALS (HELLAS)—See Royal Dutch/Shell Group of Companies; *Int'l*, pg. 1138

SHELL CHEMICALS IRELAND—See Royal Dutch/Shell Group of Companies; *Int'l*, pg. 1138

SHELL CHEMICALS NEW ZEALAND—See Royal Dutch/Shell Group of Companies; *Int'l*, pg. 1137

SHELL CHEMICALS U.K.—See Royal Dutch/Shell Group of Companies; *Int'l*, pg. 1139

SHELL CHEMICALS (ZAMBIA) LTD.—See Royal Dutch/Shell Group of Companies; *Int'l*, pg. 1136

SHELL CHILE SA COMERCIAL E INDUSTRIAL—See Royal Dutch/Shell Group of Companies; *Int'l*, pg. 1142

SHELL CHIMIE—See Royal Dutch/Shell Group of Companies; *Int'l*, pg. 1138

SHELL COAL BOTSWANA—See Royal Dutch/Shell Group of Companies; *Int'l*, pg. 1136

SHELL COLOMBIA SA—See Royal Dutch/Shell Group of Companies; *Int'l*, pg. 1142

SHELL COMPANIES IN INDONESIA—See Royal Dutch/Shell Group of Companies; *Int'l*, pg. 1139

SHELL COMPANY (HELLAS) LTD.—See Royal Dutch/Shell Group of Companies; *Int'l*, pg. 1138

THE SHELL CO. LTD.—See Royal Dutch/Shell Group of Companies; *Int'l*, pg. 1141
SHELL CO. OF GIBRALTAR LTD.—See Royal Dutch/Shell Group of Companies; *Int'l*, pg. 1138
SHELL COMPANY OF HONG KONG LTD.—See Royal Dutch/Shell Group of Companies; *Int'l*, pg. 1139
SHELL COMPANY OF PAKISTAN LTD.—See Royal Dutch/Shell Group of Companies; *Int'l*, pg. 1140
THE SHELL COMPANY OF SRI LANKA LTD.—See Royal Dutch/Shell Group of Companies; *Int'l*, pg. 1140
SHELL COMPANY OF THAILAND LTD.—See Royal Dutch/Shell Group of Companies; *Int'l*, pg. 1140
SHELL COMPANY OF THE SUDAN LTD.—See Royal Dutch/Shell Group of Companies; *Int'l*, pg. 1136
SHELL COMPANY OF TURKEY LTD.—See Royal Dutch/Shell Group of Companies; *Int'l*, pg. 1141
SHELL COMPANY OF WEST AFRICA LTD.—See Royal Dutch/Shell Group of Companies; *Int'l*, pg. 1137
SHELL COMPANY (PACIFIC ISLANDS) LTD.—See Royal Dutch/Shell Group of Companies; *Int'l*, pg. 1137
THE SHELL COMPANY (PUERTO RICO) LTD.—See Royal Dutch/Shell Group of Companies; *Int'l*, pg. 1141
THE SHELL COMPANY (WI) LTD.—See Royal Dutch/Shell Group of Companies; *Int'l*, pg. 1141
SHELL COTE D'IVOIRE—See Royal Dutch/Shell Group of Companies; *Int'l*, pg. 1137
SHELL CURACAO N.V.—See Royal Dutch/Shell Group of Companies; *Int'l*, pg. 1141
SHELL CYPRUS TRADING COMPANY LTD—See Royal Dutch/Shell Group of Companies; *Int'l*, pg. 1140
SHELL DE CABO VERDE—See Royal Dutch/Shell Group of Companies; *Int'l*, pg. 1137
SHELL DEVELOPMENT (AUSTRALIA) PTY. LTD.—Royal Dutch/Shell Group of Companies; *Int'l*, pg. 1137
SHELL DEVELOPMENT CO.—Royal Dutch/Shell Group of Companies; *Int'l*, pg. 1136
SHELL DEVELOPMENTS (HK)—See Royal Dutch/Shell Group of Companies; *Int'l*, pg. 1139
SHELL D'EXPLORATION—See Royal Dutch/Shell Group of Companies; *Int'l*, pg. 1137
SHELL DISTRIBUTION CO., INC.—See Royal Dutch/Shell Group of Companies; *Int'l*, pg. 1140
SHELL DJIBOUTI—See Royal Dutch/Shell Group of Companies; *Int'l*, pg. 1137
SHELL EASTERN PETROLEUM—See Royal Dutch/Shell Group of Companies; *Int'l*, pg. 1140
SHELL EASTERN PETROLEUM (PTE) LTD.—See Royal Dutch/Shell Group of Companies; *Int'l*, pg. 1140
SHELL ENERGY DEVELOPMENT ENTERPRISES—See Royal Dutch/Shell Group of Companies; *Int'l*, pg. 1140
SHELL ESPANA S.A.—See Royal Dutch/Shell Group of Companies; *Int'l*, pg. 1139
SHELL ETHIOPIA LTD.—See Royal Dutch/Shell Group of Companies; *Int'l*, pg. 1137
SHELL EXPLORATION & DEVELOPMENT MADAGASCAR BV—See Royal Dutch/Shell Group of Companies; *Int'l*, pg. 1137
SHELL EXPLORATION & PRODUCTION BV—See Royal Dutch/Shell Group of Companies; *Int'l*, pg. 1140
SHELL FIJI—See Royal Dutch/Shell Group of Companies; *Int'l*, pg. 1137
SHELL FORESTRY NEW ZEALAND—See Royal Dutch/Shell Group of Companies; *Int'l*, pg. 1137
SHELL FRANCAISE—See Royal Dutch/Shell Group of Companies; *Int'l*, pg. 1138
SHELL FUEL SUPPLIES—See Royal Dutch/Shell Group of Companies; *Int'l*, pg. 1141
SHELL GABON—See Royal Dutch/Shell Group of Companies; *Int'l*, pg. 1137
SHELL GAS PHILIPPINES, INC.—See Royal Dutch/Shell Group of Companies; *Int'l*, pg. 1140
SHELL GHANA SERVICES LTD.—See Royal Dutch/Shell Group of Companies; *Int'l*, pg. 1137
SHELL GUAM INC.—See Royal Dutch/Shell Group of Companies; *Int'l*, pg. 1137
SHELL HONDURAS SA—See Royal Dutch/Shell Group of Companies; *Int'l*, pg. 1141
SHELL HYDROCARBONS—See Royal Dutch/Shell Group of Companies; *Int'l*, pg. 1142
SHELL INTERNATIONAL PETROLEUM CO. LTD.—See Royal Dutch/Shell Group of Companies; *Int'l*, pg. 1139
SHELL INTERNATIONALE PETROLEUM MIJ BV—See Royal Dutch/Shell Group of Companies; *Int'l*, pg. 1135
SHELL ITALIA SPA—See Royal Dutch/Shell Group of Companies; *Int'l*, pg. 1138
SHELL IVOIRIENNE—See Royal Dutch/Shell Group of Companies; *Int'l*, pg. 1137
SHELL JAPAN LTD.—See Royal Dutch/Shell Group of Companies; *Int'l*, pg. 1139
SHELL KAGAKU K.K.—See Royal Dutch/Shell Group of Companies; *Int'l*, pg. 1139
SHELL LIBERIA LTD.—See Royal Dutch/Shell Group of Companies; *Int'l*, pg. 1137
SHELL LUXEMBOURGEOISE SA—See Royal Dutch/Shell Group of Companies; *Int'l*, pg. 1138
SHELL MALAWI LTD.—See Royal Dutch/Shell Group of Companies; *Int'l*, pg. 1136
SHELL MALAYSIA LTD—See Royal Dutch/Shell Group of Companies; *Int'l*, pg. 1140
SHELL MALAYSIA TRADING—See Royal Dutch/Shell Group of Companies; *Int'l*, pg. 1140
SHELL MALI—See Royal Dutch/Shell Group of Companies; *Int'l*, pg. 1137
SHELL MARKETING BORNEO—See Royal Dutch/Shell Group of Companies; *Int'l*, pg. 1140
SHELL MARKETING GAMBIA LTD.—See Royal Dutch/Shell Group of Companies; *Int'l*, pg. 1137
SHELL MARKETS (MIDDLE EAST) LTD.—See Royal Dutch/Shell Group of Companies; *Int'l*, pg. 1141
SHELL MAURITIUS LTD.—See Royal Dutch/Shell Group of Companies; *Int'l*, pg. 1137
SHELL MEXICO, SA DE CV—See Royal Dutch/Shell Group of Companies; *Int'l*, pg. 1141

SHELL NAMIBIA LTD.—See Royal Dutch/Shell Group of Companies; *Int'l*, pg. 1137
SHELL NEDERLAND CHEMIE—See Royal Dutch/Shell Group of Companies; *Int'l*, pg. 1135
SHELL NEDERLAND RAFFINADERIJ—See Royal Dutch/Shell Group of Companies; *Int'l*, pg. 1135
SHELL NEDERLAND VERKOOP MIJ B.V.—See Royal Dutch/Shell Group of Companies; *Int'l*, pg. 1135
SHELL NEW ZEALAND HOLDING COMPANY—See Royal Dutch/Shell Group of Companies; *Int'l*, pg. 1137
SHELL NICARAGUA S.A.—See Royal Dutch/Shell Group of Companies; *Int'l*, pg. 1141
SHELL NIGER—See Royal Dutch/Shell Group of Companies; *Int'l*, pg. 1137
SHELL OF AALBORG—See Royal Dutch/Shell Group of Companies; *Int'l*, pg. 1138
SHELL OF CASTLE DONINGTON—See Royal Dutch/Shell Group of Companies; *Int'l*, pg. 1139
SHELL OF ESBJERG—See Royal Dutch/Shell Group of Companies; *Int'l*, pg. 1138
SHELL OF GARDERMOEN—See Royal Dutch/Shell Group of Companies; *Int'l*, pg. 1139
SHELL OF STJOERDAL—See Royal Dutch/Shell Group of Companies; *Int'l*, pg. 1139
SHELL OFFSHORE—See Royal Dutch/Shell Group of Companies; *Int'l*, pg. 1142
SHELL OIL BOTSWANA—See Royal Dutch/Shell Group of Companies; *Int'l*, pg. 1136
SHELL OIL COMPANY—See Royal Dutch/Shell Group of Companies; *Int'l*, pg. 1136
SHELL OIL LESOTHO (PTY.) LTD.—See Royal Dutch/Shell Group of Companies; *Int'l*, pg. 1136
SHELL OIL NEW ZEALAND—See Royal Dutch/Shell Group of Companies; *Int'l*, pg. 1137
SHELL OIL SOUTH WEST AFRICA—See Royal Dutch/Shell Group of Companies; *Int'l*, pg. 1136
SHELL OIL SWAZILAND (PTY.) LTD.—See Royal Dutch/Shell Group of Companies; *Int'l*, pg. 1136
SHELL OLIE-OG GASUDVINDING DANMARK—See Royal Dutch/Shell Group of Companies; *Int'l*, pg. 1138
SHELL OVERSEAS SERVICES LTD—See Royal Dutch/Shell Group of Companies; *Int'l*, pg. 1141
SHELL PACIFIC ENTERPRISES LTD—See Royal Dutch/Shell Group of Companies; *Int'l*, pg. 1140
SHELL (PACIFIC ISLANDS)—See Royal Dutch/Shell Group of Companies; *Int'l*, pg. 1137
SHELL PAPUA NEW GUINEA PTY. LTD.—See Royal Dutch/Shell Group of Companies; *Int'l*, pg. 1137
SHELL PARAGUAY LTD.—See Royal Dutch/Shell Group of Companies; *Int'l*, pg. 1142
SHELL PETROLEUM DEVEL. CO. OF LIBYA BV—See Royal Dutch/Shell Group of Companies; *Int'l*, pg. 1141
THE SHELL PETROLEUM DEVELOPMENT COMPANY OF NIGERIA LTD.—See Royal Dutch/Shell Group of Companies; *Int'l*, pg. 1137
SHELL PIPE LINE CORP.—See Royal Dutch/Shell Group of Companies; *Int'l*, pg. 1136
SHELL PORTUGUESA SA—See Royal Dutch/Shell Group of Companies; *Int'l*, pg. 1139
SHELL PROSPECTING—See Royal Dutch/Shell Group of Companies; *Int'l*, pg. 1137
SHELL (PUERTO RICO)—See Royal Dutch/Shell Group of Companies; *Int'l*, pg. 1141
SHELL QUIMICA DE EL SALVADOR—See Royal Dutch/Shell Group of Companies; *Int'l*, pg. 1141
SHELL QUIMICA DE GUATEMALA—See Royal Dutch/Shell Group of Companies; *Int'l*, pg. 1141
SHELL QUIMICA DE VENEZUELA, C.A.—See Royal Dutch/Shell Group of Companies; *Int'l*, pg. 1142
SHELL RECHERCHE—See Royal Dutch/Shell Group of Companies; *Int'l*, pg. 1138
SHELL REFINING (AUSTRALIA) PTY. LTD.—See Royal Dutch/Shell Group of Companies; *Int'l*, pg. 1137
SHELL REFINING (F.O.M.) BHD.—See Royal Dutch/Shell Group of Companies; *Int'l*, pg. 1140
SHELL REPRESENTATIVE OFFICE—See Royal Dutch/Shell Group of Companies; *Int'l*, pg. 1139
SHELL RESEARCH LTD.—See Royal Dutch/Shell Group of Companies; *Int'l*, pg. 1139
SHELL ROMANIA SRL—See Royal Dutch/Shell Group of Companies; *Int'l*, pg. 1139
SHELL SEKIYU—See Royal Dutch/Shell Group of Companies; *Int'l*, pg. 1140
SHELL SEMPAKU—See Royal Dutch/Shell Group of Companies; *Int'l*, pg. 1140
SHELL SENEGAL—See Royal Dutch/Shell Group of Companies; *Int'l*, pg. 1137
SHELL SIERRA LEONE LTD.—See Royal Dutch/Shell Group of Companies; *Int'l*, pg. 1137
SHELL SOUTH AFRICA (PTY) LTD.—See Royal Dutch/Shell Group of Companies; *Int'l*, pg. 1136
SHELL SPANJE—See Royal Dutch/Shell Group of Companies; *Int'l*, pg. 1139
SHELL SPECIALTY CHEMICALS—See Royal Dutch/Shell Group of Companies; *Int'l*, pg. 1139
SHELL SURINAME VERKOOP MIJ NV—See Royal Dutch/Shell Group of Companies; *Int'l*, pg. 1142
SHELL (SWITZERLAND)—See Royal Dutch/Shell Group of Companies; *Int'l*, pg. 1139
SHELL TAIWAN LTD.—See Royal Dutch/Shell Group of Companies; *Int'l*, pg. 1140
SHELL TANKERS B.V.—See Royal Dutch/Shell Group of Companies; *Int'l*, pg. 1135
SHELL TANZANIA LTD.—See Royal Dutch/Shell Group of Companies; *Int'l*, pg. 1137
SHELL TCHAD—See Royal Dutch/Shell Group of Companies; *Int'l*, pg. 1137
SHELL TCHADIENNE—See Royal Dutch/Shell Group of Companies; *Int'l*, pg. 1137
SHELL THAILAND MANUFACTURING, LTD.—See Royal Dutch/Shell Group of Companies; *Int'l*, pg. 1140
SHELL TRADING (MIDDLE EAST)—See Royal Dutch/Shell Group of Companies; *Int'l*, pg. 1141

SHELL TUNISIENNE—See Royal Dutch/Shell Group of Companies; *Int'l*, pg. 1137
SHELL UGANDA LTD.—See Royal Dutch/Shell Group of Companies; *Int'l*, pg. 1137
SHELL UK LTD.—See Royal Dutch/Shell Group of Companies; *Int'l*, pg. 1139
SHELL UK OIL (BIRMINGHAM)—See Royal Dutch/Shell Group of Companies; *Int'l*, pg. 1139
SHELL UK OIL (STANDSTED)—See Royal Dutch/Shell Group of Companies; *Int'l*, pg. 1139
SHELL URUGUAY LTD—See Royal Dutch/Shell Group of Companies; *Int'l*, pg. 1142
SHELL VENEZUELA SA—See Royal Dutch/Shell Group of Companies; *Int'l*, pg. 1142
SHELL WEST EXPLORATION & PRODUCTION INC.—See Royal Dutch/Shell Group of Companies; *Int'l*, pg. 1142
SHELL WINNING NV—See Royal Dutch/Shell Group of Companies; *Int'l*, pg. 1135
SHELL ZIMBABWE (PRIVATE) LTD.—See Royal Dutch/Shell Group of Companies; *Int'l*, pg. 1136
SHELLER-CLIFFORD LTD.—See United Technologies Corporation; *U.S. Public*, pg. 1691
SHELLY BROS., INC.—See Brach & Brock Confections, Inc.; *U.S. Private*, pg. 163
SHELTER COMPONENTS CORPORATION—See Kevco, Inc.; *U.S. Public*, pg. 952
SHELTER DISTRIBUTION—See Kevco, Inc.; *U.S. Public*, pg. 953
SHELTER MUTUAL INSURANCE COMPANY; *U.S. Private*, pg. 992
SHELTER PRODUCTS GROUP—See Tomkins PLC; *Int'l*, pg. 1396
SHELTER PRODUCTS GROUP-WESTERN DIV.—See Tomkins PLC; *Int'l*, pg. 1398
SHENANDOAH GAS CO.—See Washington Gas Light Co.; *U.S. Public*, pg. 1741
SHENANDOAH LIFE INSURANCE COMPANY; *U.S. Private*, pg. 992
SHENANDOAH MFG. CO. INC.; *U.S. Private*, pg. 992
SHENANDOAH MILLS, INC.; *U.S. Private*, pg. 992
SHENANDOAH-VIRGINIA CORPORATION—See Norfolk Southern Corporation; *U.S. Public*, pg. 1191
SHENANGO INDUSTRIES; *U.S. Private*, pg. 992
SHENANGO VALLEY WATER CO.—See Consumers Water Company; *U.S. Public*, pg. 439
SHENMEI DAILY USE PRODUCTS LIMITED COMPANY—See The Gillette Company; *U.S. Public*, pg. 745
SHENTON HOLDINGS PRIVATE LIMITED—See Singapore Land Limited; *Int'l*, pg. 1253
SHENYANG ITT FLYGT JINBEI PUMP CO., LTD.—See ITT Industries, Inc.; *U.S. Public*, pg. 860
SHENYANG KANSAI PAINT CO., LTD.—See Kansai Paint Co., Ltd.; *Int'l*, pg. 723
SHENYANG NETS SYSTEM INTEGRATION CO., LTD.—See Toshiba Corporation; *Int'l*, pg. 1406
SHENYANG NISSAN GAS CO., LTD.—See Nippon Sanso Corporation; *Int'l*, pg. 939
SHENYANG NORTEL TELECOMMUNICATIONS CO., LTD.—See Northern Telecom Limited; *Int'l*, pg. 970
SHENYANG OFFICE—See Gunze Sangyo, Inc.; *Int'l*, pg. 579
SHENYANG YAMANOUCHI PHARMACEUTICAL CO., LTD.—See Yamanouchi Pharmaceutical Co. Ltd.; *Int'l*, pg. 1519
SHENZHEN CIC-AMERSHAM ISOTOPE CO LIMITED—See Nycomed Amersham plc; *Int'l*, pg. 993
SHENZHEN COMMUNICATION CABLE—See Kuhlman Corporation; *U.S. Public*, pg. 968
SHENZHEN-DIC CO., LTD.—See Dainippon Ink & Chemicals, Inc.; *Int'l*, pg. 372
SHENZHEN JIADIANBAO ELECTRICAL PRODUCTS CO., LTD.—See Catalina Lighting, Inc.; *U.S. Public*, pg. 314
SHENZHEN SYLVA ELECTROCHEMICAL LTD.—See GP Batteries International Ltd.; *Int'l*, pg. 537
SHEPARD CLOTHING COMPANY; *U.S. Private*, pg. 992
SHEPARD NILES, INC.; *U.S. Private*, pg. 992
SHEPARD'S—See Reed Elsevier plc; *Int'l*, pg. 1095
SHEPARD'S—See The Times Mirror Company; *U.S. Public*, pg. 1616
SHEPAUG CORPORATION; *U.S. Private*, pg. 993
SHEPHERD CONSTRUCTION CO., INC.; *U.S. Private*, pg. 993
SHEPLER'S AUSTIN—See Commercial Metals Company; *U.S. Public*, pg. 413
SHEPLER'S BEAUMONT—See Commercial Metals Company; *U.S. Public*, pg. 413
SHEPLER'S COLLEGE STATION—See Commercial Metals Company; *U.S. Public*, pg. 413
SHEPLER'S CONROE—See Commercial Metals Company; *U.S. Public*, pg. 413
SHEPLER'S CORPUS CHRISTI—See Commercial Metals Company; *U.S. Public*, pg. 413
SHEPLER'S HOUSTON SOUTH—See Commercial Metals Company; *U.S. Public*, pg. 413
SHEPLER'S HOUSTON WEST—See Commercial Metals Company; *U.S. Public*, pg. 413
SHEPLERS, INC.; *U.S. Private*, pg. 993
SHEPLER'S RIO GRANDE STEEL—See Commercial Metals Company; *U.S. Public*, pg. 413
SHEPLER'S ROUND ROCK—See Commercial Metals Company; *U.S. Public*, pg. 413
SHEPLER'S SAN ANTONIO—See Commercial Metals Company; *U.S. Public*, pg. 413
SHEPLER'S WACO—See Commercial Metals Company; *U.S. Public*, pg. 413
SHEPPARD FOODSERVICE, INC.—See Sun City Industries, Inc.; *U.S. Public*, pg. 1529
SHERATON HOTELS (ENGLAND) LIMITED—See Starwood Hotels & Resorts; *U.S. Public*, pg. 1512
SHERAZADE CONSEIL—See BDDP Group; *Int'l*, pg. 118
SHERIDAN AUSTRALIA LTD—See CS Brooks Canada Inc.; *U.S. Private*, pg. 197
SHERIDAN ELECTRONIC SYSTEMS—See The Sheridan Group; *U.S. Private*, pg. 993

MASTER INDEX TO COMPANY NAMES

SHISEIDO

Company Index

THE SHERIDAN GROUP; *U.S. Private*, pg. 993
THE SHERIDAN PRESS, INC.—See The Sheridan Group; *U.S. Private*, pg. 993
SHERLE WAGNER INTERNATIONAL, INC.—See Masco Corporation; *U.S. Public*, pg. 1054
SHERLEY GRAIN COMPANY; *U.S. Private*, pg. 993
SHERMAN & REILLY, INC.; *U.S. Private*, pg. 993
SHERMAN WIRE—See Keystone Consolidated Industries, Inc.; *U.S. Public*, pg. 955
SHERMS THUNDERBIRD MARKET; *U.S. Private*, pg. 993
THE SHERRILL CORP.—See Custom Accessories Inc.; *U.S. Private*, pg. 298
SHERWAY CENTER LIMITED—See The Canada Life Assurance Company; *Int'l*, pg. 255
SHERWIN-WILLIAMS CAYMAN ISLANDS LTD.—See The Sherwin-Williams Company; *U.S. Public*, pg. 1466
SHERWIN-WILLIAMS COMPANY RESOURCES LIMITED—See The Sherwin-Williams Company; *U.S. Public*, pg. 1466
THE SHERWIN-WILLIAMS COMPANY; *U.S. Public*, pg. 1465
SHERWIN-WILLIAMS DIVERSIFIED BRANDS, INC.—See The Sherwin-Williams Company; *U.S. Public*, pg. 1466
SHERWIN-WILLIAMS DO BRASIL INDUSTRIA E COMERCIO LIMITADA—See The Sherwin-Williams Company; *U.S. Public*, pg. 1466
SHERWIN-WILLIAMS PAINT STORES GROUP—See The Sherwin-Williams Company; *U.S. Public*, pg. 1466
SHERWIN-WILLIAMS SAUDI ARABIA LTD.—See The Sherwin-Williams Company; *U.S. Public*, pg. 1466
SHERWIN-WILLIAMS (WEST INDIES) LTD.—See The Sherwin-Williams Company; *U.S. Public*, pg. 1466
SHERWOOD—See Harsco Corporation; *U.S. Public*, pg. 793
SHERWOOD & JAMES ADVERTISING, INC.—See Union Camp Corporation; *U.S. Public*, pg. 1666
SHERWOOD CONVALESCENT HOSPITAL—See Vencor, Inc.; *U.S. Public*, pg. 1714
SHERWOOD-DAVIS & GECK—See American Home Products Corporation; *U.S. Public*, pg. 80
SHERWOOD FOOD DISTRIBUTORS; *U.S. Private*, pg. 993
SHERWOOD FOODS—See Sherwood Food Distributors; *U.S. Private*, pg. 994
THE SHERWOOD GROUP, INC.; *U.S. Public*, pg. 1466
SHERWOOD INSURANCE SERVICES, INC.—See AON Corporation; *U.S. Public*, pg. 118
SHERWOOD LUMBER CORPORATION; *U.S. Private*, pg. 994
SHERWOOD MEDICAL INDUSTRIES LTD.—See American Home Products Corporation; *U.S. Public*, pg. 82
SHERWOOD SECURITIES CORP.—See The Sherwood Group, Inc.; *U.S. Public*, pg. 1467
SHESHUNOFF INFORMATION SERVICES, INC.—See The Thomson Corporation; *U.S. Public*, pg. 1601
SHIANFU OPTICAL FIBER AND CABLES CO., LTD.—See The Furukawa Electric Co., Ltd.; *Int'l*, pg. 531
SHIANG PAO PRECISION CO., LTD.—See Citizen Watch Company, Ltd.; *Int'l*, pg. 295
SHIAWASSEE TELEPHONE COMPANY—See Telephone and Data Systems, Inc.; *U.S. Public*, pg. 1572
SHIBAURA ENGINEERING WORKS CO., LTD.—See Toshiba Corporation; *Int'l*, pg. 1403
SHIBAZAKI SEISAKUSHO LIMITED—See Aluminum Company of America; *U.S. Public*, pg. 62
THE SHIDLER GROUP; *U.S. Private*, pg. 994
SHIEFFELIN SOMERSET CO.—See Diageo Plc; *Int'l*, pg. 412
SHIEH CHI INDUSTRIAL COMPANY LTD.—See The Yokohama Rubber Co., Ltd.; *Int'l*, pg. 1521
SHIELD HEALTHCARE CENTERS—See Kobayashi Pharmaceutical Co., Ltd.; *Int'l*, pg. 740
SHIELD INSURANCE—See Spartan Stores Inc.; *U.S. Private*, pg. 1021
SHIELD SECURITY, INC.; *U.S. Private*, pg. 994
SHIELDALLOY METALLURGICAL CORPORTATION—See Metallurg, Inc.; *U.S. Private*, pg. 735
SHIKISHIMA BAKING CO., LTD.; *Int'l*, pg. 1231
SHIKMA—See American Israeli Paper Mills Ltd.; *Int'l*, pg. 75
SHILEY INCORPORATED—See Pfizer Inc.; *U.S. Public*, pg. 1284
SHILEY INTERNATIONAL—See Pfizer Inc.; *U.S. Public*, pg. 1284
SHILLCRAFT, INC.; *U.S. Private*, pg. 994
SHIMA AMERICAN CORP.—See Shima Trading Co. Ltd.; *Int'l*, pg. 1232
SHIMA TRADING CO. LTD.; *Int'l*, pg. 1231
SHIMADZU (ASIA PACIFIC) PTE. LTD.—See Shimadzu Corporation; *Int'l*, pg. 1232
SHIMADZU AUSTRALIA MANUFACTURING PTY. LTD.—See Shimadzu Corporation; *Int'l*, pg. 1232
SHIMADZU CORPORATION; *Int'l*, pg. 1232
SHIMADZU DO BRASIL REPRESENTACAO, LTDA.—See Shimadzu Corporation; *Int'l*, pg. 1232
SHIMADZU EUROPA GMBH—See Shimadzu Corporation; *Int'l*, pg. 1232
SHIMADZU ITALIA S.R.L.—See Shimadzu Corporation; *Int'l*, pg. 1232
SHIMADZU OCEANIA PTY. LTD.—See Shimadzu Corporation; *Int'l*, pg. 1232
SHIMADZU PRECISION INSTRUMENTS, INC.—See Shimadzu Corporation; *Int'l*, pg. 1232
SHIMADZU PRECISION INSTRUMENTS, INC.-MEDICAL SYSTEM DIV.—See Shimadzu Corporation; *Int'l*, pg. 1232
SHIMADZU SCIENTIFIC INSTRUMENTS, INC.—See Shimadzu Corporation; *Int'l*, pg. 1232
SHIMADZU SHANGHAI OFFICE—See Shimadzu Corporation; *Int'l*, pg. 1232
SHIMANO ADACHI CO., LTD.—See Shimano Inc.; *Int'l*, pg. 1232
SHIMANO AMERICAN CORPORATION—See Shimano Inc.; *Int'l*, pg. 1232
P.T. SHIMANO BATAM—See Shimano Inc.; *Int'l*, pg. 1232
SHIMANO BENELUX B.V.—See Shimano Inc.; *Int'l*, pg. 1233
SHIMANO CANADA LTD.—See Shimano Inc.; *Int'l*, pg. 1233
SHIMANO CENTER BICY B.V.—See Shimano Inc.; *Int'l*, pg. 1233
SHIMANO CENTER INTERBIKE N.V.—See Shimano Inc.; *Int'l*, pg. 1233
SHIMANO COMPONENTS (MALAYSIA) SDN. BHD.—See Shimano Inc.; *Int'l*, pg. 1233
SHIMANO (EUROPA) GMBH—See Shimano Inc.; *Int'l*, pg. 1233
SHIMANO FISHING TACKLE SALES CO., LTD.—See Shimano Inc.; *Int'l*, pg. 1232
SHIMANO INC.; *Int'l*, pg. 1232
SHIMANO ITALIA S.R.L.—See Shimano Inc.; *Int'l*, pg. 1233
SHIMANO (KUNSHAN) BICYCLE COMPONENTS CO., LTD.—See Shimano Inc.; *Int'l*, pg. 1233
SHIMANO (MALAYSIA) SDN. BHD.—See Shimano Inc.; *Int'l*, pg. 1233
SHIMANO RINKAI CO., LTD.—See Shimano Inc.; *Int'l*, pg. 1232
SHIMANO (SINGAPORE) PTE. LTD.—See Shimano Inc.; *Int'l*, pg. 1233
SHIMANO U.K. LTD.—See Shimano Inc.; *Int'l*, pg. 1233
SHIMANO YAMAGUCHI CO., LTD.—See Shimano Inc.; *Int'l*, pg. 1232
SHIMEX LTD.—See CODELCO Chile (Corporacion Nacional Del Cobre De Chile); *Int'l*, pg. 303
SHIMIZU AMERICA CORPORATION-ATLANTA MARIETTA OFFICE—See Shimizu Corporation; *Int'l*, pg. 1233
SHIMIZU AMERICA CORPORATION-CHICAGO OFFICE—See Shimizu Corporation; *Int'l*, pg. 1233
SHIMIZU AMERICA CORPORATION-MCALLEN OFFICE—See Shimizu Corporation; *Int'l*, pg. 1233
SHIMIZU AMERICA CORPORATION-PORTLAND OFFICE—See Shimizu Corporation; *Int'l*, pg. 1233
SHIMIZU AMERICA CORPORATION—See Shimizu Corporation; *Int'l*, pg. 1233
SHIMIZU BENELUX S.A.—See Shimizu Corporation; *Int'l*, pg. 1233
SHIMIZU C.A. GES.M.B.H.—See Shimizu Corporation; *Int'l*, pg. 1234
SHIMIZU CANADA ENGINEERING CORPORATION—See Shimizu Corporation; *Int'l*, pg. 1234
SHIMIZU CONSTRUCAO (PORTUGAL) S.A.—See Shimizu Corporation; *Int'l*, pg. 1234
SHIMIZU CORPORATION; *Int'l*, pg. 1233
SHIMIZU CORPORATION OF AUSTRALIA PTY. LTD.—See Shimizu Corporation; *Int'l*, pg. 1234
SHIMIZU (CS) SPOL. SR. O.—See Shimizu Corporation; *Int'l*, pg. 1234
SHIMIZU DEVELOPMENT (NY), INC.—See Shimizu Corporation; *Int'l*, pg. 1233
SHIMIZU EQUITIES (U.S.A.), INC.—See Shimizu Corporation; *Int'l*, pg. 1233
SHIMIZU ESPANA, S.A.-BARCELONA OFFICE—See Shimizu Corporation; *Int'l*, pg. 1234
SHIMIZU EUROPE B.V.—See Shimizu Corporation; *Int'l*, pg. 1234
SHIMIZU FRANCE S.A.—See Shimizu Corporation; *Int'l*, pg. 1234
SHIMIZU GMBH-BERLIN OFFICE—See Shimizu Corporation; *Int'l*, pg. 1234
SHIMIZU GMBH-DUSSELDORF OFFICE—See Shimizu Corporation; *Int'l*, pg. 1234
SHIMIZU GMBH-FRANKFURT OFFICE—See Shimizu Corporation; *Int'l*, pg. 1234
SHIMIZU HONG KONG CO., LTD.—See Shimizu Corporation; *Int'l*, pg. 1234
SHIMIZU HUNGARY CONSTRUCTION LTD.—See Shimizu Corporation; *Int'l*, pg. 1234
SHIMIZU INTERNATIONAL FINANCE (AUSTRALIA) LTD.-SYDNEY OFFICE—See Shimizu Corporation; *Int'l*, pg. 1234
SHIMIZU INTERNATIONAL FINANCE (UK) LTD.—See Shimizu Corporation; *Int'l*, pg. 1234
SHIMIZU INTERNATIONAL FINANCE (U.S.A.), INC.-NEW YORK OFFICE—See Shimizu Corporation; *Int'l*, pg. 1233
SHIMIZU ITALIA S.P.A.—See Shimizu Corporation; *Int'l*, pg. 1234
P.T. SHIMIZU-LAMPIRI CONSULTANTS—See Shimizu Corporation; *Int'l*, pg. 1234
SHIMIZU LAND CORPORATION—See Shimizu Corporation; *Int'l*, pg. 1233
SHIMIZU LAND CORPORATION-LOS ANGELES OFFICE—See Shimizu Corporation; *Int'l*, pg. 1233
SHIMIZU LAND CORPORATION-SAN DIEGO OFFICE—See Shimizu Corporation; *Int'l*, pg. 1233
SHIMIZU-PEREMBA SDN. BHD.—See Shimizu Corporation; *Int'l*, pg. 1234
SHIMIZU PHILIPPINE CONTRACTORS, INC.—See Shimizu Corporation; *Int'l*, pg. 1234
SHIMIZU PRECON PTE. LTD.—See Shimizu Corporation; *Int'l*, pg. 1234
SHIMIZU PROPERTIES (DEUTSCHLAND) GMBH—See Shimizu Corporation; *Int'l*, pg. 1234
SHIMIZU (UK) LTD.—See Shimizu Corporation; *Int'l*, pg. 1234
SHIMODA ELECTRIC CO., LTD.—See Sanken Electric Co., Ltd.; *Int'l*, pg. 1188
SHIMURA KAKO COMPANY, LTD.—See Inco Limited; *Int'l*, pg. 673
SHIMURA KAKO COMPANY, LTD.—See Mitsui & Co., Ltd.; *Int'l*, pg. 879
SHIN CATERPILLAR MITSUBISHI LTD.—See Caterpillar Inc.; *U.S. Public*, pg. 317
SHIN CHUN PRECISION CO., LTD.—See Citizen Watch Company, Ltd.; *Int'l*, pg. 295
SHIN-ETSU CHEMICAL CO. LTD.; *Int'l*, pg. 1234
SHIN-ETSU HANDOTAI CO. LTD.—See Shin-Etsu Chemical Co. ltd.; *Int'l*, pg. 1234
SHIN-ETSU POLYMER AMERICA, INC.—See Shin-Etsu Chemical Co. ltd.; *Int'l*, pg. 1234
SHIN-ETSU POLYMER CO. LTD.—See Shin-Etsu Chemical Co. ltd.; *Int'l*, pg. 1234
SHIN HOKKEN LTD.—See Caterpillar Inc.; *U.S. Public*, pg. 317
SHIN KONG MITSUKOSHI DEPARTMENT STORE CO., LTD.—See Mitsukoshi, Ltd.; *Int'l*, pg. 884
SHIN KONG MITSUKOSHI DEPARTMENT STORE CO. LTD. - TAIPEI STATION FRONT—See Mitsukoshi, Ltd.; *Int'l*, pg. 884
SHIN KONG MITSUKOSHI DEPARTMENT STORE CO. LTD. - KAO HSIUNG SAN TUO—See Mitsukoshi, Ltd.; *Int'l*, pg. 884
SHIN-MEITO CO., LTD.—See Nissho Iwai Corporation; *Int'l*, pg. 947
SHIN NIPPON AIR CONDITIONING ENGINEERING CO., LTD.—See Mitsui & Co., Ltd.; *Int'l*, pg. 877
SHIN NIPPON KOKI CO. LTD.; *Int'l*, pg. 1234
SHIN NISHI NIHON—See Royal Dutch/Shell Group of Companies; *Int'l*, pg. 1140
SHIN TAIWAN AGRICULTURAL MACHINERY CO., LTD.—See Kubota Corp.; *Int'l*, pg. 763
SHIN-WAKO SECURITIES INVESTMENT TRUST AND MANAGEMENT CO., LTD.—See Wako Securities Co., Ltd.; *Int'l*, pg. 1485
SHING KWAN REALTY (PTE) LIMITED—See Singapore Land Limited; *Int'l*, pg. 1253
SHINJUKU NS BUILDING CO., LTD.—See Nippon Life Insurance Co.; *Int'l*, pg. 935
SHINKO ELECTRIC CO., LTD.—See Kobe Steel, Ltd.; *Int'l*, pg. 740
SHINKO ELECTRIC INDUSTRIES CO., LTD.—See Fujitsu Limited; *Int'l*, pg. 526
SHINKO ENGINEERING CO., LTD.—See Kobe Steel, Ltd.; *Int'l*, pg. 740
SHINKO TELECOMMUNICATIONS CONSTRUCTION CO., LTD.—See The Furukawa Electric Co., Ltd.; *Int'l*, pg. 530
SHINKO WIRE CO., LTD.—See Kobe Steel, Ltd.; *Int'l*, pg. 740
SHINRYU CEMENT CORP.—See Ssangyong Business Group; *Int'l*, pg. 1291
SHINSHO CORPORATION—See Kobe Steel, Ltd.; *Int'l*, pg. 740
SHINSHU PASCO BOTTLING CO., LTD.—See Pasco Corporation; *Int'l*, pg. 1024
SHINSUNG PACKARD COMPANY, LTD.—See General Motors Corporation; *U.S. Public*, pg. 724
SHINTECH INC.—See Shin-Etsu Chemical Co. ltd.; *Int'l*, pg. 1234
SHINTO PAINT CO., LTD.—See Sumitomo Chemical Company, Ltd.; *Int'l*, pg. 1311
SHINY ENTERTAINMENT INC.—See Interplay Productions, Inc.; *U.S. Private*, pg. 573
SHINYOUNG WACOAL INC.—See Wacoal Corporation; *Int'l*, pg. 1484
SHIONOGI & CO. GMBH—See Shionogi & Co., Ltd.; *Int'l*, pg. 1235
SHIONOGI & CO., LTD.; *Int'l*, pg. 1234
SHIONOGI & CO., LTD. - DUSSELDORF—See Shionogi & Co., Ltd.; *Int'l*, pg. 1235
SHIONOGI & CO., LTD. - TAIPEI—See Shionogi & Co., Ltd.; *Int'l*, pg. 1235
SHIONOGI & CO., LTD. - LOS ANGELES—See Shionogi & Co., Ltd.; *Int'l*, pg. 1235
SHIONOGI & CO., LTD. - NEW JERSEY—See Shionogi & Co., Ltd.; *Int'l*, pg. 1235
SHIONOGI EUROPE B.V.—See Shionogi & Co., Ltd.; *Int'l*, pg. 1235
SHIONOGI FUKUOKA OFFICE—See Shionogi & Co., Ltd.; *Int'l*, pg. 1234
SHIONOGI LILLY KABUSHIKI KAISHA—See Eli Lilly and Company; *U.S. Public*, pg. 994
SHIONOGI NAGOYA OFFICE—See Shionogi & Co., Ltd.; *Int'l*, pg. 1234
SHIONOGI QUALICAPS, INC.—See Shionogi & Co., Ltd.; *Int'l*, pg. 1235
SHIONOGI QUALICAPS, S.A.—See Shionogi & Co., Ltd.; *Int'l*, pg. 1235
SHIONOGI RESEARCH LABORATORIES—See Shionogi & Co., Ltd.; *Int'l*, pg. 1235
SHIONOGI SAPPORO OFFICE—See Shionogi & Co., Ltd.; *Int'l*, pg. 1234
SHIONOGI TOKYO OFFICE—See Shionogi & Co., Ltd.; *Int'l*, pg. 1234
SHIONOGI USA, INC.—See Shionogi & Co., Ltd.; *Int'l*, pg. 1235
SHIP ANALYTICS, INC.; *U.S. Private*, pg. 994
SHIPLEY CO., LLC—See Rohm and Haas Company; *U.S. Public*, pg. 1403
SHIPLEY COMPANIES; *U.S. Private*, pg. 994
SHIPLEY EUROPE LIMITED—See Rohm and Haas Company; *U.S. Public*, pg. 1404
SHIPLEY FAR EAST LIMITED—See Rohm and Haas Company; *U.S. Public*, pg. 1404
SHIPPAMS—See Diageo Plc; *Int'l*, pg. 408
SHIRAKAWA OLYMPUS CO., LTD.—See Olympus Optical Co., Ltd.; *Int'l*, pg. 1004
SHIRMAX LEASING LTD.; *Int'l*, pg. 1235
SHIRMAX RETAIL LTD.—See Shirmax Leasing Ltd.; *Int'l*, pg. 1235
SHISEIDO (AUSTRALIA) PTY. LIMITED—See Shiseido Company Ltd.; *Int'l*, pg. 1235
SHISEIDO COMPANY LTD.; *Int'l*, pg. 1235
SHISEIDO COSMETICI (ITALIA) S.P.A.—See Shiseido Company Ltd.; *Int'l*, pg. 1235
SHISEIDO COSMETICS (AMERICA) LTD.—See Shiseido Company Ltd.; *Int'l*, pg. 1235
SHISEIDO DEUTCHLAND GMBH—See Shiseido Company Ltd.; *Int'l*, pg. 1235
SHISEIDO FRANCE S.A.—See Shiseido Company Ltd.; *Int'l*, pg. 1235

SHISEIDO N.Z. LTD.—See Shiseido Company Ltd.; *Int'l*, pg. 1235

SHISEIDO U.K. CO., LTD.—See Shiseido Company Ltd.; *Int'l*, pg. 1236

SHISSLER SEED CO.—See Groupe Limagrain; *Int'l*, pg. 566

SHIVERS TRADING & OPERATING CO., *U.S. Private*, pg. 994

SHIZUOKA CATERPILLAR MITSUBISHI CONSTRUCTION EQUIPMENT SALES, LTD.—See Caterpillar Inc.; *U.S. Public*, pg. 317

SHIZUKI ELECTRIC CORPORATION; *Int'l*, pg. 1236

SHIZUOKA BANK (EUROPE) S.A.—See Shizuoka Bank, Ltd.; *Int'l*, pg. 1236

SHIZUOKA BANK, LTD.; *Int'l*, pg. 1236

SHIZUOKA FINANCE H.K. LIMITED—See Shizuoka Bank, Ltd.; *Int'l*, pg. 1236

SHIZUOKA OKI ELECTRIC CO., LTD.—See Oki Electric Industry Company, Ltd.; *Int'l*, pg. 999

SHOALS SUPPLY, INC.—See Drew Industries Incorporated; *U.S. Public*, pg. 529

SHOBISHA CO., LTD.—See Matsuya Company Ltd.; *Int'l*, pg. 848

SHOE PAVILION; *U.S. Private*, pg. 996

THE SHOE SHOW OF ROCKY MT., INC., *U.S. Private*, pg. 996

R.M. SHOEMAKER CO.; *U.S. Private*, pg. 996

SHOFAR KOSHER FOODS—See Sara Lee Corporation; *U.S. Public*, pg. 1433

SHOGYO INTERNATIONAL CORPORATION; *U.S. Private*, pg. 996

SHOKAI FAR EAST LTD.; *U.S. Private*, pg. 996

SHOKO CHUKIN BANK; *Int'l*, pg. 1236

SHOLODGE, INC.; *U.S. Public*, pg. 1467

SHONAC CORPORATION; *U.S. Private*, pg. 996

SHONEY'S INC.; *U.S. Public*, pg. 1467

SHONEY'S RESTAURANT DIV.—See Shoney's, Inc.; *U.S. Public*, pg. 1467

SHOOK BUILDING GROUP—See Shook National Corporation; *U.S. Private*, pg. 996

SHOOK HEAVY AND ENVIRONMENTAL GROUP—See Shook National Corporation; *U.S. Private*, pg. 996

SHOOK, INCORPORATED—See Shook National Corporation; *U.S. Private*, pg. 996

SHOOK INDIANA DIVISION—See Shook National Corporation; *U.S. Private*, pg. 996

SHOOK NATIONAL CORPORATION, *U.S. Private*, pg. 996

SHOOK NORTHERN OHIO DIVISION—See Shook National Corporation; *U.S. Private*, pg. 996

SHOP 'N SAVE-MASS., INC.—See Hannaford Bros. Co.; *U.S. Public*, pg. 782

SHOP 'N SAVE WAREHOUSE FOODS, INC.—See SuperValu, Inc.; *U.S. Public*, pg. 1541

SHOP-RITE BEVERAGES, INC.—See Wakefern Food Corporation; *U.S. Private*, pg. 1146

SHOP-RITE CIGARETTES (CT)—See Wakefern Food Corporation; *U.S. Private*, pg. 1146

SHOP-RITE OF BENSALEM INC.—See Wakefern Food Corporation; *U.S. Private*, pg. 1146

SHOP RITE OF MALVERNE, INC.—See Foodarama Supermarkets, Inc.; *U.S. Public*, pg. 661

SHOP-RITE SUPERMARKETS, INC.—See Wakefern Food Corporation; *U.S. Private*, pg. 1146

SHOPKO STORES, INC.; *U.S. Public*, pg. 1467

SHOPPER PUBLISHING GROUP—See Shivers Trading & Operating Co.; *U.S. Private*, pg. 995

SHOPPERS DRUG MART, LTD.—See B.A.T Industries P.L.C.; *Int'l*, pg. 112

SHOPPERS FOOD WAREHOUSE—See Dart Group Corporation; *U.S. Public*, pg. 484

SHOPPING CENTRE GROUP—See Cambridge Shopping Centres Limited; *Int'l*, pg. 253

SHOPSMITH, INC.; *U.S. Public*, pg. 1467

SHORE LINE NEWSPAPER—See Journal Register Company; *U.S. Public*, pg. 935

SHORE LINE SHOPS, INC.—See NIPSCO Industries, Inc.; *U.S. Public*, pg. 1185

SHORELAND COMMUNICATIONS, INC.—See Motorola, Inc.; *U.S. Private*, pg. 1139

SHORELINE BANK—See Shoreline Financial Corp.; *U.S. Public*, pg. 1468

SHORELINE FINANCIAL CORP.; *U.S. Public*, pg. 1467

IRMA SHORELL, INC.—See Tri Tech Laboratories, Inc.; *U.S. Private*, pg. 1101

SHORENSTEIN COMPANY; *U.S. Private*, pg. 996

SHOREWOOD PACKAGING CORPORATION; *U.S. Public*, pg. 1468

SHOREWOOD PACKAGING CORPORATION—See Shorewood Packaging Corporation; *U.S. Public*, pg. 1468

SHOREWOOD PACKAGING CORPORATION OF CANADA, LTD.—See Shorewood Packaging Corporation; *U.S. Public*, pg. 1468

SHOREWOOD PACKAGING CORPORATION OF CANADA, LIMITED—See Shorewood Packaging Corporation; *U.S. Public*, pg. 1468

SHOREWOOD PACKAGING CORPORATION OF OREGON—See Shorewood Packaging Corporation; *U.S. Public*, pg. 1468

SHORROCK INC.—See Bell Atlantic Corporation; *U.S. Public*, pg. 203

SHORROCK MILITARY SYSTEMS INC.—See Sophus Berendsen A/S; *Int'l*, pg. 1286

SHORROCK SECURITY LTD.—See Sophus Berendsen A/S; *Int'l*, pg. 1285

SHORTS BROTHERS PLC—See Bombardier Inc.; *Int'l*, pg. 200

SHOSHONE TITLE INSURANCE & ABSTRACT COMPANY—See The First American Financial Corporation; *U.S. Public*, pg. 626

SHOUGANG NEC ELECTRONICS CO., LTD.—See NEC Corporation; *Int'l*, pg. 901

SHOWA AIRCRAFT INDUSTRY CO., LTD.—See Mitsui & Co., Ltd.; *Int'l*, pg. 878

SHOWA ALUMINUM CORP.—See Showa Denko K.K.; *Int'l*, pg. 1236

SHOWA ALUMINUM CORP. OF AMERICA—See Showa Denko K.K.; *Int'l*, pg. 1236

SHOWA BUSSAN CO., LTD.—See Snow Brand Milk Products Co. Ltd.; *Int'l*, pg. 1272

SHOWA DENKO AMERICA, INC.—See Showa Denko K.K.; *Int'l*, pg. 1237

SHOWA DENKO (EUROPE) GMBH—See Showa Denko K.K.; *Int'l*, pg. 1237

SHOWA DENKO KAWASAKI WORKS—See Showa Denko K.K.; *Int'l*, pg. 1236

SHOWA DENKO K.K.; *Int'l*, pg. 1236

SHOWA DENKO OITA WORKS—See Showa Denko K.K.; *Int'l*, pg. 1236

SHOWA DENKO SINGAPORE (PTE.) LTD.—See Showa Denko K.K.; *Int'l*, pg. 1237

SHOWA ELECTRIC WIRE & CABLE CO., LTD.—See Toshiba Corporation; *Int'l*, pg. 1403

SHOWA GATX COMPANY, LTD.—See GATX Corporation; *U.S. Public*, pg. 693

SHOWA HIGH-TECH-RENT CO., LTD.—See Kenwood Corporation; *Int'l*, pg. 730

SHOWA KANKO KAIHATSU CO., LTD.—See Suntory Ltd.; *Int'l*, pg. 1321

SHOWA LEASING CO., LTD.—See The Asahi Bank, Ltd.; *Int'l*, pg. 82

SHOWA PLASTICS (JINAN) CO. LTD.—See Showpla Asia Limited; *Int'l*, pg. 1237

SHOWA PLASTICS (SHENZHEN) CO. LTD.—See Showpla Asia Limited; *Int'l*, pg. 1237

SHOWA PRODUCTS CO., LTD.—See Sonoco Products Company; *U.S. Public*, pg. 1487

SHOWA SAVOIE—See Pechiney S.A.; *Int'l*, pg. 1032

SHOWA SHELL SEKIYU KK—See Royal Dutch/Shell Group of Companies; *Int'l*, pg. 1140

SHOWA YOKKAICHI SEKIYU CO. LTD.—See Royal Dutch/Shell Group of Companies; *Int'l*, pg. 1140

SHOWBIZ PIZZA TIME, INC.; *U.S. Public*, pg. 1468

SHOWBOAT, INCORPORATED; *U.S. Public*, pg. 1469

SHOWBOAT OPERATING CO.—See Showboat, Incorporated; *U.S. Public*, pg. 1469

SHOWCASE TECHNOLOGIES—See Platinum Equity Holdings, LLC; *U.S. Private*, pg. 872

SHOWPLA ASIA LIMITED; *Int'l*, pg. 1237

SHOWPLA BRASIL LTD.—See Showpla Asia Limited; *Int'l*, pg. 1237

SHOWPLA (DELHI) PRIVATE LIMITED—See Showpla Asia Limited; *Int'l*, pg. 1237

SHOWPLA HONG KONG LTD.—See Showpla Asia Limited; *Int'l*, pg. 1237

PT SHOWPLA INDO—See Showpla Asia Limited; *Int'l*, pg. 1237

SHOWPLA INTERNATIONAL PTE. LTD.—See Showpla Asia Limited; *Int'l*, pg. 1237

SHOWPLA (M) SDN. BHD.—See Showpla Asia Limited; *Int'l*, pg. 1237

SHOWPLA (THAILAND) CO. LTD.—See Showpla Asia Limited; *Int'l*, pg. 1237

SHOWPLA VIETNAM CO. LTD.—See Showpla Asia Limited; *Int'l*, pg. 1237

SHOWPLATRONICS (M) SDN. BHD.—See Showpla Asia Limited; *Int'l*, pg. 1237

SHOWTIME NETWORKS INC.—See National Amusements, Inc.; *U.S. Private*, pg. 779

SHOWTIME SATELLITE NETWORKS, INC.—See National Amusements, Inc.; *U.S. Private*, pg. 779

SHREDDED PRODUCTS CORP.—See Roanoke Electric Steel Corporation; *U.S. Public*, pg. 1392

SHREVE, CRUMP & LOW CO.—See Henry Birks & Sons (1993) Inc.; *Int'l*, pg. 197

SHUFORD MILLS, INC.; *U.S. Private*, pg. 996

SHUGART CORPORATION; *U.S. Private*, pg. 997

SHUNDE DONNELLY ZHEN HUA AUTOMOTIVE SYSTEMS CO. LTD.—See Donnelly Corporation; *U.S. Public*, pg. 519

SHUNT TECHNOLOGY—See Hicks, Muse, Tate & Furst Inc.; *U.S. Private*, pg. 526

SHUR-LOK CORPORATION; *U.S. Private*, pg. 997

SHUR-LOK INTERNATIONAL—See Shur-Lok Corporation; *U.S. Private*, pg. 997

SHURE BROTHERS INCORPORATED; *U.S. Private*, pg. 997

SHURE ELECTRONICS OF AZ—See Shure Brothers Incorporated; *U.S. Private*, pg. 997

SHURE, GMBH—See Shure Brothers Incorporated; *U.S. Private*, pg. 997

SHURFINE INTERNATIONAL, INC.; *U.S. Private*, pg. 997

SHURFLO PUMP MANUFACTURING CO.—See WICOR, Inc.; *U.S. Public*, pg. 1767

SHUTTERS, INC.—See Home Products International, Inc.; *U.S. Public*, pg. 832

SHUTTLELIFT, INC.—See Marine Travelift, Inc.; *U.S. Private*, pg. 703

SHUWA CORPORATION; *Int'l*, pg. 1237

SHUWA CORP. OF NEW YORK—See Shuwa Corporation; *Int'l*, pg. 1237

SHUWA INVESTMENTS CORP.—See Shuwa Corporation; *Int'l*, pg. 1237

SHUWA TRUST OF BOSTON—See Shuwa Corporation; *Int'l*, pg. 1237

SI-GLAS A/S—See Saint-Gobain; *Int'l*, pg. 1173

SIA BALTIC FEED—See Cultor Ltd.; *Int'l*, pg. 349

SIA-HANDELSGESELLSCHAFT MBH—See Schmalbach-Lubeca AG; *Int'l*, pg. 1207

SIAB ITALIA S.P.A.—See Compagnie des Machines Bull; *Int'l*, pg. 316

SIAD S.P.A.—See Praxair Inc.; *U.S. Public*, pg. 1320

SIAGARAGE S.P.A.—See Bastogi-S.p.A.; *Int'l*, pg. 170

SIAM ALGAE CO., LTD.—See Dainippon Ink & Chemicals, Inc.; *Int'l*, pg. 372

SIAM ASAHI TECHNOGLASS CO., LTD.—See The Siam Cement Public Company Limited; *Int'l*, pg. 1238

SIAM CELLULOSE CO., LTD.—See The Siam Cement Public Company Limited; *Int'l*, pg. 1238

SIAM CEMENT INDUSTRIAL LAND CO., LTD.—See The Siam Cement Public Company Limited; *Int'l*, pg. 1238

THE SIAM CEMENT PUBLIC COMPANY LIMITED; *Int'l*, pg. 1237

SIAM CHEMICAL INDUSTRY CO., LTD.—See Dainippon Ink & Chemicals, Inc.; *Int'l*, pg. 372

SIAM CITY BANK PUBLIC COMPANY LIMITED; *Int'l*, pg. 1239

SIAM CITY CHAROEN HIRE-PURCHASE (HAT YAI) CO., LTD.—See Siam City Bank Public Company Limited; *Int'l*, pg. 1239

SIAM CITY CREDIT FINANCE & SECURITIES CO., LTD.—See Siam City Bank Public Company Limited; *Int'l*, pg. 1239

SIAM CITY FACTORING CO., LTD.—See Siam City Bank Public Company Limited; *Int'l*, pg. 1239

SIAM CITY-SHOWA LEASING CO., LTD.—See Siam City Bank Public Company Limited; *Int'l*, pg. 1239

SIAM CITY SURAT LEASING CO., LTD.—See Siam City Bank Public Company Limited; *Int'l*, pg. 1239

SIAM CITY SYNDICATE FINANCE & SECURITIES CO., LTD.—See Siam City Bank Public Company Limited; *Int'l*, pg. 1239

SIAM COMPRESSOR INDUSTRY CO., LTD.—See The Siam Cement Public Company Limited; *Int'l*, pg. 1238

THE SIAM CONSTRUCTION STEEL CO., LTD.—See The Siam Cement Public Company Limited; *Int'l*, pg. 1238

SIAM ELECTRIC INDUSTRIES CO., LTD.—See Sumitomo Electric Industries, Ltd.; *Int'l*, pg. 1313

THE SIAM FIBRE-CEMENT CO., LTD.—See The Siam Cement Public Company Limited; *Int'l*, pg. 1238

SIAM FURUKAWA CO., LTD.—See The Siam Cement Public Company Limited; *Int'l*, pg. 1238

SIAM GUARDIAN GLASS CO., LTD.—See The Siam Cement Public Company Limited; *Int'l*, pg. 1238

THE SIAM GYPSUM INDUSTRY CO., LTD.—See The Siam Cement Public Company Limited; *Int'l*, pg. 1238

SIAM-HITACHI CONSTRUCTION MACHINERY CO., LTD.—See The Siam Cement Public Company Limited; *Int'l*, pg. 1238

THE SIAM IRON AND STEEL CO., LTD.—See The Siam Cement Public Company Limited; *Int'l*, pg. 1238

SIAM KABAYA CO., LTD.—See Kayaba Industry Co., Ltd.; *Int'l*, pg. 727

SIAM KIKI CO., LTD.—See Zexel Corporation; *Int'l*, pg. 1528

SIAM KRAFT INDUSTRY CO., LTD.—See The Siam Cement Public Company Limited; *Int'l*, pg. 1238

THE SIAM KUBOTA INDUSTRY CO., LTD.—See Kubota Corp.; *Int'l*, pg. 763

THE SIAM KUBOTA INDUSTRY CO., LTD.—See The Siam Cement Public Company Limited; *Int'l*, pg. 1239

SIAM LEMMERZ CO., LTD.—See The Siam Cement Public Company Limited; *Int'l*, pg. 1238

SIAM MAGOTTEAUX CO., LTD.—See The Siam Cement Public Company Limited; *Int'l*, pg. 1238

SIAM MAKRO CO., LTD.—See SHV Holdings N.V.; *Int'l*, pg. 1156

SIAM MARIWASA TOTO.—See Toto Ltd.; *Int'l*, pg. 1410

THE SIAM NAWALOHA FOUNDRY CO., LTD.—See The Siam Cement Public Company Limited; *Int'l*, pg. 1238

SIAM NEC CO., LTD.—See The Siam Cement Public Company Limited; *Int'l*, pg. 1239

SIAM PERSTORP CO., LTD.—See Perstorp AB; *Int'l*, pg. 1039

SIAM PERSTORP CO LTD—See Perstorp AB; *Int'l*, pg. 1039

THE SIAM PIPE INDUSTRY CO., LTD.—See The Siam Cement Public Company Limited; *Int'l*, pg. 1238

THE SIAM PIPE PRODUCTS CO., LTD.—See The Siam Cement Public Company Limited; *Int'l*, pg. 1238

SIAM PRINTING & PACKAGING CO., LTD.—See Toppan Printing Company, Ltd.; *Int'l*, pg. 1399

THE SIAM PULP AND PAPER CO., LTD.—See The Siam Cement Public Company Limited; *Int'l*, pg. 1238

THE SIAM SANITARY FITTINGS CO., LTD.—See The Siam Cement Public Company Limited; *Int'l*, pg. 1239

THE SIAM SANITARY FITTINGS CO., LTD.—See Toto Ltd.; *Int'l*, pg. 1410

SIAM SANITARY WARE CO., LTD.—See Toto Ltd.; *Int'l*, pg. 1410

THE SIAM SANWA INDUSTRIAL CREDIT CO., LTD.—See The Sanwa Bank Limited; *Int'l*, pg. 1190

THE SIAM SANWA TRILEASE CO., LTD.—See The Sanwa Bank Limited; *Int'l*, pg. 1190

SIAM SYNTHETIC LATEX CO., LTD.—See The Siam Cement Public Company Limited; *Int'l*, pg. 1238

SIAM TOBACCO EXPORT CORP. LTD.—See Standard Commercial Corporation; *U.S. Public*, pg. 1502

SIAM TOYOTA MANUFACTURING CO., LTD.—See The Siam Cement Public Company Limited; *Int'l*, pg. 1238

SIAM TOYOTA MANUFACTURING CO., LTD.—See Toyota Motor Corporation; *Int'l*, pg. 1414

SIAM TYRE CO., LTD.—See The Siam Cement Public Company Limited; *Int'l*, pg. 1238

SIAM TYRE INDUSTRY CO., LTD.—See The Siam Cement Public Company Limited; *Int'l*, pg. 1238

SIAM YAMATO STEEL CO., LTD.—See The Siam Cement Public Company Limited; *Int'l*, pg. 1238

SIAMAR SARL—See Royal Nedlloyd Group N.V.; *Int'l*, pg. 1145

SIAT VITA—See Eureko B.V.; *Int'l*, pg. 464

SIBAL S.A.—See Fuchs Petrolub AG Oel + Chemie; *Int'l*, pg. 519

SIBEKA—See Union Miniere; *Int'l*, pg. 1442

SIBELGAZ—See Electrabel S.A.; *Int'l*, pg. 437

SIBONEYUSA—See True North Communications Inc.; *U.S. Public*, pg. 1641

SIC PLASTICS FRANCE S.A.—See Mazzucchelli 1849 S.p.a.; *Int'l*, pg. 850

SIC PLASTICS GMBH—See Mazzucchelli 1849 S.p.a.; *Int'l*, pg. 850

SICAD S.R.L.—See Compagnie des Machines Bull; *Int'l*, pg. 318

SICAN CORP.; *U.S. Private*, pg. 997

SICHEL-WERKE GMBH—See Henkel KGaA; *Int'l*, pg. 610

SICILIANA ELECTRONICA & TELECOMUNICAZIONI S.P.A.—See Telefonaktiebolaget LM Ericsson; *Int'l*, pg. 1370

SICIT IDE S.P.A.—See Compagnie des Machines Bull; *Int'l*, pg. 318

SICIT M.T. & T. S.P.A.—See Compagnie des Machines Bull; *Int'l*, pg. 318

SICIT (SOCIETA INIZIATIVE COMMERCIALI INDUSTRIALI E TECNICE) S.P.A.—See Compagnie des Machines Bull; *Int'l*, pg. 318

THE SICO COMPANY—See First Mount Joy Corporation; *U.S. Private*, pg. 407

SICO INC.; *U.S. Private*, pg. 1239

SICO INCORPORATED; *U.S. Private*, pg. 997

SICO NORTH AMERICA INC.—See Sico Incorporated; *U.S. Private*, pg. 997

SICOAC—See ETEX; *Int'l*, pg. 430

SICOLAMARTIN INC.; *U.S. Private*, pg. 998

SICOM SpA—See IRI Istituto Ricostruzione Industriale; *Int'l*, pg. 653

SICOTEL—See Hewlett-Packard Company; *U.S. Public*, pg. 823

SICURTA 1879 ASSICURANZIONI S.P.A.—See Zurich Insurance Company; *Int'l*, pg. 1531

SID HARVEY INDUSTRIES; *U.S. Private*, pg. 998

SID TOOL CO. INC.; *U.S. Private*, pg. 998

SIDAT S.R.L.—See Freudenberg & Company; *Int'l*, pg. 506

SIDERMAR DI NAVIGAZIONE S.P.A.—See Coeclerici Group; *Int'l*, pg. 304

SIDERURGICA BARRA MANSA S.A.—See S.A. Industrias Votorantim; *Int'l*, pg. 678

SIDMAR N.V.—See Arbed S.A.; *Int'l*, pg. 79

SIDMARK SALES—See Enso Oyj; *Int'l*, pg. 458

SIDNEY RICH & ASSOCIATES—See Brown Group, Inc.; *U.S. Public*, pg. 262

SIDOBRE-SINNOVA S.A.—See Henkel KGaA; *Int'l*, pg. 614

SIDOCI—See Fujitsu Limited; *Int'l*, pg. 528

SIDWELL & COMPANY LTD.—See SLD Holdings Ltd.; *Int'l*, pg. 1160

SIEBAU SIEGENER STAHLBAUTEN GMBH—See Fried. Krupp AG; *Int'l*, pg. 509

SIEBE CONTROLS AUSTRALIA—See Siebe plc; *Int'l*, pg. 1244

SIEBE NORTH INC.—See Siebe plc; *Int'l*, pg. 1242

SIEBE PLC; *Int'l*, pg. 1240

SIEBEL—See Vendex International N.V.; *Int'l*, pg. 1462

J.E. SIEBEL & SONS COMPANY INC.—See Rhone-Poulenc S.A.; *Int'l*, pg. 1110

SIEBRET—See Bertrand Faure; *Int'l*, pg. 192

SIECOR CORPORATION—See Siemens AG; *Int'l*, pg. 1245

SIECOR GMBH—See Corning Incorporated; *U.S. Public*, pg. 449

SIECOR GMBH & CO. KG—See Corning Incorporated; *U.S. Public*, pg. 449

HENRY I. SIEGEL COMPANY, INC.; *U.S. Private*, pg. 998

SIEGENER BENELUX SA/NV—See Fried. Krupp AG; *Int'l*, pg. 508

HCH. SIEGER GMBH UND CO. KG.—See N.V. Koninklijke KNP BT; *Int'l*, pg. 757

SIEGER LTD.—See Hesta Tex AG; *Int'l*, pg. 618

SIEGER TPA LTD.—See Hesta Tex AG; *Int'l*, pg. 618

SIEGERT & CIE GMBH—See Henkel KGaA; *Int'l*, pg. 610

SIEGLING AMERICA INC.—See Forbo Holding SA; *Int'l*, pg. 497

SIEGLING AUSTRALIA PTY. LTD.—See Forbo Holding SA; *Int'l*, pg. 498

SIEGLING-AUSTRIA GES.M.B.H.—See Forbo Holding SA; *Int'l*, pg. 498

SIEGLING CANADA LTD.—See Forbo Holding SA; *Int'l*, pg. 498

SIEGLING DANMARK A/S—See Forbo Holding SA; *Int'l*, pg. 498

SIEGLING FRANCE S.A.—See Forbo Holding SA; *Int'l*, pg. 498

SIEGLING GMBH—See Forbo Holding SA; *Int'l*, pg. 498

SIEGLING IBERICA S.A.—See Forbo Holding SA; *Int'l*, pg. 498

SIEGLING ITALIA S.P.A.—See Forbo Holding SA; *Int'l*, pg. 498

SIEGLING (JAPAN) LTD.—See Forbo Holding SA; *Int'l*, pg. 498

SIEGLING MEXICO S.A. DE C.V.—See Forbo Holding SA; *Int'l*, pg. 498

SIEGLING NEDERLAND B.V.—See Forbo Holding SA; *Int'l*, pg. 498

SIEGLING (SCHWEIZ) A.G.—See Forbo Holding SA; *Int'l*, pg. 497

SIEGLING SVENSKA A.B.—See Forbo Holding SA; *Int'l*, pg. 498

SIEGRA—See ConAgra, Inc.; *U.S. Public*, pg. 429

SIELTE, S.P.A.—See Telefonaktiebolaget LM Ericsson; *Int'l*, pg. 1370

SIEMENS AB—See Siemens AG; *Int'l*, pg. 1247

SIEMENS A.E.—See Siemens AG; *Int'l*, pg. 1247

SIEMENS AG; *Int'l*, pg. 1244

SIEMENS AG OESTERREICH—See Siemens AG; *Int'l*, pg. 1247

SIEMENS A/S—See Siemens AG; *Int'l*, pg. 1247

SIEMENS AUTOMOTIVE CORPORATION—See Siemens AG; *Int'l*, pg. 1245

SIEMENS BUSINESS COMMUNICATION SYSTEMS, INC.—See Siemens AG; *Int'l*, pg. 1245

SIEMENS CANADA LTD.—See Siemens AG; *Int'l*, pg. 1247

SIEMENS COMPONENTS, INC.—See Siemens AG; *Int'l*, pg. 1245

SIEMENS COMPONENTS (PTE) LTD.—See Siemens AG; *Int'l*, pg. 1247

SIEMENS COMPONENTS SND. BHD.—See Siemens AG; *Int'l*, pg. 1247

SIEMENS CORPORATION—See Siemens AG; *Int'l*, pg. 1245

SIEMENS ELECTROCOM GMBH, KONSTANZ, GERMANY—See Siemens AG; *Int'l*, pg. 1245

SIEMENS-ELEMA AB—See Siemens AG; *Int'l*, pg. 1247

SIEMENS ENERGY & AUTOMATION INC.—See Siemens AG; *Int'l*, pg. 1245

SIEMENS FINANZIERUNGSGESELLSCHAFT FUR INFORMATIONSTECHNIK GMBH—See Siemens AG; *Int'l*, pg. 1245

P.T. SIEMENS INDONESIA, JAKARTA—See Siemens AG; *Int'l*, pg. 1247

SIEMENS K.K.—See Siemens AG; *Int'l*, pg. 1247

SIEMENS LTD—See Siemens AG; *Int'l*, pg. 1247

SIEMENS LTD.-BEIJING, CHINA—See Siemens AG; *Int'l*, pg. 1247

SIEMENS MATSUSHITA COMPONENTS GMBH & CO. KG—See Siemens AG; *Int'l*, pg. 1245

SIEMENS MEDICAL SYSTEMS, INC.—See Siemens AG; *Int'l*, pg. 1246

SIEMENS MICROELECTRONICS CENTER GMBH & CO.—See Siemens AG; *Int'l*, pg. 1245

SIEMENS NEDERLAND N.V.—See Siemens AG; *Int'l*, pg. 1247

SIEMENS NIXDORF INFORMATICA S.P.A.—See Siemens AG; *Int'l*, pg. 1245

SIEMENS NIXDORF INFORMATIESYSTEMEN BV—See Siemens AG; *Int'l*, pg. 1245

SIEMENS NIXDORF INFORMATION SYSTEMS INC.—See Siemens AG; *Int'l*, pg. 1245

SIEMENS NIXDORF INFORMATION SYSTEMS LTD.—See Siemens AG; *Int'l*, pg. 1245

SIEMENS NIXDORF INFORMATION SYSTEMS S.A.—See Siemens AG; *Int'l*, pg. 1245

SIEMENS NIXDORF INFORMATIONSSYSTEME AG—See Siemens AG; *Int'l*, pg. 1245

SIEMENS NIXDORF INFORMATIONSSYSTEME GES.M.B.H.—See Siemens AG; *Int'l*, pg. 1245

SIEMENS OSAKEYTIOF.—See Siemens AG; *Int'l*, pg. 1247

SIEMENS PAKISTAN ENGINEERING CO. LTD.—See Siemens AG; *Int'l*, pg. 1247

SIEMENS PLC—See Siemens AG; *Int'l*, pg. 1247

SIEMENS POWER CORP.—See Siemens AG; *Int'l*, pg. 1246

SIEMENS RT.—See Siemens AG; *Int'l*, pg. 1247

SIEMENS S.A.—See Siemens AG; *Int'l*, pg. 1248

SIEMENS SCHIEIZ AG—See Siemens AG; *Int'l*, pg. 1248

SIEMENS S.P.A.—See Siemens AG; *Int'l*, pg. 1248

SIEMENS TELECOMMUNICATION SYSTEMS LTD.—See Siemens AG; *Int'l*, pg. 1248

SIEMENS TRANSPORTATION SYSTEMS, INC.—See Siemens AG; *Int'l*, pg. 1246

SIEMER MILLING COMPANY; *U.S. Private*, pg. 998

SIENNA BIOTECH, INC.—See American Standard Inc.; *U.S. Public*, pg. 92

SIENOR—See Bertrand Faure; *Int'l*, pg. 192

SIEROMCO SIERRA LEONE ORE & METAL CO. LTD.—See Alusuisse-Lonza Holding Ltd.; *Int'l*, pg. 69

THE SIERRA CAPITAL COMPANIES; *U.S. Private*, pg. 998

SIERRA CAPITAL MANAGEMENT CORPORATION—See Washington Mutual Inc.; *U.S. Public*, pg. 1742

SIERRA CAST INC.—See Wyman-Gordon; *U.S. Public*, pg. 1782

SIERRA COATING TECHNOLOGIES; *U.S. Private*, pg. 998

SIERRA CONVALESCENT CENTER—See Horizon/CMS Healthcare Corporation; *U.S. Public*, pg. 837

SIERRA CRAFT, INC.—See Wolseley Plc.; *Int'l*, pg. 1512

SIERRA CREATIVE COMMUNICATIONS INC.—See Cinram Ltd.; *Int'l*, pg. 293

SIERRA HEALTH SERVICES, INC.; *U.S. Public*, pg. 1469

SIERRA HEALTHCARE OPTIONS, INC.—See Sierra Health Services, Inc.; *U.S. Public*, pg. 1469

SIERRA INC.—See Echlin Inc.; *U.S. Public*, pg. 560

SIERRA LEONE CEMENT CORP. LTD.—See Scancem AB; *Int'l*, pg. 1201

SIERRA LEONE PETROLEUM REFINING—See Royal Dutch/Shell Group of Companies; *Int'l*, pg. 1137

SIERRA ON-LINE, INC.—See Cendant Corporation; *U.S. Public*, pg. 321

SIERRA PACIFIC INDUSTRIES; *U.S. Private*, pg. 998

SIERRA PACIFIC INDUSTRIES-ARCATA DIVISION—See Sierra Pacific Industries; *U.S. Private*, pg. 998

SIERRA PACIFIC INDUSTRIES-STANDARD DIVISION—See Sierra Pacific Industries; *U.S. Private*, pg. 999

SIERRA PACIFIC POWER CO.—See Sierra Pacific Resources; *U.S. Public*, pg. 1470

SIERRA PACIFIC RESOURCES; *U.S. Public*, pg. 1470

SIERRA SEMICONDUCTOR; *U.S. Public*, pg. 1470

SIERRA SPRING WATER COMPANY—See Compagnie Generale Des Eaux; *Int'l*, pg. 322

SIERRA TECHNOLOGIES INC.; *U.S. Private*, pg. 999

SIERRA TUCSON, INC.—See NextHealth Inc.; *U.S. Public*, pg. 1181

SIERRA WEST BANCORP; *U.S. Public*, pg. 1470

SIERRA WEST BANK—See Sierra West Bancorp; *U.S. Public*, pg. 1470

SIERRACIN CORPORATION; *U.S. Private*, pg. 999

SIERRACIN/SYLMAR CORPORATION—See Sierracin Corporation; *U.S. Private*, pg. 999

SIERRACIN/TRANS TECH—See Sierracin Corporation; *U.S. Private*, pg. 999

SIERRACOM—See Sierra Technologies Inc.; *U.S. Private*, pg. 999

SIERRAPINE LIMITED; *U.S. Private*, pg. 999

SIEVAL—See Bertrand Faure; *Int'l*, pg. 192

SIFAN SYSTEMS LIMITED—See Smiths Industries plc; *Int'l*, pg. 1267

SIFASA—See Labinal SA; *Int'l*, pg. 786

SIFASA PLANT—See Labinal SA; *Int'l*, pg. 786

SIFASA SALES OFFICE—See Labinal SA; *Int'l*, pg. 786

SIFCO CUSTOM MACHINING—See Sifco Industries, Inc.; *U.S. Public*, pg. 1471

SIFCO FORGE GROUP—See Sifco Industries, Inc.; *U.S. Public*, pg. 1471

SIFCO INDUSTRIES, INC.; *U.S. Public*, pg. 1470

SIFCO SELECTIVE PLATING—See Sifco Industries, Inc.; *U.S. Public*, pg. 1471

SIFCO TURBINE COMPONENTS, LTD.—See Sifco Industries, Inc.; *U.S. Public*, pg. 1471

SIFTO CANADA, INC.—See Harris Chemical Group, Inc.; *U.S. Public*, pg. 505

SIGA, INC.; *U.S. Private*, pg. 999

SIGAL CONSTRUCTION CORP.; *U.S. Private*, pg. 999

SIGCORP, INC.; *U.S. Public*, pg. 1471

SIGES—See Sodexho S.A.; *Int'l*, pg. 1274

SIGHT AND SOUND—See Golden Books Family Entertainment Inc.; *U.S. Public*, pg. 749

SIGHT & SOUND—See Handleman Company; *U.S. Public*, pg. 780

SIGHT SYSTEMS, INC.—See Zygo Corporation; *U.S. Public*, pg. 1795

SIGLA EQUIPAMENTOS ELETRICOS LTDA.—See Jeumont-Schneider Trenformeteurs; *Int'l*, pg. 706

RUSSELL J. SIGLER INC.; *U.S. Private*, pg. 999

SIGMA—See Lagardere Groupe; *Int'l*, pg. 796

OY SIGMA AB—See Atlet AB; *Int'l*, pg. 97

SIGMA AB—See Trelleborg AB; *Int'l*, pg. 1422

SIGMA-ALDRICH CORPORATION; *U.S. Public*, pg. 1471

SIGMA-ALDRICH FS CORP.—See Sigma-Aldrich Corporation; *U.S. Public*, pg. 1472

SIGMA ALDRICH JAPAN—See Sigma-Aldrich Corporation; *U.S. Public*, pg. 1472

SIGMA-ALDRICH N.V.—See Sigma-Aldrich Corporation; *U.S. Public*, pg. 1472

SIGMA ALIMENTOS, S.A. DE C.V.—See Alfa, S.A. de C.V.; *Int'l*, pg. 56

SIGMA CHEMICAL CO.—See Sigma-Aldrich Corporation; *U.S. Public*, pg. 1472

SIGMA CHEMICAL CO., LTD.—See Sigma-Aldrich Corporation; *U.S. Public*, pg. 1472

SIGMA CHEMIE GMBH—See Sigma-Aldrich Corporation; *U.S. Public*, pg. 1472

SIGMA CHIMIE S.A.R.L.—See Sigma-Aldrich Corporation; *U.S. Public*, pg. 1472

SIGMA COATINGS B.V.—See Petrofina S.A.; *Int'l*, pg. 1044

SIGMA COATINGS, INC.—See Petrofina S.A.; *Int'l*, pg. 1044

SIGMA COATINGS S.A.—See Petrofina S.A.; *Int'l*, pg. 1044

SIGMA DESIGNS, INC.; *U.S. Public*, pg. 1472

SIGMA DIAGNOSTICS DIV.—See Sigma-Aldrich Corporation; *U.S. Public*, pg. 1472

SIGMA ELECTRONICS LIMITED—See Hanson PLC; *Int'l*, pg. 595

SIGMA INSURANCE COMPANY (BERMUDA) LTD.—See Motorola, Inc.; *U.S. Public*, pg. 1140

SIGMA INVESTMENT MANAGEMENT SYSTEMS LIMITED—See The Bank of Nova Scotia; *Int'l*, pg. 156

SIGMA ISRAEL CHEMICAL CO., LTD.—See Sigma-Aldrich Corporation; *U.S. Public*, pg. 1472

SIGMA MINES (QUEBEC) LTD.—See Placer Dome Inc.; *Int'l*, pg. 1060

SIGMA REDEVELOPMENT CORP.—See Sigma-Aldrich Corporation; *U.S. Public*, pg. 1472

SIGMA SECOND STREET REDEVELOPMENT CORP.—See Sigma-Aldrich Corporation; *U.S. Public*, pg. 1472

SIGMA-SOCIETA ITALIANA GESTIONE SISTEMA MULTI ACCESSO—See IRI Istituto Ricostruzione Industriale; *Int'l*, pg. 652

SIGMA-TAU FINANZIARIA S.P.A.; *Int'l*, pg. 1248

SIGMA UNIT TRUST MANAGERS LIMITED—See The Bank of Nova Scotia; *Int'l*, pg. 156

SIGMA VERMOEGENSVERWALTUNGS GMBH—See Commerzbank AG; *Int'l*, pg. 310

SIGMAFORM AUSTRALIA—See Raychem Corporation; *U.S. Public*, pg. 1363

SIGMAFORM (U.K.) LTD.—See Raychem Corporation; *U.S. Public*, pg. 1363

SIGMATRON, INC.—See Circuit Systems, Inc.; *U.S. Public*, pg. 374

SIGNAAL, COMMUNICATIONS—See Thomson S.A.; *Int'l*, pg. 1385

SIGNAAL SPECIAL PRODUCTS—See Thomson S.A.; *Int'l*, pg. 1385

SIGNAAL USFA—See Thomson S.A.; *Int'l*, pg. 1385

SIGNAL APPAREL COMPANY, INC.; *U.S. Public*, pg. 1472

SIGNAL ARTWEAR—See Signal Apparel Company, Inc.; *U.S. Public*, pg. 1472

SIGNAL CAPITAL CORPORATION—See Anixter International; *U.S. Public*, pg. 115

SIGNAL HILL SERVICE CENTER—See T.D. Williamson, Inc.; *U.S. Private*, pg. 1180

SIGNAL INVESTMENT & MANAGEMENT CO.—See Chattem, Inc.; *U.S. Public*, pg. 342

SIGNAL KNITWEAR—See Signal Apparel Company, Inc.; *U.S. Public*, pg. 1472

SIGNAL SCIENCE—See Allen Telecom, Inc.; *U.S. Public*, pg. 46

SIGNAL SYSTEM—See IRI Istituto Ricostruzione Industriale; *Int'l*, pg. 654

SIGNAL TRANSFORMER CO., INC.—See Insilco Corporation; *U.S. Public*, pg. 881

SIGNALBAU HUBER AG—See Robert Bosch GmbH; *Int'l*, pg. 204

SIGNATURE BRANDS USA, INC.; *U.S. Public*, pg. 1472

SIGNATURE EYEWEAR, INC.; *U.S. Public*, pg. 1473

SIGNATURE FLIGHT SUPPORT—See BBA Group plc; *Int'l*, pg. 114

THE SIGNATURE GROUP—See Montgomery Ward & Co., Inc.; *U.S. Private*, pg. 758

SIGNATURE INNS, INC.; *U.S. Public*, pg. 1473

SIGNATURE TRAVEL, INC.—See Washington Mutual Inc.; *U.S. Public*, pg. 1742

SIGNATURES—See Starcrest Products of California; *U.S. Private*, pg. 1035

SIGNBOARD HILL PRODUCTIONS—See Hallmark Cards, Inc.; *U.S. Private*, pg. 496

SIGNET GROUP PLC; *Int'l*, pg. 1248
SIGNET SCIENTIFIC CO.—See Georg Fischer Ltd.; *Int'l*, pg. 489
SIGNET STAR HOLDINGS, INC.—See W.R. Berkley Corporation; *U.S. Public*, pg. 216
SIGNET STAR REINSURANCE COMPANY—See W.R. Berkley Corporation; *U.S. Public*, pg. 216
SIGNETICS THAILAND CO., LTD.—See Philips Electronics N.V.; *Int'l*, pg. 1055
SIGNFIX LTD.—See IDEX Corporation; *U.S. Public*, pg. 862
SIGNODE—See Illinois Tool Works Inc.; *U.S. Public*, pg. 869
SIGNODE BELGIUM—See Illinois Tool Works Inc.; *U.S. Public*, pg. 869
SIGNODE BERNPAK GMBH—See Illinois Tool Works Inc.; *U.S. Public*, pg. 869
SIGNODE B.V.—See Illinois Tool Works Inc.; *U.S. Public*, pg. 869
SIGNODE CANADA—See Illinois Tool Works Inc.; *U.S. Public*, pg. 869
SIGNODE EUROPA—See Illinois Tool Works Inc.; *U.S. Public*, pg. 869
SIGNODE FASTENERS—See Illinois Tool Works Inc.; *U.S. Public*, pg. 869
SIGNODE FRANCE—See Illinois Tool Works Inc.; *U.S. Public*, pg. 869
SIGNODE HONG KONG LIMITED—See Illinois Tool Works Inc.; *U.S. Public*, pg. 869
SIGNODE INTERNATIONAL TRADING CORPORATION—See Illinois Tool Works Inc.; *U.S. Public*, pg. 869
SIGNODE KABUSHIKI KAISHA—See Illinois Tool Works Inc.; *U.S. Public*, pg. 869
SIGNODE PACKAGING SYSTEMS LIMITED—See Illinois Tool Works Inc.; *U.S. Public*, pg. 869
SIGNODE SPAIN—See Illinois Tool Works Inc.; *U.S. Public*, pg. 869
SIGNTECH USA, LTD.; *U.S. Private*, pg. 999
SIGNUM ARZNELMITTEL GMBH—See Solvay S.A.; *Int'l*, pg. 1278
SIGURD EBS LTD.—See Commerzbank AG; *Int'l*, pg. 312
SII MEGA DIAMOND—See Smith International, Inc.; *U.S. Private*, pg. 1478
SIKA CORPORATION—See Sika Finanz AG; *Int'l*, pg. 1249
SIKA FINANZ AG; *Int'l*, pg. 1248
SIKEL N.V.—See Arbed S.A.; *Int'l*, pg. 79
SIKKENS AEROSPACE FINISHERS—See Akzo Nobel N.V.; *Int'l*, pg. 1055
SIKKENS B.V.—See Akzo Nobel N.V.; *Int'l*, pg. 42
SIKKENS LINVEA SPA—See Akzo Nobel N.V.; *Int'l*, pg. 43
SIKKENS LTD.—See Akzo Nobel N.V.; *Int'l*, pg. 47
SIKORSKY AIRCRAFT—See United Technologies Corporation; *U.S. Public*, pg. 1691
SILAS CREEK MANOR—See Vencor, Inc.; *U.S. Public*, pg. 1714
FRANZ SILBERHORN GMBH & CO. KG—See Mannesmann A.G.; *Int'l*, pg. 838
FRANZ SILBERHORN HANDEL GMBH—See Mannesmann A.G.; *Int'l*, pg. 838
SILBERTECH—See Mine Safety Appliances Co.; *U.S. Public*, pg. 1115
SILBRICO CORPORATION; *U.S. Private*, pg. 1000
SILCORP LIMITED; *Int'l*, pg. 1249
SILECTRON SPA—See Chloride Group PLC; *Int'l*, pg. 287
SILENO, SOC DISTRIBUIDORA DE BEBIDAS—See Diageo Plc; *Int'l*, pg. 410
SILENTNIGHT HOLDINGS PLC; *Int'l*, pg. 1249
SILENUS INSTRUMENTS PTY LTD—See Imperial Chemical Industries PLC; *Int'l*, pg. 665
SILENUS LABORATORIES PTY LIMITED—See Imperial Chemical Industries PLC; *Int'l*, pg. 665
SILGAN CONTAINER CORP.—See Silgan Corporation; *U.S. Public*, pg. 1473
SILGAN CORPORATION; *U.S. Public*, pg. 1473
SILGAN PLASTIC CORP.—See Silgan Corporation; *U.S. Public*, pg. 1473
SILHOUETTE BOOKS—See Torstar Corporation; *Int'l*, pg. 1402
N.V. SILICAATSTEEN—See Scancem AB; *Int'l*, pg. 1199
SILICON GRAPHICS CANADA INC.—See Silicon Graphics, Inc.; *U.S. Public*, pg. 1474
SILICON GRAPHICS, INC.; *U.S. Public*, pg. 1473
SILICON GRAPHICS, LTD.—See Silicon Graphics, Inc.; *U.S. Public*, pg. 1474
SILICON GRAPHICS S.A. INTL.—See Silicon Graphics, Inc.; *U.S. Public*, pg. 1474
SILICON MATERIALS SERVICES B.V.—See Semiconductor Packaging Materials Co., Inc.; *U.S. Public*, pg. 1456
SILICON POWER CUBE CORPORATION; *U.S. Private*, pg. 1000
SILICON SYSTEMS, INC.—See Texas Instruments Incorporated; *U.S. Public*, pg. 1585
SILICON VALLEY GROUP, INC.; *U.S. Public*, pg. 1474
SILICONE ENGINEERING—See Meggitt plc; *Int'l*, pg. 853
SILICONE PRODUCTS DIV.—See General Electric Company; *U.S. Public*, pg. 711
SILICONE TECHNOLOGIES—See Bairnco Corporation; *U.S. Public*, pg. 165
SILICONES, INC.—See Hicks, Muse, Tate & Furst Inc.; *U.S. Private*, pg. 526
SILICONIX GMBH—See Daimler-Benz Aktiengesellschaft; *Int'l*, pg. 367
SILICONIX (H.K.) LTD.—See Daimler-Benz Aktiengesellschaft; *Int'l*, pg. 367
SILICONIX, INC.—See Daimler-Benz Aktiengesellschaft; *Int'l*, pg. 367
SILICONIX LTD.—See Daimler-Benz Aktiengesellschaft; *Int'l*, pg. 367
SILICONIX S.A.R.L.—See Daimler-Benz Aktiengesellschaft; *Int'l*, pg. 367
SILICONIX (TAIWAN)—See Daimler-Benz Aktiengesellschaft; *Int'l*, pg. 367
SILJA LINE AB—See NCC AB; *Int'l*, pg. 899
SILJA OY AB—See NCC AB; *Int'l*, pg. 899

SILJANS KNACKE AB—See Cultor Ltd.; *Int'l*, pg. 349
SILK AIR—See Temasek Holdings Pte. Ltd.; *Int'l*, pg. 1374
SILKOLENE FRANCE S.A.—See Fuchs Petrolub AG Oel + Chemie; *Int'l*, pg. 519
SILKOLENE LUBRICANTS PLC—See Fuchs Petrolub AG Oel + Chemie; *Int'l*, pg. 519
SILKOLENE LUBRICANTS (USA) INC.—See Fuchs Petrolub AG Oel + Chemie; *Int'l*, pg. 518
SILKOLENE PLC—See Fuchs Petrolub AG Oel + Chemie; *Int'l*, pg. 518
SILLCOCKS PLASTICS, INC.—See American Technology Corporation; *U.S. Private*, pg. 63
SILMAR RESINS—See Interplastic Corp.; *U.S. Private*, pg. 572
SILMAX, INC.—See Sumitomo Sitix Corporation; *Int'l*, pg. 1317
SILOR OPTICAL INC.—See Essilor International Compagnie Generale d'Optique; *Int'l*, pg. 462
SILOR OPTICAL OF FLORIDA—See Essilor International Compagnie Generale d'Optique; *Int'l*, pg. 462
SILTIN INDUSTRIES, INC.—See DEECO Industries; *U.S. Private*, pg. 320
SILUETT NORDIA AB—See Duni AB; *Int'l*, pg. 421
SILVANI ANTINCENDI SPA—See Williams Holdings Plc; *Int'l*, pg. 1500
SILVER BROOK REAL ESTATE DEVELOPMENT COMPANY—See Cigna Corp.; *U.S. Public*, pg. 358
SILVER BURDETT DIVISION—See National Amusements, Inc.; *U.S. Private*, pg. 778
SILVER BURDETT GINN—See National Amusements, Inc.; *U.S. Private*, pg. 778
SILVER CITY CASINO—See Circus Circus - Las Vegas; *U.S. Public*, pg. 375
SILVER CREEK MANOR NURSING CENTER—See Paragon Health Network, Inc.; *U.S. Public*, pg. 1257
SILVER DOLLAR CITY, INC.; *U.S. Private*, pg. 1000
SILVER FURNITURE CO., INC.—See Chromcraft Revington, Inc.; *U.S. Public*, pg. 352
SILVER SPRINGS CITRUS CO-OP; *U.S. Private*, pg. 1000
SILVER SPRINGS NURSING & REHABILITATION CENTER—See Horizon/CMS Healthcare Corporation; *U.S. Public*, pg. 839
SILVER STATE DISPOSAL SERVICE, INC.—See Republic Industries, Inc.; *U.S. Public*, pg. 1380
SILVER TOWNE L.P.; *U.S. Private*, pg. 1000
SILVER-WEIBULL—See Gencor Industries, Inc.; *U.S. Public*, pg. 705
SILVERADO COMMUNICATIONS CORP.—See Peoples Telephone Company, Inc.; *U.S. Public*, pg. 1276
SILVERADO CONVALESCENT HOSPITAL—See Vencor, Inc.; *U.S. Public*, pg. 1714
SILVERBROOK MANOR—See Horizon/CMS Healthcare Corporation; *U.S. Public*, pg. 837
SILVERCREST MANOR—See Horizon/CMS Healthcare Corporation; *U.S. Public*, pg. 837
SILVERDALE FACILITIES—See Corrections Corporation of America; *U.S. Public*, pg. 451
SILVERDALEN PAPER MILL—See Mo och Domsjo AB; *Int'l*, pg. 886
SILVERMAN'S DENTAL SUPPLIES INC.—See Axel Johnson AB; *Int'l*, pg. 710
SILVERSTAR LTD., S.P.A.—See Arrow Electronics, Inc.; *U.S. Public*, pg. 135
SILVERSTREAM CENTER—See Genesis Health Ventures, Inc.; *U.S. Public*, pg. 729
SILVERTON MARINE CORPORATION; *U.S. Private*, pg. 1000
SILVER-WEIBULL AB—See Gencor Industries, Inc.; *U.S. Public*, pg. 705
SILVEY CORPORATION—See General Accident Fire and Life Assurance Corporation p.l.c.; *Int'l*, pg. 543
SIMAGO, S.A.—See Jardine Matheson Holdings Limited; *Int'l*, pg. 704
SIMALU S.A.—See Pechiney S.A.; *Int'l*, pg. 1028
THE SIMBA GROUP—See Foodcorp Limited; *Int'l*, pg. 496
SIMCO—See Illinois Tool Works Inc.; *U.S. Public*, pg. 865
SIMCO, INC.—See American Electric Power Company, Inc.; *U.S. Public*, pg. 72
SIMCO JAPAN INC.—See Illinois Tool Works Inc.; *U.S. Public*, pg. 869
SIMCO (NEDERLAND) B.V.—See Illinois Tool Works Inc.; *U.S. Public*, pg. 869
SIMCOE LEAF TOBACCO COMPANY, LTD.—See Universal Corporation; *U.S. Public*, pg. 1695
SIME AIRCRAFT TYRE COMPANY SDN. BHD.—See Sime Darby Berhad; *Int'l*, pg. 1250
SIME BANK BERHAD—See Sime Darby Berhad; *Int'l*, pg. 1250
SIME DARBY BERHAD; *Int'l*, pg. 1249
SIME DIAMOND LEASING (MALAYSIA) SDN. BHD.—See The Bank of Tokyo-Mitsubishi, Ltd.; *Int'l*, pg. 158
SIME DIAMOND LEASING (MALAYSIA) SDN. BHD.—See Sime Darby Berhad; *Int'l*, pg. 1250
SIMEL S.A.—See AMP Incorporated; *U.S. Public*, pg. 9
SIMFLEX BETEILIGUNGS-GMBH—See Freudenberg & Company; *Int'l*, pg. 506
SIMFLEX GMBH & CO. KG—See Freudenberg & Company; *Int'l*, pg. 505
SIMI WINERY—See LVMH Moet Hennessy Louis Vuitton; *Int'l*, pg. 781
SIMIA AB—See Scancem AB; *Int'l*, pg. 1199
SIMIAN COMPANY, INC.—See RPM, Inc.; *U.S. Public*, pg. 1357
SIMKINS CAROLINA FOLDING BOX DIV.—See Simkins Industries, Inc.; *U.S. Private*, pg. 1000
SIMKINS CARTON DIV.-CHICAGO—See Simkins Industries, Inc.; *U.S. Private*, pg. 1000
SIMKINS CARTON DIV.-CLEVELAND—See Simkins Industries, Inc.; *U.S. Private*, pg. 1000
SIMKINS CARTON DIV.-MARIETTA—See Simkins Industries, Inc.; *U.S. Private*, pg. 1000
SIMKINS INDUSTRIES, INC.; *U.S. Private*, pg. 1000
SIMKINS MARYLAND BOARD—See Simkins Industries, Inc.; *U.S. Private*, pg. 1000

SIMKINS NEW HAVEN BOARD—See Simkins Industries, Inc.; *U.S. Private*, pg. 1000
SIMKO TICARET VE SANAYI A.S.—See Siemens AG; *Int'l*, pg. 1248
SIMMERWERK GESELLSCHAFT M.B.H.—See Freudenberg & Company; *Int'l*, pg. 507
SIMMERWERKE W. SIMMER GMBH & CO. KG—See Freudenberg & Company; *Int'l*, pg. 506
SIMMONDS PRECISION ENGINE SYSTEMS—See The B.F. Goodrich Company; *U.S. Public*, pg. 752
SIMMONS—See WPP Group plc; *Int'l*, pg. 1483
SIMMONS AIRLINES—See AMR Corporation; *U.S. Public*, pg. 9
SIMMONS AMERICAN EAGLE AIRLINES—See AMR Corporation; *U.S. Public*, pg. 10
SIMMONS BEDDING & FURNITURE (HK) LTD.—See Nifco Inc.; *Int'l*, pg. 929
SIMMONS-BOARDMAN PUBLISHING CORP.; *U.S. Private*, pg. 1000
SIMMONS COMPANY—See Investcorp International; *Int'l*, pg. 686
SIMMONS CO. LTD.—See Nifco Inc.; *Int'l*, pg. 929
SIMMONS, DURHAM & ASSOCIATES; *U.S. Private*, pg. 1000
SIMMONS JUVENILE PRODUCTS; *U.S. Private*, pg. 1001
SIMMONS OUTDOOR CORPORATION—See Blount International, Inc.; *U.S. Public*, pg. 238
SIMOGEL—See Electrabel S.A.; *Int'l*, pg. 437
SIMON ACCESS FAR EAST—See Simon Engineering plc; *Int'l*, pg. 1252
SIMON ACCESS (U.K.) LTD.—See Simon Engineering plc; *Int'l*, pg. 1251
SIMON AERIALS INC.—See Simon Engineering plc; *Int'l*, pg. 1252
SIMON AERIALS LTD.—See Simon Engineering plc; *Int'l*, pg. 1252
SIMON AG—See Bayerische Vereinsbank Group; *Int'l*, pg. 180
SIMON & ASSOCIATES; *U.S. Private*, pg. 1001
SIMON & SCHUSTER—See National Amusements, Inc.; *U.S. Private*, pg. 777
SIMON & SCHUSTER (ASIA) PTE. LTD.—See National Amusements, Inc.; *U.S. Private*, pg. 778
SIMON & SCHUSTER AUDIO—See National Amusements, Inc.; *U.S. Private*, pg. 778
SIMON & SCHUSTER CHILDREN'S PUBLISHING—See National Amusements, Inc.; *U.S. Private*, pg. 777
SIMON & SCHUSTER CONSUMER GROUP—See National Amusements, Inc.; *U.S. Private*, pg. 777
SIMON & SCHUSTER EDUCATION GROUP—See National Amusements, Inc.; *U.S. Private*, pg. 778
SIMON & SCHUSTER EDUCATION TECHNOLOGY GROUP—See National Amusements, Inc.; *U.S. Private*, pg. 778
SIMON & SCHUSTER ELEMENTARY DIVISION—See National Amusements, Inc.; *U.S. Private*, pg. 778
SIMON & SCHUSTER GENERAL REFERENCE USA—See National Amusements, Inc.; *U.S. Private*, pg. 777
SIMON & SCHUSTER INTERACTIVE—See National Amusements, Inc.; *U.S. Private*, pg. 778
SIMON & SCHUSTER INTERNATIONAL—See National Amusements, Inc.; *U.S. Private*, pg. 778
SIMON & SCHUSTER INTERNATIONAL & BUSINESS & PROFESSIONAL GROUP—See National Amusements, Inc.; *U.S. Private*, pg. 778
SIMON & SCHUSTER INTERNATIONAL (UK) LIMITED—See National Amusements, Inc.; *U.S. Private*, pg. 778
SIMON & SCHUSTER TRADE DIVISION—See National Amusements, Inc.; *U.S. Private*, pg. 777
SIMON & SCHUSTER'S CHILDREN'S PUBLISHING DIV.—See National Amusements, Inc.; *U.S. Private*, pg. 777
SIMON-ATLANTICO INC.—See Simon Engineering plc; *Int'l*, pg. 1252
SIMON AVIATION GROUND EQUIPMENT INC.—See Simon Engineering plc; *Int'l*, pg. 1252
SIMON-CARVES AUSTRALIA—See Simon Engineering plc; *Int'l*, pg. 1252
SIMON-CARVES LTD.—See Simon Engineering plc; *Int'l*, pg. 1252
SIMON-CELLA S.R.L.—See Simon Engineering plc; *Int'l*, pg. 1252
SIMON DEBARTOLO GROUP, INC.; *U.S. Public*, pg. 1474
SIMON-DIASOL—See Simon Engineering plc; *Int'l*, pg. 1251
SIMON-DUPLEX INC.—See Simon Engineering plc; *Int'l*, pg. 1251
SIMON ENGINEERING (AUSTRALIA) PTY LTD.—See Simon Engineering plc; *Int'l*, pg. 1252
SIMON ENGINEERING PLC; *Int'l*, pg. 1251
SIMON-HOLDER LTD.—See Simon Engineering plc; *Int'l*, pg. 1251
JOSEPH SIMON & SONS, INC.; *U.S. Private*, pg. 1001
SIMON LABORATORIES—See Simon Engineering plc; *Int'l*, pg. 1251
SIMON LADDER TOWERS INC.—See Simon Engineering plc; *Int'l*, pg. 1252
SIMON-LIFT GMBH—See Simon Engineering plc; *Int'l*, pg. 1252
SIMON MARKETING CONSULTING (CANADA) LTD.—See Simon Marketing, Inc.; *U.S. Private*, pg. 1001
SIMON MARKETING, INC.; *U.S. Private*, pg. 1001
SIMON MARKETING, INC.—See Simon Marketing, Inc.; *U.S. Private*, pg. 1001
SIMON MARKETING INTERNATIONAL—See Simon Marketing, Inc.; *U.S. Private*, pg. 1001
SIMON MARKETING INTERNATIONAL GMBH - FRANKFURT—See Simon Marketing, Inc.; *U.S. Private*, pg. 1001
SIMON MARKETING INTERNATIONAL GMBH - MUNICH—See Simon Marketing, Inc.; *U.S. Private*, pg. 1001
SIMON MARKETING, LTD.—See Simon Marketing, Inc.; *U.S. Private*, pg. 1001

SIMON PETROLEUM TECHNOLOGY LTD.—See Simon Engineering plc; *Int'l,* pg. 1251
SIMON-R O CORP.—See Simon Engineering plc; *Int'l,* pg. 1252
SIMON-TELELECT INC.—See Simon Engineering plc; *Int'l,* pg. 1252
SIMON UNITED STATES HOLDINGS INC.—See Simon Engineering plc; *Int'l,* pg. 1252
WILFRIED SIMON GMBH—See Mannesmann A.G.; *Int'l,* pg. 838
SIMONDS INDUSTRIES INC.; *U.S. Private,* pg. 1001
SIMONDS-SHIELDS-THEIS GRAIN CO.; *U.S. Private,* pg. 1001
SIMONIZ INTERNATIONAL PLC—See Burmah Castrol plc; *Int'l,* pg. 235
SIMONIZ USA, INC.; *U.S. Private,* pg. 1001
SIMONS PALMER DENTON CLEMMOW & JOHNSON LTD.; *Int'l,* pg. 894
SIMONSEN & SONS LIMITED—See Morgan Crucible Co. Plc; *Int'l,* pg. 894
SIMPLEX BETEILIGUNS-GMBH—See Freudenberg & Company; *Int'l,* pg. 506
SIMPLEX CONSTRUCTION CO. INC.—See Simplex Industries, Inc.; *U.S. Private,* pg. 1001
SIMPLEX INDUSTRIES, INC.; *U.S. Private,* pg. 1001
SIMPLEX INTL. TIME EQUIP. CO. LTD. (CANADA)—See Simplex Time Recorder Co.; *U.S. Private,* pg. 1002
SIMPLEX INTL. TIME EQUIP. PTY. LTD.—See Simplex Time Recorder Co.; *U.S. Private,* pg. 1002
SIMPLEX PILING LIMITED—See British Building & Engineering Appliances Plc; *Int'l,* pg. 219
SIMPLEX PRODUCTS—See K2 Inc.; *U.S. Public,* pg. 940
SIMPLEX SINO LIMITED—See Simplex Time Recorder Co.; *U.S. Private,* pg. 1002
SIMPLEX TIME RECORDER CO.; *U.S. Private,* pg. 1002
SIMPLEX TIME RECORDER CO.—See Simplex Time Recorder Co.; *U.S. Private,* pg. 1002
SIMPLICITY ENGINEERING, INC.—See Powerscreen International Plc; *Int'l,* pg. 1066
SIMPLICITY HOLDINGS INC.; *U.S. Private,* pg. 1002
SIMPLICITY MANUFACTURING, INC.; *U.S. Private,* pg. 1002
SIMPLIMATIC ENGINEERING CO.—See Crown Cork & Seal Company, Inc.; *U.S. Public,* pg. 463
J.R. SIMPLOT COMPANY; *U.S. Private,* pg. 1002
J.R. SIMPLOT COMPANY-AGRICULTURE GROUP—See J.R. Simplot Company; *U.S. Private,* pg. 1002
J.R. SIMPLOT COMPANY-DIVERSIFIED PRODUCTS GROUP—See J.R. Simplot Company; *U.S. Private,* pg. 1002
J.R. SIMPLOT COMPANY FOOD GROUP—See J.R. Simplot Company; *U.S. Private,* pg. 1002
J.R. SIMPLOT COMPANY LATHROP PLANT—See J.R. Simplot Company; *U.S. Private,* pg. 1002
A.G. SIMPSON CO. LIMITED; *Int'l,* pg. 1252
SIMPSON COUNTY BANK—See Union Planters Corporation; *U.S. Public,* pg. 1669
SIMPSON DOOR COMPANY—See Simpson Investment Co.; *U.S. Private,* pg. 1003
SIMPSON DURA-VENT CO., INC.; *U.S. Public,* pg. 1474
SIMPSON ELECTRIC CO.; *U.S. Private,* pg. 1002
SIMPSON GUMPERTZ & HEGER INC.; *U.S. Private,* pg. 1002
SIMPSON INDUSTRIES E.U.R.L. (FRANCE)—See Simpson Industries, Inc.; *U.S. Public,* pg. 1475
SIMPSON INDUSTRIES, INC.; *U.S. Public,* pg. 1474
SIMPSON INDUSTRIES, INC.—See Simpson Industries, Inc.; *U.S. Public,* pg. 1475
SIMPSON INDUSTRIES, INC. (GERMANY)—See Simpson Industries, Inc.; *U.S. Public,* pg. 1475
SIMPSON INDUSTRIES, LTDA. (BRAZIL)—See Simpson Industries, Inc.; *U.S. Public,* pg. 1475
SIMPSON INDUSTRIES S.A. DE C.V. (MEXICO)—See Simpson Industries, Inc.; *U.S. Public,* pg. 1475
SIMPSON INTERNATIONAL (UK) LTD.—See Simpson Industries, Inc.; *U.S. Public,* pg. 1475
SIMPSON INVESTMENT CO.; *U.S. Private,* pg. 1003
SIMPSON MFG. DIV.—See Simpson Industries, Inc.; *U.S. Public,* pg. 1475
SIMPSON PAPER CO.—See Simpson Investment Co.; *U.S. Private,* pg. 1003
SIMPSON PASADENA PAPER CO.—See Simpson Investment Co.; *U.S. Private,* pg. 1003
R.J. SIMPSON INTERNATIONAL, SL (SPAIN)—See Simpson Industries, Inc.; *U.S. Public,* pg. 1475
R.J. SIMPSON MFG. CO. (CANADA) LTD—See Simpson Industries, Inc.; *U.S. Public,* pg. 1475
SIMPSON REDWOOD COMPANY—See Simpson Investment Co.; *U.S. Private,* pg. 1003
SIMPSON TACOMA KRAFT CO.—See Simpson Investment Co.; *U.S. Private,* pg. 1003
SIMPSON TECHNIPARTS E.U.R.L. (FRANCE)—See Simpson Industries, Inc.; *U.S. Public,* pg. 1475
SIMPSON TIMBER CO.—See Simpson Investment Co.; *U.S. Private,* pg. 1003
SIMRAD INC.—See Simrad Norge AF; *Int'l,* pg. 1252
SIMRAD NORGE AF; *Int'l,* pg. 1252
SIMRAD OPTRONICS A/S—See Kvaerner a.s.a.; *Int'l,* pg. 770
SIMRAD OPTRONICS LTD.—See Kvaerner a.s.a.; *Int'l,* pg. 770
SIMRAX GMBH, GLEITRINGDICHTUNGEN—See Freudenberg & Company; *Int'l,* pg. 505
SIMRIT DISTRIBUTION ET CIE—See Freudenberg & Company; *Int'l,* pg. 507
SIMRIT DISTRIBUTION S.A.R.L.—See Freudenberg & Company; *Int'l,* pg. 507
SIMS DELTEC—See Smiths Industries plc; *Int'l,* pg. 1268
SIMS LEVEL 1 INC.—See Smiths Industries plc; *Int'l,* pg. 1268
SIMS MEDICAL DISTRIBUTION LIMITED—See Smiths Industries plc; *Int'l,* pg. 1267
SIMS PORTEX INC.—See Smiths Industries plc; *Int'l,* pg. 1268

SIMS PORTEX LIMITED—See Smiths Industries plc; *Int'l,* pg. 1267
SIMS PTE. LIMITED—See Smiths Industries plc; *Int'l,* pg. 1268
SIMS TRADING COMPANY LIMITED—See Jardine Matheson Holdings Limited; *Int'l,* pg. 704
SIMULA, INC.; *U.S. Public,* pg. 1475
SIMULATION DIVISION—See Evans & Sutherland Computer Corporation; *U.S. Public,* pg. 596
SIMURA—See Imetal; *Int'l,* pg. 662
THE SINCERE CO. LTD.; *Int'l,* pg. 1252
THE SINCERE COMPANY LTD. (KOWLOON BRANCH)—See The Sincere Co. Ltd.; *Int'l,* pg. 1252
THE SINCERE COMPANY (P.M.) LTD.—See The Sincere Co. Ltd.; *Int'l,* pg. 1252
THE SINCERE INSURANCE & INVESTMENT CO. LTD.—See The Sincere Co. Ltd.; *Int'l,* pg. 1252
THE SINCERE LIFE ASSURANCE CO. LTD.—See The Sincere Co. Ltd.; *Int'l,* pg. 1252
SINCLAIR/AMERITONE PAINT CORP.—See Imperial Chemical Industries PLC; *Int'l,* pg. 663
SINCLAIR COLLIS LIMITED—See Hanson PLC; *Int'l,* pg. 593
SINCLAIR OIL CORP.; *U.S. Private,* pg. 1003
SINCLAIR PAINT CO.—See Imperial Chemical Industries PLC; *Int'l,* pg. 663
SINCLAIR PRINTING & LITHO, INC.; *U.S. Private,* pg. 1003
SINDAI CO., LTD.—See NHK Spring Co., Ltd.; *Int'l,* pg. 902
SINERTECH—See Groupe Usinor; *Int'l,* pg. 572
SINGALAB PTE. LTD.—See CSA Holdings Ltd.; *Int'l,* pg. 242
SINGAPORE AIRLINES—See Temasek Holdings Pte. Ltd.; *Int'l,* pg. 1374
SINGAPORE AIRLINES LTD.—See Temasek Holdings Pte. Ltd.; *Int'l,* pg. 1374
SINGAPORE AIRPORT TERMINAL SERVICES—See Temasek Holdings Pte. Ltd.; *Int'l,* pg. 1374
SINGAPORE BANKERS CLUB PTE.—See DBS Bank Ltd.; *Int'l,* pg. 351
SINGAPORE BRITISH ENGINEERING PTE. LIMITED—See British Aerospace p.l.c.; *Int'l,* pg. 218
SINGAPORE CARBON PTE. LIMITED—See Morgan Crucible Co. Plc; *Int'l,* pg. 892
SINGAPORE ELECTRICAL STEEL SERVICES PRIVATE LTD—See Nissho Iwai Corporation; *Int'l,* pg. 949
SINGAPORE ENGINE OVERHAUL CENTRE (PTE.) LTD.—See Temasek Holdings Pte. Ltd.; *Int'l,* pg. 1374
SINGAPORE FACTORY DEVELOPMENT LTD.—See DBS Bank Ltd.; *Int'l,* pg. 351
SINGAPORE GLASS (1974) LTD.—See BTR plc; *Int'l,* pg. 129
SINGAPORE KOBE PRIVATE LIMITED—See Kobe Steel, Ltd.; *Int'l,* pg. 741
SINGAPORE LAND LIMITED; *Int'l,* pg. 1252
SINGAPORE OIL SEAL CO. (PRIVATE) LTD.—See Freudenberg & Company; *Int'l,* pg. 507
SINGAPORE OXYGEN AIR LIQUIDE PTE LTD.—See The BOC Group plc; *Int'l,* pg. 122
SINGAPORE PETROLEUM CO. (HK) LTD.—See Amoco Corporation; *U.S. Public,* pg. 102
SINGAPORE PETROLEUM CO (JAPAN) LTD.—See Amoco Corporation; *U.S. Public,* pg. 102
SINGAPORE POLYMER CORPORATION (PTE.) LTD.—See Norsk Hydro a.s; *Int'l,* pg. 964
SINGAPORE PRESS HOLDINGS LTD.; *Int'l,* pg. 1253
SINGAPORE REINSURANCE CORPORATION LIMITED; *Int'l,* pg. 1253
SINGAPORE TECHNOLOGIES PTE. LTD.; *Int'l,* pg. 1253
SINGAPORE TECHNOLOGIES SHIPBUILDING & ENGINEERING LIMITED—See Singapore Technologies Pte. Ltd.; *Int'l,* pg. 1253
SINGAPORE TOBACCO CO. (PRIVATE) CO.—See B.A.T Industries P.L.C.; *Int'l,* pg. 111
SINGAPORE TOURIST PROMOTION BOARD; *Int'l,* pg. 1253
THE SINGER COMPANY—See Semi-Tech Corporation; *Int'l,* pg. 1220
J.W. SINGER & SONS—See Delta plc; *Int'l,* pg. 391
KARL SINGER COMPANIES, INC.—See AON Corporation; *U.S. Public,* pg. 118
SINGER RETAIL DIVISION—See Fab Industries, Inc.; *U.S. Public,* pg. 603
SINGKEE CO., LTD.—See Kumagai Gumi Co., Ltd.; *Int'l,* pg. 764
THE SINGLETON OF AUCHROISK—See Diageo Plc; *Int'l,* pg. 409
SINGLETON SEAFOOD CO.—See ConAgra, Inc.; *U.S. Public,* pg. 427
SINO-AMERICAN GREAT WALL FOOD INDUSTRIES CO., LTD.—See Diageo Plc; *Int'l,* pg. 411
SINO-HEALTH LTD.—See Sinochem International Petroleum Co. Ltd.; *Int'l,* pg. 1255
SINO-SWEED PHARMACEUTICAL CORP LTD.—See Astra AB; *Int'l,* pg. 94
SINOCHEM AMERICAN HOLDINGS INC.—See Sinochem International Petroleum Co. Ltd.; *Int'l,* pg. 1255
SINOCHEM AUSTRALIA OFFICE—See Sinochem International Petroleum Co. Ltd.; *Int'l,* pg. 1255
SINOCHEM BELIZE LTD.—See Sinochem International Petroleum Co. Ltd.; *Int'l,* pg. 1255
SINOCHEM BRASIL COMERCIAL LTDA.—See Sinochem International Petroleum Co. Ltd.; *Int'l,* pg. 1255
SINOCHEM DALIAN TRAINING CENTRE—See Sinochem International Petroleum Co. Ltd.; *Int'l,* pg. 1255
SINOCHEM ELECTRONIC INFORMATION TECHNOLOGY CO. LTD.—See Sinochem International Petroleum Co. Ltd.; *Int'l,* pg. 1254
SINOCHEM FINANCE CO. LTD.—See Sinochem International Petroleum Co. Ltd.; *Int'l,* pg. 1254
SINOCHEM HAINAN CO. LTD.—See Sinochem International Petroleum Co. Ltd.; *Int'l,* pg. 1254
SINOCHEM HEBEI IMP. & EXP. CO. LTD.—See Sinochem International Petroleum Co. Ltd.; *Int'l,* pg. 1254

SINOCHEM HEILONGJIANG IMP. & EXP. CO. LTD.—See Sinochem International Petroleum Co. Ltd.; *Int'l,* pg. 1254
SINOCHEM HOTEL, GUANGZHOU—See Sinochem International Petroleum Co. Ltd.; *Int'l,* pg. 1254
SINOCHEM INTERNATIONAL ADVERTISING & EXHIBITION CO. LTD.—See Sinochem International Petroleum Co. Ltd.; *Int'l,* pg. 1254
SINOCHEM INTERNATIONAL CHEMICALS CO. LTD.—See Sinochem International Petroleum Co. Ltd.; *Int'l,* pg. 1254
SINOCHEM INTERNATIONAL CHEMICALS (HONG KONG) LTD.—See Sinochem International Petroleum Co. Ltd.; *Int'l,* pg. 1254
SINOCHEM INTERNATIONAL FERTILIZER CO. LTD.—See Sinochem International Petroleum Co. Ltd.; *Int'l,* pg. 1255
SINOCHEM INTERNATIONAL INDUSTRY CO. LTD.—See Sinochem International Petroleum Co. Ltd.; *Int'l,* pg. 1255
SINOCHEM INTERNATIONAL OIL (HONG KONG) CO., LTD.—See Sinochem International Petroleum Co. Ltd.; *Int'l,* pg. 1255
SINOCHEM INTERNATIONAL OIL (LONDON) CO. LTD.—See Sinochem International Petroleum Co. Ltd.; *Int'l,* pg. 1255
SINOCHEM INTERNATIONAL OIL (SINGAPORE) PTE. LTD.—See Sinochem International Petroleum Co. Ltd.; *Int'l,* pg. 1255
SINOCHEM INTERNATIONAL PETROLEUM CO. LTD.; *Int'l,* pg. 1254
SINOCHEM INTERNATIONAL RUBBER CO. LTD.—See Sinochem International Petroleum Co. Ltd.; *Int'l,* pg. 1255
SINOCHEM INTERTRANS CO. LTD.—See Sinochem International Petroleum Co. Ltd.; *Int'l,* pg. 1255
SINOCHEM JAPAN CO. LTD.—See Sinochem International Petroleum Co. Ltd.; *Int'l,* pg. 1255
SINOCHEM JIANGSU IMP. & EXP. CO. LTD.—See Sinochem International Petroleum Co. Ltd.; *Int'l,* pg. 1255
SINOCHEM LI YAN PING GARMENT CO.—See Sinochem International Petroleum Co. Ltd.; *Int'l,* pg. 1255
SINOCHEM LIAONING IMP. & EXP. CO. LTD.—See Sinochem International Petroleum Co. Ltd.; *Int'l,* pg. 1255
SINOCHEM MEXICO S.A. DE C.V.—See Sinochem International Petroleum Co. Ltd.; *Int'l,* pg. 1255
SINOCHEM MOSCOW CO., LTD.—See Sinochem International Petroleum Co. Ltd.; *Int'l,* pg. 1256
SINOCHEM NANDAIHE TRAINING CENTRE—See Sinochem International Petroleum Co. Ltd.; *Int'l,* pg. 1255
SINOCHEM NINGBO IMP. & EXP. CO. LTD.—See Sinochem International Petroleum Co. Ltd.; *Int'l,* pg. 1255
SINOCHEM PACIFIC INC.—See Sinochem International Petroleum Co. Ltd.; *Int'l,* pg. 1255
SINOCHEM PLASTICS CO. LTD.—See Sinochem International Petroleum Co. Ltd.; *Int'l,* pg. 1255
SINOCHEM RESEARCH INSTITUTE OF INTERNATIONAL OIL & CHEMICAL TRADE—See Sinochem International Petroleum Co. Ltd.; *Int'l,* pg. 1255
SINOCHEM R.S.A. (PTY.) LTD.—See Sinochem International Petroleum Co. Ltd.; *Int'l,* pg. 1255
SINOCHEM SEOUL OFFICE—See Sinochem International Petroleum Co. Ltd.; *Int'l,* pg. 1256
SINOCHEM SHANDONG IMP. & EXP. CO. LTD.—See Sinochem International Petroleum Co. Ltd.; *Int'l,* pg. 1255
SINOCHEM SHANGHAI IMP. & EXP. CO. LTD.—See Sinochem International Petroleum Co. Ltd.; *Int'l,* pg. 1255
SINOCHEM SHANGHAI PUDONG TRADING CO. LTD.—See Sinochem International Petroleum Co. Ltd.; *Int'l,* pg. 1255
SINOCHEM SHENZHEN INDUSTRY CO. LTD.—See Sinochem International Petroleum Co. Ltd.; *Int'l,* pg. 1255
SINOCHEM TIANJIN IMP. & EXP. CO. LTD.—See Sinochem International Petroleum Co. Ltd.; *Int'l,* pg. 1255
SINOCHEM TRADING DEVELOPMENT CO. LTD.—See Sinochem International Petroleum Co. Ltd.; *Int'l,* pg. 1255
SINOCHEM TRADING HAMBURG GMBH—See Sinochem International Petroleum Co. Ltd.; *Int'l,* pg. 1256
SINOCHEM TRADING (SINGAPORE) PTE. LTD.—See Sinochem International Petroleum Co. Ltd.; *Int'l,* pg. 1256
SINOCHEM (U.K.) LTD.—See Sinochem International Petroleum Co. Ltd.; *Int'l,* pg. 1256
SINOCHEM (U.S.A.) INC.—See Sinochem International Petroleum Co. Ltd.; *Int'l,* pg. 1255
SINOCHEM XIA MEN CO. LTD.—See Sinochem International Petroleum Co. Ltd.; *Int'l,* pg. 1255
SINOCHEM ZHU HAI CO. LTD.—See Sinochem International Petroleum Co. Ltd.; *Int'l,* pg. 1255
SINOMEC AG—See Hesta Tex AG; *Int'l,* pg. 618
SINOPEC-EBARA MACHINERY CO., LTD.—See Ebara Corporation; *Int'l,* pg. 432
SINOPEC HONEYWELL (TIANJIN) LTD.—See Honeywell Inc.; *U.S. Public,* pg. 835
SINSER HOLDING AB—See Skandia Insurance Company Limited; *Int'l,* pg. 1256
SINSER (IRELAND) LTD.—See Skandia Insurance Company Limited; *Int'l,* pg. 1258
SINSER (LUXEMBOURG) SARL—See Skandia Insurance Company Limited; *Int'l,* pg. 1258
SINTECH DIVISION—See MTS Systems Corporation; *U.S. Public,* pg. 1029
SINTED S.P.A.—See Compagnie des Machines Bull; *Int'l,* pg. 318

SINTERING TECHNOLOGIES, INC.—See Cummins Engine Company, Inc.; *U.S. Public*, pg. 468
SINTERMETAL SA—See Mannesmann A.G.; *Int'l*, pg. 835
SINTYAL OTSUKA PHARMACEUTICAL S.A—See Otsuka Pharmaceutical Co., Ltd.; *Int'l*, pg. 1014
SINUTEX S.A.R.L.—See Adidas AG; *Int'l*, pg. 25
SIOUX FALLS ARGUS LEADER—See Gannett Company, Inc.; *U.S. Public*, pg. 701
SIOUX FALLS CONSTRUCTION COMPANY; *U.S. Private*, pg. 1003
SIOUX HONEY ASSOCIATION; *U.S. Private*, pg. 1003
SIOUX MANUFACTURING CORP.; *U.S. Private*, pg. 1003
SIOUX TOOLS, INC.—See Snap-On Tools Corporation; *U.S. Public*, pg. 1480
SIOUX VALLEY RURAL TELEVISION—See Sioux Valley Southwestern Electric Association; *U.S. Private*, pg. 1004
SIOUX VALLEY SOUTHWESTERN ELECTRIC ASSOCIATION; *U.S. Private*, pg. 1004
SIOUXLAND GALVANIZING CORP.—See Leblanc Communications, Inc.; *U.S. Private*, pg. 656
SIPEX CORPORATION—See Tractebel; *Int'l*, pg. 1415
SIPING HENKEL DETERGENTS AND CLEANING PRODUCTS CO. LTD.—See Henkel KGaA; *Int'l*, pg. 614
SIPLAST CANADA INC.—See Icopal a/s; *Int'l*, pg. 659
SIPLAST ESPANA S.L.—See Icopal a/s; *Int'l*, pg. 659
SIPLAST INC.—See Icopal a/s; *Int'l*, pg. 659
SIPLAST S.A.—See Icopal a/s; *Int'l*, pg. 659
SIPLAST S.R.L.—See Icopal a/s; *Int'l*, pg. 659
SIR SPEEDY, INC.—See Franchise Services, Inc.; *U.S. Private*, pg. 423
SIRACH CAPITAL MANAGEMENT, INC.—See United Asset Management Corporation; *U.S. Public*, pg. 1674
SIRAH SDN. BHD.—See Oce-van der Grinten N.V.; *Int'l*, pg. 995
SIRIA OFFICINE MECCANICHE SPA—See Titan International, Inc.; *U.S. Public*, pg. 1619
SIRIUS REINSURANCE CORPORATION—See ABB Asea Brown Boveri (Holding) Ltd.; *Int'l*, pg. 4
SIRMA IBERICA, S.A.—See ABB Asea Brown Boveri (Holding) Ltd.; *Int'l*, pg. 6
SIRMA S.P.A.—See ABB Asea Brown Boveri (Holding) Ltd.; *Int'l*, pg. 6
SIRMAC OFFICINE MECCANICHE SPA—See Titan International, Inc.; *U.S. Public*, pg. 1619
SIROM GRAPHIC TRADING—See The Macneal-Schwendler Corp.; *U.S. Public*, pg. 1032
SIRRINE BEK ENVIRONMENTAL CO. (SBE)—See Tractebel; *Int'l*, pg. 1415
SIRTI—See Telecom Italia S.p.A.; *Int'l*, pg. 1362
SISCAT SPA—See Ascom Holding AG; *Int'l*, pg. 87
SISER LTDA.—See Hewlett-Packard Company; *U.S. Public*, pg. 823
SISKEN STEEL—See Reliance Steel & Aluminum Co.; *U.S. Public*, pg. 1375
SISO POWER PLANT—See Elkem ASA; *Int'l*, pg. 447
SISSING ELEKTROTECHNIEK B.V.—See Royal Begemann Group; *Int'l*, pg. 1133
SISTEMA ARGOS S.A.; *Int'l*, pg. 1256
SISTEMA DE AHORRO PARA EL RETIRO—See Bancomer, S.A.; *Int'l*, pg. 145
SISTEMAS DE INFORMACION DECISION C.A.—See Hewlett-Packard Company; *U.S. Public*, pg. 823
SISTEMAS DE INFORMATICA E DE MEDIDA, S.A.—See Hewlett-Packard Company; *U.S. Public*, pg. 823
SISTEMAS DE TERAPIA RESPIRATORIA S.A., INC.—See Magellan Health Services, Inc.; *U.S. Public*, pg. 1036
SISTEMAS ELECTRICOS Y CONMUTADORES, S.A. DE C.V.—See General Motors Corporation; *U.S. Public*, pg. 724
SISTEMAS ERICSSON S.A. DE C.V.—See Telefonaktiebolaget LM Ericsson; *Int'l*, pg. 1370
SISTEMAS NIFE S.A. DE C.V.—See Alcatel Alsthom Compagnie Generale D'Electricite; *Int'l*, pg. 54
SISTEMAS TECNICOS LOTERIAS DEL ESTADO (S.T.L.)—See Telefonica de Espana, S.A.; *Int'l*, pg. 1372
SISTEMAS Y TECHNICAS DE SEGURIDAD, S.A.—See The Black & Decker Corporation; *U.S. Public*, pg. 233
SISTRON LTD.—See Hewlett-Packard Company; *U.S. Public*, pg. 823
SITA—See Lyonnaise des Eaux S.A.; *Int'l*, pg. 824
SITABAC SOCIETE INDUSTRIELLE DES TABACS DU CAMEROON, S.A. (SITABAC)—See Reemtsma Cigarettenfabriken GmbH, Hamburg; *Int'l*, pg. 1101
SITE OIL COMPANY OF MISSOURI; *U.S. Private*, pg. 1004
SITE REALTY, INC.—See Pfizer Inc.; *U.S. Public*, pg. 1284
SITHE ENERGIES, INC.; *U.S. Private*, pg. 1004
SITT TATT INDUSTRIAL GASES SDN. BHD.—See Air Products and Chemicals, Inc.; *U.S. Public*, pg. 32
SITT TATT INDUSTRIAL GASES SDN. BHD.—See Air Products and Chemicals, Inc.; *U.S. Public*, pg. 32
SITT TATT INDUSTRIAL GASES SDN. BHD.—See Air Products and Chemicals, Inc.; *U.S. Public*, pg. 32
SIVA TRUCK LEASING INC.—See Badger Truck Center, Inc.; *U.S. Private*, pg. 118
SIVACO GEORGIA—See The Ivaco Group; *Int'l*, pg. 696
SIVACO NEW YORK, INC.—See The Ivaco Group; *Int'l*, pg. 696
SIVACO ONTARIO—See The Ivaco Group; *Int'l*, pg. 696
SIVACO QUEBEC—See The Ivaco Group; *Int'l*, pg. 696
SIVACO WIRE GROUP—See The Ivaco Group; *Int'l*, pg. 696
SIVALLS, INC.; *U.S. Private*, pg. 1004
SIVAQ—See Saint-Gobain; *Int'l*, pg. 1172
SIVE/YOUNG & RUBICAM L.P.—See Young & Rubicam Inc.; *U.S. Private*, pg. 1197
SIVYER STEEL CORPORATION—See Everett Smith Group, Ltd.; *U.S. Private*, pg. 1008
SIX FLAGS ASTROWORLD/SIX FLAGS WATERWORLD/ SIX FLAGS HOUSTON—See Time Warner Inc.; *U.S. Public*, pg. 1611

SIX FLAGS FIESTA TEXAS—See Time Warner Inc.; *U.S. Public*, pg. 1611
SIX FLAGS GREAT ADVENTURE THEME PARK & WILD SAFARI ANIMAL PARK—See Time Warner Inc.; *U.S. Public*, pg. 1611
SIX FLAGS GREAT AMERICA, INC.—See Time Warner Inc.; *U.S. Public*, pg. 1611
SIX FLAGS HURRICANE HARBOR—See Time Warner Inc.; *U.S. Public*, pg. 1611
SIX FLAGS MAGIC MOUNTAIN & SIX FLAGS HURRICANE HARBOR—See Time Warner Inc.; *U.S. Public*, pg. 1611
SIX FLAGS OVER GEORGIA—See Time Warner Inc.; *U.S. Public*, pg. 1612
SIX FLAGS OVER TEXAS—See Time Warner Inc.; *U.S. Public*, pg. 1612
SIX FLAGS ST. LOUIS—See Time Warner Inc.; *U.S. Public*, pg. 1612
SIX FLAGS THEME PARKS INC.—See Time Warner Inc.; *U.S. Public*, pg. 1611
600 RACING INC.—See Speedway Motorsports, Inc.; *U.S. Public*, pg. 1498
SIXTEL—See Olivetti SpA; *Int'l*, pg. 1002
SIXTH AVENUE ELECTRONICS CITY; *U.S. Private*, pg. 1004
6100 FAIRVIEW ASSOCIATES—See Cigna Corp.; *U.S. Public*, pg. 362
SIZE 5-7-9 SHOPS, INC.—See Edison Brothers Stores, Inc.; *U.S. Public*, pg. 564
SIZZLER INTERNATIONAL, INC.; *U.S. Public*, pg. 1475
SIZZLER USA, INC.—See Sizzler International, Inc.; *U.S. Public*, pg. 1475
SKADDEN, ARPS, SLATE, MEAGHER & FLOM INTERNATIONAL—See Skadden, Arps, Slate, Meagher & Flom LLP; *U.S. Private*, pg. 1004
SKADDEN, ARPS, SLATE, MEAGHER & FLOM LLP; *U.S. Private*, pg. 1004
SKAFSA KRAFTVERK I/S—See Norsk Hydro a.s; *Int'l*, pg. 961
SKAGGS TELECOMMUNICATIONS SERVICES, INC.—See American Stores Company; *U.S. Public*, pg. 93
SKALA HOME ELECTRONICS—See Thorn plc; *Int'l*, pg. 1386
SKANDIA ADVISORY COMPANY SA—See Skandia Insurance Company Limited; *Int'l*, pg. 1256
SKANDIA AFS SOUTHEAST ASIA (L) LTD.—See Skandia Insurance Company Limited; *Int'l*, pg. 1256
SKANDIA AMERICA REINSURANCE CORP., ATLANTA BRANCH OFFICE—See Skandia Insurance Company Limited; *Int'l*, pg. 1257
SKANDIA AMERICA REINSURANCE CORP., CHICAGO BRANCH OFFICE—See Skandia Insurance Company Limited; *Int'l*, pg. 1257
SKANDIA AMERICA REINSURANCE CORP., NORWALK BRANCH—See Skandia Insurance Company Limited; *Int'l*, pg. 1257
SKANDIA AMERICA REINSURANCE CORP., SAN FRANCISCO BRANCH OFFICE—See Skandia Insurance Company Limited; *Int'l*, pg. 1257
SKANDIA AMERICA REINSURANCE CORPORATION—See Skandia Insurance Company Limited; *Int'l*, pg. 1257
SKANDIA ASIA LTD.—See Skandia Insurance Company Limited; *Int'l*, pg. 1256
SKANDIA CANADA REINSURANCE COMPANY—See Skandia Insurance Company Limited; *Int'l*, pg. 1258
SKANDIA CAPITAL SERVICES—See Skandia Insurance Company Limited; *Int'l*, pg. 1256
SKANDIA COMPANIA DE ADMINISTRACION INMOBILARIA S.A.—See Skandia Insurance Company Limited; *Int'l*, pg. 1258
SKANDIA CORREDURIA DE REASEGUROS SA—See Skandia Insurance Company Limited; *Int'l*, pg. 1256
SKANDIA DIRECT OPERATIONS CORPORATION—See Skandia Insurance Company Limited; *Int'l*, pg. 1257
SKANDIA HOLDING AB—See Skandia Insurance Company Limited; *Int'l*, pg. 1256
SKANDIA HOLDING DE COLOMBIA S.A.—See Skandia Insurance Company Limited; *Int'l*, pg. 1258
SKANDIA INSURANCE COMPANY LIMITED; *Int'l*, pg. 1256
SKANDIA INSURANCE COMPANY LTD.—See Skandia Insurance Company Limited; *Int'l*, pg. 1258
SKANDIA INSURANCE (UK CONTACT OFFICE) LTD.—See Skandia Insurance Company Limited; *Int'l*, pg. 1256
SKANDIA INTERNATIONAL CONSULTING (SICON) AB—See Skandia Insurance Company Limited; *Int'l*, pg. 1256
SKANDIA INTERNATIONAL GESTION DE REASSURANCE SA—See Skandia Insurance Company Limited; *Int'l*, pg. 1256
SKANDIA INTERNATIONAL GESTION DE REASSURANCE VIE—See Skandia Insurance Company Limited; *Int'l*, pg. 1256
SKANDIA INTERNATIONAL INSURANCE CO.—See Skandia Insurance Company Limited; *Int'l*, pg. 1258
SKANDIA INTERNATIONAL INSURANCE CORPORATION—See Skandia Insurance Company Limited; *Int'l*, pg. 1256
SKANDIA INTERNATIONAL RISK MANAGEMENT (VERMONT), INC.—See Skandia Insurance Company Limited; *Int'l*, pg. 1257
SKANDIA INVESTMENT AB—See Skandia Insurance Company Limited; *Int'l*, pg. 1256
SKANDIA INVESTMENT MANAGEMENT—See Skandia Insurance Company Limited; *Int'l*, pg. 1257
SKANDIA INVESTMENT MANAGEMENT, INC.—See Skandia Insurance Company Limited; *Int'l*, pg. 1257
SKANDIA INVESTMENT MANAGEMENT LTD.—See Skandia Insurance Company Limited; *Int'l*, pg. 1257
SKANDIA LEBEN AG—See Skandia Insurance Company Limited; *Int'l*, pg. 1258

SKANDIA LEBEN HOLDING GMBH—See Skandia Insurance Company Limited; *Int'l*, pg. 1258
SKANDIA LEBENSVERSICHERUNG AG—See Skandia Insurance Company Limited; *Int'l*, pg. 1258
SKANDIA LIFE ASSURANCE CO. LTD.—See Skandia Insurance Company Limited; *Int'l*, pg. 1258
SKANDIA LIFE ASSURANCE CO. LTD. - HELSINKI—See Skandia Insurance Company Limited; *Int'l*, pg. 1256
SKANDIA LIFE ASSURANCE CO. LTD. - PARIS—See Skandia Insurance Company Limited; *Int'l*, pg. 1256
SKANDIA LIFE INSURANCE CO. (JAPAN) LTD.—See Skandia Insurance Company Limited; *Int'l*, pg. 1258
SKANDIA LIFE INSURANCE COMPANY LTD.—See Skandia Insurance Company Limited; *Int'l*, pg. 1257
SKANDIA LIFE PEP MANAGERS LTD.—See Skandia Insurance Company Limited; *Int'l*, pg. 1258
SKANDIA MARINE INSURANCE COMPANY (UK) LTD.—See Skandia Insurance Company Limited; *Int'l*, pg. 1257
SKANDIA PORTUGAL PROPRIEDADES S.A.—See Skandia Insurance Company Limited; *Int'l*, pg. 1258
SKANDIA PROPERTY (UK) LTD.—See Skandia Insurance Company Limited; *Int'l*, pg. 1258
SKANDIA S.A.—See Skandia Insurance Company Limited; *Int'l*, pg. 1258
SKANDIA SACHVERSICHERUNG AG—See Skandia Insurance Company Limited; *Int'l*, pg. 1258
SKANDIA SEGUROS DE VIDA S.A.—See Skandia Insurance Company Limited; *Int'l*, pg. 1258
SKANDIA SOCIEDAD FIDUCIARIA SA—See Skandia Insurance Company Limited; *Int'l*, pg. 1258
SKANDIA TRUST—See Skandia Insurance Company Limited; *Int'l*, pg. 1258
SKANDIA (UK) HOLDING LTD.—See Skandia Insurance Company Limited; *Int'l*, pg. 1258
SKANDIA UK INSURANCE PLC—See Skandia Insurance Company Limited; *Int'l*, pg. 1258
SKANDIA U.S. HOLDING CORPORATION—See Skandia Insurance Company Limited; *Int'l*, pg. 1257
SKANDIA U.S. INSURANCE COMPANY—See Skandia Insurance Company Limited; *Int'l*, pg. 1257
SKANDIA VERSICHERUNGS-AG—See Skandia Insurance Company Limited; *Int'l*, pg. 1258
SKANDIA VERSICHERUNGS MGMT UND SERV GMBH—See Skandia Insurance Company Limited; *Int'l*, pg. 1258
SKANDIA VIDA, S.A.—See Skandia Insurance Company Limited; *Int'l*, pg. 1258
SKANDIA VITA S.P.A.—See Skandia Insurance Company Limited; *Int'l*, pg. 1258
SKANDIABANKEN AB—See Skandia Insurance Company Limited; *Int'l*, pg. 1257
SKANDIABANKEN FONDER AB—See Skandia Insurance Company Limited; *Int'l*, pg. 1257
SKANDIALINK LIVFORSAKRINGS AB—See Skandia Insurance Company Limited; *Int'l*, pg. 1258
SKANDINAVISK BENCKISER A/S—See Joh. A. Benckiser GmbH; *Int'l*, pg. 186
SKANDINAVISK HENKEL A/S—See Henkel KGaA; *Int'l*, pg. 614
AB SKANDINAVISKA ELVERK—See Incentive AB; *Int'l*, pg. 670
SKANDINAVISKA ENSKILDA BANKEN; *Int'l*, pg. 1258
SKANDINAVISKA ENSKILDA BANKEN—See Skandinaviska Enskilda Banken; *Int'l*, pg. 1259
SKANDINAVISKA ENSKILDA BANKEN AG—See Skandinaviska Enskilda Banken; *Int'l*, pg. 1259
SKANDINAVISKA ENSKILDA BANKEN, COPENHAGEN—See Skandinaviska Enskilda Banken; *Int'l*, pg. 1259
SKANDINAVISKA ENSKILDA BANKEN CORPORATION—See Skandinaviska Enskilda Banken; *Int'l*, pg. 1259
SKANDINAVISKA ENSKILDA BANKEN-DUSSELDORF—See Skandinaviska Enskilda Banken; *Int'l*, pg. 1260
SKANDINAVISKA ENSKILDA BANKEN HELSINKI—See Skandinaviska Enskilda Banken; *Int'l*, pg. 1259
SKANDINAVISKA ENSKILDA BANKEN HONG KONG—See Skandinaviska Enskilda Banken; *Int'l*, pg. 1259
SKANDINAVISKA ENSKILDA BANKEN - MOSCOW—See Skandinaviska Enskilda Banken; *Int'l*, pg. 1259
SKANDINAVISKA ENSKILDA BANKEN OSLO—See Skandinaviska Enskilda Banken; *Int'l*, pg. 1259
SKANDINAVISKA ENSKILDA BANKEN, SINGAPORE BRANCH—See Skandinaviska Enskilda Banken; *Int'l*, pg. 1259
SKANDINAVISKA ENSKILDA BANKEN SOUTH EAST ASIA LIMITED—See Skandinaviska Enskilda Banken; *Int'l*, pg. 1260
SKANDINAVISKA ENSKILDA BANKEN, TOKYO BRANCH—See Skandinaviska Enskilda Banken; *Int'l*, pg. 1259
SKANDINAVISKA ENSKILDA BANKING, NEW YORK & CAYMAN ISLAND BRANCH—See Skandinaviska Enskilda Banken; *Int'l*, pg. 1259
AB SKANE-REPORTAGE—See Aftonbladet AB; *Int'l*, pg. 29
SKANSKA AB; *Int'l*, pg. 1260
SKANSKA ANLAGGNING AB—See Skanska AB; *Int'l*, pg. 1260
SKANSKA BOSTADER STOCKHOLM AB—See Skanska AB; *Int'l*, pg. 1260
SKANSKA BYGG AB—See Skanska AB; *Int'l*, pg. 1260
SKANSKA CAPITAL AB—See Skanska AB; *Int'l*, pg. 1260
SKANSKA DATA AB—See Skanska AB; *Int'l*, pg. 1260
SKANSKA E&C—See Skanska AB; *Int'l*, pg. 1261
SKANSKA FASTIGHETER GOTEBORG AB—See Skanska AB; *Int'l*, pg. 1260
SKANSKA FASTIGHETER RIKS AB—See Skanska AB; *Int'l*, pg. 1260
SKANSKA FASTIGHETER STOCKHOLM AB—See Skanska AB; *Int'l*, pg. 1260
SKANSKA HUNGARIA LTD.—See Skanska AB; *Int'l*, pg. 1261
SKANSKA INSTALLATION AB—See Skanska AB; *Int'l*, pg. 1260

SKANSKA INTERNATIONAL BUILDING AB—See Skanska AB; *Int'l*, pg. 1260
SKANSKA INTERNATIONAL CIVIL ENGINEERING AB—See Skanska AB; *Int'l*, pg. 1260
SKANSKA LONDON—See Skanska AB; *Int'l*, pg. 1261
SKANSKA MASKIN AB—See Skanska AB; *Int'l*, pg. 1261
SKANSKA NORR AB—See Skanska AB; *Int'l*, pg. 1260
SKANSKA ORESUND AB—See Skanska AB; *Int'l*, pg. 1261
SKANSKA OY—See Skanska AB; *Int'l*, pg. 1261
SKANSKA PREFAB AB—See Skanska AB; *Int'l*, pg. 1261
SKANSKA PROPERTY GMBH—See Skanska AB; *Int'l*, pg. 1260
SKANSKA PROPERTY HUNGARY—See Skanska AB; *Int'l*, pg. 1261
SKANSKA STALTEKNIK AB—See Skanska AB; *Int'l*, pg. 1261
SKANSKA STOCKHOLM MALARDALEN—See Skanska AB; *Int'l*, pg. 1260
SKANSKA SYD—See Skanska AB; *Int'l*, pg. 1260
SKANSKA TEKNIK AB—See Skanska AB; *Int'l*, pg. 1261
SKANSKA (U.S.A.) INC.—See Skanska AB; *Int'l*, pg. 1261
SKANSKA VAST—See Skanska AB; *Int'l*, pg. 1261
SKAPAFORS PAPER AB—See Duni AB; *Int'l*, pg. 421
ROBERT SKEELS & CO.—See Wynn's International, Inc.; *U.S. Public*, pg. 1782
SKEENA CELLULOSE INC.; *Int'l*, pg. 1261
SKEETER PRODUCTS, INC.—See MacAndrews & Forbes Holdings Inc.; *U.S. Private*, pg. 689
SKEGA AB—See Svedala Industri AB; *Int'l*, pg. 1323
OY SKEGA AB—See Svedala Industri AB; *Int'l*, pg. 1323
SKEGA CANADA LTD.—See Svedala Industri AB; *Int'l*, pg. 1323
SKEGA CHILENA S.A.—See Svedala Industri AB; *Int'l*, pg. 1323
SKEGA FAR EAST PTE. LTD.—See Svedala Industri AB; *Int'l*, pg. 1323
SKEGA GMBH—See Svedala Industri AB; *Int'l*, pg. 1323
SKEGA LTD—See Svedala Industri AB; *Int'l*, pg. 1324
SKEGA LTD.—See Svedala Industri AB; *Int'l*, pg. 1324
SKEGA MEXICANA SA DE CV—See Svedala Industri AB; *Int'l*, pg. 1324
SKEGA (PTY) LTD.—See Svedala Industri AB; *Int'l*, pg. 1324
SKEGA SA—See Svedala Industri AB; *Int'l*, pg. 1324
SKEGA SA DE CV—See Svedala Industri AB; *Int'l*, pg. 1324
SKEGA SOUTH EAST ASIA LTD.—See Svedala Industri AB; *Int'l*, pg. 1324
SKETCHLEY PLC; *Int'l*, pg. 1261
SKETCHLEY RETAIL LTD.—See Sketchley Plc; *Int'l*, pg. 1261
SKIING—See The Times Mirror Company; *U.S. Public*, pg. 1617
SKIL CANADA LTD.—See Emerson Electric Co.; *U.S. Public*, pg. 577
SKIL DENMARK A/S—See Emerson Electric Co.; *U.S. Public*, pg. 577
SKIL DEUTSCHLAND G.M.B.H.—See Emerson Electric Co.; *U.S. Public*, pg. 577
SKIL FRANCE, S.A.—See Emerson Electric Co.; *U.S. Public*, pg. 577
SKIL (GREAT BRITAIN) LTD.—See Emerson Electric Co.; *U.S. Public*, pg. 577
SKIL-INFRA S.A. DE CV—See Emerson Electric Co.; *U.S. Public*, pg. 577
SKIL-JAPAN LTD.—See Emerson Electric Co.; *U.S. Public*, pg. 577
SKIL NEDERLAND B.V.—See Emerson Electric Co.; *U.S. Public*, pg. 577
SKIL NORGE A/S—See Emerson Electric Co.; *U.S. Public*, pg. 578
SKIL POWER TOOLS N.V.—See Emerson Electric Co.; *U.S. Public*, pg. 578
SKIL SVERIGE AB—See Emerson Electric Co.; *U.S. Public*, pg. 578
SKIL VENEZOLANA S.R.L.—See Emerson Electric Co.; *U.S. Public*, pg. 578
SKILTOOLS DE MEXICO S.A. DE C.V.—See Emerson Electric Co.; *U.S. Public*, pg. 578
SKINNER CORP.; *U.S. Private*, pg. 1005
SKINNER MACARONI—See Hershey Foods Corporation; *U.S. Public*, pg. 812
SKINNER VALVE DIVISION—See Parker Hannifin Corporation; *U.S. Public*, pg. 1260
JOSEF SKIPICOL STRASSENBAUSTOFFE GMBH & CO. KG—See Philipp Holzmann AG; *Int'l*, pg. 633
SKIPJACK, INC.—See Chesapeake Utilities Corporation; *U.S. Public*, pg. 347
SKIS DYNASTAR S.A.—See Rossignol S.A.; *Int'l*, pg. 1127
SKIS ROSSIGNOL DE ESPANA S.A.—See Rossignol S.A.; *Int'l*, pg. 1127
SKODA AUTOMOBILE DEUTSCHLAND GMBH—See Volkswagen AG; *Int'l*, pg. 1475
SKODA, AUTOMOBILOVA A.S.—See Volkswagen AG; *Int'l*, pg. 1475
SKOFIN S.R.O.—See Volkswagen AG; *Int'l*, pg. 1475
SKOKIE VALLEY BEVERAGE CO.; *U.S. Private*, pg. 1005
SKOLEASE—See Volkswagen AG; *Int'l*, pg. 1475
SKOWHEGAN DIVISION—See Consumers Water Company; *U.S. Public*, pg. 360
SKY BROS. INC.—See JP Foodservice, Inc.; *U.S. Public*, pg. 918
SKY COMPUTERS, INC.—See Analogic Corporation; *U.S. Public*, pg. 109
SKY COURIER—See Airborne Freight Corporation; *U.S. Public*, pg. 33
SKY LIMITED—See Analogic Corporation; *U.S. Public*, pg. 109
SKY NETWORK TELEVISION LIMITED—See Bell Atlantic Corporation; *U.S. Public*, pg. 204
SKY SANGYO CO., LTD.—See Suntory Ltd.; *Int'l*, pg. 1321
SKYBOX INTERNATIONAL INC.—See Marvel Entertainment Group; *U.S. Public*, pg. 1052

SKYCELL COMMUNICATIONS PRIVATE LIMITED—See BellSouth Corporation; *U.S. Public*, pg. 209
SKYDYNE DIV.—See AAR Corp.; *U.S. Public*, pg. 1
SKYEPHARMA PLC; *Int'l*, pg. 1262
SKYLAND SCIENTIFIC SERVICES, INC.—See Steris Corporation; *U.S. Public*, pg. 1515
SKYLARK CO., LTD.; *Int'l*, pg. 1262
SKYLINE AUTO EXCHANGE—See Tyco International Ltd.; *U.S. Public*, pg. 1649
SKYLINE CHILI, INC.; *U.S. Public*, pg. 1475
SKYLINE CORPORATION; *U.S. Public*, pg. 1476
SKYLINE HOMES, INC.—See Skyline Corporation; *U.S. Public*, pg. 1476
SKYLINE PORT NEWARK FACILITY—See Tyco International Ltd.; *U.S. Public*, pg. 1648
SKYTEL CORP.—See Mobile Telecommunications Technologies Corp.; *U.S. Public*, pg. 1120
SKYWAY FREIGHT SYSTEMS, INC.; *U.S. Private*, pg. 1005
SKYWAY LUGGAGE CO.; *U.S. Private*, pg. 1005
SKYWAY SYSTEMS, INC.—See Skyway Freight Systems, Inc.; *U.S. Private*, pg. 1005
SKYWEST AIRLINES, INC.—See SkyWest Inc.; *U.S. Public*, pg. 1476
SKYWEST INC.; *U.S. Public*, pg. 1476
SLAB & PLATE PRODUCTS DIVISION—See The Broken Hill Proprietary Company Limited; *Int'l*, pg. 227
SLACAN—See Slater Industries Inc.; *Int'l*, pg. 1262
SLAMUB—See GIB Group; *Int'l*, pg. 533
SLANE HOSIERY MILLS, INC.; *U.S. Private*, pg. 1005
SLANT/FIN CORPORATION; *U.S. Private*, pg. 1005
SLANT-FIN, LTD./LTEE—See Slant/Fin Corporation; *U.S. Private*, pg. 1005
SLATER INDUSTRIES INC.; *Int'l*, pg. 1262
SLATER STEELS CORPORATION—See Slater Industries Inc.; *Int'l*, pg. 1263
SLATES BRAND—See Levi Strauss & Co.; *U.S. Private*, pg. 663
SLATTERY ASSOCIATES INC.—See Skanska AB; *Int'l*, pg. 1261
SLAUTTERBACK CORP.—See Nordson Corporation; *U.S. Public*, pg. 1188
SLAYBAUGH-THOMPSON, INC.—See Eclipse Inc.; *U.S. Private*, pg. 360
SLEEPECK PRINTING COMPANY; *U.S. Private*, pg. 1005
SLEEPEEZEE LIMITED; *Int'l*, pg. 1263
SLEEPY'S THE MATTRESS PROFESSIONALS; *U.S. Private*, pg. 1005
SLICK AIRCRAFT PRODUCTS—See Unison Industries; *U.S. Private*, pg. 1120
SLIM-FAST FOODS COMPANY; *U.S. Private*, pg. 1006
SLOAN CANYON SAND CO.—See CalMat Co.; *U.S. Public*, pg. 296
SLOAN FLUSHMATE—See Sloan Valve Company; *U.S. Private*, pg. 1006
THE SLOAN-MAJOR AGENCY, INC.—See Golden Enterprises Inc.; *U.S. Public*, pg. 750
SLOAN TECHNOLOGY—See Veeco Instruments, Inc.; *U.S. Public*, pg. 1711
SLOAN VALVE COMPANY; *U.S. Private*, pg. 1006
GEORGE FISCHER SLOANE, INC.—See ETEX; *Int'l*, pg. 430
SLOAN'S SUPERMARKETS, INC.—See Red Apple Companies; *U.S. Public*, pg. 915
SLOCAN FOREST PRODUCTS LTD.; *Int'l*, pg. 1263
J.T. SLOCOMB COMPANY; *U.S. Private*, pg. 1152
SLOGAN PUBLICIDAD—See Warwick Baker O'Neill; *U.S. Private*, pg. 1006
SLOTS-A-FUN, INC.—See Circus Circus - Las Vegas; *U.S. Public*, pg. 375
SLOVAK INTERNATIONAL TABAK, A.S. (S.I.T.)—See Reemtsma Cigarettenfabriken GmbH, Hamburg; *Int'l*, pg. 1101
SLUGRO S.A.—See Novartis AG; *Int'l*, pg. 985
SLUIS & GROOT ITALIA S.P.A.—See Novartis AG; *Int'l*, pg. 985
SLUIS & GROOT SEMILAS S.A.—See Novartis AG; *Int'l*, pg. 985
SLUIS & GROOT VETOMAG TERMELO ES KERESKEDO KFT.—See Novartis AG; *Int'l*, pg. 985
SMALL, PARKER & BLOSSOM—See CNB Bancshares, Inc.; *U.S. Public*, pg. 280
SMALL PARTS, INC.; *U.S. Private*, pg. 1006
SMALL PARTS, INC.-NAPCO DIVISION—See Small Parts, Inc.; *U.S. Private*, pg. 1006
SMALL SYSTEMS GROUP—See BTR plc; *Int'l*, pg. 126
SMALL TUBE PRODUCTS CO., INC.—See Wolverine Tube Inc.; *U.S. Public*, pg. 1775
SMART & FINAL—See Groupe Casino; *Int'l*, pg. 563
SMART CARDS & SYSTEMS—See DataCard Corporation; *U.S. Private*, pg. 312
SMART ENERGY SERVICES, INC.—See Central Vermont Public Service Corporation; *U.S. Public*, pg. 328
SMART MODULAR TECHNOLOGIES; *U.S. Public*, pg. 1476
SMART MONEY—See The Hearst Corporation; *U.S. Private*, pg. 1006
SMART SHIRTS (LANKA) LIMITED—See Kellwood Company; *U.S. Public*, pg. 948
SMART SHIRTS LTD.—See Kellwood Company; *U.S. Public*, pg. 948
SMART SMR, INC.—See Nextel Communications; *U.S. Public*, pg. 1181
SMARTFOODS, INC.—See PepsiCo, Inc.; *U.S. Public*, pg. 1277
SMARTRUNK SYSTEMS, INC.; *U.S. Private*, pg. 1006
SMEAD MANUFACTURING COMPANY; *U.S. Private*, pg. 1006
SMELKINSON SYSCO FOOD SERVICES, INC.—See Sysco Corporation; *U.S. Public*, pg. 1550
F.L. SMIDTH & CO. A/S—See FLS Industries A/S; *Int'l*, pg. 475
F.L. SMIDTH & CO. GMBH—See FLS Industries A/S; *Int'l*, pg. 475

F.L. SMIDTH-FULLER ENGINEERING A/S—See FLS Industries A/S; *Int'l*, pg. 475
THE PIERRE SMIRNOFF COMPANY—See Diageo Plc; *Int'l*, pg. 411
SMIT INTERNATIONALE N.V.—See Seacor Smit Inc.; *U.S. Public*, pg. 1449
A.O. SMITH CORPORATION; *U.S. Public*, pg. 1476
A.O. SMITH/UPPCO, INC.—See A.O. Smith Corporation; *U.S. Public*, pg. 1476
SMITH & BUTTERFIELD—See Champion Industries; *U.S. Public*, pg. 333
SMITH & HAWKEN—See CML Group, Inc.; *U.S. Public*, pg. 279
SMITH & MCLAURIN LIMITED—See Rexam PLC; *Int'l*, pg. 1107
SMITH & NEPHEW CASTING, INC.—See Smith & Nephew PLC; *Int'l*, pg. 1263
SMITH & NEPHEW CONSUMER PRODUCTS LTD.—See Smith & Nephew PLC; *Int'l*, pg. 1263
SMITH & NEPHEW DONJOY INC.—See Smith & Nephew PLC; *Int'l*, pg. 1263
SMITH & NEPHEW ENDOSCOPY—See Smith & Nephew PLC; *Int'l*, pg. 1263
SMITH & NEPHEW ENT—See Smith & Nephew PLC; *Int'l*, pg. 1263
SMITH & NEPHEW MEDICAL FABRICS—See Smith & Nephew PLC; *Int'l*, pg. 1263
SMITH & NEPHEW MEDICAL LTD.—See Smith & Nephew PLC; *Int'l*, pg. 1263
SMITH & NEPHEW NORTH AMERICA—See Smith & Nephew PLC; *Int'l*, pg. 1263
SMITH & NEPHEW ORTHOPEDICS—See Smith & Nephew PLC; *Int'l*, pg. 1263
SMITH & NEPHEW PLC; *Int'l*, pg. 1263
SMITH & NEPHEW REHABILITATION INC.—See Smith & Nephew PLC; *Int'l*, pg. 1263
SMITH & NEPHEW RESEARCH LTD.—See Smith & Nephew PLC; *Int'l*, pg. 1263
SMITH & NEPHEW UNITED INC.—See Smith & Nephew PLC; *Int'l*, pg. 1263
SMITH & SMITH GLASS LTD.—See International Paper Company; *U.S. Public*, pg. 904
SMITH & SONS FOODS, INC.; *U.S. Private*, pg. 1006
SMITH & WESSON CORP.—See Tomkins PLC; *Int'l*, pg. 1397
SMITH BROCAS, C.A.—See Smith International, Inc.; *U.S. Public*, pg. 1478
SMITH BROTHERS FARMS, INC.; *U.S. Private*, pg. 1007
C.D. SMITH DRUG COMPANY; *U.S. Private*, pg. 1007
C G SMITH LTD.; *Int'l*, pg. 1263
SMITH CORONA (CANADA) LTD.—See Smith Corona Corp.; *U.S. Private*, pg. 1007
SMITH CORONA CORP.; *U.S. Private*, pg. 1007
SMITH CORONA FINANCIAL DIVISION—See Smith Corona Corp.; *U.S. Private*, pg. 1007
SMITH CORONA (FRANCE) S.A.R.L.—See Smith Corona Corp.; *U.S. Private*, pg. 1007
SMITH CORONA (PTE) LTD.—See Smith Corona Corp.; *U.S. Private*, pg. 1007
SMITH CORONA S.A.—See Smith Corona Corp.; *U.S. Private*, pg. 1007
SMITH CORONA (U.K.) LTD.—See Smith Corona Corp.; *U.S. Private*, pg. 1007
E.D. SMITH; *Int'l*, pg. 1263
SMITH-EDWARDS-DUNLAP COMPANY; *U.S. Private*, pg. 1007
SMITH-EMERY COMPANY; *U.S. Private*, pg. 1007
SMITH ENGINEERING CO.—See Haden Maclellan Holdings Inc.; *Int'l*, pg. 586
SMITH ENTERPRISES; *U.S. Private*, pg. 1007
SMITH ENVIRONMENTAL TECHNOLOGIES CORP.; *U.S. Public*, pg. 1477
SMITH ENVIRONMENTAL TECHNOLOGIES CORP.—See Smith Environmental Technologies Corp.; *U.S. Public*, pg. 1477
EVERETT SMITH GROUP, LTD.; *U.S. Private*, pg. 1007
SMITH FARMS; *U.S. Private*, pg. 1008
SMITH FIBERGLASS PRODUCTS INC.—See A.O. Smith Corporation; *U.S. Public*, pg. 1477
SMITH FLOW CONTROL LIMITED—See Halma p.l.c.; *Int'l*, pg. 590
SMITH FROZEN FOODS, INC.; *U.S. Private*, pg. 1008
H.B. SMITH CO., INC.; *U.S. Private*, pg. 1008
SMITH HARDWARE COMPANY—See Distribution America; *U.S. Private*, pg. 335
SMITH HINCHMAN GRYLLS ASSOCIATES, INC.—See SmithGroup, Inc.; *U.S. Private*, pg. 1010
HOWARD SMITH PAPERS LTD—See N.V. Koninklijke KNP BT; *Int'l*, pg. 757
HOWARD SMITH SCREEN CO.—See Halliburton Company; *U.S. Public*, pg. 776
SMITH INDUSTRIES, INC.; *U.S. Private*, pg. 1008
SMITH INTERNACIONAL, S.A. DE C.V.—See Smith International, Inc.; *U.S. Public*, pg. 1478
SMITH INTERNATIONAL AUSTRALIA (PTY) LTD.—See Smith International, Inc.; *U.S. Public*, pg. 1478
SMITH INTERNATIONAL CANADA LTD.—See Smith International, Inc.; *U.S. Public*, pg. 1478
SMITH INTERNATIONAL DE ARGENTINA, S.A.—See Smith International, Inc.; *U.S. Public*, pg. 1478
SMITH INTERNATIONAL DE VENEZUELA, C.A.—See Smith International, Inc.; *U.S. Public*, pg. 1478
SMITH INTERNATIONAL DEUTSCHLAND GMBH—See Smith International, Inc.; *U.S. Public*, pg. 1478
SMITH INTERNATIONAL DO BRASIL LTDA.—See Smith International, Inc.; *U.S. Public*, pg. 1478
SMITH INTERNATIONAL FRANCE, S.A.R.L.—See Smith International, Inc.; *U.S. Public*, pg. 1478
SMITH INTERNATIONAL GULF SERVICES LIMITED—See Smith International, Inc.; *U.S. Public*, pg. 1478
SMITH INTERNATIONAL, INC.; *U.S. Public*, pg. 1478
SMITH INTERNATIONAL ITALIA, S.P.A.—See Smith International, Inc.; *U.S. Public*, pg. 1478

Company Index

SMITH INTERNATIONAL (NORTH SEA) LTD.—See Smith International, Inc.; *U.S. Public*, pg. 1478

SMITH INTERNATIONAL NORWAY A/S—See Smith International, Inc.; *U.S. Public*, pg. 1478

SMITH INTERNATIONAL SDN. BHD.—See Smith International, Inc.; *U.S. Public*, pg. 1478

SMITH INTERNATIONAL SOUTH AMERICA, INC.—See Smith International, Inc.; *U.S. Public*, pg. 1478

SMITH INVESTMENT COMPANY; *U.S. Private*, pg. 1008

J.M. SMITH CORP.; *U.S. Private*, pg. 1008

J.R. SMITH MANUFACTURING COMPANY—See Smith Industries, Inc.; *U.S. Private*, pg. 1008

J. SMITH & SONS (CLERKENWELL) LTD.—See Delta plc; *Int'l*, pg. 391

KEITH SMITH COMPANY; *U.S. Private*, pg. 1008

KELLER SMITH SUPPLY, INC.; *U.S. Private*, pg. 1008

L.B. SMITH, INC.; *U.S. Private*, pg. 1009

L.J. SMITH, INC.—See Marmac Corporation; *U.S. Private*, pg. 706

SMITH LABORATORIES, INC.—See Columbia/HCA Healthcare Corporation; *U.S. Public*, pg. 405

SMITH-LEE CO., INC.; *U.S. Private*, pg. 1009

SMITH MANAGEMENT CO., INC.; *U.S. Private*, pg. 1009

SMITH MCDONALD CORP.; *U.S. Private*, pg. 1009

SMITH METAL ARTS COMPANY, INC.—See Smith McDonald Corp.; *U.S. Private*, pg. 1009

SMITH METERS LTD.—See Hanson PLC; *Int'l*, pg. 593

SMITH MOTORS, INC.; *U.S. Private*, pg. 1009

SMITH PIPE & STEEL CO.; *U.S. Private*, pg. 1009

SMITH PREMIUM SERVICES—See J.M. Smith Corp.; *U.S. Private*, pg. 1008

SMITH RED BARON (OIL TOOLS RENTAL) LTD.—See Smith International, Inc.; *U.S. Public*, pg. 1478

SEYMOUR SMITH & SON—See Emerson Electric Co.; *U.S. Public*, pg. 575

SMITH SPECIALTY METALS—See Smith Pipe & Steel Co.; *U.S. Private*, pg. 1009

STANLEY SMITH SECURITY, INC.—See Sophus Berendsen A/S; *Int'l*, pg. 1286

SMITH SYSTEM MANUFACTURING COMPANY; *U.S. Private*, pg. 1009

DR. T.C. SMITH CO. INC.—See Bergen Brunswig Corporation; *U.S. Public*, pg. 214

SMITH TECHNOLOGIES CORP.—See Smith Environmental Technologies Corp.; *U.S. Public*, pg. 1478

T.L. SMITH DELAWARE—See T.L. Smith Machine; *U.S. Private*, pg. 1009

T.L. SMITH FLORIDA—See T.L. Smith Machine; *U.S. Private*, pg. 1009

T.L. SMITH MACHINE; *U.S. Private*, pg. 1009

T.L. SMITH MIDWEST—See T.L. Smith Machine; *U.S. Private*, pg. 1009

SMITH VALVE CORPORATION—See Tyco International Ltd.; *U.S. Public*, pg. 1651

W.H. SMITH GROUP PLC; *Int'l*, pg. 1150

W.H. SMITH CANADA LTD.—See Russel Metals Inc.; *Int'l*, pg. 1150

SMITH WHOLESALE DRUG DIV.—See J.M. Smith Corp.; *U.S. Private*, pg. 1008

WILBUR SMITH ASSOCIATES; *U.S. Private*, pg. 1009

SMITH WIRES LIMITED—See Carclo Engineering Group plc; *Int'l*, pg. 268

SMITHBOOKS—See Russel Metals Inc.; *Int'l*, pg. 1150

THE SMITHFIELD COMPANIES, INC.; *U.S. Public*, pg. 1479

SMITHFIELD FOODS, INC.; *U.S. Public*, pg. 1479

THE SMITHFIELD PACKING CO., INC.—See Smithfield Foods, Inc.; *U.S. Public*, pg. 1479

SMITHGROUP, INC.; *U.S. Private*, pg. 1010

SMITHKLINE & FRENCH (BANGLADESH) LTD.—See SmithKline Beecham plc; *Int'l*, pg. 1265

SMITHKLINE & FRENCH B.V.—See SmithKline Beecham plc; *Int'l*, pg. 1265

SMITHKLINE & FRENCH, C.A.—See SmithKline Beecham plc; *Int'l*, pg. 1265

SMITHKLINE & FRENCH INTER-AMERICAN CORP.—See SmithKline Beecham plc; *Int'l*, pg. 1265

SMITHKLINE & FRENCH INTL., GMBH—See SmithKline Beecham plc; *Int'l*, pg. 1265

SMITHKLINE & FRENCH NIGERIA, LTD.—See SmithKline Beecham plc; *Int'l*, pg. 1265

SMITHKLINE & FRENCH OF IRAN LIMITED—See SmithKline Beecham plc; *Int'l*, pg. 1265

SMITHKLINE & FRENCH PAKISTAN, LTD.—See SmithKline Beecham plc; *Int'l*, pg. 1265

SMITHKLINE & FRENCH PORTUGUESA—See SmithKline Beecham plc; *Int'l*, pg. 1265

SMITHKLINE & FRENCH (PROPRIETARY) LTD.—See SmithKline Beecham plc; *Int'l*, pg. 1265

SMITHKLINE & FRENCH, S.A.—See SmithKline Beecham plc; *Int'l*, pg. 1265

SMITHKLINE & FRENCH SWITZERLAND LTD.—See SmithKline Beecham plc; *Int'l*, pg. 1265

SMITHKLINE ANIMAL HEALTH (PROPRIETARY) LIMITED—See Pfizer Inc.; *U.S. Public*, pg. 1282

SMITHKLINE BEECHAM A.G.—See SmithKline Beecham plc; *Int'l*, pg. 1265

SMITHKLINE BEECHAM ANIMAL HEALTH (SINGAPORE) PRIVATE LIMITED—See Pfizer Inc.; *U.S. Public*, pg. 1282

SMITHKLINE BEECHAM BIOLOGICALS S.A.—See SmithKline Beecham plc; *Int'l*, pg. 1265

SMITHKLINE BEECHAM CANADA, INC.—See SmithKline Beecham plc; *Int'l*, pg. 1265

SMITHKLINE BEECHAM C.I.S.A.—See SmithKline Beecham plc; *Int'l*, pg. 1265

SMITHKLINE BEECHAM CLINICAL LABORATORIES, INC.—See SmithKline Beecham plc; *Int'l*, pg. 1264

SMITHKLINE BEECHAM CLINICAL LABORATORIES—See SmithKline Beecham plc; *Int'l*, pg. 1266

SMITHKLINE BEECHAM CONSUMER BRANDS—See SmithKline Beecham plc; *Int'l*, pg. 1264

SMITHKLINE BEECHAM CONSUMER BRANDS BV—See SmithKline Beecham plc; *Int'l*, pg. 1266

SMITHKLINE BEECHAM CONSUMER BRANDS (PTY) LTD.—See SmithKline Beecham plc; *Int'l*, pg. 1265

SMITHKLINE BEECHAM CONSUMER BRANDS SDN. BHD.—See SmithKline Beecham plc; *Int'l*, pg. 1265

SMITHKLINE BEECHAM CONSUMER HEALTHCARE—See Hoechst Aktiengesellschaft; *Int'l*, pg. 625

SMITHKLINE BEECHAM CONSUMER HEALTHCARE, U.S.—See SmithKline Beecham plc; *Int'l*, pg. 1264

SMITHKLINE BEECHAM CONSUMER PRODUCTS—See SmithKline Beecham plc; *Int'l*, pg. 1264

SMITHKLINE BEECHAM CORPORATION—See SmithKline Beecham plc; *Int'l*, pg. 1264

SMITHKLINE BEECHAM-DAUELSBERG G.M.B.H & CO.—See SmithKline Beecham plc; *Int'l*, pg. 1266

SMITHKLINE BEECHAM DE MEXICO S.A. DE C.V.—See SmithKline Beecham plc; *Int'l*, pg. 1266

SMITHKLINE BEECHAM DIERGENEESKUNDIGE PRODUCTEN B.V.—See SmithKline Beecham plc; *Int'l*, pg. 1266

SMITHKLINE BEECHAM DIVISION VETERINARIA—See SmithKline Beecham plc; *Int'l*, pg. 1266

SMITHKLINE BEECHAM FARMA B.V.—See SmithKline Beecham plc; *Int'l*, pg. 1266

SMITHKLINE BEECHAM FARMA S.A.—See SmithKline Beecham plc; *Int'l*, pg. 1266

SMITHKLINE BEECHAM ITALIA S.P.A.—See SmithKline Beecham plc; *Int'l*, pg. 1266

SMITHKLINE BEECHAM LABORATORIES—See SmithKline Beecham plc; *Int'l*, pg. 1264

SMITHKLINE BEECHAM LABORATORIES LTD.—See SmithKline Beecham plc; *Int'l*, pg. 1266

SMITHKLINE BEECHAM LABS—See SmithKline Beecham plc; *Int'l*, pg. 1265

SMITHKLINE BEECHAM (NEW ZEALAND) LTD.—See SmithKline Beecham plc; *Int'l*, pg. 1266

SMITHKLINE BEECHAM OF IRELAND LTD.—See SmithKline Beecham plc; *Int'l*, pg. 1266

SMITHKLINE BEECHAM PAKISTAN (PRIVATE) LIMITED—See SmithKline Beecham plc; *Int'l*, pg. 1266

SMITHKLINE BEECHAM PHARMA S.A.—See SmithKline Beecham plc; *Int'l*, pg. 1266

SMITHKLINE BEECHAM PHARMACEUTICALS—See SmithKline Beecham plc; *Int'l*, pg. 1264

SMITHKLINE BEECHAM PHARMACEUTICALS, EUROPEAN DIVISION—See SmithKline Beecham plc; *Int'l*, pg. 1264

SMITHKLINE BEECHAM PHARMACEUTICALS INC.—See SmithKline Beecham plc; *Int'l*, pg. 1266

SMITHKLINE BEECHAM PHARMACEUTICALS, INTERNATIONAL DIVISION—See SmithKline Beecham plc; *Int'l*, pg. 1264

SMITHKLINE BEECHAM PHARMACEUTICALS (PTE.) LTD.—See SmithKline Beecham plc; *Int'l*, pg. 1266

SMITHKLINE BEECHAM PHARMACEUTICALS (PTY.) LTD.—See SmithKline Beecham plc; *Int'l*, pg. 1266

SMITHKLINE BEECHAM PHARMACEUTICALS, RESEARCH DIVISION—See SmithKline Beecham plc; *Int'l*, pg. 1264

SMITHKLINE BEECHAM PLC; *Int'l*, pg. 1264

SMITHKLINE BEECHAM PORTUGUESA PRODUCTOS FARMACEUTICOS E QUIMICOS LDA.—See SmithKline Beecham plc; *Int'l*, pg. 1266

SMITHKLINE BEECHAM PRODUCTS FRANCE S.A.—See SmithKline Beecham plc; *Int'l*, pg. 1266

SMITHKLINE BEECHAM PRODUCTS WESTERN HEMISPHERE DIV., INTL.—See SmithKline Beecham plc; *Int'l*, pg. 1264

SMITHKLINE BEECHAM RESEARCH LIMITED—See SmithKline Beecham plc; *Int'l*, pg. 1266

SMITHKLINE BEECHAM S.A.—See SmithKline Beecham plc; *Int'l*, pg. 1266

SMITHKLINE BEECHAM SAUDE ANIMAL—See SmithKline Beecham plc; *Int'l*, pg. 1266

SMITHKLINE BEECHAM (VENEZUELA) S.A.—See SmithKline Beecham plc; *Int'l*, pg. 1266

SMITHKLINE BEECHAM YAKUHIN K.K.—See SmithKline Beecham plc; *Int'l*, pg. 1266

SMITHKLINE DIAGNOSTICS—See Beckman Instruments, Inc.; *U.S. Public*, pg. 199

B. SMITH'S (D.C.)—See Ark Restaurants Corp.; *U.S. Public*, pg. 130

SMITH'S CHEWING SWEETS MIJ. B.V.—See Van Melle N.V.; *Int'l*, pg. 1451

SMITH'S CRISPS, LTD.—See PepsiCo, Inc.; *U.S. Public*, pg. 1278

SMITHS FLOUR MILLS LTD.—See Northern Foods plc; *Int'l*, pg. 968

SMITH'S FOOD & DRUG CENTERS, INC.—See Fred Meyer Incorporated; *U.S. Public*, pg. 1103

SMITHS INDUSTRIES AEROSPACE & DEFENCE SYSTEMS LIMITED-NEWMARK—See Smiths Industries plc; *Int'l*, pg. 1267

SMITHS INDUSTRIES AEROSPACE & DEFENCE LIMITED-HEAD OFFICE—See Smiths Industries plc; *Int'l*, pg. 1267

SMITHS INDUSTRIES AEROSPACE & DEFENCE SYSTEMS LIMITED-PRODUCT SUPPORT—See Smiths Industries plc; *Int'l*, pg. 1267

SMITHS INDUSTRIES AEROSPACE & DEFENCE SYSTEMS LIMITED-BASINGSTOKE—See Smiths Industries plc; *Int'l*, pg. 1267

SMITHS INDUSTRIES AEROSPACE & DEFENCE SYSTEMS LIMITED-CIVIL SYSTEMS DIV.—See Smiths Industries plc; *Int'l*, pg. 1267

SMITHS INDUSTRIES AEROSPACE & DEFENSE SYSTEMS INC.-MALVERN—See Smiths Industries plc; *Int'l*, pg. 1268

SMITHS INDUSTRIES AEROSPACE & DEFENSE SYSTEMS INC.-WASHINGTON D.C.—See Smiths Industries plc; *Int'l*, pg. 1268

SMITHS INDUSTRIES AEROSPACE & DEFENSE SYSTEMS INC.-PRODUCT SUPPORT—See Smiths Industries plc; *Int'l*, pg. 1268

SMITHS INDUSTRIES AEROSPACE & DEFENSE SYSTEMS INC.-FINANCE DEPT.—See Smiths Industries plc; *Int'l*, pg. 1268

SMITHS INDUSTRIES AUSTRALIA PTY LIMITED-PRODUCT SUPPORT DIVISION—See Smiths Industries plc; *Int'l*, pg. 1268

SMITHS INDUSTRIES HYDRAULICS COMPANY LIMITED—See Smiths Industries plc; *Int'l*, pg. 1267

SMITHS INDUSTRIES INDUSTRIAL GROUP—See Smiths Industries plc; *Int'l*, pg. 1267

SMITHS INDUSTRIES (JAPAN) LIMITED—See Smiths Industries plc; *Int'l*, pg. 1268

SMITHS INDUSTRIES MEDICAL SYSTEMS—See Smiths Industries plc; *Int'l*, pg. 1268

SMITHS INDUSTRIES MEDICAL SYSTEMS CANADA LIMITED—See Smiths Industries plc; *Int'l*, pg. 1269

SMITHS INDUSTRIES NORTH AMERICA LIMITED—See Smiths Industries plc; *Int'l*, pg. 1269

SMITHS INDUSTRIES PLC; *Int'l*, pg. 1266

JOHN SMITH'S TADCASTER BREWERY—See Scottish & Newcastle plc; *Int'l*, pg. 1212

SMITH'S PERSONNEL SERVICE, INC.; *U.S. Private*, pg. 1010

SMITHSTOWN LIGHT ENGINEERING LTD.—See Molex Incorporated; *U.S. Public*, pg. 1123

SMITHTOWN BANCORP, INC.; *U.S. Public*, pg. 1479

SMITS' REFORM B.V.—See Nutricia BV; *Int'l*, pg. 991

BERT L. SMOKLER & CO.—See Lennar Corporation; *U.S. Public*, pg. 989

SMOOT GRAIN CO., INC.—See Archer Daniels Midland Company (ADM); *U.S. Public*, pg. 128

SMORGON A.R.C.; *Int'l*, pg. 1269

SMORGON CONSOLIDATED INDUSTRIES—See Smorgon A.R.C.; *Int'l*, pg. 1269

SMORGON CYCLONE RURAL—See Smorgon A.R.C.; *Int'l*, pg. 1269

SMORGON FENCING—See Smorgon A.R.C.; *Int'l*, pg. 1269

SMUCKER GRANDVIEW PLANT—See J.M. Smucker Company; *U.S. Public*, pg. 1480

J.M. SMUCKER COMPANY; *U.S. Public*, pg. 1480

SMUGGLERS INN OF IL, INC.—See Brierley Investments Limited; *Int'l*, pg. 216

SMURFIT CAPITAL FUNDING PLC—See Jefferson Smurfit Group p.l.c.; *Int'l*, pg. 1269

SMURFIT CARTON Y PAPEL DE MEXICO—See Jefferson Smurfit Group p.l.c.; *Int'l*, pg. 1271

SMURFIT CARTONS (CONGLETON) LTD.—See Jefferson Smurfit Group p.l.c.; *Int'l*, pg. 1271

SMURFIT CARTONS (LEEDS) LTD.—See Jefferson Smurfit Group p.l.c.; *Int'l*, pg. 1271

SMURFIT CARTONS (WITHAM) LTD.—See Jefferson Smurfit Group p.l.c.; *Int'l*, pg. 1271

SMURFIT CORRUGATED CASES (WARRINGTON) LTD.—See Jefferson Smurfit Group p.l.c.; *Int'l*, pg. 1271

SMURFIT CORRUGATED (UK) LIMITED—See Jefferson Smurfit Group p.l.c.; *Int'l*, pg. 1271

SMURFIT ESPANA, S.A.—See Jefferson Smurfit Group p.l.c.; *Int'l*, pg. 1271

SMURFIT FIBREBOARD CONVERTERS LTD.—See Jefferson Smurfit Group p.l.c.; *Int'l*, pg. 1271

SMURFIT GIFTWRAP—See Jefferson Smurfit Group p.l.c.; *Int'l*, pg. 1271

SMURFIT INTERNATIONAL B.V.—See Jefferson Smurfit Group p.l.c.; *Int'l*, pg. 1271

SMURFIT INTERNATIONAL FRANCE S.A.—See Jefferson Smurfit Group p.l.c.; *Int'l*, pg. 1271

SMURFIT INVESTMENTS U.K. LIMITED—See Jefferson Smurfit Group p.l.c.; *Int'l*, pg. 1271

SMURFIT IRELAND LIMITED—See Jefferson Smurfit Group p.l.c.; *Int'l*, pg. 1269

JEFFERSON SMURFIT CORPORATION—See Jefferson Smurfit Group p.l.c.; *Int'l*, pg. 1269

JEFFERSON SMURFIT CORPORATION (U.S.)—See Jefferson Smurfit Group p.l.c.; *Int'l*, pg. 1271

JEFFERSON SMURFIT FOLDING CARTON & BOXBOARD MILLS DIV.—See Jefferson Smurfit Group p.l.c.; *Int'l*, pg. 1270

JEFFERSON SMURFIT GROUP P.L.C.; *Int'l*, pg. 1269

JEFFERSON SMURFIT ITALIA. S.R.L.—See Jefferson Smurfit Group p.l.c.; *Int'l*, pg. 1271

SMURFIT LIMITED—See Jefferson Smurfit Group p.l.c.; *Int'l*, pg. 1271

SMURFIT MERCURIUS VERPAKKING B.V.—See Jefferson Smurfit Group p.l.c.; *Int'l*, pg. 1271

SMURFIT NEWSPRINT CORPORATION—See Jefferson Smurfit Group p.l.c.; *Int'l*, pg. 1271

SMURFIT PACKAGING CORPORATION—See Jefferson Smurfit Group p.l.c.; *Int'l*, pg. 1271

SMURFIT PACKAGING PRODUCTS—See Jefferson Smurfit Group p.l.c.; *Int'l*, pg. 1271

SMURFIT PAPER & BOX MILLS (BURNLEY) LTD.—See Jefferson Smurfit Group p.l.c.; *Int'l*, pg. 1271

SMURFIT PAPER MILLS (TAMWORTH) LTD.—See Jefferson Smurfit Group p.l.c.; *Int'l*, pg. 1271

SMURFIT PLASTIC PACKAGING DIV.—See Jefferson Smurfit Group p.l.c.; *Int'l*, pg. 1271

SMYTH, CO.; *U.S. Private*, pg. 1010

JOHN M. SMYTH CO.—See Levitz Furniture Incorporated; *U.S. Public*, pg. 990

SMYTH MANUFACTURING COMPANY—See Beacon Group; *U.S. Private*, pg. 126

SMYTHE DORWARD LAMBERT—See Omnicom Group Inc.; *U.S. Public*, pg. 1225

SMYTHSON OF BOND STREET—See John Menzies plc; *Int'l*, pg. 707

SNACK AMERICA; *U.S. Private*, pg. 1010

SNACK VENTURES EUROPE—See General Mills, Inc.; *U.S. Public*, pg. 718

SNACKS UNLIMITED DIVISION—See General Mills, Inc.; *U.S. Public*, pg. 718

SNAM INTERNATIONAL HOLDING A.G.—See ENI S.p.A.; *Int'l*, pg. 429

SNAM S.P.A.—See ENI S.p.A.; *Int'l*, pg. 428

SNAMPROGETTI INTERNATIONAL S.A.—See ENI S.p.A.; *Int'l*, pg. 429

SNAMPROGETTI S.P.A.—See ENI S.p.A.; *Int'l*, pg. 429

MASTER INDEX TO COMPANY NAMES

SOCIETE

Company Index

SNAP-ON DIAGNOSTICS—See Snap-On Tools Corporation; *U.S. Public*, pg. 1480
SNAP-ON FINANCIAL SERVICES—See Snap-On Tools Corporation; *U.S. Public*, pg. 1481
SNAP-ON INDUSTRIAL—See Snap-On Tools Corporation; *U.S. Public*, pg. 1481
SNAP-ON TOOLS—See Snap-On Tools Corporation; *U.S. Public*, pg. 1481
SNAP-ON TOOLS (AUSTRALIA) PTY. LTD.—See Snap-On Tools Corporation; *U.S. Public*, pg. 1481
SNAP-ON TOOLS CORPORATION; *U.S. Public*, pg. 1480
SNAP-ON TOOLS, GMBH—See Snap-On Tools Corporation; *U.S. Public*, pg. 1481
SNAP-ON TOOLS INTERNATIONAL, LTD.—See Snap-On Tools Corporation; *U.S. Public*, pg. 1481
SNAP-ON TOOLS JAPAN K.K.—See Snap-On Tools Corporation; *U.S. Public*, pg. 1481
SNAP-ON TOOLS LIMITED—See Snap-On Tools Corporation; *U.S. Public*, pg. 1481
SNAP-ON TOOLS NETHERLANDS B.V.—See Snap-On Tools Corporation; *U.S. Public*, pg. 1481
SNAP-ON TOOLS OF CANADA, LTD.—See Snap-On Tools Corporation; *U.S. Public*, pg. 1481
SNAP-TITE HOSE, INC.—See Snap-Tite, Inc.; *U.S. Private*, pg. 1010
SNAP-TITE, INC.; *U.S. Private*, pg. 1010
SNAP-ON WORLDWIDE, INC.—See Snap-On Tools Corporation; *U.S. Public*, pg. 1481
SNAPPER POWER EQUIPMENT—See Metromedia International Group, Inc.; *U.S. Public*, pg. 1103
SNAPPLE BEVERAGE COMPANY—See Triarc Companies, Inc.; *U.S. Public*, pg. 1635
SNAPPY AIR DISTRIBUTION PRODUCTS—See Standex International Corporation; *U.S. Public*, pg. 1506
SNAPPY CAR RENTAL, INC.; *U.S. Private*, pg. 1010
SNAVELY FOREST PRODUCTS, INC.; *U.S. Private*, pg. 1010
SNELL ACOUSTICS—See Boston Acoustics, Inc.; *U.S. Public*, pg. 246
SNELLING PERSONNEL SERVICES; *U.S. Private*, pg. 1010
SNIA U.S.A., INC.—See Fiat Auto SpA; *Int'l*, pg. 483
SNIC CO., LTD.—See NHK Spring Co., Ltd.; *Int'l*, pg. 902
SNIJBRANDCENTRUM ROERMOND—See Koninklijke Hoogovens N.V.; *Int'l*, pg. 754
SNOKIST GROWERS; *U.S. Private*, pg. 1011
SNOOK & ADERTON, INC.—See Eclipse Inc.; *U.S. Private*, pg. 360
SNORKEL—See Harbour Group Ltd.; *U.S. Private*, pg. 500
SNOW BRAND FOOD CO., LTD.—See Snow Brand Milk Products Co. Ltd.; *Int'l*, pg. 1272
SNOW BRAND MILK PRODUCTS CO. LTD.; *Int'l*, pg. 1271
SNOW BRAND PILLSBURY INC.—See Diageo Plc; *Int'l*, pg. 411
SNOW BRAND ROLLY CO., LTD.—See Snow Brand Milk Products Co. Ltd.; *Int'l*, pg. 1272
SNOW BRAND SEED CO., LTD.—See Snow Brand Milk Products Co. Ltd.; *Int'l*, pg. 1272
SNOW BRAND SHOJI CO., LTD.—See Snow Brand Milk Products Co. Ltd.; *Int'l*, pg. 1272
SNOW COUNTRY—See The New York Times Company; *U.S. Public*, pg. 1174
SNOW COUNTRY BUSINESS—See The New York Times Company; *U.S. Public*, pg. 1174
SNOWCREST PACKERS LTD.—See Nuburn Capital; *Int'l*, pg. 990
SNOWDEN RUBBER INDUSTRIES—See Trelleborg AB; *Int'l*, pg. 1423
SNOWMAX TECHNOLOGIES—See Eastman Kodak Company; *U.S. Public*, pg. 551
SNOW'S/DOXEE INC.—See Castleberry/Snow's Brands Inc.; *U.S. Private*, pg. 219
SNOWSHOE RESORT, INC.—See Intrawest Corporation; *Int'l*, pg. 685
SNUGL MFG. CO. INC.—See Berwind Corporation; *U.S. Private*, pg. 138
SNYDER BAKERY—See United States Bakery; *U.S. Private*, pg. 1124
SNYDER BERLIN—See Pro-Fac Cooperative, Inc.; *U.S. Private*, pg. 887
SNYDER COMMUNICATIONS, INC.; *U.S. Public*, pg. 1481
SNYDER-CROWN, INC.—See Snyder Industries, Inc.; *U.S. Private*, pg. 1011
SNYDER-DIAMOND; *U.S. Private*, pg. 1011
SNYDER INDUSTRIES, INC.; *U.S. Private*, pg. 1011
SNYDER OIL CORPORATION; *U.S. Public*, pg. 1481
SNYDER SOUTHEAST DIV.—See Snyder Industries, Inc.; *U.S. Private*, pg. 1011
SNYDER TANK CORP.; *U.S. Private*, pg. 1011
SNYDER'S DRUG STORES, INC.; *U.S. Private*, pg. 1011
SNYDER'S OF HANOVER, INC.; *U.S. Private*, pg. 1011
SO FRO FABRICS, INC.—See House of Fabrics, Inc.; *U.S. Public*, pg. 842
SO-LO-FOOD, INC.; *U.S. Private*, pg. 1011
SOABAR G.M.B.H.—See Avery Dennison Corporation; *U.S. Public*, pg. 154
SOABAR GRAPHICS DIVISION—See Avery Dennison Corporation; *U.S. Public*, pg. 153
SOABAR MARKING SYSTEMS LTD.—See Avery Dennison Corporation; *U.S. Public*, pg. 154
SOABAR PRODUCTS GROUP—See Avery Dennison Corporation; *U.S. Public*, pg. 153
SOABAR SYSTEMS DIVISION—See Avery Dennison Corporation; *U.S. Public*, pg. 153
SOABAR SYSTEMS (HONG KONG) LTD.—See Avery Dennison Corporation; *U.S. Public*, pg. 154
SOAP OPERA DIGEST—See Primedia Inc.; *U.S. Public*, pg. 1328
SOAP OPERA MAGAZINE—See American Media, Inc.; *U.S. Public*, pg. 87
SOAP OPERA WEEKLY—See Primedia Inc.; *U.S. Public*, pg. 1328
SOBEL NV; *Int'l*, pg. 1272
SOBELAIR S.A.—See Sabena; *Int'l*, pg. 1168
SOBELEASE N.V.—See Rabobank Nederland; *Int'l*, pg. 1082
SOBEMI N.V.—See Schmalbach-Lubeca AG; *Int'l*, pg. 1207
SOBEY INC.—See Empire Company Limited; *Int'l*, pg. 454
SOBEY LEASED PROPERTIES LIMITED—See Empire Company Limited; *Int'l*, pg. 454
SOBLAFHOR—See Accor S.A.; *Int'l*, pg. 20
M. SOBOL INC.—See Allou Health & Beauty Care, Inc.; *U.S. Public*, pg. 55
SOBOTRAM—See SNCF; *Int'l*, pg. 1164
SOC. ABIDJANISE D'EXPANSION CHIMIQUE (SAEC) SA—See Akzo Nobel N.V.; *Int'l*, pg. 43
SOC. AFRICAINE D'EXPANSION CHIMIQUE (SAEC) SA—See Akzo Nobel N.V.; *Int'l*, pg. 43
SOC. AFRICAINE DES PRODUITS CHEMIQUES, AGRICOLES ET MENAGERS SA (SAPCAM)—See Akzo Nobel N.V.; *Int'l*, pg. 43
SOCADO S.A.—See Pirelli S.p.A.; *Int'l*, pg. 1060
SOCADOUR—See Norsk Hydro a.s; *Int'l*, pg. 964
SOCAMIC STE. DE CAOUTCHOUC ET DE PRODUITS CHIMIQUES S.A.R.L.—See Saarbergwerke Aktiengesellschaft; *Int'l*, pg. 1167
SOCANAV INC.; *Int'l*, pg. 1272
SOCAPI—See Groupe GAN; *Int'l*, pg. 565
SOCAR, INC.—See Roanoke Electric Steel Corporation; *U.S. Public*, pg. 1392
SOCAR OF OHIO, INC.—See Roanoke Electric Steel Corporation; *U.S. Public*, pg. 1392
SOCARI—See Thomson S.A.; *Int'l*, pg. 1382
SOCAT L.L.C.—See Sodexho S.A.; *Int'l*, pg. 1275
SOCHATA—See SNECMA - Societe Nationale d'Etude et de Construction de Moteurs d'Aviation; *Int'l*, pg. 1166
SOCHIM COTE-D'IVOIRE SA—See Novartis AG; *Int'l*, pg. 985
SOCIAFRANCE—See The Swiss Life/Rentenanstalt Group; *Int'l*, pg. 1332
STE. SOCIDOC—See C.E.P. Communication Group; *Int'l*, pg. 239
SOCIEDAD CATALANA DE TALLERES ARTESANOS—See LVMH Moet Hennessy Louis Vuitton; *Int'l*, pg. 783
SOCIEDAD CONSTRUCTORA Y DE INVERSIONES MARTIN ZAMORA LTD.—See Corporacion MAPFRE, Compania Internacional de Reaseguros, S.A.; *Int'l*, pg. 335
SOCIEDAD DE ALMACENAJE Y TRANSPORTES S.A.—See Brambles Industries Limited; *Int'l*, pg. 212
SOCIEDAD DE PARTICIPACION Y PROMOCION EMPRESARIAL CAJA DE MADRID—See Caja de Madrid Group; *Int'l*, pg. 252
SOCIEDAD DOMINICANA DE CONSERVAS Y ALIMENTOS S.A.—See Nestle S.A.; *Int'l*, pg. 916
SOCIEDAD ESPANOLA DE AUTOMOVILES DE TURISME, S.A. (SEAT)—See Volkswagen AG; *Int'l*, pg. 1475
SOCIEDAD ESPANOLA DE FRENOS, CALEFACCION Y SENALES, S.A.—See Knorr-Bremse AG; *Int'l*, pg. 738
SOCIEDAD GENERAL DE HULES S.A.—See Solvay S.A.; *Int'l*, pg. 1279
SOCIEDAD GENERAL ESPANOLA DE LIBRERIA—See Lagardere Groupe; *Int'l*, pg. 796
SOCIEDAD GESTORA DE FUNDOS DE PENSOES SA—See Groupe GAN; *Int'l*, pg. 565
SOCIEDAD INDUSTRIAL MINERA YAMIN LTDA.—See Vista Gold Corp.; *U.S. Public*, pg. 1723
SOCIEDAD MINERA LA GRANJA S.A.—See Cambior Inc.; *Int'l*, pg. 253
SOCIEDAD NESTLE A.E.P.A.—See Nestle S.A.; *Int'l*, pg. 922
SOCIEDADE PORTUGUESA DE DESENVOLVIMENTO-QUIMICO DE MONSANTO, LIMITADA—See Monsanto Company; *U.S. Public*, pg. 1126
SOCIEDAD PORTUGUESA HONEYWELL BULL—See Compagnie des Machines Bull; *Int'l*, pg. 319
SOCIEDAD VENEZOLANA DE ELECTRIFICACION C.A. (SVECA)—See ABB Asea Brown Boveri (Holding) Ltd.; *Int'l*, pg. 3
SOCIEDADE AGRICOLA GERMINAL LTDA.—See Novartis AG; *Int'l*, pg. 985
SOCIEDADE ERICSSON DE PORTUGAL LDA.—See Telefonaktiebolaget LM Ericsson; *Int'l*, pg. 1370
SOCIEDADE GESTORA DE FUNDOS DE PENSOES DA CGD, SA—See Caixa Geral de Depositos; *Int'l*, pg. 251
SOCIEDADE PORTUGUESA DE PRODUTOS WANDER LDA.—See Novartis AG; *Int'l*, pg. 985
SOCIEDADE PORTUGUESA DOS ASCENSORES SCHINDLER LDA.—See Schindler Holding AG; *Int'l*, pg. 1205
SOCIEDADE TURISTICA DA PENINA SARL—See Granada Group PLC; *Int'l*, pg. 556
SOCIEDADE ZICKERMANN S.A.—See Knurr AG; *Int'l*, pg. 740
SOCIEDE ANONYME DE L'EXPLOITATION DE L'HOPITAL DE LA TOUR—See Columbia/HCA Healthcare Corporation; *U.S. Public*, pg. 405
SOCIETA ALFA-LAVAL, S.P.A.—See Tetra Laval Group; *Int'l*, pg. 1378
SOCIETA ASSICURATRICE INDUSTRIALE SPA (SAI)—See Groupe GAN; *Int'l*, pg. 565
SOCIETA AZIONARIA PER LA CONDOTTA DI ACQUE POTABILI S.P.A.—See ENI S.p.A.; *Int'l*, pg. 428
SOCIETA BARIO E DERIVATI, S.P.A.—See Solvay S.A.; *Int'l*, pg. 1279
SOCIETA DI BANCA SVIZZERA—See Swiss Bank Corporation; *Int'l*, pg. 1329
SOCIETA EDITRICE LOMBARDA S.E.L. S.P.A.—See Arnoldo Mondadori Editore S.p.A.; *Int'l*, pg. 888
SOCIETA EUROPEA DI EDIZONI S.P.A.—See Arnoldo Mondadori Editore S.p.A.; *Int'l*, pg. 888
SOCIETA FINANZIARIA DI PARTECIPAZIONI - SOFINPAR S.A.—See IRI Istituto Ricostruzione Industriale; *Int'l*, pg. 655
SOCIETA INDUSTRIE LIQUORISTICHE S.A.S.—See Koninklijke BolsWessanen nv; *Int'l*, pg. 751
SOCIETA INIZIATIVE INDUSTRIALI S.R.L.—See ENI S.p.A.; *Int'l*, pg. 428
SOCIETA ITAL. PER CONDOTTE D'ACQUA-ALGERIA—See IRI Istituto Ricostruzione Industriale; *Int'l*, pg. 655
SOCIETA ITAL. PER CONDOTTE D'ACQUA-EGYPT—See IRI Istituto Ricostruzione Industriale; *Int'l*, pg. 655
SOCIETA ITAL. PER CONDOTTE D'ACQUA-MOZAMBIQUE—See IRI Istituto Ricostruzione Industriale; *Int'l*, pg. 655
SOCIETA ITAL. PER CONDOTTE D'ACQUA-PORTUGAL—See IRI Istituto Ricostruzione Industriale; *Int'l*, pg. 655
SOCIETA ITALIANA ASSICURAZIONI DANNI S.P.A.—See Assicurazioni Generali S.p.A.; *Int'l*, pg. 90
SOCIETA ITALIANA ASSICURAZIONI E REASSICURAZIONI S.P.A.—See Zurich Insurance Company; *Int'l*, pg. 1531
SOCIETA ITALIANA EDITRICE STAMPATRICE S.I.E.S. S.P.A.—See Arnoldo Mondadori Editore S.p.A.; *Int'l*, pg. 888
SOCIETA ITALIANA PER IL CYNAR S.P.A.—See Koninklijke BolsWessanen nv; *Int'l*, pg. 751
SOCIETA ITALIANA PRODOTTI ALCOLLCI NATURALI SPA—See Koninklijke BolsWessanen nv; *Int'l*, pg. 753
SOCIETA ITALIANA SERVIZI AEREI MEDITERRANEI S.I.S.A.M. S.P.A.—See IRI Istituto Ricostruzione Industriale; *Int'l*, pg. 652
SOCIETA ITALO SVEDESE SEME S.P.A.—See Novartis AG; *Int'l*, pg. 985
SOCIETA MERIDIONALE ACCESSORI ELASTOMERICI S.P.A.—See Pirelli S.p.A.; *Int'l*, pg. 1058
SOCIETA PNEUMATICI PIRELLI S.P.A.—See Pirelli S.p.A.; *Int'l*, pg. 1058
SOCIETE AFRICAINE DE PROMOTION—See Hewlett-Packard Company; *U.S. Public*, pg. 823
SOCIETE ALGERIENNE D'HOTELLERIE, DE LOISIRS ET D'IMMOBILIER—See Daewoo Corporation; *Int'l*, pg. 358
SOCIETE ANF-INDUSTRIE S.A.—See Bombardier Inc.; *Int'l*, pg. 201
SOCIETE ANONYME DES EAUX MINERALES DE RIBEAUVILLE—See Nestle S.A.; *Int'l*, pg. 919
SOCIETE ANONYME FORMICA (FRANCE)—See BTR plc; *Int'l*, pg. 130
SOCIETE ANONYME FRANCAISE DE REASSURANCES—See PartnerRe Ltd.; *Int'l*, pg. 1024
SOCIETE ANONYME INDUSTRIELLE DE RESINES—See Tenneco Inc.; *U.S. Public*, pg. 1580
SOCIETE ANONYME MEDITERRANEENE DE SALAISONS—See ConAgra, Inc.; *U.S. Public*, pg. 429
SOCIETE BANCAIRE DE PARIS—See Banco Espirito Santo e Comercial de Lisboa SA; *Int'l*, pg. 142
SOCIETE BIC S.A.; *Int'l*, pg. 1272
SOCIETE BORDELAISE DE CIC—See Groupe GAN; *Int'l*, pg. 565
SOCIETE CAMEROUNAISE DE PRODUITS ALIMETAIRES, DIETETIQUES ET AUTRES (CAMAD)—See Nestle S.A.; *Int'l*, pg. 922
S.A. SOCIETE CAROLOREGIENNE DE COKEFACTION CARCOKE—See Cockerill Sambre; *Int'l*, pg. 301
S.A. SOCIETE CAROLOREGIENNE DE LAMINAGE CARLAM—See Cockerill Sambre; *Int'l*, pg. 301
SOCIETE CENTRALE DE GESTION—See Commerzbank AG; *Int'l*, pg. 312
SOCIETE CHANTILLY—See Nestle S.A.; *Int'l*, pg. 919
SOCIETE CHIMIQUE ROCHE S.A.—See Roche Holding Ltd.; *Int'l*, pg. 1121
SOCIETE CILILE IMMOBILIERE DEMAG—See Mannesmann A.G.; *Int'l*, pg. 837
SOCIETE CIVILE DE GESTION IMMOBILIERE—See AXA-UAP; *Int'l*, pg. 19
SOCIETE CIVILE IMMOBILIERE—See Castorama Dubois Investissements S.C.A.; *Int'l*, pg. 275
SOCIETE CIVILE IMMOBILIERE—See Hesta Tex AG; *Int'l*, pg. 618
SOCIETE CIVILE IMMOBILIERE BASSE-YUTZ—See Cockerill Sambre; *Int'l*, pg. 302
SOCIETE CIVILE IMMOBILIERE DE VERGEZE—See Nestle S.A.; *Int'l*, pg. 919
SOCIETE CIVILE IMMOBILIERE DU THILLAY—See Cockerill Sambre; *Int'l*, pg. 302
SOCIETE CIVILE IMMOBILIERE KUNTZIG—See Cockerill Sambre; *Int'l*, pg. 302
SOCIETE CIVILE IMMOBILIERE PLACE DE LA BELGIQUE—See Cockerill Sambre; *Int'l*, pg. 302
SOCIETE COMMERCIALE DES EAUX MINERALES DU BASSIN DE VICHY SAINT-YORRE—See Nestle S.A.; *Int'l*, pg. 919
SOCIETE COMMERCIALE DU CHAMPAGNE MERCIER—See LVMH Moet Hennessy Louis Vuitton; *Int'l*, pg. 781
SOCIETE CONDITIONNEMENT ET INDUSTRIE S.A.—See Nestle S.A.; *Int'l*, pg. 922
SOCIETE D'APPLICATION DU FLOCKAGE—See Borden, Inc.; *U.S. Private*, pg. 160
SOCIETE D'AGENCES ET DE DIFFUSION—See Lagardere Groupe; *Int'l*, pg. 793
SOCIETE D'APPLICATION DES TECHNIQUES LINDE S.A.R.L.—See Linde AG; *Int'l*, pg. 811
SOCIETE D'APPLICATIONS GENERALES D'ELECTRICITE ET DE MECHANIQUE; *Int'l*, pg. 1273
SOCIETE D'ASSURANCES SUR LA VIE ET CONTRE LES ACCIDENTS—See The Swiss Life/Rentenanstalt Group; *Int'l*, pg. 1332
SOCIETE DE BANQUE DE L'ORLEANAIS—See Generale de Banque S.A.; *Int'l*, pg. 548
SOCIETE DE BANQUE SUISSE—See Swiss Bank Corporation; *Int'l*, pg. 1329
SOCIETE DE BANQUE SUISSE (LUXEMBOURG) S.A.—See Swiss Bank Corporation; *Int'l*, pg. 1331
SOCIETE DE BANQUE SUISSE (MONACO)—See Swiss Bank Corporation; *Int'l*, pg. 1331
SOCIETE DE BANQUE SUISSE S.A.—See Swiss Bank Corporation; *Int'l*, pg. 1331
SOCIETE DE BOURSE J.P. MORGAN S.A.—See J.P. Morgan Co. Incorporated; *U.S. Public*, pg. 1131

Company Index

SOCIETE DE CONTROLE ET DE MANAGEMENT—See Lyonnaise des Eaux S.A.; *Int'l*, pg. 824
SOCIETE DE DEVELOPPEMENT DES SUPERMARCHES P.G.—See Etablissements Delhaize Freres Et Cie "Le Lion" S.A.; *Int'l*, pg. 463
SOCIETE DE DISTRIBUTION ET D'EXPORTATION AUTOMOBILES - SODEXA—See PSA Peugeot Citroen; *Int'l*, pg. 1020
SOCIETE DE GESTION DE RESTAURANTS-BARS SUR LES AUTEOROUTES SA—See Granada Group PLC; *Int'l*, pg. 556
SOCIETE DE GESTION D'INTERETS PETROLIERS (SOGEDIP)—See Compagnie Financiere de Paribas; *Int'l*, pg. 319
SOCIETE DE MAINTENANCE ET DE REPARATION DE CONTAINERS S.A.R.L.—See Hapag-Lloyd AG; *Int'l*, pg. 596
SOCIETE DE MAINTENANCE NUCLEAIRE—See Jeumont-Schneider Trenformeteurs; *Int'l*, pg. 706
SOCIETE DE PRODUITS ALIMETAIRES ET DIETETIQUES, SOPAD-NESTLE SA—See Nestle S.A.; *Int'l*, pg. 922
SOCIETE DE REASSURANCE DES RISQUES RELATIFS AUX APPLICATIONS SPATIALES (S3R)—See Arianespace SA; *Int'l*, pg. 81
SOCIETE DE REASSURANCE VALLAROCHE SA (SOREVAL)—See SNECMA - Societe Nationale d'Etude et de Construction de Moteurs d'Aviation; *Int'l*, pg. 1165
SOCIETE DE TRANSFORMATION DES MATIERES PLASTIQUES-S.T.M.P. S.A.—See Solvay S.A.; *Int'l*, pg. 1279
SOCIETE DE TRANSMISSIONS AUTOMATIQUES—See Renault; *Int'l*, pg. 1102
SOCIETE D'ENERGIE DE LA BAIE JAMES—See Hydro-Quebec; *Int'l*, pg. 640
SOCIETE DES ADHESIFS DE BELLEGARDE-AIN S.A.—See Scapa Group Plc; *Int'l*, pg. 1203
SOCIETE DES ATELIERS LOUIS VUITTON—See LVMH Moet Hennessy Louis Vuitton; *Int'l*, pg. 781
SOCIETE DES BOISSONS GAZEUSES DE VERGEZE (GARD)—See Nestle S.A.; *Int'l*, pg. 919
SOCIETE DES BOISSONS GAZEUSES DE VERGEZE—See Nestle S.A.; *Int'l*, pg. 922
SOCIETE DES BOUCHAGES, EMBALLAGES ET CONDITIONNEMENT MODERNES—See Nestle S.A.; *Int'l*, pg. 919
SOCIETE DES CIMENTS ANTILLAIS—See Lafarge S.A.; *Int'l*, pg. 790
SOCIETE DES CIMENTS DU CONGO S.A.—See Scancem AB; *Int'l*, pg. 1200
SOCIETE DES CIMENTS LIBANAIS—See Holderbank Financiers Glaris Ltd.; *Int'l*, pg. 629
SOCIETE DES EAUX MINERALES DE THONON-LES-BAINS—See Nestle S.A.; *Int'l*, pg. 919
SOCIETE DES ELECTRODES ET REFRACTAIRES "SAVOIE" (SERS)—See Pechiney S.A.; *Int'l*, pg. 1028
SOCIETE DES EMBALLAGES KEYES—See Royal Packaging Industries Van Leer B.V.; *Int'l*, pg. 1146
SOCIETE DES EMULSIONS DU PACIFIQUE—See Lyonnaise des Eaux S.A.; *Int'l*, pg. 824
SOCIETE DES ETABLISSEMENTS SCHIFFERS—See Williams Holdings Plc; *Int'l*, pg. 1500
SOCIETE DES FONDERIES D'USSEL—See Pechiney S.A.; *Int'l*, pg. 1028
SOCIETE DES MAGASINS LOUIS VUITTON-FRANCE—See LVMH Moet Hennessy Louis Vuitton; *Int'l*, pg. 781
SOCIETE DES MINES DE L'AIR (SOMAIR)—See COGEMA - Compagnie Generale des Matieres Nucleaires; *Int'l*, pg. 305
SOCIETE DES MINES DU BOURNEIX—See COGEMA - Compagnie Generale des Matieres Nucleaires; *Int'l*, pg. 305
SOCIETE DES PETROLES SHELL—See Royal Dutch/Shell Group of Companies; *Int'l*, pg. 1138
SOCIETE DES POUDRES ET PRODUITS SPECIAUX HERMILLON—See Pechiney S.A.; *Int'l*, pg. 1029
SOCIETE DES PRODUITS CHIMIQUES DU SIDOBRE-SINNOVA S.A.—See Henkel KGaA; *Int'l*, pg. 614
SOCIETE DES PRODUITS NESTLE S.A.—See Nestle S.A.; *Int'l*, pg. 916
SOCIETE DES SPECIALITES SURGELEES A LANDEVANT—See Grands Moulins de Paris S.A.; *Int'l*, pg. 556
SOCIETE DES TUBES DE VINCEY—See Groupe Usinor; *Int'l*, pg. 571
SOCIETE D'ETUDES ET DE CONSTRUCTIONS ELECTRONIQUES (SECRE)—See Jeumont-Schneider Trenformeteurs; *Int'l*, pg. 706
SOCIETE D'ETUDES ET D'INSTALLATIONS TELPHONIQUES—See Telefonaktiebolaget LM Ericsson; *Int'l*, pg. 1370
SOCIETE D'ETUDIE ET DE DEVELOPMENT DE LA PRESSE PERIODIQUE—See Lagardere Groupe; *Int'l*, pg. 793
SOCIETE D'EXPLOITATION AERONAUTIQUE—See Groupe Air France; *Int'l*, pg. 560
SOCIETE D'EXPLOITATION DES CARRIERES D'YVOIR SA—See Ballast Nedam NV; *Int'l*, pg. 135
SOCIETE D'EXPLOITATION DES MATERIELS MARTIN BAKER SEMMB (SA)—See SNECMA - Societe Nationale d'Etude et de Construction de Moteurs d'Aviation; *Int'l*, pg. 1166
SOCIETE D'EXPLOITATION DES SUPERMARCHES P.G. S.A.—See Etablissements Delhaize Freres Et Cie "Le Lion" S.A.; *Int'l*, pg. 463
SOCIETE D'IMPORTATION ET DISTRIBUTION DES AUTOMOBILES TOYOTA S.A.—See Toyota Motor Corporation; *Int'l*, pg. 1413
SOCIETE D'INVESTISSEMENT ET D'INDUSTRIALISATION DE BELFORT (SYBEL)—See Compagnie des Machines Bull; *Int'l*, pg. 316
S.A. SOCIETE D'OPERATIONS MARITIMES ET FLUVIALES S.O.M.E.F.—See Cockerill Sambre; *Int'l*, pg. 302

SOCIETE EMBALLAGES DES CEVENNES S.A.—See Abitibi-Consolidated Inc.; *Int'l*, pg. 20
SOCIETE ESPACE LEOPOLD S.A.—See Tractebel; pg. 1416
SOCIETE EUROPEENNE DE RENOVATION ET DE REPARATION INFORMATIQUE DE BELFORT (SERRIB)—See Compagnie des Machines Bull; *Int'l*, pg. 316
SOCIETE EUROPEENNE DES CARBURANTS S.A.—See Du Pont (E.I. Du Pont De Nemours & Co.); *U.S. Public*, pg. 533
SOCIETE EUROPEENNE DES MELASSES SA—See Tate & Lyle PLC; *Int'l*, pg. 1357
SOCIETE EUROPEENNE DES PRODUCTS REFRACTAIRES (SEPR)—See Saint-Gobain; *Int'l*, pg. 1175
SOCIETE EUROSUCRE S.N.C.—See Generale Sucriere SNC; *Int'l*, pg. 549
SOCIETE FINANCERE DE GENEVE—See CERUS - Compagnies Europeennes Reunies; *Int'l*, pg. 240
SOCIETE FINANCIERE D'AUTEUIL (SFA)—See Total S.A.; *Int'l*, pg. 1409
SOCIETE FINANCIERE DE DEPOTS ET DE PLACEMENTS (SOFIDEP)—See The Swiss Life/Rentenanstalt Group; *Int'l*, pg. 1332
SOCIETE FINANCIERE DE DEVELOPPEMENT—See CoreStates Financial Corp.; *U.S. Public*, pg. 447
SOCIETE FINANCIERE DES MIROIRS SFM—See Saint-Gobain; *Int'l*, pg. 1177
SOCIETE FINANCIERE ET COMMERCIALE DE CADILLAC—See Warner-Lambert Company; *U.S. Public*, pg. 1739
SOCIETE FINANCIERE ET DE DEVELOPPEMENT ALIMENTAIRE—See Grands Moulins de Paris S.A.; *Int'l*, pg. 557
SOCIETE FINANCIERE POUR LA FRANCE ET LES PAYS D'OUTRE-MER (SOFFO)—See la Compagnie de Suez; *Int'l*, pg. 313
SOCIETE FONCIERE ET FINANCIERE DE LA VILLE-L'EVEGUE—See Compagnie de Suez; *Int'l*, pg. 313
SOCIETE FRANCAISE DE PROTECTION JURIDIQUE (S.F.P.J.)—See Groupe GAN; *Int'l*, pg. 565
SOCIETE FRANCAISE DES AMORTISSEURS DE CARBON S.A.—See General Motors Corporation; *U.S. Public*, pg. 725
SOCIETE FRANCAISE DES ASCENSEURS KONE—See Kone Corporation; *Int'l*, pg. 748
SOCIETE FRANCAISE DES TECHNIQUES LUMMUS—See ABB Asea Brown Boveri (Holding) Ltd.; *Int'l*, pg. 6
SOCIETE FRANCAISE D'ORGANISATION ET DE PARTICIPATIONS—See Generale Sucriere SNC; *Int'l*, pg. 549
SOCIETE FRANCAISE LABORATOIRE ABBOTT—See Abbott Laboratories; *U.S. Public*, pg. 14
SOCIETE FRANCO-SUEDOISE DE MOTEUR'S -PRV—See AB Volvo; *Int'l*, pg. 1476
SOCIETE GABONAISE DE PRODUITS ALIMETAIRES (SOGAPRAL)—See Nestle S.A.; *Int'l*, pg. 922
SOCIETE GENERALE; *Int'l*, pg. 1273
SOCIETE GENERALE DE BANQUES AU SENEGAL—See Generale de Banque S.A.; *Int'l*, pg. 548
SOCIETE GENERALE DE BANQUES EN COTE D'IVOIRE—See Generale de Banque S.A.; *Int'l*, pg. 548
SOCIETE GENERALE DE BANQUES EN GUINEE—See Generale de Banque S.A.; *Int'l*, pg. 548
SOCIETE GENERALE DE FINANCEMENT DU QUEBEC; *Int'l*, pg. 1274
SOCIETE GENERALE DE GRANDES SOURCES BELGES S.A.—See Nestle S.A.; *Int'l*, pg. 922
SOCIETE GENERALE DE GRANDES SOURCES EAUX MINERALES—See Nestle S.A.; *Int'l*, pg. 919
SOCIETE GENERALE D'ENTREPOSAGE ET DE MANUTENTION S.R.L.—See Assicurazioni Generali S.p.A.; *Int'l*, pg. 92
SOCIETE GENERALE DES EAUX MINERALES DE VITTEL—See Nestle S.A.; *Int'l*, pg. 920
SOCIETE GENERALE EQUITIES INTERNATIONAL—See Societe, Generale; *Int'l*, pg. 1274
SOCIETE GENERALE POUR LES TECHNIQUES NOUVELLES (SGN)—See COGEMA - Compagnie Generale des Matieres Nucleaires; *Int'l*, pg. 305
SOCIETE GENERALE POUR LES TECHNIQUES NOUVELLES S.A. (SGN)—See Technip; *Int'l*, pg. 1361
SOCIETE GUADELOUPEENE DE CARTON ONDULE—See International Paper Company; *U.S. Public*, pg. 906
SOCIETE HOTELIERE PARIS VANVES—See Accor S.A.; *Int'l*, pg. 20
SOCIETE IMMOBILIERE DU PARC DE LA NQUE S.A.—See Assicurazioni Generali S.p.A.; *Int'l*, pg. 92
SOCIETE IMMOBILIERE LA MANDRAGORE S.A.—See Liebherr-International AG; *Int'l*, pg. 808
SOCIETE INDUSTRIELLE D'AUTOMATISATION BANCAIRE-SIAB S.A.—See Compagnie des Machines Bull; *Int'l*, pg. 316
SOCIETE INDUSTRIELLE D'AUTOMATISATION BANCAIRE (SIAB)—See Compagnie des Machines Bull; *Int'l*, pg. 316
SOCIETE INDUSTRIELLE DE COMBUSTIBLE NUCLEAIRE (SICN)—See COGEMA - Compagnie Generale des Matieres Nucleaires; *Int'l*, pg. 305
S.A. SOCIETE INDUSTRIELLE DE SOUVIGNY—See Cockerill Sambre; *Int'l*, pg. 302
SOCIETE INDUSTRIELLE DES MINERALS DE L'OUEST (SIMO)—See COGEMA - Compagnie Generale des Matieres Nucleaires; *Int'l*, pg. 305
SOCIETE INDUSTRIELLE D'EXPLORATION DES MOYENS DE TRANSPORT SA—See Brambles Industries Limited; *Int'l*, pg. 212
SOCIETE INDUSTRIELLE DU TITANE S.A.—See Contran Corporation; *U.S. Private*, pg. 271
SOCIETE INDUSTRIELLE ET SALINES DE BAYONNE S.A.—See Solvay S.A.; *Int'l*, pg. 1279

SOCIETE INTERNATIONALE DES HOTELS NOVOTEL—See Accor S.A.; *Int'l*, pg. 21
SOCIETE INTERNATIONALE D'INGENIERIE ET DE MAINTENANCE S.A. (2IM)—See Technip; *Int'l*, pg. 1361
SOCIETE INTERNATIONALE PIRELLI S.A.—See Pirelli S.p.A.; *Int'l*, pg. 1060
SOCIETE IVOIRIENNE DE CABLES (SICABLE)—See Pirelli S.p.A.; *Int'l*, pg. 1060
SOCIETE IVOIRIENNE DE PREFABRIQUES ET D'ACCESSOIRES INDUSTRIELS S.A.—See Nissho Iwai Corporation; *Int'l*, pg. 949
SOCIETE IVOIRIENNE POUR L'APPLICATION DE TECHNOLOGIES—See Telefonaktiebolaget LM Ericsson; *Int'l*, pg. 1370
SOCIETE KENWOOD FRANCE—See Kenwood Appliances Plc; *Int'l*, pg. 730
SOCIETE LIBANAISE DES TELEPHONES ERICSSON S.A.R.L.—See Telefonaktiebolaget LM Ericsson; *Int'l*, pg. 1370
SOCIETE LYONNAISE DES EAUX ET DE L'ECLAIRAGE—See Compagnie de Suez; *Int'l*, pg. 313
SOCIETE MAROCAINE DE MONTAGE ET D'ENTRETIEN DES ASCENSEURS "MOENA" S.A.—See Telefonaktiebolaget LM Ericsson; *Int'l*, pg. 1370
SOCIETE MAROCAINE DES ASCENSEURS SCHINDLER S.A.—See Schindler Holding AG; *Int'l*, pg. 1205
SOCIETE MARTINIQUAISE DE CARTON ONDULE—See International Paper Company; *U.S. Public*, pg. 906
SOCIETE MECANIQUE AUTOMOBILE DE L'EST—See PSA Peugeot Citroen; *Int'l*, pg. 1020
SOCIETE MEDITERRANEENNE D'EMBALLAGES—See International Paper Company; *U.S. Public*, pg. 906
SOCIETE METALLURGIQUE DE GERZAT S.A.; *Int'l*, pg. 1029
SOCIETE METALLURGIQUE DE SAINT-CHELY D'APACHER—See Groupe Usinor; *Int'l*, pg. 571
SOCIETE MINIERE DE BOUGRINE S.A.—See Metallgesellschaft AG; *Int'l*, pg. 862
SOCIETE MONSANTO S.A.—See Monsanto Company; *U.S. Public*, pg. 1126
SOCIETE NANCEIENNE VARIN-BERNIER—See Groupe GAN; *Int'l*, pg. 565
SOCIETE NATIONALE DE TELECOMMUNICATIONS—See Telefonaktiebolaget LM Ericsson; *Int'l*, pg. 1370
SOCIETE NORMANDE DE CARTON ONDULE—See International Paper Company; *U.S. Public*, pg. 906
SOCIETE NOUVELLE CELLONITE—See Borden, Inc.; *U.S. Private*, pg. 160
SOCIETE NOUVELLE DE CHIMIE INDUSTRIELLE (SNCI)—See Novartis AG; *Int'l*, pg. 986
SOCIETE NOUVELLE DES ETABLISSEMENTS MARLY FRERES SA—See Saint-Gobain; *Int'l*, pg. 1172
SOCIETE NOUVELLE DES PASTILLES DE VICHY—See Nestle S.A.; *Int'l*, pg. 919
SOCIETE NOUVELLE JULES PELLERIN SA—See Koninklijke BolsWessanen nv; *Int'l*, pg. 753
SOCIETE PETROLIERE FUCHS E.U.R.L.—See Fuchs Petrolub AG Oel + Chemie; *Int'l*, pg. 519
SOCIETE POUR LA CONVERSION DE L'URANIUM EN METAL ET EN HEXAFLUORURE—See COGEMA - Compagnie Generale des Matieres Nucleaires; *Int'l*, pg. 305
SOCIETE POUR LA VENTE DES PRODUITS CINZANO SA—See Diageo Plc; *Int'l*, pg. 410
SOCIETE POUR LE PERFECTIONNEMENT DES MATERIELS ET EQUIPEMENTS AEROSPATIAUX SA (SOPEMEA)—See SNECMA - Societe Nationale d'Etude et de Construction de Moteurs d'Aviation; *Int'l*, pg. 1165
SOCIETE POUR L'EXPORTATION DE PRODUITS NESTLE S.A.—See Nestle S.A.; *Int'l*, pg. 922
SOCIETE ROANNAISE DES PAPIERS S.A.—See Groupe Saint Louis; *Int'l*, pg. 567
SOCIETE SCHOLTES S.A.—See Merloni Elettrodomestici S.P.A.; *Int'l*, pg. 860
SOCIETE SERVICES KELLY—See Kelly Services, Inc.; *U.S. Public*, pg. 949
SOCIETE SHELL DE TUNISIE—See Royal Dutch/Shell Group of Companies; *Int'l*, pg. 1137
SOCIETE SHELL DES ANTILLES ET DA LA GUYANE FRANCAISES—See Royal Dutch/Shell Group of Companies; *Int'l*, pg. 1142
SOCIETE SHELL DU LAOS—See Royal Dutch/Shell Group of Companies; *Int'l*, pg. 1140
SOCIETE SHELL DU MAROC—See Royal Dutch/Shell Group of Companies; *Int'l*, pg. 1137
SOCIETE SHELL PACIFIQUE—See Royal Dutch/Shell Group of Companies; *Int'l*, pg. 1138
SOCIETE SPECIALISEE DANS LE MATERIEL D'IMPRIMERIE (SSMI)—See Stevens International, Inc.; *U.S. Public*, pg. 1517
SOCIETE SUISSE ACCIDENTS (FRANCE)—See The Swiss Life/Rentenanstalt Group; *Int'l*, pg. 1332
SOCIETE SUISSE-BANQUE (FRANCE)—See The Swiss Life/Rentenanstalt Group; *Int'l*, pg. 1332
SOCIETE SUISSE (FRANCE)—See The Swiss Life/Rentenanstalt Group; *Int'l*, pg. 1332
SOCIETE TOULOUSAINE DE MINOTERIE A REVEL—See Grands Moulins de Paris S.A.; *Int'l*, pg. 557
SOCIETE TUNISIENNE D'ASSURANCES ET DE REASSURANCES—See Allianz Aktiengesellschaft; *Int'l*, pg. 61
SOCIETE VENDINOISE DE DISTRIBUTION—See Etablissements Delhaize Freres Et Cie "Le Lion" S.A.; *Int'l*, pg. 463
SOCIETE VERRIERE D'ATLANTIQUE (SVA)—See Saint-Gobain; *Int'l*, pg. 1172
SOCIETE VERRIERE D'ENCAPSULATION—See Saint-Gobain; *Int'l*, pg. 1172
SOCIETE VERRIERE FRANCAISE (SVF)—See Saint-Gobain; *Int'l*, pg. 1172
SOCIETE ZAIRO-SUISSE DE PRODUITS CHIMIQUES S.A.R.L.—See Novartis AG; *Int'l*, pg. 986

SOCIETY ASSET MGMT., INC.—See Keycorp; *U.S. Public,* pg. 955
SOCIETY BANK, MICHIGAN—See Keycorp; *U.S. Public,* pg. 954
SOCIETY EQUIPMENT LEASING CORPORATION—See Keycorp; *U.S. Public,* pg. 955
SOCIETY FIRST FEDERAL SAVINGS BANK—See Keycorp; *U.S. Public,* pg. 954
SOCIETY FRANCAIS POUR LE DEVELOPMENT DE LA PORCELAINE D'ART—See Tiffany & Co.; *U.S. Public,* pg. 1609
SOCIETY INVESTMENTS, INC.—See Keycorp; *U.S. Public,* pg. 955
SOCIETY MORTGAGE COMPANY—See Keycorp; *U.S. Public,* pg. 955
SOCIETY NATIONAL BANK—See Keycorp; *U.S. Public,* pg. 954
SOCIETY NATIONAL BANK, INDIANA—See Keycorp; *U.S. Public,* pg. 954
SOCIETY NATIONAL TRUST COMPANY—See Keycorp; *U.S. Public,* pg. 955
SOCKALB G.I.E. FRANCE—See Dekalb Genetics Corporation; *U.S. Public,* pg. 493
SOCLA ITALIA (SRL)—See Danfoss A/S; *Int'l,* pg. 378
SOCLA S.A.R.L.—See Danfoss A/S; *Int'l,* pg. 378
SOCO INTERNATIONAL, INC.—See Snyder Oil Corporation; *U.S. Public,* pg. 955
SOCOBA S.R.L.—See Coeclerici Group; *Int'l,* pg. 303
SOCOFIDEX—See The Procter & Gamble Company; *U.S. Public,* pg. 1333
S.A. SOCOMETAUX—See Cockerill Sambre; *Int'l,* pg. 302
SOCOREST—See Sodexho S.A.; *Int'l,* pg. 1275
SOCREMATIC S.A.—See Sodexho S.A.; *Int'l,* pg. 278
SODAK GAMING, INC.; *U.S. Public,* pg. 1482
SODAL—See Groupe Casino; *Int'l,* pg. 563
SODAL CORPORATION—See GIB Group; *Int'l,* pg. 533
SODECA—See Groupe Air France; *Int'l,* pg. 560
SODEGAURA CHEMICAL LTD.—See Tokuyama Corporation; *Int'l,* pg. 1393
SODEM—See Castorama Dubois Investissements S.C.A.; *Int'l,* pg. 276
SODEMA—See G.T.C. Transcontinental Group Ltd.; *Int'l,* pg. 539
SODER S.A.—See Norske Skogindustrier A/S; *Int'l,* pg. 966
SODEREC INTERNATIONAL—See Laporte plc; *Int'l,* pg. 803
SODERHAMNS VERKSTADER AB—See Trelleborg AB; *Int'l,* pg. 1421
SODETAIR—See Groupe Air France; *Int'l,* pg. 560
SODETEG—See Thomson S.A.; *Int'l,* pg. 1382
SODETEG FORMATION—See Thomson S.A.; *Int'l,* pg. 1382
SODETIF—See Groupe Air France; *Int'l,* pg. 560
SODETRANS—See SNCF; *Int'l,* pg. 1165
SODEVA—See Grands Moulins de Paris S.A.; *Int'l,* pg. 557
SODEX—See Sodexho S.A.; *Int'l,* pg. 1275
SODEXHO ALASKA INC.—See Sodexho S.A.; *Int'l,* pg. 1274
SODEXHO ANGOLA S.A.—See Sodexho S.A.; *Int'l,* pg. 1275
SODEXHO A.O.—See Sodexho S.A.; *Int'l,* pg. 1275
SODEXHO ARGENTINA S.A.—See Sodexho S.A.; *Int'l,* pg. 1275
SODEXHO BELGIQUE S.A.—See Sodexho S.A.; *Int'l,* pg. 1275
SODEXHO BENIN—See Sodexho S.A.; *Int'l,* pg. 1275
SODEXHO BRASIL—See Sodexho S.A.; *Int'l,* pg. 1275
SODEXHO CAMEROUN—See Sodexho S.A.; *Int'l,* pg. 1275
SODEXHO CANADA INC.—See Sodexho S.A.; *Int'l,* pg. 1275
SODEXHO CATERING S.R.O.—See Sodexho S.A.; *Int'l,* pg. 1275
SODEXHO CHILE—See Sodexho S.A.; *Int'l,* pg. 1275
SODEXHO COLOMBIA S.A.—See Sodexho S.A.; *Int'l,* pg. 1275
SODEXHO COTE D'IVOIRE—See Sodexho S.A.; *Int'l,* pg. 1275
SODEXHO EIRING—See Sodexho S.A.; *Int'l,* pg. 1275
SODEXHO ESPANA S.A.—See Sodexho S.A.; *Int'l,* pg. 1275
SODEXHO FRANCE ECOLES-UNIVERSITES—See Sodexho S.A.; *Int'l,* pg. 1274
SODEXHO FRANCE ENTREPRISES-ADMINISTRATIONS—See Sodexho S.A.; *Int'l,* pg. 1274
SODEXHO FRANCE HOTELLERIE-SANTE—See Sodexho S.A.; *Int'l,* pg. 1274
SODEXHO GABON—See Sodexho S.A.; *Int'l,* pg. 1275
SODEXHO GHANA LTD.—See Sodexho S.A.; *Int'l,* pg. 1275
SODEXHO GUYANE—See Sodexho S.A.; *Int'l,* pg. 1275
SODEXHO HONG KONG—See Sodexho S.A.; *Int'l,* pg. 1275
SODEXHO INTERNATIONAL—See Sodexho S.A.; *Int'l,* pg. 1275
SODEXHO-ISTEK TOPLU YEMEK—See Sodexho S.A.; *Int'l,* pg. 1275
SODEXHO ITALIA SPA—See Sodexho S.A.; *Int'l,* pg. 1275
SODEXHO KAZAKHSTAN—See Sodexho S.A.; *Int'l,* pg. 1275
SODEXHO KOREA CO., LTD.—See Sodexho S.A.; *Int'l,* pg. 1275
SODEXHO LUXEMBOURG S.A.—See Sodexho S.A.; *Int'l,* pg. 1275
SODEXHO MALAYSIA SDN. BHD.—See Sodexho S.A.; *Int'l,* pg. 1275
SODEXHO MEXICO—See Sodexho S.A.; *Int'l,* pg. 1275
SODEXHO MM CATERING GMBH—See Sodexho S.A.; *Int'l,* pg. 1275
SODEXHO MONACO—See Sodexho S.A.; *Int'l,* pg. 1275
SODEXHO NIGERIA LTD.—See Sodexho S.A.; *Int'l,* pg. 1275
SODEXHO NORTH AFRICA—See Sodexho S.A.; *Int'l,* pg. 1275

SODEXHO NOUVELLE-CALEDONIE—See Sodexho S.A.; *Int'l,* pg. 1275
SODEXHO PASS CHILE-CHEQUE RESTAURANT—See Sodexho S.A.; *Int'l,* pg. 1275
SODEXHO PASS COLOMBIA—See Sodexho S.A.; *Int'l,* pg. 1275
SODEXHO PASS-GASTROTUR—See Sodexho S.A.; *Int'l,* pg. 1275
SODEXHO PASS HUNGARIA—See Sodexho S.A.; *Int'l,* pg. 1275
SODEXHO POLSKA—See Sodexho S.A.; *Int'l,* pg. 1275
SODEXHO POLYNESIE—See Sodexho S.A.; *Int'l,* pg. 1275
SODEXHO RESTORAN SERVISLERI—See Sodexho S.A.; *Int'l,* pg. 1275
SODEXHO S.A.; *Int'l,* pg. 1274
SODEXHO SERVICES (UK) LTD.—See Sodexho S.A.; *Int'l,* pg. 1275
SODEXHO USA—See Sodexho S.A.; *Int'l,* pg. 1274
SODEXHO USA CENTRAL—See Sodexho S.A.; *Int'l,* pg. 1274
SODEXHO USA SOUTH—See Sodexho S.A.; *Int'l,* pg. 1274
SODEXHO USA WEST—See Sodexho S.A.; *Int'l,* pg. 1274
SODEXHO USA-WESTCOAST HEADQUARTERS—See Sodexho S.A.; *Int'l,* pg. 1274
SODEXHO VIETNAM—See Sodexho S.A.; *Int'l,* pg. 1275
SODEXI—See Groupe Air France; *Int'l,* pg. 560
SODIAMEX INTERNATIONAL SA—See Smiths Industries plc; *Int'l,* pg. 1269
SODIEMA S.A.—See Novartis AG; *Int'l,* pg. 986
SODIF—See GIB Group; *Int'l,* pg. 533
SODIGES S.R.L.—See Assicurazioni Generali S.p.A.; *Int'l,* pg. 90
SODILY—See GIB Group; *Int'l,* pg. 534
SODIPAN BIESSARD—See Fort James Corporation; *U.S. Public,* pg. 673
SODIPAN S.A.—See Fort James Corporation; *U.S. Public,* pg. 673
SODIPI(T)—See SHV Holdings N.V.; *Int'l,* pg. 1155
SODIPRA—See Groupe Casino; *Int'l,* pg. 563
SODIPRESS—See Lagardere Groupe; *Int'l,* pg. 796
SODITHERM S.A.—See Hepworth Plc; *Int'l,* pg. 615
SODRA AG—See Sodra Cell AB; *Int'l,* pg. 1276
SODRA CELL AB; *Int'l,* pg. 1275
SODRA CELL A/S—See Sodra Cell AB; *Int'l,* pg. 1276
SODRA CELL GMBH—See Sodra Cell AB; *Int'l,* pg. 1276
SODRA CELL (UK) LTD.—See Sodra Cell AB; *Int'l,* pg. 1276
SODRA FRANCE SA—See Sodra Cell AB; *Int'l,* pg. 1276
SODRA ITALIA SRL—See Sodra Cell AB; *Int'l,* pg. 1276
SODRA NEDERLAND B.V.—See Sodra Cell AB; *Int'l,* pg. 1276
SODRA SKOGAGARNA—See Sodra Cell AB; *Int'l,* pg. 1275
SODRA TIMBER AB—See Sodra Cell AB; *Int'l,* pg. 1276
SODRAS (SOCIETE DJIBOUTIENNE DE RESTAURATION AERONOTIQUE ET DE SERVCES)—See Groupe Air France; *Int'l,* pg. 560
N.V. SOENEN BELEGGINGS-EN KREDIETKANTOOR—See Assicurazioni Generali S.p.A.; *Int'l,* pg. 92
SOFACEL S.A.—See Pechiney S.A.; *Int'l,* pg. 1032
SOFAMOR DANEK GROUP, INC.; *U.S. Public,* pg. 1482
SOFAMOR, S.N.C.—See Sofamor Danek Group, Inc.; *U.S. Public,* pg. 1482
SOFCO-MEAD, INC.; *U.S. Public,* pg. 1012
SOFERAC-FRANCESPAR—See Vector Industries, Ltd.; *Int'l,* pg. 1462
SOFIAS—See Allianz Aktiengesellschaft; *Int'l,* pg. 62
SOFIMADES—See Lagardere Groupe; *Int'l,* pg. 793
SOFIMO—See Lafarge S.A.; *Int'l,* pg. 790
SOFIN - DEALERS, S.A.—See Caja de Madrid Group; *Int'l,* pg. 252
SOFINETI—See Credit Nationale; *Int'l,* pg. 344
SOFINOV—See Caisse de depot et placement du Quebec; *Int'l,* pg. 249
SOFINPAR—See Fiat Auto SpA; *Int'l,* pg. 482
SOFOM—See Compagnie des Machines Bull; *Int'l,* pg. 316
SOFRANCE—See Labinal SA; *Int'l,* pg. 786
SOFREGAZ—See Gaz de France; *Int'l,* pg. 541
SOFRES AM, S.A.—See Telefonica de Espana, S.A.; *Int'l,* pg. 1372
SOFRIMO—See Lagardere Groupe; *Int'l,* pg. 793
SOFT SHEEN PRODUCTS, INC.; *U.S. Private,* pg. 1012
SOFTAL—See Pechiney S.A.; *Int'l,* pg. 1029
SOFTBANK CORPORATION; *Int'l,* pg. 1276
SOFTBANK HOLDINGS INC.—See Softbank Corporation; *Int'l,* pg. 1276
SOFTEC—See Lagardere Groupe; *Int'l,* pg. 793
SOFTECH, INC.; *U.S. Public,* pg. 1482
SOFTECHNICS INC.; *U.S. Private,* pg. 1012
SOFTECHNICS—See SofTechnics Inc.; *U.S. Private,* pg. 1012
SOFTECHNICS RETAIL MANAGEMENT SYSTEMS—See SofTechnics Inc.; *U.S. Private,* pg. 1012
SOFTE-LUXEMBOURG—See IRI Istituto Ricostruzione Industriale; *Int'l,* pg. 656
SOFTIMAGE INC.—See Microsoft Corporation; *U.S. Public,* pg. 1108
SOFTIMAGE S.A.R.L.—See Microsoft Corporation; *U.S. Public,* pg. 1108
SOFTIMAGE S.R.L.—See Microsoft Corporation; *U.S. Public,* pg. 1108
SOFTIMAGE (U.K.) LTD.—See Microsoft Corporation; *U.S. Public,* pg. 1108
SOFTMART, INC.; *U.S. Private,* pg. 1012
SOFTOOL DEVELOPMENT LABORATORY—See Platinum Technology, Inc.; *U.S. Public,* pg. 1309
SOFTRANS INTERNATIONAL, LTD.—See Berlitz International, Inc.; *U.S. Public,* pg. 222
SOFTRIDE, INC.—See Allsop, Inc.; *U.S. Private,* pg. 44
SOFTSOAP ENTERPRISES, INC.—See Colgate-Palmolive Company; *U.S. Public,* pg. 397
SOFTWARE AG; *Int'l,* pg. 1276
SOFTWARE AG AMERICAS, INC.; *U.S. Public,* pg. 1482

SOFTWARE AG ASIA/PACIFIC—See Software AG; *Int'l,* pg. 1277
SOFTWARE INTERFACES DEVELOPMENT LABORATORY—See Platinum Technology, Inc.; *U.S. Public,* pg. 1309
SOFTWARE PLUS INC.; *U.S. Private,* pg. 1012
SOFTWARE PLUS INC.—See Software Plus Inc.; *U.S. Private,* pg. 1012
SOFTWARE PUBLISHING CORPORATION; *U.S. Public,* pg. 1483
SOFTWARE SECURITY, INC.—See Rainbow Technologies, Inc.; *U.S. Public,* pg. 1359
SOFTWARE SPECTRUM, INC.; *U.S. Public,* pg. 1483
SOFTWARE TECHNOLOGY (SINGAPORE) PTE. LTD.—See CSA Holdings Ltd.; *Int'l,* pg. 242
SOFTWARE UNION SYSECA GMBH—See Thomson S.A.; *Int'l,* pg. 1385
SOGEBRA S.A.—See Heineken N.V.; *Int'l,* pg. 608
SOGECRED S.A.—See Banca Nazionale del Lavoro Sj.A.; *Int'l,* pg. 137
SOGEFI INDUSTRIA DE AUTOPECAS LTDA.—See AlliedSignal Inc.; *U.S. Public,* pg. 43
SOGEHO-REUNION—See Hewlett-Packard Company; *U.S. Public,* pg. 823
SOGEI DO BRASIL PUBLICIDADE LTDA.—See Sogei Inc.; *Int'l,* pg. 1277
SOGEI INC.; *Int'l,* pg. 1277
SOGEI INC.—See Sogei Inc.; *Int'l,* pg. 1277
SOGEI INC.-HIROSHIMA BRANCH—See Sogei Inc.; *Int'l,* pg. 1277
SOGEI INC.-KYOTO BRANCH—See Sogei Inc.; *Int'l,* pg. 1277
SOGEI INC.-KYUSHU BRANCH—See Sogei Inc.; *Int'l,* pg. 1277
SOGEI INC.-NAGOYA BRANCH—See Sogei Inc.; *Int'l,* pg. 1277
SOGEI INC.-OSAKA BRANCH—See Sogei Inc.; *Int'l,* pg. 1277
SOGEI INC.-SAPPORO BRANCH—See Sogei Inc.; *Int'l,* pg. 1277
SOGEI INC.-SENDAI BRANCH—See Sogei Inc.; *Int'l,* pg. 1277
SOGELERG—See Alcatel Alsthom Compagnie Generale D'Electricite; *Int'l,* pg. 54
SOGEM—See Union Miniere; *Int'l,* pg. 1442
SOGEMAT PARTICIPATIONS—See Lagardere Groupe; *Int'l,* pg. 793
SOGERAP—See Elf Aquitane; *Int'l,* pg. 445
SOGEREM—See Pechiney S.A.; *Int'l,* pg. 1029
SOGERFIN—See Bank Brussels Lambert; *Int'l,* pg. 147
SOGERISK/EGIS—See SCOR; *Int'l,* pg. 1152
SOGERMA-SOCEA—See Aerospatiale; *Int'l,* pg. 29
SOGES-FIDUCEM S.A.—See Bank Brussels Lambert; *Int'l,* pg. 147
SOGESVAL: SOCIETE EN COURS DE LIQUIDATION—See Club Mediterranee SA; *Int'l,* pg. 298
SOGETI S.A.—See Daimler-Benz Aktiengesellschaft; *Int'l,* pg. 368
SOGIL—See Sodexho S.A.; *Int'l,* pg. 1275
SOGITEC—See Dassault Aviation Group; *Int'l,* pg. 383
SOGRAPH—See Lagardere Groupe; *Int'l,* pg. 793
SOGREAH—See Alcatel Alsthom Compagnie Generale D'Electricite; *Int'l,* pg. 54
SOGRI (SOCIETE GUYANAISE DE RESTAURATION INDUSTRIELLE)—See Groupe Air France; *Int'l,* pg. 560
WALTER SOHN G.M.B.H.—See Assicurazioni Generali S.p.A.; *Int'l,* pg. 89
SOIGESTI—See GIB Group; *Int'l,* pg. 533
SOIL TEQ, INC.—See Ag-Chem Equipment Co., Inc.; *U.S. Public,* pg. 6
SOILAX DE MEXICO S.A.—See Ecolab Inc.; *U.S. Public,* pg. 562
SOILTECH, INC.—See Smith Environmental Technologies Corp.; *U.S. Public,* pg. 1478
SOJE/LONSDALE ADVERTISING INC—See Saatchi & Saatchi Advertising Worldwide; *U.S. Public,* pg. 1422
SOKNABRUKET—See Norske Skogindustrier A/S; *Int'l,* pg. 965
SOKOL & COMPANY; *U.S. Private,* pg. 1012
SOL MELIA; *Int'l,* pg. 1277
SOL MELIA AMERICA—See Sol Melia; *Int'l,* pg. 1277
SOLA BASIC AUSTRALIA LTD.—See General Signal Corporation; *U.S. Public,* pg. 727
SOLAGLAS—See Saint-Gobain; *Int'l,* pg. 1173
SOLAIR, INC.—See Banner Aerospace, Inc.; *U.S. Public,* pg. 187
SOLAR COMMUNICATIONS, INC.; *U.S. Private,* pg. 1012
SOLAR ELECTRONICA—See Hewlett-Packard Company; *U.S. Public,* pg. 823
SOLAR FASHION GMBH & CO. KG—See Hesta Tex AG; *Int'l,* pg. 618
SOLAR PLASTICS-MINNEAPOLIS—See Upper Midwest Industries, Incorporated; *U.S. Private,* pg. 1129
SOLAR PLASTICS-QUAD CITIES—See Upper Midwest Industries, Incorporated; *U.S. Private,* pg. 1129
SOLAR SCHEEPSBOUW B.V.—See Royal Begemann Group; *Int'l,* pg. 1133
SOLAR TURBINES CANADA LTD.—See Caterpillar Inc.; *U.S. Public,* pg. 317
SOLAR TURBINES INCORPORATED—See Caterpillar Inc.; *U.S. Public,* pg. 316
SOLAR TURBINES INTERNATIONAL COMPANY—See Caterpillar Inc.; *U.S. Public,* pg. 316
SOLAR TURBINES S.A.—See Caterpillar Inc.; *U.S. Public,* pg. 317
SOLAREX CORPORATION—See Amoco Corporation; *U.S. Public,* pg. 103
SOLARIUM SYSTEMS, INC.—See Apogee Enterprises, Inc.; *U.S. Public,* pg. 120
SOLARTRON LTD.—See The Roxboro Group PLC; *Int'l,* pg. 1130
SOLARTRON METROLOGY LTD.—See The Roxboro Group PLC; *Int'l,* pg. 1130

Company Index

SOLAS SHIPPING AGENCY S.R.L.—See Coeclerici Group; *Int'l*, pg. 303
SOLE CONTROL—See Recoton Corporation; *U.S. Public*, pg. 1369
SOLECTRON CALIFORNIA CORPORATION—See Solectron Corporation; *U.S. Public*, pg. 1483
SOLECTRON CORPORATION; *U.S. Public*, pg. 1483
SOLECTRON FRANCE, S.A.—See Solectron Corporation; *U.S. Public*, pg. 1483
SOLECTRON GMBH—See Solectron Corporation; *U.S. Public*, pg. 1483
SOLECTRON JAPAN, INC.—See Solectron Corporation; *U.S. Public*, pg. 1483
SOLECTRON SCOTLAND LIMITED—See Solectron Corporation; *U.S. Public*, pg. 1483
SOLECTRON TECHNOLOGY, INC.—See Solectron Corporation; *U.S. Public*, pg. 1483
SOLECTRON TECHNOLOGY SDN. BHD—See Solectron Corporation; *U.S. Public*, pg. 1483
SOLECTRON TECHNOLOGY, SDN. BHD.—See Solectron Corporation; *U.S. Public*, pg. 1483
SOLECTRON TEXAS—See Solectron Corporation; *U.S. Public*, pg. 1483
SOLECTRON WASHINGTON, INC.—See Solectron Corporation; *U.S. Public*, pg. 1483
THE SOLENDER GROUP, INC.; *U.S. Private*, pg. 1012
SOLEX S.A.—See Fiat Auto SpA; *Int'l*, pg. 482
SOLID AB—See Assa Abloy AB; *Int'l*, pg. 17
SOLID STATE DEVICES, INC.; *U.S. Private*, pg. 1012
SOLID WASTE CONTROL CORP.—See Maxon Industries, Inc.; *U.S. Private*, pg. 717
SOLIDEX—See Unitech Industries, Inc.; *U.S. Public*, pg. 1672
SOLIGAR GMBH—See AIC International, Inc.; *U.S. Private*, pg. 6
SOLIGOR U.S.A., INC.—See AIC International, Inc.; *U.S. Private*, pg. 6
SOLION—See Physician Computer Network, Inc.; *U.S. Public*, pg. 1293
SOLIS INDUSTRIAS DE ALIMENTACION S.A.—See Nestle S.A.; *Int'l*, pg. 922
SOLITEC WAFER PROCESSING, INC.; *U.S. Private*, pg. 1013
SOLKATRONIC CHEMICALS, INC.—See Air Products and Chemicals, Inc.; *U.S. Public*, pg. 31
SOLLAC—See Groupe Usinor; *Int'l*, pg. 571
GEORGE SOLLITT CONSTRUCTION; *U.S. Private*, pg. 1013
SOLO CUP COMPANY; *U.S. Private*, pg. 1013
SOLO CUP COMPANY—See Solo Cup Company; *U.S. Private*, pg. 1013
SOLOCO, INC.—See Newpark Resources, Inc.; *U.S. Public*, pg. 1179
SOLODISQUE—See Groupe Casino; *Int'l*, pg. 563
JOHN SOLOMON, INC.; *U.S. Private*, pg. 1013
SOLON MANUFACTURING COMPANY; *U.S. Private*, pg. 1013
SOLON SPRINGS TELEPHONE CO.—See Century Telephone Enterprises, Inc.; *U.S. Public*, pg. 330
SOLPLANT—See Zeneca Group Plc; *Int'l*, pg. 1524
SOLPLANT S.P.A.—See Zeneca Group Plc; *Int'l*, pg. 1526
SOLTECH—See Owens Corning; *U.S. Public*, pg. 1237
SOLTEGJO PORTUGAL—See Accor S.A.; *Int'l*, pg. 21
SOLUS OCEANEERING (MALAYSIA) SDN. BHD.—See Oceaneering International, Inc.; *U.S. Private*, pg. 1211
SOLUSOFT—See Oracle Corporation; *U.S. Public*, pg. 1228
SOLUTIA INC.; *U.S. Public*, pg. 1483
SOLUTIA INC.—See Solutia Inc.; *U.S. Public*, pg. 1484
SOLVAY—See Solvay S.A.; *Int'l*, pg. 1278
SOLVAY ALKALI GMBH—See Solvay S.A.; *Int'l*, pg. 1279
SOLVAY AMERICA INC.—See Solvay S.A.; *Int'l*, pg. 1278
SOLVAY ANIMAL HEALTH, INC.—See Solvay S.A.; *Int'l*, pg. 1277
SOLVAY AUTOMOTIVE—See Solvay S.A.; *Int'l*, pg. 1277
SOLVAY BARIUM STRONTIUM GMBH—See Solvay S.A.; *Int'l*, pg. 1279
SOLVAY CHEMIE B.V.—See Solvay S.A.; *Int'l*, pg. 1279
SOLVAY DE BRASIL S/A—See Solvay S.A.; *Int'l*, pg. 1280
SOLVAY DUPHAR B.V.—See Solvay S.A.; *Int'l*, pg. 1279
SOLVAY ENZYMES GMBH & CO—See Solvay S.A.; *Int'l*, pg. 1277
SOLVAY ENZYMES VERWALTUNGS GMBH—See Solvay S.A.; *Int'l*, pg. 1280
SOLVAY INTEROX—See Solvay S.A.; *Int'l*, pg. 1280
SOLVAY INTEROX AMERICA—See Solvay S.A.; *Int'l*, pg. 1277
SOLVAY INTEROX CHEMICALS PTY. LTD.—See Solvay S.A.; *Int'l*, pg. 1280
SOLVAY INTEROX S.A.—See Solvay S.A.; *Int'l*, pg. 1277
SOLVAY INTEROX S.P.A.—See Solvay S.A.; *Int'l*, pg. 1280
SOLVAY KUNSTSTOFFE GMBH—See Solvay S.A.; *Int'l*, pg. 1280
SOLVAY OSTERREICH AG—See Solvay S.A.; *Int'l*, pg. 1280
SOLVAY PERFORMANCE CHEMICALS—See Solvay S.A.; *Int'l*, pg. 1278
SOLVAY PHARMA DEUTSCHLAND GMBH—See Solvay S.A.; *Int'l*, pg. 1278
SOLVAY PHARMACEUTICALS, INC.—See Solvay S.A.; *Int'l*, pg. 1278
SOLVAY POLYMERS INC.—See Solvay S.A.; *Int'l*, pg. 1278
SOLVAY PORTUGAL PRODUCTOS QUIMICOS S.A.—See Solvay S.A.; *Int'l*, pg. 1277
SOLVAY S.A.; *Int'l*, pg. 1277
SOLVAY SALZ GMBH—See Solvay S.A.; *Int'l*, pg. 1280
SOLVAY SCHWEIZ S.A.—See Solvay S.A.; *Int'l*, pg. 1280
SOLVAY TECHNOLOGIES INC—See Solvay S.A.; *Int'l*, pg. 1277
SOLVAY UMWELTCHEMIE GMBH—See Solvay S.A.; *Int'l*, pg. 1278
SOLVAY VETERINARY LTD.—See Solvay S.A.; *Int'l*, pg. 1280

SOLVENTS & ENVIRONMENTAL SERVICES DIV.—See Detrex Corporation; *U.S. Public*, pg. 502
SOLVIC & CIE S.N.C.—See Solvay S.A.; *Int'l*, pg. 1277
SOLVITOL LIMITED—See Meristem plc; *Int'l*, pg. 858
SOLYMAT—See Saint-Gobain; *Int'l*, pg. 1176
SOMAPEM—See Groupe Casino; *Int'l*, pg. 563
SOMAT CORPORATION—See Premark International, Inc.; *U.S. Public*, pg. 1322
B.V. SOMEF-DAHER ROTTERDAM—See Cockerill Sambre; *Int'l*, pg. 302
SOMEFLOR SOCIETE MACANIQUE DE FLORANGE SA—See Fried. Krupp AG; *Int'l*, pg. 508
SOMERFIELD PLC; *Int'l*, pg. 1280
SOMERFIELD STORES LTD.—See Somerfield PLC; *Int'l*, pg. 1280
THE SOMERSET GROUP, INC.; *U.S. Public*, pg. 1484
SOMERSET KNITTING MILLS—See Phillips-Van Heusen Corporation; *U.S. Public*, pg. 1291
SOMERSET MILL—See Sappi Limited; *Int'l*, pg. 1193
SOMERSET PHARMACEUTICALS INC.—See Mylan Laboratories, Inc.; *U.S. Public*, pg. 1143
SOMERSET PONTIAC GMC INC.; *U.S. Private*, pg. 1013
SOMERSET RAILROAD CORP.—See New York State Electric & Gas Corporation; *U.S. Public*, pg. 1173
SOMERSET REFINERY INC.; *U.S. Private*, pg. 1013
SOMERSET SAVINGS BANK; *U.S. Public*, pg. 1484
SOMERSET STEEL—See Riggs Industries, Inc.; *U.S. Private*, pg. 930
SOMERSET TELEPHONE CO.—See Telephone and Data Systems, Inc.; *U.S. Public*, pg. 1572
SOMERSET WELDING & STEEL, INC.—See Riggs Industries, Inc.; *U.S. Private*, pg. 930
SOMERVILLE LUMBER & SUPPLY CO.—See Payless Cashways, Inc.; *U.S. Public*, pg. 1268
SOMFY S.A.—See Damart S.A.; *Int'l*, pg. 376
SOMFY SYSTEMS INC.—See Damart S.A.; *Int'l*, pg. 376
SOMIR—See Saint-Gobain; *Int'l*, pg. 1172
SOMIR AUTOVER—See Saint-Gobain; *Int'l*, pg. 1172
SOMMER & MACA INDUSTRIES, INC.; *U.S. Private*, pg. 1013
SOMMER METALCRAFT CORPORATION; *U.S. Private*, pg. 1013
SOMOCAR INTERNATIONAL N.V.—See Coeclerici Group; *Int'l*, pg. 304
SOMOCAR OVERSEAS N.V.—See Coeclerici Group; *Int'l*, pg. 304
SOMOCAR S.P.A.—See Coeclerici Group; *Int'l*, pg. 303
SOMOS GMBH—See Filterwerk Mann & Hummel GmbH; *Int'l*, pg. 484
SOMOVES SA—See Adidas AG; *Int'l*, pg. 25
SOMYCEL—See Nestle S.A.; *Int'l*, pg. 919
SON CHIEF ELECTRICS, INC.; *U.S. Private*, pg. 1014
SON CINE OPTIQUE PHOTO S.A.—See Olympus Optical Co., Ltd.; *Int'l*, pg. 1005
SONAT ENERGY SERVICES COMPANY—See Sonat Inc.; *U.S. Public*, pg. 1485
SONAT EXPLORATION COMPANY—See Sonat Inc.; *U.S. Public*, pg. 1485
SONAT EXPLORATION GOM INC.—See Sonat Inc.; *U.S. Public*, pg. 1485
SONAT INC.; *U.S. Public*, pg. 1484
SONATA LABORATORIES LTD.—See Wella Group; *Int'l*, pg. 1490
SONATECH, INC.—See Channel Technologies, Inc.; *U.S. Private*, pg. 229
SONAUTO S.A.—See Porsche AG; *Int'l*, pg. 1063
SONCO STEEL TUBE DIV., FERRUM INC.—See Jannock Limited; *Int'l*, pg. 699
SONDA LTDA.—See Digital Equipment Corporation; *U.S. Public*, pg. 508
SONDAGENS RODIO LDA.—See Empresas ICA Sociedad Controladora S.A.C.V.; *Int'l*, pg. 454
SONDERJYLLANDS ASFALTFABRIK I/S—See Icopal a/s; *Int'l*, pg. 659
SONEE HEAT TREATING—See Karsten Manufacturing Corporation; *U.S. Private*, pg. 608
SONESSON INDRETNING APS—See ACTIVE BioTech AB; *Int'l*, pg. 23
SONESSON INREDNINGAR AB—See ACTIVE BioTech AB; *Int'l*, pg. 23
SONESTA INTERNATIONAL HOTELS CORPORATION; *U.S. Public*, pg. 1485
SONEX—See Telegenix Inc.; *U.S. Private*, pg. 1073
SONGAS—See Transcanada Pipelines Limited; *Int'l*, pg. 1417
SONGGANG ELECTRONICS WIRE WORKS—See Sumitomo Electric Industries, Ltd.; *Int'l*, pg. 1313
SONIC AUTOMOTIVE, INC.; *U.S. Public*, pg. 1485
SONIC CORPORATION; *U.S. Public*, pg. 1485
SONIC COURIERS OF ARIZONA, INC.—See United Parcel Service of America, Inc.; *U.S. Private*, pg. 1123
SONIC INDUSTRIES, INC.—See Sonic Corporation; *U.S. Public*, pg. 1485
SONIC MESSENGER SERVICE—See United Parcel Service of America, Inc.; *U.S. Private*, pg. 1123
SONIC RESTAURANTS, INC.—See Sonic Corporation; *U.S. Public*, pg. 1485
SONIFORM, INC.—See MacAndrews & Forbes Holdings Inc.; *U.S. Private*, pg. 689
SONITEL S.A.—See Telefonaktiebolaget LM Ericsson; *Int'l*, pg. 1370
SONNENBERG MURPHY LEO BURNETT—See Leo Burnett Company, Inc.; *U.S. Private*, pg. 186
SONNEX INVESTMENTS (PTY) LTD—See Barlow Ltd.; *Int'l*, pg. 167
SONNICHSEN & GORTZ BAUGESELLSCHAFT MBH—See Bilfinger + Berger Bauaktiengesellschaft; *Int'l*, pg. 195
SONOCO ADHESIVES DIVISION—See Sonoco Products Company; *U.S. Public*, pg. 1486
SONOCO COLOMBIANA S.A.—See Sonoco Products Company; *U.S. Public*, pg. 1487
SONOCO CONSUMER PACKAGING GROUP—See Sonoco Products Company; *U.S. Public*, pg. 1486

SONOCO CONTAINERS, INC.—See Sonoco Products Company; *U.S. Public*, pg. 1486
SONOCO CONTAINERS OF PUERTO RICO, INC.—See Sonoco Products Company; *U.S. Public*, pg. 1486
SONOCO DE VENEZUELA C.A.—See Sonoco Products Company; *U.S. Public*, pg. 1487
SONOCO DEUTSCHLAND—See Sonoco Products Company; *U.S. Public*, pg. 1487
SONOCO ENGRAPH, INC.—See Sonoco Products Company; *U.S. Public*, pg. 1486
SONOCO ESPANA, S.A.—See Sonoco Products Company; *U.S. Public*, pg. 1487
SONOCO EUROPE, LTD.—See Sonoco Products Company; *U.S. Public*, pg. 1487
SONOCO FIBRE DRUM—See Sonoco Products Company; *U.S. Public*, pg. 1486
SONOCO FOREST PRODUCTS DIVISION—See Sonoco Products Company; *U.S. Public*, pg. 1486
SONOCO GUNTHER, S.A.—See Sonoco Products Company; *U.S. Public*, pg. 1487
SONOCO INDUSTRIAL PRODUCTS DIVISION—See Sonoco Products Company; *U.S. Public*, pg. 1486
SONOCO INTERNATIONAL DIVISION—See Sonoco Products Company; *U.S. Public*, pg. 1486
SONOCO LATIN AMERICA—See Sonoco Products Company; *U.S. Public*, pg. 1487
SONOCO LTD.—See Sonoco Products Company; *U.S. Public*, pg. 1487
SONOCO NEDERLAND B.V.—See Sonoco Products Company; *U.S. Public*, pg. 1487
SONOCO NORGE, A/S—See Sonoco Products Company; *U.S. Public*, pg. 1487
SONOCO OF PUERTO RICO, INC.—See Sonoco Products Company; *U.S. Public*, pg. 1486
SONOCO PACIFIC, LTD.—See Sonoco Products Company; *U.S. Public*, pg. 1487
SONOCO PACIFIC PTY., LTD.—See Sonoco Products Company; *U.S. Public*, pg. 1487
SONOCO PRODUCTS COMPANY; *U.S. Public*, pg. 1485
SONOCO SPECIAL PRODUCTS GROUP—See Sonoco Products Company; *U.S. Public*, pg. 1486
SONOCO U.K. LTD., INC.—See Sonoco Products Company; *U.S. Public*, pg. 1487
SONOFON—See GN Great Nordic Ltd.; *Int'l*, pg. 537
SONOMA MISSION INN & SPA; *U.S. Private*, pg. 1014
SONOMA VALLEY BANK; *U.S. Public*, pg. 1487
SONOPRESS, INC.—See Bertelsmann AG; *Int'l*, pg. 191
SONOTRON HOLDING AG—See IDB Holding Corporation; *Int'l*, pg. 644
SONY (AUSTRALIA) PTY. LIMITED—See Sony Corporation; *Int'l*, pg. 1283
SONY BROADCAST & COMMUNICATIONS LIMITED—See Sony Corporation; *Int'l*, pg. 1283
SONY COMMUNICATIONS PRODUCTS CO.—See Sony Corporation; *Int'l*, pg. 1281
SONY CORPORATION; *Int'l*, pg. 1280
SONY CORPORATION OF HONG KONG LTD.—See Sony Corporation; *Int'l*, pg. 1284
SONY CORPORATION OF PANAMA—See Sony Corporation; *Int'l*, pg. 1284
SONY CORP.-PEOPLES REPUBLIC OF CHINA—See Sony Corporation; *Int'l*, pg. 1283
SONY DEUTSCHLAND GMBH—See Sony Corporation; *Int'l*, pg. 1284
SONY DISPLAY SYSTEMS—See Sony Corporation; *Int'l*, pg. 1284
SONY ELECTRONICS—See Sony Corporation; *Int'l*, pg. 1281
SONY ENGINEERING & MANUFACTURING OF AMERICA—See Sony Corporation; *Int'l*, pg. 1284
SONY GES.M.B.H.—See Sony Corporation; *Int'l*, pg. 1284
SONY INTERNATIONAL (SINGAPORE) PTE. LTD.—See Sony Corporation; *Int'l*, pg. 1284
SONY IRELAND LTD.—See Sony Corporation; *Int'l*, pg. 1284
SONY LOGISTICS SERVICE CO.—See Sony Corporation; *Int'l*, pg. 1284
SONY LOGISTICS (SINGAPORE) PTE. LTD.—See Sony Corporation; *Int'l*, pg. 1284
SONY MAGNETIC PRODUCTS CO.—See Sony Corporation; *Int'l*, pg. 1281
SONY MICROELECTRONICS—See Sony Corporation; *Int'l*, pg. 1284
SONY MUSIC ENTERTAINMENT—See Sony Corporation; *Int'l*, pg. 1284
SONY MUSIC ENTERTAINMENT, INC.—See Sony Corporation; *Int'l*, pg. 1281
SONY MUSIC ENTERTAINMENT (JAPAN) INC.—See Sony Corporation; *Int'l*, pg. 1281
SONY MUSIC ENTERTAINMENT (UK) LIMITED—See Sony Corporation; *Int'l*, pg. 1284
SONY MUSIC INTERNATIONAL LTD.—See Sony Corporation; *Int'l*, pg. 1284
SONY MUSIC, NASHVILLE—See Sony Corporation; *Int'l*, pg. 1284
SONY PICTURES ENTERTAINMENT—See Sony Corporation; *Int'l*, pg. 1281
SONY PICTURES ENTERTAINMENT TELEVISION GROUP—See Sony Corporation; *Int'l*, pg. 1282
SONY PICTURES STUDIOS—See Sony Corporation; *Int'l*, pg. 1281
SONY PRECISION ENGINEERING CENTER (SINGAPORE) PTE. LTD.—See Sony Corporation; *Int'l*, pg. 1284
SONY PROFESSIONAL PRODUCTS CO.—See Sony Corporation; *Int'l*, pg. 1281
SONY SERVICE CO.—See Sony Corporation; *Int'l*, pg. 1284
SONY SINGAPORE PTE. LTD.—See Sony Corporation; *Int'l*, pg. 1284
SONY/TEKTRONIX CORPORATION—See Tektronix, Inc.; *U.S. Public*, pg. 1568
SONY TRANS COM SYSTEMS INC.—See Sony Corporation; *Int'l*, pg. 1281
SONY (U.K.) LTD.—See Sony Corporation; *Int'l*, pg. 1284

MASTER INDEX TO COMPANY NAMES SOUTHEASTERN

Company Index

SONY U.S.A.—See Sony Corporation; *Int'l*, pg. 1281
SONY VIDEO TAIWAN CO. LTD.—See Sony Corporation; *Int'l*, pg. 1284
SONY-WEGA PRODUKTIONS GMBH—See Sony Corporation; *Int'l*, pg. 1284
SOO LINE MILLS LIMITED—See George Weston Limited; *Int'l*, pg. 1495
SOONER PIPE & SUPPLY CORP.; *U.S. Private*, pg. 1014
SOPADE S.A.—See Tractebel; *Int'l*, pg. 1416
SOPAR PHARMA GMBH—See Ruetgers A.G.; *Int'l*, pg. 1148
SOPARCO—See ETEX; *Int'l*, pg. 430
SOPASIN (SOCIETA DI PARTECIPAZIONE SISTEMI INFORMATIVI) S.P.A.—See Compagnie des Machines Bull; *Int'l*, pg. 318
SOPE CREEK—See Superior Surgical Mfg. Co., Inc.; *U.S. Public*, pg. 1539
SOPHIE MAE DIVISION—See Gilliam Candy Brands; *U.S. Private*, pg. 454
SOPHISTICATED PRODUCTS DIV.—See Nippon Kayaku Co. Ltd.; *Int'l*, pg. 934
SOPHUS BERENDSEN A/S; *Int'l*, pg. 1284
SOPLACAS LDA—See Scancem AB; *Int'l*, pg. 1199
SOPLACHIM S.A.—See Solvay S.A.; *Int'l*, pg. 1280
SOPOMA S.R.L.—See BASF AG; *Int'l*, pg. 109
SOPORCEL-SOCIEDADE PORTUGUESA DE CELULOSE S.A.—See Groupe Saint Louis; *Int'l*, pg. 567
SOPRA BULL—See Compagnie des Machines Bull; *Int'l*, pg. 317
SOPRA S.A.—See Philip Morris Companies Inc.; *U.S. Public*, pg. 1288
SOPRADIS—See Groupe Casino; *Int'l*, pg. 563
SOPRANO S.A.—See Alcatel Alsthom Compagnie Generale D'Electricite; *Int'l*, pg. 53
SOPREDIS—See Lagardere Groupe; *Int'l*, pg. 793
SOPRELEC SA—See Laporte plc; *Int'l*, pg. 803
N.V. SOPRODAL—See Nutricia BV; *Int'l*, pg. 992
SOPROVER—See Saint-Gobain; *Int'l*, pg. 1172
SOPUR MEDIZINTECHNIK GMBH—See Sunrise Medical, Inc.; *U.S. Public*, pg. 1536
SOQUIMICA—See Hewlett-Packard Company; *U.S. Public*, pg. 823
SOR-NORGE ALUMINIUM A.S.—See Norsk Hydro a.s; *Int'l*, *pg. 961*
SORAK CO., LTD.—See KOHAP Group; *Int'l*, pg. 743
SORAL - SOR-NORGE ALUMINUM A/S—See Alusuisse-Lonza Holding Ltd.; *Int'l*, pg. 69
SORBEE INTERNATIONAL LTD.; *U.S. Private*, pg. 1014
SORBUS AG—See Bell Atlantic Corporation; *U.S. Public*, pg. 204
SORBUS B.V.—See Bell Atlantic Corporation; *U.S. Public*, pg. 204
SORBUS CANADA LIMITED—See Bell Atlantic Corporation; *U.S. Public*, pg. 204
SORBUS EUROPE, LTD.—See Bell Atlantic Corporation; *U.S. Public*, pg. 204
SORBUS FRANCE S.A.—See Bell Atlantic Corporation; *U.S. Public*, pg. 204
SORBUS GES.MBH—See Bell Atlantic Corporation; *U.S. Public*, pg. 204
SORBUS GMBH—See Bell Atlantic Corporation; *U.S. Public*, pg. 204
SORBUS ITALIA SPA—See Bell Atlantic Corporation; *U.S. Public*, pg. 204
SORBUS (U.K.) LIMITED—See Bell Atlantic Corporation; *U.S. Public*, pg. 204
SORD COMPUTER CORPORATION—See Toshiba Corporation; *Int'l*, pg. 1403
SORDONI SKANSKA CONSTRUCTION CO.—See Skanska AB; *Int'l*, pg. 1261
SOREL FORGE INC.—See Slater Industries Inc.; *Int'l*, pg. 1262
SOREMAP HENKEL GV S.A.—See Henkel KGaA; *Int'l*, pg. 614
SOREN BERGGREEN & CO. A/S—See Metsa-Serla Corporation; *Int'l*, pg. 864
SOREN BERNER A/S—See Berner Ltd.; *Int'l*, pg. 189
SORENOLIF SA—See Accor S.A.; *Int'l*, pg. 21
SORENSENS LIVS AB—See Nestle S.A.; *Int'l*, pg. 922
SORESO—See Groupe Casino; *Int'l*, pg. 563
SOREVCO INC.—See DoFasco, Inc.; *Int'l*, pg. 414
THE SORG PAPER CO.—See Wausau-Mosinee Paper Corporation; *U.S. Public*, pg. 1747
SORI (SOCIETE DE RESTAURATION INDUSTRIELLE)—See Groupe Air France; *Int'l*, pg. 560
SORIN BIOMEDICA—See Fiat Auto SpA; *Int'l*, pg. 483
SORIN BIOMEDICA AS—See Fiat Auto SpA; *Int'l*, pg. 483
SORIN BIOMEDICA LTD.—See Fiat Auto SpA; *Int'l*, pg. 483
SORIN BIOMEDICA OY—See Fiat Auto SpA; *Int'l*, pg. 483
SORIN BIOMEDICA S.P.A.—See Fiat Auto SpA; *Int'l*, pg. 483
SORMEL—See Lagardere Groupe; *Int'l*, pg. 793
SORRENTO CHEESE COMPANY, INC.—See Compagnie Laitiere BESNIER; *Int'l*, pg. 323
SOSBAM S.R.L.—See Coeclerici Group; *Int'l*, pg. 303
SOSS OF SINGAPORE PTE. LTD.—See United Dominion Industries, Ltd.; *U.S. Public*, pg. 1677
SOTAIR ITALIA—See Groupe Air France; *Int'l*, pg. 560
SOTERRA INC.—See Greif Brothers Corporation; *U.S. Public*, pg. 763
SOTEXO—See Bertrand Faure; *Int'l*, pg. 192
SOTHEBY'S ASIA—See Sotheby's Holdings Inc.; *U.S. Public*, pg. 1487
SOTHEBY'S EUROPE—See Sotheby's Holdings Inc.; *U.S. Public*, pg. 1487
SOTHEBY'S FINANCIAL SERVICES, INC.—See Sotheby's Holdings Inc.; *U.S. Public*, pg. 1487
SOTHEBY'S HOLDINGS INC.; *U.S. Public*, pg. 1487
SOTHEBY'S INC.—See Sotheby's Holdings Inc.; *U.S. Public*, pg. 1487
SOTHEBY'S INTERNATIONAL REALTY—See Sotheby's Holdings Inc.; *U.S. Public*, pg. 1487
SOTRAB—See SNCF; *Int'l*, pg. 1165
SOTRIMLO S.A.—See Assicurazioni Generali S.p.A.; *Int'l*, pg. 92
SOTUVES SA—See Adidas AG; *Int'l*, pg. 25
SOUND ADVICE, INC.; *U.S. Public*, pg. 1488
SOUND BELL ENTERPRISES CO. LTD.—See GESTRA GmbH; *Int'l*, pg. 550
SOUND ELEVATOR—See Dover Corporation; *U.S. Public*, pg. 521
SOUND QUEST—See Recoton Corporation; *U.S. Public*, pg. 1369
SOUNDCRAFT ELECTRONICS, LTD—See Harman International Industries, Inc.; *U.S. Public*, pg. 787
SOUNDESIGN CORPORATION HONG KONG LTD.—See SDI Technologies Inc.; *U.S. Private*, pg. 956
SOUNDESIGN CORPORATION JAPAN LTD.—See SDI Technologies Inc.; *U.S. Private*, pg. 956
SOURCE CAPITAL, INC.; *U.S. Public*, pg. 1488
SOURCE DU VAL SAINT LAMBERT—See Nestle S.A.; *Int'l*, pg. 919
SOURCE SERVICES CORPORATION; *U.S. Public*, pg. 1488
SOURDILLON SA—See Delta plc; *Int'l*, pg. 391
SOURDOUGH FUEL, INC.—See Arctic Slope Regional Corporation; *U.S. Private*, pg. 80
SOUS GROUPE CASTORAMA—See Castorama Dubois Investissements S.C.A.; *Int'l*, pg. 275
SOUTH AFRICAN AIRWAYS—See Transnet Ltd.; *Int'l*, pg. 1417
THE SOUTH AFRICAN BANK OF ATHENS LTD.—See National Bank of Greece S.A.; *Int'l*, pg. 907
SOUTH AFRICAN BREWERIES, LTD.; *Int'l*, pg. 1286
SOUTH AFRICAN HOSIERY COMPANY LTD.—See Sara Lee Corporation; *U.S. Public*, pg. 1435
SOUTH AFRICAN MINING COMPANY (SAPCO)—See Del Monte Royal Corporation; *Int'l*, pg. 388
SOUTH AFRICAN MOTOR CORPORATION PROPRIETARY LIMITED (SAMCOR)—See Anglo American Corporation of South Africa Limited; *Int'l*, pg. 76
SOUTH ATLANTIC EQUIPMENT, INC.—See The Dickerson Group, Inc.; *U.S. Private*, pg. 331
SOUTH ATLANTIC TRI-CITY—See Tri-City Electrical Contractors Inc.; *U.S. Private*, pg. 1100
SOUTH BAY GALLERIA, INC.—See Forest City Enterprises, Inc.; *U.S. Public*, pg. 669
SOUTH BAY TECH CENTER ASSOCIATES—See Cigna Corp.; *U.S. Public*, pg. 365
SOUTH BELOIT WATER, GAS & ELECTRIC CO.—See WPL Holdings, Inc.; *U.S. Public*, pg. 1728
SOUTH BEND PERISHABLES DIVISION—See Roundy's, Inc.; *U.S. Private*, pg. 948
SOUTH BEND PLASTICS, INC.; *U.S. Private*, pg. 1014
SOUTH BEND SCRAP & PROCESSING—See Sturgis Iron & Metal Company, Inc.; *U.S. Private*, pg. 1048
SOUTH BEND STAMPING; *U.S. Private*, pg. 1014
SOUTH CAROLINA FUEL CO., INC.—See SCANA Corporation; *U.S. Public*, pg. 1436
SOUTH CAROLINA GENERATING CO., INC.—See SCANA Corporation; *U.S. Public*, pg. 1436
SOUTH CAROLINA INSURANCE COMPANY—See The Seibels Bruce Group, Inc.; *U.S. Public*, pg. 1453
SOUTH CAROLINA MENTOR, INC.—See Magellan Health Services, Inc.; *U.S. Public*, pg. 1036
SOUTH CAROLINA NATIONAL CORPORATION—See Wachovia Corporation; *U.S. Public*, pg. 1730
SOUTH CAROLINA PIPELINE CORPORATION—See SCANA Corporation; *U.S. Public*, pg. 1436
SOUTH CAROLINA STEEL—See Commercial Metals Company; *U.S. Public*, pg. 412
SOUTH CAROLINA WSMP, INC. (SOUTH CAROLINA)—See WSMP, Inc.; *U.S. Public*, pg. 1729
SOUTH CENTRAL CO-OP; *U.S. Private*, pg. 1014
SOUTH CENTRAL CORRECTIONAL CENTER—See Corrections Corporation of America; *U.S. Public*, pg. 451
SOUTH CENTRAL FLORIDA EXPRESS, INC.—See United States Sugar Corporation; *U.S. Private*, pg. 1126
SOUTH CHARLESTON SEWAGE TREATMENT CO.—See Union Carbide Corporation; *U.S. Public*, pg. 1667
SOUTH CHARLESTON STAMPING & MANUFACTURING—See Stamford Capital; *U.S. Private*, pg. 1030
SOUTH CHICAGO RAILROAD COMPANY—See Illinois Central Corporation; *U.S. Public*, pg. 865
SOUTH CHINA INTERNATIONAL LEASING COMPANY LIMITED—See The Hokkaido Takushoku Bank, Ltd.; *Int'l*, pg. 627
THE SOUTH CHINA MORNING POST, LIMITED—See The News Corporation Limited; *Int'l*, pg. 925
SOUTH COAST SHIPPING COMPANY LIMITED—See RMC Group p.l.c.; *Int'l*, pg. 1079
SOUTH COUNTY GAS COMPANY—See Providence Energy Corporation; *U.S. Public*, pg. 1337
SOUTH COUNTY HEALTH CARE SERVICES—See Integrated Health Services, Inc.; *U.S. Public*, pg. 885
SOUTH COUNTY PRIVATE DUTY AGENCY, INC.—See Integrated Health Services, Inc.; *U.S. Public*, pg. 885
SOUTH DAYTONA MFG. DIVISION—See R.R. Donnelley & Sons Company; *U.S. Public*, pg. 518
SOUTH DEKALB—See The Rouse Company; *U.S. Public*, pg. 1408
SOUTH EAST ASIA COMPANIES—See Delta plc; *Int'l*, pg. 390
SOUTH EAST ASIA FERTILIZER COMP. (PTE.) LTD. (SEAFCO)—See BASF AG; *Int'l*, pg. 109
SOUTH EAST ASIA PETROLEUM EXPLORATION CO., LTD.—See Mitsui & Co., Ltd.; *Int'l*, pg. 877
SOUTH-EAST ASIAN PUBLISHING SERVICES UNIT—See Oxford University Press; *Int'l*, pg. 1019
SOUTH EASTERN COALFIELDS LIMITED—See Coal India Limited; *Int'l*, pg. 299
SOUTH FLORIDA LAND DIVISION—See U.S. Home Corporation; *U.S. Public*, pg. 1683
SOUTH FLORIDA RESIDENTIAL MORTGAGE CO.—See Oriole Homes Corp.; *U.S. Public*, pg. 1231
SOUTH FLORIDA TEST SERVICE—See Atlas Electric Devices Co.; *U.S. Private*, pg. 96
SOUTH FRESH FARMS; *U.S. Private*, pg. 1014
SOUTH HAVEN COIL INC.—See Humphrey Products Company; *U.S. Private*, pg. 548
SOUTH HAVEN MANOR NURSING HOME—See Paragon Health Network, Inc.; *U.S. Public*, pg. 1257
SOUTH JERSEY ENERGY CO.—See South Jersey Industries, Inc.; *U.S. Public*, pg. 1488
SOUTH JERSEY GAS CO.—See South Jersey Industries, Inc.; *U.S. Public*, pg. 1488
SOUTH JERSEY INDUSTRIES, INC.; *U.S. Public*, pg. 1488
SOUTH PACIFIC ALUMINUM—See International Paper Company; *U.S. Public*, pg. 905
SOUTH PACIFIC MERCHANT FINANCE LTD.—See Lloyds TSB Group PLC; *Int'l*, pg. 814
SOUTH PACIFIC REGIONAL MISSION—See Asian Development Bank; *Int'l*, pg. 89
SOUTH PACIFIC TYRES—See Pacific Dunlop Limited; *Int'l*, *pg. 1021*
SOUTH PADRE LAND CO.—See American General Corporation; *U.S. Public*, pg. 77
SOUTH PASADENA ASSOCIATES—See Cigna Corp.; *U.S. Public*, pg. 365
SOUTH SEAS DRILLING CO.—See Kuwait Petroleum Corporation; *Int'l*, pg. 766
SOUTH SEATTLE AUTO AUCTION—See Cox Enterprises, Inc.; *U.S. Private*, pg. 283
SOUTH SHORE HARBOUR DEVELOPMENT—See American National Insurance Company; *U.S. Public*, pg. 88
SOUTH TRUST BANK OF GEORGIA—See SouthTrust Corporation; *U.S. Public*, pg. 1492
SOUTH VALLEY NATIONAL BANK—See Pacific Capital Bancorp; *U.S. Public*, pg. 1248
SOUTH WEST WATER PLC; *Int'l*, pg. 1287
SOUTH WESTERN ONTARIO BROADCASTING INCORPORATED—See Baton Broadcasting Incorporated; *Int'l*, pg. 171
SOUTH-WESTERN PUBLISHING COMPANY—See The Thomson Corporation; *U.S. Public*, pg. 1600
THE SOUTH WESTERN RAIL ROAD CO.—See Norfolk Southern Corporation; *U.S. Public*, pg. 1191
SOUTHAM INC.—See Hollinger Inc.; *Int'l*, pg. 631
SOUTHAM MAGAZINE AND INFORMATION GROUP—See Hollinger Inc.; *Int'l*, pg. 631
SOUTHAM NEWS SERVICE—See Hollinger Inc.; *Int'l*, pg. 631
SOUTHAMPTON ASSURANCE COMPANY OF ZIMBABWE LIMITED—See Anglo American Corporation of South Africa Limited; *Int'l*, pg. 77
SOUTHBEND—See The Middleby Corporation; *U.S. Public*, pg. 1110
SOUTHCHEM; *U.S. Private*, pg. 1014
SOUTHCO DISTRIBUTING COMPANY; *U.S. Private*, pg. 1014
SOUTHCO. INC.; *U.S. Private*, pg. 1014
SOUTHCO INTERNATIONAL—See SouthCo. Inc.; *U.S. Private*, pg. 1015
SOUTHCORP APPLIANCE GROUP—See Southcorp Holdings Ltd.; *Int'l*, pg. 1287
SOUTHCORP HOLDINGS—See Southcorp Holdings Ltd.; *Int'l*, pg. 1287
SOUTHCORP HOLDINGS LTD.-MELBOURNE—See Southcorp Holdings Ltd.; *Int'l*, pg. 1287
SOUTHCORP HOLDINGS LTD.; *Int'l*, pg. 1287
SOUTHCORP PACKAGING USA, INC.—See Southcorp Holdings Ltd.; *Int'l*, pg. 1287
SOUTHCORP U.S.A., INC.—See Southcorp Holdings Ltd.; *Int'l*, pg. 1287
SOUTHCORP-WINE GROUP—See Southcorp Holdings Ltd.; *Int'l*, pg. 1287
SOUTHCORP WINES ASIA—See Southcorp Holdings Ltd.; *Int'l*, pg. 1287
SOUTHCORP WINES EUROPE—See Southcorp Holdings Ltd.; *Int'l*, pg. 1287
SOUTHCORP WINES NEW ZEALAND—See Southcorp Holdings Ltd.; *Int'l*, pg. 1287
SOUTHCORP WINES USA/CANADA—See Southcorp Holdings Ltd.; *Int'l*, pg. 1287
SOUTHDOWN CEMENT GROUP—See Southdown, Inc.; *U.S. Public*, pg. 1489
SOUTHDOWN, INC.; *U.S. Public*, pg. 1488
SOUTHEAST BEHAVIORAL SYSTEMS, INC.—See Magellan Health Services, Inc.; *U.S. Public*, pg. 1036
SOUTHEAST CORRECT CRAFT, INC.—See Correct Craft, Inc.; *U.S. Private*, pg. 277
SOUTHEAST FIRE SPRINKLER COMPANY—See S.I. Goldman Co.; *U.S. Private*, pg. 462
SOUTHEAST KINKO'S, INC.—See Kinko's Corporation; *U.S. Private*, pg. 622
SOUTHEAST MARKETING DIV.—See CUNA Mutual Insurance Society; *U.S. Private*, pg. 296
SOUTHEAST POWER CORPORATION—See The Goldfield Corporation; *U.S. Public*, pg. 750
SOUTHEAST PROPERTIES HOLDING CORPORATION, INC.—See Koger Equity Inc.; *U.S. Public*, pg. 965
SOUTHEAST REGION—See Federal Signal Corporation; *U.S. Public*, pg. 617
SOUTHEAST REGION—See MCI Communications Corp.; *U.S. Public*, pg. 1024
SOUTHEASTERN BONDED WAREHOUSES, INC.—See GATX Corporation; *U.S. Public*, pg. 691
SOUTHEASTERN COATED PRODUCTS—See Consolidated Systems, Inc.; *U.S. Private*, pg. 266
SOUTHEASTERN DEVELOPMENT COMPANY—See Southeastern Michigan Gas Enterprises, Inc.; *U.S. Public*, pg. 1489
SOUTHEASTERN FINANCIAL SERVICES, INC.—See Southeastern Michigan Gas Enterprises, Inc.; *U.S. Public*, pg. 1489

SOUTHEASTERN
DIRECTORY OF CORPORATE AFFILIATIONS
Company Index

SOUTHEASTERN FREIGHT LINES, INC.; *U.S. Private*, pg. 1015
SOUTHEASTERN MEDEQUIP, INC.; *U.S. Private*, pg. 1015
SOUTHEASTERN METAL PROCESSING—See Olympic Steel Inc.; *U.S. Public*, pg. 1221
SOUTHEASTERN METALS MANUFACTURING CO. INC—See Gibraltar Steel Corp.; *U.S. Public*, pg. 742
SOUTHEASTERN MICHIGAN GAS COMPANY—See Southeastern Michigan Gas Enterprises, Inc.; *U.S. Public*, pg. 1489
SOUTHEASTERN MICHIGAN GAS ENTERPRISES, INC.; *U.S. Public*, pg. 1489
SOUTHEASTERN NEWSPAPERS CORPORATION—See Shivers Trading & Operating Co.; *U.S. Private*, pg. 996
SOUTHEASTERN PACKAGING COMPANY—See Greif Brothers Corporation; *U.S. Public*, pg. 764
SOUTHEASTERN PENNSYLVANIA TRANSPORTATION AUTHORITY; *U.S. Private*, pg. 1015
SOUTHEASTERN PRINTING COMPANY INC.—See MasTec, Inc.; *U.S. Public*, pg. 1056
SOUTHEASTERN REALTY GROUP INC.; *U.S. Private*, pg. 1015
SOUTHEASTERN STEEL COMPANY; *U.S. Private*, pg. 1015
SOUTHEASTERN TEXTILE CO. DIV.—See Best Manufacturing, Inc.; *U.S. Private*, pg. 140
SOUTHEASTERN WISCONSIN PRODUCTS CO., INC.—See Campbell Soup Company; *U.S. Public*, pg. 299
SOUTHERN ACCENTS, INC.—See Time Warner Inc.; *U.S. Public*, pg. 1613
SOUTHERN AGRICULTURAL INSECTICIDES, INC.; *U.S. Private*, pg. 1015
SOUTHERN ALLOY OF AMERICA—See Metals USA, Inc.; *U.S. Public*, pg. 1101
SOUTHERN APPAREL CORPORATION; *U.S. Private*, pg. 1015
SOUTHERN BACK & ORTHOPAEDIC CENTER-DUNWOODY—See Vencor, Inc.; *U.S. Public*, pg. 1716
SOUTHERN BAG CORPORATION; *U.S. Private*, pg. 1015
SOUTHERN BEAUTY ENTERPRISES—See Beauty Enterprises Inc.; *U.S. Private*, pg. 128
SOUTHERN BELLE DAIRY COMPANY; *U.S. Private*, pg. 1015
SOUTHERN BEVERAGE PACKERS, INC.; *U.S. Private*, pg. 1015
SOUTHERN BRANCH—See Deutsche Babcock AG; *Int'l*, pg. 401
SOUTHERN CALIFORNIA AIR GAS—See Airgas, Inc.; *U.S. Public*, pg. 33
SOUTHERN CALIFORNIA AUTO AUCTION—See Cox Enterprises, Inc.; *U.S. Private*, pg. 282
SOUTHERN CALIFORNIA AUTO GROUP; *U.S. Private*, pg. 1016
SOUTHERN CALIFORNIA BANK—See Western Bancorp; *U.S. Public*, pg. 1758
SOUTHERN CALIFORNIA EDISON COMPANY—See Edison International; *U.S. Public*, pg. 564
SOUTHERN CALIFORNIA GAS CO.—See Pacific Enterprises; *U.S. Public*, pg. 1249
SOUTHERN CALIFORNIA GAS TOWER—See Pacific Enterprises; *U.S. Public*, pg. 1249
SOUTHERN CALIFORNIA SERVICE CENTER—See Pace Analytical Services; *U.S. Private*, pg. 829
SOUTHERN CALIFORNIA WATER COMPANY; *U.S. Public*, pg. 1489
SOUTHERN CLAY PRODUCTS INC.—See Laporte plc; *Int'l*, pg. 802
SOUTHERN COLORADO HEALTH PLAN—See Foundation Health Systems, Inc.; *U.S. Public*, pg. 678
SOUTHERN COMMUNICATIONS SERVICES—See Southern Company; *U.S. Public*, pg. 1490
SOUTHERN COMPANY; *U.S. Public*, pg. 1489
SOUTHERN COMPANY SERVICES, INC.—See Southern Company; *U.S. Public*, pg. 1490
THE SOUTHERN CONNECTICUT GAS COMPANY—See Connecticut Energy Corporation; *U.S. Public*, pg. 431
SOUTHERN CONTAINER CORPORATION; *U.S. Private*, pg. 1016
SOUTHERN COTTON OIL CO., INC.—See Archer Daniels Midland Company (ADM); *U.S. Public*, pg. 128
SOUTHERN COUNTY MUTUAL INSURANCE COMPANY—See Credit Suisse Group; *Int'l*, pg. 346
SOUTHERN CROSS INVESTMENT CO.—See Imetal; *Int'l*, pg. 662
SOUTHERN CUBIC PTY. LTD.—See Cubic Corporation; *U.S. Public*, pg. 466
SOUTHERN DEVELOPMENT AND INVESTMENT GROUP—See Southern Company; *U.S. Public*, pg. 1490
SOUTHERN DEVELOPMENT CO.—See Kansas City Southern Industries, Inc.; *U.S. Public*, pg. 944
SOUTHERN DIESEL SYSTEMS, INC.—See Twin Disc, Incorporated; *U.S. Public*, pg. 1646
SOUTHERN DIVISION—See Pameco Corp.; *U.S. Public*, pg. 1255
SOUTHERN ELECTRIC GENERATING CO.—See Southern Company; *U.S. Public*, pg. 1490
SOUTHERN ELECTRIC SUPPLY CO., INC.—See Rexel, S.A.; *Int'l*, pg. 1107
SOUTHERN ELECTRONICS CORPORATION; *U.S. Public*, pg. 1490
SOUTHERN ELECTRONICS DISTRIBUTORS INTERNATIONAL—See Southern Electronics Corporation; *U.S. Public*, pg. 1490
SOUTHERN FARM BUREAU CASUALTY INSURANCE COMPANY; *U.S. Private*, pg. 1016
SOUTHERN FINEBLANKING—See Klockner-Werke AG; *Int'l*, pg. 737
SOUTHERN FOODS GROUP; *U.S. Private*, pg. 1016
SOUTHERN FOODS, INC.; *U.S. Private*, pg. 1016
SOUTHERN FROZEN FOODS—See Pro-Fac Cooperative, Inc.; *U.S. Private*, pg. 887
SOUTHERN GAGE INC.—See Alpha Q, Inc.; *U.S. Private*, pg. 45
SOUTHERN GARDEN CITRUS PROCESSING—See United States Sugar Corporation; *U.S. Private*, pg. 1126
SOUTHERN GAS COMPANY—See Bell Atlantic Corporation; *U.S. Public*, pg. 203
SOUTHERN GOLF DISTRIBUTORS, INC.—See Putt Putt Golf Courses of America, Inc.; *U.S. Private*, pg. 896
SOUTHERN GRAPHICS SYSTEMS—See Reynolds Metals Company; *U.S. Public*, pg. 1386
SOUTHERN GRAPHITE SERVICES LIMITED—See Morgan Crucible Co. Plc; *Int'l*, pg. 891
SOUTHERN GROUP, INC.—See Kansas City Southern Industries, Inc.; *U.S. Public*, pg. 944
SOUTHERN GUARANTY INSURANCE COMPANIES—See Credit Suisse Group; *Int'l*, pg. 346
SOUTHERN HARDWOOD SAWMILL—See Georgia-Pacific Corporation; *U.S. Public*, pg. 738
SOUTHERN HEALTH SERVICES, INC.—See Coventry Corporation; *U.S. Public*, pg. 454
SOUTHERN HOSPITALITY CORPORATION—See Davco Restaurants Inc.; *U.S. Public*, pg. 488
SOUTHERN ILLINOIS AND MISSOURI BRIDGE CO.—See Union Pacific Corporation; *U.S. Public*, pg. 1668
SOUTHERN ILLINOIS RIVERBOAT CASINO CRUISE, INC.—See Players International, Inc.; *U.S. Public*, pg. 1310
SOUTHERN ILLINOISAN—See Lee Enterprises, Incorporated; *U.S. Public*, pg. 984
SOUTHERN INDIANA GAS & ELECTRIC CO.—See SIGCORP, Inc.; *U.S. Public*, pg. 1471
SOUTHERN INDIANA MINERALS, INC.—See SIGCORP, Inc.; *U.S. Public*, pg. 1471
SOUTHERN INDIANA PROPERTIES, INC.—See SIGCORP, Inc.; *U.S. Public*, pg. 1471
SOUTHERN INFORMATION SYSTEMS, INC.—See Northern Telecom Limited; *Int'l*, pg. 970
SOUTHERN INSTRUMENTS, INC.—See Jacobs Engineering Group Inc.; *U.S. Public*, pg. 921
SOUTHERN INSURANCE CO.—See Credit Suisse Group; *Int'l*, pg. 346
SOUTHERN INTERIORS—See Decorator Industries, Inc.; *U.S. Public*, pg. 491
SOUTHERN IRON & METAL CO.—See Commercial Metals Company; *U.S. Public*, pg. 413
SOUTHERN IV THERAPY, INC.—See Integrated Health Services, Inc.; *U.S. Public*, pg. 885
SOUTHERN JITNEY-JUNGLE, INC.—See Jitney-Jungle Stores of America, Inc.; *U.S. Private*, pg. 588
SOUTHERN LEASING OF KANSAS CITY, INC.—See Kansas City Southern Industries, Inc.; *U.S. Public*, pg. 944
SOUTHERN LEATHER CO., INC.; *U.S. Private*, pg. 1016
SOUTHERN LIFE AND HEALTH INSURANCE COMPANY—See Geneve Corporation; *U.S. Private*, pg. 447
THE SOUTHERN LIFE ASSOCIATION LIMITED—See Anglo American Corporation of South Africa Limited; *Int'l*, pg. 77
SOUTHERN LIFE EQUIPMENT FINANCE (PROPRIETARY) LIMITED—See Anglo American Corporation of South Africa Limited; *Int'l*, pg. 77
SOUTHERN LIFE PROPERTY HOLDINGS LIMITED—See Anglo American Corporation of South Africa Limited; *Int'l*, pg. 77
SOUTHERN LIVING, INC.—See Time Warner Inc.; *U.S. Public*, pg. 1613
SOUTHERN LIVING REAL ESTATE, INC.—See Time Warner Inc.; *U.S. Public*, pg. 1613
SOUTHERN MANUFACTURERS REP., INC.—See Klockner-Moeller GmbH; *Int'l*, pg. 736
SOUTHERN MEDICAL, INC.—See Integrated Health Services, Inc.; *U.S. Public*, pg. 885
SOUTHERN MILLS, INC.; *U.S. Private*, pg. 1016
SOUTHERN MINERAL CORPORATION; *U.S. Public*, pg. 1490
SOUTHERN MINNESOTA BEET SUGAR COOPERATIVE; *U.S. Private*, pg. 1016
SOUTHERN MISSOURI CONTAINERS INC.; *U.S. Private*, pg. 1017
SOUTHERN MORTGAGE ASSOCIATES, INC.—See Colonial Commercial Corp.; *U.S. Public*, pg. 400
SOUTHERN MORTGAGE COMPANY, INC.—See United Companies Financial Corporation; *U.S. Public*, pg. 1675
SOUTHERN NATURAL GAS COMPANY—See Sonat Inc.; *U.S. Public*, pg. 1485
SOUTHERN NEW ENGLAND TELECOMMUNICATIONS CORPORATION; *U.S. Public*, pg. 1490
THE SOUTHERN NEW ENGLAND TELEPHONE COMPANY—See Southern New England Telecommunications Corporation; *U.S. Public*, pg. 1491
SOUTHERN NUCLEAR—See Southern Company; *U.S. Public*, pg. 1490
SOUTHERN OAKS HEALTH CARE CENTER—See Horizon/CMS Healthcare Corporation; *U.S. Public*, pg. 837
SOUTHERN OHIO COAL CO.—See American Electric Power Company, Inc.; *U.S. Public*, pg. 73
SOUTHERN OHIO FABRICATORS, INC.; *U.S. Private*, pg. 1017
SOUTHERN OUTDOORS MAGAZINE—See B.A.S.S., Inc.; *U.S. Private*, pg. 106
SOUTHERN-OWNERS INSURANCE COMPANY—See Auto-Owners Insurance; *U.S. Private*, pg. 101
SOUTHERN PACIFIC BANK—See Imperial Credit Industries, Inc.; *U.S. Public*, pg. 872
SOUTHERN PACIFIC FUNDING CORPORATION—See Imperial Credit Industries, Inc.; *U.S. Public*, pg. 872
SOUTHERN PACIFIC RAIL CORPORATION—See Union Pacific Corporation; *U.S. Public*, pg. 1668
SOUTHERN PACIFIC WAREHOUSE CO.—See Union Pacific Corporation; *U.S. Public*, pg. 1668
SOUTHERN PAVING CO.—See LeGrand Johnson Construction Co.; *U.S. Private*, pg. 591
SOUTHERN PERU COPPER CORP.—See Asarco Incorporated; *U.S. Public*, pg. 138
SOUTHERN PETROLEUM EQUIPMENT CO., INC.—See Kennedy Tank & Manufacturing Co., Inc.; *U.S. Private*, pg. 614
SOUTHERN PHENIX TEXTILES, INC.—See Johnston Industries, Inc.; *U.S. Public*, pg. 933
SOUTHERN PILOT INSURANCE COMPANY—See Credit Suisse Group; *Int'l*, pg. 346
SOUTHERN PLASTICS CO.—See Bunzl PLC; *Int'l*, pg. 233
SOUTHERN POST COMPANY—See Commercial Metals Company; *U.S. Public*, pg. 412
SOUTHERN POST COMPANY-TEXAS—See Commercial Metals Company; *U.S. Public*, pg. 412
SOUTHERN POST SOUTH CAROLINA—See Commercial Metals Company; *U.S. Public*, pg. 413
SOUTHERN PROCESSORS, INC.—See Universal Corporation; *U.S. Public*, pg. 1695
SOUTHERN PROGRESS CORPORATION—See Time Warner Inc.; *U.S. Public*, pg. 1612
SOUTHERN PUMP & TANK COMPANY; *U.S. Private*, pg. 1017
SOUTHERN RAIL TERMINALS, INC.—See Norfolk Southern Corporation; *U.S. Public*, pg. 1191
SOUTHERN RAILWAY-CAROLINA DIV.—See Norfolk Southern Corporation; *U.S. Public*, pg. 1191
SOUTHERN RECLAMATION COMPANY—See Reynolds Metals Company; *U.S. Public*, pg. 1386
SOUTHERN REGION COAL TRANSPORT, INC.—See Norfolk Southern Corporation; *U.S. Public*, pg. 1191
SOUTHERN REGION INDUSTRIAL REALTY, INC.—See Norfolk Southern Corporation; *U.S. Public*, pg. 1190
SOUTHERN REGION MATERIALS SUPPLY, INC.—See Norfolk Southern Corporation; *U.S. Public*, pg. 1191
SOUTHERN REGION MOTOR TRANSPORT, INC.—See Norfolk Southern Corporation; *U.S. Public*, pg. 1191
SOUTHERN RHODE ISLAND NEWSPAPERS—See Journal Register Company; *U.S. Public*, pg. 935
SOUTHERN SERVICES INC.—See Sophus Berendsen A/S; *Int'l*, pg. 1286
SOUTHERN SIGNATURES, INC.—See Wallace Computer Services, Inc.; *U.S. Public*, pg. 1736
SOUTHERN STATES COOPERATIVE, INC.; *U.S. Private*, pg. 1017
SOUTHERN STATES STEEL COMPANY—See Commercial Metals Company; *U.S. Public*, pg. 412
SOUTHERN STATES VEHICLE AUCTION OF ATLANTA INC.—See Tyco International Ltd.; *U.S. Public*, pg. 1649
SOUTHERN STEEL COMPANY—See Phelps Tointon Inc.; *U.S. Private*, pg. 861
SOUTHERN SUN HOTEL HOLDINGS LIMITED—See South African Breweries, Ltd.; *Int'l*, pg. 1287
SOUTHERN TANK & MANUFACTURING, INC.—See Kennedy Tank & Manufacturing Co., Inc.; *U.S. Private*, pg. 614
SOUTHERN TEA CO.—See The Tetley Group Limited; *Int'l*, pg. 1377
SOUTHERN TREE SURGEONS, LTD.—See The F.A. Bartlett Tree Expert Co.; *U.S. Private*, pg. 119
SOUTHERN UNDERWRITERS, INC.—See Skandia Insurance Company Limited; *Int'l*, pg. 1257
SOUTHERN UNDERWRITERS INSURANCE COMPANY—See Credit Suisse Group; *Int'l*, pg. 346
SOUTHERN UNIFORMS DIV.—See Superior Surgical Mfg. Co., Inc.; *U.S. Public*, pg. 1539
SOUTHERN UNION COMPANY; *U.S. Public*, pg. 1491
SOUTHERN UNION GAS CO.—See Southern Union Company; *U.S. Public*, pg. 1491
SOUTHERN UTAH FUEL CO.—See The Coastal Corporation; *U.S. Public*, pg. 390
SOUTHERN WATCH & CLOCK SUPPLIES LTD.—See Lonrho plc; *Int'l*, pg. 817
SOUTHERN WINE & SPIRITS OF AMERICA INC.; *U.S. Private*, pg. 1017
SOUTHGATE FORD INC.; *U.S. Private*, pg. 1018
SOUTHLAND CORP.-BRITISH COLUMBIA DIVISION—See Ito-Yokado Co., Ltd.; *Int'l*, pg. 694
SOUTHLAND CORPORATION - CANADA NATIONAL OFFICE—See Ito-Yokado Co., Ltd.; *Int'l*, pg. 694
SOUTHLAND CORP.-PRAIRIES DIVISION—See Ito-Yokado Co., Ltd.; *Int'l*, pg. 694
THE SOUTHLAND CORPORATION—See Ito-Yokado Co., Ltd.; *Int'l*, pg. 693
SOUTHLAND FORD STERLING TRUCK; *U.S. Private*, pg. 1018
SOUTHLAND INDUSTRIES; *U.S. Private*, pg. 1018
SOUTHLAND NURSING HOME—See Paragon Health Network, Inc.; *U.S. Public*, pg. 1257
SOUTHLAND OIL COMPANY; *U.S. Private*, pg. 1018
SOUTHLAND PUBLISHING CO.—See Gannett Company, Inc.; *U.S. Public*, pg. 701
SOUTHSIDE FORD TRUCK SALES INC.; *U.S. Private*, pg. 1018
SOUTHTEC, INC.—See SouthCo. Inc.; *U.S. Private*, pg. 1015
SOUTHTECH, INC.—See Canon Inc.; *Int'l*, pg. 261
SOUTHTRUST BANK OF GEORGIA—See SouthTrust Corporation; *U.S. Public*, pg. 1492
SOUTHTRUST BANK OF NORTH CAROLINA—See SouthTrust Corporation; *U.S. Public*, pg. 1492
SOUTHTRUST CORPORATION; *U.S. Public*, pg. 1491
SOUTHTRUST DATA SERVICES, INC.—See SouthTrust Corporation; *U.S. Public*, pg. 1492
SOUTHTRUST INSURANCE AGENCY, INC.—See SouthTrust Corporation; *U.S. Public*, pg. 1492
SOUTHTRUST LEASING, INC.—See SouthTrust Corporation; *U.S. Public*, pg. 1492
SOUTHTRUST LIFE INSURANCE CO.—See SouthTrust Corporation; *U.S. Public*, pg. 1492
SOUTHTRUST MOBILE SERVICES—See SouthTrust Corporation; *U.S. Public*, pg. 1492
SOUTHTRUST MORTGAGE CORP.—See SouthTrust Corporation; *U.S. Public*, pg. 1492
SOUTHTRUST SECURITIES INC.—See SouthTrust Corporation; *U.S. Public*, pg. 1492

SOUTHWARK METAL MANUFACTURING COMPANY; *U.S. Private*, pg. 1018
SOUTHWEST AEROSPACE—See Meggitt plc; *Int'l*, pg. 853
SOUTHWEST AIRLINES CO.; *U.S. Public*, pg. 1493
SOUTHWEST BANKS, INC.—See F.N.B. Corporation; *U.S. Public*, pg. 607
SOUTHWEST CHEMICAL/SERVICES—See M.A. Hanna Company; *U.S. Public*, pg. 781
SOUTHWEST DIVERSIFIED COSCAN PARTNERSHIPS—See Brookfield Properties Corporation; *Int'l*, pg. 228
SOUTHWEST ENERGY SOLUTIONS, INC.—See UniSource Energy Corporation; *U.S. Public*, pg. 1670
SOUTHWEST EQUITY LIFE INSURANCE CO.—See AEGON N.V.; *Int'l*, pg. 27
SOUTHWEST FLORIDA PIPELINE CORP.—See GATX Corporation; *U.S. Public*, pg. 692
SOUTHWEST GAS CORPORATION; *U.S. Public*, pg. 1493
SOUTHWEST GAS TRANSMISSION COMPANY—See Southwest Gas Corporation; *U.S. Public*, pg. 1493
SOUTHWEST IN REGIONAL YOUTH VILLAGE—See Corrections Corporation of America; *U.S. Public*, pg. 451
SOUTHWEST JET FUEL CO.—See Southwest Airlines Co.; *U.S. Public*, pg. 1493
SOUTHWEST MARINE, INC.—See Carlyle Holding Corporation; *U.S. Private*, pg. 213
SOUTHWEST MARKETING DIV.—See CUNA Mutual Insurance Society; *U.S. Private*, pg. 296
SOUTHWEST MEDICAL ASSOCIATES, INC.—See Sierra Health Services, Inc.; *U.S. Public*, pg. 1470
SOUTHWEST NATIONAL BANK OF PENNSYLVANIA—See Southwest National Corporation; *U.S. Public*, pg. 1493
SOUTHWEST NATIONAL CORPORATION; *U.S. Public*, pg. 1493
SOUTHWEST OILFIELD CONSTRUCTION COMPANY—See PrimeEnergy Corporation; *U.S. Public*, pg. 1329
SOUTHWEST POWDER COATING, INC.—See Karsten Manufacturing Corporation; *U.S. Private*, pg. 608
SOUTHWEST POWER PRODUCTS—See UniSource Energy Corporation; *U.S. Public*, pg. 1670
SOUTHWEST RECREATIONAL INDUSTRIES INC.; *U.S. Private*, pg. 1018
SOUTHWEST REGION—See Federal Signal Corporation; *U.S. Public*, pg. 617
SOUTHWEST REGION—See MCI Communications Corp.; *U.S. Public*, pg. 1024
SOUTHWEST RISK SERVICES INC.—See W.R. Berkley Corporation; *U.S. Public*, pg. 215
SOUTHWEST SENIOR CARE CENTER—See Horizon/CMS Healthcare Corporation; *U.S. Public*, pg. 838
SOUTHWEST STAINLESS, L.P.—See Hughes Supply, Inc.; *U.S. Public*, pg. 847
SOUTHWEST TELEPHONE SYSTEMS, INC.—See Inter-Tel, Incorporated; *U.S. Public*, pg. 888
SOUTHWEST TITLE & TRUST COMPANY—See The First American Financial Corporation; *U.S. Public*, pg. 626
SOUTHWEST VACUUM DEVICES, INC.—See Video Display Corporation; *U.S. Public*, pg. 1720
SOUTHWEST VILLAGES—See Pacific Gateway Properties; *U.S. Public*, pg. 1250
SOUTHWEST WATER COMPANY; *U.S. Public*, pg. 1494
SOUTHWESTERN BELL MEDIA VENTURES—See SBC Communications Inc.; *U.S. Public*, pg. 1415
SOUTHWESTERN BELL MESSAGING SERVICES—See SBC Communications Inc.; *U.S. Public*, pg. 1416
SOUTHWESTERN BELL PRINTING COMPANY—See SBC Communications Inc.; *U.S. Public*, pg. 1415
SOUTHWESTERN BELL TECHNOLOGY RESOURCES—See SBC Communications Inc.; *U.S. Public*, pg. 1416
SOUTHWESTERN BELL TELECOM—See SBC Communications Inc.; *U.S. Public*, pg. 1416
SOUTHWESTERN BELL TELEPHONE CO.—See SBC Communications Inc.; *U.S. Public*, pg. 1416
SOUTHWESTERN BELL YELLOW PAGES INC.—See SBC Communications Inc.; *U.S. Public*, pg. 1415
SOUTHWESTERN CAPITAL CORPORATION—See Citizens Utilities Company; *U.S. Public*, pg. 380
SOUTHWESTERN DIE CASTING, INC.—See Baldor Electric Company; *U.S. Public*, pg. 169
SOUTHWESTERN ELECTRIC POWER CO.—See Central and South West Corporation; *U.S. Public*, pg. 324
SOUTHWESTERN ELECTRIC SERVICE CO.—See Texas Utilities Company; *U.S. Public*, pg. 1588
SOUTHWESTERN ENERGY COMPANY; *U.S. Public*, pg. 1494
SOUTHWESTERN ENERGY PIPELINE COMPANY—See Southwestern Energy Company; *U.S. Public*, pg. 1494
SOUTHWESTERN ENERGY PRODUCTION CO.—See Southwestern Energy Company; *U.S. Public*, pg. 1494
SOUTHWESTERN EXPLOSIVES—See Austin Powder Co.; *U.S. Private*, pg. 100
SOUTHWESTERN FINANCIAL CORP.—See Texas Industries, Inc.; *U.S. Public*, pg. 1585
SOUTHWESTERN FINANCIAL CORPORATION; *U.S. Private*, pg. 1018
SOUTHWESTERN FINANCIAL SERVICES CORP.—See Southwestern Financial Corporation; *U.S. Private*, pg. 1018
SOUTHWESTERN FOUNDRIES—See Crane Co.; *U.S. Public*, pg. 457
SOUTHWESTERN GAS PIPELINE, INC.—See Mitchell Energy & Development Corp.; *U.S. Public*, pg. 1117
SOUTHWESTERN GRAPHITE CO.—See Dixon Ticonderoga Company; *U.S. Public*, pg. 515
SOUTHWESTERN/GREAT AMERICAN INC.; *U.S. Private*, pg. 1018
SOUTHWESTERN INDUSTRIES, INC.; *U.S. Private*, pg. 1019
SOUTHWESTERN INVESTMENTS, INC.—See Citizens Utilities Company; *U.S. Public*, pg. 380
SOUTHWESTERN LIFE INSURANCE COMPANY—See Southwestern Financial Corporation; *U.S. Private*, pg. 1018

SOUTHWESTERN PETROLEUM CANADA LTD.—See Southwestern Petroleum Corporation; *U.S. Private*, pg. 1019
SOUTHWESTERN PETROLEUM CORPORATION; *U.S. Private*, pg. 1019
N.V. SOUTHWESTERN PETROLEUM EUROPE S.A.—See Southwestern Petroleum Corporation; *U.S. Private*, pg. 1019
SOUTHWESTERN PUBLIC SERVICE COMPANY—See New Century Energies, Inc.; *U.S. Public*, pg. 1170
SOUTHWESTERN REPROGRAPHICS INC.—See Wilco Reprographic, Inc.; *U.S. Private*, pg. 1176
SOUTHWESTERN TOBACCO CO., INC.—See Universal Corporation; *U.S. Public*, pg. 1695
SOUTHWIRE COMPANY; *U.S. Private*, pg. 1019
SOUTHWIRE SPECIALTY PRODUCTS—See Southwire Company; *U.S. Private*, pg. 1019
THE SOUTHWOOD COMPANY—See Artesian Resources Corporation; *U.S. Public*, pg. 136
SOUWESTCON PROPERTIES, INC.—See United Illuminating Company; *U.S. Public*, pg. 1679
CIA. SOUZA CRUZ INDUSTRIA E COMERCIO—See B.A.T Industries P.L.C.; *Int'l*, pg. 112
SOUZA CRUZ, S.A.—See B.A.T Industries P.L.C.; *Int'l*, pg. 112
SOVAP—See Bertrand Faure; *Int'l*, pg. 193
SOVCOR, SA—See Vishay Intertechnology, Inc.; *U.S. Public*, pg. 1722
SOVEDI BENELUX-BELGIUM—See Diageo Plc; *Int'l*, pg. 410
SOVEDI BENELUX-NEDERLAND—See Diageo Plc; *Int'l*, pg. 410
SOVEDI FRANCE—See Diageo Plc; *Int'l*, pg. 410
SOVEDYS—See Saint-Gobain; *Int'l*, pg. 1172
SOVEPER NV—See Nestle S.A.; *Int'l*, pg. 919
SOVEREIGN BANCORP, INC.; *U.S. Public*, pg. 1494
SOVEREIGN BANK F.S.B.—See Sovereign Bancorp, Inc.; *U.S. Public*, pg. 1494
SOVEREIGN BANK OF PRINCETON—See Sovereign Bancorp, Inc.; *U.S. Public*, pg. 1494
SOVEREIGN CHEMICAL INDUSTRIES LIMITED—See Laporte plc; *Int'l*, pg. 802
SOVEREIGN ENGINEERED ADHESIVE—See Sovereign Specialty Chemical, Inc.; *U.S. Private*, pg. 1019
SOVEREIGN INVESTMENT CORP.—See Sovereign Bancorp, Inc.; *U.S. Public*, pg. 1494
SOVEREIGN OIL & GAS PLC—See Neste Oy; *Int'l*, pg. 915
SOVEREIGN SPECIALTY CHEMICAL, INC.; *U.S. Private*, pg. 1019
SOVEX NATURAL FOODS—See McKee Foods Corporation; *U.S. Private*, pg. 723
SOVHENK—See Henkel KGaA; *Int'l*, pg. 614
SOVIS, SOCIETE DE VERRERIE SCIENTIFIQUE ET INDUSTRIELLE—See Saint-Gobain; *Int'l*, pg. 1172
SOWA SYSTEM CO.—See Caterpillar Inc.; *U.S. Public*, pg. 317
SOWERBY RESEARCH CENTRE—See British Aerospace p.l.c.; *Int'l*, pg. 218
SOWESTER LIMITED—See Krug International Corp.; *U.S. Public*, pg. 968
L.H. SOWLES COMPANY, INC.; *U.S. Private*, pg. 1019
L.H. SOWLES COMPANY, INC.—See L.H. Sowles Company, Inc.; *U.S. Private*, pg. 1019
SPAARBELEG—See AEGON N.V.; *Int'l*, pg. 28
SPAARBELEG N.V.—See AEGON N.V.; *Int'l*, pg. 26
SPACE CENTER, INC.—See Helmerich & Payne, Inc.; *U.S. Public*, pg. 808
SPACE & DEFENSE DIVISION—See Aerospatiale; *Int'l*, pg. 29
SPACE MASTER INTERNATIONAL; *U.S. Private*, pg. 1019
SPACE SYSTEMS/LORAL, INC.—See Loral Space & Communications; *U.S. Public*, pg. 1014
SPACECON, INC.—See Irex Corporation; *U.S. Public*, pg. 913
SPACELABS MEDICAL, INC.; *U.S. Public*, pg. 1494
SPADONE-ALFA CORPORATION—See Spadone Inc.; *U.S. Private*, pg. 1020
SPADONE INC.; *U.S. Private*, pg. 1020
SPAFAS, INC.—See Bausch & Lomb Incorporated; *U.S. Public*, pg. 195
SPAGHETTI WAREHOUSE, INC.; *U.S. Public*, pg. 1495
SPALDING—See Kohlberg Kravis Roberts & Co.; *U.S. Private*, pg. 629
SPALDING & EVENFLO COMPANIES, INC.—See Kohlberg Kravis Roberts & Co.; *U.S. Private*, pg. 629
SPALDING & EVENFLO JUVENILE FURNITURE COMPANY—See Kohlberg Kravis Roberts & Co.; *U.S. Private*, pg. 630
SPALDING AUSTRALIA PTY. LTD.—See Kohlberg Kravis Roberts & Co.; *U.S. Private*, pg. 630
SPALDING CANADA—See Kohlberg Kravis Roberts & Co.; *U.S. Private*, pg. 630
SPALDING SPORTS WORLDWIDE—See Kohlberg Kravis Roberts & Co.; *U.S. Private*, pg. 630
SPAN-AMERICA MEDICAL SYSTEMS INC.; *U.S. Public*, pg. 1495
SPAN-TRACK—See Unex Conveying Systems, Inc.; *U.S. Public*, pg. 1117
SPANAWAY LUMBER CO.—See WTD Industries, Inc.; *U.S. Public*, pg. 1730
SPANG & COMPANY; *U.S. Private*, pg. 1020
SPANG & COMPANY-BOONEVILLE PLANT—See Spang & Company; *U.S. Private*, pg. 1020
SPANG POWER CONTROL—See Spang & Company; *U.S. Private*, pg. 1020
SPANGLER CANDY COMPANY; *U.S. Private*, pg. 1020
SPANGLER INC.; *U.S. Public*, pg. 1020
SPANGLES' FLOUR MILLS OF MT. JOY—See Wilkins-Rogers Incorporated; *U.S. Private*, pg. 1176
SPANISH EXECUTIVE INFORMATION SERVICES (SEIS)—See Ketchum Communications Inc.; *U.S. Private*, pg. 617

SPANISH MEADOW NURSING CENTER—See Horizon/CMS Healthcare Corporation; *U.S. Public*, pg. 839
SPANOPTIC LIMITED—See Morgan Crucible Co. Plc; *Int'l*, pg. 892
THE SPANOS COMPANIES; *U.S. Private*, pg. 1020
SPAR AEROSPACE—See Spar Aerospace Limited; *Int'l*, pg. 1288
SPAR AEROSPACE LIMITED; *Int'l*, pg. 1287
SPAR AEROSPACE (U.K.) LIMITED—See Spar Aerospace Limited; *Int'l*, pg. 1288
SPAR AEROSPACE (U.S.) LIMITED—See Spar Aerospace Limited; *Int'l*, pg. 1288
SPAR APPLIED SYSTEMS—See Spar Aerospace Limited; *Int'l*, pg. 1288
SPAR AVIATION SERVICES—See Spar Aerospace Limited; *Int'l*, pg. 1288
SPAR BUSINESS DEVELOPMENT—See Spar Aerospace Limited; *Int'l*, pg. 1288
SPAR HANDELS AG; *Int'l*, pg. 1288
SPAR INTERNATIONALE FINANCIERING B.V.—See Spar Handels AG; *Int'l*, pg. 1288
SPAR MARKETING FORCE, INC.—See ADVO, Inc.; *U.S. Public*, pg. 23
SPAR OPERATIONS AND ENGINEERING CORPORATION—See Spar Aerospace Limited; *Int'l*, pg. 1288
SPAR SATELLITE SYSTEMS—See Spar Aerospace Limited; *Int'l*, pg. 1288
SPAR SPACE SYSTEMS—See Spar Aerospace Limited; *Int'l*, pg. 1288
SPAR (UK) LTD.; *Int'l*, pg. 1288
SPARBANKEN FASTIGHETSBYRA—See Swedbank; *Int'l*, pg. 1328
SPARBANKEN FINANS—See Swedbank; *Int'l*, pg. 1328
SPARBANKEN SVERIGE AB—See Swedbank; *Int'l*, pg. 1328
SPAREX INTERNATIONAL LTD.—See Wolseley Plc.; *Int'l*, pg. 1512
SPARKASSE GAU—See Union Bank of Switzerland; *Int'l*, pg. 1440
SPARKLETTS DRINKING WATER CORP.—See McKesson Corporation; *U.S. Public*, pg. 1073
D.R. SPARKS INSURANCE SERVICES, INC.—See Millers Mutual Insurance Assn.; *U.S. Private*, pg. 748
SPARKS FAMILY HOSPITAL—See Universal Health Services, Inc.; *U.S. Public*, pg. 1697
SPARKS STATE BANK—See Mercantile Bankshares Corporation; *U.S. Public*, pg. 1089
SPARLIV OCH SPARFOND—See Swedbank; *Int'l*, pg. 1328
SPARROWS INDUSTRIAL SERVICES, LTD.—See Sophus Berendsen A/S; *Int'l*, pg. 1285
SPARROWS OFFSHORE SERVICES LTD.—See Sophus Berendsen A/S; *Int'l*, pg. 1285
SPARTAN AUTOMATIC RETAILERS; *U.S. Private*, pg. 1020
SPARTAN INTERNATIONAL INC.; *U.S. Private*, pg. 1020
SPARTAN MILLS; *U.S. Private*, pg. 1020
SPARTAN MINERALS CORP.—See FMC Corporation; *U.S. Public*, pg. 605
SPARTAN MOTORS, INC.; *U.S. Public*, pg. 1495
SPARTAN OIL CORP.; *U.S. Private*, pg. 1020
SPARTAN PLASTICS CANADA—See Spartan International Inc.; *U.S. Private*, pg. 1020
SPARTAN SECURITY SERVICES—See Temco Service Industries; *U.S. Private*, pg. 1574
SPARTAN SECURITY SERVICES, INC.—See Temco Service Industries; *U.S. Private*, pg. 1574
SPARTAN SHOWCASE, INC.—See RHC/Spacemaster Corporation; *U.S. Public*, pg. 904
SPARTAN STORES INC.; *U.S. Private*, pg. 1021
SPARTAN TOOL—See Pettibone Corporation; *U.S. Private*, pg. 860
SPARTANBURG HERALD-JOURNAL—See The New York Times Company; *U.S. Public*, pg. 1175
SPARTANBURG STEEL PRODUCTS—See The Cypress Companies; *U.S. Private*, pg. 300
SPARTECH CORPORATION; *U.S. Public*, pg. 1495
SPARTECH PLASTICS—See Spartech Corporation; *U.S. Public*, pg. 1496
SPARTON CORPORATION; *U.S. Public*, pg. 1496
SPARTON ELECTRONICS FLORIDA, INC.—See Sparton Corporation; *U.S. Public*, pg. 1496
SPARTON ENGINEERED PRODUCTS, INC.-FLORA GROUP—See Sparton Corporation; *U.S. Public*, pg. 1496
SPARTON OF CANADA LTD.—See Sparton Corporation; *U.S. Public*, pg. 1496
SPARTON TECHNOLOGY, INC.—See Sparton Corporation; *U.S. Public*, pg. 1496
SPARTUS (HK) LTD.—See Hanson PLC; *Int'l*, pg. 595
SPARTYWOOD PRODUCTS, INC.—See Semac Industries Inc.; *U.S. Private*, pg. 983
SPATZ & CO. DEVELOPMENT—See Spatz Centers Inc.; *U.S. Private*, pg. 1021
SPATZ CENTERS INC.; *U.S. Private*, pg. 1021
SPAULDING & SLYE; *U.S. Private*, pg. 1021
SPAULDING & SLYE CONSTRUCTION CO., INC.—See Spaulding & Slye; *U.S. Private*, pg. 1021
SPAULDING COMPANY, INC.—See Semco Industries Inc.; *U.S. Private*, pg. 983
SPAV LTA.—See Bertrand Faure; *Int'l*, pg. 192
SPEA-BOLIVIA—See IRI Istituto Ricostruzione Industriale; *Int'l*, pg. 655
SPEA-IRAN—See IRI Istituto Ricostruzione Industriale; *Int'l*, pg. 655
SPEAKMAN COMPANY; *U.S. Private*, pg. 1021
SPEA-TURKEY—See IRI Istituto Ricostruzione Industriale; *Int'l*, pg. 655
SPEC HOLDINGS INC.; *U.S. Private*, pg. 1022
SPECIA—See Rhone-Poulenc S.A.; *Int'l*, pg. 1109
SPECIA COLOMBIA—See Rhone-Poulenc S.A.; *Int'l*, pg. 1114
SPECIAL DEVICES, INCORPORATED; *U.S. Public*, pg. 1496

Company Index

SPECIAL

DIRECTORY OF CORPORATE AFFILIATIONS

SPECIAL EDITIONS, LTD.—See Playboy Enterprises, Inc.; *U.S. Public*, pg. 1310
SPECIAL ERECTION SERVICES, INC.—See Construction Specialties, Inc.; *U.S. Private*, pg. 266
SPECIAL FILAMENTS ODENTON—See APEX Specialty Materials, Inc.; *U.S. Private*, pg. 77
SPECIAL MARKETS (RTVCH)—See Liz Claiborne, Inc.; *U.S. Public*, pg. 1006
SPECIAL PACKAGING, INC.—See Caraustar Industries, Inc.; *U.S. Public*, pg. 304
SPECIAL PRODUCTS DIV.—See Emerson Electric Co.; *U.S. Public*, pg. 575
SPECIAL PROGRAM MANAGEMENT, INC.—See Willis Corroon Group PLC; *Int'l*, pg. 1504
SPECIAL SERVICES COMPANY—See Bindley Western Industries, Inc.; *U.S. Public*, pg. 229
THE SPECIALISTS LTD.—See LCS Industries, Inc.; *U.S. Public*, pg. 970
SPECIALSERVICE AB—See Celsius AB; *Int'l*, pg. 277
SPECIALTIES BINDERY, INC.—See Quebecor Inc.; *Int'l*, pg. 1078
SPECIALTY BRANDS—See Burns, Philp & Company Limited; *Int'l*, pg. 237
SPECIALTY CASTINGS—See The Johnson Corporation; *U.S. Private*, pg. 591
SPECIALTY CHEMICALS DIV.—See Rhone-Poulenc S.A.; *Int'l*, pg. 1109
SPECIALTY ENVELOPE—See Miami Systems Corporation; *U.S. Private*, pg. 740
SPECIALTY EQUIPMENT COMPANIES INC.; *U.S. Public*, pg. 1496
SPECIALTY FILAMENTS INC.—See APEX Specialty Materials, Inc.; *U.S. Private*, pg. 77
SPECIALTY FILAMENTS LTD.—See APEX Specialty Materials, Inc.; *U.S. Private*, pg. 77
SPECIALTY FOODS CORPORATION; *U.S. Private*, pg. 1022
SPECIALTY FOODS INVESTMENT INL.—See Worthington Foods Inc.; *U.S. Public*, pg. 1780
SPECIALTY INDUSTRIES, INC.; *U.S. Private*, pg. 1022
SPECIALTY INSURANCE UNDERWRITERS, INC.—See Avemco Corporation; *U.S. Public*, pg. 152
SPECIALTY LIGHTING—See Luxo A/S; *Int'l*, pg. 821
SPECIALTY MANAGEMENT CO.—See Arrow International; *U.S. Private*, pg. 85
SPECIALTY POLYMERS & CHEMICALS DIVISION—See The B.F. Goodrich Company; *U.S. Public*, pg. 751
SPECIALTY PRODUCTS—See Kimberly-Clark Corporation; *U.S. Public*, pg. 958
SPECIALTY PRODUCTS AND INSULATION COMPANY—See Irex Corporation; *U.S. Public*, pg. 913
SPECIALTY PRODUCTS CENTER—See Mitsubishi Chemical Corporation; *Int'l*, pg. 871
SPECIALTY PRODUCTS GROUP—See National-Standard Co.; *U.S. Public*, pg. 1160
SPECIALTY RESTAURANTS CORPORATION; *U.S. Private*, pg. 1022
SPECIALTY STEELS—See Pechiney S.A.; *Int'l*, pg. 1032
SPECIALTY TAPES AND ADHESIVES GROUP—See Avery Dennison Corporation; *U.S. Public*, pg. 153
SPECIALTY TEXTILE PRODUCTS; *U.S. Private*, pg. 1023
SPECIALTY UNDERWRITERS, INC.—See American Financial Group; *U.S. Public*, pg. 75
SPECIALTY UNDERWRITERS REINSURANCE FACILITY—See Michigan Physicians Mutual Liability Inc.; *U.S. Private*, pg. 741
SPECIALTY WINDOW COVERINGS—See Decorator Industries, Inc.; *U.S. Public*, pg. 491
SPECIALTYCHEM PRODUCTS CORPORATION—See Bayer AG; *Int'l*, pg. 173
SPECIFICATION RUBBER PRODUCTS INC.—See American Cast Iron Pipe Co.; *U.S. Private*, pg. 52
SPEC'S MUSIC, INC.; *U.S. Public*, pg. 1497
THE SPECTATOR, HAMILTON—See Hollinger Inc.; *Int'l*, pg. 631
SPECTRA DIODE LABORATORIES—See Xerox Corporation; *U.S. Public*, pg. 1785
SPECTRA MARKETING SYSTEMS—See VNU Verenigde Nederlandse Uitgeversbedrijven B.V.; *Int'l*, pg. 1447
SPECTRA NATIONAL—See National Print Group, Inc.; *U.S. Private*, pg. 786
SPECTRA-PHYSICS AB; *Int'l*, pg. 1288
SPECTRA-PHYSICS HOLDINGS PLC—See Spectra-Physics AB; *Int'l*, pg. 1290
SPECTRA-PHYSICS, INC.—See Spectra-Physics AB; *Int'l*, pg. 1289
SPECTRA-PHYSICS LASERPLANE AB—See Spectra-Physics AB; *Int'l*, pg. 1289
SPECTRA-PHYSICS LASERPLANE INC.—See Thermo Electron Corporation; *U.S. Public*, pg. 1594
SPECTRA-PHYSICS LASERS, INC.—See Thermo Electron Corporation; *U.S. Public*, pg. 1594
SPECTRA-PHYSICS OPTICS CORP.—See Thermo Electron Corporation; *U.S. Public*, pg. 1594
SPECTRA-PHYSICS S.A.—See Spectra-Physics AB; *Int'l*, pg. 1290
SPECTRA-PHYSICS SCANNING SYSTEMS—See Spectra-Physics AB; *Int'l*, pg. 1290
SPECTRA-PHYSICS SCANNING SYSTEMS INC.—See Thermo Electron Corporation; *U.S. Public*, pg. 1594
SPECTRA-PHYSICS S.R.L.—See Spectra-Physics AB; *Int'l*, pg. 1290
SPECTRA-PHYSICS USA, INC.—See Spectra-Physics AB; *Int'l*, pg. 1289
SPECTRA-TECH—See Thermo Electron Corporation; *U.S. Public*, pg. 1593
SPECTRACE INSTRUMENTS—See Thermo Electron Corporation; *U.S. Public*, pg. 1593
SPECTRAL—See Jeumont-Schneider Trenformeteurs; *Int'l*, pg. 706
SPECTRAL TECHNOLOGY GROUP LTD.—See Nordson Corporation; *U.S. Public*, pg. 1189
SPECTRAN CORPORATION; *U.S. Public*, pg. 1497
SPECTRAN SPECIALTY OPTICS—See SpecTran Corporation; *U.S. Public*, pg. 1497
SPECTRIS MESSTECHNIK GMBH—See AGIV Group; *Int'l*, pg. 14
SPECTRIS TECHNOLOGIES, INC.—See AGIV Group; *Int'l*, pg. 14
SPECTROL ELECTRONICS CORPORATION—See The Dyson-Kissner-Moran Corporation; *U.S. Private*, pg. 351
SPECTROL RELIANCE LTD.—See The Dyson-Kissner-Moran Corporation; *U.S. Private*, pg. 352
SPECTRON DEVELOPMENT LABS—See The Titan Corporation; *U.S. Public*, pg. 1618
SPECTRONICS CORPORATION; *U.S. Private*, pg. 1024
SPECTRULITE CONSORTIUM, INC.; *U.S. Private*, pg. 1024
SPECTRUM—See American Restaurant Group, Inc.; *U.S. Private*, pg. 61
SPECTRUM ASSET MANAGEMENT, INC.—See United Asset Management Corporation; *U.S. Public*, pg. 1674
SPECTRUM CONTROL, INC.; *U.S. Public*, pg. 1497
SPECTRUM CONTROL TECHNOLOGY INC.—See Spectrum Control, Inc.; *U.S. Public*, pg. 1497
SPECTRUM DIVISION—See R & R Marketing; *U.S. Private*, pg. 902
SPECTRUM GLASS CO.—See The Clark Group; *Int'l*, pg. 296
SPECTRUM INDUSTRIES; *U.S. Private*, pg. 1024
SPECTRUM INDUSTRIES, INC.; *U.S. Private*, pg. 1024
SPECTRUM MOLDING—See Plastek Group; *U.S. Private*, pg. 870
SPECTRUM MUTUAL FUND SERVICES INC.—See Sun Life Assurance Company of Canada; *Int'l*, pg. 1319
SPECTRUM RAZOR TOOLS—See Pacific Handy Cutter, Inc.; *U.S. Private*, pg. 831
SPECTRUM SKANSKA INC.—See Skanska AB; *Int'l*, pg. 1261
SPECTRUM TECHNOLOGIES LIMITED—See British Aerospace p.l.c.; *Int'l*, pg. 218
SPECTRUM UNITED MUTUAL FUNDS, INC.—See Sun Life Assurance Company of Canada; *Int'l*, pg. 1319
SPEDIMATIFA S.R.L.—See Compagnie des Machines Bull; *Int'l*, pg. 318
SPEECH DESIGN—See Geotek Communications; *U.S. Public*, pg. 740
SPEECH DESIGN GMBH—See Geotek Communications; *U.S. Public*, pg. 740
SPEEDBIRD EXPRESS—See British Airways PLC; *Int'l*, pg. 219
SPEEDCHOICE—See People's Choice TV Corp.; *U.S. Public*, pg. 1274
SPEEDFAM CO LTD.—See SpeedFan International, Inc.; *U.S. Public*, pg. 1498
SPEEDFAM CORPORATION—See SpeedFan International, Inc.; *U.S. Public*, pg. 1498
SPEEDFAM GMBH—See SpeedFan International, Inc.; *U.S. Public*, pg. 1498
SPEEDFAM LIMITED—See SpeedFan International, Inc.; *U.S. Public*, pg. 1498
SPEEDFAN INTERNATIONAL, INC.; *U.S. Public*, pg. 1497
SPEEDLINE S.P.A.—See Amcast Industrial Corporation; *U.S. Public*, pg. 63
SPEEDLING INCORPORATED; *U.S. Private*, pg. 1024
SPEEDLING INCORPORATED—See Speedling Incorporated; *U.S. Private*, pg. 1024
SPEEDLING INCORPORATED ALAMO TRANSPLANTS DIVISION—See Speedling Incorporated; *U.S. Private*, pg. 1024
SPEEDLING INCORPORATED BUSHNELL DIVISION—See Speedling Incorporated; *U.S. Private*, pg. 1024
SPEEDLING INCORPORATED NIPOMO NURSERY—See Speedling Incorporated; *U.S. Private*, pg. 1024
SPEEDLING INCORPORATED SAN JUAN BAUTISTA NURSERY—See Speedling Incorporated; *U.S. Private*, pg. 1024
SPEEDLING INCORPORATED SUN CITY NURSERY DIVISION—See Speedling Incorporated; *U.S. Private*, pg. 1024
SPEEDO (EUROPE) LTD.—See Pentland Group PLC; *Int'l*, pg. 1036
SPEEDRACK PRODUCTS GROUP, LTD.; *U.S. Private*, pg. 1024
SPEEDRING, INC.—See Axsys Technologies, Inc.; *U.S. Public*, pg. 158
SPEEDRING SYSTEMS, INC.—See Axsys Technologies, Inc.; *U.S. Public*, pg. 158
SPEEDWAY DEVELOPMENT CORP.—See Kaiser Ventures, Inc.; *U.S. Public*, pg. 941
SPEEDWAY MOTORSPORTS, INC.; *U.S. Public*, pg. 1498
SPEEDWAY SUPERAMERICA LLC—See USX Corporation; *U.S. Public*, pg. 1662
SPEEDWING CONSULTING—See British Airways PLC; *Int'l*, pg. 219
SPEEDWING LOGICA LIMITED—See Logica Plc; *Int'l*, pg. 814
SPEEDY BRAKE & MUFFLER—See Tenneco Inc.; *U.S. Public*, pg. 1578
SPEEDY CAR-X, INC.—See Tenneco Inc.; *U.S. Public*, pg. 1578
SPEEDY MUFFLER KING, INC.—See Tenneco Inc.; *U.S. Public*, pg. 1578
SPEER COMMUNICATIONS—See TBWA Chiat/Day; *U.S. Private*, pg. 1063
SPEICHIM-PROCESSING—See Technip; *Int'l*, pg. 1360
SPEIZMAN CANADA, INC.—See Speizman Industries, Inc.; *U.S. Public*, pg. 1498
SPEIZMAN INDUSTRIES, INC.; *U.S. Public*, pg. 1498
SPEIZMAN INDUSTRIES LIMITED (EUROPE)—See Speizman Industries, Inc.; *U.S. Public*, pg. 1498
SPEKTRUM AKADEMISCHER VERLAG GMBH—See Georg von Holtzbrinck GmbH; *Int'l*, pg. 1478
SPEKTRUM DER WISSENSCHAFT VERLAGSGESELLSCHAFT MBH—See Georg von Holtzbrinck GmbH; *Int'l*, pg. 1478
SPEKTRUM FACHVERLAGE GMBH—See Georg von Holtzbrinck GmbH; *Int'l*, pg. 1478
SPELLING ENTERTAINMENT GROUP, INC.—See National Amusements, Inc.; *U.S. Private*, pg. 776
SPELLING TELEVISION—See National Amusements, Inc.; *U.S. Private*, pg. 776
SPENCE ENGINEERING CO.—See Watts Industries, Inc.; *U.S. Public*, pg. 1747
SPENCER COMPANIES INC.; *U.S. Private*, pg. 1024
SPENCER COUNTY JOURNAL-DEMOCRAT—See Landmark Communications, Inc.; *U.S. Private*, pg. 648
SPENCER DOUGLASS INSURANCE ASSOCIATES—See Frontier Insurance Group, Inc.; *U.S. Public*, pg. 685
SPENCER GIFTS, INC.—See The Seagram Company Ltd.; *Int'l*, pg. 1216
THE SPENCER GROUP INC.; *U.S. Private*, pg. 1025
J.W. SPENCER ENGINEERING LTD.—See BTR plc; *Int'l*, pg. 124
SPENCER KELLOGG—See Dainippon Ink & Chemicals, Inc.; *Int'l*, pg. 370
SPENCER MAGNET—See Landmark Communications, Inc.; *U.S. Private*, pg. 648
SPENCER PRESS, INC.; *U.S. Private*, pg. 1025
THE SPENCER TURBINE CO.; *U.S. Private*, pg. 1025
SPENCER'S INC.; *U.S. Private*, pg. 1025
SPENCO MEDICAL CORPORATION—See SBS Enterprises Inc.; *U.S. Private*, pg. 955
SPERBER-PETERMAN COMPANY—See BMW; *U.S. Private*, pg. 107
SPERLARI, S.R.L.—See Hershey Foods Corporation; *U.S. Public*, pg. 812
SPERLING & KUPFER EDITORI S.P.A.—See Arnoldo Mondadori Editore S.p.A.; *Int'l*, pg. 888
SPERLING & KUPFER S.R.L.—See Arnoldo Mondadori Editore S.p.A.; *Int'l*, pg. 888
SPERLING PAPERBACK S.R.L.—See Arnoldo Mondadori Editore S.p.A.; *Int'l*, pg. 888
SPERRHOLZ KOCH GMBH—See Westag & Getalit AG; *Int'l*, pg. 1491
THE SPERRY & HUTCHINSON COMPANY, INC.—See Leucadia National Corporation; *U.S. Public*, pg. 990
SPERRY OWENS, INC.; *U.S. Private*, pg. 1025
SPERRY RAIL SERVICES—See American Financial Group; *U.S. Public*, pg. 75
SPERRY-SUN DRILLING SERVICES DIVISION—See Dresser Industries, Inc.; *U.S. Public*, pg. 528
SPERRY TOP-SIDER, INC.—See The Stride Rite Corporation; *U.S. Public*, pg. 1525
SPFCO ERECTORS, INC.—See Southern Ohio Fabricators, Inc.; *U.S. Private*, pg. 1017
SPHERE SA—See Accor S.A.; *Int'l*, pg. 21
SPHERE SUPPLY, INC.—See Kuwait Petroleum Corporation; *Int'l*, pg. 765
SPHINX CHEMICALS—See Henkel KGaA; *Int'l*, pg. 614
SPHINX MANUFACTURING COMPANY, LTD.—See AlliedSignal Inc.; *U.S. Public*, pg. 53
SPI PROMOZIONE E. SVILUPPO IMPRENDITORIALE S.P.A.—See IRI Istituto Ricostruzione Industriale; *Int'l*, pg. 655
SPICER AXLE DIV.—See Dana Corporation; *U.S. Public*, pg. 479
SPICER CLARK-HURTH—See Dana Corporation; *U.S. Public*, pg. 479
SPICER DRIVESHAFT DIV.—See Dana Corporation; *U.S. Public*, pg. 479
SPICER EUROPE—See Dana Corporation; *U.S. Public*, pg. 480
SPICER OFF-HIGHWAY AXLE DIV.—See Dana Corporation; *U.S. Public*, pg. 479
SPICER S.A.—See Dana Corporation; *U.S. Public*, pg. 480
SPICER TRAILER PRODUCTS DIV.—See Dana Corporation; *U.S. Public*, pg. 479
SPICERS PAPER—See Amcor Limited; *Int'l*, pg. 72
SPICERS PAPER LIMITED—See Amcor Limited; *Int'l*, pg. 72
SPIDER/DMB&B—See DMB&B Communications; *U.S. Private*, pg. 305
SPIE BATIGNOLLES—See AMEC Plc; *Int'l*, pg. 16
SPIEGEL ACCEPTANCE CORPORATION—See Spiegel, Inc.; *U.S. Public*, pg. 1499
FRANZ SPIEGEL BUCH GMBH—See Georg von Holtzbrinck GmbH; *Int'l*, pg. 1478
SPIEGEL, INC.; *U.S. Public*, pg. 1498
SPIEGEL MEATS, INC.; *U.S. Private*, pg. 1025
SPIEGEL-VERLAG RUDOLF AUGSTEIN GMBH & CO.—See Bertelsmann AG; *Int'l*, pg. 190
SPIERER FRERES & CIE S.A.—See Standard Commercial Corporation; *U.S. Public*, pg. 1502
SPIERER TUTUN IHRACAT SANAUI TICARET AS—See Standard Commercial Corporation; *U.S. Public*, pg. 1502
I. SPIEWAK & SONS, INC.; *U.S. Private*, pg. 1025
SPILLERS FOODS—See Dalgety Plc; *Int'l*, pg. 376
SPILLERS MILLING—See Dalgety Plc; *Int'l*, pg. 376
SPIMA LTD—See Atlet AB; *Int'l*, pg. 97
SPIN-CAST PLASTICS, INC.—See Quixote Corporation; *U.S. Public*, pg. 1353
SPINCRAFT MASSACHUSETTS—See Standex International Corporation; *U.S. Public*, pg. 1506
SPINCRAFT WISCONSIN—See Standex International Corporation; *U.S. Public*, pg. 1506
SPINDELFABRIK SUESSEN; *Int'l*, pg. 1290
SPINHILL PROPERTIES LTD.—See Tesco PLC; *Int'l*, pg. 1376
SPINHILL PROPERTIES PLC—See Tesco PLC; *Int'l*, pg. 1376
G.R. SPINKS & CO. LTD.—See Royal Gist-Brocades N.V.; *Int'l*, pg. 1143
SPINNAKER INDUSTRIES, INC.—See Lynch Corporation; *U.S. Public*, pg. 1022
SPINNERIN INC.; *U.S. Private*, pg. 1025
SPINNSTOFFFABRIK ZEHLENDORF AG—See Hoechst Aktiengesellschaft; *Int'l*, pg. 626
SPINTAB—See Swedbank; *Int'l*, pg. 1328
SPIRALKOTE—See Fleming Packaging Corp.; *U.S. Private*, pg. 411

MASTER INDEX TO COMPANY NAMES
SSANGYONG
Company Index

SPIRE CORPORATION; *U.S. Public*, pg. 1499
SPIRE INTERNATIONAL SALES CORPORATION—See Spire Corporation; *U.S. Public*, pg. 1499
SPIRES RESTAURANTS INC.; *U.S. Private*, pg. 1026
SPIRIT CRUISES, INC.—See Sodexho S.A.; *Int'l*, pg. 1274
SPIRIT ENERGY 76—See Unocal Corporation; *U.S. Public*, pg. 1698
SPIRITE INDUSTRIES, INC.; *U.S. Private*, pg. 1026
SPIRKA MASCHINENBAU GMBH & CO. KG—See Deutsche Babcock AG; *Int'l*, pg. 399
SPIROL IND. LTD.—See Spirol International Corp.; *U.S. Private*, pg. 1026
SPIROL INTERNATIONAL CORP.; *U.S. Private*, pg. 1026
SPIROL S.A.—See Spirol International Corp.; *U.S. Private*, pg. 1026
SPIROL WEST—See Spirol International Corp.; *U.S. Private*, pg. 1026
SPIROLOX DIVISION—See Kaydon Corporation; *U.S. Public*, pg. 946
SPLENDOR FORM BRASSIERE, INC.—See New Age Intimates Inc.; *U.S. Private*, pg. 792
SPLINE GAUGES LTD.—See Danaher Corporation; *U.S. Public*, pg. 482
SPLITFIRE, INC.—See Old World Industries, Inc.; *U.S. Private*, pg. 814
SPOERLE ELECTRONIC GMBH—See Arrow Electronics, Inc.; *U.S. Public*, pg. 135
SPOM KABUSHIKI KAISHA—See Compagnie des Machines Bull; *Int'l*, pg. 316
SPONSOR'S PLAN ASSET MANAGEMENT, INC.—See Lukens Inc.; *U.S. Public*, pg. 1020
SPONTEX, INC.—See Total S.A.; *Int'l*, pg. 1409
SPONTEX S.A.—See Total S.A.; *Int'l*, pg. 1409
SPOONER INDUSTRIES LTD.—See Brunel Holdings Plc; *Int'l*, pg. 231
SPOONS—See American Restaurant Group, Inc.; *U.S. Private*, pg. 61
SPORIC AG—See Solvay S.A.; *Int'l*, pg. 1280
SPORLAN VALVE COMPANY; *U.S. Private*, pg. 1026
SPORT MART, INC.; *U.S. Public*, pg. 1499
SPORT OBERMEYER LTD., USA; *U.S. Private*, pg. 1026
SPORT-SCHECK GMBH—See Otto Versand (GmbH & Co.); *Int'l*, pg. 1014
SPORT SUPPLY GROUP, INC.; *U.S. Public*, pg. 1499
SPORTCRAFT LTD.; *U.S. Private*, pg. 1026
THE SPORTING NEWS PUBLISHING COMPANY—See The Times Mirror Company; *U.S. Public*, pg. 1616
SPORTO CORP.; *U.S. Private*, pg. 1026
SPORTS AFIELD—See The Hearst Corporation; *U.S. Private*, pg. 517
THE SPORTS AUTHORITY INC.; *U.S. Public*, pg. 1499
SPORTS ILLUSTRATED—See Time Warner Inc.; *U.S. Public*, pg. 1613
SPORTS IMPRINTS/FUN WEAR—See Littlefield, Adams & Company; *U.S. Public*, pg. 1002
SPORTS/LEISURE MAGAZINES GROUP—See The New York Times Company; *U.S. Public*, pg. 1174
THE SPORTS NETWORK (TSN)—See TSN Communications; *Int'l*, pg. 1343
THE SPORTS SECTION INC.—See BAA plc; *Int'l*, pg. 103
SPORTSERVICE CORPORATION—See Delaware North Companies, Inc.; *U.S. Private*, pg. 322
SPORTSMAN SUPPLY; *U.S. Private*, pg. 1026
THE SPORTSMAN'S GUIDE, INC.; *U.S. Public*, pg. 1499
SPORTSTYLE—See The Walt Disney Company; *U.S. Public*, pg. 513
SPORVEIS-ANNONSENE A/S—See AS OSLO Sporveier; *Int'l*, pg. 1012
SPOT BROADCASTING UNIT—See True North Communications Inc.; *U.S. Public*, pg. 1641
SPOTNAILS—See Peace Industries Inc.; *U.S. Private*, pg. 845
SPRAGUE—See Vishay Intertechnology, Inc.; *U.S. Public*, pg. 1722
SPRAGUE DEVICES, INC.—See Echlin Inc.; *U.S. Public*, pg. 561
SPRAGUE ENERGY CORP. NORTHEAST OPERATION—See Axel Johnson AB; *Int'l*, pg. 710
SPRAUGE ENERGY CORP. SOUTHEAST OPERATIONS—See Axel Johnson AB; *Int'l*, pg. 710
SPRAY-TECH, INC.; *U.S. Private*, pg. 1026
SPRAYING SYSTEMS CO.; *U.S. Private*, pg. 1026
SPRAYING SYSTEMS CO. FAR EAST—See Spraying Systems Co.; *U.S. Private*, pg. 1027
SPRAYING SYSTEMS DEUTSCHLAND GMBH—See Spraying Systems Co.; *U.S. Private*, pg. 1027
SPRAYROQ, INC.—See Insituform Technologies, Inc.; *U.S. Public*, pg. 882
SPRAYSAFE AUTOMATIC SPRINKLERS LIMITED—See Central Sprinkler Corporation; *U.S. Public*, pg. 327
SPRAYWAY, INC.—See Goldner Hawn Johnsons & Morrison Incorporated; *U.S. Private*, pg. 462
SPRECHER + SCHUH AG—See Rockwell International Corporation; *U.S. Public*, pg. 1402
SPRECHER ENERGIE AG—See Alcatel Alsthom Compagnie Generale D'Electricite; *Int'l*, pg. 55
SPRECHER & SCHUH GMBH—See Rockwell International Corporation; *U.S. Public*, pg. 1402
SPRECHER & SCHUH N. AMERICA—See Rockwell International Corporation; *U.S. Public*, pg. 1397
SPRECHER & SCHUH VERKAUF AG—See Rockwell International Corporation; *U.S. Public*, pg. 1402
THE SPRING AIR COMPANY; *U.S. Private*, pg. 1027
SPRING ARBOR DISTRIBUTORS—See Ingram Industries Inc.; *U.S. Private*, pg. 563
SPRING ENGINEERS OF HOUSTON LTD.—See SEI Holding Corp.; *U.S. Private*, pg. 956
SPRING FINANCIAL SERVICES—See Banco Popular de Puerto Rico; *U.S. Public*, pg. 176
SPRING-GREEN LAWN CARE CORPORATION; *U.S. Private*, pg. 1027
SPRING GROVE NATIONAL BANK—See Susquehanna Bancshares, Inc.; *U.S. Public*, pg. 1542
THE SPRING GROVE WATER CO.—See P.H. Glatfelter Company; *U.S. Public*, pg. 746
SPRING HILL NURSERIES CO.—See Foster & Gallagher, Inc.; *U.S. Private*, pg. 420
SPRING LAKE FEED YARD—See Friona Industries, L.P.; *U.S. Private*, pg. 429
SPRING LAKE MERCHANDISE, INC.—See Roundy's, Inc.; *U.S. Private*, pg. 948
SPRING LANE ASSOCS., INC.—See Eaton Vance Corp.; *U.S. Public*, pg. 559
SPRING MILL CORP.—See Finnaren & Haley, Inc.; *U.S. Private*, pg. 406
SPRING PROPERTIES PTY. LTD.—See Pasco Corporation; *Int'l*, pg. 1024
SPRING TOOLS COMPANY—See Peterson American Corp.; *U.S. Private*, pg. 857
SPRINGBORN TESTING & INSPECTION (EUROPE) AG—See Springborn Testing & Research, Inc.; *U.S. Private*, pg. 1027
SPRINGBORN TESTING & RESEARCH (HONG KONG) LTD.—See Springborn Testing & Research, Inc.; *U.S. Private*, pg. 1027
SPRINGBORN TESTING & RESEARCH, INC.; *U.S. Private*, pg. 1027
SPRINGBORN TESTING & RESEARCH (SINGAPORE) PTE LTD.—See Springborn Testing & Research, Inc.; *U.S. Private*, pg. 1027
SPRINGBORN TESTING & RESEARCH (TAIWAN) LTD.—See Springborn Testing & Research, Inc.; *U.S. Private*, pg. 1027
SPRINGBORN TESTING & RESEARCH (UK) LTD.—See Springborn Testing & Research, Inc.; *U.S. Private*, pg. 1027
SPRINGER-VERLAG BARCELONA—See Springer-Verlag GmbH & Co. KG; *Int'l*, pg. 1291
SPRINGER-VERLAG BUDAPEST—See Springer-Verlag GmbH & Co. KG; *Int'l*, pg. 1291
SPRINGER-VERLAG GMBH & CO. KG; *Int'l*, pg. 1291
SPRINGER-VERLAG HONG KONG—See Springer-Verlag GmbH & Co. KG; *Int'l*, pg. 1291
SPRINGER-VERLAG LONDON—See Springer-Verlag GmbH & Co. KG; *Int'l*, pg. 1291
SPRINGER-VERLAG MAILAND—See Springer-Verlag GmbH & Co. KG; *Int'l*, pg. 1291
SPRINGER-VERLAG NEW YORK INC.—See Springer-Verlag GmbH & Co. KG; *Int'l*, pg. 1291
SPRINGER-VERLAG PARIS—See Springer-Verlag GmbH & Co. KG; *Int'l*, pg. 1291
SPRINGER-VERLAG TOKYO—See Springer-Verlag GmbH & Co. KG; *Int'l*, pg. 1291
SPRINGER-VERLAG VIENNA—See Springer-Verlag GmbH & Co. KG; *Int'l*, pg. 1291
SPRINGETT COATED STONE—See RMC Group p.l.c.; *Int'l*, pg. 1080
SPRINGFIELD INSURANCE COMPANY—See Certified Grocers of California; *U.S. Private*, pg. 227
SPRINGFIELD L.D. CORP.—See Forest City Enterprises, Inc.; *U.S. Public*, pg. 669
SPRINGFIELD MANUFACTURING LLC—See S.E. Huffman Corp.; *U.S. Private*, pg. 546
SPRINGFIELD NEWS—See Lee Enterprises, Incorporated; *U.S. Public*, pg. 984
THE SPRINGFIELD NEWS LEADER—See Gannett Company, Inc.; *U.S. Public*, pg. 701
SPRINGFIELD NEWSPAPERS, INC.—See Cox Enterprises, Inc.; *U.S. Private*, pg. 281
SPRINGFIELD PRECISION INSTRUMENTS, INC.; *U.S. Private*, pg. 1027
SPRINGFIELD RELAY SYSTEMS, INC.—See Browning-Ferris Industries, Inc.; *U.S. Public*, pg. 264
SPRINGFIELD SUGAR & PROD. CO.—See SuperValu, Inc.; *U.S. Public*, pg. 1541
THE SPRINGFIELD SUN—See Landmark Communications, Inc.; *U.S. Private*, pg. 648
SPRINGHILL PAPERS DIV.—See International Paper Company; *U.S. Public*, pg. 903
SPRINGHOUSE CORPORATION—See Reed Elsevier plc; *Int'l*, pg. 1100
SPRINGS CANADA, LTD.—See Springs Industries, Inc.; *U.S. Public*, pg. 1500
SPRINGS DE MEXICO, S.A. DE C.V.—See Springs Industries, Inc.; *U.S. Public*, pg. 1500
SPRINGS INDUSTRIES, INC.; *U.S. Public*, pg. 1499
SPRINGS VALLEY MFG.—See Kimball International, Inc.; *U.S. Public*, pg. 957
SPRINGS WINDOW FASHIONS DIVISION—See Springs Industries, Inc.; *U.S. Public*, pg. 1500
THE SPRINGWALL MATTRESS CO.—See Schubert Industries Inc.; *U.S. Private*, pg. 973
SPRINKCAD—See Central Sprinkler Corporation; *U.S. Public*, pg. 327
G.W. SPRINKLER A/S—See Williams Holdings Plc; *Int'l*, pg. 1500
G.W. SPRINKLER GMBH—See Williams Holdings Plc; *Int'l*, pg. 1500
SPRINT BUSINESS—See Sprint Corporation; *U.S. Public*, pg. 1501
SPRINT CORPORATION; *U.S. Public*, pg. 1500
SPRINT INTERNATIONAL—See Sprint Corporation; *U.S. Public*, pg. 1500
SPRINT NORTH SUPPLY—See Sprint Corporation; *U.S. Public*, pg. 1501
SPRINT PARANET—See Sprint Corporation; *U.S. Public*, pg. 1501
SPRINT PCS—See Sprint Corporation; *U.S. Public*, pg. 1501
SPRINT PUBLISHING & ADVERTISING—See Sprint Corporation; *U.S. Public*, pg. 1501
SPRINT'S LOCAL TELECOMMUNICATION DIVISION—See Sprint Corporation; *U.S. Public*, pg. 1500
SPRINT'S LONG DISTANCE DIVISION—See Sprint Corporation; *U.S. Public*, pg. 1501
SPROTT OIL CO., INC.; *U.S. Private*, pg. 1027
SPRUCE FALLS INC.—See Tembec Inc.; *Int'l*, pg. 1375
SPRUCE INSURANCE LTD.—See Kemira Oy; *Int'l*, pg. 729
SPUR BELGIUM—See McKechnie PLC; *Int'l*, pg. 851
SPUR FRANCE—See McKechnie PLC; *Int'l*, pg. 851
SPUR HOLLAND—See McKechnie PLC; *Int'l*, pg. 851
SPUR REGAL-SYSTEME SRS—See McKechnie PLC; *Int'l*, pg. 851
SPUR SHELVING—See McKechnie PLC; *Int'l*, pg. 851
SPUR U.S.A. INC.—See McKechnie PLC; *Int'l*, pg. 851
SQUAMISH GAS—See BC Gas Inc.; *Int'l*, pg. 114
SQUARE BUTTE ELECTRIC COOPERATIVE—See Minnkota Power Cooperative, Inc.; *U.S. Private*, pg. 751
SQUARE D AUTOMATION PRODUCTS—See Schneider S.A.; *Int'l*, pg. 1208
SQUARE D CANADA—See Schneider S.A.; *Int'l*, pg. 1209
SQUARE D CO.—See Schneider S.A.; *Int'l*, pg. 1208
SQUARE D COMPANY—See Schneider S.A.; *Int'l*, pg. 1208
SQUARE D COMPANY ANDINA S.A.—See Schneider S.A.; *Int'l*, pg. 1209
SQUARE D COMPANY-ASSEMBLY OPERATIONS—See Schneider S.A.; *Int'l*, pg. 1208
SQUARE D COMPANY AUSTRALIA PTY. LIMITED—See Schneider S.A.; *Int'l*, pg. 1209
SQUARE D COMPANY CENTROAMERICA, S.A.—See Schneider S.A.; *Int'l*, pg. 1209
SQUARE D COMPANY (DEUTSCHLAND) GMBH—See Schneider S.A.; *Int'l*, pg. 1209
SQUARE D COMPANY ESPANA S.A.—See Schneider S.A.; *Int'l*, pg. 1209
SQUARE D COMPANY EUROPE—See Schneider S.A.; *Int'l*, pg. 1209
SQUARE D COMPANY IRELAND—See Schneider S.A.; *Int'l*, pg. 1209
SQUARE D COMPANY ITALIA, S.P.A.—See Schneider S.A.; *Int'l*, pg. 1209
SQUARE D COMPANY MANUFACTURING (THAILAND) LTD.—See Schneider S.A.; *Int'l*, pg. 1209
SQUARE D COMPANY MEXICO, S.A. DE C.V.—See Schneider S.A.; *Int'l*, pg. 1209
SQUARE D COMPANY-PACIFICO—See Schneider S.A.; *Int'l*, pg. 1208
SQUARE D COMPANY SINGAPORE PTE. LTD.—See Schneider S.A.; *Int'l*, pg. 1209
SQUARE D COMPANY UNITED KINGDOM LIMITED—See Schneider S.A.; *Int'l*, pg. 1209
SQUARE D MIDDLETOWN PLANT—See Schneider S.A.; *Int'l*, pg. 1208
SQUARE D SENECA PLANT—See Schneider S.A.; *Int'l*, pg. 1208
SQUARE D SOFTWARE LIMITED—See Marcam Solutions, Inc.; *U.S. Public*, pg. 1043
SQUARE INDUSTRIES, INC.—See Central Parking Corp.; *U.S. Public*, pg. 326
SQUARE PLUS GARAGE INC.—See Central Parking Corp.; *U.S. Public*, pg. 326
SQUARE PLUS OPERATING CORPORATION—See Central Parking Corp.; *U.S. Public*, pg. 326
SQUARE TWO GOLF INCORPORATED; *U.S. Public*, pg. 1501
SQUARE WHEELS B.V.—See Royal Begemann Group; *Int'l*, pg. 1133
SQUERI FOODSERVICE—See JP Foodservice, Inc.; *U.S. Public*, pg. 918
SQUIBB-CONTAVEC SA—See Bristol-Myers Squibb Company; *U.S. Public*, pg. 256
E.R. SQUIBB & SONS LTD.—See Bristol-Myers Squibb Company; *U.S. Public*, pg. 256
SQUIBB EUROPE INC.—See Bristol-Myers Squibb Company; *U.S. Public*, pg. 256
SQUIBB (FAR EAST) LTD.—See Bristol-Myers Squibb Company; *U.S. Public*, pg. 256
THE SQUIBB INSTITUTE FOR MEDICAL RESEARCH—See Bristol-Myers Squibb Company; *U.S. Public*, pg. 254
SQUIBB MANUFACTURING INC.—See Bristol-Myers Squibb Company; *U.S. Public*, pg. 254
SQUIBB MEDICAL SYSTEMS EUROPA GMBH—See Bristol-Myers Squibb Company; *U.S. Public*, pg. 256
SQUIBB SPA—See Bristol-Myers Squibb Company; *U.S. Public*, pg. 256
SQUIBB SURGICARE LTD.—See Bristol-Myers Squibb Company; *U.S. Public*, pg. 256
SQUIRE-COGSWELL COMPANY; *U.S. Private*, pg. 1027
SQUIRES ROBERTSON GILL; *Int'l*, pg. 1291
THE SRI MUANG INSURANCE CO., LTD.—See The Tokio Marine & Fire Insurance Company, Ltd.; *Int'l*, pg. 1392
SSANGYONG AUSTRALIA PTY., LTD.—See Ssangyong Business Group; *Int'l*, pg. 1291
SSANGYONG BUSINESS GROUP; *Int'l*, pg. 1291
SSANGYONG CEMENT INDUSTRIAL CO., LTD.—See Ssangyong Business Group; *Int'l*, pg. 1291
SSANGYONG CEMENT (SINGAPORE) LTD.—See Ssangyong Business Group; *Int'l*, pg. 1293
SSANGYONG CORPORATION—See Ssangyong Business Group; *Int'l*, pg. 1291
SSANGYONG DEVELOPMENTS PTE. LTD.—See Ssangyong Business Group; *Int'l*, pg. 1292
SSANGYONG ENG. & CONST. (M) SDN. BHD.—See Ssangyong Business Group; *Int'l*, pg. 1292
SSANGYONG ENGINEERING & CONSTRUCTION (AMERICA), INC.—See Ssangyong Business Group; *Int'l*, pg. 1292
SSANGYONG ENGINEERING & CONSTRUCTION CO., LTD.—See Ssangyong Business Group; *Int'l*, pg. 1291
SSANGYONG ENGINEERING CO., LTD.—See Ssangyong Business Group; *Int'l*, pg. 1292
SSANGYONG FINANCE INC.—See Ssangyong Business Group; *Int'l*, pg. 1292
SSANGYONG FIRE & MARINE INSURANCE CO., LTD.—See Ssangyong Business Group; *Int'l*, pg. 1292
SSANGYONG HEAVY INDUSTRIES CO., LTD.—See Ssangyong Business Group; *Int'l*, pg. 1292

SSANGYONG DIRECTORY OF CORPORATE AFFILIATIONS

Company Index

SSANGYONG (HONG KONG) CO., LTD.—See Ssangyong Business Group; *Int'l*, pg. 1291
SSANGYONG INFORMATION & COMMUNICATION CORPORATION—See Ssangyong Business Group; *Int'l*, pg. 1292
SSANGYONG INTERNATIONAL INC.—See Ssangyong Business Group; *Int'l*, pg. 1292
SSANGYONG INTERNATIONAL LTD.—See Ssangyong Business Group; *Int'l*, pg. 1292
SSANGYONG INVESTMENT & FINANCE CO., LTD.—See Ssangyong Business Group; *Int'l*, pg. 1292
SSANGYONG INVESTMENT & SECURITIES CO., LTD.—See Ssangyong Business Group; *Int'l*, pg. 1292
SSANGYONG INVESTMENT MANAGEMENT CO., LTD.—See Ssangyong Business Group; *Int'l*, pg. 1292
SSANGYONG JAPAN CORPORATION—See Ssangyong Business Group; *Int'l*, pg. 1291
SSANGYONG MOTOR COMPANY—See Ssangyong Business Group; *Int'l*, pg. 1292
SSANGYONG OIL REFINING CO. LTD.—See Ssangyong Business Group; *Int'l*, pg. 1292
SSANGYONG PACIFIC—See Ssangyong Business Group; *Int'l*, pg. 1292
SSANGYONG PAPER CO., LTD.—See Ssangyong Business Group; *Int'l*, pg. 1292
SSANGYONG PRECISION INDUSTRY CO., LTD.—See Ssangyong Business Group; *Int'l*, pg. 1292
SSANGYONG RESEARCH INSTITUTE—See Ssangyong Business Group; *Int'l*, pg. 1292
SSANGYONG RESOURCES DEVELOPMENT CO., LTD.—See Ssangyong Business Group; *Int'l*, pg. 1291
SSANGYONG RESOURCES PTY., LTD.—See Ssangyong Business Group; *Int'l*, pg. 1293
SSANGYONG SACRAMENTO LTD.—See Ssangyong Business Group; *Int'l*, pg. 1292
SSANGYONG SHIPPING CO. LTD.—See Ssangyong Business Group; *Int'l*, pg. 1292
SSANGYONG SINGAPORE PTE., LTD.—See Ssangyong Business Group; *Int'l*, pg. 1291
SSANGYONG UNI-CHARM CO., LTD.—See Ssangyong Business Group; *Int'l*, pg. 1291
SSANGYONG (U.S.A.) INC.—See Ssangyong Business Group; *Int'l*, pg. 1291
STA-RITE FOREIGN SALES CORPORATION—See WICOR, Inc.; *U.S. Public*, pg. 1767
STA-RITE INDUSTRIES, INC.—See WICOR, Inc.; *U.S. Public*, pg. 1767
STABBURET A/S—See Orkla A.S.A.; *Int'l*, pg. 1011
STABILATOR AB—See Skanska AB; *Int'l*, pg. 1261
STABILIMENTO—See IRI Istituto Ricostruzione Industriale; *Int'l*, pg. 654
STABILLUS SRL—See Mannesmann A.G.; *Int'l*, pg. 835
STABILMENTI CHIMICO FARMACEUTICI DOTT. R. RAVASINI & CIA. SPA—See Akzo Nobel N.V.; *Int'l*, pg. 45
STABILUS GMBH—See Mannesmann A.G.; *Int'l*, pg. 835
STABILUS LTD.—See Mannesmann A.G.; *Int'l*, pg. 835
STABILUS PTY. LTD.—See Mannesmann A.G.; *Int'l*, pg. 835
STABLER COMPANIES, INC.; *U.S. Private*, pg. 1028
STABLER CONSTRUCTION COMPANY—See Stabler Companies, Inc.; *U.S. Private*, pg. 1028
STACEY MOVING & STORAGE—See Planes Moving And Storage, Inc.; *U.S. Private*, pg. 869
STACEY'S/J. K. GILL RETAIL STORES—See Brodart Company; *U.S. Private*, pg. 170
STACKHOUSE INC.—See Thermo Electron Corporation; *U.S. Public*, pg. 1591
STACKIG ADVERTISING AND PUBLIC RELATIONS; *U.S. Private*, pg. 1028
STACKPOLE LIMITED—See Stackpole Ltd.; *U.S. Private*, pg. 1028
STACKPOLE LTD.; *U.S. Private*, pg. 1028
STACOENERGY PRODUCTS CO.—See Components Corporation Of America; *U.S. Private*, pg. 260
STACOSWITCH, INC.—See Components Corporation Of America; *U.S. Private*, pg. 260
STACY EQUIPMENT CO.—See Webster Industries Inc.; *U.S. Private*, pg. 1158
STADELMAN FRUIT L.L.C.; *U.S. Private*, pg. 1028
STADIUM LIMITED; *Int'l*, pg. 1293
STADTLANDER DRUG COMPANY, INC.—See Counsel Corporation; *Int'l*, pg. 338
STADTLANDER HMI—See Counsel Corporation; *Int'l*, pg. 338
STADTMUHLE CMZ ZURICH—See Coop Switzerland; *Int'l*, pg. 330
STADTSPARKASSE KOLN; *Int'l*, pg. 1293
STADTSPARKASSE MUNCHEN; *Int'l*, pg. 1293
STAENG LIMITED—See Bowthorpe plc; *Int'l*, pg. 207
STAFF BUILDERS INC.; *U.S. Public*, pg. 1501
STAFF/DMB&B—See DMB&B Communications; *U.S. Private*, pg. 305
STAFF SOURCE—See Hospital Staffing Services, Inc.; *U.S. Public*, pg. 841
STAFFING SOLUTIONS; *U.S. Private*, pg. 1028
STAFFORD-MILLER ARGENTINA S.A.—See Block Drug Company, Inc.; *U.S. Public*, pg. 237
STAFFORD-MILLER CONTINENTAL, N.V. S.A.—See Block Drug Company, Inc.; *U.S. Public*, pg. 237
STAFFORD-MILLER DE ESPANA—See Block Drug Company, Inc.; *U.S. Public*, pg. 237
STAFFORD-MILLER DE MEXICO S.A. DE C.V.—See Block Drug Company, Inc.; *U.S. Public*, pg. 237
STAFFORD-MILLER FARMACEUTICA, LTDA.—See Block Drug Company, Inc.; *U.S. Public*, pg. 237
STAFFORD-MILLER INTL., INC.—See Block Drug Company, Inc.; *U.S. Public*, pg. 237
STAFFORD-MILLER (IRELAND) LIMITED—See Block Drug Company, Inc.; *U.S. Public*, pg. 237
STAFFORD-MILLER LIMITED—See Block Drug Company, Inc.; *U.S. Public*, pg. 237
STAFFORD-MILLER LTD.—See Block Drug Company, Inc.; *U.S. Public*, pg. 237
STAFFORD-MILLER (N.Z.) LIMITED—See Block Drug Company, Inc.; *U.S. Public*, pg. 237
STAFFORD-MILLER S.R.L.—See Block Drug Company, Inc.; *U.S. Public*, pg. 237
STAFLEX/HAROTEX—See The Harodite Finishing Company Inc.; *U.S. Private*, pg. 504
STAFLEX PRODUCTS—See The C.P. Hall Company; *U.S. Private*, pg. 495
STAG BREWERY—See Anheuser-Busch Companies, Inc.; *U.S. Public*, pg. 115
STAGE STORES, INC.; *U.S. Private*, pg. 1028
STAGEBILL—See Primedia Inc.; *U.S. Public*, pg. 1328
STAHL ASIA PTE LTD—See Zeneca Group Plc; *Int'l*, pg. 1526
STAHL AUSTRALIA PTY LTD—See Zeneca Group Plc; *Int'l*, pg. 1526
STAHL BRASIL SA—See Zeneca Group Plc; *Int'l*, pg. 1526
STAHL CANADA LIMITED—See Zeneca Group Plc; *Int'l*, pg. 1526
STAHL CHEMICAL INDUSTRIES BV GMBH—See Zeneca Group Plc; *Int'l*, pg. 1526
STAHL CONSTRUCTION COMPANY—See Curran Group, Inc.; *U.S. Private*, pg. 297
STAHL DE MEXICO, S.A. DE C.V.—See Zeneca Group Plc; *Int'l*, pg. 1526
STAHL DIV.—See Berkshire Hathaway Inc.; *U.S. Public*, pg. 218
STAHL FRANCE S.A.R.L.—See Zeneca Group Plc; *Int'l*, pg. 1526
STAHL GB LIMITED—See Zeneca Group Plc; *Int'l*, pg. 1524
STAHL GMBH & CO.; *Int'l*, pg. 1293
STAHL HOLLAND B.V.—See Zeneca Group Plc; *Int'l*, pg. 1526
STAHL IBERICA, S.A.—See Zeneca Group Plc; *Int'l*, pg. 1526
STAHL INTERNATIONAL B.V.—See Zeneca Group Plc; *Int'l*, pg. 1526
STAHL ITALIA SRL—See Zeneca Group Plc; *Int'l*, pg. 1526
STAHL PORTUGUESA, LDA—See Zeneca Group Plc; *Int'l*, pg. 1526
STAHL SPECIALTY COMPANY; *U.S. Private*, pg. 1029
STAHLBAU LAVIS OFFENBACH GMBH—See Philipp Holzmann AG; *Int'l*, pg. 633
WILHELM STAHLECKER GMBH—See Spindelfabrik Suessen; *Int'l*, pg. 1290
STAHLEX GMBH—See Veba AG; *Int'l*, pg. 1459
STAHLHOCHBAU LUBBEN GMBH—See Dyckerhoff & Widmann AG; *Int'l*, pg. 423
STAHLKONTOR HAHN GMBH—See Mannesmann A.G.; *Int'l*, pg. 838
STAHLWERK THURINGEN GMBH—See Arbed S.A.; *Int'l*, pg. 79
STAHLWERKE BREMEN GMBH—See Arbed S.A.; *Int'l*, pg. 79
STAHMANN FARMS, INC.; *U.S. Private*, pg. 1029
STAINLESS ICE-TAINER CO. (SITCO)—See IMI Plc; *Int'l*, pg. 646
STAINLESS INCORPORATED; *U.S. Private*, pg. 1029
STAINLESS PRODUCTS—See The Broken Hill Proprietary Company Limited; *Int'l*, pg. 227
STAINLESS TUBULAR PRODUCTS, INC.—See Hughes Supply, Inc.; *U.S. Public*, pg. 847
STAKMORE INC.; *U.S. Private*, pg. 1029
STAL REFRIGERATION AB—See ABB Asea Brown Boveri (Holding) Ltd.; *Int'l*, pg. 7
A.E. STALEY MANUFACTURING CO.—See Tate & Lyle PLC; *Int'l*, pg. 1356
STALKER HUTCHINSON & ASSOCIATES (PTY.) LTD.—See Assicurazioni Generali S.p.A.; *Int'l*, pg. 92
STALKER HUTCHINSON SYSTEMS (PTY.) LTD.—See Assicurazioni Generali S.p.A.; *Int'l*, pg. 92
STALO CHEMICALS GMBH—See Henkel KGaA; *Int'l*, pg. 610
STAMCO-DEPIEREUX GMBH—See The Monarch Machine Tool Company; *U.S. Public*, pg. 1124
STAMCO DIV.—See The Monarch Machine Tool Company; *U.S. Public*, pg. 1124
STAMCO INDUSTRIES INC.; *U.S. Private*, pg. 1029
STAMCO (U.K.) LTD.—See The Monarch Machine Tool Company; *U.S. Public*, pg. 1124
STAMFORD CAPITAL; *U.S. Private*, pg. 1029
STAMFORD FOOD INDUSTRIES SDN. BERHAD—See Corn Products International, Inc.; *U.S. Public*, pg. 447
STAMFORD HOLDINGS B.V. (NETHERLANDS)—See Bristol-Myers Squibb Company; *U.S. Public*, pg. 256
STAMFORD HOTELS & RESORTS PTY LIMITED—See Hai Sun Hup Group Ltd.; *Int'l*, pg. 586
STAMFORD SUPERIOR DRUG CO., INC.—See Bindley Western Industries, Inc.; *U.S. Public*, pg. 229
STAMICARBON BV—See DSM N.V.; *Int'l*, pg. 354
STAMLER CORPORATION—See The Oldenburg Group Companies; *U.S. Private*, pg. 814
STAMPEN S.A.—See Commerzbank AG; *Int'l*, pg. 312
STAMPTECH—See Maclean-Fogg Co.; *U.S. Private*, pg. 692
STANBACK COMPANY; *U.S. Private*, pg. 1030
STANBEE COMPANY, INC.; *U.S. Private*, pg. 1030
STANBIC BANK BOTSWANA LIMITED—See Standard Bank Investment Corporation Limited; *Int'l*, pg. 1293
STANBIC BANK KENYA LIMITED—See Standard Bank Investment Corporation Limited; *Int'l*, pg. 1293
STANBIC BANK LESOTHO LIMITED—See Standard Bank Investment Corporation Limited; *Int'l*, pg. 1293
STANBIC BANK NAMIBIA LIMITED—See Standard Bank Investment Corporation Limited; *Int'l*, pg. 1293
STANBIC BANK SWAZILAND LIMITED—See Standard Bank Investment Corporation Limited; *Int'l*, pg. 1293
STANBIC BANK UGANDA LIMITED—See Standard Bank Investment Corporation Limited; *Int'l*, pg. 1294
STANBIC BANK ZAIRE S.Z.A.R.L.—See Standard Bank Investment Corporation Limited; *Int'l*, pg. 1294
STANBIC BANK ZAMBIA—See Standard Bank Investment Corporation Limited; *Int'l*, pg. 1294
STANBIC BANK ZIMBABWE LIMITED—See Standard Bank Investment Corporation Limited; *Int'l*, pg. 1294
STANBIC MERCHANT BANK NIGERIA LIMITED—See Standard Bank Investment Corporation Limited; *Int'l*, pg. 1294
STANCHEM INC.; *U.S. Private*, pg. 1030
STANCO METAL PRODUCTS, INC.; *U.S. Private*, pg. 1030
STANCOM HOME CENTER, INC.—See Standard Commercial Corporation; *U.S. Public*, pg. 1502
STANCOM TOBACCO CO. (MALAWI) LTD.—See Standard Commercial Corporation; *U.S. Public*, pg. 1502
STANCOM TOBACCO PACKERS (MALAWI) LTD.—See Standard Commercial Corporation; *U.S. Public*, pg. 1502
STAND-COTE INDUSTRIAL COATINGS DIV.—See Standco Industries, Inc.; *U.S. Private*, pg. 1032
STANDARD ALLOYS & MANUFACTURING—See Blue Tee Corporation; *U.S. Private*, pg. 153
STANDARD & POOR'S COMPUSTAT SERVICES, INC.—See The McGraw-Hill Companies; *U.S. Public*, pg. 1071
STANDARD & POOR'S INTERNATIONAL S.A.—See The McGraw-Hill Companies; *U.S. Public*, pg. 1072
STANDARD & POOR'S RATINGS SERVICES—See The McGraw-Hill Companies; *U.S. Public*, pg. 1071
STANDARD ARROW LTD.—See BTR plc; *Int'l*, pg. 127
STANDARD AUTOMOTIVE CORPORATION; *U.S. Private*, pg. 1030
STANDARD BANK INVESTMENT CORPORATION (ISLE OF MAN) LIMITED—See Standard Bank Investment Corporation Limited; *Int'l*, pg. 1294
STANDARD BANK INVESTMENT CORPORATION LIMITED; *Int'l*, pg. 1293
STANDARD BANK (JERSEY) LIMITED—See Standard Bank Investment Corporation Limited; *Int'l*, pg. 1294
THE STANDARD BANK OF SOUTH AFRICA—See Standard Bank Investment Corporation Limited; *Int'l*, pg. 1293
THE STANDARD BANK OF SOUTH AFRICA LIMITED—See Standard Bank Investment Corporation Limited; *Int'l*, pg. 1294
THE STANDARD BANK OF SOUTH AFRICA LIMITED REPRESENTATIVE OFFICE—See Standard Bank Investment Corporation Limited; *Int'l*, pg. 1294
STANDARD BROKERAGE SERVICES, INC.—See ABN-AMRO Holding N.V.; *Int'l*, pg. 11
STANDARD CANDY CO., INC.; *U.S. Private*, pg. 1030
STANDARD CAP & SEAL—See Sonoco Products Company; *U.S. Public*, pg. 1486
STANDARD CHARTERED ASIA LIMITED—See Standard Chartered Bank PLC; *Int'l*, pg. 1296
STANDARD CHARTERED ASIA (TAIWAN) LIMITED—See Standard Chartered Bank PLC; *Int'l*, pg. 1296
STANDARD CHARTERED AUSTRALIA LIMITED—See Standard Chartered Bank PLC; *Int'l*, pg. 1296
STANDARD CHARTERED BANK—See Standard Chartered Bank PLC; *Int'l*, pg. 1294
STANDARD CHARTERED BANK AUSTRALIA LIMITED—See Standard Chartered Bank PLC; *Int'l*, pg. 1294
STANDARD CHARTERED BANK (BAHRAIN)—See Standard Chartered Bank PLC; *Int'l*, pg. 1295
STANDARD CHARTERED BANK BOTSWANA LIMITED—See Standard Chartered Bank PLC; *Int'l*, pg. 1294
STANDARD CHARTERED BANK (BRAZIL)—See Standard Chartered Bank PLC; *Int'l*, pg. 1295
STANDARD CHARTERED BANK (CAMBODIA)—See Standard Chartered Bank PLC; *Int'l*, pg. 1295
STANDARD CHARTERED BANK CAMEROON S.A.—See Standard Chartered Bank PLC; *Int'l*, pg. 1294
STANDARD CHARTERED BANK (C.I.) LIMITED—See Standard Chartered Bank PLC; *Int'l*, pg. 1294
STANDARD CHARTERED BANK GAMBIA LTD.—See Standard Chartered Bank PLC; *Int'l*, pg. 1294
STANDARD CHARTERED BANK GHANA LTD.—See Standard Chartered Bank PLC; *Int'l*, pg. 1294
STANDARD CHARTERED BANK (INDONESIA)—See Standard Chartered Bank PLC; *Int'l*, pg. 1295
STANDARD CHARTERED BANK (IRAN)—See Standard Chartered Bank PLC; *Int'l*, pg. 1295
STANDARD CHARTERED BANK LESOTHO LIMITED—See Standard Chartered Bank PLC; *Int'l*, pg. 1295
STANDARD CHARTERED BANK (LOS ANGELES)—See Standard Chartered Bank PLC; *Int'l*, pg. 1294
STANDARD CHARTERED BANK (MACAO)—See Standard Chartered Bank PLC; *Int'l*, pg. 1295
STANDARD CHARTERED BANK, MERCHANT BANK SERVICES—See Standard Chartered Bank PLC; *Int'l*, pg. 1296
STANDARD CHARTERED BANK, MERCHANT BANKING DIVISION—See Standard Chartered Bank PLC; *Int'l*, pg. 1296
STANDARD CHARTERED BANK (MEXICO)—See Standard Chartered Bank PLC; *Int'l*, pg. 1295
STANDARD CHARTERED BANK (NEGARA BRUNEI DARUSSALAM)—See Standard Chartered Bank PLC; *Int'l*, pg. 1295
STANDARD CHARTERED BANK (NEPAL)—See Standard Chartered Bank PLC; *Int'l*, pg. 1295
STANDARD CHARTERED BANK (NEW YORK)—See Standard Chartered Bank PLC; *Int'l*, pg. 1294
STANDARD CHARTERED BANK (OMAN)—See Standard Chartered Bank PLC; *Int'l*, pg. 1295
STANDARD CHARTERED BANK (PAKISTAN)—See Standard Chartered Bank PLC; *Int'l*, pg. 1295
STANDARD CHARTERED BANK (PERU)—See Standard Chartered Bank PLC; *Int'l*, pg. 1295
STANDARD CHARTERED BANK (PHILIPPINES)—See Standard Chartered Bank PLC; *Int'l*, pg. 1295
STANDARD CHARTERED BANK PLC; *Int'l*, pg. 1294
STANDARD CHARTERED BANK (QATAR)—See Standard Chartered Bank PLC; *Int'l*, pg. 1295
STANDARD CHARTERED BANK SIERRA LEONE LTD.—See Standard Chartered Bank PLC; *Int'l*, pg. 1295
STANDARD CHARTERED BANK (SINGAPORE)—See Standard Chartered Bank PLC; *Int'l*, pg. 1295

STANDARD CHARTERED BANK (SOUTH AFRICA)—See Standard Chartered Bank PLC; *Int'l*, pg. 1295

STANDARD CHARTERED BANK (SOUTH KOREA)—See Standard Chartered Bank PLC; *Int'l*, pg. 1296

STANDARD CHARTERED BANK SWAZILAND LIMITED—See Standard Chartered Bank PLC; *Int'l*, pg. 1295

STANDARD CHARTERED BANK (SWITZERLAND)—See Standard Chartered Bank PLC; *Int'l*, pg. 1295

STANDARD CHARTERED BANK (TAIWAN)—See Standard Chartered Bank PLC; *Int'l*, pg. 1295

STANDARD CHARTERED BANK TANZANIA LIMITED—See Standard Chartered Bank PLC; *Int'l*, pg. 1295

STANDARD CHARTERED BANK (THAILAND)—See Standard Chartered Bank PLC; *Int'l*, pg. 1296

STANDARD CHARTERED BANK UGANDA LTD.—See Standard Chartered Bank PLC; *Int'l*, pg. 1295

STANDARD CHARTERED BANK (VENEZUELA)—See Standard Chartered Bank PLC; *Int'l*, pg. 1296

STANDARD CHARTERED BANK (VIETNAM)—See Standard Chartered Bank PLC; *Int'l*, pg. 1296

STANDARD CHARTERED BANK ZAMBIA LTD.—See Standard Chartered Bank PLC; *Int'l*, pg. 1295

STANDARD CHARTERED BANK ZIMBABWE LIMITED—See Standard Chartered Bank PLC; *Int'l*, pg. 1295

STANDARD CHARTERED EQUITOR GROUP LIMITED—See Standard Chartered Bank PLC; *Int'l*, pg. 1296

STANDARD CHARTERED EQUITOR TRUSTEE SINGAPORE LIMITED—See Standard Chartered Bank PLC; *Int'l*, pg. 1296

STANDARD CHARTERED ESTATE MANAGEMENT LIMITED—See Standard Chartered Bank PLC; *Int'l*, pg. 1295

STANDARD CHARTERED FINANCE (BRUNEI) BERHAD—See Standard Chartered Bank PLC; *Int'l*, pg. 1297

STANDARD CHARTERED FINANCE LIMITED—See Standard Chartered Bank PLC; *Int'l*, pg. 1297

STANDARD CHARTERED FINANCE UGANDA LIMITED—See Standard Chartered Bank PLC; *Int'l*, pg. 1297

STANDARD CHARTERED FINANCE ZIMBABWE LIMITED—See Standard Chartered Bank PLC; *Int'l*, pg. 1297

STANDARD CHARTERED FINANCIAL SERVICES LIMITED—See Standard Chartered Bank PLC; *Int'l*, pg. 1296

STANDARD CHARTERED FUTURES (SINGAPORE) PTE LIMITED—See Standard Chartered Bank PLC; *Int'l*, pg. 1295

STANDARD CHARTERED LEASING COMPANY LTD.—See Standard Chartered Bank PLC; *Int'l*, pg. 1296

STANDARD CHARTERED LEASING GMBH—See Standard Chartered Bank PLC; *Int'l*, pg. 1297

P.T. STANDARD CHARTERED LEASING—See Standard Chartered Bank PLC; *Int'l*, pg. 1297

STANDARD CHARTERED LEASING SARL—See Standard Chartered Bank PLC; *Int'l*, pg. 1297

STANDARD CHARTERED MERCHANT BANK ASIA LIMITED—See Standard Chartered Bank PLC; *Int'l*, pg. 1296

STANDARD CHARTERED MERCHANT BANK ZIMBABWE LIMITED—See Standard Chartered Bank PLC; *Int'l*, pg. 1296

P.T. STANDARD CHARTERED SECURITIES—See Standard Chartered Bank PLC; *Int'l*, pg. 1296

STANDARD CHARTERED SECURITIES ASIA LIMITED—See Standard Chartered Bank PLC; *Int'l*, pg. 1296

STANDARD CHARTERED SECURITIES INVESTMENT PTE LIMITED—See Standard Chartered Bank PLC; *Int'l*, pg. 1296

STANDARD CHARTERED SECURITIES LIMITED—See Standard Chartered Bank PLC; *Int'l*, pg. 1296

STANDARD CHARTERED THAILAND LIMITED—See Standard Chartered Bank PLC; *Int'l*, pg. 1296

STANDARD CHLORINE CLOROBEN CHEMICAL CORPORATION; *U.S. Private*, pg. 1031

STANDARD COFFEE SERVICE—See William B. Reily & Co., Inc.; *U.S. Private*, pg. 919

STANDARD COMMERCIAL CORPORATION; *U.S. Public*, pg. 1501

STANDARD COMMERCIAL (U.K.)—See Standard Commercial Corporation; *U.S. Public*, pg. 1502

STANDARD COMMUNICATIONS—See Peoples Telephone Company, Inc.; *U.S. Public*, pg. 1276

STANDARD COMMUNICATIONS CORP.—See Marantz Japan Inc.; *Int'l*, pg. 841

STANDARD CONCRETE—See Heidelberger Zement A.G.; *Int'l*, pg. 605

STANDARD CRESSALL LIMITED—See Halma p.l.c.; *Int'l*, pg. 590

STANDARD DIVISION—See Standard Motor Products Inc.; *U.S. Public*, pg. 1503

STANDARD DUPLICATING MACHINES CORP.; *U.S. Private*, pg. 1031

STANDARD ELECTRONICS, INC.; *U.S. Private*, pg. 1031

STANDARD EXAMINER; *U.S. Private*, pg. 1031

STANDARD FEDERAL BANK—See ABN-AMRO Holding N.V.; *Int'l*, pg. 10

STANDARD FLOUR CO.—See CSM N.V.; *Int'l*, pg. 244

THE STANDARD-FREEHOLDER—See Hollinger Inc.; *Int'l*, pg. 631

THE STANDARD GENERAL INSURANCE COMPANY LTD.—See Assicurazioni Generali S.p.A.; *Int'l*, pg. 92

STANDARD HAVENS—See Raytheon Company; *U.S. Public*, pg. 1365

STANDARD INDUSTRIES, INC.; *U.S. Private*, pg. 1031

STANDARD INSURANCE CO.; *U.S. Private*, pg. 1031

STANDARD-KNAPP, INC.; *U.S. Private*, pg. 1031

STANDARD LIFE & ACCIDENT INSURANCE CO.—See American National Insurance Company; *U.S. Public*, pg. 88

STANDARD LIFE ASSURANCE; *Int'l*, pg. 1297

STANDARD LOCKNUT, INC.; *U.S. Private*, pg. 1031

STANDARD LONDON (ASIA) LIMITED—See Standard Bank Investment Corporation Limited; *Int'l*, pg. 1294

STANDARD MANAGEMENT CORPORATION; *U.S. Public*, pg. 1502

STANDARD MANIFOLD COMPANY, INC.; *U.S. Private*, pg. 1031

STANDARD MANUFACTURING CO., INC.; *U.S. Private*, pg. 1031

STANDARD MARINE A/S—See SAIT-RadioHolland Group S.A.; *Int'l*, pg. 1152

STANDARD MEDICAL IMAGING, INC.; *U.S. Private*, pg. 1032

STANDARD METALS CORPORATION; *U.S. Public*, pg. 1502

STANDARD MICROSYSTEMS CORP.; *U.S. Public*, pg. 1502

STANDARD MOTOR PRODUCTS HONG KONG LIMITED—See Standard Motor Products Inc.; *U.S. Public*, pg. 1503

STANDARD MOTOR PRODUCTS INC.; *U.S. Public*, pg. 1503

STANDARD NEW YORK INC.—See Standard Bank Investment Corporation Limited; *Int'l*, pg. 1293

STANDARD PACIFIC CORP.; *U.S. Public*, pg. 1503

STANDARD PACIFIC-NO. CALIFORNIA—See Standard Pacific Corp.; *U.S. Public*, pg. 1503

STANDARD PACIFIC OF SAN DIEGO—See Standard Pacific Corp.; *U.S. Public*, pg. 1503

STANDARD PACIFIC SAVINGS, F. A.—See Standard Pacific Corp.; *U.S. Public*, pg. 1504

STANDARD-PACIFIC-TEXAS, INC.—See Standard Pacific Corp.; *U.S. Public*, pg. 1504

STANDARD PACIFIC VENTURA—See Standard Pacific Corp.; *U.S. Public*, pg. 1504

STANDARD PIPE LINE CO.—See Chevron Corporation; *U.S. Public*, pg. 348

STANDARD PLYWOODS, INC.; *U.S. Private*, pg. 1032

STANDARD PRODUCTS (CANADA) LTD.—See The Standard Products Company; *U.S. Public*, pg. 1505

THE STANDARD PRODUCTS COMPANY; *U.S. Public*, pg. 1504

STANDARD PRODUCTS INDUSTRIAL—See The Standard Products Company; *U.S. Public*, pg. 1505

STANDARD PROPERTY CORPORATION—See Highmark Inc.; *U.S. Private*, pg. 529

STANDARD PUBLISHING—See Standex International Corporation; *U.S. Public*, pg. 1506

STANDARD REGISTER-BARRINGTON—See The Standard Register Company; *U.S. Public*, pg. 1505

THE STANDARD REGISTER COMPANY; *U.S. Public*, pg. 1505

STANDARD RESEARCH CONSULTANTS—See American Appraisal Associates, Inc.; *U.S. Private*, pg. 50

STANDARD RESTAURANT EQUIPMENT CO.—See Standard Industries, Inc.; *U.S. Private*, pg. 1031

STANDARD SECURITY LIFE INSURANCE COMPANY OF NEW YORK—See Geneve Corporation; *U.S. Private*, pg. 446

STANDARD STEEL—See Freedom Forge Corporation; *U.S. Private*, pg. 425

STANDARD SUPPLY & HARDWARE CO.; *U.S. Private*, pg. 1032

STANDARD TAG MFG. CO.—See Mail-Well Inc.; *U.S. Public*, pg. 1038

STANDARD TEXTILE CO., INC.; *U.S. Private*, pg. 1032

STANDARD-THOMSON CORPORATION—See Tomkins PLC; *Int'l*, pg. 1396

THE STANDARD TIMES—See Journal Register Company; *U.S. Public*, pg. 935

P.T. STANDARD TOYO POLYMER—See Tosoh Corporation; *Int'l*, pg. 1408

P.T. STANDARD TOYO POLYMER-MERAK PLANT—See Tosoh Corporation; *Int'l*, pg. 1408

STANDARD TUBE CANADA INC.—See Jannock Limited; *Int'l*, pg. 699

STANDARD WOOL, INC.—See Standard Commercial Corporation; *U.S. Public*, pg. 1502

STANDCO CANADA, LTD.—See SPS Technologies, Inc.; *U.S. Public*, pg. 1420

STANDCO INDUSTRIES, INC.; *U.S. Private*, pg. 1032

STANDCO OILFIELD PRODUCTS DIV.—See Standco Industries, Inc.; *U.S. Private*, pg. 1032

STANDERTON BREWERY—See National Sorghum Beer Breweries Pty. Ltd. Highveld Division; *Int'l*, pg. 909

STANDEX ELECTRONICS—See Standex International Corporation; *U.S. Public*, pg. 1507

STANDEX ELECTRONICS (U.K.) LTD.—See Standex International Corporation; *U.S. Public*, pg. 1507

STANDEX HOLDINGS LIMITED—See Standex International Corporation; *U.S. Public*, pg. 1507

STANDEX INTERNATIONAL CORPORATION; *U.S. Public*, pg. 1505

STANDEX INTERNATIONAL GMBH—See Standex International Corporation; *U.S. Public*, pg. 1507

STANDEX INTERNATIONAL GMBH, MOLD-TECH SOUTH—See Standex International Corporation; *U.S. Public*, pg. 1507

STANDEX INTERNATIONAL LIMITED—See Standex International Corporation; *U.S. Public*, pg. 1507

STANDEX INTERNATIONAL S.A.—See Standex International Corporation; *U.S. Public*, pg. 1507

STANDEX INTERNATIONAL S.R.L.—See Standex International Corporation; *U.S. Public*, pg. 1507

STANDEX (IRELAND) LTD.—See Standex International Corporation; *U.S. Public*, pg. 1508

STANDING ROCK CAMPGROUND—See Commerce Group Corp.; *U.S. Public*, pg. 410

STANDUN, INC.; *U.S. Private*, pg. 1032

STANFAST, INC.—See The Standard Register Company; *U.S. Public*, pg. 1505

STANFORD TELECOMMUNICATIONS; *U.S. Public*, pg. 1508

STANGE (JAPAN) K.K.—See McCormick & Company, Incorporated; *U.S. Public*, pg. 1067

STANHOME DE MEXICO, S.A. DE C.V.—See Stanhome Inc.; *U.S. Public*, pg. 1508

STANHOME INC.; *U.S. Public*, pg. 1508

STANHOME PANAMERICANA, C.A.—See Stanhome Inc.; *U.S. Public*, pg. 1508

STANHOME S.A.—See Stanhome Inc.; *U.S. Public*, pg. 1508

STANHOME S.P.A.—See Stanhome Inc.; *U.S. Public*, pg. 1508

STANHOPE PENSION TRUST LTD.—See The General Electric Company, p.l.c.; *Int'l*, pg. 545

STANHOPE PRODUCTS COMPANY—See Brittany Corporation; *U.S. Private*, pg. 169

STANLEIGH INTERNATIONAL, INC.—See Kennington Ltd., Inc.; *U.S. Private*, pg. 615

STANLEY ACCESS TECHNOLOGIES—See The Stanley Works; *U.S. Public*, pg. 1509

STANLEY AIR TOOLS DIV.—See The Stanley Works; *U.S. Public*, pg. 1509

THE STANLEY CONSULTANTS GROUP; *U.S. Private*, pg. 1032

STANLEY CONSULTANTS, INC.—See The Stanley Consultants Group; *U.S. Private*, pg. 1033

STANLEY CUSTOMER SUPPORT DIV.—See The Stanley Works; *U.S. Public*, pg. 1509

STANLEY DESIGN-BUILD, INC.—See The Stanley Consultants Group; *U.S. Private*, pg. 1033

STANLEY DOOR SYSTEMS—See The Stanley Works; *U.S. Public*, pg. 1509

STANLEY DRYING COMPANY—See DEC International, Inc.; *U.S. Private*, pg. 301

STANLEY ENVIROMENTAL, INC.—See The Stanley Consultants Group; *U.S. Private*, pg. 1033

STANLEY FASTENING SYSTEMS—See The Stanley Works; *U.S. Public*, pg. 1509

STANLEY FURNITURE CO. INC.; *U.S. Public*, pg. 1508

STANLEY HARDWARE DIV.—See The Stanley Works; *U.S. Public*, pg. 1509

STANLEY HOME DECOR DIV.—See The Stanley Works; *U.S. Public*, pg. 1509

STANLEY HOME PRODUCTS—See CPAC, Inc.; *U.S. Public*, pg. 282

STANLEY HYDRAULIC TOOLS DIV.—See The Stanley Works; *U.S. Public*, pg. 1509

STANLEY KNIGHT CORPORATION; *U.S. Private*, pg. 1033

OWEN STANLEY FINANCIAL—See ING Groep N.V.; *Int'l*, pg. 651

STANLEY STEEMER INTERNATIONAL, INC.; *U.S. Private*, pg. 1033

STANLEY STORES, INC.; *U.S. Private*, pg. 1033

STANLEY TOOLS DIV.—See The Stanley Works; *U.S. Public*, pg. 1509

THE STANLEY WORKS; *U.S. Public*, pg. 1508

STANPAC CORP—See Standard Pacific Corp.; *U.S. Public*, pg. 1504

STANPAC PARTNERS—See Standard Pacific Corp.; *U.S. Public*, pg. 1504

STANRIC, INC.—See Standard Motor Products Inc.; *U.S. Public*, pg. 1503

STANSAND LIMITED—See The Tetley Group Limited; *Int'l*, pg. 1377

STANT CORPORATION—See Tomkins PLC; *Int'l*, pg. 1396

STANT MANUFACTURING INC.—See Tomkins PLC; *Int'l*, pg. 1397

STANTON PLC—See Saint-Gobain; *Int'l*, pg. 1177

STANTRON/PFT/EMI—See Zero Corporation; *U.S. Public*, pg. 1791

P.T. STANVAC INDONESIA—See Exxon Corporation; *U.S. Public*, pg. 603

STAODYN INC.; *U.S. Public*, pg. 1509

STAPLE COTTON COOPERATIVE ASSOCIATION; *U.S. Private*, pg. 1033

STAPLE COTTON DISCOUNT CORPORATION—See Staple Cotton Cooperative Association; *U.S. Private*, pg. 1033

STAPLES DISPOSABLES LIMITED—See James Crean PLC; *Int'l*, pg. 341

STAPLES, INC.; *U.S. Public*, pg. 1509

STAPO HOLLANDER INDUSTRIES; *U.S. Private*, pg. 1033

STAR ANCHORS & FASTENERS; *U.S. Private*, pg. 1033

STAR BALL RETAINER COMPANY OF IRELAND LTD.—See Mannesmann A.G.; *Int'l*, pg. 839

STAR BRONZE COMPANY; *U.S. Private*, pg. 1034

STAR BUFFET, INC.—See CKE Restaurants Inc.; *U.S. Public*, pg. 278

STAR BUILDING SYSTEMS—See Robertson-Ceco Corp.; *U.S. Public*, pg. 1394

STAR CHILDREN'S DRESS COMPANY, INC.; *U.S. Private*, pg. 1034

STAR CIRCUITS—See Daktronics, Inc.; *U.S. Public*, pg. 478

STAR CONTAINER, CO.—See The Tech Group; *U.S. Private*, pg. 1071

STAR CRANES—See Ederer Inc.; *U.S. Private*, pg. 363

STAR CUTTER CO.; *U.S. Private*, pg. 1034

STAR DATA SYSTEMS INC.—See The Mead Corporation; *U.S. Public*, pg. 1077

STAR EDITORIAL, INC.—See American Media, Inc.; *U.S. Public*, pg. 87

STAR EXPANSION SHIELDS LTD.—See STAR Anchors & Fasteners; *U.S. Private*, pg. 1034

STAR EXPORT SERVICES INC.—See Imperial Chemical Industries PLC; *Int'l*, pg. 664

STAR FINE FOODS, INC.; *U.S. Private*, pg. 1034

STAR FINISHING PRODUCTS, INC.—See RPM, Inc.; *U.S. Public*, pg. 1358

STAR FOOD PROCESSING, INC.; *U.S. Private*, pg. 1034

STAR FOOD PRODUCTS, INC.; *U.S. Private*, pg. 1034

STAR FURNITURE COMPANY—See Berkshire Hathaway Inc.; *U.S. Public*, pg. 221

STAR GAS CORPORATION—See Petroleum Heat & Power Co.; *U.S. Public*, pg. 1281

STAR INDUSTRIES INC.; *U.S. Private*, pg. 1034

STAR-KIST CARIBE, INC.—See H.J. Heinz Company; *U.S. Public*, pg. 806

STAR-KIST EUROPE, INC.—See H.J. Heinz Company; *U.S. Public*, pg. 807

STAR-KIST FOODS INC.—See H.J. Heinz Company; *U.S. Public*, pg. 805

STAR-KIST FOODS, INC.—See H.J. Heinz Company; *U.S. Public*, pg. 806

STAR LANGUAGE CENTER - LLC—See H.C. Miller Company; *U.S. Private*, pg. 747

STAR LUMBER & SUPPLY COMPANY, INC.; *U.S. Private*, pg. 1034

STAR MARKETS COMPANY, INC.; *U.S. Private*, pg. 1035

STAR MICRONICS CO., LTD.—See Citizen Watch Company, Ltd.; *Int'l*, pg. 294

STAR MIKRON SPA—See Mannesmann A.G.; *Int'l*, pg. 839

STAR MOBELWERK GMBH—See Stora Kopparbergs Bergslags AB; *Int'l*, pg. 1303

P.T. STAR MOTORS INDONESIA—See Daimler-Benz Aktiengesellschaft; *Int'l*, pg. 369

STAR MULTI CARE SERVICES INC.; *U.S. Public*, pg. 1510

STAR PAPER TUBE DE MEXICO, S.A. DE C.V.—See Caraustar Industries, Inc.; *U.S. Public*, pg. 304

STAR PAPER TUBE, INC.—See Caraustar Industries, Inc.; *U.S. Public*, pg. 304

STAR PUBLICATIONS—See Hollinger Inc.; *Int'l*, pg. 632

STAR RECYCLING, INC.—See Caraustar Industries, Inc.; *U.S. Public*, pg. 304

STAR SALES CO., INC.; *U.S. Private*, pg. 1035

STAR SANGYO CO., LTD.—See Suntory Ltd.; *Int'l*, pg. 1321

STAR S.P.A.—See Danone Group; *Int'l*, pg. 380

STAR STATES DEVELOPMENT CO.—See WSFS Financial Corporation; *U.S. Public*, pg. 1729

STAR-TELEGRAM NEWSPAPER, INC.—See Knight-Ridder, Inc.; *U.S. Public*, pg. 964

STAR TRANSPORTATION, INC.; *U.S. Private*, pg. 1035

STAR TRIBUNE, MINNEAPOLIS-ST. PAUL—See Cowles Media Company; *U.S. Private*, pg. 281

STAR TUBES (UK) LTD—See Rautaruukki Oy; *Int'l*, pg. 1088

STAR VIDEO ENTERTAINMENT, L.P.—See Valley Record Distributors, Inc.; *U.S. Private*, pg. 1132

STARBANC CORPORATION; *U.S. Public*, pg. 1510

STARBOARD DATA SERVICES, INC.—See Arrowhead Holding Corporation; *U.S. Private*, pg. 86

STARBOARD INDUSTRIES, INC.—See JPE, Inc.; *U.S. Public*, pg. 919

STARBRITE CORP.; *U.S. Public*, pg. 1510

STARBUCKS COFFEE COMPANY; *U.S. Public*, pg. 1510

STARCAN CORPORATION; *Int'l*, pg. 1297

STARCH AUSTRALASIA—See Bestfoods; *U.S. Public*, pg. 224

STARCH AUSTRALIA—See Goodman Fielder Limited; *Int'l*, pg. 555

H.C. STARCK GMBH—See Bayer AG; *Int'l*, pg. 172

H.C. STARCK INC.—See Bayer AG; *Int'l*, pg. 174

HERMANN C. STARCK, INC.—See Bayer AG; *Int'l*, pg. 175

STARCRAFT AUTOMOTIVE GROUP, INC.—See Starcraft Corporation; *U.S. Public*, pg. 1511

STARCRAFT CORPORATION; *U.S. Public*, pg. 1510

STARCREST OF CALIFORNIA—See Starcrest Products of California; *U.S. Private*, pg. 1035

STARCREST PRODUCTS OF CALIFORNIA; *U.S. Private*, pg. 1035

THE STARFLO CORPORATION—See The Wm. Powell Company; *U.S. Private*, pg. 877

STARK CANDY COMPANY—See UIS, Inc.; *U.S. Private*, pg. 1113

STARKE DIEKSTRA NV—See Heidemij N.V.; *Int'l*, pg. 608

STARKEY LABORATORIES, INC.; *U.S. Private*, pg. 1035

AB STARLA-WERKEN—See Tenneco Inc.; *U.S. Public*, pg. 1580

STARLUX—See Bestfoods; *U.S. Public*, pg. 225

STARMARK, INC.—See Masco Corporation; *U.S. Public*, pg. 1054

STARMARK OF VIRGINIA—See Masco Corporation; *U.S. Public*, pg. 1054

STARMET CORPORATION; *U.S. Public*, pg. 1511

STARRETT GRANITE SURFACE PLATE DIVISION—See The L.S. Starrett Company; *U.S. Public*, pg. 1511

STARRETT HRH; *U.S. Private*, pg. 1035

STARRETT INDUSTRIAL E COMERCIO LTDA.—See The L.S. Starrett Company; *U.S. Public*, pg. 1511

THE L.S. STARRETT COMPANY; *U.S. Public*, pg. 1511

L.S. STARRETT CO. LTD.—See The L.S. Starrett Company; *U.S. Public*, pg. 1511

L.S. STARRETT COMPANY OF CANADA—See The L.S. Starrett Company; *U.S. Public*, pg. 1511

STARSIGHT TELECAST, INC.—See Gemstar International Group Limited; *U.S. Public*, pg. 705

STARTEC GLOBAL COMMUNICATIONS CORPORATION; *U.S. Public*, pg. 1511

STARTER CORP.; *U.S. Public*, pg. 1511

STARVING STUDENTS, INC.; *U.S. Private*, pg. 1035

STARWOOD CAPITAL GROUP LLC; *U.S. Private*, pg. 1036

STARWOOD HOTELS & RESORTS; *U.S. Public*, pg. 1512

STARWOOD LODGING CORPORATION—See Starwood Hotels & Resorts; *U.S. Public*, pg. 1512

STAT MEDICAL EQUIPMENT, INC.—See Integrated Health Services, Inc.; *U.S. Public*, pg. 885

STATE ADVERTISING AGENCY, INC.—See Evans, Inc.; *U.S. Public*, pg. 597

STATE AUTO LIFE INSURANCE COMPANY—See Financial Industries Corp.; *U.S. Public*, pg. 622

STATE AUTO P & C—See State Automobile Mutual Insurance Co.; *U.S. Private*, pg. 1036

STATE AUTOMOBILE MUTUAL INSURANCE CO.; *U.S. Private*, pg. 1036

THE STATE BANK AND TRUST COMPANY—See Rurban Financial Corp.; *U.S. Public*, pg. 1413

STATE BANK OF INDIA; *Int'l*, pg. 1297

STATE BANK OF INDIA (CANADA)—See State Bank of India; *Int'l*, pg. 1297

STATE BANK OF STANDISH—See Citizens Banking Corporation; *U.S. Public*, pg. 379

STATE ELECTRIC SUPPLY CO.; *U.S. Private*, pg. 1036

STATE ELECTRIC SUPPLY COMPANY—See State Electric Supply Co.; *U.S. Private*, pg. 1036

STATE FAIR FOODS—See Sara Lee Corporation; *U.S. Public*, pg. 1434

STATE FARM COUNTY MUTUAL INSURANCE CO. OF TEXAS—See State Farm Mutual Automobile Insurance Company; *U.S. Private*, pg. 1036

STATE FARM FIRE AND CASUALTY CO.—See State Farm Mutual Automobile Insurance Company; *U.S. Private*, pg. 1036

STATE FARM GENERAL INSURANCE CO.—See State Farm Mutual Automobile Insurance Company; *U.S. Private*, pg. 1036

STATE FARM LIFE AND ACCIDENT ASSURANCE CO.—See State Farm Mutual Automobile Insurance Company; *U.S. Private*, pg. 1036

STATE FARM LIFE INSURANCE CO.—See State Farm Mutual Automobile Insurance Company; *U.S. Private*, pg. 1036

STATE FARM LLOYDS, INC.—See State Farm Mutual Automobile Insurance Company; *U.S. Private*, pg. 1036

STATE FARM MUTUAL AUTOMOBILE INSURANCE COMPANY; *U.S. Private*, pg. 1036

STATE FIRST NATIONAL BANK, ARKANSAS—See First Commercial Corporation; *U.S. Public*, pg. 630

STATE FIRST NATIONAL BANK, TEXAS—See First Commercial Corporation; *U.S. Public*, pg. 630

STATE GAS & OIL COMPANY DIVISION—See Uni-Marts, Inc.; *U.S. Public*, pg. 1664

STATE HOME MORTGAGE CORP.—See Lennar Corporation; *U.S. Public*, pg. 989

STATE INDUSTRIES INC.; *U.S. Private*, pg. 1036

THE STATE JOURNAL-REGISTER—See The Copley Press, Inc.; *U.S. Private*, pg. 275

THE STATE PRINTING COMPANY, INC.—See Wallace Computer Services, Inc.; *U.S. Public*, pg. 1736

THE STATE-RECORD COMPANY—See Knight-Ridder, Inc.; *U.S. Public*, pg. 964

STATE STREET AUSTRALIA LTD.—See State Street Corporation; *U.S. Public*, pg. 1513

STATE STREET BANK & TRUST CO., LONDON—See State Street Corporation; *U.S. Public*, pg. 1513

STATE STREET BANK-HONG KONG BRANCH—See State Street Corporation; *U.S. Public*, pg. 1513

STATE STREET BANK-LONDON BRANCH—See State Street Corporation; *U.S. Public*, pg. 1513

STATE STREET BANK (LUXEMBOURG) S.A.—See State Street Corporation; *U.S. Public*, pg. 1513

STATE STREET BANK & TRUST CO.—See State Street Corporation; *U.S. Public*, pg. 1513

STATE STREET BANQUE S.A.—See State Street Corporation; *U.S. Public*, pg. 1513

STATE STREET CANADA, INC.—See State Street Corporation; *U.S. Public*, pg. 1513

STATE STREET CORPORATION; *U.S. Public*, pg. 1513

STATE STREET GLOBAL ADVISORS (U.K.) LIMITED—See State Street Corporation; *U.S. Public*, pg. 1513

STATE STREET GMBH—See State Street Corporation; *U.S. Public*, pg. 1513

STATE STREET RESEARCH & MANAGEMENT COMPANY—See Metropolitan Life Insurance Co.; *U.S. Private*, pg. 738

STATE STREET RESEARCH INVESTMENT SERVICES, INC.—See Metropolitan Life Insurance Co.; *U.S. Private*, pg. 738

STATE STREET TRUST & BANKING COMPANY, LTD.—See State Street Corporation; *U.S. Public*, pg. 1513

STATE UNIVERSITY RAILROAD CO.—See Norfolk Southern Corporation; *U.S. Public*, pg. 1191

STATE VOLUNTEER MUTUAL INSURANCE CO.; *U.S. Private*, pg. 1037

STATEN ISLAND PROPERTY INC.—See Bayerische Vereinsbank Group; *Int'l*, pg. 180

STATEN ISLAND TERMINAL—See GATX Corporation; *U.S. Public*, pg. 692

STATER BROS. INC.—See Craig Corporation; *U.S. Public*, pg. 456

STATER BROTHERS HOLDINGS—See Craig Corporation; *U.S. Public*, pg. 456

STATES, INC.; *U.S. Private*, pg. 1037

STATESBORO PLANT—See Cooper Industries, Inc.; *U.S. Public*, pg. 444

STATESMAN-JOURNAL CO., INC.—See Gannett Company, Inc.; *U.S. Public*, pg. 701

STATESVILLE AUTO AUCTION—See Cox Enterprises, Inc.; *U.S. Private*, pg. 283

STATESVILLE RECORD AND LANDMARK—See Media General, Inc.; *U.S. Public*, pg. 1078

STATEWIDE MORTGAGE COMPANY—See Norwest Corporation; *U.S. Public*, pg. 1202

STATEWIDE TRANSPORT, INC.—See Vulcan Materials Company; *U.S. Public*, pg. 1726

STATEX PETROLEUM, INC.—See PS Group Holdings; *U.S. Public*, pg. 1245

STATHAM INDUSTRIES—See International Paper Company; *U.S. Public*, pg. 905

STATIM FINANCE LIMITED—See Franz Haniel & Cie, GmbH; *Int'l*, pg. 591

STATION AND CABLE SERVICES DIV.—See Jefferson-Pilot Corporation; *U.S. Public*, pg. 925

STATIONERS, INC.—See Champion Industries; *U.S. Public*, pg. 333

STATIONERY HOUSE, INC.—See American Pad and Paper Company; *U.S. Public*, pg. 89

STATIONERY HOUSE, VIP DIVISION—See American Pad and Paper Company; *U.S. Public*, pg. 89

STATIONERY PRODUCTS DIVISION—See The Gillette Company; *U.S. Public*, pg. 744

STATOIL; *Int'l*, pg. 1297

STATOIL AB—See Statoil; *Int'l*, pg. 1298

STATOIL ANGOLA—See Statoil; *Int'l*, pg. 1298

STATOIL ANTWERP NSP—See Statoil; *Int'l*, pg. 1298

STATOIL A/S KALUNDBORG—See Statoil; *Int'l*, pg. 1298

STATOIL A/S PETROKEMI—See Statoil; *Int'l*, pg. 1298

STATOIL BAKU—See Statoil; *Int'l*, pg. 1298

STATOIL BELGIUM—See Statoil; *Int'l*, pg. 1298

STATOIL, BERGEN—See Statoil; *Int'l*, pg. 1298

STATOIL, BERGEN BASE—See Statoil; *Int'l*, pg. 1298

STATOIL, BOREALIS—See Statoil; *Int'l*, pg. 1298

STATOIL CIS MOSCOW—See Statoil; *Int'l*, pg. 1298

STATOIL DANMARK A/S—See Statoil; *Int'l*, pg. 1298

STATOIL, EESTI STATOIL A/S—See Statoil; *Int'l*, pg. 1298

STATOIL ENDEN—See Statoil; *Int'l*, pg. 1298

STATOIL EUROPARTS AB—See Statoil; *Int'l*, pg. 1298

STATOIL FAR EAST PTE. LTD.—See Statoil; *Int'l*, pg. 1298

STATOIL FINLAND OY—See Statoil; *Int'l*, pg. 1298

STATOIL, FLORO—See Statoil; *Int'l*, pg. 1298

STATOIL FRANCE SA—See Statoil; *Int'l*, pg. 1298

STATOIL, HAMANG—See Statoil; *Int'l*, pg. 1298

STATOIL IRELAND, LTD.—See Statoil; *Int'l*, pg. 1298

STATOIL, KRISTIANSUND—See Statoil; *Int'l*, pg. 1298

STATOIL MARKNAD PLASTER—See Statoil; *Int'l*, pg. 1298

STATOIL, METHANOL & MTBE DIVISION—See Statoil; *Int'l*, pg. 1298

STATOIL MINERALOEL GMBH—See Statoil; *Int'l*, pg. 1298

STATOIL, MONGSTAD—See Statoil; *Int'l*, pg. 1298

STATOIL (NIGERIA) LIMITED—See Statoil; *Int'l*, pg. 1298

STATOIL NORGE AS—See Statoil; *Int'l*, pg. 1298

STATOIL NORTH AMERICA INC.—See Statoil; *Int'l*, pg. 1298

STATOIL, NORTH NORWAY—See Statoil; *Int'l*, pg. 1298

STATOIL PETROCHEMICALS—See Statoil; *Int'l*, pg. 1298

STATOIL PETROKEMI AB—See Statoil; *Int'l*, pg. 1298

STATOIL POLAND LTD.—See Statoil; *Int'l*, pg. 1298

STATOIL, RESEARCH CENTRE—See Statoil; *Int'l*, pg. 1298

STATOIL, RIGA LATVIA—See Statoil; *Int'l*, pg. 1298

STATOIL (THAILAND) LTD.—See Statoil; *Int'l*, pg. 1298

STATOIL, TRANSPORT DIVISION BYGNES—See Statoil; *Int'l*, pg. 1298

STATOIL, TRANSPORT DIVISION KARSTO—See Statoil; *Int'l*, pg. 1298

STATOIL (UK) LTD.—See Statoil; *Int'l*, pg. 1298

STATOIL VIETNAM (HO CHI MINH CITY)—See Statoil; *Int'l*, pg. 1298

STATRON AG—See Alcatel Alsthom Compagnie Generale D'Electricite; *Int'l*, pg. 54

STAUFFER CHEMICAL BELGIUM—See Zeneca Group Plc; *Int'l*, pg. 1526

STAUFFER CHEMICAL B.V.—See Zeneca Group Plc; *Int'l*, pg. 1526

STAUFFER COMMUNICATIONS, INC.—See Shivers Trading & Operating Co.; *U.S. Private*, pg. 995

D.F. STAUFFER BISCUIT CO.—See Meiji Seika Kaisha, Ltd.; *Int'l*, pg. 855

STAUFFER JAPAN, LTD.—See Akzo Nobel N.V.; *Int'l*, pg. 47

STAUFFER MEDIA SYSTEMS, INC.—See Shivers Trading & Operating Co.; *U.S. Private*, pg. 995

STAUNTON LEADER PUBLISHING CO.—See Gannett Company, Inc.; *U.S. Public*, pg. 701

STAVELEY INDUSTRIES PLC; *Int'l*, pg. 1298

STAVELEY/NDT TECHNOLOGIES INC.—See Staveley Industries PLC; *Int'l*, pg. 1299

STAVELEY SENSORS DIVISION—See Staveley Industries PLC; *Int'l*, pg. 1299

STAVELEY WEIGHING SYSTEMS CANADA, INC.—See Staveley Industries PLC; *Int'l*, pg. 1299

STAWASZ & PARTNERS/HEALTH CARE COMMUNICATIONS—See Jordan, McGrath, Case & Taylor Inc.; *U.S. Private*, pg. 599

STEADFAST INSURANCE COMPANY—See Zurich Insurance Company; *Int'l*, pg. 1530

STEADLY COMPANY—See Leggett & Platt, Incorporated; *U.S. Public*, pg. 986

STEAK AND ALE RESTAURANTS—See Metromedia Company; *U.S. Private*, pg. 736

STEAK 'N SHAKE, INC.—See Consolidated Products, Inc.; *U.S. Public*, pg. 437

STEAKLEY CHEVROLET GEO SUBARU INC.; *U.S. Private*, pg. 1037

OY STEAMSERVICE AB—See Tamrock Corp.; *Int'l*, pg. 1353

THE STEARNS & FOSTER BEDDING COMPANY—See Sealy Corporation; *U.S. Private*, pg. 979

STEARNS COMPANY LIMITED—See Stearns Enterprises, Inc.; *U.S. Private*, pg. 1037

STEARNS ENTERPRISES, INC.; *U.S. Private*, pg. 1037

STEARNS MANUFACTURING COMPANY—See K2 Inc.; *U.S. Public*, pg. 940

STEARNS PHOENIX BROADWAY—See Stearns Enterprises, Inc.; *U.S. Private*, pg. 1037

STEBBINS ENGINEERING & MFG. CO.; *U.S. Private*, pg. 1037

STECK-VAUGHN COMPANY—See Harcourt General, Inc.; *U.S. Public*, pg. 784

STECK-VAUGHN DISTRIBUTION COMPANY—See Harcourt General, Inc.; *U.S. Public*, pg. 784

STECK-VAUGHN PUBLISHING CORPORATION—See Harcourt General, Inc.; *U.S. Public*, pg. 784

STECO—See Blue Tee Corporation; *U.S. Private*, pg. 153

STEEB SOFTWARE SERVICE GMBH—See Compagnie des Machines Bull; *Int'l*, pg. 317

STEEGO CORPORATION—See Brierley Investments Limited; *Int'l*, pg. 216

STEEL CEILINGS INC.—See Airtite Contractors Inc.; *U.S. Private*, pg. 29

STEEL FORM DIV.—See Ripplewood Holdings L.L.C.; *U.S. Private*, pg. 932

STEEL, INC.; *U.S. Private*, pg. 1037

S.A. JOHN STEEL INTERNATIONAL—See Cockerill Sambre; *Int'l*, pg. 302

STEEL MOULDS LTD.—See Tarmac plc; *Int'l*, pg. 1355

STEEL OF WEST VIRGINIA, INC.; *U.S. Public*, pg. 1513

STEEL PAINTS A/S—See Jotun A/S; *Int'l*, pg. 715

THE STOP & SHOP COMPANIES, INC.—See Koninklijke Ahold NV; *Int'l*, pg. 750
STOP IN FOOD STORES—See Petroleum Marketers, Inc.; *U.S. Private*, pg. 859
STOR & LITEN AB—See KF/Konsum Coop Group; *Int'l*, pg. 718
STORA BETEILIGUNGEN GMBH—See Stora Kopparbergs Bergslags AB; *Int'l*, pg. 1302
STORA BILLERUD AB—See Stora Kopparbergs Bergslags AB; *Int'l*, pg. 1302
STORA BILLERUD PAPER GMBH—See Stora Kopparbergs Bergslags AB; *Int'l*, pg. 1302
STORA BILLERUD PAPER S.A.—See Stora Kopparbergs Bergslags AB; *Int'l*, pg. 1302
STORA BILLERUD RESEARCH—See Stora Kopparbergs Bergslags AB; *Int'l*, pg. 1302
STORA BUILDING PRODUCTS—See Stora Kopparbergs Bergslags AB; *Int'l*, pg. 1303
STORA BUILDING PRODUCTS AB—See Stora Kopparbergs Bergslags AB; *Int'l*, pg. 1302
STORA BYGGPRODUKTER AB—See Stora Kopparbergs Bergslags AB; *Int'l*, pg. 1302
STORA BYGGPRODUKTER NORGE A/S—See Stora Kopparbergs Bergslags AB; *Int'l*, pg. 1303
STORA CARBONLESS PAPER GMBH—See Stora Kopparbergs Bergslags AB; *Int'l*, pg. 1303
STORA CARTON BOARD GMBH—See Stora Kopparbergs Bergslags AB; *Int'l*, pg. 1302
STORA CELL AB—See Stora Kopparbergs Bergslags AB; *Int'l*, pg. 1303
STORA CELL NORRSUNDET AB—See Stora Kopparbergs Bergslags AB; *Int'l*, pg. 1303
STORA CORBEHEM S.A.—See Stora Kopparbergs Bergslags AB; *Int'l*, pg. 1304
STORA CORPORATE RESEARCH—See Stora Kopparbergs Bergslags AB; *Int'l*, pg. 1303
STORA DALUM A/S—See Stora Kopparbergs Bergslags AB; *Int'l*, pg. 1303
STORA FELDMUHLE AG—See Stora Kopparbergs Bergslags AB; *Int'l*, pg. 1303
STORA FELDMUHLE NORTH AMERICA COMP—See Stora Kopparbergs Bergslags AB; *Int'l*, pg. 1304
STORA FINANCE BRUSSELS S.A.—See Stora Kopparbergs Bergslags AB; *Int'l*, pg. 1303
STORA FINANCE STOCKHOLM AB—See Stora Kopparbergs Bergslags AB; *Int'l*, pg. 1303
STORA FINANCIAL SERVICES—See Stora Kopparbergs Bergslags AB; *Int'l*, pg. 1303
STORA FOREST AB—See Stora Kopparbergs Bergslags AB; *Int'l*, pg. 1303
STORA FOREST INDUSTRIES—See Stora Kopparbergs Bergslags AB; *Int'l*, pg. 1304
STORA FORS AB—See Stora Kopparbergs Bergslags AB; *Int'l*, pg. 1302
STORA GRUVON—See Stora Kopparbergs Bergslags AB; *Int'l*, pg. 1302
STORA GRYCKSBO AB—See Stora Kopparbergs Bergslags AB; *Int'l*, pg. 1303
STORA HYLTE AB—See Stora Kopparbergs Bergslags AB; *Int'l*, pg. 1304
STORA KABEL GMBH—See Stora Kopparbergs Bergslags AB; *Int'l*, pg. 1303
STORA KOPPARBERGS BERGSLAGS AB; *Int'l*, pg. 1302
STORA KVARNSVEDEN AB—See Stora Kopparbergs Bergslags AB; *Int'l*, pg. 1304
STORA LANGERBRUGGE N.V.—See Stora Kopparbergs Bergslags AB; *Int'l*, pg. 1304
STORA MERCHANT—See Stora Kopparbergs Bergslags AB; *Int'l*, pg. 1303
STORA MOLNDAL AB—See Stora Kopparbergs Bergslags AB; *Int'l*, pg. 1302
STORA NEWTON KYME LTD.—See Stora Kopparbergs Bergslags AB; *Int'l*, pg. 1302
STORA NYMOLLA AB—See Stora Kopparbergs Bergslags AB; *Int'l*, pg. 1303
STORA PAPYRUS AB—See Stora Kopparbergs Bergslags AB; *Int'l*, pg. 1303
STORA PAPYRUS INTERNATIONAL AB—See Stora Kopparbergs Bergslags AB; *Int'l*, pg. 1303
STORA PAPYRUS NETWORK AB—See Stora Kopparbergs Bergslags AB; *Int'l*, pg. 1303
STORA POWER AB—See Stora Kopparbergs Bergslags AB; *Int'l*, pg. 1303
STORA PROJECT—See NCC AB; *Int'l*, pg. 899
STORA PURCHASING & TRANSPORT AB—See Stora Kopparbergs Bergslags AB; *Int'l*, pg. 1303
STORA PURCHASING & TRANSPORT GMBH—See Stora Kopparbergs Bergslags AB; *Int'l*, pg. 1303
STORA PURCHASING & TRANSPORT—See Stora Kopparbergs Bergslags AB; *Int'l*, pg. 1303
STORA REISHOLZ GMBH—See Stora Kopparbergs Bergslags AB; *Int'l*, pg. 1303
STORA SKOGHALL—See Stora Kopparbergs Bergslags AB; *Int'l*, pg. 1302
STORA SKUTSKAR AB—See Stora Kopparbergs Bergslags AB; *Int'l*, pg. 1303
STORA SPEZIALPAPIERE GMBH—See Stora Kopparbergs Bergslags AB; *Int'l*, pg. 1303
STORA TIMBER AB—See Stora Kopparbergs Bergslags AB; *Int'l*, pg. 1303
STORA TRANSPORT (UK) LTD.—See Stora Kopparbergs Bergslags AB; *Int'l*, pg. 1303
STORA TREASURY ASIA PTE. LTD.—See Stora Kopparbergs Bergslags AB; *Int'l*, pg. 1303
STORA UETERSEN GMBH—See Stora Kopparbergs Bergslags AB; *Int'l*, pg. 1303
STORAGE AND TRANSPORT GMBH—See Migros; *Int'l*, pg. 866
STORAGE DIMENSIONS, INC.; *U.S. Public*, pg. 1522
STORAGE MANAGEMENT DIVISION—See Sterling Software, Inc.; *U.S. Public*, pg. 1516
STORAGE SYSTEMS ENGINEERING—See Handling Systems Engineering; *U.S. Private*, pg. 499

STORAGE TECHNOLOGY CORPORATION; *U.S. Public*, pg. 1522
STORAGE TECHNOLOGY DENMARK—See Storage Technology Corporation; *U.S. Public*, pg. 1523
STORAGE TECHNOLOGY FINLAND—See Storage Technology Corporation; *U.S. Public*, pg. 1523
STORAGE TECHNOLOGY GMBH—See Storage Technology Corporation; *U.S. Public*, pg. 1523
STORAGE TECHNOLOGY ITALIA S.P.A.—See Storage Technology Corporation; *U.S. Public*, pg. 1523
STORAGE TECHNOLOGY LIMITED—See Storage Technology Corporation; *U.S. Public*, pg. 1523
STORAGE TECHNOLOGY NORWAY—See Storage Technology Corporation; *U.S. Public*, pg. 1523
STORAGE TECHNOLOGY OF JAPAN LTD.—See Storage Technology Corporation; *U.S. Public*, pg. 1523
STORAGE TECHNOLOGY-PUERTO RICO—See Storage Technology Corporation; *U.S. Public*, pg. 1523
STORAGE TECHNOLOGY SWEDEN—See Storage Technology Corporation; *U.S. Public*, pg. 1523
STORAGE TECHNOLOGY SWITZERLAND AG—See Storage Technology Corporation; *U.S. Public*, pg. 1523
STORAGETEK CANADA, INC.—See Storage Technology Corporation; *U.S. Public*, pg. 1523
STORAGETEK FRANCE, S.A.—See Storage Technology Corporation; *U.S. Public*, pg. 1523
STORAGETEK NETWORK SYSTEMS GROUP—See Storage Technology Corporation; *U.S. Public*, pg. 1522
STORAGETEK PERIPHERALS—See Storage Technology Corporation; *U.S. Public*, pg. 1523
STORCK INTERNATIONAL GMBH; *Int'l*, pg. 1304
STORCK U.S.A., L.P.—See Storck International GmbH; *Int'l*, pg. 1304
STORD INTERNATIONAL A.S.—See Aker Raj Asa; *Int'l*, pg. 42
STORE EQUIPMENT, INC.—See Fleming Companies, Inc.; *U.S. Public*, pg. 653
STORE NORSKE STINNES INTERCOAL A/S—See Veba AG; *Int'l*, pg. 1461
STOREHOUSE PLC; *Int'l*, pg. 1304
STOREROOM SOLUTIONS INC.; *U.S. Private*, pg. 1045
STOREYS DECORATIVE PRODUCTS LTD.—See Borden, Inc.; *U.S. Private*, pg. 160
STORK KETELS B.V.—See Deutsche Babcock AG; *Int'l*, pg. 398
STORK N.V.; *Int'l*, pg. 1304
STORM PRODUCTS COMPANY, INC.; *U.S. Private*, pg. 1045
STORM VAN BENTEM & KLUYVER B.V.—See W.R. Grace & Co.; *U.S. Public*, pg. 756
ED STORMONT SALES—See Klockner-Moeller GmbH; *Int'l*, pg. 736
THE STORMONT ELECTRIC LIGHT & POWER COMPANY LIMITED—See Sun Life Assurance Company of Canada; *Int'l*, pg. 1319
STORNO CELLULAR SERVICES LTD.—See Motorola, Inc.; *U.S. Public*, pg. 1140
STORNO LIMITED—See Motorola, Inc.; *U.S. Public*, pg. 1140
STORZ INSTRUMENT CO.—See American Home Products Corporation; *U.S. Public*, pg. 79
STOUTLAND TELEPHONE COMPANY—See Telephone and Data Systems, Inc.; *U.S. Public*, pg. 1412
STOW DAVIS FURNITURE CO.—See Steelcase Inc.; *U.S. Private*, pg. 1038
STOWE-PHARR MILLS, INC.; *U.S. Private*, pg. 1045
STRABRUKEN AB—See NCC AB; *Int'l*, pg. 899
STRACHAN & HENSHAW LTD.—See Weir Group PLC; *Int'l*, pg. 1489
STRACHAN SHIPPING CO.; *U.S. Private*, pg. 1045
STRAFCO, INC.; *U.S. Private*, pg. 1046
STRAHMAN VALVES, INC.; *U.S. Private*, pg. 1046
STRAINSTALL ENGINEERING SERVICES LIMITED—See TT Group PLC; *Int'l*, pg. 1344
STRAITS PETROLEUM LIMITED—See Axel Johnson AB; *Int'l*, pg. 712
STRAND LIGHTING INC.—See The Rank Group PLC; *Int'l*, pg. 1087
STRAND LIGHTING LIMITED—See The Rank Group PLC; *Int'l*, pg. 1087
STRANDFLEX DIVISION—See Handy & Harman; *U.S. Public*, pg. 780
STRANO SYSCO FOODSERVICE LIMITED—See Sysco Corporation; *U.S. Public*, pg. 1345
STRATEGIC COMPENSATION ASSOCIATES—See Korn/Ferry International; *U.S. Public*, pg. 633
STRATEGIC DISTRIBUTION INC.; *U.S. Public*, pg. 1523
STRATEGIC MARKETING SERVICES LONDON—See Total Research Corporation; *U.S. Public*, pg. 1625
STRATEGIC OUTSOURCING SERVICES INC.—See Computer Horizons Corp.; *U.S. Public*, pg. 421
STRATEGIC SYSTEMS INTERNATIONAL LIMITED—See Powell Duffryn PLC; *Int'l*, pg. 1065
STRATEGIC TECHNOLOGY SERVICES—See SHL Systemhouse; *Int'l*, pg. 1154
STRATEGY XXI—See True North Diversified Companies; *U.S. Public*, pg. 1642
CLAUDIA STRATER—See Vendex International N.V.; *Int'l*, pg. 1462
THE STRATEVEST GROUP, N.A.—See Banknorth Group Inc.; *U.S. Public*, pg. 187
STRATHMORE PAPER—See International Paper Company; *U.S. Public*, pg. 903
STRATIS CORPORATION—See Phillips Plastics Corporation; *U.S. Private*, pg. 862
STRATO/INFUSAID, INC.—See Pfizer Inc.; *U.S. Public*, pg. 1284
STRATOFLEX AEROSPACE/MILITARY CONNECTORS DIV.—See Parker Hannifin Corporation; *U.S. Public*, pg. 1260
STRATOLOUNGER—See Consolidated Furniture Corporation; *U.S. Private*, pg. 265
STRATOS BOAT COMPANY, LTD.—See Greenway Partners, L.P.; *U.S. Private*, pg. 478

AB STRATOS LIMITED—See TT Group PLC; *Int'l*, pg. 1344
STRATTEC SECURITIES CORPORATION; *U.S. Public*, pg. 1523
STRATTON CORPORATION—See Intrawest Corporation; *Int'l*, pg. 685
STRATTON GROWTH FUND, INC.—See Stratton Management Company; *U.S. Private*, pg. 1046
STRATTON MANAGEMENT COMPANY; *U.S. Private*, pg. 1046
STRATTON MONTHLY DIVIDEND SHARES, INC.—See Stratton Management Company; *U.S. Private*, pg. 1046
STRATUS COMPUTER—See Stratus Computer, Inc.; *U.S. Public*, pg. 1524
STRATUS COMPUTER AB—See Stratus Computer, Inc.; *U.S. Public*, pg. 1524
STRATUS COMPUTER AG—See Stratus Computer, Inc.; *U.S. Public*, pg. 1524
STRATUS COMPUTER B.V.—See Stratus Computer, Inc.; *U.S. Public*, pg. 1524
STRATUS COMPUTER CORPORATION—See Stratus Computer, Inc.; *U.S. Public*, pg. 1524
STRATUS COMPUTER GMBH—See Stratus Computer, Inc.; *U.S. Public*, pg. 1524
STRATUS COMPUTER (HK) LTD.—See Stratus Computer, Inc.; *U.S. Public*, pg. 1524
STRATUS COMPUTER, INC.; *U.S. Public*, pg. 1524
STRATUS COMPUTER, INC.—See Stratus Computer, Inc.; *U.S. Public*, pg. 1524
STRATUS COMPUTER, LTD.—See Stratus Computer, Inc.; *U.S. Public*, pg. 1524
STRATUS COMPUTER (NZ), LTD.—See Stratus Computer, Inc.; *U.S. Public*, pg. 1524
STRATUS COMPUTER PTY, LTD.—See Stratus Computer, Inc.; *U.S. Public*, pg. 1524
STRATUS COMPUTER S.A.—See Stratus Computer, Inc.; *U.S. Public*, pg. 1524
STRATUS COMPUTER (SINGAPORE) PTE, LTD.—See Stratus Computer, Inc.; *U.S. Public*, pg. 1524
STRATUS ITALIA, S.R.L.—See Stratus Computer, Inc.; *U.S. Public*, pg. 1524
STRATUS JAPAN CO. LTD.—See Stratus Computer, Inc.; *U.S. Public*, pg. 1524
STRATUS SERVICES GROUP, INC.; *U.S. Private*, pg. 1046
STRAUBE REGIONAL CENTER LLC; *U.S. Private*, pg. 1046
STRAUSS DISCOUNT AUTO; *U.S. Private*, pg. 1046
STRAUSS 9 DE JULIO S.A.I.C.—See Imperial Chemical Industries PLC; *Int'l*, pg. 665
STRAW HAT COOPERATIVE CORP.; *U.S. Private*, pg. 1046
STRAWBERRIES INC.; *U.S. Private*, pg. 1046
STREAM—See Telecom Italia S.p.A.; *Int'l*, pg. 1363
STREAM INTERNATIONAL—See R.R. Donnelley & Sons Company; *U.S. Public*, pg. 518
STREAM INTERNATIONAL HOLDINGS INC.—See R.R. Donnelley & Sons Company; *U.S. Public*, pg. 518
STREAM INTERNATIONAL LIMITED—See R.R. Donnelley & Sons Company; *U.S. Public*, pg. 518
STREAMLIGHT INC.; *U.S. Private*, pg. 1047
STREET RETAIL, INC.—See Federal Realty Investment Trust; *U.S. Public*, pg. 616
STREETS ICE CREAM PTY. LTD.—See Unilever Plc; *Int'l*, pg. 1438
J.D. STREETT & CO., INC.; *U.S. Private*, pg. 1047
STREIF AG—See Hochtief AG; *Int'l*, pg. 623
STREIF SCHALUNGSBAU GMBH—See Hochtief AG; *Int'l*, pg. 623
STRELINGER COMPANY—See Kennametal Inc.; *U.S. Public*, pg. 951
STRETCH FILM—See AEP Industries, Inc.; *U.S. Public*, pg. 5
STRICK CORP.—See Xtra Corporation; *U.S. Public*, pg. 1787
STRICK LEASE, INC.—See Xtra Corporation; *U.S. Public*, pg. 1787
STRIDE RITE CHILDREN'S GROUP, INC.-RETAIL DIV.—See The Stride Rite Corporation; *U.S. Public*, pg. 1525
STRIDE RITE CHILDREN'S GROUP-WHOLESALE DIV.—See The Stride Rite Corporation; *U.S. Public*, pg. 1525
THE STRIDE RITE CORPORATION; *U.S. Public*, pg. 1524
STRIDE-RITE INTERNATIONAL—See The Stride Rite Corporation; *U.S. Public*, pg. 1525
STRIKE RITE MATCHES LTD.—See D.D. Bean & Sons Co.; *U.S. Private*, pg. 127
STRINGER VERONI KETCHUM ADVERTISING—See Ketchum Communications Inc.; *U.S. Private*, pg. 617
STRIP PRODUCTS—See Rautaruukki Oy; *Int'l*, pg. 1088
STRIPPIT, INC.—See IDEX Corporation; *U.S. Public*, pg. 862
STRIX INVESTMENTS LTD.—See Commerzbank AG; *Int'l*, pg. 310
STROBELGASSE 2—See Testa International; *Int'l*, pg. 1377
STROBER BROS., INC. BUILDING SUPPLY CENTERS—See Fidelity Investments (FMR Corp.); *U.S. Private*, pg. 403
STROBER BUILDING SUPPLY CENTERS, INC.—See Fidelity Investments (FMR Corp.); *U.S. Private*, pg. 403
STROBER KING BUILDING SUPPLY CENTERS, INC.—See Fidelity Investments (FMR Corp.); *U.S. Private*, pg. 403
STROBER LONG ISLAND BUILDING MATERIALS CENTERS, INC.—See Fidelity Investments (FMR Corp.); *U.S. Private*, pg. 403
STROBER NEW JERSEY BUILDING SUPPLY CENTERS, INC.—See Fidelity Investments (FMR Corp.); *U.S. Private*, pg. 403
THE STROBER ORGANIZATION, INC.—See Fidelity Investments (FMR Corp.); *U.S. Private*, pg. 403
STROBIC AIR CORP.—See Met-Pro Corporation; *U.S. Public*, pg. 1100
STROEHMANN BAKERIES—See George Weston Limited; *Int'l*, pg. 1495

STROEHMANN BAKERIES, L.C.—See George Weston Limited; *Int'l*, pg. 1495
L. STROETMANN GMBH & CO.—See Spar Handels AG; *Int'l*, pg. 1288
THE STROH BREWERY COMPANY; *U.S. Private*, pg. 1047
E. STROH GMBH—See Fried. Krupp AG; *Int'l*, pg. 514
STROMBECKER CHEMTOY DIVISION—See Strombecker Corporation; *U.S. Private*, pg. 1047
STROMBECKER CORPORATION; *U.S. Private*, pg. 1047
STROMBECKER (HK) LTD.—See Strombecker Corporation; *U.S. Private*, pg. 1047
STROMBURG GMBH—See Eckes AG; *Int'l*, pg. 433
STROMS BRUK—See Mo och Domsjo AB; *Int'l*, pg. 886
STROMSNAS BRUK AB—See Korsnas AB; *Int'l*, pg. 759
STRONG PACK CO., LTD.—See Siam City Bank Public Company Limited; *Int'l*, pg. 1239
STROTHMANN BRENNEREIEN G.M.B.H.—See Koninklijke BolsWessanen nv; *Int'l*, pg. 751
STROUD RESOURCES LTD.; *Int'l*, pg. 1304
STROUDS, INC.; *U.S. Public*, pg. 1525
THE STROUSE, ADLER COMPANY; *U.S. Private*, pg. 1047
STRUCTRON CORPORATION—See Seymour Manufacturing Company; *U.S. Private*, pg. 988
STRUCTURAL DYNAMICS RESEARCH CORP.; *U.S. Public*, pg. 1525
STRUCTURAL EUROPE—See Essef Corporation; *U.S. Public*, pg. 593
STRUCTURAL FOAM PLASTICS, INC.; *U.S. Private*, pg. 1047
STRUCTURAL INDIA PRIVATE, LIMITED—See Essef Corporation; *U.S. Public*, pg. 593
STRUCTURAL INDUSTRIES, INC.; *U.S. Private*, pg. 1048
STRUCTURAL METALS, INC.—See Commercial Metals Company; *U.S. Public*, pg. 412
STRUCTURAL NORTH AMERICA—See Essef Corporation; *U.S. Public*, pg. 593
STRUCTURAL PRODUCTS DIVISION—See Pratt Industries; *Int'l*, pg. 1066
STRUCTURAL REINFORCEMENT PRODUCTS, INC.—See H.A. Schlatter AG; *Int'l*, pg. 1206
STRUCTURE—See The Limited, Inc.; *U.S. Public*, pg. 996
STRUCTURED COMPENSATION LTD.—See Inchcape PLC; *Int'l*, pg. 671
STRUCTURED FINANCIAL CAPITAL INC.—See FCA International Ltd.; *Int'l*, pg. 471
STRUCTURED HEALTHCARE SYSTEMS, INC.—See Magellan Health Services, Inc.; *U.S. Public*, pg. 1036
STRUERS A/S—See Radiometer A/S; *Int'l*, pg. 1083
STRUERS LTD.—See Radiometer A/S; *Int'l*, pg. 1084
STRUTHERS DIVISION—See Consumers Water Company; *U.S. Public*, pg. 439
STRUTHERS INDUSTRIES INC.; *U.S. Public*, pg. 1048
STRUTHERS WELLS CORP.—See Struthers Industries Inc.; *U.S. Private*, pg. 1048
STRYDEL, INC.—See The Ohio Art Company, Inc.; *U.S. Public*, pg. 1214
STRYKER CORPORATION; *U.S. Public*, pg. 1525
STRYKER CORPORATION ENDOSCOPY—See Stryker Corporation; *U.S. Public*, pg. 1526
STRYKER FAR EAST, INC.—See Stryker Corporation; *U.S. Public*, pg. 1526
STRYKER PUERTO RICO, INC.—See Stryker Corporation; *U.S. Public*, pg. 1526
STRYKER SALES CORPORATION—See Stryker Corporation; *U.S. Public*, pg. 1526
STUART CIRCLE HOSPITAL CORPORATION—See Magellan Health Services, Inc.; *U.S. Public*, pg. 1036
D.A. STUART COMPANY; *U.S. Private*, pg. 1048
STUART DISEASE MANAGEMENT SERVICES, INC.—See Zeneca Group Plc; *Int'l*, pg. 1525
STUART ENTERTAINMENT INC.; *U.S. Public*, pg. 1526
STUART ENTERTAINMENT, S.A. DE C.V.—See Stuart Entertainment Inc.; *U.S. Public*, pg. 1526
STUART HALL CO., INC.—See Newell Co.; *U.S. Public*, pg. 1178
STUART NEWS COMPANY—See The E.W. Scripps Company; *U.S. Public*, pg. 1448
STUDER—See Harman International Industries, Inc.; *U.S. Public*, pg. 788
STUDIO CARDS LTD.—See Fine Art Developments plc; *Int'l*, pg. 485
STUDIO PIU—See Warwick Baker O'Neill; *U.S. Private*, pg. 1152
STUDIO 70—See SuperValu, Inc.; *U.S. Public*, pg. 1541
STUDLEY PRODUCTS CO.—See Nortek, Inc.; *U.S. Public*, pg. 1193
STUMPP & SCHUELE DO BRASIL INDUSTRIA E COMERCIO LIMITADA—See Barnes Group Inc.; *U.S. Public*, pg. 190
STUPP BROS., INC.; *U.S. Private*, pg. 1048
STUPP CORPORATION—See Stupp Bros, Inc.; *U.S. Private*, pg. 1048
AB STURE LJUNGDAHL—See Trelleborg AB; *Int'l*, pg. 1423
STURGE BIOCHEMICALS—See Rhone-Poulenc S.A.; *Int'l*, pg. 1113
STURGE, LIFFORD—See Rhone-Poulenc S.A.; *Int'l*, pg. 1113
STURGE S.A.—See Rhone-Poulenc S.A.; *Int'l*, pg. 1113
STURGEON ELECTRIC COMPANY—See MYR Group Inc.; *U.S. Public*, pg. 1029
STURGIS FOUNDRY CORP.—See Armstrong International, Inc.; *U.S. Private*, pg. 83
STURGIS IRON & METAL COMPANY, INC.; *U.S. Private*, pg. 1048
STURGIS IRON & METAL, ELKHART METALS DIVISION—See Sturgis Iron & Metal Company, Inc.; *U.S. Private*, pg. 1048
STURM, RUGER & CO., INC.; *U.S. Public*, pg. 1526
STURMEY-ARCHER LIMITED—See Derby International Corporation S.A.; *Int'l*, pg. 394
STUSSER ELECTRIC COMPANY—See Consolidated Electrical Distributors; *U.S. Private*, pg. 265

STUWADOORSBEDRIJF VELSERKOM BV—See Koninklijke Hoogovens N.V.; *Int'l*, pg. 754
STYLE KEUKENS B.V.—See Vorwerk & Co.; *Int'l*, pg. 1481
STYLE WEEKLY—See Landmark Communications, Inc.; *U.S. Private*, pg. 649
STYLELANDER METAL STAMPING, INC.—See Leggett & Platt, Incorporated; *U.S. Public*, pg. 986
STYRIA FEDERN GES.M.B.H.—See Voest-Alpine Stahl AG; *Int'l*, pg. 1470
STYROTECH CORP.—See Sealright Company, Inc.; *U.S. Public*, pg. 1452
STYX & LEO BURNETT—See Leo Burnett Company, Inc.; *U.S. Private*, pg. 186
SUAREZ & CLAVERA/DMB&B—See DMB&B Communications; *U.S. Private*, pg. 305
SUAREZ CORPORATION INDUSTRIES; *U.S. Private*, pg. 1048
SUB SEA INTERNATIONAL—See Dresser Industries, Inc.; *U.S. Public*, pg. 529
SUB-ZERO FREEZER CO., INC.; *U.S. Private*, pg. 1048
SUBANG JAYA MEDICAL CENTRE SDN. BHD.—See Sime Darby Berhad; *Int'l*, pg. 1250
N.V. SUBARU BENELUX S.A.—See Mitsui & Co., Ltd.; *Int'l*, pg. 879
SUBARU CANADA INC.—See Fuji Heavy Industries, Ltd.; *Int'l*, pg. 523
SUBARU CENTRAL REGION, INC.—See Fuji Heavy Industries, Ltd.; *Int'l*, pg. 523
SUBARU CREDIT CORPORATION—See Fuji Heavy Industries, Ltd.; *Int'l*, pg. 523
SUBARU DISTRIBUTOR CORP.—See Fuji Heavy Industries, Ltd.; *Int'l*, pg. 523
SUBARU FINANCIAL SERVICES, INC.—See Fuji Heavy Industries, Ltd.; *Int'l*, pg. 523
SUBARU-ISUZU AUTOMOTIVE, INC.—See Fuji Heavy Industries, Ltd.; *Int'l*, pg. 523
SUBARU-ISUZU AUTOMOTIVE, INC.—See Isuzu Motors Limited; *Int'l*, pg. 692
SUBARU LEASING CORPORATION—See Fuji Heavy Industries, Ltd.; *Int'l*, pg. 523
SUBARU MID-AMERICA, INC.—See Fuji Heavy Industries, Ltd.; *Int'l*, pg. 523
SUBARU NORTHWEST REGION—See Fuji Heavy Industries, Ltd.; *Int'l*, pg. 523
SUBARU OF AMERICA, INC.—See Fuji Heavy Industries, Ltd.; *Int'l*, pg. 523
SUBARU OF AMERICA SOUTHEAST REGION—See Fuji Heavy Industries, Ltd.; *Int'l*, pg. 523
SUBARU OF AMERICA WESTERN—See Fuji Heavy Industries, Ltd.; *Int'l*, pg. 523
SUBARU OF NEW ENGLAND, INC.—See Fuji Heavy Industries, Ltd.; *Int'l*, pg. 523
SUBARU PARTS EUROPE NV/SA—See Fuji Heavy Industries, Ltd.; *Int'l*, pg. 523
SUBARU RESEARCH & DESIGN, INC.—See Fuji Heavy Industries, Ltd.; *Int'l*, pg. 523
SUBARU SOUTHEAST REGION—See Fuji Heavy Industries, Ltd.; *Int'l*, pg. 523
SUBARU SOUTHWEST REGION—See Fuji Heavy Industries, Ltd.; *Int'l*, pg. 523
SUBARU WESTERN REGION—See Fuji Heavy Industries, Ltd.; *Int'l*, pg. 523
SUBSCRIPTION SERVICES LTD. (SSL)—See The Post Office; *Int'l*, pg. 1064
SUBSTANTIA GESELLSCHAFT M.B.H.—See Warner-Lambert Company; *U.S. Public*, pg. 1739
SUBSURFACE DEVELOPMENT COMPANY—See Ash Grove Cement Company; *U.S. Private*, pg. 88
THE SUBURBAN ADVERTISER—See Journal Register Company; *U.S. Public*, pg. 935
SUBURBAN NEWSPAPER GROUP—See Gannett Company, Inc.; *U.S. Public*, pg. 700
SUBURBAN NEWSPAPERS OF GREATER ST. LOUIS—See Journal Register Company; *U.S. Public*, pg. 935
SUBURBAN PROPANE GROUP, INC.—See SCANA Corporation; *U.S. Public*, pg. 1436
SUBURBAN PUBLICATIONS, INC.—See Journal Register Company; *U.S. Public*, pg. 935
SUBURBAN WATER SYSTEMS—See Southwest Water Company; *U.S. Public*, pg. 1494
SUBWAY FRANCHISE ADVERTISING FUND TRUST; *U.S. Private*, pg. 1048
SUBWAY JAPAN INC.—See Suntory Ltd.; *Int'l*, pg. 1321
SUCCESS DEVELOPMENT INTERNATIONAL; *U.S. Private*, pg. 1048
SUCCESSFUL FARMING MAGAZINE—See Meredith Corporation; *U.S. Public*, pg. 1094
SUCCESSFUL MEETINGS—See VNU Verenigde Nederlandse Uitgeversbedrijven B.V.; *Int'l*, pg. 1446
SUCCESSFUL MONEY MANAGEMENT SEMINARS, INC.—See ReliaStar Financial Corp.; *U.S. Public*, pg. 1376
SUCCESSORIES—See Successories, Inc.; *U.S. Private*, pg. 1049
SUCCESSORIES, INC.; *U.S. Private*, pg. 1049
SUCHARD SCHOKOLADE GES.M.B.H.—See Philip Morris Companies Inc.; *U.S. Public*, pg. 1289
SUCKER-MULLER-HACOBA GMBH & CO.—See Deutsche Babcock AG; *Int'l*, pg. 399
SUCOS REFRIGERANTES AGUAS MINERAIS INDUSTRIA E COMERCIA—See Nestle S.A.; *Int'l*, pg. 919
SUCRERIE D'AULNOIS-SOUS-LAON—See Generale Sucriere SNC; *Int'l*, pg. 549
SUCRERIE DE CAGNY—See Generale Sucriere SNC; *Int'l*, pg. 549
SUCRERIE DE ROYE—See Generale Sucriere SNC; *Int'l*, pg. 549
SUCRERIE D'EPPEVILLE/HAM—See Generale Sucriere SNC; *Int'l*, pg. 549
SUCRERIE D'ETREPAGNY—See Generale Sucriere SNC; *Int'l*, pg. 549
SUCRERIE ET DISTILLERIE DE SOUPPES OUVRE ET FILS S.A.—See Generale Sucriere SNC; *Int'l*, pg. 549
SUCROS LTD.—See Cultor Ltd.; *Int'l*, pg. 349

SUD ELECTRA GMBH—See Axel Johnson AB; *Int'l*, pg. 712
SUD ELECTRA S.A.—See Axel Johnson AB; *Int'l*, pg. 712
SUD EST S.R.L.—See Coeclerici Group; *Int'l*, pg. 303
SUD PRESSE ADMINISTRATION—See Lagardere Groupe; *Int'l*, pg. 794
SUD-WEST-KAMIN GMBH—See Redland PLC; *Int'l*, pg. 1091
SUDAMERICA DE SALUD—See Corporacion MAPFRE, Compania Internacional de Reaseguros, S.A.; *Int'l*, pg. 333
SUDAMTEX DE URUGUAY, S.A.; *Int'l*, pg. 1304
SUDARSHAN CHEMICAL INDUSTRIES LTD.—See Dainippon Ink & Chemicals, Inc.; *Int'l*, pg. 372
SUDBURY CENTER—See The Cascades Group; *Int'l*, pg. 274
SUDBURY DIVISION—See EdperBrascan Corporation; *Int'l*, pg. 433
THE SUDBURY STAR—See Hollinger Inc.; *Int'l*, pg. 631
SUDCO DEVELOPMENT CO., INC.—See The Suddath Companies; *U.S. Private*, pg. 1049
THE SUDDATH COMPANIES; *U.S. Private*, pg. 1049
SUDDATH MOVING SYSTEMS, INC.—See The Suddath Companies; *U.S. Private*, pg. 1049
SUDDATH TRANSPORTATION SERVICE—See The Suddath Companies; *U.S. Private*, pg. 1049
SUDDATH VAN LINES—See The Suddath Companies; *U.S. Private*, pg. 1049
SUDDEUTSCHE BRENNSTOFFHANDELSGESELLSCHAFT MBH—See Saarbergwerke Aktiengesellschaft; *Int'l*, pg. 1167
SUDDEUTSCHE ETNA-WERK GMBH—See Hesta Tex AG; *Int'l*, pg. 617
SUDDEUTSCHE GROSSBAUTEN GMBH—See Philipp Holzmann AG; *Int'l*, pg. 633
SUDDEUTSCHE ROHPRODUKTEN GMBH—See Fried. Krupp AG; *Int'l*, pg. 514
SUDDEUTSCHE WOHNUNGSBAU GMBH—See Hochtief AG; *Int'l*, pg. 623
SUDFACTORING GMBH—See SudwestLB; *Int'l*, pg. 1304
SUDIMMOBILIEN FONDS—See SudwestLB; *Int'l*, pg. 1304
SUDIMMOBILIEN GMBH—See SudwestLB; *Int'l*, pg. 1304
SUDKA—See SudwestLB; *Int'l*, pg. 1304
SUDKB—See SudwestLB; *Int'l*, pg. 1304
SUDKI—See SudwestLB; *Int'l*, pg. 1304
SUDKRAFT SUDDEUTSCHE KRAFTWAGEN-SPEDITIONS GMBH—See Heidelberger Zement A.G.; *Int'l*, pg. 606
SUDKRAFT VERSICHERUNGSVERMITTLUNGS GMBH—See Heidelberger Zement A.G.; *Int'l*, pg. 606
SUDKURIER GMBH—See Georg von Holtzbrinck GmbH; *Int'l*, pg. 1478
SUDLEASING GMBH—See SudwestLB; *Int'l*, pg. 1304
SUDLEASING IMMOBILIEN GMBH—See SudwestLB; *Int'l*, pg. 1305
SUDLER & HENNESSEY—See Young & Rubicam; *U.S. Private*, pg. 1197
SUDLER & HENNESSEY/GALL INC.—See Young & Rubicam Inc.; *U.S. Private*, pg. 1200
SUDLER & HENNESSEY: GALL INC.—See Young & Rubicam Inc.; *U.S. Private*, pg. 1200
SUDPETROL A.G.—See ENI S.p.A.; *Int'l*, pg. 429
SUDWESTLB; *Int'l*, pg. 1304
SUDZUCKER AG MANNHEIM/OCHSENFURT; *Int'l*, pg. 1305
SUDZUCKER GMBH—See Sudzucker AG Mannheim/Ochsenfurt; *Int'l*, pg. 1305
SUECOBRAS INDUSTRIA E COMERCIO LTDA.—See Cardo AB; *Int'l*, pg. 271
SUEDBAYERISCHES PORTLAND SIMNING ZEMENTWERK GEBR. WIESBOECK & CO. GMBH—See Heidelberger Zement A.G.; *Int'l*, pg. 605
SUEDDEUTSCHE BODENCREDITBANK AG—See Bayerische Vereinsbank Group; *Int'l*, pg. 147
SUEDWESTDEUTSCHE ROHRLEITUNGSBAU GMBH—See Hochtief AG; *Int'l*, pg. 623
SUES, YOUNG & BROWN INC.; *U.S. Private*, pg. 1049
SUESSEA MAQUIUAS S.A.—See Spindelfabrik Suessen; *Int'l*, pg. 1291
SUEZ ELECTRONICS S.A.E., ALEXANDRIA—See SAIT-RadioHolland Group S.A.; *Int'l*, pg. 1152
SUEZ NEDERLAND SECURITIES N.V.—See Compagnie de Suez; *Int'l*, pg. 314
SUFFOLK CAPITAL MANAGEMENT—See United Asset Management Corporation; *U.S. Public*, pg. 1674
SUGAR CANE GROWERS COOPERATIVE OF FLORIDA; *U.S. Private*, pg. 1049
SUGAR CREEK FOODS—See Eskimo Pie Corporation; *U.S. Public*, pg. 592
SUGAR CREEK PACKING CO.—See Sugar Creek Packing Co.; *U.S. Private*, pg. 1049
SUGAR CREEK PACKING CO.; *U.S. Private*, pg. 1049
SUGAR FOODS CORP; *U.S. Private*, pg. 1049
SUGAR VALLEY TELEPHONE CO.—See Telephone and Data Systems, Inc.; *U.S. Public*, pg. 1572
SUGARBUSH—See American Skiing Company; *U.S. Private*, pg. 62
SUGARDALE FOODS INC.—See Fresh Mark, Inc.; *U.S. Private*, pg. 62
SUGARLOAF/USA—See American Skiing Company; *U.S. Private*, pg. 62
SUGRO B.V.—See Nutricia BV; *Int'l*, pg. 991
SUHNER ELECTRONICS LTD.—See Huber & Suhner AG; *Int'l*, pg. 637
SUHNER ELEKTRONIK GMBH—See Huber & Suhner AG; *Int'l*, pg. 637
SUISSA MILLER ADVERTISING, INC.; *U.S. Private*, pg. 1049
SUISSE DE REASSURANCES (FRANCE)—See Swiss Reinsurance Company; *Int'l*, pg. 1333
SUITA INSTITUTE—See OYO Corporation; *Int'l*, pg. 1019
SUITT CONSTRUCTION COMPANY, INC.—See BE & K, Inc.; *U.S. Private*, pg. 106

SUIZA DE REASEGUROS (IBERICA) AGENCIA DE REASEGUROS, S.A.—See Swiss Reinsurance Company; *Int'l*, pg. 1333
SUIZA DE REASEGUROS S.A.—See Swiss Reinsurance Company; *Int'l*, pg. 1333
SUIZA DE RESEGUROS VENEZUELA C.A.—See Swiss Reinsurance Company; *Int'l*, pg. 1333
SUIZA FOODS CORPORATION; *U.S. Public*, pg. 1526
SUIZA RE MEXICO, S.A. DE C.V.—See Swiss Reinsurance Company; *Int'l*, pg. 1333
AB SUKAB REPRESENTATIVE OFFICE—See Axel Johnson AB; *Int'l*, pg. 712
SUKOSOL AND MAZDA ENGINEERING CO., LTD.—See Mazda Motor Corporation; *Int'l*, pg. 849
SULA SUPPLY—See Vienna Sausage Mfg. Co.; *U.S. Private*, pg. 1140
SULCUS (AUSTRALIA)—See Sulcus Computer Corp.; *U.S. Public*, pg. 1527
SULCUS COMPUTER CORP.; *U.S. Public*, pg. 1527
SULCUS INVESTMENT CORP.—See Sulcus Computer Corp.; *U.S. Public*, pg. 1527
SULCUS LAW MANAGEMENT SERVICES, INC.—See Sulcus Computer Corp.; *U.S. Public*, pg. 1527
SULLAIR ARGENTINA S.A.—See Sundstrand Corporation; *U.S. Public*, pg. 1534
SULLAIR ASIA LTD.—See Sundstrand Corporation; *U.S. Public*, pg. 1534
SULLAIR CORPORATION—See Sundstrand Corporation; *U.S. Public*, pg. 1534
SULLAIR TAIWAN LTD.—See Sundstrand Corporation; *U.S. Public*, pg. 1534
SULLIVAN & COZART INC.; *U.S. Private*, pg. 1049
SULLIVAN LONG & HAGERTY, INC.; *U.S. Private*, pg. 1050
SULLIVAN OIL COMPANY; *U.S. Private*, pg. 1050
SULLIVAN PAPER COMPANY; *U.S. Private*, pg. 1050
SULLIVAN POWELL & COMPANY LTD.—See Gallaher Limited; *Int'l*, pg. 539
SULLIVAN SYSTEMS DIV.—See Tetra Laval Group; *Int'l*, pg. 1379
SULLIVAN TRANSFER CO.—See Freeman Decorating Co.; *U.S. Private*, pg. 426
SULLYFIELD CORPORATION—See Saul Centers Inc.; *U.S. Public*, pg. 1435
SULPACO WEST—See Sullivan Paper Company; *U.S. Private*, pg. 1050
SULPHITE PULP—See Tembec Inc.; *Int'l*, pg. 1375
SULZER ARGENTINA S.A.—See Sulzer Ltd.; *Int'l*, pg. 1306
SULZER AUSTRALIA PTY. LIMITED—See Sulzer Ltd.; *Int'l*, pg. 1306
S.A. SULZER BELGIUM N.V.—See Sulzer Ltd.; *Int'l*, pg. 1306
SULZER BELGIUM S.A.—See Sulzer Ltd.; *Int'l*, pg. 1306
SULZER BETRIEBSLIEGENSCHAFTEN AG—See Sulzer Ltd.; *Int'l*, pg. 1307
SULZER BINGHAM PUMPS INC.—See Sulzer Ltd.; *Int'l*, pg. 1305
SULZER BRASIL S.A.—See Sulzer Ltd.; *Int'l*, pg. 1305
SULZER BULACHGUSS AG—See Sulzer Ltd.; *Int'l*, pg. 1307
SULZER-BURCKHARDT ENGINEERING WORKS LTD.—See Sulzer Ltd.; *Int'l*, pg. 1305
SULZER CALIQUA B.V.—See Sulzer Ltd.; *Int'l*, pg. 1306
SULZER CANADA INC.—See Sulzer Ltd.; *Int'l*, pg. 1306
SULZER CHEMTECH AG—See Sulzer Ltd.; *Int'l*, pg. 1307
SULZER CHEMTECH GMBH—See Sulzer Ltd.; *Int'l*, pg. 1308
SULZER CHEMTECH PTE. LTD.—See Sulzer Ltd.; *Int'l*, pg. 1308
SULZER DE VENEZUALA S.A.—See Sulzer Ltd.; *Int'l*, pg. 1306
SULZER DEL PERU S.A.—See Sulzer Ltd.; *Int'l*, pg. 1306
SULZER ELECTRONICS LTD.—See Sulzer Ltd.; *Int'l*, pg. 1305
SULZER ENERGY CONSULTING INC.—See Sulzer Ltd.; *Int'l*, pg. 1305
SULZER-ESCHER WYSS AG—See Sulzer Ltd.; *Int'l*, pg. 1305
SULZER-ESCHER WYSS GMBH—See Sulzer Ltd.; *Int'l*, pg. 1305
SULZER ESCHER WYSS KALTETCHNIK G.M.B.H.—See Sulzer Ltd.; *Int'l*, pg. 1306
SULZER ESPANA S.A.—See Sulzer Ltd.; *Int'l*, pg. 1306
SULZER FLOVEL HYDRO LTD.—See Sulzer Ltd.; *Int'l*, pg. 1308
SULZER FRIOTHERM LTD.—See Sulzer Ltd.; *Int'l*, pg. 1306
SULZER HOLDING GMBH—See Sulzer Ltd.; *Int'l*, pg. 1308
SULZER HYDRO AG—See Sulzer Ltd.; *Int'l*, pg. 1307
SULZER HYDRO GMBH—See Sulzer Ltd.; *Int'l*, pg. 1308
SULZER HYDRO S.A. DE C.V.—See Sulzer Ltd.; *Int'l*, pg. 1306
SULZER IMMOBILIEN AG—See Sulzer Ltd.; *Int'l*, pg. 1306
SULZER, INC.—See Sulzer Ltd.; *Int'l*, pg. 1306
SULZER INDIA LTD.—See Sulzer Ltd.; *Int'l*, pg. 1306
SULZER INDUSTRIES FRANCE S.A.—See Sulzer Ltd.; *Int'l*, pg. 1306
SULZER INFORMATIK AG—See Sulzer Ltd.; *Int'l*, pg. 1306
SULZER INFRA ANLAGEN- UND GEBAUDETECHNIK GESELLSCHAFT M.B.H—See Sulzer Ltd.; *Int'l*, pg. 1306
SULZER INFRA DEUTSCHLAND GMBH.—See Sulzer Ltd.; *Int'l*, pg. 1306
SULZER INFRA NEDERLAND B.V.—See Sulzer Ltd.; *Int'l*, pg. 1306
SULZER INFRA PORTUGAL, LTDA.—See Sulzer Ltd.; *Int'l*, pg. 1306
SULZER INFRA S.A.—See Sulzer Ltd.; *Int'l*, pg. 1306
SULZER INFRA (SCHWEIZ) AG—See Sulzer Ltd.; *Int'l*, pg. 1306
SULZER INFRA (UK)—See Sulzer Ltd.; *Int'l*, pg. 1306
SULZER INNOTEC LTD.—See Sulzer Ltd.; *Int'l*, pg. 1306
SULZER INTERNATIONAL (DEUTSCHLAND) GMBH—See Sulzer Ltd.; *Int'l*, pg. 1308

SULZER INTERNATIONAL (HONG KONG) LIMITED—See Sulzer Ltd.; *Int'l*, pg. 1306
SULZER INTERNATIONAL LTD.—See Sulzer Ltd.; *Int'l*, pg. 1306
SULZER IRAN—See Sulzer Ltd.; *Int'l*, pg. 1306
SULZER ITALIA S.P.A.—See Sulzer Ltd.; *Int'l*, pg. 1306
SULZER (JAPAN) LTD.—See Sulzer Ltd.; *Int'l*, pg. 1306
SULZER KEULS B.V.—See Sulzer Ltd.; *Int'l*, pg. 1306
SULZER KOREA LTD.—See Sulzer Ltd.; *Int'l*, pg. 1306
SULZER LTD.; *Int'l*, pg. 1305
SULZER MEDICAL TECHNOLOGY LTD.—See Sulzer Ltd.; *Int'l*, pg. 1307
SULZER METCO AG—See Sulzer Ltd.; *Int'l*, pg. 1307
SULZER METCO (BENELUX) B.V.—See Sulzer Ltd.; *Int'l*, pg. 1308
SULZER METCO (DEUTSCHLAND) GMBH—See Sulzer Ltd.; *Int'l*, pg. 1307
SULZER METCO (FRANCE) S.A.—See Sulzer Ltd.; *Int'l*, pg. 1308
SULZER METCO (JAPAN) LTD.—See Sulzer Ltd.; *Int'l*, pg. 1308
SULZER METCO (NORDEN) AB—See Sulzer Ltd.; *Int'l*, pg. 1308
SULZER METCO (SINGAPORE) PTE LTD.—See Sulzer Ltd.; *Int'l*, pg. 1308
SULZER METCO (WESTBURY) INC.—See Sulzer Ltd.; *Int'l*, pg. 1307
SULZER (MEXICO) S.A. DE C.V.—See Sulzer Ltd.; *Int'l*, pg. 1306
SULZER NEDERLAND B.V.—See Sulzer Ltd.; *Int'l*, pg. 1306
SULZER NETHERLANDS HOLDING B.V.—See Sulzer Ltd.; *Int'l*, pg. 1308
SULZER NEW ZEALAND LIMITED—See Sulzer Ltd.; *Int'l*, pg. 1306
SULZER NORGE A/S—See Sulzer Ltd.; *Int'l*, pg. 1306
SULZER PAPERTEC EUSKIRCHEN GMBH—See Sulzer Ltd.; *Int'l*, pg. 1305
SULZER PAPERTEC GMBH—See Sulzer Ltd.; *Int'l*, pg. 1305
SULZER PAPERTEC INC.—See Sulzer Ltd.; *Int'l*, pg. 1305
SULZER PAPERTEC MANCHESTER LTD.—See Sulzer Ltd.; *Int'l*, pg. 1306
SULZER PLASMA TECHNIK, INC.—See Sulzer Ltd.; *Int'l*, pg. 1307
SULZER POLSKA GMBH—See Sulzer Ltd.; *Int'l*, pg. 1306
SULZER POMPEN BENELUX B.V.—See Sulzer Ltd.; *Int'l*, pg. 1306
SULZER POMPES FRANCE S.A., MANTES-LA-JOLIE, FRANCE—See Sulzer Ltd.; *Int'l*, pg. 1306
SULZER PORTUGAL, LDA.—See Sulzer Ltd.; *Int'l*, pg. 1306
SULZER PRAHA S.R.O.—See Sulzer Ltd.; *Int'l*, pg. 1306
SULZER PUMPS LTD.—See Sulzer Ltd.; *Int'l*, pg. 1306
SULZER PUMPS (PTE) LTD.—See Sulzer Ltd.; *Int'l*, pg. 1306
SULZER RUTI GROUP—See Sulzer Ltd.; *Int'l*, pg. 1306
SULZER RUTI INC.—See Sulzer Ltd.; *Int'l*, pg. 1307
SULZER RUTI LIMITED—See Sulzer Ltd.; *Int'l*, pg. 1307
SULZER SHANGHAI ENG. AND MACH. WORKS LTD.—See Sulzer Ltd.; *Int'l*, pg. 1306
SULZER SISTEMAS E INSTALACIONES (CHILE) S.A.—See Sulzer Ltd.; *Int'l*, pg. 1306
SULZER SISTEMAS E INSTALACIONES S.A.—See Sulzer Ltd.; *Int'l*, pg. 1306
SULZER SOUTH AFRICA LTD.—See Sulzer Ltd.; *Int'l*, pg. 1306
SULZER (THAILAND) LTD.—See Sulzer Ltd.; *Int'l*, pg. 1307
SULZER THERMATEC LTD.—See Sulzer Ltd.; *Int'l*, pg. 1307
SULZER TRIEBWERKE AG—See Sulzer Ltd.; *Int'l*, pg. 1307
SULZER TURBO LTD.—See Sulzer Ltd.; *Int'l*, pg. 1305
SULZER (UK) HOLDINGS LIMITED—See Sulzer Ltd.; *Int'l*, pg. 1307
SULZER (UK) LTD.—See Sulzer Ltd.; *Int'l*, pg. 1307
SULZER (UK) PUMPS LTD.—See Sulzer Ltd.; *Int'l*, pg. 1307
SULZER USA INC.—See Sulzer Ltd.; *Int'l*, pg. 1306
SULZER WEISE GMBH—See Sulzer Ltd.; *Int'l*, pg. 1306
SULZER WINTEC LTD.—See Sulzer Ltd.; *Int'l*, pg. 1307
SULZER-WINTERTHUR GROUP—See Sulzer Ltd.; *Int'l*, pg. 1307
SULZERMEDICA GMBH—See Sulzer Ltd.; *Int'l*, pg. 1307
SULZERMEDICA GROUP—See Sulzer Ltd.; *Int'l*, pg. 1307
SULZERMEDICA JAPAN K.K.—See Sulzer Ltd.; *Int'l*, pg. 1307
SULZERMEDICA USA INC.—See Sulzer Ltd.; *Int'l*, pg. 1307
SUMARE PROCESSAMENTO E SERVICOS S.A.—See Cigna Corp.; *U.S. Public*, pg. 363
SUMBANK LIFE INSURANCE CO.—See Synovus Financial Corp.; *U.S. Public*, pg. 1549
P.T. SUMI INDO WIRING SYSTEMS—See Sumitomo Electric Industries, Ltd.; *Int'l*, pg. 1313
SUMI-PAC CONSTRUCTION CO., LTD.—See Sumitomo Electric Industries, Ltd.; *Int'l*, pg. 1313
SUMI-PAC ELECTRO-CHEMICAL CORPORATION—See Sumitomo Electric Industries, Ltd.; *Int'l*, pg. 1313
P.T. SUMIDEN SERASI WIRE PRODUCTS—See Sumitomo Electric Industries, Ltd.; *Int'l*, pg. 1313
SUMIDEN WIRE PRODUCTS CORP.—See Sumitomo Electric Industries, Ltd.; *Int'l*, pg. 1313
SUMIDEN WIRE PRODUCTS GUANGZHOU CO., LTD.—See Sumitomo Electric Industries, Ltd.; *Int'l*, pg 1313
SUMIGIN METRO INVESTMENT CORP.—See The Sumitomo Bank, Limited; *Int'l*, pg. 1310
SUMIHATSU CO., LTD.—See NHK Spring Co., Ltd.; *Int'l*, pg. 902
SUMIKA A & L INC.—See Sumitomo Chemical Company, Ltd.; *Int'l*, pg. 1311
SUMIKA-HERCULES CO. LTD.—See Hercules Incorporated; *U.S. Public*, pg. 811
SUMIKIN BUSSAN CORPORATION; *Int'l*, pg. 1308

SUMIKIN BUSSAN CORPORATION—See Sumikin Bussan Corporation; *Int'l*, pg. 1308
SUMIKIN BUSSAN INTERNATIONAL (AUSTRALIA) PTY. LTD.—See Sumikin Bussan Corporation; *Int'l*, pg. 1308
SUMIKIN BUSSAN INTERNATIONAL CORP.-CHICAGO BRANCH—See Sumikin Bussan Corporation; *Int'l*, pg. 1308
SUMIKIN BUSSAN INTERNATIONAL CORP. - FOOD DIV.—See Sumikin Bussan Corporation; *Int'l*, pg. 1308
SUMIKIN BUSSAN INTERNATIONAL CORP. - LOS ANGELES BRANCH—See Sumikin Bussan Corporation; *Int'l*, pg. 1308
SUMIKIN BUSSAN INTERNATIONAL (HK) LTD.—See Sumikin Bussan Corporation; *Int'l*, pg. 1308
SUMIKIN BUSSAN INTERNATIONAL (KOREA) CO., LTD.—See Sumikin Bussan Corporation; *Int'l*, pg. 1308
SUMIKIN BUSSAN INTERNATIONAL PTE. LTD.—See Sumikin Bussan Corporation; *Int'l*, pg. 1308
SUMIKIN BUSSAN INTERNATIONAL (THAILAND) LTD.—See Sumikin Bussan Corporation; *Int'l*, pg. 1308
SUMIKO ELECTRONICS TAIWAN CO., LTD.—See Sumitomo Metal Mining Co., Ltd.; *Int'l*, pg. 1316
SUMINISTROS GENERALES DE NUTRICON, S.A.—See Borden, Inc.; *U.S. Private*, pg. 160
SUMITOMO BAKELITE CO., LTD.—See Sumitomo Chemical Company, Ltd.; *Int'l*, pg. 1311
SUMITOMO BANK CAPITAL MARKETS, INC.—See The Sumitomo Bank, Limited; *Int'l*, pg. 1308
SUMITOMO BANK (DEUTSCHLAND) GMBH—See The Sumitomo Bank, Limited; *Int'l*, pg. 1310
SUMITOMO BANK FINANCIAL SERVICES, INC.—See The Sumitomo Bank, Limited; *Int'l*, pg. 1308
SUMITOMO BANK INVESTMENT MANAGEMENT (NEW YORK), INC.—See The Sumitomo Bank, Limited; *Int'l*, pg. 1308
SUMITOMO BANK LEASING & FINANCE, INC.—See The Sumitomo Bank, Limited; *Int'l*, pg. 1308
THE SUMITOMO BANK, LIMITED; *Int'l*, pg. 1308
THE SUMITOMO BANK, LTD.-LABUAN BRANCH—See The Sumitomo Bank, Limited; *Int'l*, pg. 1309
THE SUMITOMO BANK LTD.-LABUAN MARKETING OFFICE—See The Sumitomo Bank, Limited; *Int'l*, pg. 1309
THE SUMITOMO BANK, LTD.-AMSTERDAM REPRESENTATIVE OFFICE—See The Sumitomo Bank, Limited; *Int'l*, pg. 1309
THE SUMITOMO BANK, LTD.-ATLANTA AGENCY—See The Sumitomo Bank, Limited; *Int'l*, pg. 1309
THE SUMITOMO BANK, LTD.-BAHRAIN REPRESENTATIVE OFFICE—See The Sumitomo Bank, Limited; *Int'l*, pg. 1309
THE SUMITOMO BANK, LTD.-BANGKOK INTERNATIONAL BANKING FACILITY—See The Sumitomo Bank, Limited; *Int'l*, pg. 1309
THE SUMITOMO BANK, LTD.-BARCELONA BRANCH—See The Sumitomo Bank, Limited; *Int'l*, pg. 1309
THE SUMITOMO BANK, LTD.-BEIJING REPRESENTATIVE OFFICE—See The Sumitomo Bank, Limited; *Int'l*, pg. 1309
THE SUMITOMO BANK, LTD.-BIRMINGHAM REPRESENTATIVE OFFICE—See The Sumitomo Bank, Limited; *Int'l*, pg. 1309
THE SUMITOMO BANK, LTD.-BRUSSELS BRANCH—See The Sumitomo Bank, Limited; *Int'l*, pg. 1309
THE SUMITOMO BANK, LTD.-BUENOS AIRES REPRESENTATIVE OFFICE—See The Sumitomo Bank, Limited; *Int'l*, pg. 1309
THE SUMITOMO BANK, LTD.-CAIRO REPRESENTATIVE OFFICE—See The Sumitomo Bank, Limited; *Int'l*, pg. 1309
THE SUMITOMO BANK, LTD.-CARACAS REPRESENTATIVE OFFICE—See The Sumitomo Bank, Limited; *Int'l*, pg. 1309
THE SUMITOMO BANK, LTD.-CAYMAN BRANCH—See The Sumitomo Bank, Limited; *Int'l*, pg. 1309
THE SUMITOMO BANK, LTD.-CHICAGO BRANCH—See The Sumitomo Bank, Limited; *Int'l*, pg. 1308
THE SUMITOMO BANK, LTD.-CHONGQING REPRESENTATIVE OFFICE—See The Sumitomo Bank, Limited; *Int'l*, pg. 1309
THE SUMITOMO BANK, LTD.-DALIAN REPRESENTATIVE OFFICE—See The Sumitomo Bank, Limited; *Int'l*, pg. 1309
THE SUMITOMO BANK, LTD.-DUSSELDORF BRANCH—See The Sumitomo Bank, Limited; *Int'l*, pg. 1309
THE SUMITOMO BANK, LTD.-FRANKFURT BRANCH—See The Sumitomo Bank, Limited; *Int'l*, pg. 1309
THE SUMITOMO BANK, LTD.-GUANGZHOU BRANCH—See The Sumitomo Bank, Limited; *Int'l*, pg. 1309
THE SUMITOMO BANK, LTD.-HO CHI MINH REPRESENTATIVE OFFICE—See The Sumitomo Bank, Limited; *Int'l*, pg. 1310
THE SUMITOMO BANK, LTD.-HONG KONG BRANCH—See The Sumitomo Bank, Limited; *Int'l*, pg. 1309
THE SUMITOMO BANK, LTD.-HOUSTON AGENCY—See The Sumitomo Bank, Limited; *Int'l*, pg. 1309
THE SUMITOMO BANK, LTD.-ISTANBUL REPRESENTATIVE OFFICE—See The Sumitomo Bank, Limited; *Int'l*, pg. 1310
THE SUMITOMO BANK, LTD.-JAKARTA REPRESENTATIVE OFFICE—See The Sumitomo Bank, Limited; *Int'l*, pg. 1310
THE SUMITOMO BANK, LTD.-JOHANNESBURG REPRESENTATIVE OFFICE—See The Sumitomo Bank, Limited; *Int'l*, pg. 1310
THE SUMITOMO BANK, LTD.-KOWLOON BRANCH—See The Sumitomo Bank, Limited; *Int'l*, pg. 1309
THE SUMITOMO BANK, LTD.-KUALA LUMPUR REPRESENTATIVE OFFICE—See The Sumitomo Bank, Limited; *Int'l*, pg. 1310
THE SUMITOMO BANK, LTD.-LISBON REPRESENTATIVE OFFICE—See The Sumitomo Bank, Limited; *Int'l*, pg. 1310

Company Index

THE SUMITOMO BANK, LTD.-LONDON BRANCH—See The Sumitomo Bank, Limited; *Int'l*, pg. 1309
THE SUMITOMO BANK, LTD.-LOS ANGELES BRANCH—See The Sumitomo Bank, Limited; *Int'l*, pg. 1308
THE SUMITOMO BANK, LTD.-MADRID BRANCH—See The Sumitomo Bank, Limited; *Int'l*, pg. 1309
THE SUMITOMO BANK, LTD.-MANILA REPRESENTATIVE OFFICE—See The Sumitomo Bank, Limited; *Int'l*, pg. 1310
THE SUMITOMO BANK, LTD.-MEXICO REPRESENTATIVE OFFICE—See The Sumitomo Bank, Limited; *Int'l*, pg. 1310
THE SUMITOMO BANK, LTD.-MILAN BRANCH—See The Sumitomo Bank, Limited; *Int'l*, pg. 1309
THE SUMITOMO BANK, LTD.-MUMBAI BRANCH—See The Sumitomo Bank, Limited; *Int'l*, pg. 1309
THE SUMITOMO BANK, LTD.-NEW YORK BRANCH—See The Sumitomo Bank, Limited; *Int'l*, pg. 1309
THE SUMITOMO BANK, LTD.-PARIS BRANCH—See The Sumitomo Bank, Limited; *Int'l*, pg. 1309
THE SUMITOMO BANK, LTD.-SAN FRANCISCO BRANCH—See The Sumitomo Bank, Limited; *Int'l*, pg. 1309
THE SUMITOMO BANK, LTD.-SEATTLE REPRESENTATIVE OFFICE—See The Sumitomo Bank, Limited; *Int'l*, pg. 1309
THE SUMITOMO BANK, LTD.-SEOUL BRANCH—See The Sumitomo Bank, Limited; *Int'l*, pg. 1309
THE SUMITOMO BANK, LTD.-SHANGHAI BRANCH—See The Sumitomo Bank, Limited; *Int'l*, pg. 1309
THE SUMITOMO BANK, LTD.-SHENYANG REPRESENTATIVE OFFICE—See The Sumitomo Bank, Limited; *Int'l*, pg. 1310
THE SUMITOMO BANK, LTD.-STOCKHOLM REPRESENTATIVE OFFICE—See The Sumitomo Bank, Limited; *Int'l*, pg. 1310
THE SUMITOMO BANK, LTD.-SYDNEY REPRESENTATIVE OFFICE—See The Sumitomo Bank, Limited; *Int'l*, pg. 1310
THE SUMITOMO BANK, LTD.-TEHRAN REPRESENTATIVE OFFICE—See The Sumitomo Bank, Limited; *Int'l*, pg. 1310
THE SUMITOMO BANK, LTD.-TOKYO—See The Sumitomo Bank, Limited; *Int'l*, pg. 1308
THE SUMITOMO BANK, LTD.-VIENNA REPRESENTATIVE OFFICE—See The Sumitomo Bank, Limited; *Int'l*, pg. 1310
THE SUMITOMO BANK, LTD.-YANGON REPRESENTATIVE OFFICE—See The Sumitomo Bank, Limited; *Int'l*, pg. 1310
THE SUMITOMO BANK, LTD.-YANGPU BRANCH—See The Sumitomo Bank, Limited; *Int'l*, pg. 1309
SUMITOMO BANK OF CALIFORNIA—See The Sumitomo Bank, Limited; *Int'l*, pg. 1309
THE SUMITOMO BANK OF CANADA—See The Sumitomo Bank, Limited; *Int'l*, pg. 1309
SUMITOMO BANK OF NEW YORK TRUST COMPANY—See The Sumitomo Bank, Limited; *Int'l*, pg. 1309
SUMITOMO BANK (SCHWEIZ) AG—See The Sumitomo Bank, Limited; *Int'l*, pg. 1310
SUMITOMO BANK SECURITIES, INC.—See The Sumitomo Bank, Limited; *Int'l*, pg. 1309
SUMITOMO BAYER URETHANE CO., LTD.—See Bayer AG; *Int'l*, pg. 174
SUMITOMO CANADA LTD.—See Sumitomo Corporation; *Int'l*, pg. 1312
SUMITOMO CHEMICAL AGRO EUROPE S.A.—See Sumitomo Chemical Company, Ltd.; *Int'l*, pg. 1311
SUMITOMO CHEMICAL AMERICA, INC.—See Sumitomo Chemical Company, Ltd.; *Int'l*, pg. 1311
SUMITOMO CHEMICAL AMERICA, INC.-SAN FRANCISCO OFFICE—See Sumitomo Chemical Company, Ltd.; *Int'l*, pg. 1311
SUMITOMO CHEMICAL AMERICA, INC.-SANTA CLARA—See Sumitomo Chemical Company, Ltd.; *Int'l*, pg. 1311
SUMITOMO CHEMICAL ASIA PTE LTD.—See Sumitomo Chemical Company, Ltd.; *Int'l*, pg. 1311
SUMITOMO CHEMICAL BEJING—See Sumitomo Chemical Company, Ltd.; *Int'l*, pg. 1311
SUMITOMO CHEMICAL BELGIUM S.A./N.V.—See Sumitomo Chemical Company, Ltd.; *Int'l*, pg. 1311
SUMITOMO CHEMICAL COMPANY, LTD.; *Int'l*, pg. 1310
SUMITOMO CHEMICAL COMPANY, LTD.-MELBOURNE OFFICE—See Sumitomo Chemical Company, Ltd.; *Int'l*, pg. 1311
SUMITOMO CHEMICAL COMPANY, LTD.-WELLINGTON OFFICE—See Sumitomo Chemical Company, Ltd.; *Int'l*, pg. 1312
SUMITOMO CHEMICAL DEUTSCHLAND GMBH—See Sumitomo Chemical Company, Ltd.; *Int'l*, pg. 1312
SUMITOMO CHEMICAL DO BRASIL REPRESENTACOES LIMITADA—See Sumitomo Chemical Company, Ltd.; *Int'l*, pg. 1312
SUMITOMO CHEMICAL ENGINEERING CO., LTD.—See Sumitomo Chemical Company, Ltd.; *Int'l*, pg. 1311
SUMITOMO CHEMICAL NEDERLAND B.V.—See Sumitomo Chemical Company, Ltd.; *Int'l*, pg. 1312
SUMITOMO CHEMICAL-OSAKA—See Sumitomo Chemical Company, Ltd.; *Int'l*, pg. 1311
SUMITOMO CHEMICAL TAIWAN CO., LTD.—See Sumitomo Chemical Company, Ltd.; *Int'l*, pg. 1312
SUMITOMO CHEMICAL (U.K.) PLC—See Sumitomo Chemical Company, Ltd.; *Int'l*, pg. 1312
SUMITOMO CORPORATION; *Int'l*, pg. 1312
SUMITOMO CORPORATION OF AMERICA—See Sumitomo Corporation; *Int'l*, pg. 1312
SUMITOMO DOW LTD.—See Sumitomo Chemical Company, Ltd.; *Int'l*, pg. 1311
SUMITOMO EATON HYDRAULICS CO.-HYDRAULICS DIV.—See Eaton Corporation; *U.S. Public*, pg. 559
SUMITOMO EATON NOVA CORPORATION—See Eaton Corporation; *U.S. Public*, pg. 559

SUMITOMO ELECTRIC ASIA, LTD.—See Sumitomo Electric Industries, Ltd.; *Int'l*, pg. 1314
SUMITOMO ELECTRIC AUTOMOTIVE INC.—See Sumitomo Electric Industries, Ltd.; *Int'l*, pg. 1313
SUMITOMO ELECTRIC AUTOMOTIVE PRODUCTS (SINGAPORE) PTE., LTD.—See Sumitomo Electric Industries, Ltd.; *Int'l*, pg. 1314
SUMITOMO ELECTRIC CARBIDE, INC.—See Sumitomo Electric Industries, Ltd.; *Int'l*, pg. 1313
SUMITOMO ELECTRIC CARBIDE MANUFACTURING, INC.—See Sumitomo Electric Industries, Ltd.; *Int'l*, pg. 1313
SUMITOMO ELECTRIC COMMUNICATIONS ENGINEERING (THAILAND), LTD.—See Sumitomo Electric Industries, Ltd.; *Int'l*, pg. 1314
SUMITOMO ELECTRIC EUROPE LIMITED—See Sumitomo Electric Industries, Ltd.; *Int'l*, pg. 1314
SUMITOMO ELECTRIC EUROPE S.A. - EDGWARE—See Sumitomo Electric Industries, Ltd.; *Int'l*, pg. 1314
SUMITOMO ELECTRIC EUROPE S.A. - WALES—See Sumitomo Electric Industries, Ltd.; *Int'l*, pg. 1314
SUMITOMO ELECTRIC FINANCE NETHERLANDS B.V.—See Sumitomo Electric Industries, Ltd.; *Int'l*, pg. 1314
SUMITOMO ELECTRIC FINANCE U.K. LTD.—See Sumitomo Electric Industries, Ltd.; *Int'l*, pg. 1314
SUMITOMO ELECTRIC FINANCE U.S.A., INC.—See Sumitomo Electric Industries, Ltd.; *Int'l*, pg. 1313
SUMITOMO ELECTRIC HARDMETAL LTD.—See Sumitomo Electric Industries, Ltd.; *Int'l*, pg. 1314
SUMITOMO ELECTRIC HARTMETALL GMBH—See Sumitomo Electric Industries, Ltd.; *Int'l*, pg. 1314
SUMITOMO ELECTRIC HARTMETALLIFABRIK GMBH—See Sumitomo Electric Industries, Ltd.; *Int'l*, pg. 1314
SUMITOMO ELECTRIC INDUSTRIES, LTD.; *Int'l*, pg. 1313
SUMITOMO ELECTRIC INDUSTRIES, LTD.—See Sumitomo Electric Industries, Ltd.; *Int'l*, pg. 1314
SUMITOMO ELECTRIC INTERCONNECT PRODUCTS INC.—See Sumitomo Electric Industries, Ltd.; *Int'l*, pg. 1313
SUMITOMO ELECTRIC INTERCONNECT PRODUCTS (SINGAPORE) PTE., LTD.—See Sumitomo Electric Industries, Ltd.; *Int'l*, pg. 1314
SUMITOMO ELECTRIC INTERCONNECT PRODUCTS (M) SDN. BHD.—See Sumitomo Electric Industries, Ltd.; *Int'l*, pg. 1314
SUMITOMO ELECTRIC INTERNATIONAL (SINGAPORE) PTE. LTD.—See Sumitomo Electric Industries, Ltd.; *Int'l*, pg. 1314
SUMITOMO ELECTRIC LIGHTWAVE CORP.—See Sumitomo Electric Industries, Ltd.; *Int'l*, pg. 1313
SUMITOMO ELECTRIC MAGNET WIRE (M) SDN. BHD.—See Sumitomo Electric Industries, Ltd.; *Int'l*, pg. 1314
SUMITOMO ELECTRIC SCHRUMPF-PRODUKTE GMBH—See Sumitomo Electric Industries, Ltd.; *Int'l*, pg. 1314
SUMITOMO ELECTRIC (SINGAPORE) PTE. LTD.—See Sumitomo Electric Industries, Ltd.; *Int'l*, pg. 1314
SUMITOMO ELECTRIC SINTERED COMPONENTS (M) SDN. BHD.—See Sumitomo Electric Industries, Ltd.; *Int'l*, pg. 1314
SUMITOMO ELECTRIC (THAILAND) LTD.—See Sumitomo Electric Industries, Ltd.; *Int'l*, pg. 1314
SUMITOMO ELECTRIC U.S.A., INC.—See Sumitomo Electric Industries, Ltd.; *Int'l*, pg. 1313
SUMITOMO ELECTRIC WIRING SYSTEMS, INC.—See Sumitomo Electric Industries, Ltd.; *Int'l*, pg. 1313
SUMITOMO ELECTRIC WIRING SYSTEMS (THAILAND) LTD.—See Sumitomo Electric Industries, Ltd.; *Int'l*, pg. 1314
SUMITOMO FINANCE (ASIA) LIMITED—See The Sumitomo Bank, Limited; *Int'l*, pg. 1310
SUMITOMO FINANCE (DUBLIN) LIMITED—See The Sumitomo Bank, Limited; *Int'l*, pg. 1310
SUMITOMO FINANCE INTERNATIONAL PLC—See The Sumitomo Bank, Limited; *Int'l*, pg. 1310
SUMITOMO FINANCE (MIDDLE EAST) E.C.—See The Sumitomo Bank, Limited; *Int'l*, pg. 1310
SUMITOMO FINANCIAL FUTURES (SINGAPORE) PTE. LTD.—See The Sumitomo Bank, Limited; *Int'l*, pg. 1310
SUMITOMO HEAVY INDUSTRIES, LTD.; *Int'l*, pg. 1314
SUMITOMO HEAVY MACHINERY CORPORATION OF AMERICA—See Sumitomo Heavy Industries, Ltd.; *Int'l*, pg. 1314
SUMITOMO INTERNATIONAL FINANCE AUSTRALIA LIMITED—See The Sumitomo Bank, Limited; *Int'l*, pg. 1310
SUMITOMO LIFE INSURANCE COMPANY; *Int'l*, pg. 1315
SUMITOMO LIFE INTERNATIONAL (UK) LIMITED—See Sumitomo Life Insurance Company; *Int'l*, pg. 1315
SUMITOMO MACHINERY CORPORATION OF AMERICA—See Sumitomo Heavy Industries, Ltd.; *Int'l*, pg. 1314
SUMITOMO MARINE MGMT SERVICES—See Sumitomo Heavy Industries, Ltd.; *Int'l*, pg. 1314
SUMITOMO METAL INDUSTRIES, LTD.; *Int'l*, pg. 1315
SUMITOMO METAL MINING ARIZONA INC.—See Sumitomo Metal Mining Co., Ltd.; *Int'l*, pg. 1316
SUMITOMO METAL MINING CANADA LTD.—See Sumitomo Metal Mining Co., Ltd.; *Int'l*, pg. 1316
SUMITOMO METAL MINING CO., LTD.; *Int'l*, pg. 1316
SUMITOMO METAL MINING ELECTRONICS PARTS PTE. LTD.—See Sumitomo Metal Mining Co., Ltd.; *Int'l*, pg. 1316
SUMITOMO METAL MINING HONG KONG CO., LTD.—See Sumitomo Metal Mining Co., Ltd.; *Int'l*, pg. 1316
SUMITOMO METAL MINING OCEANIA PTY. LTD.—See Sumitomo Metal Mining Co., Ltd.; *Int'l*, pg. 1316
SUMITOMO METAL MINING SINGAPORE PTE., LTD.—See Sumitomo Metal Mining Co., Ltd.; *Int'l*, pg. 1316
SUMITOMO METAL MINING U.S.A. INC.—See Sumitomo Metal Mining Co., Ltd.; *Int'l*, pg. 1316
SUMITOMO OSAKA—See Sumitomo Metal Industries, Ltd.; *Int'l*, pg. 1315
SUMITOMO PHARMACEUTICALS CO., LTD.—See Sumitomo Chemical Company, Ltd.; *Int'l*, pg. 1311

SUMITOMO RUBBER EUROPE B.V.—See Sumitomo Rubber Industries Ltd.; *Int'l*, pg. 1317
SUMITOMO RUBBER INDUSTRIES—See Sumitomo Rubber Industries Ltd.; *Int'l*, pg. 1317
SUMITOMO RUBBER INDUSTRIES - ATLANTA—See Sumitomo Rubber Industries Ltd.; *Int'l*, pg. 1317
SUMITOMO RUBBER INDUSTRIES-BRUSSELS—See Sumitomo Rubber Industries Ltd.; *Int'l*, pg. 1317
SUMITOMO RUBBER INDUSTRIES-DUBAI—See Sumitomo Rubber Industries Ltd.; *Int'l*, pg. 1317
SUMITOMO RUBBER INDUSTRIES-JEDDAH—See Sumitomo Rubber Industries Ltd.; *Int'l*, pg. 1317
SUMITOMO RUBBER INDUSTRIES LTD.; *Int'l*, pg. 1316
SUMITOMO RUBBER INDUSTRIES-MELBOURNE—See Sumitomo Rubber Industries Ltd.; *Int'l*, pg. 1317
SUMITOMO RUBBER INDUSTRIES-PARIS—See Sumitomo Rubber Industries Ltd.; *Int'l*, pg. 1317
SUMITOMO RUBBER INDUSTRIES-TOKYO HEAD OFFICE—See Sumitomo Rubber Industries Ltd.; *Int'l*, pg. 1317
SUMITOMO RUBBER INDUSTRIES-TORONTO—See Sumitomo Rubber Industries Ltd.; *Int'l*, pg. 1317
SUMITOMO SEIKA CHEMICALS CO., LTD.—See Sumitomo Chemical Company, Ltd.; *Int'l*, pg. 1311
SUMITOMO SITIX CORPORATION; *Int'l*, pg. 1317
SUMITOMO SITIX EUROPE PLC—See Sumitomo Sitix Corporation; *Int'l*, pg. 1317
SUMITOMO SITIX SILICON, INC.—See Sumitomo Sitix Corporation; *Int'l*, pg. 1317
SUMITOMO 3M LIMITED—See 3M; *U.S. Public*, pg. 1606
SUMITOMO TRUST & BANKING CO.—See The Sumitomo Trust & Banking Co., Ltd.; *Int'l*, pg. 1318
THE SUMITOMO TRUST & BANKING CO., LTD.; *Int'l*, pg. 1317
THE SUMITOMO TRUST & BANKING CO. (U.S.A.)—See The Sumitomo Trust & Banking Co., Ltd.; *Int'l*, pg. 1317
SUMITOMO TRUST & BANKING (LUXEMBOURG) S.A.—See The Sumitomo Trust & Banking Co., Ltd.; *Int'l*, pg. 1318
SUMITOMO TRUST & BANKING (SWITZERLAND) LIMITED—See The Sumitomo Trust & Banking Co., Ltd.; *Int'l*, pg. 1318
SUMITOMO TRUST FINANCE (AUSTRALIA) LIMITED—See The Sumitomo Trust & Banking Co., Ltd.; *Int'l*, pg. 1318
SUMITOMO TRUST FINANCE (H.K.) LIMITED—See The Sumitomo Trust & Banking Co., Ltd.; *Int'l*, pg. 1318
SUMITOMO TRUST INTERNATIONAL PLC.—See The Sumitomo Trust & Banking Co., Ltd.; *Int'l*, pg. 1318
SUMITOMO TRUST MERCHANT BANK (SINGAPORE) LTD.—See The Sumitomo Trust & Banking Co., Ltd.; *Int'l*, pg. 1318
P.T. SUMITOMO WIRING SYSTEMS BATTSM INDONESIA—See Sumitomo Electric Industries, Ltd.; *Int'l*, pg. 1313
SUMITOMO-YALE CO., LTD.—See NACCO Industries, Inc.; *U.S. Public*, pg. 1150
SUMITON OFFICE—See Pinnacle Bank; *U.S. Public*, pg. 1297
SUMITRANS CORPORATION—See Sumitomo Corporation; *Int'l*, pg. 1312
SUMITRUST IVORY & SIME LIMITED—See The Sumitomo Trust & Banking Co., Ltd.; *Int'l*, pg. 1318
SUMMA FOUR, INC.; *U.S. Public*, pg. 1527
SUMMA FOUR LIMITED—See Summa Four, Inc.; *U.S. Public*, pg. 1527
SUMMA INDUSTRIES; *U.S. Public*, pg. 1527
SUMMA KUMAGAI INC.—See Kumagai Gumi Co., Ltd.; *Int'l*, pg. 764
SUMMA MILLS—See Enso Oyj; *Int'l*, pg. 457
SUMMERS GROUP—See Rexel, S.A.; *Int'l*, pg. 1108
O.C. SUMMERS LTD.—See John Laing PLC; *Int'l*, pg. 796
SUMMIT BANCORP; *U.S. Public*, pg. 1527
SUMMIT BANK—See Summit Bancorp; *U.S. Public*, pg. 1527
SUMMIT-BEERS CONSTRUCTION COMPANY—See Skanska AB; *Int'l*, pg. 1261
SUMMIT-CANADA—See American Greetings Corporation; *U.S. Public*, pg. 78
SUMMIT COMMERCIAL PROPERTY, INC.—See The Suddath Companies; *U.S. Private*, pg. 1049
SUMMIT CORPORATION OF AMERICA; *U.S. Private*, pg. 1050
SUMMIT EXPORT CORP.—See LSB Industries, Inc.; *U.S. Public*, pg. 971
SUMMIT FAMILY RESTAURANTS, INC.—See CKE Restaurants Inc.; *U.S. Public*, pg. 278
SUMMIT FOOD SERVICE DISTRIBUTORS—See Cara Operations Limited; *Int'l*, pg. 266
SUMMIT GRAVURE LTD.—See Forbo Holding SA; *Int'l*, pg. 498
SUMMIT MACHINE TOOL MFG. CORP.—See LSB Industries, Inc.; *U.S. Public*, pg. 971
SUMMIT MACHINERY CO.—See LSB Industries, Inc.; *U.S. Public*, pg. 971
THE SUMMIT MEDIA GROUP; *U.S. Private*, pg. 1050
THE SUMMIT MORTGAGE COMPANY, INC.—See Summit Bancorp; *U.S. Public*, pg. 1528
SUMMIT PLASTIC CO.—See Novartis AG; *Int'l*, pg. 974
SUMMIT PLASTIC SOLUTIONS, INC.; *U.S. Private*, pg. 1050
SUMMIT SPECIALTY CHEMICALS CORPORATION—See Sumitomo Corporation; *Int'l*, pg. 1312
SUMMIT TECHNOLOGY, INC.; *U.S. Public*, pg. 1528
SUMMIT TECHNOLOGY IRELAND—See Summit Technology, Inc.; *U.S. Public*, pg. 1529
SUMMIT TELEMARKETING—See SBC Communications Inc.; *U.S. Public*, pg. 1415
SUMMIT TOOL COMPANY; *U.S. Private*, pg. 1050
SUMOTO S.R.L.—See Ebara Corporation; *Int'l*, pg. 432
SUMTER BANK AND TRUST COMPANY—See Synovus Financial Corp.; *U.S. Public*, pg. 1549

MASTER INDEX TO COMPANY NAMES SUNCOR
Company Index

SUMTER COUNTY TIMES—See Landmark Communications, Inc.; *U.S. Private*, pg. 648
THE SUN—See The News Corporation Limited; *Int'l*, pg. 927
SUN-AD CO., LTD.—See Suntory Ltd.; *Int'l*, pg. 1321
SUN ALLIANCE USA, INC.—See Royal & Sun Alliance Insurance Group plc; *Int'l*, pg. 1131
SUN ARROW CHEMICAL CO., LTD.—See Tokuyama Corporation; *Int'l*, pg. 1394
SUN BANCORP, INC.; *U.S. Public*, pg. 1529
SUN BANK D/B/A SNYDER COUNTY TRUST COMPANY—See Sun Bancorp, Inc.; *U.S. Public*, pg. 1529
SUN BANK D/B/A WASTONTOWN NATIONAL BANK—See Sun Bancorp, Inc.; *U.S. Public*, pg. 1529
SUN BANKING CORPORATION—See Sun Life Assurance Company of Canada; *Int'l*, pg. 1319
SUN BENEFIT SERVICES COMPANY, INC.—See Sun Life Assurance Company of Canada; *Int'l*, pg. 1319
SUN BULB COMPANY, INC.; *U.S. Private*, pg. 1050
SUN CAPITAL ADVISERS, INC.—See Sun Life Assurance Company of Canada; *Int'l*, pg. 1319
SUN CHEMICAL AB—See Dainippon Ink & Chemicals, Inc.; *Int'l*, pg. 371
SUN CHEMICAL AG—See Dainippon Ink & Chemicals, Inc.; *Int'l*, pg. 371
SUN CHEMICAL A/S—See Dainippon Ink & Chemicals, Inc.; *Int'l*, pg. 371
SUN CHEMICAL COMPANY, INC.—See Sun Bulb Company, Inc.; *U.S. Private*, pg. 1050
SUN CHEMICAL CORP.—See Dainippon Ink & Chemicals, Inc.; *Int'l*, pg. 370
SUN CHEMICAL CORP. OF MICHIGAN—See Dainippon Ink & Chemicals, Inc.; *Int'l*, pg. 370
SUN CHEMICAL DE CENTRO AMERICA, S.A. DE C.V.—See Dainippon Ink & Chemicals, Inc.; *Int'l*, pg. 371
SUN CHEMICAL DE PANAMA, S.A.—See Dainippon Ink & Chemicals, Inc.; *Int'l*, pg. 371
SUN CHEMICAL DRUCKFARBEN GMBH—See Dainippon Ink & Chemicals, Inc.; *Int'l*, pg. 371
SUN CHEMICAL ECP S.A./N.V.—See Dainippon Ink & Chemicals, Inc.; *Int'l*, pg. 371
SUN CHEMICAL GROUP B.V.—See Dainippon Ink & Chemicals, Inc.; *Int'l*, pg. 370
SUN CHEMICAL HARTMANN A/S—See Dainippon Ink & Chemicals, Inc.; *Int'l*, pg. 371
SUN CHEMICAL INKS (IRELAND) LTD.—See Dainippon Ink & Chemicals, Inc.; *Int'l*, pg. 371
SUN CHEMICAL INKS S.A.—See Dainippon Ink & Chemicals, Inc.; *Int'l*, pg. 371
SUN CHEMICAL LTD.—See Dainippon Ink & Chemicals, Inc.; *Int'l*, pg. 371
SUN CHEMICAL NYOMDAFESTEK KERESKEDELMI ES GYARTO KFT—See Dainippon Ink & Chemicals, Inc.; *Int'l*, pg. 371
SUN CHEMICAL OY—See Dainippon Ink & Chemicals, Inc.; *Int'l*, pg. 371
SUN CHEMICAL PIGMENTE GMBH—See Dainippon Ink & Chemicals, Inc.; *Int'l*, pg. 371
SUN CHEMICAL PORTUGAL-TINTAS GRAFICAS S.A.—See Dainippon Ink & Chemicals, Inc.; *Int'l*, pg. 371
SUN CHEMICAL S.A.—See Dainippon Ink & Chemicals, Inc.; *Int'l*, pg. 371
SUN CHEMICAL S.A. DE C.V.—See Dainippon Ink & Chemicals, Inc.; *Int'l*, pg. 371
SUN CHEMICAL SERVIVES S.A.—See Dainippon Ink & Chemicals, Inc.; *Int'l*, pg. 371
SUN CHEMICAL SP. (Z.O.O) (LTD.)—See Dainippon Ink & Chemicals, Inc.; *Int'l*, pg. 371
SUN CHEMICAL S.P.A.—See Dainippon Ink & Chemicals, Inc.; *Int'l*, pg. 371
SUN CHEMICAL S.R.O.—See Dainippon Ink & Chemicals, Inc.; *Int'l*, pg. 371
SUN CITY EGG MARKETING, INC.—See Sun City Industries, Inc.; *U.S. Public*, pg. 1529
SUN CITY GEORGETOWN—See Del Webb Corporation; *U.S. Public*, pg. 495
SUN CITY GRAND—See Del Webb Corporation; *U.S. Public*, pg. 495
SUN CITY HILTON HEAD—See Del Webb Corporation; *U.S. Public*, pg. 495
SUN CITY INDUSTRIES, INC.; *U.S. Public*, pg. 1529
SUN CITY LAS VEGAS—See Del Webb Corporation; *U.S. Public*, pg. 495
SUN CITY MACDONALD RANCH—See Del Webb Corporation; *U.S. Public*, pg. 495
SUN CITY PALM DESERT—See Del Webb Corporation; *U.S. Public*, pg. 495
SUN CITY PALM SPRINGS—See Del Webb Corporation; *U.S. Public*, pg. 495
SUN CITY PRODUCE, INC.—See Sun City Industries, Inc.; *U.S. Public*, pg. 1529
SUN CITY REDI-MIX INC.—See Grupo Cementos de Chihuahua S.A. de C.V.; *Int'l*, pg. 573
SUN CITY ROSEVILLE—See Del Webb Corporation; *U.S. Public*, pg. 495
SUN CITY SEWER COMPANY—See Citizens Utilities Company; *U.S. Public*, pg. 380
SUN CITY SUMMERLIN—See Del Webb Corporation; *U.S. Public*, pg. 495
SUN CITY TUCSON—See Del Webb Corporation; *U.S. Public*, pg. 495
SUN CITY WATER COMPANY—See Citizens Utilities Company; *U.S. Public*, pg. 380
SUN CITY WEST—See Del Webb Corporation; *U.S. Public*, *pg. 495*
SUN CITY WEST UTILITIES COMPANY—See Citizens Utilities Company; *U.S. Public*, pg. 380
SUN COAST CLOSURES OF FLORIDA, INC.—See Sun Coast Industries, Inc; *U.S. Public*, pg. 1530
SUN COAST INDUSTRIES, INC; *U.S. Public*, pg. 1529
THE SUN CO.—See Gannett Company, Inc.; *U.S. Public*, pg. 701
SUN COMPANY, INC.; *U.S. Public*, pg. 1530
SUN DATA INC.; *U.S. Private*, pg. 1050
SUN DEW CORP.—See Investcorp International; *Int'l*, pg. 686
SUN DIAMOND GROWERS OF CALIFORNIA; *U.S. Private*, pg. 1051
SUN ELECTRIC—See Snap-On Tools Corporation; *U.S. Public*, pg. 1480
SUN ELECTRIC AUSTRIA G.M.B.H.—See Snap-On Tools Corporation; *U.S. Public*, pg. 1481
SUN ELECTRIC BELGIUM N.V.—See Snap-On Tools Corporation; *U.S. Public*, pg. 1481
SUN ELECTRIC DE MEXICO S.A. DE C.V.—See Snap-On Tools Corporation; *U.S. Public*, pg. 1481
SUN ELECTRIC DEUTSCHLAND—See Snap-On Tools Corporation; *U.S. Public*, pg. 1481
SUN ELECTRIC DO BRASIL COMERCIO E. INDUSTRIA LIMITADA—See Snap-On Tools Corporation; *U.S. Public*, pg. 1481
SUN ELECTRIC NEDERLAND, B.V. (SEN) VARODO B.V. (VRD)—See Snap-On Tools Corporation; *U.S. Public*, pg. 1481
SUN ELECTRIC SYSTEMS B.V. (SES)—See Snap-On Tools Corporation; *U.S. Public*, pg. 1481
SUN ELECTRIC U.K. LIMITED—See Snap-On Tools Corporation; *U.S. Public*, pg. 1481
SUN FINANCIAL GROUP, INC.—See GATX Corporation; *U.S. Public*, pg. 691
SUN HEALTHCARE GROUP INC.; *U.S. Public*, pg. 1530
SUN HEALTHCARE GROUP INTERNATIONAL LTD.—See Sun Healthcare Group Inc.; *U.S. Public*, pg. 1531
SUN HERALD—See Knight-Ridder, Inc.; *U.S. Public*, pg. 964
THE SUN-HERALD—See John Fairfax Holdings Limited; *Int'l*, pg. 477
SUN HILL INDUSTRIES, INC.; *U.S. Private*, pg. 1051
SUN HUNG KAI PROPERTIES LTD.; *Int'l*, pg. 1318
SUN INSURANCE CO. OF NEW YORK—See Royal & Sun Alliance Insurance Group plc; *Int'l*, pg. 1131
SUN INTERNATIONAL HOTELS LIMITED; *U.S. Public*, pg. 1531
SUN INTERNATIONAL PRODUCTION COMPANY LIMITED—See Sun Company, Inc.; *U.S. Public*, pg. 1530
SUN INVESTMENT SERVICES COMPANY—See Sun Life Assurance Company of Canada; *Int'l*, pg. 1319
SUN KWONG METAL MANUFACTURING CO. LTD.—See General Binding Corporation; *U.S. Public*, pg. 707
SUN LAND BEEF COMPANY—See Packerland Packing Co.; *U.S. Private*, pg. 833
SUN LIFE AND PROVINCIAL HOLDINGS PLC; *Int'l*, pg. 1318
SUN LIFE ASSURANCE COMPANY OF CANADA; *Int'l*, pg. 1318
SUN LIFE ASSURANCE COMPANY OF CANADA (U.K.) LIMITED—See Sun Life Assurance Company of Canada; *Int'l*, pg. 1319
SUN LIFE ASSURANCE COMPANY OF CANADA (U.S.)—See Sun Life Assurance Company of Canada; *Int'l*, pg. 1319
SUN LIFE DEALER SERVICES CORP.—See Sun Life Assurance Company of Canada; *Int'l*, pg. 1319
SUN LIFE DISTRIBUTION SERVICES INC.—See Sun Life Assurance Company of Canada; *Int'l*, pg. 1319
SUN LIFE FINANCE CORPORATION—See Sun Life Assurance Company of Canada; *Int'l*, pg. 1319
SUN LIFE FINANCIAL HOLDINGS INC.—See Sun Life Assurance Company of Canada; *Int'l*, pg. 1319
SUN LIFE INSURANCE AND ANNUITY COMPANY OF NEW YORK—See Sun Life Assurance Company of Canada; *Int'l*, pg. 1319
SUN LIFE OF CANADA—See Sun Life Assurance Company of Canada; *Int'l*, pg. 1319
SUN LIFE OF CANADA BENEFIT MANAGEMENT LIMITED—See Sun Life Assurance Company of Canada; *Int'l*, pg. 1319
SUN LIFE OF CANADA GROUP OF COMPANIES—See Sun Life Assurance Company of Canada; *Int'l*, pg. 1319
SUN LIFE OF CANADA HOME LOANS COMPANY LIMITED—See Sun Life Assurance Company of Canada; *Int'l*, pg. 1320
SUN LIFE OF CANADA INVESTMENT MANAGEMENT LIMITED—See Sun Life Assurance Company of Canada; *Int'l*, pg. 1319
SUN LIFE OF CANADA NOMINEES LIMITED—See Sun Life Assurance Company of Canada; *Int'l*, pg. 1320
SUN LIFE OF CANADA UNIT MANAGERS LIMITED—See Sun Life Assurance Company of Canada; *Int'l*, pg. 1319
SUN LIFE SAVINGS & MORTGAGE CORP.—See Sun Life Assurance Company of Canada; *Int'l*, pg. 1319
SUN LIFE TRUST COMPANY—See Sun Life Assurance Company of Canada; *Int'l*, pg. 1319
SUN-LITHO—See Morris Newspaper Corporation; *U.S. Private*, pg. 762
SUN MEDIA CORPORATION; *Int'l*, pg. 1320
SUN MEDICAL TECHNOLOGIES, INC.—See Prime Medical Services, Inc.; *U.S. Public*, pg. 1327
SUN MICRO STAMPING INC.—See Sun Microsystems, Inc.; *U.S. Public*, pg. 1531
SUN MICROSYSTEMS—See Sun Microsystems, Inc.; *U.S. Public*, pg. 1531
SUN MICROSYSTEMS AB—See Sun Microsystems, Inc.; *U.S. Public*, pg. 1531
SUN MICROSYSTEMS COMPUTER CORPORATION—See Sun Microsystems, Inc.; *U.S. Public*, pg. 1531
SUN MICROSYSTEMS EUROPE, INC.—See Sun Microsystems, Inc.; *U.S. Public*, pg. 1531
SUN MICROSYSTEMS FEDERAL INC.—See Sun Microsystems, Inc.; *U.S. Public*, pg. 1531
SUN MICROSYSTEMS FRANCE, S.A.—See Sun Microsystems, Inc.; *U.S. Public*, pg. 1531
SUN MICROSYSTEMS GMBH—See Sun Microsystems, Inc.; *U.S. Public*, pg. 1531
SUN MICROSYSTEMS IBERICA S.A.—See Sun Microsystems, Inc.; *U.S. Public*, pg. 1531
SUN MICROSYSTEMS, INC.; *U.S. Public*, pg. 1531
SUN MICROSYSTEMS ITALIA S.P.A.—See Sun Microsystems, Inc.; *U.S. Public*, pg. 1531
SUN MICROSYSTEMS LABORATORIES, INC.—See Sun Microsystems, Inc.; *U.S. Public*, pg. 1531
SUN MICROSYSTEMS LTD.—See Sun Microsystems, Inc.; *U.S. Public*, pg. 1532
SUN MICROSYSTEMS NEDERLAND, B.V.—See Sun Microsystems, Inc.; *U.S. Public*, pg. 1532
SUN MICROSYSTEMS OF AUSTRALIA PTY. LTD.—See Sun Microsystems, Inc.; *U.S. Public*, pg. 1532
SUN MICROSYSTEMS OF CALIFORNIA—See Sun Microsystems, Inc.; *U.S. Public*, pg. 1532
SUN MICROSYSTEMS OF CALIFORNIA LTD.—See Sun Microsystems, Inc.; *U.S. Public*, pg. 1532
SUN MICROSYSTEMS OF CALIFORNIA (SERVICES) LTD.—See Sun Microsystems, Inc.; *U.S. Public*, pg. 1532
SUN MICROSYSTEMS OF CANADA—See Sun Microsystems, Inc.; *U.S. Public*, pg. 1532
SUN MICROSYSTEMS, R&D—See Sun Microsystems, Inc.; *U.S. Public*, pg. 1531
SUN MICROSYSTEMS (SCHWEIZ) AG—See Sun Microsystems, Inc.; *U.S. Public*, pg. 1532
SUN MICROSYSTEMS (SUISSE) SA—See Sun Microsystems, Inc.; *U.S. Public*, pg. 1532
THE SUN NEWS—See Knight-Ridder, Inc.; *U.S. Public*, pg. 964
SUN PROCESS CONVERTING COMPANY; *U.S. Private*, pg. 1051
SUN PUBLISHING COMPANY, INC.—See Knight-Ridder, Inc.; *U.S. Public*, pg. 964
SUN RAY PRODUCTS, INC.—See Koninklijke BolsWessanen nv; *Int'l*, pg. 752
SUN REFINING & MARKETING CO. LUBES DIV.—See Sun Company, Inc.; *U.S. Public*, pg. 1530
SUN REFINING & MARKETING CO. OPERATIONS DIV.—See Sun Company, Inc.; *U.S. Public*, pg. 1530
SUN-SENTINEL COMPANY—See Tribune Company; *U.S. Public*, pg. 1636
SUN TECHNOLOGY BUSINESS—See Sun Microsystems, Inc.; *U.S. Public*, pg. 1531
SUN TIMES—See Hollinger Inc.; *Int'l*, pg. 632
THE SUN TIMES—See Hollinger Inc.; *Int'l*, pg. 631
SUN TV & APPLIANCES, INC.; *U.S. Public*, pg. 1532
SUN VALLEY CABLEVISION, INC.—See TCA Cable TV, Inc.; *U.S. Public*, pg. 1553
SUN VALLEY HEALTH CARE CENTER—See Horizon/CMS Healthcare Corporation; *U.S. Public*, pg. 839
SUN WAVE INDUSTRIAL CO.; *Int'l*, pg. 1320
SUNAC AMERICA—See Newfoundland Capital Corporation Limited; *Int'l*, pg. 924
SUNAMERICA CORPORATE FINANCE—See SunAmerica Inc.; *U.S. Public*, pg. 1533
SUNAMERICA FINANCIAL—See SunAmerica Inc.; *U.S. Public*, pg. 1533
SUNAMERICA INC.; *U.S. Public*, pg. 1532
SUNAMERICA LIFE INSURANCE COMPANY—See SunAmerica Inc.; *U.S. Public*, pg. 1533
SUNBANK CAPITAL MANAGEMENT, N.A.—See SunTrust Banks, Inc.; *U.S. Public*, pg. 1537
THE SUNBANK FAMILY OF COMPANIES, INC.—See Danaher Corporation; *U.S. Public*, pg. 482
SUNBANK JOSLYN, INC.—See Danaher Corporation; *U.S. Public*, pg. 482
SUNBEAM CORPORATION; *U.S. Public*, pg. 1533
SUNBEAM CORPORATION (CANADA) LIMITED—See Sunbeam Corporation; *U.S. Public*, pg. 1533
SUNBEAM CORPORATION LTD.—See GUD Holdings Limited; *Int'l*, pg. 539
SUNBEAM HOUSEHOLD PRODUCTS—See Sunbeam Corporation; *U.S. Public*, pg. 1533
SUNBEAM MEXICANA S.A. DE C.V.—See Sunbeam Corporation; *U.S. Public*, pg. 1533
SUNBEAM VICTA HOLDINGS LTD.—See GUD Holdings Limited; *Int'l*, pg. 539
SUNBELT BEVERAGES; *U.S. Private*, pg. 1051
SUNBELT FOOTWEAR, LTD.—See Brown Group, Inc.; *U.S. Public*, pg. 262
SUNBELT MINING CO., INC.—See Public Service Company of New Mexico; *U.S. Public*, pg. 1340
SUNBELT NATIONAL MORTGAGE CORPORATION—See First Tennessee National Corporation; *U.S. Public*, pg. 639
SUNBELT NEWSPAPERS, INC.—See Media General, Inc.; *U.S. Public*, pg. 1079
SUNBELT NURSERY GROUP INC.—See General Host Corporation; *U.S. Public*, pg. 715
SUNBELT SUPPLY CO.—See Hughes Supply, Inc.; *U.S. Public*, pg. 847
SUNBIRD BOAT CO., INC.—See Greenway Partners, L.P.; *U.S. Private*, pg. 478
SUNBRAND DIV.—See Willcox & Gibbs, Inc.; *U.S. Private*, pg. 1177
SUNBRIDGE ASSISTED LIVING—See Sun Healthcare Group Inc.; *U.S. Public*, pg. 1531
SUNBUILT HOMES, INC.—See Centex Corporation; *U.S. Public*, pg. 323
SUNBURST—See Georg von Holtzbrinck GmbH; *Int'l*, pg. 1479
SUNBURST RESORT—See Noble House Hotels and Resorts; *U.S. Private*, pg. 800
SUNBURY TEXTILES—See Furnishings International, Inc.; *U.S. Private*, pg. 432
SUNCHEMI CO., LTD.—See Miura Co., Ltd.; *Int'l*, pg. 884
SUNCITI MANUFACTURERS LTD.—See Citizen Watch Company, Ltd.; *Int'l*, pg. 295
SUNCLIPSE, INC.—See Amcor Limited; *Int'l*, pg. 72
SUNCOAST MOTION PICTURE CO.—See Musicland Group Inc.; *U.S. Public*, pg. 1142
SUNCOR DEVELOPMENT COMPANY—See Pinnacle West Capital Corporation; *U.S. Public*, pg. 1298

SUNCOR **DIRECTORY OF CORPORATE AFFILIATIONS**

Company Index

SUNCOR EXPLORATION & PRODUCTION GROUP—See Suncor Inc.; *Int'l*, pg. 1320
SUNCOR INC.; *Int'l*, pg. 1320
SUNCOR OIL SANDS GROUP—See Suncor Inc.; *Int'l*, pg. 1320
SUNDA SHELL—See Royal Dutch/Shell Group of Companies; *Int'l*, pg. 1139
SUNDAGARDAR LTD.—See Norske Skogindustrier A.S; *Int'l*, pg. 966
SUNDAY MAGAZINE NETWORK—See Metropolitan Sunday Newspapers, Inc.; *U.S. Private*, pg. 739
SUNDOR BRANDS INC.—See The Procter & Gamble Company; *U.S. Public*, pg. 1331
SUNDOWNER OFFSHORE SERVICES, INC.—See Nabors Industries, Inc.; *U.S. Public*, pg. 1149
SUNDROP—See Cadbury Schweppes p.l.c.; *Int'l*, pg. 248
SUNDS DEFIBRATOR, INC.—See UPM-Kymmene Corporation; *Int'l*, pg. 1428
SUNDS DEFIBRATOR WOODHANDLING, INC.—See UPM-Kymmene Corporation; *Int'l*, pg. 1428
SUNDSFJORD KRAFTLAG I/S—See Norsk Hydro a.s; *Int'l*, *pg. 961*
SUNDSTRAND AEROSPACE ELECTRONICS—See Sundstrand Corporation; *U.S. Public*, pg. 1533
SUNDSTRAND-AEROSPACE EUROPE—See Sundstrand Corporation; *U.S. Public*, pg. 1534
SUNDSTRAND AEROSPACE GROUP OPERATION—See Sundstrand Corporation; *U.S. Public*, pg. 1533
SUNDSTRAND AEROSPACE OPERATIONS—See Sundstrand Corporation; *U.S. Public*, pg. 1533
SUNDSTRAND AVIATION MECHANICAL—See Sundstrand Corporation; *U.S. Public*, pg. 1533
SUNDSTRAND AVIATION OPERATIONS—See Sundstrand Corporation; *U.S. Public*, pg. 1533
SUNDSTRAND CORPORATION; *U.S. Public*, pg. 1533
SUNDSTRAND ELECTRIC POWER SYSTEMS—See Sundstrand Corporation; *U.S. Public*, pg. 1533
SUNDSTRAND INTERNATIONAL CORP.—See Sundstrand Corporation; *U.S. Public*, pg. 1534
SUNDSTRAND INTERNATIONAL CORP. S.A.—See Sundstrand Corporation; *U.S. Public*, pg. 1534
SUNDSTRAND INTERNATIONAL S.A.—See Sundstrand Corporation; *U.S. Public*, pg. 1534
SUNDSTRAND PACIFIC AEROSPACE (PTE) LTD.—See Sundstrand Corporation; *U.S. Public*, pg. 1534
SUNDSTRAND POWER SYSTEMS—See Sundstrand Corporation; *U.S. Public*, pg. 1534
SUNDSTRAND SERVICE CORP.—See Sundstrand Corporation; *U.S. Public*, pg. 1534
SUNDSVALLS VERKSTADER AB—See The Black & Decker Corporation; *U.S. Public*, pg. 233
SUNDT CORP.; *U.S. Private*, pg. 1051
JAN SUNDT AS—See Keppel Corporation Limited; *Int'l*, pg. 731
SUNFLOWER—See Del Webb Corporation; *U.S. Public*, pg. 495
SUNFLOWER CARRIERS—See Crete Carrier Corp.; *U.S. Private*, pg. 289
SUNFLOWER ELECTRIC POWER CORPORATION; *U.S. Private*, pg. 1052
THE SUNFLOWER GROUP; *U.S. Private*, pg. 1052
SUNFLOWER GROUP IN-STORE SERVICES—See The Sunflower Group; *U.S. Private*, pg. 1052
SUNFLOWER MFG. CO., INC.—See United Dominion Industries, Ltd.; *U.S. Public*, pg. 1676
SUNFLOWER RACING INC.—See Hollywood Park, Inc.; *U.S. Public*, pg. 831
SUNG SAN COMPANY, LTD.—See General Motors Corporation; *U.S. Public*, pg. 724
SUNGARD ASSET MANAGEMENT SYSTEMS—See SunGard Data Systems Inc.; *U.S. Public*, pg. 1535
SUNGARD COMPUTER SERVICES GROUP—See SunGard Data Systems Inc.; *U.S. Public*, pg. 1534
SUNGARD DATA SYSTEMS INC.; *U.S. Public*, pg. 1534
SUNGARD EMPLOYEE BENEFITS SYSTEMS—See SunGard Data Systems Inc.; *U.S. Public*, pg. 1534
SUNGARD FINANCIAL SYSTEMS—See SunGard Data Systems Inc.; *U.S. Public*, pg. 1535
SUNGARD FINANCIAL SYSTEMS, INC.—See SunGard Data Systems Inc.; *U.S. Public*, pg. 1534
SUNGARD INVESTMENT SYSTEMS INC.—See SunGard Data Systems Inc.; *U.S. Public*, pg. 1535
SUNGARD MAILING SERVICES—See SunGard Data Systems Inc.; *U.S. Public*, pg. 1534
SUNGARD PLANNING SOLUTIONS INC.—See SunGard Data Systems Inc.; *U.S. Public*, pg. 1535
SUNGARD RECOVERY SERVICES GROUP—See SunGard Data Systems Inc.; *U.S. Public*, pg. 1535
SUNGARD SHAREHOLDER SYSTEMS INC.—See SunGard Data Systems Inc.; *U.S. Public*, pg. 1535
SUNGARD TECHNOLOGY SYSTEMS GROUP—See SunGard Data Systems Inc.; *U.S. Public*, pg. 1535
SUNGARD TRADING SYSTEMS GROUP—See SunGard Data Systems Inc.; *U.S. Public*, pg. 1535
SUNGARD TRUST & SHAREHOLDER SYSTEMS GROUP—See SunGard Data Systems Inc.; *U.S. Public*, *pg. 1535*
SUNGARD TRUST SYSTEMS INC.—See SunGard Data Systems Inc.; *U.S. Public*, pg. 1535
SUNGLASS HUT INTERNATIONAL; *U.S. Public*, pg. 1535
SUNGOLD DAIRIES PROPRIETARY LTD—See Philip Morris Companies Inc.; *U.S. Public*, pg. 1290
SUNGRAIN, LTD.—See Suntory Ltd.; *Int'l*, pg. 1321
SUNGROWTH CO., LTD.—See Suntory Ltd.; *Int'l*, pg. 1321
SUNHILL FOOD OF VERMONT, INC.—See Vestjyske Slagterier; *Int'l*, pg. 1464
SUNICAL LAND & LIVESTOCK DIVISION—See The Hearst Corporation; *U.S. Private*, pg. 518
SUNKIST (EUROPE) S.A.—See Sunkist Growers, Inc.; *U.S. Private*, pg. 1053
SUNKIST (FAR EAST) PROMOTION, LTD.—See Sunkist Growers, Inc.; *U.S. Private*, pg. 1053
SUNKIST GROWERS, INC.; *U.S. Private*, pg. 1052
SUNKIST PACIFIC, LTD.—See Sunkist Growers, Inc.; *U.S. Private*, pg. 1053
SUNKYONG AMERICA, INC.—See Sunkyong Industries Co.; *Int'l*, pg. 1320
SUNKYONG AMERICA, INC.-LOS ANGELES BRANCH—See Sunkyong Industries Co.; *Int'l*, pg. 1320
SUNKYONG INDUSTRIES CO.; *Int'l*, pg. 1320
SUNLAND CO., LTD.—See Mitsui & Co., Ltd.; *Int'l*, pg. 878
A/S SUNLAND-EKER PAPIRFABRIKKER—See Trelleborg AB; *Int'l*, pg. 1420
AB SUNLIGHT—See Unilever Plc; *Int'l*, pg. 1438
SUNLIGHT, AG—See Unilever Plc; *Int'l*, pg. 1438
THE SUNLIGHT SERVICE GROUP LTD.—See The Davis Service Group Plc.; *Int'l*, pg. 385
SUNLINE COACH CO., INC.; *U.S. Private*, pg. 1053
SUNLINK CORPORATION—See BellSouth Corporation; *U.S. Public*, pg. 208
SUNLITE FURNITURE—See U.S. Industries, Inc.; *U.S. Public*, pg. 1684
SUNMAC HAWAII, LTD.—See Sunkist Growers, Inc.; *U.S. Private*, pg. 1053
SUNMARK INC.—See Nestle S.A.; *Int'l*, pg. 917
SUNMED FINANCE INC.—See Sunrise Medical, Inc.; *U.S. Public*, pg. 1536
SUNNE CONTROLS DIV.—See Peco Mfg. Co., Inc.; *U.S. Private*, pg. 846
SUNNEN PRODUCTS COMPANY; *U.S. Private*, pg. 1053
SUNNILAND CORPORATION; *U.S. Private*, pg. 1053
SUNNY FRESH FOODS—See Cargill; *U.S. Private*, pg. 210
SUNNYDALE FARMS; *U.S. Private*, pg. 1053
SUNNYLAND INC.—See Smithfield Foods, Inc.; *U.S. Public*, *pg. 1479*
SUNNYLAND REFINING CO., INC.—See Kane-Miller Corp.; *U.S. Private*, pg. 607
SUNNYSIDE GOLD CORPORATION—See Echo Bay Mines Ltd.; *U.S. Public*, pg. 562
SUNOCO GROUP—See Suncor Inc.; *Int'l*, pg. 1320
SUNOCO SARNIA REFINERY—See Suncor Inc.; *Int'l*, pg. 1320
SUNPRENE CO.—See A. Schulman, Inc.; *U.S. Public*, pg. 1441
SUNPURE LTD.; *U.S. Private*, pg. 1053
SUNRACK OYODO CO., LTD.—See Nissho Iwai Corporation; *Int'l*, pg. 947
SUNRIDGE HOTEL & CONFERENCE CENTER—See Lombardi Holdings Inc.; *U.S. Private*, pg. 673
SUNRISE CARPET IND. INC.—See World Carpets, Inc.; *U.S. Private*, pg. 1190
SUNRISE DAIRY—See Hy-Vee Food Stores Incorporated; *U.S. Private*, pg. 551
SUNRISE DEVELOPMENT CO.—See Forest City Enterprises, Inc.; *U.S. Public*, pg. 669
SUNRISE ENERGY SERVICES, INC.; *U.S. Private*, pg. 1053
SUNRISE HEALTHCARE CORPORATION—See Sun Healthcare Group Inc.; *U.S. Public*, pg. 1531
SUNRISE INDUSTRIAL AUTOMATION & DESIGN—See IBT, Inc.; *U.S. Private*, pg. 553
SUNRISE LAND CO.—See Forest City Enterprises, Inc.; *U.S. Public*, pg. 670
SUNRISE LEASING CORPORATION; *U.S. Public*, pg. 1535
SUNRISE LEASING CORPORATION—See Sunrise Leasing Corporation; *U.S. Public*, pg. 1535
SUNRISE MARKETING COMMUNICATIONS LTD.—See DMB&B Communications; *U.S. Private*, pg. 305
SUNRISE MEDICAL—See Sunrise Medical, Inc.; *U.S. Public*, pg. 1536
SUNRISE MEDICAL AG—See Sunrise Medical, Inc.; *U.S. Public*, pg. 1536
SUNRISE MEDICAL B.V.—See Sunrise Medical, Inc.; *U.S. Public*, pg. 1536
SUNRISE MEDICAL CANADA INC.—See Sunrise Medical, Inc.; *U.S. Public*, pg. 1536
SUNRISE MEDICAL (FRANCE)—See Sunrise Medical, Inc.; *U.S. Public*, pg. 1536
SUNRISE MEDICAL, INC.; *U.S. Public*, pg. 1535
SUNRISE MEDICAL, INC.—See Sunrise Medical, Inc.; *U.S. Public*, pg. 1536
SUNRISE MEDICAL MOBILITY PRODUCTS—See Sunrise Medical, Inc.; *U.S. Public*, pg. 1536
SUNRISE MEDICAL PTY. LTD.—See Sunrise Medical, Inc.; *U.S. Public*, pg. 1536
SUNRISE MEDICAL RESPIRATORY PRODUCTS DIVISION—See Sunrise Medical, Inc.; *U.S. Public*, pg. 1536
SUNRISE MEDICAL S.R.L.—See Sunrise Medical, Inc.; *U.S. Public*, pg. 1536
SUNRISE MOBILITY PRODUCTS DIVISION—See Sunrise Medical, Inc.; *U.S. Public*, pg. 1536
SUNRISE NISSAN OF ORANGE PARK; *U.S. Private*, pg. 1053
SUNRISE PROPERTIES—See The Penn Traffic Company; *U.S. Public*, pg. 1271
SUNRISE RESTAURANT INC.—See Brierley Investments Limited; *Int'l*, pg. 216
SUNROC CORPORATION; *U.S. Private*, pg. 1053
SUNSET LIFE INSURANCE CO. OF AMERICA—See Kansas City Life Insurance Co.; *U.S. Public*, pg. 943
SUNSET P&A SERVICES, INC.—See Nabors Industries, Inc.; *U.S. Public*, pg. 1149
SUNSET PUBLISHING CORPORATION—See Time Warner Inc.; *U.S. Public*, pg. 1613
SUNSET RAILWAY CO.—See Union Pacific Corporation; *U.S. Public*, pg. 1668
SUNSET VILLA NURSING HOME—See Horizon/CMS Healthcare Corporation; *U.S. Public*, pg. 838
SUNSHINE ARGENTINA, INC.—See Sunshine Mining And Refining Company; *U.S. Public*, pg. 1536
SUNSHINE BISCUITS, INC.—See GF Industries, Inc.; *U.S. Private*, pg. 434
SUNSHINE BISCUITS, INC.—See Flowers Industries, Inc.; *U.S. Public*, pg. 657
SUNSHINE HAVEN—See Horizon/CMS Healthcare Corporation; *U.S. Public*, pg. 838
SUNSHINE HOME HEALTH CARE, INC.—See Integrated Health Services, Inc.; *U.S. Public*, pg. 885
SUNSHINE MINING AND REFINING COMPANY; *U.S. Public*, pg. 1536
SUNSHINE PRECIOUS METALS, INC.—See Sunshine Mining And Refining Company; *U.S. Public*, pg. 1536
SUNSHINE WSMP, INC. (FLORIDA)—See WSMP, Inc.; *U.S. Public*, pg. 1729
SUNSITES LIMITED—See Eurocamp Plc; *Int'l*, pg. 465
SUNSOFT—See Sun Microsystems, Inc.; *U.S. Public*, pg. 1531
SUNSOFT CORPORATION—See Essilor International Compagnie Generale d'Optique; *Int'l*, pg. 462
SUNSTAR INC.; *Int'l*, pg. 1320
SUNSTATES CORPORATION; *U.S. Public*, pg. 1536
SUNSTATES REALTY GROUP INC.—See Sunstates Corporation; *U.S. Public*, pg. 1536
SUNSTONE HOTEL INVESTORS, INC.; *U.S. Public*, pg. 1536
SUNSTRAND FLUID HANDLING—See Sundstrand Corporation; *U.S. Public*, pg. 1534
SUNTEC INDUSTRIES INC.; *U.S. Private*, pg. 1054
SUNTEL CORP.—See Logica Plc; *Int'l*, pg. 814
SUNTERRA GAS PROCESSING COMPANY—See Public Service Company of New Mexico; *U.S. Public*, pg. 1340
SUNTESTER (AUSTRALIA) PTY. LTD.—See Snap-On Tools Corporation; *U.S. Public*, pg. 1481
SUNTORY ADMINISTRACAO E DESENVOLVIMENTO LTDA.—See Suntory Ltd.; *Int'l*, pg. 1322
SUNTORY ALLIED LIMITED—See Allied Domecq PLC; *Int'l*, pg. 63
SUNTORY ALLIED, LTD.—See Suntory Ltd.; *Int'l*, pg. 1321
SUNTORY ALLIED LIMITED—See Suntory Ltd.; *Int'l*, pg. 1321
SUNTORY (AUST.) PTY. LTD.—See Suntory Ltd.; *Int'l*, pg. 1322
SUNTORY FOOD MANUFACTURING CO., LTD.—See Suntory Ltd.; *Int'l*, pg. 1321
SUNTORY FOODS, LTD.—See Suntory Ltd.; *Int'l*, pg. 1321
SUNTORY INTERNATIONAL CORP.—See Suntory Ltd.; *Int'l*, pg. 1321
SUNTORY KOSAN CO., LTD.—See Suntory Ltd.; *Int'l*, pg. 1321
SUNTORY LTD.; *Int'l*, pg. 1321
SUNTORY MEXICANA, S.A. DE C.V.—See Suntory Ltd.; *Int'l*, pg. 1322
SUNTORY PUBLICITY SERVICE CO., LTD.—See Suntory Ltd.; *Int'l*, pg. 1321
SUNTORY SERVICE LTD.—See Suntory Ltd.; *Int'l*, pg. 1321
SUNTORY SHOPPING CLUB, LTD.—See Suntory Ltd.; *Int'l*, pg. 1321
SUNTORY SPORTS SYSTEM, LTD.—See Suntory Ltd.; *Int'l*, pg. 1321
SUNTORY U.K. LTD.—See Suntory Ltd.; *Int'l*, pg. 1322
SUNTORY WATER GROUP, INC.—See Suntory Ltd.; *Int'l*, pg. 1321
SUNTRUST—See SunTrust Banks, Inc.; *U.S. Public*, pg. 1537
SUNTRUST BANK, ALABAMA, N.A.—See SunTrust Banks, Inc.; *U.S. Public*, pg. 1538
SUNTRUST BANK, ATLANTA—See SunTrust Banks, Inc.; *U.S. Public*, pg. 1538
SUNTRUST BANKS, INC.; *U.S. Public*, pg. 1537
SUNTRUST BANKS OF GEORGIA, INC.—See SunTrust Banks, Inc.; *U.S. Public*, pg. 1538
SUNTRUST BANKS OF TENNESSEE, INC.—See SunTrust Banks, Inc.; *U.S. Public*, pg. 1538
SUNTRUST INSURANCE COMPANY—See SunTrust Banks, Inc.; *U.S. Public*, pg. 1538
SUNTRUST MORTGAGE INC.—See SunTrust Banks, Inc.; *U.S. Public*, pg. 1538
SUNTRUST SECURITIES, INC.—See SunTrust Banks, Inc.; *U.S. Public*, pg. 1538
SUNTRUST SERVICE CORPORATION—See SunTrust Banks, Inc.; *U.S. Public*, pg. 1538
SUNWEST BANK—See West Coast Bancorp; *U.S. Public*, pg. 1755
SUNWEST BANK OF SANTA FE—See NationsBank Corporation; *U.S. Public*, pg. 1165
SUNWEST LEASING CORP. (SLC)—See West Coast Bancorp; *U.S. Public*, pg. 1755
OY SUOMEN ALLIED COLLOIDS—See Allied Colloids Group Plc.; *Int'l*, pg. 62
SUOMEN ASTRA OY—See Astra AB; *Int'l*, pg. 94
OY SUOMEN BOFORS AB—See Celsius AB; *Int'l*, pg. 278
OY SUOMEN HENKEL AB—See Henkel KGaA; *Int'l*, pg. 614
SUOMEN MSD OY—See Merck & Co., Inc.; *U.S. Public*, pg. 1092
SUOMEN NESTLE OY—See Nestle S.A.; *Int'l*, pg. 922
OY SUOMEN PLASMASCHINEN AB—See MAN Aktiengesellschaft; *Int'l*, pg. 825
SUOMEN REHU OY—See Cultor Ltd.; *Int'l*, pg. 349
SUOMEN SANDVIK OY—See Sandvik AB; *Int'l*, pg. 1187
SUOMEN 3M OY—See 3M; *U.S. Public*, pg. 1606
SUOMEN UNIPOL OY—See Oy Algol AB; *Int'l*, pg. 15
SUOMEN VESIMITTARIT OY—See Oy Algol AB; *Int'l*, pg. 15
SUPACRYL (PTY.) LTD.—See Veba AG; *Int'l*, pg. 1456
SUPAFLO TECHNOLOGIES PTY., LTD.—See Outokumpu Oyj; *Int'l*, pg. 1017
SUPER CENTER WAREHOUSE CLUB, INC.—See Wal-Mart Stores, Inc.; *U.S. Public*, pg. 1733
SUPER CHANNEL JOINT ENTERPRISE—See Hakuhodo Incorporated; *Int'l*, pg. 588
SUPER CONCRETE CORP.—See Bardon Group PLC; *Int'l*, *pg. 166*
SUPER CYCLE, INC.—See Recomp, Inc.; *U.S. Private*, pg. 914
SUPER D DRUG STORES—See Stephen LaFrance Holdings, Inc.; *U.S. Private*, pg. 642
SUPER D DRUGS ACQUISITION CO.—See Stephen LaFrance Holdings, Inc.; *U.S. Private*, pg. 642

SUPER DINING CORPORATION—See Suntory Ltd.; *Int'l*, pg. 1321
SUPER DISCOUNT MARKETS, INC.—See Etablissements Delhaize Freres Et Cie "Le Lion" S.A.; *Int'l*, pg. 463
SUPER EGO TOOLS S.A./ROTHENBERGER ESPANA—See Rothenberger Group GmbH; *Int'l*, pg. 1129
SUPER 8 MOTELS, INC.—See Cendant Corporation; *U.S. Public*, pg. 322
SUPER FOOD SERVICES, INC.—See Nash Finch Company; *U.S. Public*, pg. 1152
SUPER FRESH COMPANY—See Tengelmann Warenhandelsgesellschaft; *Int'l*, pg. 1375
SUPER G INC.—See Giant Food Inc.; *U.S. Public*, pg. 741
SUPER HOMES LTD.—See John Laing PLC; *Int'l*, pg. 796
SUPER JV S.A.—See Etablissements Delhaize Freres Et Cie "Le Lion" S.A.; *Int'l*, pg. 463
SUPER RTL—See Groupe Bruxelles Lambert S.A.; *Int'l*, pg. 562
SUPER SAGLESS CORP.—See Leggett & Platt, Incorporated; *U.S. Public*, pg. 986
SUPER SERVICES WASTE MANAGEMENT INC.—See Allied Waste Industries; *U.S. Public*, pg. 49
SUPER SKY PRODUCTS, INC.; *U.S. Private*, pg. 1054
SUPERANNUATION—See The Broken Hill Proprietary Company Limited; *Int'l*, pg. 225
SUPERBA, INC.; *U.S. Private*, pg. 1054
SUPERBREAK MINI HOLIDAYS GROUP LTD.—See Eurocamp Plc; *Int'l*, pg. 465
SUPERCUTS, INC.—See Regis Corporation; *U.S. Public*, pg. 1373
SUPERDRUG STORES PLC—See Kingfisher plc; *Int'l*, pg. 734
SUPERENVASES ENVALIC C.A.—See Reynolds Metals Company; *U.S. Public*, pg. 1387
SUPERFORM METALS—See Alcan Aluminium Limited; *Int'l*, pg. 52
SUPERGASBRAS DISTRIBUIDORA DE GAS S.A.—See SHV Holdings N.V.; *Int'l*, pg. 1156
SUPERGRIF SL—See Delta plc; *Int'l*, pg. 391
SUPERIA N.V.—See Proventus AB; *Int'l*, pg. 1072
SUPERIOR AUCTIONEERS & MARKETING, INC.; *U.S. Private*, pg. 1054
SUPERIOR BANK; *U.S. Private*, pg. 1054
SUPERIOR BLENDS, INC.—See Tyson Foods, Inc.; *U.S. Public*, pg. 1652
SUPERIOR BRANDS, INC.—See Nestle S.A.; *Int'l*, pg. 917
SUPERIOR COFFEE AND FOODS—See Sara Lee Corporation; *U.S. Public*, pg. 1434
SUPERIOR COFFEE & FOODS/HAWAII—See Buyco, Inc.; *U.S. Private*, pg. 191
SUPERIOR CONSULTANT COMPANY, INC.—See Superior Consultant Holdings Corp.; *U.S. Public*, pg. 1539
SUPERIOR CONSULTANT HOLDINGS CORP.; *U.S. Public*, pg. 1538
SUPERIOR DAIRIES, INC.—See Borden, Inc.; *U.S. Private*, pg. 158
SUPERIOR DAIRY, INC.; *U.S. Private*, pg. 1054
SUPERIOR DIE TOOL AND MACHINE COMPANY; *U.S. Private*, pg. 1054
SUPERIOR DRAPERY COMPANY; *U.S. Private*, pg. 1054
SUPERIOR EMERGENCY VEHICLES, LTD.—See Federal Signal Corporation; *U.S. Public*, pg. 617
SUPERIOR FEDERAL BANK; *U.S. Private*, pg. 1054
SUPERIOR GRAPHITE CO.; *U.S. Private*, pg. 1055
SUPERIOR GRAPHITE EUROPE, LTD.—See Superior Graphite Co.; *U.S. Private*, pg. 1055
SUPERIOR GRAPHITE LTD.—See Superior Graphite Co.; *U.S. Public*, pg. 1055
SUPERIOR GROUP, INC.; *U.S. Private*, pg. 1055
SUPERIOR INDUSTRIES INTERNATIONAL, INC.; *U.S. Public*, pg. 1539
SUPERIOR INDUSTRIES OF NEBRASKA, INC.; *U.S. Private*, pg. 1055
SUPERIOR LABEL SYSTEMS, INC.; *U.S. Private*, pg. 1055
SUPERIOR LIFE INSURANCE COMPANY—See NationsBank Corporation; *U.S. Public*, pg. 1165
SUPERIOR LINKAGE DIVISION—See Tuthill Corporation; *U.S. Private*, pg. 1111
SUPERIOR MACHINE COMPANY OF SOUTH CAROLINA, INC.; *U.S. Private*, pg. 1055
SUPERIOR MACHINE SYSTEMS—See Superior Label Systems, Inc.; *U.S. Private*, pg. 1055
SUPERIOR METAL PRINTING (HUIYANG) CO. LTD.—See Superior Metal Printing Limited; *Int'l*, pg. 1322
SUPERIOR METAL PRINTING LIMITED; *Int'l*, pg. 1322
SUPERIOR METAL PRINTING PHILIPPINES, INC.—See Superior Metal Printing Limited; *Int'l*, pg. 1322
SUPERIOR OIL CO. INC.; *U.S. Private*, pg. 1055
SUPERIOR PAPER PRODUCTS, INC.—See Ikon Office Solutions, Inc.; *U.S. Public*, pg. 864
SUPERIOR POOL PRODUCTS, INC.—See Olin Corporation; *U.S. Public*, pg. 1219
SUPERIOR PRINTING CO.; *U.S. Private*, pg. 1055
SUPERIOR REPROGRAPHICS—See Ford Graphics; *U.S. Private*, pg. 418
SUPERIOR STEEL ACQUISITION CORPORATION—See Anchor Lamina Inc.; *Int'l*, pg. 75
SUPERIOR SURGICAL MFG. CO., INC.; *U.S. Public*, pg. 1539
SUPERIOR TELECOMMUNICATIONS—See The Alpine Group, Inc.; *U.S. Public*, pg. 58
SUPERIOR THERMAL, INC.—See Eclipse Inc.; *U.S. Private*, pg. 360
SUPERIOR TUBE COMPANY; *U.S. Private*, pg. 1056
SUPERIOR VALVE COMPANY—See Amcast Industrial Corporation; *U.S. Public*, pg. 63
SUPERIOR WATER, LIGHT & POWER COMPANY—See Minnesota Power; *U.S. Public*, pg. 1116
SUPERIOR WHOLESALE DRUG CO.—See Bindley Western Industries, Inc.; *U.S. Public*, pg. 229
SUPERIOR'S BRAND MEATS—See Fresh Mark, Inc.; *U.S. Private*, pg. 427
SUPERMAR URUGUAY LIMITADA—See SGS Societe Generale de Surveillance Holding S.A.; *Int'l*, pg. 1154

SUPERMARKET CIGARETTE SALES, INC.—See Jitney-Jungle Stores of America, Inc.; *U.S. Private*, pg. 588
SUPERMARKET INSURANCE AGENCY, INC.—See Associated Wholesale Grocers, Inc.; *U.S. Private*, pg. 93
SUPERMARKET NEWS—See The Walt Disney Company; *U.S. Public*, pg. 513
SUPERMERCADOS MAYORISTAS MAKRA S.A.—See SHV Holdings N.V.; *Int'l*, pg. 1156
SUPERNAIL—See American International Industries; *U.S. Private*, pg. 57
SUPERPETZ—See Weis Markets, Inc.; *U.S. Public*, pg. 1752
SUPERPILA INDUSTRIALE S.P.A.—See Philip Morris Companies Inc.; *U.S. Public*, pg. 1290
SUPERPILA S.P.A.—See Philip Morris Companies Inc.; *U.S. Public*, pg. 1290
SUPERSHUTTLE INC.; *U.S. Private*, pg. 1056
SUPERSTATION INC.—See Time Warner Inc.; *U.S. Public*, pg. 1615
SUPERTEX, INC.; *U.S. Public*, pg. 1539
SUPERTRANSPORT—See GIB Group; *Int'l*, pg. 533
SUPERTRAPP INDUSTRIES—See Dreison International, Inc.; *U.S. Private*, pg. 342
SUPERVALU, INC.; *U.S. Public*, pg. 1540
SUPERVALU, INC.-MAINE DIV.—See SuperValu, Inc.; *U.S. Public*, pg. 1540
SUPERVALU, INC.-NORTHEASTERN REG.—See SuperValu, Inc.; *U.S. Public*, pg. 1540
SUPERVALU, INC.-ST. LOUIS DIV.—See SuperValu, Inc.; *U.S. Public*, pg. 1541
SUPERVALU, INC.-SCOTT CITY DIV.—See SuperValu, Inc.; *U.S. Public*, pg. 1541
SUPERVALU, INC.-SPOKANE DIV.—See SuperValu, Inc.; *U.S. Public*, pg. 1541
SUPERVALU, INC.-TACOMA DIV.—See SuperValu, Inc.; *U.S. Public*, pg. 1541
SUPERVALU INTERNATIONAL—See SuperValu, Inc.; *U.S. Public*, pg. 1541
SUPERVISORA DE INSTALACIONES TECNICAS SRL—See Mannesmann A.G.; *Int'l*, pg. 837
SUPERVISORY & INDUSTRIAL PROCESS CONTROL LIMITED—See N.G. Bailey & Co. Ltd.; *Int'l*, pg. 133
SUPERWOOD INC.—See Georgia-Pacific Corporation; *U.S. Public*, pg. 736
SUPPLEMENTAL INSURANCE DIVISION, INC.—See AEGON N.V.; *Int'l*, pg. 27
SUPPLY POINT, INC.—See EA Industries; *U.S. Public*, pg. 541
SUPPORT PRODUTOS NUTRICIONAIS LTDA.—See Nutricia BV; *Int'l*, pg. 992
SUPPORT SYSTEMS ASSOCIATES, INC.; *U.S. Private*, pg. 1056
SUPPORT TERMINAL SERVICES, INC.—See Kaneb Services, Inc.; *U.S. Public*, pg. 942
SUPRADIAMANT S.A.—See Smith International, Inc.; *U.S. Public*, pg. 1478
SUPRADIAMANT S.P.A.—See Smith International, Inc.; *U.S. Public*, pg. 1479
SUPRATECH SYSTEMS INC.—See Nippon Paint Company Ltd.; *Int'l*, pg. 937
SUPREMA SPECIALTIES, INC.; *U.S. Public*, pg. 1541
SUPREMA SPECIALTIES NORTHEAST, INC.—See Suprema Specialties, Inc.; *U.S. Public*, pg. 1541
SUPREME BEAUTY PRODUCTS—See Johnson Publishing Company, Inc.; *U.S. Private*, pg. 592
SUPREME CORPORATION—See Supreme Industries, Inc.; *U.S. Public*, pg. 1542
SUPREME ELECTRONICS CORP.—See Hickok Incorporated; *U.S. Public*, pg. 825
SUPREME ESTEEM LTD.—See CSA Holdings Ltd.; *Int'l*, pg. 243
SUPREME INDUSTRIES, INC.; *U.S. Public*, pg. 1541
SUPREME INTERNATIONAL CORP.; *U.S. Public*, pg. 1542
SUPREME LUMBER & MILLWORK CO.—See Lennar Corporation; *U.S. Public*, pg. 989
SUPREME MIDATLANTIC CORPORATION—See Supreme Industries, Inc.; *U.S. Public*, pg. 1542
SUPREME/MIRRO—See Newell Co.; *U.S. Public*, pg. 1178
SUPREME MURPHY CORP.—See Supreme Industries, Inc.; *U.S. Public*, pg. 1542
SUPREME SALT COMPANY LIMITED—See Tomkins PLC; *Int'l*, pg. 1396
SUPREME TRUCK BODIES OF CALIFORNIA, INC.—See Supreme Industries, Inc.; *U.S. Public*, pg. 1542
SUR ASISTENCIA—See Corporacion MAPFRE, Compania Internacional de Reaseguros, S.A.; *Int'l*, pg. 334
SURAMIC SUCOS REFRIGERANTES AGUAS MINERAIS INDUSTRIA E COMERCIO S.A.—See Nestle S.A.; *Int'l*, pg. 922
SURASSUR, S.A.—See Corporacion MAPFRE, Compania Internacional de Reaseguros, S.A.; *Int'l*, pg. 333
SURCO PRODUCTS, INC.; *U.S. Private*, pg. 1056
SURE SAVE SUPER MARKET LTD.; *U.S. Private*, pg. 1056
SURECO INC.—See Ringer Corporation; *U.S. Public*, pg. 1390
SURFACE FREIGHT CORP.—See Air Express International Corporation; *U.S. Public*, pg. 30
SURFACE SCIENCE INSTRUMENTS—See Rhone-Poulenc S.A.; *Int'l*, pg. 1111
SURFACE SCIENCE LABORATORIES—See Rhone-Poulenc S.A.; *Int'l*, pg. 1111
SURFACE TECHNOLOGIES, INC.—See Dainippon Ink & Chemicals, Inc.; *Int'l*, pg. 370
SURFACE TECHNOLOGY BUSINESS—See Engelhard Corporation; *U.S. Public*, pg. 582
SURFACE TREATMENT COMPANY N.V.—See Royal Begemann Group; *Int'l*, pg. 1134
SURFER PUBLICATIONS, INC.—See For Better Living, Inc.; *U.S. Private*, pg. 417
SURFNET BV—See KPN Koninklyke PTT Nederland NV; *Int'l*, pg. 720

SURFSIDE TOWERS II, INC.—See Forest City Enterprises, Inc.; *U.S. Public*, pg. 669
SURFSIDE VERMONT REAL ESTATE CORPORATION—See Bayerische Vereinsbank Group; *Int'l*, pg. 180
SURGECENTER OF PALO ALTO—See Vencor, Inc.; *U.S. Public*, pg. 1716
SURGICAL APPLIANCE INDUSTRIES, INC.; *U.S. Private*, pg. 1056
SURGICAL DIV.—See Gudebrod, Inc.; *U.S. Private*, pg. 486
SURGICAL INFORMATION SYSTEMS—See Allegiant Physician Services; *U.S. Private*, pg. 45
SURGICAL LASER TECHNOLOGIES, INC.; *U.S. Public*, pg. 1542
SURGICAL SPECIALTIES; *U.S. Private*, pg. 1056
SURGITEK—See Bristol-Myers Squibb Company; *U.S. Public*, pg. 253
SURIA K, S.A.—See SEPI; *Int'l*, pg. 1225
SURINAME ALUMINUM COMPANY—See Aluminum Company of America; *U.S. Public*, pg. 61
SURLEAN MEAT CO.—See Leonard & Harral Packing Co.; *U.S. Private*, pg. 660
SURPLUS WAREHOUSE-ALEXANDRIA—See E.C. Barton & Company; *U.S. Private*, pg. 119
SURPLUS WAREHOUSE-GREENVILLE—See E.C. Barton & Company; *U.S. Private*, pg. 119
SURPLUS WAREHOUSE-JACKSON—See E.C. Barton & Company; *U.S. Private*, pg. 119
SURPLUS WAREHOUSE-JONESBORO—See E.C. Barton & Company; *U.S. Private*, pg. 120
SURPLUS WAREHOUSE-LONGVIEW—See E.C. Barton & Company; *U.S. Private*, pg. 120
SURPLUS WAREHOUSE-MONROE—See E.C. Barton & Company; *U.S. Private*, pg. 120
SURPLUS WAREHOUSE-NACOGDOCHES—See E.C. Barton & Company; *U.S. Private*, pg. 120
SURPLUS WAREHOUSE-PARIS—See E.C. Barton & Company; *U.S. Private*, pg. 120
SURPLUS WAREHOUSE-SEAGOVILLE—See E.C. Barton & Company; *U.S. Private*, pg. 120
SURPLUS WAREHOUSE-TEMPLE—See E.C. Barton & Company; *U.S. Private*, pg. 120
SURPLUS WAREHOUSE-TYLER—See E.C. Barton & Company; *U.S. Private*, pg. 120
SURPLUS WAREHOUSE-WEST MEMPHIS—See E.C. Barton & Company; *U.S. Private*, pg. 120
SURPLUS WAREHOUSE-LAKE CHARLES—See E.C. Barton & Company; *U.S. Private*, pg. 119
SURVEILLANCE SYSTEMS DIV.—See Lockheed Martin Corporation; *U.S. Public*, pg. 1008
SURVEY RESEARCH ASSOCIATES—See Battelle Memorial Institute; *U.S. Private*, pg. 123
SURVEY SAMPLING, INC.; *U.S. Private*, pg. 1056
P.T. SURYA TOTO INDONESIA—See Toto Ltd.; *Int'l*, pg. 1410
SUSIE'S DEALS; *U.S. Private*, pg. 1056
SUSPA COMPART AG; *Int'l*, pg. 1322
SUSPA FRANCE SARL—See Suspa Compart AG; *Int'l*, pg. 1322
SUSPA, INC.—See Suspa Compart AG; *Int'l*, pg. 1322
SUSQUE-BANCSHARES LEASING CO., INC.—See Susquehanna Bancshares, Inc.; *U.S. Public*, pg. 1542
SUSQUE-BANCSHARES LIFE INSURANCE COMPANY—See Susquehanna Bancshares, Inc.; *U.S. Public*, pg. 1542
SUSQUEHANNA BANCSHARES, INC.; *U.S. Public*, pg. 1542
SUSQUEHANNA BANCSHARES SOUTH, INC.—See Susquehanna Bancshares, Inc.; *U.S. Public*, pg. 1543
SUSQUEHANNA DIVISION—See Consumers Water Company; *U.S. Public*, pg. 439
SUSQUEHANNA ELECTRIC CO.—See PECO Energy Company; *U.S. Public*, pg. 1268
SUSQUEHANNA POWER CO.—See PECO Energy Company; *U.S. Public*, pg. 1268
SUSQUEHANNA RADIO CORP.—See The Pfaltzgraff Co.; *U.S. Private*, pg. 860
SUSSEX CLINICAL RESEARCH CONSULTANTS LTD.—See Novartis AG; *Int'l*, pg. 986
SUSSEX GROUP, LTD.—See JG Industries, Inc.; *U.S. Public*, pg. 918
SUSSEX PUBLISHERS, INC.; *U.S. Private*, pg. 1056
SUSY CARD GMBH & CO. KG—See Herlitz PBS Aktiengesellschaft; *Int'l*, pg. 616
SUTCLIFFE CATERING GROUP LTD.—See The Peninsular and Oriental Steam Navigation Company; *Int'l*, pg. 1035
SUTER EQUIPMENT LIMITED—See Ascot Holdings Plc; *Int'l*, pg. 88
SUTHERLAND LUMBER CO.; *U.S. Private*, pg. 1057
A. SUTTER AG—See Unilever Plc; *Int'l*, pg. 1438
SUTTER AUBURN FAITH COMMUNITY HOSPITAL—See Sutter Health; *U.S. Private*, pg. 1057
SUTTER HEALTH; *U.S. Private*, pg. 1057
SUTTER HOME WINERY, INC.; *U.S. Private*, pg. 1057
SUTTLE APPARATUS CORPORATION—See Communications Systems, Inc.; *U.S. Public*, pg. 416
SUTTLE CARIBE, INC.—See Communications Systems, Inc.; *U.S. Public*, pg. 415
SUTTLE COSTA RICA S.A.—See Communications Systems, Inc.; *U.S. Public*, pg. 416
SUTTLE PRESS, INC—See Telephone and Data Systems, Inc.; *U.S. Public*, pg. 1570
SUTTON BRIDGE WHARFAGE CO. LTD.—See Simon Engineering plc; *Int'l*, pg. 1251
SUVALAN-CIA. DE PRODUTOS DE FRUTAS—See B.A.T Industries P.L.C.; *Int'l*, pg. 112
SUZHOU ESCA STEP CO. LTD.—See Schindler Holding AG; *Int'l*, pg. 1205
SUZHOU HONGDA ENZYME CO. LTD.—See Novo Nordisk A/S; *Int'l*, pg. 989
SUZHOU LANLIAN-FUJI INSTRUMENTS CO., LTD.—See Fuji Electric Co., Ltd.; *Int'l*, pg. 522
SUZHOU LITTELFUSE OVS CO. LTD.—See Littelfuse, Inc.; *U.S. Public*, pg. 1001

SUZHOU SCHINDLER ELEVATOR CO.—See Schindler
Holding AG; *Int'l*, pg. 1205
SUZHOU WATTS VALVE FACTORY—See Watts
Industries, Inc.; *U.S. Public*, pg. 1747
SUZORITE MICA PRODUCTS INC.—See Zemex
Corporation; *Int'l*, pg. 1523
SUZORITE MINERAL PRODUCTS, INC.—See Zemex
Corporation; *Int'l*, pg. 1524
SUZUKA CIRCUITLAND CO., LTD.—See Honda Motor Co.,
Ltd.; *Int'l*, pg. 634
SUZUKI AUSTRIA AUTOMOBIL HANDELS G.M.B.H.—See
Suzuki Motor Corporation; *Int'l*, pg. 1323
SUZUKI MOTOR CORPORATION; *Int'l*, pg. 1322
SUZUKI MOTORCYCLES PAKISTAN LTD.—See Suzuki
Motor Corporation; *Int'l*, pg. 1323
SVANEHOJ INTERNATIONAL A/S—See Powell Duffryn
PLC; *Int'l*, pg. 1065
SVEDALA ARBRA—See Svedala Industri AB; *Int'l*,
pg. 1324
SVEDALA A/S—See Svedala Industri AB; *Int'l*, pg.
1324
SVEDALA A/S BODO—See Svedala Industri AB; *Int'l*,
pg. 1324
SVEDALA A/S BRATTHOLMEN—See Svedala Industri AB;
Int'l, pg. 1324
SVEDALA A/S FLATASEN—See Svedala Industri AB; *Int'l*,
pg. 1324
SVEDALA A/S PLANT—See Svedala Industri AB; *Int'l*,
pg. 1324
SVEDALA AUSTRALIA—See Svedala Industri AB; *Int'l*,
pg. 1324
SVEDALA AUSTRALIA (CARRINGTON)—See Svedala
Industri AB; *Int'l*, pg. 1324
SVEDALA AUSTRALIA (GARDENVALE)—See Svedala
Industri AB; *Int'l*, pg. 1324
SVEDALA AUSTRALIA (KALGOORLIE)—See Svedala
Industri AB; *Int'l*, pg. 1324
SVEDALA AUSTRALIA (SILVERWATER)—See Svedala
Industri AB; *Int'l*, pg. 1324
SVEDALA AUSTRALIA (WELSHPOOL)—See Svedala
Industri AB; *Int'l*, pg. 1324
SVEDALA AUSTRIA—See Svedala Industri AB; *Int'l*,
pg. 1324
SVEDALA CHILE—See Svedala Industri AB; *Int'l*, pg. 1324
SVEDALA CHINA—See Svedala Industri AB; *Int'l*, pg. 1323
SVEDALA COMPACTION & PAVING—See Svedala Industri
AB; *Int'l*, pg. 1324
SVEDALA CONVEYOR BELTING—See Svedala Industri
AB; *Int'l*, pg. 1324
SVEDALA CRANES—See Svedala Industri AB; *Int'l*,
pg. 1324
SVEDALA CRUSHING & SCREENING—See Svedala
Industri AB; *Int'l*, pg. 1324
SVEDALA DANMARK—See Svedala Industri AB; *Int'l*,
pg. 1323
SVEDALA DEUTSCHALAND (MUNICH)—See Svedala
Industri AB; *Int'l*, pg. 1324
SVEDALA DEUTSCHLAND—See Svedala Industri AB; *Int'l*,
pg. 1324
SVEDALA DEUTSCHLAND (HAMBURG)—See Svedala
Industri AB; *Int'l*, pg. 1324
SVEDALA-DYNAPAC—See Svedala Industri AB; *Int'l*,
pg. 1324
SVEDALA DYNAPAC HEAVY—See Svedala Industri AB;
Int'l, pg. 1324
SVEDALA DYNAPAC LIGHT—See Svedala Industri AB;
Int'l, pg. 1324
SVEDALA ESTONIA—See Svedala Industri AB; *Int'l*,
pg. 1324
SVEDALA-FACO—See Svedala Industri AB; *Int'l*, pg. 1324
SVEDALA-FACO BELO HORIZONTE—See Svedala Industri
AB; *Int'l*, pg. 1324
SVEDALA-FACO RIO DE JANEIRO—See Svedala Industri
AB; *Int'l*, pg. 1324
SVEDALA-FACO SOROCABA—See Svedala Industri AB;
Int'l, pg. 1324
SVEDALA-FACO TABOAO DA SERRA—See Svedala
Industri AB; *Int'l*, pg. 1324
SVEDALA FIMA—See Svedala Industri AB; *Int'l*, pg. 1324
SVEDALA FLEXOWELL FOERDERSYSTEME—See
Svedala Industri AB; *Int'l*, pg. 1324
SVEDALA FOUNDRIES—See Svedala Industri AB; *Int'l*,
pg. 1324
SVEDALA FRANCE—See Svedala Industri AB; *Int'l*,
pg. 1324
SVEDALA FRANCE VITROLLES—See Svedala Industri AB;
Int'l, pg. 1323
SVEDALA FRANCE WITTENHEIM—See Svedala Industri
AB; *Int'l*, pg. 1323
SVEDALA GHANA—See Svedala Industri AB; *Int'l*,
pg. 1324
SVEDALA HONG KONG—See Svedala Industri AB; *Int'l*,
pg. 1324
SVEDALA INDIA—See Svedala Industri AB; *Int'l*, pg. 1324
SVEDALA INDIA (BANGALORE)—See Svedala Industri AB;
Int'l, pg. 1324
SVEDALA INDIA (CALCUTTA)—See Svedala Industri AB;
Int'l, pg. 1324
SVEDALA INDIA (GOA)—See Svedala Industri AB; *Int'l*,
pg. 1324
SVEDALA INDIA (MANGALORE)—See Svedala Industri
AB; *Int'l*, pg. 1324
SVEDALA INDIA (VISAKHAPATNAM)—See Svedala
Industri AB; *Int'l*, pg. 1324
SVEDALA INDUSTRI AB; *Int'l*, pg. 1323
SVEDALA INDUSTRIES CANADA—See Svedala Industri
AB; *Int'l*, pg. 1324
SVEDALA INDUSTRIES CANADA BRITISH COLUMBIA—
See Svedala Industri AB; *Int'l*, pg. 1325
SVEDALA INDUSTRIES CANADA EDMONTON—See
Svedala Industri AB; *Int'l*, pg. 1325
SVEDALA INDUSTRIES CANADA HORNBY—See Svedala
Industri AB; *Int'l*, pg. 1325
SVEDALA INDUSTRIES CANADA MISSISSAUGA—See
Svedala Industri AB; *Int'l*, pg. 1325

SVEDALA INDUSTRIES CANADA NEWFOUNDLAND—See
Svedala Industri AB; *Int'l*, pg. 1325
SVEDALA INDUSTRIES CANADA ONTARIO—See Svedala
Industri AB; *Int'l*, pg. 1325
SVEDALA INDUSTRIES CANADA QUEBEC—See Svedala
Industri AB; *Int'l*, pg. 1325
SVEDALA INDUSTRIES INC.—See Svedala Industri AB;
Int'l, pg. 1325
SVEDALA INDUSTRIES-UNIVERSAL ENGINEERING—See
Svedala Industri AB; *Int'l*, pg. 1326
SVEDALA INTERNATIONAL—See Svedala Industri AB;
Int'l, pg. 1324
SVEDALA KFT—See Svedala Industri AB; *Int'l*, pg. 1325
SVEDALA LTD.—See Svedala Industri AB; *Int'l*, pg. 1325
SVEDALA LTD. DERBY—See Svedala Industri AB; *Int'l*,
pg. 1325
SVEDALA LTD. MAGHERA—See Svedala Industri AB; *Int'l*,
pg. 1325
SVEDALA LTD. MIDDLESEX—See Svedala Industri AB;
Int'l, pg. 1325
SVEDALA LTD. PLANT—See Svedala Industri AB; *Int'l*,
pg. 1325
SVEDALA LTD. SOMERSET—See Svedala Industri AB;
Int'l, pg. 1325
SVEDALA LTD. WARWICKSHIRE—See Svedala Industri
AB; *Int'l*, pg. 1325
SVEDALA LTD. WYTHENSHAWE—See Svedala Industri
AB; *Int'l*, pg. 1325
SVEDALA MALAYSIA—See Svedala Industri AB; *Int'l*,
pg. 1325
SVEDALA MEXICO—See Svedala Industri AB; *Int'l*,
pg. 1325
SVEDALA NETHERLANDS—See Svedala Industri AB; *Int'l*,
pg. 1325
SVEDALA NEW ZEALAND—See Svedala Industri AB; *Int'l*,
pg. 1325
SVEDALA OY—See Svedala Industri AB; *Int'l*, pg. 1325
SVEDALA OY KOTKA—See Svedala Industri AB; *Int'l*,
pg. 1325
SVEDALA OY LAPPEENRANTA—See Svedala Industri AB;
Int'l, pg. 1325
SVEDALA OY OULU—See Svedala Industri AB; *Int'l*,
pg. 1325
SVEDALA OY PIEKSAMAKI—See Svedala Industri AB;
Int'l, pg. 1325
SVEDALA OY PLANT—See Svedala Industri AB; *Int'l*,
pg. 1325
SVEDALA OY TAMMERFORS—See Svedala Industri AB;
Int'l, pg. 1325
SVEDALA POLSKA—See Svedala Industri AB; *Int'l*,
pg. 1325
SVEDALA PUMPS & PROCESS—See Svedala Industri AB;
Int'l, pg. 1325
SVEDALA (PVT.) LTD.—See Svedala Industri AB; *Int'l*,
pg. 1325
SVEDALA ROBOT—See Svedala Industri AB; *Int'l*,
pg. 1325
SVEDALA RUSSIA (MOSCOW)—See Svedala Industri AB;
Int'l, pg. 1325
SVEDALA RUSSIA (ST. PETERSBURG)—See Svedala
Industri AB; *Int'l*, pg. 1325
N.V. SVEDALA S.A.—See Svedala Industri AB; *Int'l*,
pg. 1325
SVEDALA-SCHOLTZ TRANSPORTBANDTECHNIK—See
Svedala Industri AB; *Int'l*, pg. 1326
SVEDALA SKEGA—See Svedala Industri AB; *Int'l*, pg. 1324
SVEDALA SKEGA (JOHANNESBURG)—See Svedala
Industri AB; *Int'l*, pg. 1325
SVEDALA SOUTH AFRICA—See Svedala Industri AB; *Int'l*,
pg. 1325
SVEDALA SPA—See Svedala Industri AB; *Int'l*, pg. 1325
SVEDALA S.R.O.—See Svedala Industri AB; *Int'l*, pg. 1323
SVEDALA STRASSENFERTIGER—See Svedala Industri
AB; *Int'l*, pg. 1326
SVEDALA SUPERSTRUCTURES—See Svedala Industri
AB; *Int'l*, pg. 1325
SVEDALA SWITZERLAND—See Svedala Industri AB; *Int'l*,
pg. 1325
SVEDALA UKRAINE—See Svedala Industri AB; *Int'l*,
pg. 1325
SVEDALA VIETNAM—See Svedala Industri AB; *Int'l*,
pg. 1325
SVEDALA WEAR PROTECTION—See Svedala Industri AB;
Int'l, pg. 1325
SVEND MULLERS EMBALLAGEFABRIK APS—See Royal
Packaging Industries Van Leer B.V.; *Int'l*, pg. 1146
AB SVENSK LECA—See Scancem AB; *Int'l*, pg. 1200
SVENSK TEKNISK BYRA AB—See Axel Johnson AB; *Int'l*,
pg. 709
SVENSKA ALLEN CODING AB—See Smiths Industries plc;
Int'l, pg. 1269
SVENSKA BLOUNT AB—See Blount International, Inc.;
U.S. Public, pg. 239
SVENSKA BOC AB—See The BOC Group plc; *Int'l*,
pg. 122
SVENSKA CELLULOSA AKTIEBOLAGET (SCA); *Int'l*,
pg. 1326
SVENSKA DENTALINSTRUMENT AB—See Axel Johnson
AB; *Int'l*, pg. 709
SVENSKA ELGROSSIST AB SELGA—See
Telefonaktiebolaget LM Ericsson; *Int'l*, pg. 1363
SVENSKA EMISSIONSTEKNIK AB—See Johnson Matthey
Public Limited Company; *Int'l*, pg. 713
SVENSKA FODER AB—See Cultor Ltd.; *Int'l*, pg. 350
SVENSKA HANDELSBANKEN; *Int'l*, pg. 1327
SVENSKA HANDELSBANKEN BEIJING—See Svenska
Handelsbanken; *Int'l*, pg. 1327
SVENSKA HANDELSBANKEN FRANKFURT/MAIN—See
Svenska Handelsbanken; *Int'l*, pg. 1327
SVENSKA HANDELSBANKEN HONG KONG—See
Svenska Handelsbanken; *Int'l*, pg. 1327
SVENSKA HANDELSBANKEN INTERNATIONAL—See
Svenska Handelsbanken; *Int'l*, pg. 1327

SVENSKA HANDELSBANKEN LONDON—See Svenska
Handelsbanken; *Int'l*, pg. 1327
SVENSKA HANDELSBANKEN LUXEMBOURG—See
Svenska Handelsbanken; *Int'l*, pg. 1328
SVENSKA HANDELSBANKEN MANCHESTER—See
Svenska Handelsbanken; *Int'l*, pg. 1327
SVENSKA HANDELSBANKEN MARBELLA—See Svenska
Handelsbanken; *Int'l*, pg. 1327
SVENSKA HANDELSBANKEN MOSCOW—See Svenska
Handelsbanken; *Int'l*, pg. 1327
SVENSKA HANDELSBANKEN, NEW YORK—See Svenska
Handelsbanken; *Int'l*, pg. 1327
SVENSKA HANDELSBANKEN SINGAPORE—See Svenska
Handelsbanken; *Int'l*, pg. 1328
SVENSKA HANDELSBANKEN TAIPEI—See Svenska
Handelsbanken; *Int'l*, pg. 1327
SVENSKA HANDELSBANKEN TALLINN—See Svenska
Handelsbanken; *Int'l*, pg. 1327
SVENSKA HANDELSBANKEN TOKYO—See Svenska
Handelsbanken; *Int'l*, pg. 1327
SVENSKA HANDELSBANKEN ZURICH—See Svenska
Handelsbanken; *Int'l*, pg. 1327
SVENSKA HYLSFABRIKEN AB—See Royal Packaging
Industries Van Leer B.V.; *Int'l*, pg. 1146
SVENSKA JOHNSON'S VAX AB—See S.C. Johnson &
Son, Inc.; *U.S. Private*, pg. 594
SVENSKA KNACKE AB—See Novartis AG; *Int'l*, pg. 986
SVENSKA LE CARBONE A/B—See Pechiney S.A.; *Int'l*,
pg. 1032
SVENSKA NESTLE AB—See Nestle S.A.; *Int'l*, pg. 922
SVENSKA POLYSTYREN FABRIKEN AB—See Veba AG;
Int'l, pg. 1456
AB SVENSKA PRESSBYRAN—See Axel Johnson AB; *Int'l*,
pg. 709
AB SVENSKA SHELL—See Royal Dutch/Shell Group of
Companies; *Int'l*, pg. 1139
SVENSKA SKUM B.V.—See Hanson PLC; *Int'l*, pg. 595
SVENSKA SKUMSLACKNINGS AKTIEBOLAGET—See
Hanson PLC; *Int'l*, pg. 595
SVENSKA TEKNISK BYRA AB—See Axel Johnson AB;
Int'l, pg. 712
SVENSKA THAILAND LTD.—See Sandvik AB; *Int'l*,
pg. 1187
SVENSKA UNILEVER FORVALTNINGS AB—See Unilever
Plc; *Int'l*, pg. 1438
AB SVENSKA UNO-X—See Burmah Castrol plc; *Int'l*,
pg. 236
SVENSKA VOEST-ALPINE AB—See Voest-Alpine Stahl
AG; *Int'l*, pg. 1472
SVENSKT PAPPER AB—See Mo och Domsjo AB; *Int'l*,
pg. 886
SVERDRUP CIVIL, INC.—See Sverdrup Corporation; *U.S.
Private*, pg. 1057
SVERDRUP CORPORATION; *U.S. Private*, pg. 1057
SVERDRUP ENVIRONMENTAL INC.—See Sverdrup
Corporation; *U.S. Private*, pg. 1057
SVERDRUP INVESTMENTS, INC.—See Sverdrup
Corporation; *U.S. Private*, pg. 1057
SVERDRUP TECHNOLOGY, INC.—See Sverdrup
Corporation; *U.S. Private*, pg. 1057
SVETSPRODUKTER AB—See De La Rue plc; *Int'l*, pg. 388
SWADO GRAFIGROEP—See De Bussy Harms N.V.; *Int'l*,
pg. 386
SWAGELOK COMPANY; *U.S. Private*, pg. 1057
SWAIN BUILDING MATERIALS—See MBS Holding, Inc.;
U.S. Private, pg. 686
SWALLOW HOTELS LIMITED—See Vaux Group Plc; *Int'l*,
pg. 1454
SWAN HELLENIC LTD.—See The Peninsular and Oriental
Steam Navigation Company; *Int'l*, pg. 1035
SWAN HILL MILK DISTRIBUTORS PTY. LTD.—See Q.U.F.
Industries Ltd.; *Int'l*, pg. 1074
SWAN TECHNOLOGIES CORPORATION—See Compagnie
des Machines Bull; *Int'l*, pg. 317
SWANDISC AG—See Mannesmann A.G.; *Int'l*, pg. 836
SWANER HARDWOOD COMPANY, INC.; *U.S. Private*,
pg. 1057
SWANK, INC.; *U.S. Public*, pg. 1543
SWANSON—See Campbell Soup Company; *U.S. Public*,
pg. 299
W. SWANSTROM & CO. S.P.R.L.—See Norske
Skogindustrier A/S; *Int'l*, pg. 966
SWARTWOUT INDUSTRIES—See Tomkins PLC; *Int'l*,
pg. 1398
SWATCH S.A.—See SMH Swiss Corporation for Micro
Electronics & Watchmaking Indus. Ltd.; *Int'l*, pg. 1161
SWATCH TELECOM AG—See SMH Swiss Corporation for
Micro Electronics & Watchmaking Indus. Ltd.; *Int'l*,
pg. 1161
SWATCH WATCH U.S.A.—See SMH Swiss Corporation for
Micro Electronics & Watchmaking Indus. Ltd.; *Int'l*,
pg. 1161
SWAZILAND FRUIT CANNERS (PTY.) LTD.—See Nestle
S.A.; *Int'l*, pg. 922
SWECO—See Emerson Electric Co.; *U.S. Public*, pg. 574
SWECO EUROPE S.A.—See Emerson Electric Co.; *U.S.
Public*, pg. 578
SWEDBANK; *Int'l*, pg. 1328
SWEDBANK LONDON—See Swedbank; *Int'l*, pg. 1328
SWEDBANK (LUXEMBOURG) S.A.—See Swedbank; *Int'l*,
pg. 1328
SWEDBANK MARKETS—See Swedbank; *Int'l*, pg. 1328
SWEDBANK NEW YORK—See Swedbank; *Int'l*, pg. 1328
SWEDE RESCUE—See Axel Johnson AB; *Int'l*, pg. 712
SWEDEN CENTER JAPAN K.K.—See
Fastighetsaktiebolaget Hufvudstaden; *Int'l*, pg. 478
SWEDEN TABLE TENNIS AB—See Escalade Sports; *U.S.
Public*, pg. 591
SWEDISH ERICSSON COMPANY LTD.—See
Telefonaktiebolaget LM Ericsson; *Int'l*, pg. 1370
SWEDISH MATCH DO BRASIL S/A—See Swedish Match
S.A.; *Int'l*, pg. 1328
SWEDISH MATCH S.A.; *Int'l*, pg. 1328

SWEDISH MATCH S.A.—See Swedish Match S.A.; *Int'l*, pg. 1328
SWEDISH MOTOR ASSEMBLIES SDN. BHD.—See AB Volvo; *Int'l*, pg. 1477
SWEDISH RAIL SYSTEM SRS—See Scancem AB; *Int'l*, pg. 1199
SWEDISH ROYAL REFRIGERATION LTD.—See Electrolux, AB; *Int'l*, pg. 444
SWEDISH TYRE TUBE AB—See Trelleborg AB; *Int'l*, pg. 1422
SWEDOOR AB-ASTORP—See Stora Kopparbergs Bergslags AB; *Int'l*, pg. 1303
SWEDOOR AB-FORSERUM—See Stora Kopparbergs Bergslags AB; *Int'l*, pg. 1303
SWEDOOR AB-VETLANDA—See Stora Kopparbergs Bergslags AB; *Int'l*, pg. 1303
SWEDOOR A/S-GRAN—See Stora Kopparbergs Bergslags AB; *Int'l*, pg. 1303
SWEDOOR BAUELEMENTE GMBH—See Stora Kopparbergs Bergslags AB; *Int'l*, pg. 1303
SWEDPOWER AB—See Vattenfall AB; *Int'l*, pg. 1453
SWEDPOWER (THAILAND) LTD.—See Vattenfall AB; *Int'l*, pg. 1453
E.A. SWEEN COMPANY; *U.S. Private*, pg. 1058
JAKE SWEENEY AUTO LEASING, INC.—See Jake Sweeney Automotive Inc.; *U.S. Private*, pg. 1058
JAKE SWEENEY AUTOMOTIVE INC.; *U.S. Private*, pg. 1058
JAKE SWEENEY JEEP EAGLE, INC.—See Jake Sweeney Automotive Inc.; *U.S. Private*, pg. 1058
SWEET LIFE FOODS, INC.—See SuperValu, Inc.; *U.S. Public*, pg. 1541
SWEET SUE KITCHENS—See Sara Lee Corporation; *U.S. Public*, pg. 1434
SWEETHEART CUP COMPANY INC.; *U.S. Private*, pg. 1058
SWEET'S DIV.—See The McGraw-Hill Companies; *U.S. Public*, pg. 1070
THE SWEETS MIX COMPANY, INC.—See Tootsie Roll Industries, Inc.; *U.S. Public*, pg. 1621
SWEETWATER PAPER BOARD CO., INC.—See Caraustar Industries, Inc.; *U.S. Public*, pg. 304
SWENCO-WESTERN, INC.—See Swift Energy Company; *U.S. Public*, pg. 1543
SWENSEN'S ICE CREAM CO.—See Integrated Brands Inc.; *U.S. Public*, pg. 883
SWENSEN'S OF SINGAPORE PTE. LTD.—See Integrated Brands Inc.; *U.S. Public*, pg. 884
SWEPCO TUBE CORPORATION; *U.S. Private*, pg. 1058
SWEQUIPOS, S.A.—See Emerson Electric Co.; *U.S. Public*, pg. 578
SWIFLOOR SA—See Forbo Holding SA; *Int'l*, pg. 497
SWIFT ADHESIFS S.A.—See Dainippon Ink & Chemicals, Inc.; *Int'l*, pg. 370
SWIFT ADHESIVES AG—See Dainippon Ink & Chemicals, Inc.; *Int'l*, pg. 370
SWIFT ADHESIVES B.V.—See Dainippon Ink & Chemicals, Inc.; *Int'l*, pg. 370
SWIFT ADHESIVES GREECE SAIC—See Dainippon Ink & Chemicals, Inc.; *Int'l*, pg. 370
SWIFT ADHESIVES LTD.—See Dainippon Ink & Chemicals, Inc.; *Int'l*, pg. 370
SWIFT & COMPANY—See ConAgra, Inc.; *U.S. Public*, pg. 426
SWIFT AND COMPANY LTD.—See Internatio-Muller N.V.; *Int'l*, pg. 682
SWIFT AUSTRIA GMBH—See Dainippon Ink & Chemicals, Inc.; *Int'l*, pg. 370
CHUCK SWIFT SALES & LEASING; *U.S. Private*, pg. 1058
SWIFT & CO.—See ConAgra, Inc.; *U.S. Public*, pg. 426
SWIFT-COR TOOL ENGINEERING; *U.S. Private*, pg. 1058
SWIFT DENIM INC.—See Dominion Textile Inc.; *Int'l*, pg. 415
SWIFT ENERGY COMPANY; *U.S. Public*, pg. 1543
SWIFT INSTRUMENTS, INC.; *U.S. Private*, pg. 1058
SWIFT KLEBSTOFFE GMBH—See Dainippon Ink & Chemicals, Inc.; *Int'l*, pg. 370
SWIFT KLEEFSTOFFEN BVBA—See Dainippon Ink & Chemicals, Inc.; *Int'l*, pg. 370
SWIFT LEASING CO.—See Swift Transportation Co.; *U.S. Public*, pg. 1543
M. SWIFT & SONS INC.; *U.S. Private*, pg. 1059
SWIFT TEXTILES, INC.—See Dominion Textile Inc.; *Int'l*, pg. 415
SWIFT TRANSPORTATION CO.; *U.S. Public*, pg. 1543
SWIFTDRILL, INC.—See Atwood Oceanics, Inc.; *U.S. Public*, pg. 146
SWINERTON INC.; *U.S. Private*, pg. 1059
SWING-N-SLIDE CORP.; *U.S. Public*, pg. 1543
SWINGSTER COMPANY—See American Marketing Industries, Inc.; *U.S. Private*, pg. 58
SWIRE PACIFIC LIMITED; *Int'l*, pg. 1328
SWIRL, II LTD; *U.S. Private*, pg. 1059
SWISH BENELUX NV/SA—See Newmond PLC; *Int'l*, pg. 925
SWISH FRANCE SA—See Newmond PLC; *Int'l*, pg. 925
SWISH ITALIANA SRL—See Newmond PLC; *Int'l*, pg. 925
SWISH PRODUCTS LTD.—See Newmond PLC; *Int'l*, pg. 925
SWISHER COUNTY CATTLE CO.—See Friona Industries, L.P.; *U.S. Private*, pg. 429
SWISHER INTERNATIONAL GROUP, INC.; *U.S. Public*, pg. 1543
SWISS AIR TRANSPORT COMPANY LTD.—See The Swissair Group; *Int'l*, pg. 1334
SWISS ALUMINIUM AUSTRALIA LTD.—See Alusuisse-Lonza Holding Ltd.; *Int'l*, pg. 69
SWISS-AM REASSURANCE COMPANY—See Swiss Reinsurance Company; *Int'l*, pg. 1333
SWISS ARMY BRANDS, INC.; *U.S. Public*, pg. 1544
SWISS ARMY BRANDS LTD.—See Swiss Army Brands, Inc.; *U.S. Public*, pg. 1544
SWISS BANK & TRUST CORPORATION LTD.—See Swiss Bank Corporation; *Int'l*, pg. 1332

SWISS BANK CORPORATION; *Int'l*, pg. 1329
SWISS BANK CORPORATION—See Swiss Bank Corporation; *Int'l*, pg. 1329
SWISS BANK CORPORATION (CANADA)—See Swiss Bank Corporation; *Int'l*, pg. 1331
SWISS BANK CORPORATION (LUXEMBOURG) LTD.—See Swiss Bank Corporation; *Int'l*, pg. 1330
SWISS BANK CORPORATION NEDERLAND N.V.—See Swiss Bank Corporation; *Int'l*, pg. 1332
SWISS BANK CORPORATION (OVERSEAS) LTD.—See Swiss Bank Corporation; *Int'l*, pg. 1332
SWISS BANK CORPORATION (OVERSEAS) S.A.—See Swiss Bank Corporation; *Int'l*, pg. 1330
THE SWISS COLONY, INC; *U.S. Private*, pg. 1059
SWISS DAIRY—See Suiza Foods Corporation; *U.S. Public*, pg. 1527
SWISS LIFE (BELGIUM)—See The Swiss Life/Rentenanstalt Group; *Int'l*, pg. 1332
SWISS LIFE (ESPANA)—See The Swiss Life/Rentenanstalt Group; *Int'l*, pg. 1332
SWISS LIFE HOLDING—See The Swiss Life/Rentenanstalt Group; *Int'l*, pg. 1332
SWISS LIFE INTERNATIONAL SERVICES—See The Swiss Life/Rentenanstalt Group; *Int'l*, pg. 1332
SWISS LIFE INVESTMENT MANAGEMENT—See The Swiss Life/Rentenanstalt Group; *Int'l*, pg. 1332
SWISS LIFE (ITALIA)—See The Swiss Life/Rentenanstalt Group; *Int'l*, pg. 1332
SWISS LIFE (ITALIA) INFORTUNI E MALATTIE—See The Swiss Life/Rentenanstalt Group; *Int'l*, pg. 1332
SWISS LIFE (LUXEMBOURG)—See The Swiss Life/Rentenanstalt Group; *Int'l*, pg. 1332
SWISS LIFE PORTFOLIO MANAGEMENT—See The Swiss Life/Rentenanstalt Group; *Int'l*, pg. 1332
THE SWISS LIFE/RENTENANSTALT GROUP; *Int'l*, pg. 1332
SWISS LIFE (UK)—See The Swiss Life/Rentenanstalt Group; *Int'l*, pg. 1332
SWISS LIFE (UK) GROUP—See The Swiss Life/Rentenanstalt Group; *Int'l*, pg. 1332
SWISS LIFE UNIT TRUST MANAGEMENT—See The Swiss Life/Rentenanstalt Group; *Int'l*, pg. 1332
SWISS LOCOMOTIVE AND MACHINE WORKS—See Sulzer Ltd.; *Int'l*, pg. 1307
SWISS NIGERIAN CHEMICAL CO. LTD.—See Novartis AG; *Int'l*, pg. 986
SWISS PRESTIGE—See SMH Swiss Corporation for Micro Electronics & Watchmaking Indus. Ltd.; *Int'l*, pg. 1161
SWISS PRESTIGE, INC.—See Jaeger-Le Coultre; *Int'l*, pg. 697
SWISS RE AMERICA CORPORATION—See Swiss Reinsurance Company; *Int'l*, pg. 1333
SWISS RE ATRIUM CORPORATION—See Swiss Reinsurance Company; *Int'l*, pg. 1333
SWISS RE AUSTRALIA LTD.—See Swiss Reinsurance Company; *Int'l*, pg. 1333
SWISS RE BRASIL SERVICOS E PARTICIPACOES LTDA—See Swiss Reinsurance Company; *Int'l*, pg. 1333
SWISS RE CAPITAL MARKETS CORPORATIONS—See Swiss Reinsurance Company; *Int'l*, pg. 1332
SWISS RE FINANCIAL PRODUCTS—See Swiss Reinsurance Company; *Int'l*, pg. 1333
SWISS RE (ISRAEL) LTD—See Swiss Reinsurance Company; *Int'l*, pg. 1333
SWISS RE LIFE CANADA—See Swiss Reinsurance Company; *Int'l*, pg. 1333
SWISS RE LIFE COMPANY AMERICA—See Swiss Reinsurance Company; *Int'l*, pg. 1333
SWISS RE SOUTHERN AFRICA LTD.—See Swiss Reinsurance Company; *Int'l*, pg. 1333
SWISS REINSURANCE AMERICA CORPORATION—See Swiss Reinsurance Company; *Int'l*, pg. 1333
SWISS REINSURANCE COMPANY; *Int'l*, pg. 1332
SWISS REINSURANCE COMPANY-BEIJING REPRESENTATIVE OFFICE—See Swiss Reinsurance Company; *Int'l*, pg. 1333
SWISS REINSURANCE COMPANY CANADA—See Swiss Reinsurance Company; *Int'l*, pg. 1333
SWISS REINSURANCE COMPANY-HONG KONG BRANCH—See Swiss Reinsurance Company; *Int'l*, pg. 1333
SWISS REINSURANCE COMPANY-KOREA LIASON OFFICE—See Swiss Reinsurance Company; *Int'l*, pg. 1333
SWISS REINSURANCE COMPANY KUALA LUMPUR BRANCH—See Swiss Reinsurance Company; *Int'l*, pg. 1333
SWISS REINSURANCE COMPANY MANILA—See Swiss Reinsurance Company; *Int'l*, pg. 1333
SWISS REINSURANCE COMPANY-REPRESENTATIVE OFFICE TOKYO—See Swiss Reinsurance Company; *Int'l*, pg. 1333
SWISS REINSURANCE COMPANY-TAIPEI LIASON OFFICE—See Swiss Reinsurance Company; *Int'l*, pg. 1333
SWISS REINSURANCE COMPANY UK LTD.—See Swiss Reinsurance Company; *Int'l*, pg. 1333
SWISS SHIPPING AND NEPTUNE AG—See Migros; *Int'l*, pg. 866
SWISS TIMING—See SMH Swiss Corporation for Micro Electronics & Watchmaking Indus. Ltd.; *Int'l*, pg. 1161
SWISSAIR ASSOCIATED COMPANIES LTD.—See The Swissair Group; *Int'l*, pg. 1334
THE SWISSAIR GROUP; *Int'l*, pg. 1334
SWISSAM INC.—See Movado Group, Inc.; *U.S. Public*, pg. 1140
SWISSCOLOR—See Novartis AG; *Int'l*, pg. 986
SWISSCOLOR D.O.O.—See Novartis AG; *Int'l*, pg. 986
SWISSCOLOR SRL—See Novartis AG; *Int'l*, pg. 986
SWISSCOM; *Int'l*, pg. 1334
SWISSMETAL DEUTSCHLAND HANDELSGESELLSCHAFT MBH—See UMS Swiss Metalworks Holding Ltd; *Int'l*, pg. 1427

SWISSMETAL ITALIA S.R.L.—See UMS Swiss Metalworks Holding Ltd; *Int'l*, pg. 1427
SWISSMETAL PLANT DORNACH—See UMS Swiss Metalworks Holding Ltd; *Int'l*, pg. 1427
SWISS-M-TEX, L.P.; *U.S. Private*, pg. 1059
SWISSPHARMA S.A.E.—See Novartis AG; *Int'l*, pg. 986
SWISSPHARMA TAIWAN LTD.—See Novartis AG; *Int'l*, pg. 986
SWISSRE ADVISERS, INC.—See Swiss Reinsurance Company; *Int'l*, pg. 1333
SWISSRE ADVISERS (SINGAPORE) PTE. LTD.—See Swiss Reinsurance Company; *Int'l*, pg. 1333
SWISSRE ADVISERS TALLINN—See Swiss Reinsurance Company; *Int'l*, pg. 1333
SWISSRE FINANCE (BERMUDA) LTD.—See Swiss Reinsurance Company; *Int'l*, pg. 1333
SWISSRE FINANCE (US) INC.—See Swiss Reinsurance Company; *Int'l*, pg. 1333
SWISSRE INVESTMENTS (BERMUDA) LTD.—See Swiss Reinsurance Company; *Int'l*, pg. 1333
SWISSROSE INTERNATIONAL, INC.—See ConAgra, Inc.; *U.S. Public*, pg. 426
SWITCHCRAFT DE MEXICO, S.A.—See Raytheon Company; *U.S. Public*, pg. 1366
SWITCHCRAFT, INC.—See Raytheon Company; *U.S. Public*, pg. 1366
SWITCHGEAR & INSTRUMENTATION LTD.—See N.G. Bailey & Co. Ltd.; *Int'l*, pg. 133
SWITCHING SYSTEMS INTERNATIONAL—See Bowthorpe plc; *Int'l*, pg. 208
SWITZERLAND CHEESE ASSOCIATION, INC.—See Schweizerische Kaseunion AG; *Int'l*, pg. 1211
SWITZERLAND REPRASENLANZ ZURICH—See Frankfurter Sparkasse; *Int'l*, pg. 504
SWIX SPORT—See Tiedemanns - Joh.H.Andresen ANS; *Int'l*, pg. 1390
SWIX SPORT USA INC.—See Tiedemanns - Joh.H.Andresen ANS; *Int'l*, pg. 1390
SAM SWOPE AUTO GROUP, INC.; *U.S. Private*, pg. 1059
SYAR INDUSTRIES, INC.; *U.S. Private*, pg. 1059
SYBASE, INC.; *U.S. Public*, pg. 1544
SYBASE INC.—See Sybase, Inc.; *U.S. Public*, pg. 1544
SYBASE INC.-EUROPEAN HEADQUARTERS—See Sybase, Inc.; *U.S. Public*, pg. 1544
SYBEX, INC.; *U.S. Private*, pg. 1059
SYBRA, INC.—See Contran Corporation; *U.S. Private*, pg. 270
SYBRON CHEMICALS INC.; *U.S. Public*, pg. 1544
SYBRON CHEMICALS, INC.—See Sybron Chemicals Inc.; *U.S. Public*, pg. 1544
SYBRON DENTAL SPECIALTIES, INC.—See Sybron International Corporation; *U.S. Public*, pg. 1545
SYBRON INTERNATIONAL CORPORATION; *U.S. Public*, pg. 1544
SYCAMORE PLANT—See Cooper Industries, Inc.; *U.S. Public*, pg. 444
SYCAMORE SYSTEMS, INC.—See L & D Group; *U.S. Private*, pg. 638
SYCAMORE VALLEY—See BRE Properties, Inc.; *U.S. Public*, pg. 163
SYCOM SERVICES INC.—See Hadron, Inc.; *U.S. Public*, pg. 773
SYDKRAFT AB—See Veba AG; *Int'l*, pg. 1457
SYDNEY BREWERY—See Foster's Brewing Group Limited; *Int'l*, pg. 501
THE SYDNEY MORNING HERALD—See John Fairfax Holdings Limited; *Int'l*, pg. 477
SYDNEY STEEL MILL—See The Broken Hill Proprietary Company Limited; *Int'l*, pg. 227
SYDNEY WIRE MILL—See The Broken Hill Proprietary Company Limited; *Int'l*, pg. 226
SYDVED AB—See Mo och Domsjo AB; *Int'l*, pg. 887
THE SYGMA NETWORK, INC.-COLUMBUS CENTRAL DIVISION—See Sysco Corporation; *U.S. Public*, pg. 1550
THE SYGMA NETWORK, INC.-DENVER CENTRAL—See Sysco Corporation; *U.S. Public*, pg. 1551
THE SYGMA NETWORK OF PENNSYLVANIA—See Sysco Corporation; *U.S. Public*, pg. 1551
JOSEPH SYKES BROTHERS LTD.—See Carclo Engineering Group plc; *Int'l*, pg. 268
SYLAMERICA—See L'Oreal S.A.; *Int'l*, pg. 818
SYLEA HARNESS ASSEMBLY PLANT—See Labinal SA; *Int'l*, pg. 785
SYLVA INDUSTRIES LIMITED—See GP Batteries International Ltd.; *Int'l*, pg. 537
SYLVAN—See Royal Dutch/Shell Group of Companies; *Int'l*, pg. 1139
SYLVAN INC.; *U.S. Public*, pg. 1545
SYLVAN LEARNING SYSTEMS INC.; *U.S. Public*, pg. 1545
SYLVAPEN DISTRIBUIDORA S.A.C.I.Y.F.—See The Gillette Company; *U.S. Public*, pg. 745
SYMANTEC—See Symantec Corporation; *U.S. Public*, pg. 1545
SYMANTEC CORPORATION; *U.S. Public*, pg. 1545
SYMANTEC CORPORATION - BEAVERTON SITE—See Symantec Corporation; *U.S. Public*, pg. 1545
SYMANTEC K.K.—See Symantec Corporation; *U.S. Public*, pg. 1545
SYMBICOM AB—See Astra AB; *Int'l*, pg. 93
SYMBOL—See Symbol Technologies, Inc.; *U.S. Public*, pg. 1546
SYMBOL AUSTRALIA PTY. LTD.—See Symbol Technologies, Inc.; *U.S. Public*, pg. 1546
SYMBOL TECHNOLOGIES AFRICA, INC.—See Symbol Technologies, Inc.; *U.S. Public*, pg. 1546
SYMBOL TECHNOLOGIES ASIA, INC.—See Symbol Technologies, Inc.; *U.S. Public*, pg. 1546
SYMBOL TECHNOLOGIES CANADA INC.—See Symbol Technologies, Inc.; *U.S. Public*, pg. 1546
SYMBOL TECHNOLOGIES GMBH—See Symbol Technologies, Inc.; *U.S. Public*, pg. 1546
SYMBOL TECHNOLOGIES, INC.; *U.S. Public*, pg. 1546

SYMBOL DIRECTORY OF CORPORATE AFFILIATIONS

Company Index

SYMBOL TECHNOLOGIES INTERNATIONAL, INC.—See Symbol Technologies, Inc.; U.S. Public, pg. 1546
SYMBOL TECHNOLOGIES LIMITED—See Symbol Technologies, Inc.; U.S. Public, pg. 1546
SYMBOL TECHNOLOGIES, PORTABLE SYSTEMS DIVISION—See Symbol Technologies, Inc.; U.S. Public, pg. 1546
SYMBOL TECHNOLOGIES S.A.—See Symbol Technologies, Inc.; U.S. Public, pg. 1546
SYMBOL TECHNOLOGIES S.R.L.—See Symbol Technologies, Inc.; U.S. Public, pg. 1546
DAVID SYME & CO. LIMITED—See John Fairfax Holdings Limited; Int'l, pg. 477
SYMIX CIT—See Symix Systems, Inc.; U.S. Public, pg. 1547
SYMIX MALAYSIA-SDN BHD—See Symix Systems, Inc.; U.S. Public, pg. 1547
SYMIX MELBOURNE—See Symix Systems, Inc.; U.S. Public, pg. 1547
SYMIX SYSTEMS, INC.; U.S. Public, pg. 1546
SYMIX SYSTEMS, INC.-AUSTRALIA—See Symix Systems, Inc.; U.S. Public, pg. 1547
SYMIX SYSTEMS, INC.-FRANCE—See Symix Systems, Inc.; U.S. Public, pg. 1547
SYMIX SYSTEMS-NEW ZEALAND—See Symix Systems, Inc.; U.S. Public, pg. 1547
SYMMETRICOM, INC.; U.S. Public, pg. 1547
SYMONS CORPORATION—See Ripplewood Holdings L.L.C.; U.S. Private, pg. 932
SYMPLEX COMMUNICATIONS CORP.; U.S. Private, pg. 1060
SYMS CORPORATION; U.S. Public, pg. 1547
SYMSKAYA EXPLORATION, INC.—See Equity Oil Company; U.S. Public, pg. 590
SYMTRON SYSTEMS, INC.—See United Industrial Corporation; U.S. Public, pg. 1679
SYMTRONIX CORPORATION—See Tech-Sym Corporation; U.S. Public, pg. 1563
SYN STRAND INC.—See Scapa Group Plc; Int'l, pg. 1202
SYNALLOY CORPORATION; U.S. Public, pg. 1547
SYNATOM S.A.—See Electrabel S.A.; Int'l, pg. 437
SYNCHRO-START PRODUCTS, INC.—See Knowles Electronics, Inc.; U.S. Private, pg. 627
SYNCOR INTERNATIONAL CORPORATION; U.S. Public, pg. 1548
SYNDECO REALTY—See DTE Energy Company; U.S. Public, pg. 476
SYNDESIS DEVELOPMENT CORP.—See Wisconsin Energy Corporation; U.S. Public, pg. 1773
SYNDICATE SYSTEMS, INC.; U.S. Private, pg. 1060
SYNDICATED OFFICE SYSTEMS, INC.—See Tenet Healthcare Corporation; U.S. Public, pg. 1577
SYNECTICS MEDICAL AB—See Medtronic, Inc.; U.S. Public, pg. 1084
SYNERFI SA—See Generale de Banque S.A.; Int'l, pg. 547
SYNERGIE—See Havas Advertising; Int'l, pg. 601
SYNERGIE PRESSE—See EMAP Plc; Int'l, pg. 451
SYNERGIE TOKYU DMB&B LTD.—See DMB&B Communications; U.S. Private, pg. 305
SYNERGIS TECHNOLOGIES GROUP; U.S. Private, pg. 1060
SYNERGISM, INC.; U.S. Private, pg. 1060
SYNERGISTICS CHEMICALS, INC.—See The Geon Company; U.S. Public, pg. 734
SYNERGISTICS INDUSTGRIES LIMITED - PACKAGING & MEDICAL PRODUCTS—See The Geon Company; U.S. Public, pg. 734
SYNERGISTICS INDUSTRIES LIMITED—See The Geon Company; U.S. Public, pg. 734
SYNERGISTICS INDUSTRIES (NJ) INC.—See The Geon Company; U.S. Public, pg. 734
SYNERGISTICS INDUSTRIES (TX) INC.—See The Geon Company; U.S. Public, pg. 734
SYNERGY COMPUTER GRAPHICS CORPORATION—See Nippon Steel Corporation; Int'l, pg. 940
SYNERTEC, INCORPORATED—See Minnesota Power; U.S. Public, pg. 1116
SYNERTECH—See Highmark Inc.; U.S. Private, pg. 529
SYNETIC, INC.; U.S. Public, pg. 1548
SYNEX CORP.—See Berwind Corporation; U.S. Private, pg. 138
SYNFLEX DIVISION—See Furon Company; U.S. Public, pg. 689
SYNINGTON COMPANY—See Koninklijke BolsWessanen nv; Int'l, pg. 753
SYNON CORPORATION; U.S. Private, pg. 1060
SYNOPSYS, INC.; U.S. Public, pg. 1548
SYNOVUS FINANCIAL CORP.; U.S. Public, pg. 1548
SYNOVUS SECURITIES, INC.—See Synovus Financial Corp.; U.S. Public, pg. 1550
SYNRES-ALMOCO B.V.—See DSM N.V.; Int'l, pg. 354
SYNRES-ALMOCO FRANCE S.A.R.L.—See DSM N.V.; Int'l, pg. 356
SYNRES-ALMOCO UK LTD.—See DSM N.V.; Int'l, pg. 356
SYNTAX PROCESSING—See Olivetti SpA; Int'l, pg. 1002
SYNTELLECT EUROPE—See Syntellect, Inc.; U.S. Public, pg. 1550
SYNTELLECT, INC.; U.S. Public, pg. 1550
SYNTELLECT TECHNOLOGY CORP.—See Syntellect, Inc.; U.S. Public, pg. 1550
SYNTEX—See Roche Holding Ltd.; Int'l, pg. 1120
SYNTEX AGRIBUSINESS, INC.—See Roche Holding Ltd.; Int'l, pg. 1120
SYNTEX AUSTRALIA LIMITED—See Roche Holding Ltd.; Int'l, pg. 1122
SYNTEX CHEMICALS, INC.—See Roche Holding Ltd.; Int'l, pg. 1120
SYNTEX IRELAND LIMITED—See Roche Holding Ltd.; Int'l, pg. 1122
SYNTEX LATINO S.A.—See Roche Holding Ltd.; Int'l, pg. 1122
SYNTEX PHARMACEUTICALS INTERNATIONAL LIMITED—See Roche Holding Ltd.; Int'l, pg. 1122
SYNTEX PUERTO RICO, INC.—See Roche Holding Ltd.; Int'l, pg. 1122
SYNTEX S.A.—See Roche Holding Ltd.; Int'l, pg. 1122
SYNTEX S.A. DE C.V.—See Roche Holding Ltd.; Int'l, pg. 1122
SYNTHELABO PHARMACEUTICALS K.K.—See L'Oreal S.A.; Int'l, pg. 818
SYNTHELABO S.A.—See L'Oreal S.A.; Int'l, pg. 818
SYNTHELABO-TANABE CHIMIE S.A.—See Tanabe Seiyaku Co., Ltd.; Int'l, pg. 1354
SYNTHESE BV—See Akzo Nobel N.V.; Int'l, pg. 43
SYNTHOMER GMBH—See Dainippon Ink & Chemicals, Inc.; Int'l, pg. 370
SYNTHOMER, LTD.—See Dainippon Ink & Chemicals, Inc.; Int'l, pg. 370
SYNTRON ASIA PTE. LTD.—See Tech-Sym Corporation; U.S. Public, pg. 1563
SYNTRON EUROPE LIMITED—See Tech-Sym Corporation; U.S. Public, pg. 1563
SYNTRON, INC.—See Tech-Sym Corporation; U.S. Public, pg. 1563
SYQUEST TECHNOLOGY, INC.; U.S. Public, pg. 1550
THE SYRACUSE ADHESIVES COMPANY—See Laporte plc; Int'l, pg. 803
SYRACUSE SUPPLY COMPANY; U.S. Private, pg. 1060
SYRACUSE SUPPLY CONSTRUCTION & EQUIPMENT DIVISION—See Syracuse Supply Company; U.S. Private, pg. 1060
SYRACUSE SUPPLY LEASING CO., INC.—See Syracuse Supply Company; U.S. Private, pg. 1060
SYRATECH CORPORATION; U.S. Private, pg. 1060
SYREMONT S.P.A.—See Compart SpA; Int'l, pg. 324
SYRIA SHELL PETROLEUM DEVELOPMENT BV—See Royal Dutch/Shell Group of Companies; Int'l, pg. 1141
SYSABEL S.A.—See Thomson S.A.; Int'l, pg. 1385
SYSCO CORPORATION; U.S. Public, pg. 1550
SYSCO FOOD SERVICES OF CHARLOTTE, INC.—See Sysco Corporation; U.S. Public, pg. 1551
SYSCO FOOD SERVICES OF CONNECTICUT—See Sysco Corporation; U.S. Public, pg. 1551
SYSCO FOOD SERVICES OF EASTERN WISCONSIN—See Sysco Corporation; U.S. Public, pg. 1551
SYSCO FOOD SERVICES OF GRAND RAPIDS, INC.—See Sysco Corporation; U.S. Public, pg. 1551
SYSCO FOOD SERVICES OF PHILADELPHIA, INC.—See Sysco Corporation; U.S. Public, pg. 1552
SYSCO FOOD SERVICES OF SAN FRANCISCO, INC.—See Sysco Corporation; U.S. Public, pg. 1552
SYSCO FOOD SERVICES OF SOUTHEAST FLORIDA, INC.—See Sysco Corporation; U.S. Public, pg. 1552
SYSCO FOOD SERVICES OF WEST COAST FLORIDA, INC.—See Sysco Corporation; U.S. Public, pg. 1552
SYSCO INTERMOUNTAIN FOOD SERVICES, INC.—See Sysco Corporation; U.S. Public, pg. 1552
SYSCO/KONINGS WHOLESALE—See Sysco Corporation; U.S. Public, pg. 1552
SYSCO/LOUISVILLE FOOD SERVICES CO.—See Sysco Corporation; U.S. Public, pg. 1552
SYSECA—See Thomson S.A.; Int'l, pg. 1384
SYSECA CANTABRICO—See Thomson S.A.; Int'l, pg. 1384
SYSECA DE MEXICO S.A. DE CV—See Thomson S.A.; Int'l, pg. 1384
SYSECA GMBH—See Thomson S.A.; Int'l, pg. 1384
SYSECA INC.—See Thomson S.A.; Int'l, pg. 1384
SYSECA LTD—See Thomson S.A.; Int'l, pg. 1384
SYSTECH COMPUTER CORPORATION; U.S. Private, pg. 1061
SYSTECH SOLUTIONS LTD.—See Meggitt plc; Int'l, pg. 853
SYSTECON AB—See Celsius AB; Int'l, pg. 277
SYSTEM ENERGY RESOURCES, INC.—See Entergy Corporation; U.S. Public, pg. 586
SYSTEM MANAGEMENT GROUP—See Budget Group, Inc.; U.S. Private, pg. 178
SYSTEM ONE CONTROL—See Peoples Electric Contractor, Inc.; U.S. Private, pg. 851
SYSTEM PLANNING CORP.; U.S. Private, pg. 1061
SYSTEM PRODUCTS DIVISION—See Standard Microsystems Corp.; U.S. Public, pg. 1503
SYSTEM SENSOR CANADA—See Pittway Corporation; U.S. Public, pg. 1307
SYSTEM SENSOR DE MEXICO S.S. DE C.V.—See Pittway Corporation; U.S. Public, pg. 1307
SYSTEM SENSOR DIVISION—See Pittway Corporation; U.S. Public, pg. 1306
SYSTEM SENSOR LTD.—See Pittway Corporation; U.S. Public, pg. 1307
SYSTEM SERVICE DIVISION—See Cubic Corporation; U.S. Public, pg. 466
SYSTEM SOFTWARE ASSOCIATES, INC.; U.S. Public, pg. 1552
SYSTEMATIC DRILL HEAD CO. LTD.—See Haden Maclellan Holdings plc; Int'l, pg. 585
SYSTEMES Y CONNEXIONES INTEGRADES S.A. DE C.V.—See Noma Industries Limited; Int'l, pg. 955
SYSTEMHOUSE DE MEXICO S.A. DE C.V.—See SHL Systemhouse; Int'l, pg. 1154
SYSTEMHOUSE DE SUR AMERICA, C.A.—See SHL Systemhouse; Int'l, pg. 1154
SYSTEMIX, INC.—See Novartis AG; Int'l, pg. 974
SYSTEMS & COMPUTER TECHNOLOGY CORPORATION; U.S. Public, pg. 1552
SYSTEMS & ELECTRONICS INC.—See ESCO Electronics Corporation; U.S. Public, pg. 547
SYSTEMS AND PROJECTS ENGINEERING CO.—See Telefonaktiebolaget LM Ericsson; Int'l, pg. 1370
SYSTEMS & SERVICES DIV.—See Johnson Controls, Inc.; U.S. Public, pg. 932
SYSTEMS ASSEMBLY DIV.—See Dana Corporation; U.S. Public, pg. 479
SYSTEMS BIO INDUSTRIES—See Elf Aquitane; Int'l, pg. 445
SYSTEMS CAPITAL CORPORATION—See Telco Capital Corporation; U.S. Private, pg. 1073
SYSTEMS CONTROL TECHNOLOGY—See Science Applications International Corp.; U.S. Private, pg. 976
SYSTEMS DE FERMETURE S.A.—See Velcro Industries N.V.; Int'l, pg. 1462
SYSTEMS DESIGN DIVISION—See Cadence Design Systems, Inc.; U.S. Public, pg. 290
SYSTEMS DESIGN DIVISION—See Tracor, Inc.; U.S. Public, pg. 1627
SYSTEMS DEVELOPMENT LTD.—See International Business Machines Corporation; U.S. Public, pg. 897
SYSTEMS ENGINEERING DIV.—See Computer Sciences Corporation; U.S. Public, pg. 423
SYSTEMS GROUP—See Rockwell International Corporation; U.S. Public, pg. 1398
SYSTEMS INTEGRATION DIVISION—See Tracor, Inc.; U.S. Public, pg. 1627
SYSTEMS INTEGRATION, U.K.—See SHL Systemhouse; Int'l, pg. 1154
SYSTEMS MANAGEMENT & DEVELOPMENT—See Technical Aid Corporation; U.S. Private, pg. 1072
SYSTEMS MANAGEMENT GROUP—See Sterling Software, Inc.; U.S. Public, pg. 1516
SYSTEMS NORTHWEST—See Ricoh Company, Ltd.; Int'l, pg. 1114
SYSTEMS PARKING, INC.; U.S. Private, pg. 1061
SYSTEMS SOFTWARE LIMITED—See CSA Holdings Ltd.; Int'l, pg. 243
SYSTEMS STRATEGIES, INC.—See Apertus Technologies Incorporated; U.S. Public, pg. 120
SYSTEMS TAX SERVICE, INC.—See Ceridian Corporation; U.S. Public, pg. 331
SYSTER INFORMATIQUE—See Compagnie des Machines Bull; Int'l, pg. 316
SYSTHEMA VERLAG GMBH—See Georg von Holtzbrinck GmbH; Int'l, pg. 1479
SYSTRA-SOFRETU-SOFRERAIL—See SNCF; Int'l, pg. 1165
SYSTRON DONNER-INERTIAL DIVISION—See BEI Technologies, Inc.; U.S. Public, pg. 160
SYTECH—See Cummins Engine Company, Inc.; U.S. Public, pg. 468
DAVE SYVERSON LINCOLN MERCURY; U.S. Private, pg. 1061
DAVE SYVERSON TRUCK CENTER, INC.—See Dave Syverson Lincoln Mercury; U.S. Private, pg. 1061

T

T&W FINANCIAL CORPORATION; U.S. Public, pg. 1552
T B WOOD'S CANADA LTD.—See TB Wood's Corporation; U.S. Public, pg. 1562
T B WOOD'S ENERTEC LIMITED—See TB Wood's Corporation; U.S. Public, pg. 1562
T B WOOD'S INCORPORATED—See TB Wood's Corporation; U.S. Public, pg. 1562
T B WOOD'S (MEXICO) S.A. DE C.V.—See TB Wood's Corporation; U.S. Public, pg. 1562
T B WOOD'S VOLKMANN CONTROLS—See TB Wood's Corporation; U.S. Public, pg. 1562
T A HOLDINGS LIMITED; Int'l, pg. 1334
T & D METAL PRODUCTS—See L & D Group; U.S. Private, pg. 638
T&K AUTOPARTS SDN. BHD.—See Toyota Motor Corporation; Int'l, pg. 1413
T & K GLASS CO.—See BTR plc; Int'l, pg. 129
T&L OMEGA, INC.—See Omega Environmental Inc.; U.S. Public, pg. 1222
T & N INDUSTRIES, INC.—See T & N Plc; Int'l, pg. 1334
T & N PLC; Int'l, pg. 1334
T & R ELECTRIC SUPPLY COMPANY, INC.; U.S. Private, pg. 1061
T & S BRASS & BRONZE WORKS, INC.; U.S. Private, pg. 1061
T AND S SERVICOS INDUSTRIAS S/C LTDA.—See Toshiba Corporation; Int'l, pg. 1406
T&W DISPOSAL CO.—See Allied Waste Industries; U.S. Public, pg. 49
T-BAR, INC.—See General Signal Corporation; U.S. Public, pg. 727
T C MANUFACTURING COMPANY, INC.; U.S. Private, pg. 1062
T-FAL CANADA INC.—See Groupe SEB; Int'l, pg. 568
T-FAL CORPORATION—See Groupe SEB; Int'l, pg. 568
T-FAL DE MEXICO S.A. DE C.V.—See Groupe SEB; Int'l, pg. 568
T.J. MAXX—See The TJX Companies, Inc.; U.S. Public, pg. 1557
T.J. U.S. COMPANY—See Nash Finch Company; U.S. Public, pg. 1152
T-MOBIL DEUTSCHE TELEKOM MOBIL GMBH—See Deutsche Telekom AG; Int'l, pg. 407
T-NETIX, INC.; U.S. Public, pg. 1553
T-R PRINTING & PUBLISHING—See Tribune Review Publishing Co.; U.S. Private, pg. 1102
TA CONTROL A/S—See Incentive AB; Int'l, pg. 670
TA CONTROL OY—See Incentive AB; Int'l, pg. 670
TA CONTROL SYSTEM A/S—See Incentive AB; Int'l, pg. 670
TA MFG. CO.—See Esterline Technologies Corporation; U.S. Public, pg. 594
TA TRIUMPH-ADLER VERTRIEBS GMBH—See Olivetti SpA; Int'l, pg. 1004
TA WIRSBO GMBH—See Svedala Industri AB; Int'l, pg. 1324
TA-WIRSBO KFT—See Incentive AB; Int'l, pg. 669
TABC, INC.—See Toyota Motor Corporation; Int'l, pg. 1412
TABS DIRECT (OPERATING DIV.)—See Grizzard; U.S. Private, pg. 482
TAC THE ADVERTISING COMPANY LIMITED—See FCB; U.S. Private, pg. 389
TAC CONTROL AB—See Incentive AB; Int'l, pg. 670
TAC CONTROL PTE. LTD.—See Incentive AB; Int'l, pg. 670

TAC CONTROL SYSTEMS GMBH—See Incentive AB; *Int'l*, pg. 670
TAC/MEDICAL SERVICES INC.—See Technical Aid Corporation; *U.S. Private*, pg. 1072
TAC/TEMPS INC.—See Technical Aid Corporation; *U.S. Private*, pg. 1072
TAC (UK) LTD.—See Incentive AB; *Int'l*, pg. 670
TAD RESOURCES INTERNATIONAL, INC.; *U.S. Private*, pg. 1062
TAL FINANCIAL CORPORATION—See TCA Cable TV, Inc.; *U.S. Public*, pg. 1553
TAM-TRASPORTES AÉREOS REGIONAIS—See Viacao Aerea Sao Paulo S.A. (VASP); *Int'l*, pg. 1464
TAP PHARMACEUTICALS, INC.—See Takeda Chemical Industries, Ltd.; *Int'l*, pg. 1350
TASC, INC.—See Primark Corporation; *U.S. Public*, pg. 1325
TAS TVORNICA AUTOMOBILA SARAJEVO—See Volkswagen AG; *Int'l*, pg. 1475
TAUSA - TRÄSATLANTICA AGENCY USA INC.—See SEPI; *Int'l*, pg. 1224
TAV FOODS SERVICE—See Thorn Apple Valley, Inc.; *U.S. Public*, pg. 1603
TBA INDUSTRIAL PRODUCTS LTD.—See T & N Plc; *Int'l*, pg. 1334
TBAC - CANTERBURY, INC.—See Tandy Brands Accessories, Inc.; *U.S. Public*, pg. 1560
TBAC - PRINCE GARDNER, INC.—See Tandy Brands Accessories, Inc.; *U.S. Public*, pg. 1560
TBC CORPORATION; *U.S. Public*, pg. 1553
TBC DIRECT, INC.—See Trahan, Burden & Charles, Inc.; *U.S. Public*, pg. 1095
TBC FINANCIAL SERVICES—See Tasty Baking Company; *U.S. Public*, pg. 1561
TBG LIEFERBETON GMBH & CO. KG BERGSTRABE—See Dyckerhoff AG; *Int'l*, pg. 423
TBG MANAGEMENT S.A.M.; *Int'l*, pg. 1335
TBG NAUHEIMER LIEFERBETON GMBH & CO. KG—See Dyckerhoff AG; *Int'l*, pg. 423
TBG SERVICES, INC.—See TBG Management S.A.M.; pg. 1335
TBL TRANSPORTBOTEN LUDWIGSHAFEN GMBH & CO. KG—See Dyckerhoff AG; *Int'l*, pg. 423
TBM TRANSPORTBOTEN GMBH & CO. KG—See Dyckerhoff AG; *Int'l*, pg. 423
TBS-BRITANNICA CO., LTD.—See Suntory Ltd.; *Int'l*, pg. 1321
TBS GES. FUR TANK- UND BODENSCHUTZ MBH—See Fried. Krupp AG; *Int'l*, pg. 515
TBS PRODUCTIONS, INC.—See Time Warner Inc.; *U.S. Public*, pg. 1615
TBS PROPERTIES, INC.—See Time Warner Inc.; *U.S. Public*, pg. 1615
TBS SOEST—See Ballast Nedam NV; *Int'l*, pg. 134
TBV, INC.—See Victaulic Company of America; *U.S. Private*, pg. 1138
TBWA BARCELONA—See TBWA Chiat/Day; *U.S. Private*, pg. 1063
TBWA BELGIUM—See TBWA Chiat/Day; *U.S. Private*, pg. 1063
TBWA CAMPAIGN COMPANY—See TBWA Chiat/Day; *U.S. Private*, pg. 1063
TBWA CHIAT/DAY; *U.S. Private*, pg. 1062
TBWA CHIAT/DAY CHICAGO—See TBWA Chiat/Day; *U.S. Private*, pg. 1062
TBWA CHIAT/DAY DALLAS—See TBWA Chiat/Day; *U.S. Private*, pg. 1062
TBWA CHIAT/DAY FLORIDA—See TBWA Chiat/Day; *U.S. Private*, pg. 1062
TBWA CHIAT/DAY LOS ANGELES—See TBWA Chiat/Day; *U.S. Private*, pg. 1062
TBWA CHIAT/DAY NEW YORK—See TBWA Chiat/Day; *U.S. Private*, pg. 1062
TBWA CHIAT/DAY SAN FRANCISCO—See TBWA Chiat/Day; *U.S. Private*, pg. 1062
TBWA CHIAT/DAY ST. LOUIS—See TBWA Chiat/Day; *U.S. Private*, pg. 1062
TBWA CHIAT/DAY TORONTO—See TBWA Chiat/Day; *U.S. Private*, pg. 1063
TBWA CHIAT/DAY WASHINGTON, D.C.—See TBWA Chiat/Day; *U.S. Private*, pg. 1062
TBWA COPENHAGEN—See TBWA Chiat/Day; *U.S. Private*, pg. 1063
TBWA DUSSELDORF GMBH—See TBWA Chiat/Day; *U.S. Private*, pg. 1063
TBWA GERMANY—See TBWA Chiat/Day; *U.S. Private*, pg. 1063
TBWA/GGK—See TBWA Chiat/Day; *U.S. Private*, pg. 1063
TBWA GGK ZURICK; *Int'l*, pg. 1335
TBWA/H NETH-WORK—See Hakuhodo Incorporated; *Int'l*, pg. 589
TBWA HAMBURG GMBH—See TBWA Chiat/Day; *U.S. Private*, pg. 1063
TBWA INTERNATIONAL—See Hakuhodo Incorporated; *Int'l*, pg. 589
TBWA ITALIA S.P.A.—See TBWA Chiat/Day; *U.S. Private*, pg. 1063
TBWA MADRID, S.A.—See TBWA Chiat/Day; *U.S. Private*, pg. 1063
TBWA MOSCOW—See TBWA Chiat/Day; *U.S. Private*, pg. 1063
TBWA MUNICH—See TBWA Chiat/Day; *U.S. Private*, pg. 1063
TBWA OSLO—See TBWA Chiat/Day; *U.S. Private*, pg. 1063
TBWA PARIS—See TBWA Chiat/Day; *U.S. Private*, pg. 1063
TBWA PAYNE STRACEY; *Int'l*, pg. 1336
TBWA STOCKHOLM—See TBWA Chiat/Day; *U.S. Private*, pg. 1063
TC CAPITAL MANAGEMENT INC.—See The Pantry, Inc.; *U.S. Private*, pg. 837
TC SERVICES—See US 1 Industries Inc.; *U.S. Public*, pg. 1687

TCA CABLE TV, INC.; *U.S. Public*, pg. 1553
TCA MANAGEMENT COMPANY—See TCA Cable TV, Inc.; *U.S. Public*, pg. 1553
TCBY ENTERPRISES INC.; *U.S. Public*, pg. 1553
TCBY SYSTEMS, INC.—See TCBY Enterprises Inc.; *U.S. Public*, pg. 1554
TCC INDUSTRIES; *U.S. Public*, pg. 1554
TCE TELEVISION SINGAPORE PTE. LTD.—See Thomson S.A.; *Int'l*, pg. 1384
TCF AGENCY—See TCF Financial Corp.; *U.S. Public*, pg. 1554
TCF BANK ILLINOIS—See TCF Financial Corp.; *U.S. Public*, pg. 1554
TCF BANK MINNESOTA FSB—See TCF Financial Corp.; *U.S. Public*, pg. 1554
TCF BANK WISCONSIN—See TCF Financial Corp.; *U.S. Public*, pg. 1554
TCF FINANCIAL CORP.; *U.S. Public*, pg. 1554
TCF FINANCIAL SERVICES INC.—See TCF Financial Corp.; *U.S. Public*, pg. 1554
TCF FOUNDATION—See TCF Financial Corp.; *U.S. Public*, pg. 1554
TCF INSURANCE—See TCF Financial Corp.; *U.S. Public*, pg. 1554
TCF MORTGAGE CORPORATION—See TCF Financial Corp.; *U.S. Public*, pg. 1554
TCF SECURITIES—See TCF Financial Corp.; *U.S. Public*, pg. 1554
TCG INTERNATIONAL INC.; *Int'l*, pg. 1336
TCH INDUSTRIES INC.; *U.S. Private*, pg. 1063
TCI ALUMINUM; *U.S. Private*, pg. 1063
TCI CABLEVISION OF DALLAS, INC.—See TCI Communications, Inc.; *U.S. Public*, pg. 1555
TCI CABLEVISION OF WASHINGTON—See TCI Communications, Inc.; *U.S. Public*, pg. 1555
TCI COMMUNICATIONS, INC.; *U.S. Public*, pg. 1554
TCI DEVELOPMENT CORP.—See TCI Communications, Inc.; *U.S. Public*, pg. 1555
TCI ENTERPRISES, LLC—See NUI Corporation; *U.S. Public*, pg. 1148
TCI, INC.—See RPM, Inc.; *U.S. Public*, pg. 1358
TCI INTERNATIONAL INC.; *U.S. Public*, pg. 1555
TCI INTERNATIONAL SALES CORP.—See Tenneco Inc.; *U.S. Public*, pg. 1578
TCI/US WEST—See TCI Communications, Inc.; *U.S. Public*, pg. 1555
TCI WEST—See TCI Communications, Inc.; *U.S. Public*, pg. 1555
TCI WIRELESS—See TCI International Inc.; *U.S. Public*, pg. 1555
TCIL BELLSOUTH LTD.—See BellSouth Corporation; *U.S. Public*, pg. 209
TCR CORPORATION—See TransTechnology Corporation; *U.S. Public*, pg. 1632
TCV, INC.—See Conrail, Inc.; *U.S. Public*, pg. 432
TD ELECTRONICS, INC.—See Twin Disc, Incorporated; *U.S. Public*, pg. 1646
TD INDUSTRIES INC.; *U.S. Private*, pg. 1063
TD PRODUKTIONS- U. HANDELSGESELLSCHAFT S.A.—See Freudenberg & Company; *Int'l*, pg. 507
TDA ARMEMENT—See Thomson S.A.; *Int'l*, pg. 1382
TDA ARMEMENTS S.A.S.—See Daimler-Benz Aktiengesellschaft; *Int'l*, pg. 367
TDC: THE DESIGN CENTER—See Griffin Bacal Inc.; *U.S. Private*, pg. 480
TDK CORPORATION; *Int'l*, pg. 1336
TDK CORPORATION OF AMERICA—See TDK Corporation; *Int'l*, pg. 1336
TDK DALIAN CORPORATION—See TDK Corporation; *Int'l*, pg. 1336
TDK DE MEXICO S.A. DE C.V.—See TDK Corporation; *Int'l*, pg. 1337
TDK DO BRASIL IND. E COM. LTDA.—See TDK Corporation; *Int'l*, pg. 1336
TDK DO BRASIL SUZANO PLANT—See TDK Corporation; *Int'l*, pg. 1337
TDK ELECTRONICS CORPORATION—See TDK Corporation; *Int'l*, pg. 1336
TDK ELECTRONICS EUROPE GMBH—See TDK Corporation; *Int'l*, pg. 1336
TDK HONG KONG CO., LTD.—See TDK Corporation; *Int'l*, pg. 1337
TDK (MALAYSIA) SDN. BHD.—See TDK Corporation; *Int'l*, pg. 1337
TDK RECORDING MEDIA EUROPE S.A.—See TDK Corporation; *Int'l*, pg. 1337
TDK SINGAPORE (PTE.) LTD.—See TDK Corporation; *Int'l*, pg. 1337
TDK SYSTEMS DEVELOPMENT GROUP—See TDK Corporation; *Int'l*, pg. 1336
TDK TAIWAN CORP.—See TDK Corporation; *Int'l*, pg. 1337
TDK UK LTD.—See TDK Corporation; *Int'l*, pg. 1337
TDK U.S.A. CORPORATION—See TDK Corporation; *Int'l*, pg. 1336
TDN NYHETSBYRA A/S—See The A/S Norges Handels og Sjoefartstidende Group; *Int'l*, pg. 958
TDS COMPUTING SERVICES, INC.—See Telephone and Data Systems, Inc.; *U.S. Public*, pg. 1572
TDS TELECOMMUNICATIONS CORPORATION—See Telephone and Data Systems, Inc.; *U.S. Public*, pg. 1570
TDS VENTURES—See Time Warner Inc.; *U.S. Public*, pg. 1614
TDW BUILDING CORPORATION—See T.D. Williamson, Inc.; *U.S. Private*, pg. 1180
TDW DELAWARE, INC.—See T.D. Williamson, Inc.; *U.S. Private*, pg. 1180
TDW FOREIGN SALES CORP.—See T.D. Williamson, Inc.; *U.S. Private*, pg. 1180
TDW SERVICES, INC.—See T.D. Williamson, Inc.; *U.S. Private*, pg. 1180

TDW TRADING, INC.—See T.D. Williamson, Inc.; *U.S. Private*, pg. 1180
TE ENERGY SYSTEMS, INC.—See Thermo Electron Corporation; *U.S. Public*, pg. 1592
TEC CELLULAR—See Salient 3 Communications, Inc.; *U.S. Public*, pg. 1430
TEC ENERGY CORPORATION—See Thermo Electron Corporation; *U.S. Public*, pg. 1592
TEC INCORPORATED—See H.B. Fuller Company; *U.S. Public*, pg. 687
TECI—See Technip; *Int'l*, pg. 1361
TECO COAL CORP.—See TECO Energy, Inc.; *U.S. Public*, pg. 1565
TECO GENERATION INC.—See Thermo Electron Corporation; *U.S. Public*, pg. 1592
TECO TRANSPORT & TRADE CORP.—See TECO Energy, Inc.; *U.S. Public*, pg. 1565
TEL-CA-TELECOMMUNICAZIONI CALABRESE S.P.A.—See Telefonaktiebolaget LM Ericsson; *Int'l*, pg. 1370
TFA - TRANS-MARITIME FREIGHT AGENCIES B.V.—See Internatio-Muller N.V.; *Int'l*, pg. 682
TFM—See EMAP Plc; *Int'l*, pg. 452
TFP DATA SYSTEMS—See Taylor Corporation; *U.S. Private*, pg. 1070
TFX MARINE—See Teleflex Incorporated; *U.S. Public*, pg. 1570
TFX MEDICAL INC.—See Teleflex Incorporated; *U.S. Public*, pg. 1570
T.G. BATTERY CO. (CHINA) LTD.—See GP Batteries International Ltd.; *Int'l*, pg. 538
TGB TECHNISCHES GEMEINSCHAFTSBURO GMBH—See Mannesmann A.G.; *Int'l*, pg. 836
TGH HOLDINGS, LTD.—See Franklin Resources, Inc.; *U.S. Public*, pg. 680
TGI FRIDAY'S, INC.—See Carlson Companies, Inc.; *U.S. Private*, pg. 212
T.G.I. - TECNOLOGIA DEL GRUPO INI, S.A.—See SEPI; *Int'l*, pg. 1225
TGM DETECTORS INC.—See Morgan Crucible Co. Plc; *Int'l*, pg. 892
T.G.U.S. CORP.—See Taiwan Glass Industry Corp.; *Int'l*, pg. 1348
T H AGRICULTURE & NUTRITION CO. INC.—See Philips Electronics N.V.; *Int'l*, pg. 1055
TH COM—See DMB&B Communications; *U.S. Private*, pg. 305
TH PROPERTY, INC.—See Kvaerner a.s.a.; *Int'l*, pg. 774
THD, INC.—See Conseco Inc.; *U.S. Public*, pg. 433
T.H.E.—See John Menzies plc; *Int'l*, pg. 707
THF TECHNISCHER HANDEL FREUDENBERG BETEILIGUNGSGESELLSCHAFT MBH—See Freudenberg & Company; *Int'l*, pg. 506
THP UNITED ENTERPRISES—See Thyssen AG; *Int'l*, pg. 1389
TI-ACER INCORPORATED—See Acer Incorporated; *Int'l*, pg. 22
TI GROUP PLC; *Int'l*, pg. 1337
TI REYNOLDS RINGS LIMITED—See TI Group plc; *Int'l*, pg. 1338
TIC; *U.S. Private*, pg. 1064
T.I.C.-CITIZEN CO., LTD.—See Citizen Watch Company, Ltd.; *Int'l*, pg. 294
TIC GROUP LTD.—See Lennar Corporation; *U.S. Public*, pg. 989
TIC INVESTMENT CORP.—See TIC United Corporation; *U.S. Private*, pg. 1064
TIC UNITED CORPORATION; *U.S. Private*, pg. 1063
TIE SYSTEMS ARIZONA—See TIE/Communications, Inc.; *U.S. Private*, pg. 1085
TIE SYSTEMS ARKANSAS/GULFCOAST—See TIE/Communications, Inc.; *U.S. Private*, pg. 1085
TIE SYSTEMS-ATHENS—See TIE/Communications, Inc.; *U.S. Private*, pg. 1085
TIE SYSTEMS-CLEVELAND—See TIE/Communications, Inc.; *U.S. Private*, pg. 1085
TIE SYSTEMS COLORADO—See TIE/Communications, Inc.; *U.S. Private*, pg. 1085
TIE SYSTEMS-FARMINGTON HILLS—See TIE/Communications, Inc.; *U.S. Private*, pg. 1085
TIE SYSTEMS FLORIDA (NORTH)—See TIE/Communications, Inc.; *U.S. Private*, pg. 1085
TIE SYSTEMS GEORGIA—See TIE/Communications, Inc.; *U.S. Private*, pg. 1085
TIE SYSTEMS GULFCOAST—See TIE/Communications, Inc.; *U.S. Private*, pg. 1085
TIE SYSTEMS, INC. ILLINOIS—See TIE/Communications, Inc.; *U.S. Private*, pg. 1085
TIE SYSTEMS, INC. MINNESOTA—See TIE/Communications, Inc.; *U.S. Private*, pg. 1085
TIE SYSTEMS, INC. MISSISSIPPI VALLEY—See TIE/Communications, Inc.; *U.S. Private*, pg. 1085
TIE SYSTEMS, INC. NEW ENGLAND—See TIE/Communications, Inc.; *U.S. Private*, pg. 1085
TIE SYSTEMS, INC. NEW YORK—See TIE/Communications, Inc.; *U.S. Private*, pg. 1085
TIE SYSTEMS, INC. SOUTHEAST FLORIDA—See TIE/Communications, Inc.; *U.S. Private*, pg. 1085
TIE SYSTEMS-KALAMAZOO—See TIE/Communications, Inc.; *U.S. Private*, pg. 1085
TIE SYSTEMS-MANHATTAN—See TIE/Communications, Inc.; *U.S. Private*, pg. 1085
TIE SYSTEMS MID-ATLANTIC—See TIE/Communications, Inc.; *U.S. Private*, pg. 1085
TIE SYSTEMS MISSOURI—See TIE/Communications, Inc.; *U.S. Private*, pg. 1085
TIE SYSTEMS NEW MEXICO—See TIE/Communications, Inc.; *U.S. Private*, pg. 1085
TIE SYSTEMS NORTH CAROLINA—See TIE/Communications, Inc.; *U.S. Private*, pg. 1085
TIE SYSTEMS NORTHEAST—See TIE/Communications, Inc.; *U.S. Private*, pg. 1085
TIE SYSTEMS NORTHERN CALIFORNIA—See TIE/Communications, Inc.; *U.S. Private*, pg. 1085

TIE SYSTEMS NORTHWEST—See TIE/Communications, Inc.; *U.S. Private*, pg. 1085
TIE SYSTEMS OHIO—See TIE/Communications, Inc.; *U.S. Private*, pg. 1085
TIE SYSTEMS-OMAHA/DES MOINES—See TIE/Communications, Inc.; *U.S. Private*, pg. 1085
TIE SYSTEMS-PLAINVIEW—See TIE/Communications, Inc.; *U.S. Private*, pg. 1085
TIE SYSTEMS-PORTLAND—See TIE/Communications, Inc.; *U.S. Private*, pg. 1085
TIE SYSTEMS-SACRAMENTO—See TIE/Communications, Inc.; *U.S. Private*, pg. 1085
TIE SYSTEMS SOUTHERN CALIFORNIA—See TIE/Communications, Inc.; *U.S. Private*, pg. 1085
TIE SYSTEMS UTAH—See TIE/Communications, Inc.; *U.S. Private*, pg. 1085
T.I.E.C.-THE ITALIAN ECONOMIC CORPORATION—See Banca Nazionale del Lavoro SjA.; *Int'l*, pg. 136
TIFT SA—See Senior Engineering Group, plc.; *Int'l*, pg. 1223
TIG HOLDINGS, INC.; *U.S. Public*, pg. 1555
TIG INSURANCE CO.—See TIG Holdings, Inc.; *U.S. Public*, pg. 1556
TIG REINSURANCE—See TIG Holdings, Inc.; *U.S. Public*, pg. 1556
TIG TECHNOLOGIE INVESTITIONS GMBH & CO. KG—See Bayerische Vereinsbank Group; *Int'l*, pg. 180
TII CORP.—See TII Industries, Inc.; *U.S. Public*, pg. 1556
TII-DITEL—See TII Industries, Inc.; *U.S. Public*, pg. 1556
TII DOMINICANA INC.—See TII Industries, Inc.; *U.S. Public*, pg. 1556
TII ELECTRONICS, INC.—See TII Industries, Inc.; *U.S. Public*, pg. 1556
TII INDUSTRIES, INC.; *U.S. Public*, pg. 1556
TIM, INC.—See NationsBank Corporation; *U.S. Public*, pg. 1165
TIW—See Canadian Erectors Ltd.; *Int'l*, pg. 256
TIW STRESS RELIEVING—See Canadian Erectors Ltd.; *Int'l*, pg. 256
TIW WESTERN—See Canadian Erectors Ltd.; *Int'l*, pg. 256
TJ INTERNATIONAL, INC.; *U.S. Public*, pg. 1556
T.J.'S SPORTS GARDEN RESTAURANT—See Boury Enterprises; *U.S. Private*, pg. 162
THE TJX COMPANIES, INC.; *U.S. Public*, pg. 1556
TK GRAY—See PrimeSource Corporation; *U.S. Public*, pg. 1329
TKD, N.A.—See Ziebart International Corporation; *U.S. Private*, pg. 1205
T.K.G. INTERNATIONAL CORP.—See Takagi Chokoku Co., Ltd.; *Int'l*, pg. 1349
T.K.K. CO., LTD.—See Tekken Corporation; *Int'l*, pg. 1362
TKM LIMITED—See Aluminum Company of America; *U.S. Public*, pg. 62
TKT ENTERPRISE S.A.—See Deutsche Babcock AG; *Int'l*, pg. 400
TL SYSTEMS CORPORATION—See Robert Bosch GmbH; *Int'l*, pg. 205
TL VENTURES—See Safeguard Scientifics, Inc.; *U.S. Public*, pg. 1424
TLC—See Christiana Companies, Inc.; *U.S. Public*, pg. 352
TLC BEATRICE INTERNATIONAL HOLDINGS INC.; *U.S. Private*, pg. 1064
TLC GROUP, INC.—See Christiana Companies, Inc.; *U.S. Public*, pg. 352
TLP EAST—See Omnicom Group Inc.; *U.S. Public*, pg. 1224
TLPARTNERSHIP—See Omnicom Group Inc.; *U.S. Public*, pg. 1224
TLT-BABCOCK, INC.—See Deutsche Babcock AG; *Int'l*, pg. 401
TLT-ENGINEERING INDIA PVT. LTD.—See Deutsche Babcock AG; *Int'l*, pg. 401
TLT IBERPHONE—See Caja de Madrid Group; *Int'l*, pg. 252
TM CLAIMS SERVICE, INC.—See The Tokio Marine & Fire Insurance Company, Ltd.; *Int'l*, pg. 1392
TM FREIGHT BROKERS—See Tri-State Motor Transit Co.; *U.S. Private*, pg. 1101
TM MANAGEMENT SERVICES LIMITED—See The Tokio Marine & Fire Insurance Company, Ltd.; *Int'l*, pg. 1392
TMC—See WPP Group plc; *Int'l*, pg. 1482
TMC COMPANY LTD.—See Oy Nokia Ab/Nokia Group; *Int'l*, pg. 952
TMD CARAT ADVERTISING LIMITED; *Int'l*, pg. 1342
TMD DIRECT—See TMD Carat Advertising Limited; *Int'l*, pg. 1342
TMG CARIBBEAN, INC.—See Musicland Group Inc.; *U.S. Public*, pg. 1142
TMG UK DELAWARE, INC.—See Musicland Group Inc.; *U.S. Public*, pg. 1142
TMI COMMUNICATIONS INC.—See BCE Inc.; *Int'l*, pg. 116
TMK/UNITED OIL MANAGEMENT COMPANY—See Torchmark Corporation; *U.S. Public*, pg. 1623
TML METROLOGY CENTRE FOR BEDFORD—See Brown & Sharpe Manufacturing Company; *U.S. Public*, pg. 260
TML METROLOGY CENTRE FOR SCOTLAND—See Brown & Sharpe Manufacturing Company; *U.S. Public*, pg. 260
TML REED EXHIBITIONS (PTY.) LTD.-AFRICA—See Reed Elsevier plc; *Int'l*, pg. 1097
TMO HOLDINGS OF CANADA, LTD.—See Consorcio G. Grupo Dina, S.A. de C.V.; *Int'l*, pg. 326
TMP WORLDWIDE/DIRECT MARKETING SERVICES—See TMP Worldwide; *U.S. Private*, pg. 1064
TMP WORLDWIDE, INC.; *U.S. Private*, pg. 1064
TMP WORLDWIDE, INC.—See TMP Worldwide, Inc.; *U.S. Private*, pg. 1064
TMP WORLDWIDE/INTERACTIVE DIVISION—See TMP Worldwide, Inc.; *U.S. Private*, pg. 1065
TMP WORLDWIDE-INTERACTIVE/MEDSEARCH—See TMP Worldwide, Inc.; *U.S. Private*, pg. 1065
TMP WORLDWIDE LTD.—See TMP Worldwide, Inc.; *U.S. Private*, pg. 1065
TMP WORLDWIDE PTY LIMITED; *Int'l*, pg. 1342

TMP WORLDWIDE PTY LTD.—See TMP Worldwide Pty Limited; *Int'l*, pg. 1342
TMP WORLDWIDE RECRUITMENT DIVISION—See TMP Worldwide; *U.S. Private*, pg. 1065
TMP WORLDWIDE/RECRUITMENT DIVISION—See TMP Worldwide; *U.S. Private*, pg. 1065
TN ENTERTAINMENT—See True North Communications Inc.; *U.S. Public*, pg. 1641
TN MEDIA—See True North Communications Inc.; *U.S. Public*, pg. 1641
TN MEDIA INC.—See True North Communications Inc.; *U.S. Public*, pg. 1641
TN TECHNOLOGIES—See Thermo Electron Corporation; *U.S. Public*, pg. 1593
TN TECHNOLOGIES INC.—See True North Communications Inc.; *U.S. Public*, pg. 1641
TNE ADVISORS, INC.—See Metropolitan Life Insurance Co.; *U.S. Private*, pg. 738
TNE FUNDING CORPORATION—See Metropolitan Life Insurance Co.; *U.S. Private*, pg. 738
TNE INFORMATION SERVICES—See Metropolitan Life Insurance Co.; *U.S. Private*, pg. 738
TNE INVESTMENT SERVICES CORP.—See Metropolitan Life Insurance Co.; *U.S. Private*, pg. 737
TNI, INC.—See Mattel, Inc.; *U.S. Public*, pg. 1058
TNL FLIGHT SERVICES, INC.—See Trimble Navigation Limited; *U.S. Public*, pg. 1638
TNP ENTERPRISES, INC.; *U.S. Public*, pg. 1557
TNP ONE—See TNP Enterprises, Inc.; *U.S. Public*, pg. 1557
TNP OPERATING COMPANY—See TNP Enterprises, Inc.; *U.S. Public*, pg. 1557
TNT AUSTRALIA PTY. LIMITED—See TNT Limited; *Int'l*, pg. 1343
TNT HOLDING GMBH—See TNT Limited; *Int'l*, pg. 1343
TNT LIMITED; *Int'l*, pg. 1342
TNT LOGISTICS—See TNT Limited; *Int'l*, pg. 1343
TNT LOGISTICS ASIA PTE LTD—See TNT Limited; *Int'l*, pg. 1343
TNT LOGISTICS EUROPE—See TNT Limited; *Int'l*, pg. 1343
TNT LOGISTICS NORTH AMERICA—See TNT Limited; *Int'l*, pg. 1343
TNT LOGISTICS UK—See TNT Limited; *Int'l*, pg. 1343
TNT NEW ZEALAND LIMITED—See TNT Limited; *Int'l*, pg. 1343
TNT NORTH AMERICA AND CANADA INC.—See TNT Limited; *Int'l*, pg. 1343
TNT PARTICIPACOES LTDA.—See TNT Limited; *Int'l*, pg. 1343
TNT TRACO S.P.A.—See TNT Limited; *Int'l*, pg. 1343
TNT U.K. LIMITED—See TNT Limited; *Int'l*, pg. 1343
**TNT VACATIONS—See TNT Limited; *U.S. Public*, pg. 1065
TNTI—See True North Communications Inc.; *U.S. Public*, pg. 1642
T O PLASTICS, INC.; *U.S. Private*, pg. 1065
TOA-UNI CHEMICALS LTD.—See Crompton & Knowles Corporation; *U.S. Public*, pg. 460
TP MANIPULATIONS—See Senior Engineering Group, plc.; *Int'l*, pg. 1222
TPA LATIN AMERICA—See Toshiba Corporation; *Int'l*, pg. 1406
TPC CORPORATION—See PacifiCorp; *U.S. Public*, pg. 1252
TPC WIRE & CABLE—See Premier Farnell plc; *Int'l*, pg. 1068
TPLM—See Groupe Casino; *Int'l*, pg. 563
TPS—See Royal Nedlloyd Group N.V.; *Int'l*, pg. 1145
TPS PEYRARD—See Technip; *Int'l*, pg. 1360
TPS PUBLIC RELATIONS LTD.—See Shandwick International Plc; *Int'l*, pg. 1226
TPS TECHNOLOGIES INC.—See Thermo Electron Corporation; *U.S. Public*, pg. 1594
T.P.T. LTD.—See Sonoco Products Company; *U.S. Public*, pg. 1487
TPT TRANSPORTATION COMPANY—See Kirby Corporation; *U.S. Public*, pg. 962
TQM PIPELINE PARTNERSHIP—See Gaz Metropolitain & Company; *Int'l*, pg. 541
TR-METRO CHEM, INC.—See Preussag AG; *Int'l*, pg. 1071
TR NAVIGATION CORPORATION—See Trimble Navigation Limited; *U.S. Public*, pg. 1638
TRB NATIONAL SYSTEMS, INC.—See American Waste Services, Inc.; *U.S. Public*, pg. 94
TRC COMPANIES, INC.; *U.S. Public*, pg. 1557
TRC ENVIRONMENTAL SOLUTIONS, INC.—See TRC Companies, Inc.; *U.S. Public*, pg. 1558
TRC HOLDING CO. OF WASHINGTON, D.C.—See The Rouse Company; *U.S. Public*, pg. 1409
T.R.C./HONDURAS, S.A. DE C.V.—See Technology Research Corporation; *U.S. Public*, pg. 1564
TRC MARIAH ASSOCIATES, INC.—See TRC Companies, Inc.; *U.S. Public*, pg. 1558
TRI INTERNATIONAL CO.—See Tootsie Roll Industries, Inc.; *U.S. Public*, pg. 1621
TRI REALTY, INC.—See Case Corporation; *U.S. Public*, pg. 312
TRL S.A.—See Borden, Inc.; *U.S. Private*, pg. 160
TRM COPY CENTERS CORPORATION; *U.S. Public*, pg. 1558
TRMI HOLDINGS INC.—See Texaco Inc.; *U.S. Public*, pg. 1583
TRP-PROFILE UND BAUELEMENTE GMBH—See Fried. Krupp AG; *Int'l*, pg. 508
TRR CARRIERS, INC.—See Wakefern Food Corporation; *U.S. Private*, pg. 1146
TRT HOLDINGS INC.; *U.S. Private*, pg. 1065
TRT LUCENT TECHNOLOGIES—See Lucent Technologies Inc.; *U.S. Public*, pg. 1019
TRW AUTOMOTIVE ELECTRONICS GROUP—See TRW Inc.; *U.S. Public*, pg. 1558
TRW INC.; *U.S. Public*, pg. 1558
TRW INFORMATION SYSTEMS & SERVICES—See The Great Universal Stores P.L.C.; *Int'l*, pg. 557

TRW OCCUPANT RESTRAINTS SYSTEMS—See TRW Inc.; *U.S. Public*, pg. 1558
TRW SPACE & ELECTRONICS GROUP—See TRW Inc.; *U.S. Public*, pg. 1558
TRW STEERING, SUSPENSION & ENGINE GROUP—See TRW Inc.; *U.S. Public*, pg. 1558
TRW SYSTEMS INTEGRATION GROUP—See TRW Inc.; *U.S. Public*, pg. 1558
TRW VEHICLE SAFETY SYSTEMS INC.—See TRW Inc.; *U.S. Public*, pg. 1559
TS CAPITAL CORP.—See The Troy Savings Bank; *U.S. Private*, pg. 1106
TS PUBLICATIONS (FLORIDA), INC.—See Sun Media Corporation; *Int'l*, pg. 1320
T.S. TELEFONICA SISTEMAS, S.A.—See Telefonica de Espana, S.A.; *Int'l*, pg. 1372
TSB BANK SCOTLAND PLC—See Lloyds TSB Group PLC; *Int'l*, pg. 813
TSB HILL SAMUEL BANK HOLDING CO PLC—See Lloyds TSB Group PLC; *Int'l*, pg. 813
TSB TRUST CO. LTD.—See Lloyds TSB Group PLC; *Int'l*, pg. 813
TSC FILM DISTRIBUTION—See TSC Shannock Corporation; *Int'l*, pg. 1343
TSC SHANNOCK CORPORATION; *Int'l*, pg. 1343
TSC SHANNOCK CORPORATION—See TSC Shannock Corporation; *Int'l*, pg. 1343
TSE LEASING CO.—See I. Spiewak & Sons, Inc.; *U.S. Private*, pg. 1025
TSI AKTIEBOLAG—See TSI Incorporated; *U.S. Public*, pg. 1559
TSI ARGUS RESEARCH LABORATORIES & CENTER FOR PHOTOBIOLOGY—See Genzyme Corporation; *U.S. Public*, pg. 733
TSI CORPORATION—See Genzyme Corporation; *U.S. Public*, pg. 733
TSI FRANCE INC.—See TSI Incorporated; *U.S. Public*, pg. 1559
TSI GMBH—See TSI Incorporated; *U.S. Public*, pg. 1559
TSI HOLDINGS, INC.; *U.S. Private*, pg. 1066
TSI INCORPORATED; *U.S. Public*, pg. 1559
TSI MASON LABORATORIES—See Genzyme Corporation; *U.S. Public*, pg. 733
TSI WASHINGTON LABORATORIES—See Genzyme Corporation; *U.S. Public*, pg. 733
TSL—See Brite Voice Systems, Inc.; *U.S. Public*, pg. 257
TSL GROUP PLC—See Saint-Gobain; *Int'l*, pg. 1176
TSM (TELECOM SYSTEMES MOBILES)—See France Telecom; *Int'l*, pg. 503
TSN COMMUNICATIONS; *Int'l*, pg. 1343
TSO (TELEPHONE DU SUD-OUEST)—See Lagardere Groupe; *Int'l*, pg. 794
TSP INC.—See Enso Oyj; *Int'l*, pg. 457
TSP NEWSPAPERS, INC.—See The New York Times Company; *U.S. Public*, pg. 1175
TSR CONSULTING SERVICES, INC.—See TSR Inc.; *U.S. Public*, pg. 1559
TSR, INC.—See Wizards of the Coast; *U.S. Private*, pg. 1185
TSR INC.; *U.S. Public*, pg. 1559
TST/IMPRESO, INC.; *U.S. Public*, pg. 1066
TT GROUP PLC; *Int'l*, pg. 1344
TTA/NEWPORT, INC.—See Ted Thomas Associates Inc. Advertising; *U.S. Public*, pg. 1083
TTC ILLINOIS INC.; *U.S. Private*, pg. 1066
TTS CORPORATION—See Condere Corporation; *U.S. Private*, pg. 262
TTS INTERNATIONAL AS—See Charter plc; *Int'l*, pg. 283
TTX CO.; *U.S. Private*, pg. 1066
TU ELECTRIC—See Texas Utilities Company; *U.S. Public*, pg. 1588
TU-KA CELLULAR TOKYO INC.—See Nissan Motor Co., Ltd.; *Int'l*, pg. 944
TU SERVICES—See Texas Utilities Company; *U.S. Public*, pg. 1588
TUCO ANIMAL HEALTH—See Pharmacia & Upjohn, Inc.; *Int'l*, pg. 1048
T.V. & VIDEO SYSTEMS GROUP—See Sharp Corporation; *Int'l*, pg. 1228
TV GUIDE MAGAZINE—See The News Corporation Limited; *Int'l*, pg. 925
TV HOST INC.; *U.S. Private*, pg. 1066
TV KOHLENSAURE TECHNIK—See Linde AG; *Int'l*, pg. 811
T.V. OVERSEAS, S.R.L.—See Sony Corporation; *Int'l*, pg. 1282
T.V. TIMES—See Hollinger Inc.; *Int'l*, pg. 632
TVESCO, INC.; *U.S. Private*, pg. 1066
TVS BERG LTD.—See Berg Electronics; *U.S. Public*, pg. 213
TVS CHERRY PRIVATE LIMITED—See Cherry Electrical Products Corporation; *U.S. Public*, pg. 346
TVT—See Harris Corporation; *U.S. Public*, pg. 791
TVX BOHEMIA DULNI A.S.—See TVX Gold Inc.; *Int'l*, pg. 1345
TVX GOLD INC.; *Int'l*, pg. 1345
TVX HELLAS A.E.—See TVX Gold Inc.; *Int'l*, pg. 1345
TVX MINERA DE CHILE—See TVX Gold Inc.; *Int'l*, pg. 1345
TVX MINERA DEL PERU S.A.—See TVX Gold Inc.; *Int'l*, pg. 1345
TWB—See Worthington Industries, Inc.; *U.S. Public*, pg. 1780
TWC CABLE PARTNERS—See Cox Communications, Inc.; *U.S. Public*, pg. 455
TWC OF FLORIDA, INCORPORATED—See The West Company, Incorporated; *U.S. Public*, pg. 1755
TWD BALTIMORE—See Bindley Western Industries, Inc.; *U.S. Public*, pg. 229
TWI INTERNATIONAL, INC.—See Waxman Industries, Inc.; *U.S. Public*, pg. 1749
TWI INTERNATIONAL TAIWAN, INC.—See Waxman Industries, Inc.; *U.S. Public*, pg. 1749

TWP SENDIRIAN BERHAD—See Dai Nippon Printing Co., Ltd.; *Int'l*, pg. 363
TXBASE SYSTEMS, INC.—See American Software, Inc.; *U.S. Public*, pg. 91
TXEN—See Nichols Research Corporation; *U.S. Public*, pg. 1182
TXI AGGREGATE TRANSPORTATION COMPANY—See Texas Industries, Inc.; *U.S. Public*, pg. 1585
TXI AVIATION, INC.—See Texas Industries, Inc.; *U.S. Public*, pg. 1585
TXI CEMENT COMPANY—See Texas Industries, Inc.; *U.S. Public*, pg. 1585
TXI STRUCTURAL PRODUCTS, INC.—See Texas Industries, Inc.; *U.S. Public*, pg. 1585
TXI TRANSPORTATION COMPANY—See Texas Industries, Inc.; *U.S. Public*, pg. 1585
TYK CORPORATION; *Int'l*, pg. 1345
TYK REFRACTORIES CO.—See TYK Corporation; *Int'l*, pg. 1345
TA CHING MOTORS CO., LTD.—See Fuji Heavy Industries, Ltd.; *Int'l*, pg. 523
TAB ELECTRIC SUPPLY CO. INC.—See Rumsey Electric Company; *U.S. Private*, pg. 951
TAB PRODUCTS CO.; *U.S. Public*, pg. 1559
TAB PRODUCTS EUROPA B.V.—See Tab Products Co.; *U.S. Public*, pg. 1559
TAB PRODUCTS OF CANADA, LTD.—See Tab Products Co.; *U.S. Public*, pg. 1559
TAB PRODUCTS PTY. LTD.—See Tab Products Co.; *U.S. Public*, pg. 1559
TAB SALES CORP. (INTERNATIONAL)—See Tab Products Co.; *U.S. Public*, pg. 1559
TABACALERA HONDURENVA SA—See B.A.T Industries P.L.C.; *Int'l*, pg. 111
TABACALERA ISTMENA SA—See B.A.T Industries P.L.C.; *Int'l*, pg. 111
TABACALERA NICARAGUENSE S.A.—See B.A.T Industries P.L.C.; *Int'l*, pg. 111
TABACALERA, S.A.; *Int'l*, pg. 1345
TABACOS BRASILEIROS, LTDA.—See Universal Corporation; *U.S. Public*, pg. 1695
TABAPACK, S.A.—See Tabacalera, S.A.; *Int'l*, pg. 1346
TABAPRESS, S.A.—See Tang Industries Inc.; *U.S. Private*, pg. 1068
TABER METALS, INC.—See Tang Industries Inc.; *U.S. Private*, pg. 1068
TABLE PRIDE, INC.—See Flowers Industries, Inc.; *U.S. Public*, pg. 658
TABLEAU FINE ARTS MAGAZINE BV—See VNU Verenigde Nederlandse Uitgeversbedrijven B.V.; *Int'l*, pg. 1445
TABLEX, S.A. DE C.V.; *Int'l*, pg. 1346
TABOR MACHINE CO.—See Elgin National Industries, Inc.; *U.S. Private*, pg. 371
TABUCHI ELECTRIC CO., LTD.; *Int'l*, pg. 1346
TABUCHI ELECTRIC COMPANY OF AMERICA—See Tabuchi Electric Co., Ltd.; *Int'l*, pg. 1346
TABUCHI ELECTRIC DE MEXICO S.A. DE C.V.—See Tabuchi Electric Co., Ltd.; *Int'l*, pg. 1346
TABUCHI ELECTRIC U.K. LTD.—See Tabuchi Electric Co., Ltd.; *Int'l*, pg. 1346
TACA INTERNATIONAL AIRLINES, S. A.; *Int'l*, pg. 1346
TACHI-S CO., LTD.—See Nissan Motor Co., Ltd.; *Int'l*, pg. 944
TACO ALOHA, INC.—See Jardine Matheson Holdings Limited; *Int'l*, pg. 704
TACO BELL CORP.—See Tricon Global Restaurants, Inc.; *U.S. Public*, pg. 1637
TACO CABANA; *U.S. Public*, pg. 1559
TACO INCORPORATED; *U.S. Private*, pg. 1066
TACO JOHN'S INTERNATIONAL, INC.; *U.S. Private*, pg. 1066
TACONY CORPORATION; *U.S. Private*, pg. 1066
TACT HOLDING; *U.S. Private*, pg. 1067
TACTAIR FLUID CONTROLS CORP.—See Young & Franklin, Inc.; *U.S. Private*, pg. 1196
TACTECH, INC.—See Zing Technologies, Inc.; *U.S. Public*, pg. 1792
TACTYL TECHNOLOGIES, INC.—See Safeskin Corporation; *U.S. Public*, pg. 1425
TAD DAIHO INC.—See Daiko Advertising, Inc.; *Int'l*, pg. 366
TAETEL, S.L.—See Telefonica de Espana, S.A.; *Int'l*, pg. 1371
TAFA INCORPORATED—See Illinois Tool Works Inc.; *U.S. Public*, pg. 866
TAFT GROUP—See The Thomson Corporation; *U.S. Public*, pg. 1601
TAGENTREPRISE MIDT A/S—See Icopal a/s; *Int'l*, pg. 659
TAGENTREPRISE NORD A/S—See Icopal a/s; *Int'l*, pg. 659
TAGENTREPRISE OST A/S—See Icopal a/s; *Int'l*, pg. 659
TAGENTREPRISE SYD OG FYN A/S—See Icopal a/s; *Int'l*, pg. 659
TAGUS-DRAGAGENS LDA.—See Ballast Nedam NV; *Int'l*, pg. 135
LEE KIM TAH HOLDINGS LTD.; *Int'l*, pg. 1346
TAHO ENGINEERING CO., LTD.—See The Furukawa Electric Co., Ltd.; *Int'l*, pg. 531
TAI-IL MEDIA CO.; *Int'l*, pg. 1347
TAI TIEN PHARMACEUTICALS CO., LTD.—See Tanabe Seiyaku Co., Ltd.; *Int'l*, pg. 1354
TAIKO ELECTRIC WORK, LTD.—See Oki Electric Industry Company, Ltd.; *Int'l*, pg. 999
TAILLEUR INDUSTRIE—See GEODIS; *Int'l*, pg. 549
TAILOR STEEL N.V.—See Arbed S.A.; *Int'l*, pg. 79
TAILORED SOLUTIONS—See The Thomson Corporation; *U.S. Public*, pg. 1602
TAINAN SPINNING CO., LTD.; *Int'l*, pg. 1347
TAINIONKOSKI PAPER MILL—See Enso Oyj; *Int'l*, pg. 457
TAIPEI TAKASHIMAYA INTERNATIONAL CO., LTD.—See Takashimaya Company, Limited; *Int'l*, pg. 1350
TAISEI AMERICA CAPITAL FUNDING CORP.—See Taisei Corporation; *Int'l*, pg. 1347

TAISEI AMERICA CORP.—See Taisei Corporation; *Int'l*, pg. 1347
TAISEI BUILDING MAINTENANCE SERVICE CO., LTD.—See Nippon Life Insurance Co.; *Int'l*, pg. 935
TAISEI CONSTRUCTION CORP.—See Taisei Corporation; *Int'l*, pg. 1347
TAISEI CORPORATION; *Int'l*, pg. 1347
TAISEI (DEUTSCHELAND) GMBH—See Taisei Corporation; *Int'l*, pg. 1347
TAISEI EUROPE, LTD.—See Taisei Corporation; *Int'l*, pg. 1347
TAISEI HAWAII CORP.—See Taisei Corporation; *Int'l*, pg. 1347
TAISEI HOLLAND B.V.—See Taisei Corporation; *Int'l*, pg. 1347
TAISEI (MALAYSIA) SDN. BHD.—See Taisei Corporation; *Int'l*, pg. 1347
TAISEI PROPERTIES (HONG KONG) LTD.—See Taisei Corporation; *Int'l*, pg. 1347
TAISEI ROTEC CORP.—See Taisei Corporation; *Int'l*, pg. 1347
TAISEI SAUDI ARABIA CO., LTD.—See Taisei Corporation; *Int'l*, pg. 1347
TAISEI (THAILAND) CO., LTD.—See Taisei Corporation; *Int'l*, pg. 1347
TAISEI (WEST AFRICA) LTD.—See Taisei Corporation; *Int'l*, pg. 1347
TAISHO PHARMACEUTICAL CALIFORNIA INC.—See Taisho Pharmaceutical Co., Ltd.; *Int'l*, pg. 1348
TAISHO PHARMACEUTICAL CO., LTD.; *Int'l*, pg. 1348
TAISIL ELECTRONIC MATERIALS CORPORATION—See China Steel Corporation; *Int'l*, pg. 286
TAISO COMMERCE INC.—See Ajinomoto Company Inc.; *Int'l*, pg. 41
TAITO CO., LTD.—See Mitsui & Co., Ltd.; *Int'l*, pg. 878
TAITTINGER; *Int'l*, pg. 1348
TAIVAN CORP.—See Taisei Corporation; *Int'l*, pg. 1347
TAIWAN AUTOGALSS INDUSTRIES CORP.—See Taiwan Glass Industry Corp.; *Int'l*, pg. 1348
TAIWAN BRANCH OFFICE—See Mitsubishi Chemical Corporation; *Int'l*, pg. 871
TAIWAN BROTHER INDUSTRIES, LTD.—See Brother Industries, Ltd.; *Int'l*, pg. 230
TAIWAN GLASS INDUSTRY CORP.; *Int'l*, pg. 1348
TAIWAN GREEN CROSS CO. LTD.—See The Green Cross Corporation; *Int'l*, pg. 558
TAIWAN HERCULES CHEMICALS, INC.—See Hercules Incorporated; *U.S. Public*, pg. 811
TAIWAN HOKURIKU CO., LTD.—See Hokuriku Electric Industry Co., Ltd.; *Int'l*, pg. 628
TAIWAN JSP CHEMICAL CO., LTD., FACTORY—See Ajinomoto Company Inc.; *Int'l*, pg. 41
TAIWAN KANSAI PAINT CO., LTD.—See Kansai Paint Co., Ltd.; *Int'l*, pg. 723
TAIWAN KUMAGAI CO., LTD.—See Kumagai Gumi Co., Ltd.; *Int'l*, pg. 764
TAIWAN MARKETING & TRANSPORTATION DIV.—See Chinese Petroleum Corporation; *Int'l*, pg. 286
TAIWAN MEIJI CO., LTD.—See Meiji Seika Kaisha, Ltd.; *Int'l*, pg. 856
TAIWAN MORINAGA NUTRITIONAL FOODS INC.—See Morinaga Milk Industry Co., Ltd.; *Int'l*, pg. 895
TAIWAN NSK PRECISION CO.—See NSK Ltd.; *Int'l*, pg. 904
TAIWAN NALCO CHEMICAL CO LTD.—See Nalco Chemical Company; *U.S. Public*, pg. 1151
TAIWAN NISSEKI CO., LTD.—See Nippon Oil Company, Limited (NiSSEKI); *Int'l*, pg. 937
TAIWAN OBAYASHI CORPORATION—See Obayashi Corporation; *Int'l*, pg. 996
TAIWAN OTSUKA PHARMACEUTICAL CO., LTD.—See Otsuka Pharmaceutical Co., Ltd.; *Int'l*, pg. 1014
TAIWAN PETROLEUM EXPLORATION DIVISION—See Chinese Petroleum Corporation; *Int'l*, pg. 286
TAIWAN POWER COMPANY; *Int'l*, pg. 1348
TAIWAN SCOTT PAPER CORP.—See Kimberly-Clark Corporation; *U.S. Public*, pg. 960
TAIWAN SHIONOGI & CO., LTD.—See Shionogi & Co., Ltd.; *Int'l*, pg. 1235
TAIWAN TAKAGI CHOKOKU CO., LTD.—See Takagi Chokoku Co., Ltd.; *Int'l*, pg. 1349
TAIWAN TAKENAKA CO., LTD.—See Takenaka Corporation; *Int'l*, pg. 1351
TAIWAN TAKENAKA ENGINEERING CO., LTD.—See Takenaka Corporation; *Int'l*, pg. 1351
TAIWAN TANABE SEIYAKU CO., LTD.—See Tanabe Seiyaku Co., Ltd.; *Int'l*, pg. 1354
TAIWAN TOTO CO., LTD.—See Toto Ltd.; *Int'l*, pg. 1410
TAIWAN VILENE NONWOVENS COMP. LTD.—See Freudenberg & Company; *Int'l*, pg. 507
TAIWAN WACOAL CO., LTD.—See Wacoal Corporation; *Int'l*, pg. 1484
TAIWAN YAMANOUCHI PHARMACEUTICAL CO., LTD.—See Yamanouchi Pharmaceutical Co. Ltd.; *Int'l*, pg. 1519
TAIWAN YAMAZAKI CO., LTD.—See Yamazaki Baking Co., Ltd.; *Int'l*, pg. 1519
TAIYO ASSET MANAGEMENT OF AMERICA, INC.—See The Taiyo Mutual Life Insurance Co.; *Int'l*, pg. 1349
TAIYO CHEMICAL INDUSTRY CO., LTD.—See Nissho Iwai Corporation; *Int'l*, pg. 947
TAIYO INVESTMENT (JERSEY), LTD.—See The Taiyo Mutual Life Insurance Co.; *Int'l*, pg. 1349
TAIYO INVESTMENT OF CAYMAN INC.—See The Taiyo Mutual Life Insurance Co.; *Int'l*, pg. 1349
TAIYO KOGYO CORPORATION; *Int'l*, pg. 1348
TAIYO LIFE INTERNATIONAL (H.K.), LTD.—See The Taiyo Mutual Life Insurance Co.; *Int'l*, pg. 1349
TAIYO LIFE INTERNATIONAL (U.K.), LTD.—See The Taiyo Mutual Life Insurance Co.; *Int'l*, pg. 1349
TAIYO LIFE INVESTMENT (BAHAMAS), LTD.—See The Taiyo Mutual Life Insurance Co.; *Int'l*, pg. 1349
TAIYO LIFE INVESTMENT LUXEMBOURG, S.A.—See The Taiyo Mutual Life Insurance Co.; *Int'l*, pg. 1349

TAIYO LIFE REALTY OF AMERICA, INC.—See The Taiyo Mutual Life Insurance Co.; *Int'l*, pg. 1349
THE TAIYO MUTUAL LIFE INSURANCE CO.; *Int'l*, pg. 1348
TAIYO SHOKUHIN CO., LTD.—See Meiji Seika Kaisha, Ltd.; *Int'l*, pg. 855
TAIYO YUDEN COMPANY LTD.; *Int'l*, pg. 1349
TAJ INTERNATIONAL HOTELS; *U.S. Private*, pg. 1067
TAKAGI CHOKOKU CO., LTD.; *Int'l*, pg. 1349
TAKAGI CHOKOKU CO., LTD.-HAMAMATSU FACTORY—See Takagi Chokoku Co., Ltd.; *Int'l*, pg. 1349
TAKAHASHI WORKS U.S.A., INC.—See Komatsu Ltd.; *Int'l*, pg. 744
TAKAMATSU ORIKOMI CENTER, LTD.—See Daiko Advertising, Inc.; *Int'l*, pg. 366
TAKANO CO., LTD.—See NHK Spring Co., Ltd.; *Int'l*, pg. 902
TAKARA BELMONT CO., LTD.; *Int'l*, pg. 1349
TAKARA BELMONT U.S.A., INC.—See Takara Belmont Co., Ltd.; *Int'l*, pg. 1349
TAKARA STANDARD CO., LTD.—See Takara Belmont Co., Ltd.; *Int'l*, pg. 1349
TAKASHIMAYA AUSTRALIA PTY., LTD.—See Takashimaya Company, Limited; *Int'l*, pg. 1350
TAKASHIMAYA (CALIFORNIA), INC.—See Takashimaya Company, Limited; *Int'l*, pg. 1349
TAKASHIMAYA COMPANY, LIMITED; *Int'l*, pg. 1349
TAKASHIMAYA ENTERPRISES, INC. (SHIRO OF JAPAN)—See Takashimaya Company, Limited; *Int'l*, pg. 1350
TAKASHIMAYA FIFTH AVENUE CORPORATION—See Takashimaya Company, Limited; *Int'l*, pg. 1350
TAKASHIMAYA HONG KONG ENTERPRISES LIMITED—See Takashimaya Company, Limited; *Int'l*, pg. 1350
TAKASHIMAYA INTERNATIONAL FINANCE B.V.—See Takashimaya Company, Limited; *Int'l*, pg. 1350
TAKASHIMAYA (ITALIA) S.P.A.—See Takashimaya Company, Limited; *Int'l*, pg. 1350
TAKASHIMAYA MADISON AVENUE CORPORATION—See Takashimaya Company, Limited; *Int'l*, pg. 1350
TAKASHIMAYA NEW YORK, INC.—See Takashimaya Company, Limited; *Int'l*, pg. 1350
TAKASHIMAYA NIPPATSU KOGYO CO., LTD.—See NHK Spring Co., Ltd.; *Int'l*, pg. 902
TAKASHIMAYA RETAILING AUSTRALIA PTY., LTD.—See Takashimaya Company, Limited; *Int'l*, pg. 1350
TAKASHIMAYA (SINGAPORE) LTD.—See Takashimaya Company, Limited; *Int'l*, pg. 1350
TAKASHIMAYA (THAILAND) CO., LTD.—See Takashimaya Company, Limited; *Int'l*, pg. 1350
TAKASHIMAYA (UK) LTD.—See Takashimaya Company, Limited; *Int'l*, pg. 1350
TAKATTA INC.—See Highland Industries Inc.; *U.S. Private*, pg. 528
TAKEDA AMERICA, INC.—See Takeda Chemical Industries, Ltd.; *Int'l*, pg. 1350
TAKEDA BADISCHE URETHANE INDUSTRIES LTD.—See BASF AG; *Int'l*, pg. 109
TAKEDA CHEMICAL INDUSTRIES, LTD.; *Int'l*, pg. 1350
TAKEDA CHEMICAL INDUSTRIES (TAIWAN), LTD.—See Takeda Chemical Industries, Ltd.; *Int'l*, pg. 1350
TAKEDA CHEMICAL PRODUCTS USA, INC.—See Takeda Chemical Industries, Ltd.; *Int'l*, pg. 1350
TAKEDA CHEMIE THAI CO., LTD.—See Takeda Chemical Industries, Ltd.; *Int'l*, pg. 1350
TAKEDA EUROPE GMBH—See Takeda Chemical Industries, Ltd.; *Int'l*, pg. 1350
TAKEDA EUROPE RESEARCH & DEVELOPMENT CENTRE GMBH—See Takeda Chemical Industries, Ltd.; *Int'l*, pg. 1350
TAKEDA FINANCE USA, INC.—See Takeda Chemical Industries, Ltd.; *Int'l*, pg. 1350
TAKEDA FOOD PRODUCTS, LTD.—See Takeda Chemical Industries, Ltd.; *Int'l*, pg. 1350
TAKEDA IMC CHEMICAL LTD.—See Takeda Chemical Industries, Ltd.; *Int'l*, pg. 1351
P.T. TAKEDA INDONESIA—See Takeda Chemical Industries, Ltd.; *Int'l*, pg. 1351
TAKEDA ITALIA FARMACEUTICI S.P.A.—See Takeda Chemical Industries, Ltd.; *Int'l*, pg. 1351
TAKEDA KAGAKU SHIRYO CO., LTD.—See Takeda Chemical Industries, Ltd.; *Int'l*, pg. 1350
TAKEDA PHARMA GMBH—See Takeda Chemical Industries, Ltd.; *Int'l*, pg. 1351
TAKEDA (THAILAND), LTD.—See Takeda Chemical Industries, Ltd.; *Int'l*, pg. 1351
TAKEDA USA INC.—See Takeda Chemical Industries, Ltd.; *Int'l*, pg. 1350
TAKEDA VITAMIN & FOOD ASIA PTE. LTD.—See Takeda Chemical Industries, Ltd.; *Int'l*, pg. 1351
TAKEFIVE SOFTWARE, GMBH—See Integrated Systems, Inc.; *U.S. Public*, pg. 886
TAKENAKA BELGIUM S.A.—See Takenaka Corporation; *Int'l*, pg. 1351
TAKENAKA BELGIUM S.A. - FRANCE BRANCH—See Takenaka Corporation; *Int'l*, pg. 1351
TAKENAKA CIVIL ENGINEERING & CONSTRUCTION CO., LTD.—See Takenaka Corporation; *Int'l*, pg. 1351
TAKENAKA CORPORATION; *Int'l*, pg. 1351
TAKENAKA CORPORATION - HIROSHIMA BRANCH—See Takenaka Corporation; *Int'l*, pg. 1351
TAKENAKA CORPORATION - HOKKAIDO BRANCH—See Takenaka Corporation; *Int'l*, pg. 1351
TAKENAKA CORPORATION - KYUSYU BRANCH—See Takenaka Corporation; *Int'l*, pg. 1351
TAKENAKA CORPORATION - NAGOYA BRANCH—See Takenaka Corporation; *Int'l*, pg. 1351
TAKENAKA CORPORATION - TOHOKU BRANCH—See Takenaka Corporation; *Int'l*, pg. 1351
TAKENAKA CORPORATION - TOKYO OFFICE—See Takenaka Corporation; *Int'l*, pg. 1351
TAKENAKA DO BRASIL CONSTRUTORA LTDA.—See Takenaka Corporation; *Int'l*, pg. 1351

TAKENAKA EUROPE GMBH, BERLIN—See Takenaka Corporation; *Int'l*, pg. 1351
TAKENAKA EUROPE GMBH, DUSSELDORF—See Takenaka Corporation; *Int'l*, pg. 1351
TAKENAKA EUROPE GMBH, FRANKFURT—See Takenaka Corporation; *Int'l*, pg. 1351
TAKENAKA EUROPE GMBH, HAMBURG—See Takenaka Corporation; *Int'l*, pg. 1351
TAKENAKA HONG KONG LTD.—See Takenaka Corporation; *Int'l*, pg. 1351
TAKENAKA HUNGARIA KFT—See Takenaka Corporation; *Int'l*, pg. 1351
TAKENAKA (MALAYSIA) SDN. BHD., KUALA LUMPUR—See Takenaka Corporation; *Int'l*, pg. 1351
TAKENAKA (MALAYSIA) SDN. BHD., PENANG—See Takenaka Corporation; *Int'l*, pg. 1351
TAKENAKA NETHERLANDS B.V.—See Takenaka Corporation; *Int'l*, pg. 1351
TAKENAKA REAL ESTATE DEVELOPMENT CO., LTD.—See Takenaka Corporation; *Int'l*, pg. 1351
TAKENAKA SINGAPORE PTE. LTD.—See Takenaka Corporation; *Int'l*, pg. 1352
TAKENAKA (U.K.) LTD., BIRMINGHAM—See Takenaka Corporation; *Int'l*, pg. 1352
TAKENAKA (U.K.) LTD., CARDIFF—See Takenaka Corporation; *Int'l*, pg. 1352
TAKENAKA (U.K.) LTD., LONDON—See Takenaka Corporation; *Int'l*, pg. 1352
TAKENAKA (U.K.) LTD., SPAIN—See Takenaka Corporation; *Int'l*, pg. 1352
TAKENAKA (U.S.A.) CORPORATION, ATLANTA OFFICE—See Takenaka Corporation; *Int'l*, pg. 1351
TAKENAKA (U.S.A.) CORPORATION, HONOLULU OFFICE—See Takenaka Corporation; *Int'l*, pg. 1351
TAKENAKA (U.S.A.) CORPORATION, INDIANAPOLIS OFFICE—See Takenaka Corporation; *Int'l*, pg. 1351
TAKENAKA (U.S.A.) CORPORATION, LOS ANGELES OFFICE—See Takenaka Corporation; *Int'l*, pg. 1351
TAKENAKA (U.S.A.) CORPORATION, NEW YORK OFFICE—See Takenaka Corporation; *Int'l*, pg. 1351
TAKENAKA (U.S.A.) CORPORATION, PORTLAND OFFICE—See Takenaka Corporation; *Int'l*, pg. 1351
TAKENAKA (U.S.A.) CORPORATION, SAN FRANCISCO OFFICE—See Takenaka Corporation; *Int'l*, pg. 1351
TAKETA TOSHIBA ELECTRONICS CORPORATION—See Toshiba Corporation; *Int'l*, pg. 1403
TAKO BOARD MILL—See Metsa-Serla Corporation; *Int'l*, pg. 863
TAKO CARTON PLANT LTD.—See Metsa-Serla Corporation; *Int'l*, pg. 863
TAKUGIN BANK (SCHWEIZ) AG—See The Hokkaido Takushoku Bank, Ltd.; *Int'l*, pg. 627
TAKUGIN FINANCE (CAYMAN) LIMITED—See The Hokkaido Takushoku Bank, Ltd.; *Int'l*, pg. 627
TAKUGIN FINANCE INTERNATIONAL LTD.—See The Hokkaido Takushoku Bank, Ltd.; *Int'l*, pg. 627
TAKUGIN INTERNATIONAL (ASIA) LTD.—See The Hokkaido Takushoku Bank, Ltd.; *Int'l*, pg. 627
TAKUMEI KUMIAI HOLDINGS, INC.—See Stewart & Stevenson Services, Inc.; *U.S. Public*, pg. 1518
TALAVERA AT PECCOLE RANCH—See BRE Properties, Inc.; *U.S. Public*, pg. 163
TALBOOM B.V.—See Clarins; *Int'l*, pg. 296
TALBOT FINANCIAL CORPORATION—See SAFECO Corporation; *U.S. Public*, pg. 1423
TALBOTS—See AEON Group; *Int'l*, pg. 28
TALBOTS, INC.—See AEON Group; *Int'l*, pg. 28
TALC DE LUZENAC S.A.—See Rio Tinto PLC; *Int'l*, pg. 1119
TALCO—See Kennedy Manufacturing Company; *U.S. Private*, pg. 614
TALEGEN CORPORATION—See Xerox Corporation; *U.S. Public*, pg. 1784
TALENT PARTNERS—See IDC Services, Inc.; *U.S. Private*, pg. 554
TALENT TREE PERSONNEL SERVICES INC.—See Sophus Berendsen A/S; *Int'l*, pg. 1286
TALISMAN ENERGY INC.; *Int'l*, pg. 1352
TALISMAN ENERGY INC.—See Talisman Energy Inc.; *Int'l*, pg. 1352
TALISMAN ENERGY (U.K.) LIMITED—See Talisman Energy Inc.; *Int'l*, pg. 1352
TALISMAN SUGAR CORP.—See St. Joe Corp.; *U.S. Public*, pg. 1427
TALK-A-PHONE CO.; *U.S. Private*, pg. 1067
TALL TREES—See Corrections Corporation of America; *U.S. Public*, pg. 451
TALL WALL MEDIA—See Western International Media Corporation; *U.S. Private*, pg. 1166
TALLAHASSEE DEMOCRAT, INC.—See Knight-Ridder, Inc.; *U.S. Public*, pg. 964
THE TALLAHASSEE STATE BANK—See Synovus Financial Corp.; *U.S. Public*, pg. 1549
TALLAPOOSA RIVER ELECTRIC CO-OP; *U.S. Private*, pg. 1067
TALLERES RANCAGUA DIVISION—See CODELCO Chile (Corporacion Nacional Del Cobre De Chile); *Int'l*, pg. 302
TALLERES URIBARRI, S.L.—See Sunrise Medical, Inc.; *U.S. Public*, pg. 302
TALLEY DEFENSE SYSTEMS, INC.—See Carpenter Technology Corporation; *U.S. Public*, pg. 308
TALLEY INDUSTRIES, INC.—See Carpenter Technology Corporation; *U.S. Public*, pg. 307
TALLEY METALS TECHNOLOGY, INC.—See Carpenter Technology Corporation; *U.S. Public*, pg. 308
TALLEY REALTY GROUP—See Carpenter Technology Corporation; *U.S. Public*, pg. 308
TALLY INDUSTRIAL & TRADING CO. LTD.—See Selas Corporation of America; *U.S. Public*, pg. 1455
TALMADGE FARMS—See Cagle's Inc.; *U.S. Public*, pg. 292

TALMAN HOME MORTGAGE CORP. & TALMAN INSURANCE SERVICES, INC.—See ABN-AMRO Holding N.V.; *Int'l*, pg. 11
TALOCA AG—See Philip Morris Companies Inc.; *U.S. Public*, pg. 1288
TALOCA & CIA LTDA.—See Philip Morris Companies Inc.; *U.S. Public*, pg. 1289
TALOCA CAFE S/C LTDA.—See Philip Morris Companies Inc.; *U.S. Public*, pg. 1289
TALOQUIMIA, S.A.—See Hercules Incorporated; *U.S. Public*, pg. 811
TALSI BUILDING MATERIALS LTD.—See Scancem AB; *Int'l*, pg. 1201
TALTRON B.V., OMMEN—See Maxxim Medical, Inc.; *U.S. Public*, pg. 1063
TALZA LTD.—See Clarins; *Int'l*, pg. 296
TAM CERAMICS INC.—See Cookson Group plc; *Int'l*, pg. 329
TAM O'SHANTER INN—See Lawry's Restaurants, Inc.; *U.S. Private*, pg. 654
TAMA SEIMITSU CO., LTD.—See Citizen Watch Company, Ltd.; *Int'l*, pg. 294
TAMALIA—See LVMH Moet Hennessy Louis Vuitton; *Int'l*, pg. 783
TAMAM DIVISION/ELECTRONICS GROUP—See Israel Aircraft Industries Ltd.; *Int'l*, pg. 690
TAMAQUA CABLE PRODUCTS CORP.—See Draka Kabel B.V.; *Int'l*, pg. 417
TAMARACK HOMES DIV.—See Champion Enterprises, Inc.; *U.S. Public*, pg. 332
TAMARIS SA—See LVMH Moet Hennessy Louis Vuitton; *Int'l*, pg. 781
TAMARKIN CO., INC.—See Giant Eagle, Inc.; *U.S. Private*, pg. 451
TAMAROFF BUICK INC.; *U.S. Private*, pg. 1067
TAMAROFF LEASING CO.—See Tamaroff Buick Inc.; *U.S. Private*, pg. 1067
TAMARRON DIVISION—See Starwood Capital Group LLC; *U.S. Private*, pg. 1036
TAMBOUR LIMITED—See IDB Holding Corporation; *Int'l*, pg. 644
TAMBOURINE BOOKS—See The Hearst Corporation; *U.S. Private*, pg. 515
TAMBOX AB - JONKOPING FACTORY—See Enso Oyj; *Int'l*, pg. 458
TAMBOX AB - SKENE FACTORY—See Enso Oyj; *Int'l*, pg. 458
TAMBOX AB - VIKINGSTAD FACTORY—See Enso Oyj; *Int'l*, pg. 458
TAMBRANDS INC.—See The Procter & Gamble Company; *U.S. Public*, pg. 1331
TAMCO—See Ameron International Corporation; *U.S. Public*, pg. 99
TAMDHU DISTILLERY—See The Highland Distilleries Company plc; *Int'l*, pg. 619
TAMMS INDUSTRIES—See Laporte plc; *Int'l*, pg. 803
TAMMS INDUSTRIES CO.—See Laporte plc; *Int'l*, pg. 803
TAMOR CORP.—See Home Products International, Inc.; *U.S. Public*, pg. 832
TAMPA BAY MOVING SYSTEMS INC.—See Cook Moving Systems, Inc.; *U.S. Private*, pg. 273
TAMPA BAY SHIP BUILDING & REPAIR CO.; *U.S. Private*, pg. 1067
TAMPA BAY STEEL; *U.S. Private*, pg. 1067
TAMPA BAY STEEL—See Tampa Bay Steel; *U.S. Private*, pg. 1067
TAMPA ELECTRIC CO.—See TECO Energy, Inc.; *U.S. Public*, pg. 1565
TAMPA INTL. FOREST PRODUCTS, INC.—See Forest City Enterprises, Inc.; *U.S. Public*, pg. 669
TAMPA PUMP STATION—See GATX Corporation; *U.S. Public*, pg. 692
TAMPA RETAIL DIVISION—See Poe & Brown, Inc.; *U.S. Public*, pg. 1312
TAMPA TELEVISION, INC.—See Media General, Inc.; *U.S. Public*, pg. 1078
THE TAMPA TRIBUNE—See Media General, Inc.; *U.S. Public*, pg. 1079
TAMPELLA POWER AB—See Tamrock Corp.; *Int'l*, pg. 1354
TAMPELLA POWER ASIA PACIFIC PTE. LTD.—See Tamrock Corp.; *Int'l*, pg. 1354
TAMPELLA POWER CANADA, INC.—See Tamrock Corp.; *Int'l*, pg. 1354
TAMPELLA POWER CORP.—See Tamrock Corp.; *Int'l*, pg. 1353
TAMPELLA POWER INC.—See Tamrock Corp.; *Int'l*, pg. 1353
TAMPELLA POWER INC. MANUFACTURING FACILITY—See Tamrock Corp.; *Int'l*, pg. 1353
TAMPELLA POWER ST. PETERSBURG LTD.—See Tamrock Corp.; *Int'l*, pg. 1354
TAMPELLA POWER SOUTH AFRICA—See Tamrock Corp.; *Int'l*, pg. 1354
TAMPELLA-METRA—See Tamrock Corp.; *Int'l*, pg. 1354
TAMPERE SALES OFFICE & STORAGE DEPOT—See Oy Algol AB; *Int'l*, pg. 15
TAMPO INDUSTRIES INC.—See Trelleborg AB; *Int'l*, pg. 1420
TAMRA DMB&B—See DMB&B Communications; *U.S. Private*, pg. 305
TAMROCK AFRICA PTY. LTD.—See Tamrock Corp.; *Int'l*, pg. 1353
TAMROCK ARGENTINA S.A.—See Tamrock Corp.; *Int'l*, pg. 1353
TAMROCK BUREAU DE LIAISON ALGER—See Tamrock Corp.; *Int'l*, pg. 1353
TAMROCK (CHINA) LTD.—See Tamrock Corp.; *Int'l*, pg. 1353
TAMROCK CORP.; *Int'l*, pg. 1352
TAMROCK DEUSTCHLAND GMBH—See Tamrock Corp.; *Int'l*, pg. 1353
TAMROCK DRILLS—See Tamrock Corp.; *Int'l*, pg. 1352

TAMROCK DRILLS SECOMA S.A.—See Tamrock Corp.; *Int'l*, pg. 1353
TAMROCK EJC CANADA LTD.—See Tamrock Corp.; *Int'l*, pg. 1353
TAMROCK EJC CHILE S.A.—See Tamrock Corp.; *Int'l*, pg. 1353
TAMROCK EJC DE MEXICO S.A. DE C.V.—See Tamrock Corp.; *Int'l*, pg. 1353
TAMROCK EJC LTD.—See Tamrock Corp.; *Int'l*, pg. 1353
TAMROCK EJC USA INC.—See Tamrock Corp.; *Int'l*, pg. 1352
TAMROCK EQUIPAMENTOS LTDA.—See Tamrock Corp.; *Int'l*, pg. 1352
TAMROCK ESPANA S.A.—See Tamrock Corp.; *Int'l*, pg. 1353
TAMROCK FRANCE—See Tamrock Corp.; *Int'l*, pg. 1353
TAMROCK GROUP U.S.—See Tamrock Corp.; *Int'l*, pg. 1352
TAMROCK LOADERS ARA OY—See Tamrock Corp.; *Int'l*, pg. 1353
TAMROCK LOADERS EIMCO JARVIS CLARK CO. LTD.—See Tamrock Corp.; *Int'l*, pg. 1353
TAMROCK LOADERS E.M. FRANCELOADER S.A.—See Tamrock Corp.; *Int'l*, pg. 1353
TAMROCK MIDDLE EAST—See Tamrock Corp.; *Int'l*, pg. 1353
TAMROCK MOSCOW OFFICE—See Tamrock Corp.; *Int'l*, pg. 1353
TAMROCK NORGE A/S—See Tamrock Corp.; *Int'l*, pg. 1353
TAMROCK OY—See Tamrock Corp.; *Int'l*, pg. 1352
TAMROCK OY NORTHERN EUROPE—See Tamrock Corp.; *Int'l*, pg. 1352
TAMROCK PTY. LTD.—See Tamrock Corp.; *Int'l*, pg. 1353
TAMROCK REGION CIS—See Tamrock Corp.; *Int'l*, pg. 1353
TAMROCK SERVICE—See Tamrock Corp.; *Int'l*, pg. 1353
TAMROCK ZIMBABWE (PVT.) LTD.—See Tamrock Corp.; *Int'l*, pg. 1353
OY TAMROTOR AB—See Tamrock Corp.; *Int'l*, pg. 1352
TAMURA CORPORATION OF AMERICA; *U.S. Private*, pg. 1067
TAMURA CORP. OF AMERICA, MICROTRAN DIV.—See Tamura Corporation of America; *U.S. Private*, pg. 1067
P.T. TANABE-ABADI-HEADQUARTERS—See Tanabe Seiyaku Co., Ltd.; *Int'l*, pg. 1354
P.T. TANABE-ABADI-JAKARTA OFFICE—See Tanabe Seiyaku Co., Ltd.; *Int'l*, pg. 1354
TANABE EUROPE N.V.—See Tanabe Seiyaku Co., Ltd.; *Int'l*, pg. 1354
TANABE FINANCE (HOLLAND) B.V.—See Tanabe Seiyaku Co., Ltd.; *Int'l*, pg. 1354
TANABE-GLAXO S.A.—See Tanabe Seiyaku Co., Ltd.; *Int'l*, pg. 1354
TANABE GROUP SERVICE U.S.A., INC.—See Tanabe Seiyaku Co., Ltd.; *Int'l*, pg. 1354
TANABE-MARION LABORATORIES—See Tanabe Seiyaku Co., Ltd.; *Int'l*, pg. 1354
TANABE PHARMA S.A.—See Tanabe Seiyaku Co., Ltd.; *Int'l*, pg. 1354
TANABE PLANT—See Sharp Corporation; *Int'l*, pg. 1228
TANABE RESEARCH LABORATORIES U.S.A., INC.—See Tanabe Seiyaku Co., Ltd.; *Int'l*, pg. 1354
RP TANABE—See Tanabe Seiyaku Co., Ltd.; *Int'l*, pg. 1354
TANABE SEIYAKU CO., LTD.; *Int'l*, pg. 1354
TANABE SEIYAKU CO., LTD.-EUROPEAN R & D CENTER—See Tanabe Seiyaku Co., Ltd.; *Int'l*, pg. 1354
TANABE SEIYAKU CO., LTD.-INTERNATIONAL INFORMATION DIVISION—See Tanabe Seiyaku Co., Ltd.; *Int'l*, pg. 1354
TANABE SEIYAKU CO., LTD.-TOKYO—See Tanabe Seiyaku Co., Ltd.; *Int'l*, pg. 1354
TANABE SEIYAKU CO., LTD.-U.S. LIASION OFFICE—See Tanabe Seiyaku Co., Ltd.; *Int'l*, pg. 1354
TANABE SEIYAKU SINGAPORE PTE. LTD.—See Tanabe Seiyaku Co., Ltd.; *Int'l*, pg. 1354
TANABE U.S.A. INC.—See Tanabe Seiyaku Co., Ltd.; *Int'l*, pg. 1354
TANABE U.S.A., INC.-SAN DIEGO OFFICE—See Tanabe Seiyaku Co., Ltd.; *Int'l*, pg. 1354
TANAKA (THAILAND) CO., LTD.—See Nippon Sanso Corporation; *Int'l*, pg. 939
PT TANDBAM JAYA—See Haw Par Brothers International Limited; *Int'l*, pg. 603
TANDEM COMPUTERS AB—See COMPAQ Computer Corporation; *U.S. Public*, pg. 417
TANDEM COMPUTERS AG—See COMPAQ Computer Corporation; *U.S. Public*, pg. 417
TANDEM COMPUTERS AMERICAS DIV.—See COMPAQ Computer Corporation; *U.S. Public*, pg. 417
TANDEM COMPUTERS A/S—See COMPAQ Computer Corporation; *U.S. Public*, pg. 417
TANDEM COMPUTERS ASIA, LTD.—See COMPAQ Computer Corporation; *U.S. Public*, pg. 417
TANDEM COMPUTERS ASIA/PACIFIC DIV.—See COMPAQ Computer Corporation; *U.S. Public*, pg. 417
TANDEM COMPUTERS B.V.—See COMPAQ Computer Corporation; *U.S. Public*, pg. 417
TANDEM COMPUTERS CANADA LIMITED—See COMPAQ Computer Corporation; *U.S. Public*, pg. 417
TANDEM COMPUTERS DE MEXICO S.A. DE C.V.—See COMPAQ Computer Corporation; *U.S. Public*, pg. 417
TANDEM COMPUTERS EUROPEAN DIV.—See COMPAQ Computer Corporation; *U.S. Public*, pg. 417
TANDEM COMPUTERS GES.M.B.H.—See COMPAQ Computer Corporation; *U.S. Public*, pg. 418
TANDEM COMPUTERS GMBH—See COMPAQ Computer Corporation; *U.S. Public*, pg. 418
TANDEM COMPUTERS HONG KONG LTD.—See COMPAQ Computer Corporation; *U.S. Public*, pg. 418
TANDEM COMPUTERS IBERICA S.A.—See COMPAQ Computer Corporation; *U.S. Public*, pg. 418

TANDEM COMPUTERS INC.—See COMPAQ Computer Corporation; *U.S. Public,* pg. 417
TANDEM COMPUTERS INTERNATIONAL INC.—See COMPAQ Computer Corporation; *U.S. Public,* pg. 418
TANDEM COMPUTERS ITALIA S.P.A.—See COMPAQ Computer Corporation; *U.S. Public,* pg. 418
TANDEM COMPUTERS JAPAN DIV.—See COMPAQ Computer Corporation; *U.S. Public,* pg. 417
TANDEM COMPUTERS JAPAN, LTD.—See COMPAQ Computer Corporation; *U.S. Public,* pg. 418
TANDEM COMPUTERS LTD.—See COMPAQ Computer Corporation; *U.S. Public,* pg. 418
TANDEM COMPUTERS MCC—See COMPAQ Computer Corporation; *U.S. Public,* pg. 417
TANDEM COMPUTERS-NOWAY—See COMPAQ Computer Corporation; *U.S. Public,* pg. 418
TANDEM COMPUTERS S.A.—See COMPAQ Computer Corporation; *U.S. Public,* pg. 418
TANDEM COMPUTERS SA/NV—See COMPAQ Computer Corporation; *U.S. Public,* pg. 418
TANDEM NONSTOP PTY. LTD.—See COMPAQ Computer Corporation; *U.S. Public,* pg. 418
TANDEM TELECOMMUNICATIONS SYSTEMS, INC.—See COMPAQ Computer Corporation; *U.S. Public,* pg. 417
TANDY BRANDS ACCESSORIES, INC.; *U.S. Public,* pg. 1560
TANDY CABINETS—See Tandy Corporation; *U.S. Public,* pg. 1560
TANDY CABLE PRODUCTS—See Tandy Corporation; *U.S. Public,* pg. 1560
TANDY CORPORATION; *U.S. Public,* pg. 1560
TANDY ELECTRONICS ASIA—See Tandy Corporation; *U.S. Public,* pg. 1561
TANDY ELECTRONICS (CHINA) LTD.—See Tandy Corporation; *U.S. Public,* pg. 1561
TANDY INTERNATIONAL ELECTRONICS, INC.—See Tandy Corporation; *U.S. Public,* pg. 1560
TANDY LEATHER CO.—See Tandycrafts, Inc.; *U.S. Public,* pg. 1561
TANDY PACKAGING—See Tandy Corporation; *U.S. Public,* pg. 1560
TANDY SIGNS—See Tandy Corporation; *U.S. Public,* pg. 1560
TANDY TRANSPORTATION—See Tandy Corporation; *U.S. Public,* pg. 1560
TANDY WIRE & CABLE—See Tandy Corporation; *U.S. Public,* pg. 1560
TANDY WIRE FABRICATION—See Tandy Corporation; *U.S. Public,* pg. 1560
TANDYCRAFTS, INC.; *U.S. Public,* pg. 1561
THE TANEY CORPORATION; *U.S. Private,* pg. 1067
TANG INDUSTRIES INC.; *U.S. Private,* pg. 1068
TANGENT INDUSTRIES LTD.—See Esquire Radio & Electronics Inc.; *U.S. Private,* pg. 383
TANGRAM ENTERPRISE SOLUTIONS, INC.—See Safeguard Scientifics, Inc.; *U.S. Public,* pg. 1424
TANIT INTERNATIONAL—See Accor S.A.; *Int'l,* pg. 21
TANK SERVICE CO.—See Chemical Leaman Corporation; *U.S. Private,* pg. 233
TANK SERVICE, INC.—See Dover Corporation; *U.S. Public,* pg. 521
TANKSTORE PTE LTD.—See GATX Corporation; *U.S. Public,* pg. 693
TANKSYSTEME MKS GMBH—See Mannesmann A.G.; *Int'l,* pg. 839
TANNER CO.; *U.S. Private,* pg. 1068
TANNER PLATING DIV.—See Ampco-Pittsburgh Corporation; *U.S. Public,* pg. 104
TANNING RESEARCH LABS., INC.; *U.S. Private,* pg. 1068
TANO AUTOMATION, INC.—See Westwood Corporation; *U.S. Public,* pg. 1763
TANON EXPRESS—See EA Industries; *U.S. Public,* pg. 541
TANON MANUFACTURING, INC.—See EA Industries; *U.S. Public,* pg. 541
TANTEL-EOC NORMALIEN GU—See Anchor Lamina Inc.; *Int'l,* pg. 75
TANUM KOMPONENT AB—See Perstorp AB; *Int'l,* pg. 1040
TANZANIA PORTLAND CEMENT COMPANY LTD.—See Scancem AB; *Int'l,* pg. 1201
TAOKA CHEMICAL CO., LTD.—See Sumitomo Chemical Company, Ltd.; *Int'l,* pg. 1311
TAOYUAN REFINERY—See Chinese Petroleum Corporation; *Int'l,* pg. 286
TAP AIR PORTUGAL—See Transportes Aereos Portugueses; *Int'l,* pg. 1418
TAPCO INTERNATIONAL CORPORATION; *U.S. Private,* pg. 1068
TAPE & LABEL ENGINEERING—See Weber Marking Systems, Inc.; *U.S. Private,* pg. 1157
TAPE MANUFACTURING DIVISION—See 3M; *U.S. Public,* pg. 1605
TAPECOAT COMPANY—See T C Manufacturing Company, Inc.; *U.S. Private,* pg. 1062
TAPEMARK; *U.S. Private,* pg. 1068
TAPETECH TOOL CO., INC.—See AXIA Incorporated; *U.S. Private,* pg. 103
B.V. TAPIJVEREDELINGSINDUSTRIE—See Forbo Holding SA; *Int'l,* pg. 498
TAPIOLA-YHTIOT; *Int'l,* pg. 1354
TAPOCO, INC.—See Aluminum Company of America; *U.S. Public,* pg. 61
TAPPAN INTERNATIONAL SALES LTD.—See Electrolux, AB; *Int'l,* pg. 444
TAPROOT INTERACTIVE, INC.—See Devon Group, Inc.; *U.S. Public,* pg. 503
TAPTONE CONTAINER INSPECTION SYSTEMS—See Benthos, Inc.; *U.S. Public,* pg. 212
TAR RIVER COMMUNICATIONS, INC.—See Gannett Company, Inc.; *U.S. Public,* pg. 701
TARA CONSULTING NIGERIA, LTD.—See Oracle Corporation; *U.S. Public,* pg. 1229
TARA FOODS—See The Kroger Co.; *U.S. Public,* pg. 967

TARA MINES LIMITED—See Outokumpu Oyj; *Int'l,* pg. 1016
TARACORP EVANS, INC.—See Taracorp, Inc.; *U.S. Private,* pg. 1068
TARACORP IMACO, INC.—See Taracorp, Inc.; *U.S. Private,* pg. 1068
TARACORP, INC.; *U.S. Private,* pg. 1068
TARACORP INDUSTRIES, INC.—See Taracorp, Inc.; *U.S. Private,* pg. 1068
TARAS VALVE COMPANY, INC.—See Watts Industries, Inc.; *U.S. Public,* pg. 1747
TARCO; *U.S. Private,* pg. 1068
TARCO OF TEXAS, INC.—See Tarco; *U.S. Private,* pg. 1069
TARG-IT-TRONICS INC.—See Johnson Matthey Public Limited Company; *Int'l,* pg. 713
TARGET—See Lee Enterprises, Incorporated; *U.S. Public,* pg. 984
TARGET ADVERTISING AGENCY LIMITED; *Int'l,* pg. 1355
TARGET EURO RSCG—See Havas Advertising; *Int'l,* pg. 603
TARGET OILFIELD PIPE & SUPPLY COMPANY (TOPS)—See Texas Pacific Group; *U.S. Private,* pg. 1078
TARGET ROCK CORP.—See Curtiss-Wright Corp.; *U.S. Public,* pg. 470
TARGET STAMPED PRODUCTS CORP.; *U.S. Private,* pg. 1069
TARGET STORES—See Dayton Hudson Corporation; *U.S. Public,* pg. 489
TARGET TECHNOLOGY FRANCE SARL—See Meggitt plc; *Int'l,* pg. 854
TARGET TECHNOLOGY LTD.—See Meggitt plc; *Int'l,* pg. 853
TARGETBASE MARKETING—See The M/A/R/C Group; *U.S. Public,* pg. 1023
TARGETBASE MARKETING INTERNATIONAL—See The M/A/R/C Group; *U.S. Public,* pg. 1023
TARGETCOM, INC.; *U.S. Private,* pg. 1069
TARGETED GENETICS CORP.—See Immunex Corporation; *U.S. Public,* pg. 871
TARGETS-LEO BURNETT ADVERTISING—See Leo Burnett Company, Inc.; *U.S. Private,* pg. 186
TARGOR GMBH—See BASF AG; *Int'l,* pg. 105
TARGOR GMBH—See Hoechst Aktiengesellschaft; *Int'l,* pg. 624
TARIF MEDIA S.A.—See EMAP Plc; *Int'l,* pg. 451
TARIQ ALGHANIM CATERING DIVISION—See Sodexho S.A.; *Int'l,* pg. 1275
TARJETA DE CREDITO—See Bancomer, S.A.; *Int'l,* pg. 145
TARLTON CORPORATION; *U.S. Private,* pg. 1069
TARMAC (ABU DHABI) LTD.—See Tarmac plc; *Int'l,* pg. 1355
TARMAC AMERICA, INC.—See Tarmac plc; *Int'l,* pg. 1355
TARMAC CALIFORNIA, INC.—See Tarmac plc; *Int'l,* pg. 1355
TARMAC CANADA INC.—See Tarmac plc; *Int'l,* pg. 1355
TARMAC CONSTRUCTION (CARIBBEAN) LTD.—See Tarmac plc; *Int'l,* pg. 1355
TARMAC CONSTRUCTION (CONTRACTS) INTERNATIONAL LTD.—See Tarmac plc; *Int'l,* pg. 1355
TARMAC CONSTRUCTION INTL.—See Tarmac plc; *Int'l,* pg. 1355
TARMAC CONSTRUCTION LIMITED—See Tarmac plc; *Int'l,* pg. 1355
TARMAC CONSTRUCTION MAJOR PROJECTS LIMITED—See Tarmac plc; *Int'l,* pg. 1355
TARMAC FLORIDA—See Tarmac plc; *Int'l,* pg. 1355
TARMAC-LONESTAR, INC.—See Tarmac plc; *Int'l,* pg. 1355
TARMAC-MASSEY—See Tarmac plc; *Int'l,* pg. 1356
TARMAC PLC; *Int'l,* pg. 1355
TARMAC QUARRY PRODUCTS LTD.—See Tarmac plc; *Int'l,* pg. 1355
TARMAC ROADSTONE LTD.—See Tarmac plc; *Int'l,* pg. 1355
TARMAC SERVICEMASTER—See The ServiceMaster Company; *U.S. Public,* pg. 1462
TARMAC TEXAS—See Tarmac plc; *Int'l,* pg. 1356
TARMAC TOPBLOCK LIMITED—See Tarmac plc; *Int'l,* pg. 1355
TARMAC TOPMIX LIMITED—See Tarmac plc; *Int'l,* pg. 1355
TARMAC VIRGINIA, INC.—See Tarmac plc; *Int'l,* pg. 1356
TARO INDUSTRIES LIMITED—See Trimac Corporation; *U.S. Public,* pg. 1424
TARRAGON REALTY INVESTORS; *U.S. Public,* pg. 1561
TARRAGONA TERMINAL—See GATX Corporation; *U.S. Public,* pg. 693
TARRANT SERVICE, INC.; *U.S. Private,* pg. 1069
TARTAN, INC.—See Chrysler Corporation; *U.S. Public,* pg. 354
TAS PLAN, INC.—See Taisei Corporation; *Int'l,* pg. 1348
TASACIONES MADRID, S.A.—See Caja de Madrid Group; *Int'l,* pg. 252
TASCO SALES INC.—See Rice, Sangalis, Toole & Wilson; *U.S. Private,* pg. 928
TASHA; *U.S. Private,* pg. 1069
TASHKOCHAUTO—See Koc Holding A.S.; *Int'l,* pg. 742
TASMAN CHILE S.A.—See Fletcher Challenge Limited; *Int'l,* pg. 495
TASMAN FORESTRY LIMITED—See Fletcher Challenge Limited; *Int'l,* pg. 495
TASMAN LUMBER COMPANY LIMITED—See Fletcher Challenge Limited; *Int'l,* pg. 495
TASMAN PULP & PAPER COMPANY LIMITED—See Fletcher Challenge Limited; *Int'l,* pg. 495
TASMANIA ELECTRO METALLURGICAL COMPANY PTY LTD (TEMCO)—See The Broken Hill Proprietary Company Limited; *Int'l,* pg. 224
TASMANIAN ALKALOIDS PTY. LTD.—See Johnson & Johnson; *U.S. Public,* pg. 932

TASTBAU ASPHALT-STRASSEN- UND TIEFBAU GMBH—See Ruetgers A.G.; *Int'l,* pg. 1148
TASTEE FREEZ INTERNATIONAL INC.; *U.S. Private,* pg. 1069
TASTEMAKER B.V.—See Hercules Incorporated; *U.S. Public,* pg. 811
TASTEMAKER GERMANY—See Hercules Incorporated; *U.S. Public,* pg. 811
TASTEMAKER, INC.—See Hercules Incorporated; *U.S. Public,* pg. 811
TASTEMAKER K.K.—See Hercules Incorporated; *U.S. Public,* pg. 811
TASTEMAKER LTD.—See Hercules Incorporated; *U.S. Public,* pg. 811
TASTEMAKER PTE. LTD.—See Hercules Incorporated; *U.S. Public,* pg. 811
TASTEMAKER S.A.—See Hercules Incorporated; *U.S. Public,* pg. 811
TASTY BAKING COMPANY; *U.S. Public,* pg. 1561
TASTY BAKING-OXFORD—See Tasty Baking Company; *U.S. Public,* pg. 1561
TATA CONSULTANCY SERVICES—See Oracle Corporation; *U.S. Public,* pg. 1229
TATA ENGINEERING & LOCOMOTIVE CO. LTD. (TELCO)—See Daimler-Benz Aktiengesellschaft; *Int'l,* pg. 369
TATA ENGINEERING & LOCOMOTIVE CO. LTD. (TELCO)—See The Tata Iron and Steel Co. Ltd.; *Int'l,* pg. 1356
TATA HONEYWELL LTD.—See Honeywell Inc.; *U.S. Public,* pg. 835
TATA INC.—See The Tata Iron and Steel Co. Ltd.; *Int'l,* pg. 1356
THE TATA IRON AND STEEL CO. LTD.; *Int'l,* pg. 1356
TATA MCGRAW-HILL PUBLISHING CO., PRIVATE LIMITED—See The McGraw-Hill Companies; *U.S. Public,* pg. 1072
TATA OIL & MILLS COMPANY—See Unilever Plc; *Int'l,* pg. 1437
TATA TIMKEN LIMITED—See The Timken Company; *U.S. Public,* pg. 1561
TATA-YODOGAWA LTD.—See Nissho Iwai Corporation; *Int'l,* pg. 949
TATCH-A-CLEAT PRODUCTS—See Flexible Steel Lacing Company; *U.S. Private,* pg. 413
TATE ACCESS FLOORS—See International Paper Company; *U.S. Public,* pg. 905
TATE ACCESS FLOORS, INC.; *U.S. Private,* pg. 1069
TATE & LYLE PLC; *Int'l,* pg. 1356
TATEKAWA DISTRIBUTION CENTER—See Gunze Sangyo, Inc.; *Int'l,* pg. 578
TATRA BANKA, A.S.—See Raiffeisen Zentralbank Osterreich; *Int'l,* pg. 1085
TATRAREX PRECISION CASTINGS SPOL. S.R.O.—See Koninklijke Hoogovens N.V.; *Int'l,* pg. 756
TATRY OFFICINA MECCANICA S.R.L.—See The Black & Decker Corporation; *U.S. Public,* pg. 234
TATT SING SANYO ELECTRIC COMPANY LIMITED—See Sanyo Electric Co., Ltd.; *Int'l,* pg. 1193
TATTERSALLS; *Int'l,* pg. 1357
TATUM FARMS INT., INC.; *U.S. Private,* pg. 1069
P.T. TATUNG BUDI INDONESIA—See Tatung Corporation; *Int'l,* pg. 1357
TATUNG CO.—See Tatung Corporation; *Int'l,* pg. 1357
TATUNG COMPANY OF AMERICA—See Tatung Corporation; *Int'l,* pg. 1357
TATUNG CORPORATION; *Int'l,* pg. 1357
TATUNG ELECTRIC CO. OF AMERICA, INC.—See Tatung Corporation; *Int'l,* pg. 1357
TATUNG ELECTRONICS (SINGAPORE) PTE LTD.—See Tatung Corporation; *Int'l,* pg. 1357
TATUNG-FANUC ROBOTICS COMPANY—See Fanuc Ltd.; *Int'l,* pg. 477
TATUNG-FANUC ROBOTICS COMPANY—See Tatung Corporation; *Int'l,* pg. 1357
TATUNG INTERNATIONAL (DEUTSCHLAND) GMBH—See Tatung Corporation; *Int'l,* pg. 1357
TATUNG OF JAPAN, INC.—See Tatung Corporation; *Int'l,* pg. 1357
TATUNG SCIENCE & TECHNOLOGY, INC.—See Tatung Corporation; *Int'l,* pg. 1357
TATUNG TELECOM CORP.—See Tatung Corporation; *Int'l,* pg. 1357
TATUNG THAILAND COMPANY LTD.—See Tatung Corporation; *Int'l,* pg. 1357
TATUNG UK LTD.—See Tatung Corporation; *Int'l,* pg. 1357
TAU-TRON—See General Signal Corporation; *U.S. Public,* pg. 727
TAUBE/VIOLANTE, INC.; *U.S. Private,* pg. 1069
TAUBER OIL COMPANY; *U.S. Private,* pg. 1069
TAUBMAN CENTERS, INC.; *U.S. Public,* pg. 1561
TAUGBOL & OVERLAND A/S—See Aker Raj Asa; *Int'l,* pg. 42
TAUNTON CIDER COMPANY P.L.C.—See Matthew Clark Taunton, Ltd.; *Int'l,* pg. 849
TAUNTON CIDER SCOTLAND—See Matthew Clark Taunton, Ltd.; *Int'l,* pg. 849
TAUNTON DAILY GAZETTE—See Journal Register Company; *U.S. Public,* pg. 935
TAUNUS-BETON GMBH & CO. KG—See Dyckerhoff AG; *Int'l,* pg. 423
TAURUS ENERGY CO.—See Enron Corp.; *U.S. Public,* pg. 584
TAURUS ENERGY CORP.—See Enron Corp.; *U.S. Public,* pg. 584
TAURUS EXPLORATION, INC.—See Energen Corporation; *U.S. Public,* pg. 581
TAURUS TRUCKING, INC.—See Mark VII, Inc.; *U.S. Public,* pg. 1046
TAUSCHE MARTIN LONSDORF; *U.S. Private,* pg. 1069
TAVCOM, S.A.—See Caja de Madrid Group; *Int'l,* pg. 252
TAWIL ASSOCIATES INC.; *U.S. Private,* pg. 1070
TAX MANAGEMENT, INC.—See The Bureau of National Affairs, Inc.; *U.S. Private,* pg. 182

TAXANDRIA PHARMACEUTICA B.V.—See Johnson & Johnson; *U.S. Public*, pg. 932
TAY-BAN CORPORATION—See Republic Industries, Inc.; *U.S. Public*, pg. 1380
ALLEN TAYLOR & CO. LIMITED—See Boral Limited; *Int'l*, pg. 203
TAYLOR & FRANCIS—See Taylor & Francis Group Ltd.; *Int'l*, pg. 1358
TAYLOR & FRANCIS GROUP LTD.; *Int'l*, pg. 1357
TAYLOR & FRANCIS PHILADELPHIA—See Taylor & Francis Group Ltd.; *Int'l*, pg. 1358
TAYLOR & GOODMAN LTD.—See Sophus Berendsen A/S; *Int'l*, pg. 1285
TAYLOR BROS.—See Conwood Company L.P.; *U.S. Private*, pg. 272
TAYLOR BUILDING PRODUCTS COMPANY—See American Architectural Products, Inc.; *U.S. Public*, pg. 67
TAYLOR CAPITAL GROUP; *U.S. Private*, pg. 1070
TAYLOR COMPANY—See Specialty Equipment Companies Inc.; *U.S. Public*, pg. 1496
TAYLOR CONTROL S.L.—See ABB Asea Brown Boveri (Holding) Ltd.; *Int'l*, pg. 6
TAYLOR CORPORATION; *U.S. Private*, pg. 1070
D.C. TAYLOR CO.; *U.S. Private*, pg. 1070
TAYLOR HOBSON PNEUMO—See The Rank Group PLC; *Int'l*, pg. 1087
TAYLOR HOME HEALTH INC.—See Integrated Health Services, Inc.; *U.S. Public*, pg. 885
TAYLOR IMPRESSION, INC.; *U.S. Private*, pg. 1070
TAYLOR INSTRUMENT—See ABB Asea Brown Boveri (Holding) Ltd.; *Int'l*, pg. 6
TAYLOR INSTRUMENT B.V.—See ABB Asea Brown Boveri (Holding) Ltd.; *Int'l*, pg. 6
TAYLOR INSTRUMENT C.A.—See ABB Asea Brown Boveri (Holding) Ltd.; *Int'l*, pg. 6
TAYLOR INSTRUMENT COMPANY (INDIA) LTD.—See ABB Asea Brown Boveri (Holding) Ltd.; *Int'l*, pg. 6
TAYLOR INSTRUMENT FRANCE—See ABB Asea Brown Boveri (Holding) Ltd.; *Int'l*, pg. 6
TAYLOR INSTRUMENT GMBH—See ABB Asea Brown Boveri (Holding) Ltd.; *Int'l*, pg. 6
TAYLOR INSTRUMENT K.K.—See ABB Asea Brown Boveri (Holding) Ltd.; *Int'l*, pg. 6
TAYLOR INSTRUMENT LTD.—See ABB Asea Brown Boveri (Holding) Ltd.; *Int'l*, pg. 6
TAYLOR INSTRUMENT N.V.—See ABB Asea Brown Boveri (Holding) Ltd.; *Int'l*, pg. 6
TAYLOR INSTRUMENT PTE. LTD.—See ABB Asea Brown Boveri (Holding) Ltd.; *Int'l*, pg. 6
TAYLOR INSTRUMENT PTY. LTD.—See ABB Asea Brown Boveri (Holding) Ltd.; *Int'l*, pg. 6
TAYLOR INSTRUMENT S.A. DE C.V.—See ABB Asea Brown Boveri (Holding) Ltd.; *Int'l*, pg. 6
TAYLOR INSTRUMENTOS, S.A.—See ABB Asea Brown Boveri (Holding) Ltd.; *Int'l*, pg. 6
TAYLOR INSURANCE BROKERS LIMITED—See Taylor Woodrow plc; *Int'l*, pg. 1358
TAYLOR-JETT DIV.—See United States Filter Corporation; *U.S. Public*, pg. 1682
J.P. TAYLOR CO., INC.—See Universal Corporation; *U.S. Public*, pg. 1695
TAYLOR KOSMETIK G.M.B.H.—See Pfizer Inc.; *U.S. Public*, pg. 1283
TAYLOR MACHINE WORKS, INC.; *U.S. Private*, pg. 1070
TAYLOR MADE GOLF CO. INC.—See Salomon S.A.; *Int'l*, pg. 1181
TAYLOR MADE (GREAT BRITAIN) LTD.—See Salomon S.A.; *Int'l*, pg. 1181
TAYLOR MADE GROUP, INC.; *U.S. Private*, pg. 1070
TAYLOR MADE-NEW YORK—See Taylor Made Group, Inc.; *U.S. Private*, pg. 1070
TAYLOR-MORLEY, INC.; *U.S. Private*, pg. 1071
TAYLOR - MORLEY MANAGEMENT COMPANY—See Taylor-Morley, Inc.; *U.S. Private*, pg. 1071
TAYLOR OIL CO.; *U.S. Private*, pg. 1071
TAYLOR, PEARSON & CARSON DIVISION—See Acklands Limited; *Int'l*, pg. 23
TAYLOR PUBLISHING CO.—See Insilco Corporation; *U.S. Public*, pg. 881
TAYLOR RENTAL—See TruServ Corporation; *U.S. Private*, pg. 1108
TAYLOR-WHARTON GAS EQUIPMENT—See Harsco Corporation; *U.S. Public*, pg. 793
TAYLOR WOODROW (AUSTRALIA) PTY. LIMITED—See Taylor Woodrow plc; *Int'l*, pg. 1359
TAYLOR WOODROW CIVIL ENGINEERING LTD.—See Taylor Woodrow plc; *Int'l*, pg. 1358
TAYLOR WOODROW CONSTRUCTION CORP.—See Taylor Woodrow plc; *Int'l*, pg. 1359
TAYLOR WOODROW CONSTRUCTION HOLDINGS LIMITED—See Taylor Woodrow plc; *Int'l*, pg. 1358
TAYLOR WOODROW CONSTRUCTION LIMITED—See Taylor Woodrow plc; *Int'l*, pg. 1358
TAYLOR WOODROW CONSTRUCTION (MIDLANDS) LTD.—See Taylor Woodrow plc; *Int'l*, pg. 1358
TAYLOR WOODROW CONSTRUCTION (NORTHERN) LTD.—See Taylor Woodrow plc; *Int'l*, pg. 1358
TAYLOR WOODROW CONSTRUCTION (SCOTLAND) LTD.—See Taylor Woodrow plc; *Int'l*, pg. 1358
TAYLOR WOODROW CONSTRUCTION (SOUTHERN) LTD.—See Taylor Woodrow plc; *Int'l*, pg. 1358
TAYLOR WOODROW CORSER PTY. LIMITED—See Taylor Woodrow plc; *Int'l*, pg. 1358
TAYLOR WOODROW DEVELOPMENTS LTD.—See Taylor Woodrow plc; *Int'l*, pg. 1358
TAYLOR WOODROW HOMES BUILDERS PTY. LTD.—See Taylor Woodrow plc; *Int'l*, pg. 1359
TAYLOR WOODROW HOMES CALIFORNIA LIMITED—See Taylor Woodrow plc; *Int'l*, pg. 1359
TAYLOR WOODROW HOMES FLORIDA INC.—See Taylor Woodrow plc; *Int'l*, pg. 1359
TAYLOR WOODROW INDUSTRIAL ESTATES LTD.—See Taylor Woodrow plc; *Int'l*, pg. 1358

TAYLOR WOODROW INTERNATIONAL LTD.—See Taylor Woodrow plc; *Int'l*, pg. 1358
TAYLOR WOODROW INTERNATIONAL NZ LIMITED—See Taylor Woodrow plc; *Int'l*, pg. 1359
TAYLOR WOODROW INTERNATIONAL PROJECTS LTD.—See Taylor Woodrow plc; *Int'l*, pg. 1358
TAYLOR WOODROW MANAGEMENT & ENGINEERING LIMITED—See Taylor Woodrow plc; *Int'l*, pg. 1358
TAYLOR WOODROW MANAGEMENT LTD.—See Taylor Woodrow plc; *Int'l*, pg. 1359
TAYLOR WOODROW OF CALIFORNIA INC.—See Taylor Woodrow plc; *Int'l*, pg. 1359
TAYLOR WOODROW OF GHANA LIMITED—See Taylor Woodrow plc; *Int'l*, pg. 1360
TAYLOR WOODROW OF GIBRALTAR LIMITED—See Taylor Woodrow plc; *Int'l*, pg. 1360
TAYLOR WOODROW OF NIGERIA LIMITED—See Taylor Woodrow plc; *Int'l*, pg. 1360
TAYLOR WOODROW OF SAN FRANCISCO INC.—See Taylor Woodrow plc; *Int'l*, pg. 1359
TAYLOR WOODROW PLC; *Int'l*, pg. 1358
TAYLOR WOODROW PROPERTY COMPANY (GEORGIA) INC.—See Taylor Woodrow plc; *Int'l*, pg. 1359
TAYLOR WOODROW PROPERTY COMPANY LTD.—See Taylor Woodrow plc; *Int'l*, pg. 1359
TAYLOR WOODROW PROPERTY CO. OF AMERICA INC.—See Taylor Woodrow plc; *Int'l*, pg. 1359
TAYLOR WOODROW PROPERTY HOLDINGS PTY. LTD.—See Taylor Woodrow plc; *Int'l*, pg. 1360
TAYLOR WOODROW SERVICES LTD.—See Taylor Woodrow plc; *Int'l*, pg. 1359
TAYLOR WOODROW-TOWELL CO. (LLC)—See Taylor Woodrow plc; *Int'l*, pg. 1360
TAYLOR WOODROW (VICTORIA) PTY. LTD.—See Taylor Woodrow plc; *Int'l*, pg. 1360
TAYMECH LIMITED—See Taylor Woodrow plc; *Int'l*, pg. 1359
TAYMECH (U.S.A) INC.—See Taylor Woodrow plc; *Int'l*, pg. 1359
TAYSEC CONSTRUCTION LIMITED—See Taylor Woodrow plc; *Int'l*, pg. 1359
TAYSEC CONSTRUCTION LTD.—See Taylor Woodrow plc; *Int'l*, pg. 1360
TAYSEC PROPERTIES LTD.—See Taylor Woodrow plc; *Int'l*, pg. 1360
TAYSTEE BAKERIES—See Specialty Foods Corporation; *U.S. Private*, pg. 1022
TAYWOOD ENERGY SERVICES INC.—See Taylor Woodrow plc; *Int'l*, pg. 1359
TAYWOOD ENGINEERING LTD.—See Taylor Woodrow plc; *Int'l*, pg. 1359
TAYWOOD FARMS PTY. LTD.—See Taylor Woodrow plc; *Int'l*, pg. 1360
TAYWOOD HOMES LTD.—See Taylor Woodrow plc; *Int'l*, pg. 1359
TAYWOOD MINERALS INC.—See Taylor Woodrow plc; *Int'l*, pg. 1359
TAYWOOD MINING INC.—See Taylor Woodrow plc; *Int'l*, pg. 1359
TAYWOOD PLANT COMPANY LTD.—See Taylor Woodrow plc; *Int'l*, pg. 1359
TB WOOD'S CORPORATION; *U.S. Public*, pg. 1562
TCHNOFLOW TUBE-SYSTEMS GMBH—See TI Group plc; *Int'l*, pg. 1341
TE HENNEPE LIN-PACK B.V.—See Forbo Holding SA; *Int'l*, pg. 498
TE PAPAPA PAPER MILL—See International Paper Company; *U.S. Public*, pg. 905
TEA DIRECT—See Celestial Seasonings; *U.S. Public*, pg. 320
TEAC AMERICA, INC.—See Teac Corporation; *Int'l*, pg. 1360
TEAC AUSTRALIA PTY. LTD.—See Teac Corporation; *Int'l*, pg. 1360
TEAC CANADA LTD.—See Teac Corporation; *Int'l*, pg. 1360
TEAC CORPORATION; *Int'l*, pg. 1360
TEAC DEUTSCHLAND GMBH—See Teac Corporation; *Int'l*, pg. 1360
TEAC FRANCE S.A.—See Teac Corporation; *Int'l*, pg. 1360
TEAC ITALIANA S.P.A.—See Teac Corporation; *Int'l*, pg. 1360
TEAC MEXICO S.A. DE C.V.—See Teac Corporation; *Int'l*, pg. 1360
TEAC UK LTD.—See Teac Corporation; *Int'l*, pg. 1360
WM. TEACHER & SONS LIMITED—See Allied Domecq PLC; *Int'l*, pg. 63
TEACHERS INSURANCE AND ANNUITY ASSOCIATION; *U.S. Private*, pg. 1071
TEACHERS INSURANCE COMPANY—See Horace Mann Educators Corporation; *U.S. Public*, pg. 836
TEAL ELECTRONICS—See SL Industries, Inc.; *U.S. Public*, pg. 1419
TEAM EDITION APPAREL, INC.—See Woolworth Corporation; *U.S. Public*, pg. 1777
TEAM, INC.; *U.S. Public*, pg. 1562
TEAM INDUSTRIAL SERVICES, INC.—See Team, Inc.; *U.S. Public*, pg. 1562
TEAM ONE ADVERTISING—See Saatchi & Saatchi Advertising Worldwide; *U.S. Public*, pg. 1422
TEAM REHAB, INC.—See RehabCare Group, Inc.; *U.S. Public*, pg. 1373
TEAMWORK CONSTRUCTIONS PTY. LIMITED—See Taylor Woodrow plc; *Int'l*, pg. 1360
TEAMWORK CORPORATION SDN BHD—See Taylor Woodrow plc; *Int'l*, pg. 1360
TEAMWORK DEVELOPMENTS LIMITED—See Taylor Woodrow plc; *Int'l*, pg. 1360
TEAMWORK MALAYSIA SENDIRIAN BERHAD—See Taylor Woodrow plc; *Int'l*, pg. 1360
TEAMWORK SAUDI ARABIA LIMITED—See Taylor Woodrow plc; *Int'l*, pg. 1360
TEAMWORK SENDIRIAN BERHAD—See Taylor Woodrow plc; *Int'l*, pg. 1360

THE TEAROOM IN UTICA SQUARE, INC.—See Helmerich & Payne, Inc.; *U.S. Public*, pg. 808
TEBABAU GMBH—See Ruetgers A.G.; *Int'l*, pg. 1148
TEBEREBIE GOLDFIELDS, LTD.—See The Pioneer Group, Inc.; *U.S. Public*, pg. 1298
TEBODIN BV CONSULTANTS & ENGINEERS—See Hollandsche Beton Groep NV; *Int'l*, pg. 630
TECA CORPORATION—See Vickers PLC; *Int'l*, pg. 1468
TECFOR INC.—See Electrolux, AB; *Int'l*, pg. 440
TECH-AEROFOAM PRODUCTS, INC.—See Great American Industries, Inc.; *U.S. Private*, pg. 473
TECH/AID—See Technical Aid Corporation; *U.S. Private*, pg. 1072
TECH-ATLAN—See Technip; *Int'l*, pg. 1360
TECH-ATLAN - VILLENEUVE D'ASCO BRANCH—See Technip; *Int'l*, pg. 1360
TECH DATA BRASIL—See Tech Data Corporation; *U.S. Public*, pg. 1562
TECH DATA CANADA, INC.—See Tech Data Corporation; *U.S. Public*, pg. 1562
TECH DATA CORPORATION; *U.S. Public*, pg. 1562
TECH DATA EDUCATION—See Tech Data Corporation; *U.S. Public*, pg. 1562
TECH DATA FINANCE—See Tech Data Corporation; *U.S. Public*, pg. 1562
TECH DATA FRANCE—See Tech Data Corporation; *U.S. Public*, pg. 1563
TECH DATA LATIN AMERICA—See Tech Data Corporation; *U.S. Public*, pg. 1562
TECH DEVELOPMENT INC.—See Siebe plc; *Int'l*, pg. 1242
THE TECH GROUP; *U.S. Private*, pg. 1071
TECH GROUP CHICAGO, INC.—See The Tech Group; *U.S. Private*, pg. 1071
TECH GROUP PHOENIX, INC.—See The Tech Group; *U.S. Private*, pg. 1071
TECH GROUP PUERTO RICO—See The Tech Group; *U.S. Private*, pg. 1071
TECH GROUP SCOTTSDALE, INC.—See The Tech Group; *U.S. Private*, pg. 1071
TECH GROUP SINGAPORE, INC.—See The Tech Group; *U.S. Private*, pg. 1071
TECH GROUP TEMPE INC.—See The Tech Group; *U.S. Private*, pg. 1071
TECH INDUSTRIES, INC.; *U.S. Private*, pg. 1071
TECH-MET CANADA LTD.—See Emerson Electric Co.; *U.S. Public*, pg. 575
TECH MOLD—See The Tech Group; *U.S. Private*, pg. 1071
TECH/OPS SEVCON, INC.; *U.S. Public*, pg. 1563
TECH SEMICONDUCTOR SINGAPORE PTE., LTD.—See Canon Inc.; *Int'l*, pg. 262
TECH SPRAY, INC.; *U.S. Private*, pg. 1071
TECH-SYM CORPORATION; *U.S. Public*, pg. 1563
TECH SYSTEMS CORP.—See Datron Incorporated; *U.S. Private*, pg. 313
TECH-TRAN CORPORATION—See Inductotherm Industries, Inc.; *U.S. Private*, pg. 560
TECHALLOY CO., INC.—See Groupe Usinor; *Int'l*, pg. 572
TECHDYNE, INC.—See Medicore Inc.; *U.S. Public*, pg. 1080
TECHLAM SA—See SNECMA - Societe Nationale d'Etude et de Construction de Moteurs d'Aviation; *Int'l*, pg. 1166
TECHNE CORPORATION; *U.S. Public*, pg. 1563
TECHNI-THERM INC.—See Domtar Inc.; *Int'l*, pg. 416
TECHNIC INCORPORATED; *U.S. Private*, pg. 1071
TECHNICAL AID CORPORATION; *U.S. Private*, pg. 1072
TECHNICAL COATINGS CO.—See Benjamin Moore & Co.; *U.S. Private*, pg. 133
TECHNICAL ENGINEERING SERVICES LTD.—See Telefonaktiebolaget LM Ericsson; *Int'l*, pg. 1370
TECHNICAL FIELD SERVICES INTERNATIONAL—See Thomson S.A.; *Int'l*, pg. 1382
TECHNICAL IMAGE PRODUCTS, INC./DGI; *U.S. Private*, pg. 1072
TECHNICAL INFORMATION (SINTEP)—See Petrobras - Petroleo Brasileiro S.A.; *Int'l*, pg. 1042
TECHNICAL INSTRUMENT COMPANY—See Zygo Corporation; *U.S. Public*, pg. 1795
TECHNICAL MATERIALS, INC.—See Brush Wellman Inc.; *U.S. Public*, pg. 266
TECHNICAL PAPER—See Kimberly-Clark Corporation; *U.S. Public*, pg. 958
TECHNICAL RESEARCH INSTITUTE—See Obayashi Corporation; *Int'l*, pg. 995
TECHNICAL RESEARCH LABORATORY—See Kansai Paint Co., Ltd.; *Int'l*, pg. 723
TECHNICAL SERVICES DIVISION—See Tracor, Inc.; *U.S. Public*, pg. 1627
TECHNICAL SERVICES GROUP—See Namanco LLC; *U.S. Private*, pg. 773
TECHNICAL SPECIALTIES DIVISION—See FiberMark Inc.; *U.S. Public*, pg. 620
TECHNICOLOR, INC.—See Carlton Communications Plc; *Int'l*, pg. 272
TECHNICOLOR PROFESSIONAL FILM DIV.—See MacAndrews & Forbes Holdings Inc.; *U.S. Private*, pg. 689
TECHNICOLOR VIDEOCASSETTE INC.—See MacAndrews & Forbes Holdings Inc.; *U.S. Private*, pg. 689
TECHNICOMP, INC.—See Brown & Sharpe Manufacturing Company; *U.S. Public*, pg. 260
TECHNICS PLASMA GMBH PLASMA- UND LONENSTRAHLSYSTEME—See Mannesmann A.G.; *Int'l*, pg. 836
TECHNIFORM CORP.—See LSB Industries, Inc.; *U.S. Public*, pg. 971
TECHNIMAT/TDS—See General Electric Company; *U.S. Public*, pg. 711
TECHNIP; *Int'l*, pg. 1360
TECHNIP - AIX-EN-PROVENCE BRANCH—See Technip; *Int'l*, pg. 1360
TECHNIP ANLAGENBAU GMBH—See Technip; *Int'l*, pg. 1361
TECHNIP BENELUX—See Technip; *Int'l*, pg. 1361

MASTER INDEX TO COMPANY NAMES
TEKTRONIX
Company Index

TECHNIP C.I.S.—See Technip; *Int'l*, pg. 1361
TECHNIP CLE—See Technip; *Int'l*, pg. 1360
TECHNIP CLEPLAN—See Technip; *Int'l*, pg. 1361
TECHNIP-GEOPRODUCTION—See Technip; *Int'l*, pg. 1361
TECHNIP INC.—See Technip; *Int'l*, pg. 1361
TECHNIP INTERNATIONAL AG—See Technip; *Int'l*, pg. 1361
TECHNIP - LYON BRANCH—See Technip; *Int'l*, pg. 1360
TECHNIP MALAYSIA—See Technip; *Int'l*, pg. 1361
TECHNIP SAUDI ARABIA LTD.—See Technip; *Int'l*, pg. 1361
TECHNIP TIANCHEN—See Technip; *Int'l*, pg. 1361
TECHNIP TPS—See Technip; *Int'l*, pg. 1361
TECHNIP UK LTD.—See Technip; *Int'l*, pg. 1361
TECHNIPETROL—See Technip; *Int'l*, pg. 1361
TECHNISCH HANDELSBUREAU WEMEX B.V.—See Royal Begemann Group; *Int'l*, pg. 1133
TECHNISCHE GASE GMBH—See AGA AB; *Int'l*, pg. 14
TECHNISCHER HANDEL FREUDENBERG BESITZ GMBH—See Freudenberg & Company; *Int'l*, pg. 506
TECHNISCHER HANDEL FREUDENBERG KG—See Freudenberg & Company; *Int'l*, pg. 506
TECHNISH HANDELSKANTOOR LLOYD B.V.—See AAR Corp.; *U.S. Public*, pg. 2
TECHNITROL COMPONENT DIVISION—See Technitrol, Inc.; *U.S. Public*, pg. 1564
TECHNITROL, INC.; *U.S. Public*, pg. 1564
TECHNITROL INTERNATIONAL, INC.—See Technitrol, Inc.; *U.S. Public*, pg. 1564
TECHNITROL INVESTMENTS, INC.—See Technitrol, Inc.; *U.S. Public*, pg. 1564
TECHNITRON PLC.—See Oki Electric Industry Company, Ltd.; *Int'l*, pg. 1000
TECHNO CAOUTCHOUC INC.—See The Cascades Group; *Int'l*, pg. 274
TECHNO-COMMERCIAL—See GESTRA GmbH; *Int'l*, pg. 550
TECHNO DIV.—See Designatronics, Inc.; *U.S. Private*, pg. 327
TECHNO MATSUYA CO., LTD.—See Matsuya Company Ltd.; *Int'l*, pg. 848
TECHNOARBED LUXEMBOURG S.A.R.L.—See Arbed S.A.; *Int'l*, pg. 80
TECHNOCORP HOLDING S.A.—See SMH Swiss Corporation for Micro Electronics & Watchmaking Indus. Ltd.; *Int'l*, pg. 1161
TECHNODES S.A.—See Ciments Francais; *Int'l*, pg. 292
TECHNOFAN—See Labinal SA; *Int'l*, pg. 786
TECHNOFLOW IBERICA SA—See TI Group plc; *Int'l*, pg. 1341
TECHNOLOGIA MEDICA DEL CARIBE, C.A.—See Hewlett-Packard Company; *U.S. Public*, pg. 823
TECHNOLOGY FOR COMMUNICATIONS INTERNATIONAL—See TCI International Inc.; *U.S. Public*, pg. 1555
TECHNOLOGY GROUP—See Global Industrial Technologies; *U.S. Public*, pg. 748
TECHNOLOGY MANAGEMENT GROUP—See Computer Sciences Corporation; *U.S. Public*, pg. 423
TECHNOLOGY MARKETING (SECOMT)—See Petrobras - Petroleo Brasileiro S.A.; *Int'l*, pg. 1042
TECHNOLOGY RESEARCH CORPORATION; *U.S. Public*, pg. 1564
TECHNOLOGY SERVICES—See Sprint Corporation; *U.S. Public*, pg. 1501
TECHNOLOGY SOLUTIONS COMPANY (TSC); *U.S. Public*, pg. 1564
TECHNOLOGY SOLUTIONS INC.—See Weber Public Relations Worldwide; *U.S. Private*, pg. 1157
TECHNOLOGY SYSTEMS CORPORATION—See Safeguard Scientifics, Inc.; *U.S. Public*, pg. 1425
TECHNOLOGY TRANSFER INSTITUTE; *U.S. Private*, pg. 1072
TECHNOMER (PRIVATE) LTD.—See BTR plc; *Int'l*, pg. 129
TECHNOPHONE MANUFACTURING (H.K.) LTD.—See Oy Nokia Ab/Nokia Group; *Int'l*, pg. 952
TECHNOR PTY. LIMITED—See Molex Incorporated; *U.S. Public*, pg. 1123
TECHNOSERVE INTERNATIONAL CO., INC.—See JGC Corporation; *Int'l*, pg. 697
TECHNOSTAAL SCHOUTEN BV—See Tate & Lyle PLC; *Int'l*, pg. 1357
TECHNUM N.V.—See Tractebel; *Int'l*, pg. 1415
TECHOTEL, AG—See Sulcus Computer Corp.; *U.S. Public*, pg. 1527
TECHPACK INTERNATIONAL-TPI—See Pechiney S.A.; *Int'l*, pg. 1029
TECHSONIC INDUSTRIES, INC.—See Teleflex Incorporated; *U.S. Public*, pg. 1570
TECHSPACE AERO—See SNECMA - Societe Nationale d'Etude et de Construction de Moteurs d'Aviation; *Int'l*, pg. 1166
TECK CHEM COMPANY LIMITED—See Sinochem International Petroleum Co. Ltd.; *Int'l*, pg. 1256
TECK CORPORATION—See Metallgesellschaft AG; *Int'l*, pg. 862
TECKINO MANUFACTURING B.V.B.A.—See Robinson Nugent, Inc.; *U.S. Public*, pg. 1395
TECKNIT INCORPORATED; *U.S. Private*, pg. 1072
TECLA, S.A.—See Caja de Madrid Group; *Int'l*, pg. 252
TECMAR TECHNOLOGIES, INC.—See Tecmar Technologies International, Inc.; *Int'l*, pg. 1361
TECMAR TECHNOLOGIES INTERNATIONAL, INC.; *Int'l*, pg. 1361
TECMINEMET—See Imetal; *Int'l*, pg. 662
TECMISE COMPONENTES AUTOMOTIVOS S.A.—See Iochpe-Maxion S.A.; *Int'l*, pg. 688
TECNAL CORPORATION—See Enso Oyj; *Int'l*, pg. 457
TECNICA—See Hewlett-Packard Company; *U.S. Public*, pg. 823
TECNIFLO OMEGA, INC.—See Omega Environmental Inc.; *U.S. Public*, pg. 1222
TECNIMONT SPA—See Compart SpA; *Int'l*, pg. 324
TECNIQUIMIA MEXICANA S.A. DE C.V.—See Quaker Chemical Corporation; *U.S. Public*, pg. 1347
TECNOCAR GMBH—See Labinal SA; *Int'l*, pg. 786
TECNOCAR PLANT—See Labinal SA; *Int'l*, pg. 786
TECNOCAR SRL—See Labinal SA; *Int'l*, pg. 786
TECNOCERIO S.A.—See Societe BIC S.A.; *Int'l*, pg. 1273
TECNOCONFORT SA—See Bertrand Faure; *Int'l*, pg. 193
TECNOCRETO S.A. DE C.V.—See Novartis AG; *Int'l*, pg. 986
TECNOFLUOR INC.—See Fluor Corporation; *U.S. Public*, pg. 661
TECNOLOGIA MODIFICADO S.A. DE C.V.—See Caterpillar Inc.; *U.S. Public*, pg. 317
TECNOLOGIAS NEC DE MEXICO, S.A. DE C.V.—See NEC Corporation; *Int'l*, pg. 901
TECNOLOGIE PROGETTI LAVORI SPA—See Technip; *Int'l*, pg. 1361
TECNORD @ DELTA POWER CO.—See Delta Power Co.; *U.S. Private*, pg. 322
TECNOST-MAEL—See Olivetti SpA; *Int'l*, pg. 1002
TECNOVER—See Saint-Gobain; *Int'l*, pg. 1172
TECNOVIDRO INDUSTRIA, COMERCIO E REPRESENTACOES LTDA.—See Saint-Gobain; *Int'l*, pg. 1176
TECO COALBED METHANE, INC.—See TECO Energy, Inc.; *U.S. Public*, pg. 1565
TECO DIVERSIFIED, INC.—See TECO Energy, Inc.; *U.S. Public*, pg. 1565
TECO ENERGY, INC.; *U.S. Public*, pg. 1565
TECO FINANCE, INC.—See TECO Energy, Inc.; *U.S. Public*, pg. 1565
TECO INVESTMENTS, INC.—See TECO Energy, Inc.; *U.S. Public*, pg. 1565
TECO MANUFACTURING, INC.—See Team, Inc.; *U.S. Public*, pg. 1562
TECO POWER SERVICES, INC.—See TECO Energy, Inc.; *U.S. Public*, pg. 1565
TECO PROPERTIES, INC.—See TECO Energy, Inc.; *U.S. Public*, pg. 1565
TECO SCHALLSCHUTZ GMBH—See Ruetgers A.G.; *Int'l*, pg. 1148
TECOGEN INC.—See Thermo Electron Corporation; *U.S. Public*, pg. 1592
TECOM INDUSTRIES, INC.—See Tech-Sym Corporation; *U.S. Public*, pg. 1563
TECOMET-ALBUQUERQUE—See Thermo Electron Corporation; *U.S. Public*, pg. 1592
TECOMET INC.—See Thermo Electron Corporation; *U.S. Public*, pg. 1591
TECOMET-TEMPE—See Thermo Electron Corporation; *U.S. Public*, pg. 1592
TECOT ELECTRIC SUPPLY COMPANY—See Rumsey Electric Company; *U.S. Private*, pg. 951
TECPLANT INGEST—See Technip; *Int'l*, pg. 1361
TECSINTER—See Olivetti SpA; *Int'l*, pg. 1002
TECSTAR INC.; *U.S. Private*, pg. 1072
TECSYN INTERNATIONAL, INC.; *Int'l*, pg. 1361
TECSYN P.M.P. INC.—See TecSyn International, Inc.; *Int'l*, pg. 1362
TECUMSEH DO BRASIL—See Tecumseh Products Company; *U.S. Public*, pg. 1566
TECUMSEH EUROPA—See Tecumseh Products Company; *U.S. Public*, pg. 1566
TECUMSEH PRODUCTS COMPANY; *U.S. Public*, pg. 1565
TECUMSEH PRODUCTS OF CANADA LTD.—See Tecumseh Products Company; *U.S. Public*, pg. 1566
TECUMSEH PRODUCTS RESEARCH LAB.—See Tecumseh Products Company; *U.S. Public*, pg. 1566
TEDAK AB—See Charter plc; *Int'l*, pg. 281
TEDDINGTON COMPANY LIMITED—See Corning Incorporated; *U.S. Public*, pg. 449
TEDDINGTON CONTROLS LIMITED—See SLD Holdings Ltd.; *Int'l*, pg. 1160
TEDEA INC.—See IDB Holding Corporation; *Int'l*, pg. 644
TEDEC-MEIJI FARMA S.A.—See Meiji Seika Kaisha, Ltd.; *Int'l*, pg. 856
TEDECO B.V.—See Schmalbach-Lubeca AG; *Int'l*, pg. 1207
TEDECO GMBH—See Schmalbach-Lubeca AG; *Int'l*, pg. 1207
TEDECO S.A.R.L.—See Schmalbach-Lubeca AG; *Int'l*, pg. 1207
TEENFORM INC.—See Wacoal Corporation; *Int'l*, pg. 1484
TEEPAK, INC., ZURICH BRANCH—See Devro International Plc; *Int'l*, pg. 408
TEERBAU GMBH—See Ruetgers A.G.; *Int'l*, pg. 1148
TEES STORAGE COMPANY LIMITED—See GATX Corporation; *U.S. Public*, pg. 693
TEESSIDE HOLDINGS LIMITED—See Powell Duffryn PLC; *Int'l*, pg. 1065
TEFAL BELGIUM—See Groupe SEB; *Int'l*, pg. 568
TEFAL DANMARK A/S—See Groupe SEB; *Int'l*, pg. 568
TEFAL ESPANA SA—See Groupe SEB; *Int'l*, pg. 568
TEFAL ET KV SAINT PETERSBURG—See Groupe SEB; *Int'l*, pg. 568
TEFAL HANDELSGESELLSCHAFT MBH—See Groupe SEB; *Int'l*, pg. 568
TEFAL INDIA HOUSEHOLD APPLIANCES PVT. LTD.—See Groupe SEB; *Int'l*, pg. 568
TEFAL ISTANBUL—See Groupe SEB; *Int'l*, pg. 568
TEFAL ITALIA S.P.A.—See Groupe SEB; *Int'l*, pg. 568
TEFAL MEXICANA S.A. DE C.V.—See Groupe SEB; *Int'l*, pg. 568
TEFAL NEDERLAND B.V.—See Groupe SEB; *Int'l*, pg. 568
TEFAL ROWENTA PORTUGAL—See Groupe SEB; *Int'l*, pg. 568
TEFAL S.A.—See Groupe SEB; *Int'l*, pg. 569
TEFAL UK LTD.—See Groupe SEB; *Int'l*, pg. 569
TEFINA HOLDING AG—See Rieter Holdings; *Int'l*, pg. 1116
TEGA INDIA LTD—See Svedala Industri AB; *Int'l*, pg. 1324
TEGA-TECHNISCHE GASE UND GASETECHNIK GMBH—See Linde AG; *Int'l*, pg. 811
TEGEL FOODS LIMITED—See H.J. Heinz Company; *U.S. Public*, pg. 807
TEGIMENTA AG—See Roche Holding Ltd.; *Int'l*, pg. 1120
AB TEGMA—See Mine Safety Appliances Co.; *U.S. Public*, pg. 1114
TEGNER & SON AB—See Diageo Plc; *Int'l*, pg. 412
TEHDASPUU OY—See UPM-Kymmene Corporation; *Int'l*, pg. 1429
TEHNOKOM—See GESTRA GmbH; *Int'l*, pg. 550
A. TEICHERT & SON, INC.; *U.S. Private*, pg. 1072
TEICHERT LAND CO.—See A. Teichert & Son, Inc.; *U.S. Private*, pg. 1073
TEICHIKU RECORDS CO., LTD.—See Matsushita Electric Industrial Co., Ltd.; *Int'l*, pg. 846
TEIJIN LIMITED; *Int'l*, pg. 1362
TEIJIN-HERCULES LTD.—See Hercules Incorporated; *U.S. Public*, pg. 811
TEJAS GAS CORPORATION—See Royal Dutch/Shell Group of Companies; *Int'l*, pg. 1136
TEJAS GAS SYSTEMS, INC.—See Royal Dutch/Shell Group of Companies; *Int'l*, pg. 1136
TEJAS-GULF CORP.—See Royal Dutch/Shell Group of Companies; *Int'l*, pg. 1136
TEJAS HYDROCARBONS CO.—See Royal Dutch/Shell Group of Companies; *Int'l*, pg. 1136
TEJAS WESTERN OUTLET—See Luskeys Western Stores, Inc.; *U.S. Private*, pg. 681
TEJON AGRICULTURAL CORP.—See Tejon Ranch Company; *U.S. Public*, pg. 1566
TEJON FARMING COMPANY—See Tejon Ranch Company; *U.S. Public*, pg. 1566
TEJON RANCH COMPANY; *U.S. Public*, pg. 1566
TEKELEC; *U.S. Public*, pg. 1566
TEKELEC-INDIA PVT. LTD.—See Tekelec; *U.S. Public*, pg. 1566
TEKELEC, LTD.—See Tekelec; *U.S. Public*, pg. 1566
TEKGRAF, INC.; *U.S. Private*, pg. 1073
TEKIMAL ASANOR SANAYI VE TICARET A.S.—See Kone Corporation; *Int'l*, pg. 748
TEKKEN CORPORATION; *Int'l*, pg. 1362
TEKMATEX, INC.—See Marubeni Corporation; *Int'l*, pg. 845
TEKNECOMP—See Olivetti SpA; *Int'l*, pg. 1002
TEKNI-PLEX, INC.; *U.S. Private*, pg. 1073
TEKNIK MALZEME—See Bertrand Faure; *Int'l*, pg. 193
TEKNOLOGI & UTBYGGING/TECHNOLOGY & PROJECTS—See Norsk Hydro a.s; *Int'l*, pg. 961
TEKNOLON OY—See Schuttersveld Holding N.V.; *Int'l*, pg. 1210
TEKNOR APEX COMPANY; *U.S. Private*, pg. 1073
TEKNOR COLOR COMPANY—See Teknor Apex Company; *U.S. Private*, pg. 1073
TEKNOSAN AB—See Cultor Ltd.; *Int'l*, pg. 349
TEKONSHA ENGINEERING CO.—See Echlin Inc.; *U.S. Public*, pg. 560
TEKRA CORPORATION; *U.S. Private*, pg. 1073
TEKRA CORP., SOUTHEAST DIV.—See Tekra Corporation; *U.S. Private*, pg. 1073
TEKSID ALUMINUM FOUNDRY—See Fiat Auto SpA; *Int'l*, pg. 483
TEKSID, INC.—See Fiat Auto SpA; *Int'l*, pg. 483
TEKSID S.P.A.—See Fiat Auto SpA; *Int'l*, pg. 483
TEKTRONIX AB—See Tektronix, Inc.; *U.S. Public*, pg. 1567
TEKTRONIX A/S—See Tektronix, Inc.; *U.S. Public*, pg. 1567
TEKTRONIX ASIA, LIMITED—See Tektronix, Inc.; *U.S. Public*, pg. 1567
TEKTRONIX AUSTRALIA PTY. LIMITED—See Tektronix, Inc.; *U.S. Public*, pg. 1567
TEKTRONIX CANADA INC.—See Tektronix, Inc.; *U.S. Public*, pg. 1567
TEKTRONIX CHINA LTD.—See Tektronix, Inc.; *U.S. Public*, pg. 1567
TEKTRONIX DEVELOPMENT COMPANY—See Tektronix, Inc.; *U.S. Public*, pg. 1567
TEKTRONIX ENGINEERING DEVELOPMENT (INDIA) PRIVATE LIMITED—See Tektronix, Inc.; *U.S. Public*, pg. 1567
TEKTRONIX ESPANOLA S.A.-BARCELONA—See Tektronix, Inc.; *U.S. Public*, pg. 1567
TEKTRONIX ESPANOLA S.A.-MADRID—See Tektronix, Inc.; *U.S. Public*, pg. 1567
TEKTRONIX EUROPE, INC.—See Tektronix, Inc.; *U.S. Public*, pg. 1567
TEKTRONIX FEDERAL SYSTEMS, INC.—See Tektronix, Inc.; *U.S. Public*, pg. 1567
TEKTRONIX FOREIGN SALES CORPORATION—See Tektronix, Inc.; *U.S. Public*, pg. 1567
TEKTRONIX FUNDING CORPORATION—See Tektronix, Inc.; *U.S. Public*, pg. 1567
TEKTRONIX GESMBH—See Tektronix, Inc.; *U.S. Public*, pg. 1567
TEKTRONIX GMBH—See Tektronix, Inc.; *U.S. Public*, pg. 1567
TEKTRONIX HOLLAND N.V.—See Tektronix, Inc.; *U.S. Public*, pg. 1567
TEKTRONIX HOLLAND N.V.-HEERENVEEN—See Tektronix, Inc.; *U.S. Public*, pg. 1567
TEKTRONIX HONG KONG LTD.—See Tektronix, Inc.; *U.S. Public*, pg. 1567
TEKTRONIX, INC.; *U.S. Public*, pg. 1567
TEKTRONIX (INDIA) LIMITED—See Tektronix, Inc.; *U.S. Public*, pg. 1568
TEKTRONIX INDUSTRIA E COMERCIO LTDA.—See Tektronix, Inc.; *U.S. Public*, pg. 1568
TEKTRONIX INDUSTRIA E COMERCIO LTDA.-RIO—See Tektronix, Inc.; *U.S. Public*, pg. 1568
TEKTRONIX INTERNATIONAL AG—See Tektronix, Inc.; *U.S. Public*, pg. 1568
TEKTRONIX INTERNATIONAL, INC.—See Tektronix, Inc.; *U.S. Public*, pg. 1567
TEKTRONIX IRELAND LIMITED—See Tektronix, Inc.; *U.S. Public*, pg. 1568
TEKTRONIX KOREA LTD.—See Tektronix, Inc.; *U.S. Public*, pg. 1568
TEKTRONIX NEWSTAR, INC.—See Tektronix, Inc.; *U.S. Public*, pg. 1567

TEKTRONIX
DIRECTORY OF CORPORATE AFFILIATIONS
Company Index

TEKTRONIX NORGE A/S—See Tektronix, Inc.; *U.S. Public*, *pg. 1568*
TEKTRONIX N.V./S.A.—See Tektronix, Inc.; *U.S. Public*, pg. 1568
TEKTRONIX N.Z. LIMITED—See Tektronix, Inc.; *U.S. Public*, pg. 1568
TEKTRONIX OY—See Tektronix, Inc.; *U.S. Public*, pg. 1568
TEKTRONIX PROPERTIES, INC.—See Tektronix, Inc.; *U.S.* Public, pg. 1567
TEKTRONIX S.A.—See Tektronix, Inc.; *U.S. Public*, pg. 1568
TEKTRONIX S.A.-AEP—See Tektronix, Inc.; *U.S. Public*, pg. 1568
TEKTRONIX S.A. DE C.V.—See Tektronix, Inc.; *U.S. Public*, *pg. 1568*
TEKTRONIX S.A.-LN—See Tektronix, Inc.; *U.S. Public*, pg. 1568
TEKTRONIX S.A.-RENNES—See Tektronix, Inc.; *U.S. Public*, pg. 1568
TEKTRONIX S.A.-STRASBOURG—See Tektronix, Inc.; *U.S.* Public, pg. 1568
TEKTRONIX S.A.-TOULOUSE—See Tektronix, Inc.; *U.S. Public*, pg. 1568
TEKTRONIX SINGAPORE PTE. LTD.—See Tektronix, Inc.; *U.S. Public*, pg. 1568
TEKTRONIX SPA—See Tektronix, Inc.; *U.S. Public*, pg. 1568
TEKTRONIX TAIWAN LTD.-KAOHSIUNG—See Tektronix, Inc.; *U.S. Public*, pg. 1568
TEKTRONIX TAIWAN LTD.-TAIPEI—See Tektronix, Inc.; *U.S. Public*, pg. 1568
TEKTRONIX U.K. LIMITED—See Tektronix, Inc.; *U.S. Public*, pg. 1568
TEKTRONIX-VIDEO & NETWORKING DIV., GRASS VALLEY PRODUCTS—See Tektronix, Inc.; *U.S. Public*, *pg. 1567*
TEL-AD JERUSALEM STUDIO LTD.—See IDB Holding Corporation; *Int'l*, pg. 644
TEL-DRUG, INC.—See Cigna Corp.; *U.S. Public*, pg. 362
TEL MINERALWOLLE AG—See Saint-Gobain; *Int'l*, pg. 1176
TEL-SAVE HOLDINGS, INC.; *U.S. Public*, pg. 1568
TELA VERSICHERUNG AG—See Allianz Aktiengesellschaft; *Int'l*, pg. 58
TELAIR INTERNATIONAL—See Teleflex Incorporated; *U.S.* Public, pg. 1570
TELAIR INTERNATIONAL CARGO SYSTEMS—See Teleflex Incorporated; *U.S. Public*, pg. 1570
TELCEL - CHILE S.A.—See Motorola, Inc.; *U.S. Public*, pg. 1140
TELCEL S.A.—See Motorola, Inc.; *U.S. Public*, pg. 1140
TELCO CAPITAL CORP.—See R D I S Corporation; *U.S. Private*, pg. 903
TELCO CAPITAL CORPORATION; *U.S. Private*, pg. 1073
TELCO SYSTEMS, INC.; *U.S. Public*, pg. 1568
TELCOM SEMICONDUCTOR, INC.; *U.S. Public*, pg. 1569
TELDAN INFORMATION SYSTEMS—See NewsEdge Corporation; *U.S. Public*, pg. 1180
TELDIX GMBH—See Robert Bosch GmbH; *Int'l*, pg. 204
TELE-EKONOMI AB—See Aftonbladet AB; *Int'l*, pg. 29
TELE HACHETTE—See Lagardere Groupe; *Int'l*, pg. 794
TELE-MUNCHEN FERNSEH GMBH & CO.; *Int'l*, pg. 1362
TELE-QUOTE CORPORATION—See AEGON N.V.; *Int'l*, pg. 28
TELE-QUOTE, INC.—See AEGON N.V.; *Int'l*, pg. 28
TELE SCRIPPS CABLE—See The E.W. Scripps Company; *U.S. Public*, pg. 1448
TELE-TRIP COMPANY—See Mutual of Omaha Insurance Company; *U.S. Private*, pg. 770
TELEBEC LTEE—See BCE Inc.; *Int'l*, pg. 116
TELEBRAS S.A.; *Int'l*, pg. 1362
TELECABLE ASSOCIATES, INC.—See TCA Cable TV, Inc.; *U.S. Public*, pg. 1553
TELECARTERA, S.A.—See Telefonica de Espana, S.A.; *Int'l*, pg. 1371
TELECHECK SERVICES, INC.—See First Data Corporation; *U.S. Public*, pg. 631
TELECHRON OF NORTH CAROLINA, INC.; *U.S. Private*, pg. 1073
TELECOLUMBUS GMBH—See Veba AG; *Int'l*, pg. 1461
TELECOM ANALYSIS SYSTEMS—See Bowthorpe plc; *Int'l*, *pg. 208*
TELECOM CORPORATION OF NEW ZEALAND LIMITED—See Bell Atlantic Corporation; *U.S. Public*, pg. 204
TELECOM EIREANN; *Int'l*, pg. 1362
TELECOM ITALIA MOBILE—See Telecom Italia S.p.A.; *Int'l*, pg. 1363
TELECOM ITALIA S.P.A.; *Int'l*, pg. 1362
TELECOM ITALIA S.P.A.—See Telecom Italia S.p.A.; *Int'l*, pg. 1363
TELECOM SCANDINAVIA A/S—See Lagardere Groupe; *Int'l*, pg. 796
TELECOM SECURICOR CELLULAR RADIO LIMITED—See British Telecommunications plc; *Int'l*, pg. 222
TELECOM SOLUTIONS—See SymmetriCom, Inc.; *U.S. Public*, pg. 1547
TELECOM SOLUTIONS (EUROPE) LIMITED—See SymmetriCom, Inc.; *U.S. Public*, pg. 1547
TELECOM SOLUTIONS PUERTO RICO, INC.—See SymmetriCom, Inc.; *U.S. Public*, pg. 1547
TELECOMMUNICATIONS & COMPUTER TECHNOLOGIES, INC.—See Telefonaktiebolaget LM Ericsson; *Int'l*, pg. 1370
TELECOMMUNICATIONS GROUP—See Watkins-Johnson Company; *U.S. Public*, pg. 1745
TELECOMMUNICATIONS SYSTEMS—See Harris Corporation; *U.S. Public*, pg. 792
TELECOMMUNICATIONS TECHNIQUES CORP.—See Dynatech Corporation; *U.S. Public*, pg. 539
TELECOMMUNICATIONS TECHNOLOGY—See General Signal Corporation; *U.S. Public*, pg. 727
TELECOMMUNICATIONS TECHNOLOGY MIDDLE EAST INC.—See Lucent Technologies Inc.; *U.S. Public*, pg. 1018
TELECOMPONENTES ERICSSON S.A. DE C.V.—See Telefonaktiebolaget LM Ericsson; *Int'l*, pg. 1370
TELECOMSPOL SRO—See KPN Koninklyke PTT Nederland NV; *Int'l*, pg. 720
TELECOMUNICACIONES E INFORMATICA PARA CONCESIONARIOS S.A. DE C.V.—See Volkswagen AG; *Int'l*, pg. 1475
TELECOMUNICACIONES MARINAS, S.A. (TEMASA)—See Telefonica de Espana, S.A.; *Int'l*, pg. 1372
TELECORP SYSTEMS INC.—See Compagnie des Machines Bull; *Int'l*, pg. 316
TELECOURT BV—See KPN Koninklyke PTT Nederland NV; *Int'l*, pg. 721
TELECREDIT COLLECTION SERVICE—See Equifax Inc.; *U.S. Public*, pg. 588
TELECREDIT MARKETING SERVICES—See Equifax Inc.; *U.S. Public*, pg. 588
TELECREDIT SERVICE CENTER, INC.—See Equifax Inc.; *U.S. Public*, pg. 588
TELECREDIT SERVICE CORP.—See Equifax Inc.; *U.S. Public*, pg. 588
TELEDIFFUSION DE FRANCE—See France Telecom; *Int'l*, *pg. 503*
TELEDIGM—See Paradigm Communications; *U.S. Private*, pg. 838
TELEDINAMICA LDA.—See FKI Plc; *Int'l*, pg. 474
TELE-DIRECT (PUBLICATIONS) INC.—See BCE Inc.; *Int'l*, pg. 116
TELEDYNE ADVANCED MATERIALS—See Allegheny Teledyne Incorporated; *U.S. Public*, pg. 43
TELEDYNE BELGIUM S.A.—See Allegheny Teledyne Incorporated; *U.S. Public*, pg. 44
TELEDYNE BRAZIL—See Allegheny Teledyne Incorporated; *U.S. Public*, pg. 44
TELEDYNE BROWN ENGINEERING—See Allegheny Teledyne Incorporated; *U.S. Public*, pg. 43
TELEDYNE CASTING SERVICE—See Allegheny Teledyne Incorporated; *U.S. Public*, pg. 43
TELEDYNE CONTINENTAL MOTORS—See Allegheny Teledyne Incorporated; *U.S. Public*, pg. 43
TELEDYNE ELECTRONIC TECHNOLOGIES—See Allegheny Teledyne Incorporated; *U.S. Public*, pg. 43
TELEDYNE FLUID SYSTEMS—See Allegheny Teledyne Incorporated; *U.S. Public*, pg. 43
TELEDYNE FRANCE—See Allegheny Teledyne Incorporated; *U.S. Public*, pg. 44
TELEDYNE GERMANY—See Allegheny Teledyne Incorporated; *U.S. Public*, pg. 44
TELEDYNE ISRAEL—See Allegheny Teledyne Incorporated; *U.S. Public*, pg. 44
TELEDYNE ITALY—See Allegheny Teledyne Incorporated; *U.S. Public*, pg. 44
TELEDYNE JAPAN—See Allegheny Teledyne Incorporated; *U.S. Public*, pg. 44
TELEDYNE LAARS—See Allegheny Teledyne Incorporated; *U.S. Public*, pg. 43
TELEDYNE LAARS/JANDY PRODUCTS—See Allegheny Teledyne Incorporated; *U.S. Public*, pg. 43
TELEDYNE MALAYSIA—See Allegheny Teledyne Incorporated; *U.S. Public*, pg. 44
TELEDYNE PORTLAND FORGE—See Allegheny Teledyne Incorporated; *U.S. Public*, pg. 43
TELEDYNE RUSSIA—See Allegheny Teledyne Incorporated; *U.S. Public*, pg. 44
TELEDYNE RYAN AERONAUTICAL—See Allegheny Teledyne Incorporated; *U.S. Public*, pg. 43
TELEDYNE SPAIN—See Allegheny Teledyne Incorporated; *U.S. Public*, pg. 44
TELEDYNE SPECIALTY EQUIPMENT—See Allegheny Teledyne Incorporated; *U.S. Public*, pg. 44
TELEDYNE UNITED KINGDOM—See Allegheny Teledyne Incorporated; *U.S. Public*, pg. 44
TELEDYNE WATER PIK—See Allegheny Teledyne Incorporated; *U.S. Public*, pg. 44
TELEFLEX AUTOMOTIVE—See Teleflex Incorporated; *U.S.* Public, pg. 1569
TELEFLEX AUTOMOTIVE MANUFACTURING CORP.—See Teleflex Incorporated; *U.S. Public*, pg. 1569
TELEFLEX (CANADA) LTD.—See Teleflex Incorporated; *U.S. Public*, pg. 1570
TELEFLEX ELECTRICAL SYSTEMS—See Teleflex Incorporated; *U.S. Public*, pg. 1569
TELEFLEX FLUID SYSTEMS INC.—See Teleflex Incorporated; *U.S. Public*, pg. 1569
TELEFLEX INCORPORATED; *U.S. Public*, pg. 1569
TELEFLEX MARINE—See Teleflex Incorporated; *U.S. Public*, pg. 1569
TELEFLORA, LLC—See Roll International Corporation; *U.S.* Private, pg. 941
TELEFON AB LM ERICSSON BAHRAIN—See Telefonaktiebolaget LM Ericsson; *Int'l*, pg. 1370
TELEFON AB LM ERICSSON THAILAND—See Telefonaktiebolaget LM Ericsson; *Int'l*, pg. 1370
TELEFONAKTIEBOLAGET LM ERICSSON; *Int'l*, pg. 1363
TELEFONAKTIEBOLAGET LM ERICSSON BUREAUX TECHNIQUES D'ALGERIE—See Telefonaktiebolaget LM Ericsson; *Int'l*, pg. 1370
TELEFONAKTIEBOLAGET LM ERICSSON BUREAUX TECHNIQUES DE TUNISIE—See Telefonaktiebolaget LM Ericsson; *Int'l*, pg. 1370
TELEFONAKTIEBOLAGET LM ERICSSON DELAGATION TECHNIQUE DU PROJET AU MAROC—See Telefonaktiebolaget LM Ericsson; *Int'l*, pg. 1370
TELEFONAKTIEBOLAGET LM ERICSSON IRAN—See Telefonaktiebolaget LM Ericsson; *Int'l*, pg. 1370
TELEFONAKTIEBOLAGET LM ERICSSON IRAQ BRANCH—See Telefonaktiebolaget LM Ericsson; *Int'l*, pg. 1370
TELEFONAKTIEBOLAGET LM ERICSSON LIBYA BRANCH—See Telefonaktiebolaget LM Ericsson; *Int'l*, pg. 1370
TELEFONAKTIEBOLAGET LM ERICSSON MOROCCO—See Telefonaktiebolaget LM Ericsson; *Int'l*, pg. 1370
TELEFONAKTIEBOLAGET LM ERICSSON SUCURSAL EL SALVADOR—See Telefonaktiebolaget LM Ericsson; *Int'l*, pg. 1370
TELEFONAKTIEBOLAGET LM ERICSSON TECHNICAL OFFICE KUWAIT—See Telefonaktiebolaget LM Ericsson; *Int'l*, pg. 1370
TELEFONAKTIEBOLAGET LM ERICSSON TECHNICAL OFFICE OMAN—See Telefonaktiebolaget LM Ericsson; *Int'l*, pg. 1371
TELEFONAKTIEBOLAGET LM ERICSSON TECHNICAL OFFICE UAE—See Telefonaktiebolaget LM Ericsson; *Int'l*, pg. 1371
TELEFONAKTIEBOLAGET LM ERICSSON THAILAND BRANCH—See Telefonaktiebolaget LM Ericsson; *Int'l*, pg. 1371
TELEFONIA Y FINANZAS, S.A. (TELFISA)—See Telefonica de Espana, S.A.; *Int'l*, pg. 1372
TELEFONICA—See Telefonica de Espana, S.A.; *Int'l*, pg. 1372
TELEFONICA CHILE, S.A.—See Telefonica de Espana, S.A.; *Int'l*, pg. 1372
TELEFONICA DE ESPANA, S.A.; *Int'l*, pg. 1371
TELEFONICA FIAT FACTORING, S.A.—See Telefonica de Espana, S.A.; *Int'l*, pg. 1372
TELEFONICA INTERNACIONAL DE ESPANA S.A.—See Telefonica de Espana, S.A.; *Int'l*, pg. 1372
TELEFONICA INVESTIGACION Y DESARROLLO, S.A. (TIDSA)—See Telefonica de Espana, S.A.; *Int'l*, pg. 1372
TELEFONICA NORTH AMERICA, INC.—See Telefonica de Espana, S.A.; *Int'l*, pg. 1372
TELEFONICA PUBLICIDAD E INFORMAC.—See Telefonica de Espana, S.A.; *Int'l*, pg. 1372
TELEFONICA SERVICIOS MOVILES, S.A.—See Telefonica de Espana, S.A.; *Int'l*, pg. 1372
TELEFONICA SERVICIOS MULTIMEDIA, S.A.—See Telefonica de Espana, S.A.; *Int'l*, pg. 1372
TELEFONICA TELECOMUNICACIONES PUBLICAS, S.A.—See Telefonica de Espana, S.A.; *Int'l*, pg. 1372
TELEFONICA TRANSMISION DE DATOS, S.A.—See Telefonica de Espana, S.A.; *Int'l*, pg. 1372
TELEFONOS DE MEXICO S.A. DE C.V.; *Int'l*, pg. 1373
TELEFONOS ERICSSON C.A.—See Telefonaktiebolaget LM Ericsson; *Int'l*, pg. 1371
TELEFUNKEN SENDERTECHNIK GMBH—See Tech-Sym Corporation; *U.S. Public*, pg. 1563
TELEGAN GAS MONITORING LIMITED—See Halma p.l.c.; *Int'l*, pg. 590
TELEGENIX INC.; *U.S. Private*, pg. 1073
TELEGLOBE CANADA INC.—See Teleglobe, Inc.; *Int'l*, pg. 1373
TELEGLOBE, INC.; *Int'l*, pg. 1373
TELEGLOBE INSURANCE SYSTEMS—See Teleglobe, Inc.; *Int'l*, pg. 1373
TELEGLOBE INTERNATIONAL INC.—See Teleglobe, Inc.; *Int'l*, pg. 1373
TELEGLOBE MARINE INC.—See Teleglobe, Inc.; *Int'l*, pg. 1373
TELEGLOBE WORLD MOBILITY—See Teleglobe, Inc.; *Int'l*, pg. 1373
THE TELEGRAPH PLC—See Hollinger Inc.; *Int'l*, pg. 632
TELEGRAPHICS PRINTING—See Telescope Casual Furniture, Inc.; *U.S. Private*, pg. 1074
TELEINDUSTRIA ERICSSON, S.A. DE C.V.—See Telefonaktiebolaget LM Ericsson; *Int'l*, pg. 1371
TELEINFORM-GRUPPE—See Hesta Tex AG; *Int'l*, pg. 618
TELEINFORMATICA Y COMUNICACIONES, S.A.—See Telefonica de Espana, S.A.; *Int'l*, pg. 1372
TELEKEMPO C.V.—See Electrabel S.A.; *Int'l*, pg. 437
TELELUX S.A.—See Electrabel S.A.; *Int'l*, pg. 437
TELEMACH LIMITED—See GESTRA GmbH; *Int'l*, pg. 550
TELEMATCH BV—See KPN Koninklyke PTT Nederland NV; *Int'l*, pg. 720
TELEMATICS INC.—See IDB Holding Corporation; *Int'l*, pg. 643
TELEMATICS INTERNATIONAL B.V.—See IDB Holding Corporation; *Int'l*, pg. 644
TELEMATION PRODUCTIONS INC.—See USA Networks, Inc.; *U.S. Public*, pg. 1685
TELEMEDIA COMMUNICATIONS INC.—See Telemedia Inc.; *Int'l*, pg. 1373
TELEMEDIA INC.; *Int'l*, pg. 1373
TELEMOBITEL—See Telia AB; *Int'l*, pg. 1373
TELEMONTAJE ERICSSON S.A. DE C.V.—See Telefonaktiebolaget LM Ericsson; *Int'l*, pg. 1371
TELEMUNDO GROUP, INC.; *U.S. Public*, pg. 1570
TELENEX—See General Signal Corporation; *U.S. Public*, pg. 727
TELENORDIA A.B.—See British Telecommunications plc; *Int'l*, pg. 223
TELENORMA GMBH—See Robert Bosch GmbH; *Int'l*, pg. 204
TELEO COMMUNICATIONS GROUP—See Excel Communications, Inc.; *U.S. Public*, pg. 598
TELEPHONE BANK SESAM—See Skandinaviska Enskilda Banken; *Int'l*, pg. 1259
TELEPHONE AND DATA SYSTEMS, INC.; *U.S. Public*, pg. 1570
TELEPHONE DIRECTORY ADVERTISING; *U.S. Private*, pg. 1073
TELEPHONE UTILITIES OF ALASKA, INC.—See PacifiCorp; *U.S. Public*, pg. 1252
TELEPHONE UTILITIES OF EASTERN OREGON, INC.—See PacifiCorp; *U.S. Public*, pg. 1252
TELEPHONE UTILITIES OF OREGON, INC.—See PacifiCorp; *U.S. Public*, pg. 1252
TELEPHONE UTILITIES OF WASHINGTON, INC.—See PacifiCorp; *U.S. Public*, pg. 1252
TELEPHONICS CORP.—See Griffon Corp.; *U.S. Public*, pg. 766
TELEPORT COMMUNICATIONS GROUP; *U.S. Public*, pg. 1572
TELEPORT EUROPE GMBH—See Veba AG; *Int'l*, pg. 1461

TELEPROFS BV—See KPN Koninklyke PTT Nederland NV; Int'l, pg. 720
TELEQUIPOS, S.A.—See Telefonaktiebolaget LM Ericsson; Int'l, pg. 1371
TELEREP, INCORPORATED—See Cox Enterprises, Inc.; U.S. Private, pg. 282
TELEREXA LTD.—See Hewlett-Packard Company; U.S. Public, pg. 823
TELERIC PTY. LTD.—See Telefonaktiebolaget LM Ericsson; Int'l, pg. 1371
TELESAT CANADA—See BCE Inc.; Int'l, pg. 116
TELESCOPE CASUAL FURNITURE, INC.; U.S. Private, pg. 1074
TELESENSORY CORPORATION; U.S. Private, pg. 1074
TELESERVICE CORPORATION OF AMERICA—See TCA Cable TV, Inc.; U.S. Private, pg. 1553
TELESINCRO S.A.—See Compagnie des Machines Bull; Int'l, pg. 317
TELESISTEMI S.P.A.—See Compagnie des Machines Bull; Int'l, pg. 318
TELESYSTEMES—See France Telecom; Int'l, pg. 503
TELETEC SARL—See Telesensory Corporation; U.S. Private, pg. 1074
TELETRAK ADVANCED TECHNOLOGY SYSTEMS, INC.—See Helm Resources Inc.; U.S. Public, pg. 808
TELETTRA—See Alcatel Alsthom Compagnie Generale D'Electricite; Int'l, pg. 55
TELEVIDEO, INC.; U.S. Public, pg. 1572
TELEVISIE-UNIT BV—See KPN Koninklyke PTT Nederland NV; Int'l, pg. 720
TELEVISION TOKYO CHANNEL 12 LTD.—See Nihon Keizai Shimbun, Inc.; Int'l, pg. 929
TELEVITESSE SYSTEMS INCORPORATED—See Newbridge Networks Corporation; Int'l, pg. 924
BV TELEVIZIER—See VNU Verenigde Nederlandse Uitgeversbedrijven B.V.; Int'l, pg. 1445
TELEX COMMUNICATIONS, INC.; U.S. Private, pg. 1074
TELFIN S.A.—See Tractebel; Int'l, pg. 1415
TELFORD FOODS LTD.—See Koninklijke BolsWessanen nv; Int'l, pg. 753
TELIA AB; Int'l, pg. 1373
TELIVO LTD.—See Imatran Voima Oy; Int'l, pg. 661
TELLABS COMMUNICATIONS CDA—See Tellabs Operations, Inc.; U.S. Public, pg. 1573
TELLABS INTERNATIONAL, INC.—See Tellabs Operations, Inc.; U.S. Public, pg. 1573
TELLABS LTD.—See Tellabs Operations, Inc.; U.S. Public, pg. 1573
TELLABS OPERATIONS, INC.; U.S. Public, pg. 1572
TELLABS OTTAWA—See Tellabs Operations, Inc.; U.S. Public, pg. 1573
TELLABS OY—See Tellabs Operations, Inc.; U.S. Public, pg. 1573
TELLABS RESEARCH—See Tellabs Operations, Inc.; U.S. Public, pg. 1573
TELLABS ST. LAURENT TRANSPORT GROUP—See Tellabs Operations, Inc.; U.S. Public, pg. 1573
TELLABS TEXAS INC.—See Tellabs Operations, Inc.; U.S. Public, pg. 1573
TELLABS WIRELESS SYSTEMS—See Tellabs Operations, Inc.; U.S. Public, pg. 1573
TELLICO TELEPHONE COMPANY, INC.—See Telephone and Data Systems, Inc.; U.S. Public, pg. 1572
TELLUS, INC.—See Puget Sound Energy, Inc.; U.S. Public, pg. 1342
TELMA PLANT—See Labinal SA; Int'l, pg. 786
TELMA RETARDER—See Labinal SA; Int'l, pg. 786
TELMA RETARDER DEUTSCHLAND GMBH—See Labinal SA; Int'l, pg. 786
TELMA RETARDER DIVISION—See Labinal SA; Int'l, pg. 786
TELMA RETARDER ESPANA—See Labinal SA; Int'l, pg. 786
TELMA RETARDER ESPANA PLANT—See Labinal SA; Int'l, pg. 786
TELMA RETARDER ESPANA SALES—See Labinal SA; Int'l, pg. 786
TELMA RETARDER, INC.—See Labinal SA; Int'l, pg. 786
TELMA RETARDER ITALIA SRL—See Labinal SA; Int'l, pg. 786
TELMA RETARDER LTD.—See Labinal SA; Int'l, pg. 786
TELMARK, INC.—See Agway, Inc.; U.S. Private, pg. 27
TELONIC BERKELEY, INC.; U.S. Private, pg. 1074
TELOS CONSULTING SERVICES—See Telos Corporation; U.S. Public, pg. 1573
TELOS CORPORATION; U.S. Public, pg. 1573
TELOS FIELD ENGINEERING—See Telos Corporation; U.S. Public, pg. 1573
TELOS INFORMATION SYSTEMS—See Telos Corporation; U.S. Public, pg. 1573
TELOS INTERNATIONAL CORP.—See Telos Corporation; U.S. Public, pg. 1573
TELOS SYSTEMS INTEGRATION—See Telos Corporation; U.S. Public, pg. 1573
TELOS SYSTEMS SOLUTIONS—See Telos Corporation; U.S. Public, pg. 1573
TELPAR, INC.—See Moore Corporation Limited; Int'l, pg. 890
TELSCO INDUSTRIES; U.S. Private, pg. 1074
TELSI LTD.—See Siemens AG; Int'l, pg. 1248
TELSMITH, INC.—See Astec Industries, Inc.; U.S. Public, pg. 141
TELTRON TECHNOLOGIES, INC.—See Video Display Corporation; U.S. Public, pg. 1720
TELTRONICS INC.; U.S. Public, pg. 1573
TELUB AB—See Celsius AB; Int'l, pg. 277
TELUB INFORUM AB—See Celsius AB; Int'l, pg. 277
TELUB MILTEST AB—See Celsius AB; Int'l, pg. 277
TELUB TEKNIK AB—See Celsius AB; Int'l, pg. 278
TELUB TELEANLAGGNINGAR AB—See Celsius AB; Int'l, pg. 278
TELUS ADVERTISING SERVICES—See Telus Corporation; Int'l, pg. 1374
TELUS CORPORATION; Int'l, pg. 1374

TELUS MARKETING COMMUNICATIONS—See Telus Corporation; Int'l, pg. 1374
TELUS MOBILITY—See Telus Corporation; Int'l, pg. 1374
TELXON AUSTRALIA PTY. LIMITED—See Telxon Corporation; U.S. Public, pg. 1573
TELXON AUSTRALIA PTY., LTD.—See Telxon Corporation; U.S. Public, pg. 1573
N.V. TELXON BELGIUM S.A.—See Telxon Corporation; U.S. Public, pg. 1574
TELXON CANADA CORPORATION—See Telxon Corporation; U.S. Public, pg. 1574
TELXON CANADA CORPORATION, INC.—See Telxon Corporation; U.S. Public, pg. 1574
TELXON CANADA CORPORATION, LTD.—See Telxon Corporation; U.S. Public, pg. 1574
TELXON CORPORATION; U.S. Public, pg. 1573
TELXON CORPORATION—See Telxon Corporation; U.S. Public, pg. 1574
TELXON CORPORATION, BELGIUM BRANCH—See Telxon Corporation; U.S. Public, pg. 1574
TELXON CORPORATION, SINGAPORE BRANCH—See Telxon Corporation; U.S. Public, pg. 1574
TELXON CORPORATION SYSTEMS ESPANA, S.A.—See Telxon Corporation; U.S. Public, pg. 1574
TELXON FRANCE S.A.—See Telxon Corporation; U.S. Public, pg. 1574
TELXON ITALIA S.R.L.—See Telxon Corporation; U.S. Public, pg. 1574
TELXON JAPAN—See Telxon Corporation; U.S. Public, pg. 1574
TELXON LATIN AMERICA—See Telxon Corporation; U.S. Public, pg. 1574
TELXON LIMITED—See Telxon Corporation; U.S. Public, pg. 1574
TELXON MDE GMBH—See Telxon Corporation; U.S. Public, pg. 1574
TELXON-PRODUCTS DIVISION—See Telxon Corporation; U.S. Public, pg. 1573
TEMASEK HOLDINGS PTE. LTD.; Int'l, pg. 1374
TEMATI S.A. DE C.V.—See PepsiCo, Inc.; U.S. Public, pg. 1278
P.T. TEMBAGA MULIA SEMANAN (TMS)—See The Furukawa Electric Co., Ltd.; Int'l, pg. 531
TEMBEC FOREST PRODUCTS INC.—See Tembec Inc.; Int'l, pg. 1375
TEMBEC INC.; Int'l, pg. 1374
TEMBEC INC. PULP DIV.—See Tembec Inc.; Int'l, pg. 1375
TEMCA CHEMISCHE UNION GMBH—See The Procter & Gamble Company; U.S. Public, pg. 1333
TEMCO BUILDING MAINTENANCE, INC.—See Temco Service Industries; U.S. Public, pg. 1574
TEMCO EUROPE S.A.—See Temco Service Industries; U.S. Public, pg. 1574
TEMCO FIREPLACE PRODUCTS, INC.—See Temtex Industries Inc.; U.S. Public, pg. 1576
TEMCO MECHANICAL MAINTENANCE—See Temco Service Industries; U.S. Public, pg. 1574
TEMCO SERVICE INDUSTRIES; U.S. Public, pg. 1574
TEMCO SERVICE INDUSTRIES S.A.—See Temco Service Industries; U.S. Public, pg. 1574
TEMERLIN MCCLAIN—See True North Diversified Companies; U.S. Public, pg. 1642
TEMESA TECNOINDUSTRIAL MEXICANA SA DE CV—See Mannesmann A.G.; Int'l, pg. 837
TEMIC BAYERN-CHEMIE AIRBAG GMBH—See Daimler-Benz Aktiengesellschaft; Int'l, pg. 367
TEMIC MBB MIKROSYSTEME GMBH—See Daimler-Benz Aktiengesellschaft; Int'l, pg. 367
TEMIC TELEFUNKEN MICROELECTRONIC GMBH—See Daimler-Benz Aktiengesellschaft; Int'l, pg. 367
TEMKIN & TEMKIN; U.S. Private, pg. 1074
TEMLAM INC.—See Tembec Inc.; Int'l, pg. 1375
TEMP-CONTROL MECHANICAL CORP.; U.S. Private, pg. 1075
TEMPATRON LIMITED—See Siebe plc; Int'l, pg. 1241
TEMPE ELECTRONICS CENTER—See Varian Associates, Inc.; U.S. Public, pg. 1710
TEMPEL STEEL COMPANY; U.S. Private, pg. 1075
TEMPERATURE EQUIPMENT CORPORATION; U.S. Private, pg. 1075
TEMPIL INC.—See Associated Equipment Co., Inc.; U.S. Private, pg. 90
TEMPLE-INLAND FINANCIAL SERVICES, INC—See Temple-Inland Inc.; U.S. Public, pg. 1575
TEMPLE-INLAND FOREST PRODUCTS CORPORATION—See Temple-Inland Inc.; U.S. Public, pg. 1575
TEMPLE-INLAND INC.; U.S. Public, pg. 1574
TEMPLE-INLAND MORTGAGE CORPORATION—See Temple-Inland Inc.; U.S. Public, pg. 1575
TEMPLE INSURANCE COMPANY LIMITED—See Cigna Corp.; U.S. Public, pg. 360
TEMPLE Y FORJA FORTUNA S.A. DE C.V.—See Carpenter Technology Corporation; U.S. Public, pg. 308
TEMPLETON ASSET MANAGEMENT (SINGAPORE) PTE LTD.—See Franklin Resources, Inc.; U.S. Public, pg. 680
TEMPLETON FUNDS MANAGEMENT, INC.—See Franklin Resources, Inc.; U.S. Public, pg. 680
TEMPLETON GLOBAL STRATEGIC SERVICES—See Franklin Resources, Inc.; U.S. Public, pg. 680
TEMPLETON GLOBAL STRATEGIC SERVICES S.A.—See Franklin Resources, Inc.; U.S. Public, pg. 680
TEMPLETON HERITAGE LTD.—See Franklin Resources, Inc.; U.S. Public, pg. 680
TEMPLETON INVESTMENT COUNSEL, INC.—See Franklin Resources, Inc.; U.S. Public, pg. 680
TEMPLETON INVESTMENT MANAGEMENT (AUSTRALIA), LTD.—See Franklin Resources, Inc.; U.S. Public, pg. 680
TEMPLETON INVESTMENT MANAGEMENT (HONG KONG) LTD.—See Franklin Resources, Inc.; U.S. Public, pg. 680
TEMPLETON INVESTMENT MANAGEMENT, LTD.—See Franklin Resources, Inc.; U.S. Public, pg. 680

TEMPLETON INVESTMENT SERVICES, INC.—See Franklin Resources, Inc.; U.S. Public, pg. 680
TEMPLETON, KENLY & CO., INC.; U.S. Private, pg. 1075
TEMPLETON MANAGEMENT LIMITED—See Franklin Resources, Inc.; U.S. Public, pg. 680
TEMPLETON QUANTITATIVE ADVISORS—See Franklin Resources, Inc.; U.S. Public, pg. 680
TEMPO ADVERTISING, INC.—See Santa Fe Gaming Corporation; U.S. Public, pg. 1432
TEMPO ESPANA S.A. Y CIA S.E.C.—See The Procter & Gamble Company; U.S. Public, pg. 1333
TEMPO INSTRUMENT INC.—See Bowthorpe plc; Int'l, pg. 208
P.T. TEMPO NATIONAL LIFE—See National Mutual Holdings Limited; Int'l, pg. 909
TEMPO ROPARKO B.V.—See The Procter & Gamble Company; U.S. Public, pg. 1333
TEMPO SANYS S.A.—See The Procter & Gamble Company; U.S. Public, pg. 1333
TEMPO-VERTRIEBSGES FUR HYGIENISCHE ARTIKEL M.B.H—See The Procter & Gamble Company; U.S. Public, pg. 1333
TEMPORAL, S.A.—See ABB Asea Brown Boveri (Holding) Ltd.; Int'l, pg. 6
TEMPRESS—See General Signal Corporation; U.S. Public, pg. 727
TEMPS & COMPANY; U.S. Private, pg. 1075
TEMPUS SRL—See The Quaker Oats Company; U.S. Public, pg. 1348
TEMTEX INDUSTRIES INC.; U.S. Public, pg. 1575
TEMTROL, INC.—See Nortek, Inc.; U.S. Public, pg. 1193
10 MINUTE OIL CHANGE—See Pennzoil Company; U.S. Public, pg. 1272
TEN-TEN JEFFERSON CORPORATION—See Cigna Corp.; U.S. Public, pg. 361
TENAX CORPORATION—See Bespak plc; Int'l, pg. 193
TENCARVA MACHINERY CO.—See Tencarva Machinery Co., Inc.; U.S. Private, pg. 1076
TENCARVA MACHINERY COMPANY—See Tencarva Machinery Co., Inc.; U.S. Private, pg. 1076
TENCARVA MACHINERY CO.-ASHEVILLE—See Tencarva Machinery Co., Inc.; U.S. Private, pg. 1076
TENCARVA MACHINERY CO., INC.; U.S. Private, pg. 1075
TENDER LOVING CARE HOME CARE SERVICES, INC.—See Staff Builders Inc.; U.S. Public, pg. 1501
TENEL, S.A.—See Telefonaktiebolaget LM Ericsson; Int'l, pg. 1371
TENELUX—See Kaufel Group Ltd.; Int'l, pg. 725
A. TENENBAUM CO. INC.; U.S. Private, pg. 1076
TENERA ENERGY, LLC—See Tenera, Inc.; U.S. Public, pg. 1576
TENERA, INC.; U.S. Public, pg. 1576
TENERA ROCKY FLATS, LLC—See Tenera, Inc.; U.S. Public, pg. 1576
TENET HEALTHCARE CORPORATION; U.S. Public, pg. 1576
TENET HEALTHSYSTEM HEALTHCORP—See Tenet Healthcare Corporation; U.S. Public, pg. 1577
TENET HEALTHSYSTEM HOSPITALS, INC.—See Tenet Healthcare Corporation; U.S. Public, pg. 1577
TENET HEALTHSYSTEM MEDICAL, INC.—See Tenet Healthcare Corporation; U.S. Public, pg. 1577
TENGELMANN WARENHANDELSGESELLSCHAFT; Int'l, pg. 1375
TENNANT & RUTTLE DISTRIBUTION LIMITED—See James Crean PLC; Int'l, pg. 340
TENNANT & RUTTLE LIMITED—See James Crean PLC; Int'l, pg. 340
TENNANT COMPANY; U.S. Public, pg. 1577
TENNANT HOLDING B.V.—See Tennant Company; U.S. Public, pg. 1577
TENNANT KVK LTD.—See Dainippon Ink & Chemicals, Inc.; Int'l, pg. 371
TENNANT MAINTENANCE SYSTEMS, LIMITED—See Tennant Company; U.S. Public, pg. 1577
TENNECO ALASKA, INC.—See Tenneco Inc.; U.S. Public, pg. 1578
TENNECO ASSET MANAGEMENT CO.—See Tenneco Inc.; U.S. Public, pg. 1578
TENNECO ASSET PLANNING CO.—See Tenneco Inc.; U.S. Public, pg. 1578
TENNECO AUTOMOTIVE—See Tenneco Inc.; U.S. Public, pg. 1577
TENNECO AUTOMOTIVE EUROPE, INC.—See Tenneco Inc.; U.S. Public, pg. 1580
TENNECO AUTOMOTIVE TRADING COMPANY—See Tenneco Inc.; U.S. Public, pg. 1578
TENNECO AVIATION LIMITED—See Tenneco Inc.; U.S. Public, pg. 1580
S.A. TENNECO BELGIUM (POCLAIN-MONROE-PETRO-TEX) N.V.—See Tenneco Inc.; U.S. Public, pg. 1580
TENNECO CHINA TRADE INC.—See Tenneco Inc.; U.S. Public, pg. 1578
TENNECO COAL CO.—See Tenneco Inc.; U.S. Public, pg. 1579
TENNECO COAL CONVERSION CO.—See Tenneco Inc.; U.S. Public, pg. 1579
TENNECO COAL GASIFICATION CO.—See Tenneco Inc.; U.S. Public, pg. 1579
TENNECO COMMUNICATIONS CORPORTION—See Tenneco Inc.; U.S. Public, pg. 1578
TENNECO CORPORATION—See Tenneco Inc.; U.S. Public, pg. 1578
TENNECO CREDIT CORP.—See Tenneco Inc.; U.S. Public, pg. 1578
TENNECO DOMESTIC INTERNATIONAL SALES CORP.—See Tenneco Inc.; U.S. Public, pg. 1578
TENNECO EUROPE—See Tenneco Inc.; U.S. Public, pg. 1580
TENNECO FINANCIAL SERVICES, INC.—See Tenneco Inc.; U.S. Public, pg. 1578
TENNECO FOREIGN SALES CORPORATION—See Tenneco Inc.; U.S. Public, pg. 1578

TENNECO GAS MARKETING COMPANY—See Tenneco Inc.; *U.S. Public*, pg. 1579
TENNECO GAS PIPELINE GROUP—See Tenneco Inc.; *U.S. Public*, pg. 1578
TENNECO GAS PROCESSING COMPANY—See Tenneco Inc.; *U.S. Public*, pg. 1579
TENNECO GAS SUPPLY CORP.—See Tenneco Inc.; *U.S. Public*, pg. 1579
TENNECO HOLDINGS B.V.—See Tenneco Inc.; *U.S. Public*, pg. 1580
TENNECO INC.; *U.S. Public*, pg. 1577
TENNECO INSURANCE VENTURES—See Tenneco Inc.; *U.S. Public*, pg. 1578
TENNECO INTERNATIONAL FINANCE LIMITED—See Tenneco Inc.; *U.S. Public*, pg. 1580
TENNECO INTERNATIONAL INC.—See Tenneco Inc.; *U.S. Public*, pg. 1578
TENNECO INTERNATIONAL N.V.—See Tenneco Inc.; *U.S. Public*, pg. 1578
TENNECO MALROS LTD.—See Tenneco Inc.; *U.S. Public*, pg. 1580
TENNECO MANAGEMENT COMPANY—See Tenneco Inc.; *U.S. Public*, pg. 1578
TENNECO MINERALS CO.—See Tenneco Inc.; *U.S. Public*, pg. 1579
TENNECO MINERALS CO. OF AUSTRALIA INC.—See Tenneco Inc.; *U.S. Public*, pg. 1579
TENNECO NEDERLAND B.V.—See Tenneco Inc.; *U.S. Public*, pg. 1580
TENNECO NORGE, INC.—See Tenneco Inc.; *U.S. Public*, pg. 1578
TENNECO OCEAN METALS DEVELOPMENT CORP.—See Tenneco Inc.; *U.S. Public*, pg. 1578
TENNECO OIL & MINERALS OF AUSTRALIA, INC.—See Tenneco Inc.; *U.S. Public*, pg. 1580
TENNECO ORGANICS LTD.—See Tenneco Inc.; *U.S. Public*, pg. 1580
TENNECO PACKAGING—See Tenneco Inc.; *U.S. Public*, pg. 1579
TENNECO PHOSPHATE, INC.—See Tenneco Inc.; *U.S. Public*, pg. 1578
TENNECO REALTY, INC.—See Tenneco Inc.; *U.S. Public*, pg. 1578
TENNECO SNG, INC.—See Tenneco Inc.; *U.S. Public*, pg. 1579
TENNECO SPECIALTY PRODUCTS—See Tenneco Inc.; *U.S. Public*, pg. 1579
TENNECO SUDAN, INC.—See Tenneco Inc.; *U.S. Public*, pg. 1578
TENNECO SYNFUELS CO.—See Tenneco Inc.; *U.S. Public*, pg. 1578
TENNECO TRANSICOL B.V.—See Tenneco Inc.; *U.S. Public*, pg. 1580
TENNECO UNITED KINGDOM HOLDINGS LIMITED—See Tenneco Inc.; *U.S. Public*, pg. 1580
TENNECO UNITED KINGDOM, INC.—See Tenneco Inc.; *U.S. Public*, pg. 1580
TENNECO URANIUM, INC.—See Tenneco Inc.; *U.S. Public*, pg. 1579
TENNECO VENTURES,INC.—See Tenneco Inc.; *U.S. Public*, pg. 1578
TENNECO-WALKER (U.K.) LIMITED—See Tenneco Inc.; *U.S. Public*, pg. 1580
TENNESSEAN NEWSPAPERS, INC.—See Gannett Company, Inc.; *U.S. Public*, pg. 701
TENNESSEE, ALABAMA & GEORGIA RAILWAY CO.—See Norfolk Southern Corporation; *U.S. Public*, pg. 1191
TENNESSEE-AMERICAN WATER CO.—See American Water Works Company, Inc.; *U.S. Public*, pg. 95
TENNESSEE ARGENTINA, S.A.—See Tenneco Inc.; *U.S. Public*, pg. 1578
TENNESSEE BOOK COMPANY—See Ingram Industries Inc.; *U.S. Private*, pg. 563
TENNESSEE DICKEL DISTILLING CO.—See Diageo Plc; *Int'l*, pg. 412
TENNESSEE DRESSED BEEF COMPANY; *U.S. Private*, pg. 1076
TENNESSEE FARMERS CO-OP; *U.S. Private*, pg. 1076
TENNESSEE GAS MARKETING COMPANY—See Tenneco Inc.; *U.S. Public*, pg. 1579
TENNESSEE GAS TRANSMISSION CO.—See El Paso Natural Gas Co.; *U.S. Public*, pg. 567
TENNESSEE INSURANCE CO.—See Ingram Industries Inc.; *U.S. Private*, pg. 563
TENNESSEE/NEW ENGLAND PIPELINE COMPANY—See Tenneco Inc.; *U.S. Public*, pg. 1579
TENNESSEE PACKAGING—See Buckeye Corrugated Inc.; *U.S. Private*, pg. 177
TENNESSEE RAILWAY CO.—See Norfolk Southern Corporation; *U.S. Public*, pg. 1191
TENNESSEE REFINERY—See Mapco Inc.; *U.S. Public*, pg. 1042
TENNESSEE RIVER INTRASTATE GAS COMPANY—See Midcoast Energy Resources, Inc.; *U.S. Public*, pg. 1109
TENNESSEE RIVER PULP & PAPER CO.—See Tenneco Inc.; *U.S. Public*, pg. 1579
TENNESSEE TELEPHONE COMPANY—See Telephone and Data Systems, Inc.; *U.S. Public*, pg. 1572
TENNESSEE TRAILBLAZER GAS CO.—See El Paso Natural Gas Co.; *U.S. Public*, pg. 567
TENNESSEE TUBEBENDING INC.—See Morris Coupling Co.; *U.S. Private*, pg. 762
TENNESSEE VALLEY AUTHORITY; *U.S. Public*, pg. 1580
TENNESSEE VALLEY LIFE INSURANCE CO.—See NationsBank Corporation; *U.S. Public*, pg. 1163
TENNESSEE WOOLEN MILLS—See Pillowtex Corporation; *U.S. Public*, pg. 1296
TENNESSEE WSMP, INC. (TENNESSEE)—See WSMP, Inc.; *U.S. Public*, pg. 1729
TENNEY ENVIRONMENTAL; *U.S. Private*, pg. 1076
TENNEY ENVIRONMENTAL—See Tenney Environmental; *U.S. Private*, pg. 1077
TENNEY TELEPHONE CO.—See Telephone and Data Systems, Inc.; *U.S. Public*, pg. 1572

TENNIS—See The New York Times Company; *U.S. Public*, pg. 1174
TENNIS BUYER'S GUIDE—See The New York Times Company; *U.S. Public*, pg. 1174
TENNSCO CORPORATION; *U.S. Private*, pg. 1077
TENOKRON AB—See Freudenberg & Company; *Int'l*, pg. 507
TENRI LIQUID CRYSTAL DISPLAY DEVELOPMENT & GROUP—See Sharp Corporation; *Int'l*, pg. 1228
TENSID CHEMIE VERTRIEBSGESELLSCHAFT MBH—See BASF AG; *Int'l*, pg. 104
TENSION ENVELOPE CORP.; *U.S. Private*, pg. 1077
TENSOLITE COMPANY—See Carlisle Companies Incorporated; *U.S. Public*, pg. 305
TENTLER & CO., B.V.—See Standard Commercial Corporation; *U.S. Public*, pg. 1502
TENUTA S. ANNA S.R.L.—See Assicurazioni Generali S.p.A.; *Int'l*, pg. 90
TEPPAN RESTAURANTS—See Benihana, Inc.; *U.S. Public*, pg. 212
TEPPCO PARTNERS L.P.—See Duke Energy Corporation; *U.S. Public*, pg. 534
TEQUILA UK LTD.—See BDDP Group; *Int'l*, pg. 118
TER HUURNE—See Koninklijke Ahold NV; *Int'l*, pg. 749
TERA PHARMACEUTICALS—See Baxter International Inc.; *U.S. Public*, pg. 196
TERADYNE ASSEMBLY TEST/EAST DIVISION—See Teradyne, Inc.; *U.S. Public*, pg. 1581
TERADYNE ASSEMBLY TEST/WEST DIVISION—See Teradyne, Inc.; *U.S. Public*, pg. 1581
TERADYNE CIRCUITS OPERATION—See Teradyne, Inc.; *U.S. Public*, pg. 1581
TERADYNE CONNECTION SYSTEMS, INC.—See Teradyne, Inc.; *U.S. Public*, pg. 1581
TERADYNE HONG KONG LIMITED—See Teradyne, Inc.; *U.S. Public*, pg. 1581
TERADYNE, INC.; *U.S. Public*, pg. 1580
TERADYNE INDUSTRIAL/CONSUMER DIVISION—See Teradyne, Inc.; *U.S. Public*, pg. 1581
TERADYNE, K.K.—See Teradyne, Inc.; *U.S. Public*, pg. 1581
TERADYNE SEMICONDUCTOR TEST DIVISION—See Teradyne, Inc.; *U.S. Public*, pg. 1581
TERADYNE TELECOMMUNICATIONS DIVISION—See Teradyne, Inc.; *U.S. Public*, pg. 1581
TERAGLOBUS KFT—See DSM N.V.; *Int'l*, pg. 356
TERAN TBWA PUBLICIDAD—See TBWA Chiat/Day; *U.S. Private*, pg. 1063
TERANOL AG—See Roche Holding Ltd.; *Int'l*, pg. 1120
TERASAKI-NELSON LTD.—See General Signal Corporation; *U.S. Public*, pg. 727
TEREX CORPORATION; *U.S. Public*, pg. 1581
TEREX CRANES—See Terex Corporation; *U.S. Public*, pg. 1581
TEREX TRUCKS—See Terex Corporation; *U.S. Public*, pg. 1581
TERMA ELEKTRONIK AS—See Telefonaktiebolaget LM Ericsson; *Int'l*, pg. 1370
TERMAQ—See Eclipse Inc.; *U.S. Private*, pg. 361
TERME DI CRODO S.P.A.—See Koninklijke BolsWessanen nv; *Int'l*, pg. 751
TERMINAL DIVISION—See Inkel USA Corporation; *U.S. Private*, pg. 563
TERMINAL FRUTTA GENOVA S.R.L.—See Coeclerici Group; *Int'l*, pg. 304
TERMINAL FRUTTA TRIESTE S.R.L.—See Coeclerici Group; *Int'l*, pg. 304
TERMINAL GRAIN CORP.; *U.S. Private*, pg. 1077
TERMINAL INVESTMENTS, INC.—See Forest City Enterprises, Inc.; *U.S. Public*, pg. 669
TERMINAL MANAGEMENT, INC.—See Forest City Enterprises, Inc.; *U.S. Public*, pg. 669
TERMINAL RAILROAD ASSOCIATION OF ST. LOUIS—See Union Pacific Corporation; *U.S. Public*, pg. 1668
TERMINAL TECHNOLOGIES, INC.—See Serv-Tech, Inc.; *U.S. Public*, pg. 1460
TERMINALS PORTUARIAS, S.A.—See GATX Corporation; *U.S. Public*, pg. 693
THE TERMINIX INTERNATIONAL COMPANY—See The ServiceMaster Company; *U.S. Public*, pg. 1461
TERMINIX SERVICE, INC.; *U.S. Private*, pg. 1077
TERMOPLASTICI INDUSTRIA LIGURE S.P.A.—See Georg Fischer Ltd.; *Int'l*, pg. 490
TERMOSUD S.P.A.—See IRI Istituto Ricostruzione Industriale; *Int'l*, pg. 653
TEROCHEM LABORATORIES LIMITED A/K/A RAYLO CHEMICALS—See Laporte plc; *Int'l*, pg. 803
TERRA INDUSTRIES, INC.; *U.S. Public*, pg. 1581
TERRA INTERNATIONAL—See Terra Industries, Inc.; *U.S. Public*, pg. 1581
TERRA NITROGEN COMPANY, L.P.; *U.S. Public*, pg. 1581
TERRA NOVA (BERMUDA) HOLDINGS LTD.—See Cigna Corp.; *U.S. Public*, pg. 365
TERRA NOVA INSURANCE COMPANY LTD.—See Aetna Inc.; *U.S. Public*, pg. 27
TERRA TECH LABS, INC.—See Thermo Electron Corporation; *U.S. Public*, pg. 1594
TERRACE VILLA CONVALESCENT CENTER—See Vencor, Inc.; *U.S. Public*, pg. 1715
TERRAL SEED CO., INC.; *U.S. Private*, pg. 1077
TERRAM LIMITED—See BBA Group plc; *Int'l*, pg. 113
TERRASSENHAUS-BAU GMBH—See Philipp Holzmann AG; *Int'l*, pg. 633
TERRAVITA CORP.—See Del Webb Corporation; *U.S. Public*, pg. 495
TERRAZUL—See Ciments Francais; *Int'l*, pg. 292
TERRE HAUTE FIRST NATIONAL BANK—See First Financial Corporation; *U.S. Public*, pg. 634
TERRE HILL CONCRETE PRODUCTS, INC.; *U.S. Private*, pg. 1077
TERRESTRIAL MICROWAVE SERVICES DIV.—See Allen Telecom, Inc.; *U.S. Public*, pg. 46
THE TERRITORY AHEAD; *U.S. Private*, pg. 1077

TERROT STRICKMASCHINEN GMBH—See Sulzer Ltd.; *Int'l*, pg. 1307
SUSAN TERRY DIV.—See Masters, Inc.; *U.S. Private*, pg. 714
TERRY'S GROUP—See Philip Morris Companies Inc.; *U.S. Public*, pg. 1290
TERTIO GVG MBH—See Commerzbank AG; *Int'l*, pg. 310
TERUMO-BANGKOK—See Terumo Corporation; *Int'l*, pg. 1376
TERUMO CORPORATION; *Int'l*, pg. 1375
TERUMO-DUBAI—See Terumo Corporation; *Int'l*, pg. 1376
TERUMO EUROPE-MADRID—See Terumo Corporation; *Int'l*, pg. 1376
TERUMO EUROPE-ROME—See Terumo Corporation; *Int'l*, pg. 1376
TERUMO-HONG KONG—See Terumo Corporation; *Int'l*, pg. 1376
TERUMO-JAKARTA—See Terumo Corporation; *Int'l*, pg. 1376
TERUMO MEDICAL CORPORATION—See Terumo Corporation; *Int'l*, pg. 1376
TERUMO MEDICAL FACTORY—See Terumo Corporation; *Int'l*, pg. 1376
TERUMO MEDICAL-MEXICO—See Terumo Corporation; *Int'l*, pg. 1376
TERUMO MEDICAL-MIAMI—See Terumo Corporation; *Int'l*, pg. 1376
TERUMO MEDICAL-TORONTO—See Terumo Corporation; *Int'l*, pg. 1376
TERUMO RES. & DEVEL CENTER—See Terumo Corporation; *Int'l*, pg. 1376
TERUMO-SINGAPORE—See Terumo Corporation; *Int'l*, pg. 1376
TERUMO-TAIPEI—See Terumo Corporation; *Int'l*, pg. 1376
TERUYA BROS., LIMITED; *U.S. Private*, pg. 1077
TERVAKOSKI OY—See Enso Oyj; *Int'l*, pg. 456
TESA-ETIKETTENDRUCKEREI GMBH—See Beiersdorf Group; *Int'l*, pg. 182
TESA ITALIA SRL—See Brown & Sharpe Manufacturing Company; *U.S. Public*, pg. 260
TESA LEITZ GMBH—See Brown & Sharpe Manufacturing Company; *U.S. Public*, pg. 260
TESA METROLOGY LIMITED—See Brown & Sharpe Manufacturing Company; *U.S. Public*, pg. 260
TESA REFERENCE STANDARDS DIV.—See Brown & Sharpe Manufacturing Company; *U.S. Public*, pg. 260
TESA, S.A.—See Brown & Sharpe Manufacturing Company; *U.S. Public*, pg. 260
TESA SEIMITSU CO., LTD.—See Brown & Sharpe Manufacturing Company; *U.S. Public*, pg. 261
TESA TAPE INC.—See Beiersdorf Group; *Int'l*, pg. 182
TESA-WERKE OFFENBURG GMBH—See Beiersdorf Group; *Int'l*, pg. 182
TESCH INDUSTRIE- UND ROHRLEITUNGSBAU GMBH—See Bilfinger + Berger Bauaktiengesellschaft; *Int'l*, pg. 195
TESCI—See Science Applications International Corp.; *U.S. Private*, pg. 976
TESCO—See Vendex International N.V.; *Int'l*, pg. 1463
TESCO CAPITAL LTD.—See Tesco PLC; *Int'l*, pg. 1376
TESCO CO., LTD.—See Skylark Co., Ltd.; *Int'l*, pg. 1262
TESCO INSURANCE LTD.—See Tesco PLC; *Int'l*, pg. 1376
TESCO PLC; *Int'l*, pg. 1376
TESCO PROPERTY HOLDINGS LTD.—See Tesco PLC; *Int'l*, pg. 1376
TESCO STORES HONG KONG LTD.—See Tesco PLC; *Int'l*, pg. 1376
TESCO STORES LTD.—See Tesco PLC; *Int'l*, pg. 1376
TESEL INTERNATIONAL SERVICES LIMITED—See Halliburton Company; *U.S. Public*, pg. 777
TESEL OVERSEAS SERVICES LIMITED—See Halliburton Company; *U.S. Public*, pg. 777
TESEL PLC—See Halliburton Company; *U.S. Public*, pg. 777
TESEL SERVICES LIMITED—See Halliburton Company; *U.S. Public*, pg. 777
TESEL WIRELINE SERVICES LIMITED—See Halliburton Company; *U.S. Public*, pg. 777
TESHMONT CONSULTANTS INC.—See Agra Inc.; *Int'l*, pg. 31
TESMA INTERNATIONAL INC.—See Magna International Inc.; *Int'l*, pg. 830
TESORO ALASKA PETROLEUM CO.—See Tesoro Petroleum Corporation; *U.S. Public*, pg. 1582
TESORO ALASKA PIPELINE COMPANY—See Tesoro Petroleum Corporation; *U.S. Public*, pg. 1582
TESORO BOLIVIA PETROLEUM COMPANY—See Tesoro Petroleum Corporation; *U.S. Public*, pg. 1582
TESORO MARINE SERVICES—See Tesoro Petroleum Corporation; *U.S. Public*, pg. 1582
TESORO NORTHSTORE COMPANY—See Tesoro Petroleum Corporation; *U.S. Public*, pg. 1582
TESORO PETROLEUM CORPORATION; *U.S. Public*, pg. 1581
TESORO REFINING, MARKETING & SUPPLY CO.—See Tesoro Petroleum Corporation; *U.S. Public*, pg. 1582
TESSCO GROUP, INC.—See Code-Alarm, Inc.; *U.S. Public*, pg. 394
TESSCO TECHNOLOGIES, INC.; *U.S. Public*, pg. 1582
TESSENDERLO CHEMIE—See Entreprise Miniere et Chimique; *Int'l*, pg. 459
TEST AND COLIBRATION INSTRUMENTS—See AMETEK, Inc.; *U.S. Public*, pg. 100
AB TEST HOUSE LIMITED—See TT Group PLC; *Int'l*, pg. 1344
TEST & SPACE SYSTEMS DIVISION—See Tracor, Inc.; *U.S. Public*, pg. 1627
ARMANDO TESTA S.P.A.—See Testa International; *Int'l*, pg. 1377
TESTA INTERNATIONAL; *Int'l*, pg. 1376
TESTCOM, INC.—See SGS Societe Generale de Surveillance Holding S.A.; *Int'l*, pg. 1154
THE TESTOR CORPORATION—See RPM, Inc.; *U.S. Public*, pg. 1358

TESTRABAU GMBH BAUGESELLSCHAFT—See Ruetgers A.G.; *Int'l*, pg. 1148
TESTRONICS—See Gulf States, Inc.; *U.S. Private*, pg. 487
TETERBORO LEARNING CENTER—See Berkshire Hathaway Inc.; *U.S. Public*, pg. 219
TETHERCREST—See Inchcape PLC; *Int'l*, pg. 671
TETKO, INC.; *U.S. Private*, pg. 1078
THE TETLEY GROUP LIMITED; *Int'l*, pg. 1377
TETLEY USA INC.—See The Tetley Group Limited; *Int'l*, pg. 1377
TETON LAND TITLE COMPANY—See The First American Financial Corporation; *U.S. Public*, pg. 626
TETRA EUROPE LIMITED—See Severn Trent Plc; *Int'l*, pg. 1226
TETRA HEIMTIERBEDARF G.M.B.H.—See Warner-Lambert Company; *U.S. Public*, pg. 1739
TETRA LAVAL FOOD—See Tetra Laval Group; *Int'l*, pg. 1378
TETRA LAVAL GROUP; *Int'l*, pg. 1377
TETRA LAVAL INTERNATIONAL AB—See Tetra Laval Group; *Int'l*, pg. 1378
TETRA-PAK—See Tetra Laval Group; *Int'l*, pg. 1378
TETRA-PAK PROCESSING SYSTEMS—See Tetra Laval Group; *Int'l*, pg. 1379
TETRA-PAK ROMONT SA—See Tetra Laval Group; *Int'l*, pg. 1380
TETRA PLASTICS—See Nike, Inc.; *U.S. Public*, pg. 1184
TETRA TECH, INC.; *U.S. Public*, pg. 1582
TETRA TECH NUS, INC.—See Tetra Tech, Inc.; *U.S. Public*, pg. 1582
TETRA TECHNOLOGIES; *U.S. Public*, pg. 1582
TETRAETILO DE MEXICO, S.A.—See Du Pont (E.I. Du Pont De Nemours & Co.); *U.S. Public*, pg. 533
TETRAGENICS, INC.—See Montana Power Company; *U.S. Public*, pg. 1127
TETSUDO SHARYO KOGYO CO., LTD.—See Kumagai Gumi Co., Ltd.; *Int'l*, pg. 764
TETSUNA KENSETSU CO., LTD.—See Tekken Corporation; *Int'l*, pg. 1362
TETTERODE-NEDERLAND BV—See N.V. Koninklijke KNP BT; *Int'l*, pg. 757
TEUTONIA GMBH & CO. KG—See Britax International plc; *Int'l*, pg. 217
TEVA PHARMACEUTICAL INDUSTRIES LTD.; *Int'l*, pg. 1380
TEVA USA - BIOCRAFT—See Teva Pharmaceutical Industries Ltd.; *Int'l*, pg. 1380
TEVEBAU GMBH—See Ruetgers A.G.; *Int'l*, pg. 1148
TEVELO N.V.—See Electrabel S.A.; *Int'l*, pg. 437
TEVEO N.V.—See Electrabel S.A.; *Int'l*, pg. 437
TEVEOOST N.V.—See Electrabel S.A.; *Int'l*, pg. 437
TEVEWEST N.V.—See Electrabel S.A.; *Int'l*, pg. 437
TEXACO CAPITAL INC.—See Texaco Inc.; *U.S. Public*, pg. 1583
TEXACO INC.; *U.S. Public*, pg. 1582
TEXACO OVERSEAS HOLDINGS INC.—See Texaco Inc.; *U.S. Public*, pg. 1583
S.A. TEXACO PETROLEUM N.V.—See Texaco Inc.; *U.S. Public*, pg. 1584
TEXACO RESEARCH CENTER—See Texaco Inc.; *U.S. Public*, pg. 1583
TEXACO WORLDWIDE EXPLORATION & PRODUCTION—See Texaco Inc.; *U.S. Public*, pg. 1583
TEXALES LTD.—See Borden, Inc.; *U.S. Private*, pg. 160
TEXARKANA WIRE & CABLE—See Kuhlman Corporation; *U.S. Public*, pg. 968
TEXAS ALUMINUM INDUSTRIES INC.—See Metals USA, Inc.; *U.S. Public*, pg. 1101
TEXAS APPAREL—See Salant Corporation; *U.S. Public*, pg. 1429
TEXAS AUTO AUCTION SERVICES, INC.—See Cox Enterprises, Inc.; *U.S. Private*, pg. 283
TEXAS BANK N.A.—See First Banks America, Inc.; *U.S. Public*, pg. 626
TEXAS CENTRAL RAILROAD—See Birdsong Corporation; *U.S. Private*, pg. 145
TEXAS COLD FINISHED STEEL, INC.—See Commercial Metals Company; *U.S. Public*, pg. 412
TEXAS COMMERCE BANK—See The Chase Manhattan Corporation; *U.S. Public*, pg. 339
TEXAS COMMERCE BANK, N.A.—See The Chase Manhattan Corporation; *U.S. Public*, pg. 339
TEXAS COMMUNITY ANTENNAS, INC.—See TCA Cable TV, Inc.; *U.S. Public*, pg. 1553
TEXAS COPY SYSTEMS, INC.—See Ikon Office Solutions, Inc.; *U.S. Public*, pg. 864
TEXAS DIVISION—See Fuchs Petrolub AG Oel + Chemie; *Int'l*, pg. 518
TEXAS EASTERN PRODUCTS PIPELINE COMPANY, L.P.—See Duke Energy Corporation; *U.S. Public*, pg. 535
TEXAS EASTERN TRANSMISSION CORP.—See Duke Energy Corporation; *U.S. Public*, pg. 535
TEXAS EASTMAN CO.—See Eastman Chemical Company; *U.S. Public*, pg. 550
TEXAS ECOLOGISTS, INC.—See American Ecology Corporation; *U.S. Public*, pg. 71
TEXAS ELECTRIC COOPERATIVES, INC.; *U.S. Private*, pg. 1078
TEXAS FIRST SECURITIES CORP.—See PNC Bank Corp.; *U.S. Public*, pg. 1244
TEXAS GAS TRANSMISSION—See The Williams Companies, Inc.; *U.S. Public*, pg. 1769
TEXAS GENERAL INDEMNITY CO.—See American Indemnity Financial Corp.; *U.S. Public*, pg. 83
TEXAS GENERATING COMPANY—See TNP Enterprises, Inc.; *U.S. Public*, pg. 1557
TEXAS GRANITE CORP.—See Cold Spring Granite Company; *U.S. Private*, pg. 251
TEXAS HOBBY AUTO AUCTION—See Cox Enterprises, Inc.; *U.S. Private*, pg. 283
TEXAS HOLDINGS LTD.; *Int'l*, pg. 1381
TEXAS HOMESTEAD MORTGAGE CO.—See Kaufman and Broad Home Corporation; *U.S. Public*, pg. 945

TEXAS INDUSTRIAL SERVICES, INC.—See UniFirst Corporation; *U.S. Public*, pg. 1665
TEXAS INDUSTRIES, INC.; *U.S. Public*, pg. 1585
TEXAS INSTRUMENTS ADC, SEMICONDUCTOR DIV.—See Texas Instruments Incorporated; *U.S. Public*, pg. 1585
TEXAS INSTRUMENTS ASIA LTD.—See Texas Instruments Incorporated; *U.S. Public*, pg. 1586
N.V. TEXAS INSTRUMENTS BELGIUM SA—See Texas Instruments Incorporated; *U.S. Public*, pg. 1586
TEXAS INSTRUMENTS CANADA—See Texas Instruments Incorporated; *U.S. Public*, pg. 1586
TEXAS INSTRUMENTS CONSULTING—See Texas Instruments Incorporated; *U.S. Public*, pg. 1586
TEXAS INSTRUMENTS CONSUMER PRODUCTS DIV.—See Texas Instruments Incorporated; *U.S. Public*, pg. 1586
TEXAS INSTRUMENTS DEUTSCHLAND GMBH—See Texas Instruments Incorporated; *U.S. Public*, pg. 1586
TEXAS INSTRUMENTS FACILITIES, SEMICONDUCTOR—See Texas Instruments Incorporated; *U.S. Public*, pg. 1586
TEXAS INSTRUMENTS FRANCE SA—See Texas Instruments Incorporated; *U.S. Public*, pg. 1586
TEXAS INSTRUMENTS GPL—See Texas Instruments Incorporated; *U.S. Public*, pg. 1586
TEXAS INSTRUMENTS HOLLAND BV—See Texas Instruments Incorporated; *U.S. Public*, pg. 1586
TEXAS INSTRUMENTS INCORPORATED; *U.S. Public*, pg. 1585
TEXAS INSTRUMENTS INFORMATION TECHNOLOGY GROUP—See Texas Instruments Incorporated; *U.S. Public*, pg. 1586
TEXAS INSTRUMENTS INTERNATIONAL TRADE CORPORATION—See Texas Instruments Incorporated; *U.S. Public*, pg. 1586
TEXAS INSTRUMENTS ITALIA S.P.A.—See Texas Instruments Incorporated; *U.S. Public*, pg. 1586
TEXAS INSTRUMENTS JAPAN LTD.—See Texas Instruments Incorporated; *U.S. Public*, pg. 1586
TEXAS INSTRUMENTS LIMITED—See Texas Instruments Incorporated; *U.S. Public*, pg. 1586
TEXAS INSTRUMENTS LMOS, CONSUMER PRODUCTS—See Texas Instruments Incorporated; *U.S. Public*, pg. 1586
TEXAS INSTRUMENTS MATERIALS & CONTROLS GROUP—See Texas Instruments Incorporated; *U.S. Public*, pg. 1586
TEXAS INSTRUMENTS PRINTERS—See Texas Instruments Incorporated; *U.S. Public*, pg. 1586
TEXAS INSTRUMENTS SECURITY—See Texas Instruments Incorporated; *U.S. Public*, pg. 1586
TEXAS INSTRUMENTS SEMICONDUCTOR GROUP—See Texas Instruments Incorporated; *U.S. Public*, pg. 1586
TEXAS INSTRUMENTS SINGAPORE (PTE.) LTD.—See Texas Instruments Incorporated; *U.S. Public*, pg. 1586
TEXAS INSTRUMENTS (SWITZERLAND) AG—See Texas Instruments Incorporated; *U.S. Public*, pg. 1586
TEXAS IRON WORKS INC.—See Pearce Industries Inc.; *U.S. Private*, pg. 845
TEXAS-LEHIGH CEMENT CO.—See Centex Corporation; *U.S. Public*, pg. 323
TEXAS LIFE INSURANCE COMPANY—See Metropolitan Life Insurance Co.; *U.S. Private*, pg. 738
TEXAS LIME CO.—See United States Lime & Minerals; *U.S. Public*, pg. 1685
TEXAS LITHO, INC.—See Prime Medical Services, Inc.; *U.S. Public*, pg. 1327
TEXAS METAL FABRICATING—See Trinity Industries Inc.; *U.S. Public*, pg. 1639
TEXAS METAL WORKS, INC.; *U.S. Private*, pg. 1078
TEXAS MICRO, INC.; *U.S. Public*, pg. 1586
TEXAS MICROSYSTEMS INC.—See Texas Micro, Inc.; *U.S. Public*, pg. 1586
TEXAS MONTHLY, INC.—See Mediatex Communications Corporation; *U.S. Private*, pg. 727
TEXAS MOTOR SPEEDWAY—See Speedway Motorsports, Inc.; *U.S. Public*, pg. 1498
TEXAS NATIONAL BANK—See First Financial Bankshares, Inc.; *U.S. Public*, pg. 633
TEXAS, NEW MEXICO & OKLAHOMA COACHES, INC.—See Greyhound Lines, Inc.; *U.S. Public*, pg. 766
TEXAS-NEW MEXICO PIPE LINE CO.—See Texaco Inc.; *U.S. Public*, pg. 1584
TEXAS-NEW MEXICO POWER CO.—See TNP Enterprises, Inc.; *U.S. Public*, pg. 1557
TEXAS OFFSHORE PIPELINE SYSTEM, INC.—See The Coastal Corporation; *U.S. Public*, pg. 389
TEXAS PACIFIC GROUP; *U.S. Private*, pg. 1078
TEXAS PACIFIC INDEMNITY CO.—See The Chubb Corporation; *U.S. Public*, pg. 355
TEXAS PACIFIC LAND TRUST; *U.S. Public*, pg. 1586
TEXAS PETRO CHEMICALS; *U.S. Private*, pg. 1078
TEXAS POLYMER SERVICES, INC.—See A. Schulman, Inc.; *U.S. Public*, pg. 1441
TEXAS REFINERY CORP.; *U.S. Private*, pg. 1078
TEXAS RESIN—See Jones Blair Company; *U.S. Private*, pg. 596
TEXAS SUNBELT CEMENT—See Centex Corporation; *U.S. Public*, pg. 323
TEXAS TANK SHIP AGENCY, INC.—See The Coastal Corporation; *U.S. Public*, pg. 390
TEXAS TELECABLE, INC.—See TCA Cable TV, Inc.; *U.S. Public*, pg. 1553
TEXAS TELEMARKETING, INC.—See Damark International, Inc.; *U.S. Public*, pg. 478
TEXAS TRANSPORTATION CO.—See S & P Company; *U.S. Private*, pg. 954
TEXAS UTILITIES AUSTRALIA—See Texas Utilities Company; *U.S. Public*, pg. 1588
TEXAS UTILITIES COMMUNICATIONS INC.—See Texas Utilities Company; *U.S. Public*, pg. 1588
TEXAS UTILITIES COMPANY; *U.S. Public*, pg. 1586

TEXAS UTILITIES FUEL CO.—See Texas Utilities Company; *U.S. Public*, pg. 1588
TEXAS UTILITIES MINING CO.—See Texas Utilities Company; *U.S. Public*, pg. 1588
TEXAS UTILITIES PROPERTIES INC.—See Texas Utilities Company; *U.S. Public*, pg. 1588
TEXFI BLENDS DIVISION—See Texfi Industries, Inc.; *U.S. Public*, pg. 1588
TEXFI INDUSTRIES, INC.; *U.S. Public*, pg. 1588
TEXMAC, INC.—See Itochu Corporation; *Int'l*, pg. 695
TEXMARK CHEMICALS INC.—See Chemical Exchange Industries; *U.S. Private*, pg. 233
TEXON MATERIALS INC.; *U.S. Private*, pg. 1079
TEXOPRINT B.V.—See Gamma Holding N.V.; *Int'l*, pg. 540
TEXSA S.A.—See Lafarge S.A.; *Int'l*, pg. 791
TEXSTARS INC.—See BBA Group plc; *Int'l*, pg. 114
TEXTIEL TECHNIEK HAAKSBERGEN B.V.—See Scapa Group Plc; *Int'l*, pg. 1203
TEXTILE CARE SERVICES, INC.—See Sunstone Hotel Investors, Inc.; *U.S. Public*, pg. 1537
TEXTILE CHEMICAL CO., INC.—See Veba AG; *Int'l*, pg. 1458
TEXTILE IMPRESSIONS, INC.—See Itochu Corporation; *Int'l*, pg. 695
TEXTILE PRODUCTS DIV.—See Berkshire Hathaway Inc.; *U.S. Public*, pg. 217
TEXTILE RUBBER & CHEMICAL COMPANY; *U.S. Private*, pg. 1079
TEXTILEASE CORPORATION; *U.S. Private*, pg. 1079
TEXTILES DE WITTE LIETAER N.V.—See Gamma Holding N.V.; *Int'l*, pg. 540
TEXTILES MORELOS S.A. DE C.V.—See Burlington Industries, Inc.; *U.S. Public*, pg. 268
TEXTRON AUTOMOTIVE COMPANY—See Textron Inc.; *U.S. Public*, pg. 1590
TEXTRON AUTOMOTIVE INTERIORS COMPANY—See Textron Inc.; *U.S. Public*, pg. 1590
TEXTRON AUTOMOTIVE TRIM OPERATIONS—See Textron Inc.; *U.S. Public*, pg. 1590
TEXTRON CANADA LTD.—See Textron Inc.; *U.S. Public*, pg. 1590
TEXTRON COMPRESSOR COMPONENTS—See Textron Inc.; *U.S. Public*, pg. 1590
TEXTRON FINANCIAL CORPORATION—See Textron Inc.; *U.S. Public*, pg. 1590
TEXTRON INC.; *U.S. Public*, pg. 1588
TEXTRON LOGISTICS COMPANY—See Textron Inc.; *U.S. Public*, pg. 1590
TEXTRON LYCOMING—See Textron Inc.; *U.S. Public*, pg. 1589
TEXTRON MARINE & LAND SYSTEMS—See Textron Inc.; *U.S. Public*, pg. 1589
TEXTRON OPTOELECTRONICS—See Textron Inc.; *U.S. Public*, pg. 1589
TEXTRON PACIFIC LIMITED—See Textron Inc.; *U.S. Public*, pg. 1590
TEXTRON SYSTEMS—See Textron Inc.; *U.S. Public*, pg. 1589
TEXTRON SYSTEMS CORPORATION—See Textron Inc.; *U.S. Public*, pg. 1589
TEXTUEL—See BDDP Group; *Int'l*, pg. 116
THE TEXWIPE CO., INC.; *U.S. Private*, pg. 1079
TEYSSIER SERVICES—See Sodexho S.A.; *Int'l*, pg. 1275
THACKERAY CORPORATION; *U.S. Public*, pg. 1590
THAI AIRWAYS INTERNATIONAL LTD.; *Int'l*, pg. 1381
THAI AIRWAYS INTL. LTD.-CHICAGO—See Thai Airways International Ltd.; *Int'l*, pg. 1381
THAI AIRWAYS INTL. LTD.-DALLAS—See Thai Airways International Ltd.; *Int'l*, pg. 1381
THAI AIRWAYS INTL. LTD.-EL SEGUNDO—See Thai Airways International Ltd.; *Int'l*, pg. 1381
THAI AIRWAYS INTL. LTD.-NEW YORK—See Thai Airways International Ltd.; *Int'l*, pg. 1381
THAI AIRWAYS INTL. LTD.-SAN FRANCISCO—See Thai Airways International Ltd.; *Int'l*, pg. 1381
THAI AIRWAYS INTL. LTD.-TORONTO—See Thai Airways International Ltd.; *Int'l*, pg. 1381
THAI AIRWAYS INTL. LTD.-U.S. OFFICE—See Thai Airways International Ltd.; *Int'l*, pg. 1381
THAI AIRWAYS INTL. LTD.-WASHINGTON—See Thai Airways International Ltd.; *Int'l*, pg. 1381
THAI-AM TOBACCO LIMITED—See Universal Corporation; *U.S. Public*, pg. 1695
THAI BRIDGESTONE CO., LTD.—See Bridgestone Corporation; *Int'l*, pg. 214
THAI CAPROLACTAM, LTD.—See UBE Industries Ltd.; *Int'l*, pg. 1427
THAI CERAMIC CO., LTD.—See The Siam Cement Public Company Limited; *Int'l*, pg. 1238
THAI CHEMICAL & ENGINEERING CO. LTD.—See Nissho Iwai Corporation; *Int'l*, pg. 949
THAI COMPRESSOR MANUFACTURING CO., LTD.—See Mitsubishi Heavy Industries Ltd.; *Int'l*, pg. 874
THAI CONTAINERS INDUSTRY CO., LTD.—See The Siam Cement Public Company Limited; *Int'l*, pg. 1238
THAI CONTAINERS LTD.—See The Siam Cement Public Company Limited; *Int'l*, pg. 1238
THAI CONTAINERS RATCHABURI (1989) CO., LTD.—See The Siam Cement Public Company Limited; *Int'l*, pg. 1238
THAI COPPER ROD CO., LTD.—See Sumitomo Electric Industries, Ltd.; *Int'l*, pg. 1314
THAI CRT CO., LTD.—See The Siam Cement Public Company Limited; *Int'l*, pg. 1238
THAI ENGINEERING PRODUCTS CO., LTD.—See The Siam Cement Public Company Limited; *Int'l*, pg. 1238
THAI FARMERS HELLER FACTORING CO., LTD.—See The Fuji Bank, Limited; *Int'l*, pg. 521
THAI FOOD COATINGS CO.—See Newly Weds Foods Inc.; *U.S. Private*, pg. 797
THAI FOODS INTERNATIONAL CO., LTD.—See Takeda Chemical Industries, Ltd.; *Int'l*, pg. 1351
THAI FUJI FINANCE AND SECURITIES COMPANY LTD.—See The Fuji Bank, Limited; *Int'l*, pg. 521

THAI FURUKAWA UNICOMM CONSTRUCTION CO., LTD.—See The Furukawa Electric Co., Ltd.; Int'l, pg. 531
THAI GLASS INDUSTRIES LTD.—See BTR plc; Int'l, pg. 129
THAI HAKUHODO CO., LTD.—See Hakuhodo Incorporated; Int'l, pg. 589
THAI INDUSTRIAL GASSES PUBLIC CO. LTD.—See The BOC Group plc; Int'l, pg. 122
THAI INTERNATIONAL DIE MAKING CO., LTD. (TDI)—See Isuzu Motors Limited; Int'l, pg. 693
THAI INVESTMENT & SECURITIES CO. LTD.—See The Dai-Ichi Kangyo Bank, Limited; Int'l, pg. 362
THAI KABAYA INDUSTRIES CO., LTD.—See Kayaba Industry Co., Ltd.; Int'l, pg. 727
THAI KANSAI PAINT CO., LTD.—See Kansai Paint Co., Ltd.; Int'l, pg. 723
THAI KOBE WELDING CO., LTD.—See Kobe Steel, Ltd.; Int'l, pg. 741
THAI KRAFT PAPER INDUSTRY CO., LTD.—See The Siam Cement Public Company Limited; Int'l, pg. 1238
THAI MASTER BUILDERS CO. LTD.—See Novartis AG; Int'l, pg. 986
THAI MEIJI PHARMACEUTICAL CO., LTD.—See Meiji Seika Kaisha, Ltd.; Int'l, pg. 856
THAI METAL PROCESSING CO. LTD.—See The Furukawa Electric Co., Ltd.; Int'l, pg. 531
THAI NIPPON FOODS CO. LTD.—See Nippon Meat Packers, Inc.; Int'l, pg. 936
THAI NIPPON MEAT PACKERS CO., LTD.—See Nippon Meat Packers, Inc.; Int'l, pg. 936
THAI NISHIMATSU CONSTRUCTION CO., LTD.—See Nishimatsu Construction Co., Ltd.; Int'l, pg. 943
THAI NOK COMPANY LTD.—See Freudenberg & Company; Int'l, pg. 507
THAI OBAYASHI CORPORATION LIMITED—See Obayashi Corporation; Int'l, pg. 996
THAI OCEAN TRANSPORTATION—See Royal Dutch/Shell Group of Companies; Int'l, pg. 1140
THAI OIL REFINERY—See Royal Dutch/Shell Group of Companies; Int'l, pg. 1140
THAI ORIX LEASING CO., LTD.—See The Industrial Finance Corporation of Thailand; Int'l, pg. 677
THAI ORIX LEASING CO., LTD.—See Orix Corporation; Int'l, pg. 1009
THAI OTSUKA PHARMACEUTICAL CO., LTD.—See Otsuka Pharmaceutical Co., Ltd.; Int'l, pg. 1014
THAI PAPER CO., LTD.—See The Siam Cement Public Company Limited; Int'l, pg. 1239
THAI POLYETHYLENE CO., LTD.—See The Siam Cement Public Company Limited; Int'l, pg. 1239
THAI POLYPHOSPHATE & CHEMICALS CO. LTD.—See Tenneco Inc.; U.S. Public, pg. 1578
THAI SAKURA FINANCE & SECURITIES CO., LTD.—See The Industrial Finance Corporation of Thailand; Int'l, pg. 677
THAI SATO KOGYO CO., LTD.—See Sato Kogyo Co., Ltd.; Int'l, pg. 1198
THAI-SCOTT PAPER COMPANY, LTD.—See Kimberly-Clark Corporation; U.S. Public, pg. 960
THAI SHELL EXPLORATION & PRODUCTION, CO. LTD.—See Royal Dutch/Shell Group of Companies; Int'l, pg. 1140
THAI SHIMIZU CO., LTD.—See Shimizu Corporation; Int'l, pg. 1234
THAI SOLUBLE COFFEE COMPANY LTD.—See Nestle S.A.; Int'l, pg. 922
THAI SPORTS GARMENT CO., LTD.—See Mizuno Corporation; Int'l, pg. 885
THAI SUMIDEN ENGINEERING AND CONSTRUCTION CO., LTD.—See Sumitomo Electric Industries, Ltd.; Int'l, pg. 1314
THAI SUZUKI MOTOR CO., LTD.—See Suzuki Motor Corporation; Int'l, pg. 1323
THAI-SWEDISH ASSEMBLY CO. LTD.—See AB Volvo; Int'l, pg. 1476
THAI SYSTEMS CORPORATION LTD.—See International Business Machines Corporation; U.S. Public, pg. 897
THAI TAKENAKA INTERNATIONAL LTD.—See Takenaka Corporation; Int'l, pg. 1352
THAI TORAY TEXTILE MILLS PUBLIC COMPANY LIMITED—See Toray Industries, Inc.; Int'l, pg. 1400
THAI TOSHIBA ELECTRIC INDUSTRIES CO., LTD.—See Toshiba Corporation; Int'l, pg. 1406
THAI UNION PAPER CO., LTD.—See The Siam Cement Public Company Limited; Int'l, pg. 1239
THAI UNION PAPER INDUSTRY CO., LTD.—See The Siam Cement Public Company Limited; Int'l, pg. 1239
THAI WACOAL CO., LTD.—See Wacoal Corporation; Int'l, pg. 1484
THE THAI WANAPHAN CO., LTD.—See The Siam Cement Public Company Limited; Int'l, pg. 1239
THAI YAMAZAKI CO., LTD.—See Yamazaki Baking Co., Ltd.; Int'l, pg. 1519
THAILAND SMELTING & REFINING, CO. LTD.—See Royal Dutch/Shell Group of Companies; Int'l, pg. 1140
THAMES SIDE-MAYWOOD LIMITED—See Halma p.l.c.; Int'l, pg. 590
THAMES TELEVISION LTD.—See Pearson plc; Int'l, pg. 1026
THANA ONE FINANCE AND SECURITIES LIMITED—See Finance One Public Company Limited; Int'l, pg. 485
THANN ET MULHOUSE—See Millennium Chemicals Inc.; U.S. Public, pg. 1111
THATCHER ALLOYS LTD.—See Outokumpu Oyj; Int'l, pg. 1017
THAW & WALRUS, INC.—See Recreational Equipment, Inc.; U.S. Private, pg. 914
THE APEX GROUP, INC.—See ADC Telecommunications, Inc.; U.S. Public, pg. 4
THE MEDIA EDGE; U.S. Private, pg. 1079
THE SIAM FIBERGLASS CO., LTD.—See The Siam Cement Public Company Limited; Int'l, pg. 1238

THE TOKIO MARINE & FIRE INSURANCE COMPANY (U.K.) LIMITED—See The Tokio Marine & Fire Insurance Company, Ltd.; Int'l, pg. 1393
THE WORLD BANK—See The World Bank; U.S. Private, pg. 1190
DR. RER. NAT. PETER THEISS NATURWAREN—See Wella Group; Int'l, pg. 1489
THEOCHEM LABS., INC.; U.S. Private, pg. 1079
THEON CO. LTD.—See Del Laboratories, Inc.; U.S. Public, pg. 494
THERA COSMETIC GMBH—See Henkel KGaA; Int'l, pg. 610
THERADYNE CORPORATION—See Kurt Manufacturing Co. Inc.; U.S. Private, pg. 637
THERAKOS, INC.—See Johnson & Johnson; U.S. Public, pg. 929
THERANOSTIC MEDIZINELEKTRONIK GMBH—See Delft Instruments N.V.; Int'l, pg. 389
THERAPEDIC ASSOCIATES, INC.; U.S. Private, pg. 1079
THERAPY MANAGEMENT ASSOCIATES, LLC—See True North Diversified Companies; U.S. Public, pg. 1642
THERIMAGE PRODUCTS DIV.—See Avery Dennison Corporation; U.S. Public, pg. 152
THERM, INC.; U.S. Private, pg. 1079
THERM-O-DISC (CANADA) LIMITED—See Emerson Electric Co.; U.S. Public, pg. 578
THERM-O-DISC INC.—See Emerson Electric Co.; U.S. Public, pg. 573
THERMA AG—See Electrolux, AB; Int'l, pg. 444
THERMA GROSSKUCHEN AG—See Electrolux, AB; Int'l, pg. 444
THERMA-TRU CORP.; U.S. Private, pg. 1079
THERMA-TRU INDIANA MFG. OPERS.—See Therma-Tru Corp.; U.S. Private, pg. 1080
THERMA-TRU WESTERN MFG. OPERS.—See Therma-Tru Corp.; U.S. Private, pg. 1080
THERMADOR—See Masco Corporation; U.S. Public, pg. 1053
THERMAL-CARE DIV.—See MFRI Inc.; U.S. Public, pg. 1026
THERMAL CERAMICS—See Morgan Crucible Co. Plc; Int'l, pg. 894
THERMAL CERAMICS DE FRANCE S.A.—See Morgan Crucible Co. Plc; Int'l, pg. 894
THERMAL CERAMICS ESPAÑA, S.L.—See Morgan Crucible Co. Plc; Int'l, pg. 894
THERMAL CERAMICS INC.—See Morgan Crucible Co. Plc; Int'l, pg. 894
THERMAL CERAMICS ITALIANA S.R.L.—See Morgan Crucible Co. Plc; Int'l, pg. 894
THERMAL CERAMICS LIMITED—See Morgan Crucible Co. Plc; Int'l, pg. 893
THERMAL CERAMICS NEDERLAND BV—See Morgan Crucible Co. Plc; Int'l, pg. 894
THERMAL COMPONENTS, INC.—See Insilco Corporation; U.S. Public, pg. 881
THERMAL ELECTRON TECH. CO.—See Thermo Electron Corporation; U.S. Public, pg. 1593
THERMAL ENERGIES, INC.—See United Illuminating Company; U.S. Public, pg. 1679
THERMAL EQUIPMENT SYSTEMS, INC.—See Eclipse Inc.; U.S. Private, pg. 360
THERMAL INDUSTRIES, INC.—See HIG Capital Management; U.S. Private, pg. 490
THERMAL INDUSTRIES INC.—See HIG Capital Management; U.S. Private, pg. 491
THERMAL PROCESSING GROUP LTD.—See TI Group plc; Int'l, pg. 1338
THERMAL PROCESSING GROUP LTD. (CAMBRIDGE)—See TI Group plc; Int'l, pg. 1338
THERMAL PROCESSING GROUP LTD. (COVENTRY)—See TI Group plc; Int'l, pg. 1338
THERMAL PROCESSING GROUP LTD. (SHEFFIELD)—See TI Group plc; Int'l, pg. 1338
THERMAL PROCESSING GROUP LTD. (SKELMERSDALE)—See TI Group plc; Int'l, pg. 1338
THERMAL TECHNOLOGY INDUSTRIES; U.S. Private, pg. 1080
THERMAL TRANSFER CORP.—See Air & Water Technologies Corporation; U.S. Public, pg. 29
THERMALLOY, INC.—See Bowthorpe plc; Int'l, pg. 208
THERMALLOY INC.—See Bowthorpe plc; Int'l, pg. 209
THERMATOME—See Jeumont-Schneider Trenformeteurs; Int'l, pg. 706
THERMAX FUJI ELECTRIC PRIVATE LTD.—See Fuji Electric Co., Ltd.; Int'l, pg. 522
THERMAX LIMITED—See Saint-Gobain; Int'l, pg. 1173
THERMEDICS INC.—See Thermo Electron Corporation; U.S. Public, pg. 1592
THERMENDOTA, INC.—See Thermo Electron Corporation; U.S. Public, pg. 1592
THERMIC REFRACTORIES INC.—See Morgan Crucible Co. Plc; Int'l, pg. 894
THERMICE CORPORATION—See Publicker Industries Inc.; U.S. Public, pg. 1341
THERMO BLACK CLAWSON, INC.—See Thermo Electron Corporation; U.S. Public, pg. 1593
THERMO CARDIOSYSTEMS INC.—See Thermo Electron Corporation; U.S. Public, pg. 1592
THERMO CONSULTING ENGINEERS—See Thermo Electron Corporation; U.S. Public, pg. 1594
THERMO CONSULTING ENGINEERS INC.—See Thermo Electron Corporation; U.S. Public, pg. 1594
THERMO ELECTRIC (CANADA) LTD.—See Thermo Electric Co., Inc.; U.S. Private, pg. 1080
THERMO ELECTRIC CO., INC.; U.S. Private, pg. 1080
THERMO ELECTRIC GMBH—See Thermo Electric Co., Inc.; U.S. Private, pg. 1080
THERMO ELECTRIC INTL. B.V.—See Thermo Electric Co., Inc.; U.S. Private, pg. 1080
THERMO ELECTRIC INTL. LTD.—See Thermo Electric Co., Inc.; U.S. Private, pg. 1080
THERMO ELECTRIC S.A.—See Thermo Electric Co., Inc.; U.S. Private, pg. 1080

THERMO ELECTRON (CANADA)—See Thermo Electron Corporation; U.S. Public, pg. 1596
THERMO ELECTRON CORPORATION; U.S. Public, pg. 1591
THERMO ELECTRON LTD.—See Thermo Electron Corporation; U.S. Public, pg. 1596
THERMO ELECTRON NIPPON CO., LTD.—See Thermo Electron Corporation; U.S. Public, pg. 1596
THERMO ELECTRON WISCONSIN, INC.—See Thermo Electron Corporation; U.S. Public, pg. 1593
THERMO ENERGY SYSTEMS CORPORATION—See Thermo Electron Corporation; U.S. Public, pg. 1593
THERMO ENVIRONMENTAL INSTRUMENT INC.—See Thermo Electron Corporation; U.S. Public, pg. 1593
THERMO FIBERTEK, INC.—See Thermo Electron Corporation; U.S. Public, pg. 1593
THERMO INDUSTRIES INC.; U.S. Private, pg. 1080
THERMO INSTRUMENT SYSTEMS B.V.—See Thermo Electron Corporation; U.S. Public, pg. 1596
THERMO INSTRUMENT SYSTEMS (F.E.) LIMITED—See Thermo Electron Corporation; U.S. Public, pg. 1596
THERMO INSTRUMENT SYSTEMS GMBH—See Thermo Electron Corporation; U.S. Public, pg. 1596
THERMO INSTRUMENT SYSTEMS INC.—See Thermo Electron Corporation; U.S. Public, pg. 1593
THERMO JARRELL ASH CORPORATION—See Thermo Electron Corporation; U.S. Public, pg. 1594
THERMO KING CORPORATION—See Ingersoll-Rand Company; U.S. Public, pg. 877
THERMO MATERIALS—See Ceradyne, Inc; U.S. Public, pg. 330
THERMO-MIZER ENVIRONMENTAL CORP.; U.S. Public, pg. 1596
THERMO PROCESS SYSTEMS INC./CAL-DORAN METALLURGICAL, INC.—See Thermo Electron Corporation; U.S. Public, pg. 1594
THERMO PROCESS SYSTEMS INC./HOLCROFT—See Thermo Electron Corporation; U.S. Public, pg. 1594
THERMO SEPARATION PRODUCTS—See Thermo Electron Corporation; U.S. Public, pg. 1594
THERMO SOLUTIONS—See Research, Incorporated; U.S. Public, pg. 1382
THERMO-TANK-DIENST GMBH—See Fried. Krupp AG; Int'l, pg. 515
THERMO VOLTEK CORP.—See Thermo Electron Corporation; U.S. Public, pg. 1596
THERMOLASE—See Thermo Electron Corporation; U.S. Public, pg. 1595
THERMOMETRICS, INC.—See Bowthorpe plc; Int'l, pg. 208
THERMOMETRICS JAPAN CO. LTD.—See Bowthorpe plc; Int'l, pg. 209
THERMON AUSTRALIA—See Thermon Manufacturing Company; U.S. Private, pg. 1081
THERMON DEUTSCHLAND GMBH—See Thermon Manufacturing Company; U.S. Private, pg. 1081
THERMON EUROPE B.V.—See Thermon Manufacturing Company; U.S. Private, pg. 1081
THERMON FAR EAST, LTD.—See Thermon Manufacturing Company; U.S. Private, pg. 1081
THERMON FRANCE—See Thermon Manufacturing Company; U.S. Private, pg. 1081
THERMON HEAT TRACING SERVICES, INC. I—See Thermon Manufacturing Company; U.S. Private, pg. 1080
THERMON ITALIA S.P.A.—See Thermon Manufacturing Company; U.S. Private, pg. 1081
THERMON KOREA LTD.—See Thermon Manufacturing Company; U.S. Private, pg. 1081
THERMON MANUFACTURING COMPANY; U.S. Private, pg. 1080
THERMON U.K. (LTD.)—See Thermon Manufacturing Company; U.S. Private, pg. 1081
THERMOPLAST UND APPARATEBAU GMBH; Int'l, pg. 1081
THERMOPLASTICS, INC.—See Textron Inc.; U.S. Public, pg. 1590
THE THERMOS COMPANY—See Nippon Sanso Corporation; Int'l, pg. 938
THERMOS DE MEXICO S.A. DE C.V.—See Nippon Sanso Corporation; Int'l, pg. 938
THERMOS FRANCE S.A.—See Nippon Sanso Corporation; Int'l, pg. 938
THERMOS GMBH—See Nippon Sanso Corporation; Int'l, pg. 938
THERMOS LIMITED—See Nippon Sanso Corporation; Int'l, pg. 938
THERMOS PTY. LTD.—See Nippon Sanso Corporation; Int'l, pg. 939
THERMOTEC INC.—See Eclipse Inc.; U.S. Private, pg. 360
THERMOTECH SYSTEMS CORPORATION—See Gencor Industries, Inc.; U.S. Public, pg. 705
THERMOTREX—See Thermo Electron Corporation; U.S. Public, pg. 1595
THERMOTRON INDUSTRIES—See Venturedyne, Ltd.; U.S. Private, pg. 1136
THERMWELL PRODUCTS CO., INC.; U.S. Private, pg. 1081
J.E. THERRIEN, INC.—See Quebecor Inc.; Int'l, pg. 1075
THETA HOME HEALTH CARE, INC.—See Integrated Health Services, Inc.; U.S. Public, pg. 885
THETA LAND CORPORATION—See Pennsylvania Enterprises Inc.; U.S. Public, pg. 1272
THETFORD CORPORATION—See The Dyson-Kissner-Moran Corporation; U.S. Private, pg. 352
THIBAUT - COLSON - DE NEF (TCD)—See Generale de Banque S.A.; Int'l, pg. 547
RICHARD E. THIBAUT, INC.—See RPM, Inc.; U.S. Public, pg. 1358
THIBEAU—See N. Schlumberger & Cie; Int'l, pg. 1206
THIEL CHEESE CO.; U.S. Private, pg. 1081
THIELE ENGINEERING—See Barry-Wehmiller Company; U.S. Private, pg. 118
THIELE KAOLIN CO.; U.S. Private, pg. 1081

THIEMANN ARZNEIMITTEL GMBH—See Akzo Nobel N.V.; *Int'l*, pg. 45
THILMANY DIVISION—See International Paper Company; *U.S. Public*, pg. 903
THIMBLE COLLECTORS CLUB COLLECTIONS—See MBI Inc.; *U.S. Private*, pg. 685
THIN FILM TECHNOLOGY DIVISION—See Bausch & Lomb Incorporated; *U.S. Public*, pg. 194
THINGS REMEMBERED, INC.—See Cole National Corporation; *U.S. Public*, pg. 397
THINK NEW IDEAS, INC.—See Omnicom Group Inc.; *U.S. Public*, pg. 1224
THINKING MACHINES CORPORATION; *U.S. Private*, pg. 1081
THIOKOL CORPORATION; *U.S. Public*, pg. 1596
THIOKOL GOVERNMENT RELATIONS—See Thiokol Corporation; *U.S. Public*, pg. 1597
THIOKOL PROPULSION GROUP—See Thiokol Corporation; *U.S. Public*, pg. 1597
THIOKOL PUBLIC RELATIONS—See Thiokol Corporation; *U.S. Public*, pg. 1597
THIOKOL SCIENCE AND ENGINEERING—See Thiokol Corporation; *U.S. Public*, pg. 1597
THIOKOL SPACE OPERATIONS—See Thiokol Corporation; *U.S. Public*, pg. 1597
THIS END UP FURNITURE; *U.S. Private*, pg. 1081
THISCO—See Comforce Corporation; *U.S. Public*, pg. 409
THO-RO PRODUCTS, INC.—See Eagle Button Co., Inc.; *U.S. Private*, pg. 354
THOMAINFOR—See Thomson S.A.; *Int'l*, pg. 1382
THOMAS A. EDISON TECHNICAL CENTER—See Cooper Industries, Inc.; *U.S. Public*, pg. 443
THOMAS & BETTS/AMERACE—See Thomas & Betts Corporation; *U.S. Public*, pg. 1598
THOMAS & BETTS AUTOMOTIVE—See Thomas & Betts Corporation; *U.S. Public*, pg. 1597
THOMAS & BETTS CARIBE, INC.—See Thomas & Betts Corporation; *U.S. Public*, pg. 1598
THOMAS & BETTS CORPORATION; *U.S. Public*, pg. 1597
THOMAS & BETTS ELECTRONICS DIVISION—See Thomas & Betts Corporation; *U.S. Public*, pg. 1597
THOMAS & BETTS GMBH—See Thomas & Betts Corporation; *U.S. Public*, pg. 1598
THOMAS & BETTS LEHIGH LANCASTER—See Thomas & Betts Corporation; *U.S. Public*, pg. 1597
THOMAS & BETTS LTD.—See Thomas & Betts Corporation; *U.S. Public*, pg. 1598
THOMAS & BETTS MANUFACTURING LTD.—See Thomas & Betts Corporation; *U.S. Public*, pg. 1598
THOMAS & BETTS REZNOR DIVISION—See Thomas & Betts Corporation; *U.S. Public*, pg. 1598
THOMAS & HOWARD CO.; *U.S. Private*, pg. 1081
THOMAS & HOWARD CO.—See Thomas & Howard Co.; *U.S. Private*, pg. 1082
THOMAS & SKINNER, INC.; *U.S. Private*, pg. 1082
THOMAS & BETTS—See Thomas & Betts Corporation; *U.S. Public*, pg. 1598
THOMAS BUILT BUSES, INC.; *U.S. Private*, pg. 1082
THOMAS BUILT BUSES OF CANADA, LTD.—See Thomas Built Buses, Inc.; *U.S. Private*, pg. 1082
CHARLIE THOMAS DEALERSHIPS; *U.S. Private*, pg. 1082
THOMAS CONVEYOR COMPANY; *U.S. Private*, pg. 1082
THOMAS DE LA RUE LTD.—See De La Rue plc; *Int'l*, pg. 386
THOMAS ENGINEERING INC.; *U.S. Private*, pg. 1082
THOMAS EQUIPMENT LIMITED—See McCain Foods Limited; *Int'l*, pg. 850
THOMAS INDUSTRIES INC.; *U.S. Public*, pg. 1598
THOMAS JEFFERSON LIFE INSURANCE CO.—See USF&G Corporation; *U.S. Public*, pg. 1659
THOMAS LIGHTING-C&I ACCENT DIVISION—See Thomas Industries Inc.; *U.S. Public*, pg. 1599
THOMAS LIGHTING-C&I INDOOR DIVISION—See Thomas Industries Inc.; *U.S. Public*, pg. 1599
THOMAS LIGHTING-C&I OUTDOOR DIVISION—See Thomas Industries Inc.; *U.S. Public*, pg. 1599
THOMAS LIGHTING-CANADIAN DIVISION—See Thomas Industries Inc.; *U.S. Public*, pg. 1599
THOMAS LIGHTING-MILAN OPERATIONS—See Thomas Industries Inc.; *U.S. Public*, pg. 1599
THOMAS LIGHTING-SPARTA OPERS.—See Thomas Industries Inc.; *U.S. Public*, pg. 1599
THOMAS MANUFACTURING CO., INC. OF THOMASVILLE—See Masco Corporation; *U.S. Public*, pg. 1053
THOMAS PIPE & STEEL, INC.—See Harvest Partners Inc.; *U.S. Private*, pg. 508
THOMAS PUBLISHING COMPANY; *U.S. Private*, pg. 1082
THOMAS REGIONAL—See Thomas Publishing Company; *U.S. Private*, pg. 1082
ROBERT THOMAS SECURITIES, INC.—See Raymond James Financial, Inc.; *U.S. Public*, pg. 923
THOMAS STEEL STRIP CORP.—See Koninklijke Hoogovens N.V.; *Int'l*, pg. 756
SYSCO FOOD SERVICES—See Sysco Corporation; *U.S. Public*, pg. 1551
THOMAS TAIT & SONS, LTD.—See International Paper Company; *U.S. Public*, pg. 904
TED THOMAS ASSOCIATES INC. ADVERTISING; *U.S. Private*, pg. 1083
THOMAS TILLING LIMITED—See BTR plc; *Int'l*, pg. 124
THOMASON AUTO GROUP; *U.S. Private*, pg. 1083
THOMASSEN & DRIJVER-VERBLIFA N.V.—See Schmalbach-Lubeca AG; *Int'l*, pg. 1207
THOMASSEN INTERNATIONAL HOLDING B.V.—See Deutsche Babcock AG; *Int'l*, pg. 401
THOMASSEN STEWART & STEVENSON INTERNATIONAL B.V.—See Stewart & Stevenson Services, Inc.; *U.S. Public*, pg. 1518
I.C. THOMASSON ASSOCIATES, INC.; *U.S. Private*, pg. 1083
THOMASTON MILLS, INC.; *U.S. Public*, pg. 1599
THOMASVILLE ENERGY CORPORATION—See Snyder Oil Corporation; *U.S. Public*, pg. 1482

THOMASVILLE FURNITURE INDUSTRIES, INC.—See Furniture Brands International Inc.; *U.S. Public*, pg. 688
THOMASVILLE UPHOLSTERY, INC.—See Furniture Brands International Inc.; *U.S. Public*, pg. 688
THOMCAST—See Thomson S.A.; *Int'l*, pg. 1382
THOMCAST GMBH—See Thomson S.A.; *Int'l*, pg. 1385
THOMCAST INC.—See Thomson S.A.; *Int'l*, pg. 1384
THOMI & FRANCK AG—See Nestle S.A.; *Int'l*, pg. 916
THOMINTEX—See Thomson S.A.; *Int'l*, pg. 1382
THOMPACK B.V.—See AEP Industries, Inc.; *U.S. Public*, pg. 5
THOMPSON BANKWATCH, INC.—See The Thomson Corporation; *U.S. Public*, pg. 1600
THOMPSON BROS., INC.—See Ameritruck Distribution Corporation; *U.S. Private*, pg. 66
THOMPSON DIVISION—See U.S. Home Corporation; *U.S. Public*, pg. 1683
THOMPSON GMBH—See Henkel KGaA; *Int'l*, pg. 610
J. WALTER THOMPSON COMPANY—See WPP Group plc; *Int'l*, pg. 1483
THOMPSON MACHINES—See Burlington Basket Co.; *U.S. Private*, pg. 183
THOMPSON-MCCULLY ASPHALT PAVING CO.—See Thompson-McCully Co.; *U.S. Private*, pg. 1083
THOMPSON-MCCULLY CO.; *U.S. Private*, pg. 1083
THOMPSON MEDICAL COMPANY, INC.; *U.S. Public*, pg. 1083
THE THOMPSON-MINWAX COMPANY—See The Sherwin-Williams Company; *U.S. Public*, pg. 1466
THOMPSON NUTRITIONAL PRODUCTS—See Rexall Sundown Inc.; *U.S. Public*, pg. 1384
THOMPSON, SIEGEL & WALMSLEY, INC.—See United Asset Management Corporation; *U.S. Public*, pg. 1674
THOMPSON-SIEGEL GMBH—See Henkel KGaA; *Int'l*, pg. 610
THOMPSON-STARRETT CONSTRUCTION COMPANY, INC.—See Elgin National Industries, Inc.; *U.S. Private*, pg. 371
THOMPSON STEEL CO., INC.; *U.S. Public*, pg. 1083
THOMPSON TRACTOR COMPANY; *U.S. Private*, pg. 1083
W.G. THOMPSON & SONS LTD.; *Int'l*, pg. 1381
THE THOMPSON'S COMPANY—See The Sherwin-Williams Company; *U.S. Public*, pg. 1466
THOMSON & THOMSON—See The Thomson Corporation; *U.S. Public*, pg. 1601
THOMSON AUSTRALIAN HOLDINGS PTY. LTD.—See The Thomson Corporation; *U.S. Public*, pg. 1600
THOMSON BANK WATCH, INC.—See The Thomson Corporation; *U.S. Public*, pg. 1600
THOMSON BAUELEMENTE GMBH—See Thomson S.A.; *Int'l*, pg. 1385
THOMSON BOOK/REFERENCE GROUP—See The Thomson Corporation; *U.S. Public*, pg. 1600
THOMSON CANADA LIMITED—See The Thomson Corporation; *U.S. Public*, pg. 1602
THOMSON CFS-BELGIUM—See Thomson S.A.; *Int'l*, pg. 1385
THOMSON COMPANY, INC.—See Salant Corporation; *U.S. Public*, pg. 1429
THOMSON COMPETENCES—See Thomson S.A.; *Int'l*, pg. 1382
THOMSON CORPORATION OF AMERICA—See Thomson S.A.; *Int'l*, pg. 1383
THE THOMSON CORPORATION PLC—See The Thomson Corporation; *U.S. Public*, pg. 1601
THE THOMSON CORPORATION; *U.S. Public*, pg. 1599
THOMSON-CSF—See Thomson S.A.; *Int'l*, pg. 1382
THOMSON-CSF AIRSYS—See Thomson S.A.; *Int'l*, pg. 1382
THOMSON-CSF APPLICATIONS RADAR—See Thomson S.A.; *Int'l*, pg. 1382
THOMSON-CSF AUSTRIA GESMBH—See Thomson S.A.; *Int'l*, pg. 1385
THOMSON-CSF (CHILE) LTDA—See Thomson S.A.; *Int'l*, pg. 1384
THOMSON-CSF COMMUNICATIONS—See Thomson S.A.; *Int'l*, pg. 1382
THOMSON-CSF DE VENEZUELA C.A.—See Thomson S.A.; *Int'l*, pg. 1384
THOMSON-CSF DEUTSCHLAND GMBH—See Thomson S.A.; *Int'l*, pg. 1385
THOMSON-CSF ELEKTRONIK GMBH—See Thomson S.A.; *Int'l*, pg. 1385
THOMSON-CSF ELETRONICA PROFISSIONAL LTDA—See Thomson S.A.; *Int'l*, pg. 1384
THOMSON-CSF EQUIPAMENTOS DO BRASIL LTDA—See Thomson S.A.; *Int'l*, pg. 1384
THOMSON-CSF HEALTH SYSTEMS—See Thomson S.A.; *Int'l*, pg. 1385
THOMSON-CSF HELLAS A.E.—See Thomson S.A.; *Int'l*, pg. 1385
THOMSON-CSF, INC.—See Thomson S.A.; *Int'l*, pg. 1384
THOMSON-CSF MICROELECTRONIQUE—See Thomson S.A.; *Int'l*, pg. 1382
THOMSON-CSF MISSILE ELECTRONICS—See Thomson S.A.; *Int'l*, pg. 1382
THOMSON-CSF NCS FRANCE—See Thomson S.A.; *Int'l*, pg. 1382
THOMSON-CSF OPTRONIQUE—See Thomson S.A.; *Int'l*, pg. 1382
THOMSON-CSF PASSIVE COMPONENTS—See Thomson S.A.; *Int'l*, pg. 1382
THOMSON-CSF PASSIVE COMPONENTS BENELUX—See Thomson S.A.; *Int'l*, pg. 1385
THOMSON-CSF PASSIVE COMPONENTS BRAZIL LTDA—See Thomson S.A.; *Int'l*, pg. 1384
THOMSON-CSF PASSIVE COMPONENTS GMBH—See Thomson S.A.; *Int'l*, pg. 1385
THOMSON-CSF PASSIVE COMPONENTS INC.—See Thomson S.A.; *Int'l*, pg. 1384
THOMSON-CSF PASSIVE COMPONENTS ITALY S.P.A.—See Thomson S.A.; *Int'l*, pg. 1385
THOMSON-CSF RADARS & CONTRE-MESURES—See Thomson S.A.; *Int'l*, pg. 1382

THOMSON-CSF S.A.—See Thomson S.A.; *Int'l*, pg. 1383
THOMSON-CSF SECURITE—See Thomson S.A.; *Int'l*, pg. 1382
THOMSON-CSF SEMICONDUCTEURS SPECIFIQUES—See Thomson S.A.; *Int'l*, pg. 1382
THOMSON-CSF SERVICE INDUSTRIE—See Thomson S.A.; *Int'l*, pg. 1383
THOMSON-CSF SERVICES & SYSTEMES SOL SPATIAUX—See Thomson S.A.; *Int'l*, pg. 1383
THOMSON-CSF SERVICES INDUSTRIE—See Thomson S.A.; *Int'l*, pg. 1383
THOMSON-CSF SERVICES INDUSTRIE & THOMINTEX—See Thomson S.A.; *Int'l*, pg. 1383
THOMSON-CSF TECHNOLOGIES & METHODES—See Thomson S.A.; *Int'l*, pg. 1383
THOMSON DIRECTORIES—See U S West Inc.; *U.S. Public*, pg. 1689
THOMSON FACILITIES MANAGEMENT—See Thomson S.A.; *Int'l*, pg. 1383
THOMSON FINANCE LTD.—See The Thomson Corporation; *U.S. Public*, pg. 1601
THOMSON FINANCIAL SERVICES—See The Thomson Corporation; *U.S. Public*, pg. 1601
THOMSON GESTION IMMOBILIERE—See Thomson S.A.; *Int'l*, pg. 1383
THOMSON HEALTHCARE COMMUNICATIONS—See The Thomson Corporation; *U.S. Public*, pg. 1602
THOMSON HOLDINGS INC.—See The Thomson Corporation; *U.S. Public*, pg. 1601
THOMSON HOLIDAYS LTD.—See The Thomson Corporation; *U.S. Public*, pg. 1602
THOMSON INFORMATION SERVICES LTD.—See The Thomson Corporation; *U.S. Public*, pg. 1601
THOMSON INTERNATIONAL HOLDINGS LIMITED—See The Thomson Corporation; *U.S. Public*, pg. 1600
THOMSON-LCD—See Thomson S.A.; *Int'l*, pg. 1383
THOMSON-LGT (LABORATOIRE GENERALE DES TELECOMMUNICATIONS)—See Thomson S.A.; *Int'l*, pg. 1385
THOMSON MACCONNELL CADILLAC, INC.; *U.S. Private*, pg. 1084
THOMSON MICROSONICS—See Thomson S.A.; *Int'l*, pg. 1383
THOMSON MULTIMEDIA SA—See Thomson S.A.; *Int'l*, pg. 1384
THOMSON PASSIVE COMPONENTS CORP.—See Thomson S.A.; *Int'l*, pg. 1384
THOMSON PROFESSIONAL PUBLISHING—See The Thomson Corporation; *U.S. Public*, pg. 1601
THOMSON REGIONAL NEWSPAPERS LTD.—See The Thomson Corporation; *U.S. Public*, pg. 1601
THOMSON S.A.; *Int'l*, pg. 1381
THOMSON SHORTS SYSTEMES S.A.—See Thomson S.A.; *Int'l*, pg. 1383
THOMSON SINTRA ACTIVITES SOUS-MARINES—See Thomson S.A.; *Int'l*, pg. 1383
THOMSON SINTRA ASM—See Thomson S.A.; *Int'l*, pg. 1383
THOMSON SOFTWARE PRODUCTS—See Thomson S.A.; *Int'l*, pg. 1383
THOMSON TELEVISION CO. ESPANA—See Thomson S.A.; *Int'l*, pg. 1384
THOMSON TELEVISION COMPONENTS FRANCE—See Thomson S.A.; *Int'l*, pg. 1384
THOMSON TOUR OPERATIONS LTD.—See The Thomson Corporation; *U.S. Public*, pg. 1601
THOMSON TRAINING & SIMULATION—See Thomson S.A.; *Int'l*, pg. 1383
THOMSON-TRT DEFENSE—See Thomson S.A.; *Int'l*, pg. 1383
THOMSON TUBES—See Thomson S.A.; *Int'l*, pg. 1384
THOMSON TUBES ELECTRONIQUES—See Thomson S.A.; *Int'l*, pg. 1383
THOMSON TUBES ELECTRONIQUES (SIEGE)—See Thomson S.A.; *Int'l*, pg. 1383
THOMSON U.S. INC.—See The Thomson Corporation; *U.S. Public*, pg. 1601
THONET—See Shelby Williams Industries, Inc.; *U.S. Public*, pg. 1465
THOON RUAM KARN CO., LTD.—See Siam City Bank Public Company Limited; *Int'l*, pg. 1239
THOR AMERICA—See Thor Industries, Inc.; *U.S. Public*, pg. 1602
THOR CALIFORNIA, INC.—See Thor Industries, Inc.; *U.S. Public*, pg. 1602
THOR INDIANA, INC.—See Thor Industries, Inc.; *U.S. Public*, pg. 1602
THOR INDUSTRIES, INC.; *U.S. Public*, pg. 1602
THOR WEST—See Thor Industries, Inc.; *U.S. Public*, pg. 1602
THORN—See Thorn plc; *Int'l*, pg. 1386
THORN AMERICAS—See Thorn plc; *Int'l*, pg. 1385
THORN APPLE VALLEY-DELI & SMOKED MEATS DIVISION—See Thorn Apple Valley, Inc.; *U.S. Public*, pg. 1603
THORN APPLE VALLEY, INC.; *U.S. Public*, pg. 1602
THORN APPLE VALLEY-TRANSPORTATION DIVISION—See Thorn Apple Valley, Inc.; *U.S. Public*, pg. 1603
THORN AUSTRALIA PTY LTD.—See Thorn plc; *Int'l*, pg. 1386
THORN DENMARK—See Thorn plc; *Int'l*, pg. 1386
THORN EMI AUSTRALIA LIMITED—See EMI Group plc; *Int'l*, pg. 427
THORN EMI (CANADA) INC.—See EMI Group plc; *Int'l*, pg. 428
THORN EMI DANMARK A/S—See EMI Group plc; *Int'l*, pg. 428
THORN-EMI HONG KONG LTD.—See EMI Group plc; *Int'l*, pg. 428
THORN EMI INC.—See EMI Group plc; *Int'l*, pg. 427
THORN EMI (IRELAND) LIMITED—See EMI Group plc; *Int'l*, pg. 428
THORN EMI NEW ZEALAND—See EMI Group plc; *Int'l*, pg. 428

Company Index

THORN EMI SOUTH AFRICA (PTY.) LIMITED—See EMI Group plc; *Int'l*, pg. 428
THORN-ERICSSON TELECOMMUNICATIONS LIMITED—See Telefonaktiebolaget LM Ericsson; *Int'l*, pg. 1370
THORN-EUROPE—See Thorn plc; *Int'l*, pg. 1386
THORN FINLAND OY—See Thorn plc; *Int'l*, pg. 1386
THORN GROUP—See Thorn plc; *Int'l*, pg. 1385
THORN LIGHTING GROUP PLC; *Int'l*, pg. 1385
THORN NORGE A/S—See Thorn plc; *Int'l*, pg. 1386
THORN PLC; *Int'l*, pg. 1385
THORN SECURITY GROUP, LTD.; *Int'l*, pg. 1386
THORN SVENSKA AB—See Thorn plc; *Int'l*, pg. 1386
THORNDIKE PRESS—See National Amusements, Inc.; *U.S. Private*, pg. 777
THORNES—See Distribution America; *U.S. Private*, pg. 336
STANLEY THORNES (PUBLISHERS)—See Wolters Kluwer N.V.; *Int'l*, pg. 1514
THORNHILL COMPANY, INC.; *U.S. Private*, pg. 1084
THORNTON & CO. LTD.—See Dresdner Bank AG; *Int'l*, pg. 420
THORNTON OIL CORP.; *U.S. Private*, pg. 1084
THORNTONS PLC; *Int'l*, pg. 1386
THORO—See Harris Chemical Group, Inc.; *U.S. Private*, pg. 505
THOROBRED CONTAINERS INCORPORATED—See Interlock Industries, Inc.; *U.S. Private*, pg. 567
THOROUGHBRED PLASTICS CORP.—See Brown-Forman Corporation; *U.S. Public*, pg. 261
D.W. THORPE-AUSTRALIA—See Reed Elsevier plc; *Int'l*, pg. 1095
D.W. THORPE-NEW ZEALAND—See Reed Elsevier plc; *Int'l*, pg. 1095
THORSEN TRADING CO.—See Household International, Inc.; *U.S. Public*, pg. 842
THORSMAN & CO. AB—See AB Industrivarden; *Int'l*, pg. 678
THORSTENBERG MATERIALS CO., INC.—See Holderbank Financiere Glaris Ltd.; *Int'l*, pg. 1098
THOSE CHARACTERS FROM CLEVELAND, INC.—See American Greetings Corporation; *U.S. Public*, pg. 78
THOUSAND OAKS NEWS-CHRONICLE—See The E.W. Scripps Company; *U.S. Public*, pg. 1448
THRALL CAR MFG. CO.—See Duchossois Industries, Inc.; *U.S. Private*, pg. 344
THRALL ENTERPRISES, INC.; *U.S. Private*, pg. 1084
THREADNEEDLE ASSET MANAGEMENT—See B.A.T Industries P.L.C.; *Int'l*, pg. 110
THREADNEEDLE INVESTMENT MANAGERS LIMITED—See B.A.T Industries P.L.C.; *Int'l*, pg. 110
THREADNEEDLE PROPERTY FUND MANAGERS LIMITED—See B.A.T Industries P.L.C.; *Int'l*, pg. 110
THREE BRANCHES, INC.—See Carris Financial Group; *U.S. Private*, pg. 215
3COM CORPORATION; *U.S. Public*, pg. 1603
3COM CORPORATION—See 3Com Corporation; *U.S. Public*, pg. 1604
3COM, LTD.—See 3Com Corporation; *U.S. Public*, pg. 1604
3COM PERSONAL COMMUNICATIONS DIV.—See 3Com Corporation; *U.S. Public*, pg. 1604
3COM, S.A.—See 3Com Corporation; *U.S. Public*, pg. 1604
THREE D DEPARTMENTS, INC.; *U.S. Public*, pg. 1604
3 DBM, INC.—See Ducommun Incorporated; *U.S. Public*, pg. 534
III EXPLORATION CO.—See Intermountain Industries, Inc.; *U.S. Private*, pg. 568
THREE-FIVE SYSTEMS; *U.S. Public*, pg. 1604
317070 ALBERTA LTD.—See Sceptre Resources Limited; *Int'l*, pg. 1203
3I FRANCE—See 3i Group plc; *Int'l*, pg. 1386
3I SPAIN—See 3i Group plc; *Int'l*, pg. 1386
3M; *U.S. Public*, pg. 1604
3M ALASKA—See 3M; *U.S. Public*, pg. 1605
3M ARGENTINA S.A.C.I.F.I.A.—See 3M; *U.S. Public*, pg. 1606
3M A/S—See 3M; *U.S. Public*, pg. 1606
3M AUSTRALIA PTY. LTD.—See 3M; *U.S. Public*, pg. 1606
3M BELGIUM N.V./S.A.—See 3M; *U.S. Public*, pg. 1606
3M CANADA INC.—See 3M; *U.S. Public*, pg. 1606
3M CHILE S.A.—See 3M; *U.S. Public*, pg. 1606
3M CHINA LIMITED—See 3M; *U.S. Public*, pg. 1606
3M COLOMBIA S.A.—See 3M; *U.S. Public*, pg. 1606
3M COSTA RICA, S.A.—See 3M; *U.S. Public*, pg. 1606
3M CZECH REPUBLIC—See 3M; *U.S. Public*, pg. 1606
3M DEUTSCHLAND GMBH—See 3M; *U.S. Public*, pg. 1606
3M DO BRASIL LTDA.—See 3M; *U.S. Public*, pg. 1606
3M DOMINICANA S.A.—See 3M; *U.S. Public*, pg. 1606
3M (EAST) AG—See 3M; *U.S. Public*, pg. 1606
3M/ECC EUROPA BV—See Bowthorpe plc; *Int'l*, pg. 209
3M ECUADOR C.A.—See 3M; *U.S. Public*, pg. 1606
3M ESPANA S.A.—See 3M; *U.S. Public*, pg. 1606
3M FRANCE—See 3M; *U.S. Public*, pg. 1606
3M GULF LTD.—See 3M; *U.S. Public*, pg. 1606
3M HAWAII—See 3M; *U.S. Public*, pg. 1606
3M HELLAS LIMITED—See 3M; *U.S. Public*, pg. 1606
3M HONG KONG LIMITED—See 3M; *U.S. Public*, pg. 1606
3M HUNGARIA KFT.—See 3M; *U.S. Public*, pg. 1606
P.T. 3M INDONESIA—See 3M; *U.S. Public*, pg. 1606
3M INTERAMERICA, INC.—See 3M; *U.S. Public*, pg. 1606
3M INTERAMERICA, INC (TRINIDAD & TOBAGO DIV.)—See 3M; *U.S. Public*, pg. 1606
3M IRELAND LTD.—See 3M; *U.S. Public*, pg. 1606
3M ITALIA SPA—See 3M; *U.S. Public*, pg. 1607
3M KOREA LTD.—See 3M; *U.S. Public*, pg. 1607
3M MALAYSIA SDN. BERHAD—See 3M; *U.S. Public*, pg. 1607
3M MANUFACTURERA VENEZUELA S.A.—See 3M; *U.S. Public*, pg. 1607
3M MEXICO S.A. DE C.V.—See 3M; *U.S. Public*, pg. 1607
3M NEDERLAND B.V.—See 3M; *U.S. Public*, pg. 1607
3M NEW ZEALAND LTD.—See 3M; *U.S. Public*, pg. 1607
3M NORGE A/S—See 3M; *U.S. Public*, pg. 1607
3M OESTERREICH GES MBH—See 3M; *U.S. Public*, pg. 1607
3M PAKISTAN (PVT) LTD.—See 3M; *U.S. Public*, pg. 1607

3M PANAMA S.A.—See 3M; *U.S. Public*, pg. 1607
3M PERU S.A.—See 3M; *U.S. Public*, pg. 1607
3M PHILIPPINES, INC.—See 3M; *U.S. Public*, pg. 1607
3M POLAND SP. Z.O.O.—See 3M; *U.S. Public*, pg. 1607
3M PUERTO RICO, INC.—See 3M; *U.S. Public*, pg. 1605
3M RUSSIA (EAST)—See 3M; *U.S. Public*, pg. 1607
3M SANAII VE TICARET—See 3M; *U.S. Public*, pg. 1607
3M (SCHWEIZ) AG—See 3M; *U.S. Public*, pg. 1607
3M SINGAPORE PTE. LTD.—See 3M; *U.S. Public*, pg. 1607
3M SOUTH AFRICA (PTY.) LTD.—See 3M; *U.S. Public*, pg. 1607
3M SVENSKA AB—See 3M; *U.S. Public*, pg. 1607
3M TAIWAN LIMITED—See 3M; *U.S. Public*, pg. 1607
3M THAILAND LIMITED—See 3M; *U.S. Public*, pg. 1607
3M UNITED KINGDOM, PLC—See 3M; *U.S. Public*, pg. 1607
3M UNITEK CORPORATION—See 3M; *U.S. Public*, pg. 1606
3M URUGUAY—See 3M; *U.S. Public*, pg. 1607
3M ZIMBABWE (PVT.) LTD.—See 3M; *U.S. Public*, pg. 1607
3 PAGEN HANDELSGESELLSCHAFT MBH—See Otto Versand (GmbH & Co.); *Int'l*, pg. 1015
3 PAGEN VERSAND UND HANDELSGESELLSCHAFT MBH—See Otto Versand (GmbH & Co.); *Int'l*, pg. 1015
THREE QUAYS MARINE SERVICES LTD.—See The Peninsular and Oriental Steam Navigation Company; *Int'l*, pg. 1035
A THREE RIVERS FORWARDING, INC.—See Norfolk Southern Corporation; *U.S. Public*, pg. 1191
THREE RIVERS INSURANCE COMPANY—See Aluminum Company of America; *U.S. Public*, pg. 61
THREE RIVERS IRON & METAL—See Sturgis Iron & Metal Company, Inc.; *U.S. Private*, pg. 1048
THREE RIVERS REFINERY—See Ultramar Diamond Shamrock Corporation; *U.S. Public*, pg. 1663
3 SCORE, INC.—See Cadmus Communications Corporation; *U.S. Public*, pg. 291
360 DEGREES COMMUNICATIONS COMPANY; *U.S. Public*, pg. 1607
THREE STATES SUPPLY CO., INC.—See UIS, Inc.; *U.S. Private*, pg. 1113
3 SUISSES EXEMPLAIRE S.A.—See Otto Versand (GmbH & Co.); *Int'l*, pg. 1015
3 SUISSES FRANCE S.A.—See Otto Versand (GmbH & Co.); *Int'l*, pg. 1015
3 SUISSES INTERNATIONAL S.A.—See Otto Versand (GmbH & Co.); *Int'l*, pg. 1015
THREE-FIVE SYSTEMS LIMITED—See Three-Five Systems; *U.S. Public*, pg. 1604
3I GERMANY—See 3i Group plc; *Int'l*, pg. 1386
3i GROUP PLC; *Int'l*, pg. 1386
3I IBERIA DE INVERSIONES INDUSTRIALES SA—See 3i Group plc; *Int'l*, pg. 1386
3I INVESTORS IN INDUSTRY SPA—See 3i Group plc; *Int'l*, pg. 1386
3I ITALY—See 3i Group plc; *Int'l*, pg. 1386
THRESHER—See Whitbread PLC; *Int'l*, pg. 1498
THRIFTWAY, INC.—See Winn-Dixie Stores, Inc.; *U.S. Public*, pg. 1771
THRIFTY CANADA, LTD.—See Chrysler Corporation; *U.S. Public*, pg. 354
THRIFTY OIL CO.; *U.S. Private*, pg. 1084
THRIFTY RENT-A-CAR, LTD.—See Chrysler Corporation; *U.S. Public*, pg. 354
THRIFTY RENT-A-CAR SYSTEM, INC.—See Chrysler Corporation; *U.S. Public*, pg. 354
THRIFTY SYSTEM INTERNATIONAL, PTY. LTD.—See Chrysler Corporation; *U.S. Public*, pg. 354
THRIFTY WORLD HEADQUARTERS—See Chrysler Corporation; *U.S. Public*, pg. 354
THRIGE AGRO A/S—See Thrige-Titan Group; *Int'l*, pg. 1386
THRIGE ELECTRIC—See Thrige-Titan Group; *Int'l*, pg. 1387
THRIGE ELECTRIC GMBH—See Thrige-Titan Group; *Int'l*, pg. 1387
THRIGE ELECTRIC S.A.—See Thrige-Titan Group; *Int'l*, pg. 1387
THRIGE-SCOTT LTD.—See Thrige-Titan Group; *Int'l*, pg. 1387
THRIGE-TITAN A/S—See Thrige-Titan Group; *Int'l*, pg. 1387
THRIGE-TITAN GROUP; *Int'l*, pg. 1386
THRUSTMASTER, INC.; *U.S. Public*, pg. 1607
THRUWAY FASTENERS, INC.; *U.S. Private*, pg. 1084
THUGA AKTIENGESELLSCHAFT—See Veba AG; *Int'l*, pg. 1456
THUGA-KONSORTIUM BETEILIGUNGS GMBH—See Veba AG; *Int'l*, pg. 1456
THULE HOLDING GMBH—See Eldon AB; *Int'l*, pg. 436
THULE INTERNATIONAL—See Eldon AB; *Int'l*, pg. 436
THULE-KONSULT AB—See Skandia Insurance Company Limited; *Int'l*, pg. 1257
THULE LTD.—See Eldon AB; *Int'l*, pg. 436
THUMANN STAHL SERVICE GMBH & CO.—See Koninklijke Hoogovens N.V.; *Int'l*, pg. 754
THUNDER BAY TERMINALS LTD.—See Russel Metals Inc.; *Int'l*, pg. 1150
THUNDERBIRD STEEL CORPORATION—See Cameron Ashley Building Products, Inc; *U.S. Public*, pg. 298
THURINGER GEBAUDETECHNIK GMBH—See Ruhrgas Aktiengesellschaft; *Int'l*, pg. 1149
THURINGER REXROTH PNEUMATIK GMBH—See Mannesmann A.G.; *Int'l*, pg. 838
THURINGIA VERSICHERUNG AG—See AMB Aachener und Muenchener Beteiligungs-AG; *Int'l*, pg. 15
THURMAN INDUSTRIES, INC.; *U.S. Private*, pg. 1084
THYBONY WALL COVERINGS CO.; *U.S. Private*, pg. 1084
THYGESEN & BROTHER SYMASKINER A/S—See Brother Industries, Ltd.; *Int'l*, pg. 230
THYSSEN AG; *Int'l*, pg. 1387

THYSSEN A.G.—See Thyssen AG; *Int'l*, pg. 1388
THYSSEN ASCENSEURS HOLDING S.A.—See Thyssen AG; *Int'l*, pg. 1387
THYSSEN AUFZUGE GMBH—See Thyssen AG; *Int'l*, pg. 1387
THYSSEN BOETTICHER S.A.—See Thyssen AG; *Int'l*, pg. 1387
THYSSEN GUSS AG—See Thyssen AG; *Int'l*, pg. 1387
THYSSEN HANDELSUNION AG—See Thyssen AG; *Int'l*, pg. 1388
THYSSEN HANIEL LOGISTIC GMBH—See Thyssen AG; *Int'l*, pg. 1388
THYSSEN HANIEL LOGISTIC GMBH RHEINKRAFT—See Thyssen AG; *Int'l*, pg. 1388
THYSSEN HANIEL LOGISTIC INTERNATIONAL GMBH—See Thyssen AG; *Int'l*, pg. 1388
THYSSEN HANIEL LOGISTICS—See Thyssen AG; *Int'l*, pg. 1388
THYSSEN IMMOBILIEN GMBH—See Thyssen AG; *Int'l*, pg. 1388
THYSSEN INC.—See Thyssen AG; *Int'l*, pg. 1389
THYSSEN INDUSTRIE AKTIENGESELLSCHAFT—See Thyssen AG; *Int'l*, pg. 1387
THYSSEN NORDSEEWERKE GMBH—See Thyssen AG; *Int'l*, pg. 1387
THYSSEN POLYMER GMBH—See Thyssen AG; *Int'l*, pg. 1387
THYSSEN SPECIALTY STEELS, INC.—See Thyssen AG; *Int'l*, pg. 1388
THYSSEN STAHL AG—See Thyssen AG; *Int'l*, pg. 1388
THYSSEN STILL AUTO ANLAGENTECHNIK GMBH—See Thyssen AG; *Int'l*, pg. 1387
THYSSEN TELECOM A.G.—See Thyssen AG; *Int'l*, pg. 1388
THYSSEN UMFORMTECHNIK GMBH—See Thyssen AG; *Int'l*, pg. 1387
THYSSEN UMFORMTECHNIK U.K. LTD.—See Thyssen AG; *Int'l*, pg. 1387
THYSSEN WOHNSTATTEN A.G.—See Thyssen AG; *Int'l*, pg. 1388
THYSSENGAS GMBH—See Royal Dutch/Shell Group of Companies; *Int'l*, pg. 1138
TI BRAZIL INDUSTRIA E COMERICO LTDA.—See TI Group plc; *Int'l*, pg. 1342
TI POLAND SP ZO.O.—See TI Group plc; *Int'l*, pg. 1341
TIANCHI-MITEL TELECOMMUNICATIONS CORPORATION—See Mitel Corporation; *Int'l*, pg. 870
TIANJIN KOLLMORGEN INDUSTRIAL DRIVES CORP., LTD.—See Kollmorgen Corporation; *U.S. Public*, pg. 966
TIANJIN BEACON KANSAI PAINT & CHEMICALS CO., LTD.—See Kansai Paint Co., Ltd.; *Int'l*, pg. 723
TIANJIN FIGARO ELECTRONIC CO., LTD.—See Tokuyama Corporation; *Int'l*, pg. 1394
TIANJIN HENKEL DETERGENTS & CLEANING PRODUCTS CO. LTD.—See Henkel KGaA; *Int'l*, pg. 614
TIANJIN INTERNATIONAL LEASING CO., LTD.—See The Sakura Bank, Limited; *Int'l*, pg. 1181
TIANJIN JINZHU WIRING SYSTEMS CO., LTD.—See Sumitomo Electric Industries, Ltd.; *Int'l*, pg. 1314
TIANJIN KANSAI PAINT & CHEMICALS CO., LTD.—See Kansai Paint Co., Ltd.; *Int'l*, pg. 723
TIANJIN KERMA LABORATORIES—See CCL Industries, Inc.; *Int'l*, pg. 239
TIANJIN LIMING COSMETICS JOINT INDUSTRIAL CO.—See Wella Group; *Int'l*, pg. 1490
TIANJIN REPRESENTATIVE OFFICE—See The Fuji Bank, Limited; *Int'l*, pg. 520
TIANJIN-SHIMADZU HYDRAULIC EQUIPMENT CO., LTD.—See Shimadzu Corporation; *Int'l*, pg. 1232
TIANJIN TAKEDA PHARMACEUTICALS CO., LTD.—See Takeda Chemical Industries, Ltd.; *Int'l*, pg. 1351
TIANJIN TANABE SEIYAKU CO., LTD.—See Tanabe Seiyaku Co., Ltd.; *Int'l*, pg. 1354
TIANJIN TANGGU WATTS VALVE CO., LTD.—See Watts Industries, Inc.; *U.S. Public*, pg. 1747
TIANJIN TIANWEI SEASONING CO., LTD.—See Ajinomoto Company Inc.; *Int'l*, pg. 41
TIANJIN WIX FILTER CORP.—See Dana Corporation; *U.S. Public*, pg. 480
TIARA INSURANCE COMPANY—See Crown Central Petroleum Corporation; *U.S. Public*, pg. 462
TIA'S TEX-MEX RESTAURANTS—See Ruby Tuesday, Inc.; *U.S. Public*, pg. 1412
TIBSA—See Tractebel; *Int'l*, pg. 1415
TICINO SOCIETA D'ASSICURAZZIONI SULA VITA—See American International Group, Inc.; *U.S. Public*, pg. 85
TICKET-PALETTE GMBH—See Fried. Krupp AG; *Int'l*, pg. 515
TICKET SERVICIOS DO BRASIL—See Accor S.A.; *Int'l*, pg. 21
TICKETMASTER CORPORATION; *U.S. Private*, pg. 1084
TICONA POLYMERWERKE GMBH—See Hoechst Aktiengesellschaft; *Int'l*, pg. 624
TIDEL ENGINEERING, INC.—See Tidel Technologies, Inc.; *U.S. Public*, pg. 1608
TIDEL TECHNOLOGIES, INC.; *U.S. Public*, pg. 1608
TIDELANDS OIL PRODUCTION CO.; *U.S. Private*, pg. 1084
TIDEWATER COMPRESSION SERVICE, INC.—See Tidewater Inc.; *U.S. Public*, pg. 1608
TIDEWATER INC.; *U.S. Public*, pg. 1608
TIDEWATER MARINE, INC.—See Tidewater Inc.; *U.S. Public*, pg. 1608
TIDEWATER MARINE INTERNATIONAL, INC.—See Tidewater Inc.; *U.S. Public*, pg. 1608
TIDEWATER MARINE SERVICE, INC.—See Tidewater Inc.; *U.S. Public*, pg. 1608
TIDEWATER MARINE WESTERN, INC.—See Tidewater Inc.; *U.S. Public*, pg. 1608
TIDEWATER OFFSHORE SERVICES, INC.—See Tidewater Inc.; *U.S. Public*, pg. 1608

TIDEWATER PORT JACKSON MARINE PTY. LIMITED—See Brambles Industries Limited; *Int'l*, pg. 211
TIDEWATER UTILITIES, INC.—See Middlesex Water Company; *U.S. Public*, pg. 1110
TIDEX (MALAYSIA) SDN. BHD.—See Tidewater Inc.; *U.S. Public*, pg. 1608
TIDEX NIGERIA LTD.—See Tidewater Inc.; *U.S. Public*, pg. 1608
AB TIDNINGEN VI—See KF/Konsum Coop Group; *Int'l*, pg. 718
TIDY CAR INTERNATIONAL, INC.—See Ziebart International Corporation; *U.S. Private*, pg. 1205
TIE/COMMUNICATIONS, INC.; *U.S. Private*, pg. 1085
TIE RACK (CANADA) LIMITED—See Tie Rack plc; *Int'l*, pg. 1389
TIE RACK CORPORATE NECKWEAR—See Tie Rack plc; *Int'l*, pg. 1389
TIE RACK FRANCE SARL—See Tie Rack plc; *Int'l*, pg. 1389
TIE RACK PLC; *Int'l*, pg. 1389
TIE RACK TRADING LIMITED—See Tie Rack plc; *Int'l*, pg. 1389
J.L. TIEDEMANNS TOBAKSFABRIK—See Tiedemanns - Joh.H.Andresen ANS; *Int'l*, pg. 1390
TIEDEMANNS - JOH.H.ANDRESEN ANS; *Int'l*, pg. 1389
TIEFENBACH GMBH—See Akzo Nobel N.V.; *Int'l*, pg. 47
TIEL UTRECHT—See ING Groep N.V.; *Int'l*, pg. 647
TIEL UTRECHT SCHADEVERZEKERING N.V.—See ING Groep N.V.; *Int'l*, pg. 647
TIEL UTRECHT VERZEKERD SPAREN N.V.—See ING Groep N.V.; *Int'l*, pg. 647
TIEN LEE HONG CO., LTD.—See Dainippon Ink & Chemicals, Inc.; *Int'l*, pg. 372
TIEN WAH PRESS (PTE.) LTD.—See Dai Nippon Printing Co., Ltd.; *Int'l*, pg. 363
TIENDAS CHEDRAUI S.A. DE C.V.—See Grupo Comercial Chedraui S.A. de C.V.; *Int'l*, pg. 573
TIENDAS DE DESCUENTO SULTANA S.A. DE C.V.—See Organizacion Soriana S.A. de C.V.; *Int'l*, pg. 1008
TIERCE LADBROKE SA—See Ladbroke Group Plc; *Int'l*, pg. 788
TIERNAY METALS; *U.S. Private*, pg. 1085
TIERNEY & PARTNERS—See True North Communications Inc.; *U.S. Public*, pg. 1641
TIETOKESKO OY—See Kesko Ltd.; *Int'l*, pg. 732
TIFFANY & CO.; *U.S. Public*, pg. 1608
TIFFANY & CO. AG—See Tiffany & Co.; *U.S. Public*, pg. 1609
TIFFANY & CO. ICT, INC.—See Tiffany & Co.; *U.S. Public*, pg. 1609
TIFFANY & CO. INTERNATIONAL—See Tiffany & Co.; *U.S. Public*, pg. 1609
TIFFANY & CO. INTERNATIONAL (TAIWAN)—See Tiffany & Co.; *U.S. Public*, pg. 1609
TIFFANY & CO. JAPAN INC.—See Tiffany & Co.; *U.S. Public*, pg. 1609
TIFFANY & CO. K.K. (JAPAN)—See Tiffany & Co.; *U.S. Public*, pg. 1609
TIFFANY & CO. MEXICO, S.A. DE C.V.—See Tiffany & Co.; *U.S. Public*, pg. 1609
TIFFANY & CO. OF NEW YORK LIMITED—See Tiffany & Co.; *U.S. Public*, pg. 1609
TIFFANY & CO. OVERSEAS FINANCE B.V.—See Tiffany & Co.; *U.S. Public*, pg. 1609
TIFFANY & CO. PTE. LTD.—See Tiffany & Co.; *U.S. Public*, pg. 1609
TIFFANY & CO. WATCH CENTER S.A.—See Tiffany & Co.; *U.S. Public*, pg. 1609
TIFFANY EXTRUDERS, INC.; *U.S. Private*, pg. 1085
TIFFANY-FARAONE, S.P.A. (MILAN)—See Tiffany & Co.; *U.S. Public*, pg. 1609
TIFFCO JEWELERY & CHAIN CRAFTS, INC.—See Tiffany & Co.; *U.S. Public*, pg. 1609
TIFFCO KOREA, LTD.—See Tiffany & Co.; *U.S. Public*, pg. 1609
TIFFIN ENTERPRISES, INC.—See Ameriwood Industries International Inc.; *U.S. Public*, pg. 98
TIFFIN MOTOR HOMES, INC.; *U.S. Private*, pg. 1086
TIFTON ALUMINUM CO., INC.—See Aluminum Company of America; *U.S. Public*, pg. 61
P.T. TIGA MANUNGGAL SYNETHETIC INDUSTRIES—See Mitsui & Co., Ltd.; *Int'l*, pg. 880
TIGER BALM (MALAYSIA) SDN BHD—See Haw Par Brothers International Limited; *Int'l*, pg. 604
TIGER BALM (PHILIPPINES) INC.—See Haw Par Brothers International Limited; *Int'l*, pg. 604
TIGER DIRECT, INC.—See Global Direct Mail Corp; *U.S. Public*, pg. 747
TIGER DIRECT, INC. (D/B/A TIGER SOFTWARE, INC.)—See Global Direct Mail Corp; *U.S. Public*, pg. 747
TIGER ELECTRONICS, INC.; *U.S. Private*, pg. 1086
TIGER MEDICALS LTD.—See Haw Par Brothers International Limited; *Int'l*, pg. 603
TIGERFLEX CORPORATION—See Tigers Polymer Corporation; *Int'l*, pg. 1390
TIGERPOLY MANUFACTURING, INC.—See Tigers Polymer Corporation; *Int'l*, pg. 1390
TIGERS POLYMER CORPORATION; *Int'l*, pg. 1390
TIGHE INDUSTRIES, INC.; *U.S. Private*, pg. 1086
TIJDSCHRIFTEN UITGEVERS MAATSCHAPPIJ—See VNU Verenigde Nederlandse Uitgeversbedrijven B.V.; *Int'l*, pg. 1447
N.V. TIJDSCHRIFTEN VERENING VLAANDEREN—See VNU Verenigde Nederlandse Uitgeversbedrijven B.V.; *Int'l*, pg. 1447
TIKKURILA OY—See Kemira Oy; *Int'l*, pg. 729
TILBURY CEMENT COMPANY—See Heidelberger Zement A.G.; *Int'l*, pg. 606
TILBURY CONTAINER SERVICE LTD.—See The Peninsular and Oriental Steam Navigation Company; *Int'l*, pg. 1035
TILBURY DOUGLAS PLC—See Philipp Holzmann AG; *Int'l*, pg. 634

TILCON TOMASSO SERVICES INC.—See Tilcon, Inc.; *U.S. Private*, pg. 1086
TILCON, INC.; *U.S. Private*, pg. 1086
TILECERA, INC.—See The Siam Cement Public Company Limited; *Int'l*, pg. 1239
TILLAMOOK COUNTY CREAMERY ASSN.; *U.S. Private*, pg. 1086
TILLAMOOK FOOD SALES—See Tillamook County Creamery Assn.; *U.S. Private*, pg. 1086
TILLINGHAST-TOWERS PENN—See Towers Perrin; *U.S. Private*, pg. 1093
TIMA SA—See Atlet AB; *Int'l*, pg. 97
TIMAC B.V.—See Axel Johnson AB; *Int'l*, pg. 712
TIMAR (CULTURAS EM AGUA), LDA.—See Tiedemanns - Joh.H.Andresen ANS; *Int'l*, pg. 1390
TIMAR SEAFOOD A/S—See Tiedemanns - Joh.H.Andresen ANS; *Int'l*, pg. 1390
TIMBER AGENTS LTD.—See Norske Skogindustrier A.S; *Int'l*, pg. 966
TIMBER PRODUCTS CO.—See Timber Products Company, LP; *U.S. Private*, pg. 1086
TIMBER PRODUCTS COMPANY, LP; *U.S. Private*, pg. 1086
THE TIMBERLAND COMPANY; *U.S. Public*, pg. 1609
TIMBERLAND INTERNATIONAL SALES CORPORATION—See The Timberland Company; *U.S. Public*, pg. 1609
THE TIMBERLAND WORLD TRADING COMPANY—See The Timberland Company; *U.S. Public*, pg. 1609
TIMBERLINE SOFTWARE CORPORATION; *U.S. Public*, pg. 1609
TIMCO, INC.—See Aquarion Company; *U.S. Public*, pg. 126
TIMCO, INC.—See Chessco Industries, Inc.; *U.S. Private*, pg. 234
TIME—See Time Warner Inc.; *U.S. Public*, pg. 1613
TIME CANADA INC.—See Time Warner Inc.; *U.S. Public*, pg. 1615
TIME DISTRIBUTION SERVICES—See Time Warner Inc.; *U.S. Public*, pg. 1614
TIME ELECTRONICS—See Avnet, Inc.; *U.S. Public*, pg. 155
TIME, INC.—See Time Warner Inc.; *U.S. Public*, pg. 1612
THE TIME INC. BOOK COMPANY—See Time Warner Inc.; *U.S. Public*, pg. 1613
TIME INC. HEALTH—See Time Warner Inc.; *U.S. Public*, pg. 1613
TIME INDEX, INC.—See Time Systems, Inc.; *U.S. Private*, pg. 1087
TIME INSURANCE—See Fortis; *Int'l*, pg. 499
TIME-LIFE BOOKS B.V.—See Time Warner Inc.; *U.S. Public*, pg. 1615
TIME-LIFE BOOKS (EUROPE), INC.—See Time Warner Inc.; *U.S. Public*, pg. 1613
TIME-LIFE CUSTOMER SERVICE—See Time Warner Inc.; *U.S. Public*, pg. 1613
TIME-LIFE, INC.—See Time Warner Inc.; *U.S. Public*, pg. 1613
TIME-LIFE INTERNATIONAL B.V.—See Time Warner Inc.; *U.S. Public*, pg. 1615
TIME-LIFE LIBRARIES, INC.—See Time Warner Inc.; *U.S. Public*, pg. 1613
TIME-MIST DIV.—See Carpenter Technology Corporation; *U.S. Public*, pg. 308
TIME OIL COMPANY; *U.S. Private*, pg. 1086
TIME PRODUCTS, INC.—See Theochem Labs., Inc.; *U.S. Private*, pg. 1079
TIME PUBLISHING VENTURES, INC.—See Time Warner Inc.; *U.S. Public*, pg. 1613
TIME RETAIL GROUP—See Kingfisher plc; *Int'l*, pg. 734
TIME/SYSTEM DANMARK A/S—See Amer Group Ltd.; *Int'l*, pg. 73
TIME/SYSTEM FINLAND OY—See Amer Group Ltd.; *Int'l*, pg. 73
TIME/SYSTEM INTERNATIONAL A/S—See Amer Group Ltd.; *Int'l*, pg. 73
TIME/SYSTEM ITALIA S.R.L.—See Amer Group Ltd.; *Int'l*, pg. 73
TIME/SYSTEM NORGE A/S—See Amer Group Ltd.; *Int'l*, pg. 73
TIME/SYSTEM SVERIGE AB—See Amer Group Ltd.; *Int'l*, pg. 73
TIME/SYSTEM (UK) LTD.—See Amer Group Ltd.; *Int'l*, pg. 73
TIME SYSTEMS, INC.; *U.S. Private*, pg. 1086
THE TIME WARNER CABLE GROUP—See Time Warner Inc.; *U.S. Public*, pg. 1610
TIME WARNER CABLE LIBERTY DIVISION—See Time Warner Inc.; *U.S. Public*, pg. 1611
TIME WARNER CABLE OF NEW YORK CITY—See Time Warner Inc.; *U.S. Public*, pg. 1611
TIME WARNER ENTERPRISES—See Time Warner Inc.; *U.S. Public*, pg. 1611
TIME WARNER INC.; *U.S. Public*, pg. 1610
TIME WARNER PUBLISHING INC.—See Time Warner Inc.; *U.S. Public*, pg. 1614
TIME WARNER SPORTS—See Time Warner Inc.; *U.S. Public*, pg. 1611
TIME WARNER TRADE PUBLISHING—See Time Warner Inc.; *U.S. Public*, pg. 1614
TIME WOMEN'S PUBLICATIONS INC.—See Time Warner Inc.; *U.S. Public*, pg. 1614
TIMEC COMPANY; *U.S. Private*, pg. 1087
TIMEMED LABELING SYSTEMS, INC.; *U.S. Private*, pg. 1087
THE TIMES—See Gannett Company, Inc.; *U.S. Public*, pg. 700
TIMES BOOKS—See Advance Publications Inc.; *U.S. Private*, pg. 21
THE TIMES CO.—See Gannett Company, Inc.; *U.S. Public*, pg. 700
TIMES DAILY, INC.—See The New York Times Company; *U.S. Public*, pg. 1175
TIMES FIBER COMMUNICATIONS, INC.—See Kohlberg Kravis Roberts & Co.; *U.S. Private*, pg. 629

THE TIMES HERALD—See Journal Register Company; *U.S. Public*, pg. 935
THE TIMES HERALD CO.—See Gannett Company, Inc.; *U.S. Public*, pg. 701
TIMES JOURNAL PUBLISHING—See SBC Communications Inc.; *U.S. Public*, pg. 1415
THE TIMES LEADER—See Knight-Ridder, Inc.; *U.S. Public*, pg. 964
TIMES LEASING, INC.—See The New York Times Company; *U.S. Public*, pg. 1176
THE TIMES MIRROR COMPANY; *U.S. Public*, pg. 1615
TIMES MIRROR MAGAZINES, INC.—See The Times Mirror Company; *U.S. Public*, pg. 1616
TIMES-NEWS—See The New York Times Company; *U.S. Public*, pg. 1175
TIMES NEWSPAPERS LTD.—See The News Corporation Limited; *Int'l*, pg. 927
TIMES ON-LINE SERVICES, INC.—See The New York Times Company; *U.S. Public*, pg. 1174
THE TIMES-PICAYUNE PUBLISHING CORP.; *U.S. Private*, pg. 1087
TIMES PRINTING COMPANY, INC.; *U.S. Private*, pg. 1087
THE TIMES PUBLISHING CO.; *U.S. Private*, pg. 1087
TIMES PUBLISHING LIMITED; *Int'l*, pg. 1390
THE TIMES REPORTER—See Journal Register Company; *U.S. Public*, pg. 935
THE TIMES SOUTHWEST BROADCASTING, INC.—See The New York Times Company; *U.S. Public*, pg. 1173
TIMES SUPER MARKET LTD.—See Teruya Bros., Limited; *U.S. Private*, pg. 1078
TIMESAVERS INC.; *U.S. Private*, pg. 1088
TIMESFAX—See The New York Times Company; *U.S. Public*, pg. 1174
TIMESTEP CORPORATION—See Newbridge Networks Corporation; *Int'l*, pg. 924
TIMEX CORPORATION; *U.S. Private*, pg. 1088
TIMKEN ARGENTINA S.R.L.—See The Timken Company; *U.S. Public*, pg. 1617
THE TIMKEN COMPANY; *U.S. Public*, pg. 1617
TIMKEN DE MEXICO, S.A. DE C.V.—See The Timken Company; *U.S. Public*, pg. 1617
TIMKEN DO BRASIL S.A. COMERCIO E INDUSTRIA LIMITADA—See The Timken Company; *U.S. Public*, pg. 1617
TIMKEN EUROPA GMBH—See The Timken Company; *U.S. Public*, pg. 1618
TIMKEN FRANCE, SUCCURSALE DE THE TIMKEN CO.—See The Timken Company; *U.S. Public*, pg. 1618
TIMKEN ITALIA S.R.L.—See The Timken Company; *U.S. Public*, pg. 1618
TIMKEN SOUTH AFRICA PROPRIETARY LTD.—See The Timken Company; *U.S. Public*, pg. 1618
TIMLOC BUILDING PRODUCTS LTD.—See Expamet International Plc; *Int'l*, pg. 467
TIMMONS & COMPANY INC.—See WPP Group plc; *Int'l*, pg. 1483
THE TIMMS SPRING COMPANY—See Precision Products Corporation; *U.S. Private*, pg. 880
TIMPTE, INC.—See Timpte Industries, Inc.; *U.S. Private*, pg. 1088
TIMPTE INDUSTRIES, INC.; *U.S. Private*, pg. 1088
TIM'S CASCADE STYLE POTATO CHIPS—See Pro-Fac Cooperative, Inc.; *U.S. Private*, pg. 887
TIN PLATE CONTAINERS, LTD.—See Rohto Pharmaceutical Co.; *Int'l*, pg. 1126
TINE-VESTLANDSMEIERIET; *Int'l*, pg. 1390
TINGLEY RUBBER CORPORATION; *U.S. Private*, pg. 1088
TINIUS OLSEN TESTING MACHINE CO., INC.; *U.S. Private*, pg. 1088
TINO LEBENSMITTEL GMBH—See Nestle S.A.; *Int'l*, pg. 922
TINSLEY ADVERTISING; *U.S. Private*, pg. 1088
TINSLEY CORP.—See Silicon Valley Group, Inc.; *U.S. Public*, pg. 1474
H.J. TINSLEY & CO. LIMITED—See Morgan Crucible Co. Plc; *Int'l*, pg. 891
TINSLEY WIRE (SHEFFIELD) LTD.—See N.V. Bekaert S.A.; *Int'l*, pg. 185
TINTAS GRAFICAS S.A.—See BASF AG; *Int'l*, pg. 109
TINTAS ROBBIALAC S.A.—See Williams Holdings Plc; *Int'l*, pg. 1501
TINTAS YPIRANGA LTDA.—See Akzo Nobel N.V.; *Int'l*, pg. 47
TIOXIDE AUSTRALIA PROPRIETARY LIMITED—See Imperial Chemical Industries PLC; *Int'l*, pg. 665
TIOXIDE CANADA INC.—See Imperial Chemical Industries PLC; *Int'l*, pg. 665
TIOXIDE EUROPE GMBH—See Imperial Chemical Industries PLC; *Int'l*, pg. 666
TIOXIDE EUROPE LIMITED—See Imperial Chemical Industries PLC; *Int'l*, pg. 663
TIOXIDE EUROPE NV/SA—See Imperial Chemical Industries PLC; *Int'l*, pg. 666
TIOXIDE EUROPE S.A.—See Imperial Chemical Industries PLC; *Int'l*, pg. 666
TIOXIDE EUROPE SRL—See Imperial Chemical Industries PLC; *Int'l*, pg. 666
TIOXIDE GROUP LIMITED—See Imperial Chemical Industries PLC; *Int'l*, pg. 663
TIOXIDE JAPAN KK—See Imperial Chemical Industries PLC; *Int'l*, pg. 666
TIOXIDE (MALAYSIA) SDN BHD—See Imperial Chemical Industries PLC; *Int'l*, pg. 666
TIOXIDE SOUTHERN AFRICA (PTY) LTD.—See Imperial Chemical Industries PLC; *Int'l*, pg. 666
TIP TOP ICE CREAM CO. LIMITED—See Peters & Brownes Foods Ltd.; *Int'l*, pg. 1040
TIP TOP NURSERY—See General Host Corporation; *U.S. Public*, pg. 715
TIPIEL COLOMBIA—See Technip; *Int'l*, pg. 1361
TIPNESS, LTD.—See Suntory Ltd.; *Int'l*, pg. 1321
TIPPER TIE, INC.—See Dover Corporation; *U.S. Public*, pg. 520

TIPPERARY CORPORATION; *U.S. Public*, pg. 1618
TIPPERARY OIL & GAS CORP.—See Tipperary Corporation; pg. 1618
TIPPINS INCORPORATED; *U.S. Private*, pg. 1088
TIR A LOCQUES—See GIB Group; *Int'l*, pg. 534
P.T. TIRA WAHARI LESTARI—See BASF AG; *Int'l*, pg. 109
TIRAM KIMIA—See Royal Dutch/Shell Group of Companies; *Int'l*, pg. 1140
TIRE BUSINESS—See Crain Communications, Inc.; *U.S. Private*, pg. 285
TIRE MILEAGE, INCORPORATED—See Bandag, Incorporated; *U.S. Public*, pg. 177
TIROLER MAGNESIT, A.G.—See RGP Holding, Inc.; *U.S. Private*, pg. 904
TIRRENIA GAS S.P.A.—See ENI S.p.A.; *Int'l*, pg. 428
TISHMAN REALTY & CONSTRUCTION CO., INC.; *U.S. Private*, pg. 1089
TISHMAN URBAN DEVELOPMENT—See Tishman Realty & Construction Co., Inc.; *U.S. Private*, pg. 1089
TISSU CANARIAS S.A.—See Metsa-Serla Corporation; *Int'l*, pg. 864
THE TITAN CORPORATION; *U.S. Public*, pg. 1618
TITAN FRANCE SA—See Titan International, Inc.; *U.S. Public*, pg. 1619
TITAN GERMANY GMBH—See Titan International, Inc.; *U.S. Public*, pg. 1619
TITAN GLOBAL LTD.—See Construction Counsellors, Inc.; *U.S. Private*, pg. 266
TITAN HOMES DIV.—See Champion Enterprises, Inc.; *U.S. Public*, pg. 1140
THE TITAN INDUSTRIAL CORP.; *U.S. Private*, pg. 1089
TITAN INFORMATION SYSTEMS—See The Titan Corporation; *U.S. Public*, pg. 1618
TITAN INTERNATIONAL, INC.; *U.S. Public*, pg. 1618
TITAN LINKABIT—See The Titan Corporation; *U.S. Public*, pg. 1618
TITAN RESEARCH & TECHNOLOGY—See The Titan Corporation; *U.S. Public*, pg. 1618
TITAN SALES CORP.—See The Rival Company; *U.S. Public*, pg. 1391
TITAN STEEL CORP.—See The Titan Industrial Corp.; *U.S. Private*, pg. 1089
TITAN STEEL & WIRE CO., LTD.—See Kobe Steel, Ltd.; *Int'l*, pg. 741
TITAN SYSTEMS, INC.—See The Titan Corporation; *U.S. Public*, pg. 1618
TITAN TIRE CORPORATION—See Titan International, Inc.; *U.S. Public*, pg. 1618
TITAN TIRE CORPORATION OF TN—See Titan International, Inc.; *U.S. Public*, pg. 1618
TITAN TOOL, INC.—See Harbour Group Ltd.; *U.S. Private*, pg. 500
TITAN UMREIFUNGSTECHNIK GMBH—See Fried. Krupp AG; *Int'l*, pg. 509
TITAN WHEEL—See Titan International, Inc.; *U.S. Public*, pg. 1618
TITAN WHEEL CORPORATIO OF ILLINOIS—See Titan International, Inc.; *U.S. Public*, pg. 1619
TITAN WHEEL CORPORATION OF OHIO—See Titan International, Inc.; *U.S. Public*, pg. 1619
TITAN WHEEL CORPORATION OF VIRGINIA—See Titan International, Inc.; *U.S. Public*, pg. 1619
TITAN WHEEL CORPORATION OF WI—See Titan International, Inc.; *U.S. Public*, pg. 1619
TITAN WHEEL INTERNATIONAL LTD.—See Titan International, Inc.; *U.S. Public*, pg. 1619
TITAN WHEEL-PEORIA—See Titan International, Inc.; *U.S. Public*, pg. 1619
TITANIA A/S—See Contran Corporation; *U.S. Private*, pg. 271
TITANIA INSURANCE COMPANY OF AMERICA—See The Wackenhut Corporation; *U.S. Public*, pg. 1731
TITANIUM INDUSTRIES—See A. Ahlstrom Corporation; *Int'l*, pg. 34
TITANIUM INDUSTRIES, INC.—See Allegheny Teledyne Incorporated; *U.S. Public*, pg. 43
TITANIUM LTD/LTDEE—See A. Ahlstrom Corporation; *Int'l*, pg. 35
TITANIUM METALS CORPORATION—See Contran Corporation; *U.S. Public*, pg. 270
TITANUS DISTRIBUZIONE S.P.A.—See Bastogi-S.p.A.; *Int'l*, pg. 170
E.H. TITCHENER & COMPANY; *U.S. Private*, pg. 1089
TITECH-AUTOSORT—See Tiedemanns - Joh.H.Andresen ANS; *Int'l*, pg. 1390
TITEFLEX CORPORATION—See TI Group plc; *Int'l*, pg. 1340
TITEFLEX INDUSTRIAL AMERICAS—See TI Group plc; *Int'l*, pg. 1340
TITEX TOOLS LTD.—See Sandvik AB; *Int'l*, pg. 1187
TITLE INSURANCE COMPANY OF MINNESOTA—See Old Republic International Corporation; *U.S. Public*, pg. 1218
TITLEFLEX CANADA—See TI Group plc; *Int'l*, pg. 1341
TITLEFLEX EUROPE SA—See TI Group plc; *Int'l*, pg. 1341
TITLEIST & FOOT-JOY WORLDWIDE—See Fortune Brands, Inc.; *U.S. Public*, pg. 675
TITMAN GMBH—See Brunel Holdings Plc; *Int'l*, pg. 232
TITMAN TIP TOOLS—See Brunel Holdings Plc; *Int'l*, pg. 231
TITUS PRODUCTS DIV.—See Tomkins PLC; *Int'l*, pg. 1398
TIVOLI HANDELS- UN GRUNDSTUCKS GMBH & CO. OHG VERWALTUNGSZENTRUM—See Bayerische Vereinsbank Group; *Int'l*, pg. 180
TJAEREBORG STEN OG GRUS I/S—See Redland PLC; *Int'l*, pg. 1092
TLALNEPANTLA ESTADO DE MEXICO MEXICANA DE BIENES DE CAPITAL, S.A., COMBUSTION ENGINEERING, INC.—See ABB Asea Brown Boveri (Holding) Ltd.; *Int'l*, pg. 6
TOASTMASTER DE MEXICO—See Toastmaster, Inc.; *U.S. Public*, pg. 1619
TOASTMASTER, INC.; *U.S. Public*, pg. 1619

TOBACCO EXPORTERS INTERNATIONAL (USA) LIMITED—See Rothmans UK Holdings Limited; *Int'l*, pg. 1129
TOBACCO INSURANCE CO. LTD.—See B.A.T Industries P.L.C.; *Int'l*, pg. 110
TOBACCO PROCESSORS (MALAWI) LTD.—See Standard Commercial Corporation; *U.S. Public*, pg. 1502
TOBACNA LJUBLJANA D.O.O.—See Reemtsma Cigarettenfabriken GmbH, Hamburg; *Int'l*, pg. 1101
TOBER INDUSTRIES, INC.; *U.S. Private*, pg. 1089
TOBERMAN; *U.S. Private*, pg. 1089
TOBETON, SOCIETE TOGOLAISE DE BETON, S.A.—See Dyckerhoff & Widmann AG; *Int'l*, pg. 425
THE TOBIN CORPORATION—See Avis Industrial Corporation; *U.S. Private*, pg. 102
TOBLER CHOCOLAT AG—See Philip Morris Companies Inc.; *U.S. Public*, pg. 1288
TOBY RESTAURANTS LTD.—See Bass PLC; *Int'l*, pg. 170
TOC—See Long Manufacturing, Ltd.; *Int'l*, pg. 815
TOCCO, INC.—See Park-Ohio Industries, Inc.; *U.S. Public*, pg. 1259
TOCCOA METAL TECHNOLOGIES, INC.; *U.S. Private*, pg. 1089
TOCHIGI NIKON K.K.—See Nikon Corporation; *Int'l*, pg. 931
TOCKFORS VERKSTADS AB—See Telefonaktiebolaget LM Ericsson; *Int'l*, pg. 1364
TODAY'S HOMEOWNER—See The Times Mirror Company; *U.S. Public*, pg. 1617
TODAY'S KIDS—See Spang & Company; *U.S. Private*, pg. 1020
TODAY'S MAN, INC.; *U.S. Public*, pg. 1619
TODAYS TEMPORARY, INC.—See CDI Corp.; *U.S. Public*, pg. 277
TODAYS TEMPORARY, LTD.—See CDI Corp.; *U.S. Public*, pg. 277
TODCO—See Overhead Door Corporation; *U.S. Private*, pg. 823
TODD ADVERTISING AGENCY, INC.—See J.L. Todd Auction Co.; *U.S. Private*, pg. 1090
TODD & SARGENT, INC.; *U.S. Private*, pg. 1089
THE TODD-AO CORPORATION; *U.S. Public*, pg. 1619
TODD-AO/EDITWORKS—See The Todd-AO Corporation; *U.S. Public*, pg. 1619
TODD-AO EUROPE HOLDING LTD.—See The Todd-AO Corporation; *U.S. Public*, pg. 1619
TODD-AO FILMATIC LTD.—See The Todd-AO Corporation; *U.S. Public*, pg. 1619
TODD-AO HOLLYWOOD DIGITAL—See The Todd-AO Corporation; *U.S. Public*, pg. 1619
TODD-AO HOLLYWOOD DIGITAL WEST—See The Todd-AO Corporation; *U.S. Public*, pg. 1619
TODD-AO PRESERVATION SERVICES—See The Todd-AO Corporation; *U.S. Public*, pg. 1619
TODD-AO SCORING—See The Todd-AO Corporation; *U.S. Public*, pg. 1619
TODD-AO STUDIOS—See The Todd-AO Corporation; *U.S. Public*, pg. 1619
TODD-AO STUDIOS/EAST—See The Todd-AO Corporation; *U.S. Public*, pg. 1619
TODD-AO STUDIOS WEST—See The Todd-AO Corporation; *U.S. Public*, pg. 1619
TODD-AO U.K.—See The Todd-AO Corporation; *U.S. Public*, pg. 1619
TODD-AO VIDEO SERVICES—See The Todd-AO Corporation; *U.S. Public*, pg. 1619
A.M. TODD COMPANY; *U.S. Private*, pg. 1089
TODD & DUNCAN LTD.—See Dawson International PLC; *Int'l*, pg. 385
TODD ENTERPRISES—See Chem-Tainer Industries; *U.S. Private*, pg. 231
J.L. TODD AUCTION CO.; *U.S. Private*, pg. 1090
TODD JUICE PRODUCTS—See A.M. Todd Company; *U.S. Private*, pg. 1090
TODD PACIFIC SHIPYARDS CORP.; *U.S. Public*, pg. 1619
TODD PIPE & SUPPLY HAWTHORNE; *U.S. Private*, pg. 1090
TODD PIPE & SUPPLY-WEST L.A.—See Todd Pipe & Supply Hawthorne; *U.S. Private*, pg. 1090
TOERISTIEK BV—See Reed Elsevier plc; *Int'l*, pg. 1099
TOFA- TORREFACCAO DE CAFES DE PORTUGAL, S.A.R.L.—See Nestle S.A.; *Int'l*, pg. 922
TOFTE INDUSTRIER—See Norske Skogindustrier A.S; *Int'l*, pg. 966
THE TOG SHOP; *U.S. Private*, pg. 1090
TOGETHER LTD.—See Otto Versand (GmbH & Co.); *Int'l*, pg. 1015
TOGETHER PRODUCTION LTD.—See Otto Versand (GmbH & Co.); *Int'l*, pg. 1015
TOGIAK FISHERIES INC.—See Marubeni Corporation; *Int'l*, pg. 845
TOGO ET SHELL—See Royal Dutch/Shell Group of Companies; *Int'l*, pg. 1137
TOHEI CO., LTD.—See Matsuya Company Ltd.; *Int'l*, pg. 845
TOHO AMERICA INTERNATIONAL INC.—See TOHO Mutual Life Insurance Company; *Int'l*, pg. 1390
TOHO AMERICA REALTY INC.—See TOHO Mutual Life Insurance Company; *Int'l*, pg. 1390
TOHO ELECTRONICS CO., LTD.—See Oki Electric Industry Company, Ltd.; *Int'l*, pg. 999
TOHO KAGAKU KENKYUSHO CO., LTD.—See E-Z-Em, Inc.; *U.S. Public*, pg. 540
TOHO LIFE CAYMAN LTD.—See TOHO Mutual Life Insurance Company; *Int'l*, pg. 1390
TOHO LIFE INTERNATIONAL (HK) LTD.—See TOHO Mutual Life Insurance Company; *Int'l*, pg. 1390
TOHO LIFE INTERNATIONAL (UK) LTD.—See TOHO Mutual Life Insurance Company; *Int'l*, pg. 1390
TOHO LIFE LUXEMBOURG S.A.—See TOHO Mutual Life Insurance Company; *Int'l*, pg. 1390
TOHO LIFE PROPERTIES (UK) LTD.—See TOHO Mutual Life Insurance Company; *Int'l*, pg. 1390

TOHO MUTUAL LIFE INSURANCE COMPANY; *Int'l*, pg. 1390
TOHOKU CITIZEN CORPORATION—See Citizen Watch Company, Ltd.; *Int'l*, pg. 294
TOHOKU ELECTRIC POWER CO., LTD.; *Int'l*, pg. 1390
TOHOKU ELECTRIC POWER CO., LTD.-AKITA BRANCH—See Tohoku Electric Power Co., Ltd.; *Int'l*, pg. 1390
TOHOKU ELECTRIC POWER CO., LTD.-AOMORI BRANCH—See Tohoku Electric Power Co., Ltd.; *Int'l*, pg. 1390
TOHOKU ELECTRIC POWER CO., LTD.-FUKUSHIMA BRANCH—See Tohoku Electric Power Co., Ltd.; *Int'l*, pg. 1391
TOHOKU ELECTRIC POWER CO., LTD.-IWATE BRANCH—See Tohoku Electric Power Co., Ltd.; *Int'l*, pg. 1391
TOHOKU ELECTRIC POWER CO., LTD.-MIYAGI BRANCH—See Tohoku Electric Power Co., Ltd.; *Int'l*, pg. 1391
TOHOKU ELECTRIC POWER CO., LTD.-NIIGATA BRANCH—See Tohoku Electric Power Co., Ltd.; *Int'l*, pg. 1391
TOHOKU ELECTRIC POWER CO., LTD.-TOKYO BRANCH—See Tohoku Electric Power Co., Ltd.; *Int'l*, pg. 1391
TOHOKU ELECTRIC POWER CO., LTD.-YAMAGATA BRANCH—See Tohoku Electric Power Co., Ltd.; *Int'l*, pg. 1391
TOHOKU NIPPATSU CO., LTD.—See NHK Spring Co., Ltd.; *Int'l*, pg. 902
TOHOKU OKI ELECTRIC CO., LTD.—See Oki Electric Industry Company, Ltd.; *Int'l*, pg. 999
TOHOKU SEMICONDUCTOR CORPORATION—See Toshiba Corporation; *Int'l*, pg. 1403
TOHOKU SHANON CO., LTD.—See Tokuyama Corporation; *Int'l*, pg. 1394
TOHOKU YAMANOUCHI PHARMACEUTICAL CO., LTD.—See Yamanouchi Pharmaceutical Co. Ltd.; *Int'l*, pg. 1518
TOIJALA WORKS—See Rautaruukki Oy; *Int'l*, pg. 1088
TOINDUSTRIE HEISTERHOLZ ERNST RAUCH GMBH & CO. KG—See Redland PLC; *Int'l*, pg. 1091
THE TOKAI BANK, LIMITED; *Int'l*, pg. 1391
THE TOKAI BANK, LIMITED—See The Tokai Bank, Limited; *Int'l*, pg. 1391
TOKHEIM & GASBOY OF CANADA LIMITED—See Tokheim Corporation; *U.S. Public*, pg. 1620
TOKHEIM CORPORATION; *U.S. Public*, pg. 1620
TOKHEIM GMBH—See Tokheim Corporation; *U.S. Public*, pg. 1620
TOKHEIM INVESTMENT CORP.—See Tokheim Corporation; *U.S. Public*, pg. 1620
TOKHEIM LTD.—See Tokheim Corporation; *U.S. Public*, pg. 1620
TOKHEIM SO. AFRICA LTD.—See Tokheim Corporation; *U.S. Public*, pg. 1620
TOKI ELECTRIC CO., LTD.—See Toshiba Corporation; *Int'l*, pg. 1403
TOKICO LTD.; *Int'l*, pg. 1391
TOKICO (USA) INC.—See Tokico Ltd.; *Int'l*, pg. 1391
TOKIO MANAGEMENT SERVICES (ASIA) PTE. LTD.—See The Tokio Marine & Fire Insurance Company, Ltd.; *Int'l*, pg. 1392
THE TOKIO MARINE & FIRE INSURANCE COMPANY, LTD.; *Int'l*, pg. 1391
THE TOKIO MARINE & FIRE INSURANCE COMPANY (U.K.) LIMITED—See The Tokio Marine & Fire Insurance Company, Ltd.; *Int'l*, pg. 1392
TOKIO MARINE & FIRE INSURANCE COMPANY (U.K.) LIMITED—See The Tokio Marine & Fire Insurance Company, Ltd.; *Int'l*, pg. 1392
THE TOKIO MARINE & FIRE INSURANCE COMPANY (U.K.) LIMITED—See The Tokio Marine & Fire Insurance Company, Ltd.; *Int'l*, pg. 1392
THE TOKIO MARINE & FIRE INSURANCE COMPANY (SINGAPORE) PTE. LIMITED—See The Tokio Marine & Fire Insurance Company, Ltd.; *Int'l*, pg. 1392
TOKIO MARINE ASSET MANAGEMENT NEW YORK CO., LTD.—See The Tokio Marine & Fire Insurance Company, Ltd.; *Int'l*, pg. 1392
THE TOKIO MARINE CAPITAL RESEARCH LIMITED—See The Tokio Marine & Fire Insurance Company, Ltd.; *Int'l*, pg. 1393
TOKIO MARINE COMPANIA DE SEGUROS, S.A. DE C.V.—See The Tokio Marine & Fire Insurance Company, Ltd.; *Int'l*, pg. 1393
TOKIO MARINE DE VENEZUELA, C.A.—See The Tokio Marine & Fire Insurance Company, Ltd.; *Int'l*, pg. 1393
TOKIO MARINE DELAWARE CORPORATION—See The Tokio Marine & Fire Insurance Company, Ltd.; *Int'l*, pg. 1392
TOKIO MARINE EUROPE LIMITED—See The Tokio Marine & Fire Insurance Company, Ltd.; *Int'l*, pg. 1393
THE TOKIO MARINE & FIRE INSURANCE COMPANY (U.K.) LIMITED—See The Tokio Marine & Fire Insurance Company, Ltd.; *Int'l*, pg. 1392
TOKIO MARINE INTERNACIONAL SOCIEDAD ANONIMA—See The Tokio Marine & Fire Insurance Company, Ltd.; *Int'l*, pg. 1393
TOKIO MARINE INTERNATIONAL FUND (BAHAMA) COMPANY LIMITED—See The Tokio Marine & Fire Insurance Company, Ltd.; *Int'l*, pg. 1393
THE TOKIO MARINE INTERNATIONAL FUND (LUXEMBOURG) S.A.—See The Tokio Marine & Fire Insurance Company, Ltd.; *Int'l*, pg. 1393
TOKIO MARINE INVESTMENT SERVICES, LIMITED—See The Tokio Marine & Fire Insurance Company, Ltd.; *Int'l*, pg. 1393
THE TOKIO MARINE MANAGEMENT (AUSTRALIA) PTY. LTD.—See The Tokio Marine & Fire Insurance Company, Ltd.; *Int'l*, pg. 1393
TOKIO MARINE MANAGEMENT INC. - GUAM—See The Tokio Marine & Fire Insurance Company, Ltd.; *Int'l*, pg. 1392

MASTER INDEX TO COMPANY NAMES TOPPAN

Company Index

TOKIO MARINE PROPERTY LIMITED—See The Tokio Marine & Fire Insurance Company, Ltd.; *Int'l*, pg. 1393
TOKIO MARINE REALTY CO., LTD.—See The Tokio Marine & Fire Insurance Company, Ltd.; *Int'l*, pg. 1392
TOKIO MARINE SOUTH-EAST SERVICING COMPANY LIMITED—See The Tokio Marine & Fire Insurance Company, Ltd.; *Int'l*, pg. 1393
THE TOKIO (NEW YORK) CORPORATION—See The Tokio Marine & Fire Insurance Company, Ltd.; *Int'l*, pg. 1392
TOKIO RE CORPORATION—See The Tokio Marine & Fire Insurance Company, Ltd.; *Int'l*, pg. 1392
TOKO AMERICA, INC.—See Toko Inc.; *Int'l*, pg. 1393
TOKO INC.; *Int'l*, pg. 1393
TOKOROZAWA SEIMITSU CO., LTD.—See Citizen Watch Company, Ltd.; *Int'l*, pg. 294
TOKUSO TRADING CO., LTD.—See Tokuyama Corporation; *Int'l*, pg. 1394
TOKUYAMA AMERICA INC.—See Tokuyama Corporation; *Int'l*, pg. 1394
TOKUYAMA CORPORATION; *Int'l*, pg. 1393
TOKUYAMA CORPORATION-FUKUOKA BRANCH—See Tokuyama Corporation; *Int'l*, pg. 1393
TOKUYAMA CORPORATION-HIROSHIMA BRANCH—See Tokuyama Corporation; *Int'l*, pg. 1393
TOKUYAMA CORPORATION-NAGOYA BRANCH—See Tokuyama Corporation; *Int'l*, pg. 1393
TOKUYAMA CORPORATION-OSAKA BRANCH—See Tokuyama Corporation; *Int'l*, pg. 1393
TOKUYAMA CORPORATION-SAPPORO BRANCH—See Tokuyama Corporation; *Int'l*, pg. 1393
TOKUYAMA CORPORATION-SENDAI BRANCH—See Tokuyama Corporation; *Int'l*, pg. 1393
TOKUYAMA CORPORATION-TAKAMATSU BRANCH—See Tokuyama Corporation; *Int'l*, pg. 1393
TOKUYAMA EUROPE GMBH—See Tokuyama Corporation; *Int'l*, pg. 1394
TOKUYAMA FACTORY—See Tokuyama Corporation; *Int'l*, pg. 1394
TOKUYAMA READY MIXED CONCRETE CO., LTD.—See Tokuyama Corporation; *Int'l*, pg. 1394
TOKYO AGENCY OF NIPPON LIFE INSURANCE CO., LTD.—See Nippon Life Insurance Co.; *Int'l*, pg. 935
TOKYO BANKIN INDUSTRIES CO., LTD.—See Toshiba Corporation; *Int'l*, pg. 1403
TOKYO CALPIS BEVERAGES CO., LTD.—See Calpis Food Industry Co. Ltd.; *Int'l*, pg. 253
TOKYO CATERPILLAR MITSUBISHI CONSTRUCTION EQUIPMENT SALES, LTD.—See Caterpillar Inc.; *U.S. Public*, pg. 317
TOKYO CITIZEN CORPORATION—See Citizen Watch Company, Ltd.; *Int'l*, pg. 294
TOKYO COMPUTER CENTER—See The Taiyo Mutual Life Insurance Co.; *Int'l*, pg. 1348
TOKYO ELECTRIC CO., LTD.—See Toshiba Corporation; *Int'l*, pg. 1403
THE TOKYO ELECTRIC POWER CO., INC.; *Int'l*, pg. 1394
THE TOKYO ELECTRIC POWER COMPANY-LONDON—See The Tokyo Electric Power Co., Inc.; *Int'l*, pg. 1394
THE TOKYO ELECTRIC POWER COMPANY-WASHINGTON—See The Tokyo Electric Power Co., Inc.; *Int'l*, pg. 1394
TOKYO ELECTRONIC INDUSTRY CO., LTD.—See Toshiba Corporation; *Int'l*, pg. 1403
TOKYO FASHION INSTITUTE—See Matsuya Company Ltd.; *Int'l*, pg. 848
TOKYO GAS—See Tokyo Gas Co., Ltd.; *Int'l*, pg. 1394
TOKYO GAS CO., LTD.; *Int'l*, pg. 1394
TOKYO IC CO., LTD.—See Sanyo Electric Co., Ltd.; *Int'l*, pg. 1191
TOKYO IYAKUHIN CO., LTD.—See Takeda Chemical Industries, Ltd.; *Int'l*, pg. 1350
TOKYO KINZOKU CO., LTD.—See Olympus Optical Co., Ltd.; *Int'l*, pg. 1004
TOKYO LIFESTYLES INSTITUTE, INC.—See Matsuya Company Ltd.; *Int'l*, pg. 848
TOKYO-MITSUBISHI FUTURES (USA) INC.—See The Bank of Tokyo-Mitsubishi, Ltd.; *Int'l*, pg. 157
TOKYO-MITSUBISHI INTERNATIONAL (HK) LTD.—See The Bank of Tokyo-Mitsubishi, Ltd.; *Int'l*, pg. 158
TOKYO-MITSUBISHI INTERNATIONAL PLC—See The Bank of Tokyo-Mitsubishi, Ltd.; *Int'l*, pg. 158
TOKYO-MITSUBISHI INTERNATIONAL (SINGAPORE) LTD.—See The Bank of Tokyo-Mitsubishi, Ltd.; *Int'l*, pg. 158
TOKYO-MITSUBISHI SECURITIES (U.S.A.), INC.—See The Bank of Tokyo-Mitsubishi, Ltd.; *Int'l*, pg. 157
TOKYO MOTOR VEHICLE WORKS—See Mitsubishi Motors Corporation; *Int'l*, pg. 875
TOKYO MOTOR VEHICLE WORKS - MARUKO PLANT—See Mitsubishi Motors Corporation; *Int'l*, pg. 875
TOKYO MOTOR VEHICLE WORKS - NAKATSU PLANT—See Mitsubishi Motors Corporation; *Int'l*, pg. 875
TOKYO NISSAN MOTOR CO., LTD.—See Nissan Motor Co., Ltd.; *Int'l*, pg. 944
TOKYO PLANT—See Kansai Paint Co., Ltd.; *Int'l*, pg. 723
TOKYO PRINTING INK CORPORATION U.S.A—See Tokyo Printing Ink Manufacturing Co., Ltd.; *Int'l*, pg. 1394
TOKYO PRINTING INK MANUFACTURING CO., LTD.; *Int'l*, pg. 1394
TOKYO REINE, LTD.—See Kanebo, Ltd.; *Int'l*, pg. 722
TOKYO RYUKI SEIZO CO., LTD.—See Ingersoll-Rand Company; *U.S. Public*, pg. 878
TOKYO SENKO INTERNATIONAL INC.; *Int'l*, pg. 1394
TOKYO SNOW BRAND SALES CO., LTD.—See Snow Brand Milk Products Co. Ltd.; *Int'l*, pg. 1272
TOKYO SOKUHAN CO., LTD.—See Nissan Motor Co., Ltd.; *Int'l*, pg. 944
TOKYO SUBARU MOTORS CO., LTD.—See Fuji Heavy Industries, Ltd.; *Int'l*, pg. 523
TOKYO TOYO-PET MOTOR SALES CO., LTD.—See Toyota Motor Corporation; *Int'l*, pg. 1412
TOKYO TOYOTA MOTOR CO., LTD.—See Toyota Motor Corporation; *Int'l*, pg. 1412
TOKYU AGENCY INC.; *Int'l*, pg. 1394
TOKYU AGENCY INTERNATIONAL/DMB&B JAPAN—See DMB&B Communications; *U.S. Private*, pg. 305
TOKYU CORPORATION; *Int'l*, pg. 1394
TOKYU HOSPITAL—See Tokyu Corporation; *Int'l*, pg. 1395
TOLBIACHIM—See American Home Products Corporation; *U.S. Public*, pg. 82
THE TOLEDO BELT RAILWAY CO.—See Norfolk Southern Corporation; *U.S. Public*, pg. 1191
THE TOLEDO EDISON COMPANY—See FirstEnergy Corp.; *U.S. Public*, pg. 645
TOLEDO LEARNING CENTER—See Berkshire Hathaway Inc.; *U.S. Public*, pg. 219
TOLEDO MILK PROCESSING, INC.—See Seaway Food Town, Inc.; *U.S. Public*, pg. 1453
TOLEDO NORGE A/S—See Novartis AG; *Int'l*, pg. 986
TOLEDO PRECISION MACHINING DIV.—See Chrysler Corporation; *U.S. Public*, pg. 353
TOLEDO SCALE CANADA LTD.—See Novartis AG; *Int'l*, pg. 986
TOLEDO SCALE CO DE MEXICO, SA DE CV—See Novartis AG; *Int'l*, pg. 986
TOLEDO SCALE (HONG KONG) LIMITED—See Novartis AG; *Int'l*, pg. 986
TOLEDO SHIPREPAIR COMPANY—See The Manitowoc Company, Inc.; *U.S. Public*, pg. 1041
TOLEDO STAMPING & MANUFACTURING CO.—See The General Chemical Group, Inc.; *U.S. Public*, pg. 707
S.A. TOLERIES DELLOYE-MATTHIEU—See Cockerill Sambre; *Int'l*, pg. 302
TOLES IVOIRE S.A. SOCIETE DE GALVANIZATION DE TOLES EN COTE IVOIRE—See Nissho Iwai Corporation; *Int'l*, pg. 949
TOLK, INC.—See Dewberry & Davis; *U.S. Private*, pg. 329
TOLKKINEN SAWMILL—See Enso Oyj; *Int'l*, pg. 456
TOLKO INDUSTRIES LTD.; *Int'l*, pg. 1395
TOLKO MANITOBA, INC.—See Tolko Industries Ltd.; *Int'l*, pg. 1395
TOLL BROTHERS, INC.; *U.S. Public*, pg. 1620
TOLLAND SUPERMARKET, INC.—See Bozzuto's Inc.; *U.S. Public*, pg. 249
TOLLENS SA—See Lafarge S.A.; *Int'l*, pg. 789
TOLLESON LUMBER COMPANY, INC.; *U.S. Private*, pg. 1090
TOLLEY PUBLISHING LTD.—See Reed Elsevier plc; *Int'l*, pg. 1095
TOLLMAN/HUNDLEY HOTELS; *U.S. Private*, pg. 1090
TOLLYCRAFT YACHT CORPORATION; *U.S. Public*, pg. 1620
TOLMAK, INC.—See Kansas City Southern Industries, Inc.; *U.S. Public*, pg. 944
TOLMEX S.A. DE C.V.—See Cemex, S.A. de C.V.; *Int'l*, pg. 278
TOM THUMB FOOD & PHARMACY—See Randalls Food Markets, Inc.; *U.S. Private*, pg. 909
TOMADO LTD.—See N.V. Bekaert S.A.; *Int'l*, pg. 184
TOMAGO ALUMINUM COMPANY PTY. LTD.—See Pechiney S.A.; *Int'l*, pg. 1032
TOMAHAWK FARMS, INC.—See Lundy Packing Co.; *U.S. Private*, pg. 681
AB TOMAL—See Tetra Laval Group; *Int'l*, pg. 1377
TOMBIGBEE TRANSPORT CORPORATION—See Masco Corporation; *U.S. Public*, pg. 1053
TOMBSTONE PIZZA CORPORATION—See Philip Morris Companies Inc.; *U.S. Public*, pg. 1288
TOMCO AUTO PRODUCTS, INC.; *U.S. Private*, pg. 1090
TOMCO CO. LTD.—See Eclipse Inc.; *U.S. Private*, pg. 361
TOMEN AMERICA INC.—See Tomen Corporation; *Int'l*, pg. 1395
TOMEN CORPORATION; *Int'l*, pg. 1395
TOMEN TRANSPORTGERAETE GMBH—See Toyota Motor Corporation; *Int'l*, pg. 1412
TOMEN (U.K.) PLC.—See Tomen Corporation; *Int'l*, pg. 1395
TOMKINS CORPORATION—See Tomkins PLC; *Int'l*, pg. 1397
TOMKINS INDUSTRIES INC.—See Tomkins PLC; *Int'l*, pg. 1397
TOMKINS PLC; *Int'l*, pg. 1395
TOMMY HILFIGER CORPORATION; *Int'l*, pg. 1398
TOMONO AGRICA CO. LTD.—See Novartis AG; *Int'l*, pg. 986
CHAS. H. TOMPKINS CO.—See Philipp Holzmann AG; *Int'l*, pg. 633
TOMPKINS COUNTY TRUST COMPANY; *U.S. Public*, pg. 1621
TOM'S FOODS, INC.; *U.S. Private*, pg. 1090
TOMS SIERRA COMPANY; *U.S. Private*, pg. 1090
TONDEO-WERK GMBH—See Wella Group; *Int'l*, pg. 1489
TONE BROTHERS INC.—See Burns, Philp & Company Limited; *Int'l*, pg. 237
TONE COMMANDER SYSTEMS; *U.S. Private*, pg. 1090
TONEN CORPORATION; *Int'l*, pg. 1398
TONEN ENERGY INTERNATIONAL CORP.—See Tonen Corporation; *Int'l*, pg. 1399
JAMES P. TONER COMPANY, INC.—See Cigna Corp.; *U.S. Public*, pg. 358
TONERMEX S.A. DE C.V.—See Ricoh Company, Ltd.; *Int'l*, pg. 1116
TONG GUANG-NORTEL LIMITED LIABILITY COMPANY—See Northern Telecom Limited; *Int'l*, pg. 970
TONG SHING INC.—See Toray Industries, Inc.; *Int'l*, pg. 1400
TONG YANG SHL CORP.—See SHL Systemhouse; *Int'l*, pg. 1154
THE TONGAT-HULETT GROUP LIMITED—See Anglo American Corporation of South Africa Limited; *Int'l*, pg. 76
TONGLING GENERAL CONTRACTOR CO., LTD.—See Taisei Corporation; *Int'l*, pg. 1348
TONKA CORP.—See Hasbro, Inc.; *U.S. Public*, pg. 798
TONKA CORP. PTY. LTD.—See Hasbro, Inc.; *U.S. Public*, pg. 798
TONKA EUROPE, LIMITED—See Hasbro, Inc.; *U.S. Public*, pg. 798
TONKA FAR EAST LIMITED—See Hasbro, Inc.; *U.S. Public*, pg. 798
TONKA ITALIA S.P.A.—See Hasbro, Inc.; *U.S. Public*, pg. 798
TONKA PRODUCTS DIVISION—See Hasbro, Inc.; *U.S. Public*, pg. 797
TONNELLERIE GARNIER—See LVMH Moet Hennessy Louis Vuitton; *Int'l*, pg. 781
TONNELLERIE TARANSAUD—See LVMH Moet Hennessy Louis Vuitton; *Int'l*, pg. 781
TONNEMA B.V.—See CSM N.V.; *Int'l*, pg. 244
TONWERKE ERPEL WERNER E. GABLER GMBH—See Solvay S.A.; *Int'l*, pg. 1278
TOOL KING; *U.S. Private*, pg. 1091
TOOLING PRODUCTS LTD.—See Weir Group PLC; *Int'l*, pg. 1489
TOOLPRO—See Kimball International, Inc.; *U.S. Public*, pg. 957
TOOLPUSHER SUPPLY CO.—See True Companies; *U.S. Private*, pg. 1107
TOOTAL CLOTHING LTD.—See Coats Viyella plc; *Int'l*, pg. 300
TOOTAL GROUP PLC—See Coats Viyella plc; *Int'l*, pg. 300
TOOTAL TEXTILES HOLDINGS LTD.—See Coats Viyella plc; *Int'l*, pg. 300
TOOTAL TEXTILES LTD.—See Coats Viyella plc; *Int'l*, pg. 300
TOOTAL THREAD HONG KONG LTD.—See Coats Viyella plc; *Int'l*, pg. 299
TOOTAL THREAD LTD.—See Coats Viyella plc; *Int'l*, pg. 299
TOOTAL THREAD MALACCA SDN BDN—See Coats Viyella plc; *Int'l*, pg. 299
TOOTAL THREAD (PTE.) LTD.—See Coats Viyella plc; *Int'l*, pg. 299
P.T. TOOTAL THREAD WDONGSLA—See Coats Viyella plc; *Int'l*, pg. 299
THE TOOTSIE ROLL COMPANY—See Tootsie Roll Industries, Inc.; *U.S. Public*, pg. 1621
TOOTSIE ROLL INDUSTRIES, INC.; *U.S. Public*, pg. 1621
TOOTSIE ROLL MANAGEMENT, INC.—See Tootsie Roll Industries, Inc.; *U.S. Public*, pg. 1621
TOOTSIE ROLL MANUFACTURING INC.—See Tootsie Roll Industries, Inc.; *U.S. Public*, pg. 1621
TOOTSIE ROLL OF CANADA, LTD.—See Tootsie Roll Industries, Inc.; *U.S. Public*, pg. 1621
TOOTSIE ROLLS-LATIN AMERICA, INC.—See Tootsie Roll Industries, Inc.; *U.S. Public*, pg. 1621
TOOTSIETOY DIVISION—See Strombecker Corporation; *U.S. Private*, pg. 1047
TOOTSIETOY PRESCHOOL PRODUCTS DIV.—See Strombecker Corporation; *U.S. Private*, pg. 1047
TOP AIR MANUFACTURING, INC.; *U.S. Public*, pg. 1621
TOP BILLING INC.; *U.S. Private*, pg. 1091
TOP BRANDS, INC.; *U.S. Private*, pg. 1091
THE TOP FIVE CLUB, INC.—See Berkshire Hathaway Inc.; *U.S. Public*, pg. 220
TOP FLIGHT, INC.; *U.S. Private*, pg. 1091
TOP MIX CONCRETE—See Ssangyong Business Group; *Int'l*, pg. 1293
TOP OF THE WORLD HOTEL—See Arctic Slope Regional Corporation; *U.S. Private*, pg. 80
TOP OF THE WORLD VENTURES, INC—See Galesi Group; *U.S. Private*, pg. 438
TOP PRAZISIONSWERKZEUGE GMBH—See Sandvik AB; *Int'l*, pg. 1187
TOP RANK LIMITED—See The Rank Group PLC; *Int'l*, pg. 1087
TOP SANTE VOF—See VNU Verenigde Nederlandse Uitgeversbedrijven B.V.; *Int'l*, pg. 1445
TOP-SEAL CORP.—See The Tech Group; *U.S. Private*, pg. 1071
TOP TELE—See Lagardere Groupe; *Int'l*, pg. 794
TOP THERMO MFG. (MALAYSIA) SDN. BHD—See Nippon Sanso Corporation; *Int'l*, pg. 939
TOP VALUE MEDIA—See Metropolitan Sunday Newspapers, Inc.; *U.S. Private*, pg. 739
TOPA EQUITIES LTD, INC.; *U.S. Private*, pg. 1091
TOPAKA SCIENTIFIC SAFETY CO.—See Amano Corporation; *Int'l*, pg. 71
TOPCO ASSOCIATES, INC.; *U.S. Private*, pg. 1091
TOPCOMP ELEKTRONIK—See Telefonaktiebolaget LM Ericsson; *Int'l*, pg. 1363
TOPCOMP ELEKTRONIK FINLAND—See Telefonaktiebolaget LM Ericsson; *Int'l*, pg. 1371
TOPCON CORPORATION—See Toshiba Corporation; *Int'l*, pg. 1403
TOPDANMARK—See Eureko B.V.; *Int'l*, pg. 464
THE TOPEKA CAPITAL-JOURNAL—See Shivers Trading & Operating Co.; *U.S. Private*, pg. 995
TOPEKA GROUP, INCORPORATED—See Minnesota Power; *U.S. Public*, pg. 1116
TOPEKA PRODUCTION CENTER—See Hallmark Cards, Inc.; *U.S. Private*, pg. 496
TOPEKA RECYCLING CENTER—See Republic Group Incorporated; *U.S. Public*, pg. 1378
TOPEKA TELEVISION, CORP.—See Lee Enterprises, Incorporated; *U.S. Public*, pg. 984
TOPEXPRESS, LTD.—See Science Applications International Corp.; *U.S. Private*, pg. 976
TOPFLIGHT CORP.; *U.S. Private*, pg. 1091
TOPICS NEWSPAPERS—See Central Newspapers, Inc.; *U.S. Public*, pg. 326
TOPKO, TIDELANDS OIL PRODUCTION COMPANY—See Neste Oy; *Int'l*, pg. 913
TOPLINE IMPORTS, INC.; *U.S. Private*; pg. 1091
TOPLIS PAINTERS LIMITED—See Costain Group PLC; *Int'l*, pg. 337
TOPPAN CHUNGHWA ELECTRONICS CO., LTD.—See Toppan Printing Company, Ltd.; *Int'l*, pg. 1399
TOPPAN ELECTRONICS (U.S.A.), INC.—See Toppan Printing Company, Ltd.; *Int'l*, pg. 1399

TOPPAN INTERAMERICA INC.—See Toppan Printing
    Company, Ltd.; *Int'l*, pg. 1399
TOPPAN INTERAMERICA INC.-IRVINE OFFICE—See
    Toppan Printing Company, Ltd.; *Int'l*, pg. 1399
TOPPAN MOORE DATA PRODUCTS INC.—See DataCard
    Corporation; *U.S. Private*, pg. 313
TOPPAN PRINTING CO. (AMERICA), INC.—See Toppan
    Printing Company, Ltd.; *Int'l*, pg. 1399
TOPPAN PRINTING CO. (AMERICA) INC.-LOS
    ANGELES—See Toppan Printing Company, Ltd.; *Int'l*,
    pg. 1399
TOPPAN PRINTING CO. (AMERICA) INC.-NEW JERSEY—
    See Toppan Printing Company, Ltd.; *Int'l*, pg. 1399
TOPPAN PRINTING CO., (SHANGHAI) LTD.—See Toppan
    Printing Company, Ltd.; *Int'l*, pg. 1399
TOPPAN PRINTING CO., (SHENZHEN) LTD.—See Toppan
    Printing Company, Ltd.; *Int'l*, pg. 1399
TOPPAN PRINTING CO. (AUSTRALIA) PTY. LTD.—See
    Toppan Printing Company, Ltd.; *Int'l*, pg. 1399
TOPPAN PRINTING CO. (H.K.) LTD.—See Toppan Printing
    Company, Ltd.; *Int'l*, pg. 1399
TOPPAN PRINTING COMPANY, LTD.; *Int'l*, pg. 1399
TOPPAN PRINTING CO., LTD.—See Toppan Printing
    Company, Ltd.; *Int'l*, pg. 1399
TOPPAN PRINTING CO. (SINGAPORE) PTE. LTD.—See
    Toppan Printing Company, Ltd.; *Int'l*, pg. 1399
TOPPAN PRINTING CO. (UK) LTD.—See Toppan Printing
    Company, Ltd.; *Int'l*, pg. 1399
TOPPAN PRINTING GMBH—See Toppan Printing
    Company, Ltd.; *Int'l*, pg. 1399
P.T. TOPPAN PRINTING INDONESIA—See Toppan
    Printing Company, Ltd.; *Int'l*, pg. 1399
P.T. TOPPAN SAMPOERNA INDONESIA—See Toppan
    Printing Company, Ltd.; *Int'l*, pg. 1399
TOPPAN WEST, INC.—See Toppan Printing Company, Ltd.;
    Int'l, pg. 1399
TOPPS ARGENTINA S.A.—See The Topps Company, Inc.;
    U.S. Public, pg. 1622
TOPPS BRASIL LTDA.—See The Topps Company, Inc.;
    U.S. Public, pg. 1622
THE TOPPS COMPANY, INC.; *U.S. Public*, pg. 1621
TOPPS IRELAND LTD.—See The Topps Company, Inc.;
    U.S. Public, pg. 1622
TOPPS LATIN AMERICA S.A.—See The Topps Company,
    Inc.; *U.S. Public*, pg. 1622
TOPPS MEXICO, S.A. DE C.V.—See The Topps Company,
    Inc.; *U.S. Public*, pg. 1622
TOPS APPLIANCE CITY; *U.S. Public*, pg. 1622
TOPS MARKETS, INC.—See Koninklijke Ahold NV; *Int'l*,
    pg. 750
TOPS 'N BOTTOMS OF NEW YORK, INC.—See Deb
    Shops, Inc.; *U.S. Public*, pg. 491
TOPSY'S INTERNATIONAL INC.; *U.S. Private*, pg. 1092
TOPTIP (R. MULLER AG)—See Coop Switzerland; *Int'l*,
    pg. 330
TOPURA CO., LTD.—See NHK Spring Co., Ltd.; *Int'l*,
    pg. 902
TORAY COMPOSITES (AMERICA), INC.—See Toray
    Industries, Inc.; *Int'l*, pg. 1400
TORAY DEUTSCHLAND GMBH—See Toray Industries,
    Inc.; *Int'l*, pg. 1399
TORAY ENGINEERING CO., LTD.—See Toray Industries,
    Inc.; *Int'l*, pg. 1399
TORAY EUROPE LTD.—See Toray Industries, Inc.; *Int'l*,
    pg. 1400
TORAY FIBERS (THAILAND), LTD.—See Toray Industries,
    Inc.; *Int'l*, pg. 1400
TORAY INDUSTRIES (AMERICA) INC.—See Toray
    Industries, Inc.; *Int'l*, pg. 1400
TORAY INDUSTRIES (H.K.) LTD.—See Toray Industries,
    Inc.; *Int'l*, pg. 1400
TORAY INDUSTRIES, INC.; *Int'l*, pg. 1399
TORAY INDUSTRIES, INC.-BEIJING OFFICE—See Toray
    Industries, Inc.; *Int'l*, pg. 1400
TORAY INDUSTRIES, INC.-EUROPE OFFICE—See Toray
    Industries, Inc.; *Int'l*, pg. 1400
TORAY INDUSTRIES, INC.-SEOUL OFFICE—See Toray
    Industries, Inc.; *Int'l*, pg. 1400
TORAY INDUSTRIES (SINGAPORE) PTE. LTD.—See
    Toray Industries, Inc.; *Int'l*, pg. 1400
TORAY ITALIA S.R.L.—See Toray Industries, Inc.; *Int'l*,
    pg. 1400
TORAY PLASTICS (AMERICA), INC.—See Toray Industries,
    Inc.; *Int'l*, pg. 1400
TORAY RESEARCH CENTER, INC.—See Toray Industries,
    Inc.; *Int'l*, pg. 1399
TORAY TEXTILES EUROPE LTD.—See Toray Industries,
    Inc.; *Int'l*, pg. 1400
TORCAD LIMITED—See Stelco Inc.; *Int'l*, pg. 1299
TORCELLO S.R.L.—See Assicurazioni Generali S.p.A.; *Int'l*,
    pg. 90
TORCH ENERGY ADVISORS, INCORPORATED—See
    Torchmark Corporation; *U.S. Public*, pg. 1623
TORCH ENERGY CORP.—See Torchmark Corporation;
    U.S. Public, pg. 1623
TORCH OPERATING CO.—See Torchmark Corporation;
    U.S. Public, pg. 1623
TORCHINSKY ENGINEERING LTD—See Agra Inc.; *Int'l*,
    pg. 31
TORCHMARK CORPORATION; *U.S. Public*, pg. 1622
TORCHMARK INVESTMENT ADVISORY COMPANY,
    INC.—See Torchmark Corporation; *U.S. Public*,
    pg. 1623
TORCO OIL CO.; *U.S. Private*, pg. 1092
TORCON, INC.; *U.S. Private*, pg. 1092
TORESCO ENTERPRISES; *U.S. Private*, pg. 1092
TORFEACO INDUSTRIES LTD.—See Pillowtex
    Corporation; *U.S. Public*, pg. 1296
TORIN ENGINEERED BLOWERS—See BTR plc; *Int'l*,
    pg. 125
TORIN LIMITED—See Smiths Industries plc; *Int'l*, pg. 1267
TORITA CORPORATION LTD.—See IPC Corporation Ltd.;
    Int'l, pg. 651

TORK ELECTRO SISTEMAS S.A. DE C.V.—See Tork, Inc.;
    U.S. Private, pg. 1092
TORK, INC.; *U.S. Private*, pg. 1092
TORKE COFFEE ROASTING COMPANY; *U.S. Private*,
    pg. 1092
TORNADO AG—See Vorwerk & Co.; *Int'l*, pg. 1481
TORNADO S.A.—See Electrolux, AB; *Int'l*, pg. 441
TORNE-JOTUN S.A.—See Jotun A/S; *Int'l*, pg. 716
TORNET—See Swedbank; *Int'l*, pg. 1328
TORNION PAKKAUSLAVA OY—See Enso Oyj; *Int'l*,
    pg. 456
TORNOS-BECHLER S.A.—See Rothenberger Group
    GmbH; *Int'l*, pg. 1128
TORO AUSTRALIA PTY. LTD.—See The Toro Company;
    U.S. Public, pg. 1624
THE TORO COMPANY; *U.S. Public*, pg. 1623
THE TORO COMPANY IRRIGATION PRODUCTS—See
    The Toro Company; *U.S. Public*, pg. 1624
TORO CREDIT—See The Toro Company; *U.S. Public*,
    pg. 1624
TORO KANSAS—See The Toro Company; *U.S. Public*,
    pg. 1624
TORO PROBIOTIC PRODUCTS, INC.—See The Toro
    Company; *U.S. Public*, pg. 1624
TORO-WHEEL HORSE—See The Toro Company; *U.S.
    Public*, pg. 1624
TORO WORLDWIDE PARTS DISTRIBUTION CENTER—
    See The Toro Company; *U.S. Public*, pg. 1624
TOROMONT CAT—See Toromont Industries Ltd.; *Int'l*,
    pg. 1400
TOROMONT INDUSTRIES LTD.; *Int'l*, pg. 1400
TOROMONT PROCESS SYSTEMS INC.—See Toromont
    Industries Ltd.; *Int'l*, pg. 1401
TORONTO AUTO AUCTION—See Cox Enterprises, Inc.;
    U.S. Private, pg. 283
TORONTO BLUE JAYS BASEBALL CLUB, INC.—See
    Interbrew S.A.; *Int'l*, pg. 680
TORONTO CARTON CORPORATION LIMITED—See
    Shorewood Packaging Corporation; *U.S. Public*,
    pg. 1468
TORONTO DOMINION AUSTRALIA LTD.—See The
    Toronto Dominion Bank; *Int'l*, pg. 1401
THE TORONTO DOMINION BANK; *Int'l*, pg. 1401
TORONTO-DOMINION BANK (UNITED KINGDOM) LTD.—
    See The Toronto Dominion Bank; *Int'l*, pg. 1401
TORONTO DOMINION-HONG KONG BRANCH—See The
    Toronto Dominion Bank; *Int'l*, pg. 1401
TORONTO DOMINION JAPAN—See The Toronto
    Dominion Bank; *Int'l*, pg. 1401
TORONTO DOMINION SECURITIES (U.S.A.) INC.—See
    The Toronto Dominion Bank; *Int'l*, pg. 1401
TORONTO DOMINION (SOUTHEAST ASIA) LIMITED—See
    The Toronto Dominion Bank; *Int'l*, pg. 1402
TORONTO DOMINION-TAIPEI BRANCH—See The Toronto
    Dominion Bank; *Int'l*, pg. 1402
TORONTO-DOMINION (TEXAS), INC.—See The Toronto
    Dominion Bank; *Int'l*, pg. 1401
TORONTO LEARNING CENTER—See Berkshire Hathaway
    Inc.; *U.S. Public*, pg. 219
TORONTO PLANT—See Fort James Corporation; *U.S.
    Public*, pg. 672
TORONTO STAR NEWSPAPERS LTD.—See Torstar
    Corporation; *Int'l*, pg. 1402
THE TORONTO SUN PUBLISHING CORPORATION—See
    Sun Media Corporation; *Int'l*, pg. 1320
TOROTEL, INC.; *U.S. Public*, pg. 1624
TOROTEL PRODUCTS, INC.—See Torotel, Inc.; *U.S.
    Public*, pg. 1624
TORRANCE CARE CENTER—See Meritcare, Inc.; *U.S.
    Private*, pg. 733
TORRANCE COUNTY DETENTION FACILITY—See
    Corrections Corporation of America; *U.S. Public*,
    pg. 451
TORRANCE NISSAN, INC.—See Republic Industries, Inc.;
    U.S. Public, pg. 1380
TORRE COLLSEROLA, S.A.—See Telefonica de Espana,
    S.A.; *Int'l*, pg. 1372
TORRE LAZUR/WEBER HEALTHCARE PUBLIC
    RELATIONS—See Weber Public Relations Worldwide;
    U.S. Private, pg. 1157
TORREY PINES CARE CENTER—See Vencor, Inc.; *U.S.
    Public*, pg. 1715
TORRINGTON CO.-PRECISION COMPONENTS—See
    Ingersoll-Rand Company; *U.S. Public*, pg. 877
THE TORRINGTON CO.—See Ingersoll-Rand Company;
    U.S. Public, pg. 877
THE TORRINGTON COMPANY LIMITED—See Ingersoll-
    Rand Company; *U.S. Public*, pg. 878
TORRINGTON GMBH—See Ingersoll-Rand Company; *U.S.
    Public*, pg. 878
TORSTAR CORPORATION; *Int'l*, pg. 1402
TORYU CEMENT CORP.—See Ssangyong Business
    Group; *Int'l*, pg. 1291
TOS GALANTA A.S.—See Traub AG; *Int'l*, pg. 1419
TOSARA GROUP—See Forest Laboratories, Inc.; *U.S.
    Public*, pg. 670
TOSAS (PTY) LTD.—See Sasol Limited; *Int'l*, pg. 1197
TOSCANA GLAS S.P.A.—See Saint-Gobain; *Int'l*, pg. 1173
TOSCO CORPORATION; *U.S. Public*, pg. 1624
TOSCO REFINING COMPANY—See Tosco Corporation;
    U.S. Public, pg. 1625
TOSHBRO SHIMADZU LTD.—See Shimadzu Corporation;
    Int'l, pg. 1232
TOSHIBA AIR CONDITIONING CO., LTD.—See Toshiba
    Corporation; *Int'l*, pg. 1403
TOSHIBA AKITA DENKI CO., LTD.—See Toshiba
    Corporation; *Int'l*, pg. 1403
TOSHIBA AMERICA CAPITAL CORPORATION—See
    Toshiba Corporation; *Int'l*, pg. 1405
TOSHIBA AMERICA CONSUMER PRODUCTS, INC.—See
    Toshiba Corporation; *Int'l*, pg. 1405
TOSHIBA AMERICA CONSUMER PRODUCTS
    MANUFACTURING DIV.—See Toshiba Corporation;
    Int'l, pg. 1405

TOSHIBA AMERICA ELECTRONIC COMPONENTS, INC.—
    See Toshiba Corporation; *Int'l*, pg. 1405
TOSHIBA AMERICA INC.—See Toshiba Corporation; *Int'l*,
    pg. 1405
TOSHIBA AMERICA, INC.—See Toshiba Corporation; *Int'l*,
    pg. 1405
TOSHIBA AMERICA INFORMATION SYSTEMS, INC.—See
    Toshiba Corporation; *Int'l*, pg. 1405
TOSHIBA AMERICA MEDICAL SYSTEMS, INC.—See
    Toshiba Corporation; *Int'l*, pg. 1405
TOSHIBA AMERICA MRI INC.—See Toshiba Corporation;
    Int'l, pg. 1405
TOSHIBA AMERICA VENTURE CAPITAL, INC.—See
    Toshiba Corporation; *Int'l*, pg. 1405
TOSHIBA (AUSTRALIA) PTY., LTD.—See Toshiba
    Corporation; *Int'l*, pg. 1406
TOSHIBA AUTOMATION CO., LTD.—See Toshiba
    Corporation; *Int'l*, pg. 1403
TOSHIBA AVE CO. LTD.—See Toshiba Corporation; *Int'l*,
    pg. 1403
TOSHIBA BALLOTINE CO., LTD.—See Toshiba
    Corporation; *Int'l*, pg. 1403
TOSHIBA BATTERY CO., LTD.—See Toshiba Corporation;
    Int'l, pg. 1403
TOSHIBA BUILDERS APPLIANCE CO., LTD.—See Toshiba
    Corporation; *Int'l*, pg. 1403
TOSHIBA BUILDING CORPORATION—See Toshiba
    Corporation; *Int'l*, pg. 1403
TOSHIBA CAMBRIDGE RESEARCH CENTRE LTD.—See
    Toshiba Corporation; *Int'l*, pg. 1406
TOSHIBA CERAMICS CO., LTD.—See Toshiba
    Corporation; *Int'l*, pg. 1403
TOSHIBA CHEMICAL CORPORATION—See Toshiba
    Corporation; *Int'l*, pg. 1403
TOSHIBA (CHINA) CO., LTD.—See Toshiba Corporation;
    Int'l, pg. 1406
TOSHIBA CHUBU CONSUMER ELECTRONICS CO.,
    LTD.—See Toshiba Corporation; *Int'l*, pg. 1403
TOSHIBA CHUBU SERVICE & ENGINEERING CO. LTD.—
    See Toshiba Corporation; *Int'l*, pg. 1403
TOSHIBA CHUO CONSUMER ELECTRONICS CO., LTD.—
    See Toshiba Corporation; *Int'l*, pg. 1403
TOSHIBA COMPONENTS CO., LTD.—See Toshiba
    Corporation; *Int'l*, pg. 1403
TOSHIBA COMPRESSOR (TAIWAN) CORP.—See Toshiba
    Corporation; *Int'l*, pg. 1406
TOSHIBA CONSUMER PRODUCTS (THAILAND) CO.,
    LTD.—See Toshiba Corporation; *Int'l*, pg. 1406
TOSHIBA CONSUMER PRODUCTS (U.K.) LIMITED—See
    Toshiba Corporation; *Int'l*, pg. 1406
TOSHIBA CONTROL SYSTEM CORPORATION—See
    Toshiba Corporation; *Int'l*, pg. 1403
TOSHIBA CORPORATION; *Int'l*, pg. 1402
TOSHIBA CREDIT CORP.—See Toshiba Corporation; *Int'l*,
    pg. 1403
TOSHIBA DALIAN CO. LTD.—See Toshiba Corporation;
    Int'l, pg. 1406
TOSHIBA DATA DYNAMICS PTE. LTD.—See Toshiba
    Corporation; *Int'l*, pg. 1406
TOSHIBA DE MEXICO, S.A. DE C.V.—See Toshiba
    Corporation; *Int'l*, pg. 1406
TOSHIBA DE PANAMA, S.A.—See Toshiba Corporation;
    Int'l, pg. 1406
TOSHIBA DE VENEZUELA C.A.—See Toshiba Corporation;
    Int'l, pg. 1406
TOSHIBA DEVICE CORPORATION—See Toshiba
    Corporation; *Int'l*, pg. 1403
TOSHIBA DISPLAY DEVICES (THAILAND) CO., LTD.—See
    Toshiba Corporation; *Int'l*, pg. 1406
TOSHIBA DO BRASIL S.A.—See Toshiba Corporation; *Int'l*,
    pg. 1406
TOSHIBA E & S HOKKAIDO CORPORATION—See
    Toshiba Corporation; *Int'l*, pg. 1404
TOSHIBA EAST JAPAN LIFE ELECTRONICS CO., LTD.—
    See Toshiba Corporation; *Int'l*, pg. 1404
TOSHIBA ELECTRIC APPLIANCES CO., LTD.—See
    Toshiba Corporation; *Int'l*, pg. 1404
TOSHIBA ELECTROMEX, S.A. DE C.V.—See Toshiba
    Corporation; *Int'l*, pg. 1406
TOSHIBA ELECTRONIC ENGINEERING CORPORATION—
    See Toshiba Corporation; *Int'l*, pg. 1404
TOSHIBA ELECTRONIC SYSTEMS CO., LTD.—See
    Toshiba Corporation; *Int'l*, pg. 1404
TOSHIBA ELECTRONICS ASIA, LTD.—See Toshiba
    Corporation; *Int'l*, pg. 1406
TOSHIBA ELECTRONICS ASIA (SINGAPORE) PTE. LTD.—
    See Toshiba Corporation; *Int'l*, pg. 1406
TOSHIBA ELECTRONICS ESPANA S.A.—See Toshiba
    Corporation; *Int'l*, pg. 1406
TOSHIBA ELECTRONICS EUROPE GMBH—See Toshiba
    Corporation; *Int'l*, pg. 1406
TOSHIBA ELECTRONICS FRANCE S.A.R.L.—See Toshiba
    Corporation; *Int'l*, pg. 1406
TOSHIBA ELECTRONICS ITALIANA S.R.L.—See Toshiba
    Corporation; *Int'l*, pg. 1406
TOSHIBA ELECTRONICS MALAYSIA SDN. BHD.—See
    Toshiba Corporation; *Int'l*, pg. 1406
TOSHIBA ELECTRONICS SCANDINAVIA AB—See Toshiba
    Corporation; *Int'l*, pg. 1406
TOSHIBA ELECTRONICS TAIWAN CORP.—See Toshiba
    Corporation; *Int'l*, pg. 1406
TOSHIBA ELECTRONICS (UK) LTD.—See Toshiba
    Corporation; *Int'l*, pg. 1406
TOSHIBA ELEMEC CORPORATION—See Toshiba
    Corporation; *Int'l*, pg. 1404
TOSHIBA ELETEC CHUBU CORPORATION—See Toshiba
    Corporation; *Int'l*, pg. 1404
TOSHIBA ELETEC HIGASHI NIHON CORPORATION—See
    Toshiba Corporation; *Int'l*, pg. 1404
TOSHIBA ELETEC NISHINIHON CORPORATION—See
    Toshiba Corporation; *Int'l*, pg. 1404
TOSHIBA ELEVATOR & ESCALATOR SERVICE CO.,
    LTD.—See Toshiba Corporation; *Int'l*, pg. 1404

TOSHIBA ELEVATOR SALES CORPORATION—See Toshiba Corporation; *Int'l*, pg. 1404
TOSHIBA-EMI LIMITED—See EMI Group plc; *Int'l*, pg. 427
TOSHIBA-EMI LIMITED—See Toshiba Corporation; *Int'l*, pg. 1405
TOSHIBA ENGINEERING & CONSTRUCTION CO., LTD.—See Toshiba Corporation; *Int'l*, pg. 1404
TOSHIBA ENGINEERING CO., LTD.—See Toshiba Corporation; *Int'l*, pg. 1404
TOSHIBA EUROPE (I.E.) G.M.B.H.—See Toshiba Corporation; *Int'l*, pg. 1406
TOSHIBA GLASS CO., LTD.—See Toshiba Corporation; *Int'l*, pg. 1404
TOSHIBA HAWAII, INC.—See Toshiba Corporation; *Int'l*, pg. 1405
TOSHIBA HEATING APPLIANCES CO., LTD.—See Toshiba Corporation; *Int'l*, pg. 1404
TOSHIBA HOKKAIDO SERVICE & ENGINEERING CO., LTD.—See Toshiba Corporation; *Int'l*, pg. 1404
TOSHIBA INFORMATION EQUIPMENT CO., LTD.—See Toshiba Corporation; *Int'l*, pg. 1404
TOSHIBA INFORMATION SYSTEMS (JAPAN) CORPORATION—See Toshiba Corporation; *Int'l*, pg. 1404
TOSHIBA INFORMATION SYSTEMS (U.K.) LTD.—See Toshiba Corporation; *Int'l*, pg. 1406
TOSHIBA INSURANCE SERVICE CORPORATION—See Toshiba Corporation; *Int'l*, pg. 1404
TOSHIBA INTERNATIONAL CORP. INDUSTRIAL DIV.—See Toshiba Corporation; *Int'l*, pg. 1405
TOSHIBA INTERNATIONAL CORPORATION PTY., LTD.—See Toshiba Corporation; *Int'l*, pg. 1406
TOSHIBA INTERNATIONAL CORPORATION, UTILITY DIVISION—See Toshiba Corporation; *Int'l*, pg. 1405
TOSHIBA INTERNATIONAL (EUROPE) LTD.—See Toshiba Corporation; *Int'l*, pg. 1406
TOSHIBA INTERNATIONAL FINANCE (NETHERLANDS) B.V.—See Toshiba Corporation; *Int'l*, pg. 1406
TOSHIBA INTERNATIONAL FINANCE (UK) PLC—See Toshiba Corporation; *Int'l*, pg. 1406
TOSHIBA INTERNATIONAL S.C. LTDA.—See Toshiba Corporation; *Int'l*, pg. 1406
TOSHIBA IWATE DENKI CO., LTD.—See Toshiba Corporation; *Int'l*, pg. 1404
TOSHIBA KN SYSTEM CO., LTD.—See Toshiba Corporation; *Int'l*, pg. 1404
TOSHIBA KYUSHU CONSUMER ELECTRONICS CO., LTD.—See Toshiba Corporation; *Int'l*, pg. 1404
TOSHIBA KYUSHU DENKI CO., LTD.—See Toshiba Corporation; *Int'l*, pg. 1404
TOSHIBA KYUSHU SERVICES & ENGINEERING CO,. LTD.—See Toshiba Corporation; *Int'l*, pg. 1404
TOSHIBA LEASING CORPORATION—See Toshiba Corporation; *Int'l*, pg. 1404
TOSHIBA LIGHTING & TECHNOLOGY CORPORATION—See Toshiba Corporation; *Int'l*, pg. 1404
TOSHIBA LIVING SERVICE CO., LTD.—See Toshiba Corporation; *Int'l*, pg. 1404
TOSHIBA LOGISTIC SUPPORT CORPORATION—See Toshiba Corporation; *Int'l*, pg. 1404
TOSHIBA LOGISTICS CORPORATION—See Toshiba Corporation; *Int'l*, pg. 1404
TOSHIBA MACHINE CO., LTD.—See Toshiba Corporation; *Int'l*, pg. 1404
TOSHIBA MEDICAL DO BRASIL LTDA.—See Toshiba Corporation; *Int'l*, pg. 1407
TOSHIBA MEDICAL FRANCE S.A.—See Toshiba Corporation; *Int'l*, pg. 1407
TOSHIBA MEDICAL SYSTEMS AG—See Toshiba Corporation; *Int'l*, pg. 1407
TOSHIBA MEDICAL SYSTEMS CO., LTD.—See Toshiba Corporation; *Int'l*, pg. 1404
TOSHIBA MEDICAL SYSTEMS EUROPE B.V.—See Toshiba Corporation; *Int'l*, pg. 1407
TOSHIBA MEDICAL SYSTEMS GESELLSCHAFT GMBH—See Toshiba Corporation; *Int'l*, pg. 1407
TOSHIBA MEDICAL SYSTEMS GMBH—See Toshiba Corporation; *Int'l*, pg. 1407
TOSHIBA MEDICAL SYSTEMS LTD.—See Toshiba Corporation; *Int'l*, pg. 1407
TOSHIBA MEDICAL SYSTEMS NV/SA—See Toshiba Corporation; *Int'l*, pg. 1407
TOSHIBA MEDICAL SYSTEMS S.A.—See Toshiba Corporation; *Int'l*, pg. 1407
TOSHIBA MEDICAL SYSTEMS S.R.L.—See Toshiba Corporation; *Int'l*, pg. 1407
TOSHIBA MICROELECTRONICS CORPORATION—See Toshiba Corporation; *Int'l*, pg. 1404
TOSHIBA NISHI NIHON CONSUMER ELECTRONICS CO., LTD.—See Toshiba Corporation; *Int'l*, pg. 1404
TOSHIBA NISHI NIHON SERVICE & ENGINEERING CO., LTD.—See Toshiba Corporation; *Int'l*, pg. 1404
TOSHIBA OA CONSULTANTS LTD.—See Toshiba Corporation; *Int'l*, pg. 1404
TOSHIBA OF CANADA, LTD.—See Toshiba Corporation; *Int'l*, pg. 1407
TOSHIBA OSAKA BUILDING CO., LTD.—See Toshiba Corporation; *Int'l*, pg. 1404
TOSHIBA OU DENKI CO., LTD.—See Toshiba Corporation; *Int'l*, pg. 1404
TOSHIBA PHYSICAL DISTRIBUTION CO.—See Toshiba Corporation; *Int'l*, pg. 1404
TOSHIBA SALES AND SERVICES SDN. BHD.—See Toshiba Corporation; *Int'l*, pg. 1404
TOSHIBA SEMICONDUCTOR G.M.B.H.—See Toshiba Corporation; *Int'l*, pg. 1407
TOSHIBA SEMICONDUCTOR (THAILAND) CO., LTD.—See Toshiba Corporation; *Int'l*, pg. 1407
TOSHIBA SHIKOKU ELECTRIC CO., LTD.—See Toshiba Corporation; *Int'l*, pg. 1404
TOSHIBA SHOMEI PRECISION CORPORATION—See Toshiba Corporation; *Int'l*, pg. 1404
TOSHIBA SHUTOKEN SERVICE & ENGINEERING CO., LTD.—See Toshiba Corporation; *Int'l*, pg. 1404

TOSHIBA SILICONE CO., LTD.—See Toshiba Corporation; *Int'l*, pg. 1405
TOSHIBA SINGAPORE PTE., LTD.—See Toshiba Corporation; *Int'l*, pg. 1407
TOSHIBA SOUND SYSTEMS CORPORATION—See Toshiba Corporation; *Int'l*, pg. 1405
TOSHIBA STEEL TUBE CO., LTD.—See Toshiba Corporation; *Int'l*, pg. 1405
TOSHIBA SYSTEMS (FRANCE) S.A.—See Toshiba Corporation; *Int'l*, pg. 1407
TOSHIBA TECHNICAL SERVICES INTERNATIONAL CORPORATION—See Toshiba Corporation; *Int'l*, pg. 1405
TOSHIBA TECHNOLOGY DEVELOPMENT (SHANGHAI) CO., LTD.—See Toshiba Corporation; *Int'l*, pg. 1407
TOSHIBA TELECOMMUNICATION FIELD ENGINEERING CORPORATION—See Toshiba Corporation; *Int'l*, pg. 1405
TOSHIBA THAILAND CO., LTD.—See Toshiba Corporation; *Int'l*, pg. 1407
TOSHIBA TOHOKU DENKI CO., LTD.—See Toshiba Corporation; *Int'l*, pg. 1405
TOSHIBA TOHOKU SERVICE & ENGINEERING CO., LTD.—See Toshiba Corporation; *Int'l*, pg. 1405
TOSHIBA TOURIST CORPORATION—See Toshiba Corporation; *Int'l*, pg. 1405
TOSHIBA TUNGALOY CO., LTD.—See Toshiba Corporation; *Int'l*, pg. 1405
TOSHIBA (U.K.) LTD.—See Toshiba Corporation; *Int'l*, pg. 1407
TOSHIBA VISUAL-EQUIPMENT CORPORATION—See Toshiba Corporation; *Int'l*, pg. 1405
TOSHOKU AMERICA, INC.—See Toshoku Ltd.; *Int'l*, pg. 1407
TOSHOKU LTD.; *Int'l*, pg. 1407
TOSOH AMERICA, INC.—See Tosoh Corporation; *Int'l*, pg. 1407
TOSOH BELGIUM N.V.—See Tosoh Corporation; *Int'l*, pg. 1408
TOSOH CORPORATION; *Int'l*, pg. 1407
TOSOH EUROPE—See Tosoh Corporation; *Int'l*, pg. 1408
TOSOH EUROPE B.V.—See Tosoh Corporation; *Int'l*, pg. 1408
TOSOH HELLAS A.I.C.—See Tosoh Corporation; *Int'l*, pg. 1408
TOSOH MEDICS, INC.—See Tosoh Corporation; *Int'l*, pg. 1407
TOSOH SMD, INC.—See Tosoh Corporation; *Int'l*, pg. 1407
TOSOH SMD KOREA LTD.—See Tosoh Corporation; *Int'l*, pg. 1408
TOSOH USA, INC.—See Tosoh Corporation; *Int'l*, pg. 1408
TOSOH USA, INC.-NEW JERSEY OFFICE—See Tosoh Corporation; *Int'l*, pg. 1407
TOSOH USA, INC.-SAN FRANCISCO OFFICE—See Tosoh Corporation; *Int'l*, pg. 1407
TOSOHAAS COMPANY—See Tosoh Corporation; *Int'l*, pg. 1408
TOSOHAAS GMBH—See Tosoh Corporation; *Int'l*, pg. 1408
TOSTEM CORPORATION; *Int'l*, pg. 1408
TOSTMANN & DOMANN—See TBWA GGK Zurich; *Int'l*, pg. 1336
TOTAL AUDIO VISUAL SERVICES—See Caribiner International, Inc.; *U.S. Public*, pg. 305
TOTAL BEVERAGE CORPORATION—See Dart Group Corporation; *U.S. Public*, pg. 484
TOTAL CRUDE OIL TRANSPORT, INC.—See Ultramar Diamond Shamrock Corporation; *U.S. Public*, pg. 1663
TOTAL DISTRIBUTORS SUPPLY CORPORATION—See Russel Metals Inc.; *Int'l*, pg. 1150
TOTAL ENERGY SYSTEMS LIMITED—See Mining Services International, Inc.; *U.S. Public*, pg. 1115
TOTAL EXPLOITATIE EN PRODUKTIE MAATSCHAPPIJ B.K. (TEPMA)—See Total S.A.; *Int'l*, pg. 1409
TOTAL-FINA GABON S.A.—See Petrofina S.A.; *Int'l*, pg. 1044
TOTAL HOLDINGS (AUSTRALIA) PTY. LTD.—See Total S.A.; *Int'l*, pg. 1409
TOTAL INDONESIE—See Total S.A.; *Int'l*, pg. 1409
TOTAL ITALIANA SRL.—See Total S.A.; *Int'l*, pg. 1409
TOTAL MANAGEMENT SYSTEMS—See Effective Management Systems; *U.S. Public*, pg. 566
TOTAL MARINE EXPLOITATIE N.V.-TME—See Total S.A.; *Int'l*, pg. 1409
TOTAL MEXICANA—See Tyco International Ltd.; *U.S. Public*, pg. 1651
TOTAL NORGE AS—See Total S.A.; *Int'l*, pg. 1409
TOTAL OIL & GAS NEDERLAND B.V.—See Total S.A.; *Int'l*, pg. 1409
TOTAL OIL GREAT BRITAIN LTD.—See Total S.A.; *Int'l*, pg. 1409
TOTAL OIL MARINE P.L.C.-TOM—See Total S.A.; *Int'l*, pg. 1409
TOTAL OUTRE-MER—See Total S.A.; *Int'l*, pg. 1409
TOTAL PETROLEUM CANADA LTD.—See Total S.A.; *Int'l*, pg. 1409
TOTAL PETROLEUM, INC.—See Ultramar Diamond Shamrock Corporation; *U.S. Public*, pg. 1663
TOTAL PIPELINE CORPORATION—See Ultramar Diamond Shamrock Corporation; *U.S. Public*, pg. 1663
TOTAL PLASTIC INC.—See A.M. Castle & Co.; *U.S. Public*, pg. 313
TOTAL RAFFINAGE DISTRIBUTION S.A.—See Total S.A.; *Int'l*, pg. 1409
TOTAL RENAL CARE—See Total Renal Care Holdings, Inc.; *U.S. Public*, pg. 1625
TOTAL RENAL CARE HOLDINGS, INC.; *U.S. Public*, pg. 1625
TOTAL RESEARCH ARGENTINA—See Total Research Corporation; *U.S. Public*, pg. 1625
TOTAL RESEARCH CORPORATION; *U.S. Public*, pg. 1625
TOTAL S.A.; *Int'l*, pg. 1408

TOTAL SECURITY SOLUTIONS—See Borg-Warner Security Corporation; *U.S. Public*, pg. 245
TOTAL SOUTH AFRICA (PTY.) LTD.—See Total S.A.; *Int'l*, pg. 1409
TOTAL SYSTEM SERVICES, INC.—See Synovus Financial Corp.; *U.S. Public*, pg. 1550
TOTAL TRANSPORT MARITIME—See Total S.A.; *Int'l*, pg. 1409
TOTAL WALTHER FEUERSCHUTZ GMBH—See Tyco International Ltd.; *U.S. Public*, pg. 1651
TOTALGAZ—See Total S.A.; *Int'l*, pg. 1410
TOTALIZATOR SYSTEMS (UK) LIMITED—See International Lottery & Totalizator Systems, Inc.; *U.S. Public*, pg. 900
TOTEM RESOURCES CORPORATION; *U.S. Private*, pg. 1092
TOTER INCORPORATED; *U.S. Private*, pg. 1092
TOTES CANADA LTD.—See Bain Capital; *U.S. Private*, pg. 111
TOTES INCORPORATED—See Bain Capital; *U.S. Private*, pg. 111
TOTES/ISOTONER, INC.—See Sara Lee Corporation; *U.S. Public*, pg. 1433
TOTES U.K. LIMITED—See Bain Capital; *U.S. Private*, pg. 111
TOTH DESIGN; *U.S. Private*, pg. 1093
TOTH DESIGN & ADVERTISING—See Toth Design; *U.S. Private*, pg. 1093
TOTINO'S/WELLSTON—See Diageo Plc; *Int'l*, pg. 411
TOTO BEIJING BRANCH—See Toto Ltd.; *Int'l*, pg. 1410
TOTO (BEIJING) CO., LTD.—See Toto Ltd.; *Int'l*, pg. 1410
TOTO (CHINA) CO. LTD.—See Toto Ltd.; *Int'l*, pg. 1410
TOTO DALIAN CO. LTD.—See Toto Ltd.; *Int'l*, pg. 1410
TOTO GUANGZHOU BRANCH—See Toto Ltd.; *Int'l*, pg. 1410
TOTO INDUSTRIES (ATLANTA), INC.—See Toto Ltd.; *Int'l*, pg. 1410
TOTO KIKI (H.K.) LTD.—See Toto Ltd.; *Int'l*, pg. 1410
TOTO KIKI USA, INC.—See Toto Ltd.; *Int'l*, pg. 1410
TOTO KIKI USA, INC. - LOS ANGELES BRANCH—See Toto Ltd.; *Int'l*, pg. 1410
TOTO LTD.; *Int'l*, pg. 1410
TOTO SEOUL BRANCH—See Toto Ltd.; *Int'l*, pg. 1410
TOTO SHANGHAI BRANCH—See Toto Ltd.; *Int'l*, pg. 1410
TOTO SINGAPORE BRANCH—See Toto Ltd.; *Int'l*, pg. 1410
TOTO TAIPEI BRANCH—See Toto Ltd.; *Int'l*, pg. 1410
TOTO USA, INC.—See Toto Ltd.; *Int'l*, pg. 1410
TOTOKIKI (MALAYSIA) SDN.BHD.—See Toto Ltd.; *Int'l*, pg. 1410
TOTSY MANUFACTURING COMPANY, INC.; *U.S. Private*, pg. 1093
TOTTEN TUBES, INC.; *U.S. Private*, pg. 1093
TOTTON PUMPS LTD.—See Wolseley Plc.; *Int'l*, pg. 1512
TOTTORI ASAHI KOKOKUSHA, LTD.—See Daiko Advertising, Inc.; *Int'l*, pg. 366
TOTTORI SANYO ELECTRIC CO., LTD.—See Sanyo Electric Co., Ltd.; *Int'l*, pg. 1191
TOTT'S CHAMPAGNE CELLARS—See E. & J. Gallo Winery; *U.S. Private*, pg. 438
TOUCH INFOPUBLICITE INC. (INFOMERCIALS)—See BCP Group Ltd.; *Int'l*, pg. 116
TOUCHE INDUSTRIAL, S.A. DE C.V.—See Farah Incorporated; *U.S. Public*, pg. 613
TOUCHE REMNANT HOLDINGS, LTD.—See Henderson Administration Group PLC; *Int'l*, pg. 609
TOUCHSTONE SECURITIES, INC.—See The Western and Southern Life Insurance Company; *U.S. Private*, pg. 1165
TOURAINE & JACOBI GMBH—See Harpen AG; *Int'l*, pg. 597
J.J. TOUREK CO.—See Tuthill Corporation; *U.S. Private*, pg. 1111
TOURISM MALAYSIA - BANGKOK OFFICE—See Malaysia Tourism Promotion Board (MTPB); *Int'l*, pg. 833
TOURISM MALAYSIA - FRANKFURT OFFICE—See Malaysia Tourism Promotion Board (MTPB); *Int'l*, pg. 833
TOURISM MALAYSIA - HONG KONG OFFICE—See Malaysia Tourism Promotion Board (MTPB); *Int'l*, pg. 833
TOURISM MALAYSIA - JOHANNESBURG OFFICE—See Malaysia Tourism Promotion Board (MTPB); *Int'l*, pg. 833
TOURISM MALAYSIA - L.A. OFFICE—See Malaysia Tourism Promotion Board (MTPB); *Int'l*, pg. 833
TOURISM MALAYSIA - LONDON OFFICE—See Malaysia Tourism Promotion Board (MTPB); *Int'l*, pg. 833
TOURISM MALAYSIA - MILAN OFFICE—See Malaysia Tourism Promotion Board (MTPB); *Int'l*, pg. 833
TOURISM MALAYSIA - N.Y. OFFICE—See Malaysia Tourism Promotion Board (MTPB); *Int'l*, pg. 833
TOURISM MALAYSIA - OSAKA OFFICE—See Malaysia Tourism Promotion Board (MTPB); *Int'l*, pg. 833
TOURISM MALAYSIA - PARIS OFFICE—See Malaysia Tourism Promotion Board (MTPB); *Int'l*, pg. 833
TOURISM MALAYSIA - SEOUL OFFICE—See Malaysia Tourism Promotion Board (MTPB); *Int'l*, pg. 833
TOURISM MALAYSIA - SINGAPORE OFFICE—See Malaysia Tourism Promotion Board (MTPB); *Int'l*, pg. 833
TOURISM MALAYSIA - STOCKHOLM OFFICE—See Malaysia Tourism Promotion Board (MTPB); *Int'l*, pg. 833
TOURISM MALAYSIA - SYDNEY OFFICE—See Malaysia Tourism Promotion Board (MTPB); *Int'l*, pg. 833
TOURISM MALAYSIA - TOKYO OFFICE—See Malaysia Tourism Promotion Board (MTPB); *Int'l*, pg. 833
TOURISTIK ASSEKURANZ SERVICE GMBH—See Assicurazioni Generali S.p.A.; *Int'l*, pg. 89
TOURNEAU INC.; *U.S. Private*, pg. 1093
TOVAL JAPON S.A.—See Toppan Printing Company, Ltd.; *Int'l*, pg. 1399

Company Index

TOW WATER CO., INC.—See Galesi Group; *U.S. Private*, pg. 438
TOWA GIKEN CO., LTD.—See Tokuyama Corporation; *Int'l*, pg. 1394
TOWA KENSETSU CO., LTD.—See Tekken Corporation; *Int'l*, pg. 1362
TOWER AUTOMOTIVE, INC.; *U.S. Public*, pg. 1625
TOWER CITY DEVELOPMENT, INC.—See Forest City Enterprises, Inc.; *U.S. Public*, pg. 669
TOWER CITY LAND CORPORATION—See Forest City Enterprises, Inc.; *U.S. Public*, pg. 669
TOWER CITY PROPERTIES—See Forest City Enterprises, Inc.; *U.S. Public*, pg. 668
TOWER CITY VALET PARKING—See Forest City Enterprises, Inc.; *U.S. Public*, pg. 669
TOWER ELECTRONICS, INC.—See Advanced Energy Industry; *U.S. Public*, pg. 20
TOWER GROUP INTERNATIONAL—See The McGraw-Hill Companies; *U.S. Public*, pg. 1071
TOWER HOTELS, INC.—See Forest City Enterprises, Inc.; *U.S. Public*, pg. 669
TOWER LOAN OF MISSISSIPPI, INC.—See Capitol Street Corp.; *U.S. Private*, pg. 207
TOWER PRINTING COMPANY—See Wallace Computer Services, Inc.; *U.S. Public*, pg. 1736
TOWER REALTY TRUST, INC.; *U.S. Public*, pg. 1625
TOWER RECORDS—See MTS, Inc.; *U.S. Private*, pg. 688
TOWERS PERRIN; *U.S. Private*, pg. 1093
TOWERS PERRIN REINSURANCE—See Towers Perrin; *U.S. Private*, pg. 1093
TOWLE MANUFACTURING CORPORATION—See Syratech Corporation; *U.S. Private*, pg. 1061
TOWLER PRODUCTS—See The Oilgear Company; *U.S. Public*, pg. 1215
TOWN & COUNTRY—See The Hearst Corporation; *U.S. Private*, pg. 517
TOWN & COUNTRY BANK LTD.—See Australia & New Zealand Banking Group Limited; *Int'l*, pg. 98
TOWN & COUNTRY CORPORATION; *U.S. Public*, pg. 1625
TOWN & COUNTRY FINE JEWELRY GROUP, INC.—See Town & Country Corporation; *U.S. Public*, pg. 1625
TOWN & COUNTRY FORD INC.; *U.S. Private*, pg. 1093
TOWN & COUNTRY HOMES—See Cavalier Homes, Inc.; *U.S. Public*, pg. 319
TOWN & COUNTRY HOTEL—See Atlas Hotels, Inc.; *U.S. Private*, pg. 96
TOWN & COUNTRY SUPERMARKET; *U.S. Private*, pg. 1093
TOWN & COUNTRY TOURS—See Adventure Tours USA, Inc.; *U.S. Private*, pg. 23
TOWN BROOKE ASSOCIATES—See Cigna Corp.; *U.S. Public*, pg. 365
TOWN COLONY ASSOCIATES—See Cigna Corp.; *U.S. Public*, pg. 362
TOWN PUMP, INC.; *U.S. Private*, pg. 1093
TOWNE DEVELOPMENT OF HAWAII, INC.—See Zilber, Ltd.; *U.S. Private*, pg. 1206
THE TOWNE PHARMACY, INC.—See Integrated Health Services, Inc.; *U.S. Public*, pg. 885
TOWNE PROPERTIES; *U.S. Private*, pg. 1093
TOWNE REALTY, INC.—See Zilber, Ltd.; *U.S. Private*, pg. 1206
TOWNE, SILVERSTEIN, ROTTER INC.; *U.S. Private*, pg. 1093
TOWNE SQUARE FURNITURE, INC.; *U.S. Private*, pg. 1093
TOWNHOMES OF COUNTRY RUN, INC.—See Lennar Corporation; *U.S. Public*, pg. 989
TOWNSEND & BOTTUM, INC.—See Black & Veatch; *U.S. Private*, pg. 146
TOWNSEND ENGINEERING CO.; *U.S. Private*, pg. 1094
TOWNSEND HOOK LTD.—See Jefferson Smurfit Group p.l.c.; *Int'l*, pg. 1271
TOWNSENDS—See Townsends, Inc.; *U.S. Private*, pg. 1094
TOWNSENDS, INC.; *U.S. Private*, pg. 1094
TOY BIZ, INC.; *U.S. Public*, pg. 1625
TOY BIZ, INTERNATIONAL—See Toy Biz, Inc.; *U.S. Public*, pg. 1626
THE TOY FACTORY—See Pride Products, Inc.; *U.S. Private*, pg. 883
TOYMAX INTERNATIONAL INC.; *U.S. Public*, pg. 1626
TOYO ALUMINIUM K.K.—See Alcan Aluminium Limited; *Int'l*, pg. 52
TOYO BOSEKI (EUROPE) GMBH—See Toyobo Co., Ltd.; *Int'l*, pg. 1411
TOYO CORPORATION; *Int'l*, pg. 1410
TOYO ENGINEERING CORP.—See Mitsui & Co., Ltd.; *Int'l*, pg. 878
P.T. TOYO KANETSU INDONESIA—See Nissho Iwai Corporation; *Int'l*, pg. 949
TOYO-MORTON, LTD.—See Morton International, Inc.; *U.S. Public*, pg. 1136
TOYO PETROLITE CO. LTD.—See Baker Hughes Incorporated; *U.S. Public*, pg. 166
TOYO SEIKAN KAISHA, LTD.; *Int'l*, pg. 1411
TOYO SEIKAN KAISHA, LTD. (U.S.A.)—See Toyo Seikan Kaisha, Ltd.; *Int'l*, pg. 1411
TOYO TIRE & RUBBER CO., LTD.; *Int'l*, pg. 1411
TOYO TIRE (U.S.A.) CORPORATION—See Toyo Tire & Rubber Co., Ltd.; *Int'l*, pg. 1411
THE TOYO TRUST AND BANKING COMPANY, LIMITED; *Int'l*, pg. 1411
TOYO TRUST & BANKING (EUROPE) S.A.—See The Toyo Trust and Banking Company, Limited; *Int'l*, pg. 1411
TOYO TRUST & BANKING (SCHWEIZ) AG—See The Toyo Trust and Banking Company, Limited; *Int'l*, pg. 1411
TOYO TRUST ASIA LIMITED—See The Toyo Trust and Banking Company, Limited; *Int'l*, pg. 1411
TOYO TRUST AUSTRALIA LIMITED—See The Toyo Trust and Banking Company, Limited; *Int'l*, pg. 1411
TOYO TRUST BAILLIE GIFFORD LIMITED—See The Toyo Trust and Banking Company, Limited; *Int'l*, pg. 1411

TOYO TRUST COMPANY OF NEW YORK—See The Toyo Trust and Banking Company, Limited; *Int'l*, pg. 1411
TOYO TRUST INTERNATIONAL LIMITED—See The Toyo Trust and Banking Company, Limited; *Int'l*, pg. 1411
TOYOBO AMERICA INC.—See Toyobo Co., Ltd.; *Int'l*, pg. 1411
TOYOBO CO., LTD.; *Int'l*, pg. 1411
TOYOBO HONG KONG—See Toyobo Co., Ltd.; *Int'l*, pg. 1411
TOYOBO NAGOYA—See Toyobo Co., Ltd.; *Int'l*, pg. 1411
TOYOBO TOKYO—See Toyobo Co., Ltd.; *Int'l*, pg. 1411
TOYODA AUTOMATIC LOOM WORKS, LTD.—See Toyota Motor Corporation; *Int'l*, pg. 1412
TOYODA BOSHOFU CORPORATION—See Toyota Motor Corporation; *Int'l*, pg. 1412
TOYODA GOSEI CO. LTD.—See Toyota Motor Corporation; *Int'l*, pg. 1412
TOYODA MACHINE WORKS, LTD.—See Toyota Motor Corporation; *Int'l*, pg. 1412
TOYODA SPINNING & WEAVING CO., LTD.—See Toyota Motor Corporation; *Int'l*, pg. 1412
TOYODA-SULZER MANUFACTURING LTD.—See Sulzer Ltd.; *Int'l*, pg. 1307
TOYODA-SULZER SALES LTD.—See Sulzer Ltd.; *Int'l*, pg. 1307
TOYOTA ARGENTINA S.A.—See Toyota Motor Corporation; *Int'l*, pg. 1413
P.T. TOYOTA-ASTRA MOTOR—See Toyota Motor Corporation; *Int'l*, pg. 1413
TOYOTA AUTO BODY CO., LTD.—See Toyota Motor Corporation; *Int'l*, pg. 1412
TOYOTA AUTO BODY THAILAND CO., LTD.—See Toyota Motor Corporation; *Int'l*, pg. 1414
TOYOTA AUTOPARTS PHILIPPINES INC.—See Toyota Motor Corporation; *Int'l*, pg. 1413
TOYOTA CANADA INC.—See Mitsui & Co., Ltd.; *Int'l*, pg. 882
TOYOTA CANADA INC.—See Toyota Motor Corporation; *Int'l*, pg. 1414
TOYOTA CENTRAL RESEARCH & DEVELOPMENT LABORATORIES, INC.—See Toyota Motor Corporation; *Int'l*, pg. 1412
TOYOTA COROLLA AICHI CO., LTD.—See Toyota Motor Corporation; *Int'l*, pg. 1412
TOYOTA COROLLA AIHO CO., LTD.—See Toyota Motor Corporation; *Int'l*, pg. 1412
TOYOTA COROLLA CHIBA CO., LTD.—See Toyota Motor Corporation; *Int'l*, pg. 1412
TOYOTA COROLLA KANAGAWA CO., LTD.—See Toyota Motor Corporation; *Int'l*, pg. 1412
TOYOTA COROLLA NANKAI CO., LTD.—See Toyota Motor Corporation; *Int'l*, pg. 1412
TOYOTA CREDIT CANADA INC.—See Toyota Motor Corporation; *Int'l*, pg. 1413
TOYOTA DE PUERTO RICO CORP.—See Toyota Motor Corporation; *Int'l*, pg. 1412
TOYOTA DE VENEZUELA C.A.—See Toyota Motor Corporation; *Int'l*, pg. 1413
TOYOTA DEL PERU S.A.—See Toyota Motor Corporation; *Int'l*, pg. 1414
TOYOTA DEUTSCHLAND GMBH—See Toyota Motor Corporation; *Int'l*, pg. 1413
TOYOTA DO BRASIL S.A., INDUSTRIA E COMERCIO—See Toyota Motor Corporation; *Int'l*, pg. 1414
TOYOTA ESPANA, S.L.—See Toyota Motor Corporation; *Int'l*, pg. 1414
TOYOTA ESTONIA LTD.—See Amer Group Ltd.; *Int'l*, pg. 72
TOYOTA FINANCE AUSTRALIA LTD.—See Toyota Motor Corporation; *Int'l*, pg. 1414
TOYOTA FRANCE S.A.—See Toyota Motor Corporation; *Int'l*, pg. 1414
TOYOTA GABELSTAPLER DEUTSCHLAND GMBH—See Toyota Motor Corporation; *Int'l*, pg. 1414
TOYOTA (GREAT BRITAIN) LIMITED—See Toyota Motor Corporation; *Int'l*, pg. 1414
TOYOTA INDUSTRIAL EQUIPMENT EUROPE S.A.R.L.—See Toyota Motor Corporation; *Int'l*, pg. 1414
TOYOTA INDUSTRIAL EQUIPMENT MFG., INC.—See Toyota Motor Corporation; *Int'l*, pg. 1412
TOYOTA INDUSTRIAL EQUIPMENT (UK) LTD.—See Toyota Motor Corporation; *Int'l*, pg. 1414
TOYOTA KREDITBANK GMBH—See Toyota Motor Corporation; *Int'l*, pg. 1414
TOYOTA LEASING GMBH—See Toyota Motor Corporation; *Int'l*, pg. 1414
TOYOTA LEASING (THAILAND) CO., LTD.—See Toyota Motor Corporation; *Int'l*, pg. 1414
TOYOTA LIFT—See Toyota Motor Corporation; *Int'l*, pg. 1412
TOYOTA MOTOR (CHINA) LTD.—See Toyota Motor Corporation; *Int'l*, pg. 1414
TOYOTA MOTOR CORPORATE SERVICES OF NORTH AMERICA—See Toyota Motor Corporation; *Int'l*, pg. 1412
TOYOTA MOTOR CORPORATION; *Int'l*, pg. 1411
TOYOTA MOTOR CORPORATION, ATHENS REPRESENTATIVE OFFICE, C/O KASSIDOPOULOS S.A.—See Toyota Motor Corporation; *Int'l*, pg. 1413
TOYOTA MOTOR CORPORATION, AUSTRALIA LTD. (TMCA)—See Toyota Motor Corporation; *Int'l*, pg. 1414
TOYOTA MOTOR CORPORATION, AUSTRALIA OFFICE—See Toyota Motor Corporation; *Int'l*, pg. 1413
TOYOTA MOTOR CORPORATION, BAHRAIN REPRESENTATIVE OFFICE—See Toyota Motor Corporation; *Int'l*, pg. 1413
TOYOTA MOTOR CORPORATION, BEIJING REPRESENTATIVE OFFICE—See Toyota Motor Corporation; *Int'l*, pg. 1413
TOYOTA MOTOR CORPORATION, BOGOTA REPRESENTATIVE OFFICE—See Toyota Motor Corporation; *Int'l*, pg. 1413

TOYOTA MOTOR CORPORATION, CARACAS REPRESENTATIVE OFFICES—See Toyota Motor Corporation; *Int'l*, pg. 1413
TOYOTA MOTOR CORPORATION, DETROIT BRANCH—See Toyota Motor Corporation; *Int'l*, pg. 1412
TOYOTA MOTOR CORPORATION, DUBAI LIAISON OFFICE—See Toyota Motor Corporation; *Int'l*, pg. 1413
TOYOTA MOTOR CORPORATION, DURBAN REPRESENTATIVE OFFICE—See Toyota Motor Corporation; *Int'l*, pg. 1413
TOYOTA MOTOR CORPORATION, EUROPE OFFICE—See Toyota Motor Corporation; *Int'l*, pg. 1412
TOYOTA MOTOR CORPORATION, GUANGZHOU OFFICE—See Toyota Motor Corporation; *Int'l*, pg. 1413
TOYOTA MOTOR CORPORATION, JEDDAH REPRESENTATIVE OFFICE—See Toyota Motor Corporation; *Int'l*, pg. 1413
TOYOTA MOTOR CORPORATION, JOHANNESBURG REPRESENTATIVE OFFICE—See Toyota Motor Corporation; *Int'l*, pg. 1413
TOYOTA MOTOR CORPORATION, KARACHI LIAISON OFFICE—See Toyota Motor Corporation; *Int'l*, pg. 1413
TOYOTA MOTOR CORPORATION, KOLN REPRESENTATIVE OFFICE—See Toyota Motor Corporation; *Int'l*, pg. 1413
TOYOTA MOTOR CORPORATION, LONDON REPRESENTATIVE OFFICE—See Toyota Motor Corporation; *Int'l*, pg. 1413
TOYOTA MOTOR CORPORATION, NEW DELHI REPRESENTATIVE OFFICE—See Toyota Motor Corporation; *Int'l*, pg. 1413
TOYOTA MOTOR CORPORATION, PANAMA REPRESENTATIVE OFFICE—See Toyota Motor Corporation; *Int'l*, pg. 1413
TOYOTA MOTOR CORPORATION, PARIS BRANCH OFFICE, C/O S.I.D.A.T. TOYOTA FRANCE—See Toyota Motor Corporation; *Int'l*, pg. 1413
TOYOTA MOTOR CORPORATION, PORTO REPRESENTATIVE OFFICE—See Toyota Motor Corporation; *Int'l*, pg. 1413
TOYOTA MOTOR CORPORATION, SINGAPORE REPRESENTATIVE OFFICE—See Toyota Motor Corporation; *Int'l*, pg. 1413
TOYOTA MOTOR CORPORATION, SUPPLIER SUPPORT CENTER—See Toyota Motor Corporation; *Int'l*, pg. 1412
TOYOTA MOTOR CORPORATION, TAIWAN OFFICE—See Toyota Motor Corporation; *Int'l*, pg. 1413
TOYOTA MOTOR CREDIT CORP.—See Toyota Motor Corporation; *Int'l*, pg. 1413
TOYOTA MOTOR CZECH SPOL. SR.O—See Toyota Motor Corporation; *Int'l*, pg. 1413
TOYOTA MOTOR DISTRIBUTORS (IRELAND) LTD.—See Toyota Motor Corporation; *Int'l*, pg. 1413
N.V. TOYOTA MOTOR EUROPE MARKETING & ENGINEERING S.A.—See Toyota Motor Corporation; *Int'l*, pg. 1414
TOYOTA MOTOR FINANCE (NETHERLANDS) B.V.—See Toyota Motor Corporation; *Int'l*, pg. 1414
TOYOTA MOTOR FINANCE (UK) PLC—See Toyota Motor Corporation; *Int'l*, pg. 1414
TOYOTA MOTOR HUNGARY KFT.—See Toyota Motor Corporation; *Int'l*, pg. 1414
TOYOTA MOTOR ITALIA S.P.A.—See Toyota Motor Corporation; *Int'l*, pg. 1414
TOYOTA MOTOR MANAGEMENT SERVICES SINGAPORE PTE. LTD.—See Toyota Motor Corporation; *Int'l*, pg. 1414
TOYOTA MOTOR MANUFACTURING CANADA INC.—See Toyota Motor Corporation; *Int'l*, pg. 1414
TOYOTA MOTOR MANUFACTURING (UK) LTD.—See Toyota Motor Corporation; *Int'l*, pg. 1414
TOYOTA MOTOR MANUFACTURING, U.S.A., INC.—See Toyota Motor Corporation; *Int'l*, pg. 1412
TOYOTA MOTOR PHILIPPINES CORP.—See Toyota Motor Corporation; *Int'l*, pg. 1414
TOYOTA MOTOR POLAND CO., LTD. SP. ZO. O.—See Toyota Motor Corporation; *Int'l*, pg. 1414
TOYOTA MOTOR SALES AUSTRALIA LTD.—See Toyota Motor Corporation; *Int'l*, pg. 1414
TOYOTA MOTOR SALES, U.S.A., INC.—See Toyota Motor Corporation; *Int'l*, pg. 1412
TOYOTA MOTOR SVENSKA AB—See Toyota Motor Corporation; *Int'l*, pg. 1414
TOYOTA MOTOR THAILAND CO., LTD.—See Toyota Motor Corporation; *Int'l*, pg. 1414
TOYOTA MOTORSPORT GMBH—See Toyota Motor Corporation; *Int'l*, pg. 1414
TOYOTA NEW ZEALAND LTD.—See Toyota Motor Corporation; *Int'l*, pg. 1414
TOYOTA NORGE A/S—See Toyota Motor Corporation; *Int'l*, pg. 1414
TOYOTA TECHNICAL CENTER, U.S.A., INC.—See Toyota Motor Corporation; *Int'l*, pg. 1413
TOYOTA TOKYO AUTO CO., LTD.—See Toyota Motor Corporation; *Int'l*, pg. 1412
TOYOTA TOKYO COROLLA CO., LTD.—See Toyota Motor Corporation; *Int'l*, pg. 1412
TOYOTA TSUSHO CORPORATION—See Toyota Motor Corporation; *Int'l*, pg. 1412
TOYOTASA A.S.—See Sabanci Holding A.S.; *Int'l*, pg. 1168
TOYOTASA A.S.—See Toyota Motor Corporation; *Int'l*, pg. 1414
TOYS "R" US (CANADA) LTD.—See Toys "R" Us, Inc.; *U.S. Public*, pg. 1626
TOYS "R" US DEUTSCHLAND GMBH—See Toys "R" Us, Inc.; *U.S. Public*, pg. 1626
TOYS "R" US, INC.; *U.S. Public*, pg. 1626
TOYS "R" US INTERNATIONAL—See Toys "R" Us, Inc.; *U.S. Public*, pg. 1626
TOYS "R" US LIFUNG (HONG KONG) LTD.—See Toys "R" Us, Inc.; *U.S. Public*, pg. 1626
TOYS "R" US-METRO (SINGAPORE) PTE. LTD.—See Toys "R" Us, Inc.; *U.S. Public*, pg. 1626

TOYS "R" US (UK) LTD.—See Toys "R" Us, Inc.; *U.S. Public*, pg. 1626

TOYS "R" US UNITED STATES—See Toys "R" Us, Inc.; *U.S. Public*, pg. 1626

TRACE BELGIUM—See Trace Mountain Products; *U.S. Private*, pg. 1095

TRACE ELLIOT LIMITED—See Kaman Corporation; *U.S. Public*, pg. 942

TRACE INTERNATIONAL HOLDINGS, INC.; *U.S. Private*, pg. 1094

TRACE LABORATORIES CENTRAL—See Methode Electronics Inc.; *U.S. Public*, pg. 1101

TRACE LABORATORIES EAST—See Methode Electronics Inc.; *U.S. Public*, pg. 1101

TRACE MOUNTAIN PRODUCTS; *U.S. Private*, pg. 1095

TRACE OPTICAL LLC—See Cinram Ltd.; *Int'l*, pg. 293

TRACER PRODUCTS—See Spectronics Corporation; *U.S. Private*, pg. 1095

TRACINDA CORPORATION; *U.S. Private*, pg. 1024

TRACK 'N TRAIL; *U.S. Public*, pg. 1626

TRACO AB—See Axel Johnson AB; *Int'l*, pg. 709

TRACOR AEROSPACE ELECTRONICS SYSTEMS, INC.—See Tracor, Inc.; *U.S. Public*, pg. 1627

TRACOR AEROSPACE, INC.—See Tracor, Inc.; *U.S. Public*, pg. 1627

TRACOR ENTERPRISE SOLUTIONS, INC.—See Tracor, Inc.; *U.S. Public*, pg. 1627

TRACOR FLIGHT SYSTEMS, INC.—See Tracor, Inc.; *U.S. Public*, pg. 1627

TRACOR, INC.; *U.S. Public*, pg. 1627

TRACOR INFORMATION SYSTEMS COMPANY—See Tracor, Inc.; *U.S. Public*, pg. 1627

TRACOR INTEGRATED SOLUTIONS—See Tracor, Inc.; *U.S. Public*, pg. 1627

TRACOR SYSTEMS TECHNOLOGIES, INC.—See Tracor, Inc.; *U.S. Public*, pg. 1627

TRACTEBEL; *Int'l*, pg. 1414

TRACTEBEL DEVELOPMENT S.A.—See Tractebel; *Int'l*, pg. 1415

TRACTEBEL ENGINEERING INTERNATIONAL S.A.—See Tractebel; *Int'l*, pg. 1415

TRACTEBEL ENGINEERING LUXEMBOURG S.A.—See Tractebel; *Int'l*, pg. 1416

TRACTEBEL ESPAÑA S.A.—See Tractebel; *Int'l*, pg. 1416

TRACTEBEL FINANCE S.A.—See Tractebel; *Int'l*, pg. 1416

TRACTEBEL INDUSTRIE S.A.—See Tractebel; *Int'l*, pg. 1415

TRACTEBEL INGENIEUR GMBH—See Tractebel; *Int'l*, pg. 1416

TRACTEBEL PACIFIC LTD.—See Tractebel; *Int'l*, pg. 1416

TRACTION DIV.—See UAP, Inc.; *Int'l*, pg. 1426

TRACTOR ENGINEERS LIMITED—See Caterpillar Inc.; *U.S. Public*, pg. 317

TRACTOR MACHINING CO.—See Empire Southwest Co.; *U.S. Private*, pg. 375

TRACTOR SUPPLY CO.; *U.S. Public*, pg. 1627

TRACTORS MACHINERY INTERNATIONAL PTE. LTD.—See Sime Darby Berhad; *Int'l*, pg. 1251

TRACY & AVERY FOOD TOWN—See Seaway Food Town, Inc.; *U.S. Public*, pg. 1453

TRADCOR INTERNATIONAL LIMITED—See International Paper Company; *U.S. Public*, pg. 904

TRADE DIMENSIONS—See VNU Verenigde Nederlandse Uitgeversbedrijven B.V.; *Int'l*, pg. 1447

TRADE PRODUCTS—See Stuart Entertainment Inc.; *U.S. Public*, pg. 1526

TRADE PROMOTION SERVICES LTD.—See EMAP Plc; *Int'l*, pg. 451

TRADE SHOW ENTERPRISES—See I. Spiewak & Sons, Inc.; *U.S. Private*, pg. 1025

TRADE WORLD INDUSTRIAL, LTD.—See Catalina Lighting, Inc.; *U.S. Public*, pg. 314

TRADEARBED S.A.—See Arbed S.A.; *Int'l*, pg. 79

TRADEHOME SHOE STORES, INC.; *U.S. Private*, pg. 1095

TRADEMARK PRESS, INC.—See Harte-Hanks Communications, Inc.; *U.S. Public*, pg. 794

TRADEMARK RESEARCH CORPORATION—See Wolters Kluwer N.V.; *Int'l*, pg. 1513

TRADER JOE'S CO.—See TACT Holding; *U.S. Private*, pg. 1067

TRADER PUBLISHING COMPANY—See Landmark Communications, Inc.; *U.S. Private*, pg. 649

TRADESTAR INVESTMENTS, INC.—See Fiserv, Inc.; *U.S. Public*, pg. 647

TRADEWIND TECHNOLOGIES, INC.—See Justin Industries, Inc.; *U.S. Public*, pg. 937

TRADEWINDS A/S—See The A/S Norges Handels og Sjoefartstidende Group; *Int'l*, pg. 958

TRADEWINDS PTE. LTD.—See Temasek Holdings Pte. Ltd.; *Int'l*, pg. 1374

TRADICION TEXTIL, S.A.; *Int'l*, pg. 1416

TRADINCO INSTRUMENTEN-APPARATEN B.V.—See Halma p.l.c.; *Int'l*, pg. 590

TRADING PORT, INC.; *U.S. Private*, pg. 1095

TRADISCO—See GIB Group; *Int'l*, pg. 534

TRADITIONAL BEER INVESTMENTS—See South African Breweries, Ltd.; *Int'l*, pg. 1287

TRADITIONAL HOME—See Meredith Corporation; *U.S. Public*, pg. 1094

TRAFALGAR GHURKA LTD.; *U.S. Private*, pg. 1095

TRAFALGAR HOUSE CONSTRUCTION INC.—See Kvaerner a.s.a.; *Int'l*, pg. 774

TRAFALGAR HOUSE CONSTRUCTION LTD.—See Kvaerner a.s.a.; *Int'l*, pg. 773

TRAFALGAR HOUSE CORPORATE DEVELOPMENT LTD.—See Kvaerner a.s.a.; *Int'l*, pg. 773

TRAFALGAR HOUSE ENGINEERING—See Kvaerner a.s.a.; *Int'l*, pg. 773

TRAFALGAR HOUSE GROUP SERVICES LTD.—See Kvaerner a.s.a.; *Int'l*, pg. 773

TRAFALGAR HOUSE HOLDINGS INC.—See Kvaerner a.s.a.; *Int'l*, pg. 774

TRAFALGAR HOUSE INC.—See Kvaerner a.s.a.; *Int'l*, pg. 774

TRAFALGAR HOUSE OFFSHORE FABRICATORS LIMITED (PORT CLARENCE)—See Kvaerner a.s.a.; *Int'l*, pg. 773

TRAFALGAR HOUSE OFFSHORE FABRICATORS LIMITED (LINTHORPE DINSDALE)—See Kvaerner a.s.a.; *Int'l*, pg. 773

TRAFALGAR HOUSE OFFSHORE FABRICATORS LIMITED (METHIL WORKS)—See Kvaerner a.s.a.; *Int'l*, pg. 773

TRAFALGAR HOUSE PLC—See Kvaerner a.s.a.; *Int'l*, pg. 772

TRAFALGAR HOUSE PROPERTY, INC.—See Kvaerner a.s.a.; *Int'l*, pg. 774

TRAFALGAR HOUSE PROPERTY LTD.—See Kvaerner a.s.a.; *Int'l*, pg. 773

TRAFALGAR HOUSE TECHNOLOGY LIMITED (KENFIG INDUSTRIAL ESTATE)—See Kvaerner a.s.a.; *Int'l*, pg. 773

TRAFALGAR HOUSE TECHNOLOGY LIMITED (MAPLE CROSS HOUSE)—See Kvaerner a.s.a.; *Int'l*, pg. 774

TRAFALGAR HOUSE TECHNOLOGY LIMTIED (MITCHAM HOUSE)—See Kvaerner a.s.a.; *Int'l*, pg. 774

AS TRAFFIC SERVICE—See Neste Oy; *Int'l*, pg. 915

TRAFFIC WORLD—See Pearson plc; *Int'l*, pg. 1026

TRAFFORD COATED STONE—See RMC Group p.l.c.; *Int'l*, pg. 1080

TRAFFORD PARK BAKERY—See Northern Foods plc; *Int'l*, pg. 968

TRAHAN, BURDEN & CHARLES, INC.—See Trahan, Burden & Charles, Inc.; *U.S. Private*, pg. 1095

TRAHAN, BURDEN & CHARLES, INC.; *U.S. Private*, pg. 1095

TRAHAN, BURDEN & CHARLES, INC., PUBLIC RELATIONS—See Trahan, Burden & Charles, Inc.; *U.S. Private*, pg. 1095

TRAILER WHEEL & FRAME COMPANY; *U.S. Private*, pg. 1095

TRAILERS INTERNATIONAL A/S—See Eldon AB; *Int'l*, pg. 436

TRAIN KOGYO CO., LTD.—See Kosugi Sangyo Co., Ltd.; *Int'l*, pg. 759

TRAINER WORTHAM & COMPANY INCORPORATED; *U.S. Private*, pg. 1095

TRAINING SYSTEMS DIVISION—See Berkshire Hathaway Inc.; *U.S. Public*, pg. 219

TRAK AUTO CORPORATION—See Dart Group Corporation; *U.S. Public*, pg. 484

TRAK MICROWAVE CO. LTD.—See Tech-Sym Corporation; *U.S. Public*, pg. 1563

TRAK MICROWAVE CORP.—See Tech-Sym Corporation; *U.S. Public*, pg. 1563

TRAKTOR-ERSATZTEIL-GESELLSCHAFT MBH—See Fried. Krupp AG; *Int'l*, pg. 511

TRAMCO INC.—See The B.F. Goodrich Company; *U.S. Public*, pg. 752

TRAMMELL CROW COMPANY; *U.S. Public*, pg. 1628

TRAMMELL CROW INTERESTS—See Trammell Crow Company; *U.S. Public*, pg. 1628

TRAMMELL CROW RESIDENTIAL SERVICES; *U.S. Private*, pg. 1095

TRAMMOCHEM DIVISION—See Transammonia Inc.; *U.S. Private*, pg. 1096

TRAMO HOLDING INC.—See Panalpina Welttransport (Holding) AG; *Int'l*, pg. 1023

THE TRANE COMPANY-INTERNATIONAL—See American Standard Inc.; *U.S. Public*, pg. 92

THE TRANE COMPANY NORTH AMERICAN COMMERCIAL GROUP—See American Standard Inc.; *U.S. Public*, pg. 92

THE TRANE COMPANY, UNITARY PRODUCTS GROUP—See American Standard Inc.; *U.S. Public*, pg. 92

TRANS-APPAREL GROUP—See Hartmarx Corporation; *U.S. Public*, pg. 796

TRANS ASIAN INSURANCE SERVICES, INC.—See Cigna Corp.; *U.S. Public*, pg. 366

TRANS AUSTRIA GASLEITUNG GMBH—See ENI S.p.A.; *Int'l*, pg. 429

TRANS CANADA CREDIT CORPORATION—See Norwest Corporation; *U.S. Public*, pg. 1202

TRANS-CONTINENTAL LEAF TOBACCO CO. (CENTRAL AFRICA) (PRIVATE) LTD.—See Standard Commercial Corporation; *U.S. Public*, pg. 1502

TRANS EUROPEAN NATURAL GAS PIPELINE FINANCE COMPANY LIMITED—See Ruhrgas Aktiengesellschaft; *Int'l*, pg. 1149

TRANS FINANCIAL BANK—See Trans Financial, Inc.; *U.S. Public*, pg. 1628

TRANS FINANCIAL BANK, F.S.B.—See Trans Financial, Inc.; *U.S. Public*, pg. 1628

TRANS FINANCIAL BANK, N.A.—See Trans Financial, Inc.; *U.S. Public*, pg. 1628

TRANS FINANCIAL, INC.; *U.S. Public*, pg. 1628

TRANS-GENERAL LIFE & CASUALTY GROUP, INC.—See Highmark Inc.; *U.S. Private*, pg. 529

TRANS-GENERAL LIFE INSURANCE COMPANY—See Highmark Inc.; *U.S. Private*, pg. 529

TRANS-GUARD INDUSTRIES—See E.J. Brooks Company; *U.S. Private*, pg. 172

TRANS-INDIA NETWORK SYSTEMS PVT. LTD.—See Lucent Technologies Inc.; *U.S. Public*, pg. 1019

TRANS LEASING INTERNATIONAL INC.; *U.S. Public*, pg. 1628

TRANS LOUISIANA GAS CO.—See Atmos Energy Corporation; *U.S. Public*, pg. 145

TRANS-LUX CANADA LTD.—See Trans-Lux Corporation; *U.S. Public*, pg. 1629

TRANS-LUX COCTEAU CORPORATION—See Trans-Lux Corporation; *U.S. Public*, pg. 1629

TRANS-LUX CONSULTING CORPORATION—See Trans-Lux Corporation; *U.S. Public*, pg. 1629

TRANS-LUX CORPORATION; *U.S. Public*, pg. 1628

TRANS-LUX CREDIT TERMINAL CORPORATION—See Trans-Lux Corporation; *U.S. Public*, pg. 1629

TRANS-LUX EXPERIENCE CORP.—See Trans-Lux Corporation; *U.S. Public*, pg. 1629

TRANS-LUX INVESTMENT CORPORATION—See Trans-Lux Corporation; *U.S. Public*, pg. 1629

TRANS-LUX LOMA CORPORATION—See Trans-Lux Corporation; *U.S. Public*, pg. 1629

TRANS-LUX MULTIMEDIA CORP.—See Trans-Lux Corporation; *U.S. Public*, pg. 1629

TRANS-LUX PENNSYLVANIA CORPORATION—See Trans-Lux Corporation; *U.S. Public*, pg. 1629

TRANS-LUX PTY. LTD.—See Trans-Lux Corporation; *U.S. Public*, pg. 1629

TRANS-LUX SEAPORT CORPORATION—See Trans-Lux Corporation; *U.S. Public*, pg. 1629

TRANS-LUX SERVICE CORP.—See Trans-Lux Corporation; *U.S. Public*, pg. 1629

TRANS-LUX SIGN CORPORATION—See Trans-Lux Corporation; *U.S. Public*, pg. 1629

TRANS-LUX SYNDICATED PROGRAMS CORP.—See Trans-Lux Corporation; *U.S. Public*, pg. 1629

TRANS-LUX THEATRES CORPORATION—See Trans-Lux Corporation; *U.S. Public*, pg. 1629

TRANS MOUNTAIN ENTERPRISES OF BRITISH COLUMBIA LIMITED—See BC Gas Inc.; *Int'l*, pg. 114

TRANS MOUNTAIN HOLDINGS LTD.—See BC Gas Inc.; *Int'l*, pg. 114

TRANS MOUNTAIN HOUSING LTD.—See BC Gas Inc.; *Int'l*, pg. 114

TRANS MOUNTAIN OIL PIPE LINE CORP.—See BC Gas Inc.; *Int'l*, pg. 114

TRANS MOUNTAIN PETROLEUMS LTD.—See BC Gas Inc.; *Int'l*, pg. 114

TRANS MOUNTAIN PIPELINE COMPANY LTD.—See BC Gas Inc.; *Int'l*, pg. 114

TRANS OCEAN PRODUCTS, INC.—See Maruha Corporation; *Int'l*, pg. 845

TRANS-OHIO PIPELINE CO.—See Duke Energy Corporation; *U.S. Public*, pg. 535

TRANS PACIFIC INSURANCE COMPANY—See The Tokio Marine & Fire Insurance Company, Ltd.; *Int'l*, pg. 1392

TRANS-PACKET SERVICE GMBH & CO. OHG—See Royal Nedlloyd Group N.V.; *Int'l*, pg. 1145

TRANS POLYMER INTERNATIONAL N.V.—See Royal Nedlloyd Group N.V.; *Int'l*, pg. 1145

TRANS QUEBEC & MARITIMES PIPELINE—See Transcanada Pipelines Limited; *Int'l*, pg. 1417

TRANS RESOURCES, INC.; *U.S. Private*, pg. 1096

TRANS-SERVE, INC.—See Kansas City Southern Industries, Inc.; *U.S. Public*, pg. 944

TRANS-TECH, INC.—See Alpha Industries, Inc.; *U.S. Public*, pg. 57

TRANS WORLD AIRLINES, INC.; *U.S. Public*, pg. 1629

TRANS WORLD ENTERTAINMENT CORPORATION; *U.S. Public*, pg. 1629

TRANSACT TECHNOLOGIES INCORPORATED; *U.S. Public*, pg. 1629

TRANSACTION SYSTEMS ARCHITECTS, INC.; *U.S. Public*, pg. 1629

TRANSACTION TECHNOLOGY INC.—See Citicorp; *U.S. Public*, pg. 377

TRANSACTIVE CORPORATION—See GTECH Corporation; *U.S. Public*, pg. 767

TRANSALME SOCIEDADE DE REPRESENTACOES ADMINISTRACAO E ORGANIZACAO LTDA.—See Volkswagen AG; *Int'l*, pg. 1475

TRANSALPINE OELLEITUNG—See Royal Dutch/Shell Group of Companies; *Int'l*, pg. 1138

TRANSALTA CORPORATION; *Int'l*, pg. 1416

TRANSALTA ENERGY CORPORATION—See Transalta Corporation; *Int'l*, pg. 1416

TRANSALTA ENTERPRISES CORPORATION—See Transalta Corporation; *Int'l*, pg. 1416

TRANSALTA FLY ASH LTD.—See Transalta Corporation; *Int'l*, pg. 1416

TRANSALTA UTILITIES—See Transalta Corporation; *Int'l*, pg. 1416

TRANSAMERICA COMMERCIAL FINANCE CORP., INC.—See Transamerica Corporation; *U.S. Public*, pg. 1630

TRANSAMERICA CORPORATION; *U.S. Public*, pg. 1629

TRANSAMERICA FINANCE GROUP, INC.—See Transamerica Corporation; *U.S. Public*, pg. 1630

TRANSAMERICA GLASS, INC.—See TCG International Inc.; *Int'l*, pg. 1336

TRANSAMERICA HOMEFIRST, INC.—See Transamerica Corporation; *U.S. Public*, pg. 1630

TRANSAMERICA INVESTMENT SERVICES, INC.—See Transamerica Corporation; *U.S. Public*, pg. 1630

TRANSAMERICA LEASING INC.—See Transamerica Corporation; *U.S. Public*, pg. 1630

TRANSAMERICA LIFE COMPANIES—See Transamerica Corporation; *U.S. Public*, pg. 1630

TRANSAMERICA LIFE INSURANCE CO.-CANADA—See Transamerica Corporation; *U.S. Public*, pg. 1630

TRANSAMERICA REAL ESTATE INFORMATION COMPANIES—See Transamerica Corporation; *U.S. Public*, pg. 1630

TRANSAMERICA REALTY SERVICES, INC.—See Transamerica Corporation; *U.S. Public*, pg. 1630

TRANSAMERICAN NATURAL GAS CORPORATION; *U.S. Private*, pg. 1096

TRANSAMMONIA AG—See Transammonia Inc.; *U.S. Private*, pg. 1096

TRANSAMMONIA INC.; *U.S. Private*, pg. 1096

TRANSATLANTIC HOLDINGS, INC.—See American International Group, Inc.; *U.S. Public*, pg. 84

TRANSATLANTIC HOLDINGS, INC.—See American International Group, Inc.; *U.S. Public*, pg. 84

TRANSATLANTIC HOLDINGS, INC.-LONDON—See American International Group, Inc.; *U.S. Public*, pg. 85

TRANSATLANTIC HOLDINGS, INC.-TOKYO—See American International Group, Inc.; *U.S. Public*, pg. 85

TRANSATLANTIC HOLDINGS, INC.-TORONTO—See American International Group, Inc.; *U.S. Public*, pg. 85
TRANSATLANTIC REINSURANCE CO.—See American International Group, Inc.; *U.S. Public*, pg. 84
TRANSATLANTIC TRUST CORPORATION—See Northern Trust Corporation; *U.S. Public*, pg. 1197
TRANSAX DATA—See Pearson plc; *Int'l*, pg. 1026
TRANSBANQUE—See Lafarge S.A.; *Int'l*, pg. 790
TRANSBRASIL AIRLINES, INC.—See Transbrasil S.A. Linhas Aereas; *Int'l*, pg. 1416
TRANSBRASIL S.A. LINHAS AEREAS; *Int'l*, pg. 1416
TRANSBULK, INC.—See National Engineering & Contracting Co.; *U.S. Private*, pg. 782
TRANSCANADA ENERGY LTD.—See Transcanada Pipelines Limited; *Int'l*, pg. 1417
TRANSCANADA ENERGY USA INC.—See Transcanada Pipelines Limited; *Int'l*, pg. 1417
TRANSCANADA INTERNATIONAL LTD.—See Transcanada Pipelines Limited; *Int'l*, pg. 1417
TRANSCANADA PIPELINES LIMITED; *Int'l*, pg. 1416
TRANSCAPACITY, L.P.—See Eastern Utilities Associates; *U.S. Public*, pg. 550
TRANSCO INC.; *U.S. Private*, pg. 1096
TRANSCO PRODUCTS INC.—See Transco Inc.; *U.S. Private*, pg. 1096
TRANSCO RAILWAY PRODUCTS INC.—See Transco Inc.; *U.S. Private*, pg. 1096
TRANSCO REALTY INC.—See Transco Inc.; *U.S. Private*, pg. 1097
TRANSCOAST ENVELOPE CO.—See Tension Envelope Corp.; *U.S. Private*, pg. 1077
TRANSCOAT INC.—See Transco Inc.; *U.S. Private*, pg. 1097
TRANSCOMM DIVISION—See Harris Corporation; *U.S. Public*, pg. 792
TRANSCON INSURANCE LTD.—See Ford Motor Company; *U.S. Public*, pg. 667
TRANSCONTINENTAL DIGITAL SERVICES—See G.T.C. Transcontinental Group Ltd.; *Int'l*, pg. 538
TRANSCONTINENTAL GAS PIPE LINE CORP.—See The Williams Companies, Inc.; *U.S. Public*, pg. 1769
TRANSCONTINENTAL PRINTING INC.—See G.T.C. Transcontinental Group Ltd.; *Int'l*, pg. 538
TRANSCONTINENTAL PRINTING INC. - BRAMPTON—See G.T.C. Transcontinental Group Ltd.; *Int'l*, pg. 538
TRANSCONTINENTAL PRINTING INC. - CALGARY—See G.T.C. Transcontinental Group Ltd.; *Int'l*, pg. 538
TRANSCONTINENTAL PRINTING INC. - CORNWALL—See G.T.C. Transcontinental Group Ltd.; *Int'l*, pg. 538
TRANSCONTINENTAL PRINTING INC. - DRUMMONDVILLE—See G.T.C. Transcontinental Group Ltd.; *Int'l*, pg. 538
TRANSCONTINENTAL PRINTING INC. - MONTREAL—See G.T.C. Transcontinental Group Ltd.; *Int'l*, pg. 538
TRANSCONTINENTAL PRINTING INC. - OWEN SOUND—See G.T.C. Transcontinental Group Ltd.; *Int'l*, pg. 538
TRANSCONTINENTAL PRINTING INC. - SAINT-HYACINTHE—See G.T.C. Transcontinental Group Ltd.; *Int'l*, pg. 538
TRANSCONTINENTAL PRINTING INC. - TRANSMAG—See G.T.C. Transcontinental Group Ltd.; *Int'l*, pg. 538
TRANSCONTINENTAL PRINTING INC. - VANCOUVER—See G.T.C. Transcontinental Group Ltd.; *Int'l*, pg. 538
TRANSCONTINENTAL PRINTING INC. - WINNIPEG—See G.T.C. Transcontinental Group Ltd.; *Int'l*, pg. 538
TRANSCONTINENTAL PUBLICATIONS INC.—See G.T.C. Transcontinental Group Ltd.; *Int'l*, pg. 539
TRANSCONTINENTAL REALTY INVESTORS, INC.; *U.S. Public*, pg. 1630
TRANSCONTINENTAL SPORTS PUBLICATIONS—See G.T.C. Transcontinental Group Ltd.; *Int'l*, pg. 539
TRANSCOR S.A.—See Groupe Bruxelles Lambert S.A.; *Int'l*, pg. 562
TRANSCOR WASTE SERVICE, INC.—See Kimmins Corp.; *U.S. Public*, pg. 960
TRANSCORP—See Corrections Corporation of America; *U.S. Public*, pg. 451
TRANSCRYPT INTERNATIONAL; *U.S. Public*, pg. 1630
TRANSDERM LABORATORIES CORPORATION—See Health-Chem Corporation; *U.S. Public*, pg. 802
TRANSDYN CONTROLS, INC.—See Powell Industries, Inc.; *U.S. Public*, pg. 1319
TRANSELASTIC A.G.—See Forbo Holding SA; *Int'l*, pg. 497
TRANSELCO DIV.—See Ferro Corporation; *U.S. Public*, pg. 619
TRANSELECTRIC AB—See Imatran Voima Oy; *Int'l*, pg. 660
TRANSFASHION S.A.—See Royal Nedlloyd Group N.V.; *Int'l*, pg. 1144
TRANSFERTECH, INC.—See Castcraft Industries, Inc.; *U.S. Private*, pg. 219
TRANSFINITION—See G.T.C. Transcontinental Group Ltd.; *Int'l*, pg. 538
TRANSFLEET SERVICES LIMITED—See National Westminster Bank PLC; *Int'l*, pg. 911
TRANSFORMIC ELECTRONICS LIMITED—See Emess PLC; *Int'l*, pg. 453
TRANSFRUIT S.R.L.—See Coeclerici Group; *Int'l*, pg. 304
TRANSGA—See Groupe Bruxelles Lambert S.A.; *Int'l*, pg. 562
TRANSGAS DE OCCIDENTE S.A.—See Transcanada Pipelines Limited; *Int'l*, pg. 1417
TRANSGAS INC.—See Colonial Gas Company; *U.S. Public*, pg. 401
TRANSHELLENIC TOBACCO S.A.—See Standard Commercial Corporation; *U.S. Public*, pg. 1502
TRANSICO INCORPORATED; *U.S. Public*, pg. 1630
TRANSICO INC., EUROPEAN OPERATIONS—See Transico Incorporated; *U.S. Public*, pg. 1631
TRANSICO INC., KEY PAD DIV.—See Transico Incorporated; *U.S. Public*, pg. 1630
TRANSICO INC., MEMBRANE SWITCH OPERATIONS—See Transico Incorporated; *U.S. Public*, pg. 1631

TRANSICO INC., SWITCH DIVISION—See Transico Incorporated; *U.S. Public*, pg. 1631
TRANSICOIL, INC.—See Horizon Aerospace LLC; *U.S. Private*, pg. 538
TRANSIDYNE GENERAL CORPORATION—See Customedix Corporation; *U.S. Public*, pg. 298
TRANSILWRAP COMPANY, INC.; *U.S. Private*, pg. 1097
TRANSILWRAP MANUFACTURING DIVISION—See Transilwrap Company, Inc.; *U.S. Private*, pg. 1097
TRANSINKO B.V.—See Koninklijke BolsWessanen nv; *Int'l*, pg. 751
TRANSINSTRUMENTS—See IMO Industries Inc.; *U.S. Public*, pg. 857
TRANSISTEMAS S.A.—See Newbridge Networks Corporation; *Int'l*, pg. 924
TRANSISTOR DEVICES EUROPE LTD.—See Transistor Devices, Inc.; *U.S. Private*, pg. 1097
TRANSISTOR DEVICES, INC.; *U.S. Private*, pg. 1097
TRANSIT KUHLHAUSGESELLSCHAFT MBH (TKG)—See FMC Corporation; *U.S. Public*, pg. 607
TRANSIT MIX CONCRETE CO.—See Continental Materials Corporation; *U.S. Public*, pg. 441
TRANSITIONS OPTICAL, INC.—See PPG Industries, Inc.; *U.S. Public*, pg. 1245
TRANSKIMYA TICARET VE SANAYE A.S.—See Wella Group; *Int'l*, pg. 1490
TRANSKRIT CORPORATION—See National Fiberstock Corporation; *U.S. Private*, pg. 782
TRANSLOGIC CORP.—See Thyssen AG; *Int'l*, pg. 1387
TRANSMARCO LIMITED; *Int'l*, pg. 1417
TRANSMAST LTD.—See Imatran Voima Oy; *Int'l*, pg. 660
TRANSMECA TRANSMISSOES MECHANICA LDA.—See Mannesmann A.G.; *Int'l*, pg. 835
TRANSMEDIA—See G.T.C. Transcontinental Group Ltd.; *Int'l*, pg. 538
TRANSMEDIA NETWORK INC.; *U.S. Public*, pg. 1631
TRANSMISSION EPARGNE VIE—See AXA-UAP; *Int'l*, pg. 19
TRANSMIX CORPORATION—See Southdown, Inc.; *U.S. Public*, pg. 1489
TRANSMONTAIGNE—See TransMontaigne Oil Company; *U.S. Public*, pg. 1631
TRANSMONTAIGNE OIL COMPANY; *U.S. Public*, pg. 1631
TRANSNATIONAL KORN/FERRY—See Korn/Ferry International; *U.S. Private*, pg. 634
TRANSNATIONAL MOTORS INC.; *U.S. Private*, pg. 1097
TRANSNET CORPORATION; *U.S. Public*, pg. 1631
TRANSNET GROUP—See Transnet Ltd.; *Int'l*, pg. 1418
TRANSNET LTD.; *Int'l*, pg. 1417
TRANSO ENVELOPE CO./GLENDALE—See Tension Envelope Corp.; *U.S. Private*, pg. 1077
TRANSOCEAN DO BRASIL PARTIPACOES S.A.—See Assicurazioni Generali S.p.A.; *Int'l*, pg. 92
TRANSOCEAN HOLDING CORPORATION—See Assicurazioni Generali S.p.A.; *Int'l*, pg. 90
TRANSOCEAN OFFSHORE; *U.S. Public*, pg. 1631
TRANSOK, INC.—See Royal Dutch/Shell Group of Companies; *Int'l*, pg. 1136
TRANSPAC—See France Telecom; *Int'l*, pg. 503
TRANSPLANTATION & INDUSTRIAL PRODUCTS DIV.—See Analog Devices, Inc.; *U.S. Public*, pg. 108
TRANSPLATINUM SERVICE CORP.—See National Commerce Bancorporation; *U.S. Public*, pg. 1155
TRANSPO ELECTRONICS, INC.; *U.S. Private*, pg. 1097
TRANSPOLIS SCHIPHOL DIENSTEN BV—See KPN Koninklyke PTT Nederland NV; *Int'l*, pg. 720
TRANSPORT DEVELOPMENT GROUP PLC; *Int'l*, pg. 1418
TRANSPORT DIVISION—See Tokyu Corporation; *Int'l*, pg. 1395
TRANSPORT FUEL SYSTEMS (N.Z.) LIMITED—See International Paper Company; *U.S. Public*, pg. 905
TRANSPORT GRAPHICOR INC.—See Quebecor; *Int'l*, pg. 1075
TRANSPORT HOLDINGS INC.—See Conseco Inc.; *U.S. Public*, pg. 433
TRANSPORT, INC.—See Danaher Corporation; *U.S. Public*, pg. 482
TRANSPORT INSURANCE CO.—See American Financial Group; *U.S. Public*, pg. 75
TRANSPORT INTERNATIONAL POOL OF CANADA LIMITED—See General Electric Company; *U.S. Public*, pg. 713
TRANSPORT LIFE INSURANCE CO.—See Conseco Inc.; *U.S. Public*, pg. 433
TRANSPORT SYSTEMS GROUP—See ADC Telecommunications, Inc.; *U.S. Public*, pg. 4
TRANSPORT TECHNOLOGY CORP.—See Consorcio G. Grupo Dina, S.A. de C.V.; *Int'l*, pg. 326
TRANSPORT UITGEVERIJ—See Reed Elsevier plc; *Int'l*, pg. 1099
TRANSPORT USA, INC.—See The Coastal Corporation; *U.S. Public*, pg. 389
TRANSPORTACION MARITIMA MEXICANA S.A. DE C.V.; *Int'l*, pg. 1418
TRANSPORTATION CONTROLS SECTOR—See General Signal Corporation; *U.S. Public*, pg. 727
TRANSPORTATION CORP. OF AMERICA—See Duchossois Industries, Inc.; *U.S. Private*, pg. 344
TRANSPORTATION ELECTRONICS DIVISION—See Stoneridge, Inc.; *U.S. Public*, pg. 1045
TRANSPORTATION EQUIPMENT CORPORATION—See PLM International, Inc.; *U.S. Public*, pg. 1241
TRANSPORTATION EQUIPMENT GROUP—See Bombardier Inc.; *Int'l*, pg. 200
TRANSPORTATION EQUIPMENT GROUP-NORTH AMERICA—See Bombardier Inc.; *Int'l*, pg. 200
TRANSPORTATION EQUIPMENT INDEMNITY CO. LTD.—See PLM International, Inc.; *U.S. Public*, pg. 1242
TRANSPORTATION GROUP—See DSP Technology Inc.; *U.S. Public*, pg. 475
TRANSPORTATION MANUFACTURING CORPORATION—See Consorcio G. Grupo Dina, S.A. de C.V.; *Int'l*, pg. 326

TRANSPORTATION MANUFACTURING OPERATIONS, INC.—See Consorcio G. Grupo Dina, S.A. de C.V.; *Int'l*, pg. 326
TRANSPORTATION RECOVERIES INC.—See The Progressive Corporation; *U.S. Public*, pg. 1335
TRANSPORTATION SERVICES DIVISION—See The Sherwin-Williams Company; *U.S. Public*, pg. 1466
TRANSPORTATION TECHNOLOGIES, INC.; *U.S. Private*, pg. 1097
TRANSPORTES AEREOS PORTUGUESES; *Int'l*, pg. 1418
TRANSPORTS BERNIS—See SNCF; *Int'l*, pg. 1165
TRANSPORTS MOULINOIS—See SNCF; *Int'l*, pg. 1165
TRANSPORTS RAPIDES LOZERIENS—See SNCF; *Int'l*, pg. 1165
TRANSPORTS VIROLLE—See SNCF; *Int'l*, pg. 1165
TRANSPRO, INC.; *U.S. Public*, pg. 1631
TRANSQUERCY—See SNCF; *Int'l*, pg. 1165
TRANSROL S.N.C.—See AB SKF; *Int'l*, pg. 1160
TRANSTAR—See Compagnie des Machines Bull; *Int'l*, pg. 316
TRANSTAR HOLDINGS, L.P.; *U.S. Private*, pg. 1097
TRANSTATE PROPERTIES, INC.—See Union Camp Corporation; *U.S. Public*, pg. 1666
TRANSTEC ENVIRONMENTAL INC.—See American Ecology Corporation; *U.S. Public*, pg. 71
TRANSTEC PLC; *Int'l*, pg. 1418
TRANSTECH—See Rautaruukki Oy; *Int'l*, pg. 1088
TRANSTECHNOLOGY CORPORATION; *U.S. Public*, pg. 1632
TRANSTRADE (PTY) LTD.—See Transnet Ltd.; *Int'l*, pg. 1417
TRANSUS INTERMODAL L.L.C.; *U.S. Private*, pg. 1097
TRANSVER AG—See SIG Schweizersiche Industrie-Gesellschaft Holding AG; *Int'l*, pg. 1156
TRANSVET S.A.—See Royal Nedlloyd Group N.V.; *Int'l*, pg. 1144
TRANSWESTERN PIPELINE CO.—See Enron Corp.; *U.S. Public*, pg. 585
TRANSWORLD (AUSTRALIA) PTY. LTD.—See Bertelsmann AG; *Int'l*, pg. 191
TRANSWORLD HOME HEALTHCARE, INC.; *U.S. Public*, pg. 1632
TRANSWORLD INTERWEAVING AG (TIAG); *Int'l*, pg. 1418
TRANSWORLD PUBLISHERS LTD.—See Bertelsmann AG; *Int'l*, pg. 191
TRANSWORLD PUBLISHERS (NZ) LTD.—See Bertelsmann AG; *Int'l*, pg. 191
TRANSWORLD SNOWBOARDING—See The Times Mirror Company; *U.S. Public*, pg. 1617
TRANSWORLD SYSTEMS, INC.—See The Union Corporation; *U.S. Public*, pg. 1667
TRANTER, INC.—See Dover Corporation; *U.S. Public*, pg. 521
THE TRANZONIC COMPANIES; *U.S. Public*, pg. 1632
TRANZONIC INDUSTRIAL TEXTILES DIVISION—See The Tranzonic Companies; *U.S. Public*, pg. 1632
TRANZONIC PERSONAL CARE DIVISION—See The Tranzonic Companies; *U.S. Public*, pg. 1632
TRANZRAIL LIMITED—See Wisconsin Central Transportation Corporation; *U.S. Public*, pg. 1773
TRAPP FAMILY LODGE, INC.; *U.S. Private*, pg. 1098
KURT TRAPP INGENIEURBURO GMBH—See Fried. Krupp AG; *Int'l*, pg. 514
TRAPPEY'S FINE FOODS, INC.—See B&G Foods, Inc.; *U.S. Private*, pg. 105
TRAPPINGS CO.—See I. Spiewak & Sons, Inc.; *U.S. Private*, pg. 1025
TRARYDS METALL AB—See Svedala Industri AB; *Int'l*, pg. 1323
TRARYDS METALL AB—See Trelleborg AB; *Int'l*, pg. 1419
TRASE-MILLER—See MTI Vacations, Inc.; *U.S. Private*, pg. 688
TRASK-RIVER LUMBER CO.—See WTD Industries, Inc.; *U.S. Public*, pg. 1730
TRASYS S.A.—See Tractebel; *Int'l*, pg. 1415
TRATAG AB—See Korsnas AB; *Int'l*, pg. 759
TRATEL—See Ciments Francais; *Int'l*, pg. 292
TRAUB AG; *Int'l*, pg. 1419
TRAUB DREHMASCHINEN GMBH—See Traub AG; *Int'l*, pg. 1419
TRAUB-GLORIA S.R.L.—See Traub AG; *Int'l*, pg. 1419
TRAUB-HECKERT AB—See Traub AG; *Int'l*, pg. 1419
TRAUB-HECKERT AUSTRIA GMBH—See Traub AG; *Int'l*, pg. 1419
TRAUB-HECKERT BENELUX B.V.—See Traub AG; *Int'l*, pg. 1419
TRAUB-HECKERT FRANCE S.A.—See Traub AG; *Int'l*, pg. 1419
TRAUB-HECKERT IBERICA, S.A.—See Traub AG; *Int'l*, pg. 1419
TRAUB-HECKERT ITALIA S.R.L.—See Traub AG; *Int'l*, pg. 1419
TRAUB-HECKERT TECH. CENTRE (S) PTE. LTD.—See Traub AG; *Int'l*, pg. 1419
TRAUB-HECKERT UK LTD.—See Traub AG; *Int'l*, pg. 1419
TRAUB-HECKERT VERTRIEBS GMBH—See Traub AG; *Int'l*, pg. 1419
TRAUB-HERMLE CORPORATION—See Traub AG; *Int'l*, pg. 1419
TRAUBOMATIC IND. E COM. LTDA.—See Traub AG; *Int'l*, pg. 1419
TRAUTH DAIRY INC.; *U.S. Private*, pg. 1098
TRAUTMAN & SHREVE, INC.—See EMCOR Group, Inc.; *U.S. Public*, pg. 572
TRAVARU AB A. MOBERG & CO.—See Scancem AB; *Int'l*, pg. 1199
TRAVARU AB A. THOMEE—See Scancem AB; *Int'l*, pg. 1199
TRAVAUX CONSTRUCTION, INC.—See Forest City Enterprises, Inc.; *U.S. Public*, pg. 670
TRAVEL AGENCY CALAIS—See Stena Line AB; *Int'l*, pg. 1301

MASTER INDEX TO COMPANY NAMES TRIBORO
Company Index

TRAVEL AGENCY DIEPPE—See Stena Line AB; *Int'l*, pg. 1301
TRAVEL AGENCY DUNKIRK—See Stena Line AB; *Int'l*, pg. 1301
TRAVEL AGENCY LILLE—See Stena Line AB; *Int'l*, pg. 1301
TRAVEL AGENCY NORDSTADSTORGET—See Stena Line AB; *Int'l*, pg. 1300
TRAVEL AGENCY PARIS—See Stena Line AB; *Int'l*, pg. 1300
TRAVEL AGENCY STOCKHOLM—See Stena Line AB; *Int'l*, pg. 1300
TRAVEL & LEISURE—See American Express Company; *U.S. Public*, pg. 74
THE TRAVEL CHANNEL—See Landmark Communications, Inc.; *U.S. Private*, pg. 647
TRAVEL CHANNEL-LATIN AMERICA—See Landmark Communications, Inc.; *U.S. Private*, pg. 647
TRAVEL INDUSTRIES AUTOMATED SYSTEMS PTY LIMITED (TIAS)—See Air New Zealand Ltd.; *Int'l*, pg. 38
TRAVEL-NET BV—See KPN Koninklyke PTT Nederland NV; *Int'l*, pg. 720
TRAVEL PORTS OF AMERICA INC.; *U.S. Public*, pg. 1632
TRAVEL PUBLICATIONS, INC.—See The Reader's Digest Association, Inc.; *U.S. Public*, pg. 1368
TRAVEL SHOP ARHUS—See Stena Line AB; *Int'l*, pg. 1301
TRAVEL U.K.—See Landmark Communications, Inc.; *U.S. Private*, pg. 647
THE TRAVELERS ASSET MANAGEMENT INTL. CORP.—See Travelers Group; *U.S. Public*, pg. 1633
TRAVELERS EXPRESS COMPANY, INC.—See Viad Corp; *U.S. Public*, pg. 1718
TRAVELERS GROUP; *U.S. Public*, pg. 1632
THE TRAVELERS LIFE & ANNUITY CO.—See Travelers Group; *U.S. Public*, pg. 1633
THE TRAVELERS LIFE INSURANCE CO.—See Travelers Group; *U.S. Public*, pg. 1633
TRAVELERS PROPERTY CASUALTY CORP.—See Travelers Group; *U.S. Public*, pg. 1633
TRAVELING SOFTWARE INC.; *U.S. Private*, pg. 1098
TRAVELMASTER RECREATIONAL VEHICLES—See Coachmen Industries, Inc.; *U.S. Public*, pg. 388
TRAVELODGE—See Cendant Corporation; *U.S. Public*, pg. 322
TRAVELSTRENGTH LIMITED—See Commonwealth Bank Group; *Int'l*, pg. 313
TRAVIS COUNTY TITLE COMPANY—See Continental Homes Holding Corp.; *U.S. Public*, pg. 441
TRAVISA TRANSFORMADORA DEL VIDRIO S.A.—See Carl-Zeiss-Stiftung; *Int'l*, pg. 1523
TRAX MUSIC VISION LTD.—See TSC Shannock Corporation; *Int'l*, pg. 1343
TRAYCO, INC.—See Masco Corporation; *U.S. Public*, pg. 1054
TRAYCO OF S.C., INC.—See The Dyson-Kissner-Moran Corporation; *U.S. Private*, pg. 352
TRAYER PRODUCTS, INC.; *U.S. Private*, pg. 1098
TRAYLOR BROTHERS, INC.; *U.S. Private*, pg. 1098
TRAYLOR CHEMICAL & SUPPLY CO.; *U.S. Private*, pg. 1098
TREAD RUBBER PLANT—See Bandag, Incorporated; *U.S. Public*, pg. 177
TREADCO, INC.—See Arkansas Best Corporation; *U.S. Public*, pg. 131
TREADWAY CORPORATION—See Sumitomo Corporation; *Int'l*, pg. 1312
TREADWELL CORPORATION; *U.S. Private*, pg. 1098
TREASURE CHEST ADVERTISING—See Big Flower Press Holdings, Inc.; *U.S. Public*, pg. 228
TREASURE CHEST ADVERTISING CO., INC.—See Big Flower Press Holdings, Inc.; *U.S. Public*, pg. 228
TREASURE ISLAND, CORP.—See Mirage Resorts Incorporated; *U.S. Public*, pg. 1117
TREASURE ISLAND FOODMARTS INC.; *U.S. Private*, pg. 1098
TREATED WATER OUTSOURCING—See Nalco Chemical Company; *U.S. Public*, pg. 1150
TREBLA CHEMICAL COMPANY—See CPAC, Inc.; *U.S. Public*, pg. 282
TREBOR BASSETT LTD.—See Cadbury Schweppes p.l.c.; *Int'l*, pg. 248
TREDEGAR FILM PRODUCTS—See Tredegar Industries Inc.; *U.S. Public*, pg. 1634
TREDEGAR INDUSTRIES INC.; *U.S. Public*, pg. 1633
TREDI—See Entreprise Miniere et Chimique; *Int'l*, pg. 459
TREDIT TIRE & WHEEL CO.—See The Cypress Companies; *U.S. Private*, pg. 300
TREE FRESH FOODS CORP.—See Home Juice Co.; *U.S. Private*, pg. 537
TREE OF LIFE, INC.—See Koninklijke BolsWessanen nv; *Int'l*, pg. 752
TREE TOP, INC.; *U.S. Private*, pg. 1098
TREEGROVE MANAGEMENT CORP.—See Reunion Industries, Inc.; *U.S. Public*, pg. 1383
TREESOURCE, INC.—See WTD Industries, Inc.; *U.S. Public*, pg. 1729
J. TREFFILETTI & SONS, INC.; *U.S. Private*, pg. 1099
TREFICABLE PIRELLI S.N.C.—See Pirelli S.p.A.; *Int'l*, pg. 1060
TREFILARBED ARKANSAS INC.—See Arbed S.A.; *Int'l*, pg. 80
TREFILARBED BETTEMBOURG S.A.R.L—See Arbed S.A.; *Int'l*, pg. 80
TREFILARBED BISSEN S.A.R.L—See Arbed S.A.; *Int'l*, pg. 80
TREFILARBED GREMBERGEN S.A.—See Arbed S.A.; *Int'l*, pg. 80
TREFILARBED INC.—See Arbed S.A.; *Int'l*, pg. 79
TREFILARBED KOREA CO. LTD.—See Arbed S.A.; *Int'l*, pg. 80
TREFILARBED LUXEMBOURG/SAARBRUCKEN S.A.R.L.—See Arbed S.A.; *Int'l*, pg. 80
TREFILERIES DE BOURBOURG—See N.V. Bekaert S.A.; *Int'l*, pg. 184
TREFILUNION—See Groupe Usinor; *Int'l*, pg. 571
TREFIMETAUX S.A.—See KM-Europa Metal Aktiengesellschaft; *Int'l*, pg. 720
TREIBACHER CHEMISCHE WERKE AG—See Creditanstalt-Bankverein; *Int'l*, pg. 347
TREIBACHER SCHLEIFMITTEL CORP.; *U.S. Private*, pg. 1099
TREITLER-OWENS, INC.—See Owens-Illinois, Inc.; *U.S. Public*, pg. 1238
TREK BICYCLE CORPORATION—See Trek Corporation; *U.S. Private*, pg. 1099
TREK CORPORATION; *U.S. Private*, pg. 1099
TRELLBORG INDUSTRI AB—See Trelleborg AB; *Int'l*, pg. 1422
TRELLEBORG AB; *Int'l*, pg. 1419
TRELLEBORG ATLAS A/S—See Trelleborg AB; *Int'l*, pg. 1423
TRELLEBORG-BOLIDEN—See Trelleborg AB; *Int'l*, pg. 1423
TRELLEBORG BUILDING & DISTRIBUTION DIV.—See Trelleborg AB; *Int'l*, pg. 1421
TRELLEBORG FABRIEKEN B.V.—See Trelleborg AB; *Int'l*, pg. 1423
TRELLEBORG INC.—See Trelleborg AB; *Int'l*, pg. 1423
TRELLEBORG MINING & METALS DIV.—See Trelleborg AB; *Int'l*, pg. 1422
TRELLEBORG PTY. LTD.—See Trelleborg AB; *Int'l*, pg. 1423
TRELLEBORG RUBBER & PLASTICS DIV.—See Trelleborg AB; *Int'l*, pg. 1422
TRELLEBORG YSH, INC.—See Trelleborg AB; *Int'l*, pg. 1422
TRELLEBORG YSH, INC.-CARMI DIVISION—See Trelleborg AB; *Int'l*, pg. 1422
TRELLEBORG YSH, INC.-CARMI MIXING DIVISION—See Trelleborg AB; *Int'l*, pg. 1422
TRELLEBORG YSH, INC.-SANDUSKY DIVISION—See Trelleborg AB; *Int'l*, pg. 1422
TRELLEBORG YSH, INC.-WESTERN KENTUCKY DIVISION—See Trelleborg AB; *Int'l*, pg. 1422
TRELLEBORGDACK AB—See Trelleborg AB; *Int'l*, pg. 1422
TRELLEX AB—See Svedala Industri AB; *Int'l*, pg. 1324
TRELLEX AB—See Trelleborg AB; *Int'l*, pg. 1423
TREMCO, INC.—See RPM, Inc.; *U.S. Public*, pg. 1358
TREMETRICS, INC.—See Thermo Electron Corporation; *U.S. Public*, pg. 1595
TREMIX AB—See Svedala Industri AB; *Int'l*, pg. 1324
TREMIX AB—See Trelleborg AB; *Int'l*, pg. 1420
TREMONT CORPORATION—See Contran Corporation; *U.S. Private*, pg. 270
TREMONT NAIL CO.—See Maze Nails; *U.S. Private*, pg. 718
TREMPEX AB—See Saint-Gobain; *Int'l*, pg. 1173
TRENCON VUURVAST BV—See Morgan Crucible Co. Plc; *Int'l*, pg. 894
TRENCOR, INC.—See Astec Industries, Inc.; *U.S. Public*, pg. 141
TREND LABORATORIES INC.; *U.S. Public*, pg. 1634
TREND LINE CORPORATION; *U.S. Private*, pg. 1099
TREND-LINES INC.; *U.S. Private*, pg. 1099
TREND MEDIA—See Trend Laboratories Inc.; *U.S. Public*, pg. 1634
TREND OFFSET PRINTING SERVICES; *U.S. Private*, pg. 1099
TRENDMAKER HOMES INC.—See Weyerhaeuser Company; *U.S. Public*, pg. 1764
TRENDWAY CORPORATION; *U.S. Private*, pg. 1099
TRENOVA AS—See Norske Skogindustrier A.S; *Int'l*, pg. 965
TRENTON DIVISION—See Tecumseh Products Company; *U.S. Public*, pg. 1566
TRENTON MILLS—See Dyersburg Corporation; *U.S. Public*, pg. 538
TRENWICK AMERICA REINSURANCE CORPORATION—See Trenwick Group Inc.; *U.S. Public*, pg. 1634
TRENWICK GROUP INC.; *U.S. Public*, pg. 1634
H.O. TRERICE COMPANY; *U.S. Private*, pg. 1099
TRERICE TOSTO COLLIERS INTERNATIONAL; *U.S. Private*, pg. 1099
TRESSA, INC.; *U.S. Private*, pg. 1100
TRETOLITE PTY. LIMITED—See Baker Hughes Incorporated; *U.S. Public*, pg. 166
TRETORN—See Proventus AB; *Int'l*, pg. 1072
TRETORN AB—See Proventus AB; *Int'l*, pg. 1072
TRETORN A/S—See Proventus AB; *Int'l*, pg. 1072
TRETORN FORSALJNINGS AB—See Proventus AB; *Int'l*, pg. 1072
TRETORN GMBH—See Proventus AB; *Int'l*, pg. 1072
TRETORN SPORT LTD.—See Proventus AB; *Int'l*, pg. 1072
TRETORN SPORT SALES LTD.—See Proventus AB; *Int'l*, pg. 1072
TREVIRA—See Hoechst Aktiengesellschaft; *Int'l*, pg. 626
TREX MEDICAL CORPORATION—See Thermo Electron Corporation; *U.S. Public*, pg. 1595
TREXLERTOWN PROPERTIES, INC.—See Air Products and Chemicals, Inc.; *U.S. Public*, pg. 31
TRI-CAN INTERNATIONAL, LTD.—See Lynch Corporation; *U.S. Public*, pg. 1022
TRI-CAN PERFORATORS LIMITED—See Halliburton Company; *U.S. Public*, pg. 777
TRI-CHEM, INC.; *U.S. Private*, pg. 1100
TRI-CITY AUTO AUCTION, INC.—See Tyco International Ltd.; *U.S. Public*, pg. 1649
TRI-CITY BANK AND TRUST COMPANY—See First Virginia Banks, Inc.; *U.S. Public*, pg. 642
TRI-CITY ELECTRICAL CONTRACTORS INC.; *U.S. Private*, pg. 1100
TRI-CITY HERALD—See McClatchy Newspapers Inc.; *U.S. Public*, pg. 1066
TRI-CITY OLDSMOBILE INC.; *U.S. Private*, pg. 1100
TRI-CLOVER CANADA—See Tetra Laval Group; *Int'l*, pg. 1379
TRI-CLOVER INC.—See Tetra Laval Group; *Int'l*, pg. 1379
TRI-CONTINENTAL CORPORATION—See J. & W. Seligman & Co.; *U.S. Private*, pg. 982
TRI DAYTON—See Freudenberg-NOK; *U.S. Private*, pg. 428
TRI-GAS INC.—See Nippon Sanso Corporation; *Int'l*, pg. 939
TRI-GLAS—See Penda Corporation; *U.S. Private*, pg. 848
TRI-K INDUSTRIES, INC.; *U.S. Private*, pg. 1100
TRI-K LANDFILL, INC.—See Republic Industries, Inc.; *U.S. Public*, pg. 1379
TRI-LINE EXPRESSWAYS LTD.—See Russel Metals Inc.; *Int'l*, pg. 1150
TRI-LITE PLASTICS, INC.—See Bunzl PLC; *Int'l*, pg. 233
TRI-LITE PLASTICS SOUTH, INC.—See Bunzl PLC; *Int'l*, pg. 233
TRI-MANAGEMENT CORP.—See Family Inns of America, Inc.; *U.S. Private*, pg. 393
TRI-MANUFACTURING—See General Electric Company; *U.S. Public*, pg. 710
TRI-MARK INC.—See Illinois Tool Works Inc.; *U.S. Public*, pg. 866
TRI-MARK METAL CORP.; *U.S. Private*, pg. 1100
TRI-MASS., INC.—See Tootsie Roll Industries, Inc.; *U.S. Public*, pg. 1621
TRI-PALM ESTATE—See GWP, Inc.; *U.S. Private*, pg. 437
TRI PETCH ISUZU SALES CO., LTD.—See Isuzu Motors Limited; *Int'l*, pg. 693
TRI-REMANUFACTURING—See General Electric Company; *U.S. Public*, pg. 710
TRI-RUSS INTERNATIONAL (HONG KONG) LIMITED—See Russ Berrie and Company, Inc.; *U.S. Public*, pg. 223
TRI-S ENVIRONMENTAL CONSULTING—See ERD Waste Corp.; *U.S. Public*, pg. 546
TRI-S INCORPORATED—See ERD Waste Corp.; *U.S. Public*, pg. 546
TRI-STAR PICTURES, INC.—See Sony Corporation; *Int'l*, pg. 1282
TRI-STATE ARMATURE & ELECTRIC WORKS; *U.S. Private*, pg. 1100
TRI-STATE CONCRETE PRODUCTS CO., INC.—See Marley PLC; *Int'l*, pg. 843
TRI-STATE IMPROVEMENT CO.—See Cinergy Corp.; *U.S. Public*, pg. 369
TRI-STATE INSURANCE COMPANY OF MINNESOTA—See W.R. Berkley Corporation; *U.S. Public*, pg. 215
TRI-STATE LAND COMPANY—See Canadian Pacific Limited; *Int'l*, pg. 259
TRI-STATE MACK INC; *U.S. Private*, pg. 1101
TRI-STATE MOTOR TRANSIT CO.; *U.S. Private*, pg. 1101
TRI STATE STEEL CONSTRUCTION—See National Engineering & Contracting Co.; *U.S. Private*, pg. 782
TRI STATE TANK CORP.—See TSI Holdings, Inc.; *U.S. Private*, pg. 1066
TRI-STATE WHOLESALE ASSOCIATED GROCERS, INC.; *U.S. Private*, pg. 1101
TRI-SURE JAPAN LTD—See Royal Packaging Industries Van Leer B.V.; *Int'l*, pg. 1146
TRI TECH LABORATORIES, INC.; *U.S. Private*, pg. 1101
TRI TOUCH AMERICA—See Montana Power Company; *U.S. Public*, pg. 1127
TRI VALLEY GROWERS; *U.S. Private*, pg. 1101
TRIAD CHEMICAL—See Mississippi Chemical Corporation; *U.S. Public*, pg. 1117
TRIAD INTERNATIONAL MAINTENANCE CORPORATION—See Primark Corporation; *U.S. Public*, pg. 1325
TRIAD NITROGEN, INC.—See Mississippi Chemical Corporation; *U.S. Public*, pg. 1117
TRIAD PERSONNEL SERVICES—See General Employment Enterprises, Inc.; *U.S. Public*, pg. 715
TRIAD SYSTEMS CANADA LTD.—See CCI/Triad Corporation; *U.S. Private*, pg. 193
TRIAD SYSTEMS FINANCIAL CORP.—See CCI/Triad Corporation; *U.S. Private*, pg. 193
TRIANGLE BRASS MANUFACTURING; *U.S. Private*, pg. 1101
TRIANGLE DISTRIBUTING COMPANY; *U.S. Private*, pg. 1101
TRIANGLE ELECTRIC COMPANY; *U.S. Private*, pg. 1102
TRIANGLE FOOD SERVICES CO.; *U.S. Private*, pg. 1102
TRIANGLE GEOPHYSICAL CO.—See Helm Resources Inc.; *U.S. Public*, pg. 808
TRIANGLE LIFE INSURANCE—See First Citizens Banc Shares, Inc.; *U.S. Public*, pg. 629
TRIANGLE MACHINE PRODUCT CO.—See Freeway Corporation; *U.S. Private*, pg. 426
TRIANGLE MARKETING CORP.; *U.S. Private*, pg. 1102
TRIANGLE MINING EQUIPMENT CO. INC.—See FKI Plc; *Int'l*, pg. 473
TRIANGLE PACIFIC CORPORATION; *U.S. Public*, pg. 1634
TRIANGLE ROCKS PRODUCTS, INC.—See CalMat Co.; *U.S. Public*, pg. 296
TRIANGLE SERVICES, INC.; *U.S. Private*, pg. 1102
TRIANGLE SPECIAL PRODUCTS—See Audits & Surveys Worldwide; *U.S. Public*, pg. 147
TRIANGLE TOOL CO.—See Plastek Group; *U.S. Private*, pg. 870
TRIARC BEVERAGE GROUP—See Triarc Companies, Inc.; *U.S. Public*, pg. 1635
TRIARC COMPANIES, INC.; *U.S. Public*, pg. 1634
TRIARCH CORPORATION LTD.—See CoreStates Financial Corp.; *U.S. Public*, pg. 447
TRIAS SA—See Heidemij N.V.; *Int'l*, pg. 608
ETS. TRIAUD GAUVAIN S.A.—See Scapa Group Plc; *Int'l*, pg. 1202
TRIBBLE & STEPHENS CO.; *U.S. Private*, pg. 1102
TRIBONETICS CO.—See LSB Industries, Inc.; *U.S. Public*, pg. 971
TRIBORO ELECTRIC CO.; *U.S. Private*, pg. 1102

TRIBOROUGH DIRECTORY OF CORPORATE AFFILIATIONS

Company Index

TRIBOROUGH BRIDGE & TUNNEL AUTHORITY—See Metropolitan Transportation Authority; *U.S. Private*, pg. 739
THE TRIBUNE—See The Thomson Corporation; *U.S. Public*, pg. 1601
TRIBUNE BROADCASTING COMPANY—See Tribune Company; *U.S. Public*, pg. 1636
TRIBUNE COMPANY; *U.S. Public*, pg. 1635
TRIBUNE DENVER RADIO, INC.—See Tribune Company; *U.S. Public*, pg. 1636
TRIBUNE DESFOSSES—See LVMH Moet Hennessy Louis Vuitton; *Int'l*, pg. 781
TRIBUNE EDUCATION—See Tribune Company; *U.S. Public*, pg. 1636
TRIBUNE ENTERTAINMENT COMPANY—See Tribune Company; *U.S. Public*, pg. 1636
TRIBUNE MEDIA SERVICES, INC.—See Tribune Company; *U.S. Public*, pg. 1636
TRIBUNE PUBLISHING COMPANY—See Tribune Company; *U.S. Public*, pg. 1636
TRIBUNE REGIONAL PROGRAMMING INC.—See Tribune Company; *U.S. Public*, pg. 1636
TRIBUNE REVIEW PUBLISHING CO.; *U.S. Private*, pg. 1102
TRICLINICA INC.—See Lowe McAdams Healthcare; *U.S. Private*, pg. 679
TRICO COMPONENTES, S.A.—See Tomkins PLC; *Int'l*, pg. 1397
TRICO ELECTRIC CO-OP; *U.S. Private*, pg. 1102
TRICO INDUSTRIES, INC.—See Paccar Inc.; *U.S. Public*, pg. 1247
TRICO LTD.—See Tomkins PLC; *Int'l*, pg. 1397
TRICO PRODUCTS CORPORATION—See Tomkins PLC; *Int'l*, pg. 1397
TRICO PTY. LTD.—See Tomkins PLC; *Int'l*, pg. 1397
TRICO TECHNOLOGIES CORPORATION—See Tomkins PLC; *Int'l*, pg. 1397
TRICOM PAPER INTERNATIONAL B.V.—See N.V. Koninklijke KNP BT; *Int'l*, pg. 756
TRICOM SUPPLIES LTD.—See Mannesmann A.G.; *Int'l*, pg. 838
TRICON ELECTROMECHANICAL PLANT—See Tricon Industries, Inc.; *U.S. Private*, pg. 1103
TRICON GLOBAL RESTAURANTS, INC.; *U.S. Public*, pg. 1636
TRICON INDUSTRIES, INC.; *U.S. Private*, pg. 1102
TRICON RESTAURANTS INTERNATIONAL—See Tricon Global Restaurants, Inc.; *U.S. Public*, pg. 1637
TRICOR DIRECT, INC.—See W.H. Brady Co.; *U.S. Public*, pg. 250
TRICORD SYSTEMS, INC.; *U.S. Public*, pg. 1637
TRICOSAL GMBH—See Henkel KGaA; *Int'l*, pg. 610
TRIDATA INC.—See System Planning Corp.; *U.S. Private*, pg. 1061
TRIDEL ENTERPRISES INC.; *Int'l*, pg. 1423
TRIDENT ENTERPRISE LTD.—See Club Mediterranee SA; *Int'l*, pg. 298
TRIDENT FINANCIAL CORPORATION; *U.S. Private*, pg. 1103
TRIDENT MICROSYSTEMS (FAR EAST) LTD.—See Trident Microsystems, Inc.; *U.S. Public*, pg. 1637
TRIDENT MICROSYSTEMS, INC.; *U.S. Public*, pg. 1637
TRIDENT ROWAND GROUP, INC.; *U.S. Private*, pg. 1103
TRIDENT SEAFOOD CORPORATION—See ConAgra, Inc.; *U.S. Public*, pg. 429
TRIDEX CORPORATION; *U.S. Public*, pg. 1637
TRIDEX SYSTEMS LTD.—See CCI/Triad Corporation; *U.S. Private*, pg. 193
TRIDON INC.—See AT&T Corporation; *U.S. Public*, pg. 11
TRIENDA CORPORATION; *U.S. Private*, pg. 1103
TRIESTE E VENEZIA ASSICURAZIONI S.P.A.—See Assicurazioni Generali S.p.A.; *Int'l*, pg. 90
TRIFARI JEWELERS—See The Monet Group, Inc.; *U.S. Private*, pg. 757
TRIFIN B.V.—See Exor Group; *Int'l*, pg. 467
TRIFLOW LTD.—See Delta plc; *Int'l*, pg. 391
TRIGEN ENERGY CORPORATION; *U.S. Public*, pg. 1637
TRIGON ADCOTECH; *U.S. Private*, pg. 1103
TRIGON BLUE CROSS & BLUE SHIELD; *U.S. Public*, pg. 1637
TRIGON INFORMATIK AB—See Celsius AB; *Int'l*, pg. 278
TRIGON PACKAGING CORPORATION—See Sealed Air Corporation; *U.S. Public*, pg. 1451
TRIGON VISKASE PTY. LTD.—See Sealed Air Corporation; *U.S. Public*, pg. 1451
TRIKON TECHNOLOGIES INC.; *U.S. Public*, pg. 1638
TRIKONA SERVICES LTD.—See CODELCO Chile (Corporacion Nacional Del Cobre De Chile); *Int'l*, pg. 303
TRILLIUM DIGITAL DIVISION—See LTX Corporation; *U.S. Public*, pg. 972
TRILOG, INC.—See Cigna Corp.; *U.S. Public*, pg. 362
TRILON FINANCIAL CORP.—See EdperBrascan Corporation; *Int'l*, pg. 434
TRIMAC BULK TRANSPORTATION, INC.—See Trimac Corporation; *Int'l*, pg. 1424
TRIMAC CONSULTING SERVICES—See Trimac Corporation; *Int'l*, pg. 1424
TRIMAC CORPORATION; *Int'l*, pg. 1423
TRIMAC TRANSPORTATION-EASTERN DIVISION—See Trimac Corporation; *Int'l*, pg. 1424
TRIMAC TRANSPORTATION, INC.-EASTERN DIVISION—See Trimac Corporation; *Int'l*, pg. 1424
TRIMAC TRANSPORTATION SERVICES (WESTERN) INC.—See Trimac Corporation; *Int'l*, pg. 1424
TRIMAC TRANSPORTATION SYSTEM—See Trimac Corporation; *Int'l*, pg. 1424
TRIMAC TRANSPORTATION-WESTERN DIVISION—See Trimac Corporation; *Int'l*, pg. 1424
TRIMARK HOLDINGS, INC.; *U.S. Public*, pg. 1638
TRIMARK INTERACTIVE—See Trimark Holdings, Inc.; *U.S. Public*, pg. 1638
TRIMARK PICTURES—See Trimark Holdings, Inc.; *U.S. Public*, pg. 1638
TRIMARK TELEVISION—See Trimark Holdings, Inc.; *U.S. Public*, pg. 1638
TRIMAS CORPORATION—See Masco Corporation; *U.S. Public*, pg. 1054
TRIMBLE BANNER DEMOCRAT—See Landmark Communications, Inc.; *U.S. Private*, pg. 648
WM. S. TRIMBLE COMPANY, INC.; *U.S. Private*, pg. 1103
TRIMBLE NAVIGATION EUROPE LTD.—See Trimble Navigation Limited; *U.S. Public*, pg. 1638
TRIMBLE NAVIGATION INTERNATIONAL FOREIGN SALES CORPORATION—See Trimble Navigation Limited; *U.S. Public*, pg. 1638
TRIMBLE NAVIGATION INTERNATIONAL LIMITED—See Trimble Navigation Limited; *U.S. Public*, pg. 1638
TRIMBLE NAVIGATION JAPAN—See Trimble Navigation Limited; *U.S. Public*, pg. 1638
TRIMBLE NAVIGATION LIMITED; *U.S. Public*, pg. 1638
TRIMBLE NAVIGATION LTD. DEUTSCHLAND—See Trimble Navigation Limited; *U.S. Public*, pg. 1638
TRIMBLE NAVIGATION LTD., TEXAS—See Trimble Navigation Limited; *U.S. Public*, pg. 1638
TRIMBLE NAVIGATION LTD., WASHINGTON, D.C.—See Trimble Navigation Limited; *U.S. Public*, pg. 1638
TRIMEX PTY.—See Clarins; *Int'l*, pg. 296
TRIMFIT COMPANY LIMITED—See Trimfit, Inc.; *U.S. Private*, pg. 1103
TRIMFIT, INC.; *U.S. Private*, pg. 1103
TRIMFOOT COMPANY—See U.S. Industries, Inc.; *U.S. Public*, pg. 1684
TRIMIN ENTERPRISES, INC.; *Int'l*, pg. 1424
TRIMTEX CO. INC.; *U.S. Private*, pg. 1103
TRINC COMPANY—See The Ohio Art Company, Inc.; *U.S. Public*, pg. 1214
TRINE MANUFACTURING CO.—See IMPAXX, Inc.; *U.S. Private*, pg. 558
TRINIDAD BEAN & ELEVATOR CO.—See Trinidad/Benham Corp.; *U.S. Private*, pg. 1103
TRINIDAD/BENHAM CORP.; *U.S. Private*, pg. 1103
TRINIDAD FOOD PRODUCTS LTD.—See Nestle S.A.; *Int'l*, pg. 922
TRINITY CONSTRUCTION PRODUCTS—See Trinity Industries Inc.; *U.S. Public*, pg. 1639
TRINITY DIFCO—See Trinity Industries Inc.; *U.S. Public*, pg. 1639
TRINITY INDUSTRIES INC.; *U.S. Public*, pg. 1638
TRINITY LEASING—See Trinity Industries Inc.; *U.S. Public*, pg. 1639
TRINITY METAL COMPONENTS—See Trinity Industries Inc.; *U.S. Public*, pg. 1639
TRINITY RAILCAR LEASING—See Trinity Industries Inc.; *U.S. Public*, pg. 1639
TRINITY-STRUCTURAL STEEL—See Trinity Industries Inc.; *U.S. Public*, pg. 1639
TRINITY TRANSPORTATION, INC.—See Trinity Industries Inc.; *U.S. Public*, pg. 1639
TRINITY UNIVERSAL INSURANCE CO.—See Unitrin, Inc.; *U.S. Public*, pg. 1694
TRINKAUS & BURKHARDT (INTERNATIONAL) S.A.—See HSBC Holdings plc; *Int'l*, pg. 584
TRINKAUS CAPITAL MANAGEMENT—See HSBC Holdings plc; *Int'l*, pg. 584
TRINKLE SALES, INC.; *U.S. Private*, pg. 1103
TRINKS GMBH—See Nestle S.A.; *Int'l*, pg. 922
TRINOVA AEROQUIP DIV.—See Aeroquip-Vickers, Inc.; *U.S. Public*, pg. 25
TRINOVA DIVISAO VICKERS SYSTEM—See Aeroquip-Vickers, Inc.; *U.S. Public*, pg. 25
TRINOVA DO BRAZIL S.A.-DIVISAO AEROQUIP—See Aeroquip-Vickers, Inc.; *U.S. Public*, pg. 25
TRINOVA GMBH—See Aeroquip-Vickers, Inc.; *U.S. Public*, pg. 25
TRINOVA LIMITED AEROQUIP AUTOMOTIVE OPERATIONS—See Aeroquip-Vickers, Inc.; *U.S. Public*, pg. 25
TRINOVA S.A.-AEROQUIP DIV.—See Aeroquip-Vickers, Inc.; *U.S. Public*, pg. 25
TRINZIC DEVELOPMENT LABORATORY—See Platinum Technology, Inc.; *U.S. Public*, pg. 1309
TRIO-KENWOOD BRETAGNE S.A.—See Kenwood Corporation; *Int'l*, pg. 731
TRIO-KENWOOD ELECTRONICS ENGINEERING (M) SDN. BHD.—See Kenwood Corporation; *Int'l*, pg. 731
TRIO-KENWOOD EUROPE LTD.—See Kenwood Corporation; *Int'l*, pg. 731
TRIO-KENWOOD FRANCE S.A.—See Kenwood Corporation; *Int'l*, pg. 731
TRIO-KENWOOD SINGAPORE (PTE.) LTD.—See Kenwood Corporation; *Int'l*, pg. 731
TRIO-KENWOOD U.K. LIMITED—See Kenwood Corporation; *Int'l*, pg. 731
TRIO LABO CORPORATION—See Kenwood Corporation; *Int'l*, pg. 730
TRIO PRODUCTS INC.—See Ivex Packaging Corporation; *U.S. Public*, pg. 915
TRION, INC.; *U.S. Public*, pg. 1639
TRION LTD.—See Trion, Inc.; *U.S. Public*, pg. 1639
TRIOSOL, S.A.—See Solvay S.A.; *Int'l*, pg. 1279
TRIOVING A.S.—See Assa Abloy AB; *Int'l*, pg. 18
TRIPLE A SPECIALTY COMPANY; *U.S. Private*, pg. 1103
TRIPLE CROWN SERVICES COMPANY—See Conrail, Inc.; *U.S. Public*, pg. 432
TRIPLE CROWN SERVICES, INC.—See Norfolk Southern Corporation; *U.S. Public*, pg. 1192
TRIPLE D SUPPLY CORP.—See Preussag AG; *Int'l*, pg. 1070
TRIPLE F, INC.; *U.S. Private*, pg. 1104
TRIPLE S PLASTICS, INC.; *U.S. Public*, pg. 1639
TRIPLE S PLASTICS, TEXAS CENTRAL—See Triple S Plastics, Inc.; *U.S. Public*, pg. 1640
TRIPLE S PLASTICS TOOLING & TECHNOLOGY CENTRE—See Triple S Plastics, Inc.; *U.S. Public*, pg. 1640
TRIPLEJAY (PTY) LTD.—See FKI Plc; *Int'l*, pg. 474
TRIPLETT CORPORATION; *U.S. Private*, pg. 1104
TRIPLEX SAFETY GLASS LIMITED—See Pilkington Plc; *Int'l*, pg. 1056
TRIPPE MFG. CO.; *U.S. Private*, pg. 1104
TRIPTYCH CD CORP.—See G.T.C. Transcontinental Group Ltd.; *Int'l*, pg. 539
TRISCHLER CONSULT GMBH—See Heidemij N.V.; *Int'l*, pg. 608
TRISCHLER/TRIAS S.A.—See Heidemij N.V.; *Int'l*, pg. 608
TRISCHLER UND PARTNER GMBH—See Heidemij N.V.; *Int'l*, pg. 608
TRISTAR CORP.; *U.S. Public*, pg. 1640
TRISTAR INDUSTRIES LTD.—See J.M. Voith, GmbH; *Int'l*, pg. 1473
TRISTAR PICTURES—See Sony Corporation; *Int'l*, pg. 1283
TRISTAR PICTURES CENTRAL DIVISION—See Sony Corporation; *Int'l*, pg. 1283
TRISTAR PICTURES EASTERN DIVISION—See Sony Corporation; *Int'l*, pg. 1283
TRISTAR PICTURES SOUTHERN DIVISION—See Sony Corporation; *Int'l*, pg. 1283
TRISTAR PICTURES WESTERN DIVISION—See Sony Corporation; *Int'l*, pg. 1283
TRISTAR VENTURES CORPORATION—See Columbia Energy Group; *U.S. Public*, pg. 403
TRISTATE ELECTRICAL SUPPLY CO., INC.; *U.S. Private*, pg. 1104
TRI-STATE LEASING—See Tri-State Mack Inc; *U.S. Private*, pg. 1101
TRI-STATE MACK INC.—See Tri-State Mack Inc; *U.S. Private*, pg. 1101
TRITECH—See Trimin Enterprises, Inc.; *Int'l*, pg. 1424
TRITON ARGENTINA, INC.—See Triton Energy Limited; *U.S. Public*, pg. 1640
TRITON CHINA, INC. LLC-BEIJING—See Triton Energy Limited; *U.S. Public*, pg. 1640
TRITON CHINA, INC. LLC-SHEKOU—See Triton Energy Limited; *U.S. Public*, pg. 1640
TRITON COLUMBIA, INC.—See Triton Energy Limited; *U.S. Public*, pg. 1640
TRITON COMMUNICATIONS—See BDDP Group; *Int'l*, pg. 118
TRITON ECUADOR INC., LLC—See Triton Energy Limited; *U.S. Public*, pg. 1640
TRITON ENERGY LIMITED; *U.S. Public*, pg. 1640
TRITON ENGINEERING SERVICES COMPANY—See Noble Drilling Corporation; *U.S. Public*, pg. 1186
TRITON GUATEMALA—See Triton Energy Limited; *U.S. Public*, pg. 1640
TRITON INDUSTRIES, INC.; *U.S. Private*, pg. 1104
TRITON MANUFACTURING, INC.; *U.S. Private*, pg. 1104
TRITON MEDITERRANEAN OIL & GAS N.V. (ITALY)—See Triton Energy Limited; *U.S. Public*, pg. 1640
TRITON OIL CO. OF THAILAND (BANGKOK)—See Triton Energy Limited; *U.S. Public*, pg. 1640
TRITON OIL COMPANY OF THAILAND (MALAYSIA)—See Triton Energy Limited; *U.S. Public*, pg. 1640
TRITON RESOURCES UK—See Triton Energy Limited; *U.S. Public*, pg. 1640
TRIUMPH ADLER GROUP; *Int'l*, pg. 1424
TRIUMPH ADLER/ROYTYPE (UK) LTD.—See Olivetti SpA; *Int'l*, pg. 1004
TRIUMPH AIR REPAIR—See Triumph Group, Inc.; *U.S. Public*, pg. 1640
TRIUMPH GROUP, INC.; *U.S. Public*, pg. 1640
TRIUMPH INDUSTRIES—See Triumph Group, Inc.; *U.S. Public*, pg. 1641
TRIUMPH INTERNATIONAL—See Triumph International Gruppe Deutschland; *Int'l*, pg. 1424
TRIUMPH INTERNATIONAL GRUPPE DEUTSCHLAND; *Int'l*, pg. 1424
TRIUMPH MACHINE CO.—See Alamo Group, Inc.; *U.S. Public*, pg. 35
TRIUMPH PET INDUSTRIES, INC.; *U.S. Private*, pg. 1104
TRIUMPH RELEASING CORPORATION—See Sony Corporation; *Int'l*, pg. 1282
TRIUMPH RELEASING CORPORATION - CANADIAN TERRITORY—See Sony Corporation; *Int'l*, pg. 1282
TRIUMPH RELEASING CORPORATION - CENTRAL TERRITORY—See Sony Corporation; *Int'l*, pg. 1282
TRIUMPH RELEASING CORPORATION - GREAT LAKES TERRITORY—See Sony Corporation; *Int'l*, pg. 1282
TRIUMPH RELEASING CORPORATION - MID-ATLANTIC TERRITORY—See Sony Corporation; *Int'l*, pg. 1282
TRIUMPH RELEASING CORPORATION - NEW ENGLAND TERRITORY—See Sony Corporation; *Int'l*, pg. 1282
TRIUMPH RELEASING CORPORATION - NEW YORK TERRITORY—See Sony Corporation; *Int'l*, pg. 1282
TRIUMPH RELEASING CORPORATION - PACIFIC TERRITORY—See Sony Corporation; *Int'l*, pg. 1282
TRIUMPH RELEASING CORPORATION - SOUTHEASTERN TERRITORY—See Sony Corporation; *Int'l*, pg. 1282
TRIUMPH RELEASING CORPORATION - SOUTHWESTERN TERRITORY—See Sony Corporation; *Int'l*, pg. 1282
TRIUMPH TWIST DRILL CO.—See Sandvik AB; *Int'l*, pg. 1185
TRIVEST—See Biscayne Apparel Inc.; *U.S. Public*, pg. 233
TRIVEST INSURANCE NETWORK LTD.—See EdperBrascan Corporation; *Int'l*, pg. 435
TRIVOLI SYSTEMS—See International Business Machines Corporation; *U.S. Public*, pg. 896
TRIVOLI SYSTEMS INC.—See International Business Machines Corporation; *U.S. Public*, pg. 896
TRIWASTE REDUCTION SERVICES INC.—See Trimac Corporation; *Int'l*, pg. 1424
TRIWOOD, INC.—See Bassett Furniture Industries, Incorporated; *U.S. Public*, pg. 193
TRIZECHAHN CENTERS INC.—See TrizecHahn Corporation; *Int'l*, pg. 1425
TRIZECHAHN CORPORATION; *Int'l*, pg. 1424
TRIZECHAHN PROPERTIES INC.—See TrizecHahn Corporation; *Int'l*, pg. 1425

TROCADERO PARTICIPATIONS—See Alcatel Alsthom Compagnie Generale D'Electricite; *Int'l*, pg. 54
TRONCALLI MOTORS, INC.; *U.S. Private*, pg. 1104
TRONE ADVERTISING, INC.; *U.S. Private*, pg. 1104
TRONE PUBLIC RELATIONS—See Trone Advertising, Inc.; *U.S. Private*, pg. 1105
TROPAR MFG. CO., INC.; *U.S. Private*, pg. 1105
TROPHY HOLDINGS INC.; *U.S. Private*, pg. 1105
TROPIC COMMUNICATIONS INC.; *U.S. Public*, pg. 1641
TROPICAL SPORTSWEAR INTERNATIONAL; *U.S. Private*, pg. 1105
TROPICANA CASINO & RESORT—See Aztar Corporation; *U.S. Public*, pg. 159
TROPICANA DOLE BEVERAGES NORTH AMERICA—See The Seagram Company Ltd.; *Int'l*, pg. 1217
TROPICANA RESORT & CASINO—See Aztar Corporation; *U.S. Public*, pg. 159
TROPITONE FURNITURE CO. INC.; *U.S. Private*, pg. 1105
TROPONWERK GMBH & CO., KG—See Bayer AG; *Int'l*, pg. 175
TROQUELADOS ESPECIALES S.A. DE C.V.—See ABB Asea Brown Boveri (Holding) Ltd.; *Int'l*, pg. 8
ALBERT TROSTEL & SONS CO.; *U.S. Private*, pg. 1105
ALBERT TROSTEL PACKINGS LTD.—See Albert Trostel & Sons Co.; *U.S. Private*, pg. 1105
TROTTER SOFT PRETZELS, INC.—See J & J Snack Foods Corporation; *U.S. Public*, pg. 916
TROUT-BLUE CHELIAU, INC.; *U.S. Private*, pg. 1105
TROY CORPORATION; *U.S. Private*, pg. 1105
TROY MILLS, INC.; *U.S. Private*, pg. 1106
TROY MOTORS; *U.S. Private*, pg. 1106
TROY OPERATIONS—See Simpson Industries, Inc.; *U.S. Public*, pg. 1475
TROY PUBLISHING COMPANY, INC.—See Journal Register Company; *U.S. Public*, pg. 935
THE TROY SAVINGS BANK; *U.S. Private*, pg. 1106
TROY SAVINGS BANK—See The Troy Savings Bank; *U.S. Private*, pg. 1106
TROY SAVINGS BANK-ALBANY—See The Troy Savings Bank; *U.S. Private*, pg. 1106
TROY SAVINGS BANK-CLIFTON PARK—See The Troy Savings Bank; *U.S. Private*, pg. 1106
TROY SAVINGS BANK-CLIFTON PARK HANNAFORD OFFICE—See The Troy Savings Bank; *U.S. Private*, pg. 1106
TROY SAVINGS BANK-COLONIE—See The Troy Savings Bank; *U.S. Private*, pg. 1106
TROY SAVINGS BANK-EAST GREENBUSH—See The Troy Savings Bank; *U.S. Private*, pg. 1106
TROY SAVINGS BANK-GLENS FALLS—See The Troy Savings Bank; *U.S. Private*, pg. 1106
TROY SAVINGS BANK-GUILDERLAND—See The Troy Savings Bank; *U.S. Private*, pg. 1106
TROY SAVINGS BANK-HUDSON VALLEY PLAZA—See The Troy Savings Bank; *U.S. Private*, pg. 1106
TROY SAVINGS BANK-LATHAM—See The Troy Savings Bank; *U.S. Private*, pg. 1106
TROY SAVINGS BANK-MAIN OFFICE—See The Troy Savings Bank; *U.S. Private*, pg. 1106
TROY SAVINGS BANK-QUAKER ROAD—See The Troy Savings Bank; *U.S. Private*, pg. 1106
TROY SAVINGS BANK-SCHENECTADY—See The Troy Savings Bank; *U.S. Private*, pg. 1106
TROY SAVINGS BANK-WHITEHALL—See The Troy Savings Bank; *U.S. Private*, pg. 1106
TROY SB REAL ESTATE CO., INC.—See The Troy Savings Bank; *U.S. Private*, pg. 1106
TROY TELEPHONE CO., INC.—See Telephone and Data Systems, Inc.; *U.S. Public*, pg. 1572
TROYER FOODS, INC.—See Hillsdown Holdings Plc; *Int'l*, pg. 619
TROYER POTATO PRODUCTS, INC.; *U.S. Private*, pg. 1106
TRU-FIT GLOVE & HEADWEAR DIV.—See Heyman Corporation; *U.S. Private*, pg. 525
TRU-FIT PRODUCTS CORP.; *U.S. Private*, pg. 1107
TRU-FORM—See TI Group plc; *Int'l*, pg. 1338
TRU-LON PRINTED CIRCUITS (ROYSTON) LIMITED—See Spectra-Physics AB; *Int'l*, pg. 1290
TRU-SPACE—See Therma-Tru Corp.; *U.S. Private*, pg. 1080
TRU-STITCH FOOTWEAR DIV.—See Wolverine World Wide, Inc.; *U.S. Public*, pg. 1775
TRU-TEST MFG. CO.—See TruServ Corporation; *U.S. Private*, pg. 1108
TRU-TURN CORPORATION—See Hayes Wheels International, Inc.; *U.S. Private*, pg. 513
TRU-WELD GRATING, INC.; *U.S. Private*, pg. 1107
TRU-WELD LTD—See Tru-Weld Grating, Inc.; *U.S. Private*, pg. 1107
TRUCAST LTD.—See Vickers PLC; *Int'l*, pg. 1467
TRUCCHIS MARKETS; *U.S. Private*, pg. 1107
TRUCK & BUS ENGINEERING CENTER—See Mitsubishi Motors Corporation; *Int'l*, pg. 875
TRUCK CENTER SOUTH—See Tri-State Mack Inc; *U.S. Private*, pg. 1101
TRUCK COMPONENTS INC.—See Johnstown America Industries; *U.S. Public*, pg. 933
TRUCK UNDERWRITERS ASSOCIATION—See B.A.T Industries P.L.C.; *Int'l*, pg. 110
TRUCK WORLD INC.; *U.S. Private*, pg. 1107
TRUE COMPANIES; *U.S. Private*, pg. 1107
TRUE DRILLING CO.—See True Companies; *U.S. Private*, pg. 1107
TRUE GEOTHERMAL ENERGY CO.—See True Companies; *U.S. Private*, pg. 1107
TRUE LIFE; *Int'l*, pg. 1425
TRUE NORTH COMMUNICATIONS INC.; *U.S. Public*, pg. 1641
TRUE NORTH DIVERSIFIED COMPANIES; *U.S. Public*, pg. 1642
TRUE OIL CO.—See True Companies; *U.S. Private*, pg. 1107

TRUE RANCHES—See True Companies; *U.S. Private*, pg. 1107
TRUE TEMPER HARDWARE COMPANY—See Huffy Corporation; *U.S. Public*, pg. 846
TRUE TEMPER SPORTS DIVISION—See The Black & Decker Corporation; *U.S. Public*, pg. 233
TRUE WYOMING BEEF—See True Companies; *U.S. Private*, pg. 1107
TRUELOVE & MACLEAN INC.; *U.S. Private*, pg. 1107
TRUEVISION, INC.; *Int'l*, pg. 1642
TRUEVISION, INC.—See Truevision, Inc.; *U.S. Public*, pg. 1643
TRUGREEN-CHEMLAWN—See The ServiceMaster Company; *U.S. Public*, pg. 1461
TRULINE TREETEX LIMITED—See SAS Holdings Limited; *Int'l*, pg. 1152
TRUMBULL CORPORATION/P.J. DICK, INC.; *U.S. Private*, pg. 1107
TRUMBULL INVESTMENTS, INC.—See Trumbull Corporation/P.J. Dick, Inc.; *U.S. Private*, pg. 1107
THE TRUMP GROUP; *U.S. Private*, pg. 1107
THE TRUMP GROUP—See The Trump Group; *U.S. Private*, pg. 1108
TRUMP ORGANIZATION; *U.S. Private*, pg. 1108
TRUMP PLAZA OF THE PALM BEACHES; *U.S. Private*, pg. 1108
TRUMP TOWERS—See Trump Organization; *U.S. Private*, pg. 1108
TRUMPET BOOK CLUBS—See Scholastic Corporation; *U.S. Public*, pg. 1440
THE TRUMPET CLUB—See Bertelsmann AG; *Int'l*, pg. 191
TRUMPF INC.; *U.S. Private*, pg. 1108
TRUMP'S MARINA CASINO RESORT—See Trump Organization; *U.S. Private*, pg. 1108
TRUNKLINE GAS CO.—See Duke Energy Corporation; *U.S. Public*, pg. 534
TRUNKLINE LNG CO.—See Duke Energy Corporation; *U.S. Public*, pg. 535
TRUS JOIST MACMILLAN—See TJ International, Inc.; *U.S. Public*, pg. 1556
TRUS JOIST MACMILLAN LIMITED—See TJ International, Inc.; *U.S. Public*, pg. 1556
TRUS JOIST (WESTERN) LTD.—See TJ International, Inc.; *U.S. Public*, pg. 1556
TRUSCO CAPITAL MANAGEMENT—See SunTrust Banks, Inc.; *U.S. Public*, pg. 1538
TRUSERV CORPORATION; *U.S. Private*, pg. 1108
TRUSERV LUMBERYARDS/HOME CENTERS—See TruServ Corporation; *U.S. Private*, pg. 1108
THE TRUST COMPANY OF BANK OF MONTREAL—See Bank of Montreal; *Int'l*, pg. 153
TRUST COMPANY OF GEORGIA—See SunTrust Banks, Inc.; *U.S. Public*, pg. 1538
THE TRUST COMPANY OF NEW JERSEY—See The Trustcompany Bancorporation; *U.S. Public*, pg. 1643
TRUST CORPORATION OF CANADA—See Royal Bank of Canada; *Int'l*, pg. 1131
TRUST FUND ADVISORS, INC.—See ULLICO Inc.; *U.S. Private*, pg. 1116
TRUST LIFE INSURANCE COMPANY—See Torchmark Corporation; *U.S. Public*, pg. 1622
TRUSTCO BANK CORP, NY; *U.S. Public*, pg. 1643
TRUSTCO BANK, N.A.—See TrustCo Bank Corp., NY; *U.S. Public*, pg. 1643
THE TRUSTCOMPANY BANCORPORATION; *U.S. Public*, pg. 1643
TRUSTCORP—See D.A. Davidson & Co.; *U.S. Private*, pg. 314
TRUSTCORP MORTGAGE COMPANY—See 1st Source Corporation; *U.S. Public*, pg. 638
TRUSTHOASE FORTE PLC—See Bass PLC; *Int'l*, pg. 170
TRUSTMARK CORPORATION; *U.S. Public*, pg. 1643
TRUSTMARK NATIONAL BANK—See Trustmark Corporation; *U.S. Public*, pg. 1643
TRUTRAC, INC.—See Amano Corporation; *Int'l*, pg. 71
TRYGG-HANSA; *Int'l*, pg. 1425
TRYGG-HANSA INSURANCE CO. LTD.—See Trygg-Hansa; *Int'l*, pg. 1425
TSENG LABS; *U.S. Public*, pg. 1643
P.M. TSERIOTIS LTD.—See BASF AG; *Int'l*, pg. 109
TSUBAKI, INC. - ENGINEERING CHAIN DIV.—See Tsubakimoto Chain Co.; *Int'l*, pg. 1425
TSUBAKIMOTO CHAIN CO.; *Int'l*, pg. 1425
TSUCHIYA MFG. CO., LTD.—See Nissan Motor Co., Ltd.; *Int'l*, pg. 944
TSUDAKOMA CORP.; *Int'l*, pg. 1425
TSUGARU TOSHIBA ONKYO CO., LTD.—See Toshiba Corporation; *Int'l*, pg. 1405
TSUJICHO LTD.—See Suntory Ltd.; *Int'l*, pg. 1321
TSUKUBA PLANT—See Mitsubishi Chemical Corporation; *Int'l*, pg. 871
TSUMURA & CO.; *Int'l*, pg. 1425
TSUMURA INTERNATIONAL—See Tsumura & Co.; *Int'l*, pg. 1426
TSURIYOSHI CO., LTD.—See Shimano Inc.; *Int'l*, pg. 1232
TUBAC VALLEY WATER COMPANY, INC.—See Citizens Utilities Company; *U.S. Public*, pg. 380
TUBAFOR MILL INC.—See E.R. Probyn Ltd.; *Int'l*, pg. 1071
TUBAG TRASS- ZEMENT- UND STEINWERKE GMBH—See Dyckerhoff AG; *Int'l*, pg. 423
TUBE BEND—See Macristy Industries, Inc.; *U.S. Private*, pg. 693
TUBE CITY INC.; *U.S. Private*, pg. 1108
TUBE DIVISION—See Olympic Steel Inc.; *U.S. Public*, pg. 1221
TUBE-FAB LTD.—See HMI Industries; *U.S. Public*, pg. 771
TUBE FITTINGS—See Caparo Group Ltd.; *Int'l*, pg. 265
TUBE FORM, INC.—See HMI Industries; *U.S. Public*, pg. 771
TUBE PRODUCTS—See Senior Engineering Group, plc.; *Int'l*, pg. 1222
TUBE TURNS DE MEXICO, S.A.—See Sunbeam Corporation; *U.S. Public*, pg. 1533

TUBED PRODUCTS, INC.—See McCormick & Company, Incorporated; *U.S. Public*, pg. 1066
TUBETEC—See Plymouth Tube Company; *U.S. Private*, pg. 873
TUBI GHISA SPA—See Saint-Gobain; *Int'l*, pg. 1177
TUBOS DE ACERO DE MEXICO, S.A.; *Int'l*, pg. 1426
TUBOSCOPE INCORPORATED; *U.S. Public*, pg. 1643
TUBOSCOPE VETCO (DEUTCHSLAND)—See Tuboscope Incorporated; *U.S. Public*, pg. 1644
TUBULAR & EQUIPMENT SERVICES, LLC (TES)—See Bovaird Supply Co.; *U.S. Private*, pg. 162
TUBULAR SERVICES, INC.; *U.S. Private*, pg. 1108
TUBULAR STEEL INC.; *U.S. Private*, pg. 1108
TUCCHETTI—See Lettuce Entertain You Enterprises, Inc.; *U.S. Private*, pg. 661
TUCCI BENUCCH—See Lettuce Entertain You Enterprises, Inc.; *U.S. Private*, pg. 661
TUCCI MILAN—See Lettuce Entertain You Enterprises, Inc.; *U.S. Private*, pg. 662
TUCHENHAGEN GMBH; *Int'l*, pg. 1426
TUCHENHAGEN NORTH AMERICA, INC.—See Tuchenhagen GmbH; *Int'l*, pg. 1426
TUCKER FASTENERS LTD.—See The Black & Decker Corporation; *U.S. Public*, pg. 234
TUCKER GMBH—See The Black & Decker Corporation; *U.S. Public*, pg. 234
TUCKER HOUSEWARES—See Mobil Oil Corporation; *U.S. Public*, pg. 1118
TUCKER INDUSTRIES PTY. LTD.—See The Black & Decker Corporation; *U.S. Public*, pg. 235
TUCKER-ROCKY DISTRIBUTING—See LDI, Ltd.; *U.S. Private*, pg. 639
TUCKER ROCKY DISTRIBUTING—See LDI, Ltd.; *U.S. Private*, pg. 639
TUCSON ELECTRIC POWER COMPANY—See UniSource Energy Corporation; *U.S. Public*, pg. 1670
TUCSON LEARNING CENTER—See Berkshire Hathaway Inc.; *U.S. Public*, pg. 219
TUCSON NEWSPAPERS, INC.—See Gannett Company, Inc.; *U.S. Public*, pg. 701
TUCSON REALTY & TRUST CO.; *U.S. Private*, pg. 1109
TUESDAY MORNING CORPORATION; *U.S. Public*, pg. 1644
TUFF STUFF PUBLICATIONS, INC.—See Cadmus Communications Corporation; *U.S. Public*, pg. 291
TUFFY ASSOCIATES CORP.; *U.S. Private*, pg. 1109
TUFIRA S.R.I.—See Georg Fischer Ltd.; *Int'l*, pg. 490
TUFLIN AG—See Emerson Electric Co.; *U.S. Public*, pg. 578
TUFTEX—See Queen Carpet Corporation; *U.S. Private*, pg. 900
TUKKERS MILIEU-ONDERZOEK BV—See Heidemij N.V.; *Int'l*, pg. 607
TULE HUB SERVICES CO.—See Enron Corp.; *U.S. Public*, pg. 585
OY TULENKESTAVAAT TIILIET, A.B.—See RGP Holding, Inc.; *U.S. Private*, pg. 904
TULIP CORPORATION; *U.S. Private*, pg. 1109
J.M. TULL METALS CO., INC.—See Inland Steel Industries, Inc.; *U.S. Public*, pg. 879
TULL METALS DIV.—See Inland Steel Industries, Inc.; *U.S. Public*, pg. 879
TULL METALS PROCESSING DIV.—See Inland Steel Industries, Inc.; *U.S. Public*, pg. 879
TULON CO.—See Esterline Technologies Corporation; *U.S. Public*, pg. 594
TULON DE MEXICO, S.A. DE C.V.—See Esterline Technologies Corporation; *U.S. Public*, pg. 594
THE TULSA CORPORATION—See Cigna Corp.; *U.S. Public*, pg. 359
TULSA MANUFACTURING PLANT—See T.D. Williamson, Inc.; *U.S. Private*, pg. 1180
TULTEX CORPORATION; *U.S. Public*, pg. 1644
TUMWATER LUMBER CO.—See WTD Industries, Inc.; *U.S. Public*, pg. 1730
TUNBORG A/S—See Electrolux, AB; *Int'l*, pg. 443
TUNDRA BOOKS INC.—See McClelland & Stewart; *Int'l*, pg. 851
TUNDRA MESA CONSTRUCTORS—See Arctic Slope Regional Corporation; *U.S. Private*, pg. 80
TUNDRA TOURS, INC.—See Arctic Slope Regional Corporation; *U.S. Private*, pg. 80
P.T. TUNGGAL IDAMAN—See BASF AG; *Int'l*, pg. 109
TUNGSTONE BATTERIES LTD.—See BTR plc; *Int'l*, pg. 124
TUNISIE ELECTRONIQUE SARL—See Hewlett-Packard Company; *U.S. Public*, pg. 823
TUNMORE OLDSMOBILE INC.; *U.S. Private*, pg. 1109
TUNNEL REFINERIES LIMITED—See Tate & Lyle PLC; *Int'l*, pg. 1356
TUNNEL RENTAL CO., LTD.—See Caterpillar Inc.; *U.S. Public*, pg. 317
TUPELO HOME HEALTH, INC.—See Integrated Health Services, Inc.; *U.S. Public*, pg. 885
TUPMAN THURLOW CO. INC.; *U.S. Private*, pg. 1109
TUPPERWARE CORPORATION; *U.S. Public*, pg. 1644
TURBINA SOLAR S.A. DE C.V.—See Caterpillar Inc.; *U.S. Public*, pg. 316
TURBINAS SOLAR DE VENEZUELA—See Caterpillar Inc.; *U.S. Public*, pg. 316
TURBINAS Y EQUIPOS INDUSTRIALES, S.A. DE C.V.—See Sulzer Ltd.; *Int'l*, pg. 1306
TURBINE ENGINE COMPONENTS TEXTRON—See Textron Inc.; *U.S. Public*, pg. 1588
TURBO INDUSTRIES—See Dreison International, Inc.; *U.S. Private*, pg. 342
TURBO-LUFTTECHNIK GMBH—See Deutsche Babcock AG; *Int'l*, pg. 399
TURBO TECHNOLOGIA DE REPARACIONES S.A. DE C.V.—See Caterpillar Inc.; *U.S. Public*, pg. 316
TURBO-UNION LTD.—See Daimler-Benz Aktiengesellschaft; *Int'l*, pg. 367
TURBOMECA ASIA PACIFIC PTE LTD.—See Labinal SA; *Int'l*, pg. 787

Company Index

TURBOMECA AUSTRALASIA PTY LIMITED—See Labinal SA; *Int'l*, pg. 787
TURBOMECA DO BRASIL—See Labinal SA; *Int'l*, pg. 787
TURBOMECA DIVISION—See Labinal SA; *Int'l*, pg. 787
TURBOMECA ENGINE CORPORATION—See Labinal SA; *Int'l*, pg. 787
TURBOMECA GMBH—See Labinal SA; *Int'l*, pg. 787
TURBOMECA LTD.—See Labinal SA; *Int'l*, pg. 787
TURBOMECA MICROTURBO DIVISION—See Labinal SA; *Int'l*, pg. 786
TURBOMECA SUD AMERICANA—See Labinal SA; *Int'l*, pg. 787
TURBOMOTORI INTERNAZIONALE S.P.A.—See Fiat Auto SpA; *Int'l*, pg. 481
TURBONETICS ENERGY, INC.—See Mechanical Technology Inc.; *U.S. Public*, pg. 1077
TURBOSERVICES SDN BHD—See Caterpillar Inc.; *U.S. Public*, pg. 316
TURCO PRODUCTS DIVISION—See Elf Aquitane; *Int'l*, pg. 446
TUREGUM INSURANCE COMPANY—See Zurich Insurance Company; *Int'l*, pg. 1529
TURF PARADISE, INC.—See Hollywood Park, Inc.; *U.S. Public*, pg. 831
TURK & KNEITZ GMBH—See Vorwerk & Co.; *Int'l*, pg. 1480
TURK ELEKTRIK ENDUSTRISI A.S.—See Koc Holding A.S.; *Int'l*, pg. 741
TURK HENKEL A.S.—See Henkel KGaA; *Int'l*, pg. 614
TURK PHILIPS AYDINLATMA SANAYI VE TICARET A.S.—See Philips Electronics N.V.; *Int'l*, pg. 1055
TURK PHILIPS AYDINLATMA SANAYI VE TICARET A.S.—See Sabanci Holding A.S.; *Int'l*, pg. 1168
TURK PHILIPS SANAYI A.S.—See Philips Electronics N.V.; *Int'l*, pg. 1055
TURK PHILIPS SANAYI A.S.—See Sabanci Holding A.S.; *Int'l*, pg. 1168
TURK PHILIPS TICARET A.S.—See Philips Electronics N.V.; *Int'l*, pg. 1055
TURK PHILIPS TICARET A.S.—See Sabanci Holding A.S.; *Int'l*, pg. 1168
TURK PIRELLI LASTIKLER A.S.—See Pirelli S.p.A.; *Int'l*, pg. 1060
TURK SAKURA BANK A.S.—See The Sakura Bank, Limited; *Int'l*, pg. 1180
TURKELI TICARET A.S.—See Schindler Holding AG; *Int'l*, pg. 1205
TURKEY HILL DAIRY, INC.; *U.S. Private*, pg. 1109
TURKKABLO A.O.—See Oy Nokia Ab/Nokia Group; *Int'l*, pg. 954
TURKSE SHELL—See Royal Dutch/Shell Group of Companies; *Int'l*, pg. 1141
TURKU SALES OFFICE & STORAGE DEPOT—See Oy Algol AB; *Int'l*, pg. 15
TURNBULL ENTERPRISES, INC.; *U.S. Private*, pg. 1109
THE TURNER & SEYMOUR MFG. COMPANY; *U.S. Private*, pg. 1109
TURNER BIT SERVICES—See Varel Manufacturing Co.; *U.S. Private*, pg. 1134
TURNER BROADCASTING SALES, INC.—See Time Warner Inc.; *U.S. Public*, pg. 1615
TURNER BROADCASTING SYSTEM INC.—See Time Warner Inc.; *U.S. Public*, pg. 1614
TURNER CARIBE, INC.—See The Turner Corporation; *U.S. Public*, pg. 1646
TURNER/CAS LABORATORIES, INC.—See EMCON; *U.S. Public*, pg. 571
TURNER CONSTRUCTION COMPANY—See The Turner Corporation; *U.S. Public*, pg. 1645
THE TURNER CORPORATION; *U.S. Public*, pg. 1645
TURNER, DAY & WOOLWORTH HANDLE CORP.—See O.P. Link Handle Company; *U.S. Private*, pg. 669
TURNER DEVELOPMENT CORPORATION—See The Turner Corporation; *U.S. Public*, pg. 1646
TURNER ELECTRIC CORPORATION—See Valley Forge Corporation; *U.S. Public*, pg. 1705
TURNER ENTERTAINMENT COMPANY—See Time Warner Inc.; *U.S. Public*, pg. 1615
TURNER FOODS CORPORATION—See FPL Group, Inc.; *U.S. Public*, pg. 608
THE TURNER GROUP—See American Eco Corporation; *Int'l*, pg. 74
TURNER HOLDING LLC; *U.S. Private*, pg. 1109
TURNER HOLDING LLC—See Turner Holding LLC; *U.S. Private*, pg. 1109
TURNER HOME ENTERTAINMENT—See Time Warner Inc.; *U.S. Public*, pg. 1615
TURNER INDUSTRIES; *U.S. Private*, pg. 1109
TURNER INTERNATIONAL INDUSTRIES, INC.—See The Turner Corporation; *U.S. Public*, pg. 1646
TURNER INTERNATIONAL U.K. LTD.—See The Turner Corporation; *U.S. Public*, pg. 1646
TURNER LABORATORIES—See EMCON; *U.S. Public*, pg. 571
TURNER MACHINE COMPANY—See Electric Furnace Co.; *U.S. Private*, pg. 368
TURNER MARKETING, INC.—See Time Warner Inc.; *U.S. Public*, pg. 1615
TURNER MUSIC PUBLISHING, INC.—See Time Warner Inc.; *U.S. Public*, pg. 1615
TURNER NETWORK SALES—See Time Warner Inc.; *U.S. Public*, pg. 1615
TURNER NETWORK SALES, INC.—See Time Warner Inc.; *U.S. Public*, pg. 1615
TURNER NETWORK TELEVISION, INC.—See Time Warner Inc.; *U.S. Public*, pg. 1615
TURNER OMNI VENTURE, INC.—See Time Warner Inc.; *U.S. Public*, pg. 1615
TURNER/ON-SITE—See The Turner Corporation; *U.S. Public*, pg. 1646
TURNER PRIVATE NETWORKS—See Time Warner Inc.; *U.S. Public*, pg. 1614
TURNER PROGRAM SERVICES, INC.—See Time Warner Inc.; *U.S. Public*, pg. 1615

TURNER PUBLISHING, INC.—See Time Warner Inc.; *U.S. Public*, pg. 1615
TURNER RECIPROCAL ADVERTISING CORPORATION—See Time Warner Inc.; *U.S. Public*, pg. 1615
TURNER SOUTH AMERICA—See The Turner Corporation; *U.S. Public*, pg. 1646
TURNER SPORTS, INC.—See Time Warner Inc.; *U.S. Public*, pg. 1615
TURNER STEINER INTERNATIONAL—See The Turner Corporation; *U.S. Public*, pg. 1646
TURNER SUPPLY COMPANY; *U.S. Private*, pg. 1110
TURNING POINT CARE CENTER—See Universal Health Services, Inc.; *U.S. Public*, pg. 1697
TURNKEY TECHNOLOGIES, INC.; *U.S. Private*, pg. 1110
TURNKIEK HOLDING B.V.—See Internatio-Muller N.V.; *Int'l*, pg. 682
TURNTEC—See American Sporting Goods Corporation; *U.S. Private*, pg. 62
TUROVALLES, S.A.—See Vallehermoso, S.A.; *Int'l*, pg. 1447
TURTLE BAY HILTON GOLF & TENNIS RESORT—See Hilton Hotels Corporation; *U.S. Public*, pg. 829
TURTLE & HUGHES, INC.; *U.S. Public*, pg. 1110
TURTLE WAX, INC.; *U.S. Private*, pg. 1110
TURTLE WAX MANUFACTURING LTD.—See Turtle Wax, Inc.; *U.S. Private*, pg. 1110
TURULA WORKS INC.—See Outokumpu Oyj; *Int'l*, pg. 1017
TURUN SAIPPUA OY—See Unilever Plc; *Int'l*, pg. 1438
TURYAG TURKIYE YAG VE MAMULATI A.S.—See Henkel KGaA; *Int'l*, pg. 614
TUSAR, INC.—See Forest City Enterprises, Inc.; *U.S. Public*, pg. 669
THE TUSCALOOSA NEWS—See The New York Times Company; *U.S. Public*, pg. 1175
TUSCALOOSA STEEL CORP.—See British Steel Plc; *Int'l*, pg. 221
TUSCAN/LEHIGH DAIRIES LP; *U.S. Private*, pg. 1110
TUSCARORA GAS PIPELINE CO.—See Sierra Pacific Resources; *U.S. Public*, pg. 1470
TUSCARORA INCORPORATED; *U.S. Public*, pg. 1646
TUSCARORA YARNS INC.; *U.S. Private*, pg. 1110
THE TUSSAUDS GROUP LIMITED—See Pearson plc; *Int'l*, pg. 1026
TUSSENDERLO KERLEY INC.—See Hickson International Plc; *Int'l*, pg. 619
TUSTI S.A. DE C.V.—See Tootsie Roll Industries, Inc.; *U.S. Public*, pg. 1621
TUTA LABORATORIES (AUSTRALIA) PTY., LTD.—See Otsuka Pharmaceutical Co., Ltd.; *Int'l*, pg. 1014
TUTCO—See Smiths Industries plc; *Int'l*, pg. 1268
TUTHILL CORPORATION; *U.S. Private*, pg. 1110
TUTHILL PUMP—See Tuthill Corporation; *U.S. Private*, pg. 1111
TUTHILL PUMP COMPANY OF CALIFORNIA—See Tuthill Corporation; *U.S. Private*, pg. 1111
TUTOR-SALIBA CORPORATION; *U.S. Private*, pg. 1111
TUTTLE-CLICK AUTOMOBILE GROUP; *U.S. Private*, pg. 1111
TV ALABAMA, INC.—See Perpetual Corporation; *U.S. Private*, pg. 854
AB TVATTMAN TEXTIL SERVICE—See Sophus Berendsen A/S; *Int'l*, pg. 1286
TWAYNE PUBLISHERS—See National Amusements, Inc.; *U.S. Private*, pg. 777
TWEDDLE LITHO COMPANY; *U.S. Private*, pg. 1111
TWEEDS, INC.—See Hanover Direct, Inc.; *U.S. Public*, pg. 782
TWELVE ISLANDS SHIPPING COMPANY—See Diageo Plc; *Int'l*, pg. 409
TWENTIETH CENTURY FOX FILM CORP.—See The News Corporation Limited; *Int'l*, pg. 926
20TH CENTURY FOX HOME ENTERTAINMENT—See CBS Corporation; *U.S. Public*, pg. 275
20TH CENTURY INDUSTRIES; *U.S. Public*, pg. 1646
20TH CENTURY INSURANCE CO.—See 20th Century Industries; *U.S. Public*, pg. 1646
20TH CENTURY INSURANCE CO. OF ARIZONA—See American International Group, Inc.; *U.S. Public*, pg. 85
20TH CENTURY INSURANCE CO. OF ARIZONA—See 20th Century Industries; *U.S. Public*, pg. 1646
20TH CENTURY PRODUCTS DIV.—See Avery Dennison Corporation; *U.S. Public*, pg. 153
21ST CENTURY CASUALTY CO.—See 20th Century Industries; *U.S. Public*, pg. 1646
21ST VISION—See Horizon Enterprises Group LLC; *U.S. Private*, pg. 539
TWENTY GRAND OFFSHORE—See Tidewater Inc.; *U.S. Public*, pg. 1608
2929 SERVICE CORPORATION—See Old Guard Insurance Group; *U.S. Public*, pg. 1216
2110 DAVIE CORPORATION—See American Vanguard Corporation; *U.S. Public*, pg. 94
TWIL HANDLING & DISPLAY LTD.—See N.V. Bekaert S.A.; *Int'l*, pg. 184
THE TWIN CITIES TIMES/RIVERDALE FREE PRESS—See Pulitzer Publishing Company; *U.S. Public*, pg. 1343
TWIN CITY DIE CASTINGS CO.; *U.S. Private*, pg. 1111
TWIN CITY DINER—See Lettuce Entertain You Enterprises, Inc.; *U.S. Private*, pg. 662
TWIN CITY FOODS, INC.; *U.S. Private*, pg. 1111
TWIN COUNTY GROCERS, INC.; *U.S. Private*, pg. 1111
TWIN DISC (FAR EAST) LTD.—See Twin Disc, Incorporated; *U.S. Public*, pg. 1646
TWIN DISC, INCORPORATED; *U.S. Public*, pg. 1646
TWIN DISC INTL., S.A.—See Twin Disc, Incorporated; *U.S. Public*, pg. 1646
TWIN DISC ITALIA S.R.L.—See Twin Disc, Incorporated; *U.S. Public*, pg. 1647
TWIN DISC (PACIFIC) PTY. LTD.—See Twin Disc, Incorporated; *U.S. Public*, pg. 1647
TWIN DISC (SOUTH AFRICA) (PTY.) LTD.—See Twin Disc, Incorporated; *U.S. Public*, pg. 1647

TWIN DISC SPAIN, S.A.—See Twin Disc, Incorporated; *U.S. Public*, pg. 1647
TWIN PALMS CARE CENTER—See Meritcare, Inc.; *U.S. Private*, pg. 733
TWIN PINES HEALTHCARE—See Vencor, Inc.; *U.S. Public*, pg. 1715
TWIN RIVERS TEXTILE PRINTING AND FINISHING—See Guilford Mills, Inc.; *U.S. Public*, pg. 769
TWIN RIVERS TOWING CO.—See Du Pont (E.I. Du Pont De Nemours & Co.); *U.S. Public*, pg. 531
TWINCO GRAPHICS—See Twin County Grocers, Inc.; *U.S. Private*, pg. 1111
TWINCO SERVICES, INC.—See Twin County Grocers, Inc.; *U.S. Private*, pg. 1111
TWINCO TRUCKING CO., INC.—See Twin County Grocers, Inc.; *U.S. Private*, pg. 1111
TWINCRAFT, INC.; *U.S. Private*, pg. 1111
TWINE & CORDAGE MFG. CO. (PVT) LIMITED—See TT Group PLC; *Int'l*, pg. 1345
R. TWINING & CO., LTD. (UK)—See Associated British Foods plc; *Int'l*, pg. 92
TWINLOCK (IRELAND) EXPORT LIMITED—See Fortune Brands, Inc.; *U.S. Public*, pg. 675
TWINLOCK PLC—See Fortune Brands, Inc.; *U.S. Public*, pg. 675
TWINNER S.A.—See Assicurazioni Generali S.p.A.; *Int'l*, pg. 92
TWINPAK INC.—See Amcor Limited; *Int'l*, pg. 72
2AI SOCIETE NOUVELLE AUTOMATISME ET AVENIR INFORMATIQUE—See Compagnie des Machines Bull; *Int'l*, pg. 316
255 CALIFORNIA CORPORATION—See Fremont General Corporation; *U.S. Public*, pg. 681
2MA CENTRE S.A.R.L.—See Forbo Holding SA; *Int'l*, pg. 498
2-MILE COMPANY—See GATX Corporation; *U.S. Public*, pg. 692
TWO RIVERS PSYCHIATRIC HOSPITAL—See Universal Health Services, Inc.; *U.S. Public*, pg. 1697
II-VI INCORPORATED; *U.S. Public*, pg. 1647
TYBOR, S.A.—See Guilford Mills, Inc.; *U.S. Public*, pg. 769
TYCO—See Mattel, Inc.; *U.S. Public*, pg. 1058
TYCO ACQUISITIONS—See Mattel, Inc.; *U.S. Public*, pg. 1058
TYCO BACKPLANES—See Tyco International Ltd.; *U.S. Public*, pg. 1648
TYCO CANADA LTD.—See Mattel, Inc.; *U.S. Public*, pg. 1059
TYCO ENGINEERED SYSTEMS—See Tyco International Ltd.; *U.S. Public*, pg. 1648
TYCO GRINNELL ASIA PACIFIC (THAILAND) LIMITED—See Tyco International Ltd.; *U.S. Public*, pg. 1651
TYCO GRINNELL AUSTRALIA PTY LTD.—See Tyco International Ltd.; *U.S. Public*, pg. 1651
TYCO HOLDINGS CORPORATION—See Mattel, Inc.; *U.S. Public*, pg. 1058
TYCO (HONG KONG) LTD.—See Mattel, Inc.; *U.S. Public*, pg. 1059
TYCO INDUSTRIES, INC.—See Mattel, Inc.; *U.S. Public*, pg. 1059
TYCO INTERNATIONAL LTD.; *U.S. Public*, pg. 1647
TYCO INTERNATIONAL LTD.—See Tyco International Ltd.; *U.S. Public*, pg. 1648
TYCO INTERNATIONAL PTY LTD.—See Tyco International Ltd.; *U.S. Public*, pg. 1651
TYCO INVESTMENT CORP.—See Mattel, Inc.; *U.S. Public*, pg. 1058
TYCO INVESTMENTS (AUSTRALIA) LIMITED—See Tyco International Ltd.; *U.S. Public*, pg. 1651
TYCO LABORATORIES ASIA PACIFIC (S) PTE LTD.—See Tyco International Ltd.; *U.S. Public*, pg. 1651
TYCO PLAYTIME INC.—See Mattel, Inc.; *U.S. Public*, pg. 1058
TYCO PRESCHOOL—See Mattel, Inc.; *U.S. Public*, pg. 1058
TYCO PRINTED CIRCUIT GROUP—See Tyco International Ltd.; *U.S. Public*, pg. 1648
TYCO TOYS (BELGIUM) N.V.—See Mattel, Inc.; *U.S. Public*, pg. 1059
TYCO TOYS (BENELUX) N.V.—See Mattel, Inc.; *U.S. Public*, pg. 1059
TYCO TOYS (DEUTSCHLAND) GMBH—See Mattel, Inc.; *U.S. Public*, pg. 1059
TYCO TOYS ESPANA—See Mattel, Inc.; *U.S. Public*, pg. 1059
TYCO TOYS (FRANCE) S.A.—See Mattel, Inc.; *U.S. Public*, pg. 1059
TYCO TOYS, INC.—See Mattel, Inc.; *U.S. Public*, pg. 1058
TYCO TOYS (ITALY) S.P.A.—See Mattel, Inc.; *U.S. Public*, pg. 1059
TYCO TOYS (OSTERREICH) GES.M.B.H.—See Mattel, Inc.; *U.S. Public*, pg. 1059
TYCO TOYS (SCHWEIZ/SUISSE) AG/SA—See Mattel, Inc.; *U.S. Public*, pg. 1059
TYCO TOYS (UK) LTD.—See Mattel, Inc.; *U.S. Public*, pg. 1059
TYCO VALVES LIMITED—See Tyco International Ltd.; *U.S. Public*, pg. 1651
TYGAFLOR LTD.—See Chemfab Corporation; *U.S. Public*, pg. 344
TYLAN GMBH—See Millipore Corporation; *U.S. Public*, pg. 1113
TYLAN SARL—See Millipore Corporation; *U.S. Public*, pg. 1113
TYLAN (UK) LTD.—See Millipore Corporation; *U.S. Public*, pg. 1113
TYLER BANK & TRUST—See First Commercial Corporation; *U.S. Public*, pg. 630
TYLER BERLIN GMBH—See Franz Haniel & Cie, GmbH; *Int'l*, pg. 592
TYLER CORPORATION; *U.S. Public*, pg. 1651
TYLER ELEVATOR PRODUCTS, INC.; *U.S. Private*, pg. 1112
TYLER INDUSTRIES; *U.S. Private*, pg. 1112

TYLER MALL ASSOCIATES—See Cigna Corp.; *U.S. Public*, pg. 362
TYNDALE HOUSE PUBLISHERS, INC.; *U.S. Private*, pg. 1112
TYPE FILMS OF CHICAGO CO.—See Castcraft Industries, Inc.; *U.S. Private*, pg. 219
TYPE FOUNDERS OF CHICAGO—See Castcraft Industries, Inc.; *U.S. Private*, pg. 219
TYPO-GRAPHICS, INC.—See Devon Group, Inc.; *U.S. Public*, pg. 503
TYRI A/S—See Duni AB; *Int'l*, pg. 421
TYSON EXPORT SALES, INC.—See Tyson Foods, Inc.; *U.S. Public*, pg. 1652
TYSON FOODS, INC.—See Tyson Foods, Inc.; *U.S. Public*, pg. 1652
TYSON FOODS, INC.; *U.S. Public*, pg. 1652
TYSON FOODS OF TEXAS, INC.—See Tyson Foods, Inc.; *U.S. Public*, pg. 1652
TYSON'S CORNER HOTEL ASSOCIATES—See Cigna Corp.; *U.S. Public*, pg. 362
TYTON CORPORATION—See Bowthorpe plc; *Int'l*, pg. 208
TYTON HELLERMANN ASIA PACIFIC LTD.—See Bowthorpe plc; *Int'l*, pg. 209
TYTON HELLERMANN CANADA INCORPORATED—See Bowthorpe plc; *Int'l*, pg. 209
TYTON HELLERMANN DO BRASIL INDUSTRIA E COMERCIO LTDA.—See Bowthorpe plc; *Int'l*, pg. 209

U

U-HAUL INTERNATIONAL, INC.—See Amerco; *U.S. Private*, pg. 49
U-HAUL LEASING & SALES COMPANY—See Amerco; *U.S. Private*, pg. 49
U TWO CORPORATION—See UniFirst Corporation; *U.S. Public*, pg. 1665
UAB—See Groupe Bruxelles Lambert S.A.; *Int'l*, pg. 562
U.A.C. HOLDINGS LTD.—See Unilever Plc; *Int'l*, pg. 1434
UAC INTERNATIONAL LTD.—See Unilever Plc; *Int'l*, pg. 1434
UAC OF GHANA LTD.—See Unilever Plc; *Int'l*, pg. 1438
UAC OF SIERRA LEONE LTD.—See Unilever Plc; *Int'l*, pg. 1438
UAC OF TANZANIA LTD.—See Unilever Plc; *Int'l*, pg. 1438
U.A.C.-TOGO S.A.—See Gamma Holding N.V.; *Int'l*, pg. 540
UAD LABORATORIES—See Forest Laboratories, Inc.; *U.S. Public*, pg. 670
UAL CORPORATION; *U.S. Public*, pg. 1652
UAM FUND SERVICES INC.—See United Asset Management Corporation; *U.S. Public*, pg. 1674
UAM INVESTMENT SERVICES, INC.—See United Asset Management Corporation; *U.S. Public*, pg. 1674
UAM RETIREMENT PLAN SERVICES, INC.—See United Asset Management Corporation; *U.S. Public*, pg. 1674
UAP, INC.; *Int'l*, pg. 1426
UAP-NIEUWROTTERDAM LEVEN—See Groupe Bruxelles Lambert S.A.; *Int'l*, pg. 562
UAP-NIEUWROTTERDAM SCHADE—See Groupe Bruxelles Lambert S.A.; *Int'l*, pg. 562
UAP-NIEUWROTTERDAM ZORG—See Groupe Bruxelles Lambert S.A.; *Int'l*, pg. 562
UB FOODS U.S., INC.—See United Biscuits (Holdings) Plc; *Int'l*, pg. 1442
UB FROZEN & CHILLED LIMITED—See United Biscuits (Holdings) Plc; *Int'l*, pg. 1442
UB NETWORKS—See Newbridge Networks Corporation; *Int'l*, pg. 924
UBCI (TUNISIA)—See Banque Nationale de Paris; *Int'l*, pg. 163
UBE INDUSTRIES (AMERICA) INC.—See UBE Industries Ltd.; *Int'l*, pg. 1427
UBE INDUSTRIES LTD.; *Int'l*, pg. 1426
UBE INDUSTRIES LTD.-KYUSHU—See UBE Industries Ltd.; *Int'l*, pg. 1426
UBO LEVENSVERZEKERINGEN N.V.—See AEGON N.V.; *Int'l*, pg. 26
UBO SCHADEVERZEKERINGEN N.V.—See AEGON N.V.; *Int'l*, pg. 26
UBO VERZEKERINGEN—See AEGON N.V.; *Int'l*, pg. 26
U.B.R.—See Groupe GAN; *Int'l*, pg. 565
UBS ASSET MANAGEMENT LONDON LTD.—See Union Bank of Switzerland; *Int'l*, pg. 1440
UBS ASSET MANAGEMENT (NEW YORK) INC.—See Union Bank of Switzerland; *Int'l*, pg. 1440
UBS ASSET MANAGEMENT (UK) LTD.—See Union Bank of Switzerland; *Int'l*, pg. 1440
UBS AUSTRALIA LTD.—See Union Bank of Switzerland; *Int'l*, pg. 1440
UBS (EAST ASIA) LTD.—See Union Bank of Switzerland; *Int'l*, pg. 1440
UBS ITALIA INVESTIMENTI E FINANZA SPA—See Union Bank of Switzerland; *Int'l*, pg. 1440
UBS JERSEY—See Union Bank of Switzerland; *Int'l*, pg. 1440
UBS LEASING—See Union Bank of Switzerland; *Int'l*, pg. 1440
UBS LEASING AG—See Union Bank of Switzerland; *Int'l*, pg. 1440
UBS LIMITED—See Union Bank of Switzerland; *Int'l*, pg. 1440
UBS PHILLIPS & DREW INTERNATIONAL INVESTMENT LTD.—See Union Bank of Switzerland; *Int'l*, pg. 1440
UBS PHILLIPS & DREW INTL. LTD.—See Union Bank of Switzerland; *Int'l*, pg. 1440
UBS REPRESENTATIVE OFFICE—See Union Bank of Switzerland; *Int'l*, pg. 1440
UBS REPRESENTATIVE OFFICE—See Union Bank of Switzerland; *Int'l*, pg. 1441
UBS REPRESENTATIVE OFFICE—See Union Bank of Switzerland; *Int'l*, pg. 1441
UBS RESEARCH (MALAYSIA) SDN BHD—See Union Bank of Switzerland; *Int'l*, pg. 1440

UBS SECURITIES BRANCH OFFICE—See Union Bank of Switzerland; *Int'l*, pg. 1440
UBS SECURITIES (EAST ASIA) LIMITED REPRESENTATIVE OFFICE—See Union Bank of Switzerland; *Int'l*, pg. 1440
UBS SECURITIES (HONG KONG) LTD.—See Union Bank of Switzerland; *Int'l*, pg. 1440
UBS SECURITIES LLC—See Union Bank of Switzerland; *Int'l*, pg. 1440
UBS SECURITIES LTD.—See Union Bank of Switzerland; *Int'l*, pg. 1441
UBS SECURITIES (SINGAPORE) PTE. LTD.—See Union Bank of Switzerland; *Int'l*, pg. 1441
UBS SWISS LIFE LTD.—See Union Bank of Switzerland; *Int'l*, pg. 1441
UBS TRUST & BANKING LTD.—See Union Bank of Switzerland; *Int'l*, pg. 1441
UC INDUSTRIES, INC.—See Owens Corning; *U.S. Public*, pg. 1237
U.C. MOVING SERVICES, INC.—See Global Van Lines, Inc.; *U.S. Private*, pg. 458
UCAMAR SHIPPING & TRANSPORTATION CO.—See Halliburton Company; *U.S. Public*, pg. 777
UCAR PIPELINE, INC.—See Union Carbide Corporation; *U.S. Public*, pg. 1667
UCAR POLIMEROS Y QUIMICOS C.A.—See Union Carbide Corporation; *U.S. Public*, pg. 1667
UCB-BIOPRODUCTS SA—See UCB, S.A.; *Int'l*, pg. 1427
UCB PHARMA INC.—See UCB, S.A.; *Int'l*, pg. 1427
UCB PHARMA SA—See UCB, S.A.; *Int'l*, pg. 1427
UCB, S.A.; *Int'l*, pg. 1427
UCB SA CHEMICAL—See UCB, S.A.; *Int'l*, pg. 1427
UCB SA PHARMA SECTOR—See UCB, S.A.; *Int'l*, pg. 1427
UCB UMWELT CONSULT BERLIN GMBH—See Mannesmann A.G.; *Int'l*, pg. 837
UCG ENERGY CORPORATION—See Atmos Energy Corporation; *U.S. Public*, pg. 146
UCISCO INC.—See Praxair Inc.; *U.S. Public*, pg. 1320
UCM TIMBER PLC—See Norske Skogindustrier A.S.; *Int'l*, pg. 967
THE UCS GROUP—See Lagardere Groupe; *Int'l*, pg. 792
UDC GROUP HOLDINGS LIMITED—See Australia & New Zealand Banking Group Limited; *Int'l*, pg. 100
UDT SENSORS, INC.; *U.S. Private*, pg. 1112
UES, INC.; *U.S. Private*, pg. 1112
UETA, INC.—See BAA plc; *Int'l*, pg. 103
UF6 FLOURINE SPECIALTIES—See AlliedSignal Inc.; *U.S. Public*, pg. 51
UFA FILM UND FERNSEH GMBH—See Bertelsmann AG; *Int'l*, pg. 190
UFE INCORPORATED; *U.S. Private*, pg. 1112
UFE PTE LTD—See UFE Incorporated; *U.S. Private*, pg. 1112
UFP TECHNOLOGY; *U.S. Private*, pg. 1112
UGEFO—See AXA-UAP; *Int'l*, pg. 19
UGI CORPORATION; *U.S. Public*, pg. 1653
UGI ENTERPRISES—See UGI Corporation; *U.S. Public*, pg. 1653
UGI UTILITIES, INC.—See UGI Corporation; *U.S. Public*, pg. 1653
UGL, INC.—See Rieter Holdings; *Int'l*, pg. 1117
UHP HEALTHCARE; *U.S. Private*, pg. 1113
U.I.C. INSURANCE CO. LTD.—See Petrofina S.A.; *Int'l*, pg. 1043
U.I.C.A. S.P.A.—See Fiat Auto SpA; *Int'l*, pg. 481
UIP ENGINEERED PRODUCTS, INC.—See Pettibone Corporation; *U.S. Public*, pg. 860
UIS, INC.; *U.S. Private*, pg. 1113
UJB DISCOUNT BROKERAGE—See Summit Bancorp; *U.S. Public*, pg. 1528
UJB INVESTOR SERVICES COMPANY—See Summit Bancorp; *U.S. Public*, pg. 1528
U.K. PAPER PLC—See Fletcher Challenge Limited; *Int'l*, pg. 495
UK PETROLEUM PRODUCTS LTD.—See Powell Duffryn PLC; *Int'l*, pg. 1065
UM ENGINEERING—See Union Miniere; *Int'l*, pg. 1442
U.M. HOLDING LIMITED; *U.S. Private*, pg. 1113
UMB BANK COLORADO—See UMB Financial Corporation; *U.S. Public*, pg. 1654
UMB BANK OF THE WEST, N.A.—See UMB Financial Corporation; *U.S. Public*, pg. 1654
UMB COLUMBINE NATIONAL BANK—See UMB Financial Corporation; *U.S. Public*, pg. 1654
UMB FINANCIAL CORPORATION; *U.S. Public*, pg. 1653
UMB FIRST NATIONAL BANK—See UMB Financial Corporation; *U.S. Public*, pg. 1654
UMB FIRST STATE BANK OF MORRISONVILLE—See UMB Financial Corporation; *U.S. Public*, pg. 1654
UMB PROPERTIES, INC.—See UMB Financial Corporation; *U.S. Public*, pg. 1655
UMC INDUSTRIES, LTD.—See Crane Co.; *U.S. Public*, pg. 457
UMCZ—See Union Miniere; *Int'l*, pg. 1442
UMEX COMPANY—See Unilever Plc; *Int'l*, pg. 1435
UMI—See Bell & Howell Holdings; *U.S. Public*, pg. 201
UMI DATA COURIER—See Bell & Howell Holdings; *U.S. Public*, pg. 201
UMS SWISS METALWORKS HOLDING LTD; *Int'l*, pg. 1427
UMW TOYOTA MOTOR SDN. BHN.—See Toyota Motor Corporation; *Int'l*, pg. 1414
U.N. ALLOY STEEL DIV.—See Okura & Co.; *Int'l*, pg. 1001
U.N. ALLOY STEEL SALES, INC.—See Okura & Co.; *Int'l*, pg. 1001
UN GRAND CAFE'—See Lettuce Entertain You Enterprises, Inc.; *U.S. Private*, pg. 662
UN (OVERSEAS) LTD.—See United News & Media plc; *Int'l*, pg. 1443
U.N.A. CORPORATION—See Okura & Co.; *Int'l*, pg. 1001
UNAT RE, S.A.—See American International Group, Inc.; *U.S. Public*, pg. 85

UNAT, S.A.—See American International Group, Inc.; *U.S. Public*, pg. 85
UNC ACCESSORY SERVICES—See General Electric Company; *U.S. Public*, pg. 710
UNC ACCESSORY SERVICES-FLORIDA—See General Electric Company; *U.S. Public*, pg. 710
UNC ACCESSORY SERVICES-NEW YORK—See General Electric Company; *U.S. Public*, pg. 710
UNC AEROSTRUCTURES-WASHINGTON—See General Electric Company; *U.S. Public*, pg. 710
UNC AIRWORK—See General Electric Company; *U.S. Public*, pg. 710
UNC ARTEX—See General Electric Company; *U.S. Public*, pg. 710
UNC AVIATION SERVICES, INC.—See General Electric Company; *U.S. Public*, pg. 710
UNC JOHNSON TECHNOLOGY—See General Electric Company; *U.S. Public*, pg. 710
UNC LEAR SIEGLER—See General Electric Company; *U.S. Public*, pg. 710
UNELCO - UNION ELECTRICA DE CANARIAS, S.A.—See SEPI; *Int'l*, pg. 1224
UNI DISTRIBUTION CORP.—See The Seagram Company Ltd.; *Int'l*, pg. 1215
UNI-SERVICE OPERATIONS CORPORATION—See Utica Mutual Insurance Company; *U.S. Private*, pg. 1130
UNOCO—See The Walt Disney Company; *U.S. Public*, pg. 514
UNR HOME PRODUCTS DIV.—See ROHN Industries, Inc.; *U.S. Public*, pg. 1404
UNR-LEAVITT DIV.—See ROHN Industries, Inc.; *U.S. Public*, pg. 1404
UNR-ROHN DIV.—See ROHN Industries, Inc.; *U.S. Public*, pg. 1404
U.O.O., INC.—See Urban Outfitters, Inc.; *U.S. Public*, pg. 1700
UOP—See AlliedSignal Inc.; *U.S. Public*, pg. 52
U P SYSTEMS INC.—See Chloride Group PLC; *Int'l*, pg. 287
UPB OF LOUISIANA—See Union Planters Corporation; *U.S. Public*, pg. 1669
UPB OF MISSOURI—See Union Planters Corporation; *U.S. Public*, pg. 1669
UPM-KYMMENE AG—See UPM-Kymmene Corporation; *Int'l*, pg. 1430
UPM-KYMMENE BALTICA—See UPM-Kymmene Corporation; *Int'l*, pg. 1430
UPM-KYMMENE (BELGIUM) S.A./N.V.—See UPM-Kymmene Corporation; *Int'l*, pg. 1430
UPM-KYMMENE CANADA—See UPM-Kymmene Corporation; *Int'l*, pg. 1430
UPM-KYMMENE CORPORATION; *Int'l*, pg. 1427
UPM-KYMMENE DEUTSCHLAND GMBH—See UPM-Kymmene Corporation; *Int'l*, pg. 1430
UPM-KYMMENE FAR EAST PTE. LTD.—See UPM-Kymmene Corporation; *Int'l*, pg. 1430
UPM-KYMMENE FOREST PRODUCTS (HK) LTD.—See UPM-Kymmene Corporation; *Int'l*, pg. 1430
UPM-KYMMENE FRANCE S.A.—See UPM-Kymmene Corporation; *Int'l*, pg. 1430
UPM-KYMMENE IRELAND—See UPM-Kymmene Corporation; *Int'l*, pg. 1430
UPM-KYMMENE ITALIA S.R.L.—See UPM-Kymmene Corporation; *Int'l*, pg. 1430
UPM-KYMMENE - JAMSANKOSKI—See UPM-Kymmene Corporation; *Int'l*, pg. 1428
UPM-KYMMENE - KAIPOLA—See UPM-Kymmene Corporation; *Int'l*, pg. 1428
UPM-KYMMENE - KAJAANI—See UPM-Kymmene Corporation; *Int'l*, pg. 1428
UPM-KYMMENE KFT—See UPM-Kymmene Corporation; *Int'l*, pg. 1430
UPM-KYMMENE (NEDERLAND) B.V.—See UPM-Kymmene Corporation; *Int'l*, pg. 1430
UPM-KYMMENE PAPEL LDA.—See UPM-Kymmene Corporation; *Int'l*, pg. 1430
UPM-KYMMENE PAPEL S.A.—See UPM-Kymmene Corporation; *Int'l*, pg. 1430
UPM-KYMMENE PAPER DIVISION—See UPM-Kymmene Corporation; *Int'l*, pg. 1428
UPM-KYMMENE PAPER PTY LTD.—See UPM-Kymmene Corporation; *Int'l*, pg. 1430
UPM-KYMMENE PAPIER GMBH—See UPM-Kymmene Corporation; *Int'l*, pg. 1430
UPM-KYMMENE PAPIR A/S—See UPM-Kymmene Corporation; *Int'l*, pg. 1430
UPM-KYMMENE TIMBER—See UPM-Kymmene Corporation; *Int'l*, pg. 1430
UPM-KYMMENE UK PLC—See UPM-Kymmene Corporation; *Int'l*, pg. 1430
UPM-KYMMENE UK PLC-NORTHERN OFFICE—See UPM-Kymmene Corporation; *Int'l*, pg. 1431
UPM PACK—See UPM-Kymmene Corporation; *Int'l*, pg. 1430
UPN-UNITED PARAMOUNT NETWORK—See Chris-Craft Industries, Inc.; *U.S. Public*, pg. 352
UPN-UNITED PARAMOUNT NETWORK—See National Amusements, Inc.; *U.S. Private*, pg. 777
URM DEVELOPMENT CORP.—See URM Stores, Inc.; *U.S. Private*, pg. 1114
URM INSURANCE AGENCY—See URM Stores, Inc.; *U.S. Private*, pg. 1114
URM STORES, INC.; *U.S. Private*, pg. 1114
URS CORPORATION; *U.S. Public*, pg. 1655
URS GREINER—See URS Corporation; *U.S. Public*, pg. 1655
URS GREINER ENGINEERING, INC.—See URS Corporation; *U.S. Public*, pg. 1658
URS GREINER, INC.—See URS Corporation; *U.S. Public*, pg. 1658
URS GREINER, INC. MID-ATLANTIC—See URS Corporation; *U.S. Public*, pg. 1659
URS GREINER, INC. SOUTHWEST—See URS Corporation; *U.S. Public*, pg. 1659

Company Index

URS DIRECTORY OF CORPORATE AFFILIATIONS

URS GREINER INTERNATIONAL LTD.—See URS Corporation; *U.S. Public*, pg. 1659
URS LOGISTICS; *U.S. Private*, pg. 1114
U.S. FUJI ELECTRIC, INC.—See Fuji Electric Co., Ltd.; *Int'l*, *pg. 522*
US1 ALLIANCE CORP.—See National Commerce Bancorporation; *U.S. Public*, pg. 1155
USAA BUYING SERVICE—See USAA (United Services Automobile Association); *U.S. Private*, pg. 1114
USAA FEDERAL SAVINGS BANK—See USAA (United Services Automobile Association); *U.S. Private*, pg. 1114
USAA INVESTMENT MANAGEMENT CO.—See USAA (United Services Automobile Association); *U.S. Private*, pg. 1114
USAA LIFE INSURANCE CO.—See USAA (United Services Automobile Association); *U.S. Private*, pg. 1115
USAA (UNITED SERVICES AUTOMOBILE ASSOCIATION); *U.S. Private*, pg. 1114
USB PHARMA B.V.—See U.S. Bioscience, Inc.; *U.S. Public*, *pg. 1681*
USB PHARMA LTD.—See U.S. Bioscience, Inc.; *U.S. Public*, pg. 1681
USCI—See C.R. Bard, Inc.; *U.S. Public*, pg. 189
USCO, INCORPORATED—See Hughes Supply, Inc.; *U.S. Public*, pg. 847
USCS INTERNATIONAL, INC.; *U.S. Public*, pg. 1659
USDATA CORPORATION—See Safeguard Scientifics, Inc.; *U.S. Public*, pg. 1425
USECO—See Litton Industries, Inc.; *U.S. Public*, pg. 1003
USF&G CORPORATION; *U.S. Public*, pg. 1659
USF INSURANCE COMPANY—See Centris Group Inc.; *U.S. Public*, pg. 328
USF LTD.—See Aluminum Company of America; *U.S. Public*, pg. 61
USF RE INSURANCE COMPANY—See Centris Group Inc.; *U.S. Public*, pg. 328
USG ANNUITY & LIFE COMPANY—See ING Groep N.V.; *Int'l*, pg. 647
USG CORPORATION; *U.S. Public*, pg. 1660
USG INTERIORS, INC.—See USG Corporation; *U.S. Public*, *pg. 1660*
USG INTERNATIONAL—See USG Corporation; *U.S. Public*, *pg. 1660*
USHAWL, INC.—See Zeneca Group Plc; *Int'l*, pg. 1525
USLD COMMUNICATIONS CORP.—See LCI International, Inc.; *U.S. Public*, pg. 969
USNR—See Hawker Siddeley Canada Inc.; *Int'l*, pg. 604
USRB S.A.—See General Binding Corporation; *U.S. Public*, pg. 707
USS KOBE STEEL—See Kobe Steel, Ltd.; *Int'l*, pg. 741
USS-POSCO INDUSTRIES—See USX Corporation; *U.S. Public*, pg. 1662
U.S.S. SEKO WORLDWIDE; *U.S. Private*, pg. 1115
UST CAPITAL CORP.—See UST Corporation; *U.S. Public*, pg. 1660
UST CORPORATION; *U.S. Public*, pg. 1660
UST FIDUCIARY SERVICES, LTD.—See U.S. Trust Corporation; *U.S. Public*, pg. 1688
UST INC.; *U.S. Public*, pg. 1660
UST LEASING CORPORATION—See UST Corporation; *U.S. Public*, pg. 1660
UST SECURITIES CORP.—See U.S. Trust Corporation; *U.S. Public*, pg. 1688
USTC KANSAS, INC.—See Lynch Corporation; *U.S. Public*, pg. 1021
USV (P.R) DEVELOPMENT CORPORATION—See Rhone-Poulenc S.A.; *Int'l*, pg. 1111
USX CORPORATION; *U.S. Public*, pg. 1661
USX CREDIT—See USX Corporation; *U.S. Public*, pg. 1661
USX ENGINEERS & CONSULTANTS, INC.—See USX Corporation; *U.S. Public*, pg. 1662
USX FAIRFIELD WORKS—See USX Corporation; *U.S. Public*, pg. 1662
USX GARY WORKS, STEEL PRODUCTION—See USX Corporation; *U.S. Public*, pg. 1662
USX REALTY DEVELOPMENT—See USX Corporation; *U.S. Public*, pg. 1661
UTA—See Willis Corroon Group PLC; *Int'l*, pg. 1502
U.T.A. CABLE CORP.—See Lennar Corporation; *U.S. Public*, pg. 989
UTA HOLLAND PLANT—See United Technologies Corporation; *U.S. Public*, pg. 1691
UTA MILANO SPA—See Willis Corroon Group PLC; *Int'l*, pg. 1509
UTA THOMPSON PLANT—See United Technologies Corporation; *U.S. Public*, pg. 1691
UTDC SYSTEMS—See Bombardier Inc.; *Int'l*, pg. 200
UTE—See Lyonnaise des Eaux S.A.; *Int'l*, pg. 824
UTP (UNITED TECHNICAL PUBLICATIONS) DIVISION—See The Hearst Corporation; *U.S. Private*, pg. 516
UVG NEDERLAND B.V.—See Unilever Plc; *Int'l*, pg. 1438
UVP, INC.; *U.S. Private*, pg. 1115
UA WITHYA EQUIPMENT CO., LTD.—See Bangkok Bank of Commerce Ltd.; *Int'l*, pg. 146
UAB RANNILA STEEL VILNIUS—See Rautaruukki Oy; *Int'l*, *pg. 1088*
UBE EUROPE (ESPANA), S.A.—See UBE Industries Ltd.; *Int'l*, pg. 1427
UBE (HONG KONG) LTD.—See UBE Industries Ltd.; *Int'l*, pg. 1427
UBE INDUSTRIES LTD.-HIROSHIMA—See UBE Industries Ltd.; *Int'l*, pg. 1426
UBE INDUSTRIES LTD.-NAGOYA—See UBE Industries Ltd.; *Int'l*, pg. 1426
UBE INDUSTRIES LTD.-OSAKA—See UBE Industries Ltd.; *Int'l*, pg. 1426
UBE INDUSTRIES LTD.-SAPPORO—See UBE Industries Ltd.; *Int'l*, pg. 1426
UBE MACHINERY & ENGINEERING WORKS—See UBE Industries Ltd.; *Int'l*, pg. 1427
UBE OFFICE—See UBE Industries Ltd.; *Int'l*, pg. 1426
UBE (THAILAND) CO. LTD.—See UBE Industries Ltd.; *Int'l*, *pg. 1427*
UBEL B.V.—See GESTRA GmbH; *Int'l*, pg. 550
UBERLAND-ZENTRALE HELMSTEDT AG—See Veba AG; *Int'l*, pg. 1456
UBERLANDWERK LEINETAL GMBH—See Veba AG; *Int'l*, pg. 1457
UBERLANDWERK NORD HANNOVER AG—See Veba AG; *Int'l*, pg. 1457
UCAR GLOBAL ENTERPRISES INC.—See UCAR International Inc.; *U.S. Public*, pg. 1662
UCAR INTERNATIONAL INC.; *U.S. Public*, pg. 1662
U.D. IMPORTS (PROPRIETARY) LIMITED—See Diageo Plc; *Int'l*, pg. 412
UDANMAAN SACHA OY—See Imatran Voima Oy; *Int'l*, pg. 661
UDDCOMB SWEDEN AB—See Trelleborg AB; *Int'l*, pg. 1421
OY UDDEHOLM AB—See Voest-Alpine Stahl AG; *Int'l*, pg. 1472
UDDEHOLM A/S—See Voest-Alpine Stahl AG; *Int'l*, pg. 1472
UDDEHOLM GMBH.—See Voest-Alpine Stahl AG; *Int'l*, pg. 1472
UDDEHOLM KK—See Voest-Alpine Stahl AG; *Int'l*, pg. 1472
UDDEHOLM KRAFT AB—See Voest-Alpine Stahl AG; *Int'l*, pg. 1471
UDDEHOLM LIMITED—See Voest-Alpine Stahl AG; *Int'l*, pg. 1472
UDDEHOLM S.A.—See Voest-Alpine Stahl AG; *Int'l*, pg. 1472
UDDEHOLM S.P.A.—See Voest-Alpine Stahl AG; *Int'l*, pg. 1472
UDDEHOLM TOOLING AB—See Voest-Alpine Stahl AG; *Int'l*, pg. 1471
UDDEHOLM TOOLING B.V.—See Voest-Alpine Stahl AG; *Int'l*, pg. 1472
UDDEHOLM TOOLING GESMBH—See Voest-Alpine Stahl AG; *Int'l*, pg. 1472
UDDEHOLM TOOLING N.V.—See Voest-Alpine Stahl AG; *Int'l*, pg. 1472
UDDEHOLM TOOLING SVENSKA AB—See Voest-Alpine Stahl AG; *Int'l*, pg. 1471
UEBERSEEBANK AG—See American International Group, Inc.; *U.S. Public*, pg. 85
UFFICIO AFFARI QUEBEC ITALIA—See Caisse de depot et placement du Quebec; *Int'l*, pg. 249
UFFICIO DI ROMA—See IRI Istituto Ricostruzione Industriale; *Int'l*, pg. 653
UFIMA S.A.—See Fiat Auto SpA; *Int'l*, pg. 482
UFORMA SHELBY BUSINESS FORMS—See Miami Systems Corporation; *U.S. Private*, pg. 740
UGIMAG INC.—See Pechiney S.A.; *Int'l*, pg. 1029
UGIMAG RECOMA AG—See Pechiney S.A.; *Int'l*, pg. 1032
UGIMAGNETICS PTE. LTD.—See Pechiney S.A.; *Int'l*, pg. 1032
UGINE ACG (ACIERS DE CHATILLON ET GUEUGNON)—See Groupe Usinor; *Int'l*, pg. 571
UGINE ACIERS DE CHATILLON ET GUEUGNON S.A.—See Groupe Usinor; *Int'l*, pg. 571
UGINE-SAVOIE—See Groupe Usinor; *Int'l*, pg. 571
UGLY DUCKLING CORP.; *U.S. Public*, pg. 1662
GEORGE UHE CO., INC.; *U.S. Private*, pg. 1115
THE UHLMANN CO.; *U.S. Private*, pg. 1115
UITGEVERIJ GEBR. SPANJERSBERG B.V.—See Hallmark Cards, Inc.; *U.S. Private*, pg. 496
UITGEVERIJ SPAARNESTAD BV—See VNU Verenigde Nederlandse Uitgeversbedrijven B.V.; *Int'l*, pg. 1445
UITGEVERIJ VELDHUIS BV—See VNU Verenigde Nederlandse Uitgeversbedrijven B.V.; *Int'l*, pg. 1445
UITGEVERIJ WOUDESTEIN BV—See VNU Verenigde Nederlandse Uitgeversbedrijven B.V.; *Int'l*, pg. 1445
UITGEVERSMAATSCHAPPIJ DE GELDERLANDER BV—See VNU Verenigde Nederlandse Uitgeversbedrijven B.V.; *Int'l*, pg. 1445
UITGEVERSMAATSCHAPPIJ DE LIMBURGER BV—See VNU Verenigde Nederlandse Uitgeversbedrijven B.V.; *Int'l*, pg. 1445
UITGEVERSMAATSCHAPPIJ DE STEM BV—See VNU Verenigde Nederlandse Uitgeversbedrijven B.V.; *Int'l*, pg. 1445
UITGEVERSMAATSCHAPPIJ THE READER'S DIGEST N.V.—See The Reader's Digest Association, Inc.; *U.S. Public*, pg. 1368
UKRAINIAN MOBILE COMMUNICATIONS—See KPN Koninklyke PTT Nederland NV; *Int'l*, pg. 721
UKRON—See Heidemij N.V.; *Int'l*, pg. 608
UKROP'S SUPER MARKETS; *U.S. Private*, pg. 1115
ULBRICH STAINLESS STEELS & SPECIAL METALS, INC.; *U.S. Private*, pg. 1115
ULBRICH WIRE, INC.—See Ulbrich Stainless Steels & Special Metals, Inc.; *U.S. Private*, pg. 1115
ULEA OY TAIVALKOSKI SAWMILL—See Enso Oyj; *Int'l*, pg. 456
ULICO CASUALTY COMPANY—See ULLICO Inc.; *U.S. Private*, pg. 1116
ULICO INDEMNITY—See ULLICO Inc.; *U.S. Private*, pg. 1116
ULLICO INC.; *U.S. Private*, pg. 1115
ULLO INTERNATIONAL, INC.; *U.S. Private*, pg. 1116
ULLRICH COPPER, INC.—See Foster Wheeler Corporation; *U.S. Public*, pg. 677
ULLSTEIN GMBH—See Axel Springer Verlag AG; *Int'l*, pg. 102
ULSTER BANK COMMERCIAL SERVICES LIMITED—See National Westminster Bank PLC; *Int'l*, pg. 911
ULSTER BANK COMMERCIAL SERVICES (NI) LIMITED—See National Westminster Bank PLC; *Int'l*, pg. 911
ULSTER BANK DUBLIN TRUST COMPANY—See National Westminster Bank PLC; *Int'l*, pg. 912
ULSTER BANK GROUP TREASURY (INTERNATIONAL) LIMITED—See National Westminster Bank PLC; *Int'l*, pg. 912
ULSTER BANK GROUP TREASURY LIMITED—See National Westminster Bank PLC; *Int'l*, pg. 912
ULSTER BANK INSURANCE SERVICES LIMITED—See National Westminster Bank PLC; *Int'l*, pg. 911
ULSTER BANK (ISLE OF MAN) LIMITED—See National Westminster Bank PLC; *Int'l*, pg. 911
ULSTER BANK LIMITED—See National Westminster Bank PLC; *Int'l*, pg. 911
ULSTER BANK TRUST COMPANY—See National Westminster Bank PLC; *Int'l*, pg. 911
ULSTER INVESTMENT BANK LIMITED—See National Westminster Bank PLC; *Int'l*, pg. 912
ULSTER WASTE LIMITED—See RMC Group p.l.c.; *Int'l*, pg. 1079
ULTEGRA NEDERLAND B.V.—See Shimano Inc.; *Int'l*, pg. 1233
ULTI-MATE, INC.—See Molex Incorporated; *U.S. Public*, pg. 1122
ULTIMATE ELECTRONICS; *U.S. Public*, pg. 1662
ULTIMATE TECHNOLOGY CORPORATION—See Tridex Corporation; *U.S. Public*, pg. 1637
ULTIMO LTD.; *U.S. Private*, pg. 1116
ULTRA BUILDING SYSTEMS, INC.—See CFA Holding Company; *U.S. Private*, pg. 194
ULTRA ELECTRICS—See Ultra Electronics Holdings plc; *Int'l*, pg. 1431
ULTRA ELECTRONICS COMMAND & CONTROL SYSTEMS—See Ultra Electronics Holdings plc; *Int'l*, pg. 1431
ULTRA ELECTRONICS CONTROLS—See Ultra Electronics Holdings plc; *Int'l*, pg. 1431
ULTRA ELECTRONICS HOLDINGS PLC; *Int'l*, pg. 1431
ULTRA ELECTRONICS MAGNETICS—See Ultra Electronics Holdings plc; *Int'l*, pg. 1431
ULTRA ELECTRONICS OCEAN SYSTEMS—See Ultra Electronics Holdings plc; *Int'l*, pg. 1431
ULTRA ELECTRONICS SONAR & COMMUNICATIONS SYSTEMS—See Ultra Electronics Holdings plc; *Int'l*, pg. 1431
ULTRA ELECTRONICS WEAPONS SYSTEMS—See Ultra Electronics Holdings plc; *Int'l*, pg. 1431
ULTRA GMBH—See Computer Network Technology Corporation; *U.S. Public*, pg. 421
ULTRA INDUSTRIAL S.A. DE C.V.—See Clarion Co., Ltd.; *Int'l*, pg. 296
ULTRA INDUSTRIES, INC.—See Macklanburg-Duncan Co.; *U.S. Private*, pg. 692
ULTRA PAC, INC.; *U.S. Public*, pg. 1662
ULTRA TECHNOLOGIES, INC.—See Eastman Kodak Company; *U.S. Public*, pg. 551
ULTRA TOOL & PLASTICS, INC.; *U.S. Private*, pg. 1116
ULTRAFORM COMPANY—See BASF AG; *Int'l*, pg. 105
ULTRAK INC.; *U.S. Public*, pg. 1663
ULTRALIN AG—See Fuchs Petrolub AG Oel + Chemie; *Int'l*, pg. 519
ULTRAMAR DIAMOND SHAMROCK CORPORATION; *U.S. Public*, pg. 1663
ULTRASORB CHEMIKALIEN GMBH—See BASF AG; *Int'l*, pg. 104
ULTRASYSTEMS DEFENSE—See Northrop Grumman Corporation; *U.S. Public*, pg. 1199
ULTRATECH STEPPER, INC.; *U.S. Public*, pg. 1663
UMAR-UNION MARITIMA INTERNACIONAL S.A.—See Holderbank Financiere Glaris Ltd.; *Int'l*, pg. 629
UMBRO INTERNATIONAL, INC.; *U.S. Private*, pg. 1116
UMWELTSCHUTZ NORD GMBH & CO.—See Philipp Holzmann AG; *Int'l*, pg. 633
UNAFORM INC.—See Scapa Group Plc; *Int'l*, pg. 1202
UNAFORM LTD.—See Scapa Group Plc; *Int'l*, pg. 1202
UNAFORM SOUTH AFRICA (PTY) LTD.—See Scapa Group Plc; *Int'l*, pg. 1203
UNAPIX ENTERTAINMENT INC.; *U.S. Public*, pg. 1664
UNARCO MATERIAL—See Renco Group; *U.S. Private*, pg. 922
UNBRAKO DIV.—See SPS Technologies, Inc.; *U.S. Public*, pg. 1420
UNBRAKO INC.—See SPS Technologies, Inc.; *U.S. Public*, pg. 1420
UNBRAKO MEXICANA, S.A. DE C.V.—See SPS Technologies, Inc.; *U.S. Public*, pg. 1420
UNBRAKO PRODUCTS (SINGAPORE) PTE LTD.—See SPS Technologies, Inc.; *U.S. Public*, pg. 1420
UNBRAKO PTY. LTD.—See SPS Technologies, Inc.; *U.S. Public*, pg. 1420
UNCAS MANUFACTURING COMPANY; *U.S. Private*, pg. 1116
UNCLE B'S BAKERY, INC.; *U.S. Public*, pg. 1664
UNCLE BEN'S, INC.—See Mars, Incorporated; *U.S. Private*, *pg. 707*
THE UNCLE TOBY'S COMPANY LTD.—See Goodman Fielder Limited; *Int'l*, pg. 555
UNDERGROUND CONSTRUCTION CO., INC.; *U.S. Private*, pg. 1116
UNDERGROUND TECHNOLOGIES—See Thomas & Betts Corporation; *U.S. Public*, pg. 1598
UNDERLINING BV—See KPN Koninklyke PTT Nederland NV; *Int'l*, pg. 720
UNDERWATER DEFENSE SYSTEMS INTERNATIONAL—See Thomson S.A.; *Int'l*, pg. 1383
UNDERWATER WORLD SINGAPORE PTE. LTD.—See Haw Par Brothers International Limited; *Int'l*, pg. 604
UNDERWRITERS & MANAGEMENT SERVICES INC.—See Lincoln National Corporation; *U.S. Public*, pg. 998
UNDERWRITERS MANAGEMENT ASSOCIATES, INC.—See Willis Corroon Group PLC; *Int'l*, pg. 1508
UNDERWRITERS REINSURANCE—See Alleghany Corporation; *U.S. Public*, pg. 42
UNELEC S.A.—See The General Electric Company, p.l.c.; *Int'l*, pg. 546
UNEX CONVEYING SYSTEMS, INC.; *U.S. Private*, pg. 1117
UNGER COMPANY; *U.S. Private*, pg. 1117
UNI-BEAUTY LIMITED—See Wella Group; *Int'l*, pg. 1490
UNI-CARDAN NORGE A/S—See GKN plc; *Int'l*, pg. 536
UNI-DAN A/S—See Unilever Plc; *Int'l*, pg. 1438
UNI EUROPE—See AXA-UAP; *Int'l*, pg. 19

UNI-LINE DIV.—See Siebe plc; *Int'l*, pg. 1243
UNI-MARTS, INC.; *U.S. Public*, pg. 1664
OY UNI-PAK AB—See Enso Oyj; *Int'l*, pg. 456
UNI-RENTS LTD.—See Wolseley Plc.; *Int'l*, pg. 1512
UNIAO DE BANCOS BRASILEIROS S.A. (UNIBANCO); *Int'l*, pg. 1431
UNIAO DE BANCOS BRASILEIROS (UNIBANCO) (BRAZIL)—See Uniao de Bancos Brasileiros S.A. (Unibanco); *Int'l*, pg. 1431
UNIAO DE BANCOS SUICOS—See Union Bank of Switzerland; *Int'l*, pg. 1441
UNIASS ASSICURAZIONI S.P.A.—See Skandia Insurance Company Limited; *Int'l*, pg. 1256
UNIBAIL; *Int'l*, pg. 1431
UNIBETON—See Ciments Francais; *Int'l*, pg. 292
UNIBLEND SPINNERS—See Uniblend Spinners, Inc.; *U.S. Private*, pg. 1117
UNIBLEND SPINNERS, INC.; *U.S. Private*, pg. 1117
UNIBOARD CANADA INC.; *Int'l*, pg. 1431
UNIBOARD CANADA INC.-LDI DIVISION—See Uniboard Canada Inc.; *Int'l*, pg. 1431
UNIBOARD DIVISION MONT LAURIER—See Uniboard Canada Inc.; *Int'l*, pg. 1431
UNIBOARD DIVISION SAYABEC—See Uniboard Canada Inc.; *Int'l*, pg. 1431
UNIBOARD DIVISION UNIRES—See Uniboard Canada Inc.; *Int'l*, pg. 1431
UNIBOARD DIVISION VAL D'OR—See Uniboard Canada Inc.; *Int'l*, pg. 1431
UNIBUS, INC.—See Powell Industries, Inc.; *U.S. Public*, pg. 1319
UNIC S.A.—See Societe BIC S.A.; *Int'l*, pg. 1273
UNICABLES, S.A.—See General Motors Corporation; *U.S. Public*, pg. 724
UNICAL S.P.A.—See Telefonaktiebolaget LM Ericsson; *Int'l*, pg. 1371
UNICAN SECURITY SYSTEMS LTD.; *Int'l*, pg. 1432
UNICARE FINANCIAL CORP.—See Blue Cross of California; *U.S. Private*, pg. 152
UNICARE INSURANCE COMPANY—See Blue Cross of California; *U.S. Private*, pg. 152
UNICAST—See Sturm, Ruger & Co., Inc.; *U.S. Public*, pg. 1526
UNICBANK RT.—See Raiffeisen Zentralbank Osterreich; *Int'l*, pg. 1085
UNICCO SERVICE COMPANY; *U.S. Private*, pg. 1117
UNICCOMPTOIR—See GIB Group; *Int'l*, pg. 533
UNICER-UNIAO CERVEJEIRA, S.A.; *Int'l*, pg. 1432
UNICHEM—See BJ Services Company; *U.S. Public*, pg. 161
UNICHEMA CHEMICALS LTD.—See Unilever Plc; *Int'l*, pg. 1434
UNICHEMA-CHEMIE B.V.—See Unilever Plc; *Int'l*, pg. 1438
UNICHEMA CHEMIE G.M.B.H.—See Unilever Plc; *Int'l*, pg. 1438
UNICHEMA U.S.A.—See Unilever Plc; *Int'l*, pg. 1436
UNICLIFFE LIMITED—See Pfizer Inc.; *U.S. Public*, pg. 1283
UNICO BANKING GROUP—See Raiffeisen Zentralbank Osterreich; *Int'l*, pg. 1085
UNICO FINANCIAL SERVICES S.A.—See Raiffeisen Zentralbank Osterreich; *Int'l*, pg. 1085
UNICO INVESTMENT FUND—See Raiffeisen Zentralbank Osterreich; *Int'l*, pg. 1085
UNICOM—See Havas Advertising; *Int'l*, pg. 601
UNICOM CORPORATION; *U.S. Public*, pg. 1664
UNICON BETON HOLDING A/S—See FLS Industries A/S; *Int'l*, pg. 475
UNICORD PUBLIC CO. LTD.; *Int'l*, pg. 1432
UNICORP AMERICAN CORPORATION—See Unicorp Canada Corporation; *Int'l*, pg. 1433
UNICORP CANADA CORPORATION; *Int'l*, pg. 1433
UNICOVER CORPORATION; *U.S. Private*, pg. 1117
UNIDAD HERMETICA S.A.—See Electrolux, AB; *Int'l*, pg. 443
UNIDAD MOVIL DE DIAGNOSTICO—See Corporacion MAPFRE, Compania Internacional de Reaseguros, S.A.; *Int'l*, pg. 334
UNIDEN AMERICA CORPORATION—See Uniden Corporation; *Int'l*, pg. 1433
UNIDEN CORPORATION; *Int'l*, pg. 1433
UNIDESK INC.—See Compagnie des Machines Bull; *Int'l*, pg. 316
UNIDIGITAL/CARDINAL CORP.—See Unidigital Inc.; *U.S. Public*, pg. 1664
UNIDIGITAL INC.; *U.S. Public*, pg. 1664
UNIFAB INTERNATIONAL INC.; *U.S. Public*, pg. 1665
UNIFERM GMBH—See Royal Gist-Brocades N.V.; *Int'l*, pg. 1143
UNIFERM GMBH & CO.—See Royal Gist-Brocades N.V.; *Int'l*, pg. 1143
UNIFERT S.A.L.—See BASF AG; *Int'l*, pg. 109
UNIFI INC.; *U.S. Public*, pg. 1665
UNIFI INTERNATIONAL SERVICE, INC.—See Unifi Inc.; *U.S. Public*, pg. 1665
UNIFIED SYSTEMS SOLUTIONS INC.—See Computer Horizons Corp.; *U.S. Public*, pg. 421
UNIFIRST CORPORATION; *U.S. Public*, pg. 1665
UNIFIX (BELGIUM) S.A.—See Brunel Holdings Plc; *Int'l*, pg. 232
UNIFIX LTD.—See Brunel Holdings Plc; *Int'l*, pg. 231
UNIFLEX INC.—See NHK Spring Co., Ltd.; *Int'l*, pg. 902
UNIFLEX, INC.; *U.S. Public*, pg. 1665
UNIFLOW CORPORATION—See Secom General Corporation; *Int'l*, pg. 1453
UNIFLOW MANUFACTURING CO.; *U.S. Private*, pg. 1117
UNIFOIL CORPORATION; *U.S. Private*, pg. 1117
UNIFORCE INFORMATION SERVICES—See Comforce Corporation; *U.S. Public*, pg. 409
UNIFRANCK LEBENSMITTELWERKE GMBH—See Nestle S.A.; *Int'l*, pg. 922
UNIFRIDGE AG—See Electrolux, AB; *Int'l*, pg. 444
UNIFROST NAHRUNGSMITTEL GES. M.B.H.—See Unilever Plc; *Int'l*, pg. 1439
UNIFY CORPORATION; *U.S. Public*, pg. 1665

UNIGARD INDEMNITY CO.—See Credit Suisse Group; *Int'l*, pg. 345
UNIGARD INSURANCE CO.—See Credit Suisse Group; *Int'l*, pg. 345
UNIGAS—See Westcoast Energy Inc.; *Int'l*, pg. 1492
UNIGATE PLC; *Int'l*, pg. 1433
UNIGROUP, INC.; *U.S. Private*, pg. 1117
UNIGROUP WORLDWIDE, INC.—See UniGroup, Inc.; *U.S. Private*, pg. 1117
UNIHEALTH; *U.S. Private*, pg. 1117
UNIKAY S.R.L.—See Fort James Corporation; *U.S. Public*, pg. 673
UNIKIS JAPAN CO. LTD.—See Unican Security Systems Ltd.; *Int'l*, pg. 1432
UNIKOR CHEMICAL, INC.—See Crompton & Knowles Corporation; *U.S. Public*, pg. 460
UNIL-IT S.P.A.—See Unilever Plc; *Int'l*, pg. 1438
UNILAB CORPORATION—See Quest Diagnostics, Inc.; *U.S. Public*, pg. 1352
UNILAND MFG. CO., INC.—See Lakeland Industries, Inc.; *U.S. Public*, pg. 975
UNILASER—See Aerospatiale; *Int'l*, pg. 29
UNILEVER AUSTRALIA LTD.—See Unilever Plc; *Int'l*, pg. 1439
UNILEVER BECUMIJ N.V.—See Unilever Plc; *Int'l*, pg. 1439
UNILEVER CANADA LIMITED—See Unilever Plc; *Int'l*, pg. 1439
UNILEVER (COMMONWEALTH HOLDINGS) LTD.—See Unilever Plc; *Int'l*, pg. 1434
UNILEVER ESPANA S.A.—See Unilever Plc; *Int'l*, pg. 1439
UNILEVER EXPORT B.V.—See Unilever Plc; *Int'l*, pg. 1439
UNILEVER EXPORT FRANCE S.A.—See Unilever Plc; *Int'l*, pg. 1439
UNILEVER EXPORT LTD.—See Unilever Plc; *Int'l*, pg. 1434
UNILEVER FINANCIERINGS MAATSCHAPPIJ B.V.—See Unilever Plc; *Int'l*, pg. 1439
P.T. UNILEVER INDONESIA—See Unilever Plc; *Int'l*, pg. 1439
UNILEVER IS TICARET VE SANAYI TURK LIMITED SIRKETI—See Unilever Plc; *Int'l*, pg. 1439
UNILEVER NEW ZEALAND LTD.—See Unilever Plc; *Int'l*, pg. 1439
UNILEVER N.V.—See Unilever Plc; *Int'l*, pg. 1434
UNILEVER PLC; *Int'l*, pg. 1433
UNILEVER RESEARCH & DEVELOPMENT CO.—See Unilever Plc; *Int'l*, pg. 1436
UNILEVER (SCHWEIZ) AG—See Unilever Plc; *Int'l*, pg. 1439
UNILEVER SOUTH AFRICA (PTY.) LTD.—See Unilever Plc; *Int'l*, pg. 1439
UNILEVER U.K. CENTRAL RESOURCES LTD.—See Unilever Plc; *Int'l*, pg. 1434
UNILEVER U.K. HOLDINGS LTD.—See Unilever Plc; *Int'l*, pg. 1434
UNILEVER UNITED STATES INC.—See Unilever Plc; *Int'l*, pg. 1435
UNIMARK PLASTICS COMPANY—See Alltrista Corporation; *U.S. Public*, pg. 57
UNIMAS—See Groupe Casino; *Int'l*, pg. 563
UNIMAX CORP.—See Shepaug Corporation; *U.S. Private*, pg. 993
THE UNIMAX CORPORATION; *U.S. Private*, pg. 1118
UNIMED MANAGEMENT SERVICES—See UniHealth; *U.S. Private*, pg. 1118
UNIMEDIA INC.—See Hollinger Inc.; *Int'l*, pg. 632
UNIMESA CO. LTD.—See Hewlett-Packard Company; *U.S. Public*, pg. 823
UNIMET PTY LTD.—See CODELCO Chile (Corporacion Nacional Del Cobre De Chile); *Int'l*, pg. 303
UNIMETAL—See Groupe Usinor; *Int'l*, pg. 571
UNIMILLS B.V.—See Unilever Plc; *Int'l*, pg. 1439
UNIMIX—See Ciments Francais; *Int'l*, pg. 292
UNION AIR TRANSPORT DE MEXICO, S.A. DE C.V.—See Union-Transport Corporation; *U.S. Private*, pg. 1120
UNION AIR TRANSPORT GMBH—See Union-Transport Corporation; *U.S. Private*, pg. 1120
UNION AIR TRANSPORT INC.—See Union-Transport Corporation; *U.S. Private*, pg. 1120
UNION AJINOMOTO, INC.—See Ajinomoto Company Inc.; *Int'l*, pg. 41
UNION AJINOMOTO , INC., PLANT—See Ajinomoto Company Inc.; *Int'l*, pg. 41
UNION AND NHK AUTO PARTS CORP.—See NHK Spring Co., Ltd.; *Int'l*, pg. 902
UNION BANK—See The Bank of Tokyo-Mitsubishi, Ltd.; *Int'l*, pg. 157
UNION BANK & TRUST CO.—See First Financial Bancorp; *U.S. Public*, pg. 633
UNION BANK OF CALIFORNIA—See The Bank of Tokyo-Mitsubishi, Ltd.; *Int'l*, pg. 157
UNION BANK OF NORWAY; *Int'l*, pg. 1439
UNION BANK OF NORWAY INTERNATIONAL S.A.—See Union Bank of Norway; *Int'l*, pg. 1439
UNION BANK OF SWITZERLAND; *Int'l*, pg. 1439
UNION BANK OF SWITZERLAND—See Union Bank of Switzerland; *Int'l*, pg. 1441
UNION BANK OF SWITZERLAND, BEIJING REPRESENTATIVE—See Union Bank of Switzerland; *Int'l*, pg. 1441
UNION BANK OF SWITZERLAND (CANADA)—See Union Bank of Switzerland; *Int'l*, pg. 1441
UNION BANK OF SWITZERLAND, OSAKA—See Union Bank of Switzerland; *Int'l*, pg. 1441
UNION BANK OF SWITZERLAND (PANAMA) INC.—See Union Bank of Switzerland; *Int'l*, pg. 1441
UNION BANK OF SWITZERLAND, REPRESENTATIVE OFFICE—See Union Bank of Switzerland; *Int'l*, pg. 1441
UNION BANKER INSURANCE CO.—See Southwestern Financial Corporation; *U.S. Public*, pg. 1018
UNION-BAU AG—See Dyckerhoff & Widmann AG; *Int'l*, pg. 423

UNION BENEFIT LIFE INSURANCE CO.—See Conseco Inc.; *U.S. Public*, pg. 434
UNION BOILER CO.—See Concorp, Inc.; *U.S. Private*, pg. 262
UNION CAMP CORPORATION; *U.S. Public*, pg. 1665
UNION CAMP WOODLANDS DIV.—See Union Camp Corporation; *U.S. Public*, pg. 1666
UNION CARBIDE ARGENTINA S.A.I.C.S.—See Union Carbide Corporation; *U.S. Public*, pg. 1667
UNION CARBIDE ASIA LTD.—See Union Carbide Corporation; *U.S. Public*, pg. 1667
UNION CARBIDE ASIA PACIFIC INC.—See Union Carbide Corporation; *U.S. Public*, pg. 1667
UNION CARBIDE AUSTRIA GMBH—See Union Carbide Corporation; *U.S. Public*, pg. 1667
UNION CARBIDE BENELUX NV—See Union Carbide Corporation; *U.S. Public*, pg. 1667
UNION CARBIDE CHEMICALS KOREA LTD.—See Union Carbide Corporation; *U.S. Public*, pg. 1667
UNION CARBIDE COMERCIAL C.A.—See Union Carbide Corporation; *U.S. Public*, pg. 1667
UNION CARBIDE CORPORATION; *U.S. Public*, pg. 1666
UNION CARBIDE DO BRASIL S/A—See Union Carbide Corporation; *U.S. Public*, pg. 1667
UNION CARBIDE (EUROPE) S.A.—See Union Carbide Corporation; *U.S. Public*, pg. 1667
UNION CARBIDE INDONESIA PT—See Union Carbide Corporation; *U.S. Public*, pg. 1667
UNION CARBIDE INTER-AMERICA, INC.—See Union Carbide Corporation; *U.S. Public*, pg. 1667
UNION CARBIDE JAPAN K.K.—See Union Carbide Corporation; *U.S. Public*, pg. 1667
UNION CARBIDE PHILIPPINES (FAR EAST) INC.—See Union Carbide Corporation; *U.S. Public*, pg. 1667
UNION CARBIDE SOUTH AFRICA (PTY.) LTD.—See Union Carbide Corporation; *U.S. Public*, pg. 1667
UNION CEMENT CO.—See Scancem AB; *Int'l*, pg. 1201
THE UNION CENTRAL LIFE INSURANCE CO.; *U.S. Private*, pg. 1118
UNION CITY BODY COMPANY, L.P.; *U.S. Private*, pg. 1118
UNION CITY CHAIR CO.—See Brittany Corporation; *U.S. Private*, pg. 170
UNION COMMERCIAL BANK S.A.—See Standard Bank Investment Corporation Limited; *Int'l*, pg. 1294
UNION CONGOLAISE DE BANQUES—See Generale de Banque S.A.; *Int'l*, pg. 548
UNION CORPORATION—See Eclipse Inc.; *U.S. Private*, pg. 361
THE UNION CORPORATION; *U.S. Public*, pg. 1667
UNION CRISTALERA—See Saint-Gobain; *Int'l*, pg. 1176
UNION DAEWOO ENGINEERING & CONSTRUCTION CO., LTD.—See Daewoo Corporation; *Int'l*, pg. 358
UNION DE BANCOS SUIZOS—See Union Bank of Switzerland; *Int'l*, pg. 1441
UNION DE BANQUES CONGOLAISES—See Bank Brussels Lambert; *Int'l*, pg. 149
UNION DE BANQUES SUISSES—See Union Bank of Switzerland; *Int'l*, pg. 1441
UNION DE BANQUES SUISSES (LUXEMBOURG) S.A.—See Union Bank of Switzerland; *Int'l*, pg. 1441
UNION DES ASSURANCES FEDERALES—See Credit Lyonnais S.A.; *Int'l*, pg. 344
UNION DES COMBUSTIBLES "UNICO" S.A.—See Veba AG; *Int'l*, pg. 1457
UNION DEUTSCHE LEBENSMITTELWERKE G.M.B.H.—See Unilever Plc; *Int'l*, pg. 1439
UNION DRILLING DIVISION—See Equitable Resources, Inc.; *U.S. Public*, pg. 590
UNION ELECTRIC DEVELOPMENT CORPORATION—See Ameren Corporation; *U.S. Public*, pg. 66
UNION ELECTRIC STEEL CORP.—See Ampco-Pittsburgh Corporation; *U.S. Public*, pg. 103
UNION ELECTRIC STEEL N.V.—See Ampco-Pittsburgh Corporation; *U.S. Public*, pg. 104
UNION ENERGY INC.—See Westcoast Energy Inc.; *Int'l*, pg. 1492
UNION EUROPEENNE DE CIC—See Groupe GAN; *Int'l*, pg. 565
UNION GAS LIMITED—See Westcoast Energy Inc.; *Int'l*, pg. 1492
UNION GENERALE DE SAVONNERIE (UGS)—See Henkel KGaA; *Int'l*, pg. 612
UNION INDUSTRIELLE DE CREDIT (UIC)—See Groupe GAN; *Int'l*, pg. 565
UNION INDUSTRIES, INC.; *U.S. Private*, pg. 1119
UNION INSURANCE COMPANY—See W.R. Berkley Corporation; *U.S. Public*, pg. 216
THE UNION LABOR LIFE INSURANCE CO.—See ULLICO Inc.; *U.S. Private*, pg. 1116
UNION LIGHT, HEAT AND POWER CO.—See Cinergy Corp.; *U.S. Public*, pg. 369
UNION MEDICAL SUPPLY COMPANY—See Novartis AG; *Int'l*, pg. 986
UNION MINERE SERVICES & FINANCE—See Union Miniere; *Int'l*, pg. 1442
UNION MINIERE; *Int'l*, pg. 1441
UNION NAVAL DE LEVANTE, S.A.; *Int'l*, pg. 1442
UNION N.V.—See Unilever Plc; *Int'l*, pg. 1439
UNION PACIFIC CORPORATION; *U.S. Public*, pg. 1667
UNION PACIFIC MOTOR FREIGHT—See Union Pacific Corporation; *U.S. Public*, pg. 1668
UNION PACIFIC RAILROAD COMPANY—See Union Pacific Corporation; *U.S. Public*, pg. 1668
UNION PACIFIC RESOURCES COMPANY (UPRC)—See Union Pacific Corporation; *U.S. Public*, pg. 1668
UNION PACIFIC TECHNOLOGIES—See Union Pacific Corporation; *U.S. Public*, pg. 1668
UNION PAPER CO.—See Union Industries, Inc.; *U.S. Private*, pg. 1119
UNION PEN COMPANY; *U.S. Public*, pg. 1119
UNION PLANTERS BANK—See Union Planters Corporation; *U.S. Public*, pg. 1669

UNION PLANTERS BANK OF ALABAMA—See Union Planters Corporation; *U.S. Public,* pg. 1669
UNION PLANTERS BANK OF MISSISSIPPI—See Union Planters Corporation; *U.S. Public,* pg. 1669
UNION PLANTERS BANK OF NORTHWEST TENNESSEE—See Union Planters Corporation; *U.S. Public,* pg. 1669
UNION PLANTERS BANK OF WEST TENNESSEE—See Union Planters Corporation; *U.S. Public,* pg. 1669
UNION PLANTERS CORPORATION; *U.S. Public,* pg. 1668
UNION POLYMER CO., LTD.—See Nissho Iwai Corporation; *Int'l,* pg. 949
UNION POUR LE FINANCEMENT D'IMMEUBLES DESOUETES (UIS)—See Groupe GAN; *Int'l,* pg. 565
UNION PUBLICITARIA, DMB&B—See DMB&B Communications; *U.S. Private,* pg. 305
UNION PUMP (CANADA) LTD.—See Union Pump Company; *U.S. Private,* pg. 1119
UNION PUMP COMPANY; *U.S. Private,* pg. 1119
UNION QUARRIES, INC.—See Ash Grove Cement Company; *U.S. Private,* pg. 1332
THE UNION-RECORDER—See Community Newspaper Holdings Inc.; *U.S. Private,* pg. 259
UNION REINSURANCE COMPANY—See Swiss Reinsurance Company; *Int'l,* pg. 1332
UNION SEED CO.—See Land O'Lakes, Inc.; *U.S. Private,* pg. 646
UNION SPECIAL-BELGIUM—See Juki Corporation; *Int'l,* pg. 716
UNION SPECIAL (CANADA) LTD.—See Juki Corporation; *Int'l,* pg. 716
UNION SPECIAL CORP.—See Juki Corporation; *Int'l,* pg. 716
UNION SPECIAL FAR EAST LTD.—See Juki Corporation; *Int'l,* pg. 716
UNION SPECIAL-FRANCE, INC.—See Juki Corporation; *Int'l,* pg. 717
UNION SPECIAL G.M.B.H.—See Juki Corporation; *Int'l,* pg. 717
UNION SPECIAL-JAPAN LTD.—See Juki Corporation; *Int'l,* pg. 717
UNION SPECIAL (UK) LTD.—See Juki Corporation; *Int'l,* pg. 717
UNION STANDARD INSURANCE COMPANY—See W.R. Berkley Corporation; *U.S. Public,* pg. 216
UNION STANDARD OF AMERICA LIFE INSURANCE CO.—See ULLICO Inc.; *U.S. Private,* pg. 1116
UNION SUISSE COMPAGNIE GENERALE D'ASSURANCES—See Assicurazioni Generali S.p.A.; *Int'l,* pg. 92
UNION SWITCH & SIGNAL INC.—See Ansaldo Signal N.V.; *Int'l,* pg. 77
UNION TECHNIQUE INDUSTRIELLE S.A.—See Bristol-Myers Squibb Company; *U.S. Public,* pg. 256
UNION TEXAS PETROLEUM HOLDINGS; *U.S. Public,* pg. 1669
UNION-TRANSPORT—See Union-Transport Corporation; *U.S. Private,* pg. 1120
UNION-TRANSPORT (AUST) PTY LTD—See Union-Transport Corporation; *U.S. Private,* pg. 1120
UNION-TRANSPORT CORPORATION; *U.S. Private,* pg. 1119
UNION-TRANSPORT CORPORATION-BALTIMORE OFFICE—See Union-Transport Corporation; *U.S. Private,* pg. 1119
UNION-TRANSPORT CORPORATION-CHARLOTTE OFFICE—See Union-Transport Corporation; *U.S. Private,* pg. 1119
UNION-TRANSPORT CORPORATION-CLEVELAND OFFICE—See Union-Transport Corporation; *U.S. Private,* pg. 1119
UNION-TRANSPORT CORPORATION-DETROIT OFFICE—See Union-Transport Corporation; *U.S. Private,* pg. 1119
UNION-TRANSPORT CORPORATION-GREENVILLE/SPARTANBURG OFFICE—See Union-Transport Corporation; *U.S. Private,* pg. 1119
UNION-TRANSPORT CORPORATION-LOS ANGELES—See Union-Transport Corporation; *U.S. Private,* pg. 1119
UNION-TRANSPORT CORPORATION-MELVILLE OFFICE—See Union-Transport Corporation; *U.S. Private,* pg. 1119
UNION-TRANSPORT CORPORATION-MEMPHIS OFFICE—See Union-Transport Corporation; *U.S. Private,* pg. 1119
UNION-TRANSPORT CORPORATION-MINNEAPOLIS OFFICE—See Union-Transport Corporation; *U.S. Private,* pg. 1120
UNION-TRANSPORT CORPORATION-OKLAHOMA CITY OFFICE—See Union-Transport Corporation; *U.S. Private,* pg. 1120
UNION-TRANSPORT CORPORATION-ORLANDO OFFICE—See Union-Transport Corporation; *U.S. Private,* pg. 1120
UNION-TRANSPORT CORPORATION-SAINT LOUIS OFFICE—See Union-Transport Corporation; *U.S. Private,* pg. 1120
UNION-TRANSPORT CORPORATION-SALT LAKE CITY OFFICE—See Union-Transport Corporation; *U.S. Private,* pg. 1120
UNION-TRANSPORT CORPORATION-SAN JUAN OFFICE—See Union-Transport Corporation; *U.S. Private,* pg. 1120
UNION-TRANSPORT CORPORATION-SEATTLE OFFICE—See Union-Transport Corporation; *U.S. Private,* pg. 1120
UNION-TRANSPORT CORPORATION-TULSA OFFICE—See Union-Transport Corporation; *U.S. Private,* pg. 1120
UNION-TRANSPORT CORPORATION-WASHINGTON, DC OFFICE—See Union-Transport Corporation; *U.S. Private,* pg. 1120

UNION-TRANSPORT DO BRASIL LTDA—See Union-Transport Corporation; *U.S. Private,* pg. 1120
UNION-TRANSPORT (HK) LTD—See Union-Transport Corporation; *U.S. Private,* pg. 1120
UNION-TRANSPORT LTD—See Union-Transport Corporation; *U.S. Private,* pg. 1120
UNION-TRANSPORT N.V. S.A.—See Union-Transport Corporation; *U.S. Private,* pg. 1120
UNION TRUCKING CO.—See The Standard Products Company; *U.S. Public,* pg. 1505
UNION TRUST BANK—See First Financial Bancorp; *U.S. Public,* pg. 633
UNION UNDERWEAR CO., INC.—See Fruit of the Loom, Inc.; *U.S. Public,* pg. 686
UNION VERWALTUNGS- UND TREUHAND GMBH—See Bayerische Vereinsbank Group; *Int'l,* pg. 180
THE UNION WATER-POWER CO.—See Central Maine Power Company; *U.S. Public,* pg. 325
UNION WERKZEUGMASCHINENFABRIK GERA GMBH—See Metallgesellschaft AG; *Int'l,* pg. 860
UNIONBAY DIVISION—See Seattle Pacific Industries, Inc.; *U.S. Private,* pg. 980
UNIONCARE, INC.—See ULLICO Inc.; *U.S. Private,* pg. 1116
UNIONE CHIMICA MEDICAMENTI-DIFME-S.P.A.—See Solvay S.A.; *Int'l,* pg. 1279
UNIONE MEDITERRANEA DI SICURTA S.P.A.—See Assicurazioni Generali S.p.A.; *Int'l,* pg. 90
UNIONE SUBALPINA DI ASSICURAZIONI—See Allianz Aktiengesellschaft; *Int'l,* pg. 62
UNIONTOOLS, INC.—See Acorn Products, Inc.; *U.S. Public,* pg. 17
UNION-TRANSPORT—See Union-Transport Corporation; *U.S. Private,* pg. 1120
UNIPART GROUP LIMITED—See British Aerospace p.l.c.; *Int'l,* pg. 218
UNIPEN LTD.—See GATX Corporation; *U.S. Public,* pg. 693
UNIPHARMA S.A.—See Pharmacia & Upjohn, Inc.; *Int'l,* pg. 1048
UNIPHASE CORPORATION; *U.S. Public,* pg. 1670
UNIPHONE CABLES SDN. BHD.—See Sumitomo Electric Industries, Ltd.; *Int'l,* pg. 1314
UNIPHONE USHASAMA SDN. BHD.—See Sumitomo Electric Industries, Ltd.; *Int'l,* pg. 1314
UNIPLAST INDUSTRIES, INC.—See Trimin Enterprises, Inc.; *Int'l,* pg. 1424
UNIPLEX—See Oracle Corporation; *U.S. Public,* pg. 1229
UNIPOL GMBH & CO.—See Fuchs Petrolub AG Oel + Chemie; *Int'l,* pg. 519
UNIQUE CASUAL RESTAURANTS, INC.—See Compass Group plc; *Int'l,* pg. 324
UNIQUE CONCEPTS INTERNATIONAL—See Mars Advertising Co.; *U.S. Private,* pg. 707
UNIQUE MINING SYSTEMS, INC.—See The Coastal Corporation; *U.S. Public,* pg. 390
UNIREX CO., LTD.—See Tokuyama Corporation; *Int'l,* pg. 1394
UNIRISC, INC.—See AON Corporation; *U.S. Public,* pg. 117
UNIROC AB—See Atlas Copco AB; *Int'l,* pg. 96
UNIROYAL CHEMICAL B.V.—See Crompton & Knowles Corporation; *U.S. Public,* pg. 460
UNIROYAL CHEMICAL COMPANY, INC.—See Crompton & Knowles Corporation; *U.S. Public,* pg. 460
UNIROYAL CHEMICAL COMPANY, INC. (SINGAPORE)—See Crompton & Knowles Corporation; *U.S. Public,* pg. 460
UNIROYAL CHEMICAL COMPANY LIMITED—See Crompton & Knowles Corporation; *U.S. Public,* pg. 460
UNIROYAL CHEMICAL CORPORATION—See Crompton & Knowles Corporation; *U.S. Public,* pg. 459
UNIROYAL CHEMICAL JAPAN—See Crompton & Knowles Corporation; *U.S. Public,* pg. 460
UNIROYAL CHEMICAL LTD.—See Crompton & Knowles Corporation; *U.S. Public,* pg. 460
UNIROYAL CHIMICA, S.P.A.—See Crompton & Knowles Corporation; *U.S. Public,* pg. 460
UNIROYAL ENGLEBERT REIFEN GMBH—See Continental AG; *Int'l,* pg. 327
UNIROYAL ENGLEBERT TEXTILCORD S.A.—See Continental AG; *Int'l,* pg. 328
UNIROYAL ENGLEBERT TYRES LTD.—See Continental AG; *Int'l,* pg. 327
UNIROYAL GOODRICH CANADA INC.—See Compagnie Generale des Etablissements Michelin; *Int'l,* pg. 322
UNIROYAL QUIMICA, S.A.—See Crompton & Knowles Corporation; *U.S. Public,* pg. 460
UNIROYAL TECHNOLOGY CORPORATION; *U.S. Public,* pg. 1670
UNISEA FOODS, INC.—See Nippon Suisan Kaisha, Ltd.; *Int'l,* pg. 940
UNISEAL, INC.—See George Koch Sons, Inc.; *U.S. Private,* pg. 628
UNISEGUROS VIDA Y PENSIONES (UNIVYP)—See Groupe GAN; *Int'l,* pg. 565
UNISIA JECS CORPORATION—See Nissan Motor Co., Ltd.; *Int'l,* pg. 944
UNISON INDUSTRIES; *U.S. Private,* pg. 1120
UNISOURCE—See Unisource Worldwide, Inc.; *U.S. Public,* pg. 1671
UNISOURCE BUSINESS NETWORKS GMBH—See KPN Koninklyke PTT Nederland NV; *Int'l,* pg. 721
UNISOURCE BUSINESS NETWORKS NEDERLAND BV—See KPN Koninklyke PTT Nederland NV; *Int'l,* pg. 720
UNISOURCE ENERGY CORPORATION; *U.S. Public,* pg. 1670
UNISOURCE NETWORK PARTNERS BV—See KPN Koninklyke PTT Nederland NV; *Int'l,* pg. 720
UNISOURCE (NORTH EAST)—See Unisource Worldwide, Inc.; *U.S. Public,* pg. 1671
UNISOURCE NV—See KPN Koninklyke PTT Nederland NV; *Int'l,* pg. 720
UNISOURCE SATELLITE SERVICES BV—See KPN Koninklyke PTT Nederland NV; *Int'l,* pg. 721
UNISOURCE WORLDWIDE, INC.; *U.S. Public,* pg. 1670

UNISPED SPEDITION UND TRANSPORTGESELLSCHAFT MBH—See Saarbergwerke Aktiengesellschaft; *Int'l,* pg. 1167
UNI-STEEL INC.—See Metals USA, Inc.; *U.S. Public,* pg. 1101
UNISTRUT CORPORATION—See Tyco International Ltd.; *U.S. Public,* pg. 1651
UNISUN INSURANCE CO.—See Orion Capital Corporation; *U.S. Public,* pg. 1231
UNISYS AUSTRALIA LIMITED—See Unisys Corporation; *U.S. Public,* pg. 1671
UNISYS BELGIUM—See Unisys Corporation; *U.S. Public,* pg. 1672
UNISYS CANADA INC.—See Unisys Corporation; *U.S. Public,* pg. 1671
UNISYS CORPORATION; *U.S. Public,* pg. 1671
UNISYS DEUTSCHLAND GMBH—See Unisys Corporation; *U.S. Public,* pg. 1672
UNISYS ELETRONICA LTDA.—See Unisys Corporation; *U.S. Public,* pg. 1671
UNISYS ESPANA S.A.—See Unisys Corporation; *U.S. Public,* pg. 1671
UNISYS FINANCE CORPORATION—See Unisys Corporation; *U.S. Public,* pg. 1671
UNISYS FRANCE—See Unisys Corporation; *U.S. Public,* pg. 1671
UNISYS ITALIA S.P.A.—See Unisys Corporation; *U.S. Public,* pg. 1671
UNISYS LIMITED—See Unisys Corporation; *U.S. Public,* pg. 1671
UNISYS MIDWEST—See Unisys Corporation; *U.S. Public,* pg. 1671
UNISYS NEDERLAND N.V.—See Unisys Corporation; *U.S. Public,* pg. 1671
UNISYS (SCHWEIZ) A.G.—See Unisys Corporation; *U.S. Public,* pg. 1671
UNISYS SEMICONDUCTOR—See Unisys Corporation; *U.S. Public,* pg. 1671
UNISYSTEMS, INC.; *U.S. Private,* pg. 1120
UNIT CONDUIT & CONSTRUCTION—See Koninklijke Hoogovens N.V.; *Int'l,* pg. 754
UNIT CONTIFLO—See Koninklijke Hoogovens N.V.; *Int'l,* pg. 754
UNIT CORPORATION; *U.S. Public,* pg. 1672
UNIT DRILLING COMPANY—See Unit Corporation; *U.S. Public,* pg. 1672
UNIT LOGISTICS INC.—See GATX Corporation; *U.S. Public,* pg. 691
UNIT MULTI-PACK, INC.—See GATX Corporation; *U.S. Public,* pg. 691
UNIT PETROLEUM COMPANY—See Unit Corporation; *U.S. Public,* pg. 1672
UNIT PRECISIEBUIS—See Koninklijke Hoogovens N.V.; *Int'l,* pg. 754
UNIT RAIL ANCHOR COMPANY—See Varlen Corporation; *U.S. Public,* pg. 1711
UNITANK STORAGE CO. LTD.—See GATX Corporation; *U.S. Public,* pg. 693
UNITARY PRODUCTS GROUP—See York International Corporation; *U.S. Public,* pg. 1788
UNITAS CONGRES CENTER LTD.—See Merita Ltd.; *Int'l,* pg. 859
UNITECH INDUSTRIES, INC.; *U.S. Public,* pg. 1672
UNITECH PLC—See Siebe plc; *Int'l,* pg. 1241
UNITECTA ITALIANA SPA—See Williams Holdings Plc; *Int'l,* pg. 1501
UNITED ACEROS BOEHLER S.A.—See Voest-Alpine Stahl AG; *Int'l,* pg. 1472
UNITED ACQUISITION CORPORATION—See Red Apple Companies; *U.S. Private,* pg. 915
UNITED ADVERTISING PUBLICATIONS, INC.—See United News & Media plc; *Int'l,* pg. 1443
UNITED ADVERTISING PUBLICATIONS PLC—See United News & Media plc; *Int'l,* pg. 1443
UNITED AGRI PRODUCTS CO.—See ConAgra, Inc.; *U.S. Public,* pg. 426
UNITED AGRICULTURAL MERCHANTS LTD.—See Unilever Plc; *Int'l,* pg. 1434
UNITED AIR LINES CREDIT CORPORATION—See UAL Corporation; *U.S. Public,* pg. 1653
UNITED AIR LINES, INC.—See UAL Corporation; *U.S. Public,* pg. 1653
PT. UNITED AIR PRODUCTS INDONESIA—See Air Products and Chemicals, Inc.; *U.S. Public,* pg. 32
UNITED AIR SPECIALISTS, INC.—See CLARCOR, Inc.; *U.S. Public,* pg. 382
UNITED AIRCRAFT PRODUCTS—See Parker Hannifin Corporation; *U.S. Public,* pg. 1262
UNITED ALLIANT FOOD SERVICE—See Clayton, Dubilier & Rice, Inc; *U.S. Private,* pg. 244
UNITED ALUMINUM CORPORATION; *U.S. Private,* pg. 1120
UNITED AMERICAN INSURANCE CO.—See Torchmark Corporation; *U.S. Public,* pg. 1623
UNITED ARTISTS PICTURES, INC.—See Metro-Goldwyn-Mayer Inc.; *U.S. Public,* pg. 1102
UNITED ARTISTS THEATRE CIRCUITS INCORPORATED; *U.S. Private,* pg. 1120
UNITED-ASATSU INTERNATIONAL LTD.—See Asatsu Inc.; *Int'l,* pg. 86
UNITED ASSET MANAGEMENT CORPORATION; *U.S. Public,* pg. 1672
UNITED ASSET MANAGEMENT (JAPAN), INC.—See United Asset Management Corporation; *U.S. Public,* pg. 1674
UNITED ASSET MANAGEMENT-LONDON OFFICE—See United Asset Management Corporation; *U.S. Public,* pg. 1674
UNITED AUSTRALIAN AUTOMOTIVE INDUSTRIES LTD.—See General Motors Corporation; *U.S. Public,* pg. 725
UNITED AUTO GROUP, INC.—See Trace International Holdings, Inc.; *U.S. Private,* pg. 1095
UNITED AVIATION FUELS CORP.—See UAL Corporation; *U.S. Public,* pg. 1653

UNITED BANK FOR AFRICA, LTD.—See Bankers Trust New York Corporation; *U.S. Public*, pg. 186
UNITED BANKSHARES, INC.; *U.S. Public*, pg. 1674
UNITED BEVERAGES LIMITED—See James Crean PLC; *Int'l*, pg. 340
UNITED BISCUITS ASIA PACIFIC—See United Biscuits (Holdings) Plc; *Int'l*, pg. 1442
UNITED BISCUITS (HOLDINGS) PLC; *Int'l*, pg. 1442
UNITED BISCUITS (UK) LIMITED—See United Biscuits (Holdings) Plc; *Int'l*, pg. 1442
UNITED BRAKE SYSTEMS, INC.—See Echlin Inc.; *U.S. Public*, pg. 561
UNITED BROADCASTING L.P.; *U.S. Private*, pg. 1121
UNITED CAPITAL CORP.; *U.S. Public*, pg. 1674
UNITED CAPITAL CORP.—See United Capital Corp.; *U.S. Public*, pg. 1675
UNITED CAPITOL INSURANCE COMPANY—See Capsure Holdings Corp.; *U.S. Public*, pg. 303
UNITED CAPITOL INSURANCE COMPANY—See Frontier Insurance Group, Inc.; *U.S. Public*, pg. 685
UNITED CASUALTY INSURANCE COMPANY OF AMERICA—See Unitrin, Inc.; *U.S. Public*, pg. 1694
UNITED CEMENT CO.—See Holderbank Financiere Glaris Ltd.; *Int'l*, pg. 628
UNITED CHAIR, INC.—See Haworth, Inc.; *U.S. Private*, pg. 512
UNITED CHEMICAL PRODUCTS—See Mays Chemical Company; *U.S. Private*, pg. 718
UNITED CITIES GAS COMPANY—See Atmos Energy Corporation; *U.S. Public*, pg. 146
UNITED CLAYS, INC.—See Watts Blake Bearne & Co. Plc; *Int'l*, pg. 1487
UNITED COASTAL INSURANCE COMPANY—See ACMAT Corporation; *U.S. Public*, pg. 16
UNITED COATINGS, INC.—See The Sherwin-Williams Company; *U.S. Public*, pg. 1466
UNITED COGEN, INC.—See UAL Corporation; *U.S. Public*, pg. 1653
UNITED COIN MACHINE CO.—See Alliance Gaming Corporation; *U.S. Public*, pg. 47
UNITED COMPANIES FINANCIAL CORPORATION; *U.S. Public*, pg. 1675
UNITED COMPANIES INVESTOR SERVICES, INC.—See United Companies Financial Corporation; *U.S. Public*, pg. 1675
THE UNITED COMPANY; *U.S. Private*, pg. 1121
UNITED CONCORDIA COMPANIES INC.—See Highmark Inc.; *U.S. Private*, pg. 529
UNITED CONSUMER FINANCIAL SERVICES CO.—See Berkshire Hathaway Inc.; *U.S. Public*, pg. 218
UNITED CONTINENTAL STEELS LTD U.C.S.—See Cockerill Sambre; *Int'l*, pg. 302
UNITED CREDIT CORP. & PATROIT FUNDING; *U.S. Private*, pg. 1121
UNITED DAIRY FARMERS, INC.; *U.S. Private*, pg. 1121
UNITED DAIRYMEN OF ARIZONA; *U.S. Private*, pg. 1121
UNITED DEFENSE L.P.—See Carlyle Holding Corporation; *U.S. Private*, pg. 213
UNITED DESIGN CORPORATION; *U.S. Private*, pg. 1121
UNITED DISTILLERS BLENDING & BOTTLING LTD.—See Diageo Plc; *Int'l*, pg. 412
UNITED DISTILLERS CURIEL DE MARGARITA, S.A.—See Diageo Plc; *Int'l*, pg. 412
UNITED DISTILLERS PLC—See Diageo Plc; *Int'l*, pg. 412
UNITED DISTILLERS UK PLC—See Diageo Plc; *Int'l*, pg. 412
UNITED DISTILLERS USA, INC.—See Diageo Plc; *Int'l*, pg. 412
UNITED DISTRIBUTORS, INC.; *U.S. Private*, pg. 1121
UNITED DOMINION INDUSTRIES, LTD.; *U.S. Public*, pg. 1675
UNITED DOMINION REALTY TRUST, INC.; *U.S. Public*, pg. 1677
UNITED EASTERN COAL SALES CORP.—See Rochester & Pittsburgh Coal Company; *U.S. Public*, pg. 1395
UNITED ECO SYSTEMS—See American Eco Corporation; *Int'l*, pg. 74
UNITED ELECTRONICS INDUSTRIES, INC.—See United Technologies Corporation; *U.S. Public*, pg. 1690
UNITED EMPLOYERS INS.—See United Grocers Inc.; *U.S. Private*, pg. 1122
UNITED ENERGY CORPORATION—See Alabama Electric Cooperative, Inc.; *U.S. Private*, pg. 30
UNITED ENERGY INTERNATIONAL, INC.—See United Illuminating Company; *U.S. Public*, pg. 1678
UNITED ENGINE & MACHINE COMPANY; *U.S. Private*, pg. 1121
UNITED ENGINES, INC.; *U.S. Private*, pg. 1122
UNITED FAMILY LIFE INSURANCE CO.—See Fortis; *Int'l*, pg. 499
UNITED FARM FAMILY LIFE INSURANCE CO.; *U.S. Private*, pg. 1122
UNITED FARM TOOLS, INC.; *U.S. Private*, pg. 1122
UNITED FEEDS, INC.; *U.S. Private*, pg. 1122
UNITED FILTERS, INC.—See Perry Equipment Corporation; *U.S. Private*, pg. 855
UNITED FINANCIAL CASUALTY CO.—See The Progressive Corporation; *U.S. Public*, pg. 1335
UNITED FINANCIAL SERVICES, INC.—See AEGON N.V.; *Int'l*, pg. 27
UNITED FIRE & CASUALTY COMPANY; *U.S. Public*, pg. 1677
UNITED FLEXIBLE—See Senior Engineering Group, plc.; *Int'l*, pg. 1221
UNITED FOODS, INC.; *U.S. Public*, pg. 1677
UNITED GAS CO. LTD.—See UtiliCorp United Inc.; *U.S. Public*, pg. 1701
UNITED GENERAL LIFE INSURANCE—See Conseco Inc.; *U.S. Public*, pg. 433
UNITED GHS INC.—See UAL Corporation; *U.S. Public*, pg. 1653
UNITED GRAIN GROWERS LTD.; *Int'l*, pg. 1442
UNITED GRAPHICS, INC.—See Banta Corporation; *U.S. Public*, pg. 188

UNITED GROCERS INC.; *U.S. Private*, pg. 1122
UNITED GUARANTY CORP.—See American International Group, Inc.; *U.S. Public*, pg. 84
UNITED HARDWARE DISTRIBUTING CO.—See Distribution America; *U.S. Private*, pg. 335
UNITED HEALTH, INC.—See Extendicare Inc.; *Int'l*, pg. 468
UNITED HEALTHCARE CORPORATION; *U.S. Public*, pg. 1677
UNITED HEALTHCARE INSURANCE COMPANY—See United HealthCare Corporation; *U.S. Public*, pg. 1678
UNITED HEALTHCARE OF FLORIDA, INC.—See United HealthCare Corporation; *U.S. Public*, pg. 1678
UNITED HEALTHCARE OF GEORGIA, INC.—See United HealthCare Corporation; *U.S. Public*, pg. 1678
UNITED HEALTHCARE OF NEVADA, INC.—See United HealthCare Corporation; *U.S. Public*, pg. 1678
UNITED HEALTHCARE OF NORTH CAROLINA, INC.—See United HealthCare Corporation; *U.S. Public*, pg. 1678
UNITED HEALTHCARE OF OHIO, INC.—See United HealthCare Corporation; *U.S. Public*, pg. 1678
UNITED HEALTHCARE OF OREGON, INC.—See United HealthCare Corporation; *U.S. Public*, pg. 1678
UNITED HEALTHCARE OF TEXAS, INC.—See United HealthCare Corporation; *U.S. Public*, pg. 1678
UNITED HEALTHCARE OF THE MIDLANDS, INC.—See United HealthCare Corporation; *U.S. Public*, pg. 1678
UNITED HEALTHCARE OF UTAH—See United HealthCare Corporation; *U.S. Public*, pg. 1678
UNITED HEALTHCARE PLANS OF NEW ENGLAND, INC.—See United HealthCare Corporation; *U.S. Public*, pg. 1678
UNITED HEALTHCARE SERVICES, INC.—See United HealthCare Corporation; *U.S. Public*, pg. 1678
UNITED ILLUMINATING COMPANY; *U.S. Public*, pg. 1678
UNITED INDUSTRIAL CORPORATION; *U.S. Public*, pg. 1679
UNITED INSURANCE COMPANIES, INC.; *U.S. Public*, pg. 1679
UNITED INSURANCE COMPANY OF AMERICA—See Unitrin, Inc.; *U.S. Public*, pg. 1694
UNITED INSURANCE CORPORATION OF AMERICA—See Unitrin, Inc.; *U.S. Public*, pg. 1694
UNITED INTERNATIONAL FERRY FREIGHT LTD.—See Sophus Berendsen A/S; *Int'l*, pg. 1285
UNITED INVESTORS EQUITY SERVICES, INC.—See Torchmark Corporation; *U.S. Public*, pg. 1623
UNITED INVESTORS LIFE INSURANCE CO.—See Torchmark Corporation; *U.S. Public*, pg. 1623
UNITED INVESTORS MANAGEMENT COMPANY—See Torchmark Corporation; *U.S. Public*, pg. 1623
UNITED JERSEY BANK SERVICES CO—See Summit Bancorp; *U.S. Public*, pg. 1528
UNITED JERSEY CREDIT LIFE INSURANCE COMPANY—See Summit Bancorp; *U.S. Public*, pg. 1528
UNITED JERSEY LEASING COMPANY—See Summit Bancorp; *U.S. Public*, pg. 1528
UNITED JERSEY VENTURE CAPITAL, INC.—See Summit Bancorp; *U.S. Public*, pg. 1528
UNITED KINGDOM PLANT—See Cooper Industries, Inc.; *U.S. Public*, pg. 443
UNITED KNITTING, INC.—See Dyersburg Corporation; *U.S. Public*, pg. 538
UNITED LABORATORIES, INC.; *U.S. Private*, pg. 1122
UNITED LAND CORP.—See Walter Industries, Inc.; *U.S. Public*, pg. 1736
UNITED LEASING COMPANY—See Michigan Physicians Mutual Liability Inc.; *U.S. Private*, pg. 741
UNITED LEASING COMPANY, LIMITED—See The Toyo Trust and Banking Company, Limited; *Int'l*, pg. 1411
UNITED LEASING, INC.—See UniGroup, Inc.; *U.S. Private*, pg. 1117
UNITED LIFE INSURANCE COMPANY—See United Fire & Casualty Company; *U.S. Public*, pg. 1677
UNITED LITHO, INC.—See The Sheridan Group; *U.S. Private*, pg. 993
UNITED MAILING, INC.—See The Instant Web Companies; *U.S. Private*, pg. 565
UNITED MARKETING (LEICESTER) LTD.—See The Black & Decker Corporation; *U.S. Public*, pg. 234
UNITED MCGILL CORP.; *U.S. Private*, pg. 1122
UNITED MEDIA—See The E.W. Scripps Company; *U.S. Public*, pg. 1448
UNITED MEDIA CANADA—See The E.W. Scripps Company; *U.S. Public*, pg. 1448
UNITED MEDIA EUROPE/SCRIPPS—See The E.W. Scripps Company; *U.S. Public*, pg. 1448
UNITED MEDIA JAPAN—See The E.W. Scripps Company; *U.S. Public*, pg. 1448
UNITED METAL RECEPTACLE CORP.—See United Receptical, Inc.; *U.S. Public*, pg. 1124
UNITED METERING INC.—See United Water Resources; *U.S. Public*, pg. 1692
THE UNITED METHODIST PUBLISHING HOUSE; *U.S. Private*, pg. 1122
UNITED MISSOURI BANK NORTHEAST—See UMB Financial Corporation; *U.S. Public*, pg. 1654
UNITED MISSOURI BANK NORTHWEST—See UMB Financial Corporation; *U.S. Public*, pg. 1654
UNITED MISSOURI BROKERAGE SERVICES—See UMB Financial Corporation; *U.S. Public*, pg. 1655
UNITED MISSOURI CAPITAL CORPORATION—See UMB Financial Corporation; *U.S. Public*, pg. 1655
UNITED MISSOURI INSURANCE CO.—See UMB Financial Corporation; *U.S. Public*, pg. 1655
UNITED MISSOURI LEASING CORPORATION—See UMB Financial Corporation; *U.S. Public*, pg. 1655
UNITED MISSOURI MORTGAGE COMPANY—See UMB Financial Corporation; *U.S. Public*, pg. 1655
UNITED MISSOURI TRUST COMPANY OF NEW YORK—See UMB Financial Corporation; *U.S. Public*, pg. 1655
UNITED MOLASSES COMPANY—See Tate & Lyle PLC; *Int'l*, pg. 1356
UNITED NATIONAL BANCORP; *U.S. Public*, pg. 1679
UNITED NEWS & MEDIA PLC; *Int'l*, pg. 1443

UNITED OF OMAHA LIFE INSURANCE COMPANY—See Mutual of Omaha Insurance Company; *U.S. Private*, pg. 770
UNITED ORIX LEASING BERHAD—See Orix Corporation; *Int'l*, pg. 1010
UNITED OVERSEAS BANK LTD.—See United Overseas Land Limited; *Int'l*, pg. 1443
UNITED OVERSEAS LAND LIMITED; *Int'l*, pg. 1443
UNITED PACIFIC DRILLING P/L—See Imperial Chemical Industries PLC; *Int'l*, pg. 666
UNITED PACKAGING PLC—See TT Group PLC; *Int'l*, pg. 1344
UNITED PAINT CO.—See The Sherwin-Williams Company; *U.S. Public*, pg. 1466
UNITED PAPER INDUSTRIES PTE. LTD.—See United Pulp & Paper Company Limited; *Int'l*, pg. 1444
UNITED PAPER MILLS LTD.—See UPM-Kymmene Corporation; *Int'l*, pg. 1429
UNITED PARCEL SERVICE OF AMERICA, INC.; *U.S. Private*, pg. 1123
UNITED PARCEL SERVICE OF CANADA—See United Parcel Service of America, Inc.; *U.S. Private*, pg. 1123
UNITED PARKING, INC.; *U.S. Private*, pg. 1123
UNITED PARKING SERVICES, INC.—See Central Parking Corp.; *U.S. Public*, pg. 326
UNITED PIECE DYE WORKS, LP; *U.S. Private*, pg. 1123
UNITED PIPELINE SYSTEM USA, INC.—See Insituform Technologies, Inc.; *U.S. Public*, pg. 882
UNITED PIPELINE SYSTEMS, INC—See Insituform Technologies, Inc.; *U.S. Public*, pg. 882
UNITED PLANNERS' FINANCIAL SERVICES OF AMERICA—See Pacific Life Insurance Company; *U.S. Private*, pg. 831
UNITED POWER & LAND CO.—See Northern States Power Company; *U.S. Public*, pg. 1195
UNITED POWER ASSOCIATION; *U.S. Private*, pg. 1123
UNITED PRESIDENTIAL LIFE INSURANCE CO.—See Conseco Inc.; *U.S. Public*, pg. 434
UNITED PRODUCERS & CONSUMERS CO-OP; *U.S. Private*, pg. 1123
UNITED PROPERTIES; *U.S. Private*, pg. 1123
UNITED PROPERTIES GROUP—See United Water Resources; *U.S. Public*, pg. 1692
UNITED PROVINCIAL NEWSPAPERS LTD.—See United News & Media plc; *Int'l*, pg. 1443
UNITED PULP & PAPER COMPANY LIMITED; *Int'l*, pg. 1444
UNITED RAILWAY SIGNAL GROUP INC.—See ABC Rail Products Corp.; *U.S. Public*, pg. 2
UNITED RECEPTICAL, INC.; *U.S. Private*, pg. 1123
UNITED REFINING COMPANY—See Red Apple Companies; *U.S. Private*, pg. 915
UNITED REFINING INC.—See Red Apple Companies; *U.S. Private*, pg. 915
UNITED RESOURCES, INC.—See United Illuminating Company; *U.S. Public*, pg. 1678
UNITED RETAIL GROUP, INC.; *U.S. Public*, pg. 1679
UNITED SCIENCES INC.—See Bowthorpe plc; *Int'l*, pg. 208
UNITED SELF INSURED SERVICES—See Poe & Brown, Inc.; *U.S. Public*, pg. 1312
UNITED SERVICE EQUIPMENT COMPANY—See Standex International Corporation; *U.S. Public*, pg. 1507
UNITED SERVICES LIFE INSURANCE CO.—See ReliaStar Financial Corp.; *U.S. Public*, pg. 1376
UNITED SISTEMA DE TUBERIAS LTDA—See Insituform Technologies, Inc.; *U.S. Public*, pg. 882
UNITED SOLAR SYSTEMS CORP.—See Energy Conversion Devices, Inc.; *U.S. Public*, pg. 581
UNITED SOUTHERN BANK—See Union Planters Corporation; *U.S. Public*, pg. 1669
UNITED SOUTHWEST BANK—See Old National Bancorp; *U.S. Public*, pg. 1217
UNITED SPACE BOOSTERS, INC.—See United Technologies Corporation; *U.S. Public*, pg. 1690
UNITED STANDARD ASSET GROWTH CORP.—See AEGON N.V.; *Int'l*, pg. 26
US AGRI-CHEMICALS CORPORATION—See Sinochem International Petroleum Co.; *Int'l*, pg. 1255
UNITED STATES AIRLEASE, INCORPORATED—See Ford Motor Company; *U.S. Public*, pg. 664
US AIRWAYS FUEL CORPORATION—See US Airways Group, Inc.; *U.S. Public*, pg. 1680
US AIRWAYS GROUP, INC.; *U.S. Public*, pg. 1680
US AIRWAYS, INC.—See US Airways Group, Inc.; *U.S. Public*, pg. 1680
US AIRWAYS LEASING & SERVICES, INC.—See US Airways Group, Inc.; *U.S. Public*, pg. 1680
US AIRWAYS SHUTTLE; *U.S. Private*, pg. 1124
UNITED STATES ALUMINUM-CAROLINA—See International Aluminum Corporation; *U.S. Public*, pg. 895
UNITED STATES ALUMINUM CORP.—See International Aluminum Corporation; *U.S. Public*, pg. 895
UNITED STATES ALUMINUM CORP.-ILLINOIS—See International Aluminum Corporation; *U.S. Public*, pg. 895
UNITED STATES ALUMINUM CORP.-TEXAS—See International Aluminum Corporation; *U.S. Public*, pg. 895
U.S. AMADA—See Amada Co., Ltd.; *Int'l*, pg. 70
U.S. & CANADIAN FOOD PRODUCTS—See The Quaker Oats Company; *U.S. Public*, pg. 1347
UNITED STATES AUTO CLUB, MOTORING DIVISION, INC.—See Ford Motor Company; *U.S. Public*, pg. 663
U.S. AVIATION UNDERWRITERS, INC.—See General Re Corporation; *U.S. Public*, pg. 726
U.S. AXLE, INC.; *U.S. Private*, pg. 1124
THE U.S. BAIRD CORPORATION; *U.S. Private*, pg. 1124
UNITED STATES BAKERY; *U.S. Private*, pg. 1124
U.S. BANCORP; *U.S. Public*, pg. 1680
U.S. BANCORP BROKERAGE—See U.S. Bancorp; *U.S. Public*, pg. 1681

Company Index

U.S. BANCORP INSURANCE AGENCY, INC.—See U.S. Bancorp; *U.S. Public*, pg. 1681
U.S. BANCORP LEASING & FINANCIAL—See U.S. Bancorp; *U.S. Public*, pg. 1681
US BANK—See BankAmerica Corporation; *U.S. Public*, pg. 181
U.S. BANK FINANCIAL SERVICES, INC.—See U.S. Bancorp; *U.S. Public*, pg. 1681
U.S. BANK INSURANCE AGENCY—See U.S. Bancorp; *U.S. Public*, pg. 1681
U.S. BANK OF CALIFORNIA—See U.S. Bancorp; *U.S. Public*, pg. 1681
U.S. BANK OF IDAHO—See U.S. Bancorp; *U.S. Public*, pg. 1681
U.S. BANK OF UTAH—See U.S. Bancorp; *U.S. Public*, pg. 1681
U.S. BANK OF WASHINGTON N.A.—See U.S. Bancorp; *U.S. Public*, pg. 1681
US BENEFITS INSURANCE SERVICES, INC.—See Centris Group Inc.; *U.S. Public*, pg. 328
UNITED STATES BIOMEDICAL CORPORATION—See Nycomed Amersham plc; *Int'l*, pg. 992
U.S. BIOSCIENCE, INC.; *U.S. Public*, pg. 1681
U.S. BORAX INC.—See Rio Tinto PLC; *Int'l*, pg. 1119
U.S. BOTTLERS MACHINERY CO.; *U.S. Private*, pg. 1124
U.S. BRASS—See Zurn Industries, Inc.; *U.S. Public*, pg. 1794
UNITED STATES BRASS CORPORATION—See Zurn Industries, Inc.; *U.S. Public*, pg. 1795
U.S. BRICK, INC.—See Jannock Limited; *Int'l*, pg. 699
U.S. BRICK, INC.-MICHIGAN DIVISION—See Jannock Limited; *Int'l*, pg. 699
U.S. BRICK, INC.-SIPPLE BRICK DIVISION—See Jannock Limited; *Int'l*, pg. 699
U.S. BRICK-SAN ANTONIO—See Jannock Limited; *Int'l*, pg. 699
U.S. BROACH & MACHINE COMPANY—See Avis Industrial Corporation; *U.S. Private*, pg. 102
UNITED STATES BRONZE POWDERS, INC.; *U.S. Private*, pg. 1124
U.S. CAN COMPANY; *U.S. Public*, pg. 1681
UNITED STATES CELLULAR CORPORATION—See Telephone and Data Systems, Inc.; *U.S. Public*, pg. 1572
U.S. CENTRAL CREDIT UNION—See Credit Union National Association; *U.S. Private*, pg. 288
UNITED STATES CERAMIC TILE CO.; *U.S. Private*, pg. 1124
U.S. CHEM RESOURCES INC.—See Sinochem International Petroleum Co. Ltd.; *Int'l*, pg. 1255
U.S. CLEARING CORP.—See Fleet Financial Group, Inc.; *U.S. Public*, pg. 650
UNITED STATES COLD STORAGE, INC.; *U.S. Private*, pg. 1124
UNITED STATES COLD STORAGE OF CALIF.—See United States Cold Storage, Inc.; *U.S. Private*, pg. 1125
U.S. COMMERCIAL TELEPHONE CORP.—See Peoples Telephone Company, Inc.; *U.S. Public*, pg. 1276
U.S. COMPUTERS—See Hewlett-Packard Company; *U.S. Public*, pg. 815
U.S. CONTAINER DIV.—See International Paper Company; *U.S. Public*, pg. 903
UNITED STATES CORRULITE CORPORATION—See United States Sugar Corporation; *U.S. Private*, pg. 1126
U.S. DIRECT SELLING DIVISION—See Avon Products, Inc.; *U.S. Public*, pg. 156
U.S. DIVERS CO., INC.; *U.S. Private*, pg. 1125
US ECOLOGY, INC.—See American Ecology Corporation; *U.S. Public*, pg. 71
U.S. ELECTRICAL MOTOR DIVISION—See Emerson Electric Co.; *U.S. Public*, pg. 573
U.S. ELEVATOR—See Thyssen AG; *Int'l*, pg. 1387
U.S. ENGINE VALVE CORPORATION—See Eaton Corporation; *U.S. Public*, pg. 558
UNITED STATES FIDELITY & GUARANTY COMPANY—See USF&G Corporation; *U.S. Public*, pg. 1659
U.S. FILTER—See Aluminum Company of America; *U.S. Public*, pg. 61
U.S. FILTER—See United States Filter Corporation; *U.S. Public*, pg. 1682
U.S. FILTER/ARROWHEAD INC.—See United States Filter Corporation; *U.S. Public*, pg. 1682
U.S. FILTER CO., AMES—See Aluminum Company of America; *U.S. Public*, pg. 61
UNITED STATES FILTER CORPORATION; *U.S. Public*, pg. 1681
U.S. FILTER/DAVIS WATER & WASTE INDUSTRIES, INC.—See United States Filter Corporation; *U.S. Public*, pg. 1682
U.S. FILTER/PERMUTIT—See United States Filter Corporation; *U.S. Public*, pg. 1682
U.S. FILTERS CONTROL SYSTEMS—See Aluminum Company of America; *U.S. Public*, pg. 61
U.S. FINISHING—See American Fast Print, Limited; *U.S. Private*, pg. 54
UNITED STATES FIRE INSURANCE COMPANY—See Xerox Corporation; *U.S. Public*, pg. 1784
UNITED STATES FLEET LEASING, INC.—See Ford Motor Company; *U.S. Public*, pg. 664
U.S. FOOD SERVICE—See JP Foodservice, Inc.; *U.S. Public*, pg. 918
U.S. FURNITURE INDUSTRIES, INC.; *U.S. Private*, pg. 1125
U.S. GENERATING COMPANY—See PG&E Corporation; *U.S. Public*, pg. 1241
UNITED STATES GYPSUM CO.—See USG Corporation; *U.S. Public*, pg. 1660
UNITED STATES HEALTH CARE SYSTEMS OF PENNSYLVANIA, INC.—See Aetna Inc.; *U.S. Public*, pg. 26
U.S. HEALTH INSURANCE COMPANY—See Aetna Inc.; *U.S. Public*, pg. 26

U.S. HEALTHCARE, INC.—See Aetna Inc.; *U.S. Public*, pg. 26
U.S. HEALTHCARE (NEW YORK)—See Aetna Inc.; *U.S. Public*, pg. 26
U.S. HEALTHCARE OF GEORGIA, INC.—See Aetna Inc.; *U.S. Public*, pg. 27
U.S. HEALTHCARE OF NEW HAMPSHIRE, INC.—See Aetna Inc.; *U.S. Public*, pg. 27
U.S. HEALTHCARE PROPERTIES, INC.—See Aetna Inc.; *U.S. Public*, pg. 27
U.S. HOME & GARDEN INC.; *U.S. Public*, pg. 1682
U.S. HOME CORPORATION; *U.S. Public*, pg. 1682
U.S. HOME MORTGAGE CORPORATION—See U.S. Home Corporation; *U.S. Public*, pg. 1683
U.S. INDUSTRIES, INC.; *U.S. Public*, pg. 1683
US INK CORP.—See Dainippon Ink & Chemicals, Inc.; *Int'l*, pg. 370
U.S. INTEC, INC.—See GAF Corporation; *U.S. Private*, pg. 433
USLIFE ADVISERS, INC.—See American General Corporation; *U.S. Public*, pg. 77
USLIFE AGENCY SERVICES, INC.—See American General Corporation; *U.S. Public*, pg. 77
USLIFE CORPORATION—See American General Corporation; *U.S. Public*, pg. 77
USLIFE EQUITY SALES CORP.—See American General Corporation; *U.S. Public*, pg. 77
USLIFE FINANCIAL INSTITUTION MARKETING GROUP, INC.—See American General Corporation; *U.S. Public*, pg. 77
THE UNITED STATES LIFE INS. CO. IN THE CITY OF NEW YORK—See American General Corporation; *U.S. Public*, pg. 77
USLIFE INSURANCE SERVICES CORPORATION—See American General Corporation; *U.S. Public*, pg. 77
USLIFE REAL ESTATE SERVICES CORP.—See American General Corporation; *U.S. Public*, pg. 77
USLIFE SYSTEMS CORPORATION—See American General Corporation; *U.S. Public*, pg. 77
UNITED STATES LIME & MINERALS; *U.S. Public*, pg. 1684
U.S. LOCK—See Waxman Industries, Inc.; *U.S. Public*, pg. 1748
UNITED STATES LOCK & HARDWARE CO.—See York Barbell Co., Inc.; *U.S. Private*, pg. 1196
UNITED STATES LUGGAGE COMPANY; *U.S. Private*, pg. 1125
U.S. MANUFACTURING CORP.; *U.S. Private*, pg. 1125
U.S. MARINE DIV.—See Brunswick Corporation; *U.S. Public*, pg. 266
U.S. MARINE DIVISION—See Brunswick Corporation; *U.S. Public*, pg. 266
U.S. MENTAL HEALTH SYSTEMS, INC.—See Aetna Inc.; *U.S. Public*, pg. 27
UNITED STATES NAME PLATE—See La France Corporation; *U.S. Private*, pg. 640
UNITED STATES NATIONAL BANK—See Cullen/Frost Bankers, Inc.; *U.S. Public*, pg. 467
UNITED STATES NATIONAL BANK OF OREGON—See U.S. Bancorp; *U.S. Public*, pg. 1681
U.S. NEWS & WORLD REPORT—See ; *U.S. Private*, pg. 1125
USA CASUALTY COMPANY—See ULLICO Inc.; *U.S. Private*, pg. 1116
USA DETERGENTS, INC.; *U.S. Public*, pg. 1685
USA FLORAL PRODUCTS, INC.; *U.S. Public*, pg. 1685
USA NETWORK CONTROL CENTER—See USA Networks, Inc.; *U.S. Public*, pg. 1686
USA NETWORKS—See USA Networks, Inc.; *U.S. Public*, pg. 1686
USA NETWORKS, INC.; *U.S. Public*, pg. 1685
USA PETROLEUM CORPORATION; *U.S. Private*, pg. 1125
USA TODAY—See Gannett Company, Inc.; *U.S. Public*, pg. 700
USA WASTE SERVICES, INC.**; *U.S. Public*, pg. 1686
USA WEEKEND—See Gannett Company, Inc.; *U.S. Public*, pg. 701
U.S. OFFICE PRODUCTS COMPANY; *U.S. Public*, pg. 1686
U.S. OIL & REFINING CO.—See Time Oil Company; *U.S. Private*, pg. 1086
US 1 INDUSTRIES INC.; *U.S. Public*, pg. 1687
U.S. PHARMACEUTICALS—See Alpharma Inc.; *U.S. Public*, pg. 58
UNITED STATES PHYSICIANS CARE SYSTEMS, INC.—See Aetna Inc.; *U.S. Public*, pg. 27
UNITED STATES PIPE & FOUNDRY COMPANY, INC.—See Walter Industries, Inc.; *U.S. Public*, pg. 1736
U.S. PIPELINE, INC.—See Agra Inc.; *Int'l*, pg. 31
THE UNITED STATES PLAYING CARD COMPANY; *U.S. Private*, pg. 1125
U.S. PRECISION LENS INC.—See Corning Incorporated; *U.S. Public*, pg. 448
UNITED STATES PROTECTION AND INDEMNITY AGENCY, INC.—See Loews Corporation; *U.S. Public*, pg. 1011
U.S. PULP AND NEWSPRINT—See Kimberly-Clark Corporation; *U.S. Public*, pg. 959
U.S. QUALITY ALGORITHMS, INC.—See Aetna Inc.; *U.S. Public*, pg. 27
UNITED STATES REALTY & INVESTMENT CO.; *U.S. Private*, pg. 1125
U.S. REPEATING ARMS COMPANY; *U.S. Private*, pg. 1125
US REPROGRAPHICS, INC.—See Wilco Reprographic, Inc.; *U.S. Private*, pg. 1176
U.S. RING BINDER CORP.—See General Binding Corporation; *U.S. Public*, pg. 707
U.S. RING-ST. LOUIS—See General Binding Corporation; *U.S. Public*, pg. 707
U.S. SAFETY; *U.S. Private*, pg. 1125
UNITED STATES SATELLITE BROADCASTING, CO.—See Hubbard Broadcasting, Inc.; *U.S. Private*, pg. 544
U.S. SECURITY ASSOCIATES, INC.; *U.S. Private*, pg. 1126
US SERVIS; *U.S. Public*, pg. 1687

USSI—See Transaction Systems Architects, Inc.; *U.S. Public*, pg. 1629
U.S. SPECIALTY INSURANCE CO.—See Avemco Corporation; *U.S. Public*, pg. 152
U.S. STEAMSERVICE, INC.—See Tamrock Corp.; *Int'l*, pg. 1354
U.S. STEEL INTERNATIONAL, INC.—See USX Corporation; *U.S. Public*, pg. 1661
US STEEL MINING CO., INC.—See USX Corporation; *U.S. Public*, pg. 1662
US STEEL TECHNICAL CENTER—See USX Corporation; *U.S. Public*, pg. 1662
UNITED STATES SUGAR CORPORATION; *U.S. Private*, pg. 1126
U.S. SURGICAL CORP.; *U.S. Public*, pg. 1687
U.S. TAG—See Champion Industries; *U.S. Public*, pg. 333
U.S. TIMBERLANDS COMPANY, L.P.; *U.S. Public*, pg. 1688
UNITED STATES TOBACCO COMPANY—See UST Inc.; *U.S. Public*, pg. 1661
U.S. TRAILS; *U.S. Public*, pg. 1688
U.S. TRANSPARTS—See Moran Industries, Inc.; *U.S. Private*, pg. 760
USTRUST—See UST Corporation; *U.S. Public*, pg. 1660
UNITED STATES TRUST COMPANY—See UST Corporation; *U.S. Public*, pg. 1660
UNITED STATES TRUST CO. OF NEW YORK—See U.S. Trust Corporation; *U.S. Public*, pg. 1688
U.S. TRUST CORPORATION; *U.S. Public*, pg. 1688
U.S. TSUBAKI, INC.—See Tsubakimoto Chain Co.; *Int'l*, pg. 1425
U.S. TURBINE CORPORATION—See Rolls-Royce plc; *Int'l*, pg. 1127
UNITED STATES WALLBOARD MACHINERY—See The Coe Manufacturing Company; *U.S. Private*, pg. 249
U S WEST BUSINESS RESOURCES—See U S West Inc.; *U.S. Public*, pg. 1689
U S WEST CELLULAR—See U S West Inc.; *U.S. Public*, pg. 1689
U S WEST COMMUNICATIONS FEDERAL SERVICES INC.—See U S West Inc.; *U.S. Public*, pg. 1689
U S WEST COMMUNICATIONS GROUP, INC.—See U S West Inc.; *U.S. Public*, pg. 1689
U S WEST DEX—See U S West Inc.; *U.S. Public*, pg. 1689
U S WEST INC.; *U.S. Public*, pg. 1688
U S WEST MEDIA GROUP—See U S West Inc.; *U.S. Public*, pg. 1689
U.S. WOOLWORTH DIV.—See Woolworth Corporation; *U.S. Public*, pg. 1778
U.S. YELLOW PAGES—See Western International Media Corporation; *U.S. Private*, pg. 1167
UNITED STATIONERS INC.; *U.S. Public*, pg. 1689
UNITED STEEL & WIRE CO.; *U.S. Private*, pg. 1126
UNITED SUGARS CORP.—See American Crystal Sugar Company; *U.S. Private*, pg. 52
UNITED SUGARS CORP.—See Southern Minnesota Beet Sugar Cooperative; *U.S. Private*, pg. 1
UNITED SUPERMARKETS—See Hale-Halsell Company; *U.S. Private*, pg. 494
UNITED SUPERMARKETS INC.; *U.S. Private*, pg. 1126
UNITED TANKERS SERVICES PTY. LIMITED—See Brambles Industries Limited; *Int'l*, pg. 211
UNITED TECHNOLOGIES, AUTOMOTIVE—See United Technologies Corporation; *U.S. Public*, pg. 1691
UNITED TECHNOLOGIES CHEMICAL SYSTEM DIVISION—See United Technologies Corporation; *U.S. Public*, pg. 1690
UNITED TECHNOLOGIES, CHEMICAL SYSTEMS DIV.—See United Technologies Corporation; *U.S. Public*, pg. 1690
UNITED TECHNOLOGIES CHEMICAL SYSTEMS DIVISION—See United Technologies Corporation; *U.S. Public*, pg. 1690
UNITED TECHNOLOGIES CONTROL SYSTEMS—See United Technologies Corporation; *U.S. Public*, pg. 1690
UNITED TECHNOLOGIES CORPORATION; *U.S. Public*, pg. 1689
UNITED TECHNOLOGIES DIESEL SYSTEMS—See United Technologies Corporation; *U.S. Public*, pg. 1690
UNITED TECHNOLOGIES ELLIOTT—See United Technologies Corporation; *U.S. Public*, pg. 1690
UNITED TECHNOLOGIES FABRICATIONS—See United Technologies Corporation; *U.S. Public*, pg. 1690
UNITED TECHNOLOGIES FURUKAWA CORPORATION (UTF)—See The Furukawa Electric Co., Ltd.; *Int'l*, pg. 530
UNITED TECHNOLOGIES MICROELECTRONICS CENTER—See United Technologies Corporation; *U.S. Public*, pg. 1690
UNITED TECHNOLOGIES MOTOR SYSTEMS—See United Technologies Corporation; *U.S. Public*, pg. 1690
UNITED TECHNOLOGIES, NORDEN SYSTEMS LONG ISLAND—See United Technologies Corporation; *U.S. Public*, pg. 1691
UNITED TECHNOLOGIES SERVICES—See United Technologies Corporation; *U.S. Public*, pg. 1690
UNITED TECHNOLOGIES TEL MIS—See United Technologies Corporation; *U.S. Public*, pg. 1690
UNITED TELECOM SERVICES CO. LTD.—See Telefonaktiebolaget LM Ericsson; *Int'l*, pg. 1371
UNITED TRANSNET, INC.—See Corporate Express, Inc.; *U.S. Public*, pg. 449
UNITED TRANSPORT CONTAINERS LTD.—See Sophus Berendsen A/S; *Int'l*, pg. 1285
UNITED TRANSPORT SERVICES PTY. LTD.—See Brambles Industries Limited; *Int'l*, pg. 211
UNITED TRANSPORT (WA) PTY. LTD.—See Brambles Industries Limited; *Int'l*, pg. 211
UNITED UTILITIES PLC; *Int'l*, pg. 1444
UNITED VACATIONS, INC.—See UAL Corporation; *U.S. Public*, pg. 1653
UNITED VAN LINES, INC.—See UniGroup, Inc.; *U.S. Private*, pg. 1117
UNITED WASTE SYSTEMS, INC.; *U.S. Public*, pg. 1691

UNITED WATER MANAGEMENT & SERVICES—See United Water Resources; *U.S. Public,* pg. 1692
UNITED WATER MID-ATLANTIC—See United Water Resources; *U.S. Public,* pg. 1692
UNITED WATER NEW JERSEY, INC.—See United Water Resources; *U.S. Public,* pg. 1692
UNITED WATER NEW YORK—See United Water Resources; *U.S. Public,* pg. 1692
UNITED WATER RESOURCES; *U.S. Public,* pg. 1691
UNITED WATER WORKS—See United Water Resources; *U.S. Public,* pg. 1692
UNITED WHOLESALE INC.—See Spartan Stores Inc.; *U.S. Private,* pg. 1021
UNITED WIRE LIMITED—See Scapa Group Plc; *Int'l,* pg. 1202
UNITED WISCONSIN SERVICES, INC.; *U.S. Public,* pg. 1692
UNITED WORLD FILMS DIV.—See The Seagram Company Ltd.; *Int'l,* pg. 1216
UNITED WORLD LIFE INSURANCE COMPANY—See Mutual of Omaha Insurance Company; *U.S. Private,* pg. 770
UNITED WORLDWIDE CORPORATION—See UAL Corporation; *U.S. Public,* pg. 1653
UNITEL VIDEO, INC.; *U.S. Public,* pg. 1692
UNITEL VIDEO, INC. - MOBILE PRODUCTION HEADQUARTERS—See Unitel Video, Inc.; *U.S. Public,* pg. 1692
UNITEL VIDEO, INC. - STUDIO & PRODUCTION FACILITIES—See Unitel Video, Inc.; *U.S. Public,* pg. 1692
UNITEL VIDEO, INC. - STUDIO FACILITIES—See Unitel Video, Inc.; *U.S. Public,* pg. 1692
UNITEL VIDEO, INC. - STUDIO, POST-PRODUCTION & COMPUTER FACILITIES—See Unitel Video, Inc.; *U.S. Public,* pg. 1692
UNITEX LIMITED—See Smiths Industries plc; *Int'l,* pg. 1267
UNITEX OFFSHORE TRANSMISSION COMPANY—See The Coastal Corporation; *U.S. Public,* pg. 389
UNITIKA AMERICA CORP.—See Unitika Ltd.; *Int'l,* pg. 1444
UNITIKA LTD.; *Int'l,* pg. 1444
UNITIL CORPORATION; *U.S. Public,* pg. 1692
UNITIL POWER CORPORATION—See Unitil Corporation; *U.S. Public,* pg. 1692
UNITIL REALTY CORPORATION—See Unitil Corporation; *U.S. Public,* pg. 1692
UNITIL RESOURCES, INC.—See Unitil Corporation; *U.S. Public,* pg. 1692
UNITIL SERVICE CORPORATION—See Unitil Corporation; *U.S. Public,* pg. 1693
UNITIMBER AB—See Mo och Domsjo AB; *Int'l,* pg. 886
UNITOG COMPANY; *U.S. Public,* pg. 1693
UNITOG RENTAL FACILITY—See Unitog Company; *U.S. Public,* pg. 1693
UNITOL SA—See Koninklijke Hoogovens N.V.; *Int'l,* pg. 756
UNITRIN, INC.; *U.S. Public,* pg. 1693
UNITRODE CORPORATION; *U.S. Public,* pg. 1694
UNITROS—See Havas Advertising; *Int'l,* pg. 603
UNITRUCK A/S—See Atlet AB; *Int'l,* pg. 97
UNITS SETS, INC.—See Rotary Forms Press, Inc.; *U.S. Private,* pg. 947
UNITY MANUFACTURING CO.; *U.S. Private,* pg. 1126
UNITY SEWING SUPPLY DIV.—See Willcox & Gibbs, Inc.; *U.S. Private,* pg. 1177
UNIVAR EUROPE N.V.—See Royal Pakhoed NV; *Int'l,* pg. 1147
UNIVERSAL AMERICAN MORTGAGE COMPANY—See Lennar Corporation; *U.S. Public,* pg. 989
UNIVERSAL AMERICAN REALTY CORP.—See Lennar Corporation; *U.S. Public,* pg. 989
UNIVERSAL AMPHITHEATRE—See The Seagram Company Ltd.; *Int'l,* pg. 1216
UNIVERSAL BELO PRODUCTIONS—See A.H. Belo Corporation; *U.S. Public,* pg. 210
UNIVERSAL BLUEPRINT PAPER CO.—See Wilco Reprographic, Inc.; *U.S. Private,* pg. 1176
UNIVERSAL BOILERS CORP.; *U.S. Private,* pg. 1126
UNIVERSAL BUILDERS SUPPLY, INC.; *U.S. Private,* pg. 1126
UNIVERSAL CALIBRATION LABORATORIES LTD.—See Delta plc; *Int'l,* pg. 390
UNIVERSAL CITY STUDIOS (DISC), INC.—See The Seagram Company Ltd.; *Int'l,* pg. 1216
UNIVERSAL COATINGS LTD.—See Alusuisse-Lonza Holding Ltd.; *Int'l,* pg. 69
UNIVERSAL COMPOSITES-U.S.C.; *U.S. Private,* pg. 1126
UNIVERSAL CONSTRUCTION CO.—See The Turner Corporation; *U.S. Public,* pg. 1646
UNIVERSAL CONSTRUCTION COMPANY, INC.; *U.S. Private,* pg. 1127
UNIVERSAL COOPERATIVES, INC.; *U.S. Private,* pg. 1127
UNIVERSAL CORPORATION; *U.S. Public,* pg. 1694
UNIVERSAL DAIRY EQUIPMENT, INC.—See Tetra Laval Group; *Int'l,* pg. 1379
UNIVERSAL DEVELOPERS, INC.—See Commerce Group Corp.; *U.S. Public,* pg. 410
UNIVERSAL DYNAMICS, INC.—See Filterwerk Mann & Hummel GmbH; *Int'l,* pg. 484
UNIVERSAL FASTENERS INC.—See YKK Corporation; *Int'l,* pg. 1515
UNIVERSAL FIDELITY LIFE INSURANCE COMPANY; *U.S. Private,* pg. 1127
UNIVERSAL FINANCIAL SERVICES—See Universal Life Insurance Company; *U.S. Private,* pg. 1127
UNIVERSAL FLAVORS—See Universal Foods Corporation; *U.S. Public,* pg. 1695
UNIVERSAL FLAVORS CORP.—See Universal Foods Corporation; *U.S. Public,* pg. 1695
UNIVERSAL FLAVORS-U.S.A.—See Universal Foods Corporation; *U.S. Public,* pg. 1696

UNIVERSAL FLEET—See Rocor Transportation Companies Inc.; *U.S. Private,* pg. 939
UNIVERSAL FOLDING BOX COMPANY, INC.; *U.S. Private,* pg. 1127
UNIVERSAL FOODS CORPORATION; *U.S. Public,* pg. 1695
UNIVERSAL FOODS CORPORATION-BAKERY PRODUCTS DIV.—See Universal Foods Corporation; *U.S. Public,* pg. 1696
UNIVERSAL FOODS CORP.-DEHYDRATED PRODUCTS DIV.—See Universal Foods Corporation; *U.S. Public,* pg. 1696
UNIVERSAL FOODS PRODUCTS INTERNATIONAL LTD.—See Universal Foods Corporation; *U.S. Public,* pg. 1696
UNIVERSAL FOOT CARE PRODUCTS—See Henry Schein, Inc.; *U.S. Public,* pg. 1437
UNIVERSAL FOREST PRODUCTS, INC.; *U.S. Public,* pg. 1696
UNIVERSAL FURNITURE INDUSTRIES, INC.—See Furnishings International, Inc.; *U.S. Private,* pg. 432
UNIVERSAL GUARANTEE LIFE INSURANCE—See First Commonwealth Corporation; *U.S. Public,* pg. 406
THE UNIVERSAL HARDWARE AND PLASTIC FTY. LTD.—See ETEX; *Int'l,* pg. 430
UNIVERSAL HEALTH REALTY INCOME TRUST—See Universal Health Services, Inc.; *U.S. Public,* pg. 1697
UNIVERSAL HEALTH SERVICES, INC.; *U.S. Public,* pg. 1696
UNIVERSAL HOMES, INC.—See Del Webb Corporation; *U.S. Public,* pg. 495
UNIVERSAL (HONG KONG TEAKWOOD)—See Furnishings International, Inc.; *U.S. Private,* pg. 432
UNIVERSAL INDUSTRIAL PRODUCTS CO.—See United Dominion Industries, Ltd.; *U.S. Public,* pg. 1677
UNIVERSAL INSTRUMENTS CORPORATION—See Dover Corporation; *U.S. Public,* pg. 522
UNIVERSAL INSULATION, INC.—See Davenport Insulation, Inc; *U.S. Private,* pg. 314
UNIVERSAL INSURANCE CO.—See Kirby Corporation; *U.S. Public,* pg. 962
UNIVERSAL INSURANCE CO.—See The Seibels Bruce Group, Inc.; *U.S. Public,* pg. 1454
UNIVERSAL INTERNATIONAL, INC.; *U.S. Public,* pg. 1697
UNIVERSAL LAUNDRY BAGS DIV.—See Superior Surgical Mfg. Co., Inc.; *U.S. Public,* pg. 1539
UNIVERSAL LEAF EXPORT COMPANY, INC.—See Universal Corporation; *U.S. Public,* pg. 1695
UNIVERSAL LEAF FAR-EAST, LTD.—See Universal Corporation; *U.S. Public,* pg. 1695
UNIVERSAL LEAF SERVICES LTD.—See Universal Corporation; *U.S. Public,* pg. 1695
UNIVERSAL LEAF TOBACCO COMPANY, INC.—See Universal Corporation; *U.S. Public,* pg. 1694
UNIVERSAL LEAF (UK) LTD.—See Universal Corporation; *U.S. Public,* pg. 1695
UNIVERSAL LIFE INSURANCE COMPANY; *U.S. Private,* pg. 1127
UNIVERSAL MANAGEMENT CORP.—See The Rados Companies; *U.S. Public,* pg. 907
UNIVERSAL MATCHBOX GROUP—See Mattel, Inc.; *U.S. Public,* pg. 1058
UNIVERSAL MOLDING COMPANY; *U.S. Private,* pg. 1127
UNIVERSAL OPTICAL INDUSTRIES, LTD.—See Kyocera Corporation; *Int'l,* pg. 776
UNIVERSAL OVERALL COMPANY; *U.S. Private,* pg. 1127
UNIVERSAL PAPER GOODS—See Esselte AB; *Int'l,* pg. 460
UNIVERSAL PHOTONICS, INC.; *U.S. Private,* pg. 1127
UNIVERSAL PICTURES—See The Seagram Company Ltd.; *Int'l,* pg. 1216
UNIVERSAL POLYMER & RUBBER CO.—See American Industrial Partners; *U.S. Private,* pg. 56
UNIVERSAL PROMOTIONS, INC.—See Mars Advertising Co.; *U.S. Private,* pg. 707
UNIVERSAL PROPULSION CO., INC.—See Carpenter Technology Corporation; *U.S. Public,* pg. 308
UNIVERSAL PUBLIC RELATIONS INC.—See Shandwick International Plc; *Int'l,* pg. 1228
UNIVERSAL REFINING N.V.—See Daewoo Corporation; *Int'l,* pg. 358
UNIVERSAL RELAY—See Park Distributors, Inc.; *U.S. Private,* pg. 839
UNIVERSAL RESOURCES CORPORATION—See Questar Corporation; *U.S. Public,* pg. 1352
UNIVERSAL-RUNDLE CORP.—See Nortek, Inc.; *U.S. Public,* pg. 1193
UNIVERSAL SECURITIES CO., LTD.; *Int'l,* pg. 1444
UNIVERSAL SECURITY INSTRUMENTS INC.; *U.S. Public,* pg. 1697
UNIVERSAL SHOE MFG. CO.—See Craddock-Terry Inc.; *U.S. Private,* pg. 284
UNIVERSAL STANDARD HEALTHCARE, INC.; *U.S. Public,* pg. 1697
UNIVERSAL STANDARD HEALTHCARE OF DELAWARE, INC.—See Universal Standard Healthcare, Inc.; *U.S. Public,* pg. 1698
UNIVERSAL STANDARD HEALTHCARE OF MICHIGAN, INC.—See Universal Standard Healthcare, Inc.; *U.S. Public,* pg. 1698
THE UNIVERSAL STEEL CO.—See Columbia National Group, Inc.; *U.S. Private,* pg. 256
UNIVERSAL STEEL OF PENNSYLVANIA—See Columbia National Group, Inc.; *U.S. Private,* pg. 256
UNIVERSAL STEEL TUBE CO. LIMITED—See Plymouth Tube Company; *U.S. Private,* pg. 873
UNIVERSAL STUDIOS FLORIDA—See The Rank Group PLC; *Int'l,* pg. 1087
UNIVERSAL STUDIOS HOLLYWOOD—See The Seagram Company Ltd.; *Int'l,* pg. 1216
UNIVERSAL STUDIOS, INC.—See The Seagram Company Ltd.; *Int'l,* pg. 1215
UNIVERSAL STUDIOS MUSIC ENTERTAINMENT GROUP—See The Seagram Company Ltd.; *Int'l,* pg. 1215

UNIVERSAL SURETY OF AMERICA—See Capsure Holdings Corp.; *U.S. Public,* pg. 303
UNIVERSAL SUSPENSION SYSTEM—See Sybron International Corporation; *U.S. Public,* pg. 1545
UNIVERSAL TECHNOLOGY CORP.—See Schindler Holding AG; *Int'l,* pg. 1205
UNIVERSAL TELEPHONE CO. OF COLORADO—See Century Telephone Enterprises, Inc.; *U.S. Public,* pg. 330
UNIVERSAL TELEPHONE, INC.—See Century Telephone Enterprises, Inc.; *U.S. Public,* pg. 330
UNIVERSAL TELEPHONE SOUTHWEST-ARIZONA—See Century Telephone Enterprises, Inc.; *U.S. Public,* pg. 330
UNIVERSAL TITLE INSURORS, INC.—See Lennar Corporation; *U.S. Public,* pg. 989
UNIVERSAL TOOL & STAMPING—See Acme Metals Incorporated; *U.S. Public,* pg. 17
UNIVERSAL TRANSPORT—See Trimac Corporation; *Int'l,* pg. 1424
UNIVERSAL TRANSPORT GMBH—See The Peninsular and Oriental Steam Navigation Company; *Int'l,* pg. 1034
UNIVERSAL TRANSPORT OPERATIONS PTY. LTD.—See M.I.M. Holdings Ltd.; *Int'l,* pg. 827
UNIVERSAL TRANSPORT-WESTERN DIVISION—See Trimac Corporation; *Int'l,* pg. 1424
UNIVERSAL (U.K.) LIMITED—See Universal Securities Co., Ltd.; *Int'l,* pg. 1444
UNIVERSAL UNDERWRITERS INSURANCE CO.—See Zurich Insurance Company; *Int'l,* pg. 1530
UNIVERSAL UNDERWRITERS OF TEXAS—See Zurich Insurance Company; *Int'l,* pg. 1530
UNIVERSAL VOLTRONICS CORPORATION—See Thermo Electron Corporation; *U.S. Public,* pg. 1596
UNIVERSAL WILTON INC.—See Universal Corporation; *U.S. Public,* pg. 1695
UNIVERSAL WOODS, INCORPORATED—See Universal Corporation; *U.S. Public,* pg. 1695
UNIVERSALE-BAU AG—See Creditanstalt-Bankverein; *Int'l,* pg. 347
UNIVERSITY ACCOUNTING SERVICE, INC.—See Payco American Corporation; *U.S. Public,* pg. 1267
UNIVERSITY BOOK STORE; *U.S. Private,* pg. 1127
UNIVERSITY INN ASSOCIATES—See Sunstone Hotel Investors, Inc.; *U.S. Public,* pg. 1537
UNIVERSITY MECHANICAL & ENGINEERING CONTRACTORS, INC.—See EMCOR Group, Inc.; *U.S. Public,* pg. 572
UNIVERSITY NURSING CENTER—See Vencor, Inc.; *U.S. Public,* pg. 1715
UNIVERSITY OF PHOENIX—See Apollo Group, Inc.; *U.S. Public,* pg. 120
UNIVERSITY PARK DIVISION—See Consumers Water Company; *U.S. Public,* pg. 438
UNIVERSITY PRESS OF AMERICA, INC.; *U.S. Private,* pg. 1127
UNIVESCO INC.; *U.S. Private,* pg. 1128
UNIVEST FINANCIAL SERVICES, LLC; *U.S. Private,* pg. 1128
UNIVEX CORPORATION; *U.S. Private,* pg. 1128
UNIVISION LTD. PARTNERSHIP—See Chartwell Partners; *U.S. Private,* pg. 230
UNIWAX S.A.—See Unilever Plc; *Int'l,* pg. 1439
UNIWOOD DIV.—See International Paper Company; *U.S. Public,* pg. 903
UNIWORLD GROUP, INC.; *U.S. Private,* pg. 1128
UNIWORLD HISPANIC—See Uniworld Group, Inc.; *U.S. Private,* pg. 1128
UNO RESTAURANT CORPORATION; *U.S. Public,* pg. 1698
UNOC EQUIPMENT & SUPPLY L.L.C.—See Caterpillar Inc.; *U.S. Public,* pg. 316
UNOCAL AGRICULTURAL PRODUCTS GROUP—See Unocal Corporation; *U.S. Public,* pg. 1698
UNOCAL CANADA LIMITED—See Unocal Corporation; *U.S. Public,* pg. 1698
UNOCAL CARBON & MINERALS—See Unocal Corporation; *U.S. Public,* pg. 1698
UNOCAL CORPORATION; *U.S. Public,* pg. 1698
UNOCAL GEOTHERMAL OF INDONESIA LTD.—See Unocal Corporation; *U.S. Public,* pg. 1698
UNOCAL INDONESIA, LTD.—See Unocal Corporation; *U.S. Public,* pg. 1698
UNOCAL NETHERLANDS—See Unocal Corporation; *U.S. Public,* pg. 1698
UNOCAL THAILAND—See Unocal Corporation; *U.S. Public,* pg. 1698
UNOVA, INC.; *U.S. Public,* pg. 1698
UNSMOKE INTERNATIONAL—See Surco Products, Inc.; *U.S. Private,* pg. 1056
UNTERNEHMENSBETEILIGUNGS-GESELLSCHAFT FUR DIE DEUTSCHE WIRTSCHAFT—See Dresdner Bank AG; *Int'l,* pg. 418
UNTERSTUTZUNGS GESELLSCHAFT MBH DER CHEMICAL BANK—See The Chase Manhattan Corporation; *U.S. Public,* pg. 341
UNTERSTUTZUNGSKASSE DER NHW GMBH—See Mannesmann A.G.; *Int'l,* pg. 835
UNTERSTUTZUNGSKASSE DER VDO MEB UND REGELTECHNIK GMBH—See Mannesmann A.G.; *Int'l,* pg. 839
UNTERSTUTZUNGSKASSE DYWIDAG GMBH—See Dyckerhoff & Widmann AG; *Int'l,* pg. 423
UNUM—See UNUM Corporation; *U.S. Public,* pg. 1699
UNUM CORPORATION; *U.S. Public,* pg. 1699
UNUM DEVELOPMENT CORP.—See UNUM Corporation; *U.S. Public,* pg. 1699
UNUM EUROPEAN HOLDING COMPANY LIMITED—See UNUM Corporation; *U.S. Public,* pg. 1700
UNUM HOLDING COMPANY—See UNUM Corporation; *U.S. Public,* pg. 1699

Company Index

UNUM DIRECTORY OF CORPORATE AFFILIATIONS

UNUM JAPAN ACCIDENT INSURANCE COMPANY LIMITED—See UNUM Corporation; *U.S. Public*, pg. 1700
UNUM LIFE INSURANCE COMPANY OF AMERICA—See UNUM Corporation; *U.S. Public*, pg. 1699
UNUM LIMITED—See UNUM Corporation; *U.S. Public*, pg. 1700
UNUM SALES CORP.—See UNUM Corporation; *U.S. Public*, pg. 1700
U.O. FENWICK, INC.—See Urban Outfitters, Inc.; *U.S. Public*, pg. 1700
UP-RIGHT (FAR EAST) LTD.—See Up-Right, Inc.; *U.S. Private*, pg. 1128
UP-RIGHT, INC.; *U.S. Private*, pg. 1128
UP-RIGHT (IRELAND) LTD.—See Up-Right, Inc.; *U.S. Private*, pg. 1128
UP-RIGHT SCAFFOLDS LTD.—See Up-Right, Inc.; *U.S. Private*, pg. 1128
UPLAND RESOURCES, INC.—See Westvaco Corporation; *U.S. Public*, pg. 1762
THE UPPER DECK COMPANY, LLC; *U.S. Private*, pg. 1129
UPPER MERION & PLYMOUTH RAILROAD—See Lukens Inc.; *U.S. Public*, pg. 1020
UPPER MIDWEST INDUSTRIES, INCORPORATED; *U.S. Private*, pg. 1129
UPPER ROCK ISLAND COUNTY LANDFILL—See Allied Waste Industries; *U.S. Public*, pg. 49
THE UPPER ROOM; *U.S. Private*, pg. 1129
UPRIGHT—See Up-Right, Inc.; *U.S. Private*, pg. 1128
UPSON INTERNATIONAL CORP.—See Acer Incorporated; *Int'l*, pg. 22
UPSTATE MILK COOPERATIVES INC.; *U.S. Private*, pg. 1129
UPTON PRINTING CO.—See Champion Industries; *U.S. Public*, pg. 333
UPXON, INC.—See Sara Lee Corporation; *U.S. Public*, pg. 1435
URANERZ USA INC.—See Preussag AG; *Int'l*, pg. 1070
URANERZBERGBAU GMBH—See Preussag AG; *Int'l*, pg. 1070
URANIT GMBH—See Veba AG; *Int'l*, pg. 1457
URBA S.A. INDUSTRIA E COMERCIO DE AUTO PECAS—See Echlin Inc.; *U.S. Public*, pg. 561
URBAN & PARTNER—See Waverly, Inc.; *U.S. Public*, pg. 1748
URBAN & SCHWARZENBERG GMBH—See Waverly, Inc.; *U.S. Public*, pg. 1748
URBAN & VOGEL GMBH—See Waverly, Inc.; *U.S. Public*, pg. 1748
URBAN GROUP—See Cambridge Shopping Centres Limited; *Int'l*, pg. 253
URBAN OUTFITTERS CANADA, INC.—See Urban Outfitters, Inc.; *U.S. Public*, pg. 1700
URBAN OUTFITTERS, INC.; *U.S. Public*, pg. 1700
URBAN OUTFITTERS UK, LIMITE—See Urban Outfitters, Inc.; *U.S. Public*, pg. 1700
URBAN RETAIL PROPERTIES, INC.—See Urban Shopping Centers, Inc.; *U.S. Public*, pg. 1700
URBAN SHOPPING CENTERS, INC.; *U.S. Public*, pg. 1700
URBANA IBERICA, S.A.—See Telefonica de Espana, S.A.; *Int'l*, pg. 1372
URBANA LABORATORIES—See Land O'Lakes, Inc.; *U.S. Private*, pg. 646
URE PACIFIC LTD.—See Scapa Group Plc; *Int'l*, pg. 1203
UREP—See COGEMA - Compagnie Generale des Matieres Nucleaires; *Int'l*, pg. 305
URETHANES TECHNOLOGY—See Crain Communications, Inc.; *U.S. Private*, pg. 285
URLOCER, S.A.—See Vallehermoso, S.A.; *Int'l*, pg. 1447
URSCHEL LABS INCORPORATED; *U.S. Private*, pg. 1129
URSTADT BIDDLE PROPERTIES, INC.; *U.S. Public*, pg. 1700
U.S. CAN COMPANY—See U.S. Can Company; *U.S. Public*, pg. 1681
US MAGAZINE—See Wenner Media; *U.S. Private*, pg. 1162
U.S. TRUST MORTGAGE SERVICE COMPANY—See U.S. Trust Corporation; *U.S. Public*, pg. 1688
USA BROADCASTING—See USA Networks, Inc.; *U.S. Public*, pg. 1686
USA VACUUM IND. INC. LLC—See Tacony Corporation; *U.S. Private*, pg. 1067
USAG—See Groupe Strafor Facom; *Int'l*, pg. 570
USERTECH—See Ceridian Corporation; *U.S. Public*, pg. 331
USHER-WALKER GROUP LTD.—See Dainippon Ink & Chemicals, Inc.; *Int'l*, pg. 371
USIBELLI COAL MINE, INC.; *U.S. Private*, pg. 1129
USINA SAO JOSE S.A.—See S.A. Industrias Votorantim; *Int'l*, pg. 678
CIA. USINA TIUMA—See S.A. Industrias Votorantim; *Int'l*, pg. 678
USINAS SIDERURGICAS DE MINAS GERAIS S.A.—See Nissho Iwai Corporation; *Int'l*, pg. 949
USINE DE BOURGES—See Groupe Strafor Facom; *Int'l*, pg. 570
USINE DE CUSTINES—See Groupe Strafor Facom; *Int'l*, pg. 570
USINE DE WECKER S.R.L.—See Zimmermann & Jansen GmbH; *Int'l*, pg. 1529
GROUPE USINE NOUVELLE—See C.E.P. Communication Group; *Int'l*, pg. 239
USINES DEHOUSSE SA—See SNECMA - Societe Nationale d'Etude et de Construction de Moteurs d'Aviation; *Int'l*, pg. 1166
USINES & FONDERIES ARTHUR MARTIN S.A., "UFAM"—See Electrolux, AB; *Int'l*, pg. 441
USINES LAPRADE—See Groupe Usinor; *Int'l*, pg. 571
FRED USINGER, INC.; *U.S. Private*, pg. 1129
USMEDIA GROUP—See Central Valley Publishing; *U.S. Private*, pg. 225
USON CORPORATION—See Roper Industries, Inc.; *U.S. Public*, pg. 1405
USSI INGENIERIE—See COGEMA - Compagnie Generale des Matieres Nucleaires; *Int'l*, pg. 305
USTER DATASYSTEMS KK—See Hesta Tex AG; *Int'l*, pg. 618
USUI BUNDY TUBING CO. LTD.—See TI Group plc; *Int'l*, pg. 1341
UTA FINANZ UND LEASING—See ING Groep N.V.; *Int'l*, pg. 651
UTAH AUTO AUCTION—See Cox Enterprises, Inc.; *U.S. Private*, pg. 283
UTAH MEDICAL PRODUCTS, INC.; *U.S. Public*, pg. 1700
UTAH MEDICAL PRODUCTS LTD.—See Utah Medical Products, Inc.; *U.S. Public*, pg. 1700
UTAH POWER & LIGHT—See PacifiCorp; *U.S. Public*, pg. 1251
UTAH SCIENTIFIC/ARTEL—See Artel Video Systems, Inc.; *U.S. Private*, pg. 86
UTEL—See KPN Koninklyke PTT Nederland NV; *Int'l*, pg. 721
UTELL INTERNATIONAL—See Reed Elsevier plc; *Int'l*, pg. 1098
UTELL INTERNATIONAL-AUSTRALIA—See Reed Elsevier plc; *Int'l*, pg. 1098
UTELL INTERNATIONAL-BRAZIL—See Reed Elsevier plc; *Int'l*, pg. 1098
UTELL INTERNATIONAL-CANADA—See Reed Elsevier plc; *Int'l*, pg. 1098
UTELL INTERNATIONAL-CHINA—See Reed Elsevier plc; *Int'l*, pg. 1098
UTELL INTERNATIONAL-CZECH REPUBLIC—See Reed Elsevier plc; *Int'l*, pg. 1098
UTELL INTERNATIONAL-DALLAS—See Reed Elsevier plc; *Int'l*, pg. 1098
UTELL INTERNATIONAL-GERMANY—See Reed Elsevier plc; *Int'l*, pg. 1098
UTELL INTERNATIONAL-HUNGARY—See Reed Elsevier plc; *Int'l*, pg. 1098
UTELL INTERNATIONAL-OAK BROOK—See Reed Elsevier plc; *Int'l*, pg. 1098
UTELL INTERNATIONAL-OMAN—See Reed Elsevier plc; *Int'l*, pg. 1098
UTELL INTERNATIONAL-RUSSIA—See Reed Elsevier plc; *Int'l*, pg. 1099
UTELL INTERNATIONAL-SOUTH AFRICA—See Reed Elsevier plc; *Int'l*, pg. 1099
UTELL INTERNATIONAL-UNITED ARAB EMIRATES—See Reed Elsevier plc; *Int'l*, pg. 1099
UTELL INTERNATIONAL-UNITED KINGDOM—See Reed Elsevier plc; *Int'l*, pg. 1098
UTFORSKNING & PRODUKSJON—See Norsk Hydro a.s; *Int'l*, pg. 961
UTICA BOILERS INC.; *U.S. Private*, pg. 1129
UTICA LLOYDS OF TEXAS—See Utica Mutual Insurance Company; *U.S. Private*, pg. 1130
UTICA MUTUAL INSURANCE COMPANY; *U.S. Private*, pg. 1129
UTICA NATIONAL INSURANCE CO. OF TEXAS—See Utica Mutual Insurance Company; *U.S. Private*, pg. 1130
UTICA NATIONAL INSURANCE GROUP—See Utica Mutual Insurance Company; *U.S. Private*, pg. 1130
UTICA NATIONAL LIFE INSURANCE COMPANY—See Utica Mutual Insurance Company; *U.S. Private*, pg. 1130
UTICA OBSERVER-DISPATCH—See Gannett Company, Inc.; *U.S. Public*, pg. 700
UTICA SQUARE SHOPPING CENTER, INC.—See Helmerich & Payne, Inc.; *U.S. Public*, pg. 808
UTILCO GROUP—See UtiliCorp United Inc.; *U.S. Public*, pg. 1701
UTILEQUIP, INCORPORATED—See Minnesota Power; *U.S. Public*, pg. 1116
UTILICORP UNITED INC.; *U.S. Public*, pg. 1700
UTILIMASTER CORP.; *U.S. Private*, pg. 1130
UTILISATION RATIONNELLE DES GAZ—See Royal Dutch/Shell Group of Companies; *Int'l*, pg. 1138
UTILITIES ADVANCES CORPORATION—See Citizens Utilities Company; *U.S. Public*, pg. 380
UTILITIES & INDUSTRIES MANAGEMENT CORP.—See Shepaug Corporation; *U.S. Private*, pg. 993
UTILITIES CONSTRUCTION CO., INC. OF SOUTH CAROLINA; *U.S. Private*, pg. 1130
UTILITY & MUNICIPAL SERVICES, INC.—See Philadelphia Suburban Corporation; *U.S. Public*, pg. 1287
UTILITY BUSINESS SERVICES, INC.—See NUI Corporation; *U.S. Public*, pg. 1148
UTILITY DATA CORPORATION—See NIPSCO Industries, Inc.; *U.S. Public*, pg. 1185
UTILITY ENGINEERING CORPORATION—See New Century Energies, Inc.; *U.S. Public*, pg. 1170
UTILITY FINANCIAL CORP.—See Southwest Gas Corporation; *U.S. Public*, pg. 1493
UTILITY SERVICE AFFILIATES, INC.—See Middlesex Water Company; *U.S. Public*, pg. 1110
UTILITY STEEL FABRICATION, INC.—See Halter Marine Group, Inc.; *U.S. Public*, pg. 778
UTILITY TRAILER MANUFACTURING CO.; *U.S. Private*, pg. 1130
UTILITY TREE SERVICE—See The F.A. Bartlett Tree Expert Co.; *U.S. Private*, pg. 119
UTILITY VAULT CO., INC.—See CRH, plc; *Int'l*, pg. 242
UTILX CORPORATION; *U.S. Public*, pg. 1701
UTILX INTERNATIONAL PRODUCT SALES INC.—See UTILX Corporation; *U.S. Public*, pg. 1701
UTIMACO SAFEWARE AG; *Int'l*, pg. 1444
UTIMACO SAFEWARE, INC.—See Utimaco Safeware AG; *Int'l*, pg. 1444
UTIMACO SAFEWARE PLC—See Utimaco Safeware AG; *Int'l*, pg. 1444
UTLAS INTERNATIONAL—See The Thomson Corporation; *U.S. Public*, pg. 1600
UTO ALBIS AG—See Oerlikon-Buhrle Holding AG; *Int'l*, pg. 998
UTRAS—See Allianz Aktiengesellschaft; *Int'l*, pg. 62
UTSUNOMIYA MFG. DIV.—See Fuji Heavy Industries, Ltd.; *Int'l*, pg. 522
UTVECKLINGS AB—See Telefonaktiebolaget LM Ericsson; *Int'l*, pg. 1364
UTZ QUALITY FOODS, INC.; *U.S. Private*, pg. 1130
UUNET TECHNOLOGIES, INC.—See WorldCom, Inc.; *U.S. Public*, pg. 1779
UVEX SAFETY, INC.—See Bacou S.A.; *Int'l*, pg. 132
UWAJIMA CANNING CO., LTD.—See Meiji Seika Kaisha, Ltd.; *Int'l*, pg. 855
UWHARRIE ENVIRONMENTAL, INC.—See Republic Industries, Inc.; *U.S. Public*, pg. 1379
UZES—See La Meridionale des Bois et Materiaux; *Int'l*, pg. 784

V

V. MUELLER—See Allegiance Healthcare Corp.; *U.S. Public*, pg. 44
V-ONE, INC.—See Daiko Advertising, Inc.; *Int'l*, pg. 366
V&D PROJECTINRICHTING—See Vendex International N.V.; *Int'l*, pg. 1462
V&S COMUNICACOES—See Young & Rubicam Inc.; *U.S. Private*, pg. 1200
V-BAND CORPORATION; *U.S. Public*, pg. 1701
V-CREST SYSTEMS GMBH—See Volkswagen AG; *Int'l*, pg. 1473
V UND B—See Havas Advertising; *Int'l*, pg. 603
VAC DATA MANAGEMENT, INC.—See Emerson Electric Co.; *U.S. Public*, pg. 575
V.A.G. FINANCE LTD.—See Lonrho plc; *Int'l*, pg. 817
V.A.G. FINANCEMENT S.A.—See Volkswagen AG; *Int'l*, pg. 1475
V.A.G. FRANCE S.A.—See Volkswagen AG; *Int'l*, pg. 1475
V.A.G. HOLDING FINANCIERE S.A.—See Volkswagen AG; *Int'l*, pg. 1475
V.A.G. LEASING GMBH & CO. BESITZ—See Volkswagen AG; *Int'l*, pg. 1474
V.A.G. MARKETING MANAGEMENT INSTITUT GMBH—See Volkswagen AG; *Int'l*, pg. 1473
V.A.G. STOCKHOLM AB—See Volkswagen AG; *Int'l*, pg. 1476
V.A.G. SYNKO GMBH—See Volkswagen AG; *Int'l*, pg. 1473
V.A.G. TRANSPORT GMBH CO. DHG—See Volkswagen AG; *Int'l*, pg. 1473
V.A.G. (UNITED KINGDOM) LTD.—See Volkswagen AG; *Int'l*, pg. 1475
V.A.G. VERTRIEBSZENTRUM WESTFALEN GMBH—See Volkswagen AG; *Int'l*, pg. 1473
V.A.G. VERTRIEBSZENTRUM WESER-EMS GMBH—See Volkswagen AG; *Int'l*, pg. 1474
V.A.G. VERTRIEBSZENTRUM WESER-EMS GMBH U CO. KG—See Volkswagen AG; *Int'l*, pg. 1474
V.A.G. VERTRIEBSZENTRUM WESTFALEN GMBH & CO KG.—See Volkswagen AG; *Int'l*, pg. 1473
V.A.G. SVERIGE AB—See Volkswagen AG; *Int'l*, pg. 1474
VASA I/S—See Icopal a/s; *Int'l*, pg. 659
VAW ALUMINUM AG—See Viag AG; *Int'l*, pg. 1466
VAW AUSTRALIA PTY. LTD.—See Viag AG; *Int'l*, pg. 1466
VAW BELGIQUE S.A.—See Viag AG; *Int'l*, pg. 1466
VAW ITALIA S.R.L.—See Viag AG; *Int'l*, pg. 1466
VAW (UK) LTD.—See Viag AG; *Int'l*, pg. 1466
VB AUTOBATERIAS LDA.—See VARTA AG; *Int'l*, pg. 1452
VB AUTOBATTERI AB—See VARTA AG; *Int'l*, pg. 1452
VB AUTOBATTERI A/S—See VARTA AG; *Int'l*, pg. 1452
VB AUTOBATTERIE AG—See VARTA AG; *Int'l*, pg. 1452
VB AUTOBATTERIE GMBH—See VARTA AG; *Int'l*, pg. 1452
VB AUTOBATTERIE S.A.—See VARTA AG; *Int'l*, pg. 1452
VB AUTOBATTEIJEN B.V.—See VARTA AG; *Int'l*, pg. 1452
VB AUTOBATTERIEN B.V.—See VARTA AG; *Int'l*, pg. 1452
VB AUTOMOTIVE BATTERIES LTD.—See VARTA AG; *Int'l*, pg. 1452
OY VB AUTONAKUT AB—See VARTA AG; *Int'l*, pg. 1452
VB CONSULT, GESELLSCHAFT FUR MERGERS & ACQUISITIONS—See Bayerische Vereinsbank Group; *Int'l*, pg. 180
VB DIALOG GESELLSCHAFT FUR DIREKTMARKETING MBH—See Bayerische Vereinsbank Group; *Int'l*, pg. 180
VB HELLER BANK A.G.—See The Fuji Bank, Limited; *Int'l*, pg. 521
VB INTERNATIONAL FINANCE IRELAND—See Bayerische Vereinsbank Group; *Int'l*, pg. 181
VCBV COORDINATIECENTRUM N.V.—See Royal Begemann Group; *Int'l*, pg. 1134
VCF (VIDEO COMMUNICATION FRANCE)—See Groupe Bruxelles Lambert S.A.; *Int'l*, pg. 562
VCST COMPUTER SERVICES N.V.—See Royal Begemann Group; *Int'l*, pg. 1134
VCST INC.—See Royal Begemann Group; *Int'l*, pg. 1134
VCST INDUSTRIAL PRODUCTS N.V.—See Royal Begemann Group; *Int'l*, pg. 1134
VCST N.V.—See Royal Begemann Group; *Int'l*, pg. 1134
VCST SPECIAL PRODUCTS N.V.—See Royal Begemann Group; *Int'l*, pg. 1134
VCST VARIABELE TRANSMISSIE N.V.—See Royal Begemann Group; *Int'l*, pg. 1134
VDI-VERLAG GMBH—See Georg von Holtzbrinck GmbH; *Int'l*, pg. 1479
VDL GROEP BV; *Int'l*, pg. 1444
VDM HOLDING CO.—See Diebold, Incorporated; *U.S. Public*, pg. 506
VDM TECHNOLOGIES CORP.—See Fried. Krupp AG; *Int'l*, pg. 509
VDM (U.K.) LTD.—See Fried. Krupp AG; *Int'l*, pg. 509
VDO ADOLF SCHINDLING AG—See Mannesmann A.G.; *Int'l*, pg. 839
VDO ADOLF SCHINDLING BETETEILGUNGS GMBH—See Mannesmann A.G.; *Int'l*, pg. 839

VDO ANTRIEBSTECHNIK GMBH—See Mannesmann A.G.; *Int'l*, pg. 839
VDO AUSTRIA GMBH—See Mannesmann A.G.; *Int'l*, pg. 839
VDO COMPONENTS SDN.BHD.—See Mannesmann A.G.; *Int'l*, pg. 839
VDO DO BRASIL MEDIDORES LTDA.—See Mannesmann A.G.; *Int'l*, pg. 839
VDO INSTRUMENTOS SA—See Mannesmann A.G.; *Int'l*, pg. 839
VDO INSTRUMENTS AUSTRALIA PTY. LTD.—See Mannesmann A.G.; *Int'l*, pg. 839
VDO INSTRUMENTS, INC.—See Mannesmann A.G.; *Int'l*, pg. 839
VDO INSTRUMENTS LTD.—See Mannesmann A.G.; *Int'l*, pg. 839
VDO INSTRUMENTS SA—See Mannesmann A.G.; *Int'l*, pg. 839
VDO INSTRUMENTS SDN.BHD.—See Mannesmann A.G.; *Int'l*, pg. 839
VDO INSTRUMENTS SRO—See Mannesmann A.G.; *Int'l*, pg. 839
VDO KIENZLE COMERCIO E SERVICOS LTDA.—See Mannesmann A.G.; *Int'l*, pg. 839
VDO KIENZLE VERTRIEB UND SERVICE GMBH—See Mannesmann A.G.; *Int'l*, pg. 839
VDO-LUFTFAHRTGERATE WERK GMBH—See Thomson S.A.; *Int'l*, pg. 1385
VDO NEDERLAND BV—See Mannesmann A.G.; *Int'l*, pg. 839
VDO SOUTH EAST ASIA PTE. LTD.—See Mannesmann A.G.; *Int'l*, pg. 839
VDO TECHNIK AG—See Mannesmann A.G.; *Int'l*, pg. 839
VDO YAZAKI CORPORATION—See Mannesmann A.G.; *Int'l*, pg. 839
VEAG VEREINIGTE ENERGIEWERKE AG—See Veba AG; *Int'l*, pg. 1457
VEB POLYGRAPH DRUCKMACHINENWERK PLANETA RADEBEUL; *Int'l*, pg. 1445
VEM ERZ UND STAHL GMBH—See Internatio-Muller N.V.; *Int'l*, pg. 682
VEPO AANNEMINGSBEDRIJF B.V.—See Ballast Nedam NV; *Int'l*, pg. 134
VEW-VKR FERNWARMELEITUNG SHAMROCK-BOCHUM GBR—See Veba AG; *Int'l*, pg. 1460
VF ASIA LIMITED—See VF Corporation; *U.S. Public*, pg. 1702
V.F. CONSULTORES DE SELECCION Y FORMACION, S.A.—See Assicurazioni Generali S.p.A.; *Int'l*, pg. 92
VF CORPORATION; *U.S. Public*, pg. 1702
VF FACTORY OUTLET STORES—See VF Corporation; *U.S. Public*, pg. 1702
VF INTERNATIONAL—See VF Corporation; *U.S. Public*, pg. 1702
VF JEANSWEAR-EUROPE—See VF Corporation; *U.S. Public*, pg. 1702
VFT AG—See Ruetgers A.G.; *Int'l*, pg. 1148
VG ANALYTICAL LTD.—See Rhone-Poulenc S.A.; *Int'l*, pg. 1110
VG DATA SYSTEMS LTD.—See Thermo Electron Corporation; *U.S. Public*, pg. 1595
VG ELECTRONICS LTD.—See Thermo Electron Corporation; *U.S. Public*, pg. 1595
VG ELECTROVAC LTD.—See Thermo Electron Corporation; *U.S. Public*, pg. 1595
VG ELEMENTAL LTD.—See Rhone-Poulenc S.A.; *Int'l*, pg. 1110
VG EMBALLAGE—See Saint-Gobain; *Int'l*, pg. 1171
VG ENGINEERING (HASTINGS) LTD.—See Thermo Electron Corporation; *U.S. Public*, pg. 1595
VG ENGINEERING (TELFORD) LTD.—See Thermo Electron Corporation; *U.S. Public*, pg. 1595
VG GAS ANALYSIS SYSTEMS LTD.—See Thermo Electron Corporation; *U.S. Public*, pg. 1595
VG GLAS—See Saint-Gobain; *Int'l*, pg. 1173
VG INSTRUMENTS AB—See Thermo Electron Corporation; *U.S. Public*, pg. 1595
VG INSTRUMENTS ASIA LTD.—See Thermo Electron Corporation; *U.S. Public*, pg. 1595
VG INSTRUMENTS B.V.—See Thermo Electron Corporation; *U.S. Public*, pg. 1595
VG INSTRUMENTS CANADA INC.—See Thermo Electron Corporation; *U.S. Public*, pg. 1595
VG INSTRUMENTS-CHINA OFFICE—See Thermo Electron Corporation; *U.S. Public*, pg. 1595
VG INSTRUMENTS GMBH—See Thermo Electron Corporation; *U.S. Public*, pg. 1595
VG INSTRUMENTS GROUP LTD.—See Thermo Electron Corporation; *U.S. Public*, pg. 1595
VG INSTRUMENTS INC.—See Thermo Electron Corporation; *U.S. Public*, pg. 1594
VG INSTRUMENTS KOREA LTD.—See Thermo Electron Corporation; *U.S. Public*, pg. 1595
VG INSTRUMENTS PLC—See Thermo Electron Corporation; *U.S. Public*, pg. 1595
VG INSTRUMENTS SA—See Thermo Electron Corporation; *U.S. Public*, pg. 1595
VG IONEX LTD.—See Rhone-Poulenc S.A.; *Int'l*, pg. 1110
VG ISOTECH LTD.—See Rhone-Poulenc S.A.; *Int'l*, pg. 1110
VG LABORATORY SYSTEMS LTD.—See Thermo Electron Corporation; *U.S. Public*, pg. 1595
VG MASSLAB LTD.—See Rhone-Poulenc S.A.; *Int'l*, pg. 1110
VG MICROSCOPES LTD.—See Thermo Electron Corporation; *U.S. Public*, pg. 1595
VG MICROTECH LTD.—See Thermo Electron Corporation; *U.S. Public*, pg. 1595
VG MICROTRACE LTD.—See Rhone-Poulenc S.A.; *Int'l*, pg. 1111
VG PRECISION LTD.—See Thermo Electron Corporation; *U.S. Public*, pg. 1595
VG QUADRUPOLES LTD.—See Rhone-Poulenc S.A.; *Int'l*, pg. 1111

VG SCIENTIFIC LTD.—See Thermo Electron Corporation; *U.S. Public*, pg. 1595
VG SEMICON LTD.—See Thermo Electron Corporation; *U.S. Public*, pg. 1595
VG SPECIAL SYSTEMS LTD.—See Thermo Electron Corporation; *U.S. Public*, pg. 1595
VG TRITECH LTD.—See Rhone-Poulenc S.A.; *Int'l*, pg. 1111
VGF CORPORATION—See Aceto Corporation; *U.S. Public*, pg. 15
VGL INTERNATIONALE EXPEDITIE B.V.—See Royal Nedlloyd Group N.V.; *Int'l*, pg. 1145
VGL RAIL CARGO B.V.—See Royal Nedlloyd Group N.V.; *Int'l*, pg. 1145
VGL RAIL CARGO N.V.—See Royal Nedlloyd Group N.V.; *Int'l*, pg. 1145
VGL RAIL CARGO S.A.R.L.—See Royal Nedlloyd Group N.V.; *Int'l*, pg. 1145
VGM CAREER HORIZONS—See Tribune Company; *U.S. Public*, pg. 1636
VH-1/VIDEO HITS ONE—See National Amusements, Inc.; *U.S. Private*, pg. 779
V.I. CEMENT & BUILDING PRODUCTS, INC.—See Devcon International Corp.; *U.S. Public*, pg. 502
VIAG AKTIENGESELLSCHAFT—See Viag AG; *Int'l*, pg. 1466
VIAG KONZERNREVISION UND BERATUNG GMBH—See Viag AG; *Int'l*, pg. 1466
VIAG VERBINDUNGSBURO BONN—See Viag AG; *Int'l*, pg. 1466
VIL—See MetalTech International PLC; *Int'l*, pg. 862
V.I.M.G. VIAG IMMOBILIEN-MANAGEMENT GMBH—See Viag AG; *Int'l*, pg. 1466
VIMRX PHARMACEUTICALS, INC., *U.S. Public*, pg. 1702
VIR, INC.—See Allen Organ Company; *U.S. Public*, pg. 45
VITS-BLAVA TECHNOLOGIES CORPORATION—See Deutsche Babcock AG; *Int'l*, pg. 399
VITS MASCHINENBAU GMBH—See Deutsche Babcock AG; *Int'l*, pg. 399
VJ GROWERS, INC.; *U.S. Private*, pg. 1130
VKO, INC.; *U.S. Private*, pg. 1130
VL BUS ASIA (PTE) LTD.—See AB Volvo; *Int'l*, pg. 1477
V-L SERVICE LIGHTING—See Philips Electronics N.V.; *Int'l*, pg. 1055
VLSI TECHNOLOGY GMBH—See VLSI Technology, Inc.; *U.S. Public*, pg. 1703
VLSI TECHNOLOGY, INC.; *U.S. Public*, pg. 1703
VLT CORPORATION—See Vicor Corporation; *U.S. Public*, pg. 1719
VM MOTORI S.P.A.—See IRI Istituto Ricostruzione Industriale; *Int'l*, pg. 654
VM SOFTWARE DIVISION—See Sterling Software, Inc.; *U.S. Public*, pg. 1516
VMC—See Danone Group; *Int'l*, pg. 381
V.N. SOCIEDAD DE AGENCIA DE SEGUROS DE LA VASCO NAVARRA, S.A.—See Assicurazioni Generali S.p.A.; *Int'l*, pg. 92
VNU BUSINESS INFORMATION EUROPE—See VNU Verenigde Nederlandse Uitgeversbedrijven B.V.; *Int'l*, pg. 1445
VNU BUSINESS PUBLICATIONS BV—See VNU Verenigde Nederlandse Uitgeversbedrijven B.V.; *Int'l*, pg. 1445
VNU BUSINESS PUBLICATIONS ESPANA SA—See VNU Verenigde Nederlandse Uitgeversbedrijven B.V.; *Int'l*, pg. 1445
VNU BUSINESS PUBLICATIONS LTD.—See VNU Verenigde Nederlandse Uitgeversbedrijven B.V.; *Int'l*, pg. 1445
VNU DAGBLADENGROEP B.V.—See VNU Verenigde Nederlandse Uitgeversbedrijven B.V.; *Int'l*, pg. 1445
VNU MAGAZINE GROUP INTERNATIONAL BV—See VNU Verenigde Nederlandse Uitgeversbedrijven B.V.; *Int'l*, pg. 1445
VNU TIJDSCHRIFTENGROEP NEDERLAND BV—See VNU Verenigde Nederlandse Uitgeversbedrijven B.V.; *Int'l*, pg. 1445
VNU USA, INC.—See VNU Verenigde Nederlandse Uitgeversbedrijven B.V.; *Int'l*, pg. 1447
VNU VERENIGDE NEDERLANDSE UITGEVERSBEDRIJVEN B.V.; *Int'l*, pg. 1445
VNU VERKOOPGROEP BV—See VNU Verenigde Nederlandse Uitgeversbedrijven B.V.; *Int'l*, pg. 1445
VNU WORLD DIRECTORIES, N.V.—See VNU Verenigde Nederlandse Uitgeversbedrijven B.V.; *Int'l*, pg. 1447
VP BUILDINGS—See The LTV Corporation; *U.S. Public*, pg. 972
VP-SCHICKEDANZ AG—See The Procter & Gamble Company; *U.S. Public*, pg. 1333
VPC PORTUGAL LDA.—See Otto Versand (GmbH & Co.); *Int'l*, pg. 1015
VPC PROMOTION S.A.—See Otto Versand (GmbH & Co.); *Int'l*, pg. 1015
VPF B.V.—See Akzo Nobel N.V.; *Int'l*, pg. 44
VPI MIRREX CORP.—See Vinyl Plastics Incorporated; *U.S. Private*, pg. 1141
VPV EURO RSCG—See Havas Advertising; *Int'l*, pg. 603
VR/WESSON HYDRO CARBIDE—See Fansteel, Inc.; *U.S. Public*, pg. 612
VR/WESSON HYDRO CARBIDE-GULFPORT—See Fansteel, Inc.; *U.S. Public*, pg. 612
VRG ASIA PACIFIC LTD.—See N.V. Koninklijke KNP BT; *Int'l*, pg. 757
VRG BELGIE NV—See N.V. Koninklijke KNP BT; *Int'l*, pg. 757
VRG HOLDING BV—See N.V. Koninklijke KNP BT; *Int'l*, pg. 757
VRG INFORMATION SYSTEMS (UK) PLC—See N.V. Koninklijke KNP BT; *Int'l*, pg. 757
VRG INTERNATIONAL, INC.—See Roberts Pharmaceutical Corporation; *U.S. Public*, pg. 1393
VRG-PAPEL IBERICA, SA—See N.V. Koninklijke KNP BT; *Int'l*, pg. 757
VRG PAPER (HONG KONG) LTD.—See N.V. Koninklijke KNP BT; *Int'l*, pg. 757

VRG PAPER MALAYSIA SDN. BHD.—See N.V. Koninklijke KNP BT; *Int'l*, pg. 757
VRG PAPER (SINGAPORE) PTE LTD—See N.V. Koninklijke KNP BT; *Int'l*, pg. 757
VRG-PAPIER SA—See N.V. Koninklijke KNP BT; *Int'l*, pg. 757
VRG SERVIZIO CARTA SRL—See N.V. Koninklijke KNP BT; *Int'l*, pg. 757
VSA, INC.—See International Multifoods Corporation; *U.S. Public*, pg. 901
VSC-POSCO STEEL CORP. (VPS)—See Pohang Iron & Steel Co., Ltd.; *Int'l*, pg. 1062
VSH BETEILIGUNGSGESELLSCHAFT M.B.H.—See Bayerische Vereinsbank Group; *Int'l*, pg. 181
VSI CORPORATION—See The Fairchild Corporation; *U.S. Public*, pg. 610
VSI HOLDINGS, INC.; *U.S. Public*, pg. 1703
VSK GROUP—See Allied Research Corporation; *U.S. Public*, pg. 49
VSM, INC.; *U.S. Private*, pg. 1130
V.T. INC.; *U.S. Private*, pg. 1131
VTA MANAGEMENT SERVICES, INC.—See Horizon/CMS Healthcare Corporation; *U.S. Public*, pg. 839
VTEL CORPORATION; *U.S. Public*, pg. 1703
VTEL EUROPE, LTD.—See VTEL Corporation; *U.S. Public*, pg. 1703
VTF INDUSTRIES SARL—See Carl-Zeiss-Stiftung; *Int'l*, pg. 1523
VTG PAKTANK HAMBURG GMBH—See Veba AG; *Int'l*, pg. 1459
VTG USA INC.—See Preussag AG; *Int'l*, pg. 1070
VTG VEREINIGTE TANKLAGER UND TRANSPORTMITTEL GMBH—See Preussag AG; *Int'l*, pg. 1070
VTI HAMLIN OY—See Breed Technologies, Inc.; *U.S. Public*, pg. 251
VTS PROPERTIES LTD.—See Western Corporate Enterprises Inc.; *Int'l*, pg. 1494
VV-AUTO OY—See Kesko Ltd.; *Int'l*, pg. 732
VV PUBLISHING CORP.; *U.S. Private*, pg. 1131
VVB GESELLSCHAFT ZUR VERMITTLUNG VON FINANZDIENSTLEISTUNGEN MBH—See Bayerische Vereinsbank Group; *Int'l*, pg. 180
VW AUDI VERTRIEB GMBH—See Volkswagen AG; *Int'l*, pg. 1473
VW AUDI VERTRIEB GMBH & CO. VERTRIEBSZENTRUM BERLIN KG—See Volkswagen AG; *Int'l*, pg. 1473
VW AUDI VERTRIEBSZENTRUM FRANKEN GMBH & CO. KG—See Volkswagen AG; *Int'l*, pg. 1473
VW AUDI VERTRIEBSZENTRUM FRANKEN VERWALTUNGS-GMBH—See Volkswagen AG; *Int'l*, pg. 1473
VW AUDI VERTRIEBSZENTRUM GMBH—See Volkswagen AG; *Int'l*, pg. 1473
VW AUDI VERTRIEBSZENTRUM GMBH & CO. WEDEMARK KG—See Volkswagen AG; *Int'l*, pg. 1473
VW AUDI VERTRIEBSZENTRUM GMBH & CO. SUDBAYERN KG—See Volkswagen AG; *Int'l*, pg. 1473
VW AUDI VERTRIEBSZENTRUM KOLN GMBH—See Volkswagen AG; *Int'l*, pg. 1474
VW AUDI VERTRIEBSZENTRUM KOLN GMBH & CO. KG—See Volkswagen AG; *Int'l*, pg. 1474
VW AUDI VERTRIEBSZENTRUM NORD GMBH—See Volkswagen AG; *Int'l*, pg. 1474
VW AUDI VERTRIEBSZENTRUM NORD GMBH & CO. KG—See Volkswagen AG; *Int'l*, pg. 1474
VW AUDI VERTRIEBSZENTRUM RHEIN MAIN GMBH—See Volkswagen AG; *Int'l*, pg. 1474
VW AUDI VERTRIEBSZENTRUM RHEIN MAIN GMBH & CO. KG—See Volkswagen AG; *Int'l*, pg. 1474
VW AUDI VERTRIEBSZENTRUM SUD-WEST GMBH—See Volkswagen AG; *Int'l*, pg. 1474
VW AUDI VERTRIEBSZENTRUM SUD-WEST GMBH & CO. KG—See Volkswagen AG; *Int'l*, pg. 1474
VW AUDI VERTRIENSZENTRUM RHEIN-RUHR GMBH—See Volkswagen AG; *Int'l*, pg. 1474
VW AUDI VERTRIENSZENTRUM RHEIN-RUHR GMBH & CO. KG—See Volkswagen AG; *Int'l*, pg. 1474
VW AUDI VERTRIENSZENTRUM SUDBAYERN VERWALTUNGS-GMBH—See Volkswagen AG; *Int'l*, pg. 1474
VW CREDIT, INC.—See Volkswagen AG; *Int'l*, pg. 1474
VW FINANZ GMBH—See Volkswagen AG; *Int'l*, pg. 1474
VW GEDAS CONSULT GMBH—See Volkswagen AG; *Int'l*, pg. 1474
VW-GESELLSCHAFT FUR TECHNISCHE DATANVERARBEITUNGSSYSTEME MBH—See Volkswagen AG; *Int'l*, pg. 1474
VW KRAFTWERK GMBH—See Volkswagen AG; *Int'l*, pg. 1474
VW MALL, INC.—See IRT Property Company; *U.S. Public*, pg. 858
VW-VERSICHERUNGSVERMITTLUNGS-GMBH—See Volkswagen AG; *Int'l*, pg. 1474
VW-WOHNUNGS GESELLSCHAFT MBH—See Volkswagen AG; *Int'l*, pg. 1474
VWR CANLAB—See VWR Scientific Products; *U.S. Public*, pg. 1704
VWR SCIENTIFIC PRODUCTS; *U.S. Public*, pg. 1703
VWR TEXTILES & SUPPLIES, INC.—See Leggett & Platt, Incorporated; *U.S. Public*, pg. 986
VWS, INC.—See Electrolux, AB; *Int'l*, pg. 440
VXL LANDIS & STAEFA LTD.—See Landis & Staefa AG; *Int'l*, pg. 801
VAAGEN BROTHERS LUMBER, INC.; *U.S. Private*, pg. 1131
VAASA BAKERIES LTD.—See Cultor Ltd.; *Int'l*, pg. 349
VAASA SALES OFFICE—See Oy Algol AB; *Int'l*, pg. 15
VAASAMILLS LTD.—See Cultor Ltd.; *Int'l*, pg. 349
VAASANMYLLY OY—See Cultor Ltd.; *Int'l*, pg. 349
VACATION BREAK USA—See Fairfield Communities, Inc.; *U.S. Public*, pg. 611
THE VACATION STORE—See Landmark Communications, Inc.; *U.S. Private*, pg. 649

VACHON DIVISION—See Culinar Inc.; *Int'l*, pg. 348
VACTOR MFG. INC.—See Federal Signal Corporation; *U.S. Public*, pg. 617
VACU-DRY COMPANY; *U.S. Public*, pg. 1704
VACUDYNE INC.—See Altair Corporation; *U.S. Private*, pg. 46
VACUUM GENERATORS LTD.—See Thermo Electron Corporation; *U.S. Public*, pg. 1595
VACUUM METALIZING DIV.—See Crown Cork & Seal Company, Inc.; *U.S. Public*, pg. 463
VACUUMSCHMELZE GMBH—See Siemens AG; *Int'l*, pg. 1245
VADER VAST AB—See Telefonaktiebolaget LM Ericsson; *Int'l*, pg. 1364
VADIS S.P.R.L.—See Etablissements Delhaize Freres Et Cie "Le Lion" S.A.; *Int'l*, pg. 463
VAESSEN SHOEMAKER DE MEXICO—See McCormick & Company, Incorporated; *U.S. Public*, pg. 1067
VAIL ASSOCIATES, INC.—See Vail Resorts, Inc.; *U.S. Public*, pg. 1704
VAIL RESORTS, INC.; *U.S. Public*, pg. 1704
VAKUUM VULK, INC. U.S.—See Bandag, Incorporated; *U.S. Public*, pg. 177
SARL VALACIER—See Cockerill Sambre; *Int'l*, pg. 302
VALASSIS COMMUNICATIONS; *U.S. Public*, pg. 1704
VALASSIS INSERTS—See Valassis Communications, Inc.; *U.S. Public*, pg. 1704
VALCHEM AUSTRALIA PTY—See Imperial Chemical Industries PLC; *Int'l*, pg. 666
VALCOR ENGINEERING CORP.; *U.S. Private*, pg. 1131
VALE-HARMON ENTERPRISES, LTD.—See Harmon Industries, Inc.; *U.S. Public*, pg. 788
VALENCIA TERMINAL—See GATX Corporation; *U.S. Public*, pg. 693
VALENCIA Y ASOCIADOS PUBLICIDAD—See Leo Burnett Company, Inc.; *U.S. Private*, pg. 1131
ANDREW VALENTINE HOLDINGS LIMITED—See American Greetings Corporation; *U.S. Public*, pg. 78
VALENTINE RADFORD, INC.; *U.S. Private*, pg. 1131
VALEO/ACUSTAR THERMAL SYSTEMS—See Chrysler Corporation; *U.S. Public*, pg. 354
VALEO CLIMATE CONTROL—See CERUS - Compagnies Europeennes Reunies; *Int'l*, pg. 240
VALEO-CLUTCHES—See CERUS - Compagnies Europeennes Reunies; *Int'l*, pg. 240
VALEO DISTRIBUTION—See CERUS - Compagnies Europeennes Reunies; *Int'l*, pg. 240
VALEO-ELECTRONICAL SYSTEMS—See CERUS - Compagnies Europeennes Reunies; *Int'l*, pg. 240
VALEO-ELECTRONICS—See CERUS - Compagnies Europeennes Reunies; *Int'l*, pg. 240
VALEO ENGINE COOLING—See CERUS - Compagnies Europeennes Reunies; *Int'l*, pg. 240
VALEO-FRICTION MATERIALS—See CERUS - Compagnies Europeennes Reunies; *Int'l*, pg. 240
VALEO-LIGHTING—See CERUS - Compagnies Europeennes Reunies; *Int'l*, pg. 240
VALEO RESEARCH SOOAL—See CERUS - Compagnies Europeennes Reunies; *Int'l*, pg. 240
VALEO SECURITY SYSTEMS—See CERUS - Compagnies Europeennes Reunies; *Int'l*, pg. 240
VALEO WIPING SYSTEMS—See CERUS - Compagnies Europeennes Reunies; *Int'l*, pg. 240
VALER SKURLAG—See Norske Skogindustrier A.S; *Int'l*, pg. 965
VALERO ENERGY CORPORATION; *U.S. Public*, pg. 1704
VALERO MARKETING & SUPPLY COMPANY—See Valero Energy Corporation; *U.S. Public*, pg. 1704
VALERO REFINING COMPANY—See Valero Energy Corporation; *U.S. Public*, pg. 1704
VALESUL ALUMINIO—See Royal Dutch/Shell Group of Companies; *Int'l*, pg. 1142
VALEX CORP.—See Reliance Steel & Aluminum Co.; *U.S. Public*, pg. 1375
VALEXY—See Groupe Usinor; *Int'l*, pg. 571
VALEXY RHONE ALPES—See Groupe Usinor; *Int'l*, pg. 571
VALFIX FINANZ AG—See Saint-Gobain; *Int'l*, pg. 1177
VALHI, INC.—See Contran Corporation; *U.S. Private*, pg. 270
VALIANT INSURANCE COMPANY—See Zurich Insurance Company; *Int'l*, pg. 1530
OY VALITUT PALAT - READER'S DIGEST AB—See The Reader's Digest Association, Inc.; *U.S. Public*, pg. 1368
VALK MANUFACTURING COMPANY; *U.S. Private*, pg. 1131
VALLE AGORA S.A.—See Vallehermoso, S.A.; *Int'l*, pg. 1447
VALLE NORTE CARING CENTER—See Horizon/CMS Healthcare Corporation; *U.S. Public*, pg. 838
VALLEHERMOSO - CENTRO INMOBILIARIO CAJA DE MADRID, U.T.E.—See Caja de Madrid Group; *Int'l*, pg. 252
VALLEHERMOSO, S.A.; *Int'l*, pg. 1447
VALLEN CORPORATION; *U.S. Public*, pg. 1705
VALLEN SAFETY SUPPLY COMPANY—See Vallen Corporation; *U.S. Public*, pg. 1705
VALLEN SAFETY SUPPLY COMPANY, LTD.—See Vallen Corporation; *U.S. Public*, pg. 1705
VALLERIE'S TRANSPORT SERVICE, INC.; *U.S. Private*, pg. 1131
VALLET FOOD SERV INC.; *U.S. Private*, pg. 1131
VALLEY AIR—See Logan Corporation; *U.S. Private*, pg. 672
VALLEY AMERICAN BANK—See Fort Wayne National Corporation; *U.S. Public*, pg. 674
VALLEY ASPHALT CORPORATION; *U.S. Private*, pg. 1131
VALLEY BANK & TRUST; *U.S. Private*, pg. 1132
VALLEY BELL DAIRY CO.—See Borden, Inc.; *U.S. Private*, pg. 158
VALLEY COCA-COLA BOTTLING COMPANY, INC.—See Coca-Cola Enterprises Inc.; *U.S. Public*, pg. 393

VALLEY DETROIT DIESEL ALLISON; *U.S. Private*, pg. 1132
VALLEY FAIR & L.F. WIDMANN—See Schottenstein Stores Corporation; *U.S. Private*, pg. 972
VALLEY FARMS LIMITED—See McCain Foods Limited; *Int'l*, pg. 850
VALLEY FIG GROWERS—See Sun Diamond Growers of California; *U.S. Private*, pg. 1051
VALLEY FOOD DISTRIBUTORS OF NEVADA—See JP Foodservice, Inc.; *U.S. Public*, pg. 919
VALLEY FOREST RESOURCES CO.—See Villaume Industries, Inc.; *U.S. Private*, pg. 1140
VALLEY FORGE CORPORATION; *U.S. Public*, pg. 1705
VALLEY FORGE LIFE INSURANCE COMPANY—See Continental Assurance Company; *U.S. Public*, pg. 267
VALLEY FRESH, INC.; *U.S. Private*, pg. 1132
VALLEY FRESH, INC.—See Valley Fresh, Inc.; *U.S. Private*, pg. 1132
VALLEY GAS CO.—See Valley Resources, Inc.; *U.S. Public*, pg. 1706
VALLEY GAS TRANSMISSION, INC.—See Royal Dutch/Shell Group of Companies; *Int'l*, pg. 1136
VALLEY GRANDE MANOR—See Horizon/CMS Healthcare Corporation; *U.S. Public*, pg. 839
VALLEY GROUP, INC.—See Skandia Insurance Company Limited; *Int'l*, pg. 1257
VALLEY HOSPITAL MEDICAL CENTER—See Universal Health Services, Inc.; *U.S. Public*, pg. 1697
VALLEY HOUSE HEALTHCARE—See Vencor, Inc.; *U.S. Public*, pg. 1715
VALLEY IMPORTS—See W.W. Wallwork, Inc.; *U.S. Private*, pg. 1148
VALLEY INNOVATIVE MANAGEMENT SERVICE—See Trend Line Corporation; *U.S. Private*, pg. 1099
VALLEY ISLE PRODUCE, V.I.P. FOOD SERVICE; *U.S. Private*, pg. 1132
THE VALLEY LINE COMPANY—See CSX Corporation; *U.S. Public*, pg. 284
VALLEY MANOR APARTMENTS—See Vencor, Inc.; *U.S. Public*, pg. 1715
VALLEY MANOR CARE CENTER—See Meritcare, Inc.; *U.S. Private*, pg. 733
VALLEY MANUFACTURING CORPORATION—See TI Group plc; *Int'l*, pg. 1338
VALLEY MEDICAL, INC.—See Integrated Health Services, Inc.; *U.S. Public*, pg. 885
VALLEY NATIONAL BANCORP; *U.S. Public*, pg. 1705
VALLEY NATIONAL BANK—See Valley National Bancorp; *U.S. Public*, pg. 1705
VALLEY NATIONAL BANK OF CORTEZ—See Zions Bancorporation; *U.S. Public*, pg. 1793
VALLEY NATIONAL BANK—See Valley National Bancorp; *U.S. Public*, pg. 1706
VALLEY NATIONAL FINANCIAL SERVICES COMPANY—See Banc One Corporation; *U.S. Public*, pg. 173
VALLEY NATIONAL GASSES INC.; *U.S. Private*, pg. 1132
VALLEY ONIONS—See A. Duda & Sons Inc.; *U.S. Private*, pg. 344
VALLEY POINT COMMERCIAL DEVELOPMENT—See Nishimatsu Construction Co., Ltd.; *Int'l*, pg. 943
VALLEY POINT COMMERICIAL DEVELOPMENT—See Nishimatsu Construction Co., Ltd.; *Int'l*, pg. 943
VALLEY PONTIAC BUICK GMC, INC.; *U.S. Private*, pg. 1132
VALLEY PROPANE, INC.—See Valley Resources, Inc.; *U.S. Public*, pg. 1706
VALLEY RECORD DISTRIBUTORS, INC.; *U.S. Private*, pg. 1132
VALLEY RESOURCES, INC.; *U.S. Public*, pg. 1706
VALLEY RITE-MIX LIMITED—See Lafarge S.A.; *Int'l*, pg. 791
VALLEY SEED CO.—See Arizona Grains Inc.; *U.S. Private*, pg. 82
VALLEY SYSTEMS, INC.; *U.S. Public*, pg. 1706
VALLEY TIMES—See Knight-Ridder, Inc.; *U.S. Public*, pg. 964
VALLEY-TODECO, INC.—See McKechnie PLC; *Int'l*, pg. 852
VALLEYCAST, INC.—See Outokumpu Oyj; *Int'l*, pg. 1017
VALLEYDALE FOODS, INC.—See Smithfield Foods, Inc.; *U.S. Public*, pg. 1479
VALLEYFAIR—See Cedar Fair, L.P.; *U.S. Public*, pg. 319
VALLUY S.A.R.L.—See Fuchs Petrolub AG Oel + Chemie; *Int'l*, pg. 518
VALMARK INDUSTRIES, INC.—See Jordan Industries, Inc.; *U.S. Private*, pg. 598
Z.N. VALMAS & CO.—See Enso Oyj; *Int'l*, pg. 458
VALMET (ANZ) PTY. LTD.—See Valmet Corporation; *Int'l*, pg. 1448
VALMET AUTOMATION INC.—See Valmet Corporation; *Int'l*, pg. 1449
VALMET AUTOMATION INC.- FIELD INSTRUMENTS—See Valmet Corporation; *Int'l*, pg. 1449
VALMET AUTOMATION KAJAANI LTD.—See Valmet Corporation; *Int'l*, pg. 1449
VALMET-BOUSTEAD PTY. LTD.—See Valmet Corporation; *Int'l*, pg. 1449
VALMET CANADA INC.—See Valmet Corporation; *Int'l*, pg. 1448
VALMET CANADA INC. - ENERDRY—See Valmet Corporation; *Int'l*, pg. 1448
VALMET CANADA INC.-WESTERN CANADA OPERATIONS—See Valmet Corporation; *Int'l*, pg. 1448
VALMET CANADA INC., MONTREAL DIVISION—See Valmet Corporation; *Int'l*, pg. 1448
VALMET CHILE LTDA.—See Valmet Corporation; *Int'l*, pg. 1448
VALMET-COMO S.P.A.—See Valmet Corporation; *Int'l*, pg. 1448
VALMET CORPORATION; *Int'l*, pg. 1447
VALMET CORP.-BEIJING REPRESENTATIVE OFFICE—See Valmet Corporation; *Int'l*, pg. 1448
VALMET CORPORATION BOARD MACHINES—See Valmet Corporation; *Int'l*, pg. 1448

VALMET CORPORATION CALENDERS—See Valmet Corporation; *Int'l*, pg. 1448
VALMET CORPORATION FOUNDRY—See Valmet Corporation; *Int'l*, pg. 1448
VALMET CORPORATION PAPER MACHINES—See Valmet Corporation; *Int'l*, pg. 1448
VALMET CORPORATION PRINTING PAPER MACHINES—See Valmet Corporation; *Int'l*, pg. 1448
VALMET CORPORATION PRODUCTION—See Valmet Corporation; *Int'l*, pg. 1448
VALMET CORPORATION ROLL COATINGS—See Valmet Corporation; *Int'l*, pg. 1448
VALMET CORPORATION ROLL HANDLING—See Valmet Corporation; *Int'l*, pg. 1448
VALMET CORPORATION STOCK PREPARATION—See Valmet Corporation; *Int'l*, pg. 1448
VALMET DURA OY—See Valmet Corporation; *Int'l*, pg. 1448
VALMET GES.M.B.H.—See Valmet Corporation; *Int'l*, pg. 1448
VALMET-GORIZIA S.P.A.—See Valmet Corporation; *Int'l*, pg. 1448
VALMET INC.—See Valmet Corporation; *Int'l*, pg. 1448
VALMET INC.- APPLETON DIVISION—See Valmet Corporation; *Int'l*, pg. 1448
VALMET INC., CHARLOTTE DIVISION—See Valmet Corporation; *Int'l*, pg. 1448
VALMET INC.- ENERDY DIVISION—See Valmet Corporation; *Int'l*, pg. 1448
VALMET INC.- HONEYCOMB DIVISION—See Valmet Corporation; *Int'l*, pg. 1448
VALMET INC., HUDSON FALLS DIVISION—See Valmet Corporation; *Int'l*, pg. 1449
PT. VALMET INDONESIA—See Valmet Corporation; *Int'l*, pg. 1448
VALMET JAPAN CO., LTD.—See Valmet Corporation; *Int'l*, pg. 1448
VALMET-KARLSTAD AB—See Valmet Corporation; *Int'l*, pg. 1448
VALMET KOREA INC.—See Valmet Corporation; *Int'l*, pg. 1448
VALMET PAPER MACHINERY (UK) LTD.—See Valmet Corporation; *Int'l*, pg. 1448
VALMET-RAISIO OY—See Valmet Corporation; *Int'l*, pg. 1448
VALMET-ROTOMEC S.P.A.—See Valmet Corporation; *Int'l*, pg. 1449
VALMET-ROTOMEC S.P.A. AUTOMATION—See Valmet Corporation; *Int'l*, pg. 1449
VALMET SARL—See Valmet Corporation; *Int'l*, pg. 1448
VALMET (SEA) PTE LTD. PAPER MACHINERY DIVISION—See Valmet Corporation; *Int'l*, pg. 1448
VALMET SERVICE GMBH—See Valmet Corporation; *Int'l*, pg. 1448
VALMET SKANDINAVIEN AB—See Valmet Corporation; *Int'l*, pg. 1448
VALMET SVENSKA AB—See Valmet Corporation; *Int'l*, pg. 1448
VALMET TRADE PROMOTION OFFICE—See Valmet Corporation; *Int'l*, pg. 1449
VALMET VERTRIEB GMBH—See Valmet Corporation; *Int'l*, pg. 1448
VALMET-XIAN PAPER MACHINERY CO. LTD.—See Valmet Corporation; *Int'l*, pg. 1448
VALMONT—See Valmont Industries, Inc.; *U.S. Public*, pg. 1707
VALMONT FINANCIAL CORPORATION—See Chancellor Corporation; *U.S. Public*, pg. 335
VALMONT INDEMNITY CO. LTD.—See Chancellor Corporation; *U.S. Public*, pg. 335
VALMONT INDUSTRIES, INC.; *U.S. Public*, pg. 1706
VALMONT IRRIGATION DIVISION—See Valmont Industries, Inc.; *U.S. Public*, pg. 1707
VALMONT NORTHWEST—See Valmont Industries, Inc.; *U.S. Public*, pg. 1707
VALOIS OF AMERICA, INC.—See AptarGroup, Inc.; *U.S. Public*, pg. 125
VALOR—See Groupe Usinor; *Int'l*, pg. 571
VALOR ELECTRONICS, INC.—See GTI Corporation; *U.S. Public*, pg. 768
VALOR LTD.—See Newmond PLC; *Int'l*, pg. 925
VALORCAT, AGENCIA DE VALORES, S.A.—See Caixa d'Estalvis de Catalunya; *Int'l*, pg. 250
VALORES SANTANDER, S.A.—See Banco Santander; *Int'l*, pg. 144
VALPAK PTY. LTD.—See Nissho Iwai Corporation; *Int'l*, pg. 949
VALPEY-FISHER CORPORATION—See Matec Corporation; *U.S. Public*, pg. 1056
VALPEY-FISHER FREQUENCY CONTROL DIV.—See Matec Corporation; *U.S. Public*, pg. 1056
VALPEY-FISHER ULTRASOUND DIV.—See Matec Corporation; *U.S. Public*, pg. 1056
VALQUIMICA, S.A.—See Eli Lilly and Company; *U.S. Public*, pg. 994
THE VALSPAR CORPORATION; *U.S. Public*, pg. 1707
VALSPAR, INC.—See The Valspar Corporation; *U.S. Public*, pg. 1707
VALSPAR PAINTS—See The Valspar Corporation; *U.S. Public*, pg. 1707
VALTEC MINERALOEL VERTRIEBS GESELLSCHAFT—See Ashland, Inc.; *U.S. Public*, pg. 140
VALTEK/AUSTRALIA—See Flowserve Corporation; *U.S. Public*, pg. 659
VALTEK AUSTRALIA/PERTH—See Flowserve Corporation; *U.S. Public*, pg. 659
VALTEK CONTROLS, LTD.—See Flowserve Corporation; *U.S. Public*, pg. 659
VALTEK INTERNATIONAL—See Flowserve Corporation; *U.S. Public*, pg. 658
VALTEK NEW ZEALAND, LTD.—See Flowserve Corporation; *U.S. Public*, pg. 659
VALU DISCOUNT, INCORPORATED; *U.S. Private*, pg. 1132

VALU-FARE FOODS, INC.—See Hale-Halsell Company; *U.S. Private*, pg. 494
VALU-FOODS, INC.—See Hale-Halsell Company; *U.S. Private*, pg. 494
VALU FOODS INC.—See So-Lo-Food, Inc.; *U.S. Private*, pg. 1012
VALUE CARE, INC.—See Integrated Health Services, Inc.; *U.S. Public*, pg. 885
VALUE CITY DEPARTMENT STORES, INC.—See Schottenstein Stores Corporation; *U.S. Private*, pg. 972
VALUE CITY FURNITURE—See Schottenstein Stores Corporation; *U.S. Private*, pg. 972
VALUE CLOTHING COMPANY, INC.—See Farah Incorporated; *U.S. Public*, pg. 613
VALUE ENGINEERING & MANAGEMENT, INC.—See Edwards and Kelcey, Inc.; *U.S. Private*, pg. 365
VALUE LINE—See Arnold Bernhard & Co.; *U.S. Private*, pg. 137
VALUE LINE, INC.—See Arnold Bernhard & Co.; *U.S. Private*, pg. 137
VALUE LINE PUBLISHING—See Arnold Bernhard & Co.; *U.S. Private*, pg. 137
VALUE LINE SECURITIES, INC.—See Arnold Bernhard & Co.; *U.S. Private*, pg. 137
VALUE PRICED CLOTHING INC.—See Men's Wearhouse; *U.S. Public*, pg. 1086
VALUE PROPERTY TRUST; *U.S. Public*, pg. 1707
VALUE PROPERTY TRUST—See Value Property Trust; *U.S. Public*, pg. 1707
VALUE SLACKS, INC.—See Farah Incorporated; *U.S. Public*, pg. 613
VALUE STATIONERY, INC.—See American Pad and Paper Company; *U.S. Public*, pg. 89
VALVE ASSEMBLERS & MANUFACTURERES, INC.—See Dwyer Instruments Inc.; *U.S. Private*, pg. 350
VALVE DIVISION—See TRW Inc.; *U.S. Public*, pg. 1559
VALVECRAFT (PTY) LTD—See GESTRA GmbH; *Int'l*, pg. 551
VALVOLINE (AUSTRALIA) PTY. LTD.—See Ashland, Inc.; *U.S. Public*, pg. 140
VALVOLINE BELGIUM N.V.—See Ashland, Inc.; *U.S. Public*, pg. 140
VALVOLINE CANADA LTD.—See Ashland, Inc.; *U.S. Public*, pg. 140
VALVOLINE COMPANY—See Ashland, Inc.; *U.S. Public*, pg. 139
THE VALVOLINE COMPANY—See Ashland, Inc.; *U.S. Public*, pg. 139
VALVOLINE, INC.—See Ashland, Inc.; *U.S. Public*, pg. 139
VALVOLINE INSTANT OIL CHANGE, INC.—See Ashland, Inc.; *U.S. Public*, pg. 139
VALVOLINE OIL CO. GMBH—See Ashland, Inc.; *U.S. Public*, pg. 140
VALVOLINE OIL CO. LTD.—See Ashland, Inc.; *U.S. Public*, pg. 140
VALVOLINE OIL COMPANY S.P.A.—See Ashland, Inc.; *U.S. Public*, pg. 140
VALVOLINE OIL (FRANCE) S.A.R.L.—See Ashland, Inc.; *U.S. Public*, pg. 140
VALVOLINE OIL NEDERLAND B.V.—See Ashland, Inc.; *U.S. Public*, pg. 140
VALVULAS KEYSTONE DE MEXICO, S.A. DE C.V.—See Tyco International Ltd.; *U.S. Public*, pg. 1650
VALVULAS WORCESTER DE ARGENTINA S.A.—See GESTRA GmbH; *Int'l*, pg. 551
VALVULES BARBARA S.A.—See Saint-Gobain; *Int'l*, pg. 1176
VAMCO—See Valley Resources, Inc.; *U.S. Public*, pg. 1706
VAN AIR SYSTEMS, INC.—See EFCO Inc.; *U.S. Private*, pg. 354
VAN ARK CARE CENTER—See Horizon/CMS Healthcare Corporation; *U.S. Public*, pg. 838
VAN BUUREN-VAN SWAAY MARINE AIRCONDITIONING, ZOETERMEER—See Internatio-Muller N.V.; *Int'l*, pg. 681
VAN CADSAND BEHEER B.V.—See Pfizer Inc.; *U.S. Public*, pg. 1284
VAN CAMPEN BENDING TECHNICS B.V.—See Reynolds Metals Company; *U.S. Public*, pg. 1387
VAN CLEEF & ARPELS, INC.; *U.S. Private*, pg. 1707
VAN DEN BERGH & JURGENS (PTY.) LTD.—See Unilever Plc; *Int'l*, pg. 1439
VAN DEN BERGH/ANDERSON CLAYTON—See Unilever Plc; *Int'l*, pg. 1436
VAN DEN BERGH EN JURGENS B.V.—See Unilever Plc; *Int'l*, pg. 1439
VAN DEN BERGH FOODS COMPANY—See Unilever Plc; *Int'l*, pg. 1436
VAN DEN BERGH FOODS LTD.—See Unilever Plc; *Int'l*, pg. 1434
VAN DEN CIENTIFICA LTDA.—See Hewlett-Packard Company; *U.S. Public*, pg. 823
J. TH. VAN DER CAMMEN B.V.—See Deutsche Babcock AG; *Int'l*, pg. 400
VAN DEVENTER & HOCH—See The Chase Manhattan Corporation; *U.S. Public*, pg. 339
VAN DORN DEMAG CORPORATION—See Mannesmann A.G.; *Int'l*, pg. 837
VAN DYNE-CROTTY, INC.; *U.S. Private*, pg. 1132
VAN EIJLE B.V.—See Internatio-Muller N.V.; *Int'l*, pg. 682
VAN GEND & LOOS B.V.—See Royal Nedlloyd Group N.V.; *Int'l*, pg. 1145
VAN GEND & LOOS N.V.—See Royal Nedlloyd Group N.V.; *Int'l*, pg. 1145
VAN GORP CORP.—See Emerson Electric Co.; *U.S. Public*, pg. 573
VAN HEEL B.V.—See Koninklijke BolsWessanen nv; *Int'l*, pg. 751
VAN HEMELRIJCK—See GIB Group; *Int'l*, pg. 533
VAN HEUSDEN—See Vendex International N.V.; *Int'l*, pg. 1463
THE VAN HEUSEN GROUP OF COMPANIES—See Phillips-Van Heusen Corporation; *U.S. Public*, pg. 1291

VAN HEUSEN RETAIL DIVISION—See Phillips-Van Heusen Corporation; *U.S. Public*, pg. 1291
VAN KAMPEN/AMERICAN CAPITAL INC.—See Morgan Stanley Dean Witter & Co.; *U.S. Public*, pg. 1132
F VAN LANSCHOT BANKIERS NV—See National Westminster Bank PLC; *Int'l*, pg. 911
VAN LEER ARGENTINA S.A.—See Royal Packaging Industries Van Leer B.V.; *Int'l*, pg. 1146
VAN LEER AUSTRALIA PTY. LTD.—See Royal Packaging Industries Van Leer B.V.; *Int'l*, pg. 1146
VAN LEER BELGIUM B.V.—See Royal Packaging Industries Van Leer B.V.; *Int'l*, pg. 1146
VAN LEER CHILE S.A.—See Royal Packaging Industries Van Leer B.V.; *Int'l*, pg. 1146
VAN LEER CONTAINERS, INC.—See Royal Packaging Industries Van Leer B.V.; *Int'l*, pg. 1146
VAN LEER CONTAINERS (NIGERIA) PLC—See Royal Packaging Industries Van Leer B.V.; *Int'l*, pg. 1146
VAN LEER CYLINDERS SDN. BHD.—See Royal Packaging Industries Van Leer B.V.; *Int'l*, pg. 1146
VAN LEER EAST AFRICA LTD—See Royal Packaging Industries Van Leer B.V.; *Int'l*, pg. 1146
VAN LEER EGYPT L.L.C.—See Royal Packaging Industries Van Leer B.V.; *Int'l*, pg. 1146
VAN LEER ELPACK A.E.B.E.—See Royal Packaging Industries Van Leer B.V.; *Int'l*, pg. 1146
VAN LEER EMBALAGENS INDUSTRIAIS DO BRASIL LTDA.—See Royal Packaging Industries Van Leer B.V.; *Int'l*, pg. 1146
VAN LEER EMBALAGENS MOLDADAS LTDA—See Royal Packaging Industries Van Leer B.V.; *Int'l*, pg. 1146
VAN LEER ENVASES DE CENTRO AMERICA S.A.—See Royal Packaging Industries Van Leer B.V.; *Int'l*, pg. 1147
VAN LEER ENVASES DE COLOMBIA S.A.—See Royal Packaging Industries Van Leer B.V.; *Int'l*, pg. 1147
VAN LEER ENVASES DE COSTA RICA S.A.—See Royal Packaging Industries Van Leer B.V.; *Int'l*, pg. 1147
VAN LEER ENVASES DE GUATEMALA—See Royal Packaging Industries Van Leer B.V.; *Int'l*, pg. 1147
VAN LEER ENVASES-ENVASA PLAS S.A.—See Royal Packaging Industries Van Leer B.V.; *Int'l*, pg. 1147
VAN LEER ENVASES VALENCIA, C.A.—See Royal Packaging Industries Van Leer B.V.; *Int'l*, pg. 1147
VAN LEER ESPANA, S.A.—See Royal Packaging Industries Van Leer B.V.; *Int'l*, pg. 1147
VAN LEER FIBRE & PLASTIQUE FRANCE S.A.—See Royal Packaging Industries Van Leer B.V.; *Int'l*, pg. 1147
VAN LEER FLEXIBLES, INC.—See Royal Packaging Industries Van Leer B.V.; *Int'l*, pg. 1146
VAN LEER FRANCE S.A.R.L.—See Royal Packaging Industries Van Leer B.V.; *Int'l*, pg. 1147
VAN LEER (IRELAND) LTD—See Royal Packaging Industries Van Leer B.V.; *Int'l*, pg. 1147
VAN LEER ITALIA SPA—See Royal Packaging Industries Van Leer B.V.; *Int'l*, pg. 1147
VAN LEER JAMAICA LTD—See Royal Packaging Industries Van Leer B.V.; *Int'l*, pg. 1147
VAN LEER JAPAN, LTD—See Royal Packaging Industries Van Leer B.V.; *Int'l*, pg. 1147
VAN LEER (MALAYSIA) SDN. BHD.—See Royal Packaging Industries Van Leer B.V.; *Int'l*, pg. 1147
VAN LEER MAXEMBALL S.A.—See Royal Packaging Industries Van Leer B.V.; *Int'l*, pg. 1147
VAN LEER METALLIZED PRODUCTS B.V.—See Royal Packaging Industries Van Leer B.V.; *Int'l*, pg. 1146
VAN LEER METALLIZED PRODUCTS LTD.—See Royal Packaging Industries Van Leer B.V.; *Int'l*, pg. 1146
VAN LEER METALLIZED PRODUCTS (USA) LTD.—See Royal Packaging Industries Van Leer B.V.; *Int'l*, pg. 1146
VAN LEER MIMAYSAN AMBALAJ SANAYI A.S.—See Royal Packaging Industries Van Leer B.V.; *Int'l*, pg. 1147
N.V. VAN LEER MUNO S.A.—See Royal Packaging Industries Van Leer B.V.; *Int'l*, pg. 1147
VAN LEER NEDERLAND B.V.—See Royal Packaging Industries Van Leer B.V.; *Int'l*, pg. 1146
VAN LEER NEW ZEALAND LTD—See Royal Packaging Industries Van Leer B.V.; *Int'l*, pg. 1147
VAN LEER NINGBO—See Royal Packaging Industries Van Leer B.V.; *Int'l*, pg. 1147
VAN LEER OBALY A.S.—See Royal Packaging Industries Van Leer B.V.; *Int'l*, pg. 1147
VAN LEER PACKAGING SDN. BHD.—See Royal Packaging Industries Van Leer B.V.; *Int'l*, pg. 1147
VAN LEER PACKAGING SYSTEMS LTD.—See Royal Packaging Industries Van Leer B.V.; *Int'l*, pg. 1147
VAN LEER (SARAWAK) SDN. BHD.—See Royal Packaging Industries Van Leer B.V.; *Int'l*, pg. 1147
VAN LEER SERVICES B.V.—See Royal Packaging Industries Van Leer B.V.; *Int'l*, pg. 1146
VAN LEER SILESIA SP. Z.O.O.—See Royal Packaging Industries Van Leer B.V.; *Int'l*, pg. 1147
VAN LEER SINGAPORE PTE. LTD.—See Royal Packaging Industries Van Leer B.V.; *Int'l*, pg. 1147
VAN LEER SOUTH AFRICA (PTY) LTD—See Royal Packaging Industries Van Leer B.V.; *Int'l*, pg. 1147
VAN LEER SOUTH AFRICA (PTY) LTD.—See Royal Packaging Industries Van Leer B.V.; *Int'l*, pg. 1147
VAN LEER SVENSKA AB—See Royal Packaging Industries Van Leer B.V.; *Int'l*, pg. 1147
VAN LEER TAY LTD—See Royal Packaging Industries Van Leer B.V.; *Int'l*, pg. 1147
VAN LEER (UK) LTD.—See Royal Packaging Industries Van Leer B.V.; *Int'l*, pg. 1147
VAN LEER URAL—See Royal Packaging Industries Van Leer B.V.; *Int'l*, pg. 1147
VAN LEER URUGUAY—See Royal Packaging Industries Van Leer B.V.; *Int'l*, pg. 1147
VAN LEER VERPACKUNGEN GMBH—See Royal Packaging Industries Van Leer B.V.; *Int'l*, pg. 1147

VAN LEER ZIMBABWE (PRIVATE) LTD—See Royal Packaging Industries Van Leer B.V.; *Int'l*, pg. 1147
VAN LEEUWEL TUBES LTD.—See Van Leeuwen Pipe and Tube Group B.V.; *Int'l*, pg. 1450
VAN LEEUWEN BUIZEN BELGIUM BV—See Van Leeuwen Pipe and Tube Group B.V.; *Int'l*, pg. 1450
VAN LEEUWEN BUIZEN EUROPA BV—See Van Leeuwen Pipe and Tube Group B.V.; *Int'l*, pg. 1449
P. VAN LEEUWEN JR'S BUIZENHANDEL B.V.—See Van Leeuwen Pipe and Tube Group B.V.; *Int'l*, pg. 1449
VAN LEEUWEN PIPE & TUBE—See Van Leeuwen Pipe and Tube Group B.V.; *Int'l*, pg. 1450
VAN LEEUWEN PIPE & TUBE (CANADA) INC.—See Van Leeuwen Pipe and Tube Group B.V.; *Int'l*, pg. 1450
VAN LEEUWEN PIPE & TUBE CORP.—See Van Leeuwen Pipe and Tube Group B.V.; *Int'l*, pg. 1449
VAN LEEUWEN PIPE AND TUBE CORPORATION—See Van Leeuwen Pipe and Tube Group B.V.; *Int'l*, pg. 1450
VAN LEEUWEN PIPE AND TUBE EASTERN AUSTRALIA PTY. LTD.—See Van Leeuwen Pipe and Tube Group B.V.; *Int'l*, pg. 1450
VAN LEEUWEN PIPE AND TUBE (FAR EAST) PTE. LTD.—See Van Leeuwen Pipe and Tube Group B.V.; *Int'l*, pg. 1450
VAN LEEUWEN PIPE AND TUBE GROUP B.V.; *Int'l*, pg. 1449
VAN LEEUWEN PIPE AND TUBE KOREA LTD.—See Van Leeuwen Pipe and Tube Group B.V.; *Int'l*, pg. 1450
VAN LEEUWEN PIPE AND TUBE (MALAYSIA) SDN. BHD.—See Van Leeuwen Pipe and Tube Group B.V.; *Int'l*, pg. 1450
VAN LEEUWEN PIPE & TUBE OF THE SOUTHEAST, INC.—See Van Leeuwen Pipe and Tube Group B.V.; *Int'l*, pg. 1450
VAN LEEUWEN PIPE AND TUBE THAILAND LTD.—See Van Leeuwen Pipe and Tube Group B.V.; *Int'l*, pg. 1450
VAN LEEUWEN PIPE AND TUBE (THAILAND) LTD.—See Van Leeuwen Pipe and Tube Group B.V.; *Int'l*, pg. 1450
VAN LEEUWEN PIPE AND TUBE WESTERN AUSTRALIA PTY. LTD.—See Van Leeuwen Pipe and Tube Group B.V.; *Int'l*, pg. 1450
VAN LEEUWEN PIPE & TUBE CORP.—See Van Leeuwen Pipe and Tube Group B.V.; *Int'l*, pg. 1450
VAN LEEUWEN PRECISION BV—See Van Leeuwen Pipe and Tube Group B.V.; *Int'l*, pg. 1449
VAN LEEUWEN ROHREN GMBH—See Van Leeuwen Pipe and Tube Group B.V.; *Int'l*, pg. 1450
VAN LEEUWEN STAINLESS—See Van Leeuwen Pipe and Tube Group B.V.; *Int'l*, pg. 1449
VAN LEEUWEN TUBES LTD.—See Van Leeuwen Pipe and Tube Group B.V.; *Int'l*, pg. 1450
VAN LEEUWEN TUBES SA—See Van Leeuwen Pipe and Tube Group B.V.; *Int'l*, pg. 1450
VAN LEEUWEN TUBOS ESPANA S.A.E.—See Van Leeuwen Pipe and Tube Group B.V.; *Int'l*, pg. 1450
VAN MELLE AG—See Van Melle N.V.; *Int'l*, pg. 1451
VAN MELLE BRASIL LTDA.—See Van Melle N.V.; *Int'l*, pg. 1451
VAN MELLE DEUTSCHLAND GMBH—See Van Melle N.V.; *Int'l*, pg. 1451
VAN MELLE EXPORT B.V.—See Van Melle N.V.; *Int'l*, pg. 1451
VAN MELLE FAR EAST LIMITED—See Van Melle N.V.; *Int'l*, pg. 1451
VAN MELLE FAR EAST LTD.-CHINA BRANCH—See Van Melle N.V.; *Int'l*, pg. 1451
VAN MELLE-FRANCE S.A.—See Van Melle N.V.; *Int'l*, pg. 1451
VAN MELLE HOLDING GMBH—See Van Melle N.V.; *Int'l*, pg. 1451
P.T. VAN MELLE INDONESIA—See Van Melle N.V.; *Int'l*, pg. 1451
VAN MELLE INTERNATIONAL HOLDING B.V.—See Van Melle N.V.; *Int'l*, pg. 1451
VAN MELLE INTERNATIONAL TRUST B.V.—See Van Melle N.V.; *Int'l*, pg. 1451
VAN MELLE LATIN AMERICA NV—See Van Melle N.V.; *Int'l*, pg. 1451
VAN MELLE MOSCOW REPRESENTATIVE OFFICE—See Van Melle N.V.; *Int'l*, pg. 1451
VAN MELLE NEDERLAND B.V.—See Van Melle N.V.; *Int'l*, pg. 1451
VAN MELLE NEDERLAND HOLDING B.V.—See Van Melle N.V.; *Int'l*, pg. 1451
VAN MELLE NEDERLAND SERVICES B.V.—See Van Melle N.V.; *Int'l*, pg. 1451
VAN MELLE NEDERLAND VERKOOP B. V.—See Van Melle N.V.; *Int'l*, pg. 1451
VAN MELLE N.V.; *Int'l*, pg. 1450
VAN MELLE-(PHILS.) INC.—See Van Melle N.V.; *Int'l*, pg. 1451
VAN MELLE POLSKA SP. Z.O.O.—See Van Melle N.V.; *Int'l*, pg. 1451
N.V. VAN MELLE S.A.—See Van Melle N.V.; *Int'l*, pg. 1451
VAN MELLE USA, INC.—See Van Melle N.V.; *Int'l*, pg. 1451
THE VAN METRES COMPANIES; *U.S. Private*, pg. 1132
VAN NEERBOS-PCI B.V.—See Viag AG; *Int'l*, pg. 1466
VAN NIFTRIK B.V.—See Schuttersveld Holding N.V.; *Int'l*, pg. 1210
VAN NOSTRAND REINHOLD CO.—See The Thomson Corporation; *U.S. Public*, pg. 1600
VAN NUYS AIRPORT RESTAURANT CORP.—See Specialty Restaurants Corporation; *U.S. Private*, pg. 1022
VAN OMMEREN SHIPPING, INC.—See Koninklijke Van Ommeren NV; *Int'l*, pg. 758
VAN OMMEREN USA INC.—See Koninklijke Van Ommeren NV; *Int'l*, pg. 758
VAN PELT CORPORATION; *U.S. Private*, pg. 1133

VAN RAALTE DE VENEZUELA C.A.—See Fruit of the Loom, Inc.; *U.S. Public*, pg. 686
VAN RIETSCHOTEN & HOUWENS NOORD-WEST BV— See Internatio-Muller N.V.; *Int'l*, pg. 681
VAN RIETSCHOTEN & HOUWENS ZUID-WEST BV—See Internatio-Muller N.V.; *Int'l*, pg. 681
VAN ROMONDT TRADING COMPANY LTD.—See Telefonaktiebolaget LM Ericsson; *Int'l*, pg. 1371
VAN RULLEN FRERES SPRL—See Williams Holdings Plc; *Int'l*, pg. 1499
VAN SEVEREN—See Norske Skogindustrier A.S; *Int'l*, pg. 965
A/S VAN SEVEREN & CO. LTD.—See Norske Skogindustrier A.S; *Int'l*, pg. 965
VAN SOEST BV—See The Albert Fisher Group PLC; *Int'l*, pg. 491
VAN SON HOLLAND INK CORP. OF AMERICA; *U.S. Private*, pg. 1133
VAN SWAAY INTERNATIONAL CONTRACTING B.V.—See Internatio-Muller N.V.; *Int'l*, pg. 681
VAN SWAAY TOEGANGSTECHNIEK BV—See Internatio-Muller N.V.; *Int'l*, pg. 680
VAN SWAAY TRADING B.V.—See Internatio-Muller N.V.; *Int'l*, pg. 681
VAN VLISSINGEN-ANKERSMIT EXPORT MAATSCHAPPIJ B.V.—See Gamma Holding N.V.; *Int'l*, pg. 540
VAN WATERS & ROGERS—See Royal Pakhoed NV; *Int'l*, pg. 1147
VAN WATERS & ROGERS INC.—See Royal Pakhoed NV; *Int'l*, pg. 1147
VAN WATERS & ROGERS LTD.—See Royal Pakhoed NV; *Int'l*, pg. 1147
VAN ZANDBEEK/THE CORPORATE COMPANY—See BDDP Group; *Int'l*, pg. 118
VANAJA POWER PLANT—See Imatran Voima Oy; *Int'l*, pg. 660
VANCE INDUSTRIES, INC.; *U.S. Private*, pg. 1133
VANCE PUBLISHING CORPORATION; *U.S. Private*, pg. 1133
VANCO INTERNATIONAL, INC.—See Video Display Corporation; *U.S. Public*, pg. 1720
VANCOUVER ISLAND STEVEDORING CO. LTD.—See MacMillan Bloedel Limited; *Int'l*, pg. 828
VANCOUVER PORT CORPORATION—See Canada Ports Corporation; *Int'l*, pg. 255
THE VANCOUVER SUN—See Hollinger Inc.; *Int'l*, pg. 631
VANDALIA LEADER-UNION—See Landmark Communications, Inc.; *U.S. Private*, pg. 648
VANDAMME - PIE QUI CHANTE—See Danone Group; *Int'l*, pg. 380
VANDEMOORTELE N.V.; *Int'l*, pg. 1451
VANDERBILT MORTGAGE & FINANCE, INC.—See Clayton Homes, Inc.; *U.S. Public*, pg. 383
R.T. VANDERBILT COMPANY, INC.; *U.S. Private*, pg. 1133
VANDERGRIFF CHEVROLET GEO; *U.S. Private*, pg. 1133
VANFED APPRAISAL COMPANY—See Washington Mutual Inc.; *U.S. Public*, pg. 1742
VANFED INVESTMENT SERVICES, INC.—See Washington Mutual Inc.; *U.S. Public*, pg. 1742
VANFED MORTGAGE COMPANY—See Washington Mutual Inc.; *U.S. Public*, pg. 1742
VANGUARD BANK & TRUST COMPANY—See Synovus Financial Corp.; *U.S. Public*, pg. 1549
VANGUARD BINGHAMTON, INC.—See Vanguard Cellular Systems, Inc.; *U.S. Public*, pg. 1708
VANGUARD CELLULAR SYSTEMS, INC.; *U.S. Public*, pg. 1707
VANGUARD CELLULAR SYSTEMS OF SOUTH CAROLINA, INC.—See Vanguard Cellular Systems, Inc.; *U.S. Public*, pg. 1708
VANGUARD DIVISION—See Nestle S.A.; *Int'l*, pg. 917
VANGUARD ENERGY CORP.; *U.S. Private*, pg. 1133
VANGUARD FINANCIAL SERVICES—See Old Kent Financial Corporation; *U.S. Public*, pg. 1216
THE VANGUARD GROUP, INC.; *U.S. Private*, pg. 1134
VANGUARD INSTRUMENT CORP.—See Eastman Kodak Company; *U.S. Public*, pg. 551
VANGUARD PLASTICS, INC.; *U.S. Private*, pg. 1134
VANGUARD REAL ESTATE FUND II—See The Vanguard Group, Inc.; *U.S. Private*, pg. 1134
VANGUARDA COMPONENTES AUTOMOTIVOS, S.A.— See General Motors Corporation; *U.S. Public*, pg. 722
VANITY FAIR—See Advance Publications Inc.; *U.S. Private*, pg. 20
VANITY FAIR—See VF Corporation; *U.S. Public*, pg. 1702
VANLINER GROUP, INC.—See UniGroup, Inc.; *U.S. Private*, pg. 1117
VANLINER INSURANCE CO.—See UniGroup, Inc.; *U.S. Private*, pg. 1117
VANNER, INC.—See B. Elliott plc.; *Int'l*, pg. 449
VANPORT MANUFACTURING, INC.; *U.S. Private*, pg. 1134
VANPRO ASSENTOS LDA.—See Bertrand Faure; *Int'l*, pg. 193
VANS FINANCE CORPORATION—See Volkswagen AG; *Int'l*, pg. 1475
VANSTAR CORPORATION; *U.S. Public*, pg. 1708
VANTAGE COMPANIES; *U.S. Private*, pg. 1134
VANTAGE GLOBAL ADVISORS, INC.—See Lincoln National Corporation; *U.S. Public*, pg. 998
VANTAGEPARTS—See CNF Transportation Inc.; *U.S. Public*, pg. 281
VANTONA LTD.—See Coats Viyella plc; *Int'l*, pg. 299
VAPONICS INC.—See Osmonics, Inc.; *U.S. Public*, pg. 1234
VAPOR—See Westinghouse Air Brake Company; *U.S. Public*, pg. 1761
THE VAPORMATIC CO. LTD.—See Wolseley Plc.; *Int'l*, pg. 1512
VARA INTERNATONAL—See Calgon Carbon Corporation; *U.S. Public*, pg. 293
AB VARANMO GUMMIFABRIK—See Trelleborg AB; *Int'l*, pg. 1422

VARCO BEST PRODUCTS—See Varco International, Inc.; *U.S. Public*, pg. 1709
VARCO BJ DRILLING SYSTEMS—See Varco International, Inc.; *U.S. Public*, pg. 1709
VARCO BJ OIL TOOLS—See Varco International, Inc.; *U.S. Public*, pg. 1709
VARCO BJ OIL TOOLS B.V.—See Varco International, Inc.; *U.S. Public*, pg. 1709
VARCO INTERNATIONAL, INC.; *U.S. Public*, pg. 1709
VARCO-PRUDEN BUILDINGS—See United Dominion Industries, Ltd.; *U.S. Public*, pg. 1677
VARCO (U.K.) LTD. DRILLING SYSTEMS—See Varco International, Inc.; *U.S. Public*, pg. 1709
VARCO (U.K.) LTD. OIL TOOLS—See Varco International, Inc.; *U.S. Public*, pg. 1709
VAREL MANUFACTURING CO.; *U.S. Private*, pg. 1134
VARI-FORM—See TI Group plc; *Int'l*, pg. 1340
VARI-LITE INTERNATIONAL, *U.S. Public*, pg. 1709
VARI TRONICS COMPANY, INC.; *U.S. Private*, pg. 1134
THE VARIABLE ANNUITY LIFE INSURANCE CO.—See American General Corporation; *U.S. Public*, pg. 76
THE VARIABLE ANNUITY MARKETING CO.—See American General Corporation; *U.S. Public*, pg. 76
VARIAN ASSOCIATES, INC.; *U.S. Public*, pg. 1710
VARIAN AUSTRALIA PTY. LTD.—See Varian Associates, Inc.; *U.S. Public*, pg. 1710
VARIAN KOREA LTD.—See Varian Associates, Inc.; *U.S. Public*, pg. 1710
VARIAN SPA—See Varian Associates, Inc.; *U.S. Public*, pg. 1710
VARIAN-TEM LTD.—See Varian Associates, Inc.; *U.S. Public*, pg. 1710
VARIED INVESTMENTS, INC.; *U.S. Private*, pg. 1134
VARIETY MUSIC CORP. S.A.—See Philips Electronics N.V.; *Int'l*, pg. 1053
VARIETY WHOLESALERS, INCORPORATED; *U.S. Private*, pg. 1134
VARIFORM, INC.—See Nortek, Inc.; *U.S. Public*, pg. 1193
VARIG BRAZILIAN AIRLINES—See Varig Brazilian Airlines S.A.; *Int'l*, pg. 1451
VARIG BRAZILIAN AIRLINES S.A.; *Int'l*, pg. 1451
VARILUX CORPORATION—See Essilor International Compagnie Generale d'Optique; *Int'l*, pg. 462
VARITRONIC SYSTEMS, INC.—See W.H. Brady Co.; *U.S. Public*, pg. 250
VARITY DAYTON WALTHER—See LucasVarity plc; *Int'l*, pg. 820
VARITY KELSEY HAYES—See LucasVarity plc; *Int'l*, pg. 820
VARITY PERKINS—See LucasVarity plc; *Int'l*, pg. 820
VARITY ZECAL—See LucasVarity plc; *Int'l*, pg. 820
VARKAUDEN MATKATOIMISTO OY—See FinnAir Oy; *Int'l*, pg. 485
VARLEN CORPORATION; *U.S. Public*, pg. 1710
VARLEN INSTRUMENTS, INC.—See Varlen Corporation; *U.S. Public*, pg. 1711
VARNAMO ISOLERDUK—See Trelleborg AB; *Int'l*, pg. 1422
VARON—See Biscayne Apparel Inc.; *U.S. Public*, pg. 233
VARSITY INTROPA—See Riddell Sports, Inc.; *U.S. Public*, pg. 1389
VARSITY SPIRIT CORPORATION—See Riddell Sports, Inc.; *U.S. Public*, pg. 1389
VARSITY SPIRIT FASHIONS—See Riddell Sports, Inc.; *U.S. Public*, pg. 1389
VARSITY USA—See Riddell Sports, Inc.; *U.S. Public*, pg. 1389
OY VARTA AB—See VARTA AG; *Int'l*, pg. 1452
VARTA AG; *Int'l*, pg. 1451
VARTA AKU SPOL. SR.O.—See VARTA AG; *Int'l*, pg. 1452
VARTA AUTOBATERIAS S.A.—See VARTA AG; *Int'l*, pg. 1452
VARTA BATERIAS SAICYF—See VARTA AG; *Int'l*, pg. 1452
VARTA BATTERI AB—See VARTA AG; *Int'l*, pg. 1452
VARTA BATTERI A/S—See VARTA AG; *Int'l*, pg. 1452
VARTA BATTERIE AG—See VARTA AG; *Int'l*, pg. 1452
VARTA BATTERIE GES.M.B.H.—See VARTA AG; *Int'l*, pg. 1452
VARTA BATTERIE INDUSTRIALI S.P.A.—See VARTA AG; *Int'l*, pg. 1452
VARTA BATTERIE S.P.A.—See VARTA AG; *Int'l*, pg. 1452
VARTA BATTERIES—See VARTA AG; *Int'l*, pg. 1452
P.T. VARTA BATTERIES INDONESIA LTD.—See VARTA AG; *Int'l*, pg. 1452
VARTA BATTERIES PTE. LTD.—See VARTA AG; *Int'l*, pg. 1452
VARTA B.V.—See VARTA AG; *Int'l*, pg. 1452
VARTA INDUSTRIAL BATTERIES LTD.—See VARTA AG; *Int'l*, pg. 1452
VARTA INDUSTRIEBATTERIE N.V. S.A.—See VARTA AG; *Int'l*, pg. 1452
VARTA KERESKEDELMI ES SZOLGALTATO KFT.— See VARTA AG; *Int'l*, pg. 1452
VARTA LTD.—See VARTA AG; *Int'l*, pg. 1452
VARTA-PLASTIC GMBH—See VARTA AG; *Int'l*, pg. 1452
VARTA RECYCLING GMBH—See VARTA AG; *Int'l*, pg. 1452
VARTA S.A.—See VARTA AG; *Int'l*, pg. 1452
VARTA S.A. DE C.V.—See VARTA AG; *Int'l*, pg. 1452
VASA BROUGHER, INC.—See Eureko B.V.; *Int'l*, pg. 464
VASA CARE—See Eureko B.V.; *Int'l*, pg. 464
VASA FINANCE CORP.—See Eureko B.V.; *Int'l*, pg. 464
VASA LIFE INSURANCE CO.—See Eureko B.V.; *Int'l*, pg. 464
VASA NORTH AMERICA—See Eureko B.V.; *Int'l*, pg. 464
VASA NORTH ATLANTIC INSURANCE COMPANY—See Eureko B.V.; *Int'l*, pg. 464
VASA PROPERTIES—See Eureko B.V.; *Int'l*, pg. 464
VASA REALTY, INC.—See Eureko B.V.; *Int'l*, pg. 464
VASCOR—See Neptune Orient Lines Ltd.; *Int'l*, pg. 912
VASCOR, LTD.—See Neptune Orient Lines Ltd.; *Int'l*, pg. 912
VASCUTEK LIMITED—See Sulzer Ltd.; *Int'l*, pg. 1307

VASSEN ALUMINIUM BV—See Koninklijke Hoogovens N.V.; *Int'l*, pg. 753
VASTERBERGSLAGENS ELNAT AB—See Vattenfall AB; *Int'l*, pg. 1453
VATRYGGINGARFELAGID SKANDIA HF—See Skandia Insurance Company Limited; *Int'l*, pg. 1258
VATTENFALL AB; *Int'l*, pg. 1452
VATTENFALL AB—See Vattenfall AB; *Int'l*, pg. 1453
VATTENFALL A/S—See Vattenfall AB; *Int'l*, pg. 1453
VATTENFALL BOHUS-BAL ELNAT AB—See Vattenfall AB; *Int'l*, pg. 1453
VATTENFALL CENTRAL SWEDEN—See Vattenfall AB; *Int'l*, pg. 1453
VATTENFALL DEUTSCHELAND GMBH—See Vattenfall AB; *Int'l*, pg. 1453
VATTENFALL EASTERN SWEDEN—See Vattenfall AB; *Int'l*, pg. 1453
VATTENFALL ENERGIMATNING AB—See Vattenfall AB; *Int'l*, pg. 1453
VATTENFALL ENERGISYSTEM AB—See Vattenfall AB; *Int'l*, pg. 1453
VATTENFALL ENGINEERING AB—See Vattenfall AB; *Int'l*, pg. 1453
VATTENFALL ESTONIA OU—See Vattenfall AB; *Int'l*, pg. 1453
VATTENFALL EUROPEAN AFFAIRS—See Vattenfall AB; *Int'l*, pg. 1453
VATTENFALL GENERATION SERVICES AB—See Vattenfall AB; *Int'l*, pg. 1453
VATTENFALL HYDROPOWER AB—See Vattenfall AB; *Int'l*, pg. 1453
VATTENFALL LATVIA SIA—See Vattenfall AB; *Int'l*, pg. 1453
VATTENFALL LITHUANIA UAB—See Vattenfall AB; *Int'l*, pg. 1453
VATTENFALL MALARNAT AB—See Vattenfall AB; *Int'l*, pg. 1453
VATTENFALL NATURGAS AB—See Vattenfall AB; *Int'l*, pg. 1453
VATTENFALL NORRNAT AB—See Vattenfall AB; *Int'l*, pg. 1453
VATTENFALL NORTHERN SWEDEN—See Vattenfall AB; *Int'l*, pg. 1453
VATTENFALL OSTNAT AB—See Vattenfall AB; *Int'l*, pg. 1453
VATTENFALL OY—See Vattenfall AB; *Int'l*, pg. 1453
VATTENFALL POLAND SP.Z.O.O.—See Vattenfall AB; *Int'l*, pg. 1453
VATTENFALL REGIONNAT AB—See Vattenfall AB; *Int'l*, pg. 1453
VATTENFALL RINGHALS—See Vattenfall AB; *Int'l*, pg. 1453
VATTENFALL TRANSMISSION AB—See Vattenfall AB; *Int'l*, pg. 1453
VATTENFALL TREASURY AB—See Vattenfall AB; *Int'l*, pg. 1453
VATTENFALL UTVECKLING AB—See Vattenfall AB; *Int'l*, pg. 1453
VATTENFALL VARMEKRAFT—See Vattenfall AB; *Int'l*, pg. 1453
VATTENFALL VATTENKRAFT—See Vattenfall AB; *Int'l*, pg. 1453
VATTENFALL VATTERNAT AB—See Vattenfall AB; *Int'l*, pg. 1453
VATTENFALL WESTERN SWEDEN—See Vattenfall AB; *Int'l*, pg. 1453
VATTER—See Sara Lee Corporation; *U.S. Public*, pg. 1435
VAUBEL & PARTNERS LTD.—See Deutsche Bank AG; *Int'l*, pg. 405
VAUGHAN & SONS, INC.; *U.S. Private*, pg. 1134
VAUGHAN & SONS, INC. MULTI-FAMILY SALES—See Vaughan & Sons, Inc.; *U.S. Private*, pg. 1135
VAUGHAN TRANSPORT (AUSTRALIA) PTY. LTD.—See Brambles Industries Limited; *Int'l*, pg. 211
VAUGHN-HARMON LTD.—See Harmon Industries, Inc.; *U.S. Public*, pg. 788
VAUX BREWERIES LTD.—See Vaux Group Plc; *Int'l*, pg. 1454
VAUX GROUP PLC; *Int'l*, pg. 1453
VAUX INNS LTD.—See Vaux Group Plc; *Int'l*, pg. 1454
VAUXHALL MOTORS LIMITED—See General Motors Corporation; *U.S. Public*, pg. 724
VAW OF AMERICA, INC.—See Viag AG; *Int'l*, pg. 1466
VAXJO ROSTFRITT AB—See Getinge Industrier AB; *Int'l*, pg. 551
VEAM GMBH—See Litton Industries, Inc.; *U.S. Public*, pg. 1005
VEAM S.A.—See Litton Industries, Inc.; *U.S. Public*, pg. 1005
VEBA AG; *Int'l*, pg. 1454
VEBA CORPORATION—See Veba AG; *Int'l*, pg. 1461
VEBA FERNHEIZUNG CASTROP-RAUXEL GMBH—See Veba AG; *Int'l*, pg. 1460
VEBA FERNHEIZUNG DATTELN GMBH—See Veba AG; *Int'l*, pg. 1460
VEBA FERNHEIZUNG GELSENKIRCHEN-BUER GMBH— See Veba AG; *Int'l*, pg. 1460
VEBA FERNHEIZUNG GLADBECK GMBH—See Veba AG; *Int'l*, pg. 1460
VEBA FERNHEIZUNG RECKLINGHAUSEN GMBH— See Veba AG; *Int'l*, pg. 1460
VEBA FERNHEIZUNG WANNE-EICKEL GMBH—See Veba AG; *Int'l*, pg. 1460
VEBA IMMOBILIEN AG—See Veba AG; *Int'l*, pg. 1460
VEBA KRAFTWERKE RUHR AG—See Veba AG; *Int'l*, pg. 1460
VEBA OEL AG—See Veba AG; *Int'l*, pg. 1460
VEBA OEL VERTRIEB GMBH—See Veba AG; *Int'l*, pg. 1461
VEBA OIL INTERNATIONAL GMBH—See Veba AG; *Int'l*, pg. 1461
VEBA OIL TECHNOLOGIE GMBH—See Veba AG; *Int'l*, pg. 1461

VEBA POSEIDON SCHIFFAHRT GMBH—See Veba AG; *Int'l*, pg. 1461
VEBA TELECOM DEUTSCHLAND GMBH—See Veba AG; *Int'l*, pg. 1461
VEBA URBANA AG—See Veba AG; *Int'l*, pg. 1460
VEBA VERMOGENSANLAGE GMBH—See Veba AG; pg. 1461
VEBA WOHNEN AG—See Veba AG; *Int'l*, pg. 1460
VEBACOM GMBH—See Veba AG; *Int'l*, pg. 1461
VECTOR INDUSTRIES, LTD.; *Int'l*, pg. 1461
VECTOR MARINE HOLDINGS—See Vector Industries, Ltd.; *Int'l*, pg. 1461
VECTRA TECHNOLOGIES, INC.; *U.S. Public*, pg. 1711
VECTRON LABS, INC.—See Dover Corporation; *U.S. Public*, pg. 522
VECTUR ALUMINUMSTALLNINGAR—See Up-Right, Inc.; *U.S. Private*, pg. 1128
VECTUR B.V.—See Up-Right, Inc.; *U.S. Private*, pg. 1129
VECTUR GMBH—See Up-Right, Inc.; *U.S. Private*, pg. 1129
VECTUR S.A.—See Up-Right, Inc.; *U.S. Private*, pg. 1129
N.V. VECTUR S.A.—See Up-Right, Inc.; *U.S. Private*, pg. 1129
VECTURA GROUP, INC.; *U.S. Private*, pg. 1135
VEDA DESIGN GROUP—See Veridian; *U.S. Private*, pg. 1136
VEDA INCORPORATED—See Veridian; *U.S. Private*, pg. 1136
VEDA INTERNATIONAL, INC.—See Veridian; *U.S. Private*, pg. 1136
VEDA SYSTEMS, INCORPORATED—See Veridian; *U.S. Private*, pg. 1136
VEDENA B.V.—See N.V. Koninklijke KNP BT; *Int'l*, pg. 757
VEDIM SA—See UCB, S.A.; *Int'l*, pg. 1427
VEDIOR—See Vendex International N.V.; *Int'l*, pg. 1463
VEDIOR COMPUHELP—See Vendex International N.V.; *Int'l*, pg. 1463
VEDIOR FRANCE—See Vendex International N.V.; *Int'l*, pg. 1463
VEDIOR INTERNATIONAL—See Vendex International N.V.; *Int'l*, pg. 1463
VEEBMAN DIREKT—See N.V. Koninklijke KNP BT; *Int'l*, pg. 757
VEECO GMBH—See Veeco Instruments, Inc.; *U.S. Public*, pg. 1711
VEECO INSTRUMENTS, INC.; *U.S. Public*, pg. 1711
VEECO INSTRUMENTS LTD.—See Veeco Instruments, Inc.; *U.S. Public*, pg. 1711
VEECO S.A.—See Veeco Instruments, Inc.; *U.S. Public*, pg. 1711
VEEDER-ROOT COMPANY—See Danaher Corporation; *U.S. Public*, pg. 482
VEEDOL (CANADA) LTD.—See Burmah Castrol plc; *Int'l*, pg. 236
VEEDOL INTERNATIONAL LTD.—See Burmah Castrol plc; *Int'l*, pg. 235
VEENMAN KANTOORMACHINES BV—See N.V. Koninklijke KNP BT; *Int'l*, pg. 757
VEENMAN OFFICE MANAGEMENT BV—See N.V. Koninklijke KNP BT; *Int'l*, pg. 757
VEGAS ELECTRIC SUPPLY—See Consolidated Electrical Distributors; *U.S. Private*, pg. 265
VEGAS VALLEY CONVALESCENT CENTER—See Horizon/CMS Healthcare Corporation; *U.S. Public*, pg. 837
VEGETARIAN TIMES—See Cowles Media Company; *U.S. Private*, pg. 281
VEGLA VEREINIGTE GLASHANDELS-GESELLSCHAFT MBH (VGG)—See Saint-Gobain; *Int'l*, pg. 1173
VEGLA VEREINIGTE GLASWERKE GMBH—See Saint-Gobain; *Int'l*, pg. 1173
VEGLIA BORLETTI S.R.L.—See Fiat Auto SpA; *Int'l*, pg. 482
VEHICLE ASSEMBLERS NEW ZEALAND LIMITED—See Ford Motor Company; *U.S. Public*, pg. 666
VEHICLE SPARES LTD.—See Metallgesellschaft AG; *Int'l*, pg. 861
VEHICLE SYSTENIS DIVISION—See Commercial Intertech Corp.; *U.S. Public*, pg. 411
VEHIDATA, S.A.—See Corporacion MAPFRE, Compania Internacional de Reaseguros, S.A.; *Int'l*, pg. 334
VEITSILUOTO PUBLICATION PAPERS OY—See Enso Oyj; *Int'l*, pg. 457
VEL-VASK TEKSTIL SERVICE A/S—See Sophus Berendsen A/S; *Int'l*, pg. 1286
VELAN INC.—See Deutsche Babcock AG; *Int'l*, pg. 400
VELASQUES SIGARENFABRIEKEN N.V.—See B.A.T Industries P.L.C.; *Int'l*, pg. 111
VELCO—See Banco Popular de Puerto Rico; *U.S. Public*, pg. 176
VELCON FILTERS, INC.; *U.S. Private*, pg. 1135
VELCRO AUSTRALIA PTY. LTD.—See Velcro Industries N.V.; *Int'l*, pg. 1462
VELCRO CANADA INC.—See Velcro Industries N.V.; *Int'l*, pg. 1462
VELCRO EUROPE S.A.—See Velcro Industries N.V.; *Int'l*, pg. 1462
VELCRO FINANCE LTD.—See Velcro Industries N.V.; *Int'l*, pg. 1462
VELCRO GMBH—See Velcro Industries N.V.; *Int'l*, pg. 1462
VELCRO GROUP CORPORATION—See Velcro Industries N.V.; *Int'l*, pg. 1462
VELCRO HONG KONG LTD.—See Velcro Industries N.V.; *Int'l*, pg. 1462
VELCRO INDUSTRIES B.V.—See Velcro Industries N.V.; *Int'l*, pg. 1462
VELCRO INDUSTRIES N.V.; *Int'l*, pg. 1462
VELCRO ITALIA S.R.L.—See Velcro Industries N.V.; *Int'l*, pg. 1462
VELCRO LAMINATES INC.—See Velcro Industries N.V.; *Int'l*, pg. 1462
VELCRO USA INC.—See Velcro Industries N.V.; *Int'l*, pg. 1462
VELCROMEX S.A. DE C.V.—See Velcro Industries N.V.; *Int'l*, pg. 1462

VELDA FARMS—See Suiza Foods Corporation; *U.S. Public*, pg. 1527
VELLAVE DE TRANSPORTS—See SNCF; *Int'l*, pg. 1165
VELLUS SA—See N.V. Koninklijke KNP BT; *Int'l*, pg. 757
VELO LIMITED—See Dresdner Bank AG; *Int'l*, pg. 420
VELSICOL AUSTRALIA LIMITED—See Velsicol Chemical Corporation; *U.S. Private*, pg. 1135
VELSICOL CHEMICAL CORPORATION; *U.S. Private*, pg. 1135
VELSICOL CHEMICAL LIMITED—See Velsicol Chemical Corporation; *U.S. Private*, pg. 1135
VELSICOL EESTI A.S.—See Velsicol Chemical Corporation; *U.S. Private*, pg. 1135
VELVA LIQUIDS LTD.—See Simon Engineering plc; *Int'l*, pg. 1251
VELVET DRIVE TRANSMISSIONS—See Regal-Beloit Corporation; *U.S. Public*, pg. 1370
VEMALINE PRODUCTS—See Everett Charles Technologies; *U.S. Private*, pg. 386
VEMEDIA B.V.—See Solvay S.A.; *Int'l*, pg. 1279
VEMIE-VETRINAR-CHEMIE GMBH—See Akzo Nobel N.V.; *Int'l*, pg. 45
VENCARE, INCORPORATED—See Vencor, Inc.; *U.S. Public*, pg. 1715
VENCHURS PACKAGING, INC.; *U.S. Private*, pg. 1135
VENCOR, INC.; *U.S. Public*, pg. 1711
VENDEX FASHION GROUP—See Vendex International N.V.; *Int'l*, pg. 1462
VENDEX FOOD GROEP—See Vendex International N.V.; *Int'l*, pg. 1463
VENDEX INTERNATIONAL N.V.; *Int'l*, pg. 1462
VENDHALL LTD.—See Sanden Corporation; *Int'l*, pg. 1184
VENDO (BENELUX) S.A.—See Sanden Corporation; *Int'l*, pg. 1184
THE VENDO COMPANY—See Sanden Corporation; *Int'l*, pg. 1184
VENDO GMBH—See Sanden Corporation; *Int'l*, pg. 1184
VENDO IBERIA, S.A.—See Sanden Corporation; *Int'l*, pg. 1184
VENDO INTERNATIONAL DIV.—See Sanden Corporation; *Int'l*, pg. 1184
VENDO (ITALY) S.P.A.—See Sanden Corporation; *Int'l*, pg. 1184
VENDOPOLIS—See Vendex International N.V.; *Int'l*, pg. 1463
VENDOR FUNDING CO., INC.—See Bank of Ireland; *Int'l*, pg. 153
VENDRES—See La Meridionale des Bois et Materiaux; *Int'l*, pg. 784
VENEASISTENCIA C.A.—See Corporacion MAPFRE, Compania Internacional de Reaseguros, S.A.; *Int'l*, pg. 334
VENEPASTAS C.A.—See Nestle S.A.; *Int'l*, pg. 922
VENESTA INTERNATIONAL PACKAGING LIMITED—See Caradon Plc; *Int'l*, pg. 267
VENESTA PACKAGING GROUP LTD.—See Caradon Plc; *Int'l*, pg. 267
VENETA FACTORING S.P.A.—See Electrolux, AB; *Int'l*, pg. 442
VENEZIA NUOVA—See Accor S.A.; *Int'l*, pg. 21
VENEZIANA GAS S.P.A.—See ENI S.p.A.; *Int'l*, pg. 428
VENEZIANI S.P.A.—See Novartis AG; *Int'l*, pg. 986
VENEZOLANA EMPACADORA C.A.—See The East Asiatic Company Ltd. A/S; *Int'l*, pg. 431
VENGAS MARKETING COMPANY—See Stone & Webster, Incorporated; *U.S. Public*, pg. 1519
VENGAS PIPELINE COMPANY—See Stone & Webster, Incorporated; *U.S. Public*, pg. 1519
VENGROFF WILLIAMS & ASSOCIATES, INC.; *U.S. Private*, pg. 1135
VENGROFF WILLIAMS REALTY MANAGEMENT—See Vengroff Williams & Associates, Inc.; *U.S. Private*, pg. 1135
VENICE SIMPLON-ORIENT-EXPRESS LTD.—See Sea Containers Ltd.; *Int'l*, pg. 1213
VENMAR VENTILATION, INC.—See Nortek, Inc.; *U.S. Public*, pg. 1194
VENT-AXIA INC.—See Smiths Industries plc; *Int'l*, pg. 1268
VENT-AXIA LIMITED-CONTROLS DIVISION—See Smiths Industries plc; *Int'l*, pg. 1267
VENT-AXIA LTD.—See Smiths Industries plc; *Int'l*, pg. 1267
VENT-AXIA VENTILATION LIMITED—See Smiths Industries plc; *Int'l*, pg. 1269
VENTA CATALOGO S.A.—See Otto Versand (GmbH & Co.); *Int'l*, pg. 1015
VENTEK INC.—See Advanced Machine Vision Corp.; *U.S. Public*, pg. 20
VENTILEX MILIEUTECHNIEK B.V., HEERDE—See Internatio-Muller N.V.; *Int'l*, pg. 681
VENTILIZATIONUNION AB—See Trelleborg AB; *Int'l*, pg. 1422
VENTIM AB—See AB Industrivarden; *Int'l*, pg. 678
VENTLINE DIV.—See Tomkins PLC; *Int'l*, pg. 1398
VENTOMATIC SA—See FLS Industries A/S; *Int'l*, pg. 475
VENTRE PACKING COMPANY, INC.; *U.S. Private*, pg. 1135
VENTRON DIV.—See Morton International Inc.; *U.S. Public*, pg. 1135
VENTURA COASTAL CORPORATION; *U.S. Private*, pg. 1136
VENTURA COUNTY STAR-FREE PRESS—See The E.W. Scripps Company; *U.S. Public*, pg. 1448
VENTURA FOODS—See Harvest States Cooperatives; *U.S. Private*, pg. 508
VENTURA FOODS LLC—See Mitsui & Co., Ltd.; *Int'l*, pg. 879
VENTURE DISTRIBUTION COMPANY—See Stone & Webster, Incorporated; *U.S. Public*, pg. 1519
VENTURE ENGINEERING INC.—See Gradco Systems, Inc.; *U.S. Public*, pg. 757
VENTURE FURNITURE DIV.—See Furniture Brands International Inc.; *U.S. Public*, pg. 688
VENTURE PACKAGING, INC.—See Berry Plastics Corporation; *U.S. Private*, pg. 138

VENTURE PIPELINE COMPANY—See Stone & Webster, Incorporated; *U.S. Public*, pg. 1519
VENTURE PROCESSING COMPANY—See Stone & Webster, Incorporated; *U.S. Public*, pg. 1519
VENTURE RESOURCES, INC.—See Stone & Webster, Incorporated; *U.S. Public*, pg. 1519
VENTURE STORES, INC.; *U.S. Public*, pg. 1716
VENTUREDYNE, LTD.; *U.S. Private*, pg. 1136
VENTURI INC.; *U.S. Private*, pg. 1136
VENTURIAN CORP.; *U.S. Public*, pg. 1716
BEN VENUE LABORATORIES, INC.; *U.S. Private*, pg. 1136
VENUS PRE-RELEASE CENTER—See Corrections Corporation of America; *U.S. Public*, pg. 451
VERA CO., LTD.—See JGC Corporation; *Int'l*, pg. 697
VERA CRUZ CONSULTORIA TECNICA E ADMINISTRACAO DE FUNDOS S/C LTDA.—See Corporacion MAPFRE, Compania Internacional de Reaseguros, S.A.; *Int'l*, pg. 334
VERA CRUZ S.A. DE PREVIDENCIA PRIVADA—See Corporacion MAPFRE, Compania Internacional de Reaseguros, S.A.; *Int'l*, pg. 334
VERA CRUZ SEGURADORA, S.A.—See Corporacion MAPFRE, Compania Internacional de Reaseguros, S.A.; *Int'l*, pg. 334
VERA KLIPPAN AB—See Jotun A/S; *Int'l*, pg. 715
VERATEC DIVISION—See International Paper Company; *U.S. Public*, pg. 904
VERATEC JAPAN, LTD.—See International Paper Company; *U.S. Public*, pg. 906
VERATEC S.A.—See International Paper Company; *U.S. Public*, pg. 906
VERAVISION—See Ultrak Inc.; *U.S. Public*, pg. 1663
VERBA VERWALTUNGSGESELLSCHAFT MBH—See Bayerische Vereinsbank Group; *Int'l*, pg. 180
VERBATIM DO AMAZONAS INDUSTRIAL LTD.—See Eastman Kodak Company; *U.S. Public*, pg. 552
VERBATIM TAPE CORPORATION—See Mitsubishi Corporation; *Int'l*, pg. 872
VERBATIM-U.K.—See Mitsubishi Corporation; *Int'l*, pg. 872
VERCOLAC SPA—See Akzo Nobel N.V.; *Int'l*, pg. 43
VERCOOPE-UNIAO DAS ADEGAS COOPERATIVAS DA REGIAO DOS VINHOA VERDES, U.C.R.L.; *Int'l*, pg. 1463
VERDICHTER OE. G.M.B.H.—See Electrolux, AB; *Int'l*, pg. 443
VERDOME—See Danone Group; *Int'l*, pg. 381
VERDUGO RESTAURANT CORP.—See Specialty Restaurants Corporation; *U.S. Private*, pg. 1022
GEBR. VERDUIJN'S SUIKERWERKENFABRIEK B. V.—See Van Melle N.V.; *Int'l*, pg. 1451
VEREBUS ENGINEERING B.V., THE HAGUE—See Internatio-Muller N.V.; *Int'l*, pg. 680
N.V. VEREENIGDE GLASFABRIEKEN—See Danone Group; *Int'l*, pg. 381
VEREIN WEST BERATUNGSGESELLSCHAFT MBH—See Bayerische Vereinsbank Group; *Int'l*, pg. 180
VEREIN WEST OVERSEAS FINANCE (JERSEY) LTD.—See Bayerische Vereinsbank Group; *Int'l*, pg. 181
VEREINIGTE GASZAHLER-WERKSTATTEN GMBH—See Ruhrgas Aktiengesellschaft; *Int'l*, pg. 1149
VEREINIGTE KAFFEE-GROSSROSTEREIEN 'ARABIA-MIKADO' KAFFEEVERTRIEBSGES.M.B.H.—See Julius Meinl AG; *Int'l*, pg. 856
VEREINIGTE PAPIERINDUSTRIE-UND ALLGEMEINE WARENHANDELS GmbH—See Creditanstalt-Bankverein; *Int'l*, pg. 347
VEREINIGTE WEICHENBAU GMBH—See Fried. Krupp AG; *Int'l*, pg. 513
VEREINS- UND WESTBANK AG—See Bayerische Vereinsbank Group; *Int'l*, pg. 180
VEREINS- UND WESTBANK BETEILIGUNGSGESELLSCHAFT S.A.—See Bayerische Vereinsbank Group; *Int'l*, pg. 181
VEREINSBANK IMMOBILIEN VERWALTUNGS GMBH—See Bayerische Vereinsbank Group; *Int'l*, pg. 180
VEREINSBANK IN NUERNBERG AG—See Bayerische Vereinsbank Group; *Int'l*, pg. 180
VEREINSBANK INTERNATIONAL S.A.—See Bayerische Vereinsbank Group; *Int'l*, pg. 181
VEREINSBANK VICTORIA BAUSPAR AG—See Bayerische Vereinsbank Group; *Int'l*, pg. 180
VERIBEST INC.—See Intergraph Corporation; *U.S. Public*, pg. 891
VERIBEST ISRAEL—See Intergraph Corporation; *U.S. Public*, pg. 892
VERIBEST NORDIC—See Intergraph Corporation; *U.S. Public*, pg. 892
VERIDIAN; *U.S. Private*, pg. 1136
VERIFINE DAIRY PRODUCTS CORP.—See Dean Foods Company; *U.S. Public*, pg. 491
VERIFONE, INC.—See Hewlett-Packard Company; *U.S. Public*, pg. 815
VERILY ENTERPRISES, INC.—See Harcourt General, Inc.; *U.S. Public*, pg. 783
VERIN S.A.—See Suspa Compart AG; *Int'l*, pg. 1322
VERIND S.P.A.—See Durr AG; *Int'l*, pg. 422
VERISOL, S.A.—See Vallehermoso, S.A.; *Int'l*, pg. 1447
VERITAS DGC INC.; *U.S. Public*, pg. 1136
VERITAS DGC INC—See Veritas DGC Inc.; *U.S. Private*, pg. 1136
VERKEHRSBETRIEBE PEINE-SALZGITTER GMBH—See Preussag AG; *Int'l*, pg. 1070
VERKERKE REPRODUKTIES, N.V.—See Hallmark Cards, Inc.; *U.S. Private*, pg. 496
VERLAG DAS BESTE GMBH—See The Reader's Digest Association, Inc.; *U.S. Public*, pg. 1368
VERLAG DER TAGESSPIEGEL—See Georg von Holtzbrinck GmbH; *Int'l*, pg. 1479
VERLAG DR. MAX GEHLEN GMBH & CO. KG—See Georg von Holtzbrinck GmbH; *Int'l*, pg. 1479
VERLAG KREMAYR UND SCHERIAU—See Bertelsmann AG; *Int'l*, pg. 192

VERLAGSGRUPPE HANDELSBLATT GMBH—See Georg von Holtzbrinck GmbH; *Int'l,* pg. 1479
VERLEGERDIENST MUNCHEN—See Waverly, Inc.; *U.S. Public,* pg. 1748
VERMEER MANUFACTURING COMPANY; *U.S. Private,* pg. 1137
VERMEULEN HOLLANDIA BV; *Int'l,* pg. 1463
VERMEULEN-RAEMDONCK—See Bank Brussels Lambert; *Int'l,* pg. 147
VERMICULITE INDUSTRIES LTD.—See Ssangyong Business Group; *Int'l,* pg. 1293
VERMILION COUNTY DIVISION—See Consumers Water Company; *U.S. Public,* pg. 438
VERMOGENSVERWALTUNGSGESELLSCHAFT MBH— See Bayerische Vereinsbank Group; *Int'l,* pg. 181
VERMONT AMERICAN AUSTRALIA, LTD.—See Emerson Electric Co.; *U.S. Public,* pg. 578
VERMONT AMERICAN CANADA, INC.—See Emerson Electric Co.; *U.S. Public,* pg. 578
VERMONT AMERICAN CORPORATION-FOUNTAIN INN DIV.—See Emerson Electric Co.; *U.S. Public,* pg. 575
VERMONT AMERICAN TOOL CORP.—See Emerson Electric Co.; *U.S. Public,* pg. 575
VERMONT AMERICAN TOOL GROUP—See Emerson Electric Co.; *U.S. Public,* pg. 575
VERMONT ELECTRIC POWER CO., INC.—See Central Vermont Public Service Corporation; *U.S. Public,* pg. 328
VERMONT ENERGY RESOURCES, INC.—See Green Mountain Power Corporation; *U.S. Public,* pg. 761
VERMONT FASTENERS MANUFACTURING—See The Ivaco Group; *Int'l,* pg. 696
VERMONT FINANCIAL SERVICES CORP.; *U.S. Public,* pg. 1716
VERMONT GAS SYSTEMS, INC.—See Gaz Metropolitain & Company; *Int'l,* pg. 542
VERMONT GMBH—See Emerson Electric Co.; *U.S. Public,* pg. 578
VERMONT NATIONAL BANK—See Vermont Financial Services Corp.; *U.S. Public,* pg. 1716
THE VERMONT TEDDY BEAR COMPANY, INC.; *U.S. Public,* pg. 1716
VERMONT TRANSIT CO., INC.—See Greyhound Lines, Inc.; *U.S. Public,* pg. 766
VERMONT TUBBS, INC.—See Carris Financial Group; *U.S. Private,* pg. 215
VERMONT USA MACHINE TOOL GROUP—See Goldman Financial Group; *U.S. Private,* pg. 461
VERMONT YANKEE NUCLEAR POWER CORP.—See Central Vermont Public Service Corporation; *U.S. Public,* pg. 328
VERNAY LABORATORIES, INC.; *U.S. Private,* pg. 1137
VERNAY MANUFACTURING, INC.—See Vernay Laboratories, Inc.; *U.S. Private,* pg. 1137
VERNICOLOR A.G.—See The Dexter Corporation; *U.S. Public,* pg. 505
VERNITRON CONTROLS DIV.—See Axsys Technologies, Inc.; *U.S. Public,* pg. 158
VERNITRON SENSOR SYSTEMS—See Axsys Technologies, Inc.; *U.S. Public,* pg. 157
THE VERNON COMPANY; *U.S. Private,* pg. 1137
VERNON COMPUTER LEASING INC.—See Greyvest Capitol Inc.; *Int'l,* pg. 559
LILLIAN VERNON; *U.S. Public,* pg. 1716
VERNON RENTALS & LEASING INC.—See Greyvest Capitol Inc.; *Int'l,* pg. 559
VERNONS POOLS LIMITED—See Ladbroke Group Plc; *Int'l,* pg. 787
VEROC TECHNOLOGY A/S—See Jotun A/S; *Int'l,* pg. 714
VEROSOL AUSTRALIA PTY.LTD.—See Blydenstein-Willink N.V.; *Int'l,* pg. 198
VEROSOL FABRICS B.V.—See Blydenstein-Willink N.V.; *Int'l,* pg. 198
VEROSOL NEDERLAND B.V.—See Blydenstein-Willink N.V.; *Int'l,* pg. 198
VERRERIE DU LANGUEDOC ET CIE—See Nestle S.A.; *Int'l,* pg. 919
VERRERIES DE L'ORNE—See Saint-Gobain; *Int'l,* pg. 1171
VERRERIES DE SAINT-JUST—See Saint-Gobain; *Int'l,* pg. 1172
VERRERIES SOUCHEN NEUVESEL—See Danone Group; *Int'l,* pg. 381
VERSA SERVICES LTD.—See Aramark Corp.; *U.S. Private,* pg. 79
VERSAR INC.; *U.S. Public,* pg. 1717
VERSAR RISK MANAGEMENT, INC.—See Versar Inc.; *U.S. Public,* pg. 1717
VERSATECH ENGINEERING—See Mason & Hanger Corporation, Inc.; *U.S. Private,* pg. 712
VERSAX, S.A. DE C.V.—See Alfa, S.A. de C.V.; *Int'l,* pg. 56
VERSICHERUNGS-PLANER-VERMITTLUNGS G.M.B.H.— See Assicurazioni Generali S.p.A.; *Int'l,* pg. 89
VERSON DIVISION—See Allied Products Corporation; *U.S. Public,* pg. 48
VERTEC—See Saint-Gobain; *Int'l,* pg. 1171
VERTEL; *U.S. Public,* pg. 1717
VERTEL—See Vertel; *U.S. Public,* pg. 1717
VERTEX ANTENNA DIVISION—See Vertex Communications Corporation; *U.S. Public,* pg. 1718
VERTEX ANTENNENTECHNIK GMBH—See Vertex Communications Corporation; *U.S. Public,* pg. 1718
VERTEX ASIA—See Vertex Communications Corporation; *U.S. Public,* pg. 1718
VERTEX COMMUNICATIONS CORPORATION; *U.S. Public,* pg. 1717
VERTEX COMPUTER CABLE PRODUCTS; *U.S. Public,* pg. 1718
VERTEX CONTROL SYSTEMS—See Vertex Communications Corporation; *U.S. Public,* pg. 1718
VERTEX INTEGRATED SATELLITE ANTENNA TECHNOLOGY DIVISION—See Vertex Communications Corporation; *U.S. Public,* pg. 1718
VERTEX INTERNATIONAL LTD.—See Vertex Communications Corporation; *U.S. Public,* pg. 1718

VERTRETUNG DER BASF IN BELARUS—See BASF AG; *Int'l,* pg. 109
VERTRETUNG DER BASF IN DER REPUBLIK UZBEKISTAN—See BASF AG; *Int'l,* pg. 109
VERTRETUNG DER BASF IN DER RUSSISCHEN FOEDERATION—See BASF AG; *Int'l,* pg. 110
VERTRETUNG DER BASF IN DER RUSSISCHEN FOEDERATION ABT. KNOLL PHARMA—See BASF AG; *Int'l,* pg. 110
VERTRETUNG DER BASF IN DER UKRAINE—See BASF AG; *Int'l,* pg. 110
VERTRETUNG DER BASF IN KASACHSTAN—See BASF AG; *Int'l,* pg. 110
VERVIERS LOCAL HEAD OFFICE—See Bank Brussels Lambert; *Int'l,* pg. 147
VERWALTUNGSGESELLSCHAFT ATLTEN MBH—See Bayerische Vereinsbank Group; *Int'l,* pg. 180
VERWALTUNGSGESELLSCHAFT FRIEDRICH WARNKE MBH—See Mannesmann A.G.; *Int'l,* pg. 838
VERWALTUNGSGESELLSCHAFT KATHARINEHOF MBH— See Bayerische Vereinsbank Group; *Int'l,* pg. 180
VERYFINE PRODUCTS, INC.; *U.S. Private,* pg. 1137
N.V. VERZEKERINGSKANTOOR PAUL LAMIN—See Assicurazioni Generali S.p.A.; *Int'l,* pg. 92
VERZINKEREL NETZSCHKAU GMBH—See Deutsche Babcock AG; *Int'l,* pg. 400
VESCO OIL CORP.; *U.S. Private,* pg. 1138
VESPA LABORATORIES, INC.—See Chr. Hansen Holding A/S; *Int'l,* pg. 288
VESPER CORPORATION—See Arrowhead Holding Corporation; *U.S. Private,* pg. 86
VESSEL MANAGEMENT SYSTEMS COMPANY—See CSX Corporation; *U.S. Public,* pg. 284
VESSELFOREWARD LTD.—See Inchcape PLC; *Int'l,* pg. 671
VESTA DIAL FORSIKRING A/S—See Skandia Insurance Company Limited; *Int'l,* pg. 1257
VESTA FORSIKRING A/S—See Skandia Insurance Company Limited; *Int'l,* pg. 1257
VESTA FORVALTNING AS—See Skandia Insurance Company Limited; *Int'l,* pg. 1258
VESTA INSURANCE GROUP, INC.; *U.S. Public,* pg. 1718
VESTA MEDICAL, INC.—See Pfizer Inc.; *U.S. Public,* pg. 1284
VESTAL MANUFACTURING—See Walter Industries, Inc.; *U.S. Public,* pg. 1737
VESTEK SYSTEMS, INC.—See Primark Corporation; *U.S. Public,* pg. 1325
VESTER CORPORATION—See Arrowhead Holding Corporation; *U.S. Private,* pg. 86
A/S VESTFROST—See Electrolux, AB; *Int'l,* pg. 441
VESTIDURAS FRONTERIZAS, S.A. DE C.V.—See General Motors Corporation; *U.S. Public,* pg. 724
VESTISCHER VERMITTLUNGSDIENST FUR VERSICHERUNGEN GMBH—See Veba AG; *Int'l,* pg. 1454
VESTJYSKE SLAGTERIER; *Int'l,* pg. 1464
VESTOLEN GMBH—See Veba AG; *Int'l,* pg. 1461
VESTOLIT GMBH—See Veba AG; *Int'l,* pg. 1454
VESTRETUNG DES KNOLL AG—See BASF AG; *Int'l,* pg. 110
VESTRIC LTD.—See Franz Haniel & Cie, GmbH; *Int'l,* pg. 592
VESTURE CORPORATION—See R.G. Barry Corporation; *U.S. Public,* pg. 192
VESUVIUS U.S.A.—See Cookson Group plc; *Int'l,* pg. 329
VETERANS LIFE INSURANCE CO.—See AEGON N.V.; *Int'l,* pg. 26
VETERINARY COMPANIES OF AMERICA—See Colgate-Palmolive Company; *U.S. Public,* pg. 397
VETERINARY LABORATORIES, INC.—See Polydex Pharmaceuticals Limited; *Int'l,* pg. 1163
VETERINARY MEDICINE PUBLISHING CO., INC.—See The Thomson Corporation; *U.S. Public,* pg. 1600
VETRERIE ITALIANE VETR.I SPA—See Saint-Gobain; *Int'l,* pg. 1171
VETROTEX CERTAINTEED CORPORATION—See Saint-Gobain; *Int'l,* pg. 1171
VETROTEX DEUTSCHLAND GMBH—See Saint-Gobain; *Int'l,* pg. 1177
VETROTEX ESPANA SA—See Saint-Gobain; *Int'l,* pg. 1177
VETROTEX FINANCE—See Saint-Gobain; *Int'l,* pg. 1177
VETROTEX FRANCE—See Saint-Gobain; *Int'l,* pg. 1177
VETROTEX INTERNATIONAL—See Saint-Gobain; *Int'l,* pg. 1177
VETROTEX ITALIA—See Saint-Gobain; *Int'l,* pg. 1177
VETROTEX USA—See Saint-Gobain; *Int'l,* pg. 1177
VEUVE CLICQUOT IMPORT G.M.B.H.—See LVMH Moet Hennessy Louis Vuitton; *Int'l,* pg. 783
VEUVE CLICQUOT PONSARDIN—See LVMH Moet Hennessy Louis Vuitton; *Int'l,* pg. 781
VEUVE CLICQUOT (UK) LTD—See LVMH Moet Hennessy Louis Vuitton; *Int'l,* pg. 783
VEVAY DEPOSIT BANK—See First Financial Bancorp; *U.S. Public,* pg. 633
VEW-HARPEN—See Harpen AG; *Int'l,* pg. 597
VEW RESTSTOFFVERWERTUNGSGESELLSCHAFT MBH—See Harpen AG; *Int'l,* pg. 597
VEW UMWELT GMBH—See Harpen AG; *Int'l,* pg. 597
VEXA SVENSKA AB—See Celsius AB; *Int'l,* pg. 278
VI-SPRING LIMITED—See Newmond PLC; *Int'l,* pg. 925
VIA POST—See G.T.C. Transcontinental Group Ltd.; *Int'l,* pg. 538
VIA TECH PUBLISHING SOLUTIONS; *U.S. Private,* pg. 1138
VIABLE BIOPRODUCTS LTD.—See Nutricia BV; *Int'l,* pg. 902
VIACAO AEREA SAO PAULO S.A. (VASP); *Int'l,* pg. 1464
VIACOM BROADCASTING INC.—See National Amusements, Inc.; *U.S. Private,* pg. 778
VIACOM CANADA LTD.—See National Amusements, Inc.; *U.S. Private,* pg. 779
VIACOM ENTERPRISES—See National Amusements, Inc.; *U.S. Private,* pg. 779

VIACOM ENTERPRISES CANADA LTD.—See National Amusements, Inc.; *U.S. Private,* pg. 779
VIACOM ENTERTAINMENT—See National Amusements, Inc.; *U.S. Private,* pg. 778
VIACOM INC.—See National Amusements, Inc.; *U.S. Private,* pg. 775
VIACOM INTERNATIONAL INC.—See National Amusements, Inc.; *U.S. Private,* pg. 778
VIACOM INTL. LTD.—See National Amusements, Inc.; *U.S. Private,* pg. 779
VIACOM INTL. PTY. LTD.—See National Amusements, Inc.; *U.S. Private,* pg. 779
VIACOM JAPAN, INC.—See National Amusements, Inc.; *U.S. Private,* pg. 779
VIACOM NETWORKS INC.—See National Amusements, Inc.; *U.S. Private,* pg. 779
VIACOM S.A.—See National Amusements, Inc.; *U.S. Private,* pg. 779
VIACOM SATELLITE NETWORKS INC.—See National Amusements, Inc.; *U.S. Private,* pg. 779
VIACOM VIDEO-AUDIO COMUNICACOES, LTDA.—See National Amusements, Inc.; *U.S. Private,* pg. 780
VIAD CORP.; *U.S. Public,* pg. 1718
VIAD REALTY CORP.—See Viad Corp; *U.S. Public,* pg. 1718
VIAG AG; *Int'l,* pg. 1464
VIAG INTERKOM GMBH & CO.—See British Telecommunications plc; *Int'l,* pg. 223
VIAJES ECUADOR—See Accor S.A.; *Int'l,* pg. 22
VIATECH DEVELOPMENT LABORATORY—See Platinum Technology, Inc.; *U.S. Public,* pg. 1309
VIBCO INC.; *U.S. Private,* pg. 1138
VIBCO VIBRATION PRODUCTS—See Vibco Inc.; *U.S. Private,* pg. 1138
VIBORG ASFALTFABRIK I/S—See Icopal a/s; *Int'l,* pg. 659
VIBRA-METRICS, INC.—See Kingsbury, Inc.; *U.S. Public,* pg. 622
VIBRA SCREW INC.; *U.S. Public,* pg. 1138
VIBRAMETRIC—See Kingsbury, Inc.; *U.S. Public,* pg. 622
VIBRATECH, INC.—See IDEX Corporation; *U.S. Public,* pg. 862
VIBRATECHNIQUES—See Svedala Industri AB; *Int'l,* pg. 1324
VIBRATECHNIQUES STV—See Trelleborg AB; *Int'l,* pg. 1420
VIBRATION AUTOMOBILE DIVISION—See Freudenberg-NOK; *U.S. Private,* pg. 428
VIBRATION MOUNTINGS & CONTROLS, INC.—See Aeroflex Incorporated; *U.S. Public,* pg. 24
VIBRO-METER CORP.; *U.S. Private,* pg. 1138
VICASA SA—See Saint-Gobain; *Int'l,* pg. 1171
VICAT S.A.—See Heidelberger Zement A.G.; *Int'l,* pg. 606
VICEVERSA/YOUNG & RUBICAM—See Young & Rubicam Inc.; *U.S. Private,* pg. 1200
VICK INTERNATIONAL LTD.—See The Procter & Gamble Company; *U.S. Public,* pg. 1333
VICKER MEDICAL NEDERLANDS—See Vickers PLC; *Int'l,* pg. 1467
VICKERS ACTUATOR PRODUCTS—See Aeroquip-Vickers, Inc.; *U.S. Public,* pg. 24
VICKERS AIR-SHIELDS—See Vickers PLC; *Int'l,* pg. 1467
VICKERS AMD—See Aeroquip-Vickers, Inc.; *U.S. Public,* pg. 25
VICKERS INC.—See Aeroquip-Vickers, Inc.; *U.S. Public,* pg. 25
VICKERS, INCORPORATED—See Aeroquip-Vickers, Inc.; *U.S. Public,* pg. 24
VICKERS INDUSTRIAL—See Aeroquip-Vickers, Inc.; *U.S. Public,* pg. 24
VICKERS MODULAR—See Aeroquip-Vickers, Inc.; *U.S. Public,* pg. 25
VICKERS PLC; *Int'l,* pg. 1466
VICKERS POLYMOTOR—See Aeroquip-Vickers, Inc.; *U.S. Public,* pg. 25
VICKERS PRECISION MACHINING—See Vickers PLC; *Int'l,* pg. 1468
VICKERS PROPERTIES LIMITED—See Vickers PLC; *Int'l,* pg. 1467
VICKERS STERER ENGINEERING—See Aeroquip-Vickers, Inc.; *U.S. Public,* pg. 25
VICKERS SYSTEMS—See Aeroquip-Vickers, Inc.; *U.S. Public,* pg. 25
VICKERS SYSTEMS AB—See Aeroquip-Vickers, Inc.; *U.S. Public,* pg. 25
VICKERS SYSTEMS GMBH (AEROSPACE-MARINE-DEFENSE TRINOVA GMBH)—See Aeroquip-Vickers, Inc.; *U.S. Public,* pg. 25
VICKERS SYSTEMS INTERNATIONAL LTD.—See Aeroquip-Vickers, Inc.; *U.S. Public,* pg. 25
VICKERS SYSTEMS INC.—See Aeroquip-Vickers, Inc.; *U.S. Public,* pg. 25
VICKERS SYSTEMS PTE. LTD.—See Aeroquip-Vickers, Inc.; *U.S. Public,* pg. 25
VICKERS SYSTEMS S.A.—See Aeroquip-Vickers, Inc.; *U.S. Public,* pg. 25
VICKERS SYSTEMS SENDINIAN BERHAD—See Aeroquip-Vickers, Inc.; *U.S. Public,* pg. 25
VICKERS TEDECO DIV.—See Aeroquip-Vickers, Inc.; *U.S. Public,* pg. 25
VICKERS TRUCK EQUIPMENT—See Arnold Machinery Company; *U.S. Private,* pg. 84
VICKERYS HOLDINGS LTD.—See Thermo Electron Corporation; *U.S. Public,* pg. 1593
VICKSBURG PLANT—See Cooper Industries, Inc.; *U.S. Public,* pg. 444
VICOM PRODUCTION AND DISTRIBUTION CO.—See Vicorp Restaurants, Inc.; *U.S. Public,* pg. 1719
VICON, HONG KONG—See Vicon Industries, Inc.; *U.S. Public,* pg. 1719
VICON INDUSTRIES, INC.; *U.S. Public,* pg. 1719
VICON INDUSTRIES-SOUTHERN INC.—See Vicon Industries, Inc.; *U.S. Public,* pg. 1719

VICON INDUSTRIES (U.K.) LTD.—See Vicon Industries, Inc.; *U.S. Public*, pg. 1719
VICON, KOREA—See Vicon Industries, Inc.; *U.S. Public*, pg. 1719
VICON, NORWAY—See Vicon Industries, Inc.; *U.S. Public*, pg. 1719
VICON, SINGAPORE—See Vicon Industries, Inc.; *U.S. Public*, pg. 1719
VICOR CORPORATION; *U.S. Public*, pg. 1719
VICOR INTERNATIONAL—See Vicor Corporation; *U.S. Public*, pg. 1719
VICORP INTERACTIVE SYSTEMS, INC.—See Precision Systems, Inc.; *U.S. Public*, pg. 1321
VICORP, N.V.—See Precision Systems, Inc.; *U.S. Public*, pg. 1321
VICORP RESTAURANTS, INC.; *U.S. Public*, pg. 1719
VICSON S.A.—See N.V. Bekaert S.A.; *Int'l*, pg. 185
VICTAULIC COMPANY OF AMERICA; *U.S. Private*, pg. 1138
VICTAULIC COMPANY OF CANADA LIMITED—See Victaulic Company of America; *U.S. Private*, pg. 1138
VICTAULIC-EUROPE—See Victaulic Company of America; *U.S. Private*, pg. 1138
VICTAULIC FIRE SAFETY COMPANY LLC—See Victaulic Company of America; *U.S. Private*, pg. 1138
VICTAULIC INTERNATIONAL—See Victaulic Company of America; *U.S. Private*, pg. 1138
VICTAULIC TOOL COMPANY—See Victaulic Company of America; *U.S. Private*, pg. 1138
VICTOIRE TELEMATIQUE—See LVMH Moet Hennessy Louis Vuitton; *Int'l*, pg. 781
VICTOR COMPANY OF JAPAN, LTD.—See Matsushita Electric Industrial Co., Ltd.; *Int'l*, pg. 846
VICTOR CORPORATION; *U.S. Private*, pg. 1138
VICTOR HASSELBLAD AB; *Int'l*, pg. 1468
VICTOR PRODUCTS—See Dana Corporation; *U.S. Public*, pg. 480
VICTOR TECHNOLOGY; *U.S. Private*, pg. 1139
VICTOR TEMPORARY SERVICES, LTD.—See Interim Services Inc.; *U.S. Public*, pg. 892
VICTOR TUBE CORP.—See CCL Industries, Inc.; *Int'l*, pg. 239
JOSEPH VICTORI WINES, INC.; *U.S. Private*, pg. 1139
VICTORIA—See The Hearst Corporation; *U.S. Private*, pg. 517
VICTORIA CREATIONS, INC.; *U.S. Private*, pg. 1139
VICTORIA FINANCIAL CORPORATION—See USF&G Corporation; *U.S. Public*, pg. 1660
VICTORIA FIRE & CASUALTY—See USF&G Corporation; *U.S. Public*, pg. 1660
VICTORIA HALL COMPANY LIMITED—See Cigna Corp.; *U.S. Public*, pg. 363
VICTORIA HOUSE PUBLISHING, LTD.—See The Reader's Digest Association, Inc.; *U.S. Public*, pg. 1368
VICTORIA JOINERY LTD.—See John Laing PLC; *Int'l*, pg. 796
VICTORIA KAPITALANLAGEGESELLSCHAFT MBH—See Bayerische Vereinsbank Group; *Int'l*, pg. 180
VICTORIA PACKING CORPORATION; *U.S. Private*, pg. 1139
VICTORIA REGIONAL MEDICAL CENTER—See Universal Health Services, Inc.; *U.S. Public*, pg. 1697
VICTORIA STATION INC.—See A.S. Management Corporation; *U.S. Public*, pg. 8
VICTORIA-VESTA N.V.—See ING Groep N.V.; *Int'l*, pg. 651
THE VICTORIA WINE COMPANY LIMITED—See Allied Domecq PLC; *Int'l*, pg. 63
VICTORIAN CONVALESCENT HOSPITAL—See Vencor, Inc.; *U.S. Public*, pg. 1715
VICTORIA'S SECRET CATALOG—See The Limited, Inc.; *U.S. Public*, pg. 995
VICTORIA'S SECRET STORES—See The Limited, Inc.; *U.S. Public*, pg. 995
VICTORINOX—See Swiss Army Brands, Inc.; *U.S. Public*, pg. 1544
VICTORY ENVELOPE, INC.—See The Instant Web Companies; *U.S. Private*, pg. 565
VICTORY FINANCIAL GROUP, INC.; *U.S. Private*, pg. 1139
VICTORY PACKAGING; *U.S. Private*, pg. 1139
VICTORY REFRIGERATION CO. LC; *U.S. Private*, pg. 1139
VICWEST STEEL DIVISION NORTH AMERICAN BUILDING PRODUCTS—See Jannock Limited; *Int'l*, pg. 698
VICWEST STEEL SUPPLY—See Jannock Limited; *Int'l*, pg. 698
VIDA HERBAL SUPLEMENTOS ALIMENTICIOS, C.A. (VENEZUELA)—See Herbalife International of America, Inc.; *U.S. Public*, pg. 809
VIDAL SASSOON—See The Procter & Gamble Company; *U.S. Public*, pg. 1330
VIDAR, INC.; *U.S. Private*, pg. 1139
VIDCOM DMB&B—See DMB&B Communications; *U.S. Private*, pg. 305
VIDEK—See Eastman Kodak Company; *U.S. Public*, pg. 551
VIDEO CITY INC.; *U.S. Public*, pg. 1719
VIDEO COMMUNICATION & INFO. SYSTEMS DIV./ LIGHTING PRODUCTS—See Toshiba Corporation; *Int'l*, pg. 1405
VIDEO DISPLAY CORPORATION; *U.S. Public*, pg. 1720
VIDEO DISPLAY CORPORATION LIMITED—See Video Display Corporation; *U.S. Public*, pg. 1720
VIDEO ELECTRONICS DE S.A.—See Video Display Corporation; *U.S. Public*, pg. 1720
VIDEO INDIANA - WTHR—See The Dispatch Printing Company; *U.S. Private*, pg. 335
VIDEO KING GAMING SYSTEMS, INC.—See Stuart Entertainment Inc.; *U.S. Public*, pg. 1526
VIDEO LOTTERY CONSULTANTS, INC.—See Power House Technologies, Inc.; *U.S. Public*, pg. 1319
VIDEO PRODUCTS DISTRIBUTORS, INC.; *U.S. Private*, pg. 1139

VIDEO SERVICE COMPANY—See Cox Communications, Inc.; *U.S. Public*, pg. 455
VIDEO SERVICES, INC.—See Alliance Gaming Corporation; *U.S. Public*, pg. 47
VIDEO TREASURES—See Handleman Company; *U.S. Public*, pg. 780
VIDEOJET LTD.—See The General Electric Company, p.l.c.; *Int'l*, pg. 546
VIDEOJET SYSTEMS INTERNATIONAL, INC.—See The General Electric Company, p.l.c.; *Int'l*, pg. 545
VIDEOLABS, INC.; *U.S. Public*, pg. 1720
VIDEOSERVER CONNECTIONS—See VideoServer, Inc.; *U.S. Public*, pg. 1720
VIDEOSERVER, INC.; *U.S. Public*, pg. 1720
VIDEOSERVER, LIMITED—See VideoServer, Inc.; *U.S. Public*, pg. 1720
VIDEOTEX NEDERLAND BV—See KPN Koninklyke PTT Nederland NV; *Int'l*, pg. 720
VIDEOTEX OOST-BRABANT BV—See KPN Koninklyke PTT Nederland NV; *Int'l*, pg. 720
VIDEOTRON HOLDINGS PLC—See Cable and Wireless plc; *Int'l*, pg. 247
VIDEOVATION, INC.—See The Reader's Digest Association, Inc.; *U.S. Public*, pg. 1368
VIDMAR AG—See Lista Holding AG; *Int'l*, pg. 812
VIDRERIA DO MONDEGO—See Saint-Gobain; *Int'l*, pg. 1172
VIDRIERIA ARGENTINA SA—See Pilkington Plc; *Int'l*, pg. 1057
VIDRIERIAS ESPANOLAS VICASA—See Saint-Gobain; *Int'l*, pg. 1176
VIE DE FRANCE BAKERY YAMAZAKI, INC.—See Yamazaki Baking Co.; *Int'l*, pg. 1519
VIELLE COLME S.C.I.—See Etablissements Delhaize Freres Et Cie "Le Lion" S.A.; *Int'l*, pg. 463
VIENNA BEEF, LTD.—See Vienna Sausage Mfg. Co.; *U.S. Private*, pg. 1140
VIENNA REPRESENTATIVE OFFICE—See The Fuji Bank, Limited; *Int'l*, pg. 520
VIENNA SAUSAGE MFG. CO.; *U.S. Private*, pg. 1139
THE VIERA COMPANY—See A. Duda & Sons Inc.; *U.S. Private*, pg. 344
VIERO SPA—See Lafarge S.A.; *Int'l*, pg. 789
VIERVERLATEN SUGAR FACTORY—See CSM N.V.; *Int'l*, pg. 244
VIETNAM ADVERTISING CO.—See Havas Advertising; *Int'l*, pg. 602
VIETNAM CROWN VIN ALIMEX PACKAGING LTD.—See Crown Cork & Seal Company, Inc.; *U.S. Public*, pg. 465
VIETNAM MARKETING CENTER—See DMB&B Communications; *U.S. Private*, pg. 305
VIETNAM PIPE CORP.—See Pohang Iron & Steel Co., Ltd.; *Int'l*, pg. 1062
VIEW ENGINEERING—See General Motors Corporation; *U.S. Public*, pg. 721
FRIEDRICH VIEWEG & SOHN VERLAGSGESELLSCHAFT MBH—See Bertelsmann AG; *Int'l*, pg. 190
VIEWLOGIC ASIA CORPORATION—See Synopsys, Inc.; *U.S. Public*, pg. 1548
VIEWLOGIC SYSTEMS, GMBH—See Synopsys, Inc.; *U.S. Public*, pg. 1548
VIEWLOGIC SYSTEMS GROUP—See Synopsys, Inc.; *U.S. Public*, pg. 1548
VIEWLOGIC SYSTEMS, LTD.—See Synopsys, Inc.; *U.S. Public*, pg. 1548
VIEWLOGIC SYSTEMS, SARL—See Synopsys, Inc.; *U.S. Public*, pg. 1548
VIEWLOGIC SYSTEMS SRL—See Synopsys, Inc.; *U.S. Public*, pg. 1548
VIEW-MASTER, INC.—See Mattel, Inc.; *U.S. Public*, pg. 1058
VIGILANT INSURANCE CO.—See The Chubb Corporation; *U.S. Public*, pg. 355
VIGLEN LIMITED—See Viglen Technology PLC; *Int'l*, pg. 1468
VIGLEN TECHNOLOGY PLC; *Int'l*, pg. 1468
VIGORENA FEEDS, INC.—See Ridley Canada Limited; *Int'l*, pg. 1116
THE VIGORO CORPORATION—See IMC Global; *U.S. Public*, pg. 856
VIGORO INDUSTRIES, INC.—See IMC Global; *U.S. Public*, pg. 856
VIGORO INDUSTRIES, SOUTHEAST DIVISION—See IMC Global; *U.S. Public*, pg. 856
VIGORTONE AG PRODUCTS, INC.—See Tate & Lyle PLC; *Int'l*, pg. 1357
VIIALA MILL—See UPM-Kymmene Corporation; *Int'l*, pg. 1429
VIIKINKIKAAPELI OY—See Telefonaktiebolaget LM Ericsson; *Int'l*, pg. 1371
VIKERSUND TRELAST—See Norske Skogindustrier A.S.; *Int'l*, pg. 965
VIKING COFFEE OY—See ICA Handlarnas AB; *Int'l*, pg. 643
VIKING COFFEE OY—See Kesko Ltd.; *Int'l*, pg. 732
VIKING COMPUTER SERVICES—See D & K Healthcare Resources, Inc.; *U.S. Public*, pg. 472
VIKING DIRECT B.V.I.O.—See Viking Office Products; *U.S. Public*, pg. 1721
VIKING DIRECT HOLDING CO.—See Viking Office Products; *U.S. Public*, pg. 1721
VIKING DIRECT LIMITED—See Viking Office Products; *U.S. Public*, pg. 1721
VIKING DIRECT LIMITED GMBH—See Viking Office Products; *U.S. Public*, pg. 1721
VIKING DIRECT S.A.R.L.—See Viking Office Products; *U.S. Public*, pg. 1721
VIKING ELECTRONICS, INC.—See Wire-Pro Inc.; *U.S. Private*, pg. 1184
VIKING ENGRAVING CORP. INC.—See Borden, Inc.; *U.S. Private*, pg. 158
VIKING ENTERTAINMENT—See Handleman Company; *U.S. Public*, pg. 780

VIKING EXPLOSIVES & SUPPLY INC.—See Mining Services International, Inc.; *U.S. Public*, pg. 1115
VIKING FERTILIZER LTD.—See Norsk Hydro a.s; *Int'l*, pg. 964
VIKING FOREST PRODUCTS, INC.—See Forest City Enterprises, Inc.; *U.S. Public*, pg. 669
VIKING FORMED PRODUCTS—See Coachmen Industries, Inc.; *U.S. Public*, pg. 388
VIKING FOTTOY A.S.—See Orkla A.S.A.; *Int'l*, pg. 1011
VIKING FREIGHT SYSTEM, INC.—See FDX Corporation; *U.S. Public*, pg. 604
VIKING FRUIT AB—See ICA Handlarnas AB; *Int'l*, pg. 643
VIKING FRUIT AB—See Kesko Ltd.; *Int'l*, pg. 732
VIKING METALLURGICAL CORPORATION—See Firth-Rixson Inc.; *Int'l*, pg. 488
VIKING MJOENDALEN A/S—See Trelleborg AB; *Int'l*, pg. 1423
VIKING OFFICE PRODUCTS; *U.S. Public*, pg. 1720
VIKING OFFICE PRODUCTS PTY. LTD.—See Viking Office Products; *U.S. Public*, pg. 1721
VIKING PUMP, INC.—See IDEX Corporation; *U.S. Public*, pg. 862
VIKING RADIO—See EMAP Plc; *Int'l*, pg. 452
VIKING RANGE CORP.; *U.S. Private*, pg. 1140
VIKING RECREATIONAL VEHICLES, INC.—See Coachmen Industries, Inc.; *U.S. Public*, pg. 388
VIKING SEMICONDUCTOR EQUIPMENT, INC.—See Giga-Tronics Incorporated; *U.S. Public*, pg. 743
VIKING YACHT CO.; *U.S. Private*, pg. 1140
VILDSAND ASFALTFABRIK I/S—See Icopal a/s; *Int'l*, pg. 659
VILE-GOLLER, FINE ART PRINTING & LITHOGRAPHY; *U.S. Private*, pg. 1140
VILEDA ESPANA S.A.—See Freudenberg & Company; *Int'l*, pg. 507
VILEDA GMBH—See Freudenberg & Company; *Int'l*, pg. 506
VILEDA IBERICA S.A.—See Freudenberg & Company; *Int'l*, pg. 507
VILEDA IBERICA S.A., S.EN C.—See Freudenberg & Company; *Int'l*, pg. 506
VILEDA LP—See Freudenberg & Company; *Int'l*, pg. 506
VILEDA LTD.—See Freudenberg & Company; *Int'l*, pg. 507
VILENE LTD.—See Freudenberg & Company; *Int'l*, pg. 507
VILJAVUUSPALVELU OY—See Kemira Oy; *Int'l*, pg. 728
THE VILLA—See Genesis Health Ventures, Inc.; *U.S. Public*, pg. 729
VILLA BEGONIA—See Scotts Holdings Limited; *Int'l*, pg. 1213
VILLA SAN MICHELE—See Sea Containers Ltd.; *Int'l*, pg. 1213
VILLA SOUTH INC.—See Thiele Kaolin Co.; *U.S. Private*, pg. 1081
VILLADCO INC.—See Banfi Vintners; *U.S. Private*, pg. 113
VILLAGE CAR COMPANY; *U.S. Private*, pg. 1140
VILLAGE CARE CENTER—See Horizon/CMS Healthcare Corporation; *U.S. Public*, pg. 838
VILLAGE COMMON SHOPPING CENTER—See Pacific Gateway Properties; *U.S. Public*, pg. 1250
VILLAGE DISTRIBUTORS, INC.—See The Weitz Company, Inc.; *U.S. Private*, pg. 1161
VILLAGE FORD INC.; *U.S. Private*, pg. 1140
VILLAGE INN RESTAURANTS—See Vicorp Restaurants, Inc.; *U.S. Public*, pg. 1719
THE VILLAGE OF CROSS KEYS, INC.—See The Rouse Company; *U.S. Public*, pg. 1409
VILLAGE PANTRIES, INC.—See Marsh Supermarkets, Inc.; *U.S. Public*, pg. 1049
VILLAGE SQUARE NURSING CENTER—See Horizon/ CMS Healthcare Corporation; *U.S. Public*, pg. 838
VILLAGE SUPER MARKET INC.; *U.S. Public*, pg. 1721
VILLAGE TRANSPORT CORP.—See The Progressive Corporation; *U.S. Public*, pg. 1335
VILLARD BOOKS—See Advance Publications Inc.; *U.S. Private*, pg. 1140
VILLARES CORPORATION OF AMERICA—See Acos Villares S.A.; *Int'l*, pg. 23
VILLARES STEEL INTERNATIONAL BV—See Acos Villares S.A.; *Int'l*, pg. 23
VILLAUME INDUSTRIES, INC.; *U.S. Private*, pg. 1140
VILLAZON COMPANY INC.; *U.S. Private*, pg. 1140
VILLEROY & BOCH AG; *Int'l*, pg. 1468
VILLEROY & BOCH TABLEWARE, LTD.—See Villeroy & Boch AG; *Int'l*, pg. 1468
VILLEROY & BOCH (USA) INC.—See Villeroy & Boch AG; *Int'l*, pg. 1468
VILMORIN INC.—See Groupe Limagrain; *Int'l*, pg. 566
VILTER EXPORT CORP.—See Vilter Manufacturing Corporation; *U.S. Private*, pg. 1141
VILTER MANUFACTURING CORPORATION; *U.S. Private*, pg. 1140
VIMARC—See Ambac B.V.; *Int'l*, pg. 71
VIMPEX HANDELSGESELLSCHAFT MBH—See Enso Oyj; *Int'l*, pg. 458
VINAMUL LTD.—See Unilever Plc; *Int'l*, pg. 1434
VINATA INTERNATIONAL JOINT VENTURE LTD., CO.—See Taisei Corporation; *Int'l*, pg. 1348
VINCENNES NEWSPAPERS, INC.—See Central Newspapers, Inc.; *U.S. Public*, pg. 326
VINCENNES STEEL CORP.; *U.S. Private*, pg. 1141
VINCENT METAL GOODS-NORTHERN DIVISION—See Rio Algom Limited; *Int'l*, pg. 1118
VINCENT METAL GOODS-SOUTHERN DIVISION—See Rio Algom Limited; *Int'l*, pg. 1118
VINCENT METALS DIVISION—See Rio Algom Limited; *Int'l*, pg. 1118
VINCOR INTERNATIONAL; *Int'l*, pg. 1468
VINDICATOR TECHNOLOGIES; *U.S. Private*, pg. 1141
VINELAND LABORATORIES—See IGI, Inc.; *U.S. Public*, pg. 855
VINELAND TRANSIT MIX CONCRETE CO., INC.—See Scancem AB; *Int'l*, pg. 1201
VINGCARD SYSTEMS INC.—See Assa Abloy AB; *Int'l*, pg. 18

VINGMED SOUND A/S—See IDB Holding Corporation; *Int'l*, pg. 644
VINICLOR S.A.—See Solvay S.A.; *Int'l*, pg. 1280
VININGS INDUSTRIES INC.; *U.S. Private*, pg. 1141
VINK AS—See Schuttersveld Holding N.V.; *Int'l*, pg. 1210
VINK FINLAND OY—See Schuttersveld Holding N.V.; *Int'l*, pg. 1210
VINK KUNSTSTOFFE AG—See Schuttersveld Holding N.V.; *Int'l*, pg. 1210
VINK KUNSTSTOFFE GMBH & CO. K.G.—See Schuttersveld Holding N.V.; *Int'l*, pg. 1210
VINK KUNSTSTOFFEN B.V.—See Schuttersveld Holding N.V.; *Int'l*, pg. 1211
VINK N.V.—See Schuttersveld Holding N.V.; *Int'l*, pg. 1211
VINK PLAST AB—See Schuttersveld Holding N.V.; *Int'l*, pg. 1211
VINK PLAST AS—See Schuttersveld Holding N.V.; *Int'l*, pg. 1211
VINK ZAO—See Schuttersveld Holding N.V.; *Int'l*, pg. 1211
VINLAND INDUSTRIES LTD.—See Kvaerner a.s.a.; *Int'l*, pg. 770
VINNOLIT KUNSTSTOFF GMBH—See Hoechst Aktiengesellschaft; *Int'l*, pg. 626
VINSON SUPPLY COMPANY—See Sammons Enterprises, Inc.; *U.S. Private*, pg. 963
VINTAGE BLUE—See Kellwood Company; *U.S. Public*, pg. 948
VINUM INC.—See Banfi Vintners; *U.S. Private*, pg. 113
VINYL PLASTICS INCORPORATED; *U.S. Private*, pg. 1141
VINYLIUM CORP.—See HIG Capital Management; *U.S. Private*, pg. 491
VIPAC VIBRATOR AB—See Trelleborg AB; *Int'l*, pg. 1420
VIRACON/CURVLITE, INC.—See Apogee Enterprises, Inc.; *U.S. Public*, pg. 120
VIRACON, INC.—See Apogee Enterprises, Inc.; *U.S. Public*, pg. 120
VIRACON OF ILLINOIS, INC.—See Apogee Enterprises, Inc.; *U.S. Public*, pg. 120
VIRAX—See Groupe Strafor Facom; *Int'l*, pg. 570
VIRCO MFG. CORPORATION; *U.S. Public*, pg. 1721
VIRGIN HOTEL; *Int'l*, pg. 1468
VIRGIN INTERACTIVE ENTERTAINMENT INC.—See National Amusements, Inc.; *U.S. Private*, pg. 776
THE VIRGIN ISLANDS DAILY NEWS—See Gannett Company, Inc.; *U.S. Public*, pg. 702
VIRGIN MUSIC GROUP—See EMI Group plc; *Int'l*, pg. 427
VIRGIN RECORDS AMERICA INC.—See EMI Group plc; *Int'l*, pg. 427
VIRGINIA-AMERICAN WATER CO.—See American Water Works Company, Inc.; *U.S. Public*, pg. 96
VIRGINIA & SOUTHWESTERN RAILWAY CO.—See Norfolk Southern Corporation; *U.S. Public*, pg. 1191
VIRGINIA CONCRETE CO., INC.—See Florida Rock Industries, Inc.; *U.S. Public*, pg. 656
VIRGINIA ELECTRIC AND POWER COMPANY—See Dominion Resources, Inc.; *U.S. Public*, pg. 516
VIRGINIA FIBRE CORP.—See Greif Brothers Corporation; *U.S. Public*, pg. 764
VIRGINIA FIRST FINANCIAL CORP.; *U.S. Public*, pg. 1721
VIRGINIA FIRST MORTGAGE—See Virginia First Financial Corp.; *U.S. Public*, pg. 1721
VIRGINIA FIRST SAVINGS BANK, F.S.B.—See Virginia First Financial Corp.; *U.S. Public*, pg. 1721
VIRGINIA HOLDING CORPORATION—See Norfolk Southern Corporation; *U.S. Public*, pg. 1190
VIRGINIA INDONESIA COMPANY—See LASMO plc; *Int'l*, pg. 804
VIRGINIA METAL INDUSTRIES, INC.; *U.S. Private*, pg. 1141
VIRGINIA MILK PRODUCTS LIMITED—See Avonmore Waterford Group plc; *Int'l*, pg. 102
VIRGINIA MILK PRODUCTS, VIRGINIA—See Avonmore Waterford Group plc; *Int'l*, pg. 102
VIRGINIA NATURAL GAS, INC.—See Consolidated Natural Gas Company; *U.S. Public*, pg. 436
VIRGINIA OPERATIONS—See Mitsubishi Chemical Corporation; *Int'l*, pg. 871
VIRGINIA PAVING CO.—See The Lane Construction Corp.; *U.S. Private*, pg. 649
VIRGINIA SURETY CO., INC.—See AON Corporation; *U.S. Public*, pg. 118
VIRGINIA TOBACCO CO., INC.—See Universal Corporation; *U.S. Public*, pg. 1695
VIRGINIA TOURISM CORP.; *U.S. Private*, pg. 1141
VIRGINIA WSMP, INC. (VIRGINIA)—See WSMP, Inc.; *U.S. Public*, pg. 1729
THE VIRGINIAN-PILOT—See Landmark Communications, Inc.; *U.S. Private*, pg. 649
VIRGO OPTICS, INC.—See II-VI Incorporated; *U.S. Public*, pg. 1647
VIROLLE—See SNCF; *Int'l*, pg. 1165
VIRSA, INC.—See Universal Corporation; *U.S. Public*, pg. 1695
VIRSAN S.A. DE C.V.—See Virco Mfg. Corporation; *U.S. Public*, pg. 1721
THE VIRTUAL GROUP; *U.S. Private*, pg. 1141
VIRTUAL VISION, INC.—See Telxon Corporation; *U.S. Public*, pg. 1573
VIS—See Saint-Gobain; *Int'l*, pg. 1173
VISA U.S.A. INC.; *U.S. Private*, pg. 1141
VISAGE BEAUTE' COSMETICS, INC.—See MacAndrews & Forbes Holdings Inc.; *U.S. Private*, pg. 690
VISALIA ELECTRIC RAILROAD CO.—See Union Pacific Corporation; *U.S. Public*, pg. 1668
VISALIA TIMES-DELTA—See Gannett Company, Inc.; *U.S. Public*, pg. 702
VISCOSITY OIL COMPANY—See Tenneco Inc.; *U.S. Public*, pg. 1579
VISCOSUISSE—See Rhone-Poulenc S.A.; *Int'l*, pg. 1114
VISEA THORN—See Thorn plc; *Int'l*, pg. 1386
VISHAY COMPONENTS (U.K.) LTD.—See Vishay Intertechnology, Inc.; *U.S. Public*, pg. 1722

VISHAY INSTRUMENTS DIV.—See Vishay Intertechnology, Inc.; *U.S. Public*, pg. 1722
VISHAY INTERTECHNOLOGY, INC.; *U.S. Public*, pg. 1721
VISHAY ISRAEL LTD.—See Vishay Intertechnology, Inc.; *U.S. Public*, pg. 1722
VISHAY MICRO-MESURES, S.A.—See Vishay Intertechnology, Inc.; *U.S. Public*, pg. 1722
VISHAY RESISTIVE SYSTEMS—See Vishay Intertechnology, Inc.; *U.S. Public*, pg. 1722
VISHAY RESISTOR PRODUCTS—See Vishay Intertechnology, Inc.; *U.S. Public*, pg. 1722
VISIBLE CHANGES; *U.S. Private*, pg. 1141
VISIBLE CHANGES OF AUSTIN—See Visible Changes; *U.S. Private*, pg. 1141
VISIBLE CHANGES OF TEXAS—See Visible Changes; *U.S. Private*, pg. 1141
VISIBLE IMPACT TARGETS—See Crosman Corp.; *U.S. Private*, pg. 291
VISILOX SYSTEMS, INC. (VSI)—See Henkel KGaA; *Int'l*, pg. 611
VISION CABLE TIES CO.—See Applied Power Inc.; *U.S. Public*, pg. 124
VISION CENTERS—See GIB Group; *Int'l*, pg. 533
VISION-EASE LENS—See BMC Industries, Inc.; *U.S. Public*, pg. 162
VISION-EASE LENS INC.—See BMC Industries, Inc.; *U.S. Public*, pg. 162
VISION ENERGY FLORIDA, INC.—See Bell Atlantic Corporation; *U.S. Public*, pg. 203
VISION ENERGY MINNESOTA, INC.—See Bell Atlantic Corporation; *U.S. Public*, pg. 203
VISION ENERGY NORTH DAKOTA, INC.—See Bell Atlantic Corporation; *U.S. Public*, pg. 203
VISION ENERGY RESOURCES, INC.—See Bell Atlantic Corporation; *U.S. Public*, pg. 203
VISION ENERGY WISCONSIN, INC.—See Bell Atlantic Corporation; *U.S. Public*, pg. 203
VISION FACTORY PRODUCTIONS—See DMB&B Communications; *U.S. Public*, pg. 305
VISION FINANCIAL CORPORATION; *U.S. Private*, pg. 1141
VISION GROUP PLC—See Donnelly Corporation; *U.S. Public*, pg. 519
VISION ONE; *U.S. Private*, pg. 1141
VISION 7—See Lagardere Groupe; *Int'l*, pg. 794
VISIONEER, INC.; *U.S. Public*, pg. 1722
VISIONS SYSTEMS—See CSP Inc.; *U.S. Public*, pg. 283
VISKAFORS AB—See Trelleborg AB; *Int'l*, pg. 1423
VISKASE CANADA INC.—See Envirodyne Industries, Inc.; *U.S. Public*, pg. 586
VISKASE CORPORATION—See Envirodyne Industries, Inc.; *U.S. Public*, pg. 586
VISKASE UNITED KINGDOM LIMITED—See Envirodyne Industries, Inc.; *U.S. Public*, pg. 586
VISOFI S.A.—See Vorwerk & Co.; *Int'l*, pg. 1481
VISOL S.A.—See Dainippon Ink & Chemicals, Inc.; *Int'l*, pg. 371
VISPAC INC.—See VSI Holdings, Inc.; *U.S. Public*, pg. 1703
VISTA BAKERY, INC.—See Lance, Inc.; *U.S. Public*, pg. 977
VISTA CABLEVISION, INC.—See Time Warner Inc.; *U.S. Public*, pg. 1611
VISTA GOLD CORP.; *U.S. Public*, pg. 1723
VISTA GOLD HOLDINGS INC.—See Vista Gold Corp.; *U.S. Public*, pg. 1723
VISTA INSURANCE COMPANY—See Ford Motor Company; *U.S. Public*, pg. 664
VISTA INSURANCE SERVICES, INC.—See The Walt Disney Company; *U.S. Public*, pg. 514
VISTA INTERNATIONAL PACKAGING INC.—See Hormel Foods Corp.; *U.S. Public*, pg. 840
VISTA LIFE INSURANCE COMPANY OF TEXAS—See Ford Motor Company; *U.S. Public*, pg. 664
VISTA LIGHTING—See Luxo A/S; *Int'l*, pg. 821
VISTA MULTI METHOD—See Berlitz International, Inc.; *U.S. Public*, pg. 222
VISTA MULTI NATIONAL—See Berlitz International, Inc.; *U.S. Public*, pg. 222
VISTA 2000, INC.; *U.S. Private*, pg. 1142
VISTAKON JOHNSON & JOHNSON VISION PRODUCTS, INC.—See Johnson & Johnson; *U.S. Public*, pg. 929
VISTAR S.A. DE C.V.—See Moulinex S.A.; *Int'l*, pg. 896
VISUAL SERVICES INC.—See VSI Holdings, Inc.; *U.S. Public*, pg. 1703
VISUAL SIMULATION SYSTEMS DIVISION—See Berkshire Hathaway Inc.; *U.S. Public*, pg. 218
VISY PAPER INC.—See Pratt Industries; *Int'l*, pg. 1066
VITA FOOD PRODUCTS, INC.; *U.S. Private*, pg. 1142
VITA-WHEEL COMPANY—See Atlet AB; *Int'l*, pg. 97
VITACOLOR INDUSTRIES, INC.—See BASF AG; *Int'l*, pg. 110
VITACTIV AB—See Sunrise Medical, Inc.; *U.S. Public*, pg. 1536
VITAFREZE FROZEN CONFECTIONS—See Crystal Cream & Butter Company; *U.S. Private*, pg. 294
VITAL NETWORK SERVICE, INC.—See General Datacomm Industries, Inc.; *U.S. Public*, pg. 708
VITAL PHARMA, INC.—See Vital Signs, Inc.; *U.S. Public*, pg. 1723
VITAL SIGNS, INC.—See Vital Signs, Inc.; *U.S. Public*, pg. 1723
VITAL SIGNS DEUTSCHLAND, INC.—See Vital Signs, Inc.; *U.S. Public*, pg. 1723
VITAL SIGNS, INC.; *U.S. Public*, pg. 1723
VITAL SIGNS, INC.—See Vital Signs, Inc.; *U.S. Public*, pg. 1723
VITAL SIGNS MN, INC.—See Vital Signs, Inc.; *U.S. Public*, pg. 1723
VITALAIRE CORPORATION—See Air Liquide S.A.; *Int'l*, pg. 37
VITALCARE HEALTH SERVICES, INC.—See Integrated Health Services, Inc.; *U.S. Public*, pg. 885
VITALCARE OF AMERICA, INC.—See Integrated Health Services, Inc.; *U.S. Public*, pg. 885

VITALCARE OF FLORIDA, INC.—See Integrated Health Services, Inc.; *U.S. Public*, pg. 885
VITALCARE OF NEVADA, INC.—See Integrated Health Services, Inc.; *U.S. Public*, pg. 885
VITALCARE OF PENNSLYVANIA, INC.—See Integrated Health Services, Inc.; *U.S. Public*, pg. 885
VITALCARE OF TEXAS, INC.—See Integrated Health Services, Inc.; *U.S. Public*, pg. 885
VITALICIO PENSIONES, S.A. SEGUROS Y REASEGUROS—See Assicurazioni Generali S.p.A.; *Int'l*, pg. 92
VITALICO AGENCIA DE SEGUROS S.A.—See Assicurazioni Generali S.p.A.; *Int'l*, pg. 92
VITALICO ASESORIA DE PENSIONES, S.A.—See Assicurazioni Generali S.p.A.; *Int'l*, pg. 92
VITALICO SERVICIOS INFORMATICOS, S.A.—See Assicurazioni Generali S.p.A.; *Int'l*, pg. 92
VITALINK PHARMACY SERVICES, INC.—See Manor Care, Inc.; *U.S. Public*, pg. 1041
VITALITY FOODSERVICE, INC.—See Lykes Brothers Inc.; *U.S. Private*, pg. 682
VITAMILK DAIRY, INC.; *U.S. Private*, pg. 1142
VITAMIN—See Testa International; *Int'l*, pg. 1377
VITAMIN WORLD—See Nature's Bounty Inc.; *U.S. Public*, pg. 1166
VITASOY INTERNATIONAL HOLDINGS LTD.; *Int'l*, pg. 1468
VITASOY (U.S.A.) INC.—See Vitasoy International Holdings Ltd.; *Int'l*, pg. 1469
VITATECH INTERNATIONAL, INC.; *U.S. Private*, pg. 1142
VITATRON MEDICAL B.V.—See Medtronic, Inc.; *U.S. Public*, pg. 1084
VITESSE SEMICONDUCTOR CORPORATION; *U.S. Public*, pg. 1723
C.J. VITNER CO.; *U.S. Private*, pg. 1142
VITRAGES ISOLANTS D'AUVERGNE—See Saint-Gobain; *Int'l*, pg. 1172
VITRAMON, INCORPORATED—See Vishay Intertechnology, Inc.; *U.S. Public*, pg. 1722
VITRAN CORPORATION; *Int'l*, pg. 1469
VITRO-FIBRAS, S.A.—See Owens Corning; *U.S. Public*, pg. 1238
VITRO SERVICES CORPORATION—See Tracor, Inc.; *U.S. Public*, pg. 1627
VITRO, SOCIEDAD ANONIMA; *Int'l*, pg. 1469
VITRO, SOCIEDAD ANONIMA - CAPITAL GOODS—See Vitro, Sociedad Anonima; *Int'l*, pg. 1469
VITRO, SOCIEDAD ANONIMA - CHEMICAL, FIBERS & MINING—See Vitro, Sociedad Anonima; *Int'l*, pg. 1469
VITRO, SOCIEDAD ANONIMA - CONTAINERS DIV.—See Vitro, Sociedad Anonima; *Int'l*, pg. 1469
VITRO, SOCIEDAD ANONIMA - FLAT GLASS DIV.—See Vitro, Sociedad Anonima; *Int'l*, pg. 1469
VITRO, SOCIEDAD ANONIMA - GLASSWARE DIV.—See Vitro, Sociedad Anonima; *Int'l*, pg. 1469
VITROFARMA INDUSTRIA E COMERCIO DE VIDROS S.A.—See Carl-Zeiss-Stiftung; *Int'l*, pg. 1523
VITROFIL S.P.A.—See Saint-Gobain; *Int'l*, pg. 1177
VITROMATIC, S.A. DE C.V.—See Whirlpool Corporation; *U.S. Public*, pg. 1765
VITROMEX, S.A.; *Int'l*, pg. 1469
VITROSUL INDUSTRIA E COMERCIO DE VIDROS LTDA.—See Carl-Zeiss-Stiftung; *Int'l*, pg. 1523
VITRUS, INC.—See Tecumseh Products Company; *U.S. Public*, pg. 1566
VITRUVIO-LEO BURNETT—See Leo Burnett Company, Inc.; *U.S. Private*, pg. 186
VITRUVIO/LEO BURNETT—See Leo Burnett Company, Inc.; *U.S. Private*, pg. 186
VITT CORPORATION—See Toshiba Corporation; *Int'l*, pg. 1405
VITT MEDIA-CORPORATE TRADE—See Vitt Media International, Inc.; *U.S. Private*, pg. 1142
VITT MEDIA INTERNATIONAL, INC.; *U.S. Private*, pg. 1142
VITT MEDIA INTERNATIONAL, INC. - LOS ANGELES—See Vitt Media International, Inc.; *U.S. Private*, pg. 1142
VITT MEDIA-NEW MEDIA—See Vitt Media International, Inc.; *U.S. Private*, pg. 1142
VITTEL MINERALWASSER GMBH—See Nestle S.A.; *Int'l*, pg. 922
VITTEL S.A.—See Nestle S.A.; *Int'l*, pg. 922
VITTINGE TEGEL AB—See Redland PLC; *Int'l*, pg. 1092
VIVA—See Grupo Iberia; *Int'l*, pg. 575
VIVA SPECIALTY PARTNERS—See Vivra Incorporated; *U.S. Public*, pg. 1724
VIVA, VUELOS INTERNACIONALES DE VACACIONES, S.A.—See SEPI; *Int'l*, pg. 1225
VIVAGEL—See Danone Group; *Int'l*, pg. 380
VIVIAN & ELLIETTE, INC.; *U.S. Private*, pg. 1142
VIVIAN MILLWORKS; *U.S. Private*, pg. 1143
VIVIANO MACARONI CO.—See Borden, Inc.; *U.S. Private*, pg. 158
VIVITAR CANADA LIMITED—See Ricoh Company, Ltd.; *Int'l*, pg. 1116
VIVITAR CORPORATION—See Plaza Create; *Int'l*, pg. 1060
VIVITAR (EUROPE) LTD. HANIMEX-VIVITAR—See Plaza Create; *Int'l*, pg. 1061
VIVRA HEALTH ADVANTAGE, INC.—See Vivra Incorporated; *U.S. Public*, pg. 1724
VIVRA INCORPORATED; *U.S. Public*, pg. 1723
VIVRA RENAL CARE—See Vivra Incorporated; *U.S. Public*, pg. 1724
VIZDURR S.A.—See Durr AG; *Int'l*, pg. 422
VLAAMSE INVESTERINGSVENNOOTSCHAP (VIV)—See Generale de Banque S.A.; *Int'l*, pg. 547
VLIER ENGINEERING—See Applied Power Inc.; *U.S. Public*, pg. 124
VLISCO B.V.—See Gamma Holding N.V.; *Int'l*, pg. 540
VLOC—See II-VI Incorporated; *U.S. Public*, pg. 1647
VMARK ASIA-PACIFIC PTY. LTD.—See Ardent Software, Inc.; *U.S. Public*, pg. 129

VMARK SOFTWARE, LTD.—See Ardent Software, Inc.; *U.S. Public*, pg. 129

VOAC HYDRAULICS AB—See Parker Hannifin Corporation; *U.S. Public*, pg. 1264

VOAC HYDRAULICS GMBH—See Parker Hannifin Corporation; *U.S. Public*, pg. 1264

VOAC HYDRAULICS LTD.—See Parker Hannifin Corporation; *U.S. Public*, pg. 1264

VOAC HYDRAULICS S.A.—See Parker Hannifin Corporation; *U.S. Public*, pg. 1264

VOAC HYDRAULICS SPA—See Parker Hannifin Corporation; *U.S. Public*, pg. 1264

VODAFONE GROUP PLC; *Int'l*, pg. 1469

VOEST-ALPINE (AUSTRALIA) PTY. LTD.—See Voest-Alpine Stahl AG; *Int'l*, pg. 1474

VOEST-ALPINE AUSTRIA DRAHT GES.M.B.H.—See Voest-Alpine Stahl AG; *Int'l*, pg. 1470

VOEST-ALPINE HELLAS A.E.—See Voest-Alpine Stahl AG; *Int'l*, pg. 1472

VOEST-ALPINE INDUSTRIES, INC.—See Voest-Alpine Stahl AG; *Int'l*, pg. 1470

VOEST-ALPINE INDUSTRIES, INC.-STEELMAKING—See Voest-Alpine Stahl AG; *Int'l*, pg. 1470

VOEST-ALPINE INDUSTRIES, INC.-USX PROJECT OFFICE—See Voest-Alpine Stahl AG; *Int'l*, pg. 1470

VOEST-ALPINE INTERNATIONAL CORPORATION—See Voest-Alpine Stahl AG; *Int'l*, pg. 1470

VOEST-ALPINE INTERNATIONAL DE VENEZUELA C.A.—See Voest-Alpine Stahl AG; *Int'l*, pg. 1472

VOEST-ALPINE INTERTRADING GMBH—See Voest-Alpine Stahl AG; *Int'l*, pg. 1470

VOEST-ALPINE KREMS FINALTECHNIK GMBH—See Voest-Alpine Stahl AG; *Int'l*, pg. 1470

VOEST-ALPINE NORGE A/S—See Voest-Alpine Stahl AG; *Int'l*, pg. 1472

VOEST-ALPINE ROHSTOFFHANDEL GES.M.B.H.—See Voest-Alpine Stahl AG; *Int'l*, pg. 1470

VOEST-ALPINE SAUDI ARABIA LTD.—See Voest-Alpine Stahl AG; *Int'l*, pg. 1472

VOEST-ALPINE SCHIENEN GMBH—See Voest-Alpine Stahl AG; *Int'l*, pg. 1470

VOEST-ALPINE SERVICES AND TECHNOLOGIES CORP.—See Voest-Alpine Stahl AG; *Int'l*, pg. 1471

VOEST-ALPINE SERVICES AND TECHNOLOGIES CORP.-MATERIAL HANDLING EQUIPMENT—See Voest-Alpine Stahl AG; *Int'l*, pg. 1471

VOEST-ALPINE SERVICES AND TECHNOLOGIES CORP.-ROMULUS—See Voest-Alpine Stahl AG; *Int'l*, pg. 1471

VOEST-ALPINE SOUTH AFRICA (PTY.) LTD.—See Voest-Alpine Stahl AG; *Int'l*, pg. 1472

VOEST-ALPINE STAHL AG; *Int'l*, pg. 1470

VOEST-ALPINE STAHL DONAWITZ GES.M.B.H.—See Voest-Alpine Stahl AG; *Int'l*, pg. 1470

VOEST-ALPINE STAHL JUDENBURG GES.M.B.H.—See Voest-Alpine Stahl AG; *Int'l*, pg. 1470

VOEST-ALPINE STAHL LINZ GES.M.B.H.—See Voest-Alpine Stahl AG; *Int'l*, pg. 1470

VOEST-ALPINE STAHL TRAISEN GES.M.B.H.—See Voest-Alpine Stahl AG; *Int'l*, pg. 1470

VOEST-ALPINE STAHLHANDEL AG—See Voest-Alpine Stahl AG; *Int'l*, pg. 1470

VOEST-ALPINE STAHLROHR KINDBERG GES.M.B.H.—See Voest-Alpine Stahl AG; *Int'l*, pg. 1470

VOEST-ALPINE STEEL CORP.—See Voest-Alpine Stahl AG; *Int'l*, pg. 1471

VOEST-ALPINE STEEL CORP.-TUBULARS—See Voest-Alpine Stahl AG; *Int'l*, pg. 1471

VOEST-ALPINE TRADING U.S.A. CORP.—See Voest-Alpine Stahl AG; *Int'l*, pg. 1471

H.F. VOGEL GMBH ELEKTROTECHNISCHE FABRIK—See Woodhead Industries, Inc.; *U.S. Public*, pg. 1776

VOGEL POPCORN COMPANY—See ConAgra, Inc.; *U.S. Public*, pg. 427

VOGEL PUMPENFABRIK—See ITT Industries, Inc.; *U.S. Public*, pg. 861

VOGLER MOTOR COMPANY, INC.; *U.S. Private*, pg. 1143

HENRY VOGT MACHINE CO.; *U.S. Private*, pg. 1143

VOGTLIN S.A.—See GESTRA GmbH; *Int'l*, pg. 551

VOGUE MAGAZINE—See Advance Publications Inc.; *U.S. Private*, pg. 20

VOIGT & CO. BAUGESELLSCHAFT GMBH—See Skanska AB; *Int'l*, pg. 1261

VOIKKAA PAPER MILL—See UPM-Kymmene Corporation; *Int'l*, pg. 1428

VOILES GATEFF S.A.—See Societe BIC S.A.; *Int'l*, pg. 1273

VOI-SHAN/DIESSEL GMBH—See The Fairchild Corporation; *U.S. Public*, pg. 610

VOIT SPORTS, INC.; *U.S. Private*, pg. 1143

VOITH-ELIN ELECTRONIK GMBH—See J.M. Voith, GmbH; *Int'l*, pg. 1473

VOITH HYDRO, INC.—See J.M. Voith, GmbH; *Int'l*, pg. 1473

VOITH INC.—See J.M. Voith, GmbH; *Int'l*, pg. 1473

VOITH INDIA PRIVATE LTD.—See J.M. Voith, GmbH; *Int'l*, pg. 1473

J.M. VOITH AG—See J.M. Voith, GmbH; *Int'l*, pg. 1473

J.M. VOITH, GMBH; *Int'l*, pg. 1472

VOITH-KLEINWASSERKRAFT GMBH—See J.M. Voith, GmbH; *Int'l*, pg. 1473

VOITH-NOVENCO GMBH—See J.M. Voith, GmbH; *Int'l*, pg. 1473

VOITH S.A. MAQUINAS E EQUIPAMENTOS—See J.M. Voith, GmbH; *Int'l*, pg. 1473

VOITH SAFESET AB—See J.M. Voith, GmbH; *Int'l*, pg. 1473

VOITH SULZER PAPER TECHNOLOGY, NORTH AMERICA, INC.—See Sulzer Ltd.; *Int'l*, pg. 1308

VOITH SULZER PAPER TECHNOLOGY, NORTH AMERICA, INC.—See J.M. Voith, GmbH; *Int'l*, pg. 1473

VOITH SULZER PAPIERTECHNIK GMBH—See Sulzer Ltd.; *Int'l*, pg. 1307

VOITH SULZER PAPIERTECHNIK GMBH—See J.M. Voith, GmbH; *Int'l*, pg. 1473

VOITH TOLOSA S.A.—See J.M. Voith, GmbH; *Int'l*, pg. 1473

VOITH TURBO GMBH & CO. KG—See J.M. Voith, GmbH; *Int'l*, pg. 1473

VOKES LTD.—See BTR plc; *Int'l*, pg. 125

VOLCLAY LIMITED—See AMCOL International Corp.; *U.S. Public*, pg. 64

VOLCLAY STANDARD PTY. LTD.—See AMCOL International Corp.; *U.S. Public*, pg. 64

VOLEX ACCESSORIES LIMITED—See Hanson PLC; *Int'l*, pg. 593

VOLIM VOLKSWAGEN IMMOBILIEN VERNIETGESELLSCHAFT FUR VW-AUDI HANDLERBETRIEBE MBH—See Volkswagen AG; *Int'l*, pg. 1474

B.V. V/H FIRMA L.J. VOLKERS—See Veba AG; *Int'l*, pg. 1458

VOLKSFREUND-DRUCKEREI NIKOLAUS KOCH GMBH & CO. KG—See Georg von Holtzbrinck GmbH; *Int'l*, pg. 1479

VOLKSFURSORGE DEUTSCHE LEBENSVERSICHERUNG AG—See AMB Aachener und Muenchener Beteiligungs-AG; *Int'l*, pg. 16

VOLKSFURSORGE DEUTSCHE SACHVERSICHERUNG—See AMB Aachener und Muenchener Beteiligungs-AG; *Int'l*, pg. 16

VOLKSFURSORGE HOLDING AG—See AMB Aachener und Muenchener Beteiligungs-AG; *Int'l*, pg. 15

VOLKSFURSORGE KRANKENVERSICHERUNG AG—See AMB Aachener und Muenchener Beteiligungs-AG; *Int'l*, pg. 16

VOLKSWAGEN AG; *Int'l*, pg. 1473

VOLKSWAGEN AG PREUSSENELEKTRA AG OHG—See Veba AG; *Int'l*, pg. 1456

VOLKSWAGEN AKTIENGESELLSCHAFT & CO. LEASING—See Volkswagen AG; *Int'l*, pg. 1474

VOLKSWAGEN ARGENTINA S.A.—See Volkswagen AG; *Int'l*, pg. 1475

VOLKSWAGEN ASIA-PACIFIC LTD.—See Volkswagen AG; *Int'l*, pg. 1475

VOLKSWAGEN AUDI NIPPON K.K.—See Volkswagen AG; *Int'l*, pg. 1475

VOLKSWAGEN-AUDI VERTRIEBS-GMBH CHEMNITZ—See Volkswagen AG; *Int'l*, pg. 1474

VOLKSWAGEN BANK GMBH—See Volkswagen AG; *Int'l*, pg. 1474

VOLKSWAGEN-BILDUNGSNSTITUT GMBH—See Volkswagen AG; *Int'l*, pg. 1474

VOLKSWAGEN BORDNETZE GMBH—See Volkswagen AG; *Int'l*, pg. 1474

VOLKSWAGEN BRATISLAVA SPOL. S.R.O.—See Volkswagen AG; *Int'l*, pg. 1475

S.A. VOLKSWAGEN BRUXELLES N.V.—See Volkswagen AG; *Int'l*, pg. 1475

VOLKSWAGEN BRUXELLES S.A.—See Volkswagen AG; *Int'l*, pg. 1475

VOLKSWAGEN CANADA, INC.—See Volkswagen AG; *Int'l*, pg. 1475

VOLKSWAGEN COACHING GESELLSCHAFT MBH—See Volkswagen AG; *Int'l*, pg. 1474

VOLKSWAGEN COMERCIAL S.A. DE C.V.—See Volkswagen AG; *Int'l*, pg. 1475

VOLKSWAGEN DE MEXICO S.A. DE C.V.—See Volkswagen AG; *Int'l*, pg. 1475

VOLKSWAGEN DO BRASIL LTDA.—See Volkswagen AG; *Int'l*, pg. 1475

VOLKSWAGEN FINANCE AG—See Volkswagen AG; *Int'l*, pg. 1474

VOLKSWAGEN FINANCE S.A.—See Volkswagen AG; *Int'l*, pg. 1474

VOLKSWAGEN FINANCIAL SERVICES AG—See Volkswagen AG; *Int'l*, pg. 1474

VOLKSWAGEN FINANCIAL SERVICES AG & CO.—See Volkswagen AG; *Int'l*, pg. 1474

VOLKSWAGEN FINANCIAL SERVICES, S.A. DE C.V.—See Volkswagen AG; *Int'l*, pg. 1475

VOLKSWAGEN FINANCIAL SERVICES (UK) LTD.—See Volkswagen AG; *Int'l*, pg. 1475

VOLKSWAGEN GROUP UNITED KINGDOM LTD.—See Volkswagen AG; *Int'l*, pg. 1475

VOLKSWAGEN IFA PKW. GMBH.—See Volkswagen AG; *Int'l*, pg. 1476

VOLKSWAGEN INTL. FINANCE N.V.—See Volkswagen AG; *Int'l*, pg. 1475

VOLKSWAGEN INVESTMENTS LTD.—See Volkswagen AG; *Int'l*, pg. 1475

VOLKSWAGEN LEASING ANLAGEN GMBH—See Volkswagen AG; *Int'l*, pg. 1474

VOLKSWAGEN LEASING GMBH—See Volkswagen AG; *Int'l*, pg. 1474

VOLKSWAGEN LEASING S.A. DE C.V.—See Volkswagen AG; *Int'l*, pg. 1475

VOLKSWAGEN NAVARRA, S.A.—See Volkswagen AG; *Int'l*, pg. 1475

VOLKSWAGEN OF AMERICA ADMINISTRATION CENTER WEST—See Volkswagen AG; *Int'l*, pg. 1474

VOLKSWAGEN OF AMERICA, INC.—See Volkswagen AG; *Int'l*, pg. 1474

VOLKSWAGEN OF NIGERIA LTD.—See Volkswagen AG; *Int'l*, pg. 1475

VOLKSWAGEN OF SOUTH AFRICA (PTY.) LTD.—See Volkswagen AG; *Int'l*, pg. 1475

VOLKSWAGEN OVERSEAS FINANCE N.V.—See Volkswagen AG; *Int'l*, pg. 1475

VOLKSWAGEN SACHSEN GMBH—See Volkswagen AG; *Int'l*, pg. 1474

VOLKSWAGEN TRADING S.A.—See Volkswagen AG; *Int'l*, pg. 1475

VOLLAND TELEMETRY GMBH—See Bowthorpe plc; *Int'l*, pg. 209

THE VOLLRATH COMPANY, L.L.C.; *U.S. Private*, pg. 1143

VOLLRATH-KEWAUNEE PLANT—See The Vollrath Company, L.L.C.; *U.S. Private*, pg. 1143

VOLT ALPHANUMERIC PUBLICATION SYSTEMS—See Volt Information Sciences, Inc.; *U.S. Public*, pg. 1724

VOLT-AUTOLOGIC DIRECTORIES S.A.—See Volt Information Sciences, Inc.; *U.S. Public*, pg. 1724

VOLT DELTA RESOURCES, INC.—See Volt Information Sciences, Inc.; *U.S. Public*, pg. 1724

VOLT DIRECTORY SERVICES—See Volt Information Sciences, Inc.; *U.S. Public*, pg. 1724

VOLT INFORMATION SCIENCES, INC.; *U.S. Public*, pg. 1724

VOLT MANAGEMENT CORP.—See Volt Information Sciences, Inc.; *U.S. Public*, pg. 1724

VOLT SERVICES GROUP—See Volt Information Sciences, Inc.; *U.S. Public*, pg. 1724

VOLT TECHNICAL SERVICES-EAST—See Volt Information Sciences, Inc.; *U.S. Public*, pg. 1724

VOLT TECHNICAL SERVICES-WEST—See Volt Information Sciences, Inc.; *U.S. Public*, pg. 1724

VOLT TEMPORARY SERVICES—See Volt Information Sciences, Inc.; *U.S. Public*, pg. 1724

VOLT VIEWTECH, INC.—See Volt Information Sciences, Inc.; *U.S. Public*, pg. 1724

AB VOLTA—See Electrolux, AB; *Int'l*, pg. 439

VOLTA ALUMINIUM CO. LTD. (VALCO)—See Maxxam Inc.; *U.S. Public*, pg. 1063

VOLTA BREGENZ GMBH—See Electrolux, AB; *Int'l*, pg. 441

VOLTA ELECTROGENERATE VERTRIEBS GMBH—See Electrolux, AB; *Int'l*, pg. 442

VOLTA ELEKTROWAREN-VERTRIEBSGESELLSCHAFT GMBH—See Electrolux, AB; *Int'l*, pg. 441

VOLTDELTA EUROPE LIMITED—See Volt Information Sciences, Inc.; *U.S. Public*, pg. 1724

VOLTEC—See Sauer Industries, Inc.; *U.S. Private*, pg. 968

VOLTELCON—See Volt Information Sciences, Inc.; *U.S. Public*, pg. 1724

VOLTERRA S.A.—See Nippon Paper Industries Company Limited; *Int'l*, pg. 938

VOLUMATIC LIMITED—See Halma p.l.c.; *Int'l*, pg. 590

VOLUMAX S.A.—See Axel Johnson AB; *Int'l*, pg. 712

VOLUNTEER BANK—See Bancorp South Inc.; *U.S. Public*, pg. 176

VOLUNTEER ENGINEERING, INC.—See Davis Industries Inc.; *U.S. Private*, pg. 315

VOLUNTEER FABRICATORS, INC.—See The H.T. Hackney Co.; *U.S. Private*, pg. 649

VOLUNTEER LEATHER CO.—See Genesco Inc.; *U.S. Public*, pg. 728

VOLUNTEER TOOL & DIE—See State Industries Inc.; *U.S. Private*, pg. 1037

VOLVIC—See Danone Group; *Int'l*, pg. 381

AB VOLVO; *Int'l*, pg. 1476

VOLVO AND HONDA SALES & SERVICE; *U.S. Private*, pg. 1143

VOLVO CAR UK LTD.—See AB Volvo; *Int'l*, pg. 1477

VOLVO CONSTRUCTION EQUIPMENT—See AB Volvo; *Int'l*, pg. 1477

VOLVO ESPANA, S.A.—See AB Volvo; *Int'l*, pg. 1477

VOLVO EUROPEAN CORPORATE OFFICE S.A.—See AB Volvo; *Int'l*, pg. 1477

VOLVO EXCAVATORS AB—See AB Volvo; *Int'l*, pg. 1477

VOLVO GROUP FINANCE EUROPE B.V.—See AB Volvo; *Int'l*, pg. 1477

VOLVO LASTEBILER OG BUSSER NORGE AS—See AB Volvo; *Int'l*, pg. 1477

VOLVO NORGE A/S—See AB Volvo; *Int'l*, pg. 1477

VOLVO NUTZFAHRZEUGE DEUTSCHLAND GMBH—See AB Volvo; *Int'l*, pg. 1477

AB VOLVO PENTA—See AB Volvo; *Int'l*, pg. 1476

VOLVO PENTA ASIA PACIFIC CORPORATION—See AB Volvo; *Int'l*, pg. 1477

VOLVO PENTA DO BRASIL-INDUSTRIA COMERCIO DE MOTORES LTDA.—See AB Volvo; *Int'l*, pg. 1477

VOLVO PENTA ESPANA, S.A.—See AB Volvo; *Int'l*, pg. 1478

VOLVO PENTA FRANCE S.A.—See AB Volvo; *Int'l*, pg. 1478

VOLVO PENTA LATINOAMERICA S.A.—See AB Volvo; *Int'l*, pg. 1478

VOLVO PENTA U.K. LTD.—See AB Volvo; *Int'l*, pg. 1478

VOLVO PERSONVAGE DANMARK A/S—See AB Volvo; *Int'l*, pg. 1478

VOLVO SUDAMERICANA SACI—See AB Volvo; *Int'l*, pg. 1478

VOLVO TRUCKS (GREAT BRITAIN) LTD.—See AB Volvo; *Int'l*, pg. 1478

VOLVO TRUCKS (SCHWEIZ) AG—See AB Volvo; *Int'l*, pg. 1478

VOLVO VEHICULES INDUSTRIELS FRANCE S.A.—See AB Volvo; *Int'l*, pg. 1478

VOLVO VEHICULOS INDUSTRIALES ESPANA, S.A.—See AB Volvo; *Int'l*, pg. 1478

VON BROEMBSEN MARSON LEO BURNETT/HARARE—See Leo Burnett Company, Inc.; *U.S. Private*, pg. 186

VON DER HEYDT-KERSTEN & SOEHNE—See Commerzbank AG; *Int'l*, pg. 310

VON ERNST BELGIUM MANAGEMENT S.A.—See Bayerische Vereinsbank Group; *Int'l*, pg. 181

VON ERNST CAPITAL MANAGEMENT S.A.—See Bayerische Vereinsbank Group; *Int'l*, pg. 181

VON ERNST DEUTSCHLAND GESELLSCHAFT FUR VERMOGENSPLANUG MBH—See Bayerische Vereinsbank Group; *Int'l*, pg. 180

VON ERNST TRUST & CO. LTD.—See Bayerische Vereinsbank Group; *Int'l*, pg. 181

GEORG VON HOLTZBRINCK GMBH; *Int'l*, pg. 1478

VON HOUSEN MOTORS; *U.S. Private*, pg. 1143

VON ROLL AG; *Int'l*, pg. 1480

VON ROLL AG DEPARTEMENT ARMATUREN—See Von Roll AG; *Int'l*, pg. 1480

VON ROLL AG DEPARTEMENT DRUCKROHRE—See Von Roll AG; *Int'l*, pg. 1480

VON ROLL AG DEPARTEMENT MASCHINEN & FORDERTECHN—See Von Roll AG; *Int'l*, pg. 1480

VON ROLL AG DEPARTEMENT STAHLPRODUKTE—See Von Roll AG; *Int'l*, pg. 1480
VON ROLL AG DEPARTEMENT UMWELTTECHNIK—See Von Roll AG; *Int'l*, pg. 1480
VON ROLL EISEN & STAHLGIESSEREI AG—See Von Roll AG; *Int'l*, pg. 1480
VON ROLL, INC.—See Von Roll AG; *Int'l*, pg. 1480
VON ROLL MACHINERY & HANDLING SYSTEMS—See Von Roll AG; *Int'l*, pg. 1480
VONK SYSTEMS—See Internatio-Muller N.V.; *Int'l*, pg. 681
VONKDATA BV—See Internatio-Muller N.V.; *Int'l*, pg. 681
THE VONS COMPANIES, INC.—See Safeway Inc.; *U.S. Public*, pg. 1426
VORARLBERGER ZEMENTWERKE LORUNS NACHFOLGER GMBH.—See Lafarge S.A.; *Int'l*, pg. 791
VORELCO, INC.—See Volkswagen AG; *Int'l*, pg. 1474
VORELCO LTD.—See Volkswagen AG; *Int'l*, pg. 1475
VORNADO REALTY TRUST; *U.S. Public*, pg. 1725
VORTEC—See Illinois Tool Works Inc.; *U.S. Public*, pg. 865
VORWERK & CO.; *Int'l*, pg. 1480
VORWERK & CO. ELEKTROWERKE KG.—See Vorwerk & Co.; *Int'l*, pg. 1480
VORWERK & CO. INTERHOLDING GMBH.—See Vorwerk & Co.; *Int'l*, pg. 1480
VORWERK & CO. MOBELSTOFF-BETEILIGUNGSGESELLSCHAFT MBH.—See Vorwerk & Co.; *Int'l*, pg. 1480
VORWERK & CO. MOBELSTOFFWERKE GMBH. & CO. KG—See Vorwerk & Co.; *Int'l*, pg. 1480
VORWERK & CO. TEPPICH-BETEILIGUNGSGESELLSCHAFT MBH.—See Vorwerk & Co.; *Int'l*, pg. 1480
VORWERK & CO. TEPPICHWERKE GMBH. & CO. KG.—See Vorwerk & Co.; *Int'l*, pg. 1480
VORWERK & CO. THERMOMIX GMBH—See Vorwerk & Co.; *Int'l*, pg. 1480
VORWERK CARPETS LIMITED—See Vorwerk & Co.; *Int'l*, pg. 1481
VORWERK CONTEMPORA S.R.L.—See Vorwerk & Co.; *Int'l*, pg. 1481
VORWERK CS S.R.O.—See Vorwerk & Co.; *Int'l*, pg. 1481
VORWERK ESPANA S.A.—See Vorwerk & Co.; *Int'l*, pg. 1481
VORWERK FOLLETTO S.R.L.—See Vorwerk & Co.; *Int'l*, pg. 1481
VORWERK FRANCE SA—See Vorwerk & Co.; *Int'l*, pg. 1481
VORWERK GES.M.B.H.—See Vorwerk & Co.; *Int'l*, pg. 1481
VORWERK HUNGARIA KFT.—See Vorwerk & Co.; *Int'l*, pg. 1481
VORWERK INTERNATIONAL AG.—See Vorwerk & Co.; *Int'l*, pg. 1481
VORWERK (MALAYSIA) SDN BHD—See Vorwerk & Co.; *Int'l*, pg. 1481
VORWERK MEXIKO—See Vorwerk & Co.; *Int'l*, pg. 1481
VORWERK NIPPON K. K.—See Vorwerk & Co.; *Int'l*, pg. 1481
VORWERK PORTUGAL—See Vorwerk & Co.; *Int'l*, pg. 1481
VORWERK TEXTIL FRANCE S.A.R.L.—See Vorwerk & Co.; *Int'l*, pg. 1481
VORWERK (U.K.) LTD.—See Vorwerk & Co.; *Int'l*, pg. 1481
VORWERK USA INC.—See Vorwerk & Co.; *Int'l*, pg. 1481
VOSS INDUSTRIES, INC.; *U.S. Private*, pg. 1143
A/S VOSS KOMFUR SERVICE—See Electrolux, AB; *Int'l*, pg. 441
VOTAN LEO BURNETT—See Leo Burnett Company, Inc.; *U.S. Private*, pg. 186
VOTAW PRECISION TECHNOLOGIES—See Kaiser Aerospace & Electronics Corp.; *U.S. Private*, pg. 605
VOTEX GMBH—See Volkswagen AG; *Int'l*, pg. 1474
VOTRA-HYMSUN LTD—See N.V. Koninklijke KNP BT; *Int'l*, pg. 757
VOTRA (KOREA) LTD.—See N.V. Koninklijke KNP BT; *Int'l*, pg. 757
VOTRA (MALAYSIA) SDN BHD—See N.V. Koninklijke KNP BT; *Int'l*, pg. 757
VOTRA (PHILIPPINES) INC—See N.V. Koninklijke KNP BT; *Int'l*, pg. 757
VOTRA SA—See N.V. Koninklijke KNP BT; *Int'l*, pg. 757
VOTRA (SINGAPORE) PTE LTD—See N.V. Koninklijke KNP BT; *Int'l*, pg. 757
VOTRA (TAIWAN) LTD—See N.V. Koninklijke KNP BT; *Int'l*, pg. 757
VOTRA (THAILAND) CO LTD—See N.V. Koninklijke KNP BT; *Int'l*, pg. 757
THE VOUCHER CORPORATION—See Accor S.A.; *Int'l*, pg. 21
VOX MEDICA CORPORATION; *U.S. Private*, pg. 1143
VOYAGE—See Landmark Communications, Inc.; *U.S. Private*, pg. 647
VOYAGE ASSISTANCE INTERNATIONAL S.A.—See Assicurazioni Generali S.p.A.; *Int'l*, pg. 90
VOYAGER AMERICAN INSURANCE COMPANY, LTD.—See American Bankers Insurance Group, Inc.; *U.S. Public*, pg. 68
VOYAGER EMBLEMS, INC.; *U.S. Private*, pg. 1143
VOYAGER GROUP, INC.—See American Bankers Insurance Group, Inc.; *U.S. Public*, pg. 68
VOYAGER INDEMNITY INSURANCE COMPANY—See American Bankers Insurance Group, Inc.; *U.S. Public*, pg. 68
VOYAGER LIFE INSURANCE COMPANY—See American Bankers Insurance Group, Inc.; *U.S. Public*, pg. 68
VOYAGER PROPERTY AND CASUALTY INSURANCE COMPANY—See American Bankers Insurance Group, Inc.; *U.S. Public*, pg. 68
VOYAGER SERVICE PROGRAMS, INC.—See American Bankers Insurance Group, Inc.; *U.S. Public*, pg. 68

VOYAGER SERVICE WARRANTIES, INC.—See American Bankers Insurance Group, Inc.; *U.S. Public*, pg. 68
VOYAGEUR PANEL LIMITED—See Boise Cascade Corporation; *U.S. Public*, pg. 243
VOYUNGSA LTD—See N.V. Koninklijke KNP BT; *Int'l*, pg. 757
VREDESTEIN BANDEN B.V.—See Vredestein N.V.; *Int'l*, pg. 1481
VREDESTEIN CONSULTING B.V.—See Vredestein N.V.; *Int'l*, pg. 1481
VREDESTEIN EXTRUSIONS—See Vredestein N.V.; *Int'l*, pg. 1481
VREDESTEIN FIETSBANDEN B.V.—See Vredestein N.V.; *Int'l*, pg. 1481
VREDESTEIN ICOPRO B.V.—See Vredestein N.V.; *Int'l*, pg. 1481
VREDESTEIN N.V.; *Int'l*, pg. 1481
VREDESTEIN RUBBER RECYCLING B.V.—See Vredestein N.V.; *Int'l*, pg. 1481
VROOM & DREESMAN B.V.—See Vendex International N.V.; *Int'l*, pg. 1463
S.A. VULCAIN ENVIRONMENT—See Cockerill Sambre; *Int'l*, pg. 302
S.A. VULCAIN INDUSTRIE—See Cockerill Sambre; *Int'l*, pg. 302
VULCAN ASPHALT REFINING COMPANY—See Red Apple Companies; *U.S. Private*, pg. 915
VULCAN BRUNSWICK BOWLING PIN COMPANY—See Brunswick Corporation; *U.S. Public*, pg. 266
VULCAN BRUNSWICK BOWLING PIN COMPANY—See Vulcan International Corporation; *U.S. Public*, pg. 1725
VULCAN CHEMICALS—See Vulcan Materials Company; *U.S. Public*, pg. 1725
VULCAN CONSTRUCTION COMPANY—See The Weitz Company, Inc.; *U.S. Private*, pg. 1161
VULCAN CORPORATION—See Vulcan International Corporation; *U.S. Public*, pg. 1725
VULCAN-ECLIPSE (PVT) LTD.—See Eclipse Inc.; *U.S. Private*, pg. 361
VULCAN GULF COAST MATERIALS, INC.—See Vulcan Materials Company; *U.S. Public*, pg. 1726
VULCAN-HART CORP.—See Premark International, Inc.; *U.S. Public*, pg. 1322
VULCAN INC.; *U.S. Private*, pg. 1144
VULCAN INTERNATIONAL CORPORATION; *U.S. Public*, pg. 1725
VULCAN INTERNATIONAL, LTD.—See Vulcan Materials Company; *U.S. Public*, pg. 1726
VULCAN IRON WORKS, INC.; *U.S. Private*, pg. 1144
VULCAN LANDS, INC.—See Vulcan Materials Company; *U.S. Public*, pg. 1726
VULCAN LIFE INSURANCE CO.—See Conseco Inc.; *U.S. Public*, pg. 433
VULCAN MATERIALS COMPANY; *U.S. Public*, pg. 1725
VULCAN OIL & GAS COMPANY—See Atrion Corporation; *U.S. Public*, pg. 146
VULCAN PEROXIDATION SYSTEMS, INC.—See Vulcan Materials Company; *U.S. Public*, pg. 1726
VULCO SA—See Weir Group PLC; *Int'l*, pg. 1489
VULCRAFT DIV.—See Nucor Corporation; *U.S. Public*, pg. 1206
VULKAN VERWALTUNGS-UND BETEILIGUNGSGESELLSCHAFT MBH—See Heidelberger Zement A.G.; *Int'l*, pg. 606
VULNAX INTERNATIONAL LTD.—See Akzo Nobel N.V.; *Int'l*, pg. 47
VYNCKIER NV—See The General Electric Company, p.l.c.; *Int'l*, pg. 546
VYNCOLIT N.V.—See Perstorp AB; *Int'l*, pg. 1037
VYNEX S.R.L.—See Dyckerhoff AG; *Int'l*, pg. 423
VYTAHY SCHINDLER A.S.—See Schindler Holding AG; *Int'l*, pg. 1205

W

W & L MOTOR LINES, INC.—See Ameritruck Distribution Corporation; *U.S. Private*, pg. 66
W. SCHRAML SOFTWAREHAUS GMBH—See Compagnie des Machines Bull; *Int'l*, pg. 317
W & A GILBEY—See Diageo Plc; *Int'l*, pg. 409
W & A GILBEY SA—See Diageo Plc; *Int'l*, pg. 409
W & B REFRIGERATION SERVICE CO.—See Frozen Food Express Industries, Inc.; *U.S. Public*, pg. 685
W & D SECURITIES, INC.—See Jefferies Group, Inc.; *U.S. Public*, pg. 925
W. & O. BERGMANN GMBH & CO. KG—See Preussag AG; *Int'l*, pg. 1069
W & R INSURANCE AGENCY, INC. OF ALABAMA, INC.—See Torchmark Corporation; *U.S. Public*, pg. 1623
W & R INSURANCE AGENCY, INC. OF MASSACHUSETTS, INC.—See Torchmark Corporation; *U.S. Public*, pg. 1623
W & R INSURANCE AGENCY, INC. OF MONTANA, INC.—See Torchmark Corporation; *U.S. Public*, pg. 1623
W & R INSURANCE AGENCY, INC. OF NEVADA, INC.—See Torchmark Corporation; *U.S. Public*, pg. 1623
W & R INSURANCE AGENCY, INC. OF UTAH, INC.—See Torchmark Corporation; *U.S. Public*, pg. 1623
W & R INSURANCE AGENCY, INC. OF WYOMING, INC.—See Torchmark Corporation; *U.S. Public*, pg. 1623
W & R INSURANCE AGENCY OF ARKANSAS, INC.—See Torchmark Corporation; *U.S. Public*, pg. 1623
W & S DISTRIBUTORS, INC.—See Bacardi Limited; *Int'l*, pg. 132
W-B SUPPLY CO.; *U.S. Private*, pg. 1144
W-P MILLING CO., INC.—See Altair Corporation; *U.S. Private*, pg. 46
W1310/CKBY RADIO—See Rogers Communications, Inc.; *Int'l*, pg. 1124
W/A MUSIC CORPORATION—See Baton Broadcasting Incorporated; *Int'l*, pg. 171
W.A. PUBLICATIONS, INC.—See The Reader's Digest Association, Inc.; *U.S. Public*, pg. 1368

WABC-AM RADIO, INC.—See The Walt Disney Company; *U.S. Public*, pg. 512
WABC T.V.—See The Walt Disney Company; *U.S. Public*, pg. 512
WABCO-FREIGHT CAR—See Westinghouse Air Brake Company; *U.S. Public*, pg. 1761
WABCO-LOCOMOTIVE—See Westinghouse Air Brake Company; *U.S. Public*, pg. 1761
WABCO-PASSENGER TRANSIT—See Westinghouse Air Brake Company; *U.S. Public*, pg. 1761
WAG SALZGITTER WOHNUNGS-GMBH—See Preussag AG; *Int'l*, pg. 1070
WALA-TV—See USA Networks, Inc.; *U.S. Public*, pg. 1685
WALB-TV, INC., CHANNEL 10—See Gray Communications Systems, Inc.; *U.S. Public*, pg. 759
WAMZ-FM—See Clear Channel Communications, Inc.; *U.S. Public*, pg. 384
WAND TELEVISION, INC.—See AT&T Corporation; *U.S. Public*, pg. 11
WAPSA AUTO-PECAS LIMITADA—See Robert Bosch GmbH; *Int'l*, pg. 206
WARQ—See Clear Channel Communications, Inc.; *U.S. Public*, pg. 384
WAVE-TV—See Liberty Corporation; *U.S. Public*, pg. 992
WAVY-TELEVISION, INC.—See AT&T Corporation; *U.S. Public*, pg. 11
WAVZ-AM—See Clear Channel Communications, Inc.; *U.S. Public*, pg. 384
WAWS-TV—See Clear Channel Communications, Inc.; *U.S. Public*, pg. 384
WAXY (FM)—See Jefferson-Pilot Corporation; *U.S. Public*, pg. 925
W.B. HOMES, INC.—See Lennar Corporation; *U.S. Public*, pg. 989
WBAL-AM—See The Hearst Corporation; *U.S. Private*, pg. 516
WBAL DIVISION—See The Hearst Corporation; *U.S. Private*, pg. 516
WBAL-TV—See The Hearst Corporation; *U.S. Private*, pg. 516
WBAP-KSCS RADIO, INC.—See The Walt Disney Company; *U.S. Public*, pg. 512
WBB DEVON CLAYS LTD.—See Watts Blake Bearne & Co. Plc; *Int'l*, pg. 1487
WBB PACIFIC CLAYS LTD.—See Watts Blake Bearne & Co. Plc; *Int'l*, pg. 1488
WBB TECHNOLOGY LTD.—See Watts Blake Bearne & Co. Plc; *Int'l*, pg. 1487
WBBB—See Curtis Media Group; *U.S. Private*, pg. 297
WBBM-TV—See CBS Corporation; *U.S. Public*, pg. 275
WBCT-FM—See Clear Channel Communications, Inc.; *U.S. Public*, pg. 384
WBF TECHNOLOGIES—See Bertrand Faure; *Int'l*, pg. 193
WBGG-FM—See Clear Channel Communications, Inc.; *U.S. Public*, pg. 384
WBG-WOHNEN, GRUND, GESELLSCHAFT FUR WOHN-UND GEWERBEIMMOBILIEN MBH—See Viag AG; *Int'l*, pg. 1466
WBIR, INC.—See Gannett Company, Inc.; *U.S. Public*, pg. 702
WBMG-TV—See Media General, Inc.; *U.S. Public*, pg. 1078
WBNS TELEVISION & RADIO—See The Dispatch Printing Company; *U.S. Private*, pg. 335
WBT AM & WBCY FM—See Jefferson-Pilot Corporation; *U.S. Public*, pg. 926
WBTV/WBT-AM & FM—See Jefferson-Pilot Corporation; *U.S. Public*, pg. 926
WBZ RADIO—See CBS Corporation; *U.S. Public*, pg. 275
WCAU-TV—See General Electric Company; *U.S. Public*, pg. 712
WCBS-TV—See CBS Corporation; *U.S. Public*, pg. 275
WCCO-TV—See CBS Corporation; *U.S. Public*, pg. 275
WCI COMMUNITIES, INC.; *U.S. Private*, pg. 1144
WCI INTERNATIONAL COMPANY—See Electrolux, AB; *Int'l*, pg. 440
WCI MACHINE TOOLS—See Electrolux, AB; *Int'l*, pg. 440
WCI UMWELTTECHNIK GMBH FRANKFURT—See URS Corporation; *U.S. Public*, pg. 1657
WCI MACHINE TOOLS & SYSTEMS—See Electrolux, AB; *Int'l*, pg. 440
WCIV, LLC—See Perpetual Corporation; *U.S. Private*, pg. 854
WCKG, INC.—See CBS Corporation; *U.S. Public*, pg. 274
WCKT—See Clear Channel Communications, Inc.; *U.S. Public*, pg. 384
WCL RAILCARS, INC.—See Wisconsin Central Transportation Corporation; *U.S. Public*, pg. 1773
WCM CO.—See NCH Corporation; *U.S. Public*, pg. 1145
WCO PORT PROPERTIES, INC.—See The Walt Disney Company; *U.S. Public*, pg. 514
WCPO-TV—See The E.W. Scripps Company; *U.S. Public*, pg. 1448
WCPS—See Curtis Media Group; *U.S. Private*, pg. 297
WCRS—See Havas Advertising; *Int'l*, pg. 603
WCSC-TV—See Jefferson-Pilot Corporation; *U.S. Public*, pg. 926
WCVB DIVISION—See The Hearst Corporation; *U.S. Private*, pg. 516
WCVB-TV—See The Hearst Corporation; *U.S. Private*, pg. 516
WD-40 COMPANY; *U.S. Public*, pg. 1726
WD-40 COMPANY (AUSTRALIA)—See WD-40 Company; *U.S. Public*, pg. 1726
WD-40 COMPANY LTD.—See WD-40 Company; *U.S. Public*, pg. 1726
WD-40 PRODUCTS (CANADA) LTD.—See WD-40 Company; *U.S. Public*, pg. 1726
WDEF AM/FM—See Media General, Inc.; *U.S. Public*, pg. 1078
WDEF-TV—See Media General, Inc.; *U.S. Public*, pg. 1078
WDIA-AM—See Clear Channel Communications, Inc.; *U.S. Public*, pg. 384

WDIO-TV—See Hubbard Broadcasting, Inc.; *U.S. Private*, pg. 544

WDIV-TV—See The Washington Post Company; *U.S. Public*, pg. 1743

WDK, INC.—See Lindal Cedar Homes, Inc.; *U.S. Public*, pg. 999

WDS LIMITED—See Ascot Holdings Plc; *Int'l*, pg. 88

WDSU TELEVISION, INC.—See Pulitzer Publishing Company; *U.S. Public*, pg. 1344

WDTN-TV—See The Hearst Corporation; *U.S. Private*, pg. 516

WDZL CHANNEL 39—See Tribune Company; *U.S. Public*, pg. 1636

WEA CORP.—See Time Warner Inc.; *U.S. Public*, pg. 1612

WEA INTL., INC.—See Time Warner Inc.; *U.S. Public*, pg. 1612

WEA MANUFACTURING—See Time Warner Inc.; *U.S. Public*, pg. 1612

WEBN-FM—See Jacor Communications, Inc.; *U.S. Public*, pg. 922

WEFA, INC.—See Primark Corporation; *U.S. Public*, pg. 1325

WEGR—See Clear Channel Communications, Inc.; *U.S. Public*, pg. 384

WELI-AM—See Clear Channel Communications, Inc.; *U.S. Public*, pg. 384

WEN PRODUCTS, INC.; *U.S. Private*, pg. 1144

WENZ-FM—See Clear Channel Communications, Inc.; *U.S. Public*, pg. 385

WERE—See Clear Channel Communications, Inc.; *U.S. Public*, pg. 385

WESH TELEVISION, INC.—See Pulitzer Publishing Company; *U.S. Public*, pg. 1344

WEWS-TV—See The E.W. Scripps Company; *U.S. Public*, pg. 1448

WEYI, INC.—See FTSB Broadcasting; *U.S. Private*, pg. 389

WF CORROON-ALBERTA—See Willis Corroon Group PLC; *Int'l*, pg. 1502

WF CORROON-BELFAST—See Willis Corroon Group PLC; *Int'l*, pg. 1501

WF CORROON-BIRMINGHAM—See Willis Corroon Group PLC; *Int'l*, pg. 1501

WF CORROON-BRISTOL—See Willis Corroon Group PLC; *Int'l*, pg. 1501

WF CORROON CANADA INC.—See Willis Corroon Group PLC; *Int'l*, pg. 1502

WF CORROON-CARDIFF—See Willis Corroon Group PLC; *Int'l*, pg. 1501

WF CORROON-EUROPE—See Willis Corroon Group PLC; *Int'l*, pg. 1502

WF CORROON-FRANCE—See Willis Corroon Group PLC; *Int'l*, pg. 1502

WF CORROON-GLASGOW—See Willis Corroon Group PLC; *Int'l*, pg. 1501

WF CORROON-GLOBAL SUPPORT UNIT—See Willis Corroon Group PLC; *Int'l*, pg. 1502

WF CORROON-HEMEL HEMPSTEAD—See Willis Corroon Group PLC; *Int'l*, pg. 1501

WF CORROON-IPSWICH—See Willis Corroon Group PLC; *Int'l*, pg. 1501

WF CORROON-KINGSTON—See Willis Corroon Group PLC; *Int'l*, pg. 1502

WF CORROON-LONDON—See Willis Corroon Group PLC; *Int'l*, pg. 1502

WF CORROON-MANCHESTER—See Willis Corroon Group PLC; *Int'l*, pg. 1502

WF CORROON-ONTARIO—See Willis Corroon Group PLC; *Int'l*, pg. 1502

WF CORROON (PRIVATE) LIMITED—See Willis Corroon Group PLC; *Int'l*, pg. 1502

WF CORROON-READING—See Willis Corroon Group PLC; *Int'l*, pg. 1502

WF CORROON-THATCHAM—See Willis Corroon Group PLC; *Int'l*, pg. 1502

WF CORROON-UNITED KINGDOM & INTERNATIONAL—See Willis Corroon Group PLC; *Int'l*, pg. 1501

WF CORROON-VANCOUVER—See Willis Corroon Group PLC; *Int'l*, pg. 1502

WFAA-TV—See A.H. Belo Corporation; *U.S. Public*, pg. 209

WFI INTERNATIONAL, INC.; *U.S. Private*, pg. 1144

WFIE-TV—See Liberty Corporation; *U.S. Public*, pg. 992

WFLA-AM—See Jacor Communications, Inc.; *U.S. Public*, pg. 922

WFLD INC.—See The News Corporation Limited; *Int'l*, pg. 926

WFLZ-FM—See Jacor Communications, Inc.; *U.S. Public*, pg. 922

WFMY-TV—See Gannett Company, Inc.; *U.S. Public*, pg. 702

WFOR-TV CHANNEL 4—See CBS Corporation; *U.S. Public*, *pg. 275*

WFRV-TV—See CBS Corporation; *U.S. Public*, pg. 275

WFS CLEARING SERVICES—See First Union Corporation; *U.S. Public*, pg. 640

WFS FINANCIAL, INC.—See Westcorp; *U.S. Public*, pg. 1757

WFSB-TV—See The Washington Post Company; *U.S. Public*, pg. 1743

WFTC-TV—See Clear Channel Communications, Inc.; *U.S. Public*, pg. 385

WFTS-TV—See The E.W. Scripps Company; *U.S. Public*, pg. 1448

WFTV, INC.—See Cox Enterprises, Inc.; *U.S. Private*, pg. 282

WFXT-TV—See The News Corporation Limited; *Int'l*, pg. 926

WGAL-TV—See Pulitzer Publishing Company; *U.S. Public*, pg. 1344

WGBR—See Curtis Media Group; *U.S. Private*, pg. 297

W.G.C. CORP.—See Zimmerman Holdings, Inc.; *U.S. Private*, pg. 1206

WGCI-AM/FM—See Chancellor Media Corporation; *U.S. Public*, pg. 335

WGGB-TV—See Guy Gannett Communications; *U.S. Private*, pg. 439

WGM SAFETY CORPORATION—See Essilor International Compagnie Generale d'Optique; *Int'l*, pg. 462

WGME-TV—See Guy Gannett Communications; *U.S. Private*, pg. 439

WGN RADIO—See Tribune Company; *U.S. Public*, pg. 1636

WGN-TV—See Tribune Company; *U.S. Public*, pg. 1636

WGNO, INC.—See Tribune Company; *U.S. Public*, pg. 1636

WGNX, INC.—See Tribune Company; *U.S. Public*, pg. 1636

WGRV—See The News Corporation Limited; *Int'l*, pg. 926

WGST-AM—See Jacor Communications, Inc.; *U.S. Public*, pg. 923

WHAS-AM—See Clear Channel Communications, Inc.; *U.S. Public*, pg. 385

WHBF—See Lynch Corporation; *U.S. Public*, pg. 1021

WHG RESORTS & CASINOS—See Patriot American Hospitality, Inc.; *U.S. Public*, pg. 1265

WHEC-TV—See Hubbard Broadcasting, Inc.; *U.S. Private*, pg. 544

WHIO, INC.—See Cox Enterprises, Inc.; *U.S. Private*, pg. 282

WHKW-FM—See Clear Channel Communications, Inc.; *U.S. Public*, pg. 385

WHLT—See Media General, Inc.; *U.S. Public*, pg. 1078

WHNT-TV—See The New York Times Company; *U.S. Public*, pg. 1174

WHO-TV—See The New York Times Company; *U.S. Public*, pg. 1174

WHP-TV—See Clear Channel Communications, Inc.; *U.S. Public*, pg. 385

WHS—See Staveley Industries PLC; *Int'l*, pg. 1299

WHX CORPORATION; *U.S. Public*, pg. 1726

WHX ENTERTAINMENT CORPORATION—See WHX Corporation; *U.S. Public*, pg. 1726

WHYI-FM—See Clear Channel Communications, Inc.; *U.S. Public*, pg. 385

WHYN—See Clear Channel Communications, Inc.; *U.S. Public*, pg. 385

WIC ENTERTAINMENT LTD.—See WIC Western International Communications Ltd.; *Int'l*, pg. 1482

WIC RADIO LTD.—See WIC Western International Communications Ltd.; *Int'l*, pg. 1482

WIC TELEVISION LTD.—See WIC Western International Communications Ltd.; *Int'l*, pg. 1482

WIC WESTERN INTERNATIONAL COMMUNICATIONS LTD.; *Int'l*, pg. 1481

WICD-TV—See Guy Gannett Communications; *U.S. Private*, pg. 439

WICO; *U.S. Private*, pg. 1144

WICS-TV—See Guy Gannett Communications; *U.S. Private*, pg. 439

WIL RESEARCH LABORATORIES, INC.—See Great Lakes Chemical Corporation; *U.S. Public*, pg. 760

W.I.N. SYSTEMS, INC.—See Automobile Protection Corporation-APCO; *U.S. Public*, pg. 150

WINS RADIO—See CBS Corporation; *U.S. Public*, pg. 274

WIOD, INC.—See Clear Channel Communications, Inc.; *U.S. Public*, pg. 385

WIS-TV—See Liberty Corporation; *U.S. Public*, pg. 992

WISN-AM—See SFX Broadcasting Incorporated; *U.S. Public*, pg. 1418

WISN DIVISION—See The Hearst Corporation; *U.S. Private*, pg. 516

WISN-TV—See The Hearst Corporation; *U.S. Private*, pg. 516

WIXT-TV—See The Ackerley Group; *U.S. Public*, pg. 16

WIYI-FM—See The Hearst Corporation; *U.S. Private*, pg. 516

W.J. & DENNIS CO.; *U.S. Private*, pg. 1144

WJCD-FM—See Clear Channel Communications, Inc.; *U.S. Public*, pg. 385

WJHG-TV, INC., CHANNEL 7—See Gray Communications Systems, Inc.; *U.S. Public*, pg. 759

WJHL-TV—See Media General, Inc.; *U.S. Public*, pg. 1078

WJLA-TV—See Perpetual Corporation; *U.S. Private*, pg. 854

WJR-AM—See The Walt Disney Company; *U.S. Public*, pg. 512

WJRT-TV—See Lee Enterprises, Incorporated; *U.S. Public*, pg. 984

WJTV—See Media General, Inc.; *U.S. Public*, pg. 1078

WJW CONSTRUCTORS, LLC—See Joe E. Woods, Inc.; *U.S. Private*, pg. 1187

WJXT-TV—See The Washington Post Company; *U.S. Public*, pg. 1743

WJZ-TV—See CBS Corporation; *U.S. Public*, pg. 275

WK MFG. COMPANY—See K-D Lamp Company; *U.S. Private*, pg. 603

WKCI-FM—See Clear Channel Communications, Inc.; *U.S. Public*, pg. 385

WKHX-AM/WKHX-FM—See The Walt Disney Company; *U.S. Public*, pg. 512

WKJK-AM—See Clear Channel Communications, Inc.; *U.S. Public*, pg. 385

WKKV-FM—See Clear Channel Communications, Inc.; *U.S. Public*, pg. 385

WKTC—See Curtis Media Group; *U.S. Private*, pg. 297

WKY-AM—See Clear Channel Communications, Inc.; *U.S. Public*, pg. 385

WKYC-TV—See Gannett Company, Inc.; *U.S. Public*, pg. 702

WKYT-TV—See Gray Communications Systems, Inc.; *U.S. Public*, pg. 759

WLFF SA—See Accor S.A.; *Int'l*, pg. 21

WLFI-TV—See Blade Communications, Inc.; *U.S. Private*, pg. 148

WLIT-FM—See National Amusements, Inc.; *U.S. Private*, pg. 779

WLKY-AM—See Pulitzer Publishing Company; *U.S. Public*, pg. 1344

WLKY-TV—See Pulitzer Publishing Company; *U.S. Public*, pg. 1344

WLP LEASING CO.—See Wendy's International Inc.; *U.S. Public*, pg. 1754

WLP WILHELM-LEUSCHNER-PLATZ BETEILIGUNGS-GMBH—See Commerzbank AG; *Int'l*, pg. 310

WLR FOODS, INC.; *U.S. Public*, pg. 1727

WLS-AM HOLDING COMPANY, INC.—See The Walt Disney Company; *U.S. Public*, pg. 512

WLS-FM RADIO, INC.—See The Walt Disney Company; *U.S. Public*, pg. 512

WLS, INC.—See The Walt Disney Company; *U.S. Public*, pg. 512

WLS TELEVISION, INC.—See The Walt Disney Company; *U.S. Public*, pg. 512

WLT TRAVEL UK LTD—See Accor S.A.; *Int'l*, pg. 22

WLTI-FM—See National Amusements, Inc.; *U.S. Private*, pg. 779

WLTQ-FM—See SFX Broadcasting Incorporated; *U.S. Public*, pg. 1418

WLTW-FM—See National Amusements, Inc.; *U.S. Private*, pg. 779

WLUK-TV—See USA Networks, Inc.; *U.S. Public*, pg. 699

WLVI-TV—See Tribune Company; *U.S. Public*, pg. 1636

WLW-AM—See Jacor Communications, Inc.; *U.S. Public*, pg. 922

WM FINANCIAL, INC.—See Washington Mutual Inc.; *U.S. Public*, pg. 1742

WM LIFE INSURANCE COMPANY—See Washington Mutual Inc.; *U.S. Public*, pg. 1742

WM TRUST COMPANY—See Washington Mutual Inc.; *U.S. Public*, pg. 1742

WM WIRTSCHAFTS-MEDIEN AG—See Georg von Holtzbrinck GmbH; *Int'l*, pg. 480

WMAL, INC.—See The Walt Disney Company; *U.S. Public*, pg. 512

WMAR-TV—See The E.W. Scripps Company; *U.S. Public*, pg. 1448

WMAZ-WAYS RADIO—See Gannett Company, Inc.; *U.S. Public*, pg. 702

WMB DUROLINK (ZIMBABWE) (PVT.) LIMITED—See Westdeutsche Landesbank Girozentrale; *Int'l*, pg. 1493

WMC INTERNATIONAL LTD.—See Western Mining Corporation Holdings Limited; *Int'l*, pg. 1494

WMF/USA; *U.S. Private*, pg. 1144

WMRZ-WLYF-WMXJ—See Jefferson-Pilot Corporation; *U.S. Public*, pg. 926

WMS GAMES INC.—See WMS Industries Inc.; *U.S. Public*, pg. 1727

WMS GAMING INC.—See WMS Industries Inc.; *U.S. Public*, pg. 1727

WMS INDUSTRIES INC.; *U.S. Public*, pg. 1727

WMTX-AM—See Clear Channel Communications, Inc.; *U.S. Public*, pg. 385

WMTX-FM—See Clear Channel Communications, Inc.; *U.S. Public*, pg. 385

WMYK-FM—See Clear Channel Communications, Inc.; *U.S. Public*, pg. 385

WMYU-FM—See Jacor Communications, Inc.; *U.S. Public*, pg. 923

WMZQ-AM/FM—See National Amusements, Inc.; *U.S. Private*, pg. 779

W.N. BEST—See Preferred Utilities Manufacturing Corp.; *U.S. Private*, pg. 881

WNAC—See The News Corporation Limited; *Int'l*, pg. 926

WNCT-TV—See Media General, Inc.; *U.S. Public*, pg. 1078

WNCX—See Clear Channel Communications, Inc.; *U.S. Public*, pg. 385

WNEM-TV—See Meredith Corporation; *U.S. Public*, pg. 1094

WNEP-TV—See The New York Times Company; *U.S. Public*, pg. 1174

WNOE—See Clear Channel Communications, Inc.; *U.S. Public*, pg. 385

WNWS (AM) & WLYF (FM)—See Jefferson-Pilot Corporation; *U.S. Public*, pg. 926

WNY GROUP; *U.S. Private*, pg. 1144

WNYT-TV—See Hubbard Broadcasting, Inc.; *U.S. Private*, pg. 544

WNYW—See The News Corporation Limited; *Int'l*, pg. 926

WOAI-AM—See Clear Channel Communications, Inc.; *U.S. Public*, pg. 385

WOB MARKETINGKOMMUNIKATION AG; *Int'l*, pg. 1482

WOC INC.—See Waxman Industries, Inc.; *U.S. Public*, pg. 1748

WODT-AM—See Clear Channel Communications, Inc.; *U.S. Public*, pg. 385

WOFL-TV—See Meredith Corporation; *U.S. Public*, pg. 1094

WOKR-TV—See Guy Gannett Communications; *U.S. Private*, pg. 439

WOOD-AM/FM—See Clear Channel Communications, Inc.; *U.S. Public*, pg. 385

WOW—See FCAIBMZ; *Int'l*, pg. 470

WOWI-FM—See Clear Channel Communications, Inc.; *U.S. Public*, pg. 385

WP COAL COMPANY—See WHX Corporation; *U.S. Public*, pg. 1726

WP STEEL VENTURE COMPANY—See WHX Corporation; *U.S. Public*, pg. 1726

WPC LAND COMPANY—See WHX Corporation; *U.S. Public*, pg. 1726

WPCH-FM—See Jacor Communications, Inc.; *U.S. Public*, pg. 923

WPCM—See Curtis Media Group; *U.S. Private*, pg. 298

WPHL-TV, INC.—See Tribune Company; *U.S. Public*, pg. 1636

WPI TRANSPORTATION, INC.—See American Ecology Corporation; *U.S. Public*, pg. 71

WPI WASTE CARRIERS, INC.—See American Ecology Corporation; *U.S. Public*, pg. 71

WPIX, INC.—See Tribune Company; *U.S. Public*, pg. 1636

WPL HOLDINGS, INC.; *U.S. Public*, pg. 1727

WPLG-TV—See The Washington Post Company; *U.S. Public*, pg. 1743

WPLJ-FM RADIO, INC.—See The Walt Disney Company; *U.S. Public*, pg. 512

WPLT-FM—See The Walt Disney Company; *U.S. Public*, pg. 512
WPMI-TV—See Clear Channel Communications, Inc.; *U.S. Public*, pg. 385
WPMT CHANNEL 43—See Tribune Company; *U.S. Public*, pg. 1636
WPP GROUP PLC; *Int'l*, pg. 1482
WPP GROUP USA INC.—See WPP Group plc; *Int'l*, pg. 1483
WPRI-TV—See Clear Channel Communications, Inc.; *U.S. Public*, pg. 385
WPS ENERGY SERVICES, INC.—See WPS Resources Corp.; *U.S. Public*, pg. 1728
WPS LEASING, INC.—See WPS Resources Corp.; *U.S. Public*, pg. 1728
WPS POWER DEVELOPMENT, INC.—See WPS Resources Corp.; *U.S. Public*, pg. 1728
WPS RESOURCES CORP.; *U.S. Public*, pg. 1728
WPT, INC.; *U.S. Private*, pg. 1144
WPTF—See Curtis Media Group; *U.S. Private*, pg. 298
WPTV—See The E.W. Scripps Company; *U.S. Public*, pg. 1448
WPTY-TV—See Clear Channel Communications, Inc.; *U.S. Public*, pg. 385
WPVI-TV—See The Walt Disney Company; *U.S. Public*, pg. 512
WPXI INC.—See Cox Enterprises, Inc.; *U.S. Private*, pg. 282
WQAD-TV—See The New York Times Company; *U.S. Public*, pg. 1174
WQDR—See Curtis Media Group; *U.S. Private*, pg. 298
WQIK-AM—See Jacor Communications, Inc.; *U.S. Public*, pg. 923
WQIK-FM—See Jacor Communications, Inc.; *U.S. Public*, pg. 923
WQQK-FM—See Clear Channel Communications, Inc.; *U.S. Public*, pg. 385
WQUE-FM—See Clear Channel Communications, Inc.; *U.S. Public*, pg. 385
WQXI-WSTR—See Jefferson-Pilot Corporation; *U.S. Public*, pg. 926
WQXR/FM, WQEW/AM—See The New York Times Company; *U.S. Public*, pg. 1174
WRAL-TV—See Capitol Broadcasting Co., Inc.; *U.S. Private*, pg. 206
WRAW-AM—See Clear Channel Communications, Inc.; *U.S. Public*, pg. 385
WRBQ-AM—See Clear Channel Communications, Inc.; *U.S. Public*, pg. 385
WRBQ-FM—See Clear Channel Communications, Inc.; *U.S. Public*, pg. 385
W.R.C. TECHNICAL VENTURES—See W.R. Grace & Co.; *U.S. Public*, pg. 755
WREC—See Clear Channel Communications, Inc.; *U.S. Public*, pg. 385
WREG-TV—See The New York Times Company; *U.S. Public*, pg. 1174
WRFY-FM—See Clear Channel Communications, Inc.; *U.S. Public*, pg. 385
WRGB-TV—See Freedom Communication Inc.; *U.S. Private*, pg. 425
WRH WALTER REIST HOLDING AG; *Int'l*, pg. 1484
WRM, INCOPATED; *U.S. Private*, pg. 1144
WRNL-FM—See Clear Channel Communications, Inc.; *U.S. Public*, pg. 385
WROC, INC.—See FTSB Broadcasting; *U.S. Private*, pg. 389
WRQ, INC.; *U.S. Private*, pg. 1145
WRQX-FM—See The Walt Disney Company; *U.S. Public*, pg. 512
WRR ENVIRONMENTAL SERVICES CO., INC.—See The Ziegler Companies, Inc.; *U.S. Public*, pg. 1792
WRTV—See The McGraw-Hill Companies; *U.S. Public*, pg. 1070
WRVA-AM—See Clear Channel Communications, Inc.; *U.S. Public*, pg. 385
WRVQ-FM—See Clear Channel Communications, Inc.; *U.S. Public*, pg. 385
WRXL-FM—See Clear Channel Communications, Inc.; *U.S. Public*, pg. 385
WRXQ—See Clear Channel Communications, Inc.; *U.S. Public*, pg. 385
WS PUBLISHING COMPANY, INC.—See International Data Group; *U.S. Private*, pg. 570
WSA SYSTEMS & SERVICES, INC.—See Data General Corporation; *U.S. Public*, pg. 485
WSAZ-TV—See Lee Enterprises, Incorporated; *U.S. Public*, pg. 984
WSB, INC.—See Cox Enterprises, Inc.; *U.S. Private*, pg. 282
WSBA AM/FM—See The Pfaltzgraff Co.; *U.S. Private*, pg. 860
WSET INCORPORATD—See Perpetual Corporation; *U.S. Private*, pg. 854
WSFA-TV—See Liberty Corporation; *U.S. Public*, pg. 992
WSFS CREDIT CORP.—See WSFS Financial Corporation; *U.S. Public*, pg. 1729
WSFS FINANCIAL CORPORATION; *U.S. Public*, pg. 1728
WSI CORPORATION—See Primark Corporation; *U.S. Public*, pg. 1325
WSJS—See Clear Channel Communications, Inc.; *U.S. Public*, pg. 385
WSLS-TV—See Media General, Inc.; *U.S. Public*, pg. 1078
WSMP, INC.; *U.S. Public*, pg. 1729
WSOC TELEVISION, INC.—See Cox Enterprises, Inc.; *U.S. Private*, pg. 282
WSP—See Worthington Industries, Inc.; *U.S. Public*, pg. 1780
WSVY-FM—See Clear Channel Communications, Inc.; *U.S. Public*, pg. 385
WSYM-TV—See Journal Communications Inc.; *U.S. Private*, pg. 601
WTAE-AM—See SFX Broadcasting Incorporated; *U.S. Public*, pg. 1418

WTAE DIVISION—See The Hearst Corporation; *U.S. Private*, pg. 516
WTAE-TV—See The Hearst Corporation; *U.S. Private*, pg. 516
WTC INSURANCE CORP., LTD.—See International Business Machines Corporation; *U.S. Private*, pg. 898
WTD INDUSTRIES, INC.; *U.S. Public*, pg. 1729
WTIC—See Tribune Company; *U.S. Public*, pg. 1636
WTKR-TV—See The New York Times Company; *U.S. Public*, pg. 1174
WTLV-TV—See Gannett Company, Inc.; *U.S. Public*, pg. 702
WTOL-TV—See Liberty Corporation; *U.S. Public*, pg. 992
WTOV, INC.—See FTSB Broadcasting; *U.S. Private*, pg. 390
WTQR—See Clear Channel Communications, Inc.; *U.S. Public*, pg. 385
WTTG—See The News Corporation Limited; *Int'l*, pg. 926
WTTW (CHANNEL 11); *U.S. Private*, pg. 1145
WTVD-TV—See The Walt Disney Company; *U.S. Public*, pg. 512
WTVF—See Landmark Communications, Inc.; *U.S. Private*, pg. 647
WTVQ-TV (ABC) CHANNEL 36—See Media General, Inc.; *U.S. Public*, pg. 1078
WTVR-AM/FM—See Clear Channel Communications, Inc.; *U.S. Public*, pg. 385
WTWC-TV—See Guy Gannett Communications; *U.S. Private*, pg. 439
W.U.G. WOHN- UND GEWERBEBAU BETEILIGUNGS GMBH—See Bayerische Vereinsbank Group; *Int'l*, pg. 179
W.U.G. WOHN- UND GEWERBEBAU GMBH & CO. IMMOBILIEN KG—See Bayerische Vereinsbank Group; *Int'l*, pg. 179
WUSA-TV—See Gannett Company, Inc.; *U.S. Public*, pg. 702
WUTR-TV—See Media General, Inc.; *U.S. Public*, pg. 1078
WVEC-TV, INC.—See A.H. Belo Corporation; *U.S. Public*, pg. 209
WVEE-FM—See Granum Communications; *U.S. Private*, pg. 470
WVTM-TV, INC.—See General Electric Company; *U.S. Public*, pg. 712
WVTY-FM—See SFX Broadcasting Incorporated; *U.S. Public*, pg. 1418
WVUE-TV—See USA Networks, Inc.; *U.S. Public*, pg. 1685
WWB WASSERWERKS-BETEILIGUNGS GMBH—See Veba AG; *Int'l*, pg. 1456
WWBB—See Clear Channel Communications, Inc.; *U.S. Public*, pg. 385
WWBT-TV—See Jefferson-Pilot Corporation; *U.S. Public*, pg. 926
WWDM—See Clear Channel Communications, Inc.; *U.S. Public*, pg. 385
WWF-CANADA, INC.—See WWF Paper Corporation; *U.S. Private*, pg. 1145
WWF DE MEXICO, S.A. DE C.V.—See WWF Paper Corporation; *U.S. Private*, pg. 1145
WWF NATIONAL—See WWF Paper Corporation; *U.S. Private*, pg. 1145
WWF PAPER CORP.-NEW YORK—See WWF Paper Corporation; *U.S. Private*, pg. 1145
WWF PAPER CORPORATION; *U.S. Private*, pg. 1145
WWF PAPER CORPORATION - INTERNATIONAL—See WWF Paper Corporation; *U.S. Private*, pg. 1145
WWF PAPER CORPORATION - MID ATLANTIC—See WWF Paper Corporation; *U.S. Private*, pg. 1145
WWF PAPER CORPORATION - MIDWEST—See WWF Paper Corporation; *U.S. Private*, pg. 1145
WWF PAPER SALES U.K., LTD.—See WWF Paper Corporation; *U.S. Private*, pg. 1145
WWRM, INC.—See Cox Enterprises, Inc.; *U.S. Private*, pg. 282
WWRX—See Clear Channel Communications, Inc.; *U.S. Public*, pg. 385
WWT PARTNERSHIP—See Time Warner Inc.; *U.S. Public*, pg. 1614
WWT (WYTWORNIA WYROBOW TYTONIOWYCH) S.A.—See Reemtsma Cigarettenfabriken GmbH, Hamburg; *Int'l*, pg. 1101
WWW RETAIL, INC.—See Wolverine World Wide, Inc.; *U.S. Public*, pg. 1775
WWWB-TV—See The Hearst Corporation; *U.S. Private*, pg. 516
WXIA-TV—See Gannett Company, Inc.; *U.S. Public*, pg. 702
WXII-AM—See Pulitzer Publishing Company; *U.S. Public*, pg. 1344
WXII-TV—See Pulitzer Publishing Company; *U.S. Public*, pg. 1344
WXIN—See Tribune Company; *U.S. Public*, pg. 1636
WXRA—See Clear Channel Communications, Inc.; *U.S. Public*, pg. 385
WXRM—See Clear Channel Communications, Inc.; *U.S. Public*, pg. 385
WXXA-TV—See Clear Channel Communications, Inc.; *U.S. Public*, pg. 385
WXYZ TV - CHANNEL 7 OF DETROIT, INC.—See The E.W. Scripps Company; *U.S. Public*, pg. 1448
WYFF-TV—See Pulitzer Publishing Company; *U.S. Public*, pg. 1344
WYLD-AM/FM—See Clear Channel Communications, Inc.; *U.S. Public*, pg. 386
WYMT-TV—See Gray Communications Systems, Inc.; *U.S. Public*, pg. 759
WYO L.P. GAS—See Energy West Inc.; *U.S. Public*, pg. 581
WZZM—See The News Corporation Limited; *Int'l*, pg. 926
WA PEI FINANCE CO. LTD.—See Generale de Banque S.A.; *Int'l*, pg. 548
WABAG LEIPZIG GMBH WASSERTECHNISCHE ANLAGEN—See Deutsche Babcock AG; *Int'l*, pg. 399

WABAG WASSERTECHNISCHE ANLAGEN GMBH & CO. KG—See Deutsche Babcock AG; *Int'l*, pg. 399
WABASH ALLOYS DIVISION—See Connell Limited Partnership; *U.S. Private*, pg. 264
WABASH FIBRE BOX CO.—See Weston Paper & Manufacturing Co.; *U.S. Private*, pg. 1170
WABASH FIBRE BOX CO.-COLUMBIA—See Weston Paper & Manufacturing Co.; *U.S. Private*, pg. 1170
WABASH FIBRE BOX CO.-JACKSON—See Weston Paper & Manufacturing Co.; *U.S. Private*, pg. 1170
WABASH FIBRE BOX COMPANY—See Weston Paper & Manufacturing Co.; *U.S. Private*, pg. 1170
WABASH FIBRE BOX COMPANY-CHICAGO PLANT—See Weston Paper & Manufacturing Co.; *U.S. Private*, pg. 1170
WABASH FIBRE BOX COMPANY-FORT WAYNE PLANT—See Weston Paper & Manufacturing Co.; *U.S. Private*, pg. 1170
WABASH FIBRE BOX COMPANY-LEXINGTON PLANT—See Weston Paper & Manufacturing Co.; *U.S. Private*, pg. 1170
WABASH FIBRE BOX COMPANY-TERRE HAUTE PLANT—See Weston Paper & Manufacturing Co.; *U.S. Private*, pg. 1170
WABASH MAGNETICS—See The Dyson-Kissner-Moran Corporation; *U.S. Private*, pg. 351
WABASH NATIONAL CORP.; *U.S. Public*, pg. 1730
WABASH NATIONAL FINANCE CORP.—See Wabash National Corp.; *U.S. Public*, pg. 1730
WABASH PIONEER CONTAINER DIVISION—See Weston Paper & Manufacturing Co.; *U.S. Private*, pg. 1170
WABASH VALLEY LANDFILL COMPANY LTD.—See Republic Industries, Inc.; *U.S. Public*, pg. 1380
WABCO AUTOMOTIVE—See American Standard Inc.; *U.S. Public*, pg. 92
WABCO WESTINGHOUSE—See American Standard Inc.; *U.S. Public*, pg. 92
WABCO WESTINGHOUSE FERROVIARIA S.P.A.—See Cardo AB; *Int'l*, pg. 271
WABUSH MINES—See DoFasco, Inc.; *Int'l*, pg. 414
WACCAMAW CORPORATION; *U.S. Private*, pg. 1145
WACHOVIA BANK—See Wachovia Corporation; *U.S. Public*, pg. 1730
WACHOVIA BANK OF GEORGIA, N.A.—See Wachovia Corporation; *U.S. Public*, pg. 1730
WACHOVIA BANK OF NORTH CAROLINA, N.A.—See Wachovia Corporation; *U.S. Public*, pg. 1730
WACHOVIA BANK OF SOUTH CAROLINA, N.A.—See Wachovia Corporation; *U.S. Public*, pg. 1730
WACHOVIA CORPORATE SERVICES, INC.—See Wachovia Corporation; *U.S. Public*, pg. 1730
WACHOVIA CORPORATION; *U.S. Public*, pg. 1730
WACHOVIA INTERNATIONAL BANKING CORP.—See Wachovia Corporation; *U.S. Public*, pg. 1730
WACHOVIA INVESTMENTS, INC.—See Wachovia Corporation; *U.S. Public*, pg. 1730
WACHOVIA LEASING CORPORATION—See Wachovia Corporation; *U.S. Public*, pg. 1731
WACHOVIA MORTGAGE—See Wachovia Corporation; *U.S. Public*, pg. 1731
WACHOVIA MORTGAGE CO.—See Wachovia Corporation; *U.S. Public*, pg. 1731
WACKENHUT AIRLINE SERVICES, INC.—See The Wackenhut Corporation; *U.S. Public*, pg. 1731
WACKENHUT BELIZE, LTD.—See The Wackenhut Corporation; *U.S. Public*, pg. 1731
WACKENHUT CAMEROON—See The Wackenhut Corporation; *U.S. Public*, pg. 1731
WACKENHUT CENTRAL EUROPE GMBH—See The Wackenhut Corporation; *U.S. Public*, pg. 1731
WACKENHUT CHILE, S.A.—See The Wackenhut Corporation; *U.S. Public*, pg. 1731
THE WACKENHUT CORPORATION; *U.S. Public*, pg. 1731
WACKENHUT CORRECTIONS CORPORATION—See The Wackenhut Corporation; *U.S. Public*, pg. 1731
WACKENHUT DE GUATEMALA, S.A.—See The Wackenhut Corporation; *U.S. Public*, pg. 1731
WACKENHUT DE VENEZUELA, S.A.—See The Wackenhut Corporation; *U.S. Public*, pg. 1731
WACKENHUT DEL ECUADOR, S.A.—See The Wackenhut Corporation; *U.S. Public*, pg. 1731
WACKENHUT DOMINICANA, S.A.—See The Wackenhut Corporation; *U.S. Public*, pg. 1731
WACKENHUT EL SALVADOR, S.A.—See The Wackenhut Corporation; *U.S. Public*, pg. 1731
WACKENHUT INTERNATION (PANAMA), S.A.—See The Wackenhut Corporation; *U.S. Public*, pg. 1731
WACKENHUT INTL., INC.—See The Wackenhut Corporation; *U.S. Public*, pg. 1731
WACKENHUT KEIBI K.K.—See The Wackenhut Corporation; *U.S. Public*, pg. 1731
WACKENHUT MOROCCO, INC.—See The Wackenhut Corporation; *U.S. Public*, pg. 1731
WACKENHUT NUCLEAR SERVICES—See The Wackenhut Corporation; *U.S. Public*, pg. 1731
WACKENHUT OF CANADA LTD.—See The Wackenhut Corporation; *U.S. Public*, pg. 1731
WACKENHUT PARAGUAY S.R.L.—See The Wackenhut Corporation; *U.S. Public*, pg. 1732
WACKENHUT RESOURCES, INC.—See The Wackenhut Corporation; *U.S. Public*, pg. 1731
WACKENHUT, S.A.—See The Wackenhut Corporation; *U.S. Public*, pg. 1732
WACKENHUT SECURITY CYPRUS—See The Wackenhut Corporation; *U.S. Public*, pg. 1732
WACKENHUT SECURITY (HELLAS), LTD.—See The Wackenhut Corporation; *U.S. Public*, pg. 1732
WACKENHUT SECURITY (H.K.) LTD.—See The Wackenhut Corporation; *U.S. Public*, pg. 1732
WACKENHUT SERVICES, INC.—See The Wackenhut Corporation; *U.S. Public*, pg. 1732
WACKENHUT THAILAND CO., LTD.—See The Wackenhut Corporation; *U.S. Public*, pg. 1732

WACKENHUT U.K., LTD.—See The Wackenhut Corporation; *U.S. Public*, pg. 1732
WACKER-CHEMIE GMBH—See Hoechst Aktiengesellschaft; *Int'l*, pg. 625
WACKER MEXICANA, S.A. DE C.V.—See Hoechst Aktiengesellschaft; *Int'l*, pg. 625
WACKER SILICONES CORPORATION—See Hoechst Aktiengesellschaft; *Int'l*, pg. 625
WACO CHEMICAL COMPANY—See Thiele Kaolin Co.; *U.S. Private*, pg. 1081
WACO JONSEREDS AB—See Trelleborg AB; *Int'l*, pg. 1421
WACO-LIESBOSCH BETON B.V.—See Ballast Nedam NV; *Int'l*, pg. 134
WACOAL AMERICA INC.—See Wacoal Corporation; *Int'l*, pg. 1484
WACOAL CORPORATION; *Int'l*, pg. 1484
WACOAL FRANCE, S.A.—See Wacoal Corporation; *Int'l*, pg. 1484
WACOAL HONG KONG CO., LTD.—See Wacoal Corporation; *Int'l*, pg. 1484
WACOAL SINGAPORE PTE. LTD.—See Wacoal Corporation; *Int'l*, pg. 1484
WADDELL & REED ASSET MNGMT. CO.—See Torchmark Corporation; *U.S. Public*, pg. 1623
WADDELL & REED, INC.—See Torchmark Corporation; *U.S. Public*, pg. 1623
WADDELL AND REED, INC.—See Torchmark Corporation; *U.S. Public*, pg. 1623
WADDELL & REED INVESTMENT MNGMT. CO.—See Torchmark Corporation; *U.S. Public*, pg. 1623
WADDELL & REED SERVICES CO.—See Torchmark Corporation; *U.S. Public*, pg. 1623
WADDELL DISPLAY CASES DIV. OF GHENT MFG. CO.—See Ghent Manufacturing, Inc.; *U.S. Private*, pg. 450
WADDINGTON & DUVAL (HOLDINGS) LTD.—See BTR plc; *Int'l*, pg. 129
WADE GIN CO.—See Tom Wade Co.; *U.S. Private*, pg. 1146
WADE LAND CO.—See Tom Wade Co.; *U.S. Private*, pg. 1146
TOM WADE CO.; *U.S. Private*, pg. 1145
WADKIN AGENCIES—See Brunel Holdings Plc; *Int'l*, pg. 231
WADKIN PLC—See Brunel Holdings Plc; *Int'l*, pg. 231
WADSWORTH INTERNATIONAL—See The Thomson Corporation; *U.S. Public*, pg. 1600
WADSWORTH PUBLISHING CO.—See The Thomson Corporation; *U.S. Public*, pg. 1600
WAEL PHARMACY—See Hewlett-Packard Company; *U.S. Public*, pg. 823
WAELZLAGER INDUSTRIEWERKE BULLE AG—See NSK Ltd.; *Int'l*, pg. 904
WAESCHLE IDEAL PVT LTD.—See Georg Fischer Ltd.; *Int'l*, pg. 490
WAESCHLE INC.—See Georg Fischer Ltd.; *Int'l*, pg. 490
WAESCHLE MASCHINENFABRIK GMBH—See Georg Fischer Ltd.; *Int'l*, pg. 491
WAESCHLE PTE LTD.—See Georg Fischer Ltd.; *Int'l*, pg. 491
WAFABANK—See Compagnie de Suez; *Int'l*, pg. 314
WAFABANK CASABLANCA—See Compagnie de Suez; *Int'l*, pg. 314
WAFFLE HOUSE, INCORPORATED; *U.S. Private*, pg. 1146
WAGGONBAU BRUNINGHAUS GMBH—See Fried. Krupp AG; *Int'l*, pg. 509
WAGGONFABRIK TALBOT GMBH & CO. KG—See Bombardier Inc.; *Int'l*, pg. 201
WAGNER BRAKE SUBSIDIARY—See Cooper Industries, Inc.; *U.S. Public*, pg. 443
WAGNER CASTERS AND WHEELS—See E.R. Wagner Manufacturing; *U.S. Private*, pg. 1146
WAGNER CASTINGS COMPANY—See Intermet Corporation; *U.S. Public*, pg. 894
E.R. WAGNER MANUFACTURING; *U.S. Private*, pg. 1146
WAGNER FORDERTECHNIK GMBH & CO. KG—See Linde AG; *Int'l*, pg. 811
WAGNER LIGHTING PRODUCTS—See Cooper Industries, Inc.; *U.S. Public*, pg. 442
WAGNER MILLS INC.; *U.S. Private*, pg. 1146
WAGNER SPRAY TECH CORP.; *U.S. Private*, pg. 1146
WAGNER STOTT CLEARING CORP.—See Merrill Lynch & Co., Inc.; *U.S. Public*, pg. 1097
WAGNERWARE CORPORATION; *U.S. Private*, pg. 1146
WAGO & CONTROLS (INDIA) LTD.—See Bowthorpe plc; *Int'l*, pg. 209
WAGO COMPANY OF JAPAN LIMITED—See Bowthorpe plc; *Int'l*, pg. 209
WAGO CONTACT I.GR—See Bowthorpe plc; *Int'l*, pg. 209
WAGO CONTACT SA—See Bowthorpe plc; *Int'l*, pg. 209
WAGO CONTACT SARL—See Bowthorpe plc; *Int'l*, pg. 209
WAGO CORPORATION—See Bowthorpe plc; *Int'l*, pg. 209
WAGO KONTAKTTECHNIK GES MBH—See Bowthorpe plc; *Int'l*, pg. 209
WAGO KONTAKTTECHNIK GMBH—See Bowthorpe plc; *Int'l*, pg. 209
WAGO LIMITED—See Bowthorpe plc; *Int'l*, pg. 209
WAGOFI SA—See Accor S.A.; *Int'l*, pg. 22
WAGON INDUSTRIAL HOLDINGS PLC; *Int'l*, pg. 1484
WAGONS-LITS TOURISME SA—See Accor S.A.; *Int'l*, pg. 22
WAGSTAFF INC.; *U.S. Private*, pg. 1146
WAH CHANG—See Allegheny Teledyne Incorporated; *U.S. Public*, pg. 44
WAH KONG PECISION (JIANGMEN) LTD.—See Citizen Watch Company, Ltd.; *Int'l*, pg. 295
WAHEDNA/DMB&B—See DMB&B Communications; *U.S. Private*, pg. 305
WAHKIAKUM GAS CORPORATION—See Boise Cascade Corporation; *U.S. Public*, pg. 243
WAHL CLIPPER CORP.; *U.S. Private*, pg. 1146
WAHLSTROM & COMPANY—See True North Communications Inc.; *U.S. Public*, pg. 1641

WAIAHOLE IRRIGATION CO., LTD.—See JMB Realty Corporation; *U.S. Private*, pg. 578
WAILUKU AGRIBUSINESS CO., INC.—See Buyco, Inc.; *U.S. Private*, pg. 191
WAINOCO OIL & GAS COMPANY—See Wainoco Oil Corporation; *U.S. Public*, pg. 1732
WAINOCO OIL CORPORATION; *U.S. Public*, pg. 1732
WAINOCO RESOURCES, INC.—See Wainoco Oil Corporation; *U.S. Public*, pg. 1732
WAJAX (AUSTRALASIA) PTY. LTD.—See Wajax Limited; *Int'l*, pg. 1485
WAJAX INDUSTRIES LIMITED—See Wajax Limited; *Int'l*, pg. 1485
WAJAX LIMITED; *Int'l*, pg. 1484
WAJAX MANUFACTURING LIMITED—See Wajax Limited; *Int'l*, pg. 1485
WAJAX PACIFIC FIRE EQUIPMENT INC.—See Wajax Limited; *Int'l*, pg. 1485
WAKEFERN FOOD CORPORATION; *U.S. Private*, pg. 1146
WAKO BANK (SCHWEIZ) AG—See Wako Securities Co., Ltd.; *Int'l*, pg. 1485
WAKO COMPUTER SYSTEM CO., LTD.—See Wako Securities Co., Ltd.; *Int'l*, pg. 1485
WAKO ELECTRIC CO., LTD.—See Rohm Co., Ltd.; *Int'l*, pg. 1125
WAKO FINANCE CO., LTD.—See Wako Securities Co., Ltd.; *Int'l*, pg. 1485
WAKO INTERNATIONAL (EUROPE) LIMITED—See Wako Securities Co., Ltd.; *Int'l*, pg. 1485
WAKO INTERNATIONAL (HONG KONG) LIMITED—See Wako Securities Co., Ltd.; *Int'l*, pg. 1485
WAKO MERCHANT BANK (SINGAPORE) LIMITED—See Wako Securities Co., Ltd.; *Int'l*, pg. 1485
WAKO PURE CHEMICAL INDUSTRIES, LTD.—See Takeda Chemical Industries, Ltd.; *Int'l*, pg. 1350
THE WAKO RESEARCH INSTITUTE OF ECONOMICS, INC. (WRI)—See Wako Securities Co., Ltd.; *Int'l*, pg. 1485
WAKO SECURITIES (AMERICA), INC.—See Wako Securities Co., Ltd.; *Int'l*, pg. 1485
WAKO SECURITIES CO., LTD.; *Int'l*, pg. 1485
WAL MART DISTRIBUTION CENTER—See Wal-Mart Stores, Inc.; *U.S. Public*, pg. 1733
WAL-MART HOLDING CO.—See CIFRA, S.A. de C.V.; *Int'l*, pg. 241
WAL-MART HOLDING CO.—See Wal-Mart Stores, Inc.; *U.S. Public*, pg. 1733
WAL-MART HOME/SEASONAL DIV.—See Wal-Mart Stores, Inc.; *U.S. Public*, pg. 1733
WAL-MART JEWELRY DIV.—See Wal-Mart Stores, Inc.; *U.S. Public*, pg. 1733
WAL-MART MERCHANDISING DIV.—See Wal-Mart Stores, Inc.; *U.S. Public*, pg. 1733
WAL-MART PROPERTIES, INC.—See Wal-Mart Stores, Inc.; *U.S. Public*, pg. 1733
WAL-MART REALTY COMPANY—See Wal-Mart Stores, Inc.; *U.S. Public*, pg. 1733
WAL-MART SHOE DIV.—See Wal-Mart Stores, Inc.; *U.S. Public*, pg. 1733
WAL-MART SOFTLINES DIV.—See Wal-Mart Stores, Inc.; *U.S. Public*, pg. 1733
WAL-MART STORES, INC.; *U.S. Public*, pg. 1732
WALBAR INC.—See Coltec Holdings Inc; *U.S. Public*, pg. 402
WALBAR OF ARIZONA, INC.—See Coltec Holdings Inc; *U.S. Public*, pg. 402
WALBAR TURBINE COMPONENTS DIVISION—See Coltec Holdings Inc.; *U.S. Public*, pg. 402
WALBAUM—See SNCF; *Int'l*, pg. 1165
WALBRIDGE ALDINGER COMPANY; *U.S. Private*, pg. 1146
WALBRIDGE ALDINGER COMPANY—See Walbridge Aldinger Company; *U.S. Private*, pg. 1147
WALBRIDGE COATINGS, INC.—See Inland Steel Industries, Inc.; *U.S. Public*, pg. 879
WALBRO AUTOMOTIVE CORP.—See Walbro Corporation; *U.S. Public*, pg. 1733
WALBRO CORPORATION; *U.S. Public*, pg. 1733
WALCHSTADT KUNSTSTOFF GMBH—See Dyckerhoff & Widmann AG; *Int'l*, pg. 423
WALDBAUM'S SUPERMARKETS, INC.—See Tengelmann Warenhandelsgesellschaft; *Int'l*, pg. 1375
WALDEN BOOK COMPANY—See Borders Group, Inc.; *U.S. Public*, pg. 245
WALDEN HOUSE HEALTHCARE—See Vencor, Inc.; *U.S. Public*, pg. 1715
WALDEN RESIDENTIAL OPERATING PARTNERSHIP, L.P.—See Galesi Group; *U.S. Private*, pg. 438
WALDES TRUARC/INDUSTRIAL RETAINING RING—See TransTechnology Corporation; *U.S. Public*, pg. 1632
D. WALDNER COMPANY, INC.; *U.S. Private*, pg. 1147
WALDO BROS. COMPANY; *U.S. Private*, pg. 1147
WALDOM ELECTRONICS, INC.—See Katy Industries, Inc.; *U.S. Public*, pg. 944
WALDRICH COBURG INGERSOLL GMBH INC.—See Ingersoll International Inc.; *U.S. Private*, pg. 562
WALDRICH COBURG WERKZEUGMASCHINENFABRIK GMBH—See Ingersoll International Inc.; *U.S. Private*, pg. 562
WALDRICH SIEGEN INGERSOLL GMBH INC.—See Ingersoll International Inc.; *U.S. Private*, pg. 562
WALDRICH SIEGEN WERKZEUGMASCHINEN GMBH—See Ingersoll International Inc.; *U.S. Private*, pg. 562
WALGREEN CO.; *U.S. Public*, pg. 1733
WALING TOOL & DIE CO.—See E.J. Brooks Company; *U.S. Private*, pg. 172
WALK, HAYDEL & ASSOCIATES, INC.—See Hochtief AG; *Int'l*, pg. 624
WALKER & ASSOCIATES, INC.; *U.S. Private*, pg. 1147
B.B. WALKER COMPANY; *U.S. Public*, pg. 1734
WALKER DEUTSCHLAND GMBH—See Tenneco Inc.; *U.S. Public*, pg. 1580
WALKER DIE CASTING, INC.; *U.S. Private*, pg. 1147

WALKER EQUIPMENT CORP.—See Plantronics Inc.; *U.S. Public*, pg. 1308
WALKER EUROPE, INC.—See Tenneco Inc.; *U.S. Public*, pg. 1578
WALKER GROUP/CNI INC.—See WPP Group plc; *Int'l*, pg. 1483
JAMES WALKER & CO. LIMITED; *Int'l*, pg. 1485
JAMES WALKER MFG. CO.—See James Walker & Co. Limited; *Int'l*, pg. 1485
WALKER-JONES CHEVEROLET-BUICK-OLDSMOBILE INC.—See Jones Company, Inc.; *U.S. Public*, pg. 596
WALKER LUMBER & SUPPLY, INC.—See Hardwoods Of Michigan, Inc.; *U.S. Private*, pg. 502
WALKER MAGNETICS GROUP, INC.; *U.S. Private*, pg. 1147
WALKER MANUFACTURING CO.—See Tenneco Inc.; *U.S. Public*, pg. 1578
MATTHEW WALKER LTD.—See Northern Foods plc; *Int'l*, pg. 968
M.S. WALKER, INC.; *U.S. Private*, pg. 1147
WALKER NATIONAL, INC.—See Walker Magnetics Group, Inc.; *U.S. Private*, pg. 1147
O.S. WALKER CO. INC.—See Walker Magnetics Group, Inc.; *U.S. Private*, pg. 1147
WALKER-PIONEER GRAPHICS; *U.S. Private*, pg. 1147
WALKER SYSTEMS, INC.—See The Wiremold Company; *U.S. Private*, pg. 1184
WALKER WIRE & STEEL COMPANY; *U.S. Private*, pg. 1147
WALKER'S CRISPS, LTD.—See PepsiCo, Inc.; *U.S. Public*, pg. 1278
WALKERTON—See Newcor, Inc.; *U.S. Public*, pg. 1176
WALL COLMONOY CORP.; *U.S. Private*, pg. 1148
WALL DATA AUSTRALIA PTY. LTD.—See Wall Data Incorporated; *U.S. Public*, pg. 1734
WALL DATA INCORPORATED; *U.S. Public*, pg. 1734
WALL DATA JAPAN K.K.—See Wall Data Incorporated; *U.S. Public*, pg. 1734
WALL STREET DELI, INC.; *U.S. Public*, pg. 1734
THE WALL STREET JOURNAL—See Dow Jones & Company, Inc.; *U.S. Public*, pg. 524
THE WALL STREET JOURNAL EUROPE—See Dow Jones & Company, Inc.; *U.S. Public*, pg. 525
WALL TRENDS, INC.—See Solvay S.A.; *Int'l*, pg. 1278
WALLA WALLA GRAIN GROWERS, INC.; *U.S. Private*, pg. 1148
WALLA WALLA UNION BULLETIN—See Seattle Times Company; *U.S. Private*, pg. 980
WALLACE & TIERNAN CANADA, INC.—See Aluminum Company of America; *U.S. Public*, pg. 61
WALLACE & TIERNAN DE MEXICO SA DE CV—See Aluminum Company of America; *U.S. Public*, pg. 61
WALLACE & TIERNAN GMBH—See Aluminum Company of America; *U.S. Public*, pg. 61
WALLACE & TIERNAN INC.—See Aluminum Company of America; *U.S. Public*, pg. 61
WALLACE & TIERNAN PACIFIC PTY. LTD.—See Aluminum Company of America; *U.S. Public*, pg. 61
WALLACE COMPUTER SERVICES, INC.; *U.S. Public*, pg. 1735
WALLACE LABORATORIES—See Carter-Wallace, Inc.; *U.S. Public*, pg. 310
ROBERT WALLACE LIMITED—See Arnotts plc; *Int'l*, pg. 81
ROBERT WALLACE (SHIRTS) LIMITED—See Arnotts plc; *Int'l*, pg. 81
WALLACE & TIERNAN—See United Utilities plc; *Int'l*, pg. 1444
WALLBERGS FABRIKS AKTIEBOLAG—See Albany International Corp.; *U.S. Public*, pg. 37
WALLE CORPORATION; *U.S. Private*, pg. 1148
THE WALLING CO., INC.—See Eclipse Inc.; *U.S. Private*, pg. 360
WALLINGFORD PROPERTY HOLDINGS CO.—See The Unimax Corporation; *U.S. Private*, pg. 1118
A/S P. WALLMANN & CO.—See Norske Skogindustrier A.S; *Int'l*, pg. 966
WALLON IMPRIMEUR S.A.—See Nestle S.A.; *Int'l*, pg. 922
WALLPAPERS-TO-GO—See Wicks 'n Sticks, Ltd; *U.S. Private*, pg. 1175
W.W. WALLWORK, INC.; *U.S. Private*, pg. 1148
WALLWORK LEASE—See W.W. Wallwork, Inc.; *U.S. Private*, pg. 1148
WALMAN OPTICAL COMPANY; *U.S. Private*, pg. 1148
WAL-MART DISTRIBUTION CENTER—See Wal-Mart Stores, Inc.; *U.S. Public*, pg. 1733
WALNUT CREEK RESTAURANT CORP.—See Specialty Restaurants Corporation; *U.S. Private*, pg. 1022
WALNUT STREET SECURITIES, INC.—See General American Life Insurance Co.; *U.S. Private*, pg. 443
WALOP LTD.—See Citizen Watch Company, Ltd.; *Int'l*, pg. 295
WALPOLE WOODWORKERS, INC.; *U.S. Private*, pg. 1148
WALSALL CONDUITS LTD.—See Arena Lighting Ltd.; *Int'l*, pg. 80
WALSER AUTOMOTIVE GROUP; *U.S. Private*, pg. 1148
WALSER FORD INC.—See Walser Automotive Group; *U.S. Private*, pg. 1148
WALSER LEASING INC.—See Walser Automotive Group; *U.S. Private*, pg. 1148
WALSH CONSTRUCTION COMPANY—See Atkinson; *U.S. Public*, pg. 143
WALSH CONSTRUCTION CO. OF ILLINOIS—See Walsh Group; *U.S. Private*, pg. 1148
WALSH CONSTRUCTION COMPANY (WEST)—See Atkinson; *U.S. Public*, pg. 143
WALSH GROUP; *U.S. Private*, pg. 1148
WALSH INDUSTRIAL & COMMERCIAL GROUP—See Atkinson; *U.S. Public*, pg. 143
WALSH POWER GROUP—See Atkinson; *U.S. Public*, pg. 143
WALSWORTH PUBLISHING COMPANY, INC.; *U.S. Private*, pg. 1148

WALTEC AMERICAN FORGINGS, INC.—See Emco Limited; *Int'l*, pg. 453
WALTEC COMPONENTS—See Emco Limited; *Int'l*, pg. 453
WALTEC ENGINEERING—See Emco Limited; *Int'l*, pg. 453
WALTECH INC.—See Siebe plc; *Int'l*, pg. 1241
WALTER & BRUYNZEEL AG—See Electrolux, AB; *Int'l*, pg. 444
WALTER DRAKE, INC.—See Foster & Gallagher, Inc.; *U.S. Private*, pg. 421
WALTER HUNDHAUSEN GMBH & CO KG—See Fried. Krupp AG; *Int'l*, pg. 508
WALTER INDUSTRIES, INC.; *U.S. Public*, pg. 1736
JIM WALTER COMPUTER SERVICES, INC.—See Walter Industries, Inc.; *U.S. Public*, pg. 1737
JIM WALTER HOMES, INC.—See Walter Industries, Inc.; *U.S. Public*, pg. 1737
J.W. WALTER, INC.—See Walter Industries, Inc.; *U.S. Public*, pg. 1736
WALTER LAND CO.—See Walter Industries, Inc.; *U.S. Public*, pg. 1737
WALTER WERKZEUGE SALZBURG GES M.B.H. & CO.—See Rothenberger Group GmbH; *Int'l*, pg. 1129
WALTERS & WOLF; *U.S. Private*, pg. 1149
WALTHAMSTOW PLANT—See Fort James Corporation; *U.S. Public*, pg. 672
WALTON FABRIC DIVISION OF AVONDALE MILLS—See Avondale Incorporated; *U.S. Private*, pg. 103
THE WALWORTH COMPANY USA; *U.S. Private*, pg. 1149
WAMBACO & PEETERS NV—See Etablissements Delhaize Freres Et Cie "Le Lion" S.A.; *Int'l*, pg. 1454
WAMBESCO ROHSTOFFHANDELSGES. MBH—See Veba AG; *Int'l*, pg. 1458
WAMPOLE LABORATORIES—See Carter-Wallace, Inc.; *U.S. Public*, pg. 310
WAN THAI FOODS INDUSTRY CO., LTD.—See Ajinomoto Company Inc.; *Int'l*, pg. 41
WANATAH TRUCKING CO.—See Vulcan Materials Company; *U.S. Public*, pg. 1726
WANDEL & GOLTERMANN AB—See Wandel & Goltermann GmbH & Co., Elektronische Messtechnik; *Int'l*, pg. 1486
WANDEL & GOLTERMANN & CO., ARGENTINA—See Wandel & Goltermann GmbH & Co., Elektronische Messtechnik; *Int'l*, pg. 1486
WANDEL & GOLTERMANN ANDINA LTDA.—See Wandel & Goltermann GmbH & Co., Elektronische Messtechnik; *Int'l*, pg. 1486
WANDEL & GOLTERMANN BEIJING OFFICER—See Wandel & Goltermann GmbH & Co., Elektronische Messtechnik; *Int'l*, pg. 1486
WANDEL & GOLTERMANN B.V.—See Wandel & Goltermann GmbH & Co., Elektronische Messtechnik; *Int'l*, pg. 1486
WANDEL & GOLTERMANN CENTROAMERICA Y EL CARIBE—See Wandel & Goltermann GmbH & Co., Elektronische Messtechnik; *Int'l*, pg. 1486
WANDEL & GOLTERMANN DE MEXICO S.A. DE C.V.—See Wandel & Goltermann GmbH & Co., Elektronische Messtechnik; *Int'l*, pg. 1486
WANDEL & GOLTERMANN FRANCE—See Wandel & Goltermann GmbH & Co., Elektronische Messtechnik; *Int'l*, pg. 1486
WANDEL & GOLTERMANN GES.M.B.H—See Wandel & Goltermann GmbH & Co., Elektronische Messtechnik; *Int'l*, pg. 1486
WANDEL & GOLTERMANN GMBH & CO., ELEKTRONISCHE MESSTECHNIK; *Int'l*, pg. 1485
WANDEL & GOLTERMANN INC.—See Wandel & Goltermann GmbH & Co., Elektronische Messtechnik; *Int'l*, pg. 1486
WANDEL & GOLTERMANN INSTRUMENTACAO LTDA. & CIA.—See Wandel & Goltermann GmbH & Co., Elektronische Messtechnik; *Int'l*, pg. 1486
WANDEL & GOLTERMANN K.K.—See Wandel & Goltermann GmbH & Co., Elektronische Messtechnik; *Int'l*, pg. 1486
WANDEL & GOLTERMANN LTD.—See Wandel & Goltermann GmbH & Co., Elektronische Messtechnik; *Int'l*, pg. 1486
WANDEL & GOLTERMANN PTY. LTD.—See Wandel & Goltermann GmbH & Co., Elektronische Messtechnik; *Int'l*, pg. 1486
WANDEL & GOLTERMANN PVT. LTD.—See Wandel & Goltermann GmbH & Co., Elektronische Messtechnik; *Int'l*, pg. 1486
WANDEL & GOLTERMANN S.A.—See Wandel & Goltermann GmbH & Co., Elektronische Messtechnik; *Int'l*, pg. 1486
WANDEL & GOLTERMANN SALES LTD.—See Wandel & Goltermann GmbH & Co., Elektronische Messtechnik; *Int'l*, pg. 1486
WANDEL & GOLTERMANN (SCHWEIZ) AG—See Wandel & Goltermann GmbH & Co., Elektronische Messtechnik; *Int'l*, pg. 1486
WANDEL & GOLTERMANN S.R.L.-TECNOLOGIE DI MISURA ELETTRONICHE—See Wandel & Goltermann GmbH & Co., Elektronische Messtechnik; *Int'l*, pg. 1486
WANDEL & GOLTERMANN TECHNOLOGIES, INC.—See Wandel & Goltermann GmbH & Co., Elektronische Messtechnik; *Int'l*, pg. 1486
WANDER AG—See Novartis AG; *Int'l*, pg. 972
WANDER (AUSTRALIA) PTY. LTD.—See Novartis AG; *Int'l*, pg. 986
WANDER DE VENEZUELA S.A.—See Novartis AG; *Int'l*, pg. 986
WANDER GESELLSCHAFT M.B.H.—See Novartis AG; *Int'l*, pg. 986
WANDER G.M.B.H.—See Novartis AG; *Int'l*, pg. 986
WANDER INC.—See Novartis AG; *Int'l*, pg. 972
WANDER (NEDERLAND) B.V.—See Novartis AG; *Int'l*, pg. 986
WANDER PHARMA G.M.B.H.—See Novartis AG; *Int'l*, pg. 986

WANDER (PHILIPPINES) INC.—See Novartis AG; *Int'l*, pg. 986
WANDER (PORTUGAL) ALIMENTOCAO LDA.—See Novartis AG; *Int'l*, pg. 986
WANDER S.A.—See Novartis AG; *Int'l*, pg. 986
N.V. WANDER S.A.—See Novartis AG; *Int'l*, pg. 986
WANDER (SHANGHAI) NUTRITION LTD.—See Novartis AG; *Int'l*, pg. 986
WANDER (SINGAPORE) PTY. LTD.—See Novartis AG; *Int'l*, pg. 986
WANDER S.P.A.—See Novartis AG; *Int'l*, pg. 986
WANDER (THAILAND) LTD.—See Novartis AG; *Int'l*, pg. 986
WANG AUSTRALIA PTY. LTD.—See Wang Laboratories, Inc.; *U.S. Public*, pg. 1737
WANG BENELUX S.A/N.V.—See Wang Laboratories, Inc.; *U.S. Public*, pg. 1737
WANG CANADA LIMITED—See Wang Laboratories, Inc.; *U.S. Public*, pg. 1737
WANG COMPUTADORAS, INC.—See Wang Laboratories, Inc.; *U.S. Public*, pg. 1737
WANG COMPUTER KOREA, LTD.—See Wang Laboratories, Inc.; *U.S. Public*, pg. 1737
WANG COMPUTERS (PTE.) LIMITED—See Wang Laboratories, Inc.; *U.S. Public*, pg. 1737
WANG DE MEXICO, S.A. DE C.V.—See Wang Laboratories, Inc.; *U.S. Public*, pg. 1737
WANG DEUTSCHLAND GMBH—See Wang Laboratories, Inc.; *U.S. Public*, pg. 1737
WANG ESPANA, S.A.—See Wang Laboratories, Inc.; *U.S. Public*, pg. 1737
WANG EUROPE S.A./N.V.—See Wang Laboratories, Inc.; *U.S. Public*, pg. 1738
WANG EXPORT SERVICES, INC.—See Wang Laboratories, Inc.; *U.S. Public*, pg. 1738
WANG FED INC.—See Wang Laboratories, Inc.; *U.S. Public*, pg. 1737
WANG FRANCE S.A.—See Wang Laboratories, Inc.; *U.S. Public*, pg. 1738
WANG INDUSTRIAL CO., LTD.—See Wang Laboratories, Inc.; *U.S. Public*, pg. 1738
WANG IRELAND LIMITED—See Wang Laboratories, Inc.; *U.S. Public*, pg. 1738
WANG ITALIA S.P.A.—See Wang Laboratories, Inc.; *U.S. Public*, pg. 1738
WANG LABORATORIES, INC.; *U.S. Public*, pg. 1737
WANG LATIN AMERICA S.A.—See Wang Laboratories, Inc.; *U.S. Public*, pg. 1738
WANG NETHERLAND B.V.—See Wang Laboratories, Inc.; *U.S. Public*, pg. 1738
WANG NEW ZEALAND LIMITED—See Wang Laboratories, Inc.; *U.S. Public*, pg. 1738
WANG PACIFIC LIMITED—See Wang Laboratories, Inc.; *U.S. Public*, pg. 1738
WANG (SCHWEIZ) AG—See Wang Laboratories, Inc.; *U.S. Public*, pg. 1738
WANG SVENSKA AB—See Wang Laboratories, Inc.; *U.S. Public*, pg. 1738
WANG THAILAND LTD.—See Wang Laboratories, Inc.; *U.S. Public*, pg. 1738
WANG (UK) LIMITED—See Wang Laboratories, Inc.; *U.S. Public*, pg. 1738
WANGNER SYSTEMS CORPORATION—See Transworld Interweaving AG (TIAG); *Int'l*, pg. 1418
WANG'S INTERNATIONAL, INC.; *U.S. Private*, pg. 1149
WANNER Y VINYAS—See Saint-Gobain; *Int'l*, pg. 1176
WANSDYKE SECURITIES LIMITED—See SLD Holdings Ltd.; *Int'l*, pg. 1160
WANSON CO. LTD.—See FKI Plc; *Int'l*, pg. 472
WANTAGE AVENUE HOLDING COMPANY, INC.—See Selective Insurance Group, Inc; *U.S. Public*, pg. 1456
WAPT—See The News Corporation Limited; *Int'l*, pg. 926
WARATOKU STEEL CO., LTD.—See Oki Electric Industry Company, Ltd.; *Int'l*, pg. 999
WARBURG ASSET MANAGEMENT CANADA LTD.—See Swiss Bank Corporation; *Int'l*, pg. 1331
WARBURG ASSET MANAGEMENT HONG KONG LTD.—See Swiss Bank Corporation; *Int'l*, pg. 1331
WARBURG ASSET MANAGEMENT ISLE OF MAN LTD.—See Swiss Bank Corporation; *Int'l*, pg. 1331
WARBURG ASSET MANAGEMENT JAPAN LTD.—See Swiss Bank Corporation; *Int'l*, pg. 1331
WARBURG ASSET MANAGEMENT JERSEY LTD.—See Swiss Bank Corporation; *Int'l*, pg. 1331
WARBURG ASSET MANAGEMENT SINGAPORE PTE. LTD.—See Swiss Bank Corporation; *Int'l*, pg. 1331
WARBURG INVESTMENT TRUST MANAGEMENT COMPANY LTD.—See Swiss Bank Corporation; *Int'l*, pg. 1331
ASHLEY F. WARD, INC.; *U.S. Private*, pg. 1149
S.H. WARD INC.—See Vaux Group Plc; *Int'l*, pg. 1454
WARD LAKE DRILLING, INC.—See Texas Pacific Group; *U.S. Private*, pg. 1078
WARD LEONARD ELECTRIC COMPANY, INC.—See The Unimax Corporation; *U.S. Public*, pg. 1118
THE WARD MACHINERY COMPANY; *U.S. Private*, pg. 1149
WARD MANUFACTURING, INC.; *U.S. Private*, pg. 1149
WARD PRODUCTS CORPORATION; *U.S. Private*, pg. 1149
WARD SURFACING LIMITED—See RMC Group p.l.c.; *Int'l*, pg. 1081
THOS. S. WARD CONTRACTING LIMITED—See RMC Group p.l.c.; *Int'l*, pg. 1081
THOS. W. WARD ROADSTONE LIMITED—See RMC Group p.l.c.; *Int'l*, pg. 1079
WARD TRUCKING CORP.; *U.S. Private*, pg. 1149
WARDLEY BROKING SERVICES PRIVATE LIMITED—See HSBC Holdings plc; *Int'l*, pg. 584
WARDLEY FINANCIAL SERVICES LIMITED—See HSBC Holdings plc; *Int'l*, pg. 584
WARDLEY INTERNATIONAL LIMITED—See HSBC Holdings plc; *Int'l*, pg. 582

WARDS COVE PACKING COMPANY; *U.S. Private*, pg. 1149
WAREHOUSE CONCEPTS, INC.—See Raley's & Bel Air; *U.S. Private*, pg. 908
WAREHOUSE HOME FURNISHINGS DISTRIBUTOR; *U.S. Private*, pg. 1150
WAREHOUSE LENDING CORPORATION OF AMERICA—See INMC Mortgage Holdings, Inc.; *U.S. Public*, pg. 857
WAREMART INC.; *U.S. Private*, pg. 1150
EDEN WAREN G.M.B.H.—See Novartis AG; *Int'l*, pg. 982
WAREX-JESSUP, INC.—See Giant Food Inc.; *U.S. Public*, pg. 741
WARGON MILL—See Mo och Domsjo AB; *Int'l*, pg. 885
WARING & LAROSA, INC.; *U.S. Private*, pg. 1150
WARING & LAROSA DIRECT—See Waring & LaRosa, Inc.; *U.S. Private*, pg. 1150
WARING LAROSA GORDON PUBLIC RELATIONS—See Waring & LaRosa, Inc.; *U.S. Private*, pg. 1150
WARING PRODUCTS—See CTS Corporation; *U.S. Public*, pg. 286
WARM BROTHERS CONSTRUCTION COMPANY; *U.S. Private*, pg. 1150
WARMAN GROUP—See North Limited; *Int'l*, pg. 967
WARMAN INTERNATIONAL LTD.—See North Limited; *Int'l*, pg. 967
WARMETECHNIK LEICKEL GMBH—See Veba AG; *Int'l*, pg. 1460
WARMINGTON HOMES; *U.S. Private*, pg. 1150
WARN INDUSTRIES, INC.; *U.S. Private*, pg. 1150
WARNACO INC.; *U.S. Public*, pg. 1738
WARNACO INC.-INTERNATIONAL DIV.—See Warnaco Inc.; *U.S. Public*, pg. 1738
WARNACO INC.-MENSWEAR DIV.—See Warnaco Inc.; *U.S. Public*, pg. 1738
WARNACO OF CANADA LIMITED—See Warnaco Inc.; *U.S. Public*, pg. 1738
WARNER AUDIO PUBLISHING—See Time Warner Inc.; *U.S. Public*, pg. 1614
WARNER BOOKS, INC.—See Time Warner Inc.; *U.S. Public*, pg. 1614
WARNER BROS. CONSUMER PRODUCTS—See Time Warner Inc.; *U.S. Public*, pg. 1610
WARNER BROS. RECORDS, INC.—See Time Warner Inc.; *U.S. Public*, pg. 1611
WARNER BROS. STUDIOS, INC.—See Time Warner Inc.; *U.S. Public*, pg. 1611
WARNER BROS. TELEVISION, INC.—See Time Warner Inc.; *U.S. Public*, pg. 1611
WARNER CABLE COMMUNICATIONS, INC.—See Time Warner Inc.; *U.S. Public*, pg. 1611
WARNER CANDY COMPANY, INC.; *U.S. Private*, pg. 1150
WARNER-CHAPPELL MUSIC INC.—See Time Warner Inc.; *U.S. Public*, pg. 1612
WARNER-CHILCOTT LABORATORIES, INC.—See Elan Corporation Plc; *Int'l*, pg. 436
WARNER COMMUNICATIONS INC.—See Time Warner Inc.; *U.S. Public*, pg. 1611
WARNER ELECTRIC INDUSTRIAL PRODUCTS DIVISION—See Dana Corporation; *U.S. Public*, pg. 480
WARNER HOLIDAYS LIMITED—See The Rank Group PLC; *Int'l*, pg. 1087
WARNER HOME VIDEO—See Time Warner Inc.; *U.S. Public*, pg. 1611
WARNER-JENKINSON—See Universal Foods Corporation; *U.S. Public*, pg. 1696
WARNER-JENKINSON AUSTRALIA—See Universal Foods Corporation; *U.S. Public*, pg. 1696
WARNER-JENKINSON CANADA—See Universal Foods Corporation; *U.S. Public*, pg. 1696
WARNER-JENKINSON CO.—See Universal Foods Corporation; *U.S. Public*, pg. 1696
WARNER-JENKINSON COSMETIC COLORS—See Universal Foods Corporation; *U.S. Public*, pg. 1696
WARNER-JENKINSON EUROPE—See Universal Foods Corporation; *U.S. Public*, pg. 1696
WARNER-JENKINSON FRANCE—See Universal Foods Corporation; *U.S. Public*, pg. 1696
WARNER-JENKINSON NETHERLANDS—See Universal Foods Corporation; *U.S. Public*, pg. 1696
WARNER-JENKINSON S.A. DE C.V.—See Universal Foods Corporation; *U.S. Public*, pg. 1696
WARNER-LAMBERT BELGIUM N.V.—See Warner-Lambert Company; *U.S. Public*, pg. 1739
WARNER-LAMBERT CANADA, INC.—See Warner-Lambert Company; *U.S. Public*, pg. 1739
WARNER-LAMBERT COMPANY; *U.S. Public*, pg. 1738
WARNER-LAMBERT INDUSTRIA E COMERCIO LTDA—See Warner-Lambert Company; *U.S. Public*, pg. 1739
WARNER-LAMBERT INTERNATIONAL OPERATIONS—See Warner-Lambert Company; *U.S. Public*, pg. 1739
WARNER-LAMBERT K.K.—See Warner-Lambert Company; *U.S. Public*, pg. 1739
WARNER-LAMBERT PHILIPPINES, INC.—See Warner-Lambert Company; *U.S. Public*, pg. 1740
WARNER-LAMBERT (PORTUGAL) COMERCIO E INDUSTRIA LIMITADA—See Warner-Lambert Company; *U.S. Public*, pg. 1740
WARNER-LAMBERT S.A. (PROPRIETARY) LIMITED—See Warner-Lambert Company; *U.S. Public*, pg. 1740
WARNER-LAMBERT SCANDINAVIA AKTIEBOLAG—See Warner-Lambert Company; *U.S. Public*, pg. 1740
WARNER-LAMBERT (SCHWEIZ) AG—See Warner-Lambert Company; *U.S. Public*, pg. 1740
WARNER-LAMBERT SHAVING PRODUCTS GROUP—See Warner-Lambert Company; *U.S. Public*, pg. 1739
WARNER-LAMBERT—See Warner-Lambert Company; *U.S. Public*, pg. 1739
WARNER-LAMBERT VERKOOP B.V.—See Warner-Lambert Company; *U.S. Public*, pg. 1740
WARNER-LAMBERT WORLDWIDE SHAVING PRODUCTS GROUP—See Warner-Lambert Company; *U.S. Public*, pg. 1739

WARNER MUSIC GROUP, INC.—See Time Warner Inc.; *U.S. Public*, pg. 1612

WARNER MUSIC INTERNATIONAL (EUROPE) LTD.—See Time Warner Inc.; *U.S. Public*, pg. 1615

WARNER NEWHOPE ASSOCIATES—See Cigna Corp.; *U.S. Public*, pg. 362

WARNER PRESS, INC.; *U.S. Private*, pg. 1150

WARNER PRESS PUBLISHERS—See Warner Press, Inc.; *U.S. Private*, pg. 1151

WARNER PUBLISHER SERVICES, INC.—See Time Warner Inc.; *U.S. Public*, pg. 1614

WARNER SPECIAL PRODUCTS—See Time Warner Inc.; *U.S. Public*, pg. 1612

WARNER VINEYARDS; *U.S. Private*, pg. 1151

WARNER-ISHI CORPORATION—See Ishikawajima-Harima Heavy Industries Co., Ltd.; *Int'l*, pg. 689

WARNER'S—See Warnaco Inc.; *U.S. Public*, pg. 1738

WARNER'S AIGLON, S.A.—See Warnaco Inc.; *U.S. Public*, pg. 1738

WARNER'S DE MEXICO, S.A. DE C.V.—See Warnaco Inc.; *U.S. Public*, pg. 1738

WARNER'S (UNITED KINGDOM) LIMITED—See Warnaco Inc.; *U.S. Public*, pg. 1738

FRIEDRICH WARNKE GMBH & CO. KG—See Mannesmann A.G.; *Int'l*, pg. 838

WARRANTECH AUTOMOTIVE, INC.—See Warrantech Corporation; *U.S. Public*, pg. 1740

WARRANTECH CONSUMER PRODUCT SERVICES, INC.—See Warrantech Corporation; *U.S. Public*, pg. 1740

WARRANTECH CORPORATION; *U.S. Public*, pg. 1740

WARRANTECH DIRECT, INC.—See Warrantech Corporation; *U.S. Public*, pg. 1740

WARREN & SALINE RIVER RAILROAD CO.—See Potlatch Corporation; *U.S. Public*, pg. 1318

WARREN DISTRIBUTING CORP.; *U.S. Private*, pg. 1151

WARREN DISTRIBUTION, INC.; *U.S. Private*, pg. 1151

WARREN ELECTRIC COMPANY—See Warren Electric Group; *U.S. Private*, pg. 1151

WARREN ELECTRIC GROUP; *U.S. Private*, pg. 1151

WARREN ELECTRIC TELECOMMUNICATIONS-UTILITIES COMPANY—See Warren Electric Group; *U.S. Private*, pg. 1151

WARREN EQUITIES INC.; *U.S. Private*, pg. 1151

GEORGE E. WARREN CORPORATION; *U.S. Private*, pg. 1151

WARREN GORHAM LAMONT—See The Thomson Corporation; *U.S. Public*, pg. 1602

WARREN INDUSTRIES, INC.—See Rose Art Industries; *U.S. Private*, pg. 945

WARREN MANOR NURSING HOME—See Paragon Health Network, Inc.; *U.S. Public*, pg. 1257

WARREN PET PRODUCTS—See Vista 2000, Inc.; *U.S. Private*, pg. 1142

WARREN PETROLEUM COMPANY—See NGC Corporation; *U.S. Public*, pg. 1146

WARREN PLANT—See Oglebay Norton Company; *U.S. Public*, pg. 1214

WARREN PRESS, INC.—See American Pad and Paper Company; *U.S. Public*, pg. 89

WARREN PROPERTIES; *U.S. Private*, pg. 1151

WARREN PUMPS INC.—See IMO Industries Inc.; *U.S. Public*, pg. 857

WARREN RUPP, INC.—See IDEX Corporation; *U.S. Public*, pg. 862

S.D. WARREN CO.—See Sappi Limited; *Int'l*, pg. 1193

WARREN TELEPHONE CO.—See Telephone and Data Systems, Inc.; *U.S. Public*, pg. 1572

WARREN TOOL GROUP—See Wilton Corporation; *U.S. Private*, pg. 1181

WARRENS WALLER PRESS, INC.; *U.S. Private*, pg. 1151

WARRICK CONTROLS, INC.—See Danaher Corporation; *U.S. Public*, pg. 482

WARRINGTON FINANCIAL SYSTEMS INC.—See SunGard Data Systems Inc.; *U.S. Public*, pg. 1535

WARRIOR BASIN GAS COMPANY—See Atrion Corporation; *U.S. Public*, pg. 146

WARRIOR, INC.—See HarCor Energy, Inc.; *U.S. Public*, pg. 782

WARRNAMBOOL STANDARD—See John Fairfax Holdings Limited; *Int'l*, pg. 477

WARSAW MFG. DIVISION—See R.R. Donnelley & Sons Company; *U.S. Public*, pg. 519

WARSAW ORTHOPEDIC INC.—See Sofamor Danek Group, Inc.; *U.S. Public*, pg. 1482

WARSTEINER BRAUEREI HAUS CRAMER GMBH & CO.; *Int'l*, pg. 1486

WARSTEINER IMPORTERS AGENCY—See Warsteiner Brauerei Haus Cramer GmbH & Co.; *Int'l*, pg. 1486

WARTSILA DIESEL INTERNATIONAL LTD. OY—See Metra Corporation; *Int'l*, pg. 863

WARWICK BAKER O'NEILL; *U.S. Private*, pg. 1152

WARWICK FINSPA LIMITED—See EIP Group plc; *Int'l*, pg. 426

WARWICK INTERNATIONAL LTD.—See Sequa Corporation; *U.S. Public*, pg. 1459

WASA—See Eureko B.V.; *Int'l*, pg. 464

WASA G.M.B.H.—See Novartis AG; *Int'l*, pg. 986

WASA WANDER B.V.—See Novartis AG; *Int'l*, pg. 986

WASABROD AB—See Novartis AG; *Int'l*, pg. 986

WASABROD A/S—See Novartis AG; *Int'l*, pg. 986

WASATCH VILLA CONVALESCENT NURSING HOME—See Vencor, Inc.; *U.S. Public*, pg. 1715

WASCO PRODUCTS, INC.; *U.S. Private*, pg. 1152

WASHBURN DIRECT MARKETING, INC.—See Cadmus Communications Corporation; *U.S. Public*, pg. 291

WASHBURN GRAPHICS, INC.—See Cadmus Communications Corporation; *U.S. Public*, pg. 291

WASHERS, INCORPORATED; *U.S. Private*, pg. 1152

WASHINGTON ANALYSIS CORPORATION—See National Westminster Bank PLC; *Int'l*, pg. 911

WASHINGTON AREA DISTRIBUTION CENTER—See Reliable Stores, Inc.; *U.S. Private*, pg. 921

WASHINGTON BUSINESS JOURNAL, INC.—See Advance Publications Inc.; *U.S. Private*, pg. 20

WASHINGTON CRANES—See Ederer Inc.; *U.S. Private*, pg. 363

WASHINGTON CULVERT CO.—See Pitt-Des Moines, Inc.; *U.S. Public*, pg. 1305

WASHINGTON FEDERAL SAVINGS; *U.S. Public*, pg. 1740

WASHINGTON GAS ENERGY SYSTEMS, INC.—See Washington Gas Light Co.; *U.S. Public*, pg. 1741

WASHINGTON GAS LIGHT CO.; *U.S. Public*, pg. 1740

WASHINGTON HOMES, INC.; *U.S. Public*, pg. 1741

WASHINGTON HOMES, INC. OF VIRGINIA—See Washington Homes, Inc.; *U.S. Public*, pg. 1741

WASHINGTON INVENTORY SERVICE—See Huffy Corporation; *U.S. Public*, pg. 846

WASHINGTON LANGUAGE CENTER—See Berlitz International, Inc.; *U.S. Public*, pg. 222

WASHINGTON MANUFACTURING COMPANY, INC.—See Fansteel, Inc.; *U.S. Public*, pg. 612

WASHINGTON MUTUAL FEDERAL SAVINGS BANK—See Washington Mutual Inc.; *U.S. Public*, pg. 1742

WASHINGTON MUTUAL INC.; *U.S. Public*, pg. 1741

WASHINGTON MUTUAL LIFE INSURANCE SERVICES, INC.—See Washington Mutual Inc.; *U.S. Public*, pg. 1742

WASHINGTON NATIONAL INSURANCE CO.—See Conseco Inc.; *U.S. Public*, pg. 434

WASHINGTON NATIONAL LIFE INSURANCE CO. OF NEW YORK—See Columbian Mutual Life Insurance Co.; *U.S. Public*, pg. 256

WASHINGTON OPERATIONS—See Harris Corporation; *U.S. Public*, pg. 791

THE WASHINGTON POST COMPANY; *U.S. Public*, pg. 1742

THE WASHINGTON POST NATIONAL WEEKLY EDITION—See The Washington Post Company; *U.S. Public*, pg. 1743

WASHINGTON POST NEWSPAPER DIVISION—See The Washington Post Company; *U.S. Public*, pg. 1743

THE WASHINGTON POST WRITERS GROUP—See The Washington Post Company; *U.S. Public*, pg. 1743

WASHINGTON REAL ESTATE INVESTMENT TRUST; *U.S. Public*, pg. 1743

WASHINGTON SCIENTIFIC INDUSTRIES, INC.; *U.S. Public*, pg. 1744

WASHINGTON SERVICE BUREAU, INC.—See Wolters Kluwer N.V.; *Int'l*, pg. 1513

WASHINGTON SERVICES, INC.—See Washington Federal Savings; *U.S. Public*, pg. 1740

WASHINGTON SPECIALTY METALS—See Lukens Inc.; *U.S. Public*, pg. 1020

WASHINGTON SPECIALTY METALS CANADA, INC.—See Lukens Inc.; *U.S. Public*, pg. 1020

WASHINGTON SQUARE ADVISORS, INC.—See ReliaStar Financial Corp.; *U.S. Public*, pg. 1376

WASHINGTON SQUARE NURSING CENTER—See Horizon/CMS Healthcare Corporation; *U.S. Public*, pg. 838

WASHINGTON STATE APPLE COMMISSION; *U.S. Private*, pg. 1152

WASHINGTON TERMINAL COMPANY—See Amtrak-National Railroad Passenger Corp.; *U.S. Private*, pg. 69

WASHINGTON TRUST BANCORP, INC.; *U.S. Public*, pg. 1744

THE WASHINGTON TRUST COMPANY—See Washington Trust Bancorp, Inc.; *U.S. Public*, pg. 1744

THE WASHINGTON WATER POWER COMPANY; *U.S. Public*, pg. 1744

WASHOE CARE CENTER—See Horizon/CMS Healthcare Corporation; *U.S. Public*, pg. 838

WASLIC COMPANY II—See The Western and Southern Life Insurance Company; *U.S. Public*, pg. 1164

WASSALL PLC; *Int'l*, pg. 1486

WASSALL USA INC.—See Wassall Plc; *Int'l*, pg. 1486

WASSERSTEIN PERELLA GROUP, INC.—See The Nomura Securities Co., Ltd.; *Int'l*, pg. 956

WASSERSTROM COMPANY; *U.S. Private*, pg. 1152

WASTE DISPOSAL, INC.—See Browning-Ferris Industries, Inc.; *U.S. Public*, pg. 264

WASTE HANDLING SYSTEMS, INC.—See Republic Industries, Inc.; *U.S. Public*, pg. 1380

WASTE KING—See Masco Corporation; *U.S. Public*, pg. 1053

WASTE MANAGEMENT, INC.; *U.S. Public*, pg. 1744

WASTE MANAGEMENT INTERNATIONAL PLC—See Waste Management, Inc.; *U.S. Public*, pg. 1745

WASTE STREAM TECHNOLOGY, INC.—See Sevenson Environmental Services, Inc.; *U.S. Public*, pg. 1463

WASTECO, INC.—See Browning-Ferris Industries, Inc.; *U.S. Public*, pg. 264

WATER COUNTRY USA—See Anheuser-Busch Companies, Inc.; *U.S. Public*, pg. 114

WATER ENGINEERING DIVISION—See FKI Plc; *Int'l*, pg. 472

WATER ENGINEERING LTD.—See Deutsche Babcock AG; *Int'l*, pg. 399

WATER RESOURCES INTERNATIONAL, INC.—See Barnwell Industries, Inc.; *U.S. Public*, pg. 191

WATER-SIDE, INC.—See Bell Atlantic Corporation; *U.S. Public*, pg. 203

WATER STREET CORPORATION—See W.R. Grace & Co.; *U.S. Public*, pg. 755

WATER SYSTEMS GROUP—See WICOR, Inc.; *U.S. Public*, pg. 1767

WATER SYSTEMS (NC)—See State Industries Inc.; *U.S. Private*, pg. 1037

WATERBURY COMPANIES, INC.—See Carpenter Technology Corporation; *U.S. Public*, pg. 308

WATERBURY FARREL TECHNOLOGIES—See Goldman Financial Group; *U.S. Private*, pg. 461

WATERBURY HEADERS, INC.—See Seneca Falls Technology Group; *U.S. Private*, pg. 984

WATEREE TEXTILE CORP.—See Marubeni Corporation; *Int'l*, pg. 845

WATERFORD CONTINENTAL CHEESE LIMITED—See Avonmore Waterford Group plc; *Int'l*, pg. 102

WATERFORD CO-OPERATIVE DAIRY & TRADING SOCIETY LIMITED—See Avonmore Waterford Group plc; *Int'l*, pg. 102

WATERFORD CRYSTAL GALLERY LTD.—See Waterford Wedgwood Plc; *Int'l*, pg. 1487

WATERFORD CRYSTAL, INC.—See Waterford Wedgwood Plc; *Int'l*, pg. 1487

WATERFORD CRYSTAL (LIGHTINGWARE) LTD.—See Waterford Wedgwood Plc; *Int'l*, pg. 1487

WATERFORD CRYSTAL LTD.—See Waterford Wedgwood Plc; *Int'l*, pg. 1487

WATERFORD CRYSTAL U.S.A.—See Waterford Wedgwood Plc; *Int'l*, pg. 1487

WATERFORD FOODS INC.—See Avonmore Waterford Group plc; *Int'l*, pg. 102

WATERFORD FOODS INVESTMENTS LIMITED—See Avonmore Waterford Group plc; *Int'l*, pg. 102

WATERFORD FOODS IRELAND LTD.—See Avonmore Waterford Group plc; *Int'l*, pg. 102

WATERFORD FOODS LIMITED—See Avonmore Waterford Group plc; *Int'l*, pg. 102

WATERFORD FOODS USA, INC.—See Avonmore Waterford Group plc; *Int'l*, pg. 102

WATERFORD GLASS RESEARCH & DEVELOPMENT LTD.—See Waterford Wedgwood Plc; *Int'l*, pg. 1487

WATERFORD PHARMACEUTICALS LTD.—See IVAX Corporation; *U.S. Public*, pg. 915

WATERFORD WEDGWOOD PLC; *Int'l*, pg. 1487

WATERFORD WEDGWOOD UK PLC—See Waterford Wedgwood Plc; *Int'l*, pg. 1487

WATERHOUSE INVESTOR SERVICES—See The Toronto Dominion Bank; *Int'l*, pg. 1401

WATERJET CUTTING SYSTEMS DIVISION—See Ingersoll-Rand Company; *U.S. Public*, pg. 877

WATERLOO FURNITURE COMPONENTS LIMITED—See Contran Corporation; *U.S. Private*, pg. 270

WATERLOO INDUSTRIES, INC.—See Fortune Brands, Inc.; *U.S. Public*, pg. 675

WATERLOO MALTING CO., INC.—See Philip Morris Companies Inc.; *U.S. Public*, pg. 1289

WATERLOO RAILWAY COMPANY—See Illinois Central Corporation; *U.S. Public*, pg. 865

WATERLOO SERVICE COMPANY; *U.S. Private*, pg. 1152

WATERMAN S.A.—See The Gillette Company; *U.S. Public*, pg. 745

WATERMAN STEAMSHIP CORPORATION—See International Shipholding Corporation; *U.S. Public*, pg. 907

WATEROUS COMPANY—See American Cast Iron Pipe Co.; *U.S. Private*, pg. 52

WATEROUS DETROIT DIESEL-ALLISON INC.—See Wajax Limited; *Int'l*, pg. 1485

WATERS COAL COMPANY—See Alabama Electric Cooperative, Inc.; *U.S. Private*, pg. 30

WATERS CORPORATION; *U.S. Public*, pg. 1745

WATERS INSTRUMENTS, INC.; *U.S. Public*, pg. 1745

WATERVILLE TG INC.; *Int'l*, pg. 1487

WATERVILLE VALLEY SKI AREA LTD.—See American Skiing Company; *U.S. Private*, pg. 62

WATERWAY COMMUNICATIONS INC.—See CSX Corporation; *U.S. Public*, pg. 284

WATERWAY HOLDINGS, INC.—See NIPSCO Industries, Inc.; *U.S. Public*, pg. 1185

WATERWORKS EQUIPMENT CO. (WECO) DIV.—See United States Filter Corporation; *U.S. Public*, pg. 1682

WATKINS ASSOCIATED DEVELOPERS—See Watkins Associated Industries Inc.; *U.S. Private*, pg. 1153

WATKINS ASSOCIATED INDUSTRIES INC.; *U.S. Private*, pg. 1153

WATKINS CONTRACTING, INC.—See Rexx Environmental Corp.; *U.S. Public*, pg. 1384

WATKINS ENGINEERS & CONSTRUCTORS, INC.—See Dillingham Construction Corporation; *U.S. Private*, pg. 333

WATKINS INCORPORATED; *U.S. Private*, pg. 1153

WATKINS-JOHNSON COMPANY; *U.S. Public*, pg. 1745

WATKINS-JOHNSON INTERNATIONAL—See Watkins-Johnson Company; *U.S. Public*, pg. 1745

WATKINS MANUFACTURING CORP./HOT SPRING PORTABLE SPAS—See Masco Corporation; *U.S. Public*, pg. 1054

WATKINS SYSTEM INC.; *U.S. Private*, pg. 1153

WATLINGTON WATERWORKS LIMITED—See Ionics, Incorporated; *U.S. Public*, pg. 912

WATLOW ANAFAZE—See Watlow Electric Manufacturing Company; *U.S. Private*, pg. 1153

WATLOW AOV, INC.—See Watlow Electric Manufacturing Company; *U.S. Private*, pg. 1153

WATLOW BATAVIA, INC.—See Watlow Electric Manufacturing Company; *U.S. Private*, pg. 1153

WATLOW COLUMBIA, INC.—See Watlow Electric Manufacturing Company; *U.S. Private*, pg. 1153

WATLOW DE MEXICO S.A. DE C.V.—See Watlow Electric Manufacturing Company; *U.S. Private*, pg. 1153

WATLOW ELECTRIC COMPANY OF CALIFORNIA—See Watlow Electric Manufacturing Company; *U.S. Private*, pg. 1153

WATLOW ELECTRIC FOREIGN SALES CORPORATION—See Watlow Electric Manufacturing Company; *U.S. Private*, pg. 1153

WATLOW ELECTRIC MANUFACTURING COMPANY; *U.S. Private*, pg. 1153

WATLOW ELECTRIC MFG. CO. GMBH—See Watlow Electric Manufacturing Company; *U.S. Private*, pg. 1153

WATLOW FRANCE S.A.R.L.—See Watlow Electric Manufacturing Company; *U.S. Private*, pg. 1154

WATLOW GORDON—See Watlow Electric Manufacturing Company; *U.S. Private*, pg. 1153

WATLOW INDUSTRIES, INC.—See Watlow Electric Manufacturing Company; *U.S. Private*, pg. 1153

WATLOW INFRARED COMPANY—See Watlow Electric Manufacturing Company; *U.S. Private*, pg. 1153

WATLOW ITALY—See Watlow Electric Manufacturing Company; *U.S. Private,* pg. 1154
WATLOW KOREA—See Watlow Electric Manufacturing Company; *U.S. Private,* pg. 1154
WATLOW LIMITED—See Watlow Electric Manufacturing Company; *U.S. Private,* pg. 1154
WATLOW PROCESS SYSTEMS, INC.—See Watlow Electric Manufacturing Company; *U.S. Private,* pg. 1153
WATLOW ST. LOUIS, INC.—See Watlow Electric Manufacturing Company; *U.S. Private,* pg. 1153
WATLOW SINGAPORE PTE. LTD.—See Watlow Electric Manufacturing Company; *U.S. Private,* pg. 1154
WATLOW TAIWAN—See Watlow Electric Manufacturing Company; *U.S. Private,* pg. 1154
WATLOW WINONA, INC.—See Watlow Electric Manufacturing Company; *U.S. Private,* pg. 1153
WATSCO COMPONENTS, INC.—See Watsco, Inc.; *U.S. Public,* pg. 1746
WATSCO, INC.; *U.S. Public,* pg. 1745
WATSON BOWMAN ACME CORP.—See Harris Chemical Group, Inc.; *U.S. Public,* pg. 505
WATSON BROWN—See Internatio-Muller N.V.; *Int'l,* pg. 682
WATSON ELECTRIC—See Warren Electric Group; *U.S. Private,* pg. 1151
WATSON LABORATORIES, INC.—See Watson Pharmaceuticals, Inc.; *U.S. Public,* pg. 1746
WATSON PHARMACEUTICALS, INC.; *U.S. Public,* pg. 1746
R.P. WATSON CO.—See Universal Corporation; *U.S. Public,* pg. 1695
WATSON STEEL & CO. (CONSTRUCTIONAL ENGINEERS) LTD.—See AMEC Plc; *Int'l,* pg. 16
WATSON STEEL & CO. (STEELWORK) LTD.—See AMEC Plc; *Int'l,* pg. 16
WATSON WYATT WORLDWIDE; *U.S. Private,* pg. 1154
WATSON'S QUALITY TURKEY PRODUCTS, INC.; *U.S. Private,* pg. 1154
THE WATT DESIGN GROUP INC.—See Cott Corporation; *Int'l,* pg. 338
WATT PUBLISHING CO.; *U.S. Private,* pg. 1154
WATT, ROOP & CO.; *U.S. Private,* pg. 1154
WATTERS & MARTIN INC.—See Distribution America; *U.S. Private,* pg. 335
WATTIE FROZEN FOODS LIMITED—See H.J. Heinz Company; *U.S. Public,* pg. 807
J. WATTIE FOODS—See H.J. Heinz Company; *U.S. Public,* pg. 807
WATTIE'S LIMITED—See H.J. Heinz Company; *U.S. Public,* pg. 807
WATTOHM—See Imetal; *Int'l,* pg. 662
WATTS AUTOMATIC CONTROL VALVES, INC.—See Watts Industries, Inc.; *U.S. Public,* pg. 1747
WATTS BLAKE BEARNE & CO. PLC; *Int'l,* pg. 1487
WATTS BROS. (A. SUTHRELL)—See Franz Haniel & Cie, GmbH; *Int'l,* pg. 591
WATTS EUROTHERM—See Watts Industries, Inc.; *U.S. Public,* pg. 1747
WATTS FLUIDAIR—See Siebe plc; *Int'l,* pg. 1243
WATTS INDUSTRIES (CANADA) INC.—See Watts Industries, Inc.; *U.S. Public,* pg. 1747
WATTS INDUSTRIES EUROPE B.V.—See Watts Industries, Inc.; *U.S. Public,* pg. 1747
WATTS INDUSTRIES, INC.; *U.S. Public,* pg. 1746
WATTS MTR GMBH—See Watts Industries, Inc.; *U.S. Public,* pg. 1747
WATTS REGTROL—See Watts Industries, Inc.; *U.S. Public,* pg. 1746
WATTS REGULATOR CO.—See Watts Industries, Inc.; *U.S. Public,* pg. 1747
WATTS REGULATOR/WATTS ACV—See Watts Industries, Inc.; *U.S. Public,* pg. 1746
WATTYL; *Int'l,* pg. 1488
WATTYL PAINT CORPORATION—See Wattyl; *Int'l,* pg. 1488
WATTYL/CAROLINA COATINGS—See Wattyl; *Int'l,* pg. 1488
WATTYL/MCI PAINTS—See Wattyl; *Int'l,* pg. 1488
WATVEARE LTD.—See Lonrho plc; *Int'l,* pg. 817
WAUKESHA BEARINGS CORP.—See Dover Corporation; *U.S. Public,* pg. 521
WAUKESHA CHERRY-BURRELL—See United Dominion Industries, Ltd.; *U.S. Public,* pg. 1677
WAUKESHA ENGINE DIVISION—See Dresser Industries, Inc.; *U.S. Public,* pg. 528
WAUKESHA FOUNDRY INC.; *U.S. Private,* pg. 1154
WAUKESHA-PEARCE INDUSTRIES—See Pearce Industries Inc.; *U.S. Private,* pg. 845
WAUNAKEE TELEPHONE CO., INC.—See Telephone and Data Systems, Inc.; *U.S. Public,* pg. 1572
WAUPACA FOUNDRY INC.—See Thyssen AG; *Int'l,* pg. 1389
WAUSAU DAILY HERALD—See Gannett Company, Inc.; *U.S. Public,* pg. 700
WAUSAU GENERAL INSURANCE COMPANY—See Nationwide Insurance Enterprise; *U.S. Private,* pg. 789
WAUSAU HOMES, INC.; *U.S. Private,* pg. 1154
WAUSAU INSURANCE COMPANY (U.K.), LTD.—See Nationwide Insurance Enterprise; *U.S. Private,* pg. 789
WAUSAU METALS CORP.—See Apogee Enterprises, Inc.; *U.S. Public,* pg. 120
WAUSAU METALS, NANIK DIVISION—See Springs Industries, Inc.; *U.S. Public,* pg. 1500
WAUSAU-MOSINEE PAPER CORPORATION; *U.S. Public,* pg. 1747
WAUSAU-MOSINEE PAPERS EXPORT CORPORATION—See Wausau-Mosinee Paper Corporation; *U.S. Public,* pg. 1748
WAUSAU-MOSINEE PAPERS INTERNATIONAL, INC.—See Wausau-Mosinee Paper Corporation; *U.S. Public,* pg. 1748
WAUSAU-MOSINEE PAPERS SPECIALTY PAPERS GROUP—See Wausau-Mosinee Paper Corporation; *U.S. Public,* pg. 1747

WAUSAU PAPERS - PRINTING & WRITING DIV.—See Wausau-Mosinee Paper Corporation; *U.S. Public,* pg. 1747
WAUSAU SERVICE CORP.—See Nationwide Insurance Enterprise; *U.S. Private,* pg. 789
WAUSAU UNDERWRITERS INSURANCE CO.—See Nationwide Insurance Enterprise; *U.S. Private,* pg. 789
WAVE—See Worthington Industries, Inc.; *U.S. Public,* pg. 1780
WAVERLEY MINERAL CORPORATION—See Laporte plc; *Int'l,* pg. 803
WAVERLY EUROPE LTD.—See Waverly, Inc.; *U.S. Public,* pg. 1748
WAVERLY FABRICS—See F. Schumacher & Co.; *U.S. Private,* pg. 973
WAVERLY GAS/VALLEY CITIES GAS—See NUI Corporation; *U.S. Public,* pg. 1148
WAVERLY HISPANICA S.A.—See Waverly, Inc.; *U.S. Public,* pg. 1748
WAVERLY HOUSE LIMITED—See Lagardere Groupe; *Int'l,* pg. 796
WAVERLY, INC.; *U.S. Public,* pg. 1748
WAVERLY INTERNATIONAL—See Waverly, Inc.; *U.S. Public,* pg. 1748
WAVERLY PRODUCTS CO.—See The Rival Company; *U.S. Public,* pg. 1391
WAVERLY VINTNERS LIMITED—See Scottish & Newcastle plc; *Int'l,* pg. 1212
WAVETEK CORPORATION—See Wavetek Corporation; *U.S. Private,* pg. 1155
WAVETEK CORPORATION; *U.S. Private,* pg. 1154
WAVETEK EXPORT CORP.—See Wavetek Corporation; *U.S. Private,* pg. 1155
WAVETEK GMBH—See Wavetek Corporation; *U.S. Private,* pg. 1155
WAVETEK LIMITED—See Wavetek Corporation; *U.S. Private,* pg. 1155
WAVIN BV—See Royal Dutch/Shell Group of Companies; *Int'l,* pg. 1155
WAWA, INC.; *U.S. Private,* pg. 1155
WAXIE MAXIE QUALITY MUSIC CO.—See Strawberries Inc.; *U.S. Private,* pg. 1047
WAXMAN INDUSTRIES, INC.; *U.S. Public,* pg. 1748
WAXMAN USA INC.—See Waxman Industries, Inc.; *U.S. Public,* pg. 1749
WAY BO FINANCE LIMITED—See HSBC Holdings plc; *Int'l,* pg. 584
WAY CHONG FINANCE LIMITED—See HSBC Holdings plc; *Int'l,* pg. 584
WAYCROSS MOLDED PRODUCTS, INC.—See Lancaster Colony Corporation; *U.S. Public,* pg. 977
WAYCROSS PLANT, WOOD PRODUCTS DIV.—See Champion International Corp.; *U.S. Public,* pg. 334
WAYCROSSE INC.; *U.S. Private,* pg. 1155
WAYFARER TRANSIT SYSTEMS LTD.—See Meggitt plc; *Int'l,* pg. 853
WAYFOONG CREDIT LTD.—See HSBC Holdings plc; *Int'l,* pg. 584
WAYFOONG PROPERTY LIMITED—See HSBC Holdings plc; *Int'l,* pg. 584
WAYLAND (PUBLISHERS)—See Wolters Kluwer N.V.; *Int'l,* pg. 1514
WAYNE CHEMICAL CORPORATION—See Harrisons & Crosfield plc; *Int'l,* pg. 599
WAYNE COFFEE COMPANY—See Chock Full O' Nuts Corporation; *U.S. Public,* pg. 351
WAYNE DALTON CORPORATION; *U.S. Private,* pg. 1155
WAYNE DALTON OF STERLING—See Wayne Dalton Corporation; *U.S. Private,* pg. 1155
WAYNE HOME EQUIPMENT DIV.—See Berkshire Hathaway Inc.; *U.S. Public,* pg. 218
WAYNE INDEPENDENT—See Media General, Inc.; *U.S. Public,* pg. 1078
WAYNE STEEL, INC.—See Metals USA, Inc.; *U.S. Public,* pg. 1101
WAYNE WIRE CLOTH PRODUCTS, INC.; *U.S. Public,* pg. 1155
WE CARE HAIR—See The Barbers, Hairstyling for Men & Women, Inc.; *U.S. Private,* pg. 115
WE VAC PLASTICS—See E & A Industries, Inc.; *U.S. Private,* pg. 352
WEABER, INC; *U.S. Private,* pg. 1155
WEARGUARD CORP.—See Aramark Corp.; *U.S. Private,* pg. 79
WEASLER ENGINEERING INC.—See Code, Hennessy & Simmons, Inc.; *U.S. Private,* pg. 249
WEATHER BARRIER INC.—See Finnaren & Haley, Inc.; *U.S. Private,* pg. 406
THE WEATHER CHANNEL—See Landmark Communications, Inc.; *U.S. Private,* pg. 647
WEATHER-MATIC DIV.—See Telsco Industries; *U.S. Private,* pg. 1074
WEATHER TEC CORPORATION; *U.S. Private,* pg. 1155
WEATHERALL GREEN & SMITH; *Int'l,* pg. 1488
WEATHERBY HEALTH CARE; *U.S. Private,* pg. 1155
WEATHERBY, INC.; *U.S. Private,* pg. 1155
WEATHERBY LOCUMS INC.—See Weatherby Health Care; *U.S. Private,* pg. 1155
WEATHERFORD AUSTRALIA PTY. LTD.—See Weatherford Enterra Incorporated; *U.S. Public,* pg. 1750
WEATHERFORD BIN HAMODAH—See Weatherford Enterra Incorporated; *U.S. Public,* pg. 1750
WEATHERFORD CANADA LIMITED—See Weatherford Enterra Incorporated; *U.S. Public,* pg. 1750
WEATHERFORD CANADA LTD.—See Weatherford Enterra Incorporated; *U.S. Public,* pg. 1750
WEATHERFORD ENTERRA BUSINESS DEVELOPMENT GROUP, LTD.—See Weatherford Enterra Incorporated; *U.S. Public,* pg. 1750
WEATHERFORD ENTERRA INCORPORATED; *U.S. Public,* pg. 1749
WEATHERFORD ENTERRA U.S., L.P.—See Weatherford Enterra Incorporated; *U.S. Public,* pg. 1749

WEATHERFORD/ESPANA, S.A.—See Weatherford Enterra Incorporated; *U.S. Public,* pg. 1750
WEATHERFORD FRANCE, S.A.—See Weatherford Enterra Incorporated; *U.S. Public,* pg. 1750
WEATHERFORD INC.—See Weatherford Enterra Incorporated; *U.S. Public,* pg. 1750
WEATHERFORD INC.-NEW ZEALAND BRANCH—See Weatherford Enterra Incorporated; *U.S. Public,* pg. 1750
WEATHERFORD INC. P.R.C.—See Weatherford Enterra Incorporated; *U.S. Public,* pg. 1750
WEATHERFORD INC.-THAILAND—See Weatherford Enterra Incorporated; *U.S. Public,* pg. 1750
WEATHERFORD (MALAYSIA) SDN. BHD.—See Weatherford Enterra Incorporated; *U.S. Public,* pg. 1750
WEATHERFORD MEDITERRANEA S.P.A.—See Weatherford Enterra Incorporated; *U.S. Public,* pg. 1750
WEATHERFORD NATIONAL BANK—See First Financial Bankshares, Inc.; *U.S. Public,* pg. 633
WEATHERFORD NORGE, A/S—See Weatherford Enterra Incorporated; *U.S. Public,* pg. 1750
WEATHERFORD OIL TOOL CO. (1983) LTD.—See Weatherford Enterra Incorporated; *U.S. Public,* pg. 1750
WEATHERFORD OIL TOOL GMBH—See Weatherford Enterra Incorporated; *U.S. Public,* pg. 1750
WEATHERFORD OIL TOOL MIDDLE EAST LTD.—See Weatherford Enterra Incorporated; *U.S. Public,* pg. 1750
WEATHERFORD OIL TOOL NEDERLAND B.V.—See Weatherford Enterra Incorporated; *U.S. Public,* pg. 1750
WEATHERFORD OIL TOOL (PTE.) LTD.—See Weatherford Enterra Incorporated; *U.S. Public,* pg. 1750
WEATHERFORD SAUDIA ARABIA LTD.—See Weatherford Enterra Incorporated; *U.S. Public,* pg. 1750
WEATHERFORD (U.K.) LIMITED—See Weatherford Enterra Incorporated; *U.S. Public,* pg. 1750
WEATHERFORD U.K. LTD.—See Weatherford Enterra Incorporated; *U.S. Public,* pg. 1750
WEATHERFORD U.S. INC.—See Weatherford Enterra Incorporated; *U.S. Public,* pg. 1749
WEATHERFORD US INC.—See Weatherford Enterra Incorporated; *U.S. Public,* pg. 1749
WEATHERFORD U.S., INC.—See Weatherford Enterra Incorporated; *U.S. Public,* pg. 1749
WEATHERHEAD BRAKE DIV.—See Dana Corporation; *U.S. Public,* pg. 480
WEATHERLY CONSUMER PRODUCTS—See U.S. Home & Garden Inc.; *U.S. Public,* pg. 1682
WEATHERLY PRIVATE CAPITAL, INC.; *U.S. Private,* pg. 1156
WEATHERLY SECURITIES CORP.—See Weatherly Private Capital, Inc.; *U.S. Private,* pg. 1156
THE WEATHERVANE RETAIL CORP.; *U.S. Private,* pg. 1156
C. WEAVER CHEVROLET, INC.; *U.S. Private,* pg. 1156
WEAVER CONSTRUCTION, LLC; *U.S. Private,* pg. 1156
WEAVER POPCORN COMPANY, INC.; *U.S. Private,* pg. 1156
WEB GRAPHICS, INC.—See American Pad and Paper Company; *U.S. Public,* pg. 89
WEB PRESS GRAPHICS LTD.—See Quebecor Inc.; *Int'l,* pg. 1077
WEB PROCESSING EQUIP. DIV.—See P/A Industries, Inc.; *U.S. Private,* pg. 825
WEBB AUTOMOTIVE GROUP; *U.S. Private,* pg. 1156
WEBB BUILDERS HARDWARE; *U.S. Private,* pg. 1156
THE WEBB COMPANY—See Quebecor Inc.; *Int'l,* pg. 1078
WEBB-CONVEYOR COMPANY OF AUSTRALIA PTY. LTD.—See Jervis B. Webb Company; *U.S. Private,* pg. 1157
WEBB ELECTRIC CO.—See Jervis B. Webb Company; *U.S. Private,* pg. 1156
WEBB FORGING—See Jervis B. Webb Company; *U.S. Private,* pg. 1156
WEBB HEAVY-DUTY ROLLER CONVEYOR SYSTEMS—See Jervis B. Webb Company; *U.S. Private,* pg. 1156
WEBB INDIA LTD.—See Jervis B. Webb Company; *U.S. Private,* pg. 1157
JERVIS B. WEBB COMPANY; *U.S. Private,* pg. 1156
JERVIS B. WEBB COMPANY LTD.—See Jervis B. Webb Company; *U.S. Private,* pg. 1157
JERVIS B. WEBB COMPANY OF CANADA LTD.—See Jervis B. Webb Company; *U.S. Private,* pg. 1157
JERVIS B. WEBB CO. OF GEORGIA—See Jervis B. Webb Company; *U.S. Private,* pg. 1157
JERVIS B. WEBB WORLDWIDE CO.—See Jervis B. Webb Company; *U.S. Private,* pg. 1156
WEBB, MURRAY & ASSOCIATES; *U.S. Private,* pg. 1157
WEBB-TRIAX COMPANY—See Jervis B. Webb Company; *U.S. Private,* pg. 1157
WEBBER GAGE DIV.—See The L.S. Starrett Company; *U.S. Public,* pg. 1511
WEBCRAFT GAMES, INC.—See Big Flower Press Holdings, Inc.; *U.S. Public,* pg. 228
WEBCRAFT TECHNOLOGIES, INC.—See Big Flower Press Holdings, Inc.; *U.S. Public,* pg. 228
WEBER AIRCRAFT, INC.—See Groupe Zodiac; *Int'l,* pg. 572
WEBER DO BRASIL INDUSTRIA E COMERCIO LTDA.—See Fiat Auto SpA; *Int'l,* pg. 482
THE WEBER GROUP—See Weber Public Relations Worldwide; *U.S. Private,* pg. 1157
WEBER-KNAPP COMPANY—See FKI Plc; *Int'l,* pg. 473
WEBER MARKING SYSTEMS CANADA LTD.—See Weber Marking Systems, Inc.; *U.S. Private,* pg. 1157
WEBER MARKING SYSTEMS (FAR EAST) CO. LTD.—See Weber Marking Systems, Inc.; *U.S. Private,* pg. 1157
WEBER MARKING SYSTEMS, INC.; *U.S. Private,* pg. 1157
WEBER MARKING SYSTEMS LTD.—See Weber Marking Systems, Inc.; *U.S. Private,* pg. 1157

WEBER PUBLIC RELATIONS WORLDWIDE; *U.S. Private,* pg. 1157
WEBER S.P.A.—See Fiat Auto SpA; *Int'l,* pg. 483
WEBER S.R.L.—See Fiat Auto SpA; *Int'l,* pg. 482
WEBER-STEPHEN PRODUCTS CO.; *U.S. Private,* pg. 1157
WILHELM WEBER GMBH—See Borden, Inc.; *U.S. Private,* pg. 160
WEBERBANK BERLINER INDUSTRIEBANK KGAA—See Bankgesellschaft Berlin; *Int'l,* pg. 160
WEBER'S BREAD BAKERIES—See Interstate Bakeries Corporation; *U.S. Public,* pg. 909
WEBSOURCE—See Unisource Worldwide, Inc.; *U.S. Public,* pg. 1671
WEBSTER BANK—See Webster Financial Corporation; *U.S. Public,* pg. 1751
WEBSTER COMPANY, INC.—See Danfoss A/S; *Int'l,* pg. 377
WEBSTER FINANCIAL CORPORATION; *U.S. Public,* pg. 1751
WEBSTER INDUSTRIES DIV.—See Chelsea Industries, Inc.; *U.S. Private,* pg. 231
WEBSTER INDUSTRIES INC.; *U.S. Public,* pg. 1157
WEBSTER MFG. CO.—See Webster Industries Inc.; *U.S. Public,* pg. 1158
WEBSTER-PORTALLOY CHAINS, INC.—See Webster Industries Inc.; *U.S. Public,* pg. 1158
WEBSTER RESEARCH CENTER—See Xerox Corporation; *U.S. Public,* pg. 1784
WEBSTER SPRING CO., INC.—See Leggett & Platt, Incorporated; *U.S. Public,* pg. 986
WEBSTER WIRE, INC.—See Leggett & Platt, Incorporated; *U.S. Public,* pg. 986
WECHCO, INC.; *U.S. Private,* pg. 1158
WECHSLER COFFEE CORP.; *U.S. Private,* pg. 1158
WEDA PUMP AB—See Trelleborg AB; *Int'l,* pg. 1421
WEDCO HOLLAND B.V.—See ICO, Inc.; *U.S. Public,* pg. 854
WEDCO TECHNOLOGY—See ICO, Inc.; *U.S. Public,* pg. 854
WEDCO TECHNOLOGY U.K. LTD.—See ICO, Inc.; *U.S. Public,* pg. 854
WEDGE DIA-LOG—See Wedge Energy Group Inc.; *U.S. Private,* pg. 1158
WEDGE ENERGY GROUP INC.; *U.S. Private,* pg. 1158
WEDGESTONE AUTOMOTIVE CORP.—See Wedgestone Financial Inc.; *U.S. Public,* pg. 1751
WEDGESTONE FINANCIAL INC.; *U.S. Public,* pg. 1751
WEDGWOOD U.S.A.—See Waterford Wedgwood Plc; *Int'l,* pg. 1487
WEDTECH INC.—See ICO, Inc.; *U.S. Public,* pg. 854
DAVID WEEKLEY HOMES; *U.S. Private,* pg. 1158
WEEKLY READER CORP.—See Primedia Inc.; *U.S. Public,* pg. 1328
WEEKLY WORLD NEWS, INC.—See American Media, Inc.; *U.S. Public,* pg. 87
WEEKS AND LEO CO., INC.; *U.S. Private,* pg. 1158
WEEKS DAIRY FOODS, INC.—See Koninklijke BolsWessanen nv; *Int'l,* pg. 752
THE WEETABIX COMPANY, INC.—See Weetabix Limited; *Int'l,* pg. 1488
WEETABIX LIMITED; *Int'l,* pg. 1488
WEETABIX OF CANADA (MFG.) LIMITED—See Weetabix Limited; *Int'l,* pg. 1488
WEGENER COMMUNICATIONS, INC.—See Wegener Corporation; *U.S. Public,* pg. 1751
WEGENER CORPORATION; *U.S. Public,* pg. 1751
WEGMANS FOOD MARKETS, INC.; *U.S. Private,* pg. 1158
WEHCO MEDIA, INC.; *U.S. Private,* pg. 1159
WEHCO VIDEO INC.—See Wehco Media, Inc.; *U.S. Private,* pg. 1159
WEHLE ELECTRIC CO., INC.—See Westburne Inc.; *Int'l,* pg. 1492
WEHR CONSTRUCTORS INC.; *U.S. Private,* pg. 1159
WEHR CONSTRUCTORS, INC.—See Wehr Constructors Inc.; *U.S. Private,* pg. 1159
WEHRUNG FAMILY HOME CENTER—See Modern Concrete Septic Tank Company; *U.S. Private,* pg. 754
WEI-CHUAN FOODS CORPORATION; *Int'l,* pg. 1488
WEIBEL WINERY; *U.S. Private,* pg. 1159
WEICHERT COMPANY; *U.S. Private,* pg. 1159
WEICHERT INSURANCE AGENT, INC.—See Weichert Company; *U.S. Private,* pg. 1159
WEICHERT REALTORS, INC.—See Weichert Company; *U.S. Private,* pg. 1159
WEICHERT REALTY CAREER DEVELOPMENT—See Weichert Company; *U.S. Private,* pg. 1159
WEICHERT REALTY, INC.—See Weichert Company; *U.S. Private,* pg. 1159
WEI-CHUAN FOODS U.S.A.—See Wei-Chuan Foods Corporation; *Int'l,* pg. 1488
WEIDER PUBLICATIONS, INC.; *U.S. Private,* pg. 1159
WEIGH-TRONIX—See Staveley Industries PLC; *Int'l,* pg. 1299
WEIGH-TRONIX, INC.—See Staveley Industries PLC; *Int'l,* pg. 1299
WEIGHT WATCHERS FOODS CENTRAL EUROPE B.V.—See H.J. Heinz Company; *U.S. Public,* pg. 807
WEIGHT WATCHERS GOURMET FOOD COMPANY—See H.J. Heinz Company; *U.S. Public,* pg. 806
WEIGHT WATCHERS INTERNATIONAL, INC.—See H.J. Heinz Company; *U.S. Public,* pg. 806
WEIGHT WATCHERS MAGAZINE—See Time Warner Inc.; *U.S. Public,* pg. 1612
THE WEIGHTMAN GROUP; *U.S. Private,* pg. 1159
WEIL BROTHERS COTTON INC.; *U.S. Private,* pg. 1159
WEIL-MCLAIN—See United Dominion Industries, Ltd.; *U.S. Public,* pg. 1676
WEILER & COMPANY, INC.; *U.S. Private,* pg. 1160
WEILWOOD INDUSTRIES, INC.—See Santee Print Works, Inc.; *U.S. Private,* pg. 965
WEIMAN—See Bassett Furniture Industries, Incorporated; *U.S. Public,* pg. 193
WEINBRENNER SHOE COMPANY, INC.; *U.S. Private,* pg. 1160

WEINBRENNEREI SCHARLACHBERG—See A. Racke GmbH; *Int'l,* pg. 1083
WEINERS STORES, INC.; *U.S. Private,* pg. 1160
WEINGARTEN REALTY INVESTORS; *U.S. Public,* pg. 1751
WEINGUT ROBERT WEIL K.G.—See Suntory Ltd.; *Int'l,* pg. 1322
WEINIG INTL. GMBH—See Michael Weinig AG; *Int'l,* pg. 1488
MICHAEL WEINIG AG; *Int'l,* pg. 1488
MICHAEL WEINIG, INC.—See Michael Weinig AG; *Int'l,* pg. 1488
WEINSTEIN INTERNATIONAL SEAFOOD—See American Foods Group, Inc.; *U.S. Private,* pg. 54
WEIR ELECTRONICS LIMITED—See Siebe plc; *Int'l,* pg. 1241
WEIR ENGINEERING PTY. LTD.—See Weir Group PLC; *Int'l,* pg. 1489
WEIR ENVIROTECH (PTY.) LTD.—See Weir Group PLC; *Int'l,* pg. 1489
WEIR FLOWAY INC.—See Weir Group PLC; *Int'l,* pg. 1489
WEIR GROUP PLC; *Int'l,* pg. 1488
WEIR MATERIALS LTD.—See Weir Group PLC; *Int'l,* pg. 1489
WEIR PUMPS LTD.—See Weir Group PLC; *Int'l,* pg. 1489
WEIR WESTGARTH LTD.—See Weir Group PLC; *Int'l,* pg. 1489
WEIRTON STEEL CORPORATION; *U.S. Public,* pg. 1751
WEIS FOOD SERVICE—See Weis Markets, Inc.; *U.S. Public,* pg. 1752
WEIS MARKETS, INC.; *U.S. Public,* pg. 1751
N.V. WEISER EUROPE, S.A.—See Masco Corporation; *U.S. Public,* pg. 1055
WEISER INC.—See Masco Corporation; *U.S. Public,* pg. 1055
WEISER LOCK—See Masco Corporation; *U.S. Public,* pg. 1053
WEISER LOCK CO. LTD.—See Masco Corporation; *U.S. Public,* pg. 1055
WEISER LOCK DIVISION—See Masco Corporation; *U.S. Public,* pg. 1053
WEISER LOCK PTY. LTD.—See Masco Corporation; *U.S. Public,* pg. 1055
WEISER THAILAND—See Masco Corporation; *U.S. Public,* pg. 1055
WEISER (U.K.) LTD.—See Masco Corporation; *U.S. Public,* pg. 1055
WEISS GLASS TECHNOLOGIES, INC.—See Tosoh Corporation; *Int'l,* pg. 1408
WEISS GROUP.; *U.S. Private,* pg. 1160
WEISS JEWELERS—See Reliable Stores, Inc.; *U.S. Private,* pg. 921
WEISS MONEY MANAGEMENT, INC.—See Weiss Group.; *U.S. Private,* pg. 1160
WEISS RATING, INC.—See Weiss Group.; *U.S. Private,* pg. 1160
WEISS RESEARCH, INC.—See Weiss Group.; *U.S. Private,* pg. 1160
WEISS SCIENTIFIC GLASS BLOWING CO., INC.—See Tosoh Corporation; *Int'l,* pg. 1408
WEISS SHEET METAL COMPANY; *U.S. Private,* pg. 1160
WEISS, WHITTEN, STAGLIANO INC.; *U.S. Private,* pg. 1160
CARL WEISSMAN & SONS, INC.; *U.S. Private,* pg. 1160
WEISZ GRAPHICS—See Fred B. Johnston Company, Inc.; *U.S. Private,* pg. 595
THE WEITZ COMPANY, INC.; *U.S. Private,* pg. 1160
THE WEITZ COMPANY, INC.—See The Weitz Company, Inc.; *U.S. Private,* pg. 1161
WEITZ-COHEN CONSTRUCTION CO.—See The Weitz Company, Inc.; *U.S. Private,* pg. 1161
WEL-COM FINANCIAL SERVICES, INC.—See Colonial Commercial Corp.; *U.S. Public,* pg. 400
WELBECK GOLIN/HARRIS COMMUNICATIONS LTD.—See Shandwick International Plc; *Int'l,* pg. 1226
WELBILT CORPORATION—See Berisford plc; *Int'l,* pg. 188
WELBILT VARIMIXER—See Berisford plc; *Int'l,* pg. 189
WELCH FOODS INC., A COOPERATIVE—See National Grape Co-Op Association, Inc.; *U.S. Private,* pg. 784
WELCH/THOMAS VACUUM—See Thomas Industries Inc.; *U.S. Public,* pg. 1599
WELCO LUMBER COMPANY; *U.S. Private,* pg. 1161
WELCOMBE HOTEL—See Sea Containers Ltd.; *Int'l,* pg. 1213
WELCOME BREAK GROUP LIMITED—See Investcorp International; *Int'l,* pg. 686
WELCOME HOME, INC.—See Jordan Industries, Inc.; *U.S. Private,* pg. 598
WELCOME WAGON-INTL., INC.—See Cendant Corporation; *U.S. Public,* pg. 321
WELDED TUBE—See Australian National Industries Limited; *Int'l,* pg. 101
WELDED TUBE COMPANY—See Australian National Industries Limited; *Int'l,* pg. 101
WELDING PRODUCTS GROUP—See National-Standard Co.; *U.S. Public,* pg. 1161
WELDING SYSTEMS DIVISION—See ABB Asea Brown Boveri (Holding) Ltd.; *Int'l,* pg. 4
WELDON, INC.—See B. Elliott plc; *Int'l,* pg. 449
WELDON MACHINE TOOL, INC.; *U.S. Private,* pg. 1161
WELDON, WILLIAMS & LICK, INC.; *U.S. Private,* pg. 1161
WELDOTRON CORPORATION; *U.S. Public,* pg. 1752
WELDOTRON DO BRASIL—See Weldotron Corporation; *U.S. Public,* pg. 1752
WELDUN INTERNATIONAL, INC.—See Robert Bosch GmbH; *Int'l,* pg. 205
WELDWOOD OF CANADA LIMITED—See Champion International Corp.; *U.S. Public,* pg. 334
WELENCO, INC.—See OYO Corporation; *Int'l,* pg. 1019
WELL ENGINEERING AND TECHNOLOGY (GETEP)—See Petrobras - Petroleo Brasileiro S.A.; *Int'l,* pg. 1042
WELLA (AUSTRALIA) COSMETIC SUPPLIERS PTY. LTD.—See Wella Group; *Int'l,* pg. 1490

WELLA BETEILIGUNGEN AG—See Wella Group; *Int'l,* pg. 1490
WELLA CANADA INC.—See Wella Group; *Int'l,* pg. 1489
THE WELLA CORPORATION—See Wella Group; *Int'l,* pg. 1489
WELLA DUBLIN—See Wella Group; *Int'l,* pg. 1490
WELLA FRISEURBEDARF GMBH—See Wella Group; *Int'l,* pg. 1490
WELLA GROUP; *Int'l,* pg. 1489
WELLA ITALIANA—See Wella Group; *Int'l,* pg. 1490
WELLA NETHERLANDS N.V. VAN RAVENSBERG—See Wella Group; *Int'l,* pg. 1490
WELLA PARIS ETS. PELLERAY S.A.R.L.—See Wella Group; *Int'l,* pg. 1490
WELLA PORTUGAL SOCIEDADE DE COSMETICOS LUSO-ALEMA LDA.—See Wella Group; *Int'l,* pg. 1490
WELLA (SUISSE)—See Wella Group; *Int'l,* pg. 1490
WELLAND FORGE DIV.—See FKI Plc; *Int'l,* pg. 474
WELLAND PIPE LTD.—See Stelco Inc.; *Int'l,* pg. 1299
WELLBORN - CORP.—See Dunn-Edwards Corporation; *U.S. Private,* pg. 347
WELLCO ENTERPRISES, INC.; *U.S. Public,* pg. 1752
WELLCOME AG—See Glaxo Wellcome plc; *Int'l,* pg. 553
WELLCOME AUSTRALIA LTD.—See Glaxo Wellcome plc; *Int'l,* pg. 553
WELLCOME BIOFARMA SA—See Glaxo Wellcome plc; *Int'l,* pg. 553
WELLCOME COMPANY LIMITED—See Jardine Matheson Holdings Limited; *Int'l,* pg. 704
WELLCOME DANMARK A/S—See Glaxo Wellcome plc; *Int'l,* pg. 553
WELLCOME FARMACEUTICA SA—See Glaxo Wellcome plc; *Int'l,* pg. 553
WELLCOME GMBH—See Glaxo Wellcome plc; *Int'l,* pg. 553
WELLCOME ILAC URUNLERI LTD SIRKETI—See Glaxo Wellcome plc; *Int'l,* pg. 553
WELLCOME IRELAND LTD.—See Glaxo Wellcome plc; *Int'l,* pg. 553
WELLCOME KENYA LTD—See Glaxo Wellcome plc; *Int'l,* pg. 553
WELLCOME MEXICO SA DE CV—See Glaxo Wellcome plc; *Int'l,* pg. 553
WELLCOME NIGERIA LTD—See Glaxo Wellcome plc; *Int'l,* pg. 553
WELLCOME NORGE AS—See Glaxo Wellcome plc; *Int'l,* pg. 553
WELLCOME PAKISTAN LTD—See Glaxo Wellcome plc; *Int'l,* pg. 553
WELLCOME PHARMACEUTICALS BV—See Glaxo Wellcome plc; *Int'l,* pg. 553
WELLCOME PHILIPPINES INC—See Glaxo Wellcome plc; *Int'l,* pg. 553
N.V. WELLCOME S.A.—See Glaxo Wellcome plc; *Int'l,* pg. 553
WELLCOME SINGAPORE PRIVATE LTD.—See Glaxo Wellcome plc; *Int'l,* pg. 553
WELLCOME TAIWAN COMPANY LTD.—See Jardine Matheson Holdings Limited; *Int'l,* pg. 704
WELLCOME THAILAND LTD.—See Glaxo Wellcome plc; *Int'l,* pg. 553
WELLCOME ZAMBIA LTD—See Glaxo Wellcome plc; *Int'l,* pg. 553
WELLCRAFT MARINE CORP.—See Genmar Holdings, Inc.; *U.S. Private,* pg. 447
WELLENS & CO., INC.; *U.S. Private,* pg. 1161
WELLINGTON INDUSTRIES INC.; *U.S. Private,* pg. 1161
WELLINGTON INSURANCE—See ING Groep N.V.; *Int'l,* pg. 651
WELLINGTON INSURANCE COMPANY—See EdperBrascan Corporation; *Int'l,* pg. 435
WELLINGTON MANUFACTURING, INC.—See Rieter Holdings; *Int'l,* pg. 1117
WELLINGTON REGIONAL MEDICAL CENTER—See Universal Health Services, Inc.; *U.S. Public,* pg. 1697
WELLINGTON SEARS CO.—See Johnston Industries, Inc.; *U.S. Public,* pg. 933
WELLINGTON TRUST COMPANY—See BCE Inc.; *Int'l,* pg. 115
WELLMADE INDUSTRIES, INCORPORATED; *U.S. Private,* pg. 1161
WELLMAN BONDED FIBERS DIV.—See Wellman, Inc.; *U.S. Public,* pg. 1753
WELLMAN DAY PRODUCTS DIV.—See Wellman, Inc.; *U.S. Public,* pg. 1753
WELLMAN DYNAMICS CORP.—See Fansteel, Inc.; *U.S. Public,* pg. 612
WELLMAN ENGINEERING RESINS DIV.—See Wellman, Inc.; *U.S. Public,* pg. 1752
WELLMAN EXTRUSIONS, INC.—See Wellman, Inc.; *U.S. Public,* pg. 1753
WELLMAN FIBERS LTD.—See Wellman, Inc.; *U.S. Public,* pg. 1753
WELLMAN, INC.; *U.S. Public,* pg. 1752
WELLMAN INTERNATIONAL GMBH—See Wellman, Inc.; *U.S. Public,* pg. 1753
WELLMAN INTERNATIONAL LTD.—See Wellman, Inc.; *U.S. Public,* pg. 1753
WELLMAN MAN-MADE FIBERS DIV.—See Wellman, Inc.; *U.S. Public,* pg. 1753
WELLMAN NONWOVENS DIV.—See Wellman, Inc.; *U.S. Public,* pg. 1753
WELLMAN POLYMER PRODUCTS DIV.—See Wellman, Inc.; *U.S. Public,* pg. 1753
WELLMAN RECYCLING DIV.—See Wellman, Inc.; *U.S. Public,* pg. 1753
WELLMAN WOOL DIV.—See Wellman, Inc.; *U.S. Public,* pg. 1753
WELLNITE SERVICES—See Praxair Inc.; *U.S. Public,* pg. 1320
WELLPHARMA OY—See Glaxo Wellcome plc; *Int'l,* pg. 553
WELLPOINT HEALTH NETWORKS, INC.—See Blue Cross of California; *U.S. Private,* pg. 152
WELLS ALUMINUM CORP.; *U.S. Private,* pg. 1161

WELLS DIRECTORY OF CORPORATE AFFILIATIONS

Company Index

WELLS BDDP, INC.—See BDDP Group; *Int'l*, pg. 117
WELLS ELECTRONICS ASIA PTE LTD.—See Siebe plc; *Int'l*, pg. 1242
WELLS ELECTRONICS INC.—See Siebe plc; *Int'l*, pg. 1241
WELLS FARGO ALARM SERVICES, INC.—See Borg-Warner Security Corporation; *U.S. Public*, pg. 246
WELLS FARGO & COMPANY; *U.S. Public*, pg. 1753
WELLS FARGO & COMPANY—See Wells Fargo & Company; *U.S. Public*, pg. 1753
WELLS FARGO BANK—See Wells Fargo & Company; *U.S. Public*, pg. 1753
WELLS FARGO BANK, NATIONAL ASSN.—See Wells Fargo & Company; *U.S. Public*, pg. 1753
WELLS-GARDNER ELECTRONICS CORP.; *U.S. Public*, pg. 1753
WELLS JAPAN LTD.—See Siebe plc; *Int'l*, pg. 1242
WELLS MFG. CORP.—See UIS, Inc.; *U.S. Private*, pg. 1113
WELLSPRING RESOURCES, LLC—See Watson Wyatt Worldwide; *U.S. Private*, pg. 1154
WELLSPRING RESOURCES, LLC—See State Street Corporation; *U.S. Public*, pg. 1513
WELLSTREAM COMPANY—See Dresser Industries, Inc.; *U.S. Public*, pg. 528
WELLSVILLE FIRE BRICK COMPANY—See CFB Industries, Inc.; *U.S. Private*, pg. 194
WELSBACH ELECTRIC CORP.—See EMCOR Group, Inc.; *U.S. Public*, pg. 572
WELSCO INC.; *U.S. Private*, pg. 1161
WELSH CARSON ANDERSON & STOWE; *U.S. Private*, pg. 1162
WELSH FARMS, INC.; *U.S. Private*, pg. 1162
WELTMARKEN IMPORT SPIRITUOSEN UND WEINE GMBH—See Diageo Plc; *Int'l*, pg. 410
E.J. WELTON & CO. LIMITED—See Willis Corroon Group PLC; *Int'l*, pg. 1502
WELWYN COMPONENTS LIMITED—See TT Group PLC; *Int'l*, pg. 1344
WELWYN SYSTEMS LIMITED—See TT Group PLC; *Int'l*, pg. 1344
WEMADO B.V.—See Unilever Plc; *Int'l*, pg. 1439
WEMCO ENVIROTECH PUMPSYSTEMS SA—See Weir Group PLC; *Int'l*, pg. 1489
WEMCO, INC.—See Randa Corp.; *U.S. Private*, pg. 909
WEMEX ENGINEERING ASIA (PTE) LTD.—See Axel Johnson AB; *Int'l*, pg. 712
WEMEX TECHNOLOGY B.V.—See Royal Begemann Group; *Int'l*, pg. 1133
WENATCHEE MOUNTAINS, INC.—See Time Warner Inc.; *U.S. Public*, pg. 1611
WENCO INC.—See Wendy's International Inc.; *U.S. Public*, pg. 1754
WENDCO NORTHWEST LIMITED—See Wendy's International Inc.; *U.S. Public*, pg. 1754
WENDCREEK VENTURE—See Wendy's International Inc.; *U.S. Public*, pg. 1754
WENDLAND MANUFACTURING CORPORATION—See Bryan Steam Corporation; *U.S. Private*, pg. 176
WENDY CUSHING TRIMMINGS—See Conso Products Company; *U.S. Public*, pg. 434
WENDY RESTAURANT, INC.—See Wendy's International Inc.; *U.S. Public*, pg. 1754
WENDY'S CAPITAL CORPORATION—See Wendy's International Inc.; *U.S. Public*, pg. 1754
WENDY'S INTERNATIONAL INC.; *U.S. Public*, pg. 1754
WENDY'S OLD FASHIONED HAMBURGERS OF NEW YORK—See Wendy's International Inc.; *U.S. Public*, pg. 1754
WENDY'S RESTAURANTS OF CANADA INC.—See Wendy's International Inc.; *U.S. Public*, pg. 1754
WENGER CORPORATION; *U.S. Private*, pg. 1162
WENINGER INDUSTRIES DIVISION—See Jannock Limited; *Int'l*, pg. 698
WENKO COMPANY, LTD. (KOREA)—See Wendy's International Inc.; *U.S. Public*, pg. 1754
WENNER MEDIA; *U.S. Private*, pg. 1162
WENTEXAS—See Wendy's International Inc.; *U.S. Public*, pg. 1754
WENTGATE DYNAWELD INC.—See TI Group plc; *Int'l*, pg. 1337
WENTWORTH IMPORT & EXPORT LTD.—See The Albert Fisher Group PLC; *Int'l*, pg. 491
AB WERBA—See Investor AB; *Int'l*, pg. 686
WERK BAD KREUZNACH—See Klockner-Werke AG; *Int'l*, pg. 737
WERK HAMBURG—See Statoil; *Int'l*, pg. 1298
WERK HORST—See Veba AG; *Int'l*, pg. 1461
WERK MUNCHSMUNSTER—See Veba AG; *Int'l*, pg. 1461
WERK SCHOLVEN—See Veba AG; *Int'l*, pg. 1461
WERK-VERLAG—See Reed Elsevier plc; *Int'l*, pg. 1099
WERKHOF GMBH—See Standard Commercial Corporation; *U.S. Public*, pg. 1502
WERLER DRAHTWERKE GMBH & CO. KG—See N.V. Bekaert S.A.; *Int'l*, pg. 184
WERNER & PFLEIDERER AB—See Fried. Krupp AG; *Int'l*, pg. 511
OY WERNER & PFLEIDERER AB—See Fried. Krupp AG; *Int'l*, pg. 511
WERNER & PFLEIDERER AG BAKERY EQUIPMENT—See Fried. Krupp AG; *Int'l*, pg. 511
WERNER & PFLEIDERER ASIA LTD.—See Fried. Krupp AG; *Int'l*, pg. 511
WERNER & PFLEIDERER BACKTECHNIK AG—See Fried. Krupp AG; *Int'l*, pg. 511
WERNER & PFLEIDERER BACKTECHNIK VERTRIEBS-GMBH—See Fried. Krupp AG; *Int'l*, pg. 511
WERNER & PFLEIDERER CORPORATION—See Fried. Krupp AG; *Int'l*, pg. 511
WERNER & PFLEIDERER DE MEXICO S. DE R. L. DE C.V.—See Fried. Krupp AG; *Int'l*, pg. 511
WERNER & PFLEIDERER FRANCE S.A.R.L.—See Fried. Krupp AG; *Int'l*, pg. 511
WERNER & PFLEIDERER GMBH—See Fried. Krupp AG; *Int'l*, pg. 510
WERNER & PFLEIDERER GUMMITECHNIK GMBH—See Fried. Krupp AG; *Int'l*, pg. 510
WERNER & PFLEIDERER HATON B.V.—See Fried. Krupp AG; *Int'l*, pg. 511
WERNER & PFLEIDERER INC.—See Fried. Krupp AG; *Int'l*, pg. 510
WERNER & PFLEIDERER ITALIA S.R.L.—See Fried. Krupp AG; *Int'l*, pg. 511
WERNER & PFLEIDERER LEBENSMITTELTECHNIK GMBH—See Fried. Krupp AG; *Int'l*, pg. 511
WERNER & PFLEIDERER MASCHINENTECHNIK GES. MBH—See Fried. Krupp AG; *Int'l*, pg. 511
WERNER & PFLEIDERER P.V.B.A.—See Fried. Krupp AG; *Int'l*, pg. 511
WERNER & PFLEIDERER SOUTH AFRICA (PTY.) LTD.—See Fried. Krupp AG; *Int'l*, pg. 511
WERNER & PFLEIDERER (U.K.) LTD.—See Fried. Krupp AG; *Int'l*, pg. 511
WERNER BALDESSARINI DESIGN GMBH—See Hugo Boss AG; *Int'l*, pg. 637
WERNER ENTERPRISES, INC.; *U.S. Public*, pg. 1754
FRITZ WERNER MACHINE TOOLS AG—See Rothenberger Group GmbH; *Int'l*, pg. 1128
FRITZ WERNER MACHINE TOOLS INTERNATIONAL GMBH—See Rothenberger Group GmbH; *Int'l*, pg. 1128
WERNER INTERNATIONAL—See Reliance Group Holdings, Inc.; *U.S. Public*, pg. 1374
WERNERS, INC.—See Bell Atlantic Corporation; *U.S. Public*, pg. 203
WERSHOW-ASH-LEWIS; *U.S. Private*, pg. 1162
WERTHAN PACKAGING, INC.; *U.S. Private*, pg. 1162
WESALEM COMPANY—See Salem Group, Inc.; *U.S. Private*, pg. 962
WESCO DISTRIBUTION, INC.—See Clayton, Dubilier & Rice, Inc; *U.S. Private*, pg. 244
WESCO FINANCIAL CORPORATION—See Berkshire Hathaway Inc.; *U.S. Public*, pg. 217
WESCO-FINANCIAL INSURANCE COMPANY—See Berkshire Hathaway Inc.; *U.S. Public*, pg. 217
WESCON PRODUCTS COMPANY—See Latshaw Enterprises, Inc.; *U.S. Public*, pg. 979
WESER-EMS VERTRIEBSGESELLSCHAFT MBH—See Volkswagen AG; *Int'l*, pg. 1474
WESGO CERAMICS GMBH—See Morgan Crucible Co. Plc; *Int'l*, pg. 893
WESGO INC.—See Morgan Crucible Co. Plc; *Int'l*, pg. 893
WESLEY-JESSEN—See Bain Capital; *U.S. Private*, pg. 111
WESLEYAN NURSING HOME, INC.—See Vencor, Inc.; *U.S. Public*, pg. 1715
WESLEY'S QUAKER MAID ICE CREAM—See Tengelmann Warenhandelsgesellschaft; *Int'l*, pg. 1375
WESLOCK NATIONAL, INC.; *U.S. Private*, pg. 1163
WESSANEN AG—See Koninklijke BolsWessanen nv; *Int'l*, pg. 753
WESSANEN FLOUR INTERNATIONAL B.V.—See Koninklijke BolsWessanen nv; *Int'l*, pg. 751
WESSANEN MEEL B.V.—See Koninklijke BolsWessanen nv; *Int'l*, pg. 751
WESSEL HARDWARE—See Vista 2000, Inc.; *U.S. Private*, pg. 1142
WESSEL IND. LTD.—See ABB Asea Brown Boveri (Holding) Ltd.; *Int'l*, pg. 3
WESSEX ADVANCED SWITCHING PRODUCTS LTD.—See Bowthorpe plc; *Int'l*, pg. 208
WESSON/PETER PAN FOODS CO.—See ConAgra, Inc.; *U.S. Public*, pg. 428
WEST ADVERTISING/PUBLIC RELATIONS, INC.—See KOA Holdings; *U.S. Private*, pg. 603
WEST AGRO, INC.—See Tetra Laval Group; *Int'l*, pg. 1379
WEST AGRO, INC.-DES PLAINES—See Tetra Laval Group; *Int'l*, pg. 1379
THE WEST BEND CO.—See Premark International, Inc.; *U.S. Public*, pg. 1322
WEST BUILDING MATERIALS; *U.S. Private*, pg. 1163
WEST CENTRAL COOPERATIVE; *U.S. Private*, pg. 1163
WEST CHEMICAL PRODUCTS, INC.—See Wechco, Inc.; *U.S. Private*, pg. 1158
WEST CHUGOKU CATERPILLAR MITSUBISHI CONSTRUCTION EQUIPMENT SALES, LTD.—See Caterpillar Inc.; *U.S. Public*, pg. 317
WEST COAST BANCORP; *U.S. Public*, pg. 1755
WEST COAST CONVERSION CO., INC.—See Calprop Corporation; *U.S. Public*, pg. 296
WEST COAST CORRECT CRAFT, INC.—See Correct Craft, Inc.; *U.S. Private*, pg. 277
WEST COAST CREATIVE—See Devon Group, Inc.; *U.S. Public*, pg. 503
WEST COAST ENTERTAINMENT INC.; *U.S. Public*, pg. 1755
WEST COAST EXPLOSIVES—See Mining Services International, Inc.; *U.S. Public*, pg. 1115
WEST COAST LIFE INSURANCE CO.—See Protective Life Corporation; *U.S. Public*, pg. 1336
WEST COAST LIQUIDATORS, INC.—See Consolidated Stores Corp.; *U.S. Public*, pg. 437
THE WEST COMPANY ARGENTINA S.A.—See The West Company, Incorporated; *U.S. Public*, pg. 1755
THE WEST COMPANY AUSTRALIA PTY. LTD.—See The West Company, Incorporated; *U.S. Public*, pg. 1755
THE WEST COMPANY BRASIL LTDA.—See The West Company, Incorporated; *U.S. Public*, pg. 1755
THE WEST COMPANY (CUSTOM & SPECIALTY SERVICES) G.M.B.H—See The West Company, Incorporated; *U.S. Public*, pg. 1755
THE WEST COMPANY DE COLOMBIA, S.A.—See The West Company, Incorporated; *U.S. Public*, pg. 1756
THE WEST COMPANY DEUTSCHLAND—See The West Company, Incorporated; *U.S. Public*, pg. 1756
THE WEST COMPANY FRANCE, S.A.—See The West Company, Incorporated; *U.S. Public*, pg. 1756
THE WEST COMPANY GROUP LIMITED—See The West Company, Incorporated; *U.S. Public*, pg. 1756
THE WEST COMPANY HISPANIA, S.A.—See The West Company, Incorporated; *U.S. Public*, pg. 1756
THE WEST COMPANY HOLDING, G.M.B.H—See The West Company, Incorporated; *U.S. Public*, pg. 1756
THE WEST COMPANY, INCORPORATED; *U.S. Public*, pg. 1755
THE WEST COMPANY ITALIA S.R.L.—See The West Company, Incorporated; *U.S. Public*, pg. 1756
THE WEST COMPANY MEXICO, SA.DE C.V.—See The West Company, Incorporated; *U.S. Public*, pg. 1756
THE WEST COMPANY OF DELAWARE, INC.—See The West Company, Incorporated; *U.S. Public*, pg. 1755
WEST COMPANY OF KOREA LIMITED—See The West Company, Incorporated; *U.S. Public*, pg. 1756
THE WEST COMPANY OF PUERTO RICO, INC.—See The West Company, Incorporated; *U.S. Public*, pg. 1755
THE WEST COMPANY SINGAPORE PTY. LTD.—See The West Company, Incorporated; *U.S. Public*, pg. 1756
THE WEST COMPANY (UK) LTD.—See The West Company, Incorporated; *U.S. Public*, pg. 1756
THE WEST COMPANY VENEZUELA C.A.—See The West Company, Incorporated; *U.S. Public*, pg. 1756
WEST COUNTY TIMES—See Knight-Ridder, Inc.; *U.S. Public*, pg. 964
WEST DALLAS—See Salant Corporation; *U.S. Public*, pg. 1429
WEST END SYSTEMS CORPORATION—See Newbridge Networks Corporation; *Int'l*, pg. 924
FLOYD WEST & COMPANY—See H.W. Kaufman Financial Group, Inc.; *U.S. Private*, pg. 609
WEST FOOTSCRAY ENGINEERING WORKS PTY. LTD.—See Delta plc; *Int'l*, pg. 392
WEST FRASER TIMBER CO. LTD.; *Int'l*, pg. 1490
THE WEST HARRISON GAS AND ELECTRIC CO.—See Cinergy Corp.; *U.S. Public*, pg. 369
WEST HASTINGS (GMO) HOLDINGS INC.—See Confederation Life Insurance Company; *Int'l*, pg. 326
WEST HUDSON, INC. (HEALTHCARE CONSULTING SERVICES)—See Allegiance Healthcare Corp.; *U.S. Public*, pg. 45
THE WEST INDIA COMPANY OF MERCHANT BANKERS LIMITED—See The Bank of Nova Scotia; *Int'l*, pg. 156
WEST INFORMATION PUBLISHING GROUP—See The Thomson Corporation; *U.S. Public*, pg. 1602
WEST INSTRUMENTS—See Mark IV Industries Inc.; *U.S. Public*, pg. 1045
WEST INTERNATIONAL SALES CORPORATION—See The West Company, Incorporated; *U.S. Public*, pg. 1755
WEST JAPAN RAILWAY COMPANY; *Int'l*, pg. 1490
WEST JEWEL INC.; *U.S. Private*, pg. 1163
JOHN WEST FOODS LTD.—See Unilever Plc; *Int'l*, pg. 1434
WEST KENTUCKY DIVISION—See Costain Group PLC; *Int'l*, pg. 337
WEST KOOTENAY POWER—See UtiliCorp United Inc.; *U.S. Public*, pg. 1701
WEST LYNN CREAMERY, INC.—See Scangas Brothers Holdings, Inc.; *U.S. Private*, pg. 969
WEST LYNN CREAMERY REALTY CORPORATION—See Scangas Brothers Holdings, Inc.; *U.S. Private*, pg. 969
WEST MARINE, INC.; *U.S. Public*, pg. 1756
WEST MERCHANT BANK LTD.—See Westdeutsche Landesbank Girozentrale; *Int'l*, pg. 1493
WEST MERCHANT BANK LIMITED—See Westdeutsche Landesbank Girozentrale; *Int'l*, pg. 1493
WEST MERCHANT BANK LTD.—See Westdeutsche Landesbank Girozentrale; *Int'l*, pg. 1493
WEST MILL CLOTHES, H.M.C. DIV.—See West Mill Clothes, Inc.; *U.S. Private*, pg. 1163
WEST MILL CLOTHES, INC.; *U.S. Private*, pg. 1163
WEST MILL CLOTHES, TUXEDO ACCESSORIES DIV.—See West Mill Clothes, Inc.; *U.S. Private*, pg. 1163
WEST MORRIS PROPERTIES, INC.—See Quexco Incorporated; *U.S. Private*, pg. 901
WEST PALM BEACH AUTO AUCTION, INC.—See Tyco International Ltd.; *U.S. Public*, pg. 1649
WEST PALM BEACH TRAINING CENTER—See Berkshire Hathaway Inc.; *U.S. Public*, pg. 219
WEST PARK TOBACCO INC.—See Reemtsma Cigarettenfabriken GmbH, Hamburg; *Int'l*, pg. 1101
WEST PENETONE CORPORATION—See Wechco, Inc.; *U.S. Private*, pg. 1158
WEST PENETONE INC.—See Wechco, Inc.; *U.S. Private*, pg. 1158
WEST PENN POWER CO.—See Allegheny Power System, Inc.; *U.S. Public*, pg. 42
WEST PENN WIRE/CDT—See Cable Design Technologies Corporation; *U.S. Public*, pg. 287
WEST PENOBSCOT TELEGRAPH & TELEPHONE CO.—See Telephone and Data Systems, Inc.; *U.S. Public*, pg. 1572
WEST PLAINS ENERGY—See UtiliCorp United Inc.; *U.S. Public*, pg. 1701
WEST PUBLISHING CORPORATION—See The Thomson Corporation; *U.S. Public*, pg. 1602
WEST REGION—See MCI Communications Corp.; *U.S. Public*, pg. 1024
WEST RIDING WORSTED & WOOLEN MILLS LIMITED—See Coats Viyella plc; *Int'l*, pg. 299
WEST ROCKIES INC.—See Sinochem International Petroleum Co. Ltd.; *Int'l*, pg. 1255
WEST ROXBURY CRUSHED STONE CO.—See Browning-Ferris Industries, Inc.; *U.S. Public*, pg. 265
WEST SHORE ENVELOPE COMPANY, INC.; *U.S. Private*, pg. 1163
WEST TECH EXPO CORP.—See Central Newspapers, Inc.; *U.S. Public*, pg. 326
WEST TENNESSEE DETENTION FACILITY—See Corrections Corporation of America; *U.S. Public*, pg. 451
WEST TEXAS UTILITIES CO.—See Central and South West Corporation; *U.S. Public*, pg. 324

WEST TEXAS WHOLESALE SUPPLY CO.—See Distribution America; *U.S. Private,* pg. 335
WEST TORRANCE CARE CENTER—See Meritcare, Inc.; *U.S. Private,* pg. 733
WEST UNION CORPORATION; *U.S. Private,* pg. 1163
WEST VIRGINIA-AMERICAN WATER CO.—See American Water Works Company, Inc.; *U.S. Public,* pg. 96
WEST VIRGINIA CELLULAR TELEPHONE CORP.—See Vanguard Cellular Systems, Inc.; *U.S. Public,* pg. 1708
WEST VIRGINIA ELECTRIC CORP.—See Salem Group, Inc.; *U.S. Private,* pg. 962
WEST VIRGINIA POWER—See UtiliCorp United Inc.; *U.S. Public,* pg. 1701
WEST VIRGINIA PUMP & SUPPLY COMPANY—See ITT Industries, Inc.; *U.S. Public,* pg. 861
WESTAD INC.—See The Western and Southern Life Insurance Company; *U.S. Private,* pg. 1164
WESTAG & GETALIT AG; *Int'l,* pg. 1491
WESTAG WERBEAGENTUR; *Int'l,* pg. 1491
WESTAIR COMMUTER AIRLINES, INC.—See Mesa Air Group; *U.S. Public,* pg. 1099
WESTAMERICA BANCORPORATION; *U.S. Public,* pg. 1756
WESTAMERICA BANK—See Westamerica Bancorporation; *U.S. Public,* pg. 1756
WESTANA GATHERING COMPANY—See Duke Energy Corporation; *U.S. Public,* pg. 535
WESTANA GATHERING COMPANY—See Western Gas Resources, Inc.; *U.S. Public,* pg. 1759
WESTAR ENERGY—See Western Resources, Inc.; *U.S. Public,* pg. 1759
WESTAR GROUP LTD.; *Int'l,* pg. 1491
WESTAR SECURITY—See Western Resources, Inc.; *U.S. Public,* pg. 1760
WESTAT INC.; *U.S. Private,* pg. 1163
WESTBODEN-BAU UND VERWALTUNGS GMBH—See Commerzbank AG; *Int'l,* pg. 310
WESTBORN SERVICE CENTER, INC.—See The Standard Products Company; *U.S. Public,* pg. 1505
WESTBRAE NATURAL FOODS, INC.—See The Hain Food Group Inc.; *U.S. Public,* pg. 774
WESTBRAE NATURAL, INC.—See The Hain Food Group Inc.; *U.S. Public,* pg. 774
WESTBRICK LIMITED—See Tarmac plc; *Int'l,* pg. 1355
WESTBURNE INC.; *Int'l,* pg. 1491
WESTBURNE INDUSTRIAL ENTERPRISES, LTD.—See Westburne Inc.; *Int'l,* pg. 1492
WESTBURNE SUPPLY—See Westburne Inc.; *Int'l,* pg. 1492
WESTCAN CHROMALOX—See The Glen Dimplex Group; *Int'l,* pg. 554
THE WESTCAP CORPORATION—See National Western Life Insurance Company; *U.S. Public,* pg. 1161
WESTCHESTER FIRE INSURANCE COMPANY—See Xerox Corporation; *U.S. Public,* pg. 1784
WESTCHESTER LACE, INC.; *U.S. Private,* pg. 1163
WESTCHESTER PLASTICS—See AMETEK, Inc.; *U.S. Public,* pg. 100
WESTCHESTER SPECIALTY GROUP—See Fremont General Corporation; *U.S. Public,* pg. 681
WESTCO COAL CO.—See Rochester & Pittsburgh Coal Company; *U.S. Public,* pg. 1395
WESTCO FOOD SERVICE—See CSM N.V.; *Int'l,* pg. 244
WESTCO PRODUCTS, INC.—See CSM N.V.; *Int'l,* pg. 244
WESTCO PRODUCTS/SEATTLE—See CSM N.V.; *Int'l,* pg. 244
WESTCOAST CELLUFIBRE—See Canfor Corporation; *Int'l,* pg. 261
WESTCOAST ENERGY INC.; *Int'l,* pg. 1492
WESTCOAST PETROLEUM LTD.—See Westcoast Energy Inc.; *Int'l,* pg. 1492
WESTCODE INC.—See BTR plc; *Int'l,* pg. 127
WESTCODE SEMICONDUCTORS INC. (U.S.A.)—See BTR plc; *Int'l,* pg. 127
WESTCON—See Desco Corporation; *U.S. Private,* pg. 327
WESTCORP; *U.S. Public,* pg. 1756
WESTDEUTSCHE IMMOBILIENBANK—See Landesbank Rheinland-Pfalz; *Int'l,* pg. 799
WESTDEUTSCHE LANDESBANK-BRUSSELS BRANCH—See Westdeutsche Landesbank Girozentrale; *Int'l,* pg. 1493
WESTDEUTSCHE LANDESBANK (EUROPA) AG—See Westdeutsche Landesbank Girozentrale; *Int'l,* pg. 1493
WESTDEUTSCHE LANDESBANK GIROZENTRALE; *Int'l,* pg. 1492
WESTDEUTSCHE LANDESBANK GIROZENTRALE (WESTLB)—See Westdeutsche Landesbank Girozentrale; *Int'l,* pg. 1492
WESTDEUTSCHE LANDESBANK-ISTANBUL BRANCH—See Westdeutsche Landesbank Girozentrale; *Int'l,* pg. 1493
WESTDEUTSCHE LANDESBANK-MADRID BRANCH—See Westdeutsche Landesbank Girozentrale; *Int'l,* pg. 1493
WESTDEUTSCHE LANDESBANK-MILAN BRANCH—See Westdeutsche Landesbank Girozentrale; *Int'l,* pg. 1493
WESTDEUTSCHE LANDESBANK MOSCOW—See Westdeutsche Landesbank Girozentrale; *Int'l,* pg. 1494
WESTDEUTSCHE LANDESBANK POLSKA S.A.—See Westdeutsche Landesbank Girozentrale; *Int'l,* pg. 1494
WESTDEUTSCHE LANDESBANK PRAGUE—See Westdeutsche Landesbank Girozentrale; *Int'l,* pg. 1493
WESTDEUTSCHE LANDESBANK-ROTTERDAM BRANCH—See Westdeutsche Landesbank Girozentrale; *Int'l,* pg. 1493
WESTDEUTSCHE LANDESBANK (SCHWEIZ) AG—See Landesbank Rheinland-Pfalz; *Int'l,* pg. 799
WESTDEUTSCHE LANDESBANK (SCHWEIZ) AG—See Westdeutsche Landesbank Girozentrale; *Int'l,* pg. 1494
WESTDEUTSCHE MAX COCHIUS GMBH—See Fried. Krupp AG; *Int'l,* pg. 514
WESTDEUTSCHE WELLPAPPENFABRIK GMBH—See The Procter & Gamble Company; *U.S. Public,* pg. 1333
WESTDEUTSCHER VERLAG GMBH—See Bertelsmann AG; *Int'l,* pg. 190

WESTDEUTSCHES ASSEKURANZ-KONTOR GMBH—See Fried. Krupp AG; *Int'l,* pg. 512
WESTEC SECURITY INC.—See Secom Co., Ltd.; *Int'l,* pg. 1217
WESTEEL AGRICULTURAL PRODUCTS DIVISION—See Jannock Limited; *Int'l,* pg. 698
WESTEND VERLAGS- UND WERBEGESELLSCHAFT MBH—See Fried. Krupp AG; *Int'l,* pg. 513
WESTERBEKE CORPORATION; *U.S. Public,* pg. 1757
NELSON WESTERBERG, INC.; *U.S. Private,* pg. 1163
NELSON WESTERBERG OF ILLINOIS—See Nelson Westerberg, Inc.; *U.S. Private,* pg. 1164
THE WESTERFELDS; *U.S. Private,* pg. 1164
WESTERN AG-MINERALS COMPANY (MINE OFFICE)—See IMC Global; *U.S. Public,* pg. 856
WESTERN AGGREGATES, INC.—See Inco Limited; *Int'l,* pg. 672
WESTERN AGGREGATES LIMITED—See RMC Group p.l.c.; *Int'l,* pg. 1079
WESTERN ALASKA FISHERIES INC.—See Maruha Corporation; *Int'l,* pg. 845
WESTERN AMERICAN MANUFACTURING, INC.—See Waxman Industries, Inc.; *U.S. Public,* pg. 1749
THE WESTERN AND SOUTHERN LIFE INSURANCE COMPANY; *U.S. Private,* pg. 1164
WESTERN ARCTIC COAL—See Arctic Slope Regional Corporation; *U.S. Private,* pg. 80
WESTERN ASH COMPANY—See Boral Limited; *Int'l,* pg. 203
WESTERN ASSET GLOBAL MANAGEMENT—See Legg Mason, Inc.; *U.S. Public,* pg. 985
WESTERN ASSET MANAGEMENT—See Legg Mason, Inc.; *U.S. Public,* pg. 985
WESTERN ASSURANCE COMPANY—See Royal & Sun Alliance Insurance Group plc; *Int'l,* pg. 1131
WESTERN ATLAS INC.; *U.S. Public,* pg. 1756
WESTERN ATLAS INTERNATIONAL, INC.—See Western Atlas Inc.; *U.S. Public,* pg. 1757
WESTERN ATLAS LOGGING SERVICES—See Western Atlas Inc.; *U.S. Public,* pg. 1757
WESTERN ATLAS SOFTWARE—See Litton Industries, Inc.; *U.S. Public,* pg. 1004
WESTERN AUTO SUPPLY COMPANY—See Sears, Roebuck and Co.; *U.S. Public,* pg. 1452
WESTERN AUTOMOTIVE REBUILDERS—See Acklands Limited; *Int'l,* pg. 23
WESTERN BANCORP; *U.S. Public,* pg. 1757
WESTERN BEEF, INC.; *U.S. Public,* pg. 1758
WESTERN BEHAVIORAL SYSTEMS, INC.—See Magellan Health Services, Inc.; *U.S. Public,* pg. 1036
WESTERN BROADCAST SALES LTD.—See WIC Western International Communications Ltd.; *Int'l,* pg. 1482
WESTERN CARE NURSING HOME NO. 439—See Vencor, Inc.; *U.S. Public,* pg. 1715
WESTERN COAL DEVELOPMENT—See The Broken Hill Proprietary Company Limited; *Int'l,* pg. 224
WESTERN COALFIELDS LIMITED—See Coal India Limited; *Int'l,* pg. 299
WESTERN CONSUMER SERVICES, INC.—See Westcorp; *U.S. Public,* pg. 1757
WESTERN COOPERATIVE ELECTRIC ASSOCIATION, INC.; *U.S. Private,* pg. 1165
WESTERN COOPERATIVE FERTILIZERS LIMITED (WCFL)—See Saskatchewan Wheat Pool; *Int'l,* pg. 1195
WESTERN CORPORATE ENTERPRISES INC.; *Int'l,* pg. 1494
WESTERN DAIRYMEN COOPERATIVE, INC.; *U.S. Private,* pg. 1165
WESTERN DATA SYSTEMS; *U.S. Private,* pg. 1165
WESTERN DATA SYSTEMS INTL., LTD.—See Western Data Systems; *U.S. Private,* pg. 1165
WESTERN DESIGN CORPORATION—See Howden Group Plc; *Int'l,* pg. 636
WESTERN DIGITAL CORPORATION; *U.S. Public,* pg. 1758
WESTERN DIGITAL DRIVE ENGINEERING INC.—See Western Digital Corporation; *U.S. Public,* pg. 1758
WESTERN DIGITAL HONG KONG LTD.—See Western Digital Corporation; *U.S. Public,* pg. 1758
WESTERN DIGITAL MEDIA INC.—See Western Digital Corporation; *U.S. Public,* pg. 1758
WESTERN DIGITAL SINGAPORE LTD.—See Western Digital Corporation; *U.S. Public,* pg. 1758
WESTERN DIRECT—See Western International Media Corporation; *U.S. Private,* pg. 1166
WESTERN DIVISION—See Pameco Corp.; *U.S. Public,* pg. 1255
WESTERN E & P SERVICES—See Western Atlas Inc.; *U.S. Public,* pg. 1757
WESTERN ELECTRIC COMPANY—See Lucent Technologies Inc.; *U.S. Public,* pg. 1019
WESTERN ELECTROCHEMICAL COMPANY—See American Pacific Corporation; *U.S. Public,* pg. 88
WESTERN ENERGY COMPANY—See Montana Power Company; *U.S. Public,* pg. 1127
WESTERN ENTERPRISES DIV.—See Berkshire Hathaway Inc.; *U.S. Public,* pg. 218
WESTERN ENVIRONMENTAL CONTRACTING, INC.—See CalMat Co.; *U.S. Public,* pg. 296
WESTERN EXTRUSIONS; *U.S. Private,* pg. 1165
WESTERN FARM CREDIT BANK—See Federal Farm Credit Banks Funding Corporation; *U.S. Private,* pg. 398
WESTERN FILTER—See Osmonics, Inc.; *U.S. Public,* pg. 1234
WESTERN FINANCIAL AUTO LOANS, INC.—See Westcorp; *U.S. Public,* pg. 1757
WESTERN FINANCIAL BANK—See Westcorp; *U.S. Public,* pg. 1757
WESTERN FIRE EQUIP.—See Premier Farnell plc; *Int'l,* pg. 1068

WESTERN FLORIDA CELLULAR TELEPHONE CORP.—See Vanguard Cellular Systems, Inc.; *U.S. Public,* pg. 1708
WESTERN FORGE DIV.—See Emerson Electric Co.; *U.S. Public,* pg. 575
WESTERN GAS RESOURCES CANADA, INC.—See Western Gas Resources, Inc.; *U.S. Public,* pg. 1759
WESTERN GAS RESOURCES, INC.; *U.S. Public,* pg. 1758
WESTERN GAS RESOURCES STORAGE, INC.—See Western Gas Resources, Inc.; *U.S. Public,* pg. 1759
WESTERN GAS RESOURCES-LOUISIANA, INC.—See Western Gas Resources, Inc.; *U.S. Public,* pg. 1758
WESTERN GAS RESOURCES-OKLAHOMA, INC.—See Western Gas Resources, Inc.; *U.S. Public,* pg. 1758
WESTERN GEOPHYSICAL—See Western Atlas Inc.; *U.S. Public,* pg. 1757
WESTERN GEOPHYSICAL (AUSTRALIA)—See Litton Industries, Inc.; *U.S. Public,* pg. 1005
WESTERN GEOPHYSICAL (CANADA)—See Litton Industries, Inc.; *U.S. Public,* pg. 1005
WESTERN GEOPHYSICAL (GREAT BRITAIN)—See Litton Industries, Inc.; *U.S. Public,* pg. 1005
WESTERN GEOPHYSICAL (SINGAPORE)—See Litton Industries, Inc.; *U.S. Public,* pg. 1005
WESTERN GLOBE PRODUCTS, INC.—See Borden, Inc.; *U.S. Private,* pg. 158
WESTERN GRAIN, INC.; *U.S. Private,* pg. 1165
THE WESTERN GROUP; *U.S. Private,* pg. 1165
WESTERN HARBOR CROSSING PROJECT OFFICE—See Nishimatsu Construction Co., Ltd.; *Int'l,* pg. 943
WESTERN INDEMNITY INSURANCE COMPANY—See Frontier Insurance Group, Inc.; *U.S. Public,* pg. 685
WESTERN INDUSTRIES, INC.; *U.S. Private,* pg. 1165
WESTERN INTERACTIVE MEDIA—See Western International Media Corporation; *U.S. Private,* pg. 1166
WESTERN INTERNATIONAL MEDIA CORPORATION; *U.S. Private,* pg. 1165
WESTERN INTERNATIONAL MEDIA CORPORATION—See Western International Media Corporation; *U.S. Private,* pg. 1167
WESTERN INTERNATIONAL UNIVERSITY—See Apollo Group, Inc.; *U.S. Public,* pg. 120
WESTERN INTL. FOREST PRODS., INC.—See Forest City Enterprises, Inc.; *U.S. Public,* pg. 669
WESTERN KENTUCKY GAS CO.—See Atmos Energy Corporation; *U.S. Public,* pg. 146
WESTERN LAND PROPERTIES—See Lewis Homes Management Corp.; *U.S. Private,* pg. 665
WESTERN MARKETING DIV.—See CUNA Mutual Insurance Society; *U.S. Private,* pg. 296
WESTERN MEDICAL SERVICES INC.—See Western Staff Services; *U.S. Public,* pg. 1760
WESTERN METAL LATH—See Marubeni Corporation; *Int'l,* pg. 845
WESTERN MICRO TECHNOLOGY, INC.; *U.S. Public,* pg. 1759
WESTERN MINING CORPORATION HOLDINGS LIMITED; *Int'l,* pg. 1494
WESTERN MOBILE INC.—See Redland PLC; *Int'l,* pg. 1091
WESTERN MOBILE KANSAS INC.—See Redland PLC; *Int'l,* pg. 1091
WESTERN MOTIVATIONAL INCENTIVES GROUP, INC.—See Western International Media Corporation; *U.S. Private,* pg. 1167
WESTERN MULTICULTURAL GROUP—See Western International Media Corporation; *U.S. Private,* pg. 1167
WESTERN MULTIPLEX CORPORATION—See Glenayre Technologies, Inc.; *U.S. Public,* pg. 747
WESTERN NATIONAL CORPORATION—See American General Corporation; *U.S. Public,* pg. 76
WESTERN NATIONAL LIFE INSURANCE CO.—See American General Corporation; *U.S. Public,* pg. 76
WESTERN NAVIGATION GLOBAL LTD.—See Circle International Group, Inc.; *U.S. Public,* pg. 373
WESTERN NAVIGATIONAL GLOBAL LIMITED—See Circle International Group, Inc.; *U.S. Public,* pg. 373
WESTERN NEBRASKA NATIONAL BANK—See First Commerce Bancshares, Inc.; *U.S. Public,* pg. 629
WESTERN NEW MEXICO TELEPHONE CO.—See Lynch Corporation; *U.S. Public,* pg. 1022
WESTERN PACIFIC DATA SYSTEMS; *U.S. Private,* pg. 1168
WESTERN PACIFIC ROOFING; *U.S. Private,* pg. 1168
WESTERN PASSAGE EXPRESS—See United Grocers Inc.; *U.S. Private,* pg. 1122
WESTERN PENNSLYVANIA CARING FOUNDATION, INC.—See Highmark Inc.; *U.S. Private,* pg. 529
WESTERN PERMANENT SERVICES AGENCY, INC.—See Western Staff Services; *U.S. Public,* pg. 1760
WESTERN PETROLEUM COMPANY; *U.S. Private,* pg. 1168
WESTERN PIONEER LIFE INSURANCE CO.—See I.C.H. Corporation; *U.S. Public,* pg. 853
WESTERN POOL TERMINALS LIMITED—See Saskatchewan Wheat Pool; *Int'l,* pg. 1195
WESTERN POWER PRODUCTS, INC.—See Cooper Industries, Inc.; *U.S. Public,* pg. 444
WESTERN PRODUCT PLACEMENT—See Western International Media Corporation; *U.S. Private,* pg. 1167
WESTERN PRODUCTION COMPANY—See Black Hills Corporation; *U.S. Public,* pg. 236
WESTERN PULP & PAPER DIV.—See Georgia-Pacific Corporation; *U.S. Public,* pg. 736
WESTERN RECONVEYANCE COMPANY, INC.—See Westcorp; *U.S. Public,* pg. 1757
WESTERN REGION—See Komatsu Ltd.; *Int'l,* pg. 744
WESTERN REGION SALES—See Televideo, Inc.; *U.S. Public,* pg. 1572
WESTERN REGIONAL OFF TRACK BETTING; *U.S. Private,* pg. 1168
WESTERN REINSURANCE BROKERS, INC.; *U.S. Private,* pg. 1168

WESTERN **DIRECTORY OF CORPORATE AFFILIATIONS**

Company Index

WESTERN RESERVE ADMINISTRATIVE SERVICES, INC.—See Central Reserve Life Corporation; *U.S. Public*, pg. 326
WESTERN RESERVE LIFE ASSURANCE CO. OF OHIO—See AEGON N.V.; *Int'l*, pg. 27
WESTERN RESOURCES, INC.; *U.S. Public*, pg. 1759
WESTERN ROADSTONE LIMITED—See RMC Group p.l.c.; *Int'l*, pg. 1079
WESTERN SALES OFFICE—See CUNA Mutual Insurance Society; *U.S. Private*, pg. 296
WESTERN SERVICE A/S—See Western Staff Services; *U.S. Public*, pg. 1760
WESTERN SKY INDUSTRIES, INC.; *U.S. Private*, pg. 1168
WESTERN-SOUTHERN AGENCY, INC.—See The Western and Southern Life Insurance Company; *U.S. Private*, pg. 1165
WESTERN-SOUTHERN LIFE ASSURANCE CO.—See The Western and Southern Life Insurance Company; *U.S. Private*, pg. 1164
WESTERN SPECIALTY CONTAINER—See Independent Can Company; *U.S. Private*, pg. 559
WESTERN STAFF SERVICES; *U.S. Public*, pg. 1760
WESTERN STAFF SERVICES—See Western Staff Services; *U.S. Public*, pg. 1760
WESTERN STAFF SERVICES (N.Z.) LTD.—See Western Staff Services; *U.S. Public*, pg. 1760
WESTERN STAFF SERVICES PTY. LTD.—See Western Staff Services; *U.S. Public*, pg. 1760
WESTERN STAFF SERVICES (U.K.) LTD.—See Western Staff Services; *U.S. Public*, pg. 1760
WESTERN STAFF SERVICES (USA), INC.—See Western Staff Services; *U.S. Public*, pg. 1760
THE WESTERN STAR—See Hollinger Inc.; *Int'l*, pg. 632
WESTERN STAR UNDERWRITERS, INC.—See Foremost Corporation of America; *U.S. Public*, pg. 667
WESTERN STATES ASSOC.—See Metropolitan Sunday Newspapers, Inc.; *U.S. Private*, pg. 739
WESTERN STATES ENERGY—See Imperial Chemical Industries PLC; *Int'l*, pg. 664
WESTERN STATES ENVELOPE CO.; *U.S. Private*, pg. 1168
WESTERN STATES MACHINE COMPANY; *U.S. Private*, pg. 1168
WESTERN STATES PETROLEUM INC.; *U.S. Private*, pg. 1169
THE WESTERN SUGAR COMPANY—See Tate & Lyle PLC; *Int'l*, pg. 1357
WESTERN SUPPLY CORP.—See Lewis Homes Management Corp.; *U.S. Private*, pg. 666
WESTERN SURETY COMPANY—See Capsure Holdings Corp.; *U.S. Public*, pg. 303
WESTERN SYNCOAL COMPANY—See Montana Power Company; *U.S. Public*, pg. 1127
WESTERN TEMPORARY SERVICES DIV.—See Western Staff Services; *U.S. Public*, pg. 1760
WESTERN THERMAL SOILS CO.—See CalMat Co.; *U.S. Public*, pg. 296
WESTERN TIMBER CO.—See WTD Industries, Inc.; *U.S. Public*, pg. 1729
WESTERN TOWING COMPANY—See Kirby Corporation; *U.S. Public*, pg. 961
WESTERN TRUST & SAVINGS HOLDINGS LTD.—See Manulife Financial (The Manufacturers Life Insurance Company); *Int'l*, pg. 841
WESTERN UNION DATA SERVICES COMPANY, INC.—See New Valley Corporation; *U.S. Public*, pg. 1173
WESTERN UNION FINANCIAL SERVICES, INC.—See First Data Corporation; *U.S. Public*, pg. 631
WESTERN UNION INSURANCE CO.—See ING Groep N.V.; *Int'l*, pg. 651
WESTERN UNION INTERNATIONAL, INC.—See MCI Communications Corp.; *U.S. Public*, pg. 1024
WESTERN UNITED LIFE ASSURANCE COMPANY—See Metropolitan Mortgage & Securities Co., Inc.; *U.S. Private*, pg. 738
WESTERN WASTE INDUSTRIES—See USA Waste Services, Inc.; *U.S. Public*, pg. 1686
WESTERN WATERPROOFING CO. OF AMERICA, INC.—See The Western Group; *U.S. Private*, pg. 1165
WESTERN WATERPROOFING COMPANY OF AMERICA, INC.—See The Western Group; *U.S. Private*, pg. 1165
WESTERN WOOD PRODS. MFG. DIV.—See Georgia-Pacific Corporation; *U.S. Public*, pg. 736
WESTERNBANK OF PUERTO RICO; *U.S. Public*, pg. 1760
WESTERVELT LAND CO.—See Gulf States Paper Corporation; *U.S. Private*, pg. 488
WESTERWALD AG—See Saint-Gobain; *Int'l*, pg. 1172
WESTERWALDER EISEN-ROHSTOFFHANDELS-GMBH—See Fried. Krupp AG; *Int'l*, pg. 514
WESTEX, INC.—See Yellow Corporation; *U.S. Public*, pg. 1788
WESTFALENSTADION—See Harpen AG; *Int'l*, pg. 597
WESTFALL GMC TRUCK INC.; *U.S. Private*, pg. 1169
WESTFIELD COMPANIES; *U.S. Private*, pg. 1169
WESTFORD OFFICE VENTURE—See Cigna Corp.; *U.S. Public*, pg. 359
WESTGAS GMBH—See Veba AG; *Int'l*, pg. 1455
WESTGAS INTERSTATE, INC.—See New Century Energies, Inc.; *U.S. Public*, pg. 1170
WESTGATE FABRICS, INC.; *U.S. Private*, pg. 1169
WESTGATE INC.; *U.S. Private*, pg. 1169
THE WESTHALL CO.—See Signet Group plc; *Int'l*, pg. 1248
WESTHRIFT LIFE INSURANCE COMPANY—See Westcorp; *U.S. Public*, pg. 1757
WESTIM RESOURCES LTD.—See EdperBrascan Corporation; *Int'l*, pg. 435
WESTIN HOTELS & RESORTS—See Starwood Hotels & Resorts; *U.S. Public*, pg. 1512
WESTIN, INC.; *U.S. Private*, pg. 1169
WESTINGHOUSE AIR BRAKE COMPANY; *U.S. Public*, pg. 1760
WESTINGHOUSE ASIA CONTROLS CORP.—See CBS Corporation; *U.S. Public*, pg. 273
WESTINGHOUSE AUDIO INTELLIGENCE DEVICES—See CBS Corporation; *U.S. Public*, pg. 273
WESTINGHOUSE CANADA INC.—See CBS Corporation; *U.S. Public*, pg. 275
WESTINGHOUSE COMMERCIAL SECURITY—See CBS Corporation; *U.S. Public*, pg. 273
WESTINGHOUSE COMMUNICATION & INFORMATION SYSTEMS—See CBS Corporation; *U.S. Public*, pg. 273
WESTINGHOUSE COMMUNICATIONS, INC. (WESCOMM)—See CBS Corporation; *U.S. Public*, pg. 273
WESTINGHOUSE CUBIC LIMITED—See Cubic Corporation; *U.S. Public*, pg. 466
WESTINGHOUSE DE VENEZUELA S.A.—See CBS Corporation; *U.S. Public*, pg. 275
WESTINGHOUSE DO BRASIL S/A DIVISAO SERVICIOS INDUSTRIALES—See CBS Corporation; *U.S. Public*, pg. 275
WESTINGHOUSE DO BRASIL S/A ELECTROMAR DIVISION—See CBS Corporation; *U.S. Public*, pg. 275
WESTINGHOUSE DO BRASIL S/A MARINI E DAMINELLI DIVISION—See CBS Corporation; *U.S. Public*, pg. 275
WESTINGHOUSE ELECTRIC AUSTRALASIA LTD.—See CBS Corporation; *U.S. Public*, pg. 275
WESTINGHOUSE ELECTRIC AUSTRALASIA LTD.-VICTORIA DIV.—See CBS Corporation; *U.S. Public*, pg. 275
WESTINGHOUSE ELECTRIC AUSTRALASIA LTD.-W.A. DIVISION—See CBS Corporation; *U.S. Public*, pg. 275
WESTINGHOUSE ELECTRO-METALURGICA, C.A.—See CBS Corporation; *U.S. Public*, pg. 275
WESTINGHOUSE ENERGY CENTER—See CBS Corporation; *U.S. Public*, pg. 273
WESTINGHOUSE ENERGY SYSTEMS INTERNATIONAL, INC.—See CBS Corporation; *U.S. Public*, pg. 275
WESTINGHOUSE GOVERNMENT OPERATIONS—See CBS Corporation; *U.S. Public*, pg. 273
WESTINGHOUSE INDUSTRIES & TECHNOLOGIES GROUP—See CBS Corporation; *U.S. Public*, pg. 273
WESTINGHOUSE INDUSTRY SERVICES ASIA PTE. LTD.—See CBS Corporation; *U.S. Public*, pg. 275
WESTINGHOUSE INDUSTRY SERVICES-QUEENSLAND—See CBS Corporation; *U.S. Public*, pg. 275
WESTINGHOUSE MOTOR COMPANY—See CBS Corporation; *U.S. Public*, pg. 275
WESTINGHOUSE POWER GENERATION—See CBS Corporation; *U.S. Public*, pg. 273
WESTINGHOUSE POWER SYSTEMS GROUP—See CBS Corporation; *U.S. Public*, pg. 273
WESTINGHOUSE RESIDENTIAL SECURITY SYSTEMS—See CBS Corporation; *U.S. Public*, pg. 273
WESTINGHOUSE SAVANNAH RIVER CO.—See CBS Corporation; *U.S. Public*, pg. 273
WESTINGHOUSE WIRELESS SERVICES—See CBS Corporation; *U.S. Public*, pg. 273
WESTLAKE HARDWARE, INC.; *U.S. Private*, pg. 1169
WESTLAKE MEDICAL CENTER—See Universal Health Services, Inc.; *U.S. Public*, pg. 1697
WESTLAM FOODS—See Trinidad/Benham Corp.; *U.S. Private*, pg. 1103
WESTLAND SYSTEM ASSESSMENT LIMITED—See GKN plc; *Int'l*, pg. 535
WESTLAND/UTRECHT HYPOTHEEKBANK—See ING Groep N.V.; *Int'l*, pg. 647
WESTLB AUSTRALIA AND NEW ZEALAND—See Westdeutsche Landesbank Girozentrale; *Int'l*, pg. 1493
WESTLB BANGKOK—See Westdeutsche Landesbank Girozentrale; *Int'l*, pg. 1493
WESTLB-BEAL - MEXICO CITY—See Westdeutsche Landesbank Girozentrale; *Int'l*, pg. 1494
WESTLB BEIJING—See Westdeutsche Landesbank Girozentrale; *Int'l*, pg. 1493
WESTLB BERLIN BRANCH—See Westdeutsche Landesbank Girozentrale; *Int'l*, pg. 1492
WESTLB BIELEFELD BRANCH—See Westdeutsche Landesbank Girozentrale; *Int'l*, pg. 1492
WESTLB CHICAGO—See Westdeutsche Landesbank Girozentrale; *Int'l*, pg. 1493
WESTLB COLOGNE BRANCH—See Westdeutsche Landesbank Girozentrale; *Int'l*, pg. 1492
WESTLB DORTMUND BRANCH—See Westdeutsche Landesbank Girozentrale; *Int'l*, pg. 1493
WESTLB DUBAI—See Westdeutsche Landesbank Girozentrale; *Int'l*, pg. 1493
WESTLB ESSEN BRANCH—See Westdeutsche Landesbank Girozentrale; *Int'l*, pg. 1493
WESTLB EUROPA FINANZIARIA S.P.A.—See Westdeutsche Landesbank Girozentrale; *Int'l*, pg. 1494
WESTLB (FRANCE) S.A.—See Westdeutsche Landesbank Girozentrale; *Int'l*, pg. 1494
WESTLB FRANKFURT BRANCH—See Westdeutsche Landesbank Girozentrale; *Int'l*, pg. 1493
WESTLB HAMBURG BRANCH—See Westdeutsche Landesbank Girozentrale; *Int'l*, pg. 1493
WESTLB HONG KONG BRANCH—See Westdeutsche Landesbank Girozentrale; *Int'l*, pg. 1493
WESTLB (HUNGARIA) RT.—See Westdeutsche Landesbank Girozentrale; *Int'l*, pg. 1494
WESTLB INTERNATIONAL S.A.—See SudwestLB; *Int'l*, pg. 1305
WESTLB INTERNATIONAL S.A.—See Westdeutsche Landesbank Girozentrale; *Int'l*, pg. 1494
WESTLB (IRELAND) LTD.—See Westdeutsche Landesbank Girozentrale; *Int'l*, pg. 1494
WESTLB JAKARTA—See Westdeutsche Landesbank Girozentrale; *Int'l*, pg. 1493
WESTLB KIEV—See Westdeutsche Landesbank Girozentrale; *Int'l*, pg. 1493
WESTLB LONDON BRANCH—See Westdeutsche Landesbank Girozentrale; *Int'l*, pg. 1493
WESTLB LOS ANGELES—See Westdeutsche Landesbank Girozentrale; *Int'l*, pg. 1493
WESTLB NEW YORK BRANCH—See Westdeutsche Landesbank Girozentrale; *Int'l*, pg. 1493
WESTLB OSAKA—See Westdeutsche Landesbank Girozentrale; *Int'l*, pg. 1493
WESTLB ST. PETERSBURG—See Westdeutsche Landesbank Girozentrale; *Int'l*, pg. 1493
WESTLB (SCHWEIZ) AG—See SudwestLB; *Int'l*, pg. 1305
WESTLB SECURITIES PACIFIC LTD.—See Westdeutsche Landesbank Girozentrale; *Int'l*, pg. 1494
WESTLB SHANGHAI—See Westdeutsche Landesbank Girozentrale; *Int'l*, pg. 1493
WESTLB SINGAPORE BRANCH—See Westdeutsche Landesbank Girozentrale; *Int'l*, pg. 1493
WESTLB TAIPEI—See Westdeutsche Landesbank Girozentrale; *Int'l*, pg. 1493
WESTLB TOKYO BRANCH—See Westdeutsche Landesbank Girozentrale; *Int'l*, pg. 1493
WESTLB TORONTO BRANCH—See Westdeutsche Landesbank Girozentrale; *Int'l*, pg. 1493
WESTLB UK LIMITED—See Westdeutsche Landesbank Girozentrale; *Int'l*, pg. 1494
WESTLIE MOTOR COMPANY; *U.S. Private*, pg. 1169
WESTLUND INDUSTRIAL SUPPLY LTD.—See Emco Limited; *Int'l*, pg. 453
WESTMAC LTD.—See Lonrho plc; *Int'l*, pg. 817
WESTMARK GROUP HOLDINGS INC.; *U.S. Public*, pg. 1761
WESTMARK HOTELS, ALASKA—See Carnival Corporation; *U.S. Public*, pg. 306
WESTMARK MORTGAGE CORPORATION—See Westmark Group Holdings Inc.; *U.S. Public*, pg. 1761
WESTMIN TALC BV—See Western Mining Corporation Holdings Limited; *Int'l*, pg. 1494
WESTMINSTER BANK & TRUST CO. OF CARROLL COUNTY—See Mercantile Bankshares Corporation; *U.S. Public*, pg. 1089
WESTMINSTER CABLE COMPANY LIMITED—See British Telecommunications plc; *Int'l*, pg. 222
WESTMINSTER CAPITAL INC.; *U.S. Public*, pg. 1761
WESTMINSTER CONTRACTORS LTD.—See Ballast Nedam NV; *Int'l*, pg. 135
WESTMINSTER HOMES OF NORTH CAROLINA, INC.—See Washington Homes, Inc.; *U.S. Public*, pg. 1741
WESTMINSTER INSURANCE AGENCIES LIMITED—See Groupe GAN; *Int'l*, pg. 565
WESTMORELAND COAL CO.; *U.S. Public*, pg. 1761
WESTMORELAND ENERGY, INC.—See Westmoreland Coal Co.; *U.S. Public*, pg. 1761
WESTMORELAND RESOURCES, INC.—See Westmoreland Coal Co.; *U.S. Public*, pg. 1761
WESTOFEN GMBH—See Viag AG; *Int'l*, pg. 1466
WESTON AEROSPACE LTD.—See The Roxboro Group PLC; *Int'l*, pg. 1130
WESTON BAKERIES LIMITED—See George Weston Limited; *Int'l*, pg. 1495
WESTON ENGRAVING—See Schawk, Inc.; *U.S. Public*, pg. 1437
WESTON FOODS—See George Weston Limited; *Int'l*, pg. 1495
WESTON GALLERY—See Wilton Industries, Inc.; *U.S. Private*, pg. 1182
GEORGE WESTON FOODS GROUP—See Associated British Foods plc; *Int'l*, pg. 92
GEORGE WESTON LIMITED; *Int'l*, pg. 1494
WESTON INTERNATIONAL, INC.—See Roy F. Weston, Inc.; *U.S. Public*, pg. 1761
WESTON PAPER & MANUFACTURING CO.; *U.S. Private*, pg. 1169
WESTON RESOURCES—See George Weston Limited; *Int'l*, pg. 1495
ROY F. WESTON, INC.; *U.S. Public*, pg. 1761
ROY F. WESTON OF NEW YORK—See Roy F. Weston, Inc.; *U.S. Public*, pg. 1761
WESTOWER CORPORATION; *U.S. Public*, pg. 1762
WESTOWNS DISPOSAL SYSTEMS, INC.—See Browning-Ferris Industries, Inc.; *U.S. Public*, pg. 265
WESTPAC BANK - PNG LIMITED—See Westpac Banking Corporation; *Int'l*, pg. 1497
WESTPAC BANKING CORP. - TONGA—See Westpac Banking Corporation; *Int'l*, pg. 1497
WESTPAC BANKING CORPORATION; *Int'l*, pg. 1495
WESTPAC BANKING CORPORATION-ASIAN DIV.—See Westpac Banking Corporation; *Int'l*, pg. 1497
WESTPAC BANKING CORPORATION-BAHRAIN—See Westpac Banking Corporation; *Int'l*, pg. 1497
WESTPAC BANKING CORPORATION (COLUMBUS REPRESENTATIVE OFFICE)—See Westpac Banking Corporation; *Int'l*, pg. 1496
WESTPAC BANKING CORPORATION-EUROPEAN DIV.—See Westpac Banking Corporation; *Int'l*, pg. 1497
WESTPAC BANKING CORPORATION-GERMANY—See Westpac Banking Corporation; *Int'l*, pg. 1497
WESTPAC BANKING CORPORATION (JERSEY) LTD.—See Westpac Banking Corporation; *Int'l*, pg. 1497
WESTPAC BANKING CORPORATION (LOS ANGELES BRANCH)—See Westpac Banking Corporation; *Int'l*, pg. 1496
WESTPAC BANKING CORPORATION-NEW ZEALAND—See Westpac Banking Corporation; *Int'l*, pg. 1497
WESTPAC BANKING CORPORATION-PACIFIC ISLANDS DIV.—See Westpac Banking Corporation; *Int'l*, pg. 1497
WESTPAC BANKING CORPORATION (SAN FRANCISCO BRANCH)—See Westpac Banking Corporation; *Int'l*, pg. 1496
WESTPAC FINANCE ASIA LIMITED—See Westpac Banking Corporation; *Int'l*, pg. 1497
WESTPAC FINANCIAL SERVICES GROUP LIMITED—See Westpac Banking Corporation; *Int'l*, pg. 1496
WESTPAC INSURANCE SERVICES (BROKERS) LIMITED—See Westpac Banking Corporation; *Int'l*, pg. 1496
WESTPAC LIFE LIMITED—See Westpac Banking Corporation; *Int'l*, pg. 1496
WESTPAC - SOUTH AUSTRALIA—See Westpac Banking Corporation; *Int'l*, pg. 1496

WESTPEAK INVESTMENT ADVISORS, INC.—See Metropolitan Life Insurance Co.; *U.S. Private*, pg. 738
WESTPLAN INSURANCE AGENCY, INC.—See Westcorp; *U.S. Private*, pg. 1757
WESTPOINT STEVENS INC.; *U.S. Public*, pg. 1762
WESTRALIAN SANDS LIMITED—See Ishihara Sangyo Kaisha, Ltd.; *Int'l*, pg. 689
WESTREX ASIA—See Litton Industries, Inc.; *U.S. Public*, pg. 1005
WESTROC INDUSTRIES LIMITED—See BPB Industries PLC; *Int'l*, pg. 123
WESTRONICS, INC.—See Thermo Electron Corporation; *U.S. Public*, pg. 1593
WESTSHORE TERMINALS LTD.—See Westar Group Ltd.; *Int'l*, pg. 1491
WESTSTAR ENGINEERING INC.—See Amelco Corporation; *U.S. Public*, pg. 65
WESTTAX, INC.—See The Western and Southern Life Insurance Company; *U.S. Private*, pg. 1165
WESTVACO ASIA, K.K.—See Westvaco Corporation; *U.S. Public*, pg. 1762
WESTVACO CANADA, LTD.—See Westvaco Corporation; *U.S. Public*, pg. 1762
WESTVACO CORPORATION; *U.S. Public*, pg. 1762
WESTVACO DEVELOPMENT CORP.—See Westvaco Corporation; *U.S. Public*, pg. 1762
WESTVACO EUROPE, S.A.—See Westvaco Corporation; *U.S. Public*, pg. 1762
WESTVACO HONG KONG, LTD.—See Westvaco Corporation; *U.S. Public*, pg. 1763
WESTVACO PACIFIC PTY. LTD.—See Westvaco Corporation; *U.S. Public*, pg. 1763
WESTVACO SVITAVY, SPOL., S.R.O.—See Westvaco Corporation; *U.S. Public*, pg. 1763
WESTVACO WORLDWIDE DISTRIBUTION, S.A.—See Westvaco Corporation; *U.S. Public*, pg. 1763
WEST VALLEY NUCLEAR SERVICES—See CBS Corporation; *U.S. Public*, pg. 273
WESTWARD SEAFOODS, INC.—See Maruha Corporation; *Int'l*, pg. 845
WESTWAYNE, INC.; *U.S. Private*, pg. 1170
WESTWAYNE - MIAMI—See WestWayne, Inc.; *U.S. Private*, pg. 1170
WESTWAYNE - TAMPA—See WestWayne, Inc.; *U.S. Private*, pg. 1170
WESTWIND COMMUNICATIONS; *U.S. Private*, pg. 1170
WESTWOOD COMPUTER CORPORATION; *U.S. Private*, pg. 1170
WESTWOOD CORPORATION; *U.S. Public*, pg. 1763
WESTWOOD ONE ENTERTAINMENT—See Westwood One, Inc.; *U.S. Public*, pg. 1763
WESTWOOD ONE, INC.; *U.S. Public*, pg. 1763
WESTWOOD ONE RADIO NETWORKS—See Westwood One, Inc.; *U.S. Public*, pg. 1763
WESTWOOD PRODUCTS, S.A.—See Bristol-Myers Squibb Company; *U.S. Public*, pg. 256
WESTWOOD SHIPPING LINES—See Weyerhaeuser Company; *U.S. Public*, pg. 1764
WESTWOOD-SQUIBB PHARMACEUTICALS INC.—See Bristol-Myers Squibb Company; *U.S. Public*, pg. 255
WET-N-WILD, A SIX FLAGS WATER PARK—See Time Warner Inc.; *U.S. Public*, pg. 1612
THE WET SEAL, INC.; *U.S. Public*, pg. 1763
WETMORE & COMPANY—See Wallace Computer Services, Inc.; *U.S. Public*, pg. 1736
WETSEL-OVIATT LUMBER COMPANY; *U.S. Private*, pg. 1170
WETSEL SEED COMPANY—See Southern States Cooperative, Inc.; *U.S. Private*, pg. 1017
WETTERAUER TRANSPORTBETON GMBH & CO. KG—See Dyckerhoff AG; *Int'l*, pg. 423
WETTEX AB—See Freudenberg & Company; *Int'l*, pg. 506
WETTEX OY AB—See Freudenberg & Company; *Int'l*, pg. 506
WEXPRO COMPANY—See Questar Corporation; *U.S. Public*, pg. 1352
WEYBURN-BARTEL GMBH—See T & N Plc; *Int'l*, pg. 1334
WEYBURN-BARTEL, INC.—See T & N Plc; *Int'l*, pg. 1334
WEYBURN-BARTEL LTD.—See T & N Plc; *Int'l*, pg. 1334
WEYCO GROUP, INC.; *U.S. Public*, pg. 1763
WEYERHAEUSER CANADA LTD.—See Weyerhaeuser Company; *U.S. Public*, pg. 1764
WEYERHAEUSER COMPANY; *U.S. Public*, pg. 1764
WEYERHAEUSER (FAR EAST) LTD.—See Weyerhaeuser Company; *U.S. Public*, pg. 1764
WEYERHAEUSER FINANCIAL SERVICES, INC.—See Weyerhaeuser Company; *U.S. Public*, pg. 1764
WEYERHAEUSER FOREST PRODUCTS COMPANY—See Weyerhaeuser Company; *U.S. Public*, pg. 1764
WEYERHAEUSER JAPAN LTD.—See Weyerhaeuser Company; *U.S. Public*, pg. 1764
WEYERHAEUSER MORTGAGE COMPANY—See Weyerhaeuser Company; *U.S. Public*, pg. 1764
WEYERHAEUSER, S.A.—See Weyerhaeuser Company; *U.S. Public*, pg. 1764
WEYL GMBH—See Ruetgers A.G.; *Int'l*, pg. 1148
WEYMOUTH NEWS—See Gannett Company, Inc.; *U.S. Public*, pg. 702
WGM EASTMAN—See Eastman Kodak Company; *U.S. Public*, pg. 551
WHA-YO ELECTRONIC MATERIALS CORPORATION—See Sumitomo Electric Industries, Ltd.; *Int'l*, pg. 1314
WHAKATANE BOARD MILL—See International Paper Company; *U.S. Public*, pg. 905
WHALE SCIENTIFIC INC.—See Thermo Electron Corporation; *U.S. Public*, pg. 1595
WHALING INDUSTRIES, INC.; *U.S. Private*, pg. 1170
WHALING MANUFACTURING COMPANY, INC.—See Whaling Industries, Inc.; *U.S. Private*, pg. 1170
WHAM-O, INC.; *U.S. Private*, pg. 1170
WHAN GONG CO., LTD.—See Suntory Ltd.; *Int'l*, pg. 1321
WHARF HOTEL INVESTMENTS LTD.; *Int'l*, pg. 1497
WHARF MINE—See CSA Management Inc.; *Int'l*, pg. 243

WHARF RESOURCES LTD.—See CSA Management Inc.; *Int'l*, pg. 243
WHATABURGER, INC.; *U.S. Private*, pg. 1170
WHATMAN INC.—See Whatman plc; *Int'l*, pg. 1498
WHATMAN PLC; *Int'l*, pg. 1498
WHEAT FIRST BUTCHER SINGER, INC.—See First Union Corporation; *U.S. Public*, pg. 640
WHEATLAND TUBE COMPANY; *U.S. Private*, pg. 1170
THE WHEATLEY GROUP, INC.—See Avemco Corporation; *U.S. Public*, pg. 152
WHEATON COATED PRODUCTS—See Alusuisse-Lonza Holding Ltd.; *Int'l*, pg. 67
WHEATON DO BRAZIL—See Alusuisse-Lonza Holding Ltd.; *Int'l*, pg. 68
WHEATON GLASS CO.—See Alusuisse-Lonza Holding Ltd.; *Int'l*, pg. 68
WHEATON GLASS PRODUCTS—See Alusuisse-Lonza Holding Ltd.; *Int'l*, pg. 67
WHEATON INC.—See Alusuisse-Lonza Holding Ltd.; *Int'l*, pg. 67
WHEATON INJECTION MOLDING—See Alusuisse-Lonza Holding Ltd.; *Int'l*, pg. 68
WHEATON INSTRUMENTS—See Alusuisse-Lonza Holding Ltd.; *Int'l*, pg. 68
WHEATON PLASTIC CONTAINERS—See Alusuisse-Lonza Holding Ltd.; *Int'l*, pg. 68
WHEATON PLASTIC PRODUCTS—See Alusuisse-Lonza Holding Ltd.; *Int'l*, pg. 68
WHEATON RIVER MINERALS LTD.; *Int'l*, pg. 1498
WHEATON SCIENTIFIC—See Alusuisse-Lonza Holding Ltd.; *Int'l*, pg. 68
WHEATON SCIENTIFIC PRODUCTS—See Alusuisse-Lonza Holding Ltd.; *Int'l*, pg. 68
WHEATON TUBING PRODUCTS—See Alusuisse-Lonza Holding Ltd.; *Int'l*, pg. 68
WHEATON VAN LINES, INC.; *U.S. Private*, pg. 1171
WHEEL CARE RETREADING INC.—See The Cascades Group; *Int'l*, pg. 274
WHEEL TRONIC INC.—See Snap-On Tools Corporation; *U.S. Public*, pg. 1171
WHEELABRATOR TECHNOLOGIES INC.—See Waste Management, Inc.; *U.S. Public*, pg. 1745
WHEELED COACH INDUSTRIES, INC.—See Collins Industries, Inc.; *U.S. Public*, pg. 400
WHEELER BROTHERS GRAIN CO.; *U.S. Private*, pg. 1171
WHEELING CONSTRUCTION PRODUCTS, INC.—See WHX Corporation; *U.S. Public*, pg. 1726
WHEELING CORRUGATING CO.—See WHX Corporation; *U.S. Public*, pg. 1727
WHEELING DIVISION—See R.R. Donnelley & Sons Company; *U.S. Public*, pg. 519
WHEELING-EMPIRE COMPANY—See WHX Corporation; *U.S. Public*, pg. 1727
WHEELING-PITTSBURGH CAPITAL CORPORATION—See WHX Corporation; *U.S. Public*, pg. 1727
WHEELING-PITTSBURGH CORPORATION—See WHX Corporation; *U.S. Public*, pg. 1727
WHEELING-PITTSBURGH FUNDING, INC.—See WHX Corporation; *U.S. Public*, pg. 1727
WHEELING-PITTSBURGH RADIO CORPORATION—See WHX Corporation; *U.S. Public*, pg. 1727
WHEELING-PITTSBURGH STEEL CORPORATION—See WHX Corporation; *U.S. Public*, pg. 1727
WHEELING POWER COMPANY—See American Electric Power Company, Inc.; *U.S. Public*, pg. 73
WHEELOCK INC.; *U.S. Private*, pg. 1171
BUFF WHELAN CHEVROLET & GEO, INC.; *U.S. Private*, pg. 1171
WHEREHOUSE ENTERTAINMENT, INC.; *U.S. Private*, pg. 1171
WHESSOE COMPUTING SYSTEMS LTD.—See Whessoe Plc; *Int'l*, pg. 1498
WHESSOE PLC; *Int'l*, pg. 1498
WHESSOE PROJECTS LTD.—See Whessoe Plc; *Int'l*, pg. 1498
WHESSOE SYSTEMS & CONTROLS LTD.—See Whessoe Plc; *Int'l*, pg. 1498
WHESSOE VAREC—See Whessoe Plc; *Int'l*, pg. 1498
WHIBCO, INC.; *U.S. Private*, pg. 1171
WHIPP & BOURNE LTD.—See FKI Plc; *Int'l*, pg. 473
WHIPPS; *U.S. Private*, pg. 1171
WHIRLPOOL CORPORATION; *U.S. Public*, pg. 1764
WHIRLPOOL DO BRAZIL S.A.—See Whirlpool Corporation; *U.S. Public*, pg. 1765
WHIRLPOOL EUROPE B.V.—See Whirlpool Corporation; *U.S. Public*, pg. 1765
WHIRLPOOL FINANCIAL CORP.—See Whirlpool Corporation; *U.S. Public*, pg. 1765
WHISPER COMMUNICATIONS—See Safeguard Scientifics, Inc.; *U.S. Public*, pg. 1425
WHISTABLE TIMES—See EMAP Plc; *Int'l*, pg. 452
WHISTLER MOUNTAIN HOLDINGS, LIMITED—See Intrawest Corporation; *Int'l*, pg. 685
THE WHITAKER CORPORATION—See AMP Incorporated; *U.S. Public*, pg. 8
WHITBREAD BEER COMPANY—See Whitbread PLC; *Int'l*, pg. 1498
WHITBREAD INVESTMENTS LTD.—See Whitbread PLC; *Int'l*, pg. 1499
WHITBREAD PLC; *Int'l*, pg. 1498
WHITBREAD PROPERTY—See Whitbread PLC; *Int'l*, pg. 1498
WHITBREAD PUB PARTNERSHIPS—See Whitbread PLC; *Int'l*, pg. 1498
WHITBREAD RESTAURANTS & LEISURE—See Whitbread PLC; *Int'l*, pg. 1498
WHITBREAD RESTAURANTS (AUSTRALIA) LTD.—See Whitbread PLC; *Int'l*, pg. 1499
WHITBY, INC.—See UCB, S.A.; *Int'l*, pg. 1427
WHITE & LEWIS—See Willis Corroon Group PLC; *Int'l*, pg. 1502
WHITE CAP BENELUX B.V.—See Schmalbach-Lubeca AG; *Int'l*, pg. 1207

WHITE CAP DEUTSCHLAND VERTRIEBSGESELLSCHAFT MBH—See Schmalbach-Lubeca AG; *Int'l*, pg. 1207
WHITE CAP ESPANA S.L.—See Schmalbach-Lubeca AG; *Int'l*, pg. 1207
WHITE CAP EUROPE GMBH—See Schmalbach-Lubeca AG; *Int'l*, pg. 1207
WHITE CAP FRANCE S.A.R.L.—See Schmalbach-Lubeca AG; *Int'l*, pg. 1207
WHITE CAP, INC.—See Schmalbach-Lubeca AG; *Int'l*, pg. 1207
WHITE CAP INC. NORDISKA AB—See Schmalbach-Lubeca AG; *Int'l*, pg. 1207
WHITE CAP INDUSTRIES, INC.; *U.S. Public*, pg. 1765
WHITE CAP ITALIA S.R.L.—See Schmalbach-Lubeca AG; *Int'l*, pg. 1207
WHITE CAP MAGYARORSZAG KFT.—See Schmalbach-Lubeca AG; *Int'l*, pg. 1207
WHITE CAP SP.ZO.O.—See Schmalbach-Lubeca AG; *Int'l*, pg. 1207
WHITE CAP U.K. LTD.—See Schmalbach-Lubeca AG; *Int'l*, pg. 1207
WHITE CASTLE BAKERY DIVISION—See White Castle System, Inc.; *U.S. Private*, pg. 1172
WHITE CASTLE DISTRIBUTING, INC.—See White Castle System, Inc.; *U.S. Private*, pg. 1172
WHITE CASTLE INTERNATIONAL COMPANY—See White Castle System, Inc.; *U.S. Private*, pg. 1172
WHITE CASTLE SYSTEM, INC.; *U.S. Private*, pg. 1171
WHITE CONSOLIDATED INDUSTRIES, INC.—See Electrolux, AB; *Int'l*, pg. 439
DAVID WHITE, L.L.C.; *U.S. Private*, pg. 1765
WHITE ELECTRICAL CONSTRUCTION CO.; *U.S. Private*, pg. 1172
WHITE ELECTRICAL CONSTRUCTION CO.—See White Electrical Construction Co.; *U.S. Private*, pg. 1172
WHITE ELECTRICAL CONSTRUCTION CO—See White Electrical Construction Co.; *U.S. Private*, pg. 1172
WHITE ELECTRICAL CONSTRUCTION CO.—See White Electrical Construction Co.; *U.S. Private*, pg. 1172
WHITE FLASH OIL CO.—See Pugh Oil Company; *U.S. Private*, pg. 894
WHITE HEN PANTRY, INC.; *U.S. Private*, pg. 1172
WHITE IRON FILM AND VIDEO PRODUCTIONS—See Rogers Communications, Inc.; *Int'l*, pg. 1124
J.B. WHITE—See Mercantile Stores Company, Inc.; *U.S. Public*, pg. 1090
WHITE KNIGHT PRODUCTS LIMITED—See Carclo Engineering Group plc; *Int'l*, pg. 268
WHITE MARSH ENVIRONMENTAL SYSTEMS, INC.—See Middlesex Water Company; *U.S. Public*, pg. 1110
WHITE MARSH EQUITIES CORP.—See The Rouse Company; *U.S. Public*, pg. 1409
WHITE MARSH MALL, INC.—See The Rouse Company; *U.S. Public*, pg. 1409
S.A. WHITE MARTINS—See Praxair Inc.; *U.S. Public*, pg. 1320
WHITE MICROELECTRONICS—See Bowmar Instrument Corporation; *U.S. Public*, pg. 248
WHITE MOP WRINGER CO.—See White Mop Wringer Company; *U.S. Private*, pg. 1173
WHITE MOP WRINGER COMPANY; *U.S. Private*, pg. 1172
THE WHITE PASS & YUKON CORP. LIMITED—See Russel Metals Inc.; *Int'l*, pg. 1150
WHITE PASS & YUKON ROUTE—See Russel Metals Inc.; *Int'l*, pg. 1151
WHITE PASS SYSTEMS LTD.—See Russel Metals Inc.; *Int'l*, pg. 1150
WHITE PASS TRANSPORTATION LIMITED—See Russel Metals Inc.; *Int'l*, pg. 1150
WHITE PIGEON PAPER COMPANY—See Artistic Carton Company; *U.S. Private*, pg. 87
WHITE PINE SOFTWARE; *U.S. Private*, pg. 1173
WHITE RIVER CORPORATION; *U.S. Public*, pg. 1765
WHITE ROCK DISTILLERIES INC.; *U.S. Private*, pg. 1173
WHITE ROCK PRODUCTS CORP.; *U.S. Private*, pg. 1173
WHITE-RODGERS DIV., EMERSON ELECTRIC CO.—See Emerson Electric Co.; *U.S. Public*, pg. 573
WHITE ROSE DAIRY—See Di Giorgio Corporation; *U.S. Private*, pg. 330
WHITE ROSE FOOD—See Di Giorgio Corporation; *U.S. Private*, pg. 330
WHITE ROSE FROZEN FOOD—See Di Giorgio Corporation; *U.S. Private*, pg. 330
WHITE STAR STEEL—See Nashville Steel Corp.; *U.S. Private*, pg. 775
WHITE SYSTEMS, INCORPORATED—See Pinnacle Automation Inc.; *U.S. Private*, pg. 866
WHITECABLE—See Esselte AB; *Int'l*, pg. 462
WHITE-CREST DORSETT INC.—See World Carpets, Inc.; *U.S. Private*, pg. 1190
WHITEFIELD POWER & LIGHTING—See Thermo Electron Corporation; *U.S. Public*, pg. 1593
WHITEHALL BENELUX S.A.—See American Home Products Corporation; *U.S. Public*, pg. 82
WHITEHALL CORPORATION; *U.S. Public*, pg. 1765
WHITEHALL GREECE—See American Home Products Corporation; *U.S. Public*, pg. 82
WHITEHALL LABORATORIA B.V.—See American Home Products Corporation; *U.S. Public*, pg. 81
WHITEHALL LABORATORIES—See American Home Products Corporation; *U.S. Public*, pg. 81
WHITEHALL LABORATORIES LIMITED—See American Home Products Corporation; *U.S. Public*, pg. 82
WHITEHALL LABORATORIES LTD.—See American Home Products Corporation; *U.S. Public*, pg. 82
WHITEHALL LABORATORIES PTY. LIMITED—See American Home Products Corporation; *U.S. Public*, pg. 82
WHITEHALL LABORATORIOS S.A.—See American Home Products Corporation; *U.S. Public*, pg. 82
WHITEHALL MANUFACTURING INC.—See Acorn Engineering Company; *U.S. Private*, pg. 14

Company Index

WHITEHALL PORTUGAL—See American Home Products Corporation; *U.S. Public*, pg. 81

WHITEHALL PROPERTIES LIMITED—See GP Batteries International Ltd.; *Int'l*, pg. 537

WHITEHALL-ROBINS DE MEXICO, S.A. DE C.V.—See American Home Products Corporation; *U.S. Public*, pg. 82

WHITEHALL-ROBINS HEALTHCARE—See American Home Products Corporation; *U.S. Public*, pg. 80

WHITEHALL-ROBINS INC.—See American Home Products Corporation; *U.S. Public*, pg. 82

WHITEHALL-ROBINS INTERNATIONAL, INC.—See American Home Products Corporation; *U.S. Public*, pg. 80

WHITEHALL-ROBINS LABORATORIES LTD.—See American Home Products Corporation; *U.S. Public*, pg. 82

WHITEHALL SPAIN—See American Home Products Corporation; *U.S. Public*, pg. 82

WHITEHALL STREE REAL ESTATE L.P.—See Goldman, Sachs & Co.; *U.S. Private*, pg. 462

WHITEHALL SWEDEN—See American Home Products Corporation; *U.S. Public*, pg. 82

WHITEHALL VENEZUELA—See American Home Products Corporation; *U.S. Public*, pg. 81

DAVID WHITEHEAD & SONS LTD.—See Lonrho plc; *Int'l*, pg. 818

WHITEHOUSE PLANT, WOOD PRODUCTS DIV.—See Champion International Corp.; *U.S. Public*, pg. 334

WHITELEY CHEMICALS (VICTORIA) PTY. LTD.—See Electrolux, AB; *Int'l*, pg. 440

R.O. WHITESELL & ASSOCIATES, INC; *U.S. Private*, pg. 1173

THE WHITESTONE CORPORATION—See AEGON N.V.; *Int'l*, pg. 27

WHITESWAN/META—See Dowling Textile Manufacturing Co.; *U.S. Private*, pg. 342

WHITEVILLE APPAREL CORP.—See Hartmarx Corporation; *U.S. Public*, pg. 796

WHITFIELD FOODS, INC.; *U.S. Public*, pg. 1173

WHITIN ROBERTS CO.—See Damsmith Corp.; *U.S. Private*, pg. 309

WHITING CORPORATION; *U.S. Public*, pg. 1173

WHITING EQUIPMENT CANADA, INC.—See Whiting Corporation; *U.S. Public*, pg. 1173

WHITING MANUFACTURING CO., INC.; *U.S. Private*, pg. 1174

WHITING METALS, INC.—See Synalloy Corporation; *U.S. Public*, pg. 1548

THE WHITING-TURNER CONTRACTING CO.; *U.S. Private*, pg. 1174

WHITLENGE DRINK EQUIPMENT LIMITED—See Scotsman Industries, Inc.; *U.S. Public*, pg. 1445

WHITMAN CORPORATION; *U.S. Public*, pg. 1766

WHITMAN'S CANDIES, INC.—See Russell Stover Candies, Inc.; *U.S. Private*, pg. 953

WHITMIRE MICRO-GEN RESEARCH LABORATORIES INCORPORATED—See S.C. Johnson & Son, Inc.; *U.S. Private*, pg. 592

WHITMIRE MICRO-GEN RESEARCH LABORATORIES INC.—See S.C. Johnson & Son, Inc.; *U.S. Private*, pg. 592

WHITNEY CORR-PAK INTERNATIONAL, INC.—See Code, Hennessy & Simmons; *U.S. Private*, pg. 249

WHITNEY HOLDING CORPORATION; *U.S. Public*, pg. 1766

WHITNEY INTERNATIONAL—See Kyokuyo Co. Ltd.; *Int'l*, pg. 777

WHITNEY NATIONAL BANK—See Whitney Holding Corporation; *U.S. Public*, pg. 1766

W.A. WHITNEY ITALIA CO.—See Esterline Technologies Corporation; *U.S. Public*, pg. 594

W.A. WHITNEY CO.—See Esterline Technologies Corporation; *U.S. Public*, pg. 594

WHITTAKER, CLARK & DANIELS, INC.; *U.S. Private*, pg. 1174

WHITTAKER COMMUNICATIONS, INC.—See Whittaker Corporation; *U.S. Public*, pg. 1767

WHITTAKER CONTROLS, INC.—See Whittaker Corporation; *U.S. Public*, pg. 1767

WHITTAKER CORPORATION; *U.S. Public*, pg. 1766

WHITTAKER ELECTRONIC SYSTEMS—See Whittaker Corporation; *U.S. Public*, pg. 1767

WHITTAKER POWER STORAGE DIVISION—See Whittaker Corporation; *U.S. Public*, pg. 1767

WHITTAKER XYPLEX—See Whittaker Corporation; *U.S. Public*, pg. 1767

WHITTENBERG CONSTRUCTION CO.; *U.S. Private*, pg. 1174

WHITTLE COMMUNICATIONS L.P.—See Time Warner Inc.; *U.S. Public*, pg. 1614

WHIZ AUTOMOTIVE CHEMICALS DIV.—See Malco Products, Inc.; *U.S. Private*, pg. 698

WHOLE FOODS MARKET, INC.; *U.S. Public*, pg. 1767

WHOLESALE ELECTRIC SUPPLY CO.—See Hughes Supply, Inc.; *U.S. Public*, pg. 847

WHOLESALE ELECTRONIC SUPPLY; *U.S. Private*, pg. 1174

WHOLESALE GLASS FABRICATORS INC.—See Heraeus Holding GmbH; *Int'l*, pg. 616

WHOLESALE HEATING SUPPLIES—See Emco Limited; *Int'l*, pg. 453

WHOLESALE/RETAIL DIVISION—See Gold Eagle Company; *U.S. Private*, pg. 459

WHOLESALE SERVICES GROUP—See Cable and Wireless plc; *Int'l*, pg. 247

WHOLESALE SERVICES GROUP—See Sprint Corporation; *U.S. Public*, pg. 1501

WHOLESALE SUPPLY COMPANY, INC.; *U.S. Private*, pg. 1174

WHOLESALE WOOD PRODUCTS—See Lumber Group Inc.; *U.S. Private*, pg. 680

WHOLESOME DAIRY—See Borden, Inc.; *U.S. Private*, pg. 158

WHYALLA STEELWORKS—See The Broken Hill Proprietary Company Limited; *Int'l*, pg. 227

WHYBIN/TBWA—See TBWA Chiat/Day; *U.S. Private*, pg. 1063

THE WHYTE & MACKAY GROUP PLC.—See Fortune Brands, Inc.; *U.S. Public*, pg. 675

WIARTON ECHO GROUP—See Hollinger Inc.; *Int'l*, pg. 632

AB WIBE—See AB Industrivarden; *Int'l*, pg. 678

WIBROE, DUCKERT & PARTNERS—See The Lowe Group; *U.S. Private*, pg. 678

WICHITA BUSINESS JOURNAL, INC.—See Advance Publications Inc.; *U.S. Private*, pg. 20

WICHITA CESSNA LEARNING CENTER—See Berkshire Hathaway Inc.; *U.S. Public*, pg. 219

WICHITA CESSNA MAINTENANCE LEARNING CENTER—See Berkshire Hathaway Inc.; *U.S. Public*, pg. 219

THE WICHITA EAGLE AND BEACON PUBLISHING CO., INC.—See Knight-Ridder, Inc.; *U.S. Public*, pg. 964

WICHITA FALLS TIMES & RECORD NEWS—See Harte-Hanks Communications, Inc.; *U.S. Public*, pg. 794

WICHITA LEARJET LEARNING CENTER—See Berkshire Hathaway Inc.; *U.S. Public*, pg. 219

WICHITA MEDICAL CARE, INC.—See Integrated Health Services, Inc.; *U.S. Public*, pg. 885

WICHITA RAYTHEON LEARNING CENTER—See Berkshire Hathaway Inc.; *U.S. Public*, pg. 219

WICHITA RAYTHEON MAINTENANCE LEARNING CENTER—See Berkshire Hathaway Inc.; *U.S. Public*, pg. 219

WICHITA SERVICE CENTER—See Pace Analytical Services; *U.S. Private*, pg. 829

WICK BUILDING DIVISION—See Wick Building Systems; *U.S. Private*, pg. 1174

WICK BUILDING SYSTEMS; *U.S. Private*, pg. 1174

WICK PHARMA—See The Procter & Gamble Company; *U.S. Public*, pg. 1333

WICKERSHAM HUNT SCHWANTNER—See Arnold Communications, Inc.; *U.S. Private*, pg. 62

WICKES INC.—See Riverside Group, Inc.; *U.S. Public*, pg. 1391

WICKLAND CORPORATION; *U.S. Private*, pg. 1174

WICKLAND INTERNATIONAL ASIA, LTD.—See Wickland Corporation; *U.S. Private*, pg. 1175

WICKLAND OIL COMPANY, INC.—See Wickland Corporation; *U.S. Private*, pg. 1175

WICKLAND PROPERTIES—See Wickland Corporation; *U.S. Private*, pg. 1175

THE WICKMAN CORP.; *U.S. Private*, pg. 1175

WICKS HOMES DIVISION—See Wick Building Systems; *U.S. Private*, pg. 1174

WICKS 'N STICKS, LTD; *U.S. Private*, pg. 1175

WICONA BAUSYSTEME AG—See Norsk Hydro a.s; *Int'l*, pg. 964

WICONA BAUSYSTEME GMBH & CO. KG—See Norsk Hydro a.s; *Int'l*, pg. 964

WICONA BENELUX N.V.—See Norsk Hydro a.s; *Int'l*, pg. 964

WICONA DEUTSCHLAND GMBH—See Norsk Hydro a.s; *Int'l*, pg. 965

WICONA SCANDINAVIA AB—See Norsk Hydro a.s; *Int'l*, pg. 961

WICONA UK LTD.—See Norsk Hydro a.s; *Int'l*, pg. 965

WICOR, INC.; *U.S. Public*, pg. 1767

WIDAG AG—See Electrolux, AB; *Int'l*, pg. 444

WIDAROC (INDIA) LTD.—See Fried. Krupp AG; *Int'l*, pg. 510

WIDE-LITE—See The Genlyte Group Incorporated; *U.S. Public*, pg. 730

WIDE WORLD PHOTOS, INC.—See The Associated Press; *U.S. Private*, pg. 92

WIDIA HEINLEIN GMBH—See Fried. Krupp AG; *Int'l*, pg. 510

WIDIA (INDIA) LTD.—See Fried. Krupp AG; *Int'l*, pg. 510

WIDISA METAL S.A.—See FKI Plc; *Int'l*, pg. 474

WIDMER'S WINE CELLARS, INC.—See Canandaigua Wine Company, Inc.; *U.S. Public*, pg. 300

WIDNI OY—See Axel Johnson AB; *Int'l*, pg. 712

WIEDEN & KENNEDY-AMSTERDAM—See Wieden & Kennedy, Inc.; *U.S. Private*, pg. 1175

WIEDEN & KENNEDY, INC.; *U.S. Private*, pg. 1175

WIEDEN & KENNEDY-NEW YORK—See Wieden & Kennedy, Inc.; *U.S. Private*, pg. 1175

WIEGAND INDUSTRIAL-CHROMALOX—See Emerson Electric Co.; *U.S. Public*, pg. 573

THE WIEGMANN COMPANY—See Hubbell Incorporated; *U.S. Public*, pg. 845

WIELAND FINANCIAL SERVICES, INC.—See John Wieland Homes Inc.; *U.S. Private*, pg. 1175

JOHN WIELAND HOMES INC.; *U.S. Private*, pg. 1175

JOHN WIELAND HOMES OF JACKSONVILLE, INC.—See John Wieland Homes Inc.; *U.S. Private*, pg. 1175

JOHN WIELAND HOMES OF NORTH CAROLINA, INC.—See John Wieland Homes Inc.; *U.S. Private*, pg. 1175

JOHN WIELAND HOMES OF SOUTH CAROLINA, INC.—See John Wieland Homes Inc.; *U.S. Private*, pg. 1175

JOHN WIELAND HOMES OF TENESSEE, INC.—See John Wieland Homes Inc.; *U.S. Private*, pg. 1175

WIEMER UND TRACHTE—See Lyonnaise des Eaux S.A.; *Int'l*, pg. 824

WIENER ALLIANZ LEBENSVERSICHERUNGS-AG—See Allianz Aktiengesellschaft; *Int'l*, pg. 62

WIENER ALLIANZ VERSICHERUNGS-AG—See Allianz Aktiengesellschaft; *Int'l*, pg. 62

WIENERBERGER BAUSTOFFINDUSTRIE AG—See Creditanstalt-Bankverein; *Int'l*, pg. 347

WIENER-KUHLHAUS FRIGOSCANDIA GES.M.B.H.—See FMC Corporation; *U.S. Public*, pg. 607

WIENERSCHNITZEL—See Galardi Group, Inc.; *U.S. Private*, pg. 437

WIGAND CORPORATION—See Steelcase Inc.; *U.S. Private*, pg. 1038

WIGAND FABRIC WALL SYSTEMS—See Steelcase Inc.; *U.S. Private*, pg. 1038

WIGGINS ARJO IRELAND (HOLDINGS) LTD.—See Groupe Saint Louis; *Int'l*, pg. 567

WIGGINS ARJO ITALIANA SRL—See Groupe Saint Louis; *Int'l*, pg. 567

WIGGINS TEAPE (HONG KONG) LTD.—See Groupe Saint Louis; *Int'l*, pg. 567

WIGGINS TEAPE PAPER LTD.—See Groupe Saint Louis; *Int'l*, pg. 567

WIGGINS TEAPE (STATIONERY) LTD.—See Groupe Saint Louis; *Int'l*, pg. 567

WIGHTLINK LTD.—See Sea Containers Ltd.; *Int'l*, pg. 1214

WIGWAM MILLS, INC.; *U.S. Private*, pg. 1175

WIGWAM RESORT—See Kabuto Decom Inc.; *Int'l*, pg. 721

WIJKERTUNNEL BEHEER III B.V.—See Commerzbank AG; *Int'l*, pg. 312

WIKERS AB—See Celsius AB; *Int'l*, pg. 278

WIL-RICH NOBLE COMPANY—See TIC United Corporation; *U.S. Private*, pg. 1064

WILBUR CHOCOLATE CO., INC.—See Cargill; *U.S. Private*, pg. 210

WILBUR-ELLIS AGRICULTURAL—See Wilbur-Ellis Company & Connell Brothers Company; *U.S. Private*, pg. 1176

WILBUR-ELLIS COMPANY & CONNELL BROTHERS COMPANY; *U.S. Private*, pg. 1175

WILCO REPROGRAPHIC, INC.; *U.S. Private*, pg. 1176

WILCOM PRODUCTS, INC.—See NAI Technologies, Inc.; *U.S. Public*, pg. 1144

WILCOX ELECTRIC, INC.—See Thomson S.A.; *Int'l*, pg. 1384

WILCOX ENERGY COMPANY—See Callon Petroleum Company; *U.S. Public*, pg. 295

WILCOX INDUSTRIES, INC.—See Leggett & Platt, Incorporated; *U.S. Public*, pg. 987

THE WILD PAIR—See Edison Brothers Stores, Inc.; *U.S. Public*, pg. 564

THE WILDER COMPANIES; *U.S. Private*, pg. 1176

WILDER DEEM, INC.; *U.S. Private*, pg. 1176

WILDHAWK, INC.—See Northland Cranberries, Inc.; *U.S. Public*, pg. 1197

FREDERICK WILDMAN & SONS LTD.; *U.S. Private*, pg. 1176

WILDON INDUSTRIES, INC.—See BTR plc; *Int'l*, pg. 129

WILEN MANUFACTURING COMPANY, INC.; *U.S. Private*, pg. 1176

WILER AKTIENBRAUEREI—See Feldschlosschen Hurlimann Holding; *Int'l*, pg. 479

WILEY EUROPE LIMITED—See John Wiley & Sons, Inc.; *U.S. Public*, pg. 1768

JOHN WILEY & SONS, CANADA, LTD.—See John Wiley & Sons, Inc.; *U.S. Public*, pg. 1768

JOHN WILEY & SONS, INC.; *U.S. Public*, pg. 1768

JOHN WILEY & SONS, INC.—See John Wiley & Sons, Inc.; *U.S. Public*, pg. 1768

WILEY-VCH—See John Wiley & Sons, Inc.; *U.S. Public*, pg. 1768

WIL-FREDS INC.; *U.S. Private*, pg. 1176

F.A. WILHELM CONSTRUCTION CO., INC.; *U.S. Private*, pg. 1176

WILHELM KANNE GMBH & CO.—See Spar Handels AG; *Int'l*, pg. 1288

WILHELM SCHEIDT BAUUNTERNEHMUNG GMBH—See Bilfinger + Berger Bauaktiengesellschaft; *Int'l*, pg. 195

WILHELMSTAL-WERKE GMBH PAPIERSACKFABRIKEN—See Korsnas AB; *Int'l*, pg. 759

WILHOLD INC.—See American Greetings Corporation; *U.S. Public*, pg. 78

WILKINS-REGULATOR DIV.—See Zurn Industries, Inc.; *U.S. Public*, pg. 1794

WILKINS-ROGERS INCORPORATED; *U.S. Private*, pg. 1176

WILKINSON COMPANY, INC.—See Electric Furnace Co.; *U.S. Private*, pg. 368

WILL & BAUMER INCORPORATED; *U.S. Private*, pg. 1176

THE WILL-BURT COMPANY; *U.S. Private*, pg. 1177

WILLAMETTE INDUSTRIES, INC.; *U.S. Public*, pg. 1768

WILLAMETTE SALES CO.—See CNF Transportation Inc.; *U.S. Public*, pg. 281

WILLAMINA LUMBER CO. INC.—See Hampton Resources Inc.; *U.S. Private*, pg. 498

WILLARD GRAIN & FEED, INC.; *U.S. Private*, pg. 1177

WILLAWA FISHING CO.—See Marine Construction & Design Co.; *U.S. Private*, pg. 703

WILLCOX & GIBBS, INC.; *U.S. Private*, pg. 1177

WILLCOX & GIBBS, LTD.—See Willcox & Gibbs, Inc.; *U.S. Private*, pg. 1177

WILLEBROEK VASTGOED B.V.—See Royal Begemann Group; *Int'l*, pg. 1133

WILLEMSWERF V.O.F.—See Royal Nedlloyd Group N.V.; *Int'l*, pg. 1145

WILLENHALL MANUFACTURING—See Caparo Group Ltd.; *Int'l*, pg. 265

WILLENHALL STEEL STOCKHOLDERS LTD.—See Arbed S.A.; *Int'l*, pg. 79

WILLERT HOME PRODUCTS, INC.; *U.S. Private*, pg. 1177

R.C. WILLEY HOME FURNISHINGS—See Berkshire Hathaway Inc.; *U.S. Public*, pg. 221

WILLI VOEGTLIN AKTIENGESELLSCHAFT—See GESTRA GmbH; *Int'l*, pg. 551

WILLI VOEGTLIN S.A.—See GESTRA GmbH; *Int'l*, pg. 551

WILLIAM PENN LIFE INSURANCE CO. OF NEW YORK—See Legal & General Group PLC; *Int'l*, pg. 805

WILLIAM PRYM GMBH & CO. KG; *Int'l*, pg. 1499

WILLIAM WARNE LIMITED—See SLD Holdings Ltd.; *Int'l*, pg. 1160

WILLIAMHOUSE OF CALIFORNIA, INC.—See American Pad and Paper Company; *U.S. Public*, pg. 89

WILLIAMHOUSE OF COLORADO, INC.—See American Pad and Paper Company; *U.S. Public*, pg. 89

WILLIAMHOUSE OF TEXAS—See American Pad and Paper Company; *U.S. Public*, pg. 89

WILLIAMHOUSE-REGENCY, INC.—See American Pad and Paper Company; *U.S. Public*, pg. 89

WILLIAMHOUSE SALES CORPORATION—See American Pad and Paper Company; *U.S. Public*, pg. 89
WILLIAMS ADVANCED MATERIALS, INC.—See Brush Wellman Inc.; *U.S. Public*, pg. 266
WILLIAMS & COMPANY, INC.—See Superior Group, Inc.; *U.S. Private*, pg. 1055
WILLIAMS & HUMBERT LTD.—See Koninklijke BolsWessanen nv; *Int'l*, pg. 751
WILLIAMS & MACKIE—See Russel Metals Inc.; *Int'l*, pg. 1150
WILLIAMS & WILKINS ASIA PACIFIC LTD.—See Waverly, Inc.; *U.S. Public*, pg. 1748
WILLIAMS & WILKINS BOOK PUBLISHING—See Waverly, Inc.; *U.S. Public*, pg. 1748
WILLIAMS & WILKINS PERIODICAL PUBLISHING—See Waverly, Inc.; *U.S. Public*, pg. 1748
WILLIAM'S BAKERY—See United States Bakery; *U.S. Private*, pg. 1124
WILLIAMS BRIDGE CO.—See Williams Industries, Inc.; *U.S. Public*, pg. 1770
WILLIAMS BROS.—See Blue Circle Industries PLC; *Int'l*, pg. 198
WILLIAMS BROTHERS CONSTRUCTION—See Blue Circle Industries PLC; *Int'l*, pg. 198
THE WILLIAMS COMPANIES, INC.; *U.S. Public*, pg. 1769
WILLIAMS COMPANY OF ORLANDO, INC.; *U.S. Private*, pg. 1177
WILLIAMS CONSTRUCTORS—See Williams International Industries, Inc.; *U.S. Private*, pg. 1178
WILLIAMS CONTROLS, INC.; *U.S. Public*, pg. 1769
WILLIAMS CRANE & RIGGING, INC.—See Williams International Industries, Inc.; *U.S. Private*, pg. 1178
WILLIAMS DE BROE HOLDINGS LTD.—See Bank Brussels Lambert; *Int'l*, pg. 148
WILLIAMS DE BROE PANKKIIRILIIKE OY FINLAND—See Bank Brussels Lambert; *Int'l*, pg. 148
WILLIAMS DETROIT DIESEL-ALLISON MIDWEST, INC.—See The W.W. Williams Company; *U.S. Private*, pg. 1179
WILLIAMS DETROIT DIESEL-ALLISON S.E., INC.—See The W.W. Williams Company; *U.S. Private*, pg. 1179
WILLIAMS DISTRIBUTING COMPANY; *U.S. Private*, pg. 1177
DON E. WILLIAMS CO.; *U.S. Private*, pg. 1177
E.K. WILLIAMS—See The Dwyer Group, Inc.; *U.S. Public*, pg. 538
WILLIAMS ELECTRONICS GAMES, INC.—See WMS Industries Inc.; *U.S. Public*, pg. 1727
WILLIAMS EQUIPMENT CORPORATION—See Williams Industries, Inc.; *U.S. Public*, pg. 1770
WILLIAMS FAIREY ENGINEERING LTD.—See Williams Holdings Plc; *Int'l*, pg. 1500
WILLIAMS FASTENER & SUPPLY CO.—See Williams Steel & Hardware Company; *U.S. Private*, pg. 1178
WILLIAMS FIELD SERVICES—See The Williams Companies, Inc.; *U.S. Public*, pg. 1769
WILLIAMS FOODS INC.; *U.S. Private*, pg. 1178
WILLIAMS FURNACE CO.—See Continental Materials Corporation; *U.S. Public*, pg. 441
H.E. WILLIAMS, INC.; *U.S. Private*, pg. 1178
H.R. WILLIAMS INC.—See Tetko, Inc.; *U.S. Private*, pg. 1078
WILLIAMS HEALTHCARE SYSTEMS—See Standex International Corporation; *U.S. Public*, pg. 1507
WILLIAMS HOLDINGS PLC; *Int'l*, pg. 1499
WILLIAMS HOSPITALITY GROUP INC.—See Patriot American Hospitality, Inc.; *U.S. Public*, pg. 1265
WILLIAMS HOUSE OF METALS, INC.—See Superior Group, Inc.; *U.S. Private*, pg. 1055
WILLIAMS INDUSTRIES, INC.; *U.S. Public*, pg. 1769
WILLIAMS INTERNATIONAL; *U.S. Private*, pg. 1178
WILLIAMS INTERNATIONAL INDUSTRIES, INC.; *U.S. Private*, pg. 1178
J.H. WILLIAMS—See Snap-On Tools Corporation; *U.S. Public*, pg. 1481
WILLIAMS NATURAL GAS COMPANY—See The Williams Companies, Inc.; *U.S. Public*, pg. 1769
WILLIAMS PATENT CRUSHER AND PULVERIZER CO.; *U.S. Private*, pg. 1178
WILLIAMS PIPE LINE CO.—See The Williams Companies, Inc.; *U.S. Public*, pg. 1769
WILLIAMS PRINTING COMPANY—See Wallace Computer Services, Inc.; *U.S. Public*, pg. 1736
WILLIAMS-ROLLS, INC.—See Williams International; *U.S. Private*, pg. 1178
WILLIAMS SCOTSMAN GROUP, INC.—See Scotsman Holding Inc.; *U.S. Private*, pg. 977
WILLIAMS SCOTSMAN, INC.—See Scotsman Holding Inc.; *U.S. Private*, pg. 976
WILLIAMS-SONOMA, INC.; *U.S. Public*, pg. 1770
WILLIAMS STEEL ERECTION CO., INC.—See Williams Industries, Inc.; *U.S. Public*, pg. 1770
WILLIAMS STEEL & HARDWARE COMPANY; *U.S. Private*, pg. 1178
WILLIAMS STEEL & SUPPLY—See Williams Steel & Hardware Company; *U.S. Private*, pg. 1178
WILLIAMS STEEL & SUPPLY CO.—See Metals USA, Inc.; *U.S. Public*, pg. 1101
WILLIAMS TECHNOLOGIES, INC.—See The W.W. Williams Company; *U.S. Private*, pg. 1179
WILLIAMS TELECOMMUNICATIONS SYSTEMS, INC.—See The Williams Companies, Inc.; *U.S. Public*, pg. 1769
THE W.W. WILLIAMS COMPANY; *U.S. Private*, pg. 1178
WILLIAMS, WHITE & CO.; *U.S. Private*, pg. 1179
WILLIAMS WORLDWIDE; *U.S. Public*, pg. 1179
WILLIAMS WORLDWIDE—See Williams Worldwide; *U.S. Private*, pg. 1179
WILLIAMSBURG FOODS, INC.—See The Smithfield Companies, Inc.; *U.S. Public*, pg. 1479
WILLIAMSON-DICKIE MFG. CO.; *U.S. Private*, pg. 1179
WILLIAMSON INTERNATIONAL CORP.—See T.D. Williamson, Inc.; *U.S. Private*, pg. 1180
T.D. WILLIAMSON, INC.; *U.S. Private*, pg. 1179

T.D. WILLIAMSON S.A.—See T.D. Williamson, Inc.; *U.S. Private*, pg. 1180
T.D. WILLIAMSON (U.K.) LTD.—See T.D. Williamson, Inc.; *U.S. Private*, pg. 1180
WILLIAMSPORT NATIONAL BANK—See Susquehanna Bancshares, Inc.; *U.S. Public*, pg. 1543
WILLING B WIRE CORPORATION—See Handy & Harman; *U.S. Public*, pg. 780
WILLIS CORROON—See Willis Corroon Group PLC; *Int'l*, pg. 1504
WILLIS CORROON A/S—See Willis Corroon Group PLC; *Int'l*, pg. 1509
WILLIS CORROON ADMINISTRATIVE SERVICES CORPORATION—See Willis Corroon Group PLC; *Int'l*, pg. 1504
WILLIS CORROON ADMINISTRATIVE SERVICES, INC.—See Willis Corroon Group PLC; *Int'l*, pg. 1504
WILLIS CORROON ADVANCED RISK MANAGEMENT SERVICES—See Willis Corroon Group PLC; *Int'l*, pg. 1505
WILLIS CORROON AEROSPACE—See Willis Corroon Group PLC; *Int'l*, pg. 1505
WILLIS CORROON AEROSPACE-MIDWEST REGION—See Willis Corroon Group PLC; *Int'l*, pg. 1505
WILLIS CORROON AEROSPACE OF CANADA LTD.—See Willis Corroon Group PLC; *Int'l*, pg. 1509
WILLIS CORROON AEROSPACE-SOUTHWEST REGION—See Willis Corroon Group PLC; *Int'l*, pg. 1505
WILLIS CORROON AEROSPACE-WESTERN REGION—See Willis Corroon Group PLC; *Int'l*, pg. 1505
WILLIS CORROON AMERICAS—See Willis Corroon Group PLC; *Int'l*, pg. 1505
WILLIS CORROON & ASSOCIATES, INC.—See Willis Corroon Group PLC; *Int'l*, pg. 1505
WILLIS CORROON & WILLIS FABER & DUMAS LIMITED—See Willis Corroon Group PLC; *Int'l*, pg. 1509
WILLIS CORROON ASIA PACIFIC LIMITED—See Willis Corroon Group PLC; *Int'l*, pg. 1509
WILLIS CORROON CONSTRUCTION DIVISION—See Willis Corroon Group PLC; *Int'l*, pg. 1504
WILLIS CORROON CONSTRUCTION RISKS LIMITED—See Willis Corroon Group PLC; *Int'l*, pg. 1502
WILLIS CORROON CONSTRUCTION SERVICES CORP.—See Willis Corroon Group PLC; *Int'l*, pg. 1504
WILLIS CORROON CONSTRUCTION SVCS. CORP. OF FLORIDA—See Willis Corroon Group PLC; *Int'l*, pg. 1504
WILLIS CORROON CONSTRUCTION SVCS. CORP. OF CT—See Willis Corroon Group PLC; *Int'l*, pg. 1504
WILLIS CORROON CONTINENTAL EUROPE LIMITED—See Willis Corroon Group PLC; *Int'l*, pg. 1502
WILLIS CORROON CORP.—See Willis Corroon Group PLC; *Int'l*, pg. 1504
WILLIS CORROON CORP. OF ARIZONA—See Willis Corroon Group PLC; *Int'l*, pg. 1505
WILLIS CORROON CORP. OF BIRMINGHAM—See Willis Corroon Group PLC; *Int'l*, pg. 1505
WILLIS CORROON CORP. OF CALIFORNIA—See Willis Corroon Group PLC; *Int'l*, pg. 1505
WILLIS CORROON CORP. OF CHATTANOOGA—See Willis Corroon Group PLC; *Int'l*, pg. 1505
WILLIS CORROON CORP. OF EUGENE—See Willis Corroon Group PLC; *Int'l*, pg. 1505
WILLIS CORROON CORP. OF FAIRBANKS—See Willis Corroon Group PLC; *Int'l*, pg. 1505
WILLIS CORROON CORP. OF FLORIDA—See Willis Corroon Group PLC; *Int'l*, pg. 1505
WILLIS CORROON CORP. OF GEORGIA—See Willis Corroon Group PLC; *Int'l*, pg. 1506
WILLIS CORROON CORP. OF IDAHO—See Willis Corroon Group PLC; *Int'l*, pg. 1506
WILLIS CORROON CORP. OF ILLINOIS—See Willis Corroon Group PLC; *Int'l*, pg. 1506
WILLIS CORROON CORP. OF KANSAS—See Willis Corroon Group PLC; *Int'l*, pg. 1506
WILLIS CORROON CORP. OF KNOXVILLE—See Willis Corroon Group PLC; *Int'l*, pg. 1506
WILLIS CORROON CORPORATION OF LEXINGTON—See Willis Corroon Group PLC; *Int'l*, pg. 1505
WILLIS CORROON CORP. OF LOS ANGELES—See Willis Corroon Group PLC; *Int'l*, pg. 1506
WILLIS CORROON CORP. OF LOUISIANA—See Willis Corroon Group PLC; *Int'l*, pg. 1506
WILLIS CORROON CORPORATION OF LOUISVILLE—See Willis Corroon Group PLC; *Int'l*, pg. 1505
WILLIS CORROON CORP. OF MARYLAND—See Willis Corroon Group PLC; *Int'l*, pg. 1506
WILLIS CORROON CORP. OF MASSACHUSETTS—See Willis Corroon Group PLC; *Int'l*, pg. 1506
WILLIS CORROON CORP. OF MICHIGAN—See Willis Corroon Group PLC; *Int'l*, pg. 1506
WILLIS CORROON CORP. OF MINNESOTA—See Willis Corroon Group PLC; *Int'l*, pg. 1506
WILLIS CORROON CORP. OF MISSOURI—See Willis Corroon Group PLC; *Int'l*, pg. 1506
WILLIS CORROON CORP. OF MOBILE—See Willis Corroon Group PLC; *Int'l*, pg. 1506
WILLIS CORROON CORP. OF NASHVILLE—See Willis Corroon Group PLC; *Int'l*, pg. 1506
WILLIS CORROON CORP. OF NEW HAMPSHIRE—See Willis Corroon Group PLC; *Int'l*, pg. 1506
WILLIS CORROON CORP. OF NEW JERSEY—See Willis Corroon Group PLC; *Int'l*, pg. 1506
WILLIS CORROON CORP. OF NEW YORK—See Willis Corroon Group PLC; *Int'l*, pg. 1506
WILLIS CORROON CORP. OF NORTH CAROLINA—See Willis Corroon Group PLC; *Int'l*, pg. 1506
WILLIS CORROON CORP. OF NORTHERN OHIO—See Willis Corroon Group PLC; *Int'l*, pg. 1506
WILLIS CORROON CORP. OF ORANGE COUNTY—See Willis Corroon Group PLC; *Int'l*, pg. 1506
WILLIS CORROON CORPORATION OF OWENSBORO—See Willis Corroon Group PLC; *Int'l*, pg. 1505

WILLIS CORROON CORP. OF PENN.—See Willis Corroon Group PLC; *Int'l*, pg. 1507
WILLIS CORROON CORP. OF PITTSBURGH—See Willis Corroon Group PLC; *Int'l*, pg. 1507
WILLIS CORROON CORP. OF PORTLAND—See Willis Corroon Group PLC; *Int'l*, pg. 1507
WILLIS CORROON CORP. OF SACRAMENTO—See Willis Corroon Group PLC; *Int'l*, pg. 1507
WILLIS CORROON CORP. OF SAN DIEGO—See Willis Corroon Group PLC; *Int'l*, pg. 1507
WILLIS CORROON CORP. OF SAN JOSE—See Willis Corroon Group PLC; *Int'l*, pg. 1507
WILLIS CORROON CORP. OF SEATTLE—See Willis Corroon Group PLC; *Int'l*, pg. 1507
WILLIS CORROON CORP. OF SOUTH CAROLINA—See Willis Corroon Group PLC; *Int'l*, pg. 1507
WILLIS CORROON CORP. OF TEXAS—See Willis Corroon Group PLC; *Int'l*, pg. 1507
WILLIS CORROON CORP. OF UTAH—See Willis Corroon Group PLC; *Int'l*, pg. 1507
WILLIS CORROON CORP. OF VIRGINIA—See Willis Corroon Group PLC; *Int'l*, pg. 1507
WILLIS CORROON CORP. OF WASH. D.C.—See Willis Corroon Group PLC; *Int'l*, pg. 1507
WILLIS CORROON CORP. OF WESTERN MICHIGAN—See Willis Corroon Group PLC; *Int'l*, pg. 1507
WILLIS CORROON CORP. OF WISCONSIN—See Willis Corroon Group PLC; *Int'l*, pg. 1507
WILLIS CORROON CREDIT LIMITED—See Willis Corroon Group PLC; *Int'l*, pg. 1502
WILLIS CORROON DOUGLAS LIMITED—See Willis Corroon Group PLC; *Int'l*, pg. 1502
WILLIS CORROON FINANCIAL PLANNING LIMITED—See Willis Corroon Group PLC; *Int'l*, pg. 1502
WILLIS CORROON FINANCIAL SERVICES CORP.—See Willis Corroon Group PLC; *Int'l*, pg. 1504
WILLIS CORROON FRANCE SA—See Willis Corroon Group PLC; *Int'l*, pg. 1509
WILLIS CORROON GROUP PLC; *Int'l*, pg. 1501
WILLIS CORROON HARRIS MARRIAN LIMITED—See Willis Corroon Group PLC; *Int'l*, pg. 1502
WILLIS CORROON HELLAS SA—See Willis Corroon Group PLC; *Int'l*, pg. 1509
WILLIS CORROON HINTON LIMITED—See Willis Corroon Group PLC; *Int'l*, pg. 1502
WILLIS CORROON HUNGARY KFT—See Willis Corroon Group PLC; *Int'l*, pg. 1509
WILLIS CORROON, INC.—See Willis Corroon Group PLC; *Int'l*, pg. 1507
WILLIS CORROON INSPACE, INC.—See Willis Corroon Group PLC; *Int'l*, pg. 1507
WILLIS CORROON INTERNATIONAL/AMERICAS—See Willis Corroon Group PLC; *Int'l*, pg. 1507
WILLIS CORROON IRELAND LIMITED—See Willis Corroon Group PLC; *Int'l*, pg. 1509
WILLIS CORROON JAPAN LIMITED—See Willis Corroon Group PLC; *Int'l*, pg. 1509
WILLIS CORROON KENDRIKI SA—See Willis Corroon Group PLC; *Int'l*, pg. 1509
WILLIS CORROON LIMITED—See Willis Corroon Group PLC; *Int'l*, pg. 1502
WILLIS CORROON LIMITED-BERMUDA—See Willis Corroon Group PLC; *Int'l*, pg. 1509
WILLIS CORROON MANAGEMENT (CAYMAN) LTD.—See Willis Corroon Group PLC; *Int'l*, pg. 1505
WILLIS CORROON MANAGEMENT LIMITED-BERMUDA—See Willis Corroon Group PLC; *Int'l*, pg. 1509
WILLIS CORROON MANAGEMENT LIMITED-DUBLIN—See Willis Corroon Group PLC; *Int'l*, pg. 1509
WILLIS CORROON MANAGEMENT LIMITED-GUERNSEY—See Willis Corroon Group PLC; *Int'l*, pg. 1503
WILLIS CORROON MANAGEMENT LIMITED-ISLE OF MAN—See Willis Corroon Group PLC; *Int'l*, pg. 1503
WILLIS CORROON MANAGEMENT SA-LUXEMBOURG—See Willis Corroon Group PLC; *Int'l*, pg. 1509
WILLIS CORROON MANAGEMENT (VERMONT) LTD.—See Willis Corroon Group PLC; *Int'l*, pg. 1505
WILLIS CORROON MARINE & ENERGY—See Willis Corroon Group PLC; *Int'l*, pg. 1508
WILLIS CORROON MELLING INC.—See Willis Corroon Group PLC; *Int'l*, pg. 1509
WILLIS CORROON MELLING LTD.—See Willis Corroon Group PLC; *Int'l*, pg. 1509
WILLIS CORROON MIDLANDS LIMITED—See Willis Corroon Group PLC; *Int'l*, pg. 1502
WILLIS CORROON NORTH LIMITED—See Willis Corroon Group PLC; *Int'l*, pg. 1502
WILLIS CORROON OVERSEAS LTD.—See Willis Corroon Group PLC; *Int'l*, pg. 1509
WILLIS CORROON POLSKA SPOLKA AKEYJNA—See Willis Corroon Group PLC; *Int'l*, pg. 1509
WILLIS CORROON (PRIVATE) LIMITED—See Willis Corroon Group PLC; *Int'l*, pg. 1509
WILLIS CORROON PROPERTY & CASUALTY PROGRAMS DIV.—See Willis Corroon Group PLC; *Int'l*, pg. 1508
WILLIS CORROON RICHARD OLIVER PTY. LTD.—See Willis Corroon Group PLC; *Int'l*, pg. 1509
WILLIS CORROON RISK CONSULTING LIMITED—See Willis Corroon Group PLC; *Int'l*, pg. 1503
WILLIS CORROON RISK MANAGEMENT LIMITED—See Willis Corroon Group PLC; *Int'l*, pg. 1503
WILLIS CORROON SCHEUER—See Willis Corroon Group PLC; *Int'l*, pg. 1502
WILLIS CORROON SCOTLAND LIMITED—See Willis Corroon Group PLC; *Int'l*, pg. 1503
WILLIS CORROON SECRETARIAL SERVICES LIMITED-GUERNSEY—See Willis Corroon Group PLC; *Int'l*, pg. 1509
WILLIS CORROON SOUTH LIMITED—See Willis Corroon Group PLC; *Int'l*, pg. 1503
WILLIS CORROON S.R.O.—See Willis Corroon Group PLC; *Int'l*, pg. 1509

WILLIS CORROON (TAIWAN) LIMITED—See Willis Corroon Group PLC; *Int'l*, pg. 1510
WILLIS CORROON WALES LIMITED—See Willis Corroon Group PLC; *Int'l*, pg. 1503
OY WILLIS FABER AB—See Willis Corroon Group PLC; *Int'l*, pg. 1510
WILLIS FABER (AEGEAN) LIMITED—See Willis Corroon Group PLC; *Int'l*, pg. 1510
WILLIS FABER AG (ZURICH)—See Willis Corroon Group PLC; *Int'l*, pg. 1510
WILLIS FABER & DUMAS—See Willis Corroon Group PLC; *Int'l*, pg. 1510
WILLIS FABER & DUMAS (AGENCIES) LIMITED—See Willis Corroon Group PLC; *Int'l*, pg. 1503
WILLIS FABER & DUMAS LIMITED—See Willis Corroon Group PLC; *Int'l*, pg. 1503
WILLIS FABER & DUMAS LTD.—See Willis Corroon Group PLC; *Int'l*, pg. 1510
WILLIS FABER CONSULTING (FAR EAST) LTD.—See Willis Corroon Group PLC; *Int'l*, pg. 1502
WILLIS FABER EC—See Willis Corroon Group PLC; *Int'l*, pg. 1510
WILLIS FABER (FAR EAST) LIMITED—See Willis Corroon Group PLC; *Int'l*, pg. 1510
WILLIS FABER GOTHIA AB—See Willis Corroon Group PLC; *Int'l*, pg. 1510
WILLIS FABER, INC.—See Willis Corroon Group PLC; *Int'l*, pg. 1503
WILLIS FABER INSURANCE BROKERS SDN. BHD.—See Willis Corroon Group PLC; *Int'l*, pg. 1510
WILLIS FABER LIMITADA—See Willis Corroon Group PLC; *Int'l*, pg. 1510
WILLIS FABER (MALAYSIA) SDN BHD—See Willis Corroon Group PLC; *Int'l*, pg. 1510
WILLIS FABER (MIDDLE EAST) S.A.L.—See Willis Corroon Group PLC; *Int'l*, pg. 1510
WILLIS FABER NORTH AMERICA, INC.-CALIFORNIA—See Willis Corroon Group PLC; *Int'l*, pg. 1503
WILLIS FABER NORTH AMERICA, INC.-CONNECTICUT—See Willis Corroon Group PLC; *Int'l*, pg. 1503
WILLIS FABER NORTH AMERICA, INC.-FLORIDA—See Willis Corroon Group PLC; *Int'l*, pg. 1503
WILLIS FABER NORTH AMERICA, INC.-GEORGIA—See Willis Corroon Group PLC; *Int'l*, pg. 1503
WILLIS FABER NORTH AMERICA, INC.-ILLINOIS—See Willis Corroon Group PLC; *Int'l*, pg. 1503
WILLIS FABER NORTH AMERICA, INC.-NEW YORK—See Willis Corroon Group PLC; *Int'l*, pg. 1503
WILLIS FABER NORTH AMERICA, INC.-NORTH CAROLINA—See Willis Corroon Group PLC; *Int'l*, pg. 1503
WILLIS FABER NORTH AMERICA, INC.-PENNSLYVANIA—See Willis Corroon Group PLC; *Int'l*, pg. 1503
WILLIS FABER NORTH AMERICA, INC.-TENNESSEE—See Willis Corroon Group PLC; *Int'l*, pg. 1504
WILLIS FABER S.A.—See Willis Corroon Group PLC; *Int'l*, pg. 1510
WILLIS FABER (UNDERWRITING MANAGEMENT) LIMITED—See Willis Corroon Group PLC; *Int'l*, pg. 1504
WILLISTON BASIN INTERSTATE PIPELINE COMPANY—See MDU Resources Group, Inc.; *U.S. Public*, pg. 1026
WILLISTON MANUFACTURING CO.—See House of Perfection, Inc.; *U.S. Private*, pg. 542
WILLISTON TELEPHONE CO.—See Telephone and Data Systems, Inc.; *U.S. Public*, pg. 1572
WILLITTS DESIGN; *U.S. Private*, pg. 1180
WILLMOTTS LIMITED—See Ascot Holdings Plc; *Int'l*, pg. 88
WILLOUGHBY'S; *U.S. Private*, pg. 1180
WILLOWBROOK CARE CENTER, INC.—See Vencor, Inc.; *U.S. Public*, pg. 1715
THE WILLOWBROOK CORP.—See The Rouse Company; *U.S. Public*, pg. 1408
WILLOWBROOK MANOR—See Horizon/CMS Healthcare Corporation; *U.S. Public*, pg. 837
WILLS GROUP, INC.; *U.S. Private*, pg. 1180
W.D. & H.O. WILLS (AUSTRALIA) LTD.—See B.A.T Industries P.L.C.; *Int'l*, pg. 112
WILLSON STATIONERS—See Russel Metals Inc.; *Int'l*, pg. 1150
WILMER SERVICE LINE—See The Reynolds and Reynolds Company; *U.S. Public*, pg. 1385
WILMERINK & MULLER—See LVMH Moet Hennessy Louis Vuitton; *Int'l*, pg. 783
WILMINGTON HOMES, INC.—See The Rouse Company; *U.S. Public*, pg. 1409
WILMINGTON MORNING STAR—See The New York Times Company; *U.S. Public*, pg. 1175
WILMINGTON SAVINGS FUND SOCIETY (FSB)—See WSFS Financial Corporation; *U.S. Public*, pg. 1729
WILMINGTON STAR-NEWS, INC.—See The New York Times Company; *U.S. Public*, pg. 1175
WILMINGTON TRUST CORPORATION; *U.S. Public*, pg. 1770
WILMOR WAREHOUSE & SHIPPING CO., INC.—See The Hearst Corporation; *U.S. Private*, pg. 516
WILMORE COAL COMPANY—See Berwind Corporation; *U.S. Private*, pg. 138
WILMORITE, INC.; *U.S. Private*, pg. 1180
WILSEY BENNETT CO.; *U.S. Private*, pg. 1180
WILSEY BENNETT REAL ESTATE DIVISION—See Wilsey Bennett Co.; *U.S. Private*, pg. 1180
WILSEY FOODS, INC.—See Mitsui & Co., Ltd.; *Int'l*, pg. 879
WILSHIRE OIL CO. OF TEXAS; *U.S. Public*, pg. 1770
WILSHIRE OIL OF CANADA, LTD.—See Wilshire Oil Co. of Texas; *U.S. Public*, pg. 1770
WILSON & LAFLEUR, LIMITEE—See Quebecor Inc.; *Int'l*, pg. 1076
WILSON BROTHERS DRILLING CO.—See Burlington Resources Inc.; *U.S. Public*, pg. 269
WILSON COLOR—See M.A. Hanna Company; *U.S. Public*, pg. 781

WILSON CONNOLLY; *Int'l*, pg. 1510
WILSON CONVALESCENT CENTER—See Vencor, Inc.; *U.S. Public*, pg. 1715
WILSON-FIBERFIL FRANCE SA—See Akzo Nobel N.V.; *Int'l*, pg. 46
WILSON-FIBERFIL INTERNATIONAL SA—See Akzo Nobel N.V.; *Int'l*, pg. 46
WILSON-FIBERFIL SWEDEN AB—See Akzo Nobel N.V.; *Int'l*, pg. 46
WILSON FRANCE SARL—See Amer Group Ltd.; *Int'l*, pg. 73
WILSON GROUP—See BTL AB; *Int'l*, pg. 123
H. WILSON COMPANY—See EBSCO Industries, Inc.; *U.S. Private*, pg. 359
THE H.W. WILSON CO.; *U.S. Private*, pg. 1180
WILSON INDUSTRIES INC.; *U.S. Private*, pg. 1181
WILSON JAPAN, INC.—See Amer Group Ltd.; *Int'l*, pg. 73
JIM WILSON & ASSOCIATES, INC.; *U.S. Private*, pg. 1181
WILSON MACHINE KNIFE CO., INC.—See Hyde Manufacturing Co.; *U.S. Private*, pg. 551
WILSON MILLS LAND COMPANY—See The Progressive Corporation; *U.S. Public*, pg. 1335
WILSON PRODUCTS CO.; *U.S. Private*, pg. 1181
RALPH C. WILSON ENTERPRISES; *U.S. Private*, pg. 1181
RALPH WILSON PLASTICS CO.—See Premark International, Inc.; *U.S. Public*, pg. 1322
ROBERT WILSON (SINGAPORE) LIMITED—See Haw Par Brothers International Limited; *Int'l*, pg. 604
WILSON SEEDS INC.—See Land O'Lakes, Inc.; *U.S. Private*, pg. 646
WILSON SERVICE CENTER—See Carolina Steel Corporation; *U.S. Private*, pg. 214
WILSON/SHORE INSTRUMENTS—See Instron Corporation; *U.S. Public*, pg. 883
WILSON SPORTING GOODS ASIA, LTD.—See Amer Group Ltd.; *Int'l*, pg. 73
WILSON SPORTING GOODS AUSTRALIA PTY. LTD.—See Amer Group Ltd.; *Int'l*, pg. 73
WILSON SPORTING GOODS CO.—See Amer Group Ltd.; *Int'l*, pg. 73
WILSON SPORTING GOODS CO. DE MEXICO—See Amer Group Ltd.; *Int'l*, pg. 73
WILSON SPORTING GOODS CO., LTD.—See Amer Group Ltd.; *Int'l*, pg. 73
WILSON SPORTING GOODS COMPANY LIMITED—See Amer Group Ltd.; *Int'l*, pg. 73
WILSON SPORTING GOODS CS SPOL SRO—See Amer Group Ltd.; *Int'l*, pg. 73
WILSON SPORTING GOODS ESPANA, S.A.—See Amer Group Ltd.; *Int'l*, pg. 73
WILSON SPORTING GOODS EUROPE—See Amer Group Ltd.; *Int'l*, pg. 73
WILSON SPORTING GOODS GMBH—See Amer Group Ltd.; *Int'l*, pg. 73
WILSON SPORTING GOODS (MALAYSIA) SDN. BHD.—See Amer Group Ltd.; *Int'l*, pg. 73
WILSON SPORTS EQUIPMENT CANADA, INC.—See Amer Group Ltd.; *Int'l*, pg. 73
WILSON SPORTS EQUIPMENT CANADA, LTD.—See Amer Group Ltd.; *Int'l*, pg. 73
WILSON STEEL & WIRE CO.—See MCM Enterprises, Inc.; *U.S. Private*, pg. 686
WILSON SUPPLY INTERNATIONAL (U.K.) LTD.—See Wilson Industries Inc.; *U.S. Private*, pg. 1181
WILSON USA INC.—See BTL AB; *Int'l*, pg. 124
WILSONART INTERNATIONAL, INC.—See Premark International, Inc.; *U.S. Public*, pg. 1322
WILSONS THE LEATHER EXPERTS INC.; *U.S. Private*, pg. 1181
WILTIC CHEMICAL MANUFACTURING—See Genova Products, Inc.; *U.S. Private*, pg. 447
WILTON CORPORATION; *U.S. Private*, pg. 1181
WILTON INDUSTRIES, INC.; *U.S. Private*, pg. 1181
WILTON TOOL CORP.—See Wilton Corporation; *U.S. Private*, pg. 1181
WILTRON COMPANY—See Anritsu Corporation; *Int'l*, pg. 77
WILTSHIER INTERIORS (BRUNEI) SDN. BHD.—See Ballast Nedam NV; *Int'l*, pg. 134
WILTSHIRE CANADA, INC.—See McPherson's Limited; *Int'l*, pg. 852
WIM VOS INTERNATIONALE TRANSPORTEN B.V.—See Royal Nedlloyd Group N.V.; *Int'l*, pg. 1145
WIMPEY ALAWI LLC—See Tarmac plc; *Int'l*, pg. 1355
GEORGE WIMPEY & CO. (NIGERIA) LTD.—See George Wimpey PLC; *Int'l*, pg. 1510
GEORGE WIMPEY INTERNATIONAL LTD.—See George Wimpey PLC; *Int'l*, pg. 1510
GEORGE WIMPEY PLC; *Int'l*, pg. 1510
WIMPEY GROUP SERVICES LTD.—See George Wimpey PLC; *Int'l*, pg. 1510
WIMPEY HOMES HOLDINGS LTD.—See George Wimpey PLC; *Int'l*, pg. 1510
WIMPEY PROPERTY HOLDINGS LTD.—See George Wimpey PLC; *Int'l*, pg. 1510
WINCHELL'S DONUT HOUSES, L.P.—See Shato Holdings Ltd.; *Int'l*, pg. 1230
WINCHESTER CARTON CORP.—See Rock-Tenn Company; *U.S. Public*, pg. 1397
WINCHESTER ELECTRONICS—See Litton Industries, Inc.; *U.S. Public*, pg. 1003
WINCHESTER HOMES, INC.—See Weyerhaeuser Company; *U.S. Public*, pg. 1764
WINCO—See Dyna Technology Incorporated; *U.S. Private*, pg. 350
WINCOM VERSICHERUNGS-HOLDING AKTIENGESELLSCHAFT—See Commerzbank AG; *Int'l*, pg. 310
WINCUP; *U.S. Private*, pg. 1182
WIND RIVER SYSTEMS GMBH—See Wind River Systems, Inc.; *U.S. Public*, pg. 1771
WIND RIVER SYSTEMS, INC.; *U.S. Public*, pg. 1770
WIND RIVER SYSTEMS JAPAN/ASIA-PACIFIC—See Wind River Systems, Inc.; *U.S. Public*, pg. 1771

WIND RIVER SYSTEMS S.A.R.L.—See Wind River Systems, Inc.; *U.S. Public*, pg. 1771
WIND RIVER SYSTEMS SCANDANAVIA—See Wind River Systems, Inc.; *U.S. Public*, pg. 1771
WIND RIVER SYSTEMS UK LTD.—See Wind River Systems, Inc.; *U.S. Public*, pg. 1771
WINDEMULLER ELECTRIC INC.; *U.S. Private*, pg. 1182
WINDFONDS VAN MELLE B.V.—See Van Melle N.V.; *Int'l*, pg. 1451
WINDGATE PARTNERS—See Cigna Corp.; *U.S. Public*, pg. 362
THE WINDHAM COMPANY; *U.S. Private*, pg. 1182
WINDMASTER NEDERLAND B.V.—See Royal Begemann Group; *Int'l*, pg. 1134
WINDMERE CONSUMER PRODUCTS, INC.—See Windmere-Durable Holdings; *U.S. Public*, pg. 1771
WINDMERE-DURABLE HOLDINGS; *U.S. Public*, pg. 1771
WINDMERE ISLAND CLUB—See Sea Containers Ltd.; *Int'l*, pg. 1213
WINDMERE PRODS. DIV.—See Windmere-Durable Holdings; *U.S. Public*, pg. 1771
WINDMOELLER & HOELSCHER; *Int'l*, pg. 1510
WINDMOELLER & HOELSCHER—See Publishers Equipment Corporation; *U.S. Private*, pg. 1341
WINDMOELLER & HOELSCHER CORP.—See Windmoeller & Hoelscher; *Int'l*, pg. 1511
WINDMOLLER & HOLSCHER -BURO MOSKAU—See Windmoeller & Hoelscher; *Int'l*, pg. 1511
WINDMOLLER & HOLSCHER DIS TICARET A.S.—See Windmoeller & Hoelscher; *Int'l*, pg. 1511
WINDMOLLER & HOLSCHER - LIASON OFFICE—See Windmoeller & Hoelscher; *Int'l*, pg. 1511
WINDMOLLER & HOLSCHER N.V.—See Windmoeller & Hoelscher; *Int'l*, pg. 1511
WINDMOLLER & HOLSCHER AG—See Windmoeller & Hoelscher; *Int'l*, pg. 1511
WINDMOLLER & HOLSCHER BV—See Windmoeller & Hoelscher; *Int'l*, pg. 1511
WINDMOLLER & HOLSCHER DO BRASIL LTDA.—See Windmoeller & Hoelscher; *Int'l*, pg. 1511
WINDMOLLER & HOLSCHER ITALIANA S.R.L.—See Windmoeller & Hoelscher; *Int'l*, pg. 1511
WINDOW FURNISHINGS SINGAPORE PTE. LTD.—See Hunter Douglas N.V.; *Int'l*, pg. 640
WINDOWVISIONS INC.—See Lindal Cedar Homes, Inc.; *U.S. Public*, pg. 999
WINDPOINT PARTNERS; *U.S. Private*, pg. 1182
WINDSOR AIRMOTIVE—See Barnes Group Inc.; *U.S. Public*, pg. 190
WINDSOR AIRMOTIVE ASIA PTE. LTD.—See Barnes Group Inc.; *U.S. Public*, pg. 190
THE WINDSOR & HANTSPORT RAILWAY CO. LTD.—See Iron Road Railways Inc.; *U.S. Private*, pg. 575
WINDSOR ART, INC.—See Bentley International, Inc.; *U.S. Public*, pg. 212
WINDSOR COAL CO.—See American Electric Power Company, Inc.; *U.S. Public*, pg. 69
WINDSOR COURT HOTEL L.P.—See Sea Containers Ltd.; *Int'l*, pg. 1214
WINDSOR DOOR—See American Buildings Co.; *U.S. Public*, pg. 69
WINDSOR FASHIONS; *U.S. Private*, pg. 1182
WINDSOR HEALTH CARE CENTER—See Vencor, Inc.; *U.S. Public*, pg. 1715
WINDSOR HEALTHCARE LTD.—See Boehringer Ingelheim GmbH; *Int'l*, pg. 199
WINDSOR INDUSTRIES, INC.; *U.S. Private*, pg. 1182
WINDSOR INSURANCE—See American Financial Group; *U.S. Public*, pg. 75
WINDSOR MANOR—See Horizon/CMS Healthcare Corporation; *U.S. Public*, pg. 837
WINDSOR MANUFACTURING—See Barnes Group Inc.; *U.S. Public*, pg. 190
WINDSOR QUALITY FOOD CO., LTD.; *U.S. Private*, pg. 1182
WINDSOR SERVICE, INC.—See Haines Kibblehouse; *U.S. Private*, pg. 494
WINDSOR SHADE TOBACCO COMPANY, INC.; *U.S. Private*, pg. 1182
THE WINDSOR STAR—See Hollinger Inc.; *Int'l*, pg. 632
WINDY HILL PET FOOD CO.; *U.S. Private*, pg. 1182
WINDY HILL PET FOOD CO.—See Windy Hill Pet Food Co.; *U.S. Private*, pg. 1182
THE WINE ALLIANCE—See Allied Domecq PLC; *Int'l*, pg. 63
THE WINE GROUP; *U.S. Private*, pg. 1182
WINE RACK—See Vincor International; *Int'l*, pg. 1468
WINE WORLD ESTATES—See Nestle S.A.; *Int'l*, pg. 917
WINE WORLD ESTATES COMPANY—See Nestle S.A.; *Int'l*, pg. 917
WINE WORLD ESTATES, INC.—See Nestle S.A.; *Int'l*, pg. 917
WINEQUEST—See Delicato Vineyards; *U.S. Private*, pg. 322
WINFIELD LOCKS, INC.—See Masco Corporation; *U.S. Public*, pg. 1053
THE WING GROUP—See Western Resources, Inc.; *U.S. Public*, pg. 1760
WING HANG BANK LIMITED—See The Bank of New York Company, Inc.; *U.S. Public*, pg. 179
WING INDUSTRIES, INC.; *U.S. Private*, pg. 1183
WING ON FOODS CO., LTD.—See Nissin Food Products Co., Ltd.; *Int'l*, pg. 950
WINGS LUGGAGE—See Brown-Forman Corporation; *U.S. Public*, pg. 262
WINGS WEST AIRLINES—See AMR Corporation; *U.S. Public*, pg. 9
WINK DAVIS EQUIPMENT COMPANY, INC.—See Speizman Industries, Inc.; *U.S. Public*, pg. 1498
WINKELMAN STORES CREDIT CORP.—See Petrie Retail, Inc.; *U.S. Private*, pg. 858
WINKELMAN STORES, INC.—See Petrie Retail, Inc.; *U.S. Private*, pg. 858
WINKLER ADVERTISING; *U.S. Private*, pg. 1183

WINKLER FORMING—See PMC, Inc.; *U.S. Private,* pg. 827
WINMAR COMPANY—See SAFECO Corporation; *U.S. Public,* pg. 1423
THE WINN ART GROUP, LTD.—See Devon Group, Inc.; *U.S. Public,* pg. 503
WINN CORRECTIONAL CENTER—See Corrections Corporation of America; *U.S. Public,* pg. 451
WINN-DIXIE STORES, INC.; *U.S. Public,* pg. 1771
WINN DIXIE SUPERBRAND DAIRIES—See Winn-Dixie Stores, Inc.; *U.S. Public,* pg. 1771
FRANK W. WINNE & SON, INC.; *U.S. Private,* pg. 1183
WINNEBAGO ACCEPTANCE CORP.—See Winnebago Industries, Inc.; *U.S. Public,* pg. 1772
WINNEBAGO HEALTH CARE MANAGEMENT COMPANY—See Winnebago Industries, Inc.; *U.S. Public,* pg. 1772
WINNEBAGO INDUSTRIES, INC.; *U.S. Public,* pg. 1772
WINNEBAGO INTERNATIONAL CORP.—See Winnebago Industries, Inc.; *U.S. Public,* pg. 1772
WINNEBAGO R.V., INC.—See Winnebago Industries, Inc.; *U.S. Public,* pg. 1772
WINNER COMMUNICATIONS, INC.; *U.S. Private,* pg. 1183
WINNER FOOD PRODUCTS LTD.—See Nissin Food Products Co., Ltd.; *Int'l,* pg. 950
WINNERS APPAREL LTD.—See The TJX Companies, Inc.; *U.S. Public,* pg. 1557
WINNETKA FINANCIAL CENTER—See Northern Trust Corporation; *U.S. Public,* pg. 1197
WINONA DAILY NEWS—See Lee Enterprises, Incorporated; *U.S. Public,* pg. 984
WINONA KNITS; *U.S. Private,* pg. 1183
WINONA KNITTING MILLS, INC.—See Hampshire Group, Ltd.; *U.S. Public,* pg. 779
WINONA RESEARCH—See WPP Group plc; *Int'l,* pg. 1483
WINONA S.A.R.L.—See Andres Wines Ltd.; *Int'l,* pg. 76
WINPAC B.V.—See Metsa-Serla Corporation; *Int'l,* pg. 864
WINPOWER INC.—See Dyna Technology Incorporated; *U.S. Private,* pg. 350
WINROCK ENTERPRISES, INC.; *U.S. Private,* pg. 1183
WINSCHERMANN BERLIN GMBH—See Saarbergwerke Aktiengesellschaft; *Int'l,* pg. 1167
WINSCHERMANN SUED GMBH—See Saarbergwerke Aktiengesellschaft; *Int'l,* pg. 1167
WINSCHERMANN WEST GMBH—See Saarbergwerke Aktiengesellschaft; *Int'l,* pg. 1167
WINSTAR COMMUNICATIONS; *U.S. Public,* pg. 1772
WINSTAR GLOBAL PRODUCTS, INC.—See Winstar Communications; *U.S. Public,* pg. 1772
W.H. WINSTEAD COMPANY—See Universal Corporation; *U.S. Public,* pg. 1695
WINSTED PRECISION BALL CO.—See FAG Group; *Int'l,* pg. 468
WINSTON CARPET CO.—See Shaw Industries, Inc.; *U.S. Public,* pg. 1464
WINSTON CUP ILLUSTRATED—See Advance Publications Inc.; *U.S. Private,* pg. 20
WINSTON CUP SCENE—See Advance Publications Inc.; *U.S. Private,* pg. 20
HARRY WINSTON, INC.; *U.S. Private,* pg. 1183
WINSTON LEAF TOBACCO CO.—See Universal Corporation; *U.S. Public,* pg. 1695
WINSTON RESOURCES, INC.; *U.S. Public,* pg. 1772
WINSTON-SALEM CONVALESCENT CENTER—See Vencor, Inc.; *U.S. Public,* pg. 1715
WINSTON STEEL PRODUCTS CO.; *U.S. Private,* pg. 1183
WINSTON TIRE COMPANY—See J.H. Heafner Co. Inc.; *U.S. Private,* pg. 514
WINSTONE AGGREGATES LIMITED—See Fletcher Challenge Limited; *Int'l,* pg. 495
WINSTONE WALLBOARDS LIMITED—See Fletcher Challenge Limited; *Int'l,* pg. 495
WINTAI FOOD MANUFACTURERS LTD.—See Nissin Food Products Co., Ltd.; *Int'l,* pg. 950
WINTER HAVEN—See Horizon/CMS Healthcare Corporation; *U.S. Public,* pg. 839
WINTER HAVEN NEWS CHIEF—See Shivers Trading & Operating Co.; *U.S. Private,* pg. 995
WINTER VOLVO & LINCOLN MERCURY; *U.S. Private,* pg. 1183
WINTER-BOUTS B.V.—See Kemira Oy; *Int'l,* pg. 729
WINTERBURN LTD.—See Thermo Electron Corporation; *U.S. Public,* pg. 1596
WINTERLAND PRODUCTIONS—See The Seagram Company Ltd.; *Int'l,* pg. 1215
HENRI WINTERMANS' SIGARENFABRIEKEN B.V.—See B.A.T Industries P.L.C.; *Int'l,* pg. 111
WINTERS WELDING WORKS, INC.; *U.S. Private,* pg. 1183
WINTERSHALL AG—See BASF AG; *Int'l,* pg. 104
WINTERSHALL CANADA LTD.—See BASF AG; *Int'l,* pg. 110
WINTERSHALL ERDGAS BETEILIGUNGS GMBH—See BASF AG; *Int'l,* pg. 105
WINTERSHALL ERDGAS HANDELSHAUS GMBH—See BASF AG; *Int'l,* pg. 105
WINTERSHALL ERDGAS HANDELSHAUS ZUG AG—See BASF AG; *Int'l,* pg. 110
WINTERSHALL GAS GMBH—See BASF AG; *Int'l,* pg. 105
WINTERSHALL NEDERLAND B.V.—See BASF AG; *Int'l,* pg. 110
WINTERSHALL NOORDZEE B.V.—See BASF AG; *Int'l,* pg. 110
WINTERSHALL OIL AG—See BASF AG; *Int'l,* pg. 110
WINTERSHALL PETROLEUM IBERIA S.A.—See BASF AG; *Int'l,* pg. 110
WINTERTHUR LEBENSVERSICHERUNGS-GESELLSCHAFT—See Credit Suisse Group; *Int'l,* pg. 345
WINTERTHUR REINSURANCE CORPORATION OF AMERICA—See Credit Suisse Group; *Int'l,* pg. 346
WINTERTHUR SCHWEIZERISCHE VERSICHERUNGS-GESELLSCHAFT—See Credit Suisse Group; *Int'l,* pg. 345
WINTERTHUR U.S. HOLDINGS INC.—See Credit Suisse Group; *Int'l,* pg. 345

WINTHER & HEIDE'S EFTF. A/S—See Dahl International AB; *Int'l,* pg. 359
WINTHROP-ATKINS CO., INC.; *U.S. Private,* pg. 1183
WINTHROP PRINTING COMPANY, INC.; *U.S. Private,* pg. 1184
WINTRUCKS S.A.—See Etablissements Delhaize Freres Et Cie "Le Lion" S.A.; *Int'l,* pg. 463
WINTZ COMPANIES; *U.S. Private,* pg. 1184
WIPER CHECK, INC.—See Tomkins PLC; *Int'l,* pg. 1397
WIPFLI, ULLRICH, BERTELSON—See Effective Management Systems; *U.S. Public,* pg. 566
WIPRO-ACER LIMITED—See Acer Incorporated; *Int'l,* pg. 22
WIPRO INFORMATION TECHNOLOGY LIMITED—See The Macneal-Schwendler Corp.; *U.S. Public,* pg. 1032
WIRE-PRO INC.; *U.S. Private,* pg. 1184
WIRE ROPE CORPORATION OF AMERICA, INC.; *U.S. Private,* pg. 1184
WIRE TECH, INC.—See Hicks, Muse, Tate & Furst Inc.; *U.S. Private,* pg. 526
WIRELESS DATA GROUP—See Motorola, Inc.; *U.S. Public,* pg. 1139
WIRELESS NETWORK VENTURES LTD.—See Motorola, Inc.; *U.S. Public,* pg. 1140
WIRELESS NETWORKS SKYLINE - NORTHERN TELECOM CANADA LIMITED—See Northern Telecom Limited; *Int'l,* pg. 969
WIRELESS ONE NETWORK LP; *U.S. Private,* pg. 1184
WIRELESS PRODUCTS GROUP—See Watkins-Johnson Company; *U.S. Public,* pg. 1745
WIRELESS TELECOM GROUP, INC.; *U.S. Public,* pg. 1772
WIREMAKERS LIMITED—See Fletcher Challenge Limited; *Int'l,* pg. 495
THE WIREMOLD COMPANY; *U.S. Private,* pg. 1184
WIRSBO AG—See Electrolux, AB; *Int'l,* pg. 444
WIRSBO PEX GMBH—See Electrolux, AB; *Int'l,* pg. 442
WIRSBO STALROR AB—See Rautaruukki Oy; *Int'l,* pg. 1088
WIRTEN GMBH; *Int'l,* pg. 1511
WIRTH GAS EQUIPMENT, INC.—See Eclipse Inc.; *U.S. Private,* pg. 360
WIRTH LTD.—See Russel Metals Inc.; *Int'l,* pg. 1150
WIRTSCHAFS-UND PRIVATBANK—See Bayerische Vereinsbank Group; *Int'l,* pg. 181
WIRTSCHAFTSWOCHE ZEITSCHRIFTEN-VERLAGSGESELLSCHAFT M.B.H. & CO. KG—See Georg von Holtzbrinck GmbH; *Int'l,* pg. 1479
WIRTZ CORPORATION; *U.S. Private,* pg. 1184
WISAFOREST BENELUX B.V.—See UPM-Kymmene Corporation; *Int'l,* pg. 1429
WISAFOREST DEUTSCHLAND GMBH—See UPM-Kymmene Corporation; *Int'l,* pg. 1429
WISAFOREST FRANCE S.A.R.L.—See UPM-Kymmene Corporation; *Int'l,* pg. 1429
WISAFOREST OY AB—See UPM-Kymmene Corporation; *Int'l,* pg. 1429
WISAFOREST SVERIGE AB—See UPM-Kymmene Corporation; *Int'l,* pg. 1429
WISAFOREST (UK) LTD.—See UPM-Kymmene Corporation; *Int'l,* pg. 1429
WISAPAK MERTENS GMBH—See UPM-Kymmene Corporation; *Int'l,* pg. 1430
WISAPAK MULTICOATE A/S—See UPM-Kymmene Corporation; *Int'l,* pg. 1430
WISAPAK OY AB—See UPM-Kymmene Corporation; *Int'l,* pg. 1429
WISAPAK OY AB, KARHULA FACTORY—See UPM-Kymmene Corporation; *Int'l,* pg. 1429
WISAPAK OY AB, PIETARSAARI FACTORY—See UPM-Kymmene Corporation; *Int'l,* pg. 1429
WISAPAPER BENELUX B.V.—See UPM-Kymmene Corporation; *Int'l,* pg. 1430
WISCONSIN & SOUTHERN RAILROAD CO.; *U.S. Private,* pg. 1184
WISCONSIN & SOUTHERN RAILROAD COMPANY—See Wisconsin & Southern Railroad Co.; *U.S. Private,* pg. 1184
WISCONSIN AUTOMATED MACHINERY CORP.; *U.S. Private,* pg. 1184
WISCONSIN CENTRAL INTERNATIONAL, INC.—See Wisconsin Central Transportation Corporation; *U.S. Public,* pg. 1773
WISCONSIN CENTRAL LTD.—See Wisconsin Central Transportation Corporation; *U.S. Public,* pg. 1773
WISCONSIN CENTRAL TRANSPORTATION CORPORATION; *U.S. Public,* pg. 1772
WISCONSIN CONSULTAR ENGENHARIA, LTD.—See American Appraisal Associates, Inc.; *U.S. Private,* pg. 50
WISCONSIN ELECTRIC POWER COMPANY—See Wisconsin Energy Corporation; *U.S. Public,* pg. 1773
WISCONSIN ENERGY CORPORATION; *U.S. Public,* pg. 1773
WISCONSIN FINEBLANKING—See Klockner-Werke AG; *Int'l,* pg. 737
WISCONSIN GAS COMPANY—See WICOR, Inc.; *U.S. Public,* pg. 1767
WISCONSIN INSURANCE MANAGEMENT, INC.—See Associated Banc-Corp; *U.S. Public,* pg. 141
WISCONSIN LABEL CORPORATION; *U.S. Private,* pg. 1184
WISCONSIN MACHINE AND TOOL CORPORATION; *U.S. Private,* pg. 1185
WISCONSIN MICHIGAN INVESTMENT CORP.—See Wisconsin Energy Corporation; *U.S. Public,* pg. 1773
WISCONSIN PHARMACAL CO., INC.; *U.S. Private,* pg. 1185
WISCONSIN POWER & LIGHT COMPANY—See WPL Holdings, Inc.; *U.S. Public,* pg. 1728
WISCONSIN PROTECTIVE COATINGS CORP.—See RPM, Inc.; *U.S. Public,* pg. 1358
WISCONSIN PUBLIC SERVICE CORPORATION—See WPS Resources Corp.; *U.S. Public,* pg. 1728

WISCONSIN RIVER POWER CO.—See WPL Holdings, Inc.; *U.S. Public,* pg. 1728
WISCONSIN STATE JOURNAL—See Lee Enterprises, Incorporated; *U.S. Public,* pg. 984
WISCONSIN TISSUE—See Chesapeake Corporation; *U.S. Public,* pg. 347
WISCONSIN TISSUE MILLS, INC.—See Chesapeake Corporation; *U.S. Public,* pg. 347
WISCONSIN WIRE & STEEL—See Maxco, Inc.; *U.S. Public,* pg. 1061
WISDOM IMPORTS SALES CO. INC.—See Interbrew S.A.; *Int'l,* pg. 679
WISE & ASSOCIATES/S&W TECHNICAL SERVICES—See National Technical Systems, Inc.; *U.S. Public,* pg. 1161
WISE FOODS, INC.—See Borden, Inc.; *U.S. Private,* pg. 157
THE WISER OIL COMPANY; *U.S. Public,* pg. 1773
P.T. WISMA KYOEI PRINCE INDONESIA—See The Kyoei Life Insurance Co., Ltd.; *Int'l,* pg. 777
WISPARK CORPORATION—See Wisconsin Energy Corporation; *U.S. Public,* pg. 1773
WISSOTA TRADER LTD.—See Mason Shoe Mfg. Co.; *U.S. Private,* pg. 712
WISURA MINERALOLWERK GOLDGRABE & SCHEFT GMBH & CO.—See Fuchs Petrolub AG Oel + Chemie; *Int'l,* pg. 517
WISVEST CORPORATION—See Wisconsin Energy Corporation; *U.S. Public,* pg. 1773
WITBANK BREWERY—See National Sorghum Beer Breweries Pty. Ltd. Highveld Division; *Int'l,* pg. 909
WITCHER CONSTRUCTION CO.; *U.S. Private,* pg. 1185
WITCHER CONSTRUCTION COMPANY—See Dunn Industries, Inc.; *U.S. Private,* pg. 347
WITCO CANADA, INC.—See Witco Corporation; *U.S. Public,* pg. 1774
WITCO CORPORATION; *U.S. Public,* pg. 1773
WITCO ESPANA S.L.—See Witco Corporation; *U.S. Public,* pg. 1774
WITCO GMBH—See Witco Corporation; *U.S. Public,* pg. 1774
WITCO ITALIANA—See Witco Corporation; *U.S. Public,* pg. 1774
WITCO LTD.—See Witco Corporation; *U.S. Public,* pg. 1774
WITECH CORPORATION—See Wisconsin Energy Corporation; *U.S. Public,* pg. 1773
WITHERS/SUDDATH VAN LINES, INC.—See The Suddath Companies; *U.S. Private,* pg. 1049
WITT COMPANY; *U.S. Private,* pg. 1185
WITT COMPANY—See Witt Company; *U.S. Private,* pg. 1185
WITT GALVANIZING DIVISION—See Witt Company; *U.S. Private,* pg. 1185
JOSEF WITT GMBH & CO. KG.—See Otto Versand (GmbH & Co.; *Int'l,* pg. 1015
WITT PRODUCTS DIVISION—See Witt Company; *U.S. Private,* pg. 1185
WITTHAYU COMPLEX PROJECT—See Nishimatsu Construction Co., Ltd.; *Int'l,* pg. 943
WITTNAUER INTERNATIONAL, INC.—See CBS Corporation; *U.S. Public,* pg. 273
WIX DIV.—See Dana Corporation; *U.S. Public,* pg. 479
WIZARDS OF THE COAST; *U.S. Private,* pg. 1185
WOELM PHARMA GMBH & CO.—See Rhone-Poulenc S.A.; *Int'l,* pg. 1112
WOHLERT CORP.; *U.S. Private,* pg. 1185
WOHLERT DE MEXICO—See Wohlert Corp.; *U.S. Private,* pg. 1185
WOHLERT SPECIAL PRODUCTS—See Wohlert Corp.; *U.S. Private,* pg. 1185
WOHLK CONTACT-LINSEN GMBH—See Carl-Zeiss-Stiftung; *Int'l,* pg. 1523
WOHN-UND GESCHAEFTSBAUTEN GMBH—See Philipp Holzmann AG; *Int'l,* pg. 633
WOHNBAUGESELLSCHAFT NIKLAUSEN—See Georg Fischer Ltd.; *Int'l,* pg. 491
WOHNUNGSBAUGESELLSCHAFT NIEDERSACHSISCHER BRAUNKOHLENWERKE MBH—See Veba AG; *Int'l,* pg. 1456
WOLCOTT & LINCOLN, INC.; *U.S. Private,* pg. 1185
WOLF ADVERTISING LIMITED—See Wolf Mansfield Bolling Advertising Inc.; *U.S. Private,* pg. 1186
WOLF, BLOCK, SCHORR & SOLIS-COHEN; *U.S. Private,* pg. 1185
WOLF BRAND PRODUCTS—See ConAgra, Inc.; *U.S. Public,* pg. 428
WOLF-CAMPBELL PUBLIC RELATIONS—See Wolf Mansfield Bolling Advertising Inc.; *U.S. Private,* pg. 1186
WOLF CREEK NUCLEAR OPERATING CORP.—See Kansas City Power & Light Company; *U.S. Public,* pg. 943
WOLF CREEK NUCLEAR OPERATING CORP.—See Western Resources, Inc.; *U.S. Public,* pg. 1759
WOLF GROUP DIRECT—See Wolf Mansfield Bolling Advertising Inc.; *U.S. Private,* pg. 1185
WOLF GROUP PUBLIC RELATIONS—See Wolf Mansfield Bolling Advertising Inc.; *U.S. Private,* pg. 1186
HOWARD B. WOLF, INC.; *U.S. Public,* pg. 1774
WOLF KLIMATECHNIK GMBH—See Preussag AG; *Int'l,* pg. 1057
WOLF MANSFIELD BOLLING ADVERTISING INC.; *U.S. Private,* pg. 1185
WOLF MANSFIELD BOLLING ADVERTISING INC.—See Wolf Mansfield Bolling Advertising Inc.; *U.S. Private,* pg. 1186
WOLF MANUFACTURING COMPANY; *U.S. Private,* pg. 1186
WOLF RANGE CO.—See Premark International, Inc.; *U.S. Public,* pg. 1322
WOLF-TON GMBH & CO., LTD.—See Watts Blake Bearne & Co. Plc; *Int'l,* pg. 1488
WOLFE NURSERY—See General Host Corporation; *U.S. Public,* pg. 715

WOLFE DIRECTORY OF CORPORATE AFFILIATIONS

Company Index

R.E. WOLFE ENTERPRISES OF EDINBURG—See Republic Industries, Inc.; U.S. Public, pg. 1379
S.J. WOLFE DIVISION—See McDonald & Company Investments, Inc.; U.S. Public, pg. 1068
WOLFER PRINTING COMPANY; U.S. Private, pg. 1186
WOLFERMAN'S, INC.—See Sara Lee Corporation; U.S. Public, pg. 1434
WOLFF HANDELSGESELLSCHAFT & CO. GMBH—See Dyckerhoff & Widmann AG; Int'l, pg. 423
WOLFF WALSRODE AG—See Bayer AG; Int'l, pg. 175
WOLFINGTON BODY COMPANY; U.S. Private, pg. 1186
WOLF'S HEAD OIL COMPANY—See Pennzoil Company; U.S. Public, pg. 1273
JACK WOLFSKIN—See Johnson Worldwide Associates, Inc.; U.S. Public, pg. 933
WOLLARD AIRPORT EQUIPMENT CO.—See Illinois Tool Works Inc.; U.S. Public, pg. 866
WOLOHAN LUMBER CO.; U.S. Public, pg. 1774
WOLSELEY BUILDING DISTRIBUTION - EUROPE—See Wolseley Plc.; Int'l, pg. 1511
WOLSELEY CENTERS LTD.—See Wolseley Plc.; Int'l, pg. 1511
WOLSELEY PLC.; Int'l, pg. 1511
WOLSEY ELECTRONICS LIMITED—See TT Group PLC; Int'l, pg. 1344
WOLTERS KLUWER ACADEMIC PUBLISHERS—See Wolters Kluwer N.V.; Int'l, pg. 1512
WOLTERS KLUWER AUSTRALIA—See Wolters Kluwer N.V.; Int'l, pg. 1513
WOLTERS KLUWER BELGIUM—See Wolters Kluwer N.V.; Int'l, pg. 1513
WOLTERS KLUWER BUSINESS PUBLISHING—See Wolters Kluwer N.V.; Int'l, pg. 1513
WOLTERS KLUWER CENTRAL & EASTERN EUROPE—See Wolters Kluwer N.V.; Int'l, pg. 1513
WOLTERS KLUWER EDUCATIONAL ACTIVITIES—See Wolters Kluwer N.V.; Int'l, pg. 1513
WOLTERS KLUWER FRANCE—See Wolters Kluwer N.V.; Int'l, pg. 1513
WOLTERS KLUWER GERMANY—See Wolters Kluwer N.V.; Int'l, pg. 1513
WOLTERS KLUWER ITALY—See Wolters Kluwer N.V.; Int'l, pg. 1513
WOLTERS KLUWER LAW AND TAXATION—See Wolters Kluwer N.V.; Int'l, pg. 1513
WOLTERS KLUWER N.V.; Int'l, pg. 1512
WOLTERS KLUWER PROFESSIONAL TRAINING—See Wolters Kluwer N.V.; Int'l, pg. 1514
WOLTERS KLUWER SPAIN—See Wolters Kluwer N.V.; Int'l, pg. 1514
WOLTERS KLUWER SWEDEN—See Wolters Kluwer N.V.; Int'l, pg. 1514
WOLTERS KLUWER TRADE PUBLISHING—See Wolters Kluwer N.V.; Int'l, pg. 1513
WOLTERS KLUWER U.K.—See Wolters Kluwer N.V.; Int'l, pg. 1514
WOLTERS KLUWER U.S.—See Wolters Kluwer N.V.; Int'l, pg. 1513
WOLVERINE BOOT CO.—See Wolverine World Wide, Inc.; U.S. Public, pg. 1775
WOLVERINE BRAND DIV.—See Wolverine World Wide, Inc.; U.S. Public, pg. 1775
WOLVERINE GASKET & MANUFACTURING CO.—See Eagle-Picher Industries, Inc.; U.S. Private, pg. 355
WOLVERINE LEATHER DIV.—See Wolverine World Wide, Inc.; U.S. Public, pg. 1775
WOLVERINE MASSACHUSETTS CORPORATION; U.S. Private, pg. 1186
WOLVERINE PACKING CO.; U.S. Private, pg. 1186
WOLVERINE PIPE LINE CO.—See Texaco Inc.; U.S. Public, pg. 1584
WOLVERINE TELEPHONE COMPANY—See Telephone and Data Systems, Inc.; U.S. Public, pg. 1572
WOLVERINE TUBE INC.; U.S. Public, pg. 1774
WOLVERINE VINYL SIDING—See Saint-Gobain; Int'l, pg. 1171
WOLVERINE WORLD WIDE, INC.; U.S. Public, pg. 1775
WOMAN'S DAY—See Lagardere Groupe; Int'l, pg. 795
WOMEN'S HEALTH CARE SERVICES, INC.—See Integrated Health Services, Inc.; U.S. Public, pg. 885
WOMEN'S MAGAZINES GROUP—See Bertelsmann AG; Int'l, pg. 190
WOMEN'S SPORTS AND EVENT MARKETING—See Bertelsmann AG; Int'l, pg. 190
WOMEN'S WEAR DAILY—See The Walt Disney Company; U.S. Public, pg. 513
WOMETCO DE PUERTO RICO INC.—See Wometco Enterprises, Inc.; U.S. Private, pg. 1186
WOMETCO ENTERPRISES, INC.; U.S. Private, pg. 1186
WOMP'S RESTAURANT BAR & GRILL—See The Seagram Company Ltd.; Int'l, pg. 1216
WONDER STATE BOX CO.—See Southern Missouri Containers Inc.; U.S. Private, pg. 1017
WONDERLAND MUSIC CO., INC.—See The Walt Disney Company; U.S. Public, pg. 514
WONDERTEX LIMITED—See RMC Group p.l.c.; Int'l, pg. 1080
WONDERWARE CORPORATION; U.S. Public, pg. 1775
WOO YUN CO., LTD.—See Shimano Inc.; Int'l, pg. 1233
A. WOOD & SONS (DELTING)—See The Albert Fisher Group PLC; Int'l, pg. 491
WOOD COLONY MILLWORKS—See Overholtzer Church Furniture, Inc.; U.S. Private, pg. 823
E WOOD LIMITED—See Meristem plc; Int'l, pg. 858
WOOD EQUIPMENT COMPANY; U.S. Private, pg. 1186
WOOD EXPORT NEW ZEALAND (1986) LIMITED—See International Paper Company; U.S. Public, pg. 905
WOOD FOREST ASSOCIATES—See Cigna Corp.; U.S. Public, pg. 362
GARY WOOD ASSOCIATES, INC.—See Harcourt General, Inc.; U.S. Public, pg. 783
WOOD GROUP PRESSURE CONTROL; U.S. Public, pg. 1775
WOOD HILLS ASSOCIATES—See Cigna Corp.; U.S. Public, pg. 362
WOOD INDUSTRIES—See Katy Industries, Inc.; U.S. Public, pg. 944
J.R. WOOD INC.; U.S. Private, pg. 1186
WOOD MOULDING PLANT—See Georgia-Pacific Corporation; U.S. Public, pg. 738
WOOD PRODUCTS/FOREST RESOURCES/ENERGY RESOURCE DIV.—See Plum Creek Timber Co., L.P.; U.S. Public, pg. 1311
WOOD, STRUTHERS & WINTHROP MANAGEMENT CORP.—See The Equitable Companies Incorporated; U.S. Public, pg. 589
WOOD TERMINAL COMPANY—See Fortune Brands, Inc.; U.S. Public, pg. 675
THE W.B. WOOD COMPANY; U.S. Private, pg. 1186
WOODARD INC.—See CC Industries, Inc.; U.S. Private, pg. 192
WOODBANK (UK) LTD.—See Firth-Rixson Plc; Int'l, pg. 488
WOODBRIDGE CENTER, INC.—See The Rouse Company; U.S. Public, pg. 1408
WOODBRIDGE SANITARY POTTERY CORP.—See Gerber Plumbing Fixtures Corporation; U.S. Private, pg. 449
WOODBURY BUSINESS FORMS, INC.; U.S. Private, pg. 1186
THE WOODBURY TELEPHONE COMPANY—See Southern New England Telecommunications Corporation; U.S. Public, pg. 1491
WOODCHESTER INVESTMENTS PLC—See General Electric Company; U.S. Public, pg. 712
WOODCOMMERZ A.S.—See Commerzbank AG; Int'l, pg. 312
WOODCOMMERZ N.V.—See Commerzbank AG; Int'l, pg. 312
WOODCRAFT INDUSTRIES, INC.; U.S. Private, pg. 1187
WOODFIN PONTIAC-ISUZU; U.S. Private, pg. 1187
THE WOODFIN SUITE HOTELS; U.S. Private, pg. 1187
WOODGATE CONSOLIDATED INCORPORATED—See Green Tree Financial Corporation; U.S. Public, pg. 763
WOODGATE UTILITIES INCORPORATED—See Green Tree Financial Corporation; U.S. Public, pg. 763
WOODGRAIN MILLWORK; U.S. Private, pg. 1187
WOODHAVEN CARE CENTER—See Meritcare, Inc.; U.S. Private, pg. 733
WOODHEAD ASIA PTE. LTD.—See Woodhead Industries, Inc.; U.S. Public, pg. 1776
WOODHEAD CANADA LTD.—See Woodhead Industries, Inc.; U.S. Public, pg. 1776
DANIEL WOODHEAD COMPANY—See Woodhead Industries, Inc.; U.S. Public, pg. 1776
WOODHEAD DE MEXICO—See Woodhead Industries, Inc.; U.S. Public, pg. 1776
WOODHEAD INDUSTRIES, INC.; U.S. Public, pg. 1776
WOODHEAD JAPAN CORPORATION—See Woodhead Industries, Inc.; U.S. Public, pg. 1776
JONAS WOODHEAD LIMITED—See Carclo Engineering Group plc; Int'l, pg. 268
WOODHEAD SPECIALTY FABRICS—See Avondale Incorporated; U.S. Private, pg. 103
WOODLAKE SANITARY SERVICE, INC.—See Browning-Ferris Industries, Inc.; U.S. Public, pg. 265
WOODLAND BIOMASS POWER, INC.—See Thermo Electron Corporation; U.S. Public, pg. 1596
WOODLAND MOLD & TOOL COMPANY—See GP Strategies Corporation; U.S. Public, pg. 694
WOODLANDS LICENSE MANAGEMENT/FIBRE PROCUREMENT—See Fort James Corporation; U.S. Public, pg. 672
WOODLANDS MILLWORK I, LTD.—See Premdor Inc.; Int'l, pg. 1067
WOODLEY MANOR NURSING HOME—See Paragon Health Network, Inc.; U.S. Public, pg. 1257
WOODLINES SHIPPING LIMITED—See International Capital Equipment Limited; Int'l, pg. 683
WOODLORE—See Allen-Edmonds Shoe Corp.; U.S. Private, pg. 37
WOODMARK LTD.—See Norske Skogindustrier A.S; Int'l, pg. 967
WOODMARK ORIGINALS INC.—See Howard Miller; U.S. Private, pg. 747
WOODMEN ACCIDENT & LIFE CO.; U.S. Private, pg. 1187
WOODPAX LIMITED—See Enso Oyj; Int'l, pg. 458
WOODRUFF ELECTRIC CO-OP; U.S. Private, pg. 1187
WOODS EQUIPMENT COMPANY—See Code, Hennessy & Simmons, Inc.; U.S. Private, pg. 249
JOE E. WOODS, INC.; U.S. Private, pg. 1187
WOODS OF COLCHESTER LTD.—See The General Electric Company, p.l.c.; Int'l, pg. 545
WOODS OF PERTH—See Christies International plc; Int'l, pg. 290
WOODSIDE OFFSHORE PETROLEUM PTY. LTD.—See Royal Dutch/Shell Group of Companies; Int'l, pg. 1137
WOODSIDE PETROLEUM LTD.—See Royal Dutch/Shell Group of Companies; Int'l, pg. 1137
WOODSTOCK NATIONAL BANK—See Banknorth Group Inc.; U.S. Public, pg. 187
WOODSTREAM CORPORATION—See Ekco Group, Inc.; U.S. Public, pg. 566
WOODSTUFF MANUFACTURING, INC.; U.S. Private, pg. 1187
WOODWARD & DICKERSON; U.S. Private, pg. 1188
WOODWARD CABLE TV, INC.—See Time Warner Inc.; U.S. Public, pg. 1611
WOODWARD-CLYDE—See URS Corporation; U.S. Public, pg. 1656
WOODWARD-CLYDE CONSULTANTS—See URS Corporation; U.S. Public, pg. 1657
WOODWARD-CLYDE FEDERAL SERVICES—See URS Corporation; U.S. Public, pg. 1657
WOODWARD-CLYDE GROUP, INC.—See URS Corporation; U.S. Public, pg. 1655
WOODWARD-CLYDE INTERNATIONAL—See URS Corporation; U.S. Public, pg. 1657
WOODWARD-CONSTRUCTORS—See URS Corporation; U.S. Public, pg. 1657
WOODWARD GOVERNOR COMPANY; U.S. Public, pg. 1776
WOODWARD GOVERNOR COMPANY (NEW ZEALAND) LTD.—See Woodward Governor Company; U.S. Public, pg. 1776
WOODWARD GOVERNOR DE MEXICO S.A. DE C.V.—See Woodward Governor Company; U.S. Public, pg. 1776
WOODWARD GOVERNOR GERMANY GMBH—See Woodward Governor Company; U.S. Public, pg. 1777
WOODWARD GOVERNOR INDIA PVT. LTD.—See Woodward Governor Company; U.S. Public, pg. 1777
WOODY'S—See Ark Restaurants Corp.; U.S. Public, pg. 130
WOOL FILTERS INTL.—See Fruit of the Loom, Inc.; U.S. Public, pg. 686
WOOLCAN—See Woolrich, Inc.; U.S. Private, pg. 1188
WOOLF ASSOCIATES—See Arnold Communications, Inc.; U.S. Private, pg. 84
WOOLPERT; U.S. Private, pg. 1188
WOOLRICH, INC.; U.S. Private, pg. 1188
WOOLRICH STORE DIV.—See Woolrich, Inc.; U.S. Private, pg. 1188
WOOLVERTON OLDSMOBILE-G.M.C. TRUCK, INC.; U.S. Private, pg. 1188
WOOLWICH PLC; Int'l, pg. 1514
WOOLWICH SEWER COMPANY, INC.—See W.R. Grace & Co.; U.S. Public, pg. 755
WOOLWICH WATER COMPANY, INC.—See W.R. Grace & Co.; U.S. Public, pg. 755
WOOLWORTH CORPORATION; U.S. Public, pg. 1777
F.W. WOOLWORTH CO.—See Woolworth Corporation; U.S. Public, pg. 1777
F.W. WOOLWORTH CO. LIMITED, CANADA—See Woolworth Corporation; U.S. Public, pg. 1778
F.W. WOOLWORTH GMBH CO. (GERMANY)—See Woolworth Corporation; U.S. Public, pg. 1778
WOOLWORTH MEXICANA, S.A. DE C.V.—See Woolworth Corporation; U.S. Public, pg. 1778
WOOLWORTH OVERSEAS CORP.—See Woolworth Corporation; U.S. Public, pg. 1778
WOOLWORTH WORLD TRADE CORP.—See Woolworth Corporation; U.S. Public, pg. 1778
WOOLWORTHS LIMITED—See Industrial Equity Limited; Int'l, pg. 676
WOOLWORTHS (NEW ZEALAND) LTD.—See Jardine Matheson Holdings Limited; Int'l, pg. 704
WOOLWORTHS PLC—See Kingfisher plc; Int'l, pg. 734
THE WOOSTER BRUSH COMPANY; U.S. Private, pg. 1188
WOOSTER MAGIKOTER WEST DIVISION—See The Wooster Brush Company; U.S. Private, pg. 1188
WORCESTER CENTER—See Cigna Corp.; U.S. Public, pg. 362
WORCESTER CONTROLS CORP.—See BTR plc; Int'l, pg. 128
WORCESTER CONTROLS (UK) LTD.—See BTR plc; Int'l, pg. 125
THE WORCESTER INSURANCE CO.—See Harleysville Group; U.S. Public, pg. 787
THE WORCESTER PLAN, INC.—See Citicorp; U.S. Public, pg. 377
WORD, INCORPORATED—See Gaylord Entertainment Co.; U.S. Public, pg. 704
WORK AREA PROTECTION—See Stabler Companies, Inc.; U.S. Private, pg. 1028
WORK BASE, LTD.—See Herman Miller, Inc.; U.S. Public, pg. 1112
WORK/FAMILY DIRECTIONS; U.S. Private, pg. 1188
WORK 'N GEAR—See J. Baker, Inc.; U.S. Public, pg. 168
WORK WEAR CANADA—See G&K Services, Inc.; U.S. Public, pg. 690
WORKGROUP COMPUTING SHOW—See EMAP Plc; Int'l, pg. 452
WORKLON DIV.—See Superior Surgical Mfg. Co., Inc.; U.S. Public, pg. 1539
WORKSAFE, INC.—See Eastco Industrial Safety Corp.; U.S. Public, pg. 548
THE WORLD—See Pulitzer Publishing Company; U.S. Public, pg. 1343
WORLD ACCEPTANCE CORPORATION; U.S. Public, pg. 1778
WORLD AEROSPACE CORPORATION; U.S. Private, pg. 1188
WORLD AIRWAYS, INC.—See WorldCorp, Inc.; U.S. Public, pg. 1780
THE WORLD ALMANAC—See Primedia Inc.; U.S. Public, pg. 1328
THE WORLD BANK—See The World Bank; U.S. Private, pg. 1190
THE WORLD BANK; U.S. Private, pg. 1188
THE WORLD BANK—See The World Bank; U.S. Private, pg. 1190
WORLD BOOK CHILDCRAFT DIVISION—See Berkshire Hathaway Inc.; U.S. Public, pg. 218
WORLD BOOK DIRECT MARKETING—See Berkshire Hathaway Inc.; U.S. Public, pg. 218
WORLD BOOK EDUCATIONAL PRODUCTS—See Berkshire Hathaway Inc.; U.S. Public, pg. 218
WORLD BOOK FINANCE, INC.—See Berkshire Hathaway Inc.; U.S. Public, pg. 218
WORLD BOOK FINANCIAL SERVICES—See Berkshire Hathaway Inc.; U.S. Public, pg. 218
WORLD BOOK, INC.—See Berkshire Hathaway Inc.; U.S. Public, pg. 218
WORLD BOOK INTERNATIONAL—See Berkshire Hathaway Inc.; U.S. Public, pg. 218
WORLD BOOK PUBLISHING—See Berkshire Hathaway Inc.; U.S. Public, pg. 218
WORLD BRANDS DUTY FREE—See Groupe Pernod Ricard; Int'l, pg. 567
WORLD BRANDS INC.—See Topco Associates, Inc.; U.S. Private, pg. 1091

MASTER INDEX TO COMPANY NAMES WYETH-AYERST

Company Index

WORLD CARPETS, INC.; *U.S. Private*, pg. 1190
WORLD CAT LTD.—See Proventus AB; *Int'l*, pg. 1072
WORLD CLASS FILM CORPORATION; *U.S. Private*, pg. 1190
WORLD COLOR-CHICAGO DIV.—See World Color Press, Inc.; *U.S. Public*, pg. 1778
WORLD COLOR PRESS, INC.; *U.S. Public*, pg. 1778
WORLD COUNCIL OF CREDIT UNIONS—See Credit Union National Association; *U.S. Private*, pg. 288
WORLD EXPO CORPORATION—See International Data Group; *U.S. Private*, pg. 571
WORLD FASHION HOSIERY INC.—See Gunze Sangyo, Inc.; *Int'l*, pg. 579
WORLD FINANCIAL PROPERTIES, INC.—See Olympia & York Developments Ltd.; *Int'l*, pg. 1004
WORLD FINER FOODS, INC.; *U.S. Private*, pg. 1190
WORLD FLIGHT CREW SERVICES—See WorldCorp, Inc.; *U.S. Public*, pg. 1780
WORLD FUEL SERVICES, INC.—See International Recovery Corp.; *U.S. Public*, pg. 906
WORLD IMPORT CO.—See Tober Industries, Inc.; *U.S. Private*, pg. 1089
WORLD LANGUAGES SRL—See Berlitz International, Inc.; *U.S. Public*, pg. 222
WORLD LOCK CO. LTD.—See The Eastern Company; *U.S. Public*, pg. 548
WORLD MINERALS INC.—See Alleghany Corporation; *U.S. Public*, pg. 42
WORLD OIL CORP.; *U.S. Private*, pg. 1190
WORLD PACIFIC ULLENBERG CORP.—See IWI Holding Limited; *U.S. Public*, pg. 861
WORLD PUBLISHING COMPANY—See Century Publishing Company; *U.S. Private*, pg. 226
WORLD PUBLISHING COMPANY; *U.S. Private*, pg. 1190
WORLD SAVINGS BANK, FSB—See Golden West Financial Corporation; *U.S. Public*, pg. 750
WORLD SAVINGS & LOAN ASSOCIATION, FSLA—See Golden West Financial Corporation; *U.S. Public*, pg. 750
WORLD SHIPPING, INC.; *U.S. Private*, pg. 1190
WORLD STANDARD LTD.—See American Standard Inc.; *U.S. Public*, pg. 92
WORLD TABLEWARE, INC.—See Pilkington Plc; *Int'l*, pg. 1056
WORLD TOURIST—See Accor S.A.; *Int'l*, pg. 22
WORLD TRADE CENTER—See Taylor Woodrow plc; *Int'l*, pg. 1359
WORLD TRADE CENTER NORTHWEST CORPORATION—See Enron Corp.; *U.S. Public*, pg. 585
WORLD TRADE CENTRE IN LONDON LTD.—See Taylor Woodrow plc; *Int'l*, pg. 1359
WORLD TRADE & MARKETING, LTD.—See Tootsie Roll Industries, Inc.; *U.S. Public*, pg. 1621
WORLD TRADE & MARKETING LTD.—See Tootsie Roll Industries, Inc.; *U.S. Public*, pg. 1621
WORLD TRADE TRANSPORT OF VIRGINIA—See Golden Eagle Group, Inc.; *U.S. Public*, pg. 749
WORLDCOM/IDB SYSTEMS—See WorldCom, Inc.; *U.S. Public*, pg. 1779
WORLDCOM, INC.; *U.S. Public*, pg. 1779
WORLDCORP, INC.; *U.S. Public*, pg. 1779
WORLDMARK INC.—See W.H. Brady Co.; *U.S. Public*, pg. 250
WORLD'S FINEST CHOCOLATE AUSTRALIA PTY. LTD.—See World's Finest Chocolate, Inc.; *U.S. Private*, pg. 1191
WORLD'S FINEST CHOCOLATE CANADA LTD.—See World's Finest Chocolate, Inc.; *U.S. Private*, pg. 1191
WORLD'S FINEST CHOCOLATE, INC.; *U.S. Private*, pg. 1191
WORLDS OF FUN & OCEANS OF FUN—See Cedar Fair, L.P.; *U.S. Public*, pg. 319
WORLDSCOPE/DISCLOSURE, LLC—See Primark Corporation; *U.S. Public*, pg. 1325
WORLDSEC INTERNATIONAL LIMITED—See The Bank of Tokyo-Mitsubishi, Ltd.; *Int'l*, pg. 158
WORLDSERV—See GTECH Corporation; *U.S. Public*, pg. 767
WORLDVISION ENTERPRISES—See National Amusements, Inc.; *U.S. Private*, pg. 776
WORLDVISION ENTERPRISES, INC.—See National Amusements, Inc.; *U.S. Private*, pg. 776
WORLDWIDE ASSISTANCE SERVICES INC.—See Assicurazioni Generali S.p.A.; *Int'l*, pg. 90
WORLDWIDE AUTOMOTIVE INDUSTRY—See The Macneal-Schwendler Corp.; *U.S. Public*, pg. 1031
WORLDWIDE DIRECTORY PRODUCT SALES—See SBC Communications Inc.; *U.S. Public*, pg. 1415
WORLDWIDE FOOD PRODUCTS INC.; *U.S. Private*, pg. 1191
WORLDWIDE FOODS, INC.—See La Preferida, Inc.; *U.S. Private*, pg. 640
WORLDWIDE LEASING—See Illinois Tool Works Inc.; *U.S. Public*, pg. 866
WORLDWIDE MEDIA RESEARCH—See True North Communications Inc.; *U.S. Public*, pg. 1641
WORLDWIDE PAPER FACTORS INC.—See Amcor Limited; *Int'l*, pg. 72
WORLDWIDE PRODUCE, INC.—See La Preferida, Inc.; *U.S. Private*, pg. 640
WORLDWIDE QUAKER BEVERAGES—See The Quaker Oats Company; *U.S. Public*, pg. 1347
WORLDWIDE SERVICES GROUP—See BTR plc; *Int'l*, pg. 126
WORLDWIDE SPORTS & RECREATION, INC.; *U.S. Private*, pg. 1191
WORLDWIDE TELEVISION NEWS—See The Walt Disney Company; *U.S. Public*, pg. 513
WORMALD ANSUL U.K. LTD.—See Tyco International Ltd.; *U.S. Public*, pg. 1651
WORMALD AUSTRALIA PTY LIMITED—See Tyco International Ltd.; *U.S. Public*, pg. 1651
WORMALD ENGINEERING SERVICES LTD.—See Tyco International Ltd.; *U.S. Public*, pg. 1651
WORMALD ENGINEERING SYSTEMS TAIWAN LIMITED—See Tyco International Ltd.; *U.S. Public*, pg. 1651
WORMALD FIRE SYSTEMS AB—See Tyco International Ltd.; *U.S. Public*, pg. 1650
WORMALD HOLDINGS N.Z. LIMITED—See Tyco International Ltd.; *U.S. Public*, pg. 1651
WORMALD HOLDINGS U.K. LIMITED—See Tyco International Ltd.; *U.S. Public*, pg. 1651
WORMALD INTERNATIONAL (SCANDINAVIA) A/S—See Tyco International Ltd.; *U.S. Public*, pg. 1651
WORMALD ITALIANA S.P.A.—See Tyco International Ltd.; *U.S. Public*, pg. 1651
WORMALD MATHER & PLATT ESPANA S.A.—See Tyco International Ltd.; *U.S. Public*, pg. 1651
WORMALD SERVICES DE PROTECCAO CONTRA INCENDIOS LIMITADA—See Tyco International Ltd.; *U.S. Public*, pg. 1651
WORMALD SIGNALCO A/S—See Tyco International Ltd.; *U.S. Public*, pg. 1651
THE WORNICK COMPANY; *U.S. Private*, pg. 1191
WORRELL ENTERPRISES, INC.; *U.S. Private*, pg. 1191
WORSHAM SPRINKLER COMPANY; *U.S. Private*, pg. 1191
WORSLEY ALUMINA PTY. LTD.—See Reynolds Metals Company; *U.S. Public*, pg. 1387
WORSLEY COMPANIES INC.; *U.S. Private*, pg. 1191
WORTH PUBLISHER INC.—See Georg von Holtzbrinck GmbH; *Int'l*, pg. 1479
WORTHINGTON—See Worthington Industries, Inc.; *U.S. Public*, pg. 1780
WORTHINGTON CUSTOM PLASTICS—See Worthington Industries, Inc.; *U.S. Public*, pg. 1780
WORTHINGTON CYLINDER CANADA—See Worthington Industries, Inc.; *U.S. Public*, pg. 1781
WORTHINGTON CYLINDER CORPORATION—See Worthington Industries, Inc.; *U.S. Public*, pg. 1780
WORTHINGTON FOODS INC.; *U.S. Public*, pg. 1780
WORTHINGTON INDUSTRIES, INC.; *U.S. Public*, pg. 1780
WORTHINGTON STEEL CO.—See Worthington Industries, Inc.; *U.S. Public*, pg. 1780
THE WORTHINGTON STEEL COMPANY-PENNSYLVANIA—See Worthington Industries, Inc.; *U.S. Public*, pg. 1780
WORZALLA PUBLISHING CO., INC.; *U.S. Private*, pg. 1191
WOSSINGER ZEMENT—See Lafarge S.A.; *Int'l*, pg. 789
WOTTON ROADSTONE LIMITED—See RMC Group p.l.c.; *Int'l*, pg. 1079
WOTTON TRAVEL LIMITED—See Renishaw plc; *Int'l*, pg. 1103
WOVEN CLASSIC THROWS, INC.—See Crown Crafts, Inc.; *U.S. Public*, pg. 465
WOVEN PRODUCTS DIV.—See National-Standard Co.; *U.S. Public*, pg. 1161
WOZNIAK INDUSTRIES, INC.; *U.S. Private*, pg. 1192
WRAPPING SPECIALISTS PTY. LTD.—See Borden, Inc.; *U.S. Private*, pg. 160
CAROLE WREN, INC.; *U.S. Private*, pg. 1192
WREXHAM LAND COMPANY LTD.—See Schmalbach-Lubeca AG; *Int'l*, pg. 1207
WRIGHT & LOPEZ OF ALABAMA, INC.—See Patton Management, Inc.; *U.S. Private*, pg. 844
WRIGHT & LOPEZ, INC.—See Patton Management, Inc.; *U.S. Private*, pg. 843
WRIGHT & WILHELMY CO.—See Distribution America; *U.S. Private*, pg. 335
BARRY WRIGHT INTL. CORP.—See Applied Power Inc.; *U.S. Public*, pg. 124
WRIGHT-BERNET, INC.—See Ekco Group, Inc.; *U.S. Public*, pg. 566
WRIGHT BRAND FOODS, INC.; *U.S. Private*, pg. 1192
F.B. WRIGHT CO.; *U.S. Private*, pg. 1192
WRIGHT EXPRESS CORPORATION—See Cendant Corporation; *U.S. Public*, pg. 321
F.E. WRIGHT GROUP—See Lonrho plc; *Int'l*, pg. 818
G.F. WRIGHT STEEL & WIRE COMPANY; *U.S. Private*, pg. 1192
WRIGHT GROUP PUBLISHING, INC.—See Tribune Company; *U.S. Public*, pg. 1636
WRIGHT LABORATORY SERVICES, INC.—See Science Applications International Corp.; *U.S. Private*, pg. 976
WRIGHT MEDICAL TECHNOLOGY; *U.S. Private*, pg. 1192
WRIGHT PLASTIC PRODUCTS, INC.—See Maxco, Inc.; *U.S. Public*, pg. 1061
WALTER WRIGHT MAMMOET LTD.—See Royal Nedlloyd Group N.V.; *Int'l*, pg. 1144
WM. E. WRIGHT LIMITED PARTNERSHIP; *U.S. Private*, pg. 1192
WRIGLEY AUSTRIA GES.M.B.H—See Wm. Wrigley Jr. Company; *U.S. Public*, pg. 1781
WRIGLEY CANADA INC.—See Wm. Wrigley Jr. Company; *U.S. Public*, pg. 1781
WRIGLEY CHEWING GUM COMPANY LTD.—See Wm. Wrigley Jr. Company; *U.S. Public*, pg. 1781
THE WRIGLEY CO., (EAST AFRICA) LTD.—See Wm. Wrigley Jr. Company; *U.S. Public*, pg. 1781
THE WRIGLEY COMPANY (H.K.) LTD.—See Wm. Wrigley Jr. Company; *U.S. Public*, pg. 1781
WRIGLEY COMPANY, LTD., JAPAN—See Wm. Wrigley Jr. Company; *U.S. Public*, pg. 1781
THE WRIGLEY COMPANY LTD.—See Wm. Wrigley Jr. Company; *U.S. Public*, pg. 1781
THE WRIGLEY COMPANY (MALAYSIA) SDN. BHD.—See Wm. Wrigley Jr. Company; *U.S. Public*, pg. 1781
THE WRIGLEY COMPANY (N.Z.) LTD.—See Wm. Wrigley Jr. Company; *U.S. Public*, pg. 1781
THE WRIGLEY COMPANY (P.N.G.) PTY. LTD.—See Wm. Wrigley Jr. Company; *U.S. Public*, pg. 1781
THE WRIGLEY CO. PTY. LTD.—See Wm. Wrigley Jr. Company; *U.S. Public*, pg. 1781
WRIGLEY CO. S.A.—See Wm. Wrigley Jr. Company; *U.S. Public*, pg. 1781
WRIGLEY CZECHOSLOVAKIA, LTD.—See Wm. Wrigley Jr. Company; *U.S. Public*, pg. 1781
WRIGLEY HUNGARIA, LTD.—See Wm. Wrigley Jr. Company; *U.S. Public*, pg. 1781
WRIGLEY INDIA PVT. LTD.—See Wm. Wrigley Jr. Company; *U.S. Public*, pg. 1781
WRIGLEY LJUBLJANA, LTD.—See Wm. Wrigley Jr. Company; *U.S. Public*, pg. 1781
WRIGLEY N.V.—See Wm. Wrigley Jr. Company; *U.S. Public*, pg. 1781
WRIGLEY PHILIPPINES, INC.—See Wm. Wrigley Jr. Company; *U.S. Public*, pg. 1781
WRIGLEY POLAND, SP. Z.O.O.—See Wm. Wrigley Jr. Company; *U.S. Public*, pg. 1781
WRIGLEY S.A.—See Wm. Wrigley Jr. Company; *U.S. Public*, pg. 1781
WRIGLEY SCANDINAVIA AB—See Wm. Wrigley Jr. Company; *U.S. Public*, pg. 1781
OY WRIGLEY SCANDINAVIA AB—See Wm. Wrigley Jr. Company; *U.S. Public*, pg. 1781
WRIGLEY SCANDINAVIA A/S—See Wm. Wrigley Jr. Company; *U.S. Public*, pg. 1781
WRIGLEY, SPOL. S.R.O.—See Wm. Wrigley Jr. Company; *U.S. Public*, pg. 1781
WRIGLEY TAIWAN LTD.—See Wm. Wrigley Jr. Company; *U.S. Public*, pg. 1781
WM. WRIGLEY JR. COMPANY; *U.S. Public*, pg. 1781
WROUGHT WASHER MFG., INC.; *U.S. Private*, pg. 1192
WUESTENROT BANK AG—See Wuestenrot Holding GmbH; *Int'l*, pg. 1514
WUESTENROT FINANCE B.V.—See Wuestenrot Holding GmbH; *Int'l*, pg. 1514
WUESTENROT GRUNDSTUECKSVERWERTUNGS-GMBH—See Wuestenrot Holding GmbH; *Int'l*, pg. 1514
WUESTENROT HOLDING GMBH; *Int'l*, pg. 1514
WUESTENROT IMMOBILIEN GMBH—See Wuestenrot Holding GmbH; *Int'l*, pg. 1514
WUESTENROT INTERNATIONAL MANAGEMENT-GESELLSCHAFT AG—See Wuestenrot Holding GmbH; *Int'l*, pg. 1514
WUESTENROT LEBENSVERSICHERUNGS-AG—See Wuestenrot Holding GmbH; *Int'l*, pg. 1514
WUESTENROT STAEDTEBAU- UND ENTWICKLUNGSGESELLSCHAFT MBH—See Wuestenrot Holding GmbH; *Int'l*, pg. 1514
WUESTENROT STAVEBNI SPORITELNA A.S.—See Wuestenrot Holding GmbH; *Int'l*, pg. 1514
WUHAN BUNDY FLUID SYSTEMS CO. LTD.—See TI Group plc; *Int'l*, pg. 1341
WUHRLIN-SOPLAMED S.A.—See Fort James Corporation; *U.S. Public*, pg. 673
WULFRATH GROUP—See Thyssen AG; *Int'l*, pg. 1387
WUNDERLICH VERLAG—See Georg von Holtzbrinck GmbH; *Int'l*, pg. 1479
WUNDERMAN CATO JOHNSON—See Young & Rubicam Inc.; *U.S. Private*, pg. 1197
WUNDERMAN CATO JOHNSON SINGAPORE—See Dentsu Young & Rubicam Partnerships; *U.S. Private*, pg. 326
WUNDERMAN CATO JOHNSON—See Dentsu Young & Rubicam Partnerships; *U.S. Private*, pg. 326
WUNDERMAN WORLDWIDE LIMITED—See Young & Rubicam Inc.; *U.S. Private*, pg. 1199
WUNDRICH-MEISSEN GMBH—See Proventus AB; *Int'l*, pg. 1072
THE WUPHOON INSURANCE COMPANY LIMITED—See The Tokio Marine & Fire Insurance Company, Ltd.; *Int'l*, pg. 1393
THE WURLITZER COMPANY—See Baldwin Piano & Organ Company; *U.S. Public*, pg. 169
WURTH BUROBEDARF & ORGANISATION GMBH—See N.V. Koninklijke KNP BT; *Int'l*, pg. 758
PAUL WURTH S.A.—See Arbed S.A.; *Int'l*, pg. 80
WURTTEMBERGISCHE AG VERSICHERUNGS-BETEILIGUNGSGESELLSCHAFT—See Swiss Reinsurance Company; *Int'l*, pg. 1333
WURTTEMBERGISCHE ELEKTRIZITATS-AKTIENGESELLSCHAFT—See Veba AG; *Int'l*, pg. 1456
WURZBURG, INC.; *U.S. Private*, pg. 1192
WURZNER DAUERBACKWAREN GMBH; *Int'l*, pg. 1514
WUSTENROT HYPOTHEKENBANK AKTIENGESELLSCHAFT—See Wuestenrot Holding GmbH; *Int'l*, pg. 1514
WUXI-MSA SAFETY EQUIPMENT CO., LTD.—See Mine Safety Appliances Co.; *U.S. Public*, pg. 1115
WUXI OKUDA GARMENT CO. LTD.—See Gunze Sangyo, Inc.; *Int'l*, pg. 579
WUXI QUAKER CHEMICAL CO. LTD.—See Quaker Chemical Corporation; *U.S. Public*, pg. 1347
WUXI SANWA GARMENT MATERIALS CO., LTD.—See Gunze Sangyo, Inc.; *Int'l*, pg. 579
WUXI SHARP ELECTRONIC COMPONENTS CO., LTD.—See Sharp Corporation; *Int'l*, pg. 1230
WYANDOT INC.; *U.S. Private*, pg. 1193
WYANT COPORATION; *U.S. Public*, pg. 1781
WYATT CAFETERIAS INC.—See Triangle Food Services Co.; *U.S. Private*, pg. 1102
WYATT ENERGY INCORPORATED; *U.S. Private*, pg. 1193
WYATT FIELD SERVICE CO.—See Nooter Corporation; *U.S. Private*, pg. 801
THE WYCO TOOL CO.—See Racine Federated, Inc.; *U.S. Private*, pg. 906
WYDAWNICTWA PRAWNICZE PWN—See Reed Elsevier plc; *Int'l*, pg. 1095
WYETH AG—See American Home Products Corporation; *U.S. Public*, pg. 82
WYETH AUSTRALIA PTY. LTD.—See American Home Products Corporation; *U.S. Public*, pg. 82
WYETH-AYERST (ASIA) LTD.—See American Home Products Corporation; *U.S. Public*, pg. 82
WYETH-AYERST INTERNATIONAL, INC.—See American Home Products Corporation; *U.S. Public*, pg. 80

Company Index

WYETH-AYERST LABORATORIES, INC.—See American Home Products Corporation; *U.S. Public,* pg. 80
WYETH HELLAS EPE—See American Home Products Corporation; *U.S. Public,* pg. 82
WYETH (HK) LIMITED—See American Home Products Corporation; *U.S. Public,* pg. 82
WYETH (IRELAND) LIMITED—See American Home Products Corporation; *U.S. Public,* pg. 82
WYETH (JAPAN) CORPORATION—See American Home Products Corporation; *U.S. Public,* pg. 82
JOHN WYETH & BROTHER LTD.—See American Home Products Corporation; *U.S. Public,* pg. 82
JOHN WYETH & BROTHER (N.Z.) LTD.—See American Home Products Corporation; *U.S. Public,* pg. 82
JOHN WYETH (INDIA) LIMITED—See American Home Products Corporation; *U.S. Public,* pg. 82
JOHN WYETH LABORATORIES S.A.—See American Home Products Corporation; *U.S. Public,* pg. 82
WYETH LABORATORIA B.V.—See American Home Products Corporation; *U.S. Public,* pg. 82
WYETH LABORATORIES (PAKISTAN) LTD.—See American Home Products Corporation; *U.S. Public,* pg. 82
WYETH LABORATUVARLARI A.S.—See American Home Products Corporation; *U.S. Public,* pg. 82
WYETH LTD.—See American Home Products Corporation; *U.S. Public,* pg. 82
WYETH NORDISKA AB—See American Home Products Corporation; *U.S. Public,* pg. 82
WYETH-ORFI S.A.—See American Home Products Corporation; *U.S. Public,* pg. 82
WYETH-PHARMA GMBH—See American Home Products Corporation; *U.S. Public,* pg. 82
WYETH S.A.—See American Home Products Corporation; *U.S. Public,* pg. 82
WYETH S.A. DE C.V.—See American Home Products Corporation; *U.S. Public,* pg. 82
WYETH S.P.A.—See American Home Products Corporation; *U.S. Public,* pg. 82
WYETH-SUACO LABORATORIES, INC.—See American Home Products Corporation; *U.S. Public,* pg. 82
WYLE DATA SERVICES—See Veba AG; *Int'l,* pg. 1457
WYLE ELECTRONICS—See Veba AG; *Int'l,* pg. 1457
WYLE ELECTRONICS-ATLANTA—See Veba AG; *Int'l,* pg. 1457
WYLE-GINSBURY ELECTRONICS—See Veba AG; *Int'l,* pg. 1458
WYLE LABORATORIES, INC.; *U.S. Private,* pg. 1193
JEFF WYLER DEALER GROUP, INC.; *U.S. Private,* pg. 1193
JEFF WYLER OLDS, CADILLAC—See Jeff Wyler Dealer Group, Inc.; *U.S. Private,* pg. 1193
WYMAN-GORDON; *U.S. Public,* pg. 1782
WYMAN-GORDON FORGINGS—See Wyman-Gordon; *U.S. Public,* pg. 1782
WYMAN-GORDON FORGINGS INC—See Wyman-Gordon; *U.S. Public,* pg. 1782
WYMAN-GORDON FORGINGS, INC.—See Wyman-Gordon; *U.S. Public,* pg. 1782
WYMAN-GORDON INVESTMENT CASTINGS—See Wyman-Gordon; *U.S. Public,* pg. 1782
WYMAN-GORDON INVESTMENT CASTINGS, INC.—See Wyman-Gordon; *U.S. Public,* pg. 1782
WYMAN-GORDON LIMITED—See Wyman-Gordon; *U.S. Public,* pg. 1782
WYMO FUELS INC.—See Kansas City Power & Light Company; *U.S. Public,* pg. 943
WYMONDHAM OIL STORAGE COMPANY LIMITED—See GATX Corporation; *U.S. Public,* pg. 693
WYNN OIL COMPANY—See Wynn's International, Inc.; *U.S. Public,* pg. 1782
WYNN OIL (N.Z.) LIMITED—See Wynn's International, Inc.; *U.S. Public,* pg. 1783
WYNN OIL (SOUTH AFRICA)(PTY.)LTD.—See Wynn's International, Inc.; *U.S. Public,* pg. 1783
WYNN OIL (U.K.) LIMITED—See Wynn's International, Inc.; *U.S. Public,* pg. 1783
WYNN'S AUSTRALIA, PTY. LIMITED—See Wynn's International, Inc.; *U.S. Public,* pg. 1782
WYNN'S AUTOMOTIVE FRANCE—See Wynn's International, Inc.; *U.S. Public,* pg. 1783
WYNN'S BELGIUM N.V.—See Wynn's International, Inc.; *U.S. Public,* pg. 1782
WYNN'S CANADA, LTD.—See Wynn's International, Inc.; *U.S. Public,* pg. 1783
WYNN'S DEUTSCHLAND, GMBH—See Wynn's International, Inc.; *U.S. Public,* pg. 1783
WYNN'S ESPANA, S.A.—See Wynn's International, Inc.; *U.S. Public,* pg. 1783
WYNN'S FRANCE, S.A.—See Wynn's International, Inc.; *U.S. Public,* pg. 1783
WYNN'S FRICTION PROOFING DE MEXICO, S.A. DE C.V.—See Wynn's International, Inc.; *U.S. Public,* pg. 1783
WYNN'S INTERNATIONAL, INC.; *U.S. Public,* pg. 1782
WYNN'S-PRECISION (CANADA) LTD.—See Wynn's International, Inc.; *U.S. Public,* pg. 1783
WYNN'S-PRECISION FLUID SEALING DIV.—See Wynn's International, Inc.; *U.S. Public,* pg. 1783
WYNN'S-PRECISION, INC.—See Wynn's International, Inc.; *U.S. Public,* pg. 1783
WYNN'S-PRECISION (U.K.)LTD.—See Wynn's International, Inc.; *U.S. Public,* pg. 1783
WYODAK RESOURCES DEVELOPMENT CORP.—See Black Hills Corporation; *U.S. Public,* pg. 236
WYOMING CONCRETE PRODUCTS CO.—See Carder Concrete Products Co.; *U.S. Private,* pg. 208
WYOMING LAND TITLE COMPANY—See The First American Financial Corporation; *U.S. Public,* pg. 626
WYOMING MACHINERY COMPANY; *U.S. Private,* pg. 1193
A.P. WYOTT; *U.S. Private,* pg. 1193
WYSE ADVERTISING; *U.S. Private,* pg. 1193

WYSE ADVERTISING/CLEVELAND—See Wyse Advertising; *U.S. Private,* pg. 1194
WYSE DIRECT—See Wyse Advertising, *U.S. Private,* pg. 1194
WYSE TECHNOLOGY INC.; *U.S. Private,* pg. 1194
WYSEPLANT LTD.—See The Peninsular and Oriental Steam Navigation Company; *Int'l,* pg. 1035

X

X-ERGON—See NCH Corporation; *U.S. Public,* pg. 1145
X-L-CO, INC.—See Xtra Corporation; *U.S. Public,* pg. 1787
X-MARK/CDT—See Cable Design Technologies Corporation; *U.S. Public,* pg. 287
X-RITE, INCORPORATED; *U.S. Public,* pg. 1783
XATA CORPORATION; *U.S. Public,* pg. 1783
XCAN GRAIN POOL LTD.—See Saskatchewan Wheat Pool; *Int'l,* pg. 1195
XEL CORPORATION—See Salient 3 Communications, Inc.; *U.S. Public,* pg. 1430
XETA CORPORATION; *U.S. Public,* pg. 1783
XKD CORPORATION; *U.S. Private,* pg. 1194
XL CONNECT—See Intelligent Electronics, Inc.; *U.S. Public,* pg. 888
X.L. EUROPE INSURANCE—See Exel Insurance Co. Ltd.; *Int'l,* pg. 467
X.L. INSURANCE COMPANY, LTD.—See Exel Insurance Co. Ltd.; *Int'l,* pg. 467
XL VISION INC.—See Safeguard Scientifics, Inc.; *U.S. Public,* pg. 1424
XLM COMPANY—See HON Industries Inc.; *U.S. Public,* pg. 772
XRE CORPORATION—See Thermo Electron Corporation; *U.S. Public,* pg. 1595
XRL CORPORATION—See Electro Scientific Industries, Inc.; *U.S. Public,* pg. 569
XTEK, INC.; *U.S. Public,* pg. 1194
XTRA INTERNATIONAL LTD.—See Xtra Corporation; *U.S. Public,* pg. 1786
XALOY, INC.; *U.S. Private,* pg. 1194
XAMAK—See Rohm and Haas Company; *U.S. Public,* pg. 1403
XANADU DIV.—See Electroid Co.; *U.S. Private,* pg. 369
XANTOFLOR, S.A.—See Chr. Hansen Holding A/S; *Int'l,* pg. 289
XEBEC CORPORATION; *U.S. Private,* pg. 1194
XENIA L.D. CORP.—See Forest City Enterprises, Inc.; *U.S. Public,* pg. 670
XENTEK, INC.—See Taiyo Yuden Company Ltd.; *Int'l,* pg. 1349
XEROX ARGENTINA I.C.S.A.—See Xerox Corporation; *U.S. Public,* pg. 1785
XEROX BUSINESS EQUIPMENT, INC.—See Xerox Corporation; *U.S. Public,* pg. 1784
XEROX BUSINESS SERVICES—See Xerox Corporation; *U.S. Public,* pg. 1784
XEROX CANADA HOLDINGS INC.—See Xerox Corporation; *U.S. Public,* pg. 1785
XEROX CANADA LTD.—See Xerox Corporation; *U.S. Public,* pg. 1785
XEROX COLORGRAPHICS—See Xerox Corporation; *U.S. Public,* pg. 1784
XEROX COMPUTER SERVICES—See Xerox Corporation; *U.S. Public,* pg. 1784
XEROX CORPORATE RESEARCH GROUP—See Xerox Corporation; *U.S. Public,* pg. 1784
XEROX CORPORATION; *U.S. Public,* pg. 1783
XEROX CREDIT CORPORATE FINANCE DIV.—See Xerox Corporation; *U.S. Public,* pg. 1785
XEROX CREDIT CORPORATION—See Xerox Corporation; *U.S. Public,* pg. 1785
XEROX CUSTOM SYSTEMS DIVISION—See Xerox Corporation; *U.S. Public,* pg. 1784
XEROX DE CHILE S.A.—See Xerox Corporation; *U.S. Public,* pg. 1785
XEROX DE COLOMBIA S.A.—See Xerox Corporation; *U.S. Public,* pg. 1785
XEROX DE VENEZUELA, C.A.—See Xerox Corporation; *U.S. Public,* pg. 1785
XEROX DEL ECUADOR, S.A.—See Xerox Corporation; *U.S. Public,* pg. 1785
XEROX DEL PERU, S.A.—See Xerox Corporation; *U.S. Public,* pg. 1785
XEROX DIABLO SUPPLIES—See Xerox Corporation; *U.S. Public,* pg. 1784
XEROX DO BRASIL S.A.—See Xerox Corporation; *U.S. Public,* pg. 1785
XEROX DOCUMENT PROCESSING—See Xerox Corporation; *U.S. Public,* pg. 1784
XEROX ENGINEERING SYSTEMS DIVISION—See Xerox Corporation; *U.S. Public,* pg. 1784
XEROX FINANCIAL SERVICES INC.—See Xerox Corporation; *U.S. Public,* pg. 1784
XEROX FINANCIAL SERVICES LIFE INSURANCE CO.—See Xerox Corporation; *U.S. Public,* pg. 1785
THE XEROX FOUNDATION INC.—See Xerox Corporation; *U.S. Public,* pg. 1785
XEROX IMAGING SYSTEMS, INC.—See Xerox Corporation; *U.S. Public,* pg. 1785
XEROX INSTALLMENT SALES DIV.—See Xerox Corporation; *U.S. Public,* pg. 1785
XEROX INTERNATIONAL CENTER FOR TRAINING & MANAGEMENT DEVELOPMENT—See Xerox Corporation; *U.S. Public,* pg. 1785
XEROX MEDICAL SYSTEMS—See Xerox Corporation; *U.S. Public,* pg. 1784
XEROX MEXICANA S.A.—See Xerox Corporation; *U.S. Public,* pg. 1785
XEROX REAL ESTATE & GENERAL SERVICES DIVISION—See Xerox Corporation; *U.S. Public,* pg. 1785
XEROX REALTY CORPORATION—See Xerox Corporation; *U.S. Public,* pg. 1785

XEROX RESEARCH—See Xerox Corporation; *U.S. Public,* pg. 1784
XEROX SPECIAL INFORMATION SYSTEMS—See Xerox Corporation; *U.S. Public,* pg. 1784
XEROX SPECIAL MARKETS GROUP—See Xerox Corporation; *U.S. Public,* pg. 1785
XEROX TECHNIGRAPHIC PRODUCTS DIVISION—See Xerox Corporation; *U.S. Public,* pg. 1784
XEROX U.S. MARKETING GROUP—See Xerox Corporation; *U.S. Public,* pg. 1784
XERTRONIX—See Eastman Kodak Company; *U.S. Public,* pg. 551
XERXES CORPORATION; *U.S. Private,* pg. 1194
XETEL CORPORATION—See Rohm Co., Ltd.; *Int'l,* pg. 1125
XETEX, INC.—See Thermo Electron Corporation; *U.S. Public,* pg. 1594
XETRON—See Pittway Corporation; *U.S. Public,* pg. 1306
XETRON CORP.—See Northrop Grumman Corporation; *U.S. Public,* pg. 1198
XIAMEN INTERNATIONAL BANK (XIB)—See The Long-Term Credit Bank of Japan, Limited; *Int'l,* pg. 817
XIAMEN JINWOONG ENTERPRISE CO., LTD.—See Jinwoong Inc.; *Int'l,* pg. 707
XIAMEN TIGER MEDICALS CO., LTD.—See Haw Par Brothers International Limited; *Int'l,* pg. 604
XIAN-JANSSEN PHARMACEUTICAL LTD.—See Johnson & Johnson; *U.S. Public,* pg. 932
XI'AN SYSTEM SENSOR ELECTRONICS, LTD.—See Pittway Corporation; *U.S. Public,* pg. 1307
XICOR, INC.; *U.S. Public,* pg. 1785
XILINX ASIA PACIFIC—See Xilinx, Inc.; *U.S. Public,* pg. 1786
XILINX DEVELOPMENT CORPORATION—See Xilinx, Inc.; *U.S. Public,* pg. 1786
XILINX GMBH—See Xilinx, Inc.; *U.S. Public,* pg. 1786
XILINX, INC.; *U.S. Public,* pg. 1786
XILINX, INC.—See Xilinx, Inc.; *U.S. Public,* pg. 1786
XILINX K.K.—See Xilinx, Inc.; *U.S. Public,* pg. 1786
XILINX LTD.—See Xilinx, Inc.; *U.S. Public,* pg. 1786
XILINX, SARL—See Xilinx, Inc.; *U.S. Public,* pg. 1786
XLINX, INC., BOULDER—See Xilinx, Inc.; *U.S. Public,* pg. 1786
XLINX, IRELAND—See Xilinx, Inc.; *U.S. Public,* pg. 1786
XOMA CORPORATION; *U.S. Public,* pg. 1786
XOMED SURGICAL PRODUCTS—See Bristol-Myers Squibb Company; *U.S. Public,* pg. 1786
XOMOX CANADA LTD.—See Emerson Electric Co.; *U.S. Public,* pg. 578
XOMOX CORP.—See Emerson Electric Co.; *U.S. Public,* pg. 574
XOMOX K.K.—See Emerson Electric Co.; *U.S. Public,* pg. 578
XOMOX S.A. DE C.V.—See Emerson Electric Co.; *U.S. Public,* pg. 578
XOMOX U.K. LIMITED—See Emerson Electric Co.; *U.S. Public,* pg. 578
XON LEASING—See Maxon Industries, Inc.; *U.S. Private,* pg. 717
XOVIC CO. LTD.—See Hewlett-Packard Company; *U.S. Public,* pg. 823
XPELAIR LTD.—See The General Electric Company, p.l.c.; *Int'l,* pg. 545
XPLORER MOTOR HOME DIV.—See Frank Industries, Inc.; *U.S. Private,* pg. 423
XTEK CANADA, LTD.—See Xtek, Inc.; *U.S. Private,* pg. 1194
XTRA CORPORATION; *U.S. Public,* pg. 1786
XTRA, INC.—See Xtra Corporation; *U.S. Public,* pg. 1787
XTRA INC. FAR EAST/AUSTRALASIA—See Xtra Corporation; *U.S. Public,* pg. 1787
XTRA-INTERMODAL DIVISION—See Xtra Corporation; *U.S. Public,* pg. 1787
XTRA LEASE, INC.—See Xtra Corporation; *U.S. Public,* pg. 1786
XTRA SUPER FOOD CENTERS, INC.—See Pueblo Xtra International, Inc.; *U.S. Private,* pg. 894
XTRA (U.K. LEASING), LIMITED—See Xtra Corporation; *U.S. Public,* pg. 1787
XUZHOU LIEBHERR CONCRETE MACHINERY CO. LTD.—See Liebherr-International AG; *Int'l,* pg. 808
XUZHOU ROCKWELL AXLE CO., LTD.—See Rockwell International Corporation; *U.S. Public,* pg. 1402
XYROFIN OY—See Cultor Ltd.; *Int'l,* pg. 350
XYROFIN (UK) LTD.—See Cultor Ltd.; *Int'l,* pg. 350
XYVISION, INC.; *U.S. Public,* pg. 1787
XYVISION LIMITED—See Xyvision, Inc.; *U.S. Public,* pg. 1787

Y

Y&R MATTINGLY—See Dentsu Young & Rubicam Partnerships; *U.S. Private,* pg. 325
Y&R MEDELLIN—See Young & Rubicam Inc.; *U.S. Private,* pg. 1200
Y&R NEW TECHNOLOGIES—See Young & Rubicam Inc.; *U.S. Private,* pg. 1198
Y & S CANDIES—See Hershey Foods Corporation; *U.S. Public,* pg. 812
Y & S CANDIES PLANT—See Hershey Foods Corporation; *U.S. Public,* pg. 812
YDAB I HARNOSAND AB—See Celsius AB; *Int'l,* pg. 278
YKK CORPORATION; *Int'l,* pg. 1514
YKK CORPORATION OF AMERICA—See YKK Corporation; *Int'l,* pg. 1515
YKK (U.S.A.)—See YKK Corporation; *Int'l,* pg. 1515
YLA, INC.—See Perstorp AB; *Int'l,* pg. 1037
YMOS AG—See Cockerill Sambre; *Int'l,* pg. 302
YMR—See Koninklijke Ahold NV; *Int'l,* pg. 750
Y.O. MACHINERY LEASING CO., LTD.—See Orix Corporation; *Int'l,* pg. 1009
Y.P.F. GAS S.A.—See Y.P.F., S.A.; *Int'l,* pg. 1515
Y.P.F., S.A.; *Int'l,* pg. 1515

YPSI-ARBOR LANES—See Great Lakes Realty Corp.; *U.S. Private,* pg. 475
YRI (EUROPE) LTD.—See Yamaichi Securities Co., Ltd.; *Int'l,* pg. 1517
YRJ CORPORATION—See Wilco Reprographic, Inc.; *U.S. Private,* pg. 1176
YRSU B.V.—See Schmalbach-Lubeca AG; *Int'l,* pg. 1207
YSD INDUSTRIES; *U.S. Private,* pg. 1194
YSI INCORPORATED; *U.S. Private,* pg. 1195
Y.T. PACIFIC ENTERPRISES, INC. (BISTRO ICHO)—See Takashimaya Company, Limited; *Int'l,* pg. 1350
YTM INDUSTRIAL OY—See AB Industrivarden; *Int'l,* pg. 678
YTTEC AB—See Celsius AB; *Int'l,* pg. 278
YACHTING—See The Times Mirror Company; *U.S. Public,* pg. 1617
YADKIN, INC.—See Aluminum Company of America; *U.S. Public,* pg. 61
YADKIN RAILROAD CO.—See Norfolk Southern Corporation; *U.S. Public,* pg. 1191
YAFFE & COMPANY; *U.S. Private,* pg. 1195
YAHOO!, INC.; *U.S. Public,* pg. 1787
YAHYA COSTAIN LLC—See Costain Group PLC; *Int'l,* pg. 337
YALE/CHASE MATERIALS HANDLING, INC.; *U.S. Private,* pg. 1195
YALE-CORBIN CANADA LIMITED—See Williams Holdings Plc; *Int'l,* pg. 1499
YALE E KEY, INC.—See Key Energy Group Inc.; *U.S. Public,* pg. 953
YALE ELECTRONICS ASIA - PACIFIC LIMITED—See Williams Holdings Plc; *Int'l,* pg. 1499
YALE EUROPE MATERIALS HANDLING, BV—See NACCO Industries, Inc.; *U.S. Public,* pg. 1149
YALE EUROPE MATERIALS HANDLING CORPORATION LTD.—See NACCO Industries, Inc.; *U.S. Public,* pg. 1150
YALE INDUSTRIAL PRODUCTS—See Columbus McKinnon Corp.; *U.S. Public,* pg. 406
YALE SECURITY, INC.—See Williams Holdings Plc; *Int'l,* pg. 1499
YALE SECURITY PRODUCTS (HONG KONG) LTD.—See Williams Holdings Plc; *Int'l,* pg. 1499
YALE SECURITY PRODUCTS, LTD.—See Williams Holdings Plc; *Int'l,* pg. 1499
YALE SECURITY PRODUCTS S.P.A. (ITALY)—See Williams Holdings Plc; *Int'l,* pg. 1499
YALE UNIVERSITY PRESS; *U.S. Private,* pg. 1195
YAMAGATA SANKEN CO., LTD.—See Sanken Electric Co., Ltd.; *Int'l,* pg. 1188
YAMAHA CORPORATION; *Int'l,* pg. 1515
YAMAHA CREDIT CO., LTD.—See Yamaha Corporation; *Int'l,* pg. 1515
YAMAHA HALL CO., LTD.—See Yamaha Corporation; *Int'l,* pg. 1515
YAMAHA KYOHAN CO., LTD.—See Yamaha Corporation; *Int'l,* pg. 1516
YAMAHA MOTOR CO., LTD.—See Yamaha Corporation; *Int'l,* pg. 1516
YAMAHA-OLIN METAL CORPORATION—See Olin Corporation; *U.S. Public,* pg. 1220
YAMAHA PLANS CO., LTD.—See Yamaha Corporation; *Int'l,* pg. 1516
YAMAHA RECREATION CO., LTD.—See Yamaha Corporation; *Int'l,* pg. 1516
YAMAICHI ADVISORY SERVICES (MALAYSIA) SDN. BHD.—See Yamaichi Securities Co., Ltd.; *Int'l,* pg. 1517
YAMAICHI (AMERICA) FINANCE, INC.—See Yamaichi Securities Co., Ltd.; *Int'l,* pg. 1517
YAMAICHI (AMERICA) HOLDINGS, INC.—See Yamaichi Securities Co., Ltd.; *Int'l,* pg. 1517
YAMAICHI ASIA VENTURE CAPITAL PTE LTD.—See Yamaichi Securities Co., Ltd.; *Int'l,* pg. 1516
YAMAICHI ASSET MANAGEMENT (AMERICA) INC.—See Yamaichi Securities Co., Ltd.; *Int'l,* pg. 1517
YAMAICHI ASSET MANAGEMENT (ASIA) LTD.—See Yamaichi Securities Co., Ltd.; *Int'l,* pg. 1517
YAMAICHI ASSET MANAGEMENT (EUROPE) LTD.—See Yamaichi Securities Co., Ltd.; *Int'l,* pg. 1517
YAMAICHI ASSET MANAGEMENT (HONG KONG) LTD.—See Yamaichi Securities Co., Ltd.; *Int'l,* pg. 1517
YAMAICHI ASSET MANAGEMENT (SINGAPORE) PTE LTD.—See Yamaichi Securities Co., Ltd.; *Int'l,* pg. 1517
YAMAICHI AUSTRALIA LTD.—See Yamaichi Securities Co., Ltd.; *Int'l,* pg. 1517
YAMAICHI BANK (DEUTSCHLAND) GMBH—See Yamaichi Securities Co., Ltd.; *Int'l,* pg. 1517
YAMAICHI BANK-GENEVA—See Yamaichi Securities Co., Ltd.; *Int'l,* pg. 1517
YAMAICHI BANK (LUGANO)—See Yamaichi Securities Co., Ltd.; *Int'l,* pg. 1517
YAMAICHI BANK NEDERLAND CUSTODY N.V.—See Yamaichi Securities Co., Ltd.; *Int'l,* pg. 1517
YAMAICHI BANK NEDERLAND N.V.—See Yamaichi Securities Co., Ltd.; *Int'l,* pg. 1517
YAMAICHI BANK (SWITZERLAND)—See Yamaichi Securities Co., Ltd.; *Int'l,* pg. 1517
YAMAICHI BANK (U.K.) PLC—See Yamaichi Securities Co., Ltd.; *Int'l,* pg. 1517
YAMAICHI BUSINESS SERVICES CO., LTD.—See Yamaichi Securities Co., Ltd.; *Int'l,* pg. 1516
YAMAICHI CAPITAL MANAGEMENT (EUROPE) LTD.—See Yamaichi Securities Co., Ltd.; *Int'l,* pg. 1516
YAMAICHI CAPITAL MANAGEMENT (H.K.) LTD.—See Yamaichi Securities Co., Ltd.; *Int'l,* pg. 1516
YAMAICHI CAPTIAL MANAGEMENT, INC.—See Yamaichi Securities Co., Ltd.; *Int'l,* pg. 1516
YAMAICHI CAPITAL MANAGEMENT (SINGAPORE) LTD.—See Yamaichi Securities Co., Ltd.; *Int'l,* pg. 1516
YAMAICHI ECHO & CO., LTD.—See Yamaichi Securities Co., Ltd.; *Int'l,* pg. 1516
YAMAICHI ENTERPRISE CO, LTD.—See Yamaichi Securities Co., Ltd.; *Int'l,* pg. 1516

YAMAICHI FINANCE CO., LTD.—Yamaichi Securities Co., Ltd.; *Int'l,* pg. 1516
YAMAICHI FINANCIAL SERVICES INC.—See Yamaichi Securities Co., Ltd.; *Int'l,* pg. 1517
YAMAICHI FRANCE S.A.—See Yamaichi Securities Co., Ltd.; *Int'l,* pg. 1517
YAMAICHI FUTURES (H.K.) LTD.—See Yamaichi Securities Co., Ltd.; *Int'l,* pg. 1517
YAMAICHI FUTURES PTE. LTD.—See Yamaichi Securities Co., Ltd.; *Int'l,* pg. 1517
YAMAICHI GILTS LTD.—See Yamaichi Securities Co., Ltd.; *Int'l,* pg. 1517
YAMAICHI INFORMATION SYSTEMS CO., LTD.—See Yamaichi Securities Co., Ltd.; *Int'l,* pg. 1516
YAMAICHI INTERNATIONAL (AMERICA) INC.—See Yamaichi Securities Co., Ltd.; *Int'l,* pg. 1517
YAMAICHI INTERNATIONAL (AMERICA) INC.-CHICAGO BRANCH—See Yamaichi Securities Co., Ltd.; *Int'l,* pg. 1517
YAMAICHI INTERNATIONAL (AMERICA) INC.-LOS ANGELES BRANCH—See Yamaichi Securities Co., Ltd.; *Int'l,* pg. 1517
YAMAICHI INTERNATIONAL (CANADA) LIMITED/LIMITEE—See Yamaichi Securities Co., Ltd.; *Int'l,* pg. 1517
YAMAICHI INTERNATIONAL CAPITAL MANAGEMENT CO., LTD.—See Yamaichi Securities Co., Ltd.; *Int'l,* pg. 1516
YAMAICHI INTERNATIONAL (EUROPE) LTD.—See Yamaichi Securities Co., Ltd.; *Int'l,* pg. 1518
YAMAICHI INTERNATIONAL (H.K.) LTD.—See Yamaichi Securities Co., Ltd.; *Int'l,* pg. 1518
YAMAICHI INTERNATIONAL (MIDDLE EAST) E.C.—See Yamaichi Securities Co., Ltd.; *Int'l,* pg. 1518
YAMAICHI INVESTMENT TRUST MANAGEMENT CO., LTD.—See Yamaichi Securities Co., Ltd.; *Int'l,* pg. 1516
YAMAICHI ITALIA S.P.A. SOCIETA DI INTERMEDIAZIONE MOBILIARE—See Yamaichi Securities Co., Ltd.; *Int'l,* pg. 1518
YAMAICHI MERCHANT BANK—See Yamaichi Securities Co., Ltd.; *Int'l,* pg. 1518
YAMAICHI-MURRAY JOHNSTONE LTD.—See Yamaichi Securities Co., Ltd.; *Int'l,* pg. 1518
YAMAICHI OVERSEAS FINANCE N.V.—See Yamaichi Securities Co., Ltd.; *Int'l,* pg. 1518
YAMAICHI REAL ESTATE INC.—See Yamaichi Securities Co., Ltd.; *Int'l,* pg. 1518
YAMAICHI RESEARCH INSTITUTE OF SECURITIES & ECONOMICS, INC.—See Yamaichi Securities Co., Ltd.; *Int'l,* pg. 1517
YAMAICHI SECURITIES CO., LTD.; *Int'l,* pg. 1516
YAMAICHI SECURITIES CO., LTD.-TAIPEI BRANCH—See Yamaichi Securities Co., Ltd.; *Int'l,* pg. 1517
YAMAICHI SECURITIES (H.K.) LTD.—See Yamaichi Securities Co., Ltd.; *Int'l,* pg. 1518
YAMAICHI SECURITIES (SINGAPORE) PTE. LTD.—See Yamaichi Securities Co., Ltd.; *Int'l,* pg. 1518
YAMAICHI TRUST & BANK, LTD.—See Yamaichi Securities Co., Ltd.; *Int'l,* pg. 1517
YAMAICHI WORLD TOURIST INC.—See Yamaichi Securities Co., Ltd.; *Int'l,* pg. 1517
YAMAKO ELECTRIC MANUFACTURE CO., LTD.—See Oki Electric Industry Company, Ltd.; *Int'l,* pg. 999
YAMAMOTO MFG. CO., LTD.—See Citizen Watch Company, Ltd.; *Int'l,* pg. 294
YAMAMOTO MFG. (USA) INC.—See Citizen Watch Company, Ltd.; *Int'l,* pg. 295
YAMANASHI JOZO CO., LTD.—See Meiji Seika Kaisha, Ltd.; *Int'l,* pg. 855
YAMANOUCHI EUROPE B.V.—See Yamanouchi Pharmaceutical Co. Ltd.; *Int'l,* pg. 1519
YAMANOUCHI EUROPE B.V.-MANUFACTURING MEPPEL—See Yamanouchi Pharmaceutical Co. Ltd.; *Int'l,* pg. 1519
YAMANOUCHI EUROPE B.V.-RESEARCH LABORATORIES—See Yamanouchi Pharmaceutical Co. Ltd.; *Int'l,* pg. 1519
YAMANOUCHI HEALTH AND BEAUTY CO., LTD.—See Yamanouchi Pharmaceutical Co. Ltd.; *Int'l,* pg. 1518
YAMANOUCHI IRELAND CO., LTD.—See Yamanouchi Pharmaceutical Co. Ltd.; *Int'l,* pg. 1519
YAMANOUCHI MEDICAL CO., LTD.—See Yamanouchi Pharmaceutical Co. Ltd.; *Int'l,* pg. 1518
YAMANOUCHI PHARMA AB—See Yamanouchi Pharmaceutical Co. Ltd.; *Int'l,* pg. 1519
YAMANOUCHI PHARMA A/S—See Yamanouchi Pharmaceutical Co. Ltd.; *Int'l,* pg. 1519
YAMANOUCHI PHARMA B.V.-BRUSSELS—See Yamanouchi Pharmaceutical Co. Ltd.; *Int'l,* pg. 1519
YAMANOUCHI PHARMA B.V.-LEIDERDORP—See Yamanouchi Pharmaceutical Co. Ltd.; *Int'l,* pg. 1519
YAMANOUCHI PHARMA GMBH—See Yamanouchi Pharmaceutical Co. Ltd.; *Int'l,* pg. 1519
YAMANOUCHI PHARMA LDA.—See Yamanouchi Pharmaceutical Co. Ltd.; *Int'l,* pg. 1519
YAMANOUCHI PHARMA LTD.—See Yamanouchi Pharmaceutical Co. Ltd.; *Int'l,* pg. 1519
YAMANOUCHI PHARMA S.A.—See Yamanouchi Pharmaceutical Co. Ltd.; *Int'l,* pg. 1519
YAMANOUCHI PHARMA SPA—See Yamanouchi Pharmaceutical Co. Ltd.; *Int'l,* pg. 1519
YAMANOUCHI PHARMACEUTICAL CO. LTD.; *Int'l,* pg. 1518
YAMANOUCHI REAL ESTATE CO., LTD.—See Yamanouchi Pharmaceutical Co. Ltd.; *Int'l,* pg. 1518
YAMANOUCHI RESEARCH INSTITUTE (U.K.)—See Yamanouchi Pharmaceutical Co. Ltd.; *Int'l,* pg. 1519
YAMANOUCHI SANICOTT CO., LTD.—See Yamanouchi Pharmaceutical Co. Ltd.; *Int'l,* pg. 1518
YAMANOUCHI U.K. LIMTED—See Yamanouchi Pharmaceutical Co. Ltd.; *Int'l,* pg. 1519
YAMANOUCHI U.S.A. INC.—See Yamanouchi Pharmaceutical Co. Ltd.; *Int'l,* pg. 1519

YAMATAKE-HONEYWELL COMPANY LTD.—See Honeywell Inc.; *U.S. Public,* pg. 835
YAMATO TRANSPORT CO., LTD.; *Int'l,* pg. 1519
YAMATO TRANSPORT USA, INC.—See Yamato Transport Co., Ltd.; *Int'l,* pg. 1519
YAMAZAKI BAKING CO., LTD.; *Int'l,* pg. 1519
YAMAZAKI CALIFORNIA INC.—See Yamazaki Baking Co., Ltd.; *Int'l,* pg. 1519
YAMAZAKI FRANCE S.A.—See Yamazaki Baking Co., Ltd.; *Int'l,* pg. 1519
YAMAZAKI USA INC.—See Yamazaki Baking Co., Ltd.; *Int'l,* pg. 1519
YANGZHONG TEKTRONIX ELECTRONIC INSTRUMENT CO., LTD.—See Tektronix, Inc.; *U.S. Public,* pg. 1568
YANKEE ATOMIC ELECTRIC CO.—See Central Maine Power Company; *U.S. Public,* pg. 325
YANKEE ENERGY FINANCIAL SERVICES COMPANY—See Yankee Energy System, Inc.; *U.S. Public,* pg. 1787
YANKEE ENERGY PRODUCTION SERVICES, INC.—See Yankee Energy System, Inc.; *U.S. Public,* pg. 1787
YANKEE ENERGY SERVICES COMPANY—See Yankee Energy System, Inc.; *U.S. Public,* pg. 1788
YANKEE ENERGY SYSTEM, INC.; *U.S. Public,* pg. 1787
YANKEE GAS SERVICES COMPANY—See Yankee Energy System, Inc.; *U.S. Public,* pg. 1788
YANKEE GROUP RESEARCH, INC.—See Primark Corporation; *U.S. Public,* pg. 1325
YANKEE PUBLISHING INCORPORATED; *U.S. Private,* pg. 1195
YANKEE WHALER COMPANY—See Specialty Restaurants Corporation; *U.S. Private,* pg. 1023
THE YANKTON PRINTING COMPANY—See Shivers Trading & Operating Co.; *U.S. Private,* pg. 995
YANRI CWM CO., LTD.—See JGC Corporation; *Int'l,* pg. 697
YANTAI EBARA AIR CONDITIONING EQUIPMENT CO., LTD.—See Ebara Corporation; *Int'l,* pg. 432
YANTAI HUADA CHEMICALS INDUSTRY CO., LTD.—See Dainippon Ink & Chemicals, Inc.; *Int'l,* pg. 372
YANTIS CORPORATION; *U.S. Private,* pg. 1195
YAPKIM YAPI KIMYA SANAYI A.S.—See Viag AG; *Int'l,* pg. 1466
YAR COMMUNICATIONS; *U.S. Private,* pg. 1195
YAR WEST—See YAR Communications; *U.S. Private,* pg. 1195
YARDNEY TECHNICAL PRODUCTS, INC.—See Ener-Tek International Corporation; *U.S. Private,* pg. 376
YARROW SHIPBUILDERS LTD.—See The General Electric Company, p.l.c.; *Int'l,* pg. 545
YARWAY CORPORATION—See Tyco International Ltd.; *U.S. Public,* pg. 1650
YASHICA A.G.—See Kyocera Corporation; *Int'l,* pg. 776
YASHICA DO BRASIL-EXPORTACAO E INDUSTRIA LTDA.—See Kyocera Corporation; *Int'l,* pg. 776
YASHICA DO BRASIL-INDUSTRIA E COMERCIO LTDA.—See Kyocera Corporation; *Int'l,* pg. 776
YASHICA HANDELSGESELLSCHAFT MBH—See Kyocera Corporation; *Int'l,* pg. 776
YASHICA HONG KONG CO., LTD.—See Kyocera Corporation; *Int'l,* pg. 776
YASHICA, INC.—See Kyocera Corporation; *Int'l,* pg. 776
YASHICA KYOCERA GMBH—See Kyocera Corporation; *Int'l,* pg. 776
YASUDA BANK AND TRUST COMPANY (U.S.A.)—See The Yasuda Trust and Banking Co., Ltd.; *Int'l,* pg. 1520
THE YASUDA FIRE & MARINE INSURANCE COMPANY LIMITED; *Int'l,* pg. 1519
THE YASUDA FIRE & MARINE INSURANCE CO. OF AMERICA—See The Yasuda Fire & Marine Insurance Company Limited; *Int'l,* pg. 1519
YASUDA LIFE AMERICA AGENCY INC.—See Yasuda Mutual Life Insurance Co.; *Int'l,* pg. 1520
YASUDA LIFE AMERICA CAPITAL MANAGEMENT, LTD.—See Yasuda Mutual Life Insurance Co.; *Int'l,* pg. 1520
YASUDA LIFE GLOBAL INVESTMENT (JERSEY) LTD.—See Yasuda Mutual Life Insurance Co.; *Int'l,* pg. 1520
YASUDA LIFE INTERNATIONAL (HONG KONG) LTD.—See Yasuda Mutual Life Insurance Co.; *Int'l,* pg. 1520
YASUDA LIFE INTERNATIONAL INVESTMENT (B.V.I.) LTD.—See Yasuda Mutual Life Insurance Co.; *Int'l,* pg. 1520
YASUDA LIFE INTERNATIONAL (LONDON) LTD.—See Yasuda Mutual Life Insurance Co.; *Int'l,* pg. 1520
YASUDA LIFE INTERNATIONAL (SINGAPORE) LTD.—See Yasuda Mutual Life Insurance Co.; *Int'l,* pg. 1520
YASUDA MUTUAL LIFE INSURANCE CO.; *Int'l,* pg. 1519
YASUDA PROPERTIES (U.K.)—See Yasuda Mutual Life Insurance Co.; *Int'l,* pg. 1520
YASUDA REALTY AMERICA CORPORATION—See Yasuda Mutual Life Insurance Co.; *Int'l,* pg. 1520
THE YASUDA TRUST AND BANKING CO., LTD.; *Int'l,* pg. 1520
YAT YUEN HONG COMPANY LIMITED—See Hong Fok Corporation Ltd.; *Int'l,* pg. 635
YATES INVESTMENT CASTING WAX INC.—See Burmah Castrol plc; *Int'l,* pg. 234
YATSUGATAKE SNOW BRAND MILK CO., LTD.—See Snow Brand Milk Products Co. Ltd.; *Int'l,* pg. 1272
YATSUSHIRO MILL—See Nippon Paper Industries Company Limited; *Int'l,* pg. 938
YAVNIR TRADING CO. LTD.—See American Israeli Paper Mills Ltd.; *Int'l,* pg. 75
YAZAKI CORPORATION; *Int'l,* pg. 1520
YAZAKI SABANCI OTOMOTIV KABLO DONANIMI SAN. VE TIC. A.S.—See Sabanci Holding A.S.; *Int'l,* pg. 1168
YAZAKI SABANCI OTOMOTIV KABLO DONANIMI SAN. VE TIC. A.S.—See Yazaki Corporation; *Int'l,* pg. 1520
YAZOO POWER EQUIPMENT, LLC; *U.S. Private,* pg. 1195
YEAR 2K COMMUNICATIONS—See Lois/USA Inc.; *U.S. Public,* pg. 1011
YELLO-BOLE—See S.M. Frank & Co., Inc.; *U.S. Private,* pg. 424
YELLOW BOOK CO., INC.—See Multi-Local Media Corporation; *U.S. Private,* pg. 767

YELLOW BOOK OF NEW JERSEY—See Multi-Local Media Corporation; *U.S. Private,* pg. 767
YELLOW CAB CO.—See Stamford Capital; *U.S. Private,* pg. 1030
YELLOW CORPORATION; *U.S. Public,* pg. 1788
YELLOW FREIGHT SYSTEM, INC.—See Yellow Corporation; *U.S. Public,* pg. 1788
YELLOW FROG—See Domino; *Int'l,* pg. 416
YELLOW PAGES SALES LIMITED—See British Telecommunications plc; *Int'l,* pg. 222
YELLOW REDEVELOPMENT CORP.—See Yellow Corporation; *U.S. Public,* pg. 1788
THE YELLOW RIVER INTERNATIONAL LEASING CO., LTD.—See The Dai-Ichi Kangyo Bank, Limited; *Int'l,* pg. 362
YELLOW SERVICES, INC.—See Yellow Corporation; *U.S. Public,* pg. 1788
YEMEN COMPUTER COMPANY LTD.—See BASF AG; *Int'l,* pg. 110
YENKIN-MAJESTIC PAINT CORPORATION; *U.S. Private,* pg. 1195
YEO HIAP SENG LIMITED—See Orchard Parade Holdings Limited; *Int'l,* pg. 1008
YEOMANS & PARTNERS LTD.—See The Peninsular and Oriental Steam Navigation Company; *Int'l,* pg. 1035
YESAWICH, MOSS & BROWN—See Yesawich, Pepperdine & Brown; *U.S. Private,* pg. 1196
YESAWICH, PEPPERDINE & BROWN—See Yesawich, Pepperdine & Brown; *U.S. Private,* pg. 1196
YESAWICH, PEPPERDINE & BROWN; *U.S. Private,* pg. 1195
YESAWICH, PEPPERDINE & MOSS—See Yesawich, Pepperdine & Brown; *U.S. Private,* pg. 1196
YESCO ENERGY CONSULTING SERVICES, INC.—See Yankee Energy System, Inc.; *U.S. Public,* pg. 1788
YESCO INDUSTRIAL ENERGY SERVICES, INC.—See Yankee Energy System, Inc.; *U.S. Public,* pg. 1788
YESO PANAMERICANO, S.A. DE C.V.—See USG Corporation; *U.S. Public,* pg. 1660
YESOS IBERICOS—See Lafarge S.A.; *Int'l,* pg. 791
YIBITAS LAFARGE HAZIR BETON SAN. VE TIC. A.S.—See Lafarge S.A.; *Int'l,* pg. 791
YIBITAS LAFARGE ORTA ANADOLU CIMENTO SAN.VE TIC. A.S.—See Lafarge S.A.; *Int'l,* pg. 791
YMOS A.G. INDSTRIEPODUKTE—See Cockerill Sambre; *Int'l,* pg. 302
S.A. YMOS BELGIUM—See Cockerill Sambre; *Int'l,* pg. 302
YMOS (UK) LTD.—See Cockerill Sambre; *Int'l,* pg. 302
YODER OIL COMPANY INC.; *U.S. Private,* pg. 1196
YOGEN FRUZ (BARBADOS) INC.—See Yogen Fruz Worldwide Inc.; *Int'l,* pg. 1520
YOGEN FRUZ WORLDWIDE INC.; *Int'l,* pg. 1520
H.L. YOH GROUP LLC—See Day & Zimmermann, Inc.; *U.S. Private,* pg. 317
YOH HEALTH CARE SERVICES—See Day & Zimmermann, Inc.; *U.S. Private,* pg. 317
YOH SCIENTIFIC—See Day & Zimmermann, Inc.; *U.S. Private,* pg. 317
YOH STAFFING SERVICES—See Day & Zimmermann, Inc.; *U.S. Private,* pg. 317
YOKOGAWA CORPORATION OF AMERICA—See Yokogawa Electric Corporation; *Int'l,* pg. 1521
YOKOGAWA ELECTRIC CORPORATION; *Int'l,* pg. 1520
YOKOGAWA-HEWLETT-PACKARD LTD.—See Hewlett-Packard Company; *U.S. Public,* pg. 823
YOKOGAWA-KITZ-VALTEK CORP. (Y-K-V)—See Flowserve Corporation; *U.S. Public,* pg. 659
YOKOHAMA AEROQUIP KK—See The Yokohama Rubber Co., Ltd.; *Int'l,* pg. 1521
YOKOHAMA ASIA LIMITED—See Bank of Yokohama; *Int'l,* pg. 159
YOKOHAMA AUSTRIA GMBH—See The Yokohama Rubber Co., Ltd.; *Int'l,* pg. 1521
YOKOHAMA CORPORATION OF AMERICA—See The Yokohama Rubber Co., Ltd.; *Int'l,* pg. 1521
YOKOHAMA CORPORATION OF NORTH AMERICA—See The Yokohama Rubber Co., Ltd.; *Int'l,* pg. 1521
YOKOHAMA CREATIVE CENTER—See Namco Ltd.; *Int'l,* pg. 905
YOKOHAMA FRANCE S.A.—See The Yokohama Rubber Co., Ltd.; *Int'l,* pg. 1521
YOKOHAMA HPT LTD.—See The Yokohama Rubber Co., Ltd.; *Int'l,* pg. 1521
YOKOHAMA ITALIA S.P.A.—See The Yokohama Rubber Co., Ltd.; *Int'l,* pg. 1521
YOKOHAMA KIKO CO., LTD.—See NHK Spring Co., Ltd.; *Int'l,* pg. 902
YOKOHAMA MIRAI-KENKYUSHO—See Namco Ltd.; *Int'l,* pg. 905
YOKOHAMA PLANT—See Nikon Corporation; *Int'l,* pg. 931
YOKOHAMA REIFEN GMBH—See The Yokohama Rubber Co., Ltd.; *Int'l,* pg. 1521
THE YOKOHAMA RUBBER CO., LTD.—See The Yokohama Rubber Co., Ltd.; *Int'l,* pg. 1521
THE YOKOHAMA RUBBER CO., LTD.; *Int'l,* pg. 1521
YOKOHAMA SCANDINAVIA AB—See The Yokohama Rubber Co., Ltd.; *Int'l,* pg. 1521
YOKOHAMA (SUISSE) SA—See The Yokohama Rubber Co., Ltd.; *Int'l,* pg. 1521
YOKOHAMA TIRE CANADA INC.—See The Yokohama Rubber Co., Ltd.; *Int'l,* pg. 1521
YOKOHAMA TIRE CORP.—See The Yokohama Rubber Co., Ltd.; *Int'l,* pg. 1521
YOKOHAMA TIRE CORPORATION—See The Yokohama Rubber Co., Ltd.; *Int'l,* pg. 1521
YOKOHAMA TOYOPET CO., LTD.—See Toyota Motor Corporation; *Int'l,* pg. 1412
YOKOHAMA TRANSPORTATION CO., LTD.—See Nissan Motor Co., Ltd.; *Int'l,* pg. 944
YOKOHAMA TYRE AUSTRALIA PTY., LTD.—See The Yokohama Rubber Co., Ltd.; *Int'l,* pg. 1521
YOKOHAMA TYRE AUSTRALIAN PTY., LTD.—See The Yokohama Rubber Co., Ltd.; *Int'l,* pg. 1522

YOKOHAMAGOMU FINANCE EUROPE B.V.—See The Yokohama Rubber Co., Ltd.; *Int'l,* pg. 1522
YOKOYU VANTEC CORPORATION—See Nissan Motor Co., Ltd.; *Int'l,* pg. 944
YOMIKO ADVERTISING INC.; *Int'l,* pg. 1522
YONEX CO., LTD.; *Int'l,* pg. 1522
YONEX CORPORATION—See Yonex Co., Ltd.; *Int'l,* pg. 1522
YOO HOO CHOCOLATE BEVERAGE CORP.—See Groupe Pernod Ricard; *Int'l,* pg. 567
YOPLAIT USA—See General Mills, Inc.; *U.S. Public,* pg. 718
YORDAN OBEGI & CO. LTD.—See BASF AG; *Int'l,* pg. 110
THE YORK BANK AND TRUST COMPANY—See Allied Irish Banks, p.l.c.; *Int'l,* pg. 65
YORK BARBELL CO., INC.; *U.S. Private,* pg. 1196
YORK-BENIMARU CO., LTD.—See Ito-Yokado Co., Ltd.; *Int'l,* pg. 693
YORK BUILDING PRODUCTS CO., INC.; *U.S. Private,* pg. 1196
YORK INTERNATIONAL CORPORATION; *U.S. Public,* pg. 1788
YORK INTL./RECO—See York International Corporation; *U.S. Public,* pg. 1789
YORK LITHOGRAPHING—See Rogers Communications, Inc.; *Int'l,* pg. 1123
YORK MART CO., LTD.—See Ito-Yokado Co., Ltd.; *Int'l,* pg. 693
THE YORK NEWS-TIMES—See Shivers Trading & Operating Co.; *U.S. Private,* pg. 995
YORK PLANT—See Cooper Industries, Inc.; *U.S. Public,* pg. 444
YORK RESEARCH CANADA, INC.—See York Research Corporation; *U.S. Public,* pg. 1789
YORK RESEARCH CORPORATION; *U.S. Public,* pg. 1789
YORK TECHNOLOGY LTD.—See Relm Wireless Corp.; *U.S. Public,* pg. 1376
YORK TOYOTA CITY—See Toyota Motor Corporation; *Int'l,* pg. 1413
YORK WALLCOVERINGS INC.; *U.S. Private,* pg. 1196
YORK WILLIS CORROON SA—See Willis Corroon Group PLC; *Int'l,* pg. 1522
YORK WINDPOWER CORP.—See York Research Corporation; *U.S. Public,* pg. 1789
YORKRAIL INC.—See Emons Transportation Group, Inc.; *U.S. Public,* pg. 579
YORKSHIRE BANK—See National Australia Bank Limited; *Int'l,* pg. 906
YORKSHIRE BRICK COMPANY—See Franz Haniel & Cie, GmbH; *Int'l,* pg. 591
YORKSHIRE BUILDING SOCIETY; *Int'l,* pg. 1522
YORKSHIRE CHEMICALS PLC; *Int'l,* pg. 1522
YORKSHIRE GUERNSEY—See Yorkshire Building Society; *Int'l,* pg. 1522
YORKSHIRE LTD.—See Yorkshire Building Society; *Int'l,* pg. 1522
YORKSHIRE MARINE CONTAINERS LTD.—See Sea Containers Ltd.; *Int'l,* pg. 1214
YORKSHIRE POST NEWSPAPERS LTD.—See United News & Media plc; *Int'l,* pg. 1443
YORKTOWN TOOL & DIE CORPORATION; *U.S. Private,* pg. 1196
YORKTOWNE, INC.; *U.S. Private,* pg. 1196
YORKTOWNE PAPERBOARD CORP.—See The Newark Group, Inc.; *U.S. Private,* pg. 796
THE YORKVILLE PRINTING GROUP LIMITED—See G.T.C. Transcontinental Group Ltd.; *Int'l,* pg. 538
YOSEMITE CONCESSION SERVICES CO.—See The Seagram Company Ltd.; *Int'l,* pg. 1216
YOSEMITE EXPRESS CO.—See Save Mart Supermarkets; *U.S. Private,* pg. 968
YOSEMITE INSURANCE CO.—See American General Corporation; *U.S. Public,* pg. 77
YOSHITOMI-ASTRA LTD.—See Astra AB; *Int'l,* pg. 94
YOSUBA FARMS—See Maxxam Inc.; *U.S. Public,* pg. 1062
YOUGHAL CARPETS (YARNS) LTD.—See Coats Viyella plc; *Int'l,* pg. 301
YOUNG & FRANKLIN, INC.; *U.S. Private,* pg. 1196
YOUNG & RUBICAM—See Young & Rubicam Inc.; *U.S. Private,* pg. 1198
YOUNG & RUBICAM AUSTRALIA/NEW ZEALAND—See Young & Rubicam Inc.; *U.S. Private,* pg. 1198
YOUNG & RUBICAM BELGIUM S.A.—See Young & Rubicam Inc.; *U.S. Private,* pg. 1199
YOUNG & RUBICAM BOGOTA—See Young & Rubicam Inc.; *U.S. Private,* pg. 1200
YOUNG & RUBICAM BRAZIL—See Young & Rubicam Inc.; *U.S. Private,* pg. 1200
YOUNG & RUBICAM BUSINESS COMMUNICATIONS S.A.—See Young & Rubicam Inc.; *U.S. Private,* pg. 1199
YOUNG & RUBICAM C.A.—See Young & Rubicam Inc.; *U.S. Private,* pg. 1200
YOUNG & RUBICAM CALGARY—See Young & Rubicam Inc.; *U.S. Private,* pg. 1200
YOUNG & RUBICAM CHICAGO—See Young & Rubicam Inc.; *U.S. Private,* pg. 1198
YOUNG & RUBICAM COPENHAGEN—See Young & Rubicam Inc.; *U.S. Private,* pg. 1199
YOUNG & RUBICAM DAMARIS, C. POR A.—See Young & Rubicam Inc.; *U.S. Private,* pg. 1200
YOUNG & RUBICAM DETROIT—See Young & Rubicam Inc.; *U.S. Private,* pg. 1198
YOUNG & RUBICAM EUROPE—See Young & Rubicam Inc.; *U.S. Private,* pg. 1199
YOUNG & RUBICAM FINLAND—See Young & Rubicam Inc.; *U.S. Private,* pg. 1199
YOUNG & RUBICAM FINLAND OY—See Young & Rubicam Inc.; *U.S. Private,* pg. 1199
YOUNG & RUBICAM HALIFAX—See Young & Rubicam Inc.; *U.S. Private,* pg. 1200
YOUNG & RUBICAM HOLDINGS LTD.—See Young & Rubicam Inc.; *U.S. Private,* pg. 1199

YOUNG & RUBICAM HUNGARY—See Young & Rubicam Inc.; *U.S. Private,* pg. 1199
YOUNG & RUBICAM INC.; *U.S. Private,* pg. 1196
YOUNG & RUBICAM ITALIA, S.P.A.—See Young & Rubicam Inc.; *U.S. Private,* pg. 1199
YOUNG & RUBICAM LATAM (MIAMI)—See Young & Rubicam Inc.; *U.S. Private,* pg. 1198
YOUNG & RUBICAM LTD.—See Young & Rubicam Inc.; *U.S. Private,* pg. 1200
YOUNG & RUBICAM MATTINGLY, RETAIL GROUP—See Dentsu Young & Rubicam Partnerships; *U.S. Private,* pg. 325
YOUNG & RUBICAM NEW YORK—See Young & Rubicam Inc.; *U.S. Private,* pg. 1198
YOUNG & RUBICAM POLAND—See Young & Rubicam Inc.; *U.S. Private,* pg. 1199
YOUNG & RUBICAM (PORTUGAL)—See Young & Rubicam Inc.; *U.S. Private,* pg. 1199
YOUNG & RUBICAM PRAGUE—See Young & Rubicam Inc.; *U.S. Private,* pg. 1199
YOUNG & RUBICAM PUERTO RICO, INC.—See Young & Rubicam Inc.; *U.S. Private,* pg. 1198
YOUNG & RUBICAM ROMA SRL—See Young & Rubicam Inc.; *U.S. Private,* pg. 1199
YOUNG & RUBICAM S.A.—See Young & Rubicam Inc.; *U.S. Private,* pg. 1200
YOUNG & RUBICAM SAN FRANCISCO—See Young & Rubicam Inc.; *U.S. Private,* pg. 1198
YOUNG & RUBICAM/SOVERO—See Young & Rubicam Inc.; *U.S. Private,* pg. 1199
YOUNG & RUBICAM TURKEY—See Young & Rubicam Inc.; *U.S. Private,* pg. 1200
YOUNG AUTOMOTIVE GROUP—See Trace International Holdings, Inc.; *U.S. Private,* pg. 1095
BERNARD JOHNSON YOUNG INC.—See Bernard Johnson Young Inc.; *U.S. Private,* pg. 136
YOUNG BROTHERS, LTD.—See Hawaiian Electric Industries, Inc.; *U.S. Public,* pg. 800
DANIEL F. YOUNG, INC.; *U.S. Private,* pg. 1200
YOUNG DENTAL MANUFACTURING; *U.S. Private,* pg. 1201
YOUNG ELECTRIC SIGN COMPANY; *U.S. Private,* pg. 1201
YOUNG ELECTRIC SIGNS DENVER DIV.—See Young Electric Sign Company; *U.S. Private,* pg. 1201
YOUNG ELECTRIC SIGNS LAS VEGAS DIV.—See Young Electric Sign Company; *U.S. Private,* pg. 1201
YOUNG ELECTRIC SIGNS OGDEN DIVISION—See Young Electric Sign Company; *U.S. Private,* pg. 1201
YOUNG ELECTRIC SIGNS RENO DIVISION—See Young Electric Sign Company; *U.S. Private,* pg. 1201
YOUNG ELECTRIC SIGNS SALT LAKE CITY—See Young Electric Sign Company; *U.S. Private,* pg. 1201
YOUNG ENVIRONMENTAL CLEAN UP—See R.S. Young Excavating, Inc.; *U.S. Private,* pg. 1202
YOUNG GAS STORAGE COMPANY—See New Century Energies, Inc.; *U.S. Public,* pg. 1170
YOUNG-IN SCIENTIFIC CO., LTD.—See Hewlett-Packard Company; *U.S. Public,* pg. 824
JACK YOUNG ASSOCIATES; *U.S. Private,* pg. 1201
YOUNG PECAN COMPANY (A PARTNERSHIP); *U.S. Private,* pg. 1201
YOUNG PECAN COMPANY WEST, INC.—See Young Pecan Company (A Partnership); *U.S. Private,* pg. 1201
YOUNG-PHILLIPS SALES CO.; *U.S. Private,* pg. 1201
YOUNG POONG MANULIFE—See Manulife Financial (The Manufacturers Life Insurance Company); *Int'l,* pg. 841
YOUNG POONG MANULIFE INSURANCE COMPANY—See Manulife Financial (The Manufacturers Life Insurance Company); *Int'l,* pg. 841
YOUNG RADIATOR COMPANY; *U.S. Private,* pg. 1201
YOUNG REFINING CORP.; *U.S. Private,* pg. 1202
RICHARD YOUNG OFFICE PRODUCTS, INC.—See Corporate Express, Inc.; *U.S. Public,* pg. 450
RODNEY D. YOUNG INSURANCE; *U.S. Private,* pg. 1202
R.S. YOUNG EXCAVATING, INC.; *U.S. Private,* pg. 1202
YOUNG & RUBICAM BUCHAREST—See Young & Rubicam Inc.; *U.S. Private,* pg. 1199
YOUNG & RUBICAM THOLET—See Young & Rubicam Inc.; *U.S. Private,* pg. 1198
YOUNG SPRING & WIRE COMPANY—See Leggett & Platt, Incorporated; *U.S. Public,* pg. 987
YOUNG STUFF APPAREL GROUP, INC.; *U.S. Private,* pg. 1202
YOUNG SUPPLY COMPANY; *U.S. Private,* pg. 1202
YOUNG'S HOLDINGS INC.; *U.S. Private,* pg. 1202
YOUNG'S MARKET COMPANY—See Young's Holdings Inc.; *U.S. Private,* pg. 1202
YOUNGSTOWN MILLER CORP.—See GHM Industries, Inc.; *U.S. Private,* pg. 435
YOUNGSTOWN TIRE & SUPPLY COMPANY—See Ziegler Tire & Supply Company, Inc.; *U.S. Private,* pg. 1205
YOUNKERS, INC.—See Proffitt's, Inc.; *U.S. Public,* pg. 1334
YOUR MAN TOURS, INC.; *U.S. Private,* pg. 1202
YOUR STAFF, INC.—See Kelly Services, Inc.; *U.S. Public,* pg. 949
YRAJOS HERMANOS SUCESORES, S.A.—See International Data Group; *U.S. Private,* pg. 570
YU HUA LOONG TRADING SDN. BHD.—See Sinochem International Petroleum Co., Ltd.; *Int'l,* pg. 1256
YUASA CORPORATION; *Int'l,* pg. 1522
YUASA-EXIDE, INC.—See Yuasa Corporation; *Int'l,* pg. 1522
YUASA-IONICS CO., LTD.—See Ionics, Incorporated; *U.S. Public,* pg. 912
YUBA HEAT TRANSFER DIVISION—See Connell Limited Partnership; *U.S. Private,* pg. 264
THE YUCAIPA COMPANIES; *U.S. Private,* pg. 1202
YUFUTSU MILL—See Nippon Paper Industries Company Limited; *Int'l,* pg. 938
YUHAN-KIMBERLY, LTD.—See Kimberly-Clark Corporation; *U.S. Public,* pg. 960

YUKA SHELL EPOXY—See Royal Dutch/Shell Group of Companies; *Int'l*, pg. 1140
YUKON ALASKA TRANSPORT LTD.—See Lynden Incorporated; *U.S. Private*, pg. 684
THE YUKON ELECTRICAL CO. LTD.—See ATCO Group Co.; *Int'l*, pg. 95
YUKON PACIFIC CORPORATION—See CSX Corporation; *U.S. Public*, pg. 284
YUKONG FUCHS LTD.—See Fuchs Petrolub AG Oel + Chemie; *Int'l*, pg. 518
YULONG HOTEL, BEIJING—See Sinochem International Petroleum Co. Ltd.; *Int'l*, pg. 1255
YUM YUM DONUT SHOP, INC.—*U.S. Private*, pg. 1203
THE YUMA DAILY SUN—See The Thomson Corporation; *U.S. Public*, pg. 1601
YUMEX/ILC—See ILC Technology, Inc.; *U.S. Public*, pg. 856
YUNG HWA MACHINERY INDUSTRIAL CO., LTD.—See Kayaba Industry Co.; *Int'l*, pg. 727
YUSUF BIN AHMED KANOO—See BASF AG; *Int'l*, pg. 110
YUSUF BIN AHMED KANOO BASF DIVISION—See BASF AG; *Int'l*, pg. 110
YUTAKA GIKEN CO., LTD.—See Honda Motor Co., Ltd.; *Int'l*, pg. 634
YVES SAINT LAURENT PARFUMS S.A.—See Elf Aquitaine; *Int'l*, pg. 445

Z

Z. CAVARICCI INC.—See Z. Cavaricci Inc.; *U.S. Private*, pg. 1203
Z. CAVARICCI INC.; *U.S. Private*, pg. 1203
Z-SEVEN FUND, INC.; *U.S. Public*, pg. 1789
Z-SYSTEM CO., LTD.—See Miura Co., Ltd.; *Int'l*, pg. 884
ZAO NORVISTA - ST. PETERSBURG—See FinnAir Oy; *Int'l*, pg. 486
ZAO OUTOKUMPU MOSKVA—See Outokumpu Oyj; *Int'l*, pg. 1016
ZAO OUTOKUMPU ST. PETERSBURG—See Outokumpu Oyj; *Int'l*, pg. 1016
ZD PRESS—See Softbank Corporation; *Int'l*, pg. 1276
ZDS GROUPE AB—See Compagnie des Machines Bull; *Int'l*, pg. 317
ZF FRIEDRICHSHAFEN A.G.; *Int'l*, pg. 1522
ZF GREAT BRITAIN LTD.—See ZF Friedrichshafen A.G.; *Int'l*, pg. 1522
ZHCL CORP.—See Zale Corporation; *U.S. Public*, pg. 1789
ZK HOSPITAL BEDARFS GMBH—See Getinge Industrier AB; *Int'l*, pg. 552
ZMP, INC.; *U.S. Private*, pg. 1203
ZSA ZAUN-UND SICHERHEITSANLAGEN GMBH—See Plettac AG; *Int'l*, pg. 1061
ZSR CORPORATION LTD.—See Tate & Lyle PLC; *Int'l*, pg. 1357
ZAADUNIE B.V.—See Novartis AG; *Int'l*, pg. 986
H.B. ZACHRY; *U.S. Private*, pg. 1203
ZACK ELECTRONICS; *U.S. Private*, pg. 1203
ZACK ELECTRONICS/TELE-COM PRODUCTS, INC.—See Zack Electronics; *U.S. Private*, pg. 1203
ZACKY FARMS, INC.; *U.S. Private*, pg. 1203
ZACKY FOODS—See Zacky Farms, Inc.; *U.S. Private*, pg. 1203
ZADEN LABOR C.V.—See Novartis AG; *Int'l*, pg. 986
ZAHORIK CO., INC.—See AEGON N.V.; *Int'l*, pg. 28
ZAIRE MOBIL OIL—See Mobil Oil Corporation; *U.S. Public*, pg. 1119
ZAIRE SHELL—See Royal Dutch/Shell Group of Companies; *Int'l*, pg. 1137
ZALE ACQUISITION CORP.—See Zale Corporation; *U.S. Public*, pg. 1789
ZALE CORPORATION; *U.S. Public*, pg. 1789
ZALE DELAWARE, INC.—See Zale Corporation; *U.S. Public*, pg. 1789
ZALE HOLDING CO.—See Zale Corporation; *U.S. Public*, pg. 1789
ZALE LIFE INSURANCE CO.—See Zale Corporation; *U.S. Public*, pg. 1789
ZALE PUERTO RICO INC.—See Zale Corporation; *U.S. Public*, pg. 1789
ZALK JOSEPH FABRICATIONS, INC.—See Pettibone Corporation; *U.S. Private*, pg. 860
DR. LO. ZAMBELETTI S.P.A.—See SmithKline Beecham plc; *Int'l*, pg. 1266
THE ZAMOISKI CO.; *U.S. Private*, pg. 1203
ZANDA AB—See Redland PLC; *Int'l*, pg. 1092
ZANDA A/S—See Redland PLC; *Int'l*, pg. 1092
ZANDER'S CREAMERY INC.; *U.S. Private*, pg. 1203
ZANTE, INC.—See The Sands Regent; *U.S. Public*, pg. 1431
ZANTOP INTERNATIONAL AIRLINES, INC.; *U.S. Private*, pg. 1204
ZANUSSI COMPONENTI PLASTICA S.P.A.—See Electrolux, AB; *Int'l*, pg. 442
ZANUSSI ELETTRODOMESTICI S.P.A.—See Electrolux, AB; *Int'l*, pg. 442
ZANUSSI ELETTROMECCANICA S.P.A.—See Electrolux, AB; *Int'l*, pg. 442
ZANUSSI GRANDI IMPIANTI S.P.A.—See Electrolux, AB; *Int'l*, pg. 442
ZANUSSI ITALIA S.P.A.—See Electrolux, AB; *Int'l*, pg. 442
ZANUSSI METALLURGICA S.P.A.—See Electrolux, AB; *Int'l*, pg. 442
ZANUSSI VENDING S.P.A.—See Electrolux, AB; *Int'l*, pg. 442
ZAO DANFOSS—See Danfoss A/S; *Int'l*, pg. 378
ZAO KONE LIFTS—See Kone Corporation; *Int'l*, pg. 748
ZAO NIKON K.K.—See Nikon Corporation; *Int'l*, pg. 931
ZAO NORVISTA - MOSCOW—See FinnAir Oy; *Int'l*, pg. 486
ZAO SHOKUHIN CO., LTD.—See Meiji Seika Kaisha, Ltd.; *Int'l*, pg. 855
ZAPATA CORPORATION; *U.S. Public*, pg. 1789

ZAPATA HAYNIE CORP.—See Zapata Corporation; *U.S. Public*, pg. 1789
ZAPPA PLASTICS—See E.J. Brooks Company; *U.S. Private*, pg. 172
ZARDOYA OTIS SA—See United Technologies Corporation; *U.S. Public*, pg. 1691
ZAREMBA GROUP, INC.; *U.S. Private*, pg. 1204
ZAYANI COMPUTER SYSTEMS—See Hewlett-Packard Company; *U.S. Public*, pg. 824
ZAZULA PROCESS EQUIP. LTD.—See ABB Asea Brown Boveri (Holding) Ltd.; *Int'l*, pg. 6
ZEAG ZEMENTWERK LAUFFEN-ELEKTRIZITAETSWERK HEILBRONN AG—See Heidelberger Zement A.G.; *Int'l*, pg. 605
ZEBCO—See Brunswick Corporation; *U.S. Public*, pg. 265
ZEBRA TECHNOLOGIES CORPORATION; *U.S. Public*, pg. 1790
ZEDA BETEILIGUNGSGESELLSCHAFT MBH.—See Vorwerk & Co.; *Int'l*, pg. 1481
ZEDA GESELLSCHAFT FÜR DATENVERARBEITUNG UND EDV-BERATUNG MBH. & CO.—See Vorwerk & Co.; *Int'l*, pg. 1481
ZEE MEDICAL, INC.—See McKesson Corporation; *U.S. Public*, pg. 1073
ZEELAND CHEMICALS, INC.—See Cambrex Corporation; *U.S. Public*, pg. 297
ZEEPFABRIEK DE FENIX B.V.—See Unilever Plc; *Int'l*, pg. 1439
ZEHRMART INC.—See George Weston Limited; *Int'l*, pg. 1495
ZEIDLER & WIMMEL GMBH & CO.—See Philipp Holzmann AG; *Int'l*, pg. 633
ZEIDLER GMBH—See Atlet AB; *Int'l*, pg. 97
ZEIGLER COAL HOLDING COMPANY; *U.S. Public*, pg. 1790
R.L. ZEIGLER CO. INC.; *U.S. Private*, pg. 1204
CARL ZEISS—See Carl-Zeiss-Stiftung; *Int'l*, pg. 1522
CARL ZEISS CANADA LTD.—See Carl-Zeiss-Stiftung; *Int'l*, pg. 1523
CARL ZEISS JENA GMBH—See Carl-Zeiss-Stiftung; *Int'l*, pg. 1523
CARL ZEISS OPTICAL, INC.—See Carl-Zeiss-Stiftung; *Int'l*, pg. 1523
CARL ZEISS PTY. LTD. CANBERRA COMPANY—See Carl-Zeiss-Stiftung; *Int'l*, pg. 1523
CARL-ZEISS-STIFTUNG; *Int'l*, pg. 1522
ZEISS INDUSTRIELLE MESSTECHNIK GMBH—See Carl-Zeiss-Stiftung; *Int'l*, pg. 1523
ZEISS MESSGERÄTEBAU GMBH—See Carl-Zeiss-Stiftung; *Int'l*, pg. 1523
ZEITVERLAG GERD BUCERIUS GMBH—See Georg von Holtzbrinck GmbH; *Int'l*, pg. 1479
ZELHEM PLANT—See Fort James Corporation; *U.S. Public*, pg. 672
DR. TECHN. JOSEF ZELISKO GMBH—See Knorr-Bremse AG; *Int'l*, pg. 738
ZELLER CORP.; *U.S. Private*, pg. 1204
ZELLER WORLD TRADE CORPORATION—See Zeller Corp.; *U.S. Private*, pg. 1204
ZELLERBACH DIVISION—See The Mead Corporation; *U.S. Public*, pg. 1075
ZELLERS INC.—See Hudson's Bay Company; *Int'l*, pg. 637
ZELLWEGER-ECO-SYSTEME GMBH—See Hesta Tex AG; *Int'l*, pg. 618
ZELLWEGER ENERGIETECHNIK GMBH—See Hesta Tex AG; *Int'l*, pg. 618
ZELLWEGER ENERGY SYSTEMS—See Hesta Tex AG; *Int'l*, pg. 618
ZELLWEGER FINANZ AG—See Hesta Tex AG; *Int'l*, pg. 618
ZELLWEGER LTD.—See Hesta Tex AG; *Int'l*, pg. 618
ZELLWEGER LUWA—See Hesta Tex AG; *Int'l*, pg. 618
ZELLWEGER PTY. LTD.—See Hesta Tex AG; *Int'l*, pg. 618
ZELLWEGER S.A.—See Hesta Tex AG; *Int'l*, pg. 618
ZELLWEGER-SAUTER-ENERGIE S.A.—See Hesta Tex AG; *Int'l*, pg. 618
ZELLWEGER USTER AG—See Hesta Tex AG; *Int'l*, pg. 618
ZELLWEGER USTER GMBH—See Hesta Tex AG; *Int'l*, pg. 618
ZELLWEGER USTER, INC.—See Hesta Tex AG; *Int'l*, pg. 618
ZELLWEGER USTER KK—See Hesta Tex AG; *Int'l*, pg. 618
ZELTRON S.P.A.—See Electrolux, AB; *Int'l*, pg. 443
ZEMCO INDUSTRIES, INC.; *U.S. Private*, pg. 1204
ZEMENICK & WALKER, INC.—See Firstbank of Illinois Co.; *U.S. Public*, pg. 644
ZEMENTWERKE LABATLAN GMBH—See Holderbank Financiere Glaris Ltd.; *Int'l*, pg. 629
ZEMEX CORPORATION; *Int'l*, pg. 1523
ZENCO DE CHIHUAHUA, S.A. DE C.V.—See Zenith Electronics Corp.; *U.S. Public*, pg. 1790
ZENECA AG—See Zeneca Group Plc; *Int'l*, pg. 1526
ZENECA AG—See Zeneca Group Plc; *Int'l*, pg. 1526
ZENECA AG PRODUCTS—See Zeneca Group Plc; *Int'l*, pg. 1525
PT ZENECA AGRI PRODUCTS INDONESIA—See Zeneca Group Plc; *Int'l*, pg. 1526
ZENECA AGRO—See Zeneca Group Plc; *Int'l*, pg. 1526
ZENECA AGRO GMBH—See Zeneca Group Plc; *Int'l*, pg. 1526
ZENECA AGRO-PRODUTOS PARA A AGRICULTURA LDA—See Zeneca Group Plc; *Int'l*, pg. 1526
ZENECA AGRO SA—See Zeneca Group Plc; *Int'l*, pg. 1526
ZENECA AGROCHEMICALS—See Zeneca Group Plc; *Int'l*, pg. 1526
ZENECA AGROCHEMICALS AND SEEDS—See Zeneca Group Plc; *Int'l*, pg. 1524
ZENECA AGROCHEMICALS MAROC S.A.—See Zeneca Group Plc; *Int'l*, pg. 1526
ZENECA ALMATY—See Zeneca Group Plc; *Int'l*, pg. 1526
ZENECA A/S—See Zeneca Group Plc; *Int'l*, pg. 1526
ZENECA AS—See Zeneca Group Plc; *Int'l*, pg. 1526

ZENECA BIO PRODUCTS—See Zeneca Group Plc; *Int'l*, pg. 1524
ZENECA BIOCIDES—See Zeneca Group Plc; *Int'l*, pg. 1524
ZENECA BRASIL S.A.—See Zeneca Group Plc; *Int'l*, pg. 1526
ZENECA BULGARIA—See Zeneca Group Plc; *Int'l*, pg. 1526
ZENECA B.V.—See Zeneca Group Plc; *Int'l*, pg. 1526
ZENECA CHINA LTD.—See Zeneca Group Plc; *Int'l*, pg. 1526
ZENECA COLOURS—See Zeneca Group Plc; *Int'l*, pg. 1526
PT ZENECA COLOURS INDONESIA—See Zeneca Group Plc; *Int'l*, pg. 1526
ZENECA CORP.—See Zeneca Group Plc; *Int'l*, pg. 1526
ZENECA COSTA RICA, S.A.—See Zeneca Group Plc; *Int'l*, pg. 1526
ZENECA (CZ) S.R.O.—See Zeneca Group Plc; *Int'l*, pg. 1526
ZENECA DIAGNOSTICS—See Zeneca Group Plc; *Int'l*, pg. 1524
ZENECA DOMINICANA SA—See Zeneca Group Plc; *Int'l*, pg. 1526
ZENECA ELLESMERE PORT WORKS—See Zeneca Group Plc; *Int'l*, pg. 1524
ZENECA ENGINEERING—See Zeneca Group Plc; *Int'l*, pg. 1525
ZENECA FARMA—See Zeneca Group Plc; *Int'l*, pg. 1526
ZENECA GRANGEMOUTH WORKS—See Zeneca Group Plc; *Int'l*, pg. 1524
ZENECA GROUP PLC; *Int'l*, pg. 1524
ZENECA HELLAS S.A.—See Zeneca Group Plc; *Int'l*, pg. 1526
ZENECA HUDDERSFIELD WORKS—See Zeneca Group Plc; *Int'l*, pg. 1524
ZENECA HUNGARY KFT.—See Zeneca Group Plc; *Int'l*, pg. 1526
ZENECA ICI AGROCHEMICALS—See Zeneca Group Plc; *Int'l*, pg. 1526
ZENECA INC.—See Zeneca Group Plc; *Int'l*, pg. 1525
ZENECA INC. (BAYPORT)—See Zeneca Group Plc; *Int'l*, pg. 1525
ZENECA INTERNATIONAL LTD.—See Zeneca Group Plc; *Int'l*, pg. 1526
ZENECA INTERNATIONAL LTD., CUBA—See Zeneca Group Plc; *Int'l*, pg. 1526
ZENECA IRELAND LTD.—See Zeneca Group Plc; *Int'l*, pg. 1526
ZENECA KIEV—See Zeneca Group Plc; *Int'l*, pg. 1526
ZENECA KK—See Zeneca Group Plc; *Int'l*, pg. 1526
ZENECA KUBANJ—See Zeneca Group Plc; *Int'l*, pg. 1527
ZENECA MEXICAN S.A. DE C.V.—See Zeneca Group Plc; *Int'l*, pg. 1527
ZENECA MEXICANA SA DE CV—See Zeneca Group Plc; *Int'l*, pg. 1527
ZENECA MINSK—See Zeneca Group Plc; *Int'l*, pg. 1527
ZENECA NICARAGUA—See Zeneca Group Plc; *Int'l*, pg. 1527
ZENECA NV—See Zeneca Group Plc; *Int'l*, pg. 1527
ZENECA OSTERREICH GMBH—See Zeneca Group Plc; *Int'l*, pg. 1527
ZENECA OY—See Zeneca Group Plc; *Int'l*, pg. 1527
ZENECA PANAMERICANA S.A.—See BASF AG; *Int'l*, pg. 110
ZENECA PANAMERICANA S.A.—See Zeneca Group Plc; *Int'l*, pg. 1527
ZENECA PHARMA—See Zeneca Group Plc; *Int'l*, pg. 1524
ZENECA PHARMA INC.—See Zeneca Group Plc; *Int'l*, pg. 1527
ZENECA PHARMA INTERNATIONAL—See Zeneca Group Plc; *Int'l*, pg. 1527
ZENECA-PHARMA S.A.—See Zeneca Group Plc; *Int'l*, pg. 1527
ZENECA PHARMACEUTICALS—See Zeneca Group Plc; *Int'l*, pg. 1524
ZENECA PLANT SCIENCE—See Zeneca Group Plc; *Int'l*, pg. 1525
ZENECA POLAND SP. Z.O.O.—See Zeneca Group Plc; *Int'l*, pg. 1527
ZENECA PRODUTOS BIOCIENCIA, LDA—See Zeneca Group Plc; *Int'l*, pg. 1527
ZENECA RESINS—See Zeneca Group Plc; *Int'l*, pg. 1524
ZENECA RESINS BV—See Zeneca Group Plc; *Int'l*, pg. 1527
ZENECA RESINS HILLHOUSE INTERNATIONAL—See Zeneca Group Plc; *Int'l*, pg. 1524
ZENECA RESINS PTE. LTD.—See Zeneca Group Plc; *Int'l*, pg. 1527
ZENECA RESINS SA—See Zeneca Group Plc; *Int'l*, pg. 1527
ZENECA RESINS US—See Zeneca Group Plc; *Int'l*, pg. 1525
ZENECA ROMANIA—See Zeneca Group Plc; *Int'l*, pg. 1527
ZENECA SA—See Zeneca Group Plc; *Int'l*, pg. 1527
ZENECA SAIC—See Zeneca Group Plc; *Int'l*, pg. 1527
ZENECA SEEDS—See Zeneca Group Plc; *Int'l*, pg. 1524
ZENECA SEMENTES DO BRASIL—See Zeneca Group Plc; *Int'l*, pg. 1527
ZENECA SINO-PHARMA DEVELOPMENT CONSULTANCY COMPANY LIMITED—See Zeneca Group Plc; *Int'l*, pg. 1527
ZENECA SLOVAKIA S.R.O.—See Zeneca Group Plc; *Int'l*, pg. 1527
ZENECA SOPRA—See Zeneca Group Plc; *Int'l*, pg. 1527
ZENECA SOPRA SA—See Zeneca Group Plc; *Int'l*, pg. 1527
ZENECA SPECIALTIES—See Zeneca Group Plc; *Int'l*, pg. 1524
ZENECA SPECIALTIES SA—See Zeneca Group Plc; *Int'l*, pg. 1527
ZENECA SPECIALTY INKS—See Zeneca Group Plc; *Int'l*, pg. 1525

ZENECA TEXTILE COLOURS—See Zeneca Group Plc; Int'l, pg. 1527
ZENECA TURKIYE—See Zeneca Group Plc; Int'l, pg. 1527
ZENECA TURKIYE LTD. (AGROCHEMICALS)—See Zeneca Group Plc; Int'l, pg. 1527
ZENECA URUGUAY—See Zeneca Group Plc; Int'l, pg. 1527
ZENECA ZIMBABWE (PRIVATE) LIMITED—See Zeneca Group Plc; Int'l, pg. 1527
ZENGER-MILLER—See The Times Mirror Company; U.S. Public, pg. 1617
ZENIMMO N.V.—See Borden, Inc.; U.S. Private, pg. 160
ZENITH ADMINISTRATORS, INC.—See ULLICO Inc.; U.S. Private, pg. 1116
ZENITH CONSTRUCTION CO, INC.—See Jenkins & Associates; U.S. Private, pg. 585
ZENITH DATA SYSTEMS—See Compagnie des Machines Bull; Int'l, pg. 316
ZENITH DATA SYSTEMS B.V.—See Compagnie des Machines Bull; Int'l, pg. 317
ZENITH DATA SYSTEMS ESPANA S.A.—See Compagnie des Machines Bull; Int'l, pg. 317
ZENITH DATA SYSTEMS EUROPE—See Compagnie des Machines Bull; Int'l, pg. 316
ZENITH DATA SYSTEMS GMBH—See Compagnie des Machines Bull; Int'l, pg. 317
ZENITH DATA SYSTEMS INTERNATIONAL INC.—See Compagnie des Machines Bull; Int'l, pg. 317
ZENITH DATA SYSTEMS IRELAND LTD.—See Compagnie des Machines Bull; Int'l, pg. 317
ZENITH DATA SYSTEMS ITALIA S.P.A.—See Compagnie des Machines Bull; Int'l, pg. 318
ZENITH DATA SYSTEMS LTD.—See Compagnie des Machines Bull; Int'l, pg. 318
ZENITH DATA SYSTEMS N.V.—See Compagnie des Machines Bull; Int'l, pg. 318
ZENITH ELECTRONICS CORP.; U.S. Public, pg. 1790
ZENITH ELECTRONICS CORP. OF TX—See Zenith Electronics Corp.; U.S. Public, pg. 1790
ZENITH FINANCE & CONSTRUCTION CO.—See Commercial Metals Company; U.S. Public, pg. 413
ZENITH GOLDLINE PHARMACEUTICALS—See IVAX Corporation; U.S. Public, pg. 915
ZENITH MEDIA SERVICES, INC.; U.S. Private, pg. 1204
ZENITH MEDIA SERVICES, INC.—See Zenith Media Services, Inc.; U.S. Private, pg. 1204
ZENITH NATIONAL INSURANCE CORP.; U.S. Public, pg. 1790
ZENITH PRODUCTS CORP.—See Masco Corporation; U.S. Public, pg. 1054
ZENITH PUMPS DIV.—See Parker Hannifin Corporation; U.S. Public, pg. 1261
ZENITH SALES CO. DIV.—See Zenith Electronics Corp.; U.S. Public, pg. 1790
ZENITH VERSICHERUNG AG—See Alte Leipziger Versicherung Aktiengesellschaft; Int'l, pg. 66
ZENITH VIDEO TECH CORPORATION—See Zenith Electronics Corp.; U.S. Public, pg. 1790
ZENITH VIE—See Groupe GAN; Int'l, pg. 565
ZENITH WEST CORP.—See Masco Corporation; U.S. Public, pg. 1054
ZENKER-FENSTER GMBH & CO KG—See Philipp Holzmann AG; Int'l, pg. 633
ZENKER HAUSBAU GMBH & CO.—See Philipp Holzmann AG; Int'l, pg. 633
THE ZENSHINREN BANK; Int'l, pg. 1527
ZENTOX CORP.; U.S. Private, pg. 1204
ZENTOX NEPCCO—See Zentox Corp.; U.S. Private, pg. 1204
ZENTRANS, INC.—See Zenith Electronics Corp.; U.S. Public, pg. 1790
ZEOFINN OY—See J.M. Huber Corporation; U.S. Private, pg. 545
ZEOLYST INTERNATIONAL—See PQ Corporation; U.S. Private, pg. 827
ZEP EUROPE B.V.—See National Service Industries, Inc.; U.S. Public, pg. 1160
ZEP MANUFACTURING—See National Service Industries, Inc.; U.S. Public, pg. 1160
ZEP MANUFACTURING COMPANY—See National Service Industries, Inc.; U.S. Public, pg. 1160
ZEPHYER PROPERTIES, INC.—See The Mead Corporation; U.S. Public, pg. 1076
ZEPHYR INC.; U.S. Private, pg. 1204
ZEPHYR MFG. CO.—See Standun, Inc.; U.S. Private, pg. 1032
ZEPHYRHILLS WATER CORP.—See Nestle S.A.; Int'l, pg. 919
ZEPT TECHNOLOGIES—See Barry-Wehmiller Company; U.S. Private, pg. 118
ZERAND DIVISION—See Stevens International, Inc.; U.S. Public, pg. 1517
ZEREC CORP.—See Ashland, Inc.; U.S. Public, pg. 139
A. ZEREGAS SONS, INC.; U.S. Private, pg. 1204
ZERO CORPORATION; U.S. Public, pg. 1791
ZERO-MAX, INC.—See Miki Pulley Co., Ltd.; Int'l, pg. 866
ZERO PLASTICS—See Zero Corporation; U.S. Public, pg. 1791
ZERO STANTRON CABINETS—See Zero Corporation; U.S. Public, pg. 1791
SA 02 TECHNOLOGIE—See Compagnie des Machines Bull; Int'l, pg. 316
ZEROWATT S.P.A.—See Candy S.p.A.; Int'l, pg. 260
ZETA FINANZA S.P.A.—See Zurich Insurance Company; Int'l, pg. 1531
ZETA HOME HEALTH CARE, INC.—See Integrated Health Services, Inc.; U.S. Public, pg. 885
ZETEC, INC.; U.S. Private, pg. 1205
ZETRONIC S.P.A.—See Molex Incorporated; U.S. Public, pg. 1122
ALOIS ZETTLER ELECKTROTECHNISCHE FABRIK GMBH; Int'l, pg. 1528

ZEUS COMPONENTS DIVISION - INTERNATIONAL SALES DIV.—See Arrow Electronics, Inc.; U.S. Public, pg. 134
ZEXEL CORPORATION; Int'l, pg. 1528
ZEXEL CORPORATION-AKITA OFFICE—See Zexel Corporation; Int'l, pg. 1528
ZEXEL CORPORATION-AOMORI OFFICE—See Zexel Corporation; Int'l, pg. 1528
ZEXEL CORPORATION BANGKOK REPRESENTATIVE OFFICE—See Zexel Corporation; Int'l, pg. 1528
ZEXEL CORPORATION BEIJING REPRESENTATIVE OFFICE—See Zexel Corporation; Int'l, pg. 1528
ZEXEL CORPORATION HANOVER REPRESENTATIVE OFFICE—See Zexel Corporation; Int'l, pg. 1528
ZEXEL CORPORATION-HIROSHIMA—See Zexel Corporation; Int'l, pg. 1528
ZEXEL CORPORATION JAKARTA REPRESENTATIVE OFFICE—See Zexel Corporation; Int'l, pg. 1528
ZEXEL CORPORATION-KANAZAWA OFFICE—See Zexel Corporation; Int'l, pg. 1528
ZEXEL CORPORATION-KUSHIRO OFFICE—See Zexel Corporation; Int'l, pg. 1528
ZEXEL CORPORATION-MITO OFFICE—See Zexel Corporation; Int'l, pg. 1528
ZEXEL CORPORATION-NAGANO OFFICE—See Zexel Corporation; Int'l, pg. 1528
ZEXEL CORPORATION-NAGOYA—See Zexel Corporation; Int'l, pg. 1528
ZEXEL CORPORATION-NIIGATA OFFICE—See Zexel Corporation; Int'l, pg. 1528
ZEXEL CORPORATION-OKAYAMA OFFICE—See Zexel Corporation; Int'l, pg. 1528
ZEXEL CORPORATION-OSAKA—See Zexel Corporation; Int'l, pg. 1528
ZEXEL CORPORATION-SAPPORO—See Zexel Corporation; Int'l, pg. 1528
ZEXEL CORPORATION-SENDAI—See Zexel Corporation; Int'l, pg. 1528
ZEXEL CORPORATION SEOUL REPRESENTATIVE OFFICE—See Zexel Corporation; Int'l, pg. 1528
ZEXEL CORPORATION-SHIKI OFFICE—See Zexel Corporation; Int'l, pg. 1528
ZEXEL CORPORATION-SHIZUOKA OFFICE—See Zexel Corporation; Int'l, pg. 1528
ZEXEL CORPORATION TAIPEI REPRESENTATIVE OFFICE—See Zexel Corporation; Int'l, pg. 1528
ZEXEL CORPORATION-TAKAMATSU—See Zexel Corporation; Int'l, pg. 1528
ZEXEL CORPORATION-TOKYO—See Zexel Corporation; Int'l, pg. 1528
ZEXEL ILLINOIS INC.—See Zexel Corporation; Int'l, pg. 1528
ZEXEL INC.—See Zexel Corporation; Int'l, pg. 1528
ZEXEL R&D CENTER—See Zexel Corporation; Int'l, pg. 1528
ZEXEL USA CORPORATION—See Zexel Corporation; Int'l, pg. 1348
ZHONG DA ENTERPRISE CORP.—See Taisei Corporation; Int'l, pg. 1348
ZHUHAI BROTHER INDUSTRIES CO., LTD.—See Brother Industries, Ltd.; Int'l, pg. 230
ZHUHAI GOLDEN COAST WINNER FOOD PRODUCTS LTD.—See Nissin Food Products Co., Ltd.; Int'l, pg. 950
ZICCARDI & PARTNERS, INC.; U.S. Private, pg. 1205
ZICKENHUIS DIENSTEN GROEP—See Vendex International N.V.; Int'l, pg. 1463
ZIEBART CANADA, INC.—See Ziebart International Corporation; U.S. Private, pg. 1205
ZIEBART CORP.—See Ziebart International Corporation; U.S. Private, pg. 1205
ZIEBART INTERNATIONAL CORPORATION; U.S. Private, pg. 1205
ZIEGELWERKE GLEINSTATTEN CSORNA-BELED CESEREPGYARTO RT.—See Redland PLC; Int'l, pg. 1092
ZIEGELWERKE GLEINSTATTEN GMBH & CO. KG—See Redland PLC; Int'l, pg. 1092
ALFRED ZIEGLER MOLKEREI SCHLUCTERN GMBH & CO. KG—See Nutricia BV; Int'l, pg. 992
ZIEGLER ASSET MANAGEMENT, INC.—See The Ziegler Companies, Inc.; U.S. Public, pg. 1792
B.C. ZIEGLER & CO.—See The Ziegler Companies, Inc.; U.S. Public, pg. 1792
ZIEGLER CHEMICAL & MINERAL CORP.; U.S. Private, pg. 1205
ZIEGLER COLLATERALIZED SECURITIES, INC.—See The Ziegler Companies, Inc.; U.S. Public, pg. 1792
THE ZIEGLER COMPANIES, INC.; U.S. Public, pg. 1791
ZIEGLER FINANCING CORP.—See The Ziegler Companies, Inc.; U.S. Public, pg. 1792
HAROLD ZIEGLER FORD-ELKHART; U.S. Private, pg. 1205
ZIEGLER INC.; U.S. Private, pg. 1205
ZIEGLER LEASING CORP—See The Ziegler Companies, Inc.; U.S. Public, pg. 1792
ZIEGLER MEDICAL EQUIPMENT GROUP, INC.—See The Ziegler Companies, Inc.; U.S. Public, pg. 1792
ZIEGLER SECURITIES DIVISION—See The Ziegler Companies, Inc.; U.S. Public, pg. 1792
ZIEGLER THRIFT TRADING, INC.—See The Ziegler Companies, Inc.; U.S. Public, pg. 1792
ZIEGLER TIRE & SUPPLY COMPANY, INC.; U.S. Private, pg. 1205
ZIEMAN MANUFACTURING COMPANY; U.S. Private, pg. 1205
ZIFF-DAVIS BUSINESS MEDIA GROUP—See Softbank Corporation; Int'l, pg. 1276
ZIFF-DAVIS CONSUMER MEDIA GROUP—See Softbank Corporation; Int'l, pg. 1276
ZIFF-DAVIS FRANCE SARL—See Softbank Corporation; Int'l, pg. 1276
ZIFF-DAVIS GERMANY—See Softbank Corporation; Int'l, pg. 1276

ZIFF-DAVIS INTERACTIVE—See Softbank Corporation; Int'l, pg. 1276
ZIFF-DAVIS INTERNATIONAL MEDIA GROUP—See Softbank Corporation; Int'l, pg. 1276
ZIFF-DAVIS MARKETING & DEVELOPMENT—See Softbank Corporation; Int'l, pg. 1276
ZIFF-DAVIS PUBLISHING COMPANY—See Softbank Corporation; Int'l, pg. 1276
ZIFF-DAVIS TAIWAN—See Softbank Corporation; Int'l, pg. 1276
ZIFF-DAVIS U.K.—See Softbank Corporation; Int'l, pg. 1276
ZIFF INFORMATION SERVICES—See Softbank Corporation; Int'l, pg. 1276
ZIFF TECHNOLOGIES—See Softbank Corporation; Int'l, pg. 1276
ZIG-ZAG FABRIKS AB—See Electrolux, AB; Int'l, pg. 439
ZILBER, LTD.; U.S. Private, pg. 1206
AVEDIS ZILDJIAN COMPANY; U.S. Private, pg. 1206
ZIM-AMERICAN ISRAELI SHIPPING CO.; U.S. Private, pg. 1206
ZIM CONTAINER SERVICE—See Zim-American Israeli Shipping Co.; U.S. Private, pg. 1206
ZIMA CORPORATION—See Kusters Corporation; U.S. Private, pg. 637
ZIMBABWE ELECTRICITY SUPPLY AUTHORITY; Int'l, pg. 1528
ZIMBABWE PROJECT OFFICE—See Nishimatsu Construction Co., Ltd.; Int'l, pg. 943
ZIMBRA INDUSTRIA E COMERCIO LTDA.—See Bristol-Myers Squibb Company; U.S. Public, pg. 257
ZIMDAR ENTERPRISES/FRAMES UNLIMITED; U.S. Private, pg. 1206
ZIMLEAF HOLDINGS LIMITED—See Universal Corporation; U.S. Public, pg. 1695
ZIMMER AUSTRALIA PTY. LIMITED—See Bristol-Myers Squibb Company; U.S. Public, pg. 256
ZIMMER CHIRUGIE G.M.B.H.—See Bristol-Myers Squibb Company; U.S. Public, pg. 256
ZIMMER CUSTOM-MADE PACKAGING CO.—See Norse Dairy Systems; U.S. Private, pg. 802
ZIMMER, INC.—See Bristol-Myers Squibb Company; U.S. Public, pg. 254
ZIMMER INTERNATIONAL, S.A.—See Bristol-Myers Squibb Company; U.S. Public, pg. 257
ZIMMER LIMITED—See Bristol-Myers Squibb Company; U.S. Public, pg. 257
ZIMMER NEW ZEALAND LIMITED—See Bristol-Myers Squibb Company; U.S. Public, pg. 257
ZIMMER OF CANADA LIMITED—See Bristol-Myers Squibb Company; U.S. Public, pg. 257
ZIMMER ORTHOPAEDIC IMPLANT DIVISION—See Bristol-Myers Squibb Company; U.S. Public, pg. 254
ZIMMER PATIENT CARE SYSTEMS DIVISION—See Bristol-Myers Squibb Company; U.S. Public, pg. 254
ZIMMER PTE LTD.—See Bristol-Myers Squibb Company; U.S. Public, pg. 257
ZIMMER S.A.—See Bristol-Myers Squibb Company; U.S. Public, pg. 257
ZIMMER SPAIN S.A.—See Bristol-Myers Squibb Company; U.S. Public, pg. 257
ZIMMERLUND & CO.—See Amcor Limited; Int'l, pg. 72
ZIMMERMAN & PARTNERS ADVERTISING, INC.; U.S. Private, pg. 1206
ZIMMERMAN & PARTNERS ADVERTISING, INC.—See Zimmerman & Partners Advertising, Inc.; U.S. Private, pg. 1206
ZIMMERMAN HOLDINGS, INC.; U.S. Private, pg. 1206
ZIMMERMANN & JANSEN GMBH; Int'l, pg. 1528
ZIMMERMANN & JANSEN INC.—See Zimmermann & Jansen GmbH; Int'l, pg. 1528
ZIMMERMANN & JANSEN S.A. (PTY.) LTD.—See Zimmermann & Jansen GmbH; Int'l, pg. 1529
ZIN-PLAS CORPORATION—See Park Electrochemical Corporation; U.S. Public, pg. 1258
ZINC CORPORATION OF AMERICA—See Horsehead Industries, Inc.; U.S. Private, pg. 540
ZINC PRODUCTS COMPANY—See Alltrista Corporation; U.S. Public, pg. 57
ZING TECHNOLOGIES, INC.; U.S. Public, pg. 1792
ZINIZ INC.; U.S. Private, pg. 1206
ZINK & TRIEST—See A.M. Todd Company; U.S. Private, pg. 1090
JOHN ZINK CO.—See Koch Industries, Incorporated; U.S. Private, pg. 628
WM. ZINSSER & CO., INC.—See RPM, Inc.; U.S. Public, pg. 1358
ZIONS BANCORPORATION; U.S. Public, pg. 1792
ZIONS CO-OPERATIVE MERCANTILE INSTITUTION; U.S. Public, pg. 1793
ZIONS CREDIT CORPORATION—See Zions Bancorporation; U.S. Public, pg. 1793
ZIONS DATA SERVICE CO.—See Zions Bancorporation; U.S. Public, pg. 1793
ZIONS FIRST NATIONAL BANK—See Zions Bancorporation; U.S. Public, pg. 1793
ZIONS INSURANCE AGENCY, INC.—See Zions Bancorporation; U.S. Public, pg. 1793
ZIONS INVESTMENT SECURITIES, INC.—See Zions Bancorporation; U.S. Public, pg. 1793
ZIONS LIFE INSURANCE CO.—See Zions Bancorporation; U.S. Public, pg. 1793
ZIONS MORTGAGE COMPANY—See Zions Bancorporation; U.S. Public, pg. 1793
ZION'S SECURITIES CORP.—See Deseret Management Corporation; U.S. Private, pg. 327
ZIONSVILLE WATER CORPORATION—See NIPSCO Industries, Inc.; U.S. Public, pg. 1185
ZIPP INDUSTRIES; U.S. Private, pg. 1207
THE ZIPPERTUBING CO.; U.S. Private, pg. 1207
ZIPPO EUROPE S.A.—See Zippo Manufacturing Company; U.S. Private, pg. 1207
ZIPPO FRANCE S.A.—See Zippo Manufacturing Company; U.S. Private, pg. 1207

ZIPPO MANUFACTURING COMPANY; *U.S. Private*, pg. 1207

ZIPPO MANUFACTURING COMPANY OF CANADA LIMITED—See Zippo Manufacturing Company; *U.S. Private*, pg. 1207

ZIPPY MART, INC.—See Crown Central Petroleum Corporation; *U.S. Public*, pg. 462

ZIRCOTUBE—See Framatome SA; *Int'l*, pg. 503

ZITEL CORPORATION; *U.S. Public*, pg. 1793

ZITEL INTERNATIONAL CORP.—See Zitel Corporation; *U.S. Public*, pg. 1794

ZIVI S.A. CUTELARIA; *Int'l*, pg. 1529

ZODIAC HOLDINGS LTD.—See Alusuisse-Lonza Holding Ltd.; *Int'l*, pg. 69

ZODIAC PRINT PROCESSES LTD.—See Alusuisse-Lonza Holding Ltd.; *Int'l*, pg. 69

AB ZOEGAS KAFFE—See Nestle S.A.; *Int'l*, pg. 922

ZOELLER CO.; *U.S. Private*, pg. 1207

ZOLL FOOD CORP.—See ConAgra, Inc.; *U.S. Public*, pg. 426

ZOLL MEDICAL CORPORATION; *U.S. Private*, pg. 1207

ZOLLFREIZONEN-BETRIEBE GMBH—See Panalpina Welttransport (Holding) AG; *Int'l*, pg. 1023

ZOLTEK COMPANIES, INC.; *U.S. Public*, pg. 1794

ZOMBA GROUP OF COMPANIES—See Zomba Recording Corp.; *Int'l*, pg. 1529

ZOMBA PRODUCTION MUSIC (AUSTRALIA) PTY LIMITED—See Zomba Recording Corp.; *Int'l*, pg. 1529

ZOMBA RECORDING CORP.; *Int'l*, pg. 1529

THE ZONDERVAN CORPORATION—See The News Corporation Limited; *Int'l*, pg. 927

ZONE VI STUDIOS, INC.—See Calumet Photographic, Inc.; *U.S. Private*, pg. 202

ZONEX AB—See Telefonaktiebolaget LM Ericsson; *Int'l*, pg. 1364

ZONNATURA/PHARMAFOOD B.V.—See Nutricia BV; *Int'l*, pg. 991

ZOOLOGICAL SOCIETY OF SAN DIEGO; *U.S. Private*, pg. 1207

ZOOM TELEPHONICS, INC.; *U.S. Public*, pg. 1794

ZORTMAN MINING INC.—See Pegasus Gold Corporation; *U.S. Public*, pg. 1269

ZOTOS INTERNATIONAL—See Shiseido Company Ltd.; *Int'l*, pg. 1236

ZUCKERMAN-HONICKMAN INC.; *U.S. Private*, pg. 1207

ZUCO BUROSITZMOBEL AG—See Lista Holding AG; *Int'l*, pg. 812

ZUERCHER LAGERHAUS AG; *Int'l*, pg. 1529

ZUIDERHOUT B.V.—See Koninklijke BolsWessanen nv; *Int'l*, pg. 751

ZUIVELFABRIEK 'SALLAND' BV—See Koninklijke BolsWessanen nv; *Int'l*, pg. 752

ZUIVELONDERNEMING DE VIJFHEERENLANDEN B.V.—See Koninklijke BolsWessanen nv; *Int'l*, pg. 751

ZUIVELONDERNEMING DE VIJFHEERENLANDEN' B.V.—See Koninklijke BolsWessanen nv; *Int'l*, pg. 752

AG ZUM ALTEN ZEUGHAUS—See Feldschlosschen Hurlimann Holding; *Int'l*, pg. 479

C.W. ZUMBIEL COMPANY; *U.S. Private*, pg. 1207

ZUNG FU COMPANY LTD.—See Jardine Matheson Holdings Limited; *Int'l*, pg. 704

ZURICH AMERICAN INSURANCE COMPANY OF ILLINOIS—See Zurich Insurance Company; *Int'l*, pg. 1530

ZURICH AMERICAN LLOYDS—See Zurich Insurance Company; *Int'l*, pg. 1530

ZURICH-ANGLO SEGURADORA S.A.—See Zurich Insurance Company; *Int'l*, pg. 1532

ZURICH AUSTRALIAN INSURANCE LIMITED—See Zurich Insurance Company; *Int'l*, pg. 1531

ZURICH AUSTRALIAN INSURANCE LTD.—See Zurich Insurance Company; *Int'l*, pg. 1531

ZURICH AUSTRALIAN LIFE INSURANCE LIMITED—See Zurich Insurance Company; *Int'l*, pg. 1531

ZURICH BIZTOSITO RT.—See Zurich Insurance Company; *Int'l*, pg. 1532

ZURICH COMPAGNIE D'ASSURANCES—See Zurich Insurance Company; *Int'l*, pg. 1530

ZURICH COMPAGNIE D'ASSURANCES SUR LA VIE—See Zurich Insurance Company; *Int'l*, pg. 1529

ZURICH COMPANIA DE SEGUROS—See Zurich Insurance Company; *Int'l*, pg. 1531

ZURICH COMPANIA DE SEGUROS S.A.—See Zurich Insurance Company; *Int'l*, pg. 1531

ZURICH COMPANIA DE SEGUROS SOBRE LA VIDA—See Zurich Insurance Company; *Int'l*, pg. 1529

ZURICH EPARGNE—See Zurich Insurance Company; *Int'l*, pg. 1531

ZURICH EUROLIFE S.A.—See Zurich Insurance Company; *Int'l*, pg. 1531

ZURICH FORSAKRING—See Zurich Insurance Company; *Int'l*, pg. 1531

ZURICH IGUAZU COMPANIA DE SEGUROS DE RETIRO S.A.—See Zurich Insurance Company; *Int'l*, pg. 1532

ZURICH INDEMNITY COMPANY OF CANADA—See Zurich Insurance Company; *Int'l*, pg. 1531

ZURICH INSURANCE COMPANY; *Int'l*, pg. 1529

ZURICH INSURANCE COMPANY—See Zurich Insurance Company; *Int'l*, pg. 1531

ZURICH INSURANCE COMPANY (ASIA) LIMITED—See Zurich Insurance Company; *Int'l*, pg. 1532

ZURICH INSURANCE COMPANY REGIONAL REINSURANCE—See Zurich Insurance Company; *Int'l*, pg. 1532

ZURICH INSURANCE COMPANY REINSURANCE—See Zurich Insurance Company; *Int'l*, pg. 1529

ZURICH INSURANCE (GUAM), INC.—See Zurich Insurance Company; *Int'l*, pg. 1532

P.T. ZURICH INSURANCE INDONESIA—See Zurich Insurance Company; *Int'l*, pg. 1532

ZURICH INSURANCE (MALAYSIA) SDN. BHD.—See Zurich Insurance Company; *Int'l*, pg. 1532

ZURICH INSURANCE SERVICES (MIDDLE EAST) E.C.—See Zurich Insurance Company; *Int'l*, pg. 1532

ZURICH INSURANCE (SINGAPORE) PTE. LTD.—See Zurich Insurance Company; *Int'l*, pg. 1532

ZURICH INTERNATIONAL (BELGIQUE) S.A.—See Zurich Insurance Company; *Int'l*, pg. 1532

ZURICH INTERNATIONAL (BERMUDA) LTD.—See Zurich Insurance Company; *Int'l*, pg. 1532

ZURICH INTERNATIONAL DE VENEZUELA C.A. DE CORRETAJE DE REASEGUROS—See Zurich Insurance Company; *Int'l*, pg. 1532

ZURICH INTERNATIONAL (DEUTSCHLAND) VERSICHERUNGS-AKTIENGESELLSCHAFT—See Zurich Insurance Company; *Int'l*, pg. 1532

ZURICH INTERNATIONAL (ESPANA) COMPANIA DE SEGUROS Y REASEGUROS, S.A.—See Zurich Insurance Company; *Int'l*, pg. 1532

ZURICH INTERNATIONAL (FRANCE) S.A.—See Zurich Insurance Company; *Int'l*, pg. 1532

ZURICH INTERNATIONAL (ITALIA) S.P.A.—See Zurich Insurance Company; *Int'l*, pg. 1532

ZURICH INTERNATIONAL (NEDERLAND) N.V.—See Zurich Insurance Company; *Int'l*, pg. 1532

ZURICH INTERNATIONAL SERVICES (IRELAND) LIMITED—See Zurich Insurance Company; *Int'l*, pg. 1532

ZURICH INTERNATIONAL SERVICES (LUXEMBOURG) S.A.—See Zurich Insurance Company; *Int'l*, pg. 1532

ZURICH INTERNATIONAL (UK) LIMITED—See Zurich Insurance Company; *Int'l*, pg. 1532

ZURICH INVESTMENT MANAGEMENT—See Zurich Insurance Company; *Int'l*, pg. 1532

ZURICH INVESTMENT MANAGEMENT LTD.—See Zurich Insurance Company; *Int'l*, pg. 1532

ZURICH INVESTMENTGESELLSCHAFT MBH—See Zurich Insurance Company; *Int'l*, pg. 1532

ZURICH KAUTIONS-UND KREDITVERSICHERUNGS-AKTIENGESELLSCHAFT—See Zurich Insurance Company; *Int'l*, pg. 1532

ZURICH KEMPER INVESTMENTS, INC.—See Zurich Insurance Company; *Int'l*, pg. 1530

ZURICH KOSMOS VERSICHERUNGEN AG—See Zurich Insurance Company; *Int'l*, pg. 1532

ZURICH LEBENVERSICHERUNGS-GESELLSCHAFT—See Zurich Insurance Company; *Int'l*, pg. 1529

ZURICH LEVENSVERZEKERING-MAATSCHAPPIJ—See Zurich Insurance Company; *Int'l*, pg. 1529

ZURICH LIFE ASSURANCE COMPANY LIMITED—See Zurich Insurance Company; *Int'l*, pg. 1532

ZURICH LIFE INSURANCE CO. OF CANADA—See Zurich Insurance Company; *Int'l*, pg. 1532

ZURICH LIFE INSURANCE COMPANY—See Zurich Insurance Company; *Int'l*, pg. 1529

ZURICH LIFE INSURANCE COMPANY LIMITED—See Zurich Insurance Company; *Int'l*, pg. 1532

ZURICH LIFE INSURANCE COMPANY LTD.—See Zurich Insurance Company; *Int'l*, pg. 1530

ZURICH LIFE INSURANCE COMPANY OF AMERICA—See Zurich Insurance Company; *Int'l*, pg. 1530

ZURICH LIVSFORSIKRING—See Zurich Insurance Company; *Int'l*, pg. 1530

ZURICH PACIFIC INSURANCE PTY. LTD.—See Zurich Insurance Company; *Int'l*, pg. 1532

ZURICH PENSION FUND CONSULTANTS & INVESTMENTS MNGMT. LTD.—See Zurich Insurance Company; *Int'l*, pg. 1530

ZURICH POISTOVNA SLUZBY S.R.O.—See Zurich Insurance Company; *Int'l*, pg. 1532

ZURICH POJISTOVNA—See Zurich Insurance Company; *Int'l*, pg. 1531

P.T. ZURICH PSP LIFE INSURANCE INDONESIA—See Zurich Insurance Company; *Int'l*, pg. 1532

ZURICH RE (UK) LIMITED—See Zurich Insurance Company; *Int'l*, pg. 1532

ZURICH RECHTSSCHUTZVERISCHERUNGS-AKTIENGESSELLSCHAFT—See Zurich Insurance Company; *Int'l*, pg. 1532

ZURICH REINSURANCE CENTRE—See Zurich Insurance Company; *Int'l*, pg. 1530

ZURICH SHIPPING COMPANY AG—See Migros; *Int'l*, pg. 866

ZURICH UBEZPIECZENIE SERVICE SP. Z O.O.—See Zurich Insurance Company; *Int'l*, pg. 1532

ZURICH VERSICHERUNGS-AKTIENGESELLSCHAFT (DEUTSCHLAND)—See Zurich Insurance Company; *Int'l*, pg. 1532

ZURICH VERSICHERUNGS-GESELLSCHAFT—See Zurich Insurance Company; *Int'l*, pg. 1531

ZURICH VERZEKERINGEN—See Zurich Insurance Company; *Int'l*, pg. 1531

ZURICH VIDA COMPANIA DE SEGUROS S.A.—See Zurich Insurance Company; *Int'l*, pg. 1532

ZURIGO COMPAGNIA DI ASSICURAZIONI—See Zurich Insurance Company; *Int'l*, pg. 1531

ZURIGO COMPAGNIA DI ASSICURAZIONI SULLA VITA—See Zurich Insurance Company; *Int'l*, pg. 1530

ZURITEL COMPAGNIE D'ASSURANCES—See Zurich Insurance Company; *Int'l*, pg. 1532

ZURN BALKE-DURR, INC.—See Deutsche Babcock AG; *Int'l*, pg. 401

ZURN CONSTRUCTORS, INC.—See Zurn Industries, Inc.; *U.S. Public*, pg. 1795

ZURN DRAINAGE AND CONTROL SYSTEMS LTD.—See Zurn Industries, Inc.; *U.S. Public*, pg. 1795

ZURN INDUSTRIES, INC.; *U.S. Public*, pg. 1794

ZURN/NEPCO—See Zurn Industries, Inc.; *U.S. Public*, pg. 1795

ZURN PLUMBING PRODUCTS GROUP—See Zurn Industries, Inc.; *U.S. Public*, pg. 1794

ZURN THAILAND—See Zurn Industries, Inc.; *U.S. Public*, pg. 1795

ZWAAN UND CO. SAMENZUCHT G.M.B.H.—See Novartis AG; *Int'l*, pg. 986

ZWANENBERG DE MEXICO S.A.—See Unilever Plc; *Int'l*, pg. 1439

ZWEIGNIEDERLASSUNG DER ROCKWELL INTERNATIONAL GMBH—See Rockwell International Corporation; *U.S. Public*, pg. 1068

ZWEIRAD UNION GRUNDBESITZ AG—See Mannesmann A.G.; *Int'l*, pg. 835

ZWICK/ROELL GROUP; *Int'l*, pg. 1532

ZWITSERLEVEN—See The Swiss Life/Rentenanstalt Group; *Int'l*, pg. 1332

ZWJSEN B.V.—See Koninklijke Hoogovens N.V.; *Int'l*, pg. 754

ZWOLSCHE ALGEMEENE N.V.—See The Hartford Financial Services Group Inc.; *U.S. Public*, pg. 795

ZYAN, INC.—See Foster Management Co.; *U.S. Private*, pg. 421

ZYCAD G.M.B.H.—See Gatefield Corporation; *U.S. Public*, pg. 703

ZYCAD JAPAN K.K.—See Gatefield Corporation; *U.S. Public*, pg. 703

ZYGO CORPORATION; *U.S. Public*, pg. 1795

ZYLINDERKOPFFERTIGUNG EISENACH GMBH—See Volkswagen AG; *Int'l*, pg. 1474

ZYMA BENELUX S.A.—See Novartis AG; *Int'l*, pg. 986

ZYMA FARMACEUTICA PORTUGUESA LDA—See Novartis AG; *Int'l*, pg. 986

ZYMA-GEBRO ARZNEIMITTEL GMBH—See Novartis AG; *Int'l*, pg. 986

ZYMA GMBH—See Novartis AG; *Int'l*, pg. 986

ZYMA HEALTHCARE—See Novartis AG; *Int'l*, pg. 972

ZYMA-NEDERLAND—See Novartis AG; *Int'l*, pg. 986

ZYMA PHARMACEUTICA SA—See Novartis AG; *Int'l*, pg. 986

ZYMA SA—See Novartis AG; *Int'l*, pg. 972

ZYMA S.P.A—See Novartis AG; *Int'l*, pg. 986

ZYMA (UNITED KINGDOM) LIMITED—See Novartis AG; *Int'l*, pg. 986

ZYMARK CORPORATION—See Berwind Corporation; *U.S. Private*, pg. 139

ZYMOGENETICS, INC.—See Novo Nordisk A/S; *Int'l*, pg. 987

ZYNOLYTE PRODUCTS COMPANY—See Imperial Chemical Industries PLC; *Int'l*, pg. 663

BRAND NAME INDEX

A

A—Chemical Extraction Columns—Varian Associates, Inc.; *U.S. Public*, pg. 1710

AA—Engineered Sound Products; Electronic Speakers, Microphones—Peavey Electronics Corp.; *U.S. Private*, pg. 845

AAA—American Automobile Association—American Automobile Association; *U.S. Private*, pg. 50

AAA AUTOEASE—NONE—American Automobile Association; *U.S. Private*, pg. 50

AAA CAMPBOOK—Regional Camping Guidebooks—American Automobile Association; *U.S. Private*, pg. 50

AAA CITIBOOK—City Guidebooks—American Automobile Association; *U.S. Private*, pg. 50

AAA NORTH AMERICAN ROAD ATLAS—Road Atlas—American Automobile Association; *U.S. Private*, pg. 50

AAA TOURBOOK—U.S. & Canada Guidebooks—American Automobile Association; *U.S. Private*, pg. 50

AAA TRAVELBOOK—European, Caribbean & Mexico Guidebooks—American Automobile Association; *U.S. Private*, pg. 50

AAA TRIPTIK—Travel Routings & Trip Plans—American Automobile Association; *U.S. Private*, pg. 50

AAF—Filtration & Pollution Control Products—AAF McQuay, Inc.; *U.S. Private*, pg. 2

AAF AIR CONDITIONING—HVAC Products—McQuay International; *U.S. Private*, pg. 3

AAMP—Auto Sound Accessories—Recoton Corporation; *U.S. Public*, pg. 1369

AARDS—Directory—Reed Business Information Pty. Limited; *Int'l*, pg. 1094

AAS 5 FL—Atomic Absorption Spectrometer—Carl Zeiss; *Int'l*, pg. 1522

AASP—Automated Sample Preparation Instrument—Varian Associates, Inc.; *U.S. Public*, pg. 1710

AAT—Monthly Women's Magazine—The Israel Land Development Co., Ltd.; *Int'l*, pg. 691

A & B IN DESIGN—NONE—Allied Diagnostic Imaging Resources, Inc.; *U.S. Public*, pg. 282

A & D OINTMENT—Skincare—Schering-Plough Corporation; *U.S. Public*, pg. 1438

A & D OINTMENT—Skincare—Schering-Plough Healthcare Products Inc.; *U.S. Public*, pg. 1438

A & E—Cable—The Hearst Corporation; *U.S. Private*, pg. 515

A & E—Awnings & Other Products for Recreational Vehicles—White Consolidated Industries, Inc.; *Int'l*, pg. 439

A & EAGLE—Symbol—Anheuser-Busch Companies, Inc.; *U.S. Public*, pg. 113

A&M—Records & Tapes—A&M Records; *Int'l*, pg. 1052

A & M—Record Label—Philips Electronics N.V.; *Int'l*, pg. 1051

A&N STORES—Chain Stores—Sternheimer Brothers Inc.; *U.S. Private*, pg. 1042

A & P—Food Stores—The Great Atlantic & Pacific Tea Company, Inc.; *Int'l*, pg. 1375

A & P—Grocery Store—Tengelmann Warenhandelsgesellschaft; *Int'l*, pg. 1375

A & W—NONE—Cadbury Beverages; *Int'l*, pg. 248

A & W CREAM SODA—Soft Drinks—Cadbury Schweppes p.l.c.; *Int'l*, pg. 247

A & W CREAM SODA—Soft Drink—The Coca-Cola Bottling Co. of New York, Inc.; *U.S. Public*, pg. 393

A & W DIET CREAM SODA—Soft Drinks—Cadbury Schweppes p.l.c.; *Int'l*, pg. 247

A & W DIET ROOT BEER—Soft Drinks—Cadbury Schweppes p.l.c.; *Int'l*, pg. 247

A & W GREAT FOOD RESTAURANT—Fast Food Restaurant—A&W Restaurants, Inc.; *U.S. Private*, pg. 1

A&W HOT DOGS—NONE—A&W Restaurants, Inc.-Carousel Div.; *U.S. Private*, pg. 2

A & W ROOT BEER—Soft Drinks—Cadbury Schweppes p.l.c.; *Int'l*, pg. 247

A & W ROOT BEER—Soft Drink—The Coca-Cola Bottling Co. of New York, Inc.; *U.S. Public*, pg. 393

A & W ROOTBEER—Soft Drink—Grant-Lydick Beverage Co.; *U.S. Private*, pg. 470

A & Z HAYWARD—Jewelry—A&Z Hayward, Inc.; *U.S. Private*, pg. 2

ABA BANKING JOURNAL—Monthly Magazine—Simmons-Boardman Publishing Corp.; *U.S. Private*, pg. 1000

ABA 100—Diagnostic Products—Abbott Laboratories; *U.S. Public*, pg. 12

ABA 200—Diagnostic Products—Abbott Laboratories; *U.S. Public*, pg. 12

ABB MASTER—Distributed Control Systems—ABB Industrial Systems, Inc.; *Int'l*, pg. 4

ABC—Installing, Servicing & Distributing Factory Automation Equipment—General Electric Canada Inc.; *U.S. Public*, pg. 713

ABCD—Vitamins—Novo Nordisk A/S; *Int'l*, pg. 987

ABC FLEXIBLO—Air Set Coreblomatics—Beardsley & Piper, L.L.C.; *U.S. Private*, pg. 859

ABC NEWS—Syndicated Television News—ABC News, Inc.; *U.S. Public*, pg. 511

ABCO—Decorative Electrical Products—Angelo Brothers Co.; *U.S. Private*, pg. 74

ABC PACKAGING MACHINE—Packaging Equipment—ABC Packaging Machine Corp.; *U.S. Private*, pg. 3

ABD—Bearings, Oil Seals, Motor Mounts—L & S Bearing Co.; *U.S. Public*, pg. 970

A.B. DICK—Pre-Press, Press, Post-Press Equipment & Supplies, Copiers—A.B. Dick Company; *U.S. Private*, pg. 791

A.B. DICK—Reproductive Office Products—The General Electric Company, p.l.c.; *Int'l*, pg. 543

A.B. DICK—NONE—Taylor Impression, Inc.; *U.S. Private*, pg. 1070

ABE—Accelerated Benefit Election Rider—Lincoln National Corporation; *U.S. Public*, pg. 997

ABG—NONE—Ingersoll-Rand Company; *U.S. Public*, pg. 876

ABG—NONE—Pfizer Inc.; *U.S. Public*, pg. 1281

ABI—NONE—The Perkin-Elmer Corporation; *U.S. Public*, pg. 1279

ABI PRISM—NONE—The Perkin-Elmer Corporation; *U.S. Public*, pg. 1279

ABL—Automated Blood Gas Analyzer—Radiometer America Inc.; *Int'l*, pg. 1083

ABL—Bloodgas Analyzer—Radiometer A/S; *Int'l*, pg. 1083

ABO—Blood Grouping Reagents—Ortho Clinical Diagnostic Systems Inc.; *U.S. Public*, pg. 929

ABR SYSTEMS—Document Management Products—Bell & Howell Holdings; *U.S. Public*, pg. 201

ABS—Plastics—DSM N.V.; *Int'l*, pg. 352

ABS—Industrial Chemical; Cement—Hercules Chemical Co., Inc.; *U.S. Private*, pg. 523

ABS—Cement—La-Co Industries Markal Company; *U.S. Private*, pg. 640

ABS/PVC—Transition Cement—Hercules Chemical Co., Inc.; *U.S. Private*, pg. 523

ABS SAFEHULL—Dynamic Based Method for Design & Analysis of Ship Structures—American Bureau of Shipping; *U.S. Private*, pg. 51

ABS SAFENET—Life-Cycle Ship Management Ad Information Network—American Bureau of Shipping; *U.S. Private*, pg. 51

A. BYER—Juniors' Sportswear—Byer California; *U.S. Private*, pg. 191

AC—Aftermarket Products—Delphi Energy & Engine Management Systems; *U.S. Public*, pg. 719

AC—Dry Soup Mix, Bread Crumbs, Tea Mix, Grated Cheese, Season Coating Mix—4C Foods Corporation; *U.S. Private*, pg. 421

ACCTV—Video Monitors—Nellcor Puritan Bennett Incorporated; *U.S. Public*, pg. 1039

ACD—Printed Circuit Boards—Litton Industries, Inc.; *U.S. Public*, pg. 1002

ACDC—AC-DC Power Supplies/Electronic Loads—Astec America Inc.; *Int'l*, pg. 93

AC DELCO—Auto Parts—General Motors Corporation; *U.S. Public*, pg. 718

A.C.E.—Fiber—AlliedSignal Inc.; *U.S. Public*, pg. 49

ACF/VTAM—Computer System—International Business Machines Corporation; *U.S. Public*, pg. 895

AC 556—Selective Fire Automatic Rifles—Sturm, Ruger & Co., Inc.; *U.S. Public*, pg. 1526

AC 500—Card Access System which Prevents Unauthorized Entry to Any Facility—Sensormatic Electronics Corporation; *U.S. Public*, pg. 1457

AC FOAM TAPERED—Commercial Tapered Roof Insulation (Polyiso)—Atlas Roofing Corp.; *U.S. Private*, pg. 96

AC FOAM II—Commercial Roof Insulation (Polyiso)—Atlas Roofing Corp.; *U.S. Private*, pg. 96

ACG—Honeycomb Material—Hexcel Corporation; *U.S. Public*, pg. 824

ACI—Electric Motors—Cooper Industries, Inc.; *U.S. Public*, pg. 442

ACI-JEL—Therapeutic Vaginal Jelly—Ortho-McNeil Pharmaceutical Corporation; *U.S. Public*, pg. 929

ACIS—High School Travel Programs—American Institute for Foreign Study; *U.S. Private*, pg. 56

Brand Name Index

A.C. KISSLING—Sauerkraut & Meats—A.C. Kissling, Inc.; *U.S. Private*, pg. 624

ACL—Sanitizer & Bleaching Compound—Solutia Inc.; *U.S. Public*, pg. 1483

ACM—Citrus Mixes—Firmenich; *Int'l*, pg. 486

ACMI—Medical Endoscopes—Circon Corporation; *U.S. Public*, pg. 373

A. C. NIELSEN—Market Research—A.C. Nielsen Company; *U.S. Public*, pg. 1183

ACP—Accelerated Claim Processing—Health Management Systems, Inc.; *U.S. Public*, pg. 802

A-C PERFORMANCE ADDITIVES—Low-Molecular-Weight Polyethylene—AlliedSignal Inc., Engineered Materials; *U.S. Public*, pg. 51

ACR—Copper Tube, Sheet, Pipe—Kobe Steel, Ltd.; *Int'l*, pg. 740

ACR—Fastening System—Rule Industries, Inc.; *U.S. Public*, pg. 950

ACS—Surgical Sutures & Needles—Alcon Laboratories, Inc.; *Int'l*, pg. 916

A.C.T.—Hair Products—Dena Corporation; *U.S. Private*, pg. 324

AC-U-KWIK AIRPORT/FBO—Quick Reference Guide—Intertec Publishing; *U.S. Public*, pg. 1327

AD—Multiwall Paper Sack Machines—Windmoeller & Hoelscher; *Int'l*, pg. 1510

ADA—Rate Control Series—Enidine Incorporated; *U.S. Private*, pg. 377

ADC—Electronic & Electromechanical Products for Telecommunication Industry—ADC Telecommunications, Inc.; *U.S. Public*, pg. 4

ADD—NONE—Laserscope Surgical Systems; *U.S. Public*, pg. 979

ADD/STAT—NONE—Laserscope Surgical Systems; *U.S. Public*, pg. 979

AD DELHAIZE—Affiliated Grocery Stores—Etablissements Delhaize Freres Et Cie "Le Lion" S.A.; *Int'l*, pg. 462

ADM—Flours, Grains, Gasohol & Syrups—Archer Daniels Midland Company (ADM); *U.S. Public*, pg. 127

AD MAX WAGON—Car—Nissan Motor Co., Ltd.; *Int'l*, pg. 943

ADNX—Integrated Access Manager—Network Equipment Technologies, Inc.; *U.S. Public*, pg. 1168

ADP—Machinery—Hollingsworth Saco Lowell Corporation, Inc.; *U.S. Private*, pg. 535

ADP LASER STATION—Computer Hardware & Software—Automatic Data Processing, Inc.; *U.S. Public*, pg. 150

ADR PLUS—Digital Readout System for Compression Testing Machines—ELE International, Inc./Soiltest; *Int'l*, pg. 1287

ADT—Electronic Protection Systems—ADT Security Services, Inc.; *U.S. Public*, pg. 1649

ADX—Diagnostic Products—Abbott Laboratories; *U.S. Public*, pg. 12

AE—Anderson Erickson Dairy Co.—Anderson Erickson Dairy Company; *U.S. Private*, pg. 72

AEA—Auto Parts—Republic Automotive-AEA Division; *U.S. Public*, pg. 1377

AEBLE 150—Electron Beam Direct Write-on-Wafer System—Etec Systems, Inc.; *U.S. Public*, pg. 594

AEC—Sensors—Echlin Inc.; *U.S. Public*, pg. 560

AEC—Automation Electronics Corporation—Electronic Tele-Communications, Inc.; *U.S. Public*, pg. 570

A/E/C—Trade Show—Penton Publishing, Inc.; *U.S. Public*, pg. 1306

A.E.C.—Transportation Replacement Parts—Zeller Corp.; *U.S. Private*, pg. 1204

AECI—NONE—Arkansas Electric Cooperatives Inc.; *U.S. Private*, pg. 82

AEG—Household Appliances—Electrolux, AB; *Int'l*, pg. 438

AEGIS—Software—CACI International Inc; *U.S. Public*, pg. 272

AE GOETZE—Piston Prods.—T & N Plc; *Int'l*, pg. 1334

AEI—NONE—Air Express International Corporation; *U.S. Public*, pg. 30

AEI—American Enterprise Institute—American Enterprise Institute for Public Policy Research; *U.S. Private*, pg. 53

AFC—Honeycomb Material—Hexcel Corporation; *U.S. Public*, pg. 824

AFC-1—Flexible Cystoscope—Circon Corporation; *U.S. Public*, pg. 373

AFIS—Airborne Flight Information System—AlliedSignal Commercial Avionics Systems; *U.S. Public*, pg. 50

AFP—Computer Systems—International Business Machines Corporation; *U.S. Public*, pg. 895

AFRC—Ski & Sportswear—Raven Industries, Inc.; *U.S. Public*, pg. 1361

AFRC—Ski Pants—Raven Industries Sportswear Div.; *U.S. Public*, pg. 1361

AFS BIOCOMMAND—Process Control Software—New Brunswick Scientific Co., Inc.; *U.S. Public*, pg. 1169

AFT—Biochemicals—Dade Behring Inc.; *U.S. Private*, pg. 110

AFV—Filing Systems—International Envelope Company; *U.S. Public*, pg. 70

A55—Horizontal Machining Center—Makino Inc.; *Int'l*, pg. 831

"A" FLOTATION WOOL—Flotation Wool—Johns Manville Corporation; *U.S. Public*, pg. 927

A4—Camera—Konica Corporation; *Int'l*, pg. 748

AGA—Industrial Gases & Welding Equipment—AGA Gas, Inc.; *Int'l*, pg. 13

AGA—NONE—Glynwed International PLC; *Int'l*, pg. 554

AGA BURDOX—NONE—AGA Gas, Inc.; *Int'l*, pg. 13

AGA DIVATOR—NONE—AGA Gas, Inc.; *Int'l*, pg. 13

AGA THERMOLENE—NONE—AGA Gas, Inc.; *Int'l*, pg. 13

AGC—Aircraft Parts—Aircraft Gear Corporation-Arizona Division; *U.S. Private*, pg. 938

AGCO—Flow Control Products—Keystone International, Inc.; *U.S. Public*, pg. 1650

AGCO-MOUNT—Transmitter Mounting System—Anderson, Greenwood & Co.; *U.S. Public*, pg. 1650

AGFA—NONE—Taylor Impression, Inc.; *U.S. Private*, pg. 1070

AGI—Computer System—Everex Systems Inc.; *Int'l*, pg. 498

AGIL—Soybean Insecticide—Novartis; *Int'l*, pg. 972

AGMS—For Apparel Design and Production—Asahi Chemical Industry Co., Ltd.; *Int'l*, pg. 83

AGSOY—Vegetable Oil—Ag Processing Inc., A Cooperative; *U.S. Private*, pg. 26

AG SHEATHING—Plywood Exterior Cladding—Carter Holt Harvey Limited; *U.S. Public*, pg. 904

AG SOY ME—Adjuvant For Use In Agricultural Sprays—Ag Processing Inc., A Cooperative; *U.S. Private*, pg. 26

AG STAR—Livestock Equiment—Behlen Mfg. Co.; *U.S. Private*, pg. 130

A-GENT—Diagnostic Products—Abbott Laboratories; *U.S. Public*, pg. 12

A. GOODMAN & SONS—Goodman's Noodles, Spaghetti & Macaroni—A. Goodman & Sons, Inc.; *U.S. Private*, pg. 158

A GREAT TIME, EVERY TIME—NONE—Harrah's Entertainment, Inc.; *U.S. Public*, pg. 790

AHI CONTROLL-A-DOOR—Garage Door—Carter Holt Harvey Limited; *U.S. Public*, pg. 904

AHI ROLL-A-DOOR—Domestic & Commercial Roller Doors—Carter Holt Harvey Limited; *U.S. Public*, pg. 904

AHI TILT-A-DOOR—Garage Door—Carter Holt Harvey Limited; *U.S. Public*, pg. 904

AHI TILT-A-MATIC—Automatic Door Openers—Carter Holt Harvey Limited; *U.S. Public*, pg. 904

AHMSA COLOR—Painting Products—Altos Hornos de Mexico, S.A.; *Int'l*, pg. 66

AH-1S—Cobra Gunship Single Engine—Bell Helicopter Textron; *U.S. Public*, pg. 1588

AH-1W—SuperCobra Gunship Twin Engine—Bell Helicopter Textron; *U.S. Public*, pg. 1588

AHPC ETHICAL MEDICA—Pharmaceutical Products—Wyeth-Ayerst Laboratories, Inc.; *U.S. Public*, pg. 80

AHS-400—Pre-Finished Strip—Bruce Hardwood Floors; *U.S. Public*, pg. 1634

AHS-100—Pre-Finished Solid—Bruce Hardwood Floors; *U.S. Public*, pg. 1634

AHS-300—Pre-Finished Laminate—Bruce Hardwood Floors; *U.S. Public*, pg. 1634

AHS-200—Pre-Finished Laminate—Bruce Hardwood Floors; *U.S. Public*, pg. 1634

AH-64A—Helicopter—Boeing Helicopter Division; *U.S. Public*, pg. 241

AH-64D—Helicopter—Boeing Helicopter Division; *U.S. Public*, pg. 241

AHU—Photo Film—Eastman Kodak Company; *U.S. Public*, pg. 550

A. HARDY—Cognac—Paterno Imports Limited; *U.S. Private*, pg. 843

AIA-PACK—Test Cup Reagents—Tosoh Belgium N.V.; *Int'l*, pg. 1408

AIB—Finance, Leasing & Mortgage Services—Allied Irish Banks, p.l.c.; *Int'l*, pg. 64

AIC—Analysts International Corporation—Analysts International Corporation; *U.S. Public*, pg. 110

AICO—Indexing & Tabbing Products—Avery Dennison Corporation; *U.S. Public*, pg. 152

AIG—American International Group Financial Services—American International Group, Inc.; *U.S. Public*, pg. 83

AIM—Instruments—BF Goodrich Avionic Systems, Inc.; *U.S. Public*, pg. 751

AIM—Active Intermedia Measurement-Yellow Pages—NFO Research, Inc.; *U.S. Public*, pg. 1146

A-I-NET—Advanced Intelligent Network Products; Computer Programs—Lucent Technologies Inc.; *U.S. Public*, pg. 1017

AIS-IIER—Computer Based Training System—McDonnell Aircraft & Missile Systems Div.; *U.S. Public*, pg. 241

A.I.T.—Financial Inventory Mngmt. Program—Medline Industries, Inc.; *U.S. Private*, pg. 728

AIW—Steel & Supply—Alamo Industrial Group; *U.S. Private*, pg. 31

AIX—Computer Systems—International Business Machines Corporation; *U.S. Public*, pg. 895

AIX/ESA—Computer Systems—International Business Machines Corporation; *U.S. Public*, pg. 895

AIX PVME—Computer Systems—International Business Machines Corporation; *U.S. Public*, pg. 895

AIX/6000—Computer Systems—International Business Machines Corporation; *U.S. Public*, pg. 895

A IN DESIGN—NONE—Allied Diagnostic Imaging Resources, Inc.; *U.S. Public*, pg. 282

AJA LIF—Cleaning Equipment—Man-Gill Chemical Company; *U.S. Private*, pg. 699

AJ DSM—Data Speed Multiplier—Microtel International Inc.; *U.S. Public*, pg. 1108

AJ FOCUS—NONE—EMAP Business Communications Division; *Int'l*, pg. 451

AJJ SERIES—Modular Lounge Seating—Clarin; *U.S. Private*, pg. 242

AJN GUIDE—Magazine—American Journal of Nursing Company; *Int'l*, pg. 1513

AJN INTERNATIONAL NURSING INDEX—Magazine—American Journal of Nursing Company; *Int'l*, pg. 1513

A-JUST—Diagnostic Products—Abbott Laboratories; *U.S. Public*, pg. 12

AKAI—NONE—Semi-Tech Corporation; *Int'l*, pg. 1220

AKG—Microphones & Headphones—Harman International Industries, Inc.; *U.S. Public*, pg. 787

AKI—Typesetting Keyboards, Terminals, Computer Systems—Eastman Kodak Company; *U.S. Public*, pg. 550

AKI—Homebuilding Supply Stores—GIB Group; *Int'l*, pg. 532

AKU-CMC—Sodium Carboxymethyl Cellulose—Akzo Nobel N.V.; *Int'l*, pg. 42

ALA—Books—American Library Association; *U.S. Private*, pg. 58

ALBI—Safety Products—Rentokil Initial plc; *Int'l*, pg. 1285

ALBI CLAD—Fireproofing for Steel—Stanchem Inc.; *U.S. Private*, pg. 1030

A.L. HANSEN—Commercial Body & Industrial Hardware—A.L. Hansen Manufacturing Co.; *U.S. Private*, pg. 500

ALICO—American Life Insurance Co.—American International Group, Inc.; *U.S. Public*, pg. 83

ALPC 1—ASIC Microprocessor Chips—Imaging Technologies Corp.; *U.S. Public*, pg. 870

ALP-CHOLESTEROL-JIMRO—Lipoprotein-Cholesterol Test Kit—Otsuka Pharmaceutical Co., Ltd.; *Int'l*, pg. 1013

ALR—Advanced Logic Research, Inc.Trademark—Advanced Logic Research, Inc.; *U.S. Public*, pg. 703

ALS—Corporate—CACI International Inc; *U.S. Public*, pg. 272

AL 203 STAR—Ophthalmic Lens Polish—Ferro Corporation; *U.S. Public*, pg. 618

A LA CARTE—Card Case—Hugo Bosca Co., Inc.; *U.S. Private*, pg. 160

A. LINCOLN—Signature Design of All Lincoln Life Products—Lincoln National Corporation; *U.S. Public*, pg. 997

AM—Multiwall Paper Sack Machines—Windmoeller & Hoelscher; *Int'l*, pg. 1510

AMA-DRAINER—Submersible Motor Pump—KSB Aktiengesellschaft; *Int'l*, pg. 721

AMA-DURO—Submersible Motor Pump—KSB Aktiengesellschaft; *Int'l*, pg. 721

AMCI—Ameritech Mobile Communications, Inc.—Ameritech Cellular and Paging Services; *U.S. Public*, pg. 98

AMCO—Tools—American Machine & Tool Company, Inc.; *U.S. Private*, pg. 58

AMC TRADE SHOWS, LTD.—Trade Show Operating Company—AMC, Inc.; *U.S. Private*, pg. 6

A. M. CASTLE & CO—Metals Service Center, Castle Metals—A.M. Castle & Co.; *U.S. Public*, pg. 312

AMD—Merchandising Programs—AMD Industries Inc.; *U.S. Private*, pg. 6

AMD—Integrated Circuits—Advanced Micro Devices, Inc.; *U.S. Public*, pg. 21

AMF—Bowling Products—AMF Bowling Worldwide; *U.S. Private*, pg. 6

AMF—Gymnastics Equipment—Sport Supply Group, Inc.; *U.S. Public*, pg. 1499

AMI—Aircraft Seating—AMI Industries, Inc.; *U.S. Public*, pg. 401

AMI—Wholesale Express Air Courier & Airfreight Consolidator—John Menzies plc; *Int'l*, pg. 707

AML HIP—Orthopedic Product—DePuy, Inc.; *Int'l*, pg. 331

AML/2—Computer Systems—International Business Machines Corporation; *U.S. Public*, pg. 895

AMM—NONE—Adaptec, Inc.; *U.S. Public*, pg. 19

AMP—Electrical & Electronic Components—AMP Incorporated; *U.S. Public*, pg. 7

AMP—Asset Management Program—Norman Levy Associates, Inc.; *U.S. Private*, pg. 664

AM/PM—24 Hour Odor Absorber—Surco Products, Inc.; *U.S. Private*, pg. 1056

AMPS—Chemicals for Industrial Uses—The Lubrizol Corporation; *U.S. Public*, pg. 1016

AMP-TRAP—Feeder Circuits—Gould Electronics Inc., Shawmut Circuit Protection Division; *U.S. Public*, pg. 1592

AMP-TRAP É RATED—Power Fuse—Gould Electronics Inc., Shawmut Circuit Protection Division; *U.S. Public*, pg. 1592

AMP-TRAP FORM 480—Feeder Circuits with Time Delay—Gould Electronics Inc., Shawmut Circuit Protection Division; *U.S. Public*, pg. 1592

AMP-TRAP FORM 101—Semiconductor—Gould Electronics Inc., Shawmut Circuit Protection Division; *U.S. Public*, pg. 1592

AMP-TRAP II—Feeder Circuits with Time Delay—Gould Electronics Inc., Shawmut Circuit Protection Division; *U.S. Public*, pg. 1592

AMP-TRAP 2000—Time Delay Low Voltage Fuse—Gould Electronics Inc., Shawmut Circuit Protection Division; *U.S. Public*, pg. 1592

AMR—Recording, Studio, Broadcast Products—Peavey Electronics Corp.; *U.S. Private*, pg. 845

AMS—NONE—St. Jude Medical, Inc.; *U.S. Public*, pg. 1427

AMS—Automatic Microphone System—Shure Brothers Incorporated; *U.S. Private*, pg. 997

AMS ACCESS GATEWAY—NONE—American Management Systems, Inc.; *U.S. Public*, pg. 86

AMS 800—NONE—Pfizer Inc.; *U.S. Public*, pg. 1281

AMS 700 CX—NONE—Pfizer Inc.; *U.S. Public*, pg. 1281

AMS 700 ULTREX—NONE—Pfizer Inc.; *U.S. Public*, pg. 1281

AMS 650—NONE—Pfizer Inc.; *U.S. Public*, pg. 1281

AMS 600—NONE—Pfizer Inc.; *U.S. Public*, pg. 1281

AMS-2—Electronic Products—SCI Systems, Inc.; *U.S. Public*, pg. 1416

AMT—Tools & Pumps—American Machine & Tool Company, Inc.; *U.S. Private*, pg. 58

AMT—Model Kits—The Ertl Company, Inc; *U.S. Public*, pg. 1684

ANA—All Nippon Airways—All Nippon Airways Co. Ltd.; *Int'l*, pg. 57

ANA—Electronic Equipment—Eaton Corp., Aerospace & Commercial Controls Div.; *U.S. Public*, pg. 557

ANA—Rat Liver Antinuclear Antibodies Autoimmune Test System—Wampole Laboratories; *U.S. Public*, pg. 310

AND—NONE—Benetton Group S.p.A.; *Int'l*, pg. 186

ANR—Bank—Australia & New Zealand Banking Group Limited; *Int'l*, pg. 98

ANS FARM—Tires—Bridgestone/Firestone, Inc.; *Int'l*, pg. 213

ANSR—Diagnostic Products—Abbott Laboratories; *U.S. Public*, pg. 12

AO—Optical Supplies & Accessories—American Optical Corporation; *U.S. Private*, pg. 60

AOD—Pumps—ITT A-C Pump/ITT Marlow; *U.S. Public*, pg. 860

AO DEFENDER—Safety Eyewear—Aearo Company; *U.S. Private*, pg. 23

AO5 STAR—Half Mask Respirator—Aearo Company; *U.S. Private*, pg. 23

AO FORCE 55—Ophthalmic Lenses—American Optical Corporation; *U.S. Private*, pg. 60

A-OK—Surgical Knives—Alcon Laboratories, Inc.; *Int'l*, pg. 916

AOK—Cosmetics—Henkel KGaA; *Int'l*, pg. 609

AOR CLASSIC ROCK PREP—Entertainment News Programming—Westwood One, Inc.; *U.S. Public*, pg. 1763

AOS/RT32—Software—Data General Corporation; *U.S. Public*, pg. 485

AOS/VS—Software—Data General Corporation; *U.S. Public*, pg. 485

AOS/VS II—Software—Data General Corporation; *U.S. Public*, pg. 485

AO SAFETY—Safety Products—Aearo Company; *U.S. Private*, pg. 23

A.O. SMITH—Pipe & Tube—Lone Star Steel Company; *U.S. Public*, pg. 1012

AO SR99—Ophthalmic Lenses—American Optical Corporation; *U.S. Private*, pg. 60

AO TUFFMASTER—Faceshield/Headgear—Aearo Company; *U.S. Private*, pg. 23

AO XT 16—Ophthalmic Lenses—American Optical Corporation; *U.S. Private*, pg. 60

A-1—Steak Sauce—Nabisco Inc.; *U.S. Public*, pg. 1355

A-1—Steak Sauce—RJR Nabisco Holdings Corp.; *U.S. Public*, pg. 1354

A-1 BLEACH—NONE—James Austin Co.; *U.S. Private*, pg. 99

A109C—Executive Helicopter—Agusta Aerospace Corporation; *Int'l*, pg. 32

A125 SHARPLET-2—Pencil—Pentel of America, Ltd.; *Int'l*, pg. 1035

AP—Mufflers & Pipes—AP North American Aftermarket Division; *U.S. Private*, pg. 230

AP—News, Photos, & Feature Service—The Associated Press; *U.S. Private*, pg. 92

AP—Protective Coating Composition for Coating Glass or the Like—Ball Corporation; *U.S. Public*, pg. 170

A-P-A—Transport—A-P-A Transport Corp.; *U.S. Private*, pg. 2

AP BONDEZE—THEIC Modified Polyester w/Mod. Polyamide Imide & Bondable Polyester Cement—Phelps Dodge Magnet Wire Co.; *U.S. Public*, pg. 1286

APC—NONE—ETEX; *Int'l*, pg. 430

APC—Automatic Pressure Conveyor—Rapistan Demag Corp.; *Int'l*, pg. 837

API—Health Care Products—Sherwood-Davis & Geck; *U.S. Public*, pg. 80

APL—NONE—APL Limited; *Int'l*, pg. 912

APL∗PLUS—NONE—Manugistics Group, Inc.; *U.S. Public*, pg. 1042

APL2—Computer Systems—International Business Machines Corporation; *U.S. Public*, pg. 895

APL2/6000—Computer System—International Business Machines Corporation; *U.S. Public*, pg. 895

APM—Application Performance Management—Programart Corporation; *U.S. Private*, pg. 890

AP MILLENNIUM—Accounts Payable Information Systems—Dun & Bradstreet Software Services; *Int'l*, pg. 532

APN—Synthetic Rubber—Bridgestone/Firestone, Inc.; *Int'l*, pg. 213

APP—Modified Bitumen Membrane—U.S. Intec, Inc.; *U.S. Private*, pg. 433

APP-ATTACK—Diet Disc—Herbalife International of America, Inc.; *U.S. Public*, pg. 809

APP CHEMICALS—Coatings—Burmah Castrol plc; *Int'l*, pg. 234

APPN—Computer System—International Business Machines Corporation; *U.S. Public*, pg. 895

APPX—4th Generation Application Development Tool & Data Base Management System—APPX Software Inc.; *U.S. Public*, pg. 1634

AP/PLUS—Accounts Payable Software—Dun & Bradstreet Software Services; *Int'l*, pg. 532

APR—Arthritis Pain Reliever—Herbalife International of America, Inc.; *U.S. Public*, pg. 809

APS—Pacemaker Programmer—St. Jude Medical, Inc.; *U.S. Public*, pg. 1427

APS—Aerodynamic Particle Sizer—TSI Incorporated; *U.S. Public*, pg. 1559

APS/HONEYWELL—Home Security System—APS; *U.S. Public*, pg. 1297

AP 600—Indus. Asset Protection System Designed to Protect People, Property & Info.—Sensormatic Electronics Corporation; *U.S. Public*, pg. 1457

AP200 PROCESSOR—NONE—Allied Diagnostic Imaging Resources, Inc.; *U.S. Public*, pg. 282

APX—Steel Modular Enclosure Systems—Hoffman Engineering Company; *U.S. Public*, pg. 1273

A PRECEPT—Aldehyde Neutralization Protective Apparel—Isolyser Company, Inc.; *U.S. Public*, pg. 914

AQP—Hydraulic Hose—Aeroquip Corporation; *U.S. Public*, pg. 24

AQP—Hose—Aeroquip-Vickers, Inc.; *U.S. Public*, pg. 24

A-Q-TORK TONG—Speed Control System—Weatherford Enterra Incorporated; *U.S. Public*, pg. 1749

AR—Loudspeakers—Recoton Auto Corporation; *U.S. Public*, pg. 1369

A.R.A.P.—Aeronautical/Astronautical Engineering Computer Science Consulting Services—The Titan Corporation; *U.S. Public*, pg. 1618

AR (ACOUSTIC RESEARCH)—Loud Speakers—NHT; *U.S. Public*, pg. 1369

AR/ACOUSTIC RESEARCH—Cables, Connectors, & Accessories—Recoton Corporation; *U.S. Public*, pg. 1369

ARC—Midsole Cushioning Device—Avia; *U.S. Private*, pg. 62

ARC—Tire Curing Bands—Bandag, Incorporated; *U.S. Public*, pg. 177

ARC—Desk Accessories—Smith McDonald Corp.; *U.S. Private*, pg. 1009

A.R.C. WELDMESH—Fencing & Gates—Smorgon A.R.C.; *Int'l*, pg. 1269

ARC DECO—Plumbing Products—The Black & Decker Corporation; *U.S. Public*, pg. 233

ARC YELLOW—Flourescent Color—Day-Glo Color Corp.; *U.S. Public*, pg. 1357

AR-GLO—Fluorescent Additive—Spectronics Corporation; *U.S. Private*, pg. 1024

A.R.M.—Allergy Relief Caplet—Menley & James Laboratories, Inc.; *U.S. Public*, pg. 1086

AR MILLENNIUM—Accounts Receivable Software—Dun & Bradstreet Software Services; *Int'l*, pg. 532

ARO—Pumps, Tools, Hoists & Fluid Power Products—Ingersoll-Rand Company; *U.S. Public*, pg. 876

ARO—Tools & Hoists—Tool & Hoist Division; *U.S. Public*, pg. 877

AR 1—Tires—Bridgestone/Firestone, Inc.; *Int'l*, pg. 213

ART—Asphalt Residual Treating Process—Engelhard Corporation; *U.S. Public*, pg. 582

AR 2—Tires—Bridgestone/Firestone, Inc.; *Int'l*, pg. 213

A-REST—Plant Growth Regulator—The Dow Chemical Company; *U.S. Public*, pg. 522

A REVOLUTION IN SIGHT—Telecommunications Services—Lucent Technologies Inc.; *U.S. Public*, pg. 1017

ASAHI—Valves—Ryan Herco Products Corp.; *U.S. Private*, pg. 953

ASAP—Super Absorbent Polymer—AMCOL International Corp.; *U.S. Public*, pg. 63

ASAP—Automatic Service Award Program—L.G. Balfour Co., Inc.; *U.S. Private*, pg. 258

ASAP—Application Processing Software—Fair, Isaac and Company, Inc.; *U.S. Public*, pg. 609

ASAP—Presentation Graphics Software—Software Publishing Corporation; *U.S. Public*, pg. 1483

ASAP WEBSHOW—Internet Plug-In for Graphics Presentations—Software Publishing Corporation; *U.S. Public*, pg. 1483

ASAP WORDPOWER—Presentation Graphics Software—Software Publishing Corporation; *U.S. Public*, pg. 1483

AS&E-EDS—Automatic Explosives Detection Systems—American Science & Engineering, Inc.; *U.S. Public*, pg. 90

ASC—Automotive Accessories—ASC Incorporated; *U.S. Private*, pg. 8

ASCO—Solenoid Valves & Automatic Transfer Switches—Emerson Electric Co.; *U.S. Public*, pg. 572

A.S.-COR—Anti-Hypotensive—SmithKline Beecham plc; *Int'l*, pg. 1264

ASEP—Utility Load Management Equipment—American Science & Engineering, Inc.; *U.S. Public*, pg. 90

ASEP—Surgeon's Gowns—Angelica Corporation; *U.S. Public*, pg. 113

ASEP-PLUS—Surgeon's Gowns—Angelica Corporation; *U.S. Public*, pg. 113

ASF THOMAS—Air Compressors & Vacuum Pumps—Thomas Industries Inc.; *U.S. Public*, pg. 1598

AS/400—Computer Systems—International Business Machines Corporation; *U.S. Public*, pg. 895

AS/400 PERFORMANCEEDGE—Computer System—International Business Machines Corporation; *U.S. Public*, pg. 895

ASI—Worldwide Destination Services—American Sightseeing International; *U.S. Private*, pg. 61

ASI MARKET RESEARCH—Market Research Services—IDC Services, Inc.; *U.S. Private*, pg. 554

ASP—Hydrous Kaolin Aluminum Silicate Pigments—Engelhard Corporation; *U.S. Public*, pg. 582

ASPI—Software—Adaptec, Inc.; *U.S. Public*, pg. 19

ASP-IRRATOR—Suction/Irrigation Control Handle—Conmed Corporation; *U.S. Public*, pg. 431

ASR—Tires—Bridgestone/Firestone, Inc.; *Int'l*, pg. 213

ASR IV—Roof System—Pascoe Building Systems, Inc.; *U.S. Private*, pg. 842

AS/SET—Case Technology—System Software Associates, Inc.; *U.S. Public*, pg. 1552

AST—Personal Computers & Enhancement Prods.—AST Research Inc.; *Int'l*, pg. 1181

ASW—Transparent Polyvinyl Chloride Stretch Film—Reynolds Metals Company; *U.S. Public*, pg. 1385

AT—Computer Systems—International Business Machines Corporation; *U.S. Public*, pg. 895

ATAC—Auto Torque Amplification Chamber—American Honda Motor Co., Inc. Motorcycle Division; *Int'l*, pg. 634

ATA FLASH CARD—PCMCIA Cards—Epson America Inc.; *Int'l*, pg. 1219

ATAKR—Energy Source or Catheter—Medtronic, Inc.; *U.S. Public*, pg. 1082

AT&T EDI—Electronic Data Interchange—AT&T Strategy & New Service Innovations; *U.S. Public*, pg. 11

AT&T ENHANCED FAX—Broadcast Fax Service—AT&T Strategy & New Service Innovations; *U.S. Public*, pg. 11

AT&T LEARNING NETWORK—NONE—AT&T Strategy & New Service Innovations; *U.S. Public*, pg. 11

AT&T MAIL—Public E-Mail Service—AT&T Strategy & New Service Innovations; *U.S. Public*, pg. 11

ATB—Anthony's Tops & Bottoms—C.R. Anthony Company; *U.S. Private*, pg. 1029

ATC—Timers & Counters—Desco Corporation; *U.S. Private*, pg. 326

ATC—Light Bulbs—Duro-Test Corporation; *U.S. Private*, pg. 349

ATC—NONE—Staff Builders Inc.; *U.S. Public*, pg. 1501

ATC—Cable Television Opers.—Time Warner Inc.; *U.S. Public*, pg. 1610

ATC ONLINE—Calling Card—LDDS WorldCom; *U.S. Public*, pg. 1779

ATC 2000—Microscope—Leica, Inc.; *Int'l*, pg. 806

AT500—Manual Autotransfusion Machine—Medtronics Inc.; *U.S. Public*, pg. 1083

AT500P/PRP—Autotransfusion & Sequestration Machine—Medtronics Inc.; *U.S. Public*, pg. 1083

ATG-32—Applications Package—GenRad, Inc.; *U.S. Public*, pg. 731

ATG XPRESS—NONE—GenRad, Inc.; *U.S. Public*, pg. 731

ATM—Automated Teller Machine Network—Banco Popular de Puerto Rico; *U.S. Public*, pg. 175

ATM/DEBIT CARD—Twenty Four Hour Banking Service—Community Bank N.A.; *U.S. Public*, pg. 416

ATM9—Incandescent Bulb—Duro-Test Corporation; *U.S. Private*, pg. 349

ATM POP—Savings Account Exclusively for Teens Ages 12-18; Free ATM Card—Banco Popular de Puerto Rico; *U.S. Public*, pg. 175

ATN—Triple Conditioning Complex—The Dow Chemical Company; *U.S. Public*, pg. 522

ATO—Auto Fuses—Littelfuse, Inc.; *U.S. Public*, pg. 1001

AT1000—Autotransfusion Machine—Medtronics Inc.; *U.S. Public*, pg. 1083

AT750EF—Semi-Automated Autotransfusion Machine—Medtronics Inc.; *U.S. Public*, pg. 1083

AT-2000—Helicopter Transportable Drilling Rigs—Parker Drilling Company; *U.S. Public*, pg. 1259

A/T 2000 PLUS—Film Processor—Air Techniques, Inc.; *U.S. Private*, pg. 28

ATV'S BY KNAPP—Shoes—Knapp Shoes Inc.; *U.S. Private*, pg. 401

ATX RADIAL 23 DEGREES—Tires—Bridgestone/Firestone, Inc.; *Int'l*, pg. 213

A-TEX—Cotton Seamless Dampener Cover for Printing Presses—Jomac, Inc.; *U.S. Private*, pg. 595

A300—Wide Bodied Twin Jet Airliners—Airbus Industrie of North America, Inc.; *Int'l*, pg. 39

A340—Wide Bodied Long Range Airliners—Airbus Industrie of North America, Inc.; *Int'l*, pg. 39

A310—Wide Bodied Twin Jet Airliners—Airbus Industrie of North America, Inc.; *Int'l*, pg. 39

A330—Wide Bodied Twin Jet Airliners—Airbus Industrie of North America, Inc.; *Int'l*, pg. 39

A320—Narrow Bodied Twin Jet Airliners—Airbus Industrie of North America, Inc.; *Int'l*, pg. 39

A3VIP—Advanced Aircraft Avionics-Value Improvement Program—Executive Jet Aviation, Inc.; *U.S. Private*, pg. 388

A TO Z COURIERS—NONE—Rentokil Initial plc; *Int'l*, pg. 1285

A TO ZOO—Subject Access to Children's Picture Books—R.R. Bowker; *Int'l*, pg. 1096

A-2—Sporting Goods—Brunswick Bowling & Billiards Corp.; *U.S. Public*, pg. 265

A2Z SEATING—Ergonomic Seating—Domore Corporation; *U.S. Private*, pg. 339

AUCS—Automatic Clean System—Manitowoc Ice, Inc.; *U.S. Public*, pg. 1041

AUDX—Otoaccoustic Emissions Screener—Bio-Logic Systems Corp.; *U.S. Public*, pg. 230

AULT—Foods—Labatt Brewing Company Limited; *Int'l*, pg. 679

AU PRINTEMPS—Department Store—The Daiei, Inc.; *Int'l*, pg. 364

AVA—NONE—Adaptec, Inc.; *U.S. Public*, pg. 19

AVA—Laundry Detergent—Benckiser Consumer Products Inc.; *Int'l*, pg. 185

AV5000—Workstation—Data General Corporation; *U.S. Public*, pg. 485

AV400—Workstations—Data General Corporation; *U.S. Public*, pg. 485

AV4000—Workstation—Data General Corporation; *U.S. Public*, pg. 485

A-V IMPULSE SYSTEM—Foot Pump for the Reduction of Pain & Swelling & Enhanced Circulation—The Kendall Company; *U.S. Public*, pg. 1647

AV IMPULSE SYSTEM—Venous Flow Amelioration—Orthofix International N.V.; *Int'l*, pg. 1011

A-V MATIC—Automatic Sound/Filmstrip Projector—Dukane Corporation; *U.S. Private*, pg. 345

AV100—Workstation—Data General Corporation; *U.S. Public*, pg. 485

AV PLUS—Pacemaker Lead—St. Jude Medical, Inc.; *U.S. Public*, pg. 1427

AV6000—Workstation—Data General Corporation; *U.S. Public*, pg. 485

AV6220—Computer—Data General Corporation; *U.S. Public*, pg. 485

AV300—Workstations—Data General Corporation; *U.S. Public*, pg. 485

AV200—Workstations—Data General Corporation; *U.S. Public*, pg. 485

AV 220—TV Station Atomation Software—Chyron Corp.; *Int'l*, pg. 1372

AVX/KYOCERA—NONE—Milgray Electronics, Inc.; *U.S. Public*, pg. 205

AWD—Provides Common Graphical User Interface; Maintains Mainframe Function—CSC Financial Services Group; *U.S. Public*, pg. 422

AWWA—American Water Works Assn.—American Water Works Association; *U.S. Public*, pg. 94

A WORLD OF IDEAS—Corrugated Cardboard Shipping Containers—Weyerhaeuser Company; *U.S. Public*, pg. 1764

AXID—NONE—Molex Incorporated; *U.S. Public*, pg. 1121

AXY—Golf Clothing—Mizuno Corporation; *Int'l*, pg. 884

AZ—Liquid Photoresist—Hoechst Aktiengesellschaft; *Int'l*, pg. 624

A-Z/GRANT INTERNATIONAL—Sidetracking & Surface Equipment Services—Smith International, Inc.; *U.S. Public*, pg. 1478

AZO—Photographic, Paper—Eastman Kodak Company; *U.S. Public*, pg. 550

AZO-CRANBERRY—Food Supplement—PolyMedica Industries, Inc.; *U.S. Public*, pg. 1315

AZO-STANDARD—Over-the-Counter Pharmaceutical—PolyMedica Industries, Inc.; *U.S. Public*, pg. 1315

A-B-C—Asbestos Binding Compound—California Products Corp.; *U.S. Private*, pg. 201

A/E SPORT & CO.—Large Size Apparel—Shirmax Leasing Ltd.; *Int'l*, pg. 1235

AGE OF INFORMOTION—Computer software—Attachmate; *U.S. Private*, pg. 98

AAAHH! REAL MONSTERS—Chewing Gum—Amurol Confections Co.; *U.S. Public*, pg. 1781

AADVANTAGE EXTRA—Frequent Flyer Program—American Airlines, Inc.; *U.S. Public*, pg. 9

AADVANTAGE INCENTIVE MILES—Incentive and Promotion Program—American Airlines, Inc.; *U.S. Public*, pg. 9

AALBORG JUBILAEUMS AKVAVIT—Aquavit—Danisco Distillers; *Int'l*, pg. 378

AALBORG TAFFEL AKVAVIT—Aquavit—Danisco Distillers; *Int'l*, pg. 378

AALCO—NONE—Glynwed International PLC; *Int'l*, pg. 554

AAMCO—Transmissions—Aamco Transmissions, Inc.; *U.S. Private*, pg. 9

AAPAK—Packing Drums of Fiber or Fiber with Metallic Ends—Sonoco Products Company; *U.S. Public*, pg. 1485

AAPRI—Facial Scrub, Replenishing Cream & Lotion—The Gillette Company; *U.S. Public*, pg. 743

AARAU—Tennis Shoe—K-Swiss Inc.; *U.S. Public*, pg. 937

AARON ASHER—Book Imprint—The News Corporation Limited; *Int'l*, pg. 925

AARON BROTHERS—Picture Frames, Retail Art & Art Supplies—Aaron Brothers, Inc.; *U.S. Public*, pg. 1104

AARON RENTS BUSINESS EQUIPMENT—Computers, Fax Machines & Shredders—Aaron Rents, Inc.; *U.S. Public*, pg. 12

AARON RENTS CONVENTION FURNISHINGS—Short-Term Special Event Rentals—Aaron Rents, Inc.; *U.S. Public*, pg. 12

AARON RENTS FURNITURE—Office & Residential Furniture—Aaron Rents, Inc.; *U.S. Public*, pg. 12

AARON RENTS HOUSEWARES & LINENS—Sheets, Towels & Kitchen Items—Aaron Rents, Inc.; *U.S. Public*, pg. 12

AARON'S RENTAL PURCHASE—Electronics, Furniture & Appliances—Aaron Rents, Inc.; *U.S. Public*, pg. 12

AARON SELLS FURNITURE—Furniture—Aaron Rents, Inc.; *U.S. Public*, pg. 12

AARON SPELLING—Television Productions—Spelling Television; *U.S. Private*, pg. 776

AARTIK—Dinnerware—Dansk International Designs Ltd.; *U.S. Public*, pg. 261

AATLAS—Pallet Trucks—Atlas Lift Truck Rentals & Sales, Inc.; *U.S. Private*, pg. 96

ABALYN—Methyl Ester of Rosin—Hercules Incorporated; *U.S. Public*, pg. 809

ABANDERADO—Knits—Sara Lee Corporation; *U.S. Public*, pg. 1432

ABBA-ZABA—Candy—Annabelle Candy Company, Inc.; *U.S. Private*, pg. 75

ABBEY ETNA—Metalworking Machinery, Tools & Equipment—Abbey Etna Machine Company; *U.S. Private*, pg. 9

ABBI—NONE—U.S. Surgical Corp.; *U.S. Public*, pg. 1687

ABBOKINASE—Urokinase—Abbott Laboratories; *U.S. Public*, pg. 12

ABBOTT B-HCG EIA—Diagnostic Products—Abbott Laboratories; *U.S. Public*, pg. 12

ABBOTT BASE—Diagnostic Products—Abbott Laboratories; *U.S. Public*, pg. 12

ABBOTT CEA-EIA—Diagnostic Products—Abbott Laboratories; *U.S. Public*, pg. 12

ABBOTT DMS—Diagnostic Products—Abbott Laboratories; *U.S. Public*, pg. 12

ABBOTT HBE—Diagnostic Products—Abbott Laboratories; *U.S. Public*, pg. 12

ABBOTT HBE EIA—Diagnostic Products—Abbott Laboratories; *U.S. Public*, pg. 12

ABBOTT MATRIX—System for Diagnosing Allergies from a Single Blood Sample—Abbott Laboratories; *U.S. Public*, pg. 12

ABBOTT SPECTRUM—Chemical Analyzer—Abbott Laboratories; *U.S. Public*, pg. 12

ABBOTT TESTPACK—Diagnostic Products—Abbott Laboratories; *U.S. Public*, pg. 12

ABBOTTS—Milk Products—Labatt Brewing Company Limited; *Int'l*, pg. 679

ABBOTTS OLD PHILADELPHIA—Ice Cream—Labatt Brewing Company Limited; *Int'l*, pg. 679

ABBYLAND—Fresh Meats—Abbyland Foods, Inc.; *U.S. Private*, pg. 10

ABCO—Laminated Case Goods & Work-Stations—Jami, Inc.; *U.S. Private*, pg. 581

ABDOW'S FAMILY RESTAURANTS—NONE—Bickford's Family Restaurants; *U.S. Public*, pg. 545

ABDOW'S RESTAURANTS—Family Restaurants—ELXSI Corporation; *U.S. Public*, pg. 545

ABEILLE—Shoe Polishes/Waxes—Benckiser Consumer Products Inc.; *Int'l*, pg. 185

ABEL—Software—Data I/O Corporation; *U.S. Public*, pg. 486

ABEL AUTO—Car Care Products—Sara Lee Corporation; *U.S. Public*, pg. 1432

ABELCET—Amphotericin-B Liquid Complex Injection—The Liposome Company, Inc.; *U.S. Public*, pg. 1000

ABELOUR GLENLIVET—Single Malt Scotch—Austin Nichols & Co. Inc.; *Int'l*, pg. 566

ABEND-AID—Systems Software Products—Compuware Corporation; *U.S. Public*, pg. 423

ABERDEEN—Window & Bedding Products—CHF Industries, Inc.; *U.S. Private*, pg. 1094

ABERLOUR—Single Malt Scotch Whiskey—Groupe Pernod Ricard; *Int'l*, pg. 566

ABERLOUR—NONE—Austin Nichols & Co. Inc.; *Int'l*, pg. 566

ABI-INFORM—Datacourier—Bell & Howell Holdings; *U.S. Public*, pg. 201

ABITARE CABINETS—Custom Cabinetry—Crystal Cabinet Works, Inc.; *U.S. Private*, pg. 293

ABITOL—Hyroabietyl Alcohol—Hercules Incorporated; *U.S. Public*, pg. 809

ABLEWARE—Aids for Disabled—Bel-Art Products; *U.S. Private*, pg. 130

ABONDANCE—Vegetable & Flower Seed—Groupe Limagrain; *Int'l*, pg. 566

ABOUT FACE—Soft Baby Carrier—Evenflo Company, Inc.; *U.S. Public*, pg. 629

ABOVE—Electronic Instrument—Intel Corporation; *U.S. Public*, pg. 886

ABOVE THE CROWD—Recruiting Package—RE/MAX International, Inc.; *U.S. Private*, pg. 912

ABOVE THE RIM—Athletic Shoes—Reebok International Ltd.; *U.S. Public*, pg. 1369

ABOVEALL—Automatic Under Cabinet Can Opener; Can Opener Plus—National Presto Industries, Inc.; *U.S. Public*, pg. 1159

ABRASIMET—Cut Off Machine—Buehler, Limited; *U.S. Public*, pg. 574

ABRASOWELD—Electrode—The Lincoln Electric Company; *U.S. Public*, pg. 996

ABSOLUT VODKA—NONE—The Seagram Company Ltd.; *Int'l*, pg. 1214

ABSOLUTE—High Efficiency Air Filters—Farr Company; *U.S. Public*, pg. 613

ABSOLUTE PART CONTROL—Metal Forming Presses—Verson Division; *U.S. Public*, pg. 48

ABSORB-LOC—Gel Sheet—Kimberly-Clark Corporation; *U.S. Public*, pg. 958

ABSORBA—Toiletries—International Cosmetics Co., Ltd.; *Int'l*, pg. 684

ABSORBOTRON—Shock Absorber—Josam Company; *U.S. Private*, pg. 600

ABTCO EXTERIOR SHUTTERS—Injection Molded Solutions—ABT Building Products Corporation; *Int'l*, pg. 20

ABTEI—NONE—SmithKline Beecham Corporation; *Int'l*, pg. 1264

ABU-MATIC—Spin Casting Reels—Abu Garcia Inc.; *U.S. Private*, pg. 822

ABU-MATIC—Spin Casting Reels—Aritmos AB; *Int'l*, pg. 1072

ABUELITA—Hot Chocolate—The Quaker Oats Company; *U.S. Public*, pg. 1347

ABUSEABLE—Electronics—National Semiconductor Corporation; *U.S. Public*, pg. 1159

ACACIA—Dinnerware—Dansk International Designs Ltd.; *U.S. Public*, pg. 261

ACADEMIC AMERICAN ENCYCLOPEDIA—Encyclopedia—Grolier Inc.; *Int'l*, pg. 794

ACADEMIC LANKIT—Computer System—International Business Machines Corporation; *U.S. Public*, pg. 895

ACADEMIC YEAR IN AMERICA—High School Exchange Programs—American Institute for Foreign Study; *U.S. Private*, pg. 56

ACADEMIE ACCOR—Training Center—Accor S.A.; *Int'l*, pg. 20

ACADEMY—NONE—Eastman Kodak Company; *U.S. Public*, pg. 550

ACADIA PRESSBOARD—Pressboard—FiberMark Inc.; *U.S. Public*, pg. 620

ACAPULCO—Restaurants—Restaurant Associates Corporation; *U.S. Private*, pg. 924

ACAPULCO NECTARS—Fruit Nectars—Jugos del Valle, S.A. de C.V.; *Int'l*, pg. 716

ACCEL—Electrical & Fuel System Parts—Echlin Inc.; *U.S. Public*, pg. 560

ACCELADANCER—Basketball Shoes—Mizuno Corporation; *Int'l*, pg. 884

ACCELERATOR—Impact System on Drill String—Wilson Industries Inc.; *U.S. Private*, pg. 1181

ACCELEREX—Digital Accelerometer—AlliedSignal Commercial Avionics Systems; *U.S. Public*, pg. 50

ACCELL—Ion Exchange Media & Affinity Media—Millipore Corporation; *U.S. Public*, pg. 1112

ACCENT—Homes—Centex Corporation; *U.S. Public*, pg. 322

ACCENT—Loge Generator—Chyron Corp.; *Int'l*, pg. 1372

ACCENT—Post-Emergent Corn Herbicide—Du Pont (E.I. Du Pont De Nemours & Co.); *U.S. Public*, pg. 530

ACCENT—Automobile—Hyundai Motor America; *Int'l*, pg. 641

ACCENT—Craft & Hobby Paints & Finishes—Koh-I-Noor, Inc.; *U.S. Private*, pg. 629

ACCENT—Telephone—Lucent Technologies Inc.; *U.S. Public*, pg. 1017

AC' CENT—Seasoning Powders—The Pillsbury Company; *Int'l*, pg. 411

ACCENT—Bathtub Wall Kit—Plaskolite Inc.; *U.S. Private*, pg. 870

ACCENT—Cookware—Regal Ware, Inc.; *U.S. Private*, pg. 917

ACCENT BRIGHT—Quick Reference Marker—Sanford Corporation; *U.S. Public*, pg. 1178

ACCENT OAK FURNITURE—NONE—Royal Waterbeds; *U.S. Private*, pg. 949

ACCENTLINE—Display Lighting Fixtures—Fostoria Industries, Inc.; *U.S. Private*, pg. 421

ACCENTRICS—Furniture—Pulaski Furniture Corporation; *U.S. Public*, pg. 1342

ACCENTS—Bath Hardware—Amerock Corporation; *U.S. Public*, pg. 1177

ACCENTS—Area Rugs—Couristan Inc.; *U.S. Private*, pg. 279

ACCENTS—Hair Accessories—Goody Products, Inc.; *U.S. Public*, pg. 1177

ACCENTS BY JUNO—Recessed Trims—Juno Lighting, Inc.; *U.S. Public*, pg. 935

ACCENTUETTE—Sleepwear—Lanz, Inc.; *U.S. Private*, pg. 650

ACCENTUOUS—Mascara—Cosmair, Inc.; *Int'l*, pg. 818

ACCEPTOR—Plug & Receptacles—Killark Electric Manufacturing Co.; *U.S. Public*, pg. 844

ACCESNETWORK—Modems—Data Control Systems; *U.S. Public*, pg. 420

ACCESS—Pre-Paid Health Plan—Coventry Corporation; *U.S. Public*, pg. 454

ACCESS—Herbicide—The Dow Chemical Company; *U.S. Public*, pg. 522

ACCESS—Batch Controller & Flow Complete Series—ITT Barton Instruments; *U.S. Public*, pg. 860

ACCESS—Computerized System Linking Companies, Customers, and Suppliers—The Mead Corporation; *U.S. Public*, pg. 1074

ACCESS—NONE—Medline Industries, Inc.; *U.S. Private*, pg. 728

ACCESS—Computer Database—Microsoft Corporation; *U.S. Public*, pg. 1107

ACCESS—Audio/Visual Systems—Sony Electronics; *Int'l*, pg. 1281

ACCESS—NONE—Worcester Controls Corp.; *Int'l*, pg. 128

ACCESS CONTROL—NONE—Check Point Software Technologies Ltd.; *U.S. Public*, pg. 342

ACCESS CONTROL & SECURITY SYSTEMS INTEGRATION—Tabloid for Securities & Facilities Directors—Intertec Publishing; *U.S. Public*, pg. 1327

ACCESS CONTROL & SYSTEMS INTEGRATION—Monthly Publication—Intertec Publishing; *U.S. Public*, pg. 1328

ACCESS CONTROL DIRECTORY—Annual Publication—Intertec Publishing; *U.S. Public*, pg. 1328

ACCESS/EMPOWER—NONE—UB Networks; *Int'l*, pg. 924

ACCESS FOR DB2—NONE—BMC Software, Inc.; *U.S. Public*, pg. 162

ACCESS HUB—LAN Systems—Gandalf Technologies Inc.; *Int'l*, pg. 540

ACCESS MANAGER—Electronic Lock System for Pedestrian Doors—Vindicator Technologies; *U.S. Private*, pg. 1141

ACCESS MASTER—Security System—Linear Corporation; *U.S. Public*, pg. 1193

ACCESS NP—Central Office Platfrm for Switching in Storage of Voice Messages—Comverse Network Systems; *U.S. Public*, pg. 425

ACCESS/ONE—Smart Hub—Tandem Computers Inc.; *U.S. Public*, pg. 417

ACCESS/ONE—NONE—UB Networks; *Int'l*, pg. 924

ACCESS ONE BANK SYSTEM—Branchless Banking Service—Comerica Incorporated; *U.S. Public*, pg. 408

ACCESS PLUS—E-Mail Softwear—AT&T Strategy & New Service Innovations; *U.S. Public*, pg. 11

ACCESS PLUS—Automatic Meter Reading System—Badger Meter, Inc.; *U.S. Public*, pg. 164

ACCESS PRO—NONE—Linear Corporation; *U.S. Public*, pg. 1193

ACCESS REMOTE SUPPORT—NONE—GenRad, Inc.; *U.S. Public*, pg. 731

ACCESS/SECURE—NONE—UB Networks; *Int'l*, pg. 924

ACCESS60—Multiplexer—Telco Systems, Inc.; *U.S. Public*, pg. 1568

ACCESS/STAX—NONE—UB Networks; *Int'l*, pg. 924

ACCESS/TRAX—NONE—UB Networks; *Int'l*, pg. 924

ACCESS30—Multiplexer—Telco Systems, Inc.; *U.S. Public*, pg. 1568

ACCESS TO MONEY PLUS—Visa Check Card—Downey Savings & Loan Association, F.A.; *U.S. Public*, pg. 526

ACCESS 2120 & 2300—Wide Area Network Systems—Gandalf Technologies Inc.; *Int'l*, pg. 540

ACCESSMAX—Object Oriented Software for Network Based Enhanced Telecomm. Services—Comverse Network Systems; *U.S. Public*, pg. 425

ACCLAIM—Stairway Lift—Access Industries; *U.S. Private*, pg. 11

ACCLAIM—NONE—Acclaim Comics; *U.S. Public*, pg. 15

ACCLAIM—Interactive Entertainment Software—Acclaim Entertainment, Inc.; *U.S. Public*, pg. 15

ACCLAIM—Machine Warewashing Detergent—Ecolab Inc.; *U.S. Public*, pg. 562

ACCLAIM—Client Encounter Information Software—Intelligent Systems Corp.; *U.S. Public*, pg. 888

ACCLAIM—Inbound-Outbound Service—LDDS WorldCom; *U.S. Public*, pg. 1779

ACCLAIM HAIR SHINERS—Perm, Shampoos, Conditioners & Styling Aids—Zotos International; *Int'l*, pg. 1236

ACCLAIM X-TRA—Specialty Chemical—AgrEvo USA Company; *Int'l*, pg. 1203

ACCO—Stapler—ACCO Brands, Inc.; *U.S. Public*, pg. 674

ACCO—Chains—Acco Chain & Lifting Products; *Int'l*, pg. 473

ACCO—Office Products—ACCO World Corporation; *U.S. Public*, pg. 674

ACCO—Paper Fastening & Computer Accessories—Fortune Brands, Inc.; *U.S. Public*, pg. 674

ACCODATA—Computer Accessories—ACCO World Corporation; *U.S. Public*, pg. 674

ACCODATA—Office Products—Fortune Brands, Inc.; *U.S. Public*, pg. 674

ACCOLADE—NONE—Avon Products Co., Ltd.; *U.S. Public*, pg. 156

ACCOLADE—Latex Enamel—Pratt & Lambert United, Inc.; *U.S. Public*, pg. 1466

ACCOLADES—Greeting Cards & Stationery—American Greetings Corporation; *U.S. Public*, pg. 77

ACCOLATE—Pharmaceutical—Zeneca Group Plc; *Int'l*, pg. 1524

ACCOLIFT—Hoits & Trolleys—Acco Chain & Lifting Products; *Int'l*, pg. 473

ACCOLOY—Alloy Chain—Acco Chain & Lifting Products; *Int'l*, pg. 473

ACCORD—Automobile—American Honda Motor Co., Inc.; *Int'l*, pg. 634

ACCORD—Automobile—American Honda Motor Co., Inc. Automobile Sales Division; *Int'l*, pg. 634

ACCORD—Nonwoven Fabric—Kimberly-Clark Corporation; *U.S. Public*, pg. 958

ACCORDIA—Cellular Shades—Kirsch; *U.S. Public*, pg. 1176

ACCORDIA-FOLD—Drapery Hardware—Kirsch; *U.S. Public*, pg. 1176

ACCORDION—Expanding Products—ATAPCO Office Products Group; *U.S. Private*, pg. 64

ACCOS—Grocery Store—Tengelmann Warenhandelsgesellschaft; *Int'l*, pg. 1375

ACCOSOFT—Cationic-Fabric Softeners—Stepan Company; *U.S. Public*, pg. 1514

ACCOUNT PROCESSOR—Software—Bankers Systems Incorporated; *U.S. Private*, pg. 114

ACCOUNTANTS-ON-CALL—Accountant Staffing—Adecco Employment Services; *Int'l*, pg. 24

ACCOUNTANTS USA—Accounting Staffing—Western Staff Services; *U.S. Public*, pg. 1760

ACCOUNTEMPS—Specialized Temporary Financial Staffing—Robert Half International Inc.; *U.S. Public*, pg. 774

ACCPAC ACCOUNTS PAYABLE—Control & Manage Cash Disbursements—Computer Associates International, Inc.; *U.S. Public*, pg. 420

ACCPAC BPI ACCOUNTING PLUS—Micro Software—Computer Associates International, Inc.; *U.S. Public*, pg. 420

ACCPAC PLUS—Micro Software for PCs & Compatible Machines—Computer Associates International, Inc.; *U.S. Public*, pg. 420

ACCPAC PLUS ACCOUNTS RECEIVABLE—Customer Account Tracking & Cash-Management Control—Computer Associates International, Inc.; *U.S. Public*, pg. 420

ACCPRO—Enhanced Polymer Resins—Amoco Chemicals; *U.S. Public*, pg. 102

ACCPRO—Enhanced Polymer Resins—Amoco Corporation; *U.S. Public*, pg. 101

ACCRA-TEMP—Moisture Control System for Seed Cotton Cleaning & Preparation for Ginning—Continental Eagle Corporation; *U.S. Private*, pg. 267

ACCRU-SET—Refiner Control—Beloit Corporation; *U.S. Public*, pg. 789

ACCTUF—Polypropylene Impact CoPolymers—Amoco Chemicals; *U.S. Public*, pg. 102

ACCTUF—Polypropylene Impact CoPolymers—Amoco Corporation; *U.S. Public*, pg. 101

ACCU-BORE—Lock Installation Boring Tool—Ilco Unican Corp.; *Int'l*, pg. 1432

ACCU-BORE—Lock Installation Boring Tool—Unican Security Systems Ltd.; *Int'l*, pg. 1432

ACCU-CAT—Proportioning & Dispensing Machines—Graco Inc.; *U.S. Public*, pg. 756

ACCU-CHOKE—Shotgun Barrels—O.F. Mossberg & Sons, Inc.; *U.S. Private*, pg. 764

ACCU-CURVE—Thermistors—Ketema, Inc.; *U.S. Private*, pg. 604

ACCU-DERMATOME—Battery Powered Dermatone—Aesculap, Inc.; *Int'l*, pg. 29

ACCU-DOOR—Raised Panel Door System—Powermatic; *U.S. Public*, pg. 502

ACCU-FLO—Precision Metering Pump—Beckman Instruments, Inc.; *U.S. Public*, pg. 199

ACCU-FLOW—Automatic Case Depalletizer—Alvey Systems, Inc; *U.S. Private*, pg. 47

ACCU-LUBE—Metal Fluid Product—ITW Fluid Products Group; *U.S. Public*, pg. 866

ACCU-POINT—Rolling Ball Pen—The Gillette Company; *U.S. Public*, pg. 743

ACCU-PREP—Programmable Diluter & Dispenser—Beckman Instruments, Inc.; *U.S. Public*, pg. 199

ACCU-ROLL—Push/Pull Control Cable Assemblies—Teleflex Incorporated; *U.S. Public*, pg. 1569

ACCU-SORT SYSTEMS—Company Name—Accu-Sort Systems, Inc.; *U.S. Private*, pg. 11

ACCU-SPRAY—High Efficiency Spray Nozzles—Cochrane, Inc.; *U.S. Public*, pg. 456

ACCU-TEK 250 + 350—Concrete Compression Testers—ELE International, Inc./Soiltest; *Int'l*, pg. 1287

ACCU-THERM—Heat Exchanger—Paul Mueller Company; *U.S. Public*, pg. 1141

ACCU-TRAK—Measurement While Drilling—Baker Hughes INTEQ; *U.S. Public*, pg. 166

ACCU-TRIM—P.C. Flor Control Adjustment—Robert Bosch Fluid Power Corporation; *Int'l*, pg. 204

ACCU-TUNER—Electronic Components—General Instrument Corporation; *U.S. Public*, pg. 716

ACCUBALANCE—Capture Hood—TSI Incorporated; *U.S. Public*, pg. 1559

ACCUBEAD—Polystrene Filter Beads—Eastman Kodak Company; *U.S. Public*, pg. 550

ACCUBRITE—TV Picture Tubes—Thomson Consumer Electronics Inc.; *Int'l*, pg. 1383

ACCUCARE—NONE—Medline Industries, Inc.; *U.S. Private*, pg. 728

ACCUCHANGE—Coin Dispenser—Brandt, Inc.; *Int'l*, pg. 387

ACCUCHART—Chart Paper—Gould Instrument Systems, Inc.; *U.S. Public*, pg. 1592

ACCUCIRCUIT—TV Receiver Components—Thomson Consumer Electronics Inc.; *Int'l*, pg. 1383

ACCUCOLOR—TV Sets—Thomson Consumer Electronics Inc.; *Int'l*, pg. 1383

ACCUCORE—Needle—Medtronic, Inc.; *U.S. Public*, pg. 1082

ACCUDACS—Automated Telecommunications Units with Multiple Applications in Voice/Data—DSC Communications Corporation; *U.S. Public*, pg. 475

ACCUDATA—Photofinishing Apparatus—Eastman Kodak Company; *U.S. Public*, pg. 550

ACCUDIL—Zero-Dead-Volume Syringes—Hamilton Co., Inc.; *U.S. Private*, pg. 497

ACCUDRI—Sulfur Hexafluoride—AlliedSignal Inc., Engineered Materials; *U.S. Public*, pg. 51

ACCUFAX—Thermal Facsimile Papers—Perfecseal Company; *U.S. Public*, pg. 210

ACCUFIT—Computer Software—Beckman Instruments, Inc.; *U.S. Public*, pg. 199

ACCUFIX—Navigational Aids—Megapulse, Inc.; *U.S. Private*, pg. 729

ACCUFLASH—NONE—AGA Gas, Inc.; *Int'l*, pg. 13

ACCUFLASH-S—NONE—AGA Gas, Inc.; *Int'l*, pg. 13

ACCUFLASH-T—NONE—AGA Gas, Inc.; *Int'l*, pg. 13

ACCUFLOW—Piston Filler—Pneumatic Scale Corporation; *U.S. Private*, pg. 118

ACCUFORCE—Digital Gauge—AMETEK, Inc.; *U.S. Public*, pg. 99

ACCUGENE—Molecular Biology Buffers & Reagents—BioWhittaker, Inc.; *U.S. Public*, pg. 297

ACCUGLAS—Spin-On Glasses—AlliedSignal Inc.; *U.S. Public*, pg. 49

ACCUGLIDE—Package Conveying Machinery—Alvey Systems, Inc; *U.S. Private*, pg. 47

ACCUGLIDE—Taping Head, Pressure Sensitive Adhesive—3M; *U.S. Public*, pg. 1604

ACCUGLIDE PLUS—Accumulation Conveyor—Alvey Systems, Inc; *U.S. Private*, pg. 47

ACCUKOTE—Thread Dope Applicator—Weatherford Enterra Incorporated; *U.S. Public*, pg. 1749

ACCULAB—Spectrophotometer—Beckman Instruments, Inc.; *U.S. Public*, pg. 199

ACCULASER—Balancing System—Mechanical Technology Inc.; *U.S. Public*, pg. 1077

ACCULEVEL—Non-Instrumented Enzyme Immunochromatography Tests—Syntex; *Int'l*, pg. 1120

ACCULINE—Metallic Reloading Equipment—Lyman Products Corporation; *U.S. Private*, pg. 683

ACCULINK—NONE—Jason Industrial, Inc.; *U.S. Private*, pg. 583

ACCULINK—Multiplexer, FI, DSU/CSU Hardware—Paradyne; *U.S. Private*, pg. 838

ACCULITE—Photofinishing Apparatus—Eastman Kodak Company; *U.S. Public*, pg. 550

ACCULUBE—Lubricating System—Illinois Tool Works Inc.; *U.S. Public*, pg. 865

ACCUMAFLOW—Conveyors & Components—Litton Industries, Inc.; *U.S. Public*, pg. 1002

ACCUMAIL—Microcomputer Software for US Mailers—Group 1 Software, Inc.; *U.S. Public*, pg. 417

ACCUMARK—Needle Sheath—Medtronic, Inc.; *U.S. Public*, pg. 1082

ACCUMATCH—Electronic Color Matching Equipment—PPG Industries, Inc.; *U.S. Public*, pg. 1245

ACCUMATIC—TV Color Control—Thomson Consumer Electronics Inc.; *Int'l*, pg. 1383

ACCUMAX—Graphic Arts Film—Eastman Kodak Company; *U.S. Public*, pg. 550

ACCUMAX—Fiber Optic Cable & Cordage—Lucent Technologies Inc.; *U.S. Public*, pg. 1017

ACCUMEASURE SYSTEM 1500—Measuring System—Mechanical Technology Inc.; *U.S. Public*, pg. 1077

ACCUMEASURE SYSTEM 1000—Measuring System—Mechanical Technology Inc.; *U.S. Public*, pg. 1077

ACCUMESH—Skin Graft Mesher—Aesculap, Inc.; *Int'l*, pg. 29

ACCUMET—Meters—Fisher Scientific Company; *U.S. Private*, pg. 658

ACCUNET—Photographic Apparatus—Eastman Kodak Company; *U.S. Public*, pg. 550

ACCUPACTOR—Crusher—Svedala Industries Inc.; *Int'l*, pg. 1325

ACCUPIK—Automated Order Selection System—SI Handling Systems, Inc.; *U.S. Public*, pg. 1418

ACCUPLACE—Needle Guide—Medtronic, Inc.; *U.S. Public*, pg. 1082

ACCUPOWER—Brake Parts—Echlin Inc.; *U.S. Public*, pg. 560

ACCUPRIL—Pharmaceutical Product—Warner-Lambert Company; *U.S. Public*, pg. 1738

ACCURA—Cylinder Control System—AGA Ges.m.b.H.; *Int'l*, pg. 13

ACCURACY—Stationery Products—The Mead Corporation; *U.S. Public*, pg. 1074

ACCURATE—Electrical & Emission Engine System—Echlin Inc.; *U.S. Public*, pg. 560

ACCURATE METERING—Flow Meters-Sanitary—Crouch Supply Company, Inc.; *U.S. Private*, pg. 291

ACCURAY—Product/Process Control System—ABB Industrial Systems, Inc.; *Int'l*, pg. 4

ACCUREL—Specialty Chemicals—Akzo Nobel Inc.; *Int'l*, pg. 47

ACCUREL—Microporous Polymers—Akzo Nobel N.V.; *Int'l*, pg. 42

ACCURFRAME—Assembled Wirings Frames—Litton Industries, Inc.; *U.S. Public*, pg. 1002

ACCURIBBON—Fiber Optic Cable—Lucent Technologies Inc.; *U.S. Public*, pg. 1017

ACCUSAT—Stand Alone Pulse Oximeter—Datascope Corp.; *U.S. Public*, pg. 487

ACCUSENSOR—Hand-held Screening Units for On-Site Testing for Contaminants in Water—Osmonics, Inc.; *U.S. Public*, pg. 1233

ACCUSET—Energy Meter—Beckman Instruments, Inc.; *U.S. Public*, pg. 199

ACCUSPIN—Spin-On Dopants—AlliedSignal Inc., Engineered Materials; *U.S. Public*, pg. 51

ACCUSPIN—Centrifuge—Beckman Instruments, Inc.; *U.S. Public*, pg. 199

ACCUSTAT—NONE—Laserscope Surgical Systems; *U.S. Public*, pg. 979

ACCUSTROKE—Pipettes—Beckman Instruments, Inc.; *U.S. Public*, pg. 199

ACCUSWITCH—Electronic Components—General Instrument Corporation; *U.S. Public*, pg. 716

ACCUTAB—Very High Accuracy Digitizer—GTCO Corporation; *U.S. Private*, pg. 436

ACCUTECH—Golf Clubs & Balls—The Austad Company; *U.S. Public*, pg. 782

ACCUTECT—Wheel Detector—Union Switch & Signal Inc.; *Int'l*, pg. 77

ACCUTEST—Respirator Rit Test—Lensclean, Inc.; *U.S. Private*, pg. 162

ACCUTEXT—OCR Software—Xerox Imaging Systems, Inc.; *U.S. Public*, pg. 1785

ACCUTHANE—One Component Urethane Adhesive—H.B. Fuller Company; *U.S. Public*, pg. 686

ACCUTINT—TV Tint Control—Thomson Consumer Electronics Inc.; *Int'l*, pg. 1383

ACCUTINT—Color Display Circuitry—Zenith Electronics Corp.; *U.S. Public*, pg. 1790

ACCUTORR—Non-Invasive Blood Pressure Monitor With Or Without Recorder—Datascope Corp.; *U.S. Public*, pg. 487

ACCUTOUCH—Resistive Touchscreen—Elo TouchSystems, Inc.; *U.S. Public*, pg. 1362

ACCUTOUCH—TV Tuning System—Thomson Consumer Electronics Inc.; *Int'l*, pg. 1383

ACCUTRAC—Drafters—OCE-U.S.A.; *Int'l*, pg. 994

ACCUTRAK—Control & Monitoring Equipment—BetzDearborn Inc.; *U.S. Public*, pg. 226

ACCUTRAK—PH Meters—Fisher Scientific Company; *U.S. Private*, pg. 658

ACCUTRAN—Western Blot Assay Products—Schleicher & Schuell, Inc.; *Int'l*, pg. 1206

ACCUTRIM—Sheet Paper—Westvaco Corporation; *U.S. Public*, pg. 1762

ACCUTRON—Quartz Watches—Bulova Corporation; *U.S. Public*, pg. 1010

ACCUTRON—Watches—Loews Corporation; *U.S. Public*, pg. 1010

ACCUTUNE—Electronic Components—General Instrument Corporation; *U.S. Public*, pg. 716

ACCUVAC—NONE—Pfizer Inc.; *U.S. Public*, pg. 1281

ACCUVAR—Power Factor Correction System—Aerovox Inc.; *U.S. Public*, pg. 25

ACCUVIEW—Overhead Transparencies—Perfecseal Company; *U.S. Public*, pg. 210

ACCUVISION—CCD Camera—Accu-Sort Systems, Inc.; *U.S. Private*, pg. 11

ACCUWAVE—VXIbus-based Digital Subsystem for ATE Systems Integrators—GenRad, Inc.; *U.S. Public*, pg. 731

ACCUWELL—Lab Computer System—Mallinckrodt Inc.; *U.S. Public*, pg. 1039

ACE—NONE—Ace Hardware Corporation; *U.S. Private*, pg. 12

ACE—Elastic Bandages, Joint Supports, Plastic Gloves—Becton Dickinson & Company; *U.S. Public*, pg. 199

ACE—NONE—Berkley Publishing Corp.; *Int'l*, pg. 1027

ACE—NONE—Brown & Sharpe Manufacturing Company; *U.S. Public*, pg. 260

ACE—Filters—Champion Laboratories, Inc.; *U.S. Private*, pg. 1113

ACE—Lock—Chicago Lock Company; *U.S. Private*, pg. 235

ACE—Multichannel Analyzer—EG & G Ortec; *U.S. Public*, pg. 543

ACE—Gifts & Greeting Cards—Fine Art Developments plc; *Int'l*, pg. 485

ACE—Combs—Goody Products, Inc.; *U.S. Public*, pg. 1177

ACE—NONE—Procter & Gamble Venezuela, C.A.; *U.S. Public*, pg. 1332

ACE BEST BUYS—NONE—Ace Hardware Corporation; *U.S. Private*, pg. 12

ACE FIVE STAR—NONE—Ace Hardware Corporation; *U.S. Private*, pg. 12

ACE HARDWARE—NONE—Ace Hardware Corporation; *U.S. Private*, pg. 12

ACE HARDWARE AND GARDEN CENTER—NONE—Ace Hardware Corporation; *U.S. Private*, pg. 12

ACE HARDWARE COMMITTED TO A QUALITY ENVIRONMENT—NONE—Ace Hardware Corporation; *U.S. Private*, pg. 12

ACE HARDWARE - THE MORE STORE—NONE—Ace Hardware Corporation; *U.S. Private*, pg. 12

ACE HARDWARE BROWN BAG BONANZA—NONE—Ace Hardware Corporation; *U.S. Private*, pg. 12

ACE IS THE PLACE—NONE—Ace Hardware Corporation; *U.S. Private*, pg. 12

ACE IS THE PLACE WITH THE HELPFUL HARDWARE MAN—NONE—Ace Hardware Corporation; *U.S. Private*, pg. 12

ACE NEW EXPERIENCE—NONE—Ace Hardware Corporation; *U.S. Private*, pg. 12

ACE PRO—NONE—Ace Hardware Corporation; *U.S. Private*, pg. 12

ACE SEVEN STAR—NONE—Ace Hardware Corporation; *U.S. Private*, pg. 12

ACE SIL—Battery Separators—Thomas & Betts/Amerace; *U.S. Public*, pg. 1598

ACE-THREDS—Threaded Glass Joints—Ace Glass Incorporated; *U.S. Private*, pg. 12

ACE THREE STAR—NONE—Ace Hardware Corporation; *U.S. Private*, pg. 12

ACE II—Lock—Chicago Lock Company; *U.S. Private*, pg. 235

ACE 2000—NONE—Ace Hardware Corporation; *U.S. Private*, pg. 12

ACEL IMUNE—Vaccine—American Home Products Corporation; *U.S. Public*, pg. 79

ACENET—NONE—Ace Hardware Corporation; *U.S. Private*, pg. 12

ACEQUIDE—Quinapril & Diuretic, Cardiovascular—Recordati Industria Chimica e Farmaceutica S.p.A.; *Int'l*, pg. 1090

ACEQUIN—Quinapril, Antihypertensive—Recordati Industria Chimica e Farmaceutica S.p.A.; *Int'l*, pg. 1090

ACER—NONE—Acer Incorporated; *Int'l*, pg. 22

ACES—NONE—Life Technologies, Inc.; *U.S. Public*, pg. 504

ACES—Roof Engineering Software—MiTek, Inc.; *Int'l*, pg. 1106

ACESS—NONE—Pitney Bowes Inc.; *U.S. Public*, pg. 1303

ACETRON—Lubricated Polyacetate Shapes, Resins & Parts—DSM Engineering Plastic Products; *Int'l*, pg. 354

ACFB—Motor Brakes & Brake Motors—Electroid Co.; *U.S. Private*, pg. 369

ACHIEVA—Automobile—Oldsmobile Div. General Motors Corp.; *U.S. Public*, pg. 720

ACHIEVER PLAN—Checking Account Package—Standard Bank Investment Corporation Limited; *Int'l*, pg. 1293

THE ACHIEVER—Chair/Desk—Virco Mfg. Corporation; *U.S. Public*, pg. 1721

ACID MANTLE—Skin Acidifier—Bradley Pharmaceuticals; *U.S. Public*, pg. 249

ACID MANTLE—Skin Acidifier—Doak Dermatologics; *U.S. Public*, pg. 250

ACID MANTLE—Cream, Vehicle for Compatible Topical Drugs—Sandoz Pharmaceuticals Corp.; *Int'l*, pg. 974

ACIDO—Non-Asbestos Acid Free Jointing—James Walker & Co. Limited; *Int'l*, pg. 1485

ACIDRINE—Gastrointestinal Preparations—Kali-Chemie Aktiengesellschaft; *Int'l*, pg. 1278

ACINTENE—Terpenes—Arizona Chemical Div.; *U.S. Public*, pg. 901

ACINTOL—Tall Oil Products—Arizona Chemical Div.; *U.S. Public*, pg. 901

ACIPCO—Carbon Pipe & Steel Products—Thomas Pipe & Steel, Inc.; *U.S. Private*, pg. 508

ACIPEN-V—Potassium Penicillin-V Acid—Royal Gist-Brocades N.V.; *Int'l*, pg. 1142

ACLAR—Specialty Films—AlliedSignal Inc.; *U.S. Public*, pg. 49

ACLIMAT—Household Prods.—Melitta Unternehmensgruppe Bentz KG; *Int'l*, pg. 856

ACLON—Fluoropolymeno—AlliedSignal Inc.; *U.S. Public*, pg. 49

ACLOVATE—Dermatology Cream & Ointment—Glaxo Wellcome Inc.; *Int'l*, pg. 552

ACMADE INTERNATIONAL—Film Numbering Machine—J & R Film / Moviola Digital Co.; *U.S. Public*, pg. 576

ACME—Western Boots—Acme Boot Co., Inc.; *U.S. Private*, pg. 394

ACME—Canvas Covers—Acme Canvas Co., Inc.; *U.S. Private*, pg. 13

ACME—Frame Products—American Greetings Corporation; *U.S. Public*, pg. 77

ACME—Brick—Justin Industries, Inc.; *U.S. Public*, pg. 936

ACME—Chiller Barrels—Ketema, Inc.; *U.S. Private*, pg. 604

ACME—Paints & Coatings—The Sherwin-Williams Company; *U.S. Public*, pg. 1465

ACME—NONE—The Wooster Brush Company; *U.S. Private*, pg. 1188

ACME CARTOON COMPANY—NONE—The Vermont Teddy Bear Company, Inc.; *U.S. Public*, pg. 1716

ACME-GRIDLEY—NONE—DeVlieg-Bullard Inc.; *U.S. Public*, pg. 502

ACME-GRIDLEY—Multi Spindle Automatic Bar & Chucking Machine—The Machine Tool Group; *U.S. Public*, pg. 503

ACME JUICERATOR—Fruit Juices—Dynamics Corporation of America; *U.S. Public*, pg. 286

ACME MARKETS—Food Stores—Acme Markets; *U.S. Public*, pg. 93

THE ACME MOVING PICTURE GROUP—NONE—The Vermont Teddy Bear Company, Inc.; *U.S. Public*, pg. 1716

ACME UNITED—Scissors & Shears—Acme United Corporation; *U.S. Public*, pg. 17

ACME VISIBLE RECORDS—NONE—Acme Design Technology, Co.; *U.S. Private*, pg. 13

ACMED—NONE—Continental Medical Systems, Inc.; *U.S. Public*, pg. 839

ACNOMEL—Acne Medication—Menley & James Laboratories, Inc.; *U.S. Public*, pg. 1086

ACO—Precast Concrete Trench Drain—Modern Concrete Septic Tank Company; *U.S. Private*, pg. 754

ACORN—Market Segmentation System—CACI International Inc; *U.S. Public*, pg. 272

ACORN LIFESTYLES—Software—CACI International Inc; *U.S. Public*, pg. 272

ACORN STRUCTURES—PreManufactured Houses—Deck House Inc.; *U.S. Private*, pg. 320

THE ACORN—NONE—Gilmore Bros., Inc.; *U.S. Private*, pg. 454

ACOUSTA-PANE—Sound Resistant Laminated Glass Prods.—Globe-Amerada Glass Company; *U.S. Private*, pg. 458

ACOUSTEK—Sound-Deadening Shroud-Whole House Ventilator—Broan Mfg. Co., Inc.; *U.S. Public*, pg. 1193

Brand Name Index

ACOUSTI-K 27—Insulated Duct & Fittings—United McGill Corp.; *U.S. Private*, pg. 1122

ACOUSTI-SEAL—Operable Walls—Modernfold, Inc.; *U.S. Private*, pg. 755

ACOUSTIC COUNTRY—Country Music Radio Program—Westwood One Entertainment; *U.S. Public*, pg. 1763

ACOUSTIC WAVE—Music System—Bose Corporation; *U.S. Private*, pg. 160

ACOUSTICAIR—Blowers—MD Pneumatics; *U.S. Private*, pg. 1111

ACOUSTILOG—NONE—Western Atlas Logging Services; *U.S. Public*, pg. 1757

ACOUSTIMASS—Speaker Systems—Bose Corporation; *U.S. Private*, pg. 160

ACOUSTIX—Ultrasound Gel—Conmed Corporation; *U.S. Public*, pg. 431

ACOUSTIZIP—Noise Reduction Systems—The Zippertubing Co.; *U.S. Private*, pg. 1207

ACOUSTONE—Acoustical Ceiling Tile—CGC Inc.; *U.S. Public*, pg. 1660

ACOUSTONE—Acoustical Panels & Tiles—USG Corporation; *U.S. Public*, pg. 1660

ACOUSTONE—Ceiling & Wall Products—USG Interiors, Inc.; *U.S. Public*, pg. 1660

ACQUA CHILLER—Specialized Equip. for Maintaining Temp. in Salt Water Environments—American Educational Products; *U.S. Public*, pg. 71

ACQUIRE—Game—Monarch Avalon, Inc.; *U.S. Public*, pg. 1123

ACRA-VECTOR—Automatic Circuit Design—Shure Brothers Incorporated; *U.S. Private*, pg. 997

ACRALANE—Automotive Adhesives & Sealants—PPG Industries, Inc.; *U.S. Public*, pg. 1245

ACRAMATIC—CNC Control—Cincinnati Milacron U.K. Limited; *U.S. Public*, pg. 368

ACRAWAX C—Plastic Additives—Lonza Inc.; *Int'l*, pg. 67

ACRILAN—Acrylic Fiber—Monsanto Company; *U.S. Public*, pg. 1124

ACRILAN—Acrylic Fibers & Yarns—Solutia Inc.; *U.S. Public*, pg. 1483

ACRILUX—Reinforced Plastic Panels—Georgia-Pacific Corporation; *U.S. Public*, pg. 735

ACRISON—NONE—Acrison, Inc.; *U.S. Private*, pg. 14

ACRYSTEEL M—Marine Grade Acrylic Sheet—Aristech Chemical Corporation; *Int'l*, pg. 872

ACRO—Filtration Products—Gelman Sciences, Inc.; *U.S. Public*, pg. 1253

ACRO 50—Filtration Products—Gelman Sciences, Inc.; *U.S. Public*, pg. 1253

ACRO-FLEX—Non-Woven Book Binding Material—Industrial Coatings Group, Inc.; *U.S. Private*, pg. 434

ACRO FLUX—Filtration Products—Gelman Sciences, Inc.; *U.S. Public*, pg. 1253

ACRO/FUSIBLE ACRO—Interfacings—Specialty Textile Products; *U.S. Public*, pg. 1023

ACRO LC 13—Filtration Products—Gelman Sciences, Inc.; *U.S. Public*, pg. 1253

ACRO-PACK—Filtration Products—Gelman Sciences, Inc.; *U.S. Public*, pg. 1253

ACRODISC—Filtration Products—Gelman Sciences, Inc.; *U.S. Public*, pg. 1253

ACROFLOW—Filtration Products—Gelman Sciences, Inc.; *U.S. Public*, pg. 1253

ACROLC—Disposable Filtration Products—Gelman Sciences, Inc.; *U.S. Public*, pg. 1253

ACROLEX—Acrylic Polymers—Ferro Corporation; *U.S. Public*, pg. 618

ACRONAL—Polymer Dispersions & Solutions; Solid Polymers—BASF AG; *Int'l*, pg. 103

ACROPAK—Machinery—Acrometal Companies, Inc.; *U.S. Private*, pg. 14

ACROPON—Acrylic Topcoat for Appliance Industry—DeSoto Inc.; *U.S. Public*, pg. 956

ACROSOL—Polymer Dispersions & Solutions; Solid Polymers—BASF AG; *Int'l*, pg. 103

ACROSONIC—Pianos—Baldwin Piano & Organ Company; *U.S. Public*, pg. 169

ACRY-FILL—Coating Products—Columbia Paint & Coatings; *U.S. Public*, pg. 256

ACRY-FINISH—Paint—Graham Paint and Varnish Company; *U.S. Private*, pg. 468

ACRY FLOR—Patio Interior & Exterior Satin Latex Enamel—Paragon Paint & Varnish Corp.; *U.S. Private*, pg. 838

ACRY-SEAL—Coating Products—Columbia Paint & Coatings; *U.S. Private*, pg. 256

ACRY-SHIELD—Coating Products—Columbia Paint & Coatings; *U.S. Private*, pg. 256

ACRY-STAIN—Coating Products—Columbia Paint & Coatings; *U.S. Private*, pg. 256

ACRY-TUFF—Prefinished Wood Paneling—Georgia-Pacific Corporation; *U.S. Public*, pg. 735

ACRYCOTE—Isocyanate Free Acrylic Urethane Coating—Perry & Derrick Co.; *U.S. Private*, pg. 854

ACRYGLAS—Coating for Wall Paneling—Georgia-Pacific Corporation; *U.S. Public*, pg. 735

ACRYGLO—Coating—Pratt & Lambert United, Inc.; *U.S. Public*, pg. 1466

ACRYL 60—Liquid Bonding Agent—Thoro; *U.S. Private*, pg. 505

ACRYLBOND—Acrylic Latex Additive—TEC Incorporated; *U.S. Public*, pg. 687

ACRYLI-CLEAN—Professional-Quality Automotive Wax & Grease Remover—PPG Industries, Inc.; *U.S. Public*, pg. 1245

ACRYLIC—Latex Enamel—Pratt & Lambert United, Inc.; *U.S. Public*, pg. 1466

ACRYLINE 2—Dental Aid/Device (Denture)—Menley & James Laboratories, Inc.; *U.S. Public*, pg. 1086

ACRYLIQUID-40—40% Acrylamide Solution—Scientific Imaging Systems; *U.S. Public*, pg. 550

ACRYLITE—Coating—Jones Blair Co.; *U.S. Private*, pg. 596

ACRYLITE GP & FF—Acrylic Sheet—Cyro Industries; *Int'l*, pg. 1454

ACRYLITE PMMA—Acrylic Molding Compounds—Cyro Industries; *Int'l*, pg. 1454

ACRYLITE PLUS—Impact Modified Acrylic Molding Compounds—Cyro Industries; *Int'l*, pg. 1454

ACRYLITHANE C—Acrylic Coating—Jones Blair Company; *U.S. Private*, pg. 596

ACRYPLEX—Paint—Graham Paint and Varnish Company; *U.S. Private*, pg. 468

ACRYSOF—Intraocular Lenses—Alcon Laboratories, Inc.; *Int'l*, pg. 916

ACRYSTEEL—I-GP Impact Acrylic Sheet—Aristech Chemical Corporation; *Int'l*, pg. 872

ACRYSTEEL S—Solar Grade Acrylic Sheet—Aristech Chemical Corporation; *Int'l*, pg. 872

ACRYSTONE—Mineral Filled Acrylic Sheet—Aristech Chemical Corporation; *Int'l*, pg. 872

ACRYTHANE—NONE—Sico Inc.; *Int'l*, pg. 1239

ACRYTHENE—Ethylene-Methylacrylate Copolymer Resins—Millennium Petrochemicals, Inc.; *Int'l*, pg. 554

ACT—Fluoride Rinse—Johnson & Johnson; *U.S. Public*, pg. 927

ACT-O-MATIC—Shower Heads—Sloan Valve Company; *U.S. Private*, pg. 1006

ACT SERIES—Complete Hematology System Targets Physician Office Laboratories—Beckman Coulter; *U.S. Public*, pg. 199

ACT II—X-Ray Cassette Trays—Litton Industries, Inc.; *U.S. Public*, pg. 1002

ACTAIR—Airline Catering—Accor S.A.; *Int'l*, pg. 20

ACTANE—Compound For Acid Activation—Enthone-OMI, Inc.; *U.S. Public*, pg. 138

ACTAR—CPR Training Manikins—Vital Signs, Inc.; *U.S. Public*, pg. 1723

ACTIBATH—Bath Additive—The Andrew Jergens Company; *Int'l*, pg. 717

ACTIBATH—Bath Additive—Kao Corporation of America (DE); *Int'l*, pg. 717

ACTIDERM—Dermatologic Patches—Westwood-Squibb Pharmaceuticals Inc.; *U.S. Public*, pg. 255

ACTIDIL—Antihistamine—Glaxo Wellcome PLC; *Int'l*, pg. 553

ACTIFED—Antihistamine, Decongestant—Glaxo Wellcome PLC; *Int'l*, pg. 553

ACTIFED—Allergy/Cold/Flu/Sinus Medication—Warner-Lambert Consumer Healthcare; *U.S. Public*, pg. 1739

ACTIFED DAY & NIGHT MEDICINE—Cold & Allergy Medicine—Warner-Lambert Consumer Healthcare; *U.S. Public*, pg. 1739

ACTIFED PLUS—Antihistamine, Decongestant—Glaxo Wellcome PLC; *Int'l*, pg. 553

ACTIFED WITH CODEINE—Pharmaceutical Product—Glaxo Wellcome PLC; *Int'l*, pg. 553

ACTIGALL—NONE—Novartis Pharmaceuticals; *Int'l*, pg. 973

ACTILYSE—Fibrinolytic—Boehringer Ingelheim GmbH; *Int'l*, pg. 199

ACTIMETER—Automatic Replenishing Apparatus—Eastman Kodak Company; *U.S. Public*, pg. 550

ACTIMMUNE—Interferon Gamma-1b—Genentech, Inc.; *Int'l*, pg. 1120

ACTION—Carbonless Paper—Arjo Wiggins Appleton plc; *Int'l*, pg. 567

ACTION—Statistical Process Control Software Package—BetzDearborn Inc.; *U.S. Public*, pg. 226

ACTION—High-Tech & Custom Manual Wheelchair Products—Invacare Corporation; *U.S. Public*, pg. 911

ACTION—Stationery Products—The Mead Corporation; *U.S. Public*, pg. 1074

ACTION FIGHTER—Videogame—Sega of America Inc.; *Int'l*, pg. 1218

ACTION HOE—Weeding Tool—Ames Company; *U.S. Public*, pg. 1683

ACTION I/Q—Signal Conditioners—Action Instruments, Inc.; *U.S. Private*, pg. 15

ACTION I/O—Industrial Transmitters—Action Instruments, Inc.; *U.S. Private*, pg. 15

ACTION LASER 1500—Laser Printer—Epson America Inc.; *Int'l*, pg. 1219

ACTION LASER 1600—Laser Printer—Epson America Inc.; *Int'l*, pg. 1219

ACTION MAN—NONE—MB Espana, S.A.; *U.S. Public*, pg. 798

ACTION OFFICE—Desks & Tables—Herman Miller, Inc.; *U.S. Public*, pg. 1111

ACTION OFFICE ENCORE—Desks and Tables—Herman Miller Inc.; *U.S. Public*, pg. 1111

ACTION PAK—Electronic Modules for Measurement & Control—Action Instruments, Inc.; *U.S. Private*, pg. 15

ACTION PLUS—Stores—Socanav Inc.; *Int'l*, pg. 1272

ACTION PRINTER 3250—Dot Matrix Printer—Epson America Inc.; *Int'l*, pg. 1219

ACTION PRINTER 3260—Dot Matrix Printer—Epson America Inc.; *Int'l*, pg. 1219

ACTION PRINTER 2250—Dot Matrix Printer—Epson America Inc.; *Int'l*, pg. 1219

ACTION SCANNING SYSTEM—Scanner—Epson America Inc.; *Int'l*, pg. 1219

ACTION-SPECS—Safety Glasses—The Fibre-Metal Products Company; *U.S. Private*, pg. 402

ACTION SPORTS RETAILER—Magazine—Miller Freeman Inc.; *Int'l*, pg. 1443

ACTION TRACTION—Cervical & Lumbar Traction Products—Staodyn Inc.; *U.S. Public*, pg. 1509

ACTIONBAC—Carpet Backing—Amoco Chemicals; *U.S. Public*, pg. 102

ACTIONBAC—Carpet Backing—Amoco Corporation; *U.S. Public*, pg. 101

ACTIONET—Radiotelephone System—Oy Nokia Ab/Nokia Group; *Int'l*, pg. 951

ACTIONFLOR—Floor Coverings—Domco Inc.; *Int'l*, pg. 415

ACTIONPACKER—Storage Container Line—Rubbermaid Incorporated; *U.S. Public*, pg. 1411

ACTIONWRITER—Typewriter—International Business Machines Corporation; *U.S. Public*, pg. 895

ACTIPOL—Polybutenes—Amoco Corporation; *U.S. Public*, pg. 101

ACTIS—Thread Inspection—Tuboscope Incorporated; *U.S. Public*, pg. 1643

ACTISITE—Tetracycline Periodontal Fiber—Alza Corporation; *U.S. Public*, pg. 62

ACTISITE—Periodontal Fiber—The Procter & Gamble Company; *U.S. Public*, pg. 1330

ACTIV PC SKILLS LEARNING LIBRARIES—Interactive PC Skills Training Systems—ITC Learning Corp.; *U.S. Public*, pg. 859

ACTIV BASIC SKILLS LEARNING LIBRARY—Interactive Training Systems for Basic Literacy & Mathmatic Skills—ITC Learning Corp.; *U.S. Public*, pg. 859

ACTIV-8—Women's Apparel—Jacques Moret, Inc.; *U.S. Private*, pg. 580

ACTIV INVOLVE INSTRUMENTATION LEARNING LIBRARY—Interactive Training Systems for Complex Instrument, Multi-Craft—ITC Learning Corp.; *U.S. Public*, pg. 859

ACTIV LEARNING LIBRARIES—Interactive Training Systems, Programs & Administrative Software—ITC Learning Corp.; *U.S. Public*, pg. 859

ACTIV REGULATORY COMPLIANCE LIBRARY—Interactive Training Systems for OSHA Mandated Compliance Requirements—ITC Learning Corp.; *U.S. Public*, pg. 859

ACTIV TECHNICAL SKILLS LEARNING LIBRARY—Interactive Training Systems for Industrial Technical Application Skills—ITC Learning Corp.; *U.S. Public*, pg. 859

ACTIVA—Feminine Pads—Kimberly-Clark Corporation; *U.S. Public*, pg. 958

ACTIVA—Fresh Yeast—Royal Gist-Brocades N.V.; *Int'l*, pg. 1142

ACTIVAIR—NONE—Duracell International Inc.; *U.S. Public*, pg. 743

ACTIVASE—Alteplase, Recombinant, t-PA—Genentech, Inc.; *Int'l*, pg. 1120

ACTIVASE—Recombinant Fibrinolytic Enzyme—Roche Holding Ltd.; *Int'l*, pg. 1119

ACTIVATOR—Laundry Washing Machines & Parts—General Electric Canada Inc.; *U.S. Public*, pg. 713

ACTIVE—Hosiery for Women—Grupo Synkro, S.A. de C.V.; *Int'l*, pg. 576

ACTIVE DAY—Skin Care—Elizabeth Arden Company; *Int'l*, pg. 1435

ACTIVE LIFE—Ostomy Product—Bristol-Myers Squibb Company; *U.S. Public*, pg. 253

ACTIVE LIGHT—Hosiery for Women—Grupo Synkro, S.A. de C.V.; *Int'l*, pg. 576

ACTIVE MIND SERIES—NONE—Broderbund Software, Inc.; *U.S. Public*, pg. 258

ACTIVE OFFICE—MS Office Accessory Software—Software Publishing Corporation; *U.S. Public*, pg. 1483

ACTIVE PARTNER—NONE—Oxford Health Plans Inc.; *U.S. Public*, pg. 1238

ACTIVE SUPPORT—Hosiery—L'eggs Products, Inc.; *U.S. Public*, pg. 1434

ACTIVEWEAR—Jogsuits—Niches, Inc.; *U.S. Public*, pg. 1181

ACTIVIEW—Telecommunications Products—Lucent Technologies Inc.; *U.S. Public*, pg. 1017

ACTIVISION—Action/Simulation Games—Activision; *U.S. Public*, pg. 17

ACTIVISION FOR KIDS—Software Entertainment for Children—Activision; *U.S. Public*, pg. 17

ACTIVITRAX—Pacemaker—Medtronic, Inc.; *U.S. Public*, pg. 1082

ACTIVITRAX E—Pacemaker—Medtronic, Inc.; *U.S. Public*, pg. 1082

ACTIVITRAX II—Pacemaker—Medtronic, Inc.; *U.S. Public*, pg. 1082

ACTIVITY MONITOR FOR DB2—DB2 Performance Monitor—BMC Software, Inc.; *U.S. Public*, pg. 162

ACTMEDIA CARTS—Shopping Cart Mounted Displays—News America Marketing; *Int'l*, pg. 925

ACTNOW—Supermarket Co-op Coupons & Samples—News America Marketing; *Int'l*, pg. 925

ACTON—Stack Seating—American Seating Company; *U.S. Private*, pg. 61

ACTPROMOTE—Pay-for-Performance Program—News America Marketing; *Int'l*, pg. 925

ACTRADIO—In-Store Audio Advertising—News America Marketing; *Int'l*, pg. 925

ACTRAPID—Product for Diabetes Care—Novo Nordisk A/S; *Int'l*, pg. 987

ACTRON—Automotive Test Equipment—Actron Manufacturing Company; *U.S. Private*, pg. 16

ACU-METER—Water Meter—Hays Fluid Controls-Division of Romac Industries; *U.S. Private*, pg. 942

ACU-TEST—Soil Testers—Security Lawn & Garden Co.; *U.S. Private*, pg. 397

ACUATIM CREAM—Anti-Acne Vulgaris Agent—Otsuka Pharmaceutical Co., Ltd.; *Int'l*, pg. 1013

ACUBLEND—Proprietary Gas Blending Process—Scott Specialty Gases; *U.S. Private*, pg. 977

ACUCUT—NONE—Hosokawa Micron Powder Systems; *Int'l*, pg. 636

ACUDERM—Plastic Dressing—Acme United Corporation; *U.S. Public*, pg. 17

ACUDYNE—Iodine—Acme United Corporation; *U.S. Public*, pg. 17

ACUFEED—Control Equipment—BetzDearborn Inc.; *U.S. Public*, pg. 226

ACUITY—Central Monitoring System—Protocol Systems, Inc.; *U.S. Public*, pg. 1336

ACUMER—Polymer—Rohm and Haas Company; *U.S. Public*, pg. 1403

ACUPHASE—Specialized Containers—Scott Specialty Gases; *U.S. Private*, pg. 977

ACURA—Automobile—American Honda Motor Co., Inc. Automobile Sales Division; *Int'l*, pg. 634

ACURA—Valves—Watts Industries, Inc.; *U.S. Public*, pg. 1746

ACURASEE—Intraocular Lenses—Alcon Laboratories, Inc.; *Int'l*, pg. 916

ACUSHNET—Golf Equipment—Acushnet Company; *U.S. Public*, pg. 675

ACUSHNET—Titleist, Foot-Joy, Cobra—Titleist & Foot-Joy Worldwide; *U.S. Public*, pg. 675

ACUSTEK—Vacuum Motors & Blowers—AMETEK, Inc.; *U.S. Public*, pg. 99

ACUTEX—Electrohydraulic Actuators—SPX Corporation; *U.S. Public*, pg. 1420

ACUTRIM—Appetite Suppressant—Ciba Specialty Chemicals; *U.S. Public*, pg. 291

ACUTRIM—Appetite-Suppressant—Novartis; *Int'l*, pg. 972

ACUVISTA—Thermal Transfer Printer & Ribbons—Superior Label Systems, Inc.; *U.S. Private*, pg. 1055

ACUVUE—Disposable Contact Lenses—Johnson & Johnson; *U.S. Public*, pg. 927

ACUVUE—Contact Lens—Vistakon Johnson & Johnson Vision Products, Inc.; *U.S. Public*, pg. 929

ACUVUE DISPOSABLE CONTACT LENSES—Disposable Soft Contact Lenses—Vistakon Johnson & Johnson Vision Products, Inc.; *U.S. Public*, pg. 929

ACUWELD—Computer Controlled Arc Welding—Sciaky, Inc.; *U.S. Private*, pg. 862

ACXIOM—Innovative Mktg. Solutions—Acxiom Corporation; *U.S. Public*, pg. 18

AD-BUILDER—Art Illustration System—Multi-Ad Services, Incorporated; *U.S. Private*, pg. 766

AD/CYCLE—Computer Systems—International Business Machines Corporation; *U.S. Public*, pg. 895

AD-MASTER—Art Illustration System—Multi-Ad Services, Incorporated; *U.S. Private*, pg. 766

AD MATE—Pens—The Gillette Company; *U.S. Public*, pg. 743

AD PANEL—Paperboard Carriers—The Mead Corporation; *U.S. Public*, pg. 1074

AD-TYPE—Photo Paper—Eastman Kodak Company; *U.S. Public*, pg. 550

AD UPS—Cold Air Balloons—Aerostar International; *U.S. Public*, pg. 1361

ADAGEN—NONE—Enzon, Inc.; *U.S. Public*, pg. 587

ADALAT—Cardiovascular Pharmaceutical—Bayer AG; *Int'l*, pg. 171

ADALAT—Pharmaceutical—Bayer Corporation/Pharmaceutical Division; *Int'l*, pg. 173

ADALET—Cable Accesories, Cast Products Electrical Construction Materials—The Scott Fetzer Company; *U.S. Public*, pg. 217

ADALOX—Sanding Paper—Norton Company; *Int'l*, pg. 1173

ADAM—Hats—AJD; *U.S. Private*, pg. 510

ADAM-826—16-BIT High Speed Analog-Digital Converter—Analogic Corporation; *U.S. Public*, pg. 109

ADAM YORK—Unique Products—Hanover Direct Pennsylvania, Inc.; *U.S. Public*, pg. 782

ADAMAT—Defense System Quality Control Software—Dynamics Research Corporation; *U.S. Public*, pg. 539

ADAMATIC—Food Equipment—Premark International, Inc.; *U.S. Public*, pg. 1321

ADAMS—Training Simulator for Basic & Advanced Training—Balzers; *Int'l*, pg. 997

ADAMS—Medical Supplies—Becton Dickinson Primary Care Diagnostics; *U.S. Public*, pg. 199

ADAMS—Fruit Juice Concentrate—Citrus World Inc.; *U.S. Private*, pg. 241

ADAMS—Peanut Butter—Curtice Foods; *U.S. Private*, pg. 887

ADAMS—Training Simulator—Oerlikon-Contraves AG; *Int'l*, pg. 998

ADAMS—Parastiticides—SmithKline Beecham plc; *Int'l*, pg. 1264

ADAMS BEST—Vanilla Extract—Adams Extract Co., Inc.; *U.S. Private*, pg. 16

ADAMS NATURAL PEANUT BUTTER—Peanut Butter—Nalleys Fine Foods; *U.S. Private*, pg. 887

ADAMS RITE—Hardware—Adams Rite Manufacturing Co.; *U.S. Private*, pg. 17

ADAMS ROW—CLOTHING—Cliftex; *U.S. Public*, pg. 1777

ADAMS ROW—Mens Apparel—The Richman Brothers Co.; *U.S. Public*, pg. 1777

ADAPETTES FOR SENSITIVE EYES—Contact Lens Wetting Solution—Alcon Laboratories, Inc.; *Int'l*, pg. 916

ADAPTA—Plug for Conical Refiner—Harnischfeger Industries, Inc.; *U.S. Public*, pg. 788

ADAPTAFILE—Office Furniture—Lear Siegler Diversified Holdings Corp.; *U.S. Private*, pg. 655

ADAPTATIONS—Toddlers Dresses—Seibel & Stern Corp.; *U.S. Private*, pg. 981

ADAPTEC CONNECTIONS—NONE—Adaptec, Inc.; *U.S. Public*, pg. 19

ADAPTIC—Dental Restorative—Johnson & Johnson Consumer Products; *U.S. Public*, pg. 928

ADAPTIS—RF Amplifiers, Fiber-Optic Transmitters & Receivers—Scientific-Atlanta, Inc.; *U.S. Public*, pg. 1443

ADAPTORR—Downstream, Adaptive, Pressure Control System—Millipore Tylan Products; *U.S. Public*, pg. 1112

ADAPTS—Automatic Diagnostic & Probe Timing System—GenRad, Inc.; *U.S. Public*, pg. 731

ADATS—Missile System—Balzers; *Int'l*, pg. 997

ADATS—Missile System—Oerlikon-Buhrle Holding AG; *Int'l*, pg. 996

ADATS—Missile System—Oerlikon-Contraves AG; *Int'l*, pg. 998

ADCAM 100—Multichannel Analyzer System—EG & G Ortec; *U.S. Public*, pg. 543

ADCOLITE—Decals—American Decal & Mfg. Co.; *U.S. Private*, pg. 53

ADCOMP—Computer Software for Ink Jet Printers—Eastman Kodak Company; *U.S. Public*, pg. 550

ADCOTE—Packaging Adhesive—Morton International Inc.; *U.S. Public*, pg. 1135

ADD-A-CUP—NONE—The Thermos Company; *Int'l*, pg. 938

ADD-A-PAK—Diode Bridges—International Rectifier Corporation; *U.S. Public*, pg. 906

ADD-VANTAGE—Drug Delivery System & Vials & Diluent Containers—Abbott Laboratories; *U.S. Public*, pg. 12

ADD-VENT—Medication Delivery System—Quest Medical, Inc.; *U.S. Public*, pg. 1352

ADDI-CHEK—Quality Control System—Millipore Corporation; *U.S. Public*, pg. 1112

ADDIMENT—Concrete and Mortar Additives—Heidelberger Zement A.G.; *Int'l*, pg. 605

ADDIPAK—NONE—Hudson, RCI; *U.S. Private*, pg. 546

ADDISON-WESLEY—Books—Pearson plc; *Int'l*, pg. 1025

ADDITION-ELLE—Large Size Apparel—Shirmax Leasing Ltd.; *Int'l*, pg. 1235

ADDITION-ELLE LINGERIE—Large Size Lingerie—Shirmax Leasing Ltd.; *Int'l*, pg. 1235

ADDITIVE 601—Water Softener & Foam Suppressor—Ecolab Inc.; *U.S. Public*, pg. 562

ADDITROL—Bentonite Blend—AMCOL International Corp.; *U.S. Public*, pg. 63

ADDRESS SAVER—Envelopes—Tension Envelope Corp.; *U.S. Private*, pg. 1077

ADDRESS TRANSLATION—NONE—Check Point Software Technologies Ltd.; *U.S. Public*, pg. 342

ADDRESSRIGHT—NONE—Pitney Bowes Inc.; *U.S. Public*, pg. 1303

ADDSILIM—Orthodontic Products—Bristol-Myers Squibb Company; *U.S. Public*, pg. 253

ADDVENT—Pacemaker—St. Jude Medical, Inc.; *U.S. Public*, pg. 1427

ADEFLOR M RX—Vitamins & Minerals With Sodium Fluoride—Bradley Pharmaceuticals; *U.S. Public*, pg. 249

ADEFLOR M RX—Vitamins & Minerals with Sodium Fluoride—Doak Dermatologics; *U.S. Public*, pg. 250

Brand Name Index

ADELBODNER—Mineral Water—Bols Royal Distilleries; *Int'l*, pg. 751

ADEMCO—Alarm Device—Pittway Corporation; *U.S. Public*, pg. 1305

ADENOCARD—Pharmaceutical Preparations—Fujisawa U.S.A. Inc.; *Int'l*, pg. 525

ADENOSCAW—Pharmaceutical Prepaerations—Fujisawa U.S.A. Inc.; *Int'l*, pg. 525

ADES—Beverages—Bestfoods; *U.S. Public*, pg. 223

ADES—Soy Drinks—Refinerias de Maiz S.A.I.C.F.; *U.S. Public*, pg. 448

ADHESIVES AGE—News on Adhesives & Sealants—Intertec Publishing; *U.S. Public*, pg. 1327

ADHESIVES AGE—Monthly Publication—Intertec Publishing; *U.S. Public*, pg. 1328

ADHESIVES AGE DIRECTORY—Annual Publication—Intertec Publishing; *U.S. Public*, pg. 1328

ADIDAS—Sports Wear & Shoes—Adidas AG; *Int'l*, pg. 24

ADIDAS—Men's Fragrance—Coty Inc.; *Int'l*, pg. 185

ADIDAS—Men's Cosmetics—SmithKline Beecham plc; *Int'l*, pg. 1264

ADIIS—Software—CACI International Inc; *U.S. Public*, pg. 272

ADIPRENE—Liquid Castable, Sprayable & Millable Urethane—Uniroyal Chemical Company, Inc.; *U.S. Public*, pg. 460

ADIRONDACK—Athletic Equipment & Sporting Goods—Rawlings Sporting Goods Company; *U.S. Public*, pg. 1361

ADIRONDACK AMBER—Beer—The F.X. Matt Brewing Co.; *U.S. Private*, pg. 714

ADJU-LOK—Floor Lock—Faultless Nutting; *Int'l*, pg. 473

ADJUST-A-GLIDE—Rotary Carpet Brush—Flo-Pac Corporation; *U.S. Public*, pg. 414

ADJUST-A-SHORE—Adjustable Shoring System—Safway Steel Products Inc.; *Int'l*, pg. 1389

ADJUST-A-STROKE—Metering Dispensing Systems—Graco Inc.; *U.S. Public*, pg. 756

ADJUSTA-KEEPER—Adjustable Latch Keepers—Hartwell Corporation; *U.S. Private*, pg. 1168

ADJUSTA-LOCK—Security Lock-Combination—Sargent & Greenleaf, Inc.; *U.S. Private*, pg. 965

ADJUSTA-MAGIC—Adjustable Electric Beds—Leggett & Platt, Incorporated; *U.S. Public*, pg. 985

ADJUSTABLE E—Shock Absorber—Arvin Industries, Inc.; *U.S. Public*, pg. 136

ADLER—Socks—Kayser-Roth Corporation, Inc.; *Int'l*, pg. 576

ADLON—Shower Head—Interbath, Inc.; *U.S. Private*, pg. 566

ADMARK—Ink-Jet Printers—Eastman Kodak Company; *U.S. Public*, pg. 550

ADMEX—Polymeric Plasticizer—Velsicol Chemical Corporation; *U.S. Private*, pg. 1135

ADMIRAL—Maintenance Service—Admiral Maintenance Service L.P.; *U.S. Private*, pg. 17

ADMIRAL—Thread—Coats North America; *Int'l*, pg. 300

ADMIRAL—Refrigerators, Laundry Equipment, Dishwashers & Cooking Appliances—Maytag Corporation; *U.S. Public*, pg. 1064

ADMIRAL—Home Appliances—Maytag Galesburg Refrigeration Products; *U.S. Public*, pg. 1064

ADMIRAL APPLIANCES—Appliances—The Climatic Corp.; *U.S. Private*, pg. 246

ADMIRE—Lemon Aerosol Furniture Polish—Blue Cross Laboratories; *U.S. Private*, pg. 152

ADOBE ACROBAT—NONE—Adobe Systems Incorporated; *U.S. Public*, pg. 20

ADOBE DIMENSIONS—NONE—Adobe Systems Incorporated; *U.S. Public*, pg. 20

ADOBE ILLUSTRATOR—Software Program for Illustrators—Adobe Systems Incorporated; *U.S. Public*, pg. 20

ADOBE PHOTO SHOP—Photo Shop—Adobe Systems Incorporated; *U.S. Public*, pg. 20

ADOBE PREMIERE—NONE—Adobe Systems Incorporated; *U.S. Public*, pg. 20

ADOBE ROSE—Western Wear—Niches, Inc.; *U.S. Public*, pg. 1181

ADOBE STREAMLINE—NONE—Adobe Systems Incorporated; *U.S. Public*, pg. 20

ADOLFO—Handbags—Koret Pierre Cardin; *U.S. Private*, pg. 632

ADOLFO—NONE—Supreme International Corp.; *U.S. Public*, pg. 1542

ADOLFO—Fragrances—Trend Media; *U.S. Public*, pg. 1634

ADOLFO—Fragrance—Tri Tech Laboratories, Inc.; *U.S. Private*, pg. 1101

ADOLPH'S—Meat Tenderizers & Marinades; Salt Substitute—Chesebrough-Pond's; *Int'l*, pg. 1436

ADOLPH'S—Meat Tenderizers & Marinades/Salt Substitutes—Ragu Foods, Inc.; *Int'l*, pg. 1436

ADOLPHUS—Rice—American Rice Inc.; *U.S. Public*, pg. 591

ADORN—Hair Preparations—The Gillette Company; *U.S. Public*, pg. 743

ADOUR—Military Engines—Rolls-Royce Military Aero Engines Ltd.; *Int'l*, pg. 1127

ADRAS—Aircraft Data Recovery Computer System—AlliedSignal Commercial Avionics Systems; *U.S. Public*, pg. 50

ADRAY—Appliance & Photo—Adray Appliance & Photo Center, Inc.; *U.S. Private*, pg. 18

ADRIA—Pasta—Borden, Inc.; *U.S. Private*, pg. 157

ADRIA ITALIANISSIMO—Pasta—Borden, Inc.; *U.S. Private*, pg. 157

ADRIACIN—Anticancer Agents—Kyowa Hakko Kogyo Company, Ltd.; *Int'l*, pg. 778

ADRIAMYCIN—NONE—Pharmacia & Upjohn, Inc.; *Int'l*, pg. 1047

ADRIAN JORDAN—Careerwear—United Retail Group, Inc.; *U.S. Public*, pg. 1679

THE ADRIANE BERG SHOW—Talk Program—Westwood One, Inc.; *U.S. Public*, pg. 1763

ADRIEN ARPEL—Skin Care & Cosmetics—Alfin, Inc.; *U.S. Public*, pg. 40

ADSEE—Agricultural Emulsifiers—Witco Corporation; *U.S. Public*, pg. 1773

ADSORBOCARPINE—Pilocarpine Hcl—Alcon Laboratories, Inc.; *Int'l*, pg. 916

ADSORBONAC—Sodium Cloride in Hypertensity Eye Drops—Alcon Laboratories, Inc.; *Int'l*, pg. 916

ADSORBOTEAR—Artificial Tears—Alcon Laboratories, Inc.; *Int'l*, pg. 916

ADSPRAY—Small Vacuum—Advance Machine Company; *Int'l*, pg. 932

ADSTAR—Computer System—International Business Machines Corporation; *U.S. Public*, pg. 895

ADTAC—Hydrocarbon Resin—Hercules Incorporated; *U.S. Public*, pg. 809

ADTRANZ—NONE—Daimler-Benz Aktiengesellschaft; *Int'l*, pg. 366

ADTREND—Advertising Specialty Products—Golden Books Family Entertainment Inc.; *U.S. Public*, pg. 749

ADULT CONTEMPORARY/OLDIES PREP—Entertainment News Programming—Westwood One, Inc.; *U.S. Public*, pg. 1763

ADULT ROCK AND ROLL FORMAT—Rock Programming—Westwood One, Inc.; *U.S. Public*, pg. 1763

ADULT STANDARDS FORMAT—Standard Music Programming—Westwood One, Inc.; *U.S. Public*, pg. 1763

ADVAC—Small Vacuum—Advance Machine Company; *Int'l*, pg. 932

ADVACOR—NONE—FMC Corp., Lithium Division; *U.S. Public*, pg. 605

ADVANCE—Prepared Infant Formula—Abbott Laboratories; *U.S. Public*, pg. 12

ADVANCE—Floor Care Equipment—Advance Machine Company; *Int'l*, pg. 932

ADVANCE—Publications—Advance Publications Inc.; *U.S. Private*, pg. 18

ADVANCE—Gas Chlorinators—Capital Controls Company Inc.; *Int'l*, pg. 1226

ADVANCE—Pencils—Dixon Ticonderoga Company; *U.S. Public*, pg. 514

ADVANCE—Herbicide—The Dow Chemical Company; *U.S. Public*, pg. 522

ADVANCE—Cuni Resistance Alloy—Driver-Harris Company; *U.S. Public*, pg. 530

ADVANCE—NONE—Groupe Limagrain; *Int'l*, pg. 566

ADVANCE—Pregnancy Test—Ortho-McNeil Pharmaceutical Corporation; *U.S. Public*, pg. 929

ADVANCE—Ballasts—Philips Electronics North America Corporation; *Int'l*, pg. 1053

ADVANCE ARREST—Milk Replacer—Milk Specialties Company; *U.S. Private*, pg. 746

ADVANCE DYNAMIC ROM—Dynamic Splinting—EMPI, Inc.; *U.S. Public*, pg. 545

ADVANCED APPLICATION COMMUNICATION SYSTEM/2—Computer Systems—International Business Machines Corporation; *U.S. Public*, pg. 895

ADVANCED AUDIO IMAGING—Audio Systems—Zenith Electronics Corp.; *U.S. Public*, pg. 1790

ADVANCED CAPABILITY ALLIANCE—NONE—Lam Research Corporation; *U.S. Public*, pg. 975

ADVANCED CAPABILITY RAINBOW—NONE—Lam Research Corporation; *U.S. Public*, pg. 975

ADVANCED CIVILIZATION—War Game—Monarch Avalon, Inc.; *U.S. Public*, pg. 1123

ADVANCED CONSUMER LENDING SYSTEM (ACLS)—NONE—American Management Systems, Inc.; *U.S. Public*, pg. 86

THE ADVANCED CRYOSCOPES—NONE—Advanced Instruments, Inc.; *U.S. Private*, pg. 22

ADVANCED DUNGEONS & DRAGONS—Game—TSR, Inc.; *U.S. Private*, pg. 1185

ADVANCED FUNCTION PRESENTATION—Computer Systems—International Business Machines Corporation; *U.S. Public*, pg. 895

ADVANCED FUNCTION PRINTING—Computer Systems—International Business Machines Corporation; *U.S. Public*, pg. 895

ADVANCED GRAVIS—NONE—Fortune Brands, Inc.; *U.S. Public*, pg. 674

ADVANCED LABMASTER MARK III—Film Processor—Houston Fearless 76 Inc.; *U.S. Private*, pg. 542

ADVANCED NETWORK—Battery Backup—Best Power; *U.S. Private*, pg. 140

ADVANCED NETWORK PLUS—Battery Backup—Best Power; *U.S. Private*, pg. 140

THE ADVANCED OSMOMETERS—NONE—Advanced Instruments, Inc.; *U.S. Private*, pg. 22

ADVANCED PEER-TO-PEER NETWORKING—Computer System—International Business Machines Corporation; *U.S. Public*, pg. 895

ADVANCED PORTFOLIO SYSTEMS—Investment Portfolio Acctg. System—SunGard Financial Systems, Inc.; *U.S. Public*, pg. 1534

ADVANCED POWER TECHNOLOGY—NONE—Interface Electronics Corporation; *U.S. Private*, pg. 567

ADVANCED SQUAD LEADER—War Game—Monarch Avalon, Inc.; *U.S. Public*, pg. 1123

ADVANCED SYSTEM—Household Products—The Black & Decker Corporation; *U.S. Public*, pg. 233

ADVANCED THIRD REICH—Wargame—Monarch Avalon, Inc.; *U.S. Public*, pg. 1123

ADVANCED VIDEO IMAGING—Video Circuitry—Zenith Electronics Corp.; *U.S. Public*, pg. 1790

ADVANCEMAN—Remote Isolation Devices—TII Industries, Inc.; *U.S. Public*, pg. 1556

ADVANSTAR—Imaging Network—Eastman Kodak Company; *U.S. Public*, pg. 550

ADVANT—Open Control System—ABB Industrial Systems, Inc.; *Int'l*, pg. 4

ADVANT-EDGE—Cutlery—Imperial Schrade Corp.; *U.S. Public*, pg. 559

ADVANTAGE!—NONE—AST Research Inc.; *Int'l*, pg. 1181

ADVANTAGE—Photo Typesetters—AGFA EPS Division; *Int'l*, pg. 172

ADVANTAGE—Floor Tile—American Biltrite Inc.; *U.S. Public*, pg. 68

THE ADVANTAGE—Micro Proxcessor Controller Electric Fan Forced Wall Heater—Cadet Manufacturing Company; *U.S. Private*, pg. 198

ADVANTAGE—ATV Transmitter—Comark Communications, Inc.; *Int'l*, pg. 1383

ADVANTAGE—Vinyl Tile—Congoleum Corporation; *U.S. Public*, pg. 69

ADVANTAGE—NONE—Dart Transit Company; *U.S. Private*, pg. 311

ADVANTAGE—Wafer Cleaning System—Genus Inc.; *U.S. Public*, pg. 732

ADVANTAGE—Paper—Georgia-Pacific Corporation; *U.S. Public*, pg. 735

ADVANTAGE—Fireplaces—HON Industries Inc.; *U.S. Public*, pg. 772

ADVANTAGE—NONE—Molex Incorporated; *U.S. Public*, pg. 1121

ADVANTAGE—Yarn—National Spinning Co., Inc.; *U.S. Private*, pg. 786

ADVANTAGE—Toothbrushes—Oral-B Laboratories; *U.S. Public*, pg. 743

THE ADVANTAGE—Servo Roll Feed—P/A Industries, Inc.; *U.S. Private*, pg. 825

ADVANTAGE—Muffler—Walker Manufacturing Co.; *U.S. Public*, pg. 1578

ADVANTAGE—Jumbo Tissue—Wisconsin Tissue Mills, Inc.; *U.S. Public*, pg. 347

ADVANTAGE DESKTOP—NONE—American Management Systems, Inc.; *U.S. Public*, pg. 86

ADVANTAGE LIBRARIES—NONE—Broderbund Software, Inc.; *U.S. Public*, pg. 258

ADVANTAGE 24—Contraceptive Gel—Columbia Laboratories, Inc.; *U.S. Public*, pg. 405

ADVANTAGE X—Fluorescents—Philips Electronics N.V.; *Int'l*, pg. 1051

ADVANTECH—NONE—Lawter International, Inc.; *U.S. Public*, pg. 980

ADVANTEST—NONE—Advantest Corporation; *Int'l*, pg. 25

ADVANTEX—Compglass Fiber Reinforcements—Owens Corning; *U.S. Public*, pg. 1236

ADVANTIX—Advanced Photo System—Eastman Kodak Company; *U.S. Public*, pg. 550

ADVANTRA—Medicare Risk Product—Coventry Corporation; *U.S. Public*, pg. 454

ADVASERVE—NONE—FMC Corp., Lithium Division; *U.S. Public*, pg. 605

ADVASORB—NONE—FMC Corp., Lithium Division; *U.S. Public*, pg. 605

ADVENT—Helmets & Accessories—Bell Sports Corp.; *U.S. Public*, pg. 207

ADVENT—Loudspeakers—Recoton Auto Corporation; *U.S. Public*, pg. 1369

ADVENT—Speaker Series—Recoton Corporation; *U.S. Public*, pg. 1369

ADVENT—NONE—Solitec Wafer Processing, Inc.; *U.S. Private*, pg. 1013

ADVENTURE ISLAND—Water Theme Park—Busch Entertainment Corp.; *U.S. Public*, pg. 114

ADVENTURE LANDS OF AMERICA—Amusement Park—Adventure Lands of America, Inc.; *U.S. Private*, pg. 22

ADVENTURE WITH NO NAME—Role Playing—Monarch Avalon, Inc.; *U.S. Public*, pg. 1123

ADVENTURER—Household Ranges, Refrigerators & Dishwashers—General Electric Canada Inc.; *U.S. Public*, pg. 713

ADVENTURER—Motor Homes—Winnebago Industries, Inc.; *U.S. Public*, pg. 1772

ADVERBLIMPS—Helium Balloons—Aerostar International; *U.S. Public*, pg. 1361

ADVERTISER—Newspaper—The Gazette Company; *U.S. Private*, pg. 442

THE ADVERTISER—Pens for Specialty Advertising—Golden Books Family Entertainment Inc.; *U.S. Public*, pg. 749

ADVERTISING AGE—Weekly Business Newspaper—Advertising Age; *U.S. Private*, pg. 284

ADVERTISING AGE—Periodical—Crain Communications, Inc.; *U.S. Private*, pg. 284

ADVERTISING AGE INTERNATIONAL—NONE—Advertising Age; *U.S. Private*, pg. 284

ADVICE—Computer Programs for Computer-Aided Design—Lucent Technologies, Inc.; *U.S. Public*, pg. 1017

ADVIL—Analgesic Tablets And Caplets—American Home Products Corporation; *U.S. Public*, pg. 79

ADVIL—Analgesic Tablets & Caplets—Whitehall-Robins Healthcare; *U.S. Public*, pg. 80

ADVIL COLD & SINUS—Ibuprofen & Pseudoephedrine—American Home Products Corporation; *U.S. Public*, pg. 79

ADVIL COLD & SINUS—Analgesic & Decongestant Caplets—Whitehall-Robins Healthcare; *U.S. Public*, pg. 80

ADVOCACY—Patient Management—CorVel Corporation; *U.S. Public*, pg. 451

ADVOCACY ADVANTAGE—24 Hour Care & Patient Management—CorVel Corporation; *U.S. Public*, pg. 451

THE ADVOCATE—Newspaper—The Advocate; *U.S. Private*, pg. 23

ADVOCATING CARE—Tag Line—CorVel Corporation; *U.S. Public*, pg. 451

ADVOCIN—Danofloxacin—Pfizer Inc.; *U.S. Public*, pg. 1281

ADWEEK—Advertisers & Agencies—BPI Communications Inc.; *Int'l*, pg. 1446

AECO PRODUCTS—Envelopes—National Service Industries, Inc.; *U.S. Public*, pg. 1160

AEGIS—Media Theft Detection System—Anacomp Magnetics, Inc.; *U.S. Public*, pg. 107

AEGIS—NONE—Mizuno Corporation; *Int'l*, pg. 884

AER LINGUS—Airline—Aer Lingus; *Int'l*, pg. 28

AERBUS MOTOR HOME—NONE—Rexhall Industries, Inc.; *U.S. Public*, pg. 1384

AERECON—Photo Film—Eastman Kodak Company; *U.S. Public*, pg. 550

AEREX—Metal Alloy—SPS Technologies, Inc.; *U.S. Public*, pg. 1419

AERIAL—Pencils—Dixon Ticonderoga Company; *U.S. Public*, pg. 514

AERIALS—Gymnastic & Aerobic Apparel—Tighe Industries, Inc.; *U.S. Private*, pg. 1086

AERISWELD—Electrode—The Lincoln Electric Company; *U.S. Public*, pg. 996

AERMET—NONE—Carpenter Technology Corporation; *U.S. Public*, pg. 307

AERO—Motorscooter—American Honda Motor Co., Inc. Motorcycle Division; *Int'l*, pg. 634

AERO—Photo Film—Eastman Kodak Company; *U.S. Public*, pg. 550

AERO—Chocolate Confections—Nestle-Rowntree Ltd.; *Int'l*, pg. 921

AERO—Candy—Nestle S.A.; *Int'l*, pg. 915

AERO AID—Merthiolate—Graham-Field Health Products, Inc.; *U.S. Public*, pg. 757

AERO CAINE—Benzoin Compound—Graham-Field Health Products, Inc.; *U.S. Public*, pg. 757

AERO CELL—Cytology Fixative—Graham-Field Health Products, Inc.; *U.S. Public*, pg. 757

AERO CIDE—Hospital Grade Foam Cleaner & Disingectant—Graham-Field Health Products, Inc.; *U.S. Public*, pg. 757

AERO DINE—Povidone Iodine—Graham-Field Health Products, Inc.; *U.S. Public*, pg. 757

AERO FECT—Air & Surface Desinfectant—Graham-Field Health Products, Inc.; *U.S. Public*, pg. 757

AERO FREEZE—Spray Freeze Anesthetic—Graham-Field Health Products, Inc.; *U.S. Public*, pg. 757

AERO K—NONE—Lawter International, Inc.; *U.S. Public*, pg. 980

AERO M—Tradename—Aerovox Inc.; *U.S. Public*, pg. 25

AERO-MED—Oxygen Dispensing Units—Nellcor Puritan Bennett Incorporated; *U.S. Public*, pg. 1039

AERO-NEG—Photographic Process—Eastman Kodak Company; *U.S. Public*, pg. 550

AERO-90—Aerospace Test System—MTS Systems Corporation; *U.S. Public*, pg. 1028

AERO-PULSE—Air Mattress—Medline Industries, Inc.; *U.S. Private*, pg. 728

AERO PURE—Room Deodorizer—Graham-Field Health Products, Inc.; *U.S. Public*, pg. 757

AERO-SEAL—Clamp—TransTechnology Corporation; *U.S. Public*, pg. 1632

AERO SERIES—Eurostyle Hair Dryers—Remington Products Company, L.L.C.; *U.S. Private*, pg. 921

AERO SERVICE—Air & Ground Resource Survey—Litton Industries, Inc.; *U.S. Public*, pg. 1002

AERO SIL—Silicone Instrument Lubricant—Graham-Field Health Products, Inc.; *U.S. Public*, pg. 757

AERO SOLV—Adhesive Tape Remover—Graham-Field Health Products, Inc.; *U.S. Public*, pg. 757

AERO SPREAD—Sludge, Compost & Lime Spreaders—Highway Equipment Company; *U.S. Private*, pg. 529

AERO STRETCHER—Aircraft Accessories—B/E Aerospace Seating Products Group; *U.S. Public*, pg. 159

AERO THERM—Burn Spray—Graham-Field Health Products, Inc.; *U.S. Public*, pg. 757

AERO ZOIN—Tincture of Benzoin Compound—Graham-Field Health Products, Inc.; *U.S. Public*, pg. 757

AEROBID—Pharmaceutical—Forest Laboratories, Inc.; *U.S. Public*, pg. 670

AEROCAB—Trucks—Kenworth Truck Company; *U.S. Public*, pg. 1246

AEROCARB—Carbon Fiber Product—Ashland, Inc.; *U.S. Public*, pg. 138

AEROCEUTICALS—Pharmaceutical Sprays—Graham-Field Health Products, Inc.; *U.S. Public*, pg. 757

AEROCHAMBER—Pharmaceutical Product—Forest Laboratories, Inc.; *U.S. Public*, pg. 670

AEROCHROME—Photo Film—Eastman Kodak Company; *U.S. Public*, pg. 550

AEROCLEVE—Secondary Wastewater System—Eagle Industries, Inc.; *U.S. Private*, pg. 473

AEROCOLOR—Photo Film—Eastman Kodak Company; *U.S. Public*, pg. 550

AERODAG—Lubricants—Acheson Colloids Company; *U.S. Private*, pg. 12

AERODUCT—Ducting—HBD Industries, Inc.; *U.S. Private*, pg. 489

AERODYNE—Trucks—Kenworth Truck Company; *U.S. Public*, pg. 1246

AERODYNIC—Vehicle Warning Light/ Loudspeaker—Federal Signal Corporation; *U.S. Public*, pg. 616

AEROFILM—Capacitors—Aerovox Inc.; *U.S. Public*, pg. 25

AEROFILTER—EMI Filters—Aerovox Inc.; *U.S. Public*, pg. 25

AEROFIN—Heat Exchangers—Aerofin Corp.; *U.S. Public*, pg. 103

AEROFIRE—Tires—Bridgestone/Firestone, Inc.; *Int'l*, pg. 213

AEROFLEX—Electronic Components—Aeroflex Incorporated; *U.S. Public*, pg. 23

AEROFLEX—Fiber Glass Duct Liner—Owens Corning; *U.S. Public*, pg. 1236

AEROFLEX PLUS—Edge Coated Glass Fiber Duct Liner—Owens Corning; *U.S. Public*, pg. 1236

AEROFLOAT—Fly Line—Gladding Braided Products LLC; *U.S. Private*, pg. 291

AEROFLOW—Control Valves—Leslie Controls, Inc.; *U.S. Public*, pg. 1746

AEROFOIL—Capacitors—Aerovox Inc.; *U.S. Public*, pg. 25

AEROGLIDE—Grain, Rotary, Conveyor & Tower Driers, Dehydrators—Aeroglide Corporation; *U.S. Private*, pg. 24

AEROGRADE—NONE—ATMI, Inc.; *U.S. Public*, pg. 12

AEROGRAPH—Gas Chromatography Measuring Instruments—Varian Associates, Inc.; *U.S. Public*, pg. 1710

AEROGRAPHIC—Photo Film & Plates—Eastman Kodak Company; *U.S. Public*, pg. 550

AEROHAWK—Vehicle Warning Light/ Loudspeaker—Federal Signal Corporation, Signal Div.; *U.S. Public*, pg. 616

AEROHOT—Food Warmer—Duke Manufacturing Co.; *U.S. Private*, pg. 346

AEROKRAFT—Capacitors—Aerovox Inc.; *U.S. Public*, pg. 25

AEROLINEAS—Airlines—Aerolineas Argentinas; *Int'l*, pg. 575

AEROLITE—Safety Eyewear—Aearo Company; *U.S. Private*, pg. 23

AEROLITE—Binoculars & Telescopes—Swift Instruments, Inc.; *U.S. Private*, pg. 1058

AEROLITE BIRDER—Binoculars—Swift Instruments, Inc.; *U.S. Private*, pg. 1058

AEROLYTE—Drystripping Systems—Aerolyte Systems; *U.S. Private*, pg. 24

AEROLYTE MEDIA—Plastic Abrasives—Aerolyte Systems; *U.S. Private*, pg. 24

AEROLYTE PRODUCTS DIVISION—Plastic Medrid Blast Equipment from Portables to Full-Aircraft Facilities—Clemco Industries Corp.; *U.S. Private*, pg. 24

AEROMAT—Glass Fiber Duct Liner—Owens Corning; *U.S. Public*, pg. 1236

AEROMATIC—Power Factor Correction System—Aerovox Inc.; *U.S. Public*, pg. 25

AEROMAX—Capacitors—Aerovox Inc.; *U.S. Public*, pg. 25

AEROMAX—For X-Ray Tubes & Housings—Varian Associates, Inc.; *U.S. Public*, pg. 1710

AEROMET—Capacitors—Aerovox Inc.; *U.S. Public*, pg. 25

AERON—Media Management Programmable Controller—Anacomp Magnetics, Inc.; *U.S. Public*, pg. 107

AERON—Chairs—Herman Miller, Inc.; *U.S. Public*, pg. 1111

AERONCA—NONE—Magellan Aerospace Corporation; *Int'l*, pg. 829

AEROPAC—Medium & High Efficiency Air Filters for HVAC Use—Farr Company; *U.S. Public*, pg. 613

AEROPAK—Capacitors—Aerovox Inc.; *U.S. Public*, pg. 25

AEROPLANE MONTHLY—Special Interest Magazine—IPC Magazines Limited; *Int'l*, pg. 651

AEROS—Task & Operational Seating—Cramer Inc.; *U.S. Private*, pg. 285

AEROSAFE—Capacitors—Aerovox Inc.; *U.S. Public*, pg. 25

AEROSAFE—Recombination LA BAtteries for Aircrafts—Chloride Industrial Batteries Ltd.; *Int'l*, pg. 125

AEROSEAL—Containers—Beckman Instruments, Inc.; *U.S. Public*, pg. 199

AEROSITE—Safety Eyewear—Aearo Company; *U.S. Private*, pg. 23

AEROSOLV—Aerosol Can Disposal System—CRC Industries, Inc.; *U.S. Private*, pg. 138

AEROSOLVE—Centrifuge Containers & Tube Racks—Beckman Instruments, Inc.; *U.S. Public*, pg. 199

AEROSPACE—Industrial Cases—Andiamo, Inc.; *U.S. Private*, pg. 73

AEROSPACE PRECISION SYSTEMS—Automatic Riveting & Fastening Equipment—KTI; *U.S. Public*, pg. 939

AEROSPORIN—Antibiotic—Glaxo Wellcome PLC; *Int'l*, pg. 553

AEROSTAR—Hot Air Balloons—Aerostar International; *U.S. Public*, pg. 1361

AEROSTAT—Static Eliminator—Simco; *U.S. Public*, pg. 865

AEROSTOR—Capacitors—Aerovox Inc.; *U.S. Public*, pg. 25

AEROTHENE MM—Solvent—The Dow Chemical Company; *U.S. Public*, pg. 522

AEROTHENE TT—Vapor Depressant—The Dow Chemical Company; *U.S. Public*, pg. 522

AEROTWINSONIC—Vehicle Warning Light/Loudspeaker—Federal Signal Corporation, Signal Div.; *U.S. Public*, pg. 616

AEROVAR—Capacitors—Aerovox Inc.; *U.S. Public*, pg. 25

AEROVOX—Tradename—Aerovox Inc.; *U.S. Public*, pg. 25

AERRO TECHNOLOGY—Ski Poles—The Shelburne Corporation; *U.S. Private*, pg. 991

AERRONE—Pharmaceutical—The BOC Group plc; *Int'l*, pg. 121

AERUGIPEN—Antibiotics—SmithKline Beecham plc; *Int'l*, pg. 1264

AESULAP PRESTIGE ENDOSCOPIC INSTRUMENTS—NONE—Aesculap, Inc.; *Int'l*, pg. 29

AETNA—NONE—Aetna Bearing Company; *U.S. Private*, pg. 25

AETNA—Insurance—Aetna Inc.; *U.S. Public*, pg. 26

AETNA STANDARD—Industrial Machinery—Itam Tech Italimplianti, Inc.; *Int'l*, pg. 655

AFFILIATED FOOD STORES—Distr. Center Member-owned Cooperative—Affiliated Foods Cooperative Inc.; *U.S. Private*, pg. 25

THE AFFILIATES—Specialized Legal Staffing—Robert Half International Inc.; *U.S. Public*, pg. 774

AFFINITY—Pre-Finished Mouldings—ABT Building Products Corporation; *Int'l*, pg. 20

AFFINITY—Random Access Immunochemistry Analyzer—Becton Dickinson & Company; *U.S. Public*, pg. 199

AFFINITY—Tires—Bridgestone/Firestone, Inc.; *Int'l*, pg. 213

AFFINITY—Perennial Ryegrass—Green Seed Co.; *U.S. Private*, pg. 477

AFFINITY—Birthing Bed—Hillenbrand Industries, Inc.; *U.S. Public*, pg. 828

AFFINITY—Wood Clad Vinyl Windows—Lindal Cedar Homes, Inc.; *U.S. Public*, pg. 998

AFFINITY—Pacemaker—St. Jude Medical, Inc.; *U.S. Public*, pg. 1427

AFFIRMAGEN—Reagent Red Blood Cells—Ortho Clinical Diagnostic Systems Inc.; *U.S. Public*, pg. 929

AFFIX—Ergonomic Task Seating—Cramer Inc.; *U.S. Private*, pg. 285

AFFORDABLE BRAND FURNITURE—RTA Furniture—Ameriwood Industries International Inc.; *U.S. Public*, pg. 98

AFFORDABLE PORTABLE—Economy Portable Food Station—The Vollrath Company, L.L.C.; *U.S. Private*, pg. 1143

AFICIO—Digital Color Copiers—Ricoh Corporation; *Int'l*, pg. 1114

ARISTOKRAFT—Kitchen Cabinets & Bathroom Vanities—Fortune Brands, Inc.; *U.S. Public*, pg. 674

AFLABAN—Mold Inhibitor for Animal Feed—The Agricultural Group, Monsanto Company; *U.S. Public*, pg. 1125

AFLABAN—Mold Inhibitor for Animal Feed—Monsanto Company; *U.S. Public*, pg. 1124

AFRANIL—Process Chemicals & Colorants—BASF AG; *Int'l*, pg. 103

AFRICAN HONEYWOOD—Wood & Lumber Products—Georgia-Pacific Corporation; *U.S. Public*, pg. 735

AFRICATOURS—Tour Operators—Accor S.A.; *Int'l*, pg. 20

AFRIN—Nasal Spray—Schering-Plough Corporation; *U.S. Public*, pg. 1438

AFRIN—Nasal Decongestant Spray—Schering-Plough Healthcare Products Inc.; *U.S. Public*, pg. 1438

AFRINOL REPETABS—Long-Acting Nasal Decongestant—Schering-Plough Corporation; *U.S. Public*, pg. 1438

AFTA—After Shave Skin Conditioner & Pre-Electric Shave Lotion—The Mennen Company; *U.S. Public*, pg. 397

AFTATE—Athlete's Foot Treatment—Schering-Plough Corporation; *U.S. Public*, pg. 1438

AFTATE—Antifungal Preparations—Schering-Plough Healthcare Products Inc.; *U.S. Public*, pg. 1438

AFTER EIGHT—Thin Mints—Nestle Chocolate & Confection; *Int'l*, pg. 917

AFTER EIGHT—Mints—Nestle-Rowntree Ltd.; *Int'l*, pg. 921

AFTER EIGHT—Chocolate Mints—Nestle S.A.; *Int'l*, pg. 915

AFTER EIGHT—Dinner Mints—Nestle USA; *Int'l*, pg. 916

AFTER HOURS—Shoes—Johnston & Murphy Co.; *U.S. Public*, pg. 728

AFTER HOURS—Pipe Tobacco—Lane Limited; *Int'l*, pg. 1129

AFTER HOURS SPORTS—Shoes—Johnston & Murphy Co.; *U.S. Public*, pg. 728

AFTER SHOCK—Cordial—Fortune Brands, Inc.; *U.S. Public*, pg. 674

AFTER THE FALL—Fruit Juices—J.M. Smucker Company; *U.S. Public*, pg. 1480

AFTERCARE—NONE—Fermec Holdings, Ltd.; *U.S. Public*, pg. 312

AFTERMARKET BUSINESS—Trade Periodical—Advanstar Communications; *U.S. Private*, pg. 22

AFTERTHOUGHTS—Costume Jewelry, Handbags & Accessories—F.W. Woolworth Co.; *U.S. Public*, pg. 1777

AFTERTHOUGHTS/CARIMAR/RUBIN—Costume Jewelry, Handbags & Accessories—Woolworth Corporation; *U.S. Public*, pg. 1777

AFUGAN—Fungicide—Hoechst Aktiengesellschaft; *Int'l*, pg. 624

AGAIN & AGAIN—Disposable Aluminum Foil Cookware & Bakeware—Reynolds Metals Company; *U.S. Public*, pg. 1385

AGAPI—Fashion Slacks & Shorts—H. R. Kaminsky & Sons, Inc.; *U.S. Private*, pg. 606

AGAR MATIC—Agar Sterilizer—New Brunswick Scientific Co., Inc.; *U.S. Public*, pg. 1169

AGASTAT—Timing Control Devices—Thomas & Betts/Amerace; *U.S. Public*, pg. 1598

AGASTAT—Electrical Timers & Relays—Thomas & Betts Corporation; *U.S. Public*, pg. 1597

AGCO ALLIS—Tractors—AGCO Corporation; *U.S. Public*, pg. 28

AGCOSTAR—Tractors—AGCO Corporation; *U.S. Public*, pg. 28

THE AGE—NONE—John Fairfax Holdings Limited; *Int'l*, pg. 477

AGE ZONE CONTROLLER—Skin Care Treatments—Charles of the Ritz Group Ltd.; *U.S. Private*, pg. 689

AGELESS—Food Additive—FTI Foodtech International Inc.; *Int'l*, pg. 476

AGEPROOF—Papers, Vellums, Films—Dietzgen Corporation; *U.S. Private*, pg. 332

AGFA—Film—Bayer AG; *Int'l*, pg. 171

AGFA BUREAUMASTER—Photo Typesetter—AGFA EPS Division; *Int'l*, pg. 172

AGFA CATALYST—Photo Typesetter—AGFA EPS Division; *Int'l*, pg. 172

AGFACHROME—Film—Agfa-Gevaert S.A.; *Int'l*, pg. 174

AGFACOLOR—Film—Agfa-Gevaert S.A.; *Int'l*, pg. 174

AGFACOLOR—Color Negative Film—Bayer AG; *Int'l*, pg. 171

AGFASTAR—Film Processing System—Bayer AG; *Int'l*, pg. 171

AGGIES—NONE—The Bentley Agnew Group Inc.; *Int'l*, pg. 187

AGGLOMERATED—Flux—The Lincoln Electric Company; *U.S. Public*, pg. 996

AGIE—NONE—Georg Fischer Ltd.; *Int'l*, pg. 488

AGILE ENTERPRISE—Business Management consulting Services Rendered To Manufacturing Companies—Bourton Group; *U.S. Private*, pg. 162

AGIOLAX—Gastrointestinal Pharmaceutical—BYK Gulden, S.A. de C.V.; *Int'l*, pg. 66

AGITOR—Liquid Ink Pump—Graymills Corp.; *U.S. Private*, pg. 473

AGNESI—Pasta—Danone Group; *Int'l*, pg. 379

AGNEW—NONE—The Bentley Agnew Group Inc.; *Int'l*, pg. 187

AGORAL—Laxative—Warner-Lambert Company; *U.S. Public*, pg. 1738

AGREE—Shampoo, Cream Rinse & Conditioner—Dep Corporation; *U.S. Public*, pg. 500

AGREE/EXHIBIT—Insecticide—Novartis; *Int'l*, pg. 972

AGREER HAIR GELLING WATER—NONE—Shiseido Company Ltd.; *Int'l*, pg. 1235

AGRELEK—Service Package on Electrotechnology Based Solutions for Agriculture—Eskom; *Int'l*, pg. 459

AGREPT—Agricultural Chemicals—Meiji Seika Kaisha, Ltd.; *Int'l*, pg. 855

AGRI-COMP—Dairy Herd Management Computer Systems—Bou-Matic; *U.S. Private*, pg. 301

AGRI LETTER—NONE—Farm Press; *U.S. Public*, pg. 1328

AGRI-RADIAL—Tractor Tires—Universal Cooperatives, Inc.; *U.S. Private*, pg. 1127

AGRI-SUL—Chemical—Eagle-Picher Industries, Inc.; *U.S. Private*, pg. 355

AGRIBROM—Biocide—Great Lakes Chemical Corporation; *U.S. Public*, pg. 760

AGRICO—Fertilizers—Freeport-McMoRan Inc.; *U.S. Public*, pg. 680

AGRIGOLD—Corn Seed—Groupe Limagrain; *Int'l*, pg. 566

AGRINET—Agricultural Radio Network—Ray Communications, Inc.; *U.S. Private*, pg. 911

AGRIPRO BRAND—Seeds—L.L. Olds Seed Company; *U.S. Private*, pg. 814

AGRO DYNAMICS—NONE—EcoScience Corporation; *U.S. Public*, pg. 563

AGRO-MATIC—Controller—Rain Bird Sprinklers Manufacturing Corp.; *U.S. Private*, pg. 907

AGROMAC—Farm Equipment—Agromac International, Inc.; *U.S. Private*, pg. 27

AGROSIL—Soil Improvers—BASF AG; *Int'l*, pg. 103

AGROTEC—Sprayers—Agrotec, Williams Inc.; *U.S. Public*, pg. 1769

AGRUMA—Fruit Juice Concentrate without Sugar—Groupe Pernod Ricard; *Int'l*, pg. 566

AGRYLIN—Treatment for High Blood Platelets—Roberts Pharmaceutical Corporation; *U.S. Public*, pg. 1393

AGSORB—Carriers & Drying Agent—Oil-Dri Corporation of America; *U.S. Public*, pg. 1214

AGUILA—Beer—Heineken N.V.; *Int'l*, pg. 608

AGWAY—Farm & Home Supplies—Agway, Inc.; *U.S. Public*, pg. 27

AHEAD—Air Defense Gun System—Balzers; *Int'l*, pg. 997

AHEAD—Air Defense Gun System—Oerlikon-Contraves AG; *Int'l*, pg. 998

AID AUTO—Wholesale Auto Parts—Aid Auto Stores, Inc.; *U.S. Public*, pg. 29

AILEEN—Women's Clothing—Names for Dames, Inc.; *U.S. Private*, pg. 773

AILEEN PETITE—Women's Clothing—Names for Dames, Inc.; *U.S. Private*, pg. 773

AILEEN SPORT—Women's Clothing—Names for Dames, Inc.; *U.S. Private*, pg. 773

AILEEN TOO—Women's Clothing—Names for Dames, Inc.; *U.S. Private*, pg. 773

AIM—Toothpaste—Chesebrough-Pond's USA Co.; *Int'l*, pg. 1435

AIM—Computer Software Program—Datapoint Corporation; *Int'l*, pg. 384

AIM—Grocery Products—Krasdale Foods Inc.; *U.S. Private*, pg. 635

AIM N FLAME—Utility Lighter—Scripto-Tokai Corp.; *U.S. Private*, pg. 977

AIM V—NONE—Life Technologies, Inc.; *U.S. Public*, pg. 504

AIMCOR—NONE—Applied Industrial Materials Corporation; *U.S. Public*, pg. 1736

AIMPLUS—Inventory Mngmt. System—Ethicon, Inc.; *U.S. Private*, pg. 928

AIMS—NONE—Lindsay Manufacturing Company; *U.S. Public*, pg. 999

AIR BAKE—Bakeware—Mirro Company; *U.S. Public*, pg. 1177

AIR BEAR—Air Filtering Unit-Disposable Filter and Grill Mount—Trion, Inc.; *U.S. Public*, pg. 1639

AIR BLADE—Clean Mirror System—K-D Lamp Company; *U.S. Private*, pg. 603

AIR BLASTER—Activity—Tyco Toys, Inc.; *U.S. Public*, pg. 1058

AIR BOSS—Industrial Oil Mist & Air Pollution Cleaner—Trion, Inc.; *U.S. Public*, pg. 1639

AIR BRAKE—Integral to Power Master & Pile Driver Pumps for Run-Away Control—Lincoln Industrial; *U.S. Public*, pg. 1273

AIR BRUSH—Hair Dryer—Clairol, Inc.; *U.S. Public*, pg. 254

AIR BRUSH—NONE—Royal Rubber & Manufacturing Co.; *U.S. Private*, pg. 949

AIR CANADA—Air Transportation—Air Canada; *Int'l*, pg. 36

AIR CANADA—Passenger & Cargo Airline—Air Canada; *Int'l*, pg. 36

AIR CAP—Impingement Air Dryer—Harnischfeger Industries, Inc.; *U.S. Public*, pg. 788

AIR CEL—Fishing Lines, Fly, Floating—3M; *U.S. Public*, pg. 1604

AIR COMFORT—Ceiling, Window & Attic Fans—Emerson Electric Co.; *U.S. Public*, pg. 572

AIR CRUISERS—Inflatable Survival Equipment—Air Cruisers Co.; *Int'l*, pg. 572

AIR CUSIONED INLET—Headbox—Beloit Corporation; *U.S. Public*, pg. 789

AIR DIAMOND TURF—Athletic Shoe—Nike, Inc.; *U.S. Public*, pg. 1184

AIR-EVAC—Chemical Storage Container—Falcon Safety Products Inc.; *U.S. Private*, pg. 392

AIR EXPRESS—1200 Watt Dryer—Clairol, Inc.; *U.S. Public*, pg. 254

AIR FILTER TITE—Fasteners—R&B, Inc.; *U.S. Public*, pg. 1354

AIR FORCE—War Game—Monarch Avalon, Inc.; *U.S. Public*, pg. 1123

AIR FRAME—Ceiling Systems—Daw Technologies, Inc.; *U.S. Public*, pg. 489

AIR-INDIA—Airline—Air-India; *Int'l*, pg. 37

AIR JAMAICA—Airlines—Air Jamaica Ltd.; *U.S. Private*, pg. 28

AIR KING—NONE—Lasko Metal Products, Inc.; *U.S. Private*, pg. 652

AIR LEAF—Suspension—Peterbilt Motors Co.; *U.S. Public*, pg. 1247

AIR-LIFT—Work Platform—Up-Right, Inc.; *U.S. Private*, pg. 1128

AIR LITE—Athletic Equipment—Bike Athletic Co.; *U.S. Private*, pg. 143

AIR-LOC—Lighting Fixture—Juno Lighting, Inc.; *U.S. Public*, pg. 935

AIR MAX—Athletic Shoe—Nike, Inc.; *U.S. Public*, pg. 1184

AIR NEW ZEALAND—Airlines—Air New Zealand Ltd. (U.S.A.); *Int'l*, pg. 38

AIR PAC—Compressors for Construction Market—Thomas Industries Inc.; *U.S. Public*, pg. 1598

AIR-PAK—Oxygen Systems—Figgie International Inc.; *U.S. Public*, pg. 622

AIR-PAK—Breathing Apparatus—Scott Aviation; *U.S. Public*, pg. 622

AIR-PILLO—Insoles—Schering-Plough Corporation; *U.S. Public*, pg. 1438

AIR-PILLO—Insoles—Scholl U.S.A.; *U.S. Public*, pg. 1438

AIR-PLAS—Masonry Cement Additives—Westvaco Corporation; *U.S. Public*, pg. 1762

AIR PLUS—NONE—Cannon Equipment; *Int'l*, pg. 646

AIR RAM—Air Intake Moisture Eliminator—Donaldson Company, Inc.; *U.S. Public*, pg. 517

AIR RAM II—Air Intake Moisture Eliminator—Donaldson Company, Inc.; *U.S. Public*, pg. 517

AIR ROYAL—Cylinders—Conbraco Industries Inc.; *U.S. Private*, pg. 261

AIR-SAVERS—Fan Freshener Refills—Surco Products, Inc.; *U.S. Private*, pg. 1056

AIR-SCENT—Fan Air Freshener Systems—Surco Products, Inc.; *U.S. Private*, pg. 1056

AIR-SCRUBBERS—Eliminate Odors in Wastewater & Sewage—U.S. Filter/Davis Water & Waste Industries, Inc.; *U.S. Public*, pg. 1682

AIR SENTINEL—Airflow Measurement Equipment—Farr Company; *U.S. Public*, pg. 613

AIR-SHIELDS—Neonatal Intensive care Equipment—Vickers PLC; *Int'l*, pg. 1466

AIR-SPEED—Portland Cement—Essroc Cement, Corp.; *U.S. Private*, pg. 384

AIR STATION—Outdoor Products—The Black & Decker Corporation; *U.S. Public*, pg. 233

AIR STEP—Shoes—Brown Group, Inc.; *U.S. Public*, pg. 262

AIR SWEEP—Deaerator—Peterbilt Motors Co.; *U.S. Public*, pg. 1247

AIR TECH—NONE—Scotsman Industries, Inc.; *U.S. Public*, pg. 1444

AIR-TOUGH—NONE—Carpenter Technology Corporation; *U.S. Public*, pg. 307

AIR TOURS—Leisure Travel—Carnival Corporation; *U.S. Public*, pg. 306

AIR TRAC—Suspension—Peterbilt Motors Co.; *U.S. Public*, pg. 1247

AIR TRANSPORT—NONE—The Swissair Group; *Int'l*, pg. 1333

AIR TRANSPORT WORLD—Periodical—Penton Publishing, Inc.; *U.S. Public*, pg. 1306

AIR-TUFF FILM—Special Formular Plastic for Air Cargo Bags—Uniflex, Inc.; *U.S. Public*, pg. 1665

AIR VENT—NONE—Air Vent Inc.; *Int'l*, pg. 1170

AIR-WEAR—NONE—Carpenter Technology Corporation; *U.S. Public*, pg. 307

AIR WICK—Air Freshener—Reckitt & Colman plc; *Int'l*, pg. 1089

AIR WISCONSIN—Passenger Service & Freight Service—Air Wisconsin, Inc.; *U.S. Public*, pg. 1653

AIRAIL—Pneumatic Springs—Bridgestone/Firestone, Inc.; *Int'l*, pg. 213

AIRAMIC—Diffusers—Ferro Corporation; *U.S. Public*, pg. 618

AIRBAKE—Cookware—Newell Co.; *U.S. Public*, pg. 1176

AIRBAKE 2000—Cookware—Newell Co.; *U.S. Public*, pg. 1176

AIRBORNE—In-Line Skates—First Team Sports Inc.; *U.S. Public*, pg. 638

AIRBORNE CCTV—Video Monitors—Nellcor Puritan Bennett Incorporated; *U.S. Public*, pg. 1039

AIRBORNE EXPRESS—Air Express Service—Airborne Freight Corporation; *U.S. Public*, pg. 32

AIRCAP—Lawnmowers, Tillers, Edgers—Aircap Industries Corp.; *U.S. Private*, pg. 688

AIRCAP—Air Cellular Cushioning Material—Sealed Air Corporation; *U.S. Public*, pg. 1450

AIRCARES—Corporate Giving—Northwest Airlines, Inc.; *U.S. Public*, pg. 1200

AIRCO—Industrial Gases—The BOC Group Inc. (Delaware); *Int'l*, pg. 121

AIRCON—Electrically Heated Laminated Panels—PPG Industries, Inc.; *U.S. Public*, pg. 1245

AIRCON—Automatic Airline Information & Reservation—Thomson Consumer Electronics Inc.; *Int'l*, pg. 1383

AIRCRAFT BLUEBOOK—Aviation Equipment Price Guide—Intertec Publishing; *U.S. Public*, pg. 1327

AIRECTOR—Storage Racks—Jarke Corporation; *U.S. Private*, pg. 583

AIREJECTOR—Filter Pump—Fisher Scientific Company; *U.S. Private*, pg. 658

AIRELOOM—Mattresses—Chittenden & Eastman Co.; *U.S. Private*, pg. 237

AIRELUME—Clean Room Bi-Ax Unit—Guth Lighting Company; *Int'l*, pg. 821

AIRESEARCH—Products for Aircraft, Missile & Commercial Applications—AlliedSignal Aerospace; *U.S. Public*, pg. 50

AIREX—Polyvinyl Mats—Alusuisse-Lonza Holding Ltd.; *Int'l*, pg. 66

AIRFIX—Plastic Model Kits—Borden, Inc.; *U.S. Private*, pg. 157

AIRFLEX—Emulsions—Air Products and Chemicals, Inc.; *U.S. Public*, pg. 30

AIRFLEX—Mechanical Power Transmission Equipment—Airflex Div. Eaton Corp.; *U.S. Public*, pg. 556

AIRFLEX—Clutches & Brakes—Eaton Corporation; *U.S. Public*, pg. 555

AIRFLEX—Hose—HBD Industries, Inc.; *U.S. Private*, pg. 489

AIRFLOW—Radiator Fan Assemblies—Robert Bosch Corporation; *Int'l*, pg. 204

AIRFLYTE—Plaques—Tropar Mfg. Co., Inc.; *U.S. Private*, pg. 1105

AIRFOIL—Air Floatation Dryer—Thermo Fibertek, Inc.; *U.S. Public*, pg. 1593

AIRFORCE—NONE—Pfizer Inc.; *U.S. Public*, pg. 1281

AIRFUGE—Ultracentrifuge—Beckman Instruments, Inc.; *U.S. Public*, pg. 199

AIRGARD—Fume Hood Monitor—Alnor Instrument Company; *U.S. Public*, pg. 1559

AIRGRIT—Marking Unit—Matthews International Corp.; *U.S. Public*, pg. 1059

AIRGUIDE—Marine, Weather & Automotive Instruments—Johnson Worldwide Associates, Inc.; *U.S. Public*, pg. 932

AIRGUN—Guns—Crosman Airguns; *U.S. Private*, pg. 291

AIRHEADS—Chewy Fruit Candy—Van Melle N.V.; *Int'l*, pg. 1450

AIRHEADS—Candy—Van Melle USA, Inc.; *Int'l*, pg. 1451

AIRIDE—Springs—Bridgestone/Firestone, Inc.; *Int'l*, pg. 213

AIRJECTOR—Heat & Smoke Units—Swartwout Industries; *Int'l*, pg. 1398

AIRLENS—Contact Lenses—Wesley-Jessen; *U.S. Private*, pg. 111

AIRLINK—Antenna Systems—Ball Corporation; *U.S. Public*, pg. 170

AIRLINK—Commuter Partners—Northwest Airlines, Inc.; *U.S. Public*, pg. 1200

AIRLINK—Closed Circuit Television Equipment—Vicon Industries, Inc.; *U.S. Public*, pg. 1719

AIRMASTER—Circulators, Exhaust, Ceiling & Attic Fans, Roof Ventilators—Airmaster Fan Co.; *U.S. Private*, pg. 29

AIRMATE—Air Diffuser—Dry Manufacturing Co.; *U.S. Public*, pg. 1795

AIRMATE—HVAC—Eljer Plumbingware; *U.S. Public*, pg. 1794

AIRMATE—Relays & Valves—Leslie Controls, Inc.; *U.S. Public*, pg. 1746

AIRMIZER—Fuel Ratio Control—AMETEK, Inc.; *U.S. Public*, pg. 99

AIRMOULD—Gas Injection Process—Battenfeld GmbH; *Int'l*, pg. 825

AIRMOUNT—Pneumatic Springs, Isolators—Bridgestone/Firestone, Inc.; *Int'l*, pg. 213

AIROLITE—Ventilating Louvers—The Airolite Company; *U.S. Private*, pg. 29

AIRONET—Wireless LAN Communications Hardware—Telxon Corporation; *U.S. Public*, pg. 1573

AIRPAX—NONE—Philips Automotive Electronics; *Int'l*, pg. 1054

AIRPAX—Precision Controls Instruments—Philips Electronics North America Corporation; *Int'l*, pg. 1053

AIRPAX—Magnetic Circuit Breakers—Philips Electronics N.V.; *Int'l*, pg. 1051

AIRPLAY MONITORS—Magazines—BPI Communications Inc.; *Int'l*, pg. 1446

AIRPURE—Industrial Products—Email Limited; *Int'l*, pg. 450

AIRQUEST—Heating & Cooling Products—International Comfort Products Corp.; *U.S. Public*, pg. 898

AIRSEAL—Connection Sealant—Kearney Company; *U.S. Public*, pg. 444

AIRSIGNAL—Paging Service Provider—AT&T Wireless Services; *U.S. Public*, pg. 11

AIRSLIDE—Gravity Conveyor—Fuller Company; *Int'l*, pg. 475

AIRSLIDE—Covered Hopper Car—GATX Corporation; *U.S. Public*, pg. 690

AIRSPACE—Flat Glass—Guardian Industries Corp.; *U.S. Private*, pg. 485

AIRSTAR—Air Compressor—Air Techniques, Inc.; *U.S. Private*, pg. 28

AIRSTROKE—Actuators—Bridgestone/Firestone, Inc.; *Int'l*, pg. 213

AIRTEMP—Room Air Conditioning—Fedders Corp.; *U.S. Public*, pg. 614

AIRTHANE—Polyurethane Prepolymer—Air Products and Chemicals, Inc.; *U.S. Public*, pg. 30

AIRTOUCH CELLULAR—Telephone Service—AirTouch Cellular - Western Region; *U.S. Public*, pg. 34

AIRTRACE—Proprietary Exploration Technique—Barringer Technologies Inc.; *U.S. Public*, pg. 191

AIRTRON—Microwave Components—Litton Industries, Inc.; *U.S. Public*, pg. 1002

AIRVEYOR—Conveyor—Fuller Company; *Int'l*, pg. 475

AIRVOL—Polyvinyl Alcohol as an Adhesive—Air Products and Chemicals, Inc.; *U.S. Public*, pg. 30

AIRWAVE 7000—NONE—CEM Corporation; *U.S. Public*, pg. 277

AIRWAY—Compass—The Sherrill Corp.; *U.S. Private*, pg. 298

AISLE KEEPER—EAS System Devel. to Protect Hard Goods in Supermkt. & Hypermkt. Retailers—Sensormatic Electronics Corporation; *U.S. Public*, pg. 1457

AISLE-LITER—Industrial Warehouses—Guth Lighting Company; *Int'l*, pg. 821

AISLEVISION—Overhead Supermarket Promotional Directories—News America Marketing; *Int'l*, pg. 925

AIWA—Car Audio, Audio & Visual Products—Aiwa America, Inc.; *Int'l*, pg. 1280

AIXWINDOWS—Computer System—International Business Machines Corporation; *U.S. Public*, pg. 895

AJAX—Manufactured Homes—Champion Enterprises, Inc.; *U.S. Public*, pg. 332

AJAX—Cleanser—Colgate-Palmolive; *U.S. Public*, pg. 398

AJAX—Household Cleaner—Colgate-Palmolive A/S; *U.S. Public*, pg. 398

AJAX—Institutional Products—Colgate-Palmolive Co., Institutional Products Div.; *U.S. Public*, pg. 397

AJAX—Laundry Detergent—Colgate-Palmolive Company; *U.S. Public*, pg. 397

AJAX—Vertical Plunger Pumps—Gardner Denver Machinery Inc.; *U.S. Public*, pg. 703

AJAX—Heating Systems—Guthrie North America, Inc.; *Int'l*, pg. 113

AJAX—Disposer Care—Softsoap Enterprises, Inc.; *U.S. Public*, pg. 397

AJAX—Paper Cups—Westvaco Corporation; *U.S. Public*, pg. 1762

AJAX FLEXIBLE COUPLINGS—Gear Type Couplings and Spindle Couplings—Renold, Inc.; *Int'l*, pg. 1104

AJAX SHAKER—Shaker Gearbox for Vibratory Drives—Renold, Inc.; *Int'l*, pg. 1104

AJAXOMATIC—Automatic Pouring for Aluminum—Ajax Magnethermic Corp.; *Int'l*, pg. 113

AJILON—Technical Staffing—Adecco Employment Services; *Int'l*, pg. 24

AKADAMA—Plum Wine—Suntory International Corp.; *Int'l*, pg. 1321

AKADAMA—Wines—Suntory Ltd.; *Int'l*, pg. 1321

AKEBONO—Canned & Frozen Food—Nichiro Corporation; *Int'l*, pg. 928

AKERMAN—Construction Machinery—Volvo Excavators AB; *Int'l*, pg. 1477

AKNY—Jr. Sportswear-Ladies—Andrew Sports Club Inc.; *U.S. Private*, pg. 73

AKO—Toffee—Huhtamaki Oy; *Int'l*, pg. 638

AKRO—Automotive Floor Mats—Collins & Aikman Corporation; *U.S. Public*, pg. 399

AKRO-BINES—Plastic Containers—Myers Industries, Inc.; *U.S. Public*, pg. 1143

AKRO-MILS—Tradename—Myers Industries, Inc.; *U.S. Public*, pg. 1143

AKRO-ZINC BAR—NONE—Akrochem Corporation; *U.S. Private*, pg. 30

AKROCHEM—NONE—Akrochem Corporation; *U.S. Private*, pg. 30

AKROCHEX—NONE—Akrochem Corporation; *U.S. Private*, pg. 30

AKROCHLOR—NONE—Akrochem Corporation; *U.S. Private*, pg. 30

AKROFAX—NONE—Akrochem Corporation; *U.S. Private*, pg. 30

AKROFLOCK—NONE—Akrochem Corporation; *U.S. Private*, pg. 30

AKROFORM—NONE—Akrochem Corporation; *U.S. Private*, pg. 30

AKROGEL—NONE—Akrochem Corporation; *U.S. Private*, pg. 30

AKROMAG BARS—NONE—Akrochem Corporation; *U.S. Private*, pg. 30

AKROMATIC—Nozzles—Akron Brass Company; *Int'l*, pg. 1068

AKRON BRASS—Nozzles, Fittings for Fire Hoses—EEI Corporation; *Int'l*, pg. 425

AKRON BRASS—Fire Fighting Equip.—Premier Farnell; *Int'l*, pg. 1068

AKROPLAST—NONE—Akrochem Corporation; *U.S. Private*, pg. 30

AKROS—Foam & Gel Cushions & Mattresses for Therapeutic Support—Lumex Medical Products; *U.S. Public*, pg. 758

AKROSORB—NONE—Akrochem Corporation; *U.S. Private*, pg. 30

AKROSPERSE—NONE—Akrochem Corporation; *U.S. Private*, pg. 30

AKROWAX—NONE—Akrochem Corporation; *U.S. Private*, pg. 30

AKTA-VITE—NONE—Kiwi Brands Pty. Ltd.; *U.S. Public*, pg. 1434

AKTRA II—Cut-off Luminares—Wide-Lite; *U.S. Public*, pg. 730

AKUCELL—Crystallization Retarder & Moisture Binder—Akzo Nobel N.V.; *Int'l*, pg. 42

AKULON—Polyamide—Akzo Nobel N.V.; *Int'l*, pg. 42

AKZONA—Miscellaneous Chemical & Fiber Products—Akzo Nobel Inc.; *Int'l*, pg. 47

AL-TEMP I—Hand Held Pyrometer—Alnor Instrument Company; *U.S. Public*, pg. 1559

AL-TEMP II—Hand Held Pyrometer—Alnor Instrument Company; *U.S. Public*, pg. 1559

AL-TUFF—Aluminum Non-Wetting Refractories—Plibrico Co.; *U.S. Private*, pg. 872

AL-CLAD—Product Coatings—DMD; *U.S. Public*, pg. 528

AL'S AUTO SUPPLY—Trucks—Paccar Inc.; *U.S. Public*, pg. 1246

ALABAMA MANUFACTURERS REGISTER—Register—Manufacturers' News, Inc.; *U.S. Private*, pg. 700

ALACRITY—Men's Apparel—H. Freeman & Son, Inc.; *U.S. Private*, pg. 426

ALACTAMIL—Infant Formula—Bristol-Myers Squibb Company; *U.S. Public*, pg. 253

ALADDIN—Lunch Kits, Vacuum Bottles & Kerosene Lamps—Aladdin Industries, Incorporated; *U.S. Private*, pg. 30

ALADDIN—Lawn Mower Parts—Blount International, Inc.; *U.S. Public*, pg. 237

ALADDIN—Carpets & Rugs—Mohawk Industries, Inc.; *U.S. Public*, pg. 1121

ALADDIN—Lawnmower Blades—Orbex Inc.; *U.S. Public*, pg. 238

ALADDIN—Video Magnifier—Telesensory Corporation; *U.S. Private*, pg. 1074

ALADIN—Dive Computers—Johnson Worldwide Associates, Inc.; *U.S. Public*, pg. 932

ALAGA—Light & Dark Maple & Honey Corn Syrup—Whitfield Foods, Inc.; *U.S. Private*, pg. 1173

ALAMAC—Fatty Amine Acetates—Henkel Corporation; *Int'l*, pg. 610

ALAMAC—Knitted Fabrics—WestPoint Stevens Inc.; *U.S. Public*, pg. 1762

ALAMINE—Fatty Amines—Henkel Corporation; *Int'l*, pg. 610

ALAMO—Car Rental—Alamo Rent-A-Car Inc.; *U.S. Public*, pg. 1379

ALAMO BRAND—Dry Dog Foods—Alpo Pet Foods, Inc.; *Int'l*, pg. 917

ALAMO FRUIT—Gift Packages—Standex International Corporation; *U.S. Public*, pg. 1505

ALANE—Aluminum Hydride—FMC Corp., Lithium Division; *U.S. Public*, pg. 605

ALANINE—Food Additives—Nippon Kayaku Co. Ltd.; *Int'l*, pg. 934

ALARM—Air-Launched, Anti-Radar Missile—British Aerospace p.l.c.; *Int'l*, pg. 217

ALARON—Electronic & Communication Equip.—Alaron Inc.; *U.S. Private*, pg. 31

ALASKA—Airlines—Alaska Airlines, Inc.; *U.S. Public*, pg. 35

ALASKA—Anised Liquor—Groupe Pernod Ricard; *Int'l*, pg. 566

ALASKA MANUFACTURERS DIRECTORY—Directory—Manufacturers' News, Inc.; *U.S. Private*, pg. 700

ALASKAN FALLS—Bottled Drinking Water—Liqui-Box Corporation; *U.S. Public*, pg. 1000

ALATHON—High-Density Polyethylene Resins—Lyondell Petrochemical Company; *U.S. Public*, pg. 1022

ALAVAC—Vaccine for Preventive Treatment of Hay Fever—SmithKline Beecham plc; *Int'l*, pg. 1264

ALBA—Ladies Panties—Alba-Waldensian, Inc.; *U.S. Public*, pg. 35

ALBA—Dry Beverage Mixes—H.J. Heinz Company; *U.S. Public*, pg. 805

ALBA—NONE—Seiko Corporation; *Int'l*, pg. 1218

ALBA—White Mineral Oil—Witco Corporation; *U.S. Public*, pg. 1773

ALBACILLIN—Mastitis Products—Pharmacia & Upjohn; *Int'l*, pg. 1048

ALBADORA—Pasta—Borden, Inc.; *U.S. Private*, pg. 157

ALBADRY PLUS—Mastitis Products—Pharmacia & Upjohn; *Int'l*, pg. 1048

ALBAHEALTH—Healthcare Dressings—Alba-Waldensian, Inc.; *U.S. Public*, pg. 35

ALBAL—Aluminum Foil, Pans & Trays; Plastic Bags & Films—The Dow Chemical Company; *U.S. Public*, pg. 522

ALBAL L'ALUMINIUM MENAGER—Aluminum Foil, Pans & Trays—The Dow Chemical Company; *U.S. Public*, pg. 522

ALBAL STYLE—Tablecloths—The Dow Chemical Company; *U.S. Public*, pg. 522

ALBANY—Industrial Textiles—Albany Mount Vernon Dryers; *U.S. Public*, pg. 36

ALBANY—Automotive Brake Pads & Shoes—AutoZone, Inc.; *U.S. Public*, pg. 150

ALBANY TIMES UNION—Newspaper—The Hearst Corporation; *U.S. Private*, pg. 515

ALBAZIP—Plastic Bags—The Dow Chemical Company; *U.S. Public*, pg. 522

ALBEROY—Jr. Knitwear—Beldoch Industries; *U.S. Public*, pg. 519

ALBERS—NONE—Nestle USA; *Int'l*, pg. 916

ALBERT GEORGE—Greeting Cards—American Greetings Corporation; *U.S. Public*, pg. 77

ALBERT HEIJN—Food Stores—Koninklijke Ahold NV; *Int'l*, pg. 749

ALBERT ROBIN COGNAC—NONE—Star Industries, Inc.; *U.S. Private*, pg. 1034

ALBERTA CANADIAN—Blended Canadian Whiskey—Fortune Brands, Inc.; *U.S. Public*, pg. 674

ALBERTO—Cosmetics & Toiletry Products—Alberto-Culver Company; *U.S. Public*, pg. 37

ALBERTO BALSAM—Conditioner—Alberto-Culver Company; *U.S. Public*, pg. 37

ALBERTO EUROPEAN—NONE—Alberto-Culver Canada, Inc.; *U.S. Public*, pg. 38

ALBERTO FRIZZ-SOLVER—Hair Spritz—Alberto-Culver Company; *U.S. Public*, pg. 37

ALBERTO LEAVE-IN CONDITIONER—Shampoo & Conditioner—Alberto-Culver Company; *U.S. Public*, pg. 37

ALBERTO UPSIDE DOWN VOLUMIZING SPRAY—Hair Spray—Alberto-Culver Company; *U.S. Public*, pg. 37

ALBERTO VO5—NONE—Alberto-Culver Canada, Inc.; *U.S. Public*, pg. 38

ALBERTO VO5—Cosmetic & Toiletry Products—Alberto-Culver Company; *U.S. Public*, pg. 37

ALBERT'S—Wafer Cookies—R.L. Albert & Son, Inc.; *U.S. Private*, pg. 32

ALBERT'S FINEST—Salad Dressings—Ventura Foods; *U.S. Private*, pg. 508

ALBERTSON'S—Cultured Dairy Products—Philip Morris Companies Inc.; *U.S. Public*, pg. 1287

ALBERTSON'S—NONE—Albertson's, Inc.; *U.S. Public*, pg. 38

ALBION—NONE—Glynwed International PLC; *Int'l*, pg. 554

ALBOLENE—Liquifying Skin Cleanser—Menley & James Laboratories, Inc.; *U.S. Public*, pg. 1086

ALBON—Antibacterial—SmithKline Beecham plc; *Int'l*, pg. 1264

ALBORS—Stemware & Barware—Dansk International Designs Ltd.; *U.S. Public*, pg. 261

ALBOTHYL—Gynecological Pharmaceutical—BYK Gulden, S.A. de C.V.; *Int'l*, pg. 66

ALBRAZE—Heat Transfer Products—Modine Manufacturing Company; *U.S. Public*, pg. 1121

ALBUM-UNLIMITED—Office Supplies—JM Company; *U.S. Private*, pg. 577

ALBUMAX—NONE—Life Technologies, Inc.; *U.S. Public*, pg. 504

ALBUMINAR 5—Albumin (Human) U.S.P. 5%—Centeon, L.L.C.; *Int'l*, pg. 626

ALBUMINAR 25—Albumin (Human) U.S.P. 25%—Centeon, L.L.C.; *Int'l*, pg. 626

ALBUNEX—Cardiac Diagnostic Agent—Mallinckrodt Inc.; *U.S. Public*, pg. 1039

THE ALBUQUERQUE TRIBUNE—Newspaper—The E.W. Scripps Company; *U.S. Public*, pg. 1447

ALBUTEIN—NONE—Alpha Therapeutic Corp.; *Int'l*, pg. 558

ALCAINE—Proparacaine HC1—Alcon Laboratories, Inc.; *Int'l*, pg. 916

ALCAN—Aluminum Products—Alcan Aluminium Limited; *Int'l*, pg. 50

ALCAN—Aluminum Products—Alcan Aluminum Corporation; *Int'l*, pg. 50

ALCARE FOAM—Alcohol Skin Sanitizer—Calgon Vestal Laboratories; *U.S. Public*, pg. 1515

ALCATEL—NONE—Alcatel Cit (S.A.); *Int'l*, pg. 56

ALCATER—Italy—Key Handling Systems, Inc.; *U.S. Private*, pg. 618

ALCAZAR—NONE—Guinness Plc; *Int'l*, pg. 412

ALCELL—Alcohol- Based Pulping Process—Repap New Brunswick Inc.; *Int'l*, pg. 1104

ALCHROME—NONE—Carpenter Technology Corporation; *U.S. Public*, pg. 307

ALCO—Automatic & Electric Flow Controls—Emerson Electric Co.; *U.S. Public*, pg. 572

ALCO—Internal Combustion Engines & Parts—General Electric Canada Inc.; *U.S. Public*, pg. 713

ALCO—Detergents—National Starch and Chemical Company; *Int'l*, pg. 1435

ALCOA—Aluminum Prods.—Aluminum Company of America; *U.S. Public*, pg. 60

ALCOASHIP—Steamship—Alcoa Steamship Co., Inc.; *U.S. Public*, pg. 61

ALCODRILL—Polymers & Microbiocides for the Oil Field, Water Treatment, Detergent, Ect—Alco Chemical; *Int'l*, pg. 1435

ALCOGUM—Latex Thickening Chemicals—Alco Chemical; *Int'l*, pg. 1435

ALCOGUM L-SERIES—Paint, Adhesive & Paper Coating Chemicals—Alco Chemical; *Int'l*, pg. 1435

ALCOHOL FREE FRESHERNER/TONER—Cosmetics—Irma Shorell, Inc.; *U.S. Private*, pg. 1101

ALCON—Cannulas & Systitomes—Alcon Laboratories, Inc.; *Int'l*, pg. 916

ALCON—Diagnostic & Ultrasound Acessories, Stands & Supplies—Alcon Laboratories, Inc.; *Int'l*, pg. 916

ALCON—Ophthalmic Operating Room Equipment & Microscopes—Alcon Laboratories, Inc.; *Int'l*, pg. 916

ALCON—Equipment Accessories & Paks—Alcon Laboratories, Inc.; *Int'l*, pg. 916

ALCON—Pharmaceutical Products—Nestle S.A.; *Int'l*, pg. 915

ALCON CLOSURE SYSTEM, ACS—NONE—Alcon Laboratories, Inc.; *Int'l*, pg. 916

ALCON ENZYMATIC—NONE—Alcon Laboratories, Inc.; *Int'l*, pg. 916

ALCON ENZYMATIC CLEANER FOR EXTENDED WEAR—Enzymatic Contact Lens Cleaner—Alcon Laboratories, Inc.; *Int'l*, pg. 916

ALCON INSTRUMENT DELIVERY SYSTEM—Medical Instruments—Alcon Laboratories, Inc.; *Int'l*, pg. 916

ALCON OPHTHALMIC KNIFE (A-OK)—NONE—Alcon Laboratories, Inc.; *Int'l*, pg. 916

ALCON SALINE ESPECIALLY FOR SENSITIVE EYES—Contact Lens Solution—Alcon Laboratories, Inc.; *Int'l*, pg. 916

ALCON SURGICAL BLADES (ASB)—Surgical Blades—Alcon Laboratories, Inc.; *Int'l*, pg. 916

ALCON SURGICAL HAND INSTRUMENTS (ASI)—Surgical Blades—Alcon Laboratories, Inc.; *Int'l*, pg. 916

ALCOR—Private Brand Paper—The Ailing & Cory Company; *U.S. Public*, pg. 1666

ALCORD—Shoe Dressings—Henkel Corporation; *Int'l*, pg. 610

ALCOSPERSE—Soap & Detergent Additives—Alco Chemical; *Int'l*, pg. 1435

ALCOSWITCH—Electronic Switches—Thomas & Betts Corporation; *U.S. Public*, pg. 1597

ALCOTREAT—Oil Field Chemicals—Alco Chemical; *Int'l*, pg. 1435

ALDACTAZIDE—Diuretic—Searle & Co.; *U.S. Public*, pg. 1125

ALDACTAZIDE—Anti-Hypertensive—Searle Laboratories; *U.S. Public*, pg. 1125

ALDACTIZIDE—Pharmaceuticals—Monsanto Company; *U.S. Public*, pg. 1124

ALDACTONE—Pharmaceuticals—Monsanto Company; *U.S. Public*, pg. 1124

ALDACTONE—Diuretic—Searle & Co.; *U.S. Public*, pg. 1125

ALDACTONE—Anti-Hypertensive/Diuretic—Searle Laboratories; *U.S. Public*, pg. 1125

ALDAN—Synthetic Rubber & Resin Coated Fabrics—Aldan Industries; *U.S. Private*, pg. 33

ALDEN—Mail Catalogs—World Color-Chicago Div.; *U.S. Public*, pg. 1778

ALDEN NEW ENGLAND—Shoes—Alden Shoe Co., Inc.; *U.S. Private*, pg. 33

ALDEN PEDIC—Shoes—Alden Shoe Co., Inc.; *U.S. Private*, pg. 33

ALDEN USA—Shoes—Alden Shoe Co., Inc.; *U.S. Private*, pg. 33

ALDENSART—Search & Rescue Transporter—Alden Electronics, Inc.; *U.S. Private*, pg. 872

ALDEX—Lint Free Wipes & Tissues—Aldine Technologies Industries Inc.; *U.S. Private*, pg. 33

ALDI—Grocery Stores—Aldi Food Inc.; *U.S. Private*, pg. 33

ALDO—Emulsifier—Lonza Inc.; *Int'l*, pg. 67

ALDOCLOR—Methyldopa-Chlorothiazide—Merck & Co., Inc.; *U.S. Public*, pg. 1090

ALDOM—Alloy Welded Dom Tubing—Copperweld Miami Division; *Int'l*, pg. 662

ALDOMET—Methyldopa—Merck & Co., Inc.; *U.S. Public*, pg. 1090

ALDONS—Frozen Dough & Refrigerated Bread Products—Chesebrough-Pond's; *Int'l*, pg. 1436

ALDORIL—Methyldopa-Chlorothiazide—Merck & Co., Inc.; *U.S. Public*, pg. 1090

ALDOSPERSE—Emulsifier—Lonza Inc.; *Int'l*, pg. 67

ALDOSTERONE—Diagnostic Products—Abbott Laboratories; *U.S. Public*, pg. 12

ALODUR—Aluminium Oxide—Treibacher Schleifmittel Corp.; *U.S. Private*, pg. 1099

ALDUS—Desktop Publishing Software—Adobe Systems Incorporated; *U.S. Public*, pg. 20

ALDUS DIGITAL DARKROOM—Software—Adobe Systems Incorporated; *U.S. Public*, pg. 20

ALDUS FREEHAND—Software—Adobe Systems Incorporated; *U.S. Public*, pg. 20

ALDUS PAGEMAKER—Software—Adobe Systems Incorporated; *U.S. Public*, pg. 20

ALDUS PERSONAL PRESS—Software—Adobe Systems Incorporated; *U.S. Public*, pg. 20

ALDUS PERSUASION—Software—Adobe Systems Incorporated; *U.S. Public*, pg. 20

ALDUS PREPRINT—Software—Adobe Systems Incorporated; *U.S. Public*, pg. 20

ALDUS SUPER3D—Software—Adobe Systems Incorporated; *U.S. Public*, pg. 20

ALDUS SUPERCARD—Software—Adobe Systems Incorporated; *U.S. Public*, pg. 20

ALDUS SUPERPAINT—Software—Adobe Systems Incorporated; *U.S. Public*, pg. 20

ALDUTI-RUPTER—Interrupter Switch—S & C Electric Company; *U.S. Private*, pg. 954

ALEMITE—Pumps—BTR plc; *Int'l*, pg. 124

ALENTHION—Plant Protectives—DSM Chemie Linz GmbH; *Int'l*, pg. 356

ALENTISAN—Plant Protectives—DSM Chemie Linz GmbH; *Int'l*, pg. 356

ALERT—Statistical Process Control Software Package—BetzDearborn Inc.; *U.S. Public*, pg. 226

ALERT O.A.D.—Sterilization Products—Propper Manufacturing Co., Inc.; *U.S. Private*, pg. 891

ALESION—Antihistaminic—Boehringer Ingelheim GmbH; *Int'l*, pg. 199

ALESSANDRO CESARI—Jewelry—Basel Trading Company Ltd.; *Int'l*, pg. 169

ALESSE—Oral Contraceptive—American Home Products Corporation; *U.S. Public*, pg. 79

ALETE—Infant Foods & Dietetic Products—Nestle S.A.; *Int'l*, pg. 915

ALEVE—Pain Relievers—The Procter & Gamble Company; *U.S. Public*, pg. 1330

ALEVE—Pain Reliever Caplets—Procter & Gamble Pharmaceuticals, Inc.; *U.S. Public*, pg. 1331

ALEX—Acrylic Latex Caulk—DAP Inc.; *Int'l*, pg. 1486

ALEX—Mexican Food Products—Don Miguel Mexican Foods, Inc.; *U.S. Private*, pg. 339

ALEX—Brazed Aluminum Heat Exchanger—Kobe Steel, Ltd.; *Int'l*, pg. 740

ALEX DECOY LAUNCHING SYSTEM—Computer Control for Shipboard-Launched CHAFF/IR Decoy Countermeasures—L3 Communications Hycor Div.; *U.S. Public*, pg. 638

ALEX KIDD IN MIRACLE WORLD—Videogame—Sega of America Inc.; *Int'l*, pg. 1218

ALEX PLUS—Acrylic Latex Caulk Plus Silicone—DAP Inc.; *Int'l*, pg. 1486

ALEXANDER & ALEXANDER—Insurance & Financial Services—Alexander & Alexander Services Inc.; *U.S. Public*, pg. 117

ALEXANDER KEITH'S—Beer—Labatt Brewing Company Limited; *Int'l*, pg. 679

ALEXANDER SMITH—Carpets & Rugs—Mohawk Industries, Inc.; *U.S. Public*, pg. 1121

ALEXANDER ST. COLLECTION TABLE—NONE—Vecta; *U.S. Private*, pg. 1038

ALEXANDER STREET COLLECTION—Lounge & Modular Seating, ai Collection & Table—Vecta; *U.S. Private*, pg. 1038

ALEXANDER'S—Dept. Stores—Alexander's, Inc.; *U.S. Public*, pg. 1725

ALEXANDRA—Fragrances & Cosmetics—Parlux, Ltd.; *U.S. Public*, pg. 1264

ALEXANDRA DE MARKOFF—Cosmetics & Skin Care—Parlux Fragrances Inc.; *U.S. Public*, pg. 1264

ALEXANDRA DE MARKOFF—Fragrances & Cosmetics—Parlux, Ltd.; *U.S. Public*, pg. 1264

ALEXI VODKA—NONE—Star Industries Inc.; *U.S. Private*, pg. 1034

ALEXIS LICHINE—Wine—Pacific Wine Co.; *U.S. Private*, pg. 843

ALFA—Software Programs—Barrister Information Systems Corporation; *U.S. Public*, pg. 192

ALFA LAVAL AGRI—Sanitizing Cleaners & Lubricants—Crouch Supply Company, Inc.; *U.S. Private*, pg. 291

ALFA ROMEO—Automobile Parts—Alfa Romeo Distributors of North America; *Int'l*, pg. 481

ALFA ROMEO—Automobile—Fiat Auto SpA; *Int'l*, pg. 480

ALFA ROMEO—Sports Car—Fiat Auto S.p.A.; *Int'l*, pg. 481

ALFA ROMEO 145—Car—Fiat Auto Ireland Ltd.; *Int'l*, pg. 481

ALFA ROMEO 144—Car—Fiat Auto Ireland Ltd.; *Int'l*, pg. 481

ALFA ROMEO 164—Car—Fiat Auto Ireland Ltd.; *Int'l*, pg. 481

ALFARE—Food Supplement—Nestle S.A.; *Int'l*, pg. 915

ALFAROL—Agent for Osteoporosis—Chugai Pharmaceutical Co., Ltd.; *Int'l*, pg. 290

ALFATEC—Commercial Cleaning Equipment—Electrolux, AB; *Int'l*, pg. 438

ALFAX—Recording Papers—Alden Electronics, Inc.; *U.S. Private*, pg. 872

ALFAZYME—Complex for Enhancing the Feeding Value of Legume Silage—Cultor Ltd.; *Int'l*, pg. 349

ALFECU—Aminocarboxylates & Gluconates—Akzo Nobel N.V.; *Int'l*, pg. 42

ALFENTA—Pharmaceutical—Janssen Pharmaceutica, Inc.; *U.S. Public*, pg. 928

ALFERON—Resistance Alloy—Driver-Harris Company; *U.S. Public*, pg. 530

ALFERON N INJECTION—Natural Alpha Interferon—Interferon Sciences, Inc.; *U.S. Public*, pg. 694

ALFOL—Synthetic Linear Primary Alchols—Condea Vista Company; *Int'l*, pg. 325

ALFONIC—Biodegradeable Nonionics—Condea Vista Company; *Int'l*, pg. 325

ALFRAX—Refractory—The Carborundum Corporation; *Int'l*, pg. 1173

ALFUSE—Heat Transfer Products—Modine Manufacturing Company; *U.S. Public*, pg. 1121

ALGA-GRO—Biological Supplies—Carolina Biological Supply Co.; *U.S. Public*, pg. 213

ALGAETROL 76—Algacide—Harcros Chemicals Inc.; *Int'l*, pg. 598

ALGESAL—Antirheumatics—Kali-Chemie Aktiengesellschaft; *Int'l*, pg. 1278

ALGICON—Consumer Antacid—Rhone-Poulenc Rorer - U.S.; *Int'l*, pg. 1110

ALGITEC—Gastrointestinal Drug—SmithKline Beecham plc; *Int'l*, pg. 1264

ALGOFLON—PTFE—Montedison S.p.A.; *Int'l*, pg. 324

ALGOLINE—Catheter—Medtronic, Inc.; *U.S. Public*, pg. 1082

ALGOOD—Peanut Butter, No Salt Peanut Butter & Peanut Oil—Algood Food Company; *U.S. Private*, pg. 34

ALGOOD—Jams, Jellies, Preserves & Salsa—Algood Food Company; *U.S. Private*, pg. 34

ALHAMBRA—Processed, Purified Bottled Water—McKesson Corporation; *U.S. Public*, pg. 1072

ALI MILES—Original Sportswear (Upper Moderate)—Jerell, Inc.; *U.S. Private*, pg. 586

ALIANT CELLULAR TELEPHONE COMPANY—Cellular Telecommunications Services—Aliant Communications Inc.; *U.S. Public*, pg. 40

ALIANT COMMUNICATIONS—Telecommunications Services—Aliant Communications Inc.; *U.S. Public*, pg. 40

ALIANT LONG DISTANCE—Telecommunications Services—Aliant Communications Inc.; *U.S. Public*, pg. 40

ALIANT SYSTEMS—Telecommunications Products—Aliant Communications Inc.; *U.S. Public*, pg. 40

ALIAS ANIMATOR—Animation Software—Alias Wavefront; *U.S. Public*, pg. 1474

ALIAS DESIGNER—Design Software—Alias Wavefront; *U.S. Public*, pg. 1474

ALIAS FULL COLOR—Print/Color Retouch/Packaging Design Software—Alias Wavefront; *U.S. Public*, pg. 1474

ALIAS POWER ANIMATOR—Animation Software—Alias Wavefront; *U.S. Public*, pg. 1474

ALIAS SKETCH—Conceptual drawing tool for PC—Alias Wavefront; *U.S. Public*, pg. 1474

ALIAS SONATA—Architectural Design Software—Alias Wavefront; *U.S. Public*, pg. 1474

ALIAS STUDIO—Design Software—Alias Wavefront; *U.S. Public*, pg. 1474

ALIAS UPFRONT—Conceptual Architectural Design Software for PC—Alias Wavefront; *U.S. Public*, pg. 1474

ALIEN TRILOGY—Interactive Entertainment Software—Acclaim Entertainment, Inc.; *U.S. Public*, pg. 15

ALIENS—Toys—Hasbro; *U.S. Public*, pg. 797

ALIESA—Designer Chair Line—Harter; *U.S. Private*, pg. 581

ALIGAL—Protective Atmospheric Gases for Packaged Foods, Draft Beer & Wine—Air Liquide America Corporation; *Int'l*, pg. 37

ALIMAK—Hoist—Alimak Elevator Company; *U.S. Private*, pg. 34

ALIMENTOS PROCESADOS—NONE—Reed Elsevier Business Information; *Int'l*, pg. 1095

ALIMET—Methionine Hydroxy Analog/Feed Supplement—The Agricultural Group, Monsanto Company; *U.S. Public*, pg. 1125

ALIMET—Methionine Hydroxy Analog/Feed Supplement—Monsanto Company; *U.S. Public*, pg. 1124

ALIPH—Shoes, Boots, Slippers, Sandles, Socks & Sportswear—Sime Darby Berhad; *Int'l*, pg. 1249

ALIPLAST—Rehabilitation Product—Alimed, Inc.; *U.S. Private*, pg. 34

ALIPRIX—Stores—Socanav Inc.; *Int'l*, pg. 1272

ALIQUAT—Ammonium Chlorides—Henkel Corporation; *Int'l*, pg. 610

ALITALIA—Airline—Alitalia Linee Aeree Italiane S.P.A.; *Int'l*, pg. 652

ALIVE—Hosiery—Hanes Hosiery, Inc.; *U.S. Public*, pg. 1434

ALIVE NOW—Small Group Study—The Upper Room; *U.S. Public*, pg. 1129

ALKA-MINTS—Chewable Antacid Tablets—Bayer Corporation/Consumer Care Division; *Int'l*, pg. 173

ALKA-PRO—Provides Air to Treat Sewage—U.S. Filter/Davis Water & Waste Industries, Inc.; *U.S. Public*, pg. 1682

ALKA-SELTZER—Antacid—Bayer AG; *Int'l*, pg. 171

ALKA-SELTZER—NONE—Bayer Corporation; *Int'l*, pg. 172

ALKA-SELTZER—Effervescent Pain Reliever & Antacid—Bayer Corporation/Consumer Care Division; *Int'l*, pg. 173

ALKA-SELTZER ADVANCED FORMULA—Effervescent Pain Reliever & Antacid—Bayer Corporation/Consumer Care Division; *Int'l*, pg. 173

ALKA-SELTZER PLUS—NONE—Bayer Corporation; *Int'l*, pg. 172

ALKA-SELTZER PLUS—Cold Medicine—Bayer Corporation/Consumer Care Division; *Int'l*, pg. 173

ALKA-SELTZER PLUS COLD & COUGH—Cold and Cough Medicine—Bayer Corporation/Consumer Care Division; *Int'l*, pg. 173

ALKA-SELTZER PLUS NIGHT-TIME—Cold Medicine—Bayer Corporation/Consumer Care Division; *Int'l*, pg. 173

ALKA/SORB PROCESS—Dry/Wet Emission Control System For Waste Incinerators—Beco Engineering Company; *U.S. Private*, pg. 129

ALKACID—Papers—Fisher Scientific Company; *U.S. Private*, pg. 658

ALKALINE/HEAVY DUTY—NONE—RAYOVAC Corporation; *U.S. Private*, pg. 912

ALKANOL—Surfactants—Du Pont (E.I. Du Pont De Nemours & Co.); *U.S. Public*, pg. 530

ALKAT-XL—Aklylation Catalyst—BetzDearborn Inc.; *U.S. Public*, pg. 226

ALKAWET—Surfactant for Household & Industrial Products—Lonza Inc.; *Int'l*, pg. 67

ALKCO—Lighting—JJI Lighting Group Inc.; *Int'l*, pg. 821

ALKERAN—Prescription Cancer Treatment—Glaxo Wellcome PLC; *Int'l*, pg. 553

ALKETS—NONE—Lee Pharmaceuticals; *U.S. Public*, pg. 984

ALKORCELL—Sheets & Sheeting—Solvay S.A.; *Int'l*, pg. 1277

ALKYLPHENOLS—Insulating Varnishes—Schenectady International, Inc.; *U.S. Private*, pg. 969

ALL—Detergent—Lever Brothers Co.; *Int'l*, pg. 1435

ALL—Detergent—Unilever Plc; *Int'l*, pg. 1433

ALL-AMERICAN—Bottling—All American Bottling Corp.; *U.S. Private*, pg. 34

ALL-AMERICAN—Tool Storage Products—Fortune Brands, Inc.; *U.S. Public*, pg. 674

ALL-AMERICAN—Tires—The Goodyear Tire & Rubber Company; *U.S. Public*, pg. 752

ALL AMERICAN—NONE—MasterBrand Industries, Inc.; *U.S. Public*, pg. 675

ALL-AMERICAN—Sound Systems—Rauland-Borg Corporation; *U.S. Private*, pg. 911

ALL AMERICAN—Lawn Products—The Vigoro Corporation; *U.S. Public*, pg. 856

ALL AMERICAN—Tool Storage Products—Waterloo Industries, Inc.; *U.S. Public*, pg. 675

ALL AMERICAN HOMES—Manufactured Housing—Coachmen Industries, Inc.; *U.S. Public*, pg. 387

ALL AMERICAN SHOPPER—Plastic Product—Uniflex; *U.S. Public*, pg. 1665

ALL AMERICAN SYSTEMS—Metal Buildings—NCI Building Systems, Inc.; *U.S. Public*, pg. 1145

ALL-AMERICAN TEDDY BEAR—NONE—The Vermont Teddy Bear Company, Inc.; *U.S. Public*, pg. 1716

ALL AMERICAN TELEVISION—Television Production & Distribution—All American Communications, Inc.; *U.S. Public*, pg. 41

ALL AMERICANS—Cutlery—Imperial Schrade Corp.; *U.S. Private*, pg. 559

ALL-BRAN—Natural High-Fiber Cereal—Kellogg Company; *U.S. Public*, pg. 947

ALL-DAY—Colorless Finishing Powder Soft Radiants Blush—Cover Girl Cosmetics; *U.S. Public*, pg. 1330

ALL DAY LONG—Ladies Panties & Stretch Bras—Alba-Waldensian, Inc.; *U.S. Public*, pg. 35

ALL FRESH—Moist Tissues—SmithKline Beecham plc; *Int'l*, pg. 1264

ALL IN A DAY—Greeting Cards—American Greetings Corporation; *U.S. Public*, pg. 77

ALL IN ONE—Package of Wrapping Paper, Ribbon, Seals & Gift Cards—American Greetings Corporation; *U.S. Public*, pg. 77

ALL-IN-ONE—Household Products—The Black & Decker Corporation; *U.S. Public*, pg. 233

ALL-IN-ONE GREENHOUSE—Garden Products—Jiffy Products of America, Inc.; *Int'l*, pg. 706

ALL IT LEAVES IS CLEAN—Paper Towels—Georgia-Pacific Corporation; *U.S. Public*, pg. 735

ALL JUICE—100% Fruit Juice—Green Spot Packaging Inc.; *U.S. Private*, pg. 477

ALL-LAN—Electronic Interconnection System—Thomas & Betts Corporation; *U.S. Public*, pg. 1597

ALL-MARK—Marking Ink—Weber Marking Systems, Inc.; *U.S. Private*, pg. 1157

ALL NON-SKID FARM—Tires—Bridgestone/Firestone, Inc.; *Int'l*, pg. 213

ALL NON-SKID TRACTOR—Tires—Bridgestone/Firestone, Inc.; *Int'l*, pg. 213

ALL ORGANIC—Patented, Environmentally Acceptable Cooling Water Corrosion Inhibitor—Diversey Water Technologies, Inc.; *U.S. Public*, pg. 1150

ALL PARTS—Car Rental—W.W. Wallwork, Inc.; *U.S. Private*, pg. 1148

ALL PRO—Racquetball Glove—Ektelon; *U.S. Private*, pg. 884

ALL-PURPOSE MATADOR—Small Vacuum—Advance Machine Company; *Int'l*, pg. 932

ALL SEASONS—Institutional Food Service—All Seasons Services, Inc.; *U.S. Private*, pg. 35

ALL SET—Hair Care Products—DeMert & Dougherty, Inc.; *U.S. Private*, pg. 323

ALL SPORT—Scoreboard Control Consoles—Daktronics, Inc.; *U.S. Public*, pg. 478

ALL SPORT—Post-Sport Drink—PepsiCo, Inc.; *U.S. Public*, pg. 1276

ALL STAR—Sporting Goods—Brunswick Bowling & Billiards Corp.; *U.S. Public*, pg. 265

ALL STAR—Pickup Truck Bedliners—Durakon Industries, Inc.; *U.S. Public*, pg. 537

ALL STAR—Athletic Footwear—Sao Paulo Alpargatas S.A.; *Int'l*, pg. 1193

ALL STAR COLLECTION—Foot Apparel—Converse Inc.; *U.S. Public*, pg. 441

ALL STAR GAS—NONE—All Star Gas Corporation; *U.S. Private*, pg. 35

ALL STAR GOLD—Baseball Card Pages—JM Company; *U.S. Private*, pg. 577

ALL STAR 2000—Foot Apparel—Converse Inc.; *U.S. Public*, pg. 441

ALL STEER—NONE—Oshkosh Truck Corporation; *U.S. Public*, pg. 1233

ALL TERRAIN—Tires—Bridgestone/Firestone, Inc.; *Int'l*, pg. 213

ALL TERRAIN T/C—Tires—Bridgestone/Firestone, Inc.; *Int'l*, pg. 213

ALL TERRAIN T/X—Tires—Bridgestone/Firestone, Inc.; *Int'l*, pg. 213

ALL THAT JAZZ—Junior Dresses—Chorus Line Corporation; *U.S. Private*, pg. 238

ALL-TITE—Flush Fatigue Enhancing Solid Rivet—Allfast Fastening Systems, Inc.; *U.S. Private*, pg. 37

ALL TRACTION—Tires—Bridgestone/Firestone, Inc.; *Int'l*, pg. 213

ALL TRACTION CHAMPION—Tires—Bridgestone/Firestone, Inc.; *Int'l*, pg. 213

ALL TRACTION FIELD & ROAD—Tires—Bridgestone/Firestone, Inc.; *Int'l*, pg. 213

ALL TRACTION FIELD & ROAD PULLER—Tires—Bridgestone/Firestone, Inc.; *Int'l*, pg. 213

ALL TRACTION 23 DEGREES—Tires—Bridgestone/Firestone, Inc.; *Int'l*, pg. 213

ALL TRACTION UTILITY—Tires—Bridgestone/Firestone, Inc.; *Int'l*, pg. 213

ALL WAYS SOFT—Fabric Softener—The Dow Chemical Company; *U.S. Public*, pg. 522

ALL-WEATHER—Alkyd House Paints & Primer—Devoe Paint; *Int'l*, pg. 663

ALL-WEATHER—Wood Stains & Natural Wood Finish—Devoe Paint; *Int'l*, pg. 663

ALL-WEATHER—Alkyd House Paints & Primer; Wood Stains—ICI Paints; *Int'l*, pg. 664

ALLAN—Sugar Confectionery—Cadbury Schweppes p.l.c.; *Int'l*, pg. 247

ALLANTE—Ultra Luxury Car—General Motors Corporation; *U.S. Public*, pg. 718

ALLBRIGHT—Bitter/Ale—Bass PLC; *Int'l*, pg. 169

ALLBRITE—All-Purpose Degreaser/Stain Remover—Turtle Wax, Inc.; *U.S. Private*, pg. 1110

ALLCLEAR—Flowcharting Software—SPSS Inc.; *U.S. Public*, pg. 1420

ALLDATA—NONE—AutoZone, Inc.; *U.S. Public*, pg. 150

ALLEGHENY—Children's Clothing—S. Schwab Company; *U.S. Private*, pg. 974

ALLEGHENY—Printing Papers—Westvaco Corporation; *U.S. Public*, pg. 1762

ALLEGRA—Magazine—Axel Springer Verlag AG; *Int'l*, pg. 102

ALLEGRA—Antihistamine—Hoechst Marion Roussel North America; *Int'l*, pg. 625

ALLEGRA—Digital-Based Turnkey Healthcare Information System—Shared Medical Systems Corporation; *U.S. Public*, pg. 1463

ALLEGRINI—Wine—Pacific Wine Co.; *U.S. Private*, pg. 843

ALLEGRINI—Wine—Paterno Imports Limited; *U.S. Private*, pg. 843

ALLEGRO—Layout of Standard PCB, Hybrid, MCM & Advanced Components—Cadence Design Systems, Inc.; *U.S. Public*, pg. 290

ALLEGRO—Writing Paper—The Mead Corporation; *U.S. Public*, pg. 1074

ALLEGRO—Audio Speakers, Accessories—Zenith Electronics Corp.; *U.S. Public*, pg. 1790

ALLEGRO VELLUM—Writing Paper—The Mead Corporation; *U.S. Public*, pg. 1074

ALLELUIA! MUSIC—NONE—Integrity Incorporated; *U.S. Public*, pg. 886

ALLEN—Food Products—Allen Canning Company; *U.S. Private*, pg. 36

ALLEN—Organs—Allen Organ Company; *U.S. Public*, pg. 45

ALLEN—Hand Tools—Danaher Tool Group; *U.S. Public*, pg. 480

ALLEN—Chip Dips, Dairy Snacks & Desserts—Lancaster Colony Corporation; *U.S. Public*, pg. 976

ALLEN—Refrigerated Deli Products—T. Marzetti Company; *U.S. Public*, pg. 977

ALLEN & HEATH—Mixing Consoles—Harman International Industries, Inc.; *U.S. Public*, pg. 787

ALLEN-BRADLEY—Industrial Control, Communications & Computer Equipment—Rockwell Automation; *U.S. Public*, pg. 1397

ALLEN-BRADLEY—Industrial Automation Products—Rockwell International Corporation; *U.S. Public*, pg. 1397

ALLEN-EDMONDS—Men's Shoes—Allen-Edmonds Shoe Corp.; *U.S. Private*, pg. 36

ALLEN-SHERMAN-HOFF—Matl. Handling Systems—Joy Mining Machinery; *U.S. Public*, pg. 789

ALLEN TESTPRODUCTS—Diagnostic Equipment—SPX Corporation; *U.S. Public*, pg. 1420

ALLEN'S—Flavored Brandies—M.S. Walker, Inc.; *U.S. Private*, pg. 1147

ALLERCREME—Skin Care/Toiletries—Carme' Cosmeceutical Sciences, Inc.; *U.S. Private*, pg. 213

ALLERGEN INSPECTION SYSTEM—Fully Automatic—Otsuka Pharmaceutical Co., Ltd.; *Int'l*, pg. 1013

ALLERGYN—Allergy Relief Tablets—Alva/Amco Pharmacal Companies, Inc.; *U.S. Private*, pg. 47

ALLERGYSMART—Air Cleaners—Sunbeam Corporation; *U.S. Public*, pg. 1533

ALLERSHIELD—Allergy Pharmaceutical—Glaxo Wellcome PLC; *Int'l*, pg. 553

ALLERSHIELD D—Allergy Pharmaceutical—Glaxo Wellcome PLC; *Int'l*, pg. 553

ALLERTECH—NONE—BioChem Pharma Inc.; *Int'l*, pg. 196

ALLESVERLOREN ESTATE—Wine—Distillers Corporation S.A.; *Int'l*, pg. 1129

ALLEXITE—Microwave Components—Litton Industries, Inc.; *U.S. Public*, pg. 1002

ALLEY CAT—Cat Food—Ralston Purina Company; *U.S. Public*, pg. 1359

ALLFAST—Hardware—Allfast Fastening Systems, Inc.; *U.S. Private*, pg. 37

ALLIA—Sanitary Poreclain—Metra Corporation; *Int'l*, pg. 862

ALLIA—Bathroom Ceramics—Sanitec Ltd. Oy; *Int'l*, pg. 863

ALLIANCE—Table System—Howe Furniture Corporation; *U.S. Private*, pg. 543

ALLIANCE—NONE—Lam Research Corporation; *U.S. Public*, pg. 975

ALLIANCE CONSTRUCTION SOLUTIONS, INC.—Your Partner in Construction Services—Alliance Construction Solutions, Inc.; *U.S. Private*, pg. 38

ALLIANCE SEMICONDUCTOR—NONE—Interface Electronics Corporation; *U.S. Private*, pg. 567

ALLIANCEWALL—Architectural Panels—Alliance America; *U.S. Private*, pg. 37

ALLIANT—Ambulatory Care Management Software—US SerVis; *U.S. Public*, pg. 1687

ALLIED—Construction Machinery—Pubco Corporation; *U.S. Public*, pg. 1339

ALLIED CARBI-TECH—Carbide Blanks & Cutting Tools—Allied Carbi-Tech, Inc.; *U.S. Private*, pg. 38

ALLIED DUNBAR—Insurance Services & Products—B.A.T Industries P.L.C.; *Int'l*, pg. 110

ALLIED GROUP—Insurance & Related Services—Allied Mutual Insurance Company; *U.S. Private*, pg. 39

ALLIED INTERNATIONAL—NONE—NFC plc; *Int'l*, pg. 901

ALLIED VAN LINES—NONE—NFC plc; *Int'l*, pg. 901

ALLIEDSIGNAL SAFETY RESTRAINTS—Manufacturer of Seat Belts & Automotive Air Bags—Breed Technologies; *U.S. Public*, pg. 251

ALLIES—Restaurants—Marriott International, Inc.; *U.S. Public*, pg. 1047

ALLIES—Integrated Environmental Services—Philip Industrial Services Group; *Int'l*, pg. 1050

ALLIGATOR—Power Saw—The Black & Decker Corporation; *U.S. Public*, pg. 233

ALLIGATOR—Lacing & Fasteners for Conveyors, Transmission & V Belts—Flexible Steel Lacing Company; *U.S. Private*, pg. 413

ALLISION TRANSMISSION—Truck, Bus & Military Transmissions—General Motors Corporation; *U.S. Public*, pg. 718

ALLISON—Commercial & Military Engines & Industrial Product Line—Allison Engine Company Inc.; *Int'l*, pg. 1127

ALLISON—Cabinet Hardware—Amerock Corporation; *U.S. Public*, pg. 1177

ALLISON—Window Hardware & Cabinet Hardware—Newell Co.; *U.S. Public*, pg. 1176

ALLISON TRANSMISSION—Automatic Transmissions—Valley Detroit Diesel Allison; *U.S. Private*, pg. 1132

ALLMAX—Structural Blind Rivets—Allfast Fastening Systems, Inc.; *U.S. Private*, pg. 37

ALLMETAL—Stainless Steel Fasteners, Screw Machine Parts & Electronic Hardware—Allmetal Screw Products Corp.; *U.S. Private*, pg. 41

ALLNET ACCESS (R)—Gateway Calling Card Services—Frontier Communications Services; *U.S. Public*, pg. 684

ALLNET CALL DELIVERY (SM)—Specific Time-Delayed Message Delivery—Frontier Communications Services; *U.S. Public*, pg. 684

ALLNET EDGE—Commercial Services—Frontier Communications Services; *U.S. Public*, pg. 684

ALLNET 800 SERVICES—Nationwide 800 Services—Frontier Communications Services; *U.S. Public*, pg. 684

ALLNET ESP (R)—Customer-Customized Billing Management Reports—Frontier Communications Services; *U.S. Public*, pg. 684

ALLNET MOBILELINE—Cellular Service—Frontier Communications Services; *U.S. Public*, pg. 684

ALLNET PACESETTER (R)—Competitive, Flat Rate Commercial Long Distance Service—Frontier Communications Services; *U.S. Public*, pg. 684

ALLNET PREMIER ELITE (R)—Long Distance Service for Regional or City Specific Calling Patterns—Frontier Communications Services; *U.S. Public*, pg. 684

ALLNET PREMIER (R)—Long Distance Service for Regional or City Specific Calling—Frontier Communications Services; *U.S. Public*, pg. 684

ALLNET SPEEDLINK (SM)—Direct-Connect Airline, Hotel & Car Rental Thru Allnet Access (SM)—Frontier Communications Services; *U.S. Public*, pg. 684

ALLNET TELADVANCE CARD—Calling Card—Frontier Communications Services; *U.S. Public*, pg. 684

ALLNET VANTAGE (R)—WATS-Type Services for Larger Users—Frontier Communications Services; *U.S. Public*, pg. 684

ALLOMATIC—Motor Vehicle Parts & Accessories—Allomatic Products Company; *U.S. Public*, pg. 1363

ALLOY 86—Patented Duplex Stainless Steel; Highly Corrosion Resistant—Sandusky International Inc.; *U.S. Private*, pg. 964

ALLOY RODS—Welding Consumables—Esab AB; *Int'l*, pg. 281

ALLOY 75—Low Residual Stress Corrosion Resistant Duplex Stainless Steel—Sandusky International Inc.; *U.S. Private*, pg. 964

ALLOY3000—Coated Polymer Film—Tekra Corporation; *U.S. Private*, pg. 1073

ALLQUEST—AllQuest Enterprises—Philip Industrial Services Group; *Int'l*, pg. 1050

ALLRIGHT PARKING—NONE—Allright Corporation; *U.S. Private*, pg. 42

ALLROAD—Tires, Tubes—Bridgestone/Firestone, Inc.; *Int'l*, pg. 213

ALLSET—Business Forms—Crabar Business Systems; *U.S. Private*, pg. 283

ALLSORTS—Candy—Hershey Foods Corporation; *U.S. Public*, pg. 811

ALLSTATE INDEMNITY & CASUALTY INSURANCE COMPANY—Property-Liability Insurance—The Allstate Corporation; *U.S. Public*, pg. 55

ALLSTATE INSURANCE COMPANY—Multi-Line Property-Liability Insurance Company—The Allstate Corporation; *U.S. Public*, pg. 55

ALLSTATE LIFE INSURANCE CO.—Individual Life Insurance & Annuity Products—The Allstate Corporation; *U.S. Public*, pg. 55

ALLSTATE MOTOR CLUB—Emergency Road Service—The Allstate Corporation; *U.S. Public*, pg. 55

ALLSTATE REINSURANCE—Reinsurance—The Allstate Corporation; *U.S. Public*, pg. 55

ALLSTEEL—Steel Office Furniture—Allsteel, Inc.; *U.S. Public*, pg. 772

ALLT OM FESTER—Consumer Magazine—ICA Forlaget AB; *Int'l*, pg. 643

ALLT OM SOMMAREN—Consumer Magazine—ICA Forlaget AB; *Int'l*, pg. 643

ALLTEG—Chemical Cleaning—Philip Industrial Services Group; *Int'l*, pg. 1050

ALLURA—Bathtub Wall Kit—Plaskolite Inc.; *U.S. Private*, pg. 870

ALLURE—Beauty Magazine—The Conde Nast Publications Inc.; *U.S. Private*, pg. 868

ALLUVER—Chemical Reagant—Hach Company; *U.S. Public*, pg. 773

ALLVAC—NONE—Allvac; *U.S. Public*, pg. 43

ALLWEATHER ROOF & FLASHING SEALANT—Industrial Chemical—Hercules Chemical Co., Inc.; *U.S. Private*, pg. 523

ALLY—Herbicide—Du Pont (E.I. Du Pont De Nemours & Co.); *U.S. Public*, pg. 530

ALLY—Computer Software System—Unisys Corporation; *U.S. Public*, pg. 1671

ALLYMER—Polymerizable Synthetic Resin—PPG Industries, Inc.; *U.S. Public*, pg. 1245

ALLYN & BACON—Textbooks—Simon & Schuster; *U.S. Private*, pg. 777

ALLYN ST. GEORGE—Apparel—Intercontinental Branded Apparel; *U.S. Public*, pg. 796

ALLYN ST. GEORGE—Men's Apparel—Hartmarx Corporation; *U.S. Public*, pg. 795

ALMA DESK—NONE—Domore Corporation; *U.S. Private,* pg. 339

ALMADEN—Wine—Canandaigua Wine Company Div.; *U.S. Public,* pg. 300

ALMADEN—Wine—Canandaigua Wine Company, Inc.; *U.S. Public,* pg. 300

ALMANACK—Plywood, Wood, & Wood Fiber Products—Georgia-Pacific Corporation; *U.S. Public,* pg. 735

ALMAY—Cosmetics—Almay, Inc.; *U.S. Private,* pg. 689

ALMAY—Cosmetics—Revlon, Inc.; *U.S. Private,* pg. 689

ALMOND ACCENTS—Almonds—Blue Diamond Growers; *U.S. Private,* pg. 152

ALMOND/BONE PLUMBERS CAULK—Plumbing Chemical—Hercules Chemical Co., Inc.; *U.S. Private,* pg. 523

ALMOND CHOCOLATE—Chocolate Products—Meiji Seika Kaisha, Ltd.; *Int'l,* pg. 855

ALMOND COCONUT DELIGHT—Candy Bars—Tom's Foods, Inc.; *U.S. Private,* pg. 1090

ALMOND FACTS—Almonds—Blue Diamond Growers; *U.S. Private,* pg. 152

ALMOND JOY—Candy Bar—Hershey Foods Corporation; *U.S. Public,* pg. 811

THE ALMOND PEOPLE—Almonds—Blue Diamond Growers; *U.S. Private,* pg. 152

ALMOND PLEASURE—Herbal Tea Bags—Thomas J. Lipton Company; *Int'l,* pg. 1435

ALMOND ROCA—Buttercrunch—Brown & Haley; *U.S. Private,* pg. 173

ALMOND SUNSET—Herb Tea—Celestial Seasonings; *U.S. Public,* pg. 319

ALMOST FOREVER ENVELOPE—Plastic Mailers—Poly Pak America, Inc.; *U.S. Private,* pg. 875

ALNIDE—Ceramics—The Dow Chemical Company; *U.S. Public,* pg. 522

ALNO—NONE—Alno AG; *Int'l,* pg. 65

ALODINE—Metalworking Chemical—Henkel Surface Technologies; *Int'l,* pg. 610

ALOE & LANOLIN—Lotion/Soap—The Andrew Jergens Company; *Int'l,* pg. 717

ALOE E—NONE—Lee Pharmaceuticals; *U.S. Public,* pg. 984

ALOE FORMULA—Cosmetics—Tanning Research Labs., Inc.; *U.S. Private,* pg. 1068

ALOE 30-50-70—Skin Care—Yardley of London, Inc.; *Int'l,* pg. 819

THE ALOE VERA SOAP—Soap & Liquid Soap—Yardley of London, Inc.; *Int'l,* pg. 819

ALOE VESTA—Body Wash—Calgon Vestal Laboratories; *U.S. Public,* pg. 1515

ALOE 99—NONE—Lee Pharmaceuticals; *U.S. Public,* pg. 984

ALOEGEN—Skin & Hair Care Products—Levlad, Inc.; *U.S. Private,* pg. 663

ALOETTE—Aloe Based Skin Care Products—Aloette Cosmetics, Inc.; *U.S. Public,* pg. 57

ALOEWYN—Moisturizing Lotion—Stanhome Inc.; *U.S. Public,* pg. 1508

ALOMIDE .1 %—Lodoxamide Tromethamine Ophthalmic Solution—Alcon Laboratories, Inc.; *Int'l,* pg. 916

ALOND—Zopolrestat—Pfizer Inc.; *U.S. Public,* pg. 1281

ALOUETTE—Whipped Cream Cheese Based Products—BC-USA; *Int'l,* pg. 201

ALOUETTE—Whipped Cream Cheese Based Products—Bongrain Cheese USA; *Int'l,* pg. 201

ALOX—Polishing Agent for Hard & Soft Contact Lenses—Ferro Corporation; *U.S. Public,* pg. 618

ALOX—Corrosion Control Additive—RPM, Inc.; *U.S. Public,* pg. 1356

ALOXGLASS—Solid Glass Bead for Impact Blasting—Potters Industries, Inc.; *U.S. Private,* pg. 827

ALPAC—Semi-Conductor Devices—Semtech Corporation; *U.S. Public,* pg. 1456

ALPAN—Alumium Plate—Alusuisse-Lonza Holding Ltd.; *Int'l,* pg. 66

ALPEN—Hiking Shoe—K-Swiss Inc.; *U.S. Public,* pg. 937

ALPEN—Natural Cereal with Raisins & Nuts—The Weetabix Company, Inc.; *Int'l,* pg. 1488

ALPEN—Natural Cereal with Raisins & Nuts—Weetabix Limited; *Int'l,* pg. 1488

ALPHA—Men's & Boy's Shirts—Alpha Shirt Co., Inc.; *U.S. Private,* pg. 45

ALPHA—Shampoo Bowl—Belvedere Company; *U.S. Private,* pg. 1008

ALPHA—Stainless Steel Flatware—Dansk International Designs Ltd.; *U.S. Public,* pg. 261

ALPHA—Sailboat & Waveskis—Hobie Cat Company; *U.S. Private,* pg. 531

ALPHA—Hair Conditioner & Shampoo—Revlon-Realistic Professional Products, Inc.; *U.S. Private,* pg. 689

ALPHA—Alternator Regulator—Valley Forge Corporation; *U.S. Public,* pg. 1705

ALPHA ALAFLEX—Coated & Laminated Prods.—Alpha Associates, Inc.; *U.S. Private,* pg. 44

ALPHA BEDS—Electrically Operated Beds—Invacare Health Care Furnishings; *U.S. Public,* pg. 911

ALPHA-BITS—Cereal—Kraft Foods, Inc.; *U.S. Public,* pg. 1287

ALPHA-C—Seals—EG & G, Inc.; *U.S. Public,* pg. 542

ALPHA CALF FRACTION—A Culture Media Supplement for Hybridomas—HyClone Laboratories; *Int'l,* pg. 1037

ALPHA CODE—Color & Alpha Coded File Folders & Labels—Tab Products Co.; *U.S. Public,* pg. 1559

ALPHA COPY—Copy Control Terminal—Equitrac Corporation; *U.S. Public,* pg. 590

ALPHA FACTOR—Gymnastic Apparel—Tighe Industries, Inc.; *U.S. Private,* pg. 1086

ALPHA FAX—Fax Control Terminal—Equitrac Corporation; *U.S. Public,* pg. 590

ALPHA FOAMER—Surfactant—Stepan Company; *U.S. Public,* pg. 1514

ALPHA HU-AL—Indoor-Outdoor Jacketing—Alpha Associates, Inc.; *U.S. Private,* pg. 44

ALPHA HYDROX—NONE—Scott's Liquid Gold-Inc.; *U.S. Public,* pg. 1447

ALPHA IQ—Diagnostic Mammography System—Instrumentarium Imaging, Inc.; *U.S. Private,* pg. 565

ALPHA JET—Training Ground Attack Aircraft—Dassault Aviation Group; *Int'l,* pg. 383

ALPHA JET—NONE—Western Atlas Logging Services; *U.S. Public,* pg. 1757

ALPHA KERI—Shower & Bath Oil—Bristol-Myers Squibb Company; *U.S. Public,* pg. 253

ALPHA MAIL—Paging System Terminals; Voice Messaging Systems—Glenayre Technologies, Inc.; *U.S. Public,* pg. 746

ALPHA MARITEX—Marine & Power Plant Insulation Fabrics—Alpha Associates, Inc.; *U.S. Private,* pg. 44

ALPHA MICRO—Brand Name—Alpha Microsystems; *U.S. Public,* pg. 57

ALPHA PAK—Reverse Phase Columns—Millipore Corporation; *U.S. Public,* pg. 1112

ALPHA QUARTZ—High Temperature High Purity Fiber—Alpha Associates, Inc.; *U.S. Private,* pg. 44

ALPHA-REZ—NONE—Lawter International, Inc.; *U.S. Public,* pg. 980

ALPHA SERIES—Furniture—Myrtle/Mueller, A Haworth Co.; *U.S. Private,* pg. 512

ALPHA SERIES VALVE-IN-HEAD—NONE—Weather Tec Corporation; *U.S. Private,* pg. 1155

ALPHA SHIELD—Reflective Materials—Alpha Associates, Inc.; *U.S. Private,* pg. 44

ALPHA SIL—High Temperature Silica Fabric—Alpha Associates, Inc.; *U.S. Private,* pg. 44

ALPHA 16—NONE—James Hardie Industries Ltd.; *Int'l,* pg. 596

ALPHA SONIC—Lead Free Acoustical Prods.—Alpha Associates, Inc.; *U.S. Private,* pg. 44

ALPHA-STEP—Surfactant—Stepan Company; *U.S. Public,* pg. 1514

ALPHA 10—Thermally Sealed-Edge Border Wiping Cloth—The Texwipe Co., Inc.; *U.S. Private,* pg. 1079

ALPHA TRACK—Radon Detectors—Landauer, Inc.; *U.S. Public,* pg. 977

ALPHA 2 BIACTIF—Bakery Ingredients—Royal Gist-Brocades N.V.; *Int'l,* pg. 1142

ALPHA 200—Applicator, Adhesive—3M; *U.S. Public,* pg. 1604

ALPHA WELD—High Temperature Welding Fabrics—Alpha Associates, Inc.; *U.S. Private,* pg. 44

ALPHA-Z—Color Code Labels—Smead Manufacturing Company; *U.S. Private,* pg. 1006

ALPHAACCOUNTING—Software—Alpha Microsystems; *U.S. Public,* pg. 57

ALPHAACCOUNTING IN DESIGN—Software—Alpha Microsystems; *U.S. Public,* pg. 57

ALPHABASIC—Software—Alpha Microsystems; *U.S. Public,* pg. 57

ALPHA-BITS—Cereal—Philip Morris Companies Inc.; *U.S. Public,* pg. 1287

ALPHACALC—Software—Alpha Microsystems; *U.S. Public,* pg. 57

ALPHACONNECT—Software—Alpha Microsystems; *U.S. Public,* pg. 57

ALPHAFORTRAN 77—Software—Alpha Microsystems; *U.S. Public,* pg. 57

ALPHAGARD—Flat-Roof Waterproofing Prod.—The Braas Group; *Int'l,* pg. 1091

ALPHALAIN—Chinaware Body—The Homer Laughlin China Company; *U.S. Private,* pg. 653

ALPHALAN—Software—Alpha Microsystems; *U.S. Public,* pg. 57

ALPHAMAT—Needled Fiberglass Insulation Mat—Alpha Associates, Inc.; *U.S. Private,* pg. 44

ALPHAMAT—Total Conservation Mat Board—Letraset Nielsen & Bainbridge; *Int'l,* pg. 460

ALPHAMAT ARCARE—Total Cons. Matboard—Letraset Nielsen & Bainbridge; *Int'l,* pg. 460

ALPHAMOUNT—Total Conservation Mat Board—Letraset Nielsen & Bainbridge; *Int'l,* pg. 460

ALPHANATE—Solvent Detergent—Alpha Therapeutic Corp.; *Int'l,* pg. 558

ALPHANINESD—NONE—Alpha Therapeutic Corp.; *Int'l,* pg. 558

ALPHAPASCAL—Software—Alpha Microsystems; *U.S. Public,* pg. 57

ALPHAPASCAL PROGRAMMING SYSTEM—Software—Alpha Microsystems; *U.S. Public,* pg. 57

ALPHARAG—Total Conservation Mat Board—Letraset Nielsen & Bainbridge; *Int'l,* pg. 460

ALPHARJE—Software—Alpha Microsystems; *U.S. Public,* pg. 57

ALPHASERV—Software—Alpha Microsystems; *U.S. Public,* pg. 57

ALPHASET—Phenolic Foundry Resins—Borden, Inc.; *U.S. Private,* pg. 157

ALPHASORB 10—Two Ply Thermally Sealed-Edge Border Wipes—The Texwipe Co., Inc.; *U.S. Private,* pg. 1079

ALPHAWRITE—Software—Alpha Microsystems; *U.S. Public,* pg. 57

ALPHAWRITE IN DESIGN—Software—Alpha Microsystems; *U.S. Public,* pg. 57

ALPHOSYL—Pharmaceutical—Stafford-Miller Limited; *U.S. Public,* pg. 237

ALPINE—Mobile Audio Systems—Alpine Electronics of America, Inc.; *Int'l,* pg. 65

ALPINE—Asphalt Shingles—Atlas Roofing Corp.; *U.S. Private,* pg. 96

ALPINE—Powder Process Equipment, Plastic Film Mfg. Systems & Plastic Bag Machinery—Hosokawa Micron International Inc.; *Int'l,* pg. 635

ALPINE—NONE—Hosokawa Micron Powder Systems; *Int'l,* pg. 636

ALPINE—Beer—Joseph Huber Brewing Co., Inc.; *U.S. Public,* pg. 545

ALPINE—Cigarettes—Philip Morris Companies Inc.; *U.S. Public,* pg. 1287

ALPINE—Cigarettes—Philip Morris U.S.A.; *U.S. Public,* pg. 1289

ALPINE MEATS—NONE—Alpine Packing Company; *U.S. Private,* pg. 45

ALPINE MOUNTAIN—NONE—Maplehurst Farms, Inc.; *U.S. Public,* pg. 490

ALPINE WHITE—Candy Bar—Nestle Chocolate & Confection; *Int'l,* pg. 917

ALPINE WHITE—Candy Bar—Nestle S.A.; *Int'l,* pg. 915

ALPO—Premium Canned Dog Foods—Alpo Pet Foods, Inc.; *Int'l,* pg. 917

ALPO BEEF FLAVORED DINNER—Dry Dog Food—Alpo Pet Foods, Inc.; *Int'l,* pg. 917

ALPO BONES—Dog Food—Alpo Pet Foods, Inc.; *Int'l,* pg. 917

ALPO BURGERS—Dog Food—Alpo Pet Foods, Inc.; *Int'l,* pg. 917

ALPO JERKY BITS—Premium Pet Treats—Alpo Pet Foods, Inc.; *Int'l,* pg. 917

ALPO JERKY STRIPS—Premium Pet Treats—Alpo Pet Foods, Inc.; *Int'l,* pg. 917

ALPO PUPPY FOOD—Canned & Dry Puppy Food—Alpo Pet Foods, Inc.; *Int'l*, pg. 917

ALPO SNAPS—Pet Treats—Alpo Pet Foods, Inc.; *Int'l*, pg. 917

ALPO STEW BISCUITS—Dog food—Alpo Pet Foods, Inc.; *Int'l*, pg. 917

ALPREM—Infant Formula—Nestle S.A.; *Int'l*, pg. 915

ALPRO—Margarine—Vandemoortele N.V.; *Int'l*, pg. 1451

ALPROSTAR—Alprostadil, Cardiovascular—Recordati Industria Chimica e Farmaceutica S.p.A.; *Int'l*, pg. 1090

ALRECO—Aluminum & Aluminum Alloy—Reynolds Metals Company; *U.S. Public*, pg. 1385

ALSA—Desserts & Baking Aids—Bestfoods; *U.S. Public*, pg. 223

ALSACE WILLM—Alsace Wines—Frederick Wildman & Sons Ltd.; *U.S. Private*, pg. 1176

ALSEC—Aluminum Compressed Gas Cylinders—Alusuisse-Lonza Holding Ltd.; *Int'l*, pg. 66

ALSON'S—Bathroom Fittings—Masco Corporation; *U.S. Public*, pg. 1052

ALSOY—Food Supplement—Nestle S.A.; *Int'l*, pg. 915

ALSTERHAUS—Department Store—Hertie Waren- und Kaufhaus GmbH; *Int'l*, pg. 724

ALSYNOL—Printing Resin—DSM N.V.; *Int'l*, pg. 352

ALTA—NONE—Adaptec, Inc.; *U.S. Public*, pg. 19

ALTA—NONE—Howmedica, Inc.; *U.S. Public*, pg. 1282

ALTA—NONE—Pfizer Inc.; *U.S. Public*, pg. 1281

ALTA-DENA—Dairy Products—Alta-Dena Certified Dairy; *Int'l*, pg. 201

ALTA RICA—Instant Coffee—Nestle S.A.; *Int'l*, pg. 915

ALTACE—Hypertension—Hoechst Marion Roussel, Inc.; *Int'l*, pg. 624

ALTACE—Angiotensin-Converting-Enzyme Inhibitor for Hypertension & Heart Failure—Hoechst Marion Roussel North America; *Int'l*, pg. 625

ALTAI—Vodka—Groupe Pernod Ricard; *Int'l*, pg. 566

ALTAIR—Holter System—Burdick, Inc.; *U.S. Private*, pg. 181

ALTAIR—Interior Floor Tile—Monarch Tile, Inc.; *U.S. Private*, pg. 287

ALTAIR—Endpoint Detection—SpeedFan International, Inc.; *U.S. Public*, pg. 1497

ALTAIR I-300—Acrylic Sheet for Plumbingware—Aristech Chemical Corporation; *Int'l*, pg. 872

ALTAIR PLUS—Composit Laminate Acrylic Sheet—Aristech Chemical Corporation; *Int'l*, pg. 872

ALTAIRA—NONE—The Black & Decker Corporation; *U.S. Public*, pg. 233

ALTAR BRAND—Beeswax Candles—Will & Baumer Incorporated; *U.S. Private*, pg. 1176

ALTARIS—NONE—The Black & Decker Corporation; *U.S. Public*, pg. 233

ALTAWAND—Golf Club—Mizuno Corporation; *Int'l*, pg. 884

ALTEA—Economy Hotels—Accor S.A.; *Int'l*, pg. 20

ALTEC—Stereo Components—Altec Lansing Corp.; *U.S. Private*, pg. 479

ALTEC LANSING—Stereo Components—Altec Lansing Corp.; *U.S. Private*, pg. 479

ALTEC LANSING—NONE—Altec Lansing Technologies, Inc.; *U.S. Private*, pg. 479

ALTER—Insecticide—Roussel Corporation; *Int'l*, pg. 625

ALTER FOR DB2—Performance Monitor—BMC Software, Inc.; *U.S. Public*, pg. 162

ALTERA—NONE—Altera Corporation; *U.S. Public*, pg. 59

ALTERNA—Low Protein, Low Phosphorous Milk Substitute—Abbott Laboratories; *U.S. Public*, pg. 12

ALTERNATIVE—Insurance—Midland Life Insurance Co.; *U.S. Private*, pg. 744

ALTERNATIVES—Dusters—Swirl, II LTD; *U.S. Private*, pg. 1059

ALTES—NONE—The Stroh Brewery Company; *U.S. Private*, pg. 1047

ALTIER SHOE ANNEX—Discount Shoes—The Shoe Show of Rocky Mt., Inc.; *U.S. Private*, pg. 996

ALTIMA—Automobile—Nissan Motor Corporation in U.S.A.; *Int'l*, pg. 945

ALTITUDE TRAVELER—Portable Oxygen Breathing Apparatus—Nellcor Puritan Bennett Incorporated; *U.S. Public*, pg. 1039

ALTO—In the Ear Hearing Aid—Beltone Electronics Corporation; *U.S. Private*, pg. 132

ALTO—Fungicide—Novartis AG; *Int'l*, pg. 971

ALTO ESTATE—Wine—Distillers Corporation S.A.; *Int'l*, pg. 1129

ALTON/APPLIED AIR—Heating & Ventilaiton Equipment—Mestek, Inc.; *U.S. Public*, pg. 1099

ALTOS—Computer Systems—Acer/Altos Computer Systems; *Int'l*, pg. 22

ALTOSIO—Mosquito Insecticides—Novartis AG; *Int'l*, pg. 971

ALTRA—NONE—Adaptec, Inc.; *U.S. Public*, pg. 19

ALTURA—Office Seating—United Chair, Inc.; *U.S. Private*, pg. 1499

ALU-CAP—Antacid, Aluminum Hydroxide, Capsule Form—3M; *U.S. Public*, pg. 1604

ALU-REY—Aluminum Foil—Reynolds Metals Company; *U.S. Public*, pg. 1385

ALU-TAB—Antacid, Aluminum Hydroxide, Capsule Form—3M; *U.S. Public*, pg. 1604

ALUBLAST—Abrasives—IMI Plc; *Int'l*, pg. 646

ALUCOBOND—Composite Material—Alusuisse-Lonza Holding Ltd.; *Int'l*, pg. 66

ALUFIX—Flexible Food Packaging—Alusuisse-Lonza Holding Ltd.; *Int'l*, pg. 66

ALUGAL—Hot Dip Galvanized—Cockerill Sambre; *Int'l*, pg. 301

ALUGARD—Lightning Arresters—General Electric Canada Inc.; *U.S. Public*, pg. 713

ALUM-A-FILL II—Body Filler—Marson/Creative Fastener, Inc.; *U.S. Private*, pg. 708

ALUM-A-FORM—Fabricated Aluminum Products—Elixir Industries; *U.S. Private*, pg. 371

ALUM-A-LEAD—Metallic Filler—PPG Industries, Inc.; *U.S. Public*, pg. 1245

ALUMA 827—Commercial Gauge Cookware—The Vollrath Company, L.L.C.; *U.S. Private*, pg. 1143

ALUMA-FOIL—Sheet Steel—Inland Steel Industries, Inc.; *U.S. Public*, pg. 879

ALUMA-FUSE—Sheet Steel—Inland Steel Industries, Inc.; *U.S. Public*, pg. 879

ALUMA-LITE—Recreational Vehicle—Holiday Rambler; *U.S. Public*, pg. 1123

ALUMA-LOK—Hardware—Deco Products Co.; *U.S. Private*, pg. 320

ALUMA-PLATE—Protective Coating Resistant to Wear, Sliding Abrasion & Chemical Attack—Diamonite Plant; *U.S. Public*, pg. 618

ALUMA-SAND—Inert, Nonoxidizing Beads for Industrial Application—Diamonite Plant; *U.S. Public*, pg. 618

ALUMA-TI—Aluminum Coated Sheet Steel—Inland Steel Industries, Inc.; *U.S. Public*, pg. 879

ALUMA-TRAK—Aluminum Chassis Slide—Zero Corporation; *U.S. Public*, pg. 1791

ALUMAGOAL—Track & Field Equipment—Sport Supply Group, Inc.; *U.S. Public*, pg. 1499

ALUMANATION—Aluminum Coating—RPM, Inc.; *U.S. Public*, pg. 1356

ALUMAPOXY—Epoxy Coating—The Valspar Corp. Protective Coatings Div.; *U.S. Public*, pg. 1707

ALUMASCAPE—NONE—Holiday Rambler; *U.S. Public*, pg. 1123

ALUMICUBE—Lighting Diffusers—American Louver Co.; *U.S. Private*, pg. 58

ALUMIGATOR—Irrigation Equipment Center Pivot—Reinke Manufacturing Co., Inc.; *U.S. Private*, pg. 920

ALUMILINE—Electric Resistance Furnaces of the Crucible Type—Inductotherm Corp.; *U.S. Private*, pg. 560

ALUMINALL—Aluminum Paint—Henkel Corporation; *Int'l*, pg. 610

ALUMINCON—Rigid Aluminum Conduit—Reynolds Extrusion Company; *U.S. Public*, pg. 1387

ALUMINEX—Speaker Bobbins & Speakers—CTS Corporation; *U.S. Public*, pg. 285

ALUMINIZED—Aluminum Coated Sheet Steel—Inland Steel Industries, Inc.; *U.S. Public*, pg. 879

ALUMINWELD—Electrode—The Lincoln Electric Company; *U.S. Public*, pg. 996

ALUMITRAK—Aluminum Track Power & Free Conveyors—Jervis B. Webb Company; *U.S. Private*, pg. 1156

ALUMON—Aluminum Preparation—Enthone-OMI, Inc.; *U.S. Public*, pg. 138

ALUNDUM—Abrasives—Norton Company; *Int'l*, pg. 1173

ALUPAK—Radiators—IMI Plc; *Int'l*, pg. 646

ALUPENT—Bronchodilator—Boehringer Ingelheim GmbH; *Int'l*, pg. 199

ALUPENT—Bronchodilator—Boehringer Ingelheim Pharmaceuticals, Inc.; *Int'l*, pg. 199

ALUPOWER—Aluminum-Air Batteries—Yardney Technical Products, Inc.; *U.S. Private*, pg. 376

ALURA—Power Boats—Hunter Marine Corporation; *U.S. Private*, pg. 549

ALUTERM—Plastic Foam Insulation—The Dow Chemical Company; *U.S. Public*, pg. 522

ALUZINC—Hot Dip Galvanized—Cockerill Sambre; *Int'l*, pg. 301

ALVA—CD-ROM Output Services—Anacomp, Inc.; *U.S. Public*, pg. 106

ALVA TRANQUIL—Relaxant/Sleep Tablets—Alva/Amco Pharmacal Companies, Inc.; *U.S. Private*, pg. 47

ALVA TRANQUIL-SPAN—Long Acting Relaxant Caps—Alva/Amco Pharmacal Companies, Inc.; *U.S. Private*, pg. 47

ALVCO—NONE—Lawter International, Inc.; *U.S. Public*, pg. 980

ALVCO HI-SLIP—NONE—Lawter International, Inc.; *U.S. Public*, pg. 980

ALVCOLITE—NONE—Lawter International, Inc.; *U.S. Public*, pg. 980

ALVEDON—Analgestic—Astra AB; *Int'l*, pg. 93

ALVEOFACT—Natural Surfactant—Boehringer Ingelheim GmbH; *Int'l*, pg. 199

ALVINO—Pizza—Little Lady Foods, Inc.; *U.S. Private*, pg. 671

ALVITYL—Multivitamin Preparations—Kali-Chemie Aktiengesellschaft; *Int'l*, pg. 1278

ALWAYS—Feminine Protection Product—The Procter & Gamble Company; *U.S. Public*, pg. 1330

ALWAYS FRESH—Perishable Food Products—Shurfine International, Inc.; *U.S. Private*, pg. 997

ALWAYS IN TIME—NONE—Medline Industries, Inc.; *U.S. Private*, pg. 728

ALWAYS PLUS—Feminine Protection Product—The Procter & Gamble Company; *U.S. Public*, pg. 1330

ALWAYS SAVE—Extra Standard Grocery & Grocery Related Products—Associated Wholesale Grocers, Inc.; *U.S. Private*, pg. 93

ALWAYS TENDER—Pork—Hormel Foods Corp.; *U.S. Public*, pg. 840

ALWAYS 21—Foundations—The Strouse, Adler Company; *U.S. Private*, pg. 1047

ALYRANE—Pharmaceutical Anaesthetics—The BOC Group plc; *Int'l*, pg. 121

ALZAMER—Bioerodible Polymers—Alza Corporation; *U.S. Public*, pg. 62

ALZET—Osmotic Pumps—Alza Corporation; *U.S. Public*, pg. 62

AMACAST—Stainless Steel Abrasive—Ervin Industries, Inc.; *U.S. Private*, pg. 382

AMADEUS—Herbicides—Agrolinz Melamin GmbH; *Int'l*, pg. 356

AMAIR 62 PLUS—Air Filter—AAF-International; *U.S. Private*, pg. 3

AMAL—Carburetors & Flame Arresters—IMI Plc; *Int'l*, pg. 646

AMALFI—Women's Shoes—Nine West Group, Inc.; *U.S. Public*, pg. 1185

AMALOG—Inspection—Tuboscope Incorporated; *U.S. Public*, pg. 1643

AMALON—Filaments—Ketema, Inc.; *U.S. Private*, pg. 604

AMAMI—Talcum Powder & Deodorants, Shampoo, Setting Lotion—SmithKline Beecham plc; *Int'l*, pg. 1264

AMANA—Society—Amana Society, Inc.; *U.S. Private*, pg. 48

AMANA—HAC Equipment—W.A. Roosevelt Co.; *U.S. Private*, pg. 943

AMANDA STAR—Toys—Fred Meyer Stores; *U.S. Public*, pg. 1103

AMANDO—Men's Fragrance—Coty Inc.; *Int'l*, pg. 185

AMAPOLA—Flour & Corn Meal—ConAgra, Inc.; *U.S. Public*, pg. 425

AMARETTO CREME DI AMORE—NONE—Barton Brands, Ltd.; *U.S. Public*, pg. 300

AMARETTO DE SABROSO—NONE—Barton Brands, Ltd.; *U.S. Public*, pg. 300

AMARETTO DE SABROSO—Liqueur—Barton Incorporated; *U.S. Public*, pg. 300

AMARETTO DI AMORE—NONE—Barton Brands, Ltd.; *U.S. Public*, pg. 300

AMARETTO DI LORETO—Liquor—Peerless Importers, Inc.; *U.S. Private*, pg. 847

AMARI—NONE—Glynwed International PLC; *Int'l*, pg. 554

AMARILLO GLOBE-NEWS—Newspaper—Shivers Trading & Operating Co.; *U.S. Private*, pg. 994

AMARLITE ARCHITECTURAL PRODUCTS—Aluminum Doors, Entrances, Storefronts, Curtain Walls & Windows—Arch Aluminium & Glass L.C.; *U.S. Private*, pg. 79

AMARLITE OBLIQUE—Wall Slope Glazing System—Arch Aluminium & Glass L.C.; *U.S. Private*, pg. 79

AMARLITE SAFETYLINE—Aluminum Entranceway—Arch Aluminium & Glass L.C.; *U.S. Private*, pg. 79

AMARLITE THERMAFRONT—Framing System—Arch Aluminium & Glass L.C.; *U.S. Private*, pg. 79

AMARO RAMAZOTTI—Aparatif—Groupe Pernod Ricard; *Int'l*, pg. 566

AMARULA—Liquour—Distillers Corporation S.A.; *Int'l*, pg. 1129

AMARYL—Sulfonylurea Agent for Type II Diabetes—Hoechst Marion Roussel North America; *Int'l*, pg. 625

AMASTEEL—Shot Grit—Ervin Industries, Inc.; *U.S. Private*, pg. 382

AMATEUR GARDENING—Special Interest Magazine—IPC Magazines Limited; *Int'l*, pg. 651

AMATOM—Electronic Hardware—New Haven Mfg. Corp.; *U.S. Private*, pg. 793

AMATEUR PHOTOGRAPHER—Special Interest Magazine—IPC Magazines Limited; *Int'l*, pg. 651

AMAX—Match Bullets—Hornady Manufacturing Company; *U.S. Private*, pg. 539

AMAZE—Soap Product—Lever Brothers Co.; *Int'l*, pg. 1435

AMAZE—Soap Prod.—Unilever Plc; *Int'l*, pg. 1433

THE AMAZEMENT PARK—Amusement Park—Cedar Fair, L.P.; *U.S. Public*, pg. 319

AMAZIN' FRUIT—Gummy Bears—Hershey Foods Corporation; *U.S. Public*, pg. 811

AMAZING—Books—TSR, Inc.; *U.S. Private*, pg. 1185

THE AMAZING WRITING MACHINE—NONE—Broderbund Software, Inc.; *U.S. Public*, pg. 258

AMAZO II—Wet Mop with Scrubber—Stanhome Inc.; *U.S. Public*, pg. 1508

AMAZON—Water Softening & Purification Equipment—RainSoft Water Treatment Systems; *U.S. Private*, pg. 78

AMBACO—Industrial Baling Equipment—Avis Industrial Corporation; *U.S. Private*, pg. 102

AMBASSADEUR—Bait Casting Reels—Abu Garcia Inc.; *U.S. Private*, pg. 822

AMBASSADEUR—Bait Casting Reels—Aritmos AB; *Int'l*, pg. 1072

AMBASSADEUR—Aperitif—Groupe Pernod Ricard; *Int'l*, pg. 566

AMBASSADOR—Lockers—American Locker Group, Inc.; *U.S. Public*, pg. 85

AMBASSADOR—Golf Clubs—The Austad Company; *U.S. Public*, pg. 782

AMBASSADOR—Catering Trays & Bowls—Douglas Stephen Plastics, Inc.; *U.S. Private*, pg. 341

AMBASSADOR—Greeting Cards & Related Products—Hallmark Cards, Inc.; *U.S. Private*, pg. 495

AMBASSADOR—Attaches & Portfolios—United States Luggage Company; *U.S. Private*, pg. 1125

AMBER—NONE—Grolsch N.V.; *Int'l*, pg. 559

AMBER BRAND—NONE—The Smithfield Companies, Inc.; *U.S. Public*, pg. 1479

AMBER LEAF—NONE—Fortune Brands, Inc.; *U.S. Public*, pg. 674

AMBER LEAF—NONE—Gallaher Tobacco Ltd.; *Int'l*, pg. 539

AMBEREX—Yeast—Universal Foods Corporation; *U.S. Public*, pg. 1695

AMBERG—Office Products—Esselte AB; *Int'l*, pg. 459

AMBERLIGHT—NONE—Temtex Industries Inc.; *U.S. Public*, pg. 1575

AMBERLITE—NONE—CertainTeed Corporation; *Int'l*, pg. 1170

AMBERMATIC—Sunglasses—Bausch & Lomb Incorporated; *U.S. Public*, pg. 194

AMBEZYM—Enzyme Preparation—The Dow Chemical Company; *U.S. Public*, pg. 522

AMBI—Skin Care Products—Kiwi Brands; *U.S. Public*, pg. 1433

AMBI-PUR—Air Freshener—Sara Lee Corporation; *U.S. Public*, pg. 1432

AMBIANCE—Luggage—American Tourister, Inc.; *U.S. Public*, pg. 1430

AMBIANCE—Business-Class Seats—B/E Aerospace Seating Products Group; *U.S. Public*, pg. 159

AMBIANCE—NONE—Cambridge Soundworks, Inc.; *U.S. Private*, pg. 202

AMBIANCE—Fragrance—Parfums De Coeur Ltd.; *U.S. Private*, pg. 839

AMBIANCE BY HENRY KLOSS—NONE—Cambridge Soundworks, Inc.; *U.S. Private*, pg. 202

AMBIANCE BY HENRY KLOSS AND DESIGN—NONE—Cambridge Soundworks, Inc.; *U.S. Private*, pg. 202

AMBICO—Camcorder & Video Accessories—Recoton Corporation; *U.S. Public*, pg. 1369

AMBICOR—NONE—Pfizer Inc.; *U.S. Public*, pg. 1281

AMBISOME—Proprietary Liposomal Formula—Nexstar Pharmaceuticals, Inc.; *U.S. Public*, pg. 1180

AMBITROL—Coolant—The Dow Chemical Company; *U.S. Public*, pg. 522

AMBLERS—Men's Shoes—E.J. Footwear Corp.; *U.S. Public*, pg. 1684

AMBOID—Gearing—Rockwell International Corporation; *U.S. Public*, pg. 1397

AMBRA—Fine Ladies Sweaters—Winona Knitting Mills, Inc.; *U.S. Public*, pg. 779

AMBRE SOLAIRE—Sun Products—L'Oreal S.A.; *Int'l*, pg. 818

AMBRIA—NONE—Blyth Industries; *U.S. Public*, pg. 239

AMBROSIA—Dairy Desserts—Bestfoods; *U.S. Public*, pg. 223

AMBROSIA—Desserts—CPC Foods (Ireland) Ltd.; *U.S. Public*, pg. 225

AMBROSIA—Chocolate Products—Grace Cocoa/Ambrosia Chocolate; *U.S. Public*, pg. 128

AMBUSH—Perfume—Dana Perfumes Corp.; *U.S. Private*, pg. 922

AMCEL—Can Liners & Cutlery—Amcel Corp.; *U.S. Private*, pg. 48

AMCO—Rope & Twine—The American Group; *U.S. Private*, pg. 56

AMCO—Industrial Products—Email Limited; *Int'l*, pg. 450

AMCRON—Audio Electronics Export—Crown International, Inc.; *U.S. Private*, pg. 293

AMDAHL 5995—Mainframe Computer—Amdahl Corporation; *Int'l*, pg. 527

AMDRO—Insecticide—American Home Products Corporation; *U.S. Public*, pg. 79

AMECARE—Incubators—Hollister Medical Systems Division; *U.S. Private*, pg. 535

AMELETTE—Incubators—Hollister Medical Systems Division; *U.S. Private*, pg. 535

AMEN—Amenorrhea—Carnrick Laboratories, Inc.; *U.S. Private*, pg. 436

THE AMENITIES CHOICE FOR THE 90's—Toilet Articles for Hotel/Motel Distribution—Marietta Corporation; *U.S. Private*, pg. 702

THE AMENITIES SOURCE—Toilet Articles for Hotel/Motel Distribution—Marietta Corporation; *U.S. Private*, pg. 702

AMER-PLATE—Polyvinyl Chloride Sheeting—Ameron International Corporation; *U.S. Public*, pg. 98

AMER-PLATE—Polyvinyl Chloride Sheeting—Ameron Concrete & Steel Pipe Group; *U.S. Public*, pg. 99

AMERCO—Containers—American International Container, Inc.; *U.S. Private*, pg. 57

AMERCOAT—Protective Coating—Ameron Concrete & Steel Pipe Group; *U.S. Public*, pg. 99

AMERCOAT—Protective Coating—Ameron International Corporation; *U.S. Public*, pg. 98

AMERFLOC—Fluid Flocculents—Ashland, Inc.; *U.S. Public*, pg. 138

AMERFORD—Air Cargo—Amerford International Corporation; *Int'l*, pg. 1388

AMERGLOSS—Water Based Flexographic Printing Ink—American Inks & Coatings Corp.; *U.S. Private*, pg. 56

AMERGUARD—Waterborne Protective Coating—Ameron International Corporation; *U.S. Public*, pg. 98

AMERI-FLEX—Single Wall Vent Connector & Chimney Reliner for Gas Fired Appliances—American Metal Products; *U.S. Public*, pg. 1053

AMERI-FLOW—Grilles, Registers & Diffusers—American Metal Products; *U.S. Public*, pg. 1053

AMERI-FORGE—Flanges, Undercarriage—Global Industrial Technologies; *U.S. Public*, pg. 747

AMERI-GLOSS—Printed Flags—Dettra Flag Company; *U.S. Private*, pg. 328

AMERI-TEC—Chimneys & Pellet Stove Vent—American Metal Products; *U.S. Public*, pg. 1053

AMERI-VENT—Type B Gas Vent—American Metal Products; *U.S. Public*, pg. 1053

AMERICA IN THE MORNING—Morning News Magazine Program—Westwood One, Inc.; *U.S. Public*, pg. 1763

AMERICA ONLINE—Online Service—America Online Incorporated; *U.S. Public*, pg. 66

AMERICA THIS WEEK—Weekly Feature Magazine Program—Westwood One, Inc.; *U.S. Public*, pg. 1763

AMERICA WEST VACATIONS—Vacation Packaging Service—America West Airlines, Inc.; *U.S. Public*, pg. 67

AMERICA WEST'S CHAIRMAN'S CLUB—Elite Level Frequent Flyer Plan—America West Airlines, Inc.; *U.S. Public*, pg. 67

AMERICA'S FAVORITE MOVER—Mover—Interstate Van Lines, Inc.; *U.S. Private*, pg. 573

AMERICA'S NETWORK—Trade Periodical—Advanstar Communications; *U.S. Private*, pg. 22

AMERICAINE—Anesthetic Lubricant (Benzocaine)—Medeva Pharmaceuticals; *Int'l*, pg. 852

AMERICAINE OTIC—Topical Anesthetic Ear Drops (Benzocaine)—Medeva Pharmaceuticals; *Int'l*, pg. 852

AMERICAL—Ophthalmic Polish for Hard Resin Lenses—Ferro Corporation; *U.S. Public*, pg. 618

AMERICAL PLUS—Ophthalmic Polish—Ferro Corporation; *U.S. Public*, pg. 618

AMERICAN—Cranes—AmClyde Engineered Products Co., Inc.; *U.S. Public*, pg. 778

AMERICAN—Life & Accident Insurance—American General Life & Accident Insurance Co.; *U.S. Public*, pg. 76

AMERICAN—Lockers—American Locker Group, Inc.; *U.S. Public*, pg. 85

AMERICAN—Envelopes—American Mail-Well Envelope; *U.S. Public*, pg. 1038

AMERICAN—Meters—American Meter Company; *Int'l*, pg. 1149

AMERICAN—Luggage—American Tourister, Inc.; *U.S. Public*, pg. 1430

AMERICAN—Petroleum Products—Amoco Corporation; *U.S. Public*, pg. 101

AMERICAN—Peanut Butter—Clements Nut Co.; *U.S. Private*, pg. 245

AMERICAN—Beer—Pittsburgh Brewing Company; *U.S. Private*, pg. 619

AMERICAN—Woodcase Pencil—Sanford Corporation; *U.S. Public*, pg. 1178

AMERICAN ADVENTURES—Family Recreation Park—Silver Dollar City, Inc.; *U.S. Private*, pg. 1000

AMERICAN AERO—Marine Crane—Weatherford Enterra Incorporated; *U.S. Public*, pg. 1749

AMERICAN AGRICULTURIST—Farm Publication 15 Issues/Year—Farm Progress Publications; *U.S. Public*, pg. 513

AMERICAN AIRLINES—Airline—American Airlines, Inc.; *U.S. Public*, pg. 9

AMERICAN & EFIRD—Sewing Thread—Ruddick Corporation; *U.S. Public*, pg. 1412

AMERICAN ANGLER—Fishing Products—Douglas/Quikut; *U.S. Public*, pg. 217

AMERICAN ANGLER—NONE—Tandy Brands Accessories, Inc.; *U.S. Public*, pg. 1560

AMERICAN ANTHOLOGY—Riverboat Cruise Trips—American Classic Voyagers Company; *U.S. Private*, pg. 380

AMERICAN APPRAISAL ASSOCIATES—Appraisal Services—American Appraisal Associates, Inc.; *U.S. Private*, pg. 49

AMERICAN APPRAISAL CANADA—Appraisal Services—American Appraisal Associates, Inc.; *U.S. Private*, pg. 49

AMERICAN ART DIRECTORY—Directory of Art Institutions—National Register Publishing; pg. 1096

AMERICAN ARTIST—Magazine; Directories—BPI Communications Inc.; *Int'l*, pg. 1446

AMERICAN ATELIER—Dinnerware - Porcelain & Stoneware—Crystal Clear Industries; *U.S. Private*, pg. 293

AMERICAN AUTOMATIC—Towel Dispenser Cabinets—Georgia-Pacific Corporation; *U.S. Public*, pg. 735

AMERICAN BANDSTAND—Music Television Show—Dick Clark Productions, Inc.; *U.S. Public*, pg. 382

AMERICAN BANDSTAND GRILL—Restaurant—Dick Clark Productions, Inc.; *U.S. Public*, pg. 382

AMERICAN BANKER—Daily Newspaper & Reprint Service—American Banker Bond Buyer; *U.S. Public*, pg. 1600

AMERICAN BARMAG—Textile Machinery—American Barmag Co.; *U.S. Private*, pg. 51

AMERICAN BEAUTY—Greeting Cards—American Greetings Corporation; *U.S. Public*, pg. 77

AMERICAN BEAUTY—Pasta—Hershey Foods Corporation; *U.S. Public*, pg. 811

AMERICAN BEAUTY—Pasta—Hershey Pasta and Grocery Group; *U.S. Public*, pg. 812

AMERICAN BELTING LEATHER—Leather Goods—Hugo Bosca Co., Inc.; *U.S. Private*, pg. 160

AMERICAN BIG TWIN DEALER—Trade Periodical—Advanstar Communications; *U.S. Private*, pg. 22

AMERICAN BINDERY—Rebind Periodicals & Books—The American Companies, Inc.; *U.S. Private*, pg. 52

AMERICAN BLACK ACHIEVEMENT AWARDS—Television Program—Johnson Publishing Company, Inc.; *U.S. Private*, pg. 591

AMERICAN BLOWER—Blower—The Howden Fan Co.; *U.S. Private*, pg. 543

THE AMERICAN BLUES CO.—School Supplies—Union Camp Corporation; *U.S. Public*, pg. 1665

AMERICAN BOOK TRADE DIRECTORY—Directory to Retail & Antiquarian Book Dealers, Wholesalers & Distributors—R.R. Bowker; *Int'l*, pg. 1096

AMERICAN BRAKEBLOK—Brake Linings & Clutch Facings—Abex Friction Products; *U.S. Public*, pg. 443

AMERICAN BUSINESS DIRECTORIES—National Directories—American Business Information, Inc.; *U.S. Public*, pg. 69

AMERICAN BUSINESS INTERIORS—NONE—American Furniture Company; *U.S. Private*, pg. 55

AMERICAN BUSINESS PRODUCTS—Business Supplies—American Business Products, Inc.; *U.S. Public*, pg. 70

AMERICAN CARBONYL—Chemical—Air Products; *U.S. Public*, pg. 30

AMERICAN CARVER—Cutlery—General Housewares Corp.; *U.S. Public*, pg. 715

AMERICAN CITY & COUNTRY MUNICIPAL INDEX—Annual Publication—Intertec Publishing; *U.S. Public*, pg. 1328

AMERICAN CITY & COUNTY—Publication for Local Public Officials—Intertec Publishing; *U.S. Public*, pg. 1327

AMERICAN CITY & COUNTY—Monthly Publication—Intertec Publishing; *U.S. Public*, pg. 1328

AMERICAN CLASSIC—Crackers—RJR Nabisco Holdings Corp.; *U.S. Public*, pg. 1354

AMERICAN CLASSIC—Siding—Reynolds Metals Company; *U.S. Public*, pg. 1385

AMERICAN CLASSICS—Lawn & Garden Patio Accessories—American Manufacturing Company; *U.S. Private*, pg. 58

AMERICAN CLEAN CAR—Trade Journal—Crain Communications, Inc.; *U.S. Private*, pg. 284

AMERICAN COIN-OP—Trade Journal—Crain Communications, Inc.; *U.S. Private*, pg. 284

THE AMERICAN COLLECTION—NONE—Kellwood Company; *U.S. Public*, pg. 948

AMERICAN COUNTRY—Book Series—Time-Life, Inc.; *U.S. Public*, pg. 1613

AMERICAN DIRECTORY PUBLISHING—State Businesses Directories—American Business Information, Inc.; *U.S. Public*, pg. 69

AMERICAN DREAM—Motor Home—Fleetwood Enterprises, Inc.; *U.S. Public*, pg. 650

THE AMERICAN DREAM—Mattresses—Sleepy's The Mattress Professionals; *U.S. Private*, pg. 1005

AMERICAN DREAM—Vent-Free Gas Fireplaces & Logs—Temco Fireplace Products, Inc.; *U.S. Public*, pg. 1576

AMERICAN DREW—Wood Bedroom Furniture—American Drew; *U.S. Public*, pg. 974

AMERICAN DREW—Furniture—Ladd Furniture, Inc.; *U.S. Public*, pg. 974

AMERICAN DRUGGIST—Magazine—The Hearst Corporation; *U.S. Private*, pg. 515

AMERICAN DRY—Soft Drink—Polar Beverages; *U.S. Private*, pg. 873

AMERICAN DRYCLEANER—Trade Journal—Crain Communications, Inc.; *U.S. Private*, pg. 284

AMERICAN EAGLE—Ammunition—Blount International, Inc.; *U.S. Public*, pg. 237

AMERICAN EAGLE—Motor Home—Fleetwood Enterprises, Inc.; *U.S. Public*, pg. 650

AMERICAN EAGLE—Footwear—Jimlar Corporation; *U.S. Private*, pg. 587

AMERICAN EAGLE—Envelopes, Printing Paper, Envelope Paper—Westvaco Corporation; *U.S. Public*, pg. 1762

AMERICAN ECONO-THERM—NONE—Petro Chem Development Company; *U.S. Private*, pg. 858

AMERICAN ELECTRIC LIGHTING—Outdoor Lighting Products—Thomas & Betts Corporation; *U.S. Public*, pg. 1597

AMERICAN ELECTRONICS—Precision Power Electromechanical Equipment—American Electronics, Inc.; *U.S. Private*, pg. 5

THE AMERICAN ENTERPRISE—Bi-Monthly Policy Magazine—American Enterprise Institute for Public Policy Research; *U.S. Private*, pg. 53

AMERICAN EXPRESS—Charge Card Services—American Express Company; *U.S. Public*, pg. 73

AMERICAN EXPRESS CORPORATE CARD—NONE—American Express Company; *U.S. Public*, pg. 73

AMERICAN EXPRESS FINANCIAL ADVISORS—NONE—American Express Financial Advisor; *U.S. Public*, pg. 73

AMERICAN EXPRESS TRAVEL SERVICE—Travel Services—American Express Company; *U.S. Public*, pg. 73

AMERICAN EXPRESS TRAVELERS CHEQUES—Travelers Checks—American Express Company; *U.S. Public*, pg. 73

AMERICAN EXPRESS WORLD SERVICE—NONE—American Express Company; *U.S. Public*, pg. 73

AMERICAN EXPRESSIONS—Area Rugs—American Rug Craftsmen; *U.S. Public*, pg. 1121

AMERICAN FAMILY—Photo Albums—Kleer-Vu Plastics Corp.; *U.S. Public*, pg. 962

AMERICAN FAMILY BROKERAGE—Brokerage Services—American Family Mutual Insurance Co.; *U.S. Private*, pg. 53

AMERICAN FAMILY FINANCIAL SERVICES—Consumer & Home Equity Loans—American Family Mutual Insurance Co.; *U.S. Private*, pg. 53

AMERICAN FAMILY INSURANCE COMPANY—Property, Casualty & Health Insurance—American Family Mutual Insurance Co.; *U.S. Private*, pg. 53

AMERICAN FAMILY LIFE INSURANCE—Life & Related Insurance Products—American Family Mutual Insurance Co.; *U.S. Private*, pg. 53

AMERICAN FAMILY MUTUAL INSURANCE COMPANY—Property, Casualty & Health Insurance—American Family Mutual Insurance Co.; *U.S. Private*, pg. 53

AMERICAN FLYER—RV's—Cruise America, Inc.; *U.S. Private*, pg. 178

AMERICAN FLYER—Model Electric Trains—Lionel LLC; *U.S. Private*, pg. 669

AMERICAN FOUNDATION LIFE INSURANCE COMPANY—Insurance Company—Protective Life Corporation; *U.S. Public*, pg. 1336

AMERICAN GALLERIES—NONE—American Furniture Company; *U.S. Private*, pg. 55

AMERICAN GALLERY—NONE—Tandy Brands Accessories, Inc.; *U.S. Public*, pg. 1560

AMERICAN GARDEN—Dinnerware & Flatware—Tiffany & Co.; *U.S. Public*, pg. 1608

AMERICAN GENERAL—An Insurance Based Diversified Financial Co.—American General Corporation; *U.S. Public*, pg. 76

AMERICAN GENTLEMAN—Shoes—Craddock-Terry Inc.; *U.S. Private*, pg. 284

AMERICAN GIRL GEAR—Girls Cloths and Accessories—Pleasant Company; *U.S. Private*, pg. 872

AMERICAN GIRL LIBRARY—Book for Girls 7-12—Pleasant Company; *U.S. Private*, pg. 872

AMERICAN GIRL MAGAZINE—Magazine for American Girls of Today—Pleasant Company; *U.S. Private*, pg. 872

AMERICAN GIRL OF TODAY—Dolls, Doll Accessories—Pleasant Company; *U.S. Private*, pg. 872

AMERICAN GIRLS COLLECTION—Historical Dolls, Books, Doll Clothing—Pleasant Company; *U.S. Private*, pg. 872

AMERICAN GREETINGS—Greeting Cards; Date Books—American Greetings Corporation; *U.S. Public*, pg. 77

AMERICAN GREETINGS—Greeting Cards, & Gift Wrap—American Greetings U.S. Greeting Card Division; *U.S. Public*, pg. 78

AMERICAN GREETINGS WITH ROSE DESIGN—Greeting Cards; Wrapping Paper; Gift Items; Party Favors—American Greetings Corporation; *U.S. Public*, pg. 77

AMERICAN HAIR FORCE—Hair Salon—AHF Salons, Inc.; *U.S. Private*, pg. 818

AMERICAN HARDWARE MUTUAL—Insurance—American Hardware Mutual Insurance Co.; *U.S. Private*, pg. 764

AMERICAN HEALTH—Magazine—The Reader's Digest Association, Inc.; *U.S. Public*, pg. 1367

AMERICAN HERITAGE—Magazine—American Heritage Magazine; *U.S. Private*, pg. 417

AMERICAN HERITAGE ELECTRONIC DICTIONARY—Reference Work—INSO Corporation; *U.S. Public*, pg. 882

AMERICAN HISTORY—Periodical—Cowles Enthusiast Media, Inc.; *U.S. Private*, pg. 281

AMERICAN HOME FURNISHINGS—NONE—American Furniture Company; *U.S. Private*, pg. 55

AMERICAN HOME SHIELD—Home Warranty Contracts—The ServiceMaster Company; *U.S. Public*, pg. 1461

AMERICAN INGREDIENTS COMPANY—Bakery Ingredients—CSM N.V.; *Int'l*, pg. 243

AMERICAN JOURNAL OF NURSING—Magazine—American Journal of Nursing Company; *Int'l*, pg. 1513

AMERICAN LA FRANCE—Fire Apparatus—Williams Holdings Plc; *Int'l*, pg. 1499

AMERICAN LAUNDRY DIGEST—Trade Journal—Crain Communications, Inc.; *U.S. Private*, pg. 284

AMERICAN LEGEND—Apparel, Footwear & Accessories—Cherokee Inc.; *U.S. Public*, pg. 345

AMERICAN LEGEND—NONE—Karelia Tobacco Company Inc.; *Int'l*, pg. 724

AMERICAN LIBRARIES—Publication—American Library Association; *U.S. Private*, pg. 58

AMERICAN LIBRARY DIRECTORY—Reference Guide of Information on Libraries & Library-Related Organizations—R.R. Bowker; *Int'l*, pg. 1096

AMERICAN LIFT—Lift Tables—Columbus McKinnon Corp.; *U.S. Public*, pg. 405

AMERICAN LIGHTS—Cigarettes—Brown & Williamson Tobacco Corp.; *Int'l*, pg. 111

AMERICAN/M & M—Silk Screen Printing Machinery—Wisconsin Automated Machinery Corp.; *U.S. Private*, pg. 1184

AMERICAN MACHINIST—Periodical—Penton Publishing, Inc.; *U.S. Public*, pg. 1306

Brand Name Index

AMERICAN MADE—Garden Tools—Ames Company; *U.S. Public*, pg. 1683

AMERICAN MAPLE—Cutlery—General Housewares Corp.; *U.S. Public*, pg. 715

AMERICAN MARKING SYSTEMS—Marking Devices—American Marking Systems; *U.S. Private*, pg. 58

AMERICAN METAL—Air Distribution Products—Masco Corporation; *U.S. Public*, pg. 1052

AMERICAN METAL MARKET—Daily Newspaper of Metals Industry—Reed Elsevier Business Information; *Int'l*, pg. 1095

AMERICAN METALWARE—Urns & Shuttle Brewers—Grindmaster Corporation; *U.S. Private*, pg. 482

AMERICAN MUSCLE—Die Cast Vehicles—The Ertl Company, Inc; *U.S. Public*, pg. 1684

AMERICAN MUSIC AWARDS—Music Awards—Dick Clark Productions, Inc.; *U.S. Public*, pg. 382

AMERICAN NUTRITION—Cookware—Regal Ware, Inc.; *U.S. Private*, pg. 917

AMERICAN OAK—Wood Flooring Product Line—Premark International, Inc.; *U.S. Public*, pg. 1321

AMERICAN OF MARTINSVILLE—Furniture—Ladd Furniture, Inc.; *U.S. Public*, pg. 974

AMERICAN ORIGINAL—Seafoods—Clearwater Fine Foods Inc.; *Int'l*, pg. 297

AMERICAN/OSMONICS—Pumps—Ryan Herco Products Corp.; *U.S. Private*, pg. 953

AMERICAN PARK NETWORK—NONE—Meredith Corporation; *U.S. Public*, pg. 1094

AMERICAN PEANUT BUTTER—Peanut Butter—Clements Foods Co.; *U.S. Private*, pg. 245

AMERICAN PHOTO—Photography Magazine—Hachette Filipacchi Magazines Inc.; *Int'l*, pg. 794

AMERICAN PIE—Boys' Wear—Tootal Group plc; *Int'l*, pg. 300

AMERICAN PRIDE—Cutlery—General Housewares Corp.; *U.S. Public*, pg. 715

AMERICAN PRINTER—Publication on Industry & Technology Trends—Intertec Publishing; *U.S. Public*, pg. 1327

AMERICAN PROTECTION—Manufacturing & Direct Marketing of Collectibles, Home Decor & Jewelry—Roll International Corporation; *U.S. Private*, pg. 941

AMERICAN PUMP—Corrosion Resistant Pumps—Osmonics, Inc.; *U.S. Public*, pg. 1233

AMERICAN QUEEN—Riverboat—American Classic Voyagers Company; *U.S. Private*, pg. 380

AMERICAN QUILTS—Greeting Cards—American Greetings Corporation; *U.S. Public*, pg. 77

AMERICAN RED BALL—Truckline—Red Ball Corporation; *U.S. Private*, pg. 97

AMERICAN REFERENCE—Reference Books—The American Companies, Inc.; *U.S. Private*, pg. 52

AMERICAN RODDER—Magazine—Paisano Publications, Inc.; *U.S. Private*, pg. 834

AMERICAN ROYALTY—Tableware—Regal Ware, Inc.; *U.S. Private*, pg. 917

AMERICAN ROYALTY—Dinnerware—Saladmaster; *U.S. Private*, pg. 961

AMERICAN RUG—Tufted, Wovens, Border Rugs—American Rug Craftsmen; *U.S. Public*, pg. 1121

AMERICAN SALON—Trade Periodical—Advanstar Communications; *U.S. Private*, pg. 22

AMERICAN SALON'S GREEN BOOK—Trade Directory—Advanstar Communications; *U.S. Private*, pg. 22

AMERICAN SAPPHIRE—Stone Jewelery—Michael Anthony Jewelers, Inc.; *U.S. Public*, pg. 1103

AMERICAN SCHOOL & UNIVERSITY—Publication for Business & Facility Administrators—Intertec Publishing; *U.S. Public*, pg. 1327

AMERICAN SCHOOL & UNIVERSITY—Magazine—North American Publishing Company; *U.S. Private*, pg. 803

AMERICAN SEATING—Office Furniture and Theatre, Stadium and Transportation Seating—American Seating Company; *U.S. Private*, pg. 61

AMERICAN SEAWAY FOODS—Wholesale Foods—Riser Foods, Inc.; *U.S. Public*, pg. 450

AMERICAN SERIES—Merchandising System—Columbus Show Case Company; *U.S. Private*, pg. 257

AMERICAN-STANDARD—Plumbing Products—American Standard Inc.; *U.S. Public*, pg. 91

AMERICAN STANDARD INSURANCE COMPANY OF OHIO—Specialty Property & Casualty Risks—American Family Mutual Insurance Co.; *U.S. Private*, pg. 53

AMERICAN STANDARD INSURANCE COMPANY OF WISCONSIN—Specialty Property & Casualty Risks—American Family Mutual Insurance Co.; *U.S. Private*, pg. 53

AMERICAN STEEL—DBA—American Steel LLC; *U.S. Public*, pg. 1375

THE AMERICAN STOCK EXCHANGE—International Securities Exchange—The American Stock Exchange; *U.S. Private*, pg. 62

AMERICAN TECH—Process Control Equipment for the Semiconductor Industry—Halma p.l.c.; *Int'l*, pg. 589

AMERICAN TECHNICAL—Publisher of Vocational & Technical Textbooks—American Technical Publishers, Inc.; *U.S. Private*, pg. 63

AMERICAN THERAPY SERVICES—NONE—American Rehability Services, Inc.; *U.S. Public*, pg. 1257

AMERICAN TITLE CORPORATION—Title Insurance—Fidelity National Title Insurance Company of Pennsylvania; *U.S. Public*, pg. 621

AMERICAN TOOL—NONE—DeVlieg-Bullard Inc.; *U.S. Public*, pg. 502

AMERICAN TOURISTER—Luggage—American Tourister, Inc.; *U.S. Public*, pg. 1430

AMERICAN TOURISTER—Luggage—Samsonite Corporation; *U.S. Public*, pg. 1430

AMERICAN TOURISTER & DESIGN—Luggage—American Tourister, Inc.; *U.S. Public*, pg. 1430

AMERICAN TRADITION—Motor Home—Fleetwood Enterprises, Inc.; *U.S. Public*, pg. 650

AMERICAN TRADITIONAL—Deep-Grained, Staggered-Edge Shingle—GAF Premium Products, Inc.; *U.S. Private*, pg. 433

AMERICAN TRUST BOND—Bond Paper—Georgia-Pacific Corporation; *U.S. Public*, pg. 735

AMERICAN UNITED LIFE INSURANCE COMPANY—Life Insurance—American United Life Insurance Company; *U.S. Private*, pg. 64

AMERICAN UNIVERSAL—CNC Lathes—WCI Machine Tools & Systems; *Int'l*, pg. 440

AMERICAN UNIVERSAL TURNING CENTER—CNC Horizontal Lathes—WCI Machine Tools & Systems; *Int'l*, pg. 440

AMERICAN VIDEO—Greeting Cards—American Greetings Corporation; *U.S. Public*, pg. 77

AMERICAN VISION—Optical Centers—AVC/Nu-Vision, Inc.; *U.S. Public*, pg. 9

AMERICAN WAREHOUSE PLUS—NONE—American Furniture Company; *U.S. Private*, pg. 55

AMERICAN WELDING—Manufacturer Rings, Bends & Welded Assemblies—American Welding & Manufacturing Co.; *U.S. Private*, pg. 425

AMERICAN WEST—Toy—Strombecker Corporation; *U.S. Private*, pg. 1047

AMERICAN WHITE CROSS—Cotton—American Safety Razor Company; *U.S. Public*, pg. 597

AMERICAN WHITEHALL—Glassware—Indiana Glass Company; *U.S. Public*, pg. 976

AMERICAN WHOLESALE THERMOGRAPHERS—Wholesale Thermography Franchised Centers—International Center for Entrepreneurial Development, Inc.; *U.S. Private*, pg. 568

AMERICAN WILDERNESS EXPERIENCE—Site-Based Attraction—Ogden Corporation; *U.S. Public*, pg. 1213

AMERICAN WILDLIFE—NONE—Camillus Cutlery Co.; *U.S. Private*, pg. 203

AMERICAN WOODMARK—NONE—American Woodmark Corporation; *U.S. Public*, pg. 96

AMERICAN WOODWORKER—Magazine—Rodale Press, Inc.; *U.S. Private*, pg. 939

AMERICANA—Plastic Cutlery—Amcel Corp.; *U.S. Private*, pg. 48

AMERICANA—Individual Portion Products—Borden, Inc.; *U.S. Public*, pg. 157

AMERICANA—Drapery Hardware—Kirsch; *U.S. Public*, pg. 1176

AMERICANA SERIES—Wrought Iron Receptacels—United Receptical, Inc.; *U.S. Private*, pg. 1123

AMERICANA VERSATRONIC—Ranges, Refrigerators & Dishwashers for Domestic Use—General Electric Canada Inc.; *U.S. Public*, pg. 713

AMERICANO 505—Aperitif—Groupe Pernod Ricard; *Int'l*, pg. 566

AMERICARD—Greetings Cards; Gift Wrap; Paper Party Ware—American Greetings Corporation; *U.S. Public*, pg. 77

AMERICARE—Insurance—American Republic Insurance Co.; *U.S. Private*, pg. 61

AMERICA'S CHOICE—(Food Products)—The Great Atlantic & Pacific Tea Company, Inc.; *Int'l*, pg. 1375

AMERICA'S CIVIL WAR—Periodical—Cowles Enthusiast Media, Inc.; *U.S. Private*, pg. 281

AMERICA'S CORPORATE FINANCE DIRECTORY—Business Directory—National Register Publishing; *Int'l*, pg. 1096

AMERICA'S FAMILY BANK—Household Bank—Household International, Inc.; *U.S. Public*, pg. 842

AMERICA'S FAMILY VIDEO STORE—Video Rental Store Slogan—Blockbuster Entertainment Group; *U.S. Private*, pg. 775

AMERICA'S FAVORITE NEIGHBOR—NONE—Applebee's International, Inc.; *U.S. Public*, pg. 122

AMERICA'S FINEST—Cookies—Mrs. Alison's Cookie Company; *U.S. Private*, pg. 765

AMERICA'S GYM—Gym Sets—Hedstrom Corporation; *U.S. Private*, pg. 526

AMERICA'S HEALTH—Koo Koo Roo, Inc.; *U.S. Public*, pg. 966

AMERICA'S HOME FOR CAR SERVICE—Automotive Repair Services—Bridgestone/Firestone, Inc.; *Int'l*, pg. 213

AMERICA'S NEIGHBORHOOD TRADITION—NONE—Welcome Wagon-Intl., Inc.; *U.S. Public*, pg. 321

AMERICA'S PLUMBER—NONE—Roto-Rooter; *U.S. Public*, pg. 344

AMERICA'S REAL PRINTER—Printing Franchise—American Speedy Printing Centers, Inc.; *U.S. Private*, pg. 62

AMERICA'S ROLLERCOAST—Amusement Park—Cedar Fair, L.P.; *U.S. Public*, pg. 319

AMERICA'S SECOND CAR—Car Rental—Ugly Duckling Corp.; *U.S. Public*, pg. 1662

AMERICA'S STORYTELLER—Photo Products & Services—Eastman Kodak Company; *U.S. Public*, pg. 550

AMERICA'S TALKING—Cable Channel—National Broadcasting Co., Inc.; *U.S. Public*, pg. 712

AMERICA'S TIRE CO., INC.—Logo—Reinalt-Thomas Corp.; *U.S. Private*, pg. 919

AMERICA'S TROUBLESHOOTER—Sewer & Drain Cleaning Business—The Dwyer Group, Inc.; *U.S. Public*, pg. 537

AMERICATOURS—Tour Operators—Accor S.A.; *Int'l*, pg. 20

AMERICO—Janitorial Supplies—Americo Manufacturing Co., Inc.; *U.S. Private*, pg. 64

AMERICOLA—Soft Drink—Polar Beverages; *U.S. Private*, pg. 873

AMERICOLD—Compressors—Electrolux, AB; *Int'l*, pg. 438

AMERICOLD—Refrigeration Compressors—White Consolidated Industries, Inc.; *Int'l*, pg. 439

AMERIDATA—Computers, Terminals, Software & Maintenance Systems—GE Capital/IT Solutions; *U.S. Public*, pg. 711

AMERIGAMES—Equipment for Playing a Parlor Game—American Greetings Corporation; *U.S. Public*, pg. 77

AMERIGAS—Propane Products & Services—UGI Corporation; *U.S. Public*, pg. 1653

AMERIO—Contact Plate Freezer—APV Crepaco, Inc.; *Int'l*, pg. 1240

AMERISCOPE—Attitudinal & Behavioral Consumer Segmentation System—NFO Research, Inc.; *U.S. Public*, pg. 1146

AMERISPEC—Home Inspection—The ServiceMaster Company; *U.S. Public*, pg. 1461

AMERISUITES—Hotels—Prime Hospitality Corp.; *U.S. Public*, pg. 1326

AMERISURE—Insurance—Amerisure Companies; *U.S. Private*, pg. 65

AMERITAS—Insurance & Financial Services—Ameritas Life Insurance Corp.; *U.S. Private*, pg. 65

AMERITECH—NONE—Ameritech Corp.; *U.S. Public*, pg. 98

AMERITONE—Paint—Devoe & Raynolds; *Int'l*, pg. 663

AMERITONE—Paint—Grow Group, Inc.; *Int'l*, pg. 663

AMERITONE—Paint—ICI Paints; *Int'l*, pg. 664

AMERIWHITE—Chinaware—The Homer Laughlin China Company; *U.S. Private*, pg. 653

AMERLOCK—Protective Cladding—Ameron International Corporation; *U.S. Public*, pg. 98

AMEROCK—Cabinet, Bath, Window, & Door Hardware—Amerock Corporation; *U.S. Public*, pg. 1177

AMEROCK—Window Hardware & Cabinet Hardware—Newell Co.; *U.S. Public*, pg. 1176

AMEROID—Chemical—Ashland, Inc.; *U.S. Public*, pg. 138

AMERPAK—Cube Filter—AAF-International; *U.S. Private*, pg. 3

AMERSEAL—Ring Panel Filter—AAF-International; *U.S. Private*, pg. 3

AMERSHIELD—Protective Cladding—Ameron International Corporation; *U.S. Public*, pg. 98

AMERTECH—Water Based Printing—American Inks & Coatings Corp.; *U.S. Private*, pg. 56

AMERTECH II—Ink Series (Gravure & Flexo)—American Inks & Coatings Corp.; *U.S. Private*, pg. 56

AMERWOOD—Surface Treated Lumber—Georgia-Pacific Corporation; *U.S. Public*, pg. 735

AMES—Valves—Watts Industries, Inc.; *U.S. Public*, pg. 1746

AMES TAPING TOOLS—Tools for Drywall Tradesmen—AXIA Incorporated; *U.S. Private*, pg. 103

AMETEK—Electric Motors—AMETEK, Inc.; *U.S. Public*, pg. 99

AMETRICA—Paper—Georgia-Pacific Corporation; *U.S. Public*, pg. 735

AMFIPEN—Ampicillin—Royal Gist-Brocades N.V.; *Int'l*, pg. 1142

AMGARD—Security Products—Amway Corporation; *U.S. Private*, pg. 69

AMHERST—Printing Paper for Book Publishing—Georgia-Pacific Corporation; *U.S. Public*, pg. 735

AMICI—Women's Ready to Wear—RetailNet B.V.; *Int'l*, pg. 750

AMICON—SMA & Die Attach Adhesives—Emerson & Cuming Specialty Polymers; *Int'l*, pg. 1435

AMICURE—Epoxy Curatives—Air Products and Chemicals, Inc.; *U.S. Public*, pg. 30

AMICUS—Uncoated A4—Metsa-Serla Corporation; *Int'l*, pg. 863

AMIDATE—Etomidate—Abbott Laboratories; *U.S. Public*, pg. 12

AMIDOX—Surfactant—Stepan Company; *U.S. Public*, pg. 1514

AMIGASE—Amyloglucosidase for the Production of High Dextrose Syrups—Royal Gist-Brocades N.V.; *Int'l*, pg. 1142

AMIGLYDE—Antibiotic—Bristol-Myers Squibb Company; *U.S. Public*, pg. 253

AMIGO—Bananas—Chiquita Brands International, Inc.; *U.S. Public*, pg. 349

AMIKIN—Aminoglyoside—Bristol-Myers Squibb Company; *U.S. Public*, pg. 253

AMINE D—Dehydroabietylamine—Hercules Incorporated; *U.S. Public*, pg. 809

AMINO PLUS—Animal Feeds & Feed Supplies—Ag Processing Inc., A Cooperative; *U.S. Private*, pg. 26

AMINOLEBAN—Anti-Hepatic Encephalopathy—Otsuka Pharmaceutical Co., Ltd.; *Int'l*, pg. 1013

AMINOLEBAN EN—Oral Nutrition Therapy for Liver Failure—Otsuka Pharmaceutical Co., Ltd.; *Int'l*, pg. 1013

AMNIOMAX—NONE—Life Technologies, Inc.; *U.S. Public*, pg. 504

AMINOPHYLLIN—Pharmaceutical Product for Treatment of Acute Bronchial Asthma—Searle Laboratories; *U.S. Public*, pg. 1125

AMINOTRIPA—Kit for TPN—Otsuka Pharmaceutical Co., Ltd.; *Int'l*, pg. 1013

AMIPAREN—Amino Acid Solution—Otsuka Pharmaceutical Co., Ltd.; *Int'l*, pg. 1013

AMIR MOTARJEME—Catheters—Mallinckrodt Inc.; *U.S. Public*, pg. 1039

AMIRAN—NONE—Non-Reflecting Glass—Schott Glaswerke; *Int'l*, pg. 1523

AMISH KITCHEN—Egg Noodles—Lancaster Colony Corporation; *U.S. Public*, pg. 976

AMITONE—Antacid—Menley & James Laboratories, Inc.; *U.S. Public*, pg. 1086

AMITY—Leather Goods—AR Accessories Group, Inc.; *U.S. Private*, pg. 7

AMLINGS—Retail Florist—Amlings Flowerland; *U.S. Private*, pg. 66

AMLOK—Hydrant Hose Nozzle—American Cast Iron Pipe Co.; *U.S. Private*, pg. 51

AMMCO—Automotive Service Equip. & Tools—Ammco Tools, Inc.; *U.S. Public*, pg. 480

AMMCO TOOL—Brake Lathes, Lifts & Alignment—Hennessy Industries, Inc.; *U.S. Public*, pg. 481

AMMENS—Medicated Powder—Bristol-Myers Squibb Company; *U.S. Public*, pg. 253

AMMEX TAX & DUTY FREE SHOPS—U.S./Canadian Border Shops—Duty Free International, Inc.; *Int'l*, pg. 103

AMMO—Insecticide—FMC Corp., Agricultural Products Group; *U.S. Public*, pg. 605

AMMO GAS—Gas Generator—Seco Warwick Corporation; *U.S. Private*, pg. 980

AMMONYX—Surfactant—Stepan Company; *U.S. Public*, pg. 1514

AMMUNITION—20mm-30mm Calibres for Surface-to-Surface, Surface-to-Air Purposes—Balzers; *Int'l*, pg. 997

AMMUNITION—20mm - 35mm calibres—Oerlikon-Contraves AG; *Int'l*, pg. 998

AMOAID—Ammonia Inhalants—Scott Aviation; *U.S. Public*, pg. 622

AMOCAMS—Computerized Electronic Production Monitoring Equipment—Amoco Corporation; *U.S. Public*, pg. 101

AMOCO—Automotive Gasolines, Diesel Fuels, Furnace Oil—Amoco Oil Company; *U.S. Public*, pg. 102

AMOCO—Petroleum Products—Spencer Companies Inc.; *U.S. Private*, pg. 1024

AMOCO RESIN 18—Polystyrene—Amoco Corporation; *U.S. Public*, pg. 101

AMOCO SILVER—Gasoline—Amoco Corporation; *U.S. Public*, pg. 101

AMOCO SILVER—Lead Free Gasoline—Amoco Oil Company; *U.S. Public*, pg. 102

AMOCO XXV—Carpet Yarn—Amoco Corporation; *U.S. Public*, pg. 101

AMOCOR—Automobile Liner—Amoco Corporation; *U.S. Public*, pg. 101

AMODEL—Synthetic Resins—Amoco Corporation; *U.S. Public*, pg. 101

AMODEL POLYPTHALAMIDE—High Temperature Engineering Resins—Amoco Chemicals; *U.S. Public*, pg. 101

AMOLUBE—Lubricants—Amoco Corporation; *U.S. Public*, pg. 101

AMOPAVE—Geotextiles—Amoco Corporation; *U.S. Public*, pg. 101

AMOPLEX—Polypropylene Resins—Amoco Chemicals; *U.S. Public*, pg. 102

AMOR LIFT—Chip Processing Wringers—Mayfran International, Inc.; *Int'l*, pg. 1397

AMORA—Condiments—Danone Group; *Int'l*, pg. 379

AMORE—Pet food—H.J. Heinz Company; *U.S. Public*, pg. 805

AMORE—Cat Food—Star-Kist Foods Inc.; *U.S. Public*, pg. 805

AMORE—Canned Cat Food—Star-Kist Foods, Inc.; *U.S. Public*, pg. 805

AMORLINE—Bullet Resistance Entrances and Framing—Kawneer Company; *U.S. Public*, pg. 60

AMOS—Electronic Computing Equipment—Alpha Microsystems; *U.S. Public*, pg. 57

AMOXAL—Broad-Spectrum Antibiotic—SmithKline Beecham plc; *Int'l*, pg. 1264

AMOXI/CLAMOXYL—Amoxicillin—Pfizer Inc.; *U.S. Public*, pg. 1281

AMOXI-MAST—Intramammary Treatment of Mastitis—SmithKline Beecham plc; *Int'l*, pg. 1264

AMOXIL—Broad Spectrum Antibiotic—SmithKline Beecham Corporation; *Int'l*, pg. 1264

AMOXIL—Pharmaceutical Prods.—SmithKline Beecham Laboratories; *Int'l*, pg. 1264

AMOXIL—NONE—SmithKline Beecham Laboratorios Ltda.; *Int'l*, pg. 1266

AMOXIL—Anti-Infective—SmithKline Beecham plc; *Int'l*, pg. 1264

AMOXIL—Antibiotic—SmithKline Beecham Research Limited; *Int'l*, pg. 1266

AMOY—Chinese Sauces—Danone Group; *Int'l*, pg. 379

AMP-TRAP R RATED—Medium Voltage Motor Fuse—Gould Electronics Inc., Shawmut Circuit Protection Division; *U.S. Public*, pg. 1592

AUPCO—Commercial Industrial—American Metal Products; *U.S. Public*, pg. 1053

AMPCO—Alloys, Tools, Pumps—Ampco Metal Incorporated; *U.S. Private*, pg. 67

AMPCO-TRODE—Arc Welding Electrodes—Ampco Metal Incorporated; *U.S. Private*, pg. 67

AMPCO-WELD—Resistance Welding Products—Ampco Metal Incorporated; *U.S. Private*, pg. 67

AMPCOLOY—Alloys—Ampco Metal Incorporated; *U.S. Private*, pg. 67

AMPER ELASA—NONE—Amper, S.A.; *Int'l*, pg. 1372

AMPER IBERSEGUR—NONE—Amper, S.A.; *Int'l*, pg. 1372

AMPER PATOS—NONE—Amper, S.A.; *Int'l*, pg. 1372

AMPER PROGRAMAS—NONE—Amper, S.A.; *Int'l*, pg. 1372

AMPER TELEMATICA—NONE—Amper, S.A.; *Int'l*, pg. 1372

AMPEREX—Imaging Devices—Philips Electronics N.V.; *Int'l*, pg. 1051

AMPEREX—Electronics—Richardson Electronics, Ltd.; *U.S. Public*, pg. 1387

AMPERSAND—Auto Sound Accessories—Recoton Corporation; *U.S. Public*, pg. 1369

AMPHOCIL—Lipid-Complexed Ampjoterium B—Sequus Pharmaceuticals, Inc.; *U.S. Public*, pg. 1460

AMPHOSOL—Surfactant-Betaines—Stepan Company; *U.S. Public*, pg. 1514

AMPHOTEC—Lipid-Complexed Amphoterium B—Sequus Pharmaceuticals, Inc.; *U.S. Public*, pg. 1460

AMPHOTERGE—Amphoteric Surfactant—Lonza Inc.; *Int'l*, pg. 67

AMPHOTO—Books on Photography—BPI Communications Inc.; *Int'l*, pg. 1446

AMPICLOX—Anti-Infective—SmithKline Beecham plc; *Int'l*, pg. 1264

AMPICLOX—Antibiotic—SmithKline Beecham Research Limited; *Int'l*, pg. 1266

AMPINE—Industrial Particleboard—Georgia-Pacific Corporation; *U.S. Public*, pg. 735

AMPLEX—Superabrasives—Carborundum Abrasives North America; *Int'l*, pg. 1174

AMPLIFIRE—Heat Extractor—Byers Portland Willamette; *U.S. Private*, pg. 191

AMPMISER—Power Distribution Equipment—Controlled Power (CPC); *Int'l*, pg. 74

AMPROL—Amprolium—Merck & Co., Inc.; *U.S. Public*, pg. 1090

AMPROTECTION—Coccidiosis Control Program Services—Merck & Co., Inc.; *U.S. Public*, pg. 1090

AMPTRAN—Clamp-On Current Transformer—Amprobe Instrument; *U.S. Public*, pg. 1676

AMPTROL—Accessory—The Lincoln Electric Company; *U.S. Public*, pg. 996

AMREP—Land Developers & Magazine & Book Distributors—AMREP Corporation; *U.S. Public*, pg. 104

AMRES—Synthetic Resins Used in Manufacturing Paper—Georgia-Pacific Corporation; *U.S. Public*, pg. 735

AMSET—Fixative Resins—Georgia-Pacific Corporation; *U.S. Public*, pg. 735

AMSO—Alpha Microsystems Services Operations—Alpha Microsystems; *U.S. Public*, pg. 57

AMSTED INDUSTRIES—Manufacturer of Railroad Freight Car Products—Amsted Industries Incorporated; *U.S. Private*, pg. 68

AMSTEL—Beer—Heineken N.V.; *Int'l*, pg. 608

AMSTEL LIGHT—Beer—Heineken USA Inc.; *Int'l*, pg. 608

Brand Name Index

Brand Name Index

AMSTONE—Repair Products; Roof & Foundation Coatings—American Stone-Mix, Inc.; *U.S. Private*, pg. 62

AMSTRAD—NONE—Betacom Plc; *Int'l*, pg. 193

AMSYS—Paging Control System—Altec Lansing Corp.; *U.S. Private*, pg. 479

AMTECH—Electronic Identification Device—Amtech Corporation; *U.S. Public*, pg. 105

AMTEX—Latex Dipped Laboratory Grade Tubing—Minor Rubber Co., Inc.; *U.S. Private*, pg. 751

AMTOTE—Electronic Components—General Instrument Corporation; *U.S. Public*, pg. 716

AMTRAK—National Passenger Rail System—Amtrak-National Railroad Passenger Corp.; *U.S. Private*, pg. 68

AMTRAN—School & Commercial Bus—AmTran Corporation; *U.S. Public*, pg. 1167

AMTRAN CONVENTIONAL—School & Commercial Bus—AmTran Corporation; *U.S. Public*, pg. 1167

AMTRAN GENESIS—School & Commercial Bus—AmTran Corporation; *U.S. Public*, pg. 1167

AMTRAN RE—School & Commercial Bus—AmTran Corporation; *U.S. Public*, pg. 1167

AMTRAN VANGUARD—School & Commercial Bus—AmTran Corporation; *U.S. Public*, pg. 1167

AMTUFF—Can Liners—Amcel Corp.; *U.S. Private*, pg. 48

AMUSEMENT BUSINESS—Magazine; Directories—BPI Communications Inc.; *Int'l*, pg. 1446

AMWAY—Home Care Housewares & Personal Care Products—Amway Corporation; *U.S. Private*, pg. 69

AMWAY AUTO NETWORK—Auto Services—Amway Corporation; *U.S. Private*, pg. 69

AMWAY REALTY NETWORK, INC.—Realty Services—Amway Corporation; *U.S. Private*, pg. 69

AMY ALISON—Catalog Sales of American Greetings Stationery & Gift Items—Artistic Greetings, Inc.; *U.S. Public*, pg. 136

AMY BYER—Girls' (7-14) Sportswear—Byer California; *U.S. Private*, pg. 191

AMY TOO—Girls' (7-14) Dresses—Byer California; *U.S. Private*, pg. 191

AMYTAL—Amobarbital, Lilly—Eli Lilly and Company; *U.S. Public*, pg. 992

AMYTAL SODIUM—Amobarbital Sodium, Lilly—Eli Lilly and Company; *U.S. Public*, pg. 992

AN-DU-SEPTIC—Blackboard Chalks—Binney & Smith Inc.; *U.S. Private*, pg. 496

ANACHLOR—Disinfection Products—Bailey, Fischer & Porter Company; *Int'l*, pg. 449

ANACHLOR II—Dinfection Product—Bailey, Fischer & Porter Company; *Int'l*, pg. 449

ANACIN—Analgesic Tablets And Caplets—American Home Products Corporation; *U.S. Public*, pg. 79

ANACIN—Analgesic Tablets & Caplets—Whitehall-Robins Healthcare; *U.S. Public*, pg. 80

ANACONDA BOND—Bond Paper—Fort James Corporation; *U.S. Public*, pg. 670

ANADAC—Remote I/O Units—Analogic Corporation; *U.S. Public*, pg. 109

ANADEL—Color Pencils—Dixon Ticonderoga Company; *U.S. Public*, pg. 514

ANAFLUOR—Disinfection Product—Bailey, Fischer & Porter Company; *Int'l*, pg. 449

ANAFRANIL—NONE—Novartis Pharmaceuticals; *Int'l*, pg. 973

ANAIS ANAIS—Fragrance—Cosmair, Inc., Ralph Lauren Fragrance Division; *Int'l*, pg. 818

ANAIS ANAIS—Perfume—L'Oreal S.A.; *Int'l*, pg. 818

THE ANALOG ARTIST—Simulation, Layout & Verification Tools for Chip Design—Cadence Design Systems, Inc.; *U.S. Public*, pg. 290

ANALOG8—NONE—GenRad, Inc.; *U.S. Public*, pg. 731

ANALOG MASTER—NONE—NEC Electronics Inc.; *Int'l*, pg. 900

ANALOG WORKBENCH—Analog System & Board-Level Design—Cadence Design Systems, Inc.; *U.S. Public*, pg. 290

ANALYCOR—Behavioral Segmentation Program—NFO Research, Inc.; *U.S. Public*, pg. 1146

ANALYSIS—Network Mngmt. Software—Paradyne; *U.S. Private*, pg. 838

ANALYST—Motion Picture Cameras & Projectors, Video Cameras, Accessories & Recorders—Eastman Kodak Company; *U.S. Public*, pg. 550

ANALYTICAL DEVELOPMENTS—Gas Analysis Instruments based on Infra-Red Technology—Halma p.l.c.; *Int'l*, pg. 589

ANALYTICHEM—Chemical Extraction Columns—Varian Associates, Inc.; *U.S. Public*, pg. 1710

ANAMODS—3 Dimensional Models of Anatomical Organs—American Educational Products; *U.S. Public*, pg. 71

ALANAP—Herbicide—Uniroyal Chemical Company, Inc.; *U.S. Public*, pg. 460

ANANXYL—Pharmaceutical—L'Oreal S.A.; *Int'l*, pg. 818

ANAPROX—Naproxen Sodium—Roche Holding Ltd.; *Int'l*, pg. 1119

ANAPROX—Naproxen Sodium—Syntex; *Int'l*, pg. 1120

ANAREN—Microwave Assemblies, Subassemblies & Components—Anaren Microwave Inc.; *U.S. Public*, pg. 110

ANASTAR—Photographic Lenses—Eastman Kodak Company; *U.S. Public*, pg. 550

ANASTON—Photo Lenses—Eastman Kodak Company; *U.S. Public*, pg. 550

ANATRIEVE—Software—Anacomp, Inc.; *U.S. Public*, pg. 106

ANAVAC—Residual Gas Analyzer—Edwards High Vacuum, International; *Int'l*, pg. 121

ANBESOL—NONE—American Home Products Corporation; *U.S. Public*, pg. 79

ANBESOL—Antiseptic & Anesthetic Liquid & Gel—Whitehall-Robins Healthcare; *U.S. Public*, pg. 80

ANCEF—Pharmaceutical—SmithKline Beecham Corporation; *Int'l*, pg. 1264

ANCEF—Anti-Infective—SmithKline Beecham plc; *Int'l*, pg. 1264

ANCHOR—Bandshell—Anchor Industries Inc.; *U.S. Private*, pg. 71

ANCHOR—Division Servicing the Livestock Producer—Boehringer Ingelheim Animal Health Inc.; *Int'l*, pg. 199

ANCHOR—NONE—Coats Viyella plc; *Int'l*, pg. 299

ANCHOR—Beer—Heineken N.V.; *Int'l*, pg. 608

ANCHOR—Fernleaf Fern—New Zealand Dairy Board; *Int'l*, pg. 923

ANCHOR—Brushes—Philips Electronics N.V.; *Int'l*, pg. 1051

ANCHOR—Meter Sockets—Thomas & Betts Corporation; *U.S. Public*, pg. 1597

ANCHOR—Chainlink—Walpole Woodworkers, Inc.; *U.S. Private*, pg. 1148

ANCHOR BRAND—Hardware—North & Judd; *U.S. Private*, pg. 804

ANCHOR/DARLING—Valves—Flowserve Corporation; *U.S. Public*, pg. 658

ANCHOR/DARLING VALVES—Valves—BW/IP International, Inc.; *U.S. Public*, pg. 658

ANCHOR DIE CAST—Aluminum Die Cast Products—Premier Metal Products Co.; *U.S. Private*, pg. 881

ANCHOR DIE SETS—Plain Bearing & Ball Bearing Die Sets—Anchor Lamina Inc.; *Int'l*, pg. 75

ANCHOR-DOWN—Specialty Nails—Maze Nails; *U.S. Private*, pg. 718

ANCHOR FENCE—Fencing Material—Premier Metal Products Co.; *U.S. Private*, pg. 881

ANCHOR HOCKING—Glassware, Plasticware & Packaging Products—Newell Co.; *U.S. Public*, pg. 1176

ANCHOR LIBERTY ALE—Ale—Wisdom Imports Sales Co. Inc.; *Int'l*, pg. 679

ANCHOR PORTER—Porter—Wisdom Imports Sales Co. Inc.; *Int'l*, pg. 679

ANCHOR PRESS—Religious Books—Bertelsmann AG; *Int'l*, pg. 189

ANCHOR REIN—Boat Equipment—Attwood Corporation; *U.S. Private*, pg. 1038

ANCHOR STEAM BEER—Beer—Wisdom Imports Sales Co. Inc.; *Int'l*, pg. 679

ANCHOR STREAM—Beer—Labatt U.S.A.; *Int'l*, pg. 679

ANCHOR SWAN—Hoses—Mark IV Industries Inc.; *U.S. Public*, pg. 1044

ANCHOR WHEAT BEER—Beer—Wisdom Imports Sales Co. Inc.; *Int'l*, pg. 679

ANCHORLOK—Heavy-Duty Parking & Emergency Brakes—Neway Anchorlok International Inc.; *U.S. Private*, pg. 796

ANCHORPAGE—Hypertevt Indexing & Abstracting Software for Use on InterNet Worldwide Web—Innovex, Inc.; *U.S. Public*, pg. 880

ANCO—Pasta—CSM N.V.; *Int'l*, pg. 243

ANCO—Cheese—Churny Company Inc.; *U.S. Public*, pg. 1288

ANCO—Wiper Blades—Cooper Automotive Division; *U.S. Public*, pg. 443

ANCO—Windshield Wiper Products—Cooper Industries, Inc.; *U.S. Public*, pg. 442

ANCON CCL—Fixings—Newmond PLC; *Int'l*, pg. 924

ANCOR—Corrosion Inhibitor—Air Products and Chemicals, Inc.; *U.S. Public*, pg. 30

ANCRE—Beer—Heineken N.V.; *Int'l*, pg. 608

ANDANTE—NONE—Porcelanite, Inc.; *Int'l*, pg. 573

ANDARIA—Novelty Rayon Filament—Asahi Chemical Industry Co., Ltd.; *Int'l*, pg. 83

ANDEAN—Wine—Penaflor S.A.; *Int'l*, pg. 1032

ANDERLEX—Non-Woven Abrasives—Anderson Products; *U.S. Private*, pg. 1181

ANDERLEX—Brush—Wilton Corporation; *U.S. Private*, pg. 1181

ANDERLON—Brush—Wilton Corporation; *U.S. Private*, pg. 1181

ANDERSEN—Wood Window Units, Patio Doors & Roof Windows—Andersen Corporation; *U.S. Private*, pg. 71

ANDERSEN 2000 INC.—AIR POLLUTION CONTROL PRODUCTS—Crown Andersen Inc.; *U.S. Public*, pg. 462

ANDERSON—Recreational Vehicle Hardware—Anderson Industries, Inc.; *U.S. Public*, pg. 599

ANDERSON—Brushes—Wilton Corporation; *U.S. Private*, pg. 1181

ANDERSON-BARROWS—Plumbing Fixtures—Watts Industries, Inc.; *U.S. Public*, pg. 1746

ANDERSON INSTRUMENTS—Recording Instrumentation—Crouch Supply Company, Inc.; *U.S. Private*, pg. 291

ANDERSON-LITTLE—Men's & Women's Apparel & Furnishings—Woolworth Corporation; *U.S. Public*, pg. 1777

ANDERSON-LITTLE—Women's & Men's Clothing & Furnishings—F.W. Woolworth Co.; *U.S. Public*, pg. 1777

ANDERSON PRETZELS—NONE—Anderson Bakery Co., Inc.; *U.S. Private*, pg. 65

ANDES—Candy—Brach & Brock Confections, Inc.; *U.S. Private*, pg. 163

ANDES CANDIES—Mint Chocolates—Andes Candies Inc.; *U.S. Private*, pg. 163

ANDIAMO—Luggage—Andiamo, Inc.; *U.S. Private*, pg. 73

ANDIAMO—Shoes—Craddock-Terry Inc.; *U.S. Private*, pg. 284

ANDOVER TOGS—Children's Clothing—Andover Togs, Inc.; *U.S. Public*, pg. 112

ANDRE—Wine—E. & J. Gallo Winery; *U.S. Private*, pg. 438

ANDRE GASTON & CIE—Wine—Leonard Kreusch, Inc.; *U.S. Private*, pg. 635

ANDRE GIROUD—Watches—Croton Watch Company & Nationwide Time; *U.S. Private*, pg. 291

ANDRE RICHARD—Bath Accessories (Ceramics)—Springs Industries, Inc.; *U.S. Public*, pg. 1499

ANDREA ANTI-NOISE—Acitve Noise Cancellation Technology—Andrea Electronics Corporation; *U.S. Public*, pg. 112

ANDREOTTI'S—NONE—Harrah's Entertainment, Inc.; *U.S. Public*, pg. 790

ANDRES—Wine—Andres Wines Ltd.; *Int'l*, pg. 75

ANDREW BLUES—Jr. Sportswear Denim Tops—Andrew Sports Club Inc.; *U.S. Private*, pg. 73

ANDREW HARREY—NONE—Kellwood Company; *U.S. Public*, pg. 948

ANDREW JEANS—Jr. Denim Jeans-Jackests-Shorts—Andrew Sports Club Inc.; *U.S. Private*, pg. 73

ANDREW SPORTS—Jr. Sportswear (Ladies)—Andrew Sports Club Inc.; *U.S. Private*, pg. 73

ANDREWS—Dried Beef—E.W. Knauss & Son, Inc.; *U.S. Private*, pg. 626

ANDREWS ANTACID—NONE—SmithKline Beecham Corporation; *Int'l*, pg. 1264

ANDREWS LIVER SALTS—NONE—SmithKline Beecham Corporation; *Int'l*, pg. 1264

ANDREX—NONE—Kimberly-Clark Corporation; *U.S. Public*, pg. 958

ANDROID—Prescription Drug—ICN Pharmaceuticals, Inc.; *U.S. Public*, pg. 853

ANDY CAPP'S—Grain-Based Snacks—GoodMark Foods, Inc.; *U.S. Public*, pg. 751

ANDY DANDYTALE—Children's Character—Dairy Queen Corporate Store; *U.S. Public*, pg. 220

ANDYBURGER—1/4lb. Hamburger—Andy's Restaurants Inc.; *U.S. Private*, pg. 74

ANDYPAK—Child's Meal With Toy—Andy's Restaurants Inc.; *U.S. Private*, pg. 74

ANDY'S YOGURT—Frozen Yogurt Dessert—Andy's Restaurants Inc.; *U.S. Private*, pg. 74

ANECTINE—Pharmaceutical Product—Glaxo Wellcome PLC; *Int'l*, pg. 553

ANEJO—NONE—Carillon Importers, Ltd.; *Int'l*, pg. 409

ANEJO—Rum—La Tondena Distillers, Inc.; *Int'l*, pg. 785

ANEMOSTAT—Air Distribution Equipment—Dynamics Corporation of America; *U.S. Public*, pg. 286

ANEMOTHERM—Air Measuring Instruments—Anemostat Products; *U.S. Public*, pg. 286

ANEMOTHERM—Air Distribution Equipment—Dynamics Corporation of America; *U.S. Public*, pg. 286

ANEMOTRAK—Air Control Systems—Anemostat Products; *U.S. Public*, pg. 286

ANEMOTRAK—Air Distribution Equipment—Dynamics Corporation of America; *U.S. Public*, pg. 286

ANESCO—Electrical Equipment—ANESCO; *U.S. Private*, pg. 74

ANESTACON—Prescription Pharmaceutical—PolyMedica Industries, Inc.; *U.S. Public*, pg. 1315

ANEXATE—Central Nervous System Pharmaceutical—Roche Holding Ltd.; *Int'l*, pg. 1119

ANEXSIA—Pharmaceutical Prods.—SmithKline Beecham Laboratories; *Int'l*, pg. 1264

ANGEL—Records—Capitol Records, Inc.; *Int'l*, pg. 428

ANGEL—Record Label—EMI Group plc; *Int'l*, pg. 426

ANGEL BOWZ—Bows—E-Z Bowz, Inc.; *U.S. Private*, pg. 352

ANGEL DUMPLIN'—Party Goods—American Greetings Corporation; *U.S. Public*, pg. 77

ANGEL SOFT—Disposable Paper Tissues, Bathroom Tissue, Towels & Napkins—Georgia-Pacific Corporation; *U.S. Public*, pg. 735

ANGEL TREADS—Slippers—R.G. Barry Corporation; *U.S. Public*, pg. 192

ANGELICA—Uniforms & Wearing Apparel—Angelica Corporation; *U.S. Public*, pg. 113

ANGELICA-PREST—Durable-Press Garments—Angelica Corporation; *U.S. Public*, pg. 113

ANGELITE—Flour—ADM Milling Co.; *U.S. Public*, pg. 128

ANGELS BY VICTORIA'S SECRET—NONE—Victoria's Secret Stores; *U.S. Public*, pg. 995

ANGIO-CONRAY—X-Ray Contrast Media—Mallinckrodt Inc.; *U.S. Public*, pg. 1039

ANGIO-PAK—X-Ray Contrast Media—Mallinckrodt Inc.; *U.S. Public*, pg. 1039

ANGIO-SET—I.V. Catheter Placement Set—Becton Dickinson & Company; *U.S. Public*, pg. 199

ANGIOCATH—Intravenous Catheter Placement Unit—Becton Dickinson & Company; *U.S. Public*, pg. 199

ANGIODYNAMICS—NONE—E-Z-Em, Inc.; *U.S. Public*, pg. 540

ANGIOPLUS—Mobile C-Arm X-Ray—Diasonics Ultra Sound, Inc.; *Int'l*, pg. 644

ANGLAMOL—Additive Concentrates for Preparing Lubricating Compositions—The Lubrizol Corporation; *U.S. Public*, pg. 1016

ANGLE CLAMP—Booster Cables—General Cable Corporation; *Int'l*, pg. 1486

ANGLE-FLO—Angeled Conveyors—Flomaster Div.; *U.S. Public*, pg. 75

ANGLER—Camper—Fleetwood Enterprises, Inc.; *U.S. Public*, pg. 650

ANGLER'S MAIL—Special Interest Magazine—IPC Magazines Limited; *Int'l*, pg. 651

ANGLETERRE—Stainless Steel Flatware—Dansk International Designs Ltd.; *U.S. Public*, pg. 261

ANGLING PLUS—Magazine—EMAP Pursuit Publishing; *Int'l*, pg. 451

ANGLING TIMES—Magazine—EMAP Pursuit Publishing; *Int'l*, pg. 451

ANGLO—Woolens & Worsteds—Anglo Fabrics Company, Inc.; *U.S. Private*, pg. 74

ANGLO—Oil & Gas Distribution—Repsol S.A.; *Int'l*, pg. 1104

ANGLOCK—Machine Vise—Kurt Manufacturing Co. Inc.; *U.S. Private*, pg. 637

ANHEUSER-BUSCH—Beer—Anheuser-Busch Companies, Inc.; *U.S. Public*, pg. 113

ANHEUSER-BUSCH—T-Shirts & Sweatshirts—Holoubek Inc.; *U.S. Public*, pg. 536

ANHEUSER MARZEN—Beer—Anheuser-Busch Companies, Inc.; *U.S. Public*, pg. 113

ANHOLT—Ash Trays—Willert Home Products, Inc.; *U.S. Private*, pg. 1177

ANIMAL CHATTER—Greeting Cards—American Greetings Corporation; *U.S. Public*, pg. 77

ANIMAL COLLECTION—Silverplate—Dansk International Designs Ltd.; *U.S. Public*, pg. 261

ANIMALE—Fragrances—Parlux Fragrances Inc.; *U.S. Public*, pg. 1264

ANITEC—NONE—Taylor Impression, Inc.; *U.S. Private*, pg. 1070

ANJOU—Seeds—Groupe Limagrain; *Int'l*, pg. 566

THE ANN ARBOR NEWS—Newspaper—Booth Newspapers, Inc.; *U.S. Private*, pg. 157

ANN RASKAS—Gourmet Candy—Gilliam Candy Brands; *U.S. Private*, pg. 454

ANN TAYLOR—Women's Clothing, Shoes, Accessories, Fragrance & Personal Care—AnnTaylor Stores Corporation; *U.S. Public*, pg. 116

ANN TAYLOR LOFT—Women's Clothing, Shoes, Accessories, Fragrance & Personal Care—AnnTaylor Stores Corporation; *U.S. Public*, pg. 116

ANNA—Magazine—Burda Holding GmbH & Co., KG; *Int'l*, pg. 233

ANNALS OF AMERICA—Books—Encyclopaedia Britannica, Inc.; *U.S. Private*, pg. 375

ANNE COLE COLLECTION—Designer Swimwear & Covers—Cole of California; *U.S. Public*, pg. 148

ANNE KLEIN—Shoes—Schwartz & Benjamin, Inc.; *U.S. Private*, pg. 974

ANNE KLEIN—Women's Jewelry—Swank, Inc.; *U.S. Public*, pg. 1543

ANNE KLEIN COLLECTIONS—Hosiery—Pennaco Hosiery; *U.S. Public*, pg. 483

ANNE KLEIN COUTURE—Women's Jewelry—Swank, Inc.; *U.S. Public*, pg. 1543

ANNE KLEIN II—Women's Jewelry—Swank, Inc.; *U.S. Public*, pg. 1543

ANNE LESLIE—Ladies Apparel—Movie Star, Inc.; *U.S. Public*, pg. 1140

ANNETTE HIMSTEDT—Collector Dolls—Mattel, Inc.; *U.S. Public*, pg. 1057

ANNOTATIVE ECG—Chart Paper—Ludlow Corporation; *U.S. Public*, pg. 1651

ANNTAYLOR, INC.—Women's Retail Clothing Stores—AnnTaylor, Inc.; *U.S. Public*, pg. 116

ANO-KLEEN—Chemical for Metal Finishing—Haviland Enterprises; *U.S. Private*, pg. 511

ANODEFLEX—Cathodic Protection Systems for Pipes & Tanks—Raychem Corporation; *U.S. Public*, pg. 1362

ANOLINE—Linear Servo Motors—Anorad Corporation; *U.S. Private*, pg. 75

ANORIDE—X-Y Stages—Anorad Corporation; *U.S. Private*, pg. 75

ANOROUND—Rotary Stages—Anorad Corporation; *U.S. Private*, pg. 75

ANQUAMINE—Epoxy Curing Agent—Air Products and Chemicals, Inc.; *U.S. Public*, pg. 30

ANRICORIT—Corrosion Preventives—Fuchs Petrolub AG Oel + Chemie; *Int'l*, pg. 517

ANSAFONE—Phone Answering System—Dictaphone Corp.; *U.S. Private*, pg. 1045

ANSCO—Cameras—Ansco Photo-Optical Products Corp.; *Int'l*, pg. 587

ANSELL—NONE—Pacific Dunlop Limited; *Int'l*, pg. 1021

ANSELL JONES—NONE—Glynwed International PLC; *Int'l*, pg. 554

ANSELMI—Cookies & Crackers—RJR Nabisco Holdings Corp.; *U.S. Public*, pg. 1354

ANSILEX—Kaolin for Coating & Filling Paper & Board—Engelhard Corporation; *U.S. Public*, pg. 582

ANSLEY—Flat Cable & Connectors—Thomas & Betts Corporation; *U.S. Public*, pg. 1597

ANSO—Fibers—AlliedSignal Inc.; *U.S. Public*, pg. 49

ANSO FIBERS—Allied Fibers—AlliedSignal Inc., Engineered Materials; *U.S. Public*, pg. 51

ANSO V—Fibers—AlliedSignal Inc.; *U.S. Public*, pg. 49

ANSO IV—Carpet Yarn—AlliedSignal Inc.; *U.S. Public*, pg. 49

ANSO IV HP—Fibers—AlliedSignal Inc.; *U.S. Public*, pg. 49

ANSO X—Fibers—AlliedSignal Inc.; *U.S. Public*, pg. 49

ANSO-TEX—Textures Nylon—AlliedSignal Inc.; *U.S. Public*, pg. 49

ANSO V.T.E.C.—Fibers—AlliedSignal Inc.; *U.S. Public*, pg. 49

ANSTAT—Antistatic Fabrics—Herculite Products, Inc.; *U.S. Public*, pg. 802

ANSULEX—Liquid Fire Suppresant for Kitchen Hood Systems—Ansul Incorporated; *U.S. Public*, pg. 1648

ANSULITE—AFFF Foam Agent—Ansul Incorporated; *U.S. Public*, pg. 1648

ANSWER—Pregnancy & Ovulation Test Kits—Carter-Wallace, Inc.; *U.S. Public*, pg. 309

THE ANSWER—Racquetball Shoes—Ektelon; *U.S. Private*, pg. 884

ANSWER—Toiletries—The Gillette Company; *U.S. Public*, pg. 743

THE ANSWER—Universal Life Insurance—Liberty Life Insurance Company; *U.S. Public*, pg. 992

ANSWER NOW—Home Pregnancy Kit—Carter Products, Canada; *U.S. Public*, pg. 310

ANSWER PRODUCTS—NONE—LDI, Ltd.; *U.S. Private*, pg. 639

ANSWER RACING—NONE—LDI, Ltd.; *U.S. Private*, pg. 639

THE ANSWER—Telephone Answering Machines—Sony Electronics; *Int'l*, pg. 1281

ANSWERTREE—Decision Tree Software—SPSS Inc.; *U.S. Public*, pg. 1420

ANTARES—Yag Laser—Coherent, Inc.; *U.S. Public*, pg. 395

ANTEGREN—NONE—Elan Corporation Plc; *Int'l*, pg. 435

ANTELL PLANK—Pre-Finished Laminate—Bruce Hardwood Floors; *U.S. Public*, pg. 1634

ANTENNA SPECIALISTS—Communications—Allen Telecom, Inc.; *U.S. Public*, pg. 45

ANTEPAR—Prescription Drug—Glaxo Wellcome PLC; *Int'l*, pg. 553

ANTEPLEGIA—Antegrade Cardioplegia Catheter—Baxter Research Medical, Inc.; *U.S. Public*, pg. 196

ANTERIOR PAK—Surgical Instruments—Alcon Laboratories, Inc.; *Int'l*, pg. 916

ANTHEM—Tall Fescue—Green Seed Co.; *U.S. Private*, pg. 477

ANTHES FUSEE—Highway Safety Flares—Gleason Corporation; *U.S. Public*, pg. 746

ANTHIO—Insecticides—Novartis AG; *Int'l*, pg. 971

ANTHIOMIX—Insecticides—Novartis AG; *Int'l*, pg. 971

ANTHONY—Pasta Products—Borden Italian Foods; *U.S. Private*, pg. 158

ANTHONY POWER LOG—Home Log—Anthony Forest Products Co., Inc.; *U.S. Private*, pg. 76

ANTHONY POWER PLANK—Scaffold Board—Anthony Forest Products Co., Inc.; *U.S. Private*, pg. 76

ANTHONY'S—Store Signeage Logos—C.R. Anthony Company; *U.S. Private*, pg. 1029

ANTHONY'S—Pasta—Borden, Inc.; *U.S. Private*, pg. 157

ANTHRADERM—Ethical Pharmaceuticals—Rhone-Poulenc Rorer - U.S.; *Int'l*, pg. 1110

ANTHRO—Ergonomic Chair Line—Harter; *U.S. Private*, pg. 581

ANTHRO 2—Ergonomic Chair Line—Harter; *U.S. Private*, pg. 581

ANTHROCAM—NONE—FARO Technologies, Inc.; *U.S. Public*, pg. 613

ANTHROPOLOGIE—NONE—Urban Outfitters, Inc.; *U.S. Public*, pg. 1700

ANTHROSPIRIT—Ergonomic Chair Line—Harter; *U.S. Private*, pg. 581

ANTHROTEC—Anti-Inflammatory—Monsanto Company; *U.S. Public*, pg. 1124

ANTI-HUMAN GLOBULIN REAGENTS—Globulin Reagents—Ortho Clinical Diagnostic Systems Inc.; *U.S. Public*, pg. 929

ANTI-ITCH—Dermatological Products—S.C. Johnson & Son, Inc.; *U.S. Private*, pg. 592

ANTIBODY ENHANCEMENT MEDIA—Antibodies—Ortho Clinical Diagnostic Systems Inc.; *U.S. Public*, pg. 929

ANTICA TRADIZIONE—Toiletries—SmithKline Beecham plc; *Int'l*, pg. 1264

ANTIGUA—Broadloom—Couristan Inc.; *U.S. Private*, pg. 279

ANTIGUA—Cork Wall Panelling—Dodge Regupol, Inc.; *U.S. Private*, pg. 337

ANTIMINTH—NONE—Pfizer Inc.; *U.S. Public*, pg. 1281

ANTIMONY OXIDE AMSPEC SELECT—High Tint Performance Flame Retardants—Amspec Chemical Corporation; *U.S. Private*, pg. 67

ANTIMONY OXIDE KR GRADE—High Tint Performance Flame Retardants—Amspec Chemical Corporation; *U.S. Private*, pg. 67

ANTIMONY OXIDE KR GRADE SUPERFINE—Low Tint Performance Flame Retardants—Amspec Chemical Corporation; *U.S. Private*, pg. 67

ANTIMONY OXIDE LTS—Low Tint Performance Flame Retardants—Amspec Chemical Corporation; *U.S. Private*, pg. 67

ANTIPHLOGISTINE—Poultice Dressing—Medtech Inc.; *U.S. Private*, pg. 728

ANTIPHLOGISTINE RUB A-535—Topical Analgesic—Carter Products, Canada; *U.S. Public*, pg. 310

ANTIQUE BIRCH COLONIAL—Kitchen Cabinets, Vanities & Installation—Georgia-Pacific Corporation; *U.S. Public*, pg. 735

ANTIQUE FORUM—Riverboat Cruise Trips—American Classic Voyagers Company; *U.S. Private*, pg. 380

ANTISEDAN—NONE—Pfizer Inc.; *U.S. Public*, pg. 1281

ANTISPASMINA COLICA AND PROCTOLYN—Gastroenterology—Recordati Industria Chimica e Farmaceutica S.p.A.; *Int'l*, pg. 1090

ANTIVENIN—Black Widow Spider Antivenin—Merck & Co., Inc.; *U.S. Public*, pg. 1090

ANTLER—Uniforms—M. Rubin & Sons Inc.; *U.S. Private*, pg. 949

ANTLIA—Hand Pump—Schleicher & Schuell, Inc.; *Int'l*, pg. 1206

ANTOINES—Dry Pasta—A. Zeregas Sons, Inc.; *U.S. Private*, pg. 1204

ANTONELLA BOCCHINO—Grappa—Paterno Imports Limited; *U.S. Private*, pg. 843

ANTONELLI MONTEFALCO ROSSO—Italian Wine—Laird & Company; *U.S. Private*, pg. 642

ANTONELLI SAGRANTINO DI MONTEFALCO—Italian Wine—Laird & Company; *U.S. Private*, pg. 642

ANTONIN RODET—Burgundy Wines—Canandaigua Wine Co.; *U.S. Public*, pg. 300

ANTONIO Y CLEOPATRA—Domestic Cigars—Consolidated Cigar Corporation; *U.S. Private*, pg. 690

ANTORAL—Oropharyngeal Disinfectant—Recordati Industria Chimica e Farmaceutica S.p.A.; *Int'l*, pg. 1090

ANTRA—Gastrointestinal Drug—Astra AB; *Int'l*, pg. 93

ANTRIL—Human Protein to Treat Inflammatory Disorders—Amgen Boulder, Inc.; *U.S. Public*, pg. 101

ANTRON—Nylon—Du Pont (E.I. Du Pont De Nemours & Co.); *U.S. Public*, pg. 530

ANTURANE—NONE—Novartis Pharmaceuticals; *Int'l*, pg. 973

ANUSOL—Pharmaceutical Products—Warner-Lambert Company; *U.S. Public*, pg. 1738

ANUSOL—Hemmorrhoidal Cream—Warner-Lambert Consumer Healthcare; *U.S. Public*, pg. 1739

ANVAS—Automatic Noise Vibration Analysis System—GenRad, Inc.; *U.S. Public*, pg. 731

ANVIL—Stainless Steel Flatware—Dansk International Designs Ltd.; *U.S. Public*, pg. 261

ANVIL—Luggage—Zero Corporation; *U.S. Public*, pg. 1791

ANVIL F DEVICE—Logo—Formica Corporation; *Int'l*, pg. 129

ANVILBOX—Corrugated Containers—International Paper Company; *U.S. Public*, pg. 901

ANXON—Treatment of Anxiety—SmithKline Beecham plc; *Int'l*, pg. 1264

ANY WHICH WAY—Curler/Stylers—Sunbeam Household Products; *U.S. Public*, pg. 1533

ANYCARD ATM—Automated Teller Machines—Tidel Engineering, Inc.; *U.S. Public*, pg. 1608

ANYDAY—Feminine Pads—Kimberly-Clark Corporation; *U.S. Public*, pg. 958

ANYNET—Computer System—International Business Machines Corporation; *U.S. Public*, pg. 895

ANYSTREAM—Shower Heads—Speakman Company; *U.S. Public*, pg. 1021

ANYTHING ELSE IS A SUBSTITUTE—Knitwear—Wigwam Mills, Inc.; *U.S. Private*, pg. 1175

ANYTHING GOES—NONE—Rubbermaid Incorporated; *U.S. Public*, pg. 1411

ANYTIME, ANYPLACE, ANYWEAR—Shoes—Johnston & Murphy Co.; *U.S. Public*, pg. 728

ANYTIME CARDS—Greeting Cards—American Greetings Corporation; *U.S. Public*, pg. 77

ANYWHERE—UHF Remote Control for Home Satellite TV Systems—Satellite Data Networks; *U.S. Public*, pg. 716

ANYWHERE CHAIR—Pneumatic Seating—The HON Co.; *U.S. Public*, pg. 772

ANYWHERE CHAIR—Office Furniture—HON Industries Inc.; *U.S. Public*, pg. 772

AOEXPERT/MVS—Computer System—International Business Machines Corporation; *U.S. Public*, pg. 895

AOLITE—Opthalmic Lens—American Optical Corporation; *U.S. Private*, pg. 60

AOSTA—Outsole—K-Swiss Inc.; *U.S. Public*, pg. 937

AOSTE—Meats (Europe)—Sara Lee Corporation; *U.S. Public*, pg. 1432

APACHE—Five and Six Panel Farm Gates—Butler Ventamatic Corp.; *U.S. Private*, pg. 190

APACHE—Fly Bait—Security Lawn & Garden Co.; *U.S. Private*, pg. 397

APACHE LONGBOW—Helicopter—Boeing Helicopter Division; *U.S. Public*, pg. 241

APACHI—Fuels & Fuel Gases—Air Products and Chemicals, Inc.; *U.S. Public*, pg. 30

APAK—Packing Drums of Fiber or Fiber with Metal Ends—Sonoco Products Company; *U.S. Public*, pg. 1485

APATATE—B-Complex Supplement for Nutritional Deficiencies Associated With Illness—Bradley Pharmaceuticals; *U.S. Public*, pg. 249

APATATE—Liquid; Tablets; B-Complex Supplement for Nutritional Deficiencies—Doak Dermatologics; *U.S. Public*, pg. 250

APATATE FORTE—High-Potency Nutritional Supplement Containing 8 Essential Vitamins—Bradley Pharmaceuticals; *U.S. Public*, pg. 249

APATATE FORTE—High-Potency Nutritional Supplement Containing 8 Essential Vitamins—Doak Dermatologics; *U.S. Public*, pg. 250

APEC HT—Polycarbonate Thermoplastic—Bayer AG; *Int'l*, pg. 171

APECS ELECTRONIC GOVERNOR—Isochronous Device to Control Engine Speed—Synchro-Start Products, Inc.; *U.S. Private*, pg. 627

APELCO—NONE—Raytheon Marine; *U.S. Public*, pg. 1366

APERIO—Health Drink—Shiseido Company Ltd.; *Int'l*, pg. 1235

APEROL—Aperitif—Allied Domecq PLC; *Int'l*, pg. 62

APEROL—Aperitif—Barbero 1891 SpA; *Int'l*, pg. 164

APEROL JODA—Aperitif—Barbero 1891 SpA; *Int'l*, pg. 164

APEX—Heat Recovery Equipment—ABB Air Preheater Inc.; *Int'l*, pg. 3

APEX—Stove—The Canadian Coleman Co., Ltd.; *U.S. Public*, pg. 691

APEX—Screwdriver Bits, Impact Sockets & Universal Joints—Cooper Industries, Inc.; *U.S. Public*, pg. 442

APEX—Conveyor Belts—EEI Corporation; *Int'l*, pg. 425

APEX—Weightlifting Glove—Ektelon; *U.S. Private*, pg. 884

APEX—Nuclear Medicine Systems—Elscint Ltd.; *Int'l*, pg. 450

APEX—ATM-Asynchronus Transfer Mode Switch—General Datacomm Industries, Inc.; *U.S. Public*, pg. 708

APEX—Thinner—Jones Blair Company; *U.S. Private*, pg. 596

APEX—Personal Care Products—Knomark; *U.S. Private*, pg. 627

APEX—NONE—McRae Industries, Inc.; *U.S. Public*, pg. 1073

APEX—Stationery Products—The Mead Corporation; *U.S. Public*, pg. 1074

APEX—Office Supplies—Mead School & Office Products; *U.S. Public*, pg. 1074

APEX—Mushroom Growing Additive—Novartis AG; *Int'l*, pg. 971

APEX—High End Security Systems—Pittway Corporation; *U.S. Public*, pg. 1305

APEX—Large AC Induction Motors—Rockwell International Corporation; *U.S. Public*, pg. 1397

APEX—Insect Growth Regulator—Sandoz Agro, Inc.; *Int'l*, pg. 974

APEX-91—Shotshell Press—Hornady Manufacturing Company; *U.S. Private*, pg. 539

APEX II—Stove—The Canadian Coleman Co., Ltd.; *U.S. Private*, pg. 691

APEX WILDERNESS—NONE—Imperial Schrade Corp.; *U.S. Private*, pg. 559

APIEZON—High-Vacuum Oils, Greases & Waxes—Avo International; *U.S. Private*, pg. 124

APISTAN—Insecticide—Novartis AG; *Int'l*, pg. 971

APITECH—OEM Electronic & Electrohydraulic Control Devices—Applied Power Inc.; *U.S. Public*, pg. 124

APMPOWER—PC Software for Evaluating MVS Application Efficiency—Programart Corporation; *U.S. Private*, pg. 890

APOGEE—Surgical Instruments—Alcon Laboratories, Inc.; *Int'l*, pg. 916

APOLLINARIS CLASSIC—Mineral Water—Apollinaris & Schweppes Gmbh & Co.; *Int'l*, pg. 78

APOLLINARIS LEMON—Mineral Water—Apollinaris & Schweppes Gmbh & Co.; *Int'l*, pg. 78

APOLLINARIS MEDIUM—Mineral Water—Apollinaris & Schweppes Gmbh & Co.; *Int'l*, pg. 78

APOLLO—Agricultural Chemical—AgrEvo USA Company; *Int'l*, pg. 1203

APOLLO—Monitors—Akron Brass Company; *Int'l*, pg. 1068

APOLLO—Ball Valves—Associated Process Controls; *U.S. Private*, pg. 92

APOLLO—Carpet Sweeper—Bissell Inc.; *U.S. Private*, pg. 145

APOLLO—Ball Valves—Conbraco Industries Inc.; *U.S. Private*, pg. 261

APOLLO—NONE—Giddings & Lewis Sheffield Measurement Systems; *Int'l*, pg. 1389

APOLLO—Smoke & Heat Detectors for Fire Alarm Systems—Halma p.l.c.; *Int'l*, pg. 589

APOLLO—Gasoline & Kerosene—Idemitsu Kosan Co., Ltd.; *Int'l*, pg. 659

APOLLO—Software—Information Resources, Inc.; *U.S. Public*, pg. 875

APOLLO—Cationic Corn Starches—Penford Corp.; *U.S. Public*, pg. 1269

APOLLO—Water Softening & Purification Equipment—RainSoft Water Treatment Systems; *U.S. Private*, pg. 78

APOLLO—Hair Dryer—Revlon-Realistic Professional Products, Inc.; *U.S. Private*, pg. 690

APOLLO—Mobile Homes—Wick Bldg. Systems Inc. Manufactured Homes Div.; *U.S. Private*, pg. 1174

APOSTROPHE—NONE—Sears, Roebuck and Co.; *U.S. Public*, pg. 1452

APPCO—Envelopes—American Paper Group, Inc.; *U.S. Private*, pg. 60

APPEDRINE—Diet Aid—Thompson Medical Company, Inc.; *U.S. Private*, pg. 1083

APPEL—Apparel—I. Appel Corporation; *U.S. Private*, pg. 78

APPELLA—Low-Moisture Fruit—Vacu-Dry Company; *U.S. Public*, pg. 1704

APPLAUD—Ag Chemical—AgrEvo USA Company; *Int'l*, pg. 1203

APPLAUSE—1600 cc Sedan—Daihatsu Motor Corporation, Ltd.; *Int'l*, pg. 364

APPLAUSE—Honeycomb Shades—Hunter Douglas, Inc.; *Int'l*, pg. 639

APPLAUSE—Distilled Water—Sime Darby Berhad; *Int'l*, pg. 1249

APPLE—Computers—Apple Computer, Inc.; *U.S. Public*, pg. 121

APPLE—NONE—Taylor Impression, Inc.; *U.S. Private*, pg. 1070

APPLE CHIPLETS—Dried Apple Ring Snack Food—FTI Foodtech International Inc.; *Int'l*, pg. 476

APPLE CINNAMON CHEERIOS—Cereal—General Mills, Inc.; *U.S. Public*, pg. 717

APPLE CINNAMON SQUARES—Apple Cinnamon-Filled Whole Wheat Biscuits—Kellogg Company; *U.S. Public*, pg. 947

APPLE CINNAMON TOASTY O'S—Cereal—Malt-O-Meal Company; *U.S. Public*, pg. 699

APPLE COSMETICS—Cosmetics & Fragrances—Tristar Corp.; *U.S. Public*, pg. 1640

APPLE DANDY—Apple Juice—Brooklyn Bottling Co. of Milton, NY; *U.S. Private*, pg. 171

APPLE EASE—NONE—Dena Corporation; *U.S. Private*, pg. 324

APPLE GRANDE—Dessert—Taco John's International, Inc.; *U.S. Private*, pg. 1066

APPLE JACK—Chewing Tobacco—Swisher International Group, Inc.; *U.S. Public*, pg. 1543

APPLE JACKS—Ready-Sweetened Apple & Cinnamon-Flavored Cereal—Kellogg Company; *U.S. Public*, pg. 947

APPLE MUNCHIES—Low-Moisture Fruit—Vacu-Dry Company; *U.S. Public*, pg. 1704

APPLE NEWTONS—Cookies—Nabisco Inc.; *U.S. Public*, pg. 1355

APPLE PLUS—Fruit Juice—Nestle Chocolate & Confection; *Int'l*, pg. 917

APPLE RAISIN CRISP—Flakes of Rice & Rye Cereal with Apples & Raisins—Kellogg Company; *U.S. Public*, pg. 947

APPLE SLICE—Fruit Soft Drink—Pepsi-Cola Company; *U.S. Public*, pg. 1277

APPLE SPORT—Uniforms—Angelica Corporation; *U.S. Public*, pg. 113

APPLE TIME—Apple Products—Knouse Foods Inc.; *U.S. Private*, pg. 627

APPLE IIC—Personal Computer—Apple Computer, Inc.; *U.S. Public*, pg. 121

APPLE IIE—Personal Computer—Apple Computer, Inc.; *U.S. Public*, pg. 121

APPLE IIGS—Personal Computers—Apple Computer, Inc.; *U.S. Public*, pg. 121

APPLEBEE'S & DESIGN—NONE—Applebee's International, Inc.; *U.S. Public*, pg. 122

APPLEBEE'S NEIGHBORHOOD GRILL & BAR—Restaurants—Applebee's International, Inc.; *U.S. Public*, pg. 122

APPLEBEE'S NEIGHBORHOOD GRILL & BAR & DESIGN—NONE—Applebee's International, Inc.; *U.S. Public*, pg. 122

APPLESEED'S—Apparel & Gifts—Johnny Appleseed's, Inc.; *U.S. Private*, pg. 590

APPLETON—Converter Paper—Appleton Papers Inc.; *Int'l*, pg. 567

APPLI—Overlay Paper—The Mead Corporation; *U.S. Public*, pg. 1074

APPLIANCE CARE—NONE—Western Resources, Inc.; *U.S. Public*, pg. 1759

APPLICATION RESTART CONTROL—NONE—BMC Software, Inc.; *U.S. Public*, pg. 162

APPLICATION SCOREWARE—Software—Fair, Isaac and Company, Inc.; *U.S. Public*, pg. 609

APPLICATION SYSTEM/400—Computer Systems—International Business Machines Corporation; *U.S. Public*, pg. 895

APPLICATION SYSTEMS—NONE—Great Plains Manufacturing, Inc.; *U.S. Private*, pg. 475

APPLICATIONS ATLAS—Service Program—BetzDearborn Inc.; *U.S. Public*, pg. 226

APPLICATION SYSTEM/ENTRY—Computer Systems—International Business Machines Corporation; *U.S. Public*, pg. 895

APPLIED CLINICAL TRIALS—Trade Periodical—Advanstar Communications; *U.S. Private*, pg. 22

APPLIED MATHEMATICS—Textbooks that Integrate Academic Concepts with Technical Applications—Goodheart-Willcox Publisher; *U.S. Private*, pg. 464

APPLIED PRODUCTS—Industrial Cooling—Heatcraft, Inc.-Refrigeration Products Division; *U.S. Private*, pg. 659

APPRAISE—Clinical Densitometer—Beckman Instruments, Inc.; *U.S. Public*, pg. 199

APPRAISE JUNIOR—Low-Cost Densitometer—Beckman Instruments, Inc.; *U.S. Public*, pg. 199

APPSPAC—Applications Package—GenRad, Inc.; *U.S. Public*, pg. 731

APPTUNE—NONE—BMC Software, Inc.; *U.S. Public*, pg. 162

APRALAN—Animal Health—Elanco Animal Health; *U.S. Public*, pg. 993

APRALAN PREMIX—Apramycin Sulfate, Elanco—Eli Lilly and Company; *U.S. Public*, pg. 992

APRESAZIDE—NONE—Novartis Pharmaceuticals; *Int'l*, pg. 973

APRESOLINE—NONE—Novartis Pharmaceuticals; *Int'l*, pg. 973

APRIL-AIR—Humidifiers—Excelsior Manufacturing & Supply Corp.; *U.S. Private*, pg. 387

APRILAIRE—Whole-House Humidifiers—Research Products Corporation; *U.S. Private*, pg. 924

APRON—Gift Wrapping Paper—American Greetings Corporation; *U.S. Public*, pg. 77

APRON—Seed Dressing Product—Ciba Specialty Chemicals; *Int'l*, pg. 291

APRON—Seed Dressing Prod.—Novartis; *Int'l*, pg. 972

APTECON—Dispensers for Bath Tissue & Soap—Georgia-Pacific Corporation; *U.S. Public*, pg. 735

APTIN—Cardiovascular Agent, Beta-Blocker—Astra AB; *Int'l*, pg. 93

APTIVA—Personal Computer—International Business Machines Corporation; *U.S. Public*, pg. 895

APTOMIL—NONE—Milupa S.A.; *Int'l*, pg. 991

AQUA—Tub & Shower Units—Masco Corporation; *U.S. Public*, pg. 1052

AQUA-AIR—Water System Tank—A.O. Smith Corporation; *U.S. Public*, pg. 1476

AQUA-BAN—Pharmaceutical Products—Thompson Medical Company, Inc.; *U.S. Private*, pg. 1083

AQUA-BAN PLUS—Pharmaceutical Products—Thompson Medical Company, Inc.; *U.S. Private*, pg. 1083

AQUA BLASTER—Toy—Empire of Carolina, Inc.; *U.S. Public*, pg. 579

AQUA BORNE—Paint—Graham Paint and Varnish Company; *U.S. Public*, pg. 468

AQUA BOWL—Toilet Bowl Cleaner—Thetford Corporation; *U.S. Private*, pg. 352

AQUA CARE—Hand & Body Cream—Menley & James Laboratories, Inc.; *U.S. Public*, pg. 1086

AQUA CHEM—Boilers, Burners, Water Purification Equipment—Aqua-Chem Inc.; *Int'l*, pg. 824

AQUA CHEM—Swimming Pool Cleansers—Grow Group, Inc.; *Int'l*, pg. 663

AQUA CHEM—Swimming Pool Cleaners—ICI Paints; *Int'l*, pg. 664

AQUA-CLEER H-5—Drinking Water System—Culligan International Company; *U.S. Public*, pg. 467

AQUA-COIL—Waterbed Replacement mattress—Kingsdown, Inc.; *U.S. Private*, pg. 622

AQUA COOL LOGO—Bottle Water—Ionics, Incorporated; *U.S. Public*, pg. 912

AQUA CURL—Steam Hairsetter—Remington Products Company, L.L.C.; *U.S. Private*, pg. 921

AQUA EASE—Water Based Metal Cleaners—Hubbard Hall Inc.; *U.S. Private*, pg. 544

AQUA-FIBR—Corrugated—Boise Cascade Corporation; *U.S. Public*, pg. 242

AQUA FILTER—Disposable Cigarette Filter—Lee Pharmaceuticals; *U.S. Public*, pg. 984

AQUA FLECK—Multicolor - Water Based—California Products Corp.; *U.S. Private*, pg. 201

AQUA FOAM—Ensolite Foam—Stearns Manufacturing Company; *U.S. Public*, pg. 940

AQUA-FRESH—Oral Care—SmithKline Beecham plc; *Int'l*, pg. 1264

AQUA-GAUGE—NONE—Melnor Inc.; *U.S. Public*, pg. 1234

AQUA GLOSS—Paint—Pratt & Lambert United, Inc.; *U.S. Public*, pg. 1466

AQUA GUARD—Towels—Marcal Paper Mills, Inc.; *U.S. Private*, pg. 701

AQUA-GUN—NONE—Melnor Inc.; *U.S. Public*, pg. 1234

AQUA-HYDE—NONE—Lawter International, Inc.; *U.S. Public*, pg. 980

AQUA-IMAGE—Lithographic Plates, Chemicals, Equipment—Eastman Kodak Company; *U.S. Public*, pg. 550

AQUA-KEM—Liquid Holding Tank Deodorant—Thetford Corporation; *U.S. Private*, pg. 352

AQUA-KEM GREEN—Non-Toxic Liquid Holding Tank Deodorant—Thetford Corporation; *U.S. Private*, pg. 352

AQUA-KEM GREEN DRY—Non-Toxic Dry Holding Tank Deodorant—Thetford Corporation; *U.S. Private*, pg. 352

AQUA-KEM TOSS-INS—Unitized Dry Holding Tank Deodorant—Thetford Corporation; *U.S. Private*, pg. 352

AQUA-KOTE—Clay-Coated Carrier Board—Riverwood International Corporation; *U.S. Public*, pg. 1391

AQUA LAWN—Sprinkler Pump—Goulds Pumps, Incorporated; *U.S. Public*, pg. 860

AQUA-LUBE—Marine, Pool & Spa Grease—D.A. Stuart Company; *U.S. Private*, pg. 1048

AQUA LUNG—Scuba Diving Gear—U.S. Divers Co., Inc.; *U.S. Private*, pg. 1125

AQUA MAGIC—Perm Freshwater Flush Toilet—Thetford Corporation; *U.S. Private*, pg. 352

AQUA-MATE—Marine Head—Thetford Corporation; *U.S. Private*, pg. 352

AQUA MEPHYTON—Phytonadione—Merck & Co., Inc.; *U.S. Public*, pg. 1090

AQUA METER—Marine Products—Rule Industries, Inc.; *U.S. Public*, pg. 950

AQUA NET—Hairspray, Styling Aids—Chesebrough-Pond's USA Co.; *Int'l*, pg. 1435

AQUA NUCHAR—Carbonaceous Material—Westvaco Corporation; *U.S. Public*, pg. 1762

AQUA PLUS—NONE—Hudson, RCI; *U.S. Private*, pg. 546

AQUA PLUS—NONE—Lennox International Inc.; *U.S. Private*, pg. 659

AQUA-PORE—Synthetic Ion-Permeable Polymers for Use in Water Treatment—Ionics, Incorporated; *U.S. Public*, pg. 912

AQUA POWER—NONE—Morse Controls; *U.S. Public*, pg. 857

AQUA PREP—Filtration Products—Gelman Sciences, Inc.; *U.S. Public*, pg. 1253

AQUA-REZ—NONE—Lawter International, Inc.; *U.S. Public*, pg. 980

AQUA-ROYAL—Paints—Pratt & Lambert United, Inc.; *U.S. Public*, pg. 1466

AQUA-SATIN—Paints—Pratt & Lambert United, Inc.; *U.S. Public*, pg. 1466

AQUA SCOPE—Water Leak Detector—Heath Consultants Incorporated; *U.S. Private*, pg. 518

AQUA SENSOR—Water Softener—Culligan International Company; *U.S. Public*, pg. 467

AQUA SENTINEL—Coffee Makers—Regal Ware, Inc.; *U.S. Private*, pg. 917

AQUA-SHED—Rinse Aids for Metals—BetzDearborn Inc.; *U.S. Public*, pg. 226

AQUA SINK—Sinking Fly Line—Gladding Braided Products LLC; *U.S. Public*, pg. 291

AQUA SOFT—Fabric Softener & Neutralizer—Ecolab Inc.; *U.S. Public*, pg. 562

AQUA SOFT—2-Ply Toilet Tissue—Thetford Corporation; *U.S. Private*, pg. 352

AQUA-SORB—Clean Oils & Fuels From Water—Kelso Oil Company; *U.S. Private*, pg. 613

AQUA STRENGTH—Wet Strength Paper Label—Kal Grafx; *U.S. Private*, pg. 387

AQUA-TEX—Pleasure Boating Fabrics—Herculite Products, Inc.; *U.S. Public*, pg. 802

AQUA TOUR—Tire—The Kelly-Springfield Tire Company; *U.S. Public*, pg. 753

AQUA-VACTOR—Vacuum Pumps—Croll-Reynolds Company, Inc.; *U.S. Private*, pg. 290

AQUA VELVA—After Shave—Sara Lee Corporation; *U.S. Public*, pg. 1432

AQUA VELVA—Shaving Aid—SmithKline Beecham plc; *Int'l*, pg. 1264

AQUA ZYME—Enzymatic Waste Digester—Thetford Corporation; *U.S. Private*, pg. 352

AQUABASE—Autobody Refinish Paint—ICI Paints; *Int'l*, pg. 664

AQUABLOK—Coated Glass Fibers For Telecommunicatios—Owens Corning; *U.S. Public*, pg. 1236

Brand Name Index

AQUACHLORAL SUPPRETTES—Prescription Pharmaceutical—PolyMedica Industries, Inc.; *U.S. Public*, pg. 1315

AQUACLEAN—Small Vacuum—Advance Machine Company; *Int'l*, pg. 932

AQUACORR—Water Resistant Boxes Made of Corrugated Paper—Georgia-Pacific Corporation; *U.S. Public*, pg. 735

AQUACORR—Corrugating Medium—Riverwood International Corporation; *U.S. Public* pg. 1391

AQUADAG—Lubricants—Acheson Colloids Company; *U.S. Private*, pg. 12

AQUADENE—Potable Water Treatment Products—Met-Pro Corporation; *U.S. Public*, pg. 1100

AQUADEX—Waterborne Baking Enamel—The Dexter Corporation; *U.S. Public*, pg. 504

AQUAFILTER—Cigarette Holders, Disposable Filters—Scott's Liquid Gold-Inc.; *U.S. Public*, pg. 1447

AQUAFLEX—Soft Daily Wear Contact Lenses—Wesley-Jessen; *U.S. Private*, pg. 111

AQUAFOIL—Metal Pigments Fore Water Base Systems—United States Bronze Powders, Inc.; *U.S. Private*, pg. 1124

AQUAFRESH—Toothpaste—SmithKline Beecham Consumer Healthcare, U.S.; *Int'l*, pg. 1264

AQUAFRESH—Toothpaste—SmithKline Beecham Corporation; *Int'l*, pg. 1264

AQUAFRESH FLEX—Toothbrush—SmithKline Beecham Consumer Healthcare, U.S.; *Int'l*, pg. 1264

AQUAFRESH FLEX DIRECT—Toothbrush—SmithKline Beecham Corporation; *Int'l*, pg. 1264

AQUAFRESH TARTAR CONTROL—Toothpaste—SmithKline Beecham Consumer Healthcare, U.S.; *Int'l*, pg. 1264

AQUAGLOSS—High Gloss Overprint Lacquer—Raffi & Swanson, Inc.; *U.S. Private*, pg. 907

AQUAGUARD—Floor Coverings—Domco Inc.; *Int'l*, pg. 415

AQUAHEAT—NONE—Nordyne Inc.; *U.S. Public*, pg. 1193

AQUAID—NONE—Lawter International, Inc.; *U.S. Public*, pg. 980

AQUALANE—Paint—Pratt & Lambert United, Inc.; *U.S. Public*, pg. 1466

AQUALINE—Solder Paste—Alpha Metals, Inc.; *Int'l*, pg. 328

AQUALINK RS DIGITAL CONTROLS—NONE—Teledyne Laars/Jandy Products; *U.S. Public*, pg. 43

AQUALISA—Showers—Newmond PLC; *Int'l*, pg. 924

AQUALITY—Pool/Spa—Sta-Rite Water Systems; *U.S. Public*, pg. 1767

AQUALOID—Paints—Essex Chemical Corporation; *U.S. Public*, pg. 523

AQUALURE—Can Coatings—ICI Paints; *Int'l*, pg. 664

AQUALUX—NONE—Sico Inc.; *Int'l*, pg. 1239

AQUAMAGIC IV—Perm Fresh Water Toilet—Thetford Corporation; *U.S. Public*, pg. 352

AQUAMASTER RAUMA—(Rotatable Thrusters)—Vickers PLC; *Int'l*, pg. 1466

AQUAMATIC—Small Vacuum—Advance Machine Company; *Int'l*, pg. 932

AQUAMATIC—Valves for Flow Control in Water Treatment Apparatus—Osmonics, Inc.; *U.S. Public*, pg. 1233

AQUAMET—Metal Precipitation Chemicals—Alco Chemical; *Int'l*, pg. 1435

AQUAMETER—Moisture Analyzer—Beckman Instruments, Inc.; *U.S. Public*, pg. 199

AQUAMITE—Multiple Chamber ED Equipment for Demineralizing Water—Ionics, Incorporated; *U.S. Public*, pg. 912

AQUAMIX—Chemical Dispersions in Water—Harwick Standard Distribution Corporation; *U.S. Private*, pg. 509

AQUANEL—Insulating Varnishes—Schenectady International, Inc.; *U.S. Private*, pg. 969

AQUANIDE—Magnetic Material—SPS Technologies, Inc.; *U.S. Public*, pg. 1419

AQUAPART—Foundry Release Agent—Hill & Griffith Company; *U.S. Private*, pg. 529

AQUAPATCH—Roof Cement—Johns Manville Corporation; *U.S. Public*, pg. 927

AQUAPEDIC—Gel & Foam Flotation Mattresses—Graham-Field Health Products, Inc.; *U.S. Public*, pg. 757

AQUAPEL—Sizing Agent—Hercules Incorporated; *U.S. Public*, pg. 809

AQUAPHOR—Ointment & Burn Dressings—Beiersdorf, Inc.; *Int'l*, pg. 182

AQUAPLEX—Drilling Fluid Additive—Georgia-Pacific Corporation; *U.S. Public*, pg. 735

AQUAPON—Epoxy Coating, Primers & Thinners—PPG Industries, Inc.; *U.S. Public*, pg. 1245

AQUAPULSE—Marine Seismic Impulse Source—Litton Industries, Inc.; *U.S. Public*, pg. 1002

AQUAPURE—Waste Water Treatment Products—Hubbard Hall Inc.; *U.S. Private*, pg. 544

AQUARESS—Hand & Body Soap—SBS Products, Inc.; *U.S. Private*, pg. 955

AQUAREZ—Resins—Eastman Chemical Company; *U.S. Public*, pg. 550

AQUARIUS—Electric Water Coolers & Dehumidifiers—Oasis Corp.; *U.S. Private*, pg. 810

AQUARIUS—Ski Rope—Outdoor Technologies Group; *U.S. Private*, pg. 822

AQUAS MINERALES—Mineral Water—Penaflor S.A.; *Int'l*, pg. 1032

AQUASEAT—Gel Wheelchair Cushion—Graham-Field Health Products, Inc.; *U.S. Public*, pg. 757

AQUASEPT—Small Wet Electrostatic Precipitator—United McGill Corp.; *U.S. Private*, pg. 1122

AQUASPORT—Offshore Fishing Boats—Genmar Holdings, Inc.; *U.S. Private*, pg. 447

AQUASSAGER—Wet & Dry Massager—Pollenex; *U.S. Public*, pg. 1391

AQUASTAB—Chemical Additive—Eastman Chemical Company; *U.S. Public*, pg. 550

AQUASTAB—Stabilizers—Eastman Kodak Company; *U.S. Public*, pg. 550

AQUASTORM—Cleaning Systems—Electrovert; *Int'l*, pg. 328

AQUASUN—NONE—Pfizer Inc.; *U.S. Public*, pg. 1281

AQUATAC—Tackifier Resin Dispersions—Arizona Chemical Div.; *U.S. Public*, pg. 901

AQUATECH—NONE—Ganin Tire Co., Inc.; *U.S. Private*, pg. 439

AQUATENSEN—AntiHypertensive Diuretic—Wallace Laboratories; *U.S. Public*, pg. 310

AQUATEX—Pattern Glass—AFG Industries, Inc.; *Int'l*, pg. 84

AQUATHENE—Ethylene-Vinylsilane Copolymer Resins—Millennium Petrochemicals, Inc.; *Int'l*, pg. 594

AQUATHERM—NONE—Hudson, RCI; *U.S. Private*, pg. 546

AQUATINIC—Fluorescent Lamp—Duro-Test Corporation; *U.S. Public*, pg. 349

AQUATREAT—Water Treatment Chemicals—Alco Chemical; *Int'l*, pg. 1435

AQUATRED—Wet Traction Tire—The Goodyear Tire & Rubber Company; *U.S. Public*, pg. 752

AQUATREX—Multi Chamber Ultrasonic Cleaning Systems—L&R Manufacturing Co.; *U.S. Private*, pg. 638

AQUATRON—Small Vacuum—Advance Machine Company; *Int'l*, pg. 932

AQUATRON—Scientific Product-Glass—J. Bibby & Sons Plc; *Int'l*, pg. 167

AQUATRON—Electric Heater Portable—Slant/Fin Corporation; *U.S. Private*, pg. 1005

AQUEDUCT—Race Track—New York Racing Association; *U.S. Private*, pg. 795

AQUILAUN—Concentrate Delicate Fabric Wash—Stanhome Inc.; *U.S. Public*, pg. 1508

AQUIONICS—Ultraviolet Equipment for Water Sterilization & Disinfection—Halma p.l.c.; *Int'l*, pg. 589

AQUUS—Acrylic Whirlpools—Lasco Bathware; *Int'l*, pg. 1397

AR-EL—Resin Laminated Cores—Sonoco Products Company; *U.S. Public*, pg. 1485

AR-MET—Control Measurement—Brooks Instrument; *U.S. Public*, pg. 574

AR-MITE—Control Measurement—Brooks Instrument; *U.S. Public*, pg. 574

ARABESQUE—Hand Painted Ceramics—Dansk International Designs Ltd.; *U.S. Public*, pg. 261

ARABESQUE—Ceramic Wall Tile—Monarch Tile, Inc.; *U.S. Private*, pg. 287

ARAK RAZZOUK—Liqueur—Austin Nichols & Co. Inc.; *Int'l*, pg. 566

ARAL—Fuels—Burmah Castrol plc; *Int'l*, pg. 234

ARALDITE—Epoxy Resin—Ciba Specialty Chemicals; *Int'l*, pg. 291

ARALDITE—Epoxy Resin—Novartis; *Int'l*, pg. 972

ARALL—Laminates—Aluminum Company of America; *U.S. Public*, pg. 60

ARAMARK—Textile Maintenance Rental Service—Aramark Uniform Services, Inc.; *U.S. Private*, pg. 79

ARAMIS—Fragrance & Toiletries for Men—Estee Lauder Companies Inc.; *U.S. Public*, pg. 594

ARANDAS TEQUILA—Spirit—Allied Domecq PLC; *Int'l*, pg. 62

ARAPAHOE—Ceramic Wall Tile—Monarch Tile, Inc.; *U.S. Private*, pg. 287

ARAPAHOE BASIN—NONE—Ralcorp Holdings Inc.; *U.S. Public*, pg. 1359

ARATON—Roving, Strands, Mats, Chopped Fibers and Chopped Strands—Owens Corning; *U.S. Public*, pg. 1236

ARBITOR—Racquetball Eyewear—Ektelon; *U.S. Private*, pg. 884

ARBITRON—Radio Audience Measurement Rating System—The Arbitron Company; *U.S. Public*, pg. 331

ARBOR—Plywood & Paneling—Georgia-Pacific Corporation; *U.S. Public*, pg. 735

ARBOR ACRES—Breeding Stock for Broilers—Arbor Acres Farm, Inc.; *U.S. Public*, pg. 202

ARBOR DRUGS—Drugstores—Arbor Drugs, Inc.; *U.S. Public*, pg. 126

ARBOR GREEN—Tree & Lawn Care Services—The Davey Tree Expert Company; *U.S. Private*, pg. 314

ARBOR OAK—Plywood, Paneling & Roofing—Georgia-Pacific Corporation; *U.S. Public*, pg. 735

ARBORITE—Laminates for Furniture & Interior Decorating—Forbo Holding SA; *Int'l*, pg. 496

ARBOSAN—Seed Dressing Product—Novartis; *Int'l*, pg. 972

ARBOTECT—Fungicide for Dutch Elm Disease—Merck & Co., Inc.; *U.S. Public*, pg. 1090

ARBURG—Injection Molding Machines—Arburg, Inc.; *U.S. Private*, pg. 79

ARBY'S—Restaurant Chain—Triarc Companies, Inc.; *U.S. Public*, pg. 1634

ARC—Logical Computer System—Datapoint Corporation; *Int'l*, pg. 384

ARCA SWISS CAMERAS—6 x 9cm, 4" x 5", 8' x 10" Cameras—Calumet Photographic, Inc.; *U.S. Private*, pg. 202

ARCADE—Hotels—Accor S.A.; *Int'l*, pg. 20

ARCADE—Commercial Printers—Arcade Inc.; *U.S. Private*, pg. 79

ARCADE—Prefinished Wall Paneling—Georgia-Pacific Corporation; *U.S. Public*, pg. 735

ARCALOY—NONE—ESAB Welding & Cutting Products; *Int'l*, pg. 281

ARCELIK—Household Appliances—Arcelik A.S.; *Int'l*, pg. 741

ARCGATE—Data Communications Software—Datapoint Corporation; *Int'l*, pg. 384

ARCH DELUXE—Hamburger—McDonald's Corporation; *U.S. Public*, pg. 1068

ARCH PAGING—NONE—Arch Communications Group, Inc.; *U.S. Public*, pg. 127

ARCHER—Aircraft—The New Piper Aircraft, Inc.; *U.S. Private*, pg. 794

ARCHER—Antennas & Electronics—RadioShack; *U.S. Public*, pg. 1560

ARCHER DANIELS MIDLAND—Prepared Feeds & Feed Ingredients—Archer Daniels Midland Company (ADM); *U.S. Public*, pg. 127

ARCHER KIT—Hobby Kits—RadioShack; *U.S. Public*, pg. 1560

ARCHER'S—Spirits—Gilbeys of Ireland; *Int'l*, pg. 409

ARCHER'S—NONE—IDV Central Europe; *Int'l*, pg. 410

ARCHER'S—NONE—Tegner & Son AB; *Int'l*, pg. 412

ARCHER'S PEACH SCHNAPPS—NONE—GW Archer & Co.; *Int'l*, pg. 409

ARCHES—Fine Paper—Arjo Wiggins Appleton plc; *Int'l*, pg. 567

ARCHIBALD—Candy—Archibald Candy Company; *U.S. Private*, pg. 597

ARCHIFOLD—Drapery Hardware—Kirsch; *U.S. Public*, pg. 1176

ARCHITECH—Mounting Hardware Designed to Complement Surroundings—Vicon Industries, Inc.; *U.S. Public*, pg. 1719

ARCHITECTS & ENGINEERS PROTECTOR PLAN—NONE—Poe & Brown, Inc.; *U.S. Public*, pg. 1312

THE ARCHITECTS' JOURNAL—NONE—EMAP Business Communications Division; *Int'l*, pg. 451

ARCHITECTURAL CRITERION—Vinyl Composition Tyle—Kentile Operting Co.; *U.S. Private*, pg. 615

ARCHITECTURAL DIGEST—Magazine—Architectural Digest; *U.S. Private*, pg. 20

ARCHITECTURAL DIGEST—Magazine—The Conde Nast Publications Inc.; *U.S. Private*, pg. 20

ARCHITECTURAL LANDSCAPE—Lighting—JJI Lighting Group Inc.; *Int'l*, pg. 821

ARCHITECTURAL LIGHTING—Magazine—Miller Freeman Inc.; *Int'l*, pg. 1443

ARCHITECTURAL RESEARCH—NONE—EMAP Business Communications Division; *Int'l*, pg. 451

ARCHITECTURAL REVIEW—NONE—EMAP Business Communications Division; *Int'l*, pg. 451

ARCHITECTURAL TRIM—Moulded Woodwork—ABT Building Products Corporation; *Int'l*, pg. 20

ARCHITECTURE—Magazine—BPI Communications Inc.; *Int'l*, pg. 1446

ARCHITECTURE—Textbook Covering Techniques Used to Develop Working Drawings—Goodheart-Willcox Publisher; *U.S. Private*, pg. 464

ARCHITENT—Tent Fabrics—Herculite Products, Inc.; *U.S. Public*, pg. 802

ARCHITRAC—Drapery Hardware—Kirsch; *U.S. Public*, pg. 1176

ARCHIVAL MOUNT PLUS—Archival Quality Dry Mounting Colhesive—Seal Products Incorporated; *U.S. Public*, pg. 849

ARCHWAY—Cookies—Archway Cookies, Inc.; *U.S. Private*, pg. 80

ARCHWAY—Paperback Books for Young Adults & Children—Pocket Books; *U.S. Private*, pg. 777

ARCLINK—Data Communications Software—Datapoint Corporation; *Int'l*, pg. 384

ARCLIST—Microcomputer Software for US Mailers—Group 1 Software, Inc.; *U.S. Public*, pg. 417

ARCMAN-VXS—Six-Axis Welding Robots—Kobe Steel, Ltd.; *Int'l*, pg. 740

ARCNET—Local Area Network—Datapoint Corporation; *Int'l*, pg. 384

ARCNET PLUS—High Speed Area Network—Datapoint Corporation; *Int'l*, pg. 384

ARCO—Gasoline—Atlantic Richfield Company; *U.S. Public*, pg. 144

ARCO—Test Preparation—Simon & Schuster; *U.S. Private*, pg. 777

ARCO AIRE—HVAC Equipment—International Comfort Products; *U.S. Public*, pg. 898

ARCO AIRE—Heating & Cooling Products—International Comfort Products Corp.; *U.S. Public*, pg. 898

ARCOFLEX—Ungummed Paper Tape for Binding Pads, Binders & Books—FiberMark Inc.; *U.S. Public*, pg. 620

ARCOS—Welding Electrodes—Esab AB; *Int'l*, pg. 281

ARCOTE—Anti-Reflective Coatings—American Optical Corporation; *U.S. Private*, pg. 60

ARCSERVE FOR NETWARE, DOS, WINDOWS NT—Backup Software—Cheyenne; *U.S. Public*, pg. 420

ARCSERVE/OPEN—Backup Software for UNIX—Cheyenne; *U.S. Public*, pg. 420

ARCSOLO FOR WINDOWS OS/2—Backup for Stand-Alone PC's—Cheyenne; *U.S. Public*, pg. 420

ARCSTAT—Computer System Statistics Software—Datapoint Corporation; *Int'l*, pg. 384

ARCSYS—Local Area Network System Software—Datapoint Corporation; *Int'l*, pg. 384

ARCTIC—Plates—British Steel Plc; *Int'l*, pg. 220

ARCTIC BLAST—Semi-Frozen Carbonated Beverage—J & J Snack Foods Corporation; *U.S. Public*, pg. 916

ARCTIC CAPE—Fish Sticks & Portions—Frionor U.S.A. Inc.; *Int'l*, pg. 516

ARCTIC POWER—Detergent—Colgate-Palmolive Company; *U.S. Public*, pg. 397

ARCTIC SEAL—Underlayment—Herbert Malarkey Roofing Company; *U.S. Private*, pg. 698

ARCTICAR—Cryogenic Box Car—GATX Corporation; *U.S. Public*, pg. 690

ARCUS—NONE—Taylor Impression, Inc.; *U.S. Private*, pg. 1070

ARDEL—Polyarylate Resins—Amoco Corporation; *U.S. Public*, pg. 101

ARDELL—Cosmetic Accessories—American International Industries; *U.S. Private*, pg. 57

ARDELL—Knives, Blades, Scraper—Ardell Industries Inc.; *U.S. Private*, pg. 597

ARDELL BRUSH UPS—Cosmetic Brushes—American International Industries; *U.S. Private*, pg. 57

ARDEN BRAND—Homestyle Cuisine—Arden International Kitchens, Inc.; *U.S. Private*, pg. 972

ARDEN FOR MEN—Frangrance—Elizabeth Arden Company; *Int'l*, pg. 1435

ARDEN INTL. KITCHENS—Frozen Food Entrees—Arden International Kitchens, Inc.; *U.S. Private*, pg. 972

ARDENELLI'S—Italian Cuisine—Arden International Kitchens, Inc.; *U.S. Private*, pg. 972

ARDMORE—Manufactured Homes—Champion Enterprises, Inc.; *U.S. Public*, pg. 332

ARDMORE FARMS—Citrus & Fruit Juices—Ardmore Farms; *U.S. Public*, pg. 1348

ARDOR—Bond, Ledger, Mimeo, & Duplicating Papers—Georgia-Pacific Corporation; *U.S. Public*, pg. 735

ARDUAN—Pharmaceutical—Organon Inc.; *Int'l*, pg. 48

AREAMASTER—Floodlights for HPS, MV or MH Lamps—Appleton Electric Co.; *U.S. Public*, pg. 572

AREDIA—Drug for the Treatment of Tumour-Induced Hypercalcaemia & Bone Destruction—Novartis; *Int'l*, pg. 972

AREDIA—NONE—Novartis Pharmaceuticals; *Int'l*, pg. 973

ARELON—Herbicide—Hoechst Aktiengesellschaft; *Int'l*, pg. 624

AREO—Apparel—Young Stuff Apparel Group, Inc.; *U.S. Private*, pg. 1202

AREO SPORT—Apparel—Young Stuff Apparel Group, Inc.; *U.S. Private*, pg. 1202

ARGAL—Processed Meats—Sara Lee Corporation; *U.S. Public*, pg. 1432

ARGENT VODKA—NONE—Star Industries Inc.; *U.S. Private*, pg. 1034

ARGENTARIA—Financial Group—Argentaria Corporacion Bancaria de Espana, S.A.; *Int'l*, pg. 80

ARGININE GLUTAMIQUE—Treatment for Debility & Hepatic Disorders—SmithKline Beecham plc; *Int'l*, pg. 1264

ARGO—Corn Starch—Best Foods; *U.S. Public*, pg. 224

ARGO—Corn Starches; Edible Oil—Bestfoods; *U.S. Public*, pg. 223

ARGO—Corn Starch—CPC Foodservice Group; *U.S. Public*, pg. 224

ARGONAUT—Resilient Rubber Floor Tile—Burke Industries, Inc.; *U.S. Private*, pg. 183

ARGOSHIELD—Shielding Gases—The BOC Group Inc. (Delaware); *Int'l*, pg. 121

ARGOSYSTEMS—Electronic Reconnaissance Systems—ARGOSystems, Inc.; *U.S. Private*, pg. 240

ARGUS—Plasma Display Modules—Industrial Electronic Engineers, Inc.; *U.S. Private*, pg. 561

ARGUS—NONE—Landmark Graphics Corporation; *U.S. Public*, pg. 776

ARGUSTO DOLCETTO—Banfi Wine—Banfi Vintners; *U.S. Private*, pg. 113

ARGUSTO DOLCETTO D'AQUI—NONE—Castello Banfi Srl.; *U.S. Private*, pg. 113

ARGYLE—Types Of Products: Thoracic And Perfusion, Urological, & Gastrointestinal—American Home Products Corporation; *U.S. Public*, pg. 79

ARGYLE—Health Care Products—Sherwood-Davis & Geck; *U.S. Public*, pg. 80

ARGYLL—Waterproof Footwear—The Gates Rubber Company Ltd.; *Int'l*, pg. 1397

ARIA—Chip Pattern Rubber Floor Tile—Burke Industries, Inc.; *U.S. Private*, pg. 183

ARIAL—NONE—Porcelanite, Inc.; *Int'l*, pg. 573

ARIANE—Herbicide—The Dow Chemical Company; *U.S. Public*, pg. 522

ARICEPT—Donepezil—Pfizer Inc.; *U.S. Public*, pg. 1281

ARID FOAM—Small Vacuum—Advance Machine Company; *Int'l*, pg. 932

ARIDELL—Super Absorbent Polymer—AMCOL International Corp.; *U.S. Public*, pg. 63

ARIEL—Laundry Detergent—The Procter & Gamble Company; *U.S. Public*, pg. 1330

ARIEL—NONE—Procter & Gamble Espana S.A.; *U.S. Public*, pg. 1332

ARIEL—Detergent—Procter & Gamble Ltd.; *U.S. Public*, pg. 1332

ARIEL—NONE—Procter & Gamble Venezuela, C.A.; *U.S. Public*, pg. 1332

ARIES—NONE—Landmark Graphics Corporation; *U.S. Public*, pg. 776

ARIES—High Purity Loop, Disposable Cartridges—Osmonics, Inc.; *U.S. Public*, pg. 1233

ARIMAX 1000—Reaction Injection Molding Resins—Ashland, Inc.; *U.S. Public*, pg. 138

ARIMIDEX—Pharmaceutical—Zeneca Group Plc; *Int'l*, pg. 1524

ARIMUL—Agricultural Emulsifiers—Witco Corporation; *U.S. Public*, pg. 1773

ARIOSTEA—NONE—Florida Tile Industries, Inc.; *Int'l*, pg. 1322

ARIS—Business Announcement Systems—Electronic Tele-Communications, Inc.; *U.S. Public*, pg. 570

ARIS—Gloves, Knitwear, Slippers—Sara Lee Corporation; *U.S. Public*, pg. 1432

ARIS—Gloves & Knits—Totes/Isotoner, Inc.; *U.S. Public*, pg. 1433

ARISS—Cardioplegia Switch—Medtronic, Inc.; *U.S. Public*, pg. 1082

ARISTA—Sunglasses—Bausch & Lomb Incorporated; *U.S. Public*, pg. 194

ARISTA—Art Materials—Binney & Smith Inc.; *U.S. Private*, pg. 496

ARISTA—Hair Preparations—The Gillette Company; *U.S. Public*, pg. 743

ARISTALOY—Dental Amalgam—Engelhard Corporation; *U.S. Public*, pg. 582

ARISTOC—Stockings & Tights—Courtaulds Textiles Plc; *Int'l*, pg. 339

ARISTOCORT—NONE—Wyeth Australia Pty. Ltd.; *U.S. Public*, pg. 82

ARISTOCRAFT—Shoes—Johnston & Murphy Co.; *U.S. Public*, pg. 728

ARISTOCRAT—Bond Paper—The Mead Corporation; *U.S. Public*, pg. 1074

ARISTOCRAT—Preserves, Sauces—RCB Baking Company; *U.S. Public*, pg. 1354

ARISTOKRAFT—Cabinetry—Aristokraft, Inc.; *U.S. Public*, pg. 675

ARISTOKRAFT—Quality Kitchen Cabinets & Bathroom Vanities—MasterBrand Industries, Inc.; *U.S. Public*, pg. 675

ARISTON—NONE—Merloni Elettrodomestici S.P.A.; *Int'l*, pg. 860

ARISTOTLE 2000—Computer System—International Business Machines Corporation; *U.S. Public*, pg. 895

ARIZOLE—Pine Oil & Anethol—Arizona Chemical Div.; *U.S. Public*, pg. 901

ARIZONA—Public Electric Utility—APS; *U.S. Public*, pg. 1297

ARIZONA CARDINALS—Football Team—Arizona Cardinals; *U.S. Private*, pg. 81

ARIZONA JEANS CO.—Jeanswear—JC Penney Company, Inc.; *U.S. Public*, pg. 916

ARIZONA TEA—Soft Drink—Grant-Lydick Beverage Co.; *U.S. Private*, pg. 470

ARIZONA STONE—NONE—Porcelanite, Inc.; *Int'l*, pg. 573

ARIZONIAN—Steel-Belted Tire—Reinalt-Thomas Corp.; *U.S. Private*, pg. 919

ARK—Life Insurance—Allied Irish Banks, p.l.c.; *Int'l*, pg. 64

ARKALITE—Lightweight Aggregate—General Shale Products Corp.; *Int'l*, pg. 843

ARKANSAS CITY TRAVELER—Newspaper—Shivers Trading & Operating Co.; *U.S. Private*, pg. 994

Brand Name Index

ARKANSAS MANUFACTURERS REGISTER—Register—Manufacturers' News, Inc.; *U.S. Private*, pg. 700

ARKIN-Z TABLETS—Oral Cardiotonic—Otsuka Pharmaceutical Co., Ltd.; *Int'l*, pg. 1013

ARKLA—Natural Gas Utility—NorAm Energy Corp.; *U.S. Public*, pg. 843

ARKYL—Alkyl Chlorides—Akzo Nobel N.V.; *Int'l*, pg. 42

ARLBOND—Silicon Nitride-Bonded Silicon Carbide Wear Resistant Shapes—Ferro Corporation; *U.S. Public*, pg. 618

ARLCITE—Hi-Density, Hi-Alumina Wear Resistant Shapes—Ferro Corporation; *U.S. Public*, pg. 618

ARLIDIN—Ethical Pharmaceuticals—Rhone-Poulenc Rorer - U.S.; *Int'l*, pg. 1110

ARLINGTON HOUSE—Metal Household Furniture—Meadowcraft, Inc.; *U.S. Private*, pg. 725

ARLINGTON INTERNATIONAL RACECOURSE—Racecourse—The Levy Organization; *U.S. Private*, pg. 664

ARLINGTON TRACKSIDE—Restaurant—The Levy Organization; *U.S. Private*, pg. 664

ARLON—Laminated & Coated Products—Bairnco Corporation; *U.S. Public*, pg. 165

ARM & HAMMER—Household Kitchen & Laundry Products—Arm & Hammer Consumer Products; *U.S. Public*, pg. 356

ARM & HAMMER—Cleaning, Baking, Laundry Detergent & Deodorizing Products—Church & Dwight Co., Inc.; *U.S. Public*, pg. 355

ARM & HAMMER DENTAL CARE—Toothpaste, Gel & Tooth Powder—Church & Dwight Co., Inc.; *U.S. Public*, pg. 355

ARM & HAMMER PET FRESH—Carpet Deodorizer—Church & Dwight Co., Inc.; *U.S. Public*, pg. 355

ARMAC—Fatty Amine Salts—Akzo Nobel N.V.; *Int'l*, pg. 42

ARMACFLOTE—Cationic Blends—Akzo Nobel N.V.; *Int'l*, pg. 42

ARMADA—NONE—Acclaim Comics; *U.S. Public*, pg. 15

ARMAGRIP—Protective & Decorative Coatings—PPG Industries, Inc.; *U.S. Public*, pg. 1245

ARMAKLEEN—Aqueous Cleaner for Printed Wiring Assemblies—Church & Dwight Co., Inc.; *U.S. Public*, pg. 355

ARMALOY—Tool Bits, Alloy Steel Wrenches—Danaher Tool Group; *U.S. Public*, pg. 481

ARMASAFE—Recombination LA Batteries for Fighting Vehicles—Chloride Industrial Batteries Ltd.; *Int'l*, pg. 125

ARMCOR—Shrink Films—Tyco International Ltd.; *U.S. Public*, pg. 1647

ARMED AND READY IN ONE EASY MOTION—NONE—U.S. Surgical Corp.; *U.S. Public*, pg. 1687

ARMEEN—Specialty Chemicals—Akzo Nobel Inc.; *Int'l*, pg. 47

ARMEEN—Fatty Amines—Akzo Nobel N.V.; *Int'l*, pg. 42

ARMEX BLAST MEDIA—Paint Stripper—Church & Dwight Co., Inc.; *U.S. Public*, pg. 355

ARMID—Fatty Amides, Cationics—Akzo Nobel N.V.; *Int'l*, pg. 42

ARMIDE—Carbide Tipped Cutters—Danaher Tool Group; *U.S. Public*, pg. 481

ARMITAGE SHANKS—Sanitary Ware—Blue Circle Industries PLC; *Int'l*, pg. 197

ARMIX—Shortening—Armour Food Company; *U.S. Public*, pg. 427

ARMIX—Emulsifier—DeSoto Inc.; *U.S. Public*, pg. 956

ARMO—Woven Interfacings—Specialty Textile Products; *U.S. Private*, pg. 1023

ARMO-DUR—Impact Resistant Material—Shure Brothers Incorporated; *U.S. Private*, pg. 997

ARMO FLEECE—Interfacing—Specialty Textile Products; *U.S. Private*, pg. 1023

ARMO PRESS—Interfacings—Specialty Textile Products; *U.S. Private*, pg. 1023

ARMO-WOOL—Interlining—Specialty Textile Products; *U.S. Private*, pg. 1023

ARMOFILM—Water Treatment Chemicals—Akzo Nobel N.V.; *Int'l*, pg. 42

ARMOFLEXXX—Waistbanding—Specialty Textile Products; *U.S. Private*, pg. 1023

ARMOFLO—Specialty Chemicals—Akzo Nobel Inc.; *Int'l*, pg. 47

ARMOFLO—Fertilizer Anti-caking Agents—Akzo Nobel N.V.; *Int'l*, pg. 42

ARMOFLOTE—Cationic Blends—Akzo Nobel N.V.; *Int'l*, pg. 42

ARMOGARD—Oilfield Chemicals—Akzo Nobel N.V.; *Int'l*, pg. 42

ARMOHIB—Cationic Blends—Akzo Nobel N.V.; *Int'l*, pg. 42

ARMOL—Amines—Akzo Nobel N.V.; *Int'l*, pg. 42

ARMOR—NONE—Kone Corporation; *Int'l*, pg. 746

ARMOR ALL—Manufacturer Of Auto Protectants, Multi-Purpose Cleaners, Waxes & Polishes—Armor All Products Group; *U.S. Public*, pg. 387

ARMOR-COTE—Motors—Louis Allis Company; *U.S. Private*, pg. 677

ARMOR-FLEX—Portable Antenna Line—Allen Telecom Inc.; *U.S. Public*, pg. 45

ARMOR FLEX—Wheels—Faultless Nutting; *Int'l*, pg. 473

ARMOR GARD—Scratch Resident Ophthalmic Lens Treatment—Sterling Vision, Inc.; *U.S. Public*, pg. 1516

ARMOR GUARD—Motors—Louis Allis Company; *U.S. Private*, pg. 677

ARMOR LINE—Electric Motors—Louis Allis Company; *U.S. Private*, pg. 677

ARMOR PLATE—Laminated Bowling Lane Surfaces—Brunswick Corporation; *U.S. Public*, pg. 265

ARMOR SAFE COMPANY—NONE—Phelps Tointon Inc.; *U.S. Private*, pg. 860

ARMOR SEAL—Motors—Louis Allis Company; *U.S. Private*, pg. 677

ARMOR-TOUGH—NONE—Kellwood Company; *U.S. Public*, pg. 948

ARMORCAST—Telecommunication Structural Matl.—3M; *U.S. Public*, pg. 1604

ARMORCOTE—Urethane Coatings—Cook Composites & Polymers Inc.; *Int'l*, pg. 1409

ARMORED POLY-THERMALEZE 2000—THEIC Modified Polyester with modified polyamide imide overcoat—Phelps Dodge Magnet Wire Co.; *U.S. Public*, pg. 1286

ARMORKOTE—Electrical Cable—Reynolds Metals Company; *U.S. Public*, pg. 1385

ARMORWEAVE—Antenna Randome—Allen Telecom Inc.; *U.S. Public*, pg. 45

ARMOSLIP—Polymer Additives—Akzo Nobel N.V.; *Int'l*, pg. 42

ARMOSTAT—Specialty Chemicals—Akzo Nobel Inc.; *Int'l*, pg. 47

ARMOSTAT—Anti-Static Agent—Akzo Nobel N.V.; *Int'l*, pg. 42

ARMOTAN—Suspension Agents—Akzo Nobel N.V.; *Int'l*, pg. 42

ARMOTERIC—Alkyl Betaines—Akzo Nobel N.V.; *Int'l*, pg. 42

ARMOUR—Meat Products—ConAgra, Inc.; *U.S. Public*, pg. 425

ARMOUR LIGHT—Flashlights—The Canadian Coleman Co., Ltd.; *U.S. Private*, pg. 691

ARMOUR STAR—Processed Meats—Armour Food Company; *U.S. Public*, pg. 427

ARMOUR STAR—Dairy Products—ConAgra, Inc.; *U.S. Public*, pg. 425

ARMOUR STAR BEEF BOUILLON CUBES—NONE—The Dial Corporation; *U.S. Public*, pg. 505

ARMOUR STAR BEEF STEW—NONE—The Dial Corporation; *U.S. Public*, pg. 505

ARMOUR STAR BEEF TRIPE—NONE—The Dial Corporation; *U.S. Public*, pg. 505

ARMOUR STAR CHICKEN BOUILLON CUBES—NONE—The Dial Corporation; *U.S. Public*, pg. 505

ARMOUR STAR CHILI NO BEANS—NONE—The Dial Corporation; *U.S. Public*, pg. 505

ARMOUR STAR CHILI WITH BEANS—NONE—The Dial Corporation; *U.S. Public*, pg. 505

ARMOUR STAR CHOPPED BEEF—NONE—The Dial Corporation; *U.S. Public*, pg. 505

ARMOUR STAR CHOPPED HAM—NONE—The Dial Corporation; *U.S. Public*, pg. 505

ARMOUR STAR CORNED BEEF—NONE—The Dial Corporation; *U.S. Public*, pg. 505

ARMOUR STAR CORNED BEEF AND BACON HASH—NONE—The Dial Corporation; *U.S. Public*, pg. 505

ARMOUR STAR CORNED BEEF HASH—NONE—The Dial Corporation; *U.S. Public*, pg. 505

ARMOUR STAR DEVILED HAM—NONE—The Dial Corporation; *U.S. Public*, pg. 505

ARMOUR STAR DRIED BEEF—NONE—The Dial Corporation; *U.S. Public*, pg. 505

ARMOUR STAR HOT 'N SPICY VIENNA SAUSAGE—NONE—The Dial Corporation; *U.S. Public*, pg. 505

ARMOUR STAR HOT CHILI WITH BEANS—NONE—The Dial Corporation; *U.S. Public*, pg. 505

ARMOUR STAR JALAPENO VIENNA SAUSAGE—NONE—The Dial Corporation; *U.S. Public*, pg. 505

ARMOUR STAR LITE TREET—NONE—The Dial Corporation; *U.S. Public*, pg. 505

ARMOUR STAR PORK BRAINS WITH GRAVY—NONE—The Dial Corporation; *U.S. Public*, pg. 505

ARMOUR STAR POTTED MEAT—NONE—The Dial Corporation; *U.S. Public*, pg. 505

ARMOUR STAR ROAST BEEF HASH—NONE—The Dial Corporation; *U.S. Public*, pg. 505

ARMOUR STAR ROAST BEEF WITH GRAVY—NONE—The Dial Corporation; *U.S. Public*, pg. 505

ARMOUR STAR SLOPPY JOE SAUCE—NONE—The Dial Corporation; *U.S. Public*, pg. 505

ARMOUR STAR SMOKED VIENNA SAUSAGE—NONE—The Dial Corporation; *U.S. Public*, pg. 505

ARMOUR STAR TREET—NONE—The Dial Corporation; *U.S. Public*, pg. 505

ARMOUR STAR ULTIMATE CHILE LOVERS CHILE—NONE—The Dial Corporation; *U.S. Public*, pg. 505

ARMOUR STAR ULTIMATE CHILI NO BEANS—NONE—The Dial Corporation; *U.S. Public*, pg. 505

ARMOUR STAR ULTIMATE CHILI WITH BEANS—NONE—The Dial Corporation; *U.S. Public*, pg. 505

ARMOUR STAR ULTIMATE HOT CHILI WITH BEANS—NONE—The Dial Corporation; *U.S. Public*, pg. 505

ARMOUR STAR ULTIMATE TURKEY CHILI WITH BEANS—NONE—The Dial Corporation; *U.S. Public*, pg. 505

ARMOUR STAR VIENNA SAUSAGE—NONE—The Dial Corporation; *U.S. Public*, pg. 505

ARMOUR STAR VIENNA SAUSAGE IN BARBECUE SAUCE—NONE—The Dial Corporation; *U.S. Public*, pg. 505

ARMOUR STAR WESTERN STYLE CHILE WITH BEANS—NONE—The Dial Corporation; *U.S. Public*, pg. 505

ARMOUR STAR WESTERN STYLE CORNED BEEF HASH—NONE—The Dial Corporation; *U.S. Public*, pg. 505

ARMOUR THYROID—Thyroid Products, U.S.Rights Only—Forest Laboratories, Inc.; *U.S. Public*, pg. 670

ARMOUR THYROID—Ethical Pharmaceuticals—Rhone-Poulenc Rorer - U.S.; *Int'l*, pg. 1110

ARMOURFLOAT—Toughened Float Glass Products—Pilkington Australasia Limited; *Int'l*, pg. 1057

ARMOURVIEW—Toughened Float Glass Products—Pilkington Australasia Limited; *Int'l*, pg. 1057

ARMOWEFT—Interfacing—Specialty Textile Products; *U.S. Private*, pg. 1023

ARMS—NONE—Dukane Corporation; *U.S. Private*, pg. 345

ARMSTRONG—Floor Coverings, Ceiling Systems, Indus. Specialty Prods., Furniture—Armstrong World Industries, Inc.; *U.S. Public*, pg. 131

ARMSTRONG—Floor Cleaner—S.C. Johnson & Son, Inc.; *U.S. Private*, pg. 592

ARMSTRONG—Cutlery—Lifetime Hoan Corp.; *U.S. Public*, pg. 992

ARMSTRONG FORGE—Cutlery—Lifetime Hoan Corp.; *U.S. Public*, pg. 992

ARMSTRONG RIDGE—California Wines—Brown-Forman Beverages Worldwide; *U.S. Public*, pg. 261

ARMSTRONG RIDGE CALIFORNIA CHAMPAGNE—Wine—Brown-Forman Corporation; *U.S. Public*, pg. 261

ARMUL—Emulsifier—DeSoto Inc.; *U.S. Public*, pg. 956

ARMX—White Mineral Oil—Witco Corporation; *U.S. Public*, pg. 1773

ARNEEL—Fatty Nitriles—Akzo Nobel N.V.; *Int'l*, pg. 42

ARNESON—Surface Drives—Twin Disc, Incorporated; *U.S. Public*, pg. 1646

ARNI—Biscuits—Coop Switzerland; *Int'l*, pg. 329

ARNI—Swiss Chocolates—The Promotion in Motion Companies; *U.S. Private*, pg. 890

ARNIE—Headwear—AJD; *U.S. Private*, pg. 510

ARNITE—Thermoplastic Polyester—Akzo Nobel N.V.; *Int'l*, pg. 42

ARNITEL—Thermoplastic Elastomer—Akzo Nobel N.V.; *Int'l*, pg. 42

ARNOKROME—Magnetic Material—The Arnold Engineering Company; *U.S. Public*, pg. 1420

ARNOLD—Baked Goods, Breads—Bestfoods; *U.S. Public*, pg. 223

ARNOLD—Baked Goods—CPC Baking Business; *U.S. Public*, pg. 224

ARNOLD BARTON—Greeting Cards—Fine Art Developments plc; *Int'l*, pg. 485

ARNOLD PALMER—Golf Equipment & Luggage—The Arnold Palmer Golf Company; *U.S. Public*, pg. 132

ARNOLD PALMER—Apparel—Bayer Clothing Group; *U.S. Private*, pg. 124

ARNOLDS—Pickles—Dean Pickle & Specialty Products Co.; *U.S. Public*, pg. 490

ARNOMIJ—NONE—ETEX; *Int'l*, pg. 430

ARNOTTS—Department Stores Wholesalers—Arnotts plc; *Int'l*, pg. 81

ARNOX—Hard Ferrite Magnet—The Arnold Engineering Company; *U.S. Public*, pg. 1420

AROFENE—Paper Resins—Ashland, Inc.; *U.S. Public*, pg. 138

AROGRIP—Marine Adhesive—Ashland, Inc.; *U.S. Public*, pg. 138

AROMA DISC—Environmental Fragrance Records—Charles of the Ritz Group Ltd.; *U.S. Private*, pg. 689

AROMA DISC PLAYER—Environmental Fragrance Dispensers—Charles of the Ritz Group Ltd.; *U.S. Private*, pg. 689

AROMAT—Food Seasoning—Bestfoods; *U.S. Public*, pg. 223

AROMAT—Relays & Factory Automation Components—Matsushita Electric Works, Ltd.; *Int'l*, pg. 847

AROMATRAN—Measures Levels of Aromas & Odor Transmissions—Modern Controls, Inc.; *U.S. Public*, pg. 1120

AROMESENTIALS—Professional Hair Products—Freeman Cosmetic Corp.; *U.S. Private*, pg. 426

AROMOX—Ammonium Compounds—Akzo Nobel N.V.; *Int'l*, pg. 42

AROPAX—NONE—SmithKline Beecham Laboratorios Ltda.; *Int'l*, pg. 1266

AROSA—Women's Tennis Shoe—K-Swiss Inc.; *U.S. Public*, pg. 937

AROSET—Industrial Polymers—Ashland, Inc.; *U.S. Public*, pg. 138

AROTRAN—Low-Profile Resin Transfer Molding System—Ashland, Inc.; *U.S. Public*, pg. 138

ARPAN—Plant Protectives—DSM Chemie Linz GmbH; *Int'l*, pg. 356

ARPEGE—Executive Catering—Accor S.A.; *Int'l*, pg. 20

ARPEGE BY LANVIN—NONE—Cosmair, Inc.; *Int'l*, pg. 818

ARPEGGIOR—Database Publishing Software—Wall Data Incorporated; *U.S. Public*, pg. 1734

ARPOCOX—Arprinocid, Coccidiostat—Merck & Co., Inc.; *U.S. Public*, pg. 1090

ARQUAD—Specialty Chemicals—Akzo Nobel Inc.; *Int'l*, pg. 47

ARQUAD—Ammonium Compounds—Akzo Nobel N.V.; *Int'l*, pg. 42

ARR-O-LOK—Closure-Beverage Carriers—Riverwood International Corporation; *U.S. Public*, pg. 1391

ARRANGE—Hair Spray—Shaklee Corporation; *Int'l*, pg. 1518

ARRANGER—NONE—Texas Instruments Incorporated; *U.S. Public*, pg. 1585

ARRAY—Clinical Instruments & Reagents—Beckman Instruments, Inc.; *U.S. Public*, pg. 199

ARRAY—Hair Preparations—The Gillette Company; *U.S. Public*, pg. 743

ARRAY ACOUSTILOG—NONE—Western Atlas Logging Services; *U.S. Public*, pg. 1757

ARRAY PROCESSOR—Peripheral Computer Equip.—CSP Inc.; *U.S. Public*, pg. 283

ARRESTOX—Aqueous-Coated Book Cloth—Industrial Coatings Group, Inc.; *U.S. Private*, pg. 434

ARRID—Antiperspirant Deodorant—Carter Products, Canada; *U.S. Public*, pg. 310

ARRID—Deodorants & Anti Perspirants—Carter-Wallace, Inc.; *U.S. Public*, pg. 309

ARRID TEEN IMAGE—Deodorant—Carter-Wallace, Inc.; *U.S. Public*, pg. 309

ARRIVA—Pleasure Boats—Brunswick Corporation; *U.S. Public*, pg. 265

ARRIVA—Radial Tire—The Goodyear Tire & Rubber Company; *U.S. Public*, pg. 752

ARRIVA—Eye Protection—U.S. Safety; *U.S. Private*, pg. 1125

ARROSTO—NONE—Koo Koo Roo, Inc.; *U.S. Public*, pg. 966

ARROW—Remanufactured Auto Replacement Parts—Arrow Automotive Industries, Inc.; *U.S. Public*, pg. 133

ARROW—Staplers & Office Products—Arrow Fastener Co., Inc.; *U.S. Private*, pg. 85

ARROW—Storage Buildings—Arrow Group Industries, Inc.; *U.S. Private*, pg. 477

ARROW—Shirts & Men's Hoisery—Arrow Shirt Company; *Int'l*, pg. 194

ARROW—Shirts—Bidermann International S.A.; *Int'l*, pg. 194

ARROW—Machining Centre—Cincinnati Milacron U.K. Limited; *U.S. Public*, pg. 368

ARROW—Writing Instruments—Gillette Co.-Parker Pen USA; *U.S. Public*, pg. 745

ARROW—Cordials—Heublein, Inc.; *Int'l*, pg. 410

ARROW—Men's Apparel—International Cosmetics Co., Ltd.; *Int'l*, pg. 684

ARROW—Men's Underwear—Nantucket Industries, Inc.; *U.S. Public*, pg. 1151

ARROW—Aircraft—The New Piper Aircraft, Inc.; *U.S. Private*, pg. 794

ARROW—Menswear—Sao Paulo Alpargatas S.A.; *Int'l*, pg. 1193

ARROW—Children's Books—Scholastic Inc.; *U.S. Public*, pg. 1440

ARROW & GLOBE DESIGN—Computer-Enhanced Images—Litton Industries, Inc.; *U.S. Public*, pg. 1002

ARROW HAMMER—Mobile Hydraulic Hammer—East Moline Metal Products Company; *U.S. Private*, pg. 357

ARROW HART—1Wiring Devices, Specialty Switches & Industrial Controls—Cooper Industries, Inc.; *U.S. Public*, pg. 442

ARROW-HOWES—Triple-Lumen Catheter—Arrow International, Inc.; *U.S. Public*, pg. 135

ARROW-KARLAN—Balloon Cholangiography Catheterization Set—Arrow International, Inc.; *U.S. Public*, pg. 135

ARROW UNIT—Heating & Ventilation Equipment—Mestek, Inc.; *U.S. Public*, pg. 1099

ARROW-VINYL STORETTE—Collector's Edition Recycling Products—Arrow Group Industries, Inc.; *U.S. Private*, pg. 477

ARROW WOODSTOVE—Wood Stoves—HON Industries Inc.; *U.S. Public*, pg. 772

ARROWFLEX—NONE—Integrated Material Handling Company; *Int'l*, pg. 1397

ARROWGARD BLUE—Antiseptic Surface Treatment—Arrow International, Inc.; *U.S. Public*, pg. 135

ARROWHEAD—Pure Water & Water Devices—Arrowhead Mountain Spring Water Company; *Int'l*, pg. 919

ARROWHEAD—Conveyor—Integrated Material Handling Company; *Int'l*, pg. 1397

ARROWHEAD—Electrical Connectors & Plugs for Medical Apparatus—Mallinckrodt Inc.; *U.S. Public*, pg. 1039

ARROWHEAD—Bond & Safety Paper—The Mead Corporation; *U.S. Public*, pg. 1074

ARROWHEAD—Mineral Water—Nestle S.A.; *Int'l*, pg. 915

ARROWHEAD—Mountain Spring Water—The Perrier Group of America; *Int'l*, pg. 919

ARROWHEAD MILLS—Natural Foods—Arrowhead Mills, Inc.; *U.S. Private*, pg. 86

ARROWLINE—NONE—Integrated Material Handling Company; *Int'l*, pg. 1397

ARROWSTAR—NONE—Integrated Material Handling Company; *Int'l*, pg. 1397

ARROZINA—Corn Starches—Bestfoods; *U.S. Public*, pg. 223

ARSENAL—Herbicide—American Home Products Corporation; *U.S. Public*, pg. 79

ART BUSINESS NEWS—Trade Periodical—Advanstar Communications; *U.S. Private*, pg. 22

ART IRON—Fabricates Structural Steel—Art Iron, Inc.; *U.S. Private*, pg. 86

THE ART OF NEGOTIATING—Software to Prepare for Negotiations—Experience In Software, Inc.; *U.S. Private*, pg. 388

ART OF THE AGES—Porcelain Collection—The Pfaltzgraff Co.; *U.S. Private*, pg. 860

ART PARTS—NONE—Broderbund Software, Inc.; *U.S. Public*, pg. 258

ARTCARVED—NONE—Commemorative Brands, Inc.; *U.S. Private*, pg. 258

ARTCAT—Fluidizeable Contact Material—Engelhard Corporation; *U.S. Public*, pg. 582

ARTCOR—Display Boards—Amoco Corporation; *U.S. Public*, pg. 101

ARTCRAFT—Line of Craft Organizing Products—Rubbermaid Incorporated; *U.S. Public*, pg. 1411

ARTCRAFT—Mobile Homes—Wick Bldg. Systems Inc. Manufactured Homes Div.; *U.S. Private*, pg. 1174

ARTEC—Office Furniture—Kimball International, Inc.; *U.S. Public*, pg. 956

ARTFAIRE—Gift Wrappings—CPS Corporation; *U.S. Private*, pg. 422

ARTHIRITEN PM—Pain Relief Caplets—Alva/Amco Pharmacal Companies, Inc.; *U.S. Private*, pg. 47

ARTHRICARE—Arthritis Rubs—Del Pharmaceuticals, Inc.; *U.S. Public*, pg. 494

ARTHRITEN—Pain Relief Tablets—Alva/Amco Pharmacal Companies, Inc.; *U.S. Private*, pg. 47

ARTHRITIS FOUNDATION PAIN RELIEVERS—Arthritis Pain Relievers—McNeil Consumer Products Company; *U.S. Public*, pg. 928

ARTHRITIS HOT—Creme—Thompson Medical Company, Inc.; *U.S. Private*, pg. 1083

ARTHRITISCARE CENTERS OF AMERICA—Arthritis Treatment—American Healthcorp Inc.; *U.S. Public*, pg. 78

ARTHRO-FLO—Arthoscopy Irrigation System—C.R. Bard, Inc.; *U.S. Public*, pg. 189

ARTHRO-FLO—Arthroscopy Irrigation System—Davol Inc.; *U.S. Public*, pg. 189

ARTHRO-SEW—Suturing Device—U.S. Surgical Corp.; *U.S. Public*, pg. 1687

ARTHROTOME ABRADER—Orthopedic Products—Bristol-Myers Squibb Company; *U.S. Public*, pg. 253

ARTHUR—Merchandise Planning & Information Services for the Retail Industry—Comshare, Incorporated; *U.S. Public*, pg. 425

ARTHUR—Pet Food—Dalgety Plc; *Int'l*, pg. 376

ARTHUR MARTIN—Household Appliances—Electrolux, AB; *Int'l*, pg. 438

ARTHUR TREACHER'S—Fish & Chips—Arthur Treacher's, Inc.; *U.S. Public*, pg. 136

ARTHUR WOOD & SON—Chinaware—Ebeling & Reuss Company; *U.S. Private*, pg. 358

ARCTIC ICE—Frozen Fish—Louis Kemp Seafood Co.; *U.S. Public*, pg. 1652

ARTICA—NONE—Avenor, Inc.; *Int'l*, pg. 101

ARTICLAD—Pipeline Coatings—Raychem Corporation; *U.S. Public*, pg. 1362

ARTIFICIAL GRASS & INDOOR/OUTDOOR CARPET ADHESIVE—Adhesive—Pratt & Lambert United, Inc.; *U.S. Public*, pg. 1466

ARTIFICIAL PARCHMENT—Business Letterhead & Printing Grades—Crane & Co., Inc.; *U.S. Private*, pg. 286

ARTISAN—Dermatologic Lasers—Coherent, Inc.; *U.S. Public*, pg. 395

ARTISAN—NONE—DeVlieg-Bullard Inc.; *U.S. Public*, pg. 502

ARTISAN—Painting, Writing, Book & Cover Papers—Georgia-Pacific Corporation; *U.S. Public*, pg. 735

ARTISAN—Ceramic Floor Tile—Monarch Tile, Inc.; *U.S. Private*, pg. 287

THE ARTISAN COLLECTION—Solid Brass Home Hardware—H.B. Ives; *U.S. Private*, pg. 506

ARTISAN LINE—NONE—Powermatic; *U.S. Public*, pg. 502

ARTISTIC BRASS—Plumbing Fixtures—Masco Corporation; *U.S. Public*, pg. 1052

ARTISTIC SILK—NONE—Celebrity Incorporated; *U.S. Public*, pg. 319

ARTISTRY—Cosmetics—Amway Corporation; *U.S. Private*, pg. 69

ARTISTS—Color Pencils—Dixon Ticonderoga Company; *U.S. Public*, pg. 514

ARTISTS & WRITERS GUILD BOOKS—NONE—Golden Books Family Entertainment Inc.; *U.S. Public*, pg. 749

THE ARTIST'S MAGAZINE—Magazine—F & W Publications, Inc.; *U.S. Private*, pg. 388

ARTIST'S MARKET—Market Book—F & W Publications, Inc.; *U.S. Private*, pg. 388

ARTMATE—Mat Cutter—Letraset Nielsen & Bainbridge; *Int'l*, pg. 460

ARTOLEUM—Linoleum—Forbo Holding SA; *Int'l*, pg. 496

ARTONE—Text Paper—Kimberly-Clark Corporation; *U.S. Public*, pg. 958

ART'S-WAY—Farm Equipment—Art's-Way Manufacturing Co., Inc.; *U.S. Public*, pg. 136

ARTURA—Glazed Wall Tile—Florida Tile Industries, Inc.; *U.S. Public*, pg. 1322

ARTWRIGHT—NONE—Martin Universal Design, Inc.; *U.S. Private*, pg. 709

ARVINYL—Metal Laminates—Arvin Industries, Inc.; *U.S. Public*, pg. 136

ARY COOPER—Missy Contemporary Sportswear—Seattle Pacific Industries, Inc.; *U.S. Private*, pg. 980

AS-5000SRT—Measuring System—Mechanical Technology Inc.; *U.S. Public*, pg. 1077

ASACOL—Ulcerative Colitis Therapy—Procter & Gamble Pharmaceuticals, Inc.; *U.S. Public*, pg. 1331

ASACOL—NONE—SmithKline Beecham Corporation; *Int'l*, pg. 1264

ASACOL—Gastrointestinal Drug—SmithKline Beecham plc; *Int'l*, pg. 1264

ASAFLEX—Transparent Styrenic Resin—Asahi Chemical Industry Co., Ltd.; *Int'l*, pg. 83

ASBACH URALT BRANDY—Brandy—United Distillers USA, Inc.; *Int'l*, pg. 412

THE ASBURY PARK PRESS—Daily/Sunday Newspaper, Direct Mail & Travel Agency—Asbury Park Press, Inc.; *U.S. Public*, pg. 699

ASCA—Uncoated Mechanical Papers—Haindl Papier GmbH; *Int'l*, pg. 586

ASCEND—Personal Information Management System—Franklin Covey; *U.S. Public*, pg. 679

ASCENSION—Vacuum Cleaner—HMI Industries; *U.S. Public*, pg. 771

ASCENT2000—NONE—James Hardie Industries Ltd.; *Int'l*, pg. 596

ASCENTIA—NONE—AST Research Inc.; *Int'l*, pg. 1181

ASCO—Electric Power Control Products—Ascolectric Limited; *U.S. Public*, pg. 575

ASCO—Solenoid Valves—Associated Process Controls; *U.S. Private*, pg. 92

ASCO—Solenoid & Air Operated Valves & Accessories & Electrical Products—Automatic Switch Co.; *U.S. Public*, pg. 573

ASCO—Tools—Diamond Productions, Inc.; *U.S. Private*, pg. 330

ASCO/GENERAL CONTROLS COMBUSTION VALVES—NONE—Automatic Switch Co.; *U.S. Public*, pg. 573

ASCOLITE—Latex Impregnated Bookcovering—Appleton Papers Inc.; *Int'l*, pg. 567

ASCOM HASLER—NONE—Ascom Canada Limited; *Int'l*, pg. 86

ASCOT—Motorcycle—American Honda Motor Co., Inc. Motorcycle Division; *Int'l*, pg. 634

ASCOT—Nonpaper Printing Grade—Appleton Papers Inc.; *Int'l*, pg. 567

ASCOZA—Men's Tennis Shoe—K-Swiss Inc.; *U.S. Public*, pg. 937

ASCRIPTIN—Pain Reliever & Anti-Inflamatory Drug—Novartis; *Int'l*, pg. 972

ASCRIPTIN—Pain Reliever & Anti-Inflamatory Drug—Rhone-Poulenc Rorer - U.S.; *Int'l*, pg. 1110

ASCRIPTIN A/D—Consumer Analgesic—Rhone-Poulenc Rorer - U.S.; *Int'l*, pg. 1110

ASCRITPIN A/D—Consumer Analgesic—Novartis; *Int'l*, pg. 972

ASEPT-O-FLOW—Soap Dispenser—American Specialties Inc.; *U.S. Private*, pg. 62

ASEPTEX—Surgical & Dental Masks—3M; *U.S. Public*, pg. 1604

ASEPTICAR—Railcar—General Electric Capital Railcar Services; *U.S. Public*, pg. 712

ASERBINE—Cleansing Agent for Burns—SmithKline Beecham plc; *Int'l*, pg. 1264

ASGROW—Seeds—Asgrow Seed Company; *Int'l*, pg. 1048

ASGROW COAT 108—High Quality Seed Coating—Asgrow Seed Company; *Int'l*, pg. 1048

ASH PUMP—Heavy Duty Slurry Pumps—EnviroTech PumpSystems; *Int'l*, pg. 1489

ASHBACH URALT—NONE—Guinness Plc; *Int'l*, pg. 412

ASHBOURNE—Irish Cream Liquer—Marie Brizard Wines & Spirits USA; *U.S. Private*, pg. 702

ASHBOURNE—Mineral Water—Nestle S.A.; *Int'l*, pg. 915

ASHBROOKS—Home Furnishings & Accessories—Woolworth Corporation; *U.S. Public*, pg. 1777

ASHBROOKS—Linens & Kitchenware—F.W. Woolworth Co.; *U.S. Public*, pg. 1777

ASHCROFT—Gauges & Temperature Sensors—Associated Process Controls; *U.S. Private*, pg. 92

ASHCROFT—NONE—Dresser Canada, Inc.; *U.S. Public*, pg. 529

ASHCROFT—Instruments & Gauges—Dresser Industries, Inc.; *U.S. Public*, pg. 528

ASHCROFT—Lumber & Wood Products—Georgia-Pacific Corporation; *U.S. Public*, pg. 735

ASHER—Candy—Fleer-Skybox International Inc.; *U.S. Public*, pg. 1052

ASHLAND—Chemical—Ashland Chemical; *U.S. Public*, pg. 139

ASHLEY—Heating Equipment—Martin Industries, Inc. (AL); *U.S. Private*, pg. 709

ASHLEY COURT 700 SERIES—Traditional Furniture—Myrtle/Mueller, A Haworth Co.; *U.S. Private*, pg. 512

ASHLEY'S OF TEXAS—Mexican Food—Bruce Foods Corp.; *U.S. Private*, pg. 175

ASHTON—NONE—The Bentley Agnew Group Inc.; *Int'l*, pg. 187

ASHTON & PARSONS—Infants' Teething Powders—SmithKline Beecham plc; *Int'l*, pg. 1264

ASHTON DRAKE—Collectors Plates—Bradford Exchange Ltd.; *U.S. Private*, pg. 163

ASIA IMAGE—Business Magazine—Reed Elsevier Business Information; *Int'l*, pg. 1095

ASIA WEEK—Magazine—Time Warner Inc.; *U.S. Public*, pg. 1610

ASIAN HOTELIER—Asian Hospitality Trade Tabloid—Reed Elsevier Business Information; *Int'l*, pg. 1095

THE ASIAN WALL STREET JOURNAL—Daily Business & Financial Newspaper Circulated in Asia—Dow Jones & Company, Inc.; *U.S. Public*, pg. 524

THE ASIAN WALL STREET JOURNAL WEEKLY EDITION—Weekly Business & Financial Publication Circulated in the United States—Dow Jones & Company, Inc.; *U.S. Public*, pg. 524

ASICMAKER—FPGA Programmer—Gatefield Corporation; *U.S. Public*, pg. 703

ASICMASTER—Software Tools—Gatefield Corporation; *U.S. Public*, pg. 703

ASICS—Sporting Goods—ASICS Tiger Corporation; *U.S. Private*, pg. 89

ASICS TIGER—Sporting Goods—ASICS Tiger Corporation; *U.S. Private*, pg. 89

ASIETOURS—Tour Operators—Accor S.A.; *Int'l*, pg. 20

ASK A QUESTION—Omnibus Mail Service—NFO Research, Inc.; *U.S. Public*, pg. 1146

ASK ACE—NONE—Ace Hardware Corporation; *U.S. Private*, pg. 12

ASK ADVICE—NONE—First DataBank; *U.S. Private*, pg. 515

ASK RX—NONE—First DataBank; *U.S. Private*, pg. 515

ASK THE HANDYMAN WITH GLENN HAEGE—Home Repair Program—Westwood One, Inc.; *U.S. Public*, pg. 1763

ASKMARTHA—Entertainment Programming—Westwood One, Inc.; *U.S. Public*, pg. 1763

ASORBS—Investment Products—Medline Industries, Inc.; *U.S. Private*, pg. 728

ASPAC—Polystyrene Foam Loose Fill—Asahi Chemical Industry Co., Ltd.; *Int'l*, pg. 83

ASPALON—Digestive Organs Agents—Nippon Kayaku Co. Ltd.; *Int'l*, pg. 934

ASPECT—Software—Onyx Technologies Ltd.; *Int'l*, pg. 1007

ASPECTS OF LOVE—Musical—Really Useful Holdings Limited; *Int'l*, pg. 1089

ASPEN—Recycled Xerographic & Offset Paper—Boise Cascade Corporation; *U.S. Public*, pg. 242

ASPEN—Oxygen Concentrator—CAIRE, Inc.; *U.S. Private*, pg. 751

ASPEN—Men's Fragrance—Coty Inc.; *Int'l*, pg. 185

ASPEN—Cigarettes—R.J. Reynolds Tobacco Intl., Inc.; *U.S. Public*, pg. 1355

ASPEN—Home Series—Toyota Motor Corporation; *Int'l*, pg. 1411

ASPEN—Eye Protection—U.S. Safety; *U.S. Private*, pg. 1125

ASPEN CARE—Cleaning Kits—Aspen Imaging International, Inc.; *U.S. Public*, pg. 1339

ASPEN FAX—Thermal Fax Paper—Aspen Imaging International, Inc.; *U.S. Public*, pg. 1339

ASPEN FIBRE—Fuel Pellets—Villaume Industries, Inc.; *U.S. Private*, pg. 1140

ASPEN LABORATORIES—Electrosurgical Products—Conmed Corporation; *U.S. Public*, pg. 431

ASPEN RIBBONS—Cartridges—Aspen Imaging International, Inc.; *U.S. Public*, pg. 1339

ASPENCADE—Motorcycle—American Honda Motor Co., Inc. Motorcycle Division; *Int'l*, pg. 634

ASPERCREME—Pharmaceutical Products—Thompson Medical Company, Inc.; *U.S. Private*, pg. 1083

ASPERCREME HOT—Pharmaceutical Product—Thompson Medical Company, Inc.; *U.S. Private*, pg. 1083

ASPERCREME ICE—Pharmaceutical Product—Thompson Medical Company, Inc.; *U.S. Private*, pg. 1083

ASPERGUM—Sore Throat Medication—Schering-Plough Healthcare Products Inc.; *U.S. Public*, pg. 1438

ASPERHEART—Aspirin—Health Products Corporation; *U.S. Private*, pg. 514

ASPHALT STYLE TILE—1/8" Vinyl Composition Tile; 9"x9" Commercial—Kentile Operting Co.; *U.S. Private*, pg. 615

ASPHALTUM—Asphalt Varnish—Jones Blair Company; *U.S. Private*, pg. 596

ASPHERIX—Rear View Mirror—Deutsche Spezialglas AG; *Int'l*, pg. 1523

ASPHERIX—Rear-View Auto Mirror—Schott Glaswerke; *Int'l*, pg. 1523

ASPHERLITE—Opthamalic Lenses—American Optical Corporation; *U.S. Private*, pg. 60

ASPI COR—Aspirin—Health Products Corporation; *U.S. Private*, pg. 514

ASPIRA—Line of Office Furniture—Rubbermaid Incorporated; *U.S. Public*, pg. 1411

ASPIRE—Non-Prime Loan Orgigination Solutions—Fair, Isaac and Company, Inc.; *U.S. Public*, pg. 609

ASPIRIN—Pain Reliever—Bayer AG; *Int'l*, pg. 171

ASPUN—Fiber Grade Resins—The Dow Chemical Company; *U.S. Public*, pg. 522

ASSAULT—Nozzles—Akron Brass Company; *Int'l*, pg. 1068

ASSAULT—Weed Killer—Wechco, Inc.; *U.S. Private*, pg. 1158

ASSEMBLY—Magazine for Manufacturing Professionals—Reed Elsevier Business Information; *Int'l*, pg. 1095

ASSEMBLY FRIENDLY ATMIZED—Semiconductor Device Integrated Circuit, Services or Device—LSI Logic Corp.; *U.S. Public*, pg. 971

ASSENTOR—E-Mail Surveillance System—SRA International Inc.; *U.S. Private*, pg. 957

ASSERT—Herbicide—American Home Products Corporation; *U.S. Public*, pg. 79

Brand Name Index

ASSET—Magnetic Resonance—Picker International, Inc.; *Int'l*, pg. 545

ASSISA—Office Chair—Vecta; *U.S. Private*, pg. 1038

ASSISTANT SERIES—Computer Systems—International Business Machines Corporation; *U.S. Public*, pg. 895

ASSOCIATED HEALTH SERVICES—Infusion Therapy—Vivra Incorporated; *U.S. Public*, pg. 1723

ASSOCIATED HOSTS—Holding Co. of Restaurants—Associated Hosts, Inc.; *Int'l*, pg. 215

ASSOCIATED MEDICATION SERVICE—Mail Order Pharmacy Service—Vivra Incorporated; *U.S. Public*, pg. 1723

ASSOCIATED WHOLESALE GROCERS—Co-Operative Grocery Distributor—Associated Wholesale Grocers, Inc.; *U.S. Private*, pg. 93

ASSOCIATION/400—Computer Systems—International Business Machines Corporation; *U.S. Public*, pg. 895

ASSOCIATIVE INDEX METHOD—Computer Software Program—Datapoint Corporation; *Int'l*, pg. 384

ASSOCIE—Vanity Units—Matsushita Electric Works, Ltd.; *Int'l*, pg. 847

ASSURA—Car Seat—Century Products Co.; *U.S. Private*, pg. 226

ASSURANCE 50—ECG Paper—Burdick, Inc.; *U.S. Private*, pg. 181

ASSURANCE 2000—Continuous Monitor for Measuring Heart & Respiration Rates—Nellcor Puritan Bennett Incorporated; *U.S. Public*, pg. 1039

ASSURE—Specialty Paper—The Dexter Corporation; *U.S. Public*, pg. 504

ASTAR—Helicopters—American Eurocopter Corp.; *Int'l*, pg. 29

ASTAR—NONE—Sime Darby Berhad; *Int'l*, pg. 1249

ASTEC—Resistive Networks, Instruments & Meters—Emerson Electric Co.; *U.S. Public*, pg. 572

ASTEC—NONE—Milgray Electronics, Inc.; *U.S. Public*, pg. 205

ASTER—Fiber Couplers & Connectors—Thomas & Betts Corporation; *U.S. Public*, pg. 1597

ASTHMA ALLERGY CARE AMERICA—Asthma & Allergy Care Services—Vivra Incorporated; *U.S. Public*, pg. 1723

ASTHMAHALER—Aerosol Bronchodilator—Menley & James Laboratories, Inc.; *U.S. Public*, pg. 1086

ASTHMANEFRIN—Liquid Bronchodilator—Menley & James Laboratories, Inc.; *U.S. Public*, pg. 1086

ASTI CINZANO—NONE—Societe Pour la Vente des Produits Cinzano SA; *Int'l*, pg. 410

ASTI MONDORO—Sparkling Wine—Barbero 1891 SpA; *Int'l*, pg. 164

ASTI SPUMANTE—NONE—Gio. Buton S.p.a.; *Int'l*, pg. 409

ASTI SPUMANTE BANFI—NONE—Castello Banfi Srl.; *U.S. Private*, pg. 113

ASTON MARTIN—Auto—Aston Martin Lagonda of North America, Inc.; *U.S. Public*, pg. 664

ASTRA—Syringes—Astra USA, Inc.; *Int'l*, pg. 93

ASTRA—Hardware—The Black & Decker Corporation; *U.S. Public*, pg. 233

ASTRA—Business Jet—Israel Aircraft Industries Ltd.; *Int'l*, pg. 689

ASTRA—Van—Vauxhall; *U.S. Public*, pg. 724

ASTRA STERILE-PAK—Pharmaceutical Products—Astra USA, Inc.; *Int'l*, pg. 93

ASTRAD—Economic Information—Kompass International Neuenschwander SA; *Int'l*, pg. 745

ASTRAFLEX—Flexo Printing Press—Windmoeller & Hoelscher; *Int'l*, pg. 1510

ASTRAL—Building Paints for Exterior, Interior, Prof. & Retail Uses—Akzo Nobel N.V.; *Int'l*, pg. 42

ASTRAPAK—Wavesoldering System—Electrovert; *Int'l*, pg. 328

ASTRE—Service Mark—Astre Corporate Group; *U.S. Private*, pg. 93

ASTRING-O-SOL—NONE—SmithKline Beecham Research Limited; *Int'l*, pg. 1266

ASTRINGYN—Astringents for Medical Uses—The Cooper Companies, Inc.; *U.S. Public*, pg. 442

ASTRO—NONE—Astro Dairy Products Ltd.; *Int'l*, pg. 95

ASTRO—Shoes—E.J. Footwear Corp.; *U.S. Public*, pg. 1684

ASTRO—Popcorn Machine—Gold Medal Products Co.; *U.S. Private*, pg. 459

ASTRO—Tall Fescue—Green Seed Co.; *U.S. Private*, pg. 477

ASTRO-GRAPH—Digital Chart Recorders—Astro-Med, Inc.; *U.S. Public*, pg. 141

ASTRO GUM 21—Anionic Corn Starch—Penford Corp.; *U.S. Public*, pg. 1269

ASTRO GUMS—Carboxymethylated Corn Starches—Penford Corp.; *U.S. Public*, pg. 1269

ASTRO-MED—High Speed Graphic Recording Systems—Astro-Med, Inc.; *U.S. Public*, pg. 141

ASTRO POOLS—NONE—Astro-Valcour Inc.; *Int'l*, pg. 756

ASTRO POPS—Suckers—Spangler Candy Company; *U.S. Private*, pg. 1020

ASTRO-SCIENCE—Magnetic Tape Recorders—Eastman Kodak Company; *U.S. Public*, pg. 550

ASTRO STAR—Sporting Goods—Brunswick Bowling & Billiards Corp.; *U.S. Public*, pg. 265

ASTRO-TOUCH—Astronaut Style Ballpoint Pen—Eversharp Pen Co.; *U.S. Private*, pg. 386

ASTRO 2—Sporting Goods—Brunswick Bowling & Billiards Corp.; *U.S. Public*, pg. 265

ASTRO-VAC—Central Vacuum Systems—Lindsay Manufacturing Inc.; *U.S. Private*, pg. 668

ASTRO VAN—Truck—Chevrolet Motor Div. General Motors Corp.; *U.S. Public*, pg. 720

ASTRO WARRIOR—Videogame—Sega of America Inc.; *Int'l*, pg. 1218

ASTRO X—Cationic Potato Starch—Penford Corp.; *U.S. Public*, pg. 1269

ASTROCEL—Air Filter—AAF-International; *U.S. Private*, pg. 3

ASTROCOTE 75—Potato Starch—Penford Corp.; *U.S. Public*, pg. 1269

ASTRODAQ—Data Acquisition System—Astro-Med, Inc.; *U.S. Public*, pg. 141

ASTROLANE & DESIGN—Sporting Goods—Brunswick Bowling & Billiards Corp.; *U.S. Public*, pg. 265

ASTROLINE STAR DESIGN—Sporting Equipment—Brunswick Bowling & Billiards Corp.; *U.S. Public*, pg. 265

ASTRON—Pre-Engineered Metal Buildings—Commercial Intertech Corp.; *U.S. Public*, pg. 411

ASTRONAUT—Pens & Refills—Eversharp Pen Co.; *U.S. Private*, pg. 386

ASTRONOMY—Magazine—Kalmbach Publishing Co.; *U.S. Private*, pg. 606

ASTROPOL—Metal Buildings—Commercial Intertech Corp.; *U.S. Public*, pg. 411

ASTROSPEC—Industrial Safety Eyewear—Uvex Safety, Inc.; *Int'l*, pg. 132

ASTROSYN—Motors—Minebea Co., Ltd.; *Int'l*, pg. 867

ASTROTEC—Laser Transmitter & Parts—Lucent Technologies Inc.; *U.S. Public*, pg. 1017

ASTROTURF—Doormats—Solutia Inc.; *U.S. Public*, pg. 1483

ASTROTURF—Artificial Turf—Southwest Recreational Industries Inc.; *U.S. Private*, pg. 1018

ASTROTURF H-D—Heavy-Duty Matting—Solutia Inc.; *U.S. Public*, pg. 1483

ASTROX—High Alumina Ceramic Refractory—Ferro Corporation; *U.S. Public*, pg. 618

ASTRYN—Mineral Filled Polymers—Montedison S.p.A.; *Int'l*, pg. 324

ASUKA—NONE—Pfizer Inc.; *U.S. Public*, pg. 1281

ASYNCGATE—Asynchronous Communications Gateway Software—Datapoint Corporation; *Int'l*, pg. 384

ASYST—Data Analysis Software—Keithley Instruments, Inc.; *U.S. Public*, pg. 946

AT-A-GLANCE—Appointment & Record Books—The At-A-Glance Group; *U.S. Private*, pg. 295

AT-A-GLANCE ORGANIZER—Organizers—The At-A-Glance Group; *U.S. Private*, pg. 295

AT-A-GLANCE TIME MANAGEMENT SOFTWARE—Computer Software—The At-A-Glance Group; *U.S. Private*, pg. 295

AT EASE—Apparel—The Apparel Group, Ltd.; *U.S. Private*, pg. 78

AT EASE—Adult Incontinent Briefs—The Tranzonic Companies; *U.S. Public*, pg. 1632

AT EASE—Incontinent Products—Tranzonic Personal Care Division; *U.S. Public*, pg. 1632

AT EAST—Household Cleaner—Shaklee Corporation; *Int'l*, pg. 1518

AT 3D—NONE—Alliance Semiconductor Corp.; *U.S. Public*, pg. 47

AT YOUR BEST—Newsletter—Rodale Press, Inc.; *U.S. Private*, pg. 939

ATABRON—Insecticide—Ishihara Sangyo Kaisha, Ltd.; *Int'l*, pg. 689

ATALLA—Division Name & Trademark—Tandem Computers Inc.; *U.S. Public*, pg. 417

ATAR 9—Military Jet Engine—SNECMA - Societe Nationale d'Etude et de Construction de Moteurs d'Aviation; *Int'l*, pg. 1165

ATARAX-P—NONE—Pfizer Inc.; *U.S. Public*, pg. 1281

ATARAX/VISTARIL—Hyrdroxyzine—Pfizer Inc.; *U.S. Public*, pg. 1281

ATARI—Video Games, Computers—JTS Corporation; *U.S. Public*, pg. 919

ATDENIM—Women's Clothing—AnnTaylor Stores Corporation; *U.S. Public*, pg. 116

ATEBRIN—Tropical Medicine for Treatment of Malaria—Bayer AG; *Int'l*, pg. 171

ATELIER MARTEX—Bed Accessories—WestPoint Stevens Inc.; *U.S. Public*, pg. 1762

ATEMI—Fungicide—Novartis AG; *Int'l*, pg. 971

ATENOLOL—Generic Drug—American Home Products Corporation; *U.S. Public*, pg. 79

ATEX—Computerized Text Editing Products—Eastman Kodak Company; *U.S. Public*, pg. 550

ATHLETIC X-PRESS—Athletic Footwear Stores—F.W. Woolworth Co.; *U.S. Public*, pg. 1777

ATHENA—X-Ray Equipment—Fischer Imaging Corporation; *U.S. Public*, pg. 647

ATHENA—Interior Floor Tile—Monarch Tile, Inc.; *U.S. Private*, pg. 287

ATHENA—P.C. Software—Ship Analytics, Inc.; *U.S. Private*, pg. 994

ATHENA—Intensive Care Patient Monitoring System—Vickers PLC; *Int'l*, pg. 1466

ATHENA V—O/U Shotgun—Weatherby, Inc.; *U.S. Private*, pg. 1155

ATHENA IV—NONE—Weatherby, Inc.; *U.S. Private*, pg. 1155

ATHENOS—Cheese—Churny Company Inc.; *U.S. Public*, pg. 1288

ATHENS BANNER HERALD—Newspaper—Shivers Trading & Operating Co.; *U.S. Private*, pg. 994

ATHENS DAILY NEWS—Newspapers—Shivers Trading & Operating Co.; *U.S. Private*, pg. 994

ATHENS MAGAZINE—Magazine—Shivers Trading & Operating Co.; *U.S. Private*, pg. 994

ATHERMAL—Welding Protection Glass—Deutsche Spezialglas AG; *Int'l*, pg. 1523

ATHEROL—Natural Lipotropic Combination—Nature's Bounty Inc.; *U.S. Public*, pg. 1166

ATHEY—Vacuum & Mini-Mechanical Street Sweepers—Athey Products Corporation; *U.S. Public*, pg. 142

THE ATHLETE'S FOOT—Retail Stores—The Athlete's Foot Group, Inc.; *U.S. Private*, pg. 94

ATHLETIC ATTIC—Men's & Women's Athletic Apparel—Athletic Attic Retail Company; *U.S. Public*, pg. 936

ATHLETIC FILED MARKING PAINT—Paint—Mautz Paint Co.; *U.S. Private*, pg. 715

ATHLETIC LADY—Ladie's Athletic Apparel—Athletic Attic Retail Company; *U.S. Public*, pg. 936

ATHLETIC SHOE FACTORY—Athletic Footwear & Apparel—Kinney Shoe Corporation; *U.S. Public*, pg. 1777

ATHLETIC X-PRESS—Family Athletic Footwear & Apparel Stores—Woolworth Corporation; *U.S. Public*, pg. 1777

ATHLETICS WEEKLY—Magazine—EMAP Pursuit Publishing; *Int'l*, pg. 451

ATHLEX—Athlete's Foot Prevention—Sani-Mist, Inc.; *U.S. Public*, pg. 965

ATHLITE—Watches—Reebok International Ltd.; *U.S. Public*, pg. 1369

ATHLON—Fruit Drinks—Danone Group; *Int'l*, pg. 379

ATIVAN—Lorazepam - Treatment Of Anxiety—American Home Products Corporation; *U.S. Public*, pg. 79

ATIVAN—NONE—Wyeth Australia Pty. Ltd.; *U.S. Public*, pg. 82

ATIVAN—Antianxiety Agent—Wyeth-Ayerst Laboratories, Inc.; *U.S. Public*, pg. 80

ATKINS—Pickles—Dean Foods Company; *U.S. Public*, pg. 489

ATLANTA—Bath Accessories—Baldwin Hardware Corporation; *U.S. Public*, pg. 1053

ATLANTA APPAREL MART—Men's, Women's & Children's Fashions—AMC, Inc.; *U.S. Private*, pg. 6

ATLANTA BRAVES—Team Name—Atlanta National League Baseball Club, Inc.; *U.S. Public*, pg. 1614

ATLANTA BRAVES—Professional Baseball Teams—Turner Broadcasting System Inc.; *U.S. Public*, pg. 1614

ATLANTA BUSINESS CHRONICLE—Business Journal—Business First of New York, Inc.; *U.S. Private*, pg. 19

ATLANTA DAIRIES—Dairy Products—Parmalat New Atlanta Dairies; *Int'l*, pg. 1023

ATLANTA DECORATIVE ARTS CENTER—Residential & Contract Design—AMC, Inc.; *U.S. Private*, pg. 6

ATLANTA FASHION PREVIEW—Apparel & Fashion Publication—AMC, Inc.; *U.S. Private*, pg. 6

ATLANTA HAWKS—Professional Basketball Team—Turner Broadcasting System Inc.; *U.S. Public*, pg. 1614

ATLANTA MARKET DIRECTORY—Industry-Specific Directories—AMC, Inc.; *U.S. Private*, pg. 6

ATLANTA MARKET PREVIEW—Gifts Periodical & Home Furnishings Periodical—AMC, Inc.; *U.S. Private*, pg. 6

ATLANTA MERCHANDISE MART—Residential, Commercial & Contract Furnishings—AMC, Inc.; *U.S. Private*, pg. 6

ATLANTA MOTOR SPEEDWAY—NONE—Atlanta Motor Speedway; *U.S. Public*, pg. 1498

ATLANTA MOTOR SPEEDWAY—NONE—Speedway Motorsports, Inc.; *U.S. Public*, pg. 1498

ATLANTA STOVE—Heating Equipment—Martin Industries, Inc. (AL); *U.S. Private*, pg. 709

ATLANTIC—Phonograph Records—Atlantic Recording Corporation; *U.S. Public*, pg. 1611

ATLANTIC—Manufactured Homes—Champion Enterprises, Inc.; *U.S. Public*, pg. 332

ATLANTIC—Maritime Patrol Aircraft—Dassault Aviation Group; *Int'l*, pg. 383

ATLANTIC—Fine Printing—Eastern Fine Paper; *U.S. Private*, pg. 357

ATLANTIC—Petroleum Products—Sun Company, Inc.; *U.S. Public*, pg. 1530

ATLANTIC—Petroleum, Motor Oil Products—Sun Company, Inc. (R&M); *U.S. Public*, pg. 1530

ATLANTIC MASTER PLAN—Comprehensive Personal Insurance Policy—Atlantic Mutual Companies; *U.S. Private*, pg. 95

THE ATLANTIC MONTHLY MAGAZINE—Magazine—The Atlantic Monthly Magazine; *U.S. Private*, pg. 95

ATLANTIC RISK SERVICES—Alternative Risk—Atlantic Mutual Companies; *U.S. Private*, pg. 95

ATLANTIC SPORTS—Sports Radio Network Covering the Atlantic Coast—Ray Communications, Inc.; *U.S. Private*, pg. 911

ATLANTIC STEEL—Hot Rolled Rod Products—Atlantic Steel Industries, Inc.; *Int'l*, pg. 696

ATLANTIC 252—Ireland Broadcasting—CLT-UFA; *Int'l*, pg. 561

ATLANTIS—NONE—Atlantis Plastic, Inc.; *U.S. Public*, pg. 145

ATLANTIS—Watches—Baume Mercier, Inc.; *U.S. Private*, pg. 124

ATLANTIS—Broadloom—Couristan Inc.; *U.S. Private*, pg. 279

ATLAS—Hotels & Restaurants—Atlas Hotels, Inc.; *U.S. Private*, pg. 96

ATLAS—Ester-Based Leather Tanning Auxiliaries—Atlas Refinery; *U.S. Private*, pg. 96

ATLAS—Automotive Supplies—Atlas Supply Company; *U.S. Private*, pg. 96

ATLAS—Bolts—Caparo Industries Plc.; *Int'l*, pg. 265

ATLAS—Advanced Thermal Labeling System—Esselte Meto Kimball Systems; *Int'l*, pg. 460

ATLAS—Detergent—Henkel KGaA; *Int'l*, pg. 609

ATLAS—Well-Logging Services—Litton Industries, Inc.; *U.S. Public*, pg. 1002

ATLAS—Lawnmowers—MTD Products, Inc.; *U.S. Private*, pg. 688

ATLAS—Maize—Novartis; *Int'l*, pg. 972

ATLAS—Records & Cassettes—Polygram Records, Inc.; *Int'l*, pg. 1052

ATLAS—Watches, Writing Instruments—Tiffany & Co.; *U.S. Public*, pg. 1608

ATLAS—NONE—Western Atlas Logging Services; *U.S. Public*, pg. 1757

ATLAS—Fitness Products—York Barbell Co., Inc.; *U.S. Private*, pg. 1196

ATLAS AUTOMOTIVE—Automotive Accessories—General Automotive Corporation; *U.S. Private*, pg. 443

ATLAS BODY—NONE—Union City Body Company, L.P.; *U.S. Private*, pg. 1118

ATLAS COPCO—Compressors—Atlas Copco Comptec Inc.; *Int'l*, pg. 96

ATLAS COPCO ROCK TOOLS—Drill Steel Prods.—Atlas Copco AB; *Int'l*, pg. 95

ATLAS 400—Electronic Mail Switching System—France Telecom; *Int'l*, pg. 503

ATLAS LAUNCH VEHICLE—NONE—General Dynamics Corporation; *Int'l*, pg. 708

ATLAS LEATHEROIL—Oiling Off Compounds for Leather—Atlas Refinery; *U.S. Private*, pg. 96

ATLAS PEAK—Wine—The Wine Alliance; *Int'l*, pg. 63

ATLAS PEAK CALIFORNIA WINE—Wine—Allied Domecq PLC; *Int'l*, pg. 62

ATLAS SHUR-BOND—Bonded Brakes—General Automotive Corporation; *U.S. Private*, pg. 443

ATLAS/SOUND—Microphone & Equipment Stands, Accessories—Atlas/Soundolier; *U.S. Private*, pg. 64

ATLAS/SOUNDOLIER—Electronics—American Trading and Production Corporation; *U.S. Private*, pg. 63

ATLAS/SOUNDOLIER—Communication Products—Atlas/Soundolier; *U.S. Private*, pg. 64

ATLAS STEELS—Metal Products—Email Limited; *Int'l*, pg. 450

ATLAS VAN LINES—Domestic & Intl. Transportation of Household Goods; Long Distance Moving—Atlas Van Lines, Inc.; *U.S. Private*, pg. 97

ATLAS VAN LINES AGENT—NONE—Nelson Westerlay, Inc.; *U.S. Private*, pg. 1163

ATLAS WHITE—White Titanium—Warner-Jenkinson Co.; *U.S. Public*, pg. 1696

ATLAS WIRELINE SERVICES—NONE—Western Atlas Logging Services; *U.S. Public*, pg. 1757

ATLASOL—Sulphated Synthetic Oils—Atlas Refinery; *U.S. Private*, pg. 96

ATLASTAN—Synthetic Tanning Agents—Atlas Refinery; *U.S. Private*, pg. 96

ATMA—Electrical Home Appliances—Noblex Argentina S.A.C. e I.; *Int'l*, pg. 951

ATMEL—NONE—Milgray Electronics, Inc.; *U.S. Public*, pg. 205

ATMES—Mini-environments—Daw Technologies, Inc.; *U.S. Public*, pg. 489

ATMIZER—Semiconductor Device, Integrated Circuit or Services—LSI Logic Corp.; *U.S. Public*, pg. 971

ATMOS—Clock that Operates Without Batteries or Winding—Swiss Prestige, Inc.; *Int'l*, pg. 697

ATMOS—Food Emulsifiers—Witco Corporation; *U.S. Public*, pg. 1773

ATMOS 2000—Reflowsoldering System—Electrovert; *Int'l*, pg. 328

ATOLS—Die Casting Molds—Atols Tool and Mold Corp.; *U.S. Private*, pg. 97

ATOM ARC—NONE—ESAB Welding & Cutting Products; *Int'l*, pg. 281

ATOMA—Automotive Parts—Magna International Inc.; *Int'l*, pg. 829

ATOMCOMP—NONE—Thermo Jarrell Ash Corporation; *U.S. Public*, pg. 1594

ATOMIC—Alpine & Cross Country Ski Equipment—Amer Group Ltd.; *Int'l*, pg. 72

ATOMIC SPECTROSCOPY—A Perkin-Elmer Technical Publication—The Perkin-Elmer Corporation; *U.S. Public*, pg. 1279

ATOMOLAN—Metabolic Agents—Kyowa Hakko Kogyo Company, Ltd.; *Int'l*, pg. 778

ATOMSCAN—NONE—Thermo Jarrell Ash Corporation; *U.S. Public*, pg. 1594

ATORA—Food Products—Ranks Hovis McDougall Limited; *Int'l*, pg. 1395

ATRA—Pivoting Head Razors & Blades—The Gillette Company; *U.S. Public*, pg. 743

ATRA PLUS—Pivoting Head Razor & Blades—The Gillette Company; *U.S. Public*, pg. 743

ATRALAR—Protective Coating for Urethane Foam—H.B. Fuller Company; *U.S. Public*, pg. 686

ATRALOC—Surgical Needles—Ethicon, Inc.; *U.S. Public*, pg. 928

ATRIA—Business Centers—Accor S.A.; *Int'l*, pg. 20

ATRIUM—NONE—The Dress Barn, Inc.; *U.S. Public*, pg. 528

ATRIX—NONE—Beiersdorf S.A.; *Int'l*, pg. 183

ATRIXO—Handcare Product—Smith & Nephew PLC; *Int'l*, pg. 1263

ATROBAC—NONE—Pfizer Inc.; *U.S. Public*, pg. 1281

ATROHIST—NONE—Medeva PLC; *Int'l*, pg. 852

ATROPEN AUTO-INJECTOR—Pressure Activated Syringe—Meridian Medical Technology, Inc.; *U.S. Public*, pg. 1095

ATROVENT—Anticholinergic—Boehringer Ingelheim GmbH; *Int'l*, pg. 199

ATROVENT—Anticholinergic Bronchodilator—Boehringer Ingelheim Pharmaceuticals, Inc.; *Int'l*, pg. 199

ATTACHE—Brandy—Eckes AG; *Int'l*, pg. 432

ATTACHE IV—Portable Dictation Unit—Lanier Worldwide Inc.; *U.S. Public*, pg. 791

ATTACHED RESOURCE COMPUTER—Logical Computer System—Datapoint Corporation; *Int'l*, pg. 384

ATTACK—Detergent—Kao Corporation; *Int'l*, pg. 717

ATTACK—Pest Control Products—Ringer Corporation; *U.S. Public*, pg. 1390

ATTACLAY—Earth Used In Insecticide Formulations—Engelhard Corporation; *U.S. Public*, pg. 582

ATTACOTE—Attapulgite Clay for use as Anti-Caking Agent—Engelhard Corporation; *U.S. Public*, pg. 582

ATTAFLOW—Attapulgite Clay Used as a Suspending Agent in Liquid Fertilizers—Engelhard Corporation; *U.S. Public*, pg. 582

ATTAGEL—Attapulgite Clay Used as Thickener—Engelhard Corporation; *U.S. Public*, pg. 582

ATTANE—Ethylene/Octene Copolymer—The Dow Chemical Company; *U.S. Public*, pg. 522

ATTAPULGITE—Industrial Minerals—Engelhard Corp.-Quincy Operations; *U.S. Public*, pg. 582

ATTAPULGUS—Fullers Earth Having Oil & Water Absorption Properties—Engelhard Corporation; *U.S. Public*, pg. 582

ATTASORB—Low Volatile Content Fullers Earth—Engelhard Corporation; *U.S. Public*, pg. 582

ATTENDS—Paper Products—The Procter & Gamble Company; *U.S. Public*, pg. 1330

ATTENULED—Lead Sheet for Sound Control—Taracorp, Inc.; *U.S. Private*, pg. 1068

ATTENUVAX—Measles Virus Vaccine—Merck & Co., Inc.; *U.S. Public*, pg. 1090

ATTEST—Biological Monitoring Indicators & Incubators—3M; *U.S. Public*, pg. 1604

ATTIC BLANKET—Glass Fiber Insulation—Owens Corning; *U.S. Public*, pg. 1236

ATTIC BREEZE—Residential Ventilation Products—Butler Ventamatic Corp.; *U.S. Private*, pg. 190

ATTITUDES—Hair Coloring—Bristol-Myers Squibb Company; *U.S. Public*, pg. 253

ATTWOOD—Marine Accessories & Hardware—Attwood Corporation; *U.S. Private*, pg. 1038

ATWOOD & MORRILL—Industrial Valves—Atwood & Morrill Co., Inc.; *Int'l*, pg. 1489

AU BON PAIN—Croissants & Bread—Au Bon Pain Co., Inc.; *U.S. Public*, pg. 146

AU PAIR IN AMERICA—Au Pair Placement Program—American Institute for Foreign Study; *U.S. Private*, pg. 56

AUBREY—Bath Fans & Heaters—Aubrey Manufacturing Company; *U.S. Public*, pg. 1193

AUCTION—Leisure Game—Monarch Avalon, Inc.; *U.S. Public*, pg. 1123

AUDA—NONE—ETEX; *Int'l*, pg. 430

AUDAX—Loudspeakers—Harman International Industries, Inc.; *U.S. Public*, pg. 787

AUDI—Automobiles—Audi of America; *Int'l*, pg. 1474

AUDI—Automobiles—Lantzsch-Andreas Enterprises, Inc.; *U.S. Private*, pg. 650

AUDI—Auto—Loeber Motors, Inc.; *U.S. Private*, pg. 672

AUDI—Automobile—Volkswagen AG; *Int'l*, pg. 1473

AUDI A8—Automobile—Volkswagen AG; *Int'l*, pg. 1473

AUDI A8—Car—Volkswagen of America, Inc.; *Int'l*, pg. 1474

AUDI A4—Automobile—Volkswagen AG; *Int'l*, pg. 1473

AUDI A4—Car—Volkswagen of America, Inc.; *Int'l*, pg. 1474

AUDI A6—Automobile—Volkswagen AG; *Int'l*, pg. 1473

AUDI A6—Car—Volkswagen of America, Inc.; *Int'l*, pg. 1474

AUDI A3—Atuomobile—Volkswagen AG; *Int'l*, pg. 1473

AUDI CABRIOLET—Automobile—Volkswagen AG; *Int'l*, pg. 1473

AUDI CABRIOLET—Convertible Car—Volkswagen of America, Inc.; *Int'l*, pg. 1474

AUDI COUPE—Sports Car—Volkswagen AG; *Int'l*, pg. 1473

AUDIA—Radio—Clarion Corporation of America; *Int'l*, pg. 296

AUDIANT—Implantable Hearing Device—Bristol-Myers Squibb Company; *U.S. Public*, pg. 253

AUDICHRON—Announcement Systems—Electronic Tele-Communications, Inc.; *U.S. Public*, pg. 570

AUDICHRON 410—Time/Weather/Temperature Announcers—Electronic Tele-Communications, Inc.; *U.S. Public*, pg. 570

AUDIENCE INFORMATION MEASUREMENT SYSTEM (AIMS)—Market Research—Madison Newspapers, Inc.; *U.S. Public*, pg. 984

AUDIO—Home Entertainment Magazine—Hachette Filipacchi Magazines Inc.; *Int'l*, pg. 794

AUDIO ACCESS—NONE—Harman Consumer Group; *U.S. Public*, pg. 787

AUDIO CHOICE—Hearing Aids—Dahlberg, Inc.; *U.S. Public*, pg. 194

AUDIO MASTER—Industrial Communications Devices—Federal Signal Corporation, Signal Div.; *U.S. Public*, pg. 616

AUDIO MASTER—Electronic Components—Shure Brothers Incorporated; *U.S. Private*, pg. 997

AUDIO PACK—Portable Sound Systems—Actron Manufacturing Company; *U.S. Private*, pg. 16

AUDIO SCOUT—Portable Audiometer—Beltone Electronics Corporation; *U.S. Private*, pg. 132

AUDIO VAULT—Digital Audio Storage System—Broadcast Electronics, Inc.; *U.S. Private*, pg. 531

AUDIO VIDEO EXPOSITION—Hands on Experience for Customers—The Good Guys, Inc.; *U.S. Public*, pg. 750

AUDIO VISUAL CONNECTION—Computer Systems—International Business Machines Corporation; *U.S. Public*, pg. 895

AUDIO WALL—Partitions—Modernfold, Inc.; *U.S. Private*, pg. 755

AUDIOCOLOR—TV Monitors—Tatung Company of America; *Int'l*, pg. 1357

AUDIOCOM—Intercoms—Telex Communications, Inc.; *U.S. Private*, pg. 1074

AUDIOMETRICS—Electronic Product—Harris Broadcast Division; *U.S. Public*, pg. 791

AUDIOTEX—Phone Mail System—Ameritech Audiotex Services Inc.; *U.S. Public*, pg. 98

AUDIOVATION—Computer System—International Business Machines Corporation; *U.S. Public*, pg. 895

AUDIOVOX—Stereo Equipment—Audiovox Corporation; *U.S. Public*, pg. 147

AUDIOVOX—Cellular Phonest—Audiovox Corporation; *U.S. Public*, pg. 147

AUDISIO—Pasta—CSM N.V.; *Int'l*, pg. 243

AUDIT COMPASS—Compliance Database—International Technology Corporation; *U.S. Public*, pg. 907

AUDITIONS—Shoes—Craddock-Terry Inc.; *U.S. Private*, pg. 284

AUDITOR 2—Revenue Control Fee Computer for Use in Parking Operations—Federal APD, Inc.; *U.S. Public*, pg. 616

AUDIX—Telecommunications Products & Software for Voice Processing & Voice Mail—Lucent Technologies Inc.; *U.S. Public*, pg. 1017

AUDUBON—Binoculars—Swift Instruments, Inc.; *U.S. Private*, pg. 1058

AUDUTOR—Liquid Burn In—Despatch Industries; *U.S. Private*, pg. 327

AUGAT—Electronic Components—Augat, Inc.; *U.S. Public*, pg. 1597

AUGAT—Sockets—Thomas & Betts Corporation; *U.S. Public*, pg. 1597

AUGAT/ALCO—NONE—Milgray Electronics, Inc.; *U.S. Public*, pg. 205

AUGMENTIN—Antibiotics—Meiji Seika Kaisha, Ltd.; *Int'l*, pg. 855

AUGMENTIN—Anti-Infective Product—SmithKline Beecham Corporation; *Int'l*, pg. 1264

AUGMENTIN—Pharmaceutical Prods.—SmithKline Beecham Laboratories; *Int'l*, pg. 1264

AUGMENTIN—Anti-Infective—SmithKline Beecham plc; *Int'l*, pg. 1264

AUGMENTIN—Antibiotic—SmithKline Beecham Research Limited; *Int'l*, pg. 1266

AUGSBURG FORTRESS—Sunday School Curriculum, Church Bulletins, Videos, Bibles—Augsburg Fortress, Publishers; *U.S. Private*, pg. 98

AUGSBURGER—NONE—The Stroh Brewery Company; *U.S. Private*, pg. 1047

AUGUSTA CHRONICLE—Newspaper—Shivers Trading & Operating Co.; *U.S. Private*, pg. 994

AUGUSTA MAGAZINE—Magazine—Shivers Trading & Operating Co.; *U.S. Private*, pg. 994

AULT—NONE—Milgray Electronics, Inc.; *U.S. Public*, pg. 205

AULT—Foods—Parmalat Canada Ltd.; *Int'l*, pg. 1023

AULTRA-THIN—Pastes for Electronic Circuits—Ferro Corporation; *U.S. Public*, pg. 618

AUNT CLARA'S—Fruit Spreads—Nestle Chocolate & Confection; *Int'l*, pg. 917

AUNT FANNY'S—Bakery Goods—The Pillsbury Company; *Int'l*, pg. 411

AUNT JANE'S—Pickles—Dean Foods Company; *U.S. Public*, pg. 489

AUNT JEMIMA—Pancake Mix, Syrup, Corn Meal, Waffle Mix, Grits, Muffin Mixes—The Quaker Oats Company; *U.S. Public*, pg. 1347

AUNT JEMIMA BUTTERLITE—Syrup—The Quaker Oats Company; *U.S. Public*, pg. 1347

AUNT JEMIMA ENRICHED CORN MEAL—Corn Meal—The Quaker Oats Company; *U.S. Public*, pg. 1347

AUNT JEMIMA ENRICHED SELF-RISING FLOUR—Flour—The Quaker Oats Company; *U.S. Public*, pg. 1347

AUNT JEMIMA ENRICHED WHITE HOMINY GRITS—Grits—The Quaker Oats Company; *U.S. Public*, pg. 1347

AUNT JEMIMA ENRICHED WHITE HOMINY QUICK GRITS—Grits—The Quaker Oats Company; *U.S. Public*, pg. 1347

AUNT JEMIMA HOMESTYLE—Frozen Breakfast Entree—The Quaker Oats Co. of Canada Ltd.; *U.S. Public*, pg. 1348

AUNT JEMIMA JUMBO WAFFLES—Waffles—The Quaker Oats Company; *U.S. Public*, pg. 1347

AUNT JEMIMA ORIGINAL PANCAKE & WAFFLE MIX—Pancake & Waffle Mix—The Quaker Oats Company; *U.S. Public*, pg. 1347

AUNT JEMIMA PANCAKE BATTER—Frozen Pancake Batter—The Quaker Oats Company; *U.S. Public*, pg. 1347

AUNT JEMIMA SYRUP—Maple Syrup—The Quaker Oats Company; *U.S. Public*, pg. 1347

AUNT KITTY'S—Processed Soup—Hanover Foods Corporation; *U.S. Private*, pg. 499

AUNT MILLIE'S—Spaghetti Sauce—Borden, Inc.; *U.S. Private*, pg. 157

AUNT MILLIE'S—Pasta Sauces—Borden Italian Foods; *U.S. Private*, pg. 158

AUNT NELLIE'S—Canned Vegetables, Glace Fruit, Deli Salads and Sauces—The Pillsbury Company; *Int'l*, pg. 411

AUNT WICK'S—Root Beer—The Jel Sert Co.; *U.S. Private*, pg. 585

AUPAMESA—Engine System Parts—Echlin Inc.; *U.S. Public*, pg. 560

AURA—Downstream Microwave Ashers—GaSonics International; *U.S. Public*, pg. 703

AURA—NONE—Laserscope Surgical Systems; *U.S. Public*, pg. 979

AURAFILL—Dental Restorative—Johnson & Johnson Consumer Products; *U.S. Public*, pg. 928

AURAFLEX—Random Access Hormone Test & Infectious Disease Assay Clinical Analyzer—Akzo Nobel N.V.; *Int'l*, pg. 42

AURALL 292M—Superior Metal Distribution—LeaRonal, Inc.; *U.S. Public*, pg. 982

AURATONE—Acoustical Ceiling Tile—CGC Inc.; *U.S. Public*, pg. 1660

AURATONE—Acoustical Panels—USG Corporation; *U.S. Public*, pg. 1660

AURATONE—Ceiling & Wall Products—USG Interiors, Inc.; *U.S. Public*, pg. 1660

AUREX—Audio Equip.—Toshiba Corporation; *Int'l*, pg. 1402

AURIGA—CMP Tool—SpeedFan International, Inc.; *U.S. Public*, pg. 1497

AURO—Ear Drops—Del Pharmaceuticals, Inc.; *U.S. Public*, pg. 494

AURO-DRI—For Swimmer's Ear—Del Pharmaceuticals, Inc.; *U.S. Public*, pg. 494

AURODURE—24 Karat Gold Systems—LeaRonal, Inc.; *U.S. Public*, pg. 982

AUROGLEAM—Gold Electroplating Process—LeaRonal, Inc.; *U.S. Public*, pg. 982

AUROGLO 4—Acid Type Hard Bright Gold Processes—LeaRonal, Inc.; *U.S. Public*, pg. 982

AUROGLO 12—Acid Type Hard Bright Controlled Gold Process—LeaRonal, Inc.; *U.S. Public*, pg. 982

AUROJET—Specially Formulated Gold Process—LeaRonal, Inc.; *U.S. Public*, pg. 982

AURONAL—Industrial Gold Deposits—LeaRonal, Inc.; *U.S. Public*, pg. 982

AURORA—Pumps—Aurora Pump; *U.S. Public*, pg. 726

AURORA—Bathroom Tissue—Consumer Products Business; *U.S. Public*, pg. 671

AURORA—Fluorescent Lamp—Duro-Test Corporation; *U.S. Private*, pg. 349

AURORA—Tissue—Fort James Corporation; *U.S. Public*, pg. 670

AURORA—Automobile—General Motors Corporation; *U.S. Public*, pg. 718

AURORA—Off-the-Shelf Home Health Care Products Marketed through Mass Retail—Invacare Corporation; *U.S. Public*, pg. 911

AURORA—NONE—Lam Research Corporation; *U.S. Public*, pg. 975

AURORA—Automobile—Oldsmobile Div. General Motors Corp.; *U.S. Public*, pg. 720

AURORA—Gelatins, Puddings & Flan—RJR Nabisco Holdings Corp.; *U.S. Public*, pg. 1354

AURORA—Closed Circuit Television Equipment—Vicon Industries, Inc.; *U.S. Public*, pg. 1719

THE AURORA AU/90—Paint & Animation Systems—Chyron Corp.; *Int'l*, pg. 1372

THE AURORA AU/250—Paint & Animation System—Chyron Corp.; *Int'l*, pg. 1372

THE AURORA AU/240—Paint & Animation System—Chyron Corp.; *Int'l*, pg. 1372

AURORA PINK—FluorescentColor—Day-Glo Color Corp.; *U.S. Public*, pg. 1357

THE AURORA 280 CADET—Paint & Animation—Chyron Corp.; *Int'l*, pg. 1372

THE AURORA 250 GT—Paint & Animation—Chyron Corp.; *Int'l*, pg. 1372

AURORIX—Antidepressant—Roche Holding Ltd.; *Int'l*, pg. 1119

AUROSPEED—High Speed, High-Cathode Efficiencies—LeaRonal, Inc.; *U.S. Public*, pg. 982

AUROSPEED E—Cadmium Hardened Gold—LeaRonal, Inc.; *U.S. Public*, pg. 982

AUROSPOT—Specially Formulated Gold Process—LeaRonal, Inc.; *U.S. Public*, pg. 982

AUROSTRIKE GP—Dense Fine Grain Deposits—LeaRonal, Inc.; *U.S. Public*, pg. 982

AUROTAB—High Speed Hard Gold Baths—LeaRonal, Inc.; *U.S. Public*, pg. 982

AUROTECH—Gold Electroplating Solution—Lucent Technologies Inc.; *U.S. Public*, pg. 1017

AUROVEL HV—High Speed Bath—LeaRonal, Inc.; *U.S. Public*, pg. 982

AUROVEL UP 24—High Speed Bath—LeaRonal, Inc.; *U.S. Public*, pg. 982

Brand Name Index

AUSAB—Diagnostic Products—Abbott Laboratories; *U.S. Public*, pg. 12
AUSAB EIA—Diagnostic Products—Abbott Laboratories; *U.S. Public*, pg. 12
AUSCELL—Diagnostic Products—Abbott Laboratories; *U.S. Public*, pg. 12
AUSCO—Light Truck Jacks; Brakes for Off-Highway Equip. Vehicles—Ausco Products, Inc.; *U.S. Private*, pg. 299
AUSCO—Modular Buildings—James Hardie Industries Ltd.; *Int'l*, pg. 596
AUSHERMAN GP—Combine Cylinder Bars & Coulters—Great Plains Manufacturing, Inc.; *U.S. Private*, pg. 475
AUSLESE DE LUXE—NONE—British-American Tobacco (Germany) GmbH; *Int'l*, pg. 111
AUSRIA-2 125—Diagnostic Products—Abbott Laboratories; *U.S. Public*, pg. 12
AUSSIE MEGA SHAMPOO WITH PAPAYA—Shampoo—Redmond Products, Inc.; *U.S. Public*, pg. 254
AUSSIE MEGA STYLING SPRAY—Non-Aerosol & Aerosol Hair Spray—Redmond Products, Inc.; *U.S. Public*, pg. 254
AUSSIE MOIST—Shampoo—Redmond Products, Inc.; *U.S. Public*, pg. 254
AUSSIE PRODUCT NEWS—Travel Magazine—Reed Business Information Pty. Limited; *Int'l*, pg. 1094
AUSSIE STYLING GEL—Conditioner—Redmond Products, Inc.; *U.S. Public*, pg. 254
AUSTAD'S—Golf Equipment, Accessories & Apparel—Hanover Direct, Inc.; *U.S. Public*, pg. 782
AUSTEX—NONE—Castleberry/Snow's Brands Inc.; *U.S. Private*, pg. 219
AUSTIN—Cleaners & Laundry Products—James Austin Co.; *U.S. Private*, pg. 99
AUSTIN—Peanut Butter Crackers & Cookies—Austin Quality Foods; *U.S. Private*, pg. 100
THE AUSTIN COMPANY—Consultants, Designers, Engineers & Constructors—The Austin Company; *U.S. Private*, pg. 99
THE AUSTIN METHOD—Proprietary Concept of Single-Source Approach to Design, Engrng. & Constr.—The Austin Company; *U.S. Private*, pg. 99
AUSTIN REED OF REGENT STREET—Men's & Women's Clothing—Hartmarx Corporation; *U.S. Public*, pg. 795
AUSTRAL—Copper & Copper Alloy Rolled Sheet & Strip—Austral Bronze Crane Copper Limited; *Int'l*, pg. 340
AUSTRALIAN CITRIFIER—Shampoo—Redmond Products, Inc.; *U.S. Public*, pg. 254
AUSTRALIAN DOCTOR—Magazine—Reed Business Information Pty. Limited; *Int'l*, pg. 1094
AUSTRALIAN ELECTRONICS ENGINEERING—Magazine—Reed Business Information Pty. Limited; *Int'l*, pg. 1094
THE AUSTRALIAN FINANCIAL REVIEW—NONE—John Fairfax Holdings Limited; *Int'l*, pg. 477
AUSTRALIAN FUNDS MANAGEMENT INDUSTRY YEARBOOK—Directory—Reed Business Information Pty. Limited; *Int'l*, pg. 1094
AUSTRALIAN GEOGRAPHIC—Nature Magazine—John Fairfax Holdings Limited; *Int'l*, pg. 477
AUSTRALIAN HAIR SALAD—Conditioner—Redmond Products, Inc.; *U.S. Public*, pg. 254
AUSTRALIAN MINING—Magazine—Reed Business Information Pty. Limited; *Int'l*, pg. 1094
AUSTRALIAN NEWSAGENT & STATIONER—Magazine—Reed Business Information Pty. Limited; *Int'l*, pg. 1094
AUSTRALIAN 3 MINUTE MIRACLE—Conditioner—Redmond Products, Inc.; *U.S. Public*, pg. 254
AUSTRIAN ALPS—Cheese—M.H. Greenebaum, Inc.; *U.S. Private*, pg. 477
AUSTWIN—Double Glazed Units—Pilkington Australasia Limited; *Int'l*, pg. 1057
AUSZYNE—Diagnostic Products—Abbott Laboratories; *U.S. Public*, pg. 12
AUTEMP—Hot Plate—Fisher Scientific Company; *U.S. Private*, pg. 658
AUTEX—NONE—Allied Diagnostic Imaging Resources, Inc.; *U.S. Public*, pg. 282

AUTHENTIC RUGBY SHIRT—Sportshirt—Lands' End, Inc.; *U.S. Public*, pg. 977
AUTHENTICATION—NONE—Check Point Software Technologies Ltd.; *U.S. Public*, pg. 342
AUTHORITY—Herbicide—FMC Corp., Agricultural Products Group; *U.S. Public*, pg. 605
AUTO ARMOR—Rust Protection—Daubert Industries, Inc.; *U.S. Private*, pg. 313
AUTO BILD—Magazine—Axel Springer Verlag AG; *Int'l*, pg. 102
AUTO BUSINESS—NONE—EMAP Business Communications Division; *Int'l*, pg. 451
AUTO-CAP—Capacitor Controls—Fisher Pierce Division; *U.S. Public*, pg. 1250
AUTO CAPTURE—Pacemaker—St. Jude Medical, Inc.; *U.S. Public*, pg. 1427
AUTO-CHEK—Amplifier Gain Control for IR Spectrometers—The Perkin-Elmer Corporation; *U.S. Public*, pg. 1279
AUTO CLAMP—Securing Cable Into Plastic Boxes—Pass & Seymour/Legrand; *Int'l*, pg. 806
AUTO-DIP—Switches—CTS Corporation; *U.S. Public*, pg. 285
AUTO DRIVEAWAY—Vehicle Relocation Services—Auto Driveaway Co.; *U.S. Private*, pg. 100
AUTO ECOLES—NONE—EMAP France; *Int'l*, pg. 451
AUTO EXPRESS—Auto Repair Stores—Montgomery Ward & Co., Inc.; *U.S. Private*, pg. 758
AUTO-FIND—PH Meter Feature—Beckman Instruments, Inc.; *U.S. Public*, pg. 199
AUTO FLO—Humidifiers—American Metal Products; *U.S. Public*, pg. 1053
AUTO-FLO—Control Console—Medtronic, Inc.; *U.S. Public*, pg. 1082
AUTO FLOTTE—NONE—EMAP Business Communications Division; *Int'l*, pg. 451
AUTO-GAMMA—Automatic Gamma Counting System—Packard Instrument Co., Inc.; *U.S. Private*, pg. 833
AUTO-GROUND—Auto Grounding—Pass & Seymour/Legrand; *Int'l*, pg. 806
AUTO-GUIDE—Power Flanger—Lockformer Company; *U.S. Public*, pg. 1100
AUTO ICS—Automated Sample Handling System—Beckman Instruments, Inc.; *U.S. Public*, pg. 199
AUTO INFOS—NONE—EMAP France; *Int'l*, pg. 451
AUTO-INKING—Computer System—International Business Machines Corporation; *U.S. Public*, pg. 895
AUTO-ISOSET—Radioisotope Detector Feature—Beckman Instruments, Inc.; *U.S. Public*, pg. 199
AUTO-JACK—Modular Device for Telephone Network Interface—TII Industries, Inc.; *U.S. Public*, pg. 1556
AUTO LASER 500—Invisible Beam—David White, L.L.C.; *U.S. Public*, pg. 1765
AUTO LASER 500—Invisible Beam—David White, L.L.C.; *U.S. Private*, pg. 1765
AUTO LASER 1550—Invisible Beam—David White, L.L.C.; *U.S. Public*, pg. 1765
AUTO LASER 1550—Invisible Beam—David White, L.L.C.; *U.S. Private*, pg. 1765
AUTO LASER 700—Invisible Beam—David White, L.L.C.; *U.S. Public*, pg. 1765
AUTO LASER 700—Invisible Beam—David White, L.L.C.; *U.S. Private*, pg. 1765
AUTO LASER 300—Invisible Beam—David White, L.L.C.; *U.S. Public*, pg. 1765
AUTO LASER 300—Invisible Beam—David White, L.L.C.; *U.S. Private*, pg. 1765
AUTO LASER 350—Invisible Beam—David White, L.L.C.; *U.S. Public*, pg. 1765
AUTO LASER 350—Invisible Beam—David White, L.L.C.; *U.S. Private*, pg. 1765
AUTO LASER 200—Visible Beam—David White, L.L.C.; *U.S. Public*, pg. 1765
AUTO LASER 200—Visible Beam—David White, L.L.C.; *U.S. Private*, pg. 1765
AUTO LOAD—Board Handling—Universal Instruments Corporation; *U.S. Public*, pg. 522
AUTO-LOK—Filter Retainer—Donaldson Company, Inc.; *U.S. Public*, pg. 517

AUTO MECHANICS FUNDAMENTALS—Comprehensive Fundamental Automotive Mechanics Text—Goodheart-Willcox Publisher; *U.S. Private*, pg. 464
AUTO-NUTRITIONIST IV—NONE—First DataBank; *U.S. Private*, pg. 515
AUTO-OWNERS—Insurance—Auto-Owners Insurance; *U.S. Private*, pg. 100
AUTO-PAK—Sanding Materials & Accessories—3M; *U.S. Public*, pg. 1604
AUTO PANEL—Touch Up—Sherwin-Williams Diversified Brands; *U.S. Public*, pg. 1466
AUTO PLUS—NONE—EMAP France; *Int'l*, pg. 451
AUTO POWER—POWER Steering Parts—Steering and Suspension Division; *U.S. Public*, pg. 443
AUTO PROFILE—Film Guaging—Battenfeld Gloucester Engineering Co. Inc.; *U.S. Private*, pg. 123
AUTO RACING DIGEST—Magazine—Century Publishing Company; *U.S. Private*, pg. 226
AUTO-READ—pH Meter Feature—Beckman Instruments, Inc.; *U.S. Public*, pg. 199
AUTO RENTAL NEWS—NONE—Bobit Publishing Company; *U.S. Public*, pg. 154
THE AUTO SAVER—Batteries, Remanufactured Replacement Auto Parts—A.P.S.; *U.S. Public*, pg. 10
AUTO SERVICE AND REPAIR—How-To Text for Vocational Auto Mechanics Courses—Goodheart-Willcox Publisher; *U.S. Private*, pg. 464
AUTO SHUT OFF—Styling Iron—Helen of Troy Corporation; *U.S. Public*, pg. 807
AUTO SPRAY—Touch-Up Spray Paint—Sherwin-Williams Diversified Brands, Inc.; *U.S. Public*, pg. 1466
AUTO-STITCH—Feature—The Lincoln Electric Company; *U.S. Public*, pg. 996
AUTO SUTURE—Surgical Staplers—U.S. Surgical Corp.; *U.S. Public*, pg. 1687
AUTO TAG—OPA Precolumn Derivatization System—Millipore Corporation; *U.S. Public*, pg. 1112
AUTO-TEK 500—Concrete Compression Testers—ELE International, Inc./Soiltest; *Int'l*, pg. 1287
AUTO TEMP—Heater & Air Conditioning Parts—Steering and Suspension Division; *U.S. Public*, pg. 443
AUTO-TEX—Automobile Upholstering Fabrics—Guilford Mills, Inc.; *U.S. Public*, pg. 768
AUTO-TRAC—Loran C to Autopilot Interface—Benmar Marine Electronics, Inc.; *U.S. Private*, pg. 133
AUTO TRAC—Convertible Car Seat with Easy to Use Retractor—Cosco, Inc.; *U.S. Private*, pg. 277
AUTO-TRANS—Unit Load Automatic Guided Vehicles—Jervis B. Webb Company; *U.S. Private*, pg. 1156
AUTO TRUSS—Roof Engineering Software—MiTek, Inc.; *Int'l*, pg. 1106
AUTO-TRUST—Accounting System for Bank Trust Departments—SunGard Data Systems Inc.; *U.S. Public*, pg. 1534
AUTO-TUNE—Electrical & Fuel System Parts—Echlin Inc.; *U.S. Public*, pg. 560
AUTO TRUST/AT—NONE—SunGard Data Systems Inc.; *U.S. Public*, pg. 1534
AUTO-TWIN—Photocopying Apparatus—Eastman Kodak Company; *U.S. Public*, pg. 550
AUTO VANCE—Filmstrip Projector—Telex Communications, Inc.; *U.S. Private*, pg. 1074
AUTO 5—Auto Parts Store—GIB Group; *Int'l*, pg. 532
AUTO-TROL—Computer Graphic Systems—Auto-trol Technology Corporation; *U.S. Public*, pg. 148
AUTOBALANCE—Extremely High Accuracy Laboratory Scales—The Perkin-Elmer Corporation; *U.S. Public*, pg. 1279
AUTOBANK—Savings Plan Package—Standard Bank Investment Corporation Limited; *Int'l*, pg. 1293
AUTOBEND—Gauging Systems for Metal Fabricating Machine Tools—Hurco Companies, Inc.; *U.S. Public*, pg. 850
AUTOCAD—General Purpose CAD Software—Autodesk, Inc.; *U.S. Public*, pg. 148

AUTOCAD AND ITS APPLICATIONS—Guide to Applying AUTOCAD to Drafting Tasks—Goodheart-Willcox Publisher; *U.S. Private*, pg. 464

AUTOCAD DATA EXTENSION—Project Management & AutoCAD Integration Software—Autodesk, Inc.; *U.S. Public*, pg. 148

AUTOCAD DESIGNER—Parametric, Feature-Based Solid Modeling Software—Autodesk, Inc.; *U.S. Public*, pg. 148

AUTOCAD LT—2D & Basic 3D CAD Software—Autodesk, Inc.; *U.S. Public*, pg. 148

AUTOCAD MAP—Mapping & GIS Software—Autodesk, Inc.; *U.S. Public*, pg. 148

AUTOCAD TECH JOURNAL—Magazine—Miller Freeman Inc.; *Int'l*, pg. 1443

AUTOCALI—Fire Detection & Control Systems—Thorn Security Group, Ltd.; *Int'l*, pg. 1386

AUTOCALL—Fire Alarm Systems—Grinnell Fire Protection Systems; *Int'l*, pg. 1386

AUTOCALL—Fire Alarm Systems—Grinnell Fire Protection Systems; *U.S. Public*, pg. 1647

AUTOCAR—Class 8 Truck & Tractors—Volvo Truck North America, Inc.; *Int'l*, pg. 1477

AUTOCAST—Dental Lab Induction Casting Unit—3M; *U.S. Public*, pg. 1604

AUTOCLASS—Photo Printer Accessories—Eastman Kodak Company; *U.S. Public*, pg. 550

AUTOCLAVE SYSTEM GRAPHITE SHAFTS—NONE—Cobra Golf Incorporated; *U.S. Public*, pg. 675

AUTOCLAVE SYSTEM GRAPHITE SHAFTS—NONE—Fortune Brands, Inc.; *U.S. Public*, pg. 674

AUTOCOAT LV—NONE—Akzo Nobel N.V.; *Int'l*, pg. 42

AUTOCOMP—Typesetting Terminals—Eastman Kodak Company; *U.S. Public*, pg. 550

AUTOCOUNT—Typesetting Keyboards—Eastman Kodak Company; *U.S. Public*, pg. 550

AUTOCRIT—Centrifuge—Becton Dickinson Primary Care Diagnostics; *U.S. Public*, pg. 199

AUTOCUBE—Miniload Systems—SI Handling Systems, Inc.; *U.S. Public*, pg. 1418

AUTOCURE—Retread Equipment—Admiral Heintz, Inc.; *U.S. Public*, pg. 1143

AUTOCUT—Timmer Head—Stihl Inc.; *Int'l*, pg. 1301

AUTOCYTOMETER—Blood Cell Counter—Fisher Scientific Company; *U.S. Private*, pg. 658

AUTODEBUG PLUS—NONE—GenRad, Inc.; *U.S. Public*, pg. 731

AUTODELFIA—Medical Advanced TRF Diagnostics—EG & G, Inc.; *U.S. Public*, pg. 542

AUTODESK ANIMATOR STUDIO—2D Animation Software—Autodesk, Inc.; *U.S. Public*, pg. 148

AUTODESK MAPGUID—Internet/Intranet Based Mapping & GIS Software—Autodesk, Inc.; *U.S. Public*, pg. 148

AUTODESK MECHANICAL DESKTOP—2D & 3D Mechanical Design Software—Autodesk, Inc.; *U.S. Public*, pg. 148

AUTODESK MECHANICAL LIBRARY—Pick 'n' Place Parts & Comprehensive Materials Data—Autodesk, Inc.; *U.S. Public*, pg. 148

AUTODESK WORKCENTER—Technical Document & Workflow Management Software—Autodesk, Inc.; *U.S. Public*, pg. 148

AUTODESK WORLD—Geographic Data Integration & Management Tool—Autodesk, Inc.; *U.S. Public*, pg. 148

AUTOEXPRESS—NONE—Express Newspapers plc; *Int'l*, pg. 1443

AUTOFAX/MPR—NONE—SunGard Data Systems Inc.; *U.S. Public*, pg. 1534

AUTOFILM—Camera Back—Polaroid Corporation; *U.S. Public*, pg. 1313

AUTOFILM 1D—NONE—LORAD Corporation; *U.S. Public*, pg. 1595

AUTOFIT—Splice Closures—Raychem Corporation; *U.S. Public*, pg. 1362

AUTOFLEX—NONE—Gilman; *Int'l*, pg. 1389

AUTOFOM—Car Sealant—Blue Coral/Slick 50; *U.S. Public*, pg. 1348

AUTOFORM—NONE—FileNet Corporation; *U.S. Public*, pg. 622

AUTOFORUM—Magazine—Axel Springer Verlag AG; *Int'l*, pg. 102

AUTOFUSE—Auto Fuse—Littelfuse, Inc.; *U.S. Public*, pg. 1001

AUTOGAGE—NONE—Market Facts, Inc.; *U.S. Public*, pg. 1046

AUTOGLIDE—Recliners—The Berkline Corporation; *U.S. Private*, pg. 432

AUTOGRAPH—Magazine For New Car Buyers—American Automobile Association; *U.S. Private*, pg. 50

AUTOGRAPH—Women's Separates—Paul Harris Stores, Inc.; *U.S. Public*, pg. 792

AUTOGRAPH PENN—NONE—Sanford Corporation; *U.S. Public*, pg. 1178

AUTOGUIDE—X-Ray Equipment—Fischer Imaging Corporation; *U.S. Public*, pg. 647

AUTOHELM—NONE—Raytheon Marine; *U.S. Public*, pg. 1366

AUTOION—Analytical Instrument Controllers—Dionex Corporation; *U.S. Public*, pg. 510

AUTOJET—Automatic Spray Gun—Spraying Systems Co.; *U.S. Private*, pg. 1026

AUTOKON NEWS RECORDER—Wire Photo System Image Recorder—ECRM; *U.S. Private*, pg. 353

AUTOKON 1030 LASER GRAPHICS SYSTEM—Scanner/recorder/digitizer—ECRM; *U.S. Private*, pg. 353

AUTOKON 2030 LASER INPUT SCANNER—Input Scanner/Digitizer—ECRM; *U.S. Private*, pg. 353

AUTOLEASE—Leasing of Vehicles—Britax International plc; *Int'l*, pg. 216

AUTOLIFT—Heavy Lift Trucks—Plymouth Industries, Inc.; *U.S. Private*, pg. 873

AUTOLINE—Lubricating Oils & Greases—Fuchs Lubricants, Midlantic Div.; *Int'l*, pg. 518

AUTOLINE—Process Control System—Royle Systems Group; *U.S. Private*, pg. 949

AUTOLINK—HF Frequency Management System—Harris Corp., RF Communications Group Marketing Division; *U.S. Public*, pg. 792

AUTOLITE—Spark Plugs—AlliedSignal, Automotive Aftermarket; *U.S. Public*, pg. 51

AUTOLITE—NONE—AlliedSignal Canada Inc., Automotive Aftermarket; *U.S. Public*, pg. 52

AUTOLITE—Torches—BernzOmatic; *U.S. Public*, pg. 1177

AUTOLOCK—Field Stabilizer Control—Varian Associates, Inc.; *U.S. Public*, pg. 1710

AUTOLOGGER—Petroleum Engineering Services—Litton Industries, Inc.; *U.S. Public*, pg. 1002

AUTOMAGIC—Hearing Aid—Telex Communications, Inc.; *U.S. Private*, pg. 1074

AUTOMAN—Fire Detection & Control System—Ansul Incorporated; *U.S. Public*, pg. 1648

AUTOMATCHIC—Color-Matching System—Akzo Nobel N.V.; *Int'l*, pg. 42

AUTOMATE—Electric Generators for Motors & Electronic Equipment—Rockwell International Corporation; *U.S. Public*, pg. 1397

AUTOMATED CLIENT ENGAGEMENT—Windows Based Accounting Software—Computer Language Research, Inc.; *U.S. Public*, pg. 421

AUTOMATED CREDIT APPLICATION PROCESSING SYSTEM—NONE—American Management Systems, Inc.; *U.S. Public*, pg. 86

AUTOMATED GUIDE VEHICLE SYSTEMS-AGVS—Vehicle Systems—SI Handling Systems, Inc.; *U.S. Public*, pg. 1418

AUTOMATED GUIDED VEHICLE SYSTEM—Matl. Transport System—TransLogic Corp.; *Int'l*, pg. 1387

AUTOMATED MUSIC SENSOR (AMS)—Track Selection—Sony Electronics; *Int'l*, pg. 1281

AUTOMATED SYSTEM FOR ADVANCED PRINTING—Database Publishing and Electronic Printing—Group 1 Software, Inc.; *U.S. Public*, pg. 417

AUTOMATIC DRAIN RELIEF—Drain Line/Grease Trap Maintenance—Ecolab Inc.; *U.S. Public*, pg. 562

AUTOMATIC I.D. NEWS ASIA—Trade Periodical—Advanstar Communications; *U.S. Private*, pg. 22

AUTOMATIC I.D. NEWS EUROPE—Trade Periodical—Advanstar Communications; *U.S. Private*, pg. 22

AUTOMATIC I.D. NEWS LATINOAMERICA—Trade Periodical—Advanstar Communications; *U.S. Private*, pg. 22

AUTOMATIC I.D. NEWS—Trade Periodical—Advanstar Communications; *U.S. Private*, pg. 22

AUTOMATIC RADIO INTERNATIONAL—Lawn & Garden Products—Armatron International, Inc.; *U.S. Public*, pg. 131

AUTOMATIC SCORER—Sporting Goods—Brunswick Bowling & Billiards Corp.; *U.S. Public*, pg. 265

AUTOMATIC SHUT-OFF—Household Products—The Black & Decker Corporation; *U.S. Public*, pg. 233

AUTOMATIC TRU-TENSION—Paper Tension Device for Winder—Harnischfeger Industries, Inc.; *U.S. Public*, pg. 788

AUTOMATICY—Pacemaker—St. Jude Medical, Inc.; *U.S. Public*, pg. 1427

AUTOMATION—NONE—Key Handling Systems, Inc.; *U.S. Private*, pg. 618

AUTOMATRIX—Connection System—Raychem Corporation; *U.S. Public*, pg. 1362

AUTOMAX—Actuators—Flowserve Corporation; *U.S. Public*, pg. 658

AUTOMAX—Integrated Programmable Controllers & Motion Drive Systems—Rockwell International Corporation; *U.S. Public*, pg. 1397

AUTOMET—Automatic Sample Holing Grinding & Polishing Device—Buehler, Limited; *U.S. Public*, pg. 574

AUTOMIX—Adhesive Bonding System—3M; *U.S. Public*, pg. 1604

AUTOMOBILE DEALERS PROTECTOR PLAN—Insurance Package Program—Poe & Brown, Inc.; *U.S. Public*, pg. 1312

AUTOMOBILE TRANSPORTERS PROTECTOR PLAN—NONE—Poe & Brown, Inc.; *U.S. Public*, pg. 1312

AUTOMOTION—Power Recliners—The Berkline Corporation; *U.S. Private*, pg. 432

AUTOMOTIVE AFTERMARKET PROTECTOR PLAN—NONE—Poe & Brown, Inc.; *U.S. Public*, pg. 1312

AUTOMOTIVE BODY REPAIR NEWS—Publication for Professionals in the Body Shop Markets—Reed Elsevier Business Information; *Int'l*, pg. 1095

AUTOMOTIVE ENCYCLOPEDIA—Textbook Covering Fundamentals of Automobile Construction & Repair—Goodheart-Willcox Publisher; *U.S. Private*, pg. 464

AUTOMOTIVE FLEET—NONE—Bobit Publishing Company; *U.S. Private*, pg. 154

AUTOMOTIVE INDUSTRIES—Publication Serving the Automotive Original Equipment Manufacturing Segment—Reed Elsevier Business Information; *Int'l*, pg. 1095

AUTOMOTIVE MARKETING—Marketing, Trend Analysis & Research Publication—Reed Elsevier Business Information; *Int'l*, pg. 1095

AUTOMOTIVE NEWS—Newspaper—Crain Communications, Inc.; *U.S. Private*, pg. 284

AUTOMOTIVE PRODUCTION—Business to Business Magazine—Gardner Publications, Inc.; *U.S. Private*, pg. 440

AUTONET—Auto Industry Service—Conrail, Inc.; *U.S. Public*, pg. 431

AUTONET—Road Transport Services—Transnet Ltd.; *Int'l*, pg. 1417

AUTOOPERATOR—Automatic Analysis of MVS System, Subsystem, or Application Msg. & Response—Boole & Babbage, Inc.; *U.S. Public*, pg. 244

AUTOPACE—Computer Programs—Lucent Technologies Inc.; *U.S. Public*, pg. 1017

AUTOPAD—Self-Regulating Tank Heater—Raychem Corporation; *U.S. Public*, pg. 1362

AUTOPEAK—Satellite Tracking Sequence for Home Satellite TV Receiver/Descrambler—Satellite Data Networks; *U.S. Public*, pg. 716

AUTOPHASE—Computer Programs for Use With Spectrometer Systems—Varian Associates, Inc.; *U.S. Public*, pg. 1710

AUTOPHERESIS-C—Plasma Collection Device—Baxter International Inc.; *U.S. Public*, pg. 196

AUTOPHORETIC—Metalworking Chemical—Henkel Surface Technologies; *Int'l*, pg. 610

AUTOPLATEN—Diecutters—Bobst S.A.; *Int'l*, pg. 198

AUTOPLEX—Cellular Telecommunications System—Lucent Technologies Inc.; *U.S. Public*, pg. 1017

AUTOPLEX T—Treatment for Hemophilia—Nabi; *U.S. Public*, pg. 1148

AUTOPOSITIVE—Photographic Film, Paper & Plates, Photographic Developer—Eastman Kodak Company; *U.S. Public*, pg. 550

AUTOPREP—Automatic Preparatory Gas Chromatography—Varian Associates, Inc.; *U.S. Public*, pg. 1710

AUTOPROBE—Electron Microscope Analyzer—The Perkin-Elmer Corporation; *U.S. Public*, pg. 1279

AUTOPULSE—Fire Detection & Control System—Ansul Incorporated; *U.S. Public*, pg. 1648

AUTOQUEST—Market Research Products—Market Facts, Inc.; *U.S. Public*, pg. 1046

AUTOREAD 5—Machine Readable Parking System—Federal APD, Inc.; *U.S. Public*, pg. 616

AUTOROLL—Specialty Screen Printers—Autoroll Machine Co., LLC; *U.S. Private*, pg. 101

AUTOSCREEN—Photographic Film—Eastman Kodak Company; *U.S. Public*, pg. 550

AUTOSELECT—Cordless Telephones & Circuitry for Cordless Phones—Lucent Technologies Inc.; *U.S. Public*, pg. 1017

AUTOSENSE—Bar Code Scanner Stand—PSC Inc.; *U.S. Public*, pg. 1245

AUTOSEP—Blood Collection Products—Terumo Medical Corporation; *Int'l*, pg. 1376

AUTOSHIM—Automatic Gradient Control—Varian Associates, Inc.; *U.S. Public*, pg. 1710

AUTOSKETCH—Entry-Level 2D Drawing Software—Autodesk, Inc.; *U.S. Public*, pg. 148

AUTOSOLVE—For Complait Arbitration Services—American Automobile Association; *U.S. Private*, pg. 50

AUTOSPEC—Wavelength Dispersive X-ray Spectrometers—The Perkin-Elmer Corporation; *U.S. Public*, pg. 1279

AUTOSTOP—Outdoor Products—The Black & Decker Corporation; *U.S. Public*, pg. 233

AUTOSTORE—NONE—Xicor, Inc.; *U.S. Public*, pg. 1785

AUTOSURF—Surface Modeling & Surface Editing Software—Autodesk, Inc.; *U.S. Public*, pg. 148

AUTOSWITCH—Electronic Matrix Switches—Bytex Corporation; *U.S. Public*, pg. 1522

AUTOTAK—Indicator—Howell Instruments Inc.; *U.S. Private*, pg. 543

AUTOTEMP—Indicator—Howell Instruments Inc.; *U.S. Private*, pg. 543

AUTOTEST—Magazine For New Car Buyers—American Automobile Association; *U.S. Private*, pg. 50

AUTOTEST—Leak Detectors—Varian Associates, Inc.; *U.S. Public*, pg. 1710

AUTOTOUCH—Information Handling/Retrieval Equipment—Eastman Kodak Company; *U.S. Public*, pg. 550

AUTOTRACE—Heat Tracing Systems—Raychem Corporation; *U.S. Public*, pg. 1362

AUTOTRIEVE—Tote Handling System—SI Handling Systems, Inc.; *U.S. Public*, pg. 1418

AUTOTRIM—Automatic Positioning of Slitters—Beloit Lenox, Div.; *U.S. Public*, pg. 789

AUTOTRIM—Winder—Harnischfeger Industries, Inc.; *U.S. Public*, pg. 788

AUTOTROL—Control Apparatus for Regeneration or Backwash of Water Treatment Equipment—Osmonics, Inc.; *U.S. Public*, pg. 1233

AUTOTRONIC—NONE—Stuart Entertainment Inc.; *U.S. Public*, pg. 1526

AUTOTUNE—Remotely Controlled Electromechanical Automatic Shaft Positioning Mechanism—Rockwell International Corporation; *U.S. Public*, pg. 1397

AUTOVANTAGE—Total Car Ownership Program—CUC International, Inc.; *U.S. Public*, pg. 320

AUTOVIAL—Syringeless Filters—Whatman Inc.; *Int'l*, pg. 1498

AUTOVISION—Rendering & Animation Software—Autodesk, Inc.; *U.S. Public*, pg. 148

AUTOWEEK—Magazine—Crain Communications, Inc.; *U.S. Private*, pg. 284

AUTOWRAP—Self-Heating Spiral Wrap—Raychem Corporation; *U.S. Public*, pg. 1362

AUTOZONE—Automotive Products Including Batteries, Fan Belts, Engines & Hoses—AutoZone, Inc.; *U.S. Public*, pg. 150

AUTRONICS—Power Sources—Bowthorpe plc; *Int'l*, pg. 207

AVADEX—Herbicide—Monsanto Company; *U.S. Public*, pg. 1124

AVADEX BW—Herbicide—Monsanto Company; *U.S. Public*, pg. 1124

AVADEX/AVADEX BW—Herbicide—The Agricultural Group, Monsanto Company; *U.S. Public*, pg. 1125

AVAIL—NONE—Brown & Sharpe Manufacturing Company; *U.S. Public*, pg. 260

AVAIL—Office Guest Seating—Cramer Inc.; *U.S. Private*, pg. 285

AVAIL—Calcium-Intensive Vitamin—Menley & James Laboratories, Inc.; *U.S. Public*, pg. 1086

AVAILABILITY PLUS—Balance Reporting—NBD Bank (Indiana); *U.S. Public*, pg. 628

AVALANCHE—NONE—G-III Apparel Group, Ltd.; *U.S. Public*, pg. 690

AVALANCHE—Thermal Energy Storage Systems—Paul Mueller Company; *U.S. Public*, pg. 1141

AVALANCHE—Coal Car—Thrall Car Mfg. Co.; *U.S. Private*, pg. 344

AVALANCHE BLUE—NONE—Fortune Brands, Inc.; *U.S. Public*, pg. 674

AVALLO—Blended Oils—Pompeiian, Inc.; *U.S. Private*, pg. 875

AVALON—Automobile—Toyota Motor Sales, U.S.A., Inc.; *Int'l*, pg. 1412

AVANEL—Surface Active Agents for General Industrial Use—PPG Industries, Inc.; *U.S. Public*, pg. 1245

AVANT GARDE—Watches—Baume Mercier, Inc.; *U.S. Private*, pg. 124

AVANT GARDE—NONE—Luxottica Group S.p.A.; *Int'l*, pg. 822

AVANT GAUZE—Synthetic Gauze Sponges—Medline Industries, Inc.; *U.S. Private*, pg. 728

AVANTA—Paper Boards for Packaging—Metsa-Serlä Corporation; *Int'l*, pg. 863

AVANTE—Faucets, Valves & Fittings—The Black & Decker Corporation; *U.S. Public*, pg. 233

AVANTE—Writing Instruments—Union Pen Company; *U.S. Private*, pg. 1119

AVANTI—Sporting Goods—Brunswick Bowling & Billiards Corp.; *U.S. Public*, pg. 265

AVANTI—NONE—Cordis, a Johnson & Johnson Company; *U.S. Public*, pg. 928

AVANTI—Vinyl Composition Tile—Kentile Operting Co.; *U.S. Private*, pg. 641

AVANTI—Polyurethane Condoms—London International Group plc; *Int'l*, pg. 815

AVANTIS—NONE—Marcam Solutions, Inc.; *U.S. Public*, pg. 1042

AVATAR—Imagine Media—Labelon Corporation; *U.S. Private*, pg. 641

AVCOAT—NONE—Avery Dennison Corporation; *U.S. Public*, pg. 152

AVEC—Hair Spray, Shampoo, Conditioner & Styling Gel—DeMert & Dougherty, Inc.; *U.S. Private*, pg. 323

AVECREM—Boullion—Borden, Inc.; *U.S. Private*, pg. 157

AVEDA CORPORATION—NONE—Estee Lauder Companies Inc.; *U.S. Public*, pg. 594

AVEENO—Bath Products, Bar, Lotion—S.C. Johnson & Son, Inc.; *U.S. Private*, pg. 592

AVEENO—(Skin Care)—S.C. Johnson & Son, Limited; *U.S. Private*, pg. 593

AVEENO—Bath Treatment, Cleaning Bars, Shower & Bath Oil & Lotion—Rydelle Laboratories; *U.S. Private*, pg. 592

AVEENO GENTLE SKIN CLEANSER—Dermatological Products—S.C. Johnson & Son, Inc.; *U.S. Private*, pg. 592

AVEENO MOISTURIZING CREAM—Dermatological Products—S.C. Johnson & Son, Inc.; *U.S. Private*, pg. 592

AVEENO SHAVE GEL—Dermatological Products—S.C. Johnson & Son, Inc.; *U.S. Private*, pg. 592

AVEMCO—Insurance—Avemco Corporation; *U.S. Public*, pg. 151

AVENGER—Automobile—Chrysler Corporation; *U.S. Public*, pg. 352

AVENGER—(Handheld & Mobile Radios)—E.F. Johnson Radio Systems; *U.S. Public*, pg. 1630

AVENGER SORB—Petroleum Cleaning Products—Kelso Oil Company; *U.S. Private*, pg. 613

AVENIR—Furniture Components—Steelcase Inc.; *U.S. Private*, pg. 1038

AVENIR SALUT—Car—Nissan Motor Co., Ltd.; *Int'l*, pg. 943

AVENT—Baby Products—Cannon Rubber Ltd.; *Int'l*, pg. 261

AVENTYL HCI—Nortriptyline Hydrochloride, Lilly—Eli Lilly and Company; *U.S. Public*, pg. 992

THE AVENUE—Careerwear & Sportswear—United Retail Group, Inc.; *U.S. Public*, pg. 1679

AVERNA—Digestivo—Paterno Imports Limited; *U.S. Private*, pg. 843

AVERT—Virucidal Tissues—Kimberly-Clark Corporation; *U.S. Public*, pg. 958

AVERY—Self-Adhesive Labeling Products—Avery Dennison Corporation; *U.S. Public*, pg. 152

AVERY—Weighing Equipment—The General Electric Company, p.l.c.; *Int'l*, pg. 543

AVERY DENNISON—NONE—Avery Dennison Corporation; *U.S. Public*, pg. 152

AVIA—Athletic Footwear & Apparel—Avia; *U.S. Private*, pg. 62

AVIATION HISTORY—Periodical—Cowles Enthusiast Media, Inc.; *U.S. Private*, pg. 281

AVIATOR—Playing Cards—The United States Playing Card Company; *U.S. Private*, pg. 1125

AVIAX—Semduramicin—Pfizer Inc.; *U.S. Public*, pg. 1281

AVIION—Workstations & Servers—Data General Corporation; *U.S. Public*, pg. 485

AVIKRIMP—NONE—Molex Incorporated; *U.S. Public*, pg. 1121

AVIMIN—Vitamin A—Novo Nordisk A/S; *Int'l*, pg. 987

AVION—Travel Trailer—Fleetwood Enterprises, Inc.; *U.S. Public*, pg. 650

AVION—Travel Trailers—Fleetwood Travel Trailers of Nebraska, Inc.; *U.S. Public*, pg. 652

AVIOX—Oxygen Generators—Scott Aviation; *U.S. Public*, pg. 622

AVIROL—Fatty Alcohol Sulfates—Henkel Corporation; *Int'l*, pg. 610

AVIS—Car Rentals—Avis Rent A Car System, Inc.; *U.S. Public*, pg. 321

AVITEX—Softener—Du Pont (E.I. Du Pont De Nemours & Co.); *U.S. Public*, pg. 530

AVITRON—Vitamins for Pets—Carter-Wallace, Inc.; *U.S. Public*, pg. 309

AVIVA SPORTS—Sporting Goods—Mattel, Inc.; *U.S. Public*, pg. 1057

AVIZYME—Multienzyme Increases Nutritive Value of Poultry Feeds—Cultor Ltd.; *Int'l*, pg. 349

AVLOY—NONE—Avery Dennison Corporation; *U.S. Public*, pg. 152

AVMAC—Fiber Optic Connectors—Lucent Technologies Inc.; *U.S. Public*, pg. 1017

AVON—Furniture—Consolidated Furniture Corporation; *U.S. Public*, pg. 265

AVON—Tires—The Cooper Tire Company; *U.S. Public*, pg. 445

AVON—Starch Products—Goodman Fielder Limited; *Int'l*, pg. 555

AVON—Books—The Hearst Corporation; *U.S. Private*, pg. 515

AVONDALE—Marine Construction & Repairs—Avondale Industries, Inc.; *U.S. Public*, pg. 156

AVONDALE—Shipyards—Avondale Industries Inc. Shipyards Div.; *U.S. Public*, pg. 157

AVONDALE MILLS—Textiles—Walton Fabric Division of Avondale Mills; *U.S. Private*, pg. 103

AVONEX—NONE—Biogen, Inc.; *U.S. Public*, pg. 230

AWAC—Wire & Cables—Copperweld Fayetteville Division; *Int'l*, pg. 662

AWAC—Wire & Alloys—Imetal; *Int'l*, pg. 661

AWAKENINGS—Greeting Cards—American Greetings Corporation; *U.S. Public*, pg. 77

AWARD COLLECTION—Designer Faucet—Delta Faucet Corporation; *U.S. Public*, pg. 1053

AWARD METALS—Metal Products—Kaibab Industries; *U.S. Private*, pg. 605

AWARD WINNING COLLECTION—Grocery & Perishables—Shurfine International, Inc.; *U.S. Private*, pg. 997

AWETA—NONE—EcoScience Corporation; *U.S. Public*, pg. 563

AWNING MAT—Accessory—Carefree of Colorado; *U.S. Public*, pg. 217

AWNING MATE—Accessory—Carefree of Colorado; *U.S. Public*, pg. 217

AWREY—Bakery Products—Awrey Bakeries, Inc.; *U.S. Private*, pg. 103

AXE—Deodorant—Unilever Plc; *Int'l*, pg. 1433

AXEL JOHNSON—Engineered, Industrial & Electronic Products—Axel Johnson Inc.; *Int'l*, pg. 709

AXELROD—Dairy Products—Crowley Foods, Inc.; *Int'l*, pg. 752

AXENT—Interior Display—Unistrut Corporation; *U.S. Public*, pg. 1651

AXESS—NONE—Brown & Sharpe Manufacturing Company; *U.S. Public*, pg. 260

AXESS—NONE—Kompass International Neuenschwander SA; *Int'l*, pg. 745

AXIAL FLOW—Regulators—American Meter Company; *Int'l*, pg. 1149

AXIAL-FLOW—Combines—Case Corporation; *U.S. Public*, pg. 311

AXIANT—NONE—Cognos Corp.; *Int'l*, pg. 306 ·

AXID—Nizatidine, Lilly—Eli Lilly and Company; *U.S. Public*, pg. 992

AXID AR—Acid Reducer—American Home Products Corporation; *U.S. Public*, pg. 79

AXID AR—Antacid—Whitehall-Robins Healthcare; *U.S. Public*, pg. 80

AXIFLEX—Fans—The Howden Fan Co.; *U.S. Private*, pg. 543

AXIMAX—Air Moving Device—EG & G Rotron; *U.S. Public*, pg. 543

AXIOM—Golf Equipment—The Arnold Palmer Golf Company; *U.S. Public*, pg. 132

AXION—Laundry Aid—Colgate-Palmolive Company; *U.S. Public*, pg. 397

AXIOTECH—Reflected Light Telescope—Carl Zeiss; *Int'l*, pg. 1522

AXIS—Nuclear Medicine—Picker International, Inc.; *Int'l*, pg. 545

AXIS GRAPHITE—Racquetball Racquet—Ektelon; *U.S. Private*, pg. 884

AXLEMASTER—Mfg. Testing Equipment—Rockford Acromatic Product Co.; *U.S. Private*, pg. 938

AXLESS—Mine Cars—Trinity Difco; *U.S. Public*, pg. 1639

AXXENT—Communications Systems—Inter-Tel, Incorporated; *U.S. Public*, pg. 888

AXXESS—Communications System—Inter-Tel, Incorporated; *U.S. Public*, pg. 888

AXXESS 200—NONE—Intelligent Controls Inc.; *U.S. Private*, pg. 566

AXXESSORY TALK—Voice Processing System—Inter-Tel, Incorporated; *U.S. Public*, pg. 888

AYGESTIN—Generic Drug—American Home Products Corporation; *U.S. Public*, pg. 79

AYGESTIN—Progestational Agent—Wyeth-Ayerst Laboratories, Inc.; *U.S. Public*, pg. 80

AYLMER—Fruit Drinks—RJR Nabisco Holdings Corp.; *U.S. Public*, pg. 1354

AYRE CERVI-SCRAPER—Cytological Scrapers—Becton Dickinson Primary Care Diagnostics; *U.S. Public*, pg. 199

AYURA—Cosmetics—Shiseido Company Ltd.; *Int'l*, pg. 1235

AZACTAM—Monobactum Antibiotic—Bristol-Myers Squibb Company; *U.S. Public*, pg. 253

AZDEL—Engineered Plastics—General Electric Company; *U.S. Public*, pg. 709

AZDEL—Plastic Film & Sheeting—PPG Industries, Inc.; *U.S. Public*, pg. 1245

AZDONE—Pharmaceutical Products—Schwarz Pharma Manufacturing, Inc.; *Int'l*, pg. 1211

AZELEX—Topical Acne Preparation—Allergan, Inc.; *U.S. Public*, pg. 46

AZIMUTH DIPFRAC—NONE—Western Atlas Logging Services; *U.S. Public*, pg. 1757

AZIZA—NONE—Jean Philippe Fragrances, Inc.; *U.S. Public*, pg. 924

AZLOY—Engineered Plastics—General Electric Company; *U.S. Public*, pg. 709

AZLOY—Fiber Reinforced Plastic Sheeting—PPG Industries, Inc.; *U.S. Public*, pg. 1245

AZMACORT—Steroid Inhalant for Severe Asthma—Rhone-Poulenc Rorer - U.S.; *Int'l*, pg. 1110

AZMET—Engineered Plastics—General Electric Company; *U.S. Public*, pg. 709

AZMET—Fiber Reinforced Plastic Sheeting—PPG Industries, Inc.; *U.S. Public*, pg. 1245

AZOLID—Pharmaceuticals—Rhone-Poulenc Rorer - U.S.; *Int'l*, pg. 1110

AZTAR—Hotels—Aztar Corporation; *U.S. Public*, pg. 158

AZTECA—Tortillas—Azteca Foods, Incorporated; *U.S. Private*, pg. 104

AZTECA DE ORO—Brandy—Domecq Importers Inc.; *Int'l*, pg. 63

AZTEK—Paint Spraying Equipment—Eastman Kodak Company; *U.S. Public*, pg. 550

AZTEK—Airbrush & Accessories—The Testor Corporation; *U.S. Public*, pg. 1358

AZTRONIC—Inductors—Vishay Intertechnology, Inc.; *U.S. Public*, pg. 1721

AZUBI—Grocery Store—Tengelmann Warenhandelsgesellschaft; *Int'l*, pg. 1375

AZULFIDINE—Medical—Pharmacia & Upjohn Adria Laboratories; *Int'l*, pg. 1049

AZULFIDINE EN-TABS—Medical—Pharmacia & Upjohn Adria Laboratories; *Int'l*, pg. 1049

AZUMAYA—Tofu—Vitasoy (U.S.A.) Inc.; *Int'l*, pg. 1469

AZURLITE—Flat Glass—PPG Industries, Inc.; *U.S. Public*, pg. 1245

AZZARO—Perfume—Clarins; *Int'l*, pg. 295

B

B.A.C.—Company Name—Baltimore Aircoil Company; *U.S. Public*, pg. 68

B.A.C.LOGIC—Computer Control System, Control Panel—Baltimore Aircoil Company; *U.S. Private*, pg. 68

BACOUNT—Wet Deck Surface—Baltimore Aircoil Company; *U.S. Private*, pg. 68

BAL—NONE—Western Atlas Logging Services; *U.S. Public*, pg. 1757

BAPS—Biochemical Ankle Platform System—Camp Healthcare; *Int'l*, pg. 1425

B.A.S.E. TECHNOLOGY—Fertilizing System—Ringer Corporation; *U.S. Public*, pg. 1390

BASF—Magnetic Recording Media—BASF Corporation; *Int'l*, pg. 105

B.A.S.S. FISHING TECHNIQUES—Magazine—B.A.S.S., Inc.; *U.S. Private*, pg. 105

B.A.S.S. TIMES—Newspaper—B.A.S.S., Inc.; *U.S. Private*, pg. 105

BAX GLOBAL—Transportation/Logistics Services—The Pittston Company; *U.S. Public*, pg. 1305

B&B—Liqueur—Bacardi-Martini, USA, Inc.; *U.S. Private*, pg. 109

B & BURGER—Restaurants—Accor S.A.; *Int'l*, pg. 20

B&D—Accessories—The Black & Decker Corporation; *U.S. Public*, pg. 233

B&D INDUSTRY & CONSTRUCTION—Power Tools—The Black & Decker Corporation; *U.S. Public*, pg. 233

B&G—Pickles, Peppers & Relish—B&G Foods, Inc.; *U.S. Private*, pg. 105

B&G—French Wines—The Seagram Company Ltd.; *Int'l*, pg. 1214

B & L 70—Eye Care Products—Bausch & Lomb Incorporated; *U.S. Public*, pg. 194

B & M—Baked Beans & Brown Bread—The Pillsbury Company; *Int'l*, pg. 411

B & O—Prescription Pharmaceutical—PolyMedica Industries, Inc.; *U.S. Public*, pg. 1315

B & Q—Hardware & Do-It-Yourself Stores—Kingfisher plc; *Int'l*, pg. 733

B&T WEEKLY—Magazine—Reed Business Information Pty. Limited; *Int'l*, pg. 1094

B&T YEARBOOK—Advertising Directory—Reed Business Information Pty. Limited; *Int'l*, pg. 1094

BBBK, INC.—Pest Control Services—Prism Integrated Sanitation Management, Inc.; *U.S. Private*, pg. 592

BB BRAND—Adhesive Coated Paper & Cloth—Kimberly-Clark Corporation; *U.S. Public*, pg. 958

BBC—Vertical Process Cameras—Nuarc Company, Inc.; *U.S. Private*, pg. 808

BBC CLASSIC TRACKS—Rock Music Radio Program—Westwood One Entertainment; *U.S. Public*, pg. 1763

BBC CLASSIC TRACKS—Rock Programming—Westwood One, Inc.; *U.S. Public*, pg. 1763

BBC GARDENERS WORLD—NONE—BBC Magazines; *Int'l*, pg. 114

BBC GOOD FOOD—NONE—BBC Magazines; *Int'l*, pg. 114

BBC HOMES & ANTIQUES—NONE—BBC Magazines; *Int'l*, pg. 114

BBC LEARNING IS FUN—NONE—BBC Magazines; *Int'l*, pg. 114

BBC MUSIC—NONE—BBC Magazines; *Int'l*, pg. 114

BBC SPORT—NONE—BBC Magazines; *Int'l*, pg. 114

BBC VAULT-ALTERNATIVE VERSION—Music Radio Program—Westwood One Entertainment; *U.S. Public*, pg. 1763

BBC VEGETARIAN GOOD FOOD—NONE—BBC Magazines; *Int'l*, pg. 114

BBC WILDLIFE—NONE—BBC Magazines; *Int'l*, pg. 114

BBL—Diagnostic Reagents, Culture Media—Becton Dickinson & Company; *U.S. Public*, pg. 199

BBN—NONE—GTE Internetworking; *U.S. Public*, pg. 696

BBN/CLINTRACE—NONE—GTE Internetworking; *U.S. Public*, pg. 696

BBN/CLINTRIAL—NONE—GTE Internetworking; *U.S. Public*, pg. 696

BBN/CORNERSTONE—NONE—GTE Internetworking; *U.S. Public*, pg. 696

BBNS—Computer Systems—International Business Machines Corporation; *U.S. Public*, pg. 895

BBQ BAG—Single-Use, Lightable Bag of Charcoal Briquets—The Clorox Company; *U.S. Public*, pg. 386

BBW—Queen Size Hosiery—Alba-Waldensian, Inc.; *U.S. Public*, pg. 35

BBW—Builders Hardware—Triangle Brass Manufacturing; *U.S. Private*, pg. 1101

BC—Headache Powder & Tablets—Block Drug Company, Inc.; *U.S. Public*, pg. 236

B.C.—Apple Products—Knouse Foods Inc.; *U.S. Private*, pg. 627

BCA—NONE—Charan Industries, Inc.; *U.S. Private*, pg. 229

BCA—Bowling Corporation of America—Charan Industries, Inc.; *U.S. Private*, pg. 229

BCA—Blood Banking Prods.—Royal Gist-Brocades N.V.; *Int'l*, pg. 1142

B-C-BID—NONE—Lee Pharmaceuticals; *U.S. Public*, pg. 984

BCC TAP—Taper Pipe Tap—National Twist Drill Div.; *U.S. Public*, pg. 1370

BCC TAP—Type of Taper Pipe Tap—Regal-Beloit Corporation; *U.S. Public*, pg. 1370

BCD BUNN—Coffee Decanter—Bunn-O-Matic Corporation; *U.S. Public*, pg. 180

BCF BUNN—Coffee Filters—Bunn-O-Matic Corporation; *U.S. Private*, pg. 180

BCI JOIST—Precision-Engineered I-Joists—Boise Cascade Corporation; *U.S. Public*, pg. 242

BC INTERNET SERIES—UPS System—Trippe Mfg. Co.; *U.S. Private*, pg. 1104

BCN—NONE—Western Atlas Logging Services; *U.S. Public*, pg. 1757

BCOCA—Computer Systems—International Business Machines Corporation; *U.S. Public*, pg. 895

BCS—NONE—ETEX; *Int'l*, pg. 430

BCS—Board Control System—O&K Orenstein & Koppel Aktiengesellschaft; *Int'l*, pg. 516

BCW BUNN—Coffee Warmer—Bunn-O-Matic Corporation; *U.S. Public*, pg. 180

B-CAPSA I—Vaccine—Bristol-Myers Squibb Company; *U.S. Public*, pg. 253

B-D—Medical Products—Becton Dickinson & Company; *U.S. Public*, pg. 199

B.D. BAGGIES—Apparel—The Apparel Group, Ltd.; *U.S. Private*, pg. 78

BDD—Laundry Detergent—The Procter & Gamble Company; *U.S. Public*, pg. 1330

BDJ—Telecommunications Voice & Data Transmitting, Timing & Receiving—Lucent Technologies Inc.; *U.S. Public*, pg. 1017

BDK—Telecommunications Voice & Data Transmitting, Timing & Receiving—Lucent Technologies Inc.; *U.S. Public*, pg. 1017

BD LONG GRAIN—Solid Faced Construction Plywood—Carter Holt Harvey Limited; *U.S. Public*, pg. 904

B-D PRECISIONGLIDE—Needles—Becton Dickinson & Company; *U.S. Public*, pg. 199

B. DALTON—Bookstores—B. Dalton Bookseller, Inc.; *U.S. Public*, pg. 189

BEI—NONE—BEI Technologies, Inc.; *U.S. Public*, pg. 160

BEL—NONE—Bel Fuse Inc.; *U.S. Public*, pg. 200

BE RADIO—Publication on Technology & Equipment—Intertec Publishing; *U.S. Public*, pg. 1327

BES—Product & Technology Development Center—BetzDearborn Inc.; *U.S. Public*, pg. 226

BET—Television—Black Entertainment Television Holdings Inc.; *U.S. Public*, pg. 235

B-8—Automatic Coffee Brewer—Bunn-O-Matic Corporation; *U.S. Private*, pg. 180

BF—NONE—Bonney Forge Corporation; *U.S. Private*, pg. 156

BFGOODRICH PASSENGER & LIGHT TRUCK TIRES—NONE—Michelin North America (Canada) Inc.; *Int'l*, pg. 322

BFI—NONE—Browning-Ferris Industries, Inc.; *U.S. Public*, pg. 262

B.F.I.—Antiseptic Powder—Menley & James Laboratories, Inc.; *U.S. Public*, pg. 1086

BF-L—Powdered Infant Formula—Morinaga Milk Industry Co., Ltd.; *Int'l*, pg. 895

B4000—Truck—Mazda Motor of America, Inc.; *Int'l*, pg. 849

B.G.—Twist Tobaccos—Conwood Company L.P.; *U.S. Private*, pg. 272

BGC—Vaccine—BioChem Pharma Inc.; *Int'l*, pg. 196

BGF MAT—Nonwoven Fiberglass Insulation—BGF Industries Inc.; *U.S. Private*, pg. 106

B. GELAS—Armagnac—Paterno Imports Limited; *U.S. Private*, pg. 843

BHC—Securities Brokerage—BHC Securities, Inc.; *U.S. Public*, pg. 647

BIMS—Data Base Program—Barrister Information Systems Corporation; *U.S. Public*, pg. 192

B-I-N—Primer & Sealer, White Pigmented Shellac—Wm. Zinsser & Co., Inc.; *U.S. Public*, pg. 1358

B-I-N PRIMER-SEALER—Paint Primer—RPM, Inc.; *U.S. Public*, pg. 1356

BI PERFORMANCE SERVICES—Performance Improvement Focus—Schoeneckers, Inc.; *U.S. Private*, pg. 971

BIW—Electrical Cable, Wire & Connectors—BIW Cable Systems, Inc.; *Int'l*, pg. 417

B IN DESIGN—NONE—Allied Diagnostic Imaging Resources, Inc.; *U.S. Public*, pg. 282

BJ—NONE—BJ Services Company; *U.S. Public*, pg. 161

BJ—Computer Printers—Canon Inc.; *Int'l*, pg. 261

B.J. HOLLADAY—Distilled Spirits—McCormick Distilling Co.; *U.S. Private*, pg. 720

B-JUMP—NONE—Berg Electronics; *U.S. Public*, pg. 212

BK BIG FISH—Fish Sandwich—Burger King Corporation; *Int'l*, pg. 411

BK BROILER—Burger—Burger King Corporation; *Int'l*, pg. 411

BK INDUSTRIES—Ovens & Baking Equipment—Standex International Corporation; *U.S. Public*, pg. 1505

B-LINE—Components for Strut Systems—B-Line Systems, Inc.; *U.S. Public*, pg. 1471

B-LINK—DNA Synthesis Reagents—Millipore Corporation; *U.S. Public*, pg. 1112

BMD—Impulse Molding Machines Shot Blasting Equipment—Georg Fischer Disa Inc.; *Int'l*, pg. 382

BMF—Survival Knife—Fiskars-Gerber; *Int'l*, pg. 492

BMG—Compact Disc Club—Bertelsmann Inc.; *Int'l*, pg. 191

BMP RESTART—IMS DC Enhancement—BMC Software, Inc.; *U.S. Public*, pg. 162

BMR—Industrial Machinery—Pennsylvania Crusher Corp.; *U.S. Private*, pg. 850

BMTS—Burns & McDonnell Treatment System—Burns & McDonnell Engineers-Architects-Consultants; *U.S. Private*, pg. 187

BMUX—Multiplexer—Beckman Instruments, Inc.; *U.S. Public*, pg. 199

BMW—Automobiles & Motorcycles—BMW (US) Holding Corporation; *Int'l*, pg. 177

BMW—Automobiles & Motorbikes—Bayerische Motoren Werke Aktiengesellschaft; *Int'l*, pg. 177

'B' MOSCADELLO DI MONTALCINO—NONE—Castello Banfi Srl.; *U.S. Private*, pg. 113

BN—NONE—Tabacalera, S.A.; *Int'l*, pg. 1345

BNE-EUROPE—NONE—Barton Nelson Inc.; *U.S. Private*, pg. 120

B-NINE—Plant Growth Regulant—Uniroyal Chemical Company, Inc.; *U.S. Public*, pg. 460

BOA—Globe Valves—KSB Aktiengesellschaft; *Int'l*, pg. 721

BOB—Computer Equipment—Emulex Corporation; *U.S. Private*, pg. 579

B.O.S.S.—Battery Operated Spin System—Hedstrom Corporation; *U.S. Private*, pg. 526

B.O.S.S.—Brinell Optical Scanning System—NewAge Industries Inc.; *U.S. Private*, pg. 796

B.O.S.S.—Brinell Optical Scanning System—Newage Industries Inc., Testing Instruments Group; *U.S. Private*, pg. 796

BP—Holding Co.: Oil, Coal, Chemicals & Animal Feeds—BP America Inc.; *Int'l*, pg. 220

BP—British Petroleum Retail Transportation Fuels in Nine Western States—Tosco Corporation; *U.S. Public*, pg. 1624

BPCS/AS—Business Planning & Control System/Advanced Solution—System Software Associates, Inc.; *U.S. Public*, pg. 1552

BPI ENTERTAINMENT NEWS WIRE—Marketing Information Services—BPI Communications Inc.; *Int'l*, pg. 1446

BPM—Fine Paper Grades—Badger Paper Mills, Inc.; *U.S. Public*, pg. 165

BPN-THE SOURCE—Magazine—Reed Business Information Pty. Limited; *Int'l*, pg. 1094

BP OIL COMPANY—Petroleum Products—BP Oil Co.; *Int'l*, pg. 220

BPP—Buyers Protection Plan—ERA Real Estate; *U.S. Public*, pg. 321

BPR—Metal Reinforcing Compounds—PPG Industries, Inc.; *U.S. Public*, pg. 1245

BPS—Paint—The Valspar Corporation; *U.S. Public*, pg. 1707

B P SERIES—Line Printer—Dataproducts Corporation; *Int'l*, pg. 620

BQ—Cold Tablets—Bristol-Myers Squibb Company; *U.S. Public*, pg. 253

BRD—Recycling & De-inking Chemicals—Buckman Laboratories Inc.; *U.S. Private*, pg. 180

BRD—Rolling Diaphragm—Marsh Bellofram Corp.; *U.S. Private*, pg. 707

BRP—Winder—Beloit Corporation; *U.S. Public*, pg. 789

BR 700—Civil Engine—Rolls-Royce-Commercial Aero Engines Ltd.; *Int'l*, pg. 1127

BR SMOOTHIE—Beverage—Baskin-Robbins Incorporated; *Int'l*, pg. 63

BSA—Cycle—Derby International Corporation S.A.; *Int'l*, pg. 394

BS+B—Process Systems for Oil & Gas Industry—BS & B Process Systems, Inc.; *U.S. Private*, pg. 572

BSI—Helmets—Bell Sports Corp.; *U.S. Public*, pg. 207

BSL GENIE—NONE—Brammer plc; *Int'l*, pg. 212

BSS—Sterile Irrigating Solution, 250 or 500 ml—Alcon Laboratories, Inc.; *Int'l*, pg. 916

BSS—Audio Processors—Harman International Industries, Inc.; *U.S. Public*, pg. 787

BSS PLUS—Sterile Irrigating Solution—Alcon Laboratories, Inc.; *Int'l*, pg. 916

BST DIRECT—Training in Operation of Business Telephone Systems; Computer Programs—Lucent Technologies, Inc.; *U.S. Public*, pg. 1017

B SERIES—Line Printer—Dataproducts Corporation; *Int'l*, pg. 620

B-17 QUEEN OF THE SKIES—War Game—Monarch Avalon, Inc.; *U.S. Public*, pg. 1123

B SHARP—Traction Liquid—Mueller Sports Medicine, Inc.; *U.S. Private*, pg. 766

B SURE—Lubrication—Beloit Corporation; *U.S. Public*, pg. 789

BT—International Telecommunications Products & Services—British Telecommunications plc; *Int'l*, pg. 222

BTA STAT—NONE—Bard Diagnostic Sciences; *U.S. Public*, pg. 189

BTA TRAK—NONE—Bard Diagnostic Sciences; *U.S. Public*, pg. 189

BTC—Cationic-Biocidal—Stepan Company; *U.S. Public*, pg. 1514

BTR—Manufacturer of Ball Valves, Rubber Roll Coverings, Paper Machine Clothing—BTR, Inc.; *Int'l*, pg. 127

BTR—Vibration Mounts—Lord Corporation; *U.S. Private*, pg. 675

BTS—Consumer Turf Machinery—Ransomes Plc; *Int'l*, pg. 1087

B3000—Truck—Mazda Motor of America, Inc.; *Int'l*, pg. 849

B TICINO—Low-Voltage Fittings & Accessories—LeGrand S.A.; *Int'l*, pg. 805

B-12 CHEMTOOL—Carburetor Cleaner—Berryman Products, Inc.; *U.S. Private*, pg. 138

B2300—TRUCK—Mazda Motor of America, Inc.; *Int'l*, pg. 849

BUCL—Software Program—Barrister Information Systems Corporation; *U.S. Public*, pg. 192

B. V.—Wines—Beaulieu Vineyard; *Int'l*, pg. 410

BVD—Underwear & Activewear—Fruit of the Loom, Inc.; *U.S. Public*, pg. 685

BVD—Underwear—Union Underwear Co., Inc.; *U.S. Public*, pg. 686

BV FIXED RAIL VERTICAL TURNING MACHINE—CNC Vertica Lathe—WCI Machine Tools & Systems; *Int'l*, pg. 440

BWEV—Supermarket—KF/Konsum Coop Group; *Int'l*, pg. 718

BW/IP NUCLEAR VALVES—Nuclear Valves—Flowserve Corporation; *U.S. Public*, pg. 658

BW/IP VALVES—Nuclear Valves—BW/IP International, Inc.; *U.S. Public*, pg. 658

BWM—NONE—Pfizer Inc.; *U.S. Public*, pg. 1281

BW SEALS—Seals—BW/IP International, Inc.; *U.S. Public*, pg. 658

BW SEALS—Seals—Flowserve Corporation; *U.S. Public*, pg. 658

BW2—Hair Lightener—Clairol, Inc.; *U.S. Public*, pg. 254

B. WELLS-HAUTE STUFF—NONE—Tandy Brands Accessories, Inc.; *U.S. Public*, pg. 1560

BXP—Electronic Instrument—Intel Corporation; *U.S. Public*, pg. 886

BZ—Newspaper—Axel Springer Verlag AG; *Int'l*, pg. 102

BZ AM SONNTAG—Newspaper—Axel Springer Verlag AG; *Int'l*, pg. 102

BZN COMPACTS—Polycrystalline CBN—G.E. Superabrasives; *U.S. Public*, pg. 711

BABBAGE'S—Computer Software Retailer—Babbage's Etc. LLC; *U.S. Private*, pg. 108

BABBLE ON—Game—Tyco Toys, Inc.; *U.S. Public*, pg. 1058

BABIES ARE OUR BUSINESS—Baby Foods, Baby Care & Babywear—Gerber Products Company; *Int'l*, pg. 973

BABIES "R" US—Retail Baby Good Stores—Toys "R" Us, Inc.; *U.S. Public*, pg. 1626

BABIGOZ—Cosmetic Products for Babies—Nestle S.A.; *Int'l*, pg. 915

BABY ALEXANDER—Baby Dolls Design For Play—Alexander Doll Company, Inc.; *U.S. Private*, pg. 33

BABY B'GOSH—Clothing for Infants & Toddlers—OshKosh B'Gosh, Inc.; *U.S. Public*, pg. 1232

BABY BEN—Clocks—Westclox; *U.S. Private*, pg. 445

BABY B'GOSH LAYETTE—Newborn Clothing & Accessories—OshKosh B'Gosh, Inc.; *U.S. Public*, pg. 1232

BABY CAPEZIO—Baby Shoes—Jumping Jacks; *U.S. Private*, pg. 767

BABY CHECK-UP—Toys—Hasbro; *U.S. Public*, pg. 797

BABY DEER—Children's Shoes—E.J. Footwear Corp.; *U.S. Public*, pg. 1684

BABY DEER—Shoes—Trimfoot Company; *U.S. Public*, pg. 1684

BABY DEER TODDLER—Shoes—Trimfoot Company; *U.S. Public*, pg. 1684

BABY DIOR—Children's Clothes—The William Carter Company; *U.S. Private*, pg. 217

BABY FACE—Dolls—Galoob Toys, Inc.; *U.S. Public*, pg. 698

BABY FRESH WITH ULTRA GUARD—Baby Wipes—Advanced Polymer Systems; *U.S. Public*, pg. 22

BABY GET WELL—Doll—Tyco Toys, Inc.; *U.S. Public*, pg. 1058

BABY GRO—Knit Sets—Kleinert's, Inc.; *U.S. Private*, pg. 625

BABY HEAD—Baby Foods & General Merchandise for Children—Gerber Products Company; *Int'l*, pg. 973

BABY HEALTHFLOW—Baby Bottles—Johnson & Johnson Consumer Products; *U.S. Public*, pg. 928

BABY JACKS—Baby Shoes—Jumping Jacks; *U.S. Private*, pg. 767

BABY MAGIC—Baby Powder, Shampoo & Skin Lotion—The Mennen Company; *U.S. Public*, pg. 397

BABY MAGIC LITE—Baby Oil—The Mennen Company; *U.S. Public*, pg. 397

BABY MAGIC STRETCH MARK—Cocoa Butter Massage Cream—The Mennen Company; *U.S. Public*, pg. 397

BABY 'N' ME—Maternity Bra & Panties—Olga Div.; *U.S. Public*, pg. 1738

BABY NURSERS—Baby Feeding Systems—Playtex Products Corp.; *U.S. Public*, pg. 1311

BABY ORAJEL—For Teething & Cleansing Teeth—Del Pharmaceuticals, Inc.; *U.S. Public*, pg. 494

BABY RUTH—Candy Bar—Nestle Chocolate & Confection; *Int'l*, pg. 917

BABY RUTH—Candy Bar—Nestle S.A.; *Int'l*, pg. 915

BABY RUTH—Candy—Nestle USA; *Int'l*, pg. 916

BABY SHIVERS—Doll—Tyco Toys, Inc.; *U.S. Public*, pg. 1058

THE BABY SOAP—Baby & Liquid Soap—Yardley of London, Inc.; *Int'l*, pg. 819

BABY STEPS—Disposable Diapers—Kimberly-Clark Corporation; *U.S. Public*, pg. 958

BABY TENDERLOVE—Dolls—Mattel, Inc.; *U.S. Public*, pg. 1057

BABY'S OWN—Baby Products—SmithKline Beecham plc; *Int'l*, pg. 1264

BABYBEN—Clocks—General Time Corp.; *U.S. Private*, pg. 445

BABYBLUE—Resuscitator—Vital Signs, Inc.; *U.S. Public*, pg. 1723

BABYCHAM—Sparkling Perry—Matthew Clark Brands; *Int'l*, pg. 848

BABYLISS—Personal Care Products—Conair Corporation; *U.S. Private*, pg. 261

BABY'S FIRST—Baby Food—Beech-Nut Nutrition Corporation; *U.S. Public*, pg. 1359

BABY'S FIRST YEAR—Calendars, Greeting Cards & Childhood Record Books—American Greetings Corporation; *U.S. Public*, pg. 77

BABYSAFE—Baby Products—Cannon Rubber Ltd.; *Int'l*, pg. 261

BABYSAFE—Resuscitator—Vital Signs, Inc.; *U.S. Public*, pg. 1723

BABYSLING—Baby Carrier—Noel Joanna, Inc.; *U.S. Public*, pg. 465

BAC OS—Imitation Bacon Bits—General Mills, Inc.; *U.S. Public*, pg. 717

BAC-TO-BAC—NONE—Life Technologies, Inc.; *U.S. Public*, pg. 504

BACACIL/SPECTROBID—Bacampicillin—Pfizer Inc.; *U.S. Public*, pg. 1281

BACARDI—NONE—Bacardi-Martini Belgium; *U.S. Private*, pg. 109

BACARDI ANEJO—Super Premium Aged Rum—Bacardi-Martini, USA, Inc.; *U.S. Private*, pg. 109

BACARDI BREEZERS—Spirits Refresher—Bacardi-Martini, USA, Inc.; *U.S. Private*, pg. 109

BACARDI GOLD—Dark Rum—Bacardi-Martini, USA, Inc.; *U.S. Private*, pg. 109

BACARDI LIGHT-DRY—Light Rum—Bacardi-Martini, USA, Inc.; *U.S. Private*, pg. 109

BACARDI LIMON—Citrus Rum—Bacardi-Martini, USA, Inc.; *U.S. Private*, pg. 109

BACARDI MIXERS—Frozen Drink Mixers—The Minute Maid Company; *U.S. Public*, pg. 392

BACARDI RESERVE—Premium Rum—Bacardi-Martini, USA, Inc.; *U.S. Private*, pg. 109

BACARDI SELECT—Rich Rum—Bacardi-Martini, USA, Inc.; *U.S. Private*, pg. 109

BACARDI SPICE—Rum(Spice)—Bacardi-Martini, USA, Inc.; *U.S. Private*, pg. 109

BACARDI TROPICAL FRUIT MIXERS—Drink Mixer—Bacardi-Martini, USA, Inc.; *U.S. Private*, pg. 109

BACCARAT—Crystal—Baccarat (Cie des Cristalleries); *Int'l*, pg. 132

BACCARAT—Crystal—Baccarat, Inc.; *Int'l*, pg. 132

BACH—Musical Instruments—The Selmer Co., Inc.; *U.S. Public*, pg. 1514

BACHMAN—Corn Chips, Popcorn, Pretzels, Tortilla Chips—Bachman Company; *U.S. Private*, pg. 109

BACHMANN—Scaled Model Train Sets—Bachmann Industries, Inc.; *U.S. Private*, pg. 109

BACHMAN'S BY AIR—Floral & Gift Products—Bachman's, Inc.; *U.S. Private*, pg. 109

BACI—Chocolates—Perugina Brands of America; *Int'l*, pg. 917

BACIGUENT—NONE—Lee Pharmaceuticals; *U.S. Public*, pg. 984

BACITRACIN—Feed Additive—Asahi Chemical Industry Co., Ltd.; *Int'l*, pg. 83

BACK BAY BOOKS—NONE—Little, Brown & Co.; *U.S. Public*, pg. 1612

BACK CARE—NONE—Simmons Company; *Int'l*, pg. 686

BACK COUNTRY—Lumber & Wood Products—Georgia-Pacific Corporation; *U.S. Public*, pg. 735

BACK FIXER—Back Massagers—Bristol-Myers Squibb Company; *U.S. Public*, pg. 253

BACK FIXER—Back Massagers—Clairol, Inc.; *U.S. Public*, pg. 254

BACK GUARD—Full Shoe Inserts—Schering-Plough Corporation; *U.S. Public*, pg. 1438

BACK-OFF—NONE—EcoScience Corporation; *U.S. Public*, pg. 563

BACK STAGE—Magazine; Books on Theatre & Film; Directories—BPI Communications Inc.; *Int'l*, pg. 1446

BACK STAGE WEST—Magazine for Advertising Commercial Business—BPI Communications Inc.; *Int'l*, pg. 1446

BACK SUPPORTER—Mattress—The Spring Air Company; *U.S. Public*, pg. 1027

BACK THERAPY STATION—Seat in Spa—Coleman Spas, Inc.; *U.S. Private*, pg. 691

BACK TO GLAMOUR—Jewelry & Personal Accessories—Tiffany & Co.; *U.S. Public*, pg. 1608

BACK-UPS—Uninterruptible Power Supplies—American Power Conversion Corporation; *U.S. Public*, pg. 89

BACK-UPS PRO—Uninterruptible Power Supplies—American Power Conversion Corporation; *U.S. Public*, pg. 89

BACKAID—Analgesic/Diuretic—Alva/Amco Pharmacal Companies, Inc.; *U.S. Private*, pg. 47

BACKAID PM—Analgesic Tablets—Alva/Amco Pharmacal Companies, Inc.; *U.S. Private*, pg. 47

BACKER ROD—NONE—Applied Extrusion Technologies, Inc.; *U.S. Public*, pg. 122

BACKPACKER—Magazine—Rodale Press, Inc.; *U.S. Private*, pg. 939

BACKUP AND VERIFICATION FOR VSE—VSE Database Utility—BMC Software, Inc.; *U.S. Public*, pg. 162

BACKWASH—Shampoo Bowl—Belvedere Company; *U.S. Private*, pg. 1008

BACKWOODS BUCK—NONE—Wisconsin Pharmacal Co., Inc.; *U.S. Private*, pg. 1185

BACKWOODS SMOKES—Domestic Cigars—Consolidated Cigar Corporation; *U.S. Private*, pg. 690

THE BACKYARD—NONE—Broderbund Software, Inc.; *U.S. Public*, pg. 258

BACON CRUMBLES—Vegetable Toppings—McCormick/Schilling; *U.S. Public*, pg. 1066

BACON'S—Public Relations Clipping Service & Information Directories—Primedia Inc.; *U.S. Public*, pg. 1327

BACROSS—Wet Deck Surface—Baltimore Aircoil Company; *U.S. Private*, pg. 68

BACT/ALERT—Automated Blood Culture System—Akzo Nobel N.V.; *Int'l*, pg. 42

BACTEC—Medical Instruments—Becton Dickinson & Company; *U.S. Public*, pg. 199

BACTIGEN—Salmonella-Shigella Test—Wampole Laboratories; *U.S. Public*, pg. 310

BACTINE—Antiseptic—Bayer AG; *Int'l*, pg. 171

BACTINE—Skin Wound Cleanser—Bayer Corporation/Consumer Care Division; *Int'l*, pg. 173

BACTOCILL—Pharmaceutical Prods.—SmithKline Beecham Laboratories; *Int'l*, pg. 1264

BACTOCILL—Antibiotic—SmithKline Beecham plc; *Int'l*, pg. 1264

BACTOSOL—Pre-Treatment Chemicals—Clariant International Ltd.; *Int'l*, pg. 624

BACTRIM—Antibacterial Product—Roche Holding Ltd.; *Int'l*, pg. 1119

BACTROBAN—Topical Antibiotic—SmithKline Beecham Corporation; *Int'l*, pg. 1264

BACTROBAN—Anti-Infective—SmithKline Beecham plc; *Int'l*, pg. 1264

BACTROBAN—Dermatological Anti-Infective—SmithKline Beecham Research Limited; *Int'l*, pg. 1266

BACTURCULT—Kit for Bacteriuria Screen/Culture—Wampole Laboratories; *U.S. Public*, pg. 310

BAD BOY—Motorcycles—Harley-Davidson, Inc.; *U.S. Public*, pg. 786

BADA—Wheel Weights—Hennessy Industries, Inc.; *U.S. Public*, pg. 481

BADEDAS—Body Care—Sara Lee Corporation; *U.S. Public*, pg. 1432

BADEDAS—Bath Product—SmithKline Beecham plc; *Int'l*, pg. 1264

BADERBRAU—Beer—Paterno Imports Limited; *U.S. Private*, pg. 843

BADGER—Electric Powered Sweepers & Scrubbers—AAR Corp.; *U.S. Public*, pg. 1

BADGER—Rough Terrain Cranes—Avis Industrial Corporation; *U.S. Private*, pg. 102

BADGER—Hydraulic Excavators & RT Cranes—Badger Equipment Co.; *U.S. Private*, pg. 102

BADGER—Farm Equipment—Badger Farm Systems, Inc.; *U.S. Private*, pg. 748

BADGER—Farm Equip—Miller-St. Nazianz, Inc.; *U.S. Private*, pg. 748

BADGER—Engineers—Raytheon Infrastructure Incorporated; *U.S. Public*, pg. 1366

BADGER-POWHATAN—Consumer Fire Protection Products—Williams Holdings Plc; *Int'l*, pg. 1499

BADOIT—Mineral Water—Danone Group; *Int'l*, pg. 379

BAEDEKER—Reference Books—Simon & Schuster; *U.S. Private*, pg. 777

BAG'M—Can Liners—Amcel Corp.; *U.S. Private*, pg. 48

BAG'N SEASON—Seasoning—McCormick & Company, Incorporated; *U.S. Public*, pg. 1066

BAG N SEASON—Roasting Bag & Seasoning Mix—McCormick/Schilling; *U.S. Public*, pg. 1066

BAG-O-MATIC—Curing Press—McNeil & NRM., Inc.; *U.S. Private*, pg. 725

BAGEASY—Disposable Manual Resusitator—Respironics, Inc.; *U.S. Public*, pg. 1383

BAGEL BITES—Snacks—Ore-Ida Foods, Inc.; *U.S. Public*, pg. 805

BAGEL DELIGHT—Bagels—Lender's Bagel Bakery; *U.S. Public*, pg. 1288

BAGEL DOGS—Frankfurters Wrapped in Bagel Dough—Vienna Sausage Mfg. Co.; *U.S. Private*, pg. 1139

BAGEL PERFECT—Toasters with Special Bagel Feature—Toastmaster, Inc.; *U.S. Public*, pg. 1619

BAGGIES—NONE—Tandy Brands Accessories, Inc.; *U.S. Public*, pg. 1560

BAGGIES—Cooking & Storage Bags—Tenneco Packaging, Consumer Products Group; *U.S. Public*, pg. 1579

BAGGISH—Gynecological Device—The Cooper Companies, Inc.; *U.S. Public*, pg. 442

BAGGISH-TOWNSEND—Gynecological Device—The Cooper Companies, Inc.; *U.S. Public*, pg. 442

BAHA—Card Game—Mattel Games/Puzzles; *U.S. Public*, pg. 1058

BAHAMA BREEZE—Restaurant Chain—Darden Restaurants, Inc.; *U.S. Public*, pg. 483

BAHIA BREEZE—Indoor/Outdoor Casual Aluminum Furniture—Telescope Casual Furniture, Inc.; *U.S. Private*, pg. 1074

BAHN—Dog Biscuits—FTI Foodtech International Inc.; *Int'l*, pg. 476

BAHNCKE—Grocery Foods—Danisco Foods; *Int'l*, pg. 378

BAHNSON—Air Washers—Luwa Bahnson, Inc.; *U.S. Private*, pg. 682

BAILATCH—Cabinet Handle Latch—Hartwell Corporation; *U.S. Private*, pg. 1168

BAILEY—Hats—Bailey Hats; *U.S. Private*, pg. 155

BAILEY BANKS & BIDDLE—Jewelry Stores—Zale Corporation; *U.S. Public*, pg. 1789

BAILEY'S—Valves—IMI Plc; *Int'l*, pg. 646

BAILEYS—Spirits—Gilbeys of Ireland; *Int'l*, pg. 409

BAILEY'S—Original Irish Cream Liqueur—IDV North America; *Int'l*, pg. 411

BAILEYS—NONE—International Distillers Caribbean; *Int'l*, pg. 410

BAILEYS—NONE—Societe Pour la Vente des Produits Cinzano SA; *Int'l*, pg. 410

Brand Name Index

BAILEYS—NONE—Tegner & Son AB; *Int'l*, pg. 412

BAILEYS IRISH CREAM—Liquor—Dateo Import S.P.A.; *Int'l*, pg. 385

BAILEY'S IRISH CREAM—Cream Liqueur & Chocolates—Huhtamaki Oy; *Int'l*, pg. 638

BAILEY'S LIGHT—Liqueur—Grand Metropolitan Plc; *Int'l*, pg. 408

BAILEY'S LIGHT—Light Version of the Original Irish Cream Liqueur—IDV North America; *Int'l*, pg. 411

BAILEYS ORIGINAL IRISH CREAM—NONE—R & A Bailey & Co.; *Int'l*, pg. 409

BAILEYS ORIGINAL IRISH CREAM—Liqueur—Grand Metropolitan Plc; *Int'l*. pg. 408

BAILY—Fabrics—Joshua L. Baily Co., Inc.; *U.S. Private*, pg. 110

BAIN DE SOLEIL—NONE—Pfizer Inc.; *U.S. Public*, pg. 1281

BAIN DE SOLEIL—Sun Care Products—Richardson-Vicks, Inc.; *U.S. Public*, pg. 1331

BAIN DE TERRE—Perm, Shampoos, Conditioning System—Zotos International; *Int'l*, pg. 1236

BAIN-MARIE—Storage Container—Carlisle Food Service Products; *U.S. Public* pg. 305

BAINBRIDGE—Picture-Framing Products—Esselte AB; *Int'l*, pg. 459

BAITMATE—Chemical Fish Attractant—Wisconsin Pharmacal Co., Inc.; *U.S. Private*, pg. 1185

BAITSAFE BAIT STATION—NONE—LiphaTech, Inc.; *Int'l*, pg. 812

BAJA GRABBER—Racing Tires—Bridgestone/Firestone, Inc.; *Int'l*, pg. 213

BAJA RUNNER—Racing Tires—Bridgestone/Firestone, Inc.; *Int'l*, pg. 213

BAJA SPORT GRIP—Steering Wheel Covers—Superior Industries International, Inc.; *U.S. Public*, pg. 1539

BAK-A-FRY—Oven Prepared French Fries—J.R. Simplot Company; *U.S. Private*, pg. 1002

BAKE A ROO—NONE—Koo Koo Roo, Inc.; *U.S. Public*, pg. 966

BAKE AND BROIL—NONE—National Sea Products Limited; *Int'l*, pg. 909

BAKE KING—Bakery Ovens & Proofers—BKI; *U.S. Public*, pg. 1506

BAKELITE—Plastics—Union Carbide Corporation; *U.S. Public*, pg. 1666

BAKEN-ETS—Pork Skin Snack—Frito-Lay Company; *U.S. Public*, pg. 1277

BAKER—Furniture—Baker Knapp & Tubbs Inc.; *U.S. Private*, pg. 630

BAKER BRAND—Cake & Pastry Fillings—Sokol & Company; *U.S. Private*, pg. 1012

BAKER HUGHES—Process Equipment—Baker Hughes Incorporated; *U.S. Public*, pg. 165

BAKER'S CHOICE—Paper & Aluminum Cups Used in Baking—Reynolds Metals Company; *U.S. Public*, pg. 1385

BAKER'S—Small Batch Bourbon—Fortune Brands, Inc.; *U.S. Public*, pg. 674

BAKER'S—Coconut, Chocolate & Cocoa—Philip Morris Companies Inc.; *U.S. Public*, pg. 1287

BAKER'S—Supermarkets—Baker's Supermarkets, Inc.; *U.S. Public*, pg. 652

BAKERS—Coconut—Kraft Food Ingredients Corp.; *U.S. Public*, pg. 1288

BAKER'S—Chocolate Products, Shredded Coconut—Kraft Foods, Inc.; *U.S. Public*, pg. 1287

BAKER'S—Vanilla—McCormick/Schilling; *U.S. Public*, pg. 1066

BAKERS BEST—Soft Pretzels—J & J Snack Foods Corporation; *U.S. Public*, pg. 916

BAKERS BEST—Insulated Bakeware—Wilton Industries, Inc.; *U.S. Private*, pg. 1181

BAKERS BONUS—Cookies—Nabisco Inc.; *U.S. Public*, pg. 1355

BAKERS BONUS—Oatmeal Cookies—RJR Nabisco Holdings Corp.; *U.S. Public*, pg. 1354

BAKER'S FUDGETASTICS—Frozen Novelty—Kraft Foods, Inc.; *U.S. Public*, pg. 1287

BAKER'S GERMAN—Sweet Cooking Chocolate—Kraft Foods, Inc.; *U.S. Public*, pg. 1287

BAKER'S JOY—Vegetable Coating for Pans—Alberto-Culver Company; *U.S. Public*, pg. 37

BAKERS/LEEDS—Shoes—Edison Brothers Stores, Inc.; *U.S. Public*, pg. 563

BAKER'S SECRET—Bakeware—Ekco Group, Inc.; *U.S. Public*, pg. 566

BAKERS SECRET—Bakeware—Ekco Housewares, Inc.; *U.S. Public*, pg. 566

BAKERS SQUARE—Restaurants—Bakers Square Restaurants; *U.S. Public*, pg. 1719

BAKERS SQUARE—Restaurants—Vicorp Restaurants, Inc.; *U.S. Public*, pg. 1719

THE BAKERSFIELD CALIFORNIAN—Daily Newspaper—The Bakersfield Californian; *U.S. Private*, pg. 112

BAKERY PRODUCTION & MARKETING—Magazine for Professionals in the Baking Industry—Reed Elsevier Business Information; *Int'l*, pg. 1095

BAKERY PROVED—Mixes—International Multifoods Corporation; *U.S. Public*, pg. 900

BAKERY WAGON—Cookies—Mother's Cake & Cookie Co.; *U.S. Private*, pg. 1022

BAKING MAGIC—Extracts—McCormick & Company, Incorporated; *U.S. Public*, pg. 1066

BAKING SODA TOOTHPASTE—Natural Toothpaste—Health Products Corporation; *U.S. Private*, pg. 514

BAKIT—Food Products—The B. Manischewitz Company; *U.S. Private*, pg. 699

BAKOS IRON—White Iron—Webster Industries Inc.; *U.S. Private*, pg. 1157

BAL A VERSAILLES—Fragrances—Parlux Fragrances Inc.; *U.S. Public*, pg. 1264

BAL CATH—Catheter Product—Ballard Medical Products; *U.S. Public*, pg. 171

BALAN—Herbicide—The Dow Chemical Company; *U.S. Public*, pg. 522

BALANSEAL—Valve—Teledyne Fluid Systems; *U.S. Public*, pg. 43

BALANTINE—Beer & Ale—Falstaff Brewing Corporation; *U.S. Private*, pg. 955

BALBLAIR MALT SCOTCH WHISKEY—Scotch Whiskey—Allied Domecq PLC; *Int'l*, pg. 62

BALCAR—Lighting—Calumet Photographic, Inc.; *U.S. Private*, pg. 258

BALCLAD—Gold Electroplate—L.G. Balfour Co., Inc.; *U.S. Private*, pg. 258

BALCO—NONE—Carpenter Technology Corporation; *U.S. Public*, pg. 307

BALCOR—Real Estate Investment & Development—The Balcor Company; *U.S. Public*, pg. 74

BALCRANK—Lubricating Equipment—EEI Corporation; *Int'l*, pg. 425

BALDERSON INC.—Construction, Landclearing, Snow Removal—Balderson Inc.; *U.S. Public*, pg. 315

BALDERSON OVERSEA & S.A.—Construction, Landclearing, Snow Removal—Balderson Inc.; *U.S. Public*, pg. 315

BALDESSARINI—Exclusive Men's Fashions—Hugo Boss AG; *Int'l*, pg. 637

BALDOR—Industrial Electric Motors—Baldor Electric Company; *U.S. Public*, pg. 168

BALDOR MOTORS AND DRIVERS—Industrial Electric Motors—Baldor Electric Company; *U.S. Public*, pg. 168

BALDRIAN-DISPERT—Sedatives—Kali-Chemie Aktiengesellschaft; *Int'l*, pg. 1278

BALDWIN—Filters—Baldwin Filters; *U.S. Public*, pg. 381

BALDWIN—Hardware—Baldwin Hardware Corporation; *U.S. Public*, pg. 1053

BALDWIN—Pianos, Organs & Clocks—Baldwin Piano & Organ Company; *U.S. Public*, pg. 169

BALDWIN TECHNOLOGY—Press Accessory—Baldwin Technology Company, Inc.; *U.S. Public*, pg. 169

BALESTRA—Perfume—International Cosmetics Co., Ltd.; *Int'l*, pg. 684

BALFOUR—Design & Logo—L.G. Balfour Co., Inc.; *U.S. Private*, pg. 258

BALI—Game—Monarch Avalon, Inc.; *U.S. Public*, pg. 1123

BALI—Intimate Apparel—Sara Lee Corporation; *U.S. Public*, pg. 1432

BALI—Window Products—Springs Industries, Inc.; *U.S. Public*, pg. 1499

BALINIT—Machines, Machine Tools & Parts—Balzers; *Int'l*, pg. 997

BALISTO—Chocolate Covered Grain Bar—Mars, Incorporated; *U.S. Private*, pg. 707

BALITHERM—Thermal Treatment of Tools—Balzers; *Int'l*, pg. 997

BALKAMP—Automotive Products—Genuine Parts Company; *U.S. Public*, pg. 732

BALL—Home Canning Products—Alltrista Corporation; *U.S. Public*, pg. 56

BALL—Glass & Metal Containers—Ball Corporation; *U.S. Public*, pg. 170

BALL—Seed—Ball Horticultural Company; *U.S. Private*, pg. 112

BALL LINER—Rolling Ball Pen—The Pilot Pen Corp. of America; *Int'l*, pg. 1057

BALL LOUNGE 800—Lounge Seating—Vecta; *U.S. Private*, pg. 1038

BALL LOUNGE 810—Lounge Seating—Vecta; *U.S. Private*, pg. 1038

BALL MODULAR—Lounge Seating—Vecta; *U.S. Private*, pg. 1038

BALL PARK—Franks—Hygrade Food Products Corporation; *U.S. Public*, pg. 1433

BALL PARK—Hot Dogs—Sara Lee Corporation; *U.S. Public*, pg. 1432

BALL PENTEL-7—Ball Point Pen—Pentel of America, Ltd.; *Int'l*, pg. 1035

BALL PRODUCTS—Flow Measurement Equipment—The Oilgear Company; *U.S. Public*, pg. 1215

BALL SCREW ACTUATED CLUTCH—NONE—Regal-Beloit Corporation; *U.S. Public*, pg. 1370

BALLANTINE—Book Publishing—Random House, Inc.; *U.S. Private*, pg. 20

BALLARD EASI-LAV—NONE—Ballard Medical Products; *U.S. Public*, pg. 171

BALLARD MEDICAL—Medical Products & Supplies—Ballard Medical Products; *U.S. Public*, pg. 171

BALLARD MEDICAL PRODUCTS—NONE—Ballard Medical Products; *U.S. Public*, pg. 171

BALLASET—Thermally Stable Diamond Bits—Baker Hughes INTEQ; *U.S. Public*, pg. 166

BALLAST—NONE—Carpenter Technology Corporation; *U.S. Public*, pg. 307

BALLASTER—Balast Car—Trinity Difco; *U.S. Public*, pg. 1639

BALLANTINE'S WHISKY—Spirit—Allied Domecq PLC; *Int'l*, pg. 62

BALLATORE—Spumante—E. & J. Gallo Winery; *U.S. Private*, pg. 438

BALLENGER ST.—Eyeglass Frames—AVC/Nu-Vision, Inc.; *U.S. Private*, pg. 9

BALLERINA DOLL—Dolls—Tyco Toys, Inc.; *U.S. Public*, pg. 1058

BALLET—Facial Tissue, Bathroom Tissue, Cocktail & Table Napkins—Kimberly-Clark Corporation; *U.S. Public*, pg. 958

BALLET—Folding Table—Vecta; *U.S. Private*, pg. 1038

BALLINGSLOV—Kitchen & Bathroom Cabinets—Electrolux, AB; *Int'l*, pg. 438

BALLOON BOOKS—Book Imprint—Bertelsmann AG; *Int'l*, pg. 189

BALLOON ZONE—NONE—American Greetings Corporation; *U.S. Public*, pg. 77

BALLOTINI—Solid Glass Beads for Impact Blasting—Potters Industries, Inc.; *U.S. Private*, pg. 827

BALLY—Shoes, Fashion Accessories—Oerlikon-Buhrle Holding AG; *Int'l*, pg. 996

BALLY—Arcade Games—WMS Industries Inc.; *U.S. Public*, pg. 1727

BALLY—Pinball Games—Williams Electronics Games, Inc.; *U.S. Public*, pg. 1727

BALLY INC—Accessories—Bally Management; *Int'l*, pg. 998

BALLYGOWAN—Mineral Water—Allied Domecq PLC; *Int'l*, pg. 62

BALLY'S—Casino-Resorts—Hilton Hotels Corporation; *U.S. Public*, pg. 828

BALM BARR—Skin Lotions & Creams—The Mennen Company; *U.S. Public*, pg. 397

BALNEOL—Pharmaceutical Products—Solvay Pharmaceuticals, Inc.; *Int'l*, pg. 1278

BALNETAR—Water-Dispersible Emollient Tar—Westwood-Squibb Pharmaceuticals Inc.; *U.S. Public*, pg. 255

BALOMETER—Air Balancing Meter—Alnor Instrument Company; *U.S. Public*, pg. 1559

BALORAMA—Eyeware—Bausch & Lomb Incorporated; *U.S. Public*, pg. 194

BALSAM COLOR—Hair Coloring—Bristol-Myers Squibb Company; *U.S. Public*, pg. 253

BALTEK—Balsa Wood Products—Baltek Corporation; *U.S. Public*, pg. 171

BALTIBOND—Corrosion Protection System—Baltimore Aircoil Company; *U.S. Private*, pg. 68

BALTIDRIVE—Power Train—Baltimore Aircoil Company; *U.S. Private*, pg. 68

BALTIMORE BUSINESS JOURNAL—Business Journal—Business First of New York, Inc.; *U.S. Private*, pg. 19

BALTIMORE ORIOLES—Baseball Club—The Orioles, Inc.; *U.S. Private*, pg. 819

BALTOFLAKE—Marine Paint—Jotun A/S; *Int'l*, pg. 714

BALTRADE—Industrial Assembling & Installation Service for Laboratory Equipment—Balzers; *Int'l*, pg. 997

BALZERS—Vacuum Machinery Parts & Accessories—Balzers; *Int'l*, pg. 997

BAM—NONE—Bam Media; *U.S. Private*, pg. 113

BAMA—Jams & Jellies—Borden, Inc.; *U.S. Private*, pg. 157

BAMA—Shoe Care—Sara Lee Corporation; *U.S. Public*, pg. 1432

BAMA—Fruit Spreads—Welch Foods Inc., A Cooperative; *U.S. Private*, pg. 784

BAMBEC—Antiasthma Agent—Astra AB; *Int'l*, pg. 93

BAMMIES—Bay Area Music Awards—Bam Media; *U.S. Private*, pg. 113

BAN—Antiperspirant & Deodorant—Bristol-Myers Squibb Company; *U.S. Public*, pg. 253

BAN-A-STAIN—Denture Cleanser—Brimms Inc.; *U.S. Private*, pg. 169

BAN BASIC—Non-Aerosol Anti-Perspirant Spray—Bristol-Myers Squibb Company; *U.S. Public*, pg. 253

BAN CLEAR—Deodorant—Bristol-Myers Squibb Company; *U.S. Public*, pg. 253

BAN-O-DOR—Liquid Deodorant—Surco Products, Inc.; *U.S. Private*, pg. 1056

BAN-ROL—NONE—QST Industries, Inc.; *U.S. Private*, pg. 897

BAN SUPER SOLID—Anti-Perspirant Deodorant—Bristol-Myers Squibb Company; *U.S. Public*, pg. 253

BANAMINE—Nonsteroidal Anti-Inflammatory for Animals—Schering-Plough Corporation; *U.S. Public*, pg. 1438

BANANA BAGS—Storage Bags—Flex-O-Glass, Inc.; *U.S. Private*, pg. 412

BANANA BAGS—Plastic Bags—Warp Brothers; *U.S. Private*, pg. 412

BANANA BOAT—Suncare—Playtex Products Corp.; *U.S. Public*, pg. 1311

BANANA BOAT—Suncare Products—Playtex Products Inc.; *U.S. Public*, pg. 1310

BANANA BOAT—Plastic Dishes for Ice Cream—Sweetheart Cup Company Inc.; *U.S. Private*, pg. 1058

BANANA NUT CRUNCH—Breakfast Cereal—Kraft Foods, Inc.; *U.S. Public*, pg. 1287

BANANA REPUBLIC—Travel & Safari Clothes—Banana Republic; *U.S. Public*, pg. 702

BANANIA—Beverages—Bestfoods; *U.S. Public*, pg. 223

BANBURY—Internal Batch Mixer—Farrel Corporation; *U.S. Public*, pg. 614

BANC ONE WISCONSIN—Bank Holding Co.—Bank One, Wisconsin; *U.S. Public*, pg. 174

BANCES—Cigar—Villazon Company Inc.; *U.S. Private*, pg. 1140

BANCO POPULAR VISA & MASTER CARD—Credit Cards—Banco Popular de Puerto Rico; *U.S. Public*, pg. 175

BANCSTAR ACCESS & PRISM—Branch Automation Systems for Both DOS & OS/2—Broadway & Seymour, Inc.; *U.S. Public*, pg. 258

BANCTEC—Computer—BancTec, Inc.; *U.S. Public*, pg. 176

BAND-A-TAPE—Industrial Fasteners—Mid-Continent Screw Products Co.; *U.S. Private*, pg. 743

BAND-AID—Adhesive Bandage—Johnson & Johnson; *U.S. Public*, pg. 927

BAND-IT—Clamps, Banding Devices—IDEX Corporation; *U.S. Public*, pg. 862

BANDAG—Retreading Service—Bandag, Incorporated; *U.S. Public*, pg. 177

BANDERA—Western Hats—Bailey Hats; *U.S. Private*, pg. 155

BANDIT—Fragrance—Alfin, Inc.; *U.S. Public*, pg. 40

BANDIT 105.5—Swedish Broadcasting—CLT-UFA; *Int'l*, pg. 561

BANDITO DIAVOLO SPICY SAUCE—Salsa Sauce—Newman's Own, Inc.; *U.S. Private*, pg. 797

BANDOLINO—Women's Shoes—Nine West Group, Inc.; *U.S. Public*, pg. 1185

BANFF ICE—Vodka—Fortune Brands, Inc.; *U.S. Public*, pg. 674

BANFI ASTI—Sparkling Wine—Banfi Vintners; *U.S. Private*, pg. 113

BANFI BRUNELLO DI MONTALCINO—Super Premium Wine—Banfi Vintners; *U.S. Private*, pg. 113

BANFIBRUT—Sparkling Wine—Banfi Vintners; *U.S. Private*, pg. 113

BANFI BRUT—NONE—Castello Banfi Srl.; *U.S. Private*, pg. 113

BANGA—Orange Drink—Groupe Pernod Ricard; *Int'l*, pg. 566

BANGOR & AROOSTOOK—Railroad—Bangor & Aroostook Railroad Co.; *U.S. Private*, pg. 575

BANISH—Air Deodorizer—Stanhome Inc.; *U.S. Public*, pg. 1508

BANISTER—Women's Shoes—Nine West Group, Inc.; *U.S. Public*, pg. 1185

THE BANK BUSINESS BANKS—Advertising Tag Line—CVB Financial Corp.; *U.S. Public*, pg. 286

BANK LEUMI—Full Service Commercial Bank—Bank Leumi Trust Company of New York; *Int'l*, pg. 150

BANK-LOK—Locker—American Locker Security Systems, Inc.; *U.S. Public*, pg. 86

BANK MART—Banking Centers in Select Grocery Stores—Fifth Third Bancorp; *U.S. Public*, pg. 621

BANK OF BOSTON CONNECTICUT—Banking & Insurance Services—Bank of Boston Connecticut; *U.S. Public*, pg. 184

BANK OF HAWAII—NONE—Pacific Century Financial Corporation; *U.S. Public*, pg. 1248

BANK OF LAKE COUNTY—NONE—Westamerica Bancorporation; *U.S. Public*, pg. 1756

BANK OF THE HUDSON—Advertising—Bank of the Hudson; *U.S. Public*, pg. 1319

BANK OF THE WEST—Banking—Bank of the West; *Int'l*, pg. 163

BANK SYSTEMS TECHNOLOGY—Magazine—Miller Freeman Inc.; *Int'l*, pg. 1443

BANK, USA—Instructional Matl—Bell & Howell Holdings; *U.S. Public*, pg. 201

BANKERS ACCEPTANCE PORTFOLIO SYSTEM (BAPS)—NONE—American Management Systems, Inc.; *U.S. Public*, pg. 86

BANKERS' ALMANAC—Business Directory—Reed Business Information-East Grinstead; *Int'l*, pg. 1094

BANKERS CLUB BLEND—Scotch, Gin, Vodka—Laird & Company; *U.S. Private*, pg. 642

BANKERS CLUB BOURBON—Bourbon Whiskey—Laird & Company; *U.S. Private*, pg. 642

BANKGARD—Relay for Protection of Shunt Capacitor Banks—S & C Electric Company; *U.S. Private*, pg. 954

BANKING TWENTY-FOUR—ATM Product—Mercantile Bankshares Corporation; *U.S. Public*, pg. 1088

BANKLEASE—NONE—Community Bank N.A.; *U.S. Public*, pg. 1088

BANKNET—Telecommunications Network—Mastercard International, Inc.; *U.S. Private*, pg. 714

BANKPOST—NONE—American Israeli Paper Mills Ltd.; *Int'l*, pg. 74

BANKS—Beer—Hudepohl-Schoenling Brewing Company; *U.S. Private*, pg. 545

BANLICE—NONE—Pfizer Inc.; *U.S. Public*, pg. 1281

BANMINTH—Pyrantel Tartrate—Pfizer Inc.; *U.S. Public*, pg. 1281

BANNER—Spotting Scope—Bausch & Lomb Incorporated; *U.S. Public*, pg. 194

BANNER—Riflescopes & Binoculars—Bushnell Corporation; *U.S. Private*, pg. 1191

BANNER—Super Duty—CFB Industries, Inc.; *U.S. Private*, pg. 194

BANNER—Super Duty—Chicago Fire Brick Co.; *U.S. Private*, pg. 194

BANNER—Toilet Tissue—The Procter & Gamble Company; *U.S. Public*, pg. 1330

BANNER BRAND SAUSAGE MEAT—NONE—The Dial Corporation; *U.S. Public*, pg. 505

BANNER RADIO—Radio Advertising Representitive Service—Katz Media Group, Inc.; *U.S. Public*, pg. 335

BANNER STRIPED DESIGN—Motorcycle—American Honda Motor Co., Inc. Motorcycle Division; *Int'l*, pg. 634

BANNERLINE—Graphic Arts Materials—Industrial Coatings Group, Inc.; *U.S. Private*, pg. 434

BANOCIDE—Anti-Filarial—Glaxo Wellcome PLC; *Int'l*, pg. 553

BANOL—Specialty Chemical—AgrEvo USA Company; *Int'l*, pg. 1203

BANQUET—Frozen Foods—ConAgra Frozen Food Company; *U.S. Public*, pg. 427

BANQUET—Frozen Dinners—ConAgra, Inc.; *U.S. Public*, pg. 425

BANQUET—Tea—McCormick & Company, Incorporated; *U.S. Public*, pg. 1066

BANQUET MICROWAVE HOT BITES—Chicken Nuggets—ConAgra Frozen Food Company; *U.S. Public*, pg. 427

BANTA—Books, Magazines, Graphic Services—Banta Corporation; *U.S. Public*, pg. 187

BANTAM—Sporting Goods—Brunswick Bowling & Billiards Corp.; *U.S. Public*, pg. 265

BANTAM—Cameras, Photographic Accessories, Microfilmers, Photocopying Apparatus—Eastman Kodak Company; *U.S. Public*, pg. 550

BANTAM—Lightweight Fixture—GenRad, Inc.; *U.S. Public*, pg. 731

BANTAM—NONE—Mikropul Environmental Systems Div.; *Int'l*, pg. 1083

BANTAM BOOKS—Book Publisher—Bertelsmann AG; *Int'l*, pg. 189

BANTAM DOUBLEDAY DELL—Publishing—Bantam Doubleday Dell Publishing Group, Inc.; *Int'l*, pg. 191

BANTEX—Fabrics—Herculite Products, Inc.; *U.S. Public*, pg. 802

BANTU—Conditioning Hair Relaxer—Johnson Products Co., Inc.; *U.S. Public*, pg. 915

BANVEL—Herbicide—Novartis AG; *Int'l*, pg. 971

BANVEL—Herbicide—Sandoz Agro, Inc.; *Int'l*, pg. 974

BANVEL SGF—Herbicide—Sandoz Agro, Inc.; *Int'l*, pg. 974

BANZAI—War Game—Monarch Avalon, Inc.; *U.S. Public*, pg. 1123

BANZAI—Consumer Sports & Leisure Prods.—Nomaco, Inc.; *U.S. Private*, pg. 801

BANZAI—Vodka—Suntory Ltd.; *Int'l*, pg. 1321

BAOBAB TREE—NONE—American Greetings Corporation; *U.S. Public*, pg. 77

BAPCO—Aluminum Windows & Doors—Binning's Building Products, Inc.; *U.S. Public*, pg. 67

BAR-BAC—Surgeon's Gowns—Angelica Corporation; *U.S. Public*, pg. 113

BAR-BUOY—Drink Holders—Orbex Inc.; *U.S. Public*, pg. 238

BAR CODE OBJECT CONTENT ARCHITECTURE—Computer Systems—International Business Machines Corporation; *U.S. Public*, pg. 895

BAR-K—Fresh Portioned Meat—Kesterson Food Company, Inc.; *U.S. Private*, pg. 616

BAR MOBILE—Stock Transport Cart, Storage Racks—Jarke Corporation; *U.S. Private*, pg. 583

BAR NONE—Candy Bar—Hershey Chocolate U.S.A.; *U.S. Public*, pg. 812

BAR NONE—Candy Bar—Hershey Foods Corporation; *U.S. Public*, pg. 811

BAR-OX—Quick Dry Enamel—Devoe Paint; *Int'l*, pg. 663

BAR-OX—Alkyd Primer & Enamel—Grow Group, Inc.; *Int'l*, pg. 663

BAR OX—Alkyd Primer & Enamel—ICI Paints; *Int'l*, pg. 664

BAR-RUST—Ship Coating—Grow Group, Inc.; *Int'l*, pg. 663

BAR RUST—Ship Coating—ICI Paints; *Int'l*, pg. 664

BAR-S—Meat & Cheese Products—Bar-S Foods Co.; *U.S. Private*, pg. 114

BAR TENDER'S—Cocktail Mixes—Brady Enterprises, Inc.; *U.S. Private*, pg. 165

BAR WARS—Role Playing—Monarch Avalon, Inc.; *U.S. Public*, pg. 1123

BARA-MED—Hyperbaric Treatment System—Environmental Tectonics Corporation (ETC); *U.S. Public*, pg. 587

BARAGA/SQUARE SHOOTER—Rough Terrain Telescopic Lift Truck—Terex Corporation; *U.S. Public*, pg. 1581

BARAK—Missle Systems—Israel Aircraft Industries Ltd.; *Int'l*, pg. 689

BARAKA—Mineral Water—Nestle S.A.; *Int'l*, pg. 915

BARANNE—Shoe Polishes/Waxes—Benckiser Consumer Products Inc.; *Int'l*, pg. 185

BAVARIAN PRETZEL BAKERY—Retail Pretzel Shop—J & J Snack Foods Corporation; *U.S. Public*, pg. 916

BARB-LOK—Fastener Pin—Driv-Lok, Inc.; *U.S. Private*, pg. 343

BARBASOL—NONE—Pfizer Inc.; *U.S. Public*, pg. 1281

BARBECUE KING—Rotisserie Ovens—BKI; *U.S. Public*, pg. 1506

BARBECUE KING—Ovens & Baking Equipment—Standex International Corporation; *U.S. Public*, pg. 1505

BARBER—Dairy Products—Barber Dairies, Inc.; *U.S. Private*, pg. 115

BARBERANI ORVIETO CALCAIA—Italian Wine—Laird & Company; *U.S. Private*, pg. 642

BARBERANI ORVIETO CASTAGNOLO—Italian Wine—Laird & Company; *U.S. Private*, pg. 642

BARBERANI ORVIETO CLASSICO—Italian Wine—Laird & Company; *U.S. Private*, pg. 642

BARBERANI ORVIETO PULICCHIO—Italian Wine—Laird & Company; *U.S. Private*, pg. 642

BARBERO ASTI AND MOSCATO SPUMANTE—Wine—Allied Domecq PLC; *Int'l*, pg. 62

BARBERS—Full Line Ice Cream & Novelties—Barber Ice Cream Company; *U.S. Private*, pg. 115

BARBICAN—Ale—Bass PLC; *Int'l*, pg. 169

BARBICAN WITH LEMON—Ale—Bass PLC; *Int'l*, pg. 169

BARBIE—Fashion Dolls & Accessories—Mattel, Inc.; *U.S. Public*, pg. 1057

BARBIE HOLIDAY DANCE—Moving Barbie Ballroom Scene—Mr. Christmas Inc.; *U.S. Private*, pg. 765

BARBIZON—Intimate Apparel—VF Corporation; *U.S. Public*, pg. 1702

BARCALOUNGER—Lounge Chair—Consolidated Furniture Corporation; *U.S. Private*, pg. 265

BARCLAY—Cigarettes—B.A.T Industries P.L.C.; *Int'l*, pg. 110

BARCLAY—Furniture—Barclay Furniture Company; *U.S. Public*, pg. 974

BARCLAY—NONE—Barton Brands, Ltd.; *U.S. Public*, pg. 300

BARCLAY—Bourbon, Gin & Vodka—Barton Incorporated; *U.S. Public*, pg. 300

BARCLAY—Cigarettes—Brown & Williamson Tobacco Corp.; *Int'l*, pg. 111

BARCLAY—Men's Shoes—E.J. Footwear Corp.; *U.S. Public*, pg. 1684

BARCLAY—Furniture—Ladd Furniture, Inc.; *U.S. Public*, pg. 974

BARCLAY—Record Label—Philips Electronics N.V.; *Int'l*, pg. 1051

BARCLAY GENEVE—Cutlery & Flatware—Lifetime Hoan Corp.; *U.S. Public*, pg. 992

BARCLAY SERIES—Fiberglass Receptacles, Smokers' Urns Recycling Containers & Planters—United Receptical, Inc.; *U.S. Private*, pg. 1123

BARCLAYCARD—Credit Card—Barclays Bank PLC; *Int'l*, pg. 164

BARCO—Professional Apparel—Barco of California; *U.S. Private*, pg. 115

BARCO OF CALIFORNIA—Professional Apparel—Barco of California; *U.S. Private*, pg. 115

BARCO THE RIGHT IMPRESSION—Professional Apparel—Barco of California; *U.S. Private*, pg. 115

BARCODE—NONE—Intelligent Controls Inc.; *U.S. Private*, pg. 566

BARD—NONE—C.R. Bard, Inc.; *U.S. Public*, pg. 189

BARD—Heating & Air Conditioning Equipment—Bard Mfg. Co.; *U.S. Private*, pg. 116

BARD BTA—NONE—Bard Diagnostic Sciences; *U.S. Public*, pg. 189

BARD-PARKER—Surgical Blades & Scalpels—Becton Dickinson & Company; *U.S. Public*, pg. 199

BARDAC—Biocide for Germicidal Application—Lonza Inc.; *Int'l*, pg. 67

BARDAC-22—Topical Biocide—Lonza Inc.; *Int'l*, pg. 67

BARDIC—NONE—Chloride Group PLC; *Int'l*, pg. 287

BARDON—Hooks & Fittings for Wire Rope—Esco Corporation; *U.S. Private*, pg. 382

BARE BOTTOMS—Women's Shoes (Sandals)—International Seaway Trading Corporation; *U.S. Private*, pg. 572

BARE ELEGANCE—Body Shampoo—The Gillette Company; *U.S. Public*, pg. 743

BARE ESSENTIALS—Bikini Shaver—Wahl Clipper Corp.; *U.S. Private*, pg. 1146

BAREFOOT—Foot Care Line—Freeman Cosmetic Corp.; *U.S. Private*, pg. 426

BAREFOOT—Lawncare Products & Services—TruGreen-ChemLawn; *U.S. Public*, pg. 1461

BAREFOOT NAUTIQUE—Power Boat—Correct Craft, Inc.; *U.S. Private*, pg. 276

BAREN—Automotive & Industrial Batteries—Fiamm S.p.A.; *Int'l*, pg. 480

BARGAIN GARDEN—Garden Products—Jiffy Products of America, Inc.; *Int'l*, pg. 706

BARGMAN—Electrical Connectors & Lights—Echlin Inc.; *U.S. Public*, pg. 560

BARISHNIKOV—Fragrances—Parlux Fragrances Inc.; *U.S. Public*, pg. 1264

BARISOL—Wetting Agent/Dispersant—Dexter Chemical Corp.; *U.S. Private*, pg. 329

BARIVER—Chemical Reagant—Hach Company; *U.S. Public*, pg. 773

BARKEY—ID Badge Equipment & Supplies—Intelligent Controls Inc.; *U.S. Private*, pg. 566

BARKO HYDRAULIC—Log Loaders—Pettibone Corporation; *U.S. Private*, pg. 859

BARKWOOD—Vinyl Siding & Accessories—Alcoa Building Products, Inc.; *U.S. Public*, pg. 61

BARLENE—Oil Field Chemicals—Lonza Inc.; *Int'l*, pg. 67

BARLICAN—Beta-Glucanase for the Improvement of the Digestibility of Barley—Royal Gist-Brocades N.V.; *Int'l*, pg. 1142

BARLOCK—Access Control Products—Intelligent Controls Inc.; *U.S. Private*, pg. 566

BARLOX—Amine Oxide for Detergents, Shampoos, Textile Processing—Lonza Inc.; *Int'l*, pg. 67

BARNES—Non-Clog Grinder, Effluent & Sewage Ejector Pumps—Barnes Pumps, Inc.; *U.S. Public*, pg. 457

BARNES—Cutter Pump—Barnes Pumps, Inc.; *U.S. Public*, pg. 457

BARNES & NOBLE—Bookstores—Barnes & Noble Inc.; *U.S. Public*, pg. 189

BARNES & NOBLE—Imported Academic Books—Littlefield, Adams & Company; *U.S. Public*, pg. 1001

BARNESITE—Precision Polish for Glass—Ferro Corporation; *U.S. Public*, pg. 618

BARNEY'S NEW YORK—Retail Clothing Stores—Barneys Inc.; *U.S. Private*, pg. 116

BARNHARDT—Batting & Absorbent Cotton—Barnhardt Manufacturing Co.; *U.S. Private*, pg. 116

BARNMASTER—Roofing & Siding—Wheeling Corrugating Co.; *U.S. Public*, pg. 1727

BARNPLANK—Prefinished Plywood Paneling—Georgia-Pacific Corporation; *U.S. Public*, pg. 735

BARNSTEAD/THERMOLYNE—Water Purification Equip./Heating & Stirring Lab. Instruments—Sybron International Corporation; *U.S. Public*, pg. 1544

BARNUM'S ANIMAL CRACKERS—Animal Shaped Crackers—RJR Nabisco Holdings Corp.; *U.S. Public*, pg. 1354

BARNUM'S ANIMALS—Crackers—Nabisco Inc.; *U.S. Public*, pg. 1355

BARNWALL—Plywood, Lumber & Wood Products—Georgia-Pacific Corporation; *U.S. Public*, pg. 735

BAROID—Drilling Fluids—Dresser Industries, Inc.; *U.S. Public*, pg. 528

BARONET BOND—Writing & Bond Paper—The Mead Corporation; *U.S. Public*, pg. 1074

BAROQUE—Liquor—Groupe Pernod Ricard; *Int'l*, pg. 566

BAROWSKY—Breads, Bagels, Rolls, Subs—Lepage Bakery, Inc.; *U.S. Private*, pg. 660

BARQ'S—Root Beer—The Coca-Cola Company; *U.S. Public*, pg. 392

BARQUAT/HYAMINE 3500—Biocide—Lonza Inc.; *Int'l*, pg. 67

BARQUAT/UNIQUAT—Oil Field Chemicals—Lonza Inc.; *Int'l*, pg. 67

BARRACUDA—Active Ultraweight—Everest & Jennings, Inc.; *U.S. Public*, pg. 758

BARRACUDA—Conical Refiner—Harnischfeger Industries, Inc.; *U.S. Public*, pg. 788

BARRACUDA—Milling Tool—Smith International, Inc.; *U.S. Public*, pg. 1478

BARRATRON—Microwave Noise Generator—Litton Industries, Inc.; *U.S. Public*, pg. 1002

BARRATT—Sweets—Cadbury Schweppes p.l.c.; *Int'l*, pg. 247

BARRECRAFTERS—Ski Products—Barrecrafters; *U.S. Private*, pg. 991

BARREL O'FUN—Potato Chips & Snacks—Barrel O'Fun Snack Foods Co.; *U.S. Private*, pg. 118

BARREL 'O FUN—Snack Products—Borden, Inc.; *U.S. Public*, pg. 157

BARREL OF FUN—Beverage Cooler—Igloo Products Corporation; *U.S. Public*, pg. 265

BARRICADE—Anti-Bacterial Mops—Golden Star Inc.; *U.S. Private*, pg. 460

BARRIER—Jackets—Gerry Sportswear Company; *U.S. Private*, pg. 449

BARRIER—Storm Window Systems—ICI Acrylics Inc.; *Int'l*, pg. 663

BARRIER—Packs, Gowns, Scrub Apparel & Protective Goggles—Johnson & Johnson Medical, Inc.; *U.S. Public*, pg. 928

BARRIER BAGS—Food Packaging—W.R. Grace & Co.; *U.S. Public*, pg. 754

BARRIER/CAP—ATC Nickel Barrier Termination—American Technical Ceramics Corp.; *U.S. Public*, pg. 93

BARRIER PAK—Paper Containers—International Paper Company; *U.S. Public*, pg. 901

BARRINGER'S—Chocolate—Godiva Chocolatier, Inc.; *U.S. Public*, pg. 299

BARRISTER—Product Brand Name—Barrister Information Systems Corporation; *U.S. Public*, pg. 192

BARRISTER/EAGLE—Software Program—Barrister Information Systems Corporation; *U.S. Public*, pg. 192

BARRISTER/MESSAGER—Electronic Mail System—Barrister Information Systems Corporation; *U.S. Public*, pg. 192

BARRISTER/NET—Network—Barrister Information Systems Corporation; *U.S. Public*, pg. 192

BARRISTER/PUBLISHER—Document Finishing System—Barrister Information Systems Corporation; *U.S. Public*, pg. 192

BARRISTERS SCOTCH—Scotch—Laird & Company; *U.S. Private*, pg. 642

BARRNET—NONE—GTE Internetworking; *U.S. Public*, pg. 696

BARRON'S—Business & Financial Publication—Barron's The Dow Jones Business & Financial Weekly; *U.S. Public*, pg. 524

BARRON'S—Weekly Business & Financial Publication—Dow Jones & Company, Inc.; *U.S. Public*, pg. 524

BARRY—Isolators & Bearings—Barry Controls; *U.S. Public*, pg. 124

BARRY BLOWER—Commercial & Industrial Fans—AAF McQuay, Inc.; *U.S. Private*, pg. 2

BARRY CONTROLS—Vibration, Insolation Devices—Applied Power Inc.; *U.S. Public*, pg. 124

BARRY WELLS—NONE—Tandy Brands Accessories, Inc.; *U.S. Public*, pg. 1560

BARRYMORE—Bathroom Rugs & Broadloom Carpets—Peerless Carpet Corporation; *Int'l*, pg. 1032

BARRYMOUNT—Machinery & Vibration Mounts—Barry Controls; *U.S. Public*, pg. 124

BARSEAL—Bearing Seal—The Barden Corporation; *Int'l*, pg. 468

BARTELS—Pure Beer—The Lion Brewery, Inc.; *U.S. Public*, pg. 1000

BARTEMP—Bearing Seal—The Barden Corporation; *Int'l*, pg. 468

BARTER—Writing Paper & Bond Paper—The Mead Corporation; *U.S. Public*, pg. 1074

BARTEX—Barium Sulfate Pigments—Hitox Corporation of America; *U.S. Public*, pg. 829

BARTISSOL—Aperitif—Groupe Pernod Ricard; *Int'l*, pg. 566

BARTLES & JAYMES—Wine—E. & J. Gallo Winery; *U.S. Private*, pg. 438

BARTLETT—Tree Experts—The F.A. Bartlett Tree Expert Co.; *U.S. Private*, pg. 119

BARTLETT BOOST—Fertilizer for Trees & Shrubs—The F.A. Bartlett Tree Expert Co.; *U.S. Private*, pg. 119

BARTLETT MONITOR SERVICE—Integrated Pest Management—The F.A. Bartlett Tree Expert Co.; *U.S. Private*, pg. 119

BARTO—Executive Chair—Domore Corporation; *U.S. Private*, pg. 339

BARTON—NONE—Barton Brands, Ltd.; *U.S. Public*, pg. 300

BARTON—Liquors; Gin, Rum, Vodka—Barton Incorporated; *U.S. Public*, pg. 300

BARTON RESERVE—Blended Whiskey—Barton Incorporated; *U.S. Public*, pg. 300

BARTONS CANDY—Candy—Boyer Candy Company Inc.; *U.S. Private*, pg. 162

BARTON'S QT PREMIUM—Light Whiskey—Barton Incorporated; *U.S. Public*, pg. 300

BARUM—Tires—Continental AG; *Int'l*, pg. 327

BASA—Boat—Sea Ray; *U.S. Public*, pg. 266

BASACID—Dyes—BASF AG; *Int'l*, pg. 103

BASAGRAN—Crop Protection Agent—BASF AG; *Int'l*, pg. 103

BASAMID—Crop Protection Agent—BASF AG; *Int'l*, pg. 103

BASANTOL—Dyes—BASF AG; *Int'l*, pg. 103

BASCO—Automotive Equip.—Briggs & Stratton Corporation; *U.S. Public*, pg. 252

BASE HIT II—Industrial Chemical—Hercules Chemical Co., Inc.; *U.S. Private*, pg. 523

BASE RUNNER—Nucleic Acid Sequencing Instrument—Scientific Imaging Systems; *U.S. Public*, pg. 550

BASE SAS—For Data Management, Analysis, & Report Writing—SAS Institute Inc.; *U.S. Private*, pg. 966

BASE 24—Transaction Processing Software— Tandem Computers Inc.; *U.S. Public*, pg. 417

BASE 2—Cellular/PCS Base Station Equipment— Watkins-Johnson Company; *U.S. Public*, pg. 1745

BASEBALL DIGEST—Magazine—Century Publishing Company; *U.S. Private*, pg. 226

BASEBALL STRATEGY—Game—Monarch Avalon, Inc.; *U.S. Public*, pg. 1123

BASEFRAME—Paper Machine—Beloit Corporation; *U.S. Public*, pg. 789

BASEMENT BLANKET—Glass Fiber Insulation— Owens Corning; *U.S. Public*, pg. 1236

THE BASEMENT SENTRY—12-Volt Back-up Sump Pump—Zoeller Co.; *U.S. Private*, pg. 1207

BASEPAC—Turkey Feed—Hormel Foods Corp.; *U.S. Public*, pg. 840

BASES-BY-MAIL—Research Using Mail Panel— BASES Worldwide; *U.S. Private*, pg. 120

BASES LX—Line Extension Sales Forecasting— BASES Worldwide; *U.S. Private*, pg. 120

BASES I/II—New Product Sales Forecasting— BASES Worldwide; *U.S. Private*, pg. 120

BASES XRX—RX to OTC Sales Forecasting— BASES Worldwide; *U.S. Private*, pg. 120

BASEWORX—Computer Development Programs— Lucent Technologies Inc.; *U.S. Public*, pg. 1017

BASIC—Disposable Wipes, Towels & Bathroom Tissue—Kimberly-Clark Corporation; *U.S. Public*, pg. 958

BASIC—Children's Building Sets—LEGO Systems, Inc.; *Int'l*, pg. 805

BASIC—Blood Glucose Monitoring Prod.— LifeScan, Inc.; *U.S. Public*, pg. 928

BASIC—Cigarettes—Philip Morris Companies Inc.; *U.S. Public*, pg. 1287

BASIC—Cigarettes—Philip Morris U.S.A.; *U.S. Public*, pg. 1289

BASIC AMERICAN MEDICAL—Acute Care Hospitals & General Health Care Services— Columbia/HCA Healthcare Corporation; *U.S. Public*, pg. 404

BASIC COLLECTION—Teakwood—Dansk International Designs Ltd.; *U.S. Public*, pg. 261

BASIC COMPILER/2—Computer Systems— International Business Machines Corporation; *U.S. Public*, pg. 895

BASIC-D—Automatic Dishwashing Concentrate— Shaklee Corporation; *Int'l*, pg. 1518

BASIC 4—Cereal—General Mills, Inc.; *U.S. Public*, pg. 717

BASIC-G—Germicidal Cleaner—Shaklee Corporation; *Int'l*, pg. 1518

BASIC-H—Concentrated Organic Cleaner & Soil Conditioner—Shaklee Corporation; *Int'l*, pg. 1518

BASIC-I—Industrial Cleaner—Shaklee Corporation; *Int'l*, pg. 1518

BASIC-L—Laundry Concentrate—Shaklee Corporation; *Int'l*, pg. 1518

THE BASIC SOFT SEAT—Promotional Soft Seat—Sanderson Plumbing Products Inc.; *U.S. Private*, pg. 964

BASIC 2—Product Line for Small System Users— Vicon Industries, Inc.; *U.S. Public*, pg. 1719

BASIC WHITE—Powder Lighteners—Bristol-Myers Squibb Company; *U.S. Public*, pg. 253

BASIC WHITE—Hair Lightener—Clairol, Inc.; *U.S. Public*, pg. 254

BASICAM—Ducted HEPA Ceiling Modules for Cleanroom Use—Farr Company; *U.S. Public*, pg. 613

BASICS—Endoscopy System—Ballard Medical Products; *U.S. Public*, pg. 171

BASICS/DB—NONE—BMC Software, Inc.; *U.S. Public*, pg. 162

BASICSCAN—Test Generator for IEEE 1149.1- Compliant Devices—GenRad, Inc.; *U.S. Public*, pg. 731

BASIK BENCH—NONE—Kewaunee Scientific Corporation; *U.S. Public*, pg. 953

BASIL HAYDEN'S—Small Batch Bourbon— Fortune Brands, Inc.; *U.S. Public*, pg. 674

BASILEN—Dyes & Indigo—BASF AG; *Int'l*, pg. 103

BASILICA—Italian Liqueurs, Amaretto, Sambuca & Cognac—Marie Brizard Wines & Spirits USA; *U.S. Private*, pg. 702

BASIS—Preservative & Fragrance Free Skincare Products—Beiersdorf, Inc.; *Int'l*, pg. 182

BASIS—Telecommunication Switches, Controller, And Cross-Connect Devices—DSC Communications Corporation; *U.S. Public*, pg. 475

BASIS—NONE—PolyMedica Industries, Inc.; *U.S. Public*, pg. 1315

BASIX—Coated & Uncoated Paper—The Mead Corporation; *U.S. Public*, pg. 1074

BASIX—Syringe for Balloon Angioplasty—Merit Medical Systems, Inc.; *U.S. Public*, pg. 1096

BASKETBALL DIGEST—Magazine—Century Publishing Company; *U.S. Private*, pg. 226

BASKETWEAVE—Safety-Paper—Georgia-Pacific Corporation; *U.S. Public*, pg. 735

BASKIN-ROBBINS—Ice Cream—Allied Domecq PLC; *Int'l*, pg. 62

BASKIN-ROBBINS—Ice Cream & Frozen Yogurt— Baskin-Robbins Incorporated; *Int'l*, pg. 63

BASKIN 31 ROBBINS—NONE—Baskin-Robbins Canada; *Int'l*, pg. 63

BASKING LITE—Incandescent for Reptiles—Duro-Test Corporation; *U.S. Private*, pg. 349

BASO—Brand Name for Single Function Gas Valves—Johnson Controls, Inc., Controls Group; *U.S. Public*, pg. 932

BASOFIL—Heat & Flame Resistant Fiber—BASF Corporation Fiber Products Division; *Int'l*, pg. 105

BASONAT—Polymer Dispersions & Solutions; Solid Polymers—BASF AG; *Int'l*, pg. 103

BASOPLAST—Process Chemicals & Colorants— BASF AG; *Int'l*, pg. 103

BASOQUIN—Single Dose Anti-Malarial—Parke-Davis & Company, Limited; *U.S. Public*, pg. 1739

BASOTRONIC—Chemicals for the Printed Circuit Board Industry—BASF AG; *Int'l*, pg. 103

BASOVIT—Dyes—BASF AG; *Int'l*, pg. 103

BASS—Beer, Japan Only—Asahi Breweries Ltd.; *Int'l*, pg. 83

BASS—Shoes—G.H. Bass & Co.; *U.S. Public*, pg. 1291

BASS—Premium Ale—Bass PLC; *Int'l*, pg. 169

BASS—Ale—Guinness Import Company; *Int'l*, pg. 412

BASS—Footwear—Phillips-Van Heusen Corporation; *U.S. Public*, pg. 1291

BASS ALE—Ale—Bass PLC; *Int'l*, pg. 169

BASS BEST SCOTCH—Bitter—Bass PLC; *Int'l*, pg. 169

BASS BLUE—Ale—Bass PLC; *Int'l*, pg. 169

BASS EXPORT—Ale—Bass PLC; *Int'l*, pg. 169

BASS LA—Ale—Bass PLC; *Int'l*, pg. 169

BASS LIGHT—Bitter/Ale—Bass PLC; *Int'l*, pg. 169

BASS LIGHT 5 STAR—Light Mild Beer—Bass PLC; *Int'l*, pg. 169

BASS MILD—Dark Mild Beer—Bass PLC; *Int'l*, pg. 169

BASS NO 1—Strong Ale—Bass PLC; *Int'l*, pg. 169

BASS PALE ALE—Ale—Bass PLC; *Int'l*, pg. 169

BASS PLAYER—Magazine—Miller Freeman Inc.; *Int'l*, pg. 1443

BASS SPECIAL—Bitter/Ale—Bass PLC; *Int'l*, pg. 169

BASS SPECIAL BITTER—Bitters—Bass PLC; *Int'l*, pg. 169

BASSANI—Motor Vehicle Parts—Bassani Manufacturing; *U.S. Private*, pg. 122

BASSCASE—NONE—Cambridge Soundworks, Inc.; *U.S. Private*, pg. 202

BASSETT—Furniture—Bassett Furniture Industries, Incorporated; *U.S. Public*, pg. 193

BASSETT—Jellied Sweets—Cadbury Schweppes p.l.c.; *Int'l*, pg. 247

BASSETT—NONE—Royal Waterbeds; *U.S. Private*, pg. 949

BASSETT-WALKER—Sportswear—VF Corporation; *U.S. Public*, pg. 1702

BASSICK—Casters, Furniture Glides—BTR plc; *Int'l*, pg. 124

BASSICK-SACK—Furniture Hardware—BTR plc; *Int'l*, pg. 124

BASSMASTER—Magazine—B.A.S.S., Inc.; *U.S. Private*, pg. 105

BASSMASTER CLASSIC REPORT—Magazine— B.A.S.S., Inc.; *U.S. Private*, pg. 105

BASSMASTER TOP BASS DESTINATIONS— Magazine—B.A.S.S., Inc.; *U.S. Private*, pg. 105

THE BASSMASTER TOUR—Magazine—B.A.S.S., Inc.; *U.S. Private*, pg. 105

THE BASSMASTERS—TV Show—B.A.S.S., Inc.; *U.S. Private*, pg. 105

BASTA—Herbicide—Hoechst Aktiengesellschaft; *Int'l*, pg. 624

BASTION—Soil Sterilant—The Dow Chemical Company; *U.S. Public*, pg. 522

BASYNTAN—Tanning Agents, Auxiliaries & Finishes, Dyes & Pigment Finishes—BASF AG; *Int'l*, pg. 103

BATA INDUSTRIALS—Waterproof Protective Footwear—Bata Shoe Co., Inc.; *U.S. Private*, pg. 195

BATASIOLA—Italian Wines—Marie Brizard Wines & Spirits USA; *U.S. Private*, pg. 702

BATCH CONTROL FACILITY—NONE—BMC Software, Inc.; *U.S. Public*, pg. 162

BATCH TRANSACTION PROCESSOR—Batch Processing Software—Dun & Bradstreet Software Services; *Int'l*, pg. 532

BATCHELORS—Canned Soups & Vegetables— Northern Foods plc; *Int'l*, pg. 967

BATCHPAC—Modular Induction Batch Melting Systems—Inductotherm Corp.; *U.S. Private*, pg. 560

BATCHPIPES—Computer Systems—International Business Machines Corporation; *U.S. Public*, pg. 895

BATCO—Auto Parts—JPE, Inc.; *U.S. Public*, pg. 919

BATEAUX—French Magazine - Boats & Sailing— EMAP France; *Int'l*, pg. 451

BATES—Needlecraft Accessories—Coats & Clark Inc.; *Int'l*, pg. 300

BATES—Emery Boards, Clippers, Tweezers, Gift Sets—The Cook Bates Division; *Int'l*, pg. 815

BATES—Religious Gold Jewelry—Michael Anthony Jewelers, Inc.; *U.S. Public*, pg. 1103

BATES—Military Footwear—Wolverine World Wide, Inc.; *U.S. Public*, pg. 1775

BATES FLOATAWAYS—Shoes—Wolverine World Wide, Inc.; *U.S. Public*, pg. 1775

BATES FLOATERS—Shoes—Wolverine World Wide, Inc.; *U.S. Public*, pg. 1775

BATESVILLE MARBLE—Calcium Carbonate for Use in Mfrg. of Lime—United States Lime & Minerals; *U.S. Public*, pg. 1684

BATH & BODY THERAPIES—Apparel—Fred Meyer Stores; *U.S. Public*, pg. 1103

BATH FORMULA GELEE—Cosmetics—Irma Shorell, Inc.; *U.S. Private*, pg. 1101

BATH TIME—BEAUTY & Bath Accessories—Paris Presents; *U.S. Private*, pg. 839

BATHING BEAUTY—Bikini Shaver—Bristol-Myers Squibb Company; *U.S. Public*, pg. 253

BATHMATE—Radios—Thomson Consumer Electronics Inc.; *Int'l*, pg. 1383

BATHROOM PLUS MASEUR—NONE—Kiwi Brands Pty. Ltd.; *U.S. Public*, pg. 1434

BATI-SERVICE—Homebuilding/France—Kaufman and Broad Home Corporation; *U.S. Public*, pg. 944

BATINASE—Bating of Hides for Leather Industry—Royal Gist-Brocades N.V.; *Int'l*, pg. 1142

BATIROC—NONE—ETEX; *Int'l*, pg. 430

BATMAN—Toys—Hasbro; *U.S. Public*, pg. 797

BATMAN—Kenner Products—Hasbro, Inc.; *U.S. Public*, pg. 797

BATMAN FOREVER—Interactive Entertainment Software—Acclaim Entertainment, Inc.; *U.S. Public*, pg. 15

BATT PAK—Insulaton Packaging—CertainTeed Corporation; *Int'l*, pg. 1170

BATTER BOY—Bakery Equipment—Belshaw Brothers, Inc.; *Int'l*, pg. 188

BATTER DIPPED—Further-processed poultry items—Louis Kemp Seafood Co.; *U.S. Public*, pg. 1652

BATTER 'N BAKE—Chicken Mix—Kraft Foods, Inc.; *U.S. Public*, pg. 1287

BATTERGOLD—Frozen Food—Tyson Foods, Inc.; *U.S. Public*, pg. 1652

BATTERSWEET—Frozen Poultry—Tyson Foods, Inc.; *U.S. Public*, pg. 1652

BATTERY PACK—Batteries—Bright Star Industries, Inc.; *U.S. Public*, pg. 1341

BATTLE BOX—Travel Game—Mattel Games/Puzzles; *U.S. Public*, pg. 1058

BATTLE OF THE BULGE—War Game—Monarch Avalon, Inc.; *U.S. Public*, pg. 1123

BATTLESHIP—Game—Hasbro, Inc.; *U.S. Public*, pg. 797

BATTLESHIP—Game—Milton Bradley Company; *U.S. Public*, pg. 797

BAUER—Hockey Equipment—Bauer Sports Inc.; *U.S. Public*, pg. 1184

BAUER & BLACK—Supporters, Briefs, Suspensions—Becton Dickinson & Company; *U.S. Public*, pg. 199

BAUKJE—Consumer Bakery Products—CSM N.V.; *Int'l*, pg. 243

BAUKNECHT—Major Appliances—Whirlpool Corporation; *U.S. Public*, pg. 1764

BAUM—Paper Cutters—Baum USA; *Int'l*, pg. 1293

BAUM—Paper Cutters—Stahl GmbH & Co.; *Int'l*, pg. 1293

BAUM—NONE—Taylor Impression, Inc.; *U.S. Private*, pg. 1070

BAUMAN DISPOSABLADE—Fiberoptic Laryngoscope—Vital Signs, Inc.; *U.S. Public*, pg. 1723

BAUME & MERCIER—Watches—Baume Mercier, Inc.; *U.S. Private*, pg. 124

BAUMFOLDER—Paper Folding Machines—Baum USA; *Int'l*, pg. 1293

BAUMFOLDER—Paper Folding Machines—Stahl GmbH & Co.; *Int'l*, pg. 1293

BAUSCH & LOMB—Eye Care & Optical Products, Binoculars, Telescopes & Riflescopes—Bausch & Lomb Incorporated; *U.S. Public*, pg. 194

BAUSCH & LOMB ELITE—Binoculars—Bushnell Corporation; *U.S. Private*, pg. 1191

BAUSCH & LOMB ELITE—Riflescopes—Bushnell Corporation; *U.S. Private*, pg. 1191

BAUSCH & LOMB ELITE—Spotting Scopes—Bushnell Corporation; *U.S. Private*, pg. 1191

BAUSCH & LOMB MOISTURE DROPS—Eye Drops—Bausch & Lomb Incorporated; *U.S. Public*, pg. 194

BAUSCH & LOMBDIGITAL PROGRAMMABLE HEARING SYSTEM—NONE—Dahlberg, Inc.; *U.S. Public*, pg. 194

BAVARIAN CLUB—Beer—Joseph Huber Brewing Co., Inc.; *U.S. Private*, pg. 545

BAVISTIN—Crop Protection Agent—BASF AG; *Int'l*, pg. 103

BAXTER TEXT—Coated Two Side Satin Finish Paper—Great Northern Paper, Inc.; *U.S. Public*, pg. 248

BAY CITY—Milk—Q.U.F. Industries Ltd.; *Int'l*, pg. 1074

THE BAY CITY TIMES—Newspaper—Booth Newspapers, Inc.; *U.S. Private*, pg. 157

BAY SPRINGS—Comforters, Sets & Ensambles—Sunbeam Household Products; *U.S. Public*, pg. 1533

BAY TO BAY—Men's Slacks & Shorts—Tropical Sportswear International; *U.S. Private*, pg. 1105

BAYBERRY—Air Freshener—Stanhome Inc.; *U.S. Public*, pg. 1508

BAYBLEND—Flame-Retardant Plastic—Bayer AG; *Int'l*, pg. 171

BAYCHROM—Chrome Tanning Agent—Bayer AG; *Int'l*, pg. 171

BAYCLIN—Household Cleaners—Bayer AG; *Int'l*, pg. 171

BAYCOX—Poultry Vaccine—Bayer AG; *Int'l*, pg. 171

BAYER ASPIRIN—NONE—Bayer Corporation; *Int'l*, pg. 172

BAYER CANDY—Confectionery—Boyer Candy Company Inc.; *U.S. Private*, pg. 162

BAYERNLAND—Cheese—Bayernland Gmbh & Co. KG; *Int'l*, pg. 181

BAYERTITAN—White Industrial Pigment—Bayer AG; *Int'l*, pg. 171

BAYFERROX—Pigments—Bayer AG; *Int'l*, pg. 171

BAYFIELD COUNTY—NONE—Alliant Foodservice, Inc.; *U.S. Private*, pg. 244

BAYFLEX—Polyurethane Systems—Bayer AG; *Int'l*, pg. 171

BAYGON—Household Pesticides—Bayer AG; *Int'l*, pg. 171

BAYHYDROL—Water-Reducible Coating Resin—Bayer AG; *Int'l*, pg. 171

BAYLEY—Steel Windows & Security Screens—William Bayley/Folger Adam Security, Inc.; *U.S. Private*, pg. 125

BAYLINER—Boats—Brunswick Corporation; *U.S. Public*, pg. 265

BAYLITH—Molecular Sieve Zeolites—Bayer AG; *Int'l*, pg. 171

BAYMASTER—Highbay Luminaries for MV or MH Lamps—Appleton Electric Co.; *U.S. Public*, pg. 572

BAYMASTER—Marine Crane—Weatherford Enterra Incorporated; *U.S. Public*, pg. 1749

BAYMOD A—PVC-Free Plastic—Bayer AG; *Int'l*, pg. 171

BAYMYCARD/SYSCOR—Calcium Antagonist—Bayer AG; *Int'l*, pg. 171

BAYOU—All-Terrain Vehicle—Kawasaki Motors Corp., U.S.A.; *Int'l*, pg. 725

BAYPEN—Penicillin—Bayer AG; *Int'l*, pg. 171

BAYPREN—Universal Specialty Rubber—Bayer AG; *Int'l*, pg. 171

BAYSON—Non-Abrasive Scouring Cream—Bayer AG; *Int'l*, pg. 171

BAYSTAL—Latex—Bayer AG; *Int'l*, pg. 171

BAYTEC—Reactive Elastomers—Bayer AG; *Int'l*, pg. 171

BAYTHROID—Synthetic Pyrethroid—Bayer AG; *Int'l*, pg. 171

BAYTICOL—Cattle Vaccine—Bayer AG; *Int'l*, pg. 171

BAYTRIL—Antibacterial—Bayer AG; *Int'l*, pg. 171

BAYVIEW CADILLAC—Dealership—Ed Morse Automotive Group; *U.S. Private*, pg. 763

BAYWATCH—TV Program—All American Communications, Inc.; *U.S. Public*, pg. 41

THE BAZOOKA—Automatic Taper—AXIA Incorporated; *U.S. Private*, pg. 103

BAZOOKA—NONE—Cruspi S.A.; *Int'l*, pg. 348

BAZOOKA—Nozzle—The Dow Chemical Company; *U.S. Public*, pg. 522

BAZOOKA—Bubble Gum—The Topps Company, Inc.; *U.S. Public*, pg. 1621

BE A MOVIE BUFF—Video Equipment—National Video, Inc.; *U.S. Public*, pg. 1755

BE-WATERWISE—NONE—Melnor Inc.; *U.S. Public*, pg. 1234

BE YOURSELF—Maestectomy Foundations—The Strouse, Adler Company; *U.S. Private*, pg. 1047

BE-RO—NONE—Ranks Hovis McDougall Limited; *Int'l*, pg. 1395

BEACH—Disposable Decorated Tableware, Stationery Products—Golden Books Family Entertainment Inc.; *U.S. Public*, pg. 749

BEACH-AID—Burn Out of Sunburn & Jellyfish—Bethurum Research & Development, Inc.; *U.S. Private*, pg. 141

BEACH BUDDY—Fleece Beach Blanket—Dakotah, Inc.; *U.S. Public*, pg. 477

BEACH WATCH—Radio Networks—CRN International, Inc.; *U.S. Private*, pg. 197

BEACON—Herbicide—Ciba Specialty Chemicals; *Int'l*, pg. 291

BEACON—Service Stations—Ultramar Diamond Shamrock Corporation; *U.S. Public*, pg. 1663

BEACON GUARD—Frequency Detector Device—Bytex Corporation; *U.S. Public*, pg. 1522

BEACON HALL—Lumber & Wood Products—Georgia-Pacific Corporation; *U.S. Public*, pg. 735

BEACON JOURNAL—Publisher—The Beacon Journal Publishing Company; *U.S. Public*, pg. 963

BEACON-MORRIS—Heating & Ventilation Equipment—Mestek, Inc.; *U.S. Public*, pg. 1099

BEACON RAY—Electrical Revolving Light—Federal Signal Corporation; *U.S. Public*, pg. 616

BEAD & BULTON—Magazine—Kalmbach Publishing Co.; *U.S. Private*, pg. 606

BEADED—NONE—Amerimark Inc.; *U.S. Public*, pg. 1237

BEALE INMAN—NONE—Moss Bros Group PLC; *Int'l*, pg. 895

BEALL'S—Department Stores—Beall's, Inc.; *U.S. Private*, pg. 126

BEALLS—NONE—Stage Stores, Inc.; *U.S. Private*, pg. 1560

BEALL'S SIGNATURE COLLECTION—NONE—Tandy Brands Accessories, Inc.; *U.S. Public*, pg. 1560

BEAM—Fungicide—The Dow Chemical Company; *U.S. Public*, pg. 522

BEAM—Carburetors, Regulators, Fuel Lock-Offs, Adapters, Fuel Control Processors—IMPCO AirSensors Technologies; *U.S. Public*, pg. 34

BEAM—Brain Topographic Mapping System—Nicolet Analytical; *U.S. Public*, pg. 1593

BEAM—Central Vacuum Cleaning Systems—White Consolidated Industries, Inc.; *Int'l*, pg. 439

THE BEAM—Halogen Spotlight—Unity Manufacturing Co.; *U.S. Private*, pg. 1126

BEAMDIRECTOR—Industrial Laser Systems—Lumonics Inc.; *Int'l*, pg. 1314

BEAMISH—Ale—Foster's Brewing Group Limited; *Int'l*, pg. 500

BEAN CUISINE—Soups, Pasta & Beans—Reily Foods Company; *U.S. Private*, pg. 919

BEAN POD—Deli Restaurants—Pizza Haven Inc.; *U.S. Private*, pg. 868

BEAN STALK NIPPLE—Baby Bottles & Nipples—Otsuka Pharmaceutical Co., Ltd.; *Int'l*, pg. 1013

BEAN STALK ORGANIC APPLE—Apple Juice for Infants—Otsuka Pharmaceutical Co., Ltd.; *Int'l*, pg. 1013

BEAN STALK POCARI—Juice for Infants—Otsuka Pharmaceutical Co., Ltd.; *Int'l*, pg. 1013

BEAN STALK ORGANIC MOM—Beverage for Moms—Otsuka Pharmaceutical Co., Ltd.; *Int'l*, pg. 1013

BEAN'S—Sporting Specialties—L.L. Bean, Inc.; *U.S. Private*, pg. 639

BEANS MCGEE—NONE—J.G. Hook, Inc.; *U.S. Private*, pg. 538

BEAR—Golf Equipment—Nicklaus Golf Company, L.C.; *U.S. Private*, pg. 799

BEAR—Coated Abrasives, Tapes, Floor Maintenance Products—Norton Company; *Int'l*, pg. 1173

BEAR—Diagnostic Equipment—SPX Corporation; *U.S. Public*, pg. 1420

BEAR BOTTOMS—NONE—The Vermont Teddy Bear Company, Inc.; *U.S. Public*, pg. 1716

BEAR COUNSELORS—NONE—The Vermont Teddy Bear Company, Inc.; *U.S. Public*, pg. 1716

BEAR-GRAMS—NONE—The Vermont Teddy Bear Company, Inc.; *U.S. Public*, pg. 1716

BEAR-N-BRONZ—NONE—Boston Gear; *U.S. Public*, pg. 857

BEAR STEARNS—NONE—The Bear Stearns Companies Inc.; *U.S. Public*, pg. 197

BEAR-TEX—Floor Cleaning Pads—Norton Company; *Int'l*, pg. 1173

BEARCAT—Single-Action Revolvers—Sturm, Ruger & Co., Inc.; *U.S. Public*, pg. 1526
BEARCAT—Communication Equipment—Uniden America Corporation; *Int'l*, pg. 1433
BEARDSLEY—Dried Beef—E.W. Knauss & Son, Inc.; *U.S. Private*, pg. 626
BEARGUIDE—Flowmeter—Bailey, Fischer & Porter Company; *Int'l*, pg. 449
BEARITOS—Snack Foods, Canned Products—Westbrae Natural, Inc.; *U.S. Public*, pg. 774
BEAST—Household Trash Compactor—Philips Electronics N.V.; *Int'l*, pg. 1051
BEATLE YEARS—Rock Music Radio Program—Westwood One Entertainment; *U.S. Public*, pg. 1763
THE BEATLE YEARS—History of Beatles Show—Westwood One, Inc.; *U.S. Public*, pg. 1763
THE BEATLES—Clothing—Salant Corporation; *U.S. Public*, pg. 1429
BEATREME—Fat Powders—Kerry Group PLC; *Int'l*, pg. 731
BEATRICE—Consumer Products—ConAgra, Inc.; *U.S. Public*, pg. 425
BEATRIM—Fat Replacement Systems—Kerry Group PLC; *Int'l*, pg. 731
BEATS THE NAIL—All Purpose Construction Adhesive—DAP Inc.; *Int'l*, pg. 1486
BEATTIE—Corn Meal—Wilkins-Rogers Incorporated; *U.S. Private*, pg. 1176
BEAU—Electronic Components—Axsys Technologies, Inc.; *U.S. Public*, pg. 157
BEAU KREML—Hair Tonic—Menley & James Laboratories, Inc.; *U.S. Public*, pg. 1086
BEAU RIVAGE—Wine—Paterno Imports Limited; *U.S. Private*, pg. 843
BEAU RIVAGE RESORTS—Gaming Casinos & Resorts—Mirage Resorts Incorporated; *U.S. Public*, pg. 1116
BEAUCHAINE—Electronic Components—Axsys Technologies, Inc.; *U.S. Public*, pg. 157
BEAUFLAIRE—Sheet Vinyl Floor Covering—Mannington Mills, Inc.; *U.S. Private*, pg. 700
BEAULIEU VINEYARD—Wines—Grand Metropolitan Plc; *Int'l*, pg. 408
BEAULIEU VINEYARD WINES—Wine—Heublein, Inc.; *Int'l*, pg. 410
BEAULON—Zipper—YKK (U.S.A.); *Int'l*, pg. 1515
BEAUMONT ENTERPRISE—Newspaper—The Hearst Corporation; *U.S. Private*, pg. 515
BEAUTE—NONE—Revlon, Inc.; *U.S. Private*, pg. 689
BEAUTI-GLIDE—Bed Frames—Lear Siegler Diversified Holdings Corp.; *U.S. Private*, pg. 655
BEAUTICONTROL—Skin Care Products & Cosmetics—BeautiControl Cosmetics, Inc.; *U.S. Public*, pg. 198
BEAUTIFUL ANSWERS—Support Bras—Warner's; *U.S. Public*, pg. 1738
BEAUTIFUL BATH—Bath Line—Freeman Cosmetic Corp.; *U.S. Private*, pg. 426
BEAUTIFUL BROWNS—Hair Coloring—Clairol, Inc.; *U.S. Public*, pg. 254
BEAUTIFUL COLLECTION—NONE—Bristol-Myers Squibb Company; *U.S. Public*, pg. 253
BEAUTIFUL SKIN—Skin Products—Freeman Cosmetic Corp.; *U.S. Private*, pg. 426
A BEAUTIFUL WAY TO SAVE—NONE—The Cosmetic Center Inc.; *U.S. Private*, pg. 689
BEAUTY LABS—Beauty Products—Winstar Global Products, Inc.; *U.S. Public*, pg. 1772
BEAUTY LIGHTS—Makeup Mirrors—Bristol-Myers Squibb Company; *U.S. Public*, pg. 253
BEAUTY RECOVERY COMPLEX—Personal Care—Shaklee Corporation; *Int'l*, pg. 1518
BEAUTY VISION—Computer Sales Aid—Avon Products, Inc.; *U.S. Public*, pg. 155
BEAUTYGUARD—NONE—American Woodmark Corporation; *U.S. Public*, pg. 96
BEAUTYREST—Mattress—Simmons Company; *Int'l*, pg. 686
BEAUTYREST FEELINGS—Flotation Bed—Simmons Company; *Int'l*, pg. 686
BEAUTYSLEEP—Mattress—Simmons Company; *Int'l*, pg. 686
BEAUTYWARE—Building Products—Email Limited; *Int'l*, pg. 450
BEAUX RÊVES—NONE—Kellwood Company; *U.S. Public*, pg. 948
BEAUX VILLAGES—Cheese—Kraft Foods, Inc.; *U.S. Public*, pg. 1287

BEAVER—Nuts—Hershey Foods Corporation; *U.S. Public*, pg. 811
BEAVER—Heat Pump—Mitsubishi Heavy Industries Ltd.; *Int'l*, pg. 873
BEAVER FALLS—Meat products—Hatfield Quality Meats; *U.S. Private*, pg. 510
BEAVERS—Dental Burrs—Sybron International Corporation; *U.S. Public*, pg. 1544
BEAVIS & BUTTHEAD—Licensed Characters—MTV Networks; *U.S. Private*, pg. 779
BEBCO—NONE—Barton Nelson Inc.; *U.S. Private*, pg. 120
BEBERE—Fruit Juice—Jugos del Valle, S.A. de C.V.; *Int'l*, pg. 716
BECALM—Natural Aid for Tension—Nature's Bounty Inc.; *U.S. Public*, pg. 1166
BECAUSE NELLCOR CARES—NONE—Nellcor Puritan Bennett Incorporated; *U.S. Public*, pg. 1039
BECEL—Margarine—Deutsche Unilever Gmbh; *Int'l*, pg. 1436
BECEL—Margarine—FIMA-Productos Alimentares, Lda; *Int'l*, pg. 471
BECEL—Margarine—Lever Brothers Co.; *Int'l*, pg. 1435
BECEL—Margarine—Unilever Plc; *Int'l*, pg. 1433
BECK/ARNLEY WORLDPARTS—Automobile Parts for Imports—Echlin Inc.; *U.S. Public*, pg. 560
BECK'S—Beer—Dribeck Importers, Inc.; *U.S. Private*, pg. 343
BECKACITE—Resin Esters & Adducts—Arizona Chemical Div.; *U.S. Public*, pg. 901
BECKER—Automotive Stereos—Harman International Industries, Inc.; *U.S. Public*, pg. 787
BECKER—Device—Medtronic, Inc.; *U.S. Public*, pg. 1082
BECKETT—Fine Paper—International Paper Company; *U.S. Public*, pg. 901
BECKETT EXPRESSION—NONE—Beckett Papers; *U.S. Public*, pg. 903
BECK'S DARK BEER—NONE—Dribeck Importers, Inc.; *U.S. Private*, pg. 343
BECK'S FOR OKTOBERFEST—NONE—Dribeck Importers, Inc.; *U.S. Private*, pg. 343
BECK'S LIGHT BEER—NONE—Dribeck Importers, Inc.; *U.S. Private*, pg. 343
BECKY—Girlswear—Elder Manufacturing Company; *U.S. Private*, pg. 367
BECLOVENT—Asthma Treatment—Glaxo Wellcome Inc.; *Int'l*, pg. 552
BECONASE—Allergic & Non-Allergic Rhinitis Treatment—Glaxo Wellcome Inc.; *Int'l*, pg. 552
BECOPLEX—Vitamin B—Novo Nordisk A/S; *Int'l*, pg. 987
BECOTIDE/BECLOVENT—Pharmaceutical—Glaxo Wellcome plc; *Int'l*, pg. 552
BED & BREAKFAST—Reference—Simon & Schuster; *U.S. Private*, pg. 777
BED BUGS—Game—Milton Bradley Company; *U.S. Public*, pg. 797
BED O' COB—NONE—The Andersons Incorporated; *U.S. Public*, pg. 111
BEDBASE—Brass Beds—Dresher, Inc.; *U.S. Public*, pg. 986
BEDFORD—Commercial Vehicles—General Motors Corporation; *U.S. Public*, pg. 718
BEDFORD GEAR—Machining Metals—Joy Mining Machinery; *U.S. Public*, pg. 789
BEDFORD VILLAGE—Prefinished Wall Paneling—Georgia-Pacific Corporation; *U.S. Public*, pg. 735
BEDSIDE BASSINET—Bassinet—Century Products Co.; *U.S. Private*, pg. 226
BEDTIME BUDDIES—Disposable Flashlight—RAYOVAC Corporation; *U.S. Private*, pg. 912
BEE—Playing Cards—The United States Playing Card Company; *U.S. Public*, pg. 1125
BEE HIVE—Syrups—Bestfoods; *U.S. Public*, pg. 223
BEE LINE—All Models—Bee Line Company; *U.S. Private*, pg. 129
BEECH BARON—Airplane—Raytheon Aircraft Company; *U.S. Public*, pg. 1365
BEECH BONANZA—Airplane—Raytheon Aircraft Company; *U.S. Public*, pg. 1365
BEECH KING AIR—Airplane—Raytheon Aircraft Company; *U.S. Public*, pg. 1365
BEECH 1900 AIRLINER—Airplane—Raytheon Aircraft Company; *U.S. Public*, pg. 1365

BEECH-NUT—Baby Food—Beech-Nut Nutrition Corporation; *U.S. Public*, pg. 1359
BEECH-NUT—Chewing Gum—Planters Company; *U.S. Public*, pg. 1355
BEECH-NUT—NONE—Ralcorp Holdings Inc.; *U.S. Public*, pg. 1359
BEECH NUT GUM—Gum—Nabisco Inc.; *U.S. Public*, pg. 1355
BEECH STARSHIP 1—Airplane—Raytheon Aircraft Company; *U.S. Public*, pg. 1365
BEECH TREE BOOKS—Adult Books—William Morrow & Co., Inc.; *U.S. Private*, pg. 515
BEECHAM'S PILLS—Laxative—SmithKline Beecham plc; *Int'l*, pg. 1264
BEECHAMS—NONE—SmithKline Beecham Corporation; *Int'l*, pg. 1264
BEECHAMS POWDERS—Treatment for Colds & Influenza—SmithKline Beecham plc; *Int'l*, pg. 1264
BEECHJET—Airplane—Raytheon Aircraft Company; *U.S. Public*, pg. 1365
BEECHMONT AUTOMILE—NONE—Beechmont Investments Inc.; *U.S. Private*, pg. 129
BEECHMONT CHEVROLET—Chevrolet—Beechmont Investments Inc.; *U.S. Private*, pg. 129
BEECHMONT HYUNDAI—NONE—Beechmont Investments Inc.; *U.S. Private*, pg. 129
BEECHMONT ISUZU—NONE—Beechmont Investments Inc.; *U.S. Private*, pg. 129
BEECHMONT MOTORS—Volvo, Porsche, Audi—Beechmont Investments Inc.; *U.S. Private*, pg. 129
BEECHMONT TOYOTA—Toyota Inc.—Beechmont Investments Inc.; *U.S. Private*, pg. 129
BEECHNUT—Chewing Gum—Cadbury Schweppes p.l.c.; *Int'l*, pg. 247
BEEF—Publication for Beef Cattle Producers—Intertec Publishing; *U.S. Public*, pg. 1327
BEEF BITE TREATS—Premium Pet Treats—Alpo Pet Foods, Inc.; *Int'l*, pg. 917
BEEF TONIGHT—NONE—Van den Bergh Foods Company; *Int'l*, pg. 1436
BEEFAMERICA—Boxed Beef—BeefAmerica Operating Co., Inc.; *U.S. Private*, pg. 130
BEEFEATER—Restaurant—Whitbread PLC; *Int'l*, pg. 1498
BEEFEATER GIN—Gin—Allied Domecq PLC; *Int'l*, pg. 62
BEEFEATER GIN—NONE—Allied Domecq Spirits & Wine (UK) Ltd.; *Int'l*, pg. 63
BEEFSTEAK—Variety Breads—Ralston Purina Company; *U.S. Public*, pg. 1359
BEEFY-T—Cotton T-Shirts—Sara Lee Corporation; *U.S. Public*, pg. 1432
BEELINE—Electronic Mail System—Osicom Technologies Inc.; *U.S. Public*, pg. 1233
BEELINER—Collision Correction-Automotive—Bee Line Company; *U.S. Private*, pg. 129
BEEMAK—Plastics—Beemak Plastics; *U.S. Private*, pg. 598
BEEP BEEP!—Service Products—R&B, Inc.; *U.S. Public*, pg. 1354
BEEPEN-VK—Pharmaceutical Products—SmithKline Beecham Corporation; *Int'l*, pg. 1264
BEEPEN-VK—Pharmaceutical Prods—SmithKline Beecham Laboratories; *Int'l*, pg. 1264
BEEPEN-VK—Pharmaceutical—SmithKline Beecham plc; *Int'l*, pg. 1264
BEER NUTS—Glazed Nuts—Beer Nuts, Inc.; *U.S. Private*, pg. 130
BEERTENDERS—Refrigerated Beer Truck Bodies & Trailers—Kidron Inc.; *U.S. Private*, pg. 619
BEGGIN' STRIPS—Dog Treats—Ralston Purina Company; *U.S. Public*, pg. 1359
BEGINNER—Pencils—Dixon Ticonderoga Company; *U.S. Public*, pg. 514
BEHAVE—Hair Preparations—The Gillette Company; *U.S. Public*, pg. 743
BEHAVIOR BREAKTHROUGH—Education Program—Nutri/System Inc.; *U.S. Private*, pg. 859
BEHAVIOR SCAN—Test Marketing—Information Resources, Inc.; *U.S. Public*, pg. 875
BEHAVIOR SCOREWARE—Software—Fair, Isaac and Company, Inc.; *U.S. Public*, pg. 609
BEHAVIORSCOPE—NONE—Market Facts, Inc.; *U.S. Public*, pg. 1046

BEHN RIDGE MATES—Planter Attachments—Fleischer Manufacturing, Inc.; *U.S. Private*, pg. 410

BEHOLD—Hairdryers, Hairsetters—Bristol-Myers Squibb Company; *U.S. Public*, pg. 253

BEHOLD—Furniture Polish—Kiwi Brands; *U.S. Public*, pg. 1433

BEHOLD—Furniture Polish—Sara Lee Corporation; *U.S. Public*, pg. 1432

BEHOP CAFE—Liquor Stores & Lounges—Flanigan's Enterprises, Inc.; *U.S. Public*, pg. 648

BEHRING NEPHELOMETER—Analyzer—Behringwerke AG; *Int'l*, pg. 624

BEHRING NEPHELOMETER—Protein Analyzer—Dade Behring Inc.; *U.S. Private*, pg. 110

BEHRING NEPHELOMETER 100—Protein Analyzer—Dade Behring Inc.; *U.S. Private*, pg. 110

BEICH—Candies—Nestle S.A.; *Int'l*, pg. 915

BEICH—NONE—Nestle USA; *Int'l*, pg. 916

BEIJING CHEF—NONE—JP Foodservice, Inc.; *U.S. Public*, pg. 918

BEJAM—Grocery Stores—Iceland Group plc; *Int'l*, pg. 658

BEKAERT—Steel Wire & Steel Wire Prods.—N.V. Bekaert S.A.; *Int'l*, pg. 183

BEKO—Household Appiances—Arcelik A.S.; *Int'l*, pg. 741

BEL—Lithium Alkyls—FMC Corp., Lithium Division; *U.S. Public*, pg. 605

BEL-AIR VALLARTA AND CAREYES—Hotels—Grupo Sidek, S.A. de C.V.; *Int'l*, pg. 576

BEL ARBOR—California Wines—Brown-Forman Beverages Worldwide; *U.S. Public*, pg. 261

BEL ARBOR—California Wines—Brown-Forman Corporation; *U.S. Public*, pg. 261

BEL BAIE—Twin-Wire Former—Harnischfeger Industries, Inc.; *U.S. Public*, pg. 788

BEL BAPA—Coater—Harnischfeger Industries, Inc.; *U.S. Public*, pg. 788

BEL-BOND—Headbox—Beloit Corporation; *U.S. Public*, pg. 789

BEL-BOND—Top Wire Former—Harnischfeger Industries, Inc.; *U.S. Public*, pg. 788

BEL-CADD—Computer Aided Drafting System—Beloit Corporation; *U.S. Public*, pg. 789

BEL-CAM—Beloit Corporation—Beloit Corporation; *U.S. Public*, pg. 789

BEL-CHAMP—Dryer—Beloit Corporation; *U.S. Public*, pg. 789

BEL DESIGN—NONE—Bel Fuse Inc.; *U.S. Public*, pg. 200

BEL-FORM—Top Wire Former—Harnischfeger Industries, Inc.; *U.S. Public*, pg. 788

BEL FUSE—NONE—Bel Fuse Inc.; *U.S. Public*, pg. 200

BEL PAESE—Cheeses—Cucina Classica Italiana, Inc.; *U.S. Public*, pg. 1435

BEL PAESE—Cheese—Danone Group; *Int'l*, pg. 379

BEL-ROLL—Top Wire Former—Harnischfeger Industries, Inc.; *U.S. Public*, pg. 788

BEL RTL—Belgium Broadcasting—CLT-UFA; *Int'l*, pg. 561

BEL-UGA—Sanitary Paper Products—VP-Schickedanz AG; *U.S. Public*, pg. 1333

BEL-VAC—Top Wire Former—Harnischfeger Industries, Inc.; *U.S. Public*, pg. 788

BEL-AIR PATROL—Home Security—Wells Fargo Alarm Services, Inc.; *U.S. Public*, pg. 246

BELAIR—Cigarettes—B.A.T Industries P.L.C.; *Int'l*, pg. 110

BELAIR—Cigarettes—Brown & Williamson Tobacco Corp.; *Int'l*, pg. 111

BELAIRE CREEK CELLARS—Wine—Canandaigua Wine Company Div.; *U.S. Public*, pg. 300

BELARUS—Tractors—Belarus Machinery, Inc.; *Int'l*, pg. 101

BELCOBALSA—Balsa Wood for Boat Building—Baltek Corporation; *U.S. Public*, pg. 171

BELCOR—Contaminants Remover/Separator—Harnischfeger Industries, Inc.; *U.S. Public*, pg. 788

BELCOR—Intimate Apparel—VF Corporation; *U.S. Public*, pg. 1702

BELD FOIL—Aluminum Mylar Shield—Belden Inc.; *U.S. Public*, pg. 200

BELD FOIL—Aluminum Mylar Shield—Belden Wire & Cable Company; *U.S. Public*, pg. 201

BELDATA—Winding—Beloit Corporation; *U.S. Public*, pg. 789

BELDEN—NONE—Belden Inc.; *U.S. Public*, pg. 200

BELDEN—Electrical Wire & Cord Products & Electronic Cable—Cooper Industries, Inc.; *U.S. Public*, pg. 442

BELDEN/POWERPATH—Wire—Cooper Automotive Division; *U.S. Public*, pg. 443

BELDOCH POPPER—Women's Knitwear—Beldoch Industries; *U.S. Public*, pg. 519

BELEX—Heat Exchange Systems—Ashland, Inc.; *U.S. Public*, pg. 138

BELGLOSS—Gloss Calender Position—Harnischfeger Industries, Inc.; *U.S. Public*, pg. 788

BELIMITER—NONE—Bel Fuse Inc.; *U.S. Public*, pg. 200

BELIN—Biscuits, Crackers & Snacks—Danone Group; *Int'l*, pg. 379

BELL—Flavors, Fragrances & Aromatics—Bell Flavors & Fragrances; *U.S. Private*, pg. 131

BELL—Helmets—Bell Sports Corp.; *U.S. Public*, pg. 207

BELL—Milk—Dean Foods Company; *U.S. Public*, pg. 489

BELL—Helicopters—Textron Inc.; *U.S. Public*, pg. 1588

BELL—Woodworking Machinery—Wisconsin Automated Machinery Corp.; *U.S. Private*, pg. 1184

BELL & EVANS—Chicken—Farmer's Pride, Inc.; *U.S. Private*, pg. 395

BELL & GOSSETT—Pumps, Valves & Accessories, Engineered Systems & Heat Transfer Equipment—ITT Fluid Handling; *U.S. Public*, pg. 860

BELL ATLANTIC DIRECT MKTG—Marketing program—Bell Atlantic Corporation; *U.S. Public*, pg. 201

BELL ATLANTIC IQ CARD—Telephone Calling Card—Bell Atlantic Corporation; *U.S. Public*, pg. 201

BELL ATLANTIC MOBILE SYSTEMS—Mobile telephone systems—Bell Atlantic Corporation; *U.S. Public*, pg. 201

BELL ATLANTIC MOBILINK CELLULAR SERVICES—Cellular Services—Bell Atlantic Corporation; *U.S. Public*, pg. 201

BELL ATLANTIC YELLOW PAGES—Yellow pages—Bell Atlantic Corporation; *U.S. Public*, pg. 201

BELL CARTER—Jams & Jellies—Bell-Carter Foods, Inc.; *U.S. Private*, pg. 131

BELL TOWER—NONE—Crown Publishers, Inc.; *U.S. Private*, pg. 21

BELLA—Napkins—Marcal Paper Mills, Inc.; *U.S. Private*, pg. 701

BELLA VISTA—Processed Vegetables—Furman Foods, Inc.; *U.S. Private*, pg. 431

BELLA VISTA VILLAGE—Recreational and Retirement Communities—Cooper Communities, Inc.; *U.S. Private*, pg. 273

BELLAGIO—Food Products—Rykoff-Sexton, Inc.; *U.S. Public*, pg. 918

BELLAGIO RESORTS—NONE—Mirage Resorts Incorporated; *U.S. Public*, pg. 1116

BELLAVISTA—Houses—Chief Industries, Inc.; *U.S. Private*, pg. 236

BELLE CAMP—Candy—Standard Candy Co., Inc.; *U.S. Private*, pg. 1030

BELLE DES CHAMPS—Cheese—Bongrain S.A.; *Int'l*, pg. 201

BELLE KLIPSCH—Loudspeaker Systems—Klipsch, Inc.; *U.S. Public*, pg. 626

BELLE-VUE—Beer—Interbrew S.A.; *Int'l*, pg. 679

BELLERGAL-S—Drug for Nervous Tension—Sandoz Pharmaceuticals Corp.; *Int'l*, pg. 974

BELLERUE—NONE—Labatt U.S.A.; *Int'l*, pg. 679

BELLEVUE—Beauty Salon Furniture—Belvedere Company; *U.S. Private*, pg. 1008

BELLOFRAM—Precision Regulators & Transducers—Desco Corporation; *U.S. Private*, pg. 326

BELLOY—Seeds—Groupe Limagrain; *Int'l*, pg. 566

BELL'S—Seasoning—The William G. Bell Company; *U.S. Private*, pg. 165

BELL'S—Poultry Seasoning & Stuffing—Brady Enterprises, Inc.; *U.S. Private*, pg. 165

BELL'S EIGHT YEAR OLD—NONE—Guinness Plc; *Int'l*, pg. 412

BELL'S EXTRA SPECIAL—NONE—Guinness Plc; *Int'l*, pg. 412

BELLSOL—Ethyl Alcohol—Georgia-Pacific Corporation; *U.S. Public*, pg. 735

BELLSOUTH—Telecommunications—BellSouth Corporation; *U.S. Public*, pg. 207

BELLSOUTH MOBILITY—Cellular Telephone—BellSouth Corporation; *U.S. Public*, pg. 207

BELLSOUTH.NET—Internet—BellSouth Corporation; *U.S. Public*, pg. 207

BELLSOUTH TELECOMMUNICATIONS—Telecommunications—BellSouth Corporation; *U.S. Public*, pg. 207

BELMANITE—General Elastomeric Roll Cover Used in Paper Machine—Harnischfeger Industries, Inc.; *U.S. Public*, pg. 788

BELMANITE II—Elastomeric Roll Cover—Beloit Corporation; *U.S. Public*, pg. 789

BELMONT—Cigarettes—B.A.T Industries P.L.C.; *Int'l*, pg. 110

BELMONT—Dental Equipment—Koken Mfg. Co. Inc.; *Int'l*, pg. 1349

BELMONT—Photo Processing—Nashua Corporation; *U.S. Public*, pg. 1152

BELMONT—Cigarettes—Philip Morris Companies Inc.; *U.S. Public*, pg. 1287

BELMONT PARK—Race Track—New York Racing Association; *U.S. Public*, pg. 795

BELNARO PINOT NOIR—NONE—Castello Banfi Srl.; *U.S. Private*, pg. 113

BELNERO-PINOT NOIR—Red Wine—Banfi Vintners; *U.S. Private*, pg. 113

BELNIF—Cardiovascular Drug—Astra AB; *Int'l*, pg. 93

BELOC—Cardiovascular Pharmaceutical—Astra AB; *Int'l*, pg. 93

BELOIT—World-Wide Mark—Beloit Corporation; *U.S. Public*, pg. 789

BELOW ZERO PVC PLASTIC PIPE CEMENT—Industrial Chemical—Hercules Chemical Co., Inc.; *U.S. Private*, pg. 523

BELRO—Resin—Hercules Incorporated; *U.S. Public*, pg. 809

BELRUN—Dryer—Beloit Corporation; *U.S. Public*, pg. 789

BELSAW—NONE—DeVlieg-Bullard Inc.; *U.S. Public*, pg. 502

BELSEAL—Suction Roll—Beloit Corporation; *U.S. Public*, pg. 789

BELSHAW—Donut Equipment—Belshaw Brothers, Inc.; *Int'l*, pg. 188

BELSON—Professional Beauty Products—Windmere-Durable Holdings; *U.S. Public*, pg. 1771

BELTEX—Calender & Gloss Calender Position Line—Harnischfeger Industries, Inc.; *U.S. Public*, pg. 788

BELTRAC—Tension Control Applications—Harnischfeger Industries, Inc.; *U.S. Public*, pg. 788

BELTRONIC—Winder—Beloit Corporation; *U.S. Public*, pg. 789

BELVENT—Dryer—Beloit Corporation; *U.S. Public*, pg. 789

BELVILLE—Children's Building Sets—LEGO Systems, Inc.; *Int'l*, pg. 805

BELWIND—Winder—Beloit Corporation; *U.S. Public*, pg. 789

BELZER—Forged Mechanics & Industrial Hand Tools—Cooper Industries, Inc.; *U.S. Public*, pg. 442

BEMAC—Insulated Liquid-Proof Gloves—Jomac, Inc.; *U.S. Private*, pg. 595

BEMAX—Natural Wheat Germ—SmithKline Beecham plc; *Int'l*, pg. 1264

BEMBERG—Cuprammonium Rayon—Asahi Chemical Industry Co., Ltd.; *Int'l*, pg. 83

BEMIS—Paper Products—Bemis Company, Inc.; *U.S. Public*, pg. 210

BEMLIESE—Non-Woven Fabric of Cuprammonium Rayon—Asahi Chemical Industry Co., Ltd.; *Int'l*, pg. 83

BEN & JERRY'S—Ice Cream—Ben & Jerry's Homemade Inc.; *U.S. Public*, pg. 210

BEN & JERRY'S LIGHT—Ice Cream—Ben & Jerry's Homemade Inc.; *U.S. Public*, pg. 210

BEN & JERRY'S LOWFAT FROZEN YOGURT—Lowfat Frozen Yogurt—Ben & Jerry's Homemade Inc.; *U.S. Public*, pg. 210

BEN & JERRY'S PEACE POPS—Ice Cream Novelty—Ben & Jerry's Homemade Inc.; *U.S. Public*, pg. 210

BEN FRANKLIN—Domestic Cigars—Consolidated Cigar Corporation; *U.S. Private*, pg. 690

BEN FRANKLIN—Gypsum for Agricultural Application—USG Corporation; *U.S. Public*, pg. 1660

BEN FRANKLIN CRAFTS—Consumer Publ. Featuring Crafts—Sampler Publications Inc.; *U.S. Private*, pg. 963

BENADRYL—Antihistamines—Warner-Lambert Company; *U.S. Public*, pg. 1738

BENADRYL—Antihistamine, Cream & Spray—Warner-Lambert Consumer Healthcare; *U.S. Public*, pg. 1739

BENADRYL COLD—Antihistamine—Warner-Lambert Consumer Healthcare; *U.S. Public*, pg. 1739

BENADRYL COLD NIGHTIME—Nightime Antihistamine—Warner-Lambert Consumer Healthcare; *U.S. Public*, pg. 1739

BENATI—Earthmoving—New Holland Ltd.; *Int'l*, pg. 484

BENCH BRIEF—Publication—The Mead Corporation; *U.S. Public*, pg. 1074

BENCH MATE—Portable Work Bench—Marson/Creative Fastener, Inc.; *U.S. Private*, pg. 708

BENCHMARK—Boilers—Aerco International Inc.; *U.S. Private*, pg. 23

BENCHMARK—Pre-Fab Manufactured Homes—Benchmark Industries; *U.S. Private*, pg. 132

BENCHMARK—Aqueous Cleaning Consoles—Branson Ultrasonics Corp. - Precision Cleaning Div.; *U.S. Public*, pg. 574

BENCHMARK—Vinyl Siding—CertainTeed Corporation; *Int'l*, pg. 1170

BENCHMASTER—Test Equipment—Tenney Environmental; *U.S. Private*, pg. 1076

BENCHMATE—Baking Ingredients & Leaveners—Fleischmann's Yeast; *Int'l*, pg. 237

BENCKISER MIRA LANZA—Sole Detergents—Armando Testa S.p.A.; *Int'l*, pg. 1377

BENCO—Beverages—Bestfoods; *U.S. Public*, pg. 223

BEND & PEEL—Pressure Sensitive Lamination—Zimmer Custom-Made Packaging Co.; *U.S. Private*, pg. 802

BEND DOOR—Doors—Jeld-Wen, Inc.; *U.S. Private*, pg. 585

BEND/FLEX—Formable Laminate—Rogers Corporation; *U.S. Public*, pg. 1402

BENDECTIN—Antinauseant—Hoechst Marion Roussel North America; *Int'l*, pg. 625

BENDINI—Rough Terrain Mobile Cranes—Terex Corporation; *U.S. Public*, pg. 1581

BENDIX—Products for Commercial & Military Aircraft & Applications—AlliedSignal Aerospace; *U.S. Public*, pg. 50

BENDIX—Automotive Components—AlliedSignal Aftermarket Europe S.A.; *Int'l*, pg. 53

BENDIX—Brakes—AlliedSignal, Automotive Aftermarket; *U.S. Public*, pg. 51

BENDIX—NONE—AlliedSignal Canada Inc., Automotive Aftermarket; *U.S. Public*, pg. 52

BENDIX/KING—Commercial & General Aviation Avionics Products; Radio Products—AlliedSignal Aerospace; *U.S. Public*, pg. 50

BENDWAY—Metal Ducts—Callahan Mining Corporation; *U.S. Public*, pg. 394

BENE FIX—Clotting Factor—American Home Products Corporation; *U.S. Public*, pg. 79

BENEDICTINE—NONE—Bacardi-Martini Belgium; *U.S. Private*, pg. 109

BENEDICTINE—Liqueur—Bacardi-Martini, USA, Inc.; *U.S. Private*, pg. 109

BENEFICIAL CREDIT SERVICE—Credit Service—Beneficial Management Corporation; *U.S. Public*, pg. 211

BENEFICIAL INSURANCE GROUP—Consumer Credit & Related Financial Services—Beneficial Management Corporation; *U.S. Public*, pg. 211

BENEFIT—Recycled Text & Cover—Champion International Corp.; *U.S. Public*, pg. 333

BENEKE—Plumbing Supplies—Sanderson Plumbing Products Inc.; *U.S. Private*, pg. 964

BENEMID—Probenecid—Merck & Co., Inc.; *U.S. Public*, pg. 1090

BENENUTS—Grocery—Sara Lee Corporation; *U.S. Public*, pg. 1432

BENETTON—Women's, Men's & Children's Clothing—Benetton U.S.A. Corporation; *Int'l*, pg. 186

BENETTON WATCHES—Licensee—Timex Corporation; *U.S. Private*, pg. 1088

BENFORD—Dumpers & Mixers; Compacting Equipment—Powerscreen International Plc; *Int'l*, pg. 1066

BENGAL SPICE—Herb Tea—Celestial Seasonings; *U.S. Public*, pg. 319

BENGAY—NONE—Pfizer Inc.; *U.S. Public*, pg. 1281

BENIHANA—Japanese for "Red Flower", Logo for Benihana Japanese Restaurants—Benihana, Inc.; *U.S. Public*, pg. 211

BENIHANA GRILL—Retaurant—Benihana, Inc.; *U.S. Public*, pg. 211

BENIHANA OIL—Sunflower Oil—Benihana, Inc.; *U.S. Public*, pg. 211

BENJAMIN—Air Rifle—Benjamin Sheridan Co.; *U.S. Private*, pg. 291

BENJAMIN ANSEHL—Cosmetics & Perfumes—Benjamin Ansehl Company; *U.S. Private*, pg. 75

BENJAMIN MOORE—Paint, Stains & Enamels—Benjamin Moore & Co.; *U.S. Private*, pg. 133

BENLATE—Fungicide—Du Pont (E.I. Du Pont De Nemours & Co.); *U.S. Public*, pg. 530

BENNETT—NONE—Nellcor Puritan Bennett Incorporated; *U.S. Public*, pg. 1039

BENNETTS PIT COOKED BAR-B-QUE—Restaurant—WSMP, Inc.; *U.S. Public*, pg. 1729

BENNETT'S SAUCES—NONE—Dean Foods Company; *U.S. Public*, pg. 489

BENNETTS SMOKEHOUSE & SALOON—Restaurant—WSMP, Inc.; *U.S. Public*, pg. 1729

BENNIGAN'S—One of the Leading Restaurant Chains in Casual Dining Segment-223 Units—Bennigan's; *U.S. Private*, pg. 736

BENSON & HEDGES—Cigarettes—B.A.T Industries P.L.C.; *Int'l*, pg. 110

BENSON & HEDGES—NONE—British-American Tobacco (Germany) GmbH; *Int'l*, pg. 111

BENSON & HEDGES—NONE—Malaysian Tobacco Co./B.A.T. Indust.; *Int'l*, pg. 111

BENSON & HEDGES—Cigarettes—Philip Morris U.S.A.; *U.S. Public*, pg. 1289

BENSON & HEDGES DELUXE—Cigarettes—Philip Morris Companies Inc.; *U.S. Public*, pg. 1287

BENSON & HEDGES MULTIFILTER—Cigarettes—Philip Morris Companies Inc.; *U.S. Public*, pg. 1287

BENSON & HEDGES 100'S—Cigarettes—Philip Morris Companies Inc.; *U.S. Public*, pg. 1287

BENSON & HEDGES 100'S DELUXE ULTRA LIGHTS—Cigarettes—Philip Morris Companies Inc.; *U.S. Public*, pg. 1287

BENSON & HEDGES 100'S LIGHTS—Cigarettes—Philip Morris Companies Inc.; *U.S. Public*, pg. 1287

BENSON & HEDGES 100'S LIGHTS MENTHOL—Cigarettes—Philip Morris Companies Inc.; *U.S. Public*, pg. 1287

BENSON & HEDGES 100'S MENTHOL—Cigarettes—Philip Morris Companies Inc.; *U.S. Public*, pg. 1287

BENSON AND HEDGES SPECIAL FILTER—Tobacco—Fortune Brands, Inc.; *U.S. Public*, pg. 674

BENSON AND HEDGES SPECIAL FILTER—Cigarettes—Gallaher Tobacco Ltd.; *Int'l*, pg. 539

BENSON AND HEDGES SUPERKINGS—NONE—Fortune Brands, Inc.; *U.S. Public*, pg. 674

BENSON AND HEDGES SUPERKINGS—Cigarettes—Gallaher Tobacco Ltd.; *Int'l*, pg. 539

BENSON & HEDGES 100'S DELUXE ULTRA LIGHTS MENTHOL—Cigarettes—Philip Morris Companies Inc.; *U.S. Public*, pg. 1287

BENSON'S—Corn & Other Starches—Bestfoods; *U.S. Public*, pg. 223

BENSONS—Office Products—Esselte AB; *Int'l*, pg. 459

BENSON'S OLD HOME KITCHENS—Fruit Cake—Benson's, Inc.; *U.S. Private*, pg. 134

BENTASIL—NONE—Cruspi S.A.; *Int'l*, pg. 348

BENTASIL—NONE—Huhtamaki Oy; *Int'l*, pg. 638

BENTLEY—NONE—Bentley Leathers Inc.; *Int'l*, pg. 187

BENTLEY—Broadloom—Interface Inc.; *U.S. Public*, pg. 889

BENTLEY—Motor Cars—Vickers PLC; *Int'l*, pg. 1466

BENTLEY'S YORKSHIRE—Bitter—Whitbread PLC; *Int'l*, pg. 1498

BENTOMAT—Clay Liner Product—AMCOL International Corp.; *U.S. Public*, pg. 63

BENTYL—Anti-Spasmodic Drug—Hoechst Marion Roussel North America; *Int'l*, pg. 625

BENWOOD—Wood Finishes, Varnishes, Stains—Benjamin Moore & Co.; *U.S. Private*, pg. 133

BENYLIN—Cough Syrup—Warner-Lambert Company; *U.S. Public*, pg. 1738

BENYLIN—Cough Syrups—Warner-Lambert Consumer Healthcare; *U.S. Public*, pg. 1739

BENZAC—Pharmaceutical Products—Galderma Laboratories, Inc.; *Int'l*, pg. 819

BENZAC W—Pharmaceutical Products—Galderma Laboratories, Inc.; *Int'l*, pg. 819

BENZAC WASH—Pharmaceutical Products—Galderma Laboratories, Inc.; *Int'l*, pg. 819

BENZAGEL—Pharmaceutical—Dermik Laboratories, Inc.; *Int'l*, pg. 1110

BENZAMYCIN—Pharmaceutical—Dermik Laboratories, Inc.; *Int'l*, pg. 1110

BENZAMYCIN GEL—Acne Medication Combination—Dermik Laboratories, Inc.; *Int'l*, pg. 1110

BENZAMYCIN GEL—Pharmaceuticals—Rhone-Poulenc Rorer - U.S.; *Int'l*, pg. 1110

BENZEDREX—Decongestant Inhaler & Nasal Spray—Menley & James Laboratories, Inc.; *U.S. Public*, pg. 1086

BENZELMIN—Oxfendazole—Syntex; *Int'l*, pg. 1120

BENZI-PAK—Pharmaceuticals—Rhone-Poulenc Rorer - U.S.; *Int'l*, pg. 1110

BENZIGER—Wine—Glen Ellen Winery; *U.S. Private*, pg. 455

BENZODENT—Topical Oral Analgesic—Chattem, Inc.; *U.S. Public*, pg. 341

BENZODENT—Topical Oral Analgesic—Chattem, Inc., Consumer Products Division; *U.S. Public*, pg. 341

BENZODENT—Denture Ointment—Richardson-Vicks, Inc. Personal Care Products Div.; *U.S. Public*, pg. 1331

BENZOFLEX—Industrial Plasticizer—Velsicol Chemical Corporation; *U.S. Private*, pg. 1135

BENZYL TUEX—Accelerator; Rubber Chemical—Uniroyal Chemical Company, Inc.; *U.S. Public*, pg. 460

BEPEX—Powder Process Systems—Hosokawa Micron International Inc.; *Int'l*, pg. 635

BERALCAST—Light Strong Cast Material for Aerospace, Electronics, and Computer—Starmet Corporation; *U.S. Public*, pg. 1511

BERALOY—NONE—Carpenter Technology Corporation; *U.S. Public*, pg. 307

BERDEL—NONE—Luxottica Group S.p.A.; *Int'l*, pg. 822

BEREC—Batteries—Hanson PLC; *Int'l*, pg. 592

BERET—Cereal Seed Treatment—Novartis; *Int'l*, pg. 972

BERETTA—Car—Chevrolet Motor Div. General Motors Corp.; *U.S. Public*, pg. 720

BERETTA—Sports Coupe—General Motors Corporation; *U.S. Public*, pg. 718

BERG—NONE—Berg Electronics; *U.S. Public*, pg. 212

BERG—Carbon Pipe & Steel Products—Thomas Pipe & Steel, Inc.; *U.S. Private*, pg. 508

BERG/SERPENT—NONE—Berg Electronics; *U.S. Public*, pg. 212

BERGCON—NONE—Berg Electronics; *U.S. Public*, pg. 212

BERGDORF GOODMAN—Specialty Stores—Bergdorf Goodman; *U.S. Public*, pg. 785

BERGER—Paints—Sime Darby Berhad; *Int'l*, pg. 1249

BERGHOFF—Super Premium Beer—Joseph Huber Brewing Co., Inc.; *U.S. Private*, pg. 545

BERGHOFF BOCK—Super Premium Beer—Joseph Huber Brewing Co., Inc.; *U.S. Private*, pg. 545

BERGHOFF DARK—Super Premium Beer—Joseph Huber Brewing Co., Inc.; *U.S. Private*, pg. 545

BERGHOFF LIGHT—Super Premium Beer—Joseph Huber Brewing Co., Inc.; *U.S. Private*, pg. 545

BERGHOFF RED—Beer—Joseph Huber Brewing Co., Inc.; *U.S. Private*, pg. 545

BERGLANCE—NONE—Berg Electronics; *U.S. Public*, pg. 212

BERGLOK—NONE—Berg Electronics; *U.S. Public*, pg. 212

BERGPIN—NONE—Berg Electronics; *U.S. Public*, pg. 212

BERGPOST—NONE—Berg Electronics; *U.S. Public*, pg. 212

BERGSTAK—NONE—Berg Electronics; *U.S. Public*, pg. 212

BERGSTIK—NONE—Berg Electronics; *U.S. Public*, pg. 212

BERICO DRYERS—Grain Conditioning Equipment—Behlen Mfg. Co.; *U.S. Private*, pg. 130

BERIDOX—Magnetic Tape—Fuji Photo Film U.S.A., Inc.; *Int'l*, pg. 524

BERING—Cigars—Swisher International Group, Inc.; *U.S. Public*, pg. 1543

BERINGER—Wine—Nestle S.A.; *Int'l*, pg. 915

BERINGER—Vineyards—Wine World Estates Company; *Int'l*, pg. 917

BERKEL—Commercial Food Preparation Equipment—Berkel Incorporated; *Int'l*, pg. 545

BERKELEY—Cigarettes—Gallaher Tobacco Ltd.; *Int'l*, pg. 539

BERKELEY—Irrigation Pumps, Water Systems, & Wastehandling Pumps—Sta-Rite Industries, Inc.; *U.S. Public*, pg. 1767

BERKELEY—Agricultural & Turf Irrigation Pumps—Sta-Rite Water Systems; *U.S. Public*, pg. 1767

BERKELEY—NONE—WICOR, Inc.; *U.S. Public*, pg. 1767

BERKELEY SUPERKINGS—Tobacco—Fortune Brands, Inc.; *U.S. Public*, pg. 674

BERKLEY—NONE—Berkley Publishing Corp.; *Int'l*, pg. 1027

BERKLEY—Logo—Outdoor Technologies Group; *U.S. Private*, pg. 822

BERKLEY BIONIX—Rod—Outdoor Technologies Group; *U.S. Private*, pg. 822

BERKLEY BLOCKAID—Sunscreen—Outdoor Technologies Group; *U.S. Private*, pg. 822

BERKLEY ERASE—Scent Remover—Outdoor Technologies Group; *U.S. Private*, pg. 822

BERKLEY STRIKE—Fish Attractant—Outdoor Technologies Group; *U.S. Private*, pg. 822

BERKLEY VECTRA—Rod—Outdoor Technologies Group; *U.S. Private*, pg. 822

BERKO—NONE—Marley Electric Heating Company; *U.S. Public*, pg. 1676

BERKSHIRE—Furniture—Berkshire Furniture Co.; *U.S. Public*, pg. 985

BERKSHIRE—NONE—Carpenter Technology Corporation; *U.S. Public*, pg. 307

BERKSHIRE—Hosiery & Related Apparel—Mayer/Berkshire Corporation; *U.S. Private*, pg. 717

BERKSHIRE HEATSEAL—Tea Bag Paper—Kimberly-Clark Corporation; *U.S. Public*, pg. 958

BERKSHIRE HILLS—Food & Related Paper Products—Butler Wholesale Products, Inc.; *U.S. Private*, pg. 190

BERKSHIRE INTIMATES—Lingerie, Panties—Mayer/Berkshire Corporation; *U.S. Private*, pg. 717

BERKSHIRE PLACE—Hotel—Omni Hotels; *U.S. Private*, pg. 1065

BERLEI—Bras & Corsetry—Courtaulds Textiles Plc; *Int'l*, pg. 339

BERLIN—Gloves—Berlin Glove Company Ltd.; *U.S. Private*, pg. 136

BERLINER MORGENPOST—Newspaper—Axel Springer Verlag AG; *Int'l*, pg. 102

BERLITZ AND YOU—English Self-Teaching Course—Berlitz International, Inc.; *U.S. Public*, pg. 221

BERLITZ JR.—Complete Foreign Language Instruction Program—Berlitz International, Inc.; *U.S. Public*, pg. 221

BERLITZ STUDY ABROAD—Language Study in Country where It Is Spoken as a Native Language—Berlitz International, Inc.; *U.S. Public*, pg. 221

BERMISH GENUINE IRISH STOUT—Stout—Scottish & Newcastle Importers Co.; *Int'l*, pg. 1212

BERNARD—MIG Welding Torches and Accessories—Dovatech, Ltd.; *U.S. Public*, pg. 520

BERNARD—Garden Equipment—Electrolux, AB; *Int'l*, pg. 438

BERNARD MATTHEWS—NONE—Bernard Matthews PLC; *Int'l*, pg. 189

BERNARDI—Pasta Prods.—Bernardi Italian Foods; *U.S. Private*, pg. 1182

BERNARDIN—Home Canning Products—Alltrista Corporation; *U.S. Public*, pg. 56

BERNETTE—Sewing machines—Bernina Holding AG; *Int'l*, pg. 189

BERNINA—Sewing Machines—Bernina Holding AG; *Int'l*, pg. 189

BERNINA—Sewing Machines—Bernina of America Inc.; *Int'l*, pg. 189

BERNOULLI BOX—Disk Drives—Iomega Corporation; *U.S. Public*, pg. 912

BERNOULLI BOX II—Disk Drive—Iomega Corporation; *U.S. Public*, pg. 912

BERNOULLI BOX II FOR MACINTOSH—Disk Drive—Iomega Corporation; *U.S. Public*, pg. 912

BERNOULLI DRIVES—Disk Drives—Iomega Corporation; *U.S. Public*, pg. 912

BERNOULLI DUAL (44MB)—Disk Drive—Iomega Corporation; *U.S. Public*, pg. 912

BERNOULLI DUAL 90—Dual 90MB 5 1/4" External Drive—Iomega Corporation; *U.S. Public*, pg. 912

BERNOULLI INSIDER (44MB)—Internal Disk Drive—Iomega Corporation; *U.S. Public*, pg. 912

BERNOULLI INSIDER 90—90MB 5 1/4" Internal Master Drive—Iomega Corporation; *U.S. Public*, pg. 912

BERNOULLI PARTNER 90—90MB 5 1/4" Internal Slave Drive—Iomega Corporation; *U.S. Public*, pg. 912

BERNOULLI PORTABLE (44MB)—Disk Drive—Iomega Corporation; *U.S. Public*, pg. 912

BERNOULLI TRANSPORTABLE (44MB)—Disk Drive—Iomega Corporation; *U.S. Public*, pg. 912

BERNOULLI TRANSPORTABLE 90—Single 90MB 4 1/4" Exteranl Drive—Iomega Corporation; *U.S. Public*, pg. 912

BERNSTEIN'S—Liquid Dressings—Nalleys Fine Foods; *U.S. Private*, pg. 887

BERNZOMATIC—Torches—Newell Co.; *U.S. Public*, pg. 1176

BERO-SILICONE—Neutron Shielding—Reactor Experiments, Inc.; *U.S. Public*, pg. 1594

BERODUAL—Bronchodilator—Boehringer Ingelheim GmbH; *Int'l*, pg. 199

BEROL—Pens & Markers—Berol Corporation; *U.S. Public*, pg. 1178

BEROL—Writing Instruments—Empire Berol U.S.A.; *U.S. Public*, pg. 1178

BEROTEC—Bronchodilator—Boehringer Ingelheim GmbH; *Int'l*, pg. 199

BERRI-TAINER—Corrugated Containers—Georgia-Pacific Corporation; *U.S. Public*, pg. 735

BERRY BERRY KIX—Cereal—General Mills, Inc.; *U.S. Public*, pg. 717

BERRY BOX—Jams and Jellies—E.D. Smith; *Int'l*, pg. 1263

BERRY COLOSSAL CRUNCH—Sweetened Corn & Oat Cereal—Malt-O-Meal Company; *U.S. Private*, pg. 699

BERRY SPRINGS—Beverage—Q.U.F. Industries Ltd.; *Int'l*, pg. 1074

BERSANO—Spirits—Mercian Corporation; *Int'l*, pg. 858

BERSANO PIEDMONT—Wines—Canandaigua Wine Co.; *U.S. Public*, pg. 300

BERSON—Ultraviolet Equipment for Water Treatment & Disinfection—Halma p.l.c.; *Int'l*, pg. 589

BERTELSMANN—Publishing—Bertelsmann Inc.; *Int'l*, pg. 191

BERTOLINO—Processed Meat Snacks—Bridgford Foods Corporation; *U.S. Public*, pg. 252

BERTOLLI—Olive Oil, Fine Wine Vinegar—Bertolli USA, Inc.; *Int'l*, pg. 655

BERTOLLI—Olive Oil, Fine Wine Vinegar, Cookies, Chocolates—SME International; *Int'l*, pg. 655

BERTOLLI OLIVE OIL SPRAY—Olive Oil—Bertolli USA, Inc.; *Int'l*, pg. 655

BERYLLIUM COPPER—Gasket Materials—Tecknit Incorporated; *U.S. Private*, pg. 1072

BES-PAK—Plastic Bags—Chelsea Industries, Inc.; *U.S. Private*, pg. 231

BESCO—Genuine Besser Replacement Parts—Besser Company; *U.S. Private*, pg. 139

BESS—Funds Transfer System—Logica Plc; *Int'l*, pg. 814

BESS—Toilet Tissue—VP-Schickedanz AG; *U.S. Public*, pg. 1333

BEST—Locking Devices—Best Access Systems; *U.S. Public*, pg. 223

BEST—Kosher Sausage, Prepared & Smoked Meats—Best Kosher Sausage Co.; *U.S. Public*, pg. 1433

BEST—Discount Retailer—Best Products Co., Inc.; *U.S. Private*, pg. 990

BEST—Pencils & Crayons—Dixon Ticonderoga Company; *U.S. Public*, pg. 514

BEST—Fertilizer—J.R. Simplot Company; *U.S. Private*, pg. 1002

THE BEST ALWAYS COMES FROM THE HEARTH—NONE—JP Foodservice, Inc.; *U.S. Public*, pg. 918

BEST BOOKS FOR CHILDREN—Selection Guide to Children's Recreational & Curriculum-Based Reading—R.R. Bowker; *Int'l*, pg. 1096

BEST BRAND—Fertilizers—J.R. Simplot Company, Minerals & Chemicals Group; *U.S. Private*, pg. 1002

BEST BY FRUIT OF THE LOOM—Apparel for Imprinting—Fruit of the Loom, Inc.; *U.S. Public*, pg. 685

BEST CHINA—Chinaware—The Homer Laughlin China Company; *U.S. Private*, pg. 653

BEST CHOICE—Grade A Fancy Grocery & Grocery Related Items—Associated Wholesale Grocers, Inc.; *U.S. Private*, pg. 93

BEST CHOICE HEALTH CARE—Health & Beauty Care Products & General Merchandise—Associated Wholesale Grocers, Inc.; *U.S. Private*, pg. 93

BEST CHOICE VALUE CLUB—Bulk Pack Grocery Products—Associated Wholesale Grocers, Inc.; *U.S. Private*, pg. 93

BEST COUNTER—Hand Rolling Tobacco—Imperial Tobacco Group, Ltd.; *Int'l*, pg. 666

BEST ESP—Electronic Statement Preparation Software—A.M. Best Company; *U.S. Private*, pg. 139

BEST FOODS—Mayonnaise & Peanut Butters, Pastas & Desserts, Baking Aids—Bestfoods; *U.S. Public*, pg. 223

BEST JEWELRY—Jewelry—Best Products Co., Inc.; *U.S. Private*, pg. 990

BEST 'O BUTTER—Seasoning—McCormick/Schilling; *U.S. Public*, pg. 1066

BEST OF AMERICA—Line of Variable Annuity & Life Insurance Products—Nationwide Insurance Enterprise; *U.S. Private*, pg. 788

THE BEST OF THE BUDGETS—Motels—The Accor Group, Inc.; *Int'l*, pg. 21

THE BEST OF TIMES—Watches & Clocks—Woolworth Corporation; *U.S. Public*, pg. 1777

THE BEST PEOPLE—NONE—Harrah's Entertainment, Inc.; *U.S. Public*, pg. 790

BEST PRACTICES—Cost Containment Kit—U.S. Surgical Corp.; *U.S. Public*, pg. 1687

BEST RECIPES—Bi-Monthly Magazine—Ogden Publishing; *U.S. Private*, pg. 812

BEST RESULTS—Bakeware, Kitchen Tools & Gadgets—Ekco Group, Inc.; *U.S. Public*, pg. 566

BEST SELLING HOME PLANS—Home Plans Magazine—Hachette Filipacchi Magazines Inc.; *Int'l*, pg. 794

BEST VINYL—Vinyl on Particleboard—Carter Holt Harvey Limited; *U.S. Public*, pg. 904

BEST WESTERN—Hotels, Motor Inns & Resorts—Best Western International, Inc.; *U.S. Private*, pg. 140

BEST WESTERN—NONE—Sunstone Hotel Investors, Inc.; *U.S. Public*, pg. 1536

BEST WORLD BRAND—Apparel—Clothestime Stores, Inc.; *U.S. Public*, pg. 387

BEST'S KOSHER—Sausage, Cured & Smoked Meats—Bessin Corporation; *U.S. Public*, pg. 1433

BESTATIN—Antineoplastic Agents—Nippon Kayaku Co. Ltd.; *Int'l*, pg. 934

BESTCLAD—Aluminum Cladding—Biltbest Windows; *U.S. Public*, pg. 1683

BESTEST—Chemicals—The Harry Alter Company; *U.S. Private*, pg. 1075

BESTFORM—Intimate Apparel—Bestform Foundations, Inc.; *U.S. Private*, pg. 140

BESTILE—Roof Cement—Johns Manville Corporation; *U.S. Public*, pg. 927

BESTLINE—900139

BESTLINK—Value Added Timeshare System—A.M. Best Company; *U.S. Private*, pg. 139

BESTOP—NONE—Bestop, Inc.; *Int'l*, pg. 830

BESTROCK—Gypsum Base Deck Plaster—Georgia-Pacific Corporation; *U.S. Public*, pg. 735

BEST'S KOSHER—Kosher Processed Meat Products—Sara Lee Corporation; *U.S. Public*, pg. 1432

BEST'S KOSHER—NONE—Shofar Kosher Foods; *U.S. Public*, pg. 1433

BESTSELLERS & DESIGN—Greeting Cards—American Greetings Corporation; *U.S. Public*, pg. 77

BESTWALL—Gypsum Panels—Georgia-Pacific Corporation; *U.S. Public*, pg. 735

BESTWATER—Water Purification System—Shaklee Corporation; *Int'l*, pg. 1518

BESTWOOD—Veneer—Carter Holt Harvey Limited; *U.S. Public*, pg. 904

BESTWOOD MELAMINE—Low Pressure Melamine—Carter Holt Harvey Limited; *U.S. Public*, pg. 904

BETA—Hoist—Harnischfeger Industries, Inc.; *U.S. Public*, pg. 788

BETA BURNER—Baffle-Type Industrial Burner—Hauck Mfg. Co.; *U.S. Private*, pg. 510

BETA DESIGN—VCR Video Cameras, Projection TV, Video Accessories—Sony Electronics; *Int'l*, pg. 1281

BETA 58—Microphones—Shure Brothers Incorporated; *U.S. Private*, pg. 997

BETA 57—Microphones—Shure Brothers Incorporated; *U.S. Private*, pg. 997

BETA HI-FI—Video Tape Recorders, Blank & Recorded Video Tapes—Sony Electronics; *Int'l*, pg. 1281

BETA HI-FI READY—VCR—Sony Electronics; *Int'l*, pg. 1281

BETA LITE—Hydrocarbon Resin—Arizona Chemical Div.; *U.S. Public*, pg. 901

BETA 150—A Plasma Etch System used in the Manufacturing Process of Semiconductors—Photronics, Inc.; *U.S. Public*, pg. 1293

BETA QUARTZ—Dental Inserts—Lee Pharmaceuticals; *U.S. Public*, pg. 984

BETA SP—NONE—Brown & Sharpe Manufacturing Company; *U.S. Public*, pg. 260

BETA SPM—NONE—Brown & Sharpe Manufacturing Company; *U.S. Public*, pg. 260

BETA SERIES—Vocal Microphone—Shure Brothers Incorporated; *U.S. Private*, pg. 997

BETA TAC—Hydrocarbon Synthetic Resin—Arizona Chemical Div.; *U.S. Public*, pg. 901

BETA II/III DESIGN—Video Recording—Sony Electronics; *Int'l*, pg. 1281

BETA-WELD—Radiators—Modine Manufacturing Company; *U.S. Public*, pg. 1121

BETABACTYL—Antibiotic—SmithKline Beecham plc; *Int'l*, pg. 1264

BETABRACE—Reinforcing Composite—The Dow Chemical Company; *U.S. Public*, pg. 522

BETABRACE—Adhesives—Essex Chemical Corporation; *U.S. Public*, pg. 523

BETACAL—Lime Fertilizer—CSM N.V.; *Int'l*, pg. 243

BETACAM—Combination Video Camera & Video Tape Recorder—Sony Electronics; *Int'l*, pg. 1281

BETA'CTOMORAD—Medical Instrument—Capintec Inc.; *U.S. Private*, pg. 205

BETADORM—Non-Barbituate Hypnotic—Rhone-Poulenc Rorer - U.S.; *Int'l*, pg. 1110

BETAFIN—Products Made From Sugar Beets—Cultor Ltd.; *Int'l*, pg. 349

BETAGAN—Anti-Glaucome—Allergan, Inc.; *U.S. Public*, pg. 46

BETALOC—Antihypertensive/Antianginal Agent—Astra AB; *Int'l*, pg. 93

BETAMANN—Glaucoma Drug—Bausch & Lomb Incorporated; *U.S. Public*, pg. 194

BETAMATE—Structural Adhesive—The Dow Chemical Company; *U.S. Public*, pg. 522

BETAMATE—Adhesives—Essex Chemical Corporation; *U.S. Public*, pg. 523

BETAMAX—Video Cassette System—Sony Electronics; *Int'l*, pg. 1281

BETAMIX—Agricultural Chemical—AgrEvo USA Company; *Int'l*, pg. 1203

BETAMIX PROGRESS—Ag Chemical—AgrEvo USA Company; *Int'l*, pg. 1203

BETAMOVIE—Video Tape Recorder, Video Cameras & Blank Video Tapes—Sony Electronics; *Int'l*, pg. 1281

BETANEX—Agricultural Chemical—AgrEvo USA Company; *Int'l*, pg. 1203

BETAPEN VK—Penicillin—Bristol-Myers Squibb Company; *U.S. Public*, pg. 253

BETAPRENE—Olefinic Polymer—Arizona Chemical Div.; *U.S. Public*, pg. 901

BETASCAN—VCR—Sony Electronics; *Int'l*, pg. 1281

BETASCAN II—VCR with Picture Search Feature—Sony Electronics; *Int'l*, pg. 1281

BETASEAL—Urethane Sealant; Metal, Body or Glass Primer—The Dow Chemical Company; *U.S. Public*, pg. 522

BETASEAL—Sealants—Essex Chemical Corporation; *U.S. Public*, pg. 523

BETASET—Phenolic Foundry Resins—Borden, Inc.; *U.S. Public*, pg. 157

BETASKIPSCAN—VCR—Sony Electronics; *Int'l*, pg. 1281

BETASOUND—Stereo VCR—Sony Electronics; *Int'l*, pg. 1281

BETASTAY—Adhesives—Essex Chemical Corporation; *U.S. Public*, pg. 523

BETATHANE—Prepolymer; Elastomer—The Dow Chemical Company; *U.S. Public*, pg. 522

BETEX-ESP—Call Processing Platform—Precision Systems, Inc.; *U.S. Public*, pg. 1321

BETOPLAN—Film Faced Plywood for Concrete Formwork—Westag & Getalit AG; *Int'l*, pg. 1491

BETOPTIC—Betaxolol .5 % Hcl Solution—Alcon Laboratories, Inc.; *Int'l*, pg. 916

BETOPTIC—Anti-Glaucoma Product—Nestle S.A.; *Int'l*, pg. 915

BETOPTIC S—Betaxolol Hcl Suspension—Alcon Laboratories, Inc.; *Int'l*, pg. 916

BETRICING—Fats & Oils—Van den Bergh Foods Company; *Int'l*, pg. 1436

BETRIX—Cosmetics—The Procter & Gamble Company; *U.S. Public*, pg. 1330

BETRKAKE—Fats & Oils—Van den Bergh Foods Company; *Int'l*, pg. 1436

BETSY—NONE—Wisconsin Tissue Mills, Inc.; *U.S. Public*, pg. 347

BETTER & BETTER—Conditioner—Clairol, Inc.; *U.S. Public*, pg. 254

BETTER BATTER—Seafood Line—McCormick/Schilling; *U.S. Public*, pg. 1066

BETTER-BILT—Windows & Doors—Caradon Plc; *Int'l*, pg. 266

BETTER BREATHING—NONE—Oxford Health Plans Inc.; *U.S. Public*, pg. 1238

BETTER CHEDDARS—Snack Thins—Nabisco Inc.; *U.S. Public*, pg. 1355

BETTER CHEDDARS—Snack Thins—RJR Nabisco Holdings Corp.; *U.S. Public*, pg. 1354

BETTER CHOICES—Health Snacks & Meal Products—The Southland Corporation; *Int'l*, pg. 693

BETTER EARTH—Wood preservative—Osmose Wood Preserving, Inc.; *U.S. Private*, pg. 821

BETTER FOR BREAD—Flour—General Mills, Inc.; *U.S. Public*, pg. 717

BETTER GROW—Fertilizer—Sun Bulb Company, Inc.; *U.S. Private*, pg. 1050

BETTER HOMES & GARDENS—Real Estate Service—Better Homes and Gardens Real Estate Service; *U.S. Public*, pg. 1094

BETTER HOMES AND GARDENS—Magazine—Meredith Corporation; *U.S. Public*, pg. 1094

BETTER HOMES & GARDENS CRAFTS CLUB—Book—Meredith Corporation; *U.S. Public*, pg. 1094

BETTER HOMES & GARDENS SPECIAL INTEREST—Magazine—Meredith Corporation; *U.S. Public*, pg. 1094

BETTER IMPRESSIONS—Magazine—The Mead Corporation; *U.S. Public*, pg. 1074

BETTER NUTRITION—Health Magazine—Intertec Publishing; *U.S. Public*, pg. 1327

BETTER NUTRITION—Monthly Publication—Intertec Publishing; *U.S. Public*, pg. 1328

THE BETTER PRINTING PEOPLE—Printing Franchise—American Speedy Printing Centers, Inc.; *U.S. Private*, pg. 62

BETTER THAN BARE—Hosiery & Related Apparel—Mayer/Berkshire Corporation; *U.S. Private*, pg. 717

THE BETTER WAYS TO COMPUTE—Computer Time-Sharing Services—Litton Industries, Inc.; *U.S. Public*, pg. 1002

BETTER WORKSPACE FOR THE WORK PLACE—NONE—Rubbermaid Incorporated; *U.S. Public*, pg. 1411

BETTERCREME—Icing & Filling—Rich Products Corp.; *U.S. Private*, pg. 928

BETTERGRIP—Ball Point Pen—The Pilot Pen Corp. of America; *Int'l*, pg. 1057

BETTERHALF—NONE—Alliance Semiconductor Corp.; *U.S. Public*, pg. 47

BETTERWAY—Book Publisher—F & W Publications, Inc.; *U.S. Private*, pg. 388

BETTERWAY—Breads—Metz Baking Company; *U.S. Private*, pg. 1022

BETTERWAY—Breads—Metz Baking Company (WI); *U.S. Private*, pg. 1022

BETTY BROWN—Bakeries—The Penn Traffic Company; *U.S. Public*, pg. 1270

BETTY CROCKER—Foods—General Mills, Inc.; *U.S. Public*, pg. 717

BETTY CROCKER CREAMY CHILLED DESSERTS—Dessert—General Mills, Inc.; *U.S. Public*, pg. 717

BETTY LOU—Snacks—Granny Goose Foods, Inc.; *U.S. Private*, pg. 469

BETZDEARBORN KLEEN—Cleaners for Metals—BetzDearborn Inc.; *U.S. Public*, pg. 226

BEVELSIDE—Molded Hardboard—ABT Building Products Corporation; *Int'l*, pg. 20

BEVERLY—Fragrance—Jean Philippe Fragrances, Inc.; *U.S. Public*, pg. 924

THE BEVERLY HERITAGE HOTELS—Hotels—The Vagabond Inns; *U.S. Private*, pg. 558

BEVERLY HILLS—Hotel—The Beverly Hills Hotel; *U.S. Private*, pg. 142

BEVERLY HILLS—Women's Footwear—International Seaway Trading Corporation; *U.S. Private*, pg. 572

BEBAX—Correction Shoe—Camp Healthcare; *Int'l*, pg. 1425

BEXLOY—Automotive Engineering Resins—Du Pont (E.I. Du Pont De Nemours & Co.); *U.S. Public*, pg. 530

BEYOND—NONE—Alliant Foodservice, Inc.; *U.S. Private*, pg. 244

BEYOND BUTTONDOWNS—NONE—Lands' End, Inc.; *U.S. Public*, pg. 977

BEYOND CELLULAR—NONE—Nextel Communications; *U.S. Public*, pg. 1180

BEYOND COMPUTING—Computer Product—International Business Machines Corporation; *U.S. Public*, pg. 895

BEYOND DIETING- THE BONIOS PLAN—NONE—Infinicom; *U.S. Private*, pg. 561

BEYOND SUPPORT—Compression Hosiery—Futuro Inc.; *Int'l*, pg. 182

BEYOND VALOR—War Game—Monarch Avalon, Inc.; *U.S. Public*, pg. 1123

BFGOODRICH—Tires—Michelin Americas Small Tires (MAST); *Int'l*, pg. 322

BFGOODRICH—Tires—Michelin North America; *Int'l*, pg. 322

B'GOSH—Clothing—OshKosh B'Gosh, Inc.; *U.S. Public*, pg. 1232

BI-BAND—Band Saw Blades—Sandvik/Milford Corporation; *Int'l*, pg. 1185

BI-FET—Electronics—National Semiconductor Corporation; *U.S. Public*, pg. 1159

BI-K—Pharmaceuticals—Rhone-Poulenc Rorer - U.S.; *Int'l*, pg. 1110

BI-LEVEL—CPAP Device—Nellcor Puritan Bennett Incorporated; *U.S. Public*, pg. 1039

BI-LEVEL—Controls—Wide-Lite; *U.S. Public*, pg. 730

BI-LITE—Pearlescent Pigments—International Specialty Products, Inc.; *U.S. Public*, pg. 858

BI-LO—NONE—Coles Myer Ltd.; *Int'l*, pg. 306

BI-LO—Food Stores—Koninklijke Ahold NV; *Int'l*, pg. 749

BI-LO FOODS—Retail Food Outlets—The Penn Traffic Company; *U.S. Public*, pg. 1270

BI-MYCONASE—Enzyme Preparation—Royal Gist-Brocades N.V.; *Int'l*, pg. 1142

BI-O-VISION—UV Dual Wavelength Transilluminator—Spectronics Corporation; *U.S. Private*, pg. 1024

BI-PAK—Repair Adhesives—The Dexter Corporation; *U.S. Public*, pg. 504

BI-ROTOR—Control Measurement—Brooks Instrument; *U.S. Public*, pg. 574

BI-STABLE BRAKE—Pulse Brake—Electroid Co.; *U.S. Private*, pg. 369

BI-TA—Dog Biscuits—Alpo Pet Foods, Inc.; *Int'l*, pg. 917

BI-TECH—Contact Lenses—Bausch & Lomb Incorporated; *U.S. Public*, pg. 194

BI TECHNOLOGIES—NONE—Milgray Electronics, Inc.; *U.S. Public*, pg. 205

BI-TILDIEM—Pharmaceutical—L'Oreal S.A.; *Int'l*, pg. 818

BI-TRIM CAPACITORS—ATC Binary Single Layer Capacitors—American Technical Ceramics Corp.; *U.S. Public*, pg. 93

BI-VEE—Intraveneous Fluid Administration Set—Mallinckrodt Inc.; *U.S. Public*, pg. 1039

BI-STRETCH—Film Delivery System—Lantech Inc.; *U.S. Private*, pg. 650

BIACORE—NONE—Pharmacia & Upjohn, Inc.; *Int'l*, pg. 1047

BIANCHI—Hats—AJD; *U.S. Private*, pg. 510

BIANCHI—Wedding Attire—House of Bianchi, Inc.; *U.S. Private*, pg. 541

BIAS TOTAL HIP—Orthopedic Products—Bristol-Myers Squibb Company; *U.S. Public*, pg. 253

BIAVAX—Rubella & Mumps Vaccine—Merck & Co., Inc.; *U.S. Public*, pg. 1090

BIAXIN—Anti-Infective—Abbott Laboratories; *U.S. Public*, pg. 12

BIBO—Children's Clothing—Garan, Incorporated; *U.S. Public*, pg. 703

BIC—Writing Instruments, Disposable Lighters, Disposable Shavers & Sailboards—BIC Corporation; *Int'l*, pg. 1273

BIC—NONE—Societe BIC S.A.; *Int'l*, pg. 1272

BICNU—Injectable Carmustine for Palliative Treatment of Brain Tumors, Lymphomas—Bristol-Myers Squibb U.S. Pharmaceutical Group; *U.S. Public*, pg. 255

BICAP—Bipolar Cauterizer—Circon Corporation; *U.S. Public*, pg. 373

BICE—NONE—Kellwood Company; *U.S. Public*, pg. 948

BICEMOS—Bipolar With Enhanced CMOS—Integrated Device Technology, Inc.; *U.S. Public*, pg. 884

BICENTENNIAL—Beer—Falstaff Brewing Corporation; *U.S. Private*, pg. 955

BICHEM—Biological Active Seed Cultures for Groundspill & WasteTreatment—Sybron Chemicals Inc.; *Int'l*, pg. 1544

BICILLIN—Procaine & Sodium Penicillin—Royal Gist-Brocades N.V.; *Int'l*, pg. 1142

BICILLIN—Antibiotic—Wyeth-Ayerst Laboratories, Inc.; *U.S. Public*, pg. 80

BICKFORD—NONE—Giddings & Lewis Automation Technology; *Int'l*, pg. 1389

BICKFORD'S FAMILY RESTAURANTS—Restaurants—Bickford's Family Restaurants; *U.S. Public*, pg. 545

BICKFORD'S PANCAKES & FAMILY FARE—NONE—Bickford's Family Restaurants; *U.S. Public*, pg. 545

BICKFORD'S RESTAURANTS—Family Restaurants—ELXSI Corporation; *U.S. Public*, pg. 545

BICK'S—Pickles & Relishes—International Multifoods Corporation; *U.S. Public*, pg. 900

BICK'S—Pickles & Condiments—Robin Hood Multifoods Inc.; *U.S. Public*, pg. 901

BICNU—Cancer Therapy—Bristol-Myers Squibb Company; *U.S. Public*, pg. 253

BICOZENE—Cream—Sandoz Pharmaceuticals Corp.; *Int'l*, pg. 974

BICYCLE—Playing Cards—The United States Playing Card Company; *U.S. Private*, pg. 1125

BICYCLING—Magazine—Rodale Press, Inc.; *U.S. Private*, pg. 939

BIDDLE—Electrical Test & Measuring Instrument—AVO International; *Int'l*, pg. 1335

BIDETTE—Feminine Hygiene Towelette—The Clinipad Corporation; *U.S. Private*, pg. 246

BIENFANG—Art Papers & Boards—Hunt Corporation; *U.S. Public*, pg. 848

BIFENABID—Cholesterol Lowering Agent—The Dow Chemical Company; *U.S. Public*, pg. 522

BIFFI—Flow Control Products—Keystone International, Inc.; *U.S. Public*, pg. 1650

BIFIDUS—Yogurt—Morinaga Milk Industry Co., Ltd.; *Int'l*, pg. 895

BIFLEX—Annuloplasty Ring—St. Jude Medical, Inc.; *U.S. Public*, pg. 1427

BIG!—U.K. Entertainment Magazine—EMAP Metro; *Int'l*, pg. 451

BIG A—Automotive Parts—A.P.S., Inc.; *U.S. Public*, pg. 10

BIG & EASY BEER NETWORK—NONE—Newspapers First; *U.S. Public*, pg. 964

BIG & EASY HEALTHCARE NETWORK—NONE—Newspapers First; *U.S. Public*, pg. 964

BIG BALLOON—Bubble Gum—Lotte Company Ltd.; *Int'l*, pg. 819

BIG BALLOON—Bubble Gum—Lotte U.S.A., Inc.; *Int'l*, pg. 819

BIG BEAR—Supermarkets—The Penn Traffic Company; *U.S. Public*, pg. 1270

BIG BEAR PLUS—Combination Supermarket & Discount Department Store—The Penn Traffic Company; *U.S. Public*, pg. 1270

BIG BEN—Clocks—General Time Corp.; *U.S. Private*, pg. 445

BIG BEN—Puzzles—Milton Bradley Company; *U.S. Public*, pg. 797

BIG BEN—Occupational Apparel—VF Corporation; *U.S. Public*, pg. 1702

BIG BEN—Clocks—Westclox; *U.S. Private*, pg. 445

BIG BEN PUZZLES—Puzzles—Hasbro, Inc.; *U.S. Public*, pg. 797

BIG BERTHA—(Golf Club Line)—Callaway Golf Company; *U.S. Public*, pg. 294

BIG BERTHA—Paper Napkins—Erving Industries, Inc.; *U.S. Private*, pg. 382

BIG BERTHA—Dump Body Vibrators—Vibco Inc.; *U.S. Private*, pg. 1138

BIG BERTHA IRONS—(Golf Club Irons)—Callaway Golf Company; *U.S. Public*, pg. 294

BIG BERTHA PUTTERS—(Line of Golf Putters)—Callaway Golf Company; *U.S. Public*, pg. 294

BIG BERTHA TITANIUM DRIVER—(Titanium Golf Driver)—Callaway Golf Company; *U.S. Public*, pg. 294

BIG BERTHA WAR BIRD—(Graphite Shaft Golf Clubs)—Callaway Golf Company; *U.S. Public*, pg. 294

BIG BIN—Grain Storage Tanks—Behlen Mfg. Co.; *U.S. Private*, pg. 130

BIG BITE—Hot Dog Products—The Southland Corporation; *Int'l*, pg. 693

BIG BLOCK—Chocolate Bar—Hershey Chocolate U.S.A.; *U.S. Public*, pg. 812

BIG BLOCK—Candy Bar—Hershey Foods Corporation; *U.S. Public*, pg. 811

BIG BLUE—Welding & Cutting Equip.—Miller Electric Manufacturing Co.; *U.S. Public*, pg. 867

BIG BODY—Perm Rods—The Gillette Company; *U.S. Public*, pg. 743

BIG BONUS—Metric Measurement Asphalt Rooting—CertainTeed Corporation; *Int'l*, pg. 1170

BIG BOSS—Tires—Bridgestone/Firestone, Inc.; *Int'l*, pg. 213

BIG BOSS BRUISER—Tires—Bridgestone/Firestone, Inc.; *Int'l*, pg. 213

BIG BOY—Restaurants—Frisch's Restaurants, Inc.; *U.S. Public*, pg. 682

BIG BRUISERS—Large Toy Vehicles—Empire of Carolina, Inc.; *U.S. Public*, pg. 579

BIG CHIEF—Paper Tablets—The Mead Corporation; *U.S. Public*, pg. 1074

BIG CHILL—Ice Cream Maker—Salton/Maxim Housewares, Inc.; *U.S. Public*, pg. 1430

BIG CHUNK—Large Size Stew, Chili Prods.—Nalleys Fine Foods; *U.S. Private*, pg. 887

BIG CLEM—Industrial Blast Machines, Transportable—Aerolyte Systems; *U.S. Private*, pg. 24

BIG CRUNCH—Candy Bar—Nestle Chocolate & Confection; *Int'l*, pg. 917

BIG DADDY—Riveter—Marson/Creative Fastener, Inc.; *U.S. Private*, pg. 708

BIG DADDY'S—Liquor Stores & Lounges—Flanigan's Enterprises, Inc.; *U.S. Public*, pg. 648

BIG DELUXE—Hamburger Sandwich—Hardee's Food Systems, Inc.; *U.S. Public*, pg. 278

BIG DIPPER—Brashes with Foam Inserts—Sherwin-Williams Coatings Division; *U.S. Public*, pg. 1466

BIG DRUM—NONE—Life Technologies, Inc.; *U.S. Public*, pg. 504

THE BIG DUNK—Menu Item-Large Soft Drink—Dunkin' Donuts Incorporated; *Int'l*, pg. 63

BIG FOOT PIZZA—Pizza—Pizza Hut, Inc.; *U.S. Public*, pg. 1636

BIG GALS—Women's Undergarments—AGP Industrial Corporation; *Int'l*, pg. 14

BIG GRAB—Single Serve 2 oz. Packages Snacks—Frito-Lay Company; *U.S. Public*, pg. 1277

BIG GULP—Fountain Drinks—7-Eleven Stores; *Int'l*, pg. 693

BIG GULP—32 Oz. Fountain Soft Drink—The Southland Corporation; *Int'l*, pg. 693

BIG GUN—Antennas—Telex Communications, Inc.; *U.S. Private*, pg. 1074

BIG HEAT—Portable Electric Heater—Aubrey Manufacturing Company; *U.S. Public*, pg. 1193

BIG HUNK—Candy—Annabelle Candy Company, Inc.; *U.S. Private*, pg. 75

BIG INCH—Dispensing Machines—Ascom Hasler Mailing Systems, Inc.; *Int'l*, pg. 86

BIG INCH—Miniature Precision Motors—Haydon Switch & Instrument, Inc.; *U.S. Private*, pg. 513

BIG INCH MOTORS—Integral Stepper Motor & Gearbox, One Inch Diameter—Haydon Switch & Instrument, Inc.; *U.S. Private*, pg. 513

BIG JOB—Rubber Bands—HBD Industries, Inc.; *U.S. Private*, pg. 489

BIG JOHN—Sump Pump—Little Giant Pump Company; *U.S. Public*, pg. 1566

BIG JOHNS—Beans—Hunt-Wesson, Inc.; *U.S. Public*, pg. 428

BIG KICK—Loose Leaf Chewing Tobacco—Conwood Company L.P.; *U.S. Private*, pg. 272

BIG KID TRAINER—Toilet Trainer—Century Products Co.; *U.S. Private*, pg. 328

BIG LEAGUE CHEW—Shredded Bubble Gum—Amurol Confections Co.; *U.S. Public*, pg. 1781

BIG M—Supermarkets—The Penn Traffic Company; *U.S. Public*, pg. 1270

BIG M—Milk—Q.U.F. Industries Ltd.; *Int'l*, pg. 1074

BIG MAC—Sandwich—McDonald's Corporation; *U.S. Public*, pg. 1068

BIG MAC—Enclosures—TII Industries, Inc.; *U.S. Public*, pg. 1556

BIG MAC—Portable Source Captive Industrial Air Cleaner—Trion, Inc.; *U.S. Public*, pg. 1639

BIG MAMA—Pickled Sausage—GoodMark Foods, Inc.; *U.S. Public*, pg. 751

BIG MAN—Men's Clothing—Key Industries, Inc.; *U.S. Private*, pg. 618

BIG MAX—Valves—Flowserve Corporation; *U.S. Public*, pg. 658

BIG MILL—Dog Food—The Jim Dandy Co., Inc.; *Int'l*, pg. 918

BIG MINI—Camera—Konica Corporation; *Int'l*, pg. 748

BIG MO—Pencils—Dixon Ticonderoga Company; *U.S. Public*, pg. 514

BIG-MOUTH SERVERS—Plastic Beverage Server—The Vollrath Company, L.L.C.; *U.S. Private*, pg. 1143

BIG 'N CRUSTY—Bagels—Lender's Bagel Bakery; *U.S. Public*, pg. 1288

BIG 'N PRETTY—Paper Napkins—Georgia-Pacific Corporation; *U.S. Public*, pg. 735

BIG 'N SOFT—Bath Tissue—Georgia-Pacific Corporation; *U.S. Public*, pg. 735

BIG 'N THIRSTY—Paper Towels—Georgia-Pacific Corporation; *U.S. Public*, pg. 735

BIG O TIRES—Automotive Stores—Big O Tires Incorporated; *U.S. Public*, pg. 1553

THE BIG ONE—Menu Item-Large Coffee—Dunkin' Donuts Incorporated; *Int'l*, pg. 63

BIG OX—Box Blades & Scrapers—Hiniker Company; *U.S. Public*, pg. 530

THE BIG PICTURE—Financial Newsletter—KCI Communications, Inc; *U.S. Private*, pg. 784

BIG RED—All-Terrain Vehicle—American Honda Motor Co., Inc. Motorcycle Division; *Int'l*, pg. 634

BIG RED—Writing Instruments—Gillette Co.-Parker Pen USA; *U.S. Public*, pg. 745

BIG RED—Soft Drinks—Grant-Lydick Beverage Co.; *U.S. Private*, pg. 470

BIG RED—Trailway Companies—Greyhound Lines, Inc.; *U.S. Public*, pg. 765

BIG RED—Material Handling Equipment—Taylor Machine Works, Inc.; *U.S. Private*, pg. 1070

BIG RED—Industrial Cleaner—Texas Refinery Corp.; *U.S. Private*, pg. 1078

BIG RED—Chewing Gum—Wrigley Canada Inc.; *U.S. Public*, pg. 1781

BIG RED—Gum—Wm. Wrigley Jr. Company; *U.S. Public*, pg. 1781

BIG RIVER GRILLE & BREWING WORKS—Brew Pub—Rock Bottom Restaurants; *U.S. Public*, pg. 1396

BIG ROAST BEEF—Sandwich—Hardee's Food Systems, Inc.; *U.S. Public*, pg. 278

BIG SCOOP—Hard Ice Cream Cone—International Dairy Queen, Inc.; *U.S. Public*, pg. 220

BIG SMITH—NONE—Tandy Brands Accessories, Inc.; *U.S. Public*, pg. 1560

BIG STEP—Step Stool Series with Roomy Molded Steps—Cosco, Inc.; *U.S. Private*, pg. 277

BIG STICK—Fly Trap—Security Lawn & Garden Co.; *U.S. Private*, pg. 397

BIG SWITCH—Over-sized On/Off Switch—The Lamson & Sessions Co.; *U.S. Public*, pg. 976

BIG T—Restaurants—Tastee Freez International Inc.; *U.S. Private*, pg. 1069

BIG-T—Marine Steering Assemblies—Teleflex Incorporated; *U.S. Public*, pg. 1569

BIG TEE BURGER—Menu Item—Tastee Freez International Inc.; *U.S. Private*, pg. 1069

BIG THINKING IN LITTLE SIZES—Children's Shoes & Clothing—Reebok International Ltd.; *U.S. Public*, pg. 1369

BIG THREAD—Fiberglass Reinforced Plastic Piping—A.O. Smith Corporation; *U.S. Public*, pg. 1476

BIG TWIN—Pumps—Hypro Corporation; *U.S. Public*, pg. 1767

BIG VALLEY—Cattle Handling System—Behlen Mfg. Co.; *U.S. Private*, pg. 130

BIG VALLEY—Foods—Big Valley Marketing Corp.; *U.S. Private*, pg. 1186

BIG VALUE—Fabric Softener—James Austin Co.; *U.S. Private*, pg. 99

BIG WALLY—Foam Cleaner—S.C. Johnson & Son, Inc.; *U.S. Private*, pg. 592

BIG WHEEL—Ride-on Toys—Empire of Carolina, Inc.; *U.S. Public*, pg. 579

BIG WHEEL—Frozen Ice Cream Novelty—The Southland Corporation; *Int'l*, pg. 693

BIG WHEEL—All Purpose Lotion—Stanhome Inc.; *U.S. Public*, pg. 1508

BIG Y—Grocery Stores—Big Y Foods Inc.; *U.S. Private*, pg. 143

BIG YUKKERS—Greeting Cards—American Greetings Corporation; *U.S. Public*, pg. 77

BIG-A—Box Store—The Daiei, Inc.; *Int'l*, pg. 364

BIGELOW—Carpet—Fieldcrest Cannon, Inc.; *U.S. Public*, pg. 1296

BIGELOW—Carpets & Rugs—Mohawk Industries, Inc.; *U.S. Public*, pg. 1121

BIGG'S—Hypermarkets—GIB Group; *Int'l*, pg. 532

BIGHORN—Moist Smokeless Tobacco—Conwood Company L.P.; *U.S. Private*, pg. 272

BIGHORN—Sports Utility Vehicles—Isuzu Motors Limited; *Int'l*, pg. 692

BIGI—Wine—Wine World Estates Company; *Int'l*, pg. 917

BIGPICTURE—Video Phone Products—3Com Personal Communications Div.; *U.S. Public*, pg. 1604

BIKE—Athletic Apparel—Bike Athletic Co.; *U.S. Private*, pg. 143

BIKE—Magazine—EMAP Nationals; *Int'l*, pg. 451

BIKE—Publications & Productions—For Better Living, Inc.; *U.S. Private*, pg. 417

BIKE-BUOY—Drink Holders—Orbex Inc.; *U.S. Public*, pg. 238

BIKER—Magazine—Paisano Publications, Inc.; *U.S. Public*, pg. 834

BIKEXTRAS—Bicycle Accessories—Bell Sports Corp.; *U.S. Public*, pg. 207

BIKINI BABY—Bikini Shaver—Wahl Clipper Corp.; *U.S. Private*, pg. 1146

BIKINI BARE—Depilatory & Shaving Gel—Lee Pharmaceuticals; *U.S. Public*, pg. 984

BIKINI TOP—Partial Jeep Top—Bestop, Inc.; *Int'l*, pg. 830

BIL MAR—Foods—Bil Mar Foods, Inc.; *U.S. Public*, pg. 1433

BIL-MAR—Packaged Meat Products—Sara Lee Corporation; *U.S. Public*, pg. 1432

BILAR—Fruit Candy—Huhtamaki Oy; *Int'l*, pg. 638

BILD—Newspaper—Axel Springer Verlag AG; *Int'l*, pg. 102

BILD AM SONNTAG—Newspaper—Axel Springer Verlag AG; *Int'l*, pg. 102

BILD DER FRAU—Magazine—Axel Springer Verlag AG; *Int'l*, pg. 102

BILD-R-TAPE—Sealing Tape—Owens Corning; *U.S. Public*, pg. 1236

BILD-R-TAPE—Construction Tape—Owens Corning/Foamular; *U.S. Public*, pg. 1237

BILDWOCHE—Magazine—Axel Springer Verlag AG; *Int'l*, pg. 102

BILGE KING—Bilge Pump—Attwood Corporation; *U.S. Public*, pg. 1038

BILL BLASS—Sleepwear—Host Apparel, Inc.; *U.S. Private*, pg. 540

BILL BLASS—Men's Suits & Sportswear—Pincus Bros., Inc.; *U.S. Private*, pg. 865

BILL BLASS-SCARF COLLECTION—Scarves—Baar & Beards; *U.S. Private*, pg. 839

BILL ROBINSON—Menswear—Arrow Shirt Company; *Int'l*, pg. 194

BILL-TAINERS—Billfolds—DHP Limited Partnership; *U.S. Private*, pg. 302

BILL TITE—Bill Board Adhesives—Evans Adhesive Corp.; *U.S. Private*, pg. 384

BILL'S—Casino—Harrah's Entertainment, Inc.; *U.S. Public*, pg. 790

BILLBOARD—Magazine; Books on Music & Entertainment—BPI Communications Inc.; *Int'l*, pg. 1446

BILLBOARD BULLETIN—Newsletter—BPI Communications Inc.; *Int'l*, pg. 1446

BILLBOARD INFORMATION NETWORK—Marketing Information Services—BPI Communications Inc.; *Int'l*, pg. 1446

BILLBOARDBOX—Corrugated Containers—International Paper Company; *U.S. Public*, pg. 901

BILLBOARDS—Overlay Binders—Rundel Products, Inc.; *U.S. Private*, pg. 951

BILLDATS—Data Collection Apparatus, Collector, Transmitter, Switched Data Processor—Lucent Technologies Inc.; *U.S. Public*, pg. 1017

BILLDATS II—Telecommunications Data Collection Unit & Network Server—Lucent Technologies Inc.; *U.S. Public*, pg. 1017

BILLI—Process Application—Genus Inc.; *U.S. Public*, pg. 732

BILLIONAIRES—Candy—Pangburn Candy Company; *U.S. Private*, pg. 836

BILLY PACKER'S TOURNAMENT MADNESS—Sports Radio Program—Westwood One Entertainment; *U.S. Public*, pg. 1763

BILOFT—Fiber—Monsanto Company; *U.S. Public*, pg. 1124

BILTBEST—Windows—Biltbest Windows; *U.S. Public*, pg. 1683

BILTMORE & DESIGN—Envelopes—Georgia-Pacific Corporation; *U.S. Public*, pg. 735

BILTMORE FARMS—Dairy Products—Land-O-Sun Dairies, Inc.; *U.S. Private*, pg. 646

BILTRICIDE—Pharmaceutical—Bayer Corporation/Pharmaceutical Division; *Int'l*, pg. 173

BILTRITE—Shoe Repair Products—American Biltrite Inc.; *U.S. Public*, pg. 68

BILTRITE—Rubber Products—The Biltrite Corporation; *U.S. Private*, pg. 144

BIMAT—Diffusion Transfer Film—Eastman Kodak Company; *U.S. Public*, pg. 550

BIMBO—Bread—Grupo Industrial Bimbo S.A. de C.V.; *Int'l*, pg. 575

BIMET—Metals—Handy & Harman; *U.S. Public*, pg. 780

BIN BOARD—Plywood Panels—Georgia-Pacific Corporation; *U.S. Public*, pg. 735

BIND-FAST—Office Machinery—Standard Duplicating Machines Corp.; *U.S. Private*, pg. 1031

BINDEX—Transport Load Binders—Acco Chain & Lifting Products; *Int'l*, pg. 473

BINGHAMS—Meat Products—Northern Foods plc; *Int'l*, pg. 967

BINGO KING—NONE—Stuart Entertainment Inc.; *U.S. Public*, pg. 1526

BINGO QUEEN—NONE—Stuart Entertainment Inc.; *U.S. Public*, pg. 1526

BINIP—Press—Beloit Corporation; *U.S. Public*, pg. 789

BINKS—NONE—Binks Sames Corporation; *U.S. Public*, pg. 229

BINSWANGER—Real Estate Services—Binswanger; *U.S. Private*, pg. 144

BINTANG—Beer—Heineken N.V.; *Int'l*, pg. 608

BINWAL—Perimeter & Free-Standing Storage Units—Lyon Metal Products, Inc.; *U.S. Private*, pg. 638

BINY-BINY—Cosmetics—The Cosmetic Center Inc.; *U.S. Public*, pg. 689

BIO—Office Seating—American Seating Company; *U.S. Private*, pg. 61

BIO—Bifidus Yogurt—Danone Group; *Int'l*, pg. 379

BIO-ADE—Ammonia & Odor Control—DuCoa L.P.; *U.S. Private*, pg. 301

BIO BALANCE—De-Alkalizing Shampoo—Revlon-Realistic Professional Products, Inc.; *U.S. Private*, pg. 690

BIO-BLAST—NONE—EcoScience Corporation; *U.S. Public*, pg. 563

BIO-CEUTIC—Division Servicing the Veternarians—Boehringer Ingelheim Animal Health Inc.; *Int'l*, pg. 199

BIO CHANNEL—Suspended/Anchored Sports Flooring—Robbins, Inc.; *U.S. Private*, pg. 934

BIO-CHEM VALVE—Miniature Valves for Scientific Instruments—Halma p.l.c.; *Int'l*, pg. 589

BIO CLINIC—Therapeutic Mattresses—Sunrise Medical, Inc.; *U.S. Public*, pg. 1535

BIO-CONSOLE—Extracorporeal Blood Pumping Console—Medtronic, Inc.; *U.S. Public*, pg. 1082

BIO-CONSOLE—Control Console with Heart Design—Medtronic, Inc.; *U.S. Public*, pg. 1082

BIO COR—Collagen Shield—Bausch & Lomb Incorporated; *U.S. Public*, pg. 194

BIO CURVE—Cutlery—General Housewares Corp.; *U.S. Public*, pg. 715

BIO CUSHION—Suspended Maple Sports Flooring—Robbins, Inc.; *U.S. Private*, pg. 934

BIO GENTLE—Fabric Softener—Lonza Inc.; *Int'l*, pg. 67

BIO IMAGE—Digital Image Processors—Eastman Kodak Company; *U.S. Public*, pg. 550

BIO IMAGE—Software—Millipore Corporation; *U.S. Public*, pg. 1112

BIO-INERT—Membrane—Pall Corporation; *U.S. Public*, pg. 1253

BIO-KLEEN—Residue Remover—Litton Industries, Inc.; *U.S. Public*, pg. 1002

BIO-MEDICUS—Cardiopulmonary Equipment—Medtronic, Inc.; *U.S. Public*, pg. 1082

BIO-PATH—NONE—EcoScience Corporation; *U.S. Public*, pg. 563

BIO-PERFORMANCE—Skin Care—Shiseido Cosmetics (America) Ltd.; *Int'l*, pg. 1235

BIO PERM—Preservative Concentrate—Sargent-Welch Scientific Company; *U.S. Public*, pg. 1704

BIO-PREP—Membrane Systems for Treating Liquid Protein Solutions—Ionics, Incorporated; *U.S. Public*, pg. 912

BIO-PROBE—Blood Flow Monitoring System—Medtronic, Inc.; *U.S. Public*, pg. 1082

BIO-PUMP—Blood Pump—Medtronic, Inc.; *U.S. Public*, pg. 1082

BIO-SAVE—NONE—EcoScience Corporation; *U.S. Public*, pg. 563

BIO-SEAL—Sealed & Gasketed Fluorescent—Guth Lighting Company; *Int'l*, pg. 821

BIO-SOFT—Surfactant-Sulfonate—Stepan Company; *U.S. Public*, pg. 1514

BIO-SORB—I. E. Filer for Removal of Bacteria from Water—Ionics, Incorporated; *U.S. Public*, pg. 912

BIO-SOURCE—Battery Pack—Medtronic, Inc.; *U.S. Public*, pg. 1082

BIO-TERGE—Surfactant-Alpha Olefin Sulfonate—Stepan Company; *U.S. Public*, pg. 1514

BIO TRACK—Poured-in-Place Urethane—Robbins, Inc.; *U.S. Private*, pg. 934

BIO-TROL—Biocides—BetzDearborn Inc.; *U.S. Public*, pg. 226

BIO-VIAL—Liquid Scintillation Vial—Beckman Instruments, Inc.; *U.S. Public*, pg. 199

BIO-SELECTIN—Household Insecticide—Novartis; *Int'l*, pg. 972

BIOADVANCE—Beauty Recovery System—Avon Products, Inc.; *U.S. Public*, pg. 155

BIOBEST—NONE—Astro Dairy Products Ltd.; *Int'l*, pg. 95

BIOBIT—Biological Product for Control of Caterpillars—Novo Nordisk A/S; *Int'l*, pg. 987

BIOBRANE—Biosynthetic Topical Burn Dressing—Dow Hickam Pharmaceuticals Inc.; *U.S. Public*, pg. 1143

BIOCAD—Workstation That Uses Poros Media in a Computer-Aided System for Analysis—PerSeptive Biosystems, Inc.; *U.S. Public*, pg. 1279

BIOCELL—Mammary Implant—Inamed Corporation; *U.S. Public*, pg. 873

BIOCLATE—Antihemophilic Factor (Recombinant)—Centeon, L.L.C.; *Int'l*, pg. 626

BIOCLONE—Monoclonal Antibodies—Ortho Clinical Diagnostic Systems Inc.; *U.S. Public*, pg. 929

BIOCLUSIVE—Transparent Dressing—Johnson & Johnson Medical, Inc.; *U.S. Public*, pg. 928

BIOCOR—Tissue Heart Valve—St. Jude Medical, Inc.; *U.S. Public*, pg. 1427

BIOCOT—NONE—Uniroyal Chemical Company, Inc.; *U.S. Public*, pg. 460

BIOCRAFT—Pharmaceuticals—Teva USA - Biocraft; *Int'l*, pg. 1381

BIOCUBE—NONE—EG & G Environmental, Inc.; *U.S. Public*, pg. 543

BIODIET—Animal Health Products—SmithKline Beecham plc; *Int'l*, pg. 1264

BIODRY—Mastitis Products—Pharmacia & Upjohn; *Int'l*, pg. 1048

BIODYNE—Membrane—Pall Corporation; *U.S. Public*, pg. 1253

BIOEDGE—Insurance—Midland Life Insurance Co.; *U.S. Private*, pg. 744

BIOFILTER—Hemoconcentrator—Baxter Research Medical, Inc.; *U.S. Public*, pg. 196

BIOFLEX—Orthotics with Semi-Rigid Control—The Langer Biomechanics Group, Inc.; *U.S. Public*, pg. 978

BIOFLO—Fermentor—New Brunswick Scientific Co., Inc.; *U.S. Public*, pg. 1169

BIOFLUX—NONE—Akzo Nobel N.V.; *Int'l*, pg. 42

BIOFREE—Microbial Products—InterBio Inc.; *U.S. Private*, pg. 566

BIOGARD—Flush Valve Handles—Sloan Valve Company; *U.S. Private*, pg. 1006

BIOGEN—NONE—Biogen, Inc.; *U.S. Public*, pg. 230

BIOGON T—Camera Lense—Carl Zeiss; *Int'l*, pg. 1522

BIOIMPLANT—Tissue Heart Valve—St. Jude Medical, Inc.; *U.S. Public*, pg. 1427

BIOKIT—Biological Products—Carolina Biological Supply Co.; *U.S. Private*, pg. 213

BIOLYTE—Microbial Products—InterBio Inc.; *U.S. Private*, pg. 566

BIOMAG—Contrast Agent—Advanced Magnetics, Inc.; *U.S. Public*, pg. 20

BIOMEDICAL PRODUCTS—Chemical Equipment—Gordon Publications, Inc.; *Int'l*, pg. 1096

BIOMEDICAL PRODUCTS—Publication Serving the Informational Needs of Life Scientists—Reed Elsevier Business Information; *Int'l*, pg. 1095

BIOMEK—Automated Laboratory Workstation—Beckman Instruments, Inc.; *U.S. Public*, pg. 199

BIOMET—Orthopedic & Surgical Supplies—Biomet, Inc.; *U.S. Public*, pg. 231

BION TEARS—Artificial Tears—Alcon Laboratories, Inc.; *Int'l*, pg. 916

BIONAIRE—Air Cleaners & Humidifiers—The Rival Company; *U.S. Public*, pg. 1391

BIONEEM—Organic Insecticide—Ringer Corporation; *U.S. Public*, pg. 1390

BIONICK—NONE—Life Technologies, Inc.; *U.S. Public*, pg. 504

BIONIX—Biomaterials Test Systems—MTS Systems Corporation; *U.S. Public*, pg. 1028

BIOPAR FORTE—Pharmaceuticals—Rhone-Poulenc Rorer; *Int'l*, pg. 1110

BIOPATCH—Antimicrobial Dressing—Johnson & Johnson Medical, Inc.; *U.S. Public*, pg. 928

BIOPHARM—Trade Periodical—Advanstar Communications; *U.S. Private*, pg. 22

BIOPHOTO—Biological Supplies—Carolina Biological Supply Co.; *U.S. Private*, pg. 213

BIOPLUS—Biopsy Kits—Medtronic, Inc.; *U.S. Public*, pg. 1082

BIOPORE—Membrane Filter—Millipore Corporation; *U.S. Public*, pg. 1112

BIOPRIME—NONE—Life Technologies, Inc.; *U.S. Public*, pg. 504

BIOPRO—Scientific Glassware for Laboratory Use—Wheaton Inc.; *Int'l*, pg. 67

BIOPROBE—Electrode—Fisher Scientific Company; *U.S. Public*, pg. 658

BIOPTY—Urological Instrument—C.R. Bard, Inc.; *U.S. Public*, pg. 189

BIORAM—Pesticide—Roussel Corporation; *Int'l*, pg. 625

BIORAM—Pesticide—Roussel UCLAF S.A.; *Int'l*, pg. 626

BIORE—Face & Body Cleansing Agents—Kao Corporation; *Int'l*, pg. 717

BIOREVIEW—Biological Supplies—Carolina Biological Supply Co.; *U.S. Private*, pg. 213

BIOSERT—Controller Release Suppositories—KV Pharmaceutical Company; *U.S. Public*, pg. 941

BIOSOFT—Padding, Bicycle Accessories, Exercise Weights—Kimberly-Clark Corporation; *U.S. Public*, pg. 958

BIOSORB—Sutures—Alcon Laboratories, Inc.; *Int'l*, pg. 916

BIOSPECTROMETRY—Technology Relating to Biological Mass Spectrometry—PerSeptive Biosystems, Inc.; *U.S. Public*, pg. 1279

BIOSTAR—Microscope—Leica, Inc.; *Int'l*, pg. 806

BIOSTAT 1000—Kidney Dialysis System—Baxter International Inc.; *U.S. Public*, pg. 196

BIOSTIR—Scientific Glassware for Laboratory Use—Wheaton Inc.; *Int'l*, pg. 67

BIOSUN—Suncare Products—Playtex Products Inc.; *U.S. Public*, pg. 1310

BIOSURF—Iodophor for Topical Biocide—Lonza Inc.; *Int'l*, pg. 67

BIOSYN—Suture—U.S. Surgical Corp.; *U.S. Public*, pg. 1687

BIOTENE H-24—Hair Care Product—Carme' Cosmeceutical Sciences, Inc.; *U.S. Private*, pg. 213

BIOTEX—Laundry Detergent—Sara Lee Corporation; *U.S. Public*, pg. 1432

BIOTHERM—Skin Care System—Cosmair, Inc.; *Int'l*, pg. 818

BIOTHERM—NONE—L'Oreal Parfumerie; *Int'l*, pg. 819

BIOTHERM—Cosmetics—L'Oreal S.A.; *Int'l*, pg. 818

BIOTIC—Parasite Control on Sheep & Cattle—Novartis AG; *Int'l*, pg. 971

BIOTRACE—Binding Membrane—Gelman Sciences, Inc.; *U.S. Public*, pg. 1253

BIOXENO GRAFT—Graft—St. Jude Medical, Inc.; *U.S. Public*, pg. 1427

BIPAK—NONE—Allied Diagnostic Imaging Resources, Inc.; *U.S. Public*, pg. 282

BIPAP S—Airway Mngmnt. System—Respironics, Inc.; *U.S. Public*, pg. 1383

BIPAP S/T-D—Ventilatory Support System—Respironics, Inc.; *U.S. Public*, pg. 1383

BIPHETAMINE—Capsules (Amphetamine)—Medeva Pharmaceuticals; *Int'l*, pg. 852

BIRA—Office Chair—Vecta; *U.S. Private*, pg. 1038

BIRCH CREEK—Prefinished Wall Paneling—Georgia-Pacific Corporation; *U.S. Public*, pg. 735

BIRD—Machinery—Bird Machine Company; *U.S. Public*, pg. 166

BIRD—Respiratory Care Equipment—Bird Products Corporation; *U.S. Public*, pg. 1591

BIRD—Sprinkler—Rain Bird Sprinklers Manufacturing Corp.; *U.S. Private*, pg. 907

BIRD ALERT—Poultry—Tyson Foods, Inc.; *U.S. Public*, pg. 1652

BIRD KEEPER—Special Interest Magazine—IPC Magazines Limited; *Int'l*, pg. 651

BIRD SCREEN BOWL CENTRIFUGE—Combines Clarification & Dewatering—Bird Machine Company; *U.S. Public*, pg. 166

BIRD SCROLL/SCREEN CENTRIFUGE—(Dewatering Coal & Chemical)—Bird Machine Company; *U.S. Public*, pg. 166

BIRD SOLID BOWL CENTRIFUGE—Process a Variety of Slurries at High Tonnages/Hour—Bird Machine Company; *U.S. Public*, pg. 166

BIRD TILTING PAN FILTER—For Separating Large Tonnages of Material from Mother Liquor—Bird Machine Company; *U.S. Public*, pg. 166

BIRD UNIVERSAL PUSHER—Produces Very Dry Washed Cakes at High Capacities—Bird Machine Company; *U.S. Public*, pg. 166

BIRDWATCHING—Magazine—EMAP Pursuit Publishing; *Int'l*, pg. 451

BIRD-YOUNG ROTARY VACUUM FILTER—Greater Hydraulic Capacities for High Filtration Rate—Bird Machine Company; *U.S. Public*, pg. 166

BIRDERS WORLD—Magazine—Kalmbach Publishing Co.; *U.S. Private*, pg. 606

BIRDS EYE—Frozen Vegetables—Dean Foods Company; *U.S. Public*, pg. 489

BIRD'S EYE—Frozen Vegetables—Dean Foods Vegetable Company; *U.S. Public*, pg. 490

BIRDS EYE—Frozen Fruits, Vegetables, International Recipes & Stir-Fry Vegetables—Kraft Foods, Inc.; *U.S. Public*, pg. 1287

BIRDS EYE—Juices—Orange-Co., Inc.; *U.S. Public*, pg. 1229

BIRDS EYE COOL WHIP—Non-Dairy Frozen Whipped Topping, Light & Creamy Frosting—Kraft Foods, Inc.; *U.S. Public*, pg. 1287

BIRDS EYE SALADS—Pasta/Vegetable Combination—Kraft Foods, Inc.; *U.S. Public*, pg. 1287

BIRELL—Non-Alcoholic Beer—Charles Jacquin et Cie, Inc.; *U.S. Private*, pg. 580

BIRGE—Wallcoverings—Borden, Inc.; *U.S. Private*, pg. 157

BIRKEL—Pasta—Danone Group; *Int'l*, pg. 379

BIRKETT—Valves—IMI Plc; *Int'l*, pg. 646

BIRMINGHAM POST-HERALD—Newspaper—The E.W. Scripps Company; *U.S. Public*, pg. 1447

BIRNBACH WIRE—NONE—Milgray Electronics, Inc.; *U.S. Public*, pg. 205

BIRTHDAY BEAR—NONE—American Greetings Corporation; *U.S. Public*, pg. 77

THE BIRTHDAY COMPANY—NONE—American Greetings Corporation; *U.S. Public*, pg. 77

BISALLOY—Metal Products—Email Limited; *Int'l*, pg. 450

BISCOS—Cookies—Nabisco Inc.; *U.S. Public*, pg. 1355

BISCOS—Sugar Wafers & Waffle Cremes—RJR Nabisco Holdings Corp.; *U.S. Public*, pg. 1354

BISCUIT 'N GRAVY—Breakfast Biscuit—Hardee's Food Systems, Inc.; *U.S. Public*, pg. 278

BISHOP—Snack Cakes—President Baking Company; *Int'l*, pg. 1069

BISOLVON—Mucolytics—Boehringer Ingelheim GmbH; *Int'l*, pg. 199

BISON—Dairy Foods—Bison Foods Company; *U.S. Private*, pg. 1129

BISQUICK—Flour—General Mills, Inc.; *U.S. Public*, pg. 717

BISQUIT—Cognac—Groupe Pernod Ricard; *Int'l*, pg. 566

BISSELL—Floor Cleaning Needs—Bissell Inc.; *U.S. Private*, pg. 145

BISSELL—Homecare Items—Penn Champ; *U.S. Private*, pg. 145

BISSELL ONE STEP—Home Care Products—Bissell Inc.; *U.S. Private*, pg. 145

BISTAT—Bipolar Electrosurgery Generator—Conmed Corporation; *U.S. Public*, pg. 431

BISTO—Food Product—Campbell Soup Company Ltd.; *U.S. Public*, pg. 299

BISTO—Specialty Foods—Ranks Hovis McDougall Limited; *Int'l*, pg. 1395

BISTRO—Dinnerware—Dansk International Designs Ltd.; *U.S. Public*, pg. 261

BISTRO—Soups—Vienna Sausage Mfg. Co.; *U.S. Private*, pg. 1139

BISTRO COOK'S COLLECTION—Porcelain Cookware—Dansk International Designs Ltd.; *U.S. Public*, pg. 261

BISTRO 110—Restaurant—The Levy Organization; *U.S. Private*, pg. 664

BIT-O-HONEY—Candy—Nestle Chocolate & Confection; *Int'l*, pg. 917

BIT O'WAX—Oral Hygiene Aids—John O. Butler Co.; *Int'l*, pg. 1320

BIT SAVER—Float Equipment—Weatherford Enterra Incorporated; *U.S. Public*, pg. 1749

BIT-O-HONEY—Candy—Nestle USA; *Int'l*, pg. 916

BITBURGER DRIVE—Non Alcoholic Beer—Bitburger Brauerei Th. Simon GmbH; *Int'l*, pg. 197

BITBURGER LIGHT—Light Beer—Bitburger Brauerei Th. Simon GmbH; *Int'l*, pg. 197

BITBURGER PILS—Brewery—Bitburger Brauerei Th. Simon GmbH; *Int'l*, pg. 197

BITBUS—Electronic Instrument—Intel Corporation; *U.S. Public*, pg. 886

BITBUSTER—Video—LSI Logic Corp.; *U.S. Public*, pg. 971

BITELIFE—Snacking Crackers—Culinar Inc.; *Int'l*, pg. 348

BITGUARD—Ceramic Capacitors—AVX Corporation; *Int'l*, pg. 775

BITS O'MACADAMIA NUTS—Confection—Mauna Loa Macadamia Nut Corporation; *U.S. Private*, pg. 190

BITTER—NONE—Gio. Buton S.p.a.; *Int'l*, pg. 409

BITTNERS—NONE—Principal Marques Meat Co.; *Int'l*, pg. 841

BITTY BABY COLLECTION—Dolls, Doll Accessories & Books—Pleasant Company; *U.S. Private*, pg. 872

BITUMAC—Building Papers & Damp Proof Courses—Carter Holt Harvey Limited; *U.S. Public*, pg. 904

BITUMASTIC—Coating—RPM, Inc.; *U.S. Public*, pg. 1356

BITURBO—Engine—Officine A. Maserati S.p.A.; *Int'l*, pg. 482

BITUTHENE—Waterproofing—Grace Construction Products; *U.S. Public*, pg. 755

BITUTHENE—Waterproofing Membranes—W.R. Grace & Co.; *U.S. Public*, pg. 754

BIURON—Fodder Products—DSM Chemie Linz GmbH; *Int'l*, pg. 356

BIVENT—Press—Beloit Corporation; *U.S. Public*, pg. 789

BIVER—Chemical Reagant—Hach Company; *U.S. Public*, pg. 773

BIVERT—Agricultural Chemicals—Wilbur-Ellis Company & Connell Brothers Company; *U.S. Private*, pg. 1175

BIXMIX—Biscuit Mix—Pillsbury Co.; *Int'l*, pg. 411

BIZ—Laundry Product—The Procter & Gamble Company; *U.S. Public*, pg. 1330

BIZCASE—Business Software—SRA International Inc.; *U.S. Private*, pg. 957

BIZIMGAZ—Liquid Propane Gas—SHV Holdings N.V.; *Int'l*, pg. 1154

BLAC-KLAD—Culvert—Inland Steel Industries, Inc.; *U.S. Public*, pg. 879

BLACK & BEAUTIFUL—Conditioners, Hair Spray—E.T. Browne Drug Co., Inc.; *U.S. Private*, pg. 175

BLACK & DECKER—Household Appliances—Black & Decker Canada Inc.; *U.S. Public*, pg. 234

BLACK & DECKER—Tools & Accessories—The Black & Decker Corporation; *U.S. Public*, pg. 233

BLACK & DECKER HOVERMASTER—Electric Lawn & Garden Tools—The Black & Decker Corporation; *U.S. Public*, pg. 233

BLACK & DECKER QUANTUM—Power Tools—The Black & Decker Corporation; *U.S. Public*, pg. 233

BLACK & SILVER—Putty Knives, Scrapers—Hyde Manufacturing Co.; *U.S. Private*, pg. 551

BLACK & TAN—Premium Beers—The Lion Brewery, Inc.; *U.S. Public*, pg. 1000

BLACK & TAN—Beer—The F.X. Matt Brewing Co.; *U.S. Private*, pg. 714

BLACK AND WHITE—NONE—Guinness Plc; *Int'l*, pg. 412

BLACK & WHITE—Surface Coated Engraving Paper—The Mead Corporation; *U.S. Public*, pg. 1074

BLACK & WHITE—Scotch—United Distillers USA, Inc.; *Int'l*, pg. 412

BLACK ANGUS—Appliances—Son Chief Electrics, Inc.; *U.S. Private*, pg. 1014

BLACK ARMOR—Coal Tar Roofing Systems—AlliedSignal Inc., Engineered Materials; *U.S. Public*, pg. 51

BLACK BEAUTY—Poly Wheelbarrows, Sprayers, Shovels—Ames Company; *U.S. Public*, pg. 1683

BLACK BEAUTY—Sporting Goods—Brunswick Bowling & Billiards Corp.; *U.S. Public*, pg. 265

BLACK BELT—Videogame—Sega of America Inc.; *Int'l*, pg. 1218

BLACK BOTTLE—Blended Scotch Whisky—The Highland Distilleries Company plc; *Int'l*, pg. 619

BLACK BOX—Computer Equipment—Black Box Corporation of PA; *U.S. Public*, pg. 235

BLACK BRUTE—PIPES—James Hardie Industries Ltd.; *Int'l*, pg. 596

BLACK BULL—Scotch Whiskey—John Gross & Co.; *U.S. Private*, pg. 483

BLACK BUSH—Irish Whiskey—Brown-Forman Beverages Worldwide; *U.S. Public*, pg. 261

BLACK BUSH SPECIAL—Irish Whiskey—Brown-Forman Corporation; *U.S. Public*, pg. 261

BLACK BY BAINBRIDGE—Black-Core Mat Board for Framing—Letraset Nielsen & Bainbridge; *Int'l*, pg. 460

BLACK CAT—Cigarettes—Rothmans UK Holdings Limited; *Int'l*, pg. 1129

BLACK CAT IRONS—NONE—Lynx Golf, Inc.; *U.S. Private*, pg. 684

BLACK CHERRY BLAST—Black Cherry Juice Drink—Ocean Spray Cranberries, Inc.; *U.S. Private*, pg. 811

BLACK CLAWSON—Machinery—Thermo Black Clawson, Inc.; *U.S. Public*, pg. 1593

BLACK DIAMOND—Sporting Goods—Brunswick Bowling & Billiards Corp.; *U.S. Public*, pg. 265

BLACK DIAMOND—Fly Rods—Cortland Line Co., Inc.; *U.S. Private*, pg. 277

BLACK DIAMOND—Furs—Evans, Inc.; *U.S. Public*, pg. 596

BLACK DIAMOND—Industrial Footwear—Kaufman Footwear; *Int'l*, pg. 725

BLACK DIAMOND—Suspension Products for Light Trucks and Sport Utility Vehicles—Warn Industries, Inc.; *U.S. Private*, pg. 1150

BLACK DOT—Snowboard Outerwear—Pacific Trail Inc.; *U.S. Private*, pg. 673

BLACK ENTERPRISE—Magazine—Earl G. Graves, Ltd.; *U.S. Private*, pg. 471

THE BLACK-EYED PEA—Restaurant—Blackeyed Pea Restaurants Inc.; *U.S. Public*, pg. 498

BLACK FLAG—Insecticide—The Clorox Company; *U.S. Public*, pg. 386

BLACK FOREST—Beer—The F.X. Matt Brewing Co.; *U.S. Private*, pg. 714

BLACK GOLD—Sporting Goods—The Black & Decker Corporation; *U.S. Public*, pg. 233

BLACK GOLD TOUR—Outdoor Products—The Black & Decker Corporation; *U.S. Public*, pg. 233

BLACK HEART—Rum—Allied Domecq PLC; *Int'l*, pg. 62

BLACK-JACK—Roof Coatings & Cements—The Gibson-Homans Company; *U.S. Private*, pg. 451

BLACK JACK—Gin—Groupe Pernod Ricard; *Int'l*, pg. 566

BLACK JACKS—Sporting Goods—Brunswick Bowling & Billiards Corp.; *U.S. Public*, pg. 265

BLACK KNIGHT—Pipe Tobacco—Lane Limited; *Int'l*, pg. 1129

BLACK LABEL—Beer—Foster's Brewing Group Limited; *Int'l*, pg. 500

BLACK LABEL—Bacon—Hormel Foods Corp.; *U.S. Public*, pg. 840

BLACK LABEL—Beer—Sapporo Breweries Ltd.; *Int'l*, pg. 1193

BLACK LABEL—NONE—The Stroh Brewery Company; *U.S. Private*, pg. 1047

BLACK LABEL—Fragrance for Men—Yardley of London, Inc.; *Int'l*, pg. 819

BLACK LEAF—Pesticides & Insecticides—Rigo/Black Leaf; *U.S. Public*, pg. 1390

BLACK LEAF—Insecticide—Wilbur-Ellis Company & Connell Brothers Company; *U.S. Private*, pg. 1175

BLACK MAC—2-3-4 & 5 Bladed—McCauley Propeller Systems; *U.S. Public*, pg. 1589

BLACK MACHINE—Patented 2"-in-1" Frame Planters—AGCO Corporation; *U.S. Public*, pg. 28

BLACK MAGIC—Plumbing Chemical—Hercules Chemical Co., Inc.; *U.S. Private*, pg. 523

BLACK MAGIC—Blackening Products—Hubbard Hall Inc.; *U.S. Private*, pg. 544

BLACK MAGIC—Tough Glue—Miracle Adhesives; *U.S. Public*, pg. 1466

BLACK MAGIC—Chocolate Confections—Nestle-Rowntree Ltd.; *Int'l*, pg. 921

BLACK MARIA—Plug Chewing Tobaccos—Conwood Company L.P.; *U.S. Private*, pg. 272

BLACK MAX—Air Compressors—Coleman Powermate Compressors; *U.S. Private*, pg. 691

BLACK MAX—Airless Paint Spray Guns—Graco Inc.; *U.S. Public*, pg. 756

BLACK PEARL—Sporting Goods—Brunswick Bowling & Billiards Corp.; *U.S. Public*, pg. 265

BLACK RADIANCE—Cosmetics—AM Cosmetics Inc.; *U.S. Private*, pg. 6

BLACK SNOW SNOWBOARDS—Snowboards—Empire of Carolina, Inc.; *U.S. Public*, pg. 579

BLACK SWAN—Trade Paperback Books—Bertelsmann AG; *Int'l*, pg. 189

BLACK VELVET—Whiskey—Grand Metropolitan Plc; *Int'l*, pg. 408

BLACK VELVET—Canadian Whiskey—Heublein, Inc.; *Int'l*, pg. 410

BLACK VELVET—NONE—IDV Central Europe; *Int'l*, pg. 410

BLACK VELVET—NONE—Tegner & Son AB; *Int'l*, pg. 412

BLACK WATCH—Back Coated Computer Tape—3M; *U.S. Public*, pg. 1604

BLACKBIRD—Sprinklers—Rain Bird Sprinklers Manufacturing Corp.; *U.S. Private*, pg. 907

BLACKBURN—Bicycle Accessories—Bell Sports Corp.; *U.S. Public*, pg. 207

BLACKBURN—Connectors & Grounding Products—Thomas & Betts Corporation; *U.S. Public*, pg. 1597

BLACKBURN COLOR-KEYED—Electrical Connectors—Thomas & Betts Corporation; *U.S. Public*, pg. 1597

BLACKHAWK—Collision Damage Repair Systems—Hein-Werner Corporation; *U.S. Public*, pg. 805

BLACKHAWK—Single-Action Revolvers—Sturm, Ruger & Co., Inc.; *U.S. Public*, pg. 1526

BLACKHAWK LODGE—Restaurant—The Levy Organization; *U.S. Private*, pg. 664

BLACKJACK—Tongue Jacks—Dutton-Lainson Co.; *U.S. Private*, pg. 350

BLACKLINE—Reinforcing Mesh—Smorgon A.R.C.; *Int'l*, pg. 1269

BLACKOUT—Plumbing Chemical—Hercules Chemical Co., Inc.; *U.S. Private*, pg. 523

THE BLACKSTONE GROUP—Blackstone Financial Services—The Blackstone Group; *U.S. Private*, pg. 147

BLACKTOP—Athletic Shoes—Reebok International Ltd.; *U.S. Public*, pg. 1369

BLACKTRON—Children's Building Sets—LEGO Systems, Inc.; *Int'l*, pg. 805

BLADE—Small Maintenance Motor Grader—Athey Products Corporation; *U.S. Public*, pg. 142

THE BLADE—Newspaper—Blade Communications, Inc.; *U.S. Private*, pg. 147

BLADE PRO—Construction Laser Equip.—Spectra-Physics Laserplane Inc.; *U.S. Public*, pg. 1594

BLADE RUNNER—Roller Skates—Rollerblade, Inc.; *U.S. Private*, pg. 941

BLADE SAVER II—Loader Bucket Lip System—GH Hensley Industries, Inc.; *U.S. Private*, pg. 439

THE BLADE—Daily Newspaper—Toledo Blade Co.; *U.S. Private*, pg. 147

BLADEGEAR—Roller Skating Apparel & Accessories—Rollerblade, Inc.; *U.S. Private*, pg. 941

BLADES—Single-Edge & Safety Point Utility Knife Blades—Pacific Handy Cutter, Inc.; *U.S. Private*, pg. 831

BLAIR—Mail Order Services/Men's & Women's Apparel—Blair Corporation; *U.S. Public*, pg. 236

BLAIR—Cosmetics, Toiletries, Household Products & Giftware—Home Showcase Products; *U.S. Private*, pg. 1101

BLAIR—Professional Art Finishes, Fixatives & Adhesives—Loctite Corp. North American Group; *U.S. Public*, pg. 611

BLAIR BOUTIQUE—Women's Apparel—Blair Corporation; *U.S. Public*, pg. 236

BLAIR PLUS—Soil & Stain Repellent Finish—Blair Corporation; *U.S. Public*, pg. 236

BLAIR PRESS—Wash & Wear Finish for Men's & Women's Slacks—Blair Corporation; *U.S. Public*, pg. 236

BLAIR SHOPPE—Retail Home Furnishings Store Services—Blair Corporation; *U.S. Public*, pg. 236

BLAIR SHOPPER—Mail Order Services/Men's & Women's Apparel—Blair Corporation; *U.S. Public*, pg. 236

BLAIRGUARD—Water & Stain Repellent Finish for Outerwear—Blair Corporation; *U.S. Public*, pg. 236

BLAK-RAY—Long Wave Lamps—UVP, Inc.; *U.S. Private*, pg. 1115

BLAKE & MANLEY—NONE—Kellwood Company; *U.S. Public*, pg. 948

BLANC DE BOEUF—Frying Fat—Vandemoortele N.V.; *Int'l*, pg. 1451

BLANC DE FRUIT—Fruit Sparkling Wine—Groupe Pernod Ricard; *Int'l*, pg. 566

BLANCHARD—Metal Parts—Cone-Blanchard Machine Company; *U.S. Private*, pg. 262

BLANCHE—Lingerie—Warnaco Inc.; *U.S. Public*, pg. 1738

BLANKA—Laundry Additive—Benckiser Consumer Products Inc.; *Int'l*, pg. 185

BLANKE BAER—Ice Cream Flavoring—Universal Flavors-U.S.A.; *U.S. Public*, pg. 1696

BLANKET WITH A BRAIN—Electric Blankets—Sunbeam Corporation; *U.S. Public*, pg. 1533

BLANKETROL—Hyper/Hypothermia Equipment—Cincinnati Sub-Zero Products, Inc.; *U.S. Private*, pg. 240

BLANSAC BRANDY—NONE—Star Industries Inc.; *U.S. Private*, pg. 1034

BLASTCON—NONE—Berg Electronics; *U.S. Public*, pg. 212

BLATZ—Paint—Progress Paint Mfg. Co.; *U.S. Private*, pg. 890

BLATZ—NONE—The Stroh Brewery Company; *U.S. Private*, pg. 1047

BLAUCPAM—NONE—SMH Swiss Corporation for Micro Electronics & Watchmaking Indus. Ltd.; *Int'l*, pg. 1160

BLAUE QUELLEN—Mineral Water—Nestle S.A.; *Int'l*, pg. 915

BLAUER—Mens & Womens Uniform Outerwear—Blauer Manufacturing Co., Inc.; *U.S. Private*, pg. 149

BLAUNE—Hair-Coloring Rinse—Kao Corporation; *Int'l*, pg. 717

BLAUPUNKT—Car Radios—Robert Bosch Corporation; *Int'l*, pg. 204

BLAUPUNKT—Car Radios, Entertainment Electronics—Robert Bosch GmbH; *Int'l*, pg. 203

BLAW-KNOX—NONE—Blaw-Knox Construction Equipment Corporation; *U.S. Public*, pg. 877

BLAW-KONTROL—NONE—Blaw-Knox Construction Equipment Corporation; *U.S. Public*, pg. 877

BLAZE ORANGE—Fluorescent Color—Day-Glo Color Corp.; *U.S. Public*, pg. 1357

BLAZER—Crop Protection Agent—BASF AG; *Int'l*, pg. 103

BLAZER—Sport Utility—Chevrolet Motor Div. General Motors Corp.; *U.S. Public*, pg. 720

BLAZER—Truck—General Motors Corporation; *U.S. Public*, pg. 718

BLAZER—Financial Services—Great Western Consumer Finance Group; *U.S. Public*, pg. 1741

BLAZING HEARTH GRILL—NONE—Bonanza Restaurants; *U.S. Private*, pg. 736

BLECHE-WITE—White Wall Tire Cleaner—Blue Coral/Slick 50; *U.S. Public*, pg. 1348

BLEDINA—Baby Food—Danone Group; *Int'l*, pg. 379

BLEND ELEVEN—Pipe Tobacco—Lane Limited; *Int'l*, pg. 1129

BLENDED BOND—Economy Grade Single Part Stock Computer Paper—Shade/Allied, Inc.; *U.S. Public*, pg. 89

BLENDERM—Surgical Tape, Waterproof—3M; *U.S. Public*, pg. 1604

BLENDOR—Food Mixers—Dynamics Corporation of America; *U.S. Public*, pg. 286

BLENDSTICK—Touch Up Stick—DAP Inc.; *Int'l*, pg. 1486

BLENDTONE—Fine Printing Paper—Westvaco Corporation; *U.S. Public*, pg. 1762

BLENDTROL—Blending Systems—The Foxboro Company; *Int'l*, pg. 1243

BLENDY—Coffee Drink—Calpis Food Industry Co. Ltd.; *Int'l*, pg. 252

BLENDZ-ALL—Thinner—Grow Group, Inc.; *Int'l*, pg. 663

BLENDZ ALL—Thinner—ICI Paints; *Int'l*, pg. 664

BLENND—Beverage Concentrates—Byrnes & Kiefer Company; *U.S. Private*, pg. 191

BLENOXANE—Anti-Cancer Agent—Bristol-Myers Squibb Company; *U.S. Public*, pg. 253

BLENOXANE—Cytotoxic Antibiotic for Testicular Carcinoma, Lymphomas—Bristol-Myers Squibb U.S. Pharmaceutical Group; *U.S. Public*, pg. 255

BLENSIL—Heat Curable Silicone Rubber Compositions—General Electric Canada Inc.; *U.S. Public*, pg. 713

BLEO-S OINTMENT—Antineoplastic Agents—Nippon Kayaku Co. Ltd.; *Int'l*, pg. 934

BLEOMYCIN—Antineoplastic Agents—Nippon Kayaku Co. Ltd.; *Int'l*, pg. 934

BLEPH 10—Sterile Ophthalmic Solution—Allergan, Inc.; *U.S. Public*, pg. 46

BLEPHAMIDE—Sterile Ophthalmic Solution—Allergan, Inc.; *U.S. Public*, pg. 46

BLESIUS—Wine—Pacific Wine Co.; *U.S. Private*, pg. 843

BLEVINS POPCORN—Popcorn—Nalleys Fine Foods; *U.S. Private*, pg. 887

BLIND JUSTICE—Leisure Game—Monarch Avalon, Inc.; *U.S. Public*, pg. 1123

BLINK—Cleaning Device—U.S. Surgical Corp.; *U.S. Public*, pg. 1687

BLIS-TO-SOL—Foot Products—Chattem, Inc., Consumer Products Division; *U.S. Public*, pg. 341

BLISS—Yogurt Drink—Nestle S.A.; *Int'l*, pg. 915

BLISS-PRESSES—NONE—Clearing-Niagara; *U.S. Private*, pg. 196

BLISS-SALEM—Rolling Mill Machinery & Equipment;Plant Modernization & Machining Services—Bliss-Salem, Inc.; *U.S. Private*, pg. 149

BLISTERFILM—Dressings—American Home Products Corporation; *U.S. Public*, pg. 79

BLISTEX—Lip Medication—Blistex, Inc.; *U.S. Private*, pg. 149

BLISTIK—Lip Balm—Blistex, Inc.; *U.S. Private*, pg. 149

BLITZ—Surgical Instrument Cleaner & Lubricant—3M; *U.S. Public*, pg. 1604

BLITZKRIEG—War Game—Monarch Avalon, Inc.; *U.S. Public*, pg. 1123

BLIZ-WHIZ—Sno-Kone Machine—Gold Medal Products Co.; *U.S. Private*, pg. 459

BLIZZARD—Treat—American Dairy Queen Corporation; *U.S. Public*, pg. 220

BLIZZARD—Trucks & Buses—Toyota Motor Corporation; *Int'l*, pg. 1411

BLIZZARD FLAVOR TREAT—Soft Serve Ice Milk Combined with Toppings—International Dairy Queen, Inc.; *U.S. Public*, pg. 220

BLIZZARD'S HOLIDAY JAMBOREE—NONE—Broderbund Software, Inc.; *U.S. Public*, pg. 258

BLO—Butyrolactone—International Specialty Products, Inc.; *U.S. Public*, pg. 858

BLOC—Herbicide—The Dow Chemical Company; *U.S. Public*, pg. 522

BLOC-IT—Heat Absorbing Paste—La-Co Industries Markal Company; *U.S. Private*, pg. 640

BLOCADREN—Timolol Maleate—Merck & Co., Inc.; *U.S. Public*, pg. 1090

BLOCK—Plumbing Chemical—Hercules Chemical Co., Inc.; *U.S. Private*, pg. 523

BLOCK ENSEMBLE—Block-Based Routing—Cadence Design Systems, Inc.; *U.S. Public*, pg. 290

BLOCK ISLAND—NONE—Kellwood Company; *U.S. Public*, pg. 948

BLOCK-OUT—Primers—Bruning Paint Company; *U.S. Public*, pg. 176

BLOCK PREMIUM—Tax Preparation Service—H & R Block, Inc.; *U.S. Public*, pg. 770

BLOCKADE—Methyl Cellulose—The Dow Chemical Company; *U.S. Public*, pg. 522

BLOCKAID—Paint—ICI Paints; *Int'l*, pg. 664

BLOCKBUSTER—Power Tools—The Black & Decker Corporation; *U.S. Public*, pg. 233

BLOCKBUSTER VIDEO—Video Rental Retail Superstores—Blockbuster Entertainment Group; *U.S. Private*, pg. 775

BLOCKBUSTER VIDEO—Franchise Video Stores—Pueblo Xtra International, Inc.; *U.S. Private*, pg. 894

BLOCKCHECK—NONE—H & R Block, Inc.; *U.S. Public*, pg. 770

BLOCKHEAD—Game—Pressman Toy Corp.; *U.S. Private*, pg. 882

BLOCWELD—Plywood or Other Laminated Material—Georgia-Pacific Corporation; *U.S. Public*, pg. 735

BLODGETT—Baking & Roasting Ovens—The Blodgett Oven Co., Inc.; *U.S. Public*, pg. 1064

BLOMMER—Chocolate—Blommer Chocolate Co.; *U.S. Private*, pg. 150

BLONDO GEL—Hairdressing Product—Wella Group; *Int'l*, pg. 1489

BLOO—Toilet Bowl Cleaner—Sara Lee Corporation; *U.S. Public*, pg. 1432

BLOOD GROUPING REAGENTS—Grouping Reagents—Ortho Clinical Diagnostic Systems Inc.; *U.S. Public*, pg. 929

BLOODHOUND—Plug Tobacco—Brown & Williamson Tobacco Corp.; *Int'l*, pg. 111

BLOOM—Insecticide—Sara Lee Corporation; *U.S. Public*, pg. 1432

BLOOM'N BUDDIES—Greeting Cards—American Greetings Corporation; *U.S. Public*, pg. 77

BLOOMINGDALE"S—Department Stores—Bloomingdale's; *U.S. Public*, pg. 617

BLOOMINGDALE'S—Department Store—Federated Department Stores, Inc.; *U.S. Public*, pg. 617

BLOOMSBURG CRAFTSMEN—Printing—Haddon Craftsmen, Inc.; *U.S. Public*, pg. 518

BLOSSOM—Ceramic Wall Tile—Monarch Tile, Inc.; *U.S. Private*, pg. 287

BLOSSOM BRAND—Retail—Fairmont Snack Group, Inc.; *U.S. Private*, pg. 392

BLOSSOM HILL—Wines—Grand Metropolitan Plc; *Int'l*, pg. 408

BLOSSOM HILL—Wine—Heublein, Inc.; *Int'l*, pg. 410

BLOSSOM HILL—NONE—Tegner & Son AB; *Int'l*, pg. 412

BLOT-O—Industrial Chemical—Hercules Chemical Co., Inc.; *U.S. Private*, pg. 523

BLOWAVE—Permanent Wave—Revlon-Realistic Professional Products, Inc.; *U.S. Private*, pg. 690

BLOXFIL—Block Filler—Devoe Paint; *Int'l*, pg. 663

BLOXFIL—Block Filler—ICI Paints; *Int'l*, pg. 664

BLOXIDE—De-Oxidizing Weldable Primer—Tempil Inc.; *U.S. Private*, pg. 90

BLU BOTOL NATURAL WATERS—Spring & Sparkling Waters—Global Beverage Co.; *U.S. Private*, pg. 457

BLU-MOL—Hardware Products—Rule Industries, Inc.; *U.S. Public*, pg. 950

BLU-RAY—Whiteprinting Equipment, Oil Well Logger, X-Ray Duplicator—Blu-Ray; *U.S. Private*, pg. 142

BLU RIVR—Combustion Engine Heat Exchanger—Reinke Manufacturing Co., Inc.; *U.S. Private*, pg. 920

BLU TACK—NONE—Bostik Ltd.; *Int'l*, pg. 1409

BLU-WATER—Toilet Cleaner—Willert Home Products, Inc.; *U.S. Private*, pg. 1177

BLUBLOCKER—Sunglasses—JS&A Group, Inc.; *U.S. Public*, pg. 578

BLUE AIR—NONE—Merloni Elettrodomestici S.P.A.; *Int'l*, pg. 860

BLUE ANCHOR—NONE—Blue Anchor, Inc.; *U.S. Private*, pg. 150

BLUE BELL CREAMERY—Ice Cream, Frozen Snacks, Frozen Yogurt—Blue Bell Creameries, L.P.; *U.S. Private*, pg. 150

BLUE BIRD—Buses—Blue Bird Corporation; *U.S. Private*, pg. 151

BLUE BOAR HAM—Imported Hungarian Ham—Atalanta Corporation; *U.S. Private*, pg. 93

BLUE BONNET—Margarine—Nabisco Inc.; *U.S. Public*, pg. 1355

BLUE BONNET—Margarine—RJR Nabisco Holdings Corp.; *U.S. Public*, pg. 1354

BLUE BOOK—NONE—First DataBank; *U.S. Private*, pg. 515

BLUE BRAND—X-Ray Film—Eastman Kodak Company; *U.S. Public*, pg. 550

BLUE BRUTE—Pipes—James Hardie Industries Ltd.; *Int'l*, pg. 596

Brand Name Index

BLUE CHIP—AC Motors—Marathon Electric Manufacturing Corp.; *U.S. Public*, pg. 1371

BLUE CHIP—Fishing Rods and Reels—Martin Reels, A Division of Zebco; *U.S. Public*, pg. 265

BLUE CHIP STAMPS—Trading Stamps & Motivation Programs—Blue Chip Stamps; *U.S. Public*, pg. 217

BLUE CIRCLE—Cement & Aggregates—Blue Circle Industries PLC; *Int'l*, pg. 197

BLUE COLOR FILTER—Filter Cartridges—Donaldson Company, Inc.; *U.S. Public*, pg. 517

BLUE CORAL—Car Wax—Blue Coral/Slick 50; *U.S. Public*, pg. 1348

BLUE CROSS—Pressure Sensitive Tape—American Biltrite Inc.; *U.S. Public*, pg. 68

BLUE CROSS—Paper Towels—Georgia-Pacific Corporation; *U.S. Public*, pg. 735

BLUE CROSS AND BLUE SHIELD—Association—Blue Cross and Blue Shield Association; *U.S. Private*, pg. 151

BLUE CROSS OF CALIFORNIA—Health Care Plans—Blue Cross of California; *U.S. Private*, pg. 152

BLUE CROSS OF WESTERN PENNSLYVANIA—Health Care Coverage—Highmark Inc.; *U.S. Private*, pg. 528

BLUE DIAMOND BRAND—Almonds, Macadamias, Hazelnuts, Pistachios, Butter—Blue Diamond Growers; *U.S. Private*, pg. 152

BLUE GRASS—NONE—Blue Grass Quality Meats; *U.S. Private*, pg. 152

BLUE GRASS—Fragrance—Elizabeth Arden Company; *Int'l*, pg. 1435

BLUE/GREEN SHAMPOO—Shampoo—Clairol, Inc.; *U.S. Public*, pg. 254

BLUE HORSE—Pencil Tablets—The Mead Corporation; *U.S. Public*, pg. 1074

BLUE ICE—Refreezables Ice Packs—Rubbermaid Incorporated; *U.S. Public*, pg. 1411

BLUE LABEL—Floor Tile—American Biltrite Inc.; *U.S. Public*, pg. 68

BLUE LASER SHOULDER PAD—Athletic Equipment—Bike Athletic Co.; *U.S. Private*, pg. 143

BLUE LINE—Accommodative Orthotics to Protect Foot Structures—The Langer Biomechanics Group, Inc.; *U.S. Public*, pg. 978

BLUE MAX—Garage Door Opener—The Genie Company; *U.S. Private*, pg. 823

BLUE MAX—Electrode—The Lincoln Electric Company; *U.S. Public*, pg. 996

BLUE MAX—Right Angle Speed Reducer Product Line—Regal-Beloit Corporation; *U.S. Public*, pg. 1370

BLUE MESA—Apparel—Fred Meyer Stores; *U.S. Public*, pg. 1103

BLUE MIKE—Capacitors—Aerovox Inc.; *U.S. Public*, pg. 25

BLUE MOON ABBEY ALE—Micro Brew Specialty Beer—Adolph Coors Company; *U.S. Public*, pg. 445

BLUE MOON BELGIAN WHITE ALE—Micro Brew Specialty Beer—Adolph Coors Company; *U.S. Public*, pg. 445

BLUE MOON HARVEST PUMPKIN ALE—Seasonal Micro Brew Specialty Beer—Adolph Coors Company; *U.S. Public*, pg. 445

BLUE MOON HONEY BLONDE ALE—Micro Brew Specialty Beer—Adolph Coors Company; *U.S. Public*, pg. 445

BLUE MOON RASPBERRY CREAM ALE—Micro Brew Specialty Beer—Adolph Coors Company; *U.S. Public*, pg. 445

BLUE MOSS—NONE—Moss Bros Group PLC; *Int'l*, pg. 895

BLUE MOUNTAIN—Dog & Cat Food—Alpo Pet Foods, Inc.; *Int'l*, pg. 917

BLUE MOUNTAIN—Twine & Cordage—Barbour Thread, Inc.; *Int'l*, pg. 618

BLUE MOUNTAIN—NONE—The Pillsbury Company; *Int'l*, pg. 411

BLUE NOTE—Records—Capitol Records, Inc.; *Int'l*, pg. 428

BLUE NOTE—Record Label—EMI Group plc; *Int'l*, pg. 426

BLUE NUN—Wine—Schieffelin & Somerset Co.; *Int'l*, pg. 412

BLUE OX—Towing Products—Automatic Equipment Mfg. Co.; *U.S. Private*, pg. 101

BLUE OX—Wheel Tractor—FWD/Seagrave Fire Apparatus, Inc.; *U.S. Private*, pg. 390

BLUE PLATE—Mayonnaise & Cooking Oil—Reily Foods Company; *U.S. Private*, pg. 919

BLUE PLATE PEANUT BUTTER—Peanut Butter—Reily Foods Company; *U.S. Private*, pg. 919

BLUE POLY—Polymer Sealant—Blue Coral/Slick 50; *U.S. Public*, pg. 1348

BLUE RAZZ-BERRY—Candy—Charms Company; *U.S. Public*, pg. 1621

BLUE RIBBON—Rice—American Rice Inc.; *U.S. Public*, pg. 591

BLUE RIBBON—Tires—Bridgestone/Firestone, Inc.; *Int'l*, pg. 213

BLUE RIBBON—Chick Boxes—Inland Container Corporation; *U.S. Public*, pg. 1575

BLUE RIBBON—Ammonia, Bleach & Liquid Starch, Dish & Heavy Duty Laundry Detergent—Patterson Laboratories, Inc.; *U.S. Private*, pg. 843

BLUE RIBBON—French Fries—J.R. Simplot Company; *U.S. Private*, pg. 1002

BLUE RIBBON—Figs—Sun Diamond Growers of California; *U.S. Private*, pg. 1051

BLUE RIBBON IV—Tires—Bridgestone/Firestone, Inc.; *Int'l*, pg. 213

BLUE RIBBONS—Cartridges—Aspen Imaging International, Inc.; *U.S. Public*, pg. 1339

BLUE RIDGE BEADED—NONE—Amerimark Inc.; *U.S. Public*, pg. 1237

BLUE RIM—Abrasive Discs—Gardner Abrasives; *U.S. Public*, pg. 1699

BLUE-RIM—Abrasive Tools, Wheels & Discs—Litton Industries, Inc.; *U.S. Public*, pg. 1002

BLUE ROCK—Clay Targets—Remington Arms Company, Inc.; *U.S. Private*, pg. 921

BLUE SEAL—Tooling Board—Hexcel Corporation; *U.S. Public*, pg. 824

BLUE SEAL FEEDS—Animal Feed—Blue Seal Feeds, Inc.; *U.S. Private*, pg. 1134

BLUE SHIELD—Name & Emblem—Blue Shield of California; *U.S. Private*, pg. 153

BLUE SPOT—Plumbing Repair Parts—J.A. Sexauer, Inc.; *U.S. Private*, pg. 352

BLUE STAR—Prepared Frozen Foods—ConAgra Frozen Food Company; *U.S. Public*, pg. 427

BLUE STAR—Prepared Frozen Foods—ConAgra Frozen Foods; *U.S. Public*, pg. 427

BLUE STONE—Apparell—The Generra Company; *U.S. Private*, pg. 446

BLUE STREAK—Auto Products—Standard Motor Products Inc.; *U.S. Public*, pg. 1503

BLUE STREAK LABEL—Automotive Replacement Parts—Standard Motor Products Inc.; *U.S. Public*, pg. 1503

BLUE STRIPE—Abrasive Disc—Gardner Abrasives; *U.S. Public*, pg. 1699

BLUE-STRIPE—Abrasive Tools—Litton Industries, Inc.; *U.S. Public*, pg. 1002

BLUE SURF—Seafoods—Clearwater Fine Foods Inc.; *Int'l*, pg. 297

BLUE TEE—Water Well Rigs—Blue Tee Corporation; *U.S. Private*, pg. 153

BLUE TOO—Solid Automatic Bowl Cleaner—Blue Cross Laboratories; *U.S. Private*, pg. 155

BLUE TRANQUILITY—Bath Oil, Dusting Powder, Soap—Avon Products, Inc.; *U.S. Public*, pg. 155

BLUE WATER—Binoculars—E & B Marine Incorporated; *U.S. Public*, pg. 1756

BLUE WATER—Binoculars—Goldbergs Marine Distributors; *U.S. Public*, pg. 1756

BLUE WOODS—Air Freshener—Avon Products, Inc.; *U.S. Public*, pg. 155

BLUEBERRY GUM—Stick Gum—Lotte U.S.A., Inc.; *Int'l*, pg. 819

BLUEBERRY SQUARES—Blueberry-Filled Whole Wheat Biscuits—Kellogg Company; *U.S. Public*, pg. 947

BLUEBIRD—Fruit Juices And Drinks—Citrus World Inc.; *U.S. Private*, pg. 241

BLUEBIRD—Snack Cakes—Flowers Industries, Inc.; *U.S. Public*, pg. 656

BLUEBIRD—Snack Foods—Goodman Fielder Limited; *Int'l*, pg. 555

BLUEBIRD—Car—Nissan Motor Co., Ltd.; *Int'l*, pg. 943

BLUEBOARD—Plastic Foam Insulation—The Dow Chemical Company; *U.S. Public*, pg. 522

BLUEBOARD DIGEST—Newsletter—The Dow Chemical Company; *U.S. Public*, pg. 522

BLUEMAX—Disposable Sensors—Burdick, Inc.; *U.S. Private*, pg. 181

BLUEPRINT FOR SUCCESS—Broker's Business Plan—ERA Real Estate; *U.S. Public*, pg. 321

BLUESHIELD—Shielding Gas for Welding—Air Liquide America Corporation; *Int'l*, pg. 37

BLUEWATER—Yachts—Bluewater; *U.S. Private*, pg. 153

BLUEWATER—Fillets, Fish Sticks & Portions—Frionor U.S.A. Inc.; *U.S. Public*, pg. 516

BLUGARD—Cow Udder Treatment—Ecolab Inc.; *U.S. Public*, pg. 562

BLUGENE—NONE—Life Technologies, Inc.; *U.S. Public*, pg. 504

BLUNTGRIP—Anchoring Device—U.S. Surgical Corp.; *U.S. Public*, pg. 1687

BLUNTPORT—Laparoscopic Instruments—U.S. Surgical Corp.; *U.S. Public*, pg. 1687

BOAMAT—Actuated Valves—KSB Aktiengesellschaft; *Int'l*, pg. 721

BOARD RIDERS—Skiing Boats—International Seaway Trading Corporation; *U.S. Private*, pg. 572

BOARDEX—Board Cover—Dietzgen Corporation; *U.S. Private*, pg. 332

BOARDQUEST—High-Speed System Design Planning—Cadence Design Systems, Inc.; *U.S. Public*, pg. 290

BOARDWATCH—Electronic Component—Teradyne, Inc.; *U.S. Public*, pg. 1580

BOARIO—Mineral Water—Danone Group; *Int'l*, pg. 379

BOAT ANGLER—Fishing Magazine—EMAP Pursuit Publishing; *Int'l*, pg. 451

BOAT REIN—Boat Equipment—Attwood Corporation; *U.S. Private*, pg. 1038

BOAT-SUNS—Shoes—E.J. Footwear Corp.; *U.S. Public*, pg. 1684

BOATING—Boating Magazine—Hachette Filipacchi Magazines Inc.; *Int'l*, pg. 794

BOATWORKS—Sports Outerwear—Fox-Knapp; *U.S. Private*, pg. 860

BOAX—Butterfly Valves—KSB Aktiengesellschaft; *Int'l*, pg. 721

BOAXMAT—Actuated Valves—KSB Aktiengesellschaft; *Int'l*, pg. 721

BOB EVANS BURRITOS—Sausage Burritos & Ham Burritos—Bob Evans Farms, Inc. Sausage Division; *U.S. Public*, pg. 596

BOB EVANS FARM SAUSAGE—Sausage & Other Products—Bob Evans Farms, Inc. Restaurant Division; *U.S. Public*, pg. 596

BOB EVANS FARMS RESTAURANTS—Family Restaurants—Bob Evans Farms, Inc.; *U.S. Public*, pg. 596

BOB EVANS FARMS SAUSAGE—Sausage Products: Microwave Biscuit Sandwich, Burritos—Bob Evans Farms, Inc.; *U.S. Public*, pg. 596

BOB EVANS FOOD SERVICE—Food Service—Bob Evans Farms, Inc. Restaurant Division; *U.S. Public*, pg. 596

BOB EVANS GENERAL STORE & RESTAURANT—Restaurant With In-House Bakery & Gift Shop—Bob Evans Farms, Inc.; *U.S. Public*, pg. 596

BOB EVANS HARVEST SALADS—Refrigerated Deli Products—Bob Evans Farms, Inc. Restaurant Division; *U.S. Public*, pg. 596

BOB EVANS RESTAURANT & GENERAL STORE—Restaurant with In-Store Bakery & Gift Shop—Bob Evans Farms, Inc. Restaurant Division; *U.S. Public*, pg. 596

BOB EVANS RESTAURANTS—Family Restaurants—Bob Evans Farms, Inc. Restaurant Division; *U.S. Public*, pg. 596

BOB OSTROW—Meat Products—John Morrell & Co.; *U.S. Public*, pg. 1479

BOB ROSS—Publications & Art Equipment—Martin/F. Weber Company; *U.S. Private*, pg. 710

BOB TIMBONLAKE COLLECTION—NONE—Crown Crafts, Inc.; *U.S. Public*, pg. 465

BOBBI—Home Permanent—The Gillette Company; *U.S. Public*, pg. 743

BOBBI BROWN ESSENTIALS—NONE—Estee Lauder Companies Inc.; *U.S. Public*, pg. 594

BOBBIE BROOKS—Women's Clothing—Garan, Incorporated; *U.S. Public*, pg. 703

BOBBIE BROOKS—Women's Apparel—Pubco Corporation; *U.S. Public*, pg. 1339

BOBBY JONES—NONE—Callaway Golf Company; *U.S. Public*, pg. 294

BOBBY JONES—Men's Apparel—Hartmarx Corporation; *U.S. Public*, pg. 795

BOBCAT—Small Front End Loader, Trenchers, Excavators—Melroe Company; *U.S. Public*, pg. 877

BOB-CAT—Commercial Turf Machinery—Ransomes Plc; *Int'l*, pg. 1087

BOBCAT—Binocular—Swift Instruments, Inc.; *U.S. Private*, pg. 1058

BOBOLI—Bread Shells & Pizza Sauce—Bestfoods; *U.S. Public*, pg. 223

BOBOLI—Pizza Crusts—CPC Baking Business; *U.S. Public*, pg. 224

BOB'S BIG BOY—Restaurants—Marriott International, Inc.; *U.S. Public*, pg. 1047

BOBST—Printing & Converting Equipment—Bobst Group Inc.; *Int'l*, pg. 198

BOBST—Packages & Printing Machines—Bobst S.A.; *Int'l*, pg. 198

BOBST-CHAMPLAIN—Packages & Printing Machines—Bobst S.A.; *Int'l*, pg. 198

BOBST-REGISTRON—Electronic Control System—Bobst S.A.; *Int'l*, pg. 198

BOCADOR—Rum & Coladas—Charles Jacquin et Cie, Inc.; *U.S. Private*, pg. 580

BODDINGTONS—Pub Ale Draught—Labatt U.S.A.; *Int'l*, pg. 679

BODDINGTON'S—Ale—Whitbread PLC; *Int'l*, pg. 1498

BODEGAS PALACIO—Riona Wines—Canandaigua Wine Co.; *U.S. Public*, pg. 300

BODINE—Motors, Gear Motors & Motor Controls—Bodine Electric Company; *U.S. Private*, pg. 154

BODY & BOUNCE—Shampoo—Wella Group; *Int'l*, pg. 1489

BODY BASICS—Hand Massager—Pollenex; *U.S. Public*, pg. 1391

BODY BREAKTHROUGH—Activity Plan—Nutri/System Inc.; *U.S. Private*, pg. 859

BODY BUDDIES—Cereal—General Mills, Inc.; *U.S. Public*, pg. 717

BODY BUILDER—Hair-Styling Brush—Clairol, Inc.; *U.S. Public*, pg. 254

BODY BUILDERS—Hairstyling Brushes—Bristol-Myers Squibb Company; *U.S. Public*, pg. 253

BODY BULLETIN—Newsletter—Rodale Press, Inc.; *U.S. Private*, pg. 939

BODY CARE—Mattress & Box Spring Sets—Kingsdown, Inc.; *U.S. Private*, pg. 622

BODY CHAIR II—Office Seating—GF Office Furniture; *U.S. Private*, pg. 435

BODY COMFORT—Mattress & Box Spring Sets—Kingsdown, Inc.; *U.S. Private*, pg. 622

BODY DRAMA—Women's Sleepwear—Body Drama, Inc.; *U.S. Public*, pg. 1182

BODY DRAMA—Women's Sleepwear—Niches, Inc.; *U.S. Public*, pg. 1181

BODY ESSENCE—Gel & Moisturizer—Stanhome Inc.; *U.S. Public*, pg. 1508

BODY FASHIONS/INTIMATE APPAREL—Trade Periodical—Advantar Communications; *U.S. Private*, pg. 22

BODY FLOWERS—Body Spray—The Gillette Company; *U.S. Public*, pg. 743

BODY LANGUAGE—Body Massage System—Clairol, Inc.; *U.S. Public*, pg. 254

BODY LANGUAGE—NONE—Playtex Apparel, Inc.; *U.S. Public*, pg. 1433

BODY LIGHT—Body Filler—Marson/Creative Fastener, Inc.; *U.S. Private*, pg. 708

BODY LOUNGER—Home Health Care Chair—Pride Health Care, Inc.; *U.S. Private*, pg. 883

BODY MIST—Talcum Powder & Deodorant—SmithKline Beecham plc; *Int'l*, pg. 1264

BODY MOVES—Women's Apparel—Jacques Moret, Inc.; *U.S. Public*, pg. 580

BODY ON TAP—Shampoo—Bristol-Myers Squibb Company; *U.S. Public*, pg. 253

BODY PERFECT—Mattress & Box Spring Sets—Kingsdown, Inc.; *U.S. Private*, pg. 622

BODY POSTURE—Mattress & Box Spring Sets—Kingsdown, Inc.; *U.S. Private*, pg. 622

THE BODY SHOE—Walking Shoes—Wolverine World Wide, Inc.; *U.S. Public*, pg. 1775

THE BODY SHOP—Naturally-Based Toiletries—The Body Shop; *Int'l*, pg. 199

BODY SYSTEM—Mattress & Box Springd—Kingsdown, Inc.; *U.S. Private*, pg. 622

BODY TEASE—Intimate Apparel—Body Drama, Inc.; *U.S. Public*, pg. 1182

BODY-TITE—Body Hardware—R&B, Inc.; *U.S. Public*, pg. 1354

BODYFLEX—Athletic Apparel—Bike Athletic Co.; *U.S. Private*, pg. 143

BODYGARD—Pickup Truck Bedliners—Durakon Industries, Inc.; *U.S. Public*, pg. 537

BODYGUARD—Plumbing Products—The Black & Decker Corporation; *U.S. Public*, pg. 233

BODYGUARD—Car Covers—Marson/Creative Fastener, Inc.; *U.S. Private*, pg. 708

BODYSATIN N' LACE—Bras, Panties—Olga Div.; *U.S. Public*, pg. 1738

BODYSATIN STRETCH—Bras, Panties, Shapewear—Olga Div.; *U.S. Public*, pg. 1738

BODYSEARCH I—Security X-Ray System—American Science & Engineering, Inc.; *U.S. Public*, pg. 90

BODYSILK—Bras, Shapewear, Sleepwear, Panties, Daywear—Olga Div.; *U.S. Public*, pg. 1738

BODYSILK REFLECTIONS—Bras, Panties—Olga Div.; *U.S. Public*, pg. 1738

BODYWALK—Athletic Shoes—Reebok International Ltd.; *U.S. Public*, pg. 1369

BOEING—Helicopter—Boeing Helicopters; *U.S. Public*, pg. 241

THE BOEING COLLECTION BY CARRERA—Sunglasses—Optimaxx International; *U.S. Private*, pg. 818

BOFUR—Children's Books—Scholastic Inc.; *U.S. Public*, pg. 1440

BOG—NONE—Tandy Brands Accessories, Inc.; *U.S. Public*, pg. 1560

BOGE SHOCKS—Shocks—Sachs Boge of America; *Int'l*, pg. 835

BOGNER—Frangrance—Lancaster Group Worldwide; *Int'l*, pg. 185

BOH—Beer—Falstaff Brewing Corporation; *U.S. Private*, pg. 955

BOHEMIA—Beer—Labatt U.S.A.; *Int'l*, pg. 679

BOHEMIA BEER—Beer—Wisdom Imports Sales Co. Inc.; *Int'l*, pg. 679

BOHEMIAN CLUB—Beer—Joseph Huber Brewing Co., Inc.; *U.S. Private*, pg. 545

BOHEMIAN HEARTH—Variety Bread—Stroehmann Bakeries, L.C.; *Int'l*, pg. 1495

BOHEMIAN HEARTH—Baked Goods—George Weston Limited; *Int'l*, pg. 1494

BOHN—Condensing Units—EEI Corporation; *Int'l*, pg. 425

BOHN—Refrigeration Products—Heatcraft, Inc.-Refrigeration Products Division; *U.S. Private*, pg. 659

BOILEEZERS—Granules—Fisher Scientific Company; *U.S. Private*, pg. 658

BOISANGE—Cheese—BG SAS; *Int'l*, pg. 201

BOISE CASCADE—Linerboard & Corrugating Medium, All Made of Paper—Boise Cascade Corporation; *U.S. Public*, pg. 242

BOISE CASCADE SUPER SHELF—Shelving with Rounded Edge—Boise Cascade Corporation; *U.S. Public*, pg. 242

BOISE CASCADE SUPER STEP—Stair Tread—Boise Cascade Corporation; *U.S. Public*, pg. 242

BOJANGLES—Fast Food Restaurants—Bojangles' Restaraunts, Inc.; *U.S. Private*, pg. 154

BOKAR—Coffee—The Great Atlantic & Pacific Tea Company, Inc.; *Int'l*, pg. 1375

BOKAY—Flower Boxes & Brackets, Plant Tubs, Seed Flats, Window Trays, Floor Trays—Molded Fiber Glass Companies; *U.S. Private*, pg. 755

BOKS—Casual Shoes—Reebok International Ltd.; *U.S. Public*, pg. 1369

BOKU—Boxed Citrus Drinks—McCain Citrus Inc.; *Int'l*, pg. 850

BOLAN—Pastry Ingredients—Royal Gist-Brocades N.V.; *Int'l*, pg. 1142

BOLANDS—Biscuits—Irish Biscuits; *Int'l*, pg. 688

BOLD—Laundry Products—The Procter & Gamble Company; *U.S. Public*, pg. 1330

BOLD HOLD—Styling Products—Alberto-Culver Company; *U.S. Public*, pg. 37

BOLD MARK—Markers—Dixon Ticonderoga Company; *U.S. Public*, pg. 514

BOLD-3—NONE—Procter & Gamble Venezuela, C.A.; *U.S. Public*, pg. 1332

BOLD WASHER-DRYER PACKS—Combination Detergent & Fabric Softener Pouches—The Procter & Gamble Company; *U.S. Public*, pg. 1330

BOLENS—Snowthrowers, Mulching Mowers, Tractors, Riding Mowers—Garden Way, Inc.; *U.S. Private*, pg. 440

BOLERO—Intimate Apparel—VF Corporation; *U.S. Public*, pg. 1702

BOLFO—Flea & Tick Prevention—Bayer AG; *Int'l*, pg. 171

BOLLA—Italian Wines—Brown-Forman Beverages Worldwide; *U.S. Public*, pg. 261

BOLLA—Italian Wines—Brown-Forman Corporation; *U.S. Public*, pg. 261

BOLLIGER—Trademark—Bolliger, Inc.; *U.S. Private*, pg. 155

BOLOCREM—Pastry Ingredient—Royal Gist-Brocades N.V.; *Int'l*, pg. 1142

BOLS—Liquors, Liqueurs, Brandy—Bols Royal Distilleries; *Int'l*, pg. 751

BOLSTAR—Insecticide—Bayer AG; *Int'l*, pg. 171

BOLSTER—Candy—New England Confectionery Co.; *U.S. Private*, pg. 1113

BOLT—Towels—Fort James Corporation; *U.S. Public*, pg. 670

BOLT—Electronic Automotive Ignition Interrupt Systems—Millennium Technology Services, Inc.; *U.S. Private*, pg. 746

BOLT-ACTION—Sport Knives—Fiskars-Gerber; *Int'l*, pg. 492

BOLTMAKER—Machinery—National Machinery; *U.S. Private*, pg. 785

BOLTONS—Womens Apparel—A&E Stores, Inc.; *U.S. Private*, pg. 1

BOMBAY—Gin—Grand Metropolitan Plc; *Int'l*, pg. 408

BOMBAY BICYCLE CLUB—Restaurants—Associated Hosts, Inc.; *Int'l*, pg. 215

BOMBAY DRY GIN—NONE—The Bombay Spirits Company; *Int'l*, pg. 409

BOMBAY GIN—Gin—Carillon Importers, Ltd.; *Int'l*, pg. 409

BOMBAY GIN—Gin—Dateo Import S.P.A.; *Int'l*, pg. 385

BOMBAY GIN—NONE—International Distillers Caribbean; *Int'l*, pg. 410

BOMBAY SAPPHIRE—Super Premium Dry Gin—The Bombay Spirits Company; *Int'l*, pg. 409

BOMBAY SAPPHIRE—Spirits—Gilbeys of Ireland; *Int'l*, pg. 409

BOMBAY SAPPHIRE—NONE—Societe Pour la Vente des Produits Cinzano SA; *Int'l*, pg. 410

BOMBAY SAPPHIRE GIN—Super-Premium Gin—Carillon Importers, Ltd.; *Int'l*, pg. 409

BOMBER—Fishing Lures—EBSCO Industries, Inc.; *U.S. Private*, pg. 358

BOMPAN—Bakery Ingredient—Royal Gist-Brocades N.V.; *Int'l*, pg. 1142

BON-A-PETITES—Ice Cream—Good Humor/Breyers Ice Cream; *Int'l*, pg. 1435

BON AMI—NONE—Kiwi Brands Pty. Ltd.; *U.S. Public*, pg. 1434

BON APPETIT—Magazine—Bon Appetit Magazine; *U.S. Private*, pg. 20

BON APPETIT—Magazine—Conde Nast Publications; *U.S. Private*, pg. 20

BON APPETIT—Magazine—The Conde Nast Publications Inc.; *U.S. Private*, pg. 20

BON APPETIT—Trade Magazine—ICA Forlaget AB; *Int'l*, pg. 643

BON APPETIT—Food Products—McCormick & Company, Incorporated; *U.S. Public*, pg. 1066

BON APPETIT—Gourmet Food Stores—Safeway Inc.; *U.S. Public*, pg. 1426

BON BONS—Ice Cream Treats—Nestle Ice Cream Co.; *Int'l*, pg. 918

BON-BONS—NONE—Nestle USA; *Int'l*, pg. 916

BON CORE—Vinyl on Solid Wood Core—Carter Holt Harvey Limited; *U.S. Public*, pg. 904

BON-FOAM 400—Breathable Cushion Insole—Georgia-Bonded Fibers, Inc.; *U.S. Public*, pg. 734

BON JOUR—Sportswear, Jeans, Trousers, Shirts & Accessories—Bon Jour International Ltd.; *U.S. Private*, pg. 156

THE BON MARCHE—Department Store—Federated Department Stores, Inc.; *U.S. Public*, pg. 617

BON-PEL—Nonwoven—Georgia-Bonded Fibers, Inc.; *U.S. Public*, pg. 734

BON TON—NONE—Bon Ton Foods, Inc.; *U.S. Private*, pg. 65

BON VIVANT—European-Style Butter—Zander's Creamery Inc.; *U.S. Private*, pg. 1203

BONAIRE—Appliances—Southcorp Holdings Ltd.; *Int'l*, pg. 1287

BONAMIL—Baby Formula—Wyeth-Ayerst Laboratories, Inc.; *U.S. Public*, pg. 80

BONANZA—Restaurants—Bonanza Restaurants; *U.S. Private*, pg. 736

BONANZA BINGO—NONE—Stuart Entertainment Inc.; *U.S. Public*, pg. 1526

BONANZA BUS LINES—Bus Transportation—Bonanza Bus Lines, Inc.; *U.S. Private*, pg. 156

BONANZA FAMILY GRILL—NONE—Bonanza Restaurants; *U.S. Private*, pg. 736

BONAPARTE—Textile Floorcocerings—Forbo Holding SA; *Int'l*, pg. 496

BONARIL—Foundry Sand Additive—The Dow Chemical Company; *U.S. Public*, pg. 522

BOND DECK—Laminated Beams, Floor Pannels, Posts & Scaffold Planks—Carter Holt Harvey Limited; *U.S. Public*, pg. 904

BOND ELUT—Analytical Extration Columns—Varian Associates, Inc.; *U.S. Public*, pg. 1710

BOND ELUT CERTIFY—Solid Phase Extraction Columns—Varian Associates, Inc.; *U.S. Public*, pg. 1710

BOND ELUT LRC—Solid Phase Extraction Columns—Varian Associates, Inc.; *U.S. Public*, pg. 1710

BOND WOOD—Finger Jointed Timber Products—Carter Holt Harvey Limited; *U.S. Public*, pg. 904

BONDAGEL—GPC Column—Millipore Corporation; *U.S. Public*, pg. 1112

BONDAPAK—C18/Corasil LC Bulk Packing—Millipore Corporation; *U.S. Public*, pg. 1112

BONDBRITE—Metalworking Chemical—Henkel Surface Technologies; *Int'l*, pg. 610

BONDESIL—Bonded Silica Sorbents for Laboratory & Scientific Use—Varian Associates, Inc.; *U.S. Public*, pg. 1710

BONDEX—Sewing Threads—Gudebrod, Inc.; *U.S. Private*, pg. 486

BONDEX—Coatings—RPM, Inc. *U.S. Public*, pg. 1356

BONDEX—Iron On Products—Wm. E. Wright Limited Partnership; *U.S. Private*, pg. 1192

BONDEZE C—THEIC Modified Polyester with Modified Epoxy Cement—Phelps Dodge Magnet Wire Co.; *U.S. Public*, pg. 1286

BONDEZE M—THEIC Modified Polyester w/Mod. Polyamide Imide Overcoat & Polyester Cement—Phelps Dodge Magnet Wire Co.; *U.S. Public*, pg. 1286

BONDINA—Nonwovens—Freudenberg & Company; *Int'l*, pg. 505

BONDO—Auto Finishing Products—RPM, Inc.; *U.S. Public*, pg. 1356

BONDOR—Insulated Panels—James Hardie Industries Ltd.; *Int'l*, pg. 596

BONDS—NONE—Pacific Dunlop Limited; *Int'l*, pg. 1021

BONDS—Hosiery—Sara Lee Corporation; *U.S. Public*, pg. 1432

BONDSTRAND—Fiberglass Pipe & Fittings—Ameron Concrete & Steel Pipe Group; *U.S. Public*, pg. 99

BONDSTRAND—Fiberglass Pipe & Fittings—Ameron International Corporation; *U.S. Public*, pg. 98

BONDTEX—Rubber Products—Rubatex Corporation; *U.S. Private*, pg. 56

BONE ANZA—Dog Treats—Superior Brands, Inc.; *Int'l*, pg. 917

BONE-TO-PICK—Action Game—Mattel Games/Puzzles; *U.S. Public*, pg. 1058

BONESOURCE—Bone Replacement Material—Orthofix International N.V.; *Int'l*, pg. 1011

BONESOURCE—NONE—Pfizer Inc.; *U.S. Public*, pg. 1281

BONFOAM—PVC Cushion Foam—Bontex; *U.S. Public*, pg. 734

BONGO—Apparel—Clothestime Stores, Inc.; *U.S. Public*, pg. 387

BONGO KONGO—Game—Tyco Toys, Inc.; *U.S. Public*, pg. 1058

BONINE—NONE—Pfizer Inc.; *U.S. Public*, pg. 1281

BONJELA—Oral Pain-Relieving Gel—Reckitt & Colman plc; *Int'l*, pg. 1089

BONJOUR—Instant Coffee—Nestle S.A.; *Int'l*, pg. 915

BONKERS—Clothing—Harcrest International, Ltd.; *U.S. Private*, pg. 500

BONNAVILLA—Houses—Chief Industries, Inc.; *U.S. Private*, pg. 236

BONNEVILLE—Car—Pontiac-GMC Division; *U.S. Public*, pg. 720

BONNEY—Tools—Audits & Surveys Worldwide; *U.S. Public*, pg. 147

BONNIE—NONE—Pfizer Inc.; *U.S. Public*, pg. 1281

BONNIE AUGUST—Women's Apparel—Jacques Moret, Inc.; *U.S. Private*, pg. 580

BONNIE HUBBARD—Private Label Grocery—Fleming Companies, Inc.; *U.S. Public*, pg. 652

BONPEL—Nonwoven—Bontex; *U.S. Public*, pg. 734

BONTESSE—Dairy Products—Nestle Chocolate & Confection; *Int'l*, pg. 917

BONTEX—Elastomeric Fiberboard—Bontex; *U.S. Public*, pg. 734

BONTEX-COUNTOUR—Specialty Impregnated Paper—Georgia-Bonded Fibers, Inc.; *U.S. Public*, pg. 734

BONTEX 143A—Platform Material—Bontex; *U.S. Public*, pg. 734

BONTEX 101—Acrylic Belt Backing—Bontex; *U.S. Public*, pg. 734

BONTEX 36M—Belt Backing—Bontex; *U.S. Public*, pg. 734

BONTEX 350—Modified Nonwoven—Georgia-Bonded Fibers, Inc.; *U.S. Public*, pg. 734

BONTRIL—Slow Release Appetite Suppression Product—Carnrick Laboratories, Inc.; *U.S. Private*, pg. 436

BONTRIL PDM—Appetite Suppression Product—Carnrick Laboratories, Inc.; *U.S. Private*, pg. 436

BONUS—Filing System—Fellowes Manufacturing Co.; *U.S. Private*, pg. 400

BONUS—Milk Powders—Nestle S.A.; *Int'l*, pg. 915

BONUS BAG—Luggage—Lands' End, Inc.; *U.S. Public*, pg. 977

BONUS BLEND—Coffee—Reily Foods Company; *U.S. Private*, pg. 919

BONZ—Dog Snacks—Ralston Purina Company; *U.S. Public*, pg. 1359

BONZI—NONE—Uniroyal Chemical Company, Inc.; *U.S. Public*, pg. 460

BOO BERRY—Cereal—General Mills, Inc.; *U.S. Public*, pg. 717

BOODLE'S—Gin—The House of Seagram; *Int'l*, pg. 1217

BOODLES BRITISH GIN—Gin—The Seagram Company Ltd.; *Int'l*, pg. 1214

BOOK 'N TAPE—Storybooks & Tape—Golden Books Family Entertainment Inc.; *U.S. Public*, pg. 749

BOOK OF LISTS—Game—Monarch Avalon, Inc.; *U.S. Public*, pg. 1123

BOOK-OF-THE-MONTH CLUB—Club—Time Warner Inc.; *U.S. Public*, pg. 1610

THE BOOK PRINTER—Printer—McPherson's Limited; *Int'l*, pg. 852

BOOKCASES—Storage Products—GF Office Furniture; *U.S. Private*, pg. 435

BOOKER'S—Bourbon Whiskey—Fortune Brands, Inc.; *U.S. Public*, pg. 674

BOOKLIST—Publication—American Library Association; *U.S. Private*, pg. 58

BOOKMANAGER—Computer Systems—International Business Machines Corporation; *U.S. Public*, pg. 895

BOOKMASTER—Computer System—International Business Machines Corporation; *U.S. Public*, pg. 895

THE BOOKS—Book Wholesaler—John Menzies plc; *Int'l*, pg. 707

BOOKS-A-MILLION—Book Retailer—Books-A-Million, Inc.; *U.S. Public*, pg. 244

BOOKS & CULTURE—Magazine—Christianity Today, Inc.; *U.S. Private*, pg. 238

BOOKS IN PRINT—Information Source on Books Published & distributed in the United States—R.R. Bowker; *Int'l*, pg. 1096

BOOKWIRE—On-Line Book Trade Resource—Reed Elsevier Business Information; *Int'l*, pg. 1095

BOOLOON BUSTERS—Action Game—Mattel Games/Puzzles; *U.S. Public*, pg. 1058

BOOM BOOM METAL WOODS—NONE—Lynx Golf, Inc.; *U.S. Private*, pg. 684

BOONE COUNTY—Foods—Brooks Foods; *U.S. Private*, pg. 887

BOONE'S—Wine—E. & J. Gallo Winery; *U.S. Private*, pg. 438

BOONOSTER—Programmed Revolving Door—Boon Edam Inc.; *Int'l*, pg. 202

BOORUM & PEASE—Office Products—Esselte AB; *Int'l*, pg. 459

BOORUM & PEASE—Account Supplies, Bound Books, Data Binders—Esselte Corporation; *Int'l*, pg. 459

BOOST—Nutritional Product—Bristol-Myers Squibb Company; *U.S. Public*, pg. 253

BOOST—Complete Nutritional Energy Drink—Mead Johnson Nutritional Group; *U.S. Public*, pg. 254

BOOST—Nutritional Healthcare—SmithKline Beecham plc; *Int'l*, pg. 1264

BOOT HILL—Rodenticides—LiphaTech, Inc.; *Int'l*, pg. 812

BOOTH—Frozen Seafoods—National Sea Products Incorporated; *Int'l*, pg. 909

BOOTH—Frozen Fish Fillets-United States—National Sea Products Limited; *Int'l*, pg. 909

BOOTH—Commercial Beverage Dispensing Equipment—Scotsman Industries, Inc.; *U.S. Public*, pg. 1444

BOOTH S HIGH AND DRY—NONE—Guinness Plc; *Int'l*, pg. 412

BOOTH'S GIN—Gin—United Distillers USA, Inc.; *Int'l*, pg. 412

BORAL—Nuclear Shielding Material—AAR Corp.; *U.S. Public*, pg. 1

BORAL—Boron Aluminum Alloys—KB Alloys, Inc.; *U.S. Private*, pg. 249

BORATEEM DRY ALL FABRIC BLEACH—NONE—The Dial Corporation; *U.S. Public*, pg. 505

BORAXO POWDERED HAND SOAP—NONE—The Dial Corporation; *U.S. Public*, pg. 505

BORAZON CUBIC BORON NITRIDE—CBN—G.E. Superabrasives; *U.S. Public*, pg. 711

BORDEN—Dairy & Snack Products—Borden, Inc.; *U.S. Public*, pg. 157

BORDEN—NONE—Medical Meadow Gold Dairies, Inc.; *U.S. Private*, pg. 1016

BORDEN CAPS—Micro Encapsulated Oils—Firmenich; *Int'l*, pg. 486

BORDEN HOME MADE—Ice Cream—Borden, Inc.; *U.S. Private*, pg. 157

BORDEN HOME WALLCOVERINGS—Decorative Overlay Products—Borden, Inc.; *U.S. Private*, pg. 157

BORDER BREAKFAST—Breakfast Tacos—Owens Country Sausage, Inc.; *U.S. Public*, pg. 596

BORDER DESIGN—Video Equipment—National Video, Inc.; *U.S. Public*, pg. 1755

BORDER LIGHTS—Reduced Fat Mexican Fast Food—Taco Bell Corp.; *U.S. Public*, pg. 1637

BORDERLINE—Generator—Tektronix-Video & Networking Div., Grass Valley Products; *U.S. Public*, pg. 1567

BORDO—Citrus Products—Internut; *U.S. Private*, pg. 1010

BORE BACK—Design Feature For A Box Connection On Drill Collars—Smith International, Inc.; *U.S. Public*, pg. 1478

BORENS—Lamps—Luxo A/S; *Int'l*, pg. 821

BORG & BECK—Clutches—Sachs Boge of America; *Int'l*, pg. 835

BORG-WARNER—Engine & Power Transmission System Parts—Echlin Inc.; *U.S. Public*, pg. 560

BORGES—Wallcoverings—Borden, Inc.; *U.S. Private*, pg. 157

BORGHESE—Cosmetics—The Princess Marcella Borghese, Inc.; *U.S. Private*, pg. 690

BORGOCNO—Imported Brand—Banfi Vintners; *U.S. Private*, pg. 113

BORIDE—Ceramic Products—The Dow Chemical Company; *U.S. Public*, pg. 522

BORINE/SWINE—NONE—Schering-Plough Animal Health; *U.S. Public*, pg. 1438

BORLAND—Software—Borland International, Inc.; *U.S. Public*, pg. 246

BORN—Shoes—H.H. Brown Shoe Company, Inc.; *U.S. Public*, pg. 217

BORN BEAUTIFUL—Creme Hairdressing & Conditioner, Deep Conditioning Treatment & Shampoo—Clairol, Inc.; *U.S. Public*, pg. 254

BORN BLONDE—Hair Coloring—Bristol-Myers Squibb Company; *U.S. Public*, pg. 253

BORN BLONDE—Hair Coloring—Clairol, Inc.; *U.S. Public*, pg. 254

BOROFAX—Ointment—Glaxo Wellcome PLC; *Int'l*, pg. 553

BOROFLOAT—Specialty Glass Developed through Microfloat Technology—Schott Glaswerke; *Int'l*, pg. 1523

BOROGARD ZB—NONE—U.S. Borax Inc.; *Int'l*, pg. 1119

BORON—Petroleum Product—BP Oil Co.; *Int'l*, pg. 220

BOROTALCO—Talcum Powder—SmithKline Beecham plc; *Int'l*, pg. 1264

BOROVER—Chemical Reagant—Hach Company; *U.S. Public*, pg. 773

BORROUGHS—Office Furniture—Lear Siegler Diversified Holdings Corp.; *U.S. Private*, pg. 655

BORZOI—Books—Alfred A. Knopf, Inc.; *U.S. Private*, pg. 21

BORZOIVODKA—Vodka—Allied Domecq PLC; *Int'l*, pg. 62

BOSCA—Leather Goods—Hugo Bosca Co., Inc.; *U.S. Private*, pg. 160

BOSCH—Household Appliances—BS Continental S.A. Utilidades Domesticas; *Int'l*, pg. 123

BOSCH—Spark Plugs—Robert Bosch Corporation; *Int'l*, pg. 204

BOSCH—Automotive Equipment, Power Tools, Electrical Household Appliances—Robert Bosch GmbH; *Int'l*, pg. 203

BOSCH PNEUMATICS & HYDRAULICS—Pumps—Robert Bosch Fluid Power Corporation; *Int'l*, pg. 204

ROBERT BOSCH—Automotive Products—Robert Bosch Corporation; *Int'l*, pg. 204

BOSE—Loudspeakers & Electronic Equipment—Bose Corporation; *U.S. Private*, pg. 160

BOSENDORFER—Pianos—Kimball International, Inc.; *U.S. Public*, pg. 956

BOSFORD—NONE—Bacardi-Martini Belgium; *U.S. Private*, pg. 109

BOSS—NONE—Boss Manufacturing Company; *U.S. Private*, pg. 1142

BOSS—Controls/Software—The Buschman Co.; *U.S. Private*, pg. 188

THE BOSS—Cordless Hand Vac—The Eureka Company; *Int'l*, pg. 440

BOSS—Men's Business Fashions—Hugo Boss AG; *Int'l*, pg. 637

BOSS—NONE—Molex Incorporated; *U.S. Public*, pg. 1121

BOSS—Personal Care Products—Windmere-Durable Holdings; *U.S. Public*, pg. 1771

THE BOSS LITE—Cordless Vacuum—The Eureka Company; *Int'l*, pg. 440

BOSSA—Textiles—Sabanci Holding A.S.; *Int'l*, pg. 1167

BOST-BRONZ—NONE—Boston Gear; *U.S. Public*, pg. 857

BOSTFLEX—Material Handling Cables—BIW Cable Systems, Inc.; *Int'l*, pg. 417

BOSTIK—NONE—Bostik Ltd.; *Int'l*, pg. 1409

BOSTON—Contact Lens Material—Bausch & Lomb Incorporated; *U.S. Public*, pg. 194

BOSTON—Industrial Rubber Products—The Biltrite Corporation; *U.S. Private*, pg. 144

BOSTON—Sheet Rubber Products, Hoses—Dana Corporation; *U.S. Public*, pg. 479

BOSTON—Pencil Sharpeners, Air Cleaners, Paper Trimmers, Letter Openers, Lead Point—Hunt Corporation; *U.S. Public*, pg. 848

BOSTON—Pianos—Steinway & Sons; *U.S. Public*, pg. 1514

BOSTON ACOUSTICS—NONE—Boston Acoustics, Inc.; *U.S. Public*, pg. 246

BOSTON ADVANCE—Contact Lens Solutions—Bausch & Lomb Incorporated; *U.S. Public*, pg. 194

BOSTON CARVER—Extreme Carver—Boston Chicken, Inc.; *U.S. Public*, pg. 247

BOSTON CELTICS—NBA Basketball Team—Boston Celtics Limited Partnership; *U.S. Public*, pg. 246

BOSTON ENVISION—Contact Lens—Bausch & Lomb Incorporated; *U.S. Public*, pg. 194

BOSTON EQUALENS II—Contact Lens—Bausch & Lomb Incorporated; *U.S. Public*, pg. 194

BOSTON 5 STAR BRANDY—NONE—Barton Brands, Ltd.; *U.S. Public*, pg. 300

BOSTON GEAR—Gears, Drives & Speed Reducers—IMO Industries Inc.; *U.S. Public*, pg. 856

BOSTON GIN—NONE—Barton Brands, Ltd.; *U.S. Public*, pg. 300

THE BOSTON GLOBE—Daily Newspaper—The Boston Globe; *U.S. Public*, pg. 1175

THE BOSTON HERALD—Newspaper—News America Publishing Inc.; *Int'l*, pg. 925

THE BOSTON LENS—Contact Lens—Bausch & Lomb Incorporated; *U.S. Public*, pg. 194

BOSTON LIQUEURS—NONE—Barton Brands, Ltd.; *U.S. Public*, pg. 300

BOSTON MARKET—Restaurants, Carvers Sandwiches, Chicken & Hearth Products—Boston Chicken, Inc.; *U.S. Public*, pg. 247

BOSTON MARKET STORES—NONE—CKE Restaurants Inc.; *U.S. Public*, pg. 278

BOSTON RxD—Contact Lens—Bausch & Lomb Incorporated; *U.S. Public*, pg. 194

BOSTON ROTISSERIE CHICKEN—NONE—Boston Chicken, Inc.; *U.S. Public*, pg. 247

BOSTON RUM—NONE—Barton Brands, Ltd.; *U.S. Public*, pg. 300

BOSTON SCHNAPPS—NONE—Barton Brands, Ltd.; *U.S. Public*, pg. 300

BOSTON TRADERS—Mens & Womens Tops, Shirts & Sweaters—Designs, Inc.; *U.S. Public*, pg. 501

BOSTON VODKA—NONE—Barton Brands, Ltd.; *U.S. Public*, pg. 300

BOSTON WHALER—Boats, Whaler, Revenge, Outrage, Mischief, Whaler Drive—Boston Whaler, Inc.; *U.S. Public*, pg. 689

BOSTON WHALER—Boat—Sea Ray; *U.S. Public*, pg. 266

BOSTONIAN—Footwear—Clarks International; *Int'l*, pg. 296

BOSTONIAN—Shoes—Hanover Stores; *Int'l*, pg. 297

BOSTONIAN WINDSOR—Shoes—Bostonian Shoe Co.; *Int'l*, pg. 297

BOSTRIG—Oceanographic Cables—BIW Cable Systems, Inc.; *Int'l*, pg. 417

BOTANICAL—Hair Care Line—Freeman Cosmetic Corp.; *U.S. Private*, pg. 426

BOTANIX—Permanent (Fabric) Plants, Trees & Foliage—Celebrity Incorporated; *U.S. Public*, pg. 319

BOTANY 500—Apparel—Master Industries Corp.; *U.S. Private*, pg. 713

BOTNIA—Bleached & Unbleached Pulps—Metsa-Serla Corporation; *Int'l*, pg. 863

BOTTLE MASTER—Machinery for Opening & Filling Cartons, Bottle Carriers—The Mead Corporation; *U.S. Public*, pg. 1074

BOTTLEMASTER—Cartons—Mead Packaging; *U.S. Public*, pg. 1074

BOTTOM BLOWN OXYGEN CONVERTER—Refinery Process Used to Improve Precious Metal Recoveries—M.I.M. Holdings Ltd.; *Int'l*, pg. 827

BOTTOM DRIVE CENTRIFUGE—NONE—Bird Machine Company; *U.S. Public*, pg. 166

BOTTOMS UP—Booster Seat with Reversible Heights—Cosco, Inc.; *U.S. Public*, pg. 277

BOTTOMS UP—Off License Liquor Stores—Whitbread PLC; *Int'l*, pg. 1498

BOU-MATIC—Milking Equipment—Bou-Matic; *U.S. Private*, pg. 301

BOUCHARD PERE & FILS—Wines—Heublein, Inc.; *Int'l*, pg. 410

BOULARD—NONE—Bacardi-Martini Belgium; *U.S. Private*, pg. 109

BOULEVARD—NONE—Berkley Publishing Corp.; *Int'l*, pg. 1027

BOUNCE—Fabric Softener—The Procter & Gamble Company; *U.S. Public*, pg. 1330

BOUNCE WITH STAINGARD—Fabric Softener Sheets—The Procter & Gamble Company; *U.S. Public*, pg. 1330

BOUNCER III—Pitchers—Rubbermaid Incorporated; *U.S. Public*, pg. 1411

BOUNDARY—Animal Repellant—Carter-Wallace, Inc.; *U.S. Public*, pg. 309

BOUNDER—Motor Homes—Fleetwood Enterprises, Inc.; *U.S. Public*, pg. 650

BOUNTY—Confectionary—Mars Confectionery; *U.S. Private*, pg. 707

BOUNTY—Candy Bar—Mars, Incorporated; *U.S. Private*, pg. 707

BOUNTY—Paper Towels—The Procter & Gamble Company; *U.S. Public*, pg. 1330

BOUQUET D'OR—Chocalates—Cadbury Schweppes p.l.c.; *Int'l*, pg. 247

BOUQUETS—Women's Footwear—J. Baker, Inc.; *U.S. Public*, pg. 167

BOURBON—Pudding Mix—CSM N.V.; *Int'l*, pg. 243

BOURGEY MONTREUIL—NONE—GEODIS; *Int'l*, pg. 549

BOURNS INSTRUMENTS—Transducers—Bourns, Inc.; *U.S. Private*, pg. 161

BOURNS NETWORKS—Resistive Networks—Bourns, Inc.; *U.S. Private*, pg. 161

BOURNS SENSORS/CONTROLS—Panel Controls—Bourns, Inc.; *U.S. Private*, pg. 161

BOURNS TRIMPOT—Potentiometers, Resistors—Bourns, Inc.; *U.S. Private*, pg. 161

BOURNVITA—Food Drinks—Cadbury Nigeria PLC; *Int'l*, pg. 248

BOURSIN—Imported French Cheeses—Chesebrough-Pond's; *Int'l*, pg. 1436

BOUTARI—Wine—Paterno Imports Limited; *U.S. Private*, pg. 843

BOUTIQUE—Facial Tissue, Cosmetic Pads, Bathroom Tissue & Paper Napkins—Kimberly-Clark Corporation; *U.S. Public*, pg. 958

BOVA CREAM—Animal Health Care—Universal Cooperatives, Inc.; *U.S. Private*, pg. 1127

BOVAC 3—Vaccine for Dairy & Beef Cattle—SmithKline Beecham plc; *Int'l*, pg. 1264

BOVINE CALF SERUM—Bovine Serum Product—HyClone Laboratories Inc.; *Int'l*, pg. 1037

BOVISHIELD—NONE—Pfizer Inc.; *U.S. Public*, pg. 1281

BOVRIL—Beef & Vegetable Extracts & Soup Base—Bestfoods; *U.S. Public*, pg. 223

BOVRIL—Savoury Drinks—CPC Foods (Ireland) Ltd.; *U.S. Public*, pg. 225

BOW BANGLES—NONE—Claire's Stores Inc.; *U.S. Public*, pg. 381

BOW MAGIC—Ribbon Forms—3M; *U.S. Public*, pg. 1604

BOW TO STERN—Cleaners—E & B Marine Incorporated; *U.S. Public*, pg. 1756

BOW TO STERN—Cleaners—Goldbergs Marine Distributors; *U.S. Public*, pg. 1756

BOW WOW—Domestic Animal Food—Ag Processing Inc., A Cooperative; *U.S. Private*, pg. 26

BOW WOW AND MEOWS—Greeting Cards—American Greetings Corporation; *U.S. Public*, pg. 77

BOWATER—Newsprint—Bowater Incorporated; *U.S. Public*, pg. 247

BOWEN—Tools—Bowen Tools; *U.S. Public*, pg. 858

BOWENS—Lighting—Calumet Photographic, Inc.; *U.S. Private*, pg. 202

BOWER-SYLVAC—Measuring Tools—Fred V. Fowler Company, Inc.; *U.S. Private*, pg. 422

BOWERS—Measuring Tools—Fred V. Fowler Company, Inc.; *U.S. Private*, pg. 422

BOWERS—Electrical Products—Masco Corporation; *U.S. Public*, pg. 1052

BOWERS—Non-Metallic Outlet Boxes—Thomas & Betts Corporation; *U.S. Public*, pg. 1597

BOWHUNTER—Periodical—Cowles Enthusiast Media, Inc.; *U.S. Private*, pg. 281

BOWKER ANNUAL LIBRARY AND BOOK TRADE ALMANAC—Statistical Resource & Planning Guide for Book Trade Professionals—R.R. Bowker; *Int'l*, pg. 1096

BOWKER'S COMPLETE VIDEO DIRECTORY—Collection Guide Supporting Video Research/Selection/Collection Development—R.R. Bowker; *Int'l*, pg. 1096

BOWL CLEANSE—Cleaner—Ecolab Inc.; *U.S. Public*, pg. 562

BOWL FRESH—Toilet Deordorant—Willert Home Products, Inc.; *U.S. Private*, pg. 1177

BOWL 'N ALL—Cleaner & Disinfectant—The Dow Chemical Company; *U.S. Public*, pg. 522

BOWL O BEAUTY—Real Roses in Chemically Treated Water—Amlings Flowerland; *U.S. Private*, pg. 66

BOWL PATROL—Extra Strength Toilet Bowl Cleaner—Stanhome Inc.; *U.S. Public*, pg. 1508

BOWLENE—Toilet Bowl Cleaner—Malco Products, Inc.; *U.S. Private*, pg. 698

BOWLING CORPORATION OF AMERICA—Business Association—Charan Industries, Inc.; *U.S. Private*, pg. 229

BOWLING DIGEST—Magazine—Century Publishing Company; *U.S. Private*, pg. 226

BOWMAN—Milk—Dean Foods Company; *U.S. Public*, pg. 489

BOWNE—Commercial & Financial Printing—Bowne & Co., Inc.; *U.S. Public*, pg. 248

BOWYERS—Meat Products—Northern Foods plc; *Int'l*, pg. 967

BOX-FIN—Baseboard Radiation—Edwards Engineering Corporation; *U.S. Private*, pg. 365

BOXBOARD CONTAINERS INTERNATIONAL—Publication for Boxmaking & Carton Industry—Intertec Publishing; *U.S. Public*, pg. 1327

BOXER—Self-Propelled Access Platform—Simon Engineering plc; *Int'l*, pg. 1251

THE BOXER—Vitamin—Health Products Corporation; *U.S. Private*, pg. 514

BOXER TOP—Shoes—Johnston & Murphy Co.; *U.S. Public*, pg. 728

BOXSTER—Car—Porsche Cars North America, Inc.; *Int'l*, pg. 1063

BOXVELOPE—Envelopes—Tension Envelope Corp.; *U.S. Private*, pg. 1077

BOXX SEATS—School Logo Chairs—Clarin; *U.S. Private*, pg. 242

BOYD'S BOIDS—Greeting Cards—American Greetings Corporation; *U.S. Public*, pg. 77

BOYE—Art Needle Work Accessories—Boye Needle; *U.S. Private*, pg. 1192

BOYO NATURAL SPRING—NONE—Royal Waterbeds; *U.S. Private*, pg. 949

BOYO NIGHT AIR—NONE—Royal Waterbeds; *U.S. Private*, pg. 949

BRA SLETTE—Brassieres—Lady Marlene Sales Corp.; *U.S. Private*, pg. 642

BRA TOPPERS—Sport Brassieres—Lilyette Brassiere Co.; *U.S. Private*, pg. 697

BRACCACIA—Pizza—Crestar Food Products, Inc.; *U.S. Public*, pg. 805

BRACEMATE—Brace Cleaner—Reckitt & Colman plc; *Int'l*, pg. 1089

BRACH—Candy—Kraft Jacobs Suchard AG; *U.S. Public*, pg. 1288

BRACHETTO D'ACQUI—NONE—Castello Banfi Srl.; *U.S. Private*, pg. 113

BRACH'S—Candy—Brach & Brock Confections, Inc.; *U.S. Private*, pg. 163

BRACH'S PICK-A-MIX—Candy—Brach & Brock Confections, Inc.; *U.S. Private*, pg. 163

BRAD HARRISON—Connectors—Woodhead Industries, Inc.; *U.S. Public*, pg. 1776

BRAD-MULTI-ROLL—Industrial Machinery—Pennsylvania Crusher Corp.; *U.S. Private*, pg. 850

BRADEN—Power Generation Products—Jason Incorporated; *U.S. Public*, pg. 923

BRADEN—Winches—Paccar Inc.; *U.S. Public*, pg. 1246

BRADEN—Winches & Drives—PACCAR Winch Division; *U.S. Public*, pg. 1246

BRADFORD—Glasswool & Rockwool Insulation Products—CSR Limited; *Int'l*, pg. 245

BRADFORD—Resistors/Potentiometers—Vishay Intertechnology, Inc.; *U.S. Public*, pg. 1721

BRADFORD EXCHANGE—Collectors Plates—Bradford Exchange Ltd.; *U.S. Private*, pg. 163

BRADFORD INVESTMENT MANAGEMENT—NONE—J.C. Bradford & Co.; *U.S. Private*, pg. 163

BRADFORD TRUST—NONE—J.C. Bradford & Co.; *U.S. Private*, pg. 163

BRADFORD-WHITE—Gas, Electric & Oil Powered Heaters—Bradford-White Corporation; *U.S. Private*, pg. 164

BRADFORD WINDOW—NONE—CertainTeed Corporation; *Int'l*, pg. 1170

BRADINGTON-YOUNG—Recliners—Woodmark Originals Inc.; *U.S. Private*, pg. 747

BRADPACK—Modular Wash Center—Bradley Corporation; *U.S. Private*, pg. 164

BRADPACTOR—Industrial Machinery—Pennsylvania Crusher Corp.; *U.S. Private*, pg. 850

BRADSHAW'S—Honey—Sioux Honey Association; *U.S. Private*, pg. 1003

BRADSTONE—Washfountain—Bradley Corporation; *U.S. Private*, pg. 164

BRADY—Computer Books—Simon & Schuster; *U.S. Private*, pg. 777

BRAG—Container for Wipers—Kimberly-Clark Corporation; *U.S. Public*, pg. 958

BRAID-LOC—Safety Slings—Broderick & Bascom Rope Co.; *U.S. Private*, pg. 68

BRAIN ATLAS—Topographical Brain Mapping Instrument—Bio-Logic Systems Corp.; *U.S. Public*, pg. 230

BRAINERD DAILY DISPATCH—Newspaper—Shivers Trading & Operating Co.; *U.S. Private*, pg. 994

BRAINFREEZE—Television Commercial Theme—The Southland Corporation; *Int'l*, pg. 693

BRAINSTORM—Educational Software—Interplay Productions, Inc.; *U.S. Private*, pg. 572

BRAKE TECHNOLOGY—Brake Parts—Echlin Inc.; *U.S. Public*, pg. 560

BRAKEWARE—Auto Parts—JPE, Inc.; *U.S. Public*, pg. 919

BRALE—Diamond Penetrators—Wilson/Shore Instruments; *U.S. Public*, pg. 883

BRALON—Sutures—U.S. Surgical Corp.; *U.S. Public*, pg. 1687

BRAN BUDS—High-Fiber Morsels of Wheat Bran & Psyllium Cereal—Kellogg Company; *U.S. Public*, pg. 947

BRAN N' HONEY—Food Fiber—Nature's Bounty Inc.; *U.S. Public*, pg. 1166

BRANCA MENTA—NONE—Carillon Importers, Ltd.; *Int'l*, pg. 409

BRANCH—Cheese—Stella Foods Division; *U.S. Private*, pg. 1040

BRAND—Beer—Heineken N.V.; *Int'l*, pg. 608

BRAND CENTRAL—NONE—Sears, Roebuck and Co.; *U.S. Public*, pg. 1452

BRAND-REX—Electrical Cables—BICC Brand-Rex; *Int'l*, pg. 120

BRAND WARE—Flatware—World Tableware, Inc.; *Int'l*, pg. 1056

BRANDERS JEANS—Mens' & Boys Apparel—Williamson-Dickie Mfg. Co.; *U.S. Private*, pg. 1179

BRANDING AMERICA—NONE—Foodservice Director; *Int'l*, pg. 1446

BRANDON PLANK—Pre-Finished Strip—Bruce Hardwood Floors; *U.S. Public*, pg. 1634

BRANDT—Money Handling System—Brandt, Inc.; *Int'l*, pg. 387

BRANDVISION—NONE—Market Facts, Inc.; *U.S. Public*, pg. 1046

BRANDWEEK—Magazine—BPI Communications Inc.; *Int'l*, pg. 1446

BRANDY CROFT—NONE—Croft & Companhia Limitada; *Int'l*, pg. 409

BRAN'NOLA—Specialty Baked Goods, Breads—Bestfoods; *U.S. Public*, pg. 223

BRANSON—Industrial & Comml. Cleaning Equipment, Plasma Systems & Welding Equipment—Emerson Electric Co.; *U.S. Public*, pg. 572

BRANSONIC—Tabletop Ultrasonic Cleaners—Branson Ultrasonics Corp. - Precision Cleaning Div.; *U.S. Public*, pg. 574

BRANSONICS—Ultrasonic Cleaner—Branson Ultrasonics Corp.-Plastics Joining Div.; *U.S. Public*, pg. 574

BRAQUETTE—Art Equipment—Martin/F. Weber Company; *U.S. Private*, pg. 710

BRASCH TECH DATA—Technical Information Services—SPX Corporation; *U.S. Public*, pg. 1420

BRASS BOOT—Shoes—Weyco Group, Inc.; *U.S. Public*, pg. 1763

BRASS-CRAFT—Plumbing Fittings—Masco Corporation; *U.S. Public*, pg. 1052

BRASS-TITE!—Brass Unions & Fittings—R&B, Inc.; *U.S. Public*, pg. 1354

BRASSGLO—High Speed Brass Process—LeaRonal, Inc.; *U.S. Public*, pg. 982

BRASSO—Metal Cleaner—Reckitt & Colman Inc.; *Int'l*, pg. 1090

BRASSO—Metal Polishes—Reckitt & Colman plc; *Int'l*, pg. 1089

BRAT II—Blood Transfusion System—COBE Laboratories, Inc.; *Int'l*, pg. 667

BRAUD—Grape Harvesters—New Holland Ltd.; *Int'l*, pg. 484

BRAUMEISTER—Beer—Joseph Huber Brewing Co., Inc.; *U.S. Private*, pg. 545

BRAUMEISTER LIGHT—Beer—Joseph Huber Brewing Co., Inc.; *U.S. Private*, pg. 545

BRAUN—Appliances—Braun AG; *U.S. Public*, pg. 744

BRAUN—Appliances—Braun, North America; *U.S. Public*, pg. 743

BRAUN AROMASTER—Coffee Makers—Braun, North America; *U.S. Public*, pg. 743

BRAUN AROMATIC—Coffee Grinders—Braun, North America; *U.S. Public*, pg. 743

BRAUN CITROMATIC—Press Juicers—Braun, North America; *U.S. Public*, pg. 743

BRAUN CLICKER—Cordless Hair Curler—Braun, North America; *U.S. Public*, pg. 743

BRAUN DENTAL CENTER MULTIACTION ELECTRONIC IMPULSE—Electric Dental Prods.—Braun, North America; *U.S. Public*, pg. 743

BRAUN ELECTRIC RAZOR—Electric Razor—Braun, North America; *U.S. Public*, pg. 743

BRAUN HAND BLENDER—Hand Blender—The Gillette Company; *U.S. Public*, pg. 743

BRAUN INDEPENDENT 2000—Cordless Hair Curler—Braun, North America; *U.S. Public*, pg. 743

BRAUN MULTIPRACTIC—Hand Blender—Braun, North America; *U.S. Public*, pg. 743

BRAUN MULTIPRESS—Spin Juicers—Braun, North America; *U.S. Public*, pg. 743

BRAUN QUARTZ—Battery Clocks—Braun, North America; *U.S. Public*, pg. 743

BRAUN QUICKSTYLE—Electric Curlers—Braun, North America; *U.S. Public*, pg. 743

BRAUN QUICKSTYLE COMBI—Electric Curlers—Braun, North America; *U.S. Public*, pg. 743

BRAUN REFLEX CONTROL—Battery Clocks—Braun, North America; *U.S. Public*, pg. 743

BRAUN SILENTIME—Battery Clocks—Braun, North America; *U.S. Public*, pg. 743

BRAUN SLIMSTYLE—Electric Curlers—Braun, North America; *U.S. Public*, pg. 743

BRAUN VOICE CONTROL—Battery Clocks—Braun, North America; *U.S. Public*, pg. 743

BRAUNLOK—Caps—W. Braun Company; *U.S. Private*, pg. 166

BRAVA—NONE—Vauxhall; *U.S. Public*, pg. 724

BRAVADA—Multi-Purpose Vehicle—Oldsmobile Div. General Motors Corp.; *U.S. Public*, pg. 720

BRAVADO—Luggage—Andiamo, Inc.; *U.S. Private*, pg. 73

BRAVE—Motor Homes—Winnebago Industries, Inc.; *U.S. Public*, pg. 1772

BRAVISSIMO—Pizza—Little Lady Foods, Inc.; *U.S. Private*, pg. 671

BRAVO—NONE—AST Research Inc.; *Int'l*, pg. 1181

BRAVO—Pasta—Borden, Inc.; *U.S. Private*, pg. 157

BRAVO—NONE—Brown & Sharpe Manufacturing Company; *U.S. Public*, pg. 260

BRAVO—NONE—The Cessna Aircraft Co.; *U.S. Public*, pg. 1589

BRAVO—Laundry Detergent—Colgate-Palmolive Company; *U.S. Public*, pg. 397

BRAVO—Van—Fiat Auto Ireland Ltd.; *Int'l*, pg. 481

BRAVO—Grocery Products—Krasdale Foods Inc.; *U.S. Private*, pg. 635

BRAVO—Credit Card—NOVUS Services, Inc.; *U.S. Public*, pg. 1132

BRAVO—Cleansing Liquid—Nuevo Federal S.A.; *Int'l*, pg. 990

BRAVO—Front Wheel Drive Scooter—Ortho-Kinetics, Inc.; *U.S. Public*, pg. 820

BRAVO! BOSS—Upright Vacuum Cleaner—The Eureka Company; *Int'l*, pg. 440

BRAVO COFFEE—NONE—Sara Lee Corporation; *U.S. Public*, pg. 1432

BRAVO ITALIANO—Salad Dressing—Cains Foods, L.P.; *U.S. Private*, pg. 199

BRAVO OS—NONE—Brown & Sharpe Manufacturing Company; *U.S. Public*, pg. 260

BRAVO II BOSS PLUS—Upright Vac Cleaner—The Eureka Company; *Int'l*, pg. 440

BRAVOBLADES—In-Line Skates—Rollerblade, Inc.; *U.S. Private*, pg. 941

BRAVOS—Tortilla Chips—Wise Foods, Inc.; *U.S. Private*, pg. 157

BRAVOS !—Tortilla Chips—Borden, Inc.; *U.S. Private*, pg. 157

BRAWLER—Corrosion Resistant Pumps—Osmonics, Inc.; *U.S. Public*, pg. 1233

BRAWNY—Paper Towels—Consumer Products Business; *U.S. Public*, pg. 671

BRAWNY—Towels—Fort James Corporation; *U.S. Public*, pg. 670

BRAZIER—Hot Foods—International Dairy Queen, Inc.; *U.S. Public*, pg. 220

BRAZILO'S—Women's Shoes—International Seaway Trading Corporation; *U.S. Private*, pg. 572

BREAD BOX BREADMAKER—Automatic Bread Machine—Toastmaster, Inc.; *U.S. Public*, pg. 1619

BREAD DU JOUR—Bread Products—Ralston Purina Company; *U.S. Public*, pg. 1359

BREAD READY—Presliced Meats—Hormel Foods Corp.; *U.S. Public*, pg. 840

BREADMAKER'S HEARTH—Combination Breadmaker/Toaster Oven—Toastmaster, Inc.; *U.S. Public*, pg. 1619

BREADMAN—Bread Machines—Salton/Maxim Housewares, Inc.; *U.S. Public*, pg. 1430

BREADS INTERNATIONAL—Bread & Rolls—Flowers Industries, Inc.; *U.S. Public*, pg. 656

BREAK CAKES—Snacks—The Earthgrains Company; *U.S. Public*, pg. 547

BREAK'N BAKE—Pizza—Pillsbury Co.; *Int'l*, pg. 411

BREAK-THRU SAFETY TASSEL—Helps Prevent Children & Pets From being Injured—Hunter Douglas, Inc.; *Int'l*, pg. 1074

BREAKA—Milk—Q.U.F. Industries Ltd.; *Int'l*, pg. 1074

BREAKWAYS—Hotel Breaks—Vaux Group Plc; *Int'l*, pg. 1453

BREAKER MALT LAGER—Lager—Bass PLC; *Int'l*, pg. 169

BREAKERS—Juice Drink—Ocean Spray Cranberries, Inc.; *U.S. Private*, pg. 811

BREAKFAST'N FRUIT BUFFET—Morning Food Service—Eat N Park Restaurants; *U.S. Private*, pg. 358

BREAKFAST SMILE—Breakfast Special—Eat N Park Restaurants; *U.S. Private*, pg. 358

BREAKFAST YOGURT—Yogurt—Yoplait USA; *U.S. Public*, pg. 718

BREAKMATE—Compact Fountain Dispensing System—The Coca-Cola Company; *U.S. Public*, pg. 392

BREAKSTONE'S—Cultured Dairy Products—Philip Morris Companies Inc.; *U.S. Public*, pg. 1287

BREAKSTONE'S—Cultured Dairy Products—Kraft Foods Inc.; *U.S. Public*, pg. 1288

BREAST O'CHICKEN—Tuna—Star-Kist Foods Inc.; *U.S. Public*, pg. 805

BREATH GARD—Tablet that Works in the Stomach to Eliminate Bad Breath—Lee Pharmaceuticals; *U.S. Public*, pg. 984

BREATH OF SPRING—Air Freshners—Penn Champ; *U.S. Private*, pg. 145

BREATH OF SPRING—Disposable Toothbrushes—Venturi Inc.; *U.S. Private*, pg. 1136

BREATH SAVERS—Mints—Hershey Foods Corporation; *U.S. Public*, pg. 811

BREATH SAVERS—Mints—Nabisco Inc.; *U.S. Public*, pg. 1355

BREATH SAVERS—Sugar Free Mints—Planters Company; *U.S. Public*, pg. 1355

BREATH SAVERS—Sugar Free Mints—RJR Nabisco Holdings Corp.; *U.S. Public*, pg. 1354

BREATHE-MED—Microporous, Breatheable Polyurethane Tri-Laminate For EMS Clothing—Aldan Industries; *U.S. Private*, pg. 33

BREATHE-TEX—Microporous, Breatheable Polyurethane Laminate—Aldan Industries; *U.S. Private*, pg. 33

BREATHE-TEX PLUS—Hydrophilic, Breatheable, Cast Polyurethane—Aldan Industries; *U.S. Private*, pg. 33

BREATHER BAG—Vented Poly Bags—Perfecseal Company; *U.S. Public*, pg. 210

BREATHIN BRUSHED PIGSKIN—Leather—Wolverine World Wide, Inc.; *U.S. Public*, pg. 1775

BREATHLESS—To Eliminate Bad Breath—Lee Pharmaceuticals; *U.S. Public*, pg. 984

BREATHSENSOR—Disposable Airflow Thermistor—Nellcor Puritan Bennett Incorporated; *U.S. Public*, pg. 1039

BRECK CONDITIONER—NONE—The Dial Corporation; *U.S. Public*, pg. 505

BRECK HAIRSPRAY—NONE—The Dial Corporation; *U.S. Public*, pg. 505

BRECK SHAMPOO—NONE—The Dial Corporation; *U.S. Public*, pg. 505

BRECKENRIDGE—NONE—Ralcorp Holdings Inc.; *U.S. Public*, pg. 1359

BRECKENRIDGE CELLARS—Vineyard—Giumarra Vineyards; *U.S. Private*, pg. 455

BRECON CARREG—Still & Sparkling Natural Mineral Water—Spadel SA; *Int'l*, pg. 1287

BRED—Bread Improvers—Royal Gist-Brocades N.V.; *Int'l*, pg. 1142

BREDININ—Immunosuppresant—Asahi Chemical Industry Co., Ltd.; *Int'l*, pg. 83

BREEDER ENTHUSIAST—NONE—Ralston Purina Company; *U.S. Public*, pg. 1359

BREEZAIR—EVAP Coolers—Convair Cooler Corp.; *U.S. Private*, pg. 271

BREEZE—Cameras—Eastman Kodak Company; *U.S. Public*, pg. 550

BREEZE—Frozen Soft Serve Yogurt—International Dairy Queen, Inc.; *U.S. Public*, pg. 220

BREEZE—Detergent—Lever Brothers Co.; *Int'l*, pg. 1435

BREEZE—Clamps & Adapters—TransTechnology Corporation; *U.S. Public*, pg. 1632

BREEZE—Detergent—Unilever Plc; *Int'l*, pg. 1433

BREEZE MARK—Electro Mechanical Drives—Breeze Eastern; *U.S. Public*, pg. 1632

BREEZETTE—Towelettes—Clairol, Inc.; *U.S. Public*, pg. 254

BREEZEWAY—Windows—James Hardie Industries Ltd.; *Int'l*, pg. 596

BREEZIN—Men's Active Sportswear—Seattle Pacific Industries, Inc.; *U.S. Public*, pg. 980

BREMAX—Tulcbuterol—Abbott Laboratories; *U.S. Public*, pg. 12

BREMERTON SUN—J. P. Scripps Newspaper Group Dailies—The E.W. Scripps Company; *U.S. Public*, pg. 1447

BREN—Epoxy Resins—Nippon Kayaku Co. Ltd.; *Int'l*, pg. 934

BRENTWOOD—Vinyl Siding & Accessories—Alcoa Building Products, Inc.; *U.S. Public*, pg. 61

BRENTWOOD—Drapery Hardware—Kirsch; *U.S. Public*, pg. 1176

BRER RABBIT—Molasses & Syrups—Nabisco Inc.; *U.S. Public*, pg. 1355

BRER RABBIT—Molasses—RJR Nabisco Holdings Corp.; *U.S. Public*, pg. 1354

BRESLER—Ice Cream—Bresler's Industries, Inc.; *Int'l*, pg. 1520

BRESLER'S GOURMET YOGURT—Yogurt—Bresler's Industries, Inc.; *Int'l*, pg. 1520

BRESLER'S ROYALE CREMES—Ice Cream—Bresler's Industries, Inc.; *Int'l*, pg. 1520

BRESLER'S ICE CREAM—Ice Cream—Yogen Fruz Worldwide Inc.; *Int'l*, pg. 1520

BRESLER'S ROYALE LITES—Frozen Dessert—Bresler's Industries, Inc.; *Int'l*, pg. 1520

BRESTAN—Fungicide—Hoechst Aktiengesellschaft; *Int'l*, pg. 624

BRETHAIRE—NONE—Novartis Pharmaceuticals; *Int'l*, pg. 973

BRETHAID—Heat/Moisture Exchanger—Terumo Medical Corporation; *Int'l*, pg. 1376

BRETHINE—Anti-Asthmatic—Ciba Specialty Chemicals; *Int'l*, pg. 291

BRETHINE—Anti-Asthmatic—Novartis; *Int'l*, pg. 972

BRETHINE—NONE—Novartis Pharmaceuticals; *Int'l*, pg. 973

BRETTON PLACE—Women's Clothing—Cliftex; *U.S. Public*, pg. 1777

BREUITIES—Foundations—The Strouse, Adler Company; *U.S. Private*, pg. 1047

BREVERRA—Booster Seat—Century Products Co.; *U.S. Private*, pg. 226

BREVIA—Feminine Pads—Kimberly-Clark Corporation; *U.S. Public*, pg. 958

BREVIBLOC—Prescription Drug—Du Pont (E.I. Du Pont De Nemours & Co.); *U.S. Public*, pg. 530

BREVIBLOC—Esmolol HCL Injection—Ohmeda; *Int'l*, pg. 121

BREVITAL—Anesthetic—Jones Medical Industries Inc.; *U.S. Public*, pg. 933

BREW 'N GO—NONE—The Black & Decker Corporation; *U.S. Public*, pg. 233

BREW XI—Bitter/Ale—Bass PLC; *Int'l*, pg. 169

BREWER-TITCHENER—Tackle Blocks, Forgings—York Plant; *U.S. Public*, pg. 444

BREWERS—Flakes—ADM Milling Co.; *U.S. Public*, pg. 128

BREWERS AMYLIQ—Bacterial Amylase for the Liquefaction of Brewing Adjuncts—Royal Gist-Brocades N.V.; *Int'l*, pg. 1142

BREWERS FERMEX—Fungal Amylase for the Hydrolysis of Starch Remaining in Fermentation—Royal Gist-Brocades N.V.; *Int'l*, pg. 1142

BREWERS FLOW—Enzymatic Complex for Brewing with Barley—Royal Gist-Brocades N.V.; *Int'l*, pg. 1142

BREWLINE—Hose—The Goodyear Tire & Rubber Company; *U.S. Public*, pg. 752

BREYERS—Cultured Dairy Products—Kraft Foods Inc.; *U.S. Public*, pg. 1288

BRI-TOP—Vinyl Color—Mar-Hyde Corporation; *U.S. Public*, pg. 1357

BRIA—Women's Walking Shoe—K-Swiss Inc.; *U.S. Public*, pg. 937

BRIAN PULJOEY—NONE—PAXAR Corporation; *U.S. Public*, pg. 1266

BRIAR—Men's Apparel—Hartmarx Corporation; *U.S. Public*, pg. 795

BRICANYL SPACER—Bronchodilator—Astra AB; *Int'l*, pg. 93

BRICEF—Infectious Disease Therapy Product—Bristol-Myers Squibb Company; *U.S. Public*, pg. 253

BRICK OVEN—Specialty Baked Goods, Breads—Bestfoods; *U.S. Public*, pg. 223

BRICKMIX—Refractory—CFB Industries, Inc.; *U.S. Private*, pg. 194

BRICKMIX—Refractory—Chicago Fire Brick Co.; *U.S. Private*, pg. 194

BRICO—DIY Supplies & Gardening Supplies Store—GIB Group; *Int'l*, pg. 532

BRICO—Powder Metal Products—T & N Plc; *Int'l*, pg. 1334

BRICPAC—Packgin Machine System—Printpac-UEB Case Group; *U.S. Public*, pg. 905

BRIDAL ORIGINALS—Bridal Gowns, Flower Girl Dresses—S.A.S.I. Corporation; *U.S. Private*, pg. 955

BRIDAL REGISTRY—Special Purpose Savings Account With Discounts For Home Buyers—The Troy Savings Bank; *U.S. Private*, pg. 1106

BRIDE TO BE—Magazine—Reed Business Information Pty. Limited; *Int'l*, pg. 1094

BRIDEL—Dairy Products—Compagnie Laitiere BESNIER; *Int'l*, pg. 322

BRIDELICE—Dairy Products—Compagnie Laitiere BESNIER; *Int'l*, pg. 322

BRIDE'S—Magazine—The Conde Nast Publications Inc.; *U.S. Private*, pg. 20

BRIDGE BREAKER—Bin Flow Aid Devices—Hyer Industries Inc./Thayer Scale; *U.S. Private*, pg. 552

BRIDGE 96—Chromatograph Fraction Collector—Beckman Instruments, Inc.; *U.S. Public*, pg. 199

BRIDGELAM—Laminated Beams for Bridge Construction—Willamette Industries, Inc.; *U.S. Public*, pg. 1769

BRIDGEMAN—Fluid Milk Products, Ice Cream—Land O'Lakes, Inc.; *U.S. Private*, pg. 645

BRIDGEMAN'S RESTAURANTS—Ice Cream Parlors & Family Restaurants—Bridgeman's Restaurants Inc.; *U.S. Private*, pg. 167

BRIDGEPORT—Metal Working Machines—Bridgeport Machines, Inc.; *U.S. Public*, pg. 251

BRIDGEPORT—Prefinished Wall Paneling—Georgia-Pacific Corporation; *U.S. Public*, pg. 735

BRIDGES—Women's Fragrance—Tsumura International; *Int'l*, pg. 1426

BRIDGESTONE—Bicycles, Tires & Tubes—Bridgestone Cycle (U.S.A.), Inc.; *Int'l*, pg. 213

BRIDGESTONE—Tires—Bridgestone/Firestone, Inc.; *Int'l*, pg. 213

BRIDGESTONE—Tires—Bridgestone/Firestone Inc. Retail Operations; *Int'l*, pg. 213

BRIDGEWATER SPEEDY AUTO GLASS—Automotive Replacement Glass—TCG International Inc.; *Int'l*, pg. 1336

BRIDGFORD—Frozen Ready-To-Bake Bread; Beef Jerky—Bridgford Foods Corporation; *U.S. Public*, pg. 252

BRIDOU—Meats (Europe)—Sara Lee Corporation; *U.S. Public*, pg. 1432

BRIE—Canisters; Towels; T-Shirts; Stuffed Toy Figures—American Greetings Corporation; *U.S. Public*, pg. 77

BRIEFLEX—Binders & Report Covers—The Mead Corporation; *U.S. Public*, pg. 1074

BRIEFOLIO—Folder—Colad Group Inc.; *U.S. Private*, pg. 250

BRIERCREST—Mobile Home—Kit Manufacturing Company; *U.S. Public*, pg. 962

BRIGADE—Insecticide/Milticide—FMC Corp., Agricultural Products Group; *U.S. Public*, pg. 605

BRIGADE—Toilet Bowl Cleaner—The Procter & Gamble Company; *U.S. Public*, pg. 1330

BRIGADIER—NONE—Ganin Tire Co., Inc.; *U.S. Private*, pg. 439

BRIGAM'S—Ice Cream—Brigham's, Inc.; *U.S. Private*, pg. 483

BRIGGS & STRATTON—NONE—Illinois Auto Electric Co.; *U.S. Private*, pg. 557

BRIGHT AC FORMAT—Hit Song Programming—Westwood One, Inc.; *U.S. Public*, pg. 1763

BRIGHT & EARLY—Imitation Frozen Orange Juice—The Minute Maid Company; *U.S. Public*, pg. 392

BRIGHT & EASY—NONE—Ace Hardware Corporation; *U.S. Private*, pg. 12

BRIGHT BEAUTY—Spray Paints—Sherwin-Williams Diversified Brands, Inc.; *U.S. Public*, pg. 1466

BRIGHT FIELD ANALYZER (BFA)—Glass Container Inspection Device—Ball Corporation; *U.S. Public*, pg. 170

BRIGHT GIRL—Skin Cream, Lipstick, Soap—Avon Products, Inc.; *U.S. Public*, pg. 155

BRIGHT GLAZE—Glazed Ceramic Wall Tile—Florida Tile Industries, Inc.; *U.S. Public*, pg. 1322

BRIGHT GLAZE—Nominal 4″ Bright Glazed Wall Tile—United States Ceramic Tile Co.; *U.S. Private*, pg. 1124

BRIGHT LIFE—Paints—Sherwin-Williams Consumer Brands Division; *U.S. Public*, pg. 1466

BRIGHT STAR—Flashlights & Batteries—Bright Star Industries, Inc.; *U.S. Public*, pg. 1341

BRIGHT STIK—Fluorescent Lamps—General Electric Canada Inc.; *U.S. Public*, pg. 713

BRIGHTCELL—NONE—Avenor, Inc.; *Int'l*, pg. 101

BRIGHTLIFE—Sheet Vinyl Flooring—Congoleum Corporation; *U.S. Public*, pg. 69

BRIGHTON GARDENS—NONE—Marriott International, Inc.; *U.S. Public*, pg. 1047

BRIGHTON PRODUCTIONS, INC.—Production of Motion Pictures—Metromedia International Group, Inc.; *U.S. Public*, pg. 1102

BRIGHTON'S—Frozen Prepared Foods—The Earthgrains Company; *U.S. Public*, pg. 547

BRIGHTRAY—Electrical Resistance Alloys—Inco Alloys International, Inc.; *Int'l*, pg. 672

BRIGHTRAY—Alloy Series—Inco Limited; *Int'l*, pg. 672

BRIGHTS—Haircolor—Bristol-Myers Squibb Company; *U.S. Public*, pg. 253

BRIGHTS—Fruit Juices & Juice Drinks-Shelf Stable—Sundor Brands Inc.; *U.S. Public*, pg. 1331

BRIGHTWORKS—Hair Care Products—Avon Products, Inc.; *U.S. Public*, pg. 155

BRILLANCE—Lifetime Product Finish—Weiser Inc.; *U.S. Public*, pg. 1055

BRILLIANT—Brush Back Satin—Guilford Mills, Inc.; *U.S. Public*, pg. 768

BRILLIANT BLUE SR—Textile Dye—Novartis AG; *Int'l*, pg. 971

BRILLION—Farm Equipment—Brillion Iron Works, Inc.; *U.S. Public*, pg. 933

BRIM—Decaffeinated Coffee—Kraft Foods, Inc.; *U.S. Public*, pg. 1287

BRIM—Decaffeinated Coffee—Philip Morris Companies Inc.; *U.S. Public*, pg. 1287

BRIMMS—Dental Products—Brimms Inc.; *U.S. Private*, pg. 169

BRINEWELL—Trade News Magazine—The Dow Chemical Company; *U.S. Public*, pg. 522

BRING THE STARS HOME TONIGHT—Video Program—National Video, Inc.; *U.S. Public*, pg. 1755

BRINGING COLOR TO EVERYDAY BUSINESS COMMUNICATIONS—Sensitized Film & Coated Paper—The Mead Corporation; *U.S. Public*, pg. 1074

BRINGING COLOR TO EVERYDAY COMMUNICATIONS—Coated Paper & Sensitized Film—The Mead Corporation; *U.S. Public*, pg. 1074

BRINK—Mist Eliminators—Monsanto Company; *U.S. Public*, pg. 1124

BRINK & COTTON—Vise—Wilton Corporation; *U.S. Private*, pg. 1181

BRINKS—Armored Car Service—Brink's, Inc.; *U.S. Public*, pg. 1305

BRINK'S—Security Services—The Pittston Company; *U.S. Public*, pg. 1305

BRINK'S HOME SECURITY—Home Security Services—The Pittston Company; *U.S. Public*, pg. 1305

BRINTA—Breakfast Cereal—CSM N.V.; *Int'l*, pg. 243

BRIONE—Cross Court Shoe—K-Swiss Inc.; *U.S. Public*, pg. 937

BRISE—NONE—N.V. Johnson Wax Belgium S.A.; *U.S. Private*, pg. 593

BRISMET—Stainless Steel Pipe—Synalloy Corporation; *U.S. Public*, pg. 1547

BRISTOL—Cigarettes—Philip Morris Companies Inc.; *U.S. Public*, pg. 1287

BRISTEN—Basketball Shoe—K-Swiss Inc.; *U.S. Public*, pg. 937

BRISTILE—Clay Roofing Tiles, Plastic Mouldings; Vitrified Hotel Crocke—Bristile Clay Tiles, Ltd.; *Int'l*, pg. 216

BRISTOL—NONE—Bristol Hotels & Resorts; *U.S. Public*, pg. 253

BRISTOL—Cigarettes—Philip Morris U.S.A.; *U.S. Public*, pg. 1289

BRISTOL AEROSPACE—NONE—Magellan Aerospace Corporation; *Int'l*, pg. 829

BRISTOL BAR & GRILL—Restaurant—Houlihan's Restaurant Group; *U.S. Public*, pg. 841

BRISTOL HOTELS & RESORTS—NONE—Bristol Hotels & Resorts; *U.S. Public*, pg. 253

BRISTOL LANE—Sleepwear & Dresses—Lanz, Inc.; *U.S. Private*, pg. 650

BRISTOL MOTOR SPEEDWAY—NONE—Speedway Motorsports, Inc.; *U.S. Public*, pg. 1498

BRISTOL-MYERS—Pharmaceuticals—Bristol-Myers Squibb U.S. Pharmaceutical Group; *U.S. Public*, pg. 254

BRISTOL SAYBROOK—Timers/Motors—Cramer Company; *U.S. Public*, pg. 1238

BRISTOL STREET MOTORS—Motor Vehicle Dealers—Britax International plc; *Int'l*, pg. 216

BRISTOWS—Hair Products—SmithKline Beecham plc; *Int'l*, pg. 1264

BRIT TOURS—Tours—Britrail Travel International Inc.; *Int'l*, pg. 1165

BRITA—Water Filter Systems—The Clorox Company; *U.S. Public*, pg. 386

BRITANIA BY LEVI'S—Undergarments—Nantucket Industries, Inc.; *U.S. Public*, pg. 1151

BRITANNIA—Biscuits—Danone Group; *Int'l*, pg. 379

BRITANNIA—Whiskey—Montebello Brands Inc.; *U.S. Private*, pg. 758

BRITANNICA—Books & Educational Services—Encyclopaedia Britannica, Inc.; *U.S. Private*, pg. 375

BRITAPEN—Broad-Spectrum Antibiotic—SmithKline Beecham plc; *Int'l*, pg. 1264

BRITAX—Automotive Component, Child Care Products—Britax International plc; *Int'l*, pg. 216

BRITE—Voice Processing Systems—Brite Voice Systems, Inc.; *U.S. Public*, pg. 257

BRITE—Floor Polish—S.C. Johnson & Son, Inc.; *U.S. Private*, pg. 592

BRITE—Powdered Coffee Cream—Nestle Chocolate & Confection; *Int'l*, pg. 917

BRITE—Powdered Coffee Cream—Nestle S.A.; *Int'l*, pg. 915

BRITE BOND—Standard Grade Single Part Stock Computer Paper—Shade/Allied, Inc.; *U.S. Public*, pg. 89

BRITE GLAZE—Interior Wall and Countertop—Monarch Tile, Inc.; *U.S. Private*, pg. 287

BRITE LEGS—Hosiery & Related Apparel—Mayer/Berkshire Corporation; *U.S. Private*, pg. 717

BRITE LITE—Disposable Flashlights—RAYOVAC Corporation; *U.S. Public*, pg. 912

BRITE-LITE—Foodwarmers—Will & Baumer Incorporated; *U.S. Private*, pg. 1176

BRITE LITES—Truck Lighting—K-D Lamp Company; *U.S. Private*, pg. 603

BRITE MAGIC—Tough Glue—Miracle Adhesives; *U.S. Public*, pg. 1466

BRITE'N SHINY CLEANER/STRIPPER—Floor Cleaner/Stripper—Kentile Operting Co.; *U.S. Private*, pg. 615

BRITE'N SHINY FLOOR FINISH—Acrylic Floor Finish—Kentile Operting Co.; *U.S. Private*, pg. 615

BRITE-PAK—Bleach Paper & Boards—Westvaco Corporation; *U.S. Public*, pg. 1762

BRITE-STAY—Cable—Loos & Co., Inc.; *U.S. Private*, pg. 675

BRITE-TOUCH—Touch Sensitive Dimmer & Fan Speed Controls—The Lamson & Sessions Co.; *U.S. Public*, pg. 976

BRITE TOUCH—Spray Paint—Sherwin-Williams Diversified Brands, Inc.; *U.S. Public*, pg. 1466

BRITE VUE GLASS SYSTEMS—Tempered Glass and Bright Metal Entrances—Kawneer Company; *U.S. Public*, pg. 60

BRITE WALLETS—File Folders—The Mead Corporation; *U.S. Public*, pg. 1074

BRITE-GARD—Mini Halogen Light with Motion Sensor—The Lamson & Sessions Co.; *U.S. Public*, pg. 976

BRITEGARD—Clear Coating for High Wear Applications—Morton Automotive Coatings; *U.S. Public*, pg. 1135

BRITESIL—Sodium Polysilicates—PQ Corporation; *U.S. Private*, pg. 827

BRITESORB—Selective Adsorbents—PQ Corporation; *U.S. Private*, pg. 827

BRITISH AIRWAYS—Air Transportation—British Airways; *Int'l*, pg. 219

BRITISH AIRWAYS HOLIDAYS—Vacation Programs—British Airways; *Int'l*, pg. 219

BRITISH BAKER—NONE—EMAP Business Communications Division; *Int'l*, pg. 451

BRITISH HERITAGE—Periodical—Cowles Enthusiast Media, Inc.; *U.S. Private*, pg. 281

BRITISH INDICATOR—Measuring Tools—Fred V. Fowler Company, Inc.; *U.S. Private*, pg. 422

BRITISH KNIGHTS—Athletic Shoes—Jack Schwartz Shoes, Inc.; *U.S. Private*, pg. 974

BRITOS—Bite-Size Burrito Snacks—ConAgra Frozen Food Company; *U.S. Public*, pg. 427

BRITRAIL—Pass—Britrail Travel International Inc.; *Int'l*, pg. 1165

BRITTANIA—Socks—Kayser-Roth Corporation, Inc.; *Int'l*, pg. 576

BRITTANIA—War Game—Monarch Avalon, Inc.; *U.S. Public*, pg. 1123

BRITTANIA—Jeanswear—VF Corporation; *U.S. Public*, pg. 1702

BRITTANIA SPORT—Fleece Activewear—Tultex Corporation; *U.S. Public*, pg. 1644

BRITTANIA SPORTSWEAR—Apparel—Mass Market Division; *U.S. Public*, pg. 1702

BRITVIC—Soft Drinks—Whitbread PLC; *Int'l*, pg. 1498

BRIX—Charcoal—Royal Oak Enterprises, Inc.; *U.S. Private*, pg. 948

BRIXMENT—Masonry Cement—Essroc Cement, Corp.; *U.S. Private*, pg. 384

BRIXMENT-IN-COLOR—Cement—Essroc Cement, Corp.; *U.S. Private*, pg. 384

BROAD BAND DN—System Architecture—V-Band Corporation; *U.S. Public*, pg. 1701

BROADBAND SYSTEMS & DESIGN—New-Product Tabloid for Cable Television & Telecommunications Marketplace—Reed Elsevier Business Information; *Int'l*, pg. 1095

BROADCAST—Colored Copy Paper & Envelopes—Georgia-Pacific Corporation; *U.S. Public*, pg. 735

BROADCAST—Meat Products—Nestle Chocolate & Confection; *Int'l*, pg. 917

BROADCAST ENGINEERING—Publication on Broadcast Technology—Intertec Publishing; *U.S. Public*, pg. 1327

Brand Name Index

BROADCAST ENGINEERING NEWS—Magazine—Reed Business Information Pty. Limited; *Int'l*, pg. 1094

BROADCASTER PRESS—Newspaper—Shivers Trading & Operating Co.; *U.S. Private*, pg. 994

BROADCASTING & CABLE—Magazine—Reed Elsevier Business Information; *Int'l*, pg. 1095

BROADCASTING & CABLE INTERNATIONAL—Magazine—Reed Elsevier Business Information; *Int'l*, pg. 1095

BROADCOM—Electronic Components—General Instrument Corporation; *U.S. Public*, pg. 716

BROADLEAF—Lumber & Wood Products—Georgia-Pacific Corporation; *U.S. Public*, pg. 735

BROADLUME—HPS Outdoor Bracket—Guth Lighting Company; *Int'l*, pg. 821

THE BROADMOOR—Hotel—Broadmoor Hotel, Inc.; *U.S. Private*, pg. 170

BROADSIDES—Lateral Files—Steelcase Inc.; *U.S. Private*, pg. 1038

BROADSTRIKE—Herbicide—The Dow Chemical Company; *U.S. Public*, pg. 522

BROAN—Range Hoods, Ventilating Fans, Bathroom Heaters & Cabinets—Broan Mfg. Co., Inc.; *U.S. Public*, pg. 1193

BROCHURE/MAILER—Paper—PaperDirect, Inc.; *U.S. Public*, pg. 498

BROCHURE/MAILER PLUS—Paper—PaperDirect, Inc.; *U.S. Public*, pg. 498

BROCK—NONE—Brock International Inc.; *U.S. Public*, pg. 258

BROCK ACTIVITY MANAGER—Software—Brock International Inc.; *U.S. Public*, pg. 258

BROCK CONTROL SYSTEMS, INC.—NONE—Brock International Inc.; *U.S. Public*, pg. 258

BROCK CUSTOMER SERVICE ACTIVITY MANAGER—Software—Brock International Inc.; *U.S. Public*, pg. 258

BROCK DOCK—NONE—CTB International Corp.; *U.S. Public*, pg. 284

BROCK INTERNATIONAL—NONE—Brock International Inc.; *U.S. Public*, pg. 258

BROCK SALES ACTIVITY MANAGER—Software—Brock International Inc.; *U.S. Public*, pg. 258

BROCK SHUR-STEP—Bin Stairs—CTB International Corp.; *U.S. Public*, pg. 284

BROCK TELEMARKETING ACTIVITY MANAGER—Software—Brock International Inc.; *U.S. Public*, pg. 258

BROCK: "WHERE KNOWLEDGE GETS DOWN TO BUSINESS"—Corporate Slogan—Brock International Inc.; *U.S. Public*, pg. 258

BROCK'S—NONE—River Ranch Northeast, Inc.; *U.S. Private*, pg. 934

BRODERBUND—Computer Software Products—Broderbund Software, Inc.; *U.S. Public*, pg. 258

BRODERO—Pipe Coating—Dresser Industries, Inc.; *U.S. Public*, pg. 528

BROIL'N BLOT—Pans—Reynolds Metals Company; *U.S. Public*, pg. 1385

BROKEMASTER—Stock Preparation—Beloit Corporation; *U.S. Public*, pg. 789

BROKER NET—Broker Software—Metropolitan Mortgage & Securities Co., Inc.; *U.S. Private*, pg. 738

BROLIO—Italian Wines—Brown-Forman Beverages Worldwide; *U.S. Public*, pg. 261

BROLIO WINES—Wines—Brown-Forman Corporation; *U.S. Public*, pg. 261

BROLOC—Slings—Broderick & Bascom Rope Co.; *U.S. Private*, pg. 68

BROM-O-GAS—Fumigant—Great Lakes Chemical Corporation; *U.S. Public*, pg. 760

BROMAR ALASKA—NONE—Bromar Inc.; *U.S. Private*, pg. 171

BROMAR ARIZONA—NONE—Bromar Inc.; *U.S. Private*, pg. 171

BROMAR CASCADE—NONE—Bromar Inc.; *U.S. Private*, pg. 171

BROMAR FOOD SERVICE NORTH—NONE—Bromar Inc.; *U.S. Private*, pg. 171

BROMAR HAWAII—NONE—Bromar Inc.; *U.S. Private*, pg. 171

BROMAR/NBC—NONE—Bromar Inc.; *U.S. Private*, pg. 171

BROMAR NORTHERN CALIFORNIA—NONE—Bromar Inc.; *U.S. Private*, pg. 171

BROMAR OREGON—NONE—Bromar Inc.; *U.S. Private*, pg. 171

BROMAR SEATTLE—NONE—Bromar Inc.; *U.S. Private*, pg. 171

BROMAR SOUTHERN CALIFORNIA—NONE—Bromar Inc.; *U.S. Private*, pg. 171

BROMAR TRI-STATE—NONE—Bromar Inc.; *U.S. Private*, pg. 171

BROMAR UTAH/IDAHO—NONE—Bromar Inc.; *U.S. Private*, pg. 171

BROMFED—Antihistamine-Decongestant—Muro Pharmaceutical, Inc.; *U.S. Private*, pg. 767

BROMICIDE—Industrial Water Treatment—Great Lakes Chemical Corporation; *U.S. Public*, pg. 760

BRONCHENDO—NONE—SmithKline Beecham Corporation; *Int'l*, pg. 1264

BRONCHO-CATH—Endobronchial Tube—Mallinckrodt Inc.; *U.S. Public*, pg. 1039

BRONCHO-CATH—Endobronchial Tubes—Mallinckrodt Inc.; *U.S. Public*, pg. 1039

BRONCO—Herbicide—The Agricultural Group, Monsanto Company; *U.S. Public*, pg. 1125

BRONCO—Wheelbarrows—Ames Company; *U.S. Public*, pg. 1683

BRONCO—Herbicide—Monsanto Company; *U.S. Public*, pg. 1124

BRONTO—Trucks with Telescopic Platforms—Federal Signal Corporation; *U.S. Public*, pg. 616

BRONTO SKYLIFT AERIAL—NONE—Bronto Skylift Oy AB; *U.S. Public*, pg. 617

BRONZELITE—Lighting Fixtures—The Genlyte Group Incorporated; *U.S. Public*, pg. 729

BROOKFIELD—Postal Uniforms—Unitog Company; *U.S. Public*, pg. 1693

BROOKHOLLOW STRIP—Pre-Finished Strip—Bruce Hardwood Floors; *U.S. Public*, pg. 1634

BROOKLINE—Men's Shoes—E.J. Footwear Corp.; *U.S. Public*, pg. 1684

BROOKLYN—Cigarettes—SEITA, Societe Nationale D'Exploitation Industrielle des Tabacs et des Allumettes; *Int'l*, pg. 1219

BROOKLYN UNION—Gas Company—Brooklyn Union; *U.S. Public*, pg. 259

BROOKS—Catsup, Chili Beans & Tomatoes—Curtice Burns Foods; *U.S. Private*, pg. 887

BROOKS & BENTLEY—Consumer Durables—Brown-Forman Corporation; *U.S. Public*, pg. 261

BROOKS BROTHERS—NONE—Luxottica Group S.p.A.; *Int'l*, pg. 822

BROOKS-MAG—Control Measurement—Brooks Instrument; *U.S. Public*, pg. 574

BROOKSIDE PLANK—Pre-Finished Strip—Bruce Hardwood Floors; *U.S. Public*, pg. 1634

BROOKSMITE—Control Measurement—Brooks Instrument; *U.S. Public*, pg. 574

BROOMETTE—Carpet Sweeper—Bissell Inc.; *U.S. Private*, pg. 145

BROOMSTICKS—Men's Slacks—Glen Oaks Industries, Inc.; *U.S. Private*, pg. 456

BROOMWADE—Reciprocating Compressors—ComPair LeRoi; *Int'l*, pg. 1242

BROPYR—Plant Protectives—DSM Chemie Linz GmbH; *Int'l*, pg. 356

BROPYR FULLUP—Herbicides—Agrolinz Melamin GmbH; *Int'l*, pg. 356

BROSELOW/HINKLE—Pediatric Emergency System—Vital Signs, Inc.; *U.S. Public*, pg. 1723

BROSSARD—Cakes & Savory Products—Grand Metropolitan Plc; *Int'l*, pg. 408

BROSSARD—Cakes, Biscuits, Waffles—GrandMet Foods Southern Europe; *Int'l*, pg. 409

BROSSARD—Ambient, Chilled & Frozen Cakes and Gateaux—GrandMet Foods UK; *Int'l*, pg. 408

BROSSARD—Chilled & Frozen Cakes & Gateaux—GrandMet Foods UK; *Int'l*, pg. 408

BROTHER—Sewing Machines, Typewriters—Brother International Corporation; *Int'l*, pg. 229

BROTJE—Heating Equipment—Blue Circle Industries PLC; *Int'l*, pg. 197

BROUGHAM—Car—Cadillac Motor Car Division; *U.S. Public*, pg. 720

BROUWER—Comml. Turf Machinery—Ransomes Plc; *Int'l*, pg. 1087

BROVIAC—Vascular Access Catheter—Davol Inc.; *U.S. Public*, pg. 189

BROWER—Livestock & Poultry Equipment—Brower Equipment; *U.S. Private*, pg. 511

BROWER—Poultry & Livestock Equipment—Hawkeye Steel Products, Inc.; *U.S. Private*, pg. 511

BROWER PROCESSING—Equipment for Processing Birds—Hawkeye Steel Products, Inc.; *U.S. Private*, pg. 511

BROWIO TUSCAN—Wines—Canandaigua Wine Co.; *U.S. Public*, pg. 300

BROWN AIR DERMATOME—Powered Skin Grafting Instrument—Zimmer, Inc.; *U.S. Public*, pg. 254

BROWN & POLSON—Corn & Other Starches, Desserts, Baking Aids—Bestfoods; *U.S. Public*, pg. 223

BROWN & POLSON—Corn Flour—CPC Foods (Ireland) Ltd.; *U.S. Public*, pg. 225

BROWN & SHARPE—Measuring Instruments—Brown & Sharpe Manufacturing Company; *U.S. Public*, pg. 260

BROWN & SHARPE—NONE—DeVlieg-Bullard Inc.; *U.S. Public*, pg. 502

BROWN & WILLIAMSON"S SUN CURED—Plug Tobacco—Brown & Williamson Tobacco Corp.; *Int'l*, pg. 111

BROWN-BRIDGE—Adhesive Coated Paper & Cloth—Kimberly-Clark Corporation; *U.S. Public*, pg. 958

BROWN COW—Chocolate Syrup—Hershey Foods Corporation; *U.S. Public*, pg. 811

BROWN DEVILS—Fix Resistor—Ohmite Manufacturing Company; *U.S. Private*, pg. 813

BROWN EDGE—Wafers—Nabisco Inc.; *U.S. Public*, pg. 1355

BROWN GOLD—Coffee—Tetley USA Inc.; *Int'l*, pg. 1377

BROWN & HALEY SELECTIONS—Chocolate—Brown & Haley; *U.S. Private*, pg. 173

BROWN-IN-BAG—Transparent Plastic Film Bags—Reynolds Metals Company; *U.S. Public*, pg. 1385

BROWN 'N SERVE—Ham Patties & Sausages—Armour Swift Eckrich; *U.S. Public*, pg. 426

BROWNBERRY—Specialty Baked Goods, Breads—Bestfoods; *U.S. Public*, pg. 223

BROWNBUILT—Storage Systems—Email Limited; *Int'l*, pg. 450

BROWNES—Dairy Products—Peters & Brownes Foods Ltd.; *Int'l*, pg. 1040

BROWNIE—Cameras, Motion Picture Projectors, Accessories—Eastman Kodak Company; *U.S. Public*, pg. 550

BROWNING—Pulleys, Sheaves, Pillow Block Bearings—Bryant Electric Supply Company, Inc.; *U.S. Private*, pg. 177

BROWNING—Power Transmission Products—Emerson Electric Co.; *U.S. Public*, pg. 572

BROWNING—Shotguns—Herstal S.A.; *Int'l*, pg. 617

BROWNING-FERRIS INDUSTRIES, INC.—NONE—Browning-Ferris Industries, Inc.; *U.S. Public*, pg. 262

BROWN'S DIRECTORY—Trade Directory—Advanstar Communications; *U.S. Private*, pg. 22

BROWSABOUTS—Shoes—Oomphies, Inc.; *U.S. Private*, pg. 817

BROXABLET—Granular Salt, Tablet Form—Akzo Nobel N.V.; *Int'l*, pg. 42

BROXIL—Antibiotic—SmithKline Beecham plc; *Int'l*, pg. 1264

BROXO—Granular Salt—Akzo Nobel N.V.; *Int'l*, pg. 42

BROXOMATIC—Granular Salt—Akzo Nobel N.V.; *Int'l*, pg. 42

BROYHILL—NONE—Broyhill Furniture Industries, Inc.; *U.S. Public*, pg. 688

BROYHILL—Furniture—Furniture Brands International Inc.; *U.S. Public*, pg. 688

BROYHILL—NONE—Royal Waterbeds; *U.S. Private*, pg. 949

BRU—Low Sparkling Natural Mineral Water—Spadel SA; *Int'l*, pg. 1287

BRU-MASH—Dairy Feed—Labatt Brewing Company Limited; *Int'l*, pg. 679

BRU-MASH—Dairy Feed—Miracle Feeds Inc.; *U.S. Private*, pg. 432

BRUCE—Kitchen & Vanity Cabinets—Triangle Pacific Corporation; *U.S. Public*, pg. 1634

BRUCE COLD-STIK ADHESVIE—Asphalt-Based Adhesive—Bruce Hardwood Floors; *U.S. Public*, pg. 1634

BRUCE EVERBOND LP ADHESIVE—Plyable Solvent-Based Adhesive—Bruce Hardwood Floors; *U.S. Public*, pg. 1634

THE BRUCE WILLIAMS SHOW—Talk Radio Program—Westwood One Entertainment; *U.S. Public*, pg. 1763

THE BRUCE WILLIAMS SHOW—Talk Program—Westwood One, Inc.; *U.S. Public*, pg. 1763

BRUCE WILLIAM'S TRAVEL CORNER—Talk Radio Program—Westwood One Entertainment; *U.S. Public*, pg. 1763

BRUCE WILLIAM'S TRAVEL CORNER—Travel Tips Programming—Westwood One, Inc.; *U.S. Public*, pg. 1763

BRUCE'S—Southern Vegetables—Bruce Foods Corp.; *U.S. Private*, pg. 175

BRUISER—Nozzle—The Dow Chemical Company; *U.S. Public*, pg. 522

BRUISER—Corrosion Resistant Pumps—Osmonics, Inc.; *U.S. Public*, pg. 1233

BRULIN MP1793—Non Chlorinated Wipe Solvent, RTU, In Liquid & Wipes—The Brulin Corporation; *U.S. Private*, pg. 176

BRULIN 1990GD—Aqueous Detergent, Biodegradable Spray Wash—The Brulin Corporation; *U.S. Private*, pg. 176

BRUMKO MAGNETICS—Head—Magnetics Data Inc.; *U.S. Public*, pg. 695

BRUMLOW—Bathroom Rugs & Sets & Area Rugs—Peerless Carpet Corporation; *Int'l*, pg. 1032

BRUNELLO DI MONTALCINO—NONE—Castello Banfi Srl.; *U.S. Private*, pg. 113

BRUNER COMMERCIAL/INDUSTRIAL—Catalog & Specialy Engineered Water Treatment Systems—Bruner Water Treatment Systems; *U.S. Public*, pg. 467

BRUNER RESIDENTIAL—Wholesale Residential Softeners, Filters & Drinking Water Systems—Bruner Water Treatment Systems; *U.S. Public*, pg. 467

BRUNETTE—Cigarettes—Philip Morris Companies Inc.; *U.S. Public*, pg. 1287

BRUNING PAINT—Paint—Bruning Paint Company; *U.S. Private*, pg. 176

BRUNO'S—Food & Pharmacy Stores for One-Stop Shopping—Bruno's Inc.; *U.S. Public*, pg. 265

BRUNSWICK—Bowling & Billiards Equipment—Brunswick Corporation; *U.S. Public*, pg. 265

BRUNSWICK—Canned Seafood—Connors Brunswick, Inc.; *U.S. Private*, pg. 264

BRUNSWICK—Sea Food Prods.—George Weston Limited; *Int'l*, pg. 1494

BRUSH—Recorders—Gould Instrument Systems, Inc.; *U.S. Public*, pg. 1592

BRUSH N' FLOSS—NONE—Lee Pharmaceuticals; *U.S. Public*, pg. 984

BRUSH NOW—Disposable Toothbrush—Venturi Inc.; *U.S. Private*, pg. 1136

BRUSH-ON-BLUSH—Blusher—Cover Girl Cosmetics; *U.S. Public*, pg. 1330

BRUSH-PACK—Filamentary Extended-Surface Packings—Beco Engineering Company; *U.S. Private*, pg. 129

BRUSH PLUS—Shaving System—The Gillette Company; *U.S. Public*, pg. 743

BRUSH UP—Denture Cleanser—The Gillette Company; *U.S. Public*, pg. 743

BRUSH UP!—Service Products—R&B, Inc.; *U.S. Public*, pg. 1354

BRUSH WELLMAN—Beryllium Metal, Ceramic, Specialty Metal Systems& Precious Metals—Brush Wellman Inc.; *U.S. Public*, pg. 266

BRUSHLESS DC—NONE—Philips Automotive Electronics; *Int'l*, pg. 1054

BRUSHLON—Abrasive & Non-Abrasive Brush Material—3M; *U.S. Public*, pg. 1604

BRUT—Men's Fragrance, Deodorant & Toiletries—Chesebrough-Pond's USA Co.; *Int'l*, pg. 1435

BRUT—Slacks, Jeans, Shorts—The Spencer Group Inc.; *U.S. Private*, pg. 1025

BRUT & BRUT 33—Men's Underwear—Nantucket Industries, Inc.; *U.S. Public*, pg. 1151

BRUT DE POMME—Carbonated Apple Drink—Groupe Pernod Ricard; *Int'l*, pg. 566

BRUT 33—Men's Fragrance & Toiletries—Chesebrough-Pond's USA Co.; *Int'l*, pg. 1435

BRUTE—Mops, Mop Buckets, Brushes, Brooms & Trash Containers—Rubbermaid Incorporated; *U.S. Public*, pg. 1411

BRUTE—Electronic Deadbolt—Sargent & Greenleaf, Inc.; *U.S. Private*, pg. 965

BRUTE FORCE—Pressure Washers—Breuer/Tornado; *U.S. Private*, pg. 167

BRUTE POWER—Power Transmission System—Echlin Inc.; *U.S. Public*, pg. 560

THE BRUTE—Professional Rules—Arrow Fastener Co., Inc.; *U.S. Private*, pg. 85

BRUTE II—Corrosion Resistant Pumps—Osmonics, Inc.; *U.S. Public*, pg. 1233

BRUTES—Small Toy Vehicles—Empire of Carolina, Inc.; *U.S. Public*, pg. 579

BRUTUS UP—Air-operated Double Diaphragm Pump—Osmonics, Inc.; *U.S. Public*, pg. 1233

BRUYNZEEL STORAGE SYSTEMS—NONE—Electrolux, AB; *Int'l*, pg. 438

BRYAN FOODS—Meat Products—Sara Lee Corporation; *U.S. Public*, pg. 1432

BRYANT—Heating & Air Conditioning Equipment—Carrier Corp.; *U.S. Public*, pg. 1690

BRYANT—Heating & Cooling Systems—Carrier Corporation; *U.S. Public*, pg. 1689

BRYANT—Air Conditioners—The Climatic Corp.; *U.S. Private*, pg. 246

BRYANT—Heating & Air Conditioning Equipment—The Habegger Corporation; *U.S. Private*, pg. 492

BRYCE—Diesel & Fuel Injection Equipment/Agricultural & Industrial Products—Lucas Industries Inc.; *Int'l*, pg. 820

BRYCE—NONE—LucasVarity plc; *Int'l*, pg. 819

BRYCO—Automotive Aftermarket—Carfel, Inc.; *U.S. Private*, pg. 210

BRYLCREEM—Hair Care Product—Sara Lee Corporation; *U.S. Public*, pg. 1432

BRYLCREEM—Hair Styling Products, Shampoos & Conditioners—SmithKline Beecham Corporation; *Int'l*, pg. 1264

BRYLCREEM—Hair Dressing—SmithKline Beecham plc; *Int'l*, pg. 1264

BRYN MAWR—NONE—CertainTeed Corporation; *Int'l*, pg. 1170

BRYZA—Laundry Detergent—Benckiser Consumer Products Inc.; *Int'l*, pg. 185

BUB—Bath Tablets Designed to Stimulate Circulation & Relieve Fatigue—Kao Corporation; *Int'l*, pg. 717

BUBBL-EEZ—Bubble Gum—Lotte U.S.A., Inc.; *Int'l*, pg. 819

BUBBLE BEEPER—Bubble Gum—Amurol Confections Co.; *U.S. Public*, pg. 1781

BUBBLE BURGER—Gum—Fleer-Skybox International Inc.; *U.S. Public*, pg. 1052

BUBBLE DUDE—Tubed Bubble Gum—Amurol Confections Co.; *U.S. Public*, pg. 1781

BUBBLE-JET—Computer Printers—Canon Inc.; *Int'l*, pg. 261

BUBBLE JUG—Bubble Gum—Amurol Confections Co.; *U.S. Public*, pg. 1781

BUBBLE LOCKER—Bubble Gum—Amurol Confections Co.; *U.S. Public*, pg. 1781

BUBBLE MACHINE—Toy—Empire of Carolina, Inc.; *U.S. Public*, pg. 579

BUBBLE MASK—Adhesive-Coated Air Cellular Cushioning Material—Sealed Air Corporation; *U.S. Public*, pg. 1450

BUBBLE TAPE—Bubble Gum—Amurol Confections Co.; *U.S. Public*, pg. 1781

BUBBLE THING—Toy—Mattel, Inc.; *U.S. Public*, pg. 1057

BUBBLE-UP—Soft Drink—The Monarch Company, Inc.; *U.S. Private*, pg. 756

BUBBLE YUM—Gums—Nabisco Inc.; *U.S. Public*, pg. 1355

BUBBLE YUM—Bubble Gum—Planters Company; *U.S. Public*, pg. 1355

BUBBLE YUM—Bubble Gum—RJR Nabisco Holdings Corp.; *U.S. Public*, pg. 1354

BUBBLEGUMMERS—Infant Clothes—Sao Paulo Alpargatas S.A.; *Int'l*, pg. 1193

BUBBLES THE WHALE—Children's Hamper—Rubbermaid Incorporated; *U.S. Public*, pg. 1411

BUBBLICIOUS—Chewing Gum—Adams U.S.A.; *U.S. Public*, pg. 1739

BUBBLICIOUS—Chewing Gum—Warner-Lambert Company; *U.S. Public*, pg. 1738

BUBBLICIOUS GUM—Chewing Gum—Warner-Lambert K.K.; *U.S. Public*, pg. 1739

BUBBLITE—Darkroom Safe-Lights—Nuarc Company, Inc.; *U.S. Private*, pg. 808

BUCCANEER—Sporting Goods—Brunswick Bowling & Billiards Corp.; *U.S. Public*, pg. 265

BUCHANAN—Wood & Lumber Products—Georgia-Pacific Corporation; *U.S. Public*, pg. 735

BUCHANAN—Electrical Terminal Blocks & Crimping Tools—Thomas & Betts/Amerace; *U.S. Public*, pg. 1598

BUCHANAN—Electronic Terminal Blocks & Connectors—Thomas & Betts Corporation; *U.S. Public*, pg. 1597

BUCHANAN'S DE LUXE—NONE—Guinness Plc; *Int'l*, pg. 412

BUCHANANS—Scotch—United Distillers USA, Inc.; *Int'l*, pg. 412

BUCHBINDER—Device—Medtronic, Inc.; *U.S. Public*, pg. 1082

BUCHI—Evaporators—Brinkmann Instruments, Inc.; *U.S. Private*, pg. 169

BUCILLA—Yarns & Needlecraft Products—Bucilla Corporation; *U.S. Public*, pg. 352

BUCK—Cutlery—Buck Knives, Inc.; *U.S. Private*, pg. 177

BUCK TOOL—All Purpose Folding Needlenose w/ Blades & Tools 1M Handle—Buck Knives, Inc.; *U.S. Private*, pg. 177

BUCKET OF FUN—Beverage Cooler—Igloo Products Corporation; *U.S. Public*, pg. 265

BUCKEYE—Potato Chips—Borden, Inc.; *U.S. Private*, pg. 157

BUCKEYE—Power Tools & Assembly Systems—Cooper Industries, Inc.; *U.S. Public*, pg. 442

BUCKEYE—Computer & Data Processing Supplies—Pubco Corporation; *U.S. Public*, pg. 1339

BUCKEYE—Rolled Oats—The Quaker Oats Company; *U.S. Public*, pg. 1347

BUCKEYE—Cookware—Regal Ware, Inc.; *U.S. Private*, pg. 917

BUCKHORN—Beer—Pabst Brewing Co.; *U.S. Private*, pg. 954

BUCKHORN—Beer—Pabst Brewing Co./Tumwater; *U.S. Private*, pg. 954

BUCKHORN FAMILY RESTAURANT—24 Hour Restaurant—Travel Ports of America Inc.; *U.S. Public*, pg. 1632

BUCKINGHAM—Hardwood Doors—Georgia-Pacific Corporation; *U.S. Public*, pg. 735

BUCKINGHAM COLLECTION—Drapery Hardware—Kirsch; *U.S. Public*, pg. 1176

BUCKLE—Herbicide—Monsanto Company; *U.S. Public*, pg. 1124

BUCKLER—Non-Alcoholic Beer—Heineken N.V.; *Int'l*, pg. 608

BUCKLER—Non-Alcoholic Beer—Heineken USA Inc.; *Int'l*, pg. 608

BUCKLITE—Cutlery—Buck Knives, Inc.; *U.S. Private*, pg. 177

BUCKS—Cigarettes—Philip Morris Companies Inc.; *U.S. Public*, pg. 1287

BUCKS—Discount Priced Cigarettes—Philip Morris U.S.A.; *U.S. Public*, pg. 1289

BUCKWORN—Tradename—Myers Industries, Inc.; *U.S. Public*, pg. 1143

BUD—Beer—Anheuser-Busch Companies, Inc.; *U.S. Public*, pg. 113

BUD—Electronic Enclosures—Bud Industries, Inc.; *U.S. Private*, pg. 178

BUD—Beer—Central de Cervejas, S.A.; *Int'l*, pg. 279

BUD DRY—Beer—Anheuser-Busch Companies, Inc.; *U.S. Public*, pg. 113

BUD LIGHT—Beer—Anheuser-Busch Companies, Inc.; *U.S. Public*, pg. 113

BUDDIG—Meats—Carl Buddig & Company; *U.S. Private*, pg. 178

BUDDY BUDDIES—Greeting Cards—American Greetings Corporation; *U.S. Public*, pg. 77

BUDDY L—Toys—Empire of Carolina, Inc.; *U.S. Public*, pg. 579

BUDENE—Polbutadiene Rubber—The Goodyear Tire & Rubber Company; *U.S. Public*, pg. 752

BUDERUS—Household Appliances—Electrolux, AB; *Int'l*, pg. 438

BUDGET-DASD—DASD Space Budgeting & Cost Control—Boole & Babbage, Inc.; *U.S. Public*, pg. 244

BUDGET-DRI—Oil & Grease Absorbent—Oil-Dri Corporation of America; *U.S. Public*, pg. 1214

BUDGET FOLD—NONE—Wisconsin Tissue Mills, Inc.; *U.S. Public*, pg. 347

BUDGET GOURMET—Frozen Entrees—H.J. Heinz Company; *U.S. Public*, pg. 805

BUDGET GOURMET—Frozen Entrees—Kraft Foods Inc.; *U.S. Public*, pg. 1288

BUDGET GOURMET—Frozen Entrees & Dinners—Philip Morris Companies Inc.; *U.S. Public*, pg. 1287

THE BUDGET GOURMET—Frozen Entree— Weight Watchers Gourmet Food Company; *U.S. Public*, pg. 806

BUDGET RENT A CAR—Car Rental—Budget Rent A Car Corporation; *U.S. Private*, pg. 178

BUDGET RENT A TRUCK—Truck Rental—Budget Rent A Car Corporation; *U.S. Private*, pg. 178

BUDGET-TOTE—Plastic Product—Uniflex, Inc.; *U.S. Public*, pg. 1665

BUDGET WISE—Turkeys—Norbest, Inc.; *U.S. Private*, pg. 801

BUDGETEL—Economy Motels—The Marcus Corporation; *U.S. Public*, pg. 1044

BUDWEISER—Beer—Anheuser-Busch Companies, Inc.; *U.S. Public*, pg. 113

BUDWEISER ICE DRAFT—Beer—Anheuser-Busch Companies, Inc.; *U.S. Public*, pg. 113

BUEHLER/METASERV—Abrasive Cutter—Buehler, Limited; *Int'l*, pg. 574

BUENA VIDA—Tortillas—Azteca Foods, Incorporated; *U.S. Private*, pg. 104

BUENA VISTA—Restaurant—Houlihan's Restaurant Group; *U.S. Public*, pg. 841

BUENA VISTA—Premium Wines—Racke USA; *Int'l*, pg. 1083

BUENA VISTA CARNEROS—Wine—Buena Vista Winery; *Int'l*, pg. 1083

BUENA VISTA MOVIES—Movie Label—The Walt Disney Company; *U.S. Public*, pg. 511

BUENO—Avocados—Calavo Growers of California; *U.S. Private*, pg. 199

BUF-PUF—Facial Cleansing Sponge—3M; *U.S. Public*, pg. 1604

BUFF BOSS—Power Tools—The Black & Decker Corporation; *U.S. Public*, pg. 233

BUFF 'N PUFF—Greeting Cards—American Greetings Corporation; *U.S. Public*, pg. 77

BUFF NE'ER TEAR—Smooth & Rough Converting Paper—Champion International Corp.; *U.S. Public*, pg. 333

BUFFALO—Artist Color Markers—Dri Mark Products, Inc.; *U.S. Private*, pg. 342

BUFFALO—Farm Equipment—Fleischer Manufacturing, Inc.; *U.S. Private*, pg. 410

BUFFALO—China—Oneida Ltd.; *U.S. Public*, pg. 1225

BUFFALO CULTIVATOR—High Residue/No-Till/Ridge Till Cultivator—Fleischer Manufacturing, Inc.; *U.S. Private*, pg. 410

BUFFALO FLAIL SHREDDER—Shredder—Fleischer Manufacturing, Inc.; *U.S. Private*, pg. 410

BUFFALO LAW JOURNAL—Law Journal—Business First of New York, Inc.; *U.S. Private*, pg. 19

BUFFALO PATCH—Silicon Carbide Refractory Cements—Ferro Corporation; *U.S. Public*, pg. 618

BUFFALO RESIDUE CLIPPERS—Attachment for Added Residue Cutting on Buffalo Planters & Ridge Runners—Fleischer Manufacturing, Inc.; *U.S. Private*, pg. 410

BUFFALO RIDGE RUNNERS—Planter Attachments—Fleischer Manufacturing, Inc.; *U.S. Private*, pg. 410

BUFFALO ROCK—Soft Drink—Buffalo Rock Company; *U.S. Private*, pg. 179

BUFFALO SABRES—Hockey Team—Niagara Frontier Hockey, L.P.; *U.S. Private*, pg. 798

BUFFALO SCOUT II—Electronics Over Hydraulic Guidance System for Planters & Cultivators—Fleischer Manufacturing, Inc.; *U.S. Private*, pg. 410

BUFFALO SLOT PLANTER—No Till Planter—Fleischer Manufacturing, Inc.; *U.S. Private*, pg. 410

BUFFALO TILL PLANTER—Ridge Till Planter—Fleischer Manufacturing, Inc.; *U.S. Private*, pg. 410

BUFFEREZE—Prepackaged Buffers—Eastman Kodak Company; *U.S. Public*, pg. 550

BUFFERIN—Analgesic—Bristol-Myers Squibb Company; *U.S. Public*, pg. 253

BUFFET—Pet Foods—Nestle S.A.; *Int'l*, pg. 915

BUFFMASTER—Power Tools—The Black & Decker Corporation; *U.S. Public*, pg. 233

BUFLOC—Flocculating Agents—Buckman Laboratories Inc.; *U.S. Private*, pg. 180

BUFLON 2000—Wall Covering—Solvay S.A.; *Int'l*, pg. 1277

BUG CITY—Candy Tarts—Amurol Confections Co.; *U.S. Public*, pg. 1781

BUG MUGGER—Truck & Van Accessories—Kenco; *U.S. Public*, pg. 1769

BUGHOUND—NONE—GenRad, Inc.; *U.S. Public*, pg. 731

BUGLE BOY—Family Clothing—Bugle Boy Industries, Inc.; *U.S. Private*, pg. 179

BUGLE BOY—Belts—Tandy Brands Accessories, Inc.; *U.S. Public*, pg. 1560

BUGLER—Cigarette Tobacco—Brown & Williamson Tobacco Corp.; *Int'l*, pg. 111

BUGLES—Snacks—General Mills, Inc.; *U.S. Public*, pg. 717

BUGLES—NONE—Snacks Unlimited Division; *U.S. Public*, pg. 718

BUGS-BUNNY—Multiple Vitamins—Bayer Corporation/Consumer Care Division; *Int'l*, pg. 173

BUGS BUNNY—Graham Cookies—Nabisco Inc.; *U.S. Public*, pg. 1355

BUGS BUNNY—Graham Cookies—RJR Nabisco Holdings Corp.; *U.S. Public*, pg. 1354

BUGS BUNNY VITAMINS—Vitamins—Bayer AG; *Int'l*, pg. 171

BUHLER—Perfume—Rhone-Poulenc S.A.; *Int'l*, pg. 1108

BUHR—NONE—Cross Huiler; *Int'l*, pg. 1389

BUICK—Cars—General Motors Corporation; *U.S. Public*, pg. 718

BUICK CENTURY—Cars—General Motors Corporation; *U.S. Public*, pg. 718

BUICK LESABRE—Cars—General Motors Corporation; *U.S. Public*, pg. 718

BUICK PARK AVENUE—Cars—General Motors Corporation; *U.S. Public*, pg. 718

BUILDERS CHOICE—Acrylic Whirlpools—Lasco Bathware; *Int'l*, pg. 1397

BUILDERS SQUARE—Home Improvement Products—Builders Square, Inc.; *U.S. Private*, pg. 477

BUILDERS SQUARE—NONE—Kmart Corporation; *U.S. Public*, pg. 963

BUILDER'S TUBE—Construction Products—Sonoco Products Company; *U.S. Public*, pg. 1485

BUILDING DESIGN & CONSTRUCTION—Magazine Focused on the Design & Construction of Non-Residential Buildings—Reed Elsevier Business Information; *Int'l*, pg. 1095

BUILDING PACK—NONE—Meyer International PLC; *Int'l*, pg. 864

BUILDING RENOVATION—Periodical—Penton Publishing, Inc.; *U.S. Public*, pg. 1306

BUILDING SOLUTIONS—NONE—CertainTeed Corporation; *Int'l*, pg. 1170

BUILT BETTER, GUARANTEED LONGER—NONE—Calton, Inc.; *U.S. Public*, pg. 296

BUILT TO SURVIVE THE REAL WORLD—Ice Chest—Igloo Products Corporation; *U.S. Public*, pg. 265

BUITONI—Macaroni & Sphagetti—Contadina Dalla Casa Buitoni; *Int'l*, pg. 916

BUITONI—Pasta—Nestle S.A.; *Int'l*, pg. 915

BUITONI—Pasta & Sauces—Nestle USA; *Int'l*, pg. 916

BUKO—Cheese—MD Foods; *Int'l*, pg. 826

BULFINCH PRESS—NONE—Little, Brown & Co.; *U.S. Public*, pg. 1612

BULGARI—Watches & Jewelry—Bulgari Corporation of America; *Int'l*, pg. 232

BULKAN—Containers—Sealright Company, Inc.; *U.S. Public*, pg. 1451

BULKDRUM—275 Gallon Plastic Container in Steel Shell—Hoover Group, Inc.; *U.S. Private*, pg. 538

BULKDRUM II—275 Gallon Plastic Container Contained in a Fiber Box—Hoover Group, Inc.; *U.S. Private*, pg. 538

BULKEE—NONE—Medline Industries, Inc.; *U.S. Private*, pg. 728

BULKEE II—Fluffy Gauze Sponges—Medline Industries, Inc.; *U.S. Private*, pg. 728

BULKLEY DUNTON—Paper—Resource Net International; *U.S. Public*, pg. 903

BULKSERVE—Containers—Sealright Company, Inc.; *U.S. Public*, pg. 1451

BULKTOBAC—Tobacco Curing System—Gas-Fired Products, Inc.; *U.S. Private*, pg. 440

BULL—Brand Hot Sauce—Trappey's Fine Foods, Inc.; *U.S. Private*, pg. 105

BULL & HAMMAID'S—Meat Snacks—E.W. Knauss & Son, Inc.; *U.S. Private*, pg. 626

BULL CP8SMART CARD—Credit Cards—Compagnie des Machines Bull; *Int'l*, pg. 315

BULL DOG—Tape—American Biltrite Inc.; *U.S. Public*, pg. 68

BULL DOG—Rubber Lagged Head Pulleys—Portec, Inc.-Construction Equipment Div.; *U.S. Public*, pg. 1318

BULL DOG—Acrylic Primer—Premier Coatings, Inc.; *Int'l*, pg. 1488

BULL DPS—Computers—Compagnie des Machines Bull; *Int'l*, pg. 315

BULL DRIVER—Large-handled Screwdrivers—Klein Tools Inc.; *U.S. Private*, pg. 625

BULL ICE—NONE—The Stroh Brewery Company; *U.S. Private*, pg. 1047

BULL OF THE WOODS—Plug Chewing Tobacco—Conwood Company L.P.; *U.S. Private*, pg. 272

BULLARD—NONE—DeVlieg-Bullard Inc.; *U.S. Public*, pg. 502

BULLARD BVC—Vertical Chucking Machines—WCI Machine Tools & Systems; *Int'l*, pg. 440

BULLARD VTL—Machine Tools—WCI Machine Tools & Systems; *Int'l*, pg. 440

BULLARD 3000—CNC Horizontal Lathe—WCI Machine Tools & Systems; *Int'l*, pg. 440

BULLARD 6000—CNC Horizontal Lathe—WCI Machine Tools & Systems; *Int'l*, pg. 440

BULLDAWG—Power Tools—The Black & Decker Corporation; *U.S. Public*, pg. 233

BULLDOG—Cotton Flags—Dettra Flag Company; *U.S. Private*, pg. 328

BULLDOG—Pumps—Graco Inc.; *U.S. Public*, pg. 756

BULLDOG—Trailer Parts, Jacks, Couplers, Axles—The Hammerblow Corp.; *U.S. Private*, pg. 498

BULLDOG—Clips—Hunt Corporation; *U.S. Public*, pg. 848

BULLDOG—Home Hardware—Newell Co.; *U.S. Public*, pg. 1176

BULLET—Drill Bits—The Black & Decker Corporation; *U.S. Public*, pg. 233

BULLET—Cameras—Eastman Kodak Company; *U.S. Public*, pg. 550

BULLET—Pens—Eversharp Pen Co.; *U.S. Private*, pg. 386

BULLET—Herbicide—Monsanto Company; *U.S. Public*, pg. 1124

BULLET DUFFLE—Luggage—Lark Luggage Company, Inc.; *U.S. Public*, pg. 1430

BULLET PILOT-POINT—Accessories—The Black & Decker Corporation; *U.S. Public*, pg. 233

BULLET RESISTANT—Bullet Resistant Laminated Glass—Globe-Amerada Glass Company; *U.S. Private*, pg. 458

BULLETIN BOARD—Wall Linoleum—Forbo Holding SA; *Int'l*, pg. 496

BULLFROG—Sunblock & Sunscreen—Chattem, Inc.; *U.S. Public*, pg. 341

BULLFROG—Sunblock—Chattem, Inc., Consumer Products Division; *U.S. Public*, pg. 341

BULLFROG—Games Developed by UK Based Subsidiary Relating to Stories & Strategy—Electronic Arts; *U.S. Public*, pg. 569

BULLOCK—Modular Homes & Garages—Curt Bullock Builders, Inc.; *U.S. Private*, pg. 180

BULLPEN CHEW—Sunflower Seeds—RJR Nabisco Holdings Corp.; *U.S. Public*, pg. 1354

BULLS EYE—Putters—Acushnet Company; *U.S. Public*, pg. 675

BULL'S EYE—B-B-Q Sauce—Alliant Foodservice, Inc.; *U.S. Private*, pg. 244

BULL'S EYE—Flowmeter—Bailey, Fischer & Porter Company; *Int'l*, pg. 449

BULL'S-EYE—Barbecue Sauce—Kraft Foods Inc.; *U.S. Public*, pg. 1288

BULL'S EYE—Barbeque Sauces—Philip Morris Companies Inc.; *U.S. Public*, pg. 1287

BULL'S EYE—Barbeque Sauce—Ridg's Finer Foods; *U.S. Public*, pg. 1288

BULLS EYE—Shellac—Wm. Zinsser & Co., Inc.; *U.S. Public*, pg. 1358

BULLS EYE 1-2-3—Interior & Exterior Water-Based Primer-Sealer—Wm. Zinsser & Co., Inc.; *U.S. Public*, pg. 1358

BULLS-EYE PUTTERS—Golf Equipment—Fortune Brands, Inc.; *U.S. Public*, pg. 674

BULLS EYE SHELLAC—Coating—RPM, Inc.; *U.S. Public*, pg. 1356

BULMER'S WOODPECKER—Cider—Wisdom Imports Sales Co. Inc.; *Int'l*, pg. 679

BULOVA—Watches and Clocks—Bulova Corporation; *U.S. Public*, pg. 1010

BULOVA—Watches, Clocks, Timepiece Parts & Power Cells—Loews Corporation; *U.S. Public*, pg. 1010

BUMBLE BEE—Seafood Products—Bumble Bee Seafoods Inc.; *U.S. Private*, pg. 526

BUMBLE BEE TUNA—NONE—International Home Foods Inc.; *U.S. Private*, pg. 526

BUMEX—Diuretic—Roche Holding Ltd.; *Int'l*, pg. 1119

BUMINATE—Albumin (Human)—Baxter-Hyland; *U.S. Public*, pg. 196

BUMP FIGHTER—Ethnic Shaving Products—American Safety Razor Company; *U.S. Private*, pg. 597

BUMP PUMP—Rotary Pumps—Tuthill Pump; *U.S. Private*, pg. 1111

BUMPER TO BUMPER—Automotive Parts—Acklands Limited; *Int'l*, pg. 23

BUMPERS—Athletic Footwear—International Seaway Trading Corporation; *U.S. Private*, pg. 572

BUMPON—Molded Protective Shapes—3M; *U.S. Public*, pg. 1604

BUMS—Greeting Cards—American Greetings Corporation; *U.S. Public*, pg. 77

BUNBLASTER—NONE—Infinicom; *U.S. Private*, pg. 561

BUNCH O CRUNCH—Fish Sticks & Portions—Frionor U.S.A. Inc.; *Int'l*, pg. 516

BUNCHA CRUNCH—Bite-Size Candy—Nestle Chocolate & Confection; *Int'l*, pg. 917

BUNCHA CRUNCH—Candy—Nestle USA; *Int'l*, pg. 916

BUNDABERG—NONE—Guinness Plc; *Int'l*, pg. 412

BUNDLE GUARD—Plastic Film—Reynolds Metals Company; *U.S. Public*, pg. 1385

BUNDLE PACK—Facial Tissue, Bathroom Tissue, Paper Towels—Kimberly-Clark Corporation; *U.S. Public*, pg. 958

BUNDT—Baking Mold—Nordic Ware; *U.S. Private*, pg. 806

BUNDT BRAND BAKEWARE—NONE—Northland Aluminum Products, Inc.; *U.S. Private*, pg. 805

BUNDY—Musical Instruments—The Selmer Co., Inc.; *U.S. Public*, pg. 1514

BUNDY—NONE—TI Group plc; *Int'l*, pg. 1337

BUNDYWELD—Steel Tubing—Bundy North America; *Int'l*, pg. 1340

BUNGALOW—Interior Wall Paneling—Georgia-Pacific Corporation; *U.S. Public*, pg. 735

BUNKER HILL—NONE—Castleberry/Snow's Brands Inc.; *U.S. Private*, pg. 219

BUNKER HILL BRAND—Canned Meat & Meat Entrees—Bunker Hill Foods Inc.; *U.S. Private*, pg. 219

BUNKER RAMO CORP—Manufacturer of Bank Terminals & Computers—Olivetti North America; *Int'l*, pg. 1002

BUNN—NONE—Graham-Field Health Products, Inc.; *U.S. Public*, pg. 757

BUNNAHBHAIN—Single Malt Scotch—The Highland Distilleries Company plc; *Int'l*, pg. 619

BUNNY—Bread, Buns, Sweet Goods—Metz Baking Company (WI); *U.S. Private*, pg. 1022

BUNNY & ME—Children's Clothing—S. Schwab Company; *U.S. Private*, pg. 974

BUNTE—Magazine—Burda Holding GmbH & Co., KG; *Int'l*, pg. 233

BUNTON—Commercial Mowers—Bunton Division; *U.S. Public*, pg. 1589

BUOYANT—Boatwear—Stearns Manufacturing Company; *U.S. Public*, pg. 940

BURBER/CORD—Broadloom—Couristan Inc.; *U.S. Private*, pg. 279

BURBER/KNIT—Broadloom—Couristan Inc.; *U.S. Private*, pg. 279

BURBER KNIT III—Broadloom—Couristan Inc.; *U.S. Private*, pg. 279

BURBER KNIT II—Broadloom—Couristan Inc.; *U.S. Private*, pg. 279

BURBERRYS—Apparel—Arrow Shirt Company; *Int'l*, pg. 194

BURBERRYS—Men's Tailored Clothing—Hartmarx Corporation; *U.S. Public*, pg. 795

BURBERRYS FOR MEN—Fragrance—Elizabeth Arden Company; *Int'l*, pg. 1435

BURBURRYS—Apparel—Bidermann International S.A.; *Int'l*, pg. 194

BURCO—Household Appliances—The Glen Dimplex Group; *Int'l*, pg. 553

BURDA MODEN—Magazine—Burda Holding GmbH & Co., KG; *Int'l*, pg. 233

BURDINES—Department Stores—Burdines; *U.S. Public*, pg. 618

BURDINES—Department Store—Federated Department Stores, Inc.; *U.S. Public*, pg. 617

BURDOX—NONE—AGA Gas, Inc.; *Int'l*, pg. 13

THE BUREAU OF NATIONAL AFFAIRS, Inc.—Reports-Information Svcs., Books, On-Line Svcs., Databases & Training Films—The Bureau of National Affairs, Inc.; *U.S. Private*, pg. 181

BUREAULINK—NONE—American Management Systems, Inc.; *U.S. Public*, pg. 86

BUREN—Basketball Shoe—K-Swiss Inc.; *U.S. Public*, pg. 937

BURGER—Beer—Hudepohl-Schoenling Brewing Company; *U.S. Private*, pg. 545

BURGER BIG BITE—Burger Product—The Southland Corporation; *Int'l*, pg. 693

BURGER KING—Fast Food Chain—Grand Metropolitan Plc; *Int'l*, pg. 408

BURGESS-MANNING—Noise Pollution Control Stanard & Special Engineered Equip. & Prods.—Burgess Manning, Inc.; *U.S. Private*, pg. 799

BURGIT—Foot Care Products—SmithKline Beecham plc; *Int'l*, pg. 1264

BURGLAR BARS—Window Security Guard—John Sterling Corporation; *U.S. Private*, pg. 1041

BURGOYNE—Greeting Cards—Burgoyne, Inc.; *U.S. Private*, pg. 182

BURIED TREASURE—Ice Cream Products—NDS; *Int'l*, pg. 918

BURKAY—Water Heaters—A.O. Smith Corporation; *U.S. Public*, pg. 1476

BURKE—Gynecological Device—The Cooper Companies, Inc.; *U.S. Public*, pg. 442

BURKE BASE—Cove & Carpet Base—Burke Industries, Inc.; *U.S. Private*, pg. 183

THE BURKE INSTITUTE SEMINARS—Continuing Education Workshops—BASES Worldwide; *U.S. Private*, pg. 120

BURKE TREAD—Rubber Stair Treads—Burke Industries, Inc.; *U.S. Private*, pg. 183

BURKELINE ROOFING SYSTEMS—Single-Ply Membrane Roofing Systems—Burke Industries, Inc.; *U.S. Private*, pg. 183

BURLINGTON—NONE—Burlington Industries, Inc.; *U.S. Public*, pg. 268

BURLINGTON—Motor Carriers—Burlington Motor Holdings Inc.; *U.S. Private*, pg. 183

BURLINGTON—Socks—Grupo Synkro, S.A. de C.V.; *Int'l*, pg. 576

BURLINGTON HOUSE—Rugs—Burlington Industries, Inc.; *U.S. Public*, pg. 268

BURLINGTON NORTHERN—Railroad Co.—Burlington Northern Santa Fe Corporation; *U.S. Public*, pg. 268

BURLINGTON SHEER HOSIERY—Pantyhose—Kayser-Roth Corporation, Inc.; *Int'l*, pg. 576

BURLINGTON—Socks—Kayser-Roth Corporation, Inc.; *Int'l*, pg. 576

BURMA—Shaving Cream—American Safety Razor Company; *U.S. Private*, pg. 597

BURN EX—Antimony Pentoxide Flame Retardant Sysergists—PQ Corporation; *U.S. Private*, pg. 827

BURNER BUBBLE METALWOODS—Bubble Shaft Golf Woods—Taylor Made Golf Co. Inc.; *Int'l*, pg. 1181

BURNERS—Special Valves—Maxon Corporation; *U.S. Public*, pg. 716

BURNETT'S—Extracts & Flavorings—Borden, Inc.; *U.S. Public*, pg. 157

BURNETTS—Gin—The Seagram Company Ltd.; *Int'l*, pg. 1214

BURNHAM—Transportation Services—Burnham; *Int'l*, pg. 686

BURNIAM BOILERS—Heating—The Gage Company; *U.S. Private*, pg. 437

BURNS—Security Services—Borg-Warner Security Corporation; *U.S. Public*, pg. 245

BURNS & RICKER—Bagel Chips—B&G Foods, Inc.; *U.S. Public*, pg. 105

BURNS INTERNATIONAL SECURITY SERVICES—Security Services—Borg-Warner Protective Services Corporation; *U.S. Public*, pg. 245

BURO-SOL—Antiseptic Powder; Skin Care—Bradley Pharmaceuticals; *U.S. Public*, pg. 249

BURO-SOL—Antiseptic Powder—Doak Dermatologics; *U.S. Public*, pg. 250

BURONIL—Product for Treatment of Diseases of the Central Nervous System—Novo Nordisk A/S; *Int'l*, pg. 987

BURPEE—Seeds, Bulbs—W. Atlee Burpee Co.; *U.S. Private*, pg. 187

BURR-BROWN—Microelectronic Components—Burr-Brown Corporation; *U.S. Public*, pg. 270

BURR-OFF—Mechanical Deburring Tool—Cogsdill Tool Products, Inc.; *U.S. Private*, pg. 250

BURRAWAY—Mechanical Deburring Tool—Cogsdill Tool Products, Inc.; *U.S. Private*, pg. 250

BURRO—Railway Cranes—Avis Industrial Corporation; *U.S. Private*, pg. 102

BURRO—R.R. Locomotive Cranes—Badger Equipment Co.; *U.S. Private*, pg. 102

BURRY—Biscuits—George Weston Limited; *Int'l*, pg. 1494

BURSINE—Poultry Biologic—Salsbury Laboratories, Inc.; *Int'l*, pg. 1277

BURSINE—Poultry Biologic—Solvay Animal Health, Inc.; *Int'l*, pg. 1277

BURSINE—Poultry Biologic—Solvay S.A.; *Int'l*, pg. 1277

BURST OF BEAUTY—Fragranced Candle—Avon Products, Inc.; *U.S. Public*, pg. 155

BURST OF HEAT—Curler/Stylers—Sunbeam Household Products; *U.S. Public*, pg. 1533

BURST OF POWER—Hand Mixers—Sunbeam Household Products; *U.S. Public*, pg. 1533

BURT AUTOMOTIVE NETWORK—NONE—LGC Management; *U.S. Private*, pg. 639

BURT ON BROADWAY—NONE—LGC Management; *U.S. Private*, pg. 639

BURT SUVAN—NONE—LGC Management; *U.S. Private*, pg. 639

BURTON—Lamps—Luxo A/S; *Int'l*, pg. 821

BURTON RUBBER PROCESSING—Polymer Compounding—M.A. Hanna Company; *U.S. Public*, pg. 780

BURTON RUGS—Remnants—American Rug Craftsmen; *U.S. Public*, pg. 1121

BUSAN—Microbicides—Buckman Laboratories Inc.; *U.S. Private*, pg. 180

BUSBUST—Diagnostic Technique—GenRad, Inc.; *U.S. Public*, pg. 731

BUSCH—Beer—Anheuser-Busch Companies, Inc.; *U.S. Public*, pg. 113

BUSCH GARDENS TAMPA—Theme Park—Busch Entertainment Corp.; *U.S. Public*, pg. 114

BUSCH GARDENS WILLIAMSBURG—Theme Park—Busch Entertainment Corp.; *U.S. Public*, pg. 114

BUSCH LIGHT—Light Beer—Anheuser-Busch Companies, Inc.; *U.S. Public*, pg. 113

BUSCH NA—Non-Alcoholic Brew—Anheuser-Busch Companies, Inc.; *U.S. Public*, pg. 113

BUSCOPAN—Antispasmodic Drugs—Boehringer Ingelheim GmbH; *Int'l*, pg. 199

BUSH HOG—Farm Equipment—Allied Products Corporation; *U.S. Public*, pg. 48

BUSH'S BEST—Canned Vegetables—Bush Brothers & Company; *U.S. Private*, pg. 189

BUSHER—Automatic Injector—Becton Dickinson & Company; *U.S. Public*, pg. 199

BUSHMASTER—Automatic Cannon—Boeing Helicopter Division; *U.S. Public*, pg. 241

BUSHMASTER—Cannon—McDonnell Aircraft & Missile Systems Div.; *U.S. Public*, pg. 241

BUSHMILLS—Irish Whiskey—Brown-Forman Beverages Worldwide; *U.S. Public*, pg. 261

BUSHMILLS—Irish Whiskey—Brown-Forman Corporation; *U.S. Public*, pg. 261

BUSHMILLS—Irish Whiskey—Groupe Pernod Ricard; *Int'l*, pg. 566

BUSHNELL—Sports Optics—Bausch & Lomb Incorporated; *U.S. Public*, pg. 194

BUSHNELL—Binoculars—Bushnell Corporation; *U.S. Private*, pg. 1191

BUSHWHACKER—Termite Control Without Poisons—Bethurum Research & Development, Inc.; *U.S. Private*, pg. 141

BUSHWHACKER—Insect Control-Fire Ant, Roach, & Weevil and Termite Control—Bushwhacker Associates, Inc.; *U.S. Private*, pg. 141

BUSINESS AND HEALTH—Medical Publication—Medical Economics Company Inc.; *U.S. Public*, pg. 1601

BUSINESS CENTRAL EUROPE—NONE—The Economist Group Limited; *Int'l*, pg. 1026

BUSINESS CREDIT LEASING—Leasing—Schwan's Sales Enterprises; *U.S. Private*, pg. 974

BUSINESS EQUIPMENT—American Tourister—American Tourister, Inc.; *U.S. Public*, pg. 1430

BUSINESS 53—Package of Commercial Products for Small Businesses—Fifth Third Bancorp; *U.S. Public*, pg. 621

BUSINESS FIRST OF BUFFALO—Business Journal—Business First of New York, Inc.; *U.S. Private*, pg. 19

BUSINESS FIRST OF COLUMBUS—Business Journal—Business First of New York, Inc.; *U.S. Private*, pg. 19

BUSINESS FIRST OF LOUISVILLE—Business Journal—Business First of New York, Inc.; *U.S. Private*, pg. 19

BUSINESS FORMS & SYSTEMS—Magazine—North American Publishing Company; *U.S. Private*, pg. 803

BUSINESS GUARD—Insurance—American Hardware Mutual Insurance Co.; *U.S. Private*, pg. 764

BUSINESS INFO-LINE—American Business Lists—American Business Information, Inc.; *U.S. Public*, pg. 69

BUSINESS INSURANCE—Newspaper—Crain Communications, Inc.; *U.S. Private*, pg. 284

BUSINESS INTEGRATED THINKING—Telecommunications Network Design Planning & Managment Services—Lucent Technologies Inc.; *U.S. Public*, pg. 1017

THE BUSINESS JOURNAL OF CHARLOTTE—Business Journal—Business First of New York, Inc.; *U.S. Private*, pg. 19

THE BUSINESS JOURNAL OF PORTLAND—Business Journal—Business First of New York, Inc.; *U.S. Private*, pg. 19

THE BUSINESS JOURNAL—Business Journal—Business First of New York, Inc.; *U.S. Private*, pg. 19

BUSINESS MANAGEMENT PERSONNEL—Employment Agency—General Employment Enterprises, Inc.; *U.S. Public*, pg. 714

BUSINESS MARKETING—Magazine—Crain Communications, Inc.; *U.S. Private*, pg. 284

BUSINESS MERGE/PURGE—Mailing Efficiency—Group 1 Software, Inc.; *U.S. Public*, pg. 417

BUSINESS SERVER—NONE—Advanced Logic Research, Inc.; *U.S. Public*, pg. 703

BUSINESS STATION—Computer—Advanced Logic Research, Inc.; *U.S. Public*, pg. 703

BUSINESS STRATEGY—Money Game—Monarch Avalon, Inc.; *U.S. Public*, pg. 1123

BUSINESS TRANSFORMATION—Reframing And Restructuring the Company, Revitalizing the Enterprise—Gemini Consulting; *Int'l*, pg. 264

BUSINESS TRAVEL NEWS—Newspaper—Miller Freeman Inc.; *Int'l*, pg. 1443

BUSINESS VEISA 386/33—Upgradable PC—Advanced Logic Research, Inc.; *U.S. Public*, pg. 703

BUSINESSCOM—Key Systems—TIE/Communications, Inc.; *U.S. Private*, pg. 1085

BUSINESSLAND—Computer Stores & Services—Entex Information Services; *U.S. Private*, pg. 378

BUSINESSWEEK—Business Magazine—Business Week; *U.S. Public*, pg. 1069

BUSNEL—Dry Brown Apple Brandy—Groupe Pernod Ricard; *Int'l*, pg. 566

BUSPAR—Anti-Anxiety & Anti-Depression Drug—Bristol-Myers Squibb Company; *U.S. Public*, pg. 253

BUSPAR—Anti-Anxiety Agent for Mngmt. of Anxiety Disorders—Bristol-Myers Squibb U.S. Pharmaceutical Group; *U.S. Public*, pg. 255

BUSPEASE—Dispersants—Buckman Laboratories Inc.; *U.S. Private*, pg. 180

BUSS—Fuses & Fuse Accessories—Bussmann Division; *U.S. Public*, pg. 443

BUSS—Fuses & Fuse Accessories—Cooper Industries, Inc.; *U.S. Public*, pg. 442

BUSS-KNEADER—Compounding Machines—Georg Fischer Ltd.; *Int'l*, pg. 488

BUSSMAN—Fuses—Bryant Electric Supply Company, Inc.; *U.S. Private*, pg. 177

BUSTELO—Expresso—Tetley USA Inc.; *Int'l*, pg. 1377

BUSTER—NONE—Fiskars Oy AB; *Int'l*, pg. 492

BUSTER—Computer Programs for Testing Software—Lucent Technologies Inc.; *U.S. Public*, pg. 1017

BUSTER BALL—Animated Golf Ball Mascot Figure—Putt Putt Golf Courses of America, Inc.; *U.S. Private*, pg. 896

BUSTER BAR—Dessert—American Dairy Queen Corporation; *U.S. Public*, pg. 220

BUSTER BAR—Frozen Novelties—International Dairy Queen, Inc.; *U.S. Public*, pg. 220

BUSTER BAR—Harrow-Rigid Tooth—Midwest Industries, Inc.; *U.S. Private*, pg. 744

BUSTER BROWN—Shoes—Brown Group, Inc.; *U.S. Public*, pg. 262

BUSTER BROWN—Shoes—Brown Shoe Co. of Canada Ltd.; *U.S. Public*, pg. 262

BUSTER BROWN—Children's Clothes & Socks—Buster Brown Apparel, Inc.; *U.S. Private*, pg. 189

BUSTER THE TORTOISE—Children's Step Stool—Rubbermaid Incorporated; *U.S. Public*, pg. 1411

BUSY BEADS—Toy—Hasbro, Inc.; *U.S. Public*, pg. 797

BUSY BEAUTY—Permanent Wave—Revlon-Realistic Professional Products, Inc.; *U.S. Private*, pg. 690

BUTACITE—Polychemicals—Du Pont (E.I. Du Pont De Nemours & Co.); *U.S. Public*, pg. 530

BUTANOX—Ketone Peroxides—Akzo Nobel N.V.; *Int'l*, pg. 42

BUTCHER BONES—Dog Snacks—Nabisco Inc.; *U.S. Public*, pg. 1355

BUTCHER BONES—Pet Food—RJR Nabisco Holdings Corp.; *U.S. Public*, pg. 1354

THE BUTCHER COMPANY—Sale of Industrial Cleaning Supplies—The Butcher Company; *U.S. Private*, pg. 189

BUTCHER WAGON—Sausages—Hatfield Quality Meats; *U.S. Private*, pg. 510

BUTCHERS BEST—Poultry—Tyson Foods, Inc.; *U.S. Public*, pg. 1652

BUTCHER'S BLEND—Dog Foods—Ralston Purina Company; *U.S. Public*, pg. 1359

BUTEN THE PAINT & PAPER PEOPLE—Paint Stores—Buten, Division of Duron; *U.S. Private*, pg. 349

BUTERA—Retail Food Stores—Butera Finer Foods Inc.; *U.S. Private*, pg. 189

BUTERLETS—Candy—Brach & Brock Confections Inc.; *U.S. Private*, pg. 163

BUTIBEL—Gastrointestinal Anticholinergic Sedative Combination—Wallace Laboratories; *U.S. Public*, pg. 189

BUTISAN 400 SC—Crop Protection Agent—BASF AG; *Int'l*, pg. 103

BUTISAN S—Crop Protection Agent—BASF AG; *Int'l*, pg. 103

BUTISOL—Intermediate Acting Barbiturate Sedative—Wallace Laboratories; *U.S. Public*, pg. 310

BUTLER—Carpet Sweeper—Bissell Inc.; *U.S. Private*, pg. 145

BUTLER—Preventive Dentistry Aids—John O. Butler Co.; *Int'l*, pg. 1320

BUTLER—Pre-Engineered Metal Buildings—Butler Manufacturing Company; *U.S. Public*, pg. 271

BUTLER—Fine & Industrial Papers—Georgia-Pacific Corporation; *U.S. Public*, pg. 735

BUTLER—Shoe Stores—SLJ Retail LLC; *U.S. Private*, pg. 957

BUTLER CRITTERS—Child Toothbrush—John O. Butler Co.; *Int'l*, pg. 1320

BUTLER METAL BUILDINGS—Pre-fabricated Buildings—Lundy Construction Co., Inc.; *U.S. Private*, pg. 681

BUTLER SMILE CENTER—Dental Floss, Floss Threaders, Toothbrushes—John O. Butler Co.; *Int'l*, pg. 1320

BUTLER SMILE FACTORY—Dental Care Products—John O. Butler Co.; *Int'l*, pg. 1320

BUTLERS UNIFORMS—Uniforms—Dick Bruhn Incorporated; *U.S. Private*, pg. 175

BUTOFAN—Polymer Dispersions & Solutions; Solid Polymers—BASF AG; *Int'l*, pg. 103

BUTONAL—Polymer Dispersions & Solutions; Solid Polymers—BASF AG; *Int'l*, pg. 103

BUTTER BRAIDPRETZELS—Snack Food—The O'Boise Corporation; *U.S. Private*, pg. 810

BUTTER BUDS—Butter Substitute—Cumberland Packing Corp.; *U.S. Private*, pg. 295

BUTTER CHARM—Croutons—Metz Baking Company; *U.S. Public*, pg. 1022

BUTTER CHARM—Croutons—Metz Baking Company (WI); *U.S. Private*, pg. 1022

BUTTER KERNEL—Canned Vegetables—Butter Kernel Products; *U.S. Private*, pg. 393

BUTTER KERNEL—Food—Faribault Foods Inc.; *U.S. Private*, pg. 393

BUTTER POPPED CORN CAKES—Corn Cakes—The Quaker Oats Company; *U.S. Public*, pg. 1347

BUTTER PRETZELS—Pretzels—Keebler Company; *U.S. Public*, pg. 657

BUTTERBALL—Turkeys—Armour Swift Eckrich; *U.S. Public*, pg. 426

BUTTERBALL—Prepared Turkey Products—Butterball Turkey Company; *U.S. Public*, pg. 426

BUTTERBALL—Prepared Turkey Products—ConAgra, Inc.; *U.S. Public*, pg. 425

BUTTERCUP—Bread—Goodman Fielder Limited; *Int'l*, pg. 555

BUTTERCUP—NONE—Quality Bakers Australia Ltd.; *Int'l*, pg. 555

BUTTERCUP—Dry Snuff—Swisher International Group, Inc.; *U.S. Public*, pg. 1543

BUTTERCUP—Butter Blend Spread—Ventura Foods; *U.S. Private*, pg. 508

BUTTERCUP FARMS—Fresh & Frozen Chicken—Sanderson Farms, Inc.; *U.S. Public*, pg. 1430

BUTTERFIELD—Food Products—Allen Canning Company; *U.S. Private*, pg. 36

BUTTERFINGER—Candy Bar—Nestle Chocolate & Confection; *Int'l*, pg. 917

BUTTERFINGER—Candy Bar—Nestle S.A.; *Int'l*, pg. 915

BUTTERFINGER—Candy Bar—Nestle USA; *Int'l*, pg. 916

BUTTERFINGER BB'S—Bite-Size Candy—Nestle Chocolate & Confection; *Int'l*, pg. 917

BUTTERFINGER BB's—Candy—Nestle USA; *Int'l*, pg. 916

BUTTERFINGER BARS—Ice Cream Treats—Nestle Ice Cream Co.; *Int'l*, pg. 916

BUTTERFLY—Golf Clubs & Balls—Tommy Armour Golf; *U.S. Public*, pg. 1683

BUTTERFLY K—Contact Lenses—40 Fort Eye Associates; *U.S. Private*, pg. 420

BUTTERFLY LENS—Contact Lenses—40 Fort Eye Associates; *U.S. Private*, pg. 420

BUTTERICK—Patterns—Butterick Company, Inc.; *U.S. Private*, pg. 190

BUTTERLEY—Brick Products—Hanson PLC; *Int'l*, pg. 592

BUTTERMAID—Bread & Rolls—Flowers Industries, Inc.; *U.S. Public*, pg. 656

BUTTERMINT—Sugar Confectionary—Cadbury Nigeria PLC; *Int'l*, pg. 248

BUTTERNUT—Bread—Interstate Brands Corporation; *U.S. Public*, pg. 909

BUTTERWELL—Automatic Butter Melter—National Presto Industries, Inc.; *U.S. Public*, pg. 1159

BUTTON-ON—Cantilever Rack—Jarke Corporation; *U.S. Private*, pg. 583

BUTTONS—Home Entertainment Stores—Blockbuster Music; *U.S. Private*, pg. 776

BUTTREY—Supermarket Chain—Buttrey Food & Drug Company; *U.S. Public*, pg. 271

BUTVAR—Acetal Resin—Monsanto Company; *U.S. Public*, pg. 1124

BUTVAR—Resins/Adhesive Component—Solutia Inc.; *U.S. Public*, pg. 1483

BUTYCEL—Solvent—Kyowa Hakko Kogyo Company, Ltd.; *Int'l*, pg. 778

BUX EX FLUTE—Corrugated Packaging & Accessories—Danisco Pack Ltd.; *Int'l*, pg. 378

BUX SUPA-WRAP—Corrugated Packaging & Accessories—Danisco Pack Ltd.; *Int'l*, pg. 378

BUX TOG-RAIL—Corrugated Packaging & Accessories—Danisco Pack Ltd.; *Int'l*, pg. 378

BUX TOUGH-WALL—Corrugated Packaging & Accessories—Danisco Pack Ltd.; *Int'l*, pg. 378

BUXTON—Men's & Ladies Personal Leather Goods—DHP Limited Partnership; *U.S. Private*, pg. 302

BUY 'N SAVE—Food Products—Nash Finch Company; *U.S. Public*, pg. 1151

BUYER'S ASSURANCE—Service Enhancement that Extends Repair Period—American Express Company; *U.S. Public*, pg. 73

BUYERS ADVANTAGE—NONE—CUC International, Inc.; *U.S. Public*, pg. 320

BUYING CAMERAS—U.K. Photography Magazine—EMAP Apex; *Int'l*, pg. 451

BY GEORGE—Chicken Entrees—Hormel Foods Corp.; *U.S. Public*, pg. 840

BY JEEVES—Musical—Really Useful Holdings Limited; *Int'l*, pg. 1089

BYBLOS—NONE—Luxottica Group S.p.A.; *Int'l*, pg. 822

BYE FLY—Disposable Fly Trap—Security Lawn & Garden Co.; *U.S. Private*, pg. 397

BYER CALIFORNIA—Juniors' Sportswear—Byer California; *U.S. Private*, pg. 191

BYER TOO—Juniors' Dresses—Byer California; *U.S. Private*, pg. 191

BYLINE—Software—Borland International, Inc.; *U.S. Public*, pg. 246

BYNEL—Coextrudable Adhesive Resins—Du Pont (E.I. Du Pont De Nemours & Co.); *U.S. Public*, pg. 530

BYPRO—Soil Conditioner—The Mead Corporation; *U.S. Public*, pg. 1074

BYREL—Pacemaker—Medtronic, Inc.; *U.S. Public*, pg. 1082

BYRON JACKSON PUMPS—Centrifugal Pumps, Nuclear Utility Pumps & Submersible Pumps & Motors—BW/IP International, *U.S. Public*, pg. 658

BYRON JACKSON PUMPS—Centrifugal Pumps, Nuclear Utility Pumps & Submersible Pumps & Motors—Flowserve Corporation; *U.S. Public*, pg. 658

BYRON JACKSON/UNITED PUMPS—Pumps—BW/IP International, Inc.; *U.S. Public*, pg. 658

BYRON JACKSON/UNITED PUMPS—Pumps—Flowserve Corporation; *U.S. Public*, pg. 658

BYRON WINERY—NONE—Robert Mondavi Winery, Inc.; *U.S. Public*, pg. 1393

BYRONIC—Paper—Domtar Inc.; *Int'l*, pg. 416

BYRRH—Aperitif—Groupe Pernod Ricard; *Int'l*, pg. 566

BYZANCE—Perfume—Wella Group; *Int'l*, pg. 1489

C

C*—Computer Programs, Namely Compilers—Thinking Machines Corporation; *U.S. Private*, pg. 1081

CA-ACCUCHEK—Testing/Maintaining Mainframe Applications—Computer Associates International, Inc.; *U.S. Public*, pg. 420

CA-ACF2—Resource Access Control System—Computer Associates International, Inc.; *U.S. Public*, pg. 420

CA-ACF2/DB2—DB2 Resource Access Control System—Computer Associates International, Inc.; *U.S. Public*, pg. 420

CA-ACF2 GRO—Graphic Reporting for Resource Access Control System—Computer Associates International, Inc.; *U.S. Public*, pg. 420

CA-ACF2/OLC—PC-Based Workstation—Computer Associates International, Inc.; *U.S. Public*, pg. 420

CA ACF2/PC—Resource Access Control System for PC Mainframe Connectivity—Computer Associates International, Inc.; *U.S. Public*, pg. 420

CA-ACF2/SECMAN—Resource Access Control System—Computer Associates International, Inc.; *U.S. Public*, pg. 420

CA-ACP2/VIEWPOINT—Window User Interface for CA-ACF2—Computer Associates International, Inc.; *U.S. Public*, pg. 420

CA-ACTIVATOR—Automated Product Installation & Maintenance—Computer Associates International, Inc.; *U.S. Public*, pg. 420

CA-ADLIB—PC-Based Workstation & Library Management—Computer Associates International, Inc.; *U.S. Public*, pg. 420

CA-ADROIT/ASSIST—Automates the Devel. of Mainframe Concurrency Sessions for CA-ADROIT/II—Computer Associates International, Inc.; *U.S. Public*, pg. 420

CA-ADROIT/BASE—Adds Mainframe Concurrency Capabilities to CA-ADROIT/II—Computer Associates International, Inc.; *U.S. Public*, pg. 420

CA-ADROIT/CBT-AS—Sophisticated PC-Based System for Creating Highly Interactive CBT Materials—Computer Associates International, Inc.; *U.S. Public*, pg. 420

CA-ADROIT/LOOKUP—Provides Online Access to Documentation for CA Adroit/II—Computer Associates International, Inc.; *U.S. Public*, pg. 420

CA-ADROIT/II—Prods. that Automate Creation of PC Work Environment for use as Workstation—Computer Associates International, Inc.; *U.S. Public*, pg. 420

CA-ADS—High-Level Application Development Language Used with CA-IDMS/DB—Computer Associates International, Inc.; *U.S. Public*, pg. 420

CA-ADS FOR VAX—Fully Compatible VAX/VMS Implementation of CA-ADS—Computer Associates International, Inc.; *U.S. Public*, pg. 420

CA-ADS/GENERATOR—Code Generator for the CA Ads Environment—Computer Associates International, Inc.; *U.S. Public*, pg. 420

CA-ADS/PC—Fully Compatible PC Implementation of CA-ADS—Computer Associates International, Inc.; *U.S. Public*, pg. 420

CA-ADVISOR—Project Consultant System—Computer Associates International, Inc.; *U.S. Public*, pg. 420

CA-APCDDS—Report Balancing & File Validation—Computer Associates International, Inc.; *U.S. Public*, pg. 420

CA-APCDOC—Complete Production Documentation System—Computer Associates International, Inc.; *U.S. Public*, pg. 420

CA-ARCHIVER—Backup, Archive & Restore System—Computer Associates International, Inc.; *U.S. Public*, pg. 420

CA-ASM/ARCHIVE—Provides Backup, Restore & Archive Functionality for Data Sets—Computer Associates International, Inc.; *U.S. Public*, pg. 420

CA-ASM2—DASD Management System—Computer Associates International, Inc.; *U.S. Public*, pg. 420

CA-ASM/WORKSTATION—Automated Media Management Tracking System—Computer Associates International, Inc.; *U.S. Public*, pg. 420

CA-BLOCKMASTER—Automatic Reblocking Facility—Computer Associates International, Inc.; *U.S. Public*, pg. 420

CACI—Software—CACI International Inc; *U.S. Public*, pg. 272

CA-CAS—Manufacturing & Financial Management System—Computer Associates International, Inc.; *U.S. Public*, pg. 420

CA-CAS/AD—Aerospace & Defense Manufacturing—Computer Associates International, Inc.; *U.S. Public*, pg. 420

CA-CAS/AD:BOM—Bill of Material/Configuration Management—Computer Associates International, Inc.; *U.S. Public*, pg. 420

CA-CAS/AD:CCC—Standard Cost Tracking & Actual Cost Capture—Computer Associates International, Inc.; *U.S. Public*, pg. 420

CA-CAS/AD:COE—Contract/WBS Identification of Customer Orders—Computer Associates International, Inc.; *U.S. Public*, pg. 420

CA-CAS/AD:INV—Material Tracking of the Contract/WBS Level of Detail—Computer Associates International, Inc.; *U.S. Public*, pg. 420

CA-CAS/AD:MPS—Master Scheduling of Contract/WBS Level of Detail with Initial Capacity—Computer Associates International, Inc.; *U.S. Public*, pg. 420

CA-CAS/AD:MRP—Material Requirements Planning by Contract—Computer Associates International, Inc.; *U.S. Public*, pg. 420

CA-CAS/AD:PUR—Contract/WBS Identification of Purchase Requirements—Computer Associates International, Inc.; *U.S. Public*, pg. 420

CA-CAS/AD:SFC—Perform Multi-Contract Mfg. Orders & Detailed Capacity Requirements Plng.—Computer Associates International, Inc.; *U.S. Public*, pg. 420

CA-CAS:AP—Cash Disbursement Management & Reporting Facility—Computer Associates International, Inc.; *U.S. Public*, pg. 420

CA-CAS:AR—Online Credit, Collection & Receivables Management—Computer Associates International, Inc.; *U.S. Public*, pg. 420

CA-CAS:BOM—Material Billing Information for Planning & Control—Computer Associates International, Inc.; *U.S. Public*, pg. 420

CA-CAS:CCC—Cost Control for Shop Floor Labor & Inventory—Computer Associates International, Inc.; *U.S. Public*, pg. 420

CA-CAS:CFM—Rolling Demand Forecasts for Inventory Items—Computer Associates International, Inc.; *U.S. Public*, pg. 420

CA-CAS:COE—Customer Order Entry System—Computer Associates International, Inc.; *U.S. Public*, pg. 420

CA-CAS:DATA—Transaction Processing System—Computer Associates International, Inc.; *U.S. Public*, pg. 420

CA-CAS:DRP—Finished Goods Distribution Replenishment Planning—Computer Associates International, Inc.; *U.S. Public*, pg. 420

CA-CAS:EDI OPTION—A Facility that Electronically Transmits/Receives Transaction for CA-CAS—Computer Associates International, Inc.; *U.S. Public*, pg. 420

CA-CAS:FA—Fixed-Asset, Leased Prop. Maintenance Ins. Valuation & Const.-in-Prog. Mgmt—Computer Associates International, Inc.; *U.S. Public*, pg. 420

CA-CAS:GL—Fourth-Generation Online Accounting & Financial Reporting—Computer Associates International, Inc.; *U.S. Public*, pg. 420

CA-CAS:INV—Inventory Tracking, Analysis & Management—Computer Associates International, Inc.; *U.S. Public*, pg. 420

CA-CAS:MPS—Production Planning & Capacity Estimation—Computer Associates International, Inc.; *U.S. Public*, pg. 420

CA-CAS:MRP—Replenishment Planning—Computer Associates International, Inc.; *U.S. Public*, pg. 420

CA-CAS:PUR—Purchase Order Management—Computer Associates International, Inc.; *U.S. Public*, pg. 420

CA-CAS:SFC—Production Schedule & Tracking—Computer Associates International, Inc.; *U.S. Public*, pg. 420

CA-CAS:SFC DISTRIBUTED—Shop Floor Management for PC & LANS—Computer Associates International, Inc.; *U.S. Public*, pg. 420

CA-CASVISION—PC Tool Allowing Data Analysis form CA-CAS—Computer Associates International, Inc.; *U.S. Public*, pg. 420

CA-CICSORT—Full-Function Sorting Facility for CICS—Computer Associates International, Inc.; *U.S. Public*, pg. 420

CA-CIO VISION—Development Tool for Creating Executive Information Systems—Computer Associates International, Inc.; *U.S. Public*, pg. 420

CA-COLLECTION MANAGEMENT—Collection Management—Computer Associates International, Inc.; *U.S. Public*, pg. 420

CA-COMPETE—Multidimensional Modeling & Viewing—Computer Associates International, Inc.; *U.S. Public*, pg. 420

CA-CONSOL—Automated Financial Consolidation & Statement Reporting—Computer Associates International, Inc.; *U.S. Public*, pg. 420

CA-CONSOL/PC—PC-Based Consolidation System—Computer Associates International, Inc.; *U.S. Public*, pg. 420

Brand Name Index

Brand Name Index

CA-CONVERTOR—VSE to MVS Conversion System—Computer Associates International, Inc.; *U.S. Public*, pg. 420

CA-CORTANA—PC-Based Data Security System—Computer Associates International, Inc.; *U.S. Public*, pg. 420

CA-CRICKET DRAW III—Object-Oriented PostScript Drawing Program—Computer Associates International, Inc.; *U.S. Public*, pg. 420

CA-CRICKET GRAPH—Flexible Graph Creation & Customization for Business & Scientific Purposes—Computer Associates International, Inc.; *U.S. Public*, pg. 420

CA-CRICKET GRAPH III—Flexible Graph Creation & Customization for Business & Scientific Purposes—Computer Associates International, Inc.; *U.S. Public*, pg. 420

CA-CRICKET PRESENTS FOR APPLE MACINTOSH—Integrated Desktop Presentation Program—Computer Associates International, Inc.; *U.S. Public*, pg. 420

CA-CRICKET PRESENTS FOR MICROSOFT WINDOWS—Integrated Desktop Presentation Program—Computer Associates International, Inc.; *U.S. Public*, pg. 420

CA-CULPRIT—High-Volume Report Writing Language—Computer Associates International, Inc.; *U.S. Public*, pg. 420

CAD/CAM—Designing Equip. for Ovens & Furnaces—The Grieve Corporation; *U.S. Private*, pg. 480

CA-DASDCHECK—DASD Error Recovery Utility—Computer Associates International, Inc.; *U.S. Public*, pg. 420

CA-DATACOM—Integrated Solution Comprising Database & Facilities for Life Cycle Mngmt.—Computer Associates International, Inc.; *U.S. Public*, pg. 420

CA-DATACOM:CASELINK—Linkage Between CASE Tools & CA-DATACOM—Computer Associates International, Inc.; *U.S. Public*, pg. 420

CA-DATACOM/COMPLETE!—Windows Based Multi-Dimensional & Decision Tool—Computer Associates International, Inc.; *U.S. Public*, pg. 420

CA-DATACOM/CONCEPTOR—A CASE Environment Integrated with CA-DATACOM—Computer Associates International, Inc.; *U.S. Public*, pg. 420

CA-DATACOM/DB—Relational Data Base Management System—Computer Associates International, Inc.; *U.S. Public*, pg. 420

CA-DATACOM/DL1 TRANSPARENCY—Migration Software for DL/1 Applications—Computer Associates International, Inc.; *U.S. Public*, pg. 420

CA-DATACOM/PC—PC-Based Relational Database Management System—Computer Associates International, Inc.; *U.S. Public*, pg. 420

CA-DATACOM/PC LANPACK—Database Management System for LANS—Computer Associates International, Inc.; *U.S. Public*, pg. 420

CA-DATACOM/Q BY X—Windows Front-End for Workstation Accessing CA-DATACOM—Computer Associates International, Inc.; *U.S. Public*, pg. 420

CA-DATACOM SQL OPTION—Standard SQL Access to CA-DATACOM—Computer Associates International, Inc.; *U.S. Public*, pg. 420

CA-DATACOM/TDG—Test-Data Generator—Computer Associates International, Inc.; *U.S. Public*, pg. 420

CA-DATACOM/TOTAL TRANSPARENCY—Migration Software for TOTAL Applications—Computer Associates International, Inc.; *U.S. Public*, pg. 420

CA-DATACOM TRANSPARENCY FOR DB2—Enables DB2 Applications to Run Unchanged CA-DATACOM—Computer Associates International, Inc.; *U.S. Public*, pg. 420

CA-DATACOM/VSAM—Migration Software for VSAM Applications—Computer Associates International, Inc.; *U.S. Public*, pg. 420

CA-DATACOM VSE/ESA OPTION—Allows CA-DATACOM to Exploit VSE/ESA—Computer Associates International, Inc.; *U.S. Public*, pg. 420

CA-DATADICTIONARY—Active Data Dictionary, Integrated with Development Tool Set—Computer Associates International, Inc.; *U.S. Public*, pg. 420

CA-DATAMACS/II—Test Data Generator for Batch, IMS, IDMS—Computer Associates International, Inc.; *U.S. Public*, pg. 420

CA-DATAQUERY—Reporting and Query Tool for CA-DATACOM/DB—Computer Associates International, Inc.; *U.S. Public*, pg. 420

CA-DATAQUERY FOR VAX—Facility Integrating CA-DATACOM/DB with Digital VAX/VMS—Computer Associates International, Inc.; *U.S. Public*, pg. 420

CA-DATAQUERY/PC—Reporting Tool for CA-DATACOM/DB—Computer Associates International, Inc.; *U.S. Public*, pg. 420

CA-DB:cBASE—dBASE-Style Application Development System for Relational Databases—Computer Associates International, Inc.; *U.S. Public*, pg. 420

CA-DB ANALYZER FOR IMS—Static Analysis of IMS-DL/1—Computer Associates International, Inc.; *U.S. Public*, pg. 420

CA-DB:ARCHITECT—PC-Based Logical & Physical Database Design Tool—Computer Associates International, Inc.; *U.S. Public*, pg. 420

CA-DB:CASELINK—CASE Products Integration System—Computer Associates International, Inc.; *U.S. Public*, pg. 420

CA-DB/COMPLETE !—Windows Based Multidimensional & Decision Tool—Computer Associates International, Inc.; *U.S. Public*, pg. 420

CA-DB COMPRESS FOR IMS—Compacts Data for Storage—Computer Associates International, Inc.; *U.S. Public*, pg. 420

CA-DB/CONCEPTOR—A CASE Environment Integrated with CA-DB—Computer Associates International, Inc.; *U.S. Public*, pg. 420

CA-DB:EXPERT—Rule-Based Expert System Development Tool—Computer Associates International, Inc.; *U.S. Public*, pg. 420

CA-DB:EXPERT 3270 LINK—Provides CA-DB:EXPERT/VAX Realtime Access to IBM Mainframe Applications—Computer Associates International, Inc.; *U.S. Public*, pg. 420

CA-DB:EXPERT/VOICE—Development Tool Employing DECvoice for Voice Access & Response—Computer Associates International, Inc.; *U.S. Public*, pg. 420

CA-DB FOR UMX—Production Power RDBMS with FUll ANSI SQL89 Support—Computer Associates International, Inc.; *U.S. Public*, pg. 420

CA-DB FOR VAX—ANSI SQL Database with Precompilers for C, COBOL & FORTRAN—Computer Associates International, Inc.; *U.S. Public*, pg. 420

CA-DB4—Relational Database Management—Computer Associates International, Inc.; *U.S. Public*, pg. 420

CA-DB4/SCREENS—Interactive Screen Generator—Computer Associates International, Inc.; *U.S. Public*, pg. 420

CA-DB:GENERATOR/PC—Create Batch Reports & View Output Online—Computer Associates International, Inc.; *U.S. Public*, pg. 420

CA-DB:GENERATOR FOR VAX—Code Generator & Application Development System for Prof. Programmers—Computer Associates International, Inc.; *U.S. Public*, pg. 420

CA-DB GENERATOR FOR VMX—Generates C Application for UNIX and Sequential Files—Computer Associates International, Inc.; *U.S. Public*, pg. 420

CA-DB/PC CLIENT—Connectivity Between PC & CA-DB Databases—Computer Associates International, Inc.; *U.S. Public*, pg. 420

CA-DB/Q BY X—Windows Front End for Workstations Accessing CA-DB—Computer Associates International, Inc.; *U.S. Public*, pg. 420

CA-DB/RMS TRANSPARENCY—Allows Existing RMS applications to Run Unchanged Against CA-DB for VAX—Computer Associates International, Inc.; *U.S. Public*, pg. 420

CA-DB:STAR—Distributed Database Management System—Computer Associates International, Inc.; *U.S. Public*, pg. 420

CA-DB STAR/PC—Enables Applications to Transparently Retrieve Data from Mainframe—Computer Associates International, Inc.; *U.S. Public*, pg. 420

CA-DIRECTOR—Directory Management and Access Control Facility—Computer Associates International, Inc.; *U.S. Public*, pg. 420

CA-DISPATCH—Report Distribution System—Computer Associates International, Inc.; *U.S. Public*, pg. 420

CA-DISPATCH/GRAPHICS OPTIMIZER—Hardware Optimizer—Computer Associates International, Inc.; *U.S. Public*, pg. 420

CA-DISPATCH GRO—Graphic Reporting for Report Distribution—Computer Associates International, Inc.; *U.S. Public*, pg. 420

CA-DISPATCH/NOTEPAD—Centralized, Integrated Recording & Viewing of User Notes During CA—Computer Associates International, Inc.; *U.S. Public*, pg. 420

CA-DISPATCH/PC—Extends User Accessibility & Functionality of Mainframe Generated Reports—Computer Associates International, Inc.; *U.S. Public*, pg. 420

CA-DISPATCH/VIEWPOINT—Window User Interface Option to CA-Dispatch—Computer Associates International, Inc.; *U.S. Public*, pg. 420

CA-DISSPLA—FORTRAN Graphics Subroutine Library for Programmable Graphics Applications—Computer Associates International, Inc.; *U.S. Public*, pg. 420

CA-DISSPLA COBOL—COBOL Graphics Subroutine Library for Programmable Graphics Applications—Computer Associates International, Inc.; *U.S. Public*, pg. 420

CA-DISSPLA/PC—PC Component of CA-DISSPLA—Computer Associates International, Inc.; *U.S. Public*, pg. 420

CA-DL/1ONLINE FOR IMS—Online Database Editor—Computer Associates International, Inc.; *U.S. Public*, pg. 420

CA-DMS—Distribution Mngmt.—Computer Associates International, Inc.; *U.S. Public*, pg. 420

CA-DMS:CM—Aged Trial Balance, Dunning Letters & Cash Posting—Computer Associates International, Inc.; *U.S. Public*, pg. 420

CA-DMS:DCM—Integrated Warehouse Operations—Computer Associates International, Inc.; *U.S. Public*, pg. 420

CA-DMS:DRP—Finished Goods Distribution Replenishment Planning—Computer Associates International, Inc.; *U.S. Public*, pg. 420

CA-DMS:FM—Forecasting Mngmt.—Computer Associates International, Inc.; *U.S. Public*, pg. 420

CA-DMS:OM—Order Management for Medium-&-Large-Sized Companies—Computer Associates International, Inc.; *U.S. Public*, pg. 420

CA-DMS:RF—Realtime Inventory Control Through Wireless Data Communications—Computer Associates International, Inc.; *U.S. Public*, pg. 420

CA-DMS:WM—Warehouse Operations Management—Computer Associates International, Inc.; *U.S. Public*, pg. 420

CA-DOCVIEW—On-Line Documentation Facility—Computer Associates International, Inc.; *U.S. Public*, pg. 420

CA-DRIVER—JCL Management and Enhancement—Computer Associates International, Inc.; *U.S. Public*, pg. 420

CA-DUO—VSE Emulation—Computer Associates International, Inc.; *U.S. Public*, pg. 420

CA-DYNAM/B—Backup, Archive & Restore System—Computer Associates International, Inc.; *U.S. Public*, pg. 420

CA-DYNAM/D—Disk Allocation & Control System—Computer Associates International, Inc.; *U.S. Public*, pg. 420

CA-DYNAM/FAST VTOC—Improves VTOC Related Functions for VSE Shops—Computer Associates International, Inc.; *U.S. Public*, pg. 420

CA-DYNAM/FI—File & Device Independant Product—Computer Associates International, Inc.; *U.S. Public*, pg. 420

CA-DYNAM/T—Tape/Vault Management System—Computer Associates International, Inc.; *U.S. Public*, pg. 420

CA-DYNAM/TLMS—Tape/Vault Management System—Computer Associates International, Inc.; *U.S. Public*, pg. 420

CA-DYNAM/TLMS GRO—Graphic Reporting for Tape/Vault Management—Computer Associates International, Inc.; *U.S. Public*, pg. 420

CA-DYNAM/WORKSTATION—Automatic Mngmt. of Tape Inventory—Computer Associates International, Inc.; *U.S. Public*, pg. 420

CA-EARL—Report Writer—Computer Associates International, Inc.; *U.S. Public*, pg. 420

CA-EASYPROCLIB—Procedure Library Manager—Computer Associates International, Inc.; *U.S. Public*, pg. 420

CA-EDP-AUDITOR—Provides a Library of CA-CULPRIT Routines Designed for the Audit Community—Computer Associates International, Inc.; *U.S. Public*, pg. 420

CA-EFILE—Storage/Search/Retrieval of CA EMAIL Messages—Computer Associates International, Inc.; *U.S. Public*, pg. 420

CA-11—Rerun/Restart System—Computer Associates International, Inc.; *U.S. Public*, pg. 420

CA-11/DISASTER RECOVERY PLANNING—Online Tool for Developing & Testing Disaster Recovery Plans—Computer Associates International, Inc.; *U.S. Public*, pg. 420

CA-11/NOTEPAD—Centralized Integrated Recording & Viewing of User Notes Made During CA-11—Computer Associates International, Inc.; *U.S. Public*, pg. 420

CA-11/REPORTS +—Codebook of CA-11 Customizable Reports—Computer Associates International, Inc.; *U.S. Public*, pg. 420

CA-11 VIEWPOINT—Window User Interface Option to CA-11—Computer Associates International, Inc.; *U.S. Public*, pg. 420

CA-EMAIL—Electronic Mail & Information Distribution System—Computer Associates International, Inc.; *U.S. Public*, pg. 420

CA-EMAIL & COMPANION—Electronic Mail Processor—Computer Associates International, Inc.; *U.S. Public*, pg. 420

CA-EMAIL + 400—Gateway Allowing CA-EMAIL to Work with Other X 400 EMAIL Systems—Computer Associates International, Inc.; *U.S. Public*, pg. 420

CA-ESCAPE/DL1—Transparency Software for Running DL/1 Applications in Relational Manner—Computer Associates International, Inc.; *U.S. Public*, pg. 420

CA-ESCAPE/TOTAL—Transparency Software for Running Total Applications inRational Environment—Computer Associates International, Inc.; *U.S. Public*, pg. 420

CA-ESCAPE/VSAM—Transparency Software for Running VSAM Applications in Rational Environment—Computer Associates International, Inc.; *U.S. Public*, pg. 420

CA-ESTIMACS—Project Estimation System—Computer Associates International, Inc.; *U.S. Public*, pg. 420

CA-ETC—Text Processing Tool—Computer Associates International, Inc.; *U.S. Public*, pg. 420

CA-EXAMINE—System/Auditing Facility—Computer Associates International, Inc.; *U.S. Public*, pg. 420

CA-EZTEST/CICS—Online Testing & Debugging—Computer Associates International, Inc.; *U.S. Public*, pg. 420

CA-FASTDASD—DASD Performance Tool—Computer Associates International, Inc.; *U.S. Public*, pg. 420

CA 15-3—Breast Cancer Blood Test—Centocor, Inc.; *U.S. Public*, pg. 323

CA-FIS—Online, Realtime Information Mngmt. System—Computer Associates International, Inc.; *U.S. Public*, pg. 420

CA-FIXED ASSETS—Asset Control Multiple Depreciation Rates Systems—Computer Associates International, Inc.; *U.S. Public*, pg. 420

CA-FLEXISCREEN—Online Screen & Applications Development—Computer Associates International, Inc.; *U.S. Public*, pg. 420

CA-FUND ACCOUNTING—Integrated Realtime Fund Control fo the Not-For-Profit Community—Computer Associates International, Inc.; *U.S. Public*, pg. 420

CA-GENERAL LEDGER/FRS—Comprehensive Fin. Mngmt. & Reporting—Computer Associates International, Inc.; *U.S. Public*, pg. 420

CA-GKS—Level 2b Implementation of the Graphical Kernal Standard—Computer Associates International, Inc.; *U.S. Public*, pg. 420

CA-GOLDENGATE—PC-Based Integrated Information Management Tool—Computer Associates International, Inc.; *U.S. Public*, pg. 420

CA-GRAPHICS CONNECTION—Graphics MetaFILE Translator Imports CGM, HPGL, DISSPOP, GDF—Computer Associates International, Inc.; *U.S. Public*, pg. 420

CAHTS—Heat Treating Controll System—Lindberg Corporation; *U.S. Public*, pg. 999

CA-HRS—Human Resource Management—Computer Associates International, Inc.; *U.S. Public*, pg. 420

CA-HRS:APPLICANT TRACKING—Tracking & Reporting on Applicants & Applications—Computer Associates International, Inc.; *U.S. Public*, pg. 420

CA-HRS:PAYROLL—Check Issuing, Calculation & Status Maintenance—Computer Associates International, Inc.; *U.S. Public*, pg. 420

CA-HRS:PC EXTEND—PC-Based Ext. for Mainframe CA-HRS Human Resource Mngmt. Software—Computer Associates International, Inc.; *U.S. Public*, pg. 420

CA-HRS:PERSONNEL—Online, Realtime Employee Recordkeeping—Computer Associates International, Inc.; *U.S. Public*, pg. 420

CA-HRS:POSITION CONTROL—Position-Driven Online Human Resource Management—Computer Associates International, Inc.; *U.S. Public*, pg. 420

CAIRS—Computer Aided Inspection Reporting System—Oceaneering International, Inc.; *U.S. Public*, pg. 1211

CA-ICMS—End-User Information Access Tool for a Relational Environment—Computer Associates International, Inc.; *U.S. Public*, pg. 420

CA-IDEAL—Fourth-Generation Applications Development System—Computer Associates International, Inc.; *U.S. Public*, pg. 420

CA-IDEAL/CCF—Change Control Facilities for CA-IDEAL—Computer Associates International, Inc.; *U.S. Public*, pg. 420

CA-IDEAL For DB2—Program Creation & Maintenance—Computer Associates International, Inc.; *U.S. Public*, pg. 420

CA-IDEAL 400—Complete Development & Execution Environment for AS/400—Computer Associates International, Inc.; *U.S. Public*, pg. 420

CA-IDEAL/IMAGE—Allows CA-IDEAL Applications Under ACS to Control Information—Computer Associates International, Inc.; *U.S. Public*, pg. 420

CA-IDEAL/ONLINE SORT—Sorting Capabilities for CA-IDEAL—Computer Associates International, Inc.; *U.S. Public*, pg. 420

CA-IDEAL/PC—Fully Compatible PC Implementation of CA IDEAL—Computer Associates International, Inc.; *U.S. Public*, pg. 420

CA-IDMS—Integrated Solution Providing Tools for Database Mngmt. & Appl. Devel.—Computer Associates International, Inc.; *U.S. Public*, pg. 420

CA-IDMS/ADS ALIVE—Source-Level Testing & Debugging Tool—Computer Associates International, Inc.; *U.S. Public*, pg. 420

CA-IDMS/ADS TRACE—Allows Developers to Trace the Execution of CA-ADS Dialogs—Computer Associates International, Inc.; *U.S. Public*, pg. 420

CA-IDMS/APPC—Extended Communications for Cooporative Processing Under CA-IDMS/DC—Computer Associates International, Inc.; *U.S. Public*, pg. 420

CA-IDMS:CASELINK—Linkage Between CASE Tools & CA-IDMS—Computer Associates International, Inc.; *U.S. Public*, pg. 420

CA-IDMS/COMPETE!—Windows-Based Multi-Dimensional & Decision Tool—Computer Associates International, Inc.; *U.S. Public*, pg. 420

CA-IDMS/CONCEPTOR—A CASE Environment Integrated CA-IDMS—Computer Associates International, Inc.; *U.S. Public*, pg. 420

CA-IDMS/DATABASE EXTRACTOR—On-Line Utility Used to Generate Test Databases in the CA-IDMS Environment—Computer Associates International, Inc.; *U.S. Public*, pg. 420

CA-IDMS/DB—Relational Database Management System—Computer Associates International, Inc.; *U.S. Public*, pg. 420

CA-IDMS/DB ANALYZER—Physical Database Analyses & Descriptive Report Production—Computer Associates International, Inc.; *U.S. Public*, pg. 420

CA-IDMS/DB AUDIT—Detects & Corrects Error Conditions in a CA-IDMS/DBDatabase—Computer Associates International, Inc.; *U.S. Public*, pg. 420

CA-IDMS/DB REORG—CA-IDMS/DB Database Reorganization Tool—Computer Associates International, Inc.; *U.S. Public*, pg. 420

CA-IDMS/DC—High Performance Teleprocessing Monitor—Computer Associates International, Inc.; *U.S. Public*, pg. 420

CA-IDMS/DC SORT—Online Sort Utility for CICS & CA-IDMS/DC Environments—Computer Associates International, Inc.; *U.S. Public*, pg. 420

CA-IDMS/DDS—Distributed Database System—Computer Associates International, Inc.; *U.S. Public*, pg. 420

CA-IDMS/DICTIONARY MIGRATOR—Migration Utility Automating Transfer of Applications Between Dictionaries—Computer Associates International, Inc.; *U.S. Public*, pg. 420

CA-IDMS/DICTIONARY MODULE EDITOR—On-line Utility for Editing Dictionary Modules—Computer Associates International, Inc.; *U.S. Public*, pg. 420

CA-IDMS/DML ONLINE—Interactive Utility Enabling Database Retrieval & Updating Database Records—Computer Associates International, Inc.; *U.S. Public*, pg. 420

CA-IDMS/ENFORCER—Define & Maintain Enforcement Standards—Computer Associates International, Inc.; *U.S. Public*, pg. 420

CA-IDMS FOR UNIX—Completely Compatible UNIX Server Version of CA-IDMS/DB—Computer Associates International, Inc.; *U.S. Public*, pg. 420

CA-IDMS FOR VAX—Completely Compatible VAX Server Version of CA-IDMS/DB—Computer Associates International, Inc.; *U.S. Public*, pg. 420

CA-IDMS/JOURNAL ANALYZER—Comprehensive Data Analysis Facility—Computer Associates International, Inc.; *U.S. Public*, pg. 420

CA-IDMS/LOG ANALYZER—Performance Analysis & Management Tool—Computer Associates International, Inc.; *U.S. Public*, pg. 420

CA-IDMS/MASTERKEY—Task Initiation Control Facility For CA-IDMS/DC—Computer Associates International, Inc.; *U.S. Public*, pg. 420

CA-IDMS/OPTFAST—COBOL Optimization Facility for Use with DC COBOL—Computer Associates International, Inc.; *U.S. Public*, pg. 420

CA-IDMS/OPTFAST II—COBOL II Optimization Facility for use with DC COBOL II—Computer Associates International, Inc.; *U.S. Public*, pg. 420

Brand Name Index

CA-IDMS/PC—Full-Function PC-Based Version of CA-IDMS/DB for Microcomputer Environment—Computer Associates International, Inc.; *U.S. Public*, pg. 420

CA-IDMS/PC LANPACK—Database Mngmt. System for LANS—Computer Associates International, Inc.; *U.S. Public*, pg. 420

CA-IDMS/PC RUNTIME—Production Mode Execution of Applications Built in CA-IDMS/PC Dev. Environ.—Computer Associates International, Inc.; *U.S. Public*, pg. 420

CA-IDMS/PC RUNTIME SERVER—Multi-User Prod. Mode Execution of Applications in CA-IDMS/PC Dev. Environ.—Computer Associates International, Inc.; *U.S. Public*, pg. 420

CA-IDMS PERFORMANCE MONITOR—Runtime Environment Performance Data—Computer Associates International, Inc.; *U.S. Public*, pg. 420

CA-IDMS PRESSPACK—Data Compression for CA-IDMS/DB Database Records—Computer Associates International, Inc.; *U.S. Public*, pg. 420

CA-IDMS/Q BYX—Windows Front End for Workstations Accessing CA-IDMS—Computer Associates International, Inc.; *U.S. Public*, pg. 420

CA-IDMS/SP&G—Comprehensive Composition of Standards, Procedures & Guidelines—Computer Associates International, Inc.; *U.S. Public*, pg. 420

CA-IDMS/SASO—Standards Administration System Online—Computer Associates International, Inc.; *U.S. Public*, pg. 420

CA-IDMS/SCHEMA MAPPER—Batch Utility that Automatically Produces Database Structure Diagrams—Computer Associates International, Inc.; *U.S. Public*, pg. 420

CA-IDMS SQL OPTION—Standard SQL Access to CA-IDMS—Computer Associates International, Inc.; *U.S. Public*, pg. 420

CA-IDMS/TASK ANALYZER—CA-IDMS/DC Task Reporting Utility—Computer Associates International, Inc.; *U.S. Public*, pg. 420

CA-IDMS/TRANSPARENCY FOR DB2—Transparency Software Enabling DB2 Applications to Run Unchanged on CA-IDMS—Computer Associates International, Inc.; *U.S. Public*, pg. 420

CA-IDMS/UCF—Data Communications Facility for Devel. of Programs Using CA-IDMS DC—Computer Associates International, Inc.; *U.S. Public*, pg. 420

CA-IDMS VSE/E3A OPTION—Allows CA-IDMS to Exploit VSE/ESA—Computer Associates International, Inc.; *U.S. Public*, pg. 420

CA-IMPLEMENTATION WORKBENCH—PC-Based Tools—Computer Associates International, Inc.; *U.S. Public*, pg. 420

CA-IMPLEMENTATION WORKBENCH CAS/AD—PC Based Tools—Computer Associates International, Inc.; *U.S. Public*, pg. 420

CA-IMPLEMENTATION WORKBENCH CDP—PC Based Tools—Computer Associates International, Inc.; *U.S. Public*, pg. 420

CA-INFOGATE—PC-Based Integrated Tools for Communicatios & File Translation—Computer Associates International, Inc.; *U.S. Public*, pg. 420

CA-INVENTORY CONTROL—Inventory Mngmt. & Reporting—Computer Associates International, Inc.; *U.S. Public*, pg. 420

CA-ISS/THREE—Performance Analyzer and Capacity Planning Tool—Computer Associates International, Inc.; *U.S. Public*, pg. 420

CA-JARS—Resource Accounting and Chargeback System—Computer Associates International, Inc.; *U.S. Public*, pg. 420

CA-JARS/CICS—Online Monitoring and Accounting System—Computer Associates International, Inc.; *U.S. Public*, pg. 420

CA-JARS DSA—DSAD Space Accounting—Computer Associates International, Inc.; *U.S. Public*, pg. 420

CA-JARS GRO—Graphic Reporting for System Utilization—Computer Associates International, Inc.; *U.S. Public*, pg. 420

CA-JARS IDMS—Analyzing & Monitoring Tool for IDMS—Computer Associates International, Inc.; *U.S. Public*, pg. 420

CA-JARS/IMS—Analyzing & Monitoring Tool for IMS—Computer Associates International, Inc.; *U.S. Public*, pg. 420

CA-JARS INTERFACE FOR VAX—Resource Accounting & Chargeback System—Computer Associates International, Inc.; *U.S. Public*, pg. 420

CA-JARS/OLF—Added Online Functions Such as Rate Determination & Chargeback Forecast—Computer Associates International, Inc.; *U.S. Public*, pg. 420

CA-JARS/REPORT +—Codebook of CA-JARS Customizable Reports—Computer Associates International, Inc.; *U.S. Public*, pg. 420

CA-JARS/SMF—SMF Management Tool—Computer Associates International, Inc.; *U.S. Public*, pg. 420

CA-JCLCHECK—JCL Validation Program—Computer Associates International, Inc.; *U.S. Public*, pg. 420

CA-JOB COST—Cost Collection & Reporting Facility—Computer Associates International, Inc.; *U.S. Public*, pg. 420

CA JOBWATCH—Batch Execution Environment for VM—Computer Associates International, Inc.; *U.S. Public*, pg. 420

CAL—Air Transportation—Continental Airlines; *U.S. Public*, pg. 439

CALS—Computer Automated Laboratory Systems—Beckman Instruments, Inc.; *U.S. Public*, pg. 199

CA-LABOR DISTRIBUTION—Track, Report & Control Contractors' Labor Costs—Computer Associates International, Inc.; *U.S. Public*, pg. 420

CA-LIBRARIAN—Source Code Management and Change Control System—Computer Associates International, Inc.; *U.S. Public*, pg. 420

CA-LIBRARIAN/COBOLVISION—Windows BAsed COBOLAnalysis Tool—Computer Associates International, Inc.; *U.S. Public*, pg. 420

CA-LIBRARIAN/JCL VALIDATION—Automatic Syntax Checking of MVS JCL—Computer Associates International, Inc.; *U.S. Public*, pg. 420

CA-LINK—PC to Host Communications Systems—Computer Associates International, Inc.; *U.S. Public*, pg. 420

CA-LOOK—Online Performance Monitor—Computer Associates International, Inc.; *U.S. Public*, pg. 420

CAMS—Comprehensive Account Management Services—Health Management Systems, Inc.; *U.S. Public*, pg. 802

CAMS—Computer Assisted Measuring System—NewAge Industries Inc.; *U.S. Private*, pg. 796

CAM SERIES—Plaques—Tropar Mfg. Co., Inc.; *U.S. Private*, pg. 1105

CA-MASTERSTATION—Cooperative Processing Workstation for CA-General Ledger—Computer Associates International, Inc.; *U.S. Public*, pg. 420

CA-MASTERSTATION FOR DOS—Cooperative Processing Workstation for CA-General Ledger—Computer Associates International, Inc.; *U.S. Public*, pg. 420

CA-MASTERSTATION FOR OS/2—Cooperative Processing Workstation for CA-General Ledger—Computer Associates International, Inc.; *U.S. Public*, pg. 420

CA-MAZDAMON—Network Performance Monitor—Computer Associates International, Inc.; *U.S. Public*, pg. 420

CA-METACOBOL—High-Level COBOL Devel. & Maintenance System—Computer Associates International, Inc.; *U.S. Public*, pg. 420

CA-METACOBOL + /OPTFAST II—Object Code Optimization for VS COBOL II—Computer Associates International, Inc.; *U.S. Public*, pg. 420

CA-METACOBOL + /OPTFAST—Object Code Optimization for COBOL Programs—Computer Associates International, Inc.; *U.S. Public*, pg. 420

CA MIGRATE/COBOL—COBOL Upgrade & Migration to COBOL II—Computer Associates International, Inc.; *U.S. Public*, pg. 420

CA MIGRATION WORKBENCH—Assists Clients in Plng. & Analysis Phases for Upgrading CA-CAS—Computer Associates International, Inc.; *U.S. Public*, pg. 420

CA-MINDOVER—Performance Analysis & Tuning System—Computer Associates International, Inc.; *U.S. Public*, pg. 420

CA-NETMAN—Data Center Administration System—Computer Associates International, Inc.; *U.S. Public*, pg. 420

CA-NETMAN/DB—Relational Option for CA-NETMAN Users—Computer Associates International, Inc.; *U.S. Public*, pg. 420

CA-NETMAN FOR UNIX—Mngmt. of Hardware/Software at HP Sites—Computer Associates International, Inc.; *U.S. Public*, pg. 420

CA-NETMAN/OLCF—Online Customization Facility—Computer Associates International, Inc.; *U.S. Public*, pg. 420

CA-NETMAN/PC—Inventory Tracking, Analysis & Management—Computer Associates International, Inc.; *U.S. Public*, pg. 420

CA-NETMAN/REPORTS +—Codebook of CA-NETMAN Customizable Reports—Computer Associates International, Inc.; *U.S. Public*, pg. 420

CA-NETMAN/VAX—Inventory Tracking, Analysis & Management—Computer Associates International, Inc.; *U.S. Public*, pg. 420

CA-9/R +—Hardware Reliability Analysis System—Computer Associates International, Inc.; *U.S. Public*, pg. 420

CA 19-9—Pancreatic Cancer Blood Test—Centocor, Inc.; *U.S. Public*, pg. 323

CA-OLQ—Retrieval of Info. from CA-IDMS/DB Databases or Sequential Files—Computer Associates International, Inc.; *U.S. Public*, pg. 420

CA-1—Tape/Vault Management System—Computer Associates International, Inc.; *U.S. Public*, pg. 420

CA-1/COPYCAT—Optional Utilities for Tape Copy, Data Recovery, Media Replacement—Computer Associates International, Inc.; *U.S. Public*, pg. 420

CA 125—Ovarian Cancer Blood Test—Centocor, Inc.; *U.S. Public*, pg. 323

CA 125 II—NONE—Centocor, Inc.; *U.S. Public*, pg. 323

CA-1/VAX—Tape Management System—Computer Associates International, Inc.; *U.S. Public*, pg. 420

CA-1/VIEWPOINT—Window User Interface Option to CA-1—Computer Associates International, Inc.; *U.S. Public*, pg. 420

CA-1/WORKSTATION—Automatic Mngmt. of CA-1 Tape Inventory—Computer Associates International, Inc.; *U.S. Public*, pg. 420

CA-ONGUARD—Network Application Manager & Security System—Computer Associates International, Inc.; *U.S. Public*, pg. 420

CA-OPERA—Console & Message Manager—Computer Associates International, Inc.; *U.S. Public*, pg. 420

CA-OPERA/PC—PC-Based Componenet of CA-OPERA—Computer Associates International, Inc.; *U.S. Public*, pg. 420

CA-OPTIMIZER—COBOL Optimization & Debugging—Computer Associates International, Inc.; *U.S. Public*, pg. 420

CA-OPTIMIZER/COBOLVISION—Windows Based COBOL Analysis Tool—Computer Associates International, Inc.; *U.S. Public*, pg. 420

CA-OPTIMIZER/II—COBOL II Optimization & Debugging—Computer Associates International, Inc.; *U.S. Public*, pg. 420

CA-ORDER PROCESSING—Entering, Validating & Recording Sales—Computer Associates International, Inc.; *U.S. Public*, pg. 420

C-A-P—Enteric Coating Material—Eastman Chemical Company; *U.S. Public*, pg. 550

C-A-P—Enteric Coating Material, Cellulose Acetate Phthalate—Eastman Kodak Company; *U.S. Public*, pg. 550

CAPS—Central American Piggyback Service—Central Gulf Lines, Inc.; *U.S. Public*, pg. 907

CAPS—Capital Planning System Software for Site Selection and Planning—MPSI Systems Inc.; *U.S. Public*, pg. 1027

CAPS—Data Security Products—Tandem Computers Inc.; *U.S. Public*, pg. 417

CA-PANVALET/COBOLVISION—Inter-Active Anlysis Tool—Computer Associates International, Inc.; *U.S. Public*, pg. 420

CA-PLANMACS—Planning Tool for Project Estimation—Computer Associates International, Inc.; *U.S. Public*, pg. 420

CA-PLOT OPTIMIZER—High-Speed Laser Printer Device Drivers—Computer Associates International, Inc.; *U.S. Public*, pg. 420

CA-PMA/CHANGEBACK FOR VAX—Changeback Implementation, Mngmt. & Reporting—Computer Associates International, Inc.; *U.S. Public*, pg. 420

CA-PMA/CHANGEBACK—Chargeback Implementation, Management & Reporting—Computer Associates International, Inc.; *U.S. Public*, pg. 420

CA-PMA/LOOK—On-Line Performance Monitor—Computer Associates International, Inc.; *U.S. Public*, pg. 420

CA-PMA PERFORMANCE REVIEW—Analysis of MVS & Sub-System Performance—Computer Associates International, Inc.; *U.S. Public*, pg. 420

CA-POINTER EDITOR FOR IMS—Online Program for Analysis/Repair of Pointers—Computer Associates International, Inc.; *U.S. Public*, pg. 420

CA-PTFAID—Free, Online Service System for PTFs & PIBs—Computer Associates International, Inc.; *U.S. Public*, pg. 420

CA-PTFCOM—Terminal Emulation Software for CA-PTFAID—Computer Associates International, Inc.; *U.S. Public*, pg. 420

CA-PURCHASING—Full-Cycle Purchase Order Mngmt. & Control—Computer Associates International, Inc.; *U.S. Public*, pg. 420

C.A.R.S.—Syndicated Carpet/Rug Purchase Monitor—NFO Research, Inc.; *U.S. Public*, pg. 1146

CA-RAPS—CICS Printer & Spool Management—Computer Associates International, Inc.; *U.S. Public*, pg. 420

CA-RECOVERY MANAGEMENT—Recovery Mngmt.—Computer Associates International, Inc.; *U.S. Public*, pg. 420

CA-REPORTBUILD—Front-End Menu for CA-CULPRIT—Computer Associates International, Inc.; *U.S. Public*, pg. 420

CA-RMS1—Job Accounting System—Computer Associates International, Inc.; *U.S. Public*, pg. 420

CA-ROSCOE—Online Programming System—Computer Associates International, Inc.; *U.S. Public*, pg. 420

CA-ROSCOE/BULLETIN BOARD—Interactive Bulletin Board Facility Under CA-ROSCOE—Computer Associates International, Inc.; *U.S. Public*, pg. 420

CAS COLA—Glues & Adhesives—Borden, Inc.; *U.S. Private*, pg. 157

CAS COLAR—Glues & Adhesives—Borden, Inc.; *U.S. Private*, pg. 157

CASD—Cached Actuator Storage Device—Zitel Corporation; *U.S. Public*, pg. 1793

CAS/ES—NONE—CSC Financial Services Group; *U.S. Public*, pg. 422

C.A.S.H—NONE—Harrah's Entertainment, Inc.; *U.S. Public*, pg. 790

CASL—Computer Software—Attachmate; *U.S. Private*, pg. 98

CAS 200—Dual-Color Image Analysis System For Quantitative Biochemical Data—Becton Dickinson & Company; *U.S. Public*, pg. 199

CA-SCHEDULER—Automated Scheduling System—Computer Associates International, Inc.; *U.S. Public*, pg. 420

CA-SCHEDULER GRO—Graphic Reporting for Scheduling System—Computer Associates International, Inc.; *U.S. Public*, pg. 420

CA-SCHEDULER/VIEWPOINT—Window User Interface Option to CA-Scheduler—Computer Associates International, Inc.; *U.S. Public*, pg. 420

CA-SCHEDULER/VM CONNECTION—Optional Network Scheduling of VM Batch Work—Computer Associates International, Inc.; *U.S. Public*, pg. 420

CA-7—Automated Scheduling System—Computer Associates International, Inc.; *U.S. Public*, pg. 420

CA-7 FOR VAX—Automated Scheduling System—Computer Associates International, Inc.; *U.S. Public*, pg. 420

CA-7/NOTEPAD—Centralized, Integrated Recording & Viewing of User Notes Made During CA-7—Computer Associates International, Inc.; *U.S. Public*, pg. 420

CA-7/OLC—Online, Expert Assistance for CA-7 Users—Computer Associates International, Inc.; *U.S. Public*, pg. 420

CA-7/PAGER NOTIFICATION—Automatic Page or Call Capabilities—Computer Associates International, Inc.; *U.S. Public*, pg. 420

CA-7 REPORT BALANCING—Automatic Report Balancing & Verification—Computer Associates International, Inc.; *U.S. Public*, pg. 420

CA-7/REPORTS +—Codebook of CA-7 Customizable Reports—Computer Associates International, Inc.; *U.S. Public*, pg. 420

CA-7/SMART CONSOLE—Automatic Scheduling of CICS Transactions—Computer Associates International, Inc.; *U.S. Public*, pg. 420

CA-7/VIEWPOINT—Window User Interface Option to CA-7—Computer Associates International, Inc.; *U.S. Public*, pg. 420

CA-7/VM CONNECTION—Network Scheduling of VM Batch Work—Computer Associates International, Inc.; *U.S. Public*, pg. 420

CA 72-4—GastroIntestinal Cancer Blood Test—Centocor, Inc.; *U.S. Public*, pg. 323

CA-SIMPLY ACCOUNTING—Micro Software—Computer Associates International, Inc.; *U.S. Public*, pg. 420

CA-SORT/CICS—Support of Batch Sort Verb Using Native CICS Facilities for COBOL II, PL/I—Computer Associates International, Inc.; *U.S. Public*, pg. 420

CA-SPACE/MANAGER—Disk Allocation & Control System—Computer Associates International, Inc.; *U.S. Public*, pg. 420

CA-SPOOLMAN—Spool Management Facility—Computer Associates International, Inc.; *U.S. Public*, pg. 420

CA-SRAM—Sort Reentrant Access Method—Computer Associates International, Inc.; *U.S. Public*, pg. 420

CA-STRATAGEM—Corp. Plng. System, Including Date Mngmt., Reporting & Application Devel.—Computer Associates International, Inc.; *U.S. Public*, pg. 420

CA-SUPERCALC—Mainframe Spreadsheet with Graphics, Data Mngmt., Data Access & Wd. Proc.—Computer Associates International, Inc.; *U.S. Public*, pg. 420

CA-SUPERCALC/PC—Integrated Spreadsheet with Graphics & Data Management—Computer Associates International, Inc.; *U.S. Public*, pg. 420

CA-SUPERIMAGE FOR VAX—DECwindows Based Graphics Editing & Drawing Tool—Computer Associates International, Inc.; *U.S. Public*, pg. 420

CA-SUPERPROJECT—Project & Resource Management—Computer Associates International, Inc.; *U.S. Public*, pg. 420

CA-SUPERPROJECT FOR MS-DOS—Project & Resource Management—Computer Associates International, Inc.; *U.S. Public*, pg. 420

CA-SUPERPROJECT FOR VAX—Project & Rescue Management for VAX/VMS—Computer Associates International, Inc.; *U.S. Public*, pg. 420

CA-SUPERPROJECT FOR WINDOWS—Project & Resource Management—Computer Associates International, Inc.; *U.S. Public*, pg. 420

CA-SYSTEM/SCHEDULER—Automated Scheduling System—Computer Associates International, Inc.; *U.S. Public*, pg. 420

C-A-T—Cellulose Acetate Trimellitate; Enteric Coating Material—Eastman Kodak Company; *U.S. Public*, pg. 550

CATR—Cook/Chill Meal Delivery System—United Service Equipment Company; *U.S. Public*, pg. 1507

CA-TAPE/MANAGER—Tape/Vault Management System—Computer Associates International, Inc.; *U.S. Public*, pg. 420

CA-TELLAGRAF—End User Graphics for Decision-Making, Presentation & Performance—Computer Associates International, Inc.; *U.S. Public*, pg. 420

CA-TMS—Tape Management System—Computer Associates International, Inc.; *U.S. Public*, pg. 420

CA-TOP SECRET—Resource Access Control System—Computer Associates International, Inc.; *U.S. Public*, pg. 420

CA-TOP SECRET/DB2—DB2 Resource Access Control System—Computer Associates International, Inc.; *U.S. Public*, pg. 420

CA-TOP SECRET GRO—Graphic Reporting for Resource Access Control System—Computer Associates International, Inc.; *U.S. Public*, pg. 420

CA-TOP SECRET/PC—Resource Access Control System for PC Mainframe Connectivity—Computer Associates International, Inc.; *U.S. Public*, pg. 420

CA-TOP SECRET SECMAN FOR VAX—Resource Access Control System—Computer Associates International, Inc.; *U.S. Public*, pg. 420

CA-TOP SECRET/VIEWPOINT—Window User Interface for CA-TOP SECRET—Computer Associates International, Inc.; *U.S. Public*, pg. 420

CA-TRANSIT—Non-IBM COBOL to IBM Conversion System—Computer Associates International, Inc.; *U.S. Public*, pg. 420

CA-TRAPS—Quality Assurance Tool to Automate Testing & Detect Software Defects—Computer Associates International, Inc.; *U.S. Public*, pg. 420

CA-UCANDU—Data Set Management & Transfer Utility—Computer Associates International, Inc.; *U.S. Public*, pg. 420

CA-UNICENTER/II—Total Data Center Automation & Service System—Computer Associates International, Inc.; *U.S. Public*, pg. 420

CA-UNIPACK—Total Data Center Automation System—Computer Associates International, Inc.; *U.S. Public*, pg. 420

CA-UNIPACK/ANALYZER FOR CA-IDMS/DB—Tools to Evaluate System Performance—Computer Associates International, Inc.; *U.S. Public*, pg. 420

CA-UNIPACK/APC—Automated Production Control System—Computer Associates International, Inc.; *U.S. Public*, pg. 420

CA-UNIPACK/ASM—Automated Storage Management System—Computer Associates International, Inc.; *U.S. Public*, pg. 420

CA-UNIPACK/DBA FOR CA-IDMS/DB—Tools to Manage, Control, Tune & Monitor the IDMS Environment—Computer Associates International, Inc.; *U.S. Public*, pg. 420

CA-UNIPACK/DCA—Data Center Administration System—Computer Associates International, Inc.; *U.S. Public*, pg. 420

CA-UNIPACK/DEVELOPER FOR CA-IDMS/DB—A Complete Solution to the CA-IDMS/DB Development Life Cycle—Computer Associates International, Inc.; *U.S. Public*, pg. 420

CA-UNIPACK/IMS—Tools for Management & Control of the IMS/DL/I Database Environment—Computer Associates International, Inc.; *U.S. Public*, pg. 420

CA-UNIPACK/PEP—Project Estimation & Planning System—Computer Associates International, Inc.; *U.S. Public*, pg. 420

CA-UNIPACK/PMA—Performance Management & Accounting System—Computer Associates International, Inc.; *U.S. Public*, pg. 420

CA-UNIPACK/QA FOR CA-IDMS/DE—Tools to Document & Review Administrative Standards—Computer Associates International, Inc.; *U.S. Public*, pg. 420

CA-UNIPACK/SCA—Security, Control & Audit System—Computer Associates International, Inc.; *U.S. Public*, pg. 420

CA-UNIPACK VM—Total Data Center Automation System—Computer Associates International, Inc.; *U.S. Public*, pg. 420

CA-UNISERVICE/II—Online Service, Support & Training—Computer Associates International, Inc.; *U.S. Public*, pg. 420

CA-UNIVERSE—User-Oriented Relational Data Base & Applications Development System—Computer Associates International, Inc.; *U.S. Public*, pg. 420

CAV—Diesel & Fuel Injection Equip./Automotive, OE, Agricultural & Indus. Prods.—Lucas Industries Inc.; *Int'l*, pg. 820

CA-VISA—Vax Integrated Systems Administration—Computer Associates International, Inc.; *U.S. Public*, pg. 420

CA-VMAN—VTAM Security & Session Management Utility—Computer Associates International, Inc.; *U.S. Public*, pg. 420

CA-VOLLIE—Online Programming System—Computer Associates International, Inc.; *U.S. Public*, pg. 420

CA-VTERM—Security & Session Management System—Computer Associates International, Inc.; *U.S. Public*, pg. 420

C & A—Logo—Collins & Aikman Corporation; *U.S. Public*, pg. 399

C & B—Vintage Cellars—Wine World Estates Company; *Int'l*, pg. 917

C & C FOR HUMAN POTENTIAL—NONE—NEC Electronics Inc.; *Int'l*, pg. 900

C&D DEBRIS RECYCLING—Quarterly Publication—Intertec Publishing; *U.S. Public*, pg. 1327

C&H—Broad Line of Refined Sugar—Alexander & Baldwin, Inc.; *U.S. Public*, pg. 39

C & H—Sugar—California & Hawaiian Sugar Company Inc.; *U.S. Public*, pg. 39

C & T—Magazines For Members Of Auto Clubs—American Automobile Association; *U.S. Private*, pg. 50

CB—Ski & Sports Apparel—CB Sports Inc.; *U.S. Private*, pg. 192

CBA—Cement Additives—Grace Construction Products; *U.S. Public*, pg. 755

CBC—German Broadcasting—CLT-UFA; *Int'l*, pg. 561

C.B.E. TAP—Carbide Bonded Edge Tap—National Twist Drill Div.; *U.S. Public*, pg. 1370

CBI—Circuit Board Indicators—Dialight Corporation; *Int'l*, pg. 1130

CBIL—NONE—Western Atlas Logging Services; *U.S. Public*, pg. 1757

CBIPO—Computer System—International Business Machines Corporation; *U.S. Public*, pg. 895

CBK GRAPHITE RTS—Racquetball Racquet—Ektelon; *U.S. Private*, pg. 884

CB-1—Motorcycle—American Honda Motor Co., Inc. Motorcycle Division; *Int'l*, pg. 634

CBPDO—Computer System—International Business Machines Corporation; *U.S. Public*, pg. 895

CBR—Motorcycle—American Honda Motor Co., Inc. Motorcycle Division; *Int'l*, pg. 634

CBR BLACK 10—Golf Shoes—Mizuno Corporation; *Int'l*, pg. 884

CBS—Radio & Television Stations—CBS; *U.S. Public*, pg. 273

CBS-50 NIL—Bearing Steel—Latrobe Steel Company; *U.S. Public*, pg. 1617

CBS MORNING RESOURCE—Entertainment News Programming—Westwood One, Inc.; *U.S. Public*, pg. 1763

CBS-1000 M—Bearing Steel—Latrobe Steel Company; *U.S. Public*, pg. 1617

CBS RADIO NETWORKS—Over 250 News, Sports & Info. Programs—Westwood One, Inc.; *U.S. Public*, pg. 1763

CBS RADIO SPORTS NFL PACKAGE—Sports Programming—Westwood One, Inc.; *U.S. Public*, pg. 1763

CBS-600—Carburizing High Performance—Latrobe Steel Company; *U.S. Public*, pg. 1617

CBS SPECTRUM RADIO NETWORK—Entertainment News Programming—Westwood One, Inc.; *U.S. Public*, pg. 1763

CBS WORLD NEWS ROUNDUP—News Program—Westwood One, Inc.; *U.S. Public*, pg. 1763

CB SPORTS—Ski Apparel—CB North America, Inc.; *U.S. Private*, pg. 192

CB-X1/X2—Disposable Cleaning Brush—Ballard Medical Products; *U.S. Public*, pg. 171

CCA—NONE—CSC Financial Services Group; *U.S. Public*, pg. 422

CCA2—Software—CSC Financial Services Group; *U.S. Public*, pg. 422

CCC/MANAGER—Change & Configuration Management Software—Platinum Technology - Santa Barbara Laboratory; *U.S. Public*, pg. 1309

CCD—Treatment of Lower Spine Degenerative Diseases—Sofamor Danek Group, Inc.; *U.S. Public*, pg. 1482

CCH ACCESS—Legal Research System Software—CCH Incorporated; *Int'l*, pg. 1513

CCI—Motorcycles & Motor Oil—American Suzuki Motor Corporation; *Int'l*, pg. 1323

CCI—Small Arms Ammunition/Primero—Blount, Inc. Sporting Equipment Group; *U.S. Public*, pg. 238

CCI—Ammunition & Primers—Blount International, Inc.; *U.S. Public*, pg. 237

CCI—Valves—IMI Plc; *Int'l*, pg. 646

CC:MAIL—NONE—Lotus Development Corporation; *U.S. Public*, pg. 896

CC MYERS—Bridge & Highway, Land Investments—C.C. Myers, Inc.; *U.S. Private*, pg. 770

CCR 2000—Snowthrower—The Toro Company; *U.S. Public*, pg. 1623

CCS—Communication Control System—Tandem Computers Inc.; *U.S. Public*, pg. 417

C.C. SPORTS—NONE—Supreme International Corp.; *U.S. Public*, pg. 1542

C.C.T.—Company Subsidiary Name—Baltimore Aircoil Company; *U.S. Private*, pg. 68

C COMPILER PRODUCTS—Language Compilers for IBM Mainframes & Amiga DOS—SAS Institute Inc.; *U.S. Private*, pg. 966

CD—Locks Spinal Implants Together—Sofamor Danek Group, Inc.; *U.S. Public*, pg. 1482

CD—Cassette Duplicators—Telex Communications, Inc.; *U.S. Private*, pg. 245

CD-BASS—Cd to Cassette Adapters—Recoton Corporation; *U.S. Public*, pg. 1369

CD COUPLING—NONE—Zero-Max, Inc.; *Int'l*, pg. 866

CDE—Software—LSI Logic Corp.; *U.S. Public*, pg. 971

C-D EXTERIOR—Plywood for Bracing & General Use—Carter Holt Harvey Limited; *U.S. Public*, pg. 904

CD-EYE—Surgical Teaching System—Alcon Laboratories, Inc.; *Int'l*, pg. 916

CD/410—Instrument Equipment—Clayton Industries Co.; *U.S. Private*, pg. 245

CD HYDROBATH—Non-Contact Cleaner for All Types of CDs—Recoton Corporation; *U.S. Public*, pg. 1369

CDM—Coffee—Reily Foods Company; *U.S. Private*, pg. 919

CDM—Coffee—William B. Reily & Co., Inc.; *U.S. Private*, pg. 919

CD-1—CD Case & Maintenance Products—Recoton Corporation; *U.S. Public*, pg. 1369

CDOPEN—Cross Direction Profile Control Systems—Honeywell-Measurex Corporation; *U.S. Public*, pg. 833

CDP/ES—Software—CSC Financial Services Group; *U.S. Public*, pg. 422

CDRS—Conceptual Design & Rendering System; Industrial Design Product—Evans & Sutherland Computer Corporation; *U.S. Public*, pg. 595

CD READ—Documentation Manuals on CD-ROM—Tandem Computers Inc.; *U.S. Public*, pg. 417

CDSP—NONE—Texas Instruments Incorporated; *U.S. Public*, pg. 1585

CD SHOWCASE—Computer System—International Business Machines Corporation; *U.S. Public*, pg. 895

CDTECT—NONE—Pharmacia & Upjohn, Inc.; *Int'l*, pg. 1047

CDISCOURSE—Publication—The Mead Corporation; *U.S. Public*, pg. 1074

CED—Magazine of Braodband Communications—Reed Elsevier Business Information; *Int'l*, pg. 1095

CEEA—Surgical Staplers—U.S. Surgical Corp.; *U.S. Public*, pg. 1687

CEE NEWS—Publication for Electrical Contractors—Intertec Publishing; *U.S. Public*, pg. 1327

CEF—Saftey Interlocks For Access Control Valve Interlocking & Machine Guarding—Halma p.l.c.; *Int'l*, pg. 589

CEM—NONE—CEM Corporation; *U.S. Public*, pg. 277

CEM—NONE—Pfizer Inc.; *U.S. Public*, pg. 1281

CEO—Integrated Office Automation Software—Data General Corporation; *U.S. Public*, pg. 485

CEO OBJECT OFFICE—Office Automation Software—Data General Corporation; *U.S. Public*, pg. 485

CEO-TWO—Rectal Suppository—Beutlich, L.P.; *U.S. Private*, pg. 141

C.E.S.—Prescription Drug—ICN Pharmaceuticals, Inc.; *U.S. Public*, pg. 853

CEV—Contemporary English Version—American Bible Society; *U.S. Private*, pg. 51

CE-VI-SOL—Vitamin C Supplement—Mead Johnson Nutritional Group; *U.S. Public*, pg. 254

C EAGLE & SHIELD—NONE—Carpenter Technology Corporation; *U.S. Public*, pg. 307

C-F—Under Hook Lifters—Badger Equipment Co.; *U.S. Private*, pg. 102

CF&I—Carbon Pipe & Steel Products—Thomas Pipe & Steel, Inc.; *U.S. Private*, pg. 508

CFB COMMUNITY FIRST—NONE—Community First Bankshares, Inc.; *U.S. Public*, pg. 416

CFI—Stairstep Letters—Contract Freighters, Inc.; *U.S. Private*, pg. 270

CFM—Cryo-Focusing Module—O.I. Corporation; *U.S. Public*, pg. 1208

CFM56—Turbofan Engine—SNECMA - Societe Nationale d'Etude et de Construction de Moteurs d'Aviation; *Int'l*, pg. 1165

CFM-SHORT CYCLE—Computer System—International Business Machines Corporation; *U.S. Public*, pg. 895

CF MOTOR FREIGHT—Long Distance Trucking Service—Consolidated Freightways Corp.; *U.S. Public*, pg. 435

CFO MAGAZINE—NONE—The Economist Group Limited.; *Int'l*, pg. 1026

CFO VISION—Business Solution For Financial Consolodation & Reporting—SAS Institute Inc.; *U.S. Private*, pg. 966

CFS—Plenum Cable—Tensolite Company; *U.S. Public*, pg. 305

CF6-80—Turbofan Engine—SNECMA - Societe Nationale d'Etude et de Construction de Moteurs d'Aviation; *Int'l*, pg. 1165

C-5 GALAXY—Aerospace Manufacturing—Lockheed Aeronautical Systems Company; *U.S. Public*, pg. 1007

C510/C520—Trucks—Kenworth Truck Company; *U.S. Public*, pg. 1246

C/400—Computer System—International Business Machines Corporation; *U.S. Public*, pg. 895

CG—Photo Typesetters—AGFA EPS Division; *Int'l*, pg. 172

CG—NONE—Moss Bros Group PLC; *Int'l*, pg. 895

CGC—NONE—CGC Inc.; *U.S. Public*, pg. 1660

CG 1800—Golf Clubs—MacGregor Golf Company; *Int'l*, pg. 72

CGL—Cerner Graphics Language—Cerner Corporation; *U.S. Public*, pg. 331

CGM—Maritime Services—Compagnie Generale Maritime et Financiere; *Int'l*, pg. 322

CGM BORDEAUX—NONE—Compagnie Generale Maritime et Financiere; *Int'l*, pg. 322

CGM DUNKERQUE—NONE—Compagnie Generale Maritime et Financiere; *Int'l*, pg. 322

CGM LE HAVRE—NONE—Compagnie Generale Maritime et Financiere; *Int'l*, pg. 322

CGM MARSEILLE—NONE—Compagnie Generale Maritime et Financiere; *Int'l*, pg. 322

CGM SUD—NONE—Compagnie Generale Maritime et Financiere; *Int'l*, pg. 322

CGM TOUR DU MONDE—NONE—Compagnie Generale Maritime et Financiere; *Int'l*, pg. 322

CG RIA—Diagnostic Products—Abbott Laboratories; *U.S. Public*, pg. 12

CGS—Sportswear—CGS Industries, Inc.; *U.S. Private*, pg. 194

CG SCRIPT—Photo Typesetters—AGFA EPS Division; *Int'l*, pg. 172

C-GATE—Software—CACI International Inc; *U.S. Public*, pg. 272

C GRID—Electronic Components—Molex Incorporated; *U.S. Public*, pg. 1121

C-GRID S/L—Eletronic Components—Molex Incorporated; *U.S. Public*, pg. 1121

CHC SIGNATURE 2000—Software Tool—Computer Horizons Corp.; *U.S. Public*, pg. 421

CHI—Computer Software—Attachmate; *U.S. Private*, pg. 98

CHP/ES—Software—CSC Financial Services Group; *U.S. Public*, pg. 422

CHR/MODERN ROCK PREP—Modern Rock Programming—Westwood One, Inc.; *U.S. Public*, pg. 1763

CICS—Computer System—International Business Machines Corporation; *U.S. Public*, pg. 895

CICS/ESA—Computer System—International Business Machines Corporation; *U.S. Public*, pg. 895

CICS/400—Computer System—International Business Machines Corporation; *U.S. Public*, pg. 895

CICS/MVS—Computer System—International Business Machines Corporation; *U.S. Public*, pg. 895

CICS MANAGER—Comprehensive Performance Management & Reporting Tool—Boole & Babbage, Inc.; *U.S. Public*, pg. 244

CICS OS/2—Computer System—International Business Machines Corporation; *U.S. Public*, pg. 895

CICS PLAYBACK—Systems Software Product—Compuware Corporation; *U.S. Public*, pg. 423

CICS/6000—Computer System—International Business Machines Corporation; *U.S. Public*, pg. 895

CICS/VM—Computer System—International Business Machines Corporation; *U.S. Public*, pg. 895

CICS VSE—Computer System—International Business Machines Corporation; *U.S. Public*, pg. 895

CIEDS—Computer System—International Business Machines Corporation; *U.S. Public*, pg. 895

CIF—Household Cleaners—Unilever Plc; *Int'l*, pg. 1433

CIF 38—Banking Software—Jack Henry & Associates, Inc.; *U.S. Public*, pg. 808

CIF 36—Banking Software—Jack Henry & Associates, Inc.; *U.S. Public*, pg. 808

CIF 20/20—Banking Software—Jack Henry & Associates, Inc.; *U.S. Public*, pg. 808

CIHS—Cables—Tensolite Company; *U.S. Public*, pg. 305

C.I. HAYES—Electric Heat-Treating Equipment—C.I. Hayes, Inc.; *U.S. Private*, pg. 513

CII—Corporate Logo—Communications Instruments Inc.; *U.S. Private*, pg. 259

CIM ADVANTAGE—Computer System—International Business Machines Corporation; *U.S. Public*, pg. 895

CIM-PAC—IBM PC-Based Measurement & Control Software—Action Instruments, Inc.; *U.S. Private*, pg. 15

CIP—Cable—Tensolite Company; *U.S. Public*, pg. 305

CIS—Computer Inquiry Systems—Beckman Instruments, Inc.; *U.S. Public*, pg. 199

CJI & HYDROCURVE—NONE—Pilkington Barnes Hind (PBH); *U.S. Private*, pg. 111

CK-MAG—Magnetic Flowmeter—Bailey, Fischer & Porter Company; *Int'l*, pg. 449

C.K. MONDAVI—Wine—Pacific Wine Co.; *U.S. Private*, pg. 843

CK one—Men's & Women's Fragrance—Calvin Klein Cosmetics Company; *Int'l*, pg. 1435

CK PICKUP—Truck—Chevrolet Motor Div. General Motors Corp.; *U.S. Public*, pg. 720

CL—Automobile—American Honda Motor Co., Inc.; *Int'l*, pg. 634

CLC—Curl Activator & Support Lotion—The Gillette Company; *U.S. Public*, pg. 743

CL-89—Unmanned Airbourne Surveillance Systems—Bombardier Aerospace; *Int'l*, pg. 200

C. L. KIDS—Children's Shoes—Jumping Jacks; *U.S. Private*, pg. 767

CLR—Calcium, Lime & Rust Remover—Jelmar Company; *U.S. Private*, pg. 585

CLS II—NONE—Western Atlas Logging Services; *U.S. Public*, pg. 1757

CL304—Precision Ultrasonic Thickness Gage—Krautkramer-Branson, Inc.; *U.S. Public*, pg. 574

CL-289—Unmanned Airbourne Surveillance Systems—Bombardier Aerospace; *Int'l*, pg. 200

CL-215—Multi-Purpose Amphibious Aircraft—Bombardier Aerospace; *Int'l*, pg. 200

CL-227—Unmanned Airbourne Surveillance Systems—Bombardier Aerospace; *Int'l*, pg. 200

C-L-X—Metallic Sheathed Cables—The Okonite Company; *U.S. Private*, pg. 813

CLX—Computer Systems—Tandem Computers Inc.; *U.S. Public*, pg. 417

CLX/R—Computer Systems—Tandem Computers Inc.; *U.S. Public*, pg. 417

CLX 2000—Computer Systems—Tandem Computers Inc.; *U.S. Public*, pg. 417

CL-227—Unmanned Airborne Surveillance Systems—Bombardier Inc.; *Int'l*, pg. 199

CL-415—Amphibious Aircraft—Bombardier Inc.; *Int'l*, pg. 199

C-LOCK—ECG Synchronization System—Nellcor Puritan Bennett Incorporated; *U.S. Public*, pg. 1039

CMC—NONE—Connector Manufacturing Company; *U.S. Private*, pg. 264

CMC—Concrete Mixer—3ummit Performance Dist. Inc.; *U.S. Public*, pg. 1233

CMC POWER LIFT—Jack Plate for Outboard Motor Boats—Cook Manufacturing Corporation; *U.S. Private*, pg. 272

CMC TAPE TWIN—Numerical Control Computer System for CNC Machines—Cook Manufacturing Corporation; *U.S. Private*, pg. 272

CMCORP—Sales Management—Classic Markets Corp.; *U.S. Private*, pg. 244

C-MDE—Software—LSI Logic Corp.; *U.S. Public*, pg. 971

CM-88—Asphalt Emulsion Chemicals—Georgia-Pacific Corporation; *U.S. Public*, pg. 735

CMF MONITER—System Moniter for Critical System Variables: CPU, I/O, Memory & Workloads—Boole & Babbage, Inc.; *U.S. Public*, pg. 244

CM-50—High Speed Tool Speed—Latrobe Steel Company; *U.S. Public*, pg. 1617

CM-52—High Speed Tool Steel—Latrobe Steel Company; *U.S. Public*, pg. 1617

CM5—Computer Hardware—Thinking Machines Corporation; *U.S. Private*, pg. 1081

CMI—NONE—CMI Corporation; *U.S. Public*, pg. 278

C-M-I—Centrifuges—Centrifugal & Mechanical Industries; *U.S. Private*, pg. 370

CML EXCEL—COBE Membrane Lung, Oxygenator—COBE Laboratories, Inc.; *Int'l*, pg. 667

CML OIL BASE PLUS—Printing Ink—Van Son Holland Ink Corp. of America; *U.S. Private*, pg. 1133

CML VPCML—Oxygenator—COBE Laboratories, Inc.; *Int'l*, pg. 667

CM-OT—High Compressive Strength Lightweight Armored Covering—The Okonite Company; *U.S. Private*, pg. 813

CMP—Chemical Mechanical Planarization—SpeedFan International, Inc.; *U.S. Public*, pg. 1497

CM-PF—Corrugated Metal Tape Finish—The Okonite Company; *U.S. Private*, pg. 813

CM/PILOT—NONE—BMC Software, Inc.; *U.S. Public*, pg. 162

CMS—Continental Medical Systems, Inc.—Continental Medical Systems, Inc.; *U.S. Public*, pg. 839

CMS—Clinical Products—Fisher Scientific International; *U.S. Private*, pg. 658

CMS/ES—Software—CSC Financial Services Group; *U.S. Public*, pg. 422

CMS-JR—Automatic Call Sequencer—Electronic Tele-Communications, Inc.; *U.S. Public*, pg. 570

CMS-SR—Automatic Call Sequencer—Electronic Tele-Communications, Inc.; *U.S. Public*, pg. 570

CMSX-4—Single Crystal Alloy—SPS Technologies, Inc.; *U.S. Public*, pg. 1419

CM3—NONE—Scotsman Industries, Inc.; *U.S. Public*, pg. 1444

CM-300—Electronic Control System for Glass Forming—Ball Corporation; *U.S. Public*, pg. 170

CMV NEUTRAGAM—Treatment for CMV in Renal Transplants—Nabi; *U.S. Public*, pg. 1148

CMX-NETS—Data Exchange Services—NDC Tokyo Representative Office; *U.S. Public*, pg. 1156

CMX AEGIS—Editing System—Chyron Corp.; *Int'l*, pg. 1372

THE CMX OMNI—Editing Equipment—Chyron Corp.; *Int'l*, pg. 1372

CMX 3500—Editing Equipment—Chyron Corp.; *Int'l*, pg. 1372

THE CMX 3600—Editing Equipment—Chyron Corp.; *Int'l*, pg. 1372

THE CMX 300—Editing Equipment—Chyron Corp.; *Int'l*, pg. 1372

CMX 330A—Editing Equipment—Chyron Corp.; *Int'l*, pg. 1372

C-MAG—Sputter Cathode—BOC Coating Technology; *Int'l*, pg. 121

C-MAX 500 PLUS IRON—Vitamin Supplements—Otsuka Pharmaceutical Co., Ltd.; *Int'l*, pg. 1013

C-MAX MULTIVITAMINE—Vitamin Supplements—Otsuka Pharmaceutical Co., Ltd.; *Int'l*, pg. 1013

C-MAX 1000—Vitamin Supplements—Otsuka Pharmaceutical Co., Ltd.; *Int'l*, pg. 1013

CMOST—Operating System Computer Programs—Thinking Machines Corporation; *U.S. Private*, pg. 1081

CN—Disinfectant (Germicide)—Knomark, Inc.; *U.S. Private*, pg. 627

CNA—Insurance & Insurance Services—CNA Insurance Companies; *U.S. Public*, pg. 1010

CNA FINANCIAL CORP—Insurance—Loews Corporation; *U.S. Public*, pg. 1010

CNBC—Cable Television Station—CNBC; *U.S. Public*, pg. 712

CNBC—Consumer News & Business Channel—National Broadcasting Co., Inc.; *U.S. Public*, pg. 712

CNBC BUSINESS RADIO—Business Reports, Weekend Features, Week In Review—Westwood One, Inc.; *U.S. Public*, pg. 1763

C/NC GARD—Plastic Film—Reynolds Metals Company; *U.S. Public*, pg. 1385

CNC INTERTAP—Taps for International Tapping System—Regal-Beloit Corporation; *U.S. Public*, pg. 1370

CNC SIZEFINDER—Grinding Machines—Landis; *U.S. Public*, pg. 1699

CNC/XL—Taps for CNC Machining—Regal-Beloit Corporation; *U.S. Public*, pg. 1370

CNC/XM TAPS—Cobalt Taps for Computer-Numerically Controlled Machinery—Regal-Beloit Corporation; *U.S. Public*, pg. 1370

CNC/XM TAPS—Cobalt Taps for Computer-Numerically Controlled Machinery—National Twist Drill Div.; *U.S. Public*, pg. 1370

CNI—NONE—Humana Wisconsin Health Organization Insurance Corporation; *U.S. Public*, pg. 848

CNK—Paperboard—The Mead Corporation; *U.S. Public*, pg. 1074

CNM—Status Monitoring System—C-COR Electronics, Inc.; *U.S. Public*, pg. 272

CNN—Cable News Network—CNN (Cable News Network); *U.S. Public*, pg. 1614

CNN—News Network—Turner Broadcasting System Inc.; *U.S. Public*, pg. 1614

CNN AIRPORT NETWORK—NONE—CNN (Cable News Network); *U.S. Public*, pg. 1614

CNN HEADLINE NEWS—NONE—CNN (Cable News Network); *U.S. Public*, pg. 1614

CNN HEADLINE NEWS FORMAT—News Programming—Westwood One, Inc.; *U.S. Public*, pg. 1763

CNNRADIO—Newscast, Sports, Business & Entertainment Coverage—Westwood One, Inc.; *U.S. Public*, pg. 1763

CNS THIS WEEK—Community Weekly Newspapers—The Dispatch Printing Company; *U.S. Private*, pg. 334

COAXID—NONE—Molex Incorporated; *U.S. Public*, pg. 1121

COBA—Digital Seismic Recording Systems—Litton Industries, Inc.; *U.S. Public*, pg. 1002

CODAS—Digital Recording System—Litton Industries, Inc.; *U.S. Public*, pg. 1002

COPA XM—Magnetic Flowmeter—Bailey, Fischer & Porter Company; *Int'l*, pg. 449

COPA XO—Magnetic Flowmeter—Bailey, Fischer & Porter Company; *Int'l*, pg. 449

C-100 QT—Incubator—Vickers PLC; *Int'l*, pg. 1466

CP—Photo Album Pages—Command Plastic Corporation; *U.S. Public*, pg. 257

CPAC—NONE—CPAC, Inc.; *U.S. Public*, pg. 282

CPA EXAMINATION REVIEW—Audio Cassettes, Computer Programs, Books—John Wiley & Sons, Inc.; *U.S. Public*, pg. 1768

CPA MICRO-PASS—Software—John Wiley & Sons, Inc.; *U.S. Public*, pg. 1768

CPA REVIEW SYSTEM—Audio Cassettes, Computer Programs, Books—John Wiley & Sons, Inc.; *U.S. Public*, pg. 1768

C P & L—Carolina Power & Light—Carolina Power & Light Company; *U.S. Public*, pg. 306

CPC—Power Distribution Equipment—Controlled Power (CPC); *Int'l*, pg. 74

CPC—NONE—Star-Kist Foods Inc.; *U.S. Public*, pg. 805

CP-D MULTI-PURPOSE—Plywood for Bracing & General Use—Carter Holt Harvey Limited; *U.S. Public*, pg. 904

CP820—Tabletop Payphone—Landis & Staefa, Inc.; *Int'l*, pg. 800

CP-80—NONE—Polaroid Corporation; *U.S. Public*, pg. 1313

CP4000—Intelligent Telecommunications Apparatus—DSC Communications Corporation; *U.S. Public*, pg. 475

CPI—Copley Pharmaceuticals, Inc. Brand Name—Copley Pharmaceuticals, Inc.; *U.S. Public*, pg. 446

CPI—Electrical Cable—Reynolds Metals Company; *U.S. Public*, pg. 1385

CPL—Surveys—Corrpro Companies, Inc.; *U.S. Public*, pg. 451

CPM—NONE—Ingersoll-Rand Company; *U.S. Public*, pg. 876

CP MILLENNIUM—Capital Projects Information System—Dun & Bradstreet Software Services; *Int'l*, pg. 532

CP-90—NONE—Polaroid Corporation; *U.S. Public*, pg. 1313

CPO—Steel Bar Products—LaSalle Steel Company; *U.S. Public*, pg. 1181

CP1000S—Intelligent Telecommunications Apparatus—DSC Communications Corporation; *U.S. Public*, pg. 475

CPR—Rigid Systems—The Dow Chemical Company; *U.S. Public*, pg. 522

CPR—Cleaner-Polisher—La-Co Industries Markal Company; *U.S. Private*, pg. 640

CPS—Athletic Equipment—Bike Athletic Co.; *U.S. Private*, pg. 143

CPS—Uninterruptible Power Supplies—Emerson Electric Co.; *U.S. Public*, pg. 572

CP-SERIES 11—Internal Batch Mixer—Farrel Corporation; *U.S. Public*, pg. 614

CP 345T—Scanner—Linotype-Hell Company; *Int'l*, pg. 604

CP3000—Intelligent Telecommunications Apparatus—DSC Communications Corporation; *U.S. Public*, pg. 475

CP2000—Intelligent Telecommunications Apparatus—DSC Communications Corporation; *U.S. Public*, pg. 475

CPVC—Plumbing Chemical—Hercules Chemical Co., Inc.; *U.S. Private*, pg. 523

CPVC—Cement—La-Co Industries Markal Company; *U.S. Private*, pg. 640

CPX EXPRESS—Testing System—Medical Graphics Corp.; *U.S. Public*, pg. 1080

C. PLATH—Nautical & Navigation Equipment—Litton Industries, Inc.; *U.S. Public*, pg. 1002

CPLEX 400—Communication Software—Logica Plc; *Int'l*, pg. 814

C-PLUS—Laundry Detergent—Stanhome Inc.; *U.S. Public*, pg. 1508

C-PRESS—Compliant Pin Connectors—Litton Industries, Inc.; *U.S. Public*, pg. 1002

C-Q RESEARCHER—Topical Reports-Once a Week—The Times Publishing Co.; *U.S. Private*, pg. 1087

CR—Motorcycle—American Honda Motor Co., Inc. Motorcycle Division; *Int'l*, pg. 634

CR—Plastic Closures for Containers—Kerr Group, Inc.; *U.S. Public*, pg. 952

CRB-7—NONE—Carpenter Technology Corporation; *U.S. Public*, pg. 307

CR BEARINGS—Rolling Element Bearings for all Vehicles—Chicago Rawhide; *Int'l*, pg. 1157

CR BRAKEMASTER—Air Dryer for Heavy Auto Vehicles—Chicago Rawhide; *Int'l*, pg. 1157

CRC—Medical Instrument—Capintec Inc.; *U.S. Private*, pg. 205

CRG—Certified Railroad Glass—Globe-Amerada Glass Company; *U.S. Private*, pg. 458

C.R. GIBSON—Stationery; Book Publishers—C.R. Gibson Co.; *U.S. Public*, pg. 1168

CR INDUSTRIAL SEALING PRODUCTS—Sealing Products—CR Services; *Int'l*, pg. 1157

CR-I—Child Resistant Closures—Kerr Group, Inc.; *U.S. Public*, pg. 952

CRS—Cerner Rule System—Cerner Corporation; *U.S. Public*, pg. 331

CRS—Pediatric Counter Rotation Device—The Langer Biomechanics Group, Inc.; *U.S. Public*, pg. 978

CR SCOTSEAL & SCOTSEAL PLUS SEALS—Sealing Products—CR Services; *Int'l*, pg. 1157

CR SEALS & BEARINGS—Sealing Products—CR Services; *Int'l*, pg. 1157

CRT-PAC—Semi-Conductor Devices—Semtech Corporation; *U.S. Public*, pg. 1456

CR-39—Allyl Diglycol Carbonate—PPG Industries, Inc.; *U.S. Public*, pg. 1245

CR U-JOINTS—Universal Joints for Heavy Duty Vehicles—Chicago Rawhide; *Int'l*, pg. 1157

CR-WESTAINER—Plastic Containers & Closures For Pharmaceutical Products—The West Company, Incorporated; *U.S. Public*, pg. 1755

CS—Dryer—Beloit Corporation; *U.S. Public*, pg. 789

CS-CompuSearch—Management Recruiters International, Inc.; *U.S. Public*, pg. 277

CS—Oil & Gas Distribution—Repsol S.A.; *Int'l*, pg. 1104

CSA—NONE—Nutmeg Mills Inc.; *U.S. Public*, pg. 1702

CSA—Application Software—Octel Messaging Division; *U.S. Public*, pg. 1017

CSC—Steel—China Steel Corporation; *Int'l*, pg. 285

CSD/ESD—Specialty Multi-Shaft Mixers—Premier Mill Corp.; *U.S. Private*, pg. 881

CS 4000—Central Station Computer—Interactive Technologies, Inc.; *U.S. Public*, pg. 888

CSI—Printing Foils—Markem Corporation; *U.S. Private*, pg. 704

CSK—Apparel—Fred Meyer Stores; *U.S. Public*, pg. 1103

CSL LIGHTSPLICE—Fiber Optic Splicer—Lucent Technologies Inc.; *U.S. Public*, pg. 1017

CSM—Sugar—CSM N.V.; *Int'l*, pg. 243

CSO—Junior Fashions—Deb Shops, Inc.; *U.S. Public*, pg. 491

CS 100—Electronic Control System for Glass Forming Operations—Ball Corporation; *U.S. Public*, pg. 104

CSP 11—Two channel Circut—Beltone Electronics Corporation; *U.S. Private*, pg. 132

CS PRO—Copiers—Minolta Corporation; *Int'l*, pg. 869

CSS/1200—Instrument Equipment—Clayton Industries Co.; *U.S. Private*, pg. 245

CS-76—Liquid Nitrogen Delivery & Tissue Monitoring System—The Cooper Companies, Inc.; *U.S. Public*, pg. 442

CST—Controlled Start Transmission—Rockwell International Corporation; *U.S. Public*, pg. 1397

CS-3000—Blood Cell Separators—Baxter International Inc.; *U.S. Public*, pg. 196

CS-232—Custom Computer Serial Interface—Retzlaff Incorporated; *U.S. Private*, pg. 925

CS ULTIMA—Ophthalmic Needles—Ethicon, Inc.; *U.S. Public*, pg. 928

C-SAT—Text-only Satellite Messaging System—British Telecommunications plc; *Int'l*, pg. 222

C SET ++—Computer System—International Business Machines Corporation; *U.S. Public*, pg. 895

C-7B—Automatic Aerosol Dispensers—Surco Products, Inc.; *U.S. Public*, pg. 1056

C-SHUR—Oil Sight-Feed—Harnischfeger Industries, Inc.; *U.S. Public*, pg. 788

CT—Computer System—International Business Machines Corporation; *U.S. Public*, pg. 895

CTA-METRO—Sports Outerwear—Fox-Knapp; *U.S. Private*, pg. 860

CTE—Cross Tension Compensating Roll—Beloit Lenox, Div.; *U.S. Public*, pg. 789

CTE—Cross-Directional Tension Equalizing Roll—Harnischfeger Industries, Inc.; *U.S. Public*, pg. 788

CT-500—Lightweight Monorail Systems—Shepard Niles, Inc.; *U.S. Private*, pg. 992

CTG-NET—Internet-Based Communication Infrastructure—Computer Task Group, Inc. (CTG); *U.S. Public*, pg. 423

CTG-SMARTSOURCE—National Recruiting System—Computer Task Group, Inc. (CTG); *U.S. Public*, pg. 423

CTI—Christianity Today, Inc.—Christianity Today, Inc.; *U.S. Private*, pg. 238

CTI—Non-Ferrous Metal Reforging Vessels—Global Industrial Technologies; *U.S. Public*, pg. 747

CTME—Apparel—Clothestime Stores, Inc.; *U.S. Public*, pg. 387

CTOS—Business Workstation—Unisys Corporation; *U.S. Public*, pg. 1671

CTR—Tree Delimbers, Feller Bunchers—Blount International, Inc.; *U.S. Public*, pg. 237

CTS—Electronic Components—CTS Corp. Frequency Controls; *U.S. Public*, pg. 285

CTS—Bus—Champion Enterprises, Inc.; *U.S. Public*, pg. 332

CTS—Corneal Topograph System; Patented for Measuring the elevation of Cornea—PAR Technology Corporation; *U.S. Public*, pg. 1256

CTS STAR—Bus—Champion Enterprises, Inc.; *U.S. Public*, pg. 332

C.T. 3000—Moisture Analyzer—Arizona Instrument Corporation; *U.S. Public*, pg. 129

CT-TWIN—Computerized Tomograph—Elscint Ltd.; *Int'l*, pg. 450

CT/2—Computer System—International Business Machines Corporation; *U.S. Public*, pg. 895

CTX—Car Top Blocks—A.P. Green Industries, Inc.; *U.S. Public*, pg. 761

CTX—Conveyor Cooking Equipment—The Middleby Corporation; *U.S. Public*, pg. 1109

CTX—Fiberboard—Weyerhaeuser Company; *U.S. Public*, pg. 1764

C3—Microcomputer Systems—Telos Corporation; *U.S. Public*, pg. 1573

C/370—Computer System—International Business Machines Corporation; *U.S. Public*, pg. 895

C-THRU—NONE—Pfizer Inc.; *U.S. Public*, pg. 1281

C-TOWN—Grocery Products—Krasdale Foods Inc.; *U.S. Private*, pg. 635

C-TUBES—Scientific Glassware for Laboratory Use—Wheaton Inc.; *Int'l*, pg. 67

C-23 SHERPA—Military Transport Aircraft—Bombardier Inc.; *Int'l*, pg. 199

C/2—Compuer System—International Business Machines Corporation; *U.S. Public*, pg. 895

C-286 ISOLETTE—Incubator—Vickers PLC; *Int'l*, pg. 1466

CUA—Computer System—International Business Machines Corporation; *U.S. Public*, pg. 895

CU AMIGA—Computer Magazine—EMAP Images; *Int'l*, pg. 451

CUSA—NONE—Pfizer Inc.; *U.S. Public*, pg. 1281

CVC—Deposition Systems & Vacuum Components—CVC Products, Inc.; *U.S. Private*, pg. 197

CVM 4000—Vault Management System—Brandt, Inc.; *Int'l*, pg. 387

CVS—Health & Beauty Aids Stores—CVS Corp.; *U.S. Public*, pg. 287

CVS SERIES—Voltage Regulator—Best Power; *U.S. Private*, pg. 140

CVV—Fabrics—Herculite Products, Inc.; *U.S. Public*, pg. 802

C-VI-COMPLEX TABLETS—500 Mg. Vitamin C Tablets—Weider Nutrition Intl.; *U.S. Private*, pg. 1159

C-VIT—Blackcurrant Health Drink—SmithKline Beecham plc; *Int'l*, pg. 1264

CWC—Iron & Steel Castings—CWC Textron Company; *U.S. Public*, pg. 1590

C-W 85-HS RAM—Refractory—CFB Industries, Inc.; *U.S. Private*, pg. 194

C-W 85-HS RAM—Refractory—Chicago Fire Brick Co.; *U.S. Private*, pg. 194

CWF-UV—Ultraviolet Resistant Clear Wood Finish for Exterior Wood—The Flood Company; *U.S. Private*, pg. 414

CWP—Vacuum Cleaner Brushes—The Scott Fetzer Company; *U.S. Public*, pg. 217

C. W. POST—Hearty Granola Cereal—Kraft Foods, Inc.; *U.S. Public*, pg. 1287

CWS—Washroom Service & Supplies—Franz Haniel & Cie, GmbH; *Int'l*, pg. 591

CW-II—Transparent Heat-Shrinkable Thermoplastic Film—Reynolds Metals Company; *U.S. Public*, pg. 1385

CX—Clinical Analytical Instruments & Reagents—Beckman Instruments, Inc.; *U.S. Public*, pg. 199

CX—External Roller Burnishing Machine—Cogsdill Tool Products, Inc.; *U.S. Private*, pg. 250

CX—Audio Recording Cassette—3M; *U.S. Public*, pg. 1604

CX MULTI—Chemical Reagents—Beckman Instruments, Inc.; *U.S. Public*, pg. 199

C.C. SOX—Apparel—Fred Meyer Stores; *U.S. Public*, pg. 1103

CNA—Insurance & Insurance-Related Services—Continental Assurance Company; *U.S. Private*, pg. 267

CHANNELGATE—Computer Software—Attachmate; *U.S. Private*, pg. 98

COOL TOOLS—Computer Software—Attachmate; *U.S. Private*, pg. 98

CROSSFAX—Computer Software—Attachmate; *U.S. Private*, pg. 98

CROSSTALK—Computer Software—Attachmate; *U.S. Private*, pg. 98

CA RUGATE GRAPPA—Grappa—Laird & Company; *U.S. Private*, pg. 642

CA RUGATE GRAPPA RECIOTO DI SOAVE—Italian Wine—Laird & Company; *U.S. Private*, pg. 642

CA RUGATE RECIOTE DE SOAVE—Italian Dessert Wine—Laird & Company; *U.S. Private*, pg. 642

CA RUGATE SOAVE CLASSICO—Italian Wine—Laird & Company; *U.S. Private*, pg. 642

CA-VA-SEUL—Shoe Polishes/Waxes—Benckiser Consumer Products Inc.; *Int'l*, pg. 185

CAB AIR SUSPENSION—COE Cab Suspension—Peterbilt Motors Co.; *U.S. Public*, pg. 1247

CAB CUSHION—Cab Suspension System—Applied Power Inc.; *U.S. Public*, pg. 124

CAB-O-GUARD—Aqueous Silica Dispersion—Cab-o-Sil Div. Cabot Corp.; *U.S. Public*, pg. 289

CAB-O-SIL—Fumed Silica—Cab-o-Sil Div. Cabot Corp.; *U.S. Public*, pg. 289

CAB-O-SIL—Fumed Silica—Cabot Corporation; *U.S. Public*, pg. 288

CAB-O-SPERSE—Aqueous Silica Dispersion—Cab-o-Sil Div. Cabot Corp.; *U.S. Public*, pg. 289

CAB 3—Cable Marking System—Pass & Seymour/Legrand; *Int'l*, pg. 806

CABANA—NONE—Bon Ton Foods, Inc.; *U.S. Private*, pg. 65

CABANAS—Premium Cigars—Consolidated Cigar Corporation; *U.S. Private*, pg. 690

CABARET—Cover—Appleton Papers Inc.; *Int'l*, pg. 567

CABBAGE PATCH KIDS—Doll—Mattel, Inc.; *U.S. Public*, pg. 1057

CABCOR—Particleboard—Georgia-Pacific Corporation; *U.S. Public*, pg. 735

CABIN CRAFTS—Carpets—Cabin Crafts Carpets; *U.S. Public*, pg. 1464

CABIN STILL—Bourbon—Shieffelin Somerset Co.; *Int'l*, pg. 412

CABINET—Cigarettes—Reemtsma Cigarettenfabriken GmbH, Hamburg; *Int'l*, pg. 1100

CABINET AIDES—Convenience & Storage—Amerock Corporation; *U.S. Public*, pg. 1177

CABINET MAID—Cabinet Organizers—Clairson International Corp.; *U.S. Public*, pg. 575

CABINETMAKER—Magazine for Small Woodworking Shops & Distributors—Reed Elsevier Business Information; *Int'l*, pg. 1095

CABLE-ALL!—Accelerator, Clutc, Detent, Speedometer & Transhift Cables—R&B, Inc.; *U.S. Public*, pg. 1354

CABLE & WIRELESS—NONE—Cable and Wireless plc; *Int'l*, pg. 247

CABLE CALL—Security Instruments—Universal Security Instruments Inc.; *U.S. Public*, pg. 1697

CABLE CAR—Bread & Buns—Metz Baking Company (WI); *U.S. Private*, pg. 1022

CABLE CRAFT—Cables—Tuthill Corporation; *U.S. Private*, pg. 1110

CABLE DESIGN—Insulated Electrical Wires & Cables—General Cable Corporation; *Int'l*, pg. 1486

CABLECURE—Cable Renovation Service—UTILX Corporation; *U.S. Public*, pg. 1701

CABLEGUARD—Electronic Components—General Instrument Corporation; *U.S. Public*, pg. 716

CABLEGUARD—TV Tuners—Thomson Consumer Electronics Inc.; *Int'l*, pg. 1383

CABLEJET—System for Installing Fiber Optic Cable—Sherman & Reilly, Inc.; *U.S. Private*, pg. 993

CABLELINK, INC.—Manufacturer of Cable Assemblies—Robinson Nugent, Inc.; *U.S. Public*, pg. 1394

CABLELITE—UV Curable Cabling Materials—DeSoto Inc.; *U.S. Public*, pg. 956

CABLEOPTICS—Cable TV Fiber Optoelectronics—Broadband Networks Group; *U.S. Public*, pg. 716

CABLEOPTICS—AM & FM Fibre Optic Equipment—General Instrument of Canada Ltd.; *U.S. Public*, pg. 716

CABLEVISION—Business Analysis Magazine—Reed Elsevier Business Information; *Int'l*, pg. 1095

CABLEVISION—Cable Television Service—Time Warner Cable Liberty Division; *U.S. Public*, pg. 1611

CABLEWARE—Hardware—Loos & Co., Inc.; *U.S. Private*, pg. 675

CABLEWRAP—Waterproof System for Suspension Bridge Cables—Haartz-Mason, Inc.; *U.S. Public*, pg. 1358

CABMATIC—Train Control System—General Railway Signal Corp.; *Int'l*, pg. 1194

CABOFLEX—Hearing Protector—Aearo Company; *U.S. Private*, pg. 23

CABOODLES OF CALIFORNIA—Cosmetics & Beauty Products Boxes—Plano Molding Co.; *U.S. Private*, pg. 869

CABOT—Dairy Products—Cabot Creamery Co-Operative Inc.; *U.S. Private*, pg. 26

CABOT STAINS—Stains—Samuel Cabot, Inc.; *U.S. Private*, pg. 198

CABRIOLE—Fragrance—Elizabeth Arden Company; *Int'l*, pg. 1435

CACHAREL—Perfumes—Cosmair, Inc.; *Int'l*, pg. 818

CACHAREL—Perfume—L'Oreal S.A.; *Int'l*, pg. 818

CACHE VALLEY CHEESE—Natural Cheeses—Western Dairymen Cooperative, Inc.; *U.S. Private*, pg. 1165

CACHET—Fragrance—Parfums De Coeur Ltd.; *U.S. Private*, pg. 839

CACHITA—PuertoRico—Azteca Foods, Incorporated; *U.S. Private*, pg. 104

CACTUS JUICE—Interior Plant Prods.—Security Lawn & Garden Co.; *U.S. Private*, pg. 397

CACTUS/WEBCACTUS—3 Application Development—Information Builders; *U.S. Private*, pg. 561

CAD BRIDGES—NONE—Brown & Sharpe Manufacturing Company; *U.S. Public*, pg. 260

CADALYST—Trade Periodical—Advanstar Communications; *U.S. Private*, pg. 22

CADAM—Computer Aided-Design System—Stone & Webster, Incorporated; *U.S. Public*, pg. 1519

CADBURY—Chocolates—Cadbury Schweppes p.l.c.; *Int'l*, pg. 247

CADBURY—Cakes—Ranks Hovis McDougall Limited; *Int'l*, pg. 1395

CADBURY—Chocolate Confection—George Weston Limited; *Int'l*, pg. 1494

CADBURY'S—Candies—Hershey Foods Corporation; *U.S. Public*, pg. 811

CADBURY'S CARAMELLO—Candy Bar—Hershey Chocolate U.S.A.; *U.S. Public*, pg. 812

CADBURY'S CARAMELLO—Candy Bar—Hershey Foods Corporation; *U.S. Public*, pg. 811

CADBURY'S CREME EGGS—Candy—Hershey Chocolate U.S.A.; *U.S. Public*, pg. 812

CADBURY'S CREME EGGS—Easter Candies—Hershey Foods Corporation; *U.S. Public*, pg. 811

CADBURY'S DAIRY MILK—Chocolate Bar—Hershey Chocolate U.S.A.; *U.S. Public*, pg. 812

CADBURY'S DAIRY MILK—Candies—Hershey Foods Corporation; *U.S. Public*, pg. 811

CADBURY'S FRUIT & NUT—Chocolate Bar—Hershey Chocolate U.S.A.; *U.S. Public*, pg. 812

CADBURY'S FRUIT & NUT—Chocolate Bar—Hershey Foods Corporation; *U.S. Public*, pg. 811

CADBURY'S KRISP—Chocolate Bar—Hershey Foods Corporation; *U.S. Public*, pg. 811

CADBURY'S MINI EGGS—Chocolates—Hershey Chocolate U.S.A.; *U.S. Public*, pg. 812

CADBURY'S MINI EGGS—Candy—Hershey Foods Corporation; *U.S. Public*, pg. 811

CADBURY'S ROAST ALMOND—Chocolate Bar—Hershey Chocolate U.S.A.; *U.S. Public*, pg. 812

CADBURY'S ROAST ALMOND—Chocolate Bar—Hershey Foods Corporation; *U.S. Public*, pg. 811

CADCAM—NONE—EMAP Business Communications Division; *Int'l*, pg. 451

CADCO—Engineering Plastics—Cadillac Plastic & Chemical Co.; *U.S. Public*, pg. 781

CADDTRAK—Slot Tracking System—Mikohn Gaming Corporation; *U.S. Public*, pg. 1111

CADENCE—Lumber & Wood Products—Georgia-Pacific Corporation; *U.S. Public*, pg. 735

CADENCE—Magazine—Miller Freeman Inc.; *Int'l*, pg. 1443

CADET—Force Gauge—AMETEK, Inc.; *U.S. Public*, pg. 99

CADET—Blowers—Coppus Murray Group, Tuthill Corporation; *U.S. Private*, pg. 1110

CADET—Office Chair—Vecta; *U.S. Private*, pg. 1038

CADET CLASSIC—NONE—Tandy Brands Accessories, Inc.; *U.S. Public*, pg. 1560

CADILLAC—Cars—General Motors Corporation; *U.S. Public*, pg. 718

CADILLAC—Dog & Cat Foods—Menu Foods, Inc.; *U.S. Private*, pg. 731

CADILLAC CONCRETE PIPE & CULVERT—Sewer Pipe—Premarc Corporation; *U.S. Private*, pg. 881

CADILLAC PLASTIC—Distribution Plastic Shapes—M.A. Hanna Company; *U.S. Public*, pg. 780

CADMATE—Data Commnications Networking System—GenRad, Inc.; *U.S. Public*, pg. 731

CADMOLITH—Cadmium Pure Bright Red, Yellow and Orange Pigments—Millennium Inorganic Chemicals; *Int'l*, pg. 593

CADON—Engineering Thermoplastic—Monsanto Company; *U.S. Public*, pg. 1124

CADON—Engineering Thermoplastic—Solutia Inc.; *U.S. Public*, pg. 1483

CADRA—C&D Design, Drafting—Adra Systems, Inc.; *U.S. Private*, pg. 18

CADRA SOLIDS—Solid Modeling—Adra Systems, Inc.; *U.S. Private*, pg. 18

CADRE—NONE—USG Corporation; *U.S. Public*, pg. 1660

CADSCAN—Engineering Drawing Conversion Systems—Eastman Kodak Company; *U.S. Public*, pg. 550

CAEDS—Computer System—International Business Machines Corporation; *U.S. Public*, pg. 895

CAELYX—Stealth Liposome Formulation of Doxorabicin—Sequus Pharmaceuticals, Inc.; *U.S. Public*, pg. 1460

CAERE—Company Name—Caere Corporation; *U.S. Public*, pg. 291

CAESAR'S CHOICE—Food Products—Campbell Soup Company Ltd.; *U.S. Public*, pg. 299

CAESARS PALACE—Resort Hotel & Casino—Caesars Palace; *U.S. Public*, pg. 1512

CAFE AU LAIT—Food Products—Meiji Seika Kaisha, Ltd.; *Int'l*, pg. 855

CAFE BRAUR—Restaurant—The Levy Organization; *U.S. Private*, pg. 664

CAFE CHICAGO—Restaurant—The Levy Organization; *U.S. Private*, pg. 664

CAFE CLASSICS—Gourmet Creme Dessert—Bongrain Cheese USA; *Int'l*, pg. 201

CAFE DE PARIS—Sparkling Wine—Groupe Pernod Ricard; *Int'l*, pg. 566

CAFE DI AMORE—NONE—Barton Brands, Ltd.; *U.S. Public*, pg. 300

CAFE DO BRASIL—Coffee—Morinaga Milk Industry Co., Ltd.; *Int'l*, pg. 895

CAFE DU Monde—Beignets & Cafe au Lait—Duskin Co., Ltd.; *Int'l*, pg. 422

CAFE MEXICO—Frozen Mexican Foods—Schwan's Sales Enterprises; *U.S. Private*, pg. 974

CAFÉ OQUENDO—Coffee—Tetley USA Inc.; *Int'l*, pg. 1377

CAFÉ RISTRETTO—Coffee—Nestle S.A.; *Int'l*, pg. 915

CAFE ROUTE—Highway Restaurant—Accor S.A.; *Int'l*, pg. 20

CAFE SARKS—NONE—Nestle USA; *Int'l*, pg. 916

CAFE SELECT—Gourmet Flavored Coffees—The Southland Corporation; *Int'l*, pg. 693

CAFE SELECT COFFEES—NONE—7-Eleven Stores; *U.S. Private*, pg. 693

CAFE SPAGGIA—Restaurant—The Levy Organization; *U.S. Private*, pg. 664

CAFE TRAYS—Food Trays—Carlisle Food Service Products; *U.S. Public*, pg. 305

CAFERGOT—Drug for Treatment of Migraine Headaches—Sandoz Pharmaceuticals Corp.; *Int'l*, pg. 974

CAFFE SPORT ESPRESSO LIQUEUR—NONE—Carillon Importers, Ltd.; *Int'l*, pg. 409

CAFFEDRINE—Pharmaceutical Products—Thompson Medical Company, Inc.; *U.S. Private*, pg. 1083

CAFFEINE FREE COCA-COLA CLASSIC—Caffeine-free cola—The Coca-Cola Company; *U.S. Public*, pg. 392

CAFFEINE FREE DIET COKE—NONE—The Coca-Cola Company; *U.S. Public*, pg. 392

CAFFEINE-FREE DIET DR PEPPER—Caffeine-Free Diet Soft Drink—Dr Pepper/Seven Up No. America; *Int'l*, pg. 248

CAFFEINE FREE DIET PEPSI—Soft Drink—Pepsi-Cola Company; *U.S. Public*, pg. 1277

CAFFEINE-FREE DR PEPPER—Caffeine-Free Soft Drink—Dr Pepper/Seven Up No. America; *Int'l*, pg. 248

CAFFEINE FREE PEPSI—Soft Drink—Pepsi-Cola Company; *U.S. Public*, pg. 1277

CAFFEINE FREE TEA—Herb Tea—Celestial Seasonings; *U.S. Public*, pg. 319

CAFFREE—Antistain Toothpaste—Block Drug Company, Inc.; *U.S. Public*, pg. 236

CAGE & AVIARY BIRDS—Special Interest Magazine—IPC Magazines Limited; *Int'l*, pg. 651

CAGEROL—Retainer Type Roller Bearings—McGill Manufacturing Company, Inc.; *U.S. Public*, pg. 573

CALIBRA—NONE—Vauxhall; *U.S. Public*, pg. 724

CAILLER—Chocolates—Nestle Chocolate & Confection; *Int'l*, pg. 917

CAILLER—Chocolate & Confectionery—Nestle S.A.; *Int'l*, pg. 915

CAIN'S—Coffee—Cain's Coffee Co.; *U.S. Public*, pg. 351

CAIN'S—Potato Chips—Borden, Inc.; *U.S. Private*, pg. 157

CAINS—Mayonnaise, Relish, Sweet Relish, Pickles, Salad Dressing, Cocktail Sauce—Cains Foods, L.P.; *U.S. Private*, pg. 199

CAINS COUNTRY—Salad Dressing—Cains Foods, L.P.; *U.S. Private*, pg. 199

CAINS/OXFORD—Pickles—Cains Foods, L.P.; *U.S. Private*, pg. 199

CAIR—Radomes for Aircraft & Aerospace Applications—Norton Performance Plastics; *Int'l*, pg. 1174

CAIRO—Luggage—American Tourister, Inc.; *U.S. Public*, pg. 1430

CAIRO BEAUTIES—Pickles—Dean Pickles & Specialty Products; *U.S. Public*, pg. 490

CAIROX—Potassium Permanganate—Carus Chemical Company, Chemical Div.; *U.S. Private*, pg. 217

CAIROX—Chemicals—Carus Corporation; *U.S. Private*, pg. 217

CAJUN—Fiberglass Bass Boats and Fish & Ski Boats—Genmar Holdings, Inc.; *U.S. Private*, pg. 447

CAJUN CHRISTMAS/SHOPPING SPREE—Riverboat Cruise Trips—American Classic Voyagers Company; *U.S. Private*, pg. 380

CAJUN COOKIN'—Cajun Food Product—The Pillsbury Company; *Int'l*, pg. 411

CAJUN KING—Seasoning Mixes—Bruce Foods Corp.; *U.S. Private*, pg. 175

CAKE DISCHARGE FILTER—NONE—Bird Machine Company; *U.S. Public*, pg. 166

CAKE-MATE—Decorator Icing—McCormick & Company, Incorporated; *U.S. Public*, pg. 1066

CAKE MATE—Cake Decorating Icings, Gels & Decors—McCormick/Schilling; *U.S. Public*, pg. 1066

CAKEBREAD CELLARS—Super Premium California Varietal Wines—Shieffelin Somerset Co.; *Int'l*, pg. 412

CAL-CARB—Tabletting Agent for Pharmaceutical & Nutritional Tablets—Crompton & Knowles Ingredient Technology Corp.; *U.S. Public*, pg. 459

CAL-CU-DRI—Moisture Moniters & Controls (Electronic)—David Manufacturing Company (DMC); *U.S. Private*, pg. 436

CAL DI-FORM—Special Steel—Inland Steel Industries, Inc.; *U.S. Public*, pg. 879

CAL DIRECT—Weekly Direct Mail Product—The Bakersfield Californian; *U.S. Private*, pg. 112

CAL 80—Non-Fat Yogurt—Dean Foods Company; *U.S. Public*, pg. 489

CAL-EX—Decalcifying Solution—Fisher Scientific Company; *U.S. Private*, pg. 658

CAL FLORIDA—Cement Product—Puerto Rican Cement Co., Inc.; *U.S. Public*, pg. 1341

CAL HI-FORM—Special Steel—Inland Steel Industries, Inc.; *U.S. Public*, pg. 879

CAL-Q-CLUTCH—Business Case—DHP Limited Partnership; *U.S. Public*, pg. 302

CAL-SPAN—Time Release Calcium Tablet—Alva/Amco Pharmacal Companies, Inc.; *U.S. Private*, pg. 47

CAL-TAB—Tabletting Agents for Pharmaceutical & Nutritional Tablets—Crompton & Knowles Ingredient Technology Corp.; *U.S. Public*, pg. 459

CAL-TIE—Construction—CF & I Steel, L.P.; *U.S. Public*, pg. 1230

CAL-TUF—Tempered Glass Fixtures—International Aluminum Corporation; *U.S. Public*, pg. 894

CALADRYL—Anti-Itch Lotion—Warner-Lambert Consumer Healthcare; *U.S. Public*, pg. 1739

CALAN—Pharmaceuticals—Monsanto Company; *U.S. Public*, pg. 1124

CALAN—Angina Pectoris & Hypertension Treatment—Searle & Co.; *U.S. Public*, pg. 1125

CALAN—Anti-Hypertensive—Searle Laboratories; *U.S. Public*, pg. 1125

CALAN IV—Anti-Arrhythmic—Searle & Co.; *U.S. Public*, pg. 1125

CALAN SR—Pharmaceutical Product—Searle Laboratories; *U.S. Public*, pg. 1125

CALANDA—Beer—Heineken N.V.; *Int'l*, pg. 608

CALENDAR OF MEMORIES—Calendars, Greeting Cards, Printed Child Development Records—American Greetings Corporation; *U.S. Public*, pg. 77

CALANDRE—Cologne for Women—Paco Rabanne Compar; *Int'l*, pg. 1073

CALAVO—Avocados, Papaya, Mangos—Calavo Growers of California; *U.S. Private*, pg. 199

CALAVO GOLD—Papaya—Calavo Growers of California; *U.S. Private*, pg. 199

CALBERSON—NONE—GEODIS; *Int'l*, pg. 549

CALCIFEROL—NONE—Schwarz Pharma Inc.; *Int'l*, pg. 1211

CALCIJEX—Pharmaceutical—Abbott Laboratories; *U.S. Public*, pg. 12

CALCIMAR—Drug Used for Treatment of Hypercalcemea & Post-Menopausal Osteoporosis—Rhone-Poulenc Rorer - U.S.; *Int'l*, pg. 1110

CALCITONIN SANDOZ—Drug—Novartis AG; *Int'l*, pg. 971

THE CALCIUM—Energy-Packed Sandwich—Otsuka Pharmaceutical Co., Ltd.; *Int'l*, pg. 1013

CALCIUM DISODIUM VERSENATE—Calcium Disodium Edetate Prescription Drug—3M; *U.S. Public*, pg. 1604

CALCIUM 90—Direct Compression Tabletting Agents for Pharm. & Nutritional Tablets—Crompton & Knowles Ingredient Technology Corp.; *U.S. Public*, pg. 459

CALCORT—Anti-inflammatory—Hoechst Marion Roussel North America; *Int'l*, pg. 625

CALCU-DRYER—Grain Dryer—David Manufacturing Company (DMC); *U.S. Private*, pg. 436

CALCULITE—Recessed Lighting—Lightolier Division; *U.S. Public*, pg. 730

CALDEROL—Pharmaceutical—Organon Inc.; *Int'l*, pg. 48

CALDWELL—Fans, Heaters & Material Handling Systems—Chief Industries, Inc.; *U.S. Private*, pg. 236

CALDWELL'S—Vodka, Gin, Rum, Blend—M.S. Walker, Inc.; *U.S. Private*, pg. 1147

CALEFFI—Bed Linen—Caleffi S.p.A.; *Int'l*, pg. 252

CALENDER SIZE 2283—Oxidized Corn Starch—Penford Corp.; *U.S. Public*, pg. 1269

CALF-MANNA—Concentrated Ration for All Farm Animals—Manna Pro Corporation; *U.S. Private*, pg. 700

CALFORT/CALGON—Water Softener—Benckiser Consumer Products Inc.; *Int'l*, pg. 185

CALFSPAN—Treatment of Infectious Diseases In Calves—SmithKline Beecham Corporation; *Int'l*, pg. 1264

CALGON—Water Treatment Chemicals—Calgon Corporation; *Int'l*, pg. 455

CALGONIT—Automatic Dishwashing Detergent—Benckiser Consumer Products Inc.; *Int'l*, pg. 185

CALIBRATED COLORS—Colorants—Pratt & Lambert United, Inc.; *U.S. Public*, pg. 1466

CALIBRE—Polycarbonate Resin—The Dow Chemical Company; *U.S. Public*, pg. 522

CALIBRON—OEM & Private Label Products—Recoton Corporation; *U.S. Public*, pg. 1369

CALICO—Computer Software in the Nature of a Compiler & Interpreter—Lucent Technologies Inc.; *U.S. Public*, pg. 1017

CALICO—Women's Shoes—Nine West Group, Inc.; *U.S. Public*, pg. 1185

CALICO CORNERS—Retail Decorative Fabric Stores—Calico Corners; *U.S. Private*, pg. 386

CALIENTE—Tires—Bridgestone/Firestone, Inc.; *Int'l*, pg. 213

CALIENTE II—Tires—Bridgestone/Firestone, Inc.; *Int'l*, pg. 213

CALIFORNIA—Pasta, Soups, & Dry Mixes—CSM N.V.; *Int'l*, pg. 243

CALIFORNIA—Paints—California Products Corp.; *U.S. Private*, pg. 201

CALIFORNIA-ARIZONA FARM PRESS—Regional Coverage of Agricultural Industry—Intertec Publishing; *U.S. Public*, pg. 1327

CALIFORNIA/ARIZONA FARM PRESS—NONE—Intertec Publishing; *U.S. Public*, pg. 1328

CALIFORNIA CELLARS OF CHASE-LIMOGERE—Sparkling Wine—Canandaigua Wine Company Div.; *U.S. Public*, pg. 300

CALIFORNIA CLOSET COMPANY—Direct Home Selling of Closet & Workspace Organizers—Williams-Sonoma, Inc.; *U.S. Public*, pg. 1770

CALIFORNIA COLONY—Table Wines—The Beverage Source, Inc.; *U.S. Public*, pg. 591

CALIFORNIA COOPERAGE—Spa—Coleman Spas, Inc.; *U.S. Private*, pg. 691

CALIFORNIA FARMER—Farm Publication 15 Issues/Year—Farm Progress Publications; *U.S. Public*, pg. 513

CALIFORNIA FOR MEN—Fragrance—The Procter & Gamble Company; *U.S. Public*, pg. 1330

CALIFORNIA FOR WOMEN—Fragrance—The Procter & Gamble Company; *U.S. Public*, pg. 1330

CALIFORNIA MICRO DEVICES—Mfr. Integrated Circuits—California Micro Devices; *U.S. Public*, pg. 293

CALIFORNIA MICRO DEVICES—NONE—Milgray Electronics, Inc.; *U.S. Public*, pg. 205

CALIFORNIA RANCHO—Fiber-Cement Siding—GAF Premium Products, Inc.; *U.S. Private*, pg. 433

CALIFORNIA ROLLER BABY—Doll—Tyco Toys, Inc.; *U.S. Public*, pg. 1058

CALIFORNIA SADDLE LEATHER—Combination Of Leathers—Salz Leathers, Inc.; *U.S. Private*, pg. 963

CALIFORNIA SERIES—Product Line Descriptor—Kaufman and Broad Home Corporation; *U.S. Public*, pg. 944

CALIFORNIA UNITED BANK—NONE—Pacific Century Financial Corporation; *U.S. Public*, pg. 1248

CALIFORNIAN PLUS—Weekly Newspaper—The Bakersfield Californian; *U.S. Private*, pg. 112

CALIPER—Control Units—Thermo Fibertek, Inc.; *U.S. Public*, pg. 1593

CALISTOGA—Mineral Water—Nestle S.A.; *Int'l*, pg. 915

CALISTOGA—Mineral Water & Fruit Juices—The Perrier Group of America; *Int'l*, pg. 919

CALITTERA—NONE—Robert Mondavi Winery, Inc.; *U.S. Public*, pg. 1393

CALIXIN—Crop Protection Agent—BASF AG; *Int'l*, pg. 103

CALK-SCREW—Specialty Nails—Maze Nails; *U.S. Private*, pg. 718

CALL DIRECTOR—Telephone—Lucent Technologies Inc.; *U.S. Public*, pg. 1017

CALL JAM—Telecommunications Equipment—Lucent Technologies Inc.; *U.S. Public*, pg. 1017

CALL-STALKER—NONE—Lucent Technologies Inc.; *U.S. Public*, pg. 1017

CALL STAT—Business Communications—Siemens Corporation; *Int'l*, pg. 1245

CALLAGENT—Software Application used to Control how a Telephone is Answered & Directed—Centigram Communications Corporation; *U.S. Public*, pg. 323

CALLAHAN—Seeds—Groupe Limagrain; *Int'l*, pg. 566

CALLARD & BOWSER—Toffee—Philip Morris Companies Inc.; *U.S. Public*, pg. 1287

CALLAWAY—(Line of Golf Products)—Callaway Golf Company; *U.S. Public*, pg. 294

CALLAWAY—Wine—The Wine Alliance; *Int'l*, pg. 63

CALLAWAY CALIFORNIAN WINE—Wine—Allied Domecq PLC; *Int'l*, pg. 62

CALLAWAY PUTTERS—(Line of Golf Putters)—Callaway Golf Company; *U.S. Public*, pg. 294

CALLCOORDINATOR—Computer System—International Business Machines Corporation; *U.S. Public*, pg. 895

CALLCOORDINATOR/2—Computer System—International Business Machines Corporation; *U.S. Public*, pg. 895

CALLIGRAPHIC—Pens—Sanford Corporation; *U.S. Public*, pg. 1178

CALLIOPE—Designer Chair Line—Harter; *U.S. Private*, pg. 581

CALLMASTER—Digital Voice Terminal—Lucent Technologies Inc.; *U.S. Public*, pg. 1017

CALLPATH—Computer System—International Business Machines Corporation; *U.S. Public*, pg. 895

CALLPATH CICS/MVS—Computer System—International Business Machines Corporation; *U.S. Public*, pg. 895

CALLPATH CICS/VSE—Computer System—International Business Machines Corporation; *U.S. Public*, pg. 895

CALLPATH/400—Computer System—International Business Machines Corporation; *U.S. Public*, pg. 895

CALLPATH/6000—Computer System—International Business Machines Corporation; *U.S. Public*, pg. 895

CALLPATH SWITCHSERVER/2—Computer System—International Business Machines Corporation; *U.S. Public*, pg. 895

CALLPATH/2—Computer System—International Business Machines Corporation; *U.S. Public*, pg. 895

CALLUP—Computer System—International Business Machines Corporation; *U.S. Public*, pg. 895

CALLVISOR—Telecommunications Software for Private Branch Exchange Switches—Lucent Technologies Inc.; *U.S. Public*, pg. 1017

CALLWISE—Call Center Application—InteCom; *Int'l*, pg. 794

CALMOL 4—Hemorrhoidal Suppositories—Mentholatum Company; *Int'l*, pg. 1126

CALO—Pet Food—Allied Foods, Inc.; *U.S. Private*, pg. 39

CALOBAR—Goggles, Sunglasses—American Optical Corporation; *U.S. Private*, pg. 60

CALOLITE—Ophthalmic Lenses—American Optical Corporation; *U.S. Private*, pg. 60

CALOPHEN—Hot Setting Resins—Raschig GmbH; *U.S. Private*, pg. 827

CALOR—Small Household Electrical Appliances—Groupe SEB; *Int'l*, pg. 568

CALOR—Liquid Propane Gas—SHV Holdings N.V.; *Int'l*, pg. 1154

CALORIE COACHES—NONE—Physicians Weight Loss Centers, Inc.; *U.S. Private*, pg. 864

CALORIE GOURMET—Meals—Physicians Weight Loss Centers, Inc.; *U.S. Private*, pg. 864

CALORIE MATE—Balanced Food Drink—Otsuka Pharmaceutical Co., Ltd.; *Int'l*, pg. 1013

CALORIE MATE BISCUITS—Balanced Food Biscuits—Otsuka Pharmaceutical Co., Ltd.; *Int'l*, pg. 1013

THE CALORIE SHOP—Weight Loss Centers—Physicians Weight Loss Centers, Inc.; *U.S. Private*, pg. 864

CALORIE SMART—Meals—Physicians Weight Loss Centers, Inc.; *U.S. Private*, pg. 864

CALPIS—Lactic Acid Drinks—Calpis Food Industry Co. Ltd.; *Int'l*, pg. 252

CALPIS SODA—Carbonated Lactic Acid Drink—Calpis Food Industry Co. Ltd.; *Int'l*, pg. 252

CALPRO—NONE—Cleaning Solutions Group/Cello; *U.S. Public*, pg. 1466

CALSA—Bakery Ingrediants—Burns, Philp & Company Limited; *Int'l*, pg. 236

CALSAN—Calcium Stearate Dispersion for use in the Paper Industry—PPG Industries, Inc.; *U.S. Public*, pg. 1245

CALSEG—NONE—ETEX; *Int'l*, pg. 430

CALTAR LENSES—Large Format (View Camera) Lenses—Calumet Photographic, Inc.; *U.S. Private*, pg. 202

CALTON HOMES—NONE—Calton, Inc.; *U.S. Public*, pg. 296

CALTRATE—Mineral Supplement—American Home Products Corporation; *U.S. Public*, pg. 79

CALTRATE—Vitamin & Mineral Supplement—Whitehall-Robins Healthcare; *U.S. Public*, pg. 80

CALUMET—Baking Powder—Kraft Foods, Inc.; *U.S. Public*, pg. 1287

CALUMET—Baking Powder—Philip Morris Companies Inc.; *U.S. Public*, pg. 1287

CALUMET CAMERAS—4″x 5″ & 8″x 10″ View Cameras—Calumet Photographic, Inc.; *U.S. Private*, pg. 202

CALUMET LIGHT STANDS—Studio Lights Stands & Boom Assemblies—Calumet Photographic, Inc.; *U.S. Private*, pg. 202

CALUMET PROCESSORS—Nitrogen Burst Film & Print Processors—Calumet Photographic, Inc.; *U.S. Private*, pg. 202

CALUMET SINKS—Stainless Steel Darkroom Sinks, Backsplashes & Shelves—Calumet Photographic, Inc.; *U.S. Private*, pg. 202

CALVE—Dressings & Sauces—FIMA-Productos Alimentares, Lda; *Int'l*, pg. 471

CALVER—Chemical Reagant—Hach Company; *U.S. Public*, pg. 773

CALVIN—Mens Fragrance Products—Calvin Klein Cosmetics Company; *Int'l*, pg. 1435

CALVIN KLEIN—Women's Ready-to-Wear Clothing—Calvin Klein, Inc.; *U.S. Private*, pg. 202

CALVIN KLEIN HOSIERY—Pantyhose—Kayser-Roth Corporation, Inc.; *Int'l*, pg. 576

CALVIN KLEIN SPORT—Men's, Women's & Juniors Apparel—Calvin Klein, Inc.; *U.S. Private*, pg. 202

CALVIN KLEIN UNDERWEAR—Men's Underwear—Calvin Klein, Inc.; *U.S. Private*, pg. 202

CALYPSO—Rum—Barton Incorporated; *U.S. Public*, pg. 300

CALYPSO—Ice Cream—Dean Foods Company; *U.S. Public*, pg. 489

CALYPSO—Frozen Food—Southern Frozen Foods; *U.S. Private*, pg. 887

CALYPSO RUM—NONE—Barton Brands, Ltd.; *U.S. Public*, pg. 300

CAM-EL—Cam Operated Hot Stick—Kearney Company; *U.S. Public*, pg. 444

CAM-I PLUS—Ducted HEPA Ceiling Moduler for Cleanroom Use—Farr Company; *U.S. Public*, pg. 613

CAM-LOK—Hospital Equipment—Carstens Inc.; *U.S. Private*, pg. 216

CAM-LOK—Electrical Connectors—Cooper Industries, Inc.; *U.S. Public*, pg. 442

CAM-MASTER—Brakes—Rockwell International Corporation; *U.S. Public*, pg. 1397

CAM-O-FLAGE—Braided Fishing Line—Cortland Line Co., Inc.; *U.S. Private*, pg. 277

CAM-REMOTE—NONE—Matthews Studio Equipment; *U.S. Public*, pg. 1060

CAM-STAT—Heating Controls—Watsco, Inc.; *U.S. Public*, pg. 1745

CAMA—Minor Arthritic Pain Relief—Sandoz Pharmaceuticals Corp.; *Int'l*, pg. 974

CAMALOX—Consumer Antacid Pharmaceuticals—Rhone-Poulenc Rorer - U.S.; *Int'l*, pg. 1110

CAMARO—Sporting Goods—Brunswick Bowling & Billiards Corp.; *U.S. Public*, pg. 265

CAMARO—Car—Chevrolet Motor Div. General Motors Corp.; *U.S. Public*, pg. 720

CAMAY—Soap—The Procter & Gamble Company; *U.S. Public*, pg. 1330

CAMAY—Soap and Bath Products—Procter & Gamble Health & Beauty Care So. Europe; *U.S. Public*, pg. 1332

CAMAY—NONE—Procter & Gamble Venezuela, C.A.; *U.S. Public*, pg. 1332

CAMBO CAMERAS—4″ x 5″, 5″ x 7″, & 8″ x 10″ View Cameras—Calumet Photographic, Inc.; *U.S. Private*, pg. 202

CAMBO STUDIO STANDS—Camera Supports for All Format Cameras—Calumet Photographic, Inc.; *U.S. Private*, pg. 202

CAMBOLT—Fasteners—Southtec, Inc.; *U.S. Private*, pg. 1015

CAMBOROUGH—Pigs—Dalgety Plc; *Int'l*, pg. 376

CAMBRIAN—NONE—Eljer Plumbingware; *U.S. Public*, pg. 1794

CAMBRIC—NONE—Beckett Papers; *U.S. Public*, pg. 903

CAMBRIDGE—Clothing—Harcrest International, Ltd.; *U.S. Private*, pg. 500

CAMBRIDGE—Scientific Instruments—Leica, Inc.; *Int'l*, pg. 806

CAMBRIDGE—Stationery Products—The Mead Corporation; *U.S. Public*, pg. 1074

CAMBRIDGE—Office Accessories—Mead School & Office Products; *U.S. Public*, pg. 1074

CAMBRIDGE—Cigarettes—Philip Morris Companies Inc.; *U.S. Public*, pg. 1287

CAMBRIDGE—Cigarettes—Philip Morris U.S.A.; *U.S. Public*, pg. 1289

CAMBRIDGE BAY—Label—S & K Famous Brands, Inc.; *U.S. Public*, pg. 1414

CAMBRIDGE BUSINESSWARE—Stationery Products—The Mead Corporation; *U.S. Public*, pg. 1074

CAMBRIDGE LIGHTS—Cigarettes—Philip Morris Companies Inc.; *U.S. Public*, pg. 1287

CAMBRIDGE LIGHTS MENTHOL—Cigarettes—Philip Morris Companies Inc.; *U.S. Public*, pg. 1287

CAMBRIDGE LIGHTS 100'S—Cigarettes—Philip Morris Companies Inc.; *U.S. Public*, pg. 1287

CAMBRIDGE LIGHTS 100'S MENTHOL—Cigarettes—Philip Morris Companies Inc.; *U.S. Public*, pg. 1287

CAMBRIDGE 100'S ULTRA LIGHTS—Cigarette—Philip Morris Companies Inc.; *U.S. Public*, pg. 1287

CAMBRIDGE SOFTWEAR—Stationary & Business Products—The Mead Corporation; *U.S. Public*, pg. 1074

CAMBRIDGE SOUNDWORKS—NONE—Cambridge Soundworks, Inc.; *U.S. Private*, pg. 202

CAMBRIDGE SOUNDWORKS LISTENING ROOM—NONE—Cambridge Soundworks, Inc.; *U.S. Private*, pg. 202

CAMBRIDGE SOUNDWORKS PROLINE AND DESIGN—NONE—Cambridge Soundworks, Inc.; *U.S. Private*, pg. 202

CAMCO—Oilfield Equipment—Camco International Inc.; *U.S. Public*, pg. 297

CAMCO—Coiled Tubing & Nitrogen Svcs.—Camco International Inc.; *U.S. Public*, pg. 298

CAMCO—Solid & Stranded Wireline Workover Services—Camco International Inc.; *U.S. Public*, pg. 298

CAMCO PRODUCTS—Gas Lift Equip., Subsurface Safety Valves, Packers—Camco International Inc.; *U.S. Public*, pg. 298

CAMDEN—Editing Equipment—Eastman Kodak Company; *U.S. Public*, pg. 550

CAMDEN—Industrial Wire—Oneida Ltd.; *U.S. Public*, pg. 1225

CAMEL—Cigarettes—RJR Nabisco Holdings Corp.; *U.S. Public*, pg. 1354

CAMEL—Reg., Filters, Filter 100's, Filter Hard Pack, Lights Reg., Hard Pack & 100—R.J. Reynolds Tobacco Company; *U.S. Public*, pg. 1355

CAMEL—Cigarettes—R.J. Reynolds Tobacco Intl., Inc.; *U.S. Public*, pg. 1355

CAMEL SPECIAL LIGHTS—Cigarettes—R.J. Reynolds Tobacco Company; *U.S. Public*, pg. 1355

CAMELIA—Sanitary Napkins & Panty Liners—VP-Schickedanz AG; *U.S. Public*, pg. 1333

CAMELLIA—Bath Tissue—Marcal Paper Mills, Inc.; *U.S. Public*, pg. 701

CAMELOT—Cookware—Regal Ware, Inc.; *U.S. Private*, pg. 917

CAMELOT—Fittings, Quick Connect for Hose & Pipe—Serfilco, Ltd.; *U.S. Private*, pg. 985

CAMELOT EDITIONS—Books—The Hearst Corporation; *U.S. Private*, pg. 515

CAMEO—Shampoo Bowl—Belvedere Company; *U.S. Private*, pg. 1008

CAMEO—Window & Bedding Products—CHF Industries, Inc.; *U.S. Private*, pg. 1094

CAMEO—NONE—Eastman Kodak Company; *U.S. Public*, pg. 550

CAMEO—Hosiery for Women—Grupo Synkro, S.A. de C.V.; *Int'l*, pg. 576

CAMEO—Mattress & Box Spring Sets—Kingsdown, Inc.; *U.S. Private*, pg. 622

CAMEO—Interior Walls & Floors—Monarch Tile, Inc.; *U.S. Private*, pg. 287

CAMEO—Flat Latex, Semi-Gloss Latex, Semi-Gloss Oil Base Interior Finishes—Perry & Derrick Co.; *U.S. Private*, pg. 854

CAMEO—Cookies—RJR Nabisco Holdings Corp.; *U.S. Public*, pg. 1354

CAMEO—Hosiery—Sara Lee Corporation; *U.S. Public*, pg. 1432

CAMEO CRÈME—Sandwiches—Nabisco Inc.; *U.S. Public*, pg. 1355

CAMERA ART—Photography—Herff Jones Inc.; *U.S. Private*, pg. 523

CAMERA VIDEO—French Camera & Video Magazine—EMAP France; *Int'l*, pg. 451

CAMERON—Iron Works—Cameron; *U.S. Public*, pg. 298

CAMERON—Slitters-Rewinders—Kathabar Incorporated; *U.S. Private*, pg. 609

CAMERZ—Long Roll Cameras—Photo Control Corporation; *U.S. Public*, pg. 1292

CAMFLEX—Valves—Masoneilan North American Operations; *U.S. Public*, pg. 528

CAMILE—Data Acquisition & Control System—The Dow Chemical Company; *U.S. Public*, pg. 522

CAMILLUS—Pocket & Hunting Knives—Camillus Cutlery Co.; *U.S. Private*, pg. 203

CAMINO—NONE—Bacardi-Martini Belgium; *U.S. Private*, pg. 109

CAMKIT—Computer System—International Business Machines Corporation; *U.S. Public*, pg. 895

CAMLITE—Fiber Optic Connector—Siecor Corporation; *U.S. Public*, pg. 449

CAMLITE—Fiber Optic Connector—Siecor Corporation; *Int'l*, pg. 1245

CAMLOCK SYSTEMS—Lock—Chicago Lock Company; *U.S. Private*, pg. 235

CAMMS—Base Aviation Management Software—Harnischfeger Industries, Inc.; *U.S. Public*, pg. 788

CAMNET—Micro-Processor-Based Control & Monitoring Systems—Sparton Corporation; *U.S. Public*, pg. 1496

CAMP AMERICA—Camp Counselor Placement Program—American Institute for Foreign Study; *U.S. Private*, pg. 56

CAMP HYATT—Children's Program—Hyatt Hotels Corporation; *U.S. Private*, pg. 551

CAMP KITCHEN—Liquid & Propane Fuels—The Canadian Coleman Co., Ltd.; *U.S. Private*, pg. 691

CAMP TRAILS—Tents, Backpacks & Accessories—Johnson Worldwide Associates, Inc.; *U.S. Public*, pg. 932

CAMPA CHEM—Powder & Liquid Deodorant; Toilet Tissue—Thetford Corporation; *U.S. Private*, pg. 352

CAMPAIGN—Herbicide—The Dow Chemical Company; *U.S. Public*, pg. 522

CAMPBELL—Chain, Blocks, Clamps, and Fittings—Cooper Hand Tools; *U.S. Public*, pg. 444

CAMPBELL—Chain Products & Chain Connection Devices—Cooper Industries, Inc.; *U.S. Public*, pg. 442

CAMPBELL—Chain—York Plant; *U.S. Public*, pg. 444

CAMPBELL-HAUSFELD—Air Compressors—The Scott Fetzer Company; *U.S. Public*, pg. 217

CAMPBELL'S—Soups, Bean Products & Tomato Juice—Campbell Soup Company; *U.S. Public*, pg. 298

CAMPBELL'S—Food Products—Campbell Soup Company Ltd.; *U.S. Public*, pg. 299

CAMPBELL'S FRESH—Fresh Mushrooms—Campbell Soup Company; *U.S. Public*, pg. 298

CAMPEONATO—Soccer Shoes—Mizuno Corporation; *U.S. Public*, pg. 884

CAMPFIRE—Marshmallows—Borden, Inc.; *U.S. Private*, pg. 157

CAMPFIRE MARSHMALLOW PRODUCTS—NONE—International Home Foods Inc.; *U.S. Private*, pg. 526

CAMPO LEONARDO—Wine—Leonard Kreusch, Inc.; *U.S. Private*, pg. 635

CAMPOUT—Van Awning—Carefree of Colorado; *U.S. Public*, pg. 217

CAMPSA—Oil & Natural Gas Distribution—Repsol S.A.; *Int'l*, pg. 1104

CAMPUS—Clothing—Hampton Industries, Inc.; *U.S. Public*, pg. 779

CAMPUS-E1—NONE—PairGain Technologies Inc.; *U.S. Public*, pg. 1253

CAMPUS-FLEX—NONE—PairGain Technologies Inc.; *U.S. Public*, pg. 1253

CAMPUS LIFE—Magazine—Christianity Today, Inc.; *U.S. Private*, pg. 238

CAMPUS-T1—NONE—PairGain Technologies Inc.; *U.S. Public*, pg. 1253

CAMPUS-384—NONE—PairGain Technologies Inc.; *U.S. Public*, pg. 1253

CAMPUS WELCOME—NONE—Welcome Wagon-Intl., Inc.; *U.S. Public*, pg. 321

CAMPUSFUNDS—NONE—American Express Company; *U.S. Public*, pg. 73

CAMROL—Cam Followers—McGill Manufacturing Company, Inc.; *U.S. Public*, pg. 573

CAMRY—Automobile—Toyota Motor Corporation; *Int'l*, pg. 1411

CAMRY—Car—Toyota Motor Sales, U.S.A., Inc.; *Int'l*, pg. 1412

CAMTRACK—Bender—Greenlee Textron; *U.S. Public*, pg. 1589

CAMU PLUS—Chewable Vitamin C—Nature's Bounty, Inc.; *U.S. Public*, pg. 1166

CAN-DUIT—Non-Metallic Conduit Systems—The Lamson & Sessions Co.; *U.S. Public*, pg. 976

CAN-O—Dog Food—Star-Kist Foods Inc.; *U.S. Public*, pg. 805

CAN-O-MATIC—Electric Can Openers—The Rival Company; *U.S. Public*, pg. 1391

CAN-OPT—NONE—Ballard Medical Products; *U.S. Public*, pg. 171

CAN-PAK—Canned Beverages Transporter—International Container Systems; *Int'l*, pg. 685

CAN-TEX—Plastic Pipes; Conduit—Cantex Inc.; *Int'l*, pg. 1312

CANAAN—Records—Word, Incorporated; *U.S. Public*, pg. 704

CANADA DIRECT—Long Distance Service to Canada—Teleglobe, Inc.; *Int'l*, pg. 1373

CANADA DRY—NONE—Cadbury Beverages; *Int'l*, pg. 248

CANADA DRY—Soft Drinks—Cadbury Beverages North America; *Int'l*, pg. 248

CANADA DRY—Soft Drinks & Carbonated Water—Cadbury Schweppes p.l.c.; *Int'l*, pg. 247

CANADA DRY—Soft Drink—Grant-Lydick Beverage Co.; *U.S. Private*, pg. 470

CANADA DRY—Gin, Vodka—Shieffelin Somerset Co.; *Int'l*, pg. 412

CANADA MINTS—Mints—New England Confectionary Co.; *U.S. Private*, pg. 1113

CANADA TRUST—Financial Institution—Imasco Limited; *Int'l*, pg. 112

CANADIAN ON-LINE—Online Service via the Internet—Canadian Airlines Corporation; *Int'l*, pg. 255

CANADAIR JET—NONE—Bombardier Regional Aircraft Division; *U.S. Public*, pg. 242

CANADA'S WONDERLAND—Theme Park—Paramount Parks; *U.S. Private*, pg. 776

CANADIAN CLUB—Spirit—Allied Domecq PLC; *Int'l*, pg. 62

CANADIAN CLUB—Canadian Whisky—Hiram Walker; *Int'l*, pg. 63

CANADIAN CLUB—Whiskey—Hiram Walker & Sons Limited; *Int'l*, pg. 63

CANADIAN CLUB CLASSIC—Spirit—Allied Domecq PLC; *Int'l*, pg. 62

CANADIAN CLUB CLASSIC—Whiskey—Hiram Walker; *Int'l*, pg. 63

CANADIAN CLUB CLASSIC—Whiskey—Hiram Walker & Sons Limited; *Int'l*, pg. 63

CANADIAN CODE-1 PLUS—Mailing Efficiency for Canada—Group 1 Software, Inc.; *U.S. Public*, pg. 417

CANADIAN GINSENG & GRAIN—Nonalcoholic Cereal Grain Beverage—R.J. Corr Naturals, Inc.; *U.S. Private*, pg. 276

CANADIAN GOLD—Whiskey—Laird & Company; *U.S. Private*, pg. 642

CANADIAN HOST—NONE—Barton Brands, Ltd.; *U.S. Public*, pg. 300

CANADIAN HOST—Canadian Whisky—Barton Incorporated; *U.S. Public*, pg. 300

CANADIAN MIST—Canadian Whisky—Brown-Forman Beverages Worldwide; *U.S. Public*, pg. 261

CANADIAN MIST—Canadian Whiskey—Brown-Forman Corporation; *U.S. Public*, pg. 261

CANADIAN PLUS—Frequent Flyer Program—Canadian Airlines Corporation; *Int'l*, pg. 255

CANADIAN RESOURCE—CD-ROM for Mailing in Canada—Group 1 Software, Inc.; *U.S. Public*, pg. 417

CANADIAN RISE 'N SHINE BISCUITS—Biscuits—Hardee's Food Systems, Inc.; *U.S. Public*, pg. 278

CANADIAN SHITTLE—Domestic Route Brand—Canadian Airlines Corporation; *Int'l*, pg. 255

CANADIAN SUPREME—NONE—Barton Brands, Ltd.; *U.S. Public*, pg. 300

CANADIAN SUPREME—Canadian Whisky—Barton Incorporated; *U.S. Public*, pg. 300

CANADIAN UNIFORM ENTRY SYSTEM—Mailing Efficiency for Canada—Group 1 Software, Inc.; *U.S. Public*, pg. 417

CANADIER REGIONAL JET—Commercial Regional Jet—Bombardier Inc.; *Int'l*, pg. 199

CANANDAIGUA LAKE NIAGRA—Wine—Widmer's Wine Cellars, Inc.; *U.S. Public*, pg. 300

CANARD—NONE—N.V. Johnson Wax Belgium S.A.; *U.S. Private*, pg. 593

CANARD DUCHENE—NONE—LVMH Moet Hennessy Louis Vuitton; *Int'l*, pg. 779

CANARIA D'ORO—Cigars—General Cigar Company, Inc.; *U.S. Public*, pg. 708

CANARY ISLAND—Men's & Women's Travel & Vacation Apparel—Woolworth Corporation; *U.S. Public*, pg. 1777

CANARY ISLANDS—Casual Apparel for Men & Women—F.W. Woolworth Co.; *U.S. Public*, pg. 1777

CANCEL STAT—Anti-Static Fabrics—Guilford Mills, Inc.; *U.S. Public*, pg. 768

CANCER ADVANTAGE SM—Cancer Insurance—Colonial Companies, Inc.; *U.S. Public*, pg. 1699

CANDEREL—Pharmaceuticals—Monsanto Company; *U.S. Public*, pg. 1124

CANDERMYL—Pharmaceutical Products—Galderma Laboratories, Inc.; *Int'l*, pg. 819

CANADIAN LTD—NONE—Barton Brands, Ltd.; *U.S. Public*, pg. 300

CANDID—Fragrance—Avon Products, Inc.; *U.S. Public*, pg. 155

CANDIDATE—Leisure Time Election Game—Monarch Avalon, Inc.; *U.S. Public*, pg. 1123

CANDITECT—Diagnostic Culture Media—Beckman Instruments, Inc.; *U.S. Public*, pg. 199

CANDLE COMMAND CENTER—Enterprise-wide Systems Management Solutions—Candle Corporation; *U.S. Private*, pg. 204

CANDLE CORPORATION OF AMERICA—NONE—Blyth Industries; *U.S. Public*, pg. 239

CANDLE-LITE—Candles—Lancaster Colony Corporation; *U.S. Public*, pg. 976

CANDLE-LITE—Candles—Candle-Lite, A Lancaster Colony Co.; *U.S. Public*, pg. 976

CANDLEWOOD—Manufactured Homes—Champion Enterprises, Inc.; *U.S. Public*, pg. 332

CANDOLI GRAPPA ACQUAVIT DI VINACCIA—NONE—Carillon Importers, Ltd.; *Int'l*, pg. 409

CANDOLINI GRAPPA RUTA—NONE—Carillon Importers, Ltd.; *Int'l*, pg. 409

CANDOLINI GRAPPA TOKAJ RISERVA—NONE—Carillon Importers, Ltd.; *Int'l*, pg. 409

CANDU—Nuclear Reactor—Atomic Energy of Canada Ltd.; *Int'l*, pg. 97

CANDY—Household Appliances—Candy S.p.A.; *Int'l*, pg. 259

CANDY—NONE—G.D. Packaging Machinery Inc.; *Int'l*, pg. 531

CANDY CUPBOARD—Chocolates—New England Confectionery Co.; *U.S. Private*, pg. 1113

CANDY DISH—Candy—Brach & Brock Confections Inc.; *U.S. Private*, pg. 163

CANDY INDUSTRY—Trade Periodical—Advanstar Communications; *U.S. Private*, pg. 22

CANDY LAND—Game—Hasbro, Inc.; *U.S. Public*, pg. 797

CANDY LAND—Game—Milton Bradley Company; *U.S. Public*, pg. 797

CANDY MACHINE—Candy—Fleer-Skybox International Inc.; *U.S. Public*, pg. 1052

CANDY TOP—Ice Cream Bars, Nuggets & Toppings—Nestle Chocolate & Confection; *Int'l*, pg. 917

CANDYLAND—Plywood, Lumber, Wood & Wood Fiber Products—Georgia-Pacific Corporation; *U.S. Public*, pg. 735

CANDYTOPS—Candy—Nestle S.A.; *Int'l*, pg. 915

CANE PATCH—Syrup—Dean Pickles & Specialty Products; *U.S. Public*, pg. 490

CANEEL BAY—Indoor/Outdoor Casual Aluminum Furniture—Telescope Casual Furniture, Inc.; *U.S. Private*, pg. 1074

CANEI—Sparkling Wine—Groupe Pernod Ricard; *Int'l*, pg. 566

CANEI—Wine—Austin Nichols & Co. Inc.; *Int'l*, pg. 566

CANESTEN—Pharmaceutical, Cardiovascular—Bayer AG; *Int'l*, pg. 171

CANFOR—Forest Products—Canfor Corporation; *Int'l*, pg. 260

CANGURO SF600—Airplane—Agusta Aerospace Corporation; *Int'l*, pg. 32

CANIDAE—Sports Outerwear—Fox-Knapp; *U.S. Private*, pg. 860

CANIGOU—Petfood—Mars Petfoods (UNISABI); *U.S. Private*, pg. 707

CANINE CARRY OUTS—Gourmet Dog Treats—H.J. Heinz Company; *U.S. Public*, pg. 805

CANINE CARRY OUTS—Dog Treats—The Quaker Oats Company; *U.S. Public*, pg. 1347

CANLYTE—Lighting Fixtures—The Genlyte Group Incorporated; *U.S. Public*, pg. 729

CANNED HEAT—Cooking Fuel—Sterno, Inc.; *U.S. Public*, pg. 397

CANNON—Car Mats & Baby Products—Cannon Rubber Ltd.; *Int'l*, pg. 261

CANNON—Domestic Home Furnishings—Fieldcrest/Cannon Bed Fashions Division; *U.S. Public*, pg. 1296

CANNON—Bed & Bath Products—Fieldcrest Cannon, Inc.; *U.S. Public*, pg. 1296

CANNON—Socks—Grupo Synkro, S.A. de C.V.; *Int'l*, pg. 576

CANNON—Carts—IMI Plc; *Int'l*, pg. 646

CANNON—Golf Club Set—Spalding & Evenflo Companies, Inc.; *U.S. Private*, pg. 629

CANNON BALL—Plug Chewing Tobacco—Conwood Company L.P.; *U.S. Private*, pg. 272

CANNONBALL EXPRESS—Electrical Sealed Model Train Set—Bachmann Industries, Inc.; *U.S. Private*, pg. 109

CANNONDALE—Bicycles, Cycling Accessories & Apparel—Cannondale Corporation; *U.S. Public*, pg. 301

CANOE—Cologne—Dana Perfumes Corp.; *U.S. Private*, pg. 922

CANOE SPORT—Men's Fragrance—Dana Perfumes Corp.; *U.S. Private*, pg. 922

CANOGA—Vehicle Detectors—3M; *U.S. Public*, pg. 1604

CANOLA QUICK—Shoestrings, Thin Cuts, Thin Concertinas—Lamb-Weston, Inc.; *U.S. Public*, pg. 427

CANON—Computer Products—Canon Inc.; *Int'l*, pg. 261

CANON—Business Machines & Photographic Equipment—Canon (U.K.) Ltd.; *Int'l*, pg. 263

CANON—Cameras—Canon U.S.A., Inc.; *Int'l*, pg. 262

CANON—Herbicide—Monsanto Company; *U.S. Public*, pg. 1124

CANON COPIERS—Copiers—Canon U.S.A., Inc.; *Int'l*, pg. 262

CANON RC-250—Still-Image Electronic Camera—Canon U.S.A., Inc.; *Int'l*, pg. 262

CANONS DELCOUR—Rifle & Shotgun Barrels—Herstal S.A.; *Int'l*, pg. 617

CANOVEL—Canine Health Products—SmithKline Beecham plc; *Int'l*, pg. 1264

CANPLAS—NONE—ETEX; *Int'l*, pg. 430

CANSTRUT—Cable Tray Systems—Thomas & Betts Corporation; *U.S. Public*, pg. 1597

CANT LEG—Upright Truss for Selective & Drive-In Rack—Speedrack Products Group, Ltd.; *U.S. Private*, pg. 1024

CANTERBURY—Raspberry Or Orange Cream Chocolates—Brown & Haley; *U.S. Private*, pg. 173

CANTENAC BROWN—Bordeaux Wine—Frederick Wildman & Sons Ltd.; *U.S. Private*, pg. 1176

CANTERBURY—Primed Decorative Moulding System—ABT Building Products Corporation; *Int'l*, pg. 20

CANTERBURY—NONE—Blyth Industries; *U.S. Public*, pg. 239

CANTILEVER—Patented, Unique Sole Design—Avia; *U.S. Private*, pg. 62

CANTINA DEL RIO—Fine Mexican Restaurant—Bob Evans Farms, Inc. Restaurant Division; *U.S. Public*, pg. 596

CANVAS CLASSICS—Luggage—Jinwoong Inc.; *Int'l*, pg. 706

CANVAS MOUNT—Canvas Mounting Material—Seal Products Incorporated; *U.S. Public*, pg. 849

CANVASBACKS—Stationery Products—The Mead Corporation; *U.S. Public*, pg. 1074

CANVEX—Reinforced Plastic Sheeting—Raven Industries, Inc.; *U.S. Public*, pg. 1361

CANVEYOR—Cable—Loos & Co., Inc.; *U.S. Private*, pg. 675

CANYON RIVER BLUES—Denium Apparel—Sears, Roebuck and Co.; *U.S. Public*, pg. 1452

CAOTINA—Milk Modifier—Novartis AG; *Int'l*, pg. 971

CAP—NONE—CAP Gemini S.A.; *Int'l*, pg. 263

CAP COLOMBIE—Instant Coffee—Nestle S.A.; *Int'l*, pg. 915

CAP GEMINI AMERICA—Computer Services—CAP Gemini America; *Int'l*, pg. 263

CAP'N CRUNCH—Cereal—The Quaker Oats Company; *U.S. Public*, pg. 1347

CAP'N KID—Peanut Butter—Algood Food Company; *U.S. Public*, pg. 34

CAP'N PRIDE—Seafood—Rich SeaPak Corp.; *U.S. Private*, pg. 928

CAP RIA—Radioimmunoassay System—Capintec Inc.; *U.S. Private*, pg. 205

CAP-10—Navy Baseball Caps—Voyager Emblems, Inc.; *U.S. Private*, pg. 1143

CAP35—Cardotomy Reservoir & Post Operative Chest Drainage System—Gish Biomedical, Inc.; *U.S. Public*, pg. 745

CAP XPRESS—SMT Test Technique to Identify Reverse Polarized Capacitors—GenRad, Inc.; *U.S. Public*, pg. 731

CAPAC—Fuel Pumps—Avis Industrial Corporation; *U.S. Private*, pg. 102

CAPACITY SCOUT—Software Enabling Gas Users to Track Pipeline Capacity & Availability—Eastern Utilities Associates; *U.S. Public*, pg. 549

CAPACITYPRO—Computer System—International Business Machines Corporation; *U.S. Public*, pg. 895

CAPCELL—Hot Cell for Medical Use—Capintec Inc.; *U.S. Private*, pg. 205

CAPCO—Pickles & Peanut Butter—Dean Pickles & Specialty Products; *U.S. Public*, pg. 490

CAPE COD—Potato Chips—Cape Cod Potato Chip Company; *U.S. Private*, pg. 205

CAPE COD—NONE—Kellwood Company; *U.S. Public*, pg. 948

CAPE CORAL—Prefinished Wall Paneling—Georgia-Pacific Corporation; *U.S. Public*, pg. 735

CAPEHART—TV-Audio, Electronics—Luskin's, Inc.; *U.S. Private*, pg. 681

CAPELLA—Post - CMP Cleaning Tool—SpeedFan International, Inc.; *U.S. Public*, pg. 1497

CAPEWELL—Cutting Tools—Rule Industries, Inc.; *U.S. Public*, pg. 950

CAPIJECT—Blood Collection Products—Terumo Medical Corporation; *Int'l*, pg. 1376

CAPIMA—Apparel Yarns—AlliedSignal Inc.; *U.S. Public*, pg. 49

CAPIOX—Oxygenators & Accessories—Terumo Medical Corporation; *Int'l*, pg. 1376

CAPISCINT—Atherosclerotic Placque Imaging Agent—Centocor, Inc.; *U.S. Public*, pg. 323

CAPITAL—Electrical Wire & Cable—General Cable Corporation; *Int'l*, pg. 1486

CAPITAL—Aluminum Foil—Reynolds Metals Company; *U.S. Public*, pg. 1385

CAPITAL AND CODEINE SUSPENSION—Pain Reduction Product—Carnrick Laboratories, Inc.; *U.S. Private*, pg. 436

CAPITAL BOND—Writing Paper—Fox River Paper Company; *U.S. Private*, pg. 422

CAPITAL DISTRICT BUSINESS REVIEW—Business Journal—Business First of New York, Inc.; *U.S. Private*, pg. 19

THE CAPITAL TIMES—Newspaper—Madison Newspapers, Inc.; *U.S. Public*, pg. 984

CAPITAN TEQUILA—NONE—Barton Brands, Ltd.; *U.S. Public*, pg. 300

CAPITOL—Records—Capitol Records, Inc.; *Int'l*, pg. 428

CAPITOL—Record Label—EMI Group plc; *Int'l*, pg. 426

CAPITOL—Store Fixtures—RHC/Spacemaster Corporation; *U.S. Private*, pg. 904

CAPITOL GEARS—Marine Transmission—Regal-Beloit Corporation; *U.S. Public*, pg. 1370

CAPITOL IDEAS—News Program—Westwood One, Inc.; *U.S. Public*, pg. 1763

CAPITOL TRACK—Political Tracking Service—The Mead Corporation; *U.S. Public*, pg. 1074

CAPITROL—Antiseborrheic Shampoo—Westwood-Squibb Pharmaceuticals Inc.; *U.S. Public*, pg. 255

CAPKOLD—Cook-Chill System—Groen, A Dover Industries Co.; *U.S. Public*, pg. 521

CAPLET—Encapsulated Filters—Eastman Kodak Company; *U.S. Public*, pg. 550

CAPLUGS—Protects Products from Damage During Manufacturing, Storage or Shipping—Mark IV Industries Inc.; *U.S. Public*, pg. 1044

CAPLUGS—Caps & Plugs for Prod. Protection—Protective Closures Co., Inc.; *U.S. Public*, pg. 1045

CAPMAC—Molybdenum Assay Apparatus—Capintec Inc.; *U.S. Private*, pg. 205

CAPOGRO—Growing Medium—USG Corporation; *U.S. Public*, pg. 1660

CAPOTEN—ACE Inhibitor—Bristol-Myers Squibb Company; *U.S. Public*, pg. 253

CAPOTEN—Cardiovascular Drug—Bristol-Myers Squibb International; *U.S. Public*, pg. 254

CAPOZIDE—Cardiovascular Therapy Product—Bristol-Myers Squibb Company; *U.S. Public*, pg. 253

CAPOZIDE—Cardiovascular Drug—Bristol-Myers Squibb International; *U.S. Public*, pg. 254

CAPP/USA— Measuring Devices—Capp, Inc.; *U.S. Private*, pg. 207

CAPPER P-C—NONE—Glynwed International PLC; *Int'l*, pg. 554

CAPPER'S—Bi-Weekly Magazine—Ogden Publishing; *U.S. Public*, pg. 812

CAPPIO—Bottled, Iced Capucino Drink—Kraft Foods, Inc.; *U.S. Public*, pg. 1287

CAPPIO—Iced Cappuccino—Philip Morris Companies Inc.; *U.S. Public*, pg. 1287

CAPPUCCINO—Coffee-Filled Chocolates—Ferrero; *Int'l*, pg. 480

CAPPUCCINO—Coffee-Filled Chocolates—Ferrero U.S.A., Inc.; *U.S. Private*, pg. 480

CAPPUCCINO BLAST—Beverage—Baskin-Robbins Incorporated; *Int'l*, pg. 63

CAPPUCCINO EXPRES—Cappuccino/Espresso Maker—Salton/Maxim Housewares, inc.; *U.S. Public*, pg. 1430

CAPRAC—Wipe Test Counter for Medical Use—Capintec Inc.; *U.S. Private*, pg. 205

CAPRAN—Nylon Film—AlliedSignal Inc., Engineered Materials; *U.S. Public*, pg. 51

CAPRAN EMBLEM—Nylon Film—AlliedSignal Inc., Engineered Materials; *U.S. Public*, pg. 51

CAPRI—Cigarettes—B.A.T Industries P.L.C.; *Int'l*, pg. 110

CAPRI—100 Millimeter Cigarette—Brown & Williamson Tobacco Corp.; *Int'l*, pg. 111

CAPRI—Personal Care—Northern Labs, Inc.; *U.S. Private*, pg. 805

CAPRI—Recessed & Track Lighting—Thomas Industries Inc.; *U.S. Public*, pg. 1598

CAPRI SUN—Fruit Drink—Philip Morris Companies Inc.; *U.S. Public*, pg. 1287

CAPRI-SUN—Juice—Ranks Hovis McDougall Limited; *Int'l*, pg. 1395

CAPRICCI—Women's Fragrance—Accecones Ricci U.S.A., Inc.; *Int'l*, pg. 445

CAPRICE—Greeting Cards—American Greetings Corporation; *U.S. Public*, pg. 77

CAPRICE—Car—Chevrolet Motor Div. General Motors Corp.; *U.S. Public*, pg. 720

CAPRICE—Hair Care—Colgate-Palmolive Company; *U.S. Public*, pg. 397

CAPRICE—Passenger Car—General Motors Corporation; *U.S. Public*, pg. 718

CAPRICE DES DIEUX—Cheese—BG SAS; *Int'l*, pg. 201

CAPRICE DES DIEUX—Cheese—Bongrain S.A.; *Int'l*, pg. 201

CAPRO—Control Cables for Outdoor Power Equipment—Teleflex Incorporated; *U.S. Public*, pg. 1569

CAPRON—Nylon Film—AlliedSignal Inc.; *U.S. Public*, pg. 49

CAPROVLAN—Nylon—AlliedSignal Inc.; *U.S. Public*, pg. 49

CAPS—Photo Typesetters—AGFA EPS Division; *Int'l*, pg. 172

CAPSAICIN—Topical Analgesic Cream—Menley & James Laboratories, Inc.; *U.S. Public*, pg. 1086

CAPSTAN FULL—Cigarettes—Imperial Tobacco Group, Ltd.; *Int'l*, pg. 666

CAPSTAN MEDIUM—Ready Rubbed Pipe Tobacco—Imperial Tobacco Group, Ltd.; *Int'l*, pg. 666

CAPSTONE—NONE—Elcor Corporation; *U.S. Public*, pg. 567

CAPSUGEL—Encapsulated Products—Warner-Lambert Company; *U.S. Public*, pg. 1738

CAPSUHELIC—Pressure Gage—Dwyer Instruments Inc.; *U.S. Private*, pg. 350

CAPSULE-FIT—Intraocular Lenses—Alcon Laboratories, Inc.; *Int'l*, pg. 916

CAPSURE—Pacing Lead—Medtronic, Inc.; *U.S. Public*, pg. 1082

CAPSUREFIX—Lead—Medtronic, Inc.; *U.S. Public*, pg. 1082

CAPSYLITE—Track Lighting Lamps—Juno Lighting, Inc.; *U.S. Public*, pg. 935

CAPTAIN APPLEJACK—Brandy—Laird & Company; *U.S. Private*, pg. 642

CAPTAIN BLACK—Pipe Tobacco, Little Cigars, Pipe Tobacco Cigars—Lane Limited; *Int'l*, pg. 1129

CAPTAIN COOK—Food—The Daiei, Inc.; *Int'l*, pg. 364

CAPTAIN D'S—Fast Sea Food Restaurants—Captain D's Restaurant; *U.S. Public*, pg. 1467

CAPTAIN D'S—Seafood—Shoney's, Inc.; *U.S. Public*, pg. 1467

CAPTAIN MORGAN—Spiced Rum—The House of Seagram; *Int'l*, pg. 1217

CAPTAIN MORGAN—Spiced Rum—The Seagram Company Ltd.; *Int'l*, pg. 1214

CAPTAIN PRINGLE'S—Video Equipment—National Video, Inc.; *U.S. Public*, pg. 1755

CAPTAIN'S CHICKEN—Prepared Poultry—National Sea Products Limited; *Int'l*, pg. 909

CAPTAIN'S TABLE—NONE—National Sea Products Limited; *Int'l*, pg. 909

CAPTIVA—Apparel Yarns—AlliedSignal Inc.; *U.S. Public*, pg. 49

CAPTIVA—Blood Containment Device—Merit Medical Systems, Inc.; *U.S. Public*, pg. 1096

CAPTIVA SYSTEM—Instant Camera—Polaroid Corporation; *U.S. Public*, pg. 1313

CAPTIVE-AIRE—Commercial Kitchen Ventilation Hoods and Fans—Captive-Aire Systems, Inc.; *U.S. Private*, pg. 207

CAPTRO—Process Controller—Capital Controls Company Inc.; *Int'l*, pg. 1226

CAPTURE—Treatment—Christian Dior Perfumes Inc.; *Int'l*, pg. 781

CAPTURE—Insecticide/Miticide—FMC Corp., Agricultural Products Group; *U.S. Public*, pg. 605

CAPTURE THE MAGIC MOMENTS—Rental Video Players—National Video, Inc.; *U.S. Public*, pg. 1755

CAPTURED SLOT—Exhaust Muffler Accessory—Donaldson Company, Inc.; *U.S. Public*, pg. 517

CAPTUS—Thyroid Uptake System—Capintec Inc.; *U.S. Private*, pg. 205

CAR—Magazine—EMAP Nationals; *Int'l*, pg. 451

CAR AND DRIVER—Automotive Magazine—Hachette Filipacchi Magazines Inc.; *Int'l*, pg. 794

CAR BRITE—Auto Reconditioning Products—E & A Industries, Inc.; *U.S. Private*, pg. 352

CAR CRAFT—Magazine—Petersen Publishing Company, L.L.C.; *U.S. Private*, pg. 856

CAR MODELER—Magazine—Kalmbach Publishing Co.; *U.S. Private*, pg. 606

CAR STEREO REVIEW—Car Audio Equipment Magazine—Hachette Filipacchi Magazines Inc.; *Int'l*, pg. 794

CAR-X—Muffler & Brake—Speedy Car-X, Inc.; *U.S. Public*, pg. 1578

CARA LEIGH—Women's Footwear—J. Baker, Inc.; *U.S. Public*, pg. 167

CARA MIA—NONE—Artichoke Industries, Inc.; *U.S. Private*, pg. 86

CARA SHOP—Retail Giftware & Souvenirs—Cara Operations Limited; *Int'l*, pg. 266

CARADCO—Window Units—Caradco; *U.S. Public*, pg. 61

CARADCO—Windows—Jeld-Wen, Inc.; *U.S. Private*, pg. 61

CARAFATE—Ulcer Treatment—Hoechst Marion Roussel North America; *Int'l*, pg. 625

CARAFLEX—Institutional Caterer—Cara Operations Limited; *Int'l*, pg. 266

CARALUX—Motion Pictures Projectors—Eastman Kodak Company; *U.S. Public*, pg. 550

CARAMAC—Caramel Bar—Nestle-Rowntree Ltd.; *Int'l*, pg. 921

CARAMATE—Slide Projection—Telex Communications, Inc.; *U.S. Private*, pg. 1074

CARAMEL PORTER—Premium Beer—The Lion Brewery, Inc.; *U.S. Public*, pg. 1000

CARAMILK—Chocolate Bar—George Weston Limited; *Int'l*, pg. 1494

CARAVAN—Sunglasses—Bausch & Lomb Incorporated; *U.S. Public*, pg. 194

CARAVAN—NONE—The Cessna Aircraft Co.; *U.S. Public*, pg. 1589

CARAVAN—NONE—Nissan Motor Co., Ltd.; *Int'l*, pg. 943

CARAVAN—Automotive Products—Puritan/Churchill Chemical Company; *U.S. Private*, pg. 895

CARAVAN—Cast Iron Modular Boiler—Slant/Fin Corporation; *U.S. Private*, pg. 1005

CARAVELLE—Watches—Bulova Corporation; *U.S. Public*, pg. 1010

CARAVELLE WATCHES—Watches—Loews Corporation; *U.S. Public*, pg. 1010

CARB-ION—Activated Carbon for Water Treatment—Ionics, Incorporated; *U.S. Public*, pg. 912

CARB-MEDIC—Carburetor Cleaner—Radiator Specialty Company; *U.S. Private*, pg. 906

CARBATROL—NONE—Elan Corporation Plc; *Int'l*, pg. 435

CARBECIN—Treatment of Gram-Negative Bacterial Infections—SmithKline Beecham plc; *Int'l*, pg. 1264

CARBIDE COBRA—Band Saw Blades—Sandvik/Milford Corporation; *Int'l*, pg. 1185

CARBIMET—Polishing & Grinding Device—Buehler, Limited; *U.S. Public*, pg. 574

CARBITE INSERT TOUR WEDGE—Golf Wedge—Taylor Made Golf Co. Inc.; *Int'l*, pg. 1181

CARBO CLAD—Type of Carbide Tap—Regal-Beloit Corporation; *U.S. Public*, pg. 1370

CARBO GOLD—Abrasive—Carborundum Abrasives North America; *Int'l*, pg. 1174

CARBO-S.A.F.—Tire Treading Stock—Bridgestone/Firestone, Inc.; *Int'l*, pg. 213

CARBO-SORB—Luminescence Reagent—Packard Instrument Co., Inc.; *U.S. Public*, pg. 833

CARBO ZINC—Protective Coatings—Carboline Co.; *U.S. Public*, pg. 1357

CARBOCAINE—Local Anesthetics—Astra AB; *Int'l*, pg. 93

CARBOFLEX—NONE—AGA Gas, Inc.; *Int'l*, pg. 13

CARBOFLEX—Carbon Fiber Product—Ashland, Inc.; *U.S. Public*, pg. 138

CARBOFRAX—Refractory—The Carborundum Corporation; *Int'l*, pg. 1173

CARBOLINE—Coatings—RPM, Inc.; *U.S. Public*, pg. 1356

CARBOLITH—Prescription Drug—ICN Pharmaceuticals, Inc.; *U.S. Public*, pg. 853

CARBOLON—Silicon Carbide—Exolon-Esk Company; *U.S. Public*, pg. 600

CARBOMASTIC—Protective Coatings—Carboline Co.; *U.S. Public*, pg. 1357

CARBOMAT—Carbon Filled Technical Papers—FiberMark Inc.; *U.S. Public*, pg. 620

CARBON COPY—Remote Communications Software—Microcom; *U.S. Public*, pg. 417

CARBONITE—Silicon Carbide—Treibacher Schleifmittel Corp.; *U.S. Private*, pg. 1099

CARBONIZING MATTE—Printing Paper—The Mead Corporation; *U.S. Public*, pg. 1074

CARBONLESS-RECEIPT—Envelopes—Tension Envelope Corp.; *U.S. Private*, pg. 1077

CARBORUNDUM—NONE—Carbo Plc; *Int'l*, pg. 268

CARBOSORB—Industrial Products—Email Limited; *Int'l*, pg. 450

CARBOWAX—Polyethytlene—Union Carbide Corporation; *U.S. Public*, pg. 1666

CARBOXANE—Organic Phosphate Esters—Henkel Corporation; *Int'l*, pg. 610

CARBOXYDYNE—Membranes—Pall Corporation; *U.S. Public*, pg. 1253

CARBRITE—NONE—Carpenter Technology Corporation; *U.S. Public*, pg. 307

CARBY HARVEST—Bakery Mixes—Byrnes & Kiefer Company; *U.S. Private*, pg. 191

CARCHEK—Banking Product—Great Financial Bank FSB; *U.S. Private*, pg. 473

CARCO—Winches—Paccar Inc.; *U.S. Public*, pg. 1246

CARCO—Winches—PACCAR Winch Division; *U.S. Public*, pg. 1246

CARD-O-RAMA—Retail Greeting Card Shops—American Greetings Corporation; *U.S. Public*, pg. 77

CARDENE—Calcium Antagonist—Roche Holding Ltd.; *Int'l*, pg. 1119

CARDENE—Nicardipine Hydrochloride—Syntex; *Int'l*, pg. 1120

CARDENTRY—Micro-Processor Based Access Control Systems—CASI-RUSCO Inc.; *U.S. Private*, pg. 218

CARDGARD C—Card Access—ADT Security Services, Inc.; *U.S. Public*, pg. 1649

CARDHU—NONE—Guinness Plc; *Int'l*, pg. 412

CARDHU—Malt Whiskey—Schieffelin & Somerset Co.; *Int'l*, pg. 412

CARDHU UNBLENDED HIGHLAND—Malt Scotch—Shieffelin Somerset Co.; *Int'l*, pg. 412

CARDIA SALT ALTERNATIVE—A Patented Salt Alternative That Has 54% Less Sodium Than Table Salt—AMBI Inc.; *U.S. Public*, pg. 7

CARDICON SERIES—X-Ray—Picker International, Inc.; *Int'l*, pg. 545

CARDIGAN—Printing Paper—Georgia-Pacific Corporation; *U.S. Public*, pg. 735

CARDILATE—Angina-Pectoris Treatment—Glaxo Wellcome PLC; *Int'l*, pg. 553

CARDINAL—Spinning Reels—Abu Garcia Inc.; *U.S. Private*, pg. 822

CARDINAL—Office Product—American Trading and Production Corporation; *U.S. Private*, pg. 63

CARDINAL—Spinning Reels—Aritmos AB; *Int'l*, pg. 1072

CARDINAL—Bond Writing Paper—The Mead Corporation; *U.S. Public*, pg. 1074

CARDINAL—Retail Drugstore Program—Owens & Minor Inc.; *U.S. Public*, pg. 1236

CARDINAL—Red Tile Polishes—Reckitt & Colman plc; *Int'l*, pg. 1089

CARDINAL—Motor Oils & Lubricants—J.D. Streett & Co., Inc.; *U.S. Private*, pg. 1047

CARDINAL CHOICE—NONE—Cardinal Health Inc.; *U.S. Public*, pg. 304

CARDINAL COMMUNITIES—Apartment Communities In FL, GA, OH, WV, VA, MD, KY—Lexford Residential Trust; *U.S. Public*, pg. 991

CARDINAL GIFTWARE—Home Fashion Accessories—Cardinal Inc.; *U.S. Private*, pg. 208

CARDINI'S—Salad Dressing—T. Marzetti Company; *U.S. Public*, pg. 977

CARDIO/PAK—Defibrillator—Mennen Medical Inc.; *Int'l*, pg. 858

CARDIOGEN-82R—Myocardial Perfusion Agent—Bristol-Myers Squibb Company; *U.S. Public*, pg. 253

CARDIOGENERIC—Chart Paper—Ludlow Corporation; *U.S. Public*, pg. 1651

CARDIOMEGA-3—Pharmaceutical—Thompson Medical Company, Inc.; *U.S. Private*, pg. 1083

CARDIOPLEGIA PLUS—Blood Filter—Pall Corporation; *U.S. Public*, pg. 1253

CARDIORHYTHM—NONE—Medtronic, Inc.; *U.S. Public*, pg. 1082

CARDIOSENS—Disposable Sensors—Burdick, Inc.; *U.S. Private*, pg. 181

CARDIOTEC—Diagnostics—Bristol-Myers Squibb Company; *U.S. Public*, pg. 253

CARDIOVET—Canine Cardiovascular—Akzo Nobel N.V.; *Int'l*, pg. 42

CARDIO2—Testing System—Medical Graphics Corp.; *U.S. Public*, pg. 1080

CARDIZEM—Hypertension—Hoechst Marion Roussel, Inc.; *Int'l*, pg. 624

CARDIZEM—Treatment for Cardio-Vascular Conditions—Hoechst Marion Roussel North America; *Int'l*, pg. 625

CARDIZEM CD—Treatment of Hypertension & Angina—Hoechst Marion Roussel North America; *Int'l*, pg. 625

CARDIZEM INJECTABLE—Injection for Temporary Control of Rapid Heart Rate—Hoechst Marion Roussel North America; *Int'l*, pg. 625

CARDIZEM LYO-JECT—Injection—Hoechst Marion Roussel North America; *Int'l*, pg. 625

CARDIZEM SR—Release Capsules for the Treatment of Hypertension—Hoechst Marion Roussel North America; *Int'l*, pg. 625

CARDKEY—Electronic Identification Device—Amtech Corporation; *U.S. Public*, pg. 105

CARDNACOLOR—Color Proofing System—Unidigital/Cardinal Corp.; *U.S. Public*, pg. 1664

CARDS BY KRISTEN—Greeting Cards—Burgoyne, Inc.; *U.S. Private*, pg. 182

CARDURA—Doxazosin—Pfizer Inc.; *U.S. Public*, pg. 1281

CARDURA XL—Doxazosin GITS—Pfizer Inc.; *U.S. Public*, pg. 1281

CARDWELL—Machinery—The Cardwell Machine Company; *U.S. Private*, pg. 209

CARE/COM—Communications System—Executone Information Systems, Inc.; *U.S. Public*, pg. 599

CARE DO—Hair Care Products—The Wella Corporation; *Int'l*, pg. 1489

CARE-FREE—Rakes & Snow Shovels—Ames Company; *U.S. Public*, pg. 1683

CARE*FREE—Gums—Nabisco Inc.; *U.S. Public*, pg. 1355

CARE*FREE—Sugarless Gum—Planters Company; *U.S. Public*, pg. 1355

CARE FREE CHECKING—No Fee, no Minimum Balance & No Per Check Charge—The Troy Savings Bank; *U.S. Private*, pg. 1106

CARE INSTITUTE—Non-Profit Service Mark—Comprehensive Care Corporation; *U.S. Public*, pg. 419

CARE MANAGEMENT RESOURCE—Missouri PPO Product—Coventry Corporation; *U.S. Public*, pg. 454

CARE PSYCH CENTER—Service Mark for Psychiatric Programs—Comprehensive Care Corporation; *U.S. Public*, pg. 419

CARE UNIT—Service Mark for Programs for Chemical Dependency—Comprehensive Care Corporation; *U.S. Public*, pg. 419

CARE-WARE—Hospital Toilets—Acorn Engineering Company; *U.S. Private*, pg. 14

CAREBEARS—NONE—American Greetings Corporation; *U.S. Public*, pg. 77

CARECA—Soccer Shoes—Mizuno Corporation; *Int'l*, pg. 884

CAREDRAPE—Patient Warming Blankets for Operating Room Use—Mallinckrodt Inc.; *U.S. Public*, pg. 1039

CAREER CLUB—NONE—Supreme International Corp.; *U.S. Public*, pg. 1542

CAREER FASHIONS—Uniforms—Angelica Corporation; *U.S. Public*, pg. 113

CAREER 2000—Computer Lab Furniture—Spectrum Industries, Inc.; *U.S. Private*, pg. 1024

CAREERS USA—NONE—Careers USA Inc.; *U.S. Private*, pg. 209

CAREFILL—NONE—Vulcan Chemicals; *U.S. Public*, pg. 1725

CAREFOAM DX—Fire Retardant—BTR plc; *Int'l*, pg. 124

CAREFREE—Floor Tile—American Biltrite Inc.; *U.S. Public*, pg. 68

CAREFREE—Vinyl Tile—Congoleum Corporation; *U.S. Public*, pg. 69

CAREFREE—Batteries—Eagle-Picher Industries, Inc.; *U.S. Private*, pg. 355

CAREFREE—Gel Wheelchair Cushion—Graham-Field Health Products, Inc.; *U.S. Public*, pg. 757

CAREFREE—Garden Products—Jiffy Products of America, Inc.; *Int'l*, pg. 706

CAREFREE—Panty Shields—Johnson & Johnson; *U.S. Public*, pg. 927

CAREFREE—Faucets—Nortek, Inc.; *U.S. Public*, pg. 1192

CAREFREE ADD-A-ROOM—Accessory—Carefree of Colorado; *U.S. Public*, pg. 217

CAREFREE PANTY SHIELDS—Ultra Thin Pads—Personal Products Co.; *U.S. Public*, pg. 929

CAREFREE PERENNIAL GARDEN—Garden Products—Jiffy Products of America, Inc.; *Int'l*, pg. 706

CAREFREE WILDFLOWER GARDEN—Garden Products—Jiffy Products of America, Inc.; *Int'l*, pg. 706

CAREFUL AND CARING—NONE—Keyport Life Insurance Company; *U.S. Private*, pg. 666

CARELLO—Headlights—Fiat Auto SpA; *Int'l*, pg. 480

CARENET—Nursing Information System—Cerner Corporation; *U.S. Public*, pg. 331

CAREQUILT—Electric Blankets—Mallinckrodt Inc.; *U.S. Public*, pg. 1039

CARESS—Broadloom—Couristan Inc.; *U.S. Private*, pg. 279

CARESS—Bar Soap—Lever Brothers Co.; *Int'l*, pg. 1435

CARESS—Soap—Unilever Plc; *Int'l*, pg. 1433

CARESSA—Beauty Bar—Blue Cross Laboratories; *U.S. Private*, pg. 152

CARESSE—Rugs & Carpets—Glenoit Mills, Inc.; *U.S. Private*, pg. 456

CARETAKER—Wireless/Wire Voice Synthesis Security System—Interactive Technologies, Inc.; *U.S. Public*, pg. 888

CAREY—Salt—North American Salt Company; *U.S. Private*, pg. 505

CARFLEX—Liquid Tight Flexible Non-Metallic Conduit—The Lamson & Sessions Co.; *U.S. Public*, pg. 976

CARFLEX-X-FLEX—Extra-Flexible Liquidtight Nonmetallic Conduit—The Lamson & Sessions Co.; *U.S. Public*, pg. 976

CARGILL—Seeds, Salt, Poultry & Processed Meats—Cargill; *U.S. Private*, pg. 210

CARGILL—Farm Seed—Cargill Seed Div.; *U.S. Private*, pg. 210

CARGO—Beverage Chest—Igloo Products Corporation; *U.S. Public*, pg. 265

CARGO—Car—Iveco-Ford Truck Ltd.; *Int'l*, pg. 484

CARGO—Finished Pine Furnishings—Tandycrafts, Inc.; *U.S. Public*, pg. 1561

CARGO GUARD—Trailer—Dorsey Trailers, Inc.; *U.S. Public*, pg. 520

CARGO-STOP—Floor Trucks—Faultless Nutting; *Int'l*, pg. 473

CARGO VAN—Van—Toyota Motor Sales, U.S.A., Inc.; *Int'l*, pg. 1412

CARGOSEARCH I—Security X-Ray Systems—American Science & Engineering, Inc.; *U.S. Public*, pg. 90

CARGOSEARCH II—Security X-Ray Systems—American Science & Engineering, Inc.; *U.S. Public*, pg. 90

CARHARTT BROWN DUCK—Utility Clothes—Carhartt, Inc.; *U.S. Private*, pg. 210

CARHIDE—Liquid & Paste Paints—PPG Industries, Inc.; *U.S. Public*, pg. 1245

CARIBBEAN COLADA—Cranberry Pineapple Juice Drink—Ocean Spray Cranberries, Inc.; *U.S. Private*, pg. 811

CARIBBEAN SPLASH—Fruit Juice Blend—Chiquita Banana North America; *U.S. Public*, pg. 349

CARIBE—Office Seating—United Chair, Inc.; *U.S. Private*, pg. 512

CARIBES—NONE—Tabacalera, S.A.; *Int'l*, pg. 1345

CARIBOU—Camper—Fleetwood Enterprises, Inc.; *U.S. Public*, pg. 650

CARIBOU—Athletic Socks—Wigwam Mills, Inc.; *U.S. Private*, pg. 1175

CARIDEX—Caries Removal Systems—GP Strategies Corporation; *U.S. Public*, pg. 694

CARIFONE—Renters of Portable Cellular Phones to the Travel & Hospital Industry—Peoples Telephone Company, Inc.; *U.S. Public*, pg. 1275

CARINA—Automobile—Toyota Motor Corporation; *Int'l*, pg. 1411

CARINA—Intimate Apparel—VF Corporation; *U.S. Public*, pg. 1702

CARING—Dealer Sales Division—Medline Industries, Inc.; *U.S. Private*, pg. 728

CARIOCA RUM—Rum—United Distillers USA, Inc.; *Int'l*, pg. 412

CARISBROOK—Specialty Fabrics—Native Textiles; *U.S. Public*, pg. 1684

CARISTRAP WEATHERGUARD—NONE—Caristrap International Inc.; *Int'l*, pg. 271

CARITAPE—NONE—Caristrap International Inc.; *Int'l*, pg. 271

CARL ZEISS—Lenses for 35mm Cameras—Kyocera International, Inc.; *Int'l*, pg. 775

CARL ZEISS—Scientific Instruments—Carl Zeiss, Inc.; *Int'l*, pg. 1523

CARL'S JR. RESTAURANTS—Fast Food Restaurant—Carl Karcher Enterprises, Inc.; *U.S. Public*, pg. 278

CARLESS—Oil & Gas Distribution—Repsol S.A.; *Int'l*, pg. 1104

CARLING BLACK LABEL—Lager—Bass PLC; *Int'l*, pg. 169

CARLING EXTRA DRY—Lager—Bass PLC; *Int'l*, pg. 169

CARLING O'KEEFE—Beer—Foster's Brewing Group Limited; *Int'l*, pg. 500

CARLISLE—Paddles—Johnson Worldwide Associates, Inc.; *U.S. Public*, pg. 932

CARLO PELLEGRINO—Marsala—Paterno Imports Limited; *U.S. Private*, pg. 843

CARLO ROSSI—Wine—E. & J. Gallo Winery; *U.S. Private*, pg. 438

CARLO ROSSI—Wines—Carlo Rossi Vineyards; *U.S. Private*, pg. 438

CARLON—Plastic Pipe—The Lamson & Sessions Co.; *U.S. Public*, pg. 976

CARLON—All Other Products Marketed by Lamson & Sessions under Carlon Name—The Lamson & Sessions Co.; *U.S. Public*, pg. 976

CARLON P & C DUCT—Power & Communication Ducts—The Lamson & Sessions Co.; *U.S. Public*, pg. 976

CARLON PV-MOLD—Pole Riser—The Lamson & Sessions Co.; *U.S. Public*, pg. 976

CARLOS IMPERIAL—Brandy—Domecq Importers Inc.; *Int'l*, pg. 63

CARLOS MURPHY'S RESTAURANTS—Restaurant—Eateries, Inc.; *U.S. Public*, pg. 555

CARLOS I—Brandy—Domecq Importers Inc.; *Int'l*, pg. 63

CARLOS TOMASINI—NONE—Tandy Brands Accessories, Inc.; *U.S. Public*, pg. 1560

CARL'S JR. RESTAURANTS—Fast Food Restaurant—CKE Restaurants Inc.; *U.S. Public*, pg. 278

CARLSBERG—Beer (U.S.)—Anheuser-Busch Companies, Inc.; *U.S. Public*, pg. 113

CARLSBERG—Beer—UNICER-Uniao Cervejeira, S.A.; *Int'l*, pg. 1432

CARLSBERG LIGHT—Light Beer (U.S.)—Anheuser-Busch Companies, Inc.; *U.S. Public*, pg. 113

CARLSON LEASING—Equipment Leasing—Carlson Companies, Inc.; *U.S. Private*, pg. 211

CARLSON MARKETING GROUP—Marketing—Carlson Companies, Inc.; *U.S. Private*, pg. 211

CARLSON TRAVEL NETWORK—Travel Agencies—Carlson Companies, Inc.; *U.S. Private*, pg. 211

CARLSON WAGONLIT TRAVEL—Travel Planning—Carlson Wagonlit Travel; *U.S. Private*, pg. 212

CARLTON—Decorative Giftwrap Packages; Greeting Cards—American Greetings Corporation; *U.S. Public*, pg. 77

CARLTON—Cigarettes—Brown & Williamson Tobacco Corp.; *Int'l*, pg. 111

CARLTON—Beer & Malt Products—Foster's Brewing Group Limited; *Int'l*, pg. 500

CARLTON—Fruit Sparkling Wine—Groupe Pernod Ricard; *Int'l*, pg. 566

CARLTON—Paper Plates—Kimberly-Clark Corporation; *U.S. Public*, pg. 958

Brand Name Index

CARLTON COLD—Ale—Carlton & United Breweries Ltd.; *Int'l*, pg. 500

CARLTON DRAUGHT—Ale—Carlton & United Breweries Ltd.; *Int'l*, pg. 500

CARLTON LIGHT—Beer—Carlton & United Breweries Ltd.; *Int'l*, pg. 500

THE CARLTON—Hotel—The Levy Organization; *U.S. Private*, pg. 664

CARLYLE—Jewelry Retailer—Carlyle & Co. Jewelers; *U.S. Private*, pg. 213

CARLYLE—Compressors—Carrier Corporation; *U.S. Public*, pg. 1689

CARLYWARE—Melamine Dinnerware—Carlisle Food Service Products; *U.S. Public*, pg. 305

CARME—Specialty Bath—Carme' Cosmeceutical Sciences, Inc.; *U.S. Private*, pg. 213

CARMEN ADVANTAGE LIBRARY—NONE—Broderbund Software, Inc.; *U.S. Public*, pg. 258

CARMEN SANDIEGO JUNIOR DETECTIVE EDITION—NONE—Broderbund Software, Inc.; *U.S. Public*, pg. 258

CARMEN VINEYARDS—Chilean Wine—Brown-Forman Corporation; *U.S. Public*, pg. 261

CARMEN VINEYARDS CHILEAN WINES—NONE—Brown-Forman Beverages Worldwide; *U.S. Public*, pg. 261

CARMOL 40 RX—40% Carbamide Cream; RX Potent Tissue-Softener—Bradley Pharmaceuticals; *U.S. Public*, pg 249

CARMOL 40 RX—40% Carbamide Cream; RX Potent Tissue-Softener—Doak Dermatologics; *U.S. Public*, pg. 250

CARMOL HC RX—1% Hydrocortisone Acetate Cream; RX Product for Dermatological Conditions—Bradley Pharmaceuticals; *U.S. Public*, pg. 249

CARMOL HC RX—1% Hydrocortisone Acetate Cream; RX Product for Dermatological Conditions—Doak Dermatologics; *U.S. Public*, pg. 250

CARMOL-10—Deep Moisturizing Lotion; Skin Care—Bradley Pharmaceuticals; *U.S. Public*, pg. 249

CARMOL-10—Deep Moisturizing Lotion; Skin Care—Doak Dermatologics; *U.S. Public*, pg. 250

CARMOL-20—Cream; Skin Care—Bradley Pharmaceuticals; *U.S. Public*, pg. 249

CARMOL-20—Cream; Skin Care—Doak Dermatologics; *U.S. Public*, pg. 250

CARNABY'S GIN—NONE—Star Industries Inc.; *U.S. Private*, pg. 1034

CARNATION—Dairy Products, Instant Products—Nestle S.A.; *Int'l*, pg. 915

CARNATION—NONE—Nestle USA; *Int'l*, pg. 916

CARNATION ALSOY—NONE—Nestle USA; *Int'l*, pg. 916

CARNATION COCO SUPREME—NONE—Nestle USA; *Int'l*, pg. 916

CARNATION COFFEE-MATE—NONE—Nestle USA; *Int'l*, pg. 916

CARNATION 1880—NONE—Nestle USA; *Int'l*, pg. 916

CARNATION FOLLOW-UP FORMULA—NONE—Nestle USA; *Int'l*, pg. 916

CARNATION FOLLOW-UP SOY—NONE—Nestle USA; *Int'l*, pg. 916

CARNATION GOOD START—NONE—Nestle USA; *Int'l*, pg. 916

CARNATION INSTANT BREAKFAST—NONE—Nestle USA; *Int'l*, pg. 916

CARNAVAL—Ice Cream—Borden, Inc.; *U.S. Private*, pg. 157

CARNAVAL RUM—NONE—Star Industries Inc.; *U.S. Private*, pg. 1034

CARNIVAL—Brassieres, Girdles & Panty Girdles—Carnival Creations; *U.S. Private*, pg. 213

CARNIVAL—Embossed, Smooth, Vellum Offset Uncoated Paper—Champion International Corp.; *U.S. Public*, pg. 333

CARNIVAL—Disposable Plastic Flatware & Drinking Straws—Clear Shield National, Inc.; *U.S. Public*, pg. 586

CARNIVAL—Ice Cream—Dean Foods Company; *U.S. Public*, pg. 489

CARNIVAL CRUISE LINES—Cruise Line—Carnival Corporation; *U.S. Public*, pg. 306

CARNIVAL KRAFT—Envelope—Champion International Corp.; *U.S. Public*, pg. 333

CARNIVAL LIGHTS—Hair Accessories—Goody Products, Inc.; *U.S. Public*, pg. 1177

CARO—Instant Coffee—Nestle S.A.; *Int'l*, pg. 915

CAROFIBER—Corrugating Board—Sonoco Products Company; *U.S. Public*, pg. 1485

CAROID—Laxative—Mentholatum Company; *Int'l*, pg. 1126

CAROL—Electrical & Cable Wires & Accessories—General Cable Corporation; *Int'l*, pg. 1486

CAROL TANGLE PROOF—Battery Booster Cable; Parts & Fittings—General Cable Corporation; *Int'l*, pg. 1486

CAROLANS—NONE—Allied Domecq Spirits & Wine (UK) Ltd.; *Int'l*, pg. 63

CAROLANS FINEST IRISH CREAM—Irish Cream—Hiram Walker; *Int'l*, pg. 63

CAROLANS IRISH CREAM—NONE—Cantrell & Cochrane Group; *Int'l*, pg. 63

CAROLANS IRISH CREAM LIQUEUR—Liqueur—Allied Domecq PLC; *Int'l*, pg. 62

CAROLANS LIGHT—NONE—Hiram Walker; *Int'l*, pg. 63

CAROLINA—Shoes—H.H. Brown Shoe Company, Inc.; *U.S. Public*, pg. 217

CAROLINA—Rubber Rolls—HBD Industries, Inc.; *U.S. Private*, pg. 489

CAROLINA—Rice—Riviana Foods Inc.; *U.S. Public*, pg. 1392

CAROLINA—Hosiery Machinery—Speizman Industries, Inc.; *U.S. Public*, pg. 1498

CAROLINA ABSORBENT COTTON—Pharmaceutical Cotton Coil—Carolina Absorbent Cotton Co.; *U.S. Private*, pg. 117

CAROLINA DESIGNS—NONE—Blyth Industries; *U.S. Public*, pg. 239

CAROLINA DESK COMPANY—All Products—DMI Furniture Inc.; *U.S. Public*, pg. 473

CAROLINA HERRERA—NONE—Compar; *Int'l*, pg. 1073

CAROLINA HERRERA—Perfume—International Cosmetics Co., Ltd.; *Int'l*, pg. 684

CAROLINA XEROCOPY D.P.—Reprographic Papers—Weyerhaeuser Company; *U.S. Public*, pg. 1764

CAROLITE—Electrical Cords & Trouble Lights—General Cable Corporation; *Int'l*, pg. 1486

CAROLPRENE—Jacketed Electrical Cords, Insulated Electrical Portable Cord—General Cable Corporation; *Int'l*, pg. 1486

CAROL'S KITCHEN—Newsletters—Kerr Group, Inc.; *U.S. Public*, pg. 952

CARON—Knitting Yarns—Caron International; *U.S. Private*, pg. 786

CAROPAK—Biological Supplies—Carolina Biological Supply Co.; *U.S. Private*, pg. 213

CAROUGE—Basketball Shoe—K-Swiss Inc.; *U.S. Public*, pg. 937

CAROUSEL—Children's Books—Bertelsmann AG; *Int'l*, pg. 189

CAROUSEL—Slide Projectors, Trays & Projector Accessories—Eastman Kodak Company; *U.S. Public*, pg. 550

CAROUSEL—Refinished Wall Paneling—Georgia-Pacific Corporation; *U.S. Public*, pg. 735

CAROWINDS—Theme Parks—Paramount Carowinds; *U.S. Private*, pg. 279

CAROXIN—Medical Chewing Gum—Novo Nordisk A/S; *Int'l*, pg. 987

CARPANO PUNT E MES APERITIF—NONE—Carillon Importers, Ltd.; *Int'l*, pg. 409

CARPENTER—Body Works—Carpenter Industries, Inc.; *U.S. Private*, pg. 215

CARPENTER—NONE—Carpenter Technology Corporation; *U.S. Public*, pg. 307

CARPENTER AIR-HARD—NONE—Carpenter Technology Corporation; *U.S. Public*, pg. 307

CARPENTER CCM—NONE—Carpenter Technology Corporation; *U.S. Public*, pg. 307

CARPENTER EDGE TOUGH—NONE—Carpenter Technology Corporation; *U.S. Public*, pg. 307

CARPENTER FLEXCOTE—NONE—Carpenter Technology Corporation; *U.S. Public*, pg. 307

CARPENTER GLASS SEALING 49—NONE—Carpenter Technology Corporation; *U.S. Public*, pg. 307

CARPENTER HIGH PERMEABILITY 49—NONE—Carpenter Technology Corporation; *U.S. Public*, pg. 307

CARPENTER HYMU—NONE—Carpenter Technology Corporation; *U.S. Public*, pg. 307

CARPENTER INVAR—NONE—Carpenter Technology Corporation; *U.S. Public*, pg. 307

CARPENTER LOW EXPANSION 42—NONE—Carpenter Technology Corporation; *U.S. Public*, pg. 307

CARPENTER MICROMELT—NONE—Carpenter Technology Corporation; *U.S. Public*, pg. 307

CARPENTER MIRROMOLD—NONE—Carpenter Technology Corporation; *U.S. Public*, pg. 307

CARPENTER NO. 158—NONE—Carpenter Technology Corporation; *U.S. Public*, pg. 307

CARPENTER TEMPERATURE COMPENSATOR 30—NONE—Carpenter Technology Corporation; *U.S. Public*, pg. 307

CARPENTER 20 CB-3LR—NONE—Carpenter Technology Corporation; *U.S. Public*, pg. 307

CARPENTIER-EDWARDS—Tissue Heart Valves—Baxter International Inc.; *U.S. Public*, pg. 196

CARPET CARE—Rug & Room Deodorizer Shaker Box—Blue Cross Laboratories; *U.S. Private*, pg. 152

CARPET MACHINE—Cleaning Machine—Bissell Inc.; *U.S. Public*, pg. 145

CARPET MAGIC—Carpet Cleaning Supplies and Equip.—The Hartz Mountain Corp.; *U.S. Private*, pg. 508

CARPET SCENT—Rug & Room Deodorizer—Blue Cross Laboratories; *U.S. Private*, pg. 152

CARPET SCIENCE—Carpet Cleaner—S.C. Johnson & Son, Inc.; *U.S. Private*, pg. 592

CARPET SHAMPOO/SOIL GARD—Rug Shampoo—Bissell Inc.; *U.S. Private*, pg. 145

CARPETERIA—Retail of Carpets—Carpeteria, Inc.; *U.S. Private*, pg. 215

CARPETKEEPERS—Carpet Care Machines—Breuer/Tornado; *U.S. Private*, pg. 167

CARPETRIEVER—Small Vacuum—Advance Machine Company; *Int'l*, pg. 932

CARPETRON—Small Vacuum—Advance Machine Company; *Int'l*, pg. 932

CARPETWIN—Small Vacuum—Advance Machine Company; *Int'l*, pg. 932

CARQUEST—NONE—Plews/Edelmann; *Int'l*, pg. 1396

CARQUEST—Auto Parts—STRAFCO, Inc.; *U.S. Private*, pg. 1046

CARRAGAUZE—Gauze Wound Dressing—Carrington Laboratories, Inc.; *U.S. Public*, pg. 309

CARRAMERICA—Blue/Black Sans Serif Logo—CarrAmerica Realty; *U.S. Public*, pg. 308

CARRARA—Printing Paper—Georgia-Pacific Corporation; *U.S. Public*, pg. 735

CARRARA—Ornamental Structural Glass—PPG Industries, Inc.; *U.S. Public*, pg. 1245

CARREFOUR—Groceries—Carrefour; *Int'l*, pg. 272

CARRERA—Broadloom—Couristan Inc.; *U.S. Private*, pg. 279

CARRERA—Ophthalmic, Sunglasses & Goggles—Optimaxx International; *U.S. Private*, pg. 818

CARRERA—Car—Porsche Cars North America, Inc.; *Int'l*, pg. 1063

CARRIAGE—Carpets—Carriage Industries, Inc.; *U.S. Public*, pg. 514

CARRIAGE—Watches—Timex Corporation; *U.S. Private*, pg. 1088

CARRIAGE HOUSE—Lock & Bath—Amerock Corporation; *U.S. Public*, pg. 1177

CARRIAGE HOUSE—Extension House Paint—Bruning Paint Company; *U.S. Private*, pg. 176

CARRIAGE HOUSE SHINGLE—Asphalt Roofing—CertainTeed Corporation; *Int'l*, pg. 1170

CARRIBEAN CHILL—Frozen Yogurt—Alta-Dena Certified Dairy; *Int'l*, pg. 201

CARRIDEX—Bulking Agent for Low-Calorie Sweeteners—Penford Corp.; *U.S. Public*, pg. 1269

CARRIER—Heating & Air Conditioning Equip.—Carrier Corp.; *U.S. Public*, pg. 1690

CARRIER—Air Conditioning, Heating & Refrigeration—Carrier Corporation; *U.S. Public*, pg. 1689

CARRIER—Vibrating Conveyors & Process Equip.—Carrier Vibrating Equipment, Inc.; *U.S. Private*, pg. 215

CARRIER—Air Conditioners—The Climatic Corp.; *U.S. Private*, pg. 246

CARRIER—Heating & Air Conditioning Equipment—The Habegger Corporation; *U.S. Private*, pg. 492

CARRIER—War Game—Monarch Avalon, Inc.; *U.S. Public*, pg. 1123

CARRIER—Heating & Air Conditioning—United Technologies Corporation; *U.S. Public*, pg. 1689

CARRIER KOTE—Paperboard—The Mead Corporation; *U.S. Public*, pg. 1074

CARRIER TRANSICOLD—Transport Refrigeration Equipment—Carrier Corporation; *U.S. Public*, pg. 1689

CARRINGTON GELPAD—Wound Dressing Pads—Carrington Laboratories, Inc.; *U.S. Public*, pg. 309

CARRISYN—Pharmaceutical Used to Treat Tumors in Cats & Dogs—Carrington Laboratories, Inc.; *U.S. Public*, pg. 309

CARROLL SHELBY—Chili—Reily Foods Company; *U.S. Private*, pg. 919

CARROZZERIA—Car Electronics Products—Pioneer Electronic Corporation; *Int'l*, pg. 1057

CARR'S—Table Water Cracker—United Biscuits (Holdings) Plc; *Int'l*, pg. 1442

CARR'S—Table Water Crackers—United Biscuits (UK) Limited; *Int'l*, pg. 1442

CARRY CLEAN—Travel Toothbrush—Brimms Inc.; *U.S. Private*, pg. 169

CARRY-HOME COVERALL—Polyethylene Sheeting—Warp Brothers; *U.S. Private*, pg. 412

CARRYDECK—8.5 Ton Industrial Crane—Marine Travelift, Inc.; *U.S. Private*, pg. 703

CARRYFILE—Expanding Files—The Mead Corporation; *U.S. Public*, pg. 1074

CARRYHOME COVERALL—Plastic Sheeting—Flex-O-Glass, Inc.; *U.S. Private*, pg. 412

CARRYLIFT—NONE—Pettibone Corporation; *U.S. Private*, pg. 859

CARSOFOAM—Shampoo Concentrates—Lonza Inc.; *Int'l*, pg. 67

CARSON PIRIE SCOTT—Department Stores—Carson Pirie Scott & Company; *U.S. Public*, pg. 309

CARSON'S—Dried Beef—E.W. Knauss & Son, Inc.; *U.S. Private*, pg. 626

CARSONOL—Alcohol Sulfate—Lonza Inc.; *Int'l*, pg. 67

CARSONON—Nonionic Surfactants & Wetting Agents—Lonza Inc.; *Int'l*, pg. 67

CARSOQUAT—Quaternary Compound for Hair Conditioners—Lonza Inc.; *Int'l*, pg. 67

CARSOSOFT—Quaternary Compounds for Fabric Softeners—Lonza Inc.; *Int'l*, pg. 67

CARSTON—NONE—Brammer plc; *Int'l*, pg. 212

CART—Scientific Glassware for Laboratory Use—Wheaton Inc.; *Int'l*, pg. 67

CART-A-WAY—Recycling Cart—United Receptical, Inc.; *U.S. Private*, pg. 1123

CARTA—NONE—Clariant International Ltd.; *Int'l*, pg. 624

CARTA BLANCA—Beer—Labatt U.S.A.; *Int'l*, pg. 679

CARTA BLANCA BEER—Beer—Wisdom Imports Sales Co. Inc.; *Int'l*, pg. 679

CARTACOL—Specialty Chemicals—Clariant International Ltd.; *Int'l*, pg. 624

CARTAFEN—Newsprint Recycling system—Novartis AG; *Int'l*, pg. 971

CARTAFIX—Specialty Chemicals—Clariant International Ltd.; *Int'l*, pg. 624

CARTAFIX DPR LIQUID—Paper Processing Chemical—Novartis AG; *Int'l*, pg. 971

CARTALL—Material Handling Products—Peco Mfg. Co., Inc.; *U.S. Private*, pg. 846

CARTAPIP—Chemical Agent—Novartis AG; *Int'l*, pg. 971

CARTARETIN—Paper Chemicals—Novartis AG; *Int'l*, pg. 971

CARTAREX—Specialty Chemicals—Clariant International Ltd.; *Int'l*, pg. 624

CARTASEAL—Specialty Chemicals—Clariant International Ltd.; *Int'l*, pg. 624

CARTASOL—Dyes—Clariant International Ltd.; *Int'l*, pg. 624

CARTASOL—Dye—Novartis AG; *Int'l*, pg. 971

CARTE NOIRE—Coffee—Kraft Jacobs Suchard; *U.S. Public*, pg. 1290

CARTE PASTEL INTERNATIONALE—Credit Card—France Telecom; *Int'l*, pg. 503

CARTE PASTEL NATIONALE—Credit Card—France Telecom; *Int'l*, pg. 503

CARTE PASTEL SELECTION—Credit Card—France Telecom; *Int'l*, pg. 503

CARTECH—NONE—Carpenter Technology Corporation; *U.S. Public*, pg. 307

CARTEOLOL—Beta Blocker Ophthalmic Solution—Otsuka Pharmaceutical Co., Ltd.; *Int'l*, pg. 1013

CARTER—Fuel Systems—Federal-Mogul Corporation; *U.S. Public*, pg. 615

CARTER'S—Children's Clothes—The William Carter Company; *U.S. Private*, pg. 217

CARTER'S CLASSIC COLLECTION—Children's Clothes—The William Carter Company; *U.S. Private*, pg. 217

CARTER'S LITTLE PILLS—Pain Reliever—Carter Products, Canada; *U.S. Public*, pg. 310

CARTERS LITTLE PILLS—Laxative—Carter-Wallace, Inc.; *U.S. Public*, pg. 309

CARTIER—Cigarettes—Philip Morris U.S.A.; *U.S. Public*, pg. 1289

CARTON-KING—Carton Machinery—G.D. Packaging Machinery Inc.; *Int'l*, pg. 531

CARTON KOTE—Paperboard—The Mead Corporation; *U.S. Public*, pg. 1074

CARTON MASTER—Gummed Tape—Intertape Polymer Group; *Int'l*, pg. 685

CARTOON NETWORK—Entertainment Network—Turner Broadcasting System Inc.; *U.S. Public*, pg. 1614

CARTRAC—Material Handling System—SI Handling Systems, Inc.; *U.S. Public*, pg. 1418

CARTRISEAL—Mechanical Seals—Rexnord Corporation; *Int'l*, pg. 127

CARTRIX SYSTEM—Unit-dose, Disposable, Pre-filled Syringes—Meridian Medical Technology, Inc.; *U.S. Public*, pg. 1095

CARTROL—Carteolol—Abbott Laboratories; *U.S. Public*, pg. 12

CARULITE—Chemicals—Carus Corporation; *U.S. Private*, pg. 217

CARUSORB—Chemicals—Carus Corporation; *U.S. Private*, pg. 217

CARUTH PLANK—Pre-Finished Laminate—Bruce Hardwood Floors; *U.S. Public*, pg. 1634

CARVAC—Power Tools—The Black & Decker Corporation; *U.S. Public*, pg. 233

CARVEL HALL—NONE—Carvel Hall; *U.S. Private*, pg. 1061

CARVER—Yachts—Carver Boat Corp.; *U.S. Private*, pg. 447

CARVER—Home Audio Equipment—Carver Corporation; *U.S. Public*, pg. 310

CARVER—Oil Seed Processing Machinery—Carver, Inc.; *U.S. Private*, pg. 217

CARWOOD—Men's & Boy's Outerwear—Delta Apparel; *U.S. Public*, pg. 498

CARWOOD—Leisure Wear—Duck Head Apparel; *U.S. Public*, pg. 498

CARY—Spectrophotometers, Vibrating Reed Electrometers—Varian Associates, Inc.; *U.S. Public*, pg. 1710

CARY'S—Pure Maple Syrup—Borden, Inc.; *U.S. Private*, pg. 157

CARZOL—Agricultural Chemical—AgrEvo USA Company; *Int'l*, pg. 1203

CASA BONITA—Family Oriented Mexican Restaurants—Casa Bonita, Inc.; *U.S. Public*, pg. 278

CASA DE MATEUS—Jams—Bestfoods; *U.S. Public*, pg. 223

CASA DI COLORE—Hair Care Products & Haircolor—Framesi USA, Inc./Roffler Industries, Inc./Casa di Colore, Inc.; *U.S. Private*, pg. 419

CASA FIESTA—Mexican Food—Bruce Foods Corp.; *U.S. Private*, pg. 175

CASA LUPITA—Mexican Restaurant & Bar—Famous Restaurants Inc.; *U.S. Public*, pg. 393

CASA LUPITA RESTAURANTS—Restaurant—Eateries, Inc.; *U.S. Public*, pg. 555

CASA MAID—Frozen Italian Foods—Hanover Foods Corporation; *U.S. Private*, pg. 499

CASABLANCA—Fans—Casablanca Fan Co., Inc.; *U.S. Private*, pg. 549

CASABLANCA—Records & Cassettes—Polygram Records, Inc.; *Int'l*, pg. 1052

CASALINI—Liquers—M.S. Walker, Inc.; *U.S. Private*, pg. 1147

CASANOVA CHOCOLATES—Chocolates—Boyer Candy Company; *U.S. Private*, pg. 162

CASCADE—Business & Printing Papers & Market Pulp—Boise Cascade Corporation; *U.S. Public*, pg. 242

CASCADE—Beer—Carlton & United Breweries Ltd.; *Int'l*, pg. 500

CASCADE—Lift Truck Attachments—Cascade Corporation; *U.S. Public*, pg. 310

CASCADE—Manufactured Homes—Champion Enterprises, Inc.; *U.S. Public*, pg. 332

CASCADE—Direct Mail Catalogue—Fine Art Developments plc; *Int'l*, pg. 485

CASCADE—Integrated Circuit, Library Element, Circuitry—LSI Logic Corp.; *U.S. Public*, pg. 971

CASCADE—Ice Cream—Nestle S.A.; *Int'l*, pg. 915

CASCADE—Dishwasher Product—The Procter & Gamble Company; *U.S. Public*, pg. 1330

CASCADE—Window Shades—Springs Industries, Inc.; *U.S. Public*, pg. 1499

CASCADE—Mining & Chemical Machinery—Svedala Industries Inc.; *Int'l*, pg. 1325

CASCADE BLUES—Apparel—Fred Meyer Stores; *U.S. Public*, pg. 1103

CASCADE SELECT—Seafood Products—UniSea Foods, Inc.; *Int'l*, pg. 940

CASCADE SPORT—Apparel—Fred Meyer Stores; *U.S. Public*, pg. 1103

CASCADE WATER—Bottled Water—Hinckley & Schmitt, Inc.; *Int'l*, pg. 1322

CASCAMITE—Casein & Synthetic Resin Glue—Borden, Inc.; *U.S. Private*, pg. 157

CASCO—Casein & Synthetic Resin Glue—Borden, Inc.; *U.S. Private*, pg. 157

CASCO—Lighters—Casco Products Corporation; *U.S. Public*, pg. 1458

CASCOPHEN—Casein & Synthetic Resin Glue—Borden, Inc.; *U.S. Private*, pg. 157

CASCOREZ—Glues & Adhesives—Borden, Inc.; *U.S. Private*, pg. 157

CASCOSET—Casein & Synthetic Resin Glue—Borden, Inc.; *U.S. Private*, pg. 157

CASE—Disk Harrows—Case Corporation; *U.S. Public*, pg. 311

CASE—NONE—Case France S.A.; *U.S. Public*, pg. 1579

CASE—Coated & Book Papers—Case Paper Co., Inc.; *U.S. Private*, pg. 218

CASE—Data Modems—Osicom Technologies Inc.; *U.S. Public*, pg. 1233

CASE MASTER—Integral Quench Furnace—Seco Warwick Corporation; *U.S. Private*, pg. 980

CASE 1H—NONE—Case France S.A.; *U.S. Public*, pg. 1579

CASE POCLAIN—NONE—Case France S.A.; *U.S. Public*, pg. 1579

CASEBASE—Publication—Lawyers Cooperative Publishing Co.; *U.S. Public*, pg. 1602

CASEC—Powdered Protein Supplement—Mead Johnson Nutritional Group; *U.S. Public*, pg. 254

CASEY'S BIGGEST HITS—Adult Contemporary Radio Program—Westwood One Entertainment; *U.S. Public*, pg. 1763

CASEY'S BIGGEST HITS—Past Top Charting Hits Programming—Westwood One, Inc.; *U.S. Public*, pg. 1763

CASEY'S COUNTDOWN—Adult Contemporary Radio Program—Westwood One Entertainment; *U.S. Public*, pg. 1763

CASEY'S COUNTDOWN—Top Adult Hits Programming—Westwood One, Inc.; *U.S. Public*, pg. 1763

CASEY'S HOT 20—Adult Contemporary Radio Program—Westwood One Entertainment; *U.S. Public*, pg. 1763

CASEY'S HOT 20—Top 20 Countdown Programming—Westwood One, Inc.; *U.S. Public*, pg. 1763

CASEY'S TOP 40—Adult Contemporary Radio Program—Westwood One Entertainment; *U.S. Public*, pg. 1763

CASEY'S TOP 40—Countdown Top 40 Hits Programming—Westwood One, Inc.; *U.S. Public*, pg. 1763

CASH—Bubble Gum—Amurol Confections Co.; *U.S. Public*, pg. 1781

CASH—Computer Control—Harnischfeger Industries, Inc.; *U.S. Public*, pg. 788

CASH DIVIDEND—Controlled Markdown Program—Carlson Retail Marketing; *U.S. Private*, pg. 212

CASH FLOW BOOT CAMP—Financial Information Program—Success Development International; *U.S. Private*, pg. 1048

CASH-FLOW GENERATOR—Introductory Business Information Package—Success Development International; *U.S. Private*, pg. 1048

CASH MART—NONE—Harp's Food Stores, Inc.; *U.S. Private*, pg. 504

CASH-ACME—NONE—IMI Cash Valve, Inc.; *Int'l*, pg. 646

CASHIER—Coin Dispenser—Brandt, Inc.; *Int'l*, pg. 387

CASHMERE BOUQUET—Soap & Talc—Colgate-Palmolive Company; *U.S. Public*, pg. 397

CASHMILON—Acrylic Staple Fiber—Asahi Chemical Industry Co., Ltd.; *Int'l*, pg. 83

CASHMORES—NONE—Glynwed International PLC; *Int'l*, pg. 554

CASINO AZTAR—Riverboat Casinos—Aztar Corporation; *U.S. Public*, pg. 158

CASINO CASH—Game—Carlson Retail Marketing; *U.S. Private*, pg. 212

CASINO CUBAN RUM & DEVICE—Alcoholic Beverage—Sime Darby Berhad; *Int'l*, pg. 1249

CASINO JAMAICAN RUM & DEVICE—Alcoholic Beverage—Sime Darby Berhad; *Int'l*, pg. 1249

CASINOLINK—Slot Tracking System—Mikohn Gaming Corporation; *U.S. Public*, pg. 1111

CASIOTONE—Musical Instruments—Casio, Inc.; *Int'l*, pg. 274

CASIOTRON—Watch—Casio, Inc.; *Int'l*, pg. 274

CASITA—NONE—Kay Home Products, Inc.; *U.S. Public*, pg. 1258

CASITE—Fuel Additives—Hastings Manufacturing Company; *U.S. Public*, pg. 798

CASK—Champagnes & Cold Duck—Warner Vineyards; *U.S. Private*, pg. 1151

CASK GREAT LAKES COOLER—Wine Cooler—Warner Vineyards; *U.S. Private*, pg. 1151

CASLER—Performance Products—Hooker Industries; *U.S. Private*, pg. 538

CASODEX—Pharmaceutical—Zeneca Group Plc; *Int'l*, pg. 1524

CASORON—Herbicide—Uniroyal Chemical Company, Inc.; *U.S. Public*, pg. 460

CASSCO—Retail Ice—WLR Foods, Inc.; *U.S. Public*, pg. 1727

CAST COAT—Engine Paint—Sherwin-Williams Diversified Brands, Inc.; *U.S. Public*, pg. 1466

CASTALOY—Clamps & Holders—Fisher Scientific Company; *U.S. Private*, pg. 658

CASTALUM—Aluminum Finishes—PPG Industries, Inc.; *U.S. Public*, pg. 1245

CASTEEL—Heavy Duty Storage Systems—Clairson International Corp.; *U.S. Public*, pg. 575

CASTELL—Saftey Interlocks For Access Control Valve Interlocking & Machine Guarding—Halma p.l.c.; *Int'l*, pg. 589

CASTELLA—Classic, Panatella Cigars—Imperial Tobacco Group, Ltd.; *Int'l*, pg. 666

CASTELLA CLASSIC—Cigars—Hanson PLC; *Int'l*, pg. 592

CASTELLA DE VIDE—Water—UNICER-Uniao Cervejeira, S.A.; *Int'l*, pg. 1432

CASTELLARIN—Italian Wine—Marie Brizard Wines & Spirits USA; *U.S. Private*, pg. 702

CASTELLO BANFI-SUMMUS EXCELSUS—Super Premium Wines—Banfi Vintners; *U.S. Private*, pg. 113

CASTELLO VICCIO CLASSICO CHIANTI—Wine—Peerless Importers, Inc.; *U.S. Private*, pg. 847

CASTERJET—Spray Nozzle—Spraying Systems Co.; *U.S. Private*, pg. 1026

CASTETHANE—Elastomer System—The Dow Chemical Company; *U.S. Public*, pg. 522

CASTILE—Photo Typesetters—AGFA EPS Division; *Int'l*, pg. 172

CASTILLO RUM—Rum—Bacardi-Martini, USA, Inc.; *U.S. Private*, pg. 109

CASTING—Hair Care Product—Cosmair, Inc.; *Int'l*, pg. 818

CASTLE—Greeting Cards—Fine Art Developments plc; *Int'l*, pg. 485

CASTLE—Sterilizers & Lights—Getinge/Castle Inc.; *Int'l*, pg. 551

CASTLE—Breads, Buns—Metz Baking Company (WI); *U.S. Private*, pg. 1022

CASTLE—Locksmiths' Work, Safes & Cash Boxes—Sime Darby Berhad; *Int'l*, pg. 1249

CASTLE—Motion Pictures—Universal Studios Hollywood; *Int'l*, pg. 1216

CASTLE CRAFT—Clergy Vestments—Augsburg Fortress, Publishers; *U.S. Private*, pg. 98

CASTLE RIDGE—Vinyl Siding—Georgia-Pacific Corporation; *U.S. Public*, pg. 735

CASTLEBERRY'S—Harris—Castleberry/Snow's Brands Inc.; *U.S. Private*, pg. 219

CASTLEGATE—Insulated Steel Doors—Castlegate Inc.; *U.S. Private*, pg. 1067

CASTLEWICK COLLECTION—NONE—Regal Ware, Inc.; *U.S. Private*, pg. 917

CASTLOK—Hardware—Loos & Co., Inc.; *U.S. Private*, pg. 675

CASTMATE—Ceramic Additive—The Dow Chemical Company; *U.S. Public*, pg. 522

CASTOR—Rocket Motors (Class 7)—Thiokol Corporation; *U.S. Public*, pg. 1596

CASTOR—NONE—Zanussi Italia S.p.A.; *Int'l*, pg. 442

CASTOR 120—Rocket Motors (Class 7)—Thiokol Corporation; *U.S. Public*, pg. 1596

CASTORDAG—Lubricants—Acheson Colloids Company; *U.S. Private*, pg. 12

CASTRO—NONE—Krause's Furniture Inc.; *U.S. Public*, pg. 967

CASTRO CONVERTIBLES—NONE—Krause's Furniture Inc.; *U.S. Public*, pg. 967

CASTROL—Lubricants—Burmah Castrol plc; *Int'l*, pg. 234

CASTROL—Oils—Castrol North America; *Int'l*, pg. 235

CASTROL GTX—NONE—Castrol Canada Inc.; *Int'l*, pg. 235

CASTROL SUPERCLEAN—NONE—Castrol Canada Inc.; *Int'l*, pg. 235

CASTROL SYNTEC—NONE—Castrol Canada Inc.; *Int'l*, pg. 235

CASUAL CHINA BY PFALTZGRAFF—NONE—The Pfaltzgraff Co.; *U.S. Private*, pg. 860

CASUAL CONCEPTS—Wood Residential Furniture—Tandycrafts, Inc.; *U.S. Public*, pg. 1561

CASUAL CORNER—Ladies Apparel Stores—Casual Corner Group Inc.; *U.S. Private*, pg. 219

CASUAL IMAGES BY LENOX—Casual Dinnerware, Glassware, and Stainless Steel—Lenox Brands; *U.S. Private*, pg. 261

CASUALS—Facial Tissue—Kimberly-Clark Corporation; *U.S. Public*, pg. 958

CASWELL/MASSEY—Retail Fragrance Stores—Caswell-Massey Co. Ltd.; *U.S. Private*, pg. 219

CAT—Engine—Buffalo Truck Center; *U.S. Private*, pg. 179

CAT—Machinery—Caterpillar Inc.; *U.S. Public*, pg. 315

CAT-A-PHASE—Chemical reagent—ESA, Inc.; *U.S. Private*, pg. 354

CAT CHOW—Cat Food—Ralston Purina Company; *U.S. Public*, pg. 1359

CAT HOLLOW—Cider—Leonard Kreusch, Inc.; *U.S. Private*, pg. 635

CAT LIFE—Cat Foods—Pet Life Foods, Inc.; *U.S. Private*, pg. 856

CAT-TEX—Soles—American Biltrite Inc.; *U.S. Public*, pg. 68

CAT TRUCK PARTS—Truck Parts—Heintzelman's Truck Center Inc.; *U.S. Private*, pg. 519

CATA-CHEK—Catalysts—Ferro Corporation; *U.S. Public*, pg. 618

CATAFLAM—NONE—Novartis Pharmaceuticals; *Int'l*, pg. 973

CATALINA—Tomato Sauces—Alliant Foodservice, Inc.; *U.S. Private*, pg. 244

CATALINA—Swimwear—Catalina; *U.S. Public*, pg. 148

CATALINA—Cruiser—Chris-Craft Boats; *U.S. Private*, pg. 478

CATALINA—Cushioned Vinyl Floor coverings—Forbo Holding SA; *Int'l*, pg. 496

CATALINA DOUBLE CABIN—Cruiser—Chris-Craft Boats; *U.S. Private*, pg. 478

CATALIST—Business Information Directory—U S West Inc.; *U.S. Public*, pg. 1688

CATALOG—Light Weight Uncoated for Offset & Gravure—Great Northern Paper, Inc.; *U.S. Public*, pg. 248

A CATALOG FOR COOKS—Cookware Catalog—Williams-Sonoma, Inc.; *U.S. Public*, pg. 1770

CATALOG MANAGER FOR DB2—DB2 Database Administration—BMC Software, Inc.; *U.S. Public*, pg. 162

CATALOG SERVICES GROUP—Direct Marketing Services to the Catalog Industry—Metromail Corporation; *U.S. Public*, pg. 1102

CATALYST—Color Composition & Page Layout System—AGFA Division of Bayer Corporation; *Int'l*, pg. 172

CATALYX—Minerals—Feed Service Corp.; *U.S. Private*, pg. 399

CATAMOUNT—Cable Ties—Thomas & Betts Corporation; *U.S. Public*, pg. 1597

CATANIA—Broadloom—Couristan Inc.; *U.S. Private*, pg. 279

CATAPILAR—Earth Moving & Demolition Equipment—Kimmins Corp.; *U.S. Public*, pg. 960

CATAPRES—Antihypertensive Drug—Boehringer Ingelheim GmbH; *Int'l*, pg. 199

CATAPRES—Antihypertensive—Boehringer Ingelheim Pharmaceuticals, Inc.; *Int'l*, pg. 199

CATAPRES TTS—Antihypertensive—Boehringer Ingelheim Pharmaceuticals, Inc.; *Int'l*, pg. 199

CATAPULT—Athletic Shoes—L.A. Gear, Inc.; *U.S. Public*, pg. 969

CATAWBA—Hardboard Siding—Georgia-Pacific Corporation; *U.S. Public*, pg. 735

CATAWBA—Insurance Co.—South Carolina Insurance Company; *U.S. Public*, pg. 1453

CATAWBALITE—Plywood, Lumber, Wood & Wood Fiber Products—Georgia-Pacific Corporation; *U.S. Public*, pg. 735

CATCH—Perfume—Rhone-Poulenc S.A.; *Int'l*, pg. 1108

CATCH—Insecticides—Sara Lee Corporation; *U.S. Public*, pg. 1432

CATCH-ALL—Filter-Drier—Sporlan Valve Company; *U.S. Private*, pg. 1026

CATCH 'N PITCH—Disposable Fly Trap—Security Lawn & Garden Co.; *U.S. Private*, pg. 397

CATCH OF THE DAY—Frozen seafood products—Fishery Products International USA; *Int'l*, pg. 492

CATCH-ALL—Track Mat—Portec Inc., Railway Maintenance Products Div.; *U.S. Public*, pg. 1318

CATELLI—Pasta, Pasta Sauce—Borden Foods Canada; *U.S. Private*, pg. 159

CATELLI—Pasta, Pasta Sauce—Borden, Inc.; *U.S. Private*, pg. 157

CATELLI—Grocery Products—Labatt Brewing Company Limited; *Int'l*, pg. 679

CATER-TIME—Aluminum Foil Trays—Reynolds Metals Company; *U.S. Public*, pg. 1385

CATERA—Luxury Automobile—Cadillac Motor Car Division; *U.S. Public*, pg. 720

CATERAIDES—Insulated Food & Beverage Carriers—Carlisle Food Service Products; *U.S. Public*, pg. 305

CATERBOWL—Salad Packages—Tenneco Specialty Products; *U.S. Public*, pg. 1579

CATERING QUALITY—Food Products—Oscar Mayer Foods Corp.; *U.S. Public*, pg. 1288

CATERPAC—French Fries—McCain Foods Limited; *Int'l*, pg. 850

CATERPILLAR—Earth Moving Machines, Lift Trucks, Engines—Carolina Tractor & Equipment Co.; *U.S. Private*, pg. 214

CATERPILLAR—Machinery—Caterpillar Inc.; *U.S. Public*, pg. 315

CATERPILLAR—Construction Equipment & Industrial Engines—Cleveland Brothers Equipment Co., Inc.; *U.S. Private*, pg. 245

CATERPILLAR—Equipment—Powell Equipment Ltd.; *Int'l*, pg. 1066

CATERWARE—Party Platters—Tenneco Specialty Products; *U.S. Public*, pg. 1579

CATERWEDGE—Party Platters—Tenneco Specialty Products; *U.S. Public*, pg. 1579

CATES—Pickles—Dean Foods Company; *U.S. Public*, pg. 489

CATES—Pickles—Dean Pickle & Specialty Products Co.; *U.S. Public*, pg. 490

CATH-GUIDE—NONE—Hudson, RCI; *U.S. Private*, pg. 546

CATHA-COAT—Ship Coating—Grow Group, Inc.; *Int'l*, pg. 663

CATHA COAT—Ship Coating—ICI Paints; *Int'l*, pg. 664

CATHALOYS—Metal Tubing—Superior Tube Company; *U.S. Private*, pg. 1056

CATHAY PACIFIC—Airline—Swire Pacific Limited; *Int'l*, pg. 1328

CATHCAP—Central Venous Access Catheter—Gish Biomedical, Inc.; *U.S. Public*, pg. 745

CATHIVEX—Filter Unit—Millipore Corporation; *U.S. Public*, pg. 1112

CATHLON IV—I.V. Catheters—Johnson & Johnson Medical, Inc.; *U.S. Public*, pg. 928

CATHOLIC DIGEST—Magazine—Catholic Digest; *U.S. Private*, pg. 220

CATHOLIC DIGEST BOOK CLUB—Book Club—Catholic Digest; *U.S. Private*, pg. 220

CATHTEMP—Medical Catheter with Temperature Sensor—Mallinckrodt Inc.; *U.S. Public*, pg. 1039

CATHY LEE—Mass Merchant Brassieres—Lilyette Brassiere Co.; *U.S. Private*, pg. 697

CATIA—Computer Aided-Design System—Stone & Webster, Incorporated; *U.S. Public*, pg. 1519

CATIPILLAR—Engines & Parts—Great Lakes Peterbilt, GMC; *U.S. Private*, pg. 475

CATNAPPER—Reclining Chairs—Cleveland Chair Company; *U.S. Private*, pg. 579

CATNIC—Steel Linters—Caradon Plc; *Int'l*, pg. 266

CATO—Women's Specialty Apparel Store—The Cato Corporation; *U.S. Public*, pg. 318

CATO FASHIONS—Women's Specialty Apparel Stores—The Cato Corporation; *U.S. Public*, pg. 318

CATO OIL—Lubricants—Fleischli Oil Company, Inc.; *U.S. Private*, pg. 410

CATO PLUS—Women's Specialty Apparel Stores—The Cato Corporation; *U.S. Public*, pg. 318

CATOVEL—Feline Health Products—SmithKline Beecham plc; *Int'l*, pg. 1264

CATS—Sunglasses—Bausch & Lomb Incorporated; *U.S. Public*, pg. 194

CATS—Musical—Really Useful Holdings Limited; *Int'l*, pg. 1089

CAT'S PAW—Heels & Soles—American Biltrite Inc.; *U.S. Public*, pg. 68

CAT'S PAW—Shoe Repair Heels & Soles—The Biltrite Corporation; *U.S. Private*, pg. 144

CAT'S PRIDE—Scoopable Cat Litter—Oil-Dri Corporation of America; *U.S. Public*, pg. 1214

CAT'S PRIDE KAT KIT—Disposable Cat Tray with Cat Litter Inside—Oil-Dri Corporation of America; *U.S. Public*, pg. 1214

CAT'S PRIDE NATURAL—Cat Litter—Oil-Dri Corporation of America; *U.S. Public*, pg. 1214

CAT'S PRIDE PREMIUM—Cat Litter—Oil-Dri Corporation of America; *U.S. Public*, pg. 1214

CATSCAN—Cat Litter—Mars Petfoods (UNISABI); *U.S. Private*, pg. 707

CATSKILL—Plywood, Paneling, Siding, Acoustical & Roofing Tile—Georgia-Pacific Corporation; *U.S. Public*, pg. 735

CATTLE CARE—Solid Cattle Supplement—Feed Service Corp.; *U.S. Private*, pg. 399

CATTLEMASTER—Animal Vaccine—SmithKline Beecham plc; *Int'l*, pg. 1264

CAULK—Dental Supplies—Dentsply International Inc.; *U.S. Public*, pg. 498

CAVABAYA RUM—NONE—Star Industries Inc.; *U.S. Private*, pg. 1034

CAVALCADE—Slide Projectors & Photocopying Apparatus—Eastman Kodak Company; *U.S. Public*, pg. 550

CAVALIER—NONE—Aliments Flamingo; *Int'l*, pg. 57

CAVALIER—Vending Machines—Cavalier Corporation; *U.S. Private*, pg. 220

CAVALIER—Car—Chevrolet Motor Div. General Motors Corp.; *U.S. Public*, pg. 720

CAVALIER—Plywood, Lumber, Wood & Wood Fiber Products—Georgia-Pacific Corporation; *U.S. Public*, pg. 735

CAVALIER—Shoe Polish—Kiwi Brands; *U.S. Public*, pg. 1433

CAVALLINO—Tires—Bridgestone/Firestone, Inc.; *Int'l*, pg. 213

CAVENHAM—FOREST PRODUCTS—Hanson PLC; *Int'l*, pg. 592

CAVITROL—Noise Abatement Valves—Monsanto Company; *U.S. Public*, pg. 1124

CAVITRON—Surgical Equipment—Alcon Laboratories, Inc.; *Int'l*, pg. 916

CAVITRON—Dental Equipment—Dentsply International Inc.; *U.S. Public*, pg. 498

CAVVEV—Fiberglass Yachts—Genmar Holdings, Inc.; *U.S. Private*, pg. 447

CAXTON—Commercial Printers—The Caxton Printers Ltd.; *U.S. Private*, pg. 220

CAYENNE—NONE—G-III Apparel Group, Ltd.; *U.S. Public*, pg. 690

CAYMANA—NONE—Tegner & Son AB; *Int'l*, pg. 412

CD5 PLUS—Drug; Treats Graft-Versus-Host Disease—XOMA Corporation; *U.S. Public*, pg. 1786

CE-RITE—Opthalmic Polish for Glass—Ferro Corporation; *U.S. Public*, pg. 618

CEASE-FIRE—Safety Waste Receptacles—Justrite Manufacturing Company; *U.S. Public*, pg. 617

CECCHI—Imported Brands—Banfi Vintners; *U.S. Private*, pg. 113

CECIL—Robotic System for Servicing Steam Generators in Nuclear Power Plants—Foster-Miller, Inc.; *U.S. Private*, pg. 421

CECIL GEE—NONE—Moss Bros Group PLC; *Int'l*, pg. 895

CECILIA—Health Food Products—Meiji Seika Kaisha, Ltd.; *Int'l*, pg. 855

CECILIA PROTEIN JEUNE—High-Protein Products—Meiji Seika Kaisha, Ltd.; *Int'l*, pg. 855

CECLOR—Oral Antibiotic, Lilly—Eli Lilly and Company; *U.S. Public*, pg. 992

CEDA-TONE—Fiber-Cement Siding—GAF Premium Products, Inc.; *U.S. Private*, pg. 433

CEDAR BREATHER—Wood Shingle—Benjamin Obdyke, Inc.; *U.S. Private*, pg. 810

CEDAR CLASSIC—Oriented Strand Board Cedar Panels—Weyerhaeuser Forest Products Company; *U.S. Public*, pg. 1764

CEDAR CREEK—Vinyl Siding—ABT Building Products Corporation; *Int'l*, pg. 20

CEDAR HEIGHTS—Clay—Resco Products, Inc.; *U.S. Private*, pg. 924

CEDAR HOLLOW—Prefinished Wall Paneling—Georgia-Pacific Corporation; *U.S. Public*, pg. 735

CEDAR IMPRESSIONS—NONE—CertainTeed Corporation; *Int'l*, pg. 1170

CEDAR KING—Writing Instruments—Dixon Ticonderoga Company; *U.S. Public*, pg. 514

CEDAR NATURAL—Writing Instruments—Dixon Ticonderoga Company; *U.S. Public*, pg. 514

CEDAR POINT—Amusement Park—Cedar Fair, L.P.; *U.S. Public*, pg. 319

CEDAR POINT—NONE—Cedar Point; *U.S. Public*, pg. 319

CEDAR REFLECTIONS—NONE—Amerimark Inc.; *U.S. Public*, pg. 1237

CEDAR VALLEY—Cedar Products—Magla Products; *U.S. Private*, pg. 695

CEDARAPIDS—Rock Processing & Road Building Machinery—Cedarapids, Inc.; *U.S. Public*, pg. 1365

CEDARFLAME—Processed Firelogs—Duraflame, Inc.; *U.S. Public*, pg. 348

CEDARLITE—NONE—Monier Inc.; *Int'l*, pg. 1091

CEDATEX—Fiber-Cement Siding—GAF Premium Products, Inc.; *U.S. Private*, pg. 433

CEDEPAL—Surfactant—Stepan Company; *U.S. Public*, pg. 1514

CEDERBERG—Liquour—Distillers Corporation S.A.; *Int'l*, pg. 1129

CEDILANID D—Injection for Heart Failure, Atrial Fibrillation, Atrial Flutter—Sandoz Pharmaceuticals Corp.; *Int'l*, pg. 974

CEDRIC—Car—Nissan Motor Co., Ltd.; *Int'l*, pg. 943

CEDUR—Lipid Lowerer—Boehringer Mannheim GmbH; *Int'l*, pg. 331

CEEGRAPH—Neuro-Diagnostic Data Storage—Bio-Logic Systems Corp.; *U.S. Public*, pg. 230

CEEL-CO—PVC Jacketing & Fitting Covers—Johns Manville Corporation; *U.S. Public*, pg. 927

CEENU—Cancer Therapy—Bristol-Myers Squibb Company; *U.S. Public*, pg. 253

CEENU—Oral Anti-Neoplastic Agent for Treatment of Brain Tumors, Hodgkin's Disease—Bristol-Myers Squibb U.S. Pharmaceutical Group; *U.S. Public*, pg. 255

CEFACLOR—Generic Drug—American Home Products Corporation; *U.S. Public*, pg. 79

CEFADYL—Injectable Cephalosporins—Bristol-Myers Squibb Company; *U.S. Public*, pg. 253

CEFANEX—Infectious Disease Therapy Product—Bristol-Myers Squibb Company; *U.S. Public*, pg. 253

CEFAPEROS—Infectious Disease Therapy Product—Bristol-Myers Squibb Company; *U.S. Public*, pg. 253

CEFEPIME—Antibiotic—Bristol-Myers Squibb Company; *U.S. Public*, pg. 253

CEFIR—High Temp Wire—Thermo Electric Co., Inc.; *U.S. Private*, pg. 1080

CEFIRO—Car—Nissan Motor Co., Ltd.; *Int'l*, pg. 943

CEFIZOX—Pharmaceutical Preparations—Fujisawa U.S.A. Inc.; *Int'l*, pg. 525

CEFIZOX—Anti-Infective—SmithKline Beecham plc; *Int'l*, pg. 1264

CEFOBID—Cefoperazone—Pfizer Inc.; *U.S. Public*, pg. 1281

CEFTIN—Antibiotic—Glaxo Wellcome Inc.; *Int'l*, pg. 552

CEFZIL—Infectious Disease Therapy—Bristol-Myers Squibb Company; *U.S. Public*, pg. 253

CEILCOTE—Corrosion Control—Master Builders Inc.; *Int'l*, pg. 1465

CELANESE NYLON—Polyamide—Hoechst Aktiengesellschaft; *Int'l*, pg. 624

CELANEX—Thermoplastic Polyester/PBT—Hoechst Aktiengesellschaft; *Int'l*, pg. 624

CELBENIN—Antibiotic—SmithKline Beecham plc; *Int'l*, pg. 1264

CELDEK—Regrigerator Panel—Incentive AB; *Int'l*, pg. 666

CELEBRATION—Almonds—Blue Diamond Growers; *U.S. Public*, pg. 152

CELEBRATION—Sherry—Domecq Importers Inc.; *Int'l*, pg. 63

CELEBRATION—Paper Placemats in Bulk—Erving Industries, Inc.; *U.S. Private*, pg. 382

CELEBRATION—NONE—USG Corporation; *U.S. Public*, pg. 1660

CELEBRATION CAKES—Ice Cream Cake Combo—Baskin-Robbins Incorporated; *Int'l*, pg. 63

CELEBRATION EDITION—Whisky—Dunhill Scotch Whisky Sales Limited; *Int'l*, pg. 409

CELEBRATIONS—Luggage—American Tourister, Inc.; *U.S. Public*, pg. 1430

CELEBRATIONS—Particleboard—Georgia-Pacific Corporation; *U.S. Public*, pg. 735

CELEBRATIONS OF FAITH—Greeting Cards—American Greetings Corporation; *U.S. Public*, pg. 77

CELEBRITY—Canned Meats & Tuna—Atalanta Corporation; *U.S. Private*, pg. 93

CELEBRITY—Sink—Elkay Manufacturing Company; *U.S. Private*, pg. 372

CELEBRITY—High Chair—Evenflo Company, Inc.; *U.S. Private*, pg. 629

CELEBRITY—Telephones—Lucent Technologies Inc.; *U.S. Public*, pg. 1017

CELEBRITY—Home Health Care Scooter—Pride Health Care, Inc.; *U.S. Private*, pg. 883

CELEBRITY—Wood Director Chair—Telescope Casual Furniture, Inc.; *U.S. Private*, pg. 1074

CELEBRITY—Canned Meats—Vestjyske Slagterier; *Int'l*, pg. 1464

CELEBRITY—Printing Paper—Westvaco Corporation; *U.S. Public*, pg. 1762

CELEBRITY CONNECTION—Entertainment News Programming—Westwood One, Inc.; *U.S. Public*, pg. 1763

CELEBRITY DESIGNS—NONE—Celebrity Incorporated; *U.S. Public*, pg. 319

CELEBRITY SILK—NONE—Celebrity Incorporated; *U.S. Public*, pg. 319

CELENTANO BROTHERS—Frozen Foods—Celentano Bros. Inc.; *U.S. Private*, pg. 221

CELESCO—Smoke Meters—Telonic Berkeley, Inc.; *U.S. Private*, pg. 1074

CELESTA—Printing Paper—Westvaco Corporation; *U.S. Public*, pg. 1762

CELESTE FROZEN PIZZA—Frozen Pizza—The Quaker Oats Company; *U.S. Public*, pg. 1347

CELESTIAL—Inlaid Sheet Vinyl Flooring—Congoleum Corporation; *U.S. Public*, pg. 69

CELESTIAL SEASONINGS SOOTHERS—Cough Drop—Adams U.S.A.; *U.S. Public*, pg. 1739

CELESTONE—Anti-Arthritic Injection—Schering-Plough Corporation; *U.S. Public*, pg. 1438

CELESTRIUM—Jeweler's Alloy—L.G. Balfour Co., Inc.; *U.S. Private*, pg. 258

CELICA—Passenger Cars—Toyota Motor Corporation; *Int'l*, pg. 1411

CELICA—Car—Toyota Motor Sales, U.S.A., Inc.; *Int'l*, pg. 1412

CELL-AIRE—Polyethylene Foam—Sealed Air Corporation; *U.S. Public*, pg. 1450

CELL ENERGIZING COMPLEX—Cosmetics—Almay, Inc.; *U.S. Private*, pg. 689

CELL ENSEMBLE—Cell-Based Routing—Cadence Design Systems, Inc.; *U.S. Public*, pg. 290

CELL GUARD—Monitors Power & Vswr. in Cell Sites—L3 Communications Narda-Microwave Div.; *U.S. Private*, pg. 638

CELL-PORATOR—NONE—Life Technologies, Inc.; *U.S. Public*, pg. 504

CELL-TECH—Liquid Inoculant for Soybeans—LiphaTech, Inc.; *Int'l*, pg. 812

CELL-U-LOSS—Herbal Vitamin Tablets—Herbalife International of America, Inc.; *U.S. Public*, pg. 809

CELL-U-WELD—Vinyl Tabs—Smead Manufacturing Company; *U.S. Private*, pg. 1006

CELLA'S—Chocolate Covered Cherries—Tootsie Roll Industries, Inc.; *U.S. Public*, pg. 1621

CELLATE—NONE—Avenor, Inc.; *Int'l*, pg. 101

CELLCEPT—Immunosuppressant Agent—Roche Holding Ltd.; *Int'l*, pg. 1119

CELLDAX—NONE—Premisys Communications, Inc.; *U.S. Public*, pg. 1323

CELLFECTIN—NONE—Life Technologies, Inc.; *U.S. Public*, pg. 504

CELLIGEN PLUS—Cell Culture Bioreactor—New Brunswick Scientific Co., Inc.; *U.S. Public*, pg. 1169

CELLINE—Physiological Saline—Fisher Scientific Company; *U.S. Private*, pg. 658

CELLINI—Fine Watches—Rolex Watch Co. SA; *Int'l*, pg. 1126

CELLINI—Watches—Rolex Watch U.S.A., Inc.; *Int'l*, pg. 1126

CELLINK—Tower Mounted Amplifier—Allen Telecom Inc.; *U.S. Public*, pg. 45

CELLITON—Dyes for Polyester & Cellulose Acetate Fibers—BASF AG; *Int'l*, pg. 103

CELLLINK—Cell Control Software—Square D Automation Products; *Int'l*, pg. 1208

CELLMORE—Polyvinylidene Chloride Expandable Beads—Asahi Chemical Industry Co., Ltd.; *Int'l*, pg. 83

CELLO—NONE—Cleaning Solutions Group/Cello; *U.S. Public*, pg. 1466

CELLO-SEAL—Stapcock Grease—Fisher Scientific Company; *U.S. Private*, pg. 658

CELLOLYN—Synthetic Resin—Hercules Incorporated; *U.S. Public*, pg. 809

CELLOSOLVE—Solvents—Union Carbide Corporation; *U.S. Public*, pg. 1666

CELLSTAR—Terminal—Harris Corp., RF Communications Group Marketing Division; *U.S. Public*, pg. 792

CELLU-TONE—Paints—Pratt & Lambert United, Inc.; *U.S. Public*, pg. 1466

CELLUCOTTON—Beauty Coil—Kimberly-Clark Corporation; *U.S. Public*, pg. 958

CELLULAR & MOBILE INTERNATIONAL—Publication for International Industry—Intertec Publishing; *U.S. Public*, pg. 1327

CELLULAR BUSINESS—News Coverage of Cellular Radio Telephone Industry—Intertec Publishing; *U.S. Public*, pg. 1327

CELLULAR INFORMATION NETWORK—Information Source for Cellular Phone Users—Brite Voice Systems, Inc.; *U.S. Public*, pg. 257

CELLULAR INTEGRATION—NONE—Intertec Publishing; *U.S. Public*, pg. 1328

CELLULAR NUTRITION—Nutritional Program—Herbalife International of America, Inc.; *U.S. Public*, pg. 809

CELLULAR ONE—Cellular Installation & Service—AT&T Wireless Services; *U.S. Public*, pg. 11

CELLULAR ONE—Cellular Telephone—Vanguard Cellular Systems, Inc.; *U.S. Public*, pg. 1707

CELLULAR TESTED—Pacemaker—St. Jude Medical, Inc.; *U.S. Public*, pg. 1427

CELLUTENNA—Cellular Antenna Systems/Equipment—Recoton Corporation; *U.S. Public*, pg. 1369

CELLUVISC—Lubricant Opthalmic Solution—Allergan, Inc.; *U.S. Public*, pg. 46

CELODON CERAMIC SLATE—Roofing—CertainTeed Corporation; *Int'l*, pg. 1170

CELOGEN—Specialty Rubber & Chemical—Uniroyal Chemical Company, Inc.; *U.S. Public*, pg. 460

CELOTEX—Building Materials—Celotex Corporation; *U.S. Private*, pg. 221

CELSENE—Shampoo—L'Oreal S.A.; *Int'l*, pg. 818

CELSTIR—Scientific Glassware for Laboratory Use—Wheaton Inc.; *Int'l*, pg. 67

CELTECT—Antiallergic Agents—Kyowa Hakko Kogyo Company, Ltd.; *Int'l*, pg. 778

CELULON—Adhesive Sealant—Red Devil Inc.; *U.S. Private*, pg. 915

CEMAC—Office Partitions—Carter Holt Harvey Limited; *U.S. Public*, pg. 904

CEMENTHIDE—Paint Coating for Concrete, Brick, Cement & Stucco—PPG Industries, Inc.; *U.S. Public*, pg. 1245

CEMENTO PONCE—Cement Product—Puerto Rican Cement Co., Inc.; *U.S. Public*, pg. 1341

CEMENTONE—Clear Sealer—L.M. Scofield Company; *U.S. Private*, pg. 976

CEMENTSTIK—Cement—Fisher Scientific Company; *U.S. Private*, pg. 658

CEMOS—Enhanced CMOS—Integrated Device Technology, Inc.; *U.S. Public*, pg. 884

CENCARE—Auto Service—Cenex/Land O'Lakes, Inc.; *U.S. Private*, pg. 222

CENEX—Products—CENEX, Inc.; *U.S. Private*, pg. 221

CENEX—Agri Supplies—Cenex/Land O'Lakes, Inc.; *U.S. Private*, pg. 222

CENPRO 70—Soy Protein Concentrate—Central Soya Company, Inc.; *Int'l*, pg. 324

CENSYS—Programmer—Medtronic, Inc.; *U.S. Public*, pg. 1082

CENTA-FORM—Grinder—Bryant Grinder Corp.; *U.S. Private*, pg. 461

CENTAC—Air Compressors—Ingersoll-Rand Company; *U.S. Public*, pg. 876

CENTAFLEX—Power Transmission—Lovejoy Inc.; *U.S. Private*, pg. 677

CENTALIGN—Grinder—Bryant Grinder Corp.; *U.S. Private*, pg. 461

CENTAP—Anodes—Corrpro Companies, Inc.; *U.S. Public*, pg. 451

CENTAUR—Turbine Products—Solar Turbines Incorporated; *U.S. Public*, pg. 316

CENTAURI—Broadloom—Couristan Inc.; *U.S. Private*, pg. 279

CENTEIPAN—Bakery Ingredient—Royal Gist-Brocades N.V.; *Int'l*, pg. 1142

CENTENARY CASKS—Whisky—Dunhill Scotch Whisky Sales Limited; *Int'l*, pg. 409

CENTENIAL BODY—NONE—Union City Body Company, L.P.; *U.S. Private*, pg. 1118

CENTENNIAL—Flour—ADM Milling Co.; *U.S. Public*, pg. 128

CENTENNIAL—Tires—Dunlop Tire Corporation; *Int'l*, pg. 1317

CENTENNIAL—Book Cloth—Industrial Coatings Group, Inc.; *U.S. Private*, pg. 434

CENTENNIAL—Tires—Midwest Tire & Muffler, Inc.; *U.S. Private*, pg. 745

CENTENNIAL LAGER—Premium Beer—The Lion Brewery, Inc.; *U.S. Public*, pg. 1000

CENTENNIEL PLANK FLEXWOOD—Wood & Lumber Products—Georgia-Pacific Corporation; *U.S. Public*, pg. 735

CENTENNIEL 2—Plywood, Lumber, Wood & Wood Fiber Products—Georgia-Pacific Corporation; *U.S. Public*, pg. 735

CENTER FLOW—Covered Hopper Car—ACF Industries, Inc.; *U.S. Private*, pg. 556

CENTER-LOCK—Powered Pipe Threaders—Emerson Electric Co.; *U.S. Public*, pg. 572

CENTER PARCS—Holiday Villages—Scottish & Newcastle plc; *Int'l*, pg. 1211

CENTER SIMMER—Top Burner Control—Harper-Wyman Co.; *U.S. Private*, pg. 1209

CENTER STAGE—NONE—Cambridge Soundworks, Inc.; *U.S. Private*, pg. 202

CENTER STAGE BY HENRY KLOSS—NONE—Cambridge Soundworks, Inc.; *U.S. Private*, pg. 202

CENTERLINE—Motor Control Centers—Rockwell International Corporation; *U.S. Public*, pg. 1397

CENTERMARK—Peripherally Inserted Central Catheters—Johnson & Johnson Medical, Inc.; *U.S. Public*, pg. 928

CENTEX—Homes—Centex Corporation; *U.S. Public*, pg. 322

CENTEX—Soy Protein—Central Soya Company, Inc.; *Int'l*, pg. 324

CENTI-SPLINE—Combination Lock—Sargent & Greenleaf, Inc.; *U.S. Private*, pg. 965

CENTIGRAM—NONE—Centigram Communications Corporation; *U.S. Public*, pg. 323

CENTINE ROSSO DI MONTALCINO—Red Wine—Banfi Vintners; *U.S. Private*, pg. 113

CENTINE ROSSO DI MONTALCINO—NONE—Castello Banfi Srl.; *U.S. Private*, pg. 113

CENTNF—Treatment for Rheumatoid Arthritis & Inflammatory Bowel Disease—Centocor, Inc.; *U.S. Public*, pg. 323

CENTOSTAR—Textile Floorcoverings—Forbo Holding SA; *Int'l*, pg. 496

CENTRA—Private Label Merchandise—Patterson Dental Company; *U.S. Public*, pg. 1265

CENTRAC HPF—NONE—Portec Inc., Railway Maintenance Products Div.; *U.S. Public*, pg. 1318

CENTRAC LCF—NONE—Portec Inc., Railway Maintenance Products Div.; *U.S. Public*, pg. 1318

CENTRAC VHPF—NONE—Portec Inc., Railway Maintenance Products Div.; *U.S. Public*, pg. 1318

CENTRACODE—Communication Systems—General Railway Signal Corp.; *Int'l*, pg. 1194

CENTRACOTE—Vegetable Oil—Central Soya Company, Inc.; *Int'l*, pg. 324

CENTRACREME—Vegetable Oil—Central Soya Company, Inc.; *Int'l*, pg. 324

CENTRAFRY—Vegetable Oil—Central Soya Company, Inc.; *Int'l*, pg. 324

CENTRAL—Soybean Meal—Central Soya Company, Inc.; *Int'l*, pg. 324

CENTRAL—Sprinkler System—Central Sprinkler Corporation; *U.S. Public*, pg. 327

CENTRAL AMERICA—War Game—Monarch Avalon, Inc.; *U.S. Public*, pg. 1123

CENTRAL GULF LINES, INC.—Deep Sea Shipping & Cargo Transportation Services—Central Gulf Lines, Inc.; *U.S. Public*, pg. 907

CENTRAL HUDSON—Your Energy Solutions Company—Central Hudson Gas & Electric Corporation; *U.S. Public*, pg. 324

CENTRAL INSURANCE COMPANIES—Mutual Insurance—Central Mutual Insurance Co.; *U.S. Private*, pg. 223

CENTRAL LIFE—Insurance Services—American Mutual Life Holding Co.; *U.S. Private*, pg. 59

CENTRAL VERMONT RAILWAY—Freight Railroads—Grand Trunk Corporation (GTC); *Int'l*, pg. 258

CENTRAMA M PLUS—Medical Call Center Software—National Health Enhancement Systems, Inc.; *U.S. Public*, pg. 1157

CENTRAMATIC 52—Laundry Liquid Dispenser—Ecolab Inc.; *U.S. Public*, pg. 562

CENTRAMAX—Marketing Management Software—National Health Enhancement Systems, Inc.; *U.S. Public*, pg. 1157

CENTRASCAN—Building Monitoring System—ADT Security Services, Inc.; *U.S. Public*, pg. 1649

CENTRASOY—Vegetable Oil—Central Soya Company, Inc.; *Int'l*, pg. 324

CENTRAX—Pharmaceutical Products—Warner-Lambert Company; *U.S. Public*, pg. 1738

CENTREFUSE—Butt Fusion Machines—T.D. Williamson, Inc.; *U.S. Private*, pg. 1179

CENTREX—Central Office Computer Based Tele Communications—Ameritech Phone Company; *U.S. Public*, pg. 98

CENTREX—Weatherable Polymer—Monsanto Company; *U.S. Public*, pg. 1124

CENTREX—Centrfugal Filter—Schleicher & Schuell, Inc.; *Int'l*, pg. 1206

CENTREX—Weatherable Polymer—Solutia Inc.; *U.S. Public*, pg. 1483

CENTRICON—Microconcentrators—Amicon, Inc.; *U.S. Public*, pg. 1113

CENTRIFEED—Mail Orienting Machine—Pitney Bowes Inc.; *U.S. Public*, pg. 1303

CENTRIFIC—Centrifuges—Fisher Scientific Company; *U.S. Private*, pg. 658

CENTRIFLO—Membrane Cones—Amicon, Inc.; *U.S. Public*, pg. 1113

CENTRIFREE—Micropartition System—Amicon, Inc.; *U.S. Public*, pg. 1113

CENTRILINE—Electric Power Cable for Petroleum & Water Industry—Centrilift; *U.S. Public*, pg. 167

CENTRIPREP—Concentration System—Amicon, Inc.; *U.S. Public*, pg. 1113

CENTRISEP—Air Cleaners—Pall Corporation; *U.S. Public*, pg. 1253

CENTRIX—X-Ray—Picker International, Inc.; *Int'l*, pg. 545

CENTROCAP—Lecithins—Central Soya Company, Inc.; *Int'l*, pg. 324

CENTROL—Crop Consulting—CENEX, Inc.; *U.S. Private*, pg. 221

CENTROL—Lecithin—Central Soya Company, Inc.; *Int'l*, pg. 324

CENTROLENE—Lecithins—Central Soya Company, Inc.; *Int'l*, pg. 324

CENTROLEX—Lecithin—Central Soya Company, Inc.; *Int'l*, pg. 324

CENTROMATIC—Automatic Lubrication Equipment for Industry—Lincoln Industrial; *U.S. Public*, pg. 1273

CENTROMIX—Lecithins—Central Soya Company, Inc.; *Int'l*, pg. 324

CENTRONICS—NONE—Genicom Corporation; *U.S. Public*, pg. 729

CENTROPHASE—Lecithins—Central Soya Company, Inc.; *Int'l*, pg. 324

CENTROPHIL—Lecithins—Central Soya Company, Inc.; *Int'l*, pg. 324

CENTRUM—Vitamin & Mineral Supplement—American Home Products Corporation; *U.S. Public*, pg. 79

CENTRUM—Theatre Seating—American Seating Company; *U.S. Private*, pg. 61

CENTRUM—Vitamin and Mineral Supplement—Whitehall-Robins Healthcare; *U.S. Public*, pg. 80

CENTRUM JR.—Vitamin & Mineral Supplement—American Home Products Corporation; *U.S. Public*, pg. 79

CENTRUM JR.—Vitamin & Mineral Supplement—Whitehall-Robins Healthcare; *U.S. Public*, pg. 80

CENTRUM SILVER—Vitamin & Mineral Supplement—American Home Products Corporation; *U.S. Public*, pg. 79

CENTRUM SILVER—Vitamin & Mineral Supplement—Whitehall-Robins Healthcare; *U.S. Public*, pg. 80

CENTRY—Dialysis System—COBE Laboratories, Inc.; *Int'l*, pg. 667

CENTRY—Patio Doors—Morgan Products Ltd.; *U.S. Public*, pg. 1132

CENTRYSYSTEM 3—Dialysis System—COBE Laboratories, Inc.; *Int'l*, pg. 667

CENTURA—Enamel Printing Paper—Consolidated Papers, Inc.; *U.S. Public*, pg. 436

CENTURA—Actuators—Flowserve Corporation; *U.S. Public*, pg. 658

CENTURION—Goggles—Aearo Company; *U.S. Private*, pg. 23

CENTURION—Alfalfa Seed—Agway, Inc.; *U.S. Private*, pg. 27

CENTURION—NONE—American Express Company; *U.S. Public*, pg. 73

CENTURION—Rubber Roll Coverings—Samuel Bingham Co; *U.S. Private*, pg. 144

CENTURION—Carrier Chassis—Crane Carrier Company; *U.S. Private*, pg. 286

CENTURION—Hard Burned Brick—A.P. Green Industries, Inc.; *U.S. Public*, pg. 761

CENTURION—Commercial Cookware—Lincoln Foodservice Products, Inc.; *Int'l*, pg. 188

CENTURION—Motors—MagneTek, Inc.; *U.S. Public*, pg. 1037

CENTURION—Switchless Motors—Magnetek Motors & Generators; *U.S. Public*, pg. 1037

CENTURION—Smoke Detectors—Sunbeam Household Products; *U.S. Public*, pg. 1533

CENTURY—Canopy—Anchor Industries Inc.; *U.S. Private*, pg. 71

CENTURY—Automobile—Buick Motor Div. General Motors Corp.; *U.S. Public*, pg. 720

CENTURY—Children's Products & Toys—Century Products Co.; *U.S. Private*, pg. 226

CENTURY—Carrier Chassis—Crane Carrier Company; *U.S. Private*, pg. 286

CENTURY—Gold-Filled Pens & Pencils—A.T. Cross Co.; *U.S. Public*, pg. 460

CENTURY—NONE—Fuchs Lubricants, Midlantic Div.; *Int'l*, pg. 518

CENTURY—Waterproof Footwear—The Gates Rubber Company Ltd.; *Int'l*, pg. 1397

CENTURY—Air Conditioning & Heating Equipment—Heat Controller, Inc.; *U.S. Private*, pg. 518

CENTURY—Farm Chemical Sprayers—Hiniker Company; *U.S. Private*, pg. 530

CENTURY—NONE—Imperial Schrade Corp.; *U.S. Private*, pg. 559

CENTURY—Motors—MagneTek, Inc.; *U.S. Public*, pg. 1037

CENTURY—Motors—Magnetek Motors & Generators; *U.S. Public*, pg. 1037

CENTURY—B/O Compressor—Norwalk Co., Inc.; *U.S. Private*, pg. 807

CENTURY—Cigarettes—RJR Nabisco Holdings Corp.; *U.S. Public*, pg. 1354

CENTURY—25's, Lights, Filter 100's, Lights 100's Reg. & Menthol Cigarettes—R.J. Reynolds Tobacco Company; *U.S. Public*, pg. 1355

CENTURY—Automotive Batteries—Sime Darby Berhad; *Int'l*, pg. 1249

CENTURY—Boilers—H.B. Smith Co., Inc.; *U.S. Private*, pg. 1008

CENTURY AUTOMATIC DONUT SYSTEM—Bakery Equipment—Belshaw Brothers, Inc.; *Int'l*, pg. 188

CENTURY FENCE—Chain Link Fence—Century Fence Company; *U.S. Private*, pg. 226

CENTURY PLASTICS—NONE—Ingrid Division of Lawnware; *U.S. Private*, pg. 654

CENTURY 21—Real Estate Sales—Century 21 Real Estate Corp.; *U.S. Public*, pg. 321

CENTURY 21—Real Estate Franchise—HFS, Incorporated; *U.S. Public*, pg. 321

CENTURY II—Carpet Sweeper—Bissell Inc.; *U.S. Private*, pg. 145

CENTURY XL END MILLS—Rex 20 End Mills—Regal-Beloit Corporation; *U.S. Public*, pg. 1370

CENTURY YEARBOOKS—Magazines—Century Publishing Company; *U.S. Private*, pg. 226

CENTURY 21—NONE—Century 21 Agmont Real Estate, Inc.; *U.S. Private*, pg. 226

CENTURYDRAIN—Roofing & Siding—Wheeling Corrugating Co.; *U.S. Public*, pg. 1727

CEO CONNECTION—Communications Software—Data General Corporation; *U.S. Public*, pg. 485

CEOSUNIN—Anthelmintics—Kyowa Hakko Kogyo Company, Ltd.; *Int'l*, pg. 778

CEOWRITE—Word Processing Software—Data General Corporation; *U.S. Public*, pg. 485

CEPASTAT—Throat Lozenges—SmithKline Beecham Consumer Healthcare, U.S.; *Int'l*, pg. 1264

CEPHULAC—Treatment of Hepatic Coma—Hoechst Marion Roussel North America; *Int'l*, pg. 625

CEPITA—Fruit Juices—Penaflor S.A.; *Int'l*, pg. 1032

CEPSA—NONE—Compania Espanola de Petroleos, S.A. (CEPSA); *Int'l*, pg. 323

CER-VIEW—Gynecological Device—The Cooper Companies, Inc.; *U.S. Public*, pg. 442

CERA LIU—Shoe Polishes/Waxes—Benckiser Consumer Products Inc.; *Int'l*, pg. 185

CERABLANKET—NONE—Thermal Ceramics Inc.; *Int'l*, pg. 894

CERADOT—Electronic Circuit Components—CTS Corporation; *U.S. Public*, pg. 285

CERAFELT—NONE—Thermal Ceramics Inc.; *Int'l*, pg. 894

CERAFIL—NONE—Murata Manufacturing Co., Ltd.; *Int'l*, pg. 897

CERAFLEX—Exhaust System—Johns Manville Corporation; *U.S. Public*, pg. 927

CERAFLO—Microfilters—Norton Company; *Int'l*, pg. 1173

CERALAM—Ceramic Capacitors—AVX Corporation; *Int'l*, pg. 775

CERALENE-RAYNAUD—China—Baccarat (Cie des Cristalleries); *Int'l*, pg. 132

CERAM-A-SHIELD—Coil Coating System For Metal Bldg. Prods.—Akzo Nobel Coatings Inc. (KY); *Int'l*, pg. 47

CERAM-A-SIL—Coil Coating System For Metal Bldg. Prods.—Akzo Nobel Coatings Inc. (KY); *Int'l*, pg. 47

CERAM CORE—Abrasive Resistant Fiber Glass Reinforced Plastic—A.O. Smith Corporation; *U.S. Public*, pg. 1476

CERAM-GUARD—Heat Treating Coatings—A.O. Smith Corporation; *U.S. Public*, pg. 1476

CERAM-SPUN—Steel Tubing—American Cast Iron Pipe Co.; *U.S. Public*, pg. 51

CERAM-TUFF—Protective Coatings—A.O. Smith Corporation; *U.S. Public*, pg. 1476

CERAMCO—Dental Porcelain—Dentsply International Inc.; *U.S. Public*, pg. 498

CERAMCO—Polycarboxylate Cement—Johnson & Johnson Consumer Products; *U.S. Public*, pg. 928

CERAMIC—Cooling Towers—Justin Industries, Inc.; *U.S. Public*, pg. 936

CERAMIC MOSAICS—Interior and Exterior Wall & Flooring—Monarch Tile, Inc.; *U.S. Private*, pg. 287

CERAMIC ON STEEL—Cookware—General Housewares Corp.; *U.S. Public*, pg. 715

CERAMICA DOLOMITE—Bathroom Prods.—Blue Circle Industries PLC; *Int'l*, pg. 197

CERAMICRON—Pens—Pentel of America, Ltd.; *Int'l*, pg. 1035

CERAMIDE CREAM—NONE—Elizabeth Arden Company; *Int'l*, pg. 1435

CERAMITE—NONE—Elkem ASA; *Int'l*, pg. 446

CERAMO—Thermocouple—Thermo Electric Co., Inc.; *U.S. Private*, pg. 1080

CERAMVAR—NONE—Carpenter Technology Corporation; *U.S. Public*, pg. 307

CERAN—Glass-Ceramic Cooking Services—Schott Glaswerke; *Int'l*, pg. 1523

CERANEICLES—Skin Care—Elizabeth Arden Company; *Int'l*, pg. 1435

CERANINE—Textile Finishing Processing—Clariant International Ltd.; *Int'l*, pg. 624

CERAPHYL—Emollients—International Specialty Products, Inc.; *U.S. Public*, pg. 858

CERASURF—Ceramic Brick—Coors Ceramics Company; *U.S. Public*, pg. 3

CERASYNT—Emulsifiers—International Specialty Products, Inc.; *U.S. Public*, pg. 858

CERATREX—Controlled Porasity Ceramics—Osmonics, Inc.; *U.S. Public*, pg. 1233

CERATRIM—Resistors & Capacitors—CTS Corporation; *U.S. Public*, pg. 285

CERATROLS—Potentiometers—CTS Corporation; *U.S. Public*, pg. 285

CERAVAM—Ceramic Brick for Lining Pulverizers & Coal Feed Pipe, Burners—Babcock & Wilcox Co.; *U.S. Public*, pg. 1068

CERCOFORM—Ceremic Material—Flowserve Corporation; *U.S. Public*, pg. 658

CERDIP—Electronics—Kyocera Corporation; *Int'l*, pg. 775

CEREAL—Dietetic—Novartis AG; *Int'l*, pg. 971

CEREBOS—Table Salt—Ranks Hovis McDougall Limited; *Int'l*, pg. 1395

CEREC—Medical Device—Siemens Corporation; *Int'l*, pg. 1245

CEREDASE—Alglucerase Injection—Genzyme Corporation; *U.S. Public*, pg. 733

CERELAC—Infant Cereal—Nestle S.A.; *Int'l*, pg. 915

CERES—Enzyne Deactivated Grain & Flour—King Milling Company; *U.S. Private*, pg. 625

CERESOTA—Unbleached Naturally White Flour—The Uhlmann Co.; *U.S. Private*, pg. 1115

CERESOY—Soya Based Specialties—Nestle S.A.; *Int'l*, pg. 915

CERESPAN—Pharmaceuticals—Rhone-Poulenc Rorer - U.S.; *Int'l*, pg. 1110

CERESTORE—All Ceramic Crown—Johnson & Johnson Consumer Products; *U.S. Public*, pg. 928

CERETEC—Kit for Tc 99m Exametazime—Amersham Corporation; *U.S. Public*, pg. 992

CERGAL—Beer—Central de Cervejas, S.A.; *Int'l*, pg. 279

CERGO—Corporate I.D.—Certified Grocers of California; *U.S. Private*, pg. 226

CERISE—Cherries—Curtice Burns Foods; *U.S. Private*, pg. 887

CERLOX—Plastic Binding—General Binding Corporation; *U.S. Public*, pg. 707

CERMALUX—High Pressure Sodium Lighting—Philips Electronics N.V.; *Int'l*, pg. 1051

Brand Name Index

CERMAX—Lamp for Medical Endoscope & other Instruments—ILC Technology, Inc.; *U.S. Public*, pg. 856

CERNATE—Porcelain—Den-Mat Corporation; *U.S. Private*, pg. 324

CERNER COMMAND LANGUAGE—Ad Hoc Query Language—Cerner Corporation; *U.S. Public*, pg. 331

CEROCRAL—Cerebral Vasodilator—Hoechst Marion Roussel North America; *Int'l*, pg. 625

CEROX—NONE—Thermal Ceramics Inc.; *Int'l*, pg. 894

CERRUTI 1881—Fragrance—Elizabeth Arden Company; *Int'l*, pg. 1435

CERTA-EDGE—NONE—CertainTeed Corporation; *Int'l*, pg. 1170

CERTA FOIL—Insulation Cellular Plastic Board-Fal-Faced—CertainTeed Corporation; *Int'l*, pg. 1170

CERTA-SPACER—Band—CertainTeed Corporation; *Int'l*, pg. 1170

CERTA-SET—Irrigation Pipe—CertainTeed Corporation; *Int'l*, pg. 1170

CERTAFLEX—Insulated Flexible Duct—CertainTeed Corporation; *Int'l*, pg. 1170

CERTAGLASS—NONE—CertainTeed Corporation; *Int'l*, pg. 1170

CERTAIN—Bathroom Tissue—The Procter & Gamble Company; *U.S. Public*, pg. 1330

CERTAIN-TEED—NONE—CertainTeed Corporation; *Int'l*, pg. 1170

CERTALOK—Joining System—CertainTeed Corporation; *Int'l*, pg. 1170

CERTAN—Insecticide for Control of the Cibex Moth—Novartis AG; *Int'l*, pg. 971

CERTASPRAY—NONE—CertainTeed Corporation; *Int'l*, pg. 1170

CERTAVENT—Perforated Vinyl Soffit—CertainTeed Corporation; *Int'l*, pg. 1170

CERTAVIN—PVC Resin—CertainTeed Corporation; *Int'l*, pg. 1170

CERTAWRAP—Insulation-Cellular Plastic Board—CertainTeed Corporation; *Int'l*, pg. 1170

CERTI-LITE—Lighting Fixtures—Killark Electric Manufacturing Co.; *U.S. Public*, pg. 844

CERTICARE—Auto Repair Services—Amoco Corporation; *U.S. Public*, pg. 101

CERTIDUCT—NONE—Nordyne Inc.; *U.S. Public*, pg. 1193

CERTIFICATE—Fine Printing—Eastern Fine Paper; *U.S. Private*, pg. 357

CERTIFIED—Grill Parts & Accessories—W.C. Bradley Co.; *U.S. Private*, pg. 164

CERTIFIED—Generic Food Products—Certified Grocers of California; *U.S. Private*, pg. 226

CERTIFIED—Food Colors—McCormick Flavor Division-U.S.A.; *U.S. Public*, pg. 1066

CERTIFIED HARVEST KING—Agricultural Chemicals—IMC Agribusiness; *U.S. Public*, pg. 856

CERTIFIED NETWORK EXPERT (CNX)—Network Analyzing & Monitoring Software & Hardware—Network Associates, Inc.; *U.S. Public*, pg. 1168

CERTIFIED PERFECT—Jewelry—Helzberg's Diamond Shops, Inc.; *U.S. Public*, pg. 220

CERTIFIED RED LABEL—Food Products—Certified Grocers Midwest, Inc.; *U.S. Private*, pg. 226

CERTIFIER—Air Velocity Calibrator—TSI Incorporated; *U.S. Public*, pg. 1559

CERTIGARD—Car Care Franchise—Petro-Canada; *Int'l*, pg. 1041

CERTIMESH—Porous Metals—Pall Corporation; *U.S. Public*, pg. 1253

CERTINA—Watches—SMH Swiss Corporation for Micro Electronics & Watchmaking Indus. Ltd.; *Int'l*, pg. 1160

CERTINA—Hygiene Products—VP-Schickedanz AG; *U.S. Public*, pg. 1333

CERTITEST—Automated Filter Testers—TSI Incorporated; *U.S. Public*, pg. 1559

CERTO—Fruit Pectin—Kraft Foods, Inc.; *U.S. Public*, pg. 1287

CERTROCK—Gypsum Plaster—Georgia-Pacific Corporation; *U.S. Public*, pg. 735

CERTS—Breath Mints—Adams U.S.A.; *U.S. Public*, pg. 1739

CERTS—Mints—Warner-Lambert Company; *U.S. Public*, pg. 1738

CERUBIDINE—Anticancer Agent—Wyeth-Ayerst Laboratories, Inc.; *U.S. Public*, pg. 80

CERUM-C—Liquid Topical C for Wrinkles—Health Products Corporation; *U.S. Private*, pg. 514

CERVITRAK—Cervical & Lumbar Traction Products—Staodyn Inc.; *U.S. Public*, pg. 1509

CERVOXAN—Treatment of Cerebrovascular Conditions—SmithKline Beecham plc; *Int'l*, pg. 1264

CERYX—Pacemaker—Medtronic, Inc.; *U.S. Public*, pg. 1082

CESAR—Petfood—Mars Petfoods (UNISABI); *U.S. Private*, pg. 707

CESARIO—Restaurants—Accor S.A.; *Int'l*, pg. 20

CESCO—Ultrasonic Cleaning Equipment—Pegasus International Corporation; *U.S. Private*, pg. 1046

CESEM—Pulp—CSM N.V.; *Int'l*, pg. 243

CESSNA—Aircraft—The Cessna Aircraft Co.; *U.S. Public*, pg. 1589

CESTATICKET—Meal Vouchers—Accor S.A.; *Int'l*, pg. 20

CESTEX—Animal Parasiticide—SmithKline Beecham plc; *Int'l*, pg. 1264

CETABEVER—Building Paints for Exterior & Interior (Retail Uses)—Akzo Nobel N.V.; *Int'l*, pg. 42

CETACORT—Pharmaceutical Products—Galderma Laboratories, Inc.; *Int'l*, pg. 819

CETAMIDE—Sodium Sulfacetamide Ophthalmic Ointment—Alcon Laboratories, Inc.; *Int'l*, pg. 916

CETAPHIL—Pharmaceutical Products—Galderma Laboratories, Inc.; *Int'l*, pg. 819

CETAPRED—Sodium Sulfacetamide/Prednisolone Acetate Ophthalmic Ointment—Alcon Laboratories, Inc.; *Int'l*, pg. 916

CETEBE—NONE—SmithKline Beecham Corporation; *Int'l*, pg. 1264

CETRA—Office Furniture—Kimball International, Inc.; *U.S. Public*, pg. 956

CETRON—Electronics—Richardson Electronics, Ltd.; *U.S. Public*, pg. 1387

CEVI-BID—NONE—Lee Pharmaceuticals; *U.S. Public*, pg. 984

CEYLON—Porcelain Dinnerware—Dansk International Designs Ltd.; *U.S. Public*, pg. 261

CEZANI—Apparel—Phillips-Van Heusen Corporation; *U.S. Public*, pg. 1291

CH—Automatic Aerosol Dispensers & Refills—Surco Products, Inc.; *U.S. Private*, pg. 1056

CHACHAREL—NONE—L'Oreal Parfumerie; *Int'l*, pg. 819

CHADWICK—Bond Paper—The Mead Corporation; *U.S. Public*, pg. 1074

CHADWOOD—Kitchen Cabinets—Kitchen Kompact, Inc.; *U.S. Private*, pg. 624

CHAGRIN HIGHLANDS—NONE—Figgie International Inc.; *U.S. Public*, pg. 622

CHAIN LEADER—Magazine Targeting Senior Management of Chain Restaurant Companies—Reed Elsevier Business Information; *Int'l*, pg. 1095

CHAINVEYOR—Chain & Track Conveyor Systems—Litton Industries, Inc.; *U.S. Public*, pg. 1002

CHAIR EXPRESS—Seating for Bistro-Style & Fast Food Restaurants—Shelby Williams Industries, Inc.; *U.S. Public*, pg. 1464

CHAJITAS STYLE COMBO—Menu Item—Chi-Chi's Inc.; *U.S. Private*, pg. 393

CHALET—Asphalt Shingles—Atlas Roofing Corp.; *U.S. Private*, pg. 96

CHALLENGE—Laminated Composite—Chemfab Corporation; *U.S. Public*, pg. 344

CHALLENGE—Doors—Jeld-Wen, Inc.; *U.S. Private*, pg. 585

CHALLENGE—NONE—Taylor Impression, Inc.; *U.S. Private*, pg. 1070

CHALLENGE/RESPONSE—System—Tandem Computers Inc.; *U.S. Public*, pg. 417

CHALLENGER—Convertible Aluminum Hand Trucks—B & P Manufacturing; *U.S. Private*, pg. 105

CHALLENGER—Low Cost Window Series—Biltbest Windows; *U.S. Public*, pg. 1683

CHALLENGER—Business Jet—Bombardier Inc.; *Int'l*, pg. 199

CHALLENGER—Medium-Duty Bus—Champion Enterprises, Inc.; *U.S. Public*, pg. 332

CHALLENGER—Vans—Coachmen Industries, Inc.; *U.S. Public*, pg. 387

CHALLENGER—Tripod Projection Screen—Da-Lite Screen Company, Inc.; *U.S. Private*, pg. 306

CHALLENGER—Premium Cameras—Eastman Kodak Company; *U.S. Public*, pg. 550

CHALLENGER—Racquetball Glove—Ektelon; *U.S. Private*, pg. 884

CHALLENGER—Swimming Pool Pumps—Essef Corporation; *U.S. Public*, pg. 592

CHALLENGER—Land Mobile Radios—E.F. Johnson Radio Systems; *U.S. Public*, pg. 1630

CHALLENGER—Marching Drums—Ludwig Industries; *U.S. Public*, pg. 1514

CHALLENGER—Press Feeding Equipment—P/A Industries, Inc.; *U.S. Private*, pg. 825

CHALLENGER—Range—Wolf Range Co.; *U.S. Public*, pg. 1322

CHALLENGER 601—Business Jet Aircraft—Bombardier Aerospace; *Int'l*, pg. 200

CHALLENGER 2—Battle Tank—Vickers PLC; *Int'l*, pg. 1466

CHALLENGER 2000—Multi-Function, PC-Based Manifest System—Ascom Hasler Mailing Systems, Inc.; *Int'l*, pg. 86

CHALLENGER 600—Business Jet Aircraft—Bombardier Aerospace; *Int'l*, pg. 200

CHALLONER—Woodworking Machinery—Wisconsin Automated Machinery Corp.; *U.S. Private*, pg. 1184

CHAMBERLAIN—Automatic Garage Door Opener—The Chamberlain Group, Inc.; *U.S. Private*, pg. 344

CHAMBERLAIN'S GOLDEN TOUCH—Hand Lotion—Weeks And Leo Co., Inc.; *U.S. Private*, pg. 1158

CHAMBERS—Housewares & Linens Catalog—Williams-Sonoma, Inc.; *U.S. Public*, pg. 1770

CHAMBORD LIQUER ROYALE DE FRANCE—Liquor—Charles Jacquin et Cie, Inc.; *U.S. Private*, pg. 580

CHAMBOURCY—Refrigerated Products—Nestle S.A.; *Int'l*, pg. 915

CHAMBRAY—Printing & Writing Paper—Georgia-Pacific Corporation; *U.S. Public*, pg. 735

CHAMELEON—Control Products—Bailey, Fischer & Porter Company; *Int'l*, pg. 449

CHAMELEON OPEN—Protocol Analyzer—Tekelec; *U.S. Public*, pg. 1566

CHAMELEON 32 PLUS—Standard Protocol Analyzer for R&D & Evaluation Labs—Tekelec; *U.S. Public*, pg. 1566

CHAMELEON 20 PLUS—Standard Protocol Analyzer for both Lab & Field Use—Tekelec; *U.S. Public*, pg. 1566

CHAMELION SERIES—Metal Casegoods—CorryHiebert Corporation; *U.S. Public*, pg. 772

CHAMFICO—Wove Converting Paper—Champion International Corp.; *U.S. Public*, pg. 333

CHAMKOTE—Box Wrap—Champion International Corp.; *U.S. Public*, pg. 333

CHAMOIS D'OR—Cheese—Bongrain S.A.; *Int'l*, pg. 201

CHAMOMILE—Herb Tea—Celestial Seasonings; *U.S. Public*, pg. 319

CHAMP—PC-Based Mail Management System with Differential Weighing—Ascom Hasler Mailing Systems, Inc.; *Int'l*, pg. 86

CHAMP—Automotive Replacement Parts & Accessories, Service Items—Champ/Pik-A-Nut Service Line; *U.S. Public*, pg. 1503

CHAMP—Filters, Pyroil Chemicals & Additives—Champion Laboratories, Inc.; *U.S. Private*, pg. 1113

CHAMP—Instant Camera—Eastman Kodak Company; *U.S. Public*, pg. 550

CHAMP—Automotive Products—Standard Motor Products Inc.; *U.S. Public*, pg. 1503

CHAMP BURGER—NONE—Checkers Drive-In Restaurants, Inc.; *U.S. Public*, pg. 342

CHAMPAGNE—Crackers—Culinar Inc.; *Int'l*, pg. 348

CHAMPAGNE BIRCH—Wood & Lumber Products—Georgia-Pacific Corporation; *U.S. Public*, pg. 735

CHAMPAGNE BRICOUT—Champagnes—Racke USA; *Int'l*, pg. 1083

CHAMPAGNE POL ROGER—Champagne—Frederick Wildman & Sons Ltd.; *U.S. Private*, pg. 1176

CHAMPALE EXTRA DRY—NONE—The Stroh Brewery Company; *U.S. Private*, pg. 1047

CHAMPALEGOLDEN—NONE—The Stroh Brewery Company; *U.S. Private*, pg. 1047

CHAMPALE GOLDEN—NONE—The Stroh Brewery Company; *U.S. Private*, pg. 1047

CHAMPALE PINK—NONE—The Stroh Brewery Company; *U.S. Private*, pg. 1047

CHAMPFOLD—Opaque Converting Paper—Champion International Corp.; *U.S. Public*, pg. 333

CHAMPION—Line of Process Monitor/Controllers—Analogic Corporation; *U.S. Public*, pg. 109

CHAMPION—Targets—Blount International, Inc.; *U.S. Public*, pg. 237

CHAMPION—Manufactured Homes & Medium Duty Transit Buses—Champion Enterprises, Inc.; *U.S. Public*, pg. 332

CHAMPION—Spark Plugs & Glow Plugs—Champion Ignition Products; *U.S. Public*, pg. 442

CHAMPION—Bond, Mimeo, Duplicator & Xerocopy Bond Paper—Champion International Corp.; *U.S. Public*, pg. 333

CHAMPION—Air Compressors—Champion Pneumatic Machinery Co., Inc.; *U.S. Private*, pg. 228

CHAMPION—Outerwear—Champion Products Inc.; *U.S. Public*, pg. 1433

CHAMPION—Spark Plugs—Cooper Automotive Division; *U.S. Public*, pg. 443

CHAMPION—Spark Plugs, Igniters & Windshield Wiper Products—Cooper Industries, Inc.; *U.S. Public*, pg. 442

CHAMPION—Polyester Flags—Dettra Flag Company; *U.S. Private*, pg. 328

CHAMPION—Flour—Goodman Fielder Limited; *Int'l*, pg. 555

CHAMPION—For Portable Chassis Lubricators—Graco Inc.; *U.S. Public*, pg. 756

CHAMPION—Umbilical Tapes & Dental Floss—Gudebrod, Inc.; *U.S. Private*, pg. 486

CHAMPION—NONE—The Kent Company; *Int'l*, pg. 440

CHAMPION—NONE—Pacific Dunlop Limited; *Int'l*, pg. 1021

CHAMPION—NONE—Ranks Hovis McDougall Limited; *Int'l*, pg. 1395

CHAMPION—Active Wear—Sara Lee Corporation; *U.S. Public*, pg. 1432

CHAMPION—Socks—Sara Lee Sock Company; *U.S. Public*, pg. 1434

CHAMPION—Generators & Electric Plants—Winpower Inc.; *U.S. Private*, pg. 350

CHAMPION ADVERTISING PRODUCTS—Calendars—Renaissance Publishing Co., Inc.; *Int'l*, pg. 185

CHAMPION BARBELL—Physical Equipment—Aurora Electronics, Inc.; *U.S. Public*, pg. 147

CHAMPION BARBELL—Weight Lifting Equipment—Sport Supply Group, Inc.; *U.S. Public*, pg. 1499

CHAMPION 5300 SERIES—Furniture—Myrtle/Mueller, A Haworth Co.; *U.S. Private*, pg. 512

CHAMPION FOODSERVICE ROTISSERIES—Commercial 'Live' Fuel Burning Rotisseries—Hickory Specialties, Inc.; *U.S. Public*, pg. 596

CHAMPION GUIDE GRIP—Tires—Bridgestone/Firestone, Inc.; *Int'l*, pg. 213

CHAMPION JOGBRA—Intimate Activewear—Sara Lee Corporation; *U.S. Public*, pg. 1432

CHAMPION SPADE GRIP—Tires—Bridgestone/Firestone, Inc.; *Int'l*, pg. 213

CHAMPION SPADE GRIP WIRE TREAD PLY LOGGER—Tires—Bridgestone/Firestone, Inc.; *Int'l*, pg. 213

CHAMPION TTA—Bus—Champion Enterprises, Inc.; *U.S. Public*, pg. 332

CHAMPION—Car Seat—Evenflo Company, Inc.; *U.S. Private*, pg. 629

CHAMPONY—Sparkling Apple Drink—Groupe Pernod Ricard; *Int'l*, pg. 566

CHAMPS—Sporting Goods, Activewear, Leisure & Athletic Footwear—F.W. Woolworth Co.; *U.S. Public*, pg. 1777

CHAMPS SPORTING GOODS—Sporting Goods Stores—Kinney Shoe Corporation; *U.S. Public*, pg. 1777

CHAMPS SPORTS—Sporting Goods & Athletic Shoes—Champsssports; *U.S. Public*, pg. 1777

CHAMPS SPORTS—Athletic Equipment, Footwear & Apparel—Woolworth Corporation; *U.S. Public*, pg. 1777

CHAMS—Slacks, Jeans, Shorts—The Spencer Group Inc.; *U.S. Public*, pg. 1025

CHAN-TEL—Sleepwear—Lanz, Inc.; *U.S. Private*, pg. 650

CHANDLER—Refrigeration Products—Heatcraft, Inc.-Refrigeration Products Division; *U.S. Private*, pg. 659

CHANDLER EVANS—Jet Engine Fuel Control—Coltec Industries Inc.; *U.S. Public*, pg. 401

CHANGE ACCUMULATION PLUS—NONE—BMC Software, Inc.; *U.S. Public*, pg. 162

CHANGE MANAGER—NONE—BMC Software, Inc.; *U.S. Public*, pg. 162

CHANGE-O-MATIC—Garment Dispensers—Steiner Co., Inc.; *U.S. Private*, pg. 1039

CHANGING THE VISION OF FOOD SERVICE MANAGEMENT—NONE—JP Foodservice, Inc.; *U.S. Public*, pg. 918

CHANGING TIMES EDUCATION SERVICE—Career & Consumer Education—EMC Corporation; *U.S. Public*, pg. 545

CHANNEL-BASED NETWORK SOLUTIONS—Marketing Term—Computer Network Technology Corporation; *U.S. Public*, pg. 421

CHANNEL COMMANDER—Electronic Components—General Instrument Corporation; *U.S. Public*, pg. 716

CHANNEL-FREE—Circuit or Array—LSI Logic Corp.; *U.S. Public*, pg. 971

CHANNEL MASTER—Antennas—Avnet, Inc.; *U.S. Public*, pg. 155

CHANNEL MASTER—Television Antennas & Antenna Systems; Cable & Satellite Recieving Systems—Channel Master; *U.S. Private*, pg. 228

CHANNEL ONE NEWS—News Broadcast to High Schools—Primedia Inc.; *U.S. Public*, pg. 1327

CHANNEL PLUS—Telecommunications Equipment—Valley Forge Corporation; *U.S. Public*, pg. 1705

CHANNELDRAIN—Roofing & Siding—Wheeling Corrugating Co.; *U.S. Public*, pg. 1727

CHANNELDRAIN 2000—Roofing & Siding—Wheeling Corrugating Co.; *U.S. Public*, pg. 1727

CHANNELINK—Software—Computer Network Technology Corporation; *U.S. Public*, pg. 421

CHANNELLOCK BLUE—Color of Grips—Channellock, Inc.; *U.S. Private*, pg. 229

CHANNELMISER—Broadband Ethernet Interface—Zenith Electronics Corp.; *U.S. Public*, pg. 1790

CHANNELS—Programming Guide—North American Publishing Company; *U.S. Private*, pg. 803

CHANNELSPEED—Host Software—Computer Network Technology Corporation; *U.S. Public*, pg. 421

CHANNELSTREAM—Valves—Flowserve Corporation; *U.S. Public*, pg. 658

CHANNELTRON—Electron Detector—Galileo Corp.; *U.S. Public*, pg. 698

CHANSON D'EAU—Women's Fragrance—Coty Inc.; *Int'l*, pg. 185

CHANTAL—Spray Deodorants—SmithKline Beecham plc; *Int'l*, pg. 1264

CHANTECLERC—NONE—Aliments Flamingo; *Int'l*, pg. 57

CHANTILIMINUT—Pastry Ingredient—Royal Gist-Brocades N.V.; *Int'l*, pg. 1142

CHANTILLY PLACE—Dresses—Star Children's Dress Company, Inc.; *U.S. Private*, pg. 1034

CHANTRE—Brandy—Eckes AG; *Int'l*, pg. 432

CHANTRE CREAM—Cream Liquour—Eckes AG; *Int'l*, pg. 432

CHAP STICK—Lip Balm—American Home Products Corporation; *U.S. Public*, pg. 79

CHAP STICK—Lip Balm—Whitehall-Robins Healthcare; *U.S. Public*, pg. 80

CHAP-ET—Lip Conditioner—Stanback Company; *U.S. Private*, pg. 1030

CHAPARRAL BOATS—NONE—RPC Incorporated; *U.S. Public*, pg. 1356

CHAPARRAL RIDGE—NONE—Niches, Inc.; *U.S. Public*, pg. 1181

CHAPEL HILL—Home Fashions—Croscill, Inc.; *U.S. Private*, pg. 290

CHAPPARAL—Carbon Pipe & Steel Products—Thomas Pipe & Steel, Inc.; *U.S. Private*, pg. 508

CHAPPELLET—Wine—Pacific Wine Co.; *U.S. Private*, pg. 843

CHAPPIE—Chewing Gum—Cadbury Schweppes p.l.c.; *Int'l*, pg. 247

CHAPS—Sportswear—Warnaco Inc.; *U.S. Public*, pg. 1738

CHAPS BY RALPH LAUREN—Clothing—Genesco Inc.; *U.S. Public*, pg. 728

CHAPS BY RALPH LAUREN—Men's Tailored Clothing—Hartmarx Corporation; *U.S. Public*, pg. 795

CHAPS RALPH LAUREN—Formalwear For Men—West Mill Clothes, Inc.; *U.S. Private*, pg. 1163

CHAR BROIL—Gas, Charcoal & Electric Barbecue Grills—W.C. Bradley Co.; *U.S. Private*, pg. 164

CHAR FLO—Charcoal Delivery System for Use in Over-Dose Patients—Ballard Medical Products; *U.S. Public*, pg. 171

CHAR-LYNN—Hydraulic Motors—Eaton Corporation; *U.S. Public*, pg. 555

CHAR-LYNN—Hydraulic Motors—Eaton Corporation, Hydraulics Division; *U.S. Public*, pg. 557

CHARACTERS—Color Additive—Clairol, Inc.; *U.S. Public*, pg. 254

CHARADE—1000, 1300 cc 2 Box & 3 Box Sedan—Daihatsu Motor Corporation, Ltd.; *Int'l*, pg. 364

CHARAN REALTY GROUP—Business Association—Charan Industries, Inc.; *U.S. Private*, pg. 229

CHARDE—Automobile—Daihatsu America, Inc.; *Int'l*, pg. 365

CHARDON—Rubber Products—The Chardon Rubber Co.; *U.S. Private*, pg. 229

CHARGE SAFE—Automotive Booster Cables—General Cable Corporation; *Int'l*, pg. 1486

CHARGEMASTER—Static Charge Generator—Simco; *U.S. Public*, pg. 865

CHARGER—Lager—Bass PLC; *Int'l*, pg. 169

CHARGER—Tire—The Kelly-Springfield Tire Company; *U.S. Public*, pg. 753

CHARGER—Compressor for Natural Gas—Norwalk Co., Inc.; *U.S. Private*, pg. 807

CHARGER—Packaging Machine—Riverwood International Corporation; *U.S. Public*, pg. 1391

CHARGERLINK—Communication Interface—Harnischfeger Industries, Inc.; *U.S. Public*, pg. 788

CHARIOT—Children's Books, Toys, Games & Videos—Cook Communication Ministries; *U.S. Private*, pg. 272

CHARISMA—Perfumes, Cosmetics & Toiletries—Avon Products, Inc.; *U.S. Public*, pg. 155

CHARISMA—Bed & Bath—Fieldcrest Cannon, Inc.; *U.S. Public*, pg. 1296

CHARISMA—Accent Chairs—Flexsteel Industries, Inc.; *U.S. Public*, pg. 653

CHARISMA CHAIRS—Accent Chairs—Flexsteel Industries, Inc.; *U.S. Public*, pg. 653

CHARITABILITY—Donate Gifts to Lutheran Congregations, Institutions &Non-Profit Companies—Lutheran Brotherhood; *U.S. Private*, pg. 681

CHARKATE—Protective Apparel—Eastco Industrial Safety Corp.; *U.S. Public*, pg. 548

CHARLEMONT PLANK—Pre-Finished Laminate—Bruce Hardwood Floors; *U.S. Public*, pg. 1634

CHARLES & CO—Grocery Stores—Red Apple Companies; *U.S. Private*, pg. 914

CHARLES ATLAS—NONE—Charles Atlas, Ltd.; *U.S. Private*, pg. 229

CHARLES BASTION—Golf Apparel—K2 Inc.; *U.S. Public*, pg. 940

CHARLES CURTAIN—Curtains—Charles Curtain Company, Inc.; *U.S. Private*, pg. 229

CHARLES KRUG—Wine—Pacific Wine Co.; *U.S. Private*, pg. 843

CHARLES LE FRANC—Wine—Canandaigua Wine Company Div.; *U.S. Public*, pg. 300

CHARLES OF THE RITZ—Cosmetics, Fragrances, Skin Care Treatments—Charles of the Ritz Group Ltd.; *U.S. Private*, pg. 689

CHARLES OF THE RITZ—Cosmetics—Revlon, Inc.; *U.S. Private*, pg. 689

CHARLES SCHWAB INVESTMENT MANAGEMENT—Schwab Funds—Charles Schwab & Co. Inc.; *U.S. Public*, pg. 1443

Brand Name Index

CHARLESTON CHEW—Chocolate/Caramel Candies—Tootsie Roll Industries, Inc.; *U.S. Public*, pg. 1621

CHARLEY—Pens—Dixon Ticonderoga Company; *U.S. Public*, pg. 514

CHARLEY HORSE—Restaurants—Consolidated Products, Inc.; *U.S. Public*, pg. 436

CHARLEY'S PLACE—Restaurants—Houlihan's Restaurant Group; *U.S. Public*, pg. 841

CHARLIES—Frozen Specialties—Byrnes & Kiefer Company; *U.S. Private*, pg. 191

CHARLIE'S LUNCH KIT—Lunch Kit—Star-Kist Foods Inc.; *U.S. Public*, pg. 805

CHARLIE'S LUNCH KIT—NONE—Star-Kist Foods, Inc.; *U.S. Public*, pg. 806

CHARLOTTE—NONE—Falcon Products, Inc.; *U.S. Public*, pg. 611

CHARLOTTE CHARLES—Preserves, Sauces, Salad Dressings, Condiments, Baked Goods—RCB Baking Company; *U.S. Public*, pg. 1354

CHARLOTTE MOTOR SPEEDWAY—NONE—Speedway Motorsports, Inc.; *U.S. Public*, pg. 1498

CHARM GLOW—Grills—Sunbeam Corporation; *U.S. Public*, pg. 1533

CHARMERS—Deodorant Cologne—SmithKline Beecham plc; *Int'l*, pg. 1264

CHARMILLES—NONE—Georg Fischer Ltd.; *Int'l*, pg. 488

CHARMIN—Bathroom Tissue—The Procter & Gamble Company; *U.S. Public*, pg. 1330

CHARMIN CARE—Toilet Tissue—The Procter & Gamble Company; *U.S. Public*, pg. 1330

CHARMIN FREE—Bathroom Tissue—The Procter & Gamble Company; *U.S. Public*, pg. 1330

CHARMIN PLUSH—Bathroom Tissue—The Procter & Gamble Company; *U.S. Public*, pg. 1330

CHARMIN SPACE SAVER—Bathroom Tissue—The Procter & Gamble Company; *U.S. Public*, pg. 1330

CHARMS—Candy—Charms Company; *U.S. Public*, pg. 1621

CHARMS—Candy—Tootsie Roll Industries, Inc.; *U.S. Public*, pg. 1621

CHARMS BLOW POPS—Suckers—Charms Company; *U.S. Public*, pg. 1621

CHARMS BLOW POPS—Candy—Tootsie Roll Industries, Inc.; *U.S. Public*, pg. 1621

CHARMS SWEET & SOUR POPS—Suckers—Charms Company; *U.S. Public*, pg. 1621

CHARRINGTON IPA—Bitter/Ale—Bass PLC; *Int'l*, pg. 169

CHARRITO'S—Mexican Cuisine—Arden International Kitchens, Inc.; *U.S. Private*, pg. 972

CHART CADDY—Hospital Equipment—Carstens Inc.; *U.S. Private*, pg. 216

CHART-MASTER—Software—Borland International, Inc.; *U.S. Public*, pg. 246

CHARTBUSTERS—Video Selection—Blockbuster Entertainment Group; *U.S. Public*, pg. 775

CHARTER—Plywood—Georgia-Pacific Corporation; *U.S. Public*, pg. 735

CHARTER CLUB—Specialty Retail—Federated Department Stores, Inc.; *U.S. Public*, pg. 617

CHARTER MEDICAL—International Hospital Management—Magellan Health Services, Inc.; *U.S. Public*, pg. 1033

CHARTEX—Cloth Backing—Seal Products Incorporated; *U.S. Public*, pg. 849

CHARTWELLLAND—Land Subdinders/developers—Kingfisher plc; *Int'l*, pg. 733

CHARTWRITE—Pen Based Handheld Computer—Nellcor Puritan Bennett Incorporated; *U.S. Public*, pg. 1039

CHAS. H. TOMPKINS CO.—Construction Company-General Contractors—J.A. Jones, Inc.; *Int'l*, pg. 633

CHAS. T. MAIN, INC.—Engineering, Architects, Contractors—Parsons Main, Inc.; *U.S. Private*, pg. 842

CHASE—NONE—Bristol-Myers Squibb Company; *U.S. Public*, pg. 253

CHASE & SANBORN—Coffee—Philip Morris Companies Inc.; *U.S. Public*, pg. 1287

CHASE & SANBORN—Coffee—Chase & Sanborn Coffee, Inc.; *Int'l*, pg. 917

CHASE & SANBORN—Coffee—Nestle USA; *Int'l*, pg. 916

CHASE GLASTERRA—Flame Resistant Electrical Insulation—Chase Corporation; *U.S. Public*, pg. 337

CHASE LIMOGERE—Wines—Canandaigua Wine Company, Inc.; *U.S. Public*, pg. 300

CHASE-SAVER II—Closet Carrier—Josam Company; *U.S. Private*, pg. 600

CHASER—Soft Drink—Double-Cola Co.-USA; *U.S. Private*, pg. 341

CHASER—Automobile—Toyota Motor Corporation; *Int'l*, pg. 1411

CHASKA—Vodka—Marie Brizard Wines & Spirits USA; *U.S. Private*, pg. 702

CHASSIS—NONE—AmTran Corporation; *U.S. Public*, pg. 1167

CHAT—Women's Weekly Magazine—IPC Magazines Limited; *Int'l*, pg. 651

CHAT NOIR—Coffee Product—Sara Lee Corporation; *U.S. Public*, pg. 1432

CHATEAU—Drapery Hardware—Kirsch; *U.S. Public*, pg. 1176

CHATEAU—NONE—Sico Inc.; *Int'l*, pg. 1239

CHATEAU & ESTATES—Wine—Pacific Wine Co.; *U.S. Private*, pg. 843

CHATEAU CHARDON—Champagne & Sparkling Wine—Gibson Wine Company; *U.S. Private*, pg. 452

CHATEAU CLARKE & LES GRANGES—French Wines—Marie Brizard Wines & Spirits USA; *U.S. Private*, pg. 702

CHATEAU DE LA CHAIZE—Beaujolais—Seagram Chateau & Estate Wines Co.; *Int'l*, pg. 1215

CHATEAU DE PEZ—Bordeau Wine—Remy Amerique Inc.; *Int'l*, pg. 1102

CHATEAU GISCOURS—Bordeaux Wine—Remy Amerique Inc.; *Int'l*, pg. 1102

CHATEAU GLORIA—Bordeaux—Seagram Chateau & Estate Wines Co.; *Int'l*, pg. 1215

CHATEAU GREYSAC—Bordeaux—Seagram Chateau & Estate Wines Co.; *Int'l*, pg. 1215

CHATEAU LA CARDONNE—Bordeaux—Seagram Chateau & Estate Wines Co.; *Int'l*, pg. 1215

CHATEAU LA JOYA—Chilean Wine—Marie Brizard Wines & Spirits USA; *U.S. Private*, pg. 702

CHATEAU LA SALLE—Wine—Canandaigua Wine Company Div.; *U.S. Public*, pg. 300

CHATEAU LAROSE-TRINTAUDON—Bordeaux—Seagram Chateau & Estate Wines Co.; *Int'l*, pg. 1215

CHATEAU LOUDENNE—NONE—IDV France; *Int'l*, pg. 410

CHATEAU MARQUE—NONE—Wechsler Coffee Corp.; *U.S. Public*, pg. 1158

CHATEAU MERCIAN—Spirits—Mercian Corporation; *Int'l*, pg. 858

CHATEAU OLIVIER—Wine—Paterno Imports Limited; *U.S. Private*, pg. 843

CHATEAU POINT—NONE—Sico Inc.; *Int'l*, pg. 1239

CHATEAU ROTHSCHILD—Wine—Pacific Wine Co.; *U.S. Private*, pg. 843

CHATEAU ST. JEAN—Wine—Pacific Wine Co.; *U.S. Private*, pg. 843

CHATEAU STE. MICHELLE—Wine—Stimson Lane Ltd.; *U.S. Public*, pg. 1661

CHATEAU SOUVERAIN—Wine—Nestle S.A.; *Int'l*, pg. 915

CHATEAU SOUVERAIN—Wine—Wine World Estates Company; *Int'l*, pg. 917

CHATEAULET—Champagnes—Gibson Wine Company; *U.S. Private*, pg. 452

CHATEAUX SENEJAC—Bordeaux Wine—Frederick Wildman & Sons Ltd.; *U.S. Private*, pg. 1176

CHATHAM—Gin—Peerless Importers, Inc.; *U.S. Private*, pg. 847

CHATHAM INSTITUTE—NONE—Infinicom; *U.S. Private*, pg. 561

CHATILLON—Test & Calibration Instruments—AMETEK, Inc.; *U.S. Public*, pg. 99

CHATSWORTH—Individual Portion Products—Borden, Inc.; *U.S. Private*, pg. 157

CHATSWORTH—Hardwood Doors—Georgia-Pacific Corporation; *U.S. Public*, pg. 735

CHATTANOOGA—Chewing Tobacco—Swisher International Group, Inc.; *U.S. Public*, pg. 1543

CHATTANOOGA GAS COMPANY—Natural Gas Distribution—AGL Resources; *U.S. Public*, pg. 6

CHAUCER—Brand of Bookcovering—Appleton Papers Inc.; *Int'l*, pg. 567

CHAUDFONTAINE—Mineral Water—Interbrew S.A.; *Int'l*, pg. 679

CHAULK LINE—Outerwear—Russell Corporation; *U.S. Public*, pg. 1413

CHAYA—NONE—Kellwood Company; *U.S. Public*, pg. 948

CHEAF—Aerosol Filter—Crown Andersen Inc.; *U.S. Public*, pg. 462

CHEAP SHOTS—Greeting Cards—American Greetings Corporation; *U.S. Public*, pg. 77

CHECK GARD—Primer—The Sherwin-Williams Company; *U.S. Public*, pg. 1465

CHECK MARK—Glaze & Enamel Frit & Clay—Ferro Corporation; *U.S. Public*, pg. 618

CHECK✻MATE—Specialized Call-Processing System for Use in Correctional Institutions—Intllicall, Inc.; *U.S. Public*, pg. 887

CHECK PLUS—NONE—BMC Software, Inc.; *U.S. Public*, pg. 162

CHECKCARD PLUS—Banking Product—Great Financial Bank FSB; *U.S. Private*, pg. 473

CHECKCITE—Software—The Mead Corporation; *U.S. Public*, pg. 1074

CHECKERBOARD DESIGN—Bond Paper—The Mead Corporation; *U.S. Public*, pg. 1074

CHECKERS—NONE—Checkers Drive-In Restaurants, Inc.; *U.S. Public*, pg. 342

CHECKERS BURGERS, FRIES, COLAS—NONE—Checkers Drive-In Restaurants, Inc.; *U.S. Public*, pg. 342

CHECKFIRE—Fire Detection & Control System for Vehicles—Ansul Incorporated; *U.S. Public*, pg. 1648

CHECKMATE—Toxic Chemical Protection Fabric—Lakeland Industries, Inc.; *U.S. Public*, pg. 975

CHECKMATE—NONE—LumenX Company; *U.S. Public*, pg. 56

CHECKMATE—Process Controls for Aseptic Packaging Machines—The Mead Corporation; *U.S. Public*, pg. 1074

CHECKMATES—Pocket Knives—Camillus Cutlery Co.; *U.S. Private*, pg. 203

CHECKMAX—Pricing Symbol—OfficeMax; *U.S. Public*, pg. 1212

CHECKOUT CALLFREE—NONE—Catalina Marketing Corporation; *U.S. Public*, pg. 314

CHECKOUT COUPON—NONE—Catalina Marketing Corporation; *U.S. Public*, pg. 314

CHECKOUT DIRECT—NONE—Catalina Marketing Corporation; *U.S. Public*, pg. 314

CHECKOUT MESSAGE—NONE—Catalina Marketing Corporation; *U.S. Public*, pg. 314

CHECKOUT PACK—Alkaline & Heavy Duty Batteries in Packng./Displays For Store Checkout Cntr—RAYOVAC Corporation; *U.S. Private*, pg. 912

CHECKOUT PRIZES—NONE—Catalina Marketing Corporation; *U.S. Public*, pg. 314

CHECKS IN THE MAIL—Check Printing—Caradon Plc; *Int'l*, pg. 266

CHECKTRONIC—Computerized Security Document Production System—Check Technology Corporation; *U.S. Public*, pg. 342

CHED-O-MATE—Shredded Cheese Substitute Products—Borden, Inc.; *U.S. Private*, pg. 157

CHEDDAR CLASSICS—Potato Mixes—General Mills, Inc.; *U.S. Public*, pg. 717

CHEDDAR CRISPS—Finger Food—Harker's Distribution, Inc.; *U.S. Private*, pg. 502

CHEDDAR WEDGES—Cheese Crackers—RJR Nabisco Holdings Corp.; *U.S. Public*, pg. 1354

CHEE-TOS—Cheese Snacks—Frito-Lay Company; *U.S. Public*, pg. 1277

CHEE-TOS PAWS—Snack Food—Frito-Lay Company; *U.S. Public*, pg. 1277

CHEEKERS—Face Make-Up—Cover Girl Cosmetics; *U.S. Public*, pg. 1330

CHEER—Laundry Product—The Procter & Gamble Company; *U.S. Public*, pg. 1330

CHEER FREE—Unscented, Undyed Detergent—The Procter & Gamble Company; *U.S. Public*, pg. 1330

CHEER WITH COLOR GUARD—Superconcentrated Detergent—The Procter & Gamble Company; *U.S. Public*, pg. 1330

CHEERIOS—Cereal—General Mills, Inc.; *U.S. Public*, pg. 717

CHEERS—Beer—UNICER-Uniao Cervejeira, S.A.; *Int'l*, pg. 1432

CHEESE CELLAR—Restaurant—Select Restaurants, Inc.; *U.S. Private*, pg. 982

CHEESE MARKET NEWS—Weekly Newspaper Covering the Cheese, Dairy & Deli Industries—Reed Elsevier Business Information; *Int'l*, pg. 1095

CHEESE NIPS—Crackers—Nabisco Inc.; *U.S. Public*, pg. 1355

CHEESE POCOS DE CALDAS—NONE—LPC Industrias Alimenticias S.A.; *Int'l*, pg. 380

CHEESE TID-BIT—Crackers—Nabisco Inc.; *U.S. Public*, pg. 1355

CHEESE WHIZ—Processed Cheese Product—Alliant Foodservice, Inc.; *U.S. Private*, pg. 244

CHEEZ-ALL—Flavors Containing Natural Cheese Or Natural Cheese Flavor Components—McCormick Flavor Division-U.S.A.; *U.S. Public*, pg. 1066

CHEEZ DOODLES—Cheese Puffs—Clover Club Foods, Inc.; *U.S. Private*, pg. 469

CHEEZ DOODLES—Cheese & Corn Puffs—Jays Foods LLC; *U.S. Private*, pg. 584

CHEEZ DOODLES—Cheese Snacks—Wise Foods, Inc.; *U.S. Private*, pg. 157

CHEEZ-IT—Crackers—Keebler Company; *U.S. Public*, pg. 657

CHEEZ-IT—Crackers—Sunshine Biscuits, Inc.; *U.S. Private*, pg. 434

CHEEZ-IT—Crackers—Sunshine Biscuits, Inc.; *U.S. Public*, pg. 657

CHEEZ WHIZ—Pasteurized Process Cheese Products—Kraft Foods Inc.; *U.S. Public*, pg. 1288

CHEEZ WHIZ—Pasteurized Process Cheese Spread—Philip Morris Companies Inc.; *U.S. Public*, pg. 1287

CHEEZDAWGS—Dog Treats—Ralston Purina Company; *U.S. Public*, pg. 1359

CHEEZTWO—Shredded Cheese Substitute Products—Borden, Inc.; *U.S. Private*, pg. 157

CHEF—Appliances—Southcorp Holdings Ltd.; *Int'l*, pg. 1287

CHEF-AIRE—Kitchen Range Hoods—Aubrey Manufacturing Company; *U.S. Public*, pg. 1193

CHEF & BREWER—NONE—Scottish & Newcastle plc; *Int'l*, pg. 1211

CHEF-BOY-AR-DEE—Italian Foods—International Home Foods Inc.; *U.S. Private*, pg. 526

CHEF DAVID—Baked Goods—Parisian Bakeries; *U.S. Public*, pg. 909

CHEF FRANCISCO—Frozen Foods—Labatt Brewing Company Limited; *Int'l*, pg. 679

CHEF MAGIC—Hot Sauce with Garlic—Trappey's Fine Foods, Inc.; *U.S. Private*, pg. 105

CHEF MAGIC—Jalapeno Sauce—Trappey's Fine Foods, Inc.; *U.S. Private*, pg. 105

CHEF MAGIC—Steak Sauce—Trappey's Fine Foods, Inc.; *U.S. Private*, pg. 105

CHEF MAGIC—Soy Sauce—Trappey's Fine Foods, Inc.; *U.S. Private*, pg. 105

CHEF MAGIC—Worcestershire—Trappey's Fine Foods, Inc.; *U.S. Private*, pg. 105

CHEF-MATE—Food Products—Nestle USA; *Int'l*, pg. 916

CHEF PLEASER—Bacon—Hatfield Quality Meats; *U.S. Private*, pg. 510

CHEF'S CHOICE—Paper Trays—Reynolds Metals Company; *U.S. Public*, pg. 1385

CHEF SALUTO—Pizza & Snack Prods.—Pillsbury Co.; *Int'l*, pg. 411

CHEF-WAY—Oil, Shortening & Conditioned Rice—Riceland Foods, Inc.; *U.S. Private*, pg. 928

CHEF'S GALLERY—NONE—Regal Ware, Inc.; *U.S. Private*, pg. 917

CHEFARO—Home Diagnostic Products—Akzo Nobel N.V.; *Int'l*, pg. 42

CHEFMASTER—Colors—Byrnes & Kiefer Company; *U.S. Private*, pg. 191

CHEFS CHOICE—Kitchen Tools—Ekco Housewares, Inc.; *U.S. Public*, pg. 566

CHEF'S CHOICE—Oils, Mayonnaise, Mustard, Dressings, Spices & Soup Bases—Purity Products Inc.; *U.S. Private*, pg. 896

CHEF'S CHOICE—Liquid Eggs—Rose Acre Farms; *U.S. Private*, pg. 944

CHEF'S CLASSIC—Seasonings—Pacific Foods, Inc.; *U.S. Private*, pg. 831

CHEF'S EXPRESS—Restaurant—The Levy Organization; *U.S. Private*, pg. 664

CHEFS INTERNATIONAL—Corporate Name—Chefs International, Inc.; *U.S. Public*, pg. 343

CHEF'S PRIDE—Oils, Shortenings, Dresssings, Sauces—Ventura Foods LLC; *Int'l*, pg. 879

CHEF'S VARIETY—NONE—JP Foodservice, Inc.; *U.S. Public*, pg. 918

CHEF'S WOOD—Mesquite Charcoal—Tri Valley Growers; *U.S. Private*, pg. 1101

CHEIW—NONE—Huhtamaki Oy; *Int'l*, pg. 638

CHEK-MATE—Cadmium Pigments—Ferro Corporation; *U.S. Public*, pg. 618

CHEKLINK—Electronic Retail Theft Prevention System—Checkpoint Systems Inc.; *U.S. Public*, pg. 343

CHELON—Chelating Chemical—Rhone-Poulenc Basic Chemicals Co.; *Int'l*, pg. 1110

CHELSEA—Power Take-Offs, Pumps & Motors—Dana Corporation; *U.S. Public*, pg. 479

CHELSEA—ButterScotch Toffees—Meiji Seika Kaisha, Ltd.; *Int'l*, pg. 855

CHELSEA—Rose Petal Sachets—Stanhome Inc.; *U.S. Public*, pg. 1508

THE CHELSEA COLLECTION—Ladies Apparel & Gifts—Hanover Direct Pennsylvania, Inc.; *U.S. Public*, pg. 782

CHELSEA GIN—Gin—W & A Gilbey; *Int'l*, pg. 409

CHELTENHAM—Bond Paper—The Mead Corporation; *U.S. Public*, pg. 1074

CHEM FLO—Acrylic Latex Interior Flat—Paragon Paint & Varnish Corp.; *U.S. Private*, pg. 838

CHEM-KING—Mens Rain Wear—Rainfair, Inc.; *U.S. Private*, pg. 907

CHEM LUSTRE—Acrylic Latex Semi-Lustre Enamel—Paragon Paint & Varnish Corp.; *U.S. Private*, pg. 838

CHEM/METER—Hydraulically Actuated Diaphragm Metering Pumps—ChemPump; *U.S. Public*, pg. 456

CHEM-O-CONE—Enamel—Jones Blair Company; *U.S. Private*, pg. 596

CHEM-O-FEEDER—Diaphragm Pump—BIF; *U.S. Public*, pg. 726

CHEM-O-LITE—Vinyl Finish—Jones Blair Company; *U.S. Private*, pg. 596

CHEM-O-PON—Epoxy Enamel—Jones Blair Company; *U.S. Private*, pg. 596

CHEM-O-THIX—Vinyl Coating—Jones Blair Company; *U.S. Private*, pg. 596

CHEM-O-Z—Zinc Coating—Jones Blair Company; *U.S. Private*, pg. 596

CHEM-REL—Foundry Binder—Ashland, Inc.; *U.S. Public*, pg. 138

CHEM-STUD—Adhesive Anchor—Powers Fastening, Inc.; *U.S. Private*, pg. 878

CHEM-TEM—Chemically Strengthened Glass—Globe-Amerada Glass Company; *U.S. Private*, pg. 458

CHEM-VELVET—Acrylic Latex Eggshell Finish—Paragon Paint & Varnish Corp.; *U.S. Private*, pg. 838

CHEM-VENT—Filtration Products—Gelman Sciences, Inc.; *U.S. Public*, pg. 1253

CHEM-VY-KOTE—Vinyls—Grow Group, Inc.; *Int'l*, pg. 663

CHEM-VY-KOTE—Vinyls—ICI Paints; *Int'l*, pg. 664

CHEM-TREND—Lubricants—Burmah Castrol plc; *Int'l*, pg. 234

CHEMAIRE—Processor Chemical Fume Filtration System—LogEtronics Corporation; *U.S. Public*, pg. 6

CHEMAWARE—Product Information Services—The Dow Chemical Company; *U.S. Public*, pg. 522

CHEMCARE—Waste Management Services—Van Waters & Rogers; *Int'l*, pg. 1147

CHEMCOMP—Computer Program & Service—The Dow Chemical Company; *U.S. Public*, pg. 522

CHEMCON—Metering Pumps—Tuthill Pump; *U.S. Private*, pg. 1111

CHEMCRAFT—Science Kits—Tyco Toys, Inc.; *U.S. Public*, pg. 1058

CHEMCRAFT—Chemistry Sets—View-Master, Inc.; *U.S. Public*, pg. 1058

CHEMELEX—Electric Heat Tracing Systems—Raychem Corporation; *U.S. Public*, pg. 1362

CHEMET—NONE—McNeil Consumer Products Company; *U.S. Private*, pg. 928

CHEMETRON—Home Respiratory Care Products—Allied Healthcare Products, Inc.; *U.S. Public*, pg. 48

CHEMETRON—Welding Supplies & Consumables—EEI Corporation; *Int'l*, pg. 425

CHEMFAB—NONE—Chemfab Corporation; *U.S. Public*, pg. 344

CHEMFAST—Epoxies—Grow Group, Inc.; *Int'l*, pg. 663

CHEMFAST—Epoxies—ICI Paints; *Int'l*, pg. 664

CHEMFIL—Coatings, Rust Removers, Cleaning Preparations, Stripping Agents—PPG Industries, Inc.; *U.S. Public*, pg. 1245

CHEMFILM—Thin, Multi-layer Film—Chemfab Corporation; *U.S. Public*, pg. 344

CHEMFLUOR—Molded & Extruded Fluoropolymer Products—Norton Performance Plastics; *Int'l*, pg. 1174

CHEMFLUOR—Tubing—Ryan Herco Products Corp.; *U.S. Private*, pg. 953

CHEMFOS—Iron & Zinc Phosphate Solutions—PPG Industries, Inc.; *U.S. Public*, pg. 1245

CHEMGLAS—NONE—Chemfab Corporation; *U.S. Public*, pg. 344

CHEMGLAS-UVR—NONE—Chemfab Corporation; *U.S. Public*, pg. 344

CHEMGLAZE—Coatings—Lord Corporation; *U.S. Private*, pg. 675

CHEMGRIP—Treating Agents & Cement for Use with Fluoropolymers—Norton Performance Plastics; *Int'l*, pg. 1174

CHEMGUARD—Chemical Barrier Sheath—BICC Brand-Rex; *Int'l*, pg. 120

CHEMI-SCRAPER—Spatula—Fisher Scientific Company; *U.S. Private*, pg. 658

CHEMICAL EQUIPMENT—Publication for Engineers & Executives in Process Plants—Reed Elsevier Business Information; *Int'l*, pg. 1095

CHEMICAL REG-A-DEX—Regulatory Software—J.J. Keller & Associates, Inc.; *U.S. Private*, pg. 612

CHEMIGUM—Butadiene, Acrylonitrile Latices—The Goodyear Tire & Rubber Company; *U.S. Public*, pg. 752

CHEMINAX—Coaxial Cable—Raychem Corporation; *U.S. Public*, pg. 1362

CHEMINEER—Industrial Mixers—Robbins & Myers, Inc.; *U.S. Public*, pg. 1393

CHEMISTER—Containers—Fisher Scientific Company; *U.S. Private*, pg. 658

CHEMLAM—NONE—Chemfab Corporation; *U.S. Public*, pg. 344

CHEMLAM ULTRA—NONE—Chemfab Corporation; *U.S. Public*, pg. 344

CHEMLAWN—Lawn Care Products & Services—TruGreen-ChemLawn; *U.S. Public*, pg. 1461

CHEMLINK—NONE—Chemfab Corporation; *U.S. Public*, pg. 344

CHEMLOK—Rubber To Metal Adhesives—Lord Corporation; *U.S. Private*, pg. 675

CHEMMASTER—Portable Chemical Mix Tank—Houston Fearless 76 Inc.; *U.S. Private*, pg. 542

CHEMOMAT—ED Equipment for Processing Ionizable Liquids—Ionics, Incorporated; *U.S. Public*, pg. 912

CHEMOSITE—System—U.S. Surgical Corp.; *U.S. Public*, pg. 1687

CHEMOX—Chemicals—Carus Corporation; *U.S. Private*, pg. 217

CHEMPATCH—Industrial Plywood Patch Compound—ISK BioSciences; *Int'l*, pg. 689

CHEMPUMP—Leakproof Canned Motor Centrifugal Pumps—ChemPump; *U.S. Public*, pg. 456

CHEMPUTER—Computing Rules—The Perkin-Elmer Corporation; *U.S. Public*, pg. 1279

CHEMRIST—Filter Housing—Pall Corporation; *U.S. Public*, pg. 1253

CHEMSECURE—Security Paper—The Mead Corporation; *U.S. Public*, pg. 1074

CHEMSENSOR—Hand-Held Screening Units for On-Site Testing for Contaminants in Water—Osmonics, Inc.; *U.S. Public*, pg. 1233

CHEMSHEEN—Car Washing & Cleaning Composition—PPG Industries, Inc.; *U.S. Public*, pg. 1245

CHEMSTIK—NONE—Chemfab Corporation; *U.S. Public*, pg. 344

CHEMSTOP—Specialty Building Products—Tamms Industries; *Int'l*, pg. 803

CHEMSTOR—Chemical Storage Container—Falcon Safety Products Inc.; *U.S. Private*, pg. 392

CHEMSURE—Delivery Service Program—BetzDearborn Inc.; *U.S. Public*, pg. 226

CHEMTECH—Zinc Rich Primers—Pratt & Lambert United, Inc.; *U.S. Public*, pg. 1466

CHEMTOY—Toys—Strombecker Corporation; *U.S. Private*, pg. 1047

CHEMTRAK—Chemistry Controls—Medical Analysis Systems Inc.; *U.S. Private*, pg. 727

CHEMTROL—Plastic Ball & Butterfly Valves For Comml. & Indus. Applications—NIBCO, Inc.; *U.S. Private*, pg. 798

CHEMTROL—Valves—Ryan Herco Products Corp.; *U.S. Private*, pg. 953

CHEMTURE—Poured-in-Place Urethane—Robbins, Inc.; *U.S. Private*, pg. 934

CHEMTURE PLUS—Poured-in-Place Urethane—Robbins, Inc.; *U.S. Private*, pg. 934

CHENIX—Pharmaceutical Products—Solvay Pharmaceuticals, Inc.; *Int'l*, pg. 1278

CHEQUE—Birth Control for Dogs—Pharmacia & Upjohn; *Int'l*, pg. 1048

CHEQUERA POPULAR—A Checking Account with a Low Opening Balance Requirement—Banco Popular de Puerto Rico; *U.S. Public*, pg. 175

CHEROKEE—Apparel, Shoes & Accessories—Cherokee Inc.; *U.S. Public*, pg. 345

CHERRY—Switches—Cherry Electrical Products Corporation; *U.S. Public*, pg. 346

CHERRY BLOSSOM—Candy—Hershey Foods Corporation; *U.S. Public*, pg. 811

CHERRY BOMB—Mufflers—Arvin Industries, Inc.; *U.S. Public*, pg. 136

CHERRY CENTRAL—Fresh Fruits & Vegetables—Cherry Central Cooperative; *U.S. Private*, pg. 233

CHERRY COKE—Soft Drink—The Coca-Cola Company; *U.S. Public*, pg. 349

CHERRY COLA SLICE—Fruit Soft Drink—Pepsi-Cola Company; *U.S. Public*, pg. 1277

CHERRY GARCIA—Ice Cream—Ben & Jerry's Homemade Inc.; *U.S. Public*, pg. 210

CHERRY-OLA COLA—Soft Drink—Select Canfield; *U.S. Private*, pg. 982

CHERRY SEVEN-UP—Soft Drink—Dr. Pepper Co.; *Int'l*, pg. 248

CHERRY WHEAT—Premium Beer—The Lion Brewery, Inc.; *U.S. Public*, pg. 1000

CHERRYWOOD—Cutlery—General Housewares Corp.; *U.S. Public*, pg. 715

CHERRYWOOD—Rods—Outdoor Technologies Group; *U.S. Private*, pg. 822

CHERUBS—Baby Products—Playtex Products Inc.; *U.S. Public*, pg. 1310

CHERYL LYN—Pancake & Fountain Syrups—Purity Products, Inc.; *U.S. Private*, pg. 896

CHERYL TIEGS—NONE—Holt Hosiery Mills, Inc.; *U.S. Private*, pg. 536

CHESAPEAK VALLEY FARMS—Hams and Sausages—Hatfield Quality Meats; *U.S. Private*, pg. 510

CHESAPEAKE—Bay Style Seafood Seasoning—McCormick/Schilling; *U.S. Public*, pg. 1066

CHESAPEAKE—Vinyl Siding—Reynolds Metals Company; *U.S. Public*, pg. 1385

CHESAPEAKE BAGEL BAKERY—Fast Food Restaurant Specializing In Bagels, Soups & Bakery Items—AFC Enterprises; *U.S. Private*, pg. 5

CHESAPEAKE CLEAN, LANCASTER GREEN—Lawn & Garden Fertilizer—Hydro/Kirby Agri Service, Inc.; *U.S. Private*, pg. 552

CHESCO—Hex Tools—American Tool Companies, Inc.; *U.S. Private*, pg. 63

CHESDALE—Anlene Mainland—New Zealand Dairy Board; *Int'l*, pg. 923

CHESHIRE LINEN COVER—Cover Stock—FiberMark Inc.; *U.S. Public*, pg. 620

CHESS II—NONE—Western Atlas Logging Services; *U.S. Public*, pg. 1757

CHESSWOOD—Mushrooms—Ranks Hovis McDougall Limited; *Int'l*, pg. 1395

CHESTERFIELD—Cigarettes—Liggett Group Inc.; *U.S. Public*, pg. 259

CHESTERTAN BLUMENAVER BINSWANGER—Global, Cross Border Services—Binswanger; *U.S. Private*, pg. 144

CHESTNUT HILL FARMS—Seafood—Farmstead; *U.S. Private*, pg. 396

CHESTNUT RIDGE—Manufactured Homes—Champion Enterprises, Inc.; *U.S. Public*, pg. 332

CHESTY—Potato Chips—Borden, Inc.; *U.S. Private*, pg. 157

CHEVROLET—Cars, Trucks & Vans—Broadway Chevrolet; *U.S. Public*, pg. 170

CHEVROLET—Cars & Trucks—General Motors Corporation; *U.S. Public*, pg. 718

CHEVROLET—NONE—General Motors do Brasil Ltda.; *U.S. Public*, pg. 722

CHEVROLET—Motor Vehicles—Jerry Hamm Chevrolet Inc.; *U.S. Private*, pg. 497

CHEVROLET FLYER—Motor Home—Fleetwood Enterprises, Inc.; *U.S. Public*, pg. 650

CHEVROLET/GRO—Cars & Trucks—Chase Chevrolet Co., Inc.; *U.S. Private*, pg. 230

CHEVRON—Gasolines, Motor Oils & Industrial Lubricants—Chevron Corporation; *U.S. Public*, pg. 347

CHEVRON—Motion Picture Projector—Eastman Kodak Company; *U.S. Public*, pg. 550

CHEVRON—Roller Bearing End Thrust—Screw Conveyor Corp.; *U.S. Public*, pg. 977

CHEVRON—Hydraulic Seal—James Walker & Co. Limited; *Int'l*, pg. 1485

CHEVY KODIAK—Medium Duty Short Conventional Truck—Pontiac-GMC Truck Division; *U.S. Public*, pg. 720

CHEVY VAN—Truck—Chevrolet Motor Div. General Motors Corp.; *U.S. Public*, pg. 720

CHEW-EEZ—Dog Treats—Superior Brands, Inc.; *Int'l*, pg. 917

CHEW-ETS—Candy—Goldenberg Candy Company; *U.S. Public*, pg. 638

CHEW THREAD—Fiberglass Reinforced Piping—A.O. Smith Corporation; *U.S. Public*, pg. 1476

CHEWING GUM TAPE—Chewing Gum—Amurol Confections Co.; *U.S. Public*, pg. 1781

CHEWITS—Fruit Toffee—Huhtamaki Oy; *Int'l*, pg. 638

CHEWOLOGY BUBBLE GUM LAB—Chewing Gum—Amurol Confections Co.; *U.S. Public*, pg. 1781

CHEX—Cereal—General Mills, Inc.; *U.S. Public*, pg. 717

CHEX-ALL—Sterilization Products—Propper Manufacturing Co., Inc.; *U.S. Private*, pg. 891

CHEX SNACK MIX—Snacks—General Mills, Inc.; *U.S. Public*, pg. 717

CHEX SNACKS—NONE—Snacks Unlimited Division; *U.S. Public*, pg. 718

CHEX-WEAR—Chemical Resistant Floor Enamel—Benjamin Moore & Co.; *U.S. Private*, pg. 133

CHEXIT—Controlled Exit Device—Exit Device Division; *U.S. Public*, pg. 876

CHEXTRA—Debit Card—U.S. Bancorp; *U.S. Public*, pg. 1680

CHEYENNE—Ag Chemical—AgrEvo USA Company; *Int'l*, pg. 1203

CHEYENNE HSM—Data Storage Management Software—Cheyenne; *U.S. Public*, pg. 420

CHEYENNE UTILITIES—Integrated Set of Critical Server & File Management Utilities for NetWare—Cheyenne; *U.S. Public*, pg. 420

CHI CHI'S—Mexican Restaurants—Chi-Chi's Inc.; *U.S. Private*, pg. 393

CHI CHI'S—Restaurant Chain—El Torito Restaurants Inc.; *U.S. Private*, pg. 393

CHI CHI'S COCKTAILS—NONE—Barton Brands, Ltd.; *U.S. Private*, pg. 300

CHIANTI CLASSICO RISERVA—NONE—Castello Banfi Srl.; *U.S. Private*, pg. 113

CHIBROXIN—Norfloxacin—Merck & Co., Inc.; *U.S. Public*, pg. 1090

CHIBUKA—Beer—Lonrho plc; *Int'l*, pg. 817

CHIC—Women's Apparel—Henry I. Siegel Company, Inc.; *U.S. Private*, pg. 998

CHICAGO—Cutlery—Chicago Cutlery, Inc.; *U.S. Private*, pg. 716

CHICAGO—Metal Fabricating Equipment—Dreis & Krump Manufacturing Company; *U.S. Private*, pg. 342

CHICAGO BLUE—Cutlery—General Housewares Corp.; *U.S. Public*, pg. 715

CHICAGO BUSINESS DIRECTORY—Directory—Manufacturers' News, Inc.; *U.S. Private*, pg. 700

CHICAGO CUBS—Baseball Team—Chicago National League Ball Club, Inc. (Chicago Cubs); *U.S. Public*, pg. 1635

CHICAGO CUTLERY—Cutlery—General Housewares Corp.; *U.S. Public*, pg. 715

CHICAGO GRIPS—Wire, Cable Pulling Grips—Klein Tools Inc.; *U.S. Private*, pg. 625

CHICAGO-LATROBE—Drills & Reamers—Greenfield Industries Inc.; *U.S. Public*, pg. 950

CHICAGO PNEUMATIC—Air Tools—Chicago Pneumatic Tool Company; *Int'l*, pg. 96

CHICAGO READER—Newspaper—Chicago Reader, Inc.; *U.S. Private*, pg. 235

CHICAGO RIVET & MACHINE—Rivets & Rivet-Setting Equipment—Chicago Rivet & Machine Company; *U.S. Public*, pg. 348

CHICAGO SPECIALTY—Faucets & Plumbing Supplies—Fortune Brands, Inc.; *U.S. Public*, pg. 674

CHICAGO SPECIALTY—NONE—MasterBrand Industries, Inc.; *U.S. Public*, pg. 675

CHICAGO SPECIALTY—NONE—Moen Incorporated; *U.S. Public*, pg. 675

CHICAGO SWITCH—Slide & Leaf Switches—ITW Switches; *U.S. Public*, pg. 867

CHICAGO TRIBUNE—Daily Newspaper—Tribune Company; *U.S. Public*, pg. 1635

CHICK-FIL-A—Fast Food Chain Restaurants—Chick-fil-A, Inc.; *U.S. Public*, pg. 236

CHICK' N CHEDDAR—Frozen Poultry—Tyson Foods, Inc.; *U.S. Public*, pg. 1652

CHICK' N QUICK—Frozen Poultry—Tyson Foods, Inc.; *U.S. Public*, pg. 1652

CHICK' N RECIPE—Frozen Poultry—Tyson Foods, Inc.; *U.S. Public*, pg. 1652

CHICKEN BY GEORGE—Prepared Meat Product—Hormel Foods Corp.; *U.S. Public*, pg. 840

CHICKEN DESIGN—Prospect Farms—Tyson Foods, Inc.; *U.S. Public*, pg. 1652

CHICK'N EASY—Food Products—Rymer Foods Inc.; *U.S. Public*, pg. 1414

CHICKEN FILLET—Sandwich—Hardee's Food Systems, Inc.; *U.S. Public*, pg. 278

CHICKEN FLAV—Stuffing Mix—The William G. Bell Company; *U.S. Private*, pg. 165

CHICKEN FLAVOR SUPREME COUNTRY STYLE CUP-A-SOUP—Instant Soup Mix—Thomas J. Lipton Company; *Int'l*, pg. 1435

CHICKEN GLAZERS—Further-processed poultry products—Louis Kemp Seafood Co.; *U.S. Public*, pg. 1652

CHICKEN HEAD DESIGN—NONE—Koo Koo Roo, Inc.; *U.S. Public*, pg. 966

CHICKEN IN A BISKIT—Flavored Crackers—Nabisco Inc.; *U.S. Public*, pg. 1355

CHICKEN IN A BISKIT—Flavored Crackers—RJR Nabisco Holdings Corp.; *U.S. Public*, pg. 1354

CHICKEN MCNUGGETS—Entree—McDonald's Corporation; *U.S. Public*, pg. 1068

CHICKEN PLEASE—Refrigeration-Free Meal—My Own Meals, Inc.; *U.S. Private*, pg. 770

CHICKEN RAMEN—Instant Noodles—Nissin Food Products Co., Ltd.; *Int'l*, pg. 949

CHICKEN SAUCE BLENDS—Seasoning Mix—McCormick/Schilling; *U.S. Public*, pg. 1066

CHICKEN SHEET—Fabrics—Herculite Products, Inc.; *U.S. Public*, pg. 802

CHICKEN STIX—Nuggets—Hardee's Food Systems, Inc.; *U.S. Public*, pg. 278

CHICKEN TENDERS—Chicken—Burger King Corporation; *Int'l*, pg. 411

CHICKEN TENDERS—Chicken Nuggets—Burger King Corporation; *Int'l*, pg. 411

CHICKEN TONIGHT—Food Product—Chesebrough-Pond's; *Int'l*, pg. 1436

CHICKEN TONIGHT—Food Product—Van den Bergh Foods Company; *Int'l*, pg. 1436

CHICKEN TONIGHT LIGHT—Food Product—Chesebrough-Pond's; *Int'l*, pg. 1436

CHICLETS—Chewing Gum—Adams U.S.A.; *U.S. Public*, pg. 1739

CHICLETS—Chewing Gum—Warner-Lambert Company; *U.S. Public*, pg. 1738

CHIC'N CHEDDAR—Further-processed poultry products—Louis Kemp Seafood Co.; *U.S. Public*, pg. 1652

CHICO—Bananas—Chiquita Banana North America; *U.S. Public*, pg. 349

CHICO—Bananas & Related Products—Chiquita Brands International, Inc.; *U.S. Public*, pg. 349

CHICOPEE—Shop Towels, Clean Room Wipes—Chicopee Inc.; *Int'l*, pg. 113

CHICO'S—Clothing—Chico's Fas Inc; *U.S. Public*, pg. 349

CHIEF—Bins & Buildings—Chief Industries, Inc.; *U.S. Private*, pg. 236

CHIEF—Printing Paper—The Mead Corporation; *U.S. Public*, pg. 1074

CHIEFTAIN—Bond Paper—Kimberly-Clark Corporation; *U.S. Public*, pg. 958

CHIEFTAIN—Carbon Fiber Jointing—James Walker & Co. Limited; *Int'l*, pg. 1485

CHIEFTAIN—Motor Homes—Winnebago Industries, Inc.; *U.S. Public*, pg. 1772

CHIEFTAN—Carbon Fibre—James Walker & Co. Limited; *Int'l*, pg. 1485

CHIFFON—Tissue, Napkins—Fort James Corporation; *U.S. Public*, pg. 670

CHIFFON—Margarine—Nabisco Inc.; *U.S. Public*, pg. 1355

CHIHUAHUA—Beer—Labatt U.S.A.; *Int'l*, pg. 679

CHIHUAHUA BEER—Beer—Wisdom Imports Sales Co. Inc.; *Int'l*, pg. 679

CHIK'N QUICK—Further-processed poultry products—Louis Kemp Seafood Co.; *U.S. Public*, pg. 1652

CHIL-MIL—Powdered Infant Formula—Morinaga Milk Industry Co., Ltd.; *Int'l*, pg. 895

CHILD HORIZONS—Books—Ferguson Publishing Company; *U.S. Private*, pg. 401

CHILD LIFE—Magazine for Children—Benjamin Franklin Literary & Medical Society, Inc.; *U.S. Private*, pg. 133

CHILD LIFE—Children's Shoes—Jumping Jacks; *U.S. Private*, pg. 767

CHILD 2000—Funds for Ten Specific Areas—Christian Children's Fund, Inc.; *U.S. Private*, pg. 238

CHILDALERT—Relief Fund for Emergencies—Christian Children's Fund, Inc.; *U.S. Private*, pg. 238

CHILDCARE VOUCHER—Meal Vouchers—Accor S.A.; *Int'l*, pg. 20

CHILDCRAFT—Books—World Book, Inc.; *U.S. Public*, pg. 218

CHILDEUROPE—Relief Fund for Eastern Europe—Christian Children's Fund, Inc.; *U.S. Private*, pg. 238

CHILDREACH—International Development Child Sponsorship—Plan International USA, Inc.; *U.S. Private*, pg. 869

CHILDREN'S WRITER'S & ILLUSTRATOR'S MARKET—Market Book—F & W Publications, Inc.; *U.S. Private*, pg. 388

CHILDREN'S ADVIL—NONE—Whitehall-Robins Healthcare; *U.S. Public*, pg. 80

CHILDREN'S ADVIL—Children's Pain Reliever—Wyeth-Ayerst Laboratories, Inc.; *U.S. Public*, pg. 80

CHILDREN'S ADVIL SUSPENSION—NONE—American Home Products Corporation; *U.S. Public*, pg. 79

CHILDRENS BUSINESS—Business Publication—Fairchild Publications; *U.S. Public*, pg. 513

CHILDREN'S DIGEST—Magazine for Children—Benjamin Franklin Literary & Medical Society, Inc.; *U.S. Private*, pg. 133

CHILDREN'S MAGAZINE GUIDE—Index to 51 Children's Magazines for Finding Specific Articles—R.R. Bowker; *Int'l*, pg. 1096

CHILDREN'S MOTRIN—Children's Medication—McNeil Consumer Products Company; *U.S. Public*, pg. 928

CHILDREN'S MYLANTA UPSET STOMACH RELIEF—Antacid—Johnson & Johnson; *U.S. Public*, pg. 927

THE CHILDREN'S OUTLET—Children's Clothing Stores—The Children's Place Retail Stores, Inc.; *U.S. Private*, pg. 237

THE CHILDREN'S PLACE—Children's Clothing Stores & Children's Clothing—The Children's Place Retail Stores, Inc.; *U.S. Private*, pg. 237

CHILDREN'S PLAYMATE—Magazine for Children—Benjamin Franklin Literary & Medical Society, Inc.; *U.S. Private*, pg. 133

CHILDRENS PRESS—Children's Books—Childrens Press Inc.; *Int'l*, pg. 794

CHILDREN'S TYLENOL—Children's Pain Reliever—McNeil Consumer Products Company; *U.S. Public*, pg. 928

CHILDREN'S TYLENOL COLD—Children's Cold Medication—McNeil Consumer Products Company; *U.S. Public*, pg. 928

CHILDS FIRST LIBRARY OF LEARNING—Juvenile Book Series—Time-Life, Inc.; *U.S. Public*, pg. 1613

CHILD'S PLAY—Candy—Tootsie Roll Industries, Inc.; *U.S. Public*, pg. 1621

CHILDWORLD—Magazine—Christian Children's Fund, Inc.; *U.S. Public*, pg. 238

CHILI MAKIN'S—Chili Mix—Tri Valley Growers; *U.S. Private*, pg. 1101

CHILI MAN—Chili—The Milnot Company; *U.S. Private*, pg. 749

CHILI PRODUCTS—Dehydrated Products—Universal Foods Corporation; *U.S. Public*, pg. 1695

CHILI STARTER—Dry Mixes—Borden, Inc.; *U.S. Private*, pg. 157

CHILI'S GRILL & BAR—Full Service Restaurant—Brinker International, Inc.; *U.S. Public*, pg. 253

CHILL FACTOR—Newsletter—The Dow Chemical Company; *U.S. Public*, pg. 522

CHILL-VACTOR—Vacuum Pumps—Croll-Reynolds Company, Inc.; *U.S. Private*, pg. 290

CHILLRIPE—Frozen Food—Southern Frozen Foods; *U.S. Private*, pg. 887

CHILLS—Ball Point Pen—Sanford Corporation; *U.S. Public*, pg. 1178

CHILTON—Gas Cans, Oil Drain Pans—Western Industries, Inc.; *U.S. Private*, pg. 1165

CHIMECOM—Intercom Communications—The Lamson & Sessions Co.; *U.S. Public*, pg. 976

CHIMNEY LIGHT—Decorative Light Bulb—Duro-Test Corporation; *U.S. Private*, pg. 349

CHINA AIRLINES—Passenger Airline—China Airlines Ltd.; *Int'l*, pg. 284

CHINA BLACK—Pipe Tobacco—Consolidated Cigar Corp.; *U.S. Private*, pg. 690

CHINA BLACK—Pipe Tobaccos—Consolidated Cigar Corporation; *U.S. Private*, pg. 690

CHINA FOAM—Foam Trays—Amoco Chemicals; *U.S. Public*, pg. 102

CHINA FOAM—Plastic Tableware—Amoco Corporation; *U.S. Public*, pg. 101

CHINA PRIDE—Duck Sauce—Allied Old English, Inc.; *U.S. Private*, pg. 39

CHINALITE—Plastic Tableware—Amoco Corporation; *U.S. Public*, pg. 101

CHINESE SPLENDOUR—Area Rugs—Couristan Inc.; *U.S. Private*, pg. 279

CHINET—Disposable Tableware—The Chinet Co.; *Int'l*, pg. 1146

CHIP-A-ROOS—Cookies—Sunshine Biscuits, Inc.; *U.S. Private*, pg. 434

CHIP-A-ROOS—Cookies—Sunshine Biscuits, Inc.; *U.S. Public*, pg. 657

CHIP CHASERS—Snack Food—The O'Boise Corporation; *U.S. Private*, pg. 237

CHIP SUPPLY—NONE—Chip Supply Inc.; *U.S. Private*, pg. 237

CHIP TOTE—Chip Conveyor for Machine Tools—Mayfran International, Inc.; *Int'l*, pg. 1397

CHIPAWAY—Cookie—Hershey Chocolate U.S.A.; *U.S. Public*, pg. 812

CHIPCHECK—NONE—GenRad, Inc.; *U.S. Public*, pg. 731

CHIPHOG—Milling Cutter—Rogers Tool Works, Inc.; *U.S. Public*, pg. 950

CHIPICO—Pickle Products—Vienna Sausage Mfg. Co.; *U.S. Private*, pg. 1139

CHIPIE—Women's Fragrance—Coty Inc.; *Int'l*, pg. 185

CHIPITOS—Restaurant Style Tortilla Chips—Bachman Company; *U.S. Private*, pg. 109

CHIPITS—Cocoa, Baking Chocolate, Chocolate Chips—Hershey Foods Corporation; *U.S. Public*, pg. 811

CHIPLOC—Electrostatic Dissipative Bags—The Dow Chemical Company; *U.S. Public*, pg. 522

CHIPMAKER—Tooling—Federal Signal Corporation; *U.S. Public*, pg. 616

CHIPPER'S—Nuts—John B. Sanfilippo & Son, Inc.; *U.S. Public*, pg. 1431

CHIPPETTES—Solid Vegetable Flakes—Firmenich; *Int'l*, pg. 486

CHIPPEWA—Shoes & Boots—Justin Boot Company; *U.S. Public*, pg. 937

CHIPPEWA—Footwear—Justin Industries, Inc.; *U.S. Public*, pg. 936

CHIPS—Logo—Chips and Technologies, Inc.; *U.S. Public*, pg. 349

CHIPS AHOY!—Chocolate Chip Cookies—Nabisco Inc.; *U.S. Public*, pg. 1355

CHIPS AHOY!—Cookies—RJR Nabisco Holdings Corp.; *U.S. Public*, pg. 1354

CHIPS DELUXE—Cookies—Keebler Company; *U.S. Public*, pg. 657

CHIPSHOT—Electric Potato Chipper—National Presto Industries, Inc.; *U.S. Public*, pg. 1159

CHIPWICH—Ice Cream Sandwich—Chipwich Inc.; *U.S. Private*, pg. 237

CHIQUITA—Bananas—Chiquita Banana North America; *U.S. Public*, pg. 349

CHIQUITA—Bananas—Chiquita Brands International, Inc.; *U.S. Public*, pg. 349

CHIQUITA—Cameras—Eastman Kodak Company; *U.S. Public*, pg. 550

CHIQUITA JR—Smaller Sized Bananas—Chiquita Banana North America; *U.S. Public*, pg. 349

CHIQUITA JR.—Bananas—Chiquita Brands International, Inc.; *U.S. Public*, pg. 349

CHIRAT—Mayonnaise, Sauces, Mealmakers, Seasonings, Spices—Bestfoods; *U.S. Public*, pg. 223

CHIRO-SPAN—Construction Feature—King Koil Licensing Company Inc.; *U.S. Private*, pg. 621

CHIROPRACTIC—(Mattress & Box Spring)—The Springwall Mattress Co.; *U.S. Public*, pg. 973

CHIROPRACTORS PROTECTOR PLAN—NONE—Poe & Brown, Inc.; *U.S. Public*, pg. 1312

CHIROTONIC—Mattresses—Restonic Mattress Corporation; *U.S. Private*, pg. 925

CHIRPCOMM—Transmitter—BR Communications; *U.S. Public*, pg. 1555

CHIRPCOMM—Transmitter—TCI International Inc.; *U.S. Public*, pg. 1555

CHIRPSOUNDER—Tactical Frequency Mngmt. System—BR Communications; *U.S. Public*, pg. 1555

CHIRPSOUNDER—Receiver/Transmitter—TCI International Inc.; *U.S. Public*, pg. 1555

CHISHOLM—Lumber & Wood Products—Georgia-Pacific Corporation; *U.S. Public*, pg. 735

CHISWICK BITTER—Ale—Fuller, Smith & Turner Plc; *Int'l*, pg. 529

CHIVAS REGAL—Liqueur—The House of Seagram; *Int'l*, pg. 1217

CHIVAS REGAL—Scotch—The Seagram Company Ltd.; *Int'l*, pg. 1214

CHIVAS REGAL—Scotch Whiskey—Joseph E. Seagram & Sons, Inc.; *Int'l*, pg. 1215

CHIX—Foodservice Towels, Wet Wipes, Aprons, Tee Towels—Chicopee Inc.; *Int'l*, pg. 113

CHIYODA—Sake—Suntory Ltd.; *Int'l*, pg. 1321

CHLAMYDIA ANTIGEN ELISA—Test—Ortho Clinical Diagnostic Systems Inc.; *U.S. Public*, pg. 929

CHLAMYDIAZYME—Diagnostic Products—Abbott Laboratories; *U.S. Public*, pg. 12

CHLOE—Toiletries—Elizabeth Arden Company; *Int'l*, pg. 1435

CHLOR-A-VAC—Gas Induction Unit—Capital Controls Company Inc.; *U.S. Public*, pg. 1226

CHLOR-PHED—NONE—Lee Pharmaceuticals; *U.S. Public*, pg. 984

CHLOR-TERGENT—Detergent—Oakite Products, Inc.; *Int'l*, pg. 861

CHLOR-TRIMETON—Allergy Medicines—Schering-Plough Corporation; *U.S. Public*, pg. 1438

CHLOR-TRIMETON—Allergy Medicine—Schering-Plough Healthcare Products Inc.; *U.S. Public*, pg. 1438

CHLORALERT—Disinfection Product—Bailey, Fischer & Porter Company; *Int'l*, pg. 449

CHLORALERT II—Disinfection Product—Bailey, Fischer & Porter Company; *Int'l*, pg. 449

CHLORASEPTIC—Oral Antiseptic—The Procter & Gamble Company; *U.S. Public*, pg. 1330

CHLORAZENE—Purification Chemical Used to Treat Water in Hospital Hydrotherapy Units—Wisconsin Pharmacal Co., Inc.; *U.S. Private*, pg. 1185

CHLORESIUM—Pharmaceutical Products—Rystan Company, Inc.; *U.S. Private*, pg. 436

CHLORIDE—NONE—Chloride Group PLC; *Int'l*, pg. 287

CHLORINLOG—NONE—Western Atlas Logging Services; *U.S. Public*, pg. 1757

CHLORIVER—Chemical Reagant—Hach Company; *U.S. Public*, pg. 773

CHLOROMATIC—Disinfection Product—Bailey, Fischer & Porter Company; *Int'l*, pg. 449

CHLOROMYCETIN—Drug for Typhoid—Parke-Davis & Company, Limited; *U.S. Public*, pg. 1739

Brand Name Index

CHLOROPTIC—Sterile Ophthalmic Solution—Allergan, Inc.; *U.S. Public*, pg. 46

CHLOROTHALONIL—Tetrachloroisophthalonitrile—Caffaro S.p.A.; *Int'l*, pg. 248

CHLOROTHENE—Solvent—The Dow Chemical Company; *U.S. Public*, pg. 522

CHLOROWAX—Chlorinated Parafin—Occidental Chemical Corporation; *U.S. Public*, pg. 1210

CHO-SEAL—Conductive Elastomers—Chomerics Inc.; *U.S. Public*, pg. 1262

CHO-SHIELD—Conductive Coatings—Chomerics Inc.; *U.S. Public*, pg. 1262

CHOC-O-MALT—Ice Cream Product—NDS; *Int'l*, pg. 918

CHOCAPIC—Chocolate Cereal—Nestle S.A.; *Int'l*, pg. 915

CHOCK FULL O' NUTS—Coffee—Chock Full O' Nuts Corporation; *U.S. Public*, pg. 351

CHOCK FULL O' NUTS—Coffee—Chock Full O' Nuts - Food Service Div.; *U.S. Public*, pg. 351

CHOCKS—Multiple Vitamins—Bayer AG; *Int'l*, pg. 171

CHOCLAIT CHIPS—Chocolate Snack—Nestle S.A.; *Int'l*, pg. 915

CHOCLIN—Specialty Product—Lever Brothers Co.; *Int'l*, pg. 1435

CHOCLIN—Specialty Prod.—Unilever Plc; *Int'l*, pg. 1433

CHOCO BABY—Chocolate Products—Meiji Seika Kaisha, Ltd.; *Int'l*, pg. 855

CHOCO-BAKE—Unsweetened Baking Chocolate Flavor—Nestle Chocolate & Confection; *Int'l*, pg. 917

CHOCO-CREAM—Imitation Chocolate Drink—Diehl Inc.; *U.S. Private*, pg. 332

CHOCO CRUNCH—Ready-to-eat Cereal—The Quaker Oats Company; *U.S. Public*, pg. 1347

CHOCO-RIFFIC—Chocolate Drink—Dean Foods Company; *U.S. Public*, pg. 489

CHOCOLAT COOL—Chocolate—Meiji Seika Kaisha, Ltd.; *Int'l*, pg. 855

CHOCOLATE AMBER—Beer—The F.X. Matt Brewing Co.; *U.S. Private*, pg. 714

CHOCOLATE CHIP CLASSIC—Reduced Fat Cookies—Westbrae Natural, Inc.; *U.S. Public*, pg. 774

CHOCOLATE CHIP SNAPS—Cookies—Nabisco Inc.; *U.S. Public*, pg. 1355

CHOCOLATE COW—Chocolate Drink—Yoo Hoo Chocolate Beverage Corp.; *Int'l*, pg. 567

CHOCOLATE FUDGE SANDWICH—Cookie—Keebler Company; *U.S. Public*, pg. 657

CHOCOLATE GRAHAMS—Chocolate Covered Graham Crackers—Nabisco Inc.; *U.S. Public*, pg. 1355

CHOCOLATE MOUNTAIN BAR—Hard Ice Cream Novelty—International Dairy Queen, Inc.; *U.S. Public*, pg. 220

CHOCOLATE MOUSSE—NONE—Baskin-Robbins Canada; *Int'l*, pg. 63

CHOCOLATE RESOURCE—Chocolate Products—Grace Cocoa/Ambrosia Chocolate; *U.S. Public*, pg. 128

CHOCOLATE ROCKY—Gourmet Cookies—Cookie Tree Inc.; *U.S. Private*, pg. 273

CHOCOLATE SNAPS—Cookies—Nabisco Inc.; *U.S. Public*, pg. 1355

CHOCOMITE—Non-Dairy Chocolate Drink—Diehl Inc.; *U.S. Private*, pg. 332

CHOCOMITE—Non-Dairy Chocolate Flavored Beverage—Diehl Specialties International; *U.S. Private*, pg. 332

CHOCTAW—Printing Papers—Weyerhaeuser Company; *U.S. Public*, pg. 1764

CHOCTAW OFFSET GLOSS & MATTE—Lightweight Coated Papers—Weyerhaeuser Company; *U.S. Public*, pg. 1764

CHOICE—U.K. Retirement Magazine—Choice Publications Ltd; *Int'l*, pg. 451

CHOICE—Credit Card—Citibank Credit Card Marketing; *U.S. Public*, pg. 377

THE CHOICE—Dual Fuel Heat Pump—Georgia Power Co.; *U.S. Public*, pg. 1490

CHOICE ACRES—Pickles & Pepper Products—Campbell Sales; *U.S. Public*, pg. 299

CHOICE BLEND—Dog Food—H.J. Heinz Company; *U.S. Public*, pg. 805

CHOICE PLUS—NONE—Pioneer Life Insurance Co. of Illinois; *U.S. Public*, pg. 434

CHOICEPLUS—Universal Life Insurance—Colonial Companies, Inc.; *U.S. Public*, pg. 1699

CHOICES—Office Systems Furniture—Trendway Corporation; *U.S. Private*, pg. 1099

CHOICEWOOD—Finished Lumber—Weyerhaeuser Company; *U.S. Public*, pg. 1764

CHOICEWOOD—Clear Lumber & Boards—Weyerhaeuser Forest Products Company; *U.S. Public*, pg. 1764

CHOLEDYL—Bronchodilator—Warner-Chilcott Laboratories, Inc.; *Int'l*, pg. 436

CHOLOTEC—Diagnostics—Bristol-Myers Squibb Company; *U.S. Public*, pg. 253

CHOMERICS—Electronic Packaging—Chomerics Inc.; *U.S. Public*, pg. 1262

CHOOPAR—Monthly Children's Magazine—The Israel Land Development Co., Ltd.; *Int'l*, pg. 691

CHOOSY—Pet Food—Dalgety Plc; *Int'l*, pg. 376

CHOP PAK—Fiberglass Reinforcement—Johns Manville Corporation; *U.S. Public*, pg. 927

CHOPARD—Fragrance—Lancaster Group Worldwide; *Int'l*, pg. 185

CHOP HOUSE—Steakhouse & Brewhouse—Rock Bottom Restaurants; *U.S. Public*, pg. 1396

CHOPLIFTER—Videogame—Sega of America Inc.; *Int'l*, pg. 1218

CHORE—Motors—Marathon Electric Manufacturing Corp.; *U.S. Public*, pg. 1371

CHORE BOY—Pan Scourers—Reckitt & Colman Inc.; *Int'l*, pg. 1090

CHORE BOY—Scrub Sponge—Reckitt & Colman plc; *Int'l*, pg. 1089

CHORE-MATIC—Broiler Feeding System—CTB International Corp.; *U.S. Public*, pg. 284

CHOREMASTER—Paper Towels—Georgia-Pacific Corporation; *U.S. Public*, pg. 735

CHORLASTIC—Proprietary Material—Furon Company; *U.S. Public*, pg. 688

CHORUS—Telephone—France Telecom; *Int'l*, pg. 503

CHORUS—Pacemakers—L'Oreal S.A.; *Int'l*, pg. 818

CHOUINARD EQUIPMENT—Climbing & Backcountry Skiing Equip.—Lost Arrow Corporation; *U.S. Private*, pg. 676

CHOWDER STARTER—Dry Mixes—Borden, Inc.; *U.S. Private*, pg. 157

CHRIS-CRAFT—Boats—Outboard Marine Corporation; *U.S. Private*, pg. 478

CHRYSLER TOWN & COUNTRY—Minivan—Chrysler Corporation; *U.S. Public*, pg. 352

CHRISTAL RADIO—Radio Advertising Representative Service—Katz Media Group, Inc.; *U.S. Public*, pg. 335

CHRISTENSEN—Diamond Blades—Norton Company; *Int'l*, pg. 1173

CHRISTIAN ART—Church Worship Bulletins—Warner Press, Inc.; *U.S. Public*, pg. 1150

CHRISTIAN AUJARD—Men's Apparel—International Cosmetics Co., Ltd.; *Int'l*, pg. 684

CHRISTIAN BROTHERS—Wine—Grand Metropolitan Plc; *Int'l*, pg. 408

CHRISTIAN BROTHERS—Brandy—Heublein, Inc.; *Int'l*, pg. 410

CHRISTIAN DIOR—Men's Tailored Clothing—Hartmarx Corporation; *U.S. Public*, pg. 795

CHRISTIAN DIOR—Sleepwear—Host Apparel, Inc.; *U.S. Private*, pg. 540

CHRISTIAN DIOR—Ophthalmic & Sunglasses—Optimaxx International; *U.S. Private*, pg. 818

CHRISTIAN DIOR—Slacks—Trans-Apparel Group; *U.S. Public*, pg. 796

CHRISTIAN DIOR INTIMATES—Intimate Apparel—Lily of France, Inc.; *U.S. Private*, pg. 140

CHRISTIAN HISTORY—Magazine—Christianity Today, Inc.; *U.S. Public*, pg. 238

CHRISTIAN MOERLEIN—Beer—Hudepohl-Schoenling Brewing Company; *U.S. Private*, pg. 545

CHRISTIAN READER—Magazine—Christianity Today, Inc.; *U.S. Private*, pg. 238

CHRISTIAN RESOURCE CENTER—Promotional Kiosk (Consumer)—Spring Arbor Distributors; *U.S. Private*, pg. 563

CHRISTIANA—Land Development—Christiana Companies, Inc.; *U.S. Public*, pg. 352

CHRISTIANITY ONLINE—America Online Site—Christianity Today, Inc.; *U.S. Private*, pg. 238

CHRISTIANITY TODAY—Magazine—Christianity Today, Inc.; *U.S. Private*, pg. 238

CHRISTIE—Cookies, Crackers & Snacks—RJR Nabisco Holdings Corp.; *U.S. Public*, pg. 1354

CHRISTIE BRINKLEY—Women's Jewelry—Swank, Inc.; *U.S. Public*, pg. 1543

CHRISTIE'S—Shoes—Tober Industries, Inc.; *U.S. Private*, pg. 1089

CHRISTMAS BY FRANK'S—NONE—General Host Corporation; *U.S. Public*, pg. 715

CHRISTMAS CARDS BY MILES KIMBALL OF OSK KOSH—Mail Order—Miles Kimball Company; *U.S. Private*, pg. 745

THE CHRISTMAS COLLECTION—Christmas Trees, Wreaths, Foliage & Tree Trimmings—Celebrity Incorporated; *U.S. Public*, pg. 319

CHRISTMAS IN BETHLEHEM—Moving Nativity Scene—Mr. Christmas Inc.; *U.S. Private*, pg. 765

CHRISTMAS MEMORIES—Christmas Catalog—Lillian Vernon Corporation; *U.S. Public*, pg. 1716

CHRISTMAS PAST—Greeting Cards—American Greetings Corporation; *U.S. Public*, pg. 77

CHRISTOFILE—Silver—Baccarat (Cie des Cristalleries); *Int'l*, pg. 132

CHRISTOFLE—Silver Sold Retail only—Baccarat, Inc.; *Int'l*, pg. 132

CHRISTOPHER AND BANKS—Casual Sportswear—Brauns Fashions Corporation; *U.S. Public*, pg. 251

CHRISTOPHER EDWARDS—Pie—Edwards Baking Co.; *U.S. Private*, pg. 365

CHRISTY—Bathroom Textiles—Courtaulds Textiles Plc; *Int'l*, pg. 339

CHRISTY'S—Convenience Food Supplier—Christy's Markets, Inc.; *U.S. Private*, pg. 238

CHROM-O-SCOPE—Industrial Instrument—Capintec, Inc.; *U.S. Private*, pg. 205

CHROMA-CHEM—Industrial Colorant—Veba AG; *Int'l*, pg. 1454

CHROMA-KOTE—FD & C Lake Dispersion—Crompton & Knowles Ingredient Technology Corp.; *U.S. Public*, pg. 459

CHROMA LINE—Electric Discharge Lamps—General Electric Canada Inc.; *U.S. Public*, pg. 713

CHROMA-SEAL—Seal Coating for Pharmaceutical Tabs—Crompton & Knowles Ingredient Technology Corp.; *U.S. Public*, pg. 459

CHROMA-TERIC—Aqueous Colors for Enteric or Sustained Release Applications—Crompton & Knowles Ingredient Technology Corp.; *U.S. Public*, pg. 459

CHROMACOLOR—Televisions—Zenith Electronics Corp.; *U.S. Public*, pg. 1790

CHROMAFLEX—Protective, Decorative Coatings for Light Industrial Fabricated Metal Prods—PPG Industries, Inc.; *U.S. Public*, pg. 1245

CHROMAGRAM—Chromatography Sheeting & Apparatus Equipment—Eastman Kodak Company; *U.S. Public*, pg. 550

CHROMAGRAPH DC 380T—Scanner—Linotype-Hell Company; *Int'l*, pg. 604

CHROMALOX—Electric Heaters - Canada—The Glen Dimplex Group; *Int'l*, pg. 553

CHROMALOX—Electric Heating Equip.—Wiegand Industrial-Chromalox; *U.S. Public*, pg. 573

CHROMASSURE—Color Coded O-Ring Seals—Seal Group; *U.S. Public*, pg. 1262

CHROMATIC—Writing Instruments for Specialty Advertising—Golden Books Family Entertainment Inc.; *U.S. Public*, pg. 749

CHROMATICS—Lower Priced Raingear—Totes Incorporated; *U.S. Private*, pg. 111

CHROMATIX SEATING—Office Seating—The HON Co.; *U.S. Public*, pg. 772

CHROMATO-VUE—Viewing Cabinets—UVP, Inc.; *U.S. Private*, pg. 1115

CHROMATOGRAPHIC—Software—Beckman Instruments, Inc.; *U.S. Public*, pg. 199

CHROMATONE—Dispersible Colors—Crompton & Knowles Ingredient Technology Corp.; *U.S. Public*, pg. 459

CHROMAVER—Chemical Reagant—Hach Company; *U.S. Public*, pg. 773

CHROMAX—Nicr Resistance Alloy—Driver-Harris Company; *U.S. Public*, pg. 530

CHROMCRAFT—Furniture—Chromcraft Corporation; *U.S. Public*, pg. 352

CHROME—Color Reversal Paper—Konica Corporation; *Int'l*, pg. 748

CHROME CORE—NONE—Carpenter Technology Corporation; *U.S. Public*, pg. 307

CHROME-FLEX—High Temperature Resistance Cover for a Felt or Paper Carrying Roll—Harnischfeger Industries, Inc.; *U.S. Public*, pg. 788

CHROMEKILL—Reducing Hexavalent Chromium—Enthone-OMI, Inc.; *U.S. Public*, pg. 138

CHROMEL—Resistance Wire—Armada Corporation; *U.S. Private*, pg. 82

CHROMEROD—Chrome Plated Steel Bars—J.H. Roberts Industries Inc.; *U.S. Private*, pg. 935

CHROMEWEAR—Wear-Resistant Tool Steel—Allvac; *U.S. Public*, pg. 43

CHROMICOAT—Conversion Coating—Oakite Products, Inc.; *Int'l*, pg. 861

CHROMOFINE—Coloring Agent for Phthalo Blue/Greens for High Performance Pigments—Dainichiseika Colour & Chemicals Mfg. Co., Ltd.; *Int'l*, pg. 369

CHROMOGENIC—Reagents and Controls—Ortho Clinical Diagnostic Systems Inc.; *U.S. Public*, pg. 929

CHROMPLOT—Software Packages—Millipore Corporation; *U.S. Public*, pg. 1112

CHROMSPUN—Acetate Yarn—Eastman Chemical Company; *U.S. Public*, pg. 550

CHROMSPUN—Man-Made Yarn, Synthetic Staple Fiber—Eastman Kodak Company; *U.S. Public*, pg. 550

CHRONO—Herbicides—Agrolinz Melamin GmbH; *Int'l*, pg. 356

CHRONOCOM—Clocks, Communication Systems—Rauland-Borg Corporation; *U.S. Private*, pg. 911

CHRONOSPHERE—Customized Carrier Systems for Controlled Delivery of Active Ingrediants—PolyMedica Industries, Inc.; *U.S. Public*, pg. 1315

CHRONULAC—Prescription Laxitive—Hoechst Marion Roussel North America; *Int'l*, pg. 625

THE CHRYON CENTAUR—Video Adaptor Board—Chyron Corp.; *Int'l*, pg. 1372

THE CHRYON CODI SKETCHPAD—Video Graphics—Chyron Corp.; *Int'l*, pg. 1372

THE CHRYON MAX—Video Graphics—Chyron Corp.; *Int'l*, pg. 1372

THE CHRYON MAXINE—Video Graphics—Chyron Corp.; *Int'l*, pg. 1372

CHRYSALIS—Record Label—EMI Group plc; *Int'l*, pg. 426

CHRYSALIS—Records—Sony Corporation; *Int'l*, pg. 1280

CHRYSLER—Motor Vehicles & Inboard Marine Engines—Chrysler Corporation; *U.S. Public*, pg. 352

CHRYSLER CONCORDE—Car—Chrysler Corporation; *U.S. Public*, pg. 352

CHRYSLER FIFTH AVENUE—Car—Chrysler Corporation; *U.S. Public*, pg. 352

CHRYSLER IMPERIAL—Car—Chrysler Corporation; *U.S. Public*, pg. 352

CHRYSLER LE BARON CONVERTIBLE—Car—Chrysler Corporation; *U.S. Public*, pg. 352

CHRYSLER LE BARON COUPE—Car—Chrysler Corporation; *U.S. Public*, pg. 352

CHRYSLER LE BARON SEDAN—Car—Chrysler Corporation; *U.S. Public*, pg. 352

CHRYSLER LHS—Automobile—Chrysler Corporation; *U.S. Public*, pg. 352

CHRYSLER NEW YORKER SALON—Car—Chrysler Corporation; *U.S. Public*, pg. 352

CHUBBY—NONE—Pfizer Inc.; *U.S. Public*, pg. 1281

CHUCK-A-MATIC—Pneumatically Controlled Single Spindle Chucking Machine—The Machine Tool Group; *U.S. Public*, pg. 503

CHUCK E CHEESE PIZZA—Family Entertainment Centers—ShowBiz Pizza Time, Inc.; *U.S. Public*, pg. 1468

CHUCK-O-MATIC—Single Spindle Chucking Machine, Hydraulic—The Machine Tool Group; *U.S. Public*, pg. 503

CHUCK STYLE CAPPER—Capping—U.S. Bottlers Machinery Co.; *U.S. Private*, pg. 1124

CHUCK TAYLOR COLLECTION—Foot Apparel—Converse Inc.; *U.S. Public*, pg. 441

CHUCK WAGON—Dog Food—Ralston Purina Company; *U.S. Public*, pg. 1359

CHUCKLES—Candy—Huhtamaki Oy; *Int'l*, pg. 638

CHUKA—Seasoning—Ajinomoto Company Inc.; *Int'l*, pg. 40

CHUN KING—Frozen Foods—ConAgra Frozen Food Company; *U.S. Public*, pg. 427

CHUN KING—Oriental Foods—ConAgra, Inc.; *U.S. Public*, pg. 425

CHUN KING—Oriental Foods—Hunt-Wesson, Inc.; *U.S. Public*, pg. 428

CHUNCKS—Pet Food—Iams Company; *U.S. Private*, pg. 556

CHUNKY—Food Products—Campbell Soup Company Ltd.; *U.S. Public*, pg. 299

CHUNKY—Yarn—Lion Brand Yarn Co.; *U.S. Private*, pg. 669

CHUNKY—Candy—Nestle Chocolate & Confection; *Int'l*, pg. 917

CHUNKY—Candy—Nestle S.A.; *Int'l*, pg. 915

CHUNKY—Candy—Nestle USA; *Int'l*, pg. 916

CHUNKY MONKEY—Ice Cream—Ben & Jerry's Homemade Inc.; *U.S. Public*, pg. 210

CHUPA CHUPS SA—NONE—Cruspi S.A.; *Int'l*, pg. 348

CHUPI CANDY—Candy—Warner-Lambert K.K.; *U.S. Public*, pg. 1739

CHURCHILL—Grocery Sacks—Johns Manville Corporation; *U.S. Public*, pg. 927

CHURCHILL—Swim Fins—Mattel, Inc.; *U.S. Public*, pg. 1057

CHURCHILL—Swim Fins—Mattel Power Wheels; *U.S. Public*, pg. 1058

CHURCH'S—Fried Chicken Restaurants—Church's Chicken, Inc.; *U.S. Private*, pg. 5

CHURCHS' CHICKEN—Fast Food Chicken—Cara Operations Limited; *Int'l*, pg. 266

CHURCH'S CHICKEN RESTAURANT—Fast Food Restaurant Specializing in Fried Chicken—AFC Enterprises; *U.S. Private*, pg. 5

CHURNY—Cheese—Churny Company Inc.; *U.S. Public*, pg. 1288

CHUTEMASTER—Fiberglass Spiral Chutes—Flomaster Div.; *U.S. Public*, pg. 1318

CHUTES & LADDERS—Game—Hasbro, Inc.; *U.S. Public*, pg. 797

CHUTES & LADDERS—Game—Milton Bradley Company; *U.S. Public*, pg. 797

CHYMORAL—Pharmaceuticals—Rhone-Poulenc Rorer - U.S.; *Int'l*, pg. 1110

THE CHYRON CODI—Vidio System—Chyron Corp.; *Int'l*, pg. 1372

THE CHYRON IV—Video Equipment—Chyron Corp.; *Int'l*, pg. 1372

THE CHYRON INFINIT—Video Equipment—Chyron Corp.; *Int'l*, pg. 1372

THE CHYRON RGU-2—Video Equipment—Chyron Corp.; *Int'l*, pg. 1372

THE CHYRON SCRIBE FOR HDTV—Video Equipment—Chyron Corp.; *Int'l*, pg. 1372

THE CHYRON SCRIBE JR—Video Equipment—Chyron Corp.; *Int'l*, pg. 1372

THE CHYRON SCRIBE—Video Graphics Equipment—Chyron Corp.; *Int'l*, pg. 1372

THE CHYRON SUPERSCRIBE—Video Equipment—Chyron Corp.; *Int'l*, pg. 1372

CI' BELLA—Pasta Sauce—Westbrae Natural, Inc.; *U.S. Public*, pg. 774

CIBA SEEDS—Farm Seeds—CIBA Seeds; *Int'l*, pg. 973

CIBACALCIN—Pharmaceutical—Ciba Specialty Chemicals; *Int'l*, pg. 291

CIBACALCIN—Pharmaceutical—Novartis; *Int'l*, pg. 972

CIBACALCIN—NONE—Novartis Pharmaceuticals; *Int'l*, pg. 973

CIBACEN—ACE-Inhibitor for Hypertension—Novartis; *Int'l*, pg. 972

CIBACHROME—Colour Materials—Novartis; *Int'l*, pg. 972

CIBACRON F—Dye Mixtures—Novartis; *Int'l*, pg. 972

CICH FINIMETAL—Heating Equipment—Blue Circle Industries PLC; *Int'l*, pg. 197

CICORAD—NONE—Sico Inc.; *Int'l*, pg. 1239

CICROM—NONE—Acos Villares S.A.; *Int'l*, pg. 23

CICULAIRE—Ceiling Cleaners—Luwa Bahnson, Inc.; *U.S. Private*, pg. 682

CIDER SPICER—Mulling Spice—Alltrista Corporation; *U.S. Public*, pg. 56

CIDEX—Sterilizing/Disinfecting Solutions—Johnson & Johnson Medical, Inc.; *U.S. Public*, pg. 928

CIDEX 7—Disinfectant—Johnson & Johnson Consumer Products; *U.S. Public*, pg. 928

CIERA—Automobile—Oldsmobile Div. General Motors Corp.; *U.S. Public*, pg. 720

CILCO—Intraocular Lenses—Alcon Laboratories, Inc.; *Int'l*, pg. 916

CILCO EXPERT—NONE—Sico Inc.; *Int'l*, pg. 1239

CILIA—Tea Products—Melitta Unternehmensgruppe Bentz KG; *Int'l*, pg. 856

CILLIT—Hardsurface Cleaner—Benckiser Consumer Products Inc.; *Int'l*, pg. 185

CILOXAN—Ciprofloxacin HcL 0.3% As Base—Alcon Laboratories, Inc.; *Int'l*, pg. 916

CIMAREC—Binding Agent for Ceramic—The Dow Chemical Company; *U.S. Public*, pg. 522

CIMETIDINE—Generic Drug—American Home Products Corporation; *U.S. Public*, pg. 79

CIMFLEX—Silicone Bonds—Solvay S.A.; *Int'l*, pg. 1277

CIMIANTO—NONE—ETEX; *Int'l*, pg. 430

CIMLINK—System Control Software—Universal Instruments Corporation; *U.S. Public*, pg. 522

CIMOBAC—Cinoxacin—Eli Lilly Italia, S.p.A.; *U.S. Public*, pg. 994

CIMS—NONE—Landmark Graphics Corporation; *U.S. Public*, pg. 776

CIN-TEC—Control/Monitor—Cincinnati Gear Company; *U.S. Private*, pg. 240

CINCH—Agricultural—CF & I Steel, L.P.; *U.S. Public*, pg. 230

CINCH—Automobile, Aerospace, Defense, Communications & Computer Connectors—Cinch Connector Division; *Int'l*, pg. 786

CINCH—Mixes—Gilster Mary Lee Corp.; *U.S. Private*, pg. 455

CINCH—Specialty Chemicals—Klein Tools Inc.; *U.S. Private*, pg. 625

CINCH—Aeronautic-Electronic-Automotive Connector—Labinal SA; *Int'l*, pg. 785

CINCILLA—Textile Floorcoverings—Forbo Holding SA; *Int'l*, pg. 496

CINCINNATI ALL STAR—Portable Baseball Court—Robbins, Inc.; *U.S. Private*, pg. 934

CINCINNATI BUSINESS COURIER—Business Journal—Business First of New York, Inc.; *U.S. Private*, pg. 19

THE CINCINNATI ENQUIRER—Newspaper—The Cincinnati Enquirer, Inc.; *U.S. Public*, pg. 700

CINCINNATI MILACRON—Mfr. Metal Working Machinery—Cincinnati Milacron U.K. Limited; *U.S. Public*, pg. 368

THE CINCINNATI POST—Newspaper—The E.W. Scripps Company; *U.S. Public*, pg. 1447

CINCINNATI RECIPE—Cincinnati Style Chili—Skyline Chili, Inc.; *U.S. Public*, pg. 1475

CINCINNATUS-DOUBLE ARM—Mixer—Littleford Day Inc.; *U.S. Private*, pg. 671

CINDOL—Coolant for Aluminum—Houghton International Inc.; *U.S. Private*, pg. 541

CINE CHIFFRES—French Film Magazine—EMAP France; *Int'l*, pg. 451

CINE-KODAK—Motion Picture Cameras,Converter Lenses—Eastman Kodak Company; *U.S. Public*, pg. 550

CINEFLURE—X-Ray Film, Chemicals—Eastman Kodak Company; *U.S. Public*, pg. 550

CINEMA ETOILE—Ladies Lingerie—Movie Star, Inc.; *U.S. Public*, pg. 1140

CINEMA 180—Motion Picture Screen—Iwerks Entertainment; *U.S. Public*, pg. 915

CINEMAX—Pay Television Service—Home Box Office, Inc.; *U.S. Public*, pg. 1612

CINEMAX—Cable Network—Time Warner Inc.; *U.S. Public*, pg. 1610

CINEON—NONE—Eastman Kodak Company; *U.S. Public*, pg. 550

CINEPLEX ODEON THEATRES—Motion Picture Theaters—Cineplex Odeon Corporation; *Int'l*, pg. 292

CINERGI—NONE—Lawter International, Inc.; *U.S. Public*, pg. 980

CINERRIO H-LINE—Steel Wall Panel—Clestra Hauserman, Inc.; *Int'l*, pg. 569

CINERRIO I-LINE—Steel Wall Panel—Clestra Hauserman, Inc.; *Int'l*, pg. 569

CINESITE—NONE—Eastman Kodak Company; *U.S. Public*, pg. 550

CINEVIDEO PLUS—Canadian Broadcasting—CLT-UFA; *Int'l*, pg. 561

CINN∗A∗BURST—Cinnamon Flavor Gum—Adams U.S.A.; *U.S. Public*, pg. 1739

CINNABON—Cinnamon Roll Restaurants—Restaurants Unlimited; *U.S. Private*, pg. 925

CINNAMINT—Gum—Clark Gum Company; *U.S. Private*, pg. 243

CINNAMON—Topping—Lever Brothers Co.; *Int'l*, pg. 1435

CINNAMON—Topping—Unilever Plc; *Int'l*, pg. 1433

CINNAMON APPLE SPICE—Herb Tea—Celestial Seasonings; *U.S. Public*, pg. 319

CINNAMON CRISP—Cracker—Keebler Company; *U.S. Public*, pg. 657

CINNAMON N' RAISIN—Breakfast Biscuit—Hardee's Food Systems, Inc.; *U.S. Public*, pg. 278

CINNAMON ROSE—Herb Tea—Celestial Seasonings; *U.S. Public*, pg. 319

CINNAMON TEDDY BEARS—Candy—Stark Candy Company; *U.S. Private*, pg. 1113

CINNAMON TOAST CRUNCH—Cereal—General Mills, Inc.; *U.S. Public*, pg. 717

CINNAMON VIENNA—Tea—Celestial Seasonings; *U.S. Public*, pg. 319

CINQUECENTO—Car—Fiat Auto Ireland Ltd.; *Int'l*, pg. 481

CONTINENTAL CABLEVISION—NONE—MediaOne; *U.S. Public*, pg. 1688

CINTA—NONE—Kiwi Brands Pty. Ltd.; *U.S. Public*, pg. 1434

CINTA AZUL—Rice—American Rice Inc.; *U.S. Public*, pg. 591

CINTAS—Uniform Programs—Cintas Corporation; *U.S. Public*, pg. 370

CINTERNAL—Grinding Machine—Cincinnati Milacron U.K. Limited; *U.S. Public*, pg. 368

CINTI—Equa-Load-Gears—Cincinnati Gear Company; *U.S. Private*, pg. 240

CINTI-BHS—Gears—Cincinnati Gear Company; *U.S. Private*, pg. 240

CINTRA—Port Wine—Groupe Pernod Ricard; *Int'l*, pg. 566

CINTURN—Turning Centre—Cincinnati Milacron U.K. Limited; *U.S. Public*, pg. 368

CINZANO—Vermouth—Groupe Pernod Ricard; *Int'l*, pg. 566

CINZANO—NONE—IDV Central Europe; *Int'l*, pg. 410

CINZANO—NONE—Tegner & Son AB; *Int'l*, pg. 412

CINZANO ASTI & VERMOUTH—NONE—Heublein Inc.; *Int'l*, pg. 410

CINZANO BRUT—NONE—Societe Pour la Vente des Produits Cinzano SA; *Int'l*, pg. 410

CINZANO VERMOUTH—NONE—Societe Pour la Vente des Produits Cinzano SA; *Int'l*, pg. 410

CIPRO—Ciprofloxacin—Bayer Corporation/Consumer Care Division; *Int'l*, pg. 173

CIPRO IV—Pharmaceutical—Bayer Corporation/Pharmaceutical Division; *Int'l*, pg. 173

CIPRO TABLETS—Pharmaceutical—Bayer Corporation/Pharmaceutical Division; *Int'l*, pg. 173

CIPROBAY—Synthetic Antibacterial—Bayer AG; *Int'l*, pg. 171

CIPROXIN—Synthetic Antibacterial—Bayer AG; *Int'l*, pg. 171

CIPS—Tubes for Refrigeration Systems & Gas Supplies—KM-Europa Metal Aktiengesellschaft; *Int'l*, pg. 719

CIPTANE—Synthetic Precipitated Silica—PPG Industries, Inc.; *U.S. Public*, pg. 1245

CIRCLE—Form/Fill/Seal—SASIB Packaging North America; *Int'l*, pg. 1194

CIRCLE K—Convenience Stores—Tosco Corporation; *U.S. Public*, pg. 1624

CIRCLE LOGO—NONE—SunGard Data Systems Inc.; *U.S. Public*, pg. 1534

CIRCLE-O-COMFORT—Athletic Shoes—E.J. Footwear Corp.; *U.S. Public*, pg. 1684

CIRCLE O' LOVE—Jewelry—Helzberg's Diamond Shops, Inc.; *U.S. Public*, pg. 220

CIRCLE OF BEAUTY—NONE—Sears, Roebuck and Co.; *U.S. Public*, pg. 1452

CIRCLE SEAL—Valves & Regulators—Circle Seal Controls, Inc.; *U.S. Public*, pg. 1746

CIRCLE SEAL—Valves—Watts Industries, Inc.; *U.S. Public*, pg. 1746

CIRCLE TRACK—Magazine—Petersen Publishing Company, L.L.C.; *U.S. Private*, pg. 856

CIRCLE U DRY—Sausages—Armour Swift Eckrich; *U.S. Public*, pg. 426

CIRCLELOCK—NONE—Boon Edam Inc.; *Int'l*, pg. 202

CIRCLESUBE—NONE—Boon Edam Inc.; *Int'l*, pg. 202

CIRCON—Medical Video Camera—Circon Corporation; *U.S. Public*, pg. 373

CIRCOSOL—Premium Process Oil—Sun Refining & Marketing Co. Lubes Div.; *U.S. Public*, pg. 1530

CIRCUIT BOARDS—Mounts & Hardware—International Electronic Research Corp.; *U.S. Public*, pg. 286

CIRCUIT CITY—Electronics Stores—Circuit City Stores, Inc.; *U.S. Public*, pg. 374

CIRCUIT CITY SUPERSTORE—Electronics Store—Circuit City Stores, Inc.; *U.S. Public*, pg. 374

CIRCUIT SAFE—Non-Metallic Enclosures—The Lamson & Sessions Co.; *U.S. Public*, pg. 976

CIRCUIT SEEKER—Circuit Tracer—Greenlee Textron; *U.S. Public*, pg. 1589

CIRCUIT TECHNOLOGY—Microelectronics—Aeroflex Incorporated; *U.S. Public*, pg. 23

CIRCUITS ASSEMBLY—Magazine—Miller Freeman Inc.; *Int'l*, pg. 1443

CIRCUS MAXIMUS—Game—Monarch Avalon, Inc.; *U.S. Public*, pg. 1123

CIRCUSTAT—Heater—Fisher Scientific Company; *U.S. Public*, pg. 658

CIRCUTSWITCHER—Interruption & Transfer Switch—S & C Electric Company; *U.S. Private*, pg. 954

CIRKIDS—Children's Footwear—J. Baker, Inc.; *U.S. Public*, pg. 167

CIRMOSA—Drapery Hardware—Kirsch; *U.S. Public*, pg. 1176

CIRRUS—NONE—AGA Gas, Inc.; *Int'l*, pg. 13

CIRRUS—Vapor Emission Control System—AGA Ges.m.b.H.; *Int'l*, pg. 13

CIRRUS—Automobile—Chrysler Corporation; *U.S. Public*, pg. 352

CIRRUS—Office Seating—Cramer Inc.; *U.S. Private*, pg. 285

CIRRUS—Automated Teller Network—MasterCard International-Cirrus Brand; *U.S. Private*, pg. 714

CIRRUS—Glazed ceramic wall tile—Precision Die & Engineering, Inc.; *U.S. Public*, pg. 1322

CISCO—Wines—Canandaigua Wine Company, Inc.; *U.S. Public*, pg. 300

CITANEST—Local Anesthetic—Astra AB; *Int'l*, pg. 93

CITANEST—Pharmaceutical Products—Astra USA, Inc.; *Int'l*, pg. 93

CITATION—NONE—The Cessna Aircraft Co.; *U.S. Public*, pg. 1589

CITATION—Popcorn Machine—Gold Medal Products Co.; *U.S. Private*, pg. 459

CITATION—Commercial Shelving & Shop Equipment—Lear Siegler Diversified Holdings Corp.; *U.S. Private*, pg. 655

CITATION—Metal Building Panels—Reynolds Metals Company; *U.S. Public*, pg. 1385

CITATION—Airconditioners & Water Heaters—Western Auto Supply Company; *U.S. Public*, pg. 1452

CITATION—Printing Papers—Westvaco Corporation; *U.S. Public*, pg. 1762

CITATION TOOLBOX—Software Product—The Mead Corporation; *U.S. Public*, pg. 1074

CITERITE—Software Product—The Mead Corporation; *U.S. Public*, pg. 1074

CITERITE II—Software Product—The Mead Corporation; *U.S. Public*, pg. 1074

CITGO—Petroleum Products—Citgo Petroleum Corporation; *Int'l*, pg. 1045

CITGO—Petroleum Products—Spencer Companies Inc.; *U.S. Public*, pg. 1024

CITIMAP—Tourist Directory Including Road Maps—American Automobile Association; *U.S. Private*, pg. 50

CITIZEN—Handheld & Office Printing/Display Calculators—CBM America Corp.; *U.S. Private*, pg. 192

CITIZEN—Watches—Citizen Watch Co. of America, Inc.; *U.S. Private*, pg. 294

CITIZEN TV—Color Portables—CBM America Corp.; *U.S. Private*, pg. 192

CITIZENS—Insurance—Citizens Insurance Company of America; *U.S. Public*, pg. 54

CITIZENS & SOUTHERN—Banking & Financial Services—NationsBank South; *U.S. Public*, pg. 1163

CITIZENS BEST—Group Auto & Homeowners Insurance for Members of Qualified Retirement Org.—Citizens Insurance Company of America; *U.S. Public*, pg. 54

CITIZENS QUICKCHECK CARD—ATM Debit Card—CVB Financial Corp.; *U.S. Public*, pg. 286

CITODON—Analgesic—Astra AB; *Int'l*, pg. 93

CITOWETT—Crop Protection Agent—BASF AG; *Int'l*, pg. 103

CITRA COCA-COLA—Regular & Diet & Caffeine Free Diet Soft Drink—The Coca-Cola Company; *U.S. Public*, pg. 392

CITRACE—Germicidal Deodorizer—The Dow Chemical Company; *U.S. Public*, pg. 522

CITRASHINE—NONE—EcoScience Corporation; *U.S. Public*, pg. 563

CITREX—Liquid Citrus Flavors—McCormick Flavor Division-U.S.A.; *U.S. Public*, pg. 1066

CITRIKLEEN—Biodegradable Solvent/Degreaser—Wechco, Inc.; *U.S. Private*, pg. 1158

CITRIKLEEN—Biodegradable Solvent/Degreaser—West Chemical Products, Inc.; *U.S. Private*, pg. 1158

CITROCARBONATE—NONE—Lee Pharmaceuticals; *U.S. Public*, pg. 984

CITROEN—Automobile—Peugeot S.A.; *Int'l*, pg. 1020

CITROTEIN—Oral Supplement—Novartis Nutrition Corporation; *Int'l*, pg. 974

CITRUCEL—Bulk Fiber Laxative—The Dow Chemical Company; *U.S. Public*, pg. 522

CITRUCEL—Fiber Laxative—SmithKline Beecham Consumer Healthcare, U.S.; *Int'l*, pg. 1264

CITRUS AM—Orange Grapefruit Juice Drink—Ocean Spray Cranberries, Inc.; *U.S. Private*, pg. 811

CITRUS BITES—Water Ices—Good Humor/Breyers Ice Cream; *U.S. Public*, pg. 1435

CITRUS CAP—Encapsulated Citrus Flavors—McCormick Flavor Division-U.S.A.; *U.S. Public*, pg. 1066

CITRUS HILL—Orange Juice—The Procter & Gamble Company; *U.S. Public*, pg. 1330

CITRUS HILL FRESH RECIPE—Lemonade—The Procter & Gamble Company; *U.S. Public*, pg. 1330

CITRUS HILL LITE PREMIUM—Reduced Calorie Orange Juice Beverage—The Procter & Gamble Company; *U.S. Public*, pg. 1330

CITRUS HILL PLUS CALCIUM—Orange Juice—The Procter & Gamble Company; *U.S. Public*, pg. 1330

CITRUS PLUS—Fruit Juice—Nestle Chocolate & Confection; *Int'l*, pg. 917

CITRUS REFRESHERS—Juice Drinks—Ocean Spray Cranberries, Inc.; *U.S. Private*, pg. 811

CITRUS SPRING—Soft Drink—Whitbread PLC; *Int'l*, pg. 1498

CITY—NONE—Excite, Inc.; *U.S. Public*, pg. 599

CITY LOOKS SALONS INTERNATIONAL—Upscale Hair Care Salons—The Barbers, Hairstyling for Men & Women, Inc.; *U.S. Private*, pg. 115

CITY PANEL—Local Market Test Product Distribution—NFO Research, Inc.; *U.S. Public*, pg. 1146

CITY PLAZA—NONE—Swire Pacific Limited; *Int'l*, pg. 1328

CITY RADIO—Czech Republic Broadcasting—CLT-UFA; *Int'l*, pg. 561

CITY STEPS—Women's Footwear—J. Baker, Inc.; *U.S. Public*, pg. 167

CITY TAVERN—Restaurant—The Levy Organization; *U.S. Private*, pg. 664

CITYLIGHTS—Commercial Facade Lighting—Public Service Company of Oklahoma; *U.S. Public*, pg. 324

CITYLINE—Premier Information Solution—Brite Voice Systems, Inc.; *U.S. Public*, pg. 974

CITYLINE—Newspaper—The Gazette Company; *U.S. Private*, pg. 442

CITYLINK—NONE—Rentokil Initial plc; *Int'l*, pg. 1285

CIVIC—Automobile—American Honda Motor Co., Inc.; *Int'l*, pg. 634

CIVIC—Automobile—American Honda Motor Co., Inc. Automobile Sales Division; *Int'l*, pg. 634

CIVIC—Automobile—Honda Motor Co., Ltd.; *Int'l*, pg. 634

CIVIL WAR ART—NONE—Cowles Enthusiast Media, Inc.; *U.S. Private*, pg. 281

CIVIL WAR TIMES ILLUSTRATED—Periodical—Cowles Enthusiast Media, Inc.; *U.S. Private*, pg. 281

CIVILIZATION—Game—Monarch Avalon, Inc.; *U.S. Public*, pg. 1123

CLABBER GIRL—Baking Powder—Hulman & Company; *U.S. Private*, pg. 547

CLADBOARD—Melamine Panels—Domtar Inc.; *Int'l*, pg. 416

CLADMATE—Plastic Foam Insulation—The Dow Chemical Company; *U.S. Public*, pg. 522

CLAF—Packaging Reinforcement—Amoco Chemicals; *U.S. Public*, pg. 102

CLAFORAN—Infections—Hoechst Marion Roussel, Inc.; *Int'l*, pg. 624

CLAFORAN—Antibiotic for Certain Infections—Hoechst Marion Roussel North America; *Int'l*, pg. 625

CLAIBORNE—Men's Fragrance—Liz Claiborne Cosmetics, Inc.; *U.S. Public*, pg. 1006

CLAIBORNE—Men's Wear—Liz Claiborne, Inc.; *U.S. Public*, pg. 1005

CLAIBORNE—Sunglasses & Readers—Outlook Eyewear Company; *U.S. Public*, pg. 195

CLAIBORNE BOOKS—Children's Activity Books—Life-Like Products, Inc.; *U.S. Private*, pg. 666

CLAIMPANION—Computer Program for Insurance Claim Processing—Lincoln National Corporation; *U.S. Public*, pg. 997

CLAIMSFLO—NONE—American Management Systems, Inc.; *U.S. Public*, pg. 86

CLAIRE BURKE—Home Fragrance—Tsumura International; *U.S. Public*, pg. 1426

CLAIRE'S BOUTIQUES—Women's Fashion Accessories Stores—Claire's Stores Inc.; *U.S. Public*, pg. 381

CLAIRESSE—Hair Coloring—Bristol-Myers Squibb Company; *U.S. Public*, pg. 253

CLAIRESSE—Hair Coloring—Clairol, Inc.; *U.S. Public*, pg. 254

CLAIRMIST—Hair Spray—Clairol, Inc.; *U.S. Public*, pg. 254

CLAIRMIST HAIRSPRAYS—Hairspray—Bristol-Myers Squibb Company; *U.S. Public*, pg. 253

CLAIRMONT ELEGANCE—Pre-Finished Strip—Bruce Hardwood Floors; *U.S. Public*, pg. 1634

CLAIROL—Herbal Essence Creme Rinse, Conditioner & Shampoo, Balsam Color—Clairol, Inc.; *U.S. Public*, pg. 254

CLAIROL APPLIANCES—Appliances for hair—Bristol-Myers Squibb Company; *U.S. Public*, pg. 253

CLAIROL BASIC—Instant Hairsetter—Clairol, Inc.; *U.S. Public*, pg. 254

CLAIROL COLOR RENEWAL SYSTEM—Hair Color—Bristol-Myers Squibb Company; *U.S. Public*, pg. 253

CLAIROL COLOR RENEWAL SYSTEM—Hair Color—Clairol, Inc.; *U.S. Public*, pg. 254

CLAIROL CUSTOM-CARE SETTER—Hairsetter—Clairol, Inc.; *U.S. Public*, pg. 254

CLAIROL CUSTOM CARESETTER—Instant Hairsetter—Bristol-Myers Squibb Company; *U.S. Public*, pg. 253

CLAIROL DELUXE—Instant Hairsetter—Clairol, Inc.; *U.S. Public*, pg. 254

CLAIROL LOVING CARE—Hair Color—Clairol, Inc.; *U.S. Public*, pg. 254

CLAIROL NICE N EASY—Hair Color—Clairol, Inc.; *U.S. Public*, pg. 254

CLAIROL RAPIDE—Hair Dryer—Clairol, Inc.; *U.S. Public*, pg. 254

CLAIROL ULTRESS—Hair Color—Clairol, Inc.; *U.S. Public*, pg. 254

CLAIROLITE—Hair Lightener—Clairol, Inc.; *U.S. Public*, pg. 254

CLAIROXIDE—Hair Preparation—Clairol, Inc.; *U.S. Public*, pg. 254

CLAM-TROL—Mollusk Control Agent—BetzDearborn Inc.; *U.S. Public*, pg. 226

CLAMATO—NONE—Cadbury Beverages North America; *Int'l*, pg. 248

CLAMATO—Fruit Juice—Cadbury Schweppes p.l.c.; *Int'l*, pg. 247

CLAMBOAT—Clam Platter—Friendly Ice Cream Corp.; *U.S. Public*, pg. 682

CLAMOXYL—Animal Antibacterial—SmithKline Beecham plc; *Int'l*, pg. 1264

CLAMP—Wire & Cable—Times Fiber Communications, Inc.; *U.S. Private*, pg. 629

CLAMP LOCK—Fasteners—Southtec, Inc.; *U.S. Private*, pg. 1015

CLAMPZYME—Complex for Preserving Low Dry Matter Silage—Cultor Ltd.; *Int'l*, pg. 349

CLAN—Pipe Tobaccos—Consolidated Cigar Corporation; *U.S. Private*, pg. 690

CLAN—NONE—Fortune Brands, Inc.; *U.S. Public*, pg. 674

CLAN—Pipe Tobacco—Gallaher Tobacco Ltd.; *Int'l*, pg. 539

CLAN CAMPBELL—Blended Scotch Whiskey—Groupe Pernod Ricard; *Int'l*, pg. 566

CLAP—Herbicides—Agrolinz Melamin GmbH; *Int'l*, pg. 356

CLAP—Plant Protectives—DSM Chemie Linz GmbH; *Int'l*, pg. 356

CLAP SC—Herbicides—Agrolinz Melamin GmbH; *Int'l*, pg. 356

CLARA STOVER CANDIES—Candies—Russell Stover Candies, Inc.; *U.S. Private*, pg. 953

CLARCAL—Calcium Carbonate—Whittaker, Clark & Daniels, Inc.; *U.S. Private*, pg. 1174

CLARIFLOC—Polymers—AlliedSignal Inc.; *U.S. Public*, pg. 49

CLARINO—Man-Made Leather—Kuraray Co., Ltd.; *Int'l*, pg. 764

CLARINS—Skin Care, Make-Up & Perfume—Clarins; *Int'l*, pg. 295

CLARION—Bleached Earth Product—AMCOL International Corp.; *U.S. Public*, pg. 63

CLARION—Hotels & Resorts—Choice Hotels International, Inc.; *U.S. Public*, pg. 351

CLARION—Cosmetics—Clarion Cosmetics; *U.S. Public*, pg. 1330

CLARION—Hair Coloring—The Procter & Gamble Company; *U.S. Public*, pg. 1330

CLARIS DRAW—Computer Software—Claris Corporation; *U.S. Public*, pg. 121

CLARIS IMPACT—Computer Software—Claris Corporation; *U.S. Public*, pg. 121

CLARIS WORKS—Computer Software—Claris Corporation; *U.S. Public*, pg. 121

CLARITIN—Antihistamine—Schering-Plough Corporation; *U.S. Public*, pg. 1438

CLARITY—Herbicide—Sandoz Agro, Inc.; *Int'l*, pg. 974

CLARITY—Ceramic Braces—3M Unitek Corporation; *U.S. Public*, pg. 1606

CLARK—Consolidated Industries—Duellman Electric Supply, Inc.; *Int'l*, pg. 1107

CLARK—Forklifts—EEI Corporation; *Int'l*, pg. 425

CLARK—Building Products—Email Limited; *Int'l*, pg. 450

CLARK FOODSERVICE—Distr. of Paper, Plastic & Food Specialty Prods. to Restaurants, Hospitals—Clark Foodservice, Inc.; *U.S. Private*, pg. 242

CLARK GRAVE VAULTS—Metal Burial Vaults—Clark Grave Vault Co.; *U.S. Private*, pg. 243

CLARK LIFT—NONE—Clark Material Handling Company; *U.S. Private*, pg. 243

CLARKE AMERICAN—Check Printing—Caradon Plc; *Int'l*, pg. 266

CLARKS—Footwear—Clarks International; *Int'l*, pg. 296

CLARKSON/POTTER—NONE—Crown Publishers, Inc.; *U.S. Private*, pg. 21

CLARLET—NONE—Carl Zeiss Optical, Inc.; *Int'l*, pg. 1523

CLARLET SKYLET—Sunglass Lenses—Carl Zeiss; *Int'l*, pg. 1522

CLARNICO—Mints—Cadbury Schweppes p.l.c.; *Int'l*, pg. 247

CLAROSTAN—Liquid Clarifier & Flocculating Agent—LeaRonal, Inc.; *U.S. Public*, pg. 982

CLAROZINC—Liquid Clarier & Flocculatin Agent—LeaRonal, Inc.; *U.S. Public*, pg. 982

CLARVIN—Wine Clarification Chemical—Laporte plc; *Int'l*, pg. 801

CLASICO—Correspondence Papers—Kimberly-Clark Corporation; *U.S. Public*, pg. 958

CLASS—Liquid Dish Detergent—Blue Cross Laboratories; *U.S. Private*, pg. 152

CLASS—Asset Mngmt. Software System—Comdisco, Inc.; *U.S. Public*, pg. 407

CLASS—Computer Lab Furniture—Spectrum Industries, Inc.; *U.S. Private*, pg. 1024

CLASS—NONE—Western Atlas Logging Services; *U.S. Public*, pg. 1757

CLASS A-2000—Sheet Molded Cpmposite—The Budd Company; *Int'l*, pg. 1388

CLASS MATE—Stationery Products—The Mead Corporation; *U.S. Public*, pg. 1074

CLASS MATE—Filmstrip Projector—Telex Communications, Inc.; *U.S. Private*, pg. 1074

CLASS-MATIC—Retarder Yard Control System—General Railway Signal Corp.; *Int'l*, pg. 1194

CLASS STRUGGLE—Game—Monarch Avalon, Inc.; *U.S. Public*, pg. 1123

CLASSIC—NONE—Altera Corporation; *U.S. Public*, pg. 59

CLASSIC—Rotary Recorder—Bell & Howell Holdings; *U.S. Public*, pg. 201

CLASSIC—Pre-Finished Laminate—Bruce Hardwood Floors; *U.S. Public*, pg. 1634

CLASSIC—Cutlery—Buck Knives, Inc.; *U.S. Private*, pg. 460

CLASSIC—Storage Products—Clairson International Corp.; *U.S. Public*, pg. 575

CLASSIC—Gold-Filled Pens & Pencils—A.T. Cross Co.; *U.S. Public*, pg. 460

CLASSIC—Racquetball Glove—Ektelon; *U.S. Private*, pg. 884

CLASSIC—Writing Instruments—Gillette Co.-Parker Pen USA; *U.S. Public*, pg. 745

CLASSIC—Hand Held Shower Massage—Interbath, Inc.; *U.S. Private*, pg. 566

CLASSIC—Gummed Tape—Intertape Polymer Group; *Int'l*, pg. 685

CLASSIC—Commercial Closet Carriers—Josam Company; *U.S. Private*, pg. 688

CLASSIC—Tennis Shoe—K-Swiss Inc.; *U.S. Public*, pg. 937

CLASSIC—Bond Paper—Kimberly-Clark Corporation; *U.S. Public*, pg. 958

CLASSIC—Horse Feeds, Dog, Cat & Other Pet Foods—Manna Pro Corporation; *U.S. Private*, pg. 700

CLASSIC—Minicomputer Systems—Modcomp; *U.S. Public*, pg. 283

CLASSIC—Liqueurs—NWS Inc.; *U.S. Private*, pg. 772

CLASSIC—Water Ski Tow Rope—Outdoor Technologies Group; *U.S. Private*, pg. 822

CLASSIC—Roofing Shingles—Owens Corning; *U.S. Public*, pg. 1236

CLASSIC—Running Shoe—Reebok International Ltd.; *U.S. Public*, pg. 1369

CLASSIC—Potato, Fruit & Vegetable Products—J.R. Simplot Company; *U.S. Private*, pg. 1002

CLASSIC—Mobile Homes—Wick Bldg. Systems Inc. Manufactured Homes Div.; *U.S. Private*, pg. 1174

CLASSIC ACCENT—Writing Instuments—Gillette Co.-Parker Pen USA; *U.S. Public*, pg. 745

CLASSIC AMERICAN FOODS—Specialty Foods/Condiments—McCormick & Company, Incorporated; *U.S. Public*, pg. 1066

CLASSIC BABY SOFT LIQUID LAUNDRY DETERGENT—NONE—The Dial Corporation; *U.S. Public*, pg. 505

CLASSIC BIKE—Magazine—EMAP Nationals; *Int'l*, pg. 451

CLASSIC BLACK—Pens & Pencils—A.T. Cross Co.; *U.S. Public*, pg. 460

CLASSIC CARRY-OUT—Foil Packaging—Tenneco Specialty Products; *U.S. Public*, pg. 1579

CLASSIC CAR WEEKLY—Magazine—EMAP Nationals; *Int'l*, pg. 451

CLASSIC CERAMICS—Pottery—Haeger Industries, Inc.; *U.S. Private*, pg. 493

CLASSIC CHEF—Cutlery—General Housewares Corp.; *U.S. Public*, pg. 715

CLASSIC COLLECTION—Teakwood—Dansk International Designs Ltd.; *U.S. Public*, pg. 261

CLASSIC CONDOLA—NONE—MEG; *U.S. Private*, pg. 686

CLASSIC CRAFT—Entry Doors—Therma-Tru Corp.; *U.S. Private*, pg. 1079

CLASSIC CREST—Bond Paper—Kimberly-Clark Corporation; *U.S. Public*, pg. 958

CLASSIC DARK—Beer—Anheuser-Busch Companies, Inc.; *U.S. Public*, pg. 113

CLASSIC DRAFT—Beer—Pittsburgh Brewing Company; *U.S. Private*, pg. 619

CLASSIC ELEMENTS—NONE—Sears, Roebuck and Co.; *U.S. Public*, pg. 1452

CLASSIC GEM POWDER LAUNDRY DETERGENT—NONE—The Dial Corporation; *U.S. Public*, pg. 505

CLASSIC GOLD—Labels—Avery Dennison Corporation Label Group; *U.S. Public*, pg. 153

CLASSIC GOURMET—Dressings, Mayonnaise—Ventura Foods LLC; *Int'l*, pg. 879

CLASSIC MAIL—Voice Messaging System—Lucent Technologies Inc.; *U.S. Public*, pg. 1017

THE CLASSIC MOTORCYCLE—Magazine—EMAP Nationals; *Int'l*, pg. 451

CLASSIC PUREX LAUNDRY DETERGENT—NONE—The Dial Corporation; *U.S. Public*, pg. 505

CLASSIC PUREX LAUNDRY DETERGENT BLEACH ALTERNATIVE—NONE—The Dial Corporation; *U.S. Public*, pg. 505

CLASSIC PUREX LAUNDRY FABRIC SOFTENER—NONE—The Dial Corporation; *U.S. Public*, pg. 505

CLASSIC PUREX LIQUID LAUNDRY DETERGENT FREE CLEAR—NONE—The Dial Corporation; *U.S. Public*, pg. 505

CLASSIC SELECTION—House Brand—7-Eleven Stores; *Int'l*, pg. 693

THE CLASSIC SERIES—Plastic Stack Chair & Student Desks—Virco Mfg. Corporation; *U.S. Public*, pg. 1721

CLASSIC STAINLESS STEEL BY MAGNALITE—Cookware—General Housewares Corp.; *U.S. Public*, pg. 715

CLASSIC SUPREME—Room-Darkening Horizontal Blinds—Springs Industries, Inc.; *U.S. Public*, pg. 1499

CLASSIC TONES—Household Paper Goods—Orchids Paper Products Co.; *U.S. Private*, pg. 819

CLASSIC TOUCH—Vinyl Tile—Congoleum Corporation; *U.S. Public*, pg. 69

CLASSIC TOUCH—Incliner Mechanisms for Motion Upholstered Furniture—Leggett & Platt, Incorporated; *U.S. Public*, pg. 985

CLASSIC TOUCH—Adult Barrettes, Hairbands, Decorative Combs—Wilhold Inc.; *U.S. Public*, pg. 78

CLASSIC TOY TRAINS—Magazine—Kalmbach Publishing Co.; *U.S. Private*, pg. 606

CLASSIC TRAX—Slotwall—Pickering Inc.; *U.S. Private*, pg. 864

CLASSIC TREND LAUNDRY DETERGENT—NONE—The Dial Corporation; *U.S. Public*, pg. 505

CLASSIC TREND POWDER DETERGENT BLEACH ALTERNATIVE—NONE—The Dial Corporation; *U.S. Public*, pg. 505

CLASSIC VALUE—Canned Spaghetti Sauce—Chesebrough-Pond's; *Int'l*, pg. 1436

CLASSIC WALKERS—Shoes—P.W. Minor & Son, Inc.; *U.S. Private*, pg. 751

CLASSICA—Bath Accessories—Melard Manufacturing Corporation; *U.S. Private*, pg. 729

CLASSICA—Cookware—Regal Ware, Inc.; *U.S. Private*, pg. 917

CLASSICO—NONE—Borden Foods Canada; *U.S. Private*, pg. 159

CLASSICO—Italian Sauces—Borden, Inc.; *U.S. Private*, pg. 157

CLASSICO—Pasta Products & Pasta Sauces—Borden Italian Foods; *U.S. Private*, pg. 158

CLASSICO AUNT MILLIE'S—Sauce—Borden Foods Co.; *U.S. Private*, pg. 158

CLASSICO IMPORTED PASTA—Pasta—Borden Foods Co.; *U.S. Private*, pg. 158

CLASSICS—Area Rugs—Couristan Inc.; *U.S. Private*, pg. 279

CLASSIFAX—Used Tubular Inspections—Tuboscope Incorporated; *U.S. Public*, pg. 1643

CLASSIFIED ERASE—NONE—Xicor, Inc.; *U.S. Public*, pg. 1785

THE CLASSIFILER—Portfolios—The Mead Corporation; *U.S. Public*, pg. 1074

CLASSIQUE—Residential Elevator—Access Industries; *U.S. Private*, pg. 8

CLASSIQUE—Beauty Salon Furniture—Belvedere Company; *U.S. Private*, pg. 1008

CLASSIQUE—Stainless Steel Flatware—Dansk International Designs Ltd.; *U.S. Public*, pg. 261

CLASSIQUE COLLECTION—Foundations—The Strouse, Adler Company; *U.S. Private*, pg. 1047

CLASSIQUE II—NONE—Columbus Show Case Company; *U.S. Private*, pg. 257

CLASSKNIT—Fabric—E.R. Moore Co.; *U.S. Private*, pg. 759

CLASSMAKER—Hard Plastic Chair—Virco Mfg. Corporation; *U.S. Public*, pg. 1721

CLASSY CATS—Dry Cat Food—H.J. Heinz Co. of Canada Ltd.; *U.S. Public*, pg. 806

CLASSY CURL—Permanent Curl & Maintenance Prod.—Johnson Products Co., Inc.; *U.S. Public*, pg. 915

CLAST—Antiulcer—Meiji Seika Kaisha, Ltd.; *Int'l*, pg. 855

CLAUDE LEMA—Women's Apparel—International Cosmetics Co., Ltd.; *Int'l*, pg. 684

CLAUDE MICHAEL—Electronic Tools—Marshall Industries; *U.S. Public*, pg. 1051

CLAUSSEN—Pickles—Kraft Foods, Inc.; *U.S. Public*, pg. 1287

CLAUSSEN—Pickles—Kraft Foods Inc.; *U.S. Public*, pg. 1288

CLAUSSEN—Pickles—Philip Morris Companies Inc.; *U.S. Public*, pg. 1287

CLAUSTHALER—Non-Alcoholic Malt Beverage—Labatt U.S.A.; *Int'l*, pg. 679

CLAVAMOX—Animal Antibacterial—SmithKline Beecham plc; *Int'l*, pg. 1264

CLAVAMOX/SYNULOX—Amoxicillin/Clavulanic Acid—Pfizer Inc.; *U.S. Public*, pg. 1281

CLAVERSAL—NONE—SmithKline Beecham Corporation; *Int'l*, pg. 1264

CLAVERSAL—Gastrointestinal Drug—SmithKline Beecham plc; *Int'l*, pg. 1264

CLAVINOVA—Electronic Keyboard—Yamaha Corporation of America; *Int'l*, pg. 1516

CLAVODENE—Environmentally-safe Preparatin Chemicals—Dexter Chemical Corp.; *U.S. Private*, pg. 329

CLAVUCID—Antibiotic—SmithKline Beecham plc; *Int'l*, pg. 1264

CLAVULIN—NONE—SmithKline Beecham Laboratorios Ltda.; *Int'l*, pg. 1266

CLAVULIN—Antibiotic—SmithKline Beecham plc; *Int'l*, pg. 1264

CLAXTON—Ladies' Intimate Apparel—Movie Star, Inc.; *U.S. Public*, pg. 1140

THE CLAYMORE—Blended Scotch Whiskey—Fortune Brands, Inc.; *U.S. Public*, pg. 674

THE CLAYMORE—Blended Scotch Whisky—The Whyte & Mackay Group Plc.; *U.S. Public*, pg. 675

CLAYOLA—Clay—Binney & Smith Inc.; *U.S. Private*, pg. 496

CLAYTON—Manufactured Homes—Clayton Homes, Inc.; *U.S. Public*, pg. 382

CLAYTON-MARCUS—Furniture—Clayton-Marcus Company, Inc.; *U.S. Public*, pg. 975

CLAYTON MARCUS—Furniture—Ladd Furniture, Inc.; *U.S. Public*, pg. 974

CLE-BIDE—Carbide Drills—Greenfield Industries; *U.S. Public*, pg. 950

CLE-FORGE—High Speed Steel Drills—Greenfield Industries; *U.S. Public*, pg. 950

CLE-MAX—Tool Bits, Cut-Off Blades—Greenfield Industries; *U.S. Public*, pg. 950

CLEARLY CANADIAN—Soft Drink—Grant-Lydick Beverage Co.; *U.S. Private*, pg. 470

CLEAN AIR CHOICE—No-Voc Paint—ICI Paints; *Int'l*, pg. 664

CLEAN & CART—Trash Management System—Igloo Products Corporation; *U.S. Public*, pg. 265

CLEAN & CLEAR—Dermatological Products—Johnson & Johnson; *U.S. Public*, pg. 927

CLEAN & EASY—Professional Roll-On Waxing System—Inverness Corp.; *U.S. Private*, pg. 574

CLEAN CROP—Agricultural Chemicals—ConAgra, Inc.; *U.S. Public*, pg. 425

CLEAN-CUT—Steels Developed for Improved Machining Characteristics—Lukens Steel Company; *U.S. Public*, pg. 1020

CLEAN EXPRESS—Transportation & Disposal of Hazardous Waste—Clean Harbors, Inc.; *U.S. Public*, pg. 383

CLEAN EXTRACTION SYSTEM—Treatment & Recycling of Hazardous Wastes—Clean Harbors, Inc.; *U.S. Public*, pg. 383

CLEAN-FIT—Brushes—Mill-Rose Company; *U.S. Private*, pg. 746

CLEAN FIT—Plumbing, Heating & Air Conditioning Accessories—Mill-Rose Company; *U.S. Private*, pg. 746

CLEAN LASH—Mascara—Cover Girl Cosmetics; *U.S. Public*, pg. 1330

CLEAN MACHINE & DESIGN—NONE—Regal Ware, Inc.; *U.S. Private*, pg. 917

CLEAN MACHINE CAR DETAILER—Car Exterior Cleaner—Turtle Wax, Inc.; *U.S. Private*, pg. 1110

CLEAN-MASTER—Steam Cleaner—Clayton Industries Co.; *U.S. Private*, pg. 245

CLEAN-MIZER—Ball Valve, Critical Services—Worcester Controls Corp.; *Int'l*, pg. 128

CLEAN 'N CLEAR—All Purpose Cleaner—S.C. Johnson & Son, Inc.; *U.S. Private*, pg. 592

CLEAN N' STRIP—Wax—Bruce Hardwood Floors; *U.S. Public*, pg. 1634

CLEAN 'N STRIP—Non-woven Discs & Unitized Wheels for Corrosion Removal—3M; *U.S. Public*, pg. 1604

CLEAN-O-MATIC—Parts Cleaner/Degreaser—Graymills Corp.; *U.S. Private*, pg. 473

CLEAN PACKING—Collection & Disposal of Laboratory Chemicals—Clean Harbors, Inc.; *U.S. Public*, pg. 383

CLEAN-PAK—Harmonics Filter—Shizuki Electric Corporation; *Int'l*, pg. 1236

CLEAN PRINT—Carbonless Paper—Moore Corporation Limited; *Int'l*, pg. 888

CLEAN SOUND—Electronic Accessories—Recoton Corporation; *U.S. Public*, pg. 1369

CLEAN-STREAM—Food Grade Cam-op Couplings—NewAge Industries Inc.; *U.S. Private*, pg. 796

CLEANCOTTON—Cotton Thermally Sealed-Edge Border Wiper—The Texwipe Co., Inc.; *U.S. Private*, pg. 1079

CLEANFIRE—Oxy-Fuel Burner—Air Products and Chemicals, Inc.; *U.S. Public*, pg. 30

CLEANFUELS—NONE—Mesa Environmental; *U.S. Public*, pg. 1300

CLEANLINE—Solder Paste—Alpha Metals, Inc.; *Int'l*, pg. 328

CLEANROOM—Low Particulate Electronic Chemicals—Ashland, Inc.; *U.S. Public*, pg. 138

CLEANSE & BOND I—No-Mix Orthodontic Bracket Adhesive—Lee Pharmaceuticals; *U.S. Public*, pg. 984

CLEANSE & BOND II—Two-Paste Orthodontic Adhesive—Lee Pharmaceuticals; *U.S. Public*, pg. 984

CLEANSING MILK—Cosmetics—Palm Beach Beauty Products Co.; *U.S. Private*, pg. 834

CLEANSWEEP—Computer Software—Quarterdeck Corp.; *U.S. Public*, pg. 1350

CLEANTAC—Ultra Removable Labels—Moore Document Solutions; *Int'l*, pg. 890

CLEANTHROUGH—Water-Based Line of Cleaners Without CFC's—Kao Corporation; *Int'l*, pg. 717

CLEANWELDER—Oxy-Propane Welding Torch—Sycamore Plant; *U.S. Public*, pg. 444

CLEANWHITE—NONE—Avon Products Co., Ltd.; *U.S. Public*, pg. 156

CLEAR—Photographic Paper—Konica Corporation; *Int'l*, pg. 748

CLEAR 'N' CLEAN—Window/Glass Cleaning Cloth—Spontex, Inc.; *Int'l*, pg. 1409

CLEAR ADVANTAGE—NONE—Avery Dennison Corporation; *U.S. Public*, pg. 152

CLEAR AWAY—Wart Remover—Schering-Plough Corporation; *U.S. Public*, pg. 1438

CLEAR AWAY—Wart Remover—Schering-Plough Healthcare Products Inc.; *U.S. Public*, pg. 1438

CLEAR BENEFIT—Hair Preparations—The Gillette Company; *U.S. Public*, pg. 743

CLEAR BY DESIGN—Acne Medication—SmithKline Beecham Consumer Healthcare, U.S.; *Int'l*, pg. 1264

CLEAR CHOICE—Mouthwash—Bausch & Lomb Incorporated; *U.S. Public*, pg. 194

CLEAR COMPLEXION—Cosmetics—Almay, Inc.; *U.S. Private*, pg. 689

CLEAR DIFFERENCE—Hair Setting Gel—The Gillette Company; *U.S. Public*, pg. 743

CLEAR DIP—Oral Hygiene Aids—John O. Butler Co.; *Int'l*, pg. 1320

CLEAR EYES—Eye Drops—Abbott Laboratories; *U.S. Public*, pg. 12

CLEAR EYES—Eye Drops—Ross Products; *U.S. Public*, pg. 13

CLEAR 40—Clear Rigid Schedule 40 PVC Pipe—NewAge Industries Inc.; *U.S. Private*, pg. 796

CLEAR-GO—Urethane Belts—Fenner Drives; *U.S. Private*, pg. 400

CLEAR GUARD—Vinyl Protectant—Turtle Wax, Inc.; *U.S. Private*, pg. 1110

CLEAR MAGIC—All Purpose Cleaner—Blue Coral/Slick 50; *U.S. Public*, pg. 1348

CLEAR-PAK—Plastic Packaging for Wire and Cable Products—General Cable Corporation; *Int'l*, pg. 1486

CLEAR PLUMBERS CAULK—Plumbing Chemical—Hercules Chemical Co., Inc.; *U.S. Private*, pg. 523

CLEAR PROCESS—Flowcharting & Process Management—SPSS Inc.; *U.S. Public*, pg. 1420

CLEAR-SEAL—Scientific Glassware for Laboratory Use—Wheaton Inc.; *Int'l*, pg. 67

CLEAR-SELE—Coating—Rust-Oleum Corporation; *U.S. Public*, pg. 1358

CLEAR-SET—Cardiovascular Solution Administration Set—Mallinckrodt Inc.; *U.S. Public*, pg. 1039

CLEAR SPRING—Papers—Westvaco Corporation; *U.S. Public*, pg. 1762

CLEAR SPRINGS—Rainbow Trout—Clear Springs Foods, Inc.; *U.S. Private*, pg. 245

CLEAR STRIP—Blue Print Base Paper—MACtac Scranton Facility; *U.S. Public*, pg. 210

CLEAR VOICE—Hearing Aid Circuits—Beltone Electronics Corporation; *U.S. Private*, pg. 132

CLEAR WAVE—Water Conditioners—Field Controls Co.; *U.S. Private*, pg. 860

CLEAR-40—Clear Rigid Schedule 40 Pipe (PVC)—Newage Industries Inc., Plastics Technology Group; *U.S. Public*, pg. 796

CLEAR-VUE—Educational Embedments—Fisher Scientific Company; *U.S. Private*, pg. 658

CLEARADINE—Iodine Removal Pads—The Clinipad Corporation; *U.S. Private*, pg. 246

CLEARASIL—Soap & Skin Cream—Permark International (Pty.) Ltd.; *Int'l*, pg. 1036

CLEARASIL—Anti-Acne Product—The Procter & Gamble Company; *U.S. Public*, pg. 1330

CLEARASIL—Acne Medication—Richardson-Vicks, Inc.; *U.S. Public*, pg. 1331

CLEARASIL—Acne Treatment & Cleansers—Richardson-Vicks, Inc. Personal Care Products Div.; *U.S. Public*, pg. 1331

CLEARBLUE EASY—Pregnancy Test Kit—American Home Products Corporation; *U.S. Public*, pg. 79

CLEARCHANNEL LTR—Logic Trunked Radio—E.F. Johnson Radio Systems; *U.S. Public*, pg. 1630

CLEARCORE—Saturating Paper—The Mead Corporation; *U.S. Public*, pg. 1074

CLEARCUSTOMIZE—NONE—Clarify Inc.; *U.S. Public*, pg. 382

CLEARCUT—Electrosurgical Handpiece—Medtronic, Inc.; *U.S. Public*, pg. 1082

CLEARDENT—Toothbrushes & Toothpaste—Kao Corporation; *Int'l*, pg. 717

CLEARENTERPRISE—NONE—Clarify Inc.; *U.S. Public*, pg. 382

CLEAREXPRESS—NONE—Clarify Inc.; *U.S. Public*, pg. 382

CLEAREXTENSIONS—NONE—Clarify Inc.; *U.S. Public*, pg. 382

CLEARFLEX—Electrical Wire & Cable—General Cable Corporation; *Int'l*, pg. 1486

CLEARFLO—Unreinforced PVC Tubing—NewAge Industries Inc.; *U.S. Private*, pg. 796

CLEARFLO—Clear PVC Tubing-Unreinforced—Newage Industries Inc., Plastics Technology Group; *U.S. Private*, pg. 796

CLEARHELPDESK—NONE—Clarify Inc.; *U.S. Public*, pg. 382

CLEARING-NIAGARA—Presses, Press Brakes & Shears—Clearing-Niagara; *U.S. Private*, pg. 196

CLEARJEL—Starch—Unilever Plc; *Int'l*, pg. 1433

CLEARLITE—Building Products—Email Limited; *Int'l*, pg. 450

CLEARLOGISTICS—NONE—Clarify Inc.; *U.S. Public*, pg. 382

CLEARLY—Handblown Crystal, Glassware & Giftware—World Tableware, Inc.; *Int'l*, pg. 1056

CLEARMOL—Pesticides—McLaughlin Gormley King Company; *U.S. Private*, pg. 723

CLEARPLAN EASY—Ovulation Predictor—American Home Products Corporation; *U.S. Public*, pg. 79

CLEARQUALITY—NONE—Clarify Inc.; *U.S. Public*, pg. 382

CLEARSALES—NONE—Clarify Inc.; *U.S. Public*, pg. 382

CLEARSHOT—Water Filters—Eastman Kodak Company; *U.S. Public*, pg. 550

CLEARSOL GUMS—High-Oxidized Corn Starches—Penford Corp.; *U.S. Public*, pg. 1269

CLEARSOY—Food Product—Honeymead Products Co.; *U.S. Private*, pg. 537

CLEARSPAN—Wireless Data Communications System—Comptek Research, Inc.; *U.S. Public*, pg. 419

CLEARSUPPORT—NONE—Clarify Inc.; *U.S. Public*, pg. 382

CLEARTEK 2000—Touch Screens—Microtouch Systems, Inc.; *U.S. Public*, pg. 1108

CLEARVAN—Clear Imitation Vanilla—Adams Extract Co., Inc.; *U.S. Private*, pg. 16

CLEARVIEW—Sneeze Guards—Cres-Cor; *U.S. Private*, pg. 288

CLEARVIEW—NONE—Domco Inc.; *Int'l*, pg. 415

CLEARVIEW CHLAMYDIA—Chlamydia Trachomatis Antigen Test—Wampole Laboratories; *U.S. Public*, pg. 310

CLEARVIEW HCG DUO—Urine & Serum Assay—Wampole Laboratories; *U.S. Public*, pg. 310

CLEARVIEW HCG II—One-Step Chromatographic Immunoassay for Pregnancy—Wampole Laboratories; *U.S. Public*, pg. 310

CLEARVIEW STREP A—Group A Streptococcal Antigen Test—Wampole Laboratories; *U.S. Public*, pg. 310

CLEARVOICE—Hands-Free Cellular Microphone—Shure Brothers Incorporated; *U.S. Private*, pg. 997

CLECO—Electric Heavy Duty Side Fork Lift—Owen Industries, Inc.; *U.S. Private*, pg. 824

CLEEN-O-PINE—Cream & Liquid Cleansers—Reckitt & Colman plc; *Int'l*, pg. 1089

CLEENCUFF—Blood Pressure Cuffs—Vital Signs, Inc.; *U.S. Public*, pg. 1723

CLEMCO PRODUCTS DIVISION—Blast Machines, Blast Cabinets & Industrial Blast Rooms—Clemco Industries Corp.; *U.S. Private*, pg. 24

CLEMENTS—Food Products—Clements Foods Co.; *U.S. Private*, pg. 245

CLEMLITE—Lightweight Nozzles & Couplings—Aerolyte Systems; *U.S. Private*, pg. 24

CLENS—Contact Lens Care Solution—Alcon Laboratories, Inc.; *Int'l*, pg. 916

CLEOCIN—Antibiotic—Pharmacia & Upjohn; *Int'l*, pg. 1048

CLEOPATRA—Bath Soap—Colgate-Palmolive Company; *U.S. Public*, pg. 397

CLERMONT—Private Brand Paper—The Cincinnati Cordage & Paper Company; *U.S. Private*, pg. 239

CLERZ—Lubricating & Rewetting Drops—Alcon Laboratories, Inc.; *Int'l*, pg. 916

CLERZ—Contact Lens Solution—Novartis; *Int'l*, pg. 972

CLERZ—Lubricating & Rewetting Drops—Wesley-Jessen; *U.S. Private*, pg. 111

CLERZ 2—Lubricating & Rewetting Drops—Alcon Laboratories, Inc.; *U.S. Public*, pg. 916

CLEVELAND—Steam Cooking Equipment—Cleveland Range; *Int'l*, pg. 188

CLEVELAND CRANES—Cranes—Crane Manufacturing; *U.S. Private*, pg. 286

CLEVELAND HOBBING—Machine Tools—Waterbury Farrel Technologies; *U.S. Private*, pg. 461

CLEVELAND TRAMRAIL—Underhung Cranes & Monorail Systems—Shepard Niles, Inc.; *U.S. Private*, pg. 992

CLEVELAND WOOD PRODUCTS—Vacuum Cleaner Brushes—The Scott Fetzer Company; *U.S. Public*, pg. 217

CLEVELAND-CLIFFS—Mining & Holding—Cleveland-Cliffs Inc; *U.S. Public*, pg. 386

CLEVEPOST—Paper Prods.; Tubular Supports, Reinforcing Members & Cushions for Cartons—Sonoco Products Company; *U.S. Public*, pg. 1485

CLEVITE—Bearings—T & N Plc; *Int'l*, pg. 1334

CLEVITE HEAVY DUTY ENGINE PARTS—Pistons, Cylinder Sleeves/Liners, Bearings & Camshafts—Glacier Vandervell, Inc.; *Int'l*, pg. 1334

CLEVITE 77—Material for Bearings—Glacier Vandervell, Inc.; *Int'l*, pg. 1334

CLEVITE 66—Material for Bearings—Glacier Vandervell, Inc.; *Int'l*, pg. 1334

CLIC—Orange Drink—Nestle S.A.; *Int'l*, pg. 915

CLIC-LOC—Child Resistant Closures—Owens-Illinois, Inc.; *U.S. Public*, pg. 1238

CLICK—Manual Warewashing Product—Ecolab Inc.; *U.S. Public*, pg. 562

CLICK 'N CLEAN—Can Openers—The Rival Company; *U.S. Public*, pg. 1391

CLICK ART—NONE—Broderbund Software, Inc.; *U.S. Public*, pg. 258

CLICK ART 101—NONE—Broderbund Software, Inc.; *U.S. Public*, pg. 258

CLICK-IT—Padlocks—Ilco Unican Corp.; *Int'l*, pg. 1432

CLICK-IT—Padlocks—Unican Security Systems Ltd.; *Int'l*, pg. 1432

CLICKSTER—Mechanical Pencil—Sanford Corporation; *U.S. Public*, pg. 1178

CLICROLLER—Pens—Pentel of America, Ltd.; *Int'l*, pg. 1035

CLIENT/CONTACT ADMINISTRATION—Software—CSC Financial Services Group; *U.S. Public*, pg. 422

CLIENT SERIES—Business System—International Business Machines Corporation; *U.S. Public*, pg. 895

CLIENT WORD BLOCK—NONE—Keyport Life Insurance Company; *U.S. Private*, pg. 666

CLIFTON—Manufactured Homes—Champion Enterprises, Inc.; *U.S. Public*, pg. 332

CLIFTON PRECISION MOTORS—NONE—Litton Poly-Scientific; *U.S. Public*, pg. 1003

CLIFTON PRECISION PRODUCTS-CPPC—Synchros, Servo Motors—Litton Industries, Inc.; *U.S. Public*, pg. 1002

CLIMAGUARD—Exterior Coating—Spray-Tech, Inc.; *U.S. Private*, pg. 1026

CLIMALENE—Laundry Booster—Malco Products, Inc.; *U.S. Private*, pg. 698

CLIMATE COMMAMD—Packaged Terminal Air Conditioners—Slant/Fin Corporation; *U.S. Private*, pg. 1005

CLIMATE CONTROL—Refrigeration Products—Heatcraft, Inc.-Refrigeration Products Division; *U.S. Private*, pg. 659

CLIMATE GUARD—Extrusions—Reynolds Metals Company; *U.S. Public*, pg. 1385

CLIMATE SMOOTH SOLDERINGPASTE—Industrial Chemical—Hercules Chemical Co., Inc.; *U.S. Private*, pg. 523

CLIMATROL—Room Air Conditioning—Fedders Corp.; *U.S. Public*, pg. 614

CLIMATUBE—Rubber Products—Rubatex Corporation; *U.S. Private*, pg. 56

CLIMAZON—Salon Dryers—Belvedere Company; *U.S. Private*, pg. 1008

CLIMAZON—Hair Dressing Equipment—Wella Group; *Int'l*, pg. 1489

CLIMBING ROSE—Gift Wrapping Paper—American Greetings Corporation; *U.S. Public*, pg. 77

CLIN D'OEIL—Magazine—Quebecor Inc.; *Int'l*, pg. 1075

CLINAC—Medical Linear Accelerators—Varian Associates, Inc.; *U.S. Public*, pg. 1710

CLINCH—NONE—The Procter & Gamble Company; *U.S. Public*, pg. 1330

CLINCH-IT—Hair Barrettes—Goody Products, Inc.; *U.S. Public*, pg. 1177

CLINCHER—NONE—Berg Electronics; *U.S. Public*, pg. 212

CLINCHER—Ball Valves—Neles-Jamesbury Corp.; *Int'l*, pg. 1428

CLING FREE—Fabric Softener—Benckiser Consumer Products Inc.; *Int'l*, pg. 185

CLING PLUS—Adhesion Enhancer—The Dow Chemical Company; *U.S. Public*, pg. 522

CLING STRIP—Adhesive Bars—The Dow Chemical Company; *U.S. Public*, pg. 522

CLINGMASTER—Laundry Wrap Film—AEP Industries, Inc.; *U.S. Public*, pg. 4

CLINI-CARE—Pressure Ulcer Therapy System—Clinicare Systems, Inc.; *U.S. Private*, pg. 442

CLINICAL LABORATORY REFERENCE—Publication—Medical Economics Company Inc.; *U.S. Public*, pg. 1601

CLINICAL SIGNS—Magazine—Alcon Laboratories, Inc.; *Int'l*, pg. 916

CLINICSELECT—NONE—Eastman Kodak Company; *U.S. Public*, pg. 550

CLINIDINE—Iodophor, Povidone Iodine Solution—The Clinipad Corporation; *U.S. Private*, pg. 246

CLINIGLOVE—Protective Hand Lotion for Latex Dermatitis—The Clinipad Corporation; *U.S. Private*, pg. 246

CLINIGUARD—Protective Dressing Swabstick—The Clinipad Corporation; *U.S. Private*, pg. 246

CLINIPREP—Clinical Sample Filtration—Whatman Inc.; *Int'l*, pg. 1498

CLINIQUE—Beauty Products—Estee Lauder Companies Inc.; *U.S. Public*, pg. 594

CLINISCRUB—Povidone Iodine Surgical Scrub—The Clinipad Corporation; *U.S. Private*, pg. 246

CLINITUB—Clear Plastic Container Used to Soap C.A.P.D. Tubing—The Clinipad Corporation; *U.S. Private*, pg. 246

CLINIVISION—Respiratory Care Management Information System—Nellcor Puritan Bennett Incorporated; *U.S. Public*, pg. 1039

CLINIX SERIES—X-Ray—Picker International, Inc.; *Int'l*, pg. 545

CLINORIL—Sulindac—Merck & Co., Inc.; *U.S. Public*, pg. 1090

CLINORIL—Pharmaceutical—Merck Human Health Division (U.S. Human Health); *U.S. Public*, pg. 1091

CLINITEK—Urine Analyzer—Bayer Corporation/Consumer Care Division; *Int'l*, pg. 173

CLIO—Designer Chair Line—Harter; *U.S. Private*, pg. 581

CLIO—Shower Head & Hand Held Shower—Interbath, Inc.; *U.S. Private*, pg. 566

CLIP—Current Limiting Protector—G & W Electric Co.; *U.S. Private*, pg. 433

CLIP-A-MATIC—Clip Applier—U.S. Surgical Corp.; *U.S. Public*, pg. 1687

CLIP EDIT—Editorial Software—The Dartnell Corporation; *U.S. Private*, pg. 312

CLIP-GRIP—Window Clip Cellular Antennas—Allen Telecom Inc.; *U.S. Public*, pg. 45

CLIP-LOCK—Diving Knives—Fiskars-Gerber; *Int'l*, pg. 492

CLIP ROLL ELECTROFEED—Roll Forming Material—Lockformer Company; *U.S. Public*, pg. 1100

CLIP TIPS—Printed Ready to Clip Artwork—The Mead Corporation; *U.S. Public*, pg. 1074

CLIP-TITE—Beryllium Copper Shielding Gasket with a Brass Retaining Clip—Instrument Specialties Company; *U.S. Private*, pg. 565

CLIPMATE—Loose Leaf Notebook & Clipboard—The Mead Corporation; *U.S. Public*, pg. 1074

CLIPPER—Light & Medium Duty Belt Fasteners—Clipper Belt Lacer Company; *U.S. Private*, pg. 413

CLIPPER—Belt Hooks—Flexible Steel Lacing Company; *U.S. Private*, pg. 413

CLIPPER—Super Duty Fireclay—A.P. Green Industries, Inc.; *U.S. Public*, pg. 761

CLIPPER—Masonry & Concrete, Diamond Blades & Saws, & Core Drill Machines—Norton Company; *Int'l*, pg. 1173

CLIPPER—Industrial Grade Steel Shelving—Penco Products; *U.S. Private*, pg. 848

CLIPSAL—Electrical Wiring Accessories—Gold Peak Industries (Holdings) Limited; *Int'l*, pg. 537

CLIRANS—Dialysis Products—Terumo Medical Corporation; *Int'l*, pg. 1376

CLOAS—Software—CSC Financial Services Group; *U.S. Public*, pg. 422

CLOBBER—Industrial Chemical—Hercules Chemical Co., Inc.; *U.S. Private*, pg. 523

CLOCHE NOEL—Christmas Bells—Coop Switzerland; *Int'l*, pg. 329

CLOCREAM—NONE—Lee Pharmaceuticals; *U.S. Public*, pg. 984

THE CLOISTER—Resort Hotel—Sea Island Company; *U.S. Private*, pg. 977

CLOMID—Fertility Inducer—Hoechst Marion Roussel North America; *Int'l*, pg. 625

CLOMID—Clomifene-Citrate—Royal Gist-Brocades N.V.; *Int'l*, pg. 1142

CLOMYCIN—NONE—Lee Pharmaceuticals; *U.S. Public*, pg. 984

CLONEAMP—NONE—Life Technologies, Inc.; *U.S. Public*, pg. 504

CLOPARIN, CLOPAROL—Chlorinated Paraffins—Caffaro S.p.A.; *Int'l*, pg. 248

CLOPARTEN—Chlorosulphonated Paraffins—Caffaro S.p.A.; *Int'l*, pg. 248

CLOPAY—Doors, Plastic Films—Clopay Corporation; *U.S. Public*, pg. 766

CLORETS—Breath Mints & Chewing Gum—Adams U.S.A.; *U.S. Public*, pg. 1739

CLORETS—Breath Freshener—Warner-Lambert Company; *U.S. Public*, pg. 1738

CLORETS GUM—Chewing Gum—Warner-Lambert K.K.; *U.S. Public*, pg. 1739

CLOROMAT—ED Equipment for Electrodialysis of Chloride Solutions—Ionics, Incorporated; *U.S. Public*, pg. 912

CLOROX—Regular, Fresh Scent & Lemon Fresh Liquid Bleach—The Clorox Company; *U.S. Public*, pg. 386

CLOROX—Toilet Bowl Cleaner and Automatic Toilet Bowl Cleaner—The Clorox Company; *U.S. Public*, pg. 386

CLOROX CLEAN-UP—Dilutable Household Cleaner—The Clorox Company; *U.S. Public*, pg. 386

CLOROX STAIN OUT—Soil & Stain Remover—The Clorox Company; *U.S. Public*, pg. 386

CLOROX 2—Dry & Liquid All-Fabric Bleach, Lemon Fresh Liquid—The Clorox Company; *U.S. Public*, pg. 386

CLORTEX—Chlorinated Rubber—Caffaro S.p.A.; *Int'l*, pg. 248

CLOS DE BOIS — Wine—The Wine Alliance; *Int'l*, pg. 63

CLOS DU BOIS CALIFORNIAN WINE—Wine—Allied Domecq PLC; *Int'l*, pg. 62

CLOS NORMAND—Cider—Groupe Pernod Ricard; *Int'l*, pg. 566

CLOS ROBERT—California Wine—Remy Amerique Inc.; *Int'l*, pg. 1102

CLOSAN—Bathroom Care—Sara Lee Corporation; *U.S. Public*, pg. 1432

CLOSE-UP—Toothpaste—Chesebrough-Pond's USA Co.; *Int'l*, pg. 1435

CLOSERS CLUB—An Exclusive Incentive Program for Sales Professionals—Trans Leasing International Inc.; *U.S. Public*, pg. 1628

CLOSET MAID—Vinyl Coated Steel Rod Shelving, Storage Products, Closet Organizers—Clairson International Corp.; *U.S. Public*, pg. 575

CLOTH WORLD—Retail Stores Selling Fabric, Crafts & Notions—Fabri-Centers of America, Inc.; *U.S. Public*, pg. 609

CLOTHES SHAVER—Clothing Pill Remover—Windmere-Durable Holdings; *U.S. Public*, pg. 1771

CLOTHES SHOW—NONE—BBC Magazines; *Int'l*, pg. 114

CLOTHESTIME—Apparel—Clothestime Stores, Inc.; *U.S. Public*, pg. 387

CLOTTRAC—Coagulation Tester—Medtronic, Inc.; *U.S. Public*, pg. 1082

CLOUD COUNTRY—Dusting Powder, Soaps—Avon Products, Inc.; *U.S. Public*, pg. 155

CLOUD NINE—NONE—Nellcor Puritan Bennett Incorporated; *U.S. Public*, pg. 1039

CLOUD 28—NONE—Kellwood Company; *U.S. Public*, pg. 948

CLOUDS—Lumber & Wood Products—Georgia-Pacific Corporation; *U.S. Public*, pg. 735

CLOUTH OIL-EX—NONE—Clouth Gummiwerke AG; *Int'l*, pg. 297

CLOUTH-USM—NONE—Clouth Gummiwerke AG; *Int'l*, pg. 297

CLOVER BLOOM—Twist Tobacco—Conwood Company L.P.; *U.S. Private*, pg. 272

CLOVER CLUB—Corn Chips—Clover Club Foods, Inc.; *U.S. Private*, pg. 469

CLOVER CLUB—Popcorn—Clover Club Foods, Inc.; *U.S. Private*, pg. 469

CLOVER CLUB—Pretzels—Clover Club Foods, Inc.; *U.S. Private*, pg. 469

CLOVER CLUB FOODS—Potato Chips & Corn Snacks—Granny Goose Foods, Inc.; *U.S. Private*, pg. 469

CLOVER CRISP—Potato Chips—Clover Club Foods, Inc.; *U.S. Private*, pg. 469

CLOVER LEAF—Sea Food Prods.—George Weston Limited; *Int'l*, pg. 1494

CLOVER MAID—Honey—Sioux Honey Association; *U.S. Private*, pg. 1003

CLOVERBLOOM—Natural & Process Cheeses—Beatrice Cheese Co.; *U.S. Public*, pg. 426

CLOVERBLOOM—Cheese Products—ConAgra, Inc.; *U.S. Public*, pg. 425

CLOVERINE—Pharmaceuticals—Medtech Inc.; *U.S. Private*, pg. 728

CLOVERLEAF—Food Products—Bumble Bee Seafoods Inc.; *U.S. Private*, pg. 526

CLOVERLEAF—Dairy Products—Crystal Cream & Butter Company; *U.S. Private*, pg. 294

CLOVERLEAF LANE—Greeting Cards; Plates, Cups & Bowls—American Greetings Corporation; *U.S. Public*, pg. 77

CLOXAPEN—Pharmaceutical Prods.—SmithKline Beecham Laboratories; *Int'l*, pg. 1264

CLOXAPEN—Antibiotic—SmithKline Beecham plc; *Int'l*, pg. 1264

CLOZARIL—Schizophrenia Drug—Novartis AG; *Int'l*, pg. 971

CLOZARIL—Anti-Psychotic Medication—Sandoz Corporation; *Int'l*, pg. 974

CLOZARIL—Management of Severly Ill Schizophrenic Patients—Sandoz Pharmaceuticals Corp.; *Int'l*, pg. 974

CLUB—Soft Drinks & Mixers—Allied Domecq PLC; *Int'l*, pg. 62

CLUB—Chocolate Bars—Danone Group; *Int'l*, pg. 379

CLUB—Bookstores—GIB Group; *Int'l*, pg. 532

CLUB—Crackers—Keebler Company; *U.S. Public*, pg. 657

CLUB—Yogurt Drink—Nestle S.A.; *Int'l*, pg. 915

CLUB—Milk—Q.U.F. Industries Ltd.; *Int'l*, pg. 1074

CLUB—Athletic Shoe—Reebok International Ltd.; *U.S. Public*, pg. 1369

CLUB—Cast Aluminum Cookware—Regal Ware, Inc.; *U.S. Private*, pg. 917

CLUB—Cigarettes-German—R.J. Reynolds Tobacco Intl., Inc.; *U.S. Public*, pg. 1355

CLUB ALUMINUM HAMMERCRAFT WATERLESS—NONE—Regal Ware, Inc.; *U.S. Private*, pg. 917

CLUB & CHEDDAR—Cracker Snacks—Keebler Company; *U.S. Public*, pg. 657

CLUB & CONCENTRIC CIRCLES DESIGN—NONE—Regal Ware, Inc.; *U.S. Private*, pg. 917

CLUB CAST STAINLESS ALUMINUM—Cookware—Regal Ware, Inc.; *U.S. Private*, pg. 917

CLUB CLASSIC—Cookware—Regal Ware, Inc.; *U.S. Private*, pg. 917

THE CLUB COCKTAILS—Cocktail—Grand Metropolitan Plc; *Int'l*, pg. 408

THE CLUB COCKTAILS—Cocktails—Heublein, Inc.; *Int'l*, pg. 410

CLUB DUFFEL—Sport Bag—Ektelon; *U.S. Private*, pg. 884

CLUB 53—Interest-Bearing Checking Account—Fifth Third Bancorp; *U.S. Public*, pg. 621

CLUB FORME—Low Fat Cheese—Entremont S.A.; *Int'l*, pg. 458

CLUB GARD—Golf Bag—Ajay Leisure Products, Inc.; *U.S. Public*, pg. 34

CLUB HOLIDAY—Cookware—Regal Ware, Inc.; *U.S. Private*, pg. 917

CLUB HOTELS BY DOUBLETREE—Hotels—Doubletree Corporation; *U.S. Public*, pg. 1335

CLUB HOUSE—Spices, Seasonings & Specialty Food Products—McCormick Canada, Ltd.; *U.S. Public*, pg. 1067

CLUB RTL—Belgium Broadcasting—CLT-UFA; *Int'l*, pg. 561

CLUB RUN—Labels—S & K Famous Brands, Inc.; *U.S. Public*, pg. 1414

CLUB SOX—Golf Club Covers—Reliable Knitting Works; *U.S. Private*, pg. 920

CLUB TRANSATLANTIQUE—Sports Outerwear—Fox-Knapp; *U.S. Private*, pg. 860

CLUB WAGON—Van—Ford Motor Company; *U.S. Public*, pg. 661

CLUBCAST—Cookware—Regal Ware, Inc.; *U.S. Private*, pg. 917

CLUBLINK—Electronic Telecommunication Of Clubs—American Automobile Association; *U.S. Private*, pg. 50

CLUBMASTER—Sunglasses—Bausch & Lomb Incorporated; *U.S. Public*, pg. 194

CLUE—Game—Parker Brothers; *U.S. Public*, pg. 797

CLUETT CANE COLLECTION—NONE—Celebrity Incorporated; *U.S. Public*, pg. 319

CLUPAK—Extensible Paper—Clupak, Inc.; *U.S. Public*, pg. 1762

CLUSTER BOX UNIT—Parcel & Mail Receptacles—American Locker Group, Inc.; *U.S. Public*, pg. 85

CLUSTER-CLIP—Packaging Machines & Bottle Carrying Devices—The Mead Corporation; *U.S. Public*, pg. 1074

CLUSTER-PAK—Paperboard Cartons, Shipping Containers, Packaging Machines—The Mead Corporation; *U.S. Public*, pg. 1074

CLUSTER-PAK—Multiple-Unit Cartons—Mead Packaging; *U.S. Public*, pg. 1074

CLUSTER-TRAY—Paperboard Trays—The Mead Corporation; *U.S. Public*, pg. 1074

CLUSTERS—Ready-to-Eat Cereal—General Mills, Inc.; *U.S. Public*, pg. 717

CLUSTERTRAY—Cartons—Mead Packaging; *U.S. Public*, pg. 1074

CLUTCH-IN!—Clutch pilot accesories—R&B, Inc.; *U.S. Public*, pg. 1354

CLUTTER-PROOF—Office Desks—Knoll, Inc.; *U.S. Private*, pg. 627

CLYBOURN—Cartoning—SASIB Packaging North America; *Int'l*, pg. 1194

CLYDE—NONE—Pfizer Inc.; *U.S. Public*, pg. 1281

C'MON AMERICA, DRIVE OVER TO FIRESTONE—Automotive Repair Services—Bridgestone/Firestone, Inc.; *Int'l*, pg. 213

CO ACCESS—Central Office Platform for Switching in Storage of Voice Messages—Comverse Network Systems; *U.S. Public*, pg. 425

CO-DESIGNER—Software—LSI Logic Corp.; *U.S. Public*, pg. 971

CO-GESIC—NONE—Schwarz Pharma Inc.; *Int'l*, pg. 1211

CO-NECT—NONE—GTE Internetworking; *U.S. Public*, pg. 696

CO-OP—Fertilizers-Feeds & Seeds—Purdel, Cooperative Agro-Alimentaire; *Int'l*, pg. 1073

CO-OP—Automotive Products, Lubricants & Twine—Universal Cooperatives, Inc.; *U.S. Private*, pg. 1127

CO-OP ADVERTISING—Program Sourcebook—National Register Publishing; *Int'l*, pg. 1096

CO-OP-CO—Lubricant Products—Waterloo Service Company; *U.S. Private*, pg. 1152

CO-OPERATIVE—NONE—Urban Outfitters, Inc.; *U.S. Public*, pg. 1700

CO-OPERATOR—Tires—Universal Cooperatives, Inc.; *U.S. Private*, pg. 1127

CO-ORDINATES—Broadloom—Couristan Inc.; *U.S. Private*, pg. 279

CO-PILOT II—Car-Seat—Collier-Keyworth, Inc.; *U.S. Public*, pg. 985

CO-PYRONIL 2—Chlorpheniramine Maleate & Pseudoephedrine Hydrochloride, Dista—Eli Lilly and Company; *U.S. Public*, pg. 992

CO-GESIC—Pharmaceutical Product—Schwarz Pharma Manufacturing, Inc.; *Int'l*, pg. 1211

COACH—Leatherware—Coach; *U.S. Public*, pg. 1433

COACH—Leather Handbags, Belts & Access.—Sara Lee Corporation; *U.S. Public*, pg. 1432

COACHMEN—Recreational Vehicle & Vans—Coachmen Industries, Inc.; *U.S. Public*, pg. 387

COAGULATION CONTROLS—Coagulation Agents—Ortho Clinical Diagnostic Systems Inc.; *U.S. Public*, pg. 929

COAL AGE—Publication on Industry Trends—Intertec Publishing; *U.S. Public*, pg. 1327

COAL CAT—Coal Tar Epoxy Coatings—PPG Industries, Inc.; *U.S. Public*, pg. 1245

COALPACTOR—Industrial Machinery—Pennsylvania Crusher Corp.; *U.S. Private*, pg. 850

COALPORT FINE—Bone China Figurines—Waterford Wedgwood UK Plc; *Int'l*, pg. 1487

COARSE ANGLING—Special Interest Magazine—IPC Magazines Limited; *Int'l*, pg. 651

COAST—Soap—The Procter & Gamble Company; *U.S. Public*, pg. 1330

COASTAL BREEZES—Juice Drinks—Ocean Spray Cranberries, Inc.; *U.S. Private*, pg. 811

COASTAL CHEM—Agricultural & Industrial Chemicals—The Coastal Corporation; *U.S. Public*, pg. 389

COASTAL CRANBERRY—Sparkling Mineral Water—Clearly Canadian Beverage Corp.; *Int'l*, pg. 297

COASTAL FUELS MARKETING—Petroleum Products Marketing-Fuel Oil—The Coastal Corporation; *U.S. Public*, pg. 389

COASTAL GAS—Propane—The Coastal Corporation; *U.S. Public*, pg. 389

COASTAL LIVING—Bi-Monthly Magazine—Southern Progress Corporation; *U.S. Public*, pg. 1612

COASTAL MART—Retail Distribution, Gasolines, Convenience Stores—The Coastal Corporation; *U.S. Public*, pg. 389

COASTAL UNILUBE—Motor Oil, Lubricants, Greases—The Coastal Corporation; *U.S. Public*, pg. 389

COASTER—Trucks & Buses—Toyota Motor Corporation; *Int'l*, pg. 1411

COASTER BUOY—Insulated Beverage Can Holder—Orbex Inc.; *U.S. Public*, pg. 238

COASTER GEAR—Clothing & Apparel—Cedar Fair, L.P.; *U.S. Public*, pg. 319

COATED VICRYL—Polyglactin 910 Suture—Ethicon, Inc.; *U.S. Public*, pg. 928

COATED VICRYL RAPIDE—Polyglactin 910 Suture—Ethicon, Inc.; *U.S. Public*, pg. 928

COATIME—Coagulation Meter—Novo Nordisk A/S; *Int'l*, pg. 987

COATS—Specialty Threads, Sewing Accessories, Trims—Coats & Clark Inc.; *Int'l*, pg. 300

COATS—NONE—Coats Viyella plc; *Int'l*, pg. 299

COATS—Tire Changers & Wheel Balancers—Hennessy Industries, Inc.; *U.S. Public*, pg. 481

COAXIOM—Provides Telephony & Other Services, Over Hybrid Fiber Coax Network—Scientific-Atlanta, Inc.; *U.S. Public*, pg. 1443

COBALT—Men's Fragrance—Coty Inc.; *Int'l*, pg. 185

COBALT COBRA—Band Saw Blades—Sandvik/Milford Corporation; *Int'l*, pg. 1185

COBAMYDE—Vitamins—Kyowa Hakko Kogyo Company, Ltd.; *Int'l*, pg. 778

COBAN—Animal Health—Elanco Animal Health; *U.S. Public*, pg. 993

COBAN—Elastic Bandage—3M; *U.S. Public*, pg. 1604

COBAN 45 Premix—Monensin Sodium, Elanco—Eli Lilly and Company; *U.S. Public*, pg. 992

COBANIC—NONE—Carpenter Technology Corporation; *U.S. Public*, pg. 307

COBBLEHILL—Children's Hardcover Books—Penguin Putnam Inc.; *Int'l*, pg. 1027

COBBLESTONE MILL—Breads & Rolls—Flowers Industries, Inc.; *U.S. Public*, pg. 656

COBE SPECTRA—Apheresis System—COBE Laboratories, Inc.; *Int'l*, pg. 667

COBERINE—Specialty Product—Lever Brothers Co.; *Int'l*, pg. 1435

COBERINE—Speciality Prod.—Unilever Plc; *Int'l*, pg. 1433

COBOL/400—Computer System—International Business Machines Corporation; *U.S. Public*, pg. 895

COBOL/370—Computer System—International Business Machines Corporation; *U.S. Public*, pg. 895

COBOL/2—Computer System—International Business Machines Corporation; *U.S. Public*, pg. 895

COBRA—Fuel-Powered Drills—Atlas Copco AB; *Int'l*, pg. 95

COBRA—Accessories—The Black & Decker Corporation; *U.S. Public*, pg. 233

COBRA—Citizens Band Radios, Radar Detectors, Telephone Prods., Answering Systems—Cobra Electronics Corporation; *U.S. Public*, pg. 391

COBRA—Monofilament Fishing Line—Cortland Line Co., Inc.; *U.S. Private*, pg. 277

COBRA—Stretch Wrapping System—Illinois Tool Works Inc.; *U.S. Public*, pg. 865

COBRA—Automotive Products—Standard Motor Products Inc.; *U.S. Public*, pg. 1503

COBRA I & II—NONE—Datametrics Corporation; *U.S. Public*, pg. 487

COBRA T.P.A.-I—NONE—Fortune Brands, Inc.; *U.S. Public*, pg. 674

COBRA II—Gamma Counting System—Packard Instrument Co., Inc.; *U.S. Public*, pg. 833

COBRALINE MANUFACTURING CORP.—NONE—F&B Manufacturing Co.; *U.S. Private*, pg. 388

COBRALINK—Security Cable Device—Tuthill Corporation; *U.S. Private*, pg. 1110

COBREBOL—Pastry Ingredient—Royal Gist-Brocades N.V.; *Int'l*, pg. 1142

COBURN—Optical Equipment—Coburn Optical Industries Inc.; *U.S. Private*, pg. 248

COCA CASA—NONE—Cadbury Beverages; *Int'l*, pg. 248

COCA-COLA CLASSIC—Soft Drink—The Coca-Cola Bottling Co. of New York, Inc.; *U.S. Public*, pg. 393

COCA-COLA CLASSIC—Soft Drink—The Coca-Cola Company; *U.S. Public*, pg. 392

COCAT—Cracking Catalysts—Engelhard Corporation; *U.S. Public*, pg. 582

COCHONOU—Meats (Europe)—Sara Lee Corporation; *Int'l*, pg. 1432

COCIO—Chocolate Milk—Borden, Inc.; *U.S. Private*, pg. 157

COCKBURN'S SPECIAL RESERVE AND OTHER PORTS—Wine—Allied Domecq PLC; *Int'l*, pg. 62

COCKBURN'S O.V.—Scotch Whiskey—John Gross & Co.; *U.S. Private*, pg. 483

COCKBURN'S PORT—Port Wine—Frederick Wildman & Sons Ltd.; *U.S. Private*, pg. 1176

COCKSPUR RUM—NONE—International Distillers Caribbean; *Int'l*, pg. 410

COCKTAILS FOR TWO—Cocktails—Guinness Import Company; *Int'l*, pg. 412

COCKTAILS FOR TWO—Cocktails—Heublein, Inc.; *Int'l*, pg. 410

COCO LOPEZ—Cream of Coconut & Fruit Drink Mixes—Borden, Inc.; *U.S. Private*, pg. 157

THE COCOA BUTTER—Soap & Liquid Soap—Yardley of London, Inc.; *Int'l*, pg. 819

COCOA KRISPIES—Ready-Sweetened Rice Cereal with Real Cocoa—Kellogg Company; *U.S. Public*, pg. 947

COCOA PUFFS—Cereal—General Mills, Inc.; *U.S. Public*, pg. 717

COCOA ROOS—Frosted Corn Cereal Made with Real Cocoa—Malt-O-Meal Company; *U.S. Private*, pg. 699

COCONUTS MUSIC & MOVIES—Retail Music Store—Trans World Entertainment Corporation; *U.S. Public*, pg. 1629

CODA—Men's Apparel—Edison Brothers Stores, Inc.; *U.S. Public*, pg. 563

CODE-A-PHONE—Telephones and Answering Machines—Conrac Display Products; *U.S. Private*, pg. 264

CODE-ALARM—Vehicle & Home Security Systems—Code-Alarm, Inc.; *U.S. Public*, pg. 393

CODE BLUE—Resuscitator—Vital Signs, Inc.; *U.S. Public*, pg. 1723

CODE BLUE EASI-LAV—NONE—Ballard Medical Products; *U.S. Public*, pg. 171

CODE-MASTER—HID Floodlights and Lighting Fixtures—Appleton Electric Co.; *U.S. Public*, pg. 572

CODE OF BUSHIDO—War Game—Monarch Avalon, Inc.; *U.S. Public*, pg. 1123

CODE-1 INTERNATIONAL—Mailing Efficiency System—Group 1 Software, Inc.; *U.S. Public*, pg. 417

CODE/TRONIC—Access Control System—Sargent & Greenleaf, Inc.; *U.S. Private*, pg. 965

CODE WELD—Metals—Titanium Metals Corporation; *U.S. Private*, pg. 270

CODE WEST—Footwear—Genesco Inc.; *U.S. Public*, pg. 728

CODEFINDER—Medical Computer Program—3M; *U.S. Public*, pg. 1604

CODEKIT—Driveline Retrofit—York International Corporation; *U.S. Public*, pg. 1789

CODELINE—Pressure Vessell Housings—Essef Corporation; *U.S. Public*, pg. 592

CODEMPIRAL—Analgestic, Sedative—Glaxo Wellcome PLC; *Int'l*, pg. 553

CODEPAK—Reciprocating Chillers—York International Corporation; *U.S. Public*, pg. 1789

CODER IMPRESSIONS—Vinyl Siding—CertainTeed Corporation; *Int'l*, pg. 1170

Brand Name Index

CODEROLL—Metals—Titanium Metals Corporation; *U.S. Private*, pg. 270

CODETAPER—Tapes—Ascom Hasler Mailing Systems, Inc.; *Int'l*, pg. 86

CODICLEAR—NONE—Schwarz Pharma Inc.; *Int'l*, pg. 1211

CODICLEAR—Pharmaceutical Products—Schwarz Pharma Manufacturing, Inc.; *Int'l*, pg. 1211

CODIMAL—NONE—Schwarz Pharma Inc.; *Int'l*, pg. 1211

CODIMAL—Pharmaceutical Products—Schwarz Pharma Manufacturing, Inc.; *Int'l*, pg. 1211

CODIMAL-LA—Pharmaceutical Products—Schwarz Pharma Manufacturing, Inc.; *Int'l*, pg. 1211

CODIS—Analgesic—Reckitt & Colman plc; *Int'l*, pg. 1089

CODIT—Reflective Chalk—3M; *U.S. Public*, pg. 1604

CODOL—Semi-Synthetic Coolant—D.A. Stuart Company; *U.S. Private*, pg. 1048

COE—Machinery—The Coe Manufacturing Company; *U.S. Private*, pg. 249

COEUR-JOIE—Women's Fragrance—Accecones Ricci U.S.A., Inc.; *Int'l*, pg. 445

COFFEE ACCENTS—Coffee Syrups—Pacific Foods, Inc.; *U.S. Private*, pg. 831

COFFEE BUTLER—Insulated Carafe—The Thermos Company; *Int'l*, pg. 938

COFFEE BY THE POUND—Coffee—Dunkin' Donuts Incorporated; *Int'l*, pg. 63

COFFEE CRISP—Confection—Nestle-Rowntree Ltd.; *Int'l*, pg. 921

COFFEE-MATE—Powdered Cream—Nestle S.A.; *Int'l*, pg. 915

COFFEE MISER—Drip Coffeemaker—Regal Ware, Inc.; *U.S. Private*, pg. 917

COFFEE PARTNER—Chicory—William B. Reily & Co., Inc.; *U.S. Private*, pg. 919

COFFEE RICH—Non-Dairy Creamer—Rich Products Corp.; *U.S. Private*, pg. 928

COFFEE TEAK—Wood, Lumber & Wood Fiber Products—Georgia-Pacific Corporation; *U.S. Public*, pg. 735

COFFEEMASTER—Coffeemakers—Sunbeam Household Products; *U.S. Public*, pg. 1533

COFFING—Hoist—Columbus McKinnon Corp.; *U.S. Public*, pg. 405

COGEN—Software—CSC Financial Services Group; *U.S. Public*, pg. 422

COGENTIN—Benztropin Mesylate—Merck & Co., Inc.; *U.S. Public*, pg. 1090

COGITUM—Amino Acid Preparations—The Dow Chemical Company; *U.S. Public*, pg. 522

COGNAC RENAULT CARTE NOIRE EXTRA—Cognac—Groupe Pernod Ricard; *Int'l*, pg. 566

COHORT—Herbicide—The Dow Chemical Company; *U.S. Public*, pg. 522

COIL-FLEX—Seating Systems—Leggett & Platt, Incorporated; *U.S. Public*, pg. 985

COIL-FLITE—Heat Exchangers—Svedala Pumps & Process; *Int'l*, pg. 1325

COIL GUARD—Coil Rack—Jarke Corporation; *U.S. Private*, pg. 583

COIL STRIP—Self Piercing Fasteners—Maclean-Fogg Co.; *U.S. Private*, pg. 692

COILFILTER—Liquid-Solids Separation Equipment—Komline-Sanderson Engineering Corp.; *U.S. Private*, pg. 631

COILGRIP—Wire & Cable—Times Fiber Communications, Inc.; *U.S. Private*, pg. 629

COILTECH—NONE—BJ Services Company; *U.S. Public*, pg. 161

COILTEF—Coiled Teflon Tubing—NewAge Industries Inc.; *U.S. Private*, pg. 796

COILTEF—Coiled Teflon Tubing—Newage Industries Inc., Plastics Technology Group; *U.S. Private*, pg. 796

COILUBE—Coil Lubricant—Alltrista Corporation; *U.S. Public*, pg. 56

COILUBE—Electrostatic Lubricator—Ball Corporation; *U.S. Public*, pg. 170

COIN-LOK—Coin-Operated Locker—American Locker Security Systems, Inc.; *U.S. Public*, pg. 86

COKER—Corn Seed & Wheat—Northrup King Co.; *Int'l*, pg. 974

COL-R-CORN—Popcorn—Comstock Michigan Fruit; *U.S. Private*, pg. 887

COLA-UP—Jelly Candy—Meiji Seika Kaisha, Ltd.; *Int'l*, pg. 855

COLACE—Laxative—Bristol-Myers Squibb Company; *U.S. Public*, pg. 253

COLACE—Pharmaceutical for use in Softening Stools w/o Laxative Stimulation—Bristol-Myers Squibb U.S. Pharmaceutical Group; *U.S. Public*, pg. 255

COLACE—Laxative—Roberts Pharmaceutical Corporation; *U.S. Public*, pg. 1393

COLANYL—Organic Pigments—Hoechst Aktiengesellschaft; *Int'l*, pg. 624

COLAVITA—Oil, Pasta, Vegetables—Colivita USA, Inc.; *U.S. Private*, pg. 252

COLBACK—Backer for Tufted Carpets—Akzo Nobel N.V.; *Int'l*, pg. 42

COLBENEMID—Probenecid & Colchicine—Merck & Co., Inc.; *U.S. Public*, pg. 1090

COLBERT—Stainless Steel Flatware—Dansk International Designs Ltd.; *U.S. Public*, pg. 261

COLBOND—Polyester Non-woven Material—Akzo Nobel N.V.; *Int'l*, pg. 42

COLD—NONE—FileNet Corporation; *U.S. Public*, pg. 622

COLD COMFORT—Cold Pack, Medical/First Aid—3M; *U.S. Public*, pg. 1604

COLD FRONT—Grill Insert—Lund International Holdings, Inc.; *U.S. Public*, pg. 1020

COLD KITS—Various Organ Imaging Studies—Amersham Healthcare; *Int'l*, pg. 992

COLD MASTER—Cold Temperature Control—Carlisle Food Service Products; *U.S. Public*, pg. 305

COLD POWER—Detergent—Colgate-Palmolive Company; *U.S. Public*, pg. 397

COLD SHOT—Refrigerate—Radiator Specialty Company; *U.S. Private*, pg. 906

COLD SPRING GRANITE—Building Granite Company—Cold Spring Granite Company; *U.S. Private*, pg. 250

COLDCARE—NONE—Kimberly-Clark Corporation; *U.S. Public*, pg. 958

COLDER—Fittings—Ryan Herco Products Corp.; *U.S. Private*, pg. 953

COLDFLOW—Drinks Dispense—IMI Plc; *Int'l*, pg. 646

COLDFORM—Cold Formed Hollow Sections—British Steel Tubes & Pipes; *Int'l*, pg. 221

COLDSPED—European Transport of Refrigerated & Frozen Foodstuffs—BTL AB; *Int'l*, pg. 123

COLE BOSTON—Switches, Connectors & All Electrical & Electronic Items—Cole Hersee Company; *U.S. Private*, pg. 251

COLE-HAAN—Footwear—Cole-Haan; *U.S. Public*, pg. 1184

COLE OF CALIFORNIA—Missy Swim Suits—Cole of California; *U.S. Public*, pg. 148

COLEB—Cardiovascular Pharmaceutical—Astra AB; *Int'l*, pg. 93

COLEBROOK KIDS—NONE—G-III Apparel Group, Ltd.; *U.S. Public*, pg. 690

COLEMAN—Sport Footwear—Wolverine World Wide, Inc.; *U.S. Public*, pg. 1775

COLEMAN POWERMATE—Portable Electric Generators—The Coleman Company, Inc.; *U.S. Private*, pg. 690

COLEMAN POWERMATE—Electric Generators—Coleman Powermate, Inc.; *U.S. Public*, pg. 691

COLEMAN SPAS—Spas, Hot Tubs, Saunas—The Coleman Company, Inc.; *U.S. Private*, pg. 690

COLEO—Bar Soap—Colgate-Palmolive Co., Institutional Products Div.; *U.S. Public*, pg. 397

COLE'S—Soil Products—L & L Nursery Supply, Inc.; *U.S. Private*, pg. 638

COLES SUPERMARKETS—NONE—Coles Myer Ltd.; *Int'l*, pg. 306

COLESTA—Knit Shirts—Somerset Knitting Mills; *U.S. Public*, pg. 1291

COLGATE—NONE—Colgate-Palmolive; *U.S. Public*, pg. 398

COLGATE—Toothpaste, Tooth Powder—Colgate-Palmolive Company; *U.S. Public*, pg. 397

COLGATE—Toothpaste—Colgate-Palmolive Ltd.; *U.S. Public*, pg. 398

COLGATE—NONE—Colgate-Palmolive S.A.I.C.; *U.S. Public*, pg. 399

COLGATE ACTION PLUS TOOTHBRUSH—Toothbrushes—Colgate-Palmolive Company; *U.S. Public*, pg. 397

COLGATE BAKING SODA TOOTHPASTE—Toothpaste—Colgate-Palmolive Company; *U.S. Public*, pg. 397

COLGATE INSTANT SHAVE—Shaving Cream—Colgate-Palmolive Company; *U.S. Public*, pg. 397

COLGATE JUNIOR—Children's Toothbrush—Colgate-Palmolive Company; *U.S. Public*, pg. 397

COLGATE PLUS LIMITED EDITION—Toothbrushes—Colgate-Palmolive Company; *U.S. Public*, pg. 397

COLGATE SHAVE PREP—Pre-shave lotion—Colgate-Palmolive Company; *U.S. Public*, pg. 397

COLGATE TARTAR-CONTROL FORMULA—Toothpaste—Colgate-Palmolive Company; *U.S. Public*, pg. 397

COLGATE TARTAR-CONTROL MOUTH WASH—Mouthwash—Colgate-Palmolive Company; *U.S. Public*, pg. 397

COLGATE TOTAL—Toothpaste—Colgate-Palmolive Company; *U.S. Public*, pg. 397

COLGATE VIA-JET—Peridontal Irragator—Colgate Oral Pharmaceutical; *U.S. Public*, pg. 397

COLGATE WINTERFRESH—Toothpaste Gel—Colgate-Palmolive Company; *U.S. Public*, pg. 397

COLI-COUNT—Sampler—Millipore Corporation; *U.S. Public*, pg. 1112

COLI-FIRM—Confirmation Kit—Millipore Corporation; *U.S. Public*, pg. 1112

COLIBRI—Lighters—Artra Group Incorporated; *U.S. Public*, pg. 136

COLIFOAM—Pharmaceutical—Stafford-Miller Limited; *U.S. Public*, pg. 237

COLIGHT—NONE—Hanovia Colight; *Int'l*, pg. 17

COLISEUM—Plastic Case—International Container Systems; *Int'l*, pg. 685

COLISEUM BOYS—Boys Casualwear—Andrew Sports Club Inc.; *U.S. Private*, pg. 73

COLISEUM Y.M.—Young Mens-Casualwear—Andrew Sports Club Inc.; *U.S. Private*, pg. 73

COLISTIN—Feed Additive—Asahi Chemical Industry Co., Ltd.; *Int'l*, pg. 83

COLISTIN—Feed Additives & Others—Meiji Seika Kaisha, Ltd.; *Int'l*, pg. 855

COLISTIN—Animal Use—Nippon Kayaku Co. Ltd.; *Int'l*, pg. 934

COLLACUTT—NONE—Bentley Leathers Inc.; *Int'l*, pg. 187

COLLAGE—Photo Typesetters—AGFA EPS Division; *Int'l*, pg. 172

COLLAGE—Rattan Furniture—Avon Workshop Ficks Reed; *U.S. Private*, pg. 102

COLLAGEN BOOSTER LINE CONTROLLING LOTION—Skin Preparation—Avon Products, Inc.; *U.S. Public*, pg. 155

COLLAGEN PLUS—Cosmetics—Palm Beach Beauty Products Co.; *U.S. Private*, pg. 834

COLLALTO SYRAH—NONE—Castello Banfi Srl.; *U.S. Private*, pg. 113

COLLAPUR—Mfr. Collagen Prods.—Freudenberg & Company; *Int'l*, pg. 505

COLLARWEAR—Neckwear—The Apparel Group, Ltd.; *U.S. Private*, pg. 78

COLLEAGUE—Electron Infusion Pump—Baxter International Inc.; *U.S. Public*, pg. 196

COLLECT-A-CUBE—Fire Safe Steel Recycling Containers—United Receptical, Inc.; *U.S. Private*, pg. 1123

COLLECTING TOYS—Magazine—Kalmbach Publishing Co.; *U.S. Private*, pg. 606

COLLECTION—Women's Apparel—Liz Claiborne, Inc.; *U.S. Public*, pg. 1005

COLLECTION MANAGEMENT SYSTEM (CMS)—NONE—American Management Systems, Inc.; *U.S. Public*, pg. 86

COLLECTIONS—Magazine—Reed Business Information Pty. Limited; *Int'l*, pg. 1094

COLLECTIONS PROCESSING SYSTEM (CPS)—NONE—American Management Systems, Inc.; *U.S. Public*, pg. 86

THE COLLECTOR—Household Products—The Black & Decker Corporation; *U.S. Public*, pg. 233

COLLECTOR'S ITEMS—Lingerie—Warner's; *U.S. Public*, pg. 1738

COLLEGE—Shower Curtains—Springs Industries, Inc.; *U.S. Public*, pg. 1499

COLLEGE-HILL—Book Publishing—Time Warner Inc.; *U.S. Public*, pg. 1610

COLLEGE INN—Broths—Nabisco Inc.; *U.S. Public*, pg. 1355

COLLEGE INN—Broths—RJR Nabisco Holdings Corp.; *U.S. Public*, pg. 1354

COLLEGE SPORTS USA—Sports Programming—Westwood One, Inc.; *U.S. Public*, pg. 1763

COLLEGIATE CAP AND GOWN—Caps & Gowns—Herff Jones Inc.; *U.S. Private*, pg. 523

COLLEGUE—Designer Chair Line—Harter; *U.S. Private*, pg. 581

COLLETTE—Misses Sleepwear and Underwear—Miss Elaine Inc.; *U.S. Private*, pg. 752

COLLEZIONE 2 BY CORNELLIANI—Men's Apparel—Hartmarx Corporation; *U.S. Public*, pg. 795

COLLIMASTER—X-Ray Collimator—Varian Associates, Inc.; *U.S. Public*, pg. 1710

COLLINS—Navigation, Communication, Flight Control & Instrumentation Equipment—Rockwell International Corporation; *U.S. Public*, pg. 1397

COLLINS AVSAT—Satellite-Based Naviation & Communication for Aircraft—Rockwell International Corporation; *U.S. Public*, pg. 1397

COLLITEX—NONE—PAXAR Corporation; *U.S. Public*, pg. 1266

COLLOID MILL—Homogenizer & Dispenser—Premier Mill Corp.; *U.S. Private*, pg. 881

COLLUPULIN—Vegetable Protease to Prevent Hazing of Beer Kept in Cool Storage—Royal Gist-Brocades N.V.; *Int'l*, pg. 1142

COLMONOY—Hard Surfacing Alloys—Wall Colmonoy Corp.; *U.S. Private*, pg. 1148

COLODRESS—One-Piece Ostomy Pouches—Bristol-Myers Squibb Company; *U.S. Public*, pg. 253

COLOGNE EGG—NONE—Clouth Gummiwerke AG; *Int'l*, pg. 297

COLOMA—Liqueur—Suntory Ltd.; *Int'l*, pg. 1321

COLOMBO—Baking Company—San Francisco French Bread Company; *U.S. Public*, pg. 909

COLOMBO YOGURT—Yogurt—General Mills, Inc.; *U.S. Public*, pg. 717

COLOMOUSSE—Cushion Vinyl Floorcoverings—Forbo Holding SA; *Int'l*, pg. 496

COLON—Laundry Detergent—Benckiser Consumer Products Inc.; *Int'l*, pg. 185

COLONEL LEE—NONE—Barton Brands, Ltd.; *U.S. Public*, pg. 300

COLONEL LEE—Bourbon—Barton Incorporated; *U.S. Public*, pg. 300

COLONIAL—Table Salt—Cargill Salt Inc.; *Int'l*, pg. 48

COLONIAL—Bakery Products—The Earthgrains Company; *U.S. Public*, pg. 547

COLONIAL—Interior/Exterior Floor Tile—Monarch Tile, Inc.; *U.S. Private*, pg. 287

COLONIAL—Sugar—Savannah Foods & Industries, Inc.; *U.S. Public*, pg. 872

COLONIAL—Meats—Thorn Apple Valley, Inc.; *U.S. Public*, pg. 1602

COLONIAL ADVANTAGE—NONE—Colonial Gas Company; *U.S. Public*, pg. 400

COLONIAL BROACH—NONE—Cross Huller; *Int'l*, pg. 1389

COLONIAL CANDLE OF CAPE COD—NONE—Blyth Industries; *U.S. Public*, pg. 239

COLONIAL FENCE—Domed 4″ x 6″ Posts with Pockets for 2 or 3 Rails—Seaman Timber Company, Inc.; *U.S. Private*, pg. 979

COLONIAL GARDEN KITCHEN—Kitchen Supplies & Gadgets—Hanover Direct Pennsylvania, Inc.; *U.S. Public*, pg. 782

COLONIAL GARDENS KITCHEN—Specialty Catalog: Time Saving & Lifestyle Enhancing Products for Home—Hanover Direct, Inc.; *U.S. Public*, pg. 782

COLONIAL HOMES—Magazine—The Hearst Corporation; *U.S. Private*, pg. 515

COLONIAL HOMES—Magazine—Hearst Magazines Division; *U.S. Private*, pg. 516

COLONIAL PARCHMENT—Writing Papers & Bond Papers—The Mead Corporation; *U.S. Public*, pg. 1074

COLONIAL PENN—Life Insurer—Colonial Penn Group, Inc.; *U.S. Public*, pg. 990

COLONIAL RUBBER WORKS—Polymer Compounding—M.A. Hanna Company; *U.S. Public*, pg. 780

COLONIAL TRADITION—Food Service Item—Performance Food Group Company; *U.S. Public*, pg. 1278

COLONIAL WILLIAMSBURG COLLECTION—NONE—Crown Crafts, Inc.; *U.S. Public*, pg. 465

COLONIALBEEF—Wholesale Meats, Specializing in Portion Control Meat Products—Colonial Beef Co.; *U.S. Private*, pg. 253

COLONNA ARTICHOKE HEARTS—Artichokes in Oil—Colonna Bros., Inc.; *U.S. Private*, pg. 254

COLONNA BALSAMIC VINEGAR—Vinegar—Colonna Bros., Inc.; *U.S. Private*, pg. 254

COLONNA BREAD CRUMBS—Bread Crumbs—Colonna Bros., Inc.; *U.S. Private*, pg. 254

COLONNA CANNED BEANS—Red & White Kidney Beans; Chick Peas—Colonna Bros., Inc.; *U.S. Private*, pg. 254

COLONNA CANNED SOUPS—Macaroni & Bean, Lentil, Escarole & Minestrone—Colonna Bros., Inc.; *U.S. Private*, pg. 254

COLONNA FLAVORED BREAD CRUMBS—Flavored Bread Crumbs—Colonna Bros., Inc.; *U.S. Private*, pg. 254

COLONNA FLAVORED CROUTONS—Flavored Croutons—Colonna Bros., Inc.; *U.S. Private*, pg. 254

COLONNA OLIVE OIL—Olive Oil—Colonna Bros., Inc.; *U.S. Private*, pg. 254

COLONNA PARMESAN—Grated Cheese—Colonna Bros., Inc.; *U.S. Private*, pg. 254

COLONNA PLAIN CROUTONS—Croutons—Colonna Bros., Inc.; *U.S. Private*, pg. 254

COLONNA RED CLAM SAUCE—Clam Sauce—Colonna Bros., Inc.; *U.S. Private*, pg. 254

COLONNA ROASTED PEPPERS—Roasted Peppers—Colonna Bros., Inc.; *U.S. Private*, pg. 254

COLONNA ROMANO—Grated Cheese—Colonna Bros., Inc.; *U.S. Private*, pg. 254

COLONNA SPAGHETTI—Spaghetti—Colonna Bros., Inc.; *U.S. Private*, pg. 254

COLONNA SPAGHETTI SAUCE—Spaghetti Sauce—Colonna Bros., Inc.; *U.S. Private*, pg. 254

COLONNA SPICES—Spices—Colonna Bros., Inc.; *U.S. Private*, pg. 254

COLONNA STUFFING MIX—Stuffing Mix—Colonna Bros., Inc.; *U.S. Private*, pg. 254

COLONNA WHITE CLAM SAUCE—Clam Sauce—Colonna Bros., Inc.; *U.S. Private*, pg. 254

COLONNADE—Lightweight Coated Papers—Weyerhaeuser Company; *U.S. Public*, pg. 1764

COLONNADE GLOSS—Printing Papers—Weyerhaeuser Company; *U.S. Public*, pg. 1764

COLONY—Paint—The Valspar Corporation; *U.S. Public*, pg. 1707

COLONY RESORTS—Resorts—Carlson Companies, Inc.; *U.S. Private*, pg. 211

COLONY '76—Kitchen Cabinets—Georgia-Pacific Corporation; *U.S. Public*, pg. 735

COLOR ACCESS—Filing Systems—Safeguard Business Systems, Inc.; *U.S. Private*, pg. 960

COLOR ALL—Spray Paint—Sherwin-Williams Diversified Brands, Inc.; *U.S. Public*, pg. 1466

COLORBURST—Imagine Media—Labelon Corporation; *U.S. Private*, pg. 641

COLOR BY DELUXE—Motion Picture Film Processing, Video Mastering—Deluxe Laboratories, Inc.; *Int'l*, pg. 1087

COLOR BY THE FOOT—Fruit Snacks—General Mills, Inc.; *U.S. Public*, pg. 717

COLOR CART—Children's Tricycle—Hedstrom Corporation; *U.S. Public*, pg. 526

COLOR CHARM—Hair Care Products—The Wella Corporation; *Int'l*, pg. 1489

COLOR CHOICE—Haircolor—Bristol-Myers Squibb Company; *U.S. Public*, pg. 253

COLOR CONCEPTS—NONE—Celebrity Incorporated; *U.S. Public*, pg. 319

COLOR DOUGH—NONE—RPM, Inc.; *U.S. Public*, pg. 1356

COLOR DYNAMICS—Color System Consultation Services—PPG Industries, Inc.; *U.S. Public*, pg. 1245

COLOR FOAMS—Tub Blocks—Colorforms; *U.S. Public*, pg. 1625

COLOR IV—Labels—Avery Dennison Corporation Label Group; *U.S. Public*, pg. 153

COLOR IV PLUS—Labels—Avery Dennison Corporation Label Group; *U.S. Public*, pg. 153

THE COLOR GRID—Color System—Formica Corporation; *Int'l*, pg. 129

COLOR GUARD—Flea & Tick Collar—Carter-Wallace, Inc.; *U.S. Public*, pg. 309

COLOR-HOLD—Conditioning Shampoo—Clairol, Inc.; *U.S. Public*, pg. 254

COLOR KEY—Colors & Paints—Devoe Paint; *Int'l*, pg. 663

COLOR KEY COMPUTER—Computer Color Matching System—Devoe Paint; *Int'l*, pg. 663

COLOR KEY COMPUTER—Computer Color Matching System—ICI Paints; *Int'l*, pg. 664

THE COLOR KEY PROGRAM—Paints—ICI Paints; *Int'l*, pg. 664

THE COLOR KEY PROGRAM—International Color Reference—Devoe Paint; *Int'l*, pg. 663

THE COLOR KEY PROGRAM—Paints—Grow Group, Inc.; *Int'l*, pg. 663

COLOR MASTER—Filing Systems—Safeguard Business Systems, Inc.; *U.S. Private*, pg. 960

COLOR ME BEAUTIFUL—Coordinated Sportswear—International Women's Apparel Group; *U.S. Public*, pg. 796

COLOR ME PERFECT—Cosmetic Sharpeners—Sunbeam Household Products; *U.S. Public*, pg. 1533

COLOR NATURALS—Paint—ICI Paints; *Int'l*, pg. 664

COLOR PAK—Certified Food Colors—Universal Foods Corporation; *U.S. Public*, pg. 1695

COLOR PAK—Confection Processes—Warner-Jenkinson Co.; *U.S. Public*, pg. 1696

COLOR PAPER PEELABLE—Photographic Paper—Konica Corporation; *Int'l*, pg. 748

COLOR PAPER SUPER GLOSSY—Photographic Paper—Konica Corporation; *Int'l*, pg. 748

COLOR PERFECT—Hair Care Products—The Wella Corporation; *Int'l*, pg. 1489

COLOR PERFECT—Hair Colouring—Wella Group; *Int'l*, pg. 1489

COLOR PLUS—Cosmetics—Almay, Inc.; *U.S. Private*, pg. 689

COLOR + COLOR—Color System—Formica Corporation; *Int'l*, pg. 129

COLOR PURE FILTER—Trinitron Circuitry—Sony Electronics; *Int'l*, pg. 1281

COLOR QA PAPER—Photographic Paper—Konica Corporation; *Int'l*, pg. 748

COLOR SCAN—Spectromonitor—Milton Roy Company; *U.S. Public*, pg. 1534

COLOR SENTRY—Filing Systems—Safeguard Business Systems, Inc.; *U.S. Private*, pg. 960

COLOR SENTRY—TV Receivers—Zenith Electronics Corp.; *U.S. Public*, pg. 1790

COLOR SIGNAL—Specialized Security Paper—Georgia-Pacific Corporation; *U.S. Public*, pg. 735

COLOR SLIDE—NONE—Seradyn, Inc.; *Int'l*, pg. 871

COLOR SPOT—NONE—Seradyn, Inc.; *Int'l*, pg. 871

COLOR TIERS—Sheets—Formica Corporation; *Int'l*, pg. 129

COLOR TONES—Pigmented Wood Finishing Liquid—Georgia-Pacific Corporation; *U.S. Public*, pg. 735

COLOR UNION—NONE—Celebrity Incorporated; *U.S. Public*, pg. 319

COLOR VUE—NONE—Seradyn, Inc.; *Int'l*, pg. 871

COLOR ZOOM—Electronic Components—General Instrument Corporation; *U.S. Public*, pg. 716

COLOR 7—Color Photocopier—Konica Corporation; *Int'l*, pg. 748

COLORADO—Photographic Printers—Eastman Kodak Company; *U.S. Public*, pg. 550

COLORADO—Coloured Scissors—Wella Group; *Int'l*, pg. 1489

COLORADO CARNATIONS—Florist Supplies—Denver Wholesale Florists Company; *U.S. Private*, pg. 326

COLORADO RANCHER & FARMER—Monthly Publication—Farm Progress Publications; *U.S. Public*, pg. 513

COLORADO STEAKHOUSE—Restaurants—Consolidated Products, Inc.; *U.S. Public*, pg. 436

COLORAMA—Display—Eastman Kodak Company; *U.S. Public*, pg. 550

COLORAMA—Comml. & Indus. Paints—The Pervo Paint Company; *U.S. Private*, pg. 856

COLORAMA—TV Picture Tubes—Thomson Consumer Electronics Inc.; *Int'l*, pg. 1383

COLORANCE—Semi-Permanent Haircolor—Goldwell Cosmetics (USA) Inc.; *Int'l*, pg. 718

COLORART—Crayons—Dixon Ticonderoga Company; *U.S. Public*, pg. 514

COLORAXIAL—Electronic Components—General Instrument Corporation; *U.S. Public*, pg. 716

COLORAY—Inspection Equipment—Alltrista Corporation; *U.S. Public*, pg. 56

COLORBACK—Finish Restorer—Turtle Wax, Inc.; *U.S. Private*, pg. 1110

COLORBAND—Color Separation Filters—Optical Coating Laboratory, Inc.; *U.S. Public*, pg. 1227

COLORBRE—Hair Care Products—The Wella Corporation; *Int'l*, pg. 1489

COLORBRITE—Photographic Print Service—Eastman Kodak Company; *U.S. Public*, pg. 550

COLORBURST—Instant Cameras, Video Projectors—Eastman Kodak Company; *U.S. Public*, pg. 550

COLORBURST—Laser Velocity Monitor—TSI Incorporated; *U.S. Public*, pg. 1559

COLORCAST—Hi-Bulk Register Bond Litho—Champion International Corp.; *U.S. Public*, pg. 333

COLORCOAT—Coated Steel Strip—British Steel Plc; *Int'l*, pg. 220

COLORCORE—Surfacing Material—Formica Corporation; *Int'l*, pg. 129

COLORCRAFT—Memorials—Rock of Ages Corporation; *U.S. Public*, pg. 1396

COLORCURE—Concrete Sealer—L.M. Scofield Company; *U.S. Private*, pg. 976

COLOREDGE—Copy Machines—Danka Office Imaging; *U.S. Public*, pg. 551

COLOREDGE—Color Copiers, Duplicators, & Accessories, Film, Toner, & Developers—Eastman Kodak Company; *U.S. Public*, pg. 550

COLORESCENT—Cast Flat Glass with Marble Structor—Deutsche Spezialglas AG; *Int'l*, pg. 1523

COLOREX—Vinyl Floorcoverings—Forbo Holding SA; *Int'l*, pg. 496

COLORFILE SYSTEM—Color-Coded Filing System for the Automobile Dealership—The Reynolds and Reynolds Company; *U.S. Public*, pg. 1384

COLORFORMS—Vinyl Stick-Ons—Colorforms; *U.S. Public*, pg. 1625

COLORFROST—Microscope Slide—Sybron International Corporation; *U.S. Public*, pg. 1544

COLORGRAPH—Overhead Transparency Film—Polaroid Corporation; *U.S. Public*, pg. 1313

COLORGRAPHICS—Watercolor Artist Color Markers—Dri Mark Products, Inc.; *U.S. Private*, pg. 342

COLORHOLD—Haircolor—Bristol-Myers Squibb Company; *U.S. Public*, pg. 253

COLORIFIC—Color Pencils & Markers—Empire Berol U.S.A.; *U.S. Public*, pg. 1178

COLORIFIC—Plastic Bags—Reynolds Metals Company; *U.S. Public*, pg. 1385

COLORIFIC—Children's Art Materials—Sanford Corporation; *U.S. Public*, pg. 1178

COLORIFIC—Mousses & Gels—Vidal Sassoon; *U.S. Public*, pg. 1330

COLORKING—Single-Width Web Offset Press—Publishers Equipment Corporation; *U.S. Public*, pg. 1341

COLORLASTEC—Grout—TEC Incorporated; *U.S. Public*, pg. 687

COLORLINE—Food Processing Vinyl Gloves—Phoenix Medical Technology, Inc.; *U.S. Public*, pg. 1292

COLORLINK—Laser Receiving System—TSI Incorporated; *U.S. Public*, pg. 1559

COLORLITE—Cast Aluminum Cookware—Regal Ware, Inc.; *U.S. Private*, pg. 917

COLORLOK—Graphic Supplies—Dillard, A ResourceNet International Company; *U.S. Public*, pg. 901

COLORLOOM TEXTILES—Napkins, Placemats—Dansk International Designs Ltd.; *U.S. Public*, pg. 261

COLORMASTER—TV Antenna—Lance Industries; *U.S. Private*, pg. 645

COLORMASTER PLUS XF—Plus Printer—CalComp Technology, Inc.; *U.S. Public*, pg. 1007

COLORMASTER II—Film Processor—Houston Fearless 76 Inc.; *U.S. Private*, pg. 542

COLORMAX—NONE—Chr. Hansen, Inc.; *Int'l*, pg. 288

COLORMERIC—Elastomeric Coating—Consolidated Coatings Corp.; *U.S. Public*, pg. 1357

COLORMOUNT—Permanent Dry Mount Tissue—Seal Products Incorporated; *U.S. Public*, pg. 849

COLORMOUNT BOARD—Pre-Coated Mounting Board—Seal Products Incorporated; *U.S. Public*, pg. 849

COLOROZO—Table Salt—Akzo Nobel N.V.; *Int'l*, pg. 42

COLORQUARTZ—Flooring Aggregate—3M; *U.S. Public*, pg. 1604

COLORQUEST—Toys—Strombecker Corporation; *U.S. Private*, pg. 1047

COLORS—Cameras—Eastman Kodak Company; *U.S. Public*, pg. 550

COLORS BY ALEXANDER JULIAN—Sleepwear—Host Apparel, Inc.; *U.S. Private*, pg. 540

COLORSCAPE—Photo Typesetter—AGFA EPS Division; *Int'l*, pg. 172

COLORSEAL—Hair Color Rinse—Clairol, Inc.; *U.S. Public*, pg. 254

COLORSNAPS—Snap-in insert for Displawall Panels—Marlite; *U.S. Public*, pg. 705

COLORSOURCE—1671

COLORSQUEEZE—Software—Eastman Kodak Company; *U.S. Public*, pg. 550

COLORTAC—Transluscent Pressure Sensitive Film—Signtech USA, Ltd.; *U.S. Public*, pg. 999

COLORTEX—Household Paper Goods—Orchids Paper Products Co.; *U.S. Private*, pg. 819

COLORTILE—Roofing Tiles—Carter Holt Harvey Limited; *U.S. Public*, pg. 904

COLORTRAK—TV Receivers—Thomson Consumer Electronics Inc.; *Int'l*, pg. 1383

COLORTYME—Rent-To-Own Stores—ColorTyme, Inc.; *U.S. Private*, pg. 255

COLORVIEW—COMPUTER MONITOR—International Business Machines Corporation; *U.S. Public*, pg. 895

COLORVIVE TECHNICARE—Hair Color—Cosmair, Inc.; *Int'l*, pg. 818

COLORWARE—NONE—Regal Ware, Inc.; *U.S. Private*, pg. 917

COLORWATCH—Photofinishing Quality Monitoring System—Eastman Kodak Company; *U.S. Public*, pg. 550

COLORWELD—Prepainted Metal—Reynolds Metals Company; *U.S. Public*, pg. 1385

COLORWORKS—Manicure Implements—The Cook Bates Division; *Int'l*, pg. 815

COLORWORKS—Spray Paints—Sherwin-Williams Diversified Brands, Inc.; *U.S. Public*, pg. 1466

COLORWORLD—Paints—Sime Darby Berhad; *Int'l*, pg. 1249

COLOSSAL CRUNCH—Sweetened Corn & Oat Cereal—Malt-O-Meal Company; *U.S. Private*, pg. 699

COLOSSUS—Software—CSC Financial Services Group; *U.S. Public*, pg. 422

COLOSSUS—Games—Mikohn Gaming Corporation; *U.S. Public*, pg. 1111

COLOURINGS—Cosmetic Range—The Body Shop International; *Int'l*, pg. 199

COLOURS & SCENTS—Discount Retail Cosmetic Stores—The Cosmetic Center Inc.; *U.S. Private*, pg. 689

COLOURS BY ALEXANDER JULIAN—Watches, Men's Jewelry, Belts, Suspenders & Leather Accessories—Swank, Inc.; *U.S. Public*, pg. 1543

COLOURSTEP—Vinyl Floorcoverings—Forbo Holding SA; *Int'l*, pg. 496

COLOVINYL—Vinyl Floorcoverings—Forbo Holding SA; *Int'l*, pg. 496

COLPO-PNEUMO OCCLUDER—Gynecological Device—The Cooper Companies, Inc.; *U.S. Public*, pg. 442

COLRING—Cable Ties—Pass & Seymour/Legrand; *Int'l*, pg. 806

COLSON—Cable Ties—Pass & Seymour/Legrand; *Int'l*, pg. 806

COLT—Wheelbarrows—Ames Company; *U.S. Public*, pg. 1683

COLT 45—NONE—The Stroh Brewery Company; *U.S. Private*, pg. 1047

COLTEC—Automotive Products—Coltec Industries Inc.; *U.S. Public*, pg. 401

COLTINA—Hard Food Goods—The Daiei, Inc.; *Int'l*, pg. 364

COLTRON—Polyester Non-woven Material—Akzo Nobel N.V.; *Int'l*, pg. 42

COLUMBIA—Exercise Equip. & School Furniture—Columbia Manufacturing Inc.; *U.S. Private*, pg. 255

COLUMBIA—Economy Grade Vinyl Electrical Tape—Plymouth Rubber Company, Inc.; *U.S. Public*, pg. 1311

COLUMBIA—Vinyl Siding—Reynolds Metals Company; *U.S. Public*, pg. 1385

COLUMBIA—Record Label—Sony Corporation; *Int'l*, pg. 1280

COLUMBIA—Records—Sony Music Entertainment, Inc.; *Int'l*, pg. 1281

COLUMBIA—Dry Pasta—A. Zeregas Sons, Inc.; *U.S. Private*, pg. 1204

COLUMBIA/CBS RECORD & TAPE CLUB—Records & Audio Cassettes—Columbia Pictures; *Int'l*, pg. 1281

COLUMBIA CEMENT—Adhesives—Burmah Castrol plc; *Int'l*, pg. 234

COLUMBIA COLLECTION—Ranges, Refrigerators, Dishwashers, Clothes Washers & Dryers—General Electric Canada Inc.; *U.S. Public*, pg. 734

COLUMBIA CREST—Wine—Stimson Lane Ltd.; *U.S. Public*, pg. 1661

COLUMBIA HOUSE—Record Label—Columbia House Music Club; *Int'l*, pg. 1281

COLUMBIA HOUSE—Records—Sony Corporation; *Int'l*, pg. 1280

COLUMBIA HOUSE MUSIC CLUB—Retail Mail Order Records & CDs—Columbia House Music Club; *Int'l*, pg. 1281

COLUMBIA HOUSE VIDEO & DISC CLUB—Videos—Columbia Pictures; *Int'l*, pg. 1281

COLUMBIA HOUSE VIDEO CLUB—Retail Mail Order Videos—Columbia House Music Club; *Int'l*, pg. 1281

COLUMBIA HOUSE VIDEO LIBRARY—Videos—Columbia House Music Club; *Int'l*, pg. 1281

COLUMBIA PICTURES—Motion Picture Production & Distribution—Columbia Pictures; *Int'l*, pg. 1281

COLUMBIA PICTURES—Movies—Sony Corporation; *Int'l*, pg. 1280

COLUMBIA PICTURES TELEVISION—Television Production & Distribution—Columbia TriStar Television; *Int'l*, pg. 1282

COLUMBIA TRI-STAR HOME VIDEO—Home Video Movies—Sony Pictures Studios; *Int'l*, pg. 1283

COLUMBIAN—Envelopes & Printing Papers—Westvaco Corporation; *U.S. Public*, pg. 1762

COLUMBIAN—Envelopes—Westvaco Corporation-Envelope Div.; *U.S. Public*, pg. 1762

COLUMBIAN—Vise—Wilton Corporation; *U.S. Private*, pg. 1181

COLUMBO—Yogurt—Yoplait USA; *U.S. Public*, pg. 718

COLUMBUS—Carpet—Columbus Mills, Inc.; *U.S. Private*, pg. 256

THE COLUMBUS DISPATCH—Daily Newspaper—The Dispatch Printing Company; *U.S. Private*, pg. 334

COLVECCHID-SYRAH—Red Wine—Banfi Vintners; *U.S. Private*, pg. 113

COLYTE—NONE—Schwarz Pharma Inc.; *Int'l*, pg. 1211

COM-FLEX—Spectacle Temples—U.S. Safety; *U.S. Private*, pg. 1125

COM KEY—Key Telephone System—Lucent Technologies Inc.; *U.S. Public*, pg. 1017

COM-PACK—Microfilm Cartridge—Eastman Kodak Company; *U.S. Public*, pg. 550

THE COM-PAK—Electric Fan Forced Wall Heater—Cadet Manufacturing Company; *U.S. Private*, pg. 198

COM-PRESS—Press—Harnischfeger Industries, Inc.; *U.S. Public*, pg. 788

COMAR—Fuels—Burmah Castrol plc; *Int'l*, pg. 234

COMARE—Professional Beauty Products—Windmere-Durable Holdings; *U.S. Public*, pg. 1771

COMARE ELITE COLLECTION—NONE—Comare Products; *U.S. Public*, pg. 1771

COMB COMPANY—NONE—Damark International, Inc.; *U.S. Public*, pg. 478

COMBAT—Boron Nitride—The Carborundum Corporation; *Int'l*, pg. 1173

COMBAT—Ant & Roach Bait Stations & Aerosols—The Clorox Company; *U.S. Public*, pg. 386

COMBAX—Combustion Boats—Fisher Scientific Company; *U.S. Private*, pg. 658

COMBI—Bender—Greenlee Textron; *U.S. Public*, pg. 1589

COMBI—Chiropractic Tables & Multi-Therapy Systems—Standex International Corporation; *U.S. Public*, pg. 1505

COMBI-CORE MACHINE—Core Equipment—Georg Fischer Disa Inc.; *Int'l*, pg. 382

COMBIBATCH—Additives—Clariant International Ltd.; *Int'l*, pg. 624

COMBIBLOC—Packaging—Southcorp Holdings Ltd.; *Int'l*, pg. 1287

COMBIBLOC ASEPTIC—Aseptic Carton Packaging System For Liquid Food Products—PKL Verpackungssysteme GmbH; *Int'l*, pg. 1020

COMBIFERT—Fertilizers—DSM Chemie Linz GmbH; *Int'l*, pg. 356

COMBIHESIVE—Two-Piece Ostomy Product—Bristol-Myers Squibb Company; *U.S. Public*, pg. 253

COMBINASE—Feed Additives & Others—Meiji Seika Kaisha, Ltd.; *Int'l*, pg. 855

COMBITARD—Product for Diabetes Care—Novo Nordisk A/S; *Int'l*, pg. 987

COMBO—Magazine—Century Publishing Company; *U.S. Private*, pg. 226

COMBO—Musical Instruments—Ludwig Industries; *U.S. Public*, pg. 1514

COMBO—NONE—Vauxhall; *U.S. Public*, pg. 724

COMBO CADDY—Tabletop Entree Server—The Vollrath Company, L.L.C.; *U.S. Private*, pg. 1143

THE COMBO CARTRIDGE—Videogames—Sega of America Inc.; *Int'l*, pg. 1218

COMBO-CYCLER—Recycling Container—United Receptical, Inc.; *U.S. Private*, pg. 1123

COMBO-PAK—Aluminum Foil Containers & Lids—Reynolds Metals Company; *U.S. Public*, pg. 1385

COMBO TOOTH—Band Saw Blades—Sandvik/Milford Corporation; *Int'l*, pg. 1185

COMBOJET—Traveling Cleaners—Luwa Bahnson, Inc.; *U.S. Private*, pg. 682

COMBOMAT—General Purpose Fiber Glass—PPG Industries, Inc.; *U.S. Public*, pg. 1245

COMBOS—Snack—M&M/Mars; *U.S. Private*, pg. 707

COMBOS—Pretzel Snacks—Mars, Incorporated; *U.S. Private*, pg. 707

COMBRACO—Ball Valves—Associated Process Controls; *U.S. Private*, pg. 92

COMBU-CHANGER—Regenerative Oxidizers—ABB Air Preheater Inc.; *Int'l*, pg. 3

COMBUSOC—Process in which Combustible Elements are Extracted—Saint-Gobain; *Int'l*, pg. 1170

COMBUSTIONEER—Heaters & Furnaces—The Will-Burt Company; *U.S. Private*, pg. 1177

COMCAST—Cable Television—Comcast Corporation; *U.S. Public*, pg. 406

COMCOM—Computerized Typesetting—Haddon Craftsmen, Inc.; *U.S. Public*, pg. 518

COME 'N GET IT—Dog Food—Nestle S.A.; *Int'l*, pg. 915

COME RIDE WITH US—Division Slogan—American Honda Motor Co., Inc. Motorcycle Division; *Int'l*, pg. 634

COME WALK WITH US—NONE—Rocky Shoes & Boots, Inc.; *U.S. Public*, pg. 1402

COMED—NONE—ComEd; *U.S. Public*, pg. 1664

COMEDY CENTRAL—Cable Network—Viacom Inc.; *U.S. Public*, pg. 775

COMERCIAL MEXICANO—General Merchandise Store—Controladora Comercial Mexicana, S.A. de C.V.; *Int'l*, pg. 328

COMERICA—Holding Company for Commerical Banks—Comerica Incorporated; *U.S. Public*, pg. 408

COMERIMART—Supermarket Branches—Comerica Incorporated; *U.S. Public*, pg. 408

COMET—Flour—ADM Milling Co.; *U.S. Public*, pg. 128

COMET—Instant Rice Mixes—American Rice Inc.; *U.S. Public*, pg. 591

COMET—Rice—Comet Ventures, Inc.; *U.S. Public*, pg. 591

COMET—Electricals—Kingfisher plc; *Int'l*, pg. 733

COMET—Ice Cream Cones, Cups & Sugar Cones—Nabisco Inc.; *U.S. Public*, pg. 1355

COMET—Cleaner—The Procter & Gamble Company; *U.S. Public*, pg. 1330

COMET BATHROOM CLEANER—Foam Bathroom Cleaner—The Procter & Gamble Company; *U.S. Public*, pg. 1330

COMET LIQUID—Household Cleaner—The Procter & Gamble Company; *U.S. Public*, pg. 1330

COMET SERIES—Trucks—DAF Trucks N.V.; *U.S. Public*, pg. 1247

COMETTE—Microfilm Reader—Bell & Howell Holdings; *U.S. Public*, pg. 201

COMFEES—Diapers—Dryper's Corp.; *U.S. Private*, pg. 344

COMFORT—Latex Gloves—Magla Products; *U.S. Private*, pg. 695

COMFORT—Electric Irons—Sunbeam Household Products; *U.S. Public*, pg. 1533

COMFORT-AIR—Respirator—U.S. Safety; *U.S. Private*, pg. 1125

COMFORT-AIRE—Heating & Air Conditioning Equipment—Heat Controller, Inc.; *U.S. Private*, pg. 518

COMFORT & BEAUTY—NONE—Kimberly-Clark Corporation; *U.S. Public*, pg. 958

COMFORT ASSURED—Heat Pump Installations—Virginia Electric and Power Company; *U.S. Public*, pg. 516

COMFORT-CARRY SHOULDER STRAP—Comfortable Carrying System—Hartmann Luggage & Leather Goods Group; *U.S. Public*, pg. 261

COMFORT CASUALS—Brassieres—Lilyette Brassiere Co.; *U.S. Private*, pg. 697

COMFORT CHOICE—Mattress With One Foam Side for Infants, One Spring Side for Toddlers—Cosco, Inc.; *U.S. Private*, pg. 277

COMFORT CORE—Comfort Technology Footwear—Georgia/Durango Boot Company; *U.S. Public*, pg. 1684

COMFORT-E—Low Emissivity Glass—AFG Industries, Inc.; *Int'l*, pg. 84

COMFORT-EASE—Respirators—U.S. Safety; *U.S. Private*, pg. 1125

COMFORT EYES—VG Prescription Eyewear—Aearo Company; *U.S. Private*, pg. 23

COMFORT-GLO—Infrared Heating Units—General Electric Canada Inc.; *U.S. Public*, pg. 713

COMFORT GUARD—Mattress & Box Spring Sets—Kingsdown, Inc.; *U.S. Private*, pg. 622

COMFORT INNS—Main Stay Suites (Extended Stay Hotels)—Choice Hotels International, Inc.; *U.S. Public*, pg. 351

COMFORT KING—Mattress—Georgia Tent & Awning Inc.; *U.S. Private*, pg. 448

COMFORT MAKER—HVAC Equipment—International Comfort Products; *U.S. Public*, pg. 898

COMFORT MASK—Cleanroom Face Mask—The Texwipe Co., Inc.; *U.S. Private*, pg. 1079

COMFORT PLUS—Cushioned Gripped Garden Tools—Ames Company; *U.S. Public*, pg. 1683

COMFORT QUILT—Incontinence Products—Blessings Corporation; *U.S. Private*, pg. 1179

COMFORT-RAY—Infrared Heating Units—General Electric Canada Inc.; *U.S. Public*, pg. 713

COMFORT RIDE—NONE—Cosco, Inc.; *U.S. Private*, pg. 277

COMFORT-SET—Thermostats for Heating & Air Conditioning—White-Rodgers Div., Emerson Electric Co.; *U.S. Public*, pg. 573

COMFORT SOUND—Hearing Aid—Telex Communications, Inc.; *U.S. Private*, pg. 1074

COMFORT SUITES—Min Stay Suites (Extended Stay Hotels)—Choice Hotels International, Inc.; *U.S. Public*, pg. 351

COMFORT TREAD—Footrest (for office)—Rubbermaid Incorporated; *U.S. Public*, pg. 1411

COMFORTASK—NONE—The HON Co.; *U.S. Public*, pg. 772

COMFORTEX—Breathable Polyurethane Coating—Raffi & Swanson, Inc.; *U.S. Private*, pg. 907

COMFORTEX—Rubber Products—Rubatex Corporation; *U.S. Public*, pg. 56

COMFORTFLEECE—Fleece Products for the Home—Dakotah, Inc.; *U.S. Public*, pg. 477

COMFORTINE—Pharmaceuticals—Rhone-Poulenc Rorer - U.S.; *Int'l*, pg. 1110

COMFORTMAKER—Heating & Cooling Prods.—International Comfort Products Corp.; *U.S. Public*, pg. 898

COMFORTO—Seating—Haworth, Inc.; *U.S. Private*, pg. 511

COMFY—Slippers-Women's & Men's—Daniel Green Co.; *U.S. Private*, pg. 477

COMGAP—Electronic Components—General Instrument Corporation; *U.S. Public*, pg. 716

COMHIST—Anti-Allergy Drug—Roberts Pharmaceutical Corporation; *U.S. Public*, pg. 1393

THE COMIC STRIP—Greeting Cards—American Greetings Corporation; *U.S. Public*, pg. 77

COMING EVENT—Maternity & Large Size Apparel—Shirmax Leasing Ltd.; *Int'l*, pg. 1235

COMING HOME—Logo—Lands' End, Inc.; *U.S. Public*, pg. 977

COMING HOME WITH LANDS' END—Logo—Lands' End, Inc.; *U.S. Public*, pg. 977

COMING HOME WITH LANDS' END DIRECT MERCHANTS—Logo—Lands' End, Inc.; *U.S. Public*, pg. 977

COMITE—Insecticide—Uniroyal Chemical Company, Inc.; *U.S. Public*, pg. 460

COMM—Cut-Sized Printing Paper—Georgia-Pacific Corporation; *U.S. Public*, pg. 735

COMM KIT—Computer Programs Enabling a Host Computer to Interface Externally—Lucent Technologies Inc.; *U.S. Public*, pg. 1017

COMMAND—Outdoor Products—The Black & Decker Corporation; *U.S. Public*, pg. 233

COMMAND—Herbicide—FMC Corp., Agricultural Products Group; *U.S. Public*, pg. 605

COMMAND—NONE—Pfizer Inc.; *U.S. Public*, pg. 1281

COMMAND 1—Survival Knives—Fiskars-Gerber; *Int'l*, pg. 492

COMMAND PERFORMANCE—Floor Finish—Calgon Vestal Laboratories; *U.S. Public*, pg. 1515

COMMAND PERFORMANCE—TV Receivers—Thomson Consumer Electronics Inc.; *Int'l*, pg. 1383

COMMANDER—Diagnostic Instrument—Abbott Laboratories; *U.S. Public*, pg. 12

COMMANDER—Cable TV Headend Equipment—Broadband Networks Group; *U.S. Public*, pg. 716

COMMANDER—Digital Intercon Systems—Chyron Corp.; *Int'l*, pg. 1372

COMMANDER—High Pressure Jet Spray Cleaning Machines—Graco Inc.; *U.S. Public*, pg. 756

COMMANDER—Hose—HBD Industries, Inc.; *U.S. Private*, pg. 489

COMMANDER—Wireless Security System—Interactive Technologies, Inc.; *U.S. Public*, pg. 888

COMMANDER—Scissors Lift Work Platform—JLG Industries, Inc.; *U.S. Public*, pg. 918

COMMANDER—Lavatory & Sink Fittings—Speakman Company; *U.S. Private*, pg. 1021

COMMANDER—Hairbrush—Stanhome Inc.; *U.S. Public*, pg. 1508

COMMANDER—Range—Wolf Range Co.; *U.S. Public*, pg. 1322

COMMANDER BUDGET—Enterprise Budget Preparation System—Comshare, Incorporated; *U.S. Public*, pg. 425

COMMANDER BUDGETPLUS—Client/Server, Multidimensional Budgeting System—Comshare, Incorporated; *U.S. Public*, pg. 425

COMMANDER DECISION—Client/Server Multidimensional Decision Support System—Comshare, Incorporated; *U.S. Public*, pg. 425

COMMANDER DECISIONWEB—Web-Based Decision Support System—Comshare, Incorporated; *U.S. Public*, pg. 425

COMMANDER FDC—Financial Data Collection, Consolidation & Reporting—Comshare, Incorporated; *U.S. Public*, pg. 425

COMMANDER V—Electronic Components—General Instrument Corporation; *U.S. Public*, pg. 716

COMMANDER-4—Portable Boat Horn—Falcon Safety Products Inc.; *U.S. Private*, pg. 392

COMMANDER IV—Electronic Components—General Instrument Corporation; *U.S. Public*, pg. 716

COMMANDER OLAP—Enterprise Information System Client/Server Applications—Comshare, Incorporated; *U.S. Public*, pg. 425

COMMANDER YACHT—Yacht—Chris-Craft Boats; *U.S. Private*, pg. 478

COMMANDO—Dry Cell Hand Lantern—Koehler Manufacturing Company; *U.S. Public*, pg. 706

COMMANDO—Wheeled & Tracked Armored Vehicle—Textron Inc.; *U.S. Public*, pg. 1588

COMMANDO—Envelopes—Westvaco Corporation; *U.S. Public*, pg. 1762

COMMANDO BY JACK YOUNG—Military & Police Sweaters—Jack Young Associates; *U.S. Private*, pg. 1201

COMMENT ON THE NEWS—News Stories Programming—Westwood One, Inc.; *U.S. Public*, pg. 1763

COMMERCE BANCSHARES—Banking Service—Commerce Bancshares, Inc.; *U.S. Public*, pg. 409

THE COMMERCIAL APPEAL—Publication (Daily & Sunday)—Memphis Publishing Co.; *U.S. Public*, pg. 1448

THE COMMERCIAL APPEAL—Newspaper—The E.W. Scripps Company; *U.S. Public*, pg. 1447

COMMERCIAL CAM—Motion Control Equipment—Emerson Electric Co.; *U.S. Public*, pg. 572

COMMERCIAL CARRIER JOURNAL—Magazine Covering Motor Vehicle Fleets—Reed Elsevier Business Information; *Int'l*, pg. 1095

COMMERCIAL CLIMATE SYSTEMS—Heat Pumps—APS; *U.S. Public*, pg. 1297

COMMERCIAL CREDIT—Financial Services—Commercial Credit Company; *U.S. Public*, pg. 1633

COMMERCIAL IGNITION—Ignition Parts—Echlin Inc.; *U.S. Public*, pg. 560

COMMERCIAL METALS—Manufacturing of Metals—Commercial Metals Company; *U.S. Public*, pg. 411

COMMERCIAL PICK-UP TRUCK PRODUCTS—NONE—The Crown Divisions; *U.S. Public*, pg. 1631

COMMERCIAL PROPERTY NEWS—Magazine—Miller Freeman Inc.; *Int'l*, pg. 1443

COMMERCIAL QUALITY—Cutlery—General Housewares Corp.; *U.S. Public*, pg. 715

COMMERCIAL REAL ESTATE SOUTH—Industry News—Intertec Publishing; *U.S. Public*, pg. 1327

COMMERCIAL SECURITIES—Personal Loans & Financing—Great Western Consumer Finance Group; *U.S. Public*, pg. 1741

COMMERCIAL 210 M—Professional Dry Mounting/Laminating Press—Seal Products Incorporated; *U.S. Public*, pg. 849

COMMERCIAL VAN INTERIOR CONVERSIONS—Factory Ship Through—The Crown Divisions; *U.S. Public*, pg. 1631

COMMERCIAL VAN INTERIOR EQUIPMENT—Fabrication—The Crown Divisions; *U.S. Public*, pg. 1631

COMMERCIAL PROTECTOR POLICY—A Comprehensive Package for the Small to Medium Size Business Owner—Peerless Insurance Company; *Int'l*, pg. 648

COMMFONE—Electrical Fire Alarm/Voice System—Federal Signal Corporation, Signal Div.; *U.S. Public*, pg. 616

COMMITMENTS—NONE—Market Facts, Inc.; *U.S. Public*, pg. 1046

COMMNET—Protocol Test Module—GenRad, Inc.; *U.S. Public*, pg. 731

COMMODORE—Cruises—Commodore Holdings; *U.S. Public*, pg. 414

COMMODORE—Pleasure Boat Name—Regal Marine Industries Inc.; *U.S. Private*, pg. 917

COMMON SENSE OAT BRAN FLAKES—Flakes of Natural Oat Bran Cereal—Kellogg Company; *U.S. Public*, pg. 947

COMMON SENSE OAT BRAN WAFFLES—Frozen Waffles—Kellogg Company; *U.S. Public*, pg. 947

COMMON SENSE TERM—Life Insurance—Travelers Group; *U.S. Public*, pg. 1632

COMMON USER ACCESS—Computer System—International Business Machines Corporation; *U.S. Public*, pg. 895

COMMONVIEW—Computer System—International Business Machines Corporation; *U.S. Public*, pg. 895

COMMONWEALTH—Life Insurance—Providian Agency Group; *Int'l*, pg. 27

COMMONWEALTH EDISON—Regional Electric Utility—ComEd; *U.S. Public*, pg. 1664

COMMONWEALTH VA PLUS—Variable Annuity Product—The Life Insurance Co. of Virginia; *U.S. Public*, pg. 712

COMMPUTER—Electronic Instrument—Intel Corporation; *U.S. Public*, pg. 886

COMMS. NETWORK—Magazine—Reed Business Information Pty. Limited; *Int'l*, pg. 1094

COMMSWITCH—Telecommunications Switching System—Datapoint Corporation; *Int'l*, pg. 384

COMMUNI-CORE—Computer Furniture—Hunt Corporation; *U.S. Public*, pg. 848

COMMUNICATION CABLE, INC.—NONE—Communication Cable, Inc.; *U.S. Public*, pg. 968

COMMUNICATION SYSTEMS DESIGN—Magazine—Miller Freeman Inc.; *Int'l*, pg. 1443

COMMUNICATIONS—NONE—Intertec Publishing; *U.S. Public*, pg. 1328

COMMUNICATIONS DATA SERVICES—Subscription Services—The Hearst Corporation; *U.S. Private*, pg. 515

COMMUNICATIONS INTERNATIONAL—NONE—EMAP Business Communications Division; *Int'l*, pg. 451

COMMUNICATIONS SYSTEMS—Textbooks Introducing a Variety of Ways Technology is Used in Communication—Goodheart-Willcox Publisher; *U.S. Private*, pg. 464

COMMUNICATIONS WEEK—Newspaper—CMP Media, Inc.; *U.S. Public*, pg. 279

COMMUNICATIONS WEEK INTERNATIONAL—Newspaper—CMP Media, Inc.; *U.S. Public*, pg. 279

COMMUNICATOR—Markers & Ballpoint Pens—Dri Mark Products, Inc.; *U.S. Private*, pg. 342

COMMUNICATOR—Printing Paper—Georgia-Pacific Corporation; *U.S. Public*, pg. 735

COMMUNICOLOR—Direct Response Printing—The Standard Register Company; *U.S. Public*, pg. 1505

COMMUNISOFT—Word Processing Software—CD Products, Inc.; *U.S. Public*, pg. 276

COMMUNITY—Silverware—Oneida Ltd.; *U.S. Public*, pg. 1225

COMMUNITY BANK, N.A.—Banking Services—Community Bank N.A.; *U.S. Public*, pg. 416

COMMUNITY BANKER SERVICES CORP—NONE—Westamerica Bancorporation; *U.S. Public*, pg. 1756

COMMUNITY PARTNERSHIP—NONE—The Stop & Shop Companies, Inc.; *Int'l*, pg. 750

COMMUTE-TACHE—Luggage—Hartmann Luggage & Leather Goods Group; *U.S. Public*, pg. 261

COMMUTER—Tires—Bridgestone/Firestone, Inc.; *Int'l*, pg. 213

COMMUTERS—Shoes—Bostonian Shoe Co.; *Int'l*, pg. 297

COMNET III—NONE—CACI International Inc; *U.S. Public*, pg. 272

COMNET II.5—Simulation Modeling System—CACI International Inc; *U.S. Public*, pg. 272

COMP-FAST—Composite Fasteners—SPS Technologies, Inc.; *U.S. Public*, pg. 1419

COMP-LINK—Computer Peripheral Products—Integra Technologies Corp.; *U.S. Private*, pg. 565

COMP-TITE—Composite Fasteners—SPS Technologies, Inc.; *U.S. Public*, pg. 1419

COMP-U-CARD—Electronic Shopping Service—CUC International, Inc.; *U.S. Public*, pg. 320

COMP-U-STORE—Electronic Shopping Service—CUC International, Inc.; *U.S. Public*, pg. 320

COMPAC—Semi-Conductor Devices—Semtech Corporation; *U.S. Public*, pg. 1456

COMPAC ENG—Liquid Level Devices—Ryan Herco Products Corp.; *U.S. Private*, pg. 953

COMPAC 3—Portable Thermometers—Land Instruments International Ltd.; *Int'l*, pg. 798

COMPACLINE—Closed Circuit Television Equipment—Vicon Industries, Inc.; *U.S. Public*, pg. 1719

COMPACT—Suction Pumps—Hollister Medical Systems Division; *U.S. Private*, pg. 535

COMPACT—Water Heaters—Patterson-Kelley Company; *U.S. Public*, pg. 793

COMPACT—Electric Irons—Sunbeam Household Products; *U.S. Public*, pg. 1533

COMPACT 400—Water Heaters—Patterson-Kelley Company; *U.S. Public*, pg. 793

COMPACT 100—Filter Integrity Tester—Pall Corporation; *U.S. Public*, pg. 1253

COMPACT PROVER—Control Measurement—Brooks Instrument; *U.S. Public*, pg. 574

COMPACTA—Shock-Proof Faeces Lifting Plant—KSB Aktiengesellschaft; *Int'l*, pg. 721

COMPACTALL—Domestic Machines for Compressing & Bagging Domestic Refuse—General Electric Canada Inc.; *U.S. Public*, pg. 713

COMPACTED ARRAY—Circuit—LSI Logic Corp.; *U.S. Public*, pg. 971

COMPACTED ARRAY PLUS—Circuit—LSI Logic Corp.; *U.S. Public*, pg. 971

COMPACTION COMMANDER—NONE—Brillion Iron Works, Inc.; *U.S. Public*, pg. 933

COMPACTROL—Pharmaceutical Excipient—Penford Corp.; *U.S. Public*, pg. 1269

COMPACTS—Grounds Equipment—Excel Industries, Inc.; *U.S. Public*, pg. 387

COMPACTUS—Materials-handling Equipment—Electrolux, AB; *Int'l*, pg. 438

COMPAK—Van Storage Systems—Lyon Metal Products, Inc.; *U.S. Private*, pg. 638

COMPAKTA—Insulating Foams—Heidelberger Zement A.G.; *Int'l*, pg. 605

COMPANION—Enteral Device—Abbott Laboratories; *U.S. Public*, pg. 12

COMPANION—Canine Vaccine—Bayer AG; *Int'l*, pg. 171

COMPANION—Recreational Vehicles—Kit Manufacturing Company; *U.S. Public*, pg. 962

COMPANION—Oxygen Supply Systems—Nellcor Puritan Bennett Incorporated; *U.S. Public*, pg. 1039

COMPANION—Communications System—Northern Telecom; *Int'l*, pg. 969

COMPANION—NONE—Northern Telecom Limited; *Int'l*, pg. 968

COMPANION—Search & Order System (Electronic)—Spring Arbor Distributors; *U.S. Private*, pg. 563

COMPANION ANIMAL PHARMACEUTICALS—NONE—Schering-Plough Animal Health; *U.S. Public*, pg. 1438

COMPANION PLUS—Enhanced Search & Order System (Computerized)—Spring Arbor Distributors; *U.S. Private*, pg. 563

COMPANY—Magazine—The National Magazine Company Ltd.; *U.S. Private*, pg. 518

COMPANY OF AMERICA—NONE—Provident Mutual Life Insurance Co.; *U.S. Private*, pg. 891

THE COMPANY STORE—Upscale Direct Marketing of Down Comforters & Home Products—Hanover Direct, Inc.; *U.S. Public*, pg. 782

COMPAQ—Computers—COMPAQ Computer Corporation; *U.S. Public*, pg. 417

COMPAQ PORTABLE III—Computer—COMPAQ Computer Corporation; *U.S. Public*, pg. 417

COMPAQ PRESARIO—Computer—COMPAQ Computer Corporation; *U.S. Public*, pg. 417

COMPARE FOR DB2—NONE—BMC Software, Inc.; *U.S. Public*, pg. 162

COMPARERITE—Software—The Mead Corporation; *U.S. Public*, pg. 1074

COMPAS—Generic Company Reference—American Computer Assembly/Compas; *Int'l*, pg. 36

COMPAS—Business Continuity Planning Software—Comdisco, Inc.; *U.S. Public*, pg. 407

COMPASS—Shoes—G.H. Bass & Co.; *U.S. Public*, pg. 1291

COMPASS—Station Automation Software—Chyron Corp.; *Int'l*, pg. 1372

COMPASS—Communication System—Executone Information Systems, Inc.; *U.S. Public*, pg. 599

COMPASS—Economic Information—Kompass International Neuenschwander SA; *Int'l*, pg. 745

COMPASS COLLABORATIVE—MRPII with Multimedia—Western Data Systems; *U.S. Private*, pg. 1165

COMPASS CONTRACT—MRPII Software—Western Data Systems; *U.S. Private*, pg. 1165

COMPATIBAG—Bags for Use In Rubber Compounding—Reynolds Metals Company; *U.S. Public*, pg. 1385

COMPATIBLE SOFT BUSINESS CASES—Business Cases—Lark Luggage Company, Inc.; *U.S. Public*, pg. 1430

COMPAX DIL BLANKS—Polycrystalline Diamond—G.E. Superabrasives; *U.S. Public*, pg. 711

COMPAZINE—Pharmaceutical—SmithKline Beecham Corporation; *Int'l*, pg. 1264

COMPAZINE—Neurosciences—SmithKline Beecham plc; *Int'l*, pg. 1264

COMPCARE—Service Mark—Comprehensive Care Corporation; *U.S. Public*, pg. 419

COMPCORE—Fiberglass Core for Reels—Glassmaster Company; *U.S. Public*, pg. 745

COMPET—Reinforced Fibers—AlliedSignal Inc.; *U.S. Public*, pg. 49

COMPETE—NONE—Market Facts, Inc.; *U.S. Public*, pg. 1046

COMPETE—Herbicide—Rohm and Haas Company; *U.S. Public*, pg. 1403

COMPETITOR—Blowers—MD Pneumatics; *U.S. Private*, pg. 1111

COMPHEALTH—NONE—Continental Medical Systems, Inc.; *U.S. Public*, pg. 839

COMPIMIDE—Bismaleimide Resins—Shell Chemical Co.; *Int'l*, pg. 1136

COMPLAMIN—Cardiopulmonary Drug—SmithKline Beecham plc; *Int'l*, pg. 1264

COMPLEAT—Tube Feeding—Novartis Nutrition Corporation; *Int'l*, pg. 974

COMPLEMENTS—Vertical Blinds—Hunter Douglas, Inc.; *Int'l*, pg. 639

COMPLEMENTS—Glassware—Indiana Glass Company; *U.S. Public*, pg. 976

COMPLEMENTS—Colored Contact Lenses—Wesley-Jessen; *U.S. Private*, pg. 111

COMPLETE—Contact Lens Care Product—Allergan, Inc.; *U.S. Public*, pg. 46

COMPLETE—Furniture Polish—S.C. Johnson & Son, Inc.; *U.S. Private*, pg. 592

COMPLETE—Toothpaste—The Procter & Gamble Company; *U.S. Public*, pg. 1330

COMPLETE—Denture Cleanser & Toothpaste—Richardson-Vicks, Inc. Personal Care Products Div.; *U.S. Public*, pg. 1331

COMPLETE BRAN FLAKES—Bran Cereal—Kellogg Company; *U.S. Public*, pg. 947

THE COMPLETE FAT UNIT GUIDE—U.K. Health Magazine—EMAP Elan; *Int'l*, pg. 451

COMPLETE HEAT—Heat & Hot Water System—Lennox International Inc.; *U.S. Private*, pg. 659

COMPLETE HOME—Data Base of National Home Improvement & Maintenance Services—CUC International, Inc.; *U.S. Public*, pg. 320

COMPLEX BLUE—Water-based Cleaner/Degreaser—CRC Industries, Inc.; *U.S. Private*, pg. 138

COMPLEX 15—Face Cream, Hand & Body Cream & Hand & Body Lotion—Schering-Plough Corporation; *U.S. Public*, pg. 1438

COMPLEX 15—Skincare—Schering-Plough Healthcare Products Inc.; *U.S. Public*, pg. 1438

COMPLIANCE PLUS—Waste Water Treatment System—Ionics, Incorporated; *U.S. Public*, pg. 912

COMPLIMENT—Cooking Sauce—The Pillsbury Company; *Int'l*, pg. 411

COMPLIMENTS—Note Pads, Paper & Holder, Writing Paper & Envelopes, Pen & Pencil Holders—American Greetings Corporation; *U.S. Public*, pg. 77

COMPLY—Foam Tip Earmolds & Sound Tubes—3M; *U.S. Public*, pg. 1604

COMPO-CAST—Hammers—The Stanley Works; *U.S. Public*, pg. 1508

COMPOFLOW—Microprocessor Based Air Velocity Dust—Alnor Instrument Company; *U.S. Public*, pg. 1559

COMPOMAC—Emulsion—Raschig GmbH; *U.S. Private*, pg. 827

COMPONENTS—NONE—Lotus Development Corporation; *U.S. Public*, pg. 896

COMPONETICS—Stock Components—W. Braun Company; *U.S. Private*, pg. 166

COMPOOL—Swimming Pool Controls & Valves—Essef Corporation; *U.S. Public*, pg. 592

COMPOSER—Programmable Hearing Aid—Beltone Electronics Corporation; *U.S. Private*, pg. 132

COMPOSER—NONE—Texas Instruments Incorporated; *U.S. Public*, pg. 1585

COMPOSER 2000—Programmable Hearing Aid—Beltone Electronics Corporation; *U.S. Private*, pg. 132

COMPOSITE EDGE—Natural Gas Tanks for Vehicles—Pressed Steel Tank Co., Inc.; *U.S. Private*, pg. 882

COMPOSITE-FILTER—Gas Turbine Filter—Donaldson Company, Inc.; *U.S. Public*, pg. 517

COMPOSITIONS—Rattan Furniture—Avon Workshop Ficks Reed; *U.S. Private*, pg. 102

COMPOSITIONS—NONE—CertainTeed Corporation; *Int'l*, pg. 1170

COMPOSITZ—Silicon Insulators—Maclean-Fogg Co.; *U.S. Private*, pg. 692

COMPOUND W—NONE—Whitehall-Robins Healthcare; *U.S. Public*, pg. 80

COMPOZ—Nighttime Sleep Aid—Medtech Inc.; *U.S. Private*, pg. 728

COMPRESS 110S—Starter Dry Mounting/Laminating Press—Seal Products Incorporated; *U.S. Public*, pg. 849

COMPRESSION POLYMERS—Pumps—Ryan Herco Products Corp.; *U.S. Private*, pg. 953

COMPRESSO-DRI—Air Compressors—Air Techniques, Inc.; *U.S. Private*, pg. 28

COMPRO—Commercial Cabinetry—Crystal Cabinet Works, Inc.; *U.S. Private*, pg. 293

COMPROTENN—Compressor Protection System—Tenney Environmental; *U.S. Private*, pg. 1076

COMPTON'S ENCYCLOPEDIA—Books—Encyclopaedia Britannica, Inc.; *U.S. Private*, pg. 375

COMPTON'S MULTIMEDIA—Encyclopedia—Encyclopaedia Britannica, Inc.; *U.S. Private*, pg. 375

COMPU-COURSE 2000—Autopilot Systems—Benmar Marine Electronics, Inc.; *U.S. Private*, pg. 133

COMPU-COURSE 220—Autopilot Systems—Benmar Marine Electronics, Inc.; *U.S. Private*, pg. 133

COMPU-LOGIC—Over Head Crane Control System—Whiting Corporation; *U.S. Private*, pg. 1173

COMPU-LOK—Computer-Controlled Lockers—American Locker Security Systems, Inc.; *U.S. Public*, pg. 86

COMPU-SONIC—Ultrasonic Meters—Badger Meter, Inc.; *U.S. Public*, pg. 164

COMPU-TORQUE—Dynamometers—M&W; *U.S. Public*, pg. 35

COMPU-LOK—Computer Controlled Lockers—American Locker Group, Inc.; *U.S. Public*, pg. 85

COMPUBLEND—Building Maintenance/Cleaning Chemicals System—3M; *U.S. Public*, pg. 1604

COMPUCHARGE—Power Electronic Charging System—C&D Charter Power Systems; *U.S. Public*, pg. 271

COMPUCOLOR—Color & Numerically Coded File Folders & Labels—Tab Products Co.; *U.S. Public*, pg. 1559

COMPUCOM SYSTEMS—Computer Reseller—Safeguard Scientifics, Inc.; *U.S. Public*, pg. 1424

COMPUDAT—Computer Service—Shivers Trading & Operating Co.; *U.S. Private*, pg. 994

COMPUDOSE—Animal Health—Elanco Animal Health; *U.S. Public*, pg. 993

COMPUGRAPHIC—Phote Typesetters—AGFA EPS Division; *Int'l*, pg. 172

COMPUGRAPHIC/UNIVERSAL—Photo Typesetters—AGFA EPS Division; *Int'l*, pg. 172

COMPUHEAT—Heat Loss Program—Gas-Fired Products, Inc.; *U.S. Private*, pg. 440

COMPULATOR—Scientific Glassware for Laboratory Use—Wheaton Inc.; *Int'l*, pg. 67

COMPULIFT—Crane Overload Warning System—Litton Industries, Inc.; *U.S. Public*, pg. 1002

COMPUMOTOR—Electromechanical Controls—Parker Hannifin Corporation; *U.S. Public*, pg. 1259

COMPUPAK—All Risk Computer Package—Harleysville Group; *U.S. Public*, pg. 786

COMPURITE—Ink Jet Printing—Moore Document Solutions; *Int'l*, pg. 890

COMPUSA PC—Built-to-Order Personal Computers—CompUSA; *U.S. Public*, pg. 420

COMPUSET—Software Module—Beckman Instruments, Inc.; *U.S. Public*, pg. 199

COMPUSET—NONE—Plantronics Inc.; *U.S. Public*, pg. 1308

COMPUSHIELD—Superior Conductive Coatings for Plastic Computer & Electronic Enclosure—Elcor Corporation; *U.S. Public*, pg. 567

COMPUSPENSE—Scientific Glassware for Laboratory Use—Wheaton Inc.; *Int'l*, pg. 67

COMPUTER ACQUIRE—Microcomputer Games—Monarch Avalon, Inc.; *U.S. Public*, pg. 1123

COMPUTER-AIDED DRAFTING—ComprehensiveTextbook Covering Hardware, Operation & Language of CAD—Goodheart-Willcox Publisher; *U.S. Private*, pg. 464

COMPUTER-AIDED ENGINEERING—Periodical—Penton Publishing, Inc.; *U.S. Public*, pg. 1306

COMPUTER & VIDEO GAMES—Games Magazine—EMAP Images; *Int'l*, pg. 451

COMPUTER ASSISTED COLLECTION SYSTEM/PLUS (CACPLUS)—NONE—American Management Systems, Inc.; *U.S. Public*, pg. 86

COMPUTER BILO—Magazine—Axel Springer Verlag AG; *Int'l*, pg. 102

COMPUTER CITY—Computer Stores-Commercial—Tandy Corporation; *U.S. Public*, pg. 1560

COMPUTER CLOCK BATTERIES—Alkaline Battery for Personal Computers—RAYOVAC Corporation; *U.S. Private*, pg. 912

COMPUTER CORP. OF AMERICA—Computer Software—Computer Corporation of America; *U.S. Private*, pg. 260

COMPUTER DATA SYSTEMS—Data Processing Services—Computer Data Systems, Inc.; *U.S. Public*, pg. 28

COMPUTER DEALER—Laboratory Equipment—Gordon Publications, Inc.; *Int'l*, pg. 1096

COMPUTER DIPLOMACY—Microcomputer Game—Monarch Avalon, Inc.; *U.S. Public*, pg. 1123

COMPUTER GRAPHICS—Decorative, Pressure-Sensitive Tape—Spartan International Inc.; *U.S. Private*, pg. 1020

THE COMPUTER INSIDE—Sales Slogan—Intel Corporation; *U.S. Public*, pg. 886

COMPUTER-PAK—Continuous Envelopes—Georgia-Pacific Corporation; *U.S. Public*, pg. 735

COMPUTER PRODUCTS INC.—NONE—Milgray Electronics, Inc.; *U.S. Public*, pg. 205

COMPUTER RENAISSANCE—Buys, Sells, Trades & Consigns Used & New Computer Equipment—Grow Biz International, Inc.; *U.S. Public*, pg. 767

COMPUTER RESELLER NEWS—Newspaper—CMP Media, Inc.; *U.S. Public*, pg. 279

COMPUTER RETAIL WEEK—Newspaper—CMP Media, Inc.; *U.S. Public*, pg. 279

COMPUTER STATIS PRO BASEBALL—Microcomputer Game—Monarch Avalon, Inc.; *U.S. Public*, pg. 1123

COMPUTER TELEPHONY INTEGRATION—Voice with Data Products and Systems Integration Services—Rockwell Switching Systems Div.; *U.S. Public*, pg. 1398

COMPUTER THIRD REICH—Microcomputer Games—Monarch Avalon, Inc.; *U.S. Public*, pg. 1123

COMPUTERIZED PNEUMATIC TUBE SYSTEM—Matl. Transport System—TransLogic Corp.; *Int'l*, pg. 1387

COMPUTERLAND—Computer Stores—Vanstar Corporation; *U.S. Public*, pg. 1708

COMPUTERVISION—CAE Systems & Software—Parametric Technology Corporation; *U.S. Public*, pg. 1257

COMPUTERWATCH—Computer Data Programs—Lucent Technologies Inc.; *U.S. Public*, pg. 1017

COMPUTERWORLD—Magazine—Computerworld, Inc.; *U.S. Private*, pg. 569

COMPUTHERM—Thermal Micro Imager—Barnes Engineering; *U.S. Public*, pg. 542

COMPUTIME—Medication Repackaging System—TimeMed Labeling Systems, Inc.; *U.S. Private*, pg. 1087

COMPUTING TODAY—Magazine—Christianity Today, Inc.; *U.S. Private*, pg. 238

Brand Name Index

COMPUTRAC—NONE—Arizona Instrument Corporation; *U.S. Public*, pg. 129

COMPUTRACE—Computer Design Programs for Steam & Electric Tracing—Thermon Manufacturing Company; *U.S. Private*, pg. 1080

COMPUWARE CICS—Systems Software Products—Compuware Corporation; *U.S. Public*, pg. 423

COMPUWELDER—NONE—D.C. Taylor Co.; *U.S. Private*, pg. 1070

COMPUWRITER—Photo Typesetters—AGFA EPS Division; *Int'l*, pg. 172

COMQUIP—Computer Equipment—Communications Equipment Co.; *U.S. Public*, pg. 276

COMSAT—Communications Satellite Corp.—COMSAT Corporation; *U.S. Public*, pg. 424

COMSKILL LEARNING CENTERS—Franchise—ITC Learning Corp.; *U.S. Public*, pg. 859

COMSONICS—Corporate Logo—ComSonics, Inc.; *U.S. Private*, pg. 260

COMSPHERE—Data Communication Hardware—Paradyne; *U.S. Private*, pg. 838

COMSTAR—Motorcycle—American Honda Motor Co., Inc. Motorcycle Division; *Int'l*, pg. 634

COMSTOCK—Fillings & Toppings—Comstock Michigan Fruit; *U.S. Private*, pg. 887

COMSTOCK—Thank You & Wilderness—Comstock Michigan Fruit; *U.S. Private*, pg. 887

COMSTOCK—Pie Fillings—Curtice Burns Foods; *U.S. Private*, pg. 887

COMSTRON—Frequency Synthesizers—Aeroflex Incorporated; *U.S. Public*, pg. 23

COMTEC—NONE—BJ Services Company; *U.S. Public*, pg. 161

COMTECH—Hydropneumatic &I Expansion Pressure Vessel—Essef Corporation; *U.S. Public*, pg. 592

COMTRAK—Commutating Encoder—BEI Sensors and Systems Company; *U.S. Public*, pg. 160

COMTREX—Cold Medicine—Bristol-Myers Squibb Company; *U.S. Public*, pg. 253

COMTRO—Incinerators (Solid Waste)—Seco Warwick Corporation; *U.S. Private*, pg. 980

COMUNICACIONES—Trade Periodical—Advanstar Communications; *U.S. Private*, pg. 22

COMUS—Software—SBE, Inc.; *U.S. Public*, pg. 1416

CON-AIRE—Water Pressure Tanks—Sta-Rite Water Systems; *U.S. Public*, pg. 1767

CON-DOR—Entrance Tile—Pawling Corporation; *U.S. Private*, pg. 844

CON SEP2000—NONE—Mayfran International, Inc.; *Int'l*, pg. 1397

CON-SERV—Rubber Products—Rubatex Corporation; *U.S. Private*, pg. 56

CON-TACT—Decorative Coverings—Rubbermaid Incorporated; *U.S. Public*, pg. 1411

CON-TORQ—T-Nuts—North & Judd; *U.S. Private*, pg. 804

CONACURE—Curing Agents—Conap Inc.; *U.S. Private*, pg. 261

CONAGRA DAIRY PRODUCTS CO.—Armour Star, Armour Cloverbloom, Miss Wisconsin, Miss New York & Decker—ConAgra, Inc.; *U.S. Public*, pg. 425

CONAGRA DELI COMPANY—World's Fare—ConAgra, Inc.; *U.S. Public*, pg. 425

CONAGRA FRESH MEATS CO.—Fresh Meats—ConAgra, Inc.; *U.S. Public*, pg. 425

CONAGRA FROZEN FOODS—Banquet, Armour, Morton's, Patio, Chun King, Award & Blue Star—ConAgra, Inc.; *U.S. Public*, pg. 425

CONAGRA PET PRODUCTS CO.—Pet Products—ConAgra, Inc.; *U.S. Public*, pg. 425

CONAGRA PROCESSED MEAT CO.—Armour, Decker & Webber Farms—ConAgra, Inc.; *U.S. Public*, pg. 425

CONAIR—Personal Care Products—Conair Corporation; *U.S. Private*, pg. 261

CONAIRPHONES—Telephones—Conair Corporation; *U.S. Private*, pg. 261

CONAN—NONE—Berg Electronics; *U.S. Public*, pg. 212

CONAP—Electrical Insulating Coating; Uncured Modified Urethane Resin—Conap Inc.; *U.S. Private*, pg. 261

CONAPOXY—Epoxy Resin Systems—Conap Inc.; *U.S. Private*, pg. 261

CONAR—Pharmaceutical Products—SmithKline Beecham Corporation; *Int'l*, pg. 1264

CONAR—Pharmaceutical Prods.—SmithKline Beecham Laboratories; *Int'l*, pg. 1264

CONAR—Relief Medicine for Coughs & Congestion—SmithKline Beecham plc; *Int'l*, pg. 1264

CONASPRAY—Two Component Polyurethane Elastomer—Conap Inc.; *U.S. Private*, pg. 261

CONASTIC—Bonding Adhesive—Conap Inc.; *U.S. Private*, pg. 261

CONATHANE—Urethane Resin Systems—Conap Inc.; *U.S. Private*, pg. 261

CONBRACO—Ball Valves—Conbraco Industries Inc.; *U.S. Private*, pg. 261

CONCENSYS—Panel Systems—The HON Co.; *U.S. Public*, pg. 772

CONCENTRIC CIRCLES—NONE—Regal Ware, Inc.; *U.S. Private*, pg. 917

CONCENTRIX—Cookware—Newell Co.; *U.S. Public*, pg. 1176

CONCENTRX—Seating—Steelcase Inc.; *U.S. Private*, pg. 1038

CONCEPT—NONE—Beckett Papers; *U.S. Public*, pg. 903

CONCEPT—Tires—Bridgestone/Firestone, Inc.; *Int'l*, pg. 213

CONCEPT—Fishing Lines, Fly, Floating & Sinking—3M; *U.S. Public*, pg. 1604

CONCEPT IV MH—Headbox—Beloit Corporation; *U.S. Public*, pg. 789

CONCEPT 90—Boats—Chris-Craft Boats; *U.S. Private*, pg. 478

CONCEPT SLICE—Disposable Arthroscopic Blades—Bristol-Myers Squibb Company; *U.S. Public*, pg. 253

CONCEPT 32—Lumber, Wood & Wood Fiber Products—Georgia-Pacific Corporation; *U.S. Public*, pg. 735

CONCEPT III—Headbox—Harnischfeger Industries, Inc.; *U.S. Public*, pg. 788

CONCEPT XXI—Tires—Bridgestone/Firestone, Inc.; *Int'l*, pg. 213

CONCEPT II—Major Appliances-Namely Refrigerators, Ranges, Dishwashers, Washers, Dryers—General Electric Canada Inc.; *U.S. Public*, pg. 713

CONCEPT TWO DUAL ALTUS—Tungsten—Novellus Systems, Inc.; *U.S. Public*, pg. 1204

CONCEPT TWO SEQUEL—NONE—Novellus Systems, Inc.; *U.S. Public*, pg. 1204

CONCEPT 2000—Fixtures—Gibson Greetings, Inc.; *U.S. Public*, pg. 742

CONCEPTOS INT'L—Hispanic Division—Tinsley Advertising; *U.S. Private*, pg. 1088

CONCEPTROL—Contraceptive—Johnson & Johnson; *U.S. Public*, pg. 927

CONCEPTROL—Contraceptive Gel—Ortho-McNeil Pharmaceutical Corporation; *U.S. Public*, pg. 929

CONCEPTROL—Contraceptive Inserts—Ortho-McNeil Pharmaceutical Corporation; *U.S. Public*, pg. 929

CONCEPTS—Lumber, Wood & Wood Fiber Products—Georgia-Pacific Corporation; *U.S. Public*, pg. 735

CONCERT—Binoculars—Bausch & Lomb Incorporated; *U.S. Public*, pg. 194

CONCERT SERIES—Postscript Fonts—Linotype-Hell Company; *Int'l*, pg. 604

CONCERTO—Document Imaging Systems—Anacomp, Inc.; *U.S. Public*, pg. 106

CONCERTO—Compositing Software—Chyron Corp.; *Int'l*, pg. 1372

CONCERTO—Dinnerware—Dansk International Designs Ltd.; *U.S. Public*, pg. 261

CONCERTO—Automobile—Honda Motor Co., Ltd.; *Int'l*, pg. 634

CONCHA—NONE—Hudson, RCI; *U.S. Private*, pg. 546

CONCHA Y TORO—Varietal Wines—Banfi Vintners; *U.S. Private*, pg. 113

CONCHAPAK—NONE—Hudson, RCI; *U.S. Private*, pg. 546

CONCHATHERM—NONE—Hudson, RCI; *U.S. Private*, pg. 546

CONCIEVE—Human Fertility Products—Quidel Corporation; *U.S. Public*, pg. 1352

CONCISE—Crown Build-up Material, Dental Restorative, Two-paste System, Enamel Bond, —3M; *U.S. Public*, pg. 1604

CONCO—Paper Products—Paper Enterprises, Inc.; *U.S. Private*, pg. 837

CONCORD—Minature Furniture—Cardinal Inc.; *U.S. Private*, pg. 208

CONCORD—Manufactured Homes—Champion Enterprises, Inc.; *U.S. Public*, pg. 332

CONCORD—Watches—Movado Group, Inc.; *U.S. Public*, pg. 1140

CONCORD PROCESSORS—Computers—Concord EFS, Inc.; *U.S. Public*, pg. 429

CONCORDE—Tires—The Goodyear Tire & Rubber Company; *U.S. Public*, pg. 752

CONCORDE—Folding Conference Tables—Howe Furniture Corporation; *U.S. Private*, pg. 543

CONCORDE—Surgical Staplers—U.S. Surgical Corp.; *U.S. Public*, pg. 1687

CONCORDE EXPRESS—Air Cargo Handling Services—John Menzies plc; *Int'l*, pg. 707

CONCORDE GRAPHITE—Racquetball Racquet—Ektelon; *U.S. Private*, pg. 884

CONCORDE LIGHTLY SPARKLING BRITISH WINE—Sparkling British Wine—Matthew Clark Brands; *Int'l*, pg. 848

CONCORDER—Computer System—Corrpro Companies, Inc.; *U.S. Public*, pg. 451

CONCOURS—Ceramic Floor Tile—Monarch Tile, Inc.; *U.S. Private*, pg. 287

CONCRETE PRODUCTS—Publication for Administrative & Production Mngmt.—Intertec Publishing; *U.S. Public*, pg. 1327

CONCRETE SAVER—Coatings—Rust-Oleum Corporation; *U.S. Private*, pg. 1358

CONCURRENT ASSOCIATIVITY—NONE—Structural Dynamics Research Corp.; *U.S. Public*, pg. 1525

CONCURRENT READWRITE—NONE—Xicor, Inc.; *U.S. Public*, pg. 1785

CONCURRENT REORG FOR DB2—NONE—BMC Software, Inc.; *U.S. Public*, pg. 162

CONCURRENT REORG FOR IMS—NONE—BMC Software, Inc.; *U.S. Public*, pg. 162

CONCURRENT TRANSFORMATION—Implementing Effective Information Systems While Reengineering Bus. Proc.—Gemini Consulting; *Int'l*, pg. 264

CONCYCLE—Recycled Enamel Coated Printing Paper—Consolidated Papers, Inc.; *U.S. Public*, pg. 436

CONDE NAST—Magazine Publisher—The Conde Nast Publications Inc.; *U.S. Private*, pg. 20

CONDE NAST—Travel Magazine—Conde Nast Traveler; *U.S. Private*, pg. 20

CONDE NAST TRAVELER—Magazine—Advance Publications Inc.; *U.S. Private*, pg. 18

CONDE NAST TRAVELER—Magazine—The Conde Nast Publications Inc.; *U.S. Private*, pg. 20

CONDE NET—Magazine—The Conde Nast Publications Inc.; *U.S. Private*, pg. 20

CONDESA—Upholstery Fabrics—Amoco Corporation; *U.S. Public*, pg. 101

CONDESS—Hair Shampoos & Conditioners—SmithKline Beecham plc; *Int'l*, pg. 1264

CONDI—Executive Furniture—American Seating Company; *U.S. Private*, pg. 61

CONDIMIX—Seasonings, Spices—Bestfoods; *U.S. Public*, pg. 223

CONDIMIX—NONE—Nestle USA; *Int'l*, pg. 916

CONDITION—Shampoo—Bristol-Myers Squibb Company; *U.S. Public*, pg. 253

CONDITION—Hair Treatment,Shampoo,Hair Spray, Beauty Pack Treatment,Styling Mousse, Gel—Clairol, Inc.; *U.S. Public*, pg. 254

CONDITION II—After Shampoo Treatment—Bristol-Myers Squibb Company; *U.S. Public*, pg. 253

CONDITION II—Instant After Shampoo Treatment—Clairol, Inc.; *U.S. Public*, pg. 254

CONDITIONADE—Feed Conditioner—Oil-Dri Corporation of America; *U.S. Public*, pg. 1214

CONDOR—Theft Prevention System—Checkpoint Systems Inc.; *U.S. Public*, pg. 343

CONDOR—NONE—Fortune Brands, Inc.; *U.S. Public*, pg. 674

CONDOR—Pipe Tobacco—Gallaher Tobacco Ltd.; *Int'l*, pg. 539

CONDOR—NONE—Milgray Electronics, Inc.; *U.S. Public*, pg. 205

CONDOR—NONE—Molex Incorporated; *U.S. Public*, pg. 1121

CONDOR—Binoculars—Swift Instruments, Inc.; *U.S. Private*, pg. 1058

CONDOR I & II—NONE—Datametrics Corporation; *U.S. Public*, pg. 487

CONDUCT-O-FIL—Conductive Particles—Potters Industries, Inc.; *U.S. Private*, pg. 827

CONDUCT-TITE!—Electrical Parts & Supplies—R&B, Inc.; *U.S. Public*, pg. 1354

CONDUCTAFLEX—Flexible Hosing for Vaccum Cleaners—Smiths Industries plc; *Int'l*, pg. 1266

CONDUCTROX—Conductor Paste—Ferro Corporation; *U.S. Public*, pg. 618

CONE BUSTER—Milling Tool—Smith International, Inc.; *U.S. Public*, pg. 1478

CONE DRIVE—Worm Gear Set, Speed Reducers—Textron Inc.; *U.S. Public*, pg. 1588

CONE FLOWER—Print Design—Liberty PLC; *Int'l*, pg. 807

CONE-O-CORN—Container—Gold Medal Products Co.; *U.S. Private*, pg. 459

CONE SPORTSWEAR—NONE—Cone Mills Corporation; *U.S. Public*, pg. 430

THE CONE WITH THE CURL ON TOP—Ice Milk Product in a Cone—International Dairy Queen, Inc.; *U.S. Public*, pg. 220

CONEJET—Spray Nozzle—Spraying Systems Co.; *U.S. Private*, pg. 1026

CONEX—Two Axis Dynamically Tuned Gyroscope—Kearfott Guidance & Navigation Corp.; *U.S. Private*, pg. 93

CONEX GYRO—Gyroscope—Kearfott Guidance & Navigation Corp.; *U.S. Private*, pg. 93

CONFECTIONS—Glassware—Indiana Glass Company; *U.S. Public*, pg. 976

CONFESS—Fragrance—Parfums De Coeur Ltd.; *U.S. Private*, pg. 839

CONFETTI—Almonds—Blue Diamond Growers; *U.S. Private*, pg. 152

CONFETTI—Glazed Ceramic Wall Tile—Florida Tile Industries, Inc.; *U.S. Public*, pg. 1322

CONFETTI—Writing, Text & Cover Paper—Fox River Paper Company; *U.S. Private*, pg. 422

CONFETTI—Pantiliners—Kimberly-Clark Corporation; *U.S. Public*, pg. 958

CONFETTI—Glazed ceramic wall tile—Precision Die & Engineering, Inc.; *U.S. Private*, pg. 1322

CONFEZIONI RISERVA/LUCIANO FRANZONI—Career Apparel—Hartmarx Corporation; *U.S. Public*, pg. 795

CONFI-SCAN—Carbonless Paper—Appleton Papers Inc.; *Int'l*, pg. 567

CONFIDELLE—Home Pregnancy Kit—Carter Products, Canada; *U.S. Public*, pg. 310

CONFIDENCE—Incontinence Products—Blessings Corporation; *U.S. Private*, pg. 1179

CONFIDENT—Denture Adhesive—Block Drug Company, Inc.; *U.S. Public*, pg. 236

CONFIRM—Insecticide—Rohm and Haas Company; *U.S. Public*, pg. 1403

CONFIRM—Validation Tab Products, Document Security—3M; *U.S. Public*, pg. 1604

CONFLAT—Metallic Vacuum Sealing Flanges—Varian Associates, Inc.; *U.S. Public*, pg. 1710

CONFORM—Athletic Equipment—Bike Athletic Co.; *U.S. Private*, pg. 143

CONFORMABLE—NONE—Belden Inc.; *U.S. Public*, pg. 200

CONFORMASK—High Conformance Solder Mask System—Morton International Inc.; *U.S. Public*, pg. 1134

CONFRONT—Herbicide—The Dow Chemical Company; *U.S. Public*, pg. 522

CONGESPIRIN—Children's Cold Remedy—Bristol-Myers Squibb Company; *U.S. Public*, pg. 253

CONGESTAC—Cold Medication—Menley & James Laboratories, Inc.; *U.S. Public*, pg. 1086

CONGO—Chocolate Milk—Borden, Inc.; *U.S. Private*, pg. 157

CONGOLEUM—Sheet Vinyl—American Biltrite Inc.; *U.S. Public*, pg. 68

CONGRESS—Playing Cards—The United States Playing Card Company; *U.S. Private*, pg. 1125

CONGRESSIONAL MONITOR—Daily Update on Congressional Activity—The Times Publishing Co.; *U.S. Private*, pg. 1087

CONGRESSIONAL QUATERLY—Weekly Report & Analysis—The Times Publishing Co.; *U.S. Private*, pg. 1087

CONGRESSIONAL RECORD SCANNER—Daily—The Times Publishing Co.; *U.S. Private*, pg. 1087

CONICAL—Tooth Equipment for Earthmoving Buckets—Esco Corporation; *U.S. Private*, pg. 382

CONICAL—Mining & Chemical Machinery—Svedala Industries Inc.; *Int'l*, pg. 1325

CONIEL—Agent for Hypertension & Angina—Kyowa Hakko Kogyo Company, Ltd.; *Int'l*, pg. 778

CONIMEX—Sauces, Mealmakers—Bestfoods; *U.S. Public*, pg. 223

CONMAG—Sputter Coating Guns—Varian Associates, Inc.; *U.S. Public*, pg. 1710

CONMAX—Nickel Fiber Filled Silicone—Tecknit Incorporated; *U.S. Private*, pg. 1072

CONMED—Electrosurgical Devices—Conmed Corporation; *U.S. Public*, pg. 431

CONMEMORATIVO—Tequila—Domecq Importers Inc.; *Int'l*, pg. 63

CONMET—Aluminum Foundry Prods., Truck & Trailer Hubs & Diesel Fuel Water Separator—Consolidated Metco, Inc.; *U.S. Public*, pg. 1710

CONN CREEK—Wine—Stimson Lane Ltd.; *U.S. Public*, pg. 1661

CONNAISSEUR—Writing Instruments—Sheaffer Inc.; *Int'l*, pg. 542

CONNAISSEUR—Sea Food Prods.—George Weston Limited; *Int'l*, pg. 1494

CONNECT FOUR—Game—Milton Bradley Company; *U.S. Public*, pg. 797

CONNECTCONTROL—NONE—Check Point Software Technologies Ltd.; *U.S. Public*, pg. 342

CONNECTFIRST—First Class for the Price of Coach—Northwest Airlines, Inc.; *U.S. Public*, pg. 1200

CONNECTICUT GENERAL—Insurance—Cigna Corp.; *U.S. Public*, pg. 356

CONNECTICUT MAGAZINE—Magazine—Communications International (NY); *U.S. Private*, pg. 259

CONNECTICUT MANUFACTURERS REGISTER—Register—Manufacturers' News, Inc.; *U.S. Private*, pg. 700

CONNECTICUT SPECIALTY INSURANCE—Special Programs—Orion Capital Companies, Inc.; *U.S. Public*, pg. 1231

CONNECTION MACHINE—Computers & Electronically Prerecorded Computer Programs—Thinking Machines Corporation; *U.S. Private*, pg. 1081

CONNEXIONS—Dictation/Telephone-Based Voice Processing Systems—Dictaphone Corp.; *U.S. Private*, pg. 1045

CONNIE—Shoes—Brown Group, Inc.; *U.S. Public*, pg. 262

CONNOISSEUR—Business Stationery—Arjo Wiggins Appleton plc; *Int'l*, pg. 567

CONNOISSEUR—Cutlery—Russell Harrington Cutlery Inc.; *U.S. Private*, pg. 551

CONNOISSEUR—Food Products—Rykoff-Sexton, Inc.; *U.S. Public*, pg. 918

CONNORS—Sea Food Prods.—George Weston Limited; *Int'l*, pg. 1494

CONOLITE—Laminated Plastic Sheets—Pioneer Plastics Corporation; *U.S. Private*, pg. 867

CONOLON—Fishing Rods—Aritmos AB; *Int'l*, pg. 1072

CONOMATIC—Metal Parts—Cone-Blanchard Machine Company; *U.S. Private*, pg. 262

CONOPTIC—Clear PU Potting/Casting Resins—Conap Inc.; *U.S. Private*, pg. 261

CONQUEROR—Business Stationery—Arjo Wiggins Appleton plc; *Int'l*, pg. 567

CONQUEST—Commercial Upright Vacuum Cleaner—Hoover Company; *U.S. Public*, pg. 1065

CONRAD-AMERICAN—Grain Bins—Hawkeye Steel Products, Inc.; *U.S. Private*, pg. 511

CONRAD INTERNATIONAL—Hotels/Casino Resorts—Hilton Hotels Corporation; *U.S. Public*, pg. 828

CONRAY—Iophthalmic Acid—Mallinckrodt Inc.; *U.S. Public*, pg. 1039

CONRAY—X-Ray Contrast Media—Mallinckrodt Inc.; *U.S. Public*, pg. 1039

CONSTELLATION CLEANING SYSTEM—Cleaning Line In Prep Room of Textile Mills—Continental Eagle Corporation; *U.S. Private*, pg. 267

CONSENSYS—Office Furniture—HON Industries Inc.; *U.S. Public*, pg. 772

CONSER-TILL—Tillage Equip.—Case Corporation; *U.S. Public*, pg. 311

CONSERV—Paper Napkins, Covers & Placemats—Erving Industries, Inc.; *U.S. Private*, pg. 382

CONSERVATIONIST—Water Heaters & Electric Motors—A.O. Smith Corporation; *U.S. Public*, pg. 1476

CONSERVATOR—Gas Furnaces—Lennox International Inc.; *U.S. Private*, pg. 659

CONSERVBAG—Trash Bags—Brawny Plastics West; *U.S. Public*, pg. 166

CONSERVE—Herbicide—The Dow Chemical Company; *U.S. Public*, pg. 522

CONSERVE—Breathing Gas Filter—Pall Corporation; *U.S. Public*, pg. 1253

CONSERVER—Combustion Management Systems—Bailey Controls Company; *Int'l*, pg. 654

CONSERVISION—Energy Conservation Program—Virginia Electric and Power Company; *U.S. Public*, pg. 516

CONSIL—Silver Alloy—Handy & Harman; *U.S. Public*, pg. 780

CONSIL—Conductive Elastomer—Tecknit Incorporated; *U.S. Private*, pg. 1072

CONSO—NONE—Conso Products Company; *U.S. Public*, pg. 434

CONSO-GARD—Single Ply Roofing Systems—Consolidated Coatings Corp.; *U.S. Public*, pg. 1357

CONSO GLOSS—Enamel Printing Paper—Consolidated Papers, Inc.; *U.S. Public*, pg. 436

CONSO-LASTIC—Rubberized Roofcoating—Consolidated Coatings Corp.; *U.S. Public*, pg. 1357

CONSOLES PLUS—Computer Gaming Magazine—EMAP France; *Int'l*, pg. 451

CONSOLIDATED—Safety & Safety Relief Valves—Dresser Industries, Inc.; *U.S. Public*, pg. 528

CONSOLIDATED AMERICAN—Insurance Company—South Carolina Insurance Company; *U.S. Public*, pg. 1453

CONSOLIDATED FREIGHTWAYS CORPORATION OF DELAWARE—Long Distance Trucking Service—Consolidated Freightways Corp.; *U.S. Public*, pg. 435

CONSOLIDATED-GOODYEAR COATINGS—Paints & Waterproofing Compounds, Roofing Systems—Consolidated Coatings Corp.; *U.S. Public*, pg. 1357

CONSOLIDATED NATURAL GAS—Public Utility Holding Co.—Consolidated Natural Gas Company; *U.S. Public*, pg. 435

CONSOLIDATED PAPER COMPANY—Redistributor—Paper Enterprises, Inc.; *U.S. Private*, pg. 837

CONSOLITE—Paints & Waterproofing Compounds, Roofing Systems—Consolidated Coatings Corp.; *U.S. Public*, pg. 1357

CONSOLITH GLOSS—Recycled Enamel Printing Paper—Consolidated Papers, Inc.; *U.S. Public*, pg. 436

CONSOPLY—Built-Up Roof System—Consolidated Coatings Corp.; *U.S. Public*, pg. 1357

CONSORT—Grooming Products for Men—Alberto-Culver Company; *U.S. Public*, pg. 37

CONSORT PRO-PLUS—Conditioning Shampoo—Alberto-Culver Company; *U.S. Public*, pg. 37

CONSOTROL—Indicating & Recording Recording Remote Control Stations—The Foxboro Company; *Int'l*, pg. 1243

CONSOWEB BRILLIANT—Enamel Printing Paper—Consolidated Papers, Inc.; *U.S. Public*, pg. 436

CONSTA METRIC—High/Low Pressure Pumps—Thermo Separation Products; *U.S. Public*, pg. 1594

CONSTA VAC—NONE—Stryker Corporation; *U.S. Public*, pg. 1525

CONSTA-VOLT—Battery Chargers—La Marche Mfg. Co.; *U.S. Private*, pg. 640

CONSTANT PRIDE—Floor Coverings—Domco Inc.; *Int'l*, pg. 415

CONSTANT TORQUE—Clamp—TransTechnology Corporation; *U.S. Public*, pg. 1632

CONSTANT TOUCH—Telephone Voice Messaging Systems; Automated Message System—Glenayre Technologies, Inc.; *U.S. Public*, pg. 746

Brand Name Index

CONSTANTEMP—Water Heater—Leslie Controls, Inc.; *U.S. Public*, pg. 1746

CONSTELLATION—Sporting Goods—Brunswick Bowling & Billiards Corp.; *U.S. Public*, pg. 265

CONSTELLATION—Motor Yachts—Chris-Craft Boats; *U.S. Private*, pg. 478

CONSTELLATION—Marine/Weather Instrument—Swift Instruments, Inc.; *U.S. Private*, pg. 1058

CONSTITUTION—Pencils—Dixon Ticonderoga Company; *U.S. Public*, pg. 514

CONSTITUTION—Plywood & Wood Products—Georgia-Pacific Corporation; *U.S. Public*, pg. 735

CONSTITUTION—Marine/Clock—Swift Instruments, Inc.; *U.S. Private*, pg. 1058

CONSTRUCT—Business Reengineering Methodology Integrating StrategyOpers. & Info. Sys.—Gemini Consulting; *Int'l*, pg. 264

CONSTRUCTION CONTRACTOR—Magazine—Reed Business Information Pty. Limited; *Int'l*, pg. 1094

CONSTRUCTION CONTRACTOR SPEC. GUIDE—Magazine—Reed Business Information Pty. Limited; *Int'l*, pg. 1094

CONSTRUCTION EQUIPMENT—Magazine Providing Information About Equipment, Trucks & Related Products—Reed Elsevier Business Information; *Int'l*, pg. 1095

CONSTRUCTION GOLD—NONE—Timberline Software Corporation; *U.S. Public*, pg. 1609

CONSTRUCTION KING—Fork Lifts & Backhoe/Loaders—Case Corporation; *U.S. Public*, pg. 311

CONSTRUCTOR—Self-Propelled Access Platform—Simon Engineering plc; *Int'l*, pg. 1251

CONSUL—Fruits—Chiquita Brands International, Inc.; *U.S. Public*, pg. 349

CONSULTANTS BUREAU—English Translations of Soviet Texts—Plenum Publishing Corporation; *U.S. Public*, pg. 1311

CONSULTING-SPECIFYING ENGINEER—Magazine for Engineers Who Design Mechanical/Electrical Systems—Reed Elsevier Business Information; *Int'l*, pg. 1095

CONSUMER CLEAN—NONE—Avery Dennison Corporation; *U.S. Public*, pg. 152

CONSUMER COPY—Bond Copy Paper, Mimeograph Copy Paper & Offset Copy—Georgia-Pacific Corporation; *U.S. Public*, pg. 735

CONSUMER MAIL PANEL—NONE—Market Facts, Inc.; *U.S. Public*, pg. 1046

CONSUMERS—Frozen Foods—Hanover Foods Corporation; *U.S. Private*, pg. 499

CONSUMERS CAR CARE—Extended Service Product for Autos—Consumers Financial Corporation; *U.S. Public*, pg. 437

CONSUMERS FINANCIAL GROUP—NONE—Consumers Financial Corporation; *U.S. Public*, pg. 437

CONSUMET—NONE—Carpenter Technology Corporation; *U.S. Public*, pg. 307

CONTAC—Cold Cough Remedy—SmithKline Beecham Consumer Healthcare, U.S.; *Int'l*, pg. 1264

CONTAC—NONE—SmithKline Beecham Corporation; *Int'l*, pg. 1264

CONTAC—Coughs, Colds & Influenza Treatment—SmithKline Beecham plc; *Int'l*, pg. 1264

CONTACT—Cement—DAP Inc.; *Int'l*, pg. 1486

CONTACT AMBIANCE—Telephone—France Telecom; *Int'l*, pg. 503

CONTACT LASER DELIVERY SYSTEMS—NONE—Surgical Laser Technologies, Inc.; *U.S. Public*, pg. 1542

CONTACTASOAK—Contact Lens Solution—Novartis; *Int'l*, pg. 972

CONTACTASOL—Contact Lens Solution—Novartis; *Int'l*, pg. 972

CONTACTOR—Welding Tip—Brush Research Manufacturing Company; *U.S. Private*, pg. 176

CONTADINA—Culinary Products—Nestle S.A.; *Int'l*, pg. 915

CONTADINA DALLA CASA BUITONI—Tomato Paste & Sauce—Nestle USA; *Int'l*, pg. 916

CONTADINA PASTA READY—NONE—Nestle USA; *Int'l*, pg. 916

CONTADINA PIZZA SQUEEZE—NONE—Nestle USA; *Int'l*, pg. 916

CONTADINA RECIPE READY—NONE—Nestle USA; *Int'l*, pg. 916

CONTAINER MATIC—Heat Sealing Machinery for Lids—Reynolds Metals Company; *U.S. Public*, pg. 1385

CONTAINS—Contamination Barrier Products—Medtronic, Inc.; *U.S. Public*, pg. 1082

CONTAMEX—Treatment of Anxiety—SmithKline Beecham plc; *Int'l*, pg. 1264

CONTAX—35 mm Cameras—Kyocera International, Inc.; *Int'l*, pg. 775

CONTAX—Cameras—Yashica, Inc.; *Int'l*, pg. 776

CONTAX G1—Autofocus Pocket Camera—Carl Zeiss; *Int'l*, pg. 1522

CONTAX SLR—Camera—Carl Zeiss; *Int'l*, pg. 1522

CONTE—NONE—Societe BIC S.A.; *Int'l*, pg. 1272

CONTE DI CAVOUR—Wines—Barbero 1891 SpA; *Int'l*, pg. 164

CONTECH—Automotive Parts-Die Castings—SPX Corporation; *U.S. Public*, pg. 1420

CONTEF—Convoluted Flexible Teflon Tubing—NewAge Industries Inc.; *U.S. Private*, pg. 796

CONTEF—Convoluted Teflon Tubing—Newage Industries Inc., Plastics Technology Group; *U.S. Private*, pg. 796

CONTEMPO LIGHTER—Lighter—Zippo Manufacturing Company; *U.S. Private*, pg. 1207

CONTEMPORARY—Refrigerator & Freezer—Foster Refrigerator Corporation; *U.S. Private*, pg. 421

CONTEMPORARY LONG-TERM CARE—Nursing Home Care—Bill Communications, Inc.; *Int'l*, pg. 1446

CONTEMPORARY MAPLE—Laminated 3" Plank-Square Edge—Robbins, Inc.; *U.S. Private*, pg. 934

CONTEMPORARY OB/GYN—Medical Publication—Medical Economics Company Inc.; *U.S. Public*, pg. 1601

CONTEMPORARY PARQUET—Solid Parquet-Fingerblock—Robbins, Inc.; *U.S. Private*, pg. 934

CONTEMPORARY PEDIATRICS—Medical Publication—Medical Economics Company Inc.; *U.S. Public*, pg. 1601

CONTEMPORARY PLANK—Laminated 3" Plank Flooring-Eased Edge—Robbins, Inc.; *U.S. Private*, pg. 934

CONTEMPORARY STRIP—Solid 2 1/4" Strip-Beveled Edge—Robbins, Inc.; *U.S. Private*, pg. 934

CONTEMPORARY SURGERY—NONE—Bobit Publishing Company; *U.S. Private*, pg. 154

CONTEMPORARY UROLOGY—Medical Publication—Medical Economics Company Inc.; *U.S. Public*, pg. 1601

CONTEMPOS—Shoes—Craddock-Terry Inc.; *U.S. Private*, pg. 284

CONTEMPRA—Costume Jewelry—Artra Group Incorporated; *U.S. Public*, pg. 136

CONTEMPRA—Furniture—Fisher Scientific Company; *U.S. Private*, pg. 658

CONTENDER—Hose & Conveyer Belting—The Goodyear Tire & Rubber Company; *U.S. Public*, pg. 752

CONTENT SECURITY—NONE—Check Point Software Technologies Ltd.; *U.S. Public*, pg. 342

CONTENTS—Cosmetic Organizers—Rubbermaid Incorporated; *U.S. Public*, pg. 1411

CONTESSA—Ranges, Refrigerators, Dishwashers, Clothes Washers & Dryers—General Electric Canada Inc.; *U.S. Public*, pg. 713

CONTEXT—Systems Furniture—Steelcase Inc.; *U.S. Private*, pg. 1038

CONTHERM—Scraped-Surface Heat Exchangers—Alfa Laval Inc.; *Int'l*, pg. 1378

CONTI—Soap With Olive Oil—Menley & James Laboratories, Inc.; *U.S. Public*, pg. 1086

CONTI—Hair Shampoo & Soap—SmithKline Beecham plc; *Int'l*, pg. 1264

CARLA CONTI—Hosiery for Women—Grupo Synkro, S.A. de C.V.; *Int'l*, pg. 576

CONTICO—Janitorial Supplies & Storage Containers—Contico International, Inc.; *U.S. Private*, pg. 267

CONTINENTAL—Household Appliances—BS Continental S.A. Utilidades Domesticas; *Int'l*, pg. 123

CONTINENTAL—Boiler—The Bethlehem Corporation; *U.S. Public*, pg. 225

CONTINENTAL—Tires—Continental AG; *Int'l*, pg. 327

CONTINENTAL—Insurance—The Continental Corporation; *U.S. Public*, pg. 1011

CONTINENTAL—Tires—Continental General Tire, Inc.; *Int'l*, pg. 327

CONTINENTAL—Military Engines for Tanks—General Dynamics Land Systems Div.; *U.S. Public*, pg. 709

CONTINENTAL—Gasoline & Diesel Engines—Harley Industries, Inc.; *U.S. Public*, pg. 880

CONTINENTAL—Drapery Hardware—Kirsch; *U.S. Public*, pg. 1176

CONTINENTAL—Chocolate Confectionery—Thorntons PLC; *Int'l*, pg. 1386

CONTINENTAL AIRLINES, INC—Air Transportation—Continental Airlines; *U.S. Public*, pg. 439

CONTINENTAL/BESPRESS—Balling Press—Continental Eagle Corporation; *U.S. Private*, pg. 267

CONTINENTAL CHAFER—Food Chafer—The Vollrath Company, L.L.C.; *U.S. Private*, pg. 1143

THE CONTINENTAL DIAMOND COLLECTION—Jewelry—Helzberg's Diamond Shops, Inc.; *U.S. Public*, pg. 220

CONTINENTAL EXPRESS—Air Transportation—Continental Airlines; *U.S. Public*, pg. 439

CONTINENTAL EXPRESS—Commercial Airline—Continental Express; *U.S. Public*, pg. 439

CONTINENTAL MICRONESIA, INC.—Air Transportation—Continental Airlines; *U.S. Public*, pg. 439

CONTINENTAL PLAZA—Hotels—Grupo Sidek, S.A. de C.V.; *Int'l*, pg. 576

CONTINENTAL SATELLITE—NONE—MediaOne; *U.S. Public*, pg. 1688

CONTINOUS PROCESSING SYSTEMS—Fault-Tolerant Computer Architecture—Stratus Computer, Inc.; *U.S. Public*, pg. 1524

CONTINU-MATIC—Continuous Form Stencils—Weber Marking Systems, Inc.; *U.S. Private*, pg. 1157

CONTINUOUS COLOR—Lipstick—Cover Girl Cosmetics; *U.S. Public*, pg. 1330

CONTINUUM—NONE—Lam Research Corporation; *U.S. Public*, pg. 975

CONTINUUM—Cable Headend Control Software & Equipment—Scientific-Atlanta, Inc.; *U.S. Public*, pg. 1443

CONTINUUM—Office Chairs—Steelcase Wood Div.; *U.S. Private*, pg. 1038

CONTINUUM—On-Line Transaction Processing Systems—Stratus Computer, Inc.; *U.S. Public*, pg. 1524

CONTINUUM—Lithium Thionyl Chloride Batteries—Yardney Technical Products, Inc.; *U.S. Private*, pg. 376

CONTINUUM AEC—Cooling Water Treatment—BetzDearborn Inc.; *U.S. Public*, pg. 226

CONTIROD—Copper Wire Rod—Union Miniere; *Int'l*, pg. 1441

CONTITECH—Technical Products—Continental AG; *Int'l*, pg. 327

CONTOUR—Cellulose Synthic Fiber—Bontex; *U.S. Public*, pg. 734

CONTOUR—Vinyl & Paper Wallcoverings—Forbo Holding SA; *Int'l*, pg. 496

CONTOUR—Car—Ford Motor Company; *U.S. Public*, pg. 661

CONTOUR—Cellulose Synthetic Fiber Compound Flexible Insole—Georgia-Bonded Fibers, Inc.; *U.S. Public*, pg. 734

CONTOUR—Jellied Resin—Marson/Creative Fastener, Inc.; *U.S. Private*, pg. 708

CONTOUR—Slimming Diet Drink—Novartis AG; *Int'l*, pg. 971

CONTOUR-PAK—Carrier—Owens-Illinois, Inc.; *U.S. Public*, pg. 1238

CONTOUR 35—Cosmetics—Irma Shorell, Inc.; *U.S. Private*, pg. 1101

CONTOURKORE—Balsa Wood for Boat Building—Baltek Corporation; *U.S. Public*, pg. 171

CONTOURS—NONE—Rubbermaid Incorporated; *U.S. Public*, pg. 1411

CONTRACOOL—Extruder Cooling—Battenfeld Gloucester Engineering Co. Inc.; *U.S. Private*, pg. 123

CONTRACT DESIGN—Magazine—Miller Freeman Inc.; *Int'l*, pg. 1443

CONTRACT 21—Broadloom—Couristan Inc.; *U.S. Private*, pg. 279

CONTRACTING BUSINESS—Periodical—Penton Publishing, Inc.; *U.S. Public*, pg. 1306

CONTRACTOR—Magazine for Air-Conditioning, Heating, Plumbing & Mechanical Contractors—Reed Elsevier Business Information; *Int'l*, pg. 1095

CONTRACTOR TOUGH & DESIGN—Electrical Extension Cords—General Cable Corporation; *Int'l*, pg. 1486

CONTRACTOR'S ONE MINUTE—Varnisher & Paint Stripper—Nasco Industries Inc.; *U.S. Private*, pg. 774

CONTRACTOR'S SERIES OF PAINT SOLVENTS—Varnisher & Paint Stripper—Nasco Industries Inc.; *U.S. Private*, pg. 774

CONTRAST HCG—One Step Pregnancy Test—Genzyme Diagnostics, Medix Biotech; *U.S. Public*, pg. 733

CONTRAST MONO—Quick Test for Mononucleusis—Genzyme Diagnostics, Medix Biotech; *U.S. Public*, pg. 733

CONTRAST STREP A—Rapid Test for Strep A—Genzyme Diagnostics, Medix Biotech; *U.S. Public*, pg. 733

CONTRASTS—Booklets Promoting Fine Printing Papers—Georgia-Pacific Corporation; *U.S. Public*, pg. 735

CONTREAT—NONE—Aqua Care Systems Inc.; *U.S. Public*, pg. 126

CONTREX—Mineral Water—Nestle S.A.; *Int'l*, pg. 915

CONTROL—Cat Litter—The Clorox Company; *U.S. Public*, pg. 386

CONTROL—Disposable Gowns, Surgical Drapes—Kimberly-Clark Corporation; *U.S. Public*, pg. 958

CONTROL—Diet Aid—Thompson Medical Company, Inc.; *U.S. Private*, pg. 1083

CONTROL—Concentrate Teat Dip—3M; *U.S. Public*, pg. 1604

CONTROL-A-FLO—Water Conserving Cartridge for Faucets—The Chicago Faucet Co.; *U.S. Private*, pg. 234

CONTROL ENGINEERING—Magazine for Engineers—Reed Elsevier Business Information; *Int'l*, pg. 1095

CONTROL ENGINEERING INTERNATIONAL—Magazine for Engineers in the International Market—Reed Elsevier Business Information; *Int'l*, pg. 1095

CONTROL-FLO—Water Heaters—Patterson-Kelley Company; *U.S. Public*, pg. 793

CONTROL LINE—Disconnect Motor Starters & Pushbutton Stations—The Lamson & Sessions Co.; *U.S. Public*, pg. 976

CONTROL MASTER—Process Controller—Analogic Corporation; *U.S. Public*, pg. 109

CONTROL MASTER—NONE—Executive Software; *U.S. Private*, pg. 388

CONTROL MASTER—Heat Control—National Presto Industries, Inc.; *U.S. Public*, pg. 1159

CONTROL RELEASE—Needle Suture—Ethicon, Inc.; *U.S. Public*, pg. 928

CONTROLLED COMBUSTION—Donut Fryer—Belshaw Brothers, Inc.; *Int'l*, pg. 188

CONTROLLED FINISHING SYSTEM—Power Tools—The Black & Decker Corporation; *U.S. Public*, pg. 233

CONTROLLED MAGNETIC—Electronic Components—Shure Brothers Incorporated; *U.S. Private*, pg. 997

CONTROLLER—Racquetball Glove—Ektelon; *U.S. Private*, pg. 884

CONTROLLER—Controlling Devices—Veeder-Root Company; *U.S. Public*, pg. 482

CONTROLLING INTEREST—Equipment as Unit for Parlor Game—American Greetings Corporation; *U.S. Public*, pg. 77

CONTROLTAC—Pressure Activated Films, Colored Vinyl Film—3M; *U.S. Public*, pg. 1604

CONTROLWARE II—Control Products—Bailey, Fischer & Porter Company; *Int'l*, pg. 449

CONTVEX—Mineral Water—Eckes AG; *Int'l*, pg. 432

CONVAIR—EVAP Coolers—Convair Cooler Corp.; *U.S. Private*, pg. 271

CONVAP—Scraped-Surface Evaporators—Alfa Laval Inc.; *Int'l*, pg. 1378

CONVECTAIR—Furnace—Selas Corporation of America; *U.S. Public*, pg. 1454

CONVECTION COMBO—Combination Steamer-Oven—Groen, A Dover Industries Co.; *U.S. Public*, pg. 521

CONVECTRON—Electric Heter Portable—Slant/Fin Corporation; *U.S. Public*, pg. 1005

CONVENIENT FOOD MART—Food Mart—Convenient Food Mart, Inc.; *U.S. Private*, pg. 271

CONVENIENT FOOD MART—Convenience Stores—Dairy Mart Convenience Stores, Inc.; *U.S. Public*, pg. 476

CONVENIENT FOOD MARTS—Food Marts—Dairy Mart Southeast; *U.S. Public*, pg. 476

CONVERSANT—Interactive Voice Information System—Lucent Technologies Inc.; *U.S. Public*, pg. 1017

CONVERSE—Athletic Footwear—Sao Paulo Alpargatas S.A.; *Int'l*, pg. 1193

CONVERSION MODEL—Market Research Products—Market Facts, Inc.; *U.S. Public*, pg. 1046

CONVERTAMATIC—Small Vacuum—Advance Machine Company; *Int'l*, pg. 932

CONVERTAPIPE—Hose—HBD Industries, Inc.; *U.S. Private*, pg. 489

CONVERTIBLE—Upright Vacuum Cleaner—Hoover Company; *U.S. Public*, pg. 1065

THE CONVERTIBLE—NONE—Life Technologies, Inc.; *U.S. Public*, pg. 504

CONVERTIBLE CUTTING BOARDS—Cutting Boards—General Housewares Corp.; *U.S. Public*, pg. 715

CONVERTIBLES—Sunglass System—Polaroid Corporation; *U.S. Public*, pg. 1313

CONVERTING MAGAZINE—Publication on Converting Paper/Paperboard/Film/Foil to Packaging Products—Reed Elsevier Business Information; *Int'l*, pg. 1095

CONVERTORS—Disposable, Non-Woven Products for Use in Hospitals—Allegiance Healthcare Corp.; *U.S. Public*, pg. 44

CONVEX C3 & C4—Series Computers—Convex Technology Center - Hewlett-Packard; *U.S. Public*, pg. 815

CONVOCAN—Containers—Sealright Company, Inc.; *U.S. Public*, pg. 1451

CONVOFLEX—Continous Convoluted Teflon Tubing—Bunnell Plastics Division; *U.S. Public*, pg. 689

CONVOLEX—Irradiated Tubing—Raychem Corporation; *U.S. Public*, pg. 1362

CONVOY—Tires—Bridgestone/Firestone, Inc.; *Int'l*, pg. 213

CONVOY—Gummed Tape—Intertape Polymer Group; *Int'l*, pg. 685

CONWAY—Dressing for Salads—Conway Import Co. Inc.; *U.S. Private*, pg. 272

CONWOOD—Loose Leaf Chewing Tobaccos—Conwood Company L.P.; *U.S. Private*, pg. 272

CONZ—Syringe Tip Filters—Whatman Inc.; *Int'l*, pg. 1498

CONZELO—Salad Dressings—Ridg's Finer Foods; *U.S. Public*, pg. 1288

COOK—Consumer Paint—Davis Paint Company; *U.S. Private*, pg. 315

COOK MACHINERY—Cableing Equip.—The Entwistle Company; *U.S. Private*, pg. 378

COOK-OFF—Chili—International Home Foods Inc.; *U.S. Private*, pg. 526

COOKDO—Seasoning Mixes—Ajinomoto Company Inc.; *Int'l*, pg. 40

COOKER BAR & GRILL—NONE—Cooker Restaurant Corporation; *U.S. Public*, pg. 442

COOKIE BLAST—Microwaveable Oatmeal—The Quaker Oats Company; *U.S. Public*, pg. 1347

COOKIE BREAK—Vanilla Creme Sandwich—RJR Nabisco Holdings Corp.; *U.S. Public*, pg. 1354

COOKIE CRISP—NONE—Ralcorp Holdings Inc.; *U.S. Public*, pg. 1359

COOKIE JAR—Pipe Tobacco—Lane Limited; *Int'l*, pg. 1129

COOKIE JAR CLASSIC—Reduced Fat Cookies—Westbrae Natural, Inc.; *U.S. Public*, pg. 774

COOKIE KING—Flour—ADM Milling Co.; *U.S. Public*, pg. 128

COOKIES 'N FUDGE—Fudge Striped Shortbread—RJR Nabisco Holdings Corp.; *U.S. Public*, pg. 1354

COOKIES 'N FUDGE—Cookies—Nabisco Inc.; *U.S. Public*, pg. 1355

COOKIES 'N' MINT—Chocolate Bar—Hershey Foods Corporation; *U.S. Public*, pg. 811

COOKIES WITH M&MS—Refrigerated Cookie Dough—Pillsbury Co.; *Int'l*, pg. 411

COOKIETREE COOKIES—Cookies & Cookie Dough—Cookie Tree Inc.; *U.S. Private*, pg. 273

COOKIN' BAG—Cooking Bag Entrees—ConAgra Frozen Food Company; *U.S. Public*, pg. 427

COOKIN' GOOD—Frozen Poultry—Perdue Farms Incorporated; *U.S. Private*, pg. 852

COOKIN' GOOD—Fresh & Frozen Chicken, Chicken Items & Turkeys—Perdue Farms, Inc.; *U.S. Private*, pg. 852

COOKING & CRAFTS BOOK CLUB—Book Club—Book of the Month Club; *U.S. Public*, pg. 1612

COOKING LIGHT—Bi-Monthly Magazine—Southern Progress Corporation; *U.S. Public*, pg. 1612

COOKING LIGHT—Magazine—Time Warner Inc.; *U.S. Public*, pg. 1610

COOKING-TONE—Stainless Steel Cookware—Regal Ware, Inc.; *U.S. Public*, pg. 917

COOKMASTER—Frypan—Sunbeam Household Products; *U.S. Public*, pg. 1533

COOK'S AMERICAN CHAMPAGNE—Champagne—Canandaigua Wine Company Div.; *U.S. Public*, pg. 300

COOK'S CAPTAIN'S RESERVE—Wine—Canandaigua Wine Company Div.; *U.S. Public*, pg. 300

COOKS CLUB—NONE—Lechters, Inc.; *U.S. Public*, pg. 983

COOKS SPK—Wines—Canandaigua Wine Company, Inc.; *U.S. Public*, pg. 300

COOKS VAR—Wines—Canandaigua Wine Company, Inc.; *U.S. Public*, pg. 300

COOL—Antiperspirant Deodorants—SmithKline Beecham plc; *Int'l*, pg. 1264

COOL—Computer Software—Sterling Software, Inc.; *U.S. Public*, pg. 1516

COOL-A-PED—Foot Treatment—Stanhome Inc.; *U.S. Public*, pg. 1508

COOL ACE—Scientific Glassware for Laboratory Use—Wheaton Inc.; *Int'l*, pg. 67

COOL-AID!—Air conditioning O-ring Gaskets, Valves, Tubes & Switches—R&B, Inc.; *U.S. Public*, pg. 1354

COOL-AIR—Mens Rain Wear—Rainfair, Inc.; *U.S. Private*, pg. 907

COOL & FRUITY—Drink Mixes—McCormick/Schilling; *U.S. Public*, pg. 1066

COOL ATTIC—Residential Ventilation Products—Butler Ventamatic Corp.; *U.S. Private*, pg. 190

COOL BREEZE—Wines—Canandaigua Wine Company, Inc.; *U.S. Public*, pg. 300

COOL CAM—Instant Camera—Polaroid Corporation; *U.S. Public*, pg. 1313

COOL CHARM—Antiperspirant Deodorants—SmithKline Beecham plc; *Int'l*, pg. 1264

COOL CREATIONS—Ice Cream Treats—Nestle Ice Cream Co.; *Int'l*, pg. 918

COOL CREATIONS—NONE—Nestle USA; *Int'l*, pg. 916

COOL EDGE GRILL—Griddle with Cool Touch Perimeter—Toastmaster, Inc.; *U.S. Public*, pg. 1619

COOL MINT LISTERINE—Antiseptic Mouthwash—Warner-Lambert Consumer Healthcare; *U.S. Public*, pg. 1739

COOL N FRESH—Pre-Sweetened Drink Mixes & Ice Tea—Hormel Foods Corp.; *U.S. Public*, pg. 840

COOL RANCH DORITOS—Corn Chips—Frito-Lay Company; *U.S. Public*, pg. 1277

COOL SACK—Lunch Kit—Igloo Products Corporation; *U.S. Public*, pg. 265

COOL SPEED—Cutting & Grinding Fluids—Daubert Industries, Inc.; *U.S. Private*, pg. 313

COOL-TEX—Surgical Gowns—Medline Industries, Inc.; *U.S. Private*, pg. 728

COOL TWIST—Cones & Sundaes—Hardee's Food Systems, Inc.; *U.S. Public*, pg. 278

COOL WHIP—Topping—Philip Morris Companies Inc.; *U.S. Public*, pg. 1287

COOLABAH—White Wine—Groupe Pernod Ricard; *Int'l*, pg. 566

COOLANOL—Cooling Fluids—Monsanto Company; *U.S. Public,* pg. 1124

COOLANOL—Dielectric Coolant—Solutia Inc.; *U.S. Public,* pg. 1483

COOLBEAM—Heat/Light Separation Mirrors—Optical Coating Laboratory, Inc.; *U.S. Public,* pg. 1227

COOLCUT—Abrasive Disc—Gardner Abrasives; *U.S. Public,* pg. 1699

COOLDADDY—Electric Deep Fryer—National Presto Industries, Inc.; *U.S. Public,* pg. 1159

COOLMAX—Fabric—Du Pont (E.I. Du Pont De Nemours & Co.); *U.S. Public,* pg. 530

COOLPAK—Precooler—Research Products Corporation; *U.S. Private,* pg. 274

COOLPURE—"Cool Pasteurize" Fluid Foods—Maxwell Technologies, Inc.; *U.S. Public,* pg. 1061

COOLSHIELD—Helmut—The Lincoln Electric Company; *U.S. Public,* pg. 996

COOLTEMP—Cold Therapy System—Cincinnati Sub-Zero Products, Inc.; *U.S. Private,* pg. 240

COOLTONG—Holder—The Lincoln Electric Company; *U.S. Public,* pg. 996

COOMBS CONTROL—Reagent Red Blood Cells—Ortho Clinical Diagnostic Systems Inc.; *U.S. Public,* pg. 929

COOPER—Hockey Equipment—Bauer Sports Inc.; *U.S. Public,* pg. 1184

COOPER—Thermometers—Cooper Instrument Corp.; *U.S. Private,* pg. 274

COOPER—Automobile & Truck Tires, Inner Tubes, Reinforced Hoses & Other Auto Parts—Cooper Tire & Rubber Company; *U.S. Public,* pg. 445

COOPER—Tires—The Cooper Tire Company; *U.S. Public,* pg. 445

COOPER—Baseball Products—Irwin Toy Ltd.; *Int'l,* pg. 688

COOPER HGP—Rigid Gas-Permeable Daily-Wear Contact Lens—The Cooper Companies, Inc.; *U.S. Public,* pg. 442

COOPER VAC—Smoke Evacuator—The Cooper Companies, Inc.; *U.S. Public,* pg. 442

COOPER WEYMOUTH PETERSON—Stock Feeding Equipment for the Metal Forming Industry—Mestek, Inc.; *U.S. Public,* pg. 1099

COOPERCLEAR—Daily-Wear Soft Contact Lens—The Cooper Companies, Inc.; *U.S. Public,* pg. 442

COOPERSTOWN ASH—Lumber & Wood Products—Georgia-Pacific Corporation; *U.S. Public,* pg. 735

COOPERSURGICAL SMOKE EVACUATION SYSTEM 6080—Air Purification Equipment—The Cooper Companies, Inc.; *U.S. Public,* pg. 442

COOPERTHIN—Daily-Wear Soft Contact Lens—The Cooper Companies, Inc.; *U.S. Public,* pg. 442

COORDINATES—Luggage—Hartmann Luggage & Leather Goods Group; *U.S. Public,* pg. 261

COORS—Beer, Japan Only—Asahi Breweries Ltd.; *Int'l,* pg. 83

COORS—No-Alcohol Beer—Adolph Coors Company; *U.S. Public,* pg. 445

COORS—Restaurant China & Cookware—Standex International Corporation; *U.S. Public,* pg. 1505

COORS BREWING—T-Shirts & Sweatshirts—Holoubek Inc.; *U.S. Private,* pg. 536

COORS DRY—Dry Beer—Adolph Coors Company; *U.S. Public,* pg. 445

COORS EXTRA GOLD—Premium Beer—Adolph Coors Company; *U.S. Public,* pg. 445

COORS LIGHT—Low-Calorie Premium Beer—Adolph Coors Company; *U.S. Public,* pg. 445

COORSH—NONE—Principal Marques Meat Co.; *Int'l,* pg. 841

COOSAPRESS—Printing Paper—Kimberly-Clark Corporation; *U.S. Public,* pg. 958

COOSAPRESTIGE—Printing Paper—Kimberly-Clark Corporation; *U.S. Public,* pg. 958

COOSAPRIME—Printing Paper—Kimberly-Clark Corporation; *U.S. Public,* pg. 958

COOTIE—Game—Milton Bradley Company; *U.S. Public,* pg. 797

COOYMANS—Advocaat Liqueur—Groupe Pernod Ricard; *Int'l,* pg. 566

COPAL—Switches & Receptacles—Eagle Electric Mfg. Co., Inc.; *U.S. Public,* pg. 354

COPCO—Fashion Kitchenware—Wilton Industries, Inc.; *U.S. Private,* pg. 1181

COPE—Expansion Process for Claus & Sulfur Recovery Units—Air Products and Chemicals, Inc.; *U.S. Public,* pg. 30

COPE—Analgesic—Mentholatum Company; *Int'l,* pg. 1126

COPELAND—Compressors—Copeland Corporation Ltd.; *U.S. Public,* pg. 576

COPELAND—HVAC Compressor—Emerson Electric Co.; *U.S. Public,* pg. 572

COPENHAGEN—NONE—United States Tobacco Company; *U.S. Public,* pg. 1661

COPIESOLUTION—Recycled Content White Papers—Avenor, Inc.; *Int'l,* pg. 101

COPIS—NONE—Berg Electronics; *U.S. Public,* pg. 212

THE COPLEY PRESS—Daily Newspapers—The Copley Press, Inc.; *U.S. Private,* pg. 275

COPON—Industrial Coatings—Meristem plc; *Int'l,* pg. 858

COPOZIDE—Ace Inhibitor—Bristol-Myers Squibb Company; *U.S. Public,* pg. 253

COPPER-ALLOY—Special Steels—Inland Steel Industries, Inc.; *U.S. Public,* pg. 879

COPPER CANYON—Bicycle Accessories—Bell Sports Corp.; *U.S. Public,* pg. 207

COPPER CLIFF—Milk Products—Labatt Brewing Company Limited; *Int'l,* pg. 679

COPPER COAT—Copper Tank Lining—Precision Parts Corp.; *U.S. Private,* pg. 879

COPPER FREE—Welding Wire—National-Standard Co.; *U.S. Public,* pg. 1160

COPPER GLEAM PC—Bright Acid Copper Process—LeaRonal, Inc.; *U.S. Public,* pg. 982

COPPER GLEAM PCM—Bright Acid Copper Process—LeaRonal, Inc.; *U.S. Public,* pg. 982

COPPER GLEAM RG 10—Bright Acid Copper—LeaRonal, Inc.; *U.S. Public,* pg. 982

COPPER LINE—DC Power Supply—Best Power; *U.S. Private,* pg. 140

COPPER-NU—Metal Cleaner—Litton Industries, Inc.; *U.S. Public,* pg. 1002

COPPER PLUS—Spark Plug—Champion Ignition Products; *U.S. Public,* pg. 442

COPPER PLUS—Spark Plugs—Cooper Automotive Division; *U.S. Public,* pg. 443

COPPER-PLUS—Grounding Connector for Bushings/Terminators—O-Z/Gedney Co.; *U.S. Public,* pg. 727

COPPER TOP—NONE—Duracell International Inc.; *U.S. Public,* pg. 743

COPPER-TROL—Corrosion Inhibitor—BetzDearborn Inc.; *U.S. Public,* pg. 226

COPPERCLAD—Anti-Fouling Coating—Ferro Corporation; *U.S. Public,* pg. 618

COPPERHEAD—Airgun Ammunition—Crosman Airguns; *U.S. Private,* pg. 291

COPPERHEAD—Cider—Matthew Clark Brands; *Int'l,* pg. 848

COPPERSOL—Wire & Cable—Times Fiber Communications, Inc.; *U.S. Private,* pg. 629

COPPERSPLINE—Wire & Cable—Times Fiber Communications, Inc.; *U.S. Private,* pg. 629

COPPERTONE—Waterproof Suntan, Sunscreen & Sunblock Products & Sunnless Tanning Lotions—Schering-Plough Corporation; *U.S. Public,* pg. 1438

COPPERTONE—Sun Care Products—Schering-Plough Healthcare Products Inc.; *U.S. Public,* pg. 1438

COPPERTONE KIDS—Six-Hour Waterproof Sunblock Lotions—Schering-Plough Corporation; *U.S. Public,* pg. 1438

COPPERTONE KIDS—Sun Protection Products—Schering-Plough Healthcare Products Inc.; *U.S. Public,* pg. 1438

COPPERTONE SPORT—Sweatproof Dry Lotion Sunscreen & Sunblock Products—Schering-Plough Corporation; *U.S. Public,* pg. 1438

COPPERWELD—Copper-Clad Wire & Strand—Copperweld Bimetallics Products Co.; *Int'l,* pg. 662

COPPERWELD—Wire—Copperweld Fayetteville Division; *Int'l,* pg. 662

COPPERWELD—Tubing—Imetal; *Int'l,* pg. 661

COPPRITE—Animal Health Products—SmithKline Beecham plc; *Int'l,* pg. 1264

COPPUS—Turbine & Portable Ventilation Equipment—Tuthill Corporation; *U.S. Private,* pg. 1110

COPR-TRODE—Arc Welding Electrodes—Ampco Metal Incorporated; *U.S. Private,* pg. 67

COPS—Electronics—National Semiconductor Corporation; *U.S. Public,* pg. 1159

COPY CLUB—Digital Copying Center—International Center for Entrepreneurial Development, Inc.; *U.S. Private,* pg. 568

COPY FAX—Thermal Facsimilie Paper—Nashua Corporation; *U.S. Public,* pg. 1152

COPY PLUS FOR DB2—DB2 Database Utility—BMC Software, Inc.; *U.S. Public,* pg. 162

COPY VIEW—Communication Products—Arkwright, Inc; *Int'l,* pg. 994

COPYCODE—Shelf Marking Label—Avery Dennison Corporation; *U.S. Public,* pg. 152

COPYETTE 1 & 1—Cassette Copiers—Telex Communications, Inc.; *U.S. Private,* pg. 1074

COPYETTE 1 & 3—Cassette Copiers—Telex Communications, Inc.; *U.S. Private,* pg. 1074

COPYFLEX—Semi-Moist Diazo Supplies—OCE-U.S.A.; *Int'l,* pg. 994

COPYMAX—Store-Within-Store Print & Copy Service—OfficeMax; *U.S. Public,* pg. 1212

COPYPRINTER—Digital Duplicators—Gestetner Holdings PLC; *Int'l,* pg. 1114

COPYRITE—Premium No. 4—Badger Paper Mills, Inc.; *U.S. Public,* pg. 165

COPYRUN—Chemical Carbonless Copy Paper—Georgia-Pacific Corporation; *U.S. Public,* pg. 735

COPYSOURCE—Marketing Program—Ikon Office Solutions, Inc.; *U.S. Public,* pg. 862

COPYSOURCE—Copier Paper—Unisource; *U.S. Public,* pg. 1671

COPYSTAR—NONE—Mita Copystar America Inc.; *Int'l,* pg. 870

COPYSTAR—Copying Machine—Mita Industrial Company, Ltd.; *Int'l,* pg. 870

COQUI MALT LIQUOR—NONE—The Stroh Brewery Company; *U.S. Private,* pg. 1047

COR-GEL—Medical ECG Electrolyte Cream—Burdick, Inc.; *U.S. Private,* pg. 181

COR-LOC—Seating System—Nemschoff Chairs, Inc.; *U.S. Private,* pg. 791

COR-O-BATE—Corrosion Inhibitor Paper—Fort James Corporation; *U.S. Public,* pg. 670

COR-PAK—Heat Recovery Equipment; Thermal & Catalytic Oxidizers—ABB Air Preheater Inc.; *Int'l,* pg. 3

COR-PAK—Oxidizers—ABB Inc.; *Int'l,* pg. 3

COR-TEN—Special Steel—Inland Steel Industries, Inc.; *U.S. Public,* pg. 879

CORAB—Diagnostic Products—Abbott Laboratories; *U.S. Public,* pg. 12

CORABOND—Adhesives for Motor Vehicle Assembly & Maintenance—PPG Industries, Inc.; *U.S. Public,* pg. 1245

CORACTEN—NONE—Medeva PLC; *Int'l,* pg. 852

CORAL—Hand Dishwashing Detergent—Benckiser Consumer Products Inc.; *Int'l,* pg. 185

CORAL—Seafood Products—Bumble Bee Seafoods Inc.; *U.S. Private,* pg. 526

CORAL—Installation for Lighting, Heating, Steam Generating & Cooking—Sime Darby Berhad; *Int'l,* pg. 1249

CORALURE—Pre-Printed Laminated Boxes—Georgia-Pacific Corporation; *U.S. Public,* pg. 735

CORASIL—LC Bulk Packing—Millipore Corporation; *U.S. Public,* pg. 1112

CORATOP—Fungicide—Novartis; *Int'l,* pg. 972

CORBEL—Crop Protection Agent—BASF AG; *Int'l,* pg. 103

CORBERO—NONE—Electrolux, AB; *Int'l,* pg. 438

CORBETT CANYON VINEYARDS—Varietal Wines—The Wine Group; *U.S. Private,* pg. 1182

CORBIN—Hardware—The Black & Decker Corporation; *U.S. Public,* pg. 233

CORBY'S CANADIAN—Blended Whisky—Barton Incorporated; *U.S. Public,* pg. 300

CORBY'S RESERSE—Blended Whisky—Barton Incorporated; *U.S. Public,* pg. 300

CORBY'S—NONE—Barton Brands, Ltd.; *U.S. Public,* pg. 300

CORCARE—PPO—CorVel Corporation; *U.S. Public,* pg. 451

CORCARE RX—Pharmacy Network—CorVel Corporation; *U.S. Public,* pg. 451

CORCOM—Radio Frequency Interference Filters—Corcom, Inc.; *U.S. Public,* pg. 446

CORDAIR—Private Brand Paper—The Cincinnati Cordage & Paper Company; *U.S. Private*, pg. 239

CORDAMEX—Textile & Indus. Rayon—CYDSA S.A.; *Int'l*, pg. 246

CORDARONE—Antiarrhythmia Drug—American Home Products Corporation; *U.S. Public*, pg. 79

CORDARONE—Antiarrhythmic Agent—Wyeth-Ayerst Laboratories, Inc.; *U.S. Public*, pg. 80

CORDARONE I.V.—Antiarrhymia Drug—American Home Products Corporation; *U.S. Public*, pg. 79

CORDAX—NONE—Giddings & Lewis Sheffield Measurement Systems; *Int'l*, pg. 1389

CORDECK—Corrugated Shipping Pallets—Stone Container Corporation; *U.S. Public*, pg. 1520

CORDENKA—Viscose Rayon—Akzo Nobel N.V.; *Int'l*, pg. 42

CORDGUARD—Disposable Umbilical Blood Sampling System—Utah Medical Products, Inc.; *U.S. Public*, pg. 1700

CORDIALLY YOURS CHERRIES—Candy—Brach & Brock Confections Inc.; *U.S. Private*, pg. 163

CORDO—Lacquer Coatings—Ferro Corporation; *U.S. Public*, pg. 618

CORDOBOND—Plastic Resin Adhesive—Ferro Corporation; *U.S. Public*, pg. 618

CORDOMATIC—Retractable Cord Reels—Klein Tools Inc.; *U.S. Private*, pg. 625

CORDON—Stainless Steel Flatware—Dansk International Designs Ltd.; *U.S. Public*, pg. 261

CORDON BLEU—NONE—Regal Ware, Inc.; *U.S. Private*, pg. 917

CORDOVA—Recreational Vehicles—Kit Manufacturing Company; *U.S. Public*, pg. 962

CORDSPUN—Dress Goods Fabric—Dan River Inc.; *U.S. Public*, pg. 478

CORDURA—Nylon—Du Pont (E.I. Du Pont De Nemours & Co.); *U.S. Public*, pg. 530

CORDX—Private Brand Paper—The Cincinnati Cordage & Paper Company; *U.S. Private*, pg. 239

CORE BANKING—NONE—HongKong Bank of Canada; *Int'l*, pg. 583

CORE-BRIGHT—NONE—ESAB Welding & Cutting Products; *Int'l*, pg. 281

CORE-CHILL—Vacuum Pumps—Croll-Reynolds Company, Inc.; *U.S. Private*, pg. 290

CORE 2544—Laser Beam Lithography System—Etec Systems, Inc.; *U.S. Public*, pg. 594

CORE-VENT—Dental Implants—Dentsply International Inc.; *U.S. Public*, pg. 498

CORECOM—Petroleum Engineering Services—Litton Industries, Inc.; *U.S. Public*, pg. 1002

COREDIL—Polyurethane Insulating Panels—The Dow Chemical Company; *U.S. Public*, pg. 522

COREG—NONE—SmithKline Beecham Corporation; *Int'l*, pg. 1264

COREGA—Denture Adhesive Powder—Block Drug Company, Inc.; *U.S. Public*, pg. 236

COREGARD—Low Invasion Coring System—Baker Hughes INTEQ; *U.S. Public*, pg. 166

COREGUN—NONE—Western Atlas Logging Services; *U.S. Public*, pg. 1757

CORELLE—Dinnerware—Corning Incorporated; *U.S. Public*, pg. 448

COREMASTER—Heavy Duty Core Barrel for Highly Deviated Holes—Baker Hughes INTEQ; *U.S. Public*, pg. 166

CORES LOG—Core Analysis Evaluation—Litton Industries, Inc.; *U.S. Public*, pg. 1002

CORESTATES FINANCIAL—Financial Services—CoreStates Financial Corp.; *U.S. Public*, pg. 446

COREWARE—Library—LSI Logic Corp.; *U.S. Public*, pg. 971

COREWELD—NONE—ESAB Welding & Cutting Products; *Int'l*, pg. 281

COREZYN—Resin—Interplastic Corp.; *U.S. Private*, pg. 572

CORFLEX—Bolts & Screws—Continental/Midland, Inc.; *U.S. Private*, pg. 268

CORFLEX—Pipe Coating—Ferro Corporation; *U.S. Public*, pg. 618

CORFLO—NONE—Applied Extrusion Technologies, Inc.; *U.S. Public*, pg. 122

CROFT PARTICULAR—NONE—Croft Sherry; *Int'l*, pg. 409

CORFU—Broadloom—Couristan Inc.; *U.S. Private*, pg. 279

CORGARD—Ace Inhibitor—Bristol-Myers Squibb Company; *U.S. Public*, pg. 253

CORGARD—Beta-Blocking Agent for Management of Hypertension—Bristol-Myers Squibb U.S. Pharmaceutical Group; *U.S. Public*, pg. 255

CORGI—Book Publishing—Bertelsmann AG; *Int'l*, pg. 189

CORIA—Edible Casing—Devro-Teepak, Inc.; *Int'l*, pg. 408

CORIAN—Building Products—Du Pont (E.I. Du Pont De Nemours & Co.); *U.S. Public*, pg. 530

CORICIDIN—Decongestant Tablets—Schering-Plough Corporation; *U.S. Public*, pg. 1438

CORICIDIN—Cold/Flu Medicine—Schering-Plough Healthcare Products Inc.; *U.S. Public*, pg. 1438

CORICIDIN D—Decongestant Tablets—Schering-Plough Corporation; *U.S. Public*, pg. 1438

CORINNIS—Distilled Bottled Water—Hinckley & Schmitt, Inc.; *Int'l*, pg. 1322

CORINTHIAN—Instruments Providing Depth, Speed, Distance, Wind Information for Sailboat—Datamarine International, Inc.; *U.S. Public*, pg. 486

CORK DRY GIN—Dry Gin—Groupe Pernod Ricard; *Int'l*, pg. 566

CORKEN—Pumps & Compressors—IDEX Corporation; *U.S. Public*, pg. 862

CORMATIC—Washroom Tissue, Paper Towels, Soaps & Dispensers—Georgia-Pacific Corporation; *U.S. Public*, pg. 735

CORMATIC AIRE—Room Air Freshener & Dispensers—Georgia-Pacific Corporation; *U.S. Public*, pg. 735

CORN BURSTS—Crunchy Sweetened Popped-Up Corn Cereal—Malt-O-Meal Company; *U.S. Private*, pg. 699

CORN FLAKE CRUMBS—Topping—Kellogg Company; *U.S. Public*, pg. 947

CORN POPS—Ready-Sweetened Puffed Corn Cereal—Kellogg Company; *U.S. Public*, pg. 947

CORN SILK—Cosmetics—Chattem, Inc., Consumer Products Division; *U.S. Public*, pg. 341

CORN SILK OIL—Absorbent Liquid Make-Up—Chattem, Inc., Consumer Products Division; *U.S. Public*, pg. 341

CORN SKIS—Snack Products—The Quaker Oats Company; *U.S. Public*, pg. 1347

CORN TOTAL—Cereal—General Mills, Inc.; *U.S. Public*, pg. 717

CORNADO—Commercial Poppers—Gold Medal Products Co.; *U.S. Private*, pg. 459

CORNELIUS—Comml. Ice & Beverage Systems—IMI Cornelius, Inc. (IA); *Int'l*, pg. 646

CORNELIUS—Drinks Dispense—IMI Plc; *Int'l*, pg. 646

CORNER BAKERY—Breadmaker/Dessert Maker—Toastmaster, Inc.; *U.S. Public*, pg. 1619

CORNER CURL DESIGN—Photo Products & Services—Eastman Kodak Company; *U.S. Public*, pg. 550

CORNER STORE—Convenience Store with Gasoline Outlets—Ultramar Diamond Shamrock Corporation; *U.S. Public*, pg. 1663

CORNERSTONE—Transmission Products—Northern Telecom; *Int'l*, pg. 969

CORNERSTONE—NONE—Northern Telecom Limited; *Int'l*, pg. 968

CORNERSTONE—Floor Sealer/Finish—3M; *U.S. Public*, pg. 1604

CORNERSTONE LIFE—Whole Life Product—MSI Insurance Companies; *U.S. Private*, pg. 688

CORNETTO—Ice Cream Dessert—Unilever Plc; *Int'l*, pg. 1433

CORNIANI—NONE—G.D. Packaging Machinery Inc.; *Int'l*, pg. 531

CORNIES—Cheese Puffs—Borden, Inc.; *U.S. Private*, pg. 157

CORNING—Cookware—Corning Incorporated; *U.S. Public*, pg. 448

CORNING WARE—Cookware—Corning Incorporated; *U.S. Public*, pg. 448

CORNNUTS—Crunch Corn Snacks—RJR Nabisco Holdings Corp.; *U.S. Public*, pg. 1354

CORNQUISTOS—Snack Product—Mars, Incorporated; *U.S. Private*, pg. 707

CORNSILK—Cosmetics Line—Chattem, Inc.; *U.S. Public*, pg. 341

CORNSTALKERS—NONE—Rocky Shoes & Boots, Inc.; *U.S. Public*, pg. 1402

CORNWALL COATED CARD—Paper—Domtar Inc.; *Int'l*, pg. 416

CORNZYME—Complex for Enhancing the Feeding Value of Corn Silage—Cultor Ltd.; *Int'l*, pg. 349

CORO—Jewelry—Richton International Corporation; *U.S. Public*, pg. 1389

CORO-FOAM—Foam—Cook Composites & Polymers Inc.; *Int'l*, pg. 1409

COROC—Resins—Cook Composites & Polymers Inc.; *Int'l*, pg. 1409

COROCRAFT—Jewelry—Richton International Corporation; *U.S. Public*, pg. 1389

COROGOLD—Jewelry—Richton International Corporation; *U.S. Public*, pg. 1389

COROLLA—Automobile—Toyota Motor Corporation; *Int'l*, pg. 1411

COROLLA—Car—Toyota Motor Sales, U.S.A., Inc.; *Int'l*, pg. 1412

COROLLA II—Passenger Cars—Toyota Motor Corporation; *Int'l*, pg. 1411

CORONA—Corn Mills—RJR Nabisco Holdings Corp.; *U.S. Public*, pg. 1354

CORONA—Automobile—Toyota Motor Corporation; *Int'l*, pg. 1411

CORONA—Utility Maintenance Services—Westmoreland Coal Co.; *U.S. Public*, pg. 1761

CORONA EXTRA—Mexican Beer—Barton Beers, Ltd.; *U.S. Public*, pg. 300

CORONA EXTRA—Mexican Beer—Barton Incorporated; *U.S. Public*, pg. 300

CORONA LIGHT—Beer—Barton Beers, Ltd.; *U.S. Public*, pg. 300

CORONA MAGENTA—Fluorescent Color—Day-Glo Color Corp.; *U.S. Public*, pg. 1357

CORONADO—Jewelry—Uncas Manufacturing Company; *U.S. Private*, pg. 1116

CORONADO SST—Text & Cover Paper—Fox River Paper Company; *U.S. Private*, pg. 422

CORONATION—Aluminum Cookware—Regal Ware, Inc.; *U.S. Private*, pg. 917

CORONATION—Printing Paper—Westvaco Corporation; *U.S. Public*, pg. 1762

CORONET—Sporting Goods—Brunswick Bowling & Billiards Corp.; *U.S. Public*, pg. 265

CORONET—Film & Video—Coronet/MTI; *U.S. Private*, pg. 863

CORONET—Bathroom & Facial Tissue, Paper Towels & Napkins—Georgia-Pacific Corporation; *U.S. Public*, pg. 735

CORONET—Passenger Tires—Pirelli Armstrong Tire Corporation; *Int'l*, pg. 1058

CORONET (STYLIZED)—NONE—Regal Ware, Inc.; *U.S. Private*, pg. 917

CORONET PRINTS—Bathroom Tissue—Georgia-Pacific Corporation; *U.S. Public*, pg. 735

CORONITA—Beer—Barton Beers, Ltd.; *U.S. Public*, pg. 300

CORONOL—Electrical Wires, Cables & Conductors—General Electric Canada Inc.; *U.S. Public*, pg. 713

CORPORATE CARD—Charge Card Services—American Express Company; *U.S. Public*, pg. 73

CORPORATE CARD—NONE—American Express Service Europe Ltd.; *U.S. Public*, pg. 74

THE CORPORATE COMMUNICATORS—Div. Offering Media & Crisis Communication Trng., Plng. & Implementation—HMS Partners; *U.S. Private*, pg. 491

CORPORATE FINANCE—Publication—Financial World Partners; *U.S. Private*, pg. 404

CORPORATE FINANCE SOURCEBOOK—Business Directory—National Register Publishing; *Int'l*, pg. 1096

CORPORATE LINK—Teleconferencing System—Shure Brothers Incorporated; *U.S. Private*, pg. 997

CORPORATE NAVIGATOR—Survey Service—ScanTron Corporation; *U.S. Public*, pg. 786

CORPOTASIN CI—Potassium Supplement—SmithKline Beecham plc; *Int'l*, pg. 1264

CORPS DIPLOMATIQUE—Cigars—Lane Limited; *Int'l*, pg. 1129

CORPUS—NONE—LPC Industrias Alimenticias S.A.; *Int'l*, pg. 380

CORRECT COMFORT—Bedding—The Stearns & Foster Bedding Company; *U.S. Private*, pg. 979

CORRECTENGLISH—Proofing Tools - ESL Grammar Correction System—INSO Corporation; *U.S. Public*, pg. 882

CORRECTEXT GRAMMAR CORRECTION SYSTEM—Proofing Tool—INSO Corporation; *U.S. Public*, pg. 882

CORRECTOL—Laxatives—Schering-Plough Corporation; *U.S. Public*, pg. 1438

CORRECTOL—Laxative—Schering-Plough Healthcare Products Inc.; *U.S. Public*, pg. 1438

CORRESPOND—Bond Paper—The Mead Corporation; *U.S. Public*, pg. 1074

CORRESPOND RECYCLED 25% COTTON—Recycled Cotton Writing Paper—Gilbert Paper; *U.S. Public*, pg. 1074

CORRESPOND 25% COTTON—Cotton Fiber Writing Paper—Gilbert Paper; *U.S. Public*, pg. 1074

CORROSTOP—NONE—Sico Inc.; *Int'l*, pg. 1239

CORRSHIELD—Inhibitor—BetzDearborn Inc.; *U.S. Public*, pg. 226

CORRTEF—Corrugated Flexible Teflon Tubing—NewAge Industries Inc.; *U.S. Private*, pg. 796

CORRTEF—Corrugated Teflon Tubing—Newage Industries Inc., Plastics Technology Group; *U.S. Private*, pg. 796

CORRU KOTE—Paperboard—The Mead Corporation; *U.S. Public*, pg. 1074

CORRY JAMESTOWN—Office Furniture—HON Industries Inc.; *U.S. Public*, pg. 772

CORRYHIEBERT—Metal Office Furniture—CorryHiebert Corporation; *U.S. Public*, pg. 772

CORSA—Automobile—Toyota Motor Corporation; *Int'l*, pg. 1411

CORSA—NONE—Vauxhall; *U.S. Public*, pg. 724

CORSAF—Inhibitor Concentrate—The Dow Chemical Company; *U.S. Public*, pg. 522

CORSAIR—Oil Well Servicing Rigs—Crane Carrier Company; *U.S. Private*, pg. 286

CORSAIR—High Speed Tool Steel—Latrobe Steel Company; *U.S. Public*, pg. 1617

CORSAVAN—NONE—Vauxhall; *U.S. Public*, pg. 724

CORSAVER—Paper Roll Core Plugs—Westvaco Corporation; *U.S. Public*, pg. 1762

CORSICA—Car—Chevrolet Motor Div. General Motors Corp.; *U.S. Public*, pg. 720

CORSICA—Rugs—Couristan Inc.; *U.S. Private*, pg. 279

CORSINI—Jewelry—Uncas Manufacturing Company; *U.S. Private*, pg. 1116

CORSODYL—NONE—SmithKline Beecham Corporation; *Int'l*, pg. 1264

CORSON—Quicklime, Hydrated Lime & Construction Lime—Corson Lime Company; *U.S. Public*, pg. 1685

CORT—Carry-On Receiver/Transmitter—Megapulse, Inc.; *U.S. Private*, pg. 729

CORT-DOME—Pharmaceutical—Bayer Corporation/Pharmaceutical Division; *Int'l*, pg. 173

CORTAID—Pharmaceutical Product—Pharmacia & Upjohn; *Int'l*, pg. 1048

CORTAL—NONE—SmithKline Beecham Research Limited; *Int'l*, pg. 1266

CORTE SANT 'ALDA AMARONE—Italian Wine—Laird & Company; *U.S. Private*, pg. 642

CORTE SANT 'ALDA VALPOLICELLA—Italian Wine—Laird & Company; *U.S. Private*, pg. 642

CORTE SANT'ALDA RECIOTO DELLA VALPOLICELLA—Italian Wine—Laird & Company; *U.S. Private*, pg. 642

CORTE SANT'ALDA VALPOLICELLA MITHAS—Italian Wine—Laird & Company; *U.S. Private*, pg. 642

CORTE SANT'ALDA VALPOLICELLA SUPERIORE—Italian Wine—Laird & Company; *U.S. Private*, pg. 642

CORTEM—Conductive Motor Brush Springs—Toledo Commutator Co.; *U.S. Private*, pg. 623

CORTENEMA—Pharmaceutical Products—Solvay Pharmaceuticals, Inc.; *Int'l*, pg. 1278

CORTEXX—Shampoo & Conditioner—Alberto-Culver Company; *U.S. Public*, pg. 37

CORTIFOAM—NONE—Schwarz Pharma Inc.; *Int'l*, pg. 1211

CORTINA—NONE—British-American Tobacco (Germany) GmbH; *Int'l*, pg. 111

CORTISPORIN—Ear, Eye, Skin Prescription—Glaxo Wellcome PLC; *Int'l*, pg. 553

CORTIZONE—NONE—Pfizer Inc.; *U.S. Public*, pg. 1281

CORTIZONE EXTERNAL—Anal Itch Relief Creme—Thompson Medical Company, Inc.; *U.S. Private*, pg. 1083

CORTIZONE-5—Anti-Itch Creme—Thompson Medical Company, Inc.; *U.S. Private*, pg. 1083

CORTIZONE FOR KIDS—Anti-Itch Creme—Thompson Medical Company, Inc.; *U.S. Private*, pg. 1083

CORTIZONE-10—Anti-Itch Creme—Thompson Medical Company, Inc.; *U.S. Private*, pg. 1083

CORTLAND—Dacron Trolling Line—Cortland Line Co., Inc.; *U.S. Private*, pg. 277

CORTONE—Cortisone Acetate—Merck & Co., Inc.; *U.S. Public*, pg. 1090

CORTROL—Boiler Water Corrosion Inhibitors—BetzDearborn Inc.; *U.S. Public*, pg. 226

CORTROSYN—Pharmaceutical—Organon Inc.; *Int'l*, pg. 48

CORUM—Watches—Movado Group, Inc.; *U.S. Public*, pg. 1140

CORVEL—Powder Coating Systems to Protect the Internal Surfaces of Gas & Oil Pipes—Morton International Inc.; *U.S. Public*, pg. 1134

CORVETTE—Car—Chevrolet Motor Div. General Motors Corp.; *U.S. Public*, pg. 720

CORVETTE VAC—Hand Vac—The Eureka Company; *Int'l*, pg. 440

CORVO—Wine—Paterno Imports Limited; *U.S. Private*, pg. 843

CORZIDE—Cardiovascular Therapy Product—Bristol-Myers Squibb Company; *U.S. Public*, pg. 253

CORZIDE—Beta-Blocking Agent & Diuretic For the Treatment of Hypertension—Bristol-Myers Squibb U.S. Pharmaceutical Group; *U.S. Public*, pg. 255

CORZYME—Diagnostic Products—Abbott Laboratories; *U.S. Public*, pg. 12

COSCAN DAVIDSON HOMES—Home Builder—Brookfield Homes; *Int'l*, pg. 228

COSCO—Fire Protection Systems—Cosco Fire Protection Inc.; *U.S. Public*, pg. 1795

COSCO—Folding Furniture, Housewares—Cosco, Inc.; *U.S. Private*, pg. 277

COSESSION & MODEM SHARE—Remote Communications—Artisoft, Inc.; *U.S. Public*, pg. 136

COSMA—Automotive Parts—Magna International Inc.; *Int'l*, pg. 829

COSME' PUF—Cotton Rounds—American White Cross; *U.S. Public*, pg. 694

COSMEGEN—Dactinomycin—Merck & Co., Inc.; *U.S. Public*, pg. 1090

COSMETAN—Sunglasses, Lenses, Frames—American Optical Corporation; *U.S. Private*, pg. 60

COSMETCO—Men's Grooming Prods. & Manicure Implements—The Cook Bates Division; *Int'l*, pg. 815

THE COSMETIC CENTER—Discount Retail Cosmetic Stores—The Cosmetic Center Inc.; *U.S. Private*, pg. 689

COSMIC—Cosmetics—International Cosmetics Co., Ltd.; *Int'l*, pg. 684

COSMIC—Main Distributing Frame—Lucent Technologies Inc.; *U.S. Public*, pg. 1017

COSMIC CALF—A Fortified Bovine Calf Serum—HyClone Laboratories Inc.; *Int'l*, pg. 1037

COSMIC WESTERN CLOTHING—Western Clothing—Swatch Watch U.S.A.; *Int'l*, pg. 1161

COSMICAR—Security Camera Lens—Asahi Optical Co., Ltd.; *Int'l*, pg. 85

COSMICAR—Television Optic—Pentax Corporation; *Int'l*, pg. 85

COSMO—Clock Radios, Alarm Clocks, Wall Clocks, Telephones, Task Lighting Products—Cosmo Communications Corporation; *U.S. Public*, pg. 451

COSMOLINE—Rust Preventive—Houghton International Inc.; *U.S. Private*, pg. 541

COSMOLON—Hook & Loop Fastener—YKK (U.S.A.); *Int'l*, pg. 1515

COSMOPOLITAN—Electric Screen—Da-Lite Screen Company, Inc.; *U.S. Private*, pg. 306

COSMOPOLITAN—Magazine—The Hearst Corporation; *U.S. Private*, pg. 515

COSMOPOLITAN—Magazine—Hearst Magazines Division; *U.S. Private*, pg. 516

COSMOPOLITAN—Magazine—The National Magazine Company Ltd.; *U.S. Private*, pg. 518

COSMOPOLITAN—Shower Heads—Speakman Company; *U.S. Private*, pg. 1021

COSMOS—Beauty Salon Furniture—Belvedere Company; *U.S. Private*, pg. 1008

COSMOS—TV Broadcasting—Cosmos Broadcasting Corp.; *U.S. Public*, pg. 992

COSMOS—Management System for Tracking Packages—FDX Corporation; *U.S. Public*, pg. 603

COSMOS—Budget Escorted Tours to Britain, Europe, USA, Canada & Hawaii—Globus & Cosmos; *U.S. Public*, pg. 458

COSNG—Electronic Identification Device—Amtech Corporation; *U.S. Public*, pg. 105

COSORB PROCESS—Production—KTI Group B.V.; *Int'l*, pg. 837

COSOURCING—NONE—Electronic Data Systems Corporation; *U.S. Public*, pg. 569

COSPEC—Remote Sensor—Barringer Technologies Inc.; *U.S. Public*, pg. 191

COSSACK—Men's Haircare Products—Carter-Wallace, Inc.; *U.S. Public*, pg. 309

COSSACK—NONE—Guinness Plc; *Int'l*, pg. 412

COSSACK—Vodka & Gin—M.S. Walker, Inc.; *U.S. Private*, pg. 1147

COST CUTTERS FAMILY HAIR CARE SHOPS—Value Price Beauty Salons—The Barbers, Hairstyling for Men & Women, Inc.; *U.S. Private*, pg. 115

COST PROBE—NONE—First DataBank; *U.S. Private*, pg. 515

COSTA CRUISES—Cruise Line—Carnival Corporation; *U.S. Public*, pg. 306

COSTA DEL SOL—Dinnerware—Dansk International Designs Ltd.; *U.S. Public*, pg. 261

COSTA DO SOL ROSE—Wine—M.S. Walker, Inc.; *U.S. Private*, pg. 1147

COSTER ENGINEERING—Water Purification & Vending Machines-Municipal, Industrial & Commercial—Hiniker Company; *U.S. Private*, pg. 530

COSTIMATOR SYSTEM—Computer-Aided Cost Estimating for Metal Working Mfrs.—Manufacturers Technologies, Inc.; *U.S. Private*, pg. 701

COSYFLOR—Cushion Vinyl Floorcoverings—Forbo Holding SA; *Int'l*, pg. 496

COSWORTH—High Performance Engines & Precision Alloy Castings—Vickers PLC; *Int'l*, pg. 1466

COSY COMFORT—Electric Blanket—The Glen Dimplex Group; *Int'l*, pg. 553

COT-1-DNA—NONE—Life Technologies, Inc.; *U.S. Public*, pg. 504

COTAZYM—Pharmaceutical—Organon Inc.; *Int'l*, pg. 48

COTAZYM-S—Pharmaceutical—Organon Inc.; *Int'l*, pg. 48

COTE D'OR—Chocolate—Kraft Jacobs Suchard AG; *U.S. Public*, pg. 1288

COTE D'OR—Chocolate—Kraft Jacobs Suchard; *U.S. Public*, pg. 1290

COTE D'OR—Chocolate Bar—Philip Morris Companies Inc.; *U.S. Public*, pg. 1287

COTE D'OR—Chemicals for Electro Plating—Technic Incorporated; *U.S. Private*, pg. 1071

COTILLION—Fragrance—Avon Products, Inc.; *U.S. Public*, pg. 155

COTRAN—Proprietary Airborne Mineral Systems—Barringer Technologies Inc.; *U.S. Public*, pg. 191

COTRAN—Pharmaceutical Grade Transfer Adhesive—3M; *U.S. Public*, pg. 1604

COTT—NONE—Cadbury Beverages; *Int'l*, pg. 248

COTTAGE—Interior Prefinished 3-Ply Plywood Paneling—Georgia-Pacific Corporation; *U.S. Public*, pg. 735

COTTAGE FRIES—Potato Chips—Borden, Inc.; *U.S. Private*, pg. 157

COTTAGE FRIES—Potato Chips—Wise Foods, Inc.; *U.S. Private*, pg. 157

COTTAGE HEARTH—Bakery Items—Certified Grocers of California; *U.S. Private*, pg. 226

COTTMAN—Transmission Systems—Cottman Transmission Systems, Inc.; *U.S. Private*, pg. 278

COTTON BOLL—Twist Tobaccos—Conwood Company L.P.; *U.S. Private*, pg. 272

COTTON CORDELL—Fishing Lures—EBSCO Industries, Inc.; *U.S. Private*, pg. 358

COTTON EXPRESS—Pickers—Case Corporation; *U.S. Public*, pg. 311

COTTON GROVE—Apparel—Merchant Capital Group Ltd.; *U.S. Private*, pg. 732

COTTON SUPPLY COMPANY—Men's & Women's Cotton Apparel—Woolworth Corporation; *U.S. Public*, pg. 1777

COTTON'S BREAD—Bread—Interstate Brands Corporation; *U.S. Public*, pg. 909

COTTONETTES—Cosmetic Squares, Rounds, Swabs—American White Cross; *U.S. Public*, pg. 694

COTTOSINT—Fabric Hand Modifier—Henkel Corporation; *Int'l*, pg. 610

COTY 24—Lipstick—Coty Inc.; *Int'l*, pg. 185

COUCH-RITE II—Cylinder Machine Couch Roll—Beloit Corporation; *U.S. Public*, pg. 789

COUGAR—Focus Lock Binoculars—Swift Instruments, Inc.; *U.S. Private*, pg. 1058

COUGAR—Printing Papers—Weyerhaeuser Company; *U.S. Public*, pg. 1764

COUGAR NATURAL OPAQUE TEXT & COVER—Printing Papers—Weyerhaeuser Company; *U.S. Public*, pg. 1764

COUGAR OPAQUE-LASER GUARANTEED—Electronic Publishing Papers—Weyerhaeuser Company; *U.S. Public*, pg. 1764

COUGAR OPAQUE TEXT & COVER—Printing Papers—Weyerhaeuser Company; *U.S. Public*, pg. 1764

COUGH CAPS—Cough Capsules—SmithKline Beecham plc; *Int'l*, pg. 1264

COULARRAY—Electrochemical detector—ESA, Inc.; *U.S. Private*, pg. 354

COULEUR RICH—Hydrating Lipstick—Cosmair, Inc.; *Int'l*, pg. 818

COULOCHEM—Electrochemical detector—ESA, Inc.; *U.S. Private*, pg. 354

COUNSELOR—Scales—Newell Co.; *U.S. Public*, pg. 1176

COUNSELOR/BORG SCALES—Scales—Sunbeam Corporation; *U.S. Public*, pg. 1533

COUNT CHOCULA—Cereal—General Mills, Inc.; *U.S. Public*, pg. 717

COUNT IMPERIAL—Sporting Goods—Brunswick Bowling & Billiards Corp.; *U.S. Public*, pg. 265

COUNT PUSHKIN—Vodka—Distillers Corporation S.A.; *Int'l*, pg. 1129

COUNT-ALL—Automatic Bacterial Colony Counter—Fisher Scientific Company; *U.S. Private*, pg. 658

COUNTER—Insecticide—American Home Products Corporation; *U.S. Public*, pg. 79

COUNTER CAP—Plastic Cups—The West Company, Incorporated; *U.S. Public*, pg. 1755

COUNTER CAP WITH DESIGN—Plastic Caps—The West Company, Incorporated; *U.S. Public*, pg. 1755

COUNTER MATE—Plastic Grocery Bags—Sonoco Products Company; *U.S. Public*, pg. 1485

COUNTER POINT—Indoor Illuminated Sign Series—American Sign & Marketing Services, Inc.; *U.S. Public*, pg. 1309

COUNTERBOY—Tape Dispensing Machines—Ascom Hasler Mailing Systems, Inc.; *Int'l*, pg. 86

COUNTERLINE—Retail Centers for Electr-Mechanical Products—Johnson Controls, Inc., Controls Group; *U.S. Public*, pg. 932

COUNTERPAIN—NONE—Bristol-Myers Squibb Company; *U.S. Public*, pg. 253

COUNTERPAK—Check Out Counter Bags—Tenneco Packaging, Consumer Products Group; *U.S. Public*, pg. 1579

COUNTERPOINT—Automatic Tag Deactivation Equipment—Checkpoint Systems Inc.; *U.S. Public*, pg. 343

COUNTERPOINT—Magazine—Reed Business Information Pty. Limited; *Int'l*, pg. 1094

COUNTERSAVER—Microwave Ovens—General Electric Canada Inc.; *U.S. Public*, pg. 713

COUNTESS—Currency Counter—Brandt, Inc.; *Int'l*, pg. 387

COUNTESS—Vans—Coachmen Industries, Inc.; *U.S. Public*, pg. 387

COUNTESS—Conditioning Shampoos—SmithKline Beecham plc; *Int'l*, pg. 1264

COUNTESS ISSERLYN—Cosmetics—Charles of the Ritz Group Ltd.; *U.S. Private*, pg. 689

COUNTRY ACCENTS—Rugs—Couristan Inc.; *U.S. Private*, pg. 279

COUNTRY AMERICA—Magazine—Meredith Corporation; *U.S. Public*, pg. 1094

COUNTRY BEST—Potatoes—Agway, Inc.; *U.S. Private*, pg. 27

COUNTRY BLEND—Chewing Tobacco—Swisher International Group, Inc.; *U.S. Public*, pg. 1543

COUNTRY BREEZE—Perfume—Avon Products, Inc.; *U.S. Public*, pg. 155

COUNTRY BUFFET—Buffet Restaurants in Colorado—Buffets, Inc.; *U.S. Public*, pg. 267

COUNTRY CANE—Sugar—Refined Sugars, Inc.; *Int'l*, pg. 699

COUNTRY CASUAL—Rattan Furniture—Avon Workshop Ficks Reed; *U.S. Private*, pg. 102

COUNTRY CAT—Cat Food—Triple F, Inc.; *U.S. Private*, pg. 1104

COUNTRY CHURN—Margarine—Alliant Foodservice, Inc.; *U.S. Private*, pg. 244

COUNTRY CLOTHES—Women's Apparel—Pendleton Woolen Mills, Inc.; *U.S. Private*, pg. 848

COUNTRY CLUB—Fertilizer—Lebanon Seaboard Corporation; *U.S. Private*, pg. 656

COUNTRY CLUB—Malt Liquor—Pearl Brewing Company; *U.S. Private*, pg. 954

COUNTRY CLUB BOURBON—Bourbon Whiskey—Laird & Company; *U.S. Private*, pg. 642

COUNTRY CLUB HOTELS—Hotels—Whitbread PLC; *Int'l*, pg. 1498

COUNTRY COLOR—Paint—Pratt & Lambert United, Inc.; *U.S. Public*, pg. 1466

COUNTRY COLORS COLLECTION—Authentic Folk Colors in Paints & Dyes—Koh-I-Noor, Inc.; *U.S. Private*, pg. 629

COUNTRY COMPANIES—Insurance—Country Life Insurance Company; *U.S. Private*, pg. 278

COUNTRY CORN FLAKES—Breakfast Foods—General Mills, Inc.; *U.S. Public*, pg. 717

COUNTRY COTTAGE—Frozen & Chilled Fruit & Vegetables—The Albert Fisher Group PLC; *Int'l*, pg. 491

COUNTRY COTTONS—Apparel—Cross Creek Apparel, Inc.; *U.S. Public*, pg. 1413

COUNTRY COUNTDOWN USA—Country Music Radio Program—Westwood One Entertainment; *U.S. Public*, pg. 1763

COUNTRY COUNTDOWN USA—Country Music Programming—Westwood One, Inc.; *U.S. Public*, pg. 1763

COUNTRY COURT—Rattan Furniture—Avon Workshop Ficks Reed; *U.S. Private*, pg. 102

COUNTRY COUSINS—Figurines—Stanhome Inc.; *U.S. Public*, pg. 1508

COUNTRY CRISP—Potato Chips—Clover Club Foods, Inc.; *U.S. Private*, pg. 469

COUNTRY CRISP FOODS—Potato Chips & Corn Snacks—Granny Goose Foods, Inc.; *U.S. Private*, pg. 469

COUNTRY CROCK—Margarine—Unilever Plc; *Int'l*, pg. 1433

COUNTRY CROCK CHEESE—Cheese Product Spread—Chesebrough-Pond's; *Int'l*, pg. 1436

COUNTRY CUPBOARD—Fragrance, Dusting Powder—Avon Products, Inc.; *U.S. Public*, pg. 155

COUNTRY CUPBOARD—Meats—Carl Buddig & Company; *U.S. Private*, pg. 178

COUNTRY DAYBREAK—Eggs—Rose Acre Farms; *U.S. Private*, pg. 944

COUNTRY FAIR—Rattan Furniture—Avon Workshop Ficks Reed; *U.S. Private*, pg. 102

COUNTRY GARDEN—Rugs—Couristan Inc.; *U.S. Private*, pg. 279

COUNTRY GENERAL STORES—Retailer—ConAgra, Inc.; *U.S. Public*, pg. 425

COUNTRY GOLD SATURDAY NIGHT—Country Music Radio Program—Westwood One Entertainment; *U.S. Public*, pg. 1763

COUNTRY GOLD SATURDAY NIGHT—Country Music Programming—Westwood One, Inc.; *U.S. Public*, pg. 1763

COUNTRY HARVEST—Crackers—Culinar Inc.; *Int'l*, pg. 348

COUNTRY HARVEST—NONE—Weston Bakeries Limited; *Int'l*, pg. 1495

COUNTRY HARVEST—Baked Goods—George Weston Limited; *Int'l*, pg. 1494

COUNTRY HEARTH—Baking Goods—The Earthgrains Company; *U.S. Public*, pg. 547

COUNTRY HEARTH—Bread, Rolls & Croutons—Metz Baking Company; *U.S. Private*, pg. 1022

COUNTRY HEARTH—Bread, Rolls, Croutons—Metz Baking Company (WI); *U.S. Private*, pg. 1022

COUNTRY HOE-DOWN—Greeting Cards, Invtns., Thank You Notes, Caldrs.,Party Goods & Decorations—American Greetings Corporation; *U.S. Public*, pg. 77

COUNTRY HOME—Magazine—Country Home Magazine; *U.S. Public*, pg. 1094

COUNTRY HOME—Magazine—Meredith Corporation; *U.S. Public*, pg. 1094

COUNTRY HOMES & INTERIORS—Home Interest Magazine—IPC Magazines Limited; *Int'l*, pg. 651

COUNTRY HOSPITALITY—Franchised Family Chain—Country Kitchen International, Inc.; *U.S. Private*, pg. 624

COUNTRY INN—Vegetable & Rice Dishes—Uncle Ben's, Inc.; *U.S. Private*, pg. 707

COUNTRY INN PASTA & SAUCE—Pasta—Uncle Ben's, Inc.; *U.S. Private*, pg. 707

COUNTRY JOURNAL—Periodical—Cowles Enthusiast Media, Inc.; *U.S. Private*, pg. 281

COUNTRY JUNCTION—Telephones—Lucent Technologies Inc.; *U.S. Public*, pg. 1017

COUNTRY KENNEL—Dog Food—Triple F, Inc.; *U.S. Private*, pg. 1104

COUNTRY KITCHEN—Pancake Syrup—Kraft Foods, Inc.; *U.S. Public*, pg. 1287

COUNTRY KITCHEN—Bread Rolls, Donuts, English Muffins, Brown & Serve—Lepage Bakery, Inc.; *U.S. Private*, pg. 660

COUNTRY KITCHEN—Syrup—Philip Morris Companies Inc.; *U.S. Public*, pg. 1287

COUNTRY KITCHEN RESTAURANTS—Restaurants—Carlson Companies, Inc.; *U.S. Private*, pg. 211

COUNTRY LIFE—Country Pursuits & Property Magazine—IPC Magazines Limited; *Int'l*, pg. 651

COUNTRY LIVING—Magazine—The Hearst Corporation; *U.S. Private*, pg. 515

COUNTRY LIVING—Magazine—Hearst Magazines Division; *U.S. Private*, pg. 516

COUNTRY LIVING—Magazine—The National Magazine Company Ltd.; *U.S. Private*, pg. 518

COUNTRY LODGING BY CARLSON—(Limited Service Hotels)—Country Kitchen International, Inc.; *U.S. Private*, pg. 624

COUNTRY LOFT—Acrylic Enamel Spray & Brush On Paints—Sherwin-Williams Diversified Brands, Inc.; *U.S. Public*, pg. 1466

COUNTRY MA...—...Dean Pickles & Specialty Products...; *U.S. Public*, pg. 490

COUNTRY MANOR—Perry—Matthew Clark Brands; *Int'l*, pg. 848

COUNTRY MANOR—Food Products—P & C Food Markets, Inc.; *U.S. Public*, pg. 1270

COUNTRY MORNING—Margarine & Spread—Land O'Lakes, Inc.; *U.S. Private*, pg. 645

COUNTRY NATURAL—Cosmetics, Skin Care—Avon Products, Inc.; *U.S. Public*, pg. 155

COUNTRY OAK—PVC Coated Aluminum Siding—Alcoa Building Products, Inc.; *U.S. Public*, pg. 61

COUNTRY PEACH SPICE—Herb Tea—Celestial Seasonings; *U.S. Public*, pg. 319

COUNTRY PLACE—Plywood, Lumber, Wood & Wood Fiber Products—Georgia-Pacific Corporation; *U.S. Public*, pg. 735

COUNTRY PREP—Entertainment News Programming—Westwood One, Inc.; *U.S. Public*, pg. 1763

COUNTRY PRIDE—Poultry—ConAgra, Inc.; *U.S. Public*, pg. 425

COUNTRY PRIDE—Poultry—ConAgra Poultry Co.; *U.S. Public*, pg. 427

COUNTRY PRIDE—NONE—Ranks Hovis McDougall Limited; *Int'l*, pg. 1395

COUNTRY RASPBERRY—Sparkling Mineral Water—Clearly Canadian Beverage Corp.; *Int'l*, pg. 297

COUNTRY SAMPLER—Consumer Magazine Featuring Handcrafted Items—Sampler Publications Inc.; *U.S. Private*, pg. 963

COUNTRY SAMPLER'S COUNTRY BUSINESS—Business Publication for Small Retail Stores—Sampler Publications Inc.; *U.S. Private*, pg. 963

COUNTRY SAMPLER'S DECORATING IDEAS—Consumer Magazine Featuring Do-It-Yourself Home Decorating Projects—Sampler Publications Inc.; *U.S. Private*, pg. 963

Brand Name Index

COUNTRY SAMPLER'S WEST—Consumer Magazine Featuring Western Decorating—Sampler Publications Inc.; *U.S. Private*, pg. 963

COUNTRY SIX PACK—Seasonal—Westwood One Entertainment; *U.S. Public*, pg. 1763

COUNTRY SIX PACK—Country Music Programming—Westwood One, Inc.; *U.S. Public*, pg. 1763

COUNTRY SKILLET—Frozen Chicken—ConAgra Frozen Food Company; *U.S. Public*, pg. 427

COUNTRY SKILLET—Catfish, Poultry, Eggs—ConAgra, Inc.; *U.S. Public*, pg. 425

COUNTRY SOPHISTICATES—Womens' Apparel—Pendleton Woolen Mills, Inc.; *U.S. Private*, pg. 848

COUNTRY SPECIAL EVENTS—Live Country Event Programming—Westwood One, Inc.; *U.S. Public*, pg. 1763

COUNTRY SPLIT—NONE—Quality Bakers New Zealand Ltd.; *Int'l*, pg. 556

COUNTRY SQUIRE—Telephones—Lucent Technologies, Inc.; *U.S. Public*, pg. 1017

COUNTRY SQUIRE—Truck Tires—Universal Cooperatives, Inc.; *U.S. Private*, pg. 1127

THE COUNTRY SQUIRE—Spicy Beef Pattie—Harker's Distribution, Inc.; *U.S. Private*, pg. 502

COUNTRY STORE—Instant Mashed Potatoes—Borden, Inc.; *U.S. Public*, pg. 157

COUNTRY SUBURBAN—Women's Apparel—Hartmarx Corporation; *U.S. Public*, pg. 795

COUNTRY TIME—NONE—Cadbury Beverages; *Int'l*, pg. 248

COUNTRY TIME—Lemonade—Cadbury Schweppes p.l.c.; *Int'l*, pg. 247

COUNTRY TIME—Soft Drink Mix—Philip Morris Companies Inc.; *U.S. Public*, pg. 1287

COUNTRY TIME DRINK MIX—Soft Drink—Grant-Lydick Beverage Co.; *U.S. Private*, pg. 470

COUNTRY TIME LEMONADE—Lemonade—The Coca-Cola Bottling Co. of New York, Inc.; *U.S. Public*, pg. 393

COUNTRY TIME LEMONADE—Soft Drink—Grant-Lydick Beverage Co.; *U.S. Private*, pg. 470

COUNTRY TOUCH—Clothing—Harcrest International, Ltd.; *U.S. Private*, pg. 500

COUNTRY TRADITIONALS—Men's Apparel—Pendleton Woolen Mills, Inc.; *U.S. Private*, pg. 848

COUNTRY WALKING—Magazine—EMAP Pursuit Publishing; *Int'l*, pg. 451

COUNTRY WEEKLY—Newspaper—American Media, Inc.; *U.S. Public*, pg. 87

COUNTRY WOODS—Custom Made Wood Blinds—Hunter Douglas, Inc.; *Int'l*, pg. 639

COUNTRY'S CUTTING EDGE—Country Music Radio Program—Westwood One Entertainment; *U.S. Public*, pg. 1763

COUNTRY'S CUTTING EDGE—Country Music Programming—Westwood One, Inc.; *U.S. Public*, pg. 1763

COUNTRYS DELIGHT—Food Products—Certified Grocers Midwest, Inc.; *U.S. Private*, pg. 226

COUNTRY'S INSIDE TRAK—Country Music Radio Program—Westwood One Entertainment; *U.S. Public*, pg. 1763

COUNTRY'S INSIDE TRAK—Stars of Country Music Programming—Westwood One, Inc.; *U.S. Public*, pg. 1763

COUNTRYSIDE—Salads—Hormel Foods Corp.; *U.S. Public*, pg. 840

COUNTY FAIR—Plywood, Lumber, Wood & Wood Fiber Products—Georgia-Pacific Corporation; *U.S. Public*, pg. 735

COUNTY LINE—Cheese—ConAgra, Inc.; *U.S. Public*, pg. 425

COUNTY MARKET—Retail Grocery—Covington Foods, Inc.; *U.S. Private*, pg. 280

COUNTY POST STORES—Retail Stores—Quality Stores Inc.; *U.S. Private*, pg. 899

COUNTY SEAT—Retail Clothing Stores—County Seat Stores, Inc.; *U.S. Private*, pg. 279

COUNTY SQUIRE—Manufactured Homes—Clayton Homes, Inc.; *U.S. Public*, pg. 382

COUPE FIAT—Car—Fiat Auto Ireland Ltd.; *Int'l*, pg. 481

COUPLED PLASMA—NONE—Lam Research Corporation; *U.S. Public*, pg. 975

COUPLES—Greeting Cards, Gift Wrap Paper & Ceramic Plates—American Greetings Corporation; *U.S. Public*, pg. 77

COUPOLET—Fittings—Bonney Forge Corporation; *U.S. Private*, pg. 156

COURAGE—Bitter Ale—Foster's Brewing Group Limited; *Int'l*, pg. 500

COURCHEVEL—Neckwear—The Apparel Group, Ltd.; *U.S. Private*, pg. 78

COURIER—Inserter—Bell & Howell Holdings; *U.S. Public*, pg. 201

COURIER—Tires—Bridgestone/Firestone, Inc.; *Int'l*, pg. 213

THE COURIER—NONE—Life Technologies, Inc.; *U.S. Public*, pg. 504

COURIER-JOURNAL—Newspaper—The Courier-Journal Louisville Times Co.; *U.S. Public*, pg. 700

COURIER PAK—Overnight Envelope for Documents—FDX Corporation; *U.S. Public*, pg. 603

COURSE SETTER 21—Autopilot Systems—Benmar Marine Electronics, Inc.; *U.S. Private*, pg. 133

COURSE SETTER 21R—Autopilot Systems—Benmar Marine Electronics, Inc.; *U.S. Private*, pg. 133

COURT CHAMPION—Sport Bag—Ektelon; *U.S. Private*, pg. 884

COURT SOURCE—Sporting Goods—Nixdorff Krein Industries Inc.; *U.S. Private*, pg. 799

COURTE - PAILLE—Restaurants—Accor S.A.; *Int'l*, pg. 20

COURTESY COACH—Pick-Up Vehicle—Thrifty Rent-a-Car System, Inc.; *U.S. Public*, pg. 354

COURTLAND—Coated Offset Matte—Champion International Corp.; *U.S. Public*, pg. 333

COURTLAND GLOSS—Coated Web—Champion International Corp.; *U.S. Public*, pg. 333

COURTLAND MATTE—Coated Web—Champion International Corp.; *U.S. Public*, pg. 333

COURTOIS—Musical Instruments—G. Leblanc Corporation; *U.S. Private*, pg. 656

COURTYARD BY MARRIOTT—Hotel Chain—Marriott International, Inc.; *U.S. Public*, pg. 1047

COURTYARD BY MARRIOTT—NONE—Sunstone Hotel Investors, Inc.; *U.S. Public*, pg. 1536

COURTYARD CLUB—NONE—Marriott International, Inc.; *U.S. Public*, pg. 1047

COURVOISIER COGNACS—Liqueur—Allied Domecq PLC; *Int'l*, pg. 62

COUSINS SUBS—Uniquely Prepared Submarine Sandwiches—Cousins Submarines; *U.S. Private*, pg. 280

COUSINS SUBS—Wearable Clothing Line—Cousins Submarines; *U.S. Private*, pg. 280

COVA—Decorative Films—Forbo Holding SA; *Int'l*, pg. 496

COVANDUR—NONE—Carpenter Technology Corporation; *U.S. Public*, pg. 307

COVENTRY—Corporate Trademark—Coventry Corporation; *U.S. Public*, pg. 454

COVENTRY—Holding Company—Del Webb's Coventry Homes; *U.S. Public*, pg. 495

COVENTRY—Lightweight Coated Publishing Papers—Weyerhaeuser Company; *U.S. Public*, pg. 1764

COVENTRY & CASE—NONE—American Woodmark Corporation; *U.S. Public*, pg. 96

COVER CAT—Cat Box Filler—Golden Cat Corporation; *U.S. Public*, pg. 1360

COVER GIRL—Cosmetics—The Procter & Gamble Company; *U.S. Public*, pg. 1330

COVER GIRL COSMETICS—NONE—Procter & Gamble Cosmetics Co.; *U.S. Public*, pg. 1330

COVER GIRL POWDER—Liquid, Pressed & Tube—Cover Girl Cosmetics; *U.S. Public*, pg. 1330

COVER-PAD—Sterile Surgical Dressings—Beiersdorf, Inc.; *Int'l*, pg. 182

COVER PERFECT—Paint—ICI Paints; *Int'l*, pg. 664

COVER-ROLL—Adhesive Gauze—Beiersdorf, Inc.; *Int'l*, pg. 182

COVER-ROLL STRETCH—Non-Woven Bandages—Beiersdorf, Inc.; *Int'l*, pg. 182

COVER-STAIN—Oil Base Primer-Sealer—Wm. Zinsser & Co., Inc.; *U.S. Public*, pg. 1358

COVER-STRIP—Wound Closure Stripe—Beiersdorf, Inc.; *Int'l*, pg. 182

COVER-UP—Protective Apparel—Eastco Industrial Safety Corp.; *U.S. Public*, pg. 548

COVER YOUR OWN—Buttons—Prym-Dritz Corporation; *Int'l*, pg. 1499

COVERAGEPLUS—NONE—QUALCOMM; *U.S. Public*, pg. 1348

COVERALL—Polyethylene Sheeting—Warp Brothers; *U.S. Private*, pg. 412

COVERLET—Dressings—Beiersdorf, Inc.; *Int'l*, pg. 182

COVERLET O.R.—Adhesive Surgical Dressings—Beiersdorf, Inc.; *Int'l*, pg. 182

COVERLIGHT—Protective Coverings Coated Fabrics—Reeves International; *U.S. Private*, pg. 507

COVEROHM—Resistor Paste—Ferro Corporation; *U.S. Public*, pg. 618

COVERT—Snaps—York Plant; *U.S. Public*, pg. 444

COVI-OX—Mixed Tocopherols, Antioxidant—Henkel Corporation; *Int'l*, pg. 610

COVINGTON FARMS—Fresh & Frozen Chicken—Sanderson Farms, Inc.; *U.S. Public*, pg. 1430

COVINGTON LTD INC—Jeans—Game Winner, Inc.; *U.S. Private*, pg. 280

COVITOL—Vitamin E Products—Henkel Corporation; *Int'l*, pg. 610

COVO—Shortening—Lever Brothers Co.; *Int'l*, pg. 1435

COVO—Shortening—Unilever Plc; *Int'l*, pg. 1433

COWARD-MCCANN—Books—The Putnam & Grosset Group; *Int'l*, pg. 1027

COWBOY DESIGN—Solder in Wire Form—Litton Industries, Inc.; *U.S. Public*, pg. 1002

COWLES—Syndicate—The Hearst Corporation; *U.S. Private*, pg. 515

COWLES BUSINESS MEDIA—Business to Business Magazines—Cowles Media Company; *U.S. Private*, pg. 280

COWLES ENTHUSIASTS—Special Interest Magazines—Cowles Media Company; *U.S. Private*, pg. 280

COX—Pressure Treaded Wood Products—Cox Wood Preserving Co.; *U.S. Private*, pg. 283

COX—Instruments—Ketema, Inc.; *U.S. Private*, pg. 604

COX—Turbine Meters—Schutte & Koerting Division; *U.S. Private*, pg. 604

COXISTAC—Salinomycin—Pfizer Inc.; *U.S. Public*, pg. 1281

COYOTE—Performance Headers—Hooker Industries; *U.S. Private*, pg. 538

COYOTE—Tequila—The House of Seagram; *Int'l*, pg. 1217

COZY CHUMS—Greeting Cards—American Greetings Corporation; *U.S. Public*, pg. 77

COZY COTTAGE—Children's Bed—Rubbermaid Incorporated; *U.S. Public*, pg. 1411

COZY COUPE—NONE—Rubbermaid Incorporated; *U.S. Public*, pg. 1411

COZY KITTENS—Greeting Cards—American Greetings Corporation; *U.S. Public*, pg. 77

CRAB DELIGHTS—Surimi Analog Items—Louis Kemp Seafood Co.; *U.S. Public*, pg. 1652

CRAB DELIGHTS—Imitation Crab Meat—Louis Kemp Seafood Company; *U.S. Public*, pg. 1652

CRABTREE—Electrical Products—Hanson PLC; *Int'l*, pg. 592

CRACK-BACK—Films Coating—Avery Dennison Corporation; *U.S. Public*, pg. 152

CRACKA DIP—Dairy Products—Q.U.F. Industries Ltd.; *Int'l*, pg. 1074

CRACKER BARREL—Cheese—Kraft Foods Inc.; *U.S. Public*, pg. 1288

CRACKER BARREL—Cheese—Philip Morris Companies Inc.; *U.S. Public*, pg. 1287

CRACKER BARREL OLD COUNTRY STORE—Combination Restaurants & Gift Shops—Cracker Barrel Old Country Store, Inc.; *U.S. Public*, pg. 455

CRACKER JACK—NONE—Borden Foods Canada; *U.S. Private*, pg. 159

CRACKER JACK—NONE—Borden Foods Co.; *U.S. Private*, pg. 158

CRACKER JACK—Carmel Popcorn & Nuts—Borden, Inc.; *U.S. Private*, pg. 157

CRACKER KING—Flour—ADM Milling Co.; *U.S. Public*, pg. 128

CRACKLIN' OAT BRAN—Ready-Sweetened High-Fiber Cereal with Oat & Wheat Bran—Kellogg Company; *U.S. Public*, pg. 947

CRAFT—Eraser—Dixon Ticonderoga Company; *U.S. Public*, pg. 514

THE CRAFT WORKS—Craft Store—Genovese Drug Stores, Inc.; *U.S. Public*, pg. 730

CRAFTERGUITARS—Guitars—Hohner/HSS Inc.; *U.S. Private*, pg. 533

CRAFTERS GALLERY—Needlework & Crafts—Mary Maxim, Inc.; *U.S. Private*, pg. 716

CRAFTEX MILLS—Upholstery Materials—Craftex Mills Inc. of Pennsylvania; *U.S. Private*, pg. 284

CRAFTMARK—Exterior Aluminum Siding, Soffit & Facing—Reynolds Metals Company; *U.S. Public*, pg. 1385

CRAFTMASTER—Water Heaters—Southcorp Holdings Ltd.; *Int'l*, pg. 1287

CRAFTMATIC—Adjustable Beds—Craftmatic Industries, Inc.; *U.S. Private*, pg. 284

CRAFTSMAN—Plywood—Georgia-Pacific Corporation; *U.S. Public*, pg. 735

CRAFTSMAN—Power Tools—Ryobi Motor Products; *Int'l*, pg. 1151

CRAFTSMAN—NONE—Sears, Roebuck and Co.; *U.S. Public*, pg. 1452

CRAFTSMAN—Printing Paper—Westvaco Corporation; *U.S. Public*, pg. 1762

CRAFTSMAN II—Lumber & Wood Products—Georgia-Pacific Corporation; *U.S. Public*, pg. 735

CRAGAR—Wheels—Cragar Industries, Inc.; *U.S. Public*, pg. 456

CRAGAR LITE—Wheels—Cragar Industries, Inc.; *U.S. Public*, pg. 456

CRAGGANMORE—NONE—Guinness Plc; *Int'l*, pg. 412

CRAIN COMPUTER SERVICES—Computerized Subscription Services—Crain Communications, Inc.; *U.S. Private*, pg. 284

CRAIN NEWS SERVICE—News & Feature Service—Crain Communications, Inc.; *U.S. Private*, pg. 284

CRAIN'S CHICAGO BUSINESS—Newspaper—Crain Communications, Inc.; *U.S. Private*, pg. 284

CRAIN'S CLEVELAND BUSINESS—Newspaper—Crain Communications, Inc.; *U.S. Private*, pg. 284

CRAIN'S DETROIT BUSINESS—Newspaper—Crain Communications, Inc.; *U.S. Private*, pg. 284

CRAIN'S NEW YORK BUSINESS—Newspaper—Crain Communications, Inc.; *U.S. Private*, pg. 284

CRAIN'S LIST RENTAL SERVICE—Subscription List Rental Service—Crain Communications, Inc.; *U.S. Private*, pg. 284

CRAISINS—Sweetened Dried Cranberries—Ocean Spray Cranberries, Inc.; *U.S. Private*, pg. 811

CRAN—Cranberry Juice Drinks—Ocean Spray Cranberries, Inc.; *U.S. Private*, pg. 811

CRAN B-Q—Barbecue Sauce—Ocean Spray Cranberries, Inc.; *U.S. Private*, pg. 811

CRAN CURRANT—Black Currant Cranberry Juice Drink—Ocean Spray Cranberries, Inc.; *U.S. Private*, pg. 811

CRAN ORANGE—Cranberry Orange Juice Drink—Ocean Spray Cranberries, Inc.; *U.S. Private*, pg. 811

CRANAPPLE—Cranberry Apple Drink, Low Calorie Drink—Ocean Spray Cranberries, Inc.; *U.S. Private*, pg. 811

CRANBERRY—NONE—Celestial Seasonings; *U.S. Public*, pg. 319

CRANBERRY COVE—Herb Tea—Celestial Seasonings; pg. 319

CRANBLUEBERRY—Blueberry Cranberry Drink—Ocean Spray Cranberries, Inc.; *U.S. Private*, pg. 811

CRANCHERRY—Cranberry Cherry Drink—Ocean Spray Cranberries, Inc.; *U.S. Private*, pg. 811

CRANE—Potato Chips—Borden, Inc.; *U.S. Private*, pg. 157

CRANE CREST—Business Letterhead & Printing Grades—Crane & Co., Inc.; *U.S. Private*, pg. 286

CRANE-FOIL—Flexible Graphite—John Crane Mechanical Seals; *Int'l*, pg. 1339

CRANEGLAS—Glass Fiber Paper—Crane & Co., Inc.; *U.S. Private*, pg. 286

CRANEMASTER—Cranes—Abell-Howe Company; *U.S. Private*, pg. 10

CRANES BOND—Business Letterhead & Printing Grades—Crane & Co., Inc.; *U.S. Private*, pg. 286

CRANFRUIT—Sauces—Ocean Spray Cranberries, Inc.; *U.S. Private*, pg. 811

CRANGEL—Cranberry Softgels—Ocean Spray Cranberries, Inc.; *U.S. Private*, pg. 811

CRANGRAPE—Grape Cranberry Drink—Ocean Spray Cranberries, Inc.; *U.S. Private*, pg. 811

CRANICOT—Cranberry Apricot Juice Drink—Ocean Spray Cranberries, Inc.; *U.S. Private*, pg. 811

CRANK-UPS—Tower for Antenna—Telex Communications, Inc.; *U.S. Private*, pg. 1074

CRANORANGE—Cranberry Orange Relish—Ocean Spray Cranberries, Inc.; *U.S. Private*, pg. 811

CRANORANGE—Cranberry Orange Sauce—Ocean Spray Cranberries, Inc.; *U.S. Private*, pg. 811

CRANRASPBERRY—Raspberry Cranberry Drink—Ocean Spray Cranberries, Inc.; *U.S. Private*, pg. 811

CRANRASPBERRY—Cranberry Raspberry Jellied Sauce—Ocean Spray Cranberries, Inc.; *U.S. Private*, pg. 811

CRANSTRAWBERRY—Cranberry Strawberry Juice Drink—Ocean Spray Cranberries, Inc.; *U.S. Private*, pg. 811

CRANTASIA—NONE—Ocean Spray Cranberries, Inc.; *U.S. Private*, pg. 811

CRANTASTIC—Cranberry Based Fruit Punch Drink—Ocean Spray Cranberries, Inc.; *U.S. Private*, pg. 811

CRAPPIEMATIC—Crappie Fishing System Including Rods and Reels—Martin Reels, A Division of Zebco; *U.S. Public*, pg. 265

CRAQUINETTE—Cracker—Danone Group; *Int'l*, pg. 379

CRATE & BARREL—Specialty Housewares Stores—Euromarket Designs, Inc.; *U.S. Private*, pg. 384

CRATEC—Glass Fibers Chopped Strands—Owens Corning; *U.S. Public*, pg. 1236

CRATEC PLUS—Chopped Strand Mat—Owens Corning; *U.S. Public*, pg. 1236

CRATHCO—Beverage Dispenser—Grindmaster Corporation; *U.S. Private*, pg. 482

CRAVAT BY MR. R—NONE—Tandy Brands Accessories, Inc.; *U.S. Public*, pg. 1560

CRAVE THE WAVE—NONE—Ocean Spray Cranberries, Inc.; *U.S. Private*, pg. 811

CRAVEN—Cigarettes—Rothmans UK Holdings Limited; *Int'l*, pg. 1129

CRAWDAD—Fishing Boat—The Canadian Coleman Co., Ltd.; *U.S. Private*, pg. 691

CRAWDAD XT—Fishing Boat—The Canadian Coleman Co., Ltd.; *U.S. Private*, pg. 691

CRAWFORD'S—Scotch—Shieffelin Somerset Co.; *Int'l*, pg. 412

CRAY—Supercomputers—Cray Research; *U.S. Public*, pg. 1473

CRAY J90—NONE—Silicon Graphics, Inc.; *U.S. Public*, pg. 1473

CRAY T90—NONE—Silicon Graphics, Inc.; *U.S. Public*, pg. 1473

CRAY T3E—NONE—Silicon Graphics, Inc.; *U.S. Public*, pg. 1473

CRAYOLA—Crayons, Chalks, Clay, Markers, Activity Sets—Binney & Smith Inc.; *U.S. Private*, pg. 496

CRAYOLA—Crayons, Markers, Coloured Pencils, Activity Kits, Craft Paint—Binney & Smith Ltd.; *U.S. Private*, pg. 496

CRAYOLA—Crayons & Markers—Hallmark Cards, Inc.; *U.S. Private*, pg. 495

CRAYOLA CRAFT—Kits and Modelling Refills—Binney & Smith Ltd.; *U.S. Private*, pg. 496

CRAYOLA PRE SCHOOL—Art Material & Kits—Binney & Smith Ltd.; *U.S. Private*, pg. 496

CRAZY BABY—Styling Wand—Clairol, Inc.; *U.S. Public*, pg. 254

CRAZY BREAD—Bread Brushed with Garlic Spread & Parmesan Cheese—Little Caesar Enterprises, Inc.; *U.S. Private*, pg. 671

CRAZY BRUSH—Dry Soft Styler—Clairol, Inc.; *U.S. Public*, pg. 254

CRAZY COW—Juice Blend—Alta-Dena Certified Dairy; *Int'l*, pg. 201

CRAZY CURL—Styling Wands & Brushes—Bristol-Myers Squibb Company; *U.S. Public*, pg. 253

CRAZY DUCK—Hairdryer—Salton/Maxim Housewares, Inc.; *U.S. Public*, pg. 1430

CRAZY KIWI PASSION—NONE—Ocean Spray Cranberries, Inc.; *U.S. Private*, pg. 811

CRAZY SPRAY CAN—Bubble Gum—Fleer-Skybox International Inc.; *U.S. Public*, pg. 1052

CRAZY TWIRL—Curling Iron—Clairol, Inc.; *U.S. Public*, pg. 254

CRAZY WORLD—Greeting Cards—American Greetings Corporation; *U.S. Public*, pg. 77

CREAM CORN STARCH—NONE—The Dial Corporation; *U.S. Public*, pg. 505

CREAM OF RICE—Cereal—RJR Nabisco Holdings Corp.; *U.S. Public*, pg. 1354

CREAM OF TOMATO COUNTRY STYLE CUP-A-SOUP—Instant Soup Mix—Thomas J. Lipton Company; *Int'l*, pg. 1435

CREAM OF WHEAT—Cereal-Instant, Mix 'n Eat, Quick & Regular—Nabisco Inc.; *U.S. Public*, pg. 1355

CREAM OF WHEAT—Hot Cereal—RJR Nabisco Holdings Corp.; *U.S. Public*, pg. 1354

CREAMALIN—NONE—SmithKline Beecham Research Limited; *Int'l*, pg. 1266

CREAMETTE—Pasta/Noodles—Borden Foods Co.; *U.S. Private*, pg. 158

CREAMETTE—Pasta—Borden, Inc.; *U.S. Private*, pg. 157

CREAMETTE—Pasta Products—Borden Italian Foods; *U.S. Private*, pg. 158

CREAMLAND—Milk—Dean Foods Company; *U.S. Public*, pg. 489

CREAMSICLE BRAND—Ice Pops & Bars—Good Humor/Breyers Ice Cream; *Int'l*, pg. 1435

CREAMY CHICKEN FLAVOR VEGETABLE COUNTRY STYLE SOUP—Cup-A-Soup—Thomas J. Lipton Company; *Int'l*, pg. 1435

CREAMY DELUXE—Frosting—General Mills, Inc.; *U.S. Public*, pg. 717

CREAMY WHEAT—Hot Cereal—The Quaker Oats Company; *U.S. Public*, pg. 1347

CREANIT—Plastic Prods.—Rohm GmbH; *Int'l*, pg. 1454

CREAP—Cream Powder for Coffee—Morinaga Milk Industry Co., Ltd.; *Int'l*, pg. 895

CREATACARD—NONE—American Greetings Corporation; *U.S. Public*, pg. 77

CREATE—Service Mark—BASF Corporation Fiber Products Division; *Int'l*, pg. 105

CREATE-A-PRINT—Self Contained Enlargement Center—Eastman Kodak Company; *U.S. Public*, pg. 550

CREATE 'N COLOR—Children's Rubber Stampers—Mattel Games/Puzzles; *U.S. Public*, pg. 1058

CREATING A HIGHER STANDARD—Slogan—Cadillac Motor Car Division; *U.S. Public*, pg. 720

CREATIONS—Cosmetics Line—Stanhome Inc.; *U.S. Public*, pg. 1508

CREATIONS AROMATIQUES—Fragrances—Creations Aromatiques, Inc.; *Int'l*, pg. 173

CREATIVE—Greeting Cards—Fine Art Developments plc; *Int'l*, pg. 485

CREATIVE ADVANTAGE LIBRARY—NONE—Broderbund Software, Inc.; *U.S. Public*, pg. 258

CREATIVE CORNER—Greeting Cards, Stationery, Party Goods & Gift Wrap—American Greetings Corporation; *U.S. Public*, pg. 77

CREATIVE EXPRESSIONS—Specialty Products—Restonic Mattress Corporation; *U.S. Private*, pg. 925

CREATIVE FUN & LEARNING CENTER—Display Stands—The Mead Corporation; *U.S. Public*, pg. 1074

CREATIVE LOAN—Five Year Step Rate Consumer Loan for Personal & Auto Borrowings—The Troy Savings Bank; *U.S. Private*, pg. 1106

CREATIVE PAPERS—Stationery, Gift Wrap, Greeting Cards, Playing Cards—C.R. Gibson Co.; *U.S. Public*, pg. 1168

CREATIVE PUBLICATIONS—Educational Materials—Creative Publications; *U.S. Private*, pg. 288

CREATIVE WORKS—NONE—Fiskars Oy AB; *Int'l*, pg. 492

CREATIVELY YOURS—Curtains—Robertson Factories, Inc.; *U.S. Private*, pg. 936

CREATIVITY COLLECTION—NONE—Martin Universal Design, Inc.; *U.S. Private*, pg. 709

CREATOR—Toy—Toymax International Inc.; *U.S. Public*, pg. 1626

CRECS—Potato Chips—Borden, Inc.; *U.S. Private*, pg. 157

CREDA—Cooker—The General Electric Company, p.l.c.; *Int'l*, pg. 543

CREDIT—Electronic Instrument—Intel Corporation; *U.S. Public*, pg. 886

CREDIT CARD GUARDIAN—NONE—CUC International, Inc.; *U.S. Public*, pg. 320

CREDITABLE—Credit Application Scorecard—Fair, Isaac and Company, Inc.; *U.S. Public*, pg. 609

CREDITDESK—Application Processing Software—Fair, Isaac and Company, Inc.; *U.S. Public*, pg. 609

CREDITGARD—Services Provided for Card Holders—American Automobile Association; *U.S. Private*, pg. 50

CREDITQUOTE—Service—Fair, Isaac and Company, Inc.; *U.S. Public*, pg. 609

CREDO—Saw blades & Power Tool Accessories—Vermont American Tool Corp.; *U.S. Public*, pg. 575

CREEK CLUB—Fishing Lines—EBSCO Industries, Inc.; *U.S. Private*, pg. 358

CREEPY CRAWLERS—Toy—Toymax International Inc.; *U.S. Public*, pg. 1626

CRELAN—Powder Coating Resins—Bayer AG; *Int'l*, pg. 171

CREMALIN—NONE—Lee Pharmaceuticals; *U.S. Public*, pg. 984

CREME DE BRIE—Spreadable Brie—Bongrain Cheese USA; *Int'l*, pg. 201

CREME FRAICHE—Cooking Cream—BC-USA; *Int'l*, pg. 201

CREME FRAICHE—Cooking Cream—Bongrain Cheese USA; *Int'l*, pg. 201

CREME POCKETS—NONE—Drake Bakeries, Inc.; *Int'l*, pg. 349

CREME RELAXER—Hair Straightener—Revlon-Realistic Professional Products, Inc.; *U.S. Private*, pg. 690

CREMEDAS—Skin Care Products—SmithKline Beecham plc; *Int'l*, pg. 1264

CREMODAN—Functional Systems—Danisco Ingredients; *Int'l*, pg. 378

CREMODAN—Dairy Stabilizer System—Danisco Ingredients USA, Inc.; *Int'l*, pg. 378

CREMOGEMA—Corn & Other Starches—Bestfoods; *U.S. Public*, pg. 223

CREMOGEN—Fragrance—Haarmann & Reimer Corp.; *Int'l*, pg. 173

CREMORA—Non-Dairy Creamer—Borden, Inc.; *U.S. Private*, pg. 157

CREMORA LITE—Non-Dairy Creamer with No Tropical Oils—Borden, Inc.; *U.S. Private*, pg. 157

CREO-TERPIN—Cough Suppressant—Medtech Inc.; *U.S. Private*, pg. 728

CREON—Gastrointestinal Preparations—Kali-Chemie Aktiengesellschaft; *Int'l*, pg. 1278

CREON—Pharmaceutical Product—Solvay Pharmaceuticals, Inc.; *Int'l*, pg. 1278

CREORD—Real Estate Service—Accor S.A.; *Int'l*, pg. 20

CREPEPLUS—Paper Creping Aids—BetzDearborn Inc.; *U.S. Public*, pg. 226

CREPESET—Nylon—BASF Corporation Fiber Products Division; *Int'l*, pg. 105

CRES-COR—Mobile Food Service Equipment—Cres-Cor; *U.S. Private*, pg. 288

CRESCENT—Wrenches, Pilers,and Screwdrivers/Nutdrivers—Cooper Hand Tools; *U.S. Public*, pg. 444

CRESCENT—Tools—Cooper Industries, Inc.; *U.S. Public*, pg. 442

CRESCENT—Adjustable Wrenches, Pliers & Screwdrivers—Cooper Industries, Inc.; *U.S. Public*, pg. 442

CRESCENT—Industrial & Household Cutting Blades—Crescent Manufacturing Company; *U.S. Private*, pg. 289

CRESCENT—Automobile Harness, Battery Cable Leads & Hi-Tension Ignition Cable—General Cable Corporation; *Int'l*, pg. 1486

CRESCENT—Lighting Fixtures—The Genlyte Group Incorporated; *U.S. Public*, pg. 729

CRESCENT—Spices, Extracts, Seasoning Mixes—McCormick/Schilling; *U.S. Public*, pg. 1066

CRESCENT—Corsets—NCC Industries, Inc.; *U.S. Private*, pg. 697

CRESCENT—Valves—The Wm. Powell Company; *U.S. Private*, pg. 877

CRESCENT—Retaining Ring—Waldes Truarc/Industrial Retaining Ring; *U.S. Public*, pg. 1632

CRESCENT SOX—Athletic Socks—Wigwam Mills, Inc.; *U.S. Private*, pg. 1175

CRESLINE—Plastic Pipe & Fittings—Cresline Plastic Pipe Co. Inc.; *U.S. Private*, pg. 289

CRESOPUR—Plant Protectives—DSM Chemie Linz GmbH; *Int'l*, pg. 356

CRESSIDA—Car—Toyota Motor Sales, U.S.A., Inc.; *Int'l*, pg. 1412

CREST—Toothpaste—The Procter & Gamble Company; *U.S. Public*, pg. 1330

CREST—Toothpaste—Procter & Gamble Venezuela, C.A.; *U.S. Public*, pg. 1332

CREST—Writing Instruments—Sheaffer Inc.; *Int'l*, pg. 542

CREST BAKING SODA—Baking Soda—The Procter & Gamble Company; *U.S. Public*, pg. 1330

CREST COMPLETE—Toothbrush—The Procter & Gamble Company; *U.S. Public*, pg. 1330

CREST DEEP SWEEP—Toothbrush—The Procter & Gamble Company; *U.S. Public*, pg. 1330

CREST FOR KIDS—Mint Gel Toothpaste—The Procter & Gamble Company; *U.S. Public*, pg. 1330

CREST HOMES—Manufactured Housing—Schult Homes Corporation; *U.S. Public*, pg. 1442

CREST-KUT—Precision Cutting Tool—Regal-Beloit Corporation; *U.S. Public*, pg. 1370

CREST SUPER COOL—Kid's Toothpaste—The Procter & Gamble Company; *U.S. Public*, pg. 1330

CRESTA—Wall Paper Base Materials—Metsa-Serla Corporation; *Int'l*, pg. 863

CRESTA—Automobile—Toyota Motor Corporation; *Int'l*, pg. 1411

CRESTAR—Bank—Crestar Bank; *U.S. Public*, pg. 458

CRESTCLAD—Wood & Aluminum Clad Windows—SNE Enterprises, Inc.; *U.S. Public*, pg. 1193

CRESTED BUTTE—Ski Resort—Crested Butte Mountain Resort, Inc.; *U.S. Private*, pg. 289

CRESTLINE—Hollow Handle Buffetware—The Vollrath Company, L.L.C.; *U.S. Private*, pg. 1143

CRESTLINER—Aluminum Boats—Genmar Holdings, Inc.; *U.S. Private*, pg. 447

CRESTWOOD—NONE—American Woodmark Corporation; *U.S. Public*, pg. 96

CRESTWOOD—Vinyl Siding—Reynolds Metals Company; *U.S. Public*, pg. 1385

CREUSLI—Granola Bars—The Quaker Oats Company; *U.S. Public*, pg. 1347

CREW—Car—Nissan Motor Co., Ltd.; *Int'l*, pg. 943

CRIADA—Pasta Sauce—Borden, Inc.; *U.S. Private*, pg. 157

CRIBARI—Wine & Sparkling Wine—Canandaigua Wine Company Div.; *U.S. Public*, pg. 300

CRIBARI—Wines—Canandaigua Wine Company, Inc.; *U.S. Public*, pg. 300

CRICKET—Skin Stapler—U.S. Surgical Corp.; *U.S. Public*, pg. 1687

CRICKET—Industrial Safety Eyewear—Uvex Safety, Inc.; *Int'l*, pg. 132

CRICKET BOX—Prepasted Vinyl Coated Strippable Wallcovering—York Wallcoverings Inc.; *U.S. Private*, pg. 1196

CRICKET LANE—NONE—Kellwood Company; *U.S. Public*, pg. 948

CRICKLES—Pickles—Cains Foods, L.P.; *U.S. Private*, pg. 199

CRIMPMASTER—Scientific Glassware for Laboratory Use—Wheaton Inc.; *Int'l*, pg. 67

CRINO—Powder Milk—Agropur; *Int'l*, pg. 31

CRINOLINE—Toiletries—Avon Products, Inc.; *U.S. Public*, pg. 155

CRINONE—Progesterone—American Home Products Corporation; *U.S. Public*, pg. 79

CRINONE—Vaginal Progesterone Prod.—Columbia Laboratories, Inc.; *U.S. Public*, pg. 405

CRISA—Handblown Crystal, Glassware & Giftware—World Tableware, Inc.; *Int'l*, pg. 1056

CRISAN—Hair Care Products—Wella Group; *Int'l*, pg. 1489

CRISCO—Shortening—The Procter & Gamble Company; *U.S. Public*, pg. 1330

CRISP—Corporate Banking Sales & Relationship Profitability Management—Broadway & Seymour, Inc.; *U.S. Public*, pg. 258

CRISP N TASTY CRUST—Pizza—Pillsbury Co.; *Int'l*, pg. 411

CRISPERS—Frozen Potatoes—Ore-Ida Foods, Inc.; *U.S. Public*, pg. 805

CRISPIX—Crisp Cross of Corn & Rice Cereal—Kellogg Company; *U.S. Public*, pg. 947

CRISPURA—Shoestrings, Thin Cuts, Wedge Cuts, QQQ's—Lamb-Weston, Inc.; *U.S. Public*, pg. 427

CRISPURA—French Fries—Universal Foods Corporation; *U.S. Public*, pg. 1695

CRISPY BAKES—Potato Products—H.J. Heinz Company; *U.S. Public*, pg. 805

CRISPY CRITTERS—Ready-to-Eat Cereal—Kraft Foods, Inc.; *U.S. Public*, pg. 1287

CRISPY CROWNS—Frozen Potatoes—Ore-Ida Foods, Inc.; *U.S. Public*, pg. 805

CRISPY CRUNCH—Chocolate Bar—George Weston Limited; *Int'l*, pg. 1494

CRISPY CURLS—Seasoned, Curled Fries—Hardee's Food Systems, Inc.; *U.S. Public*, pg. 278

CRISPY CUTS—Pickles—Cains Foods, L.P.; *U.S. Private*, pg. 199

CRISPY-Q FRIES—Potato Products—Universal Foods Corporation; *U.S. Public*, pg. 1695

CRISPY RICE—Cereal—Malt-O-Meal Company; *U.S. Private*, pg. 699

CRISPY SNACKS—NONE—Drake Bakeries, Inc.; *Int'l*, pg. 349

CRISPY WHEATIES'N RAISINS—Cereal—General Mills, Inc.; *U.S. Public*, pg. 717

CRISPYWRAP—Plastic Packaging—W.R. Grace & Co.; *U.S. Public*, pg. 754

CRISS—Wine Cooler—Eckes AG; *Int'l*, pg. 432

CRISSCUT FRIES—Natural, Natural Thick, Private Reserve, Original Recipe Seasoned—Lamb-Weston, Inc.; *U.S. Public*, pg. 427

CRISTAL—NONE—Beiersdorf S.A.; *Int'l*, pg. 183

CRISTAL—Beer—UNICER-Uniao Cervejeira, S.A.; *Int'l*, pg. 1432

CARLA CRISTALDI—Women's Footwear—J. Baker, Inc.; *U.S. Public*, pg. 167

CRITERIA—Conditioning Systems—Reliability Incorporated; *U.S. Public*, pg. 1373

CRITERION—Fabrics—Dan River Inc.; *U.S. Public*, pg. 478

CRITERION—Seating—Steelcase Inc.; *U.S. Private*, pg. 1038

CRITERION SOLIDS—Vinyl Composition Tile—Kentile Operting Co.; *U.S. Private*, pg. 615

CRITERION 3x8—Key System—Vidar, Inc.; *U.S. Private*, pg. 1139

CRITERION II—Large Center Cartoners—R.A. Jones & Co. Inc.; *U.S. Private*, pg. 597

CRITICAL CARE NUTRITIONALS—Nutritional Supplements for Critical Care Patients—Mead Johnson Nutritional Group; *U.S. Public*, pg. 254

CRITICAP—Filtration Products—Gelman Sciences, Inc.; *U.S. Public*, pg. 1253

CRITICARE—Adult Vitamins—Bristol-Myers Squibb Company; *U.S. Public*, pg. 253

CRITICS' CHOICE VIDEO—Catalog—Playboy Enterprises, Inc.; *U.S. Public*, pg. 1309

CRITIKON—NONE—Johnson & Johnson; *U.S. Public*, pg. 927

CRITIKON—Blood Pressure Cuffs—Johnson & Johnson Medical, Inc.; *U.S. Public*, pg. 928

CRITIQUE—Business System—International Business Machines Corporation; *U.S. Public*, pg. 895

CRIZAL—Coatings—Essilor International Compagnie Generale d'Optique; *Int'l*, pg. 462

CROCHET DIGEST—Crafts Publications—House of White Birches, Inc.; *U.S. Private*, pg. 542

CROCHET WORLD—Crafts Magazine—House of White Birches, Inc.; *U.S. Private*, pg. 542

CROCHET WORLD SPECIALS—Crafts Magazine—House of White Birches, Inc.; *U.S. Private*, pg. 542

CROCHETMASTER—Crochet Kit—Wm. E. Wright Limited Partnership; *U.S. Private*, pg. 1192

CROCK-GRILL—NONE—The Rival Company; *U.S. Public*, pg. 1391

CROCK-ETTE—Slow Cooker—The Rival Company; *U.S. Public*, pg. 1391

CROCK-POT—Slow Cooker—The Rival Company; *U.S. Public*, pg. 1391

CRODON—Hard Chrome PlatedDiesel Engine Cylinder Liners—Elcor Corporation; *U.S. Public*, pg. 567

CROFT—Ale—Falstaff Brewing Corporation; *U.S. Private*, pg. 955

CROFT CLASSIC AMONTILLADO—NONE—Croft Sherry; *Int'l*, pg. 409

CROFT DELICADO FINO—NONE—Croft Sherry; *Int'l*, pg. 409

CROFT ORIGINAL—Wine Spirits—Grand Metropolitan Plc; *Int'l*, pg. 408

CROFT ORIGINAL PALE CREAM—NONE—Croft Sherry; *Int'l*, pg. 409

CROFT PALO CORTADO—NONE—Croft Sherry; *Int'l*, pg. 409

CROFT PORT—NONE—Societe Pour la Vente des Produits Cinzano SA; *Int'l*, pg. 410

CROFT PORTS—NONE—Croft & Companhia Limitada; *Int'l*, pg. 409

CROFT SHERRY—NONE—Societe Pour la Vente des Produits Cinzano SA; *Int'l*, pg. 410

CROISIERES PAQUET—Cruises—Accor S.A.; *Int'l*, pg. 20

CROISSANT PASTRY PIZZA—Pizza—Pepperidge Farm, Incorporated; *U.S. Public*, pg. 299

CROKY—Snacks—United Biscuits (Holdings) Plc; *Int'l*, pg. 1442

CROKY—Snacks—United Biscuits (UK) Limited; *Int'l*, pg. 1442

CROMAC—Vinyl Impregnated Gloves—Jomac, Inc.; *U.S. Private*, pg. 595

CROMALOY—Resistance Wires—IMI Plc; *Int'l*, pg. 646

CROPMATE—Fertilizer—ConAgra, Inc.; *U.S. Public*, pg. 425

CROSBY—Industrial Valves & Gauges—FMC-Crosby Valve, Inc.; *U.S. Public*, pg. 605

CROSCILL—Home Fashions—Croscill, Inc.; *U.S. Private*, pg. 290

CROSS—NONE—Cross Huller; *Int'l*, pg. 1389

CROSS—Corn Meal—Wilkins-Rogers Incorporated; *U.S. Private*, pg. 1176

CROSS & TRECKER—NONE—Cross Huller; *Int'l*, pg. 1389

CROSS COUNTRY—Luggage—American Tourister, Inc.; *U.S. Public*, pg. 1430

CROSS COUNTRY PLUS—Luggage—American Tourister, Inc.; *U.S. Public*, pg. 1430

CROSS COUNTRY II—Luggage—American Tourister, Inc.; *U.S. Public*, pg. 1430

CROSS CREEK—Apparel—Cross Creek Apparel, Inc.; *U.S. Public*, pg. 1413

CROSS CREEK—Premium Placket Shirts—Russell Corporation; *U.S. Public*, pg. 1413

CROSS CREEK PRO COLLECTION—Apparel—Cross Creek Apparel, Inc.; *U.S. Public*, pg. 1413

CROSS FIRE—Oscillating Warning Light—Federal Signal Corporation, Signal Div.; *U.S. Public*, pg. 616

CROSS-LOK—Snaps—Outdoor Technologies Group; *U.S. Private*, pg. 822

CROSS REFERENCE—Collaborative Gas Analysis—Scott Specialty Gases; *U.S. Private*, pg. 977

CROSS STITCH & COUNTRY CRAFTS—Magazine—Meredith Corporation; *U.S. Public*, pg. 1094

CROSS-STITCH PLUS—Crafts Publication—House of White Birches, Inc.; *U.S. Private*, pg. 542

CROSS STITCH SAMPLER—Consumer Magazine Featuring Needlework Projects—Sampler Publications Inc.; *U.S. Private*, pg. 963

CROSS YOUR HEART—NONE—Playtex Apparel, Inc.; *U.S. Public*, pg. 1433

CROSSBAR—Bar Code Data Collection Network—Intermec Technologies Corporation; *U.S. Public*, pg. 1699

CROSSBOW—Herbicide—The Dow Chemical Company; *U.S. Public*, pg. 522

CROSSCHECK—Aseptic Packaging Machines—The Mead Corporation; *U.S. Public*, pg. 1074

CROSSE & BLACKWELL—Sauces—Nestle S.A.; *Int'l*, pg. 915

CROSSE & BLACKWELL—Sauces, Soups, Jellies, Specialty Items—Nestle USA; *Int'l*, pg. 916

CROSSE & BLACKWELL—Imports—Wine World Estates Company; *Int'l*, pg. 917

CROSSFIN—Inner Grooved Tubes—KM-Europa Metal Aktiengesellschaft; *Int'l*, pg. 719

CROSSFIRE—Wood Veneers—Georgia-Pacific Corporation; *U.S. Public*, pg. 735

CROSSFIRE—Game—Milton Bradley Company; *U.S. Public*, pg. 797

CROSSFIRE—Pesticide-Insecticide—Roussel Corporation; *Int'l*, pg. 625

CROSSFIRE—Pesticide-Insecticide—Roussel UCLAF S.A.; *Int'l*, pg. 626

THE CROSSING NETWORK—Instinet's After-Hours Match—Instinet Corporation; *Int'l*, pg. 1106

CROSSLAND—Manufactured Homes—Clayton Homes, Inc.; *U.S. Public*, pg. 382

CROSSLOCK—New DBL or Single Locking Folding Knife—Buck Knives, Inc.; *U.S. Private*, pg. 177

CROSSMEN—Men's Fragrance—Coty Inc.; *Int'l*, pg. 185

CROSSROADS—NONE—Sears, Roebuck and Co.; *U.S. Public*, pg. 1452

CROSSROADS FURNITURE—Furniture—Rhodes, Inc.; *U.S. Public*, pg. 805

CROSSTUNE—Surfboard Foams—The Dow Chemical Company; *U.S. Public*, pg. 522

CROSSWIND—Street Sweeper—Elgin Sweeper Company; *U.S. Public*, pg. 617

CROTON—Watches—Croton Watch Company & Nationwide Time; *U.S. Private*, pg. 291

CROTON AQUATIC—Watches—Croton Watch Company & Nationwide Time; *U.S. Private*, pg. 291

CROUCH & FITZGERALD—Leather Goods—Lenox, Incorporated; *U.S. Public*, pg. 261

CROUSE-HINDS—Explosive Proof Fittings—Bryant Electric Supply Company, Inc.; *U.S. Private*, pg. 177

CROUSE-HINDS—Industrial Electrical Switching Equipment, Fittings, Enclosures & Lighting—Cooper Industries, Inc.; *U.S. Public*, pg. 442

CROUTETTES—Herb-Seasoned Stuffing Mix—Kellogg Company; *U.S. Public*, pg. 947

CROW CONSTRUCTION COMPANY—Construction Company-General Contractors—J.A. Jones, Inc.; *Int'l*, pg. 633

CROWCON—Gas Detection Instruments—Halma p.l.c.; *Int'l*, pg. 589

CROWLEY—Dairy Products—Crowley Foods, Inc.; *Int'l*, pg. 752

CROWLEY—Dairy Products—Koninklijke BolsWessanen nv; *Int'l*, pg. 750

CROWLEY AMERICAN TRANSPORT—Intl. Liner Cargo Service—Crowley Maritime Corporation; *U.S. Private*, pg. 292

CROWLEY MARINE SERVICES—Worldwide Special Marine Contract Transportation—Crowley Maritime Corporation; *U.S. Private*, pg. 292

CROWLEY MARITIME—Marine Cargo Transportation Services—Crowley Maritime Corporation; *U.S. Private*, pg. 292

CROWLEY MILNER & COMPANY—Department Stores—Crowley, Milner & Company; *U.S. Public*, pg. 461

CROWN—Automotive—Allen Telecom, Inc.; *U.S. Public*, pg. 45

CROWN—Self-Priming Centrifugal & Trash Pumps & Packaged Lift Stations—Barnes Pumps, Inc.; *U.S. Public*, pg. 457

CROWN—Wallcovering—Borden, Inc.; *U.S. Public*, pg. 157

CROWN—Tanks—Crown Andersen Inc.; *U.S. Public*, pg. 462

CROWN—Books—Crown Books Corporation; *U.S. Public*, pg. 484

CROWN—Petroleum Products—Crown Central Petroleum Corporation; *U.S. Public*, pg. 462

CROWN—Audio Electronics Domestic—Crown International, Inc.; *U.S. Private*, pg. 293

CROWN—NONE—Crown Publishers, Inc.; *U.S. Private*, pg. 21

CROWN—Investment Plans—Derbyshire Building Society; *Int'l*, pg. 394

CROWN—Jacks—The Hammerblow Corp.; *U.S. Private*, pg. 498

CROWN—Cruise Ship—Norwegian Cruise Line; *U.S. Private*, pg. 808

CROWN—Children's Books—Random House, Inc.; *U.S. Private*, pg. 20

CROWN—Paints—Sime Darby Berhad; *Int'l*, pg. 1249

CROWN—Flush Valves—Sloan Valve Company; *U.S. Private*, pg. 1006

CROWN ACHIEVEMENT—Pipe Tobacco—Lane Limited; *Int'l*, pg. 1129

CROWN ARISTOCRAFT—Shoes—Johnston & Murphy Co.; *U.S. Public*, pg. 728

CROWN BRAND—Syrups—Bestfoods; *U.S. Public*, pg. 223

CROWN BRANDS—Foods—Ventura Foods; *U.S. Private*, pg. 508

CROWN CLUB—Shirts & Sweaters—King Louie International; *U.S. Private*, pg. 621

CROWN COLLECTION—Mattress & Box Spring—Kingsdown, Inc.; *U.S. Private*, pg. 622

CROWN COMFORT—Mattress & Box Spring Sets—Kingsdown, Inc.; *U.S. Private*, pg. 622

CROWN CORK & SEAL—Manufacturer of Packaging Products to Consumer Marketing Companies—Crown Cork & Seal Company, Inc.; *U.S. Public*, pg. 462

CROWN CRAFTS—NONE—Crown Crafts, Inc.; *U.S. Public*, pg. 465

CROWN DESIGN—NONE—Stuart Entertainment Inc.; *U.S. Public*, pg. 1526

CROWN DIAMOND—NONE—Sico Inc.; *Int'l*, pg. 1239

CROWN FAB—Parts for Trucks, Off-Highway Equipment & Telephone Communs. Equipment—The Crown Divisions; *U.S. Public*, pg. 1631

CROWN-FLEXXX—Interfacings—Specialty Textile Products; *U.S. Private*, pg. 1023

CROWN GEAR—Angle Gear Drives—Zero-Max, Inc.; *Int'l*, pg. 866

CROWN IMPERIAL—Mattresses & Box Springs—Kingsdown, Inc.; *U.S. Private*, pg. 622

CROWN JEWEL—Sporting Goods—Brunswick Bowling & Billiards Corp.; *U.S. Public*, pg. 265

CROWN LAGER—Lager Ale—Carlton & United Breweries Ltd.; *Int'l*, pg. 500

CROWN MATS—Entrance & Anti-Fatigue—Ludlow Composites Corporation; *U.S. Public*, pg. 680

CROWN NEOLITE—Soles & Heels—The Goodyear Tire & Rubber Company; *U.S. Public*, pg. 752

CROWN PILOT—Crackers—Nabisco Inc.; *U.S. Public*, pg. 1355

CROWN PILOT—Crackers—RJR Nabisco Holdings Corp.; *U.S. Public*, pg. 1354

CROWN PRINCE—Canned Seafood—Crown Prince, Inc. (CA); *U.S. Private*, pg. 293

CROWN ROYAL—Liquor—The House of Seagram; *Int'l*, pg. 1217

CROWN ROYAL—Canadian Whisky—The Seagram Company Ltd.; *Int'l*, pg. 1214

CROWN SEAL—Double Acting Piston Seal—Macrotech Plyseal, Inc.; *U.S. Private*, pg. 693

CROWN SHOES—Name Brand & Cancellation Shoe—Shonac Corporation; *U.S. Private*, pg. 996

CROWN STERLING—Scotch—Peerless Importers, Inc.; *U.S. Private*, pg. 847

CROWN-TEXXX—Interlinings—Specialty Textile Products; *U.S. Private*, pg. 1023

CROWN THIN BOILING—Acid-Modified Corn Starches—Penford Corp.; *U.S. Public*, pg. 1269

CROWN III—Coal—Freeman Energy Corporation; *U.S. Public*, pg. 709

CROWN TOP—Heat Exchangers for Solar Heating Systems—Reynolds Metals Company; *U.S. Public*, pg. 1385

CROWN TRADE PAPERBACKS—NONE—Crown Publishers, Inc.; *U.S. Private*, pg. 21

CROWN II—Fly Reel—Cortland Line Co., Inc.; *U.S. Private*, pg. 277

CROWN II—Coal—Freeman Energy Corporation; *U.S. Public*, pg. 709

CROWN VICTORIA—Car—Ford Motor Company; *U.S. Public*, pg. 661

CROWN-WEFT—Weft-Insertion Interfacings—Specialty Textile Products; *U.S. Private*, pg. 1023

CROWN WINDSOR—Shoes—Bostonian Shoe Co.; *Int'l*, pg. 297

CROWN-X—Mobile Convection Ovens, Food Preparation Equipment—Cres-Cor; *U.S. Private*, pg. 288

CROWN ZELLERBACH—Printing Papers—Fort James Corporation; *U.S. Public*, pg. 670

CROWNE PLAZA—Hotels—Holiday Inn Worldwide; *Int'l*, pg. 170

CROWN'S OF LONDON—Cigarettes—Brown & Williamson Tobacco Corp.; *Int'l*, pg. 111

CROWS—Candy—Tootsie Roll Industries, Inc.; *U.S. Public*, pg. 1621

CROXLEY—Puzzles—Milton Bradley Company; *U.S. Public*, pg. 797

CRUISE AIR—Class A Motor Home—Georgie Boy Manufacturing, Inc.; *U.S. Public*, pg. 388

CRUISE AIR III—Class A Motor Home—Georgie Boy Manufacturing, Inc.; *U.S. Public*, pg. 388

CRUISE MASTER—Class A Motor Home—Georgie Boy Manufacturing, Inc.; *U.S. Public*, pg. 388

CRUISE PAL—Accessories—Hunter Marine Corporation; *U.S. Private*, pg. 549

CRUISE TRAVEL—Magazine—Century Publishing Company; *U.S. Private*, pg. 226

CRUISELINK—NONE—Northwest Airlines, Inc.; *U.S. Public*, pg. 1200

CRUISERS—Portfolios & Binders—The Mead Corporation; *U.S. Public*, pg. 1074

CRUM AND FORSTER—Casualty & Property Insurance—Talegen Corporation; *U.S. Public*, pg. 1784

CRUNCH—Chocolate & Confectionery—Nestle S.A.; *Int'l*, pg. 915

CRUNCH—Candy—Nestle USA; *Int'l*, pg. 916

CRUNCH 'N YOGURT—Yogurt—Yoplait USA; *U.S. Public*, pg. 718

CRUNCH 'N MUNCH—Popcorn/Peanut Candy—International Home Foods Inc.; *U.S. Private*, pg. 526

CRUNCH TATORS—Extra Crunchy Potato Chips—Frito-Lay Company; *U.S. Public*, pg. 1277

CRUNCHIE—Chocolate Bar—George Weston Limited; *Int'l*, pg. 1494

CRUNCHY BRAN—Cereal—The Quaker Oats Company; *U.S. Public*, pg. 1347

CRUNCHY CORN BRAN—Cereal—The Quaker Oats Company; *U.S. Public*, pg. 1347

CRUNCHY MEALS—Pet food—H.J. Heinz Company; *U.S. Public*, pg. 805

CRUNCHY MEALS—Dry Cat Food—Star-Kist Foods, Inc.; *U.S. Public*, pg. 806

CRUNCHY RICE BRAN—Ready-to-Eat Cereal—The Quaker Oats Company; *U.S. Public*, pg. 1347

CRUSADER—RADIATOR VALVES—Crane Limited U.K.; *U.S. Public*, pg. 458

CRUSADER—High Speed Tool Steel—Latrobe Steel Company; *U.S. Public*, pg. 1617

CRUSADER—Fish Line—Outdoor Technologies Group; *U.S. Private*, pg. 822

CRUSH—Soda—Cadbury Beverages; *Int'l*, pg. 248

CRUSH—Soft Drinks—Cadbury Beverages North America; *Int'l*, pg. 248

CRUSH—Soft Drinks—Cadbury Schweppes p.l.c.; *Int'l*, pg. 247

CRUSHED LEAF—Writing, Text & Cover Paper—Fox River Paper Company; *U.S. Private*, pg. 422

CRUSKEN—Fiber Product—Novo Nordisk A/S; *Int'l*, pg. 987

CRISTAL ALKEN—Beer—Danone Group; *Int'l*, pg. 379

CRUSTBUSTER—Farm Tillage Equipment—Crustbuster, Inc.; *U.S. Private*, pg. 293

CRUTCHFIELD'S—Flour—Wilkins-Rogers Incorporated; *U.S. Private*, pg. 1176

CRUXITE—Safety Lens—American Optical Corporation; *U.S. Private*, pg. 60

CRUZCAMPO—NONE—Guinness Plc; *Int'l*, pg. 412

CRUZEIRO—Water—Central de Cervejas, S.A.; *Int'l*, pg. 279

CRYO-LITE—Fibrous Blanket—Johns Manville Corporation; *U.S. Public*, pg. 927

CRYO-QUICK—Food Freezers—Air Products and Chemicals, Inc.; *U.S. Public*, pg. 30

CRYO-SURG—Nitrogen Delivery System—The Cooper Companies, Inc.; *U.S. Public*, pg. 442

CRYO-TEK—Plumbing Chemical—Hercules Chemical Co., Inc.; *U.S. Private*, pg. 523

CRYOLAB—Cryogenic Valves—Circle Seal Controls, Inc.; *U.S. Public*, pg. 1746

CRYOTACT—Electrical Connectors—Raychem Corporation; *U.S. Public*, pg. 1362

CRYOTECH—Frozen Mouse Embryos & Hamster Ova—Bausch & Lomb Incorporated; *U.S. Public*, pg. 194

CRYOTIGER—Liquid Nitrogen Temperature Cryogenic RefrigerationSystems—Intermagnetics General Corporation; *U.S. Public*, pg. 893

CRYOTIGHT—Cryogenic High-Performance Valves—Fisher Controls International, Inc.; *U.S. Public*, pg. 573

CRYOVAC—Plastic Packaging Materials & Equipment—W.R. Grace & Co.; *U.S. Public*, pg. 754

CRYPTO—LA Test—Wampole Laboratories; *U.S. Public*, pg. 310

CRYSCOAT—Conversion Coating—Oakite Products, Inc.; *Int'l*, pg. 861

CRYSEL—Acrylic Fiber—CYDSA S.A.; *Int'l*, pg. 246

CRYSTAL—Mints & Hard Candies—Cadbury Schweppes p.l.c.; *Int'l*, pg. 247

CRYSTAL—Dairy Products—Crystal Cream & Butter Company; *U.S. Private*, pg. 294

CRYSTAL—Interactive Seismic Interpretation System—Litton Industries, Inc.; *U.S. Public*, pg. 1002

CRYSTAL BAY—Soft Drink—Beverage Canners International Corp.; *U.S. Private*, pg. 106

CRYSTAL BAY—Emery Cloth Coated Abrasives—3M; *U.S. Public*, pg. 1604

CRYSTAL CABINETS—Custom Cabinets—Crystal Cabinet Works, Inc.; *U.S. Private*, pg. 293

CRYSTAL CLEAN—Condiment—Diamond Crystal Specialty Foods, Inc.; *U.S. Private*, pg. 330

CRYSTAL CLEAR—Incandescent Lamps—General Electric Canada Inc.; *U.S. Public*, pg. 713

CRYSTAL CLEAR—Clear Spray Coating—Sherwin-Williams Diversified Brands, Inc.; *U.S. Public*, pg. 1466

CRYSTAL CLEAR CHANDELIERS—Lighting Fixtures & Chandeliers—Crystal Clear Industries; *U.S. Private*, pg. 293

CRYSTAL COLOR—Plastic Film—Reynolds Metals Company; *U.S. Public*, pg. 1385

CRYSTAL COMFORT—Beverage—Brown-Forman Corporation; *U.S. Public*, pg. 261

CRYSTAL CRUISES—Luxury Cruise Operator—Crystal Cruises, Inc.; *Int'l*, pg. 941

CRYSTAL DECANTER—Whisky—Dunhill Scotch Whisky Sales Limited; *Int'l*, pg. 409

CRYSTAL FARMS—Refrigerated Grocery Products—Michael Foods, Inc.; *U.S. Public*, pg. 1103

CRYSTAL-GARD—Ironing Board Covers—Magla Products; *U.S. Private*, pg. 695

CRYSTAL GEYSER—Sparkling Mineral Water—Crystal Geyser; *U.S. Private*, pg. 294

CRYSTAL GEYSER ALPINE SPRING WATER—Spring Water—Otsuka Pharmaceutical Co., Ltd.; *Int'l*, pg. 1013

CRYSTAL GEYSER JUICE SQUEEZE—Natural Soda & Juice Product—Crystal Geyser; *U.S. Private*, pg. 294

CRYSTAL GLAZE—Glazed Ceramic Wall and Bathroom Floor Tile—Florida Tile Industries, Inc.; *U.S. Public*, pg. 1322

CRYSTAL GLAZE—Glazed Ceramic Tile—Porcelanite, Inc.; *Int'l*, pg. 573

CRYSTAL GLAZE—Glazed ceramic wall and bathroom floor tile—Precision Die & Engineering, Inc.; *U.S. Public*, pg. 1322

CRYSTAL HARMONY—Cruise Ship—Crystal Cruises, Inc.; *Int'l*, pg. 941

CRYSTAL LIGHT—NONE—Cadbury Beverages; *Int'l*, pg. 248

CRYSTAL LIGHT—Powdered Soft Drink—Kraft Foods, Inc.; *U.S. Public*, pg. 1287

CRYSTAL LIGHT—Frozen Novelties—Philip Morris Companies Inc.; *U.S. Public*, pg. 1287

CRYSTAL LIGHT COOL 'N CREAMY—Frozen Dessert—Kraft Foods, Inc.; *U.S. Public*, pg. 1287

CRYSTAL PACK—Plastic Containers—Amoco Chemicals; *U.S. Public*, pg. 102

CRYSTAL PALACE—NONE—Barton Brands, Ltd.; *U.S. Public*, pg. 300

CRYSTAL-PANE—Window Material—Warp Brothers; *U.S. Private*, pg. 412

CRYSTAL PEPSI—Soft Drink—Pepsi-Cola Company; *U.S. Public*, pg. 1277

CRYSTAL PEPSI—Soft Drink—PepsiCo, Inc.; *U.S. Public*, pg. 1276

CRYSTAL PLACE—Gin & Vodka—Barton Incorporated; *U.S. Public*, pg. 300

CRYSTAL PLEAT—Window Shades—Springs Industries, Inc.; *U.S. Public*, pg. 1499

CRYSTAL PURE—Bleaching & Sanitizing Compound—Monsanto Company; *U.S. Public*, pg. 1124

CRYSTAL SPRING—Spring Water—Danone Group; *Int'l*, pg. 379

CRYSTAL SUGAR—Sugar—American Crystal Sugar Company; *U.S. Private*, pg. 52

CRYSTAL SYMPHONY—Cruise Ship—Crystal Cruises, Inc.; *Int'l*, pg. 941

CRYSTAL TIPS—Automatic Ice Making Equipment—Scotsman Industries, Inc.; *U.S. Public*, pg. 1444

CRYSTAL TISSUE—Manufacturer Commercial & Specialty Tissues—The Crystal Tissue Co.; *U.S. Private*, pg. 294

CRYSTAL TONES—Nominal 4" & Hexagon with Glazed Lace Waterspot Surface—United States Ceramic Tile Co.; *U.S. Private*, pg. 1124

CRYSTAL TREASURES—24% Full Lead Crystal Rocking Characters—Princess House, Inc.; *U.S. Public*, pg. 399

CRYSTAL WALK—Floor Coverings—Domco Inc.; *Int'l*, pg. 415

CRYSTAL WAVE—Microwave Products—Tupperware Corporation; *U.S. Public*, pg. 1644

CRYSTAL WEDDING—Rolled Oats & Wheat Flour—The Quaker Oats Company; *U.S. Public*, pg. 1347

CRYSTAL WHITE—Detergent—Colgate-Palmolive Company; *U.S. Public*, pg. 397

CRYSTALFLOR—Floor Coverings—Domco Inc.; *Int'l*, pg. 415

CRYSTALLON—Wrapping Paper—Fort James Corporation; *U.S. Public*, pg. 670

CRYSTALON—Tumbler—Carlisle Food Service Products; *U.S. Public*, pg. 305

CRYSTAR—Ceramic Kiln Furniture, Recrystallized Silicon Carbide—Norton Company; *Int'l*, pg. 1173

CRYSTEX—Rubber Chemicals—Akzo Nobel Inc.; *Int'l*, pg. 47

CRYSTEX—Insoluable Sulfur—Akzo Nobel N.V.; *Int'l*, pg. 42

CRYSTEX—Rubber Industry, Tire Mfr.—Kali-Chemie Aktiengesellschaft; *Int'l*, pg. 1278

CRYSTIN—C2S White Cover—Appleton Papers Inc.; *Int'l*, pg. 567

CRYSTODIGIN—Digitoxin, Lilly—Eli Lilly and Company; *U.S. Public*, pg. 992

CRYSTOLON—Abrasives, Etc.—Norton Company; *Int'l*, pg. 1173

CRYSTON—Nitride Bonded Silicon Carbide—Norton Company; *Int'l*, pg. 1173

CRYULE—Scientific Glassware for Laboratory Use—Wheaton Inc.; *Int'l*, pg. 67

CUB FOODS—Supermarkets—Cub Foods Stores; *U.S. Public*, pg. 1541

CUB LITE—Cutlery—Buck Knives, Inc.; *U.S. Private*, pg. 177

"CUBE OF LIGHTS" LOGO—for Computer Manuals—Thinking Machines Corporation; *U.S. Private*, pg. 1081

CUBE SERIES—Desks—GF Office Furniture; *U.S. Private*, pg. 435

CUBICUT—Coated Abrasives—3M; *U.S. Public*, pg. 1604

CUBITAINER—Vacuum-Formed Products—Hedwin Corporation; *Int'l*, pg. 1278

CUBITRON—Ceramic Aluminum Oxide Abrasive Material—3M; *U.S. Public*, pg. 1604

CUDDL DUDS—Warm Underwear—O'Bryan Brothers Inc.; *U.S. Private*, pg. 810

CUDDLE BUNNIES—Greeting Cards, Stationery & Party Goods—American Greetings Corporation; *U.S. Public*, pg. 77

CUDDLE TUB—Bath Tub—Century Products Co.; *U.S. Private*, pg. 226

CUDEC—Bright Acid Copper Plating—LeaRonal, Inc.; *U.S. Public*, pg. 982

CUE LOK—Slide Recall Feature—Telex Communications, Inc.; *U.S. Private*, pg. 1074

CUES, INC.—Sewer Inspection & Repair Equipment—ELXSI Corporation; *U.S. Public*, pg. 545

CUFFABLE—Blood Pressure Cuffs—Vital Signs, Inc.; *U.S. Public*, pg. 1723

CUISINART—Food Processors, Cookware—Cuisinart Inc.; *U.S. Private*, pg. 261

CUISINE—Food Product—Alliant Foodservice, Inc.; *U.S. Private*, pg. 244

CUISINE LEGERE—Dietary Dinners—Nestle S.A.; *Int'l*, pg. 915
CULINARY COLLECTIONS—Knives—Servotronics, Inc.; *U.S. Public*, pg. 1462
CULINARY PALETTE—Housewares—Stanhome Inc.; *U.S. Public*, pg. 1508
CULINET—Aluminum Foil, Pans & Trays—The Dow Chemical Company; *U.S. Public*, pg. 522
CULINOVA—Refrigerated Dinners—Kraft Foods, Inc.; *U.S. Public*, pg. 1287
CULINOX—Salt—Morton Salt; *U.S. Public*, pg. 1135
CULLMAN—Mouldings—Cullman Products Corporation; *U.S. Private*, pg. 294
CULLUM—Hardfacing—Tuboscope Incorporated; *U.S. Public*, pg. 1643
CULMINAL—Methylcellulose—Hercules Incorporated; *U.S. Public*, pg. 809
CULP—Upholstery Fabrics & Ticking—Culp, Inc.; *U.S. Public*, pg. 467
CULTISPHER—Macroporous Microcarriers—HyClone Laboratories Inc.; *Int'l*, pg. 1037
CULTURTEK—Pipets—Fisher Scientific Company; *U.S. Private*, pg. 658
CUMBERLAND—Twist Tobaccos—Conwood Company L.P.; *U.S. Private*, pg. 272
CUMMINS—Engine—Buffalo Truck Center; *U.S. Private*, pg. 179
CUMMINS—Engines & Parts—Great Lakes Peterbilt, GMC; *U.S. Private*, pg. 475
CUMMINS ENGINE—Cummins Diesel Engines—Cummins Engine Company, Inc.; *U.S. Public*, pg. 467
CUMMUNS TRUCK PARTS—Truck Parts—Heintzelman's Truck Center Inc.; *U.S. Private*, pg. 519
CUMULUS—NONE—AGA Gas, Inc.; *Int'l*, pg. 13
CUMULUS—Vapor Emission Control System—AGA Ges.m.b.H.; *Int'l*, pg. 13
CUNAPSOL—Wood Preservative—ISK BioSciences; *Int'l*, pg. 689
CUNARD LINE—Cruise Ships—Cunard Line Ltd.; *Int'l*, pg. 773
CUNE—Wine—Wine World Estates Company; *Int'l*, pg. 917
CUNIP—Alloy—Handy & Harman; *U.S. Public*, pg. 780
CUORE—850 cc 2 Box Sedan—Daihatsu Motor Corporation, Ltd.; *Int'l*, pg. 364
CUP-A-SOUP—Instant Soup—Lever Brothers Co.; *Int'l*, pg. 1435
CUP-A-SOUP—Instant Soup—Unilever Plc; *Int'l*, pg. 1433
CUP-AT-A-TIME—CoffeeMaker—The Black & Decker Corporation; *U.S. Public*, pg. 233
CUP FINAL—Ice Cream Flavour-Finishing—Royal Gist-Brocades N.V.; *Int'l*, pg. 1142
CUP NOODLE—Instant Noodles in a Cup—Nissin Food Products Co., Ltd.; *Int'l*, pg. 949
CUP NOODLES—Instant Noodles—Nissin Foods (U.S.A.) Co. Ltd.; *Int'l*, pg. 949
CUPAC—Semi-Conductor Devices—Semtech Corporation; *U.S. Public*, pg. 1456
CUPHANGER—NONE—Imperial Schrade Corp.; *U.S. Private*, pg. 559
CUPL-UP—Storage Racks—Jarke Corporation; *U.S. Private*, pg. 583
CUPRIMINE—Penicillamine—Merck & Co., Inc.; *U.S. Public*, pg. 1090
CUPRINOL—Stain/Preservative—The Sherwin-Williams Company; *U.S. Public*, pg. 1465
CUPRODINE—Metalworking Chemical—Henkel Surface Technologies; *Int'l*, pg. 610
CUPRON—NONE—Carpenter Technology Corporation; *U.S. Public*, pg. 307
CUPROPHAN—Membranes for Medical Applications—Akzo Nobel N.V.; *Int'l*, pg. 42
CUPROTHERM—Hot Water Underfloor Heating Systems—KM-Europa Metal Aktiengesellschaft; *Int'l*, pg. 719
CUPROXAT—Plant Protectives—DSM Chemie Linz GmbH; *Int'l*, pg. 356
CURAD—NONE—Colgate-Palmolive S.A.I.C.; *U.S. Public*, pg. 399
CURAD—Bandages—Futuro Inc.; *Int'l*, pg. 182
CURE/81—Hams—Hormel Foods Corp.; *U.S. Public*, pg. 840
CUREMASTER—Hams—Hormel Foods Corp.; *U.S. Public*, pg. 840

CURESAN—Insolubilizer for Paper Making Applications—PPG Industries, Inc.; *U.S. Public*, pg. 1245
CURFEW—Herbicide—The Dow Chemical Company; *U.S. Public*, pg. 522
CURFEW—Apparel—Fred Meyer Stores; *U.S. Public*, pg. 1103
CURIOUS CATS—Greeting Cards—American Greetings Corporation; *U.S. Public*, pg. 77
CURITAS—NONE—Colgate-Palmolive S.A.I.C.; *U.S. Public*, pg. 399
CURITHANE—Urethane Rigids Catalysts & Epoxy Curing Agents—The Dow Chemical Company; *U.S. Public*, pg. 522
CURITY—Incontinence Products—Futuro Inc.; *Int'l*, pg. 182
CURITY—Surgical Dressings—The Kendall Company; *U.S. Public*, pg. 1647
CURIX—Medical Film for Traditional X-Ray Imaging—AGFA Division of Bayer Corporation; *Int'l*, pg. 172
CURL FREE—Curl Relaxer—The Gillette Company; *U.S. Public*, pg. 743
CURL-OIL MOISTURE BALANCER—Oil Restorative & Curl Revitalizer for Hair—The Gillette Company; *U.S. Public*, pg. 743
CURL-TECHNICS—Hairsetter—Bristol-Myers Squibb Company; *U.S. Public*, pg. 253
CURLAX—Hair Products—Dena Corporation; *U.S. Private*, pg. 324
CURLER CONSOLE—Hair Setters—Sunbeam Household Products; *U.S. Public*, pg. 1533
CURLEY QQQ FRIES—Curley QQQ's, Oven QQQ's, Western Spicy QQQ's, Western Medium QQQ's—Lamb-Weston, Inc.; *U.S. Public*, pg. 427
CURLIER FRERES—Bordeaux Wines—Frederick Wildman & Sons Ltd.; *U.S. Private*, pg. 1176
CURLMASTER—Curling Iron—Windmere-Durable Holdings; *U.S. Public*, pg. 1771
CURLY PERM—Ethnic Hair Care Products—Johnson Products Co., Inc.; *U.S. Public*, pg. 915
CUROSURF—Drug to Treat Respitory Distress Syndrome; Surfactant—Ares-Serono S.A.; *Int'l*, pg. 80
CURRENCY—Smooth & Embossed Paper—Appleton Papers Inc.; *Int'l*, pg. 567
CURRENT—Stationery & Gifts—Current, Inc.; *U.S. Public*, pg. 498
CURRENT—Computer System—International Business Machines Corporation; *U.S. Public*, pg. 895
CURRENTROL—Accessory—The Lincoln Electric Company; *U.S. Public*, pg. 996
CURRETAB—Pharmaceutical Product—Solvay Pharmaceuticals, Inc.; *Int'l*, pg. 1278
CURRIES—Metal Doors & Frames—Essex Industries, Inc.; *Int'l*, pg. 18
CURRINT 80 SERIES—Universal Life Insurance—Pan-American Life Insurance Company; *U.S. Private*, pg. 836
CURRYS—Retail Consumer Electronics Stores—Dixons Group plc; *Int'l*, pg. 413
CURTAIL—Small Grain Herbicide—The Dow Chemical Company; *U.S. Public*, pg. 522
CURTAIN CALL COSTUMES—Dance Apparel—Tighe Industries, Inc.; *U.S. Private*, pg. 1086
CURTIN MATHESON SCIENTIFIC—Clinical Products—Fisher Scientific International; *U.S. Private*, pg. 658
CURTIS—Compressors—Curtis-Toledo, Inc.; *U.S. Private*, pg. 298
CURTIS—Computer Products—Esselte Corporation; *Int'l*, pg. 459
CURTIS—Printing Papers—Fort James Corporation; *U.S. Public*, pg. 670
CURTIS—Creations—Uncas Manufacturing Company; *U.S. Private*, pg. 1116
CURTIS FARM—Milk, Dairy Products—Q.U.F. Industries Ltd.; *Int'l*, pg. 1074
CURTIS MATHES—Electronic Home Entertainment Prods.—Curtis Mathes Corporation; *U.S. Public*, pg. 1057
CURTIS MATHES—Premium Quality Home Electronics—Curtis Mathes Holding Corp.; *U.S. Public*, pg. 1057
CURTIS SWANN—Greeting Cards—Burgoyne, Inc.; *U.S. Private*, pg. 182
CURTIS WHISKY—Spirit—Allied Domecq PLC; *Int'l*, pg. 62

CURTMAN—Jewelry—Uncas Manufacturing Company; *U.S. Private*, pg. 1116
CURVATURA—NONE—USG Corporation; *U.S. Public*, pg. 1660
CURVE-CLEAN—Denture Brush—Brimms Inc.; *U.S. Private*, pg. 169
CURVE'N BODY—Perm Rods—The Gillette Company; *U.S. Public*, pg. 743
CURVED ARROW DESIGN—Instant Cameras & Film—Eastman Kodak Company; *U.S. Public*, pg. 550
CURVER—Plastic Prods.—DSM N.V.; *Int'l*, pg. 352
CURVET—Farm Building—Behlen Mfg. Co.; *U.S. Private*, pg. 130
CURY Q—Extension Cords—General Cable Corporation; *Int'l*, pg. 1486
CUSENIER—Syrup—Groupe Pernod Ricard; *Int'l*, pg. 566
CUSH-N-AIRE—Seating—National Seating Co.; *U.S. Private*, pg. 786
CUSH 'N TOW—Floor Trucks—Faultless Nutting; *Int'l*, pg. 473
CUSHION DRIVE—Fluid Coupling—Reuland Electric Company; *U.S. Private*, pg. 925
CUSHION-EDGE—Embossing—James Burn Intl.; *U.S. Private*, pg. 1506
CUSHION/FLEX—Goggle—U.S. Safety; *U.S. Private*, pg. 1125
CUSHION-FOLD—Laminates of Aluminum Foil Bonded to Paper—Reynolds Metals Company; *U.S. Public*, pg. 1385
CUSHION GANG—Disk Harrows—Case Corporation; *U.S. Public*, pg. 311
CUSHION GRIP—Hunting Knives—Fiskars-Gerber; *Int'l*, pg. 492
CUSHION GRIP—Rod Handle—Outdoor Technologies Group; *U.S. Private*, pg. 822
CUSHION LIFT—Cushion Lift Chair—Ortho-Kinetics, Inc.; *U.S. Private*, pg. 820
CUSHION-LOCK REGLETS—Hardware—Dayton Superior Corporation; *U.S. Private*, pg. 931
CUSHION ROLL—Knitwear—Wigwam Mills, Inc.; *U.S. Private*, pg. 1175
CUSHION TOP—Knitwear—Wigwam Mills, Inc.; *U.S. Private*, pg. 1175
CUSHIONAIR—Felt—Central/Shippee, Inc.; *U.S. Private*, pg. 224
CUSHIONAIRE—Bakeware—Mirro Company; *U.S. Public*, pg. 1177
CUSHIONAIRE—Cookware—Newell Co.; *U.S. Public*, pg. 1176
CUSHIONFLOR—Sheet Vinyl Flooring—Congoleum Corporation; *U.S. Public*, pg. 69
CUSHIONFLOR—Cushioned Vinyl Floor Covering—Forbo Holding SA; *Int'l*, pg. 496
CUSHMAN—NONE—DeVlieg-Bullard Inc.; *U.S. Public*, pg. 502
CUSHMAN—Industrial Vehicles—Harley Industries, Inc.; *U.S. Public*, pg. 880
CUSHMAN—Lawn & Garden Equipment—Ransomes-Cushman-Ryan; *Int'l*, pg. 1088
CUSHMAN—Indus. & Comml. Vehicles; Comml. Turf Machinery—Ransomes Plc; *Int'l*, pg. 1087
CUSSONS FOR MEN—Men's Toiletries—Cussons (U.K.) LTD.; *Int'l*, pg. 1024
CUSTAMINE—Chemicals—Westvaco Corporation; *U.S. Public*, pg. 1762
CUSTARD STYLE—Yogurt—Yoplait USA; *U.S. Public*, pg. 718
CUSTODIAN—Locksmiths' Work, Safes & Cash Boxes—Sime Darby Berhad; *Int'l*, pg. 1249
CUSTOM—Binocular—Bausch & Lomb Incorporated; *U.S. Public*, pg. 194
CUSTOM—Binoculars—Bushnell Corporation; *U.S. Private*, pg. 1191
CUSTOM—Permanent Wave—Revlon-Realistic Professional Products, Inc.; *U.S. Private*, pg. 690
CUSTOM AGE 625 PLUS—NONE—Carpenter Technology Corporation; *U.S. Public*, pg. 307
CUSTOM AIR HANDLING UNITS—NONE—Niagara Blower Company; *U.S. Private*, pg. 798
CUSTOM ALUMINUM—Vacuum Formed Plastics—Elixir Industries; *U.S. Private*, pg. 371
CUSTOM BAGGING—Fertilizer—Hydro/Kirby Agri Service, Inc.; *U.S. Private*, pg. 552
CUSTOM CARE—Hair Conditioner—Clairol, Inc.; *U.S. Public*, pg. 254

Brand Name Index

Brand Name Index

CUSTOM CARE—Alternating Pressure Mattress, Dynamic Mattress & Wheelchair Cushion—Span-America Medical Systems Inc.; *U.S. Public*, pg. 1495

CUSTOM CARE SETTER—Tighter Curls Hair Setter & Rollers—Clairol, Inc.; *U.S. Public*, pg. 254

CUSTOM CARE-USA—Health Insurance—Blue Cross and Blue Shield Association; *U.S. Private*, pg. 151

CUSTOM CLUB INTERNATIONAL—Apparel—Phillips-Van Heusen Corporation; *U.S. Public*, pg. 1291

CUSTOM COLLECTION—Hosiery—Pennaco Hosiery; *U.S. Public*, pg. 483

CUSTOM COLOR—Pencils—Dixon Ticonderoga Company; *U.S. Public*, pg. 514

CUSTOM CURL—Beauty Products—Windmere-Durable Holdings; *U.S. Public*, pg. 1771

CUSTOM DESIGNS—Waterbed Linens—Springs Industries, Inc.; *U.S. Public*, pg. 1499

CUSTOM FIT SEATING—Ergonomic Seating—Domore Corporation; *U.S. Private*, pg. 339

CUSTOM FOODS—NONE—Crestar Food Products, Inc.; *U.S. Public*, pg. 805

CUSTOM 450—NONE—Carpenter Technology Corporation; *U.S. Public*, pg. 307

CUSTOM 455—NONE—Carpenter Technology Corporation; *U.S. Public*, pg. 307

CUSTOM-FYL—Activated Carbon and Filter Purification Products—FiberMark, Inc.; *U.S. Public*, pg. 620

CUSTOM HOISTS—Telescopic & Pistonrod Hydraulic Cylinders—Standex International Corporation; *U.S. Public*, pg. 1505

CUSTOM HOME ELECTRONICS—NONE—Bobit Publishing Company; *U.S. Private*, pg. 154

CUSTOM HOUSE GUIDE—Magazine—North American Publishing Company; *U.S. Private*, pg. 803

CUSTOM KOTE—Coated Board—The Mead Corporation; *U.S. Public*, pg. 1074

CUSTOM LTD.—Sporting Goods—Brunswick Bowling & Billiards Corp.; *U.S. Public*, pg. 265

CUSTOM-MATIC—Sporting Equipment—Brunswick Bowling & Billiards Corp.; *U.S. Public*, pg. 265

CUSTOM NOVA—Pens for Specialty Advertising—Golden Books Family Entertainment Inc.; *U.S. Public*, pg. 749

CUSTOM PAK—Surgical Kits—Alcon Laboratories, Inc.; *Int'l*, pg. 916

CUSTOM PLANK—Heavy Sized Planks for Shelving & General Use—Carter Holt Harvey Limited; *U.S. Public*, pg. 904

CUSTOM PROTECTION OFFICER—Specially Selected & Trained Security Officer—The Wackenhut Corporation; *U.S. Public*, pg. 1731

CUSTOM ROLLED—Coil—United Aluminum Corporation; *U.S. Private*, pg. 1120

CUSTOM SEALDON—NONE—CertainTeed Corporation; *Int'l*, pg. 1170

CUSTOM VINYLS—Decorative Panels—Patrick Industries Inc.; *U.S. Public*, pg. 1264

CUSTOMARK—Service Mark-Labels—Markem Corporation; *U.S. Private*, pg. 704

CUSTOMCARE—Computer Software System—Unisys Corporation; *U.S. Public*, pg. 1671

CUSTOMCRAFT—Shoes—Schwartz & Benjamin, Inc.; *U.S. Private*, pg. 974

CUSTOMER ACCOUNT MANAGEMENT SYSTEM (CAMS)—NONE—American Management Systems, Inc.; *U.S. Public*, pg. 86

CUSTOMERQ—Customer Support, Help Desk, Call Tracking Solutions—Quintus Corporation; *U.S. Private*, pg. 901

CUSTOMER SATISFACTION GUARANTEE—NONE—Pitney Bowes Inc.; *U.S. Public*, pg. 1303

CUSTOMER SERVICE SOLUTION—Sewer Technology Focuses on Call Center Customer Service—Broadway & Seymour, Inc.; *U.S. Public*, pg. 258

CUSTOMFLOR—Floor Coverings—Domco Inc.; *Int'l*, pg. 415

CUSTOMLINE—Beauty Salon Furniture—Belvedere Company; *U.S. Private*, pg. 1008

CUSTOMLINE—Patient Chart Racks—Carstens Inc.; *U.S. Private*, pg. 216

CUSTOMPAC—Computer System—International Business Machines Corporation; *U.S. Public*, pg. 895

CUSTOMPRINTS—Imprinted Paper Tableware—Golden Books Family Entertainment Inc.; *U.S. Public*, pg. 749

CUSTOMSPEC—Commercial Rotogravure Vinyl Flooring—Mannington Resilient Floors; *U.S. Private*, pg. 700

CUSTOMWEAVE CARPETS—Carpet—World Carpets, Inc.; *U.S. Private*, pg. 1190

CUSTOMWOOD—Sheet Medium Density Fibreboard—Carter Holt Harvey Limited; *U.S. Public*, pg. 904

CUSTOMWOOD DOOR JAMBS—Door Jamb Sets—Carter Holt Harvey Limited; *U.S. Public*, pg. 904

CUSTOMWOOD MOULDINGS—Moisture-Resistant Mouldings—Carter Holt Harvey Limited; *U.S. Public*, pg. 904

THE CUT—Music Radio Program—Westwood One Entertainment; *U.S. Public*, pg. 1763

THE CUT—New Songs Programming—Westwood One, Inc.; *U.S. Public*, pg. 1763

CUT ABOVE—Under Cabinet Can Opener—The Rival Company; *U.S. Public*, pg. 1391

CUT EVEREST—NONE—Hudepohl-Schoenling Brewing Company; *U.S. Private*, pg. 545

CUT-N-FRY—Bakery Equipment—Belshaw Brothers, Inc.; *Int'l*, pg. 188

CUT-RITE—Scissors—Fiskars Oy AB; *Int'l*, pg. 492

CUT-RITE—Waxed Paper—Reynolds Metals Company; *U.S. Public*, pg. 1385

CUTCHER—Canned Seafood Products—Borden, Inc.; *U.S. Private*, pg. 157

CUTEX—Nail Polish Remover—Chesebrough-Pond's USA Co.; *Int'l*, pg. 1435

CUTEXCOLOR QUICK—Nail Enamel & Treatment Prods.—Chesebrough-Pond's USA Co.; *Int'l*, pg. 1435

CUTEXCOLOR SPLASH—Lipstick—Chesebrough-Pond's USA Co.; *Int'l*, pg. 1435

CUTEXSTRONG NAIL—Nail Enamel & Treatment Prods.—Chesebrough-Pond's USA Co.; *Int'l*, pg. 1435

CUTICURA—Sensitive Skin Care Products—Dep Corporation; *U.S. Public*, pg. 500

CUTISINCASING—NONE—Devro-Teepak, Inc.; *Int'l*, pg. 408

CUTIVATE—Dermatology Cream & Ointment—Glaxo Wellcome Inc.; *Int'l*, pg. 552

CUTLASS CIERA—Automobile—Oldsmobile Div. General Motors Corp.; *U.S. Public*, pg. 720

CUTLASS CRUISER—Station Wagon—Oldsmobile Div. General Motors Corp.; *U.S. Public*, pg. 720

CUTLASS SUPREME—Automobile—Oldsmobile Div. General Motors Corp.; *U.S. Public*, pg. 720

CUTLER HAMMER—Refrigeration Controls—Eaton Corporation Automotive Controls Division; *U.S. Public*, pg. 557

CUTLER-HAMMER—Switches, Relays, Circuit Breakers & Pushbottons—Eaton Corporation Commercial Controls Division; *U.S. Public*, pg. 556

CUTLER SPORTS—Decorated Knitwear—VF Corporation; *U.S. Public*, pg. 1702

CUTLER-HAMMER—Electrical & Electronic Equip.—Eaton Corporation; *U.S. Public*, pg. 555

CUTLESS—Turf Growth Regulator—The Dow Chemical Company; *U.S. Public*, pg. 522

CUTOVER DEVICE—Simpler Means of SS7 Installation—Tekelec; *U.S. Public*, pg. 1566

CUTQUICK—Powere Cut Off Saw—Stihl Inc.; *Int'l*, pg. 1301

CUTRITE—Woodworking Coated Abrasives—3M; *U.S. Public*, pg. 1604

CUTSAW—Power Tools—The Black & Decker Corporation; *U.S. Public*, pg. 233

CUTTER—Insect Repellent—Bayer AG; *Int'l*, pg. 171

THE CUTTING CENTER—Kitchen Cutlery Organizer—M. Kamenstein, Inc.; *U.S. Private*, pg. 606

CUTTY SARK—Scotch—Hiram Walker; *Int'l*, pg. 63

CUTWELD—NONE—Harris Calorific Co.; *U.S. Public*, pg. 996

CUTWELDER—NONE—Harris Calorific Co.; *U.S. Public*, pg. 996

CUVAISON—Wine—Pacific Wine Co.; *U.S. Private*, pg. 843

CYANASORB—Proprietary, Environmental—Coeur D'Alene Mines Corporation; *U.S. Public*, pg. 394

CYANIVER—Chemical Reagant—Hach Company; *U.S. Public*, pg. 773

CYBER LAW—Communication Cable(Category Five)—Southwire Company; *U.S. Private*, pg. 1019

CYBER9385—NONE—Trident Microsystems, Inc.; *U.S. Public*, pg. 1637

CYBER9382—NONE—Trident Microsystems, Inc.; *U.S. Public*, pg. 1637

CYBER9320—NONE—Trident Microsystems, Inc.; *U.S. Public*, pg. 1637

CYBERGUARD—Firewall—CyberGuard Corporation; *U.S. Public*, pg. 470

CYBERPRISE—Internet Server—Wall Data Incorporated; *U.S. Public*, pg. 1734

CYBEX—Rehabilitation & Fitness—Lumex Medical Products; *U.S. Public*, pg. 758

CYBORG SOLUTION SERIES SOFTWARE—Payroll, Human Resources & Fixed Assets Software—Cyborg Systems, Inc.; *U.S. Private*, pg. 299

CYCARE—Medical Data Processing—HBO & Company/Cycare Business Group; *U.S. Public*, pg. 770

CYCLAMATIC-DOK-LOK—Self-Cycling Levelers—Rite-Hite Corporation; *U.S. Private*, pg. 933

CYCLE—Dog Food—H.J. Heinz Company; *U.S. Public*, pg. 805

CYCLE—NONE—Star-Kist Foods Inc.; *U.S. Public*, pg. 805

CYCLE—Canned & Dry Dog Food—Star-Kist Foods, Inc.; *U.S. Public*, pg. 806

CYCLE PRODUCTS—Bicycle Accessories—Bell Sports Corp.; *U.S. Public*, pg. 207

CYCLE SPORT—Sports Magazine—IPC Magazines Limited; *Int'l*, pg. 651

CYCLE WORLD—Motorcycle Magazine—Hachette Filipacchi Magazines Inc.; *Int'l*, pg. 794

CYCLEAN—Filter Material—Kimberly-Clark Corporation; *U.S. Public*, pg. 958

CYCLELOG—Time Schedule Stations—The Foxboro Company; *Int'l*, pg. 1243

CYCLETECH—Bicycle Accessories—Bell Sports Corp.; *U.S. Public*, pg. 207

CYCLING WEEKLY—Sports Magazine—IPC Magazines Limited; *Int'l*, pg. 651

CYCLO AIR—Planters—Case Corporation; *U.S. Public*, pg. 311

CYCLO-INDEX—Motion Control Systems—Leggett & Platt, Incorporated; *U.S. Public*, pg. 985

CYCLO/PHRAM—Diaphragm Pumps—BIF; *U.S. Public*, pg. 726

CYCLO-MIXER—Mixer—Becton Dickinson Primary Care Diagnostics; *U.S. Public*, pg. 199

CYCLOBLOWER—Rotary Lobe Blower—Gardner Denver Machinery Inc.; *U.S. Public*, pg. 703

CYCLOCHM—Wax—Witco Corporation; *U.S. Public*, pg. 1773

CYCLOFLOW—Air Cleaner—Donaldson Company, Inc.; *U.S. Public*, pg. 517

CYCLOGEL—Wax—Witco Corporation; *U.S. Public*, pg. 1773

CYCLOGYL—Cyclopentolate HC1; Pharmaceutical—Alcon Laboratories. Inc.; *Int'l*, pg. 916

CYCLOKONE—Air Cleaner—Donaldson Company, Inc.; *U.S. Public*, pg. 517

CYCLOMYDRIL—Cyclopentolate HC1; Pharmaceutical—Alcon Laboratories. Inc.; *Int'l*, pg. 916

CYCLONE—Fragrance & Cosmetics—Avon Products, Inc.; *U.S. Public*, pg. 155

CYCLONE—Outdoor Products—The Black & Decker Corporation; *U.S. Public*, pg. 233

CYCLONE—Ducting—HBD Industries, Inc.; *U.S. Private*, pg. 489

CYCLONE—Lawn & Garden Tools—Huffy Corporation; *U.S. Public*, pg. 846

CYCLONE—Scanning Machine—Renishaw plc; *Int'l*, pg. 1103

CYCLONE—Computer Systems—Tandem Computers Inc.; *U.S. Public*, pg. 417

CYCLONE/R—Computer Systems—Tandem Computers Inc.; *U.S. Public*, pg. 417

CYCLONOX—Ketone Peroxides—Akzo Nobel N.V.; *Int'l*, pg. 42

CYCLOPAC—Air Cleaner—Donaldson Company, Inc.; *U.S. Public*, pg. 517

CYCLOPAL—Sizing Agents—Akzo Nobel N.V.; *Int'l*, pg. 42

CYCLOPS—Portable Thermometers—Land Instruments International Ltd.; *Int'l*, pg. 798

CYCLOPS—Interactive Pointer System—Proxima Corporation; *U.S. Public*, pg. 1339

CYCLOPTIC—Microscope—Leica, Inc.; *Int'l*, pg. 806

CYCLOSAL—Insecticides—Nippon Kayaku Co. Ltd.; *Int'l*, pg. 934

CYCLUS—Designer Chair Line—Harter; *U.S. Private*, pg. 581

CYCOLOR—Sensitized Film, Copying Equipment, Photocopies, Printers, Slide Printers—The Mead Corporation; *U.S. Public*, pg. 1074

CYCRIN—Generic Drug—American Home Products Corporation; *U.S. Public*, pg. 79

CYCRIN—Progestational Agent—Wyeth-Ayerst Laboratories, Inc.; *U.S. Public*, pg. 80

CYDECTIN—Veterinary Pharmaceuticals—American Home Products Corporation; *U.S. Public*, pg. 79

CYLINDER CITY—Hydraulic Cylinder Mfr.—Commercial Intertech Corp.; *U.S. Public*, pg. 411

CYLINDICATOR—Proximity Switches—Namco Controls Corporation; *U.S. Public*, pg. 482

CYLOK—Cyanoacrylatic Adhesives—Lord Corporation; *U.S. Private*, pg. 675

CYLSONIC—Ultrasonic Wire Cleaner—Branson Ultrasonics Corp. - Precision Cleaning Div.; *U.S. Public*, pg. 574

CYMEVENE—Ganciclovir, Antiviral—Recordati Industria Chimica e Farmaceutica S.p.A.; *Int'l*, pg. 1090

CYMEVENE—Antiviral Agent—Roche Holding Ltd.; *Int'l*, pg. 1119

CYMEVENE—Ganciclovir Sodium—Syntex; *Int'l*, pg. 1120

CYPOXY—Cycloaliphatic Epoxy Resin Insulation System—S & C Electric Company; *U.S. Private*, pg. 954

CYPOXYLATED—Devices Employing S&C Cypoxy Resin System—S & C Electric Company; *U.S. Private*, pg. 954

CYPRESS GARDENS—Orange Juice, Beverage Bases & Tea—Orange-Co., Inc.; *U.S. Public*, pg. 1229

CYREL—Photo Polymer Flexographic Printing Plates—Du Pont (E.I. Du Pont De Nemours & Co.); *U.S. Public*, pg. 530

CRYO-GRIND—Recycling Process—Air Products and Chemicals, Inc.; *U.S. Public*, pg. 30

CYRO-LOCK—Mixer System—Pfaudler, Inc.; *U.S. Public*, pg. 1393

CYRO-TRIM—Cryogenic Deflashing—Air Products and Chemicals, Inc.; *U.S. Public*, pg. 30

CYROLITE—Acrylic Based Multipolymer Compound—Cyro Industries; *Int'l*, pg. 1454

CYROLON ZX—Poly Carbonate Sheet—Cyro Industries; *Int'l*, pg. 1454

CYROSCAN—Datalogging System for Cryogenic Applications—ITT Barton Instruments; *U.S. Public*, pg. 860

CYRUS CLARK—Cotton & Chintz—Cyrus Clark Co., Inc.; *U.S. Private*, pg. 242

CYSTAGON—Treatment for Nephropathic Cystinosis—Mylan Laboratories, Inc.; *U.S. Public*, pg. 1143

CYSTO-CONRAY—X-Ray Contrast Media—Mallinckrodt Inc.; *U.S. Public*, pg. 1039

CYSTOGRAFIN—Diagnostics—Bristol-Myers Squibb Company; *U.S. Public*, pg. 253

CYSTOSPAZ—Prescription Pharmaceutical—PolyMedica Industries, Inc.; *U.S. Public*, pg. 1315

CYSTOSPAZ-M—NONE—PolyMedica Industries, Inc.; *U.S. Public*, pg. 1315

CYTODEX—Biotechnology—Pharmacia & Upjohn Adria Laboratories; *Int'l*, pg. 1049

CYTOFLUOR—Fluorescence Scanning Instruments & Reagents for Monitoring Cell Behavior—PerSeptive Biosystems, Inc.; *U.S. Public*, pg. 1279

CYTOGAM—Cytomegalovirus Immune Globulin Intravenous (Human)—MedImmune, Inc.; *U.S. Public*, pg. 1081

CYTOGUARD—Vial Adapter—Meridian Medical Technology, Inc.; *U.S. Public*, pg. 1095

CYTOLASE—Pectinase Enzymes for Clarification & Filtration of Fruit Juices—Royal Gist-Brocades N.V.; *Int'l*, pg. 1142

CYTOLOGY BRUSH—Medical Brush which gathers cell samples—Ballard Medical Products; *U.S. Public*, pg. 171

CYTOMEL—Thyroid Hormone—Jones Medical Industries Inc.; *U.S. Public*, pg. 933

CYTOPREP—Fixature—Fisher Scientific Company; *U.S. Private*, pg. 658

CYTORONABSOLUTE—Laser Flow Cytometry System—Ortho Clinical Diagnostic Systems Inc.; *U.S. Public*, pg. 929

CYTOTEC—Pharmaceuticals—Monsanto Company; *U.S. Public*, pg. 1124

CYTOTEC—Ulcer Medication—Searle & Co.; *U.S. Public*, pg. 1125

CYTOTEC—Ulcer Preventitive—Searle Laboratories; *U.S. Public*, pg. 1125

CYTOVENE—Ganciclovir Sodium—Syntex; *Int'l*, pg. 1120

CYTOXAN—Anti-Cancer Agent—Bristol-Myers Squibb Company; *U.S. Public*, pg. 253

CYTOXAN—Alkylating Agent used with other Neoplstic Drugs—Bristol-Myers Squibb U.S. Pharmaceutical Group; *U.S. Public*, pg. 255

CYTRADREN—NONE—Novartis Pharmaceuticals; *Int'l*, pg. 973

CZARINAVODKA—NONE—Barton Brands, Ltd.; *U.S. Public*, pg. 300

D

D—Hydraulic Turbines—General Electric Canada Inc.; *U.S. Public*, pg. 713

D—Plastic Pipe & Fittings—Phillips Petroleum Company; *U.S. Public*, pg. 1290

DAA—Chemical Compounds, Specific Monomeric Chemical Intermediates—The Lubrizol Corporation; *U.S. Public*, pg. 1016

DAAB—Adjustable Downhole Motor—Baker Hughes INTEQ; *U.S. Public*, pg. 166

DAF—Light, Medium & Heavy Trucks—DAF Trucks N.V.; *U.S. Public*, pg. 1247

DA-LITE—Projection Screens—Da-Lite Screen Company, Inc.; *U.S. Private*, pg. 306

DA-LITE/ORAVISUAL—Easels, Lecterns, Communication Cabinets, Credenzas & Scheduling Boards—Da-Lite Screen Company, Inc.; *U.S. Private*, pg. 306

DA-LITE/WELT—Background Stands—Da-Lite Screen Company, Inc.; *U.S. Private*, pg. 306

DAP—Caulks & Sealants—DAP Inc.; *Int'l*, pg. 1486

DASC—Direct Air Support Central—Comptek Research, Inc.; *U.S. Public*, pg. 419

DASD ADVISOR—Msrmnt. & Anal. of DASD Perf. to Ident. & Correct Causes of I/O Degradation—Boole & Babbage, Inc.; *U.S. Public*, pg. 244

DASD MANAGER FOR DB2—DB2 Database Administration—BMC Software, Inc.; *U.S. Public*, pg. 162

DASD MANAGER PLUS—NONE—BMC Software, Inc.; *U.S. Public*, pg. 162

DASL—Computer Programming Language—Datapoint Corporation; *Int'l*, pg. 384

DASP—Data Communications System—Datapoint Corporation; *Int'l*, pg. 384

DAT SERVICES (DIAL-A-TRUCK)—Communications for Trucking Industry—Data Transmission Network Corporation; *U.S. Public*, pg. 486

DA-TEX—Rear Projection Screen—Da-Lite Screen Company, Inc.; *U.S. Private*, pg. 306

D&D—Golf Ball—MacGregor Golf Company; *Int'l*, pg. 72

D & N—Stylized D & N Logo is a Registered Mark of D & N Bank—D & N Financial Corporation; *U.S. Public*, pg. 472

D & P—Rock Candy Products—Gravymaster Inc.; *U.S. Private*, pg. 471

DB—Spectrophotometer—Beckman Instruments, Inc.; *U.S. Public*, pg. 199

DBASE IV—Software—Borland International, Inc.; *U.S. Public*, pg. 246

DBASE MAC—Software—Borland International, Inc.; *U.S. Public*, pg. 246

DBASE III PLUS—Software—Borland International, Inc.; *U.S. Public*, pg. 246

DBASE III PLUS LAN PACK—Software—Borland International, Inc.; *U.S. Public*, pg. 246

DBA-XPERT—Database Administration Tool Set For Oracle—Compuware Corporation; *U.S. Public*, pg. 423

DBADVANTAGE—Database System—Fair, Isaac and Company, Inc.; *U.S. Public*, pg. 609

DB-BATCH-FE—Software—Tandem Computers Inc.; *U.S. Public*, pg. 417

DB DIRECTOR—Base Station Antenna—Allen Telecom Inc.; *U.S. Public*, pg. 45

DB GREEN L—Liquid Small Grains, Seed Treatment—Agsco, Inc.; *U.S. Private*, pg. 27

D.B. KAPLAN'S—Restaurant—The Levy Organization; *U.S. Private*, pg. 664

DBMS—Magazine—Miller Freeman Inc.; *Int'l*, pg. 1443

DBMS/COPY PLUS—Option to SPSS/PC+—SPSS Inc.; *U.S. Public*, pg. 1420

DBN—Diesel Engine Oil Additives—The Lubrizol Corporation; *U.S. Public*, pg. 1016

DB2—Computer System—International Business Machines Corporation; *U.S. Public*, pg. 895

DB2/400—Computer System—International Business Machines Corporation; *U.S. Public*, pg. 895

DB2/6000—Computer System—International Business Machines Corporation; *U.S. Public*, pg. 895

DB2/2—Computer System—International Business Machines Corporation; *U.S. Public*, pg. 895

DB VAULT—Computer Programs—Lucent Technologies Inc.; *U.S. Public*, pg. 1017

DBX—Compressors & Limiters—Harman International Industries, Inc.; *U.S. Public*, pg. 787

DC—Golf Ball—MacGregor Golf Company; *Int'l*, pg. 72

DCA—Computer Peripherals—Attachmate; *U.S. Private*, pg. 98

DCA—NONE—Donnelly Corporation; *U.S. Public*, pg. 519

DCA—Designer Classic Alternative—Tristar Corp.; *U.S. Public*, pg. 1640

DCAP—Decoupling Capacitors—AVX Corporation; *Int'l*, pg. 775

DCADVANTAGE—Computer Software—Attachmate; *U.S. Private*, pg. 98

DC COMICS—Comic Book—DC Comics, Inc.; *U.S. Public*, pg. 1614

DCE—Dust Control Equipment—BTR plc; *Int'l*, pg. 124

DCI—Golf Clubs—Acushnet Company; *U.S. Public*, pg. 675

DCI—Golf Clubs—Titleist & Foot-Joy Worldwide; *U.S. Public*, pg. 675

DCI STARSHIP METALS—NONE—Acushnet Company; *U.S. Public*, pg. 675

DCI STARSHIP METALS—Golf Clubs—Fortune Brands, Inc.; *U.S. Public*, pg. 674

DCI SYSTEM SIX—Distributed Control Instrumentation—Bailey, Fischer & Porter Company; *Int'l*, pg. 449

DCM 24—Digital Loop Carrier—Vidar, Inc.; *U.S. Private*, pg. 1139

DCP/88—Computer Equipment—Emulex Corporation; *U.S. Public*, pg. 579

DCRSI—Instrumentation Recorders—Ampex Corporation; *U.S. Public*, pg. 104

DCS "THE BAG"—Alternate Delivery—The Dispatch Printing Company; *U.S. Private*, pg. 334

DCT—Professional Television Equipment—Ampex Corporation; *U.S. Public*, pg. 104

DC TAYLOR CO—NONE—D.C. Taylor Co.; *U.S. Private*, pg. 1070

DC 3000 SERIES—High End Color Systems—Linotype-Hell Company; *Int'l*, pg. 604

DCU 3200—Control Product—Bailey, Fischer & Porter Company; *Int'l*, pg. 449

DCX—Communications Processor—Osicom Technologies Inc.; *U.S. Public*, pg. 1233

D. COMM—NONE—The Economist Group Limited; *Int'l*, pg. 1026

D-CON—Pest Control—Reckitt & Colman Inc.; *Int'l*, pg. 1090

D-CON—Pest Control—Reckitt & Colman plc; *Int'l*, pg. 1089

DD—Disc Refiner—Harnischfeger Industries, Inc.; *U.S. Public*, pg. 788

DDAVP—Pharmaceuticals—Rhone-Poulenc Rorer - U.S.; *Int'l*, pg. 1110

DDC—NONE—Detroit Diesel Corp.; *U.S. Private*, pg. 850

DDEC—NONE—Detroit Diesel Corp.; *U.S. Private*, pg. 850

DDI—Liquid Aliphatic Diisocyanate—Henkel Corporation; *Int'l*, pg. 610

DDNAM—Communications Software—Tandem Computers Inc.; *U.S. Public*, pg. 417

DDR 10—Digital Data Recorder—Westronics, Inc.; *U.S. Public*, pg. 1593

DDR 10 MULTIBAND—Digital Data Recorder—Westronics, Inc.; *U.S. Public*, pg. 1593

D-DAY—Game—Monarch Avalon, Inc.; *U.S. Public*, pg. 1123

DE—Device—The Dow Chemical Company; *U.S. Public*, pg. 522

DE & SE TINTS—Printing Paper—The Mead Corporation; *U.S. Public*, pg. 1074

DEC USER—NONE—EMAP Business Communications Division; *Int'l*, pg. 451

D.E.H.—Epoxy Hardeners—The Dow Chemical Company; *U.S. Public*, pg. 522

D.E.N.—Epoxy Novolacs—The Dow Chemical Company; *U.S. Public*, pg. 522

DENA—Electronic Equipment—Eaton Corp., Aerospace & Commercial Controls Div.; *U.S. Public*, pg. 557

DEP—Image Intensifiers—Delft Instruments N.V.; *Int'l*, pg. 388

DEP—Styling & Hair Care Products—Dep Corporation; *U.S. Public*, pg. 500

DEP FOR MEN—Gels & Hair Sprays—Dep Corporation; *U.S. Public*, pg. 500

D.E.R.—Epoxy Resins—The Dow Chemical Company; *U.S. Public*, pg. 522

DE-STA-CO—Industrial & Production Hardware; Blower Housings—De-Sta-Co, A Dover Resources Co.; *U.S. Public*, pg. 521

DE VIBRATOR—Boring Bars—Kennametal Inc.; *U.S. Public*, pg. 950

DE-VO-KO—Alkyd & Latex Finishes—Devoe Paint; *Int'l*, pg. 663

DE-VO-PRO—Contractor Product Line of Paints—Devoe Paint; *Int'l*, pg. 663

DE-VO-TEX—Texture Coating—Devoe Paint; *Int'l*, pg. 663

D-8—Photographic Developers—Eastman Kodak Company; *U.S. Public*, pg. 550

D-88—Photographic Developers—Eastman Kodak Company; *U.S. Public*, pg. 550

D-11—Photographic Developers—Eastman Kodak Company; *U.S. Public*, pg. 550

DFA—Filters—Pall Corporation; *U.S. Public*, pg. 1253

DFDSM—Computer System—International Business Machines Corporation; *U.S. Public*, pg. 895

DF/EMCONTROL—Electromagnetic Compliance—Cadence Design Systems, Inc.; *U.S. Public*, pg. 290

DF1—NONE—Life Technologies, Inc.; *U.S. Public*, pg. 504

DFS—Surgical Staplers—U.S. Surgical Corp.; *U.S. Public*, pg. 1687

DFSMSDFP—Computer System—International Business Machines Corporation; *U.S. Public*, pg. 895

DFSMS—Computer System—International Business Machines Corporation; *U.S. Public*, pg. 895

DFSMSDSS—Computer System—International Business Machines Corporation; *U.S. Public*, pg. 895

DFSMSHSM—Computer System—International Business Machines Corporation; *U.S. Public*, pg. 895

DFSMS/MVS—Computer System—International Business Machines Corporation; *U.S. Public*, pg. 895

DFSMSRMM—Computer System—International Business Machines Corporation; *U.S. Public*, pg. 895

DFSMS/VM—Computer System—International Business Machines Corporation; *U.S. Public*, pg. 895

DF/SIGNOISE—Signal Integrity—Cadence Design Systems, Inc.; *U.S. Public*, pg. 290

DFSORT—Computer System—International Business Machines Corporation; *U.S. Public*, pg. 895

DF/THERMAX—Thermal—Cadence Design Systems, Inc.; *U.S. Public*, pg. 290

DF/VIABLE—Reliability—Cadence Design Systems, Inc.; *U.S. Public*, pg. 290

DFX-8000—Dot Matrix Printer—Epson America Inc.; *Int'l*, pg. 1219

DFX-5000+—Dot Matrix Printer—Epson America Inc.; *Int'l*, pg. 1219

D-FILM—Shrinkable Film—Grace Packaging; *U.S. Public*, pg. 755

D/FLEX—Inspiratory Filter—Nellcor Puritan Bennett Incorporated; *U.S. Public*, pg. 1039

D-FOR-ICE—Ice Cream Ingredients—Royal Gist-Brocades N.V.; *Int'l*, pg. 1142

D4—Record Cleaning Systems/Products—Recoton Corporation; *U.S. Public*, pg. 1369

DGD—Power Tools & Assembly Systems—Cooper Industries, Inc.; *U.S. Public*, pg. 442

DG/RDOS—Software—Data General Corporation; *U.S. Public*, pg. 485

DGS—Chemical Reagents—Beckman Instruments, Inc.; *U.S. Public*, pg. 199

DG 32—Digital Electroencephalograph—Vickers PLC; *Int'l*, pg. 1466

DG TRIM PRODUCTS—Automotive Interior Trim—Indian Head Industries Inc.; *U.S. Private*, pg. 559

DG/UX—Software—Data General Corporation; *U.S. Public*, pg. 485

DH—NONE—Life Technologies, Inc.; *U.S. Public*, pg. 504

DHD—Hammer Drive, Masonry Anchor—Gunnebo Fastening Corp.; *U.S. Private*, pg. 488

DHE 45—Migrane Analgesic Nasal Spray—Novartis AG; *Int'l*, pg. 971

DHE-45—Vascular/Migraine Headache Pharmaceutical—Sandoz Pharmaceuticals Corp.; *Int'l*, pg. 974

DH11S—NONE—Life Technologies, Inc.; *U.S. Public*, pg. 504

DH5—NONE—Life Technologies, Inc.; *U.S. Public*, pg. 504

DH5A—NONE—Life Technologies, Inc.; *U.S. Public*, pg. 504

DH5AF—NONE—Life Technologies, Inc.; *U.S. Public*, pg. 504

DH5AMCR—NONE—Life Technologies, Inc.; *U.S. Public*, pg. 504

DH5AFIQ—NONE—Life Technologies, Inc.; *U.S. Public*, pg. 504

DHL—Worldwide Express—DHL Airways, Inc.; *U.S. Private*, pg. 302

DHL—International Air Express—DHL Worldwide Express; *U.S. Private*, pg. 301

DH10B—NONE—Life Technologies, Inc.; *U.S. Public*, pg. 504

DH10BAC—NONE—Life Technologies, Inc.; *U.S. Public*, pg. 504

DH12S—NONE—Life Technologies, Inc.; *U.S. Public*, pg. 504

DHW—Yeast—Burns, Philp & Company Limited; *Int'l*, pg. 236

D I C ENTERPRISES—Animation TV Shows—DIC Entertainment; *U.S. Public*, pg. 513

D-I-D—Closures for Pharmaceutical Containers Made Primarily of Metal & Plastic—The West Company, Incorporated; *U.S. Public*, pg. 1755

DIF—Wallpaper Stripper—Wm. Zinsser & Co,. Inc.; *U.S. Public*, pg. 1358

DIS—Instrumentation & Data Recording—Ampex Corporation; *U.S. Public*, pg. 104

DK—Spectrophotometric Apparatus—Beckman Instruments, Inc.; *U.S. Public*, pg. 199

DK ENERGY SERVICES—Integrated Well Services & Project Management—Dresser Industries, Inc.; *U.S. Public*, pg. 528

DK-50—Photographic Developers—Eastman Kodak Company; *U.S. Public*, pg. 550

DK-50R—Photographic Developers—Eastman Kodak Company; *U.S. Public*, pg. 550

DKNY COVERINGS—Hosiery—Sara Lee Corporation; *U.S. Public*, pg. 1432

DKS—NONE—James Hardie Industries Ltd.; *Int'l*, pg. 596

DK-60A—Photographic Developers—Eastman Kodak Company; *U.S. Public*, pg. 550

DK-60ATR—Photographic Developers—Eastman Kodak Company; *U.S. Public*, pg. 550

DKTH—Techno Home Fashion Products—Dakotah, Inc.; *U.S. Public*, pg. 477

DL—Foam Trays—Amoco Chemicals; *U.S. Public*, pg. 102

DL—Winches, Oilers, Fence Splicers—Dutton-Lainson Co.; *U.S. Private*, pg. 350

DL—Key Blanks—Ilco Unican Corp.; *Int'l*, pg. 1432

DL—Key Blanks—Unican Security Systems Ltd.; *Int'l*, pg. 1432

DLC-100—Tires—Bridgestone/Firestone, Inc.; *Int'l*, pg. 213

DL-50—NONE—Molex Incorporated; *U.S. Public*, pg. 1121

DLP—NONE—Medtronic, Inc.; *U.S. Public*, pg. 1082

DLP—NONE—Texas Instruments Incorporated; *U.S. Public*, pg. 1585

DLRO—Digital Low Resistance Ohmmeters—Avo International; *U.S. Private*, pg. 9

D'LITE—Lo Calorie/No Sugar Pies—Bakers Square Restaurants; *U.S. Public*, pg. 1719

D LOGO—Environmental Control Appartus—Donaldson Company, Inc.; *U.S. Public*, pg. 517

D-LUX—Protective Coating—Lucent Technologies Inc.; *U.S. Public*, pg. 1017

DMA—Herbicide—The Dow Chemical Company; *U.S. Public*, pg. 522

DMC 4032—Half-Page Printer—Datametrics Corporation; *U.S. Public*, pg. 487

DMC-I—Microprocessor Control for Oildraulic Elevators—Dover Elevator Systems, Inc.; *U.S. Public*, pg. 521

DMC 1900—Color Thermal Printer—Datametrics Corporation; *U.S. Public*, pg. 487

DMC 1600—Printers—Datametrics Corporation; *U.S. Public*, pg. 487

DMC 1200—Environmental Dot Matrix Printer—Datametrics Corporation; *U.S. Public*, pg. 487

DMCS—NONE—Structural Dynamics Research Corp.; *U.S. Public*, pg. 1525

DMD—Piping Specialties—Dresser Industries, Inc.; *U.S. Public*, pg. 528

DME—Navigational Equipment—Wilcox Electric, Inc.; *Int'l*, pg. 1384

DM4—Ultrasonic Thickness Gauge—Krautkramer-Branson, Inc.; *U.S. Public*, pg. 574

DMI—All Products—DMI Furniture Inc.; *U.S. Public*, pg. 473

DMI, INC.—Farm Equipment Sales & Service—Adair Feed & Grain Company; *U.S. Private*, pg. 16

DMJ—NONE—Donnelly Corporation; *U.S. Public*, pg. 519

DM1—NONE—Life Technologies, Inc.; *U.S. Public*, pg. 504

DMS—Switcher for Public Networks—BCE Inc.; *Int'l*, pg. 114

DMS—Ultrasonic Thickness Gauge—Krautkramer-Branson, Inc.; *U.S. Public*, pg. 574

DMS—Telephone Products—Northern Telecom; *Int'l*, pg. 969

DMS—Telephone Switching Equip.—Northern Telecom Limited; *Int'l*, pg. 968

DMS/ES—Software—CSC Financial Services Group; *U.S. Public*, pg. 422

DMS-MTX—Telecommunications—Northern Telecom Limited; *Int'l*, pg. 968

DMS-100/200—NONE—Northern Telecom Limited; *Int'l*, pg. 968

DMS-10—Telecommunications—Northern Telecom Limited; *Int'l*, pg. 968

DMS-250—NONE—Northern Telecom Limited; *Int'l*, pg. 968

DMWD—Retrievable, Directional Measurement While Drilling—Baker Hughes INTEQ; *U.S. Public*, pg. 166

DMX—Footwear Cushioning Technology—Reebok International Ltd.; *U.S. Public*, pg. 1369

DNA—Allopops—Apollinaris & Schweppes Gmbh & Co.; *Int'l*, pg. 78

DNA TYPING GRADE—Proof Positive of Quality & Design—Life Technologies, Inc.; *U.S. Public*, pg. 504

DNC—Telecommunication Computer Hardware—Northern Telecom Limited; *Int'l*, pg. 968

DNG—Digital Network Gateway—Northern Telecom Limited; *Int'l*, pg. 968

DNR—Electronics—National Semiconductor Corporation; *U.S. Public*, pg. 1159

DNS—Distributed Name Service Software—Tandem Computers Inc.; *U.S. Public*, pg. 417

DNX—Digital Telecommunications Cross Connect System—Northern Telecom Limited; *Int'l*, pg. 968

D-19—Photographic Developers—Eastman Kodak Company; *U.S. Public*, pg. 550

D.O.C.—Optical—D.O.C. Optics Corporation; *U.S. Private*, pg. 305

D.O.C. EYEWORLD—Optical Centers—D.O.C. Optics Corporation; *U.S. Public*, pg. 305

D.O.C. OPTICAL CENTERS—Optical Centers—D.O.C. Optics Corporation; *U.S. Private*, pg. 305

DOD—Professional Electronics—Harman International Industries, Inc.; *U.S. Public*, pg. 787

DOM—Hardware—The Black & Decker Corporation; *U.S. Public*, pg. 233

DOS3270—Computer Software—Attachmate; *U.S. Private*, pg. 98

DOT—Directional Orientation Tool—Baker Hughes INTEQ; *U.S. Public*, pg. 166

D100 WHITEPRINTER—Printer—Dietzgen Corporation; *U.S. Private*, pg. 332

DPC—Curing Process—Bandag, Incorporated; *U.S. Public*, pg. 177

D/P CELL—Flow & Liquid Level Transmitter—The Foxboro Company; *Int'l*, pg. 1243

DPIC COMPANIES—Professional Liability—Orion Capital Companies, Inc.; *U.S. Public*, pg. 1231

DPIL—NONE—Western Atlas Logging Services; *U.S. Public*, pg. 1757

DPN—Telecommunications Digital Switch—Northern Telecom Limited; *Int'l*, pg. 968

DPN-100—Data Packet Switching—BCE Inc.; *Int'l*, pg. 114

DP/90 PLUS—NONE—SunGard Data Systems Inc.; *U.S. Public*, pg. 1534

DPP—Disposable Plotter Pens—Koh-I-Noor, Inc.; *U.S. Private*, pg. 629

DPR—Depolymerized Rubber & Compounds—Hardman Division of Harcros Chemicals, Inc.; *Int'l*, pg. 598

DPS 8—Data Processing System—Bull HN Information Systems Inc.; *Int'l*, pg. 316

DPS 8000—Data Processing System—Bull HN Information Systems Inc.; *Int'l*, pg. 316

DPS 88—Data Processing System—Bull HN Information Systems Inc.; *Int'l*, pg. 316

DPS 9000—Data Processing System—Bull HN Information Systems Inc.; *Int'l*, pg. 316

DPS 90—Data Processing System—Bull HN Information Systems Inc.; *Int'l*, pg. 316

DPS 7—Data Processing System—Bull HN Information Systems Inc.; *Int'l*, pg. 316

DPS 7000—Data Processing System—Bull HN Information Systems Inc.; *Int'l*, pg. 316

DPS 6—Data Processing System—Bull HN Information Systems Inc.; *Int'l*, pg. 316

DPX—Sport Performance Sterndrive—Volvo Penta of the Americas, Inc.; *Int'l*, pg. 1477

DPX/20—Data Processing System—Bull HN Information Systems Inc.; *Int'l*, pg. 316

DPX/2—Data Processing System—Bull HN Information Systems Inc.; *Int'l*, pg. 316

DPROP—Computer System—International Business Machines Corporation; *U.S. Public*, pg. 895

DQ CHIPPER SANDWICH—Frozen Novelties—International Dairy Queen, Inc.; *U.S. Public*, pg. 220

DQ HOMESTYLE ULTIMATE BURGER—Bacon Cheeseburger—International Dairy Queen, Inc.; *U.S. Public*, pg. 220

DQ WICH—Frozen Novelties—International Dairy Queen, Inc.; *U.S. Public*, pg. 220

DR—Flotation Machines—Svedala Pumps & Process; *Int'l*, pg. 1325

DRB—NONE—Western Atlas Logging Services; *U.S. Public*, pg. 1757

DRDA—Computer System—International Business Machines Corporation; *U.S. Public*, pg. 895

DRP—Generators—Dresser-Rand Sales; *U.S. Public*, pg. 529

DRT—Paging System Infrastructure Equipment; Computer Programs for Paging—Glenayre Technologies, Inc.; *U.S. Public*, pg. 746

DRX—Bar Code Data Reconstruction (software)—Accu-Sort Systems, Inc.; *U.S. Private*, pg. 11

DS—Amylase Reagent—Beckman Instruments, Inc.; *U.S. Public*, pg. 199

DSA-20—Drywall Adhesive—Pratt & Lambert United, Inc.; *U.S. Public*, pg. 1466

DSB—Barrier Screw—Davis Standard Corporation; *U.S. Public*, pg. 459

DSBM-T—Feed Screw—Davis Standard Corporation; *U.S. Public*, pg. 459

DSC NEXOS—Computer Programs—DSC Communications Corporation; *U.S. Public*, pg. 475

DSD—Drives—MagneTek, Inc.; *U.S. Public*, pg. 1037

DS/EXPRESS—Computer Software—Attachmate; *U.S. Private*, pg. 98

DSF—Reader/Printer—Bell & Howell Holdings; *U.S. Public*, pg. 201

DS-50—NONE—Molex Incorporated; *U.S. Public*, pg. 1121

DSIS—Orthotics for Hyper Pronation—The Langer Biomechanics Group, Inc.; *U.S. Public*, pg. 978

DSLK—Disposable Sealkleen Filter Assembly—Pall Corporation; *U.S. Public*, pg. 1253

DSM—NONE—Lam Research Corporation; *U.S. Public*, pg. 975

DSM—NONE—LORAD Corporation; *U.S. Public*, pg. 1595

DSM—Double Side Machine—SpeedFam International, Inc.; *U.S. Public*, pg. 1497

DST—Data Storage Products—Ampex Corporation; *U.S. Public*, pg. 104

D700 SERIES—NONE—Detroit Diesel Corp.; *U.S. Private*, pg. 850

D-76—Photographic Developers—Eastman Kodak Company; *U.S. Public*, pg. 550

D-76R—Photographic Developers—Eastman Kodak Company; *U.S. Public*, pg. 550

D-SHIELD—Communication Cables—General Cable Corporation; *Int'l*, pg. 1486

D-16—Photographic Developers—Eastman Kodak Company; *U.S. Public*, pg. 550

D'STAT—Record Table/Static Eliminators—Recoton Corporation; *U.S. Public*, pg. 1369

DTE—Clinical Chemistry Products—Eastman Kodak Company; *U.S. Public*, pg. 550

DTF—Digital Tape Format High-Capacity Data Storage Devices—DRS Technologies, Inc.; *U.S. Public*, pg. 474

DTN AGDAILY—Communications for Agribusiness—Data Transmission Network Corporation; *U.S. Public*, pg. 486

DTNAUTO—Communications Linking Auto Auctions & Auto Dealers—Data Transmission Network Corporation; *U.S. Public*, pg. 486

DTNERGY—Communications for the Oil & Natural Gas Industries—Data Transmission Network Corporation; *U.S. Public*, pg. 486

DTN FARMDAYTA—Communication for Agribusiness—Data Transmission Network Corporation; *U.S. Public*, pg. 486

DTN FIRSTRATE—Communications for the Morgage Industry—Data Transmission Network Corporation; *U.S. Public*, pg. 486

DTNIRON—Communications for the Farm Implement Dealer—Data Transmission Network Corporation; *U.S. Public*, pg. 486

DTN MISSING CHILDREN INFORMATION CENTER (MCIC)—Communications for Missing & Endangered Children—Data Transmission Network Corporation; *U.S. Public*, pg. 486

DTN PRO SERVICES—Enhanced Communication for Agribusiness—Data Transmission Network Corporation; *U.S. Public*, pg. 486

DTN PRODUCE—Communications for Produce Industry—Data Transmission Network Corporation; *U.S. Public*, pg. 486

DTN REAL TIME—Communications for the Real Time Financial Industry—Data Transmission Network Corporation; *U.S. Public*, pg. 486

DTN SPECTRUM—Communications for Financial Industry—Data Transmission Network Corporation; *U.S. Public*, pg. 486

DTNSTANT—Agriculture Ticker Service—Data Transmission Network Corporation; *U.S. Public*, pg. 486

DTN WALL STREET—Communications for the Financial Industry—Data Transmission Network Corporation; *U.S. Public*, pg. 486

DTN WEATHER CENTER—Communication for Weather-Dependent Industries—Data Transmission Network Corporation; *U.S. Public*, pg. 486

DT100—Clinical Chemistry Products—Eastman Kodak Company; *U.S. Public*, pg. 550

DTP—Books—Dell Publishing; *Int'l*, pg. 191

DT-PLUS—Clinical Chemistry Products—Eastman Kodak Company; *U.S. Public*, pg. 550

DTSC—Clinical Chemistry Products—Eastman Kodak Company; *U.S. Public*, pg. 550

DT60—Clinical Chemistry Products—Eastman Kodak Company; *U.S. Public*, pg. 550

DTX—NONE—ECI Telecom Ltd.; *Int'l*, pg. 643

D-TIPPER PIPETTES—Microprocessor controlled automated pipetting system—Medical Laboratory Automation, Inc.; *U.S. Private*, pg. 727

D-TR DOOR—Airport Door to Deter Unauthorized Entry—Jervis B. Webb Company; *U.S. Private*, pg. 1156

D-TRANS—Electrotransport System—Alza Corporation; *U.S. Public*, pg. 62

D-TRANS—Pesticides—McLaughlin Gormley King Company; *U.S. Public*, pg. 723

DU—Spectrophotometer—Beckman Instruments, Inc.; *U.S. Public*, pg. 199

DVC—Looseleaf Binders—Via Tech Publishing Solutions; *U.S. Private*, pg. 1138

DVL—Close Clearance Connector Chimney System—Simpson Dura-Vent Co., Inc.: *U.S. Public*, pg. 1474

DVM NEWSMAGAZINE—Trade Periodical—Advanstar Communications; *U.S. Private*, pg. 22

DVS—NONE—Chr. Hansen, Inc.; *Int'l*, pg. 288

DV-38—85% Alumina Brick—A.P. Green Industries, Inc.; *U.S. Public*, pg. 761

DWF—Window Film—The Dow Chemical Company; *U.S. Public*, pg. 522

DWM COPELAND—Compressors—Copeland Corporation Ltd.; *U.S. Public*, pg. 576

DX—Suspension Systems—CGC Inc.; *U.S. Public*, pg. 1660

DX—NONE—Kiwi Brands Pty. Ltd.; *U.S. Public*, pg. 1434

DX—Golf Clubs—MacGregor Golf Company; *Int'l*, pg. 72

DX—TI/E1 TDM Network Multiplexerx—Telematics Inc.; *Int'l*, pg. 643

DX—NONE—USG Corporation; *U.S. Public*, pg. 1660

DX DESIGN—Photgraphic Films—Eastman Kodak Company; *U.S. Public*, pg. 550

DXI—Communications Worstation—V-Band Corporation; *U.S. Public*, pg. 1701

DXP—Digital Telephone Systems—Comdial Corporation; *U.S. Public*, pg. 407

DXT—Computer System—International Business Machines Corporation; *U.S. Public*, pg. 895

DXT/D1—Computer System—International Business Machines Corporation; *U.S. Public*, pg. 895

DX-XXX—Unix-Based Network Service Hardware Systems—Datapoint Corporation; *Int'l*, pg. 384

DYC—Grocery Products—Goodman Fielder Limited; *Int'l*, pg. 555

DO3 SYSTEMS—Open Plan Systems—Domore Corporation; *U.S. Private*, pg. 339

D-ZERTA—Desserts & Reduced Calorie Whipped Topping Mix—Kraft Foods, Inc.; *U.S. Public*, pg. 1287

DABCO—Catalysts—Air Products and Chemicals, Inc.; *U.S. Public*, pg. 30

D'AC—Lighting—JJI Lighting Group Inc.; *Int'l*, pg. 821

DACOBAS—Industrial Furniture—Knurr AG; *Int'l*, pg. 739

DACOM—Facsimile Equipment—Ricoh Corporation; *Int'l*, pg. 1114

DACOMATIC—Photo Film, Processing Chemicals—Eastman Kodak Company; *U.S. Public*, pg. 550

DACON—Deformed Steel Bars—Kobe Steel, Ltd.; *Int'l*, pg. 740

DACONIL—Agricultural Chemical—Novartis AG; *Int'l*, pg. 971

DACOR—Scuba & Skin Diving Equipment—Dacor Corporation; *U.S. Private*, pg. 306

DACRON—Polyester—Du Pont (E.I. Du Pont De Nemours & Co.); *U.S. Public*, pg. 530

DACSCAN—Telecommunications Netwrok Controllers Located in a Central Office—Lucent Technologies Inc.; *U.S. Public*, pg. 1017

DACSMATE—Computer Programs—Lucent Technologies Inc.; *U.S. Public*, pg. 1017

DACTA—Educational Sets—LEGO Systems, Inc.; *Int'l*, pg. 805

DADDIES—Tomato Ketchup—Danone Group; *Int'l*, pg. 379

DADDY WHACKER—Insect Control—Bushwhacker Associates, Inc.; *U.S. Private*, pg. 141

DAD'S—Soft Drink—Grant-Lydick Beverage Co.; *U.S. Private*, pg. 470

DAD'S—Cookies—Mrs. Alison's Cookie Company; *U.S. Private*, pg. 765

DAD'S CHUNX—Pet Food—Dad's Products Co., Inc.; *U.S. Private*, pg. 306

DAD'S DOG FOODS—Dog Food—Dad's Products Co., Inc.; *U.S. Private*, pg. 306

DAD'S ECON-O-METS—Pet Food—Dad's Products Co., Inc.; *U.S. Private*, pg. 306

DAD'S MEAL—NONE—Dad's Products Co., Inc.; *U.S. Private*, pg. 306

DAD'S ROOT BEER—Soft Drink—The Monarch Company, Inc.; *U.S. Private*, pg. 756

DAG—Lubricants—Acheson Colloids Company; *U.S. Private*, pg. 12

DAGLAS—Polyester and Glass Fiber Wrapped—Phelps Dodge Magnet Wire Co.; *U.S. Public*, pg. 1286

DAHL—Diesel Filter/Separtors—Baldwin Filters; *U.S. Public*, pg. 381

DAI DAY—Chinese Condiments—Allied Old English, Inc.; *U.S. Private*, pg. 39

DAICOLOR—Pigment for Plastic Coloring Agents—Dainichiseika Colour & Chemicals Mfg. Co., Ltd.; *Int'l*, pg. 369

DAIEI—Superstore—The Daiei, Inc.; *Int'l*, pg. 364

DAIEI CONVENIENCE SYSTEMS—Convenience Store—The Daiei, Inc.; *Int'l*, pg. 364

DAILEY—Pickles—Dean Pickle & Specialty Products Co.; *U.S. Public*, pg. 490

DAILY—NONE—Iveco-Ford Truck Ltd.; *Int'l*, pg. 484

DAILY CFR—On-Line Services—The Washington Post Company; *U.S. Public*, pg. 1742

DAILY EXPRESS—NONE—Express Newspapers plc; *Int'l*, pg. 1443

THE DAILY GRINDER—Seasoning Appliance—McCormick/Schilling; *U.S. Public*, pg. 1066

DAILY HERALD—Newspaper—Paddock Publications, Inc.; *U.S. Private*, pg. 833

DAILY-JOURNAL—Daily Newspaper—The Record-Journal Publishing Company; *U.S. Private*, pg. 914

DAILY MIRROR—NONE—Mirror Group plc; *Int'l*, pg. 869

DAILY NEWS RECORD—Business Publication—Fairchild Publications; *U.S. Public*, pg. 513

THE DAILY OKLAHOMAN—Daily Newspaper—The Daily & Sunday Oklahoman; *U.S. Private*, pg. 813

DAILY PRESS—Daily Newspaper—Tribune Company; *U.S. Public*, pg. 1635

DAILY RACING FORM—Newspaper of the Thoroughbred Horseracing Industry—Primedia Inc.; *U.S. Public*, pg. 1327

DAILY RECORD—NONE—Mirror Group plc; *Int'l*, pg. 869

DAILY ROASTERS—NONE—Koo Koo Roo, Inc.; *U.S. Public*, pg. 966

DAILY'S—Fruit Juices—Koninklijke BolsWessanen nv; *Int'l*, pg. 750

DAILY STAR—NONE—Express Newspapers plc; *Int'l*, pg. 1443

DAILY VARIETY—Daily Newspaper of the Entertainment Industry—Reed Elsevier Business Information; *Int'l*, pg. 1095

DAIMON—NONE—Duracell International Inc.; *U.S. Public*, pg. 743

DAIPYROXIDE—Coloring Agent for Calcined Pigments—Dainichiseika Colour & Chemicals Mfg. Co., Ltd.; *Int'l*, pg. 369

DAIRI-FRESH—Dairy & Ice Cream Products—Publix Supermarkets Inc.; *U.S. Private*, pg. 893

DAIRY BELLE—Dairy Products—Hilland Dairy Company; *U.S. Private*, pg. 879

DAIRY BOX—Chocolate Confections—Nestle-Rowntree Ltd.; *Int'l*, pg. 921

DAIRY CHARM—Milk & Ice Cream—Mid-America Dairymen, Inc.; *U.S. Private*, pg. 743

DAIRY FOODS—Magazine Serving Professionals in the Dairy Processing Industry—Reed Elsevier Business Information; *Int'l*, pg. 1095

DAIRY FRESH—Dairy Products—Crystal Cream & Butter Company; *U.S. Private*, pg. 294

DAIRY FRESH—Ice Cream—Kemps Foods, Inc.; *Int'l*, pg. 752

DAIRY MART—Convenience Stores—Dairy Mart Convenience Stores, Inc.; *U.S. Public*, pg. 476

DAIRY PRO—Material Handling Equipment for Dairy Industry—Cannon Equipment; *Int'l*, pg. 646

DAIRY QUEEN—Dessert—American Dairy Queen Corporation; *U.S. Public*, pg. 220

DAIRY QUEEN—Soft Service Ice Milk Product—International Dairy Queen, Inc.; *U.S. Public*, pg. 220

DAIRY QUEEN/BRAZIER—Fast Food Restaurants—American Dairy Queen Corporation; *U.S. Public*, pg. 220

DAIRY SWEET—Sweetened Condensed Milk—The Milnot Company; *U.S. Private*, pg. 749

DAIRY WISE—Milk—Q.U.F. Industries Ltd.; *Int'l*, pg. 1074

DAIRYLEA—Processed Cheese—Philip Morris Companies Inc.; *U.S. Public*, pg. 1287

DAIRYMATE—Milk & Cream Substitute—The Pillsbury Company; *Int'l*, pg. 411

DAIRYPAK—Dairy Containers—Champion International Corp.; *U.S. Public*, pg. 333

DAISCOAT—Coloring Agent for Aqueous Coatings—Dainichiseika Colour & Chemicals Mfg. Co., Ltd.; *Int'l*, pg. 369

DAISY—Disposable Lady's Shaver—The Gillette Company; *U.S. Public*, pg. 743

DAISY—Tricycle—Roadmaster/Brunswick; *U.S. Public*, pg. 265

DAISY CHAIN—Redundant Switching Method for Electronic Products Used in Communications—Comtech Telecommunications Corp.; *U.S. Public*, pg. 425

DAISY COUNTRY—Complete Line Of Western Toy Guns—Daisy Manufacturing Company, Inc.; *U.S. Private*, pg. 308

DAISY PLUS—Disposable Shaver—The Gillette Company; *U.S. Public*, pg. 743

DAISYFRESH—Personal Products—Sara Lee Corporation; *U.S. Public*, pg. 1432

DAISYTEK—NONE—Daisytek International Corporation; *U.S. Public*, pg. 477

DAKON—Photo Lenses—Eastman Kodak Company; *U.S. Public*, pg. 550

DAKOTA—Ag Chemical—AgrEvo USA Company; *Int'l*, pg. 1203

DAKOTA—NONE—M. Fine & Sons Manufacturing Co., Inc.; *U.S. Private*, pg. 405

DAKOTA—Sunflower Seeds—Pioneer Hi-Bred International, Inc.; *U.S. Public*, pg. 1298

DAKOTA CASE—Jewelry Boxes—Scotchman Industries, Inc.; *U.S. Private*, pg. 636

DAKOTA FARMER—NONE—Farm Progress Publications; *U.S. Public*, pg. 513

DAKOTA HEARTH—Frozen Bread Dough—Rhodes International, Inc.; *U.S. Private*, pg. 927

DAKOTA MAID—Bakery Flour—North Dakota Mill & Elevator Association; *U.S. Private*, pg. 804

DAKOTAH—NONE—Dakotah, Inc.; *U.S. Public*, pg. 477

DAKOTAH LUXE—Luxe Products for the Home—Dakotah, Inc.; *U.S. Public*, pg. 477

DAKOTAH OUTDOORS—Outdoor Fabrics, Including Pillows & Cushion Covers—Dakotah, Inc.; *U.S. Public*, pg. 477

DAKSTATS—Sports Results & Statistics Software—Daktronics, Inc.; *U.S. Public*, pg. 478

DAL RECCOLTO—Oil, Pasta, Vegetables—Colivita USA, Inc.; *U.S. Private*, pg. 252

DALE—Resistors/Potentiometers—Vishay Intertechnology, Inc.; *U.S. Public*, pg. 1721

DALE FARM—Dairy Products & Ice Cream—Northern Foods plc; *Int'l*, pg. 967

DALE/INCOR—NONE—Dale Industries Inc.; *U.S. Private*, pg. 308

DALEY—Pickles—Dean Foods Company; *U.S. Public*, pg. 489

DALGETY—Animal Feed—Dalgety Plc; *Int'l*, pg. 376

DALLAIRE—Milk Production—Labatt Brewing Company Limited; *Int'l*, pg. 679

DALLAS—Bath Accessories—Baldwin Hardware Corporation; *U.S. Public*, pg. 1053

DALLAS—Sunglasses—Bausch & Lomb Incorporated; *U.S. Public*, pg. 194

THE DALLAS BUSINESS JOURNAL—Business Journal—Business First of New York, Inc.; *U.S. Private*, pg. 19

DALLAS SEMICONDUCTOR—Semiconductor—Interface Electronics Corporation; *U.S. Private*, pg. 567

DALLAS SEMICONDUCTOR—NONE—Milgray Electronics, Inc.; *U.S. Public*, pg. 205

THE DALMORE—Scotch Whiskey—Fortune Brands, Inc.; *U.S. Public*, pg. 674

THE DALMORE—SINGLE MALT SCOTCH WHISKY—The Whyte & Mackay Group Plc.; *U.S. Public*, pg. 675

DALPAD—Coalescing Agent—The Dow Chemical Company; *U.S. Public*, pg. 522

DALWHINNIE—NONE—Guinness Plc; *Int'l*, pg. 412

DAMARK—NONE—Damark International, Inc.; *U.S. Public*, pg. 478

DAMARK INTERNATIONAL, INC.—NONE—Damark International, Inc.; *U.S. Public*, pg. 478

DAMASCUS PIPE—Stainless Pipe—Damascus Bishop Tube Co.; *Int'l*, pg. 842

DAMATIC—Industrial Process Instrumentation Equipment & Automation Sys.—Valmet Corporation; *Int'l*, pg. 1447

DAMMINIX—Provides Protection Against Deer Ticks—Ecolab Inc.; *U.S. Public*, pg. 562

DAMON—Apparel—The Apparel Group, Ltd.; *U.S. Private*, pg. 78

DAMPLAY—Sound Absorbing Steel Plate—Kobe Steel, Ltd.; *Int'l*, pg. 740

DAN DEE—Potato Chips, Pretzels & Corn Snacks Prods.—Troyer Potato Products, Inc.; *U.S. Private*, pg. 1106

DAN KLORIX—Disinfectant—Colgate-Palmolive Company; *U.S. Public*, pg. 397

DAN-LOC—NONE—The Flexitallic Group, Inc.; *U.S. Private*, pg. 413

DAN POST—Western Boots—Acme Boot Co., Inc.; *U.S. Private*, pg. 394

DAN-PRESS—Fabrics—Dan River Inc.; *U.S. Public*, pg. 478

DAN RATHER REPORTING—News Program—Westwood One, Inc.; *U.S. Public*, pg. 1763

DAN'UP—Liquid Yogurt—Danone Group; *Int'l*, pg. 379

DAN'UP—NONE—LPC Industrias Alimenticias S.A.; *Int'l*, pg. 380

DANA BUCHMAN—Women's Apparel—Liz Claiborne, Inc.; *U.S. Public*, pg. 1005

DANA DESIGN—Backpacks & Hydration Systems—K2 Inc.; *U.S. Public*, pg. 940

DANAHER—Holding Co.—Danaher Corporation; *U.S. Public*, pg. 480

DANBURY—Suspenders, Belts, Neckties & Small Leather Accessories—Gem-Dandy, Inc.; *U.S. Private*, pg. 442

DANBURY APPAREL—Ladies' Lingerie—Gem-Dandy, Inc.; *U.S. Private*, pg. 442

DANCE MIX—NONE—Quality Music; *Int'l*, pg. 1075

DANCE MIX USA—NONE—Quality Music; *Int'l*, pg. 1075

DANCE TRAXX—International Music Programming—Westwood One, Inc.; *U.S. Public*, pg. 1763

DANCIN—Hair Care Products—Wella Group; *Int'l*, pg. 1489

DANCING WATERS—Sprinklers—Rain Bird Sprinklers Manufacturing Corp.; *U.S. Private*, pg. 907

DAND-O-LINE—Wire—Elco Textron; *U.S. Public*, pg. 1590

DANDEE—Bread & Rolls—Flowers Industries, Inc.; *U.S. Public*, pg. 656

DANDRUFF CONTROL PERT PLUS—Shampoo—The Procter & Gamble Company; *U.S. Public*, pg. 1330

DANDUX—Canvas Goods—C.R. Daniels, Inc.; *U.S. Private*, pg. 310

DANDY—Vegetable—A. Duda & Sons Inc.; *U.S. Private*, pg. 344

DANETTE—Yogurt—Danone Group; *Int'l*, pg. 379

DANETTE—NONE—LPC Industrias Alimenticias S.A.; *Int'l*, pg. 380

DANFORTH—Marine Products—Rule Industries, Inc.; *U.S. Public*, pg. 950

DANFRUT—NONE—LPC Industrias Alimenticias S.A.; *Int'l*, pg. 380

D'ANGLAS—Cosmetics—L'Oreal S.A.; *Int'l*, pg. 818

DANIEL DEFASSON—Perfume—International Cosmetics Co., Ltd.; *Int'l*, pg. 684

DANIEL GREEN—Slippers—Daniel Green Co.; *U.S. Private*, pg. 477

DANILASE—Anti-Inflammatory—Novo Nordisk A/S; *Int'l*, pg. 987

DANIMALS—Yogurt—The Dannon Co.; *Int'l*, pg. 379

DANINO—Yougurts & Desserts—Q.U.F. Industries Ltd.; *Int'l*, pg. 1074

DANIPROL—Analgesic—Novo Nordisk A/S; *Int'l*, pg. 987

DANIS—Hardware—The Danis Companies; *U.S. Private*, pg. 310

DANISH BAKERY—Bakery Items—Publix Supermarkets Inc.; *U.S. Private*, pg. 893

DANISH CROWN—Canned Hams—M.H. Greenebaum, Inc.; *U.S. Private*, pg. 477

DANISH ORCHARDS—Processed Fruit Products—Danisco Foods; *Int'l*, pg. 378

DANNON—Yogurt—The Dannon Co.; *Int'l*, pg. 379

DANNON—Yogurt—Danone Group; *Int'l*, pg. 379

DANNON—Natural Spring Water—Great Brands of Europe; *Int'l*, pg. 381

DANNON DOUBLE DELIGHTS—Yogurt—The Dannon Co.; *Int'l*, pg. 379

DANNON LIGHT—Yogurt and Frozen Yogurt—The Dannon Co.; *Int'l*, pg. 379

DANNON LIGHT—Low-Fat Yogurt—Danone Group; *Int'l*, pg. 379

DANNON MINIPACK—Yogurt—The Dannon Co.; *Int'l*, pg. 379

DANONE—Yogurt—Danone Group; *Int'l*, pg. 379

DANONE—Yogurts & Desserts—Q.U.F. Industries Ltd.; *Int'l*, pg. 1074

DANONE—Yogurt Product—George Weston Limited; *Int'l*, pg. 1494

DANONINHO—Yogurt—Danone Group; *Int'l*, pg. 379

DANONINHO—NONE—LPC Industrias Alimenticias S.A.; *Int'l*, pg. 380

DANSEN CONTEMPORARY—Contemporary Sofas & Chairs—Woodmark Originals Inc.; *U.S. Private*, pg. 747

DANSK—Tableware & Housewares—Lenox, Incorporated; *U.S. Public*, pg. 261

DANSK INTERNATIONAL DESIGNS—China, Cryatal, Flatware, Cookware, Etc.—Brown-Forman Corporation; *U.S. Public*, pg. 261

DANSKIN LEGWEAR—Tights & Socks—Pennaco Hosiery; *U.S. Public*, pg. 483

DANSTORM—Fabrics—Dan River Inc.; *U.S. Public*, pg. 478

DANSUKKER—Sugar, Sugar Grain & Instant Sugar—Danisco Sugar; *Int'l*, pg. 378

DANTEX—Synthetic Products—C.R. Daniels, Inc.; *U.S. Private*, pg. 310

DANTIFOLD—Disposable Paper Products—Wisconsin Tissue Mills, Inc.; *U.S. Public*, pg. 347

DANTOBROM—Water Treatment Chemicals—Lonza Inc.; *Int'l*, pg. 67

DANTOCHLOR—Water Treatment Chemicals—Lonza Inc.; *Int'l*, pg. 67

DANTOGARD—Preservatives for Microbiological Control—Lonza Inc.; *Int'l*, pg. 67

DANTOGARD PLUS—Preservatives for Microbiological Control—Lonza Inc.; *Int'l*, pg. 67

DANTRIUM CAPSULES—Skeletal Muscle Relaxant & MH Preventative—Procter & Gamble Pharmaceuticals, Inc.; *U.S. Public*, pg. 1331

DANTWILL—Fabrics—Dan River Inc.; *U.S. Public*, pg. 478

DANUFIL—Flame-Retardant Fibres—Hoechst Aktiengesellschaft; *Int'l*, pg. 624

DANUSER—Large Equipment—Danuser Machine Co.; *U.S. Private*, pg. 310

DANVERN—Paint Nozzle—Sherwin-Williams Diversified Brands, Inc.; *U.S. Public*, pg. 1466

DANY—Yogurt—Danone Group; *Int'l*, pg. 379

DANY—NONE—LPC Industrias Alimenticias S.A.; *Int'l*, pg. 380

DANY—Yogurts & Desserts—Q.U.F. Industries Ltd.; *Int'l*, pg. 1074

DAPRAL—Mild Shampoo Thickener—Akzo Nobel N.V.; *Int'l*, pg. 42

DARA—Pharmaceutical Products—Galderma Laboratories, Inc.; *Int'l*, pg. 819

DARA MICHELLE—Women's Fashion Accessories Stores—Claire's Stores Inc.; *U.S. Public*, pg. 381

DARAGEN—Pharmaceutical Products—Galderma Laboratories, Inc.; *Int'l*, pg. 819

DARAMAX—Fermentation Process Aids—BetzDearborn Inc.; *U.S. Public*, pg. 226

DARAN—Industrial Chemicals & Paper Coatings—Hampshire Chemical Corp.; *U.S. Private*, pg. 498

DARANIDE—Dichlorphenamide—Merck & Co., Inc.; *U.S. Public*, pg. 1090

DARAPRIM—Antimalarial Prescription Drug—Glaxo Wellcome PLC; *Int'l*, pg. 553

DARASPRAY—Paper Making Aids—BetzDearborn Inc.; *U.S. Public*, pg. 226

DARATAK—Industrial Chemicals—Hampshire Chemical Corp.; *U.S. Private*, pg. 498

DARBY THE DRAGON—NONE—Broderbund Software, Inc.; *U.S. Public*, pg. 258

DARCO—Activated Carbons—American Norit Co. Inc.; *Int'l*, pg. 958

DARCO—Gen. Carbon Name—NORIT N.V.; *Int'l*, pg. 958

DARDA—Racing Cars & Sets—Life-Like Products, Inc.; *U.S. Private*, pg. 666

DARE TO DRESS—NONE—Kellwood Company; *U.S. Public*, pg. 948

DAREX—Container Sealing Compounds—W.R. Grace & Co.; *U.S. Public*, pg. 754

DAREX—Textile Print Blankets—Polyfibron Technologies Corp.; *U.S. Private*, pg. 875

DARFRESH—Plastic Packaging—W.R. Grace & Co.; *U.S. Public*, pg. 754

DARI-KOOL—Bulk Milk Cooling Systems—Bou-Matic; *U.S. Private*, pg. 301

DARI-LITE—Low Fat/Non-Fat Dairy Products—Darigold, Inc.; *U.S. Private*, pg. 311

DARI-PRO—Milk Replacers—Ralston Purina Company; *U.S. Public*, pg. 1359

DARICON—Pharmaceutical Prods.—SmithKline Beecham Laboratories; *Int'l*, pg. 1264

DARIGOLD—Dairy Products—Darigold, Inc.; *U.S. Private*, pg. 311

DARILOID—Alginate Blend—The NutraSweet Kelco Company; *U.S. Public*, pg. 1125

DARILOID 100—Xanthan Gum Blend—The NutraSweet Kelco Company; *U.S. Public*, pg. 1125

DARILOID 300—Xanthan Gum Blend—The NutraSweet Kelco Company; *U.S. Public*, pg. 1125

DARITEEN—Flavors—Haarmann & Reimer Corp.; *Int'l*, pg. 173

DARK EMPEROR—Game—Monarch Avalon, Inc.; *U.S. Public*, pg. 1123

DARK N' RICH—Wax—Bruce Hardwood Floors; *U.S. Public*, pg. 1634

DARK SIDE, THE—Greeting Cards—American Greetings Corporation; *U.S. Public*, pg. 77

DARLIE—Toothpaste—Colgate-Palmolive Company; *U.S. Public*, pg. 397

DARLYN—Chemical Fabric—Chemfab Corporation; *U.S. Public*, pg. 344

DARRICK—Toiletries—Avon Products, Inc.; *U.S. Public*, pg. 155

DARRYL'S—Restaurants—Houlihan's Restaurant Group; *U.S. Public*, pg. 841

DART—Book Stores, Auto Parts & Accessories—Dart Group Corporation; *U.S. Public*, pg. 484

DART—Depth, Speed, Distance, Time and Water Temperature—Datamarine International, Inc.; *U.S. Public*, pg. 486

DARTMOUTH—Manufactured Homes—Champion Enterprises, Inc.; *U.S. Public*, pg. 332

DARTY—Electricals—Kingfisher plc; *Int'l*, pg. 733

DARVOCET-N—Propoxyphene Napsylate With Acetaminophen, Lilly—Eli Lilly and Company; *U.S. Public*, pg. 992

DARVON—Propoxyphene Hydrochloride, Lilly—Eli Lilly and Company; *U.S. Public*, pg. 992

DARVON COMPOUND—Propoxyphene Hydrochloride, Aspirin & Caffeine, Lilly—Eli Lilly and Company; *U.S. Public*, pg. 992

DARVON COMPOUND-65—Propoxyphene Hydrochloride, Aspirin & Caffeine, Lilly—Eli Lilly and Company; *U.S. Public*, pg. 992

DARVON-N—Propoxyphene Napsylate, Lilly—Eli Lilly and Company; *U.S. Public*, pg. 992

DARVON-N WITH A.S.A.—Propoxyphene Napsylate With Aspirin, Lilly—Eli Lilly and Company; *U.S. Public*, pg. 992

DARVON WITH A.S.A—Propoxyphene Hydrochloride With Aspirin, Lilly—Eli Lilly and Company; *U.S. Public*, pg. 992

DARWIN—Computer Programs for use in Microcomputers Recorded on Magnetic Discs—Thinking Machines Corporation; *U.S. Private*, pg. 1081

DAS HAUS—Magazine—Burda Holding GmbH & Co., KG; *Int'l*, pg. 233

DASCO—RP Water Soluble Rust Preventive—D.A. Stuart Company; *U.S. Private*, pg. 1048

DASCOLENE—Cutting Fluids & Lubricants—D.A. Stuart Company; *U.S. Private*, pg. 1048

DASCOOL—Coolant—D.A. Stuart Company; *U.S. Private*, pg. 1048

DASH—Aircraft—The Boeing Company; *U.S. Public*, pg. 239

DASH—NONE—Oshkosh Truck Corporation; *U.S. Public*, pg. 1233

DASH—Laundry Product—The Procter & Gamble Company; *U.S. Public*, pg. 1330

DASH—Detergent—Procter & Gamble Espana S.A.; *U.S. Public*, pg. 1332

DASH VIII—8-Channel Portable Recorder—Astro-Med, Inc.; *U.S. Public*, pg. 141

DASH IV—4-Channel Portable Recorder—Astro-Med, Inc.; *U.S. Public*, pg. 141

DASH 'O LEMON—Seafood Seasoning—McCormick/Schilling; *U.S. Public*, pg. 1066

DASH II MT—2-Channel Chart Recorder—Astro-Med, Inc.; *U.S. Public*, pg. 141

DASHER/486—Family Personal Computer System—Data General Corporation; *U.S. Public*, pg. 485

DASHER/386—Family Personal Computer Systems—Data General Corporation; *U.S. Public*, pg. 485

DASHER/286—Family Personal Computer System—Data General Corporation; *U.S. Public*, pg. 485

DASIN—Pharmaceutical Prods.—SmithKline Beecham Laboratories; *Int'l*, pg. 1264

DASKOR—Insecticide—The Dow Chemical Company; *U.S. Public*, pg. 522

DASM ON-LINE—Multimedia Knowledge Base—Analogic Corporation; *U.S. Public*, pg. 109

DATA ACCELERATOR—NONE—BMC Software, Inc.; *U.S. Public*, pg. 162

DATA CARD—NONE—Taylor Impression, Inc.; *U.S. Private*, pg. 1070

DATA CENTER—Stationery Products—The Mead Corporation; *U.S. Public*, pg. 1074

DATA CENTRAL—Establishment & Training for Computer-based Information Retrieval Systems—The Mead Corporation; *U.S. Public*, pg. 1074

DATA COLLECTION EDITION—Computer Product—International Business Machines Corporation; *U.S. Public*, pg. 895

DATA CONTROL SYSTEMS—Telemetry—Data Control Systems; *U.S. Public*, pg. 420

DATA DEFENDER—Office Products—HON Industries Inc.; *U.S. Public*, pg. 772

DATA FILES—Stationery Products—The Mead Corporation; *U.S. Public*, pg. 1074

DATA FLEX—Cable—Rockbestos-Suprenant Cable Corp.; *U.S. Private*, pg. 938

DATA-FRAME—CRT Display Format—Eastman Kodak Company; *U.S. Public*, pg. 550

DATA GAGE—Market Research Products—Market Facts, Inc.; *U.S. Public*, pg. 1046

DATA GRAPH—Laboratories Software—Beckman Instruments, Inc.; *U.S. Public*, pg. 199

DATA-GUARD—Coated and Embossed Pressboard—FiberMark Inc.; *U.S. Public*, pg. 620

DATA HUB—NONE—Detroit Diesel Corp.; *U.S. Private*, pg. 850

DATA INDUSTRIAL—Flow Meter—Datamarine International, Inc.; *U.S. Public*, pg. 486

DATA JUNCTION—Microcomputer Software for US Mailers—Group 1 Software, Inc.; *U.S. Public*, pg. 417

DATA LEADER—Laboratories Software—Beckman Instruments, Inc.; *U.S. Public*, pg. 199

DATA LIBRARY—Integrated Library System Software—Datapoint Corporation; *Int'l*, pg. 384

DATA MATH—Laboratories Software—Beckman Instruments, Inc.; *U.S. Public*, pg. 199

DATA MEDIA—Filing Cabinets—Tab Products Co.; *U.S. Public*, pg. 1559

DATA OPTIMIZER—NONE—BMC Software, Inc.; *U.S. Public*, pg. 162

DATA PACKER FOR DB2—DASD Data Compression—BMC Software, Inc.; *U.S. Public*, pg. 162

DATA PACKER/IMS—DASD Data Compression—BMC Software, Inc.; *U.S. Public*, pg. 162

DATA-PAK—Filing System—Fellowes Manufacturing Co.; *U.S. Private*, pg. 400

DATA PIPELINE—Electronic Instrument—Intel Corporation; *U.S. Public*, pg. 886

DATA PLOT—Laboratories Software—Beckman Instruments, Inc.; *U.S. Public*, pg. 199

DATA*SAFE—Data Encryptor—Microtel International Inc.; *U.S. Public*, pg. 1108

DATA*SAT—High-Speed Satellite Terminal—Rockwell International Corporation; *U.S. Public*, pg. 1397

DATA 6100—Ultra High Precision Waveform Analyzer—Analogic Corporation; *U.S. Public*, pg. 109

DATA TRANSPORTER—PC Ready Receptor Feature—Beckman Instruments, Inc.; *U.S. Public*, pg. 199

DATA 2020—Polynomial Waveform Generator—Analogic Corporation; *U.S. Public*, pg. 109

DATA-VAULT—Computer Shipping & Carrying Cases—Plastic Reel Corp. of America; *U.S. Private*, pg. 871

DATA View—Communication Products—Arkwright, Inc; *Int'l*, pg. 994

DATA-XPERT—NONE—Compuware Corporation; *U.S. Public*, pg. 423

DATA-PAC—Binder Files—Master Craft Corp.; *Int'l*, pg. 267

DATABASE INTEGRITY PLUS—NONE—BMC Software, Inc.; *U.S. Public*, pg. 162

DATABASE PROGRAMMING & DESIGN—Magazine—Miller Freeman Inc.; *Int'l*, pg. 1443

DATABASE 2—Software—International Business Machines Corporation; *U.S. Public*, pg. 895

DATABASE 2 OS/400—Software—International Business Machines Corporation; *U.S. Public*, pg. 895

DATABASE VERIFIER—NONE—BMC Software, Inc.; *U.S. Public*, pg. 162

DATACAPTURE—Microfilm—Eastman Kodak Company; *U.S. Public*, pg. 550

DATACENTRAL—Computer Software Systems—Unisys Corporation; *U.S. Public*, pg. 1671

DATACHECK—Data Management System for Blood Gas Quality Control—Radiometer America Inc.; *Int'l*, pg. 1083

DATACLEAR—Data Cable—Champlain Cable Corp.; *Int'l*, pg. 637

DATACOPY—Bond, Xerographic Bond—Champion International Corp.; *U.S. Public*, pg. 333

DATADESIGNS—Database Marketing System—Group 1 Software, Inc.; *U.S. Public*, pg. 417

DATAFILE—Color Coded Filing Systems—Applied Power Inc.; *U.S. Public*, pg. 124

DATAFLEX—Flexible Circuit Boards—Freudenberg & Company; *Int'l*, pg. 505

DATAFLO—NONE—Worcester Controls Corp.; *Int'l*, pg. 128

DATAFORM—Computer Programming Language—Datapoint Corporation; *Int'l*, pg. 384

DATAGLANCE—Computer System—International Business Machines Corporation; *U.S. Public*, pg. 895

DATAGRAF—Computer Based Data Acquisition Recording Product with Real Time Monitor—Gould Instrument Systems, Inc.; *U.S. Public*, pg. 1592

DATAGRAPHIX—COM Systems, Duplicators—Anacomp, Inc.; *U.S. Public*, pg. 106

DATAGUIDE—Informational & Instructional Guides—Eastman Kodak Company; *U.S. Public*, pg. 550

DATAGUIDE—Computer System—International Business Machines Corporation; *U.S. Public*, pg. 895

DATAGYR 1000—Meter Translation System—Landis & Staefa, Inc.; *Int'l*, pg. 800

DATAHUB—Computer System—International Business Machines Corporation; *U.S. Public*, pg. 895

DATAKEEPER—NONE—Kronos Incorporated; *U.S. Public*, pg. 967

DATAKIT—Virtual Circuit Switch—Lucent Technologies Inc.; *U.S. Public*, pg. 1017

DATAKODE—Magnetic Recording Coatings for Photographic Films—Eastman Kodak Company; *U.S. Public*, pg. 550

DATALAN—PC Network Operating System Software—Datapoint Corporation; *Int'l*, pg. 384

DATALIFT—Microcomputer Product—Group 1 Software, Inc.; *U.S. Public*, pg. 417

DATALINE—Computer Supplies—Esselte AB; *Int'l*, pg. 459

DATALINK—Data Transfer & Terminal Emulation Package—GenRad, Inc.; *U.S. Public*, pg. 731

DATALLIANCE—Computer Program for Insurance Underwriting & Risk Management—Lincoln National Corporation; *U.S. Public*, pg. 997

DATALOG—Data Processing Facsimile Equipment—Litton Industries, Inc.; *U.S. Public*, pg. 1002

DATAMARK—Microprocessor-based Ticketing Terminal—International Lottery & Totalizator Systems, Inc.; *U.S. Public*, pg. 900

DATAMARK FLIPPER—PC-Based Ticketing Terminal—International Lottery & Totalizator Systems, Inc.; *U.S. Public*, pg. 900

DATAMETRICS—Pressure & Flow Instrumentation—Edwards High Vacuum, International; *Int'l*, pg. 121

DATAMITE—Data Logger—Thermo Electric Co., Inc.; *U.S. Private*, pg. 1080

DATAMOVER—Wireless Data Communications System—Comptek Research, Inc.; *U.S. Public*, pg. 419

DATAMYTE—Quality Data Acquisition Devices—Rockwell Automation; *U.S. Public*, pg. 1397

DATAMYTE—Factory Data Collection & Monitoring Systems—Rockwell International Corporation; *U.S. Public*, pg. 1397

DATAOPTIC IMAGING SYSTEMS—Digital Image Capture & Storage Systems—DRS Technologies, Inc.; *U.S. Public*, pg. 474

DATAPAC—Data Collector—IRD Mechanalysis, Inc. (U.S.A.); *U.S. Public*, pg. 789

DATAPAGE—NONE—Brown & Sharpe Manufacturing Company; *U.S. Public*, pg. 260

DATAPAK—Photo Film—Eastman Kodak Company; *U.S. Public*, pg. 550

DATAPLATE—NONE—Fred B. Johnston Company, Inc.; *U.S. Private*, pg. 595

DATAPOINT—Gen. Purpose Bus. Computer Systems—Datapoint Corporation; *Int'l*, pg. 384

DATAPOLL—Data Communications Software System—Datapoint Corporation; *Int'l*, pg. 384

DATAPORT—NONE—LORAD Corporation; *U.S. Public*, pg. 1595

DATAPRO INFORMATION SERVICES GROUP—Publisher of Info Services for EDP & Office Automation Products—Datapro Information Services Grp.; *U.S. Public*, pg. 1070

DATAPROPAGATOR—Computer System—International Business Machines Corporation; *U.S. Public*, pg. 895

DATARAM—Mini-Computer Related Products—Dataram Corporation; *U.S. Public*, pg. 487

DATAREACH—NONE—BMC Software, Inc.; *U.S. Public*, pg. 162

DATAREFRESHER—Computer System—International Business Machines Corporation; *U.S. Public*, pg. 895

DATARESCUE—Data Recovery Service & Floppy Disk—Polaroid Corporation; *U.S. Public*, pg. 1313

DATARIBBON—Printer Ribbon—Dataproducts Corporation; *Int'l*, pg. 620

DATARIM—Network Interface Hardware—Datapoint Corporation; *Int'l*, pg. 384

DATASAFE—Recombination Lead Acid Batteries for Telecommunications—Chloride Industrial Batteries Ltd.; *Int'l*, pg. 125

DATASCAN—Datalogging System for Gas & Chemical Applications—ITT Barton Instruments; *U.S. Public*, pg. 860

DATASELECT—Switches—CTS Corporation; *U.S. Public*, pg. 285

DATASENSOR—Reusable Pulse Oximetry Sensor—Datascope Corp.; *U.S. Public*, pg. 487

DATASERVICE—Specialty Chemicals Information Catalogs—Eastman Kodak Company; *U.S. Public*, pg. 550

DATASHARE—Multi-User Computer System—Datapoint Corporation; *Int'l*, pg. 384

DATASHOW—Electronic Projection Equipment, Accessories—Eastman Kodak Company; *U.S. Public*, pg. 550

DATASORT—Computer Software Program—Datapoint Corporation; *Int'l*, pg. 384

DATASOUTH—Printers—Datasouth Computer Corporation; *U.S. Public*, pg. 267

DATASTAR—Enterprise-Wide Gateway—Apertus Technologies Incorporated; *U.S. Public*, pg. 119

DATASTAR—Digital PBX System—TIE/Communications, Inc.; *U.S. Private*, pg. 1085

DATASTRUCTURE SERIES—Computer System—International Business Machines Corporation; *U.S. Public*, pg. 895

DATATAPE—Magnetic Tape Transport Recording & Playback Systems—Eastman Kodak Company; *U.S. Public*, pg. 550

DATATRAC—Diagnostic Products—Abbott Laboratories; *U.S. Public*, pg. 12

DATATRACE—Information Retrieval & Reporting System—GenRad, Inc.; *U.S. Public*, pg. 731

DATATRACE—Temperature Recorder—Mesa Laboratories, Inc.; *U.S. Public*, pg. 1099

DATATRADE—Computer System—International Business Machines Corporation; *U.S. Public*, pg. 895

DATATWIST—NONE—Belden Wire & Cable Company; *U.S. Public*, pg. 201

DATATWIST 350—NONE—Belden Inc.; *U.S. Public*, pg. 200

DATAVIEW—Statistical Control Software—NewAge Industries Inc.; *U.S. Private*, pg. 796

DATAVIEW—Statistical Control Software—Newage Industries Inc., Testing Instruments Group; *U.S. Private*, pg. 796

DATAVUE—NONE—Acme Design Technology, Co.; *U.S. Private*, pg. 13

DATAXCELLERATOR—Cable Modem—Scientific-Atlanta, Inc.; *U.S. Public*, pg. 1443

DATOS—NONE—Brown & Sharpe Manufacturing Company; *U.S. Public*, pg. 260

DATREX—NONE—Western Atlas Logging Services; *U.S. Public*, pg. 1757

DATRIL—Non-Asprin Pain Reliever—Bristol-Myers Squibb Company; *U.S. Public*, pg. 253

DATUM—Precision Instruments—Datum Inc.; *U.S. Public*, pg. 488

DAUBOND—Adhesive—Daubert Industries, Inc.; *U.S. Private*, pg. 313

DAUN—Bathroom Tissue—Kimberly-Clark Corporation; *U.S. Public*, pg. 958

DAUNOXOME—Proprietary Liposomal Formula—Nexstar Pharmaceuticals, Inc.; *U.S. Public*, pg. 1180

DAUNTLESS—Writing Papers & Bond Papers—The Mead Corporation; *U.S. Public*, pg. 1074

DAUNTLESS—War Game—Monarch Avalon, Inc.; *U.S. Public*, pg. 1123

DAUPHIN—Helicopter—American Eurocopter Corp.; *Int'l*, pg. 29

DAUPHIN—Seating—Carter Holt Harvey Limited; *U.S. Public*, pg. 904

DAVAC—Dry Gummed Paper—Nashua Corporation; *U.S. Public*, pg. 1152

THE DAVE ROSS SHOW—News Program—Westwood One, Inc.; *U.S. Public*, pg. 1763

DAVE'S—Cigarettes—Philip Morris U.S.A.; *U.S. Public*, pg. 1289

DAVEY TREE—Tree & Lawn Care Services—The Davey Tree Expert Company; *U.S. Private*, pg. 314

DAVID—Radio Automation—Harman International Industries, Inc.; *U.S. Public*, pg. 787

DAVID—NONE—Nestle USA; *Int'l*, pg. 916

DAVID BROOKS—NONE—Kellwood Company; *U.S. Public*, pg. 948

DAVID DART—NONE—Kellwood Company; *U.S. Public*, pg. 948

DAVID ESSEL-ALIVE!—Talk Radio Program—Westwood One Entertainment; *U.S. Public*, pg. 1763

DAVID ESSEL-ALIVE!—Talk Radio Show—Westwood One, Inc.; *U.S. Public*, pg. 1763

DAVID HARRISON—Clothing—Harcrest International, Ltd.; *U.S. Private*, pg. 500

DAVID MOSS—NONE—Moss Bros Group PLC; *Int'l*, pg. 895

DAVID WHITE—Surveying Instruments & Lasers—David White, L.L.C.; *U.S. Public*, pg. 1765

DAVID WHITE—Surveying Instruments & Lasers—David White, L.L.C.; *U.S. Private*, pg. 1765

DAVIDOFF—Fragrance—Lancaster Group Worldwide; *Int'l*, pg. 185

DAVIDOFF—Cigarettes—Reemtsma Cigarettenfabriken GmbH, Hamburg; *Int'l*, pg. 1100

DAVIDS—NONE—Petrie Retail, Inc.; *U.S. Private*, pg. 858

DAVINCI—Imported Italian Pasta & Related Products—World Finer Foods, Inc.; *U.S. Private*, pg. 1190

DAVIS—Consumer Paint—Davis Paint Company; *U.S. Private*, pg. 315

DAVIS—NONE—Giddings & Lewis Automation Technology; *Int'l*, pg. 1389

DAVIS—Baking Powder—Nabisco Inc.; *U.S. Public*, pg. 1355

DAVIS—Baking Products—RJR Nabisco Holdings Corp.; *U.S. Public*, pg. 1354

DAVIS CUP—Tennis Equipment—Mizuno Corporation; *Int'l*, pg. 884

DAVIS-GERMANTOWN—Stabilizers—Goodman Fielder Limited; *Int'l*, pg. 555

DAVIS INDUSTRIAL—Coating—Davis Paint Company; *U.S. Private*, pg. 315

DAVISON—Fluid Cracking & Emission Control Catalysts—W.R. Grace & Co.; *U.S. Public*, pg. 754

DAVITAMON—Vitamins & Minerals—Akzo Nobel N.V.; *Int'l*, pg. 42

DAVOL RELIA VAC—Wound Drain & Closed Wound Suction Evacuator—C.R. Bard, Inc.; *U.S. Public*, pg. 189

DAVOL SYSTEM 5000—Electro Surgical Generator—C.R. Bard, Inc.; *U.S. Public*, pg. 189

DAVSHEP—Bulk Water Meters—Davies Shephard Pty. Ltd.; *Int'l*, pg. 2

DAVSON—In/Out Personnel System—Rubbermaid Incorporated; *U.S. Public*, pg. 1411

DAWN—Photo Typesetters—AGFA EPS Division; *Int'l*, pg. 172

DAWN—Detergent—The Procter & Gamble Company; *U.S. Public*, pg. 1330

DAWN BUTTER—Butter Spread—Kerry Group PLC; *Int'l*, pg. 731

DAWN FRESH MILK—Drinking Milk—Kerry Group PLC; *Int'l*, pg. 731

DAWN HI & LO—Drinking Milk—Kerry Group PLC; *Int'l*, pg. 731

DAWN LIGHT BUTTER—Butter Spread—Kerry Group PLC; *Int'l*, pg. 731

DAXAD—Industrial Chemicals—Hampshire Chemical Corp.; *U.S. Private*, pg. 498

DAY & NIGHT—Heating & Air Conditioning Equipment—Carrier Corp.; *U.S. Public*, pg. 1690

DAY & NIGHT—Air Conditioning & Heating—Carrier Corporation; *U.S. Public*, pg. 1689

DAY-BRITE—Commercial & Industrial Lighting—Thomas Industries Inc.; *U.S. Public*, pg. 1598

DAY-BRITE—Lighting—Thomas Lighting-C&I Indoor Divison; *U.S. Public*, pg. 1599

DAY-CHEM—Chemical for Concrete Construction—Dayton Superior Corporation; *U.S. Private*, pg. 931

DAY CRADLE—Molded Carrier with Rocking Action—Cosco, Inc.; *U.S. Private*, pg. 277

DAY-GLO—Fluorescent Colors—Day-Glo Color Corp.; *U.S. Public*, pg. 1357

DAY-GLO—Fluorescent Colors—RPM, Inc.; *U.S. Public*, pg. 1356

DAY MARK II NAUTA—Mixer—Littleford Day Inc.; *U.S. Private*, pg. 671

DAY MATT—Mattress Specifically for Day Bed Use—Kingsdown, Inc.; *U.S. Private*, pg. 622

DAY NURSE—NONE—SmithKline Beecham Corporation; *Int'l*, pg. 1264

DAY NURSE—Coughs, Colds & Influenza Product—SmithKline Beecham plc; *Int'l*, pg. 1264

DAY-SPAN—Water Capsules—Alva/Amco Pharmacal Companies, Inc.; *U.S. Private*, pg. 47

DAY SPRING—Records—Word, Incorporated; *U.S. Public*, pg. 704

DAY-TIMER—Personal Organizers & Time Management Products—Fortune Brands, Inc.; *U.S. Public*, pg. 674

DAY-TIMERS—Time Management Systems—ACCO World Corporation; *U.S. Public*, pg. 674

DAY-TREADS—Safety Footwear—Alba-Waldensian, Inc.; *U.S. Public*, pg. 35

DAYBRITE—Lighting Products—Thomas Lighting-Sparta Opers.; *U.S. Public*, pg. 1599

DAYCARE DAYTIME—Colds Medicine Liquid & Caplets—Richardson-Vicks, Inc., Health Care Products; *U.S. Public*, pg. 1331

DAYCO—Automotive & Industiral Products—Dayco Products Inc.; *U.S. Public*, pg. 1045

DAYCO—Belts & Hoses—Mark IV Automotive Canada Inc.; *U.S. Public*, pg. 1045

DAYCO—Hose, Belts—Mark IV Industries Inc.; *U.S. Public*, pg. 1044

DAYCO—Tubing—Ryan Herco Products Corp.; *U.S. Private*, pg. 953

DAYFRESH—Feminine Pads—Kimberly-Clark Corporation; *U.S. Public*, pg. 958

DAYLIGHTER—Vertical Stat Camera—GraphLine Inc.; *U.S. Private*, pg. 471

DAYLITE BLUE—Tinted Light Bulb—Duro-Test Corporation; *U.S. Private*, pg. 349

DAYMATRIX—Metering Central Systems—Eastern Utilities Associates; *U.S. Public*, pg. 549

DAYMAX—Lamp for Motion Picture Studio & Television Sports Lighting—ILC Technology, Inc.; *U.S. Public*, pg. 856

DAYMAX—Mixer—Littleford Day Inc.; *U.S. Private*, pg. 671

DAYQUIL—Cold Medication—The Procter & Gamble Company; *U.S. Public*, pg. 1330

DAYS HOTELS—Hotels—Days Inns of America, Inc.; *U.S. Public*, pg. 321

DAYS INN—Motels—Days Inns of America, Inc.; *U.S. Public*, pg. 321

DAYS INN OF AMERICA—Hotel Chain—HFS, Incorporated; *U.S. Public*, pg. 321

DAYS SUITES—Suite Hotels—Days Inns of America, Inc.; *U.S. Public*, pg. 321

DAYSPRING CARDS—Christian Greeting Cards—Cook Communication Ministries; *U.S. Private*, pg. 272

DAYSTAR NOVA—LCD Display Modules—Industrial Electronic Engineers, Inc.; *U.S. Private*, pg. 561

DAYSTOPS—Motels—Days Inns of America, Inc.; *U.S. Public*, pg. 321

DAYTIMERS—Women's Footwear—J. Baker, Inc.; *U.S. Public*, pg. 167

DAYTON—Tires—Bridgestone/Firestone, Inc.; *Int'l*, pg. 213

DAYTON—Tires—Dayton Tire Company; *Int'l*, pg. 213

DAYTON—Motors, Fans, Heaters & Lighting—W.W. Grainger, Inc.; *U.S. Public*, pg. 758

DAYTON HUDSON—Department Store—The Department Store Division of Dayton Hudson Corporation; *U.S. Public*, pg. 489

DAYTON WALTHER—Wheel & Brake Products—LucasVarity Inc.; *Int'l*, pg. 820

DAYTON WALTHER—NONE—LucasVarity plc; *Int'l*, pg. 819

DAYTON WALTHER—Truck Components—Varity Dayton Walther; *Int'l*, pg. 820

DAYTONA—Tires—Bridgestone/Firestone, Inc.; *Int'l*, pg. 213

DAYTONA—Accessories—Echlin Inc.; *U.S. Public*, pg. 560

DAYTONA RADIAL GT—Tires—Bridgestone/Firestone, Inc.; *Int'l*, pg. 213

DAYTONA RADIAL H/R—Tires—Bridgestone/Firestone, Inc.; *Int'l*, pg. 213

DAYTONA RADIAL RLT—Tires—Bridgestone/Firestone, Inc.; *Int'l*, pg. 213

DAYTONA RADIAL S/R—Tires—Bridgestone/Firestone, Inc.; *Int'l*, pg. 213

DAYTONA RADIAL STAG—Tires—Bridgestone/Firestone, Inc.; *Int'l*, pg. 213

DAYTONA SPORT 70—Tires—Bridgestone/Firestone, Inc.; *Int'l*, pg. 213

DAYTONA SPORT 60—Tires—Bridgestone/Firestone, Inc.; *Int'l*, pg. 213

DAYTONA SUPER STAG—Tires—Bridgestone/Firestone, Inc.; *Int'l*, pg. 213

DAYTONIAN—Tires—Bridgestone/Firestone, Inc.; *Int'l*, pg. 213

DC VISTAR—12V & 24V DC Flood Light (Metal Halide)—The Will-Burt Company; *U.S. Private*, pg. 1177

DE-AIREX—Defoamer—Houghton International Inc.; *U.S. Private*, pg. 541

DE BEUKELAER—Biscuits—Danone Group; *Int'l*, pg. 379

DE FRIESCH VLAG—Sugar Syrup—CSM N.V.; *Int'l*, pg. 243

DE HAVILLAND—Aircraft—The Boeing Company; *U.S. Public*, pg. 239

DE HAVILLAND DASH 8—NONE—Bombardier Regional Aircraft Division; *U.S. Public*, pg. 242

DEJEAN'S—Canned Seafood Products—Borden, Inc.; *U.S. Private*, pg. 157

DE KEIZER BITTER—Spirit—Allied Domecq PLC; *Int'l*, pg. 62

DE LAVAL—Centrifuges—Alfa Laval Inc.; *Int'l*, pg. 1378

DE NEVE—Skiwear—Raven Industries, Inc.; *U.S. Public*, pg. 1361

DE NEVE—Ski Pants—Raven Industries Sportswear Div.; *U.S. Public*, pg. 1361

DE RUIJTER—Sweet Sandwich Fillings—CSM N.V.; *Int'l*, pg. 243

DE SANDER SCREEN—Vibrating Screen With End Tensioned Wires—Portec, Inc.-Construction Equipment Div.; *U.S. Public*, pg. 1318

DESOCLEAN—Solvent & Cleaner—DeSoto Inc.; *U.S. Public*, pg. 956

DESOFORM—Primary & Topcoat Coating for Prepainted Appliance Coil—DeSoto Inc.; *U.S. Public*, pg. 956

DESOLITE—UV & EB Curable Coating—DeSoto Inc.; *U.S. Public*, pg. 956

DESONATE—Anionic Surfactant—DeSoto Inc.; *U.S. Public*, pg. 956

DESONIC—Non-Ionic Surfactant—DeSoto Inc.; *U.S. Public*, pg. 956

DESONOL—Anionic Surfactant—DeSoto Inc.; *U.S. Public*, pg. 956

DESOTHANE SERIES 1000—Aircraft Topcoat, Polyurethane—DeSoto Inc.; *U.S. Public*, pg. 956

DE TUINEN—Drug & Beauty Chain Stores—Koninklijke Ahold NV; *Int'l*, pg. 749

DE VILBISS—Respiratory Equipment—Sunrise Medical, Inc.; *U.S. Public*, pg. 1535

DE-VO-KO—Alkyd & Latex Finishes—ICI Paints; *Int'l*, pg. 664

DE-VO-LAC—Lacquers—Devoe Paint; *Int'l*, pg. 663

DE-VO-LAC—Lacquers—ICI Paints; *Int'l*, pg. 664

DE-VO-PRO—Contractor Product Line of Paints—ICI Paints; *Int'l*, pg. 664

DE-VO-TEX—Texture Coating—ICI Paints; *Int'l*, pg. 664

DE ZAAN—Cocoa Products—Grace Cocoa/Ambrosia Chocolate; *U.S. Public*, pg. 128

DE ZEEUWSCH BOERIN—Sugar Syrup—CSM N.V.; *Int'l*, pg. 243

DEAD RIVER—Petroleum & Real Estate—Dead River Company; *U.S. Private*, pg. 318

DEALER BUSINESS—Publication for New Car Dealerships—Intertec Publishing; *U.S. Public*, pg. 1327

DEALER EQUIPMENT AND SERVICES—Dealer Equipment Programs—SPX Corporation; *U.S. Public*, pg. 1420

DEALER GUARD—Insurance—American Hardware Mutual Insurance Co.; *U.S. Private*, pg. 764

DEALER PAK—Fasteners—R&B, Inc.; *U.S. Public*, pg. 1354

DEALERNEWS—Trade Periodical—Advanstar Communications; *U.S. Private*, pg. 22

DEALER'S PRIDE—Dog Food—Ralston Purina Company; *U.S. Public*, pg. 1359

DEALERSCOPE MERCHANDISING—Magazine—North American Publishing Company; *U.S. Private*, pg. 803

DEALS DIGEST—Online Promotion News Service—Advanstar Communications; *U.S. Private*, pg. 22

DEAN—Dairy Products—Dean Foods Company; *U.S. Public*, pg. 489

DEAN—Kosher Poultry—Empire Kosher Poultry, Inc.; *U.S. Private*, pg. 374

DEAN—Pumps—Met-Pro Corporation; *U.S. Public*, pg. 1100

DEAN—Heat Exchangers—Tranter, Inc.; *U.S. Public*, pg. 521

DEAN—Fryers & Filtration Systems—Welbilt Corporation; *Int'l*, pg. 188

DEAN ENAMEL—Paint—Paragon Paint & Varnish Corp.; *U.S. Private*, pg. 838

DEAN FAT FREE—Dairy Products—Dean Foods Company; *U.S. Public*, pg. 489

DEAN LIGHT—Dairy Products—Dean Foods Company; *U.S. Public*, pg. 489

DEAN WITTER—Financial Services—Dean Witter, Discover & Co.; *U.S. Public*, pg. 1132

DEANSGATE—Labels—S & K Famous Brands, Inc.; *U.S. Public*, pg. 1414

DEAR CAROL—Newsletters—Kerr Group, Inc.; *U.S. Public*, pg. 952

DEARBORN BRASS—Faucets & Plumbing Supplies—Fortune Brands, Inc.; *U.S. Public*, pg. 674

DEARBORN BRASS—NONE—MasterBrand Industries, Inc.; *U.S. Public*, pg. 675

DEARBORN BRASS—NONE—Moen Incorporated; *U.S. Public*, pg. 675

DEARFOAMS—Slippers & Various Thermal Heated Products—R.G. Barry Corporation; *U.S. Public*, pg. 192

DEARTEK—Detackification Products—BetzDearborn Inc.; *U.S. Public*, pg. 226

DEATH PROBE—Fire Ant Applicator—Security Lawn & Garden Co.; *U.S. Private*, pg. 397

DEB—Retail Junior Fashions & Accessories Shops—Deb Shops, Inc.; *U.S. Public*, pg. 491

DEB PLUS—Fashions—Deb Shops, Inc.; *U.S. Public*, pg. 491

DEBBIE REYNOLDS' CASINO—Casino—Jackpot Enterprises, Inc.; *U.S. Public*, pg. 920

DEBBIE'S FAMOUS GRANOLA—Granola—RCB Baking Company; *U.S. Public*, pg. 1354

DEBOLES—Organic and Natural Pasta Products—Arrowhead Mills, Inc.; *U.S. Public*, pg. 86

DEBRA LUBELL—Apparel—The Apparel Group, Ltd.; *U.S. Private*, pg. 78

DEBRIDAT—Antispasmodic—SmithKline Beecham plc; *Int'l*, pg. 1264

DEBRON 811—Waterborne Nonstick Coatings—The Dexter Corporation; *U.S. Public*, pg. 504

DEBRON 711—Waterborne Nonstick Coatings—The Dexter Corporation; *U.S. Public*, pg. 504

DEBROX—Ear Drops—SmithKline Beecham Consumer Healthcare, U.S.; *Int'l*, pg. 1264

DEBUT—Pre-Finished Laminate—Bruce Hardwood Floors; *U.S. Public*, pg. 1634

DEBUT—Computer Assisted Research Services—The Mead Corporation; *U.S. Public*, pg. 1074

DEC-A-TRIM—Leather-grained Vinyl Film—Fasson Films; *U.S. Public*, pg. 153

DEC-KING—Fasteners—Illinois Tool Works Inc.; *U.S. Public*, pg. 865

DECA-DURABOLIN—Pharmaceutical—Organon Inc.; *Int'l*, pg. 48

DECA-TRAN—Curret Transducer For Amprobe Analog AC Ammeter—Amprobe Instrument; *U.S. Public*, pg. 1676

DECADE SHOWCASE WITH ENDURACOTE—Two sided steel door with painted hardware—Raynor Garage Doors; *U.S. Private*, pg. 912

DECADRON—Dexamethasome—Merck & Co., Inc.; *U.S. Public*, pg. 1090

DECALTAL—Tanning Agents, Auxiliaries & Finishes, Dyes & Pigment Finishes—BASF AG; *Int'l*, pg. 103

DECAP—Dispensing System for Water Cables—Liqui-Box Corporation; *U.S. Public*, pg. 1000

DECARBONIZER—Soak Tank Kitchenware—Ecolab Inc.; *U.S. Public*, pg. 562

DECARBONIZER MXP—Soaking Solution—Ecolab Inc.; *U.S. Public*, pg. 562

DECATHLON—Vinyl Tile—Congoleum Corporation; *U.S. Public*, pg. 69

DECATHLON—Sports Game—Monarch Avalon, Inc.; *U.S. Public*, pg. 1123

DECATHLON—Zipper—YKK (U.S.A.); *Int'l*, pg. 1515

DECCA LONDON—Recod Label—Philips Electronics N.V.; *Int'l*, pg. 1051

DECCO—Industrial Solenoid—Detroit Coil Company; *U.S. Private*, pg. 328

DECHLORANE—Flame Retardant—Occidental Chemical Corporation; *U.S. Public*, pg. 1210

DECHOLIN TABLETS—Pharmaceutical—Bayer Corporation/Pharmaceutical Division; *Int'l*, pg. 173

DECIMAL SQUARES—Vinyl Squares Used to Teach All Decimal Concepts—American Educational Products; *U.S. Public*, pg. 71

DECIS—Ag Chemical—AgrEvo USA Company; *Int'l*, pg. 1203

DECIS—Insecticide—Hoechst Aktiengesellschaft; *Int'l*, pg. 624

DECISION—Blood Serum Controls—Beckman Instruments, Inc.; *U.S. Public*, pg. 199

DECISION ADVANTAGE—Computer Systems—Sequent Computer Systems, Inc.; *U.S. Public*, pg. 1459

DECISION DATA—NONE—IIS Intelligent Information Systems Ltd.; *Int'l*, pg. 645

DECISION/SQL—Computer Software for Processing of Complex Queries—Thinking Machines Corporation; *U.S. Private*, pg. 1081

DECISION SYSTEMS—NONE—Market Facts, Inc.; *U.S. Public*, pg. 1046

DECISIONMARK—NONE—The Gazette Company; *U.S. Private*, pg. 442

DECK & DOCK—Outdoor Wood Furniture—Telescope Casual Furniture, Inc.; *U.S. Private*, pg. 1074

DECK BLADE—Carbide Circular Saw Blade—The Disston Co.; *U.S. Private*, pg. 950

DECK HOUSE—Premanufactured Houses—Deck House Inc.; *U.S. Private*, pg. 320

DECK-LOCK—Metal Nails & Screws—Georgia-Pacific Corporation; *U.S. Public*, pg. 735

DECK PROTECTOR—Outdoor Wood Protector—Armor All Products Group; *U.S. Public*, pg. 387

DECK THE WALLS—Retail Stores Featuring Prints, Posters & Custom Framing—Wicks 'n Sticks, Ltd; *U.S. Private*, pg. 1175

DECKCARE—CCA Wood Protector—ISK BioSciences; *Int'l*, pg. 689

DECKER—Processed Meats—Armour Food Company; *U.S. Public*, pg. 427

DECKGUN—Power Tools—The Black & Decker Corporation; *U.S. Public*, pg. 233

DECLANS FINNIANS—Irish Figurines, Each With A Stone From The Blarney Stone Quarry In Ireland—Roman, Inc.; *U.S. Private*, pg. 942

DECO—Plastic Organizers—Esselte Corporation; *Int'l*, pg. 459

DECO ACCENTS BY IVES—Colored Epoxy Coated Aluminum Hardware—H.B. Ives; *U.S. Private*, pg. 506

DECOBRITE—NONE—Lawter International, Inc.; *U.S. Public*, pg. 980

DECODE—Software Enables Determination of Protein & Peptide Sequences using Voyager—PerSeptive Biosystems, Inc.; *U.S. Public*, pg. 1279

DECOGLAZE—Epoxy Enamel—Jones Blair Company; *U.S. Private*, pg. 596

DECOLITE—Structural Panels—Baltek Corporation; *U.S. Public*, pg. 171

DECOLLETE—Fragrance—Merle Norman Cosmetics, Inc.; *U.S. Private*, pg. 733

DECOMA—Automotive Parts—Magna International Inc.; *Int'l*, pg. 829

DECONAMINE CX LIQUID—Liquid Antitussive/Expectorant—Bradley Pharmaceuticals; *U.S. Public*, pg. 249

DECONAMINE CX LIQUID—Liquid Antitussive/Expectorant—Doak Dermatologics; *U.S. Public*, pg. 250

DECONAMINE CX TABLETS—Antitussive/Expectorant—Bradley Pharmaceuticals; *U.S. Public*, pg. 249

DECONAMINE CX TABLETS—Antitussive/Expectorant—Doak Dermatologics; *U.S. Public*, pg. 250

DECONAMINE CHEWABLE TABLETS—Chewable Tablets; Pediatric Antihistamine/Decongestant—Bradley Pharmaceuticals; *U.S. Public*, pg. 249

DECONAMINE CHEWABLE TABLETS—Pediatric Antihistamine/Decongestant—Doak Dermatologics; *U.S. Public*, pg. 250

DECONAMINE DYE-FREE SYRUP—Dye-Free Syrup; Liquid Antihistamine/Decongestant—Bradley Pharmaceuticals; *U.S. Public*, pg. 249

DECONAMINE DYE-FREE SYRUP—Liquid Antihistamine/Decongestant—Doak Dermatologics; *U.S. Public*, pg. 250

DECONAMINE DYE-FREE TABLETS—Antihistamine/Decongestant—Bradley Pharmaceuticals; *U.S. Public*, pg. 249

DECONAMINE DYE-FREE TABLETS—Antihistamine/Decongestant—Doak Dermatologics; *U.S. Public*, pg. 250

DECONAMINE SR CAPSULES—SR Capsules; Sustained Release Antihistamine Decongestant—Bradley Pharmaceuticals; *U.S. Public*, pg. 249

DECONAMINE SR CAPSULES—Sustained Release Antihistamine Decongestant—Doak Dermatologics; *U.S. Public*, pg. 250

DECONSAL—NONE—Medeva PLC; *Int'l*, pg. 852

DECOPOL—NONE—Lawter International, Inc.; *U.S. Public*, pg. 980

DECOR—Embossed Pattern Sheet Steel—Inland Steel Industries, Inc.; *U.S. Public*, pg. 879

DECOR—Bathtub Wall Kit—Plaskolite Inc.; *U.S. Private*, pg. 870

DECOR—Tape Dispenser—3M; *U.S. Public*, pg. 1604

DECOR DELIGHTS—Cake Decors—McCormick/Schilling; *U.S. Public*, pg. 1066

DECOR WALL—Covering—American Felt & Filter; *U.S. Private*, pg. 54

DECORA—Cabinetry—Aristokraft, Inc.; *U.S. Public*, pg. 675

DECORA—Kitchen Cabinets & Bathroom Vanities—Fortune Brands, Inc.; *U.S. Public*, pg. 674

DECORA—Wiring Devices—Leviton Mfg. Co., Inc.; *U.S. Private*, pg. 663

DECORA—NONE—MasterBrand Industries, Inc.; *U.S. Public*, pg. 675

DECORATION CHEZ SOI—Magazine—Quebecor Inc.; *Int'l*, pg. 1075

DECORATIVE ARTIST'S WORKBOOK—Magazine—F & W Publications, Inc.; *U.S. Private*, pg. 388

DECORATIVE INSERTS—Glazed Border Design 4 1/4" & 6" Wall Tiles in Foral, Herb & Other Designs—United States Ceramic Tile Co.; *U.S. Private*, pg. 1124

DECORATIVE WOODCRAFTS—Magazine—Meredith Corporation; *U.S. Public*, pg. 1094

DECORATOR—Paint—Jones Blair Company; *U.S. Private*, pg. 596

DECORATOR SERIES—Switches & Recepatcles—Pass & Seymour/Legrand; *Int'l*, pg. 806

DECORETTE—Home Decoration—RetailNet B.V.; *Int'l*, pg. 750

DECORETTE—Decorative Ribbons—3M; *U.S. Public*, pg. 1604

DECORTISYL—Corticosteroid Hormone—SmithKline Beecham Research Limited; *Int'l*, pg. 1266

DECOSTA—Fresh Sausage—Kayem Foods, Inc.; *U.S. Public*, pg. 610

DECOTEX—Design Engineered Coated Textiles—ATHOL Corporation; *U.S. Private*, pg. 94

DECOTHERM—NONE—Lawter International, Inc.; *U.S. Public*, pg. 980

DECRA—Roofing Tiles based upon Galvanized Steel—Icopal a/s; *Int'l*, pg. 658

DECRA ROOFING COATINGS—Roofing Tiles—Carter Holt Harvey Limited; *U.S. Public*, pg. 904

DECRABOND—Roofing Tiles—Carter Holt Harvey Limited; *U.S. Public*, pg. 904

DECRASHIELD—NONE—ICI Paints; *Int'l*, pg. 664

DECRATREND—NONE—ICI Paints; *Int'l*, pg. 664

DECTOMAX—Doramectin—Pfizer Inc.; *U.S. Public*, pg. 1281

DEE GEE—Casual Footwear—Daniel Green Co.; *U.S. Private*, pg. 477

DEE ZEE—Automotive Running Boards—Lancaster Colony Corporation; *U.S. Public*, pg. 976

DEEGAN—Chimes—Yamaha Corporation of America; *Int'l*, pg. 1516

DEEP BLUE—Tuna—Camerican International; *U.S. Public*, pg. 426

DEEP-DOWN—Topical Analgesic—SmithKline Beecham plc; *Int'l*, pg. 1264

DEEP GREEN—Lawn Products—The Vigoro Corporation; *U.S. Public*, pg. 856

DEEP HEAT—Heating Pads—Pollenex; *U.S. Public*, pg. 1391

DEEP MAGIC—Cleansing Lotions & Moisturizers—The Gillette Company; *U.S. Public*, pg. 743

DEEP 'N DELICIOUS—Pizza, Cake—McCain Foods Limited; *Int'l*, pg. 850

DEEP-REACH—Double Scissors Mechanism—The Raymond Corporation; *U.S. Public*, pg. 123

DEEP ROCK—Bottled Water—Hinckley & Schmitt, Inc.; *Int'l*, pg. 1322

DEEP ROOT—Planters—W. Atlee Burpee Co.; *U.S. Private*, pg. 187
DEEP SKID—Tires—Bridgestone/Firestone, Inc.; *Int'l*, pg. 213
DEEP TREAD—Tires—Bridgestone/Firestone, Inc.; *Int'l*, pg. 213
DEEP WOODS—Fragrance—Avon Products, Inc.; *U.S. Public*, pg. 155
DEEP WOODS OFF!—Insect Repellent—S.C. Johnson & Son, Inc.; *U.S. Private*, pg. 592
DEEP WOODS OFF! for SPORTSMAN—Repellents—S.C. Johnson & Son, Inc.; *U.S. Private*, pg. 592
DEEP Z SEAL—Double Lip Rod Seal—Macrotech Plyseal, Inc.; *U.S. Private*, pg. 693
DEEPLATES—Paper Plates—The Mead Corporation; *U.S. Public*, pg. 1074
DEEPTONE DENIM—NONE—Cone Mills Corporation; *U.S. Public*, pg. 430
DEEPWATER—Weather Modification Chemicals—Deepwater Chemicals, Inc.; *Int'l*, pg. 1395
DEER ISLE—NONE—New England Stone Industries, Inc.; *U.S. Private*, pg. 793
DEERBROOK INSURANCE—Property-Liability Insurance—The Allstate Corporation; *U.S. Public*, pg. 55
DEERFIELD—Tartar Sauce & Design—Cains Foods, L.P.; *U.S. Private*, pg. 199
DEERFIELD—Metal Stampings—Deerfield Manufacturing Co., Inc.; *U.S. Private*, pg. 1044
DEERFIELD CONNECTOR—Electrical Connector—Ilsco; *U.S. Private*, pg. 558
DEERING ICE CREAM—NONE—Deering Ice Cream, Inc.; *U.S. Private*, pg. 403
DEERSKIN—Wood Pulp & Writing Papers—Westvaco Corporation; *U.S. Public*, pg. 1762
DEFENDER—Mufflers—Arvin Industries, Inc.; *U.S. Public*, pg. 136
DEFENDER—Hood Protectors—Lund International Holdings, Inc.; *U.S. Public*, pg. 1020
DEFENDER—Nitrous Oxide Alarm—Nellcor Puritan Bennett Incorporated; *U.S. Public*, pg. 1039
DEFENDER—Crash, Fire & Rescue Vehicles—Simon Engineering plc; *Int'l*, pg. 1251
DEFENDER 8000—Computer Access System—Axent Technologies; *U.S. Public*, pg. 157
DEFENDER 5000—Computer Access System—Axent Technologies; *U.S. Public*, pg. 157
DEFENDER 1000—Computer Access System—Axent Technologies; *U.S. Public*, pg. 157
DEFENDER 6000—Computer Access System—Axent Technologies; *U.S. Public*, pg. 157
DEFENDER II—Computer Access System—Axent Technologies; *U.S. Public*, pg. 157
DEFENDERS—Fire Safe Step-Can Line—United Receptical, Inc.; *U.S. Private*, pg. 1123
DEFENSE FORCE—Complete Line Of Replica Military Toy Guns—Daisy Manufacturing Company, Inc.; *U.S. Private*, pg. 308
DEFIANT—NONE—Linear Corporation; *U.S. Public*, pg. 1193
DEFINITELY DONUTS—Donut Shop—Cara Operations Limited; *Int'l*, pg. 266
DEFINITION—Liquid/Styling Products—Goldwell Cosmetics (USA) Inc.; *Int'l*, pg. 718
DEFINITION-PERM—NONE—Goldwell Cosmetics (USA) Inc.; *Int'l*, pg. 718
DEFINITY—Telecommunications Switching Apparatus & System—Lucent Technologies Inc.; *U.S. Public*, pg. 1017
DEFRA—Roofing Paper—Raschig GmbH; *U.S. Private*, pg. 827
DEFROSTERS—Boots—Kaufman Footwear; *Int'l*, pg. 725
DEGELMAN—Farm Machinery & Parts—Degelman Industries Ltd.; *Int'l*, pg. 388
DEGREASER—Cleaning Solution—Stanhome Inc.; *U.S. Public*, pg. 1508
DEGREASER PLUS—Concentrated Laundry Soil & Stain Remover—Stanhome Inc.; *U.S. Public*, pg. 1508
DEGREE—Antiperspirant & Deodorant—Helene Curtis Industries, Inc.; *Int'l*, pg. 1434
DEHESIVE—Paper Release Coating—Wacker Silicones Corporation; *Int'l*, pg. 625
DEHYBOR—Anhydrous Borax—U.S. Borax Inc.; *Int'l*, pg. 1119
DEITERMANN—Products for Roofing; Products & Systems for Laying Tile—Heidelberger Zement A.G.; *Int'l*, pg. 605

DEK-PRO-TECH—Wood Preservative—Monsey-Bakor; *U.S. Private*, pg. 757
DEKADOOR—Hardboard—Georgia-Pacific Corporation; *U.S. Public*, pg. 735
DEKAFILM—Microfilm Reader Accessories—Eastman Kodak Company; *U.S. Public*, pg. 550
DEKALB—Seed, Swine—Dekalb Genetics Corporation; *U.S. Public*, pg. 493
DEKALEATHER—Hardboard—Georgia-Pacific Corporation; *U.S. Public*, pg. 735
DEKALUX—Fiber Composition Board—Georgia-Pacific Corporation; *U.S. Public*, pg. 735
DEKATILE—Hardboard—Georgia-Pacific Corporation; *U.S. Public*, pg. 735
DEKORON—Wire & Cable—Furon Company; *U.S. Public*, pg. 688
DEKOPAS—Material Fpr Prototypes—Raschig GmbH; *U.S. Private*, pg. 827
DEKORIT—Cast Resinsfor Machinery—Raschig GmbH; *U.S. Private*, pg. 827
DEKORIT—Decorative Laminate Faced Doors & Frames—Westag & Getalit AG; *Int'l*, pg. 1491
DEKSWOOD—Cleaner & Brightener for Weathered & Dirty Exterior Wood—The Flood Company; *U.S. Private*, pg. 414
DEKTAK—Metrology Systems—Veeco Instruments, Inc.; *U.S. Public*, pg. 1711
DEKTAK 3030—Surface Profiler—Sloan Technology; *U.S. Public*, pg. 1711
DEKTAK II A—Surface Profiler—Sloan Technology; *U.S. Public*, pg. 1711
DEKTOL—Photo Developer—Eastman Kodak Company; *U.S. Public*, pg. 550
DEKTOMATIC—Photographic Chemicals—Eastman Kodak Company; *U.S. Public*, pg. 550
DEKUYPER—Cordial—Fortune Brands, Inc.; *U.S. Public*, pg. 674
DEL DESTINO—Olive Oil—Atalanta Corporation; *U.S. Private*, pg. 93
DEL MAR—NONE—Del Mar Avionics; *U.S. Private*, pg. 321
DEL MONTE—Canned Vegetable Products—Del Monte Foods; *U.S. Private*, pg. 321
DEL MONTE—Beverages, Canned Fruits & Vegetables, Pudding Cups & Tomato Products—RJR Nabisco Holdings Corp.; *U.S. Public*, pg. 1354
DEL-PAK—Plastic Containers & Lids—Reynolds Metals Company; *U.S. Public*, pg. 1385
DEL REY—Book Publishing—Random House, Inc.; *U.S. Private*, pg. 20
DEL-SEAL—Acrylic Automotive Coatings—PPG Industries, Inc.; *U.S. Public*, pg. 1245
DEL SOL—Automobile—American Honda Motor Co., Inc.; *Int'l*, pg. 634
DEL TERRA—Processed Vegetables—Furman Foods, Inc.; *U.S. Private*, pg. 431
DEL WEBB—Land Developers—Del Webb Corporation; *U.S. Public*, pg. 494
DELAC—Rubber Chemical—Uniroyal Chemical Company, Inc.; *U.S. Public*, pg. 460
DELACORTE PRESS—Book Publisher—Bertelsmann AG; *Int'l*, pg. 189
DELACORTE PRESS—Books—Dell Publishing; *Int'l*, pg. 191
DELACRE—Frozen Entrees, Cookies, Pastries & Chocolates—Campbell Soup Company; *U.S. Public*, pg. 298
DELAFORCE—NONE—Tegner & Son AB; *Int'l*, pg. 412
DELATESTRYL—Testosterone Prod. for Treatment of Breast Cancer & Testosterone Deficiency—Bristol-Myers Squibb U.S. Pharmaceutical Group; *U.S. Public*, pg. 255
DELAVAN—Gas Turbine Prods.—Coltec Industries Inc.; *U.S. Public*, pg. 401
DELAWARE—Ribbons—Delaware Ribbon Manufacturers, Inc.; *U.S. Private*, pg. 322
DELAWARE—Titling Equipment—Eastman Kodak Company; *U.S. Public*, pg. 550
DELAWARE MANUFACTURERS REGISTER—Register—Manufacturers' News, Inc.; *U.S. Private*, pg. 700
DELAYED EXTRACTION TECHNOLOGY—Enhancement Enables Voyager to Sequence Biomolecules—PerSeptive Biosystems, Inc.; *U.S. Public*, pg. 1279
DELCAP—Unit Dispensing Cap—Ortho-McNeil Pharmaceutical Corporation; *U.S. Public*, pg. 929

DELCLEAR—Acrylic Urethane Coatings—PPG Industries, Inc.; *U.S. Public*, pg. 1245
DELCO/BOSE—Audio System—Delco Electronics Corporation; *U.S. Public*, pg. 720
DELCO ETR—Electronically Tuned Receiver—Delco Electronics Corporation; *U.S. Public*, pg. 720
DELCO LOC—Radio Theft Deterrent—Delco Electronics Corporation; *U.S. Public*, pg. 720
DELCOTRON—Generators—Delphi Energy & Engine Management Systems; *U.S. Public*, pg. 719
DELECTA-DELICIOUS—Frozen Foods—Tyson Foods; *U.S. Public*, pg. 1652
DELECTA-RAY—Frozen Foods—Tyson Foods, Inc.; *U.S. Public*, pg. 1652
DELECTRA—Cologne & Toiletries—Avon Products, Inc.; *U.S. Public*, pg. 155
D'ELEGANCE—Decorative Plumbing Fittings—Speakman Company; *U.S. Private*, pg. 1021
DELESTROGEN—Pharmaceutical—Bristol-Myers Squibb Company; *U.S. Public*, pg. 253
DELESTROGEN—Hormonal Product—Bristol-Myers Squibb U.S. Pharmaceutical Group; *U.S. Public*, pg. 255
DELETION FACTORY—NONE—Life Technologies, Inc.; *U.S. Public*, pg. 504
DELEX—Two Handled Faucet—Delta Faucet Corporation; *U.S. Public*, pg. 1053
DELFEN—NONE—Johnson & Johnson; *U.S. Public*, pg. 927
DELFEN—Contraceptive Foam—Ortho-McNeil Pharmaceutical Corporation; *U.S. Public*, pg. 929
DELFIA—Medical Diagnostic System—EG & G, Inc.; *U.S. Public*, pg. 542
DELFIELD—NONE—Scotsman Industries, Inc.; *U.S. Public*, pg. 1444
DELFLOC—Retention Aid—Hercules Incorporated; *U.S. Public*, pg. 809
DELGADO—Gift Wrap—Fine Art Developments plc; *Int'l*, pg. 485
DELGARD ALUMINUM ORNAMENTAL FENCE—Decorative Fences—Delair Group, L.L.C.; *U.S. Private*, pg. 47
DELGLO—Acrylic Automotive Coatings—PPG Industries, Inc.; *U.S. Public*, pg. 1245
DELHAIZE "LE LION"—Supermarket Chain—Etablissements Delhaize Freres Et Cie "Le Lion" S.A.; *Int'l*, pg. 462
THE DELI AT PUBLIX—Deli Items—Publix Supermarkets Inc.; *U.S. Private*, pg. 893
DELI CAT—Cat Food—Ralston Purina Company; *U.S. Public*, pg. 1359
DELI CENTRAL—NONE—7-Eleven Stores; *Int'l*, pg. 693
DELI CENTRAL—Sandwiches—The Southland Corporation; *Int'l*, pg. 693
DELI KING—Hot & Cold Cases—BKI; *U.S. Public*, pg. 1506
DELI READY—Food Service Poultry Items—Tyson Foods, Inc.; *U.S. Public*, pg. 1652
DELI WARE—Servingware—Carlisle Food Service Products; *U.S. Public*, pg. 305
DELIAL—Body Care Products—Bayer AG; *Int'l*, pg. 171
DELICARE—Fine Fabric Wash—Benckiser Consumer Products Inc.; *Int'l*, pg. 185
DELICATO—Popular Premium Wines—Delicato Vineyards; *U.S. Private*, pg. 322
DELICE DE FRANCE—Brie & Camembert—Bongrain Cheese USA; *Int'l*, pg. 201
DELICIOUS—Preserves & Jellies—Clements Foods Co.; *U.S. Private*, pg. 245
DELICIOUS—Foods—Labatt Brewing Company Limited; *Int'l*, pg. 679
DELICO—Baby Swiss, Smoked Baby Swiss, Feta Cheese—BC-USA; *Int'l*, pg. 201
DELICO—Baby Swiss, Smoked Baby Swiss, Feta Cheese—Bongrain Cheese USA; *Int'l*, pg. 201
DELINAISE—Mustard/Mayo Sandwich Spread—Cains Foods, L.P.; *U.S. Private*, pg. 199
DELINE—NONE—Sadia Group; *Int'l*, pg. 1168
DELISLE—Yogurts—Danone Group; *Int'l*, pg. 379
DELISO—Footwear—Brown Group, Inc.; *U.S. Public*, pg. 262
DELIX—Hypertension—Hoechst Marion Roussel, Inc.; *Int'l*, pg. 624
DELL—Books—Dell Publishing; *Int'l*, pg. 191
DELL COMPUTER—Personal Computers—Dell Computer Corporation; *U.S. Public*, pg. 495

DELL PUBLISHING—Book Publishers—Bertelsmann AG; *Int'l*, pg. 189

DELLA NOTTE—Liqueur—Grand Metropolitan Plc; *Int'l*, pg. 408

DELMAR—Yearbooks & Photography—Herff Jones Inc.; *U.S. Private*, pg. 523

DELMARK—Food Service—Novartis Nutrition Corporation; *Int'l*, pg. 974

DELMARVA POWER & LIGHT—Public Utility—Delmarva Power & Light Company; *U.S. Public*, pg. 430

DELMONICO—Foods—Delmonico Foods; *U.S. Public*, pg. 812

DELMONICO—Pasta—Hershey Foods Corporation; *U.S. Public*, pg. 811

DELMOOR—Grocery Bags—Johns Manville Corporation; *U.S. Public*, pg. 927

DELNET—NONE—Applied Extrusion Technologies, Inc.; *U.S. Public*, pg. 122

DELOX—Abrasives—IMI Plc; *Int'l*, pg. 646

DELPIANO WHITIN ROBERTS—NONE—Whitin Roberts Co.; *U.S. Private*, pg. 309

DELRIN—Acetal Resins—Du Pont (E.I. Du Pont De Nemours & Co.); *U.S. Public*, pg. 530

DELROYD—NONE—Boston Gear; *U.S. Public*, pg. 857

DELROYD—Speed Reducers—IMO Industries Inc.; *U.S. Public*, pg. 856

DELSEY—Bathroom Tissues—Kimberly-Clark Corporation; *U.S. Public*, pg. 958

DELSEYS—Mexican Food Products—Wilson Products Co.; *U.S. Private*, pg. 1181

DELSPECTIN—Spectinomycin—Royal Gist-Brocades N.V.; *Int'l*, pg. 1142

DELSTAR—Resin-Based Finishes—PPG Industries, Inc.; *U.S. Public*, pg. 1245

DELSYM—Cough Medicine—Johnson & Johnson; *U.S. Public*, pg. 927

DELSYM—Extended-Release Suspension (Dextromethorphan Polistirex)—Medeva Pharmaceuticals; *Int'l*, pg. 852

DELTA—Dampener—Baldwin Technology Company, Inc.; *U.S. Public*, pg. 169

DELTA—Software Program—Barrister Information Systems Corporation; *U.S. Public*, pg. 192

DELTA—NONE—Brown & Sharpe Manufacturing Company; *U.S. Public*, pg. 260

DELTA—Books—Dell Publishing; *Int'l*, pg. 191

DELTA—Air Transportation—Delta Air Lines, Inc.; *U.S. Public*, pg. 497

DELTA—T-Shirts, Fleece—Delta Apparel; *U.S. Public*, pg. 498

DELTA—Truck, Auto, Home Storage Boxes—Delta Consolidated Industries, Inc. (Co. Headquarters); *U.S. Public*, pg. 481

DELTA—Single Handle Faucet—Delta Faucet Corporation; *U.S. Public*, pg. 1053

DELTA—Mobile Two-Way Radios for Police, Fire Fighting, Ambulance, Taxi,Industrial—General Electric Canada Inc.; *U.S. Public*, pg. 713

DELTA—Household Tissue Products—Georgia-Pacific Corporation; *U.S. Public*, pg. 735

DELTA—Syrups, Molasses & Mustard—Griffin Manufacturing Co.; *U.S. Private*, pg. 481

DELTA—Rice—Lever Brothers Co.; *Int'l*, pg. 1435

DELTA—Plumbing Fixtures—Masco Corporation; *U.S. Public*, pg. 1052

DELTA—Device—Medtronic, Inc.; *U.S. Public*, pg. 1082

DELTA—Industrial Automotive Coating—PPG Industries, Inc.; *U.S. Public*, pg. 1245

DELTA—Woodworking Equipment—Pentair, Inc.; *U.S. Public*, pg. 1273

DELTA—Protector Module—Porta Systems Corp.; *U.S. Public*, pg. 1317

DELTA—Rice—Unilever Plc; *Int'l*, pg. 1433

DELTA AGRICULTURAL DIGEST—NONE—Intertec Publishing; *U.S. Public*, pg. 1328

DELTA AGRICULTURAL DIGEST—NONE—Farm Press; *U.S. Public*, pg. 1328

DELTA FARM PRESS—Coverage of Production Agriculture—Intertec Publishing; *U.S. Public*, pg. 1327

DELTA FARM PRESS—NONE—Intertec Publishing; *U.S. Public*, pg. 1328

DELTA IMS—IMS DC Enhancement—BMC Software, Inc.; *U.S. Public*, pg. 162

DELTA MEDICAL—Medication Delivery System—Quest Medical, Inc.; *U.S. Public*, pg. 1352

DELTA PAC—Differential Temp. Fire Detection System—Kidde-Fenwal, Inc.; *Int'l*, pg. 1500

DELTA PAK—Chromatography System—Millipore Corporation; *U.S. Public*, pg. 1112

DELTA PREP—3000 Preparative Liquid & Chromatography System—Millipore Corporation; *U.S. Public*, pg. 1112

DELTA PRIDE—Farm Raised Catfish—Delta Pride Catfish, Inc.; *U.S. Private*, pg. 322

DELTA QUEEN—Riverboat—American Classic Voyagers Company; *U.S. Private*, pg. 380

DELTA SP—NONE—Brown & Sharpe Manufacturing Company; *U.S. Public*, pg. 260

DELTA 16 DIGITAL—Diagnostic Mammography System—Instrumentarium Imaging, Inc.; *U.S. Private*, pg. 565

DELTA SKYMILES—NONE—American Express Company; *U.S. Public*, pg. 73

DELTA II—Launch Vehicle—McDonnell Aircraft & Missile Systems Div.; *U.S. Public*, pg. 241

DELTADYNE—Filter Monitor—Pall Corporation; *U.S. Public*, pg. 1253

DELTAFLEX—Power Transmissions—Lovejoy Inc.; *U.S. Private*, pg. 677

DELTAFORCE PORT—Wine—Dateo Import S.P.A.; *Int'l*, pg. 385

DELTAGRAPH—Charting & Spreadsheet Software—SPSS Inc.; *U.S. Public*, pg. 1420

DELTAL—Floor Coverings—Domco Inc.; *Int'l*, pg. 415

DELTAMAT—Chair Mat—Rubbermaid Incorporated; *U.S. Public*, pg. 1411

DELTASIL—Electrical Wire & Cable—General Electric Canada Inc.; *U.S. Public*, pg. 713

DELTAWALL—Material for Bearings—Glacier Vandervell, Inc.; *Int'l*, pg. 1334

DELTEC—Computer Power Supply Systems—Fiskars Oy AB; *Int'l*, pg. 492

DELTHANE—Catalytic Additives for Automotive Paint—PPG Industries, Inc.; *U.S. Public*, pg. 1245

DELTIS—Information Related Products—Olympus Optical Co., Ltd.; *Int'l*, pg. 1004

DELTON—Pit & Fissure Sealant—Johnson & Johnson Consumer Products; *U.S. Public*, pg. 928

DELTRAN—Blood Pressure Monitor/Transducer—Utah Medical Products, Inc.; *U.S. Public*, pg. 1700

DELTRON—Automotive Coating Compositions—PPG Industries, Inc.; *U.S. Public*, pg. 1245

DELUX BLEACHED OAK—Bath Accessories—Melard Manufacturing Corporation; *U.S. Private*, pg. 729

DELUX OAK—Bath Accessories—Melard Manufacturing Corporation; *U.S. Private*, pg. 729

DELUX PRODUCTIONS—Luxembourg Broadcasting—CLT-UFA; *Int'l*, pg. 561

DELUX SOLID BRASS—Bath Accessories—Melard Manufacturing Corporation; *U.S. Private*, pg. 729

DELUXE—Shower Wall Kit—Plaskolite Inc.; *U.S. Private*, pg. 870

DELUXE—Permanent Marker—Sanford Corporation; *U.S. Public*, pg. 1178

DELUXE—Roller Ball Pens—Sanford Corporation; *U.S. Public*, pg. 1178

DELUXE—Saw Blades—Vermont American Tool Corp.; *U.S. Public*, pg. 575

DELUXE—NONE—Weatherby, Inc.; *U.S. Private*, pg. 1155

DELUXE CHAMPION—Tires—Bridgestone/Firestone, Inc.; *Int'l*, pg. 213

DELUXE DIPLOMACY—Game—Monarch Avalon, Inc.; *U.S. Public*, pg. 1123

DELUXE FLAIR CHAIR—High Chair with Exclusive Hugger Back Feature—Cosco, Inc.; *U.S. Private*, pg. 277

DELUXE GRAHAMS—Cookie—Keebler Company; *U.S. Public*, pg. 657

DELUXE QUARTER—1/4 Pound Cheeseburger—Dairy Queen Corporate Store; *U.S. Public*, pg. 220

DELUXE ROLLPAC—Road Machinery-Compactor—Rosco Manufacturing Co.; *U.S. Private*, pg. 944

DELUXE SKIP-BO—Card Game—Mattel Games/Puzzles; *U.S. Public*, pg. 1058

DELUXE SQUARE RIGGER—Luggage—Lands' End, Inc.; *U.S. Public*, pg. 977

DELUXE UNO—Card Games—Mattel Games/Puzzles; *U.S. Public*, pg. 1058

DELUXE WHIZ BANG—Pop Corn Machine—Gold Medal Products Co.; *U.S. Private*, pg. 459

DELVAN—Synthetic Print Thickener—Dexter Chemical Corp.; *U.S. Private*, pg. 329

DELVO-CRETE—Cement Hydration Control Chemical—Novartis AG; *Int'l*, pg. 971

DELVO-X-PRESS—Tests to Determine Antibiotic Residues in Milk—Royal Gist-Brocades N.V.; *Int'l*, pg. 1142

DELVOCID—Enzyme to Prevent Molding of Cheese, Refermentation of Beverages—Royal Gist-Brocades N.V.; *Int'l*, pg. 1142

DELVOTEST—Tests for Detection of Antibiotic Residues in Milk—Royal Gist-Brocades N.V.; *Int'l*, pg. 1142

DELWEVE—NONE—Applied Extrusion Technologies, Inc.; *U.S. Public*, pg. 122

DEM GEO—NONE—Brown & Sharpe Manufacturing Company; *U.S. Public*, pg. 260

DEM-KOTE—Spray Paint—W.W. Grainger, Inc.; *U.S. Public*, pg. 758

DEMAK'UP—Make-Up Remover Pads—VP-Schickedanz AG; *U.S. Public*, pg. 1333

DEMAND CHAIN VOYAGER—Software System—American Software, Inc.; *U.S. Public*, pg. 91

DEMARK'S—Pipe Tobaccos—Consolidated Cigar Corporation; *U.S. Private*, pg. 690

DEMCO—Power Transmission Belts—W.W. Grainger, Inc.; *U.S. Public*, pg. 758

DEMCO-BOUND—Book Binding—Demco Inc.; *U.S. Private*, pg. 323

DEMCOTE—Adhesive—Demco Inc.; *U.S. Private*, pg. 323

DEMERT NAIL DRYER—Nail Polish Dryer Aerosol—DeMert & Dougherty, Inc.; *U.S. Private*, pg. 323

DEMERT TRAVEL SHAVE—Personal Care Travel Kit—DeMert & Dougherty, Inc.; *U.S. Private*, pg. 323

DEMET'S—French Thin Mints—Nestle-Rowntree Ltd.; *Int'l*, pg. 921

DEMETRE—Ski-Sweaters—Gerry Sportswear Company; *U.S. Private*, pg. 449

DEMETS—Chocolates—Nestle Chocolate & Confection; *Int'l*, pg. 917

DEMETS—Confections—Nestle S.A.; *Int'l*, pg. 915

DEMEURES ET CHATEAUX—French Women's Interest Magazine—EMAP France; *Int'l*, pg. 451

DEMI LOAF—Frozen Bread Dough—Bridgford Foods Corporation; *U.S. Public*, pg. 252

DEMI-REGROTON—Pharmaceuticals—Rhone-Poulenc Rorer - U.S.; *Int'l*, pg. 1110

DEMIDEKK—Opaque Stain—Jotun A/S; *Int'l*, pg. 714

DEMING—Pumps—Crane Deming Pumps; *U.S. Public*, pg. 457

DEMING'S—Canned Salmon—Peter Pan Seafoods, Inc.; *Int'l*, pg. 928

DEMISTER—Mist Eliminators—Koch Otto H. York Co., Inc.; *U.S. Private*, pg. 628

DEMOGRAPHIC CODING SYSTEM—Database Marketing—Group 1 Software, Inc.; *U.S. Public*, pg. 417

DEMON—Motor Cars—Life-Like Products, Inc.; *U.S. Private*, pg. 666

DEMPSEY'S—Ale—Joseph Huber Brewing Co., Inc.; *U.S. Private*, pg. 545

DEMPSTER DINOSAUR—Hydraulic Tilting Frame—Dempster Equipment; *U.S. Private*, pg. 1089

DEMPSTER DUMPSTER—Hoist Unit—Dempster Equipment; *U.S. Private*, pg. 1089

DEMTROL—Crude Oils Demulsifiers—The Dow Chemical Company; *U.S. Public*, pg. 522

DEMULEN—Oral Contraceptive—Monsanto Company; *U.S. Public*, pg. 1124

DEMULEN—Oral Contraceptive—Searle & Co.; *U.S. Public*, pg. 1125

DEMULEN—Pharmaceutical Products—Searle Laboratories; *U.S. Public*, pg. 1125

DEMULEN 1/35—Oral Contraceptive—Searle & Co.; *U.S. Public*, pg. 1125

DENA-VIE—Hair Products—Dena Corporation; *U.S. Private*, pg. 324

DENAKA—Vodka—Allied Domecq PLC; *Int'l*, pg. 62

DENAN—Lipid-lowering Drug—Boehringer Ingelheim GmbH; *Int'l*, pg. 199

DENDRITIC—Salt—Morton Salt; *U.S. Public*, pg. 1135

DENEUVE—Fragrance—Avon Products, Inc.; *U.S. Public*, pg. 155

DENFLEX—NONE—Dennis Chemical Co., Inc.; *U.S. Private*, pg. 324

DENICOTEA—Cigarette Holders & Filters—Lane Limited; *Int'l*, pg. 1129

DENNIS MILLER LIVE—Monologue Highlight Program—Westwood One, Inc.; *U.S. Public*, pg. 1763

DENNISONS—Chili—International Home Foods Inc.; *U.S. Private*, pg. 526

DENNY—Fresh & Canned Mushrooms—Bestfoods; *U.S. Public*, pg. 223

DENNY PORK—Pork Products—Kerry Group PLC; *Int'l*, pg. 731

DENNY'S—Eating Place—Advantica Restaurant Group, Inc.; *U.S. Public*, pg. 23

DENNY'S—Restaurants—Denny's, Inc.; *U.S. Public*, pg. 23

DENNY'S—24 Hr. Family Restaurant—BR Associates, Inc.; *U.S. Private*, pg. 107

DENOREX—NONE—American Home Products Corporation; *U.S. Public*, pg. 79

DENOREX—Medicated Shampoo—Whitehall-Robins Healthcare; *U.S. Public*, pg. 80

DENQUEL—Toothpaste—The Procter & Gamble Company; *U.S. Public*, pg. 1330

DENQUEL—Sensitive Teeth Toothpaste—Richardson-Vicks, Inc. Personal Care Products Div.; *U.S. Public*, pg. 1331

DENS-CORE—Core for Fire Resistant Door—Georgia-Pacific Corporation; *U.S. Public*, pg. 735

DENS-COTE—Gypsum Composition Board & Plaster in Powder Form—Georgia-Pacific Corporation; *U.S. Public*, pg. 735

DENS-DECK—Gypsum Board—Georgia-Pacific Corporation; *U.S. Public*, pg. 735

DENS-GLASS—Fiberglass-Faced Gypsum Sheathing—Georgia-Pacific Corporation; *U.S. Public*, pg. 735

DENS-SHIELD—Gypsum Board—Georgia-Pacific Corporation; *U.S. Public*, pg. 735

DENSCAL—Gypsum Plaster for Construction—Georgia-Pacific Corporation; *U.S. Public*, pg. 735

DENSFLOR—Gypsum Flooring Compound—Georgia-Pacific Corporation; *U.S. Public*, pg. 735

DENSILOG—NONE—Western Atlas Logging Services; *U.S. Public*, pg. 1757

DENSITE—Gypsum Plaster for Construction—Georgia-Pacific Corporation; *U.S. Public*, pg. 735

DENSWALL—Gypsum Wall & Ceiling Texture—Georgia-Pacific Corporation; *U.S. Public*, pg. 735

DENT-X—Dental X-ray Line—AFP Imaging Corporation; *U.S. Public*, pg. 6

DENTA SWAB POLY-PLUS—NONE—Ballard Medical Products; *U.S. Public*, pg. 171

DENTAGARD—Toothpaste—Colgate-Palmolive Company; *U.S. Public*, pg. 397

DENTAL—Scotch & Sweet Snuffs—Conwood Company L.P.; *U.S. Private*, pg. 272

DENTAL C.—Toothbrush—International Cosmetics Co., Ltd.; *Int'l*, pg. 684

DENTAL CENTER—Dental Tools—The Gillette Company; *U.S. Public*, pg. 743

DENTASWAB—NONE—Ballard Medical Products; *U.S. Public*, pg. 171

DENTCO—Entry Control Systems—Detex Corporation; *U.S. Private*, pg. 327

DENTIN—Bonding Agent—Johnson & Johnson Consumer Products; *U.S. Public*, pg. 928

DENTIST PREFERRED—Tooth Brushes—Health Products Corporation; *U.S. Private*, pg. 514

DENTLOCK—NONE—Lee Pharmaceuticals; *U.S. Public*, pg. 984

DENTLOCK—Denture Adhesive—Medtech Inc.; *U.S. Private*, pg. 728

DENTO-DRAIN—Compressor Drain Valve—Air Techniques, Inc.; *U.S. Private*, pg. 28

DENTO-DRI—Compressed Air Dryers—Air Techniques, Inc.; *U.S. Private*, pg. 28

DENTOTAPE—Dental Floss—Johnson & Johnson Consumer Products; *U.S. Public*, pg. 928

DENTROL—Denture Adhesive—Block Drug Company, Inc.; *U.S. Public*, pg. 236

DENTSURE—Denture Rinse—Pfizer Inc.; *U.S. Public*, pg. 1281

DENTU-CREME—Toothpaste for Dentures—Block Drug Company, Inc.; *U.S. Public*, pg. 236

DENTU-GEL—Toothpaste for Dentures—Block Drug Company, Inc.; *U.S. Public*, pg. 236

DENTUR-EZE—Denture Liner—Blistex, Inc.; *U.S. Private*, pg. 149

DENTURE RINSE—NONE—Pfizer Inc.; *U.S. Public*, pg. 1281

DENTURITE—Denture Cushion—Brimms Inc.; *U.S. Private*, pg. 169

DENTYNE—Chewing Gum—Adams U.S.A.; *U.S. Public*, pg. 1739

DENTYNE—Chewing Gum—Warner-Lambert Company; *U.S. Public*, pg. 1738

DENTYNE ICE—Chewing Gum—Warner-Lambert Company; *U.S. Public*, pg. 1738

DENVER—Densitometers, Film Editing Equipment—Eastman Kodak Company; *U.S. Public*, pg. 550

DENVER—Mineral Processing & Solid-Liquid Separation Equipment & Pumps—Svedala Pumps & Process; *Int'l*, pg. 1325

DENVER AND TREFOIL DESIGN—The Denver Logo—Svedala Pumps & Process; *Int'l*, pg. 1325

DENVER BUSINESS JOURNAL—Business Journal—Business First of New York, Inc.; *U.S. Private*, pg. 19

DENVER ORION—Pumps—Svedala Pumps & Process; *Int'l*, pg. 1325

DEOXIDINE—Metalworking Chemical—Henkel Surface Technologies; *Int'l*, pg. 610

DEOXO—Catalytic Purifiers—Engelhard Corporation; *U.S. Public*, pg. 582

DEOXSULF—NONE—Reactive Metals & Alloys Corporation (REMACOR); *U.S. Private*, pg. 913

DEPAKENE—Central Nervous System Agents—Kyowa Hakko Kogyo Company, Ltd.; *Int'l*, pg. 778

DEPAKOTE—Devalproex Sodium Antiepileptic—Abbott Laboratories; *U.S. Public*, pg. 12

DEPARTURE—Small Volume Industrial Fabric Filter—United McGill Corp.; *U.S. Private*, pg. 1122

DEPARTURES—Magazine—American Express Company; *U.S. Public*, pg. 73

DEPARTURES—Magazine—American Express Publishing Corporation; *U.S. Public*, pg. 74

DEPASAN—Cardiovascular Preparations—Kali-Chemie Aktiengesellschaft; *Int'l*, pg. 1278

DEPAZ—Rum—Paterno Imports Limited; *U.S. Private*, pg. 843

DEPEN—Severe Rheumatoid Arthritis—Wallace Laboratories; *U.S. Public*, pg. 310

DEPEND—Incontinence Products—Kimberly-Clark Corporation; *U.S. Public*, pg. 958

DEPENDABLES—Luggage—American Tourister, Inc.; *U.S. Public*, pg. 1430

DEPENDO-COPY—Paper for Use in Copying—Georgia-Pacific Corporation; *U.S. Public*, pg. 735

DEPLOY—Herbicide—Monsanto Company; *U.S. Public*, pg. 1124

DEPO-PROVERA—Contraceptive—Pharmacia & Upjohn; *Int'l*, pg. 1048

DEPOCILLIN—Procaine Penicillin—Royal Gist-Brocades N.V.; *Int'l*, pg. 1142

DEPOLAB—Deposition Summarizing—Interim Services Inc.; *U.S. Public*, pg. 892

DEPONIT—NONE—Schwarz Pharma Inc.; *Int'l*, pg. 1211

DEPOSIPAC 2000—Security Deposit Bags—John H. Harland Company; *U.S. Public*, pg. 785

DEPOSIT GUARANTY GOLF CLASSIC—NONE—Deposit Guaranty Corp.; *U.S. Public*, pg. 500

DEPRAMIN—Depressants in Ore Flotation—Akzo Nobel N.V.; *Int'l*, pg. 42

DEPROL—Antidepressant/tranquilizer—Wallace Laboratories; *U.S. Public*, pg. 310

DEPTH-O-MATIC—Mono—Outdoor Technologies Group; *U.S. Private*, pg. 822

DEQUACAINE—NONE—Boots Healthcare International; *Int'l*, pg. 202

DEQUADIN—NONE—Boots Healthcare International; *Int'l*, pg. 202

DEQUEST—Water Treating Chemical—Monsanto Company; *U.S. Public*, pg. 1124

DER LOWENBRAU—Beer, Japan Only—Asahi Breweries Ltd.; *Int'l*, pg. 83

DERAKANE—Vinyl Ester Resin—The Dow Chemical Company; *U.S. Public*, pg. 522

DERBY—Cigarette—Philip Morris Companies Inc.; *U.S. Public*, pg. 1287

DERBY—Converence Tables—Vecta; *U.S. Private*, pg. 1038

THE DERBYSHIRE—Financial & Insurance Services—Derbyshire Building Society; *Int'l*, pg. 394

DERBYSHIRE—Hardwood Doors—Georgia-Pacific Corporation; *U.S. Public*, pg. 735

THE DERBYSHIRE CAPITAL RESERVE—Investment Plans—Derbyshire Building Society; *Int'l*, pg. 394

THE DERBYSHIRE DEAL CHECK—Mortgages—Derbyshire Building Society; *Int'l*, pg. 394

DERBYSHIRE DIRECT—Mortgage Distribution—Derbyshire Building Society; *Int'l*, pg. 394

THE DERBYSHIRE HARVESTER—Equity Release Mortgage Plans—Derbyshire Building Society; *Int'l*, pg. 394

DERBYSHIRE LIFE—Financial & Insurance Services—Derbyshire Building Society; *Int'l*, pg. 394

DERBYSHIRE MANX BOND—Insurance & Financial Services—Derbyshire Building Society; *Int'l*, pg. 394

THE DERBYSHIRE MEMBERLOAN—Personal Loan Plans—Derbyshire Building Society; *Int'l*, pg. 394

THE DERBYSHIRE MONEYLINK—ATM Card Account—Derbyshire Building Society; *Int'l*, pg. 394

DERBYSHIRE MORTGAGECOVER—Financial & Insurance Services—Derbyshire Building Society; *Int'l*, pg. 394

THE DERBYSHIRE PAYMENTSCOVER—Mortgage Payment Protection Plan—Derbyshire Building Society; *Int'l*, pg. 394

THE DERBYSHIRE TOTAL HOMECOVER—Insurance—Derbyshire Building Society; *Int'l*, pg. 394

DERBYSURE—General Marketing—Derbyshire Building Society; *Int'l*, pg. 394

DERIFIL—Pharmaceutical Products—Rystan Company, Inc.; *U.S. Private*, pg. 436

DERIPHAT—Amphoteric Surfactants—Henkel Corporation; *Int'l*, pg. 610

DERMA—Dyes—Clariant International Ltd.; *Int'l*, pg. 624

DERMA-GEL—Wound Care Products—Medline Industries, Inc.; *U.S. Private*, pg. 728

DERMA KLENZ—Hand Cleaner & Lotion—Ecolab Inc.; *U.S. Public*, pg. 562

DERMA TOUCH—NONE—Medline Industries, Inc.; *U.S. Private*, pg. 728

DERMABRASE/35—Cosmetics—Irma Shorell, Inc.; *U.S. Private*, pg. 1101

DERMALIGHT PL—Leather Dye—Novartis AG; *Int'l*, pg. 971

DERMAPULSE—Medical Electrical Device Use to Treat Decubitus Ulcers—Staodyn Inc.; *U.S. Public*, pg. 1509

DERMAREST—Anti-Itch Medication—Del Pharmaceuticals, Inc.; *U.S. Public*, pg. 494

DERMASSAGE—Dishwashing Liquid—Colgate-Palmolive Company; *U.S. Public*, pg. 397

DERMASTAT—NONE—Laserscope Surgical Systems; *U.S. Public*, pg. 979

DERMATOLOGY TIMES—Trade Periodical—Advanstar Communications; *U.S. Private*, pg. 22

DERMOLATE—Skin Cream—Schering-Plough Corporation; *U.S. Public*, pg. 1438

DERMOVAN—Pharmaceutical Products—Galderma Laboratories, Inc.; *Int'l*, pg. 819

DERON—Hydraulics—National Mine Service, Inc.; *Int'l*, pg. 280

DEROSAL—Fungicide—Hoechst Aktiengesellschaft; *Int'l*, pg. 624

DERUSTO—Rust Preventative Paint—DAP Inc.; *Int'l*, pg. 1486

DES—NONE—Brown & Sharpe Manufacturing Company; *U.S. Public*, pg. 260

DES OWEN—Pharmaceutical Products—Galderma Laboratories, Inc.; *Int'l*, pg. 819

DESPHOS—Phosphate Esters—DeSoto Inc.; *U.S. Public*, pg. 956

DESCENTE—NONE—Descente America Inc.; *Int'l*, pg. 395

DESCHAUX BRANDY—Spirits—Leonard Kreusch, Inc.; *U.S. Private*, pg. 635

Brand Name Index

DESCO—Handkerchiefs—Honey Fashions Ltd.; *U.S. Private*, pg. 537

DESCO—Wall & Floor Surfacings—Master Builders Inc.; *Int'l*, pg. 1465

DESCOTE—Microencapsulated Vitamin, Mineral & Active Pharmaceutical Raw Matls.—KV Pharmaceutical Company; *U.S. Public*, pg. 941

DESERT BOOT—Shoes—Clark Shoe Co.; *Int'l*, pg. 297

DESERT DRY—Economical Grade of Redwood—Louisiana Pacific Corporation; *U.S. Public*, pg. 1015

DESERT FOX—Hose—The Goodyear Tire & Rubber Company; *U.S. Public*, pg. 752

DESERT SANDS—Vinyl Composition Tile—Kentile Operting Co.; *U.S. Private*, pg. 615

DESERT WIND—Toiletry—Shaklee Corporation; *Int'l*, pg. 1518

DESFERAL—Anti-Asthmatic—Ciba Specialty Chemicals; *Int'l*, pg. 291

DESFERAL—Anti-Asthmatic—Novartis; *Int'l*, pg. 972

DESFERAL—NONE—Novartis Pharmaceuticals; *Int'l*, pg. 973

DESICAL—Lime Dispersions—Harwick Standard Distribution Corporation; *U.S. Private*, pg. 509

DESICOOLER—Desiccator—Fisher Scientific Company; *U.S. Private*, pg. 658

DESICOTE—Water-Repellent Coating—Beckman Instruments, Inc.; *U.S. Public*, pg. 199

DESIGN—Hair Care Products—Wella Group; *Int'l*, pg. 1489

DESIGN-AN-EMBLEM—Needlework—A-B Emblem Div. of Conrad Industries, Inc.; *U.S. Private*, pg. 2

DESIGN-DUKE—Sporting Goods—Brunswick Bowling & Billiards Corp.; *U.S. Public*, pg. 265

DESIGN ENGINEERING—Factory—Gordon Publications, Inc.; *Int'l*, pg. 1096

DESIGN EXPRESSIONS—Photo Albums—C.R. Gibson Co.; *U.S. Public*, pg. 1168

DESIGN FREEDOM—Perm, Shampoos, Styling Aids, Conditioners—Zotos International; *Int'l*, pg. 1236

DESIGN GUILD—Handmade & Machine-Made Glass & Lead Crystal—Crystal Clear Industries; *U.S. Private*, pg. 293

DESIGN KETTLE—Stainless Steel—Dansk International Designs Ltd.; *U.S. Public*, pg. 261

DESIGN LINE—Decorator Telephone—Lucent Technologies Inc.; *U.S. Public*, pg. 1017

DESIGN NEWS—News Magazine for Design Engineers—Reed Elsevier Business Information; *Int'l*, pg. 1095

DESIGN RIBBON AND DESIGN—Ribbon—American Greetings Corporation; *U.S. Public*, pg. 77

DESIGN SEATING—Designer Seating Products—Domore Corporation; *U.S. Private*, pg. 339

DESIGN STUDIO—Decorative Ribbon—American Greetings Corporation; *U.S. Public*, pg. 77

DESIGN TRENDS—Drapery Hardware—Kirsch; *U.S. Public*, pg. 1176

DESIGN 2—Art Materials—Sanford Corporation; *U.S. Public*, pg. 1178

DESIGN WITH LIGHT COLLECTION—Candleholders, Silverplate & Crystal—Dansk International Designs Ltd.; *U.S. Public*, pg. 261

DESIGNACOLOR—Color Display Accessories—PPG Industries, Inc.; *U.S. Public*, pg. 1245

DESIGNAR—Glass Assembly System—Carter Holt Harvey Limited; *U.S. Public*, pg. 904

DESIGNAR—Toughened Safety Glass Entrance-Ways—Pilkington Australasia Limited; *Int'l*, pg. 1057

DESIGNARE—Plybent Wood Chair—Sauder Manufacturing Corporation; *U.S. Private*, pg. 967

DESIGNBOW & DESIGN—Bows—American Greetings Corporation; *U.S. Public*, pg. 77

DESIGNER CAREFREE—Vinyl Tile—Congoleum Corporation; *U.S. Public*, pg. 69

THE DESIGNER DIAMOND COLLECTION—Jewelery—Helzberg's Diamond Shops, Inc.; *U.S. Public*, pg. 220

DESIGNER IMPOSTERS—Women's Body Sprays & Fragrances—Parfums De Coeur Ltd.; *U.S. Private*, pg. 839

DESIGNER IMPOSTERS—Men's Body Sprays & Fragrances—Parfums De Coeur Ltd.; *U.S. Private*, pg. 839

DESIGNER LINE—Metallic Finish Receptacles & Planters—United Receptical, Inc.; *U.S. Private*, pg. 1123

DESIGNER MORTGAGE—Customized Fixed & Adjustable Mortgage Program—The Troy Savings Bank; *U.S. Private*, pg. 1106

DESIGNER SERIES—Recreational Vehicles—Jayco Inc.; *U.S. Private*, pg. 583

DESIGNER SERIES—Indash Car Stereos—Kraco Enterprises, Inc.; *U.S. Private*, pg. 634

DESIGNER SERIES—Stationary Products—The Mead Corporation; *U.S. Public*, pg. 1074

DESIGNER SERIES—Cabinets—Tab Products Co.; *U.S. Public*, pg. 1559

DESIGNER SPORT GRIP—Steering Wheel Covers—Superior Industries International, Inc.; *U.S. Public*, pg. 1539

THE DESIGNER—Magazine—North American Publishing Company; *U.S. Private*, pg. 803

DESIGNER WALL—Steel Wall Panel—Clestra Hauserman, Inc.; *Int'l*, pg. 569

DESIGNERS CHOICE—Nominal 4″ Bright Glazed Wall Tile with 3/4″ x 6″ Accent Strips Available—United States Ceramic Tile Co.; *U.S. Private*, pg. 1124

DESIGNERS COLLECTION—Greeting Cards; Gift Wrap, Ribbons & Bows—American Greetings Corporation; *U.S. Public*, pg. 77

DESIGNERS ORIGINALS—Sweaters—Hampshire Group, Ltd.; *U.S. Public*, pg. 778

DESIGNER'S TOUCH—Carpet—Lees Carpets; *U.S. Public*, pg. 268

DESIGNLINE—Orthotics for Men's & Women's Dress Shoes—The Langer Biomechanics Group, Inc.; *U.S. Public*, pg. 978

DESIGNMASTER—All-Digital Color Electronic Pre-Press System—Eastman Kodak Company; *U.S. Public*, pg. 550

DESIGNMATE—Pen Plotter—CalComp Technology; *U.S. Public*, pg. 1007

DESIGNMATE—Packaging Systems—Sanderson Plumbing Products Inc.; *U.S. Private*, pg. 964

DESIGNPRINTS—Greeting Cards, Invit. & Anncmnt., Thank U Notes, Calenders, Party Goods—American Greetings Corporation; *U.S. Public*, pg. 77

DESIGNSELECTION—Pocket Binoculars—Carl Zeiss; *Int'l*, pg. 1522

DESIGNSTUDIO—Greeting Cards, Invit. & Anncmnt., Thank U Notes, Calenders, & Party Goods—American Greetings Corporation; *U.S. Public*, pg. 77

DESIGNWARE—Greeting Cards, Inv. & Anncmnt. Forms, Thank U Notes, Calndrs, Party Goods—American Greetings Corporation; *U.S. Public*, pg. 77

DESIGNWORKS,THE—Greeting Cards, Inv. & Announcement, Thank U Notes, Calenders, Party Goods—American Greetings Corporation; *U.S. Public*, pg. 77

DESIGNWRAP—Paper-Decorative Wrapping Paper, Packaging Material, Cartons, Boxes, Tags—American Greetings Corporation; *U.S. Public*, pg. 77

DESIGNWRAP 'N TRIM & DESIGN—Gift Wrap Paper, Matching Note or Gift Cards, Bow & Ribbons Sold As A Unit—American Greetings Corporation; *U.S. Public*, pg. 77

DESINTE—NONE—Acos Villares S.A.; *Int'l*, pg. 23

DESITIN/DAILY CARE—NONE—Pfizer Inc.; *U.S. Public*, pg. 1281

THE DESK ORGANIZER—Desk-Top Supply Organizer & Other Stationery Items—M. Kamenstein, Inc.; *U.S. Private*, pg. 606

DESK SCENES—Paper Pads—The Mead Corporation; *U.S. Public*, pg. 1074

DESKETTE—Desk Set—Dixon Ticonderoga Company; *U.S. Public*, pg. 514

DESKPRO 486-50L—Personal Computer—COMPAQ Computer Corporation; *U.S. Public*, pg. 417

DESKPRO 386/20e—Personal Computer—COMPAQ Computer Corporation; *U.S. Public*, pg. 417

DESKSTAR—Computer Application Processor—Datapoint Corporation; *Int'l*, pg. 384

DESKTOP BUILDING—Computer Aided Design Program—Weyerhaeuser Forest Products Company; *U.S. Public*, pg. 1764

DESKTOP GENERATION—Desktop Micro Computer—Data General Corporation; *U.S. Public*, pg. 485

DESKTOP PDM—NONE—Structural Dynamics Research Corp.; *U.S. Public*, pg. 1525

DESKTOP PROJECTOR—LCD Projector—Proxima Corporation; *U.S. Public*, pg. 1339

DESMA—Injection Molding Machines—Klockner-Werke AG; *Int'l*, pg. 736

DESMODUR—Polyurethane Coatings—Bayer AG; *Int'l*, pg. 171

DESMOPHEN—Polyurethane Coatings—Bayer AG; *Int'l*, pg. 171

DESOBRY—Cakes, Biscuits, Waffles—GrandMet Foods Southern Europe; *Int'l*, pg. 409

DESOGEN—Oral Contraceptive—Akzo Nobel N.V.; *Int'l*, pg. 42

DESOGEN—Pharmaceutical—Organon Inc.; *Int'l*, pg. 48

DESOMEEN—Ethoxylated Amines—Witco Corporation; *U.S. Public*, pg. 1773

DESPARD—Interchangeable Switches, Receptacles & Pilot Lights—Pass & Seymour/Legrand; *Int'l*, pg. 806

DESQUAM-E—Acne & Oily Skin Care Aids—Westwood-Squibb Pharmaceuticals Inc.; *U.S. Public*, pg. 255

DESQUAM-X—Benzoyl Pexoride Preparation—Bristol-Myers Squibb Company; *U.S. Public*, pg. 253

DESQUAM-X—Acne & Oily Skin Care Aids—Westwood-Squibb Pharmaceuticals Inc.; *U.S. Public*, pg. 255

DESQUIEN—Multitasking Product—Quarterdeck Corp.; *U.S. Public*, pg. 1350

DESSERTS—Culinary Publication—House of White Birches, Inc.; *U.S. Private*, pg. 542

DESTAB—Direct Compression Products—KV Pharmaceutical Company; *U.S. Public*, pg. 941

DESTINATION—Fragrance & Personal Care Products—AnnTaylor Stores Corporation; *U.S. Public*, pg. 116

DESTINY—Computer Program, Software—Lucent Technologies Inc.; *U.S. Public*, pg. 1017

DESTINY—Women's Fragrance—Marilyn Miglin, L.P.; *U.S. Private*, pg. 745

DESTINY—Pleasure Boat Name—Regal Marine Industries Inc.; *U.S. Private*, pg. 917

DESTINY HOMES—Mobile Homes—Oakwood Homes Corporation; *U.S. Public*, pg. 1209

DESTONATE—Feed Additives & Others—Meiji Seika Kaisha, Ltd.; *Int'l*, pg. 855

DESTROYIT—Paper Shredders & Paper Balers—Michael Business Machines Corporation; *U.S. Private*, pg. 740

DESULCO—Carbon Alloy—Superior Graphite Co.; *U.S. Private*, pg. 1054

DESYREL—Antidepressant—Bristol-Myers Squibb Company; *U.S. Public*, pg. 253

DESYREL—Pharmaceutical Product for Symptoms of Depression—Bristol-Myers Squibb U.S. Pharmaceutical Group; *U.S. Public*, pg. 255

DET-TRONICS—Electronic Equip.—Detector Electronics Corporation; *Int'l*, pg. 1500

DETAC—Pitch Control Technology—BetzDearborn Inc.; *U.S. Public*, pg. 226

DETACHABLE PLUS—Hair Clipper—Andis Company; *U.S. Private*, pg. 73

DETACLAD—NONE—Dynamic Materials Corporation; *U.S. Public*, pg. 539

DETACOUPLE—NONE—Dynamic Materials Corporation; *U.S. Public*, pg. 539

DETAFORM—NONE—Dynamic Materials Corporation; *U.S. Public*, pg. 539

DETAIL—Herbicide—American Home Products Corporation; *U.S. Public*, pg. 79

DETAILS—Magazine—The Conde Nast Publications Inc.; *U.S. Private*, pg. 20

DETAN-ESCONDTE—NONE—Alimentation Couche Tard Inc.; *Int'l*, pg. 57

DETECT-A-FIRE—Fire Detector—Kidde-Fenwal, Inc.; *Int'l*, pg. 1500

DETECT-ASE—Chemical Reagent—Beckman Instruments, Inc.; *U.S. Public*, pg. 199

DETECT-HIV—Diagnostic Kit—BioChem Pharma Inc.; *Int'l*, pg. 196

DETECT-HTLV—Diagnostic Kit—BioChem Pharma Inc.; *Int'l*, pg. 196

DETECTO—Scales—Detecto Scale Company; *U.S. Private*, pg. 209

DETECTO-LITE—Neon Tester—Eagle Electric Mfg. Co., Inc.; *U.S. Private*, pg. 354

DETECTO-PAK—Flame Ionization Gas Leak Detector—Heath Consultants Incorporated; *U.S. Private*, pg. 518

DETECTOR II—Tape Cleaner—Anacomp Magnetics, Inc.; *U.S. Public*, pg. 107

DETECTRIC—Culture Growth Medium—Beckman Instruments, Inc.; *U.S. Public*, pg. 199

DETER—Family Toiletries—Amway Corporation; *U.S. Private*, pg. 69

DETERGENT 101—Liquid Warewashing Detergent—Ecolab Inc.; *U.S. Public*, pg. 562

DETERMINATOR—Recreational Products—The Black & Decker Corporation; *U.S. Public*, pg. 233

DETOUR—Dog, Rabbit, Deer, Squirrel & Bat Repellent—Security Lawn & Garden Co.; *U.S. Private*, pg. 397

DETRIANA—Wood Frame Side Chair, ai Collection—Vecta; *U.S. Private*, pg. 1038

DETROIT DIESEL—Diesel Engines—Valley Detroit Diesel Allison; *U.S. Public*, pg. 1132

DETROIT—Engine—Buffalo Truck Center; *U.S. Private*, pg. 179

DETROIT DIESEL—NONE—Detroit Diesel Corp.; *U.S. Private*, pg. 850

DETROIT DIESEL—Parts—Great Lakes Peterbilt, GMC; *U.S. Private*, pg. 475

DETROIT DIESEL & SPINNING ARROWS DESIGN—NONE—Detroit Diesel Corp.; *U.S. Private*, pg. 850

DETROIT DIESEL ENGINES—NONE—Detroit Diesel Corp.; *U.S. Private*, pg. 850

DETROIT DIESEL TRUCK PARTS—Truck Parts—Heintzelman's Truck Center Inc.; *U.S. Private*, pg. 519

DETROIT DIESEL WITHIN SPINNING ARROW DESIGN—NONE—Detroit Diesel Corp.; *U.S. Private*, pg. 850

DETROIT FREE PRESS—Newspaper—Detroit Newspapers; *U.S. Public*, pg. 965

DETROIT GASKET—Full Line of Domestic & Import Auto Engine & Marine Gaskets—Indian Head Industries Inc.; *U.S. Private*, pg. 559

DETROIT MONTHLY—Magazine—Crain Communications, Inc.; *U.S. Private*, pg. 284

DETTOL—Antiseptics—Reckitt & Colman plc; *Int'l*, pg. 1089

DETTOL DEEP FRESH—Foam Bath, Shower Soap, Shower Gel—Reckitt & Colman plc; *Int'l*, pg. 1089

DETTOX—Anti-Bacterial Cleanser—Reckitt & Colman plc; *Int'l*, pg. 1089

DEUCE—NONE—Callaway Golf Company; *U.S. Public*, pg. 294

DEUCE—Socks & Knitted Headwear—Wigwam Mills, Inc.; *U.S. Private*, pg. 1175

DEUTSCH—High-Precision Oil & Air Filters (Automotive)—AutoZone, Inc.; *U.S. Public*, pg. 150

DEUTSCH—NONE—Milgray Electronics, Inc.; *U.S. Public*, pg. 205

DEUTSCHE GRAMMOPHON—Classical Records—Philips Electronics N.V.; *Int'l*, pg. 1051

DEUTSCHE GRAMMOPHON—Records & Cassettes—Polygram Records, Inc.; *Int'l*, pg. 1052

DEUTZ—Liquid & Air Cooled High Speed Engines—Deutz AG; *Int'l*, pg. 407

DEUTZ—Diesel Engines—Harley Industries, Inc.; *U.S. Public*, pg. 880

DEUTZ—Diesel Engines—McDonald Equipment Co.; *U.S. Private*, pg. 721

DEUTZ MWM—Medium to Large Sized Gas & Diesel Engines—Deutz AG; *Int'l*, pg. 407

DEVCHEM—Coating—Grow Group, Inc.; *Int'l*, pg. 663

DEVCHEM—Coatings—ICI Paints; *Int'l*, pg. 664

DEVCHLOR—Chlorinated Rubber Coating—Grow Group, Inc.; *Int'l*, pg. 663

DEVCHLOR—Chlorinated Rubber Coating—ICI Paints; *Int'l*, pg. 664

DEVCO—Coal Mining & Distribution—Cape Breton Development Corporation; *Int'l*, pg. 265

DEVELOPERS@WORK—Program for Third Party Software Developers—Mitel Corporation; *Int'l*, pg. 870

DEVELOPMATE—Computer System—International Business Machines Corporation; *U.S. Public*, pg. 895

DEVELOPURE—Water Purification Filters—Osmonics, Inc.; *U.S. Public*, pg. 1233

DEVIL DOGS—Snack Cakes—Drake Bakeries, Inc.; *Int'l*, pg. 349

DEVIL MOUNTAIN—Microbrew—The Seagram Company Ltd.; *Int'l*, pg. 1214

DEVILLE—Car—Cadillac Motor Car Division; *U.S. Public*, pg. 720

DEVIMCO—Wholesale Equipment Suppliers—Accor S.A.; *Int'l*, pg. 20

DEVLIEG—NONE—DeVlieg-Bullard Inc.; *U.S. Public*, pg. 502

DEVO'ZINE—Devotional Magazine for Teens—The Upper Room; *U.S. Private*, pg. 1129

DEVOE—Paint—Devoe & Raynolds; *Int'l*, pg. 663

DEVOE—Trade Sales Paint—Devoe Paint; *Int'l*, pg. 663

DEVOE—Trade Sales Paint—Grow Group, Inc.; *Int'l*, pg. 663

DEVOE—Trade Sales Paint—ICI Paints; *Int'l*, pg. 664

DEVON—NONE—CertainTeed Corporation; *Int'l*, pg. 1170

DEVON—Book Cloth—Industrial Coatings Group, Inc.; *U.S. Private*, pg. 434

DEVON—NONE—SunGard Data Systems Inc.; *U.S. Public*, pg. 1534

THE DEVON SYSTEM—NONE—SunGard Data Systems Inc.; *U.S. Public*, pg. 1534

DEVON SYSTEMS INTERNATIONAL—NONE—SunGard Data Systems Inc.; *U.S. Public*, pg. 1534

DEVONSHEER—Snack Crackers, Bread Crumbs—Bestfoods; *U.S. Public*, pg. 223

DEVONSHIRE CROWN LIQUOUR—Liquour—Charles Jacquin et Cie, Inc.; *U.S. Private*, pg. 580

DEVOS-LEMMENS—Pickles, Sauces, Mustard, Mayonnaise—Campbell Soup Company; *U.S. Public*, pg. 298

DEVOTEE—Women's Fragrance—Avon Products, Inc.; *U.S. Public*, pg. 155

DEVRAN—Coating—Grow Group, Inc.; *Int'l*, pg. 663

DEVRAN—Coating—ICI Paints; *Int'l*, pg. 664

DEVRO COLLAGEN CASING—NONE—Devro-Teepak, Inc.; *Int'l*, pg. 408

DEVRY—Technical Colleges—DeVry Institutes; *U.S. Public*, pg. 503

DEW FLEX—Mono—Outdoor Technologies Group; *U.S. Private*, pg. 822

DEW POINTER—Measuring Device—Alnor Instrument Company; *U.S. Public*, pg. 1559

DEWALT—Radial Arm Saw—The Black & Decker Corporation; *U.S. Public*, pg. 233

DEWAR'S WHITE LABEL—Gin—Guinness Import Company; *Int'l*, pg. 412

DEWAR'S WHITE LABEL—NONE—Guinness Plc; *Int'l*, pg. 412

DEWCEL—Humidity Measuring Element—The Foxboro Company; *Int'l*, pg. 1243

DEWCO—Industrial Supplies—Don E. Williams Co.; *U.S. Private*, pg. 1177

DEWEESE—Womens Swimsuits—Beach Patrol Inc.; *U.S. Private*, pg. 125

DEWKIST—Pickles & Syrup—Dean Pickles & Specialty Products; *U.S. Public*, pg. 490

DEXA—Butterfly Valves—KSB Aktiengesellschaft; *Int'l*, pg. 721

DEXACORT RESPIHALER—NONE—Medeva PLC; *Int'l*, pg. 852

DEXACORT TURBINAIRE—NONE—Medeva PLC; *Int'l*, pg. 852

DEXASONE—Prescription Drug—ICN Pharmaceuticals, Inc.; *U.S. Public*, pg. 853

DEXATRIM—Diet Aid—Thompson Medical Company, Inc.; *U.S. Public*, pg. 1083

DEXSTAR—Silicone Polyester Coating—The Dexter Corporation; *U.S. Public*, pg. 504

DEXTER—Shoes—Dexter Shoe Company; *U.S. Public*, pg. 217

DEXTER—Chef Knives—Hyde Manufacturing Co.; *U.S. Private*, pg. 551

DEXTER—Cutlery—Russell Harrington Cutlery Inc.; *U.S. Private*, pg. 551

DEXTER/RUSSELL—Cutlery—Russell Harrington Cutlery Inc.; *U.S. Private*, pg. 551

DEXTEX—Specialty Papers—The Dexter Corporation; *U.S. Public*, pg. 504

DEXTRO-ENERGEN—Quick Energy Products—Bestfoods; *U.S. Public*, pg. 223

DEXTRO-PAK—Cartridge—Millipore Corporation; *U.S. Public*, pg. 1112

DEXTROPUR—Quick Energy Products—Bestfoods; *U.S. Public*, pg. 223

DEXTROSOL—Pure Crystallized Dextrose for Food & Medicinal Purposes—Bestfoods; *U.S. Public*, pg. 223

DEY-LUTE—Unique Drug Formulations—Dey Laboratories Inc.; *Int'l*, pg. 812

DEY-PAK—Unique Packaging Type—Dey Laboratories Inc.; *Int'l*, pg. 812

DEY-VIAL—Unique Packaging Type—Dey Laboratories Inc.; *Int'l*, pg. 812

DEZIGNRITE—Paint & Paint Sundries Retailers—PRO Group, Inc.; *U.S. Private*, pg. 887

DEZURIK—Valves—DEZurik; *U.S. Public*, pg. 726

DI—Drugstore Chain—Etablissements Delhaize Freres Et Cie "Le Lion" S.A.; *Int'l*, pg. 462

DI-CUP—Dicumyl Peroxide—Hercules Incorporated; *U.S. Public*, pg. 809

DI-ELYTE—Non-Metallic Wire—Glastic Corporation; *Int'l*, pg. 740

DI-GEL—Antacid & Antigas Tablets & Liquid—Schering-Plough Corporation; *U.S. Public*, pg. 1438

DI-GEL—Antacid—Schering-Plough Healthcare Products Inc.; *U.S. Public*, pg. 1438

DI GIORNO—Fresh Pastas & Sauces—Kraft Foods Inc.; *U.S. Public*, pg. 1288

DI LUSSO—Genoa Sausage—Hormel Foods Corp.; *U.S. Public*, pg. 840

DI-NA-CAL—Labels—Jefferson Smurfit Group p.l.c.; *Int'l*, pg. 1269

DI PARMA—Fresh Pasta—Borden, Inc.; *U.S. Private*, pg. 157

DI SARONNO AMARETTO—Liqueur—Grand Metropolitan Plc; *Int'l*, pg. 408

DI SARONNO AMARETTO—Liqueur—IDV North America; *Int'l*, pg. 411

DI-SHIELD—Aluminum Can Forming Lubricants—D.A. Stuart Company; *U.S. Public*, pg. 1048

DI-TAB—Tabletting Excipients—Rhone-Poulenc Basic Chemicals Co.; *Int'l*, pg. 1110

DIAB-A-THOTICS—Orthotics for Those with "At Risk" Diabetic Conditions—The Langer Biomechanics Group, Inc.; *U.S. Public*, pg. 978

DIABETA—Diabetes—Hoechst Marion Roussel, Inc.; *Int'l*, pg. 624

DIABETA—Oral Blood-Glucose-Lowering Drug for Diabetes—Hoechst Marion Roussel North America; *Int'l*, pg. 625

DIABETES TREATMENT CENTERS OF AMERICA—Diabetes Treatment Centers—American Healthcorp Inc.; *U.S. Public*, pg. 78

DIABINESE—Chlorpropamide—Pfizer Inc.; *U.S. Public*, pg. 1281

DIABLITOS—Deviled Meat Spreads—The Pillsbury Company; *Int'l*, pg. 411

DIABON—Graphite—Hoechst Aktiengesellschaft; *Int'l*, pg. 624

DIACRYL—Resin Raw Materials—Akzo Nobel N.V.; *Int'l*, pg. 42

DIADORA—Athletic Footwear & Apparel—Diadora America, Inc.; *U.S. Private*, pg. 330

DIAGLUTO—Agglutination Reading Device—Beckman Instruments, Inc.; *U.S. Public*, pg. 199

DIAGNOSTIC CHALLENGE—Newsletter Sections about Diagnostic Imaging—Mallinckrodt Inc.; *U.S. Public*, pg. 1039

DIAGNOSTIC HYSTEROSCOPY REDI-KIT—Surgical Prepatory Kits—The Cooper Companies, Inc.; *U.S. Public*, pg. 442

DIAGNOSTIC IMAGING—Magazine—Miller Freeman Inc.; *Int'l*, pg. 1443

DIAGNOSTIC IMAGING INTERNATIONAL—Magazine—Miller Freeman Inc.; *Int'l*, pg. 1443

DIAGRAM-MASTER—Software—Borland International, Inc.; *U.S. Public*, pg. 246

DIAL—Children's Hardcover Books—Penguin Putnam Inc.; *Int'l*, pg. 1027

DIAL-A-CELL—Membrane Laboratory Electrolytic Equipment—Ionics, Incorporated; *U.S. Public*, pg. 912

DIAL-A-LITE—Lamps—Eagle Electric Mfg. Co., Inc.; *U.S. Private*, pg. 354

DIAL A MATTRESS—Mattress Delivery Service—Dial A Mattress USA; *U.S. Private*, pg. 330

DIAL-A-TEMP—Heated Cabinets—Foster Refrigerator Corporation; *U.S. Private*, pg. 421

DIAL-A-TIME—Oscillating Sprinkler With Timer—L.R. Nelson Corporation; *U.S. Private*, pg. 790

DIAL BAR SOAP—NONE—The Dial Corporation; *U.S. Public*, pg. 505

DIAL BUDGET—Discount Grocery Stroes—Etablissements Delhaize Freres Et Cie "Le Lion" S.A.; *Int'l*, pg. 462

DIAL MASSAGE—Massager Shower—Pollenex; *U.S. Public*, pg. 1391

DIAL-O-MATIC—Luggage—Hartmann Luggage & Leather Goods Group; *U.S. Public*, pg. 261

DIAL PLUS BAR SOAP—NONE—The Dial Corporation; *U.S. Public*, pg. 505

DIAL PLUS BODY WASH—NONE—The Dial Corporation; *U.S. Public*, pg. 505

DIAL PRESS—NONE—Dell Publishing; *Int'l*, pg. 191

DIAL SET—Adjustable Boring Bars—Kennametal Inc.; *U.S. Public*, pg. 950

DIAL-TAPER—Tape Machine—Marsh Company; *U.S. Private*, pg. 707

DIAL ULTRA SKIN CARE BAR SOAP—NONE—The Dial Corporation; *U.S. Public*, pg. 505

DIAL ULTRA SKIN CARE BODY WASH—NONE—The Dial Corporation; *U.S. Public*, pg. 505

DIAL ULTRA SKIN CARE LIQUID SOAP—NONE—The Dial Corporation; *U.S. Public*, pg. 505

DIALATCH—Container Latch—Hartwell Corporation; *U.S. Private*, pg. 1168

DIALCO—Electronic Components—Dialight Corporation; *Int'l*, pg. 1130

DIALGRADE—Construction Laser Equipment—Spectra-Physics Laserplane Inc.; *U.S. Public*, pg. 1594

DIALOG—Electrical Control System—R.A. Jones & Co. Inc.; *U.S. Private*, pg. 597

DIALOG—Intercom System, Electronic Multi-Link Intercom—Lucent Technologies Inc.; *U.S. Public*, pg. 1017

DIALPAK—Contraceptive—Johnson & Johnson; *U.S. Public*, pg. 927

DIALPAK—Tablet Dispenser—Ortho-McNeil Pharmaceutical Corporation; *U.S. Public*, pg. 929

DIALUDID HP—Pharmaceuticals—Knoll Pharmaceutical Company; *Int'l*, pg. 105

DIAM—Fatty Diamines—Henkel Corporation; *Int'l*, pg. 610

DIAMANTE—Automobile—Mitsubishi Motor Sales of America, Inc.; *Int'l*, pg. 875

DIAMON—Diagnostic Monitor—GenRad, Inc.; *U.S. Public*, pg. 731

DIAMON DEB—Salon Professional Manicure Products—The Cook Bates Division; *Int'l*, pg. 815

DIAMONAIR—Fine Jewelry—Diamonair; *U.S. Public*, pg. 1003

DIAMONAIR—Simulated Diamond Jewelry—Litton Industries, Inc.; *U.S. Public*, pg. 1002

DIAMOND—Tools—Audits & Surveys Worldwide; *U.S. Public*, pg. 147

DIAMOND—CO2 Laser—Coherent, Inc.; *U.S. Public*, pg. 395

DIAMOND—Horseshoes, Farrier Tools, Pliers, and Wrenches—Cooper Hand Tools; *U.S. Public*, pg. 444

DIAMOND—Pliers & Wrenches—Cooper Industries, Inc.; *U.S. Public*, pg. 442

DIAMOND—Matches, Toothpicks, Clothes Pins & Plastic Cutlery—Diamond Brands, Inc.; *U.S. Private*, pg. 330

DIAMOND—Roller & Conveyor Chains—Diamond Chain Company; *U.S. Private*, pg. 68

DIAMOND—Electronics—Diamond Electronics, Inc.; *U.S. Public*, pg. 1663

DIAMOND—Service—The Dow Chemical Company; *U.S. Public*, pg. 522

DIAMOND—Kitchen & Bathroom Cabinets—Electrolux, AB; *Int'l*, pg. 438

DIAMOND—Foil—Reynolds Metals Co., Consumer Products Div.; *U.S. Public*, pg. 1386

DIAMOND—Rolls & Laminated Sheets of Aluminous Metal Foil—Reynolds Metals Company; *U.S. Public*, pg. 1385

DIAMOND—Walnuts, Pecans, Filberts, Brazil Nuts, Mixed Nuts—Sun Diamond Growers of California; *U.S. Private*, pg. 1051

DIAMOND—Cabinets—White Consolidated Industries, Inc.; *U.S. Public*, pg. 439

DIAMOND A—Canned Food—Agripac Inc.; *U.S. Private*, pg. 26

DIAMOND-BACK—Mirror Back Coatings—PPG Industries, Inc.; *U.S. Public*, pg. 1245

DIAMOND BRAND SOYBEAN—NONE—Garst Seed Company; *U.S. Private*, pg. 1524

DIAMOND COAT—Film Laminating Process—Colad Group Inc.; *U.S. Private*, pg. 250

DIAMOND COAT—Protective & Decorative Coatings—PPG Industries, Inc.; *U.S. Public*, pg. 1245

DIAMOND CRYSTAL—Salt Product Line—Akzo Nobel N.V.; *Int'l*, pg. 42

DIAMOND CRYSTAL—Condiments—Diamond Crystal Specialty Foods, Inc.; *U.S. Private*, pg. 330

DIAMOND DELUXE—Paper Plates—Tenneco Specialty Products; *U.S. Public*, pg. 1579

DIAMOND DESIGN—Metal Caps, Lids, Closures & Liners for Containers—The West Company, Incorporated; *U.S. Public*, pg. 1755

DIAMOND DUO—Spread/Blanket—Medline Industries, Inc.; *U.S. Private*, pg. 728

DIAMOND ESSENCE—Diamonds—Ranjit Corporation; *U.S. Private*, pg. 909

DIAMOND F—Lighting Fixtures—The Genlyte Group Incorporated; *U.S. Public*, pg. 729

DIAMOND FLEUR—Cologne & Toiletries—Avon Products, Inc.; *U.S. Public*, pg. 155

DIAMOND FLEX—Protective & Decorative Coatings—PPG Industries, Inc.; *U.S. Public*, pg. 1245

DIAMOND GRIT—Abrasive—Carborundum Abrasives North America; *Int'l*, pg. 1174

DIAMOND J.—Boots—Justin Boot Company; *U.S. Public*, pg. 937

DIAMOND LIQUI-TOOL—NONE—Audits & Surveys Worldwide; *U.S. Public*, pg. 147

DIAMOND LOGO (SYNTEQ)—Hydraulic Filter—Donaldson Company, Inc.; *U.S. Public*, pg. 517

DIAMOND OFFSHORE DRILLING, INC.—Offshore Drilling—Loews Corporation; *U.S. Public*, pg. 1010

DIAMOND PARK FINE JEWELERS—Leased Department Stores—Zale Corporation; *U.S. Public*, pg. 1789

DIAMOND PASTA—Pasta—Goodman Fielder Limited; *Int'l*, pg. 555

DIAMOND REFLECTIONS—Watches—Baume Mercier, Inc.; *U.S. Private*, pg. 124

DIAMOND SCOT—NONE—Tommy Armour Golf; *U.S. Public*, pg. 1683

DIAMOND SHAKERS—Disposables—Diamond Crystal Specialty Foods, Inc.; *U.S. Private*, pg. 330

DIAMOND WALNUT OIL—Nut Oil—Sun Diamond Growers of California; *U.S. Private*, pg. 1051

DIAMOND WOOD STAIN—NONE—The Flecto Co., Inc.; *U.S. Private*, pg. 410

DIAMOND WORLD REVIEW—Trade Publication on the International Diamond Industry—Reed Elsevier Business Information; *Int'l*, pg. 1095

DIAMONDCOAT—Deluxe Nonstick Finish—National Presto Industries, Inc.; *U.S. Public*, pg. 1159

DIAMONDITE—Jewelry—Richton International Corporation; *U.S. Public*, pg. 1389

DIAMONDS & EMERALDS—Fragrance—Parfums International Ltd.; *Int'l*, pg. 1435

DIAMONDS & RUBIES—Fragrance—Parfums International Ltd.; *Int'l*, pg. 1435

DIAMONDS & SAPPHIRES—Fragrance—Parfums International Ltd.; *Int'l*, pg. 1435

DIAMONITE—Ceramic Products—Diamonite Plant; *U.S. Public*, pg. 618

DIAM'S—Hosiery—Sara Lee Corporation; *U.S. Public*, pg. 1432

DIANA—Art Needle Work Accessories—Wm. E. Wright Limited Partnership; *U.S. Private*, pg. 1192

DIANA MARCO—NONE—Petrie Retail, Inc.; *U.S. Private*, pg. 858

DIANODIC—Scale Inhibitor—BetzDearborn Inc.; *U.S. Public*, pg. 226

DIANOL—Resin Raw Material—Akzo Nobel N.V.; *Int'l*, pg. 42

DIAGNOSTIC LINK—NONE—Detroit Diesel Corp.; *U.S. Private*, pg. 850

DIAPER GUARD—Therapeutic Rash Ointment—Del Pharmaceuticals, Inc.; *U.S. Public*, pg. 494

DIAPID—Nasal Spray—Sandoz Pharmaceuticals Corp.; *Int'l*, pg. 974

DIAR-AID—Tablets—Thompson Medical Company, Inc.; *U.S. Private*, pg. 1083

DIARAD—Medical Instrument—Capintec Inc.; *U.S. Private*, pg. 205

DIASORB—Diarrhea Medication—Columbia Laboratories, Inc.; *U.S. Public*, pg. 405

DIASTAR—Microscope—Leica, Inc.; *Int'l*, pg. 806

DIASTAT—NONE—Elan Corporation Plc; *Int'l*, pg. 435

DIAZINON—Insecticides—Nippon Kayaku Co. Ltd.; *Int'l*, pg. 934

DIAZO—Film Duplicators—Houston Fearless 76 Inc.; *U.S. Private*, pg. 542

DIAZO BASE—Blue Print Base Paper—MACtac Scranton Facility; *U.S. Public*, pg. 210

DIAZO CHROME—Diazo Film—Fort James Corporation; *U.S. Public*, pg. 670

DIB CABLE—Duplex Intrabuilding Cable—Siecor Corporation; *U.S. Public*, pg. 449

DIB CABLE—Duplex Intrabuilding Cable—Siecor Corporation; *Int'l*, pg. 1245

DIBETA—Insecticide—Abbott Laboratories; *U.S. Public*, pg. 12

DIBLOCIN—Cardiovascular Drug—Astra AB; *Int'l*, pg. 93

DIC—NONE—GS Societa Generale Supermercati; *Int'l*, pg. 186

DICETEL—Gastrointestinal Pharmaceutical—BYK Gulden, S.A. de C.V.; *Int'l*, pg. 66

DICETEL—Gastrointestinal Preparations—Kali-Chemie Aktiengesellschaft; *Int'l*, pg. 1278

DICHROLGHT—Color Filters—Balzers; *Int'l*, pg. 997

DICINI—Jewelry—Richton International Corporation; *U.S. Public*, pg. 1389

DICKIES—Mens' & Boys Apparel—Williamson-Dickie Mfg. Co.; *U.S. Private*, pg. 1179

DICKINSON'S—Preserves—J.M. Smucker Company; *U.S. Public*, pg. 1480

DICOFLUID—Plant Protectives—DSM Chemie Linz GmbH; *Int'l*, pg. 356

DICOM—Educational Programs—Eastman Kodak Company; *U.S. Public*, pg. 550

DICON—Designation, Routing & Connection of Conductors & Electrical Apparatus—General Electric Canada Inc.; *U.S. Public*, pg. 713

DICONIX—Ink-Jet Printers, Computers, Printing Papers & Computerized Printing—Eastman Kodak Company; *U.S. Public*, pg. 550

DICOPUR—Plant Protectives—DSM Chemie Linz GmbH; *Int'l*, pg. 356

DICTAMATION—Portable & Desktop Cassette Systems—Dictaphone Corp.; *U.S. Private*, pg. 1045

DICTAMITE—Dictaphone Portable Recorders—Dictaphone Corp.; *U.S. Private*, pg. 1045

DICTIONARY OF CULTURAL LITERACY—Reference Work—INSO Corporation; *U.S. Public*, pg. 882

DICURAN—Herbicide—Novartis; *Int'l*, pg. 972

DIDONO—NONE—AGA Gas, Inc.; *Int'l*, pg. 13

DIDRONEL—Abnormal Calcium Metabolism Regulator—Procter & Gamble Pharmaceuticals, Inc.; *U.S. Public*, pg. 1331

DIDRONEL I.V. INFUSION—Drug for Treatment of Hypercalcemia—MGI PHARMA INC.; *U.S. Public*, pg. 1026

DIE BUNTE SPAR MARKE—NONE—Spar Handels AG; *Int'l*, pg. 1288

DIE SPARSAMEN—NONE—Spar Handels AG; *Int'l*, pg. 1288

DIE WELT—Newspaper—Axel Springer Verlag AG; *Int'l*, pg. 102

DIEBELS ALKOHOLFREI—Beer—Diebels Private Brewery; *Int'l*, pg. 413

DIEBELS ALT—Beer—Diebels Private Brewery; *Int'l*, pg. 413

DIEBELS LIGHT—Beer—Diebels Private Brewery; *Int'l*, pg. 413

DIEBOLD—Corporate Name—Diebold, Incorporated; *U.S. Public*, pg. 506

DIEHARD—NONE—Sears, Roebuck and Co.; *U.S. Public*, pg. 1452

DIELECTRIC MATERIALS—Mounts & Hardware—International Electronic Research Corp.; *U.S. Public*, pg. 286

DIELECTRITE—Thermoset Polyester Molding Compound—Industrial Dielectrics, Inc.; *U.S. Private*, pg. 560

DIELEKTROL I—Dielectric Fluids in Electrical Capacitors—General Electric Canada Inc.; *U.S. Public*, pg. 713

DIELEKTROL III—Dielectric Fluids for Electrical Capacitors & Dielectirc Filled Capacitors—General Electric Canada Inc.; *U.S. Public*, pg. 713

DIELEKTROL II—Dielectric Fluids in Electrical Capacitors—General Electric Canada Inc.; *U.S. Public*, pg. 713

DIENITE—Polybutadiene Thermosetting Resins—Bridgestone/Firestone, Inc.; *Int'l*, pg. 213

DIESEL TECHNOLOGY CORP AND LOGO—NONE—Detroit Diesel Corp.; *U.S. Private*, pg. 850

DIESEL-TONE—Fuel Conditioner—Radiator Specialty Company; *U.S. Private*, pg. 906

DIESELDRIVE—Inboard Engines—Stewart & Stevenson Services, Inc.; *U.S. Public*, pg. 1517

DIESELJET—Inboard Engines—Stewart & Stevenson Services, Inc.; *U.S. Public*, pg. 1517

DIESELTUNE—Specialty Service Tools—SPX Corporation; *U.S. Public*, pg. 1420

DIESELWELD—Steel Tubing—Bundy North America; *Int'l*, pg. 1340

DIET APPLE SLICE—Diet Fruit Soft Drink—Pepsi-Cola Company; *U.S. Public*, pg. 1277

DIET BARQ'S—Root Beer—The Coca-Cola Company; *U.S. Public*, pg. 392

DIET CENTER—Weight Loss Center—Diet Center Worldwide, Inc.; *U.S. Private*, pg. 864

DIET CHASER—Soft Drink—Double-Cola Co.-USA; *U.S. Private*, pg. 341

DIET CHERRY CHOCOLATE FUDGE—Soft Drink—Select Canfield; *U.S. Private*, pg. 982

DIET CHERRY COKE—Diet Soft Drink—The Coca-Cola Company; *U.S. Public*, pg. 392

DIET CHERRY COLA SLICE—Diet Fruit Soft Drink—Pepsi-Cola Company; *U.S. Public*, pg. 1277

DIET CHOCOLATE FUDGE—Soft Drink—Select Canfield; *U.S. Private*, pg. 982

DIET COKE—Diet Soft Drink—The Coca-Cola Bottling Co. of New York, Inc.; *U.S. Public*, pg. 393

DIET COKE—NONE—The Coca-Cola Company; *U.S. Public*, pg. 392

DIET CRYSTAL PEPSI—Soft Drink—Pepsi-Cola Company; *U.S. Public*, pg. 1277

DIET DOUBLE-COLA—Soft Drink—Double-Cola Co.-USA; *U.S. Private*, pg. 341

DIET DR PEPPER—Soft Drink—Dr Pepper/Seven Up No. America; *Int'l*, pg. 248

DIET FROSTED—Cereal—The Quaker Oats Company; *U.S. Public*, pg. 1347

DIET KIT—Food Service Kits—Diamond Crystal Specialty Foods, Inc.; *U.S. Private*, pg. 330

DIET LITE—Yogurts & Desserts—Q.U.F. Industries Ltd.; *Int'l*, pg. 1074

DIET MAID—Sugarless Ice Cream Substitute—Hilland Dairy Company; *U.S. Private*, pg. 879

DIET MELLO YELLO—Diet Soft Drink—The Coca-Cola Company; *U.S. Public*, pg. 392

DIET PEPSI—Soft Drink—Pepsi-Cola Company; *U.S. Public*, pg. 1277

DIET PEPSI—Soft Drink—Pepsi-Co. International; *U.S. Public*, pg. 1277

DIET PEPSI FREE—Caffeine Free Diet Cola—Pepsi-Cola Company; *U.S. Public*, pg. 1277

DIET RITE—Soft Drink—Triarc Companies, Inc.; *U.S. Public*, pg. 1634

DIET 7 UP—Soft Drink—Cadbury Schweppes p.l.c.; *Int'l*, pg. 247

DIET SEVEN-UP—Soft Drink—Dr. Pepper Co.; *Int'l*, pg. 248

DIET SKI—Soft Drink—Double-Cola Co.-USA; *U.S. Private*, pg. 341

DIET SKINNY WAIST—Foundations—The Strouse, Adler Company; *U.S. Public*, pg. 1047

DIET SLICE—Lemon-Lime Caffeine Free Soft Drink—Pepsi-Cola Company; *U.S. Public*, pg. 1277

DIET SPRITE—Diet Soft Drink—The Coca-Cola Company; *U.S. Public*, pg. 392

DIET SQUIRT—Soft Drinks—Cadbury Schweppes p.l.c.; *Int'l*, pg. 247

DIET VERNORS—Soft Drinks—Cadbury Schweppes p.l.c.; *Int'l*, pg. 247

DIETENE—Dietary Products—Novartis Nutrition Corporation; *Int'l*, pg. 974

DIEZANO—NONE—Bierbrauerei Fohrenburg; *Int'l*, pg. 194

DIEZIME—Cefodizime, Antibiotic—Recordati Industria Chimica e Farmaceutica S.p.A.; *Int'l*, pg. 1090

DIEZLINGER—NONE—Bierbrauerei Fohrenburg; *Int'l*, pg. 194

DIFFRIENT—Tables—Howe Furniture Corporation; *U.S. Public*, pg. 543

DIFFSTAK—Diffusion Pumping System—Edwards High Vacuum, International; *Int'l*, pg. 121

DIFFUSAIRE—Odor Control System—Surco Products, Inc.; *U.S. Private*, pg. 1056

DIFFUSION—Cologne & Toiletries—Avon Products, Inc.; *U.S. Public*, pg. 155

DIFFUSIT—Wood Preservative—BASF AG; *Int'l*, pg. 103

DIFLUCAN/DIFLUCAN VC—Fluconazole—Pfizer Inc.; *U.S. Public*, pg. 1281

DIFLUCAN ONE—NONE—Pfizer Inc.; *U.S. Public*, pg. 1281

DIG-EZY—Shovels & Post Hole Diggers—Ames Company; *U.S. Public*, pg. 1683

DIGESDAHL—Digestion Module—Hach Company; *U.S. Public*, pg. 773

DIGGER FLAKE—Pipe Tobacco—Imperial Tobacco Group, Ltd.; *Int'l*, pg. 666

DIGI-CAL-II—Thermocouple Temperature Indicator—Analogic Corporation; *U.S. Public*, pg. 109

DIGI INTERNATIONAL—Communications & Networking Products—Digi International Inc.; *U.S. Public*, pg. 506

DIGI-PULSNORMA—Cardiovascular Preparations—Kali-Chemie Aktiengesellschaft; *Int'l*, pg. 1278

DIGI-TELL—Tank Gauge & Leak Detection—Preferred Utilities Manufacturing Corp.; *U.S. Private*, pg. 881

DIGIBIND—Pharmaceutical Product—Glaxo Wellcome PLC; *Int'l*, pg. 553

DIGIBRIDGE—NONE—GenRad, Inc.; *U.S. Public*, pg. 731

DIGICABLE—Digital Subscriber Terminals—Broadband Networks Group; *U.S. Public*, pg. 716

DIGICALL—Wireless Local Loop System—Aydin Corporation; *U.S. Public*, pg. 158

DIGICEPT—Announcement Systems—Electronic Tele-Communications, Inc.; *U.S. Public*, pg. 570

DIGICEPT 2000—Announcement Systems—Electronic Tele-Communications, Inc.; *U.S. Public*, pg. 570

DIGICEPT 2002—Announcement System—Electronic Tele-Communications, Inc.; *U.S. Public*, pg. 570

DIGICHEM—Automatic Titration Analyzer—Ionics, Incorporated; *U.S. Public*, pg. 912

DIGICIPHER—Digital Compression Technology—Broadband Networks Group; *U.S. Public*, pg. 716

DIGICON—Hand Held Pyrometer—Alnor Instrument Company; *U.S. Public*, pg. 1559

DIGICOUNT—Digital Displays—Litton Industries, Inc.; *U.S. Public*, pg. 1002

DIGICOURSE—Sensing Devices & Related Equip.—The Laitram Corporation; *U.S. Private*, pg. 643

DIGIFAX—Transmission Systems—Litton Industries, Inc.; *U.S. Public*, pg. 1002

DIGIGLOBIN—Hemoglobinometer—Fisher Scientific Company; *U.S. Private*, pg. 658

DIGIGRAPHX—Ink Jet Media—Transilwrap Company, Inc.; *U.S. Private*, pg. 1097

DIGIKOTE—Thermal Laminating Film for Ink Jet—Transilwrap Company, Inc.; *U.S. Private*, pg. 1097

DIGILINE—Linear Converters—Litton Industries, Inc.; *U.S. Public*, pg. 1002

DIGILINE ARROW—Linear Converters—Litton Industries, Inc.; *U.S. Public*, pg. 1002

DIGILOOP—NONE—ECI Telecom Ltd.; *Int'l*, pg. 643

DIGIMATIC—NONE—Amprobe Instrument; *U.S. Public*, pg. 1676

DIGIMATIC—Clock Radios—Sony Electronics; *Int'l*, pg. 1281

DIGIMETRY—Computer Acquisition & Interface Apparatus—Beckman Instruments, Inc.; *U.S. Public*, pg. 199

DIGIPROX—Ground Proximity Warning System—Litton Industries, Inc.; *U.S. Public*, pg. 1002

DIGISCALE—Encoders—Litton Industries, Inc.; *U.S. Public*, pg. 1002

DIGISCAN—NONE—Brown & Sharpe Manufacturing Company; *U.S. Public*, pg. 260

DIGISEC—Encoders—Litton Industries, Inc.; *U.S. Public*, pg. 1002

DIGISTAR—Planetarium System—Evans & Sutherland Computer Corporation; *U.S. Public*, pg. 595

DIGISTATION—Test System—GenRad, Inc.; *U.S. Public*, pg. 731

DIGISYN—Encoders—Litton Industries, Inc.; *U.S. Public*, pg. 1002

DIGIT—Lead Pencil—Sanford Corporation; *U.S. Public*, pg. 1178

DIGITAIR—End-of-Train System—Union Switch & Signal Inc.; *Int'l*, pg. 77

DIGITAK—Encoders—Litton Industries, Inc.; *U.S. Public*, pg. 1002

DIGITAL—Computer—Digital Equipment Corporation; *U.S. Public*, pg. 507

DIGITAL AND PREPRESS LINKS—Supplement to American Printer—Intertec Publishing; *U.S. Public*, pg. 1327

DIGITAL BOOK SYSTEM—NONE—Franklin Electronic Publishers, Inc.; *U.S. Public*, pg. 679

DIGITAL CITY CHICAGO—Local On-Line Information Sources—Tribune Company; *U.S. Public*, pg. 1635

DIGITAL CITY HAMPTON ROADS—Local On-Line Information Sources—Tribune Company; *U.S. Public*, pg. 1635

DIGITAL CITY ORLANDO—Local On-Line Information Sources—Tribune Company; *U.S. Public*, pg. 1635

DIGITAL CITY SOUTH FLORIDA—Local On-Line Information Sources—Tribune Company; *U.S. Public*, pg. 1635

DIGITAL DATA MANAGEMENT SYSTEM—NONE—The Black & Decker Corporation; *U.S. Public*, pg. 233

DIGITAL DESIGN & PRODUCTION—Digital Graphics Magazine—Reed Elsevier Business Information; *Int'l*, pg. 1095

DIGITAL ES—NONE—Magnetrol International; *U.S. Private*, pg. 696

DIGITAL EZ—NONE—Magnetrol International; *U.S. Private*, pg. 696

DIGITAL EXPRESS—Centralized Voice Processing Computers—Dictaphone Corp.; *U.S. Private*, pg. 1045

DIGITAL LIGHT PROCESSING—NONE—Texas Instruments Incorporated; *U.S. Public*, pg. 1585

DIGITAL LINEAR ACTUATORS—NONE—Philips Automotive Electronics; *Int'l*, pg. 1054

DIGITAL LINK—NONE—Digital Link Corporation; *U.S. Public*, pg. 508

DIGITAL SOLUTIONS—NONE—SunGard Data Systems Inc.; *U.S. Public*, pg. 1534

DIGITAL WORLD—Digital Communication Systems—Northern Telecom Limited; *Int'l*, pg. 968

DIGITALK—Voice Compression Technology for Modems—Rockwell International Corporation; *U.S. Public*, pg. 1397

DIGITEC—Digital Panel Meters—Desco Corporation; *U.S. Private*, pg. 326

DIGITECH—Telephone System—Comdial Corporation; *U.S. Public*, pg. 407

DIGITECH—Signal Processors—Harman International Industries, Inc.; *U.S. Public*, pg. 787

DIGITEK—Closed Circuit Television Equipment—Vicon Industries, Inc.; *U.S. Public*, pg. 1719

DIGITENN—Test Equipment—Tenney Environmental; *U.S. Private*, pg. 1076

DIGITRAC—Mfg. Testing Equipment—Rockford Acromatic Product Co.; *U.S. Private*, pg. 938

DIGITRAC—Train Location System—Union Switch & Signal Inc.; *U.S. Public*, pg. 1534

DIGITRONIC—Solid State Temperature Controller—Despatch Industries; *U.S. Private*, pg. 327

DIGNOCON—NONE—Berg Electronics; *U.S. Public*, pg. 212

DIGOXIN RIABEAD—Diagnostic Products—Abbott Laboratories; *U.S. Public*, pg. 12

DIJICOMP—Computer Software for Ink Jet-Printers—Eastman Kodak Company; *U.S. Public*, pg. 550

DIJIT—Ink Jet Printers, Computers, Printing Paper & Computerized Printing—Eastman Kodak Company; *U.S. Public*, pg. 550

DIJONNAISE—Creamy Mustard Blend—Bestfoods; *U.S. Public*, pg. 223

DIKONE—NONE—Western Atlas Logging Services; *U.S. Public*, pg. 1757

DILANLE—NONE—AGA Gas, Inc.; *Int'l*, pg. 13

DILANTIN—Anticonvulsant—Warner-Lambert Company; *U.S. Public*, pg. 1738

DILATRATE-SR—NONE—Schwarz Pharma Inc.; *Int'l*, pg. 1211

DILATTO—Domestic Grated Cheese—Suprema Specialties, Inc.; *U.S. Public*, pg. 1541

DILAUDID—Pharmaceuticals—Knoll Pharmaceutical Company; *Int'l*, pg. 105

DILECTRIX—NONE—Chemfab Corporation; *U.S. Public*, pg. 344

DILEMMAS—Game—Monarch Avalon, Inc.; *U.S. Public*, pg. 1123

DILL—Tire Valves—Air Control Products; *U.S. Public*, pg. 556

DILLON'S—Mexican Food Products—Wilson Products Co.; *U.S. Private*, pg. 1181

DILLY BAR—Frozen Novelties—International Dairy Queen, Inc.; *U.S. Public*, pg. 220

DILLYWICH—Frozen Novelties—International Dairy Queen, Inc.; *U.S. Public*, pg. 220

DILU-VIAL—Blood Dilution Vial—Elkay Products, Inc.; *U.S. Public*, pg. 372

DILUMAT—Dispensing Apparatus—Fisher Scientific Company; *U.S. Private*, pg. 658

DILZEM—Cardiovascular Products—Warner-Lambert Company; *U.S. Public*, pg. 1738

DIM—Hosiery—Sara Lee Corporation; *U.S. Public*, pg. 1432

DIME—Corporate Logo—The Dime Savings Bank of New York; *U.S. Public*, pg. 509

DIME BRAND—Sweetened Condensed Filled Dairy Blend—Borden, Inc.; *U.S. Private*, pg. 157

DIMENSIA—TV Receivers—Thomson Consumer Electronics Inc.; *Int'l*, pg. 1383

DIMENSION—Clinical Chemistry System—Du Pont (E.I. Du Pont De Nemours & Co.); *U.S. Public*, pg. 530

DIMENSION—Delivery Body or Trailer—Hackney and Sons, Inc.; *U.S. Private*, pg. 1097

DIMENSION—Upright Vacuum—Hoover Company; *U.S. Public*, pg. 1065

DIMENSION—Canoes & Kayaks—Johnson Worldwide Associates, Inc.; *U.S. Public*, pg. 932

DIMENSION—Herbicide—Monsanto Company; *U.S. Public*, pg. 1124

DIMENSION—Multi-Loop Digital Controller—Research, Incorporated; *U.S. Public*, pg. 1382

DIMENSION—Herbicide—Rohm and Haas Company; *U.S. Public*, pg. 1403

DIMENSIONS—Sheet Vinyl Flooring—Congoleum Corporation; *U.S. Public*, pg. 69

DIMETALLIC—Metals Passivators for Refining—BetzDearborn Inc.; *U.S. Public*, pg. 226

DIMETANE—NONE—American Home Products Corporation; *U.S. Public*, pg. 79

DIMETANE—Cough/Cold Medication—Wyeth-Ayerst Laboratories, Inc.; *U.S. Public*, pg. 80

DIMETAPP—Tablets, Caplets, Elixir, Extentabs: Relieve Cold, Allergy, And Flu—American Home Products Company; *U.S. Public*, pg. 79

DIMETAPP ADULT—Cold, Allergy & Flu Relief Tablets, Caplets & Elixir—Whitehall-Robins Healthcare; *U.S. Public*, pg. 80

DIMETAPP PEDIATRIC—NONE—Whitehall-Robins Healthcare; *U.S. Public*, pg. 80

DIMETCOTE—Zinc Coatings—Ameron Concrete & Steel Pipe Group; *U.S. Public*, pg. 99

DIMETCOTE—Zinc Coatings—Ameron International Corporation; *U.S. Public*, pg. 98

DIMEZONE—Photo Developing Agent—Eastman Kodak Company; *U.S. Public*, pg. 550

DIMILIN—Insecticide—Uniroyal Chemical Company, Inc.; *U.S. Public*, pg. 460

DIMITRI VODKA—Spirit—Allied Domecq PLC; *Int'l*, pg. 62

DIMODAN—Emulsifiers—Danisco Ingredients; *Int'l*, pg. 378

DIMODAN—Food Emulsifier—Danisco Ingredients USA, Inc.; *Int'l*, pg. 378

DIMON—Tobacco—DIMON, Incorporated; *U.S. Public*, pg. 509

DIMONIQUE—Cubic Zirconia—L.G. Balfour Co., Inc.; *U.S. Private*, pg. 258

DIMPLE FIFTEEN YEAR OLD—NONE—Guinness Plc; *Int'l*, pg. 412

DIMPLEX—Household Appliances—The Glen Dimplex Group; *Int'l*, pg. 553

DIMS—NONE—Landmark Graphics Corporation; *U.S. Public*, pg. 776

DIMUL—Mullite Refractories—Ferro Corporation; *U.S. Public*, pg. 618

DINAFOLD—NONE—Wisconsin Tissue Mills, Inc.; *U.S. Public*, pg. 347

DINAIRE—NONE—Dinaire Corp.; *U.S. Private*, pg. 334

DINAMAP—Blood Pressure Monitors—Johnson & Johnson; *U.S. Public*, pg. 927

DINAMAP—Patient Monitoring—Johnson & Johnson Medical, Inc.; *U.S. Public*, pg. 928

DINER—Foods—Brooks Foods; *U.S. Private*, pg. 887

DINERS CLUB—Charge Card Service—Diners Club Inc.; *U.S. Public*, pg. 377

DING DONGS—Snack Cake—Ralston Purina Company; *U.S. Public*, pg. 1359

DINGO—Casual & Dress Boots—Acme Boot Co., Inc.; *U.S. Private*, pg. 394

DINGO—Training Wear—Mizuno Corporation; *Int'l*, pg. 884

DINI 10—Digital Levels for Surveying—Carl Zeiss; *Int'l*, pg. 1522

DINI 20—Digital Level for Surveyors—Carl Zeiss; *Int'l*, pg. 1522

DINING LITE—Calorie Controlled Frozen Foods—ConAgra Frozen Food Company; *U.S. Public*, pg. 427

DINING LITE—Calorie Controlled Frozen Foods—ConAgra Frozen Foods; *U.S. Public*, pg. 427

DINING TREAT—Prepared Frozen Foods—ConAgra Frozen Food Company; *U.S. Public*, pg. 427

DINING TREAT—Prepared Frozen Foods—ConAgra Frozen Foods; *U.S. Public*, pg. 427

DINITROL—NONE—EMS-Togo; *Int'l*, pg. 981

DINITROL—Motor Vehicle Maintenance Chemical—Novartis AG; *Int'l*, pg. 971

DINNEFORD'S—Infants' Gripe Mixture—SmithKline Beecham plc; *Int'l*, pg. 1264

DINNER BELL—Meat Products—John Morrell & Co.; *U.S. Public*, pg. 1479

DINNER ON US CLUB—NONE—CUC International, Inc.; *U.S. Public*, pg. 320

DINNER SENSATIONS—Main Dish Mixes—General Mills, Inc.; *U.S. Public*, pg. 717

DINNER SUPREME—Frozen Dinners—Nestle S.A.; *Int'l*, pg. 915

DINO-RIDERS—Boys Action Figures—Tyco Toys, Inc.; *U.S. Public*, pg. 1058

DINO'S—Spagetti Sauces—Ventre Packing Company, Inc.; *U.S. Private*, pg. 1135

DINOSAUR—Refrigerated Cookie Dough—Pillsbury Co.; *Int'l*, pg. 411

DINOSAURS OF THE LOST WORLD—Leisure Game—Monarch Avalon, Inc.; *U.S. Public*, pg. 1123

DINTY MOORE—Canned Stews, Hash, Prepared Entrees—Hormel Foods Corp.; *U.S. Public*, pg. 840

DIOCALM—Stomach/Indigestion Remedy—SmithKline Beecham plc; *Int'l*, pg. 1264

DIODE-LITE—LED Panel Mount Indicators—Dialight Corporation; *Int'l*, pg. 1130

DIOK—NONE—Carpenter Technology Corporation; *U.S. Public*, pg. 307

DIOLEN—Synthetic Filament Yarn—Akzo Nobel N.V.; *Int'l*, pg. 42

DIOR—Make-Up Products—Christian Dior Perfumes Inc.; *Int'l*, pg. 781

DIORESSENCE—Women's Fragrance—Christian Dior Perfumes Inc.; *Int'l*, pg. 781

DIORISSIMO—Women's Fragrence—Christian Dior Perfumes Inc.; *Int'l*, pg. 781

DIOSTATE D—NONE—Lee Pharmaceuticals; *U.S. Public*, pg. 984

DIOX-BLOK—Chemically Inert Powder Which Prevents Dioxin Formation—Beco Engineering Company; *U.S. Private*, pg. 129

DIP-ALARM—Indicators—Projects Unlimited, Inc.; *U.S. Private*, pg. 890

DIP CLASSICS—Seasoning Mixes—McCormick/Schilling; *U.S. Public*, pg. 1066

DIP-FLASH—Indicators—Projects Unlimited, Inc.; *U.S. Private*, pg. 890

DIP/LOC—Electronic Equipment—Everett Charles Technologies; *U.S. Private*, pg. 386

DIP N CRISP—Seafood Line—McCormick/Schilling; *U.S. Public*, pg. 1066

DIPEL—Biological Insecticide—Abbott Laboratories; *U.S. Public*, pg. 12

DIPENTENE No. 122—Terpene Liquid—Hercules Incorporated; *U.S. Public*, pg. 809

DIPENTUM—Pharmaceuticals—Pharmacia & Upjohn Adria Laboratories; *Int'l*, pg. 1049

DIPGUARD—Ceramic Capacitors—AVX Corporation; *U.S. Public*, pg. 775

DIPHOS—Product for the Treatment of Paget's Disease—Boehringer Mannheim GmbH; *Int'l*, pg. 331

DIPLOG—NONE—Western Atlas Logging Services; *U.S. Public*, pg. 1757

DIPLOMA—Cosmetics—Henkel KGaA; *Int'l*, pg. 609

DIPLOMACY—Game—Monarch Avalon, Inc.; *U.S. Public*, pg. 1123

DIPLOMAT—Plotter Materials—Dietzgen Corporation; *U.S. Public*, pg. 332

DIPLOMAT—Sleepwear—Host Apparel, Inc.; *U.S. Private*, pg. 540

DIPLOMAT—Framed Decorator Switch—Pass & Seymour/Legrand; *Int'l*, pg. 806

DIPLOMAT ALPINI—Confectionery—Thorntons PLC; *Int'l*, pg. 1386

DIPPIN STIK—Rod—Outdoor Technologies Group; *U.S. Private*, pg. 822

DIPPITY DO—Hair Styling Preparations—The Gillette Company; *U.S. Public*, pg. 743

DIPPS—Ready-to-eat Cereal Derived Snack Bars—The Quaker Oats Company; *U.S. Public*, pg. 1347

DIPPY CANOES—Snacks—The Quaker Oats Company; *U.S. Public*, pg. 1347

DIPRINOVET—Antibacterial Agent—Mallinckrodt Inc.; *U.S. Public*, pg. 1039

DIPRIVAN—Pharmaceutical—Zeneca Group Plc; *Int'l*, pg. 1524

DIPROLENE—High-Potency Topical Steroid—Schering-Plough Corporation; *U.S. Public*, pg. 1438

DIPROLENE AF—High-Potency Advanced Formula Topical Steroid Cream—Schering-Plough Corporation; *U.S. Public*, pg. 1438

DIPROSONE—High-Potency Topical Steroid—Schering-Plough Corporation; *U.S. Public*, pg. 1438

DIPSY DOODLES—Rippled Corn Chips—Borden, Inc.; *U.S. Private*, pg. 157

DIPTAPE—NONE—Gems Sensors; *U.S. Public*, pg. 481

DIRAME—Pain Killing Pharmaceutical—Roberts Pharmaceutical Corporation; *U.S. Public*, pg. 1393

DIREC-TROL—Valves—Snap-Tite, Inc.; *U.S. Private*, pg. 1010

DIRECT—Convenience Stores—E-Z Serve Convenience Stores, Inc.; *U.S. Public*, pg. 540

DIRECT—Convenience Stores—E-Z Serve Corp.; *U.S. Public*, pg. 540

DIRECT—NONE—Kiwi Brands Pty. Ltd.; *U.S. Public*, pg. 1434

DIRECT-A-PRINT—Photographic Paper—Eastman Kodak Company; *U.S. Public*, pg. 550

DIRECT-A-PRINT—Photographic Color Paper—Eastman Kodak Company; *U.S. Public*, pg. 550

DIRECT ACCESS—Track Selection—Sony Electronics; *Int'l*, pg. 1281

DIRECT DRIVE—Circuit or Array—LSI Logic Corp.; *U.S. Public*, pg. 971

DIRECT FUELS—Fuel Wholesaling & Processing—FFP Marketing Company, Inc.; *U.S. Public*, pg. 604

DIRECT LINE—Toiletries—Avon Products, Inc.; *U.S. Public*, pg. 155

DIRECT LINE—Import Product Line—Fraenkel Company; *U.S. Private*, pg. 423

DIRECT MARKETING MARKET PLACE—Business Directory—National Register Publishing; *Int'l*, pg. 1096

DIRECT REPAY—Servicing—SLM Holding Corp.; *U.S. Public*, pg. 1419

DIRECT SCRIPT—NONE—Oxford Health Plans Inc.; *U.S. Public*, pg. 1238

DIRECT TORQ—Engine Torque Control—Rockwell International Corporation; *U.S. Public*, pg. 1397

DIRECT VENT—Gas Stove Venting—Simpson Dura-Vent Co., Inc.; *U.S. Public*, pg. 1474

DIRECTAIR—Valves—Schrader Bellows Division; *U.S. Public*, pg. 1261

DIRECTCARE—NONE—JP Foodservice, Inc.; *U.S. Public*, pg. 918

DIRECTCARE MEALS MENUS AND MORE—NONE—JP Foodservice, Inc.; *U.S. Public*, pg. 918

DIRECTCONNECT—Prescription Drug Plan—PCS Health Systems, Inc.; *U.S. Public*, pg. 993

DIRECTONE—Industrial Horn—Federal Signal Corporation; *U.S. Public*, pg. 616

DIRECTONE—Electrical Fire Alarm/Voice System—Federal Signal Corporation, Signal Div.; *U.S. Public*, pg. 616

DIRECTOR II—School Communication Systems—Rauland-Borg Corporation; *U.S. Private*, pg. 911

DIRECTORY OF CORPORATE AFFILIATIONS—Business Directory—National Register Publishing; *U.S. Public*, pg. 1096

DIRECTOVALVE—Control Valve—Spraying Systems Co.; *U.S. Private*, pg. 1026

DIRECTRAC—Automated Delivery Management System—Directory Distributing Associates, Inc.; *U.S. Private*, pg. 334

DIRECTSET—Photo Typesetters—AGFA EPS Division; *Int'l*, pg. 172

DIRECTTALK—Computer System—International Business Machines Corporation; *U.S. Public*, pg. 895

DIRECTTALK/6000—Computer System—International Business Machines Corporation; *U.S. Public*, pg. 895

DIRECTTALK/2—Computer System—International Business Machines Corporation; *U.S. Public*, pg. 895

DIRECTWRITE—NONE—Xicor, Inc.; *U.S. Public*, pg. 1785

DIREKTALURE—Photographic Paper—Eastman Kodak Company; *U.S. Public*, pg. 550

DIRESUL—Cellulose Fibers—Clariant International Ltd.; *Int'l*, pg. 624

DIRESUL—RDT Dye—Novartis AG; *Int'l*, pg. 971

DRIPAK—Air Filter—AAF-International; *U.S. Private*, pg. 3

DIRT ALERT—Filter—Pall Corporation; *U.S. Public*, pg. 1253

DIRT DEVIL—Vacuum Cleaners—Royal Appliance Mfg. Co.; *U.S. Public*, pg. 1410

DIRT ERASER—Mobile Dust Collection Unit—The Spencer Turbine Co.; *U.S. Private*, pg. 1025

DIRT FINDER—Upright Vacuum Cleaner—Hoover Company; *U.S. Public*, pg. 1065

DIRT RIDER—Magazine—Petersen Publishing Company, L.L.C.; *U.S. Private*, pg. 856

DIRT-TERGENT—Powder Cleaners—Graco Inc.; *U.S. Public*, pg. 756

DIRTBUSTER—Household Product—The Black & Decker Corporation; *U.S. Public*, pg. 233

DIRTEX—Cleaner, Powder, Liquid & Spray—The Savogran Company; *U.S. Private*, pg. 968

DIRTY DOGS—Greeting Cards—American Greetings Corporation; *U.S. Public*, pg. 77

DISAMATIC—Molding—Georg Fischer Disa Inc.; *Int'l*, pg. 382

DISASTER PLAN/90—Microcomputer Software for Recovery Planning—SunGard Data Systems Inc.; *U.S. Public*, pg. 1534

DISBURSEMATE—Transaction Processing System Software and Control Terminals—Equitrac Corporation; *U.S. Public*, pg. 590

DISC—Conference Tables—Vecta; *U.S. Private*, pg. 1038

DISC DESIGN—NONE—Pall Corporation; *U.S. Public*, pg. 1253

DISC GO ROUND—Buys & Sells Used & New CDs—Grow Biz International, Inc.; *U.S. Public*, pg. 767

DISC MASTER—Machinery—Gardner Abrasives; *U.S. Public*, pg. 1699

DISCACHE—Disc Caching Feature—Quantum Corporation; *U.S. Public*, pg. 1350

DISCFLO—Disposable Filter Assembly—Pall Corporation; *U.S. Public*, pg. 1253

DISCJET—Spray Nozzle—Spraying Systems Co.; *U.S. Private*, pg. 1026

DISCKIT—NONE—Laserscope Surgical Systems; *U.S. Public*, pg. 979

DISCKPAC—Electronic Components—General Instrument Corporation; *U.S. Public*, pg. 716

DISCLOSURE—Financial Information Svcs.—Disclosure Incorporated; *U.S. Public*, pg. 1325

DISCMAN—Portable Compact Discplayers—Sony Electronics; *Int'l*, pg. 1281

DISCO—Software—Veritas DGC Inc; *U.S. Private*, pg. 1136

DISCO-CHEF—Mixer Attachments—Sunbeam Household Products; *U.S. Public*, pg. 1533

DISCOCHECK—Valves—GESTRA GmbH; *Int'l*, pg. 549

DISCOSTAR—Hair Care Products—Wella Group; *Int'l*, pg. 1489

DISCOUNT POINTS—Controlled Markdown Program—Carlson Retail Marketing; *U.S. Private*, pg. 212

DISCOUNT RECORDS—Pre-Recorded Audio & Video Tapes, Blank Tapes & Accessories—Musicland Group Inc.; *U.S. Public*, pg. 1142

DISCOUNT TIRE CO., INC.—Logo—Reinalt-Thomas Corp.; *U.S. Private*, pg. 919

DISCOUNT TIRE DIRECT—Logo—Reinalt-Thomas Corp.; *U.S. Private*, pg. 919

DISCOVER—Sheet Vinyl Flooring—Congoleum Corporation; *U.S. Public*, pg. 69

DISCOVER CARD—Credit Card—Dean Witter, Discover & Co.; *U.S. Public*, pg. 1132

DISCOVER CARD—Financial Services & Credit Card—NOVUS Services, Inc.; *U.S. Public*, pg. 1132

DISCOVER DCA—Computer Software—Attachmate; *U.S. Private*, pg. 98

DISCOVER/EDUCATION—Computer System—International Business Machines Corporation; *U.S. Public*, pg. 895

DISCOVER SATELLITE TELEVISION—Satellite Receiving Systems & Components—Zenith Electronics Corp.; *U.S. Public*, pg. 1790

DISCOVERER—Telescopes, Binoculars—Bushnell Corporation; *U.S. Private*, pg. 1191

DISCOVERY—Veterinary Pharmaceuticals—American Home Products Corporation; *U.S. Public*, pg. 79

DISCOVERY—Seminar Series—Beckman Instruments, Inc.; *U.S. Public*, pg. 199

DISCOVERY—Four Wheel Drive Vehicle—British Aerospace p.l.c.; *Int'l*, pg. 217

DISCOVERY—Manufactured Homes—Champion Enterprises, Inc.; *U.S. Public*, pg. 332

DISCOVERY—Motor Home—Fleetwood Enterprises, Inc.; *U.S. Public*, pg. 650

DISCOVERY—Software—Veritas DGC Inc; *U.S. Private*, pg. 1136

DISCOVERY CHANNEL—Cable Network Channel—Discovery Networks, Inc.; *U.S. Private*, pg. 334

THE DISCOVERY INTERACTIVE LIBRARY—Interactive Videodiscs—Coronet/MTI; *U.S. Private*, pg. 863

DISCOVISION—Licensing—Discovision Associates; *Int'l*, pg. 1057

DISCUS—Training Programs—Eastman Kodak Company; *U.S. Public*, pg. 550

DISCUS ATHLETIC—Fleece Apparel for Sporting Goods Market—Tultex Corporation; *U.S. Public*, pg. 1644

DISCWASHER—Care & Maintenance Accessories—Recoton Corporation; *U.S. Public*, pg. 1369

DISEASE STATE MANAGEMENT—Medical Wellness Management Services—Comprehensive Care Corporation; *U.S. Public*, pg. 419

DISEÑO—Clothing—Carrefour; *Int'l*, pg. 272

DISKECTER—Therauputic Cutting Instrument—Sofamor Danek Group, Inc.; *U.S. Public*, pg. 1482

DISKEEPER—Defragmentation Software—Executive Software; *U.S. Private*, pg. 388

DISKEEPER FOR WINDOWS NT—Defragmenter for NT Systems—Executive Software; *U.S. Private*, pg. 388

DISKFLEX—Flexible Circuit Boards—Freudenberg & Company; *Int'l*, pg. 505

DISKLAVIER—Piano—Yamaha Corporation; *Int'l*, pg. 1515

DISKLAVIER—Digital Piano—Yamaha Corporation of America; *Int'l*, pg. 1516

DISKRIBE—Computer Software Marker—Sanford Corporation; *U.S. Public*, pg. 1178

DISNEY—Shoes—Brown Group, Inc.; *U.S. Public*, pg. 262

DISNEY—T-Shirt—Holoubek Inc.; *U.S. Private*, pg. 536

DISNEY—Infant & Pre-School Products—Mattel, Inc.; *U.S. Public*, pg. 1057

DISNEY CHANNEL—Pay Television Channel—The Walt Disney Company; *U.S. Public*, pg. 511

DISNEY CINEMA CLASSICS—Licensee—Timex Corporation; *U.S. Private*, pg. 1088

DISNEY FROZEN TREATS—Ice Pops & Ice Cream—Good Humor/Breyers Ice Cream; *Int'l*, pg. 1435

DISNEYLAND—Amusement Park—The Walt Disney Company; *U.S. Public*, pg. 511

DISOGRIN—Rubber Seal—Freudenberg-NOK; *U.S. Private*, pg. 427

DISOGRIN—Mfr. Polyurethane Seals & Molded Parts—Freudenberg NOK; *Int'l*, pg. 505

DISPARO—Insecticides—The Dow Chemical Company; *U.S. Public*, pg. 522

DISPATCH CONSUMER SERVICES—Commercial Printing—The Dispatch Printing Company; *U.S. Private*, pg. 334

DISPEN-SI-MATIC—Less Than Full Case Order Selection System—SI Handling Systems, Inc.; *U.S. Public*, pg. 1418

DISPENSALL—Household Clothes Washing Machines—General Electric Canada Inc.; *U.S. Public*, pg. 713

DISPENSAPAK—Patient Kit—Beckman Instruments, Inc.; *U.S. Public*, pg. 199

DISPENSE-A-LINER—Vinyl Liners—Witt Company; *U.S. Private*, pg. 1185

DISPERGAN—Plastic-Dispersion Glues—PKL Verpackungssysteme GmbH; *Int'l*, pg. 1020

DISPERSALL—Conical Deflaker—Harnischfeger Industries, Inc.; *U.S. Public*, pg. 788

DISPERSALLOY—Dispersed Phase Alloy—Johnson & Johnson Consumer Products; *U.S. Public*, pg. 928

DISPLAWALL—Slotted Merchandising Panels—Marlite; *U.S. Private*, pg. 705

DISPLAY SAFE—Dispensing Device—Calmar Inc.; *U.S. Private*, pg. 201

DISPLAYMAKER—Electronic Projection Equipment—Eastman Kodak Company; *U.S. Public*, pg. 550

DISPLAYPHONE—Combined Voice & Data Telecommunication Terminal—Northern Telecom Limited; *Int'l*, pg. 968

DISPLAYWRITE—Software—International Business Machines Corporation; *U.S. Public*, pg. 895

DISPLAYWRITE ASSISTANT—Software—International Business Machines Corporation; *U.S. Public*, pg. 895

DISPORT—Sporting Goods—GIB Group; *Int'l*, pg. 532

DISPOSA-COVER—Disposable Cover for Hyperthermia Blankets—Cincinnati Sub-Zero Products, Inc.; *U.S. Private*, pg. 240

DISPOSA-DERM—Gynecological Device—The Cooper Companies, Inc.; *U.S. Public*, pg. 442

DISPOSA-HOOD—Newborn Environmental Control Device—Utah Medical Products, Inc.; *U.S. Public*, pg. 1700

DISPOSAL DEPOT—Blood Waste Management Bag—Merit Medical Systems, Inc.; *U.S. Public*, pg. 1096

DISPOSALL—Domestic Machines for Cutting or Grinding Garbage—General Electric Canada Inc.; *U.S. Public*, pg. 713

DISPOSER CARE—Cleans & Deoderizes Garbage Disposals—Wisconsin Pharmacal Co., Inc.; *U.S. Private*, pg. 1185

DISPRIN—Analgesic—Reckitt & Colman plc; *Int'l*, pg. 1089

DISPRO—Logic Analyzer—GenRad, Inc.; *U.S. Public*, pg. 731

DISPROL—Analgesic—Reckitt & Colman plc; *Int'l*, pg. 1089

Brand Name Index

DISQ—Audio Processing & Recording Equipment—Lucent Technologies Inc.; *U.S. Public*, pg. 1017

DISRUPT—Control Release Dispenser—Hercon Environmental Corporation; *U.S. Public*, pg. 802

DISSOLVE—Dry Water Soluble Selective Herbicide—Riverdale Chemical Co.; *U.S. Private*, pg. 934

DISSOLVINE—Sequestering Agents—Akzo Nobel N.V.; *Int'l*, pg. 42

DISTAFF LINEN—Business Letterhead & Printing Grades—Crane & Co., Inc.; *U.S. Private*, pg. 286

DISTAFLEX—Catheter—Medtronic, Inc.; *U.S. Public*, pg. 1082

DISTLINER—NONE—Chemfab Corporation; *U.S. Public*, pg. 344

DISTRANEURIN—Pharmaceutical for Central Nervous System—Astra AB; *Int'l*, pg. 93

DISTRIBUTED APPLICATION ENVIRONMENT—Computer System—International Business Machines Corporation; *U.S. Public*, pg. 895

DISTRIBUTED AUTOMATION EDITION—Computer System—International Business Machines Corporation; *U.S. Public*, pg. 895

DISTRIBUTED DATABASE CONNECTION SERVICES/2—Computer System—International Business Machines Corporation; *U.S. Public*, pg. 895

DISTRIBUTED RELATIONAL DATABASE ARCHITECTURE—Computer System—International Business Machines Corporation; *U.S. Public*, pg. 895

DISTRIBUTED SNIFFER SYSTEM—Network Analyzing & Monitoring Hardware & Software—Network Associates, Inc.; *U.S. Public*, pg. 1168

DISTRIBUTION—Magazine Providing Editorial Concerning Intermodal Freight Transportation—Reed Elsevier Business Information; *Int'l*, pg. 1095

DISTRIBUTION 2000—Computer Hardware & Software—Automatic Data Processing, Inc.; *U.S. Public*, pg. 150

D'ITALIANO—NONE—Weston Bakeries Limited; *Int'l*, pg. 1495

DITCH WITCH—NONE—Charles Machine Works, Inc.; *U.S. Private*, pg. 230

DITEL—Logo—TII Industries, Inc.; *U.S. Public*, pg. 1556

DITERA—Insecticide—Abbott Laboratories; *U.S. Public*, pg. 12

DITHANE—Fungicide—Rohm and Haas Company; *U.S. Public*, pg. 1403

DITHERFINA—NONE—Alliance Semiconductor Corp.; *U.S. Public*, pg. 47

DITO SAMA—Food-service Equipment—Electrolux, AB; *Int'l*, pg. 438

DITROPAN—Antispasmodic & Anticholinergic—Hoechst Marion Roussel North America; *Int'l*, pg. 625

DITTO—Dinnerware—Dansk International Designs Ltd.; *U.S. Public*, pg. 261

DITZ-LAC—Automobile Finishes—PPG Industries, Inc.; *U.S. Public*, pg. 1245

DITZ-O—Wax & Grease Remover—PPG Industries, Inc.; *U.S. Public*, pg. 1245

DITZCO—Liquid Paints & Paint Enamels—PPG Industries, Inc.; *U.S. Public*, pg. 1245

DITZLER—Decorative & Protective Coatings—PPG Industries, Inc.; *U.S. Public*, pg. 1245

DIULO—Antihypertensive Diuretic—Monsanto Company; *U.S. Public*, pg. 1124

DIULO—Long-Acting Diuretic—Searle & Co.; *U.S. Public*, pg. 1125

DIUREX—Water Pills & Caplets—Alva/Amco Pharmacal Companies, Inc.; *U.S. Private*, pg. 47

DIUREX LONG ACTING—Water Capsules—Alva/Amco Pharmacal Companies, Inc.; *U.S. Private*, pg. 47

DIUREX MPR—Menstrual Pain Relief Medicine—Alva/Amco Pharmacal Companies, Inc.; *U.S. Private*, pg. 47

DIUREX-2—Water Pills With Iron—Alva/Amco Pharmacal Companies, Inc.; *U.S. Private*, pg. 47

DIURIL—Chlorothiazide—Merck & Co., Inc.; *U.S. Public*, pg. 1090

DIUTENSEN—Anti Hypertensive—Wallace Laboratories; *U.S. Public*, pg. 310

DIVA—Plastic Cutlery—Amcel Corp.; *U.S. Private*, pg. 48

DIVA—Interactive Verification—Cadence Design Systems, Inc.; *U.S. Public*, pg. 290

DIVERCTI—Fully Integrated Agent Desktop Solution—Rockwell Switching Systems Div.; *U.S. Public*, pg. 1398

DIVERGATOR—Grizzly—Royer Industries, Inc.; *Int'l*, pg. 1066

DIVERCO—NONE—Diversco, Inc.; *U.S. Private*, pg. 336

DIVERSIFLEX—Hose—The Goodyear Tire & Rubber Company; *U.S. Public*, pg. 752

DIVERSION—Magazine—The Hearst Corporation; *U.S. Private*, pg. 515

DIVERSIPHASE—Wireless Electronics—Shure Brothers Incorporated; *U.S. Private*, pg. 997

DIVERSITY MASTER—Base Station Antenna—Allen Telecom Inc.; *U.S. Public*, pg. 45

DIVIDEND INVESTMENT PLUS—Automatic Dividend Reinvestment Service—Quick & Reilly, Inc.; *U.S. Public*, pg. 650

DIVIDEND REINVESTMENT PLUS—Dividend Reinvestment Service—The Quick & Reilly Group Inc.; *U.S. Public*, pg. 650

DIVIDOSE—Pharmaceutical Product—Bristol-Myers Squibb Company; *U.S. Public*, pg. 253

DIVINA OF SWITZERLAND—Fashion—Basel Trading Company Ltd.; *Int'l*, pg. 169

DIVINE NINE—NONE—Callaway Golf Company; *U.S. Public*, pg. 294

DIVINYCELL—Cellular Construction Plastics & Military Camouflage Nets—Incentive AB; *Int'l*, pg. 666

DIXAN—Detergent—Henkel KGaA; *Int'l*, pg. 609

DIXECON—Solid Carbide Rotary File—National Twist Drill Div.; *U.S. Public*, pg. 1370

DIXECON—Solid Carbide Rotary File—Regal-Beloit Corporation; *U.S. Public*, pg. 1370

DIXIE—Cups & Plates—Consumer Products Business; *U.S. Public*, pg. 671

DIXIE—NONE—Dixie Dairy Company; *U.S. Private*, pg. 337

DIXIE—Yarns—The Dixie Group, Inc.; *U.S. Public*, pg. 514

DIXIE—Cups & Plates—Fort James Corporation; *U.S. Public*, pg. 670

DIXIE—Window Covering Product—Hunter Douglas N.V.; *Int'l*, pg. 639

DIXIE—Bedroom & Dining Room Furniture—Masco Corporation; *U.S. Public*, pg. 1052

DIXIE BASIN STREET ALE—Beer—Dixie Brewing Co., Inc.; *U.S. Private*, pg. 336

DIXIE BEER—Beer—Dixie Brewing Co., Inc.; *U.S. Private*, pg. 336

DIXIE BLACKENED VOODOO LAGER—Lager Beer—Dixie Brewing Co., Inc.; *U.S. Private*, pg. 336

DIXIE CARBIDE—Sold Under Regal Cutting Tools & National—Regal-Beloit Corporation; *U.S. Public*, pg. 1370

DIXIE CRIMSON VOODOO ALE—Ale—Dixie Brewing Co., Inc.; *U.S. Private*, pg. 336

DIXIE CRYSTALS—Sugar—Savannah Foods & Industries, Inc.; *U.S. Public*, pg. 872

DIXIE DYNA-DRILL—Solid Carbide Drill—National Twist Drill Div.; *U.S. Public*, pg. 1370

DIXIE DYNA-DRILLS—Solid Carbide Drills—Regal-Beloit Corporation; *U.S. Public*, pg. 1370

DIXIE DYNA-MILL—Solid Carbide End Mill—National Twist Drill Div.; *U.S. Public*, pg. 1370

DIXIE DYNA-MILLS—Square End Ball End Mills—Regal-Beloit Corporation; *U.S. Public*, pg. 1370

DIXIE DYNA-REAMER—Solid Carbide Reamer—National Twist Drill Div.; *U.S. Public*, pg. 1370

DIXIE DYNA-REAMERS—Solid Carbide Reamers—Regal-Beloit Corporation; *U.S. Public*, pg. 1370

DIXIE HOUSE—Restaurant—Blackeyed Pea Restaurants Inc.; *U.S. Public*, pg. 498

DIXIE JAZZ AMBER LIGHT—Light Beer—Dixie Brewing Co., Inc.; *U.S. Private*, pg. 336

DIXIE/MARATHON—Paper & Plastic Products—Consumer Products Business; *U.S. Public*, pg. 671

DIXIE-NARCO—Bottle & Can Vending Equipment, Currency Validators & Bill Changers—Maytag Corporation; *U.S. Public*, pg. 1064

DIXIE PEACH—Cosmetics—Lander Co., Inc.; *U.S. Private*, pg. 647

DIXIE VANILLA—Cookies—Sunshine Biscuits, Inc.; *U.S. Private*, pg. 434

DIXIE VANILLA—Cookies—Sunshine Biscuits, Inc.; *U.S. Public*, pg. 657

DIXIE WHITE MOOSE—Dessert Beer—Dixie Brewing Co., Inc.; *U.S. Private*, pg. 336

DIXON ZTR—Mowers—Blount International, Inc.; *U.S. Public*, pg. 237

DIXONS—Retail Consumer Electronics Stores—Dixons Group plc; *Int'l*, pg. 413

DO ALL—Tools—DOALL Company; *U.S. Private*, pg. 337

DO IT BEST—NONE—Hardware Wholesalers, Inc.; *U.S. Private*, pg. 502

DO IT CENTER—Hardware—Hardware Wholesalers, Inc.; *U.S. Private*, pg. 502

DO IT EXPRESS—NONE—Hardware Wholesalers, Inc.; *U.S. Private*, pg. 502

DO-NUT KING—Fryer—BKI; *U.S. Public*, pg. 1506

DO YOU KNOW ME?—Charge Card Services—American Express Company; *U.S. Public*, pg. 73

DOAK—Dermatology Products; Mostly Coal Tar Based Therapies—Bradley Pharmaceuticals; *U.S. Public*, pg. 249

DOAK—Dermatology Products; Mostly Coal Tar Based Therapies—Doak Dermatologics; *U.S. Public*, pg. 250

DOAK TERASEPTIC—Skin Cleanser—Doak Dermatologics; *U.S. Public*, pg. 250

DOANE—Pet Foods—Doane Products Co.; *U.S. Private*, pg. 337

DOAN'S PILLS—Backache Medicine—Ciba Specialty Chemicals; *Int'l*, pg. 291

DOBER—Industrial Chemicals—Dober Chemical Corp.; *U.S. Private*, pg. 337

DOBUTREX—Dobutamine Hydrochloride Cardiovascular Agent, Lilly—Eli Lilly and Company; *U.S. Public*, pg. 992

DOBUTREX—Dobutamin HCI—Eli Lilly Italia, S.p.A.; *U.S. Public*, pg. 994

"DOC BEAR"—Healthcare USA-Medicaid Mascot—Coventry Corporation; *U.S. Public*, pg. 454

DOC KENNEDY—Dry Dog Food—H.J. Heinz Co. of Canada Ltd.; *U.S. Public*, pg. 806

DOC-LT—Gel Documentation Equipment—UVP, Inc.; *U.S. Private*, pg. 1115

DOC1—Electronic Documentation System—Group 1 Software, Inc.; *U.S. Public*, pg. 417

DOCKERS—NONE—Genesco Inc.; *U.S. Public*, pg. 728

DOCKERS BRAND—Men's, Women's & Children's Apparel—Levi Strauss & Co.; *U.S. Private*, pg. 662

DOCKMASTER—Bulk Delivery Trailer or Body—Hackney and Sons, Inc.; *U.S. Private*, pg. 1097

DOCKSTOCKER—Stand Up-End Contro Vehicle—The Raymond Corporation; *Int'l*, pg. 123

DOCTOR—Blades—Thermo Fibertek, Inc.; *U.S. Public*, pg. 1593

DOCTRONICS—Electronic Repair Shops—Montgomery Ward & Co., Inc.; *U.S. Private*, pg. 758

DOCU-LOK—Envelopes—Westvaco Corporation; *U.S. Public*, pg. 1762

DOCU-LOPE—Envelopes—Westvaco Corporation; *U.S. Public*, pg. 1762

DOCUCLIP—NONE—H.C. Miller Company; *U.S. Private*, pg. 747

DOCUMAIL—Mail Sorter—Bell & Howell Holdings; *U.S. Public*, pg. 201

DOCUMAX—Printers—Datasouth Computer Corporation; *U.S. Public*, pg. 267

DOCUMENT RETRIEVAL ASSISTANT—Computer System—International Business Machines Corporation; *U.S. Public*, pg. 895

DOCUTEL OLIVETTI—Typewriters, Personal Computers—Olivetti SpA; *Int'l*, pg. 1002

DOCUTROL II—Universal Control Module—Circon Corporation; *U.S. Public*, pg. 373

DODGE—Fasteners—The Black & Decker Corporation; *U.S. Public*, pg. 233

DODGE—Mechanical Coupling Bearings—Rockwell Automation; *U.S. Public*, pg. 1397

DODGE CARAVAN—Minivan—Chrysler Corporation; *U.S. Public*, pg. 352

DODGE CITY DAILY GLOBE—Newspaper—Shivers Trading & Operating Co.; *U.S. Private*, pg. 994

DODGE COLT—Car—Chrysler Corporation; *U.S. Public*, pg. 352

DODGE COLT VISTA—Wagon—Chrysler Corporation; *U.S. Public*, pg. 352

DODGE DAKOTA—Pickup Truck—Chrysler Corporation; *U.S. Public*, pg. 352

DODGE DAYTONA—Car—Chrysler Corporation; *U.S. Public*, pg. 352

DODGE DYNASTY—Car—Chrysler Corporation; *U.S. Public*, pg. 352

DODGE GRAND CARAVAN—Truck—Chrysler Corporation; *U.S. Public*, pg. 352

DODGE INTREPID—Car—Chrysler Corporation; *U.S. Public*, pg. 352

DODGE MINI RAM VAN—Truck—Chrysler Corporation; *U.S. Public*, pg. 352

DODGE RAM—Pickup Truck—Chrysler Corporation; *U.S. Public*, pg. 352

DODGE RAM 50—Pickup Truck—Chrysler Corporation; *U.S. Public*, pg. 352

DODGE RAM WAGON & VAN—Truck—Chrysler Corporation; *U.S. Public*, pg. 352

DODGE RAMCHARGER—Sport Utility—Chrysler Corporation; *U.S. Public*, pg. 352

DODGE SHADOW—Car—Chrysler Corporation; *U.S. Public*, pg. 352

DODGE SPIRIT—Car—Chrysler Corporation; *U.S. Public*, pg. 352

DODGE STEALTH—Car—Chrysler Corporation; *U.S. Public*, pg. 352

DODGE VIPER—High-Performance Automobile—Chrysler Corporation; *U.S. Public*, pg. 352

DODIE—Baby Care—Polive/Tricosteril; *U.S. Public*, pg. 673

DOERR—Breakmotors—Emerson Electric Co.; *U.S. Public*, pg. 572

DOERR STOP BRAKEMOTOR—Energy Bank High Efficency Motors—Emerson Motor Company; *U.S. Public*, pg. 573

DOG—Phonograph (Picture) TV Sets—Thomson Consumer Electronics Inc.; *Int'l*, pg. 1383

DOG CHOW—Dog Food—Ralston Purina Company; *U.S. Public*, pg. 1359

DOG LIFE—Dog Foods—Pet Life Foods, Inc.; *U.S. Private*, pg. 856

DOG MAGIC—Power-and Free Trolley Systems—Jervis B. Webb Company; *U.S. Private*, pg. 1156

DOGEROO—Hot Dog Machine—Gold Medal Products Co.; *U.S. Private*, pg. 459

DOK-LOK—Vehicle Restraint—Rite-Hite Corporation (WI); *U.S. Private*, pg. 933

DOK-LOK—Vehicle Restraints—Rite-Hite Corporation; *U.S. Private*, pg. 933

DOLAN—Polyacrylonitrilye Fibres—Hoechst Aktiengesellschaft; *Int'l*, pg. 624

DOLBI CASHIER—NONE—Windsor Art, Inc.; *U.S. Public*, pg. 212

DOLCELATTE—Gorgonzola—Cucina Classica Italiana, Inc.; *U.S. Public*, pg. 1435

DOLE—Fresh Produce & Dried Fruits & Nuts—Dole Citrus & Dole Deciduous; *U.S. Public*, pg. 515

DOLE—Fresh Produce Citrus & Fruit—Dole Food Company, Inc.; *U.S. Public*, pg. 515

DOLE—NONE—Dole Packaged Food Company; *U.S. Public*, pg. 515

DOLE—Electromechanical & Electronic Appliances & Automotive Controls—Eaton Corporation; *U.S. Public*, pg. 555

DOLE—Automotive & Appliance Controls—Eaton Corporation Automotive Controls Division; *U.S. Public*, pg. 557

DOLE FROZEN NOVELTIES—NONE—Nestle Ice Cream Co.; *Int'l*, pg. 918

DOLE JUICES—Juices—Dole Food Company, Inc.; *U.S. Public*, pg. 515

DOLE JUICES—Natural Juices—Tropicana Dole Beverages North America; *Int'l*, pg. 1217

DOLE SALADS—Salads—Dole Food Company, Inc.; *U.S. Public*, pg. 515

DOLER—Power Tools & Assembly Systems—Cooper Industries, Inc.; *U.S. Public*, pg. 442

DOLISOS—Homeopathy Products—Groupe Limagrain; *Int'l*, pg. 566

DOLL COLLECTOR'S PRICE GUIDE—Price Guide—House of White Birches, Inc.; *U.S. Private*, pg. 542

DOLL DESIGNS—Crafts Publication—House of White Birches, Inc.; *U.S. Private*, pg. 542

DOLL READER—NONE—Cowles Enthusiast Media, Inc.; *U.S. Private*, pg. 281

DOLL WORLD—Doll Magazine—House of White Birches, Inc.; *U.S. Private*, pg. 542

DOLLAR BARGAIN—Bargain Stores—G B Stores; *U.S. Private*, pg. 972

DOLLAR GENERAL STORES—Discount Retail Stores—Dollar General Corporation; *U.S. Public*, pg. 515

DOLLAR RENT A CAR—Tradename—Dollar Rent A Car; *U.S. Public*, pg. 354

DOLLMAKER—Periodical for Collectors & Crafters of Dolls—Meredith Corporation; *U.S. Public*, pg. 1094

DOLLS & FLOWERS—Bathroom Tissue—Georgia-Pacific Corporation; *U.S. Public*, pg. 735

DOLLY MADISON—Cake—Interstate Brands Corporation; *U.S. Public*, pg. 909

DOLLYWOOD—Dolly Parton's Smoky Mountain Heritage Park—Silver Dollar City, Inc.; *U.S. Private*, pg. 1000

DOLMAR—Engine Tools—Makita Corporation; *Int'l*, pg. 831

DOLMIO—Italian Foods—Master Foods; *U.S. Private*, pg. 707

DOLOBID—Pharmaceutical—Merck Human Health Division (U.S. Human Health); *U.S. Public*, pg. 1091

DOLPHIN—NONE—National R.V., Inc.; *U.S. Public*, pg. 1159

DOLPHIN—Mens Rain Wear—Rainfair, Inc.; *U.S. Private*, pg. 907

DOLPHIN—Flush Valves—Sloan Valve Company; *U.S. Private*, pg. 1006

DOLPHIN—Focus Lock Binoculars—Swift Instruments, Inc.; *U.S. Private*, pg. 1058

DOLPHIN BOOK CLUB—Book Club—Book of the Month Club; *U.S. Public*, pg. 1612

DOLPHIN BOOKS—Book Imprint—Bertelsmann AG; *Int'l*, pg. 189

DOM PERIGNON—NONE—LVMH Moet Hennessy Louis Vuitton; *Int'l*, pg. 779

DOM PERIGNON—French Tete de Cuvee Champagne—Schieffelin & Somerset Co.; *Int'l*, pg. 412

DOM RUINART—Champagne—Schieffelin & Somerset Co.; *Int'l*, pg. 412

DOMAFOAM—Laminated Insulation Panel—The Dow Chemical Company; *U.S. Public*, pg. 522

DOMAIN—NONE—Elcor Corporation; *U.S. Public*, pg. 567

DOMAIN/DACS—Centralized Client/Workstation Security Management—Utimaco Safeware, Inc.; *Int'l*, pg. 1444

DOMAINE—Burgundy Wines—Frederick Wildman & Sons Ltd.; *U.S. Private*, pg. 1176

DOMAINE ARMAND ROUSSEAU—Red Burgundy Wines—Frederick Wildman & Sons Ltd.; *U.S. Private*, pg. 1176

DOMAINE CHANDON—NONE—LVMH Moet Hennessy Louis Vuitton; *Int'l*, pg. 779

DOMAINE CHANDON—Sparkling Wine—Schieffelin & Somerset Co.; *Int'l*, pg. 412

DOMAINE D'OR—Wine—Andres Wines Ltd.; *Int'l*, pg. 75

DOMAINE DUJAC—Red Burgundy Wines—Frederick Wildman & Sons Ltd.; *U.S. Private*, pg. 1176

DOMAINE ST. MICHELLE—Wine—Stimson Lane Ltd.; *U.S. Public*, pg. 1661

DOMAINES CORDIER—Bordeaux—Seagram Chateau & Estate Wines Co.; *Int'l*, pg. 1215

DOMANI—Shoes—Johnston & Murphy Co.; *U.S. Public*, pg. 728

DOME—Lid for Home Canning Jars—Alltrista Corporation; *U.S. Public*, pg. 56

DOME PASTE—Pharmaceutical—Bayer Corporation/Pharmaceutical Division; *Int'l*, pg. 173

DOMECHARGER—One Hour Fast Charger—Sanyo Energy (U.S.A.) Corporation; *Int'l*, pg. 1191

DOMECQ—Sherry—Allied Domecq PLC; *Int'l*, pg. 62

DOMECQ—Sherry—Domecq Importers Inc.; *Int'l*, pg. 63

DOMESTIC—Condensate Handling Equipment, Boiler Feed Units & Centrifugal Pumps—ITT Fluid Handling; *U.S. Public*, pg. 860

DOMESTICATIONS—Specialty Home Textiles Catalog—Hanover Direct, Inc.; *U.S. Public*, pg. 782

DOMESTICATIONS—Home Decorating—Hanover Direct Pennsylvania, Inc.; *U.S. Public*, pg. 782

DOMESTOS—Household Cleaners—Unilever Plc; *Int'l*, pg. 1433

DOMETIC—Leisure Products—Electrolux, AB; *Int'l*, pg. 438

DOMETIC—Products for Recreational Vehicles—White Consolidated Industries, Inc.; *Int'l*, pg. 439

DOMINICAN BUNDLES—Premium Cigars—Consolidated Cigar Corporation; *U.S. Private*, pg. 690

DOMINICK'S—Food Products—Dominick's Finer Foods; *U.S. Private*, pg. 1202

DOMINION—Non-Woven Group—Dominion Textile Inc.; *Int'l*, pg. 415

DOMINION—Hydraulic Pump Machinery—General Electric Canada Inc.; *U.S. Public*, pg. 713

DOMINION—Shoes—Genesco Inc.; *U.S. Public*, pg. 728

DOMINION—Food Store—The Great Atlantic & Pacific Tea Company, Inc.; *Int'l*, pg. 1375

DOMINION ENGINEERING—Hydraulic Turbines—General Electric Canada Inc.; *U.S. Public*, pg. 713

DOMINION LIFE—Excess Interest Whole Life Product—The Life Insurance Co. of Virginia; *U.S. Public*, pg. 712

DOMINO—Matches—Diamond Brands, Inc.; *U.S. Private*, pg. 330

DOMINO—Sugar Products—Domino Sugar Corporation; *Int'l*, pg. 1356

DOMINO—NONE—Lotus Development Corporation; *U.S. Public*, pg. 896

DOMINO—Sugars—Tate & Lyle PLC; *Int'l*, pg. 1356

DOMINO—Portable Reading Machine—Telesensory Corporation; *U.S. Private*, pg. 1074

DOMINO APPLICATIONS—NONE—Lotus Development Corporation; *U.S. Public*, pg. 896

DOMINO RALLY—Game—Pressman Toy Corp.; *U.S. Private*, pg. 882

DOMINO'S—Pizza—Domino's Pizza Inc.; *U.S. Private*, pg. 339

DOMINUS—California Wine—Seagram Chateau & Estate Wines Co.; *Int'l*, pg. 1215

DOMITOR—NONE—Pfizer Inc.; *U.S. Public*, pg. 1281

DOMO PANN—Dust Cloths—The Dow Chemical Company; *U.S. Public*, pg. 522

DOMOCLEAN—House Mark—The Dow Chemical Company; *U.S. Public*, pg. 522

DOMOL—Pharmaceutical—Bayer Corporation/Pharmaceutical Division; *Int'l*, pg. 173

DOMONET—Cleaning Products—The Dow Chemical Company; *U.S. Public*, pg. 522

DOMOPAK—House Mark—The Dow Chemical Company; *U.S. Public*, pg. 522

DOMOPAK DRINK—Ice Cube Bags—The Dow Chemical Company; *U.S. Public*, pg. 522

DOMOPAK STRIP—Dispenser—The Dow Chemical Company; *U.S. Public*, pg. 522

DOMOPAK ZIP—Napkin Dispenser—The Dow Chemical Company; *U.S. Public*, pg. 522

DOMORE—Office Furniture—Domore Corporation; *U.S. Private*, pg. 339

DOMUS—Department Stores—KF/Konsum Coop Group; *Int'l*, pg. 718

DOMWIRE—Steel Reinforcing Mesh—Smorgon A.R.C.; *Int'l*, pg. 1269

DON—Brake Friction Materials—BBA Friction LTD.; *Int'l*, pg. 112

DON ALLESON—Athletic Wear—Don Alleson, Inc.; *U.S. Private*, pg. 339

DON & MIKE—Talk Radio Program—Westwood One Entertainment; *U.S. Public*, pg. 1763

DON & MIKE—Talk Radio Program—Westwood One, Inc.; *U.S. Public*, pg. 1763

DON COSSACK—Vodka—M.S. Walker, Inc.; *U.S. Private*, pg. 1147

DON CRIQUI ON SPORTS—Sports Radio Program—Westwood One Entertainment; *U.S. Public*, pg. 1763

DON CRIQUI ON SPORTS—Sports Commentary Program—Westwood One, Inc.; *U.S. Public*, pg. 1763

DON DIEGO—Premium Cigars—Consolidated Cigar Corporation; *U.S. Private*, pg. 690

DON LOPER—Belts & Billfolds—Tandy Brands Accessories, Inc.; *U.S. Public*, pg. 1560

DON MARTINO—Pizza—Crestar Food Products, Inc.; *U.S. Public*, pg. 805

DON MIGUEL—Cigars—Consolidated Cigar Corporation; *U.S. Private*, pg. 690

DON MIGUEL—Mexican Food Products—Don Miguel Mexican Foods, Inc.; *U.S. Private*, pg. 339

DON PABLO—Pipe Tobacco—Lane Limited; *Int'l*, pg. 1129

DON PEDRO—Brandy—Domecq Importers Inc.; *Int'l*, pg. 63

DON 1500—Combine—Belarus Machinery, Inc.; *Int'l*, pg. 101

DON'T BREAK THE ICE—Game—Milton Bradley Company; *U.S. Public*, pg. 797

DON'T START WITHOUT US—Medical Instruments—Mallinckrodt Inc.; *U.S. Public*, pg. 1039

DONACLONE—Air Cleaner—Donaldson Company, Inc.; *U.S. Public*, pg. 517

DONALD BROOKS—Clothing—Genesco Inc.; *U.S. Public*, pg. 728

DONALD DUCK—100% Pure Fruit Juices—Citrus World Inc.; *U.S. Private*, pg. 241

DONALD DUCK SOUP—Soup—Nestle S.A.; *Int'l*, pg. 915

DONALDSON—Air Cleaner & Exhaust; Oil Filtration Products & Acessory—McDonald Equipment Co.; *U.S. Private*, pg. 721

DONALDSON—Environmental Control Apparatus—Donaldson Company, Inc.; *U.S. Public*, pg. 517

DONASONIC—Gas Turbine Intake Silencer—Donaldson Company, Inc.; *U.S. Public*, pg. 517

DONASPIN—Pre-Cleaner—Donaldson Company, Inc.; *U.S. Public*, pg. 517

DONBEI—Instant Japanese Noodles in a Cup—Nissin Food Products Co., Ltd.; *Int'l*, pg. 949

DONCASTER—Dresses & Sportswear—Tanner Co.; *U.S. Private*, pg. 1068

DONCASTER CUSTOM—Taylor Made Dresses & Sportswear—Tanner Co.; *U.S. Private*, pg. 1068

DONKIN—NONE—Carbo Plc; *Int'l*, pg. 268

DONLEE ENERGY SYSTEMS—CombustionSystems—Donlee Technologies Inc.; *U.S. Private*, pg. 339

DONN—Suspension Systems—CGC Inc.; *U.S. Public*, pg. 1660

DONNA KARAN—Designer Fashions—Donna Karan; *U.S. Public*, pg. 517

DONNA KARAN—Hosiery—Sara Lee Corporation; *U.S. Public*, pg. 1432

DONNA KARAN COSMETICS—NONE—Estee Lauder Companies Inc.; *U.S. Public*, pg. 594

DONNA MUSIC PUBLICATIONS—Music Publishing (Theatrical)—Metromedia International Group, Inc.; *U.S. Public*, pg. 1102

DONNAGEL—NONE—American Home Products Corporation; *U.S. Public*, pg. 79

DONNAGEL—Pharmaceutical Products—Wyeth-Ayerst Laboratories, Inc.; *U.S. Public*, pg. 80

DONNELLY—NONE—Donnelly Corporation; *U.S. Public*, pg. 519

DONNKENNY—Sportswear—Donnkenny, Inc.; *U.S. Public*, pg. 519

DONNY MAC—Greeting Cards—Fine Art Developments plc; *Int'l*, pg. 485

DONOR ADULT BOVINE SERUM—Bovine Serum—HyClone Laboratories Inc.; *Int'l*, pg. 1037

DONOR EQUINE SERUM—Equine Serum—HyClone Laboratories Inc.; *Int'l*, pg. 1037

DONSON—Building Products—Email Limited; *Int'l*, pg. 450

DON'T DO BUSINESS WITHOUT IT—Corporate Card Services—American Express Company; *U.S. Public*, pg. 73

DON'T LEAVE HOME WITHOUT IT—Charge Card Services—American Express Company; *U.S. Public*, pg. 73

DON'T LEAVE HOME WITHOUT THEM—Traveler's Cheque Services—American Express Company; *U.S. Public*, pg. 73

DON'T LEAVE HOME WITHOUT US—Travel Services—American Express Company; *U.S. Public*, pg. 73

DONUT—Cakes—Allied Domecq PLC; *Int'l*, pg. 62

DONUT MINI MATIC—Bakery Equipment—Belshaw Brothers, Inc.; *Int'l*, pg. 188

DONUT ROBOT MARK V—Bakery Machinery—Belshaw Brothers, Inc.; *Int'l*, pg. 188

DONUT ROBOT MARK IX—Bakery Equipment—Belshaw Brothers, Inc.; *Int'l*, pg. 188

DOO DADS—Snacks—Nabisco Inc.; *U.S. Public*, pg. 1355

DOODLE ART—Children's Learn & Color Kits—Price Stern Sloan Inc.; *Int'l*, pg. 1215

DOOR CRAFT—Doors—Jeld-Wen, Inc.; *U.S. Private*, pg. 585

DOORMAN—Doors—Morgan Products Ltd.; *U.S. Public*, pg. 1132

DOORMATE—Locksets—Unican Security Systems Ltd.; *Int'l*, pg. 1432

DOPAMIN—Treatment of Shock—Kali-Chemie Aktiengesellschaft; *Int'l*, pg. 1278

DOPAMINE—Pharmaceutical Products—Astra USA, Inc.; *Int'l*, pg. 93

DOPP—Travel Kits & Business Cases—DHP Limited Partnership; *U.S. Private*, pg. 302

DORADO—Mobile Homes—Wick Bldg. Systems Inc. Manufactured Homes Div.; *U.S. Private*, pg. 1174

DORAL—Sedative, U.S. Marketing—Carter-Wallace, Inc.; *U.S. Public*, pg. 309

DORAL—Cigarettes—RJR Nabisco Holdings Corp.; *U.S. Public*, pg. 1354

DORAL—Filter, Menthol, 100's Filter & Menthol, Full Flavor 85's & 100's, Ultra Lt—R.J. Reynolds Tobacco Company; *U.S. Public*, pg. 1355

DORAL—Cigarettes-Middle East—R.J. Reynolds Tobacco Intl., Inc.; *U.S. Public*, pg. 1355

DORAL—Hypnotic—Wallace Laboratories; *U.S. Public*, pg. 310

DORAL—Mobile Homes—Wick Bldg. Systems Inc. Manufactured Homes Div.; *U.S. Private*, pg. 1174

DORCHESTER—Cigarettes-United Kingdom—R.J. Reynolds Tobacco Intl., Inc.; *U.S. Public*, pg. 1355

DORCOL—Children's Cough Syrup, Decongestant Liquid, Liquid Cold Formula—Sandoz Pharmaceuticals Corp.; *Int'l*, pg. 974

DOREM I—Cologne & Toiletries—Avon Products, Inc.; *U.S. Public*, pg. 155

DORF—Building Products—Email Limited; *Int'l*, pg. 450

DORFILE—Shelving Systems—Newell Co.; *U.S. Public*, pg. 1176

DORIAN GREY—Hosiery for Women—Grupo Synkro, S.A. de C.V.; *Int'l*, pg. 576

DORIDEN—Pharmaceuticals—Rhone-Poulenc Rorer - U.S.; *Int'l*, pg. 1110

DORIS—Software—CACI International Inc; *U.S. Public*, pg. 272

DORITOS—Tortilla Chips—Frito-Lay Company; *U.S. Public*, pg. 1277

DORLASTEN—Elastic Fiber—Bayer AG; *Int'l*, pg. 171

DORMAN—Natural & Process Cheeses—Beatrice Cheese Co.; *U.S. Public*, pg. 426

DORMAN—Fasteners—R&B, Inc.; *U.S. Public*, pg. 1354

DORMEYER—Industrial Electric Equipment—Dormeyer Industries; *U.S. Private*, pg. 340

DORMICUM—Anesthetic—Roche Holding Ltd.; *Int'l*, pg. 1119

DORMOSEDAN—Equine Sedative/Analgesic—SmithKline Beecham plc; *Int'l*, pg. 1264

DORNE & MARGOLIN—Antennas & Electronic Reserve Equipment—Metex Corporation; *U.S. Public*, pg. 1674

DORNER—Conveyers—Dorner Manufacturing Corp.; *U.S. Private*, pg. 340

DORNEY PARK & WILDWATER KINGDOM—Amusement Park—Cedar Fair, L.P.; *U.S. Public*, pg. 319

DORNIER—NONE—Daimler-Benz Aktiengesellschaft; *Int'l*, pg. 366

DOROTENNIS—NONE—Fila Sport S.p.A.; *Int'l*, pg. 484

DORR-OLIVER—Processing Equipment & Systems—Dorr-Oliver Incorporated; *Int'l*, pg. 839

DORSET FOODS—Frozen Uncooked Savoury Prods.—Northern Foods plc; *Int'l*, pg. 967

DORSET PRESS—Publishing Imprint—Barnes & Noble Direct; *U.S. Public*, pg. 189

DORSEY—Trailers—Dorsey Trailers, Inc.; *U.S. Public*, pg. 520

DORVILLE—Brandy—Groupe Pernod Ricard; *Int'l*, pg. 566

DORYX—Antibiotic—Warner-Chilcott Laboratories, Inc.; *Int'l*, pg. 436

DOS EQUIS—Mexican Beer—Guinness Import Company; *Int'l*, pg. 412

DOS EQUIS—Beer—Labatt U.S.A.; *Int'l*, pg. 679

DOS HERMANOS—Mexican Restaurante & Cantina—The Levy Organization; *U.S. Private*, pg. 664

DOS REALES TEQUILA—NONE—Carillon Importers, Ltd.; *Int'l*, pg. 409

DOSEMASTER—Disinfection Product—Bailey, Fischer & Porter Company; *Int'l*, pg. 449

DOSETTE—Unit-of-Use , Ampul, Vial & Cartridge Injectable Dosage Forms—Elkins-Sinn, Inc.-Lederle; *U.S. Public*, pg. 79

DOSETTE—Cartridge Unit—Wyeth-Ayerst Laboratories, Inc.; *U.S. Public*, pg. 80

DOSGATE—Computer Software System—Datapoint Corporation; *Int'l*, pg. 384

DOSIA—Laundry Detergent—Benckiser Consumer Products Inc.; *Int'l*, pg. 185

DOSSERVER—Computer Software System—Datapoint Corporation; *Int'l*, pg. 384

DOT.TEN—Hardware that Conforms to the IEEE 1101.10 Standard—Electronic Solutions; *U.S. Public*, pg. 1791

DOT-X—Vide Monitor—Dotronix, Inc.; *U.S. Public*, pg. 520

DOTCO—Pneumatic Tools—Cooper Industries, Inc.; *U.S. Public*, pg. 442

DOTTI—NONE—Kellwood Company; *U.S. Public*, pg. 948

DOUBLE AGENT—Industrial Chemical—Hercules Chemical Co., Inc.; *U.S. Private*, pg. 523

DOUBLE BARREL—Combination Aggregate Dryer/Mixer Center—Astec Industries, Inc.; *U.S. Public*, pg. 141

DOUBLE BUBBLE—Gum—Fleer-Skybox International Inc.; *U.S. Public*, pg. 1052

DOUBLE/BUBBLE—Package for 2-Part Epoxies—Hardman Division of Harcros Chemicals, Inc.; *Int'l*, pg. 598

DOUBLE CHECK—Color Proofing System—Eastman Kodak Company; *U.S. Public*, pg. 550

DOUBLE CHECK—Dual Technology-A PIR/Microwave Detector—Linear Corporation; *U.S. Public*, pg. 1193

DOUBLE-COLA—Soft Drink—Double-Cola Co.-USA; *U.S. Private*, pg. 341

DOUBLE COVER—Liquid & Paste Paints—PPG Industries, Inc.; *U.S. Public*, pg. 1245

DOUBLE D—Stock Preparation—Beloit Corporation; *U.S. Public*, pg. 789

DOUBLE DANDERINE—Pharmaceuticals—Medtech Inc.; *U.S. Private*, pg. 728

DOUBLE DEVILLE—NONE—Checkers Drive-In Restaurants, Inc.; *U.S. Public*, pg. 342

DOUBLE DIAMOND—Beer—Barton Beers, Ltd.; *U.S. Public*, pg. 300

DOUBLE DIAMOND—Beef—Cargill; *U.S. Private*, pg. 210

DOUBLE DIP CRUNCH—Ready-Sweetened Corn & Rice Cereal with Real Nuts & Honey—Kellogg Company; *U.S. Public*, pg. 947

DOUBLE-DRY—Soft Drink—Double-Cola Co.-USA; *U.S. Private*, pg. 341

DOUBLE DUTY—Blowers—Coppus Murray Group, Tuthill Corporation; *U.S. Private*, pg. 1110

DOUBLE EAGLE—Tires—The Goodyear Tire & Rubber Company; *U.S. Public*, pg. 752

DOUBLE EAGLE 141—Saw Gin Stand for Ginning Seed Cotton—Continental Eagle Corporation; *U.S. Public*, pg. 267

DOUBLE EDGE—NONE—H.C. Miller Company; *U.S. Public*, pg. 747

DOUBLE EXPOSURE—Shirts Jackets Mens—M. Rubin & Sons Inc.; *U.S. Private*, pg. 949

DOUBLE-FLUFF—Household Paper Goods—Orchids Paper Products Co.; *U.S. Private*, pg. 819

DOUBLE FRUIT—NONE—J.M. Smucker Company; *U.S. Public*, pg. 1480

DOUBLE-H BOOTS—NONE—H.H. Brown Shoe Company, Inc.; *U.S. Public*, pg. 217

DOUBLE HEADER—NONE—Carpenter Technology Corporation; *U.S. Public*, pg. 307

DOUBLE LOK-BACK TRAPPER—Hunting Knife—Camillus Cutlery Co.; *U.S. Private*, pg. 203

DOUBLE MAXIM—Brown Ale—Vaux Group Plc; *Int'l*, pg. 1453

DOUBLE POWER ALL—Liquid Detergent—Lever Brothers Co.; *Int'l*, pg. 1435

DOUBLE POWER SURF—Liquid Detergent—Lever Brothers Co.; *Int'l*, pg. 1435

DOUBLE POWER WISK—Liquid Detergent—Lever Brothers Co.; *Int'l*, pg. 1435

DOUBLE Q—Canned Salmon—Peter Pan Seafoods, Inc.; *Int'l*, pg. 928

DOUBLE SCRUB—Surgical Scrub Brush—Ballard Medical Products; *U.S. Public*, pg. 171

DOUBLE-SEAL—Ball Valves—Neles-Jamesbury Corp.; *Int'l*, pg. 1428

DOUBLE SIX M-2—High Speed Tool Steel— Latrobe Steel Company; *U.S. Public*, pg. 1617

DOUBLE SURE—Grocery Sacks—Johns Manville Corporation; *U.S. Public*, pg. 927

DOUBLE TOP—Frozen Pizza—Tombstone Pizza Corporation; *U.S. Public*, pg. 1288

DOUBLE WALL—Stainless Steelware—The Canadian Coleman Co., Ltd.; *U.S. Private*, pg. 691

DOUBLE WALL—Steel Wall Panel—Clestra Hauserman, Inc.; *Int'l*, pg. 569

DOUBLE-X—Photo Film—Eastman Kodak Company; *U.S. Public*, pg. 550

DOUBLEANDY—1/2lb. Hamburger—Andy's Restaurants Inc.; *U.S. Private*, pg. 74

DOUBLEDAY—Publishers—Bertelsmann AG; *Int'l*, pg. 189

DOUBLEDAY—Election Materials & Supplies— Standex International Corporation; *U.S. Public*, pg. 1505

DOUBLEDAY BOOK CLUB—NONE—Doubleday Direct; *Int'l*, pg. 191

DOUBLEDUTY—Loader Cutting Edges—Bucyrus Blades Inc.; *U.S. Private*, pg. 383

DOUBLEMINT—Chewing Gum—Wrigley Canada Inc.; *U.S. Public*, pg. 1781

DOUBLEMINT—Gum—Wm. Wrigley Jr. Company; *U.S. Public*, pg. 1781

DOUBLETREE GUEST SUITES—Hotels— Doubletree Corporation; *U.S. Public*, pg. 1335

DOUBLETREE HOTELS—Hotels—Doubletree Corporation; *U.S. Public*, pg. 1335

DOUBLETREE RESORTS—Hotels—Doubletree Corporation; *U.S. Public*, pg. 1335

DOUGLAS—Vacuum Cleaner—Douglas/Quikut; *U.S. Public*, pg. 217

DOUGLAS-COOKER—High Shear Cooker Corn Starches—Penford Corp.; *U.S. Public*, pg. 1269

DOUGLAS-ENZYME—Enzyme-Converting Corn Starches—Penford Corp.; *U.S. Public*, pg. 1269

DOUGLAS PRODUCTS—Vacuum Cleaners, Wet/ Dry Vacs, Hand Held Vacs—The Scott Fetzer Company; *U.S. Public*, pg. 217

DOUINUS—Wine—Pacific Wine Co.; *U.S. Private*, pg. 843

DOULTON—Bathroom Sanitaryware—Caradon Plc; *Int'l*, pg. 266

DOUVILLE—Baked Goods—Grocers Baking Co.; *U.S. Private*, pg. 482

DOUWE EGBERTS—Coffee, Tea & Tobacco Prods.—Sara Lee Corporation; *U.S. Public*, pg. 1432

DOVE—Bar Soap & Detergent—Lever Brothers Co.; *Int'l*, pg. 1435

DOVE—Ice Cream Bars—M&M/Mars; *U.S. Private*, pg. 707

DOVE—Soap & Dishwashing Liquid—Unilever Plc; *Int'l*, pg. 1433

DOVE BAR—NONE—M&M/Mars; *U.S. Private*, pg. 707

DOVE CHOCOLATE—NONE—M&M/Mars; *U.S. Private*, pg. 707

DOVEBAR—Chocolate Bar—Mars, Incorporated; *U.S. Private*, pg. 707

DOVER—Flour—Dover Industries Limited; *Int'l*, pg. 417

DOVER FARMS—Frozen Whipped Toppings— Kraft Foods, Inc.; *U.S. Public*, pg. 1287

DOW BATHROOM CLEANER—Bathroom Cleaner—DowBrands, L.P.; *U.S. Public*, pg. 523

DOW CORNING—NONE—Dow Corning Corporation; *U.S. Public*, pg. 523

DOW (in Diamond)—For all Dow Products & Services—The Dow Chemical Company; *U.S. Public*, pg. 522

DOW JONES—NONE—Dow Jones & Company, Inc.; *U.S. Public*, pg. 524

THE DOW JONES AVERAGES—Stock Indices— Dow Jones & Company, Inc.; *U.S. Public*, pg. 524

DOW JONES INTERACTIVE—Electronic News Retrieval Service—Dow Jones & Company, Inc.; *U.S. Public*, pg. 524

DOW JONES MARKETS—Computerized Financial Information Systems—Dow Jones Telerate Holdings, Inc.; *U.S. Public*, pg. 525

DOW OVEN CLEANER—Oven Cleaner— DowBrands, L.P.; *U.S. Public*, pg. 523

DOWANOL—Glycol Ether Products—The Dow Chemical Company; *U.S. Public*, pg. 522

DOWCAL—Heat Transfer Agents—The Dow Chemical Company; *U.S. Public*, pg. 522

DOWCLENE—Drycleaning Solution—The Dow Chemical Company; *U.S. Public*, pg. 522

DOWCLOR—Drycleaning Solvent—The Dow Chemical Company; *U.S. Public*, pg. 522

DOWCO—Pesticides—The Dow Chemical Company; *U.S. Public*, pg. 522

DOWEL—Doors—Weyerhaeuser Forest Products Company; *U.S. Public*, pg. 1764

DOWEX—Ion Exchange Resins—The Dow Chemical Company; *U.S. Public*, pg. 522

DOWEX MARATHON—Ion Exchange Resins—The Dow Chemical Company; *U.S. Public*, pg. 522

DOWEX MONOSPHERE—Tough Gel Resins—The Dow Chemical Company; *U.S. Public*, pg. 522

DOWFAX—Surfactant—The Dow Chemical Company; *U.S. Public*, pg. 522

DOWFLAKE—Calcium Chloride Flake—The Dow Chemical Company; *U.S. Public*, pg. 522

DOWFROST—Heat Transfer Agent—The Dow Chemical Company; *U.S. Public*, pg. 522

DOWFROTH—Propylene Glycol—The Dow Chemical Company; *U.S. Public*, pg. 522

DOWICIDE—Antimicrobials—The Dow Chemical Company; *U.S. Public*, pg. 522

DOWICIL—Antimicrobials—The Dow Chemical Company; *U.S. Public*, pg. 522

DOWLEX—Polyolefin Resin—The Dow Chemical Company; *U.S. Public*, pg. 522

DOWN CHRISTMAS LANE—Greeting Cards; Gift Wrap & Trims; Gift Boxes—American Greetings Corporation; *U.S. Public*, pg. 77

DOWN-E-SOF—Tissue—Fort James Corporation; *U.S. Public*, pg. 670

DOWN EAST TIMBERLANDS—Real Estate—The Hearst Corporation; *U.S. Private*, pg. 515

DOWN TO EARTH—Environmental Products— Reckitt & Colman plc; *Int'l*, pg. 1089

DOWNFLO—Air Filtration & Contaminant Collection System—Donaldson Company, Inc.; *U.S. Public*, pg. 517

DOWNRIGHT—Products for Asphalt—The Dow Chemical Company; *U.S. Public*, pg. 522

DOWNY—Fabric Softener—The Procter & Gamble Company; *U.S. Public*, pg. 1330

DOWNYFLAKE—Breakfast Item—The Pillsbury Company; *Int'l*, pg. 411

DOWPER—Drycleaning Solvent—The Dow Chemical Company; *U.S. Public*, pg. 522

DOWTHERM—Heat Transfer Fluid & Diesel Coolant—The Dow Chemical Company; *U.S. Public*, pg. 522

DOWTY—NONE—TI Group plc; *Int'l*, pg. 1337

DOXIL—Stealth Liposome Formulation of Doxorubicin—Sequus Pharmaceuticals, Inc.; *U.S. Public*, pg. 1460

DOXOME—Liposomal Formulation of Doxorubicin—Nexstar Pharmaceuticals, Inc.; *U.S. Public*, pg. 1180

DOXSEE—Clam Products—Snow's/Doxee Inc.; *U.S. Private*, pg. 219

DOXSEE CLAM PRODUCTS—NONE— Castleberry/Snow's Brands Inc.; *U.S. Private*, pg. 219

DR BAKERS ASPIRIN—NONE—Health Products Corporation; *U.S. Private*, pg. 514

DR. BALLARD'S—Pet Foods—Nestle S.A.; *Int'l*, pg. 915

DR BEST—NONE—SmithKline Beecham Corporation; *Int'l*, pg. 1264

DR. BEST—Oral Care—SmithKline Beecham plc; *Int'l*, pg. 1264

DR. DENTON—Sleeping Garments, Sweaters, Robes, Underwear—Salant Childrens Apparel Group; *U.S. Public*, pg. 1429

DR. DENTON—Clothing—Salant Corporation; *U.S. Public*, pg. 1429

DR. DOBBS JOURNAL—Magazine—Miller Freeman Inc.; *Int'l*, pg. 1443

DR. FULLER—Mattresses—Restonic Mattress Corporation; *U.S. Private*, pg. 925

DR. GJUST FOR TEENS—Mattresses & Box Springs for Teenagers—Kingsdown, Inc.; *U.S. Private*, pg. 622

DR. GOODBONES—Juvenile Mattress & Box Springs—Kingsdown, Inc.; *U.S. Private*, pg. 622

DR. GRIP—Ball Point Pen—The Pilot Pen Corp. of America; *Int'l*, pg. 1057

DR. HANDS—Teething Lotion—Medtech Inc.; *U.S. Private*, pg. 728

DR. KOCH'S—Fruit Juices—Eckes AG; *Int'l*, pg. 432

DR. KOCH'S MINIKAL—Fruit Juices—Eckes AG; *Int'l*, pg. 432

DR. MANN PHARMA—Non-Prescription Medications—Bausch & Lomb Incorporated; *U.S. Public*, pg. 194

DR. MCGILLICUDDY'S—Mentholmint Schnapps— The Seagram Company Ltd.; *Int'l*, pg. 1214

DR. PEPPER—Soft Drink—Buffalo Rock Company; *U.S. Private*, pg. 179

DR. PEPPER—NONE—Cadbury Beverages; *Int'l*, pg. 248

DR PEPPER—Soft Drink—The Coca-Cola Bottling Co. of New York, Inc.; *U.S. Public*, pg. 393

DR PEPPER—Soft Drink—Dr. Pepper Co.; *Int'l*, pg. 248

DR PEPPER—Soft Drink—Dr Pepper/Seven Up No. America; *Int'l*, pg. 248

DR. RUMNEY'S—Snuff—Imperial Tobacco Group, Ltd.; *Int'l*, pg. 666

DR SCHOLL'S—Shoes—Brown Group, Inc.; *U.S. Public*, pg. 262

DR. SCHOLL'S—Foot Care Products—Schering-Plough Corporation; *U.S. Public*, pg. 1438

DR. SCHOLL'S—Footcare—Schering-Plough Healthcare Products Inc.; *U.S. Public*, pg. 1438

DR SCHOLL'S—Foot Products—Scholl U.S.A.: *U.S. Public*, pg. 1438

DR. TEST—NONE—GenRad, Inc.; *U.S. Public*, pg. 731

DR. WELLS—Soft Drink—The Monarch Company, Inc.; *U.S. Private*, pg. 756

DR WHITES—Feminine Hygiene Products—Smith & Nephew PLC; *Int'l*, pg. 1263

DR. HANDS—NONE—Lee Pharmaceuticals; *U.S. Public*, pg. 984

DRACULA—Physical Verification—Cadence Design Systems, Inc.; *U.S. Public*, pg. 290

DRAFT SEAL—Weatherstripping—W.J. & Dennis Co.; *U.S. Private*, pg. 1144

DRAFTING FOR INDUSTRY—Textbook Covering Drafting Fundamentals & Advanced Design Techniques—Goodheart-Willcox Publisher; *U.S. Private*, pg. 464

DRAFTITE—Weather Strip—The Standard Products Company; *U.S. Public*, pg. 1504

DRAFTRITE—Measuring Instrument—Bacharach Inc.; *U.S. Private*, pg. 109

DRAFTY—Beer—Sapporo Breweries Ltd.; *Int'l*, pg. 1193

DRAFTY BLACK—Beer—Sapporo Breweries Ltd.; *Int'l*, pg. 1193

DRAG—Valves—IMI Plc; *Int'l*, pg. 646

DRAG RACING—Magazine—Petersen Publishing Company, L.L.C.; *U.S. Private*, pg. 856

DRAGANON—Nootropic Agent—Roche Holding Ltd.; *Int'l*, pg. 1119

DRAGNET—Termiticide—FMC Corp., Agricultural Products Group; *U.S. Public*, pg. 605

DRAGON—Cutter Suction Dredge—Ellicott Machine Corporation International; *U.S. Private*, pg. 372

DRAGON—Pentium PC—Ssangyong Business Group; *Int'l*, pg. 1291

DRAGON—Publishing—TSR, Inc.; *U.S. Private*, pg. 1185

DRAGON FLYZ—Flying Action Figures—Galoob Toys, Inc.; *U.S. Public*, pg. 698

DRAGON SEAL—Dry Wine—Groupe Pernod Ricard; *Int'l*, pg. 566

DRAGONHUNT—Fantasy Game—Monarch Avalon, Inc.; *U.S. Public*, pg. 1123

DRAGONLANCE CHRONICLES—Novels—TSR, Inc.; *U.S. Private*, pg. 1185

DRAGONLANCE LEGENDS—Novels—TSR, Inc.; *U.S. Private*, pg. 1185

DRAGONSWITCH—NONE—UB Networks; *Int'l*, pg. 924

DRAIN PUMP—Wastewater Pumping System—Zoeller Co.; *U.S. Private*, pg. 1207

DRAIN VALVE LUBRICANT—Holding Tank Lubricant—Thetford Corporation; *U.S. Private*, pg. 352

DRAINCLAD—NONE—Owens-Corning Canada; *U.S. Public*, pg. 1237

DRAINO—NONE—S.C. Johnson & Son, Limited; *U.S. Private*, pg. 593

DRAINOSAUR—Water Removal System—Little Giant Pump Company; *U.S. Public*, pg. 1566

DRAINTAINER—Oil Recycling Pan—Rubbermaid Incorporated; *U.S. Public*, pg. 1411

DRAKE'S—Snack Cakes—Culinar Inc.; *Int'l*, pg. 348

DRAKEOL—Mineral Oils—Penreco; *U.S. Public*, pg. 1273

DRAKKAR NOIR—Fragrance for Men—Cosmair, Inc.; *Int'l*, pg. 818

DRAKKAR NOIR—Fragrance—Cosmair, Inc., Ralph Lauren Fragrance Division; *Int'l*, pg. 818

DRALON—Synthetic Fiber—Bayer AG; *Int'l*, pg. 171

DRALORIC—Resistors/Potentiometers—Vishay Intertechnology, Inc.; *U.S. Public*, pg. 1721

DRAM—Computer Peripherals—Micron Technology Inc.; *U.S. Public*, pg. 1105

DRAMA TONE—Colorants—ICI Paints; *Int'l*, pg. 664

DRAMAMINE—Motion Sickness Medication—Pharmacia & Upjohn; *Int'l*, pg. 1048

DRAMBUIE—Liqueur—Hiram Walker; *Int'l*, pg. 63

DRAN-LOGGER—NONE—Dranetz-BMI; *U.S. Private*, pg. 1144

DRAN-VIEW—NONE—Dranetz-BMI; *U.S. Private*, pg. 1144

DRAN-SCAN—Electrical Technology—Dranetz-BMI; *U.S. Private*, pg. 1144

DRANETZ—Electrical Technology—Dranetz-BMI; *U.S. Private*, pg. 1144

DRANO—Drain Openers—Bristol-Myers Squibb Company; *U.S. Public*, pg. 253

DRANO—Bathroom Care—S.C. Johnson & Son, Inc.; *U.S. Private*, pg. 592

DRAUGHT BASS—Ale—Bass PLC; *Int'l*, pg. 169

DRAUGHT GUINESS IN CANS—NONE—Guinness Plc; *Int'l*, pg. 412

DRAUGHT GUINNESS—Stout—Guinness Import Company; *Int'l*, pg. 412

DRAUGHT GUINNESS—NONE—Guinness Plc; *Int'l*, pg. 412

DRAW APPLAUSE—Software—Borland International, Inc.; *U.S. Public*, pg. 246

DRAWING ASSISTANT—Software—International Business Machines Corporation; *U.S. Public*, pg. 895

DRAWINGBOARD III—Digitizer—CalComp Technology, Inc.; *U.S. Public*, pg. 1007

DRAWINGMASTER—Direct Imaging Plotters—CalComp Technology, Inc.; *U.S. Public*, pg. 1007

DRAWINGSLATE II—Graphics Tablots—CalComp Technology, Inc.; *U.S. Public*, pg. 1007

DRAWMASTER—Software—International Business Machines Corporation; *U.S. Public*, pg. 895

DRAWSOL—Drawing Compound—D.A. Stuart Company; *U.S. Private*, pg. 1048

DRAXIMOX—Amoxicillin—Novo Nordisk A/S; *Int'l*, pg. 987

DREADNAUGHT—Bond Paper—The Mead Corporation; *U.S. Public*, pg. 1074

DREAM BUILDERS—Blocks—Tyco Toys, Inc.; *U.S. Public*, pg. 1058

DREAM CANDY—Peanut Butter Bar—Sorbee International Ltd.; *U.S. Private*, pg. 1014

DREAM-EZE—Solid Carbide Drill/Reamer Combination—National Twist Drill Div.; *U.S. Public*, pg. 1370

DREAM-EZE—Solid Carbide Drill/Reamer Combination—Regal-Beloit Corporation; *U.S. Public*, pg. 1370

DREAM LINE—Clock Radio/Phone—Sony Electronics; *Int'l*, pg. 1281

DREAM MACHINE—Upright Carpet Extractor—The Eureka Company; *Int'l*, pg. 440

DREAM MACHINE—Clock Radios—Sony Electronics; *Int'l*, pg. 1281

DREAM-MAKERS—National Art Education Program—Binney & Smith Inc.; *U.S. Private*, pg. 496

DREAM RIDE—Infant Car Bed/Car Seat—Cosco, Inc.; *U.S. Private*, pg. 277

DREAM WEAVE—Durable-Use Nonwoven Materials—Kimberly-Clark Corporation; *U.S. Public*, pg. 958

DREAM WHIP—Whipped Topping Mix—Kraft Foods, Inc.; *U.S. Public*, pg. 1287

DREAM WHIP—Whipped Topping—Philip Morris Companies Inc.; *U.S. Public*, pg. 1287

DREAMLAND—Electrical Appliances—Newmond PLC; *Int'l*, pg. 924

DREAMPERKS—Auction with Worldforks Flyer Miles—Northwest Airlines, Inc.; *U.S. Public*, pg. 1200

DREAMSPACE—Patio Enclosures—Thermal Industries, Inc.; *U.S. Private*, pg. 490

DREAMWEAR LINGERIE—Ladies Apparel—Movie Star, Inc.; *U.S. Public*, pg. 1140

DREAMWOOD—Windows—Thermal Industries, Inc.; *U.S. Private*, pg. 490

DRECO—Drilling Rigs—National-Oilwell/Dreco; *U.S. Public*, pg. 1158

DREEMS INTERNATIONAL—Cosmetics—Sentinel Consumer Products, Inc.; *U.S. Private*, pg. 984

DREFT—Laundry Product—The Procter & Gamble Company; *U.S. Public*, pg. 1330

DREHER—Brandy—Grand Metropolitan Plc; *Int'l*, pg. 408

DREHER—Beer—Heineken N.V.; *Int'l*, pg. 608

DREMEL—Compact Power Bench Tools & Hand Held Rotary Power Tools—Emerson Electric Co.; *U.S. Public*, pg. 572

DRESINATE—Rosin Soaps—Hercules Incorporated; *U.S. Public*, pg. 809

DRESINOL—Resin Dispersions—Hercules Incorporated; *U.S. Public*, pg. 809

DRESS ALL—Fats & Oils—Van den Bergh Foods Company; *Int'l*, pg. 1436

DRESS BARN—NONE—The Dress Barn, Inc.; *U.S. Public*, pg. 528

DRESS UPS—Shoes—P.W. Minor & Son, Inc.; *U.S. Private*, pg. 751

DRESSEN-BARNES ELECTRONICS—Electromechanical Equipment—American Electronics, Inc.; *U.S. Private*, pg. 5

DRESSER—Construction Equipment—Komatsu America International Company; *Int'l*, pg. 744

DRESSER OIL TOOLS—Completion & Production Systems—Dresser Industries, Inc.; *U.S. Public*, pg. 528

DRESSER-RAND—Compressors, Turbines & Generators—Dresser Industries, Inc.; *U.S. Public*, pg. 528

DRESSFLEX—Custom Orthotic for High-Heel Wearers—The Langer Biomechanics Group, Inc.; *U.S. Public*, pg. 978

DREST GEL—Pharmaceuticals—Rhone-Poulenc Rorer - U.S.; *Int'l*, pg. 1110

DREW—Specialty Chemicals for Water & Fuel Treatments—Drew Industrial; *U.S. Public*, pg. 139

DREW—Slings—Macwhyte Co.; *U.S. Private*, pg. 68

DREW CHEMICALS—Chemicals—Ashland, Inc.; *U.S. Public*, pg. 138

DREWMULSE—Organic Chemicals—Stepan Company; *U.S. Public*, pg. 1514

DREWPOL—Organic Chemicals—Stepan Company; *U.S. Public*, pg. 1514

DREXEL—Furniture—Drexel Heritage Furnishings Inc.; *U.S. Private*, pg. 432

DREXEL—Furniture—Masco Corporation; *U.S. Public*, pg. 1052

DREXEL STUDIO—NONE—Drexel Heritage Furnishings Inc.; *U.S. Private*, pg. 432

DREYER'S—Ice Cream—Dreyer's Grand Ice Cream, Inc.; *U.S. Public*, pg. 529

DRGFINDER—Medical Computer Program—3M; *U.S. Public*, pg. 1604

DRI-CAL—Registered Label—Dri-Print Foils Inc.; *U.S. Private*, pg. 343

DRI-CONTROL—Valves—Valcor Engineering Corp.; *U.S. Private*, pg. 1131

DRI-DON—Fabrics—Dan River Inc.; *U.S. Public*, pg. 478

DRI EVERLAST TILE—Tile Building Products—Dodge Regupol, Inc.; *U.S. Private*, pg. 337

DRI-FILM—Organo-Silicon Halides or Mixtures for Water-Repellent Organic/Inorg. Matl.—General Electric Canada Inc.; *U.S. Public*, pg. 713

DRI-FLO—Dried Molasses & Honey—Crompton & Knowles Ingredient Technology Corp.; *U.S. Public*, pg. 459

DRI-KEM—Dri-Holding Tank Deodorant—Thetford Corporation; *U.S. Private*, pg. 352

DRI-KLEAR—Cellulose Polymer Coating—Crompton & Knowles Ingredient Technology Corp.; *U.S. Public*, pg. 459

DRI-LOC—Absorbant Meat-Packaging Pads—Sealed Air Corporation; *U.S. Public*, pg. 1450

DRI-MASTER—Paper Towel Dispenser—Georgia-Pacific Corporation; *U.S. Public*, pg. 735

DRI-PRINT—Office Machinery—Standard Duplicating Machines Corp.; *U.S. Private*, pg. 1031

DRI-SEALS—Spray-Dried Fragrances & Encapsulated Spray-Dried Flavors—Crompton & Knowles Ingredient Technology Corp.; *U.S. Public*, pg. 459

DRI-SOLONOID—Valves—Valcor Engineering Corp.; *U.S. Private*, pg. 1131

DRI-STAT—Dry Reagents—Beckman Instruments, Inc.; *U.S. Public*, pg. 199

DRI-SWEET—Corn Syrup Solids—Roquette America Inc.; *U.S. Private*, pg. 944

DRIBACK—Dry-Base Labels—Moore Document Solutions; *Int'l*, pg. 890

DRIBOND—Adhesive—Eastman Chemical Company; *U.S. Public*, pg. 550

DRICOID—Alginate Emulsifier Blend—The NutraSweet Kelco Company; *U.S. Public*, pg. 1125

DRICOID 200—Xanthan Gum/Emulsifier Blend—The NutraSweet Kelco Company; *U.S. Public*, pg. 1125

DRICON—Fire Retardant Treated Wood—Hickson Corporation; *Int'l*, pg. 619

DRIE STERREN GENEVER—Spirit—Allied Domecq PLC; *Int'l*, pg. 62

DRIEHOEK—Cakes, Biscuits, Waffles—GrandMet Foods Southern Europe; *Int'l*, pg. 409

DRIFTER—Sweater—Lands' End, Inc.; *U.S. Public*, pg. 977

DRIFTER—Confections—Nestle-Rowntree Ltd.; *Int'l*, pg. 921

DRIGEST—Biotechnology—Pharmacia & Upjohn Adria Laboratories; *Int'l*, pg. 1049

DRIL-FLEX—Self-Drilling Fasteners—Elco Textron; *U.S. Public*, pg. 1590

DRIL-KWICK—Self Drilling Screws—Parker Kalon; *U.S. Public*, pg. 233

DRILCO—Tubular Services—Smith International, Inc.; *U.S. Public*, pg. 1478

DRILKWICK—Fasteners—The Black & Decker Corporation; *U.S. Public*, pg. 233

DRILLMINDER—Bit Dispenser—American Tool Companies, Inc.; *U.S. Private*, pg. 63

DRILLMINDER PLUS—Bit Dispenser—American Tool Companies, Inc.; *U.S. Private*, pg. 63

DRILLUNIT—NONE—Cross Huller; *Int'l*, pg. 1389

DRIMAGEN—Dyeing Chemicals—Clariant International Ltd.; *Int'l*, pg. 624

DRIMAREN—Cellulose Fibers—Clariant International Ltd.; *Int'l*, pg. 624

DRIMARENE—Dyes—Novartis AG; *Int'l*, pg. 971

DRINK BUOY—Insulated Tumbler—Orbex Inc.; *U.S. Public*, pg. 238

DRINK-UP—Boat Accessories—Attwood Corporation; *U.S. Private*, pg. 1038

DRINKWATER—Bakery Flour—Cargill Flour Div.; *U.S. Private*, pg. 210

DRIP-CHECK—Automotive Aluminium Sealer—3M; *U.S. Public*, pg. 1604

DRIP-MATIC—Caffeine-Free Coffee—Kraft Foods, Inc.; *U.S. Public*, pg. 1287

DRIP-O-MATIC—Drip Dispenser—Surco Products, Inc.; *U.S. Private*, pg. 1056

DRIPRINT—Diazo Products: Papers, Vellums, Films—Dietzgen Corporation; *U.S. Private*, pg. 332

DRISTAN—Decongestant And Analgesic Tablets And Caplets—American Home Products Corporation; *U.S. Public*, pg. 79

DRISTAN—Decongestant & Analgesic Tablets & Caplets—Whitehall-Robins Healthcare; *U.S. Public*, pg. 80

DRISTAN SPRAYS—Decongestant & Analgesic Sprays & Pumps—Whitehall-Robins Healthcare; *U.S. Public*, pg. 80

DRITZ—Sewing Notions & Art Needlework—Prym-Dritz Corporation; *Int'l*, pg. 1499

DRIVAL—Chemical—Air Products; *U.S. Public*, pg. 30

DRIVE—Anti-Perspirants & After Shave—The Gillette Company; *U.S. Public*, pg. 743

DRIVE—Expansion Bolt—Powers Fastening, Inc.; *U.S. Private*, pg. 878

DRIVE-N-GO—NONE—Packaging Resources, Incorporated; *U.S. Private*, pg. 833

DRIVERS DINER—Restaurants at Truck Stops—FFP Marketing Company, Inc.; *U.S. Public*, pg. 604

DRIVER'S FRESH—NONE—Huhtamaki Oy; *Int'l*, pg. 638

DRIVERS TRAVEL MARTS—Truck Stops—FFP Marketing Company, Inc.; *U.S. Public*, pg. 604

DRIVETRAIN PLUS—Total On-Highway Drivetrain—Rockwell International Corporation; *U.S. Public*, pg. 1397

DRIXORAL—12 Hour Decongestant; Liquicaps, Tablets & Syrup—Schering-Plough Corporation; *U.S. Public*, pg. 1438

DRIXORAL—Cold/Flu, Allergy & Cough Products—Schering-Plough Healthcare Products Inc.; *U.S. Public*, pg. 1438

DRIZORB—NONE—The Andersons Incorporated; *U.S. Public*, pg. 111

DRONTAL—Tapeworm & Roundworm Control—Bayer AG; *Int'l*, pg. 171

DROP CABLE—NONE—Times Fiber Communications, Inc.; *U.S. Private*, pg. 629

DROPLET SYMBOL—Liquid Reagents—Beckman Instruments, Inc.; *U.S. Public*, pg. 199

DROPP—Agricultural Chemical—AgrEvo USA Company; *Int'l*, pg. 1203

DROPTELLA—Candies—Van Melle N.V.; *Int'l*, pg. 1450

DROSTE—Cocoa Powder & Chocolate Pastilles—CSM N.V.; *Int'l*, pg. 243

DROSTY-HOF—Wine—Distillers Corporation S.A.; *Int'l*, pg. 1129

DRUG & COSMETIC INDUSTRY—Trade Periodical—Advanstar Communications; *U.S. Private*, pg. 22

DRUG EMPORIUM OF ARIZONA—Retail Drug Stores—Drug Emporium of Arizona; *U.S. Private*, pg. 343

DRUG SAVING CENTRES—Drug Stores—Socanav Inc.; *Int'l*, pg. 1272

DRUG TOPICS—Medical Publication—Medical Economics Company Inc.; *U.S. Public*, pg. 1601

DRUG TOPICS RED BOOK—Medical Publication—Medical Economics Company Inc.; *U.S. Public*, pg. 1601

DRUGSEAL—Drug Packaging Press—Seal Products Incorporated; *U.S. Public*, pg. 849

DRUMDEAN—Heat Exchangers—Tranter, Inc.; *U.S. Public*, pg. 521

DRUMOCHTER—Scotch Whiskey—John Gross & Co.; *U.S. Private*, pg. 483

DRUMSTICK—Ice Cream Treats—Nestle Ice Cream Co.; *Int'l*, pg. 918

DRUMSTICK—Ice Cream Treat—Nestle USA; *Int'l*, pg. 916

DRY—Anti-Perspirant—Cussons (U.K.) LTD.; *Int'l*, pg. 1024

DRY & GO—Nail Enamel—Cosmair, Inc.; *Int'l*, pg. 818

DRY DOCK—Shoes—E.J. Footwear Corp.; *U.S. Public*, pg. 1684

DRY EYE THERAPY—Eye Drops—Bausch & Lomb Incorporated; *U.S. Public*, pg. 194

DRY FOOT—Socks & Knitted Headwear—Wigwam Mills, Inc.; *U.S. Public*, pg. 1175

DRY GUY—Adjustable Styling Dryer—Clairol, Inc.; *U.S. Public*, pg. 254

DRY IDEA—Anti-Perspirant—The Gillette Company; *U.S. Public*, pg. 743

DRY JOYS—Golf Shoes—Titleist & Foot-Joy Worldwide; *U.S. Public*, pg. 675

DRY LABO SYSTEM—Blood Sample Analysis System—Konica Corporation; *Int'l*, pg. 748

THE DRY LOOK—Hair Syling Preparations—The Gillette Company; *U.S. Public*, pg. 743

DRY MATE—Plastic Grocer Sacks—Sonoco Products Company; *U.S. Public*, pg. 1485

THE DRY PREPRESS BY POLAROID—NONE—Polaroid Corporation; *U.S. Public*, pg. 1313

DRY STICK BRUSH—Curler/Stylers—Sunbeam Household Products; *U.S. Public*, pg. 1533

DRY STICK I—Curler/Stylers—Sunbeam Household Products; *U.S. Public*, pg. 1533

DRY TECH—NONE—Polaroid Corporation; *U.S. Public*, pg. 1313

DRY-UR-FLY—Fishing Line—Cortland Line Co., Inc.; *U.S. Private*, pg. 277

DRY WEAR—Rainwear—Stearns Manufacturing Company; *U.S. Public*, pg. 940

DRYBLOT—Enzyme Overlay Membrane—Eastman Kodak Company; *U.S. Public*, pg. 550

DRYBREW—Brewing Method—Anheuser-Busch Companies, Inc.; *U.S. Public*, pg. 113

DRYCURE—Vulcanizing System—Royle Systems Group; *U.S. Private*, pg. 949

DRYFLO—Mist Collector—Donaldson Company, Inc.; *U.S. Public*, pg. 517

DRYGOLIN—NONE—Jotun A/S; *Int'l*, pg. 714

DRYJET—NONE—Polaroid Corporation; *U.S. Public*, pg. 1313

DRYJOYS—Shoes—Acushnet Company; *U.S. Public*, pg. 675

DRYJOYS—Golf Shoes—Fortune Brands, Inc.; *U.S. Public*, pg. 674

DRYMASTER—Laundry Dryers—Ecolab Inc.; *U.S. Public*, pg. 562

DRYPER'S—Diapers—Dryper's Corp.; *U.S. Private*, pg. 344

DRYTECH—Superabsorbent—The Dow Chemical Company; *U.S. Public*, pg. 522

DRYULE—Scientific Glassware for Laboratory Use—Wheaton Inc.; *Int'l*, pg. 67

DRYVIT—NONE—RPM, Inc.; *U.S. Public*, pg. 1356

DTERMINATOR—Telephone Terminal Block Systems—Raychem Corporation; *U.S. Public*, pg. 1362

DTERMINATOR 2—NONE—Raychem Corporation; *U.S. Public*, pg. 1362

DU-ALL—Drains, Refills & Recycles Antifreeze—Wynn's International, Inc.; *U.S. Public*, pg. 1782

DU CHEF SYL—Bouillons, Sauces, Mealmakers—Bestfoods; *U.S. Public*, pg. 223

DU RI DU BU—Dress Shoes—Mizuno Corporation; *Int'l*, pg. 884

DU-RO VITRES ET ACCESSOIRES D'AUTO—Retail ARG Sales—TCG International Inc.; *Int'l*, pg. 1336

DUA-LUX—Bathroom Tissue—Georgia-Pacific Corporation; *U.S. Public*, pg. 735

DUADACIN—Capsules; Antipyretic/Analgesic/Decongestant—Bradley Pharmaceuticals; *U.S. Public*, pg. 249

DUADACIN—Capsules; Antipyretic/Analgesic/Decongestant—Doak Dermatologics; *U.S. Public*, pg. 250

DUAL ACTION—Floor Scrub Brush—Flo-Pac Corporation; *U.S. Private*, pg. 414

DUAL ADJUST HEAD—Car Stereo Tapehead—Sony Electronics; *Int'l*, pg. 1281

DUAL-D—Communications Cables—General Cable Corporation; *Int'l*, pg. 1486

DUAL-D SCREENED—Shielded Communication Cable—General Cable Corporation; *Int'l*, pg. 1486

DUAL-DECK—Video Cassette Recorders—Go-Video, Inc.; *U.S. Public*, pg. 748

DUAL-DOKLIFT/LEVELER—Combination Hydraulic Scissors Lift & Hydraulic Dock Leveler—Rite-Hite Corporation; *U.S. Private*, pg. 933

DUAL DUTY PLUS—Home Sewing Thread—Coats & Clark Inc.; *Int'l*, pg. 300

DUAL DUTY XTRA—Thread—Coats North America; *Int'l*, pg. 300

DUAL FOIL MICRO SCREEN—Electric Shavers—Remington Products Company, L.L.C.; *U.S. Private*, pg. 921

DUAL LOCK—Fasteners—Southtec, Inc.; *U.S. Private*, pg. 1015

DUAL-LOK—Combined Lift/Leveler—Rite-Hite Corporation (WI); *U.S. Private*, pg. 933

DUAL-MELT—Batch Melting Power Supply—Inductotherm Corp.; *U.S. Private*, pg. 560

DUAL-PNEUMATIC—In-Space Atomizing Humidification Equipment—Herrmidifier Co., Inc.; *U.S. Public*, pg. 1639

DUAL POWER—Uninterruptible Power Supplies—Hayes Corporation, Regional Office; *U.S. Public*, pg. 801

DUAL SEAL—High Performance Dynamic Beam, Lip Seal Fittings—Titeflex Corporation; *Int'l*, pg. 1340

DUAL SHIELD—NONE—ESAB Welding & Cutting Products; *Int'l*, pg. 281

DUAL SHIELD WEATHER BARRIER—Weather Strip—The Standard Products Company; *U.S. Public*, pg. 1504

DUAL SURFACE—Floor Scrub Brush—Flo-Pac Corporation; *U.S. Private*, pg. 414

DUAL-SWITCH—Power Switching—Inductotherm Corp.; *U.S. Private*, pg. 560

DUAL TRACK—Rotary Shaver—Remington Products Company, L.L.C.; *U.S. Private*, pg. 921

DUAL-TRAK—Batch Melting Power Supply—Inductotherm Corp.; *U.S. Private*, pg. 560

DUAL WAVE—Microwave Ovens—General Electric Canada Inc.; *U.S. Public*, pg. 713

DUAL WHEEL EXCAVATOR—Underwater Bucketwheel Cutter—Ellicott Machine Corporation International; *U.S. Private*, pg. 372

DUALAY—Periodic Reversal of a Conductor Lay-Up in a Multi-Conductor Assembly—The Okonite Company; *U.S. Private*, pg. 813

DUALCON—NONE—Molex Incorporated; *U.S. Public*, pg. 1121

DUALEX—Transducer Protector Unit—Millipore Corporation; *U.S. Public*, pg. 1112

DUALITE—Signs—Dualite Inc.; *U.S. Private*, pg. 344

DUALITE—Polymeric Microspheres—Pierce & Stevens Corp.; *U.S. Private*, pg. 1019

DUALITE—Coating—Pratt & Lambert United, Inc.; *U.S. Public*, pg. 1466

DUALL—Corrosion Resistant Scrubbers & Fans—Met-Pro Corporation; *U.S. Public*, pg. 1100

DUALOCK—Protection Security Systems—Audiovox Corporation; *U.S. Public*, pg. 147

DUALPLEX—Tires—Bridgestone/Firestone, Inc.; *Int'l*, pg. 213

DUALSPORT—Motorcycle—American Suzuki Motor Corporation; *Int'l*, pg. 1323

DUALSTOR—Computer System—International Business Machines Corporation; *U.S. Public*, pg. 895

DUBARRY—Cosmetics—Carme' Cosmeceutical Sciences, Inc.; *U.S. Private*, pg. 213

DUBIX-DE SOUZA—Industrial Laundry Equipment—Electrolux, AB; *Int'l*, pg. 438

DUBL-DUTY—Wet/Dry Hand Vac—Hoover Company; *U.S. Public*, pg. 1065

DUBL-PANL—Stressed-Skin Building Systems—Behlen Mfg. Co.; *U.S. Private*, pg. 130

DUBLINER—NONE—Tegner & Son AB; *Int'l*, pg. 412

DUBLINER AND SHERIDAN'S—NONE—R & A Bailey & Co.; *Int'l*, pg. 409

DUBLO—Hot Water Storage—IMI Plc; *Int'l*, pg. 646

DUBOIS—Specialty Cleaning Compounds—DuBois Chemicals; *Int'l*, pg. 1437

DUBON—Canned Vegetables—Bush Brothers & Company; *U.S. Private*, pg. 189

DUBONNET—Aperitif—Groupe Pernod Ricard; *Int'l*, pg. 566

DUBOX—NONE—Berg Electronics; *U.S. Public*, pg. 212

DUBUQUE—Deli Sliced Sandwich Meat Slices—Hormel Foods Corp.; *U.S. Public*, pg. 840

DUCADOS—NONE—Tabacalera, S.A.; *Int'l*, pg. 1345

DUCAIR—Bath Products—Tsumura International; *Int'l*, pg. 1426

DUCANE—Gas Grills—The Climatic Corp.; *U.S. Private*, pg. 246

DUCATO—Car—Fiat Auto Ireland Ltd.; *Int'l*, pg. 481

DUCHE DE LONGUEVILLE—Cider—Groupe Pernod Ricard; *Int'l*, pg. 566

DUCK BUTTER—Industrial Chemical—Hercules Chemical Co., Inc.; *U.S. Private*, pg. 523

DUCK HEAD—Men's & Boy's Sportswear—Delta Woodside Industries, Inc.; *U.S. Public*, pg. 497

DUCK HEAD—Casual & Leisure Apparel—Duck Head Apparel; *U.S. Public*, pg. 498

DUCK-PAK—Sporting Goods—Brunswick Bowling & Billiards Corp.; *U.S. Public*, pg. 265

DUCKS UNLIMITED—NONE—Tandy Brands Accessories, Inc.; *U.S. Public*, pg. 1560

DUCKWALL-ALCO—Retail Chain—Duckwall-Alco Stores, Inc.; *U.S. Public*, pg. 533

DUCT-D-FUSER—Air Terminal—United McGill Corp.; *U.S. Private*, pg. 1122

DUCT FAS—Adhesives for Attaching Insulation Metal—H.B. Fuller Company; *U.S. Public*, pg. 686

DUCTILE—NONE—Glynwed International PLC; *Int'l*, pg. 554

DUCTILLITE—Tin Plate—WHX Corporation; *U.S. Public*, pg. 1726

DUCTLINER—Air Conditioning Insulation—Carter Holt Harvey Limited; *U.S. Public*, pg. 904

DUCTPIC—Cable—Lucent Technologies Inc.; *U.S. Public*, pg. 1017

DUCTWRAP—Industrial Insulation—Carter Holt Harvey Limited; *U.S. Public*, pg. 904

DUDLEY—Baseball Equipment—Spalding & Evenflo Companies, Inc.; *U.S. Private*, pg. 629

DUET—Presentation Scanner—PSC Inc.; *U.S. Public*, pg. 1245

DUETT—Shampoos—Wella Group; *Int'l*, pg. 1489

DUETTE—Luggage—American Tourister, Inc.; *U.S. Public*, pg. 1430

DUETTE—Window Covering Product—Hunter Douglas N.V.; *Int'l*, pg. 639

DUETTE DUOLITE—Honeycomb Shades With Two Fabrics on The Same Headrail—Hunter Douglas, Inc.; *Int'l*, pg. 639

DUETTE EASYGLIDE—NONE—Hunter Douglas, Inc.; *Int'l*, pg. 639

DUETTE EASYRISE SHADES—Honeycomb Shades With Clutch-and-Pulley Mechanism for Easy Operation—Hunter Douglas, Inc.; *Int'l*, pg. 639

DUETTE ECLIPSE—Black-Out Fabric with a Metallized Core—Hunter Douglas, Inc.; *Int'l*, pg. 639

DUETTE HONEYCOMB SHADES—Honeycomb Shades—Hunter Douglas, Inc.; *Int'l*, pg. 639

DUETTE PHENOMENA III—Triple Honeycomb Shades for Maximum Energy Efficiency—Hunter Douglas, Inc.; *Int'l*, pg. 639

DUETTE SIMPLICITY SHADES—Manual Hardware System for Skylights or Slanted Windows—Hunter Douglas, Inc.; *Int'l*, pg. 639

DUETTE SKYRISE SHADES—Special Application for Skylights or Slanted Shades—Hunter Douglas, Inc.; *Int'l*, pg. 639

DUETTE SMART SHADE—Curved Track System for Vertical or Horizontal Application—Hunter Douglas, Inc.; *Int'l*, pg. 639

DUETTE VERTIGLIDE—Vertical Honeycomb Shades—Hunter Douglas, Inc.; *Int'l*, pg. 639

DUEX—Film Cassettes—Eastman Kodak Company; *U.S. Public*, pg. 550

DUFF—Mixes—Gilster Mary Lee Corp.; *U.S. Private*, pg. 455

DUFF-NORTON—Jacks—Duff-Norton; *U.S. Public*, pg. 406

DUFFY'S—Removers—W.M. Barr & Co., Inc.; *U.S. Private*, pg. 117

DUFRAIS—Vinegars—Nestle S.A.; *Int'l*, pg. 915

DUK-IT—Smoking Receptacles—Smith McDonald Corp.; *U.S. Private*, pg. 1009

DUKE—Sporting Goods—Brunswick Bowling & Billiards Corp.; *U.S. Public*, pg. 265

DUKE—Cutlery—Buck Knives, Inc.; *U.S. Private*, pg. 177

DUKE CITY—Soft Lumber—Hanson PLC; *Int'l*, pg. 592

DUKE ENERGY—NONE—Duke Energy Corporation; *U.S. Public*, pg. 534

DUKE'S GIN AND DEVICE—Alcoholic Beverage—Sime Darby Berhad; *Int'l*, pg. 1249

DULAMEL—Interior Solvent Enamel—Benjamin Moore & Co.; *U.S. Private*, pg. 133

DULCIA—Cosmetic—L'Oreal S.A.; *Int'l*, pg. 818

DULCIORA—Sugar Confectionery—Cadbury Schweppes p.l.c.; *Int'l*, pg. 247

DULCITOS—Italian Pepperoncini—Trappey's Fine Foods, Inc.; *U.S. Private*, pg. 105

DULCOLAX—Laxative—Boehringer Ingelheim GmbH; *Int'l*, pg. 199

DULCOLAX—Laxative—Boehringer Ingelheim Italia S.p.A.; *Int'l*, pg. 199

DULUTH, WINNIPEG & PACIFIC RAILWAY—Freight Railroads—Grand Trunk Corporation (GTC); *Int'l*, pg. 258

DULUX—Finishes—Du Pont (E.I. Du Pont De Nemours & Co.); *U.S. Public*, pg. 530

DULUX—Paint—ICI Paints; *Int'l*, pg. 664

DULUX—Fluorescent Lamps—Siemens Corporation; *Int'l*, pg. 1245

DULUX ENDURANCE—Paint—ICI Paints; *Int'l*, pg. 664

DULUX INSPIRATIONS—Paint—ICI Paints; *Int'l*, pg. 664

DUM-DUM—Suckers—Spangler Candy Company; *U.S. Private*, pg. 1020

DUMAURIER—Cigarettes—Imasco Limited; *Int'l*, pg. 112

DUMMY—Confections—Van Melle N.V.; *Int'l*, pg. 1450

DUMOR—Animal Feeds—Tractor Supply Co.; *U.S. Public*, pg. 1627

DUMORE—Industrial Power Equipment—Dumore Corporation; *U.S. Private*, pg. 346

DUMP MASTER—Front Loading Refuse Truck—Dempster Equipment; *U.S. Private*, pg. 1089

DUN & BRADSTREET—Credit Services—Dun & Bradstreet; *U.S. Public*, pg. 535

DUN-BRITE—Metallic Colors—Dunmore Corporation; *U.S. Private*, pg. 346

DUN-CHROME—Metallized Films—Dunmore Corporation; *U.S. Private*, pg. 346

DUN-FAB—Metallized Fabrics—Dunmore Corporation; *U.S. Private*, pg. 346

DUN GUARD—Security Transfer Films—Dunmore Corporation; *U.S. Private*, pg. 346

DUN-KOTE—Special Coatings on Films—Dunmore Corporation; *U.S. Private*, pg. 346

DUN-LAM—Laminations for Industry—Dunmore Corporation; *U.S. Private*, pg. 346

DUN-LAR—Stainproof, Weatherable Films—Dunmore Corporation; *U.S. Private*, pg. 346

DUN-MET—Metallized Films for Aerospace—Dunmore Corporation; *U.S. Private*, pg. 346

DUN-NOVEL—Metallized PVC—Dunmore Corporation; *U.S. Private*, pg. 346

DUN-ORO—Gold Colored Films—Dunmore Corporation; *U.S. Private*, pg. 346

DUN-PRINT—Print Patterns, Custom Designs—Dunmore Corporation; *U.S. Private*, pg. 346

DUN-QUICK—Rapid Delivery Stock Films—Dunmore Corporation; *U.S. Private*, pg. 346

DUN-RAY—Solar & Energy Control Films—Dunmore Corporation; *U.S. Private*, pg. 346

DUN-SPUN—Metallized Non-Wovens—Dunmore Corporation; *U.S. Private*, pg. 346

DUN-STRIPE—Metallic Stripe Patterns—Dunmore Corporation; *U.S. Private*, pg. 346

DUN-THANE—Ployurethane Transfer Films—Dunmore Corporation; *U.S. Private*, pg. 346

DUN-TRAN—Metallic Transfers—Dunmore Corporation; *U.S. Private*, pg. 346

DUNCAN—Towing Products—Automatic Equipment Mfg. Co.; *U.S. Private*, pg. 101

DUNCAN—Toys—Duncan Toys Company; *U.S. Private*, pg. 409

DUNCAN—Electricity Meters—Landis & Staefa, Inc.; *Int'l*, pg. 800

DUNCAN ELECTRONICS—Potentiometers—BEI Sensors and Systems Company; *U.S. Public*, pg. 160

DUNCAN HINES—Prepared Mixes, Cookies, Frosting—The Procter & Gamble Company; *U.S. Public*, pg. 1330

DUNCANS SCOTCH—NONE—Star Industries Inc.; *U.S. Private*, pg. 1034

DUNE—Deodorant—The Gillette Company; *U.S. Public*, pg. 743

DUNES—Men's Shoes—E.J. Footwear Corp.; *U.S. Public*, pg. 1684

DUNFEY'S TAVERN—Restaurant—Omni Hotels; *U.S. Private*, pg. 1065

DUNGEONS & DRAGONS—Game—TSR, Inc.; *U.S. Private*, pg. 1185

DUNHEATH SCOTCH—Scotch—Laird & Company; *U.S. Private*, pg. 642

DUNHILL—Pipes & Smokers Accessories—Lane Limited; *Int'l*, pg. 1129

DUNHILL—Cigarettes—Rothmans UK Holdings Limited; *Int'l*, pg. 1129

DUNHILL CANARY ISLAND CIGARS—Cigars—Lane Limited; *Int'l*, pg. 1129

DUNHILL DOMINICAN—Cigars—Lane Limited; *Int'l*, pg. 1129

DUNHILL EARLY MORNING—Pipe Tobacco—Lane Limited; *Int'l*, pg. 1129

DUNHILL ELIZABETHAN MIXTURE—Pipe Tobacco—Lane Limited; *Int'l*, pg. 1129

DUNHILL GOLDEN HOURS—Pipe Tobacco—Lane Limited; *Int'l*, pg. 1129

DUNHILL LIGHT FLAKE—Pipe Tobacco—Lane Limited; *Int'l*, pg. 1129

DUNHILL LONDON MIXTURE—Pipe Tobacco—Lane Limited; *Int'l*, pg. 1129

DUNHILL MILD AROMATIC—Pipe Tobacco—Lane Limited; *Int'l*, pg. 1129

DUNHILL MILD BLEND—Pipe Tobacco—Lane Limited; *Int'l*, pg. 1129

DUNHILL MY MIXTURE 1129

DUNHILL NIGHTCAP—Pipe Tobacco—Lane Limited; *Int'l*, pg. 1129

DUNHILL NO.1 TOBACCO COLLECTION—Tobacco—Lane Limited; *Int'l*, pg. 1129

DUNHILL OLD MASTER—Scotch Whiskey—Grand Metropolitan Plc; *Int'l*, pg. 408

DUNHILL OLD MASTER—NONE—J&B Scotland; *Int'l*, pg. 410

DUNHILL PROFESSIONAL SEARCH—Employment Service—Dunhill Personnel System, Inc.; *U.S. Public*, pg. 1746

DUNHILL RUBBED FLAKE—Pipe Tobacco—Lane Limited; *Int'l*, pg. 1129

DUNHILL STANDARD MIXTURE—Pipe Mixture—Lane Limited; *Int'l*, pg. 1129

DUNHILL TEMPORARY SYSTEMS—Temporary Employment Service—Dunhill Personnel System, Inc.; *U.S. Public*, pg. 1746

DUNHILL-THE "ROYAL YACHT" MIXTURE—Pipe Tobacco—Lane Limited; *Int'l*, pg. 1129

DUNHILL TIN SAMPLER—Tobacco—Lane Limited; *Int'l*, pg. 1129

DUNHILL VIRGINIA READY RUBBED—Pipe Tobacco—Lane Limited; *Int'l*, pg. 1129

DUNKAROOS—Cookies with Frosting—General Mills, Inc.; *U.S. Public*, pg. 717

DUNKIN' DONUTS—Donut Shop Chain—Allied Domecq PLC; *Int'l*, pg. 62

DUNKIN' DONUTS CEREAL—Breakfast Cereal—Dunkin' Donuts Incorporated; *Int'l*, pg. 63

DUNKIN' DECAF—Decaffinated Coffee—Dunkin' Donuts Incorporated; *Int'l*, pg. 63

DUNLOP—Tires—Dunlop Tire Corporation; *Int'l*, pg. 1317

DUNLOP—NONE—Pacific Dunlop Limited; *Int'l*, pg. 1021

DUNLOP MAX 300 I—Tennis Racket—BTR plc; *Int'l*, pg. 124

DUNLOP MAX 200G—Tennis Racket—BTR plc; *Int'l*, pg. 124

DUNLOP MAXFLI—Golf Balls—BTR plc; *Int'l*, pg. 124

DUNLOPILLO—Beds—BTR plc; *Int'l*, pg. 124

DUNLOPLAN—Flooring—BTR plc; *Int'l*, pg. 124

DUNMORE—Engineered Films—Dunmore Corporation; *U.S. Private*, pg. 346

DUNNE & COLE—Apparel—Fred Meyer Stores; *U.S. Public*, pg. 1103

DUNNEWOOD—Wines—Canandaigua Wine Company, Inc.; *U.S. Public*, pg. 300

DUNNEWOOD VINEYARDS & WINERY—Wine—Canandaigua Wine Company Div.; *U.S. Public*, pg. 300

DUNOVER PLACE—Booklets for Home Imorovement Ideas—Georgia-Pacific Corporation; *U.S. Public*, pg. 735

DUO—High Security Locks—The Eastern Company; *U.S. Public*, pg. 548

DUO—Eyelash Adhesive—Menley & James Laboratories, Inc.; *U.S. Public*, pg. 1086

DUO-BOND—Glass-Mount Antennas—Allen Telecom Inc.; *U.S. Public*, pg. 45

DUO-BOND—Fastener Coatings—Duo-Fast Corporation; *U.S. Private*, pg. 347

DUO CORR—Corrugated Paper Medium & Corrugated Paperboard—Georgia-Pacific Corporation; *U.S. Public*, pg. 735

DUO-DUOMETER—Floor Squeege—White Mop Wringer Company; *U.S. Private*, pg. 1172

DUO-FAST—Nailers & Staplers—Duo-Fast Corporation; *U.S. Private*, pg. 347

DUO-GLASS—Coated Abrasive, Glass Polishing/Seaming—3M; *U.S. Public*, pg. 1604

DUO-LEAD PACK—X-ray Film Pack—Eastman Kodak Company; *U.S. Public*, pg. 550

DUO-MATIC—Temperature Regulators—Leslie Controls, Inc.; *U.S. Public*, pg. 1746

DUO-MEDIHALER—Isoproterenol Hydrochloride Phenylephrine Bitartrate, Prescription Drug—3M; *U.S. Public*, pg. 1604

DUO-OPTIC—Printing, Writing & Test-Scoring Paper—The Mead Corporation; *U.S. Public*, pg. 1074

DUO PAK—Cartons—White Cap, Inc.; *Int'l*, pg. 1207

DUO-PLY—Decorative Paper—The Mead Corporation; *U.S. Public*, pg. 1074

DUO RECORD—Sterilization Products—Propper Manufacturing Co., Inc.; *U.S. Private*, pg. 891

DUO RIB—Tires—Bridgestone/Firestone, Inc.; *Int'l*, pg. 213

DUO-SYNCRO-Chairs—Chairs—Knoll, Inc.; *U.S. Private*, pg. 627

DUO-TAPTITE—Bolts & Screws—Continental/Midland, Inc.; *U.S. Private*, pg. 268

DUO-TRACH KIT—Pharmaceutical Products—Astra USA, Inc.; *Int'l*, pg. 93

DUO-TUBE—Naso-Gastric Feeding Tube—Quest Medical, Inc.; *U.S. Public*, pg. 1352

DUOBOND—Coaxial Cable—Belden Inc.; *U.S. Public*, pg. 200

DUOBOND—Coaxial Cable—Belden Wire & Cable Company; *U.S. Public*, pg. 201

DUOBOX—Electrical Cranes & Hoists—American Crane & Equipment Corp.; *U.S. Private*, pg. 52

DUOCON—Adjustable Radiographic Cones for Therapeutic Use—Varian Associates, Inc.; *U.S. Public*, pg. 1710

DUODERM—Wound Care Products—Bristol-Myers Squibb Company; *U.S. Public*, pg. 253

DUODOZEN—Paperboard Article Carriers—The Mead Corporation; *U.S. Public*, pg. 1074

DUODOZEN—Cartons—Mead Packaging; *U.S. Public*, pg. 1074

DUOFILM—Liquid Wart Remover—Schering-Plough Corporation; *U.S. Public*, pg. 1438

DUOFILM—Wart Preparation—Schering-Plough Healthcare Products Inc.; *U.S. Public*, pg. 1438

DUOFOIL—Double Sided Foil Tape for Coaxial Cable—Belden Inc.; *U.S. Public*, pg. 200

DUOFOIL—Double Sided Foil Tape for Coaxial Cable—Belden Wire & Cable Company; *U.S. Public*, pg. 201

DUOFONE—Telephone Equipment—RadioShack; *U.S. Public*, pg. 1560

DUOGRAN—Herbicides—Agrolinz Melamin GmbH; *Int'l*, pg. 356

DUOGRAN—Plant Protectives—DSM Chemie Linz GmbH; *Int'l*, pg. 356

DUOGRANOL—Herbicides—Agrolinz Melamin GmbH; *Int'l*, pg. 356

DUOMAC—Fatty Diamine Salts—Akzo Nobel N.V.; *Int'l*, pg. 42

DUOMAT—Photo Developer—Eastman Kodak Company; *U.S. Public*, pg. 550

DUOMEEN—Plasticisers—Akzo Nobel N.V.; *Int'l*, pg. 42

DUOMET—Belt Surfacer—Buehler, Limited; *U.S. Public*, pg. 574

DUOPLANT—Gel Wart Remover—Schering-Plough Corporation; *U.S. Public*, pg. 1438

DUOPLANT—Wart Preparation—Schering-Plough Healthcare Products Inc.; *U.S. Public*, pg. 1438

DUOPLY—NONE—Clouth Gummiwerke AG; *Int'l*, pg. 297

DUOPROP—Sterndrive—Volvo Penta of the Americas, Inc.; *Int'l*, pg. 1477

DUOSIL—Wire Mesh & Silicone—Tecknit Incorporated; *U.S. Private*, pg. 1072

DUOSTAT—Grapaic Arts Products—GraphLine Inc.; *U.S. Private*, pg. 471

DUOTECT—Pressure Switch—Dwyer Instruments Inc.; *U.S. Private*, pg. 350

DUOTHERM—RV Air Conditioning—White Consolidated Industries, Inc.; *Int'l*, pg. 439

DUOTOUR—NONE—Boon Edam Inc.; *Int'l*, pg. 202

DUOVEC—Multidirectional Vector Magnetization—ITW Magnaflux; *U.S. Public*, pg. 866

DUOVISC—Viscoelastic Solution—Alcon Laboratories, Inc.; *Int'l*, pg. 916

DUPACO—Smoked Meats—BeefAmerica Operating Co., Inc.; *U.S. Private*, pg. 130

DUPAGE COUNTY (IL) BUSINESS DIRECTORY—Directory—Manufacturers' News, Inc.; *U.S. Private*, pg. 700

DUPE ELIMINATOR—Microcomputer Software for US Mailers—Group 1 Software, Inc.; *U.S. Public*, pg. 417

DUPEL—Electrode Devices—EMPI, Inc.; *U.S. Public*, pg. 545

DUPEN—Catheter—C.R. Bard, Inc.; *U.S. Public*, pg. 189

DUPHALAC—Lactulose Mixture Against Obstipation—Novo Nordisk A/S; *Int'l*, pg. 987

DUPHALAC—Pharmaceutical Product—Solvay Pharmaceuticals, Inc.; *Int'l*, pg. 1278

DUPLATE—Flat Glass—PPG Industries, Inc.; *U.S. Public*, pg. 1245

DUPLEX—Compact, Coaxial Loudspeaker—Altec Lansing Corp.; *U.S. Private*, pg. 479

DUPLEX—Tire—Bridgestone/Firestone, Inc.; *Int'l*, pg. 213

DUPLEX—Packaging Board—Stora Billerud AB; *Int'l*, pg. 1302

DUPLEX ND—Tires—Bridgestone/Firestone, Inc.; *Int'l*, pg. 213

DUPLEX 2000—Tires—Bridgestone/Firestone, Inc.; *Int'l*, pg. 213

DUPLI-COLOR—Aerosol—The Sherwin-Williams Company; *U.S. Public*, pg. 1465

DUPLI-COLOR—Automotive Aerosols—Pegasus International Corporation; *U.S. Private*, pg. 1046

DUPLI-COLOR—Spray & Touch Up Paints—Sherwin-Williams Diversified Brands, Inc.; *U.S. Public*, pg. 1466

DUPLICAL—Decals—American Decal & Mfg. Co.; *U.S. Private*, pg. 53

DUPLICUT—Surgical Instruments—Alcon Laboratories, Inc.; *Int'l*, pg. 916

DUPLIMATIC—Vertical Injection Molding Machines—Package Machinery Co.; *U.S. Private*, pg. 832

DUPLITIZE—X-Ray Film—Eastman Kodak Company; *U.S. Public*, pg. 550

DUPLO—Preschool Building Sets—LEGO Systems, Inc.; *Int'l*, pg. 805

DUPLOSAN—Crop Protection Agent—BASF AG; *Int'l*, pg. 103

DUPONOL—Surfactants—Du Pont (E.I. Du Pont De Nemours & Co.); *U.S. Public*, pg. 530

DUR-A-FRAME—NONE—The Thermos Company; *Int'l*, pg. 938

DURA-BLACK—Stovepipe & Fittings—Simpson Dura-Vent Co., Inc.; *U.S. Public*, pg. 1474

DURA-CAGE—CageLayer System or Cages—CTB International Corp.; *U.S. Public*, pg. 284

DURA-COAT—Antenna Finish—Allen Telecom Inc.; *U.S. Public*, pg. 45

DURA-CON—Antenna Coatings—Allen Telecom Inc.; *U.S. Public*, pg. 45

DURA/CONNECT—Gas Vent-Single Wall System—Simpson Dura-Vent Co., Inc.; *U.S. Public*, pg. 1474

DURA CONVERTIBLE SYSTEMS—Convertible Top Systems—Collins & Aikman Corporation; *U.S. Public*, pg. 399

DURA-CUBE—Water Softener Salt—Cargill Salt Inc.; *Int'l*, pg. 48

DURA-DISC—Wet Disc Brakes—Rockwell International Corporation; *U.S. Public*, pg. 1397

DURA EDGE—Cutlery—Imperial Schrade Corp.; *U.S. Private*, pg. 559

DURA-FLEX—Professional Antennas—Allen Telecom Inc.; *U.S. Public*, pg. 45

DURA-FLO—Power Steering Pumps—Steering and Suspension Division; *U.S. Public*, pg. 443

DURA-FOIL—Mat—Johns Manville Corporation; *U.S. Public*, pg. 927

DURA-FORM—NONE—Carpenter Technology Corporation; *U.S. Public*, pg. 307

DURA-FRESH—NONE—EcoScience Corporation; *U.S. Public*, pg. 563

DURA-GLAS—Glass Containers—Owens-Illinois, Inc.; *U.S. Public*, pg. 1238

DURA-GLAS—Swimming Pool Pumps—Sta-Rite Water Systems; *U.S. Public*, pg. 1767

DURA-GLASS—Fiberglass Mats—Johns Manville Corporation; *U.S. Public*, pg. 927

DURA-GRIND—Scientific Glassware for Laboratory Use—Wheaton Inc.; *Int'l*, pg. 67

DURA-INK—NONE—La-Co Industries Markal Company; *U.S. Private*, pg. 640

DURA KING—Sporting Goods—Brunswick Bowling & Billiards Corp.; *U.S. Public*, pg. 265

DURA-LINE—Electric Coreless Induction Furnaces—Inductotherm Corp.; *U.S. Private*, pg. 560

DURA-LITE—Nylon Flags—Dettra Flag Company; *U.S. Private*, pg. 328

DURA-LITE—Plastic Resin for Trash Bags—Reynolds Metals Company; *U.S. Public*, pg. 1385

DURA-LOK—Rings for Binders—Carstens Inc.; *U.S. Private*, pg. 216

DURA LOOP—NONE—Royal Rubber & Manufacturing Co.; *U.S. Private*, pg. 949

DURA-LUSTER CLEANER—Cleaner for Urethane Floors—Bruce Hardwood Floors; *U.S. Public*, pg. 1634

DURA-LUSTER FRESH FINISH—Urethane Dressing—Bruce Hardwood Floors; *U.S. Public*, pg. 1634

DURA-MASTER—Brakes—Rockwell International Corporation; *U.S. Public*, pg. 1397

DURA-NAP—NONE—Medline Industries, Inc.; *U.S. Private*, pg. 728

DURA PANL—Opaque Fiberglass Reinforced Plastic for Industrial/Corrosive Uses—Sequentia Inc.; *U.S. Public*, pg. 985

DURA-PLATE EPOXY—Mastic, Epoxy—Pratt & Lambert United, Inc.; *U.S. Public*, pg. 1466

DURA-PLUS 2100—Triple Wall Chimney System—Simpson Dura-Vent Co., Inc.; *U.S. Public*, pg. 1474

DURA POX EPOXY—Mastic, Epoxy—Pratt & Lambert United, Inc.; *U.S. Public*, pg. 1466

DURA-RAIL—Platform Side & End Rail—The Knapheide Mfg. Co.; *U.S. Private*, pg. 626

DURA-RIB—Roof & Wall Panel—Star Building Systems; *U.S. Public*, pg. 1394

DURA-SKRIM—Polyeth Sheeting—Raven Industries, Inc.; *U.S. Public*, pg. 1361

DURA-SPRAY—Pistol Nozzle—L.R. Nelson Corporation; *U.S. Private*, pg. 790

DURA-STONE—Sculpture Material—Austin Productions, Inc.; *U.S. Private*, pg. 100

DURA-TAB—Fire Brick—CFB Industries, Inc.; *U.S. Private*, pg. 194

DURA-TAB—Fire Brick—Chicago Fire Brick Co.; *U.S. Private*, pg. 194

DURA-TABLE—Ironing Table—Magla Products; *U.S. Private*, pg. 695

DURA-TORQUE—Shovels—UnionTools, Inc.; *U.S. Public*, pg. 17

DURA-TRED—Floor Marks & Finish—Johns Manville Corporation; *U.S. Public*, pg. 927

DURA-TRIM—Fabric—Narrow Fabric Industries, Inc.; *U.S. Private*, pg. 774

DURA-VENT—Type B Gas Vent—Simpson Dura-Vent Co., Inc.; *U.S. Public*, pg. 1474

DURA-Y—Multi Site Sensor—Nellcor Puritan Bennett Incorporated; *U.S. Public*, pg. 1039

DURA-COLOR—Coaxial Antennae Cable—General Cable Corporation; *Int'l*, pg. 1486

DURABACK—Release Papers used for Label Backing—Weyerhaeuser Company; *U.S. Public*, pg. 1764

DURABAKE—Switchgear Enclosure Finish—S & C Electric Company; *U.S. Private*, pg. 954

DURABEAM—Flashlight—Duracell International Inc.; *U.S. Public*, pg. 743

DURABELT—NONE—Clouth Gummiwerke AG; *Int'l*, pg. 297

DURABLE—Record Keeping Products—ATAPCO Office Products Group; *U.S. Private*, pg. 64

DURABLE CAST ALUMINUM & DESIGN COOKWARE—NONE—Regal Ware, Inc.; *U.S. Private*, pg. 917

DURABLE POWER—Uninteruptible Power Systems—International Power Machines Corporation; *Int'l*, pg. 126

DURABLOCK—Manometer—Dwyer Instruments Inc.; *U.S. Private*, pg. 350

DURABOLIN—Pharmaceutical—Organon Inc.; *Int'l*, pg. 48

DURABOND—NONE—CGC Inc.; *U.S. Public*, pg. 1660

DURABOND—Adhesives—DAP Inc.; *Int'l*, pg. 1486

DURABOND—Mortars, Mastics & Grouts—USG Corporation; *U.S. Public*, pg. 1660

DURABOOT—C.V. Boots—Rockford Acromatic Product Co.; *U.S. Private*, pg. 938

DURABRITE—Clear & Metallic Coatings—PPG Industries, Inc.; *U.S. Public*, pg. 1245

DURABUTE—High Voltage Electrical Distribution Protection Equipment—General Electric Canada Inc.; *U.S. Public*, pg. 713

DURACAP—Polyvinyl Chloride Resins—The Geon Company; *U.S. Public*, pg. 733

DURACARB—Hydroxyl Terminated Polycarbonate—PPG Industries, Inc.; *U.S. Public*, pg. 1245

DURACEL—Air Filter—AAF-International; *U.S. Private*, pg. 3

DURACELL—Batteries—Duracell International Inc.; *U.S. Public*, pg. 743

DURACLEAR—Labels—Avery Dennison Corporation Label Group; *U.S. Public*, pg. 153

DURACLEAR—Display Material—Eastman Kodak Company; *U.S. Public*, pg. 550

DURACLIP—Presentation Binders—ATAPCO Office Products Group; *U.S. Private*, pg. 64

DURACOLOR—NONE—Burlington Industries, Inc.; *U.S. Public*, pg. 268

DURACOLOR—Interior & Exterior Latex House, Wall & Trim Paint—PPG Industries, Inc.; *U.S. Public*, pg. 1245

DURACON—NONE—Howmedica, Inc.; *U.S. Public*, pg. 1282

DURACON—NONE—Pfizer Inc.; *U.S. Public*, pg. 1281

DURACRETE—Cement Board—CGC Inc.; *U.S. Public*, pg. 1660

DURACRON—Thermosetting Acrylic Coatings—PPG Industries, Inc.; *U.S. Public*, pg. 1245

DURACRYL—Chemical Reagent—ESA, Inc.; *U.S. Private*, pg. 354

DURACRYL—Acrylic Coatings, Thinners & Sealers—PPG Industries, Inc.; *U.S. Public*, pg. 1245

DURACT—Non-Narcotic Analgesic—American Home Products Corporation; *U.S. Public*, pg. 79

DURACURVE—Heat Exchanger—Lennox International Inc.; *U.S. Private*, pg. 659

DURAD—TFE/Polyimide Wire—Champlain Cable Corp.; *Int'l*, pg. 637

DURADENE—Synthetic Rubber—Bridgestone/Firestone, Inc.; *Int'l*, pg. 213

DURADIANT—Burner—Selas Corporation of America; *U.S. Public*, pg. 1454

DURADOR—Double Acting Doors—Clark Door Co., Inc.; *U.S. Private*, pg. 242

DURAEDGE—NONE—Crescent Manufacturing Company; *U.S. Private*, pg. 289

DURAFAXX—Engine Filter/Fluid Testing—Donaldson Company, Inc.; *U.S. Public*, pg. 517

DURAFELT—Felt—Central/Shippee, Inc.; *U.S. Private*, pg. 224

DURAFILL—Filling Agent—Akzo Nobel N.V.; *Int'l*, pg. 42

DURAFIN—Photo Developer & Replenisher—Eastman Kodak Company; *U.S. Public*, pg. 550

DURAFLAME—Processed Firelogs—Duraflame, Inc.; *U.S. Private*, pg. 348

DURAFLEX—Processing Trays, Photographic Film—Eastman Kodak Company; *U.S. Public*, pg. 550

DURAFLEX—Resins—Shell Chemical Co.; *Int'l*, pg. 1136

DURAFLEX—Gas Relining System—Simpson Dura-Vent Co., Inc.; *U.S. Public*, pg. 1474

DURAFLO—Photographic Chemicals—Eastman Kodak Company; *U.S. Public*, pg. 550

DURAFLO II—Heparin Treatment—Baxter Research Medical, Inc.; *U.S. Public*, pg. 196

DURAFOAM—Electrical Transmission Cable—General Cable Corporation; *Int'l*, pg. 1486

DURAFON—Anti-Fog Coating—Aearo Company; *U.S. Private*, pg. 23

DURAFORM—Oxygen Transducer System—Nellcor Puritan Bennett Incorporated; *U.S. Public*, pg. 1039

DURAGESIC—Pharmaceutical—Janssen Pharmaceutica, Inc.; *U.S. Public*, pg. 928

DURAGESIC—NONE—Johnson & Johnson; *U.S. Public*, pg. 927

DURAGLAS—NONE—The Flexitallic Group, Inc.; *U.S. Private*, pg. 413

DURAGLOSS—Automatic Floor Burnisher—The Kent Company; *Int'l*, pg. 440

DURAGRAPHIC—Printing Process—Avery Dennison Corporation; *U.S. Public*, pg. 152

DURAGRAPHIC—Labels—Avery Dennison Corporation Label Group; *U.S. Public*, pg. 153

DURAGRAPHIC—Decorative Coatings—PPG Industries, Inc.; *U.S. Public*, pg. 1245

DURAKOTA—Semolina—North Dakota Mill & Elevator Association; *U.S. Public*, pg. 804

DURAL LINER—Stainless Steel Chimney Liner—Simpson Dura-Vent Co., Inc.; *U.S. Public*, pg. 1474

DURALACE—Nonwoven Fabric—Chicopee Inc.; *Int'l*, pg. 113

DURALAR—Protective Coating for Urethane Foam—H.B. Fuller Company; *U.S. Public*, pg. 686

DURALASH—Eyelashes & Accessories—American International Industries; *U.S. Private*, pg. 57

DURALAST—Automotive Hard Parts Including Starters, Alternators & Brakes—AutoZone, Inc.; *U.S. Public*, pg. 150

DURALAST—NONE—Chemfab Corporation; *U.S. Public*, pg. 344

DURALCAN—Metal Matrix Composite—Alcan Aluminium Limited; *Int'l*, pg. 50

DURALIFE—High-Efficiency Lube Filters—Donaldson Company, Inc.; *U.S. Public*, pg. 517

DURALIFE II—Air Filter—Donaldson Company, Inc.; *U.S. Public*, pg. 517

DURALINE—Overlay Paper—The Mead Corporation; *U.S. Public*, pg. 1074

DURALINER—Truck Bed Liners—Durakon Industries, Inc.; *U.S. Public*, pg. 537

DURALINGUAL—Dentition Alloy Accessories—3M; *U.S. Public*, pg. 1604

DURALINK—Hexamethylene Bisthiosulfate Disodium Salt Dihydrate—Monsanto Company; *U.S. Public*, pg. 1124

DURALINK—Hexamethylene Bisthiosulfate Disodium Salt Dihydrate—Solutia Inc.; *U.S. Public*, pg. 1483

DURALITE—Air Cleaner—Donaldson Company, Inc.; *U.S. Public*, pg. 517

DURALITE ENVELOPES—NONE—Poly Pak America, Inc.; *U.S. Private*, pg. 875

DURALITE MAILERS—NONE—Poly Pak America, Inc.; *U.S. Private*, pg. 875

DURALITE-60—Fire Brick—CFB Industries, Inc.; *U.S. Private*, pg. 194

DURALITE-60—Fire Brick—Chicago Fire Brick Co.; *U.S. Private*, pg. 194

DURALITH—NONE—LucasVarity plc; *Int'l*, pg. 819

DURALUME—Screen Frames—Autoroll Machine Co., LLC; *U.S. Private*, pg. 101

DURALUX—Marine Coatings—Progress Paint Mfg. Co.; *U.S. Private*, pg. 890

DURALYN—NONE—Cordis, a Johnson & Johnson Company; *U.S. Public*, pg. 928

DURAMAG—Engine System Parts—Echlin Inc.; *U.S. Public*, pg. 560

DURAMAL—Special Treated Iron—Webster Industries Inc.; *U.S. Private*, pg. 1157

DURAMAT—NONE—Durakon Industries, Inc.; *U.S. Public*, pg. 537

DURAMATE—NONE—Berg Electronics; *U.S. Public*, pg. 212

DURAMAX—Lube Filter—Donaldson Company, Inc.; *U.S. Public*, pg. 517

DURAMIC—Diaphragms—American Meter Company; *Int'l*, pg. 1149

DURAMID—Cage Layer System or Cages—CTB International Corp.; *U.S. Public*, pg. 284

DURAMID—Gland Packing—James Walker & Co. Limited; *Int'l*, pg. 1485

DURAMORPH—Preservative-Free Morphine Sulfate Injection, USP—Elkins-Sinn, Inc.-Lederle; *U.S. Public*, pg. 79

DURAMUNE—Veterinary Pharmaceuticals—American Home Products Corporation; *U.S. Public*, pg. 79

DURAN—Borosilicate Glass—Schott Glaswerke; *Int'l*, pg. 1523

DURANAR—Heat-Curing Resin-Based Coatings—PPG Industries, Inc.; *U.S. Public*, pg. 1245

DURANE—Polyurethane Coatings—Raffi & Swanson, Inc.; *U.S. Private*, pg. 907

DURANEST—Local Anesthetic—Astra AB; *Int'l*, pg. 93

DURANEST—Pharmaceutical Products—Astra USA, Inc.; *Int'l*, pg. 93

DURANGO—Private Label Hispanic Grocery Products—Banner Wholesale Grocers, Inc.; *U.S. Private*, pg. 114

DURANGO—NONE—Porcelanite, Inc.; *Int'l*, pg. 573

DURANGO BOOT—Adult & Kids Western Boots—Georgia/Durango Boot Company; *U.S. Public*, pg. 1684

DURANGO FARM & RANCH—Footwear—Georgia/Durango Boot Company; *U.S. Public*, pg. 1684

DURANGO TRUCK'N BOOTS—Footwear—Georgia/Durango Boot Company; *U.S. Public*, pg. 1684

DURANT—Counting & Measuring Instruments—Cutler-Hammer Products; *U.S. Public*, pg. 556

DURANT—Counting & Controlling Instruments—Eaton Corporation; *U.S. Public*, pg. 555

DURAPAK—Liquid Coated GC Packing—Millipore Corporation; *U.S. Public*, pg. 1112

DURAPANE—Tempered Glass—Gemtron Corporation; *Int'l*, pg. 1523

DURAPHRAM—Diaphragms—Osmonics, Inc.; *U.S. Public*, pg. 1233

DURAPINE—Pressure Treaded Decking Products—Cox Wood Preserving Co.; *U.S. Private*, pg. 283

DURAPIPE-S.LP—NONE—Glynwed International PLC; *Int'l*, pg. 554

DURAPLANK—NONE—Safway Steel Products Inc.; *U.S. Public*, pg. 1389

DURAPLUS—C.V. Boots—Rockford Acromatic Product Co.; *U.S. Private*, pg. 938

DURAPLUS—Chemicals—Volvo Penta of the Americas, Inc.; *Int'l*, pg. 1477

DURAPORE—Membrane, Cartridge—Millipore Corporation; *U.S. Public*, pg. 1112

DURAPORE—Surgical Tape, Heavy Duty—3M; *U.S. Public*, pg. 1604

DURAPRINT—Urethane Squeegee—Autoroll Machine Co., LLC; *U.S. Private*, pg. 101

DURAPRINT—Fabric Labels—Markem Corporation; *U.S. Private*, pg. 704

DURAROME—Solid Flavors—Firmenich; *Int'l*, pg. 486

DURASCALE—Drafting Machin Scales—OCE-U.S.A.; *Int'l*, pg. 994

DURASCRUB—Automatic Scrubbers—The Kent Company; *Int'l*, pg. 440

DURASEAL—Mechanical Seals—Flowserve Corporation; *U.S. Public*, pg. 658

DURASEAL—Tempered Glass—Gemtron Corporation; *Int'l*, pg. 1523

DURASEAL—Notebook Binder—The Mead Corporation; *U.S. Public*, pg. 1074

DURASEAL—Splices—Raychem Corporation; *U.S. Public*, pg. 1362

DURASENSOR—Pressure-Mounted Oxygen Transducer—Nellcor Puritan Bennett Incorporated; *U.S. Public*, pg. 1039

DURASHARP—Scissors—Fiskars Oy AB; *Int'l*, pg. 492

DURASOFT—Contact Lenses—Wesley-Jessen; *U.S. Private*, pg. 111

DURASOFT COLORS—Contact Lenses—Wesley-Jessen; *U.S. Private*, pg. 111

DURASOFT COLORS LENS CARE SYSTEM—Solutions for Tinted & Colored Soft Contact Lenses—Wesley-Jessen; *U.S. Private*, pg. 111

DURASOFT 3 FLEXIWEAR—Soft Contact Lenses—Wesley-Jessen; *U.S. Private*, pg. 111

DURASOLE—Men's Shoes—E.J. Footwear Corp.; *U.S. Public*, pg. 1684

DURASORB—Saturating Kraft Paperboard—Westvaco Corporation; *U.S. Public*, pg. 1762

DURAPSIN—Roller Tool Materials—DSM Engineering Plastic Products; *Int'l*, pg. 354

DURASPORT—Sport Utility Liner—Durakon Industries, Inc.; *U.S. Public*, pg. 537

DURASPRAY—Fireproofing for Steel—Stanchem Inc.; *Int'l*, pg. 1030

DURASTAT—Industrial Manufacturing Chemicals—PPG Industries, Inc.; *U.S. Public*, pg. 1245

DURASWEEP—NONE—The Kent Company; *Int'l*, pg. 440

DURATEARS NATURALE—Ocular Lubricant Ointment—Alcon Laboratories, Inc.; *Int'l*, pg. 916

DURATEC—NONE—ETEX; *Int'l*, pg. 430

DURATHERM—Thermal Bar Code Labels—Intermec Technologies Corporation; *U.S. Public*, pg. 1699

DURATION—NONE—Nellcor Puritan Bennett Incorporated; *U.S. Public*, pg. 1039

DURATION—Rolled Rubber Sheet—Robbins, Inc.; *U.S. Private*, pg. 934

DURATION—Over-the-Counter Nasal Spray—Schering-Plough Corporation; *U.S. Public*, pg. 1438

DURATION—Nasal Decongestant Spray—Schering-Plough Healthcare Products Inc.; *U.S. Public*, pg. 1438

DURATION PLUS—Rolled Rubber Sheet Over Pad—Robbins, Inc.; *U.S. Private*, pg. 934

DURATOOL—Pocket & Hunting Knives—Camillus Cutlery Co.; *U.S. Private*, pg. 203

DURATRAC—Carpet Extractors—The Kent Company; *Int'l*, pg. 440

DURATRANS—Photo Film—Eastman Kodak Company; *U.S. Public*, pg. 550

DURATREX—Sintered Stainless Steel Cartridge Filters—Osmonics, Inc.; *U.S. Public*, pg. 1233

DURATROL—Household Flea Spray—3M; *U.S. Public*, pg. 1604

DURATRUNK—Pickup Truck Toolbox—Durakon Industries, Inc.; *U.S. Public*, pg. 537

DURATUBE—Heat Exchanger—Lennox International Inc.; *U.S. Public*, pg. 659

DURATYPE 240—Keyboard Lettering System—Kroy Inc.; *U.S. Public*, pg. 1339

DURATYPE 240 SE—Keyboard Lettering System—Kroy Inc.; *U.S. Public*, pg. 1339

DURAVINYL—Vinyl Tile—American Biltrite Inc.; *U.S. Public*, pg. 68

DURAWEB—Printing Papers—Kimberly-Clark Corporation; *U.S. Public*, pg. 958

DURAY—Cosmetic & Travel Accessories—Goody Products, Inc.; *U.S. Public*, pg. 1177

DURAZONE—Antiozonant—Uniroyal Chemical Company, Inc.; *U.S. Public*, pg. 460

DURBER—Steel Plates—British Steel Plc; *Int'l*, pg. 220

DURCO—Equipment—Flowserve Corporation; *U.S. Public*, pg. 658

DURCO-CAST—Equipment—Flowserve Corporation; *U.S. Public*, pg. 658

DURCO-D—Equipment—Flowserve Corporation; *U.S. Public*, pg. 658

DURCOMETER—Metering Pumps—Flowserve Corporation; *U.S. Public*, pg. 658

DURCON—Alloys—Flowserve Corporation; *U.S. Public*, pg. 658

DURCOPUMP—Pumps—Flowserve Corporation; *U.S. Public*, pg. 658

DURESTER—Engineering Products—Arkwright, Inc; *Int'l*, pg. 994

DURETHAN—Polyamide Resin—Bayer AG; *Int'l*, pg. 171

DURETHANE—Polyurethane Coatings & Finishes—PPG Industries, Inc.; *U.S. Public*, pg. 1245

DUREX—Latex Condoms—London International Group plc; *Int'l*, pg. 815

DUREZ—Phenolic Resins & Molding Compounds—Occidental Chemical Corporation; *U.S. Public*, pg. 1210

DURFRESH—Plastic Packaging—Grace Packaging; *U.S. Public*, pg. 755

DURICEF—Oral Cephalosporin—Bristol-Myers Squibb Company; *U.S. Public*, pg. 253

DURICEF—Pharmaceutical Prod. for Infections, Tonsillitis & Pharyngitis—Bristol-Myers Squibb U.S. Pharmaceutical Group; *U.S. Public*, pg. 255

DURICHLOR—Alloys—Flowserve Corporation; *U.S. Public*, pg. 658

DURIRON—Equipment—Flowserve Corporation; *U.S. Public*, pg. 658

DURITE—Coated Abrasives—Norton Company; *Int'l*, pg. 1173

DURKEE—Herbs & Spices—Burns, Philp & Company Limited; *Int'l*, pg. 236

DURKEE SPICES/SEASONINGS—NONE—Tone Brothers Inc.; *Int'l*, pg. 237

DURKEX—Fats & Oils—Van den Bergh Foods Company; *Int'l*, pg. 1436

DURKEX 500—Fats and Oils—Van den Bergh Foods Company; *Int'l*, pg. 1436

DURKO—Fats & Oils—Van den Bergh Foods Company; *Int'l*, pg. 1436

DURKOPP—Sewing Machines—Durkopp Adler AG; *Int'l*, pg. 468

DURLOK—Locknuts—SPS Technologies, Inc.; *U.S. Public*, pg. 1419

DURO—Adhesive—Loctite Corp. North American Group; *Int'l*, pg. 611

DURO—Paper & Paperboard—Sonoco Products Company; *U.S. Public*, pg. 1485

DURO-BOARD—Roof Insulation—Johns Manville Corporation; *U.S. Public*, pg. 927

DURO-CORES—Wound Paper Tubes—Sonoco Products Company; *U.S. Public*, pg. 1485

DURO-LAST—Roofing System—Duro-Last Roofing, Inc.; *U.S. Public*, pg. 349

DURO ZONE—Forced Air Zone Control Dampers & Panels—Duro Dyne Corporation; *U.S. Private*, pg. 349

DURO-M—Flame Retardant Papers—Wausau-Mosinee Paper Corporation; *U.S. Public*, pg. 1747

DUROCHOLOR—Chemical Products—Haviland Enterprises; *U.S. Private*, pg. 511

DUROCK—Cement Board—CGC Inc.; *U.S. Public*, pg. 1660

DUROCK—Cement Board—USG Corporation; *U.S. Public*, pg. 1660

DUROCRETE—Paint—Swire Pacific Limited; *Int'l*, pg. 1328

DUROFLEX—Offset Printing Blankets—Reeves International; *Int'l*, pg. 507

DUROFLOW—Displacement Blowers—Gardner Denver Machinery Inc.; *U.S. Public*, pg. 703

DUROGRAPHIC—Photo Typesetters—AGFA EPS Division; *Int'l*, pg. 172

DUROI—Bread—Groupe Limagrain; *Int'l*, pg. 566

DUROID—Industrial Roofing Membrane—Domtar Inc.; *Int'l*, pg. 416

DUROID—Microwave Laminate—Rogers Corporation; *U.S. Public*, pg. 1402

DUROLENE—Wound Paper Tubes—Sonoco Products Company; *U.S. Public*, pg. 1485

DUROLL—Calender Roll Cover Used in Yankee Paper Machine—Harnischfeger Industries, Inc.; *U.S. Public*, pg. 788

DUROLOK—Adhesive—Unilever Plc; *Int'l*, pg. 1433

DURON—Paper Tubes—Sonoco Products Company; *U.S. Public*, pg. 1485

DURONET—Extruded Plastic Net—Nalle Plastics Inc.; *U.S. Private*, pg. 773

DUROPIPE—Bituminized Fibre Pipes—Sonoco Products Company; *U.S. Public*, pg. 1485

DUROS—Human Implantable System—Alza Corporation; *U.S. Public*, pg. 62

DUROSET—Resin—Unilever Plc; *Int'l*, pg. 1433

DUROWELD—Impregnated Paper Cones & Tubes—Sonoco Products Company; *U.S. Public*, pg. 1485

DUROX—Paper & Paperboard—Sonoco Products Company; *U.S. Public*, pg. 1485

DURRAX—Pharmaceuticals—Rhone-Poulenc Rorer - U.S.; *Int'l*, pg. 1110

DURSBAN—Insecticide—The Dow Chemical Company; *U.S. Public*, pg. 522

DURSBEL—Insecticide—The Dow Chemical Company; *U.S. Public*, pg. 522

DURST—Farm Irrigation Drives—Regal-Beloit Corporation; *U.S. Public*, pg. 1370

DURYEAS—Corn Starch, Corn Flour & Corn Starch for Laundry—Bestfoods; *U.S. Public*, pg. 223

DUSCHDAS—Body Care Products—Sara Lee Corporation; *U.S. Public*, pg. 1432

DUSCHDAS—Shower Product—SmithKline Beecham plc; *Int'l*, pg. 1264

DUSPATALIN—Antipasmodic—Novo Nordisk A/S; *Int'l*, pg. 987

DUSSEK CAMPBELL—Coatings—Burmah Castrol plc; *Int'l*, pg. 234

DUST-CAT—Media Filtration—United Air Specialists, Inc.; *U.S. Public*, pg. 382

DUST DEMON—Disposable Respirator—Aearo Company; *U.S. Private*, pg. 23

DUST FOE—Pre-Filter—Donaldson Company, Inc.; *U.S. Public*, pg. 517

DUST FORCE—Premium Dust Mop—Rubbermaid Incorporated; *U.S. Public*, pg. 1411

DUST-HOG—Dust Collector—United Air Specialists, Inc.; *U.S. Public*, pg. 382

DUST MANNET—NONE—Euroclean; *Int'l*, pg. 440

DUST MASTER—Dustless FD&C Dye—Warner-Jenkinson Co.; *U.S. Public*, pg. 1696

DUST-OFF—Magnesium Chloride for Dust Control—Cargill Salt; *U.S. Private*, pg. 210

DUST-OFF PLUS—Precise Dusting of Negatives, Camera & Lab Equip. & Computers—Falcon Safety Products Inc.; *U.S. Private*, pg. 392

DUST-OFF PRO SYSTEM—Implement to Remove Dust from Records & Stero Equipment—Falcon Safety Products Inc.; *U.S. Private*, pg. 392

DUSTAC—Anti-Corrosion Chemicals for Roads—Georgia-Pacific Corporation; *U.S. Public*, pg. 735

DUSTAC—Pillow Blocks—The Torrington Co.; *U.S. Public*, pg. 877

DUSTBUSTER—Hand Held Vacuum—The Black & Decker Corporation; *U.S. Public*, pg. 233

DUSTBUSTER POWERPRO—Household Products—The Black & Decker Corporation; *U.S. Public*, pg. 233

DUSTER—Cover—Bestop, Inc.; *Int'l*, pg. 830

DUSTER PLUS—Wax-Free Cleaner—S.C. Johnson & Son, Inc.; *U.S. Private*, pg. 592

DUSTMASTER—Dust Control—Mapco Natural Gas Liquids Inc.; *U.S. Public*, pg. 1042

DUSTMASTER—Color Products—Universal Foods Corporation; *U.S. Public*, pg. 1695

DUSTRET A—Dry Potato Seed Treatment—Agsco, Inc.; *U.S. Private*, pg. 27

DUSTTRAK—Aerosol Monitor—TSI Incorporated; *U.S. Public*, pg. 1559

DUTCH BOY—Paints & Coatings—The Sherwin-Williams Company; *U.S. Public*, pg. 1465

DUTCH BOY—Solders—Taracorp, Inc.; *U.S. Private*, pg. 1068

DUTCH BRAND—Gloss Oil, Gloss Latex, Flat Latex, Exterior Finishes—Perry & Derrick Co.; *U.S. Private*, pg. 854

DUTCH FARMS—Frozen Foods—Hanover Foods Corporation; *U.S. Private*, pg. 499

DUTCH GIRL—Apple Butter & Jellies—J.M. Smucker Company; *U.S. Public*, pg. 1480

DUTCH HARBOR—Seafood Products—UniSea Foods, Inc.; *Int'l*, pg. 940

DUTCH MAID—Pasta—Borden, Inc.; *U.S. Private*, pg. 157

DUTCH MASTERS—Pipe Tobacco—Consolidated Cigar Corp.; *U.S. Private*, pg. 690

DUTCH MASTERS—Domestic Cigars—Consolidated Cigar Corporation; *U.S. Private*, pg. 690

DUTCH MASTERS CAVENDISH—Pipe Tobaccos—Consolidated Cigar Corporation; *U.S. Private*, pg. 690

DUTCH QUALITY HOUSE—Meat—Continental Grain Company; *U.S. Private*, pg. 268

DUTCH STANDARD—NONE—Harrison Paint Corp.; *U.S. Private*, pg. 506

DUTCH TREATS—Domestic Cigars—Consolidated Cigar Corporation; *U.S. Private*, pg. 690

DUTCHIE—Soft Pretzels—J & J Snack Foods Corporation; *U.S. Public*, pg. 916

DUTTON CHILDRENS—Children's Harcover Books—Penguin Putnam Inc.; *Int'l*, pg. 1027

DUTTON & NAL—Adult Hardcover Books—Penguin Putnam Inc.; *Int'l*, pg. 1027

DUVAL—NONE—Bacardi-Martini Belgium; *U.S. Private*, pg. 109

DUVOID—Urological Drug—Roberts Pharmaceutical Corporation; *U.S. Public*, pg. 1393

DUYVIS—Grocery Products—Sara Lee Corporation; *U.S. Public*, pg. 1432

D'VERSIBIT—Flexible Bit System—Greenlee Textron; *U.S. Public*, pg. 1589

DWYER—Pressure Switch—Dwyer Instruments Inc.; *U.S. Private*, pg. 350

DY-O-DERM—Pharmaceutical Products—Galderma Laboratories, Inc.; *Int'l*, pg. 819

DYALL—NONE—Lawter International, Inc.; *U.S. Public*, pg. 980

DYALON—NONE—Lawter International, Inc.; *U.S. Public*, pg. 980

DYATRON—NONE—SunGard Data Systems Inc.; *U.S. Public*, pg. 1534

DYAZIDE—Potassium Sparing Dieuretic for Cardiovascular—SmithKline Beecham Corporation; *Int'l*, pg. 1264

DYAZIDE—Cardiopulmonary Drug—SmithKline Beecham plc; *Int'l*, pg. 1264

DYAZIDE—Diuretic—SmithKline Beecham Research Limited; *Int'l*, pg. 1266

DYCILL—Pharmaceutical Prods.—SmithKline Beecham Laboratories; *Int'l*, pg. 1264

DYCILL—Antibiotic—SmithKline Beecham plc; *Int'l*, pg. 1264

DYCLEER—Herbicide—Sandoz Agro, Inc.; *Int'l*, pg. 974

DYCLONE—Pharmaceutical Products—Astra USA, Inc.; *Int'l*, pg. 93

DYCOR—Mass Spectrometer—AMETEK, Inc.; *U.S. Public*, pg. 99

DYDEX—Lignosulfonate Dye Dispersant Extender—Georgia-Pacific Corporation; *U.S. Public*, pg. 735

DYEMATREX—Protein Screening Kits—Amicon, Inc.; *U.S. Public*, pg. 1113

DYGRATYL—Vitamin D-Derivative—Novo Nordisk A/S; *Int'l*, pg. 987

DYKEN—Winding Machinery—Wisconsin Automated Machinery Corp.; *U.S. Private*, pg. 1184

DYMACEL—Casual Shoes—Jack Schwartz Shoes, Inc.; *U.S. Private*, pg. 974

DYMELOR—Acetohexamide, Lilly—Eli Lilly and Company; *U.S. Public*, pg. 992

DYMEREX—Modified Rosin—Hercules Incorporated; *U.S. Public*, pg. 809

DYMETROL—Elastomeric Tape—Du Pont (E.I. Du Pont De Nemours & Co.); *U.S. Public*, pg. 530

DYMIST—Aerosol Valve—Risdon Corporation; *U.S. Public*, pg. 463

DYMO—Labeling, Office Supplies—Esselte AB; *Int'l*, pg. 459

DYMO—Electronic and Embossing Labeling Systems—Esselte Corporation; *Int'l*, pg. 459

DYMORIG—Power Tools—Milwaukee Electric Tool Corp.; *Int'l*, pg. 96

DYN-AU-TURN—Vertica Tureet Lathe—WCI Machine Tools & Systems; *Int'l*, pg. 440

DYN-O-MISER—Ball Valve, High Pressure—Worcester Controls Corp.; *Int'l*, pg. 128

DYNA—Trucks & Buses—Toyota Motor Corporation; *Int'l*, pg. 1411

DYNA—Generators and Accessories—WINCO; *U.S. Private*, pg. 350

DYNA-BELT—Oil Skimmer—Ferguson International, Inc.; *U.S. Private*, pg. 401

DYNA BILT—NONE—Burtman Iron Works, Inc.; *U.S. Private*, pg. 188

DYNA CLEAN—Electric Vacuums & Rug Shampooers—Bissell Inc.; *U.S. Private*, pg. 145

DYNA-CUT—Well Abandonment System—Smith International, Inc.; *U.S. Public*, pg. 1478

DYNA-DAMP—Vibration & Sound Dampening—Lord Corporation; *U.S. Private*, pg. 675

DYNA-DECK—Railroad Shock & Vibration Mounts—Lord Corporation; *U.S. Private*, pg. 675

DYNA-DECK—Screening—Telsmith, Inc.; *U.S. Public*, pg. 141

DYNA-DISC—Oil skimmer—Ferguson International, Inc.; *U.S. Private*, pg. 401

DYNA DRIVE—Tillage System—M&W; *U.S. Public*, pg. 35

DYNA FLEX—Beam Delivery Systems—Laser Power Corporation; *U.S. Private*, pg. 652

DYNA-FLEX—Vibratory Conveyors—TCC Industries; *U.S. Public*, pg. 1554

DYNA GLIDE—Motorcycles—Harley-Davidson, Inc.; *U.S. Public*, pg. 786

DYNA GRIP—Muffler Clamps—Heckethorn Mfg. Company, Inc.; *U.S. Private*, pg. 519

DYNA-LOCK—All-In-One Brackets—Bristol-Myers Squibb Company; *U.S. Public*, pg. 253

DYNA-MITE—Self-Propelled Aerial Work Platform—Mayville Engineering Co., Inc.; *U.S. Private*, pg. 718

DYNA MITE—Small Video & Audio Routing Switchers—Meret Communications; *U.S. Public*, pg. 1233

DYNA-POISE—Autopsy Table with Electro-Mechanical Adjustments—The Jewett Refrigerator Co., Inc.; *U.S. Private*, pg. 952

DYNA-SCRUB—Abrasive Rotary Brush for Scrubbing—Flo-Pac Corporation; *U.S. Private*, pg. 414

DYNA SEALS—Rubber to Metal Seals—Wynn's-Precision, Inc.; *U.S. Public*, pg. 1783

DYNA-STAR—Hydraulically Powered Lubrication Pumps—Graco Inc.; *U.S. Public*, pg. 756

DYNA STOP—Electronic Brake—Reuland Electric Company; *U.S. Private*, pg. 925

DYNA-TORK—Nut Runner—Chicago Pneumatic Tool Company; *Int'l*, pg. 96

DYNA-MIX—Stirrer—Fisher Scientific Company; *U.S. Private*, pg. 658

DYNABAC—NONE—Eli Lilly and Company; *U.S. Public*, pg. 992

DYNABOLT—Mortise Deadbolt—Unican Security Systems Ltd.; *Int'l*, pg. 1432

DYNABUS—Communication Business—Tandem Computers Inc.; *U.S. Public*, pg. 417

DYNABUS+—Business Interprocessor—Tandem Computers Inc.; *U.S. Public*, pg. 417

DYNAC II—Centrifuge—Becton Dickinson Primary Care Diagnostics; *U.S. Public*, pg. 199

DYNACELL—Diesel Engine AirIntake Filter—Farr Company; *U.S. Public*, pg. 613

DYNACELL—Cell Growth System—Millipore Corporation; *U.S. Public*, pg. 1112

DYNACHARGE—NONE—Duracell International Inc.; *U.S. Public*, pg. 743

DYNACIRC—Antihypertensive—Novartis AG; *Int'l*, pg. 971

DYNACIRC—Management of Hypertension—Sandoz Pharmaceuticals Corp.; *Int'l*, pg. 974

DYNACLAD—NONE—Dynamic Materials Corporation; *U.S. Public*, pg. 539

DYNACOR—NONE—Medline Industries, Inc.; *U.S. Private*, pg. 728

DYNACOUPLE—NONE—Dynamic Materials Corporation; *U.S. Public*, pg. 539

DYNADOME—Pressure Regulating Dome Type Valves—Circle Seal Controls, Inc.; *U.S. Public*, pg. 1746

DYNAFLEX—Modified Bitumen Base Flashing—Johns Manville Corporation; *U.S. Public*, pg. 927

DYNAFLEX—Elastomeric Flexible Couplings—Lord Corporation; *U.S. Private*, pg. 675

DYNAFLEX—NONE—Pfizer Inc.; *U.S. Public*, pg. 1281

DYNAFLEX COUPLINGS—Couplings—Lord Corporation, Mechanical Products Division; *U.S. Private*, pg. 676

DYNAFLOW—High Pressure Hand & Relief Valves—Circle Seal Controls, Inc.; *U.S. Public*, pg. 1746

DYNAFOCAL—Aircraft Engine Mounts & Access.—Lord Corporation; *U.S. Private*, pg. 675

DYNAFOCAL MOUNTS—Mounts—Lord Corporation, Mechanical Products Division; *U.S. Private*, pg. 676

DYNAFOLD—Paper Folder—Michael Business Machines Corporation; *U.S. Private*, pg. 740

DYNAFORCE—HVAC Equipment—Mestek, Inc.; *U.S. Public*, pg. 1099

DYNAFORM—NONE—Dynamic Materials Corporation; *U.S. Public*, pg. 539

DYNAGRIP—Handle—Becton Dickinson & Co., Massachusetts Div.; *U.S. Public*, pg. 199

DYNAGUARD—Alternating Pressure Mattress—Span-America Medical Systems Inc.; *U.S. Public*, pg. 1495

DYNAKAP—Modified Bitumen Roofing—Johns Manville Corporation; *U.S. Public*, pg. 927

DYNALIFT—Telescopic Handlers—Gehl Company; *U.S. Public*, pg. 704

DYNALINK—Database Access System—Fair, Isaac and Company, Inc.; *U.S. Public*, pg. 609

DYNALITE—NONE—RPM, Inc.; *U.S. Public*, pg. 1356

DYNALLOY—Manganese Silicon Bronze—Mueller Industries, Inc.; *U.S. Public*, pg. 1141

DYNALOCK—NONE—Dynamic Materials Corporation; *U.S. Public*, pg. 539

DYNALOCK—Anterior Spinal Fixation System—Sofamor Danek Group, Inc.; *U.S. Public*, pg. 1482

DYNALYTE—Outdoor Products—The Black & Decker Corporation; *U.S. Public*, pg. 233

DYNAMAG—Magnetic Lock—Exit Device Division; *U.S. Public*, pg. 876

DYNAMAR—Polymer Processing Additive—3M; *U.S. Public*, pg. 1604

DYNAMRK—Coated Plastics for Signs—3M; *U.S. Public*, pg. 1604

DYNAMASK KM—Photoimageable Solder Masks—Morton International, Inc.; *U.S. Public*, pg. 1134

DYNAMATCH—Merge/Purge Service—Fair, Isaac and Company, Inc.; *U.S. Public*, pg. 609

DYNAMATIC—Clutches, Brakes, Drives, Controls & Dynamometers—Eaton Corporation; *U.S. Public*, pg. 555

DYNAMAX—Footwear Cushioning Technology—Reebok International Ltd.; *U.S. Public*, pg. 1369

DYNAMAX—X-Ray Tubes & Housings—Varian Associates, Inc.; *U.S. Public*, pg. 1710

DYNAMENTAL—NONE—The Timken Company; *U.S. Public*, pg. 1617

DYNAMIC—Outdoor Products—The Black & Decker Corporation; *U.S. Public*, pg. 233

DYNAMIC—Footwear Cushioning Technology—Reebok International Ltd.; *U.S. Public*, pg. 1369

DYNAMIC COLOR—Trinitron Circuitry—Sony Electronics; *Int'l*, pg. 1281

DYNAMIC FOCUS—Trinitron Circuitry—Sony Electronics; *Int'l*, pg. 1281

DYNAMIC GOLD—Outdoor Products—The Black & Decker Corporation; *U.S. Public*, pg. 233

DYNAMIC HOMES—Homes—Dynamic Homes, Inc.; *U.S. Public*, pg. 538

DYNAMIC INCUBATOR—Diagnostic Products—Abbott Laboratories; *U.S. Public*, pg. 12

DYNAMIC MINUTE MART—Convenience Stores—FFP Marketing Company; *U.S. Public*, pg. 604

DYNAMIC NAVIGATOR—NONE—Structural Dynamics Research Corp.; *U.S. Public*, pg. 1525

DYNAMIC OFFICE BALANCER—Electronic Echo Canceler for use with Telephone Systems—DSC Communications Corporation; *U.S. Public*, pg. 475

DYNAMIC PICTURE—Trinitron Circuitry—Sony Electronics; *Int'l*, pg. 1281

DYNAMIC POSTURE CHAIR—Children's Posture Chair—Ortho-Kinetics, Inc.; *U.S. Private*, pg. 820

DYNAMIC PRESS CONTROLLER—NONE—Dukane Corporation; *U.S. Private*, pg. 345

DYNAMIC TRACKING—Electrically Operated Apparatus for VCR Tracking—Sony Electronics; *Int'l*, pg. 1281

DYNAMIC-TENSION—Method of Training—Charles Atlas, Ltd.; *U.S. Private*, pg. 229

DYNAMICRON—Video Tape Cassette—Sony Electronics; *Int'l*, pg. 1281

DYNAMINO—Animal Feeds & Feed Supplies—Ag Processing Inc., A Cooperative; *U.S. Private*, pg. 26

DYNAMISAN—Pharmaceutical—Novartis AG; *Int'l*, pg. 971

DYNAMIT NOBEL—Pistol & Revolver Cartridges—EEI Corporation; *Int'l*, pg. 425

DYNAMO—Laundry—Colgate-Palmolive Co., Institutional Products Div.—*U.S. Public*, pg. 397

DYNAMO—Pump for Swimming Pool Accessories—Essef Corporation; *U.S. Public*, pg. 592

DYNAMO—Scooter—Pride Health Care, Inc.; *U.S. Private*, pg. 883

DYNAMO ACTION PLUS—Laundry Detergent—Colgate-Palmolive Company; *U.S. Public*, pg. 397

DYNAPAR—Digital Sensing, Monitoring & Control Equipment—Chicago Pneumatic Tool Company; *Int'l*, pg. 96

DYNAPATH DELTA SERIES—Computer Numerical Controls System—Hurco Companies, Inc.; *U.S. Public*, pg. 850

DYNAPEN—Infectious Disease Therapy—Bristol-Myers Squibb Company; *U.S. Public*, pg. 253

DYNAPERT—Electronic Assembly Equipment—The Black & Decker Corporation; *U.S. Public*, pg. 233

DYNAPOISE—Autopsy Table-Electro-Mechanical—Ruslander & Sons, Inc.; *U.S. Private*, pg. 952

DYNAPOL—Monomer & Coating Resin—Veba AG; *Int'l*, pg. 1454

DYNAPOUR—Automatic Pouring for Aluminum—Ajax Magnethermic Corp.; *Int'l*, pg. 113

DYNAPOWER—Arc Welding Cable—General Cable Corporation; *Int'l*, pg. 1486

DYNAPRECIPITOR—Paint Spray Booth—Binks Sames Corporation; *U.S. Public*, pg. 229

DYNAPRO—NONE—Milgray Electronics, Inc.; *U.S. Public*, pg. 205

DYNAPULSE—Electronic Tubes to Controlling Apparatus—Varian Associates, Inc.; *U.S. Public*, pg. 1710

DYNAPUMP—Economical Leakproof Canned Motor Centrifugal Pumps—ChemPump; *U.S. Public*, pg. 456

DYNAROHR—Aircraft Acoustic Structures—Rohr, Inc.; *U.S. Public*, pg. 751

DYNASCOPE—Image Tubes—Varian Associates, Inc.; *U.S. Public*, pg. 1710

DYNASPHERE—Bearings—Lear Siegler Diversified Holdings Corp.; *U.S. Private*, pg. 655

DYNASTAR—Skis—Rossignol Ski Co.; *Int'l*, pg. 1127

DYNASTY—Passenger & Cargo Services—China Airlines Ltd.; *Int'l*, pg. 284

DYNASTY—Inlaid Sheet Vinyl Flooring—Congoleum Corporation; *U.S. Public*, pg. 69

DYNASTY—Printing Paper—Georgia-Pacific Corporation; *U.S. Public*, pg. 735

DYNASTY—Video Routing Switchers—Meret Communications; *U.S. Public*, pg. 1233

DYNASTY—Bedding—The Stearns & Foster Bedding Company; *U.S. Private*, pg. 979

DYNASTY ONE—Dacron Robewear—Guilford Mills, Inc.; *U.S. Public*, pg. 768

DYNATEL—Locator, Cable, Identifier, Cable & Conductor—3M; *U.S. Public*, pg. 1604

DYNATUP—Impact Testing—Wilson/Shore Instruments; *U.S. Public*, pg. 883

DYNAVAR—Surge Arrestors—Hubbell Incorporated; *U.S. Public*, pg. 844

DYNAVAR—Surge Arresters—The Ohio Brass Co.; *U.S. Public*, pg. 845

DYNAVECTION—Jumbo Finned Heating Element—Slant/Fin Corporation; *U.S. Private*, pg. 1005

DYNAWHITE—Printing Paper—Weyerhaeuser Company; *U.S. Public*, pg. 1764

DYNEEMA—Fibre—DSM N.V.; *Int'l*, pg. 352

DYNETIC—Phonograph Cartridges—Shure Brothers Incorporated; *U.S. Public*, pg. 997

DYNIX—Operating Systems—Sequent Computer Systems, Inc.; *U.S. Public*, pg. 1459

DYNIX/PTX—Operating Systems—Sequent Computer Systems, Inc.; *U.S. Public*, pg. 1459

DYNO MAX PERFORMANCE EXHAUST—Muffler—Walker Manufacturing Co.; *U.S. Public*, pg. 1578

DYNO-MITE—Car Seat/Baby Carrier—Spalding & Evenflo Companies, Inc.; *U.S. Private*, pg. 629

DYNOPTICS—Video, Audio, & Fiberoptic Transmission—Meret Communications; *U.S. Public*, pg. 1233

DYNOTIE—Nylon Locking Duct Tie—Duro Dyne Corporation; *U.S. Private*, pg. 349

DYNOVA—Acrylic Fiber—Bayer AG; *Int'l*, pg. 171

DYPENOL—Mercerizing Assistant—Dexter Chemical Corp.; *U.S. Private*, pg. 329

DYPROTEX—Diaper Rash Ointment—Blistex, Inc.; *U.S. Private*, pg. 149

DYRA TORQUE—Tractor Tires—The Goodyear Tire & Rubber Company; *U.S. Public*, pg. 752

DYRENIUM—Cardiopulmonary Drug—SmithKline Beecham plc; *Int'l*, pg. 1264

DYSAN—Floppy Disks—Anacomp, Inc.; *U.S. Public*, pg. 106

DYSPAMET—Gastrointestinal Drug—SmithKline Beecham plc; *Int'l*, pg. 1264

DYTA-URESE—Cardiopulmonary Drug—SmithKline Beecham plc; *Int'l*, pg. 1264

DYTAC—Cardiopulmonary Drug—SmithKline Beecham plc; *Int'l*, pg. 1264

DYTEL—Red Leak Detective—Du Pont (E.I. Du Pont De Nemours & Co.); *U.S. Public*, pg. 530

DYTEX—Dye Tubes—Sonoco Products Company; *U.S. Public*, pg. 1485

DYTRON XL—Thermoplastic Elastomer—Monsanto Company; *U.S. Public*, pg. 1124

DYVEL—Herbicide—Sandoz Agro, Inc.; *Int'l*, pg. 974

E

EM-30—Gynecological Device—The Cooper Companies, Inc.; *U.S. Public*, pg. 442

E/A—Seats—B/E Aerospace Seating Products Group; *U.S. Public*, pg. 159

EA—EA Engineering, Science & Technology—EA Engineering, Science & Technology, Inc.; *U.S. Public*, pg. 540

EAC—NONE—Brazos Sportswear Inc.; *U.S. Public*, pg. 251

EAD—Custom Designed Motors, Fans & Blowers—Eastern Air Devices, Inc.; *U.S. Private*, pg. 357

EA EASY-DIST SYSTEM—EA Engineering, Science & Technology—EA Engineering, Science & Technology, Inc.; *U.S. Public*, pg. 540

EA FINANCIAL, INC.—EA Engineering, Scinece & Technology—EA Engineering, Science & Technology, Inc.; *U.S. Public*, pg. 540

EA GLOBAL, INC.—EA Engineering, Science & Technology—EA Engineering, Science & Technology, Inc.; *U.S. Public*, pg. 540

EA INTERNATIONAL, INC.—EA Engineering, Science & Technology—EA Engineering, Science & Technology, Inc.; *U.S. Public*, pg. 540

E. A. MILLER—Meat Processing—E.A. Miller Company; *U.S. Public*, pg. 428

EAO—Switches—EAO Switch Corporation; *Int'l*, pg. 444

EAO—Switches—Elektro-Apparatebau Olten AG; *Int'l*, pg. 444

E.A.R.—Hearing Protection—Aearo Company; *U.S. Private*, pg. 23

E.A.R. CLASSIC—Foam Ear Plugs—Aearo Company; *U.S. Private*, pg. 23

EAS—Earnings Analysis System Software—Hogan Systems, Inc.; *U.S. Public*, pg. 422

EASL—Computer Text Editing Software—Datapoint Corporation; *Int'l*, pg. 384

EA SIEST—Interactive Modeling Tool Kit—Evans & Sutherland Computer Corporation; *U.S. Public*, pg. 595

EA SPORTS—Computer & Video Games Relating to Sports—Electronic Arts; *U.S. Public*, pg. 569

E. & J. Brandy—Brandy—E. & J. Gallo Winery; *U.S. Public*, pg. 438

E & S—Computers, Components, Peripherals—Evans & Sutherland Computer Corporation; *U.S. Public*, pg. 595

EB ALLOY—Glass Mold Components—McInnes Steel Company; *U.S. Private*, pg. 722

EBBI—NONE—Molex Incorporated; *U.S. Public*, pg. 1121

E-B EMULSA-BOND—Bonding Agent for Latex Paint—The Flood Company; *U.S. Private*, pg. 414

E.B. EVANS—Ice Cream Topping—J.M. Smucker Company; *U.S. Public*, pg. 1480

E B 5—Cosmetic Company Specializing in Creams & Lotions—EB5 Corporation; *U.S. Private*, pg. 353

EBI COMPANIES—Workers Compensation—Orion Capital Companies, Inc.; *U.S. Public*, pg. 1231

EBM/PABST—NONE—Milgray Electronics, Inc.; *U.S. Public*, pg. 205

EBV-VCA—Mono Test System—Wampole Laboratories; *U.S. Public*, pg. 310

E BAG—Shrinkable Plastic Bag—Grace Packaging; *U.S. Public*, pg. 755

EC—NONE—IMO Pump; *U.S. Public*, pg. 857

ECDEL—Elastomer, Copolyester, Flexible Polyester, Flexible CoPolyester, Elastomer—Eastman Kodak Company; *U.S. Public*, pg. 550

EC4U—NONE—Kellwood Company; *U.S. Public*, pg. 948

ECKD—Computer System—International Business Machines Corporation; *U.S. Public*, pg. 895

ECMO—Heater—Cincinnati Sub-Zero Products, Inc.; *U.S. Private*, pg. 240

EC PLUS—Blood Filter—Pall Corporation; *U.S. Public*, pg. 1253

ECRM TRANSPARENCY SCANNER—High Resolution Transparency Scanner—ECRM; *U.S. Private*, pg. 353

ECS—Automotive Refinish Coatings—PPG Industries, Inc.; *U.S. Public*, pg. 1245

EC-SERIES—CNC Wire-Cut EDM—Makino Inc.; *Int'l*, pg. 831

ECT—Internal Fracture Fixation Systems—Bristol-Myers Squibb Company; *U.S. Public*, pg. 253

ECAP—Capillary Electrophoresis Tubes, Accessories & Reagents—Beckman Instruments, Inc.; *U.S. Public*, pg. 199

EDA/SQL—Data Access Products—Information Builders; *U.S. Public*, pg. 561

ED BETA VTR—Video Player—Sony Electronics; *Int'l*, pg. 1281

EDC SYSTEMS—Drive Systems—Electronic Drives and Controls; *U.S. Private*, pg. 370

EDE—Generation, Transmission & Distribution of Electricity—The Empire District Electric Company; *U.S. Public*, pg. 579

EDIF INTERFACE—NONE—GenRad, Inc.; *U.S. Public*, pg. 731

EDI-NET—Electronic Data Interchange System—British Telecommunications plc; *Int'l*, pg. 222

EDI*NET—Electronic Data Interchange—McDonnell Aircraft & Missile Systems Div.; *U.S. Public*, pg. 241

EDI/SET—Electronic Data Interchange/Software Enabling Technology—System Software Associates, Inc.; *U.S. Public*, pg. 1552

EDI 2000—Computer Hardware & Software—Automatic Data Processing, Inc.; *U.S. Public*, pg. 150

EDI-XPRESS—Data Communication Svc. Facilitating the Ordering & Delivery of Merchandise—General Electric Canada Inc.; *U.S. Public*, pg. 713

EDL—Lamps—Luxo A/S; *Int'l*, pg. 821

EDN—Magazine Supplying Information on Electronic Products, Technology & Design—Reed Elsevier Business Information; *Int'l*, pg. 1095

EDN ASIA—Magazine Serving Electronics Engineers in Asia's Market—Reed Elsevier Business Information; *Int'l*, pg. 1095

EDNC SERIES—CNC Ram-Type EDM—Makino Inc.; *Int'l*, pg. 831

EDN CHINA—Magazine Serving China's Electronic Equipment Manufacturing Industry—Reed Elsevier Business Information; *Int'l*, pg. 1095

EDN EUROPE—Magazine Serving Electronics Engineers in Europe's Market—Reed Elsevier Business Information; *Int'l*, pg. 1095

EDN PRODUCTS EDITION—Publication of New Products for Engineers in the ElectronicManufacturing Market—Reed Elsevier Business Information; *Int'l*, pg. 1095

EDS—Seating Systems—Interkal, Inc.; *Int'l*, pg. 759

E.D. SMITH—Pie Filling—E.D. Smith; *Int'l*, pg. 1263

EDX-P—Packet Switching Systems—Siemens Corporation; *Int'l*, pg. 1245

E-DISK—Effects Memory System Enhancement—Tektronix-Video & Networking Div., Grass Valley Products; *U.S. Public*, pg. 1567

EEA—Stapler—U.S. Surgical Corp.; *U.S. Public*, pg. 1687

EE-ZEE ADE—Imitation Fruit-Like Drinks—Gold Medal Products Co.; *U.S. Private*, pg. 459

EE-ZEE SNO-KONE CONCENTRATE—Premeasured Concentrate—Gold Medal Products Co.; *U.S. Private*, pg. 459

EMC DIRECTORY—NONE—Intertec Publishing; *U.S. Public*, pg. 1328

E! ENTERTAINMENT RADIO—Talk Radio Program—Westwood One Entertainment; *U.S. Public*, pg. 1763

E! ENTERTAINMENT RADIO—Entertainment News Programming—Westwood One, Inc.; *U.S. Public*, pg. 1763

EFCO—Building Products—Email Limited; *Int'l*, pg. 450

EFG—Glazing Systems—PPG Industries, Inc.; *U.S. Public*, pg. 1245

EFS—Extruded Flexible Sheet Heat Transfer Cement—Thermon Manufacturing Company; *U.S. Public*, pg. 1080

EFS WEBFILE—Turnkey Document Image Management Solution for the Worldwide Web—Excalibur Technologies Corporation; *U.S. Public*, pg. 598

EFX—Elliptical Fitness Cross Trainers—Precor, Inc.; *U.S. Public*, pg. 1322

E5—Drug; Treats Documented Gram-Negative Sepsis—XOMA Corporation; *U.S. Public*, pg. 1786

E-FORM—Electronic Tax Form Service—Computer Language Research, Inc.; *U.S. Public*, pg. 421

E45—NONE—Boots Healthcare International; *Int'l*, pg. 202

EGA—Glues & Adhesives—Borden, Inc.; *U.S. Private*, pg. 157

E-GRAM—Electropherogram—Thermo Separation Products; *U.S. Public*, pg. 1594

EIS—Brake Parts—Standard Motor Products Inc.; *U.S. Public*, pg. 1503

EISA MULTICHANNEL—NONE—Adaptec, Inc.; *U.S. Public*, pg. 19

EISA SCSI MASTER—NONE—Adaptec, Inc.; *U.S. Public*, pg. 19

Brand Name Index

Brand Name Index

EISA WIDE SCSI—NONE—Adaptec, Inc.; *U.S. Public*, pg. 19

EI-70—Outdoor Products—The Black & Decker Corporation; *U.S. Public*, pg. 233

EIU—Economist Intelligence Unit—The Economist Group Limited; *Int'l*, pg. 1026

EJ—Shoes—E.J. Footwear Corp.; *U.S. Public*, pg. 1684

E.J. BROOKS—Security Seals & Sealing Devices—E.J. Brooks Company; *U.S. Private*, pg. 172

EJ GYM—Athletic Shoes—E.J. Footwear Corp.; *U.S. Public*, pg. 1684

EJ PRO—Athletic Shoes—E.J. Footwear Corp.; *U.S. Public*, pg. 1684

EJ200—Military Engine—Rolls-Royce Military Aero Engines Ltd.; *Int'l*, pg. 1127

E-JAY—Athletic Shoes—E.J. Footwear Corp.; *U.S. Public*, pg. 1684

E. JOVEN—Mens' & Boys' Apparel—Farah Incorporated; *U.S. Public*, pg. 612

E.K. CAMPBELL—Heaters—Thomas & Betts Corporation; *U.S. Public*, pg. 1597

E.K. CAMPBELL—HVAC Products—Thomas & Betts Reznor Division; *U.S. Public*, pg. 1598

EKWIP—Filter Papers—Internatio-Muller N.V.; *Int'l*, pg. 680

E.L. FUDGE—Cookies—Keebler Company; *U.S. Public*, pg. 657

ELG—Recycling of Stainless Steel for Industry—Franz Haniel & Cie, GmbH; *Int'l*, pg. 591

ELMD500—Transportable Autotransfusion Machine—Medtronics Inc.; *U.S. Public*, pg. 1083

ELU—Power Tools—The Black & Decker Corporation; *U.S. Public*, pg. 233

E LOGO-FUEL ECONOMY—MUFFLER—Donaldson Company, Inc.; *U.S. Public*, pg. 517

EM—Magazine—Johnson Publishing Company, Inc.; *U.S. Private*, pg. 591

EMALJ—Paints—Masury Paint; *U.S. Public*, pg. 1707

EMC PRODUCTIONS—Custom Audio, Video & Computer Diskette Production & Duplication Services—EMC Corporation; *U.S. Public*, pg. 545

EMC PUBLISHING—School Books & Programs—EMC Corporation; *U.S. Public*, pg. 545

EMGE—Processed Meats—Cargill; *U.S. Private*, pg. 210

EMI—Records—Capitol Records, Inc.; *Int'l*, pg. 428

EMI—Record label—EMI Group plc; *Int'l*, pg. 426

EMI AMERICA—Records—Capitol Records, Inc.; *Int'l*, pg. 428

EMI/RFI—Power Line Filters—Standex International Corporation; *U.S. Public*, pg. 1505

EMMI—Yogurt—Morinaga Milk Industry Co., Ltd.; *Int'l*, pg. 895

EM 906—Zoom Electron Microscope—Carl Zeiss; *Int'l*, pg. 1522

EMO—NONE—Western Atlas Logging Services; *U.S. Public*, pg. 1757

EMS—Enhanced Mobility System—AM General Corporation; *U.S. Private*, pg. 922

EMS—Anti-Embolism Stockings—Medline Industries, Inc.; *U.S. Private*, pg. 728

EMS—Blood Pressure Monitor—Meridian Medical Technology, Inc.; *U.S. Public*, pg. 1095

EMS—Environmental Monitoring of Underground Storage Tanks—Tidel Engineering, Inc.; *U.S. Public*, pg. 1608

EMS VENDING SYSTEMS—Business Computers, Software & Services to Vending Opers.—Effective Management Systems; *U.S. Public*, pg. 565

EMT—Tracheal Tubes—Mallinckrodt Inc.; *U.S. Public*, pg. 1039

EMW GROSCHOPP—Motors & Reducers—Groschopp, Inc.; *Int'l*, pg. 559

E-MEM—Effects Memory System—Tektronix-Video & Networking Div., Grass Valley Products; *U.S. Public*, pg. 1567

E-MIL DEVICE—Scientific Product-Glass—J. Bibby & Sons Plc; *Int'l*, pg. 167

E-MYCIN—Pharmaceuticals—Knoll Pharmaceutical Company; *Int'l*, pg. 105

ENEX—Luxembourg Broadcasting—CLT-UFA; *Int'l*, pg. 561

ENI—RF Amplifiers—ENI; *U.S. Private*, pg. 354

ENP—Extended Nip Press—Harnischfeger Industries, Inc.; *U.S. Public*, pg. 788

EOCF/2—Computer System—International Business Machines Corporation; *U.S. Public*, pg. 895

EOCN—Epoxy Resins—Nippon Kayaku Co. Ltd.; *Int'l*, pg. 934

E-O-D BUCKET—Mining Equipment—Atlas Copco Wagner Inc.; *Int'l*, pg. 96

EOS—Opthalmic Microscope—Alcon Laboratories, Inc.; *Int'l*, pg. 916

E-ONE—Fire Engines—Federal Signal Corporation; *U.S. Public*, pg. 616

EPB—Vinyl Oxiranes—Eastman Chemical Company; *U.S. Public*, pg. 550

EPC—Epoxy Powder Coating Compounds—Georgia-Pacific Corporation; *U.S. Public*, pg. 735

EPCO—Food Racks—Standex International Corporation; *U.S. Public*, pg. 1505

EPI—Paint Waste Recycling—Meridian National Corporation; *U.S. Public*, pg. 1095

E.P.I.—Containment Systems—The Will-Burt Company; *U.S. Private*, pg. 1177

EPI-LINE—Catheter—Medtronic, Inc.; *U.S. Public*, pg. 1082

EPP—NONE—Lam Research Corporation; *U.S. Public*, pg. 975

E*P*S*—Timing Belts—PIC Design; *U.S. Private*, pg. 864

EPS-200—Photo Typesetters—AGFA EPS Division; *Int'l*, pg. 172

EP SERIES COPIERS—Copiers—Minolta Corporation; *Int'l*, pg. 869

E.P.T.—Home Pregnancy Test—Warner-Lambert Company; *U.S. Public*, pg. 1738

E.P.T.—Home Pregnancy Test—Warner-Lambert Consumer Healthcare; *U.S. Public*, pg. 1739

E-PACK—Reticulated-Pellet Fibrous Packing—Beco Engineering Company; *U.S. Private*, pg. 129

E-PACK—Procedure Kit—Ethicon, Inc.; *U.S. Public*, pg. 928

E.PLUS—Package Water/Water Heater—Aerco International Inc.; *U.S. Private*, pg. 23

E-PLUS—Motors—MagneTek, Inc.; *U.S. Public*, pg. 1037

E-PLUS—Energy Efficient Motors—Magnetek Motors & Generators; *U.S. Public*, pg. 1037

E-PLUS SPEED ENGINEERED—Motors—Magnetek Motors & Generators; *U.S. Public*, pg. 1037

E-PLUS III—Motors—MagneTek, Inc.; *U.S. Public*, pg. 1037

ERA—Real Estate Franchise—HFS, Incorporated; *U.S. Public*, pg. 321

ERC—Cargo Hooks & Suspension Systems—Breeze Eastern; *U.S. Public*, pg. 1632

ERC—Conduit—Electron Beam Technologies; *U.S. Private*, pg. 370

ERI—Shoe Polish—Sara Lee Corporation; *U.S. Public*, pg. 1432

ERK—Emergency Restoration Kits—Siecor Corporation; *U.S. Public*, pg. 449

ERK—Emergency Restoration Kits—Siecor Corporation; *Int'l*, pg. 1245

ERTL—Steel Trucks & Cars; Miniature Die-Cast Vehicles—The Ertl Company, Inc; *U.S. Public*, pg. 1684

E.R. WAGNER—Casters—Wagner Casters and Wheels; *U.S. Private*, pg. 1146

ERYC—Antibiotic—Warner-Chilcott Laboratories, Inc.; *Int'l*, pg. 436

E-RAID—NONE—IIS Intelligent Information Systems Ltd.; *Int'l*, pg. 645

E-ROV—Remotely Operated Vehicle—Benthos, Inc.; *U.S. Public*, pg. 212

ES—Reagents & Reagent Kits—Beckman Instruments, Inc.; *U.S. Public*, pg. 199

ES—Reagent Test Kits—Beckman Instruments, Inc.; *U.S. Public*, pg. 199

ESA—Company name—ESA, Inc.; *U.S. Private*, pg. 354

ESAP—Computer System—International Business Machines Corporation; *U.S. Public*, pg. 895

ESA/390—Computer System—International Business Machines Corporation; *U.S. Public*, pg. 895

ESA/370—Computer System—International Business Machines Corporation; *U.S. Public*, pg. 895

E.S.B.—Ale—Fuller, Smith & Turner Plc; *Int'l*, pg. 529

ES/C—Software—CSC Financial Services Group; *U.S. Public*, pg. 422

ESD—Electronic Test Equipment—Hayes Corporation, Regional Office; *U.S. Public*, pg. 801

ES-800C PRO—Scanning System—Epson America Inc.; *Int'l*, pg. 1219

ES/4381—Computer System—International Business Machines Corporation; *U.S. Public*, pg. 895

ESI—Laser Systems—Electro Scientific Industries, Inc.; *U.S. Public*, pg. 568

ESIG-4000—Visual Simulation System—Evans & Sutherland Computer Corporation; *U.S. Public*, pg. 595

ESIG-3000—Visual Simulation System—Evans & Sutherland Computer Corporation; *U.S. Public*, pg. 595

ESIG-2000—Visual Simulation Systems—Evans & Sutherland Computer Corporation; *U.S. Public*, pg. 595

ESI PRODUCTS—Pharmaceutical Products—Wyeth-Ayerst Laboratories, Inc.; *U.S. Public*, pg. 80

ESI-3D—Motion Picture Projector with Enhanced Spatial Effects—Iwerks Entertainment; *U.S. Public*, pg. 915

ES/9000—Computer System—International Business Machines Corporation; *U.S. Public*, pg. 895

ES/9370—Computer System—International Business Machines Corporation; *U.S. Public*, pg. 895

ESP—Pediatric Antibiotic—Barr Laboratories Inc.; *U.S. Public*, pg. 191

ESP—Computer Software Feature—Beckman Instruments, Inc.; *U.S. Public*, pg. 199

E.S.P.—Hotel Reservation—Omni Hotels; *U.S. Private*, pg. 1065

ESP—Single Part Epoxy—Permabond International; *Int'l*, pg. 1435

ESP-DX—Telephone system—Inter-Tel, Incorporated; *U.S. Public*, pg. 888

ESP EASY SURFACE PREP—Wipe On/Wipe Off Surface Cleaner—The Flood Company; *U.S. Private*, pg. 414

ESRIG—Radar Image Generators—Evans & Sutherland Computer Corporation; *U.S. Public*, pg. 595

ESS—Engine Synchro Shift Transmission—Rockwell International Corporation; *U.S. Public*, pg. 1397

ESSO—NONE—Imperial Oil Limited; *U.S. Public*, pg. 602

ES/3090—Computer System—International Business Machines Corporation; *U.S. Public*, pg. 895

ESV—Graphics Workstation—Evans & Sutherland Computer Corporation; *U.S. Public*, pg. 595

E-SCAN—X-Ray Imaging Technology—EG & G Astrophysics; *U.S. Public*, pg. 543

E-SCAN—Specialty X-Ray Equipment—EG & G, Inc.; *U.S. Public*, pg. 542

E. SCHWAB—NONE—Charles Schwab & Co. Inc.; *U.S. Public*, pg. 1443

E/SERIES—Statistical Multiplexer Data Concentrator—Ascom Timeplex; *Int'l*, pg. 86

E78 PLUS—Computer Software—Attachmate; *U.S. Private*, pg. 98

E-6 ECK—Design Mark for Photographic Technical Advice—Eastman Kodak Company; *U.S. Public*, pg. 550

E-SMART—Electronic Wiring Devices—Eagle Electric Mfg. Co., Inc.; *U.S. Private*, pg. 354

E.T.—Records—Universal Studios, Inc.; *Int'l*, pg. 1215

ETA—Snacks—Danone Group; *Int'l*, pg. 379

ETA—Margarine, Mayonnaise—Goodman Fielder Limited; *Int'l*, pg. 555

ETAP—Economy Hotels—Accor S.A.; *Int'l*, pg. 20

ETC—NONE—Environmental Tectonics Corporation (ETC); *U.S. Public*, pg. 587

ETC—Terminals—Molex Incorporated; *U.S. Public*, pg. 1121

ETE WATCH—Patented Software Tool for Managing Application Response Time—Candle Corporation; *U.S. Private*, pg. 204

ETG—Emulation Toolset for GENESIS—GenRad, Inc.; *U.S. Public*, pg. 731

ET MOSCH—Hats—Hermes International; *Int'l*, pg. 617

Brand Name Index

ETO-ABATOR—Ethylene Oxide Removal Device—Donaldson Company, Inc.; *U.S. Public*, pg. 517

ETS—Communications Networks—American Financial Group; *U.S. Public*, pg. 75

ETS—NONE—Evans & Sutherland Computer Corporation; *U.S. Public*, pg. 595

ETS—Automated Urine Toxicology Analyzer—Syntex; *Int'l*, pg. 1120

ETV-ELECTRONIC TV HOST—PC Based Interactive Program Guide Enables User to Sort Genre for Viewing—TV Host Inc.; *U.S. Private*, pg. 1066

E3 SERIES—Miniature Records—Westronics, Inc.; *U.S. Public*, pg. 1593

E-TRANS—Electrotransport System—Alza Corporation; *U.S. Public*, pg. 62

E 2—NONE—Nikon Inc.; *Int'l*, pg. 931

E-250—Truck—Ford Motor Company; *U.S. Public*, pg. 661

E2 POT—NONE—Xicor, Inc.; *U.S. Public*, pg. 1785

E2 PROMS—NONE—Xicor, Inc.; *U.S. Public*, pg. 1785

E 2 S—NONE—Nikon Inc.; *Int'l*, pg. 931

EUI—NONE—LucasVarity plc; *Int'l*, pg. 819

EVA—Electronic Equipment—Eaton Corp., Aerospace & Commercial Controls Div.; *U.S. Public*, pg. 557

EVAC—Vacuum Pumps—Varian Associates, Inc.; *U.S. Public*, pg. 1710

EWSD—Public Telephone Digital Switching Systems—Siemens Corporation; *Int'l*, pg. 1245

EWSIP—Electronic Warefare Standardization & Improvement Program—Comptek Research, Inc.; *U.S. Public*, pg. 419

EXPZ 180—Tennis Rackets—Mizuno Corporation; *Int'l*, pg. 884

EXR—Motion Picture Films—Eastman Kodak Company; *U.S. Public*, pg. 550

EXR—Industrial X-Ray Tubes—Litton Industries, Inc.; *U.S. Public*, pg. 1002

EXT—Computer Systems—Tandem Computers Inc.; *U.S. Public*, pg. 417

E-Z—Wire Devices—Eagle Electric Mfg. Co., Inc.; *U.S. Private*, pg. 354

E-Z ALARM—Clock Radio—Sony Electronics; *Int'l*, pg. 1281

EZ-AUDIO—Software—Adaptec, Inc.; *U.S. Public*, pg. 19

E-Z BAKE—Flour—ADM Milling Co.; *U.S. Public*, pg. 128

EZ BEND—Conduit Bending Equipment—The Lamson & Sessions Co.; *U.S. Public*, pg. 976

E-Z BETA—VCR—Sony Electronics; *Int'l*, pg. 1281

EZ BRAND—Sewing Notions—EZ International; *U.S. Private*, pg. 1192

E Z BREAK—High Temperature Anti-Seize & Lubricating Compound—La-Co Industries Markal Company; *U.S. Private*, pg. 640

E-Z BREAKER—Concrete Breaking Machines—Chief Industries, Inc.; *U.S. Private*, pg. 236

E-Z-CAT DRY—Oral Contrast Mediums for CT Scans—E-Z-Em, Inc.; *U.S. Public*, pg. 540

E-Z CHECK—Circuit Tester—Ideal Industries, Inc.; *U.S. Private*, pg. 557

E-Z CLEAN—Coated Products for Wash Down—Rockwell International Corporation; *U.S. Public*, pg. 1397

EZ CLEAN—Dust Cloth—Stanhome Inc.; *U.S. Public*, pg. 1508

E-Z-CUT—Plate—Joseph T. Ryerson & Son, Inc.; *U.S. Public*, pg. 879

E-Z DECK WASH WOOD RESTORER—Wood Restorer—Armor All Products Group; *U.S. Public*, pg. 387

EZ DRY—Rinse Additive—Ecolab Inc.; *U.S. Public*, pg. 562

E-Z-EM—Medical Products—E-Z-Em, Inc.; *U.S. Public*, pg. 540

E-Z EXPLANATIONS—Compliance Explanations—J.J. Keller & Associates, Inc.; *U.S. Private*, pg. 612

EZF—Connectors—Raychem Corporation; *U.S. Public*, pg. 1362

EZ FEATURE MILL—Off-Line Programming Software—Bridgeport Machines, Inc.; *U.S. Public*, pg. 251

E-Z FEET—Slippers—R.G. Barry Corporation; *U.S. Public*, pg. 192

EZ-FIRE—Heating System for Aluminum, Non-Ferrous Metals—Air Products and Chemicals, Inc.; *U.S. Public*, pg. 30

EZ-FLO—Flowing Arch Expansion Joint—Garlock Sealing Technologies; *U.S. Public*, pg. 402

E-Z-FLOW—Angiographic Catherers—E-Z-Em, Inc.; *U.S. Public*, pg. 540

E-Z FOIL—Aluminum Cookware—Tenneco Specialty Products; *U.S. Public*, pg. 1579

E-Z 4 WHEELER—Luggage—Lark Luggage Company, Inc.; *U.S. Public*, pg. 1430

EZ GRIP—Connectors—Raychem Corporation; *U.S. Public*, pg. 1362

E-Z GROUND—Receptacles—Eagle Electric Mfg. Co., Inc.; *U.S. Private*, pg. 354

EZ GUARD—RV Accessories—Superior Industries International, Inc.; *U.S. Public*, pg. 1539

E-Z-HD—Upper G.I. Oral Contrast Medium—E-Z-Em, Inc.; *U.S. Public*, pg. 540

E-Z HOLD—NONE—Life Technologies, Inc.; *U.S. Public*, pg. 504

E-Z JECT—NONE—Electronic Solutions; *U.S. Public*, pg. 1791

E Z KLEEN—Furnace Filter—Research Products Corporation; *U.S. Private*, pg. 924

E-Z-LINK—Electronics—National Semiconductor Corporation; *U.S. Public*, pg. 1159

EZ-LINK—Fiber Optic Communication System—Tektronix-Video & Networking Div., Grass Valley Products; *U.S. Public*, pg. 1567

EZ LOADER PRODUCTS—NONE—E Z Loader Corporate; *U.S. Private*, pg. 352

E-Z LUBE—Lubricating Oil—Bachmann Industries, Inc.; *U.S. Private*, pg. 109

EZMT—NONE—Rubbermaid Incorporated; *U.S. Public*, pg. 1411

E-Z MATE—Couplers—Bachmann Industries, Inc.; *U.S. Private*, pg. 109

E-Z-MATE—Pneumatic Quick Coupler—Parker Hannifin Corp., Quick Coupling Div.; *U.S. Public*, pg. 1260

EZ MELT, FILL & FILTER—Bakery Equipment—Belshaw Brothers, Inc.; *Int'l*, pg. 188

E-Z MOUNT INSTALLATION—Drop Side Contractor Body—The Knapheide Mfg. Co.; *U.S. Private*, pg. 626

EZO—Denture Cushion—Medtech Inc.; *U.S. Private*, pg. 728

E-Z-ON—Hinge Feature—Sanderson Plumbing Products Inc.; *U.S. Private*, pg. 964

E-Z ON/E-Z OFF—Hinge Feature—Sanderson Plumbing Products Inc.; *U.S. Private*, pg. 964

EZ1—Controller/Integrator—Nuarc Company, Inc.; *U.S. Private*, pg. 808

EZ-1 INFUSION PUMP—Deliver Prescribed Doses of Drugs & Fluids Automatically to Patients—Medex Inc.; *U.S. Public*, pg. 689

EZ PAINTR—Painting Supplies—EZ Paintr Corp.; *U.S. Public*, pg. 1177

E-Z-PAQUE—Upper G.I. Oral Contrast Medium—E-Z-Em, Inc.; *U.S. Public*, pg. 540

EZ PATH—Powerpath CNC Lathes—Bridgeport Machines, Inc.; *U.S. Public*, pg. 251

E-Z PULL—Rubber Stoppers—The West Company, Incorporated; *U.S. Public*, pg. 1755

EZRIDER—NONE—Blaw-Knox Construction Equipment Corporation; *U.S. Public*, pg. 877

E Z ROOF—Self Adhering Single Ply Roofing—Consolidated Coatings Corp.; *U.S. Public*, pg. 1357

E-Z SAMPLER—Scientific Glassware for Laboratory Use—Wheaton Inc.; *Int'l*, pg. 67

EZ SAT—Satellite Tracking Sequence for Home Satellite TV Receiver/Descramblers—Satellite Data Networks; *U.S. Public*, pg. 716

E-Z SCAN—Large Format Digital Scanners—Eastman Kodak Company; *U.S. Public*, pg. 550

EZ-SCSI—Software—Adaptec, Inc.; *U.S. Public*, pg. 19

EZ-SCSI LITE—NONE—Adaptec, Inc.; *U.S. Public*, pg. 19

E-Z SEAL—Wood Preservers & Waterproof Sealer—The Gibson-Homans Company; *U.S. Private*, pg. 451

E-Z SERVE—Convenience Stores—E-Z Serve Convenience Stores, Inc.; *U.S. Public*, pg. 540

E-Z SERVE—Convenience Stores—E-Z Serve Corp.; *U.S. Public*, pg. 540

E Z SET—Package Conveying Machinery—Alvey Systems, Inc; *U.S. Public*, pg. 47

EZ SHOPPER—3-Wheel Scooter Grocery Cart—Ortho-Kinetics, Inc.; *U.S. Private*, pg. 820

EZ SIDER—RV Accessories—Superior Industries International, Inc.; *U.S. Public*, pg. 1539

EZ SLIDER—RV Accessories—Superior Industries International, Inc.; *U.S. Public*, pg. 1539

EZ SURF—CNC Grinder—Bridgeport Machines, Inc.; *U.S. Public*, pg. 251

E-Z-SYTE—Dustless Chalk—Binney & Smith Inc.; *U.S. Private*, pg. 496

EZ TOPPS—NONE—Rubbermaid Incorporated; *U.S. Public*, pg. 1411

E-Z TRACK SYSTEM—NONE—Bachmann Industries, Inc.; *U.S. Private*, pg. 109

EZ TRAK—Explorer, Discovery Torq-Cut 22—Bridgeport Machines, Inc.; *U.S. Public*, pg. 251

EZ TWIST—Connectors—Raychem Corporation; *U.S. Public*, pg. 1362

E-Z VIAL—Scientific Glassware for Laboratory Use—Wheaton Inc.; *Int'l*, pg. 67

EZ WAXER—Wax Applicator—Stanhome Inc.; *U.S. Public*, pg. 1508

EZ WELD—Adhesive—RPM, Inc.; *U.S. Public*, pg. 1356

E-Z WIRE—Copal Switches & Receptacles—Eagle Electric Mfg. Co., Inc.; *U.S. Private*, pg. 354

EZ WRAP—Stretch Film—Brawny Plastics West; *U.S. Public*, pg. 166

E-PLAN—Electronic Banking That Operates Through ATM—Standard Bank Investment Corporation Limited; *Int'l*, pg. 1293

E-Z BOWMAKER—Bow Maker—E-Z Bowz, Inc.; *U.S. Private*, pg. 352

E-Z BOWZ—Bows—E-Z Bowz, Inc.; *U.S. Private*, pg. 352

E-Z WHEELER—Luggage—Lark Luggage Company, Inc.; *U.S. Public*, pg. 1430

EASY-SCANNER—Bar Code Scanning System—Caere Corporation; *U.S. Public*, pg. 291

EADIE'S KITCHEN & MARKET—Restaurant—The Levy Organization; *U.S. Private*, pg. 664

EADS WATER—Bottle Water—Hinckley & Schmitt, Inc.; *Int'l*, pg. 472

EAGALINE—Wall Plates—Eagle Electric Mfg. Co., Inc.; *U.S. Private*, pg. 354

EAGER BEAVER—Trailer & Trucks—Eager Beaver; *U.S. Private*, pg. 354

EAGLE—Garden Tools—Ames Company; *U.S. Public*, pg. 1683

EAGLE—Sweeper—Elgin Sweeper Company; *U.S. Public*, pg. 617

EAGLE—Pencils—Empire Berol U.S.A.; *U.S. Public*, pg. 1178

EAGLE—Street Sweeper—Federal Signal Corporation; *U.S. Public*, pg. 616

EAGLE—High-Performance Tires—The Goodyear Tire & Rubber Company; *U.S. Public*, pg. 752

EAGLE—Bus—Greyhound Lines, Inc.; *U.S. Public*, pg. 765

EAGLE—Various Balls, Balloons, Lawn Games—Hedstrom Corporation; *U.S. Private*, pg. 526

EAGLE—NONE—Lowrance Electronics, Inc.; *U.S. Public*, pg. 1015

EAGLE—NONE—Molex Incorporated; *U.S. Public*, pg. 1121

EAGLE—Roof Coating Products—Monsey-Bakor; *U.S. Public*, pg. 757

EAGLE—Ice Cream—Riser Foods, Inc.; *U.S. Private*, pg. 450

EAGLE—Fungicide—Rohm and Haas Company; *U.S. Public*, pg. 1403

EAGLE—Woodcase Pencil—Sanford Corporation; *U.S. Public*, pg. 1178

EAGLE—Self Propelled Access Platform—Simon Engineering plc; *Int'l*, pg. 1251

EAGLE—STP—Tekelec; *U.S. Public*, pg. 1566

EAGLE—Valves—Watts Industries, Inc.; *U.S. Public*, pg. 1746

EAGLE BOND FLOORING ADHESIVE—Adhesives—Pratt & Lambert United, Inc.; *U.S. Public*, pg. 1466

EAGLE BRAND—NONE—Borden Foods Canada; *U.S. Public*, pg. 159

EAGLE BRAND—Sweetened Condensed Milk; Home-Style Ice Cream—Borden, Inc.; *U.S. Private*, pg. 157

EAGLE BRAND—Caramels & Candy Coating—New England Confectionery Co.; *U.S. Private*, pg. 1113

EAGLE BRAND MILK—NONE—Borden Foods Co.; *U.S. Private*, pg. 158

EAGLE CANYON—Pickled Pig's Feet—GoodMark Foods, Inc.; *U.S. Public*, pg. 751

EAGLE COUNTRY MARKET—NONE—Eagle Food Centers, Inc.; *U.S. Public*, pg. 547

Brand Name Index

EAGLE EYE—Electronic Faucets—The Chicago Faucet Co.; *U.S. Private*, pg. 234
EAGLE OTTAWA LEATHER—Leather Products—Albert Trostel & Sons Co.; *U.S. Private*, pg. 1105
EAGLE PERFORMANCE SYSTEMS—Fitness—Lumex Medical Products; *U.S. Public*, pg. 758
EAGLE PREMIER—Car—Chrysler Corporation; *U.S. Public*, pg. 352
EAGLE SAVERS' CARD—NONE—Eagle Food Centers, Inc.; *U.S. Public*, pg. 547
EAGLE SCAN—Computer Product—International Business Machines Corporation; *U.S. Public*, pg. 895
EAGLE SERIES—Recreational Vehicles & Vans—Jayco Inc.; *U.S. Private*, pg. 583
EAGLE SNACKS—NONE—The Procter & Gamble Company; *U.S. Public*, pg. 1330
EAGLE SUMMIT—Car—Chrysler Corporation; *U.S. Public*, pg. 352
EAGLE TALON—Car—Chrysler Corporation; *U.S. Public*, pg. 352
EAGLE II DELINTER—Delinting Cotton Seed for Oil Mills—Continental Eagle Corporation; *U.S. Private*, pg. 267
EAGLE VISION—Car—Chrysler Corporation; *U.S. Public*, pg. 352
EAGLE'S EYE—Magazine—Paisano Publications, Inc.; *U.S. Private*, pg. 834
EAGLEMOTIVE—Fan Clutches—Mark IV Industries Inc.; *U.S. Public*, pg. 1044
EAGLET—Binoculars—Swift Instruments, Inc.; *U.S. Private*, pg. 1058
EAMES—Chairs—Herman Miller, Inc.; *U.S. Public*, pg. 1111
EAR CAPS—Hearing Protector—Aearo Company; *U.S. Private*, pg. 23
EARGAGE—Ear Measuring Device—Aearo Company; *U.S. Private*, pg. 23
EARL-GLO—Fabrics—Balson-Hercules Ltd.; *Int'l*, pg. 326
EARL GREY—Tea—Celestial Seasonings; *U.S. Public*, pg. 319
EARL MAY SEED & NURSERY—Flower Seeds & Nursery Supplies—Earl May Seed & Nursery L.c.; *U.S. Private*, pg. 356
EARL OF WELDON—NONE—Karelia Tobacco Company Inc.; *Int'l*, pg. 724
EARL SCHEIB—Automobile Paint Shops—Earl Scheib, Inc.; *U.S. Public*, pg. 1437
EARLE SWENSEN'S ALL-NATURAL—Custom Combinations Ice Cream—Swensen's Ice Cream Co.; *U.S. Public*, pg. 883
EARLE SWENSEN'S ALL NATURAL LIGHT—Light Ice Cream—Swensen's Ice Cream Co.; *U.S. Public*, pg. 883
EARLY AMERICAN LIFE—Periodical—Cowles Enthusiast Media, Inc.; *U.S. Private*, pg. 281
EARLY BIRD SERVICE—Automotive Repair Services—Bridgestone/Firestone, Inc.; *Int'l*, pg. 213
EARLY CALIFORNIA—Ripe Olives—Campbell Soup Company; *U.S. Public*, pg. 298
EARLY LEARNING CENTRE—Retailer of Quality Eductional Toys, Games & Books—John Menzies plc; *Int'l*, pg. 707
EARLY RECOVERY—Collection Program—I.C. System, Inc.; *U.S. Private*, pg. 553
EARLY RISER—Planters—Case Corporation; *U.S. Public*, pg. 311
EARLY SPRING—Plywood, Lumber, Wood & Wood Fiber Products—Georgia-Pacific Corporation; *U.S. Public*, pg. 735
EARLY TIMES—Old Style Kentucky Whiskey—Brown-Forman Beverages Worldwide; *U.S. Public*, pg. 261
EARLY TIMES—Whisky—Brown-Forman Corporation; *U.S. Public*, pg. 261
EARLY WORLD OF LEARNING—School Readiness Program—World Book, Inc.; *U.S. Public*, pg. 218
EARSET—Earphone—Telex Communications, Inc.; *U.S. Private*, pg. 1074
EARTH—Magazine—Kalmbach Publishing Co.; *U.S. Private*, pg. 606
EARTH BORN—Shampoo—The Gillette Company; *U.S. Public*, pg. 743
EARTH GRAINS—Natural Bread & Rolls—The Earthgrains Company; *U.S. Public*, pg. 547
EARTH HARVEST—Variety Bread—Stroehmann Bakeries, L.C.; *Int'l*, pg. 1495

EARTH HARVEST—Baked Goods—George Weston Limited; *Int'l*, pg. 1494
EARTH MARK—Recycled Envelope Products—Griffin Envelope, Inc.; *U.S. Public*, pg. 1038
EARTH MATTERS—NONE—Tandy Brands Accessories, Inc.; *U.S. Public*, pg. 1560
EARTH METAL—Tillage Parts—Case Corporation; *U.S. Public*, pg. 311
EARTH SCIENCE VIDEO LAB—Multimedia Activity Kits for Earth Science Studies—American Educational Products; *U.S. Public*, pg. 71
EARTH STALKERS—Cologne—Avon Products, Inc.; *U.S. Public*, pg. 155
EARTHFIRE—Women's Fragrance—Avon Products, Inc.; *U.S. Public*, pg. 155
EARTHMASTER—Tillage Systems—M&W; *U.S. Public*, pg. 35
EARTHMOVER TIRES & TUBES—NONE—Michelin North America (Canada) Inc.; *Int'l*, pg. 322
EARTH'S BEST—Baby Food—H.J. Heinz Company; *U.S. Public*, pg. 805
EARTHWISE—Office Products—Esselte AB; *Int'l*, pg. 459
EARTHWORKS—D.E. Filter with Ring-Lok Access—Jacuzzi Bros., Jacuzzi, Inc.; *U.S. Public*, pg. 1684
EASAMATIC—Microfilm Reader & Access., Index Cards—Eastman Kodak Company; *U.S. Public*, pg. 550
EASCO—Aluminum—Easco Inc.; *U.S. Public*, pg. 548
EASE—Automation Simplification System—Applied Materials, Inc.; *U.S. Public*, pg. 123
EASE SPORT—NONE—Kellwood Company; *U.S. Public*, pg. 948
EASI-AIR—Respirator Cartridge Replacement—3M; *U.S. Public*, pg. 1604
EASI-LAV—Closed Gastric Lavage System—Ballard Medical Products; *U.S. Public*, pg. 171
EAST ISLAND—NONE—Bloomingdale's; *U.S. Public*, pg. 617
EAST TEXAS FAIR PEAS—Food Products—Allen Canning Company; *U.S. Private*, pg. 36
EASTACEL—Cellulose Resin—Eastman Kodak Company; *U.S. Public*, pg. 550
EASTACHROME—Fiber; Staple Fiber—Eastman Kodak Company; *U.S. Public*, pg. 550
EASTACOAT—Polymeric Materials—Eastman Chemical Company; *U.S. Public*, pg. 550
EASTACRYL—Acrylic Polymer—Eastman Chemical Company; *U.S. Public*, pg. 550
EASTALITE—Polyester—Eastman Chemical Company; *U.S. Public*, pg. 550
EASTALLOY—Plastics—Eastman Chemical Company; *U.S. Public*, pg. 550
EASTAPAK—Bottle Polymer; Copolyester—Eastman Chemical Company; *U.S. Public*, pg. 550
EASTAPURE—Plasticizer—Eastman Chemical Company; *U.S. Public*, pg. 550
EASTAR—Polyester; Copolyester—Eastman Chemical Company; *U.S. Public*, pg. 550
EASTBAY—Diesel Yachts—GB Holdings; *Int'l*, pg. 531
EASTCOM—Communications Software—Eastman Kodak Company; *U.S. Public*, pg. 550
EASTEK—Water-Based Polymers—Eastman Chemical Company; *U.S. Public*, pg. 550
EASTEK—Aqueous Polymer; Inks—Eastman Kodak Company; *U.S. Public*, pg. 550
EASTERN NEWS DISTRIBUTORS—Magazine & Book Distribution—The Hearst Corporation; *U.S. Private*, pg. 515
EASTERN SAFETY—Safety Products—Aearo Company; *U.S. Private*, pg. 23
EASTERS—Retail Grocery Stores—Nash Finch Company; *U.S. Public*, pg. 1151
EASTLIGHT—Storage Products—ACCO World Corporation; *U.S. Public*, pg. 674
EASTLIGHT—Office Products—Fortune Brands, Inc.; *U.S. Public*, pg. 674
EASTMAN—Photo Film, Cameras & Equipment, Yarns, Chemicals, Plastics, Vitamins—Eastman Kodak Company; *U.S. Public*, pg. 550
EASTMAN—Plumbing Supplies & Connectors—Eljer Plumbingware; *U.S. Public*, pg. 1794
EASTMAN AQ—Water Dispersible Polymers—Eastman Kodak Company; *U.S. Public*, pg. 550

EASTMAN AQ—Water-Dispersible Polymers—Eastman Chemical Company; *U.S. Public*, pg. 550
EASTMAN HOUSE—Bedding-Upholstery—Chittenden & Eastman Co.; *U.S. Private*, pg. 237
EASTMAN RADIO—Radio Advertising Representitive Service—Katz Media Group, Inc.; *U.S. Public*, pg. 335
EASTOBOND—Synthetic Adhesives—Eastman Chemical Company; *U.S. Public*, pg. 550
EASTOBOND—Adhesives—Eastman Kodak Company; *U.S. Public*, pg. 550
EASTOBRITE—Optical Brightener—Eastman Chemical Company; *U.S. Public*, pg. 550
EASTOFLEX—Amorphous Polyolefins—Eastman Chemical Company; *U.S. Public*, pg. 550
EASTONE—Fountain Solution Extender—Eastman Chemical Company; *U.S. Public*, pg. 550
EASTONE—Dyes—Eastman Kodak Company; *U.S. Public*, pg. 550
EASTOTAC—Hydrocarbon Resin—Eastman Chemical Company; *U.S. Public*, pg. 550
EASTOTAC—Hydrocarbon Resin—Eastman Kodak Company; *U.S. Public*, pg. 550
EASTRON—Eastern Style Water Closet—Josam Company; *U.S. Private*, pg. 600
EASTSIDE LINCOLNMERCURY—Lincoln-Mercury—Beechmont Investments Inc.; *U.S. Private*, pg. 129
EASTWEST RECORDS—NONE—Atlantic Recording Corporation; *U.S. Public*, pg. 1611
EASY-SET—Truss Equipment—MiTek, Inc.; *Int'l*, pg. 1106
EASY—Trigger Sprayer—The Dow Chemical Company; *U.S. Public*, pg. 522
EASY ACCESS—Packaging—Ethicon, Inc.; *U.S. Public*, pg. 928
EASY ACCESS—NONE—Life Technologies, Inc.; *U.S. Public*, pg. 504
EASY ACCESS—Plumbing Wall Panel—Sloan Valve Company; *U.S. Private*, pg. 1006
EASY-AIRE—Seating—National Seating Co.; *U.S. Private*, pg. 786
EASY BREADS—Dessert—General Mills, Inc.; *U.S. Public*, pg. 717
EASY CAP—End Tidal CO2 Detector—Nellcor Puritan Bennett Incorporated; *U.S. Public*, pg. 1039
EASY CARE—Service Contract—Automobile Protection Corporation-APCO; *U.S. Public*, pg. 150
EASY CARE—Paints—PPG Industries, Inc.; *U.S. Public*, pg. 1245
EASY CHECK—Checking Service—NBD Bank (Indiana); *U.S. Public*, pg. 628
EASY CHEESE—Cheese Spreads—Nabisco Inc.; *U.S. Public*, pg. 1355
EASY-COMB - EASY-SET—Hair Setting Lotion—Clairol, Inc.; *U.S. Public*, pg. 254
EASY CONNECT—Piping—Baltimore Aircoil Company; *U.S. Public*, pg. 68
EASY-EDGE—Lawn Edging—Flex-O-Glass, Inc.; *U.S. Private*, pg. 412
EASY-EDGE—Lawn Edging—Warp Brothers; *U.S. Private*, pg. 412
EASY EGGS—UHT Liquid Eggs—Michael Foods, Inc.; *U.S. Public*, pg. 1103
EASY FEAST—NONE—Jerome Foods Inc.; *U.S. Private*, pg. 586
EASY FILE—Optical Filing System—Lanier Worldwide Inc.; *U.S. Public*, pg. 791
EASY FINISH—Coating—RPM, Inc.; *U.S. Public*, pg. 1356
EASY-FLO—Brazing Alloy—Handy & Harman; *U.S. Public*, pg. 780
EASY GO—Computerized Tax Processing—Computer Language Research, Inc.; *U.S. Public*, pg. 421
EASY GRIP—Mechanical Goods—Moeller Products Co., Inc.; *U.S. Private*, pg. 755
EASY-GRIP—Tube & Partition Surface—Sonoco Products Company; *U.S. Public*, pg. 1485
EASY-GROW—Plastic Garden Mulch—Warp Brothers; *U.S. Private*, pg. 412
EASY GROW GREENHOUSE—Garden Products—Jiffy Products of America, Inc.; *Int'l*, pg. 706
EASY-IVY—Eliminate All Signs of Poison Ivy Osk & Sumac—Bethurum Research & Development, Inc.; *U.S. Private*, pg. 141

EASY LIVING—NONE—Sears, Roebuck and Co.; *U.S. Public*, pg. 1452

EASY MASK—Masking Tape—Daubert Industries, Inc.; *U.S. Private*, pg. 313

EASY MIX COFFEE CAKE—Cake Mix—The Quaker Oats Company; *U.S. Public*, pg. 1347

EASY MIX CORN BREAD—Bread Mix—The Quaker Oats Company; *U.S. Public*, pg. 1347

EASY-OFF—Crayons—Binney & Smith Inc.; *U.S. Private*, pg. 496

EASY-OFF—Adhesives for Easy Removal—Ferro Corporation; *U.S. Public*, pg. 618

EASY OFF—Oven & Window Cleaner—Reckitt & Colman Inc.; *Int'l*, pg. 1090

EASY ON—Spray Starch—Reckitt & Colman Inc.; *Int'l*, pg. 1090

EASY-ON—Storm Window Kit—Warp Brothers; *U.S. Private*, pg. 412

EASY PAVE—Bridge Membrane—Royston Laboratories; *U.S. Public*, pg. 337

EASY PAY—Money Services—New Valley Corporation; *U.S. Public*, pg. 1173

EASY PAY—Money Services—Western Union Financial Services, Inc.; *U.S. Public*, pg. 631

EASY PURE—Deionization System—Barnstead/Thermolyne Corporation; *U.S. Public*, pg. 1545

EASY-PUSH—Metering Faucets—Speakman Company; *U.S. Private*, pg. 1021

EASY RIDER—Lawn Cart—Rubbermaid Incorporated; *U.S. Public*, pg. 1411

EASY-SEAL—Filter Bags—American Felt & Filter; *U.S. Private*, pg. 54

EASY SEARCH—Formulated Search Library & Software—The Mead Corporation; *U.S. Public*, pg. 1074

EASY SHIP—Customer Automation—DHL Worldwide Express; *U.S. Private*, pg. 301

EASY SHOT—NONE—Concord Camera Corporation; *U.S. Public*, pg. 429

EASY-SPARE—Spare Tire Carrier—Dutton-Lainson Co.; *U.S. Private*, pg. 350

EASY SPIRIT—Women's Shoes—Nine West Group, Inc.; *U.S. Public*, pg. 1185

EASY STEEL—Cutlery—General Housewares Corp.; *U.S. Public*, pg. 715

EASY STEER—Front Axles—Rockwell International Corporation; *U.S. Public*, pg. 1397

EASY-STOP—Trailer Antilock Braking System—Rockwell International Corporation; *U.S. Public*, pg. 1397

EASY TALK—Radio Communicators & Telephone Headsets—Nady Systems, Inc.; *U.S. Private*, pg. 773

EASY-TITE—Faucet Washers & Valve Packings—J.A. Sexauer, Inc.; *U.S. Private*, pg. 352

EASY TRADE—Interactive Touch-Tone Telephone Trading System—The Quick & Reilly Group Inc.; *U.S. Public*, pg. 650

EASY TRADE—Touch-tone Telephone Trading Service—Quick & Reilly, Inc.; *U.S. Public*, pg. 650

EASY TUGGER—Puller—Greenlee Textron; *U.S. Public*, pg. 1589

EASY-TUNE—Control Products—Bailey, Fischer & Porter Company; *Int'l*, pg. 449

EASY TURN—Luggage—American Tourister, Inc.; *U.S. Public*, pg. 1430

EASY 2%—Lowfat, Lower Lactose Milk—Dean Foods Company; *U.S. Public*, pg. 489

EASY WALL—Shower Wall Kit—Plaskolite Inc.; *U.S. Private*, pg. 870

EASY WAY—Paint—Plasti-Kote Company Inc.; *U.S. Private*, pg. 870

EASY WIPES—Disposable Cloth—Magla Products; *U.S. Private*, pg. 695

EASY-WRITER—Toy Typewriters—Empire of Carolina, Inc.; *U.S. Public*, pg. 579

EASY-OFF—Oven Cleaner—Reckitt & Colman plc; *Int'l*, pg. 1089

EASY-ON—Ironing Aid—Reckitt & Colman plc; *Int'l*, pg. 1089

EASYBAKE OVEN—Kenner Products—Hasbro, Inc.; *U.S. Public*, pg. 797

EASYCUT—Plastic Tubing & Pipe Cutter—NewAge Industries Inc.; *U.S. Private*, pg. 796

EASYCUT—Plastic Tubing Cutter—Newage Industries Inc., Plastics Technology Group; *U.S. Private*, pg. 796

EASYEST—Automatic Program Generator—Keithley Instruments, Inc.; *U.S. Public*, pg. 946

EASYGREEN—Seeds—Green Seed Co.; *U.S. Private*, pg. 477

EASYLIMS—Computer Software—Beckman Instruments, Inc.; *U.S. Public*, pg. 199

EASYLINK MAIL—Public E-Mail Service—AT&T Strategy & New Service Innovations; *U.S. Public*, pg. 11

EASYPLEAT—Drapery Tapes & Hooks—Kirsch; *U.S. Public*, pg. 1176

EASYPOXY—Epoxy Adhesives—Conap Inc.; *U.S. Private*, pg. 261

EASYRIDERS—Magazine—Paisano Publications, Inc.; *U.S. Private*, pg. 834

EASYSTRIKE—Business Product—International Business Machines Corporation; *U.S. Public*, pg. 895

EASYVUE—Copy Holder—Rubbermaid Incorporated; *U.S. Public*, pg. 1411

EASYWALL—Bathtub Wall Kit—Plaskolite Inc.; *U.S. Private*, pg. 870

EASYXPRESS—Household Products—The Black & Decker Corporation; *U.S. Public*, pg. 233

EAT-A-SNAX—Sandwich Crackers—Tom's Foods, Inc.; *U.S. Private*, pg. 1090

EAT-MORE—Candy—Hershey Foods Corporation; *U.S. Public*, pg. 811

EAT N PARK—Restaurants—Eat N Park Restaurants; *U.S. Private*, pg. 358

EATING RIGHT—Frozen Dessert—Kraft Foods, Inc.; *U.S. Public*, pg. 1287

EATON—Typing Papers—The At-A-Glance Group; *U.S. Private*, pg. 295

EATON—Automotive & Appliance Controls—Eaton Corporation Automotive Controls Division; *U.S. Public*, pg. 557

EATON—High-Carbon Steel, Heat-Treated Wire Wound Retaining Rings—Eaton Corporation, Engineered Fasteners Division; *U.S. Public*, pg. 556

EATON—Hydrostatic Transmissions—Eaton Corporation, Hydraulics Division; *U.S. Public*, pg. 557

EATON—Axles & Brakes—Eaton Corporation, Truck Components Operations-North America; *U.S. Public*, pg. 557

EATON—Fasteners—Engineered Fasteners Div.; *U.S. Public*, pg. 557

EATON ENGINE VALVES—Engine Valves—Eaton Corporation, Engine Components Division; *U.S. Public*, pg. 556

EATON FULLER—Heavy-Duty Truck Transmissions—Eaton Corporation; *U.S. Public*, pg. 555

EATON FULLER—Transmissions—Eaton Corporation, Truck Components Operations-North America; *U.S. Public*, pg. 557

EATON ROADRANGER—Truck Component Sales, Service & Training—Eaton Corporation; *U.S. Public*, pg. 555

EAU DE GUERLAIN—Fragrance—Guerlain S.A.; *Int'l*, pg. 780

EAU JEUNE—Perfume—L'Oreal S.A.; *Int'l*, pg. 818

EAU SAUVAGE—Men's Fragrence—Christian Dior Perfumes Inc.; *Int'l*, pg. 781

EAVESHIELD—Fiberglas Underlay—Domtar Inc.; *Int'l*, pg. 416

EAZY—Computer Equipment—Black Box Corporation of PA; *U.S. Public*, pg. 235

EBARA—NONE—Ebara Corporation; *Int'l*, pg. 431

EBERHARD—Locking Devices—The Eastern Company; *U.S. Public*, pg. 548

EBERHARD—Truck & Trailer Hardware—Eberhard Manufacturing; *U.S. Public*, pg. 548

EBERLINE INSTRUMENT—Manufacturer Radiation Detection & Measurement Equipment—Eberline Instrument Corporation; *U.S. Public*, pg. 1593

EBONE—Cosmetics—Johnson Publishing Company, Inc.; *U.S. Private*, pg. 591

EBONOL—Salts For Blackening & Coloring Metals—Enthone-OMI, Inc.; *U.S. Public*, pg. 138

EBONY—Magazine—Johnson Publishing Company, Inc.; *U.S. Private*, pg. 591

EBONY/JETSHOWCASE—Television Show—Johnson Publishing Company, Inc.; *U.S. Private*, pg. 591

EBONY RICH—Hosiery & Related Apparel—Mayer/Berkshire Corporation; *U.S. Private*, pg. 717

EBONY SUPREME—Hosiery & Related Apparel—Mayer/Berkshire Corporation; *U.S. Private*, pg. 717

ECAT—Position Emission Tomography—Siemens Corporation; *Int'l*, pg. 1245

THE ECCENTRIC—NONE—HomeTown Communications Network, Inc.; *U.S. Private*, pg. 537

ECCOBOND—One & Two Component Adhesives—Emerson & Cuming Specialty Polymers; *Int'l*, pg. 1435

ECCOCOAT—One & Two Component Conformal Coatings for Electronics—Emerson & Cuming Specialty Polymers; *Int'l*, pg. 1435

ECDEL—Exible Copolyester; Polyester—Eastman Chemical Company; *U.S. Public*, pg. 550

ECFORMS—Business Product—International Business Machines Corporation; *U.S. Public*, pg. 895

ECHELON—Zipper—YKK (U.S.A.); *Int'l*, pg. 1515

ECHINACEA—NONE—Celestial Seasonings; *U.S. Public*, pg. 319

ECHINACEA COLD SEASON—Blend with Echinacea—Celestial Seasonings; *U.S. Public*, pg. 319

ECHLIN—Electrical & Fuel System Parts—Echlin Inc.; *U.S. Public*, pg. 560

ECHO—Cross-Linking Agents—Hercules Incorporated; *U.S. Public*, pg. 809

ECHO SEARCH—InterNet Search Engine Enhancement—Innovex, Inc.; *U.S. Public*, pg. 880

ECHO VIDEO—Duplicators—TSC Shannock Corporation; *Int'l*, pg. 1343

ECHOS VEDETTES—Newspaper—Quebecor Inc.; *Int'l*, pg. 1075

ECHOTEL—Ultrasonic Level Switches & Transmitters—Magnetrol International; *U.S. Private*, pg. 696

ECHOVISION—Automotive Obstacle Detection Systems—Armatron International, Inc.; *U.S. Public*, pg. 131

ECHTER NORDHAUSER—Schnaps—Eckes AG; *Int'l*, pg. 432

ECKADAMS—Office & Institutional Furniture—EAC Corporation; *U.S. Private*, pg. 353

ECKERD DRUG—Retail Drug Stores—Eckerd Corporation; *U.S. Public*, pg. 917

ECKES EDELKIRSCH—Cherry Liqueur—Eckes AG; *Int'l*, pg. 432

ECKES EDELKIRSCH CHOCOLAT—Chocolat—Eckes AG; *Int'l*, pg. 432

ECKES EDELKIRSCH CREAM—Cherry Cream Liqueur—Eckes AG; *Int'l*, pg. 432

ECKES PRIVAT BRAND—Brandy—Eckes AG; *Int'l*, pg. 432

ECKES TRAUBENSAFT—Fruit Juice—Eckes AG; *Int'l*, pg. 432

ECLECTIC—Classroom Seating—Clarin; *U.S. Private*, pg. 242

ECLIPS—NONE—Western Atlas Logging Services; *U.S. Public*, pg. 1757

ECLIPSE—Downdraft Range Ventilation—Broan Mfg. Co., Inc.; *U.S. Public*, pg. 1193

ECLIPSE—Electrocardiograph—Burdick, Inc.; *U.S. Private*, pg. 181

ECLIPSE—Dispersion Polymers—Calgon Corporation; *Int'l*, pg. 455

ECLIPSE—Herbicide—The Dow Chemical Company; *U.S. Public*, pg. 522

ECLIPSE—Indus. Latches—The Eastern Company; *U.S. Public*, pg. 548

ECLIPSE—Silicon Carbide Refractory Line—A.P. Green Industries, Inc.; *U.S. Public*, pg. 761

ECLIPSE—Surgical Group—Medline Industries, Inc.; *U.S. Private*, pg. 728

ECLIPSE—Fine Pitch Circuit Board Printer—Millennium Technology Services, Inc.; *U.S. Private*, pg. 746

ECLIPSE—Automobile—Mitsubishi Motor Sales of America, Inc.; *Int'l*, pg. 875

ECLIPSE—Program Vehicle—Mitsubishi Motor Sales of America, Inc.; *Int'l*, pg. 875

ECLIPSE—Magnetic Resonance—Picker International, Inc.; *Int'l*, pg. 545

ECLIPSE—Party Platters—Tenneco Specialty Products; *U.S. Public*, pg. 1579

ECLIPSE—Floodlights—Wide-Lite; *U.S. Public*, pg. 730

ECLIPSE CANDLES—NONE—Blyth Industries; *U.S. Public*, pg. 239

ECLIPSE MV—Computer—Data General Corporation; *U.S. Public*, pg. 485
ECLIPSE MV/30000—Computer—Data General Corporation; *U.S. Public*, pg. 485
ECLIPSE MV/3500 DC—Computer—Data General Corporation; *U.S. Public*, pg. 485
ECLIPSE MV/40000—Computer—Data General Corporation; *U.S. Public*, pg. 485
ECLIPSE MV/5500 DC—Computer—Data General Corporation; *U.S. Public*, pg. 485
ECLIPSE MV/9500—Computer—Data General Corporation; *U.S. Public*, pg. 485
ECLIPSE NON-STICK—Cookware—General Housewares Corp.; *U.S. Public*, pg. 715
ECLIPSE STYLING COVERS—Headlight, Side Window & Taillight Covers—Lund International Holdings, Inc.; *U.S. Public*, pg. 1020
ECLIPSEMOBILE ELECTRONICS—Advanced Mobile Autosound Equipment—Fujitsu Ten Corp. of America; *Int'l*, pg. 526
ECO—Air Filter-Engine—Farr Company; *U.S. Public*, pg. 613
ECO—Towels—Marcal Paper Mills, Inc.; *U.S. Private*, pg. 701
ECO CHEMIE—Voltammetric Instruments—Brinkmann Instruments, Inc.; *U.S. Private*, pg. 169
ECO-TEMP—Low-Temperature Warewashing Rental & Service Program—Ecolab Inc.; *U.S. Public*, pg. 562
ECO II—Truck Air Filter—Farr Company; *U.S. Public*, pg. 613
ECO-TY—Ink for Synthetic Paper—Raffi & Swanson, Inc.; *U.S. Private*, pg. 907
ECOBRITE—Silver Ink—Raffi & Swanson, Inc.; *U.S. Private*, pg. 907
ECOCHARGEBACK—NONE—Compuware Corporation; *U.S. Public*, pg. 423
ECOCOOL—Cutting Fluids—Fuchs Petrolub AG Oel + Chemie; *Int'l*, pg. 517
ECODEX—Spray System—The Dexter Corporation; *U.S. Public*, pg. 504
ECOGLOSS—Water Reducible Gloss Ink (and Extender)—Raffi & Swanson, Inc.; *U.S. Private*, pg. 907
ECOLO CHIEF—Wastewater Treament System—Chief Industries, Inc.; *U.S. Private*, pg. 236
ECOLOGIZER—Air & Water Purification—Talley Industries, Inc.; *U.S. Public*, pg. 307
ECOLUBE—NONE—Carpenter Technology Corporation; *U.S. Public*, pg. 307
ECOMET—Low-Price Polishing & Grinding Machine—Buehler, Limited; *U.S. Public*, pg. 574
ECON—NONE—Richfood Holdings, Inc.; *U.S. Public*, pg. 1388
ECON-O-TILE—Hardboard Paneling—Georgia-Pacific Corporation; *U.S. Public*, pg. 735
ECON-O-MITE—Ball Valves—Worcester Controls Corp.; *Int'l*, pg. 128
ECONA—Cooking Oil Which Gives Food a Light, Non-Greasy Flavor—Kao Corporation; *Int'l*, pg. 717
ECONAX—Tap Fittings & Sanitaryware—Sime Darby Berhad; *Int'l*, pg. 1249
ECONMOD—Economic Model Comoputer Program—The Dow Chemical Company; *U.S. Public*, pg. 522
ECONO-CABLE—NONE—Berg Electronics; *U.S. Public*, pg. 212
ECONO-CLAD—Prebound Paperback Book—The American Companies, Inc.; *U.S. Private*, pg. 52
ECONO-CORD—Plastic Product—Uniflex, Inc.; *U.S. Public*, pg. 1665
ECONO-FLO—Water Conserving Spout Outlet—The Chicago Faucet Co.; *U.S. Private*, pg. 234
ECONO FOIL—Foil Laminated Paper—Hazen Paper Company; *U.S. Private*, pg. 514
ECONO-LINER—Brake Lining—Rockwell International Corporation; *U.S. Public*, pg. 1397
ECONO-LITE—Electric Incandenscent Light Bulbs—General Electric Canada Inc.; *U.S. Public*, pg. 713
ECONO LODGES—Hotels—Choice Hotels International, Inc.; *U.S. Public*, pg. 351
ECONO PAK—Packaged Fasteners—Bulldog VSI; *U.S. Public*, pg. 1176
ECONO-POP—Popcorn Machine—Gold Medal Products Co.; *U.S. Private*, pg. 459
ECONO PROOF BOX—Bakery Equipment—Belshaw Brothers, Inc.; *Int'l*, pg. 188

ECONO RAM—Cylinder—Schrader Bellows Division; *U.S. Public*, pg. 1261
ECONO/TAB—Carbonless Copy Paper—The Mead Corporation; *U.S. Public*, pg. 1074
ECONO-TAPE—Contact Materials—Engelhard Corporation; *U.S. Public*, pg. 582
ECONO-TOTE—Plastic Product—Uniflex, Inc.; *U.S. Public*, pg. 1665
ECONO-TRAP—NONE—Berg Electronics; *U.S. Public*, pg. 212
ECONO-VAULT—NONE—Uniflex, Inc.; *U.S. Public*, pg. 1665
ECONO-CON—NONE—Berg Electronics; *U.S. Public*, pg. 212
ECONOBOARD—Liner Board Backing for Hardboard Face Veneer Paneling—Georgia-Pacific Corporation; *U.S. Public*, pg. 735
ECONOCASE—Heated Instrument—Thermon Manufacturing Company; *U.S. Private*, pg. 1080
ECONOCELL—Industrial Products—Email Limited; *Int'l*, pg. 450
ECONOFOLD—Paper Napkins—Georgia-Pacific Corporation; *U.S. Public*, pg. 735
ECONOFOODS—Retail Grocery Stores—Nash Finch Company; *U.S. Public*, pg. 1151
ECONOLINE—Truck—Ford Motor Company; *U.S. Public*, pg. 661
ECONOLINER—Roof & Wall Insulation—Johns Manville Corporation; *U.S. Public*, pg. 927
ECONOLOPE—Correspondence & Mailing Envelopes—Georgia-Pacific Corporation; *U.S. Public*, pg. 735
ECONOMART—Retail Grocery Store—Nash Finch Company; *U.S. Public*, pg. 1151
ECONOMASTER—Soap Dispenser—Steiner Co., Inc.; *U.S. Private*, pg. 1039
ECONOMATE—Equipment & Salad Bars—Duke Manufacturing Co., Inc.; *U.S. Private*, pg. 346
ECONOMATIC—Paper Towel Dispenser—Georgia-Pacific Corporation; *U.S. Public*, pg. 735
ECONOMAX—Banded & Coated Abrasives—Norton Company; *Int'l*, pg. 1173
ECONOMIE—Home, Health, & Beauty Products—The Jean Coutu Group (PJC) Inc.; *Int'l*, pg. 340
THE ECONOMIST NEWSPAPER—NONE—The Economist Group Limited; *Int'l*, pg. 1026
ECONOMITE—Residential & Commercial Heating Equip.—Midco International Inc.; *U.S. Private*, pg. 744
ECONOMIZER—Grain Spreaders—David Manufacturing Company (DMC); *U.S. Private*, pg. 436
ECONOMIZER—Interior Door Units—Georgia-Pacific Corporation; *U.S. Public*, pg. 735
ECONOMY—Solid Waste Compaction Equipment—Avis Industrial Corporation; *U.S. Private*, pg. 102
ECONOMY—Mailing Bags—Bemis Company, Inc.; *U.S. Public*, pg. 210
ECONOMY—Convenience Stores—FFP Marketing Company, Inc.; *U.S. Public*, pg. 604
ECONOMY 2-DAY SERVICE—2 Day Delivery Service—FDX Corporation; *U.S. Public*, pg. 603
ECONOPAK—Culture Test Kit—Beckman Instruments, Inc.; *U.S. Public*, pg. 199
ECONOPAK—Wavesoldering System—Electrovert; *Int'l*, pg. 328
ECONOPRED—Prednisolone Acetete Ophthalmic Suspension—Alcon Laboratories, Inc.; *Int'l*, pg. 916
ECONOPRED PLUS—Prednisolone Acetate—Alcon Laboratories, Inc.; *Int'l*, pg. 916
ECONOPRESS—Filter—American Felt & Filter; *U.S. Private*, pg. 54
ECONOPURE—RO Unit—Osmonics, Inc.; *U.S. Public*, pg. 1233
ECONOSERV—Paper Napkins—Georgia-Pacific Corporation; *U.S. Public*, pg. 735
ECONOSOURCE—Marketing Program—Ikon Office Solutions, Inc.; *U.S. Public*, pg. 862
ECONOSOURCE—Copy Paper DP 1671
ECONOTEMP—Laboratory Ovens—Fisher Scientific Company; *U.S. Private*, pg. 658
ECONOTIG—Welding & Cutting Equip.—Miller Electric Manufacturing Co.; *U.S. Public*, pg. 867
ECONOTRACE—Parallel Heating Cables—Thermon Manufacturing Company; *U.S. Private*, pg. 1080
ECONOTRON—Closet Carrier—Josam Company; *U.S. Private*, pg. 600

ECONOVENT—Heat Exchanger—Incentive AB; *Int'l*, pg. 666
ECOPAPER—Water-Reducible Ink Extender—Raffi & Swanson, Inc.; *U.S. Private*, pg. 907
ECOSCIENCE—NONE—EcoScience Corporation; *U.S. Public*, pg. 563
ECOSCRUBS—Uniforms—Angelica Corporation; *U.S. Public*, pg. 113
ECOSMOOTH—Water Reducible Ink (and Extender)—Raffi & Swanson, Inc.; *U.S. Private*, pg. 907
ECOSOFT—Towels & Tissues—Bay West Paper Corp. Towel & Tissue Div.; *U.S. Public*, pg. 1747
ECOSOFT—Recycled Towel & Tissue Products—Wausau-Mosinee Paper Corporation; *U.S. Public*, pg. 1747
ECOSOLUTION—NONE—Avenor, Inc.; *Int'l*, pg. 101
ECOSPERSE—Water Reducible Ink—Raffi & Swanson, Inc.; *U.S. Private*, pg. 907
ECOSPRAY—Fitment—W. Braun Company; *U.S. Private*, pg. 166
ECOSTIK—Adhesive—Laporte plc; *Int'l*, pg. 801
ECOSYS—Environmental Equipment—ATMI, Inc.; *U.S. Public*, pg. 12
ECOSYS—Home & Office Page Printers—Kyocera International, Inc.; *Int'l*, pg. 775
ECOTE—NONE—Urban Outfitters, Inc.; *U.S. Public*, pg. 1700
ECOTRIN—Aspirin for Arthritis—SmithKline Beecham Consumer Healthcare, U.S.; *Int'l*, pg. 1264
ECOTRIN—NONE—SmithKline Beecham Corporation; *Int'l*, pg. 1264
ECOTRIN—Analgesic—SmithKline Beecham plc; *Int'l*, pg. 1264
ECOVISION—Integrated Software Package for Visual Follow up Environmental Data—Electrabel S.A.; *Int'l*, pg. 436
ECOWRITER—Woodcase Pencil—Sanford Corporation; *U.S. Public*, pg. 1178
ECSAINE—Man-Made Suede—Toray Industries, Inc.; *Int'l*, pg. 1399
ECSTASY—Mattress & Box Spring Sets—Kingsdown, Inc.; *U.S. Private*, pg. 622
ECTO PLUS—Ectoparasiticide—Ciba Specialty Chemicals; *Int'l*, pg. 291
ECTO PLUS—Ectoparasiticide—Novartis; *Int'l*, pg. 972
ECTOMIN—Ectoparasiticide—Novartis; *Int'l*, pg. 972
ED BURNETT CONSULTANTS INC—Mailing Lists—Database America Companies; *U.S. Private*, pg. 312
ED MORSE CADILLAC/DELRAY—Dealership—Ed Morse Automotive Group; *U.S. Private*, pg. 763
ED MORSE CADILLAC/TAMPA—Dealership—Ed Morse Automotive Group; *U.S. Private*, pg. 763
EDCLIFF INSTRUMENTS—Pressure Sensors—BEI Sensors and Systems Company; *U.S. Public*, pg. 160
EDDIE BAUER—Weekend & Outdoor Men's & Women's Wear—Spiegel, Inc.; *U.S. Public*, pg. 1498
EDDIE BAUER ADVENTURER—Men's Cologne and Toiletries—Eddie Bauer, Inc.; *U.S. Public*, pg. 1499
EDDY'S—Bread—Interstate Brands Corporation; *U.S. Public*, pg. 909
EDECRIN—Ethacrynic Acid—Merck & Co., Inc.; *U.S. Public*, pg. 1090
EDELBROCK—Auto Equip.—Edelbrock Corp.; *U.S. Public*, pg. 563
EDELMANN—NONE—Plews/Edelmann; *Int'l*, pg. 1396
EDEN—Dinnerware—Dansk International Designs Ltd.; *U.S. Private*, pg. 261
EDEN ROC—Champagne—E. & J. Gallo Winery; *U.S. Private*, pg. 438
EDENTEC—NONE—Nellcor Puritan Bennett Incorporated; *U.S. Public*, pg. 1039
EDENTRACE—Recording System—Nellcor Puritan Bennett Incorporated; *U.S. Public*, pg. 1039
EDENTRACE II—Recording System—Nellcor Puritan Bennett Incorporated; *U.S. Public*, pg. 1039
EDENTRACE II PLUS—Portable Sleep Apnea Recording System—Nellcor Puritan Bennett Incorporated; *U.S. Public*, pg. 1039

EDENTREND—Memory Module—Nellcor Puritan Bennett Incorporated; *U.S. Public*, pg. 1039

EDERER—Cranes—Ederer Inc.; *U.S. Private*, pg. 363

EDEX—NONE—Schwarz Pharma Inc.; *Int'l*, pg. 1211

EDGE—Bowling Ball—Brunswick Bowling & Billiards Corp.; *U.S. Public*, pg. 265

EDGE—NONE—Countrywide Home Loans Inc.; *U.S. Public*, pg. 452

EDGE—Shaving Gel—S.C. Johnson & Son, Inc.; *U.S. Private*, pg. 592

EDGE—(Shave Preparation)—S.C. Johnson & Son, Limited; *U.S. Private*, pg. 593

EDGE—Cymbals—Avedis Zildjian Company; *U.S. Private*, pg. 1206

THE EDGE IN ELECTRONICS—Electronics Stores—Tandy Corporation; *U.S. Public*, pg. 1560

EDGE SHAVING GEL SENSITIVE SKIN WITH NATURAL ALOE—Shaving Gel—S.C. Johnson & Son, Inc.; *U.S. Private*, pg. 592

EDGE SOOTHING AFTER SHAVE WITH ALOE—After Shave Lotion—S.C. Johnson & Son, Inc.; *U.S. Private*, pg. 592

THE EDGE—Servo Roll Feed—P/A Industries, Inc.; *U.S. Private*, pg. 825

EDGEFIELD—Pressure Treaded Decking Products—Cox Wood Preserving Co.; *U.S. Private*, pg. 283

EDGESEAL—Glass Sealant—PPG Industries, Inc.; *U.S. Public*, pg. 1245

EDGEWORTH—Pipe Tobacco—Lane Limited; *Int'l*, pg. 1129

EDICON—Image Processing Products—Eastman Kodak Company; *U.S. Public*, pg. 550

EDIFOAM—Durable, Wear-Resistant Polyurethane System; Prolongs Athletic Shoe Life—Kao Corporation; *Int'l*, pg. 717

EDILIT—NONE—ETEX; *Int'l*, pg. 430

EDIQUIP—Film Editing Equipment—J & R Film / Moviola Digital Co.; *U.S. Private*, pg. 576

EDISON—Lighting—Cooper Industries, Inc.; *U.S. Public*, pg. 442

EDISON CAPITAL—NONE—Edison International; *U.S. Public*, pg. 564

EDISON EV—NONE—Edison International; *U.S. Public*, pg. 564

EDISON INTERNATIONAL—NONE—Edison International; *U.S. Public*, pg. 564

EDISON MISSION ENERGY—NONE—Edison International; *U.S. Public*, pg. 564

EDISON SELECT—NONE—Edison International; *U.S. Public*, pg. 564

EDISON SOURCE—NONE—Edison International; *U.S. Public*, pg. 564

EDITION—Printing Paper—Georgia-Pacific Corporation; *U.S. Public*, pg. 735

EDITIONS—Apparel—Phillips-Van Heusen Corporation; *U.S. Public*, pg. 1291

EDITWRITER—Photo Typesetters—AGFA EPS Division; *Int'l*, pg. 172

EDLUND—Can Openers, Scales, Slicers, Knife Sharpening Equip.—Edlund Company, Inc.; *U.S. Private*, pg. 364

EDMUND—Scientific Equipment—Edmund Scientific Company; *U.S. Private*, pg. 364

EDOMAE—Beer—Asahi Breweries Ltd.; *Int'l*, pg. 83

EDUCATION/EXPRESS—Computer System—International Business Machines Corporation; *U.S. Public*, pg. 895

EDUCATION....MEDTRONIC'S INVESTMENT IN YOU—Training Programs—Medtronic, Inc.; *U.S. Public*, pg. 1082

EDUCTAIR—Liquid-Solids Separation Equipment—Komline-Sanderson Engineering Corp.; *U.S. Private*, pg. 631

EDUCTROL—Educator Chemical Feed System—Diversey Water Technologies, Inc.; *U.S. Public*, pg. 1150

EDUQUEST—Computer System—International Business Machines Corporation; *U.S. Public*, pg. 895

EDWARD D. JONES—Securities Brokerage Firm—Edward Jones; *U.S. Private*, pg. 597

EDWARD DON—Food Service Equip., Furnishings & Supplies—Edward Don & Company; *U.S. Private*, pg. 339

EDWARD G. ROBINSON—Pipe Tobaccos—Consolidated Cigar Corporation; *U.S. Private*, pg. 690

EDWARDS—Frozen Pies—Edwards Baking Co.; *U.S. Private*, pg. 365

EDWARDSVILLE INTELLIGENCER—Newspaper—The Hearst Corporation; *U.S. Private*, pg. 515

EDY'S FROZEN YOGURT INSPIRATIONS—Frozen Confection—Dreyer's Grand Ice Cream, Inc.; *U.S. Public*, pg. 529

EDY'S GRAND ICE CREAM—Ice Cream—Dreyer's Grand Ice Cream, Inc.; *U.S. Public*, pg. 529

EECO KEYPAD—NONE—Transico Incorporated; *U.S. Public*, pg. 1630

EECO SWITCH—NONE—Transico Incorporated; *U.S. Public*, pg. 1630

EEPN—Periodical—Penton Publishing, Inc.; *U.S. Public*, pg. 1306

EEZ-THRU—Oral Hygiene Aids—John O. Butler Co.; *Int'l*, pg. 1320

EEZE OFF—Waffle Mold—Gold Medal Products Co.; *U.S. Private*, pg. 459

EFACT—Computerized Energy Management Analysis Program—Johnson Controls, Inc., Controls Group; *U.S. Public*, pg. 932

EFAMOL—Dietary Supplement—Novo Nordisk A/S; *Int'l*, pg. 987

EFEXOR—NONE—Wyeth Australia Pty. Ltd.; *U.S. Public*, pg. 82

EFFECTO—Paint—Pratt & Lambert United, Inc.; *U.S. Public*, pg. 1466

EFFECTONE—Undercoater—Jones Blair Company; *U.S. Private*, pg. 596

EFFECTS—Dimmers, Fan Controls, Switches & Photocell Controls—The Lamson & Sessions Co.; *U.S. Public*, pg. 976

EFFERDENT—Denture Cleaner—Warner-Lambert Company; *U.S. Public*, pg. 1738

EFFERDENT—Denture Cleanser—Warner-Lambert Consumer Healthcare; *U.S. Public*, pg. 1739

EFFERGRIP—Denture Adhesive—Warner-Lambert Company; *U.S. Public*, pg. 1738

EFFEX—Floodlights—Wide-Lite; *U.S. Public*, pg. 730

EFFEX SERIES FLOODLIGHT—NONE—Wide-Lite; *U.S. Public*, pg. 730

EFFEXOR—Anti-depressant—American Home Products Corporation; *U.S. Public*, pg. 79

EFFEXOR—Pharmaceutical Products—Wyeth-Ayerst Laboratories, Inc.; *U.S. Public*, pg. 80

EFFEXOR XR—Anti-Depressant—American Home Products Corporation; *U.S. Public*, pg. 79

EFFI—Low Fat Spread—Unilever Plc; *Int'l*, pg. 1433

EFFLUENT—NONE—Sta-Rite Industries, Inc.; *U.S. Public*, pg. 1767

EFIDAC—Decongestant—Novartis; *Int'l*, pg. 972

EFTEK—NONE—Dynamic Materials Corporation; *U.S. Public*, pg. 539

EGEKVIST—Danish, Donuts & Sweet Goods—Metz Baking Company; *U.S. Private*, pg. 1022

EGEKVIST—Danish, Donuts, Bread, Buns, Sweet Goods—Metz Baking Company (WI); *U.S. Private*, pg. 1022

EGERMEIER'S—Bible Story Book—Warner Press, Inc.; *U.S. Private*, pg. 1150

EGG BEATERS—99% Real Egg Product—Nabisco Inc.; *U.S. Public*, pg. 1355

EGG MAKER—Poultry Feeds—Manna Pro Corporation; *U.S. Private*, pg. 700

EGG MCMUFFIN—Sandwich—McDonald's Corporation; *U.S. Public*, pg. 1068

EGGBEATER—Bladed PDC—Baker Hughes INTEQ; *U.S. Public*, pg. 166

EGGHEAD—Computer & Software Retailer—Egghead, Inc.; *U.S. Public*, pg. 566

EGGLAND'S BEST—Eggs Products—Eggland's Best, Inc.; *U.S. Private*, pg. 366

EGGO—Frozen Waffles—Kellogg Company; *U.S. Public*, pg. 947

EGGO CINNAMON TOAST WAFFLES—Snack Food—Kellogg Company; *U.S. Public*, pg. 947

EGGSTRO'DNAIRE—Alternative Egg Product—Novartis Nutrition Corporation; *Int'l*, pg. 974

EGRET—Binoculars—Swift Instruments, Inc.; *U.S. Private*, pg. 1058

EHAPARIN—Sizing Agents—Akzo Nobel N.V.; *Int'l*, pg. 42

883 PLUS—NONE—Carpenter Technology Corporation; *U.S. Public*, pg. 307

855—Golf Clubs—Tommy Armour Golf; *U.S. Public*, pg. 1683

845 S—Golf Clubs—Tommy Armour Golf; *U.S. Public*, pg. 1683

841 PLUS—IEEE 841 Motor—U.S. Electrical Motor Division; *U.S. Public*, pg. 573

800-BASKETS—Gift-Giving Service—800-FLOWERS, Inc.; *U.S. Private*, pg. 366

800-CANDIES—Gift-Giving Service—800-FLOWERS, Inc.; *U.S. Private*, pg. 366

883B/RETS—Electronics—National Semiconductor Corporation; *U.S. Public*, pg. 1159

883S/RETS—Electronics—National Semiconductor Corporation; *U.S. Public*, pg. 1159

800-FLOWERS—Flower Delivery Service—800-FLOWERS, Inc.; *U.S. Private*, pg. 366

800-GOODIES—Gift-Giving Service—800-FLOWERS, Inc.; *U.S. Private*, pg. 366

800-LAS-FLORES—Flower Delivery Service—800-FLOWERS, Inc.; *U.S. Private*, pg. 366

820 TABLES—Conference Tables—Vecta; *U.S. Private*, pg. 1038

800 UNI-DEN PRESS—Baling Press for Baling Cotton Lint—Continental Eagle Corporation; *U.S. Private*, pg. 267

8-MOP—Prescription Drug—ICN Pharmaceuticals, Inc.; *U.S. Public*, pg. 853

EIGHT O'CLOCK—Coffee—The Great Atlantic & Pacific Tea Company, Inc.; *Int'l*, pg. 1375

810—Heavy Duty Trucks—Isuzu Motors Limited; *Int'l*, pg. 692

8000 SERIES—Serial Dot Matrix Printers—Dataproducts Corporation; *Int'l*, pg. 620

8000 SERIES—Bar Code Card/Badge Readers—Intelligent Controls Inc.; *U.S. Private*, pg. 566

8300—Page Layout & Copy Processing Systems—G.E. Harris Energy Control Systems, LLC; *U.S. Public*, pg. 712

8028—Photocopier—Konica Corporation; *Int'l*, pg. 748

18-8 BOAT RUB RAIL—NONE—Carpenter Technology Corporation; *U.S. Public*, pg. 307

18-18 PLUS—NONE—Carpenter Technology Corporation; *U.S. Public*, pg. 307

1881—Silverware—Oneida Ltd.; *U.S. Public*, pg. 1225

1886's—Domestic Cigars—Consolidated Cigar Corporation; *U.S. Private*, pg. 690

EIGHTEEN HOUR—NONE—Playtex Apparel, Inc.; *U.S. Public*, pg. 1433

1847 ROGERS BROS.—Flatware—Syratech Corporation; *U.S. Private*, pg. 1060

18K—Catheters—Medtronic, Inc.; *U.S. Public*, pg. 1082

1830—Game—Monarch Avalon, Inc.; *U.S. Public*, pg. 1123

80 ALUMINA—High Alumina Brick—A.P. Green Industries, Inc.; *U.S. Public*, pg. 761

8520 TAPE OPTIMIZER—Data Compresser—Anacomp Magnetics; *U.S. Public*, pg. 107

8400 UNIDEN PRESS—Economical Universal Density Baling Press—Continental Eagle Corporation; *U.S. Private*, pg. 267

80 SERIES—Handheld Multimeters—Fluke Corporation; *U.S. Public*, pg. 659

8700/8800 SERIES—Furniture—Myrtle/Mueller, A Haworth Co.; *U.S. Private*, pg. 512

8600 SERIES—Furniture—Myrtle/Mueller, A Haworth Co.; *U.S. Private*, pg. 512

8600X—Fully Addressable Baseband Set-Top Terminal With Descrambler—Scientific-Atlanta, Inc.; *U.S. Public*, pg. 1443

EIGHTY-EIGHT—Automobile—Oldsmobile Div. General Motors Corp.; *U.S. Public*, pg. 720

EIKONIX—Imaging Products—Eastman Kodak Company; *U.S. Public*, pg. 550

EINSTEIN MOOMJY-THE CARPET DEPARTMENT STORE—Retail Floor Covering—Einstein Moomjy Inc.; *U.S. Private*, pg. 366

EJECTOR—Cooling Tower—Baltimore Aircoil Company; *U.S. Private*, pg. 68

EKALUX—Cotton Herbicide—Novartis AG; *Int'l*, pg. 971

EKCO—Bakeware, Kitchen Tools & Gadgets—Ekco Group, Inc.; *U.S. Public*, pg. 566

EKCO BAKEWARE—Bakeware—Ekco Housewares, Inc.; *U.S. Public*, pg. 566

EKCOTHERM PLUS—Paperboard for Oven Cooking—Tenneco Specialty Products; *U.S. Public*, pg. 1579

EKSTATIC—Electro Copy Paper—Fort James Corporation; *U.S. Public*, pg. 670

EKSTROM—Meter Socket Adapters & Testing Devices—Ekstrom Industries, Inc.; *U.S. Private*, pg. 172

EKTA-CLEAR—Anti-Fogging Wax for Eyewear—Ektelon; *U.S. Private*, pg. 884

EKTABROME—Photo Paper—Eastman Kodak Company; *U.S. Public*, pg. 550

EKTACHEM—Blood Analysis Equipment & Chemicals—Eastman Kodak Company; *U.S. Public*, pg. 550

EKTACHROME—Color Photo Film, Paper, Transparencies & Chemicals—Eastman Kodak Company; *U.S. Public*, pg. 550

EKTACHROME-X—Color Photographic Film—Eastman Kodak Company; *U.S. Public*, pg. 550

EKTACOLOR—Color Photo Film, Paper, Apparatus & Chemicals—Eastman Kodak Company; *U.S. Public*, pg. 550

EKTAFAX—Thermal Copying Apparatus, Heat Sensitive & Copy Papers—Eastman Kodak Company; *U.S. Public*, pg. 550

EKTAFICHE—Microfilm Duplicator—Eastman Kodak Company; *U.S. Public*, pg. 550

EKTAFLEX—Photographic Paper, Film, Apparatus & Chemicals—Eastman Kodak Company; *U.S. Public*, pg. 550

EKTAFLO—Photo Processing Chemicals—Eastman Kodak Company; *U.S. Public*, pg. 550

EKTAGRAPHIC—Motion Picture, Slide Projectors & Other Audiovisual Apparatus—Eastman Kodak Company; *U.S. Public*, pg. 550

EKTALINE—Photo Paper, Chemicals & Apparatus—Eastman Kodak Company; *U.S. Public*, pg. 550

EKTALITE—Field Lens, Projection Screens & Microfilm Readers—Eastman Kodak Company; *U.S. Public*, pg. 550

EKTALITH—Copying Equipment, Photo Paper, Copy Paper Chemicals—Eastman Kodak Company; *U.S. Public*, pg. 550

EKTALOG—Photofinishing Tape Cassette & Terminals—Eastman Kodak Company; *U.S. Public*, pg. 550

EKTALURE—Photo Paper—Eastman Kodak Company; *U.S. Public*, pg. 550

EKTALUX—Light Filters—Eastman Kodak Company; *U.S. Public*, pg. 550

EKTAMARK—Photographic Film & Chemicals—Eastman Kodak Company; *U.S. Public*, pg. 550

EKTAMAT—Radiographic Film—Eastman Kodak Company; *U.S. Public*, pg. 550

EKTAMATE—Photo Paper, Lenses, Microfilm Equipment—Eastman Kodak Company; *U.S. Public*, pg. 550

EKTAMATIC—Photo Paper & Chemicals, Processing Apparatus—Eastman Kodak Company; *U.S. Public*, pg. 550

EKTAMITE—Flash Lighting Apparatus—Eastman Kodak Company; *U.S. Public*, pg. 550

EKTANAR—Photo Lenses—Eastman Kodak Company; *U.S. Public*, pg. 550

EKTANON—Photo Lenses—Eastman Kodak Company; *U.S. Public*, pg. 550

EKTAPAN—Photo Film—Eastman Kodak Company; *U.S. Public*, pg. 550

EKTAPHOR—Automated Electrophoresis systems—Eastman Kodak Company; *U.S. Public*, pg. 550

EKTAPLUS—Printers—Eastman Kodak Company; *U.S. Public*, pg. 550

EKTAPRESS—Photographic Film—Eastman Kodak Company; *U.S. Public*, pg. 550

EKTAPRINT—Xerographic Copier—Eastman Kodak Company; *U.S. Public*, pg. 550

EKTAPRO—Cassettes, Lenses, Motion Analyzers, Processors, Solvent—Eastman Kodak Company; *U.S. Public*, pg. 550

EKTAR—Synthetic Resins , Photographic Lenses & Film—Eastman Kodak Company; *U.S. Public*, pg. 550

EKTASCAN—Imaging Scanning Equipment, Film & Software—Eastman Kodak Company; *U.S. Public*, pg. 550

EKTASOLVE—Industrial Solvents—Eastman Kodak Company; *U.S. Public*, pg. 550

EKTASOUND—Motion Picture Sound Camera & Projectors—Eastman Kodak Company; *U.S. Public*, pg. 550

EKTASPEED—X-ray Film—Eastman Kodak Company; *U.S. Public*, pg. 550

EKTATHERM—Video Print Cartridges, Paper, Etc.—Eastman Kodak Company; *U.S. Public*, pg. 550

EKTAVISION—Televison Monitors—Eastman Kodak Company; *U.S. Public*, pg. 550

EKTAVOLT—Photographic Film & Chemicals—Eastman Kodak Company; *U.S. Public*, pg. 550

EKTAWRITE—Film Folios—Eastman Kodak Company; *U.S. Public*, pg. 550

EKTOBAN—Ectoparasiticides—Novartis; *Int'l*, pg. 972

EKTON—Photo Lenses—Eastman Kodak Company; *U.S. Public*, pg. 550

EKTONOL—Photo Developer—Eastman Kodak Company; *U.S. Public*, pg. 550

EKTRA—Cameras—Eastman Kodak Company; *U.S. Public*, pg. 550

EKTRALITE—Cameras—Eastman Kodak Company; *U.S. Public*, pg. 550

EKTRAMAX—Cameras—Eastman Kodak Company; *U.S. Public*, pg. 550

EKTRON—Electronic Flash Processing Chemicals—Eastman Kodak Company; *U.S. Public*, pg. 550

EL AL ISRAEL AIRLINES—NONE—El Al Israel Airlines, Ltd.; *Int'l*, pg. 435

EL APOSENTO ALTO—The Upper Room for Spanish Speaking People—The Upper Room; *U.S. Private*, pg. 1129

EL CHARRITO—Mexican Food Products—Don Miguel Mexican Foods, Inc.; *U.S. Private*, pg. 339

EL CHARRITO—Frozen Mexican Dinners & Prepared Foods—The Earthgrains Company; *U.S. Public*, pg. 547

EL CHICO—Restaurants—El Chico Restaurants, Inc.; *U.S. Private*, pg. 283

EL CONDOR—Tequila—Montebello Brands Inc.; *U.S. Private*, pg. 758

EL CONDOR—Candles—Nuevo Federal S.A.; *Int'l*, pg. 990

EL DORADO—Corn & Tortilla Chips—Borden, Inc.; *U.S. Private*, pg. 157

EL DORADO—Avocados—Calavo Growers of California; *U.S. Private*, pg. 199

EL DORADO—Area Rugs—Couristan Inc.; *U.S. Private*, pg. 279

EL GALEON—Trademark for Edible Foods—H.J. Baker & Bro., Inc.; *U.S. Private*, pg. 112

EL MARKO—Markers—The Gillette Company; *U.S. Public*, pg. 743

EL MOLINO—Dips, Sauces & Spices—Borden, Inc.; *U.S. Private*, pg. 157

EL MONTEREY—Frozen Mexican Food—Ruiz Food Products, Inc.; *U.S. Public*, pg. 951

EL PASO HERALD-POST—Newspaper—The E.W. Scripps Company; *U.S. Public*, pg. 1447

EL PICO—Removers—W.M. Barr & Co., Inc.; *U.S. Private*, pg. 117

EL PICO—Expresso—Tetley USA Inc.; *Int'l*, pg. 1377

EL POLLO LOCO—Eating Place—Advantica Restaurant Group, Inc.; *U.S. Public*, pg. 22

EL POLLO LOCO—Restaurants—El Pollo Loco; *U.S. Public*, pg. 23

EL PRODUCTO—Domestic Cigars—Consolidated Cigar Corporation; *U.S. Private*, pg. 690

EL-RIO—Assorted Mexican Food Products—World Finer Foods, Inc.; *U.S. Private*, pg. 1190

EL RODEO—Whole Milk Powder—Borden, Inc.; *U.S. Private*, pg. 157

EL TORITO—Restaurant Chain—El Torito Restaurants Inc.; *U.S. Private*, pg. 393

EL TORO—Seasonings, Peppers, Corn Husks—McCormick/Schilling; *U.S. Public*, pg. 1066

EL TORO TEQUILA—NONE—Barton Brands, Ltd.; *U.S. Public*, pg. 300

EL TRELLIS—Cigars—Swisher International Group, Inc.; *U.S. Public*, pg. 1543

EL TRIUNFO—Premium Cigars—Consolidated Cigar Corporation; *U.S. Private*, pg. 690

ELAN—Frozen Yogurt—Brigham's, Inc.; *U.S. Private*, pg. 483

ELAN—Frozen Yogurt—Elan Foods; *U.S. Private*, pg. 484

ELAN BY BARCO—Professional Apparel—Barco of California; *U.S. Private*, pg. 115

ELANTE—Motor Homes—Winnebago Industries, Inc.; *U.S. Public*, pg. 1772

ELANTRA—Automobile—Hyundai Motor America; *Int'l*, pg. 641

ELAST-HONE—External Surface Finishing Abrasive Disc—Brush Research Manufacturing Company; *U.S. Private*, pg. 176

ELASTAN—Polyurethane Systems—BASF AG; *Int'l*, pg. 103

ELASTENE—Polymer—Rohm and Haas Company; *U.S. Public*, pg. 1403

ELASTIMOLD—Electrical Connectors—Thomas & Betts/Amerace; *U.S. Public*, pg. 1598

ELASTIMOLD—Power Connectors & Accessories—Thomas & Betts Corporation; *U.S. Public*, pg. 1597

ELASTOCOAT—Polyurethane Systems—BASF AG; *Int'l*, pg. 103

ELASTOFLEX—Polyurethane Systems—BASF AG; *Int'l*, pg. 103

ELASTOFOAM—Polyurethane Systems—BASF AG; *Int'l*, pg. 103

ELASTOFOAM—Oriented Wires In Soft Silicone Sponge—Tecknit Incorporated; *U.S. Private*, pg. 1072

ELASTOLIT—Polyurethane Systems—BASF AG; *Int'l*, pg. 103

ELASTOLLAN—Polyurethane Systems—BASF AG; *Int'l*, pg. 103

ELASTOMERIC TECHNOLOGIES—Electronic Connectors—Thomas & Betts Corporation; *U.S. Public*, pg. 1597

ELASTOMET—Oriented Wires In Silicone—Tecknit Incorporated; *U.S. Private*, pg. 1072

ELASTOMULL—Elastic Gauze Bandages—Beiersdorf, Inc.; *Int'l*, pg. 182

ELASTOPAL—Polyurethane Systems—BASF AG; *Int'l*, pg. 103

ELASTOPAN S—Polyurethane Systems—BASF AG; *Int'l*, pg. 103

ELASTOPLAST—Bandages—Beiersdorf, Inc.; *Int'l*, pg. 182

ELASTOPLAST—First Aid Dressing—Smith & Nephew PLC; *Int'l*, pg. 1263

ELASTOPOR F—Polyurethane Systems—BASF AG; *Int'l*, pg. 103

ELASTRATOR—Sheep Docker & Castrator—Nasco Modesto; *U.S. Private*, pg. 446

ELATE—Diisocyanate—Akzo Nobel N.V.; *Int'l*, pg. 42

ELATEC—Pacemakers—L'Oreal S.A.; *Int'l*, pg. 818

ELAVIL—Amitriptyline Hydrochloride—Merck & Co., Inc.; *U.S. Public*, pg. 1090

ELBA—Broadloom—Couristan Inc.; *U.S. Private*, pg. 279

ELBA-MOBIL—Materials-handling Equipment—Electrolux, AB; *Int'l*, pg. 438

ELBECO—Uniform Shirts & Trousers—Elbeco Incorporated; *U.S. Private*, pg. 367

ELBOLET—Fittings—Bonney Forge Corporation; *U.S. Private*, pg. 156

ELBRODUR—Electrode Materials for Resistance Welding—KM-Europa Metal Aktiengesellschaft; *Int'l*, pg. 719

ELCAMINO—NONE—Seats Incorporated; *U.S. Private*, pg. 410

ELCATONIN—Vitamin—SmithKline Beecham plc; *Int'l*, pg. 1264

ELCITONIN—Agent for Bone Metabolism—Asahi Chemical Industry Co., Ltd.; *Int'l*, pg. 83

ELCO CONNECTORS—NONE—Milgray Electronics, Inc.; *U.S. Public*, pg. 205

ELCOM—Brushless DC Motors—Penn Engineering & Manufacturing Corp.; *U.S. Public*, pg. 1269

ELDEPRYL—Treatment for the Late Stages of Parkinson's Disease; 50% via Somerset—Mylan Laboratories, Inc.; *U.S. Public*, pg. 1143

ELDER-BEERMAN—Retail Department Stores—The Elder-Beerman Stores Corp.; *U.S. Private*, pg. 367

ELDERADO—Boyswear—Elder Manufacturing Company; *U.S. Private*, pg. 367

ELDERS—Grain, Meat, Beer—Foster's Brewing Group Limited; *Int'l*, pg. 500

ELDON CRESTMONT—Desktop Accessories Line—Rubbermaid Incorporated; *U.S. Public*, pg. 1411

ELDOPAQUE—Prescription Drug—ICN Pharmaceuticals, Inc.; *U.S. Public*, pg. 853

ELDOQUINE—NONE—ICN Pharmaceuticals, Inc.; *U.S. Public*, pg. 853

ELDORADO—Car—Cadillac Motor Car Division; *U.S. Public*, pg. 720

ELDORADO—NONE—Seats Incorporated; *U.S. Private*, pg. 410

ELDORADO VIP—NONE—Seats Incorporated; *U.S. Private*, pg. 410

ELECROGATOR—Irrigation Equipment Center Pivot—Reinke Manufacturing Co., Inc.; *U.S. Private*, pg. 920

ELECT-AIRE—NONE—Nordyne Inc.; *U.S. Public*, pg. 1193

ELECTIVE ELEMENTS-1—Open Plan Office Furniture—Steelcase Wood Div.; *U.S. Private*, pg. 1038

ELECTONE—Home Organ—Yamaha Corporation of America; *Int'l*, pg. 1516

ELECTOTE—Horizontal Transport System—The Raymond Corporation; *Int'l*, pg. 123

ELECTRA—Automobile—Buick Motor Div. General Motors Corp.; *U.S. Public*, pg. 720

ELECTRA—Crucibles—Ferro Corporation; *U.S. Public*, pg. 618

ELECTRA 800—Automatic Coagulation Timer—Medical Laboratory Automation, Inc.; *U.S. Private*, pg. 727

ELECTRA 1400C—Automatic Coagulation Analyzer—Ortho Clinical Diagnostic Systems Inc.; *U.S. Public*, pg. 929

ELECTRA GLIDE—Motorcycles—Harley-Davidson, Inc.; *U.S. Public*, pg. 786

ELECTRA MAGIC—Recirculating Toilet—Thetford Corporation; *U.S. Private*, pg. 352

ELECTRA-MATIC—Coffee—Kraft Foods, Inc.; *U.S. Public*, pg. 1287

ELECTRA 900—Random Access Photo-Optical Clot Detection System—Medical Laboratory Automation, Inc.; *U.S. Private*, pg. 727

ELECTRA 900C—Random Access Photo-Optical Clot Detection System—Medical Laboratory Automation, Inc.; *U.S. Private*, pg. 727

ELECTRA 1000C—Automated Coagulation Analyzer—Medical Laboratory Automation, Inc.; *U.S. Private*, pg. 727

ELECTRA-PLOT—Dielectric Media for Electrostatic Plotter—Dietzgen Corporation; *U.S. Private*, pg. 332

ELECTRA 750—Semi-Automated Coagulation Analyzer—Medical Laboratory Automation, Inc.; *U.S. Private*, pg. 727

ELECTRA 700—Fully Automated Coagulation Analyzer—Medical Laboratory Automation, Inc.; *U.S. Private*, pg. 727

ELECTRA 1600C—Automated Coagulation Analyzer—Medical Laboratory Automation, Inc.; *U.S. Private*, pg. 727

ELECTRA 1600C—Automatic Coagulation Analyzer—Ortho Clinical Diagnostic Systems Inc.; *U.S. Public*, pg. 929

ELECTRA-SAVER—Air Compressors—Gardner Denver Machinery Inc.; *U.S. Public*, pg. 703

ELECTRA-SCREW—Air Compressors—Gardner Denver Machinery Inc.; *U.S. Public*, pg. 703

ELECTRACK—Monorail Gearbox—Regal-Beloit Corporation; *U.S. Public*, pg. 1370

ELECTRADOME—NONE—Evans & Sutherland Computer Corporation; *U.S. Public*, pg. 595

ELECTRAFLASH 141—Flashing Light—Federal Signal Corporation, Signal Div.; *U.S. Public*, pg. 616

ELECTRAK—Electronic Transportation Controls—Warner Electric Industrial Products Division; *U.S. Public*, pg. 480

ELECTRARAY 225—Rotating Warning Light—Federal Signal Corporation, Signal Div.; *U.S. Public*, pg. 616

ELECTRASOL—Automatic Dishwashing Detergent—Benckiser Consumer Products Inc.; *Int'l*, pg. 185

ELECTRIC AVENUE—Appliance & Electronic Stores—Montgomery Ward & Co., Inc.; *U.S. Private*, pg. 758

ELECTRIC BEACH—Junior Swimwear—Jantzen; *U.S. Public*, pg. 1702

ELECTRIC EAR—Mining & Chemical Machinery—Svedala Industries Inc.; *Int'l*, pg. 1325

ELECTRIC RACING—Racing—Tyco Toys, Inc.; *U.S. Public*, pg. 1058

ELECTRIC TRACK VEHICLE SYSTEM—Matl. Transport System—TransLogic Corp.; *Int'l*, pg. 1387

ELECTRIC TRAINS—Trains—Tyco Toys, Inc.; *U.S. Public*, pg. 1058

ELECTRICAL CONSTRUCTION & MAINTENANCE—Publication on Electrical Systems—Intertec Publishing; *U.S. Public*, pg. 1327

ELECTRICAL MARKETING—Twice Monthly Newsletter—Intertec Publishing; *U.S. Public*, pg. 1327

ELECTRICAL WHOLESALING—Information on Business Trends—Intertec Publishing; *U.S. Public*, pg. 1327

ELECTRICAL WORLD—Magazine—Reed Business Information Pty. Limited; *Int'l*, pg. 1094

ELECTRICAL WORLD BUYERS' GUIDE—Directory—Reed Business Information Pty. Limited; *Int'l*, pg. 1094

ELECTRICHEQUE—Gift Certificates—Public Service Company of Oklahoma; *U.S. Public*, pg. 324

ELECTRICWELD—Steel Tubing—Bundy North America; *Int'l*, pg. 1340

ELECTRIM—Torque/Force Gauges—AMETEK, Inc.; *U.S. Public*, pg. 99

ELECTRISIL—Silicone Rubber Paste for Use as a Sealant in Wire & Cable Manufacture—General Electric Canada Inc.; *U.S. Public*, pg. 713

ELECTRO-AIR—Electronic Air Cleaners—White-Rodgers Div., Emerson Electric Co.; *U.S. Public*, pg. 573

ELECTRO BRAND—NONE—Electro Brand, Inc.; *U.S. Private*, pg. 368

ELECTRO/CONNECT—Manufactured Wiring System—Thomas Industries Inc.; *U.S. Public*, pg. 1598

ELECTRO/CONNECT—Wiring—Thomas Lighting-C&I Indoor Divison; *U.S. Public*, pg. 1599

ELECTRO-CRAFT—Motion Control Products House Mark—Rockwell International Corporation; *U.S. Public*, pg. 1397

ELECTRO-GEL—Electrolyte Gel—Conmed Corporation; *U.S. Public*, pg. 431

ELECTRO IMAGE—Electrodepositable Photoresist Coating—PPG Industries, Inc.; *U.S. Public*, pg. 1245

ELECTRO-MAXX—NONE—Morse Controls; *U.S. Public*, pg. 857

ELECTRO-METRICS—Test Instruments & Measuring Equipment—Hayes Corporation, Regional Office; *U.S. Public*, pg. 801

ELECTRO-MOTIVE—Diesel Engines—Valley Detroit Diesel Allison; *U.S. Private*, pg. 1132

ELECTRO NIT—Knitted Wire Mesh—Instrument Specialties Company; *U.S. Private*, pg. 565

ELECTRO-STEAM—Valve—Hays Fluid Controls-Division of Romac Industries; *U.S. Private*, pg. 942

ELECTRO-THERM—Thermoplastic Printing Media—Ferro Corporation; *U.S. Public*, pg. 618

ELECTRO-THRED—Anti-theft Target—Sentry Technology Corp.; *U.S. Public*, pg. 1458

ELECTRO-THERM—Electronic Instruments—Cooper Instrument Corp.; *U.S. Private*, pg. 274

ELECTROCARDIOCORDER—NONE—Del Mar Avionics; *U.S. Private*, pg. 321

ELECTRODAG—Conductive Coatings—Acheson Colloids Company; *U.S. Private*, pg. 12

ELECTROFLO—Valve—Hays Fluid Controls-Division of Romac Industries; *U.S. Private*, pg. 942

ELECTROGRAPHIC—Computer System—International Business Machines Corporation; *U.S. Public*, pg. 895

ELECTROLET—Electric Projection Screen—Da-Lite Screen Company, Inc.; *U.S. Private*, pg. 306

ELECTROLET—Conduit Fitting—Killark Electric Manufacturing Co.; *U.S. Public*, pg. 844

ELECTROLOG—NONE—Western Atlas Logging Services; *U.S. Public*, pg. 1757

ELECTROLOSS—Filterline Wire—Raychem Corporation; *U.S. Public*, pg. 1362

ELECTROLUX—NONE—Zanussi Italia S.p.A.; *Int'l*, pg. 442

ELECTROLUX-WASCATOR—Industrial Laundry Equipment—Electrolux, AB; *Int'l*, pg. 438

ELECTROMAT—ED Equip. for Use by Mfrs. & Industrial Companies of Food/Chemical—Ionics, Incorporated; *U.S. Public*, pg. 912

ELECTROMAX—Self Tuning Controller—Honeywell, Inc.; *U.S. Public*, pg. 834

ELECTROMAX—NONE—Life Technologies, Inc.; *U.S. Public*, pg. 504

ELECTROMELT—Heat-Tracing System—Raychem Corporation; *U.S. Public*, pg. 1362

ELECTROMET—Electrolytic Polisher & Etcher—Buehler, Limited; *U.S. Public*, pg. 574

ELECTROMITE—Valve—Hays Fluid Controls-Division of Romac Industries; *U.S. Private*, pg. 942

ELECTROMODE—Electric Heaters - USA—The Glen Dimplex Group; *Int'l*, pg. 553

ELECTRONI-CORD—Tires—Bridgestone/Firestone, Inc.; *Int'l*, pg. 213

ELECTRONIC ARTS—Computer & Video Games relating to Stories, Action, Strategy & Simulation—Electronic Arts; *U.S. Public*, pg. 569

ELECTRONIC BUSINESS—Management Magazine for the Electronics Industry—Reed Elsevier Business Information; *Int'l*, pg. 1095

ELECTRONIC BUSINESS ASIA—Managment Magazine for the Electronics Industry in Asia/Pacific Region—Reed Elsevier Business Information; *Int'l*, pg. 1095

ELECTRONIC BUYERS' NEWS—Newspaper—CMP Media, Inc.; *U.S. Public*, pg. 279

ELECTRONIC COMPONENT NEWS—Product News Magazine for Professionals in the Electronics Equipment Market—Reed Elsevier Business Information; *Int'l*, pg. 1095

ELECTRONIC DESIGN—Periodical—Penton Publishing, Inc.; *U.S. Public*, pg. 1306

ELECTRONIC ENCYCLOPEDIA—Electronic Encyclopedia—Franklin Electronic Publishers, Inc.; *U.S. Public*, pg. 679

ELECTRONIC ENGINEERING TIMES—Newspaper—CMP Media, Inc.; *U.S. Public*, pg. 279

ELECTRONIC ENGINEERS MASTER CATALOG—Book—The Hearst Corporation; *U.S. Private*, pg. 515

ELECTRONIC FIRE COMMANDER—NONE—Detroit Diesel Corp.; *U.S. Private*, pg. 850

ELECTRONIC HOLY BIBLE—King James & Revised Standard Versions—Franklin Electronic Publishers, Inc.; *U.S. Public*, pg. 679

ELECTRONIC INDUSTRY TELEPHONE DIRECTORY (EITD)—Phone/Fax Listings for Companies in the Electronics Marketplace—Reed Elsevier Business Information; *Int'l*, pg. 1095

ELECTRONIC LEARNING—Publications For Computer Instruction K-12; 8 Issues/Yr.—Scholastic Inc.; *U.S. Public*, pg. 1440

ELECTRONIC MARKETPLACE—Computer System—International Business Machines Corporation; *U.S. Public*, pg. 895

ELECTRONIC MEDIA—Newspaper—Crain Communications, Inc.; *U.S. Private*, pg. 284

ELECTRONIC MESSAGE SERVICE—Electronic Message System Software—Datapoint Corporation; *Int'l*, pg. 384

ELECTRONIC NEWS—Weekly Technology News Publication—Reed Elsevier Business Information; *Int'l*, pg. 1095

ELECTRONIC PACKAGING & PRODUCTION—Magazine Covering Design & Production of Electronic Equipment—Reed Elsevier Business Information; *Int'l*, pg. 1095

ELECTRONIC PRODUCTS MAGAZINE—Magazine—The Hearst Corporation; *U.S. Private*, pg. 515

ELECTRONICS NEWS—Magazine—Reed Business Information Pty. Limited; *Int'l*, pg. 1094

THE ELECTRONICS SOURCE BOOK—Publication for Corporate Purchasing Agents—Intertec Publishing; *U.S. Public*, pg. 1327

ELECTROPACK—Electrosurgical Supplies Kit—Conmed Corporation; *U.S. Public*, pg. 431

ELECTROPHOTOMETER—Photoelectric Colorimeter—Fisher Scientific Company; *U.S. Private*, pg. 658

ELECTROPILE—Weather Strip—The Standard Products Company; *U.S. Public*, pg. 1504

Brand Name Index

ELECTROSHIELD MONITORING SYSTEM—NONE—Pfizer Inc.; *U.S. Public*, pg. 1281

ELECTROSILVER—Photographic Processing Chemicals—Eastman Kodak Company; *U.S. Public*, pg. 550

ELECTROSPEED—Variable Speed (Frequency) Motor Controller—Centrilift; *U.S. Public*, pg. 167

ELECTROTORQUE—Control—Harnischfeger Industries, Inc.; *U.S. Public*, pg. 788

ELECTROTRAY—Cable Tray Systems—Thomas & Betts Corporation; *U.S. Public*, pg. 1597

ELEDON—Infant Foods & Dietetic Products—Nestle S.A.; *Int'l*, pg. 915

ELEFANTEN—Childrens Shoes—Freudenberg & Company; *Int'l*, pg. 505

ELEGANCE—Paper Napkins, Placemats & Covers with Plastic Backing—Erving Industries, Inc.; *U.S. Private*, pg. 382

ELEGANCE—Socks—Grupo Synkro, S.A. de C.V.; *Int'l*, pg. 576

ELEGANCE—Glassware—Indiana Glass Company; *U.S. Public*, pg. 976

ELEGANCE—Fabric Painting Dye—Koh-I-Noor, Inc.; *U.S. Private*, pg. 629

ELEGANCE—Bathtub Wall Kit—Plaskolite Inc.; *U.S. Private*, pg. 870

ELEGANCE—Cookware—Regal Ware, Inc.; *U.S. Private*, pg. 917

ELEGANCE—NONE—Rubbermaid Incorporated; *U.S. Public*, pg. 1411

ELEGANT IMPRINTS—Note Cards & Envelopes—American Greetings Corporation; *U.S. Public*, pg. 77

ELEGANTE—Paint—Graham Paint and Varnish Company; *U.S. Private*, pg. 468

ELEGENCE IN AWARDS & GIFTS—Line Name—R.S. Owens; *U.S. Private*, pg. 824

ELEK-TRO-CUT—Electrostatically Coated Abrasives—3M; *U.S. Private*, pg. 1604

ELEKTRA—Racquetball Racquet—Head USA, Inc.; *U.S. Private*, pg. 514

ELEKTRIKBROOM—Vacuum Cleaner—Oreck Manufacturing Company; *U.S. Private*, pg. 819

ELEKTRO HELIOS—NONE—Electrolux, AB; *Int'l*, pg. 438

ELEKTROSERVE—Advisory Service on Energy Applications in the Commercial Sector—Eskom; *Int'l*, pg. 459

ELEKTROWISE—Advisory Service to Electrified Customers in the Private Sector—Eskom; *Int'l*, pg. 459

ELEMENTS—Shoes—Bostonian Shoe Co.; *Int'l*, pg. 297

ELEMENTS—Office Accessories—Empire Berol U.S.A.; *U.S. Public*, pg. 1178

ELEMENTS—Glassware—Syratech Corporation; *U.S. Private*, pg. 1060

ELENA—Laundry Detergent—Benckiser Consumer Products Inc.; *Int'l*, pg. 185

ELEPHANT—Malt Liquor (U.S.)—Anheuser-Busch Companies, Inc.; *U.S. Public*, pg. 113

ELEPHANT—Portland Cement Type I—The Siam Cement Public Company Limited; *Int'l*, pg. 1237

ELEVATION—Liquid Volumizer—The Dow Chemical Company; *U.S. Public*, pg. 522

ELEY—Sporting Ammunition—IMI Plc; *Int'l*, pg. 646

ELF—Light Duty Trucks—Isuzu Motors Limited; *Int'l*, pg. 692

ELFAB—Pressure Relief Devices—Halma p.l.c.; *Int'l*, pg. 589

ELFACOS—Consistency Regulator for Cosmetic Emulsions—Akzo Nobel N.V.; *Int'l*, pg. 42

ELFAN—Fatty Acid Soap—Akzo Nobel N.V.; *Int'l*, pg. 42

ELFANOL—Detergent—Akzo Nobel N.V.; *Int'l*, pg. 42

ELFAPUR—Dishwasher Detergents—Akzo Nobel N.V.; *Int'l*, pg. 42

ELGIN—Clocks—Elgin National Industries, Inc.; *U.S. Private*, pg. 370

ELGIN WATCH INTERNATIONAL—Mfr. Watches—Elgin Watch Company; *U.S. Private*, pg. 371

ELIDOS—Industrial Furniture—Knurr AG; *Int'l*, pg. 739

ELIMINATOR—Belt Fasteners—Clipper Belt Lacer Company; *U.S. Private*, pg. 413

ELIMINATOR—Belt Cleaning Systems—Flexible Steel Lacing Company; *U.S. Private*, pg. 413

ELIMINATOR—Cable Terminators—G & W Electric Co.; *U.S. Private*, pg. 433

ELIMINATOR—Ball Valves—Neles-Jamesbury Corp.; *Int'l*, pg. 1428

ELIMINATOR—Insulation System—Owens Corning; *U.S. Public*, pg. 1236

ELIMINATOR—Antennas—Telex Communications, Inc.; *U.S. Private*, pg. 1074

ELIMINATOR—Trash Bags—Tenneco Packaging, Consumer Products Group; *U.S. Public*, pg. 1579

ELIMINATORS—Sewage & Wastewater Pumps—Little Giant Pump Company; *U.S. Public*, pg. 1566

ELIMOBIL—Mobile Workplace System—Knurr AG; *Int'l*, pg. 739

ELI'S—Cheesecake & Muffins—Eli's Cheese Cake Company; *U.S. Private*, pg. 371

ELISABETH—Women's Apparel—Liz Claiborne, Inc.; *U.S. Public*, pg. 1005

ELITE—Scooters—American Honda Motor Co., Inc. Motorcycle Division; *Int'l*, pg. 634

ELITE—Professional Hair Dryer—Andis Company; *U.S. Private*, pg. 73

ELITE—Binoculars—Bausch & Lomb Incorporated; *U.S. Public*, pg. 194

ELITE—NONE—Berg Electronics; *U.S. Public*, pg. 212

ELITE—Binoculars & Spotting Scopes—Bushnell Corporation; *U.S. Public*, pg. 1191

ELITE—Photographic Paper—Eastman Kodak Company; *U.S. Public*, pg. 550

ELITE—Air Cleaners & Valve Covers—Edelbrock Corp.; *U.S. Public*, pg. 563

ELITE—Paint—Graham Paint and Varnish Company; *U.S. Private*, pg. 468

ELITE—Racquetball Racquet—Head USA, Inc.; *U.S. Private*, pg. 514

ELITE—Upright Vacuum Cleaner—Hoover Company; *U.S. Private*, pg. 1065

ELITE—Massage Shower Head—Interbath, Inc.; *U.S. Private*, pg. 566

ELITE—Recreational Vehicles—Kit Manufacturing Company; *U.S. Public*, pg. 962

ELITE—NONE—Lennox International Inc.; *U.S. Private*, pg. 659

ELITE—Dressing—Lever Brothers Co.; *Int'l*, pg. 1435

ELITE—Pacemaker—Medtronic, Inc.; *U.S. Public*, pg. 1082

ELITE—Refrigerated Products—Nestle S.A.; *Int'l*, pg. 915

ELITE—High End Home Audio & Video—Pioneer Electronics (USA) Inc.; *Int'l*, pg. 1058

ELITE—Bathtub Wall Kit—Plaskolite Inc.; *U.S. Private*, pg. 870

ELITE—Lotion Soap—SBS Products, Inc.; *U.S. Private*, pg. 955

ELITE—Dressing—Unilever Plc; *Int'l*, pg. 1433

ELITE—Skin Stapler—U.S. Surgical Corp.; *U.S. Public*, pg. 1687

ELITE—Fitness Products—York Barbell Co., Inc.; *U.S. Private*, pg. 1196

ELITE LINE—Brass Plated Beds—Dresher, Inc.; *U.S. Public*, pg. 986

ELITE PREMIUM—Pies—Bakers Square Restaurants; *U.S. Public*, pg. 1719

ELITE SERIES—X-Ray—Picker International, Inc.; *Int'l*, pg. 545

ELITE TEX—Fabric for Professional Wear Products—Medline Industries, Inc.; *U.S. Private*, pg. 728

ELITE TIMER—In-Wall Interval Time Switch—Tork, Inc.; *U.S. Private*, pg. 1092

ELITE II—Pacemaker—Medtronic, Inc.; *U.S. Public*, pg. 1082

ELIZABETH SHAW—Chocolates & Truffles—Huhtamaki Oy; *Int'l*, pg. 638

ELJAY—Rock Processing Machinery—Cedarapids, Inc.; *U.S. Public*, pg. 1365

ELJER—Plumbingware—Eljer Plumbingware; *U.S. Public*, pg. 1794

THE ELK EDGE—NONE—Elcor Corporation; *U.S. Public*, pg. 567

ELK HUNGER II—Sleeping Bags—The Canadian Coleman Co., Ltd.; *U.S. Private*, pg. 691

ELK RIDGE VINEYARDS—Varietal Wines—Gibson Wine Company; *U.S. Private*, pg. 452

ELK ULTRA-WRAP—NONE—Elcor Corporation; *U.S. Public*, pg. 567

ELKE DAG HAARSPOELING—Hair Conditioner—Colgate-Palmolive Company; *U.S. Public*, pg. 397

ELKE'S BISCUIT—Biscuits & Cakes—Northern Foods plc; *Int'l*, pg. 967

ELKEM MICROSILICA—NONE—Elkem ASA; *Int'l*, pg. 446

ELKHORN—Camper—Fleetwood Enterprises, Inc.; *U.S. Public*, pg. 650

ELLA—Feminine Pads—Kimberly-Clark Corporation; *U.S. Public*, pg. 958

ELLANAR—Jewelry Cleaner—L&R Manufacturing Co.; *U.S. Private*, pg. 638

ELLE—Magazine—Burda Holding GmbH & Co., KG; *Int'l*, pg. 233

ELLE—U.K. Women's Magazine—EMAP Elan; *Int'l*, pg. 451

ELLE—Fashion Magazine—Hachette Filipacchi Magazines Inc.; *Int'l*, pg. 794

ELLE—Women's Apparel—International Cosmetics Co., Ltd.; *Int'l*, pg. 684

ELLE BISTRO—Magazine—Burda Holding GmbH & Co., KG; *Int'l*, pg. 233

ELLE DECOR—Architecture & Interior Design Magazine—Hachette Filipacchi Magazines Inc.; *Int'l*, pg. 794

ELLE DECORATION—Magazine—Burda Holding GmbH & Co., KG; *Int'l*, pg. 233

ELLE DECORATION—U.K.Home Decorating Magazine—EMAP Elan; *Int'l*, pg. 451

ELLE TOP MODEL—Magazine—Burda Holding GmbH & Co., KG; *Int'l*, pg. 233

ELLENERGIE—NONE—Avon Products Co., Ltd.; *U.S. Public*, pg. 156

ELLER DIGITAL IMAGING—Poster Printing Service—Eller Media Company; *U.S. Public*, pg. 383

ELLER DIMENSION—Outdoor Structure Supplier—Eller Media Company; *U.S. Public*, pg. 383

ELLICOT—NONE—Ellicott Machine Corporation International; *U.S. Private*, pg. 372

ELLINGTON—Bookcovering—Appleton Papers Inc.; *Int'l*, pg. 567

ELMAGCO BRAKE—Drawworks Brakes—Baylor Company; *Int'l*, pg. 1134

ELMER'S—Glues, Cements, Building Adhesives, Sealants, Wood Filler—Borden, Inc.; *U.S. Private*, pg. 157

ELMIRON—Pharmaceutical for Treatment of Cystitis—IVAX Corporation; *U.S. Public*, pg. 914

ELOCON—Mid-Potency Topical Corticosteroid—Schering-Plough Corporation; *U.S. Public*, pg. 1438

ELON—Photo Developing Agent—Eastman Kodak Company; *U.S. Public*, pg. 550

ELONEX—PC Hardware—Onyx Technologies Ltd.; *Int'l*, pg. 1007

ELONGASE—NONE—Life Technologies, Inc.; *U.S. Public*, pg. 504

ELOPRAM—Citalopram, Antidepressant—Recordati Industria Chimica e Farmaceutica S.p.A.; *Int'l*, pg. 1090

ELOTEX—Powdered Resins—National Starch and Chemical Company; *Int'l*, pg. 1435

ELPAR—NONE—Elwell-Parker Limited; *U.S. Private*, pg. 373

ELPH—Digital Thermocouple Indicator—Thermo Electric Co., Inc.; *U.S. Private*, pg. 1080

ELPOR—Vitreous Component for Printed Circuits—Ferro Corporation; *U.S. Public*, pg. 618

ELSINORE—Stainless Steel Flatware—Dansk International Designs Ltd.; *U.S. Private*, pg. 261

ELSINORE—Operators of Hotels & Casinos—Elsinore Corporation; *U.S. Public*, pg. 570

ELSPAR-L—Asparaginase—Merck & Co., Inc.; *U.S. Public*, pg. 1090

ELSTER—Industrial Products—Email Limited; *Int'l*, pg. 450

ELTAC—Household appliances—Basel Trading Company Ltd.; *Int'l*, pg. 169

ELU-QUIK—DNA Purification Kit—Schleicher & Schuell, Inc.; *Int'l*, pg. 1206

ELUTIP-D—Reverse-Phase Mini-Column—Schleicher & Schuell, Inc.; *Int'l*, pg. 1206

ELUTIP-R—Reverse-Phase Mini Column—Schleicher & Schuell, Inc.; *Int'l*, pg. 1206

ELUTRAP—Electro-Separation Device—Schleicher & Schuell, Inc.; *Int'l*, pg. 1206

ELVACITE—Acrylic Resins—Du Pont (E.I. Du Pont De Nemours & Co.); *U.S. Public*, pg. 530

ELWELL-PARKER—Industrial Material-Moving Equipment—Elwell-Parker Limited; *U.S. Private*, pg. 373

ELY & WALKER—Men's Shirts—Oxford Industries, Inc.; *U.S. Public*, pg. 1239

ELYSEES—Cameras—Eastman Kodak Company; *U.S. Public*, pg. 550

EMABOND—Specialty Electromagnetic Adhesive Compounds, Equipment & Technology—Ashland, Inc.; *U.S. Public*, pg. 138

EMACO—Restoration Products—Master Builders Inc.; *Int'l*, pg. 1465

EMATIC—Guide Bars—Stihl Inc.; *Int'l*, pg. 1301

EMBASSY—Beauty Salon Furniture—Belvedere · Company; *U.S. Private*, pg. 1008

EMBASSY—Catering Trays & Bowls—Douglas Stephen Plastics, Inc.; *U.S. Private*, pg. 341

EMBASSY—No.1 Mild King Size Filter Cigarettes—Imperial Tobacco Group, Ltd.; *Int'l*, pg. 666

EMBASSY—Economic Information—Kompass International Neuenschwander SA; *Int'l*, pg. 745

EMBASSY—Laces & Trims—Wm. E. Wright Limited Partnership; *U.S. Private*, pg. 1192

EMBASSY SQUARE—Clothing—Cliftex; *U.S. Public*, pg. 1777

EMBASSY SUITES—Hotels—Promus Hotel Corporation; *U.S. Public*, pg. 1335

EMBECO—Grouts & Mortars—Master Builders Inc.; *Int'l*, pg. 1465

EMBEDDED ARRAY—Circuit—LSI Logic Corp.; *U.S. Public*, pg. 971

EMBEDDED INTERNET—NONE—Wind River Systems, Inc.; *U.S. Public*, pg. 1770

EMBEDDED SYSTEMS PROGRAMMING—Magazine—Miller Freeman Inc.; *Int'l*, pg. 1443

EMBEGUARD—Polymer Floors—Master Builders Inc.; *Int'l*, pg. 1465

EMBER-GLO—Restaurant Cooking Equip.—Midco International Inc.; *U.S. Private*, pg. 744

EMBERS—Charcoal Hardwood Briquets—Embers Charcoal Company, Inc.; *U.S. Private*, pg. 373

EMBERS—ERISA Reporting & Performance Measurement—SunGard Data Systems Inc.; *U.S. Public*, pg. 1534

EMBROIDERY/MONOGRAM BUSINESS—Magazine—Miller Freeman Inc.; *Int'l*, pg. 1443

EMCAT-30—Moving Bed Cracking Catalysts—Engelhard Corporation; *U.S. Public*, pg. 582

EMCEE—System & Broadcast Equipment Sales—Emcee Broadcast Products, Inc.; *U.S. Public*, pg. 570

EMCO—Commercial Outdoor Lighting—Thomas Industries Inc.; *U.S. Public*, pg. 1598

EMCODEL—Pharmaceutical Excipient—Penford Corp.; *U.S. Public*, pg. 1269

EMCOMPASS—Test Data Management System—GenRad, Inc.; *U.S. Public*, pg. 731

EMCOMPRESS—Pharmaceutical Excipient—Penford Corp.; *U.S. Public*, pg. 1269

EMCOR—Modular Enclosures—Crenlo, Inc.; *U.S. Private*, pg. 288

EMCOSOY—Soy Fiber Disintegrant—Penford Corp.; *U.S. Public*, pg. 1269

EMDEX—Pharmaceutical Excipient—Penford Corp.; *U.S. Public*, pg. 1269

EMERALAIR—Jewelry—Litton Industries, Inc.; *U.S. Public*, pg. 1002

EMERALD—Area Rug—Couristan Inc.; *U.S. Private*, pg. 279

EMERALD—X-Ray Tubes—Litton Industries, Inc.; *U.S. Public*, pg. 1002

EMERALD—Peat Moss—Premier CDN Enterprises Ltd.; *Int'l*, pg. 1067

EMERALD BAY—Tents, Backpacks, & Sleeping Bags—Jinwoong Inc.; *Int'l*, pg. 706

EMERALD CAS FOR WINDOWS—Accounting Software—Moscom Corporation; *U.S. Public*, pg. 1136

EMERALD CREAM—Coffee—Superior Coffee and Foods; *U.S. Public*, pg. 1434

EMERAUDE—Fragrance—Coty Inc.; *Int'l*, pg. 185

EMERCHROME—Floor Hardener—L.M. Scofield Company; *U.S. Private*, pg. 976

EMERGENCY—NONE—Bobit Publishing Company; *U.S. Private*, pg. 154

EMERGENCY ALARM STATION—Safety Alarms—Falcon Safety Products Inc.; *U.S. Private*, pg. 392

EMERSON—Electronic Components—Emerson Radio Corp.; *U.S. Public*, pg. 578

EMERSON QUIET KOOL—Room Air Condition & Dehumidifiers—Fedders Corp.; *U.S. Public*, pg. 614

EMETROL—NONE—Pharmacia & Upjohn; *Int'l*, pg. 1048

EMETROL—Pharmaceuticals for Nausea, Vomiting—Rhone-Poulenc Rorer - U.S.; *Int'l*, pg. 1110

EMFLON—Filters—Pall Corporation; *U.S. Public*, pg. 1253

EMFLON II—Filters—Pall Corporation; *U.S. Public*, pg. 1253

EMHART FASTENING TEKNOLOGIES—NONE—The Black & Decker Corporation; *U.S. Public*, pg. 233

EMHART GLASS—Glass Container-Making Machinery—The Black & Decker Corporation; *U.S. Public*, pg. 233

EMIFIL—NONE—Murata Manufacturing Co., Ltd.; *Int'l*, pg. 897

EMILY ROSE—Dresses—Star Children's Dress Company, Inc.; *U.S. Public*, pg. 1034

EMINASE—Treatment for Coronary Turombosis—Roberts Pharmaceutical Corporation; *U.S. Public*, pg. 1393

EMINASE—Thrombolytic to Dissolve Blood Clots—SmithKline Beecham Corporation; *Int'l*, pg. 1264

EMINASE—Cardiopulmonary Drug—SmithKline Beecham plc; *Int'l*, pg. 1264

EMIT—Enzyme Immunoassay Reagent Tests—Syntex; *Int'l*, pg. 1120

EMKAY—Fleet Leasing—Emkay, Inc.; *U.S. Private*, pg. 374

EMKAY—Candles—Muench-Kreuzer Candle Company; *U.S. Private*, pg. 766

EMLA—Topical Anesthetic—Astra AB; *Int'l*, pg. 93

EMLA—NONE—Astra USA, Inc.; *Int'l*, pg. 93

EMMCO—Industrial Products—Email Limited; *Int'l*, pg. 450

EMMENTAL—NONE—Schweizerische Kaseunion AG; *Int'l*, pg. 1211

EMMETS—NONE—R & A Bailey & Co.; *Int'l*, pg. 409

EMMETS—Liqueur—Grand Metropolitan Plc; *Int'l*, pg. 408

EMMETS—Cream Liqueur—IDV North America; *Int'l*, pg. 411

EMMI—Emission Microscope—Barnes Engineering; *U.S. Public*, pg. 542

EMMISSION-GENERAL—Ball Valve—Neles-Jamesbury Corp.; *Int'l*, pg. 1428

EMMISSION-PAK—Ball Valve Seal—Neles-Jamesbury Corp.; *Int'l*, pg. 1428

EMMVEO—Industrial Products—Email Limited; *Int'l*, pg. 450

EMMY—Wood Frame Side Chair, ai Collection—Vecta; *U.S. Private*, pg. 1038

EMOLICA MEDICATED BATH ESSENCE—Bath Additive Containing Skin Moisturizers Effective Against Eczema—Kao Corporation; *Int'l*, pg. 717

EMORIN—Diaper Film—Solutia Inc.; *U.S. Public*, pg. 1483

EMPAQUES LATINOAMERICANOS—Bimonthly Spanish-Language Publication—Intertec Publishing; *U.S. Public*, pg. 1327

EMPEROR NORTON—NONE—San Francisco French Bread Company; *U.S. Public*, pg. 909

EMPERORS CHOICE—Herb Tea—Celestial Seasonings; *U.S. Public*, pg. 319

EMPHASIS—Mask for Corneal Surgery—Summit Technology, Inc.; *U.S. Public*, pg. 1528

EMPI—Medical Electronic Access.—EMPI, Inc.; *U.S. Public*, pg. 545

EMPIRAL—Analgesic, Sedative—Glaxo Wellcome PLC; *Int'l*, pg. 553

EMPIRE—Insecticide—The Dow Chemical Company; *U.S. Public*, pg. 522

EMPIRE—U.K. Entertainment Magazine—EMAP Metro; *Int'l*, pg. 451

EMPIRE—Pencils & School Supplies—Empire Berol U.S.A.; *U.S. Public*, pg. 1178

EMPIRE—Diamonds & Jewelry—Empire Diamond Corporation; *U.S. Private*, pg. 374

EMPIRE—Insurance—Empire Insurance Group; *U.S. Public*, pg. 990

EMPIRE—Kosher Poultry—Empire Kosher Poultry, Inc.; *U.S. Private*, pg. 374

EMPIRE—High Duty Firebrick—A.P. Green Industries, Inc.; *U.S. Public*, pg. 761

EMPIRE—Electric Housewares—The Metal Ware Corp.; *U.S. Private*, pg. 734

EMPIRE SYSTEM—NONE—Berg Electronics; *U.S. Public*, pg. 212

EMPIREGAS—NONE—All Star Gas Corporation; *U.S. Private*, pg. 35

EMPIRELAC—Paints—Essex Chemical Corporation; *U.S. Public*, pg. 523

EMPIRES IN ARMS—Game—Monarch Avalon, Inc.; *U.S. Public*, pg. 1123

EMPIRIN—Analgesic, Antipyretic—Glaxo Wellcome PLC; *Int'l*, pg. 553

EMPIRIN WITH CODEINE—Analgesic, Antipyretic with Codeine—Glaxo Wellcome PLC; *Int'l*, pg. 553

EMPORE—Reactive Membrane Technology—3M; *U.S. Public*, pg. 1604

EMPORIO ARMANI—NONE—Luxottica Group S.p.A.; *Int'l*, pg. 822

EMPRAZIL—Pharmaceutical Product—Glaxo Wellcome PLC; *Int'l*, pg. 553

EMPRESS—Canned Food Products—Mitsui Foods, Inc.; *U.S. Public*, pg. 879

EMPRESS LOUNGE—International Business Class—Canadian Airlines Corporation; *Int'l*, pg. 255

EMPRESS-30—Free-flowing Castable—A.P. Green Industries, Inc.; *U.S. Public*, pg. 761

EMPRESS-27—Free-flowing Castable—A.P. Green Industries, Inc.; *U.S. Public*, pg. 761

EMRALON—Lubricants—Acheson Colloids Company; *U.S. Private*, pg. 12

EMRICH—Danish, Donuts, Bread, Buns, Sweet Goods—Metz Baking Company (WI); *U.S. Private*, pg. 1022

EMSAC—NONE—Elkem ASA; *Int'l*, pg. 446

EMULAN—Emulsifiers—BASF AG; *Int'l*, pg. 103

EMULEX—Computer Equipment—Emulex Corporation; *U.S. Public*, pg. 579

EMULLO—Nitrocellulose Lacquer Emulsions For Leather—Henkel Corporation; *Int'l*, pg. 610

EMULSI-PHOS—Cheese Emulsifier—Solutia Inc.; *U.S. Public*, pg. 1483

EMVELOP—Wax Matrix for Controlled-Release Tablets—Penford Corp.; *U.S. Public*, pg. 1269

EN GARDE—Anti-Bacterial Finish—Guilford Mills, Inc.; *U.S. Public*, pg. 768

EN VISION CT—Injection System—Medrad, Inc.; *Int'l*, pg. 1204

ENABLE—NONE—Rohm and Haas Company; *U.S. Public*, pg. 1403

ENABLE—Program Generator Software—Tandem Computers Inc.; *U.S. Public*, pg. 417

ENAMELESCENT—For Nacreous Pigments—Ferro Corporation; *U.S. Public*, pg. 618

ENAMELITE—Tooth-Coating Resin—Lee Pharmaceuticals; *U.S. Public*, pg. 984

ENAMELITH—Printing Paper—The Mead Corporation; *U.S. Public*, pg. 1074

ENARAX—Pharmaceutical Prods.—SmithKline Beecham Laboratories; *Int'l*, pg. 1264

ENATHENE—Ethylene N-Butyl Acrylate Copolymer Resins—Millennium Petrochemicals, Inc.; *Int'l*, pg. 594

ENBOND—Metal Cleaner—Enthone-OMI, Inc.; *U.S. Public*, pg. 138

ENCAPRIN—Aspirin—The Procter & Gamble Company; *U.S. Public*, pg. 1330

ENCAPSULON—Medical Devices—Teleflex Incorporated; *U.S. Public*, pg. 1569

ENCARE—Pharmaceutical Products—Thompson Medical Company, Inc.; *U.S. Private*, pg. 1083

ENCHANTE—NONE—Kellwood Company; *U.S. Public*, pg. 948

ENCHANTED ISLE—Cruise Ship—Commodore Holdings; *U.S. Public*, pg. 414

ENCHANTED SEAS—Cruise Ship—Commodore Holdings; *U.S. Public*, pg. 414

ENCLAD—Bulk Thermocouple Stock—Engelhard Corporation; *U.S. Public*, pg. 582

ENCLOSED KNIFE BLOCK—Cutlery—General Housewares Corp.; *U.S. Public*, pg. 715

ENCODER—Encoders—Litton Industries, Inc.; *U.S. Public*, pg. 1002

ENCODER SYSTEMSDIVISION—Encoders—BEI Sensors and Systems Company; *U.S. Public*, pg. 160

ENCOER—High Coercivity Magnetic Striped Cards—Schlumberger Malco Inc.; *Int'l*, pg. 1206

ENCOMPASS—Fuel Management & Environmental Compliance System—Arizona Instrument Corporation; *U.S. Public*, pg. 129

ENCOMPASS—Work Flow Analysis Service—Eastman Kodak Company; *U.S. Public*, pg. 550

ENCOMPASS—Information Management System—Parsons Power Group, Inc.; *U.S. Private*, pg. 841

ENCOMPASS—Distributed Data Base Management System—Tandem Computers Inc.; *U.S. Public*, pg. 417

ENCORE—System II Chemistry Analyzer—BioChem ImmunoSystems, Inc.; *Int'l*, pg. 196

ENCORE—NONE—Consolidated Papers, Inc.; *U.S. Public*, pg. 436

ENCORE—NONE—Electro Brand, Inc.; *U.S. Private*, pg. 368

ENCORE—Travel Savings Club—Encore Marketing International, Inc.; *U.S. Public*, pg. 580

ENCORE—Parts—Harnischfeger Industries, Inc.; *U.S. Public*, pg. 788

ENCORE—Roller Ball Pen—Pentel of America, Ltd.; *Int'l*, pg. 1035

ENCORE—Magazine—Reed Business Information Pty. Limited; *Int'l*, pg. 1094

ENCORE—Magazine & Directory—Reed Business Information Pty. Limited; *Int'l*, pg. 1094

ENCORE 90—Open Systems Computer System—Encore Computer Corporation; *U.S. Public*, pg. 580

ENCORE 91—Computer System—Encore Computer Corporation; *U.S. Public*, pg. 580

ENCORE 93—Computer System—Encore Computer Corporation; *U.S. Public*, pg. 580

ENCORE RSX—Real Time Computer System—Encore Computer Corporation; *U.S. Public*, pg. 580

ENCORE TRAVEL CENTER—Travel Agency Services—Encore Marketing International, Inc.; *U.S. Public*, pg. 580

ENCORLINER—100% Recycled Linerboard—Gaylord Container Corporation; *U.S. Public*, pg. 704

ENCORPACK—High Recycled Fiber Content Packaging—Gaylord Container Corporation; *U.S. Public*, pg. 704

ENCOUNTER—NONE—American Management Systems, Inc.; *U.S. Public*, pg. 86

ENCOUNTER—Class A Motor Home—Georgie Boy Manufacturing, Inc.; *U.S. Public*, pg. 388

ENCRYPTION/VIRTUAL PRIVATE NETWORKS—NONE—Check Point Software Technologies Ltd.; *U.S. Public*, pg. 342

ENCYCLOPEDIA AMERICANA—Encyclopedia—Grolier Inc.; *Int'l*, pg. 794

END-FLO—Rotary Vacuum Drum Filter—Svedala Pumps & Process; *Int'l*, pg. 1325

END-LICE—Pediculicide—Thompson Medical Company, Inc.; *U.S. Private*, pg. 1083

END SMOKE—Smoke Odor Removal System—Surco Products, Inc.; *U.S. Private*, pg. 1056

THE END—Briefs—Warner's; *U.S. Public*, pg. 1738

ENDA-BUG—Insecticide—Stanhome Inc.; *U.S. Public*, pg. 1508

ENDAL HD—Pharmaceutical—Forest Laboratories, Inc.; *U.S. Public*, pg. 670

ENDEASOR—NONE—Holiday Rambler; *U.S. Public*, pg. 1123

ENDEX—Resin—Hercules Incorporated; *U.S. Public*, pg. 809

ENDICOTT JOHNSON—Footwear—E.J. Footwear Corp.; *U.S. Public*, pg. 1684

ENDLESS POWER—Transistorized Uninterruptible Power Systems (UPS)—International Power Machines Corporation; *Int'l*, pg. 126

ENDLESS QUEST—Books—TSR, Inc.; *U.S. Private*, pg. 1185

ENDLESS SUMMER—Tomato—DNAP Holding Corp.; *Int'l*, pg. 454

ENDLESS VACATION—Subscription Magazine—Resort Condominiums International; *U.S. Public*, pg. 322

ENDO A—NONE—Allied Diagnostic Imaging Resources, Inc.; *U.S. Public*, pg. 282

ENDO BABCOCK—Laparoscopic Instruments—U.S. Surgical Corp.; *U.S. Public*, pg. 1687

ENDO BOWEL—Laparoscopic Instruments—U.S. Surgical Corp.; *U.S. Public*, pg. 1687

ENDO CATCH—Laparoscopic Instruments—U.S. Surgical Corp.; *U.S. Public*, pg. 1687

ENDO CLINCH—Laparoscopic Instruments—U.S. Surgical Corp.; *U.S. Public*, pg. 1687

ENDO CLIP—Laparoscopic Clip Appliers—U.S. Surgical Corp.; *U.S. Public*, pg. 1687

ENDO CLOSE—Suturing Device—U.S. Surgical Corp.; *U.S. Public*, pg. 1687

ENDO DISSECT—Laparoscopic Instruments—U.S. Surgical Corp.; *U.S. Public*, pg. 1687

ENDO GAS—Gas Generator—Seco Warwick Corporation; *U.S. Private*, pg. 980

ENDO GAUGE—Laparoscopic Instruments—U.S. Surgical Corp.; *U.S. Public*, pg. 1687

ENDO GIA—Laparoscopic Surgical Staplers—U.S. Surgical Corp.; *U.S. Public*, pg. 1687

ENDO GRASP—Laparoscopic Instruments—U.S. Surgical Corp.; *U.S. Public*, pg. 1687

ENDO-GUARD—NONE—Ballard Medical Products; *U.S. Public*, pg. 171

ENDO HERNIA—Laparoscopic Surgical Staplers—U.S. Surgical Corp.; *U.S. Public*, pg. 1687

ENDO LUNG—Laparoscopic Instruments—U.S. Surgical Corp.; *U.S. Public*, pg. 1687

ENDO MINI-RETRACT—Laparoscopic Instruments—U.S. Surgical Corp.; *U.S. Public*, pg. 1687

ENDO MINI-SHEARS—Laparoscopic Instruments—U.S. Surgical Corp.; *U.S. Public*, pg. 1687

ENDO PEANUT—NONE—U.S. Surgical Corp.; *U.S. Public*, pg. 1687

ENDO RETRACT—Instrument—U.S. Surgical Corp.; *U.S. Public*, pg. 1687

ENDO RETRACT MAXI—Laparoscopic Instruments—U.S. Surgical Corp.; *U.S. Public*, pg. 1687

ENDO SCIZ—Laparoscopic Instruments—U.S. Surgical Corp.; *U.S. Public*, pg. 1687

ENDO SHEARS—Laparoscopic Instruments—U.S. Surgical Corp.; *U.S. Public*, pg. 1687

ENDO SLIDE—Laparoscopic Instruments—U.S. Surgical Corp.; *U.S. Public*, pg. 1687

ENDO STITCH—Suturing Device—U.S. Surgical Corp.; *U.S. Public*, pg. 1687

ENDO TA—Laparoscopic Instruments—U.S. Surgical Corp.; *U.S. Public*, pg. 1687

ENDO UNIVERSAL—Stapler—U.S. Surgical Corp.; *U.S. Public*, pg. 1687

ENDOCAINE—NONE—Ballard Medical Products; *U.S. Public*, pg. 171

ENDOKNOT—Suture & Pre-Tied Suture—Ethicon, Inc.; *U.S. Public*, pg. 928

ENDOLIVE 3D—Video Laparoscopy System—Carl Zeiss; *Int'l*, pg. 1522

ENDOLOOP—Chromic or Plain Gut Ligature—Ethicon, Inc.; *U.S. Public*, pg. 928

ENDOPATH—NONE—Johnson & Johnson; *U.S. Public*, pg. 927

ENDOPOUCH—Specimen Retrieval Bag—Ethicon, Inc.; *U.S. Public*, pg. 928

ENDOSTAT—NONE—Laserscope Surgical Systems; *U.S. Public*, pg. 979

ENDOTAC—Implantable Defibrillation Lead—Guidant Corporation-Cardiac Rhythm Management Group; *U.S. Public*, pg. 768

ENDOTECH—In-Line Skates—K2 Inc.; *U.S. Public*, pg. 940

ENDOTROL—Medico-Surgical Tubes & Appliances—Mallinckrodt Inc.; *U.S. Public*, pg. 1039

ENDOVATIONS—NONE—Ballard Medical Products; *U.S. Public*, pg. 171

ENDOVIDEO V—Medical Video Camera—Circon Corporation; *U.S. Public*, pg. 373

ENDOX—Rust Remover—Enthone-OMI, Inc.; *U.S. Public*, pg. 138

ENDPOINT PLUS—NONE—Lam Research Corporation; *U.S. Public*, pg. 975

ENDSEAL—Grooved Pipe Coupling Gasket For Lined Pipe End Preparation—Victaulic Company of America; *U.S. Private*, pg. 1138

ENDUR—Elastomer Product—Rogers Corporation; *U.S. Public*, pg. 1402

ENDURA—Rubber Flooring—The Biltrite Corporation; *U.S. Private*, pg. 144

ENDURA—High Density Polyethelene Carts—Luxor; *U.S. Private*, pg. 359

ENDURA—Industrial Flame Retardant Composition—PPG Industries, Inc.; *U.S. Public*, pg. 1245

ENDURACELL—NONE—Pfizer Inc.; *U.S. Public*, pg. 1281

ENDURAGLO—Decorative Gold Processes—LeaRonal, Inc.; *U.S. Public*, pg. 982

ENDURANCE—Sheet Vinyl Flooring—Congoleum Corporation; *U.S. Public*, pg. 69

ENDURANCE—Paint & Stain—ICI Paints; *Int'l*, pg. 664

EDURANCE—Conductivity Sensors—Rosemount Analytical, Uniloc Div.; *U.S. Public*, pg. 574

ENDURATEX—Coil-coated material—Material Sciences Corporation; *U.S. Public*, pg. 1056

ENDURE—Cold Process Roofing System—Monsey-Bakor; *U.S. Private*, pg. 757

ENDURO—Hoists—Shepard Niles, Inc.; *U.S. Private*, pg. 992

ENDURO-FLITE—Formed Piano Hinge Conveyor—Webster Industries Inc.; *U.S. Private*, pg. 1157

ENDURO RACER—Videogame—Sega of America Inc.; *Int'l*, pg. 1218

ENDURON—Methyclothiazide—Abbott Laboratories; *U.S. Public*, pg. 12

ENDURONYL—Methyclothiazide & Deserpidine—Abbott Laboratories; *U.S. Public*, pg. 12

ENDUST—Furniture Polish—Bristol-Myers Squibb Company; *U.S. Public*, pg. 253

ENDUST—Furniture Polish—Kiwi Brands; *U.S. Public*, pg. 1433

ENDUST—Furniture Polish—Sara Lee Corporation; *U.S. Public*, pg. 1432

ENDUSTERS—Dust Wipes—Bristol-Myers Squibb Company; *U.S. Public*, pg. 253

ENDWIT—Zipper—YKK (U.S.A.); *Int'l*, pg. 1515

ENEMY IN SIGHT—Game—Monarch Avalon, Inc.; *U.S. Public*, pg. 1123

ENERGEN—Energy Holding Company—Energen Corporation; *U.S. Public*, pg. 581

ENERGEN—Energy-Maintenance Drink—Otsuka Pharmaceutical Co., Ltd.; *Int'l*, pg. 1013

ENERGEX—Synthetic Wall System—Polymer Plastics Corporation; *U.S. Private*, pg. 875

ENERGIE 5—Bakery Ingredients—Royal Gist-Brocades N.V.; *Int'l*, pg. 1142

ENERGIE 5 VITEX—Bakery Ingredient—Royal Gist-Brocades N.V.; *Int'l*, pg. 1142

ENERGITE—Highway Crash Barrel—Quixote Corporation; *U.S. Public*, pg. 1353

ENERGIX-B—Pharmaceutical—SmithKline Beecham Corporation; *Int'l*, pg. 1264

ENERGIZER—Batteries & Lighting Products—Eveready Battery Co.; *U.S. Public*, pg. 1360

ENERGIZER—Batteries—Ralston Purina Company; *U.S. Public*, pg. 1359

ENERGIZER—Mattresses—Therapedic Associates, Inc.; *U.S. Private*, pg. 1079

ENERGY & MOTION—Women's Apparel—Jacques Moret, Inc.; *U.S. Private*, pg. 580

ENERGY BANK—Economic Development Program—Unitil Corporation; *U.S. Public*, pg. 1692

ENERGY CENTER—Prewired Electrical Outlet Strip—General Cable Corporation; *Int'l*, pg. 1486

ENERGY EFFICIENT—Machine Tools—Seneca Falls Technology Group; *U.S. Private*, pg. 984

ENERGY ENGINEERED—Electrical Equipment—MagneTek, Inc.; *U.S. Public*, pg. 1037

ENERGY ENGINEERED—Motors—Magnetek Motors & Generators; *U.S. Public*, pg. 1037

ENERGY GUARD—Doors—Morgan Products Ltd.; *U.S. Public*, pg. 1132

ENERGY-GUARD—Aluminum Windows—Reynolds Metals Company; *U.S. Public*, pg. 1385

ENERGY-MAX—Monitoring & Control System—Eastman Kodak Company; *U.S. Public*, pg. 550

ENERGY MISER—Fan System—Baltimore Aircoil Company; *U.S. Private*, pg. 68

ENERGY MISER—Water Heaters—Rheem Water Heater; *Int'l*, pg. 1022

ENERGY MIZER—Ball Valve Steam Service—Worcester Controls Corp.; *Int'l*, pg. 128

ENERGY SAVER HOME—Energy-efficient Homes—Virginia Electric and Power Company; *U.S. Public*, pg. 516

ENERGY SAVING PRODUCTS—Home & Industry Access.—Energy Brokers Guild; *U.S. Private*, pg. 376

ENERGY SHIELD—Residential Polyiso Foam Insulation—Atlas Roofing Corp.; *U.S. Private*, pg. 96

ENERGY USA—Energy Related Products & Services—Bay State Gas Company; *U.S. Public*, pg. 196
ENERGY USER NEWS—Business-News Tabloid—Reed Elsevier Business Information; *Int'l*, pg. 1095
ENERGY USER NEWS DIGEST—Publication—Reed Elsevier Business Information; *Int'l*, pg. 1095
ENERGYMATE—Power Pack—National Presto Industries, Inc.; *U.S. Public*, pg. 1159
ENERGYONE—Electric & Gas Energy Products & Services—UtiliCorp United Inc.; *U.S. Public*, pg. 1700
ENERIX-B—Vaccine—SmithKline Beecham Research Limited; *Int'l*, pg. 1266
ENERPAC—Tools & Equipment for Industry & Construction—Applied Power Inc.; *U.S. Public*, pg. 124
ENERSCAN—Vapor Concentration Controller—Despatch Industries; *U.S. Private*, pg. 327
ENERTEC—Batteries & Feedthroughs—Medtronic, Inc.; *U.S. Public*, pg. 1082
THE ENESCO TREASURY OF CHRISTMAS ORNAMENTS—Registered Trademark of Enesco Corporation-Christmas Ornaments—Stanhome Inc.; *U.S. Public*, pg. 1508
ENFALAC—Infant Formula—Bristol-Myers Squibb Company; *U.S. Public*, pg. 253
ENFAMIL—Infant Formula—Bristol-Myers Squibb Company; *U.S. Public*, pg. 253
ENFAMIL—Infant Formula—Mead Johnson Nutritional Group; *U.S. Public*, pg. 254
ENFAMIL HUMAN MILK FORTIFIER—Powdered Supplement Added to Preterm Human Milk fed to Premature Infants—Mead Johnson Nutritional Group; *U.S. Public*, pg. 254
ENFANT—Toiletries—International Cosmetics Co., Ltd.; *Int'l*, pg. 684
ENFAPRO—Infant Formula—Bristol-Myers Squibb Company; *U.S. Public*, pg. 253
ENFLEX III—Coating—Pratt & Lambert United, Inc.; *U.S. Public*, pg. 1466
ENFORCER—K-Band Radar System—Federal Signal Corporation, Signal Div.; *U.S. Public*, pg. 616
THE ENFORCER—Carpet Backing & Adhesives—The Dow Chemical Company; *U.S. Public*, pg. 522
ENFORM—Report Writer Software—Tandem Computers Inc.; *U.S. Public*, pg. 417
ENGALOY—Brazing Alloys—Engelhard Corporation; *U.S. Public*, pg. 582
ENGCON—Energy Constancy Option for Tracker System—Keithley Instruments Inc.-Radiation Measurements Div.; *U.S. Public*, pg. 946
ENGEDURA—Fresh Yeast—Royal Gist-Brocades N.V.; *Int'l*, pg. 1142
ENGELBURGER—NONE—Bierbrauerei Fohrenburg; *Int'l*, pg. 194
ENGER KRESS—Leather Goods—Enger-Kress Company; *U.S. Private*, pg. 376
ENGERIX-B—Hepatitis B Vaccine—SmithKline Beecham plc; *Int'l*, pg. 1264
ENGEVITA—Inactive Dried Yeast for Spice Mixes, as Protein & B-Vitamin Source—Royal Gist-Brocades N.V.; *Int'l*, pg. 1142
ENGINATOR—Engine Generating System—Waukesha Engine Division; *U.S. Public*, pg. 528
ENGINE BRITE—Degreaser/Cleaner—Radiator Specialty Company; *U.S. Private*, pg. 906
ENGINEERED BY ROCKPORT—Athletic Shoes—Reebok International Ltd.; *U.S. Public*, pg. 1369
ENGINEERED RELIABILITY—Over Head Crane—Whiting Corporation; *U.S. Private*, pg. 1173
ENGINEERED WOOD—Laminated Wood Products—Anthony Forest Products Co., Inc.; *U.S. Private*, pg. 76
ENGINEERING & MINING JOURNAL—Publication on New Mines & Plants—Intertec Publishing; *U.S. Public*, pg. 1327
ENGLANDER—Bedding—Schottenstein Stores Corporation; *U.S. Private*, pg. 972
ENGLANDER SLEE—Sleep Products—Fraenkel Company; *U.S. Private*, pg. 423
ENGLISH BREAKFAST—Tea—Celestial Seasonings; *U.S. Public*, pg. 319
ENGLISH LACE—Wood & Lumber Products—Georgia-Pacific Corporation; *U.S. Public*, pg. 735

ENGLISH LACE—Fragrance—Yardley of London, Inc.; *Int'l*, pg. 819
ENGLISH LAVENDER—Bath Crystals, Spray Cologne, Perfume—Yardley of London, Inc.; *Int'l*, pg. 819
ENGLISH OVALS—Cigarettes—Philip Morris Companies Inc.; *U.S. Public*, pg. 1287
ENGLISH SPRING—Fragrance—Yardley of London, Inc.; *Int'l*, pg. 819
ENGLISH WOMAN'S WEEKLY—Magazine—Reed Business Information Pty. Limited; *Int'l*, pg. 1094
ENGOMATIC—Switchgear & Control System—Waukesha Engine Division; *U.S. Public*, pg. 528
ENGRAVOGRAPH—Engraving Machines—New Hermes Incorporated; *U.S. Private*, pg. 793
ENHANCE—NONE—Beckett Papers; *U.S. Public*, pg. 903
ENHANCE—Catheter Coating—Medtronic, Inc.; *U.S. Public*, pg. 1082
ENHANCED CREDIT—NONE—CUC International, Inc.; *U.S. Public*, pg. 320
THE ENHANCER—Urethane Carpet Backing—The Dow Chemical Company; *U.S. Public*, pg. 522
ENICOTE—Protective Coating—Enidine Incorporated; *U.S. Private*, pg. 377
ENIGMA—Fragrances—Charles of the Ritz Group Ltd.; *U.S. Private*, pg. 689
ENISIZE—Shock Absorber Sizing Program—Enidine Incorporated; *U.S. Private*, pg. 377
ENJOLI—Fragrances—Charles of the Ritz Group Ltd.; *U.S. Private*, pg. 689
ENJOUE MUSK—Cologne Spray—Stanhome Inc.; *U.S. Public*, pg. 1508
ENKA—Miscellaneous Textile & Fiber Products—Akzo Nobel Inc.; *Int'l*, pg. 47
ENKA—Synthetic Filament Yarn—Akzo Nobel N.V.; *Int'l*, pg. 42
ENKADRAIN—Drainage Matl. for Bldgs.—Akzo Nobel N.V.; *Int'l*, pg. 42
ENKAFILL—Synthetic Chamois Leathers; Household Cloths—Akzo Nobel N.V.; *Int'l*, pg. 42
ENKAID—Anti-Arrythmia—Bristol-Myers Squibb Company; *U.S. Public*, pg. 253
ENKALON—Polyamide—Akzo Nobel N.V.; *Int'l*, pg. 42
ENKAMAT—Synthetic Mat for Soil Stabilization—Akzo Nobel N.V.; *Int'l*, pg. 42
ENKEL—NONE—Baldwin Technology Company, Inc.; *U.S. Public*, pg. 169
ENLON—Edrophonium Chloride Injection, USP—Ohmeda; *Int'l*, pg. 121
ENLON-PLUS—Edrophonium Chloride, USP & Atrophine Sulfate, USP—Ohmeda; *Int'l*, pg. 121
ENMARK—Service Station Brand—Colonial Oil Industries; *U.S. Private*, pg. 253
ENNIS—Business Forms—Ennis Business Forms, Inc.; *U.S. Public*, pg. 583
ENO—NONE—SmithKline Beecham Corporation; *Int'l*, pg. 1264
ENO—Stomach/Indigestion Remedy—SmithKline Beecham plc; *Int'l*, pg. 1264
ENOTS—Tubes, Tube Fittings, Pneumatic Cylinders, Valves—IMI Plc; *Int'l*, pg. 646
ENOVID—Pharmaceutical—Searle & Co.; *U.S. Public*, pg. 1125
ENOZ—Moth Preventives—Willert Home Products, Inc.; *U.S. Private*, pg. 1177
ENPAC—Animal Feeds—Hormel Foods Corp.; *U.S. Public*, pg. 840
ENPLATE—Electroless Plating Baths—Enthone-OMI, Inc.; *U.S. Public*, pg. 138
ENPROX—Environmental Protection Prod.—Oakite Products, Inc.; *Int'l*, pg. 861
ENRAF—Tank Gauging—Delft Instruments N.V.; *Int'l*, pg. 388
ENRAF NONIUS—Physiothepray—Delft Instruments N.V.; *Int'l*, pg. 388
ENRICH—Hair Care Products—American International Industries; *U.S. Private*, pg. 57
ENRICHING LIFE THROUGH BIOMEDICAL TECHNOLOGY—Training Program—Medtronic, Inc.; *U.S. Public*, pg. 1082
ENRICO SERGIO—Women's Footwear—J. Baker, Inc.; *U.S. Public*, pg. 167
ENRICO'S—Spaghetti Sauce & Salsa—Ventre Packing Company, Inc.; *U.S. Private*, pg. 1135
ENRO—Apparel—The Apparel Group, Ltd.; *U.S. Private*, pg. 78

ENSCO—Oil & Gas Service—Ensco International Incorporated (ENSCO); *U.S. Public*, pg. 585
ENSELE—Tower Coatings—Rust-Oleum Corporation; *U.S. Public*, pg. 1358
ENSEMBLE—Place & Route Solutions for Gate, Cell, Block & Mixed Designs—Cadence Design Systems, Inc.; *U.S. Public*, pg. 290
ENSEMBLE—NONE—Cambridge Soundworks, Inc.; *U.S. Private*, pg. 202
ENSEMBLE—Plastic Heads—Ludwig Industries; *U.S. Public*, pg. 1514
ENSEMBLE BY HENRY KLOSS—NONE—Cambridge Soundworks, Inc.; *U.S. Private*, pg. 202
ENSEMBLE BY HENRY KLOSS AND DESIGN—NONE—Cambridge Soundworks, Inc.; *U.S. Private*, pg. 202
ENSERCH—Natural Gas and Oil Exploration and Production—ENSERCH Corporation; *U.S. Public*, pg. 1587
ENSIGN—Binoculars—Bushnell Corporation; *U.S. Private*, pg. 1191
ENSIMAX—For Efficient & Safe Silage—Cultor Ltd.; *Int'l*, pg. 349
ENSOLITE—Rubber Products—Rubatex Corporation; *U.S. Private*, pg. 56
ENSOLITE—Closed-Cell Foam—Uniroyal Technology Corporation; *U.S. Public*, pg. 1670
ENSONIC AUDIO PCI—PC Sound Cards—Ensoniq; *U.S. Private*, pg. 377
ENSTRIP—Selective Stripping for Plated Metal Coatings—Enthone-OMI, Inc.; *U.S. Public*, pg. 138
ENSURE—Adult Medical Nutritional—Abbott Laboratories; *U.S. Public*, pg. 12
ENSURE—Liquid Nutrition—Ross Products; *U.S. Public*, pg. 13
ENSURE—Reflective Sheeting—3M; *U.S. Public*, pg. 1604
ENTARA—Vandelism Protection—Kawneer Company; *U.S. Public*, pg. 60
ENTEK—Tarnish Preventative—Enthone-OMI, Inc.; *U.S. Public*, pg. 138
ENTENMANN'S—Sweet Baked Goods—Bestfoods; *U.S. Public*, pg. 223
ENTENMANN'S—Sweet Baked Goods—CPC Baking Business; *U.S. Public*, pg. 224
ENTERO-VU—Small Bowel Oral Contrast Medium—E-Z-Em, Inc.; *U.S. Public*, pg. 540
ENTEROVAX—Poultry Vaccine—Schering-Plough Corporation; *U.S. Public*, pg. 1438
ENTERPRISE—Induction Casting—Air Techniques, Inc.; *U.S. Private*, pg. 28
ENTERPRISE—Open Application Interface Product—Comdial Corporation; *U.S. Public*, pg. 407
ENTERPRISE—Paint—The Valspar Corporation; *U.S. Public*, pg. 1707
ENTERPRISE CAR SALES—NONE—Enterprise Rent-A-Car Company; *U.S. Private*, pg. 377
ENTERPRISE DATA ACCESS/SQL—A Client/ Server Family of Products for Heterogeneous Data Access—Information Builders; *U.S. Private*, pg. 561
ENTERPRISE EXCHANGE—Local Area Network Interconnect Modules—Zenith Electronics Corp.; *U.S. Public*, pg. 1790
ENTERPRISE FLEET SERVICES—NONE—Enterprise Rent-A-Car Company; *U.S. Private*, pg. 377
THE ENTERPRISE GROUP—Mutual Fund Family—The Mutual Life Insurance Company of New York; *U.S. Private*, pg. 769
ENTERPRISE/INTEGRATOR—Tool for Development of Solutions to Integrations—Apertus Technologies Incorporated; *U.S. Public*, pg. 119
ENTERPRISE RENT-A-CAR—NONE—Enterprise Rent-A-Car Company; *U.S. Private*, pg. 377
ENTERPRISE SOLUTIONS BY CONTINUUM—Software—CSC Financial Services Group; *U.S. Public*, pg. 422
ENTERPRISE SYSTEM/4381—Computer System—International Business Machines Corporation; *U.S. Public*, pg. 895
ENTERPRISE SYSTEM/9000—Computer System—International Business Machines Corporation; *U.S. Public*, pg. 895
ENTERPRISE SYSTEM/3090—Computer System—International Business Machines Corporation; *U.S. Public*, pg. 895

ENTERPRISE SYSTEMS ARCHITECTURE/390—Computer System—International Business Machines Corporation; *U.S. Public*, pg. 895

ENTERPRISE SYSTEMS ARCHITECTURE/370—Computer System—International Business Machines Corporation; *U.S. Public*, pg. 895

ENTERPRISE SYSTEMS CONNECTION ARCHITECTURE—Computer System—International Business Machines Corporation; *U.S. Public*, pg. 895

ENTERPRISE SYSTEM/9370—Computer System—International Business Machines Corporation; *U.S. Public*, pg. 895

ENTERPRISECHANNEL—Channel Extension Hardware—Network Systems Corporation; *U.S. Public*, pg. 1522

ENTERPRIZE—Imaging & Information Management Platform—Information & Engineering Technology; *U.S. Private*, pg. 351

ENTERTAINER—Customized Pay Per View Listing Guides Distributed Monthly by Cable Systems—TV Host Inc.; *U.S. Private*, pg. 1066

ENTERTAINMENT—Coupon Books—Entertainment Publications, Inc.; *U.S. Public*, pg. 320

THE ENTERTAINMENT—Distributor of Audio & Video Home Entertainment Products—John Menzies plc; *Int'l*, pg. 707

ENTERTAINMENT NEWSFEED—Entertainment News Programming—Westwood One, Inc.; *U.S. Public*, pg. 1763

ENTERTAINMENT PUBLICATIONS—Discount Coupon Programs—CUC International, Inc.; *U.S. Public*, pg. 320

THE ENTERTAINMENT REPORT—Entertainment News Programming—Westwood One, Inc.; *U.S. Public*, pg. 1763

ENTERTAINMENT UK—Home Entertainment Products—Kingfisher plc; *Int'l*, pg. 733

ENTERTAINMENT WEEKLY—Magazine—Time Warner Inc.; *U.S. Public*, pg. 1610

ENTEX—NONE—NorAm Energy Corp.; *U.S. Public*, pg. 843

ENTEX—Respiratory Congestion Relief—Procter & Gamble Pharmaceuticals, Inc.; *U.S. Public*, pg. 1331

ENTEX PSE—Respiratory Relief—Procter & Gamble Pharmaceuticals, Inc.; *U.S. Public*, pg. 1331

ENTHOBRITE—Zinc Cadmium & Copper Brightener—Enthone-OMI, Inc.; *U.S. Public*, pg. 138

ENTHOL—Metal Cleaners—Enthone-OMI, Inc.; *U.S. Public*, pg. 138

ENTHONICS—Research Service—Enthone-OMI, Inc.; *U.S. Public*, pg. 138

ENTHOX—Conversion Coatings—Enthone-OMI, Inc.; *U.S. Public*, pg. 138

ENTICEMENTS—NONE—Kellwood Company; *U.S. Public*, pg. 948

ENTOCORT—Gastrointestinal Drug—Astra AB; *Int'l*, pg. 93

ENTRAP—Vinyl Floor Mat—3M; *U.S. Public*, pg. 1604

ENTREFINOS—NONE—Tabacalera, S.A.; *Int'l*, pg. 1345

ENTREMONT—Cheese—Entremont S.A.; *Int'l*, pg. 458

ENTRUST—Adult Incontinence Products—McKesson Corporation; *U.S. Public*, pg. 1072

ENUCLENE—Lubricating Solution—Alcon Laboratories, Inc.; *Int'l*, pg. 916

ENVACOR—Diagnostic Test—Abbott Laboratories; *U.S. Public*, pg. 12

ENVACOR HTLV III—Diagnostic Test—Abbott Laboratories; *U.S. Public*, pg. 12

ENVELOK—Folios—The Mead Corporation; *U.S. Public*, pg. 1074

ENVEX—High Performance Plastics—Rogers Corporation; *U.S. Public*, pg. 1402

ENVIRACRYL—Powder Coating Composition—PPG Industries, Inc.; *U.S. Public*, pg. 1245

ENVIREX—Industrial Machinery—Envirex Inc.; *U.S. Public*, pg. 61

ENVIRO-CHOICE—NONE—Ace Hardware Corporation; *U.S. Private*, pg. 12

ENVIRO-GUARD—Coating—Pratt & Lambert United, Inc.; *U.S. Public*, pg. 1466

ENVIRO-MATE—Leather-Like Book Binding Material—Industrial Coatings Group, Inc.; *U.S. Private*, pg. 434

ENVIRO-MATE—Plastic Grocery Bags—Sonoco Products Company; *U.S. Public*, pg. 1485

ENVIRO-PRIME—Electrodeposition Coatings—PPG Industries, Inc.; *U.S. Public*, pg. 1245

ENVIRO SEAL—Valve Packing—Fisher Controls International, Inc.; *Int'l*, pg. 573

ENVIRO TUFF—Plastic Packaging—Poly Pak America, Inc.; *U.S. Private*, pg. 875

ENVIROBASE—Paints—PPG Industries, Inc.; *U.S. Public*, pg. 1245

ENVIROCRON—Electrodeposition Coatings—PPG Industries, Inc.; *U.S. Public*, pg. 1245

ENVIROFLEX—NONE—The Flexitallic Group, Inc.; *U.S. Private*, pg. 413

ENVIROFUGE 2000—Centrifugal Unit—Reuter Manufacturing Inc.; *U.S. Public*, pg. 1383

ENVIROGRAPHIC—Recycled Papers—Badger Paper Mills, Inc.; *U.S. Public*, pg. 165

ENVIROGUARD—Food Processing Fixtures—Guth Lighting Company; *Int'l*, pg. 821

ENVIROLITH—Recycled Paper Label—Kal Grafx; *U.S. Public*, pg. 387

ENVIROMAT—Waste Water Treatment System—Ionics, Incorporated; *U.S. Public*, pg. 912

ENVIRON—Transportable Suite for Specialized Electronic & Medical Diagnostic Equip.—Dynamics Corporation of America; *U.S. Public*, pg. 286

ENVIRON—Air Conditioning—James Hardie Industries Ltd.; *Int'l*, pg. 596

ENVIRON—Water Reducible Coating Composition—PPG Industries, Inc.; *U.S. Public*, pg. 1245

ENVIRONMENT—NONE—Kimberly-Clark Corporation; *U.S. Public*, pg. 958

ENVIRONMENTAL NEWS DIGEST—Periodical Of Environmental Pollution Info—American Automobile Association; *U.S. Private*, pg. 50

ENVIRONMENTAL SELF ASSESSMENT PROGRAM—Computer System—International Business Machines Corporation; *U.S. Public*, pg. 895

ENVIRONMENTAL SOLUTIONS—Trade Periodical—Advantar Communications; *U.S. Private*, pg. 22

ENVIRONMENTAL TECHNOLOGY, INC.—Country Fresh Cat Litter—Professional Apartment Management, Inc.; *U.S. Private*, pg. 889

ENVIRONMENTS 20/20—Freestanding Desking System—CorryHiebert Corporation; *U.S. Public*, pg. 772

ENVIROQ—Company Name—Enviroq; *U.S. Public*, pg. 881

ENVIROQUAT SPRAY—Aerosal Spray Disinfectant & Deodorizer—Calgon Vestal Laboratories; *U.S. Public*, pg. 1515

ENVIRORESEARCH—Electronic Air Cleaners—Windmere-Durable Holdings; *U.S. Public*, pg. 1771

ENVIROSENSE—Plastic Packaging—Poly Pak America, Inc.; *U.S. Private*, pg. 875

ENVIROSTAR—Zinc-Free Chemical Floor Product Line—Pioneer/Eclipse Corp.; *Int'l*, pg. 71

ENVIROSTAT—Static Eliminator—Simco; *U.S. Public*, pg. 865

ENVIROTRAK—Laboratory Controls—Anemostat Products; *U.S. Public*, pg. 286

ENVIROTRAK—Air Distribution Equipment—Dynamics Corporation of America; *U.S. Public*, pg. 286

ENVIROWATCH—NONE—Eastman Kodak Company; *U.S. Public*, pg. 550

ENVISION—Contact Lens—Bausch & Lomb Incorporated; *U.S. Public*, pg. 194

ENVISION—Object-Oriented Programming Software—LTX Corporation; *U.S. Public*, pg. 972

ENVISION—NONE—Lam Research Corporation; *U.S. Public*, pg. 975

ENVISTA—NT Server—Amdahl Corporation; *Int'l*, pg. 527

ENVOID—Oral Contraceptive—Monsanto Company; *U.S. Public*, pg. 1124

ENVOL—White Mineral Oil—Witco Corporation; *U.S. Public*, pg. 1773

ENVOY—NONE—Cordis, a Johnson & Johnson Company; *U.S. Public*, pg. 928

ENVOY—Towels—Fort James Corporation; *U.S. Public*, pg. 670

ENVOY—Electronic Pocket Organizer—Motorola, Inc.; *U.S. Public*, pg. 1136

ENVOY—Data Communications System—Tandem Computers Inc.; *U.S. Public*, pg. 417

ENVOY—Manual Wheelchair—Theradyne Corporation; *U.S. Private*, pg. 637

ENVOY 100—Electronic Mail Service—BCE Inc.; *Int'l*, pg. 114

ENVUE—Still Store Systems—Chyron Corp.; *Int'l*, pg. 1372

ENWAVE—Application-Specific System-Level Design Suites—Cadence Design Systems, Inc.; *U.S. Public*, pg. 290

ENZIMAX—Laundry Powder Soaps—Nuevo Federal S.A.; *Int'l*, pg. 990

ENZIO—NONE—Crestar Food Products, Inc.; *U.S. Public*, pg. 805

ENZO ANGIOLINI—Women's Shoes & Accessories—Nine West Group, Inc.; *U.S. Public*, pg. 1185

ENZON—NONE—Enzon, Inc.; *U.S. Public*, pg. 587

ENZY-SIZE—Alpha-Amylase, for the Preparation of Starch Based Paper Coatings—Royal Gist-Brocades N.V.; *Int'l*, pg. 1142

ENZYGNOST—Diagnostic Test Kit—Behringwerke AG; *Int'l*, pg. 624

ENZYGRAPHIC WEB—Non-Radioactive System to Detect Enzyme Activity—Scientific Imaging Systems; *U.S. Public*, pg. 550

EOLIKI—Liquor & Ouzo—Groupe Pernod Ricard; *Int'l*, pg. 566

EPACE—X-Ray Equipment—Fischer Imaging Corporation; *U.S. Public*, pg. 647

EPDM—Rubber—DSM N.V.; *Int'l*, pg. 352

EPECO—Electric Power Equipment Co.—Electric Power Equipment Co.; *U.S. Private*, pg. 368

EPIAMART—Non-steroidal Cream for Skin Rashes—Shiseido Company Ltd.; *Int'l*, pg. 1235

EPIC—Thread—Coats North America; *Int'l*, pg. 300

EPIC—High Style Faucet—Delta Faucet Corporation; *U.S. Public*, pg. 1053

EPIC—NONE—Everest & Jennings, Inc.; *U.S. Public*, pg. 758

EPIC—Toiletries—The Gillette Company; *U.S. Public*, pg. 743

EPIC—NONE—LucasVarity plc; *Int'l*, pg. 819

EPIC—Liquid Photoimageable Solder Mask—Morton International Inc.; *U.S. Public*, pg. 1134

EPIC—Records—Sony Corporation; *Int'l*, pg. 1280

EPIC—Records—Sony Music Entertainment, Inc.; *Int'l*, pg. 1281

EPIC SOUNDTRAX—Recording Label—Sony Music Entertainment, Inc.; *Int'l*, pg. 1281

EPIC III—Supervisory Temperature Control System—Davis Standard Corporation; *U.S. Public*, pg. 459

EPIC XTRA—Thread—Coats North America; *Int'l*, pg. 300

EPICS—PostScript-Compatible Composition System—Prepress Solutions, Inc.; *U.S. Private*, pg. 882

EPICURE—Paper Towels & Napkins—Georgia-Pacific Corporation; *U.S. Public*, pg. 735

EPICURE—NONE—H.J. Heinz Company Australia Ltd.; *U.S. Public*, pg. 807

EPIFOAM—NONE—Schwarz Pharma Inc.; *Int'l*, pg. 1211

EPIGRADE—Source Requests—ATMI, Inc.; *U.S. Public*, pg. 12

EPILINK—Epoxy Curing Agent—Akzo Nobel N.V.; *Int'l*, pg. 42

EPILOG—NONE—Western Atlas Logging Services; *U.S. Public*, pg. 1757

EPINAL—Ophthalmic Preparation—Alcon Laboratories, Inc.; *Int'l*, pg. 916

EPION—Semiconductor Devices—Solid State Devices, Inc.; *U.S. Private*, pg. 1012

EPIPEN AUTO-INJECTOR—Epinephrine for Self-Administration—Meridian Medical Technology, Inc.; *U.S. Public*, pg. 1095

EPISENSE—Source Reagents—ATMI, Inc.; *U.S. Public*, pg. 12

EPISODES—Magazine—ABC, Inc; *U.S. Public*, pg. 511

EPISODES—Tour Operators—Accor S.A.; *Int'l*, pg. 20

EPISTAR—Microscope—Leica, Inc.; *Int'l*, pg. 806

EPITHERM—Lasers—Excel Technology, Inc.; *U.S. Public*, pg. 599

EPITOME—Electrosurgical Scalpel with Ceramic Care—Utah Medical Products, Inc.; *U.S. Public*, pg. 1700

EPITRONICS—Epitaxial Materials—ATMI, Inc.; *U.S. Public*, pg. 12

EPIX XL—Electrode Device—EMPI, Inc.; *U.S. Public*, pg. 545

EPO-KWICK—Fast Curing Epoxy Mounting Compound—Buehler, Limited; *U.S. Public*, pg. 574

EPOCAP—Two-Part Epoxy Compounds—Hardman Division of Harcros Chemicals, Inc.; *Int'l*, pg. 598

EPOCEL—Filters—Pall Corporation; *U.S. Public*, pg. 1253

EPOCH 480—Magnetic Computer Tape—Anacomp Magnetics, Inc.; *U.S. Public*, pg. 107

EPOCH-MTC—Magnetic Tape Cartridge—Anacomp Magnetics, Inc.; *U.S. Public*, pg. 107

EPOCH MTCH—Magnetic Tape Cartridge—Anacomp Magnetics, Inc.; *U.S. Public*, pg. 107

EPOCH 2000—Off-the-Shelf Satellite Command & Control System—Integral Systems, Inc.; *U.S. Public*, pg. 883

EPOCRETE—Two-Part Epoxy Concrete Materials—Hardman Division of Harcros Chemicals, Inc.; *Int'l*, pg. 598

EPOCURE—Epoxy Curing Agents—Hardman Division of Harcros Chemicals, Inc.; *Int'l*, pg. 598

EPOGEN—Recombinant Erythropoietin Treatment of Anemia of Chronic Renal Failure—Amgen Inc.; *U.S. Public*, pg. 100

EPOGIN—Agent for Anemin Associated with Chronic Renal Failure—Chugai Pharmaceutical Co., Ltd.; *Int'l*, pg. 290

EPOGIN—Erythropoietin—Genetics Institute, Inc.; *U.S. Public*, pg. 79

EPOLENE—Waxes—Eastman Chemical Company; *U.S. Public*, pg. 550

EPOLENE—Synthetic Resins & Waxes, Polyethylene Waxes—Eastman Kodak Company; *U.S. Public*, pg. 550

EPOMET—Mounting Compound—Buehler, Limited; *U.S. Public*, pg. 574

EPON—Resins—Shell Chemical Co.; *Int'l*, pg. 1136

EPON CURING AGENTS—Accelerators—Shell Chemical Co.; *Int'l*, pg. 1136

EPON HPT—Resins & Curing Agents—Shell Chemical Co.; *Int'l*, pg. 1136

EPOSET—Two-Part Epoxy Compounds—Hardman Division of Harcros Chemicals, Inc.; *Int'l*, pg. 598

EPOSOLVE—Solvent for Epoxy Clean-Up—Hardman Division of Harcros Chemicals, Inc.; *Int'l*, pg. 598

EPOST—NONE—Deutsche Post AG; *Int'l*, pg. 407

EPOWELD—Two-Part Epoxy Compound—Hardman Division of Harcros Chemicals, Inc.; *Int'l*, pg. 598

EPOXI-PATCH—Structural Bonding Adhesives—The Dexter Corporation; *U.S. Public*, pg. 504

EPOXSTEEL—Epoxy Coating—RPM, Inc.; *U.S. Public*, pg. 1356

EPOXY RUST-MATE—Rust Inhibiting Paint—Zynolyte Products Company; *Int'l*, pg. 663

EPOXY TABS—NONE—La-Co Industries Markal Company; *U.S. Private*, pg. 640

EPOXYCOP—Anti-Fouling Paints & Coatings—Rule Industries, Inc.; *U.S. Public*, pg. 950

EPOXYN—Lab Furniture Tops—Fisher Scientific Company; *U.S. Private*, pg. 658

EPPENDORF—Pipettes & Centrifuges—Brinkmann Instruments, Inc.; *U.S. Private*, pg. 169

EPREX—NONE—Johnson & Johnson; *U.S. Public*, pg. 927

EPROMETER—UV Meter—Spectronics Corporation; *U.S. Private*, pg. 1024

EPSILON—Direct Marketing & Computer Services—Epsilon; *U.S. Public*, pg. 74

EPSILON—Direct Marketing & Computer Services—Epsilon/West; *U.S. Public*, pg. 74

EPSON—Computer Products—Monsanto Company; *U.S. Public*, pg. 1124

EPSON—NONE—Seiko Epson Corporation; *Int'l*, pg. 1219

EPURE COLLECTION—Sinks—Vance Industries, Inc.; *U.S. Private*, pg. 1133

EQUA—Chairs—Herman Miller, Inc.; *U.S. Public*, pg. 1111

EQUA-TEMP—Combustion System—Harrop Industries, Inc.; *U.S. Private*, pg. 506

EQUAL—Artificial Sweetner—Monsanto Company; *U.S. Public*, pg. 1124

EQUAL—Low Calorie Tabletop Sweetener—The NutraSweet Company; *U.S. Public*, pg. 1125

EQUAL—Aspartame—NutraSweet International, Ltd.; *U.S. Public*, pg. 1125

EQUAL—OTC Low-Calorie Tabletop Sweetener Made With NutraSweet—Searle Laboratories; *U.S. Public*, pg. 1125

EQUAL TIME—Greeting Cards—American Greetings Corporation; *U.S. Public*, pg. 77

EQUALENS—Contact Lens Materials—Bausch & Lomb Incorporated; *U.S. Public*, pg. 194

EQUALIZER—Level Payment Plan—APS; *U.S. Public*, pg. 1297

EQUALIZER—Bearing Protector—Garlock Sealing Technologies; *U.S. Public*, pg. 402

EQUALIZER—Blowers—MD Pneumatics; *U.S. Private*, pg. 1111

EQUALIZER—Doctor—Thermo Fibertek, Inc.; *U.S. Public*, pg. 1593

EQUIBOND—Insulated Panels—James Hardie Industries Ltd.; *Int'l*, pg. 596

EQUINADER—Horse Feed—Manna Pro Corporation; *U.S. Private*, pg. 700

EQUINE—NONE—Schering-Plough Animal Health; *U.S. Public*, pg. 1438

EQUINOX—Sleeping Bags—The Canadian Coleman Co., Ltd.; *U.S. Private*, pg. 194

EQUINOX—Insulated Panels—James Hardie Industries Ltd.; *Int'l*, pg. 596

EQUITE—Cleansing Line—Christian Dior Perfumes Inc.; *Int'l*, pg. 781

EQUITHERM—Machinery—Gardner Abrasives; *U.S. Public*, pg. 1699

EQUITRAC—Registered Tradename of Company—Equitrac Corporation; *U.S. Public*, pg. 590

EQUITRAC'S PROFESSIONAL INTERNET CLIENT (E.P.I.C.)—Internet Tracking—Equitrac Corporation; *U.S. Public*, pg. 590

EQUITY—Communications System—Executone Information Systems, Inc.; *U.S. Public*, pg. 599

EQULINE—High Performance Operable Vents—Kawneer Company; *U.S. Public*, pg. 60

EQVALAN—Animal Health Pharmaceuticals—Merial Ltd.; *U.S. Public*, pg. 1092

EQVALAN—Animal Health Pharmaceuticals—Merial Ltd.; *Int'l*, pg. 1109

ERA—Laundry Detergent—The Procter & Gamble Company; *U.S. Public*, pg. 1330

ERA—Integrated Computer Systems Marketed to Automobile Dealers—The Reynolds and Reynolds Company; *U.S. Public*, pg. 1384

ERA PLUS—Detergent—The Procter & Gamble Company; *U.S. Public*, pg. 1330

ERAS-EVER—Pens—Dixon Ticonderoga Company; *U.S. Public*, pg. 514

ERASCO—Frozen & Ready Made Meals—Grand Metropolitan Plc; *Int'l*, pg. 408

ERASCO—Soups & Ready Meals—GrandMet Foods GmbH; *Int'l*, pg. 409

ERASE-ITT—Sewage Odor Counteractant—Surco Products, Inc.; *U.S. Private*, pg. 1056

ERASER MATE—Pens & Refills—The Gillette Company; *U.S. Public*, pg. 743

ERAWAN—Portland Cement Type III—The Siam Cement Public Company Limited; *Int'l*, pg. 1237

ERECTOMATIC—Shelving—Penco Products; *U.S. Private*, pg. 848

ERECTOR—Erector Sets—View-Master, Inc.; *U.S. Public*, pg. 1058

EREM—Tools—Audits & Surveys Worldwide; *U.S. Public*, pg. 147

EREM—Electronics Pliers, Cutters, and Tweezers—Cooper Hand Tools; *U.S. Public*, pg. 444

EREM—Precision Cutters & Tweezers—Cooper Industries, Inc.; *U.S. Public*, pg. 442

ERGAMISOL—Pharmaceutical—Janssen Pharmaceutica, Inc.; *U.S. Public*, pg. 928

ERGAMISOL—NONE—Johnson & Johnson; *U.S. Public*, pg. 927

ERGO-BENCH—(Adj. Height Bench)—Lyon Metal Products, Inc.; *U.S. Private*, pg. 638

ERGO 2000—Scraping & Spreading Tools—Red Devil Inc.; *U.S. Private*, pg. 915

ERGODENTAL—Dental & Lab Seating—3M; *U.S. Public*, pg. 1604

ERGOLSTAK—Wire-Frame Stacking Chairs—United Chair, Inc.; *U.S. Private*, pg. 512

ERGON 2—Chairs—Herman Miller, Inc.; *U.S. Private*, pg. 1111

ERGONOMIC DESIGN—Remote Controls—Zenith Electronics Corp.; *U.S. Public*, pg. 1790

ERGOVISION—Diagnostic System—Essilor International Compagnie Generale d'Optique; *Int'l*, pg. 462

ERICKSON—Toolholding & Workholding Devices—Kennametal Inc.; *U.S. Public*, pg. 950

ERICKSON'S—Combo Food & Drug—Erickson's Diversified Corp.; *U.S. Private*, pg. 381

ERICSSON—Electrical Wire, Cable & Access.—Ericsson, Inc.; *Int'l*, pg. 1364

ERIE—Forging Equip.—Erie Press Systems; *U.S. Private*, pg. 353

ERIE SCIENTIFIC—Laboratory Prods.—Sybron International Corporation; *U.S. Public*, pg. 1544

ERIEZ—Magnetics—Eriez Magnetics; *U.S. Private*, pg. 381

ERISTOFF—NONE—Bacardi-Martini Belgium; *U.S. Private*, pg. 109

ERIUM—Permanent Magnetic Power Source—Eriez Magnetics; *U.S. Private*, pg. 381

ERLANGER—Fabrics—Balson-Hercules Ltd.; *Int'l*, pg. 326

ERRAZURIZ—NONE—Robert Mondavi Winery, Inc.; *U.S. Public*, pg. 1393

ERTHROCIN—Erythromycin—Abbott Laboratories; *U.S. Public*, pg. 12

ERVEVAX—Vaccine—SmithKline Beecham Research Limited; *Int'l*, pg. 1266

ERYCETTE—Topical Solution Pledgets—Ortho-McNeil Pharmaceutical Corporation; *U.S. Public*, pg. 929

ERYGEL—Topical Erythomycin Gel—Allergan, Inc.; *U.S. Public*, pg. 46

ERYTRHRO-PAK—Pharmaceuticals—Rhone-Poulenc Rorer - U.S.; *Int'l*, pg. 1110

ESAB—Welding Machines & Equipment—Esab AB; *Int'l*, pg. 281

ESAB-HANCOCK—Gas, Plasma & Laser Cutting—Esab AB; *Int'l*, pg. 281

ESAB OK—Welding Electrodes—Esab AB; *Int'l*, pg. 281

ESCALOL—Sunscreens—International Specialty Products, Inc.; *U.S. Public*, pg. 858

ESCASCOPE—Electon Microscope—VG Instruments plc; *U.S. Public*, pg. 1595

ESCADRILLE—Casual Slacks—Trans-Apparel Group; *U.S. Public*, pg. 796

ESCALIN—Animal Production Enhancer—SmithKline Beecham plc; *Int'l*, pg. 1264

ESCALOL 557—Sunscreen—Mallinckrodt Inc.; *U.S. Public*, pg. 1039

ESCALOL 507—Sunscreen—Mallinckrodt Inc.; *U.S. Public*, pg. 1039

ESCANABA ENAMEL—Printing Paper—The Mead Corporation; *U.S. Public*, pg. 1074

ESCANABA RED BUCK PULP—Wood Pulp—The Mead Corporation; *U.S. Public*, pg. 1074

ESCAPE—Women's Fragrance—Calvin Klein Cosmetics Company; *U.S. Public*, pg. 1435

ESCAPE ARTIST—Escape Respirator—Aearo Company; *U.S. Private*, pg. 23

ESCAPE FOR MEN—Mens' Fragrance—Calvin Klein Cosmetics Company; *Int'l*, pg. 1435

ESCO—Elevators—Esco Elevator Corp.; *U.S. Private*, pg. 383

ESCON—Computer System—International Business Machines Corporation; *U.S. Public*, pg. 895

ESCON XDF—Computer System—International Business Machines Corporation; *U.S. Public*, pg. 895

ESCOR—Tegra Super-Cell Screening Technology—Prepress Solutions, Inc.; *U.S. Private*, pg. 882

ESCORT—Luggage—American Tourister, Inc.; *U.S. Public*, pg. 1430

ESCORT—Herbicide—The Dow Chemical Company; *U.S. Public*, pg. 522

ESCORT—Motion Picture Camera—Eastman Kodak Company; *U.S. Public*, pg. 550

ESCORT—Pocket Knives—Fiskars-Gerber; *Int'l*, pg. 492

ESCORT—Car—Ford Motor Company; *U.S. Public*, pg. 661

ESCORT—Stationery Products—The Mead Corporation; *U.S. Public*, pg. 1074

ESCORT—Flea & Tick Collars & Sprays—Schering-Plough Corporation; *U.S. Public*, pg. 1438

Brand Name Index

ESEETAC—NONE—Barton Nelson Inc.; *U.S. Private*, pg. 120

ESGIC—Pharmaceutical—Forest Laboratories, Inc.; *U.S. Public*, pg. 670

ESGIC PLUS—Pharmaceutical—Forest Laboratories, Inc.; *U.S. Public*, pg. 670

ESIDRIX—NONE—Novartis Pharmaceuticals; *Int'l*, pg. 973

ESIMIL—NONE—Novartis Pharmaceuticals; *Int'l*, pg. 973

ESKIMO—Ice Cream—Morinaga Milk Industry Co., Ltd.; *Int'l*, pg. 895

ESKIMO PIE—Stick & Stickless Ice Cream Bars & Half Gallons—Eskimo Pie Corporation; *U.S. Public*, pg. 592

ESMERON—Muscle Relaxant—Akzo Nobel N.V.; *Int'l*, pg. 42

ESOPE—Hard Gas-Permeable Lens—Essilor International Compagnie Generale d'Optique; *Int'l*, pg. 462

ESOTERICA—Medical Skin-Care—SmithKline Beecham plc; *Int'l*, pg. 1264

ESPECIAL—Tequila—Domecq Importers Inc.; *Int'l*, pg. 63

ESPECIALLY YOU—Ladies Apparel—Movie Star, Inc.; *U.S. Public*, pg. 1140

ESPLANADE—Floor Coverings—Domco Inc.; *Int'l*, pg. 415

ESPASMO-SILIDRON—Antispasmodic for Gastric Distress—SmithKline Beecham plc; *Int'l*, pg. 1264

ESPRE—Recreational Vehicle—Kit Manufacturing Company; *U.S. Public*, pg. 962

ESPREE—Wheel Cleaner—Blue Coral/Slick 50; *U.S. Public*, pg. 1348

EXPRESO—A 3 Transaction Facilities with Teller, Phone Connections & Extended Hours—Banco Popular de Puerto Rico; *U.S. Public*, pg. 175

ESPRESSIMO—Espresso Machine—Grindmaster Corporation; *U.S. Private*, pg. 482

ESPRIT—Women's Hoisery—Arrow Shirt Company; *Int'l*, pg. 194

ESPRIT—Non-Alcoholic Sparkling Juice & Water—Canandaigua Wine Company, Inc.; *U.S. Public*, pg. 300

ESPRIT—Women's & Children's Clothing, Accessories & Footwear—Esprit de Corp.; *U.S. Private*, pg. 383

ESPRIT—Computer Terminals—Esprit Systems, Inc.; *U.S. Private*, pg. 383

ESPRIT—High Fidelity Sound Apparatus—Sony Electronics; *Int'l*, pg. 1281

ESPRIT—Motorcycle Parts & Acces.—Tucker Rocky Distributing; *U.S. Private*, pg. 639

ESQUIRE—Magazine—The Hearst Corporation; *U.S. Private*, pg. 515

ESQUIRE—Magazine—Hearst Magazines Division; *U.S. Private*, pg. 516

ESQUIRE—Socks—Kayser-Roth Corporation, Inc.; *Int'l*, pg. 576

ESQUIRE—Watches—Movado Group, Inc.; *U.S. Public*, pg. 1140

ESQUIRE—Magazine—The National Magazine Company Ltd.; *U.S. Private*, pg. 518

ESQUIRE/NICHOLS—Toys—Strombecker Corporation; *U.S. Private*, pg. 1047

ESSAR—NONE—Lawter International, Inc.; *U.S. Public*, pg. 980

ESSE—Watermark in Bond Paper—The Mead Corporation; *U.S. Public*, pg. 1074

ESSE BY GILBERT-COVER—Recycled Paper—Gilbert Paper; *U.S. Public*, pg. 1074

ESSE BY GILBERT-TEXT—Recycled Paper—Gilbert Paper; *U.S. Public*, pg. 1074

ESSE BY GILBERT-WRITING—Recycled Paper—Gilbert Paper; *U.S. Public*, pg. 1074

ESSENCE—Luggage—American Tourister, Inc.; *U.S. Public*, pg. 1430

ESSENCE—Ceramic Wall Tile—Monarch Tile, Inc.; *U.S. Private*, pg. 287

ESSENCE—Glazed ceramic wall tile—Precision Die & Engineering, Inc.; *U.S. Public*, pg. 1322

ESSENTIAL BALANCE—Multiple Vitamins for Adults—Pharmavite Corp.; *U.S. Private*, pg. 860

THE ESSENTIAL COLLECTION—Beauty Products—DeMert & Dougherty, Inc.; *U.S. Private*, pg. 323

ESSENTIAL COLORS—Acrylic Paints—Koh-I-Noor, Inc.; *U.S. Private*, pg. 629

ESSENTIALS—Women's General Interest Magazine—IPC Magazines Limited; *Int'l*, pg. 651

ESSENTIALS—Surgical, Medical, Dental & Vetinary Instruments & Apparatus—Sime Darby Berhad; *Int'l*, pg. 1249

ESSENTIALS—Watches—Timex Corporation; *U.S. Private*, pg. 1088

ESSENTIALS FOR HOME—NONE—Damark International, Inc.; *U.S. Public*, pg. 478

ESSERA—Upholstery Yarn—Amoco Chemicals; *U.S. Public*, pg. 102

ESSEX CORPORATION—NONE—CUC International, Inc.; *U.S. Public*, pg. 320

ESSICK—NONE—MultiQuip, Inc.; *Int'l*, pg. 695

ESSKAY—Meat Packer—Esskay; *U.S. Public*, pg. 1479

ESSKAY—Processed Meats—Smithfield Foods, Inc.; *U.S. Public*, pg. 1479

ESSLINGER PREMIUM—Beer—The Lion Brewery, Inc.; *U.S. Public*, pg. 1000

ESSO—Petroleum Products—Exxon Corporation; *U.S. Public*, pg. 601

ESTABEX—Bactericidel Fungicide—Akzo Nobel N.V.; *Int'l*, pg. 42

ESTAFLEX—Plasticisers—Akzo Nobel N.V.; *Int'l*, pg. 42

ESTANE—Thermoplastic Polyurethane—Kyowa Hakko Kogyo Company, Ltd.; *Int'l*, pg. 778

ESTAR—Film Base—Eastman Kodak Company; *U.S. Public*, pg. 550

ESTAR—Thereapeutic Tar Gel—Westwood-Squibb Pharmaceuticals Inc.; *U.S. Public*, pg. 255

ESTAR-AH—Film Base—Eastman Kodak Company; *U.S. Public*, pg. 550

ESTATE—Drapery Hardware—Kirsch; *U.S. Public*, pg. 1176

ESTATE CHERRY—Prefinished Wall Paneling—Georgia-Pacific Corporation; *U.S. Public*, pg. 735

ESTATE OAK—Prefinished Wall Paneling—Georgia-Pacific Corporation; *U.S. Public*, pg. 735

ESTEE—Diet Control Products—The Hain Food Group Inc.; *U.S. Public*, pg. 774

ESTEE LAUDER—Cosmetics—Estee Lauder Companies Inc.; *U.S. Public*, pg. 594

ESTEEM—Automobile—American Suzuki Motor Corporation; *Int'l*, pg. 1323

ESTEEM—Inlaid Sheet Vinyl Flooring—Congoleum Corporation; *U.S. Public*, pg. 69

ESTEEM—MRI System—Elscint Ltd.; *Int'l*, pg. 450

ESTEEM WAGON—Automobile—American Suzuki Motor Corporation; *Int'l*, pg. 1323

ESTEK—Semiconductor Products—Eastman Kodak Company; *U.S. Public*, pg. 550

ESTER-MID—Insulated Wire—General Electric Canada Inc.; *U.S. Public*, pg. 713

ESTERLON—Filaments—Ketema, Inc.; *U.S. Private*, pg. 604

ESTERON—Herbicide—The Dow Chemical Company; *U.S. Public*, pg. 522

ESTETIC—Prepainted Steel—Cockerill Sambre; *Int'l*, pg. 301

ESTHER WILLIAMS SWIMMING POOL—Swimming Pool—Delair Group, L.L.C.; *U.S. Private*, pg. 47

ESTIVIN II EYE PAK—Sterile, Single-Use Ophthalmic Drops—Alcon Laboratories, Inc.; *Int'l*, pg. 916

ESTOTEK—Polyester Plastic, Thermoplastic Olefin Elastomer—Eastman Kodak Company; *U.S. Public*, pg. 550

ESTRACE—Oral Estrogen Product—Bristol-Myers Squibb Company; *U.S. Public*, pg. 253

ESTRACE—Estrogen Product—Bristol-Myers Squibb U.S. Pharmaceutical Group; *U.S. Public*, pg. 255

ESTRACE—Hormone Replacement Therapy—Roberts Pharmaceutical Corporation; *U.S. Public*, pg. 1393

ESTRADERM—Estradiol Transdermal System—Ciba Specialty Chemicals; *Int'l*, pg. 291

ESTRADERM—NONE—Novartis Pharmaceuticals; *Int'l*, pg. 973

ESTRADERM TTS—Patch for the Treatment of Menopausal Disorders—Novartis; *Int'l*, pg. 972

ESTRATAB—Pharmaceutical Products—Solvay Pharmaceuticals, Inc.; *Int'l*, pg. 1278

ESTRATEST—Pharmaceutical Products—Solvay Pharmaceuticals, Inc.; *Int'l*, pg. 1278

ESTRATEST H.S.—Pharmaceutical Products—Solvay Pharmaceuticals, Inc.; *Int'l*, pg. 1278

ESTRELLA DEL SUR—NONE—Guinness Plc; *Int'l*, pg. 412

ESTRING—NONE—Pharmacia & Upjohn, Inc.; *Int'l*, pg. 1047

ESTROBOND—Plasticizers—Eastman Chemical Company; *U.S. Public*, pg. 550

ESTROBOND—Additives for Thermoplastics—Eastman Kodak Company; *U.S. Public*, pg. 550

ESTROFEM—Product for Gynaecological Use—Novo Nordisk A/S; *Int'l*, pg. 987

ESTRON—Acetate Yarn—Eastman Chemical Company; *U.S. Public*, pg. 550

ESTRON—Cigarette Filter Tow—Eastman Kodak Company; *U.S. Public*, pg. 550

ETABLOC—Close-Coupled Pump—KSB Aktiengesellschaft; *Int'l*, pg. 721

ETACHROM B—Close-Coupled Pump—KSB Aktiengesellschaft; *Int'l*, pg. 721

ETACHROM N—Annular Casing Pump—KSB Aktiengesellschaft; *Int'l*, pg. 721

ETADURIN—Tissue Softners—Akzo Nobel N.V.; *Int'l*, pg. 42

ETHALLOY—Needle Alloy—Ethicon, Inc.; *U.S. Public*, pg. 928

ETATHERM-M—Volute Casing Pumps—KSB Aktiengesellschaft; *Int'l*, pg. 721

ETAZET—Volute Casing Pumps—KSB Aktiengesellschaft; *Int'l*, pg. 721

ETCH-A-SKETCH—Toys—The Ohio Art Company, Inc.; *U.S. Public*, pg. 1214

ETERNAFLEX—Caulks & Sealants—The Gibson-Homans Company; *U.S. Private*, pg. 451

ETERNALUX—NONE—Blyth Industries; *U.S. Public*, pg. 239

ETERNAWALL—Gypsum Wallboard—Georgia-Pacific Corporation; *U.S. Public*, pg. 735

ETERNIT INDUSTRIES—NONE—ETEX; *Int'l*, pg. 430

ETERNITY—Women's Fragrance—Calvin Klein Cosmetics Company; *Int'l*, pg. 1435

ETERNITY FOR MEN—Men's Fragrance Products—Calvin Klein Cosmetics Company; *Int'l*, pg. 1435

ETERPLAST SANAYL—NONE—ETEX; *Int'l*, pg. 430

ETHACALC—Computer Programs—The Dow Chemical Company; *U.S. Public*, pg. 522

ETHAFOAM—Polyethylene Foam—The Dow Chemical Company; *U.S. Public*, pg. 522

ETHAN ALLEN—Home Furnishings—Ethan Allen, Inc.; *U.S. Public*, pg. 595

ETHATROL KITS—Clinical Chemistry Reagents—Dade Behring Inc.; *U.S. Private*, pg. 110

ETHEL M—Chocolate Liqueur—Mars, Incorporated; *U.S. Private*, pg. 707

ETHER START—NONE—Detroit Diesel Corp.; *U.S. Private*, pg. 850

ETHERSTREAMER—Business Product—International Business Machines Corporation; *U.S. Public*, pg. 895

ETHI-PACK—Pre-cut Sutures—Ethicon, Inc.; *U.S. Public*, pg. 928

ETHIBOND—Polyester Sutures—Ethicon, Inc.; *U.S. Public*, pg. 928

ETHICARE—NONE—Staff Builders Inc.; *U.S. Public*, pg. 1501

ETHICON—Wound Closure Prods.—Ethicon, Inc.; *U.S. Public*, pg. 928

ETHICON—NONE—Johnson & Johnson; *U.S. Public*, pg. 927

ETHIGUARD—Blunt Point Needle—Ethicon, Inc.; *U.S. Public*, pg. 928

ETHILON—Nylon Suture—Ethicon, Inc.; *U.S. Public*, pg. 928

ETHOCEL—Ethylcellulose Resin—The Dow Chemical Company; *U.S. Public*, pg. 522

ETHODUOMEEN—Ethoxylated Fatty Diamines, Cationics Detergents—Akzo Nobel N.V.; *Int'l*, pg. 42

ETHOFAT—Fatty Acids—Akzo Nobel N.V.; *Int'l*, pg. 42

ETHOMEEN—Specialty Chemicals—Akzo Nobel Inc.; *Int'l*, pg. 47

ETHOMEEN—Amines—Akzo Nobel N.V.; *Int'l*, pg. 42

ETHOMID—Nionionics—Akzo Nobel N.V.; *Int'l*, pg. 42

ETHOQUAD—Specialty Chemicals—Akzo Nobel Inc.; *Int'l*, pg. 47

ETHOQUAD—Anti-Static Agents—Akzo Nobel N.V.; *Int'l*, pg. 42

ETHOSPACE—Interiors—Herman Miller, Inc.; *U.S. Public*, pg. 1111

ETHRANE—Enflurane—Abbott Laboratories; *U.S. Public*, pg. 12

ETHRANE—Pharmaceutical Anaesthetics—The BOC Group plc; *Int'l*, pg. 121

ETHRANE—Enflurane, USP—Ohmeda; *Int'l*, pg. 121

ETHYOL—Selective Cytoprotective Agent—U.S. Bioscience, Inc.; *U.S. Public*, pg. 1681

ETIENNE AIGNER—NONE—Etienne Aigner; *U.S. Private*, pg. 384

ETIENNE AIGNER—NONE—The Hartstone Group PLC; *Int'l*, pg. 599

ETIENNE AIGNER—Designer Line Apparel—Phillips-Van Heusen Corporation; *U.S. Public*, pg. 1291

ETINGAL—Process Chemicals & Colorants—BASF AG; *Int'l*, pg. 103

ETNA—Petroleum Prods.—Mobil Oil Corporation; *U.S. Public*, pg. 1118

ETONIC—Athletic Shoes—Aritmos AB; *Int'l*, pg. 1072

ETONIC—Athletic Shoes—Etonic Tretorn; *U.S. Private*, pg. 629

ETONIC—Athletic Shoes—Tretorn AB; *Int'l*, pg. 1072

ETORKI—Cheese—Bongrain S.A.; *Int'l*, pg. 201

ETOS—Drugs & Beauty Chain Stores—Koninklijke Ahold NV; *Int'l*, pg. 749

ETRAFON—Anti-Depressant/Anti-Anxiety Tablets—Schering-Plough Corporation; *U.S. Public*, pg. 1438

ETRI—NONE—Milgray Electronics, Inc.; *U.S. Public*, pg. 205

EUCALYPTAMINT—Arthritis Pain Reliever—Ciba Specialty Chemicals; *Int'l*, pg. 291

EUCERIN—Unscented Moisturizers—Beiersdorf, Inc.; *Int'l*, pg. 182

EUCLID—Rigid Haulers—Euclid Hitachi; *Int'l*, pg. 622

EUCO—Logo—The Euclid Chemical Company; *U.S. Public*, pg. 1358

EUDRAGIT—Pharma-Polymers—Rohm GmbH; *Int'l*, pg. 1454

EUGLUCON—Pharmaceutical—Boehringer Mannheim GmbH; *Int'l*, pg. 331

EUIPAN—Anaesthetic—Bayer AG; *Int'l*, pg. 171

EUKANUBA—Pet Food—Iams Company; *U.S. Private*, pg. 556

EULEXIN—Advanced Prostate Cancer Treatment—Schering-Plough Corporation; *U.S. Public*, pg. 1438

EUNOVA—NONE—SmithKline Beecham Corporation; *Int'l*, pg. 1264

EUNOVA—Vitamin & Tonic—SmithKline Beecham plc; *Int'l*, pg. 1264

EUPERGIT—Pharma-Polymers—Rohm GmbH; *Int'l*, pg. 1454

EURAIL—NONE—Rail Europe Inc.; *Int'l*, pg. 1165

EURECAT—Specialty Chemicals—Akzo Nobel Inc.; *Int'l*, pg. 47

EUREKA—Sulphated Natural Oils—Atlas Refinery; *U.S. Private*, pg. 96

EUREKA—Vacuum Cleaner—Electrolux, AB; *Int'l*, pg. 438

EUREKA—Vacuum Cleaner—The Eureka Company; *Int'l*, pg. 440

EUREKA!—Tents, Backpacks & Accessories—Johnson Worldwide Associates, Inc.; *U.S. Public*, pg. 932

EUREKA—X-Ray Tubes—Litton Industries, Inc.; *U.S. Public*, pg. 1002

EUREKA—Vacuum Cleaners—National Union Electric Corp.; *Int'l*, pg. 440

EUREKA—Wooden Chests, Silverware Chests, Jewelry Boxes & Humidors—Reed & Barton Corporation; *U.S. Private*, pg. 916

EUREKA—Vacuum Cleaners—White Consolidated Industries, Inc.; *Int'l*, pg. 439

EUREKA EXPRESS—Power Team Vacuum Cleaner—The Eureka Company; *Int'l*, pg. 440

EUREKA WORLD VAC—Upright Vacuum Cleaner—The Eureka Company; *Int'l*, pg. 440

EUREST—International Catering—Accor S.A.; *Int'l*, pg. 20

EURO BED—Wallbed—Sico Incorporated; *U.S. Private*, pg. 997

EURO BLUE—NONE—Rubbermaid Incorporated; *U.S. Public*, pg. 1411

EURO COLLECTIONS—Cosmetics & Fragrances—Tristar Corp.; *U.S. Public*, pg. 1640

EURO-KLEEN—Gynecological Device—The Cooper Companies, Inc.; *U.S. Public*, pg. 442

EURO-NOMIC—Ergonomic Style Office Seating—Globe Business Furniture, Inc.; *U.S. Private*, pg. 512

EURO-STYLE—Advertising, Broadcast Service—CRN International, Inc.; *U.S. Private*, pg. 197

EURO TECH—Truck—Iveco-Ford Truck Ltd.; *Int'l*, pg. 484

EURO-35—Cameras—Eastman Kodak Company; *U.S. Public*, pg. 550

EURO TRAKKER—Truck—Iveco-Ford Truck Ltd.; *Int'l*, pg. 484

EURO-TURF—NONE—Farm Press; *U.S. Public*, pg. 1328

EUROCLEAN—Commercial Cleaning Equipment—Electrolux, AB; *Int'l*, pg. 438

EUROCLEAN—NONE—White Consolidated Industries, Inc.; *Int'l*, pg. 439

EURODIP—Epucamide—Witco Corporation; *U.S. Public*, pg. 1773

EUROFLEX—Spring Loaded PTFE Seal—James Walker & Co. Limited; *Int'l*, pg. 1485

EUROLINE—Bath Accessories—Melard Manufacturing Corporation; *U.S. Private*, pg. 729

EUROMA—Herbs & Spices—Burns, Philp & Company Limited; *Int'l*, pg. 236

EUROMARK—Model of Bolt Action Rifle—Weatherby, Inc.; *U.S. Private*, pg. 1155

EUROMARKETING—Newsletter—Crain Communications, Inc.; *U.S. Private*, pg. 284

EUROMASTER—Professional Hair Dryer—Andis Company; *U.S. Private*, pg. 73

EUROMERCATO—NONE—GS Societa Generale Supermercati; *Int'l*, pg. 186

EUROMET—Automatic Preparation Head—Buehler, Limited; *U.S. Public*, pg. 574

EUROPA—Chimneys—Eljer Plumbingware; *U.S. Public*, pg. 1794

EUROPA SEA CRUISES—Ocean liner—Europa Cruises Corporation; *U.S. Public*, pg. 595

EUROPA SEA KRUZ—Tradname—Europa Cruises Corporation; *U.S. Public*, pg. 595

EUROPA SKY—Ocean Liner—Europa Cruises Corporation; *U.S. Public*, pg. 595

EUROPA STAR—Ocean Liner—Europa Cruises Corporation; *U.S. Public*, pg. 595

EUROPA STRDANCER—Vessel—Europa Cruises Corporation; *U.S. Public*, pg. 595

EUROPA SUN—Ocean Liner—Europa Cruises Corporation; *U.S. Public*, pg. 595

EUROPAINTS—Paints Manufactured Using German Components—Earl Scheib, Inc.; *U.S. Public*, pg. 1437

EUROPASS—NONE—Cordis, a Johnson & Johnson Company; *U.S. Public*, pg. 928

EUROPASS—NONE—Rail Europe Inc.; *Int'l*, pg. 1165

EUROPCAR—Car Rental—Accor S.A.; *Int'l*, pg. 20

EUROPEAN BAKER—NONE—EMAP Business Communications Division; *Int'l*, pg. 451

EUROPEAN BIC—Perfumes—BIC Corporation; *Int'l*, pg. 1273

EUROPEAN DESIGNER LINE—Enamel Finished Steel Receptacles with Mirror Brass Accents—United Receptical, Inc.; *U.S. Private*, pg. 1123

EUROPEAN MYSTIQUE—Hair Products—Dena Corporation; *U.S. Private*, pg. 324

EUROPEAN RUBBER JOURNAL—Periodical—Crain Communications, Inc.; *U.S. Private*, pg. 284

EUROPEAN STYLE—NONE—Nestle USA; *Int'l*, pg. 916

EUROPEAN VOICE—NONE—The Economist Group Limited.; *Int'l*, pg. 1026

EUROPLAST—NONE—ETEX; *Int'l*, pg. 430

EUROPOX—Epoxy Resins—Witco Corporation; *U.S. Public*, pg. 1773

EUROSPORT—NONE—Weatherby, Inc.; *U.S. Private*, pg. 1155

EUROSTAR—Truck—Iveco-Ford Truck Ltd.; *Int'l*, pg. 484

EUROSTAR—NONE—Rail Europe Inc.; *Int'l*, pg. 1165

EUROSTYLERS—Brushes—Wilhold Inc.; *U.S. Public*, pg. 78

EUROTAN—Running Track-Urethane—Southwest Recreational Industries Inc.; *U.S. Private*, pg. 1018

EUROTUNNEL—Tunnel Connecting UK & France—The Eurotunnel Group; *Int'l*, pg. 466

EUROWAY—Travel Trailer—Fleetwood Enterprises, Inc.; *U.S. Public*, pg. 650

EUVITOL—NONE—SmithKline Beecham Corporation; *Int'l*, pg. 1264

EUVITOL—Topical/Skincare—SmithKline Beecham plc; *Int'l*, pg. 1264

EVA—Women's Weekly Magazine—IPC Magazines Limited; *Int'l*, pg. 651

EVAC—Sanitary Sewage Systems—Metra Corporation; *Int'l*, pg. 862

EVAC—Vacuum Sewage Systems—Sanitec Ltd. Oy; *Int'l*, pg. 863

EVACTOR—Vacuum Pumps—Croll-Reynolds Company, Inc.; *U.S. Private*, pg. 290

EVADE—Herbicide—The Dow Chemical Company; *U.S. Public*, pg. 522

EVAL—Ethylene-Vinyl Alcohol Copolymer—Kuraray Co., Ltd.; *Int'l*, pg. 764

EVALUATION AMERICAINE DU CANADA—Appraisal Services—American Appraisal Associates, Inc.; *U.S. Private*, pg. 49

EVAN PICONE—Career Sportswear—Jones Apparel Group, Inc.; *U.S. Public*, pg. 933

EVAN-PICONE—Women's Shoes—Nine West Group, Inc.; *U.S. Public*, pg. 1185

EVANGELINE—Grocery Bags—Johns Manville Corporation; *U.S. Public*, pg. 927

EVANGELINE MAID—Bread & Rolls—Flowers Industries, Inc.; *U.S. Public*, pg. 656

EVANOHM—NONE—Carpenter Technology Corporation; *U.S. Public*, pg. 307

EVANOVA—Tennis Wear—Mizuno Corporation; *Int'l*, pg. 884

EVANS-BLACK—Carpet—Evans-Black Carpet Mills; *U.S. Public*, pg. 1464

EVANS COLLECTION—Furs—Evans, Inc.; *U.S. Public*, pg. 596

EVANS TEMPCON—Heating & Air Conditioning Products—Evans Tempcon Inc.; *U.S. Private*, pg. 7

THE EVANSVILLE COURIER—Newspaper—The E.W. Scripps Company; *U.S. Public*, pg. 1447

EVE—Translucent Printing Film—Appleton Papers Inc.; *Int'l*, pg. 567

EVE—Cigarettes—Liggett Group Inc.; *U.S. Public*, pg. 259

EVE BYER—Girls' (4-6x) Sportswear—Byer California; *U.S. Public*, pg. 191

EVE TOO—Girls (4-6X) Dresses—Byer California; *U.S. Public*, pg. 191

EVEN BAKE—Insulated Bakeware—Wilton Industries, Inc.; *U.S. Private*, pg. 1181

EVENAIR—Duct Boosters—Field Controls Co.; *U.S. Private*, pg. 860

EVENEDGE—NONE—H.C. Miller Company; *U.S. Private*, pg. 747

EVENFLO—Fluid Surge Dampener—Graco Inc.; *U.S. Public*, pg. 756

EVENFLO—Baby Equipment—Spalding & Evenflo Companies, Inc.; *U.S. Private*, pg. 629

EVENMIST—Humidifiers—Field Controls Co.; *U.S. Private*, pg. 860

EVENRUN—Abrasive Bands Or Belts—3M; *U.S. Public*, pg. 1604

EVENSPUN YARNS—For Open End Yarns—Harriet & Henderson Yarns, Inc.; *U.S. Private*, pg. 504

EVENTEMP—Temperature Regulators—Leslie Controls, Inc.; *U.S. Public*, pg. 1746

EVENTING—Equestrian Magazine—IPC Magazines Limited; *Int'l*, pg. 651

EVER AFTER—Cologne & Toiletries—Avon Products, Inc.; *U.S. Public*, pg. 155

EVER CLEAN—Clumping Cat Litter—First Brands Corporation; *U.S. Public*, pg. 626

EVER-FLEX—Innerspring Assemblies for Mattresses—Leggett & Platt, Incorporated; *U.S. Public*, pg. 985

EVER FRESH—Fruit Freshener—Borden, Inc.; *U.S. Private*, pg. 157

EVER-READY—Shaving Brushes—American Safety Razor Company; *U.S. Private*, pg. 597

EVER READY—Desk Calendars—The At-A-Glance Group; *U.S. Private*, pg. 295

EVER-ROLL—Rubber Flooring—Dodge Regupol, Inc.; *U.S. Private*, pg. 337

EVER-SERV—Bathroom Tissue—Georgia-Pacific Corporation; *U.S. Public*, pg. 735

EVER-SOFT—Ion Exchange Water Softeners, Filter & Activated Carbon Apparatus—Ionics, Incorporated; *U.S. Public*, pg. 912

EVERBAN—Pesticides—McLaughlin Gormley King Company; *U.S. Private*, pg. 723

EVERCANE—Sugar—Savannah Foods & Industries, Inc.; *U.S. Public*, pg. 872

EVERCIDE—Pesticides—McLaughlin Gormley King Company; *U.S. Private*, pg. 723

EVERCO—Heating & air Conditioning Products—Cooper Industries, Inc.; *U.S. Public*, pg. 442

EVERCO—Heater & Air Conditioner Parts, Power Steering Parts, Brass Fittings—Steering and Suspension Division; *U.S. Public*, pg. 443

EVERDUR—Tubing Access.—Outokumpu American Brass Co.; *Int'l*, pg. 1016

EVEREADY—Batteries & Lighting Products—Eveready Battery Co.; *U.S. Public*, pg. 1360

EVEREADY—Batteries—Ralston Purina Company; *U.S. Public*, pg. 1359

EVEREST—Windows & Doors—Caradon Plc; *Int'l*, pg. 266

EVEREST—Carpet—Columbus Mills, Inc.; *U.S. Private*, pg. 256

EVEREST—Bleached Board—International Paper Company; *U.S. Public*, pg. 901

EVEREST—NONE—Porcelanite, Inc.; *Int'l*, pg. 573

Everest & Jennings—Wheelchair—Everest & Jennings, Inc.; *U.S. Public*, pg. 758

EVEREST ELITE—NONE—Kellwood Company; *U.S. Public*, pg. 948

EVEREST RE—NONE—Everest Reinsurance Holdings; *U.S. Public*, pg. 597

EVERETT—Piano—Yamaha Corporation of America; *Int'l*, pg. 1516

EVEREX—Computer Peripherals—Everex Systems Inc.; *Int'l*, pg. 498

EVEREX STEP—Computers—Everex Systems Inc.; *Int'l*, pg. 498

EVEREX TEMPO—Computer Systems—Everex Systems Inc.; *Int'l*, pg. 498

EVERFLEX—Industrial Chemicals—Hampshire Chemical Corp.; *U.S. Private*, pg. 498

EVERFRESH—Fruit Juices—Everfresh Beverages Inc.; *U.S. Public*, pg. 1153

EVERFRESH—Clumping/Clay Litter—First Brands Corporation; *U.S. Public*, pg. 626

EVERFRESH PREMIUM LIGHT—Sparkling Fruit Juice—Everfresh Beverages Inc.; *U.S. Public*, pg. 1153

EVERGLADES CYPRESS—Manufactured Paneling—Georgia-Pacific Corporation; *U.S. Public*, pg. 735

EVERGREEN—Feeds—Evergreen Mills Inc.; *U.S. Private*, pg. 1134

EVERGREEN—Writing, Text & Cover Paper—Fox River Paper Company; *U.S. Private*, pg. 422

EVERITE—Glaze Powder—Mallet & Co.; *U.S. Private*, pg. 698

EVERLAST—Sporting Goods—Everlast Sports Manufacturing Corp.; *U.S. Private*, pg. 386

EVERLITE—Super Clear Fiberglass Reinforced Plastic Solar Collectors—Sequentia Inc.; *U.S. Private*, pg. 985

EVERNEW—PVC Fencing—CertainTeed Corporation; *Int'l*, pg. 1170

EVERNU—Cover—National Presto Industries, Inc.; *U.S. Public*, pg. 1159

EVERS—NONE—Huhtamaki Oy; *Int'l*, pg. 638

EVERSCENT—Splashes/Deodorants—Tristar Corp.; *U.S. Public*, pg. 1640

EVERSHARP—Pens & Refills—Eversharp Pen Co.; *U.S. Private*, pg. 386

EVERSOFT—Golf Gloves—The Austad Company; *U.S. Public*, pg. 782

EVERSOFT—Hand & Body Lotion—The Andrew Jergens Company; *Int'l*, pg. 717

EVERSTIK—Dry Gum Paper—Eastern Fine Paper; *U.S. Private*, pg. 357

EVERSTRAIT—Door Systems—Pease Industries, Inc.; *U.S. Public*, pg. 845

EVERTITE—Vinyl Ring Binders—Via Tech Publishing Solutions; *U.S. Public*, pg. 1138

EVERTRON—Solid State Power Supply—Everbrite, Inc.; *U.S. Private*, pg. 386

EVERTRON 223—Solid State Power Supply—Everbrite, Inc.; *U.S. Private*, pg. 386

EVERWATCH—Fume Hood Monitor—TSI Incorporated; *U.S. Public*, pg. 1559

EVERWOOD—Composite Wood Blinds—Hunter Douglas, Inc.; *Int'l*, pg. 639

EVERY-DAY—Office Furniture—HON Industries Inc.; *U.S. Public*, pg. 772

EVERY DAY—Powdered Milk—Nestle S.A.; *Int'l*, pg. 915

EVERY-DAY CHAIR—Pneumatic Seating—The HON Co.; *U.S. Public*, pg. 772

EVERY DAY EVERY ITEM—NONE—One Price Clothing Stores, Inc.; *U.S. Public*, pg. 1225

EVERY STEP—NONE—Premier, Inc.; *U.S. Private*, pg. 647

EVERYDAY—Children's Disposable Diapers—The Tranzonic Companies; *U.S. Public*, pg. 1632

EVERYDAY LIVING—Apparel—Fred Meyer Stores; *U.S. Public*, pg. 1103

EVERYMAN LIBRARY—Classic Books—Alfred A. Knopf, Inc.; *U.S. Private*, pg. 21

EVERYSTEP FOOT POWDER—Shoe & Foot Deodorant—Advanced Polymer Systems; *U.S. Public*, pg. 22

EVERYSUN—Suntan Preparations—Permark International (Pty.) Ltd.; *Int'l*, pg. 1036

EVERYTHING RUBBERMAID—Laboratory Store (Research & Retail)—Rubbermaid Incorporated; *U.S. Public*, pg. 1411

EVIAN—Mineral Water—Danone Group; *Int'l*, pg. 379

EVIAN—Natural Spring Water—Great Brands of Europe; *Int'l*, pg. 381

EVIDENCE/VISITOR—Locker—American Locker Group, Inc.; *U.S. Public*, pg. 85

EVIN—Margarine—Sabanci Holding A.S.; *Int'l*, pg. 1167

EVINRUDE—Outboard Boat Motors, Parts & Access., Electric Fishing Motors—Outboard Marine Corporation; *U.S. Private*, pg. 478

EVIS—Laser Equipment—Newport Corporation; *U.S. Public*, pg. 1179

EVISECT—Toxin—Novartis AG; *Int'l*, pg. 971

EVITAL—Herbicide—Sandoz Agro, Inc.; *Int'l*, pg. 974

EVLAST—Powder Coatings—Eastman Kodak Company; *U.S. Public*, pg. 550

ENVIROTHANE—(Secondary Containment Coating)—The Valspar Corp. Protective Coatings Div.; *U.S. Public*, pg. 1707

EVO—Office Seating—American Seating Company; *U.S. Private*, pg. 61

EVOLUTION—NONE—Advanced Logic Research, Inc.; *U.S. Public*, pg. 703

EVOLUTION—Luxury Vinyl Tile—Congoleum Corporation; *U.S. Public*, pg. 69

EVOLUTION—Skincare—Guerlain, Inc.; *Int'l*, pg. 780

EVOLUTION—NONE—Kewaunee Scientific Corporation; *U.S. Public*, pg. 953

EVOLUTION—Durable-Use Nonwoven Materials—Kimberly-Clark Corporation; *U.S. Public*, pg. 958

EVOLUTION 3—Nonwoven Material—Kimberly-Clark Corporation; *U.S. Public*, pg. 958

EVOLUTION TWO—Nonwoven Material—Kimberly-Clark Corporation; *U.S. Public*, pg. 958

EVOLUTIONS—Wood & Lumber Products—Georgia-Pacific Corporation; *U.S. Public*, pg. 735

EVON—Nuts—John B. Sanfilippo & Son, Inc.; *U.S. Public*, pg. 1431

EVSCO PHARMACEUTICALS—Veterinary Pharmaceuticals—IGI, Inc.; *U.S. Public*, pg. 855

EVTECH—Powder Coatings—Eastman Kodak Company; *U.S. Public*, pg. 550

EVYAN PERFUMES—Fragrance—Parfums International Ltd.; *Int'l*, pg. 1435

EWOS—NONE—Suomen Rehu Oy; *Int'l*, pg. 349

EX LAX—Laxative—Novartis AG; *Int'l*, pg. 971

EX-LAX—Chocolated Laxative Tablets, Regular Strength, Extra Gentle, Maximum Relief—Sandoz Pharmaceuticals Corp.; *Int'l*, pg. 974

EX-O-FIT—Fitness Shoe—Reebok International Ltd.; *U.S. Public*, pg. 1369

EX/PRESS AM-4—Swing Arm Transfer Press—Seal Products Incorporated; *U.S. Public*, pg. 849

EX-SERT—Backplane System—Reliability Incorporated; *U.S. Public*, pg. 1373

EXA LUB—Oils & Greases—Mallet & Co.; *U.S. Private*, pg. 698

EXAC—Machining Stock—Norton Performance Plastics; *Int'l*, pg. 1174

EXACHEM—Chemical Pump With Canned Motor—KSB Aktiengesellschaft; *Int'l*, pg. 721

EXACT—Control Configurator—The Foxboro Company; *Int'l*, pg. 1243

EXACT—NONE—Premier, Inc.; *U.S. Private*, pg. 647

EXACT MEDICATED CLEANSER—Acnee Medication—Advanced Polymer Systems; *U.S. Public*, pg. 22

EXACT-O-BOARD—Board Type Liner—Johns Manville Corporation; *U.S. Public*, pg. 927

EXACT-O-MAT—Blanket Type Liner—Johns Manville Corporation; *U.S. Public*, pg. 927

EXACT TINTED CREAM—Acne Medication—Advanced Polymer Systems; *U.S. Public*, pg. 22

EXACT VANISHING CREAM—Acne Medication—Advanced Polymer Systems; *U.S. Public*, pg. 22

EXACT WEIGHT—Industrial Scales—Exact Equipment Corporation; *U.S. Private*, pg. 387

EXACTA—Rubber & Plastic Hardness Testers—NewAge Industries Inc.; *U.S. Private*, pg. 796

EXACTA—Plastic Hardness Tester—Newage Industries Inc., Testing Instruments Group; *U.S. Private*, pg. 796

EXACTRA—Close Tolerance Screen Printers—Autoroll Machine Co., LLC; *U.S. Private*, pg. 101

EXAGE—Bicycle—Shimano Inc.; *Int'l*, pg. 1232

EXAMINE—Computer Programs, Software—Lucent Technologies Inc.; *U.S. Public*, pg. 1017

EXANE—Cable—Rockbestos-Supranant Cable Corp.; *U.S. Private*, pg. 938

EXAPAK—Recording Media—Exabyte Corporation; *U.S. Public*, pg. 597

EXAR—Insulated Wire—Champlain Cable Corp.; *Int'l*, pg. 637

EXAR—NONE—Milgray Electronics, Inc.; *U.S. Public*, pg. 205

EXAR-PLUS—Insulated Wire—Champlain Cable Corp.; *Int'l*, pg. 637

EXATAPE—Recording Media—Exabyte Corporation; *U.S. Public*, pg. 597

EXATIN—Insecticides—Novartis AG; *Int'l*, pg. 971

EXCALIBUR—Needles & Sutures—Alcon Laboratories, Inc.; *Int'l*, pg. 916

EXCALIBUR—Toiletries—Avon Products, Inc.; *U.S. Public*, pg. 155

EXCALIBUR—Electrosurgery Generator—Conmed Corporation; *U.S. Public*, pg. 431

EXCALIBUR—Upright Vacuum Cleaner—The Eureka Company; *Int'l*, pg. 440

EXCALIBUR—NONE—GenRad, Inc.; *U.S. Public*, pg. 731

EXCALIBUR—Scotch Whiskey—John Gross & Co.; *U.S. Private*, pg. 483

EXCALIBUR—Pen & Pencils—Pentel of America, Ltd.; *Int'l*, pg. 1035

EXCALIBUR—Apparel—I. Spiewak & Sons, Inc.; *U.S. Private*, pg. 1025

EXCALIBUR EFS—Electronic Filing Software—Excalibur Technologies Corporation; *U.S. Public*, pg. 598

EXCEDRIN—Analgesic—Bristol-Myers Squibb Company; *U.S. Public*, pg. 253

EXCEDRIN DUAL—Analgesic/Antacid—Bristol-Myers Squibb Company; *U.S. Public*, pg. 253

EXCEDRIN EXTRA-STRENGTH—Analgesic—Bristol-Myers Squibb Company; *U.S. Public*, pg. 253

EXCEDRIN P.M.—Nightime Analgesic Tablets—Bristol-Myers Squibb Company; *U.S. Public*, pg. 253

EXCEED—Machine Warewashing Detergent—Ecolab Inc.; *U.S. Public*, pg. 562

EXCEL—Beef—Cargill; *U.S. Private*, pg. 210

EXCEL—Fiberglass Sportboats—Genmar Holdings, Inc.; *U.S. Public*, pg. 447

EXCEL—Building Automation—Honeywell Inc.; *U.S. Public*, pg. 833

EXCEL—Automobile—Hyundai Motor America; *Int'l*, pg. 641

EXCEL—Carbonless Paper—The Mead Corporation; *U.S. Public*, pg. 1074

EXCEL—Spreadsheet Software—Microsoft Corporation; *U.S. Public*, pg. 1107

EXCEL—Food Products—P & C Food Markets, Inc.; *U.S. Public*, pg. 1270

EXCEL—Chewing Gum—Wrigley Canada Inc.; *U.S. Public*, pg. 1781

EXCEL-GRO—Water Soluable Plant Food—Bachman's, Inc.; *U.S. Private*, pg. 109

EXCEL HR—High Resolution Ink Jet Printer—Videojet Systems International, Inc.; *Int'l*, pg. 545

EXCEL 178I—Small Character Ink Jet Printer—Videojet Systems International, Inc.; *Int'l*, pg. 545

EXCEL SERIES 100—Ink Jet Printer—Videojet Systems International, Inc.; *Int'l*, pg. 545

EXCEL SERIES 170I—Ink Jet Printer—Videojet Systems International, Inc.; *Int'l*, pg. 545

EXCEL SERIES 270I—Ink Jet Printer—Videojet Systems International, Inc.; *Int'l*, pg. 545

EXCEL VII—NONE—The Cessna Aircraft Co.; *U.S. Public*, pg. 1589

EXCEL X—NONE—The Cessna Aircraft Co.; *U.S. Public*, pg. 1589

EXCEL/P—Ink Jet Printer—Videojet Systems International, Inc.; *Int'l*, pg. 545

EXCELAR—Graphics System—W.H. Brady Co.; *U.S. Public*, pg. 250

EXCELASE—Digestive Enzyme—Meiji Seika Kaisha, Ltd.; *Int'l*, pg. 855

EXCELENE—Cutting & Grinding Oils—D.A. Stuart Company; *U.S. Private*, pg. 1048

EXCELINE—Lighting Fixtures—The Genlyte Group Incorporated; *U.S. Public*, pg. 729

EXCELIS—NONE—The First American Financial Corporation; *U.S. Public*, pg. 624

EXCELL—Storage & Retrieval Machine—Harnischfeger Industries, Inc.; *U.S. Public*, pg. 788

EXCELL—Foods—URM Stores, Inc.; *U.S. Private*, pg. 1114

EXCELLED—NONE—Excelled Sheepskin & Leather Coat Corporation; *U.S. Private*, pg. 387

EXCELLENCE—Hair Color—Cosmair, Inc.; *Int'l*, pg. 818

EXCELLENCY—Men's Apparel—International Cosmetics Co., Ltd.; *Int'l*, pg. 684

EXCELLO—Ribbon—American Greetings Corporation; *U.S. Public*, pg. 77

EXCELMARK FINANCIAL SERVICES, INC.—NONE—California State Bank-La Habra; *U.S. Public*, pg. 294

EXCELO—NONE—Carpenter Technology Corporation; *U.S. Public*, pg. 307

EXCELOAM—Packaged Potting Soil—Bachman's, Inc.; *U.S. Private*, pg. 109

EXCELON—Duct Connector Fabric—Duro Dyne Corporation; *U.S. Private*, pg. 349

EXCELSIOR—Imported Hungarian Ham—Atalanta Corporation; *U.S. Private*, pg. 93

EXCELSIOR—Compact Disc Products—Musicland Group Inc.; *U.S. Public*, pg. 1142

EXCELSIOR—Industrial Safety Eyewear—Uvex Safety, Inc.; *Int'l*, pg. 132

EXCELSIOR—Mobile Homes—Wick Bldg. Systems Inc. Manufactured Homes Div.; *U.S. Private*, pg. 1174

EXCEPTOR—NONE—BMC Software, Inc.; *U.S. Public*, pg. 162

EXCHANGE—Interface to SNA Networks—Tandem Computers Inc.; *U.S. Public*, pg. 417

EXCHANGEMAX—Telecommunications Products & Accessories—Lucent Technologies Inc.; *U.S. Public*, pg. 1017

EXCIMERHORIZONS—Educational Services—Alcon Laboratories, Inc.; *Int'l*, pg. 916

EXCITE—NONE—Excite, Inc.; *U.S. Public*, pg. 599

EXCITRON—High Power Electron Beam Accelerator—Maxwell Technologies, Inc.; *U.S. Public*, pg. 1061

EXCLAMATION—Vinyl Tile—Congoleum Corporation; *U.S. Public*, pg. 66

EXCLAMATION—Fragrance—Coty Inc.; *Int'l*, pg. 185

EXCLAY—Lightweight Aggregates—Scancem AB; *Int'l*, pg. 1198

EXCLUSIVE—High End Audio Products—Pioneer Electronic Corporation; *Int'l*, pg. 1057

EXCLUSIVELY YOU—Weight Management Program—Diet Center Worldwide, Inc.; *U.S. Private*, pg. 864

EXCLUSIVELY YOURS BY SUBTRACT—Control Garments—True Form Intimate Apparel; *U.S. Private*, pg. 697

EXCLUSIVES-LIQUID/FINISH LINE—NONE—Goldwell Cosmetics (USA) Inc.; *Int'l*, pg. 718

EXEC*SAT—Commercial Satellite Terminal—Rockwell International Corporation; *U.S. Public*, pg. 1397

EXECJET—Computer Printer—International Business Machines Corporation; *U.S. Public*, pg. 895

EXECTALK/EXECTALK PLUS—Desktop Voice Processing Systems—Dictaphone Corp.; *U.S. Private*, pg. 1045

EXECU-FIT HEALTH PROGRAMS—Health & Wellness Programs—PacifiCare Health Systems, Inc.; *U.S. Public*, pg. 1250

EXECU-LINE—Office Supplies—JM Company; *U.S. Private*, pg. 577

EXECUCAR—Executive Ride Services—Supershuttle Inc.; *U.S. Private*, pg. 1056

EXECUSTATION—Computer Programs—Litton Industries, Inc.; *U.S. Public*, pg. 1002

EXECUTECH—Telephone System—Comdial Corporation; *U.S. Public*, pg. 407

EXECUTIVE—Ophthalmic Lenses—American Optical Corporation; *U.S. Private*, pg. 60

EXECUTIVE—Envelopes for High-Speed Mail Processing—Westvaco Corporation-Envelope Div.; *U.S. Public*, pg. 1762

EXECUTIVE BROKER—NONE—Countrywide Home Loans Inc.; *U.S. Public*, pg. 452

EXECUTIVE COLLECTION—Shoes—Johnston & Murphy Co.; *U.S. Public*, pg. 728

EXECUTIVE COMFORT SERVICE—Rental Service—Thrifty Rent-a-Car System, Inc.; *U.S. Public*, pg. 354

EXECUTIVE DECISION—Game—Monarch Avalon, Inc.; *U.S. Public*, pg. 1123

EXECUTIVE FEMALE—Publication—The National Association for Female Executives, Inc.; *U.S. Private*, pg. 691

EXECUTIVE LIMITED—Clubs/Balls—Spalding Sports Worldwide; *U.S. Private*, pg. 630

EXECUTIVE MIXTURE—Pipe Tobacco—Lane Limited; *Int'l*, pg. 1129

EXECUTIVE PROTECTION SYSTEM—User-Friendly Alarm—Holmes Protection Group, Inc.; *U.S. Public*, pg. 1649

EXECUTIVE PUTTERS—Golf Clubs—Spalding Sports Worldwide; *U.S. Private*, pg. 630

EXECUTIVE SERVICE PLAN—Hotel & Awards Program for Business Travelers & Bus. Travel Planners—Omni Hotels; *U.S. Private*, pg. 1065

EXECUTIVE SOUFFLE—Sporting Goods—Brunswick Bowling & Billiards Corp.; *U.S. Public*, pg. 265

EXECUTIVE STYLE—Envelopes—Westvaco Corporation; *U.S. Public*, pg. 1762

EXECUWRITER—Phototypesetters—AGFA EPS Division; *Int'l*, pg. 172

EXEL—Computerized Tomographs—Elscint Ltd.; *Int'l*, pg. 450

EXEL LOGISTICS—NONE—NFC plc; *Int'l*, pg. 901

EXELDERM—Dermatological Therapy—Bristol-Myers Squibb Company; *U.S. Public*, pg. 253

EXELDERM—Sulconazole Nitrate—Syntex; *Int'l*, pg. 1120

EXELDERM—Topical Antifungal—Westwood-Squibb Pharmaceuticals Inc.; *U.S. Public*, pg. 255

EXEMPLAR—SPP—Convex Technology Center - Hewlett-Packard; *U.S. Public*, pg. 815

EXERSAUCER—Exercise & Entertainment Center—Evenflo Company, Inc.; *U.S. Private*, pg. 629

EXERSAUCER BABY PLAY GYM—Play Gym—Evenflo Company, Inc.; *U.S. Private*, pg. 629

EXERSAUCER DELUXE—Exercise & Entertainment Center—Evenflo Company, Inc.; *U.S. Private*, pg. 629

EXERSAUCER JR.—Exercise & Entertainment Center—Evenflo Company, Inc.; *U.S. Private*, pg. 629

EXERSTRESS—NONE—Del Mar Avionics; *U.S. Private*, pg. 321

EXETER—Canned Meat Products—Campbell Soup Company; *U.S. Public*, pg. 298

EXETER—NONE—Pfizer Inc.; *U.S. Public*, pg. 1281

EXHIBITEX—Presses & Material for Laminating—Seal Products Incorporated; *U.S. Public*, pg. 849

EXIDE—Batteries—Exide Corporation; *U.S. Public*, pg. 600

EXIDE—Uninterruptible Power Supplies—Exide Electronics Group, Inc.; *Int'l*, pg. 126

EXIDE—NONE—Yuasa-Exide, Inc.; *Int'l*, pg. 1522

EXITO!—Spanish Language News Weeklies & Educational Materials—Tribune Company; *U.S. Public*, pg. 1635

EXLINE—NONE—ECI Telecom Ltd.; *Int'l*, pg. 643

EXO GAS—Gas Generator—Seco Warwick Corporation; *U.S. Private*, pg. 980

EXOCAINE PLUS—Arthritis Rub—Del Pharmaceuticals, Inc.; *U.S. Public*, pg. 494

EXOLITE NO DRIP—Acrylic Double-Skinned Sheet—Cyro Industries; *Int'l*, pg. 1454

EXOLON—Aluminum Oxide—Exolon-Esk Company; *U.S. Public*, pg. 600

EXOSTAR—Muffler—Arvin Industries, Inc.; *U.S. Public*, pg. 136

EXOSURF NEONATAL—Pharmaceutical Product—Glaxo Wellcome PLC; *Int'l*, pg. 553

EXOTECH—In-Line Skates—K2 Inc.; *U.S. Public*, pg. 940

EXOTIQUES—NONE—Comare Products; *U.S. Public*, pg. 1771

EXPAN-DESK—Office Furniture—Knoll, Inc.; *U.S. Private*, pg. 627

EXPAND—Intraocular Lenses—Alcon Laboratories, Inc.; *Int'l*, pg. 916

EXPAND—Networking Software System—Tandem Computers Inc.; *U.S. Public*, pg. 417

EXPAND-O-FLASH—Expansion Joint Covers—Johns Manville Corporation; *U.S. Public*, pg. 927

EXPAND-O-FLEX—Joint Covers—Johns Manville Corporation; *U.S. Public*, pg. 927

EXPAND-O-GARD—Joint Covers—Johns Manville Corporation; *U.S. Public*, pg. 927

EXPAND-O-GUTTER—Joint Covers—Johns Manville Corporation; *U.S. Public*, pg. 927

EXPAND-O-MATICS—Inside Elastic Waistband—Haggar Corporation; *U.S. Public*, pg. 774

EXPAND-TITE—Engine Expansion Plugs—R&B, Inc.; *U.S. Public*, pg. 1354

EXPANDA DECK—Mocular Mezzanine Systems—Penco Products; *U.S. Private*, pg. 848

EXPANDABLES—Stationary Products—The Mead Corporation; *U.S. Public*, pg. 1074

EXPANDER—Microphone—Telex Communications, Inc.; *U.S. Private*, pg. 1074

EXPANDO SEAL—Seals—W. Braun Company; *U.S. Private*, pg. 166

EXPECTING—Magazine—Gruner + Jahr USA Publishing, Inc.; *Int'l*, pg. 190

EXPEDITE—Business Product—International Business Machines Corporation; *U.S. Public*, pg. 895

EXPEDITE—Nucleic Acid Synthesis System for Solid-Phase Sysnthesis of DNA, RNA & PNA—PerSeptive Biosystems, Inc.; *U.S. Public*, pg. 1279

EXPEDITION—Parka—Lands' End, Inc.; *U.S. Public*, pg. 977

EXPEDITOR—Machine Readable Identification Card—Lucent Technologies Inc.; *U.S. Public*, pg. 1017

EXPENSELINK—Outsourced Travel Expense Mangement Solution Featuring PC Reporting—Gelco Information Network, Inc.; *U.S. Private*, pg. 442

EXPERIENCES—NONE—Provigo Inc.; *Int'l*, pg. 1072

EXPERT—Sewing Machine System—Aisin Seiki Co. Ltd.; *Int'l*, pg. 39

EXPERT—NONE—Brown & Sharpe Manufacturing Company; *U.S. Public*, pg. 260

EXPERT—Software—Exabyte Corporation; *U.S. Public*, pg. 597

EXPERT—Multi-Instrument, GPC, Bridge & Chromatography Software—Millipore Corporation; *U.S. Public*, pg. 1112

EXPERT EYES—Eyeliners, Shadows, Mascaras—Maybelline, Inc.; *Int'l*, pg. 819

EXPERTEAM—Promotional Programs—Eastman Kodak Company; *U.S. Public*, pg. 550

EXPLENDIDO—NONE—Alliant Foodservice, Inc.; *U.S. Private*, pg. 244

EXPLORA, HMX—Network Computers—Network Computing Devices, Inc.; *U.S. Public*, pg. 1168

EXPLORATOY—Mass Market Science Activity Kits—Educational Insights, Inc.; *U.S. Public*, pg. 565

EXPLORE/EDUCATION—Computer Product—International Business Machines Corporation; *U.S. Public*, pg. 895

EXPLORER—Binoculars—Bausch & Lomb Incorporated; *U.S. Public*, pg. 194

EXPLORER—Electromyography System—Bio-Logic Systems Corp.; *U.S. Public*, pg. 230

EXPLORER—Auto Booster Seat for Older Child—Cosco, Inc.; *U.S. Private*, pg. 277

EXPLORER—Cameras—Eastman Kodak Company; *U.S. Public*, pg. 550

EXPLORER—Truck—Ford Motor Company; *U.S. Public*, pg. 661

EXPLORER—4 Wheel Scooter—Ortho-Kinetics, Inc.; *U.S. Private*, pg. 820

EXPLORER—MP&G Notebook Chipset—Sigma Designs, Inc.; *U.S. Public*, pg. 1472

EXPLORER II—X-Ray—Picker International, Inc.; *Int'l*, pg. 545

EXPLOTAB—Pharmaceutical Excipient—Penford Corp.; *U.S. Public*, pg. 1269

EXPO—Automobile—Mitsubishi Motor Sales of America, Inc.; *Int'l*, pg. 875

EXPO—Dry Erase Markers & Accesories—Sanford Corporation; *U.S. Public*, pg. 1178

EXPO LRV—Program Vehicle—Mitsubishi Motor Sales of America, Inc.; *Int'l*, pg. 875

EXPO II—Low Odor, Dry Erase Markers & Accessories—Sanford Corporation; *U.S. Public*, pg. 1178

EXPORT "A"—Cigarettes-Canada—R.J. Reynolds Tobacco Intl., Inc.; *U.S. Public*, pg. 1355

EXPORT STONES—Export—Bass PLC; *Int'l*, pg. 169

EXPORTSS—Loan Servicing—SLM Holding Corp.; *U.S. Public*, pg. 1419

EXPOSTAR—Automatic Shutter Control—Leica, Inc.; *Int'l*, pg. 806

EXPOSURES—Mail Order—Miles Kimball Company; *U.S. Private*, pg. 745

EXPRESS—NONE—Advanced Logic Research, Inc.; *U.S. Public*, pg. 703

EXPRESS—Ear Plugs—Aearo Company; *U.S. Private*, pg. 23

EXPRESS—Software-Enterprise-Wide Connectivity—Apertus Technologies Incorporated; *U.S. Public*, pg. 119

EXPRESS—Machine—Ascom Hasler Mailing Systems, Inc.; *Int'l*, pg. 86

EXPRESS—Fine Fabric Wash—Benckiser Consumer Products Inc.; *Int'l*, pg. 185

EXPRESS—Lavatory System—Bradley Corporation; *U.S. Private*, pg. 164

EXPRESS—Manual Warewashing Product—Ecolab Inc.; *U.S. Public*, pg. 562

EXPRESS—Free-Flowing Self-Leveling Castables—A.P. Green Industries, Inc.; *U.S. Public*, pg. 761

EXPRESS—Dental Registration Material, Vinyl Polysiloxane—3M; *U.S. Public*, pg. 1604

EXPRESS CARD—Business & Announcement Card Printing Machines—Photo-Me International plc; *Int'l*, pg. 1055

EXPRESS CHECK—NONE—SunGard Data Systems Inc.; *U.S. Public*, pg. 1534

EXPRESS COMMANDER—TV Remote Control—Sony Electronics; *Int'l*, pg. 1281

EXPRESS CRUISERS—Cruisers—Chris-Craft Boats; *U.S. Private*, pg. 478

EXPRESS FIVE—NONE—Life Technologies, Inc.; *U.S. Public*, pg. 504

EXPRESS GRILL—Portable, Foldable Charcoal Grill—Porcelain Metals Corp.; *U.S. Private*, pg. 876

THE EXPRESS LINE—Free Distribution Newspaper—Guard Publishing Company; *U.S. Private*, pg. 485

EXPRESS MEALS—Toaster Oven—Sunbeam Household Products; *U.S. Public*, pg. 1533

EXPRESS MOVIE CARD—Video Program—National Video, Inc.; *U.S. Public*, pg. 1755

EXPRESS 1 STOP—Convenience Stores—Sullivan Oil Company; *U.S. Private*, pg. 1050

EXPRESS PERSONNEL SERVICE—Private Employment Agency—Staffing Solutions; *U.S. Private*, pg. 1028

EXPRESS QUOTE—Consumer Information Source—The Progressive Corporation; *U.S. Public*, pg. 1334

EXPRESS SR—Motorcycle—American Honda Motor Co., Inc. Motorcycle Division; *Int'l*, pg. 634

EXPRESS SERIES—Car Stereo—Sony Electronics; *Int'l*, pg. 1281

EXPRESS SET—Hairsetters—Remington Products Company, L.L.C.; *U.S. Private*, pg. 921

EXPRESS STATION—Office Furniture—HON Industries Inc.; *U.S. Public*, pg. 772

EXPRESS TALK—Automatic Voice Delivery System—Dictaphone Corp.; *U.S. Private*, pg. 1045

EXPRESS TEMPORARY SERVICE—Temporary Help Contractor—Staffing Solutions; *U.S. Private*, pg. 1028

EXPRESS TRUCK—Expedited Coast-to-Coast Transportation Service—Skyway Freight Systems, Inc.; *U.S. Private*, pg. 1005

EXPRESS TUNING—TV Tuning System—Sony Electronics; *Int'l*, pg. 1281

EXPRESS II—Motorcycle—American Honda Motor Co., Inc. Motorcycle Division; *Int'l*, pg. 634

EXPRESSA 2200—Brewer's Yeast Extract—Royal Gist-Brocades N.V.; *Int'l*, pg. 1142

EXPRESSDATE—Customer Service—Westvaco Corporation; *U.S. Public*, pg. 1762

EXPRESSFREIGHTER—Fastest Routing for Inbound Shipments to U.S. from Major Trading Centers—FDX Corporation; *U.S. Public*, pg. 603

EXPRESSION—NONE—Beckett Papers; *U.S. Public*, pg. 903

EXPRESSIONS—Bathroom Cabinets—Broan Mfg. Co., Inc.; *U.S. Public*, pg. 1193

EXPRESSIONS—Decorative Faucets—The Chicago Faucet Co.; *U.S. Private*, pg. 234

EXPRESSIONS—Paneling, Plywood, Siding, Roofing & Ceiling Tile—Georgia-Pacific Corporation; *U.S. Public*, pg. 735

EXPRESSIONS—Bathtub Wall Kit—Plaskolite Inc.; *U.S. Private*, pg. 870

EXPRESSIONS—Indoor Planters—Rubbermaid Incorporated; *U.S. Public*, pg. 1411

EXPRESSIONS FROM HALLMARK—NONE—Hallmark Cards, Inc.; *U.S. Private*, pg. 495

EXPRESSNET—NONE—American Express Company; *U.S. Public*, pg. 73

EXPRESSO—Polymer Point Pens—Sanford Corporation; *U.S. Public*, pg. 1178

EXPRESSWAY—Multiplexers—Microtel International Inc.; *U.S. Public*, pg. 1108

EXPRESSWAY—Carbonless Paper—Nashua Corporation; *U.S. Public*, pg. 1152

EXQUISITE FORM—Women's Undergarments—AGP Industrial Corporation; *Int'l*, pg. 14

EXQUISITE FORMS—Bras—Bestform Foundations, Inc.; *U.S. Private*, pg. 140

EXRAD—Insulated Wire—Champlain Cable Corp.; *Int'l*, pg. 637

EXTAND—NONE—GEODIS; *Int'l*, pg. 549

EXTARDER—Exhaust Brake—Jacobs Vehicle Equipment Company; *U.S. Public*, pg. 481

EXTEK—Duplicators/Cameras—Houston Fearless 76 Inc.; *U.S. Private*, pg. 542

EXTEMPO—Chafers—Sterno, Inc.; *U.S. Public*, pg. 397

EXTEND—Rust Destroyer—Loctite Corp. North American Group; *Int'l*, pg. 611

EXTEND—Rust Treatment—Loctite Corporation; *Int'l*, pg. 611

EXTEND—Telescoping Conveyor—Santa Rosa Steel Forming, Inc.; *U.S. Private*, pg. 965

EXTEND-A-CELL—Cell Enhancer—Allen Telecom Inc.; *U.S. Public*, pg. 45

EXTEND A PHONE—Communication Equipment—Uniden America Corporation; *Int'l*, pg. 1433

EXTENDA-PEN—Pen—Dixon Ticonderoga Company; *U.S. Public*, pg. 514

EXTENDAFLO—Filter—American Felt & Filter; *U.S. Private*, pg. 54

EXTENDAHOE—Extending Back Hoe—Case Corporation; *U.S. Public*, pg. 311

EXTENDED BUFFER MANAGER FOR CICS—NONE—BMC Software, Inc.; *U.S. Public*, pg. 162

EXTENDED BUFFER MANAGER FOR DB2—NONE—BMC Software, Inc.; *U.S. Public*, pg. 162

EXTENDED BUFFER MANAGER FOR IMS—NONE—BMC Software, Inc.; *U.S. Public*, pg. 162

EXTENDED LIFE DISPOSABLES—IV Filter—Pall Corporation; *U.S. Public*, pg. 1253

EXTENDED NIP—Press—Harnischfeger Industries, Inc.; *U.S. Public*, pg. 788

EXTENDED SERVICES—Computer Product—International Business Machines Corporation; *U.S. Public*, pg. 895

EXTENDED SERVICES FOR OS/2—Computer Product—International Business Machines Corporation; *U.S. Public*, pg. 895

EXTENDED TERMINAL ASSIST—NONE—BMC Software, Inc.; *U.S. Public*, pg. 162

EXTENDO-DIE—NONE—Carpenter Technology Corporation; *U.S. Public*, pg. 307

EXTENSA—Computer Product—Texas Instruments Incorporated; *U.S. Public*, pg. 1585

EXTERN—Telephones—Lucent Technologies Inc.; *U.S. Public*, pg. 1017

EXTINGUISHSURE—Fire Sprinkler Piping System—George Fischer Sloane, Inc.; *Int'l*, pg. 430

EXTOL—Medical Equipment—Burdick, Inc.; *U.S. Private*, pg. 181

EXTRA—Chewing Gum—Wrigley Canada Inc.; *U.S. Public*, pg. 1781

EXTRA—Sugar Free Gum & Bubble Gum—Wm. Wrigley Jr. Company; *U.S. Public*, pg. 1781

EXTRA CRISP—Pickle Spice & Pickle Mix—Kerr Group, Inc.; *U.S. Public*, pg. 952

EXTRA DEPTH—Shoes—P.W. Minor & Son, Inc.; *U.S. Private*, pg. 751

EXTRA DEPTH EXECUTIVES—Shoes—P.W. Minor & Son, Inc.; *U.S. Private*, pg. 751

EXTRA FRUIT—NONE—J.M. Smucker Company; *U.S. Public*, pg. 1480

EXTRA-HELPING—Frozen Entrees—ConAgra Frozen Food Company; *U.S. Public*, pg. 427

EXTRA-LEAN—Meat & Cheese Products—Bar-S Foods Co.; *U.S. Private*, pg. 114

EXTRA LIFE—Batteries—Bridgestone/Firestone, Inc.; *U.S. Public*, pg. 213

EXTRA LONGCORD—Irons—The Black & Decker Corporation; *U.S. Public*, pg. 233

EXTRA PERFORMANCE—Thermostats—Robertshaw Tennessee; *Int'l*, pg. 1243

EXTRA STRENGTH ALKA SELTZER—Antacid & Pain Reliever—Bayer Corporation/Consumer Care Division; *Int'l*, pg. 173

EXTRA STRENGTH ASCRIPTIN—Analgesic—Rhone-Poulenc Rorer - U.S.; *Int'l*, pg. 1110

EXTRA STRENGTH BUFFERIN—Analgesic—Bristol-Myers Squibb Company; *U.S. Public*, pg. 253

EXTRA STRENGTH DATRIL—Non-Aspirin Pain Reliever—Bristol-Myers Squibb Company; *U.S. Public*, pg. 253

EXTRA TASTY CRISPY CHICKEN—Menu Item—Kentucky Fried Chicken Corporation (KFC); *U.S. Public*, pg. 1636

EXTRA TRACTION LUG—Tires—Bridgestone/Firestone, Inc.; *Int'l*, pg. 213

EXTRA WINTER FRESH—Sugar Free Gum—Wm. Wrigley Jr. Company; *U.S. Public*, pg. 1781

EXTRAPAN—Bakers' Sundries—Royal Gist-Brocades N.V.; *Int'l*, pg. 1142

EXTRAVITE—Liquid Iron/Vitamin Product—SmithKline Beecham plc; *Int'l*, pg. 1264

EXTREMELY GENTLE SOFTLINER—Eye Pencils—Cover Girl Cosmetics; *U.S. Public*, pg. 1330

EXTREMULTUS—Power Transmission & Material Handling Belts—Forbo Holding SA; *Int'l*, pg. 496

EXTREN—Pultrusions—Ryan Herco Products Corp.; *U.S. Private*, pg. 953

EXTRIN—Bakery Flavors—Crompton & Knowles Ingredient Technology Corp.; *U.S. Public*, pg. 459

EXTRION—Implantation Machines—Varian Associates, Inc.; *U.S. Public*, pg. 1710

EXTROVERT—Cologne & Toiletries—Avon Products, Inc.; *U.S. Public*, pg. 155

EXTRU-FORM—Industrial Fasteners—Mid-Continent Screw Products Co.; *U.S. Private*, pg. 743

EXTRU-PLAS—Industrial Fasteners—Mid-Continent Screw Products Co.; *U.S. Private*, pg. 743

EXTRUDITE—Phosphate Coatings—Detrex Corporation; *U.S. Public*, pg. 501

EXXCELL—Vascular Graft—Meadox Medicals, Inc.; *U.S. Public*, pg. 247

EXXON—Petroleum Prodsucts—Exxon Corporation; *U.S. Public*, pg. 601

EXXON—Retail Transportation Fuels in Arizona—Tosco Corporation; *U.S. Public*, pg. 1624

EXXON OIL—Lubricants—Fleischli Oil Company, Inc.; *U.S. Private*, pg. 410

EXXPOL—Catalysts—Exxon Corporation; *U.S. Public*, pg. 601

EYE-DENT—Medical Surgical Tubes & Appliances—Mallinckrodt Inc.; *U.S. Public*, pg. 1039

EYE DEVICE—Electrical & Scientific Apparatus—The Cooper Companies, Inc.; *U.S. Public*, pg. 442

EYE GEAR—Sunglasses—Goody Products, Inc.; *U.S. Public*, pg. 1177

EYE-MO—NONE—SmithKline Beecham Research Limited; *Int'l*, pg. 1266

EYE-PAK—Sterile, Single-Use Ophthalmic Drapes—Alcon Laboratories, Inc.; *Int'l*, pg. 916

EYE POPPERS—Sour Gumball—Huhtamaki Oy; *Int'l*, pg. 638

EYE-SAVER—Safety Eye Washes—Speakman Company; *U.S. Private*, pg. 1021

EYE-SHAPED DESIGN—Opthalmic Apparatus, Accessories, Preparations—The Cooper Companies, Inc.; *U.S. Public*, pg. 442

EYE-STREAM—Balanced-Salt Eye Irrigating Solution—Alcon Laboratories, Inc.; *Int'l*, pg. 916

EYEBROW & LINER PENCIL—Eye Pencils—Cover Girl Cosmetics; *U.S. Public*, pg. 1330

EYECATCHERS—Hosiery & Related Apparel—Mayer/Berkshire Corporation; *U.S. Private*, pg. 717

EYEDEAS—Newsletter—AVC/Nu-Vision, Inc.; *U.S. Private*, pg. 9

EYELINE—Safety Glasses—The Fibre-Metal Products Company; *U.S. Private*, pg. 402

EYEMAP—Corneal Analysis System—Alcon Laboratories, Inc.; *Int'l*, pg. 916

EYES FIRST—Optical Centers—AVC/Nu-Vision, Inc.; *U.S. Private*, pg. 9

EYESITE—Video Call Center—InteCom; *Int'l*, pg. 794

EYEWEAR—Business/Fashion Magazine for Dispensers of Eyewear and Eye Care Products—Reed Elsevier Business Information; *Int'l*, pg. 1095

EZ CAM—Off-Line Programming Software—Bridgeport Machines, Inc.; *U.S. Public*, pg. 251

EZ-CASE PLUS—Database Publishing and Electronic Printing—Group 1 Software, Inc.; *U.S. Public*, pg. 417

EZ-LETTER—Database Publishing and Electronic Printing—Group 1 Software, Inc.; *U.S. Public*, pg. 417

EZ-PLY—Hand-held Labeling Dispenser—Esselte Meto Kimball Systems; *Int'l*, pg. 460

EZ-6—Mailing Efficiency for Canada—Group 1 Software, Inc.; *U.S. Public*, pg. 417

EZCHROM—Chromotagraphy Data System—Shimadzu Scientific Instruments, Inc.; *Int'l*, pg. 1232

EZTEIL—Coolers—The Coleman Company, Inc.; *U.S. Private*, pg. 690

EZY-OUT—Screw Extractors—Greenfield Industries; *U.S. Public*, pg. 950

F

FA—Polysulfide Rubber—Morton International Inc.; *U.S. Public*, pg. 1135

FAA—Business Product—International Business Machines Corporation; *U.S. Public*, pg. 895

FACS—NONE—Lam Research Corporation; *U.S. Public*, pg. 975

FAM—Free Abrasive Machine—SpeedFan International, Inc.; *U.S. Public*, pg. 1497

FA MILLENNIUM—Fixed Asset Information System—Dun & Bradstreet Software Services; *Int'l*, pg. 532

F.A.O. SCHWARZ—Retail Children's Toys—F.A.O. Schwarz; *Int'l*, pg. 750

FA/PLUS—Fixed Assets Software—Dun & Bradstreet Software Services; *Int'l*, pg. 532

FA-SET—Flass to Front Framing with Silicon Glazing Options—Kawneer Company; *U.S. Public*, pg. 60

FAT—Plated & Coated Circuit Boards—Litton Industries, Inc.; *U.S. Public*, pg. 1002

F&P SURGEBUSTER—Disinfection Product—Bailey, Fischer & Porter Company; *Int'l*, pg. 449

F & T LIFE—Life Insurance—Farmers and Traders Life Insurance Co.; *U.S. Public*, pg. 394

FBI—Security Systems—Pittway Corporation; *U.S. Public*, pg. 1305

FB PETITE—NONE—Stage Stores, Inc.; *U.S. Private*, pg. 1028

FBR—Industrial Machinery—Pennsylvania Crusher Corp.; *U.S. Private*, pg. 850

FCS—Control Products—Bailey, Fischer & Porter Company; *Int'l*, pg. 449

F. CHAUVENET—Wine—Paterno Imports Limited; *U.S. Private*, pg. 843

F-CIM—Control Products—Bailey, Fischer & Porter Company; *Int'l*, pg. 449

FDC—Fiber Distribution Center—Siecor Corporation; *U.S. Public*, pg. 449

FDC—Fiber Distribution Center—Siecor Corporation; *Int'l*, pg. 1245

FDG 1000—NONE—Brown & Sharpe Manufacturing Company; *U.S. Public*, pg. 260

FDG 3000—NONE—Brown & Sharpe Manufacturing Company; *U.S. Public*, pg. 260

FDG 2000—NONE—Brown & Sharpe Manufacturing Company; *U.S. Public*, pg. 260

FDM—Magazine Serving Professionals in the Furniture Market—Reed Elsevier Business Information; *Int'l*, pg. 1095

FDS—Feminine Deodorant—Alberto-Culver Company; *U.S. Public*, pg. 37

FDX 106—Vertical F Series Copy Mill—Makino Inc.; *Int'l*, pg. 831

FDX 128—Vertical F Series Copy Mill—Makino Inc.; *Int'l*, pg. 831

FDX 220—Vertical F Series Copy Mill—Makino Inc.; *Int'l*, pg. 831

FE-TRACIN & DESIGN—Material for Supplying Trace Minerals to Trees—Georgia-Pacific Corporation; *U.S. Public*, pg. 735

FF—Tips for Paint Spray Guns—Graco Inc.; *U.S. Public*, pg. 756

FFE—Fire & Safety Equipment—James Hardie Industries Ltd.; *Int'l*, pg. 596

FF JET—Marine Propulsion—Vickers PLC; *Int'l*, pg. 1466

FFS—Federal Financial System; Accounting System for Federal Government Agencies—American Management Systems, Inc.; *U.S. Public*, pg. 86

FFST—Computer System—International Business Machines Corporation; *U.S. Public*, pg. 895

FFST/400—Computer System—International Business Machines Corporation; *U.S. Public*, pg. 895

FFST/MVS—Computer System—International Business Machines Corporation; *U.S. Public*, pg. 895

FFST/3990—Computer System—International Business Machines Corporation; *U.S. Public*, pg. 895

FFST/2—Computer System—International Business Machines Corporation; *U.S. Public*, pg. 895

FIP—NONE—NEC Electronics Inc.; *Int'l*, pg. 900

F 5—NONE—Nikon Inc.; *Int'l*, pg. 931

F-500—Hair Coloring Computer—Revlon Manufacturing Facilities; *U.S. Private*, pg. 690

F-560—Tires—Bridgestone/Firestone, Inc.; *Int'l*, pg. 213

F 5 SLR—NONE—Nikon Inc.; *Int'l*, pg. 931

FG 1 2 3—Fixed Window System for Punched Openings—Kawneer Company; *U.S. Public*, pg. 60

FHE—Home Video Entertainment—LIVE Entertainment Inc.; *U.S. Private*, pg. 671

FHM—U.K. Entertainment Magazine—EMAP Metro; *Int'l*, pg. 451

FHMA—Frequency Hopping Spread Spectrum Technology—Geotek Communications; *U.S. Public*, pg. 739

FIDS—Integrated Circui—EXAR Corporation; *U.S. Public*, pg. 597

FIFTE—NONE—SunGard Data Systems Inc.; *U.S. Public*, pg. 1534

FI LANA—Acrylic Fibers—Monsanto Company; *U.S. Public*, pg. 1124

F.I.P—Fensecure—Glynwed International PLC; *Int'l*, pg. 554

FIT—Fast Installation Technique—Victaulic Company of America; *U.S. Private*, pg. 1138

FJ44—Military Engine—Rolls-Royce Military Aero Engines Ltd.; *Int'l*, pg. 1127

F. KORBEL & BROS.—BRANDY—Heck Cellars Winery; *U.S. Private*, pg. 632

FLST HERITAGE SOFTAIL—Motorcycle—Harley-Davidson, Inc.; *U.S. Public*, pg. 786

FL-70—Detergent—Fisher Scientific Company; *U.S. Private*, pg. 658

FM—Boilers & Heaters—Babcock & Wilcox Co.; *U.S. Public*, pg. 1068

FM—Disposable Loading Units—U.S. Surgical Corp.; *U.S. Public*, pg. 1687

FM ELEMENTS—Apparel—Fred Meyer Stores; *U.S. Public*, pg. 1103

FML FORTE—Sterile Ophthalmic Solution—Allergan, Inc.; *U.S. Public*, pg. 46

FML-S—Sterile Opthalmic Solution—Allergan, Inc.; *U.S. Public*, pg. 46

FMS-TECHNOLOGY—Flexible Manufacturing Cells & Systems—Durriesscharmann, AG; *Int'l*, pg. 860

FMS 300—Marine Fuel Management—Benmar Marine Electronics, Inc.; *U.S. Private*, pg. 133

FM SPLASH—Apparel—Fred Meyer Stores; *U.S. Public*, pg. 1103

FM20—Meter Probe—Radix Corporation; *U.S. Private*, pg. 906

F-M-V—Food Products—Fred Meyer Stores; *U.S. Public*, pg. 1103

FNC106—Vertical Machining Center—Makino Inc.; *Int'l*, pg. 831

FNC 178—Vertical Machining Center—Makino Inc.; *Int'l*, pg. 831

FNC128—Vertical Machining Center—Makino Inc.; *Int'l*, pg. 831

FNC74—Vertical Machining Center—Makino Inc.; *Int'l*, pg. 831

FNC60—Vertical Machining Center—Makino Inc.; *Int'l*, pg. 831

FN HERSTAL—Military Small Arms & Ammunition—Herstal S.A.; *Int'l*, pg. 617

FOSC 100—Fiber-Optic Splice Closure Systems—Raychem Corporation; *U.S. Public*, pg. 1362

F O V—NONE—LVMH Moet Hennessy Louis Vuitton; *Int'l*, pg. 779

FOX—Fiber Optic Extension—Tandem Computers Inc.; *U.S. Public*, pg. 417

F ON A MEDALLION—Tires, Automotive Repair Services—Bridgestone/Firestone, Inc.; *Int'l*, pg. 213

F1—Hybrid Flower Seeds—Pan-American Seed Co.; *U.S. Private*, pg. 112

F-150—Truck—Ford Motor Company; *U.S. Public*, pg. 661

FP40—Portable Printer—Radix Corporation; *U.S. Private*, pg. 906

F.P.I.—Frozens Seafood Products—Fishery Products International Ltd.; *Int'l*, pg. 492

FPJ—Aluminum Wheels-Europe—LucasVarity Inc.; *Int'l*, pg. 820

F.P. PRODUCTIONS—Production of Motion Pictures—Metromedia International Group, Inc.; *U.S. Public*, pg. 1102

FP-10 ROOF VENT—Solar Operated—Johns Manville Corporation; *U.S. Public*, pg. 927

FP20—Add-on Printer—Radix Corporation; *U.S. Private*, pg. 906

FR CHEM-FREE—Flame Resistant Fabric—Guilford Mills, Inc.; *U.S. Public*, pg. 768

F.R.E.D.—Stereo Decoders & Speaker Systems—Recoton Corporation; *U.S. Public*, pg. 1369

FR480—Tires—Bridgestone/Firestone, Inc.; *Int'l*, pg. 213

F R H—Machinery—Plymouth Industries, Inc.; *U.S. Private*, pg. 873

FRR—Commerical Truck—American Isuzu Motors Inc.; *Int'l*, pg. 692

FR-S—Synthetic Rubber—Bridgestone/Firestone, Inc.; *Int'l*, pg. 213

FR680—Tires—Bridgestone/Firestone, Inc.; *Int'l*, pg. 213

FSL—NONE—Fossil Inc.; *U.S. Private*, pg. 420

FSQ—Computer Software Feature—Beckman Instruments, Inc.; *U.S. Public*, pg. 199

Brand Name Index

FSR—Commercial Truck—American Isuzu Motors Inc.; *Int'l*, pg. 692

FSR—Tires—Bridgestone/Firestone, Inc.; *Int'l*, pg. 213

FS20—Add-on Laser Scanner—Radix Corporation; *U.S. Private*, pg. 906

F-SERIES—Truck—Ford Motor Company; *U.S. Public*, pg. 661

F-SERIES—Vertical Copy Mill—Makino Inc.; *Int'l*, pg. 831

F-16 FIGHTING FALCON—Videogame—Sega of America Inc.; *Int'l*, pg. 1218

FTA-ABS—Syphilis Test System—Wampole Laboratories; *U.S. Public*, pg. 310

FTA-ABS-DS—Syphilis Test System—Wampole Laboratories; *U.S. Public*, pg. 310

FTD—Florist Delivery Assn.—FTD, Inc./Florists Transworld Delivery, Inc.; *U.S. Private*, pg. 389

F.T.E.—Plant Food Fertilizer—Ferro Corporation; *U.S. Public*, pg. 618

FTR—Commercial Truck—American Isuzu Motors Inc.; *Int'l*, pg. 692

FTX—Twin Screw Extruder—Farrel Corporation; *U.S. Public*, pg. 614

FTX—Unix Operating System—Stratus Computer, Inc.; *U.S. Public*, pg. 1524

FTZ—Connectors—Ilsco; *U.S. Private*, pg. 558

F 3—SLR Camera—Nikon Inc.; *Int'l*, pg. 931

F-TRAN—Control Products—Bailey, Fischer & Porter Company; *Int'l*, pg. 449

F-290—Tires—Bridgestone/Firestone, Inc.; *Int'l*, pg. 213

FWD—Trucks—FWD/Seagrave Fire Apparatus, Inc.; *U.S. Private*, pg. 390

FWD AMERICA—Refuse Chassis—FWD/Seagrave Fire Apparatus, Inc.; *U.S. Private*, pg. 390

FWDOS—Dos Hand Held—Radix Corporation; *U.S. Private*, pg. 906

FW60—Hand-Held Computer—Radix Corporation; *U.S. Private*, pg. 906

FX—Mechanical Leak Detectors—Marley Pump; *U.S. Public*, pg. 1676

FX-870—Dot Matrix Printer—Epson America Inc.; *Int'l*, pg. 1219

FX-1170—Dot Matrix Printer—Epson America Inc.; *Int'l*, pg. 1219

F.X. LASALLE—Shoe Stores—Brown Group, Inc.; *U.S. Public*, pg. 262

FX SERIES—Speaker Systems—Kraco Enterprises, Inc.; *U.S. Private*, pg. 634

FYI NEWSALERT—Information Service—AT&T Strategy & New Service Innovations; *U.S. Public*, pg. 11

FAAM—Licorice—Cadbury Schweppes p.l.c.; *Int'l*, pg. 247

FAB—Detergent—Colgate-Palmolive Company; *U.S. Public*, pg. 397

FAB-SILK—Styling Lotion—Revlon-Realistic Professional Products, Inc.; *U.S. Private*, pg. 690

FAB ULTRA—Detergent—Colgate-Palmolive Company; *U.S. Public*, pg. 397

FABERGE LUNETTES—Eyewear—Logo of the Americas; *Int'l*, pg. 462

FABIA—Still Mineral Water—Sangemini S.p.A.; *Int'l*, pg. 1188

FABLON—Self-Adhesive Decorative Products—Forbo Holding SA; *Int'l*, pg. 496

FABRASORB—Acoustical Liner Fabric—Chemfab Corporation; *U.S. Public*, pg. 344

FABRETTE—Window Covering Product—Hunter Douglas N.V.; *Int'l*, pg. 639

FABRI-CENTER—Punch Press—Strippit, Inc.; *U.S. Public*, pg. 862

FABRI-LOK—Splice For Coated Abrasive Belts—3M; *U.S. Public*, pg. 1604

FABRI-TECH—Fabric Protection—The W.B. Wood Company; *U.S. Private*, pg. 1186

FABRI-TEK—Connectors & Back Panels—CTS Corporation; *U.S. Public*, pg. 285

FABRI-TEK—Connectors & Backpanels—CTS Corporation-Connector Division; *U.S. Public*, pg. 285

FABRIC FUN—Art Supplies—Pentel of America, Ltd.; *Int'l*, pg. 1035

FABRICARE—Automatic Clothes Washer & Dryers—General Electric Canada Inc.; *U.S. Public*, pg. 713

FABRICATOR—Punch Press—Strippit, Inc.; *U.S. Public*, pg. 862

FABRICLAND, INC.—Retail Chain of Sewing Supplies Stores—House of Fabrics, Inc.; *U.S. Public*, pg. 842

FABRICOST SYSTEM—Computer-Aided Cost Estimating for Sheet-Metal, Assembly, Fabrication—Manufacturers Technologies, Inc.; *U.S. Private*, pg. 701

FABRICRAFT—Peel n' Stick Fabrics—Rubbermaid Incorporated; *U.S. Public*, pg. 1411

FABRICUT—Openmesh Web Coated Abrasives—3M; *U.S. Public*, pg. 1604

FABRIGLIDE—Textile Lubricant—Dow Corning Corporation; *U.S. Public*, pg. 523

FABRIMET—Fabricated Piping Systems—Synalloy Corporation; *U.S. Public*, pg. 1547

FABRINET—Geotextile Fabric—Gundle/SLT Environmental, Inc.; *U.S. Public*, pg. 769

FABRIPULSE—Fabric Dust Collector—AAF-International; *U.S. Private*, pg. 3

FABRITANK—Embankment Supported Tank—American Fuel Cell & Coated Fabrics Co. (Amfuel); *U.S. Private*, pg. 55

FABULAND—Children's Building Sets—LEGO Systems, Inc.; *Int'l*, pg. 805

FABULAXER—Hair Straightener—Revlon-Realistic Professional Products, Inc.; *U.S. Private*, pg. 690

FABULON—Floor Finish—Pierce & Stevens Corp.; *U.S. Private*, pg. 1019

FABULON—Varnish—Pratt & Lambert United, Inc.; *U.S. Public*, pg. 1466

FABULON—Fabric Re-Texturizer—Reckitt & Colman plc; *Int'l*, pg. 1089

FABULON—Paints & Coatings—The Sherwin-Williams Company; *U.S. Public*, pg. 1465

FABULOSO—Cleaner—Colgate-Palmolive Company; *U.S. Public*, pg. 397

FAC-FINDERS—Office Products—Dixon Ticonderoga Company; *U.S. Public*, pg. 514

FACE-A-GLOW—Cosmetics—Avon Products, Inc.; *U.S. Public*, pg. 155

FACE-GUARD—Razor Blades—American Safety Razor Company; *U.S. Private*, pg. 597

FACE OFF—News Program—Westwood One, Inc.; *U.S. Public*, pg. 1763

FACE THE NATION—News Forum Program—Westwood One, Inc.; *U.S. Public*, pg. 1763

FACER—High Density Overlay Paper—The Mead Corporation; *U.S. Public*, pg. 1074

FACET—Crop Protection Agent—BASF AG; *Int'l*, pg. 103

FACET—Filters—Mark IV Industries Inc.; *U.S. Public*, pg. 1044

FACET SC—Crop Protection Agent—BASF AG; *Int'l*, pg. 103

FACETS—Wood Case Goods—Herman Miller, Inc.; *U.S. Public*, pg. 1111

FACETTE—Barware—Dansk International Designs Ltd.; *U.S. Public*, pg. 261

FACEWELD—Electrode—The Lincoln Electric Company; *U.S. Public*, pg. 996

FACIAL FIRMING GEL—Cosmetics—Irma Shorell, Inc.; *U.S. Private*, pg. 1101

FACIAL FLUFFS—Household Paper Goods—Orchids Paper Products Co.; *U.S. Private*, pg. 819

FACIL—Camera—Eastman Kodak Company; *U.S. Public*, pg. 550

FACILE—Fabric—Springs Industries, Inc.; *U.S. Public*, pg. 1499

THE FACILITATOR—Multi-Funded Annuity—New York Life Insurance Company; *U.S. Private*, pg. 794

FACILITIES DESIGN & MANAGEMENT—Magazine—Miller Freeman Inc.; *Int'l*, pg. 1443

FACILITIES MANAGEMENT SYSTEM FMS—NONE—American Management Systems, Inc.; *U.S. Public*, pg. 86

FACILITY WALL—Steel Wall Panel—Clestra Hauserman, Inc.; *Int'l*, pg. 569

FACOM—Hand Tools—SK Hand Tool Corp.; *Int'l*, pg. 570

FACSCAN—Flow Cytometry—Becton Dickinson & Company; *U.S. Public*, pg. 199

FACSCOUNT—Clinical System Providing Absolute Counts for Monitoring HIV Patients—Becton Dickinson & Company; *U.S. Public*, pg. 199

FACSIMILE SUPPORT/400—Business Product—International Business Machines Corporation; *U.S. Public*, pg. 895

FACSORT—Benchtop Cell Sorter—Becton Dickinson & Company; *U.S. Public*, pg. 199

FACSPREP—System to Automate Preparation of Tissue Samples—Becton Dickinson & Company; *U.S. Public*, pg. 199

FACSTAR—Cell Sorter—Becton Dickinson & Company; *U.S. Public*, pg. 199

FACT PLUS—Pregnancy Test—Ortho-McNeil Pharmaceutical Corporation; *U.S. Public*, pg. 929

FACTAIR—Diffuser—United McGill Corp.; *U.S. Private*, pg. 1122

FACTER 8000—Computer Terminal—Eagle-Picher Industries, Inc.; *U.S. Private*, pg. 355

FACTOR ASSAY—Reagents—Ortho Clinical Diagnostic Systems Inc.; *U.S. Public*, pg. 929

FACTORY-DIRECT SPEAKER WALL—NONE—Cambridge Soundworks, Inc.; *U.S. Private*, pg. 202

FACTORY EQUIPMENT NEWS—Magazine—Reed Business Information Pty. Limited; *Int'l*, pg. 1094

FACTORY LINE—Wiring Systems—Matsushita Electric Works, Ltd.; *Int'l*, pg. 847

FACTORYMAX—Industrial Computer Workstations—Rockwell International Corporation; *U.S. Public*, pg. 1397

FACTS—Fast Airtron Computer Testing Service—Airtron; *U.S. Public*, pg. 1003

FACTS IN FIVE—Game—Monarch Avalon, Inc.; *U.S. Public*, pg. 1123

FACTSNOW—Electronic Training Services—Alcon Laboratories, Inc.; *Int'l*, pg. 916

FACULTY—Carpet—Lees Carpets; *U.S. Public*, pg. 268

FADAL—NONE—Fadal Engineering Company, Inc.; *Int'l*, pg. 1389

FADE BLADE—Special Clipper Blade For Cutting Fade—Andis Company; *U.S. Private*, pg. 73

FADE-OMETER—Accelerated Light Fastness Test Chamber—Atlas Electric Devices Co.; *U.S. Private*, pg. 96

FADE-SAFE—Ultra Violet Filtered Laminated Glass—Globe-Amerada Glass Company; *U.S. Private*, pg. 458

FADEX—Dyeing Chemicals—Clariant International Ltd.; *Int'l*, pg. 624

FAFLON—Lined Bearings—Fafnir Div. of Torrington Co.; *U.S. Public*, pg. 877

FAFNIR—NONE—Ingersoll-Rand Company; *U.S. Public*, pg. 876

FAFNIR—Bearings—The Torrington Co.; *U.S. Public*, pg. 877

FAG—Automobile Parts—Echlin Inc.; *U.S. Public*, pg. 560

FAGORUTIN—NONE—SmithKline Beecham Corporation; *Int'l*, pg. 1264

FAGORUTIN—Vitamin & Tonic—SmithKline Beecham plc; *Int'l*, pg. 1264

FAHRENHEAT—NONE—Marley Electric Heating Company; *U.S. Public*, pg. 1676

FAHRENHEIT—Men's Fragrance—Christian Dior Perfumes Inc.; *Int'l*, pg. 781

FAIL-SAFE—Vandal-Resistant Lighting Fixtures—Cooper Industries, Inc.; *U.S. Public*, pg. 442

FAILSAFE—Escalator Safety Device—Electroid Co.; *U.S. Private*, pg. 369

FAILSAFE—Desktop Monitoring System—International Power Machines Corporation; *Int'l*, pg. 126

FAIR—Rail Anchors—Portec Inc., Railway Maintenance Products Div.; *U.S. Public*, pg. 1318

FAIR, ISAAC—NONE—Fair, Isaac and Company, Inc.; *U.S. Public*, pg. 609

FAIR PLAY—Fly Line—Cortland Line Co., Inc.; *U.S. Private*, pg. 277

FAIRBANKS MORSE—Diesel Engines—Coltec Industries, Inc.; *U.S. Public*, pg. 401

FAIRCHILD NEWS SERVICE—Wire Service—Fairchild Publications; *U.S. Public*, pg. 513

THE FAIRCHILD SYNDICATE—Business Text Service—Fairchild Publications; *U.S. Public*, pg. 513

FAIRFAX—Wood & Lumber Products—Georgia-Pacific Corporation; *U.S. Public*, pg. 735

FAIRFIELD INN—Motels—Fairfield Inn; *U.S. Public*, pg. 1048

FAIRFIELD INN BY MARRIOTT—Hotel Chain—Marriott International, Inc.; *U.S. Public*, pg. 1047

FAIRLADY Z—Car—Nissan Motor Co., Ltd.; *Int'l*, pg. 943

FAIRLEE—Fruit Juice—FTI Foodtech International Inc.; *Int'l*, pg. 476

FAIRMONT HOTEL—Hotel—The Fairmont Hotels; *U.S. Private*, pg. 391

FAIRMOUNT—Hardwood Doors—Georgia-Pacific Corporation; *U.S. Public*, pg. 735

FAIRVIEW—Liqueur—White Rock Distilleries Inc.; *U.S. Private*, pg. 1173

FAIRWAY GREEN—Lawn Fertilizer—The Vigoro Corporation; *U.S. Public*, pg. 856

FAIRWAY OUTDOOR ADVERTISING—Outdoor Advertising—Shivers Trading & Operating Co.; *U.S. Private*, pg. 994

FAIRWINDS—NONE—Brothers Gourmet Coffees, Inc.; *U.S. Public*, pg. 259

FAIRY—NONE—Procter & Gamble Espana S.A.; *U.S. Public*, pg. 1332

FAISCA—NONE—Lancers; *Int'l*, pg. 411

FAITHFUL—Grooming Products for Dogs—Avon Products, Inc.; *U.S. Public*, pg. 155

FALCON—Ophthalmic Products—Alcon Laboratories, Inc.; *Int'l*, pg. 916

FALCON—Laboratory Product—Becton Dickinson & Company; *U.S. Public*, pg. 199

FALCON—Tires—Bridgestone/Firestone, Inc.; *Int'l*, pg. 213

FALCON—Business Jets—Dassault Aviation Group; *Int'l*, pg. 383

FALCON—Furniture Mfg.—Falcon Products, Inc.; *U.S. Public*, pg. 611

FALCON—Print Trimmer—Falcon Safety Products Inc.; *U.S. Private*, pg. 392

FALCON—Catheter—Medtronic, Inc.; *U.S. Public*, pg. 1082

FALCON—Scissor Lift Access Platform—Simon Engineering plc; *Int'l*, pg. 1251

FALCON—Men's Hairspray—SmithKline Beecham plc; *Int'l*, pg. 1264

FALCON—Focus Lock Binoculars—Swift Instruments, Inc.; *U.S. Private*, pg. 1058

FALCON 50EX—Executive Jet Aircraft—Dassault Falcon Jet Corp.; *Int'l*, pg. 383

FALCON-FORSHEDA LINE MASTERS—Mooring Compensator—Falcon Safety Products Inc.; *U.S. Private*, pg. 392

FALCON 2000—Executive Jet Aircraft—Dassault Falcon Jet Corp.; *Int'l*, pg. 383

FALCON 900B—Executive Jet Aircraft—Dassault Falcon Jet Corp.; *Int'l*, pg. 383

FALCON 900EX—Executive Jet Aircraft—Dassault Falcon Jet Corp.; *Int'l*, pg. 383

FALK—Power Drives—The Falk Corporation; *U.S. Public*, pg. 1534

FALLS—Poultry Products—National Foods Inc.; *U.S. Public*, pg. 429

FALSTAFF—Beer—Falstaff Brewing Corporation; *U.S. Private*, pg. 955

FALU—Crispbread—Novartis AG; *Int'l*, pg. 971

FAMA—Margarine—Vandemoortele N.V.; *Int'l*, pg. 1451

FAMAR—Baby Care Products—Sara Lee Corporation; *U.S. Public*, pg. 1432

FAMILIA—Cereal—Novartis Nutrition Corporation; *Int'l*, pg. 974

FAMILIE & CO.—Magazine—Axel Springer Verlag AG; *Int'l*, pg. 102

FAMILINA—Cocoas—Meiji Seika Kaisha, Ltd.; *Int'l*, pg. 855

FAMILY—Coolers—The Canadian Coleman Co., Ltd.; *U.S. Private*, pg. 691

FAMILY—Casual Clothing—Gitano Fashions Ltd.; *U.S. Public*, pg. 686

FAMILY BAKERY—Coffee Maker—Regal Ware, Inc.; *U.S. Private*, pg. 917

FAMILY BARGAIN CENTERS—Department Stores—General Textiles; *U.S. Private*, pg. 445

FAMILY CIRCLE—Magazine—The Family Circle, Inc.; *Int'l*, pg. 190

FAMILY CIRCLE—Women's General Interest Magazine—IPC Magazines Limited; *Int'l*, pg. 651

FAMILY DOLLAR—Retail Discount Stores—Family Dollar Stores, Inc.; *U.S. Public*, pg. 612

FAMILY FAVORITES—Cookies—Nabisco Inc.; *U.S. Public*, pg. 1355

FAMILY FUDGE BROWNIES—Brownie Mix—General Mills, Inc.; *U.S. Public*, pg. 717

THE FAMILY HANDYMAN—Magazine—The Reader's Digest Association, Inc.; *U.S. Public*, pg. 1367

FAMILY HEALTH—NONE—AAH Pharmaceuticals Limited; *Int'l*, pg. 591

FAMILY INNS OF AMERICA—Motels, Restaurants & Lounges—Family Inns of America, Inc.; *U.S. Private*, pg. 392

FAMILY PHARMACY—Private Label Vitamins, Health & Beauty Products—AmeriSource Health Corp.; *U.S. Public*, pg. 96

FAMILY PRIDE—Turkeys—Norbest, Inc.; *U.S. Private*, pg. 801

FAMILY SIZE FLO-THRU—Tea Bags—Thomas J. Lipton Company; *Int'l*, pg. 1435

FAMILY THRIFT CENTER—Retail Grocery Stores—Nash Finch Company; *U.S. Public*, pg. 1151

FAMILY TRADITION—Turkeys—Norbest, Inc.; *U.S. Private*, pg. 801

FAMILY TREE MAKER DELUXE EDITION II—NONE—Broderbund Software, Inc.; *U.S. Public*, pg. 258

FAMILY WAYS—Pharmaceutical Products—Wyeth-Ayerst Laboratories, Inc.; *U.S. Public*, pg. 80

FAMILYFINDER INDEX—NONE—Broderbund Software, Inc.; *U.S. Public*, pg. 258

FAMOSA—Cookies & Crackers—RJR Nabisco Holdings Corp.; *U.S. Public*, pg. 1354

FAMOTIDINE—Prescription Drug—ICN Pharmaceuticals, Inc.; *U.S. Public*, pg. 853

FAMOUS—Footwear—Famous Footwear; *U.S. Public*, pg. 262

FAMOUS—Chocolate Wafers & Cookie Assortment—Nabisco Inc.; *U.S. Public*, pg. 1355

FAMOUS AMOS—Chocolate Chip Cookies—President Baking Company; *Int'l*, pg. 1069

FAMOUS-BARR—Department Store—Famous-Barr; *U.S. Public*, pg. 1063

FAMOUS-BARR—Department Stores—The May Department Stores Company; *U.S. Public*, pg. 1063

FAMOUS BRANDS—Housewares—Lechters, Inc.; *U.S. Public*, pg. 983

FAMOUS CLASSICS—Greeting Cards—American Greetings Corporation; *U.S. Public*, pg. 77

FAMOUS FISH CO.—Restaurant and Bar—Famous Restaurants Inc.; *U.S. Private*, pg. 393

FAMOUS FLAVOR—Sausages—Parks LLC; *U.S. Private*, pg. 840

FAMOUS FOOTWEAR—Shoe Stores—Brown Group, Inc.; *U.S. Public*, pg. 262

FAMOUS FOR STEAKBURGERS—Restaurants—Consolidated Products, Inc.; *U.S. Public*, pg. 436

FAMOUS FOR STEAKBURGERS—Restaurants—Steak 'n Shake, Inc.; *U.S. Public*, pg. 437

THE FAMOUS GROUSE—Scotch—Heublein, Inc.; *Int'l*, pg. 410

THE FAMOUS GROUSE—Blended Scotch Whisky—The Highland Distilleries Company plc; *Int'l*, pg. 619

THE FAMOUS GROUSE SCOTCH—Scotch—Heublein Inc.; *Int'l*, pg. 410

FAMOUS READING ANTHRACITE—Anthracite Coal—Reading Anthracite Co.; *U.S. Private*, pg. 913

FAMVIR—NONE—SmithKline Beecham Corporation; *Int'l*, pg. 1264

FAMVIR—Anti-Infective—SmithKline Beecham plc; *Int'l*, pg. 1264

FAMVIR—Antiviral—SmithKline Beecham Research Limited; *Int'l*, pg. 1266

FANCI FULL—Rinse—Revlon Manufacturing Facilities; *U.S. Public*, pg. 690

FANCI TONE—Tint—Revlon Manufacturing Facilities; *U.S. Public*, pg. 690

FANCY CONDIMENTS—Sweet Pepper Relish, Mustard Pickle, Onion Relish, Green Tomato Picalilli—Cains Foods, L.P.; *U.S. Private*, pg. 199

FANCY CUTS—Decorative Shingles—Shakertown 1992, Inc.; *Int'l*, pg. 296

FANCY CUTS—Decorative Shingles—Spectrum Glass Co.; *Int'l*, pg. 296

FANCY FEAST—Cat Food—Nestle S.A.; *Int'l*, pg. 915

FANCY FINGERS—False Nail Tips, Nail Glue & Press-On Nails—Lee Pharmaceuticals; *U.S. Public*, pg. 984

FANFARES—Shoes—Brown Group, Inc.; *U.S. Public*, pg. 262

FANFOLD—Insulation—Owens Corning/Foamular; *U.S. Public*, pg. 1237

FANMATE—NONE—Blyth Industries; *U.S. Public*, pg. 239

FANMIX—Gas Burners—Coppus Murray Group, Tuthill Corporation; *U.S. Private*, pg. 1110

FANNIE MAY—Candies & Ice Cream—Archibald Candy Company; *U.S. Private*, pg. 597

FANNY FARMER—Candies & Ice Cream—Archibald Candy Company; *U.S. Private*, pg. 597

FANNY FARMER—Candy Shops—Great Lakes Confectionery; *Int'l*, pg. 865

FANSIDAR—Antimalarial Agent—Roche Holding Ltd.; *Int'l*, pg. 1119

FANSIMEF—Antimalarial—Roche Holding Ltd.; *Int'l*, pg. 1119

FANSPRAY—Paint Nozzle Pattern—Sherwin-Williams Diversified Brands, Inc.; *U.S. Public*, pg. 1466

FANTA—Office Chairs & Tray Tables—All-Luminum Products, Inc.; *U.S. Private*, pg. 34

FANTA-Z—Webbing Effect Spray—Zynolyte Products Company; *Int'l*, pg. 663

FANTAS-STICK—Curler/Stylers—Sunbeam Household Products; *U.S. Public*, pg. 1533

FANTASIA—Bakery Products—International Multifoods Corporation; *U.S. Public*, pg. 900

FANTASIA—NONE—North America Foods; *U.S. Public*, pg. 901

FANTASIA—Crystal Dinnerware—Princess House, Inc.; *U.S. Public*, pg. 399

FANTASTIC SAM'S—Family Hair Cutters—FS Concepts, Inc.; *U.S. Private*, pg. 818

FANTASTICO—Deodorizing Cleaner/Bilingual Label—Blue Cross Laboratories; *U.S. Private*, pg. 152

FANTASTIK—Cleaner—The Dow Chemical Company; *U.S. Public*, pg. 522

FANTASTIK—Spray Cleaner—DowBrands, L.P.; *U.S. Public*, pg. 523

FANTASY—Stationery Products—The Mead Corporation; *U.S. Public*, pg. 1074

FANTASY ZONE—Videogame—Sega of America Inc.; *Int'l*, pg. 1218

FAR AWAY—Women's Fragrance—Avon Products, Inc.; *U.S. Public*, pg. 155

FAR EASTERN ECONOMIC REVIEW—Magazine—Dow Jones & Company, Inc.; *U.S. Public*, pg. 524

FAR-GO—Herbicide—The Agricultural Group, Monsanto Company; *U.S. Public*, pg. 1125

FAR-GO—Herbicide—Monsanto Company; *U.S. Public*, pg. 1124

FAR NORTH CASEMENT—Window—Scherer Bros. Lumber Company; *U.S. Private*, pg. 970

FAR-TRIEVE—Automated Contracting Systems Software—CACI International Inc; *U.S. Public*, pg. 272

FARADAY—Fire Alarm Systems—Faraday, Inc.; *Int'l*, pg. 1246

FARAH—Men's, Young Men's, & Women's Apparel—Farah Incorporated; *U.S. Public*, pg. 612

FARAONE—Jewelry & Watches—Tiffany & Co.; *U.S. Public*, pg. 1608

FARBERWARE—Cutlery, Kitchen Gadgets & BBQ Cutting Boards—Lifetime Hoan Corp.; *U.S. Public*, pg. 992

FARBERWARE—NONE—Syratech Corporation; *U.S. Private*, pg. 1060

FARDILEX—Stretch Film—DSM N.V.; *Int'l*, pg. 352

FARIAS—NONE—Tabacalera, S.A.; *Int'l*, pg. 1345

FARIBO—All Faribault Prods.—Faribault Woolen Mill Co.; *U.S. Private*, pg. 394

FARLEY—Jellies, Chocolate & Fruit Snacks—Farley Candy Company; *U.S. Private*, pg. 397

FARLEYS—Hard Cider—Gibson Wine Company; *U.S. Private*, pg. 452

FARM BUREAU—Insurance—Southern Farm Bureau Casualty Insurance Company; *U.S. Private*, pg. 1016

FARM CHUNK—Cookies—Pepperidge Farm, Incorporated; *U.S. Public*, pg. 299

FARM FOODS—A Line of Healthy Soy-Based Frozen Desserts, Pizza & Single-Serve Items—The Hain Food Group Inc.; *U.S. Public*, pg. 774

FARM FORUM—Magazine—Case Corporation; *U.S. Public*, pg. 311

FARM FRESH—Grocery Store—Farm Fresh, Inc.; *U.S. Public*, pg. 1388

FARM FRESH—NONE—Victoria Packing Corporation; *U.S. Private*, pg. 1139

FARM FRESH BUTTER—Butter—Plymouth Creameries, Inc.; *U.S. Public*, pg. 872

FARM FUTURES—Monthly Magazine Providing Agricultural Business Information—Miller Publishing Co.; *U.S. Public*, pg. 513

FARM/IMPLEMENT—Tires—Bridgestone/Firestone, Inc.; *Int'l*, pg. 213

FARM INDUSTRY NEWS—Business Newsin Farm Industry—Intertec Publishing; *U.S. Public*, pg. 1327

FARM MART—Farm Supply Distributors/Retailers—PRO Group, Inc.; *U.S. Private*, pg. 887

FARM MASTER—Shoes—E.J. Footwear Corp.; *U.S. Public*, pg. 1684

FARM PRESS PUBLICATIONS—NONE—Farm Press; *U.S. Public*, pg. 1328

FARM PROGRESS PUBLICATIONS—Periodicals for the Working Farmer—Farm Progress Publications; *U.S. Public*, pg. 513

FARM PROGRESS SHOW—Trade Show—Farm Progress Publications; *U.S. Public*, pg. 513

FARM-RATED—Single Phase IHP Motors—Magnetek Motors & Generators; *U.S. Public*, pg. 1037

FARM RICH—Non-Dairy Creamer—Rich Products Corp.; *U.S. Private*, pg. 928

FARM RICH—Vegetables—Rich SeaPak Corp.; *U.S. Private*, pg. 928

FARM-ROD—Field Tile Cleaner—Roto-Rooter; *U.S. Public*, pg. 344

FARM SPECIAL—Tires—Bridgestone/Firestone, Inc.; *Int'l*, pg. 213

FARM STORES—Gasoline Stations & Grocery Stores—Farm Stores; *U.S. Private*, pg. 394

FARM TIRE L—Tires—Bridgestone/Firestone, Inc.; *Int'l*, pg. 213

FARMAN'S—Pickles & Sauerkraut—Curtice Burns Foods; *U.S. Private*, pg. 887

FARMASTER—Gates, S&K Tanks, Feeders—Behlen Mfg. Co.; *U.S. Private*, pg. 130

FARMER BOY—Meat Prods.—Worldwide Food Products Inc.; *U.S. Private*, pg. 1191

FARMER JACK—Food Stores—The Great Atlantic & Pacific Tea Company, Inc.; *Int'l*, pg. 1375

THE FARMER—NONE—Farm Progress Publications; *U.S. Public*, pg. 513

FARMERS FURNITURE COMPANY—Furniture—Warehouse Home Furnishings Distributor; *U.S. Private*, pg. 1150

FARMERS MUTUAL—Insurance on Crops; Poultry, Reinsurance—Farmers Mutual Hail Insurance Co. of Iowa; *U.S. Private*, pg. 395

FARMER'S PRIDE—Natural Chicken—Farmer's Pride, Inc.; *U.S. Private*, pg. 395

FARMHAND—Loaders—AGCO Corporation; *U.S. Public*, pg. 28

FARMINGTON—Lumber & Wood Products—Georgia-Pacific Corporation; *U.S. Public*, pg. 735

FARMLAND—Pork Products—Farmland Foods, Inc.; *U.S. Private*, pg. 396

FARMLAND FOODS—Pork Products—Farmland Industries, Inc.; *U.S. Private*, pg. 395

FARMORUBICIN—NONE—Pharmacia & Upjohn, Inc.; *Int'l*, pg. 1047

FARMSTEAD—Dairy Prods.—Crowley Foods, Inc.; *Int'l*, pg. 752

FARNAM—Sealing Systems—Coltec Industries Inc.; *U.S. Public*, pg. 401

FARNAM—Veterinary Pharmaceuticals—Farnam Companies, Inc.; *U.S. Private*, pg. 396

FAROARM—NONE—FARO Technologies, Inc.; *U.S. Public*, pg. 613

FAROUCHE—Women's Fragrance—Accecones Ricci U.S.A., Inc.; *Int'l*, pg. 445

FARRAND—Transducers & Electronics—Ruhle Companies, Inc.; *U.S. Private*, pg. 950

FARRAND SELCA SYSTEMS—CNC Machine Controls—Ruhle Companies, Inc.; *U.S. Private*, pg. 950

FARRAR, STRAUS & GIROUX—Books—Farrar, Straus & Giroux, Inc.; *Int'l*, pg. 1479

FARREL—NONE—Farrel Corporation; *U.S. Public*, pg. 614

FARRELL—Steamship Service—Farrell Lines Incorporated; *U.S. Private*, pg. 397

FARRIS—Valves—Teledyne Fluid Systems; *U.S. Public*, pg. 43

FARRISERVO—Valves—Teledyne Fluid Systems; *U.S. Public*, pg. 43

FARROW & HUMPHREYS—Toiletries—International Cosmetics Co., Ltd.; *Int'l*, pg. 684

FARROWSURE—NONE—Pfizer Inc.; *U.S. Public*, pg. 1281

FARROWSURE—Animal Vaccine—SmithKline Beecham plc; *Int'l*, pg. 1264

FAS-LOC—Quick Change Toolholder—Air Gage Company; *U.S. Public*, pg. 1676

FASCAL—Cast Vinyls—Avery Dennison Corporation; *U.S. Public*, pg. 152

FASCAL—Calendered & Cast Film—Fasson Films; *U.S. Public*, pg. 153

FASCIA—Ready-Made Frames—Letraset Nielsen & Bainbridge; *Int'l*, pg. 460

FASCINATION—Printing Paper—Westvaco Corporation; *U.S. Public*, pg. 1762

FASCLEAR—NONE—Avery Dennison Corporation; *U.S. Public*, pg. 152

FASCLEAR—Clear Label Film—Fasson Films; *U.S. Public*, pg. 153

FASCLING—Static Cling Vinyl Film—Fasson Films; *U.S. Public*, pg. 153

FASCO—Electronic Printers & Fabric Labels—PAXAR Corporation; *U.S. Public*, pg. 1266

FASCOPY—High Quality Self Adhesive for use in Copy Machines—Avery Dennison Corporation; *U.S. Public*, pg. 152

FASFILM—Films for Roll Label Converters—Fasson Films; *U.S. Public*, pg. 153

FASHION—Writing Instruments—Sheaffer Inc.; *Int'l*, pg. 542

FASHION AIRE—Hair Dryers—Sunbeam Household Products; *U.S. Public*, pg. 1533

FASHION BAR—NONE—Stage Stores, Inc.; *U.S. Private*, pg. 1028

FASHION BOW—Ready Made Bows of Ribbon for Gift Wrapping—American Greetings Corporation; *U.S. Public*, pg. 77

FASHION BUG—Junior, Misses Apparel & Large Size Apparel—Charming Shoppes, Inc.; *U.S. Public*, pg. 335

FASHION BUG PLUS—Large Size Women's Apparel—Charming Shoppes, Inc.; *U.S. Public*, pg. 335

FASHION FAIR—Cosmetics—Johnson Publishing Company, Inc.; *U.S. Private*, pg. 591

FASHION FLEX—Women's Shoes—E.J. Footwear Corp.; *U.S. Public*, pg. 1684

FASHION FLORALS—Brushes—Wilhold Inc.; *U.S. Public*, pg. 78

FASHION GAL—Women's Retail Specialty Store—Gateway Apparel, Inc.; *U.S. Private*, pg. 441

FASHION GALAXY—Ladies Apparel—Hanover Direct Pennsylvania, Inc.; *U.S. Public*, pg. 782

FASHION HOUSE—Wallcoverings—Borden, Inc.; *U.S. Private*, pg. 157

FASHION LOCKER—Paperboard Displayer—The Mead Corporation; *U.S. Public*, pg. 1074

FASHION MAGIC—Gift Wrap—American Greetings Corporation; *U.S. Public*, pg. 77

FASHION MAGIC—Party Goods—American Greetings U.S. Greeting Card Division; *U.S. Public*, pg. 78

FASHION MAGIC—Activity—Tyco Toys, Inc.; *U.S. Public*, pg. 1058

FASHION MOOD—Fragrance—Jean Philippe Fragrances, Inc.; *U.S. Public*, pg. 924

FASHION PLEAT—Window Shades—Springs Industries, Inc.; *U.S. Public*, pg. 1499

FASHION SCOOPS—Panties—Olga Div.; *U.S. Public*, pg. 1738

FASHION SEAL—Uniforms—Superior Surgical Mfg. Co., Inc.; *U.S. Public*, pg. 1539

FASHION 10—Women's Shoes—E.J. Footwear Corp.; *U.S. Public*, pg. 1684

FASHION-TREADS—Safety Footwear—Alba-Waldensian, Inc.; *U.S. Public*, pg. 35

FASHION TRENDS—Drapery Hardware—Kirsch; *U.S. Public*, pg. 1176

FASHION WRITE—Envelopes—The Mead Corporation; *U.S. Public*, pg. 1074

FASHIONAIRE—Career Apparel—Hartmarx Corporation; *U.S. Public*, pg. 795

FASHIONATION—Women's Retail Specialty Store—Gateway Apparel, Inc.; *U.S. Private*, pg. 441

FASHIONMATE—Packaging System—Sanderson Plumbing Products Inc.; *U.S. Private*, pg. 964

FASIGYN—Tinidazole—Pfizer Inc.; *U.S. Public*, pg. 1281

FASINEX—Veterinary Pharmaceutical—Ciba Specialty Chemicals; *Int'l*, pg. 291

FASINEX—Veterinary Pharmaceutical—Novartis; *Int'l*, pg. 972

FASROLL—NONE—Avery Dennison Corporation; *U.S. Public*, pg. 152

FASS-DRI—Coating—Maintenance, Inc.; *Int'l*, pg. 1068

FASSATI—Table Wine—Paterno Imports Limited; *U.S. Private*, pg. 843

FASSBIND EAUX-DE-VIE—Liqueur—Paterno Imports Limited; *U.S. Private*, pg. 843

FASSON—Adhesives—Avery Dennison Corporation; *U.S. Public*, pg. 152

FAST—Structure Portable Fabric Buildings—Anchor Industries Inc.; *U.S. Private*, pg. 71

FAST—Functional & Streee Testing—GenRad, Inc.; *U.S. Public*, pg. 731

FAST—Flux & Solder—La-Co Industries Markal Company; *U.S. Private*, pg. 640

FAST BAKS—Athletic Shoes—C.R. Anthony Company; *U.S. Private*, pg. 1029

FAST-BALL—Lubrication Transfer Pumps—Graco Inc.; *U.S. Public*, pg. 756

FAST BILL—NONE—Integra Technologies Corp.; *U.S. Private*, pg. 565

FAST CAP—NONE—Johnson & Johnson; *U.S. Public*, pg. 927

FAST CASH—NONE—Integra Technologies Corp.; *U.S. Private*, pg. 565

FAST CLEAN—Oil Industry Services—Serv-Tech, Inc.; *U.S. Public*, pg. 1460

FAST-CUT—Steels Developed for Improved Machining Characteristics—Lukens Steel Company; *U.S. Public*, pg. 1020

FAST DRAW—Oil Industry Services—Serv-Tech, Inc.; *U.S. Public*, pg. 1460

FAST DRY—Marker—La-Co Industries Markal Company; *U.S. Private*, pg. 640

FAST FARE—Convenience Stores—Crown Central Petroleum Corporation; *U.S. Public*, pg. 462

FAST/FLEX—Baseboard Connectors—Slant/Fin Corporation; *U.S. Private*, pg. 1005

FAST FLO—Pumps—Graco Inc.; *U.S. Public*, pg. 756

FAST-FOLD—Portable Folding Screen—Da-Lite Screen Company, Inc.; *U.S. Private*, pg. 306

FAST FORWARD—NONE—Forstmann & Company, Inc.; *U.S. Public*, pg. 670

FAST 4000—NONE—Integra Technologies Corp.; *U.S. Private*, pg. 565

FAST GRAPH—Computer Programs for Problem Mapping Applications—Thinking Machines Corporation; *U.S. Private*, pg. 1081

FAST LANE—Stationery Items—The Mead Corporation; *U.S. Public*, pg. 1074

FAST LOK—Hose Clamps—Deco Products Co.; *U.S. Private*, pg. 320

FAST MAILER—One Way Mailers Continuous—Hano Document Printers, Inc.; *U.S. Public*, pg. 1686

FAST MAX—C-Store Name—Kocolene Oil Corp.; *U.S. Private*, pg. 629

FAST 'N EASY—Pre-Cooked Meats; Bacon—Hormel Foods Corp.; *U.S. Public*, pg. 840

FAST-ON—Electrical Outlet Boxes & Retaining Clips—The Lamson & Sessions Co.; *U.S. Public*, pg. 976

FAST ORANGE—Hand Cleaner—Loctite Corp. North American Group; *Int'l*, pg. 611

FAST-PAK—Angiography Kit—Mallinckrodt Inc.; *U.S. Public*, pg. 1039

FAST-PATCH—Defibrillation Electrodes—Physio-Control Corporation; *U.S. Public*, pg. 1294

FAST PATH ANALYZER/EP—NONE—BMC Software, Inc.; *U.S. Public*, pg. 162

FAST PATH REORG/EP—NONE—BMC Software, Inc.; *U.S. Public*, pg. 162

FAST REORG FACILITY—NONE—BMC Software, Inc.; *U.S. Public*, pg. 162

FAST REORG FACILITY/EP—NONE—BMC Software, Inc.; *U.S. Public*, pg. 162

FAST TAP—Quick Deilivery of Special Taps—National Twist Drill Div.; *U.S. Public*, pg. 1370

FAST TAP—Quick Delivery of Special Taps—Regal-Beloit Corporation; *U.S. Public*, pg. 1370

FAST-TAX—Computerized Tax Processing Software—Computer Language Research, Inc.; *U.S. Public*, pg. 421

FAST TRACK—High Speed Vision Inspection Equipment—Alltrista Corporation; *U.S. Public*, pg. 56

FAST TRACK—Retractable Ball-Point Pen—The Pilot Pen Corp. of America; *Int'l*, pg. 1057

FAST TRAXX—Radio Control—Tyco Toys, Inc.; *U.S. Public*, pg. 1058

FAST WRAP—Orthopedic Software—Camp Healthcare; *Int'l*, pg. 1425

FASTABLE—Surgical Table—Diasonics Ultra Sound, Inc.; *Int'l*, pg. 644

FASTACH—Vibrating Screed For Paving Machines—Cedarapids, Inc.; *U.S. Public*, pg. 1365

FASTAPE—Tape—Demco Inc.; *U.S. Private*, pg. 323

FASTATEMENT—Semi-Automatic Billing System—Pitney Bowes Inc.; *U.S. Public*, pg. 1303

FASTBACK—Cabspoiler—Lund International Holdings, Inc.; *U.S. Public*, pg. 1020

FASTBANK—ATM Network—U.S. Bancorp; *U.S. Public*, pg. 1680

FASTBLT—Graphics Controller—LSI Logic Corp.; *U.S. Public*, pg. 971

FASTBOND—Construction/cabinetry Contact Cements—3M; *U.S. Public*, pg. 1604

FASTCELL—Performance Library—GenRad, Inc.; *U.S. Public*, pg. 731

FASTCHECK—NONE—Life Technologies, Inc.; *U.S. Public*, pg. 504

FASTCLASS—Rental Service—Thrifty Rent-a-Car System, Inc.; *U.S. Public*, pg. 354

FASTECH—NONE—Berg Electronics; *U.S. Public*, pg. 212

FASTEETH—Denture Adhesive Powder—Richardson-Vicks, Inc. Personal Care Products Div.; *U.S. Public*, pg. 1331

FASTEK—Filter Separation Equipment & Materials—Eastman Kodak Company; *U.S. Public*, pg. 550

FASTEK—Membranes—Osmonics, Inc.; *U.S. Public*, pg. 1233

FASTEN MATES—Plastic Buckles—YKK (U.S.A.); *Int'l*, pg. 1515

FASTEN-PAK—Industrial Fasteners—Mid-Continent Screw Products Co.; *U.S. Private*, pg. 743

FASTENAL—NONE—Fastenal Company; *U.S. Public*, pg. 614

FASTEST—Array—LSI Logic Corp.; *U.S. Public*, pg. 971

FASTFAX—High-Speed Digital Facsimile System—Litton Industries, Inc.; *U.S. Public*, pg. 1002

FASTFILL—PC Graphics Chip—LSI Logic Corp.; *U.S. Public*, pg. 971

FASTFIT—Interior Wood Door—Premdor Inc.; *Int'l*, pg. 1066

FASTFUNDS—Prescription Drug Plan—PCS Health Systems, Inc.; *U.S. Public*, pg. 993

FASTIN—Pharmaceutical Prods.—SmithKline Beecham Laboratories; *Int'l*, pg. 1264

FASTIN—Treatment of Obesity—SmithKline Beecham plc; *Int'l*, pg. 1264

FASTITE—Pipe Joint—American Cast Iron Pipe Co.; *U.S. Private*, pg. 51

FASTLAC—Paints—Essex Chemical Corporation; *U.S. Public*, pg. 523

FASTLINE 24 HOUR BANKING—Phone Banking Service—U.S. Bancorp; *U.S. Public*, pg. 1680

FASTLINK—Wireless System—Radionics, Inc.; *U.S. Public*, pg. 501

FASTLOCK—Plastic Roof Panels—Icopal a/s; *Int'l*, pg. 658

FASTNET—Ladies & Childrens Clothes—Arnotts plc; *Int'l*, pg. 81

FASTOOL—Epoxy Casting System—CIBA Specialty Chemicals; *Int'l*, pg. 291

FASTPATH—Electronic Instrument—Intel Corporation; *U.S. Public*, pg. 886

FASTRAC—Shower—Bradley Corporation; *U.S. Private*, pg. 164

FASTRAC—Building Materials—Jewell Building Systems; *U.S. Private*, pg. 587

FASTRADE—Trading Information System—Logica Plc; *Int'l*, pg. 814

FASTRAK—Hourly Service Between MSP & ORD—Northwest Airlines, Inc.; *U.S. Public*, pg. 1200

FASTREF—Business Product—International Business Machines Corporation; *U.S. Public*, pg. 895

FASTRIV—Process for Fastening Metal Parts with Rivets—Clayhithe P.L.C.; *Int'l*, pg. 297

FASTSERVICE—Business Product—International Business Machines Corporation; *U.S. Public*, pg. 895

FASTTOOL—NONE—Fastenal Company; *U.S. Public*, pg. 614

FASTTRACK—Data Analysis and Reporting Software—Fair, Isaac and Company, Inc.; *U.S. Public*, pg. 609

FASTTRACK—Data Collector—IRD Mechanalysis, Inc. (U.S.A.); *U.S. Public*, pg. 789

FASTTRACK—NONE—Pitney Bowes Inc.; *U.S. Public*, pg. 1303

FAT BATTS—Fibreglass Building Blanket, Acoustic Pannels, Duct Liners—Carter Holt Harvey Limited; *U.S. Public*, pg. 904

FAT CAT—Motorcycle—American Honda Motor Co., Inc. Motorcycle Division; *Int'l*, pg. 634

FAT CATS—Greeting Cards—American Greetings Corporation; *U.S. Public*, pg. 77

FAT FREDDIE—Meat Snacks—Carl Buddig & Company; *U.S. Private*, pg. 178

FAT FREE—Frozen Desserts—Borden, Inc.; *U.S. Private*, pg. 157

FAT FREE—Yogurt—Yoplait USA; *U.S. Public*, pg. 718

FAT-FREE NEWTONS—Cookies—Nabisco Inc.; *U.S. Public*, pg. 1355

FAT-HEAD—Specialty Nails—Maze Nails; *U.S. Private*, pg. 718

FATE—NONE—Fate S.A.; *Int'l*, pg. 478

FATHER & SON—Men's Shoes—E.J. Footwear Corp.; *U.S. Public*, pg. 1684

FATHOMETER—Depth Sounder—Raytheon Company; *U.S. Public*, pg. 1364

FATIGUE PROOF—Steel Bar Products—LaSalle Steel Company; *U.S. Public*, pg. 1181

FATIGUEPROOF—Type of Cold Finished Steel Bar—Quanex Corporation; *U.S. Public*, pg. 1349

FAUCET WATER FILTER—Faucet Mounted Fiter—Pollenex; *U.S. Public*, pg. 1391

FAULT FITER—Electronic Power Fuse—S & C Electric Company; *U.S. Private*, pg. 954

FAULT TAMER—Electronic Power Fuse—S & C Electric Company; *U.S. Private*, pg. 954

FAULTLESS—Rubber Sundries—Abbott Laboratories; *U.S. Public*, pg. 12

FAULTLESS—Casters, Wheels & Chair Controls—Faultless Caster; *Int'l*, pg. 473

FAVOR—Furniture Polish—S.C. Johnson & Son, Inc.; *U.S. Private*, pg. 592

FAVORIT—Textile Floorcoverings—Forbo Holding SA; *Int'l*, pg. 496

FAVORITE—Oil & Grease Absorbent—Oil-Dri Corporation of America; *U.S. Public*, pg. 1214

FAWCETT—Book Publishing—Random House, Inc.; *U.S. Private*, pg. 20

FAWICK—(Industrial Clutches & Brakes)—Airflex Div. Eaton Corp.; *U.S. Public*, pg. 556

FAX MAX—Imagine Media—Labelon Corporation; *U.S. Private*, pg. 641

FAX 150—Facimile Machine—Konica Corporation; *Int'l*, pg. 748

FAX 285—Facimile Machine—Konica Corporation; *Int'l*, pg. 748

FAX 500—Facimile Machine—Konica Corporation; *Int'l*, pg. 748

FAX/MODEM CARD—PCMCIA Cards—Epson America Inc.; *Int'l*, pg. 1219

FAXAGENT—Fax Processing—Octel Messaging Division; *U.S. Public*, pg. 1017

FAXAIDE—Facsimile Apparatus—Zenith Electronics Corp.; *U.S. Public*, pg. 1790

FAXALYZER—Facsimile Diagnostic System—Lucent Technologies Inc.; *U.S. Public*, pg. 1017

FAXASAK—Restaurants—Consolidated Products, Inc.; *U.S. Public*, pg. 436

FAXASAK—Restaurants—Steak 'n Shake, Inc.; *U.S. Public*, pg. 437

FAXBROADCAST—Fax Processing—Octel Messaging Division; *U.S. Public*, pg. 1017

FAXCALL—Voice Processing & Application Software—Octel Messaging Division; *U.S. Public*, pg. 1017

FAXCONCENTRATOR—Business Product—International Business Machines Corporation; *U.S. Public*, pg. 895

FAXLINK—Facsimile Software—Tandem Computers Inc.; *U.S. Public*, pg. 417

FAXLYNK—International Facsimile Service & Hand-Delivered Fax Documents—DHL Worldwide Express; *U.S. Private*, pg. 301

FAXMATE—Low Cost Marine Weather Chart Recorder—Alden Electronics, Inc.; *U.S. Private*, pg. 872

FAXON—Magazine Subscription—The Faxon Company, Inc.; *Int'l*, pg. 385

FAXSERVE—Facsimile Software—Cheyenne; *U.S. Public*, pg. 420

FAXSHARE—Fax Server—Mitek Systems, Inc.; *U.S. Public*, pg. 1117

FAXSOLUTION—NONE—Avenor, Inc.; *Int'l*, pg. 101

FAXSTATION—Fax Processing—Octel Messaging Division; *U.S. Public*, pg. 1017

FAXWRITER—Facsimile Unit—Lanier Worldwide Inc.; *U.S. Public*, pg. 791

FAYGO—Soft Drink—Faygo Beverages, Inc.; *U.S. Public*, pg. 1153

FAZI-BATTAGLIA—Wine—Paterno Imports Limited; *U.S. Private*, pg. 843

FAZOLI'S—Italian Restaurant—Seed Restaurant Group, Inc.; *U.S. Private*, pg. 981

FAZOR—NONE—Uniroyal Chemical Company, Inc.; *U.S. Public*, pg. 460

FEATHER—Lamp-Low Voltage—George Kovacs Lighting, Inc.; *U.S. Public*, pg. 634

FEATHER-FLO—Eye/Face-Wash Fountains & Showers—Haws Drinking Faucet Co.; *U.S. Private*, pg. 512

FEATHER TOUCH—Stuffed Toy Figures—American Greetings Corporation; *U.S. Public*, pg. 77

FEATHERED FRIEND—Bird Food—Agway, Inc.; *U.S. Public*, pg. 27

FEATHERLITE—Rolling Steel Service Door—Raynor Garage Doors; *U.S. Private*, pg. 912

FEATHERWEIGHT—Bicycles—Bridgestone/Firestone, Inc.; *Int'l*, pg. 213

FEATHERWEIGHT—Special Dietary Prods.—Novartis Nutrition Corporation; *Int'l*, pg. 974

FEATURBILT—Crane—Harnischfeger Industries, Inc.; *U.S. Public*, pg. 788

FECTOIDS—Safety Eyewear—Aearo Company; *U.S. Public*, pg. 23

FEDAHIST—NONE—Schwarz Pharma Inc.; *Int'l*, pg. 1211

FEDAHIST GYROCAPS—NONE—Schwarz Pharma Inc.; *Int'l*, pg. 1211

FEDDERS—Room Air Conditioning—Fedders Corp.; *U.S. Public*, pg. 614

FEDERAL—Ammunition—Blount International, Inc.; *U.S. Public*, pg. 1209

FEDERAL—Paperboard & Paper Products—Imperial Bondware Corp.; *U.S. Public*, pg. 903

FEDERAL—Washing Soap—Nuevo Federal S.A.; *Int'l*, pg. 990

FEDERAL CARTRIDGE—Sporting Ammunition—Federal Cartridge Co.; *U.S. Public*, pg. 239

FEDERAL FINANCIAL SYSTEM (FFS)—NONE—American Management Systems, Inc.; *U.S. Public*, pg. 86

FEDERAL INTERNATIONAL—Floor Care—The Valspar Corporation; *U.S. Public*, pg. 1707

FEDERAL-MOGUL—Engine Bearings, Bushings & Washers, Chassis Products—Federal-Mogul Corporation; *U.S. Public*, pg. 615

FEDERAL PROPELLER—Commercial Marine Propellers—Michigan Wheel Corporation; *U.S. Private*, pg. 741

FEDEX—Brand Name—FDX Corporation; *U.S. Public*, pg. 603

FEDEX ASIAONE—NONE—FDX Corporation; *U.S. Public*, pg. 603

FEDEX DROPBOX—NONE—FDX Corporation; *U.S. Public*, pg. 603

FEDEX EXPRESSFREIGHTER—NONE—FDX Corporation; *U.S. Public*, pg. 603

FEDEX FIRST OVERNIGHT—NONE—FDX Corporation; *U.S. Public*, pg. 603

FEDEX INTERNATIONAL ECONOMY—NONE—FDX Corporation; *U.S. Public*, pg. 603

FEDEX INTERNATIONAL PRIORITY—Custom-cleared pickup & Delivery of Smaller Shipments Between Canada & US—FDX Corporation; *U.S. Public*, pg. 603

FEDEX INTERNATIONAL PRIORITY PLUS—Overnight Delivery to Major Centers in Europe & Brazil—FDX Corporation; *U.S. Public*, pg. 603

FEDEX POWERSHIP—NONE—FDX Corporation; *U.S. Public*, pg. 603

FEDEX POWERSHIP 3—NONE—FDX Corporation; *U.S. Public*, pg. 603

FEDEX POWERSHIP 2—NONE—FDX Corporation; *U.S. Public*, pg. 603

FEDEX PRIORITY OVERNIGHT—Next Business Day Delivery by 10:30 a.m. of Smaller Shipments—FDX Corporation; *U.S. Public*, pg. 603

FEDEX SAMEDAY—NONE—FDX Corporation; *U.S. Public*, pg. 603

FEDEX SHIPSITE—NONE—FDX Corporation; *U.S. Public*, pg. 603

FEDEX STANDARD OVERNIGHT—Delivery Service—FDX Corporation; *U.S. Public*, pg. 603

FEDEX WORLD SERVICE CENTER—NONE—FDX Corporation; *U.S. Public*, pg. 603

FEDEXPRESS—NONE—FDX Corporation; *U.S. Public*, pg. 603

FEDRAZIL—Decongestant—Glaxo Wellcome PLC; *Int'l*, pg. 553

FEED & WEED—Lawn Food—The Chas. H. Lilly Co.; *U.S. Private*, pg. 667

FEED ADDITIVE COMPENDEUM—Directory—Farm Progress Publications; *U.S. Public*, pg. 513

FEED STUFFS—Farm Publication—Farm Progress Publications; *U.S. Public*, pg. 513

FEEDFORWARD—Electronic Components—General Instrument Corporation; *U.S. Public*, pg. 716

FEEDRAIL—Electrical Connector—Thomas & Betts/Amerace; *U.S. Public*, pg. 1598

FEEDRAIL—Power Supply Systems—Thomas & Betts Corporation; *U.S. Public*, pg. 1597

FEEL FREE—Deodorant—The Gillette Company; *U.S. Public*, pg. 743

FEEL GOOD FOOD—NONE—Koo Koo Roo, Inc.; *U.S. Public*, pg. 966

FEEL THE QUALITY ENJOY THE SAVINGS—Rental Cars—Thrifty Rent-a-Car System, Inc.; *U.S. Public*, pg. 354

THE FEELING NEVER ENDS—Trade Mark—FTD, Inc./Florists Transworld Delivery, Inc.; *U.S. Private*, pg. 389

FEELINGS—Perfumed Body Spray—SmithKline Beecham plc; *Int'l*, pg. 1264

FEELS SO LIVELY—Perm—Zotos International; *Int'l*, pg. 1236

FEEN-A-MINT—Laxatives—Schering-Plough Corporation; *U.S. Public*, pg. 1438

FEEN-A-MINT—Laxative—Schering-Plough Healthcare Products Inc.; *U.S. Public*, pg. 1438

FEESABILITY—Trust Accounting Software—MCRB Service Bureau, Inc.; *U.S. Private*, pg. 686

FEET RELIEF—Foot Bath—Pollenex; *U.S. Public*, pg. 1391

FEINTOOL—Fine-Blanking Presses & Fine-Blanking Tools—Feintool International Holding AG; *Int'l*, pg. 479

FEIST—Port Wine—Groupe Pernod Ricard; *Int'l*, pg. 566

FEL-O-VAX—Veterinary Pharmaceuticals—American Home Products Corporation; *U.S. Public*, pg. 79

FELBATOL—Antiepileptic—Wallace Laboratories; *U.S. Public*, pg. 310

FELDENE—Piroxicam—Pfizer Inc.; *U.S. Public*, pg. 1281

FELDENE FDDF—Piroxicam—Pfizer Inc.; *U.S. Public*, pg. 1281

FELDINI—NONE—Supreme International Corp.; *U.S. Public*, pg. 1542

FELGERIAS BUEBAS—NONE—Vercoope-Uniao Das Adegas Cooperativas da Regiao Dos Vinhoa Verdes, U.C.R.L.; *Int'l*, pg. 1463

FELIX—Pet Food—Dalgety Plc; *Int'l*, pg. 376

FELIX—Grocery Products—Sara Lee Corporation; *U.S. Public*, pg. 1432

FELOCELL—Animal Vaccine—SmithKline Beecham plc; *Int'l*, pg. 1264

FELS NAPTHA BAR SOAP—NONE—The Dial Corporation; *U.S. Public*, pg. 505

FELSTED—Push-Pull Cable & Controls—Eaton International Corp.; *U.S. Public*, pg. 558

FELSTED—Cables & Controls—Furon Company; *U.S. Public*, pg. 688

FELTAN—Felt—American Felt & Filter; *U.S. Private*, pg. 54

FELTASTIC—Felt—American Felt & Filter; *U.S. Private*, pg. 54

FELTWEAVE—Printing Paper—Georgia-Pacific Corporation; *U.S. Public*, pg. 735

FEMCARE—Value-Priced Brand for Vaginal Yeast Infections—Schering-Plough Corporation; *U.S. Public*, pg. 1438

FEMFLEX—Femoral Catheter—Baxter Research Medical, Inc.; *U.S. Public*, pg. 196

FEMFRESH—NONE—Boots Healthcare International; *Int'l*, pg. 202

FEMINESSE—Vaginal Odor—Columbia Laboratories, Inc.; *U.S. Public*, pg. 405

FEMIRON—Vitamin Supplement For Women—Menley & James Laboratories, Inc.; *U.S. Public*, pg. 1086

FEMME—Perfume—Wella Group; *Int'l*, pg. 1489

FEMME PLUS—Magazine—Quebecor Inc.; *Int'l*, pg. 1075

FEMPOTANE—Vitamins—Health Products Corporation; *U.S. Private*, pg. 514

FEMS—Feminine Napkins, Tampons—Kimberly-Clark Corporation; *U.S. Public*, pg. 958

FEMSTAT—Butoconazole Nitrate—Syntex; *Int'l*, pg. 1120

FENCE PRO—Wood Fence Nails—MMI Products, Inc.; *U.S. Private*, pg. 687

FENCIR—Inflammation & Tissue Repair—SmithKline Beecham plc; *Int'l*, pg. 1264

FENDER—Guitars, Amplifiers, Strings, Sound Reinforcement—Fender Musical Instruments; *U.S. Private*, pg. 400

FENDER MATE—Boat Fender—Attwood Corporation; *U.S. Private*, pg. 1038

FENDI ASJA—Fragrance—Elizabeth Arden Company; *Int'l*, pg. 1435

FENDT—Tractors—AGCO Corporation; *U.S. Public*, pg. 28

FENESHIELD—Fiber Glass Yarn—PPG Industries, Inc.; *U.S. Public*, pg. 1245

FENESTRA—Door Products—The Marmon Group, Inc.; *U.S. Private*, pg. 706

FENJAL—Bath Additives & Soap—SmithKline Beecham plc; *Int'l*, pg. 1264

FENLIN—Total Shoulder System—Bristol-Myers Squibb Company; *U.S. Public*, pg. 253

FENN—Mfr. of Aircraft Engines & Parts—Fenn Manufacturing Co.; *U.S. Public*, pg. 1676

FENOXYPEN—Penicillin V—Novo Nordisk A/S; *Int'l*, pg. 987

FENURIL—NONE—Pharmacia & Upjohn, Inc.; *Int'l*, pg. 1047

FENZIA—Label—S & K Famous Brands, Inc.; *U.S. Public*, pg. 1414

FEOSOL—Iron Therapy—SmithKline Beecham Consumer Healthcare, U.S.; *Int'l*, pg. 1264

FEOSOL—Iron Supplement—SmithKline Beecham Research Limited; *Int'l*, pg. 1266

FER-IN-SOL—Iron Supplement for Prevention & Treatment of Iron Deficiency Anemia—Mead Johnson Nutritional Group; *U.S. Public*, pg. 254

FERAG—Forwarding & Processing Systems for Printing Industry—WRH Walter Reist Holding AG; *Int'l*, pg. 1484

FERDI FROG—Greeting Cards—American Greetings Corporation; *U.S. Public*, pg. 77

FERENKA—Steelcord—Akzo Nobel N.V.; *Int'l*, pg. 42

FERIDEX—Contrast Agent—Advanced Magnetics, Inc.; *U.S. Public*, pg. 20

FERMALOX—Pharmaceuticals—Rhone-Poulenc Rorer - U.S.; *Int'l*, pg. 1110

FERMEC—NONE—Fermec Holdings, Ltd.; *U.S. Public*, pg. 312

FERMICHAMP—Wine Yeasts—Royal Gist-Brocades N.V.; *Int'l*, pg. 1142

FERMIOL—Active Dried Yeast for the Production of Alcohol—Royal Gist-Brocades N.V.; *Int'l*, pg. 1142

FERMIPAN—Fresh & Instant Dry Yeast—Royal Gist-Brocades N.V.; *Int'l*, pg. 1142

FERMIVIN—Wine Yeasts—Royal Gist-Brocades N.V.; *Int'l*, pg. 1142

FERMIX—Plant Micronutrient Fertilizer—Georgia-Pacific Corporation; *U.S. Public*, pg. 735

FERMPRESS—Manual Bottle Capper—The West Company, Incorporated; *U.S. Public*, pg. 1755

FERN BRATTEN FOR MELROSE—NONE—Kellwood Company; *U.S. Public*, pg. 948

FERNET BRANCA—Liqueur—Carillon Importers, Ltd.; *Int'l*, pg. 409

FERODO—Disc Brake Pads, Linings—T & N Plc; *Int'l*, pg. 1334

FERON—Natural Interferon-B Preparation—Toray Industries, Inc.; *Int'l*, pg. 1399

FEROZA—1600 cc (Petrol) 4WD—Daihatsu Motor Corporation, Ltd.; *Int'l*, pg. 364

FERRALL ON THE BENCH—Talk Radio Program—Westwood One Entertainment; *U.S. Public*, pg. 1763

FERRALL ON THE BENCH—Sport Talk Program—Westwood One, Inc.; *U.S. Public*, pg. 1763

FERRALN—Pastes for Electronics—Ferro Corporation; *U.S. Public*, pg. 618

FERRARA—Italian Specialty Food Imports—Colivita USA, Inc.; *U.S. Private*, pg. 252

FERRARELLE—Carbonated Water—Danone Group; *Int'l*, pg. 379

FERRARI—Automobile—Ferrari North America, Inc.; *Int'l*, pg. 483

FERRARI—Automobile—Fiat Auto SpA; *Int'l*, pg. 480

FERRARI—Perfume—International Cosmetics Co., Ltd.; *Int'l*, pg. 684

FERRARI—Wine—Pacific Wine Co.; *U.S. Private*, pg. 843

FERRARI-CORONO—Wine—Pacific Wine Co.; *U.S. Private*, pg. 843

FERRARIA—NONE—Fiskars Oy AB; *Int'l*, pg. 492

FERRARIS—Piston—Tomkins PLC; *Int'l*, pg. 1395

FERRELL NORTH AMERICA—Trading—Ferrellgas Partners, L.P.; *U.S. Public*, pg. 618

FERRELLGAS INC—Bottled Gas—Ferrellgas Partners, L.P.; *U.S. Public*, pg. 618

FERRENE—Electronic Thermoplastic Compound—Ferro Corporation; *U.S. Public*, pg. 618

FERRERO ROCHER—Fine Hazlenut Chocolates—Ferrero; *Int'l*, pg. 480

FERRERO ROCHER—Fine Hazlenut Chocolates—Ferrero U.S.A., Inc.; *Int'l*, pg. 480

FERREX—High Gloss Mineral-Filled Polypropylene—Ferro Corporation; *U.S. Public*, pg. 618

FERRISELTZ—MRI Contrasting Agent for GI Tract—Otsuka Pharmaceutical Co., Ltd.; *Int'l*, pg. 1013

FERRIZYME—Ela Diagnostic Products—Abbott Laboratories; *U.S. Public*, pg. 12

FERRO PICKLE PILLS—Chemicals in Pickling Baths—Ferro Corporation; *U.S. Public*, pg. 618

FERRO TIC—Alloy Bonded Carbides—Alloy Technology International Inc.; *U.S. Private*, pg. 42

FERRO-CURE—Rubber Compounding Additives—Ferro Corporation; *U.S. Public*, pg. 618

FERROCAP—Precious Metal Pastes—Ferro Corporation; *U.S. Public*, pg. 618

FERROCK—NONE—CertainTeed Corporation; *Int'l*, pg. 1170

FERROCON—Conductive Thermoplastic—Ferro Corporation; *U.S. Public*, pg. 618

FERROCOTE—Corrosion Preventives for Ferrous & Non-Ferrous Metals—Quaker Chemical Corporation; *U.S. Public*, pg. 1346

FERROFLEX—Thermoplastic Olefin-Based Elastomers—Ferro Corporation; *U.S. Public*, pg. 618

FERROFLO—Thermoplastic Lubricated Compound—Ferro Corporation; *U.S. Public*, pg. 618

FERROFLUIDIC—Rotary & Exclusion Seals—Ferrofluidics Corporation; *U.S. Public*, pg. 620

FERROFORM—Antioxidants—Novo Nordisk A/S; *Int'l*, pg. 987

FERROMANITE—Sillimanite Refractory—Ferro Corporation; *U.S. Public*, pg. 618

FERROMARK—Rotary & Exclusion Seals—Ferrofluidics Corporation; *U.S. Public*, pg. 620

FERROMATIK—Injection Molding Machines—Klockner-Werke AG; *Int'l*, pg. 736

FERROMETIC—Rotary & Exclusion Seals—Ferrofluidics Corporation; *U.S. Public*, pg. 620

FERROPAK—Thermoplastic Packaging Compounds—Ferro Corporation; *U.S. Public*, pg. 618

FERROPHOS—Pigment—Occidental Chemical Corporation; *U.S. Public*, pg. 1210

FERROSAN D-DROPS—Vitamin D for Infants—Novo Nordisk A/S; *Int'l*, pg. 987

FERROSIL—Fused Silica Refractories—Ferro Corporation; *U.S. Public*, pg. 618

FERROSOUND—Audio Ferro Fluids—Ferrofluidics Corporation; *U.S. Public*, pg. 620

FERROTRON—Magnetic Synthetic Resin—DSM Engineering Plastic Products; *Int'l*, pg. 354

FERROVER—Chemical Reagant—Hach Company; *U.S. Public*, pg. 773

FERROWELD—Electrode—The Lincoln Electric Company; *U.S. Public*, pg. 996

FERROXCUBE—Linear Ferrite Materials—Philips Components; *Int'l*, pg. 1054

FERROZINE—Chemical Reagant—Hach Company; *U.S. Public*, pg. 773

FERRY—Electrical Parts—General Cable Corporation; *Int'l*, pg. 1486

FERRY—Alloy—Inco Limited; *Int'l*, pg. 672

FERRY-MORSE—Packet Vegetable & Flower Seeds & Packaged Lawn Seed—Advance Seed Co.; *Int'l*, pg. 566

FERRY MORSE—Seeds—Groupe Limagrain, *Int'l*, pg. 566

FERRY-MORSE—Vegetable Seed & Home Garden Seed Prods.—Ferry-Morse Seed Company; *Int'l*, pg. 566

FERT—Fertilizer—The Chas. H. Lilly Co.; *U.S. Private*, pg. 667

FERT-O-BATCHER—Weight Tank & Mixing System—Ferguson International, Inc.; *U.S. Private*, pg. 401

FERTILE BAG—Potting Soil—Premier Brands, Inc.; *Int'l*, pg. 1068

FERZEA HA—Topical Xeroderma Pigmentosa Treatment—Shiseido Company Ltd.; *Int'l*, pg. 1235

FES-CORE—Roof Insulation—Johns Manville Corporation; *U.S. Public*, pg. 927

FESCANT PLUS—Cant Strip—Johns Manville Corporation; *U.S. Public*, pg. 927

FESCO BOARD—Roof Insulations—Johns Manville Corporation; *U.S. Public*, pg. 927

FESCO DRI-DECK—Roof Insulator—Johns Manville Corporation; *U.S. Public*, pg. 927

FESCO FOAM—Roof Insulations—Johns Manville Corporation; *U.S. Public*, pg. 927

FESTAIOLA—Pasta—Danone Group; *Int'l*, pg. 379

FESTAL—Canned Vegetables—Owatonna Canning Company; *U.S. Public*, pg. 349

FESTIVA—Area Rugs—Couristan Inc.; *U.S. Private*, pg. 279

FESTIVAL—Ice Cream—Barber Ice Cream Company; *U.S. Private*, pg. 115

FESTIVAL—Dairy Products—Quality Chekd Dairies, Inc.; *U.S. Private*, pg. 898

FESTIVE FIXINGS—Decorations—McCormick & Company, Incorporated; *U.S. Public*, pg. 1066

FESTIVE FIXINGS—Decors—McCormick/Schilling; *U.S. Public*, pg. 1066

FETAL BOVINE SERUM—Bovine Serum—HyClone Laboratories Inc.; *Int'l*, pg. 1037

FETAL FILE—Chart Paper—Ludlow Corporation; *U.S. Public*, pg. 1651

FETALCLONE—Bovine Serum Products Optimized for Various Cell Lines—HyClone Laboratories Inc.; *Int'l*, pg. 1037

FETALSCREEN—Screening Test—Ortho Clinical Diagnostic Systems Inc.; *U.S. Public*, pg. 929

FETFE—Chemical Resistant 'O' Rings—Ace Glass Incorporated; *U.S. Private*, pg. 12

FETRILON—Micronutrient Fertilizer—BASF AG; *Int'l*, pg. 103

FETZER VINEYARDS—Wines—Brown-Forman Beverages Worldwide; *U.S. Public*, pg. 261

FETZER VINEYARDS—California Wines—Brown-Forman Corporation; *U.S. Public*, pg. 261

FEUDAL—Game—Monarch Avalon, Inc.; *U.S. Public*, pg. 1123

FEUTRON—Felt Filter Media—American Felt & Filter; *U.S. Private*, pg. 54

FEVARIN—Antidepressant—Novo Nordisk A/S; *Int'l*, pg. 987

FEVER—27', 32' & 38' Sport Boats—Fountain Powerboat Industries, Inc.; *U.S. Public*, pg. 678

FEXFOIL—Electrical Cable—General Cable Corporation; *Int'l*, pg. 1486

FFV FAMOUS FOODS OF VIRGINIA—Biscuits—George Weston Limited; *Int'l*, pg. 1494

FI-LANA—Acrylic Fiber—Solutia Inc.; *U.S. Public*, pg. 1483

FIAM—NONE—Kone Corporation; *Int'l*, pg. 746

FIAMM—Automotive, Industrial & Household Batteries & Automobile horns—Fiamm S.p.A.; *Int'l*, pg. 480

FIAMM-GS—Consumer Batteries—Fiamm S.p.A.; *Int'l*, pg. 480

FIAT—NONE—Fiat Auto Belgio SA; *Int'l*, pg. 481

FIAT—Cars—Fiat Auto Ireland Ltd.; *Int'l*, pg. 481

FIAT—Automobile—Fiat Auto SpA; *Int'l*, pg. 480

FIAT-ALLIS—Earthmoving—New Holland Ltd.; *Int'l*, pg. 484

FIAT-HITACHI—Earthmoving—New Holland Ltd.; *Int'l*, pg. 484

FIATAGRI—Tractors, Combines, Hay & Forage—New Holland Ltd.; *Int'l*, pg. 484

FIATALLIS—Construction & Earth Moving Equipment—Fiatallis North America, Inc.; *Int'l*, pg. 483

FIBE-MINI—Health Beverage—Otsuka Pharmaceutical Co., Ltd.; *Int'l*, pg. 1013

FIBE MINI PLUS—Health Beverage—Otsuka Pharmaceutical Co., Ltd.; *Int'l*, pg. 1013

FIBER CLASSIC—Insulated Fiberglass Entry Doors—Therma-Tru Corp.; *U.S. Private*, pg. 1079

FIBER FACE—Hardboard Panels—Georgia-Pacific Corporation; *U.S. Public*, pg. 735

FIBER-FULL—Diet Aid—Thompson Medical Company, Inc.; *U.S. Private*, pg. 1083

FIBER HEALTH—Diet Caps—Health Products Corporation; *U.S. Private*, pg. 514

FIBER MATE—Fiber Optics Module—ADC Telecommunications, Inc.; *U.S. Public*, pg. 4

FIBER ONE—Cereal—General Mills, Inc.; *U.S. Public*, pg. 717

FIBER PLAN—Nutritional Products—Shaklee Corporation; *Int'l*, pg. 1518

FIBER-PLY—Plywood Panels—Georgia-Pacific Corporation; *U.S. Public*, pg. 735

FIBER-SHAKE—Fiber-Cement Siding—GAF Premium Products, Inc.; *U.S. Private*, pg. 433

FIBER-WEB—Industrial Filter—Donaldson Company, Inc.; *U.S. Public*, pg. 517

FIBER-AIRE—Roof Ventilator—Swartwout Industries; *Int'l*, pg. 1398

FIBERAID—NONE—Elkem ASA; *Int'l*, pg. 446

FIBERALL—Laxative—Ciba Specialty Chemicals; *Int'l*, pg. 291

FIBERBOND—Fiber Gypsum Panels—Louisiana Pacific Corporation; *U.S. Public*, pg. 1015

FIBERCON—NONE—American Home Products Corporation; *U.S. Public*, pg. 79

FIBERCON—Supplement—Whitehall-Robins Healthcare; *U.S. Public*, pg. 80

FIBERCOR—Particleboard—Georgia-Pacific Corporation; *U.S. Public*, pg. 735

FIBERESIN—Decorative Laminated Particle Board & Wood Composites—Fiberesin Industries Inc.; *U.S. Private*, pg. 402

FIBERFRAX—Ceramic Fiber—The Carborundum Corporation; *Int'l*, pg. 1173

FIBERGLAS—Glass Fiber Insulation—Owens Corning; *U.S. Public*, pg. 1236

FIBERGLIDE—Self-Lubricating Bearings—Lear Siegler Diversified Holdings Corp.; *U.S. Private*, pg. 655

FIBERGRAFIX—Telecommunications Network Design Software—Lucent Technologies Inc.; *U.S. Public*, pg. 1017

FIBERGUIDE—Management System—ADC Telecommunications, Inc.; *U.S. Public*, pg. 4

FIBERIL—Mfr. of Polishing Pads & Lenses—Freudenberg & Company; *Int'l*, pg. 505

FIBERLEC—Northern Kraft Medium & High Density Electrical Insulation—FiberMark Inc.; *U.S. Public*, pg. 620

FIBERLIFE—NONE—Laserscope Surgical Systems; *U.S. Public*, pg. 979

FIBERLINE—Pulping Systems—Beloit Corporation; *Int'l*, pg. 789

FIBERLINE—Fiber Optics Insulating System—Royle Systems Group; *U.S. Private*, pg. 949

FIBERLOC—Felt—The Felters Company; *U.S. Private*, pg. 400

FIBERLOC—Polyvinyl Chloride Resins—The Geon Company; *U.S. Public*, pg. 733

FIBERLOY—Polymer Base Material & Fiber—Rogers Corporation; *U.S. Public*, pg. 1402

FIBERLUME—Aluminum Coating—Gulf States Asphalt Company, Inc.; *U.S. Private*, pg. 487

FIBEROCK—Paperboard Shipping Baskets—Weyerhaeuser Company; *U.S. Public*, pg. 1764

FIBERONI—High Fiber Pasta—Borden, Inc.; *U.S. Private*, pg. 157

FIBEROPTIC PRODUCT NEWS—New Product Tabloid for Users of Fiberoptic Products, Services & Technology—Reed Elsevier Business Information; *Int'l*, pg. 1095

FIBERPACK—Optical Fiber Splicing Systems—Raychem Corporation; *U.S. Public*, pg. 1362

FIBERPAK—Shipping Drums—Sonoco Products Company; *U.S. Public*, pg. 1485

FIBERSITE—NONE—Gems Sensors; *U.S. Public*, pg. 481

FIBERSOURCE—Tube Feeding—Novartis Nutrition Corporation; *Int'l*, pg. 974

FIBERSTRUCT—Fibrous Enrng. Constructions—American Felt & Filter; *U.S. Private*, pg. 54

FIBERWISE—Flakes of Whole Grain Wheat, Oat Bran & Psyllium Cereal—Kellogg Company; *U.S. Public*, pg. 947

FIBERWOOD—Panel—Weyerhaeuser Forest Products Company; *U.S. Public*, pg. 1764

FIBERWORLD—Multimedia Telecommunications Network—Northern Telecom Limited; *Int'l*, pg. 968

FIBERZYM KIT—Kit for Analysis of Dietary Fiber—Novo Nordisk A/S; *Int'l*, pg. 987

FIBLAST—Trafermin—Scios Inc.; *U.S. Public*, pg. 1444

FIBO—Lightweight Aggregates—Scancem AB; *Int'l*, pg. 1198

FIBR-NOTES—Technical Publication—Buehler, Limited; *U.S. Public*, pg. 574

FIBRA-CEL—Cell Support Matrix—New Brunswick Scientific Co., Inc.; *U.S. Public*, pg. 1169

FIBRAL—Polishing Pads & Lenses—Freudenberg & Company; *Int'l*, pg. 505

FIBRALLOY—NONE—Carpenter Technology Corporation; *U.S. Public*, pg. 307

FIBRATEX—Non Woven—Carborundum Abrasives North America; *Int'l*, pg. 1174

FIBRE GOODNESS—Bread & Rolls—Stroehmann Bakeries, L.C.; *Int'l*, pg. 1495

FIBRE GOODNESS—NONE—Weston Bakeries Limited; *Int'l*, pg. 1494

FIBRE GOODNESS—Baked Goods—George Weston Limited; *Int'l*, pg. 1494

FIBRE NATURALE—Bulk Forming Laxative Tablets—Alva/Amco Pharmacal Companies, Inc.; *U.S. Private*, pg. 47

FIBRE PLUS—Fibreglas Underlay—Domtar Inc.; *Int'l*, pg. 416

FIBRE TRIM—Health Food—Ferrosan International A/S; *Int'l*, pg. 987

FIBRE TRIM—Fiber Product—Novo Nordisk A/S; *Int'l*, pg. 987

FIBREMASTER—Conical Refiner—Harnischfeger Industries, Inc.; *U.S. Public*, pg. 788

FIBRENE—Nonmetallic Material—Webster Industries Inc.; *U.S. Private*, pg. 1157

FIBREPLEX—Bulk Storage Containers—Longview Fibre Company; *U.S. Public*, pg. 1013

FIBRESINOL—Glass Fibres—Raschig GmbH; *U.S. Private*, pg. 827

FIBREX—Nonwoven Nickel Fiber Product—National-Standard Co.; *U.S. Public*, pg. 1160

FIBRICOL—Dressing—Johnson & Johnson Medical, Inc.; *U.S. Public*, pg. 928

FIBRILLA—Hostess Trays—Molded Fiber Glass Companies; *U.S. Private*, pg. 755

FIBRIM—Soy Fiber—Ralston Purina Company; *U.S. Public*, pg. 1359

FIBRINDEX—Reagents—Ortho Clinical Diagnostic Systems Inc.; *U.S. Public*, pg. 929

FIBRLOK—Splicing Trays & Tools—3M; *U.S. Public*, pg. 1604

FIBRMET—Optical Fiber Polisher—Buehler, Limited; *U.S. Public*, pg. 574

FIBRPOL—Optical Fiber Polishing System—Buehler, Limited; *U.S. Public*, pg. 574

FICKS FEATURES—Rattan Furniture—Avon Workshop Ficks Reed; *U.S. Private*, pg. 102

FICOLL—Biotechnology—Pharmacia & Upjohn Adria Laboratories; *Int'l*, pg. 1049

FICOLL-PAQUE—Biotechnology—Pharmacia & Upjohn Adria Laboratories; *Int'l*, pg. 1049

FIDDLE FADDLE—Snack Prod.—Novartis Nutrition Corporation; *Int'l*, pg. 974

FIDDLE STICKS—Scented Water Color Pens—Sanford Corporation; *U.S. Public*, pg. 1178

FIDELIO—Property Managment Systems—Micros Systems Inc.; *U.S. Public*, pg. 1106

FIDELITY—Coal—Freeman Energy Corporation; *U.S. Public*, pg. 709

FIDELO—Telephone—France Telecom; *Int'l*, pg. 503

FIDJI—Perfume—L'Oreal S.A.; *Int'l*, pg. 818

FIDO DIDO—Activewear—Sao Paulo Alpargatas S.A.; *Int'l*, pg. 1193

THE FIELD—Country Pursuits & Property Magazine—IPC Magazines Limited; *Int'l*, pg. 651

FIELD—Draft Controls—Spartan Tool; *U.S. Private*, pg. 860

FIELD & STREAM—Mens Apparel—Gordon & Ferguson of Delaware, Inc.; *U.S. Private*, pg. 465

FIELD ACTIVITY MANAGER—Software—Brock International Inc.; *U.S. Public*, pg. 258

FIELD ACTIVITY MATERIAL MANAGEMENT SYSTEM (FAMMS)—NONE—American Management Systems, Inc.; *U.S. Public*, pg. 86

FIELD & STREAM—Socks—Sara Lee Sock Company; *U.S. Public*, pg. 1434

FIELD & STREAM—Magazine—Times Mirror Magazines, Inc.; *U.S. Public*, pg. 1616

FIELD FLOWERS—Fragrance—Avon Products, Inc.; *U.S. Public*, pg. 155

FIELD FORMULA—Dog Formula—The Jim Dandy Co., Inc.; *Int'l*, pg. 918

FIELD FRESH—NONE—The Andersons Incorporated; *U.S. Public*, pg. 111

FIELD LOK—Gaskets—United States Pipe & Foundry Company, Inc.; *U.S. Public*, pg. 1736

FIELD MASTER—Dog Food—Ralston Purina Company; *U.S. Public*, pg. 1359

FIELD & ROAD—Tires—Bridgestone/Firestone, Inc.; *Int'l*, pg. 213

FIELDBROOK—Vinyl Siding—ABT Building Products Corporation; *Int'l*, pg. 20

FIELDCREST—Milk—Dean Foods Company; *U.S. Public*, pg. 489

FIELDCREST—Domestic Home Furnishings—Fieldcrest/Cannon Bed Fashions Division; *U.S. Public*, pg. 1296

FIELDCREST—Bath & Bed Products—Fieldcrest Cannon, Inc.; *U.S. Public*, pg. 1296

FIELDERS—Bakery Products—Goodman Fielder Limited; *Int'l*, pg. 555

FIELDES—NONE—Quality Bakers Australia Ltd.; *Int'l*, pg. 555

FIELDGATE—Cheese Products—First District Association; *U.S. Private*, pg. 406

FIELDGUARD—Artillery Fire Direction System—Oerlikon-Contraves AG; *Int'l*, pg. 998

FIELDJACK—Training Wear—Mizuno Corporation; *Int'l*, pg. 884

FIELDMASTER—NONE—Sears, Roebuck and Co.; *U.S. Public*, pg. 1452

FIELDS—Commercial Stencil Inlaid Flooring—Mannington Resilient Floors; *U.S. Private*, pg. 700

FIELDSTONE—Cabinetry—Masco Corporation; *U.S. Public*, pg. 1052

FIELDVUE—Instruments—Fisher Controls International, Inc.; *U.S. Public*, pg. 573

FIESTA—Patio Canopy—Anchor Industries Inc.; *U.S. Private*, pg. 71

FIESTA—Mexican-Style Soups—Campbell Soup Company; *U.S. Public*, pg. 298

FIESTA—Awning—Carefree of Colorado; *U.S. Public*, pg. 217

FIESTA—Camera—Eastman Kodak Company; *U.S. Public*, pg. 550

FIESTA—Snack Cakes—Ferrero; *Int'l*, pg. 480

FIESTA—Snack Cakes—Ferrero U.S.A., Inc.; *Int'l*, pg. 480

FIESTA—Chinaware & Stainless Flatware—The Homer Laughlin China Company; *U.S. Private*, pg. 653

FIESTA—Cake—McCain Foods Limited; *Int'l*, pg. 850

FIESTA—Seasoning—McCormick & Company, Incorporated; *U.S. Public*, pg. 1066

FIESTA—Chocolate Candy—RJR Nabisco Holdings Corp.; *U.S. Public*, pg. 1354

FIESTA—Hot Dog Grills, Roll Warmers, Toasters, Cheesemelters, Elec. Conveyer Ovens—Vulcan-Hart Corp.; *U.S. Public*, pg. 1322

FIESTA MART—NONE—Fiesta Mart Inc.; *U.S. Private*, pg. 403

15-15LC—NONE—Carpenter Technology Corporation; *U.S. Public*, pg. 307

FIFTH AVENUE—Women's Fragrance—Avon Products, Inc.; *U.S. Public*, pg. 155

FIFTH AVENUE—Show Cases—Columbus Show Case Company; *U.S. Private*, pg. 257

5TH AVENUE—Candies—Hershey Foods Corporation; *U.S. Public*, pg. 811

5th AVENUE—Candy Bar—Luden's Inc.; *U.S. Public*, pg. 812

FIFTH AVENUE CRYSTAL LTD.—Handmade & Machine-Made Glass & Lead Crystal—Crystal Clear Industries; *U.S. Private*, pg. 293

FIFTH AVENUE PLANK—Laminated 3-5-7" Plank-Beveled—Robbins, Inc.; *U.S. Private*, pg. 934

5TH FLEET—Game—Monarch Avalon, Inc.; *U.S. Public*, pg. 1123

FIFTH QUARTER—Steak House—Shoney's, Inc.; *U.S. Public*, pg. 1467

FIFTH THIRD EQUITY LINE—Personal Line of Credit—Fifth Third Bancorp; *U.S. Public*, pg. 621

THE 5TH VITAL SIGN—NONE—Nellcor Puritan Bennett Incorporated; *U.S. Public*, pg. 1039

THE 5TH VITAL SIGN & HEART DESIGN—NONE—Nellcor Puritan Bennett Incorporated; *U.S. Public*, pg. 1039

5830—Film Image Recorder for Series 4000/5000 Image Controllers—Prepress Solutions, Inc.; *U.S. Private*, pg. 882

5500—Film Image Recorder for Series 4000/5000 Image Controllers—Prepress Solutions, Inc.; *U.S. Private*, pg. 882

5510—Plain-Paper Recorder for Series 4000/5000 or Series 6000—Prepress Solutions, Inc.; *U.S. Private*, pg. 882

5510E—Plain-Paper PostScript Imagesetter—Prepress Solutions, Inc.; *U.S. Private*, pg. 882

5960E—Large-Format Imagesetting System—Prepress Solutions, Inc.; *U.S. Private*, pg. 882

5100—Plain-Paper Recorder for Series 4000/5000 or Series 6000—Prepress Solutions, Inc.; *U.S. Private*, pg. 882

5100E—Plain-Paper PostScript Imagesetter—Prepress Solutions, Inc.; *U.S. Private*, pg. 882

50+ CERAMIC TILE ADHESIVE—Adhesives—Pratt & Lambert United, Inc.; *U.S. Public*, pg. 1466

5700 CALIBRATOR—Electronic Calibration Equipment—Fluke Corporation; *U.S. Public*, pg. 659

57 STREET—Toiletries—Avon Products, Inc.; *U.S. Public*, pg. 155

5630—Film Image Recorder for Series 4000/5000 image Controllers—Prepress Solutions, Inc.; *U.S. Private*, pg. 882

5060W—Plain-Paper Recorder for Series 4000/5000 or Series 6000—Prepress Solutions, Inc.; *U.S. Private*, pg. 882

5300B—Film Image Recorder for Series 3000 Software RIP—Prepress Solutions, Inc.; *U.S. Private*, pg. 882

5300E—Film Image Recorder for Series 4000/5000 Image Controllers—Prepress Solutions, Inc.; *U.S. Private*, pg. 882

5287—NONE—Eastman Kodak Company; *U.S. Public*, pg. 550

FIGARO—Pet Food—Bumble Bee Seafoods Inc.; *U.S. Private*, pg. 282

FIGARO—Liquid Barbecue Smoke—The Figaro Company, Inc.; *U.S. Private*, pg. 404

FIGGIE—NONE—Figgie International Inc.; *U.S. Public*, pg. 622

FIGGIE PROPERTIES—NONE—Figgie International Inc.; *U.S. Public*, pg. 622

FIGURINES & COLLECTIBLES—NONE—Cowles Enthusiast Media, Inc.; *U.S. Public*, pg. 281

FIKE—Fire Protection Systems—Fike Corporation; *U.S. Private*, pg. 404

FILA—NONE—Fila Sport S.p.A.; *Int'l*, pg. 484

FILA—Shoes—Fila USA; *Int'l*, pg. 484

FILA FITNESS—Beauty Products—Charles of the Ritz Group Ltd.; *U.S. Private*, pg. 689

FILARC—Welding Electrodes—Esab AB; *Int'l*, pg. 281

FILARE—Writing, Text & Cover Paper—Fox River Paper Company; *U.S. Private*, pg. 422

FILARIBITS—Diethylcarbamazine—Pfizer Inc.; *U.S. Public*, pg. 1281

FILARIBITS—Heartworm & Intestinal Worm Control Medicine for Dogs—SmithKline Beecham Corporation; *Int'l*, pg. 1264

FILARIBITS—Animal Parasiticide—SmithKline Beecham plc; *Int'l*, pg. 1264

FILE-AID—Systems Software Products—Compuware Corporation; *U.S. Public*, pg. 423

FILE SEARCH—Document Management Products—Bell & Howell Holdings; *U.S. Public*, pg. 201

FILE SECURE—Software—Exabyte Corporation; *U.S. Public*, pg. 597

FILE TRACKER—Barcode Systems—Tab Products Co.; *U.S. Public*, pg. 1559

FILEMAKER PRO—Computer Software—Claris Corporation; *U.S. Public*, pg. 121

FILEMASTER—Document Management Products—Bell & Howell Holdings; *U.S. Public*, pg. 201

FILENE'S—Department Stores—The May Department Stores Company; *U.S. Public*, pg. 1063

FILENET—NONE—FileNet Corporation; *U.S. Public*, pg. 622

FILET-O-FISH—Sandwich—McDonald's Corporation; *U.S. Public*, pg. 1068

FILEX—Filing Cabinets & Desks—Martin Industries, Inc. (AL); *U.S. Private*, pg. 709

FILING ASSISTANCE—Business Product—International Business Machines Corporation; *U.S. Public*, pg. 895

FILKO—Automotive Products—Standard Motor Products Inc.; *U.S. Public*, pg. 1503

FILKO AUTOMOTIVE PRODUCTS—NONE—F&B Manufacturing Co.; *U.S. Private*, pg. 388

FILKO/COBRA, INC.—NONE—F&B Manufacturing Co.; *U.S. Private*, pg. 388

FILL-MAG—Magnetic Flowmeter—Bailey, Fischer & Porter Company; *Int'l*, pg. 449

FILL-RITE—Pumps—Tuthill Corporation; *U.S. Private*, pg. 1110

FILL-RITE—Electric Gas Pumps—Tuthill Pump; *U.S. Private*, pg. 1111

FILLE D'EVE—Women's Fragrance—Accecones Ricci U.S.A., Inc.; *Int'l*, pg. 445

FILLER—Potato Chips—Borden, Inc.; *U.S. Private*, pg. 157

FILLERUP—Automotive Body Filler—PPG Industries, Inc.; *U.S. Public*, pg. 1245

FILLES D'AUJOURD'HUI—Magazine—Quebecor Inc.; *Int'l*, pg. 1075

FILM/FLASH—Newsletter—Eastman Kodak Company; *U.S. Public*, pg. 550

FILM FONTS—2" Film Alphabets—Castcraft Industries, Inc.; *U.S. Private*, pg. 219

FILM FYTER—Windshield Towels—Bay West Paper Corp. Towel & Tissue Div.; *U.S. Public*, pg. 1747

THE FILM IN THE FAMILIAR YELLOW BOX—Photographic film—Eastman Kodak Company; *U.S. Public*, pg. 550

THE FILM THAT'S A CAMERA—Photo Film/Camera Combination—Eastman Kodak Company; *U.S. Public*, pg. 550

FILMATIC—X-Ray Film Processors—Varian Associates, Inc.; *U.S. Public*, pg. 1710

FILMCELL—Wood Pulp—Avenor, Inc.; *Int'l*, pg. 101

FILMCORE—NONE—H.C. Miller Company; *U.S. Private*, pg. 747

FILMEX—Alcohol Solvents—Millennium Petrochemicals, Inc.; *Int'l*, pg. 594

FILMEX—Tuber, Cast Film Line—Windmoeller & Hoelscher; *Int'l*, pg. 1510

FILMTEC—Membranes & Membrane Modules—The Dow Chemical Company; *U.S. Public*, pg. 522

FILODORO—Hosiery—Sara Lee Corporation; *U.S. Public*, pg. 1432

FILPAC—Flexible Packaging Materials—Filpac, Inc.; *Int'l*, pg. 233

FILQUIK—Centrifugal Thrower—Svedala Bulk Materials Handling Engineered Products; *Int'l*, pg. 1326

FILTER-COUNT—Pseudocumene-Based Cocktail—Packard Instrument Co., Inc.; *U.S. Private,* pg. 833

FILTER DRYER—NONE—Bird Machine Company; *U.S. Public,* pg. 166

FILTER-FLO—Laundry Washing Machinery—General Electric Canada Inc.; *U.S. Public,* pg. 713

FILTER-MEDIA—Air Pollution Control Equipment & Systems—Hosokawa Micron International Inc.; *Int'l,* pg. 635

FILTER PLUS—Filters—Pall Corporation; *U.S. Public,* pg. 1253

FILTER QUEEN—Vacuum Cleaners—HMI Industries; *U.S. Public,* pg. 771

FILTER-SEP—Filter Vessel—Perry Equipment Corporation; *U.S. Private,* pg. 855

FILTER TEX—Filtration Cartiges Used in Filter Vessels—Perry Equipment Corporation; *U.S. Private,* pg. 855

FILTERAY—UV Absorbing Clear Coats—Day-Glo Color Corp.; *U.S. Public,* pg. 1357

FILTERMATE—NONE—Blyth Industries; *U.S. Public,* pg. 239

FILTERMATIC MAKER—Cigarette Rolling Tobacco—Consolidated Cigar Corporation; *U.S. Private,* pg. 690

FILTERMATIC SUPPLIES—Cigarette Rolling Tobacco—Consolidated Cigar Corporation; *U.S. Private,* pg. 690

FILTERSPUN ACCUWOUND—Wound Filter Media—Serfilco, Ltd.; *U.S. Private,* pg. 985

FILTERTEK—Filters—Filtertek Inc.; *U.S. Public,* pg. 546

FILTERVENT—NONE—Air Vent Inc.; *Int'l,* pg. 1170

FILTERVENT—Ridge Vent—CertainTeed Corporation; *Int'l,* pg. 1170

FILTERWELD—Welding Protection—Aearo Company; *U.S. Public,* pg. 23

FILTEX—Industrial Filter Bags—Hosokawa Micron International Inc.; *Int'l,* pg. 635

FILTRAN—Automotive Transmission Filter—SPX Corporation; *U.S. Public,* pg. 1420

FILTRASE—Bacterial Glucanase for Beer Filtration—Royal Gist-Brocades N.V.; *Int'l,* pg. 1142

FILTRATOR—Filtration Device—Fisher Scientific Company; *U.S. Private,* pg. 658

FILTRENE—Industrial Products—Email Limited; *Int'l,* pg. 450

FILTRESSE—Surgical Smoker Handler & Filter—Utah Medical Products, Inc.; *U.S. Public,* pg. 1700

FILTRETE—Filter Media—3M; *U.S. Public,* pg. 1604

FILTREX—Disposable Semipermeable Membrane Filter—Millipore Corporation; *U.S. Public,* pg. 1112

FILTROBA—NONE—Bird Machine Company; *U.S. Public,* pg. 166

FILTRON—Interference Filters—Del Global Technologies; *U.S. Public,* pg. 493

FILTRON—Surgical Mask—3M; *U.S. Public,* pg. 1604

FILTRONA—Cigarette Filters—Filtrona Richmond Company; *Int'l,* pg. 232

FILTROROLL—Industrial Products—Email Limited; *Int'l,* pg. 450

FILTROS—Silica Porous Ceramic Shapes—Ferro Corporation; *U.S. Public,* pg. 618

FILTROS 35—Electrolytic Diaphragms—Ferro Corporation; *U.S. Public,* pg. 618

FILTRUBA—Centrifuges—Ketema, Inc.; *U.S. Private,* pg. 604

FILUMA—Garage Doors—Wayne Dalton of Sterling; *U.S. Private,* pg. 1155

FIN-FAN—Heat Exchangers—McDermott International, Inc.; *U.S. Public,* pg. 1067

FIN-FLITE—Heat Exchangers—Svedala Pumps & Process; *Int'l,* pg. 1325

FINA—Petroleum Products, Petrochemicals & Plastics—Fina, Inc.; *Int'l,* pg. 1044

FINA—Oil Prods., Chemicals, Lubricants & Specialties—Petrofina S.A.; *Int'l,* pg. 1043

FINACILLIN—Antibiotic—SmithKline Beecham plc; *Int'l,* pg. 1264

FINAL NET—Hair Spray—Bristol-Myers Squibb Company; *U.S. Public,* pg. 253

FINAL NET—Hair Spray—Clairol, Inc.; *U.S. Public,* pg. 254

FINAL ONE—Solution Used in Conjunction with a Permanent Wave Product—Revlon-Realistic Professional Products, Inc.; *U.S. Private,* pg. 690

FINAL SHINE—Hair Spray—Clairol, Inc.; *U.S. Public,* pg. 254

FINAL TOUCH—Dryer Sheets—Lever Brothers Co.; *Int'l,* pg. 1435

FINAL TOUCH—Aluminum Skirting for Mobile Homes—Reynolds Metals Company; *U.S. Public,* pg. 1385

FINALE—Specialty Chemical—AgrEvo USA Company; *Int'l,* pg. 1253

FINALE—Hair Spray—Bristol-Myers Squibb Company; *U.S. Public,* pg. 253

FINALIST—Sporting Goods—Brunswick Bowling & Billiards Corp.; *U.S. Public,* pg. 265

FINALS—Competetive Swimwear—The Finals, Inc.; *U.S. Private,* pg. 404

FINANCIAL APPLICATION ARCHITECTURE—Computer System—International Business Machines Corporation; *U.S. Public,* pg. 895

FINANCIAL COLLECTION AGENCIES-FCA—NONE—FCA International Ltd.; *Int'l,* pg. 470

FINANCIAL CORPORATION—NONE—Pacific Century Financial Corporation; *U.S. Public,* pg. 1248

FINANCIAL MANAGER—Software Program—Barrister Information Systems Corporation; *U.S. Public,* pg. 192

FINANCIAL TIMES—Newspaper—The Financial Times Ltd.; *Int'l,* pg. 1025

FINANCIAL TIMES—Newspapers—Pearson plc; *Int'l,* pg. 1025

FINANCIAL TRADER—Magazine—Miller Freeman Inc.; *Int'l,* pg. 1443

FINANCIAL WORLD—Publication—Financial World Partners; *U.S. Private,* pg. 404

FINAST—Food Stores—FINAST; *Int'l,* pg. 750

FINCH—Paper—Finch, Pruyn & Co., Inc.; *U.S. Private,* pg. 405

FINCOR—NONE—Boston Gear; *U.S. Public,* pg. 857

FINCOR—Adjustable Speed Drives—IMO Industries Inc.; *U.S. Public,* pg. 856

FINDLATERS—Scotch—Marie Brizard Wines & Spirits USA; *U.S. Private,* pg. 702

FINDLATERS 12 YEAR OLD—Scotch—Marie Brizard Wines & Spirits USA; *U.S. Private,* pg. 702

FINDUS—Frozen Foods—Nestle S.A.; *Int'l,* pg. 915

FINE BOUCHE—Cheese—BG SAS; *Int'l,* pg. 201

FINE BOUCHE—Low - Fat Cheese—Bongrain S.A.; *Int'l,* pg. 201

FINE CUISINE—Frozen Dinners—Nestle S.A.; *Int'l,* pg. 915

FINE/LINE—Hydronic Baseboard—Slant/Fin Corporation; *U.S. Public,* pg. 1005

FINE-RITER—Writing Instruments—Union Pen Company; *U.S. Private,* pg. 1119

FINE WOOD—Floor Care—S.C. Johnson & Son, Inc.; *U.S. Private,* pg. 592

FINEFLUTE—High Quality Lithography Laminated to Single-Face Corrugated—F.N. Burt Company, Inc.; *U.S. Private,* pg. 188

FINELINE STEEL—Process for Producing Clean, Low Sulfur, Shape-Controlled Plate Steels—Lukens Steel Company; *U.S. Public,* pg. 1020

FINELON—Yarn—Lion Brand Yarn Co.; *U.S. Private,* pg. 669

FINEPAK—Fast Food Containers—Carter Holt Harvey Limited; *U.S. Public,* pg. 904

FINERY BY FREEMAN—Men's Apparel—H. Freeman & Son, Inc.; *U.S. Private,* pg. 426

FINES FACE—Particle Board—Georgia-Pacific Corporation; *U.S. Public,* pg. 735

FINESCALE—Magazine—Kalmbach Publishing Co.; *U.S. Private,* pg. 606

FINESSE—Rangehoods—Broan Mfg. Co., Inc.; *U.S. Public,* pg. 1193

FINESSE—Broadloom—Couristan Inc.; *U.S. Private,* pg. 279

FINESSE—Hair Care Line—Helene Curtis Industries, Inc.; *U.S. Public,* pg. 1434

FIN'ESSE—Vascular Graft—Meadox Medicals, Inc.; *U.S. Public,* pg. 247

FINESSE—Electrosurgical Generator With Integrated Smoke Evacuator—Utah Medical Products, Inc.; *U.S. Public,* pg. 1700

FINESSE-IT—Automotive Paint Repair System—3M; *U.S. Public,* pg. 1604

FINEST—Food—Faribault Foods Inc.; *U.S. Private,* pg. 393

THE FINEST GIFT—Nuts—John B. Sanfilippo & Son, Inc.; *U.S. Public,* pg. 1431

FINEST IN THE FIELD—Athletic Equipment & Sporting Goods—Rawlings Sporting Goods Company; *U.S. Public,* pg. 1361

FINESTONE—Synthetic Building Coatings—K2 Inc.; *U.S. Public,* pg. 940

FINESTRA—Side Chair—Vecta; *U.S. Private,* pg. 1038

FINGER PINKIES—Hand Cleaners—The Gillette Company; *U.S. Public,* pg. 743

FINI—Fresh Pasta & Cold Cuts—Philip Morris Companies Inc.; *U.S. Public,* pg. 1287

FINISH—Automatic Dishwashing Detergent—Benckiser Consumer Products Inc.; *Int'l,* pg. 185

FINISH LINE—Toiletries—Avon Products, Inc.; *U.S. Public,* pg. 155

FINISH/THOMPSON—Pumps—Ryan Herco Products Corp.; *U.S. Private,* pg. 953

FINISH 2001—Car Wax—Turtle Wax, Inc.; *U.S. Private,* pg. 1110

FINISHED TOUCH—Vinyl Mounting Blocks & Vents—ABT Building Products Corporation; *Int'l,* pg. 20

FINISHEEN—Conditioner & Sheen Spray—Revlon-Realistic Professional Products, Inc.; *U.S. Private,* pg. 690

FINISHLINE—Doors—John S. Frey Enterprises; *U.S. Private,* pg. 687

FINK—NONE—Urban Outfitters, Inc.; *U.S. Public,* pg. 1700

FINLANDIA VODKA—Vodka—Heublein Inc.; *Int'l,* pg. 410

FINLANDIA VODKAS—Vodka—Brown-Forman Beverages Worldwide; *U.S. Public,* pg. 261

FINLEY—Coffee—Superior Coffee and Foods; *U.S. Public,* pg. 1434

FINNAIR—Air Line—FINNAIR; *Int'l,* pg. 485

FINNALINE—Pigmented Powdered Leather Finish Concentrate—Henkel Corporation; *Int'l,* pg. 610

FINNCRISP—Thin Crackerbread—Cultor Ltd.; *Int'l,* pg. 349

FINNIGAN MAT—Mass Spectrometer Products—Finnigan Corporation; *U.S. Public,* pg. 1591

FINNSTIM—Bioproduct for Fish Feed—Cultor Ltd.; *Int'l,* pg. 349

FINO II (P-1)—Interfacings—Specialty Textile Products; *U.S. Private,* pg. 1023

FINOVA—NONE—The FINOVA Group Inc.; *U.S. Public,* pg. 624

FINOVA FINANCIAL INNOVATORS—Money Lender—The FINOVA Group Inc.; *U.S. Public,* pg. 624

FINSEAL—Seal-Weatherstripping With 'Hi-Fin+—Schlegel Corporation; *Int'l,* pg. 128

FINSOLU—Benzoic Ester—Witco Corporation; *U.S. Public,* pg. 1773

FINYL BOND—NONE—TEC Incorporated; *U.S. Public,* pg. 687

FIOR DI VITE—Aperitif—Groupe Pernod Ricard; *Int'l,* pg. 566

FIORICET—Relief of Symptom of Tension Headache—Sandoz Pharmaceuticals Corp.; *Int'l,* pg. 974

FIORINAL—Pharmaceutical—Novartis AG; *Int'l,* pg. 971

FIORINAL C11—Relief of Symptom of Tension Headache—Sandoz Pharmaceuticals Corp.; *Int'l,* pg. 974

FIRCRAFT—Industrial Quality Particleboard—Willamette Industries, Inc.; *U.S. Public,* pg. 1769

FIRE—Fragrance—Jean Philippe Fragrances, Inc.; *U.S. Public,* pg. 924

FIRE & ICE 2000—Motor Oil—Shell Oil Company; *Int'l,* pg. 1136

FIRE-BALL—Pumps—Graco Inc.; *U.S. Public,* pg. 756

FIRE CHIEF—Fire Doors—Clark Door Co., Inc.; *U.S. Private,* pg. 242

FIRE CHIEF—Publication for Fire Personnel—Intertec Publishing; *U.S. Public,* pg. 1327

FIRE FIGHTERS—Self-Extinguishing Waste Receptacles—United Receptical, Inc.; *U.S. Private,* pg. 1123

FIRE-FILE—Insulated Files—Knoll, Inc.; *U.S. Private,* pg. 627

FIRE-GLASS III—Shingles—Johns Manville Corporation; *U.S. Public*, pg. 927

FIRE-GUARD—Doors—Morgan Products Ltd.; *U.S. Public*, pg. 1132

FIRE GUARD—Protective Equip.—Schwab Corp.; *U.S. Private*, pg. 974

FIRE LITE—Alarms—Fire Lite Alarms, Inc./Notifier Co.; *U.S. Public*, pg. 1306

FIRE-LITE—Commercial Fire Alarm Systems—Pittway Corporation; *U.S. Public*, pg. 1305

FIRE-LITE—Pavement Markers—Thomas & Betts/Amerace; *U.S. Public*, pg. 1598

FIRE MAN—Fire Doors—Clark Door Co., Inc.; *U.S. Private*, pg. 242

FIRE ORANGE—Fluorescent Color—Day-Glo Color Corp.; *U.S. Public*, pg. 1357

FIRE PLEX—Fire Alarm System—Rauland-Borg Corporation; *U.S. Private*, pg. 911

FIRE RIBBON—Fire Starter—Mautz Paint Co.; *U.S. Private*, pg. 715

FIRE-SEAL—Smoke/Fire Stop Fitting for Donduit/Cable—O-Z/Gedney Co.; *U.S. Public*, pg. 727

FIRE-TROL—Fire Retardant Chemicals—Erly Industries, Inc.; *U.S. Public*, pg. 591

FIRE WATCH—Product Series—Faraday, Inc.; *Int'l*, pg. 1246

FIRE WATER SCHNAPPS—Liqueur—White Rock Distilleries Inc.; *U.S. Private*, pg. 1173

FIREBALL—Sporting Goods—Brunswick Bowling & Billiards Corp.; *U.S. Public*, pg. 265

FIREBALL—Electrical Revolving Light—Federal Signal Corporation; *U.S. Public*, pg. 616

FIREBALL—Liqueur—Marie Brizard Wines & Spirits USA; *U.S. Private*, pg. 702

FIREBALL—Valve Series 727—Victaulic Company of America; *U.S. Private*, pg. 1138

FIREBAN—NONE—Uniroyal Chemical Company, Inc.; *U.S. Public*, pg. 460

FIREBAR—Electric Heating Element, Tubular—Watlow Electric Manufacturing Company; *U.S. Private*, pg. 1153

FIREBERD—NONE—Dynatech Corporation; *U.S. Public*, pg. 539

FIREBIRD—Car—Pontiac-GMC Division; *U.S. Public*, pg. 720

FIREBRAKE ZB—NONE—U.S. Borax Inc.; *Int'l*, pg. 1119

FIRECHIEF—Matches—Diamond Brands, Inc.; *U.S. Private*, pg. 330

FIRECHIEF—Monthly Publication—Intertec Publishing; *U.S. Public*, pg. 1328

FIREDAM—Endothermic Fire Protection Caulk—3M; *U.S. Public*, pg. 1604

FIREDEX—Fire Detection Equipment—JSB Electrical PLC; *Int'l*, pg. 453

FIREDOME—Fire Helmuts—E.D. Bullard Company; *U.S. Private*, pg. 180

FIREFLY—Illuminated Reader & Illuminated Opera Glass—Swift Instruments, Inc.; *U.S. Private*, pg. 1058

FIREGARD—Rolling Fire Door—Cornell Iron Works, Inc.; *U.S. Private*, pg. 276

FIREGUARD—Technical Papers—MACtac Scranton Facility; *U.S. Public*, pg. 210

FIREGUARD—Fire Retardant Fabrics—Springs Industries, Inc.; *U.S. Public*, pg. 1499

FIREHAWK—Tires—Bridgestone/Firestone, Inc.; *Int'l*, pg. 213

FIREHAWK FTX—Tires—Bridgestone/Firestone, Inc.; *Int'l*, pg. 213

FIREHAWK GT—Tires—Bridgestone/Firestone, Inc.; *Int'l*, pg. 213

FIREHAWK GTA—Tires—Bridgestone/Firestone, Inc.; *Int'l*, pg. 213

FIREHAWK GTX—Tires—Bridgestone/Firestone, Inc.; *Int'l*, pg. 213

FIREHAWK LH—Tires—Bridgestone/Firestone, Inc.; *Int'l*, pg. 213

FIREHAWK SS—Tires—Bridgestone/Firestone, Inc.; *Int'l*, pg. 213

FIREHAWK SVX—Tires—Bridgestone/Firestone, Inc.; *Int'l*, pg. 213

FIREHAWK SZ—Tires—Bridgestone/Firestone, Inc.; *Int'l*, pg. 213

FIREHAWK 670—Tires—Bridgestone/Firestone, Inc.; *Int'l*, pg. 213

FIREHAWK 660—Tires—Bridgestone/Firestone, Inc.; *Int'l*, pg. 213

FIREHAWK SV—Tires—Bridgestone/Firestone, Inc.; *Int'l*, pg. 213

FIREKING—NONE—Fire King International, Inc.; *U.S. Private*, pg. 406

FIREKING III—Shingles—Johns Manville Corporation; *U.S. Public*, pg. 927

FIRELAKE—Aluminum Flake Powder—United States Bronze Powders, Inc.; *U.S. Private*, pg. 1124

FIRELARM—Fire Alarm Control Panel—Federal Signal Corporation, Signal Div.; *U.S. Public*, pg. 616

FIRELIGHT—Interior Wall Paneling—Georgia-Pacific Corporation; *U.S. Public*, pg. 735

FIRELITE—Fireplace—HON Industries Inc.; *U.S. Public*, pg. 772

FIRELOCK—Rigid Fire Protection Coupling—Victaulic Company of America; *U.S. Private*, pg. 1138

FIREMASTER 642—Flame Regardants—Great Lakes Chemical Corporation; *U.S. Public*, pg. 760

FIREPAC 360—Fire Detector—Kidde-Fenwal, Inc.; *Int'l*, pg. 1500

FIREPLI—Flame Retardant Paper—The Mead Corporation; *U.S. Public*, pg. 1074

FIREPLUG—Candy—Fleer-Skybox International Inc.; *U.S. Public*, pg. 1052

FIREPOWER—War Game—Monarch Avalon, Inc.; *U.S. Public*, pg. 1123

FIREROD—Electrical Heating Elements, Cartridge, H-T—Watlow Electric Manufacturing Company; *U.S. Private*, pg. 1153

FIRESHIELD—Insulated Files—The HON Co.; *U.S. Public*, pg. 772

FIRESIDE—Paperback Books—Simon & Schuster; *U.S. Public*, pg. 777

FIRESIDE BY PETERSON—Smoking Accessories—Consolidated Cigar Corporation; *U.S. Private*, pg. 690

FIRESTART—Processed Firestarter—Duraflame, Inc.; *U.S. Private*, pg. 348

FIRESTONE—Tires—Bridgestone/Firestone Inc. Retail Operations; *Int'l*, pg. 213

FIRESTONE—Automotive, Rubber, Roofing Products & Services, Car Rental Services—Bridgestone/Firestone, Inc.; *Int'l*, pg. 213

FIRESTONE CHAMPION—Tires—Bridgestone/Firestone, Inc.; *Int'l*, pg. 213

FIRESTONE FRIGITONE—Antifreeze—Bridgestone/Firestone, Inc.; *Int'l*, pg. 213

FIRESTONE SUPREME—Batteries—Bridgestone/Firestone, Inc.; *Int'l*, pg. 213

FIRESTONE TRANSPORT—Tires—Bridgestone/Firestone, Inc.; *Int'l*, pg. 213

FIRESTOP—Plasterboard—Georgia-Pacific Corporation; *U.S. Public*, pg. 735

FIRETECH 2000—NONE—Temtex Industries Inc.; *U.S. Public*, pg. 1575

FIRETEST—Fire-rated Paneling—Marlite; *U.S. Private*, pg. 705

FIRETRAC—NONE—Del Mar Avionics; *U.S. Private*, pg. 321

FIREWALL-1—NONE—Check Point Software Technologies Ltd.; *U.S. Public*, pg. 342

FIREWALL 111—Power & Control Cable—Rockbestos-Suprenant Cable Corp.; *U.S. Private*, pg. 938

FIREWORKS—Jewelry Collection—Tiffany & Co.; *U.S. Public*, pg. 1608

THE FIREWORKS FACTORY—Restaurant—The Levy Organization; *U.S. Private*, pg. 664

FIREZONE R—Appendix R Nuclear Cable—Rockbestos-Suprenant Cable Corp.; *U.S. Private*, pg. 938

FIRLOK—Particleboard Underlayment—Willamette Industries, Inc.; *U.S. Public*, pg. 1769

FIRM-O-PEDIC—Mattress & Box Spring Sets—Kingsdown, Inc.; *U.S. Private*, pg. 622

FIRMA-RAIL—Plastics—Joseph T. Ryerson & Son, Inc.; *U.S. Public*, pg. 879

FIRMALINE—Plastics—Joseph T. Ryerson & Son, Inc.; *U.S. Public*, pg. 879

FIRMENICH—Fragrances—Firmenich Incorporated; *Int'l*, pg. 486

FIRMS—Electronic Component—Teradyne, Inc.; *U.S. Public*, pg. 1580

FIROMATIC—Valves & Security Prods.—Highfield Manufacturing Co.; *Int'l*, pg. 127

FIRST—Women's Fragrance—Sanofi Beaute, Inc.; *Int'l*, pg. 445

FIRST ALERT—NONE—First Alert, Inc.; *U.S. Private*, pg. 406

FIRST ALERT—Exercises for Success in School Testing—Houghton Mifflin Company; *U.S. Public*, pg. 841

FIRST ALERT PROFESSIONAL—Security Systems—Pittway Corporation; *U.S. Public*, pg. 1305

FIRST AMERICAN APPRAISAL SERVICES—NONE—The First American Financial Corporation; *U.S. Public*, pg. 624

FIRST AMERICAN CREDCO—Credit Reporting—The First American Financial Corporation; *U.S. Public*, pg. 624

FIRST AMERICAN EQUITY LOAN SERVICES—NONE—The First American Financial Corporation; *U.S. Public*, pg. 624

FIRST AMERICAN FIELD SERVICES—NONE—The First American Financial Corporation; *U.S. Public*, pg. 624

FIRST AMERICAN FLOOD DATA SERVICES—Flood Compliance Services—The First American Financial Corporation; *U.S. Public*, pg. 624

FIRST AMERICAN HOME BUYERS PROTECTION—Home Warranties for Re-Sale Homes—The First American Financial Corporation; *U.S. Public*, pg. 624

FIRST AMERICAN REAL ESTATE TAX SERVICE—Tax Reporting, Certification, Outsourcing—The First American Financial Corporation; *U.S. Public*, pg. 624

FIRST AMERICAN TITLE—Title Insurance—The First American Financial Corporation; *U.S. Public*, pg. 624

FIRST AMERICAN TRUST—Trust Services—The First American Financial Corporation; *U.S. Public*, pg. 624

FIRST BUSINESS—TV Daily Business News Program—Nation's Business; *U.S. Private*, pg. 788

FIRST CARD—Credit Card—Svenska Handelsbanken; *Int'l*, pg. 1327

FIRST CHOICE—U.K.—CLT-UFA; *Int'l*, pg. 561

FIRST CHOICE—Metal Building Materials, Paper Goods & Clothing—Weyerhaeuser Company; *U.S. Public*, pg. 1764

FIRST COAT—Primer Paint—USG Corporation; *U.S. Public*, pg. 1660

FIRST DATABANK—Pharmaceutical Data—The Hearst Corporation; *U.S. Private*, pg. 515

FIRST DATABANK BLUE BOOK—Book—The Hearst Corporation; *U.S. Private*, pg. 515

FIRST EVER—Graduation Gowns for Kindergarten Children—E.R. Moore Co.; *U.S. Private*, pg. 759

FIRST FAILURE SUPPORT TECHNOLOGY—Computer System—International Business Machines Corporation; *U.S. Public*, pg. 895

FIRST FAILURE SUPPORT TECHNOLOGY/400—Computer System—International Business Machines Corporation; *U.S. Public*, pg. 895

FIRST FAILURE SUPPORT TECHNOLOGY/MVS—Computer System—International Business Machines Corporation; *U.S. Public*, pg. 895

FIRST FAILURE SUPPORT TECHNOLOGY/3990—Computer System—International Business Machines Corporation; *U.S. Public*, pg. 895

FIRST FAILURE SUPPORT TECHNOLOGY/2—Computer System—International Business Machines Corporation; *U.S. Public*, pg. 895

FIRST FEDERAL SAVINGS & LOAN ASSOC. OF ROCHESTER—Financial Institution—Imasco Limited; *Int'l*, pg. 112

FIRST FLIGHT—Golf Equipment—The Arnold Palmer Golf Company; *U.S. Public*, pg. 132

1ST FOODS—Baby Fruits, Vegetables, Cereals & Juices—Gerber Products Company; *Int'l*, pg. 973

FIRST FORM—Concrete Forming Panels—Weyerhaeuser Forest Products Company; *U.S. Public*, pg. 1764

FIRST FUTURES—NONE—SunGard Data Systems Inc.; *U.S. Public*, pg. 1534

FIRST GAMES—Pre-School Games—Colorforms; *U.S. Public*, pg. 1625

FIRST GEAR—Stationery Products, Portfolios & Backpacks—The Mead Corporation; *U.S. Public*, pg. 1074

FIRST INTERSTATE BANK OF CALIFORNIA—Bank—First Interstate Bank of California; *U.S. Public*, pg. 1753

FIRST INTERSTATE BANK OF OREGON—Bank—First Interstate Bank of Oregon, N.A.; *U.S. Public*, pg. 1753

FIRST INTERSTATE BANK OF WASHINGTON—Bank—First Interstate Bank of Washington, N.A.; *U.S. Public*, pg. 1753

FIRST LADY—Beauty Salon & Barber Shop Furniture—Belvedere Company; *U.S. Private*, pg. 1008

FIRST LIGHT—News Program—Westwood One, Inc.; *U.S. Public*, pg. 1763

FIRST MATE—Disinfectant Cleaner—Stanhome Inc.; *U.S. Public*, pg. 1508

FIRST MATE CONCENTRATE—Cleaner—Stanhome Inc.; *U.S. Public*, pg. 1508

FIRST PERSON SINGULAR—NONE—Lands' End, Inc.; *U.S. Public*, pg. 977

FIRST PRIZE—Foods—Ventura Foods; *U.S. Private*, pg. 508

FIRST PROTECTIVE INSURANCE GROUP—Insurance Company—Protective Life Corporation; *U.S. Public*, pg. 1336

FIRST PUZZLES—Pre-School Puzzles—Colorforms; *U.S. Public*, pg. 1625

FIRST RATE—Flow Totalizer—ITT Barton Instruments; *U.S. Public*, pg. 860

FIRST RESPONSE—Home Pregnancy Kit—Carter Products, Canada; *U.S. Public*, pg. 310

FIRST RESPONSE—Pregnancy & Ovulation Test Kits—Carter-Wallace, Inc.; *U.S. Public*, pg. 309

FIRST ROAD—Simulation System—MTS Systems Corporation; *U.S. Public*, pg. 1028

FIRST STEP—NONE—Howmedica, Inc.; *U.S. Public*, pg. 1282

FIRST TEMP GENIUS—Tympanic & Filac Predictive Thermometers—American Home Products Corporation; *U.S. Public*, pg. 79

FIRST TENNESSEE—Bank Holding Company—First Tennessee National Corporation; *U.S. Public*, pg. 638

FIRST-TIME-RIGHT—Prototype, Design—LSI Logic Corp.; *U.S. Public*, pg. 971

FIRST TOUCH—Static Control Pad/Mat—3M; *U.S. Public*, pg. 1604

THE FIRST YEARS—Childrens Products—The First Years Inc.; *U.S. Public*, pg. 642

FIRSTEEL—Steel Strip—Lonrho plc; *Int'l*, pg. 817

FIRSTELLER—ATM Services—Pacific Capital Bancorp; *U.S. Public*, pg. 1247

FIRTH CLEVELAND—NONE—Glynwed International PLC; *Int'l*, pg. 554

FISAN—Cleaning Prods. For Food Indus.—Oakite Products, Inc.; *Int'l*, pg. 861

FISCHBEIN—Bag Closing Equipment—AXIA Incorporated; *U.S. Private*, pg. 103

FISCHER—Beer—Heineken N.V.; *Int'l*, pg. 608

FISERV—Financial Data Service—Fiserv, Inc.; *U.S. Public*, pg. 647

FISH HAB—Artificial Habitat—Outdoor Technologies Group; *U.S. Private*, pg. 822

FISH'N HATCH—Coolers—The Canadian Coleman Co., Ltd.; *U.S. Private*, pg. 691

FISH-N-TACKLE—Coolers—The Canadian Coleman Co., Ltd.; *U.S. Private*, pg. 691

FISHAMAJIG—Fish Sandwich—Friendly Ice Cream Corp.; *U.S. Public*, pg. 682

FISHER—Control Valves, Process Instrumentation—Associated Process Controls; *U.S. Private*, pg. 92

FISHER—Cheese Substitute Products—Borden, Inc.; *U.S. Private*, pg. 157

FISHER—Various Special Machines including Injected Metal—Fisher Gauge Limited; *Int'l*, pg. 491

FISHER—Scientific Products—Fisher Scientific International; *U.S. Private*, pg. 658

FISHER—Skylights—Fisher Skylights, Inc.; *U.S. Private*, pg. 408

FISHER—Materials Handling Equip.—NVF Company; *U.S. Private*, pg. 772

FISHER—Nuts—The Procter & Gamble Company; *U.S. Public*, pg. 1330

FISHER—NONE—John B. Sanfilippo & Son, Inc.; *U.S. Public*, pg. 1431

FISHER—Audio Systems—Sanyo Electric Co., Ltd.; *Int'l*, pg. 1190

FISHER—NONE—Sanyo Espana S.A.; *Int'l*, pg. 1192

FISHER—Portable Audio, Televisions, Video Cassette Recorders—Sanyo Fisher Company; *Int'l*, pg. 1191

FISHER BOY—Frozen Seafoods—National Sea Products Incorporated; *Int'l*, pg. 909

FISHER BOY—Frozen Fish Fillets-United States—National Sea Products Limited; *Int'l*, pg. 909

FISHER GUIDE—Lighting and Vehicle Hardware Components—General Motors Corporation; *U.S. Public*, pg. 718

FISHER JET-DRI—Lab Glassware Dryer—Fisher Scientific Company; *U.S. Private*, pg. 658

FISHER-PRICE—Toys—Fisher-Price Spielwaren GmbH; *U.S. Public*, pg. 1058

FISHER-PRICE—Toys & Children's Products—Mattel, Inc.; *U.S. Public*, pg. 1057

FISHER-PRICE CHILDREN'S TOILETRIES—Children's Bath Products—S.C. Johnson & Son, Inc.; *U.S. Private*, pg. 592

FISHER RADIO-SEATTLE—NONE—Fisher Broadcasting Inc.; *U.S. Public*, pg. 648

FISHER RECORDALL—Lab Recorders—Fisher Scientific Company; *U.S. Private*, pg. 658

FISHERBRAND—Scientific Products—Fisher Scientific Company; *U.S. Private*, pg. 658

FISHERCAST—Small Precise Zinc Alloy Die Castings—Fisher Gauge Limited; *Int'l*, pg. 491

FISHERMAN'S FILLET—Sandwich—Hardee's Food Systems, Inc.; *U.S. Public*, pg. 278

FISHERMAN'S FRIEND—Pharmaceuticals—Bristol-Myers Squibb Company; *U.S. Public*, pg. 253

FISHER'S—NONE—Fischer Packing Co.; *Int'l*, pg. 201

FISHERTECH—I.M.A. & Fixturblok Equip. Div.—Fisher Gauge Limited; *Int'l*, pg. 491

FISHERY PRODUCTS INTERNATIONAL—Frozen Seafood Products—Fishery Products International USA; *Int'l*, pg. 492

FISHIN' PARTNER—Tackle Box—Outdoor Technologies Group; *U.S. Private*, pg. 822

FISHING MACHINE—Marine Products; Boats & Canoes—Sea Nymph Inc.; *U.S. Private*, pg. 478

FISHING TACKLE RETAILER—Magazine—B.A.S.S., Inc.; *U.S. Private*, pg. 105

FISHIPPER—Corrugated Paperboard Shipping Containers—Georgia-Pacific Corporation; *U.S. Public*, pg. 735

FISHKEEPING ANSWERS—Pet Magazine—EMAP Pursuit Publishing; *Int'l*, pg. 451

FISKARS—NONE—Fiskars Oy AB; *Int'l*, pg. 492

FISKE—NONE—Advanced Instruments, Inc.; *U.S. Private*, pg. 22

FISSAN—Baby Care—Sara Lee Corporation; *U.S. Public*, pg. 1432

FISSAN—Baby Products—SmithKline Beecham plc; *Int'l*, pg. 1264

FIT—Shrinkable Tubing—Alpha Wire Company; *U.S. Public*, pg. 201

FIT-AL—Hardware Products—Rule Industries, Inc.; *U.S. Public*, pg. 950

FIT 'N EASY—Skinless & Boneless Poultry—Perdue Farms Incorporated; *U.S. Private*, pg. 852

FIT 'N TRIM—Dog Food—Ralston Purina Company; *U.S. Public*, pg. 1359

FIT PREGNANCY—Magazine—Weider Publications, Inc.; *U.S. Private*, pg. 1159

FITALL—Fuse Links—Kearney Company; *U.S. Public*, pg. 444

FITNESSTRAINER—Line of Health Equipment—Paramount Fitness Corp.; *U.S. Private*, pg. 838

FITS YOUR MOOD—Brassieres—Lilyette Brassiere Co.; *U.S. Private*, pg. 697

FITTING PRETTY—Hosiery—Hanes Hosiery, Inc.; *U.S. Public*, pg. 1434

FITTING ROOMS—NONE—MEG; *U.S. Private*, pg. 686

FITZ AND FLOYD—Home Fragrance—Tsumura International; *Int'l*, pg. 1426

FIVE—NONE—Brown & Sharpe Manufacturing Company; *U.S. Public*, pg. 260

FIVE ALIVE—Chilled, Aseptic & Frozen Concentrated Refreshment Beverages—The Coca-Cola Company; *U.S. Public*, pg. 392

5 ALIVE—Card Game—Mattel Games/Puzzles; *U.S. Public*, pg. 1058

FIVE ALIVE—Refreshment Beverages—The Minute Maid Company; *U.S. Public*, pg. 392

5-BENZAGEL—Pharmaceuticals—Rhone-Poulenc Rorer - U.S.; *Int'l*, pg. 1110

FIVE BROTHER—NONE—M. Fine & Sons Manufacturing Co., Inc.; *U.S. Private*, pg. 405

FIVE BROTHERS PREMIUM PASTA SAUCE—Pasta Sauce—Van den Bergh Foods Company; *Int'l*, pg. 1436

5 DAY—Deodorant/Antiperspirant—Menley & James Laboratories, Inc.; *U.S. Public*, pg. 1086

FIVE DIAMOND—Credit Card Services—American Automobile Association; *U.S. Public*, pg. 50

550 MUSIC—Records—Sony Music Entertainment, Inc.; *Int'l*, pg. 1281

540 TABLES—Conference Tables—Vecta; *U.S. Private*, pg. 1038

500 SPORT GRIP—Steering Wheel Covers—Superior Industries International, Inc.; *U.S. Public*, pg. 1539

500 II SERIES—Table System—Howe Furniture Corporation; *U.S. Private*, pg. 543

FIVE O'CLOCK—Gin & Vodka—Laird & Company; *U.S. Private*, pg. 642

FIVE ROSES—Grocery Products—Labatt Brewing Company Limited; *Int'l*, pg. 679

5-7-9 SHOPS—Junior's Apparel—Edison Brothers Stores, Inc.; *U.S. Public*, pg. 563

570 SERIES—Office Seating—GF Office Furniture; *U.S. Private*, pg. 435

FIVE SPRINGS—Bottled Water—Hinckley & Schmitt, Inc.; *Int'l*, pg. 1322

FIVE STAR—Stationery Products, Portfolios & Backpacks—The Mead Corporation; *U.S. Public*, pg. 1074

FIVE STAR—Passenger Tires—Pirelli Armstrong Tire Corporation; *Int'l*, pg. 1058

FIVE STAR AMERICAN—Blended Whiskey—Laird & Company; *U.S. Private*, pg. 642

5-STAR MEATS—NONE—Eagle Food Centers, Inc.; *U.S. Public*, pg. 547

FIVE STAR SEAL—Seals—Flowserve Corporation; *U.S. Public*, pg. 658

FIVE STAR SEALS—Seals—BW/IP International, Inc.; *U.S. Public*, pg. 658

535—Civil Engine—Rolls-Royce-Commercial Aero Engines Ltd.; *Int'l*, pg. 1127

5000 SERIES—Network Mngmt. Systems—Osicom Technologies Inc.; *U.S. Public*, pg. 1233

5010 MFD—Multifunctional-Copier, Fax, Laser Printer—Lanier Worldwide Inc.; *U.S. Public*, pg. 791

524 G/H—Civil Engine—Rolls-Royce-Commercial Aero Engines Ltd.; *Int'l*, pg. 1127

FIVE U-NIQUE—NONE—Brown & Sharpe Manufacturing Company; *U.S. Public*, pg. 260

5 UP—Women's Apparel—International Cosmetics Co., Ltd.; *Int'l*, pg. 684

FIX—Dehydrated Seasonings—Nestle S.A.; *Int'l*, pg. 915

FIX-A-DRINK—Drink Mixes—Borden, Inc.; *U.S. Private*, pg. 157

FIX-A-LEAK—Roof Coating Products—Monsey-Bakor; *U.S. Private*, pg. 757

FIXALL—Paint—Progress Paint Mfg. Co.; *U.S. Private*, pg. 890

FIXODENT—Denture Adhesives—The Procter & Gamble Company; *U.S. Public*, pg. 1330

FIXODENT—Denture Adhesive—Richardson-Vicks, Inc. Personal Care Products Div.; *U.S. Public*, pg. 1331

FIXTURBLOK—Orienting & Positioning Sys for Difficult to Clamp Parts—Fisher Gauge Limited; *Int'l*, pg. 491

FIXTUREMATE—NONE—GenRad, Inc.; *U.S. Public*, pg. 731

FIXTURES FURNITURE—Institutional, Office & Hospitality, Seating & Tables—Jami, Inc.; *U.S. Private*, pg. 581

FLA-VOR-AID—Soft Drink Powder—The Jel Sert Co.; *U.S. Private*, pg. 585

FLA-VOR-ICE—Frozen Confection—The Jel Sert Co.; *U.S. Private*, pg. 585

FLAGG—Shoes—Genesco Inc.; *U.S. Public*, pg. 728

FLAGS—Men's Sortswear—Hartmarx Corporation; *U.S. Public*, pg. 795

FLAGSHIP—Carbon Paper—Ko-Rec-Type; *U.S. Private*, pg. 117

FLAGYL—Pharmaceuticals—Monsanto Company; *U.S. Public*, pg. 1124

FLAGYL—Anti-Infective—Searle Laboratories; *U.S. Public*, pg. 1125

Brand Name Index

FLAGYL IV—Anti-infective—Searle Laboratories; *U.S. Public*, pg. 1125

FLAGYL IV—Anti-Microbial—Searle & Co.; *U.S. Public*, pg. 1125

FLAHERTY—Chipspreader—Rosco Manufacturing Co.; *U.S. Private*, pg. 944

FLAIR—Indoor Illuminated Sign Series—American Sign & Marketing Services, Inc.; *U.S. Public*, pg. 1309

FLAIR—Homes—Centex Corporation; *U.S. Public*, pg. 322

FLAIR—Motor Home—Fleetwood Enterprises, Inc.; *U.S. Public*, pg. 650

FLAIR—Decorative Electric Lamp Bulbs—General Electric Canada Inc.; *U.S. Public*, pg. 713

FLAIR—Paper Napkins & Tissues—Georgia-Pacific Corporation; *U.S. Public*, pg. 735

FLAIR—Porous Point & Plastic Point Pens—The Gillette Company; *U.S. Public*, pg. 743

FLAIR—Disposable Household Towels—Kimberly-Clark Corporation; *U.S. Public*, pg. 958

FLAIR—11 1/2" Dolls, Clothes & Accessories—Totsy Manufacturing Company, Inc.; *U.S. Private*, pg. 1093

FLAIR—Ash Trays—Willert Home Products, Inc.; *U.S. Private*, pg. 1177

FLAIR CHAIR—High Chair with Tray that Swings to Either Side of Chair—Cosco, Inc.; *U.S. Private*, pg. 277

FLAK—Hockey Equipment—Bauer Sports Inc.; *U.S. Public*, pg. 1184

FLAK—Athletic Shoes—L.A. Gear, Inc.; *U.S. Public*, pg. 969

FLAKE FACE NOVOPLY—Plywood—Georgia-Pacific Corporation; *U.S. Public*, pg. 735

FLAKE-OFF—Paint Remover-Dry—Mar-Hyde Corporation; *U.S. Public*, pg. 1357

FLAKEGLAS—Foliated Glass—Owens Corning; *U.S. Public*, pg. 1236

FLAKO—Mixes—The Quaker Oats Company; *U.S. Public*, pg. 1347

FLAMARREST—NONE—Belden Inc.; *U.S. Public*, pg. 200

FLAME—Bicycles—Bridgestone/Firestone, Inc.; *Int'l*, pg. 213

FLAME-AWAY—Flame Retardent Bulletin-Board—Dodge Regupol, Inc.; *U.S. Private*, pg. 337

FLAME BLOCKER—Flame Retardant Thermoformable Coated Fabric—Uniroyal Technology Corporation; *U.S. Public*, pg. 1670

FLAME-GLO—Cosmetics—Naturistics; *U.S. Public*, pg. 494

FLAME GLOW—Cosmetics—Del Laboratories, Inc.; *U.S. Public*, pg. 494

FLAME-GUARD—Gypsum—Weyerhaeuser Forest Products Company; *U.S. Public*, pg. 1764

FLAME MASTER—Cooking Controls—Robertshaw Controls Company; *Int'l*, pg. 1243

FLAME SET—Cooking Controls—Robertshaw Controls Company; *Int'l*, pg. 1243

FLAMENCO—Premium Cigars—Consolidated Cigar Corporation; *U.S. Private*, pg. 690

FLAMEPROOF LHC—Flame Retardant Wood Preservative—Osmose Wood Preserving, Inc.; *U.S. Private*, pg. 821

FLAMESCAN—Burner Flame Monitor—Land Instruments International Ltd.; *Int'l*, pg. 798

FLAMESEAL-FSP—Fire Stop Putty—O-Z/Gedney, Nelson Firestop Products; *U.S. Public*, pg. 726

FLAMESTOP—Foil Insulation—Carter Holt Harvey Limited; *U.S. Public*, pg. 904

FLAMETITE—Integral Silicone Fire Sleeve—Titeflex Corporation; *Int'l*, pg. 1340

FLAMEX D—Welding Cutting Fuel—Mapco Natural Gas Liquids Inc.; *U.S. Public*, pg. 1042

FLAMGLO FIRESTARTERS—Barbecue Fire Starter Cubes—Weber-Stephen Products Co.; *U.S. Private*, pg. 1157

FLAMIN'HOT—Jalapeno Potato Chips—Frito-Lay Company; *U.S. Public*, pg. 1277

FLAMINGO—NONE—Aliments Flamingo; *Int'l*, pg. 57

FLAMINGO—Casino-Resorts—Hilton Hotels Corporation; *U.S. Public*, pg. 828

FLAMINOX—Detergent—Fisher Scientific Company; *U.S. Private*, pg. 658

FLAN—Adhesive Flannel—Sentinel Consumer Products, Inc.; *U.S. Private*, pg. 984

FLANAX—Naproxen Sodium—Syntex; *Int'l*, pg. 1120

FLANBY—Caramel Coated Flan—Nestle S.A.; *Int'l*, pg. 915

FLANDRIA GARDEN—Lawn Mowers—Aritmos AB; *Int'l*, pg. 1072

FLANGE-TYTE—Gaskets—United States Pipe & Foundry Company, Inc.; *U.S. Public*, pg. 1736

FLANGETTE—Metal Housed Units—Fafnir Div. of Torrington Co.; *U.S. Public*, pg. 877

FLANGETTE UNIT—Bearing Housed Unit—The Torrington Co.; *U.S. Public*, pg. 877

FLANIE—Ladies Wear—Kosugi Sangyo Co., Ltd.; *Int'l*, pg. 759

FLANIGAN'S—Liquor Stores & Lounges—Flanigan's Enterprises, Inc.; *U.S. Public*, pg. 648

FLANKDRIVE—Wrenching Systems—Snap-On Tools Corporation; *U.S. Public*, pg. 1480

FLANTADIN—Anti-inflammatory—Hoechst Marion Roussel North America; *Int'l*, pg. 625

FLAPJACK—Syrup—Dean Pickles & Specialty Products; *U.S. Public*, pg. 490

FLARE COLLECTION—Teakwood—Dansk International Designs Ltd.; *U.S. Public*, pg. 261

FLARE EDITIONS—Book—The Hearst Corporation; *U.S. Private*, pg. 515

FLARE-UP-TAMERS—Stainless Channels (Angles) for Gas Grills to Replace Lava Rocks—Vance Industries, Inc.; *U.S. Private*, pg. 1133

FLAREX—Fluoromethasone Acetate—Alcon Laboratories, Inc.; *U.S. Public*, pg. 43

FLASH—NONE—Brown & Sharpe Manufacturing Company; *U.S. Public*, pg. 260

FLASH—Spirometry System—Burdick, Inc.; *U.S. Private*, pg. 181

FLASH—Magazine—Paisano Publications, Inc.; *U.S. Private*, pg. 834

FLASH FOAM—NONE—Ballard Medical Products; *U.S. Public*, pg. 171

FLASH GUARD—NONE—Harris Calorific Co.; *U.S. Public*, pg. 996

FLASH LEGS—Women's Hosiery—Hampshire Hosiery, Inc.; *U.S. Public*, pg. 778

FLASHBLAST—Surface Preparation—Maxwell Technologies, Inc.; *U.S. Public*, pg. 1061

THE FLASHES—Newspapers—Shivers Trading & Operating Co.; *U.S. Private*, pg. 994

FLASHFUN—Cameras—Eastman Kodak Company; *U.S. Public*, pg. 550

FLASHJET—Paint Stripping—Maxwell Technologies, Inc.; *U.S. Public*, pg. 1061

FLASHLOGIC—NONE—Altera Corporation; *U.S. Public*, pg. 59

FLASHMAN—Flashing Stop Sign (Hand-Held)—Millennium Technology Services, Inc.; *U.S. Private*, pg. 746

FLASHMITE—Camera—Eastman Kodak Company; *U.S. Public*, pg. 550

FLASHPOINT: GOLAN—War Game—Monarch Avalon, Inc.; *U.S. Public*, pg. 1123

FLAT FIGHTER—Tire Puncture Sealant—Bridgestone/Firestone, Inc.; *Int'l*, pg. 213

FLAT OUT—Conventional Gummed Paper—Brown-Bridge; *U.S. Public*, pg. 1022

FLAT OUT—Adhesive Coated Paper & Cloth—Kimberly-Clark Corporation; *U.S. Public*, pg. 958

FLAT PACK—Storage Racks—Jarke Corporation; *U.S. Private*, pg. 583

FLAT PAK—Fuses—Littelfuse, Inc.; *U.S. Public*, pg. 1001

FLAT-ROUND—Mechanical Bond Radiator—Young Radiator Company; *U.S. Private*, pg. 1201

FLAT STACK—Low Profile Transformer—Tamura Corp. of America, Microtran Div.; *U.S. Private*, pg. 1067

FLAT TOP—War Game—Monarch Avalon, Inc.; *U.S. Public*, pg. 1123

FLAT-TRAC—Dynamic Tire & Wheel Test System—MTS Systems Corporation; *U.S. Public*, pg. 1028

FLATJET—Spray Nozzle—Spraying Systems Co.; *U.S. Private*, pg. 1026

FLAV-O-RICH—Milk, Ice Cream & Fresh Dairy Products—Mid-America Dairymen, Inc.; *U.S. Private*, pg. 743

FLAV-R-PAC—Vegetables—Norpac Foods, Inc.; *U.S. Public*, pg. 802

FLAVACOL—Seasoning Salt—Gold Medal Products Co.; *U.S. Private*, pg. 459

FLAVEL—NONE—Glynwed International PLC; *Int'l*, pg. 554

FLAVETTE—Soft Drink—The Monarch Company, Inc.; *U.S. Private*, pg. 756

FLAVODAN—Enzymes, Flavourings & Antioxidants—Danisco Ingredients; *Int'l*, pg. 378

FLAVOMYCIN—Animal Health Products—Hoechst Aktiengesellschaft; *Int'l*, pg. 624

FLAVOR-CAP—Flavors & Spices—McCormick Flavor Division-U.S.A.; *U.S. Public*, pg. 1066

FLAVOR FRY—NONE—Alliant Foodservice, Inc.; *U.S. Private*, pg. 244

FLAVOR GUARD—Food Wrapping Paper—Fort James Corporation; *U.S. Public*, pg. 670

FLAVOR HOUSE—Snacks—Flavor House Products, Inc.; *U.S. Private*, pg. 410

FLAVOR-KIST—Crackers & Cookies—Schulze & Burch Biscuit Company; *U.S. Private*, pg. 973

FLAVOR-LOCK—Coffeemakers—Sunbeam Household Products; *U.S. Public*, pg. 1533

FLAVOR REDI FILLETS—Foodservice Poultry Items—Louis Kemp Seafood Co.; *U.S. Public*, pg. 1652

FLAVOR REDI IQF—Foodservice Frozen Items—Louis Kemp Seafood Co.; *U.S. Public*, pg. 1652

FLAVOR ROLLS—Candy—Tootsie Roll Industries, Inc.; *U.S. Public*, pg. 1621

FLAVOR ROLLS—Candy—World Trade & Marketing, LTD.; *U.S. Public*, pg. 1621

FLAVOR-SET POINT—Meal Place—Nutri/System Inc.; *U.S. Private*, pg. 859

FLAVOR SNACKS—Pet Foods—RJR Nabisco Holdings Corp.; *U.S. Public*, pg. 1354

FLAVORCELL—Food Processor Product—McCormick & Company, Incorporated; *U.S. Public*, pg. 1066

FLAVORITE—Stainless Steel Cookware—Regal Ware, Inc.; *U.S. Private*, pg. 917

FLAVORMAX—NONE—Regal Ware, Inc.; *U.S. Private*, pg. 917

FLAVORSUM—Coffee—Superior Coffee and Foods; *U.S. Public*, pg. 1434

FLAWLESS FLUSH—Makeup—Elizabeth Arden Company; *Int'l*, pg. 1435

FLAX—Pattern Glass—AFG Industries, Inc.; *Int'l*, pg. 84

FLEC-IT—Granite-Like Spray Finish—Zynolyte Products Company; *Int'l*, pg. 663

FLECK STONE—Paint—Plasti-Kote Company Inc.; *U.S. Private*, pg. 870

FLECO—Forestry & Land Clearing Attachments—Balderson Inc.; *U.S. Public*, pg. 315

FLECTOL—Rubber-Processing Compound—Monsanto Company; *U.S. Public*, pg. 1124

FLECTOL—Rubber Antioxidant—Solutia Inc.; *U.S. Public*, pg. 1483

FLEECY—Fabric Softener—Colgate-Palmolive Company; *U.S. Public*, pg. 397

FLEET—Proprietary Medicines—C. B. Fleet Co., Inc.; *U.S. Private*, pg. 410

FLEET BABYLAX—Proprietary Medicine—C. B. Fleet Co., Inc.; *U.S. Private*, pg. 410

FLEET BUSINESS LINE—Business Credit Line—Fleet National Bank; *U.S. Public*, pg. 649

FLEET CAR—NONE—EMAP Business Communications Division; *Int'l*, pg. 451

FLEET DEALER—NONE—EMAP Business Communications Division; *Int'l*, pg. 451

FLEET INDUSTRIER—NONE—Magellan Aerospace Corporation; *Int'l*, pg. 829

FLEET LINE—Personal Line of Credit—Fleet National Bank; *U.S. Public*, pg. 649

FLEET NEWS—NONE—EMAP Business Communications Division; *Int'l*, pg. 451

FLEET ONE—Consolidated Bank Account—Fleet National Bank; *U.S. Public*, pg. 649

FLEET OWNER—Publication for Truck Fleet Operators—Intertec Publishing; *U.S. Public*, pg. 1327

FLEET PLUS—Checking Account Package—Fleet National Bank; *U.S. Public*, pg. 649

FLEET 24—ATM Card—Fleet National Bank; *U.S. Public*, pg. 649

FLEETLINE—Cleaning Prods. For Transportation Indus.—Oakite Products, Inc.; *Int'l*, pg. 861

FLEETLINE INC—NONE—Dart Transit Company; *U.S. Private*, pg. 311

FLEETLINE SPORT GRIP—Steering Wheel Covers—Superior Industries International, Inc.; *U.S. Public*, pg. 1539

FLEETWELD—Electrode—The Lincoln Electric Company; *U.S. Public*, pg. 996

FLEETWOOD—Car—Cadillac Motor Car Division; *U.S. Public*, pg. 720

FLEETWOOD—Luxury Car—General Motors Corporation; *U.S. Public*, pg. 718

FLEETWOOD—Refrigerated Food Market Equipment—Jordon Commercial Refrigerator Co.; *U.S. Private*, pg. 599

FLEISCHMANN'S—Yeast—Burns, Philp & Company Limited; *Int'l*, pg. 236

FLEISCHMANN'S—NONE—Barton Brands, Ltd.; *U.S. Public*, pg. 300

FLEISCHMANN'S—Yeast—Fleischmann's Yeast; *Int'l*, pg. 237

FLEISCHMANN'S—Margarine, Corn Oil Margarine—Nabisco Inc.; *U.S. Public*, pg. 1355

FLEISCHMANNS EGG BEATERS—Egg Substitute—RJR Nabisco Holdings Corp.; *U.S. Public*, pg. 1354

FLEISCHMANN'S PREFERRED—NONE—Barton Brands, Ltd.; *U.S. Public*, pg. 300

FLEISCHMANN'S YEAST—NONE—Tone Brothers Inc.; *Int'l*, pg. 237

FLEMINGS—Intl. Broking, Investment Bankers, Money Management & Stock Exchanges—Robert Fleming, Inc.; *Int'l*, pg. 493

FLEMINGS OATEN PRODUCTS—Breakfast Cereals—Goodman Fielder Limited; *Int'l*, pg. 555

FLETCHERS CASTORIA—Laxative—Mentholatum Company; *Int'l*, pg. 1126

FLEUR DE FLEURS—Women's Fragrance—Accecones Ricci U.S.A., Inc.; *Int'l*, pg. 445

FLEUR DE LAIT—Cream Cheese Based Products—BC-USA; *Int'l*, pg. 201

FLEUR DE LAIT—Cream Cheese Based Products—Bongrain Cheese USA; *Int'l*, pg. 201

FLEUR DE LAIT LIGHT—Light Cream Cheese Based Products—Bongrain Cheese USA; *Int'l*, pg. 201

FLEUR-DE-LIS SYMBOL—Cards, Gift Wrap, Misc. Paper Products—Gibson Greetings, Inc.; *U.S. Public*, pg. 742

FLEUR DU CAP—Wine—Distillers Corporation S.A.; *Int'l*, pg. 1129

FLEX—NONE—Altera Corporation; *U.S. Public*, pg. 59

FLEX—Balsam Shampoo & Conditioner—Revlon-Realistic Professional Products, Inc.; *U.S. Private*, pg. 690

FLEX—Magazine—Weider Publications, Inc.; *U.S. Private*, pg. 1159

FLEX-A-DRIVE—Double Input Center Pivot Irrigation Final Drive—Regal-Beloit Corporation; *U.S. Public*, pg. 1370

FLEX-A-MATIC—Writing Instruments—Union Pen Company; *U.S. Private*, pg. 1119

FLEX-A-MOUNT—Center Pivot Irrigation Center Drive—Regal-Beloit Corporation; *U.S. Public*, pg. 1370

FLEX-A-SEAL—Secondary Seal for Tank Floating Roofs—Matrix Service Company; *U.S. Public*, pg. 1057

FLEX-A-SPAN—Primary Seal for Tank Floating Roofs—Matrix Service Company; *U.S. Public*, pg. 1057

FLEX-A-SWIVEL—Floating Roof Drain Swivel Joint—Matrix Service Company; *U.S. Public*, pg. 1057

FLEX-A-TROL—Scanner—Tocco, Inc.; *U.S. Public*, pg. 1259

FLEX-ALL 454—Pain Relieving Gel—Chattem, Inc.; *U.S. Public*, pg. 341

FLEX-ALL 454—Analgesic—Chattem, Inc., Consumer Products Division; *U.S. Public*, pg. 341

FLEX-AUGER—Feed Delivery System or Conveying System—CTB International Corp.; *U.S. Public*, pg. 284

FLEX-BAC—Floor Coverings—Domco Inc.; *Int'l*, pg. 415

FLEX BAGS—Extruded Plastic Net—Nalle Plastics Inc.; *U.S. Private*, pg. 773

FLEX-BAND—Closures—Owens-Illinois, Inc.; *U.S. Public*, pg. 1238

FLEX BEAM—Farm Tools—UnionTools, Inc.; *U.S. Public*, pg. 17

FLEX-BOLT—Sandwich Mounts—Lord Corporation; *U.S. Private*, pg. 675

FLEX-CAN—Pouch—Reynolds Metals Company; *U.S. Public*, pg. 1385

FLEX-CARE FOR SENSITIVE EYES—Sterile Solution for Rinsing & Storage of Soft Contact Lenses—Alcon Laboratories, Inc.; *Int'l*, pg. 916

FLEX-CLASS—Versatile Geometry Seats—B/E Aerospace Seating Products Group; *U.S. Public*, pg. 159

FLEX-COM—Electrical Connectors—Litton Industries, Inc.; *U.S. Public*, pg. 1002

FLEX CONTROL—Electric Shaver—The Gillette Company; *U.S. Public*, pg. 743

FLEX-E-FILL—Machines for Packaging Food Products—Sweetheart Cup Company Inc.; *U.S. Private*, pg. 1058

FLEX-E-FORM—Machines for Forming Paper Food Containers—Sweetheart Cup Company Inc.; *U.S. Private*, pg. 1058

FLEX 8000—NONE—Altera Corporation; *U.S. Public*, pg. 59

FLEX-EL—ECG Electrodes—Conmed Corporation; *U.S. Public*, pg. 431

FLEX-FORM—Concrete Forming System—Symons Corporation; *U.S. Private*, pg. 932

FLEX-GAGE—Hardware for SPC & Machine Control—Air Gage Company; *U.S. Public*, pg. 1676

FLEX-GRIP—Flexable Coppectoks—Ace Glass Incorporated; *U.S. Private*, pg. 12

FLEX-GUARD—Metal Backed Brushes Used as Machine Guards and Containments Seals—Felton Brush Inc.; *U.S. Private*, pg. 400

FLEX-GUARD—Extruded Plastic Net—Nalle Plastics Inc.; *U.S. Private*, pg. 773

FLEX-HONE TOOL—Flexible Cylinder Hone—Brush Research Manufacturing Company; *U.S. Private*, pg. 176

FLEX-I-DRAIN—Flexible Roof Drains—Johns Manville Corporation; *U.S. Public*, pg. 927

FLEX-I-MID—Polyimide Coated Circuit Materials—Rogers Corporation; *U.S. Public*, pg. 1402

FLEX-I-VISION—Hanging Folders—Smead Manufacturing Company; *U.S. Private*, pg. 1006

FLEX-IN-LINE—Concentric Shart Helical Gear Speedreducers—Regal-Beloit Corporation; *U.S. Public*, pg. 1370

FLEX-LAG—Pulley Lagging—Flexible Steel Lacing Company; *U.S. Public*, pg. 413

FLEX-LIGHT—Solid Printing Plate—Polyfibron Technologies Corp.; *U.S. Private*, pg. 875

FLEX-LOC—Hose—HBD Industries, Inc.; *U.S. Private*, pg. 489

FLEX-LOCK—Limit Switches—Namco Controls Corporation; *U.S. Public*, pg. 482

FLEX-LOK—Boltless River Crossing Joint—American Cast Iron Pipe Co.; *U.S. Private*, pg. 51

FLEX NET—Coaxial Headend Amplifier—C-COR Electronics, Inc.; *U.S. Public*, pg. 272

FLEX NODE—AM Fiber Optic Node—C-COR Electronics, Inc.; *U.S. Public*, pg. 272

FLEX-O—Covers—James Burn Intl.; *U.S. Public*, pg. 1506

FLEX-O-BAG—Plastic Bags—Flex-O-Glass, Inc.; *U.S. Private*, pg. 412

FLEX-O-BAGS—Plastic Bags—Warp Brothers; *U.S. Private*, pg. 412

FLEX-O-FILM—Plastic Packaging Film—Flex-O-Glass, Inc.; *U.S. Private*, pg. 412

FLEX-O-GLASS—Window Material—Flex-O-Glass, Inc.; *U.S. Private*, pg. 412

FLEX-O-GLASS—Window Material—Warp Brothers; *U.S. Private*, pg. 412

FLEX-O-GLAZE—Rigid Plastic Glazing—Flex-O-Glass, Inc.; *U.S. Private*, pg. 412

FLEX-O-GLAZE—Rigid Plastic Glazing—Warp Brothers; *U.S. Private*, pg. 412

FLEX-O-LATORS, INC.—Automotive Seating Systems—Leggett & Platt, Incorporated; *U.S. Public*, pg. 985

FLEX-O-PANE—Window Material—Warp Brothers; *U.S. Private*, pg. 412

FLEX-O-TWIST—Fish Tape—Greenlee Textron; *U.S. Public*, pg. 1589

FLEX-PLUS BLUE—Electrical Non-Metallic Tubing—The Lamson & Sessions Co.; *U.S. Public*, pg. 976

FLEX POISE—Scales—Ferguson International, Inc.; *U.S. Private*, pg. 401

FLEX-RING—Restrained Joint Pipe—American Cast Iron Pipe Co.; *U.S. Private*, pg. 51

FLEX-SIL—Battery Separators—Thomas & Betts/Amerace; *U.S. Public*, pg. 1598

FLEX SPLITTER—BX Cutter—Greenlee Textron; *U.S. Public*, pg. 1589

FLEX-SPREADER—Spreader Roller—Samuel Bingham Co; *U.S. Private*, pg. 144

FLEX-TECH—Modular Furniture System—Kewaunee Scientific Corporation; *U.S. Public*, pg. 953

FLEX 10K—NONE—Altera Corporation; *U.S. Public*, pg. 59

FLEX 3—Stationery Products—The Mead Corporation; *U.S. Public*, pg. 1074

FLEX-TITE—Interior Insulating Window—Plaskolite Inc.; *U.S. Private*, pg. 870

FLEX-TRUNK—Fume Exhauster—Donaldson Company, Inc.; *U.S. Public*, pg. 517

FLEX TUBE—U-Tube Manometer—Dwyer Instruments Inc.; *U.S. Private*, pg. 350

FLEX-2000—Sheet Molded Composite—The Budd Company; *Int'l*, pg. 1388

FLEX-VENT—Oil Ring Part—Hastings Manufacturing Company; *U.S. Public*, pg. 798

FLEX-WRAP—Extruded Plastic Net—Nalle Plastics Inc.; *U.S. Private*, pg. 773

FLEX-X—Flexible Natural Gas Transportation Expansion Program—Duke Energy International, L.L.C.; *U.S. Public*, pg. 534

FLEX-LUBE—Motor Oils—Coastal Refining & Marketing; *U.S. Public*, pg. 390

FLEXA—Building Paints for Exterior & Interior (Retail Uses)—Akzo Nobel N.V.; *Int'l*, pg. 42

FLEXA-MIX—Magnetic Stirrers—Fisher Scientific Company; *U.S. Private*, pg. 658

FLEXACLEAN—Food Industry Gearbox—Regal-Beloit Corporation; *U.S. Public*, pg. 1370

FLEXACON—Flexible Food Packaging—Alusuisse-Lonza Holding Ltd.; *Int'l*, pg. 66

FLEXACRON—Protective & Decorative Coatings for Wood & Vinyl Surfaces—PPG Industries, Inc.; *U.S. Public*, pg. 1245

FLEXAFRAME—Frame Supports—Fisher Scientific Company; *U.S. Private*, pg. 658

FLEXAGUIDE—Flexible Waveguide—Airtron; *U.S. Public*, pg. 1003

FLEXAGUIDE—Flexible Microwave Waveguide—Litton Industries, Inc.; *U.S. Public*, pg. 1002

FLEXALID—Flexible Food Packaging—Alusuisse-Lonza Holding Ltd.; *Int'l*, pg. 66

FLEXALINE—Standard Gearbox with Modular Design/Applications—Regal-Beloit Corporation; *U.S. Public*, pg. 1370

FLEXALITE—Electronic Lighting Controls—Gold Peak Industries (Holdings) Limited; *Int'l*, pg. 537

FLEXALUM—Window Covering Product—Hunter Douglas N.V.; *Int'l*, pg. 639

FLEXAN—Ultra-Thin, Highly Flexible Film Wand Dressing—Dow Hickam Pharmaceuticals Inc.; *U.S. Public*, pg. 1143

FLEXANAR—Flexible Coating for Metal & Plastic Surfaces—PPG Industries, Inc.; *U.S. Public*, pg. 1245

FLEXANGLE—Slotted steel angle—Hynes Industries Inc.; *U.S. Private*, pg. 552

FLEXAR—Integrated Circuit—EXAR Corporation; *U.S. Public*, pg. 597

FLEXATEL—Telephone Accessories—Gold Peak Industries (Holdings) Limited; *Int'l*, pg. 537

FLEXATHENE—Thermoplastic Olefins—Millennium Petrochemicals, Inc.; *Int'l*, pg. 594

FLEXATIVE—Elastomeric Coating Additive—PPG Industries, Inc.; *U.S. Public*, pg. 1245

FLEXATRON—Insulating/padding Material For Matresses & Upholstery—Kingsdown, Inc.; *U.S. Private*, pg. 622

FLEXAUST—Flexible Hose—Callahan Mining Corporation; *U.S. Public*, pg. 394

FLEXBAR—Machine Tool Accessories—Pegasus International Corporation; *U.S. Private*, pg. 1046

FLEXBASE—Flexible Copperclad Laminate—Sheldahl, Inc.; *U.S. Public*, pg. 1465

FLEXBOLT MOUNTS—Mounts—Lord Corporation, Mechanical Products Division; *U.S. Private*, pg. 676

FLEXBOND—Polyvinyl Acetate Copolymer Emulsions—Air Products and Chemicals, Inc.; *U.S. Public*, pg. 30

FLEXCO—Conveyor Belt Fasteners—Flexible Steel Lacing Company; *U.S. Public*, pg. 413

Brand Name Index

FLEXCOMM—In-Flight Direct Communication System—AlliedSignal Commercial Avionics Systems; *U.S. Public*, pg. 50

FLEXCONNECT—LAN Integration—GE Capital/IT Solutions; *U.S. Public*, pg. 711

FLEXCOR—Flexible Wire Mesh Holding Devices—Pass & Seymour/Legrand; *Int'l*, pg. 806

FLEXCORD—Paper Covered Wire—Leggett & Platt, Incorporated; *U.S. Public*, pg. 985

FLEXCORE—Semiconductor Device—LSI Logic Corp.; *U.S. Public*, pg. 971

FLEXCRYL—Acrylic Emulsions—Air Products and Chemicals, Inc.; *U.S. Public*, pg. 30

FLEXDERM—Ultra-Thin, Highly Comfortable Polyurethane Foam Adhesive Dressing—Dow Hickam Pharmaceuticals Inc.; *U.S. Public*, pg. 1143

FLEXDOCK—Hose—The Goodyear Tire & Rubber Company; *U.S. Public*, pg. 752

FLEXEAL—High Temperature Cage—The Barden Corporation; *Int'l*, pg. 468

FLEXEES—Foundation Garments—True Form Intimate Apparel; *U.S. Private*, pg. 697

FLEXERIL—Cyclobenzaprine—Merck & Co., Inc.; *U.S. Public*, pg. 1090

FLEXEVIL—Pharmaceutical—Merck Human Health Division (U.S. Human Health); *U.S. Public*, pg. 1091

FLEXFAB—NONE—Flexfab Horizons International, Inc.; *U.S. Private*, pg. 412

FLEXFACE—Reinforced Vinyl for Flexible Display Sign Faces—Signtech USA, Ltd.; *U.S. Private*, pg. 999

FLEXFAST—Couplings—Flexible Technologies Inc.; *Int'l*, pg. 1267

FLEXFILL—Electrical Wire & Cable—General Cable Corporation; *Int'l*, pg. 1486

FLEXFLO—Regulators—Grove Valve & Regulator Company; *U.S. Private*, pg. 484

FLEXFLYTE—Hose—Flexible Technologies Inc.; *Int'l*, pg. 1267

FLEXGEL—Filling Compound; Electrical Telecommunications Cable—Lucent Technologies Inc.; *U.S. Public*, pg. 1017

FLEXGLASS—Flexible Sheet Material—Georgia-Pacific Corporation; *U.S. Public*, pg. 735

FLEXGUARD—Electronic Wire & Cable—General Cable Corporation; *Int'l*, pg. 1486

FLEXGUARD—Paper Tamper-Evident Lids—Sweetheart Cup Company Inc.; *U.S. Private*, pg. 1058

FLEXHARD—Epoxy—Pratt & Lambert United, Inc.; *U.S. Public*, pg. 1466

FLEXI-FIRE—Propane Torch—Sycamore Plant; *U.S. Public*, pg. 444

FLEXI FLO—Bulk Commodity Service—Conrail, Inc.; *U.S. Public*, pg. 431

FLEXI-LITES BY FLEXEES—Control Garments—True Form Intimate Apparel; *U.S. Private*, pg. 697

FLEXI-STAR—Disposable/Reusable Half Mask—Aearo Company; *U.S. Private*, pg. 23

FLEXI-VAN—Chassis—Flexi-Van Leasing, Inc.; *U.S. Private*, pg. 413

FLEXIBELT—Liquid-Solids Separation Equipment—Komline-Sanderson Engineering Corp.; *U.S. Private*, pg. 631

FLEXIBLE ADVANCED MATERIALS—NONE—Chemfab Corporation; *U.S. Public*, pg. 344

FLEXIBLE CONTROL STRATEGY—Control Products—Bailey, Fischer & Porter Company; *Int'l*, pg. 449

FLEXIBLE ENGINEERED MATERIALS—NONE—Chemfab Corporation; *U.S. Public*, pg. 344

FLEXIBLE FLYER—Sleds—Brunswick Corporation; *U.S. Public*, pg. 265

FLEXIBLE FLYER—Snow Sleds—Flexible Flyer Toys; *U.S. Private*, pg. 412

FLEXIBLE FLYER—Sleds—Roadmaster/Brunswick; *U.S. Public*, pg. 265

FLEXIBLE MIN-K—Insulation—Johns Manville Corporation; *U.S. Public*, pg. 927

FLEXIBLE MONITORING—Vital Signs Monitoring System—Protocol Systems, Inc.; *U.S. Public*, pg. 1336

FLEXIBLOMATICS—Core Machines—Beardsley & Piper, L.L.C.; *U.S. Private*, pg. 859

FLEXIBOS—Backup Embossing Roll Cover—Harnischfeger Industries, Inc.; *U.S. Public*, pg. 788

FLEXIBOS II—Backup Embossing—Beloit Corporation; *U.S. Public*, pg. 789

FLEXIBUS—Device-Specific Adaptor—GenRad, Inc.; *U.S. Public*, pg. 731

FLEXICARB—NONE—The Flexitallic Group, Inc.; *U.S. Private*, pg. 413

FLEXICLEAR—Autobody Seam Sealer—3M; *U.S. Public*, pg. 1604

FLEXICOLOR—Photo Processing Chemicals—Eastman Kodak Company; *U.S. Public*, pg. 550

FLEXICUT—TFE Based Expandable Piston Rings—John Crane Mechanical Seals; *Int'l*, pg. 1339

FLEXIFLO—Felt—American Felt & Filter; *U.S. Private*, pg. 54

FLEXIFLO II—Enteral Feeding System—Abbott Laboratories; *U.S. Public*, pg. 12

FLEXIGUARD—Electronic Controller—Amot Controls Corporation; *U.S. Public*, pg. 1405

FLEXIKRON—Adjustable Timer—Union Switch & Signal Inc.; *Int'l*, pg. 77

FLEXILAYER—Flexible-Rigid Multilayer Circuit—Parlex Corporation; *U.S. Public*, pg. 1264

FLEXIPANEL—Electric Tank Heating Pads—Thermon Manufacturing Company; *U.S. Private*, pg. 1080

FLEXIS—Office Seating—United Chair, Inc.; *U.S. Private*, pg. 512

FLEXISENSOR—Pulse Oximetry Sensor—Datascope Corp.; *U.S. Public*, pg. 487

FLEXITALLIC—NONE—The Flexitallic Group, Inc.; *U.S. Private*, pg. 413

FLEXITE—NONE—The Flexitallic Group, Inc.; *U.S. Private*, pg. 413

FLEXJOINT—Caulking Compound—Elf Atochem North America, Inc.; *Int'l*, pg. 445

FLEXKING—Ducting—HBD Industries, Inc.; *U.S. Private*, pg. 489

FLEXKLEER—Paint Booth Coating Composition—PPG Industries, Inc.; *U.S. Public*, pg. 1245

FLEXLOC—Self Locking Nuts—SPS Technologies, Inc.; *U.S. Public*, pg. 1419

FLEXLOGIC—NONE—Altera Corporation; *U.S. Public*, pg. 59

FLEXMETL—Laminated Panel—Georgia-Pacific Corporation; *U.S. Public*, pg. 735

FLEXO—Film Clips—Eastman Kodak Company; *U.S. Public*, pg. 550

FLEXOGEN—Vinyl Garden Hose—Vermont American Tool Corp.; *U.S. Public*, pg. 575

FLEXOLINE—NONE—Acme Design Technology, Co.; *U.S. Private*, pg. 13

FLEXONICS—Expansion Joints, Compensator, Flexible Metal Hose, Ducting & Connectors—Senior Flexonics Inc.; *Int'l*, pg. 1222

FLEXOPLATE—Transformer Radiators—Tranter, Inc.; *U.S. Public*, pg. 521

FLEXOPRINT—Newsprint—Champion International Corp.; *U.S. Public*, pg. 333

FLEXOWELL—Inclined/Vertical Conveyors—Svedala Bulk Materials Handling Engineered Products; *Int'l*, pg. 1326

FLEXPAK—Corrugated Containers—Westvaco Corporation; *U.S. Public*, pg. 1762

FLEXPHY—LAN Interface Modules—GTI Corporation; *U.S. Public*, pg. 767

FLEXPICK/SOFTPICK—Automatic Order Picking Systems—ElectroCom Automation L.P.; *Int'l*, pg. 1244

FLEXPREP—Software Program For Microlab Instruments—Hamilton Co., Inc.; *U.S. Private*, pg. 497

FLEXPULSE—Hose—The Goodyear Tire & Rubber Company; *U.S. Public*, pg. 752

FLEXSEAL—Laminated Safety Glass—PPG Industries, Inc.; *U.S. Public*, pg. 1245

FLEXSIL—Refractory Cloth Filters—AMETEK, Inc.; *U.S. Public*, pg. 99

FLEXSTEEL—Fine Upholstered Furniture—Flexsteel Industries, Inc.; *U.S. Public*, pg. 653

FLEXSTRENGTH—Hose—HBD Industries, Inc.; *U.S. Private*, pg. 489

FLEXSTRIP—Flexible Interconnects—Thomas & Betts Corporation; *U.S. Public*, pg. 1597

FLEXTERM—Cable Terminals—Lucent Technologies Inc.; *U.S. Public*, pg. 1017

FLEXTEST—Digital Servo Controller—MTS Systems Corporation; *U.S. Public*, pg. 1028

FLEXTHANE—Acrylic/Urethane Dispersions—Air Products and Chemicals, Inc.; *U.S. Public*, pg. 30

FLEXTIE—Flexible Terminal Interface Equip. for 56-KBPS Networks—California Microwave, Inc.; *U.S. Public*, pg. 293

FLEXTIP PLUS—Epidural Catheter for Administering Regional Anesthesia—Arrow International, Inc.; *U.S. Public*, pg. 135

FLEXWEAR—Industrial Uniform Shirts—UniFirst Corporation; *U.S. Public*, pg. 1665

FLEXWORD—Voice Messaging Computer Programs—Lucent Technologies Inc.; *U.S. Public*, pg. 1017

FLEXWRAP—Pipe Insulation—Carter Holt Harvey Limited; *U.S. Public*, pg. 904

FLEXZAN—Spyroflex—PolyMedica Industries, Inc.; *U.S. Public*, pg. 1315

FLEXZONE—Antiozonant—Uniroyal Chemical Company, Inc.; *U.S. Public*, pg. 460

FLIC—Paper Towel Dispensers—The Dow Chemical Company; *U.S. Public*, pg. 522

FLICK-A-SWITCH—Refrigerator—Foster Refrigerator Corporation; *U.S. Public*, pg. 421

FLICKER—Ladies Shaver—American Safety Razor Company; *U.S. Private*, pg. 597

FLIGHT CUSTOM II—Aviation Tires—The Goodyear Tire & Rubber Company; *U.S. Public*, pg. 752

FLIGHT DECK U.S.A.—Outerwear for Men & Boys—I. Spiewak & Sons, Inc.; *U.S. Private*, pg. 1025

FLIGHT EAGLE—Aviation Tires—The Goodyear Tire & Rubber Company; *U.S. Public*, pg. 752

FLIGHT LEADER—Aviation Tires—The Goodyear Tire & Rubber Company; *U.S. Public*, pg. 752

FLIGHT LEADER—Game—Monarch Avalon, Inc.; *U.S. Public*, pg. 1123

FLIGHT RADIAL—Aviation Tires—The Goodyear Tire & Rubber Company; *U.S. Public*, pg. 752

FLIGHT SPECIAL II—Aviation Tires—The Goodyear Tire & Rubber Company; *U.S. Public*, pg. 752

FLIGHT TESTED—Gymnastic Apparel—Tighe Industries, Inc.; *U.S. Private*, pg. 1086

FLIGHT2SYSTEM—Cockpit Display System—Rockwell International Corporation; *U.S. Public*, pg. 1397

FLIGHTFUND—Frequent Flyer Program—America West Airlines, Inc.; *U.S. Public*, pg. 67

FLIGHTLINK—NONE—Cable and Wireless plc; *Int'l*, pg. 247

FLIGHTSAFETY INTERNATIONAL—Aviation & Marine Consultant & Training—FlightSafety International Inc.; *U.S. Public*, pg. 218

FLIK FLAK—Watches—SMH Swiss Corporation for Micro Electronics & Watchmaking Indus. Ltd.; *Int'l*, pg. 1160

FLING—Sporting Goods—Brunswick Bowling & Billiards Corp.; *U.S. Public*, pg. 265

FLING—Combined Film and Camera—Eastman Kodak Company; *U.S. Public*, pg. 550

FLINN & DREFFEIN—Industrial Furnaces & Process Control Systems—Flinn & Dreffein Engineering Co.; *U.S. Private*, pg. 413

FLINT—Cutlery, Kitchen Tools, Beaters, Can Opener—Ekco Housewares, Inc.; *U.S. Public*, pg. 566

FLINT & WALLING—Water Pumps—Masco Corporation; *U.S. Public*, pg. 1052

THE FLINT JOURNAL—Newspaper—Booth Newspapers, Inc.; *U.S. Private*, pg. 157

FLINTSTONE VITAMINS—Vitamins—Bayer AG; *Int'l*, pg. 171

FLINTSTONES—Multiple Vitamins—Bayer Corporation/Consumer Care Division; *Int'l*, pg. 173

FLIP—Vacuum Fluorescent Display Modules—Industrial Electronic Engineers, Inc.; *U.S. Private*, pg. 561

FLIP CHART—Flip Chart Marker—Sanford Corporation; *U.S. Public*, pg. 1178

FLIP-FILE—Office Supplies—JM Company; *U.S. Private*, pg. 577

FLIP-IT—Games—Mikohn Gaming Corporation; *U.S. Public*, pg. 1111

FLIP-IT—Tile—Pawling Corporation; *U.S. Private*, pg. 844

FLIP LID—Weatherproof Cover—Pass & Seymour/Legrand; *Int'l*, pg. 806

FLIP-LOC—Seating System—Nemschoff Chairs, Inc.; *U.S. Private*, pg. 791

FLIP 'N' FRY—Sea Food Product—George Weston Limited; *Int'l*, pg. 1494

FLIP-OFF—Closures For Use on Containers For Medicaments—The West Company, Incorporated; *U.S. Public*, pg. 1755

FLIP OFF TRADE DRESS WITH TARGET RING—Closures For Use on Containers For Medicaments—The West Company, Incorporated; *U.S. Public*, pg. 1755

FLIP OFF TRADE DRESS WITHOUT TARGET RING—Closures For Use on Containers For Medicaments—The West Company, Incorporated; *U.S. Public*, pg. 1755

FLIP STICK—Industrial Chemical—Hercules Chemical Co., Inc.; *U.S. Private*, pg. 523

FLIP TEAR—Metal & Non-Metal Closures For Use on Containers for Medicaments—The West Company, Incorporated; *U.S. Public*, pg. 1755

FLIP-TOP—Lid (on feed bin)—CTB International Corp.; *U.S. Public*, pg. 284

FLIP-TOP—Bender—Greenlee Textron; *U.S. Public*, pg. 1589

FLIP/TOP—Platemakers—Nuarc Company, Inc.; *U.S. Private*, pg. 808

FLIP-UPS—Greeting Cards—American Greetings Corporation; *U.S. Public*, pg. 77

FLIPPEN—Valves—Watts Industries, Inc.; *U.S. Public*, pg. 1746

FLIPPER—Walking Sandals—Bangkok Athletic Co., Ltd.; *Int'l*, pg. 146

FLIPSIDERS—Game—Milton Bradley Company; *U.S. Public*, pg. 797

FLIRTS—Sleepwear—Donnkenny, Inc.; *U.S. Public*, pg. 519

FLISELINA—Non-Woven Textile for the Apparel Industry—Freudenberg & Company; *Int'l*, pg. 505

FLIT—Insecticide—Exxon Corporation; *U.S. Public*, pg. 601

FLITE STAR—Residential Garage Door Opener—Raynor Garage Doors; *U.S. Private*, pg. 912

FLITECOMM—Voice Communications for Air Traffic Control—AlliedSignal Commercial Avionics Systems; *U.S. Public*, pg. 50

FLITEFONE—In-Flight Air-to-Ground Communication System—AlliedSignal Commercial Avionics Systems; *U.S. Public*, pg. 50

FLITEMASK—Oxygen Masks—Nellcor Puritan Bennett Incorporated; *U.S. Public*, pg. 1039

FLIX—Added Value Service—Showtime Networks Inc.; *U.S. Private*, pg. 779

FLO-CLEAN—Coated Filter Media—American Felt & Filter; *U.S. Private*, pg. 54

FLO-FRE—Flowability Aid—Oil-Dri Corporation of America; *U.S. Public*, pg. 1214

FLO-GARD—Synthetic Precipitated Silica Flow Conditioner & Anticaking Agent for Salt—PPG Industries, Inc.; *U.S. Public*, pg. 1245

FLO-MANAGER—Control System—Rain Bird Sprinklers Manufacturing Corp.; *U.S. Private*, pg. 907

FLO-MATIC—Cosmetics/Mascara—Merle Norman Cosmetics, Inc.; *U.S. Private*, pg. 733

FLO-METER—Pressure-Sensitive IV Labels—TimeMed Labeling Systems, Inc.; *U.S. Private*, pg. 1087

FLO-MO—Emulsifiers—DeSoto Inc.; *U.S. Public*, pg. 956

FLO-MO—Agricultural Emulsifiers—Witco Corporation; *U.S. Public*, pg. 1773

FLO-RITE—Paste Solder—Litton Industries, Inc.; *U.S. Public*, pg. 1002

FLO-SCINT—Liquid Scintillation Solutions—Packard Instrument Co., Inc.; *U.S. Private*, pg. 833

FLO-SCOPE—Gas Mixer—Selas Corporation of America; *U.S. Public*, pg. 1454

FLO-SEPTOR—Waste Receivers—Josam Company; *U.S. Private*, pg. 600

FLO-SET—Roof Drains—Josam Company; *U.S. Private*, pg. 600

FLO-SOAR—Milking Claw—Bou-Matic; *U.S. Private*, pg. 301

FLO-SOFT—NONE—Ace Hardware Corporation; *U.S. Private*, pg. 12

FLO-TEMP—Shampoo Bowl Fixture—Belvedere Company; *U.S. Private*, pg. 1008

FLO-THRU—Tea Bags—Thomas J. Lipton Company; *Int'l*, pg. 1435

FLO-THRU THREAD CLEANER—Thread Cleaner—Weatherford Enterra Incorporated; *U.S. Public*, pg. 1749

FLO-VAC—Suction Unit & Belt—Harnischfeger Industries, Inc.; *U.S. Public*, pg. 788

FLO-WATCH—Meters—BIF; *U.S. Public*, pg. 726

FLOAM—Toys—Mattel, Inc.; *U.S. Public*, pg. 1057

FLOAT GLASS—Quality Flat Glass—Pilkington Australasia Limited; *Int'l*, pg. 1057

FLOATING FLOORS—Access Floor Systems—Tate Access Floors, Inc.; *U.S. Private*, pg. 1069

FLOATING SEAL—Valves—Valcor Engineering Corp.; *U.S. Private*, pg. 1131

FLOCO—Positive Displacement Meter—ITT Barton Instruments; *U.S. Public*, pg. 860

FLODIL—Cardiovascular Pharmaceutical—Astra AB; *Int'l*, pg. 93

FLOETROL—Latex Paint Additive—The Flood Company; *U.S. Public*, pg. 414

FLOHWEG DECANTER—NONE—Dorr-Oliver Incorporated; *Int'l*, pg. 839

FLOJEL—Starch—Unilever Plc; *Int'l*, pg. 1433

FLOLAN—Renal Dialysis—Glaxo Wellcome PLC; *Int'l*, pg. 553

FLOMASTER—NONE—Flomaster Div.; *U.S. Public*, pg. 1318

FLOMATIC—Photo Processing Chemicals—Eastman Kodak Company; *U.S. Public*, pg. 550

FLOODGATE-1—NONE—Check Point Software Technologies Ltd.; *U.S. Public*, pg. 342

FLOODJET—Spray Nozzle—Spraying Systems Co.; *U.S. Private*, pg. 1026

FLOOR COVERING WEEKLY—Magazine—The Hearst Corporation; *U.S. Private*, pg. 515

FLOOR SUCKER—Utility Pump—Zoeller Co.; *U.S. Private*, pg. 1207

FLOOR-TRACK—Refrigerator—Foster Refrigerator Corporation; *U.S. Public*, pg. 421

FLOORKEEPERS—Automatic Scrubbers—Breuer/Tornado; *U.S. Private*, pg. 167

FLOORMACHINES—Vacuum Cleaners—Breuer/Tornado; *U.S. Private*, pg. 167

FLOORMATE—Plastic Foam Insulation—The Dow Chemical Company; *U.S. Public*, pg. 522

FLOORMAX—Commercial Floor Machine—Hoover Company; *U.S. Public*, pg. 1065

FLOORPLANNER—Software—LSI Logic Corp.; *U.S. Public*, pg. 971

FLOORSHURE—Slip Resistant Finish—Pioneer/Eclipse Corp.; *Int'l*, pg. 71

FLOORSOURCE—Raised Floor Boxes—Walker Systems, Inc.; *U.S. Private*, pg. 1184

FLOORSPLY—Plywood for Flooring—Carter Holt Harvey Limited; *U.S. Public*, pg. 904

FLOPTICAL DRIVE—HOT = Holographic Optical Technology—Iomega Corporation; *U.S. Public*, pg. 912

FLOQUIL—Hobby/Leisure Products—RPM, Inc.; *U.S. Public*, pg. 1356

FLOR—Fabric Softener—Benckiser Consumer Products Inc.; *Int'l*, pg. 185

FLOR-EVER—Sheet Vinyl Flooring—Congoleum Corporation; *U.S. Public*, pg. 69

FLORA—Dinnerware—Dansk International Designs Ltd.; *U.S. Private*, pg. 261

FLORA—Margarine—FIMA-Productos Alimentares, Lda; *Int'l*, pg. 471

FLORA—Additive-Free Food Products—Unilever Plc; *Int'l*, pg. 1433

FLORA FREY—NONE—Groupe Limagrain; *Int'l*, pg. 566

FLORA-GUARD—Heating for Greenhouses—Modine Manufacturing Company; *U.S. Public*, pg. 1121

FLORA HI—Flowers of Hawaii—Flowers of Hawaii; *U.S. Private*, pg. 415

FLORA LACE COLLECTION—NONE—Celebrity Incorporated; *U.S. Public*, pg. 319

FLORAFIBER—Acidophilus & Fiber Tablets—Herbalife International of America, Inc.; *U.S. Public*, pg. 809

FLORACASH—Electronic Point Of Sale Credit Card Processing—Florafax International, Inc.; *U.S. Public*, pg. 654

FLORAFREE—Antiseptic Lotion Soap—SBS Products, Inc.; *U.S. Private*, pg. 955

FLORAL PORTRAITS—Greeting Cards—American Greetings Corporation; *U.S. Public*, pg. 77

FLORAMOR—Flowers—DIMON, Incorporated; *U.S. Public*, pg. 509

FLORANID—Slow-Release Fertilizer—BASF AG; *Int'l*, pg. 103

FLORASENSE—NONE—Blyth Industries; *U.S. Public*, pg. 239

FLORE—NONE—Compar; *Int'l*, pg. 1073

FLORENAMEL—Enamel—ICI Paints; *Int'l*, pg. 664

FLORENCE V VOGUE—NONE—Luxottica Group S.p.A.; *Int'l*, pg. 822

FLORENTINE—Glass & Wood Bifold Door—Wing Industries, Inc.; *U.S. Private*, pg. 1183

FLORET—Air Velocity Measurement Instrument—Bacharach Inc.; *U.S. Private*, pg. 109

FLORET—Flykiller—Reckitt & Colman plc; *Int'l*, pg. 1089

FLORETTE—Area Rugs—Couristan Inc.; *U.S. Private*, pg. 279

FLOREX—Pattern Glass—AFG Industries, Inc.; *Int'l*, pg. 84

FLORHIDE—Ready-Mixed Liquid Paint—PPG Industries, Inc.; *U.S. Public*, pg. 1245

FLORIDA CITRUS—Juice—Labatt Brewing Company Limited; *Int'l*, pg. 679

FLORIDA GOLD—NONE—Stuart Entertainment Inc.; *U.S. Public*, pg. 1526

FLORIDA GROVE AND VEGETABLE MANAGMENT—NONE—Farm Press; *U.S. Public*, pg. 1328

FLORIDA MANUFACTURERS REGISTER—Register—Manufacturers' News, Inc.; *U.S. Private*, pg. 700

FLORIDA PANTHERS—Hockey Team—Florida Panthers Holdings, Inc.; *U.S. Public*, pg. 654

FLORIDA TILE—Ceramic Tile—Premark International, Inc.; *U.S. Public*, pg. 1321

FLORIDA TIMES UNION—Newspaper—Shivers Trading & Operating Co.; *U.S. Private*, pg. 994

FLORIDA'S NATURAL BRAND—Premium, Not-From-Concentrate Juices—Citrus World Inc.; *U.S. Private*, pg. 241

FLORIDAGOLD—Line of 100% Florida OJ—Lykes Brothers Inc.; *U.S. Private*, pg. 682

FLORIGEL—Industrial Chemical-A-Gel-HVM—Engelhard Corp.-Quincy Operations; *U.S. Public*, pg. 582

FLORIGEL H-Y—Industrial Chemical-A-GEL-HVM—Engelhard Corp.-Quincy Operations; *U.S. Public*, pg. 582

FLORIGOLD—Citrus Fruits—Sealed-Sweet Growers, Inc.; *U.S. Private*, pg. 978

FLORIMEX—Flowers—DIMON, Incorporated; *U.S. Public*, pg. 509

FLORIO MARSALA—Wine—IDV North America; *Int'l*, pg. 411

FLORITE—Air Velocity Measurement Instrument—Bacharach Inc.; *U.S. Private*, pg. 109

FLORONE—Pharmaceutical—Dermik Laboratories, Inc.; *Int'l*, pg. 1110

FLORONE CREAM—Pharmaceuticals—Rhone-Poulenc Rorer - U.S.; *Int'l*, pg. 1110

FLORONE E—Pharmaceutical—Dermik Laboratories, Inc.; *Int'l*, pg. 1110

FLORSHEIM COMFORTECH—Walking Shoe for Men—Florsheim Group Inc.; *U.S. Public*, pg. 656

FLORSHEIM FROGS—Golf Shoes—Florsheim Group Inc.; *U.S. Public*, pg. 656

FLORSHEIM OUTDOORSMAN—Performance Men's Shoes—Florsheim Group Inc.; *U.S. Public*, pg. 656

FLORSHEIM SHOES—Shoes for Men—Florsheim Group Inc.; *U.S. Public*, pg. 656

FLORASYNTH—Flavor & Fragrance Compounds—Florasynth Inc.; *Int'l*, pg. 173

FLOSSMATE—Oral Hygiene Aids—John O. Butler Co.; *Int'l*, pg. 1320

FLOSSUGAR—Ready Mix Extra Coarse Sugar—Gold Medal Products Co.; *U.S. Private*, pg. 459

FLOSWEET—Sugar—Refined Sugars, Inc.; *Int'l*, pg. 699

FLOTATION ALL TERRAIN—Tires—Bridgestone/Firestone, Inc.; *Int'l*, pg. 213

FLOTATION 23 DEGREES—Tires—Bridgestone/Firestone, Inc.; *Int'l*, pg. 213

FLOTEC—Water Products—Sta-Rite Industries, Inc.; *U.S. Public*, pg. 1767

FLOTEC—Drainers, Sump Pumps—Sta-Rite Water Systems; *U.S. Public*, pg. 1767

FLOTEC—NONE—WICOR, Inc.; *U.S. Public*, pg. 1767

FLOTECT—Flow Switches—Dwyer Instruments Inc.; *U.S. Private*, pg. 350

FLOTECTOR—Internal Graft Locater—Baxter Research Medical, Inc.; *U.S. Public*, pg. 196

FLOTRAC—NONE—CertainTeed Corporation; *Int'l*, pg. 1170

FLOTREX—Pleated Membrane Cartridge Filters—Osmonics, Inc.; *U.S. Public*, pg. 1233

FLOTRONICS—Filters & Coalescing Device—Osmonics, Inc.; *U.S. Public*, pg. 1233

FLOVA—Italian—Performance Food Group Company; *U.S. Public*, pg. 1278

FLOVUE—Final Control System—Fisher Controls International, Inc.; *U.S. Public*, pg. 573

FLOW-BY—NONE—Nellcor Puritan Bennett Incorporated; *U.S. Public*, pg. 1039

FLOW COATED—Soybean Meal—Central Soya Company, Inc.; *Int'l*, pg. 324

FLOW GEMINI—Health & Environmental Software—GRC International, Inc.; *U.S. Public*, pg. 695

FLOW KOTE—Ready-Mixed Paints—PPG Industries, Inc.; *U.S. Public*, pg. 1245

FLOW MANUFACTURING—Software System—American Software, Inc.; *U.S. Public*, pg. 91

FLOW MATE—Effluent Pump—Zoeller Co.; *U.S. Private*, pg. 1207

FLOW RACK—Storage Rack—Rapistan Demag Corp.; *Int'l*, pg. 837

FLOWCATOR—Underground Tracking System for Drilling—UTILX Corporation; *U.S. Public*, pg. 1701

THE FLOWER CLUB—Joint Marketing Alliance with Numerous Fortune 500 Companies—Florafax International, Inc.; *U.S. Public*, pg. 654

FLOWER CRACKER—Interior Plant Prods.—Security Lawn & Garden Co.; *U.S. Private*, pg. 397

FLOWER OF THE MONTH—Garden Stock by Mail—Michigan Bulb Company; *U.S. Private*, pg. 421

FLOWEROCK—Volcanic Rock for Landscaping—MWCA; *U.S. Public*, pg. 804

FLOWERS—Baked Goods—Flowers Industries, Inc.; *U.S. Public*, pg. 656

FLOWERS—Bitter—Whitbread PLC; *Int'l*, pg. 1498

FLOWERS BY BACHMANS—Free-Standing Flower Markets—Bachman's, Inc.; *U.S. Private*, pg. 109

FLOWLINE—Level Controls—Ryan Herco Products Corp.; *U.S. Private*, pg. 953

FLOWMARK—Business Product—International Business Machines Corporation; *U.S. Public*, pg. 895

FLOWMASTER—Valve—East Jordan Iron Works; *U.S. Private*, pg. 356

FLOWMASTER—Software—Flow International Corporation; *U.S. Public*, pg. 656

FLOWMASTER—Explosive Grade Ammonium Nitrate—PCS Nitrogen; *Int'l*, pg. 1064

FLOWMOLE—Guided Drilling for Utility Replacement—UTILX Corporation; *U.S. Public*, pg. 1701

FLOWPRO—Material Handling Agents—BetzDearborn Inc.; *U.S. Public*, pg. 226

FLOWRATOR—Rotameter Flowmeters—Bailey, Fischer & Porter Company; *Int'l*, pg. 449

FLOWS—Osmonics RO Design Program—Osmonics, Inc.; *U.S. Public*, pg. 1233

FLOWTITE—Glass Fiber Reinforced Plastic Manholes and Pipe—Owens Corning; *U.S. Public*, pg. 1236

FLOWTRAN—Chemical Process Simulation System—Monsanto Company; *U.S. Public*, pg. 1124

FLOWTRON—Lawn & Garden Prods.—Armatron International, Inc.; *U.S. Public*, pg. 131

FLOXAPEN—NONE—SmithKline Beecham Corporation; *Int'l*, pg. 1264

FLOXAPEN—Anti-Infective—SmithKline Beecham plc; *Int'l*, pg. 1264

FLOXIN—NONE—Johnson & Johnson; *U.S. Public*, pg. 927

FLOXIN—Tablets—Ortho-McNeil Pharmaceutical Corporation; *U.S. Public*, pg. 929

FLOXIN I.V.—NONE—Ortho-McNeil Pharmaceutical Corporation; *U.S. Public*, pg. 929

FLUARIX—NONE—SmithKline Beecham Corporation; *Int'l*, pg. 1264

FLUCAM—Ampiroxicam—Pfizer Inc.; *U.S. Public*, pg. 1281

FLUF—Fabric Softener—The Dow Chemical Company; *U.S. Public*, pg. 522

FLUFF-UP—Rug Shampoo—The Dow Chemical Company; *U.S. Public*, pg. 522

FLUFF-OUT—Facial Tissue—Marcal Paper Mills, Inc.; *U.S. Private*, pg. 701

FLUFFICUFF—Blood Pressure Cuffs—Vital Signs, Inc.; *U.S. Private*, pg. 1723

FLUFFO—Shortening—The Procter & Gamble Company; *U.S. Public*, pg. 1330

FLUFFY—Concentrated Fabric Softener—Blue Cross Laboratories; *U.S. Private*, pg. 152

FLUFFY REFILL—Fabric Softener Refill 21.5-oz Carton—Blue Cross Laboratories; *U.S. Private*, pg. 152

FLUID ACTION SOLDER FLUX—Industrial Chemical—Hercules Chemical Co., Inc.; *U.S. Private*, pg. 523

FLUID CONSERVATION SYSTEMS—Equipment for Detecting Underground Water Leaks—Halma p.l.c.; *Int'l*, pg. 589

FLUID-CORE ROLL—Temperature Controlled Roll with Double Shell—Harnischfeger Industries, Inc.; *U.S. Public*, pg. 788

FLUID FLEX—Fats & Oils—Van den Bergh Foods Company; *Int'l*, pg. 1436

FLUID MANAGEMENT—Fluid Dispensing, Metering & Mixing Equipment—IDEX Corporation; *U.S. Public*, pg. 862

FLUID POWER SERVICE CENTER—Periodical—Penton Publishing, Inc.; *U.S. Public*, pg. 1306

FLUID-TITE—PVC Pipe—CertainTeed Corporation; *Int'l*, pg. 1170

FLUID-SHAFT—Electric Motors—Reuland Electric Company; *U.S. Private*, pg. 925

FLUIDAIR—Air Compressors—IMI Plc; *Int'l*, pg. 646

FLUIDIC FLARE—Refiner & Process Waste Gas Burner—NAO, Inc.; *U.S. Private*, pg. 771

FLUIDIZER—Size Reduction of Granular Material—Ferguson International, Inc.; *U.S. Private*, pg. 401

FLUIDSHIELD—Surgical Mask—Kimberly-Clark Tecnol; *U.S. Public*, pg. 959

FLUNARL—Cardiovascular Agents—Kyowa Hakko Kogyo Company, Ltd.; *Int'l*, pg. 778

FLUOBOND—Bondable PTFE—James Walker & Co. Limited; *Int'l*, pg. 1485

FLUOGRAF—Gland Packing—James Walker & Co. Limited; *Int'l*, pg. 1485

FLUOLION—PTFE Components—James Walker & Co. Limited; *Int'l*, pg. 1485

FLUOMERIC—Mercury Vapor Lamp—Duro-Test Corporation; *U.S. Private*, pg. 349

FLUOR—Engrng., Construction & Diversified Services—Fluor Daniel Inc.; *U.S. Public*, pg. 660

FLUOR-O-PAC—Emergency Lighting—MagneTek Lighting Products Group; *U.S. Public*, pg. 1037

FLUORAD—Fluorochemical Surfactants—3M; *U.S. Public*, pg. 1604

FLUOREL—Fluoroelastomer—3M; *U.S. Public*, pg. 1604

FLUORESCEIN—Sodium Ophthalmic Solution—Alcon Laboratories, Inc.; *Int'l*, pg. 916

FLUORESCITE—Sodium Fluorescein Injection—Alcon Laboratories, Inc.; *Int'l*, pg. 916

FLUORGLAS—PTFE/Glass—Furon Fluorglas Products; *U.S. Public*, pg. 689

FLUORIGARD—Dental Rinses—Colgate-Palmolive Company; *U.S. Public*, pg. 397

FLUORINERT—Electronic Liquids—3M; *U.S. Public*, pg. 1604

FLUORIVER—Chemical Reagant—Hach Company; *U.S. Public*, pg. 773

FLUORO-URACIL ROCHE—Anti Cancer Drug—Roche Holding Ltd.; *Int'l*, pg. 1119

FLUORODYNE—Filters—Pall Corporation; *U.S. Public*, pg. 1253

FLUOROFLEX—Rigid Gas-Permeable Daily Wear Contact Lens—The Cooper Companies, Inc.; *U.S. Public*, pg. 442

FLUOROFLEX UV—Contact Lenses—The Cooper Companies, Inc.; *U.S. Public*, pg. 442

FLUOROFLOOD—Outdoor Lighting Fixtures—General Electric Canada Inc.; *U.S. Public*, pg. 713

FLUOROGARD—Cartridge Filter—Millipore Corporation; *U.S. Public*, pg. 1112

FLUOROGLIDE—TFE Fluoropolymer Spray Film—Norton Performance Plastics; *Int'l*, pg. 1174

FLUOROGOLD—Proprietary Materials—Furon Company; *U.S. Public*, pg. 688

FLUOROLASE RARE EARTH DOPED FIBER—Enhanced Fluoride Fiber—Galileo Corp.; *U.S. Public*, pg. 698

FLUOROLOYS—Proprietary Materials—Furon Company; *U.S. Public*, pg. 688

FLUOROLUBES—Lubricants—Occidental Chemical Corporation; *U.S. Public*, pg. 1210

FLUORON—NONE—Lawter International, Inc.; *U.S. Public*, pg. 980

FLUOROPA—Amino Acid Analysis Reagent—Dionex Corporation; *U.S. Public*, pg. 510

FLUOROPORE—Membrane Filter—Millipore Corporation; *U.S. Public*, pg. 1112

FLUOROSINT—Filled PTFE Shapes & Parts—DSM Engineering Plastic Products; *Int'l*, pg. 354

FLUOTHANE—Pharmaceutical—Zeneca Group Plc; *Int'l*, pg. 1524

FLURAN—Fluoroelastomer Tubing—Norton Performance Plastics; *Int'l*, pg. 1174

FLURO—Photo Lenses—Eastman Kodak Company; *U.S. Public*, pg. 550

FLURO-SPRAY—Light Bulb—Duro-Test Corporation; *U.S. Private*, pg. 349

FLURODIZE—Fluoropolymer Coating for Architectural Aluminum—DeSoto Inc.; *U.S. Public*, pg. 956

FLUROPON—Fluropolymer Coating for Architectural Metal—DeSoto Inc.; *U.S. Public*, pg. 956

FLUROSPOT—X-Ray Film—Eastman Kodak Company; *U.S. Public*, pg. 550

FLUROSTAR—Polyvinylidine Polyester Coating—The Dexter Corporation; *U.S. Public*, pg. 504

FLUROTEC—Vial Stoppers—The West Company, Incorporated; *U.S. Public*, pg. 1755

FLUROTHANE—Thick Film Coating for Agricultural Metal—DeSoto Inc.; *U.S. Public*, pg. 956

FLUSHIELD—Vaccine—American Home Products Corporation; *U.S. Public*, pg. 79

FLUSHLINE—NONE—Kawneer Company; *U.S. Public*, pg. 60

FLUSHLOK—Insulated Sash & Division Bar Window Units—PPG Industries, Inc.; *U.S. Public*, pg. 1245

FLUSHSEAL—Grooved Pipe Coupling Gasket—Victaulic Company of America; *U.S. Private*, pg. 1138

FLUTEX—Pattern Glass—AFG Industries, Inc.; *Int'l*, pg. 84

FLUTTER—Mucus Clearance Device—Nellcor Puritan Bennett Incorporated; *U.S. Public*, pg. 1039

FLUVAC—Veterinary Pharmaceuticals—American Home Products Corporation; *U.S. Public*, pg. 79

FLUVIRAL—NONE—BioChem Pharma Inc.; *Int'l*, pg. 196

FLUVIRIN—NONE—Medeva PLC; *Int'l*, pg. 852

FLUX-RITE 90—Soldering Flux—La-Co Industries Markal Company; *U.S. Private*, pg. 640

FLUXARTEN—Peripheral Vasodilator—SmithKline Beecham plc; *Int'l*, pg. 1264

FLUZONE—Influenza Vaccine—Connaught Laboratories, Inc.; *Int'l*, pg. 1109

FLXIBLE—Transit Buses—General Automotive Corporation; *U.S. Private*, pg. 443

FLXIBLE METRO—Transit Bus—General Automotive Corporation; *U.S. Private*, pg. 443

FLY—NONE—Brown & Sharpe Manufacturing Company; *U.S. Public*, pg. 260

FLY FISHERMAN—Periodical—Cowles Enthusiast Media, Inc.; *U.S. Private*, pg. 281

FLY SNIPER—Fly Control—Security Lawn & Garden Co.; *U.S. Private*, pg. 397

FLY STOP—Fly Trap—Security Lawn & Garden Co.; *U.S. Private*, pg. 397

FLY WATE—Fishing Rods, Reels and Line—Martin Reels, A Division of Zebco; *U.S. Public*, pg. 265

FLYER—Tires—Bridgestone/Firestone, Inc.; *Int'l*, pg. 213

FLYER—Tripod Projection Screen—Da-Lite Screen Company, Inc.; *U.S. Private*, pg. 306

FLYER'S—Men's Slacks & Shorts—Tropical Sportswear International; *U.S. Private*, pg. 1105

FLYERS—Spicy Chicken Wings—Tyson Foods, Inc.; *U.S. Public*, pg. 1652

FLYING—Aviation Magazine—Hachette Filipacchi Magazines Inc.; *Int'l*, pg. 794

FLYING ALONE—Brochures For Parents Of Children Traveling Alone—American Automobile Association; *U.S. Private*, pg. 50

FLYING COLORS—Sunglasses—Bausch & Lomb Incorporated; *U.S. Public*, pg. 194

FLYING COLORS—Collection of White Faucets & Fixtures—The Black & Decker Corporation; *U.S. Public*, pg. 233

FLYING DUTCHMAN—Pipe Tobaccos—Consolidated Cigar Corporation; *U.S. Private*, pg. 690

FLYING HORSE—NONE—Cruspi S.A.; *Int'l*, pg. 348

FLYMO—Garden Equipment—Electrolux, AB; *Int'l*, pg. 438

FOAM CARE—Surgical Hand Scrub—Ballard Medical Products; *U.S. Public*, pg. 171

FOAM CARE DOUBLE SCRUB—NONE—Ballard Medical Products; *U.S. Public*, pg. 171

FOAM CAST—Process that Utilizes Foam Patterns to Produce Castings—Waukesha Foundry Inc.; *U.S. Private*, pg. 1154

FOAM CAT—Systems for Spraying Insulating Foam—Graco Inc.; *U.S. Public*, pg. 756

FOAM LOCK—Foamboard Adhesive—Miracle Adhesives; *U.S. Public*, pg. 1466

FOAM-TROL—Antifoaming Agents—BetzDearborn Inc.; *U.S. Public*, pg. 226

FOAMATIC—Small Vacuum—Advance Machine Company; *Int'l*, pg. 932

FOAMBRAKE—Defoaming Agent for Paper Making Applications—PPG Industries, Inc.; *U.S. Public*, pg. 1245

FOAMDET—Detergent—Oakite Products, Inc.; *Int'l*, pg. 861

FOAMFLEX—Doorstrip—Essex Specialty Products; *U.S. Public*, pg. 523

FOAMGRIP—Anchoring Device—U.S. Surgical Corp.; *U.S. Public*, pg. 1687

FOAMIZER—Device For Foam Washing Vehicles—Oakite Products, Inc.; *Int'l*, pg. 861

FOAMPRO—Automatic Foam Proportioner—Hypro Corporation; *U.S. Public*, pg. 1767

FOAMPRO—NONE—WICOR, Inc.; *U.S. Public*, pg. 1767

FOAMSEALR—ESB Polyethylene Foam Insulation—Owens Corning; *U.S. Public*, pg. 1236

FOAMSEALR—Sill Plate Gasket—Owens Corning/Foamular; *U.S. Public*, pg. 1237

FOAMTREAD—Slippers—Kaufman Footwear; *Int'l*, pg. 725

FOAMULAR—Extruded Polystyrene Insulation Sheets—Owens Corning; *U.S. Public*, pg. 1236

FOAMULAR—Insulation—Owens Corning/Foamular; *U.S. Public*, pg. 1237

FOAMY—Shave Preparations—The Gillette Company; *U.S. Public*, pg. 743

FOCAL—Contemporary Door Trim Halve—Triangle Brass Manufacturing; *U.S. Private*, pg. 1101

FOCAUDIT—An Auditing System—Information Builders; *U.S. Private*, pg. 561

FOCMAN—Project Management System—Information Builders; *U.S. Private*, pg. 561

FOCUS—Comml. Security System—ADT Security Services, Inc.; *U.S. Public*, pg. 1649

FOCUS—Crop Protection Agent—BASF AG; *Int'l*, pg. 103

FOCUS—Magazine—Burda Holding GmbH & Co., KG; *Int'l*, pg. 233

FOCUS—Dialyzers—Fresenius Medical Care (North America); *Int'l*, pg. 505

FOCUS—4 GL for Developing Information Management Applications—Information Builders; *U.S. Private*, pg. 561

FOCUS—Office Furniture—Kimball International, Inc.; *U.S. Public*, pg. 956

FOCUS—Nonwoven Fabric—Kimberly-Clark Corporation; *U.S. Public*, pg. 958

FOCUS—Slide Lighting Control—The Lamson & Sessions Co.; *U.S. Public*, pg. 976

FOCUS—NONE—Life Technologies, Inc.; *U.S. Public*, pg. 504

FOCUS—Contact Lenses—Novartis; *Int'l*, pg. 972

FOCUS—Fiber Optic Connection Universal System—Porta Systems Corp.; *U.S. Public*, pg. 1317

FOCUS/ELS—Executive Information Systems—Information Builders; *U.S. Private*, pg. 561

FOCUS FEATURE—On-line Retrieval Feature—The Mead Corporation; *U.S. Public*, pg. 1074

FOCUS FOR WINDOWS—4 GL PC Based Application Development System for Database Management—Information Builders; *U.S. Private*, pg. 561

FOCUS SERIES—Furniture—Myrtle/Mueller, A Haworth Co.; *U.S. Private*, pg. 512

FOCUS 3—Heater—The Canadian Coleman Co., Ltd.; *U.S. Private*, pg. 691

FOCUS 12—Heaters—The Canadian Coleman Co., Ltd.; *U.S. Private*, pg. 691

FOCUSVIEW—NONE—UB Networks; *Int'l*, pg. 924

FODEN—Trucks—Paccar Inc.; *U.S. Public*, pg. 1246

FODOR—Travel Books—Random House, Inc.; *U.S. Private*, pg. 20

FODOR'S—Travel Guides—Fodor's Travel Publications, Inc.; *U.S. Private*, pg. 21

FODUCT—Flexible Conduit—Aeroquip-Vickers, Inc.; *U.S. Public*, pg. 24

FOG PACER—Suspension Insulator—Lapp Insulator Company; *U.S. Private*, pg. 473

FOGA—Aluminum Profiles—Foga System International AB; *Int'l*, pg. 496

FOGA SYSTEM—Extruded Aluminum Profiles for Exhibit Industry—Foga Systems; *Int'l*, pg. 496

FOGEL—Freezers & Refrigerators—Jordon Commercial Refrigeration Co.; *U.S. Private*, pg. 599

FOGJET—Spray Nozzle—Spraying Systems Co.; *U.S. Private*, pg. 1026

FOHO FOR OILY HAIR ONLY—Shampoo & Rinse—The Gillette Company; *U.S. Public*, pg. 743

FOHRENBURGER—NONE—Bierbrauerei Fohrenburg; *Int'l*, pg. 194

FOIBEX VA—Herbicide—Novartis; *Int'l*, pg. 972

FOIL-FAST—Adhesive Anchor—Powers Fastening, Inc.; *U.S. Private*, pg. 878

FOILCLAD—Spirally Wound Composite Cans—Reynolds Metals Company; *U.S. Public*, pg. 1385

FOILFLAKE—Aluminum—United States Bronze Powders, Inc.; *U.S. Private*, pg. 1124

FOILLE—First Aid & Burn Products—Blistex, Inc.; *U.S. Private*, pg. 149

FOLD-AWAY—Electric Slicer—The Rival Company; *U.S. Public*, pg. 1391

FOLD KRAFT—Paperboard—The Mead Corporation; *U.S. Public*, pg. 1074

FOLD 'N GO—Playard—Century Products Co.; *U.S. Private*, pg. 226

FOLD N' GO—Folding Handle Hair Dryer—Andis Company; *U.S. Private*, pg. 73

FOLDAMAX—Table-Top Folding Machine—Pitney Bowes Inc.; *U.S. Public*, pg. 1303

FOLDERVIEW—NONE—FileNet Corporation; *U.S. Public*, pg. 622

FOLDING HUNTER—Cutlery—Buck Knives, Inc.; *U.S. Private*, pg. 177

FOLDOOR—Folding Partitions—Holcomb & Hoke Mfg. Company, Inc.; *U.S. Private*, pg. 533

FOLDOVER—Greeting Cards Invits. & Anncmnts., Thank U Notes, Calendars, & Party Goods—American Greetings Corporation; *U.S. Public*, pg. 77

FOLDUR—Converting Paper—Champion International Corp.; *U.S. Public*, pg. 333

FOLEX—Merphos Defoliant—Rhone-Poulenc S.A.; *Int'l*, pg. 1108

FOLEY—Kitchen Tools & Gadgets—Mirro Company; *U.S. Public*, pg. 1177

FOLEY—Cookware—Newell Co.; *U.S. Public*, pg. 1176

FOLEY-BELSAW—Tool Maintenance Equip.—Foley-Belsaw Company; *U.S. Private*, pg. 416

FOLEY'S—Department Stores—Foley's; *U.S. Public*, pg. 1063

FOLEY'S—Department Stores—The May Department Stores Company; *U.S. Public*, pg. 1063

FOLGERS—Coffees—The Folger Coffee Company; *U.S. Public*, pg. 1331

FOLGERS COFFEE SINGLES—Single Serve Coffee Bags—The Procter & Gamble Company; *U.S. Public*, pg. 1330

FOLGERS GOURMET SUPREME—Coffee—The Procter & Gamble Company; *U.S. Public*, pg. 1330

FOLHAMINUT—Pastry Ingredient—Royal Gist-Brocades N.V.; *Int'l*, pg. 1142

FOLIA-FEED—Plant Growth Stimulant—The Dow Chemical Company; *U.S. Public*, pg. 522

FOLIAFUME—Pesticide—Roussel Corporation; *Int'l*, pg. 625

FOLIAFUME—Pesticide—Roussel UCLAF S.A.; *Int'l*, pg. 626

FOLIES—NONE—LPC Industrias Alimenticias S.A.; *Int'l*, pg. 380

FOLIFERT—Fertilizers—DSM Chemie Linz GmbH; *Int'l*, pg. 356

FOLIO—Software—The Mead Corporation; *U.S. Public*, pg. 1074

FOLIO—Catalogue—Saks Fifth Avenue; *U.S. Public*, pg. 1429

FOLIO PREVIEWS—Software—The Mead Corporation; *U.S. Public*, pg. 1074

FOLIO VIEWS—Software—The Mead Corporation; *U.S. Public*, pg. 1074

FOLIOTRONIC—Computerized Security Document Finishing System—Check Technology Corporation; *U.S. Public*, pg. 342

FOLKLORE—Lumber & Wood Products—Georgia-Pacific Corporation; *U.S. Public*, pg. 735

FOLLOW THE LEADER—Slogan—American Honda Motor Co., Inc. Motorcycle Division; *Int'l*, pg. 634

FOLONARI—Wine—Frederick Wildman & Sons Ltd.; *U.S. Private*, pg. 1176

FOLTENE—Hair Supplement—International Cosmetics Co., Ltd.; *Int'l*, pg. 684

FOLTENE HAIR CARE SYSTEM—Hair Care—Conair Corporation; *U.S. Private*, pg. 261

FOMADS—Business Forms Mngmt. & Distr. System—The Standard Register Company; *U.S. Public*, pg. 1505

FOMBLIN—Perfluorinated Polyether Fluids—Montedison S.p.A.; *Int'l*, pg. 324

FOME-COR—Extruded Polystyrene Foam Board—Monsanto Company; *U.S. Public*, pg. 1124

FOND DE CAVE—Cabernet Sauvignon/Chardonnay—Penaflor S.A.; *Int'l*, pg. 1032

FONDANMINUT—Pastry Ingredient—Royal Gist-Brocades N.V.; *Int'l*, pg. 1142

FONDO—Acrylic Leather Finish—Henkel Corporation; *Int'l*, pg. 610

FONE BUX—Prepaid Calling Cards—Fone America, Inc.; *U.S. Public*, pg. 661

FONEAMERICARD—Prepaid Calling Cards—Fone America, Inc.; *U.S. Public*, pg. 661

FONT STRIP STRUCTURE—Photo Typesetters—AGFA EPS Division; *Int'l*, pg. 172

FONT VELLA—Mineral Water—Danone Group; *Int'l*, pg. 379

FONTAMINI HEIRLOOM NATIVITIES—Imported Italian Nativity; Figures & Nativity Village Structures—Roman, Inc.; *U.S. Private*, pg. 942

FONTANA—Records—Philips Electronics N.V.; *Int'l*, pg. 1051

FONTANA CANDIDA—Italian Wines—Brown-Forman Beverages Worldwide; *U.S. Public*, pg. 261

FONTANA CANDIDA—Italian Wines—Brown-Forman Corporation; *U.S. Public*, pg. 261

FONTANA FREDDA—Italian Wines—Brown-Forman Corporation; *U.S. Public*, pg. 261

FONTANAFREDDA—Italian Wines—Brown-Forman Beverages Worldwide; *U.S. Public*, pg. 261

FONTANELLE CHARDONNAY—NONE—Castello Banfi Srl.; *U.S. Private*, pg. 113

FONTANELLE-CABERNET SAUVIGNON—Red Wine—Banfi Vintners; *U.S. Private*, pg. 113

FOOD & BEVERAGE—Cleaning Products—Food & Beverage; *U.S. Public*, pg. 562

FOOD & WINE—Magazine—American Express Company; *U.S. Public*, pg. 73

FOOD & WINE—Magazine—American Express Publishing Corporation; *U.S. Public*, pg. 74

FOOD BONANZA—Retail Grocery Stores—Nash Finch Company; *U.S. Public*, pg. 1151

FOOD CARNIVAL—Grocery Store—Farm Fresh, Inc.; *U.S. Public*, pg. 1388

FOOD CITY—Grocery Stores—URM Stores, Inc.; *U.S. Private*, pg. 1114

FOOD CLUB—Dry Groceries—Topco Associates, Inc.; *U.S. Private*, pg. 1091

FOOD EMPORIUM—Food Stores—The Great Atlantic & Pacific Tea Company, Inc.; *Int'l*, pg. 1375

THE FOOD EMPORIUM—Food Store—The Food Emporium; *Int'l*, pg. 1375

FOOD ENGINEERING—Magazine Covering Packaging & Processing Technology—Reed Elsevier Business Information; *Int'l*, pg. 1095

FOOD ENGINEERING INTERNATIONAL—Magazine Targeting Food & Beverage Industry in Europe & Asia—Reed Elsevier Business Information; *Int'l*, pg. 1095

FOOD FAIR—Grocery Store—Bruno's Inc.; *U.S. Public*, pg. 265

FOOD FOLKS—Retail Grocery Stores—Nash Finch Company; *U.S. Public*, pg. 1151

FOOD FOLKS & FUN—Advertising Slogan—McDonald's Corporation; *U.S. Public*, pg. 1068

FOOD FOR FRIENDS—NONE—The Stop & Shop Companies, Inc.; *Int'l*, pg. 750

FOOD FORMULATING—Magazine Providing Information for Formulators in Food & Beverage Industry—Reed Elsevier Business Information; *Int'l*, pg. 1095

FOOD GIANT—NONE—GES Inc.; *U.S. Private*, pg. 434

FOOD LION—Grocery Stores—Food Lion, Inc.; *Int'l*, pg. 463

FOOD MACHINERY DIVISION—NONE—The Cardwell Machine Company; *U.S. Private*, pg. 209

FOOD MANAGEMENT—Periodicals—Penton Publishing, Inc.; *U.S. Public*, pg. 1306

FOOD MANUFACTURING—New-Product Tabloid—Reed Elsevier Business Information; *Int'l*, pg. 1095

FOOD MARKETING—Wholesale Groceries—SuperValu, Inc.-Food Marketing Div.; *U.S. Public*, pg. 1540

FOOD MASTER—Annual Hardbound Reference Source—Reed Elsevier Business Information; *Int'l*, pg. 1095

FOOD PAVILION—Supermarkets—Associated Grocers, Inc.; *U.S. Private*, pg. 90

FOOD PRIDE—Retail Grocery Stores—Nash Finch Company; *U.S. Public*, pg. 1151

FOOD PROCESSOR—Magazine—Reed Business Information Pty. Limited; *Int'l*, pg. 1094

FOOD SERVICE—Fruit & Vegetable Container Line of Products—Spartech Plastics; *U.S. Public*, pg. 1496

FOOD TOWN—NONE—Seaway Food Town, Inc.; *U.S. Public*, pg. 1452

FOOD WORLD—Grocery Store—Bruno's Inc.; *U.S. Public*, pg. 265

FOODANE—Meat Products—Vestjyske Slagterier; *Int'l*, pg. 1464

FOODMAX—Upscale Super-Warehouse Grocery Store—Bruno's Inc.; *U.S. Public*, pg. 265

FOODS—NONE—Lever Brothers West Indies Ltd.; *Int'l*, pg. 1437

FOODSERVICE DIRECTOR—Business Publication—Bill Communications, Inc.; *Int'l*, pg. 1446

THE FOODSERVICE DISTRIBUTOR—Periodical—Penton Publishing, Inc.; *U.S. Public*, pg. 1306

FOODSERVICE EQUIPMENT & SUPPLIES—Magazine for Dealers, Distributors & Designers of Foodservice Facilities—Reed Elsevier Business Information; *Int'l*, pg. 1095

FOOT CHARGERS—Foot Massagers—Bristol-Myers Squibb Company; *U.S. Public*, pg. 253

FOOT COMFORT—Foot Preparations—Scholl U.S.A.; *U.S. Public*, pg. 1438

FOOT CUSHION—NONE—Royal Rubber & Manufacturing Co.; *U.S. Private*, pg. 949

FOOT FIXER—Air Massage—Clairol, Inc.; *U.S. Public*, pg. 254

FOOT GUARD—Deodorant—The Gillette Company; *U.S. Public*, pg. 743

FOOT JOY—Shoes, Gloves, Accessories—Titleist & Foot-Joy Worldwide; *U.S. Public*, pg. 675

FOOT-JOY CLASSICS—Shoes, Gloves & Socks—Acushnet Company; *U.S. Public*, pg. 675

FOOT-JOY CLASSICS—Golf Shoes—Fortune Brands, Inc.; *U.S. Public*, pg. 674

FOOT LOCKER—Footwear & Sports Apparel—Foot Locker; *U.S. Public*, pg. 1777

FOOT LOCKER—Athletic Footwear & Apparel—Woolworth Corporation; *U.S. Public*, pg. 1777

FOOT RELIEF ZONE—Section in Spa—Coleman Spas, Inc.; *U.S. Private*, pg. 691

FOOT SCENE—Shoes—Genesco Inc.; *U.S. Public*, pg. 728

FOOT SPA—Foot Massagers—Bristol-Myers Squibb Company; *U.S. Public*, pg. 253

FOOT SPA WHIRL—Foot Bath with Massage—Remington Products Company, L.L.C.; *U.S. Private*, pg. 921

FOOTBALL DIGEST—Magazine—Century Publishing Company; *U.S. Private*, pg. 226

FOOTBALL STRATEGY—Game—Monarch Avalon, Inc.; *U.S. Public*, pg. 1123

FOOTE-JONES—Standard & Custom Gear Drives—Foote-Jones/Illinois Gear; *U.S. Public*, pg. 1370

FOOTGARDS—Disposable Plastic Shoe Covers—Handgards Inc.; *U.S. Private*, pg. 499

FOOTNOTES—Hosiery & Related Apparel—Mayer/Berkshire Corporation; *U.S. Private*, pg. 717

FOOTPRINT—Office Furniture—Kimball International, Inc.; *U.S. Public*, pg. 956

FOOTQUARTERS—Brand Name Family Shoe Stores—Woolworth Corporation; *U.S. Public*, pg. 1777

FOOTWEAR NEWS—Business Publication—Fairchild Publications; *U.S. Public*, pg. 513

FOOTYFAB—Steel Reinforcing Mesh—Smorgon A.R.C.; *Int'l*, pg. 1269

FOR A GOOD LOOK—Photographic Papers—Eastman Kodak Company; *U.S. Public*, pg. 550

FOR ALL YOU'RE WORTH!—Recruiting Package—RE/MAX International, Inc.; *U.S. Private*, pg. 912

FOR ATHLETIC USE ONLY—High Performance, Functional Athletic Shoes—Avia; *U.S. Private*, pg. 62

FOR EVER—Floor Wax—Grow Group, Inc.; *Int'l*, pg. 663

FOR FEET THAT COMPETE—Socks—Wigwam Mills, Inc.; *U.S. Private*, pg. 1175

FOR HEAT'S SAKE—Plumbing Chemical—Hercules Chemical Co., Inc.; *U.S. Private*, pg. 523

FOR THE FINISHING TOUCH—Beloit Lenox—Beloit Corporation; *U.S. Public*, pg. 789

FOR THE TIMES OF YOUR LIFE—Photographic Films & Paper—Eastman Kodak Company; *U.S. Public*, pg. 550

FORAL RESIN—Rosin Ester—Hercules Incorporated; *U.S. Public*, pg. 809

FORANE—Isoflurane—Abbott Laboratories; *U.S. Public*, pg. 12

FORANE—Pharmaceutical Anaesthetics—The BOC Group plc; *Int'l*, pg. 121

FORANE—Refrigerants & Foaming Agents & Amines—Elf Atochem North America, Inc.; *Int'l*, pg. 445

FORANE—Isoflurane, USP—Ohmeda; *Int'l*, pg. 121

FORASOL—Oil Service Supply—Forasol S.A.; *Int'l*, pg. 496

FORAY—Dry Chemical Agent—Ansul Incorporated; *U.S. Public*, pg. 1648

FORAY 48.B—Biological Product for Control of Forestry Pests—Novo Nordisk A/S; *Int'l*, pg. 987

FORBES—Magazine—Forbes, Inc.; *U.S. Private*, pg. 417

FORBIDDEN—Eau de Parfum—Dana Perfumes Corp.; *U.S. Private*, pg. 922

FORBO—Floor & Wallcoverings—Forbo Holding SA; *Int'l*, pg. 496

FORBON—Vulcanized Fibre—NVF Company; *U.S. Private*, pg. 772

FORCE—Outboard Motors—Brunswick Corporation; *U.S. Public*, pg. 265

FORCE—Fitness Products—York Barbell Co., Inc.; *U.S. Private*, pg. 1196

FORCE ARGON—NONE—Pfizer Inc.; *U.S. Public*, pg. 1281

FORCE EZ—NONE—Pfizer Inc.; *U.S. Public*, pg. 1281

FORCE-FEED LOADER—Self-Propelled Belt Loader—Athey Products Corporation; *U.S. Public*, pg. 142

FORCE 5—Warewashing Detergents & Dispenser—Ecolab Inc.; *U.S. Public*, pg. 562

FORCE 40—NONE—Pfizer Inc.; *U.S. Public*, pg. 1281

FORCE 4—Tires—Bridgestone/Firestone, Inc.; *Int'l*, pg. 213

FORCE FX—NONE—Pfizer Inc.; *U.S. Public*, pg. 1281

FORCE GSU—NONE—Pfizer Inc.; *U.S. Public*, pg. 1281

FORCE OUTBOARD MOTORS—Outboard Motors—Mercury Marine; *U.S. Public*, pg. 265

FORCE 30—NONE—Pfizer Inc.; *U.S. Public*, pg. 1281

FORCE 300—NONE—Pfizer Inc.; *U.S. Public*, pg. 1281

FORCE 10,000—Concrete Strength Enhancer—W.R. Grace & Co.; *U.S. Public*, pg. 754

FORD—Tractors—New Holland Ltd.; *Int'l*, pg. 484

FORD BACON & DAVIS—Engineers & Contractors—Ford, Bacon & Davis Companies Inc.; *Int'l*, pg. 401

FORD EXPEDITION—Truck—Ford Motor Company; *U.S. Public*, pg. 661

FORD STEEL—Abrasive Resistant Wearalloy Bars—EEI Corporation; *Int'l*, pg. 425

FORD TRUCKS—Trucks—Heintzelman's Truck Center Inc.; *U.S. Private*, pg. 519

FORD'S—Insecticides & Herbicides—Roussel Corporation; *Int'l*, pg. 625

FORE!—Golf Magazine—EMAP Pursuit Publishing; *Int'l*, pg. 451

FORE—Fungicide—Rohm and Haas Company; *U.S. Public*, pg. 1403

FORECAST—Lighting Fixtures—The Genlyte Group Incorporated; *U.S. Public*, pg. 729

FOREGROUND MUSIC ONE—Satellite Delivered Origional Artist Music—Muzak Limited Partnership; *U.S. Private*, pg. 222

FORELLI—Sportswear—United Retail Group, Inc.; *U.S. Public*, pg. 1679

FOREMAN/FOURMAN—All-Terrain Vehicles—American Honda Motor Co., Inc. Motorcycle Division; *Int'l*, pg. 634

FOREMOST—Wallcoverings—Borden, Inc.; *U.S. Private*, pg. 157

FOREMOST—Company Name—Foremost Corporation of America; *U.S. Public*, pg. 667

FOREST—Fasteners—Caparo Industries Plc.; *Int'l*, pg. 265

FOREST—Crude Oil & Natural Gas Exploration and Production—Forest Oil Corporation; *U.S. Public*, pg. 670

FOREST FRESH—Pine, Hardwood & Cypress Bark Pieces—Georgia-Pacific Corporation; *U.S. Public*, pg. 735

FOREST LINES INC.—Deep Sea Shipping Services—Central Gulf Lines, Inc.; *U.S. Public*, pg. 907

FOREST PURE—Hair, Body & Bath—Levlad, Inc.; *U.S. Private*, pg. 663

FOREST RIDGE—Vinyl Siding—Georgia-Pacific Corporation; *U.S. Public*, pg. 735

FORESTER 1870—Bourbon Whiskey—Brown-Forman Beverages Worldwide; *U.S. Public*, pg. 261

FORESTGLO—Paneling—Weyerhaeuser Forest Products Company; *U.S. Public*, pg. 1764

FORESTRY SPECIAL—Tires—Bridgestone/Firestone, Inc.; *Int'l*, pg. 213

FORESTRY SPECIAL WIRE TREAD PLY—Tires—Bridgestone/Firestone, Inc.; *Int'l*, pg. 213

FORETHOUGHT—Funeral Plans—Hillenbrand Industries, Inc.; *U.S. Public*, pg. 828

FOREVA—Hosiery for Women—Grupo Synkro, S.A. de C.V.; *Int'l*, pg. 576

FOREVER—Batteries—Bridgestone/Firestone, Inc.; *Int'l*, pg. 213

FOREVER FREE—Greeting Cards—American Greetings Corporation; *U.S. Public*, pg. 77

FOREVER YOURS—NONE—IWI Holding Limited; *U.S. Public*, pg. 861

FOREVER YOURS—Frozen Novelty Ice Cream Dessert—M&M/Mars; *U.S. Private*, pg. 707

FOREVER YOURS—Jewelry—World Pacific Ullenberg Corp.; *U.S. Public*, pg. 861

FOREVERFLEX—NONE—Krause's Furniture Inc.; *U.S. Public*, pg. 967

FOREX—Foamed Panels—Alusuisse-Lonza Holding Ltd.; *Int'l*, pg. 66

FORGE—Herbicide—Monsanto Company; *U.S. Public*, pg. 1124

FORGE—Books—St. Martins Press, Inc.; *Int'l*, pg. 1479

FORGET IT—Batteries—Universal Cooperatives, Inc.; *U.S. Private*, pg. 1127

FORGET ME NOT—NONE—American Greetings Corporation; *U.S. Public*, pg. 77

FORGET-ME-NOT—Greeting Cards—American Greetings U.S. Greeting Card Division; *U.S. Public*, pg. 78

FORGETEMP—Roll Forged Steel—Bucyrus Blades Inc.; *U.S. Private*, pg. 383

FORGING—Periodical—Penton Publishing, Inc.; *U.S. Public*, pg. 1306

FORGIVENESS IS IN OUR SOLES—NONE—Callaway Golf Company; *U.S. Public*, pg. 294

FORGOTTEN REALMS—Books & Games—TSR, Inc.; *U.S. Private*, pg. 1185

FORILIN—Product for the Treatment of Infections—Novo Nordisk A/S; *Int'l*, pg. 987

FORKER—NONE—Daimler-Benz Aktiengesellschaft; *Int'l*, pg. 366

FORLENE—Herbicide—The Dow Chemical Company; *U.S. Public*, pg. 522

FORM-A-DRAIN—PVC Foundation Drainings System—CertainTeed Corporation; *Int'l*, pg. 1170

FORM-A-GASKET—Sealant—Loctite Corp. North American Group; *Int'l*, pg. 611

FORM-A-THREAD—Silicone—Loctite Corporation; *Int'l*, pg. 611

FORM & FUNCTION—Stationery; Calendars; Picture Frames; Mugs; File Boxes—American Greetings Corporation; *U.S. Public*, pg. 77

FORM-FIT—Latex Gloves—Magla Products; *U.S. Private*, pg. 695

FORMAGG—Lactose & Chloresterol Free Cheese Substitute—Galaxy Food Company; *U.S. Public*, pg. 697

FORMALDEFRESH—Odorless Formaldehyde—Fisher Scientific Company; *U.S. Private*, pg. 658

FORMALL—Super Plastic Forming Material—Alusuisse-Lonza Holding Ltd.; *Int'l*, pg. 66

FORMATIONS—Shelving—Weyerhaeuser Forest Products Company; *U.S. Public*, pg. 1764

FORMAX—Animal Feed—ConAgra, Inc.; *U.S. Public*, pg. 425

FORMAX—Machinery—National Machinery; *U.S. Private*, pg. 785

FORMAX PLUS—Machinery—National Machinery; *U.S. Private*, pg. 785

FORMBOND—Enamelled Wire—General Electric Canada Inc.; *U.S. Public*, pg. 713

FORMBY—Refinishing Prods.—The Thompson's Company; *U.S. Public*, pg. 1466

FORMED PRODUCTS—Tater Roundabouts, Tater Puffs, Tri-Patties, Side O'Brown's—Lamb-Weston, Inc.; *U.S. Public*, pg. 427

FORMEX—Electrical Wires, Cables & Conductors—General Electric Canada Inc.; *U.S. Public*, pg. 713

FORMFLOW—Registers—The Standard Register Company; *U.S. Public*, pg. 1505

FORMFOLD—Business Form Paper—Georgia-Pacific Corporation; *U.S. Public*, pg. 735

FORMIC—Business Forms Mngmt. Service—The Standard Register Company; *U.S. Public*, pg. 1505

FORMICA—Laminates—CSR Limited; *Int'l*, pg. 245

FORMICA—Laminate & Adhesives—Formica Corporation; *Int'l*, pg. 129

FORMICA BRAND—High Pressure Laminate—California Panel & Veneer Company; *U.S. Private*, pg. 201

FORMIVAR—Acetal Resin—Monsanto Company; *U.S. Public*, pg. 1124

FORMOL—Business Forms Mngmt. System—The Standard Register Company; *U.S. Public*, pg. 1505

FORMPAC—Foam Trays—W.R. Grace & Co.; *U.S. Public*, pg. 754

FORMRUN—Printing Paper—Georgia-Pacific Corporation; *U.S. Public*, pg. 735

FORMS—Commercial Stencil Inlaid Flooring—Mannington Resilient Floors; *U.S. Private*, pg. 700

FORMS PROFESSIONAL—Magazine—North American Publishing Company; *U.S. Private*, pg. 803

FORMSPRAG—Overrunning Clutches—Warner Electric Industrial Products Division; *U.S. Public*, pg. 480

FORMU-3—Weight Reduction System—Form-You-3 International, Inc.; *U.S. Private*, pg. 418

FORMULA—Refuse Disposal Bodies—Heil Environmental Industries; *U.S. Public*, pg. 520

FORMULA—Tires—Pirelli Armstrong Tire Corporation; *Int'l*, pg. 1058

FORMULA—NONE—Sico Inc.; *Int'l*, pg. 1239

FORMULA 40—Herbicide—The Dow Chemical Company; *U.S. Public*, pg. 522

FORMULA 44—Cough Syrup—Richardson-Vicks, Inc., Health Care Products; *U.S. Public*, pg. 1331

FORMULA 405—Skin Care Prods.; Acne & Suncare Prods.; Shampoo & Conditioner; Nail Oil—Doak Dermatologics; *U.S. Public*, pg. 250

FORMULA 405 A-H-A—Alpha Hydroxy Acid Skin Care—Doak Dermatologics; *U.S. Public*, pg. 250

FORMULA 409—All Purpose Spray Cleaner—The Clorox Company; *U.S. Public*, pg. 386

FORMULA 405—Variety of Topical Products for the Skin, Hair & Nails—Bradley Pharmaceuticals; *U.S. Public*, pg. 249

FORMULA 405 A-H-A—Alpha Hydroxy Acid Skin Care—Bradley Pharmaceuticals; *U.S. Public*, pg. 249

FORMULA 1—Shock Mount for CB Antenna—Allen Telecom Inc.; *U.S. Public*, pg. 45

FORMULA I—Clinical Chemistry Reagent & Service Mark—Beckman Instruments, Inc.; *U.S. Public*, pg. 199

FORMULA ONE—NONE—Forstmann & Company, Inc.; *U.S. Public*, pg. 670

FORMULA 2589—Chemical Reagent—Hach Company; *U.S. Public*, pg. 773

FORMULA 2533—Chemical Reagent—Hach Company; *U.S. Public*, pg. 773

FORMULA ZP II—Anti-Dandruff Shampoo—Revlon-Realistic Professional Products, Inc.; *U.S. Private*, pg. 690

FORMULA I—Nutritional Products—Shaklee Corporation; *Int'l*, pg. 1518

FORMULA 36—Wallboard Adhesive—Ohio Sealants Inc.; *Int'l*, pg. 802

FORMULA 38—Drywall Construction Adhesive—Ohio Sealants Inc.; *Int'l*, pg. 802

FORMULA 815GD—Aqueous Detergent, Biodegradable; Immersion/Ultrasonic—The Brulin Corporation; *U.S. Private*, pg. 176

FORMULARY—Trade Periodical—Advanstar Communications; *U.S. Private*, pg. 22

FORMULATED SHELL—Gasoline—Shell Oil Company; *Int'l*, pg. 1136

FORMULE 1—Budget Hotels—Accor S.A.; *Int'l*, pg. 20

FORMVAR—Polyvinyl Formal Resin—Solutia Inc.; *U.S. Public*, pg. 1483

FORMVELOPE—Envelopes—Tension Envelope Corp.; *U.S. Private*, pg. 1077

FORON—Polyester—Clariant International Ltd.; *Int'l*, pg. 624

FORON—Dyes—Novartis AG; *Int'l*, pg. 971

FORON RD—Dyes—Novartis AG; *Int'l*, pg. 971

FORPAN—Decorative Paper Overlay—Uniboard Canada Inc.; *Int'l*, pg. 1431

FORCHNER—Horse Health Care Products—Farnam Companies, Inc.; *U.S. Private*, pg. 396

FORSTER—Toothpicks, Plastic Cutlery, Clothes Pins, Rope, Crafts—Diamond Brands, Inc.; *U.S. Private*, pg. 330

FORSTMANN—NONE—Forstmann & Company, Inc.; *U.S. Public*, pg. 670

FORT DODGE—Veterinary Products—Fort Dodge Animal Health; *U.S. Public*, pg. 79

FORTA—Nutritional Supplements—Abbott Laboratories; *U.S. Public*, pg. 12

FORTAFIL CARBON FIBERS—NONE—Akzo Nobel Fortafil Fibers Inc.; *Int'l*, pg. 48

FORTAZ—Antibiotic—Glaxo Wellcome Inc.; *Int'l*, pg. 552

FORTE—Automatic Drafting Pencil—Pentel of America, Ltd.; *Int'l*, pg. 1035

FORTE—Dental Laboratory Alloy—3M; *U.S. Public*, pg. 1604

FORTE 18—NONE—Pfizer Inc.; *U.S. Public*, pg. 1281

FORTE HOTELS—Hotels—Travelodge; *U.S. Public*, pg. 322

FORTE 30—NONE—Pfizer Inc.; *U.S. Public*, pg. 1281

FORTEFITE—Printing, Converting, Specialty, Wrapping, Writing & Book Paper—Georgia-Pacific Corporation; *U.S. Public*, pg. 735

FORTHEFUNOFIT—Advertising & Promotion Phrase—Putt Putt Golf Courses of America, Inc.; *U.S. Private*, pg. 896

FORTIC—Hot Water Storage—IMI Plc; *Int'l*, pg. 646

FORTIMICIN—Antibiotics—Kyowa Hakko Kogyo Company, Ltd.; *Int'l*, pg. 778

FORTIS—Banking, Insurance, Investments & Financial Services—Fortis, Inc.; *Int'l*, pg. 499

FORTRAN/400—Computer System—International Business Machines Corporation; *U.S. Public*, pg. 895

FORTRAN/2—Computer System—International Business Machines Corporation; *U.S. Public*, pg. 895

FORTRESS—Saftey Interlocks For Access Control Valve Interlocking& Machine Guarding—Halma p.l.c.; *Int'l*, pg. 589

FORTRESS—NONE—Pfizer Inc.; *U.S. Public*, pg. 1281

FORTRON—Polyphenylensulphide/PPS—Hoechst Aktiengesellschaft; *Int'l*, pg. 624

FORTUM/FORTAZ—Pharmaceutical—Glaxo Wellcome plc; *Int'l*, pg. 552

FORTUNA—Cigarettes—Philip Morris Companies Inc.; *U.S. Public*, pg. 1287

FORTUNA—NONE—Tabacalera, S.A.; *Int'l*, pg. 1345

FORTUNE—Enamel Coated Printing Paper—Consolidated Papers, Inc.; *U.S. Public*, pg. 436

FORTUNE—Cigarettes—Philip Morris Companies Inc.; *U.S. Public*, pg. 1287

FORTUNE—Magazine—Time Warner Inc.; *U.S. Public*, pg. 1610

FORTUNE—Stacking Chairs—United Chair, Inc.; *U.S. Private*, pg. 512

FORTUNE BOOK CLUB—Book Club—Book of the Month Club; *U.S. Public*, pg. 1612

40E—Aluminum Alloy—Frontier Foundry, Inc.; *U.S. Private*, pg. 430

4800-SERIES—Wan & Lan Access Products—Osicom Technologies Inc.; *U.S. Public*, pg. 1233

45 TO 3600 SERIES—Trucks—DAF Trucks N.V.; *U.S. Public*, pg. 1247

4012—Color Ink Jet Printer for Series 3000 Software RIP—Prepress Solutions, Inc.; *U.S. Private*, pg. 882

FORUM—Solid Vinyl Tile—Congoleum Corporation; *U.S. Public*, pg. 69

FORUM—Magazine—General Media International Inc.; *U.S. Private*, pg. 444

FORUM—Hotels—Inter-Continental Hotels & Resorts Corporation; *Int'l*, pg. 1178

FORUM II—Vinyl Tile—Congoleum Corporation; *U.S. Public*, pg. 69

FORWARD—Medium Duty Trucks—Isuzu Motors Limited; *Int'l*, pg. 692

FORWAY—Machine Bolt Expansion Shield—Gunnebo Fastening Corp.; *U.S. Private*, pg. 488

FOS—Signaling Devices—Faraday, Inc.; *Int'l*, pg. 1246

FOS-FLO—Brazing Alloy—Handy & Harman; *U.S. Public*, pg. 780

FOSCARINI—Contemporary Lighting Fixtures—IL International Inc.; *U.S. Public*, pg. 855

FOSCAVIR—Antibiotic—Astra AB; *Int'l*, pg. 93

FOSECO—Mettallurigical Chemicals—Foseco Plc; *Int'l*, pg. 234

FOSGATE-AUDIONICS—Audio Products—Harman International Industries, Inc.; *U.S. Public*, pg. 787

FOSMICIN—Antibiotics—Meiji Seika Kaisha, Ltd.; *Int'l*, pg. 855

FOSONE—Loudspeaker Systems—Polk Audio, Inc.; *U.S. Public*, pg. 1315

FOSROC—Construction Chemicals—Foseco Plc; *Int'l*, pg. 234

FOSROC EXPANDITE—Sealants—Burmah Castrol plc; *Int'l*, pg. 234

FOSSEYS—NONE—Coles Myer Ltd.; *Int'l*, pg. 306

FOSSIL—NONE—Fossil Inc.; *U.S. Private*, pg. 420

FOSTER—Adhesive Materials & Coatings—H.B. Fuller Company; *U.S. Public*, pg. 686

FOSTER—Food Equipment—Premark International, Inc.; *U.S. Public*, pg. 1321

FOSTER WHEELER ENVIRONMENTAL CORPORATION—NONE—Foster Wheeler Environmental Corporation; *U.S. Public*, pg. 677

FOSTER'S LAGER—Australian Beer—Carlton & United Breweries Ltd.; *Int'l*, pg. 500

FOSTER'S LIGHT—Light Beer—Carlton & United Breweries Ltd.; *Int'l*, pg. 500

FOSTER'S SPECIAL BITTER—Bitter Ale—Carlton & United Breweries Ltd.; *Int'l*, pg. 500

FOSTERCOAT 2020—Pipe Coatings—L.B. Foster Company; *U.S. Public*, pg. 675

FOSTERGE—Organic Phosphate Esters—Henkel Corporation; *Int'l*, pg. 610

FOSTERS—Beer, Japan Only—Asahi Breweries Ltd.; *Int'l*, pg. 83

FOSTER'S—Lager Beer—Foster's Brewing Group Limited; *Int'l*, pg. 500

FOSTER'S—Beer—Philip Morris Companies Inc.; *U.S. Public*, pg. 1287

FOSTERS FREEZE—Ice Cream—Fosters Freeze International, Inc.; *U.S. Public*, pg. 677

FOSTERWELD—Spiral Weld Pipe—L.B. Foster Company; *U.S. Public*, pg. 675

FOSTEX—Acne Treatment—Bristol-Myers Squibb Company; *U.S. Public*, pg. 253

FOSTEX—Alkylphosphonic Acids & Salts—Henkel Corporation; *Int'l*, pg. 610

FOSTEX—Acne & Oily Skin Care Aids—Westwood-Squibb Pharmaceuticals Inc.; *U.S. Public*, pg. 255

FOSTORIA—Radiant Heating Equipment—Fostoria Industries, Inc.; *U.S. Private*, pg. 421

FOSTORIA—Glass—Lancaster Colony Corporation; *U.S. Public*, pg. 976

FOSTORIA—Glass—Lancaster Glass Corporation; *U.S. Public*, pg. 977

FOSTRIL—Drying Lotion for Acne—Westwood-Squibb Pharmaceuticals Inc.; *U.S. Public*, pg. 255

FOTEC—NONE—ETEX; *Int'l*, pg. 430

FOTOFLAT—Removal Dry Mount Tissue—Seal Products Incorporated; *U.S. Public*, pg. 849

FOTRESS—Locksmiths' Work, Safes & Cash Boxes—Sime Darby Berhad; *Int'l*, pg. 1249

FOTURAN—Photosensitive Lithium Silicate Glass—Schott Glaswerke; *Int'l*, pg. 1523

FOUNDERS—Furniture—Thomasville Furniture Industries, Inc.; *U.S. Public*, pg. 688

FOUNDRISEL—NONE—Elkem ASA; *Int'l*, pg. 446

FOUNDRY MANAGEMENT & TECHNOLOGY—Periodical—Penton Publishing, Inc.; *U.S. Public*, pg. 1306

FOUNTAIN PENTEL—Pens—Pentel of America, Ltd.; *Int'l*, pg. 1035

4X4—Pickup Truck—Toyota Motor Sales, U.S.A., Inc.; *Int'l*, pg. 1412

4X2—Pickup Truck—Toyota Motor Sales, U.S.A., Inc.; *Int'l*, pg. 1412

4C—Bread Crumbs, Tea Mix, Lemonade, Grated Cheese, Season Coating Mix—4C Foods Corporation; *U.S. Private*, pg. 421

4C CRUM'N BAKE—Crumb Mix—4C Foods Corporation; *U.S. Private*, pg. 421

4C +—Anti Fog, Anti Scratch, Anti UV Scratch Resistant Coating—Uvex Safety, Inc.; *Int'l*, pg. 132

4-D—Four Directional Motion—The Raymond Corporation; *Int'l*, pg. 123

4DAY—Tire Stores—4Day Tire Stores; *U.S. Private*, pg. 424

481 COLLET STEEL—NONE—Carpenter Technology Corporation; *U.S. Public*, pg. 307

486—Microprocessor—Intel Corporation; *U.S. Public*, pg. 886

444—Fly Lines—Cortland Line Co., Inc.; *U.S. Private*, pg. 277

444 LAZERLINE—Fly Lines—Cortland Line Co., Inc.; *U.S. Private*, pg. 277

444 SL—Fly Lines—Cortland Line Co., Inc.; *U.S. Private*, pg. 277

400—Computer System—International Business Machines Corporation; *U.S. Public*, pg. 895

400 SERIES—Vans—DAF Trucks N.V.; *U.S. Public*, pg. 1247

400 SERIES—Sedgefield Collection—Myrtle/Mueller, A Haworth Co.; *U.S. Private*, pg. 512

407—Seven Place Single Engine Helicopter—Bell Helicopter Textron; *U.S. Public*, pg. 1588

406 CS—CombatScout Single Engine, Four Bladed—Bell Helicopter Textron; *U.S. Public*, pg. 1588

430—Nine Place Twin Engine, 4 Bladed Helicopter—Bell Helicopter Textron; *U.S. Public*, pg. 1588

412—15 Place Four Bladed, Twin Engine Helicopter—Bell Helicopter Textron; *U.S. Public*, pg. 1588

4 IN 1—Task Force—Case Corporation; *U.S. Public*, pg. 311

4-IN-1—Carseat/Stroller—Century Products Co.; *U.S. Private*, pg. 226

4 N 1—Multiblade Driver—Hold-E-Zee, Ltd.; *U.S. Private*, pg. 229

4 IN 1—Brushes—Mill-Rose Company; *U.S. Private*, pg. 746

FOUR-IN-ONE—Curling Iron/Brush—Sunbeam Household Products; *U.S. Public*, pg. 1533

FOUR KIT—Eye Shadows—Cover Girl Cosmetics; *U.S. Public*, pg. 1330

FOUR MONKS—Pipe Tobacco—Lane Limited; *Int'l*, pg. 1129

4 MOST—Crushing Machine—Svedala Industries-Universal Engineering; *Int'l*, pg. 1326

4 O'CLOCK—Office Seating—Vecta; *U.S. Private*, pg. 1038

FOUR POINTS HOTELS—NONE—ITT Sheraton Corporation; *U.S. Public*, pg. 1512

4 - QUART—Cheese—Land O'Lakes, Inc.; *U.S. Private*, pg. 645

FOUR QUEENS BLEND—Whiskey—Laird & Company; *U.S. Private*, pg. 642

FOUR RIVERS—Riverboat Cruise Trips—American Classic Voyagers Company; *U.S. Private*, pg. 380

FOUR ROSES—Whisky—The Seagram Company Ltd.; *Int'l*, pg. 1214

4 RUNNER—Sport Utility—Toyota Motor Sales, U.S.A., Inc.; *Int'l*, pg. 1412

FOUR SEASONS—Tires—Bridgestone/Firestone, Inc.; *Int'l*, pg. 213

FOUR SEASONS—Hotels & Resorts—Four Seasons Hotels & Resorts; *Int'l*, pg. 502

FOUR SEASONS—Greenhouses—Four Seasons Solar Products Corp.; *U.S. Private*, pg. 422

FOUR SEASONS—Pipe Tobacco—Lane Limited; *Int'l*, pg. 1129

FOUR SEASONS—Paint—M.A.B. Paints; *U.S. Private*, pg. 175

FOUR SEASONS—Auto Air Conditioning—Standard Motor Products Inc.; *U.S. Public*, pg. 1503

FOUR SEASONS HOTELS & RESORTS—NONE—Four Seasons Hotels Inc.; *Int'l*, pg. 502

FOUR SEASONS SUNROOMS—Sunrooms—Four Seasons Solar Products Corp.; *U.S. Private*, pg. 422

417—Apparel—Phillips-Van Heusen Corporation; *U.S. Public*, pg. 1291

4-SITE—Electronic Instrument—Intel Corporation; *U.S. Public*, pg. 886

FOUR SLIDE—NONE—The U.S. Baird Corporation; *U.S. Private*, pg. 1124

FOUR-SQUARE—X-Ray Cassettes—Spectronics Corporation; *U.S. Private*, pg. 1024

4-SQUARE—Rough and Dressed Lumber—Weyerhaeuser Company; *U.S. Public*, pg. 1764

4-SQUARE—Lumber—Weyerhaeuser Forest Products Company; *U.S. Public*, pg. 1764

4-SURE—Door Gates—Gerry Baby Products Company; *U.S. Private*, pg. 629

4 TEL—Line Tester—Teradyne, Inc.; *U.S. Public*, pg. 1580

431-X MERCURY VAPOR ANALYZER—NONE—Arizona Instrument Corporation; *U.S. Public*, pg. 129

4085X—Wafer Probers—Electroglas, Inc.; *U.S. Public*, pg. 727

4080X—Wafer Probers—Electroglas, Inc.; *U.S. Public*, pg. 727

4100 SERIES—Conveyers—Dorner Manufacturing Corp.; *U.S. Private*, pg. 340

4000 SERIES—Carpet Tile—Interface Inc.; *U.S. Public*, pg. 889

4060X—Wafer Probers—Electroglas, Inc.; *U.S. Public*, pg. 727

FOUR TRAX—All Terrain Vehicles—American Honda Motor Co., Inc. Motorcycle Division; *Int'l*, pg. 634

427—Seven Place Twin Engine Helicopter—Bell Helicopter Textron; *U.S. Public*, pg. 1588

FOUR WAY—Nasal Spray—Bristol-Myers Squibb Company; *U.S. Public*, pg. 253

4-WAY—Rolled Steel Floor Plate—Inland Steel Industries, Inc.; *U.S. Public*, pg. 879

4-WAY—Demoisturant, General Purpose Aerosol Lubricant—3M; *U.S. Public*, pg. 1604

4 WAY STOP—NONE—Rocky Shoes & Boots, Inc.; *U.S. Public*, pg. 1402

4-WAY STRIP MILL PLATE COILS—Hot Rolled Steel—Inland Steel Industries, Inc.; *U.S. Public*, pg. 879

4-WHEEL & OFF-ROAD—Magazine—Petersen Publishing Company, L.L.C.; *U.S. Private*, pg. 856

FOUR WHEELER—Magazine—General Media International Inc.; *U.S. Private*, pg. 444

FOUR WINNS—Boats—Outboard Marine Corporation; *U.S. Private*, pg. 478

4-X—Photo Film—Eastman Kodak Company; *U.S. Public*, pg. 550

FOUR-S—Restaurant & Institutional Breads—Four-S Baking Company; *U.S. Private*, pg. 422

FOURCAS HOSTEN—Bordeaux Wine—Frederick Wildman & Sons Ltd.; *U.S. Private*, pg. 1176

14K—Catheters—Medtronic, Inc.; *U.S. Public*, pg. 1082

FOWLER—Measuring Tools—Fred V. Fowler Company, Inc.; *U.S. Private*, pg. 422

FOWLER—NONE—James Hardie Industries Ltd.; *Int'l*, pg. 596

FOWLER'S FURNITURE CENTER—Furniture—Rhodes, Inc.; *U.S. Public*, pg. 805

FOWLERS WEE HEAVY—Strong Ale—Bass PLC; *Int'l*, pg. 169

FOX—Television Network—Fox Broadcasting Company (FBC); *Int'l*, pg. 926

FOX—Process Computer—The Foxboro Company; *Int'l*, pg. 1243

FOX—Guns—Savage Arms Inc.; *U.S. Public*, pg. 968

FOX—Car—Volkswagen of America, Inc.; *Int'l*, pg. 1474

FOX & JACOBS—Homes—Centex Corporation; *U.S. Public*, pg. 322

FOX BRADY—Road Sanding Equipment, Tailgates, Body Sanders & Cup Sanders—Hiniker Company; *U.S. Private*, pg. 530

FOX-KNAPP—Sports Outerwear—Fox-Knapp; *U.S. Private*, pg. 860

FOX-O-POL—Liquid Components For Rigid Polyurethane Foams—DSM N.V.; *Int'l*, pg. 352

FOX RIDGE HOMES—NONE—NVR, Inc.; *U.S. Public*, pg. 1148

FOX RIVER—Writing Paper—Fox River Paper Company; *U.S. Private*, pg. 422

FOX RIVER OPAQUE—Writing Paper—Fox River Paper Company; *U.S. Private*, pg. 422

FOX RIVER SELECT—Writing Paper—Fox River Paper Company; *U.S. Private*, pg. 422

FOX'S—Glacier Mints—Nestle-Rowntree Ltd.; *Int'l*, pg. 921

FOX'S—Biscuits—Northern Foods plc; *Int'l*, pg. 967

FOXCROFT—Apparel—The Apparel Group, Ltd.; *U.S. Private*, pg. 78

FOXES—Candy Rolls, Cookie Wafers—F&F Foods; *U.S. Private*, pg. 388

FOXNET—Communication Link—The Foxboro Company; *Int'l*, pg. 1243

FOXPRO—Computer Database—Microsoft Corporation; *U.S. Public*, pg. 1107

FOXS—Medical Equipment—Nellcor Puritan Bennett Incorporated; *U.S. Public*, pg. 1039

FOXY POXY—Epoxy—Krazy Glue Inc.; *U.S. Private*, pg. 158

FRA-O-FORM—NONE—Fraser Papers, Inc.; *Int'l*, pg. 434

FRACAS—Fragrance—Alfin, Inc.; *U.S. Public*, pg. 40

FRACLOG—NONE—Western Atlas Logging Services; *U.S. Public*, pg. 1757

FRACTAL FIBEROPTICS—High Quality, Improved Optical Performance Fiber Optics—Galileo Corp.; *U.S. Public*, pg. 698

FRACTION BARS—Unique Vinyl Strips for Teaching All Fraction Concepts—American Educational Products; *U.S. Public*, pg. 71

FRADIOMYCIN—Antibiotic Preparations—Nippon Kayaku Co. Ltd.; *Int'l*, pg. 934

FRAENKEL BEDDING COMPANY—Mattress—Fraenkel Company; *U.S. Private*, pg. 423

FRAENKEL DINING—Dining Products—Fraenkel Company; *U.S. Private*, pg. 423

FRAG GUARD—Fragmentation Prevention Utility—Executive Software; *U.S. Private*, pg. 388

FRAGMATOME—Surgical Needles & Instruments—Alcon Laboratories, Inc.; *Int'l*, pg. 916

FRAGRANCE BURST—Fragrance Sampling Technique—3M; *U.S. Public*, pg. 1604
FRAGRANCE ORIGINALS BY MRS. BAKER—NONE—Blyth Industries; *U.S. Public*, pg. 239
FRAM—Filters—AlliedSignal, Automotive Aftermarket; *U.S. Public*, pg. 51
FRAM—NONE—AlliedSignal Canada Inc., Automotive Aftermarket; *U.S. Public*, pg. 52
FRAMAC—Office Chairs—Carter Holt Harvey Limited; *U.S. Public*, pg. 904
FRAME SCENE—Frames, Framing Services & Photographic Prints—F.W. Woolworth Co.; *U.S. Public*, pg. 1777
FRAME TRAY—Jigsaw Puzzles—Golden Books Family Entertainment Inc.; *U.S. Public*, pg. 749
FRAMEKIT—Easy-to-Assemble Frames—Letraset Nielsen & Bainbridge; *Int'l*, pg. 460
FRAMES UNLIMITED—Picture Frame Stores—Zimdar Enterprises/Frames Unlimited; *U.S. Private*, pg. 1206
FRAMESI—Hair Care Products & Haircolor, For Chemically Treated Hair—Framesi USA, Inc./Roffler Industries, Inc./Casa di Colore, Inc.; *U.S. Private*, pg. 419
FRAMESTEEL—Building Materials—Jewell Building Systems; *U.S. Private*, pg. 587
FRAMEWORK—Systems—American Seating Company; *U.S. Private*, pg. 61
FRAMEWORK III—Software—Borland International, Inc.; *U.S. Public*, pg. 246
FRAMEWORK II—Software—Borland International, Inc.; *U.S. Public*, pg. 246
FRAMEWORKS—NONE—TJ International, Inc.; *U.S. Public*, pg. 1556
FRAMEWORKS—Wall System—Trus Joist MacMillan; *Int'l*, pg. 829
FRAMEWORKS—Wall System—Trus Joist MacMillan; *U.S. Public*, pg. 1556
FRAMEX—Windows—James Hardie Industries Ltd.; *Int'l*, pg. 596
FRAMEXPRESS—Frame Relay Networking System—Network Equipment Technologies, Inc.; *U.S. Public*, pg. 1168
FRANCE—Compressor Components—Coltec Industries Inc.; *U.S. Public*, pg. 401
FRANCE DIRECT—Long Distance—France Telecom; *Int'l*, pg. 503
FRANCESCA CARETTI—NONE—Kellwood Company; *U.S. Public*, pg. 948
FRANCESCO SMALTO—Perfume—International Cosmetics Co., Ltd.; *Int'l*, pg. 684
FRANCISCAN—Wine—Andres Wines Ltd.; *Int'l*, pg. 75
FRANCISCAN—China—Waterford Crystal, Inc.; *Int'l*, pg. 1487
FRANCISCAN—Dinnerware & Giftware—Waterford Wedgwood UK Plc; *Int'l*, pg. 1487
FRANCISCAN BURGUNDY—Wine—Peller Wines of California; *Int'l*, pg. 76
FRANCISCAN CHABLIS—Wine—Peller Wines of California; *Int'l*, pg. 76
FRANCISCO—Bread & Rolls—CPC Baking Business; *U.S. Public*, pg. 224
FRANCO-AMERICAN—Gravies & Pasta—Campbell Soup Company; *U.S. Public*, pg. 298
FRANCOIS LABET CABERNET—French Wine—Laird & Company; *U.S. Private*, pg. 642
FRANCOIS LABET CHARDONNAY—French Wine—Laird & Company; *U.S. Private*, pg. 642
FRANCOIS LABET MERLOT—French Wine—Laird & Company; *U.S. Private*, pg. 642
FRANCOIS LABET SYRAH—French Wine—Laird & Company; *U.S. Private*, pg. 642
FRANGELICO—Liqueur—Allied Domecq PLC; *Int'l*, pg. 62
FRANGELICO—Liqueur—Barbero 1891 SpA; *Int'l*, pg. 164
FRANK-A-MATIC—Food Equipment—Townsend Engineering Co.; *U.S. Private*, pg. 1094
FRANK COOPER—Jellies, Jams & Other Spreads—Bestfoods; *U.S. Public*, pg. 223
FRANK LEWIS—Fruit Gift Packages—Standex International Corporation; *U.S. Public*, pg. 1505
FRANK 'N STUFF—Food Products—Hormel Foods Corp.; *U.S. Public*, pg. 840
FRANK'S—NONE—General Host Corporation; *U.S. Public*, pg. 715
FRANK'S SUPERCRAFTS—NONE—General Host Corporation; *U.S. Public*, pg. 715
FRANK SCHOONMAKER—Selections—Seagram Chateau & Estate Wines Co.; *Int'l*, pg. 1215

FRANK THOMAS 'BIG HURT 'BASEBALL—Interactive Entertainment Software—Acclaim Entertainment, Inc.; *U.S. Public*, pg. 15
FRANK'S NURSERY & CRAFTS—Stores—General Host Corporation; *U.S. Public*, pg. 715
FRANKEN BERRY—Cereal—General Mills, Inc.; *U.S. Public*, pg. 717
FRANKLIN—Bread & Rolls—Franklin Baking Co., Inc.; *U.S. Private*, pg. 424
FRANKLIN—NONE—Franklin Electronic Publishers, Inc.; *U.S. Public*, pg. 679
FRANKLIN—Batting Glove—Franklin Sports, Inc.; *U.S. Private*, pg. 424
FRANKLIN ELECTRIC—Motor—Franklin Electric Co., Inc.; *U.S. Public*, pg. 679
FRANKLIN LIFE INSURANCE—Life Insurance & Annuity Prods.—The Franklin Life Insurance Company; *U.S. Public*, pg. 76
THE FRANKLIN MINT—Collectibles—The Franklin Mint; *U.S. Private*, pg. 941
THE FRANKLIN—Insurance—The Franklin Life Insurance Company; *U.S. Public*, pg. 76
FRANKLIN'S PRINTING—Printing Center—International Center for Entrepreneurial Development, Inc.; *U.S. Private*, pg. 568
FRANKLINS—NONE—Petrie Retail, Inc.; *U.S. Private*, pg. 858
FRANK'S—Canned Foods—The Fremont Co.; *U.S. Private*, pg. 426
FRANK'S KIDS CORNER—NONE—General Host Corporation; *U.S. Public*, pg. 715
FRANK'S RED HOT—Food Sauces—Reckitt & Colman Inc.; *Int'l*, pg. 1090
FRANRICA—Aseptic Processing Equipment & Systems—FMC FoodTech/Fran Rica; *U.S. Public*, pg. 605
FRANSK—Dinnerware—Dansk International Designs Ltd.; *U.S. Public*, pg. 261
FRANTZ—Hardware Products—Wayne Dalton of Sterling; *U.S. Private*, pg. 1155
FRANZ—Breads—United States Bakery; *U.S. Private*, pg. 1124
FRANZIA WINETAPS—Table Wines—The Wine Group; *U.S. Private*, pg. 1182
FRAPPUCCINO—Coffee Drink—Starbucks Coffee Company; *U.S. Public*, pg. 1510
FRASER—Paper—Fraser Papers, Inc.; *Int'l*, pg. 434
FRASER-JOHNSTON—Air Conditioning Products—York International Corporation; *U.S. Public*, pg. 1789
FRASER-JOHNSTON—Air Conditioners & Furnaces—Unitary Products Group; *U.S. Public*, pg. 1788
FRE-CUT—Loading Retardant Coating for Abrasive Surface—3M; *U.S. Public*, pg. 1604
FRE-HEATER—Hot Water Heating System—Paul Mueller Company; *U.S. Public*, pg. 1141
FRED BEAR—Apparel & Food—Fred Meyer Stores; *U.S. Public*, pg. 1103
FRED GANG'S—Restaurants—Golden Corral Corporation; *U.S. Private*, pg. 575
FRED HAYMAN BEVERLY HILLS—Fragrances—Parlux Fragrances Inc.; *U.S. Public*, pg. 1264
FRED LUXURY EYEWEAR—Eyewear—Logo of the Americas; *Int'l*, pg. 462
FRED MEYER—Aparel, Home, Food—Fred Meyer Stores; *U.S. Public*, pg. 1103
FRED MEYER—General Merchandise—Fred Meyer Stores; *U.S. Public*, pg. 1103
FRED P. OTT—Restaurants—Houlihan's Restaurant Group; *U.S. Public*, pg. 841
FREDELLE—Women Shoe Stores—Kinney Shoe Corporation; *U.S. Public*, pg. 1777
FREDERICH THE GREAT—War Game—Monarch Avalon, Inc.; *U.S. Public*, pg. 1123
FREDERICIA—Stemware—Dansk International Designs Ltd.; *U.S. Public*, pg. 261
FREDERICK'S OF HOLLYWOOD—Retail & Mail-Order Women's Fashions & Specialty Items—Frederick's of Hollywood, Inc.; *U.S. Private*, pg. 424
FREE-AIR—Air Pumps—E.D. Bullard Company; *U.S. Private*, pg. 180
FREE & LOVELY—Antidandruff Foam—SmithKline Beecham plc; *U.S. Public*, pg. 1264
FREE BREAKFAST & DESIGN—Promotion—Regal Ware, Inc.; *U.S. Private*, pg. 917
FREE-CUT INVAR 36—NONE—Carpenter Technology Corporation; *U.S. Public*, pg. 307

FREE KAST—Refractory Castable—CFB Industries, Inc.; *U.S. Private*, pg. 194
FREE KAST—Refractory Castable—Chicago Fire Brick Co.; *U.S. Private*, pg. 194
FREE-LOCK—Compression Hip Fixation System—Bristol-Myers Squibb Company; *U.S. Public*, pg. 253
FREE MARKET PARTNERS—On-Line Multiple Merchant, Frequent Shopper Program—Provident Financial Group, Inc.; *U.S. Public*, pg. 1338
FREE 'N EASY—Shampoo—The Gillette Company; *U.S. Public*, pg. 743
FREE PEOPLE—NONE—Urban Outfitters, Inc.; *U.S. Public*, pg. 1700
FREE POINT—Large Format 3D Digitizer—GTCO Corporation; *U.S. Private*, pg. 436
FREEDAY—Line of Thin-Film Type Sanitary Napkins—Kao Corporation; *Int'l*, pg. 717
FREEDENT—Chewing Gum—Wrigley Canada Inc.; *U.S. Public*, pg. 1781
FREEDENT—Gum—Wm. Wrigley Jr. Company; *U.S. Public*, pg. 1781
FREEDOM—Vinyl Cladding—Biltbest Windows; *U.S. Public*, pg. 1683
FREEDOM—Box Awning—Carefree of Colorado; *U.S. Public*, pg. 217
FREEDOM—NONE—Erickson Oil Products, Inc.; *U.S. Private*, pg. 381
FREEDOM—(Disc Couplings)—The Falk Corporation; *U.S. Public*, pg. 1534
FREEDOM—Feminine Pads—Kimberly-Clark Corporation; *U.S. Public*, pg. 958
FREEDOM—Camera—Minolta Corporation; *Int'l*, pg. 869
FREEDOM—Herbicide—Monsanto Company; *U.S. Public*, pg. 1124
FREEDOM—Canned Iced Coffee—PepsiCo, Inc.; *U.S. Public*, pg. 1276
FREEDOM ANNUITY—NONE—Keyport Life Insurance Company; *U.S. Private*, pg. 666
FREEDOM BACK—Bras—Olga Div.; *U.S. Public*, pg. 1738
FREEDOM FIT—Incontinence Products—Blessings Corporation; *U.S. Private*, pg. 1179
FREEDOM GRAPHICS—NONE—Evans & Sutherland Computer Corporation; *U.S. Public*, pg. 595
FREEDOM HOMES—Mobile Homes—Oakwood Homes Corporation; *U.S. Public*, pg. 1209
FREEDOM LINE—Barrier-Free and Assisted-Care Bath Fixtures—Lasco Bathware; *Int'l*, pg. 1397
FREEDOM OF CHOICE—747 & 550 Series Ring Shank Designs—L.G. Balfour Co.; *U.S. Private*, pg. 258
FREEDOM PHONE—Phone Line—Original Equipment Division; *U.S. Public*, pg. 1416
FREEDOM PHONE—Telephone Equip.—SBC Communications Inc.; *U.S. Public*, pg. 1415
FREEDOM PLAN—NONE—Oxford Health Plans Inc.; *U.S. Public*, pg. 1238
FREEDOM SERIES—NONE—Evans & Sutherland Computer Corporation; *U.S. Public*, pg. 595
THE FREEDOM SERIES—Plastic Stack Chair—Virco Mfg. Corporation; *U.S. Public*, pg. 1721
FREEDOM SIX—Platform-Based Motion Simulation—Iwerks Entertainment; *U.S. Public*, pg. 915
FREEDOM SPLINTS—Splints—Alimed, Inc.; *U.S. Private*, pg. 34
FREEFOAM—Foam Extrusion Process—Royle Systems Group; *U.S. Private*, pg. 949
FREELINE—Cordless Telephone—Sony Electronics; *Int'l*, pg. 1281
FREELINER—Printers—Datasouth Computer Corporation; *U.S. Public*, pg. 267
FREEMAN PROFESSIONAL—Hair & Skin Care Products—Freeman Cosmetic Corp.; *U.S. Private*, pg. 426
FREESTYLE—Swim Pool Products—Harcros Chemicals Inc.; *U.S. Public*, pg. 598
FREESTYLE—Children's Building Sets—LEGO Systems, Inc.; *Int'l*, pg. 805
FREESTYLE—Valve—Medtronic, Inc.; *U.S. Public*, pg. 1082
FREESTYLE—Aerobic Shoe—Reebok International Ltd.; *U.S. Public*, pg. 1369
FREESTYLE—Lounge Seating & Tables—United Chair, Inc.; *U.S. Private*, pg. 512
FREEWAY—Women's Apparel—International Cosmetics Co., Ltd.; *Int'l*, pg. 684

FREEWHEELERS—Luggage—American Tourister, Inc.; *U.S. Public*, pg. 1430

FREEZE—Magazine—Times Mirror Magazines, Inc.; *U.S. Public*, pg. 1616

FREEZE-TITE—Freezer Wrap—Polyvinyl Films, Inc.; *U.S. Private*, pg. 875

FREEZEFRAME—Video Image Recorder—Polaroid Corporation; *U.S. Public*, pg. 1313

FREEZER QUEEN—Frozen Prepared Foods—Freezer Queen Foods Inc.; *Int'l*, pg. 340

FREEZETTE—NONE—Ingrid Division of Lawnware; *U.S. Private*, pg. 654

FREEZGARD—Pipe Heater Freeze Protection—Raychem Corporation; *U.S. Public*, pg. 1362

FREEZLOC—Plastic Freezer Wrap—The Dow Chemical Company; *U.S. Public*, pg. 522

FREEZOMINT—Mint Cream—Groupe Pernod Ricard; *Int'l*, pg. 566

FREIGHT LINER—NONE—Daimler-Benz Aktiengesellschaft; *Int'l*, pg. 366

FREIGHT MISER—3 Day Delivery Service—Danzas Corporation; *Int'l*, pg. 382

FREIGHTLINER—Diesel Trucks & Tractors—Freightliner Corp.; *Int'l*, pg. 368

FREIHOFER'S—Bread & Sweet Baked Goods—CPC Baking Business; *Int'l*, pg. 224

FREIHOFER'S—Sweet Baked Products & Breads—Bestfoods; *U.S. Public*, pg. 223

FREIZEIT REVUE—Magazine—Burda Holding GmbH & Co., KG; *Int'l*, pg. 233

FREKOTE—Mold Release Agents—The Dexter Corporation; *U.S. Public*, pg. 504

FREM—Plastic Molded Products—Ekco Group, Inc.; *U.S. Public*, pg. 566

FREMLINS—Bitters—Whitbread PLC; *Int'l*, pg. 1498

FREMONT—Insurance—Fremont General Corporation; *U.S. Public*, pg. 681

THE FRENCH COLLECTION—Toy Stuffed Animals—American Greetings Corporation; *U.S. Public*, pg. 77

THE FRENCH MANICURE—Press-On Nails—Lee Pharmaceuticals; *U.S. Public*, pg. 984

FRENCH PIES—Layers of Pastry—Meiji Seika Kaisha, Ltd.; *Int'l*, pg. 855

FRENCH QUARTER—Lumber & Wood Products—Georgia-Pacific Corporation; *U.S. Public*, pg. 735

FRENCH TOAST—NONE—Tandy Brands Accessories, Inc.; *U.S. Public*, pg. 1560

FRENCH TOAST CRUNCH—Cereal—General Mills, Inc.; *U.S. Public*, pg. 717

FRENCH'S—Mustard, Worcestershire Sauce—Reckitt & Colman Inc.; *Int'l*, pg. 1090

FRENCH'S—Mustard—Reckitt & Colman plc; *Int'l*, pg. 1089

FREND—Prewash Treatment—Reckitt & Colman plc; *Int'l*, pg. 1089

FREON—Refrigerants, Solvents—Du Pont (E.I. Du Pont De Nemours & Co.); *U.S. Public*, pg. 530

FREOSTAT—Uniforms—Angelica Corporation; *U.S. Public*, pg. 113

FREQUENT FLYER—Luggage—American Tourister, Inc.; *U.S. Public*, pg. 1430

FRESCA—Soft Drink Flavors—The Coca-Cola Company; *U.S. Public*, pg. 392

FRESCARINI—Salty Fresh Pastry—LPC Industrias Alimenticias S.A.; *Int'l*, pg. 380

FRESCATTI—Summer-Only Hotels—Aritmos AB; *Int'l*, pg. 1072

FRESCAVENA—Powdered Oat Drink—The Quaker Oats Company; *U.S. Public*, pg. 1347

FRESCO MAGIC—Wet Tissues—The Dow Chemical Company; *U.S. Public*, pg. 522

FRESCOBALDI—Wine—Paterno Imports Limited; *U.S. Private*, pg. 843

FRESCOLAT—Fragrance—Haarmann & Reimer Corp.; *Int'l*, pg. 173

FRESH ADVANTAGE—Pre-Cut Produce—Performance Food Group Company; *U.S. Public*, pg. 1278

FRESH AIR—Deodorizers—Reynolds Metals Company; *U.S. Public*, pg. 1385

THE FRESH ALTERNATIVE TO FAST FOOD—NONE—Koo Koo Roo, Inc.; *U.S. Public*, pg. 966

FRESH & CLEAN—Pet Shampoo—Carter-Wallace, Inc.; *U.S. Public*, pg. 309

FRESH APPLE—Greeting Cards—American Greetings Corporation; *U.S. Public*, pg. 77

FRESH-AS-A-BABY—Odor Neutralizer—Surco Products, Inc.; *U.S. Private*, pg. 1056

FRESH COMFORT—Detachable Mattress Pillow Top—Kingsdown, Inc.; *U.S. Private*, pg. 622

FRESH CREATIONS—Frozen Dinners—Kraft Foods, Inc.; *U.S. Public*, pg. 1287

FRESH DECK—Deck Cleaning Preparation—PPG Industries, Inc.; *U.S. Public*, pg. 1245

FRESH EXPRESS—Pizza—Crestar Food Products, Inc.; *U.S. Public*, pg. 805

FRESH EXPRESSIONS—Women's Undergarments—AGP Industrial Corporation; *Int'l*, pg. 14

FRESH FELINERS—Odor Preventing Catbox Liner Pad—Softsoap Enterprises, Inc.; *U.S. Public*, pg. 397

FRESH FROST—Hair Coloring—Clairol, Inc.; *U.S. Public*, pg. 254

FRESH GOURMET—Seasoning Mix—McCormick/Schilling; *U.S. Public*, pg. 1066

FRESH GUY—Cloth Towels—Chicopee Inc.; *Int'l*, pg. 113

FRESH HOLD—Hair Spray—Clairol, Inc.; *U.S. Public*, pg. 254

FRESH LASH—Mascara—Maybelline, Inc.; *Int'l*, pg. 819

FRESH LENS—Frequent Lens Replacement Program—Bausch & Lomb Incorporated; *U.S. Public*, pg. 194

FRESH-LOCK—Resalable Plastic Bag—Reynolds Metals Company; *U.S. Public*, pg. 1385

FRESH MARKET SQUARE—NONE—Harrah's Entertainment, Inc.; *U.S. Public*, pg. 790

FRESH MUSK—Fragrances—Charles of the Ritz Group Ltd.; *U.S. Public*, pg. 689

FRESH 'N LIGHT—Dairy Products—Land-O-Sun Dairies, Inc.; *U.S. Private*, pg. 646

FRESH 'N' MINTY—Mouthwash in Sample-Size Bottles for Hotel/Motel Distribution—Marietta Corporation; *U.S. Private*, pg. 702

FRESH 'N READY—Desserts—Rich Products Corp.; *U.S. Private*, pg. 928

FRESH'ND AIRE—Air Cleaners—Sunbeam Household Products; *U.S. Public*, pg. 1533

FRESH-O-MATIC—Food Steamers—Lincoln Foodservice Products, Inc.; *Int'l*, pg. 188

FRESH SCENTS—Air Freshener—Stanhome Inc.; *U.S. Public*, pg. 1508

FRESH SOURCE—Water Purification—Sunbeam Corporation; *U.S. Public*, pg. 1533

FRESH START—Detergent—Colgate-Palmolive Company; *U.S. Public*, pg. 397

FRESH START BAKERIES—Buns & Muffins—Campbell Soup Company; *U.S. Public*, pg. 298

FRESH STEP—Cat Litter—The Clorox Company; *U.S. Public*, pg. 386

FRESH STEP—Scented Comfort Insoles—Schering-Plough Corporation; *U.S. Public*, pg. 1438

FRESH-STEP—Time-Release Fragrance Insole—Scholl U.S.A.; *U.S. Public*, pg. 1438

FRESH STEP SCOOP—Scoopable Cat Litter—The Clorox Company; *U.S. Public*, pg. 386

FRESH TOPS—NONE—Rubbermaid Incorporated; *U.S. Public*, pg. 1411

FRESH-TRAK—Reclosable Closures for Plastic Bags—Reynolds Metals Company; *U.S. Public*, pg. 1385

FRESH-X-CHANGER—Heat Recovery Ventilator—United Air Specialists, Inc.; *U.S. Public*, pg. 382

FRESHBURST LISTERINE—Mouthwash—Warner-Lambert Consumer Healthcare; *U.S. Public*, pg. 1739

FRESHLIKE—Frozen Vegetables—Dean Foods Company; *U.S. Public*, pg. 489

FRESHLIKE—Frozen & Canned Vegetables—Dean Foods Vegetable Company; *U.S. Public*, pg. 490

FRESHLITE—Canned Vegetables—Dean Foods Vegetable Company; *U.S. Public*, pg. 490

FRESHPAK—Gas Blends for Food Packaging—Air Products and Chemicals, Inc.; *U.S. Public*, pg. 30

FRESHRAP WAXED PAPERS—Specialty Waxed Papers—Badger Paper Mills, Inc.; *U.S. Public*, pg. 165

FRESHWORLD FARMS—Tomatoes, Carrots & Sweet Peppers—DNAP Holding Corp.; *Int'l*, pg. 454

FRESSY—Waterless Shampoo—Shiseido Company Ltd.; *Int'l*, pg. 1235

FRETEX—Shoes Beds Made from Frelen—Freudenberg & Company; *Int'l*, pg. 505

FREUDENBERG MEGULASTIK—Mechanical Dampers—Freudenberg & Company; *Int'l*, pg. 505

FREUDIAN SLIPS—Greeting Cards—American Greetings Corporation; *U.S. Public*, pg. 77

FREUNDIN—Magazine—Burda Holding GmbH & Co., KG; *Int'l*, pg. 233

FREYMILLER—Long Distance Trucking Services—AmeriTruck Refrigerated Transport, Inc.; *U.S. Private*, pg. 66

FRI-D'OR—Frozen Processed Potato Products—Danisco Foods; *Int'l*, pg. 378

FRIAR TUBB—Stuffed Toy Figures; Canisters; Towels; T-Shirts—American Greetings Corporation; *U.S. Public*, pg. 77

FRIAR TUCK SHIRTS—Clergy Shirts—Augsburg Fortress, Publishers; *U.S. Private*, pg. 98

FRIBBLE—Ice Milk Drink—Friendly Ice Cream Corp.; *U.S. Public*, pg. 682

FRICG FR-12—Environmentally Acceptable Replacement Refrigerant for AC Systems—Intermagnetics General Corporation; *U.S. Public*, pg. 893

FRICTION-GARD—Cable Pulling Lubricant—The Lamson & Sessions Co.; *U.S. Public*, pg. 976

FRICTION TECH—Brake Parts—Echlin Inc.; *U.S. Public*, pg. 560

FRIDAY—Weekly General Interest Men's Magazine—Kodansha Ltd.; *Int'l*, pg. 742

FRIEDLAND—Door Chimes—Caradon Plc; *Int'l*, pg. 266

FRIELE—Coffee—Sara Lee Corporation; *U.S. Public*, pg. 1432

FRIENDLY—Ice Cream, Restaurants, Sherbet—Friendly Ice Cream Corp.; *U.S. Public*, pg. 682

FRIENDLY BIG BEEF—Hamburger Sandwich—Friendly Ice Cream Corp.; *U.S. Public*, pg. 682

THE FRIENDLY CONFINES & SIDEWALK CAFE—Restaurant—The Levy Organization; *U.S. Private*, pg. 664

FRIENDLY FRANK—Frankfurter Sandwich—Friendly Ice Cream Corp.; *U.S. Public*, pg. 682

FRIENDLY HOLIDAYS—Travel Tours—Friendly Holidays Inc.; *U.S. Private*, pg. 428

FRIENDS—Baked Beans & Brown Bread—The Pillsbury Company; *Int'l*, pg. 411

FRIENDSHIP—Photographic Printing Services—Eastman Kodak Company; *U.S. Public*, pg. 550

FRIENDSHIP—Cottage Cheese, Sour Cream, Yogurt, Farmer Cheese, Buttermilk—Friendship Dairies, Inc.; *U.S. Private*, pg. 429

FRIENDSHIP FAVORITES—Giftware—Home Showcase Products; *U.S. Private*, pg. 1101

FRIES—CrissCut Fries, Twister Fries, Thin Cuts, Regular Cuts, WaveLength Fries—Lamb-Weston, Inc.; *U.S. Public*, pg. 427

FRIGID—Fans—Frigid Products, Inc.; *U.S. Private*, pg. 883

FRIGIDAIRE—Major Appliances—Electrolux, AB; *Int'l*, pg. 438

FRIGIDAIRE—Major Appliances—Email Limited; *Int'l*, pg. 450

FRIGIDAIRE—Appliances—Frigidaire Home Products; *Int'l*, pg. 439

FRIGIDAIRE—Major Appliances—White Consolidated Industries, Inc.; *Int'l*, pg. 439

FRIGIDAIRE—NONE—Zanussi Italia S.p.A.; *Int'l*, pg. 442

FRIGITRONICS—Freon & Nitrous Oxide Cryosurgical Equipment—The Cooper Companies, Inc.; *U.S. Public*, pg. 442

FRIGODAN—Frozen Vegetables, Soups & Sauces—Danisco Foods; *Int'l*, pg. 378

FRIGOR—Chocolates—Nestle S.A.; *Int'l*, pg. 915

FRIGOSNIFF—Gas Leak Detectors—Balzers; *Int'l*, pg. 997

FRIONOR—Fish & Seafood Prods.—Frionor A/S; *Int'l*, pg. 516

FRIONOR—Fillets, Fishsticks & Portions—Frionor U.S.A. Inc.; *Int'l*, pg. 516

FRIS—Vodka—Jim Walker; *Int'l*, pg. 63

FRISBEE—Flying Disc—Mattel, Inc.; *U.S. Public*, pg. 1057

FRISBEE—Flying Discs—Mattel Power Wheels; *U.S. Public*, pg. 1058

FRISCH'S—Restaurants—Frisch's Restaurants, Inc.; *U.S. Public*, pg. 682

FRISCO—Frozen Foods & Ice Cream—Nestle S.A.; *Int'l*, pg. 915

FRISCO BREAKFAST—Sandwich—Hardee's Food Systems, Inc.; *U.S. Public*, pg. 278

FRISCO BURGER—Hamburger Sandwich—Hardee's Food Systems, Inc.; *U.S. Public*, pg. 278

FRISCO GRILLED CHICKEN—Chicken Sandwich—Hardee's Food Systems, Inc.; *U.S. Public*, pg. 278

FRISIA—Marshmallow Sweets—Cadbury Schweppes p.l.c.; *Int'l*, pg. 247

FRISKIES MASTER'S CHOICE—NONE—Nestle USA; *Int'l*, pg. 916

FRISKIES—Pet Foods—Nestle S.A.; *Int'l*, pg. 915

FRISKIES—Pet Food—Nestle USA; *Int'l*, pg. 916

FRISKIES ALPO—NONE—Nestle USA; *Int'l*, pg. 916

FRISKIES CHEF'S BLEND—NONE—Nestle USA; *Int'l*, pg. 916

FRISKIES CHEW-EEZ—NONE—Nestle USA; *Int'l*, pg. 916

FRISKIES CHEW-EEZ BONE-ANZA—NONE—Nestle USA; *Int'l*, pg. 916

FRISKIES CHEW-EEZ STICKS—NONE—Nestle USA; *Int'l*, pg. 916

FRISKIES COME 'N GET IT—NONE—Nestle USA; *Int'l*, pg. 916

FRISKIES DR. BALLARD—NONE—Nestle USA; *Int'l*, pg. 916

FRISKIES FANCY FEAST—NONE—Nestle USA; *Int'l*, pg. 916

FRISKIES KITTEN—NONE—Nestle USA; *Int'l*, pg. 916

FRISKIES MIGHTY DOG—NONE—Nestle USA; *Int'l*, pg. 916

FRISKIES MIGHTY DOG SENIOR—NONE—Nestle USA; *Int'l*, pg. 916

FRISKIES PRIME STREAKS—NONE—Nestle USA; *Int'l*, pg. 916

FRISKIES PRIME STRIPS—NONE—Nestle USA; *Int'l*, pg. 916

FRISKIES SENIOR—NONE—Nestle USA; *Int'l*, pg. 916

FRISKIES SPECIAL DIET—NONE—Nestle USA; *Int'l*, pg. 916

FRISKIES WAGTIME—NONE—Nestle USA; *Int'l*, pg. 916

FRISUMO—Soft Drinks—UNICER-Uniao Cervejeira, S.A.; *Int'l*, pg. 1432

FRITO-LAY—Snack Foods—PepsiCo, Inc.; *U.S. Public*, pg. 1276

FRITOS—Corn Chips—Frito-Lay Company; *U.S. Public*, pg. 1277

FRITOS NON-STOP NACHO—Corn Chips—Frito-Lay Company; *U.S. Public*, pg. 1277

FRITOS WILD N' MILD RANCH—Corn Chips—Frito-Lay Company; *U.S. Public*, pg. 1277

FRITZI—Misses Sportswear—Fritzi of California Manufacturing Corp.; *U.S. Private*, pg. 429

FROG FEAST—Game—Tyco Toys, Inc.; *U.S. Public*, pg. 1058

FROLIC—Pet Food—Mars Petfoods (UNISABI); *U.S. Private*, pg. 707

FROM MINE TAILINGS—NONE—Coeur D'Alene Mines Corporation; *U.S. Public*, pg. 394

FROM SCHOOL TO WORK—Textbooks Designed to Help Students Make Transitions from Classroom to Jobs—Goodheart-Willcox Publisher; *U.S. Private*, pg. 464

FROM THE VALLEYS OF CALIFORNIA—Almonds—Blue Diamond Growers; *U.S. Private*, pg. 152

FROMASE—Microbial Rennet for Cheese-Making—Royal Gist-Brocades N.V.; *Int'l*, pg. 1142

FROMMELT—Dock Shelters—Rite-Hite Corporation (WI); *U.S. Private*, pg. 933

FROMMER—Reference—Simon & Schuster; *U.S. Private*, pg. 777

FRONE—Native Beta Interferon—Ares-Serono S.A.; *Int'l*, pg. 80

FRONT AND REAR LOAD CARRIER—Shock Absorbers—Arvin Industries, Inc.; *U.S. Public*, pg. 136

FRONT CAPITAL SYSTEMS—NONE—SunGard Data Systems Inc.; *U.S. Public*, pg. 1534

FRONT PAGE—Prepaid Pagers—Fone America, Inc.; *U.S. Public*, pg. 661

FRONT ROW—Operating Stool—Bristol-Myers Squibb Company; *U.S. Public*, pg. 253

FRONT RUNNER—Hood Shield—Lund International Holdings, Inc.; *U.S. Public*, pg. 1020

FRONT STREET—Prefinished Wall Paneling—Georgia-Pacific Corporation; *U.S. Public*, pg. 735

FRONTIER—Household Paper Goods—Orchids Paper Products Co.; *U.S. Private*, pg. 819

FRONTIER—Herbicide—Sandoz Agro, Inc.; *Int'l*, pg. 974

FRONTIER FUELS—Fuels—Fleischli Oil Company, Inc.; *U.S. Private*, pg. 410

FROOT LOOPS—Ready-Sweetened Fruit-Flavored Cereal—Kellogg Company; *U.S. Public*, pg. 947

FROSLITE—NONE—Medline Industries, Inc.; *U.S. Private*, pg. 728

FROST—Drink Mixes—McCormick/Schilling; *U.S. Public*, pg. 1066

FROST KING—Consumer Prods.—Thermwell Products Co., Inc.; *U.S. Private*, pg. 1081

FROST LINE—Snow Tools—Bissell Inc.; *U.S. Private*, pg. 145

FROST LINE—Plate Steel for Low Temperature Applications—Lukens Steel Company; *U.S. Public*, pg. 1020

FROST-LITE—Transluscent White Laminated Glass—Globe-Amerada Glass Company; *U.S. Private*, pg. 458

FROST 'N TIP—Haircolor—Bristol-Myers Squibb Company; *U.S. Public*, pg. 253

FROSTAR—Frozen Treats & Desserts—J & J Snack Foods Corporation; *U.S. Public*, pg. 916

FROSTBAN—Natural Pesticide—DNAP Holding Corp.; *Int'l*, pg. 454

FROSTBRITE MATTE—Enamel Printing Paper—Consolidated Papers, Inc.; *U.S. Public*, pg. 436

FROSTED CHEERIOS—Cereal—General Mills, Inc.; *U.S. Public*, pg. 717

FROSTED KRISPIES—Ready-Sweetened Rice Cereal—Kellogg Company; *U.S. Public*, pg. 947

FROSTED MINI-WHEATS—Lightly Sweetened Shredded Whole Wheat Biscuits—Kellogg Company; *U.S. Public*, pg. 947

FROSTED TOASTY O'S—Cereal—Malt-O-Meal Company; *U.S. Private*, pg. 699

FROSTEX—Pipe Heater Freeze Protection—Raychem Corporation; *U.S. Public*, pg. 1362

FROSTICK—Ice Cream Novelties—Borden, Inc.; *U.S. Private*, pg. 157

FROSTIE—Root Beer—The Monarch Company, Inc.; *U.S. Private*, pg. 756

FROSTING PRIDE—Frozen Toppings—Presto Food Products, Inc.; *U.S. Public*, pg. 1527

FROSTINGS—Lingerie—Warner's; *U.S. Public*, pg. 1738

FROTH PAK—Two-Component Urethane Foam—Flexible Products Company; *U.S. Private*, pg. 412

FROTH PAK—Poly-Urethane Foam Insulation & Sealing—Insta-Foam Products, Inc.; *U.S. Private*, pg. 412

FROTH TOP—Milk—Q.U.F. Industries Ltd.; *Int'l*, pg. 1074

FROWNCIDE—Fungicide—Ishihara Sangyo Kaisha, Ltd.; *Int'l*, pg. 689

FROZEN COAL CRACKER—Industrial Machinery—Pennsylvania Crusher Corp.; *U.S. Private*, pg. 850

FROZEN RITE—Frozen Rolls & Biscuits—Bridgford Foods Corporation; *U.S. Public*, pg. 252

FROZFRUIT—NONE—Frozfruit Corporation; *U.S. Private*, pg. 430

FRUCHTZWERGE—Yogurt—Danone Group; *Int'l*, pg. 379

FRUCO—Mayonnaise, Seasonings, Spices, Beverages—Bestfoods; *U.S. Public*, pg. 223

FRUEN—Oat Products & Horse Feeds—ConAgra, Inc.; *U.S. Public*, pg. 425

FRUGAL FRANK'S—Brand-Name Footwear at Promotional Prices—F.W. Woolworth Co.; *U.S. Public*, pg. 1777

FRUIT & NUT—Candies—Hershey Foods Corporation; *U.S. Public*, pg. 811

FRUIT BARS—NONE—Snacks Unlimited Division; *U.S. Public*, pg. 718

FRUIT BASKET—Candy—Brach & Brock Confections Inc.; *U.S. Private*, pg. 163

FRUIT BOUNTY—Glassware—Indiana Glass Company; *U.S. Public*, pg. 976

FRUIT BY THE FOOT—Fruit Snack—General Mills, Inc.; *U.S. Public*, pg. 717

FRUIT CREST—Fruit Spreads & Fruit Juices—Nestle Chocolate & Confection; *Int'l*, pg. 917

FRUIT FLAVORED TOASTY O'S—Cereal—Malt-O-Meal Company; *U.S. Private*, pg. 699

FRUIT FRESH—Fruit Protector—Alltrista Corporation; *U.S. Public*, pg. 56

FRUIT GALAXY—Low-Moisture Fruit—Vacu-Dry Company; *U.S. Public*, pg. 1704

FRUIT INN—Juice Drink—Calpis Food Industry Co. Ltd.; *Int'l*, pg. 252

FRUIT JELL—Jelling Agent—Alltrista Corporation; *U.S. Public*, pg. 56

FRUIT-LINE—Ice Cream—Unilever Plc; *Int'l*, pg. 1433

FRUIT N FIBRE—Presweetened Cereal—Kraft Foods, Inc.; *U.S. Public*, pg. 1287

FRUIT NATURALS—Canned Fruit—Del Monte Foods; *U.S. Private*, pg. 321

FRUIT OF THE LOOM—Underwear, Activewear & Socks—Fruit of the Loom, Inc.; *U.S. Public*, pg. 685

FRUIT OF THE LOOM—Underwear—Union Underwear Co., Inc.; *U.S. Public*, pg. 686

FRUIT OF THE LOOM CASUALWEAR—Activewear—Fruit of the Loom, Inc.; *U.S. Public*, pg. 685

FRUIT-OF-THE-MONTH CLUB—Monthly Shipments of Fruit—Harry and David; *Int'l*, pg. 1518

FRUIT PATCH—Fresh & Processed Fruits & Vegetables—Cherry Central Cooperative; *U.S. Private*, pg. 233

FRUIT ROLL-UPS—Snacks—General Mills, Inc.; *U.S. Public*, pg. 717

FRUIT ROLL UPS—NONE—Snacks Unlimited Division; *U.S. Public*, pg. 718

FRUIT SCOOPS—NONE—Nestle USA; *Int'l*, pg. 916

FRUIT SNACK MAKER—Activity—Tyco Toys, Inc.; *U.S. Public*, pg. 1058

FRUIT SNACKERS—Real Fruit Snack—Brach & Brock Confections Inc.; *U.S. Private*, pg. 163

FRUIT SNACKS—Real Fruit Snacks; Teenage Mutant Ninja Turtle & Michael Jordan Varieties—Farley Candy Company; *U.S. Private*, pg. 397

FRUIT STRING THING—Snack Food—General Mills, Inc.; *U.S. Public*, pg. 717

FRUIT STRIPE—Gums—Nabisco Inc.; *U.S. Public*, pg. 1355

FRUIT STRIPE—Chewing Gum—Planters Company; *U.S. Public*, pg. 1355

FRUIT SWIRL BARS—NONE—Snacks Unlimited Division; *U.S. Public*, pg. 718

FRUIT TAPE—Chewing Gum—Amurol Confections Co.; *U.S. Public*, pg. 1781

FRUIT-TELLA—Candies—Van Melle N.V.; *Int'l*, pg. 1450

FRUITAGE—99% Fruit SoftServe—J.M. Smucker Company; *U.S. Public*, pg. 1480

FRUITFUL BRAN—Flakes of Wheat Bran Cereal with Raisins, Dates, Apples, Peaches & Honey—Kellogg Company; *U.S. Public*, pg. 947

FRUITLAND—Fruit Juices—Krier Foods, Inc.; *U.S. Private*, pg. 636

FRUITOPIA—NONE—The Coca-Cola Company; *U.S. Public*, pg. 392

FRUITY MARSHMALLOW KRISPIES—Frosted Rice Cereal with Fruit-Flavored Marshmallow Bits—Kellogg Company; *U.S. Public*, pg. 947

FRULIX—Snack Cakes—Culinar Inc.; *Int'l*, pg. 348

FRUTAPON—Plant Protectives—DSM Chemie Linz GmbH; *Int'l*, pg. 356

FRUTSI—Children's Fruit Juice Drink—Jugos del Valle, S.A. de C.V.; *Int'l*, pg. 716

FRY KING—Pressure Fryers—BKI; *U.S. Public*, pg. 1506

FRYBABY—Electric Deep Fryer—National Presto Industries, Inc.; *U.S. Public*, pg. 1159

FRYDADDY—Electric Deep Fryer—National Presto Industries, Inc.; *U.S. Public*, pg. 1159

FRYE BOOT COMPANY—Footwear—Jimlar Corporation; *U.S. Private*, pg. 587

THE FRYE CO.—Shoes & Boots—The Frye Company; *U.S. Private*, pg. 430

FRYING SAUCER—Rolling Machines—Gold Medal Products Co.; *U.S. Private*, pg. 459

FRYMASTER—Fryers, Pasta Cookers & Filtration Systems—Welbilt Corporation; *Int'l*, pg. 188

Brand Name Index

FRY'S—Chocolate—Cadbury Schweppes p.l.c.; *Int'l*, pg. 247

FUDDRUCKERS—Restaurants—Fuddruckers, Inc.; *Int'l*, pg. 325

FUDGE STICKS—Cookies—Keebler Company; *U.S. Public*, pg. 657

FUDGE STRIPES—Cookies—Keebler Company; *U.S. Public*, pg. 657

FUDGSICLE BRAND—Fudge Pops & Bars—Good Humor/Breyers Ice Cream; *Int'l*, pg. 1435

FUEL FIGHTER—Tires—Bridgestone/Firestone, Inc.; *Int'l*, pg. 213

FUEL MISER—Engine System—Echlin Inc.; *U.S. Public*, pg. 560

FUEL OIL SLUDGE TREAT—Industrial Chemical—Hercules Chemical Co., Inc.; *U.S. Private*, pg. 523

FUEL-SOLV—Fireside Additive—BetzDearborn Inc.; *U.S. Public*, pg. 226

FUELMASTER +—Heat Pump Control System—Lennox International Inc.; *U.S. Private*, pg. 659

FUELSAFE—Insulated Fuel Tank—Ace Tank & Equipment Co.; *U.S. Private*, pg. 12

FUGAZY INTERNATIONAL—Travel & Air Services—Fugazy International Corporation; *U.S. Private*, pg. 430

FUGUE—Tables—Howe Furniture Corporation; *U.S. Private*, pg. 543

FUJI—Film, Photographic Equip. & Supplies—Fuji Photo Film U.S.A., Inc.; *Int'l*, pg. 524

FUJI—NONE—Taylor Impression, Inc.; *U.S. Private*, pg. 1070

FUJI—Stacking Side Chair, ai Collection—Vecta; *U.S. Private*, pg. 1038

FUJI FILM—Photographic Supplies—Fuji Photo Film U.S.A., Inc.; *Int'l*, pg. 524

FUJICA—Photographic Supplies—Fuji Photo Film U.S.A., Inc.; *Int'l*, pg. 524

FUJICHROME—Photographic Supplies—Fuji Photo Film U.S.A., Inc.; *Int'l*, pg. 524

FUJICOLOR—Photographic Supplies—Fuji Photo Film U.S.A., Inc.; *Int'l*, pg. 524

FUJIGRAPH—Reprographic Supplies—Fuji Photo Film U.S.A., Inc.; *Int'l*, pg. 524

FUJILITH—Graphic Arts Supplies—Fuji Photo Film U.S.A., Inc.; *Int'l*, pg. 524

FUJINON—Photographic Supplies—Fuji Photo Film U.S.A., Inc.; *Int'l*, pg. 524

FUJITSU—Cellular Telephones—Fujitsu Ten Corp. of America; *Int'l*, pg. 526

FUJITSU—NONE—Milgray Electronics, Inc.; *U.S. Public*, pg. 205

FUJITSU MICROELECTRONICS—Electronic Components—Interface Electronics Corporation; *U.S. Private*, pg. 567

FUJITSU TEN—Sound Entertainment, OEM Prods., Stereos, Speakers, Amplifiers, TV's, VCR's—Fujitsu Ten Corp. of America; *Int'l*, pg. 526

FUJIX—Electronic Products—Fuji Photo Film U.S.A., Inc.; *Int'l*, pg. 524

FUL-LY—Women's Undergarments—AGP Industrial Corporation; *Int'l*, pg. 14

FUL-O-MITE—Exterior Insulation Finish System—TEC Incorporated; *U.S. Public*, pg. 687

FUL-VUE—Windshield Washer Solvent—Patterson Laboratories, Inc.; *U.S. Private*, pg. 843

FULACOLOR—Paper Coating Clay—Laporte plc; *Int'l*, pg. 801

FULACRYL—Acrylic Latex Caulk—H.B. Fuller Company; *U.S. Public*, pg. 686

FULAPRENE—Industrial Adhesive/Sealant—H.B. Fuller Company; *U.S. Public*, pg. 686

FULATEX—Polymers—H.B. Fuller Company; *U.S. Public*, pg. 686

FULBAR—Conical Refiner Filling—Harnischfeger Industries, Inc.; *U.S. Public*, pg. 788

FULFLO SPECIALTIES—Valves—Gusher Pumps, Inc.; *U.S. Private*, pg. 488

FULL AUTHORITY—Software Products—The Mead Corporation; *U.S. Public*, pg. 1074

FULL COMFORT—Bras—Warner's; *U.S. Public*, pg. 1738

FULL-FILL—Antifreeze/Coolant—The Dow Chemical Company; *U.S. Public*, pg. 522

FULL-FIT—Sepralators—Osmonics, Inc.; *U.S. Public*, pg. 1233

FULL FLAVOR—Hollywood—Souza Cruz, S.A.; *Int'l*, pg. 112

FULL FLEX—Mortar—TEC Incorporated; *U.S. Public*, pg. 687

FULL IMPACT—Software—Borland International, Inc.; *U.S. Public*, pg. 246

FULL MEAL DEAL—Hot Foods—American Dairy Queen Corporation; *U.S. Public*, pg. 220

FULL MEAL DEAL—Combination Meal—International Dairy Queen, Inc.; *U.S. Public*, pg. 220

FULL'N SOFT—Dry/Mist Curler Set—Sunbeam Household Products; *U.S. Public*, pg. 1533

FULL PACK—Refuse Bodies—Heil Environmental Industries; *U.S. Public*, pg. 520

FULL PAINT—Software—Borland International, Inc.; *U.S. Public*, pg. 246

FULL POWER—Small Electrical Equipment—General Cable Corporation; *Int'l*, pg. 1486

A FULL SERVICE BANK—Member Banks—The American Bankers Association; *U.S. Private*, pg. 51

FULL SMART—NONE—Molex Incorporated; *U.S. Public*, pg. 1121

FULL SMART PLUS—NONE—Molex Incorporated; *U.S. Public*, pg. 1121

FULL SPECTRUM—Greeting Cards—American Greetings Corporation; *U.S. Public*, pg. 77

FULL VALUE—Private Label Over-the-Counter Products—Avatex Corporation; *U.S. Public*, pg. 151

FULL VIEW—Control Measurement—Brooks Instrument; *U.S. Public*, pg. 574

FULL WRITE PROFESSIONAL—Software—Borland International, Inc.; *U.S. Public*, pg. 246

FULL-POUR—NONE—H.B. Fuller Company; *U.S. Public*, pg. 686

FULLBACK—Envelope Gum—H.B. Fuller Company; *U.S. Public*, pg. 686

FULLER—Dust Collector—Fuller Company; *Int'l*, pg. 475

FULLER-O'BRIEN—NONE—ICI Paints; pg. 664

FULLER'S—Glue—H.B. Fuller Company; *U.S. Public*, pg. 686

FULLJET—Spray Nozzle—Spraying Systems Co.; *U.S. Private*, pg. 1026

FULLREZ—Starch Additives—H.B. Fuller Company; *U.S. Public*, pg. 686

FULLSEAL—Envelope Gum—H.B. Fuller Company; *U.S. Public*, pg. 686

FULLSPACE—Filing Systems—Lundia Div. of MII, Inc.; *U.S. Private*, pg. 680

FULTON—Sundry Items—Pratt & Lambert United, Inc.; *U.S. Public*, pg. 1466

FULTORK—Motor—Fisher Scientific Company; *U.S. Public*, pg. 658

FULVICIN P/G—Oral Antifungal Tablets—Schering-Plough Corporation; *U.S. Public*, pg. 1438

FULVICIN-U/F—Oral Antifungal Tablets—Schering-Plough Corporation; *U.S. Public*, pg. 1438

FUMAGALLI—Wheels—Rockwell International Corporation; *U.S. Public*, pg. 1397

FUMAGALLI'S—Men's Apparel—Hartmarx Corporation; *U.S. Public*, pg. 795

FUMARON—Fodder Products—DSM Chemie Linz GmbH; *Int'l*, pg. 356

FUME ERASER—Mobile Welding Fume Extractions Unit—The Spencer Turbine Co.; *U.S. Private*, pg. 1025

FUME-GATOR—NONE—United Air Specialists, Inc.; *U.S. Public*, pg. 382

FUN BOX—Ice Cream & Water Ices—Good Humor/Breyers Ice Cream; *Int'l*, pg. 1435

FUN DIP—NONE—Nestle USA; *Int'l*, pg. 916

FUN MOVERS—Motorhomes with Garages—Cruise America, Inc.; *U.S. Private*, pg. 178

FUN PAK—Ready-to-Eat Cereal in Six Single-Serving Packages—Kellogg Company; *U.S. Public*, pg. 947

FUN + FASHION—Fashionable Apparel for Men & Women—F.W. Woolworth Co.; *U.S. Public*, pg. 1777

FUN RADIO—France Broadcasting—CLT-UFA; *Int'l*, pg. 561

FUN SAVER—Motion Picture Camera—Eastman Kodak Company; *U.S. Public*, pg. 550

FUN STUFF—Household Tissue Paper Goods—Orchids Paper Products Co.; *U.S. Private*, pg. 819

FUN-TAK—Adhesive—DAP Inc.; *Int'l*, pg. 1486

FUN THAT LASTS—NONE—Rubbermaid Incorporated; *U.S. Public*, pg. 1411

FUN-TOUCH 2—NONE—Nikon Inc.; *Int'l*, pg. 931

FUN TUBE—Recreational Rubber Tubes—Bridgestone/Firestone, Inc.; *Int'l*, pg. 213

FUN WITH A PURPOSE—Descriptive Phrase—Highlights for Children, Inc.; *U.S. Private*, pg. 528

THE FUN ZONE—Magazine—Highlights for Children, Inc.; *U.S. Private*, pg. 528

FUNA—Soups, Sauces, Spices—Bestfoods; *U.S. Public*, pg. 223

FUNBRELLA—20' Diameter Umbrella—Anchor Industries Inc.; *U.S. Private*, pg. 71

FUNCTIONPAC—Business Product—International Business Machines Corporation; *U.S. Public*, pg. 895

FUND TRAC—NONE—SunGard Data Systems Inc.; *U.S. Public*, pg. 1534

FUNDADOR—Brandy—Domecq Importers Inc.; *Int'l*, pg. 63

FUND'MENTALS—School Supplies—Empire Berol U.S.A.; *U.S. Public*, pg. 1178

FUNELAIRE—Filtering Aid—Fisher Scientific Company; *U.S. Private*, pg. 658

FUNGALS—Girls' Underwear—Fruit of the Loom, Inc.; *U.S. Public*, pg. 685

FUNGICLEAR—Nail Revitalizer Liquid—Alva/Amco Pharmacal Companies, Inc.; *U.S. Private*, pg. 47

FUNGICURE—Anti-Fungal Liquid—Alva/Amco Pharmacal Companies, Inc.; *U.S. Private*, pg. 47

FUNGIZONE—Infectious Disease Therapy—Bristol-Myers Squibb Company; *U.S. Public*, pg. 253

FUNGLASSES—Card Game—Mattel Games/Puzzles; *U.S. Public*, pg. 1058

FUNGUS RESISTANT—NONE—CertainTeed Corporation; *Int'l*, pg. 1170

FUNGUSBUSTER—Asphalt Shingle—CertainTeed Corporation; *Int'l*, pg. 1170

FUNK UHR—Magazines—Axel Springer Verlag AG; *Int'l*, pg. 102

FUNK & WAGNALLS—29-Volume Adult Encyclopedia—Primedia Inc.; *U.S. Public*, pg. 1328

FUNNEL—Cake Insert Pan—Gold Medal Products Co.; *U.S. Private*, pg. 459

FUNNEL CAKE FACTORY—Funnel Cake—J & J Snack Foods Corporation; *U.S. Public*, pg. 916

FUNNIES & DESIGN—Greeting Cards—American Greetings Corporation; *U.S. Public*, pg. 77

FUNNY BONES—Snack Cakes—Drake Bakeries, Inc.; *Int'l*, pg. 349

FUNNY CHEW CHEWS—Childrens Vitamin—Health Products Corporation; *U.S. Private*, pg. 514

FUNNY FACE—Drink Mix—Brady Enterprises, Inc.; *U.S. Private*, pg. 165

FUNPALS—Boys' Underwear—Fruit of the Loom, Inc.; *U.S. Public*, pg. 685

FUNSAVER—Disposable Camera—Eastman Kodak Company; *U.S. Public*, pg. 550

FUNSOFT—CD-Rom & Other Multimedia Software—John Menzies plc; *Int'l*, pg. 707

FUNTIME—Cameras—Eastman Kodak Company; *U.S. Public*, pg. 550

FUNYUNS—Onion Rings—Frito-Lay Company; *U.S. Public*, pg. 1277

FUNYUNS TASTY RANCH—Onion Rings—Frito-Lay Company; *U.S. Public*, pg. 1277

FURACIN—Treatment of Burn Wounds—Roberts Pharmaceutical Corporation; *U.S. Public*, pg. 1393

FURADAN—Insecticide/Nematicide—FMC Corp., Agricultural Products Group; *U.S. Public*, pg. 605

FURADANTIN—Urinary Tract Antibacterial—Procter & Gamble Pharmaceuticals, Inc.; *U.S. Public*, pg. 1331

FURALAC—Corrosion-Resistant Mortar—Elf Atochem North America, Inc.; *Int'l*, pg. 445

FURMANO'S—Processed Vegetables—Furman Foods, Inc.; *U.S. Private*, pg. 431

FURMAN'S—Processed Vegetables—Furman Foods, Inc.; *U.S. Private*, pg. 431

FURNITURE MEDIC—On-Site Furniture Repair & Restoration—The ServiceMaster Company; *U.S. Public*, pg. 1461

FURNITURE/TODAY—Weekly Newspaper—Reed Elsevier Business Information; *Int'l*, pg. 1095

FURNITUREMAX—Store-Within-Store Furniture Needs—OfficeMax; *U.S. Public*, pg. 1212

FUROXONE—Treatment of Gastrointestinal Infections—Roberts Pharmaceutical Corporation; *U.S. Public*, pg. 1393

FURRER-JACOT—Jewelry—Basel Trading Company Ltd.; *Int'l*, pg. 169

FURST BISMARCK QUELLE—Mineral Water—Nestle S.A.; *Int'l*, pg. 915

FURTHER PROCESS POULTRY—NONE—Aliments Flamingo; *Int'l*, pg. 57

FURTULON—Anticancer Agent—Roche Holding Ltd.; *Int'l*, pg. 1119

FUTURENET—Software—Data I/O Corporation; *U.S. Public*, pg. 486

FURY—Insecticide—FMC Corp., Agricultural Products Group; *U.S. Public*, pg. 605

FURY IN THE WEST—War Game—Monarch Avalon, Inc.; *U.S. Public*, pg. 1123

FURYS—Ball Point Pen—Sanford Corporation; *U.S. Public*, pg. 1178

FUSE-O-LINK—Hardware—Clark Door Co., Inc.; *U.S. Private*, pg. 242

FUSEAL—Plastic Acid Waste System—Ryan Herco Products Corp.; *U.S. Private*, pg. 953

FUSEAL—Polypropylene Electric Resistance Coil Fused Pipe & Fittings—George Fischer Sloane, Inc.; *Int'l*, pg. 430

FUSHION TIP—Rod—Outdoor Technologies Group; *U.S. Private*, pg. 822

FUSIBLE P-91—Interfacings—Specialty Textile Products; *U.S. Private*, pg. 1023

FUSION—Ergonomic Task Seating—Cramer Inc.; *U.S. Private*, pg. 285

FUSION—Multi-Dimensional Data Base—Information Builders; *U.S. Private*, pg. 561

FUSION FINISH—Manufacturing Process for Hardboard Siding—ABT Building Products Corporation; *Int'l*, pg. 20

FUSION 4000 PLUS—Dry Mounting Adhesive—Seal Products Incorporated; *U.S. Public*, pg. 849

FUSION 2000—Trademark—Eaton Corporation, Semi-Conductor; *U.S. Public*, pg. 557

FUSISTOR—Current Control Fuse—S & C Electric Company; *U.S. Private*, pg. 954

FUSITE—Hermetically Sealed Connectors—Emerson Electric Co.; *U.S. Public*, pg. 572

FUSOR—Epoxy Adhesive—Lord Corporation; *U.S. Private*, pg. 675

FUTABA—Vacuum Fluorescent Display, Keyboard—Futaba Corporation; *Int'l*, pg. 531

FUTURA—PH Electrodes—Beckman Instruments, Inc.; *U.S. Public*, pg. 199

FUTURA—Recycled Enamel Coated Printing Paper—Consolidated Papers, Inc.; *U.S. Public*, pg. 436

FUTURA—Communication System—Executone Information Systems, Inc.; *U.S. Public*, pg. 599

FUTURA—High Temperature Jet Dyeing Machine—Gaston County Dyeing Machine Co.; *U.S. Private*, pg. 441

FUTURA—Canister Vacuum Cleaner—Hoover Company; *U.S. Public*, pg. 1065

FUTURA—Feminine Pads—Kimberly-Clark Corporation; *U.S. Public*, pg. 958

FUTURA—Miniature Switch Mechanisms & Faceplates—The Lamson & Sessions Co.; *U.S. Public*, pg. 976

FUTURA—Binders—Master Craft Corp.; *Int'l*, pg. 267

FUTURA—Plastic Electrical Wall Plates—Mulberry Metal Products, Inc.; *U.S. Private*, pg. 766

FUTURA—Portable Electric Heater—Slant/Fin Corporation; *U.S. Private*, pg. 1005

FUTURA—Industrial Goggles—Uvex Safety, Inc.; *Int'l*, pg. 132

FUTURA II—Air Cooled Hair Dryer—Revlon-Realistic Professional Products, Inc.; *U.S. Private*, pg. 690

FUTURE—Floor Polish—S.C. Johnson & Son, Inc.; *U.S. Private*, pg. 592

FUTURE—(Floor Polish)—S.C. Johnson & Son, Limited; *U.S. Public*, pg. 593

THE FUTURE ACCESS—Computer Furniture—Virco Mfg. Corporation; *U.S. Public*, pg. 1721

FUTURE CELL—Soft Foam—Future Foam, Inc.; *U.S. Private*, pg. 433

FUTURE PAC—Packaging Foam—Future Foam, Inc.; *U.S. Private*, pg. 433

FUTURE STAT—Anti Static Foam—Future Foam, Inc.; *U.S. Private*, pg. 433

FUTURECHOICE SM—Long-Term Care Rider on Universal Life Insurance—Colonial Companies, Inc.; *U.S. Public*, pg. 1699

FUTURMILL—NONE—DeVlieg-Bullard Inc.; *U.S. Public*, pg. 502

FUTURO—Elastic Braces & Patient Aids—Futuro Inc.; *Int'l*, pg. 182

FUTURO SPORT—NONE—Futuro Inc.; *Int'l*, pg. 182

FUZERE—Thermoform Packaging—Filtertek Inc.; *U.S. Public*, pg. 546

FUZZ BUTTONS—Mesh Contacts—Tecknit Incorporated; *U.S. Private*, pg. 1072

FUZZY FRIENDS—Greeting Cards—American Greetings Corporation; *U.S. Public*, pg. 77

FYARSTOR—Flame Retardants—Witco Corporation; *U.S. Public*, pg. 1773

FYBOGEL—Natural Fibre Bulking Agent—Reckitt & Colman plc; *Int'l*, pg. 1089

FYBROC—Corrosion Resistant Fiberglass Pumps—Met-Pro Corporation; *U.S. Public*, pg. 1100

FYE-FOR YOUR ENTERTAINMENT—Retail Music & Video Store—Trans World Entertainment Corporation; *U.S. Public*, pg. 1629

FYNNON CALCIUM—Treatment of Rheumatic Pain—SmithKline Beecham plc; *Int'l*, pg. 1264

FYNNON SALT—Treatment of Rheumatic Pain—SmithKline Beecham plc; *Int'l*, pg. 1264

FYR-LACE—Electronic Lacing Tape—Gudebrod, Inc.; *U.S. Private*, pg. 486

FYRITE—Measuring Instrument—Bacharach Inc.; *U.S. Private*, pg. 109

FYTOSTREP—Prod. to Prevent Mildew on Roses & Plant Bacterial Diseases—Royal Gist-Brocades N.V.; *Int'l*, pg. 1142

G

G—Bond Paper—The Mead Corporation; *U.S. Public*, pg. 1074

GA—Computer System—General Automation, Inc.; *U.S. Public*, pg. 706

GA—Gladiator Fire Truck Chassis—Spartan Motors, Inc.; *U.S. Public*, pg. 1495

GAD—Valve Trim—Copes-Vulcan Inc.; *U.S. Private*, pg. 274

GAF GAFGLAS PLY 6—Conventional Roll Roofing—Building Materials Corporation of America; *U.S. Private*, pg. 433

G & FEATHER DESIGN—Letterhead Design Competition—The Mead Corporation; *U.S. Public*, pg. 1074

G & G—NONE—Petrie Retail, Inc.; *U.S. Private*, pg. 858

G & H EXPORIT—Insulation—Saint-Gobain; *Int'l*, pg. 1170

G & H ISOVER—Insulation—Saint-Gobain; *Int'l*, pg. 1170

G & H SILLEN—Insulation—Saint-Gobain; *Int'l*, pg. 1170

G & O—Automotive—Allen Telecom, Inc.; *U.S. Public*, pg. 45

GB—Electrical Construction Tools—Applied Power Inc.; *U.S. Public*, pg. 124

GBC—Punch Machines—General Binding Corporation; *U.S. Public*, pg. 707

GBC—NONE—Taylor Impression, Inc.; *U.S. Private*, pg. 1070

GBC 1-STEP—Desktop Binding System—General Binding Corporation; *U.S. Public*, pg. 707

GB500—Motorcycle—American Honda Motor Co., Inc. Motorcycle Division; *Int'l*, pg. 634

GB MAXI—Hypermarkets—GIB Group; *Int'l*, pg. 532

GB SUPER—Supermarkets—GIB Group; *Int'l*, pg. 532

GCC—Products for Electrical & Communications Industry—General Cable Corporation; *Int'l*, pg. 1486

GCM—Generator Condition Monitor—Environment/One Corporation; *U.S. Public*, pg. 586

GCP SERIES—Paint Spray Booth Additives—BetzDearborn Inc.; *U.S. Public*, pg. 226

GCS—Ski Gloves—The Grandoe Corp.; *U.S. Private*, pg. 469

G-CRYL—Acrylic Resin—Henkel Corporation; *Int'l*, pg. 610

G-CURE—Acrylic Resin—Henkel Corporation; *Int'l*, pg. 610

GDC—NONE—General Datacomm Industries, Inc.; *U.S. Public*, pg. 708

GDDM—Computer System—International Business Machines Corporation; *U.S. Public*, pg. 895

GDLH—Rotating Deformed Spines to Align with Implanted Hardware—Sofamor Danek Group, Inc.; *U.S. Public*, pg. 1482

GDS—Gas Turbine Filter System—Donaldson Company, Inc.; *U.S. Public*, pg. 517

GDX—Gas Turbine Air Filter System—Donaldson Company, Inc.; *U.S. Public*, pg. 517

GE ANSWER CENTER—Telemarketing Service—General Electric Company; *U.S. Public*, pg. 709

GEC—Electrical Products—The General Electric Company, p.l.c.; *Int'l*, pg. 543

GEC-MARCONI—Electronic Systems & Components—The General Electric Company, p.l.c.; *Int'l*, pg. 543

G.E. CAPITAL—Financial Services Company—G.E. Capital Commercial Real Estate Financing; *U.S. Public*, pg. 712

GEHE—NONE—Franz Haniel & Cie, GmbH; *Int'l*, pg. 591

GEM—BUTTERFLY VALVES—Crane Limited U.K.; *U.S. Public*, pg. 458

GEM—Aluminum Foil—Reynolds Metals Company; *U.S. Public*, pg. 1385

GE90—Turbofan Engine—SNECMA - Societe Nationale d'Etude et de Construction de Moteurs d'Aviation; *Int'l*, pg. 1165

GE REWARDS MASTERCARD—Credit Card Service—General Electric Company; *U.S. Public*, pg. 709

GF—Metal Office Furniture—GF Office Furniture Ltd.; *U.S. Private*, pg. 434

G.F.—Valves, Pipes & Fittings—Ryan Herco Products Corp.; *U.S. Private*, pg. 953

GF/GIROFLEX COLLECTION—Ergonomic Seating—GF Office Furniture; *U.S. Private*, pg. 435

GFI—Tubing Sets—Alcon Laboratories, Inc.; *Int'l*, pg. 916

GF100K—FPGA Family of Parts—Gatefield Corporation; *U.S. Public*, pg. 703

GFP—Corporate Logo—Gas-Fired Products, Inc.; *U.S. Private*, pg. 440

GFS—Xanthan Gum Blend—The NutraSweet Kelco Company; *U.S. Public*, pg. 1125

GF 250 F—FPGA Family of Parts—Gatefield Corporation; *U.S. Public*, pg. 703

GF 260 F—FPGA Family of Parts—Gatefield Corporation; *U.S. Public*, pg. 703

GF 200 F—FPGA Family of Parts—Gatefield Corporation; *U.S. Public*, pg. 703

G-FET—Centrifuge-Based Dynamic Flight Simulator—Environmental Tectonics Corporation (ETC); *U.S. Public*, pg. 587

G-50—AG Sprinklers—Weather Tec Corporation; *U.S. Private*, pg. 1155

GG-CEN—NONE—Schwarz Pharma Inc.; *Int'l*, pg. 1211

THE G. GORDON LIDDY SHOW—Talk Radio Program—Westwood One Entertainment; *U.S. Public*, pg. 1763

THE G. GORDON LIDDY SHOW—Talk Show—Westwood One, Inc.; *U.S. Public*, pg. 1763

GHDL—GenRad Hardware Description for Language—GenRad, Inc.; *U.S. Public*, pg. 731

GIA—Surgical Staplers—U.S. Surgical Corp.; *U.S. Public*, pg. 1687

GIA 50 PREMIUM—Surgical Staplers—U.S. Surgical Corp.; *U.S. Public*, pg. 1687

GIA 90 PREMIUM—Surgical Staplers—U.S. Surgical Corp.; *U.S. Public*, pg. 1687

G.I. JOE— Action Figure—Hasbro; *U.S. Public*, pg. 797

G.I. JOE—Action Figures—Hasbro, Inc.; *U.S. Public*, pg. 797

GIVN—NONE—Cable and Wireless plc; *Int'l*, pg. 247

GL—Motorcycle—American Honda Motor Co., Inc. Motorcycle Division; *Int'l*, pg. 634

GL1100—Motorcycle—American Honda Motor Co., Inc. Motorcycle Division; *Int'l*, pg. 634

GL1100-GOLDWING—Motorcycle—American Honda Motor Co., Inc. Motorcycle Division; *Int'l*, pg. 634

GL1100-INTERSTATE—Motorcycle—American Honda Motor Co., Inc. Motorcycle Division; *Int'l*, pg. 634

Brand Name Index

GL500I SILVER WING INTERSTATE—Motorcycle—American Honda Motor Co., Inc. Motorcycle Division; *Int'l*, pg. 634

GL500 SILVER WING—Motorcycle—American Honda Motor Co., Inc. Motorcycle Division; *Int'l*, pg. 634

GLH 943

GLM—Welder—The Lincoln Electric Company; *U.S. Public*, pg. 996

GL MILLENNIUM—General Ledger Information System—Dun & Bradstreet Software Services; *Int'l*, pg. 532

GL/PLUS—General Ledger Software—Dun & Bradstreet Software Services; *Int'l*, pg. 532

GLR—Gravity Lumbar Reduction—Camp Healthcare; *Int'l*, pg. 1425

GLS—Fiberglass & Plastics Distributors—GLS Corporation; *U.S. Private*, pg. 435

GLX-12—Business Telephone System—Inter-Tel, Incorporated; *U.S. Public*, pg. 888

G-LAB—High G-Onset Human Centrifuge—Environmental Tectonics Corporation (ETC); *U.S. Public*, pg. 587

GMAC—Financial Services—General Motors Acceptance Corporation (GMAC); *U.S. Public*, pg. 719

GMC—Truck—Buffalo Truck Center; *U.S. Private*, pg. 179

GMC—Medium Duty Trucks—Great Lakes Peterbilt, GMC; *U.S. Private*, pg. 475

GMC & CHEVY PICKUP TRUCKS—Compact & Full Size Light Duty 1/2 Thru One-Ton—Pontiac-GMC Truck Division; *U.S. Public*, pg. 720

GMC & CHEVY SCHOOL BUS—School Bus Chassis—Pontiac-GMC Truck Division; *U.S. Public*, pg. 720

GMC & CHEVY SUBURBAN—Light Duty MPV—Pontiac-GMC Truck Division; *U.S. Public*, pg. 720

GMC FORWARD—Light & Medium Duty Cab-Over-Engine—Pontiac-GMC Truck Division; *U.S. Public*, pg. 720

GMC JIMMY—Compact & Full Size Light Duty, Sports/Utility—Pontiac-GMC Truck Division; *U.S. Public*, pg. 720

GMC RALLY WAGON—Light Duty Passenger Van—Pontiac-GMC Truck Division; *U.S. Public*, pg. 720

GMC SAFARI—Mid Sized People Mover & Cargo Mover Van—Pontiac-GMC Truck Division; *U.S. Public*, pg. 720

GMC SIERRA—Cars—General Motors Corporation; *U.S. Public*, pg. 718

GMC TOP KICK—Medium Duty Short Conventional Truck—Pontiac-GMC Truck Division; *U.S. Public*, pg. 720

GMC TRUCKS—Trucks—General Motors Corporation; *U.S. Public*, pg. 718

GMC VALUE VAN—Forward Control Chassis—Pontiac-GMC Truck Division; *U.S. Public*, pg. 720

GMC VANDURA—Light Duty Commercial Van—Pontiac-GMC Truck Division; *U.S. Public*, pg. 720

GML—Mixes—Gilster Mary Lee Corp.; *U.S. Private*, pg. 455

GM MASTERCARD—Credit Card—General Motors Acceptance Corporation (GMAC); *U.S. Public*, pg. 719

GMTV MAGAZINE—NONE—IPC Magazines Limited; *Int'l*, pg. 651

G.M. TIDDY'S—Canadian Liqueur—Marie Brizard Wines & Spirits USA; *U.S. Private*, pg. 702

GMX-48—Business Telephone System—Inter-Tel, Incorporated; *U.S. Public*, pg. 888

G-MAX—Floating Spacers—Beckman Instruments, Inc.; *U.S. Public*, pg. 199

G-MAXX 2010—Bevel Gear Cutting System—Gleason Corporation; *U.S. Public*, pg. 746

G-METRIC—Tires—The Goodyear Tire & Rubber Company; *U.S. Public*, pg. 752

GNA—Insurance Services—Weyerhaeuser Company; *U.S. Public*, pg. 1764

GNS—Value Added Data Communications Systems—British Telecommunications plc; *Int'l*, pg. 222

GN-6—Microbiological Analysis—Gelman Sciences, Inc.; *U.S. Public*, pg. 1253

GP—Large Variety of Batteries—GP Batteries International Ltd.; *Int'l*, pg. 537

GPC—Cigarettes—Brown & Williamson Tobacco Corp.; *Int'l*, pg. 111

GPCRC—Plastic Child-Resistant Caps—Kerr Group, Inc.; *U.S. Public*, pg. 952

GPD—Drives—MagneTek, Inc.; *U.S. Public*, pg. 1037

GPI—NONE—Zygo Corporation; *U.S. Public*, pg. 1795

GP-LAM—Laminated Veneer Lumber—Georgia-Pacific Corporation; *U.S. Public*, pg. 735

GP N.S.I. BOARD & DESIGN—Paperboard Cartons—Georgia-Pacific Corporation; *U.S. Public*, pg. 735

GP 100—Double-Action Revolver—Sturm, Ruger & Co., Inc.; *U.S. Public*, pg. 1526

G-P PANELBOARD—Wall Paneling—Georgia-Pacific Corporation; *U.S. Public*, pg. 735

GP PLUS & DESIGN—Linerboard & Corrugated Boxes—Georgia-Pacific Corporation; *U.S. Public*, pg. 735

G.P. PUTNAM'S SONS—Books—The Putnam & Grosset Group; *Int'l*, pg. 1027

GPS—NONE—Wilcox Electric, Inc.; *Int'l*, pg. 1384

GPSC—Plastic Prescription Snap Caps—Kerr Group, Inc.; *U.S. Public*, pg. 952

GPSI—Communications Adapter—Nellcor Puritan Bennett Incorporated; *U.S. Public*, pg. 1039

GP SORENSEN—Automotive Products—Standard Motor Products Inc.; *U.S. Public*, pg. 1503

GPTI—General Purpose Tester Interface—GenRad, Inc.; *U.S. Public*, pg. 731

GPV—Plastic Prescription Vials—Kerr Group, Inc.; *U.S. Public*, pg. 952

G-PAC—Wood Moulding Packaged in Bundles—Georgia-Pacific Corporation; *U.S. Public*, pg. 735

GQDS—Database Management Software—GRC International, Inc.; *U.S. Public*, pg. 695

GR—Almond & White Automatic Coffee Brewer—Bunn-O-Matic Corporation; *U.S. Private*, pg. 180

GR—NONE—GenRad, Inc.; *U.S. Public*, pg. 731

GR8—Corn Seeds—Groupe Limagrain; *Int'l*, pg. 566

GRF-1000—Fly Rod—Cortland Line Co., Inc.; *U.S. Private*, pg. 277

GR-PAL—GenRad's Programmer's Application Language—GenRad, Inc.; *U.S. Public*, pg. 731

GRXPERT—NONE—GenRad, Inc.; *U.S. Public*, pg. 731

GS—NONE—GS Societa Generale Supermercati; *Int'l*, pg. 186

GSC—Gymnastics Equipment—Sport Supply Group, Inc.; *U.S. Public*, pg. 1499

GS & DESIGN—Cardboard Boxes—Georgia-Pacific Corporation; *U.S. Public*, pg. 735

GSE CONDUCTIVE—Conductive Surface HDPE—Gundle/SLT Environmental, Inc.; *U.S. Public*, pg. 769

GSE CURTAIN WALL—Barrier System—Gundle/SLT Environmental, Inc.; *U.S. Public*, pg. 769

GSE HD—Polyethylene Liner—Gundle/SLT Environmental, Inc.; *U.S. Public*, pg. 769

GSE HDT—Polyethylene Textured Lining Sheet—Gundle/SLT Environmental, Inc.; *U.S. Public*, pg. 769

GSE HDW—Multilayered, High Density Polyethylene Liner with Reflective Surface—Gundle/SLT Environmental, Inc.; *U.S. Public*, pg. 769

GSE HYPERFLEX FR—Flame Retardant Smooth HDPE—Gundle/SLT Environmental, Inc.; *U.S. Public*, pg. 769

GSE HYPERNET—High Density, Conductive Polyethylene Liner—Gundle/SLT Environmental, Inc.; *U.S. Public*, pg. 769

GSE ULTRAFLEX—VFPE Polyethylene—Gundle/SLT Environmental, Inc.; *U.S. Public*, pg. 769

GSE WHITE TEXTURED—White Surface HDPE—Gundle/SLT Environmental, Inc.; *U.S. Public*, pg. 769

GSM—NONE—SunGard Data Systems Inc.; *U.S. Public*, pg. 1534

GSM-T—GSM Network Diagnostic Tool—Tekelec; *U.S. Public*, pg. 1566

GSP—Heat-Shrinkable, Transparent Polyvinyl Chloride Film—Reynolds Metals Company; *U.S. Public*, pg. 1385

GSR—Tires—Bridgestone/Firestone, Inc.; *Int'l*, pg. 213

G.S.R.—Plastic Pipe & Fittings—Ryan Herco Products Corp.; *U.S. Private*, pg. 953

GSR—Thermoplastic Pipe, Valves & Fittings—George Fischer Sloane, Inc.; *Int'l*, pg. 430

GS-700—General Service Control Valves—Copes-Vulcan Inc.; *U.S. Private*, pg. 274

GST—Laminates—Glasteel Industrial Laminates; *U.S. Private*, pg. 45

GT—Outboard Motors—Johnson Outboards Marine Corp.; *U.S. Private*, pg. 478

GTC PAGE/PARTY—Paging System—Gai-Tronics Corporation; *U.S. Public*, pg. 1430

GTECH—Computer-Based On-Line Lottery Systems—GTECH Corporation; *U.S. Public*, pg. 767

GTO—Bicycles—Bridgestone/Firestone, Inc.; *Int'l*, pg. 213

GTO—Sporting Goods—Brunswick Bowling & Billiards Corp.; *U.S. Public*, pg. 265

GTP—Absorbent Track Mat—Portec Inc., Railway Maintenance Products Div.; *U.S. Public*, pg. 1318

GT 21—Trimmer—Hoffco/Comet Industries, Inc.; *U.S. Private*, pg. 532

GT 211A—Trimmer—Hoffco/Comet Industries, Inc.; *U.S. Private*, pg. 532

GT-II SPORT GRIP—Steering Wheel Covers—Superior Industries International, Inc.; *U.S. Public*, pg. 1539

GTX—Motor Oil—Castrol North America; *Int'l*, pg. 235

G-III—NONE—G-III Apparel Group, Ltd.; *U.S. Public*, pg. 690

G-III OUTERWEAR COMPANY STORE—NONE—G-III Apparel Group, Ltd.; *U.S. Public*, pg. 690

G20—Automobile—Nissan Motor Corporation in U.S.A.; *Int'l*, pg. 945

G2—Application Server—Gensym Corporation; *U.S. Public*, pg. 731

G-2—Corporate Name—LSI Logic Corp.; *U.S. Public*, pg. 971

G-U-M—Oral Hygiene Aids—John O. Butler Co.; *Int'l*, pg. 1320

GUTS—NONE—Brazos Sportswear Inc.; *U.S. Public*, pg. 251

GWP, INC.—Real Estate Sales & Property Management—GWP, Inc.; *U.S. Private*, pg. 437

G. WASHINGTON—Broth & Seasoning—International Home Foods Inc.; *U.S. Private*, pg. 526

GX-5000—NONE—Mitel Corporation; *Int'l*, pg. 870

GX-120—Business Telephone System—Inter-Tel, Incorporated; *U.S. Public*, pg. 888

GXT—NONE—Berg Electronics; *U.S. Public*, pg. 212

GXT150L—Computer System—International Business Machines Corporation; *U.S. Public*, pg. 895

GXT150M—Computer System—International Business Machines Corporation; *U.S. Public*, pg. 895

GXT1000—Computer System—International Business Machines Corporation; *U.S. Public*, pg. 895

GRNET—High-Speed, Baseband Local Area Network—GenRad, Inc.; *U.S. Public*, pg. 731

GTV-6—Sports Car—Fiat Auto S.p.A.; *Int'l*, pg. 481

GEMNI—Mixed Level Verilog Simulator—IKOS Systems, Inc.; *U.S. Public*, pg. 864

GABRIEL—Shock Absorbers—Arvin Industries, Inc.; *U.S. Public*, pg. 136

GABRIEL—Missle System—Israel Aircraft Industries Ltd.; *Int'l*, pg. 689

GABRIELLE—Hosiery for Women—Grupo Synkro, S.A. de C.V.; *Int'l*, pg. 576

GACO—Coatings & Linings—Haartz-Mason, Inc.; *U.S. Public*, pg. 1358

GADCO—Garage Doors—Merchant Capital Group Ltd.; *U.S. Private*, pg. 732

GADD—NONE—Glynwed International PLC; *Int'l*, pg. 554

GADGET ORGANIZER—Revolving Kitchen Caddy Organizer—M. Kamenstein, Inc.; *U.S. Private*, pg. 606

GAFTEMP—Roof Insulation—International Specialty Products, Inc.; *U.S. Public*, pg. 858

GAGGENAU—Household Appliances—Gaggenau USA Corporation; *U.S. Private*, pg. 437

GAIN—Prepared Infant Formula—Abbott Laboratories; *U.S. Public*, pg. 12

GAIN—NONE—Avenmore Waterford Foods plc; *Int'l*, pg. 102

GAIN—Laundry Products—The Procter & Gamble Company; *U.S. Public*, pg. 1330

GAINER—Pet Foods—Ag Processing Inc., A Cooperative; *U.S. Private*, pg. 26

GAINES BURGERS—Dog Food—H.J. Heinz Company; *U.S. Public*, pg. 805

GAINES CYCLE—Dog Food—The Quaker Oats Company; *U.S. Public*, pg. 1347

GAINES CYCLE BISCUITS—Dog Treats—The Quaker Oats Company; *U.S. Public*, pg. 1347

GAINES GRAVY TRAIN—Dog Food—H.J. Heinz Company; *U.S. Public*, pg. 805

GAINESBURGERS—Dog Food—The Quaker Oats Company; *U.S. Public*, pg. 1347

GAINSBOROUGH—Writing, Text & Cover Paper—Fox River Paper Company; *U.S. Private*, pg. 422

GAINT GAITHER—Scarfs—Baar & Beards; *U.S. Private*, pg. 839

GALA—Towels—Fort James Corporation; *U.S. Public*, pg. 670

GALA—Beverages—Sancor Cooperativas Unidas Limitadas; *Int'l*, pg. 1183

GALACTIC—Cameras—Eastman Kodak Company; *U.S. Public*, pg. 550

GALAFLEX—NONE—Pfizer Inc.; *U.S. Public*, pg. 1281

GALAK—Chocolate Bars—Nestle S.A.; *Int'l*, pg. 915

GALANT—Automobile—Mitsubishi Motor Sales of America, Inc.; *Int'l*, pg. 875

GALARDI—Wienerschnitzel, Original Hamburger Stand & Weldons—Galardi Group, Inc.; *U.S. Private*, pg. 437

GALAX—Synthetic Crystal—AlliedSignal Inc.; *U.S. Public*, pg. 49

GALAXIA—NONE—Porcelanite, Inc.; *Int'l*, pg. 573

GALAXY—NONE—Galaxy Food Company; *U.S. Public*, pg. 697

GALAXY—Writing Paper & Envelopes—Georgia-Pacific Corporation; *U.S. Public*, pg. 735

GALAXY—Hose—The Goodyear Tire & Rubber Company; *U.S. Public*, pg. 752

GALAXY—Top & Base Program—Howe Furniture Corporation; *U.S. Private*, pg. 543

GALAXY—Flame-Resistant Vinyl Sign Material—Industrial Coatings Group, Inc.; *U.S. Private*, pg. 434

GALAXY—Business Jet—Israel Aircraft Industries Ltd.; *Int'l*, pg. 689

GALAXY—NONE—Lasko Metal Products, Inc.; *U.S. Private*, pg. 652

GALAXY—Cigarettes—Philip Morris Companies Inc.; *U.S. Public*, pg. 1287

GALAXY—Automatic Call Distributor—Rockwell International Corporation; *U.S. Public*, pg. 1397

GALAXY—Automatic Call Distributor—Rockwell Switching Systems Div.; *U.S. Public*, pg. 1398

GALAXY—Cast Iron Gas Boiler—Slant/Fin Corporation; *U.S. Private*, pg. 1005

GALAXY ARTHROSCOPES—Low-Cost, High-Quality Arthroscopes—Galileo Corp.; *U.S. Public*, pg. 698

GALAXY EXCHANGE—Internetwork Communication Server—Zenith Electronics Corp.; *U.S. Public*, pg. 1790

GALAXY III—Preamplifiers—Blonder-Tongue Laboratories, Inc.; *U.S. Public*, pg. 237

GALBANI—Cheeses & Prosciutto—Cucina Classica Italiana, Inc.; *U.S. Public*, pg. 1435

GALBANI—Cheese—Danone Group; *Int'l*, pg. 379

GALBEST—Hot Dip Galvanized—Cockerill Sambre; *Int'l*, pg. 301

GALCO—NONE—Aliments Flamingo; *Int'l*, pg. 57

GALDEN—Perfluorinated Polyether Fluids—Montedison S.p.A.; *Int'l*, pg. 324

GALE—Book Publishers—Gale Research Inc.; *U.S. Public*, pg. 1600

GALECRON—Herbicide—Novartis; *Int'l*, pg. 972

GALEN—Microscope—Leica, Inc.; *Int'l*, pg. 806

GALERIE—Coated Papers & Graphic Boards—Metsa-Serla Corporation; *Int'l*, pg. 863

GALFAN—NONE—Cockerill Sambre; *Int'l*, pg. 301

GALIGHER PUMPS—Heavy Duty Slurry Pumps—EnviroTech PumpSystems; *Int'l*, pg. 1489

GALILEE BOOKS—Book Imprint—Bertelsmann AG; *Int'l*, pg. 189

GALILEO—Italian Specialty Meats—Gallo/Galileo Salame; *U.S. Public*, pg. 1433

GALILEO—Meat Products—Sara Lee Corporation; *U.S. Public*, pg. 1432

GALILEO ARTHROSCOPE SYSTEM—NONE—Galileo Corp.; *U.S. Public*, pg. 698

GALION—Construction Equipment—Komatsu America International Company; *Int'l*, pg. 744

GALL & GALL—Liquor Chain Stores—Koninklijke Ahold NV; *Int'l*, pg. 749

GALL-TOUGH—NONE—Carpenter Technology Corporation; *U.S. Public*, pg. 307

GALLANT—Herbicide—The Dow Chemical Company; *U.S. Public*, pg. 522

GALLERY—Herbicide—The Dow Chemical Company; *U.S. Public*, pg. 522

GALLERY—Photo Albums—Eastman Kodak Company; *U.S. Public*, pg. 550

GALLERY—Menswear Updated Line—Haggar Corporation; *U.S. Public*, pg. 774

GALLERY—Plastic Cups & Lids—Sweetheart Cup Company Inc.; *U.S. Private*, pg. 1058

GALLERY—High-Fashion Brand-Name Women's Shoes—Woolworth Corporation; *U.S. Public*, pg. 1777

GALLERY CAFE—Restaurant—The Levy Organization; *U.S. Private*, pg. 664

GALLERY EIGHT KIT—Eye Shadows—Cover Girl Cosmetics; *U.S. Public*, pg. 1330

GALLERY SERIES—NONE—Helen of Troy Corporation; *U.S. Public*, pg. 807

GALLERY SERIES—Interior Wall and Countertop Tile—Monarch Tile, Inc.; *U.S. Private*, pg. 287

GALLERY 2000—Digital Picture Library—Logica Plc; *Int'l*, pg. 814

GALLIA—Skin Care—Permark International (Pty.) Ltd.; *Int'l*, pg. 1036

GALLINA BLANCA—Dry Soup Mixes—Borden, Inc.; *U.S. Private*, pg. 157

GALLO—Olive Oil—FIMA-Productos Alimentares, Lda; *Int'l*, pg. 471

GALLO—Wines, Vermouth—E. & J. Gallo Winery; *U.S. Private*, pg. 438

GALLO DESIGN—NONE—Villeroy & Boch AG; *Int'l*, pg. 1468

GALLO OF SONOMA—NONE—E. & J. Gallo Winery; *U.S. Private*, pg. 438

GALLO SALAME—Italian Specialty Meats—Gallo/Galileo Salame; *U.S. Public*, pg. 1433

GALLO SALAME—Meat Products—Sara Lee Corporation; *U.S. Public*, pg. 1432

GALLOWAYS—NONE—Pfizer Inc.; *U.S. Public*, pg. 1281

GALP—Products Commercialized by Petrogal—Petrogal, s.a.; *Int'l*, pg. 1044

GALV-A-GARD—Fence & Border—Gilbert & Bennett Manufacturing Company; *U.S. Private*, pg. 453

GALV-A-WELD—Cages—CTB International Corp.; *U.S. Public*, pg. 284

GALVA-KOTE—Galvanized Coating—The Valspar Corp. Protective Coatings Div.; *U.S. Public*, pg. 1707

GALVALUME—Gym Set Feature—Hedstrom Corporation; *U.S. Private*, pg. 526

GALVATITE—Sheet Steel—British Steel Plc; *Int'l*, pg. 220

GALVEX—Exposed Quality Sheet Steel—Inland Steel Industries, Inc.; *U.S. Public*, pg. 879

GALVICON—Paint—Pratt & Lambert United, Inc.; *U.S. Public*, pg. 1466

GALVINOLEUM—Galvanized Metal Coating—Rust-Oleum Corporation; *U.S. Public*, pg. 1358

GALVOLINE—Galvanic Anodes Magnesium—The Dow Chemical Company; *U.S. Public*, pg. 522

GALVOMAG—Galvanic Anodes Magnesium—The Dow Chemical Company; *U.S. Public*, pg. 522

GALVOPAK—Backfill for Anodes—The Dow Chemical Company; *U.S. Public*, pg. 522

GALVOROD—Galvanic Anodes Magnesium—The Dow Chemical Company; *U.S. Public*, pg. 522

GAMA GLOBULIN—Pharmaceutical Product—Baxter-Hyland; *U.S. Public*, pg. 196

GAMAL—Polishing Access.—Fisher Scientific Company; *U.S. Private*, pg. 658

GAMBLER SERIES KNIVES—NONE—Camillus Cutlery Co.; *U.S. Private*, pg. 203

GAMCO—Chrome Plated Zinc Coatings—Masco Corporation; *U.S. Public*, pg. 1052

GAME BOY—Portable Video Entertainment System—Konami Corporation of America Inc.; *Int'l*, pg. 746

GAME BOY—Hand-Held Video Game—Nintendo Company, Ltd.; *Int'l*, pg. 932

GAME BOY POCKET—Portable Videogame Hardware Unit—Nintendo of America; *Int'l*, pg. 932

GAME DEVELOPER—Magazine—Miller Freeman Inc.; *Int'l*, pg. 1443

GAME OF GOOD COOKING—Game—Monarch Avalon, Inc.; *U.S. Public*, pg. 1123

GAME OF LIFE—Game—Hasbro, Inc.; *U.S. Public*, pg. 797

GAME OF TRIVIA—Leisure Time Game—Monarch Avalon, Inc.; *U.S. Public*, pg. 1123

THE GAME—Headwear, Athletic Wear, Liscensed Products—Russell Corporation; *U.S. Public*, pg. 1413

GAME TIME—Manufacturer of Playground & Recreational Equipment—Game Time, Inc.; *U.S. Public*, pg. 1543

GAME WINNER—Hunting & Outdoor Clothing—Game Winner, Inc.; *U.S. Private*, pg. 280

GAMECOCK—Syrup—Dean Pickles & Specialty Products; *U.S. Public*, pg. 490

GAMECRAFT—Field Hockey, Soccer & Table Tennis Equipment—Sport Supply Group, Inc.; *U.S. Public*, pg. 1499

THE GAMES—Distributor of Nintendo Products in the United Kingdom—John Menzies plc; *Int'l*, pg. 707

GAMES ARCADE—Card Game—Mattel Games/Puzzles; *U.S. Public*, pg. 1058

GAMES FOR GROWING—Preschool Card, Board & Floor Games—Mattel Games/Puzzles; *U.S. Public*, pg. 1058

GAMIM UNE N—Intravenous Immune Globulin Concentrate—Bayer AG; *Int'l*, pg. 171

GAMMA—Barrier Containers—American National Can Company; *Int'l*, pg. 1029

GAMMA—Fuel Additive—The Lubrizol Corporation; *U.S. Public*, pg. 1016

GAMMA-GUN—NONE—Western Atlas Logging Services; *U.S. Public*, pg. 1757

GAMMA NAIL—NONE—Pfizer Inc.; *U.S. Public*, pg. 1281

GAMMAGARD—Immune Globulin Intravenous (Human)—Baxter-Hyland; *U.S. Public*, pg. 196

GAMMAGARD—Immune Globulin—Baxter International Inc.; *U.S. Public*, pg. 196

GAMMAR IM—Immune Serum Globulin (Human) USP—Centeon, L.L.C.; *Int'l*, pg. 626

GAMMAR PIV—Immune Globulin Intravenous (Human Lyophilized)—Centeon, L.L.C.; *Int'l*, pg. 626

GAMMATRACE—Gamma Ray Detectors—Barringer Technologies Inc.; *U.S. Public*, pg. 191

GAMMEL DANSK BITTER DRAM—NONE—Danisco Distillers; *Int'l*, pg. 378

GAMMIMUNE N—Pharmaceutical—Bayer Corporation/Pharmaceutical Division; *Int'l*, pg. 173

GAMULIN RH—Immune Globulin Human—Centeon, L.L.C.; *Int'l*, pg. 626

GANCIA—Wine—Paterno Imports Limited; *U.S. Private*, pg. 843

GANDALF XPRESS—Remote Access & Concentration—Gandalf Technologies Inc.; *Int'l*, pg. 540

GANDY'S—Milk—Dean Foods Company; *U.S. Public*, pg. 489

GANEX—Alkylated Vinylpyrrolidone Polymers—International Specialty Products, Inc.; *U.S. Public*, pg. 858

GANGSTER TOWN—Videogame—Sega of America Inc.; *Int'l*, pg. 1218

GANGSTERS—Leisure Time Board Game—Monarch Avalon, Inc.; *U.S. Public*, pg. 1123

GANT—Sportswear-Sportshirts, Sweaters, Knits, Pants & Dress Shirts—Gant; *U.S. Public*, pg. 1291

GANTNER—Women's Swimwear—Tighe Industries, Inc.; *U.S. Private*, pg. 1086

GANTNER OF CALIFORNIA—Women's Swimwear—Tighe Industries, Inc.; *U.S. Private*, pg. 1086

GANTOS—Women's Retail Stores—Gantos Inc.; *U.S. Public*, pg. 702

GANTREZ—Vinyl Ether Polymers—International Specialty Products, Inc.; *U.S. Public*, pg. 858

THE GAP—Retail Clothing Store—The Gap, Inc.; *U.S. Public*, pg. 702

GAP-KAP—Capacitors—Philips Components; *Int'l*, pg. 1054

GAPS—Home-study Courses—American Passage Media Corporation; *U.S. Private*, pg. 60

GAPWRAP—Air Infiltration Barrier—Benjamin Obdyke, Inc.; *U.S. Private*, pg. 810

GAR-KENYON—Hydraulic Valves—New Haven Mfg. Corp.; *U.S. Private*, pg. 793

GARACIN—Oral Swine Antibiotic—Schering-Plough Corporation; *U.S. Public*, pg. 1438

GARAMYCIN—Broad-Spectrum Antibiotic Injectables, Topicals & Opthalmics—Schering-Plough Corporation; *U.S. Public*, pg. 1438

GARAN BY MARITA—Women's Sportswear—Garan, Incorporated; *U.S. Public*, pg. 703

THE GARAN MAN—Men's Sportswear—Garan, Incorporated; *U.S. Public*, pg. 703

GARANIMALS—Color Related Tops & Bottoms for Children—Garan, Incorporated; *U.S. Public*, pg. 703

GARB-O-FLAKES—Garbage Pail Deodorant—Surco Products, Inc.; *U.S. Private*, pg. 1056

GARBIT—Exotic Dishes—Danone Group; *Int'l*, pg. 379

GARCIA Y VEGA—Cigars—General Cigar Company, Inc.; *U.S. Public*, pg. 708

GARCIA'S MEXICAN RESTAURANTS—Restaurant—Eateries, Inc.; *U.S. Public*, pg. 555

GARCIA'S MEXICAN RESTAURANTS—Mexican Restaurant & Bar—Famous Restaurants Inc.; *U.S. Private*, pg. 393

GARCY—Store Fixtures—RHC/Spacemaster Corporation; *U.S. Private*, pg. 904

GARD—Hair Care—Colgate-Palmolive Company; *U.S. Public*, pg. 397

GARDCO—Commercial Outdoor Lighting—Thomas Industries Inc.; *U.S. Public*, pg. 1598

GARDEN ANSWERS—U.K. Gardening Magazine—EMAP Apex; *Int'l*, pg. 451

GARDEN BOUQUET—Area Rug—Couristan Inc.; *U.S. Private*, pg. 279

GARDEN CLUB—Preserves, Jellies, Salad Dressing, Mustard, Vinegar, Syrup, Apple Butter—Clements Foods Co.; *U.S. Private*, pg. 245

GARDEN CLUB—Vinegar—Clements Nut Co.; *U.S. Private*, pg. 245

GARDEN CLUB—Peanut Butter—Clements Nut Co.; *U.S. Private*, pg. 245

GARDEN CRISPS—Snacks—Nabisco Inc.; *U.S. Public*, pg. 1355

GARDEN CRISPS—Vegetable Crackers—RJR Nabisco Holdings Corp.; *U.S. Public*, pg. 1354

GARDEN DEVILS—NONE—Fiskars Oy AB; *Int'l*, pg. 492

GARDEN FARE—Seasoning Mixes—McCormick/Schilling; *U.S. Public*, pg. 1066

GARDEN GREATS—Garden Products—Jiffy Products of America, Inc.; *Int'l*, pg. 706

GARDEN MASTER—Lawn & Garden Distributors/Retailers—PRO Group, Inc.; *U.S. Private*, pg. 887

GARDEN NEWS—U.K. Gardening Magazine—EMAP Apex; *Int'l*, pg. 451

THE GARDEN PARTY—Produce Packaging—Tenneco Specialty Products; *U.S. Public*, pg. 1579

GARDEN PRIDE—Lawnmowers—Southland Mower Corp.; *U.S. Private*, pg. 1144

GARDEN RAILWAYS—Magazine—Kalmbach Publishing Co.; *U.S. Private*, pg. 606

GARDEN SCENE—Planterware, Macrame Plant Hangers—Duraco Products, Inc.; *U.S. Private*, pg. 348

GARDEN SCENE BIRD FEEDERS—Five Feeders of Geometric Design with 10lb Seed Capacity—Duraco Products, Inc.; *U.S. Private*, pg. 348

GARDEN SOLUTIONS—Garden Stock by Mail—Michigan Bulb Company; *U.S. Private*, pg. 421

GARDEN SOUP COMPANY—NONE—The Smithfield Companies, Inc.; *U.S. Public*, pg. 1479

THE GARDEN—U.K. Gardening Magazine—EMAP Apex; *Int'l*, pg. 451

GARDEN TRADE NEWS—U.K. Gardening Magazine—EMAP Apex; *Int'l*, pg. 451

GARDEN TRADE NEWS—NONE—EMAP Business Communications Division; *Int'l*, pg. 451

GARDENELLA—Indoor/outdoor Casual Aluminum Furniture—Telescope Casual Furniture, Inc.; *U.S. Private*, pg. 1074

GARDENER'S EDEN—Retail & Mail Order Decorative Items For Home & Garden—Williams-Sonoma, Inc.; *U.S. Public*, pg. 1770

GARDENER'S GUIDE—Book Series—Time-Life, Inc.; *U.S. Public*, pg. 1613

GARDENFARE—Food Products—McCormick & Company, Incorporated; *U.S. Public*, pg. 1066

GARDEX—Armored Type MC Cable—Rockbestos-Suprenant Cable Corp.; *U.S. Private*, pg. 938

GARDGLAS—Plastic Sheets—Bunzl Extrusion; *Int'l*, pg. 232

GARDNER—Machinery & Abrasive Discs—Gardner Abrasives; *U.S. Public*, pg. 1699

GARDNER—Grinding Wheels & Machines—Litton Industries, Inc.; *U.S. Public*, pg. 1002

GARDNER—Bread, Buns & Sweet Goods—Metz Baking Company; *U.S. Private*, pg. 1022

GARDNER—Bread, Buns, Sweet Goods—Metz Baking Company (WI); *U.S. Private*, pg. 1022

GARDNER-DENVER—Pneumatic Tools, Hoists, Assembly Machinery, Pumps, Drills & Drilling Equip—Cooper Industries, Inc.; *U.S. Public*, pg. 442

GARDNER-DENVER—Air Compressors—Gardner Denver Machinery Inc.; *U.S. Public*, pg. 703

GARDNER G H SERIES—Abrasive Discs—Gardner Abrasives; *U.S. Public*, pg. 1699

GARDNER GV SERIES—Abrasive Discs—Gardner Abrasives; *U.S. Public*, pg. 1699

GARDNER SUPERABRASIVES—Abrasive Discs—Gardner Abrasives; *U.S. Public*, pg. 1699

GARDNER'S GRIP—Rubber Products—Rubatex Corporation; *U.S. Private*, pg. 56

GARDRIN—Enprostil—Syntex; *Int'l*, pg. 1120

GARDRINE—Enprostil—Syntex; *Int'l*, pg. 1120

GARDS—Children's Disposable Diapers—The Tranzonic Companies; *U.S. Public*, pg. 1632

GARDS—Sanitary Napkins—Tranzonic Personal Care Division; *U.S. Public*, pg. 1632

GARED SPORTS—Sporting Goods—Nixdorff Krein Industries Inc.; *U.S. Private*, pg. 799

GARFIELD'S—Restaurant & Pub—Eateries, Inc.; *U.S. Public*, pg. 555

GARLAND—Cooking Equip.—Garland Commercial Ranges, Ltd.; *Int'l*, pg. 189

GARLAND—Ranges & Ovens—Welbilt Corporation; *Int'l*, pg. 188

GARLIC—NONE—Celestial Seasonings; *U.S. Public*, pg. 319

GARLOCK—Gasketing, Seals, Packings, Bearings—Coltec Industries Inc.; *U.S. Public*, pg. 401

GARLOCK—Mechanical Packing—Garlock Sealing Technologies; *U.S. Public*, pg. 402

GARLON—Industrial Herbicide—The Dow Chemical Company; *U.S. Public*, pg. 522

GARNIER—Haircare Product—L'Oreal S.A.; *Int'l*, pg. 818

GARRETT—Products for Aircraft, Missile, Commercial Applications—AlliedSignal Aerospace; *U.S. Public*, pg. 50

GARST—Seeds—Garst Seed Company; *Int'l*, pg. 1524

GARTH GRAPHIC—Photo Typesetters—AGFA EPS Division; *Int'l*, pg. 172

GARUDA—Tents—K2 Inc.; *U.S. Public*, pg. 940

GARY JENKINS—Art Materials—Martin/F. Weber Company; *U.S. Private*, pg. 710

THE GAS COMPANY—Gas Utility & Propane Distribution—BHP Hawaii, Inc.; *Int'l*, pg. 225

GAS EXPRESS—Retail Gasoline Chain—BHP Hawaii, Inc.; *Int'l*, pg. 225

GAS-GLO—Fluorescent Additive—Spectronics Corporation; *U.S. Private*, pg. 1024

GAS-MAGNUM—Shock Absorbers—Monroe Auto Equipment Co.; *U.S. Public*, pg. 1577

GAS-MATIC—Shocks & Struts—Monroe Auto Equipment Co.; *U.S. Public*, pg. 1577

GAS-POINTER—Measuring Instrument—Bacharach Inc.; *U.S. Private*, pg. 109

GAS-RACK—Gas Cylinder Storage—Jarke Corporation; *U.S. Private*, pg. 583

GAS RYDER—Shock Absorbers & Struts—Arvin Industries, Inc.; *U.S. Public*, pg. 136

GAS RYDER LT—Shock Absorbers—Arvin Industries, Inc.; *U.S. Public*, pg. 136

GAS/SPEC—Solvents & Services—The Dow Chemical Company; *U.S. Public*, pg. 522

GAS WATCHERS—Association Services—American Automobile Association; *U.S. Private*, pg. 50

GAS-X—Anti-Gas Tablets, Cherry & Peppermint Creme Flavor, Extra Strength Tablets—Sandoz Pharmaceuticals Corp.; *Int'l*, pg. 974

GASBOY—Mfr. of Card Reader System for Gas Stations—Tokheim Corporation; *U.S. Public*, pg. 1620

GASCARD—Fuel Management systems—Fleischli Oil Company, Inc.; *U.S. Private*, pg. 410

GASCO—Gas Utility—Gasco, Inc.; *Int'l*, pg. 225

GASES & WELDING DISTRIBUTOR—Periodical—Penton Publishing, Inc.; *U.S. Public*, pg. 1306

GASFIRE—Household Appliances—Candy S.p.A.; *Int'l*, pg. 259

GASGUARD—Gas Cabinets for Electronic Industry—Air Products and Chemicals, Inc.; *U.S. Public*, pg. 30

GASK-O-SEAL—Engineered Metal/Rubber Combined Seal—Seal Group; *U.S. Public*, pg. 1262

GASKET-LOCK REGLETS—Hardware—Dayton Superior Corporation; *U.S. Private*, pg. 931

GASKLEEN—NONE—Pall Corporation; *U.S. Public*, pg. 1253

GASKLEEN III—Filter Assembly—Pall Corporation; *U.S. Public*, pg. 1253

GASLIGHT—Lumber & Wood Products—Georgia-Pacific Corporation; *U.S. Public*, pg. 735

GASPAC—Seals—BW/IP International, Inc.; *U.S. Public*, pg. 658

GASPAC—Seals—Flowserve Corporation; *U.S. Public*, pg. 658

GASPAK—Laboratory Products—Becton Dickinson & Company; *U.S. Public*, pg. 199

GASTIGHT—Teflon-Tipped Plunger Syringes—Hamilton Co., Inc.; *U.S. Private*, pg. 497

GASTITE—Flexible Gas Piping—Titeflex Corporation; *Int'l*, pg. 1340

GASTOBAC—Tobacco Curing System—Gas-Fired Products, Inc.; *U.S. Private*, pg. 440

GASTON DE LAGRANGE—NONE—Bacardi-Martini.Belgium; *U.S. Private*, pg. 109

GASTON 824—Knit Fabrics Dyeing Machine—Gaston County Dyeing Machine Co.; *U.S. Private*, pg. 441

GASTRIN—Diagnostic Products—Abbott Laboratories; *U.S. Public*, pg. 12

GASTROCCULT—Test for Gastric Occult Blood & pH—Beckman Instruments, Inc.; *U.S. Public*, pg. 199

GASTROCROM—Capsules (Cromolyn Sodium, USP)—Medeva Pharmaceuticals; *U.S. Private*, pg. 852

GASTROGRAFIN—Diagnostics—Bristol-Myers Squibb Company; *U.S. Public*, pg. 253

GASTROLOC—Gastrointestinal Drug—Astra AB; *Int'l*, pg. 93

GASTROLYTE—Pharmaceuticals—Rhone-Poulenc Rorer - U.S.; *Int'l*, pg. 1110

GASTROMARK—Contrast Agent—Advanced Magnetics, Inc.; *U.S. Public*, pg. 20

GASTROMARK—Diagnostic Agents for Medical Applications—Mallinckrodt Inc.; *U.S. Public*, pg. 1039

GASTRONOOM—Institutional Food Wholesalers—SHV Holdings N.V.; *Int'l*, pg. 1154

GASTRONORM—Refrigerator—Foster Refrigerator Corporation; *U.S. Private*, pg. 421

GASTROZEPIN—Anti-Ulcer Drug—Boehringer Ingelheim GmbH; *Int'l*, pg. 199

GATE-COTE—Gate or Fountain Roll Cover—Harnischfeger Industries, Inc.; *U.S. Public*, pg. 788

GATE ENSEMBLE—Place & Route Engine—Cadence Design Systems, Inc.; *U.S. Public*, pg. 290

GATEHOUSE—Prefinished Wall Paneling—Georgia-Pacific Corporation; *U.S. Public*, pg. 735

GATEKEEPER—Tailgate Protector—Lund International Holdings, Inc.; *U.S. Public*, pg. 1020

GATES—Belts & Hoses—The Gates Corporation; *Int'l*, pg. 1396

GATEWAY—Manufactured Homes—Champion Enterprises, Inc.; *U.S. Public*, pg. 332

GATEWAY—Communications System—Executone Information Systems, Inc.; *U.S. Public*, pg. 599

GATOR—Battery Operated Crimper—Greenlee Textron; *U.S. Public*, pg. 1589

GATOR FOOD STORES—Grocery Stores with SS Gasoline—Presto Food Stores, Inc.; *U.S. Private*, pg. 882

GATOR GRIP—Plugs & Connectors—General Electric Canada Inc.; *U.S. Public*, pg. 713

GATORADE—Thirst Quenching Beverage—The Quaker Oats Company; *U.S. Public*, pg. 1347

GATORADE—Beverage—Stokely-Van Camp, Inc.; *U.S. Public*, pg. 1348

GATORADE—Beverage—Worldwide Quaker Beverages; *U.S. Public*, pg. 1347

GATORADE CITRUS COOLER—Thirst Quenching Beverage—The Quaker Oats Company; *U.S. Public*, pg. 1347

GATORADE FROST—Thirst Quenching Drink—The Quaker Oats Company; *U.S. Public*, pg. 1347

GATORADE LIGHT—Thirst Quenching Beverage—The Quaker Oats Company; *U.S. Public*, pg. 1347

GATORBOX—Single Serving Package of Gatorade—The Quaker Oats Company; *U.S. Public*, pg. 1347

GATORLODE—Thirst Quencher with Carbohydrates—The Quaker Oats Company; *U.S. Public*, pg. 1347

GATORPRO—Sports Nutrition Supplement—The Quaker Oats Company; *U.S. Public*, pg. 1347

GATSBY—Sunglasses—Bausch & Lomb Incorporated; *U.S. Public*, pg. 194

GATTUSO—Pizza & Pasta Sauce—Borden, Inc.; *U.S. Private*, pg. 157

GATTUSO—NONE—Campbell Soup Company Ltd.; *U.S. Public*, pg. 299

GATTUSO—Pickles & Relishes—International Multifoods Corporation; *U.S. Public*, pg. 900

GATTUSO—Pickles & Condiments—Robin Hood Multifoods Inc.; *U.S. Public*, pg. 901

GAULOISES—NONE—British-American Tobacco (Germany) GmbH; *Int'l*, pg. 111

GAULOISES—Cigarettes—SEITA, Societe Nationale D'Exploitation Industrielle des Tabacs et des Allumettes; *Int'l*, pg. 1219

GAUNTLET—Two in One Glove—Horace Small Apparel Company; *Int'l*, pg. 635

GAUTIERCOGNAC—Cognac—Marie Brizard Wines & Spirits USA; *U.S. Private*, pg. 702

GAVILANS—Mail Order House—Starcrest Products of California; *U.S. Private*, pg. 1035

GAVIOTA—Women's Lingerie—Body Drama, Inc.; *U.S. Public*, pg. 1182

GAVIOTA—Fertilizer—C. Brewer & Company, Limited; *U.S. Private*, pg. 190

GAVISCON—Gastric Reflux Suppressant—Reckitt & Colman plc; *Int'l*, pg. 1089

GAVISCON—Antacid—SmithKline Beecham Consumer Healthcare, U.S.; *Int'l*, pg. 1264

GAVISCON—NONE—SmithKline Beecham Corporation; *Int'l*, pg. 1264

GAVISCON—Antacid—SmithKline Beecham plc; *Int'l*, pg. 1264

GAY 90'S—Popcorn Machine—Gold Medal Products Co.; *U.S. Private*, pg. 459

GAYELORD HAUSER—Health Foods—Danone Group; *Int'l*, pg. 379

GAYLORD—Broadcasting—Gaylord Broadcasting Co.; *U.S. Public*, pg. 704

GAYLORD—Container—Gaylord Container Corporation; *U.S. Public*, pg. 704

GAYLORD HANDLE BAG—Grocery Sack With Handles—Gaylord Container Corporation; *U.S. Public*, pg. 704

GAYMERS OLDE ENGLISH—Cider—Matthew Clark Brands; *Int'l*, pg. 848

GAZELLE—Cycle—Derby International Corporation S.A.; *Int'l*, pg. 394

THE GAZETTE—Newspaper—The Gazette Company; *U.S. Private*, pg. 442

GAZETTE DATABASE SERVICES—NONE—The Gazette Company; *U.S. Private*, pg. 442

GEAR—Drives, Bearings—Blount International, Inc.; *U.S. Public*, pg. 237

GEAR KIDS—Children's Wear—Seibel & Stern Corp.; *U.S. Private*, pg. 981

GEAR UP—Fortified Juice Blend—R.J. Corr Naturals, Inc.; *U.S. Private*, pg. 276

GEAR-UP!—Flywheels, Ring Gears & Flex Plates—R&B, Inc.; *U.S. Public*, pg. 1354

GEARBOX—Business Product—International Business Machines Corporation; *U.S. Public*, pg. 895

GEARED MTRS.—NONE—Philips Automotive Electronics; *Int'l*, pg. 1054

GEARFLEX—Shafting & Couplings—General Electric Canada Inc.; *U.S. Public*, pg. 713

GEARMATIC—Winches—Paccar Inc.; *U.S. Public*, pg. 1246

GEARMATIC—Winches—PACCAR Winch Division; *U.S. Public*, pg. 1246

GEBHARDT—Mexican Food—ConAgra, Inc.; *U.S. Public*, pg. 425

GEE BEE—Discount Dept. Store—G B Stores; *U.S. Private*, pg. 972

GEE YOUR HAIR SMELLS TERRIFIC—Shampoo & Conditioner—The Andrew Jergens Company; *Int'l*, pg. 717

GEHKA—Art & Cosmetic Brushes—Koh-I-Noor, Inc.; *U.S. Private*, pg. 629

GEHL—Farm & Construction Machinery—Gehl Company; *U.S. Public*, pg. 704

GEISER'S—Potato Chips & Other Snacks—Borden, Inc.; *U.S. Private*, pg. 157

GEISHA—Canned & Frozen Foods—Nozaki America, Inc.; *Int'l*, pg. 990

GEISHA—Canned Food—Nozaki & Company Ltd.; *Int'l*, pg. 990

GEISLER—Pet Products—ConAgra, Inc.; *U.S. Public*, pg. 425

GEL-MIX—NONE—Life Technologies, Inc.; *U.S. Public*, pg. 504

GEL SET—Hair Care—Palm Beach Beauty Products Co.; *U.S. Private*, pg. 834

GEL STAIN—NONE—The Flecto Co., Inc.; *U.S. Private*, pg. 410

GELATTI—Colognes, Moisturizing Creams, Toilet Soaps, Parfums—Nuevo Federal S.A.; *Int'l*, pg. 990

GELCO TRAVEL MANAGER—A Complete Modular System for Government Travel & Travel Management—Gelco Information Network, Inc.; *U.S. Private*, pg. 442

GELEX—Turbidity Standard—Hach Company; *U.S. Public*, pg. 773

GELLA—Reenterable Encapsulant Compound, Moisture/Electrical Protection Telecommun—3M; *U.S. Public*, pg. 1604

GELMATCH—Image Analysis Software Packages—UVP, Inc.; *U.S. Private*, pg. 1115

GELMATE—Variable Intensity Light Source—Beckman Instruments, Inc.; *U.S. Public*, pg. 199

GELOCAST—Unna Boot—Beiersdorf, Inc.; *Int'l*, pg. 182

GELOXIDE—Hair Preparation—Clairol, Inc.; *U.S. Public*, pg. 254

GELOY—Engineered Plastics—General Electric Company; *U.S. Public*, pg. 709

GELRITE—Gellan Gum—The NutraSweet Kelco Company; *U.S. Public*, pg. 1125

GELSEQ—Image Analysis Software Packages—UVP, Inc.; *U.S. Private*, pg. 1115

GELSONS—Supermarkets—Arden Group, Inc.; *U.S. Public*, pg. 128

GELSTADIP—Animal Health Products—SmithKline Beecham plc; *Int'l*, pg. 1264

GELTEK—Sealants—Raychem Corporation; *U.S. Public*, pg. 1362

GELUSIL—Antacid—Warner-Lambert Company; *U.S. Public*, pg. 1738

GELUSOL—NONE—Lawter International, Inc.; *U.S. Public*, pg. 980

GELVA—Multipolymer Solutions & Emulsions—Monsanto Company; *U.S. Public*, pg. 1124

GELVA—Polyvinyl Acetate Resin—Solutia Inc.; *U.S. Public*, pg. 1483

GEM—Razor Blades—American Safety Razor Company; *U.S. Public*, pg. 597

GEM—Tubular Products—British Steel Plc; *Int'l*, pg. 220

GEM—Interior/Exterior Paint—Buten, Division of Duron; *U.S. Private*, pg. 349

GEM—Emery Boards, Clippers, Tweezers, Gift Sets, Scissors—The Cook Bates Division; *Int'l*, pg. 815

GEM—Rugs—Couristan Inc.; *U.S. Private*, pg. 279

GEM—Generic Emulation Module—GenRad, Inc.; *U.S. Public*, pg. 731

GEM—System Software—Novell Inc.; *U.S. Public*, pg. 1203

GEM—Helicopter Engine—Rolls-Royce Military Aero Engines Ltd.; *Int'l*, pg. 1127

GEM-COAL—Ceramic Grill Briquettes—Ferro Corporation; *U.S. Public*, pg. 618

GEM SPORT—Steel R.V. Pickup Caps—Gem Top Mfg., Inc.; *U.S. Private*, pg. 443

GEMAX—Engineered Plastics—General Electric Company; *U.S. Public*, pg. 709

GEMBASE—4GL Application Development System—Ross Systems, Inc.; *U.S. Public*, pg. 1406

GEMCO—Controls—MagneTek, Inc.; *U.S. Public*, pg. 1037

GEMEAZ CUSIN—Restaurants—Accor S.A.; *Int'l*, pg. 20

GEMFLOR—Floor Coverings—Domco Inc.; *Int'l*, pg. 415

GEMGLAZE—Floor Coverings—Domco Inc.; *Int'l*, pg. 415

GEMGLO—Floor Coverings—Domco Inc.; *Int'l*, pg. 415

GEMINI—Monitors—Akron Brass Company; *Int'l*, pg. 1068

GEMINI—Dual Crucible Electron Beam Source—BOC Coating Technology; *Int'l*, pg. 121

GEMINI—All-Floor Sweeper—Bissell Inc.; *U.S. Private*, pg. 145

GEMINI—Sporting Goods—Brunswick Bowling & Billiards Corp.; *U.S. Public*, pg. 265

GEMINI—NONE—CAP Gemini S.A.; *Int'l*, pg. 263

GEMINI—Dehulling Machinery—Carver, Inc.; *U.S. Private*, pg. 217

GEMINI—Trademark—Eaton Corporation, Semi-Conductor; *U.S. Public*, pg. 557

GEMINI—Laundry Detergent—Ecolab Inc.; *U.S. Public*, pg. 562

GEMINI—Systems & Equipment for Controlling Tension in a Flexible Sheet Material—General Electric Canada Inc.; *U.S. Public*, pg. 713

GEMINI—Paper & Boards—Georgia-Pacific Corporation; *U.S. Public*, pg. 735

GEMINI—Hose—The Goodyear Tire & Rubber Company; *U.S. Public*, pg. 752

GEMINI—Twin Wheel Caster—ITW Plastiglide; *U.S. Public*, pg. 867

GEMINI—Graphic Communications System—Lucent Technologies Inc.; *U.S. Public*, pg. 1017

GEMINI—Blankets—Medline Industries, Inc.; *U.S. Private*, pg. 728

GEMINI—Fire Fighting Equip.—Premier Farnell; *Int'l*, pg. 1068

GEMINI—NMR Spectrometers & Computer Programs—Varian Associates, Inc.; *U.S. Public*, pg. 1710

GEMINI HOUSE—Rings—Litton Industries, Inc.; *U.S. Public*, pg. 1002

GEMINI 6—Two-Seat Platform-Based Simulator—Iwerks Entertainment; *U.S. Public*, pg. 915

GEMLITE—Lamps—Lava World International/Haggerty Enterprises, Inc.; *U.S. Private*, pg. 653

GEMMA—Intimate Apparel—VF Corporation; *U.S. Public*, pg. 1702

GEMOLD—Computer Software for Mold Design & Manufacture—General Electric Canada Inc.; *U.S. Public*, pg. 713

GEMS—Level & Flow Sensors—IMO Industries Inc.; *U.S. Public*, pg. 856

GEMSTONE—Thermoset Polyester Microwave Cook & Bakeware—Nordic Ware; *U.S. Private*, pg. 806

GEMSTONE—Transaction SuperSystems—VeriFone, Inc.; *U.S. Public*, pg. 815

GEMZAR—NONE—Eli Lilly and Company; *U.S. Public*, pg. 992

GEN-GUARD—Pigment-Coated & Embossed Genuine Pressboard—FiberMark Inc.; *U.S. Public*, pg. 620

GEN III—Fuel Additive—The Lubrizol Corporation; *U.S. Public*, pg. 1016

GEN.S SYSTEM—Top of the Line Hematology Analyzer for High Volume Laboratories—Beckman Coulter; *U.S. Public*, pg. 199

GENAMID—Epoxy Coreactants—Henkel Corporation; *Int'l*, pg. 610

GENAPOL—Surfactants—Hoechst Aktiengesellschaft; *Int'l*, pg. 624

GENBLOCK—Biotechnology—Pharmacia & Upjohn Adria Laboratories; *Int'l*, pg. 1049

GENDAI—Monthly General Interest Men's Magazine—Kodansha Ltd.; *Int'l*, pg. 742

GENDEX—X-Ray Systems—Del Global Technologies; *U.S. Public*, pg. 493

GENDEX—Dental & Medical X-Ray Equipment & Supplies—Dentsply International Inc.; *U.S. Public*, pg. 498

GENECOL 99—Antidiarrheal Oral Vaccine (Equine & Bovine)—Schering-Plough Corporation; *U.S. Public*, pg. 1438

GENELCAN—Time Sales Financing, Loans, Leasing & Mortgage Financing—General Electric Canada Inc.; *U.S. Public*, pg. 713

GENELINE—Pulse-Field Electrophoresis Apparatus—Beckman Instruments, Inc.; *U.S. Public*, pg. 199

GENELISA—Software Program—Beckman Instruments, Inc.; *U.S. Public*, pg. 199

GENENTECH—Pharmaceuticals—Genentech, Inc.; *Int'l*, pg. 1120

GENERAIL—Remote Switch Control—General Railway Signal Corp.; *Int'l*, pg. 1194

GENERAL—Sunglass—Bausch & Lomb Incorporated; *U.S. Public*, pg. 194

GENERAL—Tires—Continental AG; *Int'l*, pg. 327

GENERAL—Tires—Continental General Tire, Inc.; *Int'l*, pg. 327

GENERAL—Microwave Test Equipment & Components—General Microwave Corporation; *U.S. Public*, pg. 717

GENERAL—Tools—General Tools Mfg., Co. Inc.; *U.S. Private*, pg. 445

GENERAL—Tours—General Tours Inc.; *U.S. Private*, pg. 445

GENERAL-AIRE—Drum Type Power Humidifier—General Filters, Inc.; *U.S. Private*, pg. 444

GENERAL APPRAISAL—Services of Appraisal & Valuation of Tangible & Intangible Property—American Appraisal Associates, Inc.; *U.S. Private*, pg. 49

GENERAL BUSINESS CORPORATION—NONE—Fund American Enterprises Holdings, Inc.; *U.S. Public*, pg. 688

GENERAL ELECTRIC—Major Appliances—G.E. Appliances; *U.S. Public*, pg. 710

GENERAL EMPLOYMENT—Employment Agency—General Employment Enterprises, Inc.; *U.S. Public*, pg. 714

GENERAL FOODS INTERNATIONAL—Coffee—Philip Morris Companies Inc.; *U.S. Public*, pg. 1287

GENERAL IONICS LOGO—Ion Exchange Water Softeners, Filters & Demineralizers—Ionics, Incorporated; *U.S. Public*, pg. 912

GENERAL MICROWAVE—NONE—General Microwave Corporation; *U.S. Public*, pg. 717

GENERAL NUTRITION—Retail Health Foods—General Nutrition Centers; *U.S. Public*, pg. 725

GENERAL NUTRITION—Vitamins—General Nutrition, Inc.; *U.S. Public*, pg. 725

GENERAL RADIO—NONE—GenRad, Inc.; *U.S. Public*, pg. 731

GENERAL RADIO CO.—NONE—GenRad, Inc.; *U.S. Public*, pg. 731

GENERAL SHALE—Clay Bricks—Marley PLC; *Int'l*, pg. 843

GENERAL SLICING—Slicers, Mixers, Grinders, Processors & Food Service Equipment Carts—General Slicing/Red Goat Disposers; *U.S. Public*, pg. 1506

GENERAL SLICING—Commercial Slicing Appliances—Standex International Corporation; *U.S. Public*, pg. 1505

THE GENERAL—Magazine—Monarch Avalon, Inc.; *U.S. Public*, pg. 1123

GENERAL TIME—Clocks—General Time Corp.; *U.S. Private*, pg. 445

GENERALE DE RESTAURATION—Institutional Catering—Accor S.A.; *Int'l*, pg. 20

GENERALIZED SELECTION PLUS—Database Marketing—Group 1 Software, Inc.; *U.S. Public*, pg. 417

GENERATION—Dinnerware—Dansk International Designs Ltd.; *U.S. Public*, pg. 261

GENERATION—Metals—Generation Metals Corp.; *U.S. Private*, pg. 446

GENERATION—Rodenticides—LiphaTech, Inc.; *Int'l*, pg. 812

GENERATION 3—Vacuum Cleaner—Berkshire Hathaway Inc.; *U.S. Public*, pg. 217

GENERATION ZEL—NONE—Provigo Inc.; *Int'l*, pg. 1072

GENERATIONS—Vinyl Siding and Vinyl Windows—Owens Corning; *U.S. Public*, pg. 1236

GENEROID—Gearing—Rockwell International Corporation; *U.S. Public*, pg. 1397

GENEROL—Phytosterols—Henkel Corporation; *Int'l*, pg. 610

GENERON—Air Separation Systems—The Dow Chemical Company; *U.S. Public*, pg. 522

GENERRA—Sportswear & Accessories—The Generra Company; *U.S. Private*, pg. 446

GENESEE BEER—Beer—Genesee Corporation; *U.S. Public*, pg. 728

GENESEE BOCK—Beer—Genesee Corporation; *U.S. Public*, pg. 728

GENESEE CREAM ALE—Ale—Genesee Corporation; *U.S. Public*, pg. 728

GENESEE LIGHT—Beer—Genesee Corporation; *U.S. Public*, pg. 728

GENESEE NA—Non-Alcoholic Malt Beverage—Genesee Corporation; *U.S. Public*, pg. 728

GENESEE 12 HORSE—Ale—Genesee Corporation; *U.S. Public*, pg. 728

GENESIS—Luggage—American Tourister, Inc.; *U.S. Public*, pg. 1430

GENESIS—Carpets—Amoco Corporation; *U.S. Public*, pg. 101

GENESIS—School & Commercial Bus—AmTran Corporation; *U.S. Public*, pg. 1167

GENESIS—Plastic Hose—Callahan Mining Corporation; *U.S. Public*, pg. 394

GENESIS—Vinyl Window—CertainTeed Corporation; *Int'l*, pg. 1170

GENESIS—NONE—Clark Material Handling Company; *U.S. Private*, pg. 243

GENESIS—GenRad's Environment for Strategy Independent Software—GenRad, Inc.; *U.S. Public*, pg. 731

GENESIS—Tennis Racquet—Head USA, Inc.; *U.S. Private*, pg. 514

GENESIS—Analog to Digital Conversion—Meret Communications; *U.S. Public*, pg. 1233

GENESIS—Cylindrical Blankets—Reeves International; *U.S. Private*, pg. 507

GENESIS—Print & Apply Equipment—Superior Label Systems, Inc.; *U.S. Private*, pg. 1055

GENESIS—Gas Barbeques—Weber-Stephen Products Co.; *U.S. Private*, pg. 1157

GENESOLV—Fluorocarbon Solvents—AlliedSignal Inc., Engineered Materials; *U.S. Public*, pg. 51

GENESPECTROMETRY—Technology for Fast, Accurate Detection of Genomic Sequences & Mutations—PerSeptive Biosystems, Inc.; *U.S. Public*, pg. 1279

GENESYS—Generator Sets—Magnetek Motors & Generators; *U.S. Public*, pg. 1037

GENETICIN—NONE—Life Technologies, Inc.; *U.S. Public*, pg. 504

GENETRAPPER—NONE—Life Technologies, Inc.; *U.S. Public*, pg. 504

GENETRON—Flurocarbons—AlliedSignal Inc.; *U.S. Public*, pg. 49

GENETRON CYDSA—Refrigeration & Repellent Gas—CYDSA S.A.; *Int'l*, pg. 246

GENETRON 113—Refrigerant Gas—AlliedSignal Inc., Engineered Materials; *U.S. Public*, pg. 51

GENEVA—GenRad's Extended VXIbus Architecture—GenRad, Inc.; *U.S. Public*, pg. 731

GENEVA—Carbon Pipe & Steel Products—Thomas Pipe & Steel, Inc.; *U.S. Private*, pg. 508

GENEVA CLUB—NONE—Stuart Entertainment Inc.; *U.S. Public*, pg. 1526

GENEVA GENERICS—Generic Pharmaceutical Co.-Wholesale & Direct—Geneva Pharmaceuticals, Inc.; *Int'l*, pg. 973

GENEVA LOGO—NONE—GenRad, Inc.; *U.S. Public*, pg. 731

GENEZAPPER—Electroporation System—Scientific Imaging Systems; *U.S. Public*, pg. 550

GEMFIBROZIL—Generic Drug—American Home Products Corporation; *U.S. Public*, pg. 79

GENGLIDE—Bearing Seal—General Bearing Corp.; *U.S. Public*, pg. 706

GENICOM—Electronic Components—Genicom Corporation; *U.S. Public*, pg. 729

GENIE—Heavy Duty Detergents—Colgate-Palmolive Company; *U.S. Public*, pg. 397

GENIE—Gate Opener & Wet/Dry Shop Vacuum—The Genie Company; *U.S. Private*, pg. 823

GENIE—Door Operator Systems—Overhead Door Corporation; *U.S. Private*, pg. 822

GENIE—Garage Door Openers—Philips Electronics N.V.; *Int'l*, pg. 1051

GENIE—Color Video Magnifier—Telesensory Corporation; *U.S. Public*, pg. 1074

GENIE CHAIN DRIVE—NONE—The Genie Company; *U.S. Private*, pg. 823

GENIE GARAGE DOOR OPENER—NONE—The Genie Company; *U.S. Private*, pg. 823

GENIE PRO—Garage Door Opener—The Genie Company; *U.S. Private*, pg. 823

GENIE PRO MAX—Garage Door Opener—The Genie Company; *U.S. Private*, pg. 823

GENIE PRO SCREW DRIVE—Garage Door Opener—The Genie Company; *U.S. Private*, pg. 823

GENIE SCREW DRIVE—Garage Door Opener—The Genie Company; *U.S. Private*, pg. 823

GENIE STEALTH—Garage Door Opener—The Genie Company; *U.S. Private*, pg. 823

GENIGRAPHICS—NONE—In Focus Systems, Inc.; *U.S. Public*, pg. 873

GENIMUNE—Drug; Treats Rheumatoid Arthritis & Autoimmune Disease—XOMA Corporation; *U.S. Public*, pg. 1786

GENISYS—Programmable Controller—Union Switch & Signal Inc.; *Int'l*, pg. 77

GENIUS—Electronic Instrument—Intel Corporation; *U.S. Public*, pg. 886

THE GENIUS IS IN THE DETAILS—Photographic Film—Eastman Kodak Company; *U.S. Public*, pg. 550

GENKENE—Electrical Cables & Wires—General Cable Corporation; *Int'l*, pg. 1486

GENLECO—Leather Pastes And Non Resinated Pigments—Henkel Corporation; *Int'l*, pg. 610

GENNY—NONE—Luxottica Group S.p.A.; *Int'l*, pg. 822

GENNY ICE—Beer—Genesee Corporation; *U.S. Public*, pg. 728

GENOA—Fresh Sausage—Kayem Foods, Inc.; *U.S. Private*, pg. 610

GENOPTIC—Sterile Ophthalmic Solution—Allergan, Inc.; *U.S. Public*, pg. 46

GENOTHERM—Polypropylene—Hoechst Aktiengesellschaft; *Int'l*, pg. 624

GENOTROPIN—NONE—Pharmacia & Upjohn, Inc.; *Int'l*, pg. 1047

GENOVESE—Drug Stores—Genovese Drug Stores, Inc.; *U.S. Public*, pg. 730

GENRAD—NONE—GenRad, Inc.; *U.S. Public*, pg. 731

GENRAD CAT SYSTEM—NONE—GenRad, Inc.; *U.S. Public*, pg. 731

GENRALOGIC—Emulator—General Railway Signal Corp.; *Int'l*, pg. 1194

GENSIL—Silicone Rubber Compound for Wire & Cable Insulation—General Electric Canada Inc.; *U.S. Public*, pg. 713

GENTEMP—Generation Temperature Monitor System—Westronics, Inc.; *U.S. Public*, pg. 1593

GENTEX—Automotive Component Supplier/Manufacturer—Gentex Corporation; *U.S. Public*, pg. 731

GENTLE BEND—Package or Packaging—Ethicon, Inc.; *U.S. Public*, pg. 928

GENTLE CREATURES—Greeting Cards—American Greetings Corporation; *U.S. Public*, pg. 77

GENTLE EXPRESSIONS—NONE—Graham-Field Health Products, Inc.; *U.S. Public*, pg. 757

GENTLE-FLO—Catheters—Mallinckrodt Inc.; *U.S. Public*, pg. 1039

GENTLE HEARTS—Greeting Cards—American Greetings Corporation; *U.S. Public*, pg. 77

GENTLE JUICE—Juice—Beech-Nut Nutrition Corporation; *U.S. Public*, pg. 1359

GENTLE LIFT—Home Health Care Chair—Pride Health Care, Inc.; *U.S. Private*, pg. 883

GENTLE LIGHTS—Hair Lightener—Clairol, Inc.; *U.S. Public*, pg. 254

GENTLE MOMENTS—Greeting Cards—American Greetings Corporation; *U.S. Public*, pg. 77

GENTLE ORANGE—Herbal Tea Bags—Thomas J. Lipton Company; *Int'l*, pg. 1435

GENTLE TOUCH—Two-Piece Ostomy Postoperative System—Bristol-Myers Squibb Company; *U.S. Public*, pg. 253

GENTLE TOUCH—Soap—The Andrew Jergens Company; *Int'l*, pg. 717

GENTLE TOUCH—Mixers & Mixer Speed Controls—Sunbeam Household Products; *U.S. Public*, pg. 1533

GENTLE TOUCH FREQUENT REPLACEMENT LENSES—NONE—Pilkington Barnes Hind (PBH); *U.S. Private*, pg. 111

GENTLE TREATMENT—Hair Relaxer & Maintenance Prod.—Johnson Products Co., Inc.; *U.S. Public*, pg. 915

GENTLEMAN JACK—Whiskey—Jack Daniels Distillery; *U.S. Public*, pg. 261

GENTLEMAN JACK RARE—Tennessee Whiskey—Brown-Forman Corporation; *U.S. Public*, pg. 261

GENTLEMAN JACK RARE TENNESSEE—Whiskey—Brown-Forman Beverages Worldwide; *U.S. Public*, pg. 261

GENTLEMEN'S QUARTERLY—Magazine—The Conde Nast Publications Inc.; *U.S. Private*, pg. 20

GENTLEMAN'S HOME—NONE—Drexel Heritage Furnishings Inc.; *U.S. Private*, pg. 432

GENTLEMAN'S SPEYSIDE BLEND—Whisky—Dunhill Scotch Whisky Sales Limited; *Int'l*, pg. 409

GENTOCIN—Broad-Spectrum Antibiotic (Equine & Bovine)—Schering-Plough Corporation; *U.S. Public*, pg. 1438

GENTOCIN—Otic Solution (Canine & Feline)—Schering-Plough Corporation; *U.S. Public*, pg. 1438

GENTOCIN DURAFILM—Opthalmic Soloution (Canine & Feline)—Schering-Plough Corporation; *U.S. Public*, pg. 1438

GENU—Carrageenan & Pectins—Hercules Incorporated; *U.S. Public*, pg. 809

GENUINE BRASS, LUSTRE BRASS—Fashion Beds—Leggett & Platt, Incorporated; *U.S. Public*, pg. 985

GENUINE FIESTA ACCESSORIES—Accessories For Chinaware—The Homer Laughlin China Company; *U.S. Private*, pg. 653

GENUINE KIDS—Clothing—OshKosh B'Gosh, Inc.; *U.S. Public*, pg. 1232

GENUINE PRESSBOARD—Type I Pressboard—FiberMark Inc.; *U.S. Public*, pg. 620

GENURIN—Flavoxate, Urology—Recordati Industria Chimica e Farmaceutica S.p.A.; *Int'l*, pg. 1090

GENUS—Company Name—Genus Inc.; *U.S. Public*, pg. 732

GENVAKODE—Track Circuit/Communicaitons Systems—General Railway Signal Corp.; *Int'l*, pg. 1194

GEO INFO SYSTEMS—Trade Periodical—Advantar Communications; *U.S. Private*, pg. 22

GEO-MARKETING—Software—CACI International Inc; *U.S. Public*, pg. 272

GEO-MATT—Foam Overlay—Span-America Medical Systems Inc.; *U.S. Public*, pg. 1495

GEO-NET 2000—Position & Information Exchange System—Rockwell International Corporation; *U.S. Public*, pg. 1397

GEO STAR—GPS and Laser Controls—Spectra-Physics Laserplane Inc.; *U.S. Public*, pg. 1594

GEOBLOCK—Plastic Paving Blocks—Reynolds Metals Company; *U.S. Public*, pg. 1385

GEOCODING PRODUCTS—NONE—MapInfo Corp.; *U.S. Public*, pg. 1042

GEOCON—Access Control System—CASI-RUSCO Inc.; *U.S. Private*, pg. 218

GEODE—Complex Inorganic Color Pigments—Ferro Corporation; *U.S. Public*, pg. 618

GEODIS—NONE—GEODIS; *Int'l*, pg. 549

GEODOLITE—Construction Laser Equip.—Spectra-Physics Laserplane Inc.; *U.S. Public*, pg. 1594

GEOFFERY BEENE—Designer Line Apparel—Phillips-Van Heusen Corporation; *U.S. Public*, pg. 1291

GEOFFREY BOEHMCHOCOLATES—Confectionery—Boyer Candy Company Inc.; *U.S. Private*, pg. 162

GEOFFREY BEENE—Men's Suits—Oxford Industries, Inc.; *U.S. Public*, pg. 1239

GEOFFREY BEENE BOWLING GREEN—Men's Fragrance—Sanofi Beaute, Inc.; *Int'l*, pg. 445

GEOFFREY BEENE GREY FLANNEL—Men's Fragrance—Sanofi Beaute, Inc.; *Int'l*, pg. 445

GEOFLEX—Roof Coating—RPM, Inc.; *U.S. Public*, pg. 1356

GEOGPG RTF—Computer System—International Business Machines Corporation; *U.S. Public*, pg. 895

GEOGPG/6000—Computer System—International Business Machines Corporation; *U.S. Public*, pg. 895

GEOGRAPHIC & GEO DEMOGRAPHIC—NONE—MapInfo Corp.; *U.S. Public*, pg. 1042

GEOGRAPHIC CODING PLUS—Database Marketing—Group 1 Software, Inc.; *U.S. Public*, pg. 417

GEOGRAPHIX—NONE—Landmark Graphics Corporation; *U.S. Public*, pg. 776

GEOIMAGES—Computer-Enhanced Imagery—Litton Industries, Inc.; *U.S. Public*, pg. 1002

GEOLAN—NONE—UB Networks; *Int'l*, pg. 924

GEOLAST—Thermoplastic Elastomer—Monsanto Company; *U.S. Public*, pg. 1124

GEOLAST—Thermoplastic Elastomer—Solutia Inc.; *U.S. Public*, pg. 1483

GEOMANAGER—Computer System—International Business Machines Corporation; *U.S. Public*, pg. 895

GEOMANAGER/6000—Computer System—International Business Machines Corporation; *U.S. Public*, pg. 895

GEOMATCH—Software—CACI International Inc; *U.S. Public*, pg. 272

GEOMETRIC—Taps, Dies & Guages—Greenfield Industries Inc.; *U.S. Public*, pg. 950

GEON—Polyvinyl Chloride Resins—The Geon Company; *U.S. Public*, pg. 733

GEOPRENE—Electrical Wire & Cable—General Electric Canada Inc.; *U.S. Public*, pg. 713

GEOREAD—Software—CACI International Inc; *U.S. Public*, pg. 272

GEORG JENSEN—Silver—Royal Copenhagen A/S; *Int'l*, pg. 1134

GEORGE DICKEL NO TWELVE—NONE—Guinness Plc; *Int'l*, pg. 412

GEORGE FISCHER—Valves, Pipe & Fittings—Ryan Herco Products Corp.; *U.S. Private*, pg. 953

GEORGE KILLIAN'S—Beer—Heineken N.V.; *Int'l*, pg. 608

GEORGE KOVACS—Lighting Fixtures—George Kovacs Lighting, Inc.; *U.S. Private*, pg. 634

GEORGES RECH—Designer Clothes & Accessories—Courtaulds Textiles Plc; *Int'l*, pg. 339

GEORGETOWN—Bath Accessories—Baldwin Hardware Corporation; *U.S. Public*, pg. 1053

GEORGETOWN—Plumbing Products—The Black & Decker Corporation; *U.S. Public*, pg. 233

GEORGETTE KLINGER—Hair Care Products & Skin Care Cosmetics & Salons—Georgette Klinger, Inc.; *U.S. Private*, pg. 626

GEORGI GIN—NONE—Star Industries Inc.; *U.S. Private*, pg. 1034

GEORGI VODKA—NONE—Star Industries Inc.; *U.S. Private*, pg. 1034

GEORGIA—Canvas Products—Georgia Tent & Awning Co.; *U.S. Private*, pg. 448

GEORGIA BANANAS N' CREAM—Liqueur—NWS Inc.; *U.S. Private*, pg. 772

GEORGIA BOOT—Boots & Shoes—Georgia/Durango Boot Company; *U.S. Public*, pg. 1684

GEORGIA COFFEE—Canned Iced Coffee—The Coca-Cola Company; *U.S. Public*, pg. 392

GEORGIA FARM & RANCH—Boots—Georgia/Durango Boot Company; *U.S. Public*, pg. 1684

GEORGIA INDUSTRIAL FOOTWEAR—Safety & Non-Safety Work Footwear—Georgia/Durango Boot Company; *U.S. Public*, pg. 1684

GEORGIA MANUFACTURERS REGISTER—Register—Manufacturers' News, Inc.; *U.S. Private*, pg. 700

GEORGIA NATURAL GAS COMPANY—Natural Gas Distribution—AGL Resources; *U.S. Public*, pg. 6

GEORGIA-PACIFIC—Paper Towels, Bath Tissue, Soap & Dispensers, Building Products—Georgia-Pacific Corporation; *U.S. Public*, pg. 735

GEORGIA PEACHES N'CREAM—Liqueur—NWS Inc.; *U.S. Private*, pg. 772

GEORGIA STRAWBERRY CHEESECAKE N' CREAM—Liqueur—NWS Inc.; *U.S. Private*, pg. 772

GEORGIAN—Bath Tissue—Georgia-Pacific Corporation; *U.S. Public*, pg. 735

GEORIM—NONE—UB Networks; *Int'l*, pg. 924

GEOSAFARI—Electronic Learning Aid—Educational Insights, Inc.; *U.S. Public*, pg. 565

GEOSCOPE—NONE—Market Facts, Inc.; *U.S. Public*, pg. 1046

GEOSITE—Safety Eyewear—Aearo Company; *U.S. Private*, pg. 23

GEOSWITCH—NONE—UB Networks; *Int'l*, pg. 924

GEOSYSTEMS—Plastic Paving Blocks & Ground Support—Reynolds Metals Company; *U.S. Public*, pg. 1385

GEOTRIEVE-THE SOFTWARE BUSINESS—Software—CACI International Inc; *U.S. Public*, pg. 272

GEOVIEW—NONE—UB Networks; *Int'l*, pg. 924

GEOWEB—Plastic Ground Support—Reynolds Metals Company; *U.S. Public*, pg. 1385

GERAHEALTH TABS—Vitamins—Health Products Corporation; *U.S. Private*, pg. 514

GERAMONT—Cheese—BG SAS; *Int'l*, pg. 201

GERAMONT—Cheese—Bongrain S.A.; *Int'l*, pg. 201

GERARD—Metal Roof Tiles—Alcan Aluminium Limited; *Int'l*, pg. 50

GERARD—Cheese—BG SAS; *Int'l*, pg. 201

GERARD SUPEROOF—Roofing Tiles—Carter Holt Harvey Limited; *U.S. Public*, pg. 904

GERBER—Knives—Fiskars Oy AB; *Int'l*, pg. 492

GERBER—Baby Foods, Baby Care & Babywear—Gerber Products Company; *Int'l*, pg. 973

GERBER BABY FORMULA—Infant Formulas—Bristol-Myers Squibb Company; *U.S. Public*, pg. 253

GERBER LIFE—Insurance—Gerber Products Company; *Int'l*, pg. 973

GERBER SCIENTIFIC INCORPORATED—NONE—Gerber Scientific, Inc.; *U.S. Public*, pg. 740

GEREF—Growth Hormone Releasing Factor—Ares-Serono S.A.; *Int'l*, pg. 80

GERHARD SCHULZ—Wine & Spirits—Leonard Kreusch, Inc.; *U.S. Private*, pg. 635

GERIATRIC PHARMATON—Vitamin—Boehringer Ingelheim GmbH; *Int'l*, pg. 199

GERIATRICS—Trade Periodical—Advanstar Communications; *U.S. Private*, pg. 22

GERITOL—Vitamins—SmithKline Beecham Consumer Healthcare, U.S.; *Int'l*, pg. 1264

GERITOL—Vitamins—SmithKline Beecham Corporation; *Int'l*, pg. 1264

GERITOL—Vitamin & Tonic—SmithKline Beecham plc; *Int'l*, pg. 1264

GERM-CHEK—Antiseptic Dressings—Hercon Laboratories Corp.; *U.S. Public*, pg. 802

GERM-FIGHTER—Antimicrobial Treated Rigid Plastic Liners—United Receptical, Inc.; *U.S. Private*, pg. 1123

GERM-TROL—Concentrate Disinfectant Cleaner—Stanhome Inc.; *U.S. Public*, pg. 1508

GERM-X—Disinfectant Spray—Stanhome Inc.; *U.S. Public*, pg. 1508

GERMA BEN—Cosmetic Preservatives—International Specialty Products, Inc.; *U.S. Public*, pg. 858

GERMAINE MONTEIL—Cosmetics—Revlon, Inc.; *U.S. Private*, pg. 689

GERMALL—Cosmetic Preservatives—International Specialty Products, Inc.; *U.S. Public*, pg. 858

GERMANIN—Tropical Medicine for Treatment of Sleeping Sickness—Bayer AG; *Int'l*, pg. 171

GERMANTOWN—Food Ingredients—Goodman Fielder Limited; *Int'l*, pg. 555

GERMOLENE—Topical/Skincare—SmithKline Beecham plc; *Int'l*, pg. 1264

GERMOLOIDS—Topical/Skincare—SmithKline Beecham plc; *Int'l*, pg. 1264

GERRITY LUMBER—NONE—Wickes Inc.; *U.S. Public*, pg. 1391

GERRY—Infant Prods.—Gerry Baby Products Company; *U.S. Private*, pg. 629

GERSTENSLAGER—Automotive Stampings—The Gerstenslager Company; *U.S. Public*, pg. 1780

GERVAIS—Cheese—Danone Group; *Int'l*, pg. 379

GESSNER—Dry Finishing & Other Textile Industry Equipment—GHM Industries, Inc.; *U.S. Private*, pg. 435

GESTETNER—Office Equipment—Gestetner Holdings PLC; *Int'l*, pg. 1114

GESTETNER COPYSTATION—Copiers—Gestetner Corporation; *Int'l*, pg. 1115

GESTETNER FAXSTATION—Facsimilie Machines—Gestetner Corporation; *Int'l*, pg. 1115

GESTETNER PRINTSTATION—Digital Duplicators—Gestetner Corporation; *Int'l*, pg. 1115

GESTRA—Steam Traps, Check Valves—GESTRA GmbH; *Int'l*, pg. 549

GET IT ROTO-ROOTER RIGHT—Slogan—Roto-Rooter; *U.S. Public*, pg. 344

GET MET IT PAYS—Company Advertising Slogan—Metropolitan Life Insurance Co.; *U.S. Private*, pg. 737

GET OFF MY GARDEN—Dog and Cat Repellent—Security Lawn & Garden Co.; *U.S. Private*, pg. 397

GET SET—Hair Set—Alberto-Culver Company; *U.S. Public*, pg. 37

GETALIT—Decorative Laminates (HPL)—Westag & Getalit AG; *Int'l*, pg. 1491

GETAWAY—Men's Apparel—International Cosmetics Co., Ltd.; *Int'l*, pg. 684

GETTA HAIRCUT—Home Hair Clipper Kit—Andis Company; *U.S. Private*, pg. 73

GETTY—Petroleum Products—Getty Petroleum Marketing Inc.; *U.S. Public*, pg. 740

GETTY MART—Convenience Food Stores—Getty Petroleum Marketing Inc.; *U.S. Public*, pg. 740

GETTYSBURG—Game—Monarch Avalon, Inc.; *U.S. Public*, pg. 1123

GEVALIA—Coffee—Philip Morris Companies Inc.; *U.S. Public*, pg. 1287

GEVALIA KAFFEE—Coffee Import Service—Kraft Foods, Inc.; *U.S. Public*, pg. 1287

GEVRIL—Watches—Basel Trading Company Ltd.; *Int'l*, pg. 169

GEWURZTALER—Spiced Biscuits—Coop Switzerland; *Int'l*, pg. 329

GEYER-MCALLISTER—Periodicals & Publications—Geyer-McAllister Publications, Inc.; *U.S. Private*, pg. 450

GHENT—Mfr. Visual Communications Aids—Ghent Manufacturing, Inc.; *U.S. Private*, pg. 450

GHIBLI—NONE—Brown & Sharpe Manufacturing Company; *U.S. Public*, pg. 260

GHOST—Bass Drum Pedal—Ludwig Industries; *U.S. Public*, pg. 1514

GHOST HOUSE—Videogame—Sega of America Inc.; *Int'l*, pg. 1218

GHOSTWRITER—Invisible Ink & Developer—Sanford Corporation; *U.S. Public*, pg. 1178

THE GHURKA COLLECTION—Luggage & Handbags—Trafalgar Ghurka Ltd.; *U.S. Private*, pg. 1095

GIANNI—Spagetti Sauces—Ventre Packing Company, Inc.; *U.S. Private*, pg. 1135

GIANT—Food Stores & Pharmacies—Giant Food Inc.; *U.S. Public*, pg. 741

GIANT—Food Stores—Koninklijke Ahold NV; *Int'l*, pg. 749

GIANT EAGLE—Wholesale Grocery Prods.—Giant Eagle, Inc.; *U.S. Private*, pg. 449

GIANT KISS—Chocolate—Hershey Foods Corporation; *U.S. Public*, pg. 811

GIANT SANDWICHES—Ice Cream—Good Humor/Breyers Ice Cream; *Int'l*, pg. 1435

GIANT STEEL RADIAL—Tires—Bridgestone/Firestone, Inc.; *Int'l*, pg. 213

GIANT VAC—Blowers & Vacuums—Frost Company; *U.S. Private*, pg. 430

GIANT VOICE—Outdoor Warning System—Altec Lansing Corp.; *U.S. Public*, pg. 479

GIBBERELLIN—Plant-Growth Regulator—Meiji Seika Kaisha, Ltd.; *Int'l*, pg. 855

GIBBONS—Premium Beer & Ale—The Lion Brewery, Inc.; *U.S. Public*, pg. 1000

GIBBS—Processed Food—Hanover Foods Corporation; *U.S. Private*, pg. 499

GIBCO—NONE—Life Technologies, Inc.; *U.S. Public*, pg. 504

GIBCO BBL—NONE—Life Technologies, Inc.; *U.S. Public*, pg. 504

GIBCO SQUARE—NONE—Life Technologies, Inc.; *U.S. Public*, pg. 504

GIBCOWARE—NONE—Life Technologies, Inc.; *U.S. Public*, pg. 504

GIBRALTAR—Strong Spring—Cargill Flour Div.; *U.S. Private*, pg. 210

GIBRALTAR—Manufactured Homes—Champion Enterprises, Inc.; *U.S. Public*, pg. 332

GIBRALTAR—Versatile Stone-Like Surfacing Material—Premark International, Inc.; *U.S. Public*, pg. 1321

GIBSON—Appliances—The Climatic Corp.; *U.S. Private*, pg. 246

GIBSON—Major Appliances—Electrolux, AB; *Int'l*, pg. 438

GIBSON—Appliances—Frigidaire Home Products; *Int'l*, pg. 439

GIBSON—Appliance—Gibson Appliances; *Int'l*, pg. 439

GIBSON—Greeting Cards—Gibson Greetings, Inc.; *U.S. Public*, pg. 742

GIBSON—Major Appliances—White Consolidated Industries, Inc.; *Int'l*, pg. 439

GIBSON VINEYARDS—Wines—Gibson Wine Company; *U.S. Private*, pg. 452

GIDDINGS & LEWIS—NONE—Automation Control; *Int'l*, pg. 1389

GIEN—Dinnerware—Baccarat, Inc.; *Int'l*, pg. 132

GIEVES & HAWKES—Men's Apparel—Hartmarx Corporation; *U.S. Public*, pg. 795

GIEVES & HAWKES—Clothing—Hickey-Freeman/Bobby Jones; *U.S. Public*, pg. 795

GIFT CHEQUE—Money Service—American Express Company; *U.S. Public*, pg. 73

THE GIFT OF ENTERTAINMENT—Advertising Slogan—Blockbuster Entertainment Group; *U.S. Private*, pg. 775

GIFT & STATIONERY BUSINESS—Magazines—Miller Freeman Inc.; *Int'l*, pg. 1443

GIFTS & GOOD WISHES—Greeting Cards & Gift Items—American Greetings Corporation; *U.S. Public*, pg. 77

GIGA-TRONICS—Microwave Signal Generators—Giga-Tronics Incorporated; *U.S. Public*, pg. 742

GIGAHUB—High-Performance LAM Distrb. & Switching—N Base Communications; *U.S. Public*, pg. 1027

GIGGLE POPS—Children's Novelties—Kemps Foods, Inc.; *Int'l*, pg. 752

GIGI—Greeting Cards; Ceramic Figurines & Plates—American Greetings Corporation; *U.S. Public*, pg. 77

THE GIL GROSS SHOW—Talk Show—Westwood One, Inc.; *U.S. Public*, pg. 1763

GILA DUCT—Galvanized Steel Conduit With PE Jacket—Tamaqua Cable Products Corp.; *Int'l*, pg. 417

GILBANE—Construction Management—Gilbane Building Company; *U.S. Private*, pg. 452

GILBERT—Bond Paper—The Mead Corporation; *U.S. Public*, pg. 1074

GILBERT COTTON—Writing Papers—The Mead Corporation; *U.S. Public*, pg. 1074

GILBERT COVER RECYCLED—Recycled, Laid, Wove Plate Finish Paper—Gilbert Paper; *U.S. Public*, pg. 1074

GILBERT COVERS—Laid, Wove, Plate Finish Cover Paper—Gilbert Paper; *U.S. Public*, pg. 1074

GILBERT ECO—Bond Paper—The Mead Corporation; *U.S. Public*, pg. 1074

GILBERT 50% COTTON—Cotton Fiber Paper—Gilbert Paper; *U.S. Public*, pg. 1074

GILBERT 100% COTTON—Cotton Fiber Paper—Gilbert Paper; *U.S. Public*, pg. 1074

GILBERT OXFORD—Writing, Text, Cover Paper—Gilbert Paper; *U.S. Public*, pg. 1074

GILBERT RECYCLED—Recycled Bond Paper—The Mead Corporation; *U.S. Public*, pg. 1074

GILBERT 25% COTTON—Cotton Fiber Paper—Gilbert Paper; *U.S. Public*, pg. 1074

GILBERT WRITING—Stationery Products—The Mead Corporation; *U.S. Public*, pg. 1074

GILBEY'S—Gin—Grand Metropolitan Plc; *Int'l*, pg. 408

GILBEY'S—Vodka/Gin—Fortune Brands, Inc.; *U.S. Public*, pg. 674

GILBEY'S—NONE—Tegner & Son AB; *Int'l*, pg. 412

GILBEY'S ANTIQUE GIN—Gin—W & A Gilbey; *Int'l*, pg. 409

GILBEY'S GIN—Spirits—Gilbeys of Ireland; *Int'l*, pg. 409

GILBEY'S GIN—NONE—International Distillers Caribbean; *Int'l*, pg. 410

GILBEY'S GIN—NONE—Societe Pour la Vente des Produits Cinzano SA; *Int'l*, pg. 410

GILBEY'S LONDON DRY GIN—Gin—W & A Gilbey; *Int'l*, pg. 409

GILCLEAR—Translucent Paper-Light, Medium & Heavy Grades—Gilbert Paper; *U.S. Public*, pg. 1074

GILCLEAR—Transparentized papers—The Mead Corporation; *U.S. Public*, pg. 1074

GILCREST—Bond Paper—The Mead Corporation; *U.S. Public*, pg. 1074

GILCREST BOND—Laid Finish Writing & Cover Paper—Gilbert Paper; *U.S. Public*, pg. 1074

GILDA MARX—Activewear—Bestform Foundations, Inc.; *U.S. Private*, pg. 140

GILDA MARX INCORPORATED—Clothing—Gilda Marx Inc.; *U.S. Private*, pg. 710

GILLAB—RFP Countertops—M.C. Gill Corporation; *U.S. Private*, pg. 453

GILLARD'S—Pies, Sausages & Other Products—GrandMet Foods UK; *Int'l*, pg. 408

GILLCORE—Aramid Paper Honey Comb Core and Aluminum Honey Comb core—M.C. Gill Corporation; *U.S. Private*, pg. 453

GILLESPIE—Woodcare & Artist's Supplies—W.M. Barr & Co., Inc.; *U.S. Private*, pg. 117

GILLETTE—Shave Creams, Blades, Razors—The Gillette Company; *U.S. Public*, pg. 743

GILLETTE—Razor Blades—Gillette UK Ltd.; *U.S. Public*, pg. 745

GILLETTE ANTI-PERSPIRANT—Anti-perspirant—The Gillette Company; *U.S. Public*, pg. 743

GILLETTE BLUE BLADES—Blades—The Gillette Company; *U.S. Public*, pg. 743

GILLETTE SERIES COOL WAVE—Men's Grooming Products—The Gillette Company; *U.S. Public*, pg. 743

GILLETTE SERIES WILD RAIN—Men's Grooming Products—The Gillette Company; *U.S. Public*, pg. 743

GILLETTE SUPER BLUE BLADES—Blades—The Gillette Company; *U.S. Public*, pg. 743

GILLETTE SUPER-SPEED—Razor—The Gillette Company; *U.S. Public*, pg. 743

GILLFLOOR—Passenger & Cargo Compartment Flooring for Commercial Aircraft—M.C. Gill Corporation; *U.S. Private*, pg. 453

GILLFOAM—Structural Foam, Primarily for Use in Commercial Aircraft—M.C. Gill Corporation; *U.S. Private*, pg. 453

GILLINER—Cargo Liner for Commercial Aircraft—M.C. Gill Corporation; *U.S. Private*, pg. 453

GILLNETTERS BEST—Canned Salmon—Peter Pan Seafoods, Inc.; *Int'l*, pg. 928

GILLPATCH—Cargo Liner Repair Patches for Commercial Aircraft—M.C. Gill Corporation; *U.S. Private*, pg. 453

GILMORE—Envelopes—Gilmore Envelope Corp.; *U.S. Private*, pg. 454

GILMOUR—Pistol-grip Water Nozzle & Garden Sprayers—Vermont American Tool Corp.; *U.S. Public*, pg. 575

GILPLEX—Coating—Jones Blair Co.; *U.S. Private*, pg. 596

GILROY FARMS—Garlic, Produce Items—McCormick/Schilling; *U.S. Public*, pg. 1066

GILUSTENON—Cardiovascular Preparations—Kali-Chemie Aktiengesellschaft; *Int'l*, pg. 1278

GIMINI—Cameras—Eastman Kodak Company; *U.S. Public*, pg. 550

GIN AND JUICE—Citrus Juice & Gin—The House of Seagram; *Int'l*, pg. 1217

GINA COSMETICS—Cosmetics—Tristar Corp.; *U.S. Public*, pg. 1640

GINA PETERS—NONE—Kellwood Company; *U.S. Public*, pg. 948

GINEBRA SAN MIGUEL—Gin—La Tondena Distillers, Inc.; *Int'l*, pg. 785

GINGER TREE—Prepasted Vinyl Coated Strippable Wallcovering—York Wallcoverings Inc.; *U.S. Private*, pg. 1196

GINGHAM—Food Products—Certified Grocers of California; *U.S. Private*, pg. 226

GINGISS—Formalwear/Accessories- Rental/Sales—Gingiss International; *U.S. Private*, pg. 455

GINGISS FORMALWEAR—Formalwear Rental & Sales Stores—Gingiss International; *U.S. Private*, pg. 455

GINGSENG PLUS—Herb Tea—Celestial Seasonings; *U.S. Public*, pg. 319

GINI—Soft Drinks—Cadbury Schweppes p.l.c.; *Int'l*, pg. 247

GINKGO BILOBA—NONE—Celestial Seasonings; *U.S. Public*, pg. 319

GINKGO BILOBA—Conference Table Series—Vecta; *U.S. Private*, pg. 1038
GINKGO SHARP—Blend with Ginkgo Biloba—Celestial Seasonings; *U.S. Public*, pg. 319
GINOZIN—Pure Ginseng & Ginseng with Vitamins & Minerals—Novo Nordisk A/S; *Int'l*, pg. 987
GINSENG—NONE—Celestial Seasonings; *U.S. Public*, pg. 319
GINSENG ENERGY—Blend with Ginseng—Celestial Seasonings; *U.S. Public*, pg. 319
GINSENG RUSH—Soft Drink—R.J. Corr Naturals, Inc.; *U.S. Private*, pg. 276
GINSTAR—Ag Chemical—AgrEvo USA Company; *Int'l*, pg. 1203
GINSU—Knife Set—Douglas/Quikut; *U.S. Public*, pg. 217
GIO DE GIORGIO ARMANI—Women's Fragrance—Cosmair, Inc.; *Int'l*, pg. 818
GIOIA—Pasta—Borden, Inc.; *U.S. Private*, pg. 157
GIOIA—Pasta Products—Borden Italian Foods; *U.S. Private*, pg. 158
GIORGIO ARMANI—Fragrances for Men & Women—Cosmair, Inc.; *Int'l*, pg. 818
GIORGIO ARMANI—Men's & Women's Fragrances—Cosmair, Inc., Ralph Lauren Fragrance Division; *Int'l*, pg. 818
GIORGIO ARMANI—NONE—L'Oreal Parfumerie; *Int'l*, pg. 819
GIORGIO ARMANI—NONE—Luxottica Group S.p.A.; *Int'l*, pg. 822
GIRARDS—Salad Dressing—T. Marzetti Company; *U.S. Public*, pg. 977
GIRL TALK—Game—Golden Books Family Entertainment Inc.; *U.S. Public*, pg. 749
GIRLING—Hydraulic Brake Products for Automotive, Industrial & Agricultural Use—Lucas Industries Inc.; *Int'l*, pg. 820
GIRLOON—Carpeting, Upholstery Velvet, Decoration Velvet—Girmes GmbH; *Int'l*, pg. 552
GIRLS OF PENTHOUSE—Magazine—General Media International Inc.; *U.S. Private*, pg. 444
GIRLTALK—NONE—BBC Magazines; *Int'l*, pg. 114
GIRMI—NONE—Moulinex S.A.; *Int'l*, pg. 896
GIRO—Bicycle Helmets—Bell Sports Corp.; *U.S. Public*, pg. 207
GIRO—Tequila—Domecq Importers Inc.; *Int'l*, pg. 63
GIROD—Measuring Tools—Fred V. Fowler Company, Inc.; *U.S. Private*, pg. 422
GIRPI—NONE—ETEX; *Int'l*, pg. 430
GISELE DENIS—Color Cosmetics—Coty Inc.; *Int'l*, pg. 185
GISLAVED—Tires—Continental AG; *Int'l*, pg. 327
GISTEX—Primary Grown Yeast Extracts for the Food Industry—Royal Gist-Brocades N.V.; *Int'l*, pg. 1142
GITANES—Cigarettes—SEITA, Societe Nationale D'Exploitation des Tabacs et des Allumettes; *Int'l*, pg. 1219
GITANO—Casual Clothing—Gitano Fashions Ltd.; *U.S. Public*, pg. 686
GIUBIASCO—Floor Coverings—Forbo Holding SA; *Int'l*, pg. 496
GIUGIARO—NONE—Luxottica Group S.p.A.; *Int'l*, pg. 822
GIUMARRA—Vineyards—Giumarra Vineyards; *U.S. Private*, pg. 455
GIVENCHY—Liscensed Name Brand Watch—Jan Bell Marketing Inc.; *U.S. Public*, pg. 207
GIVENCHY—Small Leather Goods & Handbags—Koret Pierre Cardin; *U.S. Private*, pg. 632
GIVENCHY—Hosiery—Pennaco Hosiery; *U.S. Public*, pg. 483
GIVENCHY LUNETTES—Eyewear—Logo of the Americas; *Int'l*, pg. 462
GLACIER—Coated Printing Paper—The Mead Corporation; *U.S. Public*, pg. 1074
GLACIER—Bearings—T & N Plc; *Int'l*, pg. 1334
GLACIER BAR—Ice Cream Novelties—Borden, Inc.; *U.S. Private*, pg. 157
GLACIER PAK—Paperboard Cartons—Georgia-Pacific Corporation; *U.S. Public*, pg. 735
GLACIER SPRINGS WATER—Bottled Water—Beverage Canners International Corp.; *U.S. Private*, pg. 106
GLACIER'S EDGE—Sporting—Fred Meyer Stores; *U.S. Public*, pg. 1103
GLACIERVAN—Refrigerated Truck Body—Kidron Inc.; *U.S. Private*, pg. 619

GLAD—Plastic Wrap & Bags—First Brands Corporation; *U.S. Public*, pg. 626
GLAD-LOCK—Zipper Food Bags—First Brands Corporation; *U.S. Public*, pg. 626
GLADDING—Cordage & Rope—Gladding Braided Products LLC; *U.S. Private*, pg. 291
GLADE—Air Freshener—S.C. Johnson & Son, Inc.; *U.S. Private*, pg. 592
GLADE—Air Care—S.C. Johnson & Son, Limited; *U.S. Private*, pg. 593
GLADE AEROSOL—Air Care—S.C. Johnson & Son, Inc.; *U.S. Private*, pg. 592
GLADE BASICS SPRAY—Air Care—S.C. Johnson & Son, Inc.; *U.S. Private*, pg. 592
GLADE BASICS CARPET & ROOM DEODORIZER—Air Care—S.C. Johnson & Son, Inc.; *U.S. Private*, pg. 592
GLADE CLIP-ONS—Air Care—S.C. Johnson & Son, Inc.; *U.S. Private*, pg. 592
GLADE COUNTRY POTTERY—Air Freshener—S.C. Johnson & Son, Inc.; *U.S. Private*, pg. 592
GLADE LASTING MIST—Air Care—S.C. Johnson & Son, Inc.; *U.S. Private*, pg. 592
GLADE LIGHT—Air Freshener—S.C. Johnson & Son, Inc.; *U.S. Private*, pg. 592
GLADE NEUTRALIZER—Air Care—S.C. Johnson & Son, Inc.; *U.S. Private*, pg. 592
GLADE PLUG-INS—Air Care—S.C. Johnson & Son, Inc.; *U.S. Private*, pg. 592
GLADE POTPOURRI—Air Freshener—S.C. Johnson & Son, Inc.; *U.S. Private*, pg. 592
GLADE POTPOURRI CARPET & ROOM DEODORIZER—Air Care—S.C. Johnson & Son, Inc.; *U.S. Private*, pg. 592
GLADE POTPOURRI SOLID—Air Care—S.C. Johnson & Son, Inc.; *U.S. Private*, pg. 592
GLADE POTPOURRI SPRAY—Air Care—S.C. Johnson & Son, Inc.; *U.S. Private*, pg. 592
GLADE II—Air Freshener—S.C. Johnson & Son, Inc.; *U.S. Private*, pg. 592
GLADIATOR—High Alumina Phosbonded Brick—A.P. Green Industries, Inc.; *U.S. Public*, pg. 761
GLADIATOR—War Game—Monarch Avalon, Inc.; *U.S. Public*, pg. 1123
GLADWEG—De-Icing Salt—Akzo Nobel N.V.; *Int'l*, pg. 42
GLAESEL—Stringed Instruments—The Selmer Co., Inc.; *U.S. Public*, pg. 1514
GLAMAPYNE—Laminated Board—CSR Limited; *Int'l*, pg. 245
GLAMIN—NONE—Pharmacia & Upjohn, Inc.; *Int'l*, pg. 1047
GLAMINATE—Multilayer Tubes—American National Can Company; *Int'l*, pg. 1029
GLAMOR—Paint—Jones Blair Company; *U.S. Private*, pg. 596
GLAMORISE—Brassieres, Girdles & Foundation Garments—Glamorise Foundations, Inc.; *U.S. Private*, pg. 455
GLAMOUR—Magazine—The Conde Nast Publications Inc.; *U.S. Private*, pg. 20
GLAMOUR KITTY—Kitty Litter—Laporte plc; *Int'l*, pg. 801
GLAMOURSUIT—Shapewear—Olga Div.; *U.S. Public*, pg. 1738
GLANCE—NONE—Brown & Sharpe Manufacturing Company; *U.S. Public*, pg. 260
GLANDOSANE—Mouth Moisturizer—Bradley Pharmaceuticals; *U.S. Public*, pg. 249
GLANDOSANE—Mouth Moisturizer—Doak Dermatologics; *U.S. Public*, pg. 250
GLARE CARE—Stationery Products—The Mead Corporation; *U.S. Public*, pg. 1074
GLARE DEFENDER—Anti Glare Filter—Optical Coating Laboratory, Inc.; *U.S. Public*, pg. 1227
GLARE/GUARD—Visual Displays Antiglare Panels For CRT'S—Optical Coating Laboratory, Inc.; *U.S. Public*, pg. 1227
GLARE LESS—Anti-Reflective Coating—AVC/Nu-Vision, Inc.; *U.S. Private*, pg. 9
GLARE TAMER—Photochromatics—AVC/Nu-Vision, Inc.; *U.S. Private*, pg. 9
GLAREFREE—Electrochromic Mirror—Donnelly Corporation; *U.S. Public*, pg. 519
GLARESTOPPER—NONE—Donnelly Corporation; *U.S. Public*, pg. 519
GLAS-CLAD—NONE—The Sherwin-Williams Company; *U.S. Public*, pg. 1465
GLASBAC—Backing for Carpeting—Interface Inc.; *U.S. Public*, pg. 889

GLASBASE—Fiberglass Felt—Johns Manville Corporation; *U.S. Public*, pg. 927
GLASCLAD—NONE—Owens-Corning Canada; *U.S. Public*, pg. 1237
GLASCOTE—Water Heaters—A.O. Smith Corporation; *U.S. Public*, pg. 1476
GLASFLEX—Acrylic Rods & Tubes for Lighting Fixtures, Furniture & Optical Lenses—Uniroyal Technology Corporation; *U.S. Public*, pg. 1670
GLASKAP—Built-Up Roofing—Johns Manville Corporation; *U.S. Public*, pg. 927
GLASLINK—NONE—Donnelly Corporation; *U.S. Public*, pg. 519
GLASLOCK—Roofing Shingles—Owens Corning; *U.S. Public*, pg. 1236
GLASPLY—Premier Fiberglass Relt—Johns Manville Corporation; *U.S. Public*, pg. 927
GLASROD—Pultruded Rod—Glastic Corporation; *Int'l*, pg. 740
GLASS & MORE—Glass & Appliance Cleaner—Blue Cross Laboratories; *U.S. Private*, pg. 152
GLASS ARTS—Glass Furniture—International Aluminum Corporation; *U.S. Public*, pg. 894
GLASS BRITE—Glass Cleaner—Blue Cross Laboratories; *U.S. Private*, pg. 152
GLASS EXPRESS—Foam Glass & Surface Cleaner—Stanhome Inc.; *U.S. Public*, pg. 1508
GLASS-O-NET—Reinforced Window Material—Warp Brothers; *U.S. Private*, pg. 412
GLASS PLUS—Cleaner—The Dow Chemical Company; *U.S. Public*, pg. 522
GLASS PLUS—Glass & Multi-Surface Cleaner—DowBrands, L.P.; *U.S. Public*, pg. 523
GLASS THANE—Mat—Johns Manville Corporation; *U.S. Public*, pg. 927
GLASSCAN—Image Digitizing—Galileo Corp.; *U.S. Public*, pg. 698
GLASSDEK—Forming Board—Johns Manville Corporation; *U.S. Public*, pg. 927
GLASSES EXPRESS—Optician Services—AVC/Nu-Vision, Inc.; *U.S. Private*, pg. 9
GLASSEX—Surface Cleaner—Reckitt & Colman plc; *Int'l*, pg. 1089
GLASSFYRE—Glass Firescreen Enclosures—Byers Portland Willamette; *U.S. Private*, pg. 191
GLASSGUARD—Asphalt Roofing Shingle with Fiberglass Base—CertainTeed Corporation; *Int'l*, pg. 1170
GLASSKOTE—Transparent Coating for Flexible Display Sign Faces—Signtech USA, Ltd.; *U.S. Private*, pg. 999
GLASSMASTER—Asphalt Shingles—Atlas Roofing Corp.; *U.S. Private*, pg. 96
GLASSMASTER—Boats, Antenas, Monofilaments, Flexible & Electronic Controls, Composites—Glassmaster Company; *U.S. Public*, pg. 745
GLASSMAX—NONE—Life Technologies, Inc.; *U.S. Public*, pg. 504
GLASSPROTEX—Fire-Rated Door & Wall Space—O'Keeffe's, Inc.; *U.S. Private*, pg. 813
GLASSROOT—Fiber Glass Rovings for Soil Stabilization & Erosion Control—PPG Industries, Inc.; *U.S. Public*, pg. 1245
GLASSTEX—Asphalt Roofing Shingle with Fiberglass Base—CertainTeed Corporation; *Int'l*, pg. 1170
GLASSTEX—V-Belts—HBD Industries, Inc.; *U.S. Private*, pg. 489
GLASSVENT—Concealed Vent for Storegront Use—Kawneer Company; *U.S. Public*, pg. 60
GLASTEEL—Process Equipment—Pfaudler, Inc.; *U.S. Public*, pg. 1393
GLASTHERM—Thermal Insulating Sheet—Glastic Corporation; *Int'l*, pg. 740
GLASTIC—Fiberglass Reinforced Plastics—Glastic Corporation; *Int'l*, pg. 740
GLASTITE—Flexible Base Flashing—Johns Manville Corporation; *U.S. Public*, pg. 927
GLASTRAC—Electronic Information Display Systems—PPG Industries, Inc.; *U.S. Public*, pg. 1245
GLASTRON—Fiberglass Boats—Genmar Holdings, Inc.; *U.S. Private*, pg. 447
GLASTRON—Boats—Glastron Boats; *U.S. Private*, pg. 447
GLASTRON/CARLSON—Boats—Glastron Boats; *U.S. Private*, pg. 447
GLAUCON—Epinephrine Hydrochloride Solution—Alcon Laboratories, Inc.; *Int'l*, pg. 916

GLAXO—Ethical Pharmaceuticals—Glaxo Wellcome Inc.; *Int'l*, pg. 552

GLAYVA—Scotch Liquer—Marie Brizard Wines & Spirits USA; *U.S. Private*, pg. 702

GLAYZE—Primer Putty—Marson/Creative Fastener, Inc.; *U.S. Private*, pg. 708

GLAZ—Designing Gel—The Dow Chemical Company; *U.S. Public*, pg. 522

GLAZED PENTA—Chemical—Vulcan Chemicals; *U.S. Public*, pg. 1725

GLAZEGUARD—Building Panels—Weyerhaeuser Company; *U.S. Public*, pg. 1764

GLEAM—Gift Wrap Paper—American Greetings Corporation; *U.S. Public*, pg. 77

GLEAM RITE LR—Liquid Brightener & Cleaner—LeaRonal, Inc.; *U.S. Public*, pg. 982

GLEAMLIGHTS—Votive Candles—Will & Baumer Incorporated; *U.S. Private*, pg. 1176

GLEANER—Rotary Combines—AGCO Corporation; *U.S. Public*, pg. 28

GLEASON WHEELS—Wheels: Lawn & Garden, Industrial Casters, Pneumatic & Solid Rubber—Gleason Corporation; *U.S. Public*, pg. 746

GLEEM—Toothpaste—The Procter & Gamble Company; *U.S. Public*, pg. 1330

GLEESON FLO VAC—Suction Irrigation Instrument—Conmed Corporation; *U.S. Public*, pg. 431

GLEN—Household Appliances—The Glen Dimplex Group; *Int'l*, pg. 553

GLEN CLOVA—Scotch—Marie Brizard Wines & Spirits USA; *U.S. Private*, pg. 702

GLEN COULL—Scotch Whiskey—John Gross & Co.; *U.S. Private*, pg. 483

GLEN COVE PLANK—Pre-Finished Laminate—Bruce Hardwood Floors; *U.S. Public*, pg. 1634

GLEN ELLEN—Wine—Glen Ellen Winery; *U.S. Private*, pg. 455

GLEN ELLEN—Wines—Grand Metropolitan Plc; *Int'l*, pg. 408

GLEN ELLEN—NONE—Tegner & Son AB; *Int'l*, pg. 412

GLEN ELLEN WINES—Wine—Heublein, Inc.; *Int'l*, pg. 410

GLEN-GERY—Face & Paving Brick—Glen-Gery Corporation; *Int'l*, pg. 658

GLEN ORD—NONE—Guinness Plc; *Int'l*, pg. 412

GLEN ORD—Scotch—United Distillers USA, Inc.; *Int'l*, pg. 412

GLEN RAVEN—Canvas Fabrics—Glen Raven Mills, Inc.; *U.S. Private*, pg. 456

GLENARA—Fabric—Glenoit Mills, Inc.; *U.S. Private*, pg. 456

GLENAYRE—Infrastructure Equipment & Systems—Glenayre Technologies, Inc.; *U.S. Public*, pg. 746

GLENAYRE—Advanced Wireless Communications Products—TCG International Inc.; *Int'l*, pg. 1336

GLENAYREPAGE—Advanced Wireless Communications Systems—TCG International Inc.; *Int'l*, pg. 1336

GLENBARD REAMERS—Presicion Cutting Tools—Regal-Beloit Corporation; *U.S. Public*, pg. 1370

GLENBROOK—Lumber & Wood Products—Georgia-Pacific Corporation; *U.S. Public*, pg. 735

GLENBROOK LIFE—Life Insurance & Savings—The Allstate Corporation; *U.S. Public*, pg. 55

GLENCOE—Tillage Equipment, Planters—AGCO Corporation; *U.S. Public*, pg. 28

GLENDINNING—Marine Engine Synchronizers—Valley Forge Corporation; *U.S. Public*, pg. 1705

THE GLENDRONACH SINGLE MALT—12 & 15 Year Old Scotch—Allied Domecq PLC; *Int'l*, pg. 62

THE GLENDRONACH SINGLE MALT SCOTCH—Scotch—Hiram Walker; *Int'l*, pg. 63

GLENEAGLES—Weatherwear—Hartmarx Corporation; *U.S. Public*, pg. 795

GLENEAGLES—Hospital—Parkway Holdings Limited; *Int'l*, pg. 1023

GLENFARCLAS—Scotch Whisky—Barton Incorporated; *U.S. Public*, pg. 300

GLENFIDDICH—Spirits—Mercian Corporation; *Int'l*, pg. 858

GLENGOYNE—Single Malt Scotch—Paterno Imports Limited; *U.S. Private*, pg. 843

GLENKINCHIE—NONE—Guinness Plc; *Int'l*, pg. 412

GLENLIVET—Scotch—The House of Seagram; *Int'l*, pg. 1217

THE GLENLIVIT—Scotch—The Seagram Company Ltd.; *Int'l*, pg. 1214

THE GLENLIVET—Scotch Whiskey—Joseph E. Seagram & Sons, Inc.; *Int'l*, pg. 1215

GLENMOOR—Screw Machine Prods.—Ilsco; *U.S. Private*, pg. 558

GLENMORANGIE—Single Highland Malt Scotch—Brown-Forman Corporation; *U.S. Public*, pg. 261

GLENMORANGIE SINGLE HIGHLAND MALT SCOTCH—Scotch Whiskey—Brown-Forman Beverages Worldwide; *U.S. Public*, pg. 261

GLENMORE—NONE—Barton Brands, Ltd.; *U.S. Public*, pg. 300

GLENNET—Advanced Wireless Communications Systems—TCG International Inc.; *Int'l*, pg. 1336

GLENTEX—Scarves & Accessories—Honey Fashions Ltd.; *U.S. Private*, pg. 537

GLENTURRET—Single Malt Scotch—The Highland Distilleries Company plc; *Int'l*, pg. 619

GLENWOOD POST—Newspaper—Shivers Trading & Operating Co.; *U.S. Private*, pg. 994

GLIBENESE/GLUCOTROL—Glipizide—Pfizer Inc.; *U.S. Public*, pg. 1281

GLID—Paint—ICI Paints; *Int'l*, pg. 664

GLID-GUARD—Coating—ICI Paints; *Int'l*, pg. 664

GLID-THANE—Coating—ICI Paints; *Int'l*, pg. 664

GLID-TONE—Stain—ICI Paints; *Int'l*, pg. 664

GLID-ZINC—Paint—ICI Paints; *Int'l*, pg. 664

GLID-SHIELD—Paint—ICI Paints; *Int'l*, pg. 664

GLID-THANE—Paint—ICI Paints; *Int'l*, pg. 664

GLID-TILE—Paint—ICI Paints; *Int'l*, pg. 664

GLIDDEN—Paint—ICI Paints; *Int'l*, pg. 664

GLIDE GUARD—Gym Set Feature—Hedstrom Corporation; *U.S. Private*, pg. 526

GLIDE-ON—Paint—ICI Paints; *Int'l*, pg. 664

GLIDE/PACK—Industrial Air Filtering Apparatus—Farr Company; *U.S. Public*, pg. 613

GLIDE RAIL—Adjustable Wall Mounting System—Alsons Corporation; *U.S. Public*, pg. 1053

GLIDE-TRAC—Stationary Items—The Mead Corporation; *U.S. Public*, pg. 1074

GLIDEWIRE—Guidewires—Terumo Medical Corporation; *Int'l*, pg. 1376

GLIFARELAX-T—Neuro-Muscular—SmithKline Beecham Research Limited; *Int'l*, pg. 1266

GLIMPSE—NONE—Brown & Sharpe Manufacturing Company; *U.S. Public*, pg. 260

GLIS'N—Instant Haircolor & Shampoo—Revlon-Realistic Professional Products, Inc.; *U.S. Private*, pg. 690

GLISTEN—Dishwasher Cleanser—Superior Brands, Inc.; *Int'l*, pg. 917

GLISTER—Oral Care Products—Amway Corporation; *U.S. Private*, pg. 69

GLITTER GLOBE—Decorative Light Bulb—Duro-Test Corporation; *U.S. Private*, pg. 349

GLITTER MAGIC—Yarn—Lion Brand Yarn Co.; *U.S. Private*, pg. 669

GLITZI—Household Pad—Freudenberg & Company; *Int'l*, pg. 505

GLO-AWAY—UV-Fluorescent Additive Cleaner-Remover—Spectronics Corporation; *U.S. Private*, pg. 1024

GLO BAY—HID Industrial Lighting—Stonco Genlyte; *U.S. Public*, pg. 730

GLO-COAT—Floor Polish—S.C. Johnson & Son, Inc.; *U.S. Private*, pg. 592

GLO-CRAFT—UV Lights & Accessories—Day-Glo Color Corp.; *U.S. Public*, pg. 1357

GLO-JUICE—Phosphorescent Marking Dye—Scientific Imaging Systems; *U.S. Public*, pg. 550

GLO-DOODLER—Glo-Slate—Colorforms; *U.S. Public*, pg. 1625

GLO- PLUG—Extension Cord—Southwire Company; *U.S. Private*, pg. 1019

GLO-RITER—Picture Maker—Colorforms; *U.S. Public*, pg. 1625

GLOAG'S GIN—Gin—The Highland Distilleries Company plc; *Int'l*, pg. 619

GLOBAL—Canned & Frozen Foods—Basic Food International Inc.; *U.S. Private*, pg. 121

GLOBAL ASSIST—Emergency or Legal aid to Cardmembers—American Express Company; *U.S. Public*, pg. 73

GLOBAL CITYVOICE—NONE—Cable and Wireless plc; *Int'l*, pg. 247

GLOBAL DESIGN NEWS—International News Magazine for Design Engineers—Reed Elsevier Business Information; *Int'l*, pg. 1095

GLOBAL INTELLIGENT VIRTUAL NETWORK—NONE—Cable and Wireless plc; *Int'l*, pg. 247

GLOBAL LINK—Pre-paid Calling Card—Peoples Telephone Company, Inc.; *U.S. Public*, pg. 1275

GLOBAL MANAGED DATA SERVICE—NONE—Cable and Wireless plc; *Int'l*, pg. 247

GLOBAL MANAGED PRIVATE LINE—NONE—Cable and Wireless plc; *Int'l*, pg. 247

GLOBAL MANAGED ROUTER SERVICE—NONE—Cable and Wireless plc; *Int'l*, pg. 247

GLOBAL SECURITIES MANAGER—NONE—SunGard Data Systems Inc.; *U.S. Public*, pg. 1534

GLOBAL SWITCH—Digital Central Office Switch—Mitel Corporation; *Int'l*, pg. 870

GLOBAL TELEPHONY—Publication for International Telecommunications—Intertec Publishing; *U.S. Public*, pg. 1327

GLOBAL TOTAL SHOULDER SYSTEM—Orthopedic Product—DePuy, Inc.; *Int'l*, pg. 331

GLOBAL TRADE—Magazine—North American Publishing Company; *U.S. Private*, pg. 803

GLOBAL VAN LINES—Long Distance Moving Services—Global Van Lines, Inc.; *U.S. Private*, pg. 458

GLOBAL VIDEOPHONE STANDARD—Videophones—Lucent Technologies Inc.; *U.S. Public*, pg. 1017

GLOBAL WORKS—Multi-Processor Computers—Thinking Machines Corporation; *U.S. Private*, pg. 1081

GLOBE—Food Service Pie Fillings—Comstock Michigan Fruit; *U.S. Private*, pg. 887

GLOBE—NONE—Keng Hua Paper Products Co., Inc.; *Int'l*, pg. 729

GLOBE—High Precision Miniature Electric Motors—Labinal SA; *Int'l*, pg. 785

GLOBE A-1—Pasta—Borden, Inc.; *U.S. Private*, pg. 157

GLOBE A-1—Pasta Products—Borden Italian Foods; *U.S. Private*, pg. 158

GLOBE BOOK COMPANY—Publishers—Simon & Schuster; *U.S. Private*, pg. 777

GLOBE DESIGN—NONE—Berg Electronics; *U.S. Public*, pg. 212

THE GLOBE DEVICE—NONE—Cable and Wireless plc; *Int'l*, pg. 247

GLOBE MASTER—Mass merchandiser type globe—Replogle Globes, Inc.; *U.S. Private*, pg. 923

GLOBE PEQUOT—Book Publisher & Distribution—Shivers Trading & Operating Co.; *U.S. Private*, pg. 994

GLOBE-WEIS—Filing Supplier—ATAPCO Office Products Group; *U.S. Private*, pg. 64

GLOBESAT—Satellite Business Service—Teleglobe, Inc.; *Int'l*, pg. 1373

GLOBETRADER—NONE—Elof Hansson AB; *Int'l*, pg. 595

GLOBEVIEW—Telecommunications Products—Lucent Technologies Inc.; *U.S. Public*, pg. 1017

GLOBI—Supermarket—GIB Group; *Int'l*, pg. 532

GLOCK—9mm Parabellum Pistol—EEI Corporation; *Int'l*, pg. 425

GLOCOIL—Heating Elements—Eagle Electric Mfg. Co., Inc.; *U.S. Private*, pg. 354

GLORIA—Car—Nissan Motor Co., Ltd.; *Int'l*, pg. 943

GLORIA—Milk Products—RJR Nabisco Holdings Corp.; *U.S. Public*, pg. 1354

GLORIA—White Mineral Oil—Witco Corporation; *U.S. Public*, pg. 1773

GLORIA VANDERBILT—Frangrances—Cosmair, Inc.; *Int'l*, pg. 818

GLORIA'S MOMENTS—Greeting Cards—American Greetings Corporation; *U.S. Public*, pg. 77

GLORIOUS GRAYS—Hair Coloring—Clairol, Inc.; *U.S. Public*, pg. 254

GLORY—Mammography—Elscint Ltd.; *Int'l*, pg. 450

GLORY—Rug Cleaner—S.C. Johnson & Son, Inc.; *U.S. Private*, pg. 592

GLOSETTE—Peanuts & Raisins—Hershey Foods Corporation; *U.S. Public*, pg. 811

GLOSSER BROS.—Dept. Store—G B Stores; *U.S. Private*, pg. 972

GLOSSIES—Intimate Apparel—Lily of France, Inc.; *U.S. Private*, pg. 140

GLOSSMASTER—Gloss Calender Roll Cover—Harnischfeger Industries, Inc.; *U.S. Public*, pg. 788

GLOSSTONE—Color Coated Paper & Paperboard—Hazen Paper Company; *U.S. Private*, pg. 514

GLOUCESTER—Marine Product—Rule Industries, Inc.; *U.S. Public*, pg. 950

GLOBE-WEIS—Office Products—American Trading and Production Corporation; *U.S. Private*, pg. 63

GLOW CUBE—Reflected Light Displays—Daktronics, Inc.; *U.S. Public*, pg. 478

GLOW IN THE DARK—Vinyl Tape—Hanovia Colight; *Int'l*, pg. 17

GLOWING STAR—Food Products—Rykoff-Sexton, Inc.; *U.S. Public*, pg. 918

GLU-BIRD—Glue—DAP Inc.; *Int'l*, pg. 1486

GLU GLU—Fruit Drink—Jugos del Valle, S.A. de C.V.; *Int'l*, pg. 716

GLU-ON—Adhesive—DAP Inc.; *Int'l*, pg. 1486

GLUCKS REVUE—Magazine—Burda Holding GmbH & Co., KG; *Int'l*, pg. 233

GLUCOMETER—Blood Monitor—Bayer AG; *Int'l*, pg. 171

GLUCOMETER II—Blood Glucose Meter—Bayer Corporation/Consumer Care Division; *Int'l*, pg. 173

GLUCOMETER M—Blood Glucose Meter WithMemory—Bayer Corporation/Consumer Care Division; *Int'l*, pg. 173

GLUCOPHAGE—Antihyperglycemic—The Dow Chemical Company; *U.S. Public*, pg. 522

GLUCOTROL XL—Glipizide GITS—Pfizer Inc.; *U.S. Public*, pg. 1281

GLUG—Odorless Drain Opener—Hercules Chemical Co., Inc.; *U.S. Private*, pg. 523

GLUMAL—Gastrointestinal Agents—Kyowa Hakko Kogyo Company, Ltd.; *Int'l*, pg. 778

GLUMIN—Gastrointestinal Agents—Kyowa Hakko Kogyo Company, Ltd.; *Int'l*, pg. 778

GLUTAMAX—NONE—Life Technologies, Inc.; *U.S. Public*, pg. 504

GLUTOFAC—Vitamin/Mineral Supplement for Replenishing Nutrients in Patients—Bradley Pharmaceuticals; *U.S. Public*, pg. 249

GLUTOFAC—Caplets; Vitamin/Mineral Supplement for Replenishing Nutrients in Patients—Doak Dermatologics; *U.S. Public*, pg. 250

GLUTOFAC-ZX—Prescription High-Potency Multivitamin & Multimineral Supplement—Bradley Pharmaceuticals; *U.S. Public*, pg. 249

GLUTOFAC-ZX—Capsules; Prescription High-Potency Multivitamin & Multimeral Supplement—Doak Dermatologics; *U.S. Public*, pg. 250

THE GLUTTON—Abrasive Materials Pumps—Graco Inc.; *U.S. Public*, pg. 756

GLY-MIRACLE—Skin Care—Palm Beach Beauty Products Co.; *U.S. Private*, pg. 834

GLY-OXIDE—Mouth Rinse—SmithKline Beecham Consumer Healthcare; *U.S. Int'l*, pg. 1264

GLYCACIL—NONE—Lonza Inc.; *Int'l*, pg. 67

GLYCINE—Food Additives—Nippon Kayaku Co. Ltd.; *Int'l*, pg. 934

GLYCO—Engine bearings, bushings, washers—Federal-Mogul Corporation; *U.S. Public*, pg. 615

GLYCO—Babbit Metal—Joseph T. Ryerson & Son, Inc.; *U.S. Public*, pg. 879

GLYCOLUBE—Textile Chemicals—Lonza Inc.; *Int'l*, pg. 67

GLYCOMER—Suture—U.S. Surgical Corp.; *U.S. Public*, pg. 1687

GLYCON—Glycerin, Sorbital for Humectancy In Food, Tobacco, Toothpaste—Lonza Inc.; *Int'l*, pg. 67

GLYCOSPERSE—Emulsifier & Water Treatment Chemical—Lonza Inc.; *Int'l*, pg. 67

GLYCOSTAT—Plastic Additives—Lonza Inc.; *Int'l*, pg. 67

GLYCOWAX—Defoamer Wax For Water Treatment—Lonza Inc.; *Int'l*, pg. 67

GLYDANT—Preservatives for Microbiological Control—Lonza Inc.; *Int'l*, pg. 67

GLYDANT PLUS—Preservatives for Microbiological Control—Lonza Inc.; *Int'l*, pg. 67

GLYSOLID—Hand Cream—SmithKline Beecham plc; *Int'l*, pg. 1264

GLYTEX—Textile Chemicals—Lonza Inc.; *Int'l*, pg. 67

GMORPHIC-80—Excipient—Eastman Chemical Company; *U.S. Public*, pg. 550

GNOME—Helicopter Engine—Rolls-Royce Military Aero Engines Ltd.; *Int'l*, pg. 1127

GO-ANYWHERE—Grill—Weber-Stephen Products Co.; *U.S. Private*, pg. 1157

GO-CARD—Smart Card—Cubic Corporation; *U.S. Public*, pg. 466

GO - CAT—Cat Food—Nestle S.A.; *Int'l*, pg. 915

GO LIGHTS—Carlton, Free—Souza Cruz, S.A.; *Int'l*, pg. 112

GO TO THE HEAD OF CLASS—Game—Milton Bradley Company; *U.S. Public*, pg. 797

GO-VIDEO—Video Cassette Recorder—Go-Video, Inc.; *U.S. Public*, pg. 748

GO WEST—Slug Baits—The Chas. H. Lilly Co.; *U.S. Private*, pg. 667

GOAL—Sports Magazine—IPC Magazines Limited; *Int'l*, pg. 651

GOAL—Herbicide—Rohm and Haas Company; *U.S. Public*, pg. 550

GOLD MAKER—Feed For Cattle—Ag Processing Inc., A Cooperative; *U.S. Private*, pg. 26

GOANNA—Reinforcing Bar Chairs—Smorgon A.R.C.; *Int'l*, pg. 1269

GODAS—Telecommunications Services—Lucent Technologies Inc.; *U.S. Public*, pg. 1017

GODDARD'S—Household Products—Northern Labs, Inc.; *U.S. Private*, pg. 805

GODDESS—Bras, Girdles—Goddess Bra Company; *U.S. Private*, pg. 458

GODET—NONE—R & A Bailey & Co.; *Int'l*, pg. 409

GODFATHER'S—Pizza—Godfather's Pizza, Inc.; *U.S. Private*, pg. 458

GODIVA—Candy—Campbell Soup Company; *U.S. Public*, pg. 298

GODIVA—Chocolates—Godiva Chocolatier, Inc.; *U.S. Public*, pg. 299

GODIVA—Liqueur—The House of Seagram; *Int'l*, pg. 1217

GODIVA LIQUEUR—NONE—The Seagram Company Ltd.; *Int'l*, pg. 1214

GOD'S IN HIS HEAVEN—Calendars & Greeting Cards—American Greetings Corporation; *U.S. Public*, pg. 77

GODS WORD TODAY—Magazine—Catholic Digest; *U.S. Private*, pg. 220

GOEBEL—Beer—The Stroh Brewery Company; *U.S. Private*, pg. 1047

GOEDEHOOP ESTATE—Wine—Distillers Corporation S.A.; *Int'l*, pg. 1129

GOERLICH'S—Mufflers & Pipes—AP North American Aftermarket Division; *U.S. Private*, pg. 230

GOETZ PALE—Near Beer—Pearl Brewing Company; *U.S. Private*, pg. 954

GOFOR—Trailer-Mounted Access Platform—Simon Engineering plc; *Int'l*, pg. 1251

GOING FOR THE GLITZ—NONE—Stuart Entertainment Inc.; *U.S. Public*, pg. 1526

GOL—Compact Car—Volkswagen AG; *Int'l*, pg. 1473

GLOBUS-GATEWAY—First Class Escorted Tours to Britain, Europe, Orient, USA & Australia—Globus & Cosmos; *U.S. Private*, pg. 458

GOLD—Beer—Danone Group; *Int'l*, pg. 379

GOLD—Photographic Film—Eastman Kodak Company; *U.S. Public*, pg. 550

GOLD—Instant Coffee—Nestle S.A.; *Int'l*, pg. 915

GOLD—Low Fat Spread—Unigate PLC; *Int'l*, pg. 1433

GOLD—Logistics for Aerospace of Defense—Western Pacific Data Systems; *U.S. Private*, pg. 1168

GOLD BAND—Scientific Glassware for Laboratory Use—Wheaton Inc.; *Int'l*, pg. 67

GOLD BLOCK—Pipe Tobacco—Hanson PLC; *Int'l*, pg. 592

GOLD BLOCK—Pipe Tobacco—Imperial Tobacco Group, Ltd.; *Int'l*, pg. 666

GOLD BOND—Ice Cream & Water Ices—Good Humor/Breyers Ice Cream; *Int'l*, pg. 1435

GOLD BOND—Gypsum Wallboard & Related Products—National Gypsum Company; *Int'l*, pg. 790

GOLD BOND—Foods—Ventura Foods; *U.S. Private*, pg. 508

GOLD BOND STAMP—Trading Stamps, Gift Merchandise, Retail Promotion—Carlson Retail Marketing; *U.S. Private*, pg. 212

GOLD C/SAVINGS SPREE—Coupon Books—Entertainment Publications, Inc.; *U.S. Public*, pg. 320

GOLD CARD—Charge Card Services—American Express Company; *U.S. Public*, pg. 73

GOLD CARD—NONE—American Express Service Europe Ltd.; *U.S. Public*, pg. 74

GOLD-CLAD—Chemicals for Electro Plating—Technic Incorporated; *U.S. Private*, pg. 1071

GOLD COAST—Wine—Andres Wines Ltd.; *Int'l*, pg. 75

GOLD COAST—Cigarettes-Middle East—R.J. Reynolds Tobacco Intl., Inc.; *U.S. Public*, pg. 1355

GOLD COAT—Metallic Marker—Sanford Corporation; *U.S. Public*, pg. 1178

GOLD CONNECTION—Video & Audio Cables—Recoton Corporation; *U.S. Public*, pg. 1369

GOLD CREST—Insecticides—Roussel Corporation; *Int'l*, pg. 625

GOLD CROWN—Remote Mounted Aircraft Electronics—AlliedSignal Commercial Avionic Systems; *U.S. Public*, pg. 50

GOLD CROWN—Sporting Goods—Brunswick Bowling & Billiards Corp.; *U.S. Public*, pg. 265

GOLD CROWN—Paint—Sime Darby Berhad; *Int'l*, pg. 1249

GOLD CROWN—Liqueur—White Rock Distilleries Inc.; *U.S. Private*, pg. 1173

GOLD CUP—Socks—Kayser-Roth Corporation, Inc.; *Int'l*, pg. 576

GOLD DRAGON—Band Saw Blades—Sandvik/Milford Corporation; *Int'l*, pg. 1185

GOLD EAGLE—NONE—Harlequin Enterprises Ltd.; *Int'l*, pg. 1402

GOLD EAGLE LEAK STOPPERS—NONE—Gold Eagle Company; *U.S. Private*, pg. 459

GOLD-FISH—Fish Tape—Ideal Industries, Inc.; *U.S. Private*, pg. 557

GOLD K BILD—Manufacturer of Photographic Prints—Eastman Kodak Company; *U.S. Public*, pg. 550

GOLD KING—Frozen Food—Southern Frozen Foods; *U.S. Private*, pg. 887

GOLD KIST FARMS—Fresh, Frozen & Further Processed Poultry—Gold Kist, Inc.; *U.S. Private*, pg. 459

GOLD LABEL—Cigars—General Cigar Company, Inc.; *U.S. Public*, pg. 708

GOLD LABEL—Fresh Pork—The Smithfield Packing Co., Inc.; *U.S. Public*, pg. 1479

GOLD LEAF—NONE—Martin/F. Weber Company; *U.S. Private*, pg. 710

GOLD LEAF COLLECTION—NONE—Celebrity Incorporated; *U.S. Public*, pg. 319

GOLD LINE—DC Power Supply—Best Power; *U.S. Private*, pg. 140

GOLD MASTERCARD CARD—Prestige Card—Mastercard International, Inc.; *U.S. Private*, pg. 714

GOLD MEDAL—Wallcoverings—Borden, Inc.; *U.S. Private*, pg. 157

GOLD MEDAL—Flour & Baking Mixes—General Mills, Inc.; *U.S. Public*, pg. 717

GOLD MEDAL RECREATIONAL PRODUCTS—NONE—Barbour Thread, Inc.; *Int'l*, pg. 618

GOLD METAL—Gold-Tone Electric Curling Irons—Andis Company; *U.S. Private*, pg. 73

GOLD-N-FRESH—Poultry—Farmstead; *U.S. Private*, pg. 396

GOLD-N-FRESH—Retail Poultry Products—Seaboard Corporation; *U.S. Public*, pg. 1448

GOLD N GEMS—Fine Jewelry Stores—Montgomery Ward & Co., Inc.; *U.S. Private*, pg. 758

GOLD' N HONEY—Poultry Frozen—Tyson Foods, Inc.; *U.S. Public*, pg. 1652

GOLD-N-HOT—Personal Care Products—Windmere-Durable Holdings; *U.S. Public*, pg. 1771

GOLD'N LITE—Franks—Hormel Foods Corp.; *U.S. Public*, pg. 840

GOLD N'PLUMP—NONE—JFC Inc.; *U.S. Private*, pg. 577

Brand Name Index

GOLD-N-SWEET—Butter Blend Margarine, Aerosol Pan Coating—Ventura Foods LLC; *Int'l*, pg. 879

GOLD PEAK—Batteries—Gold Peak Industries (Holdings) Limited; *Int'l*, pg. 537

GOLD PLUS—Outdoor Products—The Black & Decker Corporation; *U.S. Public*, pg. 233

GOLD PLUS—Enhanced Immunogold Staining—Eastman Kodak Company; *U.S. Public*, pg. 550

GOLD+—Corrosion-Resistant Screws—Elco Textron; *U.S. Public*, pg. 1590

GOLD RIBBON—Hams—Hatfield Quality Meats; *U.S. Private*, pg. 510

GOLD RIVER—Wood Pulp, Newsprint—Avenor, Inc.; *Int'l*, pg. 101

GOLD RIVER—Moist Snuff Smokeless Tobacco—Swisher International Group, Inc.; *U.S. Public*, pg. 1543

GOLD SEAL—Interior/Exterior Paint—Buten, Division of Duron; *U.S. Private*, pg. 349

GOLD SEAL—Vineyards—Canandaigua Wine Co.; *U.S. Public*, pg. 300

GOLD SEAL—Tooling Board—Hexcel Corporation; *U.S. Public*, pg. 824

GOLD SEAL—Curtain Rods—Kirsch; *U.S. Public*, pg. 1176

GOLD SEAL PINS—Hot Melt Insulation Fasteners—Duro Dyne Corporation; *U.S. Private*, pg. 349

GOLD SHIELD—Retail Nut Packages—Pacific Foods, Inc.; *U.S. Private*, pg. 831

GOLD STRAND—Insect Screening—New York Wire Co.; *U.S. Private*, pg. 795

GOLD TOE—Hosiery—Arrow Shirt Company; *Int'l*, pg. 194

GOLD TOE—Hosiery—Bidermann International S.A.; *Int'l*, pg. 194

GOLD WING—Motorcycle—American Honda Motor Co., Inc. Motorcycle Division; *Int'l*, pg. 634

GOLDBERG—Film & Tape Reels—J & R Film / Moviola Digital Co.; *U.S. Private*, pg. 576

GOLDBERGER—Dolls—Goldberger Doll Mfg. Company, Inc.; *U.S. Private*, pg. 459

GOLDCARE 65—Medical Plan fo Seniors—Humana Health Chicago, Inc.; *U.S. Public*, pg. 847

GOLDCREST—Greeting Cards—American Greetings U.S. Greeting Card Division; *U.S. Public*, pg. 78

GOLDCREST—25% Cotton Fiber Paper—Unisource; *U.S. Public*, pg. 1671

GOLDE—Sunroof Systems—Rockwell International Corporation; *U.S. Public*, pg. 1397

GOLDE 50—Life Insurance—Old American Insurance Co.; *U.S. Public*, pg. 943

GOLDEN—Children's Books & Other Products—Golden Books Family Entertainment Inc.; *U.S. Public*, pg. 749

GOLDEN—Fruit Juice—Nestle Chocolate & Confection; *Int'l*, pg. 917

GOLDEN ALMOND—Chocolate Bar—Hershey Chocolate U.S.A.; *U.S. Public*, pg. 812

GOLDEN ALMOND—Chocolate Bar—Hershey Foods Corporation; *U.S. Public*, pg. 811

GOLDEN ALMOND NUGGETS—Chocolates—Hershey Chocolate U.S.A.; *U.S. Public*, pg. 812

GOLDEN ALMOND NUGGETS—Chocolates—Hershey Foods Corporation; *U.S. Public*, pg. 811

GOLDEN ALMOND SOLITAIRES—Chocolate Covered Almonds—Hershey Chocolate U.S.A.; *U.S. Public*, pg. 812

GOLDEN ALMOND SOLITAIRES—Chocolate Covered Almonds—Hershey Foods Corporation; *U.S. Public*, pg. 811

GOLDEN APPLE—Book Publishing—Bertelsmann AG; *Int'l*, pg. 189

GOLDEN ARCHES—McDonald's Symbol & Logo—McDonald's Corporation; *U.S. Public*, pg. 1068

GOLDEN BEAR—Cable—Loos & Co., Inc.; *U.S. Private*, pg. 675

GOLDEN BEAR—Golf Equipment—MacGregor Golf Company; *Int'l*, pg. 72

GOLDEN BEER—Beer—Central de Cervejas, S.A.; *Int'l*, pg. 279

GOLDEN BOOK—Children's Books—Golden Books Family Entertainment Inc.; *U.S. Public*, pg. 749

GOLDEN BOOK MUSIC VIDEOS—Children's Videos—Golden Books Family Entertainment Inc.; *U.S. Public*, pg. 749

GOLDEN BOOK 'N TAPE—Children's Books with Audio Cassette—Golden Books Family Entertainment Inc.; *U.S. Public*, pg. 749

GOLDEN BOOK'N TAPE—Book & Audio Cassette Set—Golden Books Publishing; *U.S. Public*, pg. 749

GOLDEN BOOK STEP AHEAD VIDEOS—Children's Educational Videos—Golden Books Family Entertainment Inc.; *U.S. Public*, pg. 749

GOLDEN BOOK VIDEO—Pre-Recorded Children's Home Videocassettes—Golden Books Publishing; *U.S. Public*, pg. 749

GOLDEN BOOK VIDEOS—Children's Videos—Golden Books Family Entertainment Inc.; *U.S. Public*, pg. 749

GOLDEN BOOKS—Children's Story Books, Color Activity Books—Golden Books Publishing; *U.S. Public*, pg. 749

GOLDEN BRASS—Low Concentration Brass Plating—LeaRonal, Inc.; *U.S. Public*, pg. 982

GOLDEN BRIDGE—Cigarettes-China—R.J. Reynolds Tobacco Intl., Inc.; *U.S. Public*, pg. 1355

GOLDEN BROWN—Pre-Cooked & Browned Sausage—Jones Dairy Farm; *U.S. Private*, pg. 596

GOLDEN CANOLA—Canola Oil—Mallet & Co.; *U.S. Private*, pg. 698

GOLDEN CHOICE—Medicare HMO—Sierra Health Services, Inc.; *U.S. Public*, pg. 1469

GOLDEN CHOICE—Wines & Spirits—Vendex International N.V.; *Int'l*, pg. 1462

GOLDEN COMFORT—Orthotics for Adults 50+—The Langer Biomechanics Group, Inc.; *U.S. Public*, pg. 978

GOLDEN CORRAL FAMILY STEAK HOUSES—Restaurant—Investors Management Corp.; *U.S. Private*, pg. 574

GOLDEN CRÈME—Dairy & Bakery Items—Certified Grocers of California; *U.S. Private*, pg. 226

GOLDEN CRISP—Potato Chips—Bachman Company; *U.S. Private*, pg. 109

GOLDEN CRISP—Breakfast Cereal—Kraft Foods, Inc.; *U.S. Public*, pg. 1287

GOLDEN CROWN—Food Products—Rykoff-Sexton, Inc.; *U.S. Public*, pg. 918

GOLDEN DAYS—NONE—H.J. Heinz Company Australia Ltd.; *U.S. Public*, pg. 807

GOLDEN DIPT—NONE—McCormick & Company, Incorporated; *U.S. Public*, pg. 1066

GOLDEN DIPT—Seafood Seasoning, Sauce, Soup & Condiments—McCormick/Schilling; *U.S. Public*, pg. 1066

GOLDEN DOT—Fishing Line—Gladding Braided Products LLC; *U.S. Private*, pg. 291

GOLDEN EAGLE EXTRACTOR—Final Extractor Cleaner/Feeder Preparing Cotton to be Ginned—Continental Eagle Corporation; *U.S. Private*, pg. 267

GOLDEN EAGLE SERIES—Lint Cleaner—Continental Eagle Corporation; *U.S. Private*, pg. 267

GOLDEN EAGLE SERIES 161—Saw Gin—Continental Eagle Corporation; *U.S. Private*, pg. 267

GOLDEN EXTRA—Body Filler—Marson/Creative Fastener, Inc.; *U.S. Private*, pg. 708

GOLDEN FALCON—Tires & Tubes—Bridgestone/Firestone, Inc.; *Int'l*, pg. 213

GOLDEN FITNESS—Orthotics for Active Adults 50+—The Langer Biomechanics Group, Inc.; *U.S. Public*, pg. 978

GOLDEN FLAKE—Snack Foods—Golden Flake Snack Foods, Inc.; *U.S. Public*, pg. 750

GOLDEN FLEECE—Outerwear & Apparel—I. Spiewak & Sons, Inc.; *U.S. Private*, pg. 1025

GOLDEN FRIES—Frozen Potatoes—Ore-Ida Foods, Inc.; *U.S. Public*, pg. 805

GOLDEN FRUIT—Cookies—Sunshine Biscuits, Inc.; *U.S. Private*, pg. 434

GOLDEN FRUIT—Cookies—Sunshine Biscuits, Inc.; *U.S. Public*, pg. 657

GOLDEN GALLEY—Seafood Flavors—Crompton & Knowles Ingredient Technology Corp.; *U.S. Public*, pg. 459

GOLDEN GATE—Pickled Specialties—Star Fine Foods, Inc.; *U.S. Private*, pg. 1034

GOLDEN GIRL—Margarine—Lever Brothers Co.; *Int'l*, pg. 1435

GOLDEN GIRL—Margarine—Unilever Plc; *Int'l*, pg. 1433

GOLDEN GLO—Turkey—Jerome Foods Inc.; *U.S. Private*, pg. 586

GOLDEN GLOW—Oil—Mallet & Co.; *U.S. Private*, pg. 698

GOLDEN GLUTEN—Animal Feed—Ag Processing Inc., A Cooperative; *U.S. Private*, pg. 26

GOLDEN GRAHAMS—Cereal—General Mills, Inc.; *U.S. Public*, pg. 717

GOLDEN GRAHAMS TREATS—Snacks—General Mills, Inc.; *U.S. Public*, pg. 717

GOLDEN GRAIN—Rice & Pasta Products—The Quaker Oats Company; *U.S. Public*, pg. 1347

GOLDEN GRAIN ALCOHOL—NONE—Barton Brands, Ltd.; *U.S. Public*, pg. 300

GOLDEN GRAIN/MISSION PASTA—Dry Pasta—Golden Grain Company; *U.S. Public*, pg. 1348

GOLDEN GRIDDLE—Syrups—Best Foods; *U.S. Public*, pg. 224

GOLDEN GRIDDLE—Syrups—Bestfoods; *U.S. Public*, pg. 223

GOLDEN GRIP—Sporting Goods—Brunswick Bowling & Billiards Corp.; *U.S. Public*, pg. 265

GOLDEN GUIDE—Science & Nature Books—Golden Books Publishing; *U.S. Public*, pg. 749

GOLDEN HEARTH—Bread & Buns—Metz Baking Company; *U.S. Private*, pg. 1022

GOLDEN HEARTH—Bread, Buns—Metz Baking Company (WI); *U.S. Private*, pg. 1022

GOLDEN HEARTH—Bread & Rolls—National Baking; *U.S. Private*, pg. 1022

GOLDEN INVESTOR—Golf Equipment—RAM Golf Corporation; *U.S. Private*, pg. 908

GOLDEN JERSEY—Milk & Ice Cream—Hygeia Dairy Co., Inc.; *U.S. Private*, pg. 552

GOLDEN JET—NONE—Western Atlas Logging Services; *U.S. Public*, pg. 1757

GOLDEN LIGHTS—Cigarette—Lorillard Tobacco Company; *U.S. Public*, pg. 1011

GOLDEN LUXURY—Gift Wrap & Trim; Greeting Cards; Gift Boxes—American Greetings Corporation; *U.S. Public*, pg. 77

GOLDEN MARK—Tires—Universal Cooperatives, Inc.; *U.S. Private*, pg. 1127

GOLDEN MUSIC—Children's Cassette Tapes—Golden Books Publishing; *U.S. Public*, pg. 749

GOLDEN NUGGET—NONE—Mirage Resorts Incorporated; *U.S. Public*, pg. 1116

GOLDEN PILSENER—Beer—The F.X. Matt Brewing Co.; *U.S. Private*, pg. 714

GOLDEN PINE—Lumber & Plywood—Johns Manville Corporation; *U.S. Public*, pg. 927

GOLDEN PLACENTA—Hair Care—Palm Beach Beauty Products Co.; *U.S. Private*, pg. 834

GOLDEN PRESS—NONE—Golden Books Family Entertainment Inc.; *U.S. Public*, pg. 749

GOLDEN PRIDE—Ale—Fuller, Smith & Turner Plc; *Int'l*, pg. 529

GOLDEN PRO—Golf Equipment—RAM Golf Corporation; *U.S. Private*, pg. 908

GOLDEN PUFFS—Presweetened Puffed Wheat—Malt-O-Meal Company; *U.S. Private*, pg. 699

GOLDEN QUILL—Letterhead Design Competition—The Mead Corporation; *U.S. Public*, pg. 1074

GOLDEN RAM—Golf Clubs & Balls—RAM Golf Corporation; *U.S. Private*, pg. 908

GOLDEN REY—Food Products—Rykoff-Sexton, Inc.; *U.S. Public*, pg. 918

GOLDEN RIDGES—Potato Chips—Bachman Company; *U.S. Private*, pg. 109

GOLDEN ROTISSERIE CHICKEN—Restaurant—IHOP Corp.; *U.S. Public*, pg. 862

GOLDEN RULE—Lumber Stores Program—Distribution America; *U.S. Private*, pg. 335

GOLDEN RULE LUMBER CENTERS—Retail Lumber Yards—United Hardware Distributing Co.; *U.S. Private*, pg. 335

GOLDEN SADDLE—Gold Overlay On Celestrium—L.G. Balfour Co., Inc.; *U.S. Private*, pg. 258

GOLDEN SCOT—Golf Clubs—Tommy Armour Golf; *U.S. Private*, pg. 1683

GOLDEN SEEK 'N' SOUND—NONE—Golden Books Family Entertainment Inc.; *U.S. Public*, pg. 749

GOLDEN SHORE—Seafood—King & Prince Seafood Corporation; *U.S. Private*, pg. 620

GOLDEN SHRED—Marmalade—Ranks Hovis McDougall Limited; *Int'l*, pg. 1395

GOLDEN SING ALONG—NONE—Golden Books Family Entertainment Inc.; *U.S. Public*, pg. 749

GOLDEN SOFT—Margarine—Borden, Inc.; *U.S. Private*, pg. 157

GOLDEN SOUND STORY—NONE—Golden Books Family Entertainment Inc.; *U.S. Public*, pg. 749

GOLDEN SOURCE—Pet Foods—Ag Processing Inc., A Cooperative; *U.S. Private*, pg. 26

GOLDEN SPIKE—NONE—Bachmann Industries, Inc.; *U.S. Private*, pg. 109

GOLDEN STAR—Turkey, Canned Hams, Canned Boneless Hams, Smoked Hams—Armour Food Company; *U.S. Public*, pg. 427

GOLDEN STATE—Almonds—Blue Diamond Growers; *U.S. Private*, pg. 152

GOLDEN STATE—Mobile Home—Kit Manufacturing Company; *U.S. Public*, pg. 962

GOLDEN STATE MUTUAL—Life Insurance—Golden State Mutual Life Insurance Company; *U.S. Private*, pg. 461

GOLDEN STEP AHEAD—Children's Learning Series—Golden Books Family Entertainment Inc.; *U.S. Public*, pg. 749

GOLDEN STEP AHEAD PLUS—Children's Workbooks, Flash Cards & Learning Boards—Golden Books Family Entertainment Inc.; *U.S. Public*, pg. 749

GOLDEN SUN—Animal Feeds—Golden Sun Feeds, Inc.; *U.S. Private*, pg. 895

GOLDEN TALKING TALES—NONE—Golden Books Family Entertainment Inc.; *U.S. Public*, pg. 749

GOLDEN III—Chocolate Bar—Hershey Chocolate U.S.A.; *U.S. Public*, pg. 812

GOLDEN III—Chocolate Bar—Hershey Foods Corporation; *U.S. Public*, pg. 811

GOLDEN TOUR—Golf Equipment—RAM Golf Corporation; *U.S. Private*, pg. 908

GOLDEN TRI CUT—Hacksaw Blades—Klein Tools Inc.; *U.S. Private*, pg. 625

GOLDEN VELVET—Cheese—Land O'Lakes, Inc.; *U.S. Private*, pg. 645

GOLDEN VIRGINIA—Handrolling Tobacco—Hanson PLC; *Int'l*, pg. 592

GOLDEN VIRGINIA—Hand Rolling Tobacco—Imperial Tobacco Group, Ltd.; *Int'l*, pg. 666

GOLDEN WAVE—Potato Chips—Troyer Potato Products, Inc.; *U.S. Private*, pg. 1106

GOLDEN WEST HOMES—Mobile Homes—Oakwood Homes Corporation; *U.S. Public*, pg. 1209

GOLDENAIR—Hose—HBD Industries, Inc.; *U.S. Private*, pg. 489

GOLDENBERG PEANUT CHEWS—Candy—Goldenberg Candy Company; *U.S. Private*, pg. 461

GOLDENCRAFT—Children's Books—Childrens Press Inc.; *Int'l*, pg. 794

GOLDENROD—Fuel Filters—Dutton-Lainson Co.; *U.S. Private*, pg. 350

GOLDENRULE STORE—Building Center—Frederick Trading Company; *U.S. Private*, pg. 335

GOLDENS—High Quality Audio/Video Cables—Recoton Corporation; *U.S. Public*, pg. 1369

GOLDET—NONE—Carl Zeiss Optical, Inc.; *Int'l*, pg. 1523

GOLDIE—NONE—Golden Books Family Entertainment Inc.; *U.S. Public*, pg. 749

GOLDIE—NONE—Pfizer Inc.; *U.S. Public*, pg. 1281

GOLDILOCKS—Cable—Loos & Co., Inc.; *U.S. Private*, pg. 675

GOLDILOCKS—Pan Cleaner—Reckitt & Colman plc; *Int'l*, pg. 1089

GOLDLINE—Servomotors, Power Amplifiers & Power Supplies—Kollmorgen Corporation; *U.S. Public*, pg. 965

GOLDLINK—Audio/Video Connector Plates & Accessories—Atlas/Soundolier; *U.S. Private*, pg. 64

GOLDMAN SACHS—Security Brokers—Goldman, Sachs & Co.; *U.S. Private*, pg. 462

GOLDRITE—NONE—Martin/F. Weber Company; *U.S. Private*, pg. 710

GOLDSCHLAGER—Spirits—Gilbeys of Ireland; *Int'l*, pg. 409

GOLDSCHLAGER—Cinnamon Schnapps—IDV North America; *Int'l*, pg. 411

GOLDSCHLAGER—NONE—Tegner & Son AB; *Int'l*, pg. 412

GOLDSCHLAGER SCHNAPPS—NONE—Grand Metropolitan Plc; *Int'l*, pg. 408

GOLDSMITH'S—Department Store—Federated Department Stores, Inc.; *U.S. Public*, pg. 617

GOLDSTAR—Automotive Aftermarket—Carfel, Inc.; *U.S. Private*, pg. 210

GOLDSTAR—Sugar—Tate & Lyle PLC; *Int'l*, pg. 1356

GOLDSTEIN—Frozen Cakes & Gateaux—GrandMet Foods GmbH; *Int'l*, pg. 409

GOLDWELL—Hair Care Products—Goldwell A.G.; *Int'l*, pg. 717

GOLDWELL—Hair Care Products—Goldwell Cosmetics (USA) Inc.; *Int'l*, pg. 718

GOLF—Magazine—Times Mirror Magazines, Inc.; *U.S. Public*, pg. 1616

GOLF—Automobile—Volkswagen AG; *Int'l*, pg. 1473

GOLF-BUOY—Drink Holders—Orbex Inc.; *U.S. Public*, pg. 238

GOLF CLUB—Fragrance—Jean Philippe Fragrances, Inc.; *U.S. Public*, pg. 924

GOLF DAY—Golf Equip.—Trend-Lines Inc.; *U.S. Private*, pg. 1099

GOLF EUROPEEN—French Golfing Magazine—EMAP France; *Int'l*, pg. 451

GOLF FOR WOMEN—Periodical—Meredith Corporation; *U.S. Public*, pg. 1094

GOLF GTI—Automobile—Volkswagen AG; *Int'l*, pg. 1473

GOLF INDUSTRY NEWS—Golf Magazine—EMAP Pursuit Publishing; *Int'l*, pg. 451

GOLF MONHTLY—Sports Magazine—IPC Magazines Limited; *Int'l*, pg. 651

GOLF PRIDE—Golf Grips—Eaton Corporation; *U.S. Public*, pg. 555

GOLF PRO—Business Publication—Fairchild Publications; *U.S. Public*, pg. 513

THE GOLF SPOT—Golf Program—Westwood One, Inc.; *U.S. Public*, pg. 1763

GOLF WEEKLY—Golf Magazine—EMAP Pursuit Publishing; *Int'l*, pg. 451

GOLF WORLD—Golf Magazine—EMAP Pursuit Publishing; *Int'l*, pg. 451

GOLIN/HARRIS—NONE—Shandwick International Plc; *Int'l*, pg. 1226

GOLPANOL—Specialty Chemicals for the Electropating Industry—BASF AG; *Int'l*, pg. 103

GOLTIX—Beet Herbicide—Bayer AG; *Int'l*, pg. 171

GOMCO—Portable Suction Equipment—Allied Healthcare Products, Inc.; *U.S. Public*, pg. 48

GOMOLJAK BLOCK—Masonry & Block Supply—Glen-Gery Corporation; *Int'l*, pg. 658

GONAL-F—Recombinant Follicle Stimilating Hormone—Ares-Serono S.A.; *Int'l*, pg. 80

GONIOCOLOR—Special-Effect Lacquers Measurement Device—Carl Zeiss; *Int'l*, pg. 1522

GONIOSCOPIC PRISM SOLUTION—Hydroxyethylcellulose—Alcon Laboratories, Inc.; *Int'l*, pg. 916

GONNELLA—French Bread & Rolls—Gonnella Baking Co.; *U.S. Private*, pg. 463

GONOZYME—Diagnostic Products—Abbott Laboratories; *U.S. Public*, pg. 12

GONZALES BYASS—Sherry & Brandy—Heublein Inc.; *Int'l*, pg. 410

GOO GOO CLUSTER—Chocolate Bar—Standard Candy Co., Inc.; *U.S. Private*, pg. 1030

GOOBER—Peanut Butter & Jelly Combination—J.M. Smucker Company; *U.S. Public*, pg. 1480

GOOBERS—Candy—Nestle Chocolate & Confection; *Int'l*, pg. 917

GOOBERS—Candy—Nestle S.A.; *Int'l*, pg. 915

GOOBERS—Candy—Nestle USA; *Int'l*, pg. 916

GOOCH—Foods—Gooch Foods, Inc.; *U.S. Public*, pg. 128

GOOD & PLENTY—Candy—Huhtamaki Oy; *Int'l*, pg. 638

GOOD ADVICE—Special Line of Painting Prods.—Premier Coatings, Inc.; *Int'l*, pg. 1488

GOOD ADVICE FROM GOOD HOUSEKEEPING—Practical Advice News Programming—Westwood One, Inc.; *U.S. Public*, pg. 1763

GOOD BEDROOM—Bedroom Furniture—Good Companies; *U.S. Private*, pg. 463

GOOD BUDDIES—Fruit Drinks—Green Spot Packaging Inc.; *U.S. Private*, pg. 477

GOOD CENTS APARTMENT—Energy Effecient Construction Program—Public Service Company of Oklahoma; *U.S. Public*, pg. 324

GOOD CENTS COMMERCIAL—Energy Efficient Construction & Reprofit Program—Public Service Company of Oklahoma; *U.S. Public*, pg. 324

GOOD CENTS HEAT PUMP—Maintenance Rebate Program—Public Service Company of Oklahoma; *U.S. Public*, pg. 324

GOOD CENTS HOME—Program to Certify Energy Efficiency of Residential Dwellings—Georgia Power Co.; *U.S. Public*, pg. 1490

GOOD CENTS IMPROVED HOME—Residential Energy Efficient Improvement Program—Public Service Company of Oklahoma; *U.S. Public*, pg. 324

GOOD CENTS INCENTIVE—Cash Payments for High Efficiency Heat Pump Changeouts—Public Service Company of Oklahoma; *U.S. Public*, pg. 324

GOOD CENTS NEW HOME—Energy Efficient Construction Program—Public Service Company of Oklahoma; *U.S. Public*, pg. 324

GOOD CENTS PRICE—Option for Certified Structures—Public Service Company of Oklahoma; *U.S. Public*, pg. 324

GOOD CHOICE—Food & Related Paper Products—Butler Wholesale Products, Inc.; *U.S. Private*, pg. 190

GOOD DAY—NONE—Albertson's, Inc.; *U.S. Public*, pg. 38

GOOD FOOD—Magazine—Good Food Magazine; *Int'l*, pg. 925

GOOD GRIPS—Kitchen Tools—General Housewares Corp.; *U.S. Public*, pg. 715

THE GOOD GUYS—Electronic Stores—The Good Guys, Inc.; *U.S. Public*, pg. 750

GOOD HOUSEKEEPING—Magazine—Good Housekeeping; *U.S. Private*, pg. 517

GOOD HOUSEKEEPING—Magazine—The Hearst Corporation; *U.S. Private*, pg. 515

GOOD HOUSEKEEPING—Magazine—Hearst Magazines Division; *U.S. Private*, pg. 516

GOOD HOUSEKEEPING—Magazine—The National Magazine Company Ltd.; *U.S. Private*, pg. 518

GOOD HUMOR—Ice Cream Products—Good Humor/Breyers Ice Cream; *Int'l*, pg. 1435

GOOD IDEAS—R.T.A. Furniture—Good Companies; *U.S. Private*, pg. 463

GOOD LOOK—Photographic Papers—Eastman Kodak Company; *U.S. Public*, pg. 550

GOOD MEASURE—Household Product—Bristol-Myers Squibb Company; *U.S. Public*, pg. 253

GOOD MORNING—Marmalade—J.M. Smucker Company; *U.S. Public*, pg. 1480

GOOD N' NATURAL—Vitamin Products—Nature's Bounty Inc.; *U.S. Public*, pg. 1166

GOOD NEWS—Twin Blade Disposable Razors & Toiletries—The Gillette Company; *U.S. Public*, pg. 743

GOOD NEWS—Confections—Nestle-Rowntree Ltd.; *Int'l*, pg. 921

GOOD NEWS BAG—Recycled Paper Bags—Stone Container Corporation; *U.S. Public*, pg. 1520

GOOD NEWS PIVOT PLUS—Disposable Shavers—The Gillette Company; *U.S. Public*, pg. 743

GOOD OLD DAYS—Nostalgia Magazine—House of White Birches, Inc.; *U.S. Private*, pg. 542

GOOD OLD DAYS SPECIAL ISSUES—Nostolgia Magazine—House of White Birches, Inc.; *U.S. Private*, pg. 542

GOOD ONE—Milk—Q.U.F. Industries Ltd.; *Int'l*, pg. 1074

GOOD SEASONS—Salad Dressing Mix—Kraft Foods, Inc.; *U.S. Public*, pg. 1287

GOOD SEASONS—Salad Dressings—Philip Morris Companies Inc.; *U.S. Public*, pg. 1287

GOOD SENSE—Plastic Tableware, Storage Bars—Chelsea Industries, Inc.; *U.S. Private*, pg. 231

GOOD TABLES—Occasional Furniture—Good Companies; *U.S. Private*, pg. 463

GOOD THINGS COOKIN, BREAKFAST, LUNCH & DINNER—Restaurant—IHOP Corp.; *U.S. Public*, pg. 862

GOOD VALUE—Private Label Grocery, Perishables & Frozen Foods—Fleming Companies, Inc.; *U.S. Public*, pg. 652

GOOD VIBES—Musical Instruments Mallets—Ludwig Industries; *U.S. Public*, pg. 1514

THE GOOD WATER PEOPLE—Service Mark; Construction, Installation, Maintenance of ED Equip.—Ionics, Incorporated; *U.S. Public*, pg. 912

GOOD WEEKEND—Lifestyle Magazine—John Fairfax Holdings Limited; *Int'l*, pg. 477

GOODALL—Commercial Mowers—Bunton Division; *U.S. Public*, pg. 1589

GOODALL'S—Salad Dressings & Seasonings—Bestfoods; *U.S. Public*, pg. 223

GOODALL'S—Table Sauces, Dressings, Mayonnaise, Herbs & Spices—CPC Foods (Ireland) Ltd.; *U.S. Public*, pg. 225

GOODFORM 11—Seating—GF Office Furniture; *U.S. Private*, pg. 435

GOODHOST—Coffee—Nestle S.A.; *Int'l*, pg. 915

GOODIES—Candy—Hershey Foods Corporation; *U.S. Public*, pg. 811

GOODLOE—NONE—Koch Otto H. York Co., Inc.; *U.S. Private*, pg. 628

GOODMAN'S—Pasta—Borden, Inc.; *U.S. Private*, pg. 157

GOODNIGHT—Nasal CPAP System—Nellcor Puritan Bennett Incorporated; *U.S. Public*, pg. 1039

GOODSPICE—Upscale Line of Herbs & Seasonings—M. Kamenstein, Inc.; *U.S. Private*, pg. 606

GOODWIN WEAVERS—NONE—Crown Crafts, Inc.; *U.S. Public*, pg. 465

GOODY—Hair Products—Goody Products, Inc.; *U.S. Public*, pg. 1177

GOODYEAR—NONE—Pacific Dunlop Limited; *Int'l*, pg. 1021

GOOSE EGGS—Easter Molded Milk Balls—New England Confectionery Co.; *U.S. Private*, pg. 1113

GORDON—Manufacturers Temperature Measurement Equipment—Watlow Gordon; *U.S. Private*, pg. 1153

GORDON PLASTICS—NONE—Plastigage Corporation; *U.S. Private*, pg. 871

GORDON'S GIN—Gin—United Distillers USA, Inc.; *Int'l*, pg. 412

GORDON'S VODKA—Vodka—United Distillers USA, Inc.; *Int'l*, pg. 412

GORDON'S—NONE—Guinness Plc; *Int'l*, pg. 412

GORDONS—London Dry Gin—La Tondena Distillers, Inc.; *Int'l*, pg. 785

GORDON'S JEWELERS—Jewelry Stores—Zale Corporation; *U.S. Public*, pg. 1789

GORE TEX—All-Weather Fabric—W.L. Gore & Associates, Inc.; *U.S. Private*, pg. 465

GORE-TEX—Fabric—The Timberland Company; *U.S. Public*, pg. 1609

GORGES—NONE—Gorges/Quik-To-Fix Foods; *U.S. Private*, pg. 465

GORHAM—Silver, Crystal & China—Brown-Forman Corporation; *U.S. Public*, pg. 261

GORHAM—Silverware—Dansk International Designs Ltd.; *U.S. Public*, pg. 261

GORHAM—Crystal, Sterling, Silverplated, Stainless Steel Flatware, Stemware & Gifts—Lenox Brands; *U.S. Public*, pg. 261

GORHAM—Crystal, China, Sterling, Stainless Flatware—Lenox, Incorporated; *U.S. Public*, pg. 261

GORILLA—Hose—The Goodyear Tire & Rubber Company; *U.S. Public*, pg. 752

GORILLA BAGS—Luggage—American Tourister, Inc.; *U.S. Public*, pg. 1430

GORILLA GRIP—Luggage Hardware—American Tourister, Inc.; *U.S. Public*, pg. 1430

GORILLA LOGO—Luggage—American Tourister, Inc.; *U.S. Public*, pg. 1430

GORILLABAND—Band Saw Blades—Sandvik/Milford Corporation; *Int'l*, pg. 1185

GORSHED—Golf Shoes—Mizuno Corporation; *Int'l*, pg. 884

GORTIFLEX—Machine Tool Covers—A&A Manufacturing Co.; *U.S. Private*, pg. 1

GORTITE—Machine Tool Covers—A&A Manufacturing Co.; *U.S. Private*, pg. 1

GORTON SELECT—Prepared Frozen Fish Filets—The Gorton Group; *Int'l*, pg. 1434

GORTON'S FISH MARKETFRESH—Frozen Fish Fillets—The Gorton Group; *Int'l*, pg. 1434

GORTRAC—Cable & Hose Carriers—A&A Manufacturing Co.; *U.S. Private*, pg. 1

GORTUBE—Cable & Hose Carriers—A&A Manufacturing Co.; *U.S. Private*, pg. 1

GOSLING TAPES—Tapes for Window Treatments—EZ International; *U.S. Private*, pg. 1192

GOSLING'S BLACK SEAL—Rum—Barton Incorporated; *U.S. Public*, pg. 300

GOSLING'S BLACK SEAL—Bermuda Rum—Marie Brizard Wines & Spirits USA; *U.S. Private*, pg. 702

GOSS—Web Offset Printing Presses—Goss Graphic Systems; *U.S. Private*, pg. 466

GOSSAMER BAY—NONE—E. & J. Gallo Winery; *U.S. Private*, pg. 438

GOSSARD—Bras & Co-ordinated Lingerie—Courtaulds Textiles Plc; *Int'l*, pg. 339

GOSYSTEM—Microcomputer Tax System for Accounting Firms—Computer Language Research, Inc.; *U.S. Public*, pg. 421

GOTHIC—Chinaware—The Homer Laughlin China Company; *U.S. Private*, pg. 653

GOTTA GO POTTY—Toilet Trainer—Century Products Co.; *U.S. Private*, pg. 226

GOTTCHAS—Greeting Cards—American Greetings Corporation; *U.S. Public*, pg. 77

GOTTLIEB—Dairy Products—Crowley Foods, Inc.; *Int'l*, pg. 752

GOURMET—Magazine—The Conde Nast Publications Inc.; *U.S. Private*, pg. 20

GOURMET—Sink—Elkay Manufacturing Company; *U.S. Private*, pg. 372

GOURMET—Magazine—Gourmet; *U.S. Private*, pg. 20

GOURMET—Garden Products—Jiffy Products of America, Inc.; *Int'l*, pg. 706

GOURMET—Petfood—Nestle S.A.; *Int'l*, pg. 915

GOURMET—Domestic Ranges and Cooktops—Wolf Range Co.; *U.S. Public*, pg. 1322

GOURMET BAKER—NONE—North America Foods; *U.S. Public*, pg. 901

GOURMET FOODS—Cajun Sunshine Wine & Pepper Sauce, Etc.—Reily Foods Company; *U.S. Private*, pg. 919

GOURMET GOLD—(100% Soy Oil) Shoestrings, Thin Cuts, Regular Cut, Steak House Fries—Lamb-Weston, Inc.; *U.S. Public*, pg. 427

GOURMET GRID—BBQ Grilltop Grilling Accessories—Porcelain Metals Corp.; *U.S. Private*, pg. 876

GOURMET SELECTION—Specialty Frozen Foods—Louis Kemp Seafood Co.; *U.S. Public*, pg. 1652

GOURMET SELECTION—Fresh Poultry—Tyson Foods, Inc.; *U.S. Public*, pg. 1652

THE GOURMET'S COMPANION—Magazine—John Wiley & Sons, Inc.; *U.S. Public*, pg. 1768

GOVERNAIR—Air Conditioners—Nortek, Inc.; *U.S. Public*, pg. 1192

GOVERNMENT COMPUTER NEWS—Magazine—The Washington Post Company; *U.S. Public*, pg. 1742

GOVERNMENT EMPLOYEES INSURANCE COMPANY—Insurance Company—Government Employees Insurance Co. (GEICO); *U.S. Public*, pg. 220

GOVERNMENT EQUIPMENT NEWS—Magazine—Reed Business Information Pty. Limited; *Int'l*, pg. 1094

GOVERNMENT PRODUCT NEWS—Periodical—Penton Publishing, Inc.; *U.S. Public*, pg. 1306

GOYA—Food Products—Goya Foods, Inc.; *U.S. Private*, pg. 468

GOYEN—Appliances—Southcorp Holdings Ltd.; *Int'l*, pg. 1287

GPS WORLD—Trade Periodical—Advanstar Communications; *U.S. Private*, pg. 22

GRABBAG—Software—The Mead Corporation; *U.S. Public*, pg. 1074

GRABBER—NONE—Blaw-Knox Construction Equipment Corporation; *U.S. Public*, pg. 877

GRABBER—Chair Mats—General Electric Canada Inc.; *U.S. Public*, pg. 713

THE GRABBER—Sporting Equipment—Brunswick Bowling & Billiards Corp.; *U.S. Public*, pg. 265

THE GRABBER—Cellulose Sponge—Spontex, Inc.; *Int'l*, pg. 1409

GRABBIN GRASSHOPPERS—Game—Tyco Toys, Inc.; *U.S. Public*, pg. 1058

GRABER—Window Products—Springs Industries, Inc.; *U.S. Public*, pg. 1499

GRACE—Clothing—Kosugi Sangyo Co., Ltd.; *Int'l*, pg. 759

GRACIAL—NONE—Akzo Nobel N.V.; *Int'l*, pg. 42

GRACIAS—Cheese Sauces—Comstock Michigan Fruit; *U.S. Private*, pg. 887

GRACIAS—Super Pop & Pops Rite—Comstock Michigan Fruit; *U.S. Private*, pg. 887

GRAD—Stationary Items—The Mead Corporation; *U.S. Public*, pg. 1074

GRAD G—Stationery Items—The Mead Corporation; *U.S. Public*, pg. 1074

GRADAL—NONE—Carl Zeiss Optical, Inc.; *Int'l*, pg. 1523

GRADE PRO—Construction Laser Equipment—Spectra-Physics Laserplane Inc.; *U.S. Public*, pg. 1594

GRADLINK—Data Parser—GenRad, Inc.; *U.S. Public*, pg. 731

GRADUATE—NONE—Life Technologies, Inc.; *U.S. Public*, pg. 504

GRADUATES—Toddler Foods & Toddler Care—Gerber Products Company; *Int'l*, pg. 973

GRADY'S AMERICAN GRILL—Upscale Full Service Restaurant—Brinker International, Inc.; *U.S. Public*, pg. 253

GRADY'S AMERICAN GRILL—Restaurant—Quality Dining Inc.; *U.S. Public*, pg. 1349

GRAF/PEN—Sonic Digitizer—GTCO Corporation; *U.S. Private*, pg. 436

GRAFCO—NONE—Graham-Field Health Products, Inc.; *U.S. Public*, pg. 757

GRAFFITI—Cameras—Eastman Kodak Company; *U.S. Public*, pg. 550

GRAFIKLEEN—Ink Cleaners-Printing—West Chemical Products, Inc.; *U.S. Private*, pg. 1158

GRAHAM—Wood Doors—Essex Industries, Inc.; *Int'l*, pg. 18

GRAHAM—Paint—Graham Paint and Varnish Company; *U.S. Private*, pg. 468

GRAHAM & GUNN LTD—Men's Clothing—Hartmarx Corporation; *U.S. Public*, pg. 795

GRAHAMAIRE—Air Cooled Condenser—Graham Corporation; *U.S. Public*, pg. 757

GRAHAMS—Cracker—Keebler Company; *U.S. Public*, pg. 657

GRAIN BELT—Beer—Minnesota Brewing Company; *U.S. Public*, pg. 1115

GRAIN BIN—Variety Bread—Stroehmann Bakeries, L.C.; *Int'l*, pg. 1495

GRAIN FLOW WITH CALCUDRI—In Bin Grain Dryer With Cal-Cu-Dry—David Manufacturing Company (DMC); *U.S. Private*, pg. 436

GRAIN HOG—Cycolac Scoop—Ames Company; *U.S. Public*, pg. 1683

GRAINFIELDS—Cereals—The Weetabix Company, Inc.; *Int'l*, pg. 1488

GRAINGERS—Multigrain Snacks—Borden, Inc.; *U.S. Private*, pg. 157

GRALAB—Timers—Dimco-Gray Company; *U.S. Private*, pg. 333

GRAM—Refrigerator Compressors & Freezers—EEI Corporation; *Int'l*, pg. 425

GRAM-PAC—Reagent Pockets—Fisher Scientific Company; *U.S. Private*, pg. 658

GRAMERCY—Wallcovering, Fabrics—F. Schumacher & Co.; *U.S. Private*, pg. 973

GRAMERCY PICTURES—Movie Distributor—Gramercy Pictures; *U.S. Private*, pg. 468

GRAMPAN—Bakers' Sundries—Royal Gist-Brocades N.V.; *Int'l*, pg. 1142

GRAN CHAMPION—Tires—Bridgestone/Firestone, Inc.; *Int'l*, pg. 213

GRAN CINZANO—NONE—Gio. Buton S.p.a.; *Int'l*, pg. 409

GRAN MELIA—NONE—Sol Melia; *Int'l*, pg. 1277

GRAN MOVE—1500 cc 2 Box—Daihatsu Motor Corporation, Ltd.; *Int'l*, pg. 364

GRAN-O-ROC—Top Press Roll Cover—Harnischfeger Industries, Inc.; *U.S. Public*, pg. 788

GRANARY—Bread—Ranks Hovis McDougall Limited; *Int'l*, pg. 1395

GRANCOURT GSTAAD—Tennis Shoe—K-Swiss Inc.; *U.S. Public*, pg. 937

GRAND AM—Car—Pontiac-GMC Division; *U.S. Public*, pg. 720

GRAND ANDY—3/4lb. Hamburger—Andy's Restaurants Inc.; *U.S. Private*, pg. 74

GRAND AUTO—Trucks—Paccar Inc.; *U.S. Public*, pg. 1246

GRAND BANKS—Diesel Cruiser—GB Holdings; *Int'l*, pg. 531

GRAND BANKS—Yachts—Grand Banks Yachts, Ltd.; *Int'l*, pg. 531

GRAND BANKS OUTFITTERS—Clothing—Harcrest International, Ltd.; *U.S. Private*, pg. 500

GRAND BAY HOTELS—Exclusive Collection of Grand Luxe Hotels With Five-Star Rating—Carnival Hotels & Casinos; *U.S. Public*, pg. 1265

GRAND BUFFET—All-You-Can-Eat Buffet—Ponderosa Steakhouse; *U.S. Private*, pg. 736

GRAND CARAVAN—NONE—The Cessna Aircraft Co.; *U.S. Public*, pg. 1589

GRAND DUKE—Imported Food Products—World Finer Foods, Inc.; *U.S. Private*, pg. 1190

GRAND FINALE—Catalogue—Harcourt General, Inc.; *U.S. Public*, pg. 782

GRAND HAVEN—Sofa/Chairs—Flexsteel Industries, Inc.; *U.S. Public*, pg. 653

GRAND ISLAND INDEPENDENT—Newspaper—Shivers Trading & Operating Co.; *U.S. Private*, pg. 994

GRAND'ITALIA—Italian Food—Danone Group; *Int'l*, pg. 379

GRAND LIFESTYLES—Bank Preferred Account Promotions—Bankers Systems Incorporated; *U.S. Private*, pg. 114

GRAND MACNISH—Scotch—Domecq Importers Inc.; *Int'l*, pg. 63

GRAND MANOR—Asphalt Roofing—CertainTeed Corporation; *Int'l*, pg. 1170

GRAND MANSION—NONE—Rubbermaid Incorporated; *U.S. Public*, pg. 1411

GRAND MANSION COLLECTIBLES—NONE—Rubbermaid Incorporated; *U.S. Public*, pg. 1411

GRAND MARNIER—Liqueur—Schieffelin & Somerset Co.; *Int'l*, pg. 412

GRAND MARNIER LIQUOR—Liquor—Dateo Import S.P.A.; *Int'l*, pg. 385

GRAND MARQUIS—Car—Ford Motor Company; *U.S. Public*, pg. 661

GRAND MASTER—Switch Machine—General Railway Signal Corp.; *Int'l*, pg. 1194

GRAND MERE—Coffee—Kraft Jacobs Suchard; *U.S. Public*, pg. 1290

GRAND MONARCH—Golf Clothing—Mizuno Corporation; *Int'l*, pg. 884

GRAND MONARCH XA—Golf Clubs—Mizuno Corporation; *Int'l*, pg. 884

GRAND OLD PARR TWELVE YEAR OLD—NONE—Guinness Plc; *Int'l*, pg. 412

GRAND PANAX—NONE—Carillon Importers, Ltd.; *Int'l*, pg. 409

GRAND PASSAGE—Doors—Georgia-Pacific Corporation; *U.S. Public*, pg. 735

GRAND PRIX—Passenger Car—General Motors Corporation; *U.S. Public*, pg. 718

GRAND PRIX—Car—Pontiac-GMC Division; *U.S. Public*, pg. 720

GRAND PRIX—Glazed Ceramic Tile—Porcelanite, Inc.; *Int'l*, pg. 573

GRAND RAPIDS—Carpet Sweeper—Bissell Inc.; *U.S. Private*, pg. 145

THE GRAND RAPIDS PRESS—Newspaper—Booth Newspapers, Inc.; *U.S. Private*, pg. 157

GRAND SLAM—Golf Clubs & Ball Bats—Hillerich & Bradsby Co.; *U.S. Private*, pg. 530

GRAND TOUR—Soft Baby Carrier—Evenflo Company, Inc.; *U.S. Private*, pg. 629

GRAND TRAVERSE—Fresh & Processed Fruit & Vegetables—Cherry Central Cooperative; *U.S. Private*, pg. 233

GRAND TRUCK WESTERN RAILROAD—Freight Railroads—Grand Trunk Corporation (GTC); *Int'l*, pg. 258

GRAND UNION—Supermarkets—The Grand Union Company; *U.S. Public*, pg. 758

GRANDADDY'S—Snack Foods—Wyandot Inc.; *U.S. Private*, pg. 1193

GRANDE—Tires—Bridgestone/Firestone, Inc.; *Int'l*, pg. 213

GRANDMA—Kosher Foods—Rokeach Food Distributing Inc.; *U.S. Private*, pg. 940

GRANDMA BESSIES—Ice Tea, Lemonade—Farmland Dairies; *U.S. Private*, pg. 395

GRANDMA'S—Molasses—Cadbury Beverages; *Int'l*, pg. 248

GRANDMA'S—Molasses—Cadbury Beverages North America; *Int'l*, pg. 248

GRANDMA'S—Fruit Cake—Metz Baking Company; *U.S. Private*, pg. 1022

GRANDMA'S—Seasonings—Williams Foods Inc.; *U.S. Private*, pg. 1178

GRANDMA'S BEST—Knitting Yarns—Caron International; *U.S. Private*, pg. 786

GRANDMA'S BRAND—Cookies—Frito-Lay Company; *U.S. Public*, pg. 1277

GRANDMA'S TUMMY MINT—Herb Tea—Celestial Seasonings; *U.S. Public*, pg. 319

GRANDMOTHER REMEMBERS—Diaries & Family Record Books—American Greetings Corporation; *U.S. Public*, pg. 77

GRANDOE—Dress Gloves—The Grandoe Corp.; *U.S. Private*, pg. 469

GRANDPA—NONE—SmithKline Beecham Corporation; *Int'l*, pg. 1264

GRANDPA—Analgesic—SmithKline Beecham plc; *Int'l*, pg. 1264

GRANDS!—Refrigerated Biscuits—The Pillsbury Company; *Int'l*, pg. 411

GRANDS REPORTAGES—French Travel Magazine—EMAP France; *Int'l*, pg. 451

GRANDY'S—Fast Food Restaurant Chain—Grandy's, Inc.; *U.S. Private*, pg. 61

GRANDY'S—Fast Food Chicken—BR Associates, Inc.; *U.S. Private*, pg. 107

GRANGER—High Frequency Antennas—Andrew Corporation; *U.S. Public*, pg. 112

GRANIT BRONZ—Bronze & Granite Products for the Memorial Industry—Cold Spring Granite Company; *U.S. Private*, pg. 250

GRANITE—Converting Paper—Champion International Corp.; *U.S. Public*, pg. 333

GRANITE STATE—Specialty Machine Equip.—Granite State Manufacturing Co.; *U.S. Private*, pg. 36

GRANITEWARE II—Cookware—General Housewares Corp.; *U.S. Public*, pg. 715

GRANITEX—Concrete Floor Sealer—Devoe Paint; *Int'l*, pg. 663

GRANITEX—Concrete Floor Sealer—ICI Paints; *Int'l*, pg. 664

GRANITO—NONE—Porcelanite, Inc.; *Int'l*, pg. 573

GRANJA—Consumer Turf Machinery—Ransomes Plc; *Int'l*, pg. 1087

GRANLON—Hot Melt Adhesive Systems—Norton Performance Plastics; *Int'l*, pg. 1174

GRANNING AIR SUSPENSION—NONE—Fluidrive Inc.; *U.S. Private*, pg. 415

GRANNY—Greeting Cards—American Greetings Corporation; *U.S. Public*, pg. 77

GRANNY GOOSE—Snack Foods—Granny Goose Foods, Inc.; *U.S. Private*, pg. 469

GRANNY'S—Tarts—Culinar Inc.; *Int'l*, pg. 348

GRANNY'S—Fruit Wines—Adams Wine Co.; *U.S. Private*, pg. 17

GRANNY'S BLOOMERS—Interior Plant Prods.—Security Lawn & Garden Co.; *U.S. Private*, pg. 397

GRANOCYTE—Neutropenia Treatment—Chugai Pharmaceutical Co., Ltd.; *Int'l*, pg. 290

GRANODINE—Metalworking Chemical—Henkel Surface Technologies; *Int'l*, pg. 610

GRANPAPPY—Electric Deep Fryer—National Presto Industries, Inc.; *U.S. Public*, pg. 1159

GRANPECHER—NONE—GW Archer & Co.; *Int'l*, pg. 409

GRANPOMIER—NONE—GW Archer & Co.; *Int'l*, pg. 409

GRANSIL—Granulated Ferrosilicon—Elkem ASA; *Int'l*, pg. 446

GRANTREE—Furniture Rental—Globe Furniture Rentals; *U.S. Private*, pg. 458

GRANT'S ALES—NONE—Stimson Lane Ltd.; *U.S. Public*, pg. 1661

GRANT'S FARM—Bread—The Earthgrains Company; *U.S. Public*, pg. 547

GRANT'S FARMS ESSENTIALS—Bread—The Earthgrains Company; *U.S. Public*, pg. 547

GRANUFINK—NONE—SmithKline Beecham Corporation; *Int'l*, pg. 1264

GRANUFINK—Stimulant—SmithKline Beecham plc; *Int'l*, pg. 1264

GRANULEX—Rx Topical Wound Spray for Chronic Ulcers—Dow Hickam Pharmaceuticals, Inc.; *U.S. Public*, pg. 1143

GRANULON—Spray-On Surfacing Material—Formica Corporation; *Int'l*, pg. 129

GRANUSIL—Fired Crushed Stone for Use in Construction Industry—General Electric Canada Inc.; *U.S. Public*, pg. 713

GRANY—Granola Snack—Danone Group; *Int'l*, pg. 379

GRAPE KING—Grape Juice—Giumarra Vineyards; *U.S. Private*, pg. 455

GRAPE NUTS—Breakfast Cereal—Kraft Foods, Inc.; *U.S. Public*, pg. 1287

GRAPEFRUIT DIET TABS—Natural Vitamin Pill—Health Products Corporation; *U.S. Private*, pg. 514

GRAPETEE—Soft Drink—Grant-Lydick Beverage Co.; *U.S. Private*, pg. 470

GRAPETTE—Soft Drink—The Monarch Company, Inc.; *U.S. Private*, pg. 756

GRAPH-AIR—Cold Work Die Steel—Latrobe Steel Company; *U.S. Public*, pg. 1617

GRAPH-COP—Paints & Coatings for Marine Use—Rule Industries, Inc.; *U.S. Public*, pg. 950

GRAPH-COTE—Paints & Coatings for Marine Use—Rule Industries, Inc.; *U.S. Public*, pg. 950

GRAPH-MO—Cold Work Die Steel—Latrobe Steel Company; *U.S. Public*, pg. 1617

GRAPHER—Graphical Evaluation Software—Harnischfeger Industries, Inc.; *U.S. Public*, pg. 788

GRAPHIC ARTS CERTIFIED—Photo Typesetters—AGFA EPS Division; *Int'l*, pg. 172

GRAPHIC ARTS FUNDAMENTALS—Textbook Covering Processes & Techniques Used in the Graphics Industry—Goodheart-Willcox Publisher; *U.S. Private*, pg. 464

GRAPHIC ARTS MONTHLY—Magazine for Buyers of Printing Equipment/Supplies at Commercial Operations—Reed Elsevier Business Information; *Int'l*, pg. 1095

GRAPHIC COMMUNICATIONS—Printing Technology Textbook—Goodheart-Willcox Publisher; *U.S. Private*, pg. 464

GRAPHIC DESIGNER'S BOOK CLUB—Book Club—F & W Publications, Inc.; *U.S. Private*, pg. 388

GRAPHICA—Wood Veneer—Georgia-Pacific Corporation; *U.S. Public*, pg. 735

GRAPHICOLOR—NONE—Avery Dennison Corporation; *U.S. Public*, pg. 152

GRAPHIGS—Software—International Business Machines Corporation; *U.S. Public*, pg. 895

GRAPHICS—Glazed Ceramic Tile—Porcelanite, Inc.; *Int'l*, pg. 573

GRAPHICS ASSISTANT—Software—International Business Machines Corporation; *U.S. Public*, pg. 895

GRAPHICWEAVE—Printing Paper—Georgia-Pacific Corporation; *U.S. Public*, pg. 735

GRAPHIKORE—Sign Panels—Baltek Corporation; *U.S. Public*, pg. 171

GRAPHLET—Pencil—Pentel of America, Ltd.; *Int'l*, pg. 1035

GRAPHLINE—Graphic Arts Products—GraphLine Inc.; *U.S. Private*, pg. 471

GRAPHLITE—Running Shoe Technology—Reebok International Ltd.; *U.S. Public*, pg. 1369

GRAPHPACK—Software Program For Microlab Instruments—Hamilton Co., Inc.; *U.S. Private*, pg. 497

GRAPHSIZE—Specialty Chemicals—Akzo Nobel Inc.; *Int'l*, pg. 47

GRAPHSIZE—Pulp & Paper Chemicals—Akzo Nobel N.V.; *Int'l*, pg. 42

GRAPHTOL—Pigments—Clariant International Ltd.; *Int'l*, pg. 624

GRAPICO—Soft Drink—Buffalo Rock Company; *U.S. Private*, pg. 179

GRAPPA DI BRUNELLO—NONE—Castello Banfi Srl.; *U.S. Private*, pg. 113

GRAPPA DI MOSCADELLO—NONE—Castello Banfi Srl.; *U.S. Private*, pg. 113

GRAPPLE—Contractor's Mechanical Grapple—Allied Construction Products, Inc.; *U.S. Public*, pg. 1339

GRAPPLER—Power-Fuse Handling Fitting—S & C Electric Company; *U.S. Private*, pg. 954

GRASIS—Guyed & Selfsupporting Towers—Andrew Corporation; *U.S. Public*, pg. 112

GRASSHOPPERS—Footwear—The Keds Corporation; *U.S. Public*, pg. 1525

GRASSHOPPERS—Footwear—The Stride Rite Corporation; *U.S. Public*, pg. 1524

Brand Name Index

GRASSZYME—Complex for Enhancing Feeding Value of Grass Silage—Cultor Ltd.; *Int'l,* pg. 349

GRATESTRIP—Caustic-Type Paint Stripper for Impolymerized Paint—PPG Industries, Inc.; *U.S. Public,* pg. 1245

GRAU—Heavy Duty Brake System Parts—Echlin Inc.; *U.S. Public,* pg. 560

GRAVABELT—Liquid-Solids Separation Equipment—Komline-Sanderson Engineering Corp.; *U.S. Private,* pg. 631

GRAVATRONIX—Natural Gas Instrumentation—Badger Meter, Inc.; *U.S. Public,* pg. 164

GRAVEL INFUSER—Sand Control—Baker Hughes Incorporated; *U.S. Public,* pg. 165

GRAVELMASTER—Crushing Machine—Svedala Industries-Universal Engineering; *Int'l,* pg. 1326

GRAVIBLEND—Blending System—K-Tron International, Inc.; *U.S. Public,* pg. 938

GRAVITY—Fragrance—Coty Inc.; *Int'l,* pg. 185

GRAVITY GEAR—Lifestyle—L.A. Gear, Inc.; *U.S. Public,* pg. 969

GRAVOFLEX—Laminated Engravable Plastic—New Hermes Incorporated; *U.S. Private,* pg. 793

GRAVOPLY—Laminated Engravable Plastic—New Hermes Incorporated; *U.S. Private,* pg. 793

GRAVY MASTER—Gravy, Seasoning & Browning Sauce—Gravymaster Inc.; *U.S. Private,* pg. 471

GRAVY TRAIN—NONE—Star-Kist Foods Inc.; *U.S. Public,* pg. 805

GRAY—NONE—Giddings & Lewis Automation Technology; *Int'l,* pg. 1389

GRAY/BRONZE—Float Glass—AFG Industries, Inc.; *Int'l,* pg. 84

GRAY-SEAL—Paint & Industrial Maintenance Coatings—Progress Paint Mfg. Co.; *U.S. Private,* pg. 890

GRAYBARNET—Computer Ordering—Graybar Electric Company, Inc.; *U.S. Public,* pg. 472

GRAYHIDE—Synthetic Blended Glove—Jomac, Inc.; *U.S. Private,* pg. 595

GRAYHOUND—Road-Paving Machines—Cedarapids, Inc.; *U.S. Public,* pg. 1365

GRAYLINE—Space-Savers—Grayline Housewares; *U.S. Private,* pg. 472

GRAYLITE—Gray Tinted Flat Glass—PPG Industries, Inc.; *U.S. Public,* pg. 1245

GRAYS BY GARY WASSERMAN—Clothing—Genesco Inc.; *U.S. Public,* pg. 728

GRAYS BY GARY WASSERMAN—Men's Tailored Clothing—Hartmarx Corporation; *U.S. Public,* pg. 795

GRAYS SPORTING JOURNAL—Magazine—Shivers Trading & Operating Co.; *U.S. Private,* pg. 994

GRAYSON CELLARS—Varietal Wines—The Beverage Source, Inc.; *U.S. Public,* pg. 591

GRAZEMASTER—Herbicide—The Dow Chemical Company; *U.S. Public,* pg. 522

GRAZER—Front-Cut Commercial Mowers—Ingersoll Equipment Co., Inc.; *Int'l,* pg. 1129

GRAZIA—General Iterest Women's Magazine—Kodansha Ltd.; *Int'l,* pg. 742

GRAZIN IN THE BRASS—Full Service Restaurants—Holly's Inc.; *U.S. Private,* pg. 535

GRAZIOSI—Wine—Leonard Kreusch, Inc.; *U.S. Private,* pg. 635

GRAZON—Herbicide—The Dow Chemical Company; *U.S. Public,* pg. 522

GREASE MONKEY—10 Minute Lube & Oil Pros—Grease Monkey International Inc.; *U.S. Public,* pg. 759

GREASE RELIEF—All Purpose Degreaser & Cleaner—The Dow Chemical Company; *U.S. Public,* pg. 522

GREASE RELIEF—Household Cleaner—DowBrands, L.P.; *U.S. Public,* pg. 1479

THE GREASEMAN SHOW—Talk Radio Program—Westwood One Entertainment; *U.S. Public,* pg. 1763

THE GREASEMAN SHOW—Comedy Show—Westwood One, Inc.; *U.S. Public,* pg. 1763

GREASESTRIP—Heavy Duty Liquid Degreaser—Ecolab Inc.; *U.S. Public,* pg. 562

GREAT—Meat Products—Gwaltney of Smithfield, Ltd.; *U.S. Public,* pg. 1479

GREAT—Guard Rail Energy Absorbing Terminal—Quixote Corporation; *U.S. Public,* pg. 1353

GREAT AMERICAN—Rubber Prods., Electronic Components, Household Appliances, Swimwear—Great American Industries, Inc.; *U.S. Public,* pg. 473

GREAT AMERICAN—Management & Investments—Great American Management & Investment, Inc.; *U.S. Public,* pg. 473

GREAT AMERICAN BEAR SERIES W/DESIGN—Stuffed Toy Figures—American Greetings Corporation; *U.S. Public,* pg. 77

GREAT AMERICAN BLUEBERRIES—Blueberries—Michigan Blueberry Growers Assn.; *U.S. Private,* pg. 740

GREAT AMERICAN DRUG STORES—Drug Stores—Genovese Drug Stores, Inc.; *U.S. Public,* pg. 730

THE GREAT AMERICAN TEDDY BEAR—NONE—The Vermont Teddy Bear Company, Inc.; *U.S. Public,* pg. 1716

GREAT BASEBALL—Videogame—Sega of America Inc.; *Int'l,* pg. 1218

GREAT BASKETBALL—Videogame—Sega of America Inc.; *Int'l,* pg. 1218

GREAT BEAR—Mineral Water—Nestle S.A.; *Int'l,* pg. 915

GREAT BEAR—Mineral Water—The Perrier Group of America; *Int'l,* pg. 919

GREAT BEARSPRING—Commercial & Industrial Refrigeration Equip. & Drinking Water—Great Bear Spring Company; *Int'l,* pg. 919

GREAT BEGINNINGS—Meat Chunks & Gravy—Hormel Foods Corp.; *U.S. Public,* pg. 840

GREAT BODY—Shampoo w/Protein & Conditioner—Clairol, Inc.; *U.S. Public,* pg. 254

GREAT BOOKS OF THE WESTERN WORLD—Books—Encyclopaedia Britannica, Inc.; *U.S. Private,* pg. 375

GREAT CLIPS—Hair Cut Franchise—Great Clips, Inc.; *U.S. Public,* pg. 473

GREAT COLOR—Make Up—Elizabeth Arden Company; *Int'l,* pg. 1435

GREAT DANE—Trailers—Great Dane Trailers, Inc.; *U.S. Private,* pg. 1030

GREAT DAY—Men's Hair Coloring—Clairol, Inc.; *U.S. Public,* pg. 254

THE GREAT DEAL COMPANY—NONE—Damark International, Inc.; *U.S. Public,* pg. 478

GREAT DEAL PACK—NONE—Damark International, Inc.; *U.S. Public,* pg. 478

GREAT DISHES—Cookware—Regal Ware, Inc.; *U.S. Private,* pg. 917

GREAT EARTH—Health Food/Vitamin Stores—Great Earth Distribution; *U.S. Private,* pg. 386

GREAT EXPECTATIONS PRECISION HAIRCUTTERS—Precision Haircutting & Customized Perming for Men & Women—Cutco Industries, Inc.; *U.S. Public,* pg. 470

GREAT FEELINGS—Permanent Wave—Revlon-Realistic Professional Products, Inc.; *U.S. Private,* pg. 690

GREAT FOOTBALL—Videogame—Sega of America Inc.; *Int'l,* pg. 1218

THE GREAT FRAME UP—Frame Stores—The Great Frame Up Systems, Inc.; *U.S. Private,* pg. 473

GREAT GLANCES—Portfolios—The Mead Corporation; *U.S. Public,* pg. 1074

GREAT GRAINS—Multi-Grain Breakfast Cereal—Kraft Foods, Inc.; *U.S. Public,* pg. 1287

GREAT GUACAMOLE—Dips—McCormick/Schilling; *U.S. Public,* pg. 1066

GREAT ICE HOCKEY—Videogame—Sega of America Inc.; *Int'l,* pg. 1218

GREAT IMPRESSIONS—Sauces, Salad Dressings, Vinegars, Olive Oils, Fruit Soups, Mustard—RCB Baking Company; *U.S. Public,* pg. 1354

GREAT LAKES—Blueberries—Michigan Blueberry Growers Assn.; *U.S. Private,* pg. 740

GREAT LAKES 50—NONE—Great Lakes Financial Resources, Inc.; *U.S. Private,* pg. 474

GREAT LASH—Mascara—Maybelline, Inc.; *Int'l,* pg. 819

GREAT LIFE—Paints—Sherwin-Williams Consumer Brands Division; *U.S. Public,* pg. 1466

GREAT NORTHWEST—Apparel—Fred Meyer Stores; *U.S. Public,* pg. 1103

GREAT OCEAN—Canned Goods—Camerican International; *U.S. Public,* pg. 426

GREAT PLAINS—Grain Drills & No-Till Hitches—Great Plains Manufacturing, Inc.; *U.S. Private,* pg. 475

GREAT PLAINS—Black Powder Bullets—Hornady Manufacturing Company; *U.S. Private,* pg. 539

GREAT PLAINS—Muzzle Loading Rifle—Lyman Products Corporation; *U.S. Private,* pg. 683

GREAT POSSIBILITIES—Magazine for Home Improvement & Ideas—Georgia-Pacific Corporation; *U.S. Public,* pg. 735

GREAT REWARDS—Servicing—SLM Holding Corp.; *U.S. Public,* pg. 1419

GREAT SHAKES—Foot Massager—Wahl Clipper Corp.; *U.S. Private,* pg. 1146

GREAT SHAPES—NONE—CertainTeed Corporation; *Int'l,* pg. 1170

GREAT SOCCER—Videogame—Sega of America Inc.; *Int'l,* pg. 1218

GREAT STARTS—Breakfast Entrees—Campbell Soup Company; *U.S. Public,* pg. 298

GREAT STARTS—NONE—Swanson; *U.S. Public,* pg. 299

GREAT STATE—Economic Development Program—Public Service Company of Oklahoma; *U.S. Public,* pg. 324

GREAT STATES—Worker's Compensation—PacifiCare Health Systems, Inc.; *U.S. Public,* pg. 1250

THE GREAT STEAMBOAT RACE—Riverboat Cruise Trips—American Classic Voyagers Company; *U.S. Private,* pg. 380

THE GREAT STUDENT DESIGNER AWARDS—Competition for Letterhead Design—The Mead Corporation; *U.S. Public,* pg. 1074

GREAT STUFF—One Component Urethane Sealant—Flexible Products Company; *U.S. Private,* pg. 412

GREAT STUFF—Poly-Urethane Foam Insulation & Sealing—Insta-Foam Products, Inc.; *U.S. Private,* pg. 412

GREAT SUNBELT—Blueberries—Michigan Blueberry Growers Assn.; *U.S. Private,* pg. 740

GREAT TIME—Clocks—Westclox; *U.S. Private,* pg. 445

GREAT VACATIONS INTERNATIONAL—Time Share Marketing Company—New Mexico & Arizona Land Co.; *U.S. Public,* pg. 1172

GREAT VIBRATIONS—Hand Held Shower Massage—Interbath, Inc.; *U.S. Private,* pg. 566

GREAT VOLLEYBALL—Videogame—Sega of America Inc.; *Int'l,* pg. 1218

GREAT WESTERN—Champagne, Varietals, & Dessert Wines—Canandaigua Wine Co.; *U.S. Public,* pg. 300

GREAT WOODS—Prefinished Wall Paneling—Georgia-Pacific Corporation; *U.S. Public,* pg. 735

GREATEST HITS—Stationery Products—The Mead Corporation; *U.S. Public,* pg. 1074

GREATEST SHOW ON EARTH—Entertainment Advertisement—Feld Productions; *U.S. Private,* pg. 399

THE GREATEST SHOW ON EARTH!—Circus—Ringling Bros., Barnum & Bailey Combined Shows, Inc.; *U.S. Private,* pg. 400

GREATWHITE—Coper, Laser Printer—Union Camp Corporation; *U.S. Public,* pg. 1665

GRECIAN FORMULA—Hair Coloring Product—Combe Incorporated; *U.S. Private,* pg. 257

GREDAG—Lubricants—Acheson Colloids Company; *U.S. Private,* pg. 12

GREEN APE—NONE—Boss Manufacturing Company; *U.S. Private,* pg. 1142

GREEN BAND—Abrasive Discs—Gardner Abrasives; *U.S. Public,* pg. 1699

GREEN BAND—Abrasive Discs—Litton Industries, Inc.; *U.S. Public,* pg. 1002

GREEN CHARGER—Fertilizer—Southern States Cooperative, Inc.; *U.S. Private,* pg. 1017

GREEN CORPS—Abrasive Discs & Sheets—3M; *U.S. Public,* pg. 1604

GREEN CREST—Insecticides, Herbicides & Fertilizers—Roussel Corporation; *Int'l,* pg. 625

GREEN DOT—Electrode—The Lincoln Electric Company; *U.S. Public,* pg. 996

GREEN GIANT—Food—Grand Metropolitan Plc; *Int'l,* pg. 408

GREEN GIANT—Canned & Frozen Sweetcorn—GrandMet Foods Southern Europe; *Int'l,* pg. 409

GREEN GIANT—Canned & Frozen Vegetables—GrandMet Foods UK; *Int'l,* pg. 408

GREEN GIANT—Canned, Frozen, Fresh Vegetables; Beans; Pasta & Rice Side Dishes—The Pillsbury Company; *Int'l*, pg. 411

GREEN GOLD—Fertilizer—Lebanon Seaboard Corporation; *U.S. Private*, pg. 656

GREEN GRANITE—Cover for Press Section, Size Press & Breaker Stack—Harnischfeger Industries, Inc.; *U.S. Public*, pg. 788

GREEN LABEL—Imagine Media—Labelon Corporation; *U.S. Public*, pg. 641

GREEN LABEL—Specialty Foods—Ranks Hovis McDougall Limited; *Int'l*, pg. 1395

GREEN LITE—Reflective Pavement Striping Powder & Striping Equipment—3M; *U.S. Public*, pg. 1604

GREEN MINT—Mouth Wash—Block Drug Company, Inc.; *U.S. Public*, pg. 236

GREEN MOUNTAIN—Coffee Filters—Green Mountain Coffee Roasters, Inc.; *U.S. Public*, pg. 761

GREEN RIM—Abrasive Discs—Gardner Abrasives; *U.S. Public*, pg. 1699

GREEN RIM—Abrasive Discs—Litton Industries, Inc.; *U.S. Public*, pg. 1002

GREEN SEAS—NONE—H.J. Heinz Company Australia Ltd.; *U.S. Public*, pg. 807

GREEN SLIME—Chewing Gum—Amurol Confections Inc.; *U.S. Public*, pg. 1781

GREEN SPOT—Fruit Drinks—Green Spot Packaging Inc.; *U.S. Public*, pg. 477

GREEN STRIPE—Fleet Engine Products—The Gates Rubber Company; *Int'l*, pg. 1396

GREEN TEA EXTRACT—NONE—Celestial Seasonings; *U.S. Public*, pg. 319

GREEN THREAD—Fiberglass Reinforced Plastic Piping—A.O. Smith Corporation; *U.S. Public*, pg. 1476

GREEN THUMB—Registered Art—Lawn Doctor Inc.; *U.S. Private*, pg. 653

GREEN TREE—Canned Hams—M.H. Greenebaum, Inc.; *U.S. Private*, pg. 477

GREENAL—High Alumina Brick—A.P. Green Industries, Inc.; *U.S. Public*, pg. 761

GREENBERG BOOKS—Books—Kalmbach Publishing Co.; *U.S. Private*, pg. 606

GREENBERG SHOWS—Consumer Shows—Kalmbach Publishing Co.; *U.S. Private*, pg. 606

GREENBRIER PARK—Rattan Furniture—Avon Workshop Ficks Reed; *U.S. Private*, pg. 102

GREENBURN—Combustion Improver Additive—Ethyl Corporation; *U.S. Public*, pg. 595

GREENCARB—Tar Impregnated, Coked Brick—A.P. Green Industries, Inc.; *U.S. Public*, pg. 761

GREENCAST—Castables—A.P. Green Industries, Inc.; *U.S. Public*, pg. 761

GREENEVILLE PRESS—NONE—American Greetings Corporation; *U.S. Public*, pg. 77

GREENFIELD—Cookies & Brownies—Campbell Soup Company; *U.S. Public*, pg. 298

GREENFIELD—Herbicide—The Dow Chemical Company; *U.S. Public*, pg. 522

GREENFIELD—Company Tradename—Greenfield Industries Inc.; *U.S. Public*, pg. 950

GREENGUN—Plastic Gunning Refractory—A.P. Green Industries, Inc.; *U.S. Public*, pg. 761

GREENHILL—Crackers—Fine Art Developments plc; *Int'l*, pg. 485

GREENHOUSE—Restaurant—Sonesta International Hotels Corporation; *U.S. Public*, pg. 1485

GREENIE—Grounding Wire Connector—Ideal Industries, Inc.; *U.S. Private*, pg. 557

GREENKLEEN—Aluminum Resistant Insulating Castable—A.P. Green Industries, Inc.; *U.S. Public*, pg. 761

GREENKON—Castables—A.P. Green Industries, Inc.; *U.S. Public*, pg. 761

GREENLEE—BX Cutter—Greenlee Textron; *U.S. Public*, pg. 1589

GREENLEE—Contractor Tools & Equip.—Textron Inc.; *U.S. Public*, pg. 1588

GREENLITE—Insulating Firebrick—A.P. Green Industries, Inc.; *U.S. Public*, pg. 761

GREENLITE EXPRESS—Free-flowing Insulating Castables—A.P. Green Industries, Inc.; *U.S. Public*, pg. 761

GREENMARK—Foods, Non-Foods, General Merchandise—Topco Associates, Inc.; *U.S. Private*, pg. 1091

GREENMUL—High Alumina Brick—A.P. Green Industries, Inc.; *U.S. Public*, pg. 761

GREENPAK—Plastic—A.P. Green Industries, Inc.; *U.S. Public*, pg. 761

GREENPRO—Garden Prod.—Lebanon Seaboard Corporation; *U.S. Private*, pg. 656

GREENRIVER—Boots & Waders—E.J. Footwear Corp.; *U.S. Public*, pg. 1684

GREENROD—Closed Cell Polyethelene Rod for Comml. Use—Nomaco, Inc.; *U.S. Private*, pg. 801

GREENS—Ice Cream—Kemps Foods, Inc.; *Int'l*, pg. 752

GREENS MASTER—Institutional Mower—The Toro Company; *U.S. Public*, pg. 1623

GREENSET—Mortar—A.P. Green Industries, Inc.; *U.S. Public*, pg. 761

GREENSKEEPER—Fertilizer—Lebanon Seaboard Corporation; *U.S. Private*, pg. 656

GREENSLEEVES—Shrink-fit Seamless Dampening Cover for Printing Presses—Jomac, Inc.; *U.S. Private*, pg. 595

GREENTOP—Gas Ball Valves—A.Y. McDonald Industries, Inc.; *U.S. Public*, pg. 721

GREENVIEW—Fertilizer—Lebanon Seaboard Corporation; *U.S. Private*, pg. 656

GREENWICH AIR SERVICES—Aviation Maintenance Base—Greenwich Air Services; *U.S. Public*, pg. 710

GREENWICH MILLS—Mfr. of Coffee, Tea & Dry Drink Mix—Chock Full O' Nuts - Food Service Div.; *U.S. Public*, pg. 351

GREENWILLOW—Books—The Hearst Corporation; *U.S. Private*, pg. 515

GREENWILLOW BOOKS—Juvenile Books—William Morrow & Co., Inc.; *U.S. Private*, pg. 515

GREENWOOD—Beets—Comstock Michigan Fruit; *U.S. Private*, pg. 887

GREENWOOD—Silver Floss—Comstock Michigan Fruit; *U.S. Private*, pg. 887

GREETING CANS—Gift Canisters of Popcorn—The Popcorn Factory; *U.S. Private*, pg. 421

GREGG—Food Products—A.E. Staley Manufacturing Co.; *Int'l*, pg. 1356

GREGG'S—Foodservice Products—Borden, Inc.; *U.S. Private*, pg. 157

GREGG'S GOLD-N-SOFT—Margarine—A.E. Staley Manufacturing Co.; *Int'l*, pg. 1356

GREGORY AND THE HOT AIR BALLOON—NONE—Broderbund Software, Inc.; *U.S. Public*, pg. 258

GREG'S—Cookies—President Baking Company; *Int'l*, pg. 1069

GREIF—Shipping Containers & Creative Packaging—Greif Brothers Corporation; *U.S. Public*, pg. 763

GREIF—Men's Tailored Clothing—Hartmarx Corporation; *U.S. Public*, pg. 795

GREITER—NONE—Johnson & Johnson; *U.S. Public*, pg. 927

GREMLINS—Carmel/Chocolate/Pecan Candy—Brown & Haley; *U.S. Private*, pg. 173

GRENADIER—Tires—Bridgestone/Firestone, Inc.; *Int'l*, pg. 213

GRESEN—Pumps, Control Valves, Filters—Dana Corporation; *U.S. Public*, pg. 479

GRESEN—Hydraulic Cylinders—Dana Corporation; *U.S. Public*, pg. 479

GRESEN—Pumps, Motors—Dana Corporation; *U.S. Public*, pg. 479

GRETCHEN—Greeting Cards—American Greetings Corporation; *U.S. Public*, pg. 77

GRETCHEN GRANT—Frozen Hors d'oeuvres—Van den Bergh Foods Company; *Int'l*, pg. 1436

GRETZKY 802—Roller Hockey Products—First Team Sports Inc.; *U.S. Public*, pg. 638

GREY KRAFT—Envelope—Champion International Corp.; *U.S. Public*, pg. 333

GREY POUPON—Mustards—Nabisco Inc.; *U.S. Public*, pg. 1355

GREY POUPON—Mustard—RJR Nabisco Holdings Corp.; *U.S. Public*, pg. 1354

GREY-ROCK—Brake Parts—Echlin Inc.; *U.S. Public*, pg. 560

THE GREY-TECH—Collection Cookware—Regal Ware, Inc.; *U.S. Private*, pg. 917

GREY-TECH COLLECTION—Aluminum Cookware—Regal Ware, Inc.; *U.S. Private*, pg. 917

GREY WATER ODOR CONTROL—Grey Water Holding Tank Deodorant—Thetford Corporation; *U.S. Private*, pg. 352

GREYHOUND—Transportation Line—Greyhound Lines, Inc.; *U.S. Public*, pg. 765

GREYHOUND—Intercity Bus Transportation—Greyhound Lines, Inc.; *U.S. Public*, pg. 765

GREYLOCK—Stock Preparation—Beloit Corporation; *U.S. Public*, pg. 789

GRIBETZ—Quilting & Cutting Machinery—Leggett & Platt, Incorporated; *U.S. Public*, pg. 985

GRID—NONE—AST Research Inc.; *Int'l*, pg. 1181

GRID PATTERN REED VALVE—Motorcycle—American Honda Motor Co., Inc. Motorcycle Division; *Int'l*, pg. 634

GRIDPAK—Antennas—Andrew Corporation; *U.S. Public*, pg. 112

GRIEF—Apparel—Genesco Inc.; *U.S. Public*, pg. 728

GRIESEDIECK—Beer—Falstaff Brewing Corporation; *U.S. Private*, pg. 955

GRIEVE—Ovens & Furnaces—The Grieve Corporation; *U.S. Private*, pg. 480

GRIFCOTE—Concrete Release Agents—Hill & Griffith Company; *U.S. Private*, pg. 529

GRIFFIN, LUCKY DUTCH, RAIDER & PRIZE TAKER—NONE—Griffin Manufacturing Co.; *U.S. Private*, pg. 481

GRIFFIN'S—Biscuits—Danone Group; *Int'l*, pg. 379

GRIFFITH—Downhole Tools—National-Oilwell/Dreco; *U.S. Public*, pg. 1158

GRIFULVIN V—Tablets—Ortho-McNeil Pharmaceutical Corporation; *U.S. Public*, pg. 929

GRIFULVIN V—Suspension—Ortho-McNeil Pharmaceutical Corporation; *U.S. Public*, pg. 929

GRIGIO TERLA—Perfume—International Cosmetics Co., Ltd.; *Int'l*, pg. 684

GRILL—Flavors—Kraft Food Ingredients Corp.; *U.S. Public*, pg. 1288

GRILL BITS—NONE—Star-Kist Foods, Inc.; *U.S. Public*, pg. 806

GRILL MATES—Seasoning—McCormick/Schilling; *U.S. Public*, pg. 1066

GRILL STIX—NONE—Star-Kist Foods, Inc.; *U.S. Public*, pg. 806

GRILL TIME—Charcoal—Royal Oak Enterprises, Inc.; *U.S. Private*, pg. 948

GRILLED CHICKEN SALAD DELUXE—Salad—McDonald's Corporation; *U.S. Public*, pg. 1068

THE GRILLER—Indoor Grill—Regal Ware, Inc.; *U.S. Private*, pg. 917

GRILLMASTER—Processed Meats—Hygrade Food Products Corporation; *U.S. Public*, pg. 1433

GRILLMASTER—Grills—Sunbeam Corporation; *U.S. Public*, pg. 1533

GRILLWORKS—Cutlery—General Housewares Corp.; *U.S. Public*, pg. 715

GRIME STOPPER—Service Products—R&B, Inc.; *U.S. Public*, pg. 1354

GRIND-O-MAT—Manual Grinder—The Rival Company; *U.S. Public*, pg. 1391

GRINDER PUMP—Low Pressure Sewer Systems—Environment/One Corporation; *U.S. Public*, pg. 586

GRINDMASTER—Coffee Grinders & Brewers—Grindmaster Corporation; *U.S. Private*, pg. 482

GRINDOX—Enzymes, Flavorings & Antioxidants—Danisco Ingredients; *Int'l*, pg. 378

GRINDSTED—Stabilizers—Danisco Ingredients; *Int'l*, pg. 378

GRINDSTED—Pectin, Alginate, LBG, Carrageenan Flavor, Enzyme—Danisco Ingredients USA, Inc.; *Int'l*, pg. 378

GRINDSTED CITREM—Food Emulsifier—Danisco Ingredients USA, Inc.; *Int'l*, pg. 378

GRINDSTED LACTEM—Food Emulsifier—Danisco Ingredients USA, Inc.; *Int'l*, pg. 378

GRINDSTED PGE—Food Emulsifier—Danisco Ingredients USA, Inc.; *Int'l*, pg. 378

GRINDSTED PGME—Food Emulsifier—Danisco Ingredients USA, Inc.; *Int'l*, pg. 378

GRINDSTED PS—Food Emulsifier—Danisco Ingredients USA, Inc.; *Int'l*, pg. 378

GRINDSTED STS & SMS—Food Emulsifier—Danisco Ingredients USA, Inc.; *Int'l*, pg. 378

GRINNELL—Fire Protection Products—Tyco International Ltd.; *U.S. Public*, pg. 1647

GRINNELL-SAUNDERS—Pipe Fittings—Grinnell Corporation; *U.S. Public*, pg. 1651

GRINNER BECHER—Dairy Products—Nestle S.A.; *Int'l*, pg. 915

Brand Name Index

GRIP—Conference Tables, ai Collection—Vecta; *U.S. Private*, pg. 1038

GRIP-IT—Strap & Chain Wrenches—Klein Tools Inc.; *U.S. Private*, pg. 625

GRIP-IT—Notebook Binders—The Mead Corporation; *U.S. Public*, pg. 1074

GRIP-IT SPINE & DESIGN—Binders—The Mead Corporation; *U.S. Public*, pg. 1074

GRIP LINER—NONE—Rubbermaid Incorporated; *U.S. Public*, pg. 1411

GRIP LOCK SYSTEM—Handbag System—Hartmann Luggage & Leather Goods Group; *U.S. Public*, pg. 261

GRIP-LUG—Grouser Bar—Allied Construction Products, Inc.; *U.S. Public*, pg. 1339

GRIP-MAT—Non-Slip Linen—Warp Brothers; *U.S. Private*, pg. 412

GRIP N'SERV SPOODLE II—Plastic Portion Control Server—The Vollrath Company, L.L.C.; *U.S. Private*, pg. 1143

GRIP-O-MATIC—Tools—SPX Corporation; *U.S. Public*, pg. 1420

GRIP SEAL—Envelopes—Westvaco Corporation; *U.S. Public*, pg. 1762

GRIP STRIP—Office Supplies—JM Company; *U.S. Private*, pg. 577

GRIP-TITE—Clip on Beryllium Copper Shielding Gasket—Instrument Specialties Company; *U.S. Private*, pg. 565

GRIP-TITE—Barettes for Fine Hair—Wilhold Inc.; *U.S. Public*, pg. 78

GRIPCO—Fasteners—The Black & Decker Corporation; *U.S. Public*, pg. 233

GRIPLET—NONE—Berg Electronics; *U.S. Public*, pg. 212

GRIPPER—Ceramic Golf Cleats—Coors Ceramics Company; *U.S. Public*, pg. 3

GRIPPER—Children's Toothbrush—Oral-B Laboratories; *U.S. Public*, pg. 743

GRIPPIT—Paper Adhesive—Sanford Corporation; *U.S. Public*, pg. 1178

GRIPRING—Retaining Ring—Waldes Truarc/ Industrial Retaining Ring; *U.S. Public*, pg. 1632

GRIPS-ALL—Envelopes—Westvaco Corporation; *U.S. Public*, pg. 1762

GRIPSTAY—Specialty Nails—Maze Nails; *U.S. Private*, pg. 718

GRIPTITE—Belting—HBD Industries, Inc.; *U.S. Private*, pg. 489

GRIPWELL—Handles—Hartwell Corporation; *U.S. Private*, pg. 1168

GRIS-PEG—Antifungal Tablets—Allergan, Inc.; *U.S. Public*, pg. 46

GRISANTI'S—Italian Restaurants—Grisanti, Inc.; *U.S. Private*, pg. 482

GRISEOFULVIN—Pharmaceutical Raw Materials— Nippon Kayaku Co. Ltd.; *Int'l*, pg. 934

GRISETIN—Antibiotic Preparations—Nippon Kayaku Co. Ltd.; *Int'l*, pg. 934

GRISSOL—Dry Bread Products—Culinar Inc.; *Int'l*, pg. 348

GRISTEDES—Grocery Stores—Red Apple Companies; *U.S. Private*, pg. 914

GRIT—Bi-Weekly Magazine—Ogden Publishing; *U.S. Private*, pg. 812

GRIT O' COB—NONE—The Andersons Incorporated; *U.S. Public*, pg. 111

GRIZZLY—Construction Tools—Klein Tools Inc.; *U.S. Private*, pg. 625

GRAND HYATT SEOUL—Korea's Most Prestigious Businessmen's Preferred Hotel— Grand Hyatt Seoul; *U.S. Private*, pg. 551

GRO & SHO—Electric Light Bilbs for Horticulture Use—General Electric Canada Inc.; *U.S. Public*, pg. 713

GRO-CELL—Garden Products—Jiffy Products of America, Inc.; *Int'l*, pg. 706

GRO-CELL GREENHOUSE—Garden Products— Jiffy Products of America, Inc.; *Int'l*, pg. 706

GRO-COATED—Field Seeds—Interstate Payco Seed Company; *U.S. Private*, pg. 573

GRO-DOME—Garden Products—Jiffy Products of America, Inc.; *Int'l*, pg. 706

GRO-TONE—Lawn Products—The Vigoro Corporation; *U.S. Public*, pg. 856

GROCER'S PRIDE—NONE—Richfood Pennsylvania; *U.S. Public*, pg. 1389

GROCERY PRO—Material Handling Equipment for Grocery Industry—Cannon Equipment; *Int'l*, pg. 646

THE GROCERY STORE—Convenience Stores— Farm Fresh, Inc.; *U.S. Public*, pg. 1388

GRODAN—NONE—EcoScience Corporation; *U.S. Public*, pg. 563

GROHE—Faucets & Shower Heads—Friedrich Grohe Armaturenfabrik GmbH & Co.; *Int'l*, pg. 559

GROKO—Frozen Vegetables, Potato Croquettes— Campbell Soup Company; *U.S. Public*, pg. 298

GROKO—Frozen Vegetables, Soups & Sauces— Danisco Foods; *Int'l*, pg. 378

GROLIER—Encyclopedias & Reference Materials—Grolier Inc.; *Int'l*, pg. 794

GROLSCH—Dutch Beer—Grolsch Importers Inc.; *Int'l*, pg. 559

GROLSCH—Pilsner Beer—Grolsch N.V.; *Int'l*, pg. 559

GROOM'N'EDGE—Outdoor Products—The Black & Decker Corporation; *U.S. Public*, pg. 233

GROOMEX—Animal Grooming Vacuum—HMI Industries; *U.S. Private*, pg. 771

GROOMSMAN—Cordless Beard & Mustache Trimmer—Wahl Clipper Corp.; *U.S. Private*, pg. 1146

GROOT VERBRUIK AHOLD—Food Distribution— Koninklijke Ahold NV; *Int'l*, pg. 749

GROOVE—Uncoated Embossed Paper—Champion International Corp.; *U.S. Public*, pg. 333

GROOVERS—Potato Chips—Borden, Inc.; *U.S. Private*, pg. 157

GROOVIES—Sporting Goods—Brunswick Bowling & Billiards Corp.; *U.S. Public*, pg. 265

GROSAFE—Plant Protection Carbon—NORIT N.V.; *Int'l*, pg. 958

GROSCHOPP—FHP Electric Motors, Gearmotors & Reducers—Groschopp & Co. GmbH EMW Elektromotoren-Feinbauwerk; *Int'l*, pg. 559

GROSJEAN—Dairy Products—Compagnie Laitiere BESNIER; *Int'l*, pg. 322

GROSS—Baked Sweet Snacks—Borden, Inc.; *U.S. Private*, pg. 157

GROSSET & DUNLAP—Books—The Putnam & Grosset Group; *Int'l*, pg. 1027

GROSSMANN—Chilled Salads—Bestfoods; *U.S. Public*, pg. 223

GROSVENOR—Cutlery & Silverware— McPherson's Limited; *Int'l*, pg. 852

GROTE—Vehicular Safety Lighting Products— Grote Industries; *U.S. Private*, pg. 483

GROUND GRIP—Tires—Bridgestone/Firestone, Inc.; *Int'l*, pg. 213

GROUND PROBE—Earth Resistivity Tester— Amprobe Instrument; *U.S. Public*, pg. 1676

GROUND ROUND—Family-Type Restaurants— Ground Round Inc.; *U.S. Public*, pg. 766

GROUND-TITE—Liquidtight Conduit Fittings with Integral Cast Lug for External Grounding—O-Z/ Gedney Co.; *U.S. Public*, pg. 727

GROUNDS MAINTENANCE—Publication for Grounds Care Practitioners—Intertec Publishing; *U.S. Public*, pg. 1327

GROUNDSKEEPER—Vacuums for Leaf & Yard Debris Removal—Highway Equipment Company; *U.S. Private*, pg. 529

GROUNDSKEEPER CARE—Tree & Lawn Care Services—The Davey Tree Expert Company; *U.S. Private*, pg. 314

GROUNDSMASTER—Institutional Mower—The Toro Company; *U.S. Public*, pg. 1623

GROUP ALTERNATIVES—Voluntary Group Life, Disability, Universal Life, Term & Stop Loss— American United Life Insurance Company; *U.S. Private*, pg. 64

GROUP ONE ANESTHESIA—NONE—Continental Medical Systems, Inc.; *U.S. Public*, pg. 839

GROUP ONE ANESTHESIA PLUS DESIGN— NONE—Continental Medical Systems, Inc.; *U.S. Public*, pg. 839

GROUP ONE NURSING—NONE—Continental Medical Systems, Inc.; *U.S. Public*, pg. 839

GROUP ONE THERAPY—NONE—Continental Medical Systems, Inc.; *U.S. Public*, pg. 839

GROUP RESOURCE—Newsletter Containing Insurance/Reinsurance Articles—Lincoln National Corporation; *U.S. Public*, pg. 997

GROUP 10—Heater & Air Conditioning Parts— Steering and Suspension Division; *U.S. Public*, pg. 443

GROVE—Valves & Actuators—Dresser Industries, Inc.; *U.S. Public*, pg. 528

GROVE AVENUE—Women's Sportswear— Catherines Stores Corporation; *U.S. Public*, pg. 317

GROVE/MANLIFT—Self Propelled Aerial Work Platforms—Grove WorldWide; *Int'l*, pg. 593

GROWERS RESERVE—100% Indian River Grapefruit Juice—Ocean Spray Cranberries, Inc.; *U.S. Private*, pg. 811

GROWING AWARENESS—NONE—Farm Press; *U.S. Public*, pg. 1328

GROWING PROFITS—Publication—Georgia-Pacific Corporation; *U.S. Public*, pg. 735

GROWING UP—Picture & Story Books—Golden Books Family Entertainment Inc.; *U.S. Public*, pg. 749

GROWING UP—Registered Trademark of Enesco Corporation for Figures—Stanhome Inc.; *U.S. Public*, pg. 1508

GROWISE RADIO NETWORK—Garden Radio Talk Show—Ray Communications, Inc.; *U.S. Private*, pg. 911

GROWMASTER—Hybrid & Varietal Seeds & Fertilizer—Southern States Cooperative, Inc.; *U.S. Private*, pg. 1017

GROWTH—Publication—Georgia-Pacific Corporation; *U.S. Public*, pg. 735

GROWTH POTENTIAL INTERFEROMETER— NONE—Zygo Corporation; *U.S. Public*, pg. 1795

GROWTH STOCK WINNERS—Financial Newsletter—KCI Communications, Inc; *U.S. Private*, pg. 784

GROWTTH—Get Rid of Waste Through Team Harmony—Freudenberg-NOK; *U.S. Private*, pg. 427

GRRIP—Plumbing Chemical—Hercules Chemical Co., Inc.; *U.S. Private*, pg. 523

GRRIP LITE—Plumbing Chemical—Hercules Chemical Co., Inc.; *U.S. Private*, pg. 523

GRRRAVY—Dog Foods—Ralston Purina Company; *U.S. Public*, pg. 1359

GRUMBACHER—Art Materials—Koh-I-Noor, Inc.; *U.S. Private*, pg. 629

GRUMMAN—Boats—Outboard Marine Corporation; *U.S. Public*, pg. 478

GRUNDIG ROLTRONIC PRO—Electric Shaver— Parks Products, Inc.; *U.S. Private*, pg. 840

GRUNDKORN—Fertilizers—DSM Chemie Linz GmbH; *Int'l*, pg. 356

GRUTILITIES—NONE—GenRad, Inc.; *U.S. Public*, pg. 731

GRUVEX—Carbide Groving Inserts—Allied Carbi-Tech, Inc.; *U.S. Private*, pg. 38

GRUVLOCK—Butterfly Valve—Kennedy Valve; *U.S. Private*, pg. 725

GRUVLOK—Fittings & Couplings—Grinnell Corporation; *U.S. Public*, pg. 1651

GRUYERE—Cheese—Schweizerische Kaseunion AG; *Int'l*, pg. 1211

GRYO STACK—NONE—AGA Gas, Inc.; *Int'l*, pg. 13

GSTAAD—Tennis Shoe—K-Swiss Inc.; *U.S. Public*, pg. 937

GUAIFED—Expectorant-Decongestant—Muro Pharmaceutical, Inc.; *U.S. Private*, pg. 767

GUAIMAX-D—NONE—Schwarz Pharma Inc.; *Int'l*, pg. 1211

GUAIMAX-D—Pharmaceutical Products—Schwarz Pharma Manufacturing, Inc.; *Int'l*, pg. 1211

GUARANTEED DELIVERY—Service Guarantee— DHL Worldwide Express; *U.S. Private*, pg. 301

GUARANTEED TOUGH—Power Tools—The Black & Decker Corporation; *U.S. Public*, pg. 233

GUARANTEED.PERIOD.—Guarantee—Lands' End, Inc.; *U.S. Public*, pg. 977

GUARANTY CALL—NONE—Deposit Guaranty Corp.; *U.S. Public*, pg. 500

GUARANTY CHEK—NONE—Deposit Guaranty Corp.; *U.S. Public*, pg. 500

GUARANTY FIRST—NONE—Deposit Guaranty Corp.; *U.S. Public*, pg. 500

GUARANTY GOLD—NONE—Deposit Guaranty Corp.; *U.S. Public*, pg. 500

GUARANTY LINK—NONE—Deposit Guaranty Corp.; *U.S. Public*, pg. 500

GUARANTY SELECT—NONE—Deposit Guaranty Corp.; *U.S. Public*, pg. 500

GUARD—Wallcoverings—Borden, Inc.; *U.S. Private*, pg. 157

GUARD-PAK—Precolumn Insert & Module, Anion Kit & Inserts—Millipore Corporation; *U.S. Public*, pg. 1112

GUARD-RITE—Protective Railing System—Rite-Hite Corporation; *U.S. Private*, pg. 933

GUARD-SEAL—Closures—White Cap, Inc.; *Int'l*, pg. 1207

GUARDIAN—Combustion Scrubber—ATMI, Inc.; *U.S. Public*, pg. 12

GUARDIAN—Eye Glass Holder—Brimms Inc.; *U.S. Private*, pg. 169

GUARDIAN—Plastic Guideposts—Bunzl Extrusion; *Int'l*, pg. 232

GUARDIAN—Fall Arrestor Gear—Columbus McKinnon Corp.; *U.S. Public*, pg. 405

GUARDIAN—Warewashing Detergents & Dispenser—Ecolab Inc.; *U.S. Public*, pg. 562

GUARDIAN—Survival Knives—Fiskars-Gerber; *Int'l*, pg. 492

GUARDIAN—Pumps—Flowserve Corporation; *U.S. Public*, pg. 658

GUARDIAN—FEP-Lined Expansion Joint—Garlock Sealing Technologies; *U.S. Public*, pg. 402

GUARDIAN—Wires, Cables & Cords—General Cable Corporation; *Int'l*, pg. 1486

GUARDIAN—Scraper Matting - Carpet—Golden Star Inc.; *U.S. Private*, pg. 460

GUARDIAN—Fire Hydrant—Kennedy Valve; *U.S. Private*, pg. 725

GUARDIAN—Sectional Residential Garage Doors—McKee Door, Inc.; *U.S. Public*, pg. 69

GUARDIAN—Standard Quiet Lockers—Penco Products; *U.S. Private*, pg. 848

GUARDIAN—Filtration System—Serfilco, Ltd.; *U.S. Private*, pg. 985

GUARDIAN—Locksmiths' Work, Safes & Cash Boxes—Sime Darby Berhad; *Int'l*, pg. 1249

GUARDIAN—Ambulatory Aids & Bath Safety Products—Sunrise Medical, Inc.; *U.S. Public*, pg. 1535

GUARDIAN—Operating Systems—Tandem Computers Inc.; *U.S. Public*, pg. 417

GUARDIAN INSURE—Machine Warewashing Detergent—Ecolab Inc.; *U.S. Public*, pg. 562

GUARDIAN 90—Operating System—Tandem Computers Inc.; *U.S. Public*, pg. 417

GUARDIAN SAFETY—Flat Glass—Guardian Industries Corp.; *U.S. Private*, pg. 485

THE GUARDIAN—Insurance—The Guardian Life Insurance Company of America; *U.S. Private*, pg. 486

GUARDIAWN—awning—Carefree of Colorado; *U.S. Public*, pg. 217

GUARDLINE—Audiotex Information Service Accessed by Touchtone Phone—Guard Publishing Company; *U.S. Private*, pg. 485

GUARDNET—Domain Name With Home Page in Development—Guard Publishing Company; *U.S. Private*, pg. 485

GUARDSMAN—Battery Line for Specialized UPS Applications—C&D Charter Power Systems; *U.S. Public*, pg. 271

GUARDSMAN—Watchman's Clocks—Detex Corporation; *U.S. Private*, pg. 327

GUARDSMAN—Shingles—Johns Manville Corporation; *U.S. Public*, pg. 927

GUARDSMAN—Herbicide—Sandoz Agro, Inc.; *Int'l*, pg. 974

GUARDSMARK—Security Systems & Services—Guardsmark, Inc.; *U.S. Private*, pg. 486

GUARTEC—Gum Products—Henkel Corporation; *Int'l*, pg. 610

GUCCI—Shoes—Guccio Gucci S.p.A.; *Int'l*, pg. 686

GUDELACE—Electronic Lacing Tape—Gudebrod, Inc.; *U.S. Private*, pg. 486

GUESS—Women's Jeans—Guess ?, Inc.; *U.S. Public*, pg. 768

GUESS?—Undergarments—Nantucket Industries, Inc.; *U.S. Public*, pg. 1151

GUESS SPORTSWEAR—NONE—Guess ?, Inc.; *U.S. Public*, pg. 768

GUESS WHO?—Game—Milton Bradley Company; *U.S. Public*, pg. 797

GUESS?—Women's Jewelry Men's Personnel Leather—Swank, Inc.; *U.S. Public*, pg. 1543

GUEST—Battery Chargers, Spotlights & Safety Lights—Valley Forge Corporation; *U.S. Public*, pg. 1705

GUEST RANCH—Paper Towels, Paper Napkins, Bathroom Tissue & Facial Tissue—Georgia-Pacific Corporation; *U.S. Public*, pg. 735

GUEST READY—Food Products—Rymer Foods Inc.; *U.S. Public*, pg. 1414

GUEST STACKER—Stackable Side Chair—CorryHiebert Corporation; *U.S. Public*, pg. 772

GUEST STACKER—NONE—The HON Co.; *U.S. Public*, pg. 772

GUILTLESS INDULGENCE—Fat Free, Low Fat Cookies—Cookie Tree Inc.; *U.S. Private*, pg. 273

GUIDE GRIP—Tires—Bridgestone/Firestone, Inc.; *Int'l*, pg. 213

GUIDE GRIP 3-RIB—Tires—Bridgestone/Firestone, Inc.; *Int'l*, pg. 213

GUIDE TO DIPLOMACY—Booklet—Monarch Avalon, Inc.; *U.S. Public*, pg. 1123

GUIDE TO GOOD FOOD—Textbook for Management & Preparation of Food—Goodheart-Willcox Publisher; *U.S. Private*, pg. 464

GUIDE TO NEW AUSTRALIAN BOOKS—Directory—Reed Business Information Pty. Limited; *Int'l*, pg. 1094

GUIDELINE—Solder Paste—Alpha Metals, Inc.; *Int'l*, pg. 328

GUIDEMASTER—Electric Hose Guide—Hannay Reels; *U.S. Private*, pg. 499

GUIDEROL—Full Complement Roller Bearings—McGill Manufacturing Company, Inc.; *U.S. Public*, pg. 573

GUIDEX TYPE II PRESSBOARD—Type Two Pressboard—FiberMark Inc.; *U.S. Public*, pg. 620

GUIGOZ—Dietetic Products—Nestle S.A.; *Int'l*, pg. 915

GUILD—Acoustic Guitars—Fender Musical Instruments; *U.S. Private*, pg. 400

GUILD—Jigsaw Puzzles—Golden Books Family Entertainment Inc.; *U.S. Public*, pg. 749

GUILD HOUSE—Candles—American Greetings Corporation; *U.S. Public*, pg. 77

GUILD HOUSE—Candles, Greeting Cards—American Greetings U.S. Greeting Card Division; *U.S. Public*, pg. 78

GUILDWARE—Plastic Cutlery—Sweetheart Cup Company Inc.; *U.S. Private*, pg. 1058

GUILDWAY TIMBER STRUCTURES—Timber Frame—Meyer International PLC; *Int'l*, pg. 864

GUILFORD—Appointment Books—The At-A-Glance Group; *U.S. Private*, pg. 295

GUILFORD—Fabrics & Wallcoverings—Guilford of Maine, Inc.; *U.S. Public*, pg. 889

GUILFORD OF MAINE—Fabrics—Interface Inc.; *U.S. Public*, pg. 889

GUILLAUME M. DUMONS—Wine—Andres Wines Ltd.; *Int'l*, pg. 75

GUILMARK—Recreational Van Conversion Fabrics—Guilford Mills, Inc.; *U.S. Public*, pg. 768

GUINNESS—Stout—Guinness Import Company; *Int'l*, pg. 412

GUINNESS DRAUGHT BITTER—NONE—Guinness Plc; *Int'l*, pg. 412

GUINNESS EXTRA STOUT—NONE—Guinness Plc; *Int'l*, pg. 412

GUINNESS FOREIGN EXTRA STOUT—NONE—Guinness Plc; *Int'l*, pg. 412

GUINNESS GOLD—Golden Lager—Guinness Import Company; *Int'l*, pg. 412

GUINNESS ORIGINAL—NONE—Guinness Plc; *Int'l*, pg. 412

GUITAR PLAYER—Magazine—Miller Freeman Inc.; *Int'l*, pg. 1443

GULDEN'S—Mustard—International Home Foods Inc.; *U.S. Private*, pg. 526

GULF—Power—Gulf Power Company; *U.S. Public*, pg. 1490

GULF BELLE—Shrimp & Oysters—The Pillsbury Company; *Int'l*, pg. 411

GULF-SEAL—Cements & Coatings—Gulf States Asphalt Company, Inc.; *U.S. Private*, pg. 487

GULF STATES—Utilities—Entergy Gulf States, Inc.; *U.S. Public*, pg. 586

GULFBRITE—Market Pulp—Boise Cascade Corporation; *U.S. Public*, pg. 242

GULFMASTER—Marine Crane—Weatherford Enterra Incorporated; *U.S. Public*, pg. 1749

GULFSTREAM—Seafood—King & Prince Seafood Corporation; *U.S. Private*, pg. 620

GULFSTREM CORPORATE—Business Jet & SRA-4—Gulfstream Aerospace Corporation; *U.S. Private*, pg. 419

GUM-DIPPED—Tires—Bridgestone/Firestone, Inc.; *Int'l*, pg. 213

GUM DROPS—Men's & Women's Footwear—J. Baker, Inc.; *U.S. Public*, pg. 167

GUMMI SAVERS—Candy—Nabisco Inc.; *U.S. Public*, pg. 1355

GUMP'S—Retail Specialty Gift Stores—Gump's; *U.S. Public*, pg. 782

GUMP'S—Upscale Catalog-Exclusive Gifts—Hanover Direct, Inc.; *U.S. Public*, pg. 782

GUNDLACH-BUNDSCHU—Wine—Pacific Wine Co.; *U.S. Private*, pg. 843

GUNDRY—Retrograde Cannula—Medtronic, Inc.; *U.S. Public*, pg. 1082

GUNDSEAL—Polyethelyne Liner Laminated to a Layer of Bentonite Clay—Gundle/SLT Environmental, Inc.; *U.S. Public*, pg. 769

GUNG HO—War Game—Monarch Avalon, Inc.; *U.S. Public*, pg. 1123

GUNITE—Truck Components—Gunite Corporation; *U.S. Public*, pg. 933

GUNJET—Spray Gun—Spraying Systems Co.; *U.S. Private*, pg. 1026

GUNK—Cleaning Compound, Degreaser—Radiator Specialty Company; *U.S. Private*, pg. 906

GUNKING—Computerized Variable-Beam Laser Sighting System—Oerlikon-Contraves AG; *Int'l*, pg. 998

GUNMASTER—Gun Cases—Delta Consolidated Industries, Inc. (Co. Headquarters); *U.S. Public*, pg. 481

GUNNEBO—Wire & Wire Products, Fencing—Gunnebo Industrier AB; *Int'l*, pg. 578

GUNS & AMMO—Magazine—Petersen Publishing Company, L.L.C.; *U.S. Private*, pg. 856

GUNSTAR—Compact Fire Control System—Oerlikon-Contraves AG; *Int'l*, pg. 998

GUNSTONES—Christmas Puddings & Pies—Northern Foods plc; *Int'l*, pg. 967

GUNZO—Monthly Japanese Literary Magazine—Kodansha Ltd.; *Int'l*, pg. 742

GUPPIES—Fish-Shaped Candy Tablets—Nestle Chocolate & Confection; *Int'l*, pg. 917

GUPPIES—Fish-Shaped Candy Tablets—Nestle S.A.; *Int'l*, pg. 915

GUPPIES—Crackers—Snack America; *U.S. Private*, pg. 1010

GURLEY'S—Cookies, Candy & Confectionary Items—Metz Baking Company (WI); *U.S. Private*, pg. 1022

GUSHER PUMPS—Pumps—Gusher Pumps, Inc.; *U.S. Private*, pg. 488

GUSHERS—Fruit Snacks—General Mills, Inc.; *U.S. Public*, pg. 717

GUSTAV—Barware—Dansk International Designs Ltd.; *U.S. Public*, pg. 261

GUSTO—Dining House—Skylark Co., Ltd.; *Int'l*, pg. 1262

GUTH—Lighting—JJI Lighting Group Inc.; *Int'l*, pg. 821

GUTHION—Insecticide—Bayer AG; *Int'l*, pg. 171

GUTTALAX—Laxative—Boehringer Ingelheim Italia S.p.A.; *Int'l*, pg. 199

GUTTER HELMET—Gutter Protection—American Metal Products; *U.S. Public*, pg. 1053

GUY-A-WIRE—Wire—Elco Textron; *U.S. Public*, pg. 1590

GUY CARPENTER—Reinsurance Broking Services—Marsh & McLennan Companies, Inc.; *U.S. Public*, pg. 1048

GUY F. ATKINSON—Heavy, Civil Construction & Manufacturing Operations—Atkinson; *U.S. Public*, pg. 143

GUY LAROCHE—Perfumes—Cosmair, Inc.; *Int'l*, pg. 818

GUY LAROCHE—Men's Apparel—International Cosmetics Co., Ltd.; *Int'l*, pg. 684

GUY LAROCHE—Women's Apparel—International Cosmetics Co., Ltd.; *Int'l*, pg. 684

GUY LAROCHE—Perfume—L'Oreal S.A.; *Int'l*, pg. 818

GUYS AND DOLLS—Permanent Wave Setting Solution—Revlon-Realistic Professional Products, Inc.; *U.S. Private*, pg. 690

GUY'S FOODS—Snack Foods—Family Smacks, Inc.; *U.S. Private*, pg. 393

GUZZLER—Vacuum Trucks—Federal Signal Corporation; *U.S. Public*, pg. 616

Brand Name Index

GUZZLER—Industrial Vacuum—Philip Industrial Services Group; *Int'l*, pg. 1050

GWALTNEY—Meat Products—Gwaltney of Smithfield, Ltd.; *U.S. Public*, pg. 1479

GWALTNEY—Processed Meats—Smithfield Foods, Inc.; *U.S. Public*, pg. 1479

GYLON—Gasketing—Garlock Sealing Technologies; *U.S. Public*, pg. 402

GYMCORK—Cork Flooring—Dodge Regupol, Inc.; *U.S. Private*, pg. 337

GYNE-ELECTRODE—Uterus Resectioning Instruments—The Cooper Companies, Inc.; *U.S. Public*, pg. 442

GYNE-LOTRIMIN—Vaginal Yeast Infection Antifungal—Schering-Plough Corporation; *U.S. Public*, pg. 1438

GYNE-LOTRIMIN—Vaginal Anti-Fungal—Schering-Plough Healthcare Products Inc.; *U.S. Public*, pg. 1438

GYNE-MOISTRIN—Moisturizing Gel for Vaginal Dryness—Schering-Plough Corporation; *U.S. Public*, pg. 1438

GYNE-MOISTRIN—Vaginal Moisturizer—Schering-Plough Healthcare Products Inc.; *U.S. Public*, pg. 1438

GYNE-RESECTOSCOPE—Uterus Resectioning Equipment—The Cooper Companies, Inc.; *U.S. Public*, pg. 442

GYNECORT—Feminine Cream Medication—Combe Incorporated; *U.S. Private*, pg. 257

GYNECURE—NONE—Pfizer Inc.; *U.S. Public*, pg. 1281

GYNESTREL—Naproxen Sodium, Gynecology—Recordati Industria Chimica e Farmaceutica S.p.A.; *Int'l*, pg. 1090

GYNO-ELECTRODE—Uterus Resectioning Instruments—The Cooper Companies, Inc.; *U.S. Public*, pg. 442

GYNO-RESECTOSCOPE—Uterus Resectioning Equipment—The Cooper Companies, Inc.; *U.S. Public*, pg. 442

GYNOL—NONE—Johnson & Johnson; *U.S. Public*, pg. 927

GYNOL II—Contraceptive Jelly—Ortho-McNeil Pharmaceutical Corporation; *U.S. Public*, pg. 929

GYNOL II—Extra Strength—Ortho-McNeil Pharmaceutical Corporation; *U.S. Public*, pg. 929

GYP-GRIP—Screws—Georgia-Pacific Corporation; *U.S. Public*, pg. 735

GYPORE—Plasterboard—Scancem AB; *Int'l*, pg. 1198

GYPROC—Gypsom Board—Domtar Inc.; *Int'l*, pg. 416

GYPROCK—Plasterboard—CSR Limited; *Int'l*, pg. 245

GYRASPHERE—Rock Crushers—Telsmith, Inc.; *U.S. Public*, pg. 141

GYRO—Motorscooters—American Honda Motor Co., Inc. Motorcycle Division; *Int'l*, pg. 634

GYRO—Shaving Cream—The Gillette Company; *U.S. Public*, pg. 743

GYRO LIFT—Lifting Device for Precast Concrete—Richmond Screw Anchor Company; *U.S. Private*, pg. 932

GYRO TILT PLUS—Lifting Device for Concrete Walls—Richmond Screw Anchor Company; *U.S. Private*, pg. 932

GYROCHIP—NONE—BEI Technologies, Inc.; *U.S. Public*, pg. 160

GYROCHIP—NONE—Systron Donner-Inertial Division; *U.S. Public*, pg. 160

GYROFLEX GYRO—Gyroscope—Kearfott Guidance & Navigation Corp.; *U.S. Private*, pg. 93

GYROL—Fluid Drive—The Howden Fan Co.; *U.S. Private*, pg. 543

GYROLAB—Spatial Orientation Trainer—Environmental Tectonics Corporation (ETC); *U.S. Public*, pg. 587

GYROLTROL—Control of Fluid Drives—The Howden Fan Co.; *U.S. Private*, pg. 543

GYROSCAN—Imaging Systems—Philips Electronics N.V.; *Int'l*, pg. 1051

GYROSIM—Dynamic Flight Simulator—Environmental Tectonics Corporation (ETC); *U.S. Public*, pg. 587

GYROSTAR—NONE—Murata Manufacturing Co., Ltd.; *Int'l*, pg. 897

GYROTOR—Mining & Chemical Machinery—Svedala Industries Inc.; *Int'l*, pg. 1325

GYROTORY—Biological Shakers—New Brunswick Scientific Co., Inc.; *U.S. Public*, pg. 1169

H

HACMP/6000—Computer System—International Business Machines Corporation; *U.S. Public*, pg. 895

HAK—Vegetables & Fruit In Glass Jars—CSM N.V.; *Int'l*, pg. 243

HAK EXTRA—Vegetables in Glass Jars—CSM N.V.; *Int'l*, pg. 243

HAZ-EX—Hazardous Exposure Computer Model—Ecology and Environment, Inc.; *U.S. Public*, pg. 562

HAZ STOR—Safety Building—Federal Signal Corporation; *U.S. Public*, pg. 616

H&C CONCRETE STAIN AND SEALERS—Paints & Coatings—The Sherwin-Williams Company; *U.S. Public*, pg. 1465

H&K—Metal Products—Harrington & King; *U.S. Private*, pg. 504

H & R BLOCK—Income Tax Preparation—H & R Block, Inc.; *U.S. Public*, pg. 770

H B—Cigarettes—B.A.T Industries P.L.C.; *Int'l*, pg. 110

HB—NONE—British-American Tobacco (Germany) GmbH; *Int'l*, pg. 111

H.B. FULLER—Adhesives—H.B. Fuller Company; *U.S. Public*, pg. 686

HBC ELISA—Test System—Ortho Clinical Diagnostic Systems Inc.; *U.S. Public*, pg. 929

HB-40—Plasticizer—Monsanto Company; *U.S. Public*, pg. 1124

HB-40—Plasticizer—Solutia Inc.; *U.S. Public*, pg. 1483

HB-METER—Analytical Instrument—Leica, Inc.; *Int'l*, pg. 806

HBO—Pay Television Service—Home Box Office, Inc.; *U.S. Public*, pg. 1612

HBO CHAMPIONSHIP BOXING—Sports Radio Program—Westwood One Entertainment; *U.S. Public*, pg. 1763

HBR—NONE—Applied Extrusion Technologies, Inc.; *U.S. Public*, pg. 122

HBSAG ELISA—Test System—Ortho Clinical Diagnostic Systems Inc.; *U.S. Public*, pg. 929

H.B. SCOTT'S—Loose Leaf Chewing Tobacco—Conwood Company L.P.; *U.S. Private*, pg. 272

H-BIG—Hepatitis B Immune Globulin—Nabi; *U.S. Public*, pg. 1148

H-BIG IV—NONE—Nabi; *U.S. Public*, pg. 1148

HC—Horizontal Core Air Cooled Heat Exchangers—Young Radiator Company; *U.S. Private*, pg. 1201

HCF—Photographic Film—Eastman Kodak Company; *U.S. Public*, pg. 550

HCF7—Photographic Film—Eastman Kodak Company; *U.S. Public*, pg. 550

HCHs—Hygroscopic Condensor Humidifiers—Vital Signs, Inc.; *U.S. Public*, pg. 1723

HCI—Host Command Interface Applications Package—Mitel Corporation; *Int'l*, pg. 870

HC-110—Photographic Developer & Replenisher—Eastman Kodak Company; *U.S. Public*, pg. 550

HCP—Photographic Film—Eastman Kodak Company; *U.S. Public*, pg. 550

HCV 3.0 ELISA—Test System—Ortho Clinical Diagnostic Systems Inc.; *U.S. Public*, pg. 929

H-CIG IV—NONE—Nabi; *U.S. Public*, pg. 1148

HDC—Filters—Pall Corporation; *U.S. Public*, pg. 1253

HDC II—Filters—Pall Corporation; *U.S. Public*, pg. 1253

HDF—Photographic Film—Eastman Kodak Company; *U.S. Public*, pg. 550

HDF7—Photographic Film—Eastman Kodak Company; *U.S. Public*, pg. 550

HDK—NONE—Hokuriku Electric Industry Co., Ltd.; *Int'l*, pg. 627

HD SERIES—Analog Router—Chyron Corp.; *Int'l*, pg. 1372

HD-3000 STL HYDRAULIC LEVELER—Fully-Hydraulic Dock Leveler with Automatic Safe-T-Lip Vehicle Barrier—Rite-Hite Corporation; *U.S. Private*, pg. 933

HDW—Merchant Shipbuilding—Howaldtswerke-Deutsche Werft AG; *Int'l*, pg. 1069

H DESIGN—Motorcycle—American Honda Motor Co., Inc. Motorcycle Division; *Int'l*, pg. 634

"H" DESIGN—Luggage—Hartmann Luggage & Leather Goods Group; *U.S. Public*, pg. 261

HEA—High Efficiency Antireflection Coating—Optical Coating Laboratory, Inc.; *U.S. Public*, pg. 1227

HED ARZI—Record Label—The Israel Land Development Co., Ltd.; *Int'l*, pg. 691

HFC FIELD COMMANDER—Cultivator—Brillion Iron Works, Inc.; *U.S. Public*, pg. 933

H F SECURITE—Safety Interlocks—Halma p.l.c.; *Int'l*, pg. 589

HFZ—Cracking Catalysts—Engelhard Corporation; *U.S. Public*, pg. 582

H. FREEMAN—Men's Apparel—H. Freeman & Son, Inc.; *U.S. Private*, pg. 426

HGTV—NONE—Home & Garden Television; *U.S. Public*, pg. 1447

H.H. BROWN—Shoes—H.H. Brown Shoe Company, Inc.; *U.S. Public*, pg. 217

H. H. SCOTT—Electronic Components—Emerson Radio Corp.; *U.S. Public*, pg. 578

H.H. WEST—Shoes—H.H. Brown Shoe Company, Inc.; *U.S. Public*, pg. 217

H. HOOGENDOORN—NONE—EcoScience Corporation; *U.S. Public*, pg. 563

H-I—Rockets—Mitsubishi Heavy Industries Ltd.; *Int'l*, pg. 873

HI/AK—Variable Speed D.C. Motor Drives—General Electric Canada Inc.; *U.S. Public*, pg. 713

HIAB—General Cargo Cranes—Partek Corporation; *Int'l*, pg. 1024

HIG—Acquired Asset—Communications Instruments Inc.; *U.S. Private*, pg. 259

HIPEC—Materials for Hitech Applications—Dow Corning Corporation; *U.S. Public*, pg. 523

HIQU 32—NONE—Chips and Technologies, Inc.; *U.S. Public*, pg. 349

HIQV 64—NONE—Chips and Technologies, Inc.; *U.S. Public*, pg. 349

HIQ VIDEO—NONE—Chips and Technologies, Inc.; *U.S. Public*, pg. 349

H.I.S.—Jeans—Henry I. Siegel Company, Inc.; *U.S. Private*, pg. 998

HIT—Home Interface Terminal—Sony Electronics; *Int'l*, pg. 1281

HIV IG—HIV Immune Globulin—Nabi; *U.S. Public*, pg. 1148

HIV-1 ELSIA—Test System—Ortho Clinical Diagnostic Systems Inc.; *U.S. Public*, pg. 929

HIV-1/HIV-2—Synthetic Peptides—BioChem Pharma Inc.; *Int'l*, pg. 196

H.K. PORTER—Bolt and Cable Cutters—Cooper Hand Tools; *U.S. Public*, pg. 444

H.K. PORTER—Hand & Hydraulic Cutting & Crimping Tools—Cooper Industries, Inc.; *U.S. Public*, pg. 442

H.K. PORTER—NONE—Cooper Tools; *U.S. Public*, pg. 444

HL-1—Rail Lubricators—Portec Inc., Railway Maintenance Products Div.; *U.S. Public*, pg. 1318

HM/CAP—Immunoassay Test—E-Z-Em, Inc.; *U.S. Public*, pg. 540

HME—Heat & Moisture Exchanger—Ballard Medical Products; *U.S. Public*, pg. 171

HMMWV—M998 Series Military Tactical Wheeled Vehicle—AM General Corporation; *U.S. Private*, pg. 922

HMO TEXAS—HMO—Sierra Health Services, Inc.; *U.S. Public*, pg. 1469

HMO-USA—Health Insurance—Blue Cross and Blue Shield Association; *U.S. Private*, pg. 151

HMS BUYERTRACK—Customer Follow Up Program—Homeowners Group, Inc.; *U.S. Public*, pg. 832

HMS REFNET—Referral Networking System—Homeowners Group, Inc.; *U.S. Public*, pg. 832

HMS RISK MANAGEMENT SYSTEM—Liability Prevention & Management Tools—Homeowners Group, Inc.; *U.S. Public*, pg. 832

HMS SELLERTRACK—Listing & Risk Management Tool—Homeowners Group, Inc.; *U.S. Public*, pg. 832

HM7—Ariene 4 Engine—SNECMA - Societe Nationale d'Etude et de Construction de Moteurs d'Aviation; *Int'l*, pg. 1165

HMT DIRECTORY—NONE—Intertec Publishing; *U.S. Public*, pg. 1328

HMV—Music Retailer—EMI Group plc; *Int'l*, pg. 426

HNA, HEALTHCARE NETWORK ARCHITECTURE—Architecture for Cerner's—Cerner Corporation; *U.S. Public*, pg. 331

H-O—Hot Cereals—GFA Brands, Inc.; *U.S. Private*, pg. 435

HOF—Nautical Shoe—K-Swiss Inc.; *U.S. Public*, pg. 937

H.O.G.—Enthusiast Club—Harley-Davidson, Inc.; *U.S. Public*, pg. 786

H ORISKY—Men's Apparel—Hartmarx Corporation; *U.S. Public*, pg. 795

HP—Multipolymer Sheet—Cyro Industries; *Int'l*, pg. 1454

HP—Sauces—Danone Group; *Int'l*, pg. 379

HPC—NONE—Berg Electronics; *U.S. Public*, pg. 212

HP DESKJET PLUS—Printer—Hewlett-Packard Company; *U.S. Public*, pg. 813

HP DESKWRITER—Printer—Hewlett-Packard Company; *U.S. Public*, pg. 813

HP-80—High Pressure Washer—Clayton Industries Co.; *U.S. Private*, pg. 245

HPIC—Anion Chromatography Columns—Dionex Corporation; *U.S. Public*, pg. 510

HPL—Bowling Products—AMF Bowling Worldwide; *U.S. Private*, pg. 6

HPL—Latex—The Dow Chemical Company; *U.S. Public*, pg. 522

HP LASERJET—Printer—Hewlett-Packard Company; *U.S. Public*, pg. 813

HP LASERJET IIII SI—Printer—Hewlett-Packard Company; *U.S. Public*, pg. 813

HP LASERJET III—Printer—Hewlett-Packard Company; *U.S. Public*, pg. 813

HP LASERJET III D—Printer—Hewlett-Packard Company; *U.S. Public*, pg. 813

HP LASERJET III P—Printer—Hewlett-Packard Company; *U.S. Public*, pg. 813

HP LASERJET III SI—Printer—Hewlett-Packard Company; *U.S. Public*, pg. 813

HP LASERJET II D—Printer—Hewlett-Packard Company; *U.S. Public*, pg. 813

HP LASERJET II P—Printer—Hewlett-Packard Company; *U.S. Public*, pg. 813

HP MINER—Hose—The Goodyear Tire & Rubber Company; *U.S. Public*, pg. 752

HPN—Hydrogenation Catalyst—Engelhard Corporation; *U.S. Public*, pg. 582

HP OFFICE JET—Printer, Fax & Copier—Hewlett-Packard Company; *U.S. Public*, pg. 813

HP 100—Industrial Air Filter—Farr Company; *U.S. Public*, pg. 613

HP PAINTJET—Printer—Hewlett-Packard Company; *U.S. Public*, pg. 813

HP SCANJET—Computer Scanner—Hewlett-Packard Company; *U.S. Public*, pg. 813

HP SCANJET II CX—Scanner—Hewlett-Packard Company; *U.S. Public*, pg. 813

HP SCANJET II P—Scanner—Hewlett-Packard Company; *U.S. Public*, pg. 813

HPTS—Computer System—International Business Machines Corporation; *U.S. Public*, pg. 895

HP THINKJET—Printer—Hewlett-Packard Company; *U.S. Public*, pg. 813

HP-2—Riveter—Marson/Creative Fastener, Inc.; *U.S. Private*, pg. 708

HP 200—Industrial Air Filter—Farr Company; *U.S. Public*, pg. 613

HP 2000—Tires—Bridgestone/Firestone, Inc.; *Int'l*, pg. 213

HP VECTRA—Personal Computer—Hewlett-Packard Company; *U.S. Public*, pg. 813

HPX—Fasteners—R&B, Inc.; *U.S. Public*, pg. 1354

H-R—Sterile Lubricating Jelly—Carter-Wallace, Inc.; *U.S. Public*, pg. 309

HRC—Honda Racing Corporation—American Honda Motor Co., Inc. Motorcycle Division; *Int'l*, pg. 634

HRD—Zinc Products—Zinc Corporation of America; *U.S. Private*, pg. 540

HRF—Plastic Film—Reynolds Metals Company; *U.S. Public*, pg. 1385

HRH—Honeycomb Materials—Hexcel Corporation; *U.S. Public*, pg. 824

HR M APPLICANT FLOW—Human Resources Software—Dun & Bradstreet Software Services; *Int'l*, pg. 532

HR M BENEFITS ADMINISTRATION—Human Resources Software—Dun & Bradstreet Software Services; *Int'l*, pg. 532

HR M PAYROLL—Payroll Software—Dun & Bradstreet Software Services; *Int'l*, pg. 532

HR M PERSONNEL—Personnel Software—Dun & Bradstreet Software Services; *Int'l*, pg. 532

HR M POSITION CONTROL—Human Resources Software—Dun & Bradstreet Software Services; *Int'l*, pg. 532

HR M SAFETY AND HEALTH—Human Resources Software—Dun & Bradstreet Software Services; *Int'l*, pg. 532

HR MILLENNIUM—Human Resources Information System—Dun & Bradstreet Software Services; *Int'l*, pg. 532

HR-97—Enhanced Aluminum Front Surface Mirrors—Optical Coating Laboratory, Inc.; *U.S. Public*, pg. 1227

HRP—Photographic Developer—Eastman Kodak Company; *U.S. Public*, pg. 550

HRP—Honeycomb Material—Hexcel Corporation; *U.S. Public*, pg. 824

HR SERIES—NONE—Detroit Diesel Corp.; *U.S. Private*, pg. 850

HRTI—Thermal Rating Data—American Precision Industries Inc.; *U.S. Public*, pg. 90

HR VISION SOFTWARE—Human ResourceManagement—SAS Institute Inc.; *U.S. Private*, pg. 966

HS—NONE—Procter & Gamble Espana S.A.; *U.S. Public*, pg. 1332

HSC—Silicon Carbide—Superior Graphite Co.; *U.S. Private*, pg. 1054

HSM—Transparent Plastic Film Packaging—Reynolds Metals Company; *U.S. Public*, pg. 1385

HS-100 (M42)—High Speed Tool Steel—Latrobe Steel Company; *U.S. Public*, pg. 1617

HSR—High Speed Precision Sheeter—Beloit Lenox, Div.; *U.S. Public*, pg. 789

HSRA—Rinse Additive—Ecolab Inc.; *U.S. Public*, pg. 562

HSV ANTIGEN ELISA—Test—Ortho Clinical Diagnostic Systems Inc.; *U.S. Public*, pg. 929

HSV-I—Herpes Antibodies Test System—Wampole Laboratories; *U.S. Public*, pg. 310

HSV-II—Herpes Antibodies Test System—Wampole Laboratories; *U.S. Public*, pg. 310

H. SALT ESQ.—Fish & Chips—H. Salt of Southern California, Inc.; *U.S. Public*, pg. 489

H. SALT SEAFOOD GALLEY—Restaurant—H. Salt of Southern California, Inc.; *U.S. Private*, pg. 489

H-SERIES—Die/Mold Machining Center—Makino Inc.; *Int'l*, pg. 831

H-1700—Adult Oxygenator—C.R. Bard, Inc.; *U.S. Public*, pg. 189

HT—Kaolin for use in The Paper Industry—Engelhard Corporation; *U.S. Public*, pg. 582

HT—Metallic—Gudebrod, Inc.; *U.S. Private*, pg. 486

HTC—High Torque Centerwind Winder—Harnischfeger Industries, Inc.; *U.S. Public*, pg. 788

HTC BI-WIND—Duplex Winder—Beloit Lenox, Div.; *U.S. Public*, pg. 789

HTH—Pool Prods.—Olin Corporation; *U.S. Public*, pg. 1218

HTLV-I/II—Western Blot Kit—Ortho Clinical Diagnostic Systems Inc.; *U.S. Public*, pg. 929

HTP—Press—Beloit Corporation; *U.S. Public*, pg. 789

HTPM—Press—Beloit Corporation; *U.S. Public*, pg. 789

HTP-2—Iron Oxide Dispersants—BetzDearborn Inc.; *U.S. Public*, pg. 226

H.T.R.—Polymer—U.S. Surgical Corp.; *U.S. Public*, pg. 1687

HTS—Surround Sound Decoders—Shure Brothers Incorporated; *U.S. Private*, pg. 997

H.T.S.—Ignition Wire—Standard Motor Products Inc.; *U.S. Public*, pg. 1503

HTSH—Diagnostic Products—Abbott Laboratories; *U.S. Public*, pg. 12

HTSH RIABEAD—Diagnostic Products—Abbott Laboratories; *U.S. Public*, pg. 12

HTX—High-Heat Compounds—The Geon Company; *U.S. Public*, pg. 733

HTX—Glass Fibers, Strands, Rovings & Mats—PPG Industries, Inc.; *U.S. Public*, pg. 1245

H-1300—Infant/Pediatric Oxygenator—C.R. Bard, Inc.; *U.S. Public*, pg. 189

H-330—Tires—Bridgestone/Firestone, Inc.; *Int'l*, pg. 213

H2 OFF—Water Rinsing Paint Remover—The Savogran Company; *U.S. Private*, pg. 968

H2OIL-BASE—Interior & Exterior Oil-Based Primer & Sealer—Wm. Zinsser & Co., Inc.; *U.S. Public*, pg. 1358

H. UPMANN—Premium Cigars—Consolidated Cigar Corporation; *U.S. Private*, pg. 690

HVCMOS—High Voltage Complementary Metal Oxide Semiconductor—Supertex, Inc.; *U.S. Public*, pg. 1539

HWAT—Heating Cable—Raychem Corporation; *U.S. Public*, pg. 1362

HWI—Hardware Wholesaler—Hardware Wholesalers, Inc.; *U.S. Private*, pg. 502

HWS—Transparent Polyvinyl Chloride Film—Reynolds Metals Company; *U.S. Public*, pg. 1385

HYQ PTFE—Flow Control Component—Osmonics, Inc.; *U.S. Public*, pg. 1233

HY-TEC—Allergy Diagnostics—Hycor Biomedical, Inc.; *U.S. Public*, pg. 851

HZ-1—Catalyst & Catalyst Support—Engelhard Corporation; *U.S. Public*, pg. 582

HZ-PLUS—Cracking Catalyst—Engelhard Corporation; *U.S. Public*, pg. 582

HAMILTON BEACH—Blenders, Food Processors, Mixers, Can Openers & Small Electric Appliances—NACCO Industries, Inc.; *U.S. Public*, pg. 1149

Heinz—Condiments—H.J. Heinz Co. of Canada Ltd.; *U.S. Public*, pg. 806

HAAGEN-DAZS—Ice Cream—Grand Metropolitan Plc; *Int'l*, pg. 408

HAAGEN-DAZS—Superpremium Ice Cream—GrandMet Foods GmbH; *Int'l*, pg. 409

HAAGEN-DAZS—Superpremium Ice Cream—GrandMet Foods Southern Europe; *Int'l*, pg. 409

HAAGEN-DAZS—Ice Cream Pints, Mini-Cups, Stick Bars & Frozen Yoghurt—GrandMet Foods UK; *Int'l*, pg. 408

HAAGEN-DAZS—Ice Cream—The Haagen-Dazs Company Inc.; *Int'l*, pg. 411

HAAGEN-DAZS—Premium Ice Cream & Frozen Yogurt Products—The Pillsbury Company; *Int'l*, pg. 411

HAAGEN-DAZS SNACK BARS—Bite Size Ice Cream Bars—The Haagen-Dazs Company Inc.; *Int'l*, pg. 411

HAAKE BECK NON-ALCOHOLIC BREW—NONE—Dribeck Importers, Inc.; *U.S. Private*, pg. 343

HAARTZ-MASON—Rubber Coated Fabrics—Haartz-Mason, Inc.; *U.S. Private*, pg. 1358

HABAND—Men's & Women's Wear—The Haband Co.; *U.S. Private*, pg. 492

HABERDASHER—Women's Suits & Separates—Paul Harris Stores, Inc.; *U.S. Public*, pg. 792

HABERDASHERY—Women's Clothing—The Leslie Fay Companies, Inc.; *U.S. Public*, pg. 989

HABITANT—Canned Soups, Fresh Mushrooms, Marinated Products—Campbell Soup Company; *U.S. Public*, pg. 298

HABITANT—Food Products—Campbell Soup Company Ltd.; *U.S. Public*, pg. 299

HABITANT—Pickles & Relishes—International Multifoods Corporation; *U.S. Public*, pg. 900

HABITANT—Grocery Products—Labatt Brewing Company Limited; *Int'l*, pg. 679

HABITANT—Pickles & Condiments—Robin Hood Multifoods Inc.; *U.S. Public*, pg. 901

HABITAT—Ceramic Wall Tile—Monarch Tile, Inc.; *U.S. Private*, pg. 287

HABITROL—Smoking Cessation Patch—Novartis; *Int'l*, pg. 972

HACAR—Film—AlliedSignal Inc.; *U.S. Public*, pg. 49

HACH—Company Logo—Hach Company; *U.S. Public*, pg. 773

HACH ONE—pH Electrode—Hach Company; *U.S. Public*, pg. 773

HACKNEY—Refrigerated Truck Bodies & Trailers—Kidron Inc.; *U.S. Private*, pg. 619

HACKNEY AND SONS—Beverage Truck Bodies & Trailers—Transportation Technologies, Inc.; *U.S. Private*, pg. 1097

Brand Name Index

HACKNEY BROTHERS—Refrigerated Truck Bodies—Transportation Technologies, Inc.; *U.S. Private*, pg. 1097

HACKY SACK—Footbag—Mattel, Inc.; *U.S. Public*, pg. 1057

HACKY SACK—Footbag—Wham-O, Inc.; *U.S. Private*, pg. 1170

HACO—Driers—The Harry Alter Company; *U.S. Private*, pg. 1075

HADAR—White Woodfree paper for Books, Copybooks, Office Use, Stationar—American Israeli Paper Mills Ltd.; *Int'l*, pg. 74

HADAR BULKY—NONE—American Israeli Paper Mills Ltd.; *Int'l*, pg. 74

HADAR PAZ—Recycled for Printing & Office Use—American Israeli Paper Mills Ltd.; *Int'l*, pg. 74

HADASUI—Moisturizer—Shiseido Company Ltd.; *Int'l*, pg. 1235

HADCO—Lighting Fixtures—The Genlyte Group Incorporated; *U.S. Public*, pg. 729

HADDON CRAFTSMEN, INC.—Book Bindery—Haddon Craftsmen, Inc.; *U.S. Public*, pg. 518

HAEGER—Pottery—Haeger Industries, Inc.; *U.S. Private*, pg. 493

HAEGER FLORAL—Pottery—Haeger Industries, Inc.; *U.S. Private*, pg. 493

HAFFENREFFER—Beer—Falstaff Brewing Corporation; *U.S. Private*, pg. 955

HAG—Coffee—Philip Morris Companies Inc.; *U.S. Public*, pg. 1287

HAGGAR—Menswear—Tandy Brands Accessories, Inc.; *U.S. Public*, pg. 1560

HAGGAR STUFF—NONE—Tandy Brands Accessories, Inc.; *U.S. Public*, pg. 1560

HAGGAR 2 IN 1 REV.—NONE—Tandy Brands Accessories, Inc.; *U.S. Public*, pg. 1560

HAGGLUNDS DENISON—Hydraulic Pumps & Valves—Denison Hydraulics, Inc.; *U.S. Private*, pg. 324

HAGUKUMI—(Powdered Infant Formula)—Morinaga Milk Industry Co., Ltd.; *Int'l*, pg. 895

HAIG—NONE—Guinness Plc; *Int'l*, pg. 412

HAIN—A Full Line of Over 200 Natural Food Products—The Hain Food Group Inc.; *U.S. Public*, pg. 774

HAINES HUNTER—Boats—Outboard Marine Corporation; *U.S. Private*, pg. 478

HAIR—Women's Special Interest Magazine—IPC Magazines Limited; *Int'l*, pg. 651

HAIR & BODY—Shampoo—Wella Group; *Int'l*, pg. 1489

HAIR PROTEIN BUILDER—Permanent Wave & Shampoo—Revlon-Realistic Professional Products, Inc.; *U.S. Private*, pg. 690

HAIR SAVER—Hair Care—Palm Beach Beauty Products Co.; *U.S. Private*, pg. 834

HAIR-SO-NEW—Creme Rinse—Clairol, Inc.; *U.S. Public*, pg. 254

HAIR THERAPY—Hair Care—Palm Beach Beauty Products Co.; *U.S. Private*, pg. 834

HAIRCRAFTERS—Full-Service Hair Care Salons—Cutco Industries, Inc.; *U.S. Public*, pg. 470

HAKAPHOS—Nutrient Salts—BASF AG; *Int'l*, pg. 103

HALAMID—Disinfectants—Akzo Nobel N.V.; *Int'l*, pg. 42

HALAR—Polyethylene Chlorotrifluoroethylene—Montedison S.p.A.; *Int'l*, pg. 324

HALBA—Chocolate—Coop Switzerland; *Int'l*, pg. 329

HALCION—Prescription Sleeping Aid—Pharmacia & Upjohn; *Int'l*, pg. 1048

HALDENGUT—Beer—Heineken N.V.; *Int'l*, pg. 608

HALDOL CONCENTRATE—NONE—Ortho-McNeil Pharmaceutical Corporation; *U.S. Public*, pg. 929

HALDOL DECANOTE INJECTION—NONE—Ortho-McNeil Pharmaceutical Corporation; *U.S. Public*, pg. 929

HALDOL TABLETS—NONE—Ortho-McNeil Pharmaceutical Corporation; *U.S. Public*, pg. 929

HALE—Valves—Watts Industries, Inc.; *U.S. Public*, pg. 1746

HALE PRODUCTS—Fire Pumps—IDEX Corporation; *U.S. Public*, pg. 862

HALEX—Die Casting—The Scott Fetzer Company; *U.S. Public*, pg. 217

HALEX—NONE—Lawter International, Inc.; *U.S. Public*, pg. 980

HALF PACK—Refuse Bodies—Heil Environmental Industries; *U.S. Public*, pg. 520

ROBERT HALF—Specialized Full-Time Financial Staffing—Robert Half International Inc.; *U.S. Public*, pg. 774

HALF TREAD LOADER DOZER—Tires—Bridgestone/Firestone, Inc.; *Int'l*, pg. 213

HALFAN—NONE—SmithKline Beecham Corporation; *Int'l*, pg. 1264

HALFAN—Anti-Infective—SmithKline Beecham plc; *Int'l*, pg. 1264

HALITE—De-Icing Salt—Cargill Salt Inc.; *Int'l*, pg. 48

HALITE—NONE—Lawter International, Inc.; *U.S. Public*, pg. 980

HALL—China—The Hall China Company; *U.S. Private*, pg. 494

HALL BRITE—Sun Screen Additives—The C.P. Hall Company; *U.S. Private*, pg. 495

HALL OF HANOVER—Gifts & Ladies Apparel—Hanover Direct Pennsylvania, Inc.; *U.S. Public*, pg. 782

HALL STAR—Personal Care Additives—The C.P. Hall Company; *U.S. Private*, pg. 495

HALL TRESS—Hair Care Additives—The C.P. Hall Company; *U.S. Private*, pg. 495

HALL VERSIPOWER—Dual Powered Orthopedic Instruments—Bristol-Myers Squibb Company; *U.S. Public*, pg. 253

HALLCOTE—Pigmented Slab Dips—The C.P. Hall Company; *U.S. Private*, pg. 495

HALLEY'S BIBLE HANDBOOK—Religious Reference Book—The Zondervan Corporation; *Int'l*, pg. 927

HALLMARK—Greeting Cards & Related Prods.—Hallmark Cards, Inc.; *U.S. Private*, pg. 495

HALLMARK SHANGLE—Asphalt Roofing—CertainTeed Corporation; *Int'l*, pg. 1170

HALLOWELL—Shaft Collars—SPS Technologies, Inc.; *U.S. Public*, pg. 1419

HALLS—Cough Drops—Adams U.S.A.; *U.S. Public*, pg. 1739

HALLS—Cough Drops—Warner-Lambert Company; *U.S. Public*, pg. 1738

HALLS CANDY—Candy—Warner-Lambert K.K.; *U.S. Public*, pg. 1739

HALO—Recessed & Track Lighting—Cooper Industries, Inc.; *U.S. Public*, pg. 442

HALO CELL—Exclusion Seals—Norton Performance Plastics; *Int'l*, pg. 1174

HALOCARBON—Oil, Grease & Wares—Halocarbon Products Corp.; *U.S. Private*, pg. 496

HALOFRESH—Nylon Filament—AlliedSignal Inc.; *U.S. Public*, pg. 49

HALOG—Dermatological Therapy—Bristol-Myers Squibb Company; *U.S. Public*, pg. 253

HALOG—Topical Steroid—Westwood-Squibb Pharmaceuticals Inc.; *U.S. Public*, pg. 255

HALON—Fluropolymero—AlliedSignal Inc.; *U.S. Public*, pg. 49

HALON—Fire Extinguishing Compounds—Great Lakes Chemical Corporation; *U.S. Public*, pg. 760

HALON 1211—Fire Extinguishers—Falcon Safety Products Inc.; *U.S. Private*, pg. 392

HALOSPOR—Antibiotic—Novartis; *Int'l*, pg. 972

HALOTEX—Cream & Solution Antifungel Agent—Westwood-Squibb Pharmaceuticals Inc.; *U.S. Public*, pg. 255

HALPASOL—Low Aromatic Hydrocarbon Solvents—Haltermann AG; *Int'l*, pg. 590

HALPER BROS—Imported Ski & Apres Ski Headwear, Scarves, Fashion Gloves—Reliable Knitting Works; *U.S. Private*, pg. 920

HALSA—Shampoo & Conditioner—Dep Corporation; *U.S. Public*, pg. 500

HALSA HAIR SPRAY—Hair Care Products—Dep Corporation; *U.S. Public*, pg. 500

HALSA MOUSSE—Hair Care Products—Dep Corporation; *U.S. Public*, pg. 500

HALSA SWEDISH BOTANICAL—Hair Care Products—Dep Corporation; *U.S. Public*, pg. 500

HALSO—Solvent—Occidental Chemical Corporation; *U.S. Public*, pg. 1210

HALSTED PRESS—Books—John Wiley & Sons, Inc.; *U.S. Public*, pg. 1768

HALSTON—Fragrances—Halston Enterprises, Inc.; *U.S. Private*, pg. 690

HALSTON—Men & Ladies Wear—Kosugi Sangyo Co., Ltd.; *Int'l*, pg. 759

HALSTON LIMITED—Fragrance—Halston Enterprises, Inc.; *U.S. Private*, pg. 690

HALSTON NIGHT—Fragrance—Halston Enterprises, Inc.; *U.S. Private*, pg. 690

HALTERMANN—Toll Distillation—Haltermann AG; *Int'l*, pg. 590

HALTEX—Alumina Trihydrate Filler Pigment—Hitox Corporation of America; *U.S. Public*, pg. 829

HALTRAN—NONE—Lee Pharmaceuticals; *U.S. Public*, pg. 984

HAM'N CHEESE'N BISCUIT—Sandwich—Owens Country Sausage, Inc.; *U.S. Public*, pg. 596

HAMADA—NONE—Taylor Impression, Inc.; *U.S. Private*, pg. 1070

HAMAMATSU—Photosensitive Devices & Special Lamps—Hamamatsu Corp.; *U.S. Private*, pg. 497

HAMBRECHT & QUIST—Investment Banker—Hambrecht & Quist LLC.; *U.S. Public*, pg. 778

HAMBURGER ABENDBLATT—Newspaper—Axel Springer Verlag AG; *Int'l*, pg. 102

HAMBURGER HELPER—Main Dish Mixes—General Mills, Inc.; *U.S. Public*, pg. 717

HAMBURGER UNIVERSITY—Management Training School for McDonalds—McDonald's Corporation; *U.S. Public*, pg. 1068

HAMILTON—Pianos—Baldwin Piano & Organ Company; *U.S. Public*, pg. 169

HAMILTON—Web Fed Printing & Collating Machinery—Hamilton Division; *U.S. Public*, pg. 1517

HAMILTON—Lamps—RDM Sports Group; *U.S. Public*, pg. 1354

HAMILTON—Watches—SMH Swiss Corporation for Micro Electronics & Watchmaking Indus. Ltd.; *Int'l*, pg. 1160

HAMILTON BEACH—Small Appliances—Hamilton Beach/Proctor-Silex, Inc.; *U.S. Public*, pg. 1149

HAMILTON BEACH—Blenders, Food Processors, Mixers, Can Openers; Small Electrical Appliances—NACCO Industries, Inc.; *U.S. Public*, pg. 1149

HAMILTON EASY KARV—Meat Products—The Smithfield Packing Co., Inc.; *U.S. Public*, pg. 1479

HAMILTON PARK—NONE—CertainTeed Corporation; *Int'l*, pg. 1170

HAMILTON PRECISION METALS—Strip & Foil—Pegasus International Corporation; *U.S. Private*, pg. 1046

HAMILTON STANDARD—Propellers, Space Suits, Jet Engine Controls—United Technologies Corporation; *U.S. Public*, pg. 1689

HAMILTON'S—Processed Meats—Smithfield Foods, Inc.; *U.S. Public*, pg. 1479

HAMLET—NONE—Fortune Brands, Inc.; *U.S. Public*, pg. 674

HAMLET—Cigars—Gallaher Tobacco Ltd.; *Int'l*, pg. 539

HAMLET MINIATURES—NONE—Fortune Brands, Inc.; *U.S. Public*, pg. 674

HAMLET MINIATURES—NONE—Gallaher Tobacco Ltd.; *Int'l*, pg. 539

HAMLIN—NONE—Hamlin, Inc.; *U.S. Public*, pg. 251

HAMM'S—Beer—Pabst Brewing Co.; *U.S. Private*, pg. 954

HAMM'S—Beer—Pabst Brewing Co./Tumwater; *U.S. Private*, pg. 954

HAMM'S DRAUGHT—Beer—Pabst Brewing Co.; *U.S. Private*, pg. 954

HAMM'S LIGHT—Beer—Pabst Brewing Co./Tumwater; *U.S. Private*, pg. 954

HAMM'S SPECIAL LIGHT—Beer—Pabst Brewing Co.; *U.S. Private*, pg. 954

HAMMACHER, SCHLEMMER—Houseware & Gift Store—Hammacher, Schlemmer & Co., Inc.; *U.S. Private*, pg. 497

HAMMER—Radio Control—Tyco Toys, Inc.; *U.S. Public*, pg. 1058

HAMMER HEAD—Drywall Tools—Hyde Manufacturing Co.; *U.S. Private*, pg. 551

HAMMERED—Pattern Glass—AFG Industries, Inc.; *Int'l*, pg. 84

HAMMERGUN—Power Tools—The Black & Decker Corporation; *U.S. Public*, pg. 233

HAMMERLOK—Mechanical Coupling Link Rigger—Columbus McKinnon Corp.; *U.S. Public*, pg. 405

HAMMERMASTER—Crusher—Svedala Industries-Universal Engineering; *Int'l*, pg. 1326

HAMMERMILL—Reprographic and Printing Papers—International Paper Company; *U.S. Public*, pg. 901

HAMMOND—Elevating & Conveying Equip.—Screw Conveyor Corp.; *U.S. Private*, pg. 977

HAMP-ENE—Chemicals—Hampshire Chemical Corp.; *U.S. Private*, pg. 498

HAMP-EX—Industrial Chemicals—Hampshire Chemical Corp.; *U.S. Private*, pg. 498

HAMP-OL—Chemicals—Hampshire Chemical Corp.; *U.S. Private*, pg. 498

HAMPDEN—NONE—Carpenter Technology Corporation; *U.S. Public*, pg. 307

HAMPOSYL—Industrial Chemicals—Hampshire Chemical Corp.; *U.S. Private*, pg. 498

HAMPSHIRE—Industrial Chemicals—Hampshire Chemical Corp.; *U.S. Private*, pg. 498

HAMPSHIRE-DESIGNERS—Sweaters, Skirts & Slacks—Designers Knitting Mills; *U.S. Public*, pg. 778

HAMPTON—Bath Accessories—Baldwin Hardware Corporation; *U.S. Public*, pg. 1053

HAMPTON—Watches—Baume Mercier, Inc.; *U.S. Private*, pg. 124

HAMPTON—NONE—Sunstone Hotel Investors, Inc.; *U.S. Public*, pg. 1536

HAMPTON INN—Suites—Promus Hotel Corporation; *U.S. Public*, pg. 1335

HAMPTON MANOR FRYTIME—Lamb Weston—Lamb-Weston, Inc.; *U.S. Public*, pg. 427

HAMPTON II—Wicker Furniture—Avon Workshop Ficks Reed; *U.S. Private*, pg. 102

HAMPTON II—Office Chair—Vecta; *U.S. Private*, pg. 1038

HANCOCK—Fabrics—Hancock Fabrics, Inc.; *U.S. Public*, pg. 779

HANCOCK—Heart Valves—Medtronic, Inc.; *U.S. Public*, pg. 1082

HANCOCK—NONE—Sico Inc.; *Int'l*, pg. 1239

HANCOCK PLANK—Pre-Finished Laminate—Bruce Hardwood Floors; *U.S. Public*, pg. 1634

HAND AID—Wrist SUpports—Kimberly-Clark Tecnol; *U.S. Public*, pg. 959

HAND HELPERS—Latex Gloves—Magla Products; *U.S. Private*, pg. 695

HAND-L-BAG—Plastic Product—Uniflex, Inc.; *U.S. Public*, pg. 1665

HAND-MASKER—Painting Masker—3M; *U.S. Public*, pg. 1604

HAND SAVERS—Gloves—Playtex Products Corp.; *U.S. Public*, pg. 1311

HAND TAPER—Tape Machine—Marsh Company; *U.S. Private*, pg. 707

HAND-TROL—Electrosurgery Pencil—Conmed Corporation; *U.S. Public*, pg. 431

HANDAR—Company Name—TSI Incorporated; *U.S. Public*, pg. 1559

HANDBOOK OF FOODSERVICE DISTRIBUTION—Annually Published Handbook—ID Magazine; *Int'l*, pg. 1446

HANDCRAFT—Professional Applicators—Sherwin-Williams Coatings Division; *U.S. Public*, pg. 1466

HANDGARDS—Disposable Plastic Gloves—Handgards Inc.; *U.S. Private*, pg. 499

HANDGUNS—Magazine—Petersen Publishing Company, L.L.C.; *U.S. Private*, pg. 856

HANDHUGGERS—Beginners Products—Sanford Corporation; *U.S. Public*, pg. 1178

HANDI-BAG—Plastic Bags—Chelsea Industries, Inc.; *U.S. Private*, pg. 231

HANDI-CHEM—NONE—Allied Diagnostic Imaging Resources, Inc.; *U.S. Public*, pg. 282

HANDI-LITER—Lighting Fixtures—Guth Lighting Company; *Int'l*, pg. 821

HANDI-PAK—Ready-to-Eat Cereal in Eight Single-Serving Packages—Kellogg Company; *U.S. Public*, pg. 947

HANDI-PIK—Crane—Harnischfeger Industries, Inc.; *U.S. Public*, pg. 788

HANDI-SCRUBB—Soap—Georgia-Pacific Corporation; *U.S. Public*, pg. 735

HANDI-SNACKS—Snack Food—Kraft Foods Inc.; *U.S. Public*, pg. 1288

HANDI-SWABS—Cotton Swabs—Reynolds Metals Company; *U.S. Public*, pg. 1385

HANDI WIPES—Reusable Cloths—Colgate-Palmolive Company; *U.S. Public*, pg. 397

HANDI-WRAP—Plastic Film—The Dow Chemical Company; *U.S. Public*, pg. 522

HANDI-WRAP—Food Storage Wrap—DowBrands, L.P.; *U.S. Public*, pg. 523

HANDI-WRAP II—Plastic Film—The Dow Chemical Company; *U.S. Public*, pg. 522

HANDI-HOLD—Spatula—Fisher Scientific Company; *U.S. Private*, pg. 658

HANDICHECK—Checking Service—NBD Bank (Indiana); *U.S. Public*, pg. 628

HANDIMATCH—Portable Computer Color Matching System—Devoe Paint; *Int'l*, pg. 663

HANDIMATCH—Portable Computer Color Matching System—ICI Paints; *Int'l*, pg. 664

HANDIMET—Abrasive Strip Grinder—Buehler, Limited; *U.S. Public*, pg. 574

HANDIMOUNT—Biological Supplies—Carolina Biological Supply Co.; *U.S. Private*, pg. 213

HANDIWIPES—Disposable Cleaning Cloths—Softsoap Enterprises, Inc.; *U.S. Public*, pg. 397

HANDIWIRE—Extention Cords, Drop Lights—Essex International, Inc.; *U.S. Public*, pg. 593

HANDLE-IT—Office Mobile Storage Systems—Tab Products Co.; *U.S. Public*, pg. 1559

THE HANDLE—Instant Camera—Eastman Kodak Company; *U.S. Public*, pg. 550

HANDLEMAN—Phonographic Records, Tapes, Books, Video Cassettes Computer Software—Handleman Company; *U.S. Public*, pg. 779

HANDLE2—Instant Camera—Eastman Kodak Company; *U.S. Public*, pg. 550

HANDMACHER—Women's Apparel—Hartmarx Corporation; *U.S. Public*, pg. 795

HANDMACHER—Suits—International Women's Apparel Group; *U.S. Public*, pg. 796

HANDS DOWN—Game—Milton Bradley Company; *U.S. Public*, pg. 797

HANDSAN—Hand Cream—Wella Group; *Int'l*, pg. 1489

HANDSDOWN—Manicure Towels, Nail Wipers—Kimberly-Clark Corporation; *U.S. Public*, pg. 958

HANDSOME REWARDS—Mail Order House—Starcrest Products of California; *U.S. Private*, pg. 1035

HANDWASH—Control Inc. in & Sold as a Component Part of a Clothes Washing Machine—General Electric Canada Inc.; *U.S. Public*, pg. 713

HANDWRITTEN FONTS—NONE—Broderbund Software, Inc.; *U.S. Public*, pg. 258

HANDY ALUMIBRAZE—Brazing Aluminum—Handy & Harman; *U.S. Public*, pg. 780

HANDY ANDY—Repair Part Assortments—J.A. Sexauer, Inc.; *U.S. Public*, pg. 352

HANDY BUFFER—Power Buffer—The Black & Decker Corporation; *U.S. Public*, pg. 233

HANDY CUTTERS—Carton Cutters—Pacific Handy Cutter, Inc.; *U.S. Private*, pg. 831

HANDY FILL—Pepper Pouch—McCormick & Company, Incorporated; *U.S. Public*, pg. 1066

HANDY-FLUX—Flux for Brazing—Handy & Harman; *U.S. Public*, pg. 780

HANDY FUEL—Canned Heat—Colgate-Palmolive Co., Institutional Products Div.; *U.S. Public*, pg. 397

HANDY HERMAN—Manually-Propelled Aerial Work Platform—Mayville Engineering Co., Inc.; *U.S. Private*, pg. 718

HANDY HOOKS—Hardware—Knape & Vogt Mfg. Co.; *U.S. Public*, pg. 963

HANDY LAZERBLADE KNIFE—Art Knife—Pacific Handy Cutter, Inc.; *U.S. Private*, pg. 831

HANDY-LINE—Promotional Cigar Cutters & Torches—Pacific Handy Cutter, Inc.; *U.S. Private*, pg. 831

HANDY-PAC—Electronic Wire & Cable—General Cable Corporation; *Int'l*, pg. 1486

HANDY PACK—Special Type of Plastic Molded Put-up for Twine, Rope, Cords & Clotheslines—Crowe Rope Industries L.L.C.; *U.S. Private*, pg. 291

HANDY SOUND—Electronic Instruments—Yamaha Corporation of America; *Int'l*, pg. 1516

HANDY STEAMER—Food Steamer/Rice Cooker—The Black & Decker Corporation; *U.S. Public*, pg. 233

HANDYBLENDER—Power Blender—The Black & Decker Corporation; *U.S. Public*, pg. 233

HANDYCAM—Video Camera—Sony Electronics; *Int'l*, pg. 1281

HANDYCHOPPER—Mincer/Chopper—The Black & Decker Corporation; *U.S. Public*, pg. 233

HANDYDRIVER—NONE—The Black & Decker Corporation; *U.S. Public*, pg. 233

HANDYMAN—Tools—The Stanley Works; *U.S. Public*, pg. 1508

HANDYMIXER—Power Mixer—The Black & Decker Corporation; *U.S. Public*, pg. 233

HANDYPOST—Yard Posts—Universal Industrial Products Co.; *U.S. Public*, pg. 1677

HANDYSERIES—Household Products—The Black & Decker Corporation; *U.S. Public*, pg. 233

HANDYSKIN-HANDYCOAT—NONE—Cockerill Sambre; *Int'l*, pg. 301

HANDYXPRESS—Household Products—The Black & Decker Corporation; *U.S. Public*, pg. 233

HANES—Hosiery—Hanes Hosiery, Inc.; *U.S. Public*, pg. 1434

HANES—Hosiery & Underwear for Men & Boys—Sara Lee Corporation; *U.S. Public*, pg. 1432

HANES—Socks—Sara Lee Sock Company; *U.S. Public*, pg. 1434

HANES ALIVE—Pantyhose—Hanes Hosiery, Inc.; *U.S. Public*, pg. 1434

HANES HER WAY—Hosiery—Sara Lee Corporation; *U.S. Public*, pg. 1432

HANES HER WAY—Coordinate Knitwear—Sara Lee Hosiery; *U.S. Public*, pg. 1434

HANES HER WAY—Socks—Sara Lee Sock Company; *U.S. Public*, pg. 1434

HANES SOFT STEPS—Footwear—Sara Lee Hosiery; *U.S. Public*, pg. 1434

HANES TOO—Hosiery—Hanes Hosiery, Inc.; *U.S. Public*, pg. 1434

HANES TOO—Hosiery—Sara Lee Corporation; *U.S. Public*, pg. 1432

HANG TEN—Footwear—Genfoot Inc.; *Int'l*, pg. 549

HANG-UP—Wall Mounted Hair Dryer—Andis Company; *U.S. Private*, pg. 73

HANGIN' ON THE RIM—NONE—Brazos Sportswear Inc.; *U.S. Public*, pg. 251

HANIMEX—Cameras—Gestetner Holdings PLC; *Int'l*, pg. 1114

HANLEY—Pilsner Beer—Falstaff Brewing Corporation; *U.S. Private*, pg. 955

HANNA—Commercial Machinery & Equip.—Hanna Corporation; *U.S. Private*, pg. 231

HANNA-BARBERA CARTOONS—NONE—Turner Broadcasting System Inc.; *U.S. Public*, pg. 1614

HANNA-BARBERA—Motion Picture Films—Hanna-Barbera Productions, Inc.; *U.S. Public*, pg. 1614

HANNAFORD FOOD AND DRUG—Retail Food & Drug Stores—Hannaford Bros. Co.; *U.S. Public*, pg. 781

HANNAH & HOGG—Liquors—NWS Inc.; *U.S. Private*, pg. 772

HANNAY REELS—Reels—Hannay Reels; *U.S. Private*, pg. 499

HANNCOCK'S HB—Bitter—Bass PLC; *Int'l*, pg. 169

HANNIBAL—NONE—Pfizer Inc.; *U.S. Public*, pg. 1281

HANNIBAL COURIER POST—Newspaper—Shivers Trading & Operating Co.; *U.S. Private*, pg. 994

HANOVER—Footwear—Clarks International; *Int'l*, pg. 296

HANOVER—Processed & Frozen Foods—Hanover Foods Corporation; *U.S. Private*, pg. 499

HANOVER—Fire & Casualty Insurance Company—The Hanover Insurance Company; *U.S. Public*, pg. 54

HANOVER—Shoes—Hanover Stores; *Int'l*, pg. 297

HANOVER HOUSE—Novelties & Housewares Catalog—Hanover Direct, Inc.; *U.S. Public*, pg. 782

HANOVER HOUSE—Gift Items & Catalogs—Hanover Direct Pennsylvania, Inc.; *U.S. Public*, pg. 782

HANOVER SLATE—Vinyl Composition Tile—Kentile Operting Co.; *U.S. Private*, pg. 615

HANOVIA—Ultraviolet Equipment for Water Treatment & Disinfection—Halma p.l.c.; *Int'l*, pg. 589

HANOVIA—Lamps—Hanovia Colight; *Int'l*, pg. 17

HANSA—Organic Pigments—Hoechst Aktiengesellschaft; *Int'l*, pg. 624

Brand Name Index

HANSAGLAST—NONE—Beiersdorf S.A.; *Int'l*, pg. 183
HANSEN—Couplings—Tuthill Corporation; *U.S. Private*, pg. 1110
HANSON—Taps, Dies & Drill Bits—American Tool Companies, Inc.; *U.S. Private*, pg. 63
HANSON INDUSTRIES—Meat Packing—Hanson North America; *Int'l*, pg. 593
HANSON SCALE CO.—Scales—Sunbeam Corporation; *U.S. Public*, pg. 1533
HANUTA—Chocolate Bars—Ferrero; *Int'l*, pg. 480
HANY—Missy Division-Ladies—Andrew Sports Club Inc.; *U.S. Private*, pg. 73
HAPMAN—Bulk Handling Conveyors & Systems—Prab, Inc.; *U.S. Public*, pg. 1319
HAPPINESS—Foam-In Hair Color—Clairol, Inc.; *U.S. Public*, pg. 254
HAPPY CABANA—Portable Play Yard—Evenflo Company, Inc.; *U.S. Private*, pg. 629
HAPPY CAMPER—Portable Play Yard—Evenflo Company, Inc.; *U.S. Private*, pg. 629
HAPPY CAT—Cat Food—Ralston Purina Company; *U.S. Public*, pg. 1359
HAPPY CHEF—NONE—Allen Canning Company; *U.S. Private*, pg. 36
HAPPY DAYS—High Chair—Evenflo Company, Inc.; *U.S. Private*, pg. 629
HAPPY ENDING—Ice Cream Dessert—Friendly Ice Cream Corp.; *U.S. Public*, pg. 682
HAPPY FACE—Cleansing Lotion—The Gillette Company; *U.S. Public*, pg. 743
HAPPY FACTOR—Information Technology & Services—The Black & Decker Corporation; *U.S. Public*, pg. 233
HAPPY GO LIGHTLY—Shoes—P.W. Minor & Son, Inc.; *U.S. Private*, pg. 751
HAPPY HOLIDAY—Christmas Trees—Happy Holiday Tree Farms; *U.S. Private*, pg. 254
HAPPY HOLIES—Greeting Cards—American Greetings Corporation; *U.S. Public*, pg. 77
HAPPY JACK—Syrup—Borden, Inc.; *U.S. Private*, pg. 157
HAPPY KIDS—Pickles, Peanut Butter & Syrup—Dean Pickles & Specialty Products; *U.S. Public*, pg. 490
HAPPY MEAL—Children's Meal—McDonald's Corporation; *U.S. Public*, pg. 1068
HAPPY SHOPPER—Groceries—Booker PLC; *Int'l*, pg. 202
HAPPY TIME—Ice Cream & Related Items—Certified Grocers of California; *U.S. Private*, pg. 226
HAR TECH—Agency Automation System—Harleysville Group; *U.S. Public*, pg. 786
HARBIL—Fluid Mixing, Metering Equipment—IDEX Corporation; *U.S. Public*, pg. 862
HARBINGER—Carpets & Rugs—Mohawk Industries, Inc.; *U.S. Public*, pg. 1121
HARBISON-WALKER—Refractory Products—Global Industrial Technologies; *U.S. Public*, pg. 747
HARBOR MASTER—NONE—R&B, Inc.; *U.S. Public*, pg. 1354
HARBOR ONE—Mens' & Boys Apparel—Williamson-Dickie Mfg. Co.; *U.S. Private*, pg. 1179
HARBORMASTER—Telescopes—Bushnell Corporation; *U.S. Private*, pg. 1191
HARBORTOWN—Aluminum Siding—Reynolds Metals Company; *U.S. Public*, pg. 1385
HARBOUR CLASSICS—NONE—Tandy Brands Accessories, Inc.; *U.S. Public*, pg. 1560
HARCO—Safety Check Paper—John H. Harland Company; *U.S. Public*, pg. 785
HARD AS NAILS—Nail Hardner—Sally Hansen; *U.S. Public*, pg. 494
HARD BODY—Toys—Strombecker Corporation; *U.S. Private*, pg. 1047
HARD BOILED—Hard Hats—E.D. Bullard Company; *U.S. Private*, pg. 180
HARD FLEX—High Grade Saw Blades—Lawson Products, Inc.; *U.S. Public*, pg. 980
HARD HAT—Industrial Spray Coatings—Rust-Oleum Corporation; *U.S. Public*, pg. 1358
HARDBODY—Handheld Pen-Based Mobile Ruggedized Computer—Texas Micro, Inc.; *U.S. Public*, pg. 1586
HARDCARD—Hard Disk Expansion Board for Personal Computers—Quantum Corporation; *U.S. Public*, pg. 1350

HARDEN—Furniture Co—Harden Furniture Company; *U.S. Private*, pg. 501
HARDHEAD FLAIR—Plastic Tip Pens—The Gillette Company; *U.S. Public*, pg. 743
HARDI DUX—Hot Water System—James Hardie Industries Ltd.; *Int'l*, pg. 596
HARDIBACKER—Fibre Cement Building Products—James Hardie Industries Ltd.; *Int'l*, pg. 596
HARDIBRACE—Internal Lining—James Hardie Industries Ltd.; *Int'l*, pg. 596
HARDIFENCE—Internal Lining—James Hardie Industries Ltd.; *Int'l*, pg. 596
HARDIGLAZE—Fibre Cement Building Boards—James Hardie Industries Ltd.; *Int'l*, pg. 596
HARDIKOTE—Gypsum—James Hardie Industries Ltd.; *Int'l*, pg. 596
HARDIPANEL—Insulated Panels—James Hardie Industries Ltd.; *Int'l*, pg. 596
HARDIPLANK—Fibre Cement Building Products—James Hardie Industries Ltd.; *Int'l*, pg. 596
HARDIPLAS—PVC Pipe—James Hardie Industries Ltd.; *Int'l*, pg. 596
HARDIPRIME—Fibre Cement Building Boards—James Hardie Industries Ltd.; *Int'l*, pg. 596
HARDISHAKE—Fibre Cement Building Products—James Hardie Industries Ltd.; *Int'l*, pg. 596
HARDISOFT—Fibre Cement Building Products—James Hardie Industries Ltd.; *Int'l*, pg. 596
HARDITEX—Fibre Cement Building Products—James Hardie Industries Ltd.; *Int'l*, pg. 596
HARDITUBE—PVC Pipe—James Hardie Industries Ltd.; *Int'l*, pg. 596
HARDIWALL—NONE—James Hardie Industries Ltd.; *Int'l*, pg. 596
HARDNOSE—Bumper Cover—Lund International Holdings, Inc.; *U.S. Public*, pg. 1020
HARDSET—Heat Curing Hard Rubber Compound—Hardman Division of Harcros Chemicals, Inc.; *Int'l*, pg. 598
HARDWARE CONFIGURATION DEFINITION—Computer Product—International Business Machines Corporation; *U.S. Public*, pg. 895
HARDWARE HANK—Retail Hardware Stores—United Hardware Distributing Co.; *U.S. Private*, pg. 335
HARDWARE UNIVERSITY—NONE—Ace Hardware Corporation; *U.S. Private*, pg. 12
HARDWEAR—Hard Steel Plate for Abrasion Resistent Application—Lukens Steel Company; *U.S. Public*, pg. 1020
HARDWICK—Ranges—Maytag Corporation; *U.S. Public*, pg. 1064
HARDWICK CLOTHES—Clothing—Hardwick Clothes Inc.; *U.S. Private*, pg. 502
HARDWICK STOVE—Gas—Maytag Cleveland Cooking Products; *U.S. Public*, pg. 1064
HARDWIRE—Low Cost, High Volume Non-Reprogrammable FPGA—Xilinx, Inc.; *U.S. Public*, pg. 1786
HARDWOOD HOUSE—Wood Office Furniture—Allsteel, Inc.; *U.S. Public*, pg. 772
HARDY—Shoes—Genesco Inc.; *U.S. Public*, pg. 728
HAREM—Rugs & Carpets—Glenoit Mills, Inc.; *U.S. Private*, pg. 456
HARGRAVE—Vise—Wilton Corporation; *U.S. Private*, pg. 1181
HARGRO PACKAGING—Flexible Packaging Products—Hargro Enterprises, Inc.; *U.S. Private*, pg. 502
HARIBO—NONE—Cruspi S.A.; *Int'l*, pg. 348
HARIG—Machine Tools—Harig Products; *U.S. Public*, pg. 252
HARK—NONE—GTE Internetworking; *U.S. Public*, pg. 696
HARKER'S FLAV-R-CUT—Swiss Steak, Beef Fritters, Kabob Meat & Steaks—Harker's Distribution, Inc.; *U.S. Private*, pg. 502
HARKER'S PREMIUM-CUT—Steaks—Harker's Distribution, Inc.; *U.S. Private*, pg. 502
HARKER'S TEND-R-CUT—Steaks—Harker's Distribution, Inc.; *U.S. Private*, pg. 502
HARLAN MACHINERY—Laminating Presses—Patrick Industries Inc.; *U.S. Public*, pg. 1264
HARLEQUIN—NONE—Harlequin Enterprises Ltd.; *Int'l*, pg. 1402
HARLEQUIN HISTORICALS—Romance Paperbacks—Silhouette Books; *Int'l*, pg. 1402

HARLEY DAVIDSON—Manufacturer of Motorcycles, Motorcycle Clothing & Accessories—Harley-Davidson Motor Company; *U.S. Public*, pg. 786
HARLEY-DAVIDSON—T-Shirts, Sweatshirts, Suspenders, Caps & Transfers—Holoubek Inc.; *U.S. Private*, pg. 536
HARLEY-DAVIDSON—Cigarettes—Lorillard Tobacco Company; *U.S. Public*, pg. 1011
HARLEY-DAVIDSON WATCHES—NONE—Bulova Corporation; *U.S. Public*, pg. 1010
HARLEY, MOTOR CLOTHES—Clothing—Harley-Davidson, Inc.; *U.S. Public*, pg. 786
HARMAN KARDON—Components—Harman Consumer Group; *U.S. Public*, pg. 787
HARMAN KARDON—Electronic Components—Harman International Industries, Inc.; *U.S. Public*, pg. 787
HARMON HOMES—NONE—United Advertising Publications, Inc.; *Int'l*, pg. 1443
HARMONALYZER—Powerline Harmonic Power Analyzer—Amprobe Instrument; *U.S. Public*, pg. 1676
HARMONIZER—Positive Pressure Ventilation Unit—CTB International Corp.; *U.S. Public*, pg. 284
HARMONIZER—Scale Stabilizing Software—Weigh-Tronix, Inc.; *Int'l*, pg. 1299
HARMONIZERS—2X6 Liners Silk Screened Design—Monarch Tile, Inc.; *U.S. Private*, pg. 287
HARMONY—NONE—Ace Hardware Corporation; *U.S. Private*, pg. 12
HARMONY—NONE—Crown Publishers, Inc.; *U.S. Private*, pg. 21
HARMONY—Women's Apparel—International Cosmetics Co., Ltd.; *Int'l*, pg. 684
HARMONY—Telephone Sets—Northern Telecom Limited; *Int'l*, pg. 968
HARMONY—Book Imprint—Random House, Inc.; *U.S. Private*, pg. 20
HARNOIS—Cookies—RJR Nabisco Holdings Corp.; *U.S. Public*, pg. 1354
HAROSYN—Brushless Resolver—API Harowe; *U.S. Public*, pg. 90
HAROT—Kosher Poultry—Empire Kosher Poultry, Inc.; *U.S. Private*, pg. 374
HARP—Lager—Guinness Import Company; *Int'l*, pg. 412
HARP LAGER—NONE—Guinness Plc; *Int'l*, pg. 412
HARP'S FOOD STORE—Retail Groceries—Harp's Food Stores, Inc.; *U.S. Private*, pg. 504
HARPER—Clothing—Harcrest International, Ltd.; *U.S. Private*, pg. 500
HARPER & ROW—Publisher—HarperCollins Publishers; *Int'l*, pg. 926
HARPER PAPERBACKS—Books—HarperCollins Publishers; *Int'l*, pg. 926
HARPER PRISM—Books—HarperCollins Publishers; *Int'l*, pg. 926
HARPER'S BAZAAR—Magazine—The Hearst Corporation; *U.S. Private*, pg. 515
HARPER'S BAZAAR—Magazine—Hearst Magazines Division; *U.S. Private*, pg. 516
HARPERS—Metal Office Furniture—Kimball International, Inc.; *U.S. Public*, pg. 956
HARPERS & QUEEN—Magazine—The National Magazine Company Ltd.; *U.S. Private*, pg. 518
HARPIC—Lavatory Cleaners—Reckitt & Colman plc; *Int'l*, pg. 1089
HARPOON—Metal Chip Conveyors—Prab, Inc.; *U.S. Public*, pg. 1319
HARRAH'S—Casino—Harrah's Entertainment, Inc.; *U.S. Public*, pg. 790
HARRAH'S JAZZ CASINO—NONE—Harrah's Entertainment, Inc.; *U.S. Public*, pg. 790
HARRAH'S NORTHERN STAR—NONE—Harrah's Entertainment, Inc.; *U.S. Public*, pg. 790
HARRIER—Military Aircraft—British Aerospace p.l.c.; *Int'l*, pg. 217
HARRIER—NONE—Datametrics Corporation; *U.S. Public*, pg. 487
HARRINGTON—Ham—Harrington's of Vermont, Inc.; *U.S. Private*, pg. 504
HARRINGTONS—NONE—Glynwed International PLC; *Int'l*, pg. 554
HARRIS—Canned Crabmeat—Borden, Inc.; *U.S. Private*, pg. 157
HARRIS—Seafood Soups—Bunker Hill Foods Inc.; *U.S. Private*, pg. 219

HARRIS—NONE—Castleberry/Snow's Brands Inc.; *U.S. Private*, pg. 219

HARRIS—Paint—Grow Group, Inc.; *Int'l*, pg. 663

HARRIS—NONE—Harris Calorific Co.; *U.S. Public*, pg. 996

HARRIS—Digital Telephone Systems—Harris Corp., Digital Telephone Systems Div.; *U.S. Public*, pg. 791

HARRIS—Shear—Harris Waste Mgmt. Group, Inc.; *Int'l*, pg. 473

HARRIS—Paint—ICI Paints; *Int'l*, pg. 664

HARRIS—Coffee & Tea—Sara Lee Corporation; *U.S. Public*, pg. 1432

HARRIS ADACOMNETWORK SERVICES—NONE—Genicom Corporation; *U.S. Public*, pg. 729

HARRIS DEVLIN ASSOCIATES—NONE—SunGard Data Systems Inc.; *U.S. Public*, pg. 1534

HARRIS FORD—Isuzu—Harris Ford, Inc.; *U.S. Private*, pg. 506

HARRIS/GALANTE—Porous Hip—Bristol-Myers Squibb Company; *U.S. Public*, pg. 253

HARRIS TEETER—Grocery Stores—Ruddick Corporation; *U.S. Public*, pg. 1412

HARRISON—Radiator—General Motors Corporation; *U.S. Public*, pg. 718

HARRY AND DAVID—Fruit & Gift Mail Order—Harry and David; *Int'l*, pg. 1518

HARRY WINSTON—Precious Jewels—Harry Winston, Inc.; *U.S. Private*, pg. 1183

HART—Publishers—Banta Publications Group; *U.S. Public*, pg. 188

HART SCHAFFNER & MARX—Men's Apparel—Hartmarx Corporation; *U.S. Public*, pg. 795

HARTCO—Hardwood Flooring—Premark International, Inc.; *U.S. Public*, pg. 1321

HARTE-HANKS—Communications—Harte-Hanks Communications, Inc.; *U.S. Public*, pg. 793

HARTER—Trade Style-Corp.—Harter; *U.S. Private*, pg. 581

HARTER—Ergonomic Office Seating—Jami, Inc.; *U.S. Private*, pg. 581

HARTEX—Pale Crepe Rubber & Latex Rubber—Bridgestone/Firestone, Inc.; *Int'l*, pg. 213

HARTFIELD'S—NONE—Petrie Retail, Inc.; *U.S. Private*, pg. 858

HARTFORD—Glass Machinery—The Black & Decker Corporation; *U.S. Public*, pg. 233

THE HARTFORD STAG—NONE—The Hartford Financial Services Group Inc.; *U.S. Public*, pg. 794

HARTLAND-HORSES—Model—Steven Manufacturing Co.; *U.S. Private*, pg. 1042

HARTLEY—NONE—Canandaigua Wine Company Div.; *U.S. Public*, pg. 300

HARTLEY & PARKER SCOTCH—NONE—Star Industries Inc.; *U.S. Private*, pg. 1034

HARTLEY BRANDY—NONE—Barton Brands, Ltd.; *U.S. Public*, pg. 300

HARTMAN—Division—Communications Instruments Inc.; *U.S. Private*, pg. 259

HARTMAN—Unitload System—SI Handling Systems, Inc.; *U.S. Public*, pg. 1418

HARTMAN LUGGAGE—Luggage & Business Cases—Brown-Forman Corporation; *U.S. Public*, pg. 261

HARTMANN—Luggage—Hartmann Luggage & Leather Goods Group; *U.S. Public*, pg. 261

HARTMANN—Luggage & Leather Goods—Lenox, Incorporated; *U.S. Public*, pg. 261

THE HARTMANN INTERNATIONAL—Luggage—Hartmann Luggage & Leather Goods Group; *U.S. Public*, pg. 261

HART'S—Milk—Dean Foods Company; *U.S. Public*, pg. 489

HARTS—Discount Department Stores—The Penn Traffic Company; *U.S. Public*, pg. 1270

HARTZ—Pet Supplies—The Hartz Mountain Corp.; *U.S. Private*, pg. 508

HARVARD—NONE—Software Publishing Corporation; *U.S. Public*, pg. 1483

HARVARD CHART XL—Graphical Charting Software—Software Publishing Corporation; *U.S. Public*, pg. 1483

HARVARD GRAPHICS—Presentation Graphics Software—Software Publishing Corporation; *U.S. Public*, pg. 1483

HARVARD SPOTLIGHT—Presenting Support Software—Software Publishing Corporation; *U.S. Public*, pg. 1483

HARVEST—Records—Capitol Records, Inc.; *Int'l*, pg. 428

HARVEST—Plywood, Lumber, Wood, & Wood Fiber Products—Georgia-Pacific Corporation; *U.S. Public*, pg. 735

HARVEST CRISPS—Crackers—Nabisco Inc.; *U.S. Public*, pg. 1355

HARVEST CRISPS—Snack Crackers—RJR Nabisco Holdings Corp.; *U.S. Public*, pg. 1354

HARVEST CRUNCH—Cereal—The Quaker Oats Company; *U.S. Public*, pg. 1347

HARVEST DAY—NONE—Eagle Food Centers, Inc.; *U.S. Public*, pg. 547

HARVEST FOODS—Grocery Stores—URM Stores, Inc.; *U.S. Private*, pg. 1114

HARVEST GRAIN N NUT—Menu Item—IHOP Corp.; *U.S. Public*, pg. 862

HARVEST LANE—Preserves—RCB Baking Company; *U.S. Public*, pg. 1354

HARVEST MOON—Foods—Seneca Foods Corporation; *U.S. Public*, pg. 1456

HARVEST RECIPE—Bread—Roman Meal Company; *U.S. Private*, pg. 942

HARVEST SPICE—Herb Tea—Celestial Seasonings; *U.S. Public*, pg. 319

HARVEST VALUE—NONE—JP Foodservice, Inc.; *U.S. Public*, pg. 918

HARVESTERS—Domestic Cigars—Consolidated Cigar Corporation; *U.S. Private*, pg. 690

HARVESTORE—Crop Storage Systems—A.O. Smith Corporation; *U.S. Public*, pg. 1476

HARVEY—Sterilizers—Barnstead/Thermolyne Corporation; *U.S. Public*, pg. 1545

HARVEY—Chemiclave Sterilizers—Getinge/Castle Inc.; *Int'l*, pg. 551

FRED HARVEY—Resorts—Amfac, Inc.; *U.S. Private*, pg. 577

HARVEY'S—Hamburger Restaurants—Cara Operations Limited; *Int'l*, pg. 266

HARVEYS BRISTOL CREAM—Sherry—Allied Domecq PLC; *Int'l*, pg. 62

HARVEY'S BRISTOL CREAM—Sherry—Harveys of Bristol Limited; *Int'l*, pg. 63

HARVEYS BRISTOL DRY—Sherry—Allied Domecq PLC; *Int'l*, pg. 62

HARVEYS BRISTOL MILK—Sherry—Allied Domecq PLC; *Int'l*, pg. 62

HARVEYS CLUBAMONTLLADO—Sherry—Allied Domecq PLC; *Int'l*, pg. 62

HARVEYS DUNE—Sherry—Allied Domecq PLC; *Int'l*, pg. 62

HARVEYS ISIS—Sherry—Allied Domecq PLC; *Int'l*, pg. 62

HARVEYS MADERA—Wine—Allied Domecq PLC; *Int'l*, pg. 62

HARVEYS NO. 1 RANGE—Wine—Allied Domecq PLC; *Int'l*, pg. 62

HARVIKRAFT—Laminated Packaging—Carter Holt Harvey Limited; *U.S. Public*, pg. 904

HARWOOD VISUALS—Conference & Training Room Furniture—Furniture Group Industries; *U.S. Private*, pg. 432

HASBRO—NONE—MB Espana, S.A.; *U.S. Public*, pg. 798

HASH ROUNDS—Breakfast Potatoes—Hardee's Food Systems, Inc.; *U.S. Public*, pg. 278

HASK PLACENTA—Hair Treatment—Hask Toiletries; *U.S. Private*, pg. 509

HASKEL—Pumps, Gas Booster & Related Access.—Haskel International, Inc.; *U.S. Public*, pg. 798

HASLER—Heavy Duty Feeders—K-Tron International, Inc.; *U.S. Public*, pg. 938

HASSELBLAD—Cameras, Lenses, Magazines—Hasselblad USA, Inc.; *Int'l*, pg. 1468

HASTELLOY—Metals Class 6—Haynes International, Inc.; *U.S. Public*, pg. 801

HASTING—Tool Line—Hastings Manufacturing Company; *U.S. Public*, pg. 798

HATFIELD—Fresh Pork, Hams, Bacon, Sausage—Hatfield Quality Meats; *U.S. Private*, pg. 510

HATHAWAY—Scotch Whiskey—John Gross & Co.; *U.S. Private*, pg. 483

HATHAWAY—Shirts & Sportswear—C.F. Hathaway; *U.S. Private*, pg. 510

HATTERAS—Spa Light—Essef Corporation; *U.S. Public*, pg. 592

HATTERAS—Yachts and Convertible Fishing Boats—Genmar Holdings, Inc.; *U.S. Private*, pg. 447

HATTERAS—Yachts—Hatteras Yachts; *U.S. Private*, pg. 447

HATZ—Diesel Engines—Harley Industries, Inc.; *U.S. Public*, pg. 880

HAUCK PULSE FIRING SYSTEM—Burner Control & Management Combustion System—Hauck Mfg. Co.; *U.S. Private*, pg. 510

HAUTE CUISINE—Food Service—Campbell Soup Company; *U.S. Public*, pg. 298

HAVAB—Diagnostic Products—Abbott Laboratories; *U.S. Public*, pg. 12

HAVAB EIA—Diagnostic Products—Abbott Laboratories; *U.S. Public*, pg. 12

HAVAB-M—Diagnostic Products—Abbott Laboratories; *U.S. Public*, pg. 12

HAVAB-M EIA—Diagnostic Products—Abbott Laboratories; *U.S. Public*, pg. 12

HAVABLACK—Chemical Products—Haviland Enterprises; *U.S. Private*, pg. 511

HAVABOND—Chemical Products—Haviland Enterprises; *U.S. Private*, pg. 511

HAVAHART—Non-toxic Pest Control: Mouse & Rat Traps, Molded & Cage Traps—Ekco Group, Inc.; *U.S. Public*, pg. 566

HAVAHART—Caring Control for Small Animals—Woodstream Corporation; *U.S. Public*, pg. 566

HAVAIANAS—Sandals—Sao Paulo Alpargatas S.A.; *Int'l*, pg. 1193

HAVANA CLUB—Cuban Rum—Groupe Pernod Ricard; *Int'l*, pg. 566

HAVANITOS—Cigars—SEITA, Societe Nationale D'Exploitation Industrielle des Tabacs et des Allumettes; *Int'l*, pg. 1219

HAVASOL—Chemical Products—Haviland Enterprises; *U.S. Private*, pg. 511

HAVASTRIP—Chemical Products—Haviland Enterprises; *U.S. Private*, pg. 511

HAVE A MEAL TO YOUR HEALTH—NONE—Koo Koo Roo, Inc.; *U.S. Public*, pg. 966

HAVE-DESK-WILL-TRAVEL—Office Supplies—JM Company; *U.S. Private*, pg. 577

HAVEG—Corrosion-Resistant Matl.—AMETEK, Inc.; *U.S. Public*, pg. 99

HAVEN GRIPS—Wire, Cable Pulling Grips—Klein Tools Inc.; *U.S. Private*, pg. 625

HAVEN'T YOU DONE WITHOUT A TORO LONG ENOUGH?—Advertising Slogan—The Toro Company; *U.S. Public*, pg. 1623

HAVILAND—Fine China, Distribution Only—Baccarat, Inc.; *Int'l*, pg. 132

HAVILAND—Chocolate Candy—Borden, Inc.; *U.S. Private*, pg. 157

HAVILAND—NONE—New England Confectionery Co.; *U.S. Private*, pg. 1113

HAVOLINE—Motor Oil—Texaco Inc.; *U.S. Public*, pg. 1582

HAVRIX—NONE—SmithKline Beecham Corporation; *Int'l*, pg. 1264

HAVRIX—Vaccine—SmithKline Beecham plc; *Int'l*, pg. 1264

HAVRIX—Vaccine—SmithKline Beecham Research Limited; *Int'l*, pg. 1266

HAWAII MANUFACTURERS DIRECTORY—Directory—Manufacturers' News, Inc.; *U.S. Private*, pg. 700

HAWAIIAN—Airlines—Hawaiian Airlines, Inc.; *U.S. Public*, pg. 799

HAWAIIAN ISLAND POPS—NONE—Amurol Confections Co.; *U.S. Public*, pg. 1781

HAWAIIAN PUNCH—Soft Drink—Grant-Lydick Beverage Co.; *U.S. Private*, pg. 470

HAWAIIAN PUNCH—Line of Juices—The Procter & Gamble Company; *U.S. Public*, pg. 1330

HAWAIIAN TROPIC—Skin Care Cosmetics—Tanning Research Labs., Inc.; *U.S. Private*, pg. 1068

HAWAII'S OWN—Fruit Drinks—C. Brewer & Company, Limited; *U.S. Private*, pg. 190

HAWK—Motorcycle—American Honda Motor Co., Inc. Motorcycle Division; *Int'l*, pg. 634

HAWK—After Shave & Cologne—The Mennen Company; *U.S. Public*, pg. 397

HAWK—NONE—Molex Incorporated; *U.S. Public*, pg. 1121

HAWK—NONE—Oshkosh Truck Corporation; *U.S. Public*, pg. 1233

HAWK—Binoculars—Swift Instruments, Inc.; *U.S. Private*, pg. 1058

HAWK-I—Programmable Logic Controller—Amot Controls Corporation; *U.S. Public*, pg. 1405

HAWKEN—Moist Smokeless Tobacco—Conwood Company L.P.; *U.S. Private*, pg. 272

HAWKER 800—Airplane—Raytheon Aircraft Company; *U.S. Public*, pg. 1365

HAWKER HORIZON—Airplane—Raytheon Aircraft Company; *U.S. Public*, pg. 1365

HAWKER 1000—Airplane—Raytheon Aircraft Company; *U.S. Public*, pg. 1365

HAWKEYE—Hampers—Burlington Basket Co.; *U.S. Private*, pg. 183

HAWKEYE—Cameras—Eastman Kodak Company; *U.S. Public*, pg. 550

HAWKEYE—Revolver—Sturm, Ruger & Co., Inc.; *U.S. Public*, pg. 1526

HAWTHORNE—Plywood, Lumber, Wood & Wood Fiber Products—Georgia-Pacific Corporation; *U.S. Public*, pg. 735

HAY & FORAGE GROWER—Bi-Annual Publication—Intertec Publishing; *U.S. Public*, pg. 1327

HAYAT—Bottled Water—Sabanci Holding A.S.; *Int'l*, pg. 1167

HAYES ESP—Communications Accelerator—Hayes Microcomputer Products, Inc.; *U.S. Public*, pg. 801

HAYESCONNECT—Modem Sharing Software—Hayes Microcomputer Products, Inc.; *U.S. Public*, pg. 801

HAYNES—Metals Class 6—Haynes International, Inc.; *U.S. Public*, pg. 801

HAYS—Power Transmission—Echlin Inc.; *U.S. Public*, pg. 560

HAYWARD—Pools—Hayward Industries, Inc.; *U.S. Private*, pg. 513

HAYWARD—Pipe Tobacco—Lane Limited; *Int'l*, pg. 1129

HAYWARD—Valves—Ryan Herco Products Corp.; *U.S. Private*, pg. 953

HAYWOOD—Premium Wines—Racke USA; *Int'l*, pg. 1083

HAYWOOD WINERY—NONE—Buena Vista Winery; *Int'l*, pg. 1083

HAZARDMASTER—Faceshields/Headgear—Aearo Company; *U.S. Private*, pg. 23

HAZE—Air Fresheners—Reckitt & Colman plc; *Int'l*, pg. 1089

HAZEL—Office Product—American Trading and Production Corporation; *U.S. Private*, pg. 63

HAZEL—Business Accessories—ATAPCO Office Products Group; *U.S. Private*, pg. 64

HAZEL BISHOP—Cosmetics & Hair Care Products—Hazel Bishop International; *U.S. Private*, pg. 514

HAZEN—Air Preheater—ABB Inc.; *Int'l*, pg. 3

HAZLUX—Hazardous & Adverse Location Lighting—Thomas & Betts Corporation; *U.S. Public*, pg. 1597

HAZYME—Amyarase Used to Hydrolize Starch in Fruits for Fruit Juices—Royal Gist-Brocades N.V.; *Int'l*, pg. 1142

HEAD—Skiing, Tennis & Golf Equipment—Head USA, Inc.; *U.S. Private*, pg. 514

HEAD & CHEST—Decongestant—The Procter & Gamble Company; *U.S. Public*, pg. 1330

HEAD & SHOULDERS—Shampoo—The Procter & Gamble Company; *U.S. Public*, pg. 1330

HEAD & SHOULDERS—Haircare Products—Procter & Gamble (Health & Beauty Care) Limited; *U.S. Public*, pg. 1332

HEAD & SHOULDERS DRY SCALP—Shampoo—The Procter & Gamble Company; *U.S. Public*, pg. 1330

HEAD LOCK—Musical Instruments—Ludwig Industries; *U.S. Public*, pg. 514

HEADLAND TECHNOLOGY—Corporate Name—LSI Logic Corp.; *U.S. Public*, pg. 971

HEADLAND TECHNOLOGY LOGO DESIGN—Corporate Logo—LSI Logic Corp.; *U.S. Public*, pg. 971

HEADLINE NEWS—News Network—Turner Broadcasting System Inc.; *U.S. Public*, pg. 1614

HEADLINER—NONE—Venture Stores, Inc.; *U.S. Public*, pg. 1716

HEADLINES—Domestic Cigars—Consolidated Cigar Corporation; *U.S. Private*, pg. 690

HEADLINES—Antidandruff Shampoo & Conditioner—SmithKline Beecham plc; *Int'l*, pg. 1264

HEADMASTERS/TASKFORCE—Wet/Dry Vacuums—Breuer/Tornado; *U.S. Private*, pg. 167

HEADS UP—Hair Grooms—The Gillette Company; *U.S. Public*, pg. 743

HEAF—Aerosol Filter—Crown Andersen Inc.; *U.S. Public*, pg. 462

HEAL RELIEF—Consolidation—SLM Holding Corp.; *U.S. Public*, pg. 1419

HEAL REWARDS—Consolidation—SLM Holding Corp.; *U.S. Public*, pg. 1419

HEAL-SEAL STIK—NONE—La-Co Industries Markal Company; *U.S. Private*, pg. 640

HEALD COLLEGES—Professional Schools—Heald Colleges; *U.S. Private*, pg. 514

HEALON—Pharmaceuticals—Pharmacia & Upjohn Adria Laboratories; *Int'l*, pg. 1049

HEALON—NONE—Pharmacia & Upjohn, Inc.; *Int'l*, pg. 1047

HEALTH—Soaps—Health Products Corporation; *U.S. Private*, pg. 514

HEALTH—Consumer Women's Healthy Lifestyle Publication—Time Inc. Health; *U.S. Public*, pg. 1613

HEALTH-A-DAY—Vitamins—Health Products Corporation; *U.S. Private*, pg. 514

HEALTH ADVANTAGE INC—Diabetes Management—Vivra Incorporated; *U.S. Public*, pg. 1723

HEALTH AIRE—Humidifiers—Pollenex; *U.S. Public*, pg. 1391

HEALTH & HEATHER—Natural Remedies—Novo Nordisk A/S; *Int'l*, pg. 987

HEALTH ASSURANCE—Pennsylvania PPO Product—Coventry Corporation; *U.S. Public*, pg. 454

HEALTH ASSURANCE HMO—Ohio HMO Product—Coventry Corporation; *U.S. Public*, pg. 454

HEALTH AT HOME—Blood Pressure Monitors, Digital Thermometers,—Sunbeam Household Products; *U.S. Public*, pg. 1533

HEALTH BODY-BUILDER PROTEIN—Vitamin-Health Products Corporation; *U.S. Private*, pg. 514

HEALTH CENTER—Mattress—The Spring Air Company; *U.S. Private*, pg. 1027

HEALTH CLUB—Massagers & Whirlpool Bath—Pollenex; *U.S. Public*, pg. 1391

HEALTH CODER—Thermal Code Labeling System—TimeMed Labeling Systems, Inc.; *U.S. Private*, pg. 1087

HEALTH COMFORT—Mattress—The Spring Air Company; *U.S. Private*, pg. 1027

HEALTH DIET LIFE—Food Products—Rykoff-Sexton, Inc.; *U.S. Public*, pg. 918

HEALTH/FITNESS BUSINESS—Magazine—Miller Freeman Inc.; *Int'l*, pg. 1443

HEALTH GARD—Toilet Seat Covers—The Tranzonic Companies; *U.S. Public*, pg. 1632

HEALTH HAIR—Vitamins—Health Products Corporation; *U.S. Private*, pg. 514

HEALTH INSURANCE CLAIM FORMS—Claim Forms—TFP Data Systems; *U.S. Private*, pg. 1070

HEALTH MANAGEMENT TECHNOLOGY—Information Technology Publication—Intertec Publishing; *U.S. Public*, pg. 1327

HEALTH MANAGEMENT TECHNOLOGY—NONE—Intertec Publishing; *U.S. Public*, pg. 1328

HEALTH MART—Pharmacy Franchise—McKesson U.S. Health Care; *U.S. Public*, pg. 1073

HEALTH-O-METER—Scales—Signature Brands USA, Inc.; *U.S. Public*, pg. 1472

HEALTH PLAN OF NEVADA—HMO—Sierra Health Services, Inc.; *U.S. Public*, pg. 1469

HEALTH SAVER—NONE—CUC International, Inc.; *U.S. Public*, pg. 320

HEALTH-TEX—Children's Apparel—VF Corporation; *U.S. Public*, pg. 1702

HEALTH-TEX—Children's Apparel—Healthtex; *U.S. Public*, pg. 1702

HEALTHBEAT—Member Newsletter—Humana Health Chicago, Inc.; *U.S. Public*, pg. 847

HEALTHBEE—Vitamins—Health Products Corporation; *U.S. Private*, pg. 514

HEALTHCARE—Sanitary Disposal Service—Rentokil Initial plc; *Int'l*, pg. 1285

HEALTHCARE—Medical Air Systems—Squire-Cogswell Company; *U.S. Private*, pg. 1027

HEALTHCRAFTS—Vitamins & Minerals—Novo Nordisk A/S; *Int'l*, pg. 987

HEALTHDEX—Health Services—Hooper Holmes Corporation; *U.S. Public*, pg. 835

HEALTHFLEX—NONE—Blue Cross and Blue Shield of Massachusetts; *U.S. Private*, pg. 151

HEALTHFLEX—Orthotics for an Active Lifestyle; Aerobics—The Langer Biomechanics Group, Inc.; *U.S. Public*, pg. 978

HEALTHKNIT—Underwear—Delta Apparel; *U.S. Public*, pg. 498

HEALTHMART—Franchised Drugstore Chain—Avatex Corporation; *U.S. Public*, pg. 151

HEALTHMASTER—Fitness Products—Roadmaster/Brunswick; *U.S. Public*, pg. 265

HEALTHTALK—Medical News Program—Westwood One, Inc.; *U.S. Public*, pg. 1763

HEALTHTEAM—NONE—Graham-Field Health Products, Inc.; *U.S. Public*, pg. 757

HEALTHY BAKE—NONE—National Sea Products Limited; *Int'l*, pg. 909

HEALTHY BALANCE—Frozen Dinners—ConAgra, Inc.; *U.S. Public*, pg. 425

HEALTHY CATCH—NONE—National Sea Products Limited; *Int'l*, pg. 909

HEALTHY CHOICE—Frozen Entrees—ConAgra Frozen Food Company; *U.S. Public*, pg. 427

HEALTHY CHOICE—Frozen Dinners—ConAgra, Inc.; *U.S. Public*, pg. 425

HEALTHY FAVORITES—Snacks—Kraft Foods Inc.; *U.S. Public*, pg. 1288

HEALTHY MIND HEALTHY BODY—NONE—Oxford Health Plans Inc.; *U.S. Public*, pg. 1238

HEALTHY PORTION—Further-processed Poultry Items—Louis Kemp Seafood Co.; *U.S. Public*, pg. 1652

HEALTHY RECIPES—Low-Sodium & Low-Fat Shelf Stable Entrees—Novartis Nutrition Corporation; *Int'l*, pg. 974

HEALTHY REQUEST—Soup—Campbell Soup Company; *U.S. Public*, pg. 298

HEALTHY U.S.A.—Foodservice Items—Performance Food Group Company; *U.S. Public*, pg. 1278

HEARD ON THE STREET—Column Heading—Dow Jones & Company, Inc.; *U.S. Public*, pg. 524

HEARGUARD—Ear Plugs—Aearo Company; *U.S. Private*, pg. 23

HEARING AID—NONE—RAYOVAC Corporation; *U.S. Private*, pg. 912

HEARING INSTRUMENTS—Trade Periodical—Advanstar Communications; *U.S. Private*, pg. 22

HEARSAY—Family Game—Mattel Games/Puzzles; *U.S. Public*, pg. 1058

HEARST ANIMATION PRODUCTIONS—T.V. Production—The Hearst Corporation; *U.S. Private*, pg. 515

HEARST BOOKS—Books—The Hearst Corporation; *U.S. Private*, pg. 515

HEARST BOOKS—Adult Books—William Morrow & Co., Inc.; *U.S. Private*, pg. 515

HEARST BOOKS INTERNATIONAL—Books—The Hearst Corporation; *U.S. Private*, pg. 515

HEARST ENTERTAINMENT DISTRIBUTION—T.V. Distribution—The Hearst Corporation; *U.S. Private*, pg. 515

HEARST ENTERTAINMENT PRODUCTIONS—T.V. Production—The Hearst Corporation; *U.S. Private*, pg. 515

HEARST NEW MEDIA & TECHNOLOGY—Ineractive Media—The Hearst Corporation; *U.S. Private*, pg. 515

HEARST NEWS SERVICE—News Wire Service—The Hearst Corporation; *U.S. Private*, pg. 515

HEARST REALTIES—Real Estate—The Hearst Corporation; *U.S. Private*, pg. 515

HEART—Shampoo—The Gillette Company; *U.S. Public*, pg. 743

HEART BEAT—Table Spread—GFA Brands, Inc.; *U.S. Private*, pg. 435

HEART HEALTH—Blend with Garlic & other Herbs—Celestial Seasonings; *U.S. Public*, pg. 319

HEART INTERFACE—Power Inverters—Valley Forge Corporation; *U.S. Public*, pg. 1705

HEART-OF-PINK—Roofing Shingles—Owens Corning; *U.S. Public*, pg. 1236

HEART OF ROCA—Buttercrunch—Brown & Haley; *U.S. Private*, pg. 173

HEART OF THE HIDE—Baseball Gloves—Rawlings Sporting Goods Company; *U.S. Public*, pg. 1361

HEART OF VALUES—Service Mark—D & W Food Centers, Inc.; *U.S. Private*, pg. 300

HEART SMART—NONE—Health Products Corporation; *U.S. Private*, pg. 514

HEART TO HEART—Soft Carrier—Cosco, Inc.; *U.S. Private*, pg. 277

HEARTGARD 30—Ivermectin-Antiparastic for Dogs—Merck & Co., Inc.; *U.S. Public*, pg. 1090

HEARTGARD-30—Animal Health Pharmaceuticals—Merial Ltd.; *U.S. Public*, pg. 1092

HEARTGARD-30—Animal Health Pharmaceuticals—Merial Ltd.; *Int'l*, pg. 1109 ·

HEARTGARD-30 PLUS—Animal Health Pharmaceuticals—Merial Ltd.; *U.S. Public*, pg. 1092

HEARTGARD-30 PLUS—Animal Health Pharmaceuticals—Merial Ltd.; *Int'l*, pg. 1109

HEARTH ESSENTIALS—Fireplace Tools & Accessories—Duraflame, Inc.; *U.S. Private*, pg. 348

HEARTH FARMS—Variety Bread—Stroehmann Bakeries, L.C.; *Int'l*, pg. 1495

HEARTH FARMS—Baked Goods—George Weston Limited; *Int'l*, pg. 1494

HEARTHLOGG—Fire Logs—First Brands Corporation; *U.S. Public*, pg. 626

HEARTHROBS—Greeting Cards—American Greetings Corporation; *U.S. Public*, pg. 77

HEARTHSTEADSHINGLE—Asphalt Roofing—CertainTeed Corporation; *Int'l*, pg. 1170

HEARTLAND—Cutlery & Flatware—Lifetime Hoan Corp.; *U.S. Public*, pg. 992

HEARTLAND NATURAL CEREAL—Cereal—The Pillsbury Company; *Int'l*, pg. 411

HEARTLINE—Disposable Sensors—Burdick, Inc.; *U.S. Private*, pg. 181

HEARTLINE—Gift Items—Hallmark Cards, Inc.; *U.S. Private*, pg. 495

HEART'S DELIGHT—Nectars—Nestle Chocolate & Confection; *Int'l*, pg. 917

HEARTSHEAD—NONE—CertainTeed Corporation; *Int'l*, pg. 1170

HEARTSWOOD—Fighting Varietal Wines—Delicato Vineyards; *U.S. Private*, pg. 322

HEARTWOOD—Engineering Strand Lumber—Weyerhaeuser Forest Products Company; *U.S. Public*, pg. 1764

HEARTY BRAND—Dog Food—Manna Pro Corporation; *U.S. Private*, pg. 700

HEARTY CHEWS—Dog Treats—Ralston Purina Company; *U.S. Public*, pg. 1359

HEARTY CHICKEN NOODLE BOWL-A-SOUP—Soup—Thomas J. Lipton Company; *Int'l*, pg. 1435

THE HEARTY HOLIDAY COLLECTION—NONE—Broderbund Software, Inc.; *U.S. Public*, pg. 258

HEARTY NOODLES—Food Product—Campbell Soup Company Ltd.; *U.S. Public*, pg. 299

HEAT BEATER—NONE—Clairol, Inc.; *U.S. Public*, pg. 254

HEAT DEFIER 11—Seamless Cotton Heat Glove—Jomac, Inc.; *U.S. Private*, pg. 595

HEAT KILLER—Fans & Blowers—Coppus Murray Group, Tuthill Corporation; *U.S. Private*, pg. 1110

HEAT MAX—Cookware—Newell Co.; *U.S. Public*, pg. 1176

HEAT ON DEMAND—Induction Heat Process—Aladdin Synergetics, Inc.; *U.S. Private*, pg. 31

HEAT SEAL—Electronic Device—The Bergquist Company; *U.S. Private*, pg. 135

HEAT SENTRY—Residential Ventilation Products—Butler Ventamatic Corp.; *U.S. Private*, pg. 190

HEAT SINKS—Insulating Components—International Electronic Research Corp.; *U.S. Public*, pg. 286

HEAT SMART—Energy Comparison Program—Aerco International Inc.; *U.S. Private*, pg. 23

HEAT STROKES—Portfolios—The Mead Corporation; *U.S. Public*, pg. 1074

HEAT THRUSTER—Portable Heater—The Black & Decker Corporation; *U.S. Public*, pg. 233

HEAT-TRAK—Electric Ladle & Crucible Heaters—Inductotherm Corp.; *U.S. Private*, pg. 560

HEATBAN—Roof Paint—Jones Blair Company; *U.S. Private*, pg. 596

HEATCASE II—Compact, Cordless Heat Unit for Disinfection of Contact Lenses—Wesley-Jessen; *U.S. Private*, pg. 111

HEATDISH—Parabolic Electric Heater—National Presto Industries, Inc.; *U.S. Public*, pg. 1159

HEATFLON—Heating Panels for Corrosive Liquid Applications—Norton Performance Plastics; *Int'l*, pg. 1174

HEATH BAR—Candy—Huhtamaki Oy; *Int'l*, pg. 638

HEATHER CREAM LIQUER—NONE—Barton Brands, Ltd.; *U.S. Public*, pg. 300

HEATHER-GLO—Liqueur—Montebello Brands Inc.; *U.S. Private*, pg. 758

HEATHER HILL—Plywood, Lumber, Wood & Wood Fiber Products—Georgia-Pacific Corporation; *U.S. Public*, pg. 735

HEALILATOR—Fireplaces—HON Industries Inc.; *U.S. Public*, pg. 772

HEATING/PIPING/AIR CONDITIONING—Periodical—Penton Publishing, Inc.; *U.S. Public*, pg. 1306

HEATRAE SAIDIA—Water Heating—Newmond PLC; *Int'l*, pg. 924

HEATRITE—Furnace—Nordyne Inc.; *U.S. Public*, pg. 1193

HEATWARE—NONE—Ingrid Division of Lawnware; *U.S. Private*, pg. 654

HEATWORKS—Power Tools—The Black & Decker Corporation; *U.S. Public*, pg. 233

HEATWRINGER—Heat Recovery Unit—Lennox International Inc.; *U.S. Private*, pg. 659

HEAVEN—Ice Cream—Nestle USA; *Int'l*, pg. 916

HEAVEN ICE CREAM BARS—NONE—Nestle Ice Cream Co.; *Int'l*, pg. 918

HEAVENLY TRUFFLE—Confectionery—Thorntons PLC; *Int'l*, pg. 1386

HEAVENWOOD—NONE—Callaway Golf Company; *U.S. Public*, pg. 294

HEAVY DUTY DEEP TREAD—Tires—Bridgestone/Firestone, Inc.; *Int'l*, pg. 213

HEAVY DUTY LOW BOY—Tires—Bridgestone/Firestone, Inc.; *Int'l*, pg. 213

HEAVY DUTY MAINTENANCE—High Gloss Oil Base Rust Inhibitive for Interior & Exterior Use—Perry & Derrick Co.; *U.S. Private*, pg. 854

HEAVY DUTY TRANSPORT—Tires—Bridgestone/Firestone, Inc.; *Int'l*, pg. 213

HEAVY-HAULER—Heavy-Duty Platform Model—The Knapheide Mfg. Co.; *U.S. Private*, pg. 626

HEAVY-HAULER JR—Heavy Duty Platform Model—The Knapheide Mfg. Co.; *U.S. Private*, pg. 626

HEAVY MAGNUM—Enhanced Velocity Ammunition—Hornady Manufacturing Company; *U.S. Private*, pg. 539

HEAVY METAL—Heavy Duty Portable Chairs—Clarin; *U.S. Private*, pg. 242

HEAVYGUARD—Roof Insulation—The Dow Chemical Company; *U.S. Public*, pg. 522

HEAVYHANDS—Hand-Held Exercise Equipment—Empire of Carolina, Inc.; *U.S. Public*, pg. 579

HEAVYWIPES—Disposable Cleaning Cloths—Softsoap Enterprises, Inc.; *U.S. Public*, pg. 397

HEBREW NATIONAL—Food Products—National Foods Inc.; *U.S. Public*, pg. 429

HECALI—NONE—Grupo Elektra S.A. de C.V.; *Int'l*, pg. 573

HECCOLON—Turkish Emery—Treibacher Schleifmittel Corp.; *U.S. Private*, pg. 1099

HECHINGER—Hardware Prods.—Hechinger Company Investors II, L.P.; *U.S. Private*, pg. 477

HECHT'S—Department Stores—Hecht's; *U.S. Public*, pg. 1063

HECHT'S—Department Stores—The May Department Stores Company; *U.S. Public*, pg. 1063

HECKERS—Unbleached Naturally White Flour—The Uhlmann Co.; *U.S. Private*, pg. 1115

HECKERT—Horizontal & Vertical Machining Centers—Traub AG; *Int'l*, pg. 1419

HECO—Relays & Circuit Breakers—Eaton Corporation-Heinemann Products, Commercial Controls Division; *U.S. Public*, pg. 557

HECO—Home Loudspeakers—Recoton Corporation; *U.S. Public*, pg. 1369

HEDDON—Fishing Lures—EBSCO Industries, Inc.; *U.S. Private*, pg. 358

HEDEX—NONE—SmithKline Beecham Corporation; *Int'l*, pg. 1264

HEDGE HOG—Electric Lawn & Garden Tools—The Black & Decker Corporation; *U.S. Public*, pg. 233

HEDGEROW HELL—War Game—Monarch Avalon, Inc.; *U.S. Public*, pg. 1123

HEDGES—Gas, Electric & Oil Powered Heaters—Bradford-White Corporation; *U.S. Private*, pg. 164

HEDLINER—Vacuum Formed Prods.—Hedwin Corporation; *Int'l*, pg. 1278

HEDPAK—Blow Molded Containers—Hedwin Corporation; *Int'l*, pg. 1278

HEDRUM—Blow Moulded Prods.—Hedwin Corporation; *Int'l*, pg. 1278

HEDTAINER—Vacuum Formed Prods.—Hedwin Corporation; *Int'l*, pg. 1278

HEELCARE—Sandals—Bangkok Athletic Co., Ltd.; *Int'l*, pg. 146

HEET—NONE—Gold Eagle Company; *U.S. Private*, pg. 459

HEET—Men's & Women's Sportswear—Seattle Pacific Industries, Inc.; *U.S. Private*, pg. 980

HEETSHEET—Vessel Heating Unit.—Thermon Manufacturing Company; *U.S. Private*, pg. 1080

HEFFERITE—Cutlery—Lifetime Hoan Corp.; *U.S. Public*, pg. 992

HEFTY—Disposable Cups & Dishes—Mobil Oil Corporation; *U.S. Public*, pg. 1118

HEFTY BAGS—Trash Bags—Mobil Oil Corporation; *U.S. Public*, pg. 1118

HEFTY BAGS—Trash Bags—Tenneco Packaging, Consumer Products Group; *U.S. Public*, pg. 1579

HEFTY DESIGNS—Waste Baskets—Mobil Land Development Corporation; *U.S. Public*, pg. 1118

HEHR—Windows—Hehr International Inc.; *U.S. Private*, pg. 519

HEHR GLASS CO—Tempered Glass—Hehr International Inc.; *U.S. Private*, pg. 519

HEHR POWERLINE—Alternators—Hehr International Inc.; *U.S. Private*, pg. 519

HEIDELBERG—Salad Dressings—Bestfoods; *U.S. Public*, pg. 223

HEIDELBERGER DAMMSYSTEME—Insulation Panels—Heidelberger Zement A.G.; *Int'l*, pg. 605

HEIDELBERGER FORMENGIPS—Industrial Modelling Gypsum—Heidelberger Zement A.G.; *Int'l*, pg. 605

HEIDELBERGER PUTZSYSTEME—Plasters & Mortars—Heidelberger Zement A.G.; *Int'l*, pg. 605

HEIDI—Bakery—Giant Food Inc.; *U.S. Public*, pg. 741

HEIDOLPH—Mixers—Brinkmann Instruments, Inc.; *U.S. Private*, pg. 169

HEIFETZ—Pickles—Dean Foods Company; *U.S. Public*, pg. 489

HEIFETZ—Food Prods.—Dean Pickle & Specialty Products Co.; *U.S. Public*, pg. 490

HEIL—HVAC Equipment—International Comfort Products; *U.S. Public*, pg. 898

HEIL—Heating & Cooling Prods.—International Comfort Products Corp.; *U.S. Public*, pg. 898

HEINEKEN—Pilsener Beer—Cervejarias Kaiser Brasil Ltda.; *Int'l*, pg. 279

HEINEKEN—Beer—Heineken N.V.; *Int'l*, pg. 608

HEINEKEN—Beer—Heineken USA Inc.; *Int'l*, pg. 608

HEINEKEN—Lager—Whitbread PLC; *Int'l*, pg. 1498

HEINE'S BLEND—Pipe Tobaccos—Consolidated Cigar Corporation; *U.S. Private*, pg. 690

HEINKE—NONE—J.M. Smucker Company; *U.S. Public*, pg. 1480

HEINZ—Baby Food, Beans, Mustard, Seafood Cocktail & Barbecue Sauce—H.J. Heinz Company; *U.S. Public*, pg. 805

HEINZ—NONE—H.J. Heinz Company Australia Ltd.; *U.S. Public*, pg. 807

HEINZ—Product Line Name—H.J. Heinz Company, Limited; *U.S. Public*, pg. 806

HEINZ DEEPFRIES—Frozen Potatoes—Ore-Ida Foods, Inc.; *U.S. Public*, pg. 805

HEINZ 57—Steak Sauce—H.J. Heinz Company; *U.S. Public*, pg. 805

HEINZ KETCHUP—Ketchup—H.J. Heinz Company; *U.S. Public*, pg. 805

HEINZ LITE—Ketchup—H.J. Heinz Company; *U.S. Public*, pg. 805

HEINZEL'S—Cakes, Cheesecakes, Desserts—Ranks Hovis McDougall Limited; *Int'l*, pg. 1395

HEIRESS—Luxury Lotion Soap—SBS Products, Inc.; *U.S. Private*, pg. 955

HEIRLOOM—Manicure Gift Sets—The W.E. Bassett Company; *U.S. Private*, pg. 122

HEIRLOOM—Silverware—Oneida Ltd.; *U.S. Public*, pg. 1225

HEISE—NONE—Dresser Canada, Inc.; *U.S. Public*, pg. 529

HEISE—Instruments & Gauges—Dresser Industries, Inc.; *U.S. Public*, pg. 528

HEKTOWRITER—Business Product—International Business Machines Corporation; *U.S. Public*, pg. 895

HELABIT—Plastic for Permanent Road Markings—Raschig GmbH; *U.S. Private*, pg. 827

HELABITOL—Road Marking Paint—Raschig GmbH; *U.S. Private*, pg. 827

HELEN OF TROY—Professional Hair Care Appliances—Helen of Troy Corporation; *U.S. Public*, pg. 807

HELEN OF TROY—Ladies Apparel—Movie Star, Inc.; *U.S. Public*, pg. 1140

HELENA RUBINSTEN—NONE—L'Oreal Parfumerie; *Int'l*, pg. 819

HELENE CURTIS—Cosmetics—Rhone-Poulenc S.A.; *Int'l*, pg. 1108

HELI-HOIST—Helicopter Transportable Drilling Rigs—Parker Drilling Company; *U.S. Public*, pg. 1259

HELIAN—Trademark—Helian Health Group, Inc.; *U.S. Public*, pg. 1715

HELIAX—Coaxial Cable and Elliptical Waveguide—Andrew Corporation; *U.S. Public*, pg. 112

HELICOIL—Mechanical Fastening Systems—The Black & Decker Corporation; *U.S. Public*, pg. 233

HELICON—Gearing—Illinois Tool Works Inc.; *U.S. Public*, pg. 865

HELIFLOW—Spiral Tube Heat Exchanger—Graham Corporation; *U.S. Public*, pg. 757

HELILOK—Tooth Equipment for Earthmoving Buckets—Esco Corporation; *U.S. Private*, pg. 382

HELIMATE—NONE—AGA Gas, Inc.; *Int'l*, pg. 13

HELIMATE—Balloon Gas, Equipment & Services—AGA Ges.m.b.H.; *Int'l*, pg. 13

HELIOS—Measuring Tools—Fred V. Fowler Company, Inc.; *U.S. Private*, pg. 422

HELIOS—Digital Dry-Process Imaging Systems—Polaroid Corporation; *U.S. Public*, pg. 1313

HELIOS—Cutting Machine—Strippit, Inc.; *U.S. Public*, pg. 862

HELIOSTAR 2000—Gravure Printing Press—Windmoeller & Hoelscher; *Int'l*, pg. 1510

HELIOZ—Carpets & Rugs—Mohawk Industries, Inc.; *U.S. Public*, pg. 1121

HELIX—Motorscooter—American Honda Motor Co., Inc. Motorcycle Division; *Int'l*, pg. 634

HELIX—NONE—DC Comics, Inc.; *U.S. Public*, pg. 1614

HELIX—Paperback Books—Littlefield, Adams & Company; *U.S. Public*, pg. 1001

HELIX—Flexible Screw Conveyors—Prab, Inc.; *U.S. Public*, pg. 1319

HELIX 2000—Helical Reducers & Gear Motors—Regal-Beloit Corporation; *U.S. Public*, pg. 1370

HELIXATE—Antihemophilic Factor (Recombinant)—Centeon, L.L.C.; *Int'l*, pg. 626

HELLAS—Chocolate—Huhtamaki Oy; *Int'l*, pg. 638

HELLER—Plastic Model Kits—Borden, Inc.; *U.S. Private*, pg. 157

HELLERMANN—Fixing & Securing Components—Bowthorpe plc; *Int'l*, pg. 207

HELLESENS—NONE—Duracell International Inc.; *U.S. Public*, pg. 743

HELLMANN'S—Mayonnaise—CPC Foods (Ireland) Ltd.; *U.S. Public*, pg. 225

HELLMANN'S & BEST FOODS—Mayonnaise—CPC Foodservice Group; *U.S. Public*, pg. 224

HELLMANN'S—Mayonnaise, Seasonings & Spices, Salad Dressings—Bestfoods; *U.S. Public*, pg. 223

HELLMANN'S—Mayonnaise & Salad Dressings—Refinerias de Maiz S.A.I.C.F.; *U.S. Public*, pg. 448

HELLMANN'S/BEST FOODS—Mayonnaise—Best Foods; *U.S. Public*, pg. 224

HELLMANN'S/BEST FOODS DIJONNAISE—Mustard—Best Foods; *U.S. Public*, pg. 224

HELLO—Biscuits—Danone Group; *Int'l*, pg. 379

HELLO HEAVEN—Website—Catholic Digest; *U.S. Private*, pg. 220

HELLY-HANSEN—Outerwear—Helly-Hansen (US), Inc.; *Int'l*, pg. 1010

HELLY-TECH—Fabric—Helly-Hansen A/S; *Int'l*, pg. 1010

HELLY-TECH—Rainwear—Helly-Hansen (US), Inc.; *Int'l*, pg. 1010

HELMITIN—Adhesives—Forbo Holding SA; *Int'l*, pg. 496

HELMSLEY—Lodging, Restaurants & Food Service—Helmsley Enterprises, Inc.; *U.S. Private*, pg. 521

HELOSAN—Asceptic Hand Lotion—Cultor Ltd.; *Int'l*, pg. 349

HELP—CB Radios—Thomson Consumer Electronics Inc.; *Int'l*, pg. 1383

HELP!—Specialty Parts—R&B, Inc.; *U.S. Public*, pg. 1354

HELPBUY—Business Product—International Business Machines Corporation; *U.S. Public*, pg. 895

HELPCENTER—Computer Product—International Business Machines Corporation; *U.S. Public*, pg. 895

HELPCLUB—Computer Product—International Business Machines Corporation; *U.S. Public*, pg. 895

THE HELPFUL HARDWARE MAN—NONE—Ace Hardware Corporation; *U.S. Private*, pg. 12

HELPING HANDS—NONE—Derbyshire Building Society; *Int'l*, pg. 394

HELPING PEOPLE MANAGE A BUSINESS CALLED LIFE—Microprocessors & Smart Cards—Lucent Technologies Inc.; *U.S. Public*, pg. 1017

HELPING YOU STAY IN POWER—Sales Slogan—Exide Electronics Group, Inc.; *Int'l*, pg. 126

HELPLEARN—Computer Product—International Business Machines Corporation; *U.S. Public*, pg. 895

HELPMATE—Plastic Grocery Sacks—Sonoco Products Company; *U.S. Public*, pg. 1485

HELPMATE JR.—Plastic Grocery Sack—Sonoco Products Company; *U.S. Public*, pg. 1485

HELPMATE 3000—Plastic Grocery Sack—Sonoco Products Company; *U.S. Public*, pg. 1485

HELPS—Cough Suppressant Tablets—Hershey Chocolate U.S.A.; *U.S. Public*, pg. 812

HELPS—Cough Suppressant Tablets—Hershey Foods Corporation; *U.S. Public*, pg. 811

HELPS—Cough/Throat Drops—Luden's Inc.; *U.S. Public*, pg. 812

HELPWARE—Computer Product—International Business Machines Corporation; *U.S. Public*, pg. 895

HELUVA GOOD—Cheese, Salsa, Dips, Sour Cream, Dairy & Horseradish Prods.—Heluva Good Cheese Inc.; *Int'l*, pg. 752

HELUVA GOOD CHEESE—Cheese Products—Koninklijke BolsWessanen nv; *Int'l*, pg. 750

HELZBERG—Diamonds—Helzberg's Diamond Shops, Inc.; *U.S. Public*, pg. 220

HELZBERG LIMITED EDITION—Jewelry—Helzberg's Diamond Shops, Inc.; *U.S. Public*, pg. 220

HEMACAROTID PATCH—Collagen Coated Knitted Polyester Vascular Patch—Datascope Corp.; *U.S. Public*, pg. 487

HEMACOL—Absorbable Collagen Hemostat Pad—Datascope Corp.; *U.S. Public*, pg. 487

HEMADYNE—Membrane—Pall Corporation; *U.S. Public*, pg. 1253

HEMAFLO 2—Venous Compression Therapy—Camp Healthcare; *Int'l*, pg. 1425

HEMAMAN—Advertising Character—Ruslander & Sons, Inc.; *U.S. Private*, pg. 952

HEMASHIELD—Vascular Graft—Meadox Medicals, Inc.; *U.S. Public*, pg. 247

HEMATALL—Reagent System for Blood Cell Counting—Fisher Scientific Company; *U.S. Private*, pg. 658

HEMATROL—Blood Controls—Hycor Biomedical, Inc.; *U.S. Public*, pg. 851

HEMELING LAGER—Lager—Bass PLC; *Int'l*, pg. 169

HEMESELECT—Immunochemical Reagents & Test Kit for Human Globulin in Feces—Beckman Instruments, Inc.; *U.S. Public*, pg. 199

HEMINEVRIN—Pharmaceutical for CNS—Astra AB; *Int'l*, pg. 93

HEMISODIUM—Ionophores—Eastman Kodak Company; *U.S. Public*, pg. 550

HEMO—Chocolate Drink Mix—Borden, Inc.; *U.S. Private*, pg. 157

HEMO-RO—Water System—Millipore Corporation; *U.S. Public*, pg. 1112

HEMO-SEAL—Needle Suture—Ethicon, Inc.; *U.S. Public*, pg. 928

HEMOCCULT—Occult Blood Test—Beckman Instruments, Inc.; *U.S. Public*, pg. 199

HEMOCCULT II—In Vitro Diagnostic Test—Beckman Instruments, Inc.; *U.S. Public*, pg. 199

HEMOCLIP—Surgical Device—Bristol-Myers Squibb Company; *U.S. Public*, pg. 253

HEMOFIL—Pharmaceutical Prod.—Baxter-Hyland; *U.S. Public*, pg. 196

HEMOFIL M—Antihemophilic Factor—Baxter-Hyland; *U.S. Public*, pg. 196

HEMOFIL M—Clotting Factor For Hemophiliacs—Baxter International Inc.; *U.S. Public*, pg. 196

HEMOGARD—Blood Collection Tube Stopper—Becton Dickinson & Company; *U.S. Public*, pg. 199

HEMOKART—Hemoperfusion Cartridge for Drug Overdose—Fresenius Medical Care (North America); *Int'l*, pg. 505

HEMOPAD—Topical Hemostat—Astra USA, Inc.; *Int'l*, pg. 93

HEMOPHOTOMETER—Measuring Instrument—Fisher Scientific Company; *U.S. Private*, pg. 658

HEMOPUMP—Circulatory Assist Pump—Medtronic, Inc.; *U.S. Public*, pg. 1082

HEMORID—NONE—Pfizer Inc.; *U.S. Public*, pg. 1281

HEMOTHERM—Hyper/Hypthermia Equipment—Cincinnati Sub-Zero Products, Inc.; *U.S. Private*, pg. 240

HEMOVAC HYDROCOAT—Wound Drains—Bristol-Myers Squibb Company; *U.S. Public*, pg. 253

HEMOXIMETER—Hemoglobin, Oxygen Saturation Meter—Radiometer America Inc.; *Int'l*, pg. 1083

HENCOL—Switches, Connectors & All Electrical & Electronic Items—Cole Hersee Company; *U.S. Private*, pg. 251

HENDRIX—Medium Voltage Cable—Thomas & Betts/Amerace; *U.S. Public*, pg. 1598

HENKE—Roller Mills & Feed Wagons—Fleischer Manufacturing, Inc.; *U.S. Private*, pg. 410

HENKEL KGAA—Industrial Chemicals, Household & Car Care Supplies—Henkel KGaA; *Int'l*, pg. 609

HENKELL—Sparkling Wine—Paterno Imports Limited; *U.S. Private*, pg. 843

HENNA N' PLACENTA—Hair Treatment—Hask Toiletries; *U.S. Private*, pg. 509

HENNALUCENT—Hair Care Products—American International Industries; *U.S. Private*, pg. 57

HENNESSY—NONE—LVMH Moet Hennessy Louis Vuitton; *Int'l*, pg. 779

HENNESSY—Apparel—Phillips-Van Heusen Corporation; *U.S. Public*, pg. 1291

HENNESSY—Cognac—Schieffelin & Somerset Co.; *Int'l*, pg. 412

HENNINGSEN—Food Prods.—Henningsen Foods, Inc.; *Int'l*, pg. 1074

HENNY PENNY—Shell Eggs (For State of Arizona Only)—McAnally Enterprises, Inc.; *U.S. Private*, pg. 718

HENRAD—Boilers & Radiators—Caradon Plc; *Int'l*, pg. 266

HENREDON—Bedroom, Dining Room & Upholstered Furniture—Henredon Furniture Industries, Inc.; *U.S. Private*, pg. 432

HENREDON—Furniture—Masco Corporation; *U.S. Public*, pg. 1052

HENRI MARCHANT—Champagne—Canandaigua Wine Co.; *U.S. Public*, pg. 300

HENRI NESTLE PREMIUM CHOCOLATES—Gold-Wrapped Chocolates—Nestle Chocolate & Confection; *Int'l*, pg. 917

HENRI WINTERMAN'S—Cigars (Distributed by Imperial in the UK)—Imperial Tobacco Group, Ltd.; *Int'l*, pg. 666

HENRI WINTERMANN—Premium Cigars—Consolidated Cigar Corporation; *U.S. Private*, pg. 690

HENRI WINTERMANS—Cigars—Hanson PLC; *Int'l*, pg. 592

HENRI'S—Dressings—Bestfoods; *U.S. Public*, pg. 223

HENRY—Bakery Ingredients—CSM N.V.; *Int'l*, pg. 243

HENRY CLAY—Premium Cigars—Consolidated Cigar Corporation; *U.S. Private*, pg. 690

HENRY GRETHEL—Men's Apparel—Hartmarx Corporation; *U.S. Public*, pg. 795

HENRY GRETHEL—Men's Wear—The Manhattan Shirt Co.; *U.S. Public*, pg. 1429

HENRY HOUSE—Fresh & Further-processed pork items—Louis Kemp Seafood Co.; *U.S. Public*, pg. 1652

HENRY LINK—Wicker Household Furniture—Lexington Furniture Industries; *U.S. Private*, pg. 432

HENRY WEINHARD'S BLACKBERRY WHEAT—NONE—The Stroh Brewery Company; *U.S. Private*, pg. 1047

HENRY WEINHARD'S AMBER ALE—NONE—The Stroh Brewery Company; *U.S. Private*, pg. 1047

HENRY WEINHARD'S HAZELNUT STOUT—NONE—The Stroh Brewery Company; *U.S. Private*, pg. 1047

HENTEX—Food Prods.—Henningsen Foods, Inc.; *Int'l*, pg. 1074

HEP-LOCK—Heparin Lock Flush Solution, USP—Elkins-Sinn, Inc.-Lederle; *U.S. Public*, pg. 79

HEP-LOCK U/P—Preservative-Free Heparin Lock Flush Solution, USP—Elkins-Sinn, Inc.-Lederle; *U.S. Public*, pg. 79

HEPA-CLEAR—Air Purifier—Slant/Fin Corporation; *U.S. Private*, pg. 1005

HEPAGENE—NONE—Medeva PLC; *Int'l*, pg. 852

HEPARIN—Generic Drug—American Home Products Corporation; *U.S. Public*, pg. 79

HEPBURN SPA—Seltzer Water—Cadbury Schweppes p.l.c.; *Int'l*, pg. 247

HEPCHECK—Disposable Filter—Pall Corporation; *U.S. Public*, pg. 1253

HEPCON—Coating—Medtronic, Inc.; *U.S. Public*, pg. 1082

HEPPINGER—Water for Sportsmen & Active People—Apollinaris & Schweppes Gmbh & Co.; *Int'l*, pg. 78

HEPTAVAX—Pharmaceutical—Merck Human Health Division (U.S. Human Health); *U.S. Public*, pg. 1091

HEPTAVAX B—Plasma Hepatitis B Vaccine—Merck & Co., Inc.; *U.S. Public*, pg. 1090

HEPTEX—Enzymatically Treated Feed Ingredient—Cultor Ltd.; *Int'l*, pg. 349

HERA—Print Design—Liberty PLC; *Int'l*, pg. 807

HERACILLIN—Antibiotic—Astra AB; *Int'l*, pg. 93

HERALD SQUARE—Party Goods, Gifts, Stationery & Greeting Cards—F.W. Woolworth Co.; *U.S. Public*, pg. 1777

HERALD SQUARE PARTY SHOP—Party Goods, Gifts, Stationery & Greeting Cards—Woolworth Corporation; *U.S. Public*, pg. 1777

HERB-LAX—Nutritional Products—Shaklee Corporation; *Int'l*, pg. 1518

HERB MAGIC—Pourable Salad Dressing—Reily Foods Company; *U.S. Private*, pg. 919

HERB-OX—Broths & Seasonings—Hormel Foods Corp.; *U.S. Public*, pg. 840

HERBA-TAN—Sun Screen Prods.—Herbalife International of America, Inc.; *U.S. Public*, pg. 809

HERBAL ALOE—Drink—Herbalife International of America, Inc.; *U.S. Public*, pg. 809

HERBAL DEEP CLEAN—Shampoo—Revlon-Realistic Professional Products, Inc.; *U.S. Private*, pg. 690

HERBAL ESSENCE—Hair Care Products—Clairol, Inc.; *U.S. Public*, pg. 254

HERBAL EXTRACTS—NONE—Celestial Seasonings; *U.S. Public*, pg. 319

HERBALIFE WEIGHT CONTROL—Flavored Protein Drink Mix—Herbalife International of America, Inc.; *U.S. Public*, pg. 809

HERBALIFELINE—Marine Source Liquid Complex Capsules—Herbalife International of America, Inc.; *U.S. Public*, pg. 809

HERBCRAFT—NONE—Kellwood Company; *U.S. Public*, pg. 948

HERBCRAFT II—NONE—Kellwood Company; *U.S. Public*, pg. 948

HERBAL ESSENCE—Hair Care Product—Bristol-Myers Squibb Company; *U.S. Public*, pg. 253

HERBERGER'S—Department Stores—G.R. Herberger's, Inc.; *U.S. Public*, pg. 1333

HERBERT—Cannulated Bone Screw—Bristol-Myers Squibb Company; *U.S. Public*, pg. 253

HERBESSER—Diltiazem, Calcium Antagonist—Tanabe Seiyaku Co., Ltd.; *Int'l*, pg. 1354

HERBISSIMO—Cologne—Dana Perfumes Corp.; *U.S. Private*, pg. 922

HERBOL—Automobile Refinishes & Coatings; Powder Paints & House Paints—BASF AG; *Int'l*, pg. 103

HERC ALLOY—Grade 80 Chain—Columbus McKinnon Corp.; *U.S. Public*, pg. 405

HERCAL—Masonry Cement—Juan Minetti S.A.; *Int'l*, pg. 869

HERCO—Pine Oil—Hercules Incorporated; *U.S. Public*, pg. 809

HERCOFLEX—Plasticizer—Hercules Incorporated; *U.S. Public*, pg. 809

HERCOFROTH—Frother—Hercules Incorporated; *U.S. Public*, pg. 809

HERCOLUBE—Synthetic Ester—Hercules Incorporated; *U.S. Public*, pg. 809

HERCOLYN—Hydrogenated Ester of Rosin—Hercules Incorporated; *U.S. Public*, pg. 809

HERCON—NONE—Hercon Laboratories Corp.; *U.S. Public*, pg. 802

HERCON—Sizing Emulsion—Hercules Incorporated; *U.S. Public*, pg. 809

HERCOSETT—Synthetic Resin—Hercules Incorporated; *U.S. Public*, pg. 809

HERCOSOL—Resinous Solution—Hercules Incorporated; *U.S. Public*, pg. 809

HERCUFLEX—Coated Glass Fiber & Yarn for Building & Industrial Use—PPG Industries, Inc.; *U.S. Public*, pg. 1245

HERCULES—Internal Combustion Engine—Hercules Engine Company; *U.S. Private*, pg. 523

HERCULES—Tires & Tread Rubber—The Hercules Tire & Rubber Company; *U.S. Private*, pg. 523

HERCULES—Hot Water Storage—IMI Plc; *Int'l*, pg. 646

HERCULES—LED Displays—Industrial Electronic Engineers, Inc.; *U.S. Private*, pg. 561

HERCULES—Aerospace Manufacturing—Lockheed Aeronautical Systems Company; *U.S. Public*, pg. 1007

HERCULES—Tires—Midwest Tire & Muffler, Inc.; *U.S. Private*, pg. 745

HERCULES—Portland Cement—Juan Minetti S.A.; *Int'l*, pg. 869

HERCULES—Chemical—Warner-Jenkinson Co.; *U.S. Public*, pg. 1696

HERCULES—Fitness Products—York Barbell Co., Inc.; *U.S. Private*, pg. 1196

HERCULES AEROSPACE—Advanced Electronic Systems—Alliant Techsystems (Aerospace Division); *U.S. Public*, pg. 47

HERCULES FOR HANDS—Industrial Chemical—Hercules Chemical Co., Inc.; *U.S. Private*, pg. 523

HERCULES 2400—Smokeless Powder—Hercules Incorporated; *U.S. Public*, pg. 809

HERCULES 2000—Lift—Pride Health Care, Inc.; *U.S. Private*, pg. 883

HERCULEX—Fabrics—Herculite Products, Inc.; *U.S. Public*, pg. 802

HERCULITE—Fabrics—Herculite Products, Inc.; *U.S. Public*, pg. 802

HERCULITE—Tempered & Semitempered Sheet, Flat & Shaped Glass—PPG Industries; *U.S. Public*, pg. 1245

HERCULITE AUSTENITIC PROTECTION FABRICS—Fabrics—Herculite Products, Inc.; *U.S. Public*, pg. 802

HERCULOCK—Padlocks—Ilco Unican Corp.; *Int'l*, pg. 1432

HERCULON—Olefin Fiber—Hercules Incorporated; *U.S. Public*, pg. 809

HERCUVIT—Glass-Baed Crystalline Materials for Industrial Arts Applications—PPG Industries, Inc.; *U.S. Public*, pg. 1245

HERE'S HEALTH—U.K. Health Magazine—EMAP Elan; *Int'l*, pg. 451

HERESITE—Protective Coating—Heresite Protective Coatings Inc.; *U.S. Private*, pg. 523

HERESY II—Loudspeaker Systems—Klipsch, Inc.; *U.S. Private*, pg. 626

HERFSTBOK—NONE—Grolsch N.V.; *Int'l*, pg. 559

HERITAGE—Last Survivor Whole Life Insurance—American United Life Insurance Company; *U.S. Private*, pg. 64

HERITAGE—Furniture—Drexel Heritage Furnishings Inc.; *U.S. Private*, pg. 432

HERITAGE—Buffet Equipment & Salad Bars—Duke Manufacturing Co., Inc.; *U.S. Private*, pg. 346

HERITAGE—Nylon Wallets—Enger-Kress Company; *U.S. Private*, pg. 376

HERITAGE—Men's Fragrance—Guerlain, Inc.; *Int'l*, pg. 780

HERITAGE—Low Tar Cigarettes—Lorillard Tobacco Company; *U.S. Public*, pg. 1011

HERITAGE—Latex & Alkyd Interior & Exterior Floor Paint—Paragon Paint & Varnish Corp.; *U.S. Private*, pg. 838

HERITAGE—Cooking Utensils—Regal Ware, Inc.; *U.S. Private*, pg. 917

HERITAGE—Vinyl Siding—Reynolds Metals Company; *U.S. Public*, pg. 1385

HERITAGE & DESIGN—NONE—Regal Ware, Inc.; *U.S. Private*, pg. 917

HERITAGE BLOSSOM—Porcelain Dinnerware—Princess House, Inc.; *U.S. Public*, pg. 399

HERITAGE COLLECTION—Church Worship Bulletins for the Black Church—Warner Press, Inc.; *U.S. Private*, pg. 1150

HERITAGE EDITION—NONE—Melnor Inc.; *U.S. Public*, pg. 1234

HERITAGE LEATHERS—Leather Goods—Enger-Kress Company; *U.S. Private*, pg. 376

HERITAGE SLATE—Replacement for Slate—GAF Premium Products, Inc.; *U.S. Private*, pg. 433

HERITAGE SQUARE—Pre-Finished Laminate—Bruce Hardwood Floors; *U.S. Public*, pg. 1634

HERITAGE U.S.A.—Sportswear—Heritage Sportswear; *U.S. Public*, pg. 1472

HERITAGE U.S.A.—Sweaters & Knit Shirts—Signal Apparel Company, Inc.; *U.S. Public*, pg. 1472

HERMAN—Shoes, Boots—Jos. M. Herman Shoe Co.; *U.S. Private*, pg. 524

HERMAN MILLER—Office Furniture—Herman Miller, Inc.; *U.S. Public*, pg. 1111

HERMAN SURVIVORS—Shoes, Boots—Jos. M. Herman Shoe Co.; *U.S. Private*, pg. 524

HERMES AVIATION—NONE—Mercury Air Group Inc.; *U.S. Public*, pg. 1092

HERMET—Temperature Indicating Labels—La-Co Industries Markal Company; *U.S. Private*, pg. 640

HERMETEK—Fibre or Cardboard Tubes for Cartridges for Sealants/Adhesives—Sonoco Products Company; *U.S. Public*, pg. 1485

HERMETICOOL—Test Equipment—Tenney Environmental; *U.S. Private*, pg. 1076

HERMITAGE—Lumber & Wood Products—Georgia-Pacific Corporation; *U.S. Public*, pg. 735

HERMLE—Universal Milling Machines—Traub AG; *Int'l*, pg. 1419

HEROES IN A HALF SHELL—Card Game—Mattel Games/Puzzles; *U.S. Public*, pg. 1058

HERON—Long Range Mission U.A.V.—Israel Aircraft Industries Ltd.; *Int'l*, pg. 689

HEROS—Wooden Toys—Life-Like Products, Inc.; *U.S. Private*, pg. 666

HERRADURA—Tequila—The House of Seagram; *Int'l*, pg. 1217

HERRERA FOR MEN—NONE—Compar; *Int'l*, pg. 1073

HERRICANE—Process Steam Humidification Equipment—Herrmidifier Co., Inc.; *U.S. Public*, pg. 1639

HERRINGBONE—Hand Painted Ceramics—Dansk International Designs Ltd.; *U.S. Public*, pg. 261

HERRINGSTRIP—Pre-Finished Laminate—Bruce Hardwood Floors; *U.S. Public*, pg. 1634

Brand Name Index

HERRMIDICOOL—In-Duct Atomizing Humidification Equipment—Herrmidifier Co., Inc.; *U.S. Public*, pg. 1639

HERRMIDIFIER—Humidification Equipment—Herrmidifier Co., Inc.; *U.S. Public*, pg. 1639

HERRTRONIC—Steam Generating Humidification Equipment—Herrmidifier Co., Inc.; *U.S. Public*, pg. 1639

HERRUD—Meats—Thorn Apple Valley, Inc.; *U.S. Public*, pg. 1602

HERS—Shaving Cream—Medtech Inc.; *U.S. Private*, pg. 728

HERSHEL'S DELI—Sandwich Shop—Cara Operations Limited; *Int'l*, pg. 266

HERSHEY-ETS—Chocolate Candies—Hershey Chocolate U.S.A.; *U.S. Public*, pg. 812

HERSHEY-ETS—Candy—Hershey Foods Corporation; *U.S. Public*, pg. 811

HERSHEY'S—Cocoa, Syrup, Chocolate Chips, Chocolate Milk, Milk Chocolate Bar—Hershey Chocolate U.S.A.; *U.S. Public*, pg. 812

HERSHEY'S—Milk Chocolate Bar With & Without Almonds—Hershey Foods Corporation; *U.S. Public*, pg. 811

HERSHEY'S HUGS—Chocolate—Hershey Foods Corporation; *U.S. Public*, pg. 811

HERSHEY'S CHOCOLATE DRINK—Chocolate Drink w/Aseptic BoxPackaging—Hershey Foods Corporation; *U.S. Public*, pg. 811

HERSHEY'S CHOCOLATE SHOPPE—Fudge Toppings—Hershey Foods Corporation; *U.S. Public*, pg. 811

HERSHEY'S KISS—Chocolate—Hershey Chocolate U.S.A.; *U.S. Public*, pg. 812

HERSHEY'S KISSES—Chocolates—Hershey Chocolate U.S.A.; *U.S. Public*, pg. 812

HERSHEY'S KISSES—Chocolates—Hershey Foods Corporation; *U.S. Public*, pg. 811

HERSHEY'S KISSES WITH ALMONDS—Chocolates with Almonds—Hershey Foods Corporation; *U.S. Public*, pg. 811

HERSHEY'S MINIATURES—Chocolate Bars—Hershey Chocolate U.S.A.; *U.S. Public*, pg. 812

HERSHEY'S MINIATURES—Chocolate Bars—Hershey Foods Corporation; *U.S. Public*, pg. 811

HERSHEY'S NEW TRAIL—Granola Bar—Hershey Foods Corporation; *U.S. Public*, pg. 811

HERSHEY'S PREMIUM—Baking Chocolate—Hershey Foods Corporation; *U.S. Public*, pg. 811

HERSHEY'S PUDDING—Regular & Sugar-Free Refrigerated Puddings—Hershey Foods Corporation; *U.S. Public*, pg. 811

HERSHEY'S SYRUP—Chocolate Syrup & Chocolate Milk Mix—Hershey Foods Corporation; *U.S. Public*, pg. 811

HERSHEY'S TOP SCOTCH—Butterscotch syrup—Hershey Foods Corporation; *U.S. Public*, pg. 811

HERTA—Delicatessen Items—Nestle S.A.; *Int'l*, pg. 915

HERTIE—Department Store—Hertie Waren-und Kaufhaus GmbH; *Int'l*, pg. 724

HERTTA—Mineral Feed—Cultor Ltd.; *Int'l*, pg. 349

HERTZ—Vehicle & Equipment Rental—The Hertz Corporation; *U.S. Public*, pg. 664

HESS—Franchised Service Stations—Amerada Hess Corporation; *U.S. Public*, pg. 65

HESS ENGINEERING, INC.—Wheel & Rim Technologies—Hess Engineering Inc.; *U.S. Private*, pg. 524

HESS MART—Convenience Stores—Amerada Hess Corporation; *U.S. Public*, pg. 65

HESS-SUNDWIG—Ferrous & Non Ferrous Reduction Mills; Shape Systems; Processing Lines—Hess Engineering Inc.; *U.S. Private*, pg. 524

HESSTON—Hay Tools & Forage Equipment—AGCO Corporation; *U.S. Public*, pg. 28

HESTRON—Heat Strenghtened Glass—PPG Industries, Inc.; *U.S. Public*, pg. 1245

HETERO-CAVITY MOLDING—Interchangeable Custom Tools & Custom Injection Molding—Security Plastics, Inc.; *U.S. Private*, pg. 981

HETZEL—NONE—Fortune Brands, Inc.; *U.S. Public*, pg. 674

HEUBLEIN—Wines & Spirits—Grand Metropolitan Plc; *Int'l*, pg. 408

HEUBLEIN COCKTAILS—Cocktails—Heublein, Inc.; *Int'l*, pg. 410

HEUDEBERT—Toasted Bread—Danone Group; *Int'l*, pg. 379

HEUGA—Floor Coverings—Interface Inc.; *U.S. Public*, pg. 889

HEVI-HITTER—Mechanical Drilling Jar—Baker Hughes INTEQ; *U.S. Public*, pg. 166

HEVI-LIFT—Hoist—Harnischfeger Industries, Inc.; *U.S. Public*, pg. 788

HEVI-WATE—Drill Pipe—Smith International, Inc.; *U.S. Public*, pg. 1478

HEX-A-FIELD—NONE—Life Technologies, Inc.; *U.S. Public*, pg. 504

HEX NOSE—Spring Plunger—Vlier Engineering; *U.S. Public*, pg. 124

HEXABOND—Adhesive System—Hexcel Corporation; *U.S. Public*, pg. 824

HEXABRIX—Oixaglic Acid—Mallinckrodt Inc.; *U.S. Public*, pg. 1039

HEXADRIVE—Power Transmission—Lovejoy Inc.; *U.S. Private*, pg. 677

HEXADROL—Pharmaceutical—Organon Inc.; *Int'l*, pg. 48

HEXAGON—Screws, Bolts & Nuts—Precision Fasteners Ltd.; *U.S. Public*, pg. 1420

HEXAGONE—Central Kitchen Facilities—Accor S.A.; *Int'l*, pg. 20

HEXALEN—Oral Cytotoxic Drug—U.S. Bioscience, Inc.; *U.S. Public*, pg. 1681

HEXALITE—Cushioning System—Reebok International Ltd.; *U.S. Public*, pg. 1369

HEXALON—NONE—Lawter International, Inc.; *U.S. Public*, pg. 980

HEXAVER—Chemical Reagant—Hach Company; *U.S. Public*, pg. 773

HEXCELITE—Adhesive System—Hexcel Corporation; *U.S. Public*, pg. 824

HEXENE-1—NONE—Sasol Alpha Olefins; *Int'l*, pg. 1196

HEXFET-MOSFET—Power Transistor—International Rectifier Corporation; *U.S. Public*, pg. 906

HEXOLOY—Silicon Carbide—The Carborundum Corporation; *Int'l*, pg. 1173

HEY THAT'S ME—NONE—American Greetings Corporation; *U.S. Public*, pg. 77

HEYDAY BAR—Fudge, Caramel & Peanut Bar—RJR Nabisco Holdings Corp.; *U.S. Public*, pg. 1354

HI ACE—Trucks & Buses—Toyota Motor Corporation; *Int'l*, pg. 1411

HI-AL-RAM-G—Refractory—CFB Industries, Inc.; *U.S. Private*, pg. 194

HI-AL-RAM-G—Refractory—Chicago Fire Brick Co.; *U.S. Private*, pg. 194

HI-BRAU—Beer—Joseph Huber Brewing Co., Inc.; *U.S. Private*, pg. 545

HI BROW FUNNY BOOKS—Books—American Greetings Corporation; *U.S. Public*, pg. 77

HI BROWS—Greeting Cards—American Greetings Corporation; *U.S. Public*, pg. 77

HI-BROWS—Studio Greeting Cards—American Greetings U.S. Greeting Card Division; *U.S. Public*, pg. 78

HI-BULK—Braided Fishing Line—Cortland Line Co., Inc.; *U.S. Private*, pg. 277

HI-C—Fruit Drinks—The Coca-Cola Company; *U.S. Public*, pg. 392

HI-C—High Carbon Spring Steel—Minerallac Co.; *U.S. Private*, pg. 750

HI-C—Fruit Drinks—The Minute Maid Company; *U.S. Public*, pg. 392

HI-CALCIUM—Milk—Borden, Inc.; *U.S. Private*, pg. 157

HI-CELL—Lint Cleaning Machinery—Carver, Inc.; *U.S. Private*, pg. 217

HI COLOR—Color Coated Paper & Paperboard—Hazen Paper Company; *U.S. Private*, pg. 514

HI-CONE—Multipack Carrier—Illinois Tool Works Inc.; *U.S. Public*, pg. 865

HI-COUNT—Paper Towels—Kimberly-Clark Corporation; *U.S. Public*, pg. 958

HI-D—Urethane Roller Cover—Samuel Bingham Co; *U.S. Private*, pg. 144

HI-D—Synthetic Coolants—D.A. Stuart Company; *U.S. Private*, pg. 1048

HI-DRI—Paper Towels—Kimberly-Clark Corporation; *U.S. Public*, pg. 958

HI DRUM—2 Drum Racks—Jarke Corporation; *U.S. Public*, pg. 583

HI-F—High Voltage Porcelain Insulators—Lapp Insulator Company; *U.S. Private*, pg. 473

HI-FAX—Thermoplastic Olefins—Montedison S.p.A.; *Int'l*, pg. 324

HI-FLEX—Sheet Molding Composite—The Budd Company; *Int'l*, pg. 1388

HI-FLO—Extended Surface Bag-Type Air Filters—Farr Company; *U.S. Public*, pg. 613

HI FLO—Filtration Products—Gelman Sciences, Inc.; *U.S. Public*, pg. 1253

HI-FLO-CO-AX—Vapor Recovery Hose—HBD Industries, Inc.; *U.S. Private*, pg. 489

HI-FORM—High Strength, Low Alloy Steels—Inland Steel Industries, Inc.; *U.S. Public*, pg. 879

HI-FREQ—Accessory—The Lincoln Electric Company; *U.S. Public*, pg. 996

HI-FRUCTOSE—High Fructose Corn Syrup 42—Roquette America Inc.; *U.S. Private*, pg. 944

HI-G—Diagnostic Products—Abbott Laboratories; *U.S. Public*, pg. 12

HI GREEN—Fertilizer—PCS Phosphate - Raleigh; *Int'l*, pg. 1064

HI-HO—Crackers—Keebler Company; *U.S. Public*, pg. 657

HI-HO—Crackers—Sunshine Biscuits, Inc.; *U.S. Private*, pg. 434

HI-HO—Crackers—Sunshine Biscuits, Inc.; *U.S. Public*, pg. 657

HI-IMPULSE—Hose—Aeroquip-Vickers, Inc.; *U.S. Public*, pg. 24

HI-JACKER—Radio Control—Tyco Toys, Inc.; *U.S. Public*, pg. 1058

HI-LEMON—A Citrus-Flavored Candy with Vitamin C—Meiji Seika Kaisha, Ltd.; *Int'l*, pg. 855

HI LIFE—Screens—Laubeck Corporation/Cross; *U.S. Private*, pg. 652

HI LINE—Paper Napkins, Bath Tissue & Paper Towels—Georgia-Pacific Corporation; *U.S. Public*, pg. 735

HI-LINE—Hardware—Joslyn Corporation; *U.S. Public*, pg. 481

HI-LINE—Power Line Maintenance Tools—Kearney Company; *U.S. Public*, pg. 444

HI-LITE—Lamps—Eagle Electric Mfg. Co., Inc.; *U.S. Private*, pg. 354

HI-LITE—Fastening Sytem—Hi-Shear Industries Inc.; *U.S. Public*, pg. 824

HI-LITE—Polymer Insulators—The Ohio Brass Co.; *U.S. Public*, pg. 845

HI LITE—TV Picture Tubes—Thomson Consumer Electronics Inc.; *Int'l*, pg. 1383

HI-LO—Pulper—Harnischfeger Industries, Inc.; *U.S. Public*, pg. 788

HI-LO—Tracheal Tube—Mallinckrodt Inc.; *U.S. Public*, pg. 1039

HI-LO—Imaging System—Nuarc Company, Inc.; *U.S. Private*, pg. 808

HI-LO JET—Tracheal Tubes—Mallinckrodt Inc.; *U.S. Public*, pg. 1039

HI-LO-TEMP—Temperature Monitoring Systems—Mallinckrodt Inc.; *U.S. Public*, pg. 1039

HI-LUX—Trucks & Buses—Toyota Motor Corporation; *Int'l*, pg. 1411

HI-MAN—Special Steels—Inland Steel Industries, Inc.; *U.S. Public*, pg. 879

HI-MATIC—Photo Developer, Stop Bath & Fixer—Eastman Kodak Company; *U.S. Public*, pg. 550

HI MILER—Bias Truck Tires—The Goodyear Tire & Rubber Company; *U.S. Public*, pg. 752

HI-PAC—Hydraulic Hose—Aeroquip Corporation; *U.S. Public*, pg. 24

HI-PAC—Hose—Aeroquip-Vickers, Inc.; *U.S. Public*, pg. 24

HI PERFORMANCE—Shelving—Penco Products; *U.S. Private*, pg. 848

HI-PHI—Amino Acid Analysis Buffers—Dionex Corporation; *U.S. Public*, pg. 510

HI-POLYMER—Lead—Pentel of America, Ltd.; *Int'l*, pg. 1035

HI-POWER—NONE—Gates Europe; *Int'l*, pg. 1396

HI-PRO—Dry Dog Food—Ralston Purina Company; *U.S. Public*, pg. 1359

HI-PROTEIN—Milk—Borden, Inc.; *U.S. Private*, pg. 157

HI PUR—Filtration Products—Gelman Sciences, Inc.; *U.S. Public*, pg. 1253

HI-Q—Powder Coatings—Ferro Corporation; *U.S. Public*, pg. 618

HI-Q'S—Greeting Cards—American Greetings Corporation; *U.S. Public*, pg. 77

HI-RES—Hi Resolution Ink Jet—Marsh Company; *U.S. Private*, pg. 707

HI-RISE—Hinge Feature—Sanderson Plumbing Products Inc.; *U.S. Private*, pg. 964

HI-RISER—Loading Towers—Ferguson International, Inc.; *U.S. Private*, pg. 401

HI SHOCK 60—NONE—Carpenter Technology Corporation; *U.S. Public*, pg. 307

HI-SIL—Silicas for Plastics, Rubber & Insecticide Applications—PPG Industries, Inc.; *U.S. Public*, pg. 1245

HI-SPEED—Portland Cement—Essroc Cement, Corp.; *U.S. Private*, pg. 384

HI-SPEED—NONE—Kiwi Brands Pty. Ltd.; *U.S. Public*, pg. 1434

HI-SPEEDPOWER—Spindle—Bryant Grinder Corp.; *U.S. Private*, pg. 461

HI STRENGTH TRU-GUIDE—Gas Lift Mandrels—Halliburton Energy Services; *U.S. Public*, pg. 776

HI-STYLE—Necked-In Aerosol Container—U.S. Can Company; *U.S. Public*, pg. 522

HI-SWEET—High Fructose Corn Syrup 55—Roquette America Inc.; *U.S. Private*, pg. 944

HI-T GRAY—Float Glass—AFG Industries, Inc.; *Int'l*, pg. 84

HI-TECH—Coatings—Seymour of Sycamore, Inc.; *U.S. Private*, pg. 988

HI-TECH WELLATON—Hair Dyeing Product—Wella Group; *Int'l*, pg. 1489

HI-TEMP—High Temperature Expansion Screw Conveyors—Thomas Conveyor Company; *U.S. Private*, pg. 1082

HI-TOR SPECIAL DIETS—Dog & Cat Food—Triumph Pet Industries, Inc.; *U.S. Private*, pg. 1104

HI-TORQUE—Clamp—TransTechnology Corporation; *U.S. Public*, pg. 1632

HI-TRACTOR—Sprayer/Detasseling Equipment—Hagie Manufacturing Co.; *U.S. Private*, pg. 493

HI-TRI—Solvent—The Dow Chemical Company; *U.S. Public*, pg. 522

HI-TUFF—NONE—JPS Elastomerics Corp.; *U.S. Private*, pg. 578

HI-TUFF/EP—NONE—JPS Elastomerics Corp.; *U.S. Private*, pg. 578

HI-VIZ—NONE—Lawter International, Inc.; *U.S. Public*, pg. 980

HI-WAY—Truck Mounted Municipal De-Icing Spreaders—Highway Equipment Company; *U.S. Private*, pg. 529

HI-WAY AUTUMNMATE 720—Leaf Collection Unit—Highway Equipment Company; *U.S. Private*, pg. 529

HI-WAY FIDELITY SERIES—Radio—Clarion Corporation of America; *Int'l*, pg. 296

HI WEAR 64—NONE—Carpenter Technology Corporation; *U.S. Public*, pg. 307

HI YIELD PRINTKOTE—Coated Paperboard—Westvaco Corporation; *U.S. Public*, pg. 1762

HI-Z—Gamma Oryzanol Preparation—Otsuka Pharmaceutical Co., Ltd.; *Int'l*, pg. 1013

HI-TEN—Carbon Steel Wrenches—Danaher Tool Group; *U.S. Public*, pg. 481

HIAWATHA OFFSET—Printing Paper—The Mead Corporation; *U.S. Public*, pg. 1074

HIAWATHA PREMIUM—Printing Paper—The Mead Corporation; *U.S. Public*, pg. 1074

HIBERNATE—NONE—Life Technologies, Inc.; *U.S. Public*, pg. 504

HIBERNIA NATIONAL BANK—NONE—Hibernia Corporation; *U.S. Public*, pg. 825

HIBERNIA PEOPLE FOR GOOD GOVERNMENT—NONE—Hibernia Corporation; *U.S. Public*, pg. 825

HIBITANE—Pharmaceutical—Zeneca Group Plc; *Int'l*, pg. 1524

HIBOY SELF PROPELLED SPRAYER—Sprayer—Hahn Equipment Co.; *U.S. Public*, pg. 1624

HIBTITER—Vaccine—American Home Products Corporation; *U.S. Public*, pg. 79

HICKEY FREEMAN—Men's Apparel—Hartmarx Corporation; *U.S. Public*, pg. 795

HICKEY-FREEMAN—Clothing—Hickey-Freeman/ Bobby Jones; *U.S. Public*, pg. 795

HICKMAN—Vascular Access Catheter—Davol Inc.; *U.S. Public*, pg. 189

HICKOK—Belts & Billfolds—Tandy Brands Accessories, Inc.; *U.S. Public*, pg. 1560

HICKORY—Polo Shirt—Mizuno Corporation; *Int'l*, pg. 884

HICKORY BRAND—Premium Hickory Charcoal Briquet—Hickory Specialties, Inc.; *U.S. Public*, pg. 596

HICKORY CHAIR—Furniture—Furniture Brands International Inc.; *U.S. Public*, pg. 688

HICKORY FARMS—Specialty Food—Hickory Farms, Inc.; *U.S. Private*, pg. 525

HICKORY HILL—Sausage—Armour Swift Eckrich; *U.S. Public*, pg. 426

HICKORY SPECIALTIES—Charcoal, Smoke Flavorings, Grilling Products—Bob Evans Farms, Inc. Restaurant Division; *U.S. Public*, pg. 596

HINCKLEY & SCHMITT—Bottled Water—Hinckley & Schmitt, Inc.; *Int'l*, pg. 1322

HICOM—Terminal—Harris Corp., RF Communications Group Marketing Division; *U.S. Public*, pg. 792

HID-N-LOK—Tile—Pawling Corporation; *U.S. Private*, pg. 844

HID-N-AIRE—Wall Blower—Swartwout Industries; *Int'l*, pg. 1398

HIDDEN ADVANTAGE BY FLEXEES—Control Garments—True Form Intimate Apparel; *U.S. Private*, pg. 697

HIDDEN AGENDA—Outerwear for Men & Boys—I. Spiewak & Sons, Inc.; *U.S. Private*, pg. 1025

HIDDEN COMFORT—High Heel Accessories & Insoles—Schering-Plough Corporation; *U.S. Public*, pg. 1438

HIDDEN COMFORT—Half-Insole—Scholl U.S.A.; *U.S. Public*, pg. 1438

HIDDEN GLIDES—NONE—American Woodmark Corporation; *U.S. Public*, pg. 96

HIDDEN VALLEY—Bottled Salad Dressings, Dry Salad Dressings, Party Dip Mixes—The Clorox Company; *U.S. Public*, pg. 386

HIDDEN VALLEY LOW-FAT—Cholesterol-Free, Low Fat Salad Dressings—The Clorox Company; *U.S. Public*, pg. 386

HIDDEN VALLEY SALAD CRISPINS—Seasoned Mini-Croutons—The Clorox Company; *U.S. Public*, pg. 386

HIDE-A-DISC—Air Freshener—Surco Products, Inc.; *U.S. Private*, pg. 1056

HIDE-A-SHELF—Merchandising Display—The Mead Corporation; *U.S. Public*, pg. 1074

HIDE-A-WAY—Candy—Brach & Brock Confections Inc.; *U.S. Public*, pg. 163

HIDEAWAY HARDWARE—Gym Set Feature—Hedstrom Corporation; *U.S. Private*, pg. 526

HIEBERT—Office Furniture—HON Industries Inc.; *U.S. Public*, pg. 772

HIFEVER—Clothing—Vendex International N.V.; *Int'l*, pg. 1462

HIFLEX—Icing Powders—Mallet & Co.; *U.S. Private*, pg. 698

HIGAIN—NONE—PairGain Technologies Inc.; *U.S. Public*, pg. 1253

HIGGINS INK—Drawing Inks—Sanford Corporation; *U.S. Public*, pg. 1178

HIGH ABILITY—NONE—Check Point Software Technologies Ltd.; *U.S. Public*, pg. 342

HIGH ALUMINA PLASTIC—Plastic—A.P. Green Industries, Inc.; *U.S. Public*, pg. 761

HIGH BANKED SPEEDWAY—Race Set—Tyco Toys, Inc.; *U.S. Public*, pg. 1058

HIGH COTTON—Premium Sportswear—Russell Corporation; *U.S. Public*, pg. 1413

HIGH DEFINITION—NONE—Elcor Corporation; *U.S. Public*, pg. 567

HIGH DENSITY PLUS—Electronic Component—Teradyne, Inc.; *U.S. Public*, pg. 1580

HIGH DESIGN—Hip & Ridge—Herbert Malarkey Roofing Company; *U.S. Private*, pg. 698

HIGH ENDURANCE—Cellular Phone Batteries—VARTA Batteries Inc.; *Int'l*, pg. 1452

HIGH-FIDELITY—Mirrors & Specialty Flat & Curved Glass—PPG Industries, Inc.; *U.S. Public*, pg. 1245

HIGH-FLO—Pump—Graco Inc.; *U.S. Public*, pg. 756

HIGH FLYER—Industrial Safety Eyewear—Uvex Safety, Inc.; *Int'l*, pg. 132

HIGH GRADE WESTERN WEAR—Men's Apparel—Pendleton Woolen Mills, Inc.; *U.S. Private*, pg. 848

HIGH HAIR—Hair Care Products—Wella Group; *Int'l*, pg. 1489

HIGH-K—Shell & Tube Heat Exchangers—Baltimore Aircoil Company; *U.S. Private*, pg. 68

HIGH LIFE—Foods—Ventura Foods; *U.S. Private*, pg. 508

HIGH-LIGHTS—Wood Blinds—Kirsch; *U.S. Public*, pg. 1176

HIGH-LINE—Photo Developer—Eastman Kodak Company; *U.S. Public*, pg. 550

HIGH LINER—Frozen Seafoods—National Sea Products Incorporated; *Int'l*, pg. 909

HIGH LINER—Frozen & Canned Seafood—National Sea Products Limited; *Int'l*, pg. 909

HIGH-LITES—Lighting—JJI Lighting Group Inc.; *Int'l*, pg. 821

HIGH MOMENTUM—Burner—Hauck Mfg. Co.; *U.S. Private*, pg. 510

HIGH NOON—Lumber & Wood Products—Georgia-Pacific Corporation; *U.S. Public*, pg. 735

HIGH-PER MIZER—Ball Valve, High Temperature—Worcester Controls Corp.; *Int'l*, pg. 128

HIGH POINT—Coffees—The Folger Coffee Company; *U.S. Public*, pg. 1331

HIGH POINT—Office Seating—HON Industries Inc.; *U.S. Public*, pg. 772

HIGH PROTEIN 28—Dog Food—H.J. Heinz Company; *U.S. Public*, pg. 805

HIGH RIDGE—Lumber & Wood Products—Georgia-Pacific Corporation; *U.S. Public*, pg. 735

HIGH-STAK—Filing System—Fellowes Manufacturing Co.; *U.S. Private*, pg. 400

HIGH TOUCH—Hairdressing Salon Equipment—Wella Group; *Int'l*, pg. 1489

HIGH VOLTAGE—Music Radio Program—Westwood One Entertainment; *U.S. Public*, pg. 1763

HIGH VOLTAGE—Rock Program—Westwood One, Inc.; *U.S. Public*, pg. 1763

HIGH VOLTAGE MODULES—Semi-Conductor Devices—Semtech Corporation; *U.S. Public*, pg. 1456

HIGHFALLS BREWING COMPANY—Beer—Genesee Corporation; *U.S. Public*, pg. 728

HIGHGATE MILD—Dark Mild Beer—Bass PLC; *Int'l*, pg. 169

HIGHGATE OLD ALE—Ale—Bass PLC; *Int'l*, pg. 169

HIGHLAND—Vinyl Plastic Electrical Tape, Pressure Sensitive Adhesive Tape—3M; *U.S. Public*, pg. 1604

HIGHLAND BOLT & NUT—NONE—MNP Corp.; *U.S. Private*, pg. 687

HIGHLAND HICKORY—Plywood, Paneling Siding & Roofing—Georgia-Pacific Corporation; *U.S. Public*, pg. 735

HIGHLAND HOUSE—NONE—Broyhill Furniture Industries, Inc.; *U.S. Public*, pg. 688

HIGHLAND HOUSE—Furniture—Furniture Brands International Inc.; *U.S. Public*, pg. 688

HIGHLAND HOUSE—Mattress & Box Spring Sets—Kingsdown, Inc.; *U.S. Private*, pg. 622

HIGHLAND INTERNATIONAL—NONE—MNP Corp.; *U.S. Private*, pg. 687

HIGHLAND MIST—Scotch Whisky—Barton Incorporated; *U.S. Public*, pg. 300

HIGHLAND MIST SCOTCH—NONE—Barton Brands, Ltd.; *U.S. Public*, pg. 300

HIGHLAND PARK—Scotch Whiskey—John Gross & Co.; *U.S. Private*, pg. 483

HIGHLAND PARK—Single Malt Scotch—The Highland Distilleries Company plc; *Int'l*, pg. 619

HIGHLANDER—Sportshirt—Lands' End, Inc.; *U.S. Public*, pg. 977

HIGHLIGHT—Sheet Vinyl Flooring—Congoleum Corporation; *U.S. Public*, pg. 69

HIGHLIGHTING—Haircolor—Bristol-Myers Squibb Company; *U.S. Public*, pg. 253

HIGHLIGHTS—Adult Barrettes, Ponytail Holders, Hairbands, Decorative Combs—Wilhold Inc.; *U.S. Public*, pg. 78

HIGHLIGHTS FOR CHILDREN—Magazine—Highlights for Children, Inc.; *U.S. Private*, pg. 528

HIGHLIGHTS IN LEAD CRYSTAL—Full Lead Crystal Giftware—Princess House, Inc.; *U.S. Public*, pg. 399

HIGHLINER—Canned Sea Food Products—Borden, Inc.; *U.S. Public*, pg. 157

HIGHLOAF—Flour—Dover Industries Limited; *Int'l*, pg. 417

HIGH'S—Dairy Store Chain—The Southland Corporation; *Int'l*, pg. 693

HIGLASS—Glass Reinforced Polymers—Montedison S.p.A.; *Int'l*, pg. 324

HIJACKERS—Shock Absorbers—Arvin Industries, Inc.; *U.S. Public*, pg. 136

HIJET PICKUP—1000 cc Cab Truck—Daihatsu Motor Corporation, Ltd.; *Int'l*, pg. 364

HIJET VAN—1000 cc 1 Box Van—Daihatsu Motor Corporation, Ltd.; *Int'l*, pg. 364

HILCO—Optical Prods. & Accessories—The Hilsinger Co. L.P.; *U.S. Private*, pg. 530

HILITE—Polymer Insulators—Hubbell Incorporated; *U.S. Public*, pg. 844

HILITER—Ultrasound Enhancement Needles—Medtronic, Inc.; *U.S. Public*, pg. 1082

HILL-ROM COMPOSER—Nurse Communications System Using Digital Audio Technology—Hillenbrand Industries, Inc.; *U.S. Public*, pg. 828

HILL'S—Pet Products—Colgate-Palmolive Company; *U.S. Public*, pg. 168

HILLBILLY—Jeans—Master Industries Corp.; *U.S. Private*, pg. 713

HILLBILLY—Bread—Metz Baking Company; *U.S. Private*, pg. 1022

HILLBILLY—Bread—Metz Baking Company (WI); *U.S. Private*, pg. 1022

HILLCRAFT—Upholstery Line—Fraenkel Company; *U.S. Private*, pg. 397

HILLE—Seating—Carter Holt Harvey Limited; *U.S. Public*, pg. 904

HILLEBRAND—Wine—Andres Wines Ltd.; *Int'l*, pg. 75

HILLS—Department Stores—Hills Stores Co.; *U.S. Public*, pg. 828

HILLS BROS.—Coffee—Nestle S.A.; *Int'l*, pg. 915

HILLS BROS.—Coffee—Nestle USA; *Int'l*, pg. 916

HILLS OF WESTCHESTER—Candy—Boyer Candy Company Inc.; *U.S. Private*, pg. 162

HILLS PHARMACY—NONE—AAH plc; *Int'l*, pg. 591

HILLSDALE DAILY NEWS—Newspaper—Shivers Trading & Operating Co.; *U.S. Private*, pg. 994

HILLSHIRE FARM—Packaged Meats & Processed Meat Products—Hillshire Farm & Kahn's; *U.S. Public*, pg. 1433

HILLSHIRE FARM—Processed Meat Products—Hillshire Farm Company; *U.S. Public*, pg. 1433

HILLSHIRE FARM—Meat Products—Sara Lee Corporation; *U.S. Public*, pg. 1432

HILLSHIRE LITE—Reduced Calorie Smoked Sausage—Hillshire Farm Company; *U.S. Public*, pg. 1433

HILLSIDE—NONE—Brothers Gourmet Coffees, Inc.; *U.S. Public*, pg. 259

HILLSIDE—Plywood, Paneling, Siding, Roofing & Acoustical Tile—Georgia-Pacific Corporation; *U.S. Public*, pg. 735

HILLTOP HEARTH—NONE—JP Foodservice, Inc.; *U.S. Public*, pg. 918

HILTON—NONE—Castleberry/Snow's Brands Inc.; *U.S. Private*, pg. 219

HILTON—Hotels—Hilton Hotels Corporation; *U.S. Public*, pg. 828

HILTON—NONE—Sunstone Hotel Investors, Inc.; *U.S. Public*, pg. 1536

HILTON BARDEN INNS—Hotels—Hilton Hotels Corporation; *U.S. Public*, pg. 828

HILTON HEAD NEWS—Newspaper—Shivers Trading & Operating Co.; *U.S. Private*, pg. 994

HILTON USA—Apparel—K2 Inc.; *U.S. Public*, pg. 940

HILTON'S—Oyster Stews—Borden, Inc.; *U.S. Private*, pg. 157

HILTON'S—Seafood Soups—Bunker Hill Foods Inc.; *U.S. Private*, pg. 219

HIMALAYA—Computer/Server Systems—Tandem Computers Inc.; *U.S. Public*, pg. 417

HIMELINE—Non-Metallic Enclosures—The Lamson & Sessions Co.; *U.S. Public*, pg. 976

HIMSELF THE ELF—Greeting Cards—American Greetings Corporation; *U.S. Public*, pg. 77

HINDS—NONE—SmithKline Beecham Corporation; *Int'l*, pg. 1264

HINE—NONE—LVMH Moet Hennessy Louis Vuitton; *Int'l*, pg. 779

HINE—Cognac—Schieffelin Somerset Co.; *Int'l*, pg. 412

HINE COGNAC—Cognac—Veuve Clicquot Ponsardin; *Int'l*, pg. 781

HINEX-R—Enteral Alimentation—Otsuka Pharmaceutical Co., Ltd.; *Int'l*, pg. 1013

HINEX-V—Balanced Food Drink—Otsuka Pharmaceutical Co., Ltd.; *Int'l*, pg. 1013

HINGE-FLEX—Innerspring Assemblies for Mattresses—Leggett & Platt, Incorporated; *U.S. Public*, pg. 985

HINGE LOCK—Fasteners—Southtec, Inc.; *U.S. Private*, pg. 1015

HINIKER—Rowcrop & Field Cultivators, Cedars, Ridge Clearing Equipment & Shredders—Hiniker Company; *U.S. Private*, pg. 530

HIONIC-FLUOR—Pseudocumene-Based Cocktail—Packard Instrument Co., Inc.; *U.S. Private*, pg. 833

HIOTROL BOTTOMSIDE—Industrial Deodorant—Ferro Corporation; *U.S. Public*, pg. 618

HIOTROL TOPSIDE—Industrial Deodorant—Ferro Corporation; *U.S. Public*, pg. 618

HIP HUGGER—Laundry Basket Contoured for Easy Carrying on the Hip—Rubbermaid Incorporated; *U.S. Public*, pg. 1411

HIP VAC—NONE—Euroclean; *Int'l*, pg. 440

HIPACK—Glass Coating—Alltrista Corporation; *U.S. Public*, pg. 56

HIPAK—Glass Release Coatings—Ball Corporation; *U.S. Public*, pg. 170

HIPEC—Engineered Plastics—General Electric Company; *U.S. Public*, pg. 709

HIPER—Pin Card—LTX Corporation; *U.S. Public*, pg. 972

HIPERBATCH—Computer Product—International Business Machines Corporation; *U.S. Public*, pg. 895

HIPERCO—NONE—Carpenter Technology Corporation; *U.S. Public*, pg. 307

HIPERFORM—Refrigeration System—Paul Mueller Company; *U.S. Public*, pg. 1141

HIPERNOM—NONE—Carpenter Technology Corporation; *U.S. Public*, pg. 307

HIPERSORTING—Computer Product—International Business Machines Corporation; *U.S. Public*, pg. 895

HIPERSPACE—Computer Product—International Business Machines Corporation; *U.S. Public*, pg. 895

HIPERSTATION—On-Line Software Testing Product With Strong Batch & IMS Capabilities—Compuware Corporation; *U.S. Public*, pg. 423

HIPHASE—Rosin Emulsion Size—Hercules Incorporated; *U.S. Public*, pg. 809

HIPOTRONICS—Power Supplies & Test Equip.—Hipotronics, Inc.; *U.S. Public*, pg. 844

HIPOX—High Pressure Oxidation Systems—GaSonics International; *U.S. Public*, pg. 703

HIPPOCRATES—Physician Journal—Time Inc. Health; *U.S. Public*, pg. 1613

HIPPURAN—Sodium Ortho-Iodohippurate, Etc.—Mallinckrodt Inc.; *U.S. Public*, pg. 1039

HIRAM WALKER—Cordials & Fruit Flavored Brandies—Hiram Walker; *Int'l*, pg. 63

HIRAM WALKER CORDIALS—Spirit—Allied Domecq PLC; *Int'l*, pg. 62

HIRAM WALKER'S BRANDY—Brandy—Hiram Walker; *Int'l*, pg. 63

HIRDA—Cathodic Protection—Corrpro Companies, Inc.; *U.S. Public*, pg. 451

HIRES—Root Beer—Cadbury Beverages; *Int'l*, pg. 248

HIRES—Soft Drink—Cadbury Beverages North America; *Int'l*, pg. 248

HIRES—Root Beer—Cadbury Schweppes p.l.c.; *Int'l*, pg. 247

HIRES—Soft Drink—Grant-Lydick Beverage Co.; *U.S. Private*, pg. 470

HIRES ROOT BEER—Soft Drink—The Procter & Gamble Company; *U.S. Public*, pg. 1330

HIRSH ADD-A-CLOSET—Garment Racks—Hirsh Company; *U.S. Public*, pg. 963

HIRSH CUSTOM CABINET—Modular Cabinet System—Hirsh Company; *U.S. Public*, pg. 963

HIRSH CUSTOM CLOSET—Modular Closet System—Hirsh Company; *U.S. Public*, pg. 963

HIRSH CUTTERS EDGE—Cutting Guide—Hirsh Company; *U.S. Public*, pg. 963

HIRSH FOLDING LAUNDRY CADDY—Folding Laundry Caddy—Hirsh Company; *U.S. Public*, pg. 963

HIRSH-GIBRALTER—Steel Shelving—Hirsh Company; *U.S. Public*, pg. 963

HIRSH MINI STACKERS—Mini Stackable Organizers—Hirsh Company; *U.S. Public*, pg. 963

HIRSH-SAWTABLE—Portable Folding Sawtable—Hirsh Company; *U.S. Public*, pg. 963

HIRSH STORAGE CABINETS—Wood Storage Cabinets—Hirsh Company; *U.S. Public*, pg. 963

HIRSH WORK CENTERS—Workbench Center—Hirsh Company; *U.S. Public*, pg. 963

HIRSH WORK'N STORAGE SYSTEM—Storage Cabinets—Hirsh Company; *U.S. Public*, pg. 963

HIRULOG—NONE—Biogen, Inc.; *U.S. Public*, pg. 230

HIRUNDO—NONE—Merloni Elettrodomestici S.P.A.; *Int'l*, pg. 860

HIS EMINENCE'S CHOICE PORTS—NONE—Delaforce Sons & Ca Vinhos Lda.; *Int'l*, pg. 409

HIS MASTER'S VOICE—Music Retailing—EMI Group plc; *Int'l*, pg. 426

HIS MASTER'S VOICE—TV Sets—Thomson Consumer Electronics Inc.; *Int'l*, pg. 1383

HISMANAL—Pharmaceutical—Janssen Pharmaceutica, Inc.; *U.S. Public*, pg. 928

HISMANAL—Prescription Antihistamine—Johnson & Johnson; *U.S. Public*, pg. 927

HISTALET FORTE—Pharmaceutical Products—Solvay Pharmaceuticals, Inc.; *Int'l*, pg. 1278

HISTALET SYRUP—Pharmaceutical Products—Solvay Pharmaceuticals, Inc.; *Int'l*, pg. 1278

HISTALET X SYRUP—Pharmaceutical Products—Solvay Pharmaceuticals, Inc.; *Int'l*, pg. 1278

HISTALET X TABLETS—Pharmaceutical Products—Solvay Pharmaceuticals, Inc.; *Int'l*, pg. 1278

HISTASPAN-D—Pharmaceuticals—Rhone-Poulenc Rorer - U.S.; *Int'l*, pg. 1110

HISTASPAN PLUS—Pharmaceuticals—Rhone-Poulenc Rorer - U.S.; *Int'l*, pg. 1110

HISTO PREP—Histological Tissue Processing Equip—Fisher Scientific Company; *U.S. Private*, pg. 658

HISTO-CENTER—Tissue Embedding Unit For Preparation of Histological Specimans—Fisher Scientific Company; *U.S. Private*, pg. 658

HISTOMATIC—Tissue Processing Apparatus—Fisher Scientific Company; *U.S. Private*, pg. 658

HISTORIC TRAVELER—Periodical—Cowles Enthusiast Media, Inc.; *U.S. Private*, pg. 281

THE HISTORY CHANNEL—History Channel—The Hearst Corporation; *U.S. Private*, pg. 515

HISTOSTAT-50—Feed Additives—Salsbury Laboratories, Inc.; *Int'l*, pg. 1277

HISTOSYSTEM—Antibody Kit—E-Z-Em, Inc.; *U.S. Public*, pg. 540

HIT OR MISS—Women's Clothing Stores—Hit or Miss, Inc.; *U.S. Private*, pg. 531

HITACHI—Electronic Components—Hitachi America, Ltd.; *Int'l*, pg. 622

HITACHI—Televisions, Radios, Tape Recorders, Stereo Components, Hi Fi Components—Hitachi Home Electronics; *Int'l*, pg. 621

HITACHI—Power Tools—Hitachi Koki U.S.A. Ltd.; *Int'l*, pg. 620

HITACHI—TV's, Audio Equipment, VTR's—Hitachi, Ltd.; *Int'l*, pg. 621

HITACHI—NONE—Milgray Electronics, Inc.; *U.S. Public*, pg. 205

HITACHI—Hitachi Data Systems—Sand Technology Systems; *Int'l*, pg. 1183

HITCH-HIKER—Portable Ground Fault Circuit Interrupter—Pass & Seymour/Legrand; *Int'l*, pg. 806

HITCH WORLD—Moving Aid—U-Haul International, Inc.; *U.S. Private*, pg. 49

HITE-MASTER—Self-Propelled Aerial Work Platform—Mayville Engineering Co., Inc.; *U.S. Private*, pg. 718

HITEC—Performance Additives—Ethyl Corporation; *U.S. Public*, pg. 595

HITEMITE—Self-Propeller Access Platform—Simon Engineering plc; *Int'l*, pg. 1251

HITENSO—Tubing Access.—Outokumpu American Brass Co.; *Int'l*, pg. 1016

HITOX—Titanium Dioxide Pigment—Hitox Corporation of America; *U.S. Public*, pg. 829

HITRADIO VERONICA—Luxembourg Broadcasting—CLT-UFA; *Int'l*, pg. 561

HITSCHLER—NONE—Cruspi S.A.; *Int'l*, pg. 348

HIVID—Oncology & Virology Pharmaceutical—Roche Holding Ltd.; *Int'l*, pg. 1119

HIWAY-WIPE—Paper Towels—Georgia-Pacific Corporation; *U.S. Public*, pg. 735

HO HOS—Snack Cake—Ralston Purina Company; *U.S. Public*, pg. 1359

HO-PAC—Vibratory Mounted Compactor/Driver—Allied Construction Products, Inc.; *U.S. Public*, pg. 1339

HO-RAM—Pneumatic Mounted Breaker—Allied Construction Products, Inc.; *U.S. Public*, pg. 1339

HOBART—Food Equipment—Premark International, Inc.; *U.S. Public*, pg. 1321

HOBART—Welding Machines—Welsco Inc.; *U.S. Private*, pg. 1161

HOBART BROTHERS—Arc Welding Systems, Ind. Battery Chargers, Aircraft Ground Power Units—Hobart Brothers Co.; *U.S. Public*, pg. 866

HOBAS—PVC Pipe—James Hardie Industries Ltd.; *Int'l*, pg. 596

HOBBIES & IDEAS—Stationary Products—The Mead Corporation; *U.S. Public*, pg. 1074

HOBBS—Meters, Mechanical Devices—BTR plc; *Int'l*, pg. 124

HOBBS—Meters, Switches, Lamp Assemblies—Hobbs Corporation; *Int'l*, pg. 127

HOBBY—Cameras—Eastman Kodak Company; *U.S. Public*, pg. 550

HOBBY CRAFT—1/2 oz., 2 oz., & 3 oz. Spray Paint—Koh-I-Noor, Inc.; *U.S. Private*, pg. 629

HOBBY-PAC—Photographic Chemicals—Eastman Kodak Company; *U.S. Public*, pg. 550

HOBIE/CATS—Catamarans—Hobie Cat Company; *U.S. Private*, pg. 531

HOBOURN—Steering & Suspension Components—Echlin Inc.; *U.S. Public*, pg. 560

HOCHTALER—Wine—Andres Wines Ltd.; *Int'l*, pg. 75

HOCKEY DIGEST—Magazine—Century Publishing Company; *U.S. Private*, pg. 226

HOCUT—Metal Machining Coolants—Houghton International Inc.; *U.S. Private*, pg. 541

HODGES—Shelving Mfg.—Falcon Products, Inc.; *U.S. Public*, pg. 611

HOEGAARDEN—Wheat Beer—Interbrew S.A.; *Int'l*, pg. 679

HOEGAARDEN—Beer—Labatt U.S.A.; *Int'l*, pg. 679

HOERAUF—Packaging, Paper Cup & Letter File Covering Machines—Spindelfabrik Suessen; *Int'l*, pg. 1290

HOERAUF GVA—Yarn Conditioning Plant—Spindelfabrik Suessen; *Int'l*, pg. 1290

HOFELS—Vitamins & Food Supplements—Hanson PLC; *Int'l*, pg. 592

HOFFER—Intraocular Lenses—Alcon Laboratories, Inc.; *Int'l*, pg. 916

HOFFMAN—Gas, Electric & Oil Powered Heaters—Bradford-White Corporation; *U.S. Private*, pg. 164

HOFFMAN—Cheese—Churny Company Inc.; *U.S. Public*, pg. 1288

HOFFMAN—Condensate Handling Equipment—ITT Fluid Handling; *U.S. Public*, pg. 860

HOFFMAN—Electrical Enclosures—Pentair, Inc.; *U.S. Public*, pg. 1273

HOFFMAN—NONE—Pfizer Inc.; *U.S. Public*, pg. 1281

HOFFMAN—Food Products—York Barbell Co., Inc.; *U.S. Private*, pg. 1196

HOFFMAN HOUSE—Specialty Sauces & Salad Dressings—Dean Foods Company; *U.S. Public*, pg. 489

HOFFMAN HOUSE—Food Prods.—Dean Pickle & Specialty Products Co.; *U.S. Public*, pg. 490

HOFFMAN-LA ROCHE—Pharmaceuticals & Consumer Chemicals—Hoffmann-La Roche Inc.; *Int'l*, pg. 1120

HOFFMAN MODULATION CONTRAST SYSTEM—Viewing System for Microscopes—Slant/Fin Corporation; *U.S. Private*, pg. 1005

HOFFMAN SEEDS—Planting Seeds—Hoffman Seeds, Inc.; *U.S. Private*, pg. 532

HOFFMAN SPECIALTIES—Steam Specialties—ITT Fluid Handling; *U.S. Public*, pg. 860

HOFFMANS—NONE—Guinness Plc; *Int'l*, pg. 412

HOFLER—Seeds—The Dow Chemical Company; *U.S. Public*, pg. 522

HOFMANN MENU—Frozen Ready Meals—GrandMet Foods GmbH; *Int'l*, pg. 409

HOGAN SYSTEMS PLUS DESIGN—Software—Hogan Systems, Inc.; *U.S. Public*, pg. 422

HOGAN UMBRELLA SYSTEM PLUS DESIGN—Banking Applications Software—Hogan Systems, Inc.; *U.S. Public*, pg. 422

HOGATE'S—Restaurants—Houlihan's Restaurant Group; *U.S. Public*, pg. 841

HOHES C—Orange Juice—Eckes AG; *Int'l*, pg. 432

HOHNER—Harmonicas, Accordions, Guitars—Hohner/HSS Inc.; *U.S. Private*, pg. 533

HOISTALOY—Load Chain—Columbus McKinnon Corp.; *U.S. Public*, pg. 405

HOKUOHM—NONE—Hokuriku Electric Industry Co., Ltd.; *Int'l*, pg. 627

HOL HUGGER—Anchors—Hilti Inc.; *Int'l*, pg. 620

HOLADAY—RF Radiation, Microwave Oven & Leakage Meters—Bowthorpe plc; *Int'l*, pg. 207

HOLD—Cough Suppressant Lozenge—Menley & James Laboratories, Inc.; *U.S. Public*, pg. 1086

HOLD—Helium Operated Leak Detector—Weatherford Enterra Incorporated; *U.S. Public*, pg. 1749

HOLD & CLEAN—Hair Preparations—The Gillette Company; *U.S. Public*, pg. 743

HOLD-E-ZEE—Screw Holding Screwdriver—Channellock, Inc.; *U.S. Private*, pg. 229

HOLD-E-ZEE—Screw Driver—Hold-E-Zee, Ltd.; *U.S. Private*, pg. 229

HOLD EVERYTHING—Home & Office Organizers, Retail & Mail Order—Williams-Sonoma, Inc.; *U.S. Public*, pg. 1770

HOLD TIGHT—Hair Spray Solution—Revlon-Realistic Professional Products, Inc.; *U.S. Private*, pg. 690

HOLD TITE—Cable Staples—E.H. Titchener & Company; *U.S. Private*, pg. 1089

HOLD-ZIT—Rubber Straps & Fasteners—Radiator Specialty Company; *U.S. Private*, pg. 906

HOLDENS—Passenger Cars & Light Comml. Vehicles—General Motors Corporation; *U.S. Public*, pg. 718

HOLDER—Sailboats—Hobie Cat Company; *U.S. Private*, pg. 531

HOLDTITE—Tube Connectors for Medico-Surgical Tubes—Mallinckrodt Inc.; *U.S. Public*, pg. 1039

HOLE HAMMER—Pneumatic Inpact Tool—McLaughlin Manufacturing Company; *U.S. Private*, pg. 724

HOLE HAWG—Power Tools—Milwaukee Electric Tool Corp.; *Int'l*, pg. 96

HOLE-HOG—Piercing Tool—Allied Construction Products, Inc.; *U.S. Public*, pg. 1339

HOLE IN THE HEAD—NONE—Callaway Golf Company; *U.S. Public*, pg. 294

HOLE SHOOTERS—Power Tools—Milwaukee Electric Tool Corp.; *Int'l*, pg. 96

HOLEMASTER—Rotary Drilling Rigs—The George E. Failing Company; *U.S. Private*, pg. 153

HOLEPROOF—NONE—Pacific Dunlop Limited; *Int'l*, pg. 1021

HOLFORM—Concrete Sleeves—The Lamson & Sessions Co.; *U.S. Public*, pg. 976

HOLGA—Office Furniture—HON Industries Inc.; *U.S. Public*, pg. 772

HOLGUN—Power Tools—The Black & Decker Corporation; *U.S. Public*, pg. 233

HOLIDAY—Tires—Bridgestone/Firestone, Inc.; *Int'l*, pg. 213

HOLIDAY—Insecticide—The Clorox Company; *U.S. Public*, pg. 386

HOLIDAY—Beer—Joseph Huber Brewing Co., Inc.; *U.S. Private*, pg. 545

HOLIDAY—Pipe Tobacco—Lane Limited; *Int'l*, pg. 1129

HOLIDAY—Luggage—Monarch Luggage Co. Inc.; *U.S. Private*, pg. 757

HOLIDAY ACTIVITY FUN PAK—NONE—Broderbund Software, Inc.; *U.S. Public*, pg. 258

HOLIDAY AT THE CAROUSEL—Carousel—Mr. Christmas Inc.; *U.S. Private*, pg. 765

HOLIDAY COACH—Vehicle Conversions—Starcraft Corporation; *U.S. Public*, pg. 1510

HOLIDAY CONNECTION—Cookware—Regal Ware, Inc.; *U.S. Private*, pg. 917

HOLIDAY EXPRESS—Hotels—Holiday Inn Worldwide; *U.S. Public*, pg. 170

HOLIDAY FIESTA—Tires—Bridgestone/Firestone, Inc.; *Int'l*, pg. 213

HOLIDAY FROM HELLMANN'S—Dressings—Bestfoods; *U.S. Public*, pg. 223

HOLIDAY GLAZE—Ham—Hormel Foods Corp.; *U.S. Public*, pg. 840

HOLIDAY HARVEST—Cranberry Sauce—Ocean Spray Cranberries, Inc.; *U.S. Private*, pg. 811

HOLIDAY HOME—Home—Fred Meyer Stores; *U.S. Public*, pg. 1103

HOLIDAY INN—NONE—Sunstone Hotel Investors, Inc.; *U.S. Public*, pg. 1536

HOLIDAY JUICE—NONE—Labatt Brewing Company Limited; *Int'l*, pg. 679

HOLIDAY RAMBLER—Recreational Vehicle—Holiday Rambler; *U.S. Public*, pg. 1123

HOLIDAY RAMBLER—Motorhomes & Towable Recreational Vehicles—Monaco Coach Corporation; *U.S. Public*, pg. 1123

HOLIDAY SCENTSABLES—Control Release Dispensers—Hercon Environmental Corporation; *U.S. Public*, pg. 802

HOLIDAY TREATS—Ice Cream—Good Humor/Breyers Ice Cream; *Int'l*, pg. 1435

HOLIDAY WORKSHOP—Seasonal Items—Syratech Corporation; *U.S. Private*, pg. 1060

HOLIDAYS—Candy—Mars, Incorporated; *U.S. Private*, pg. 707

HOLIDAYS NEWS SERVICE—Holiday Travel Information—American Automobile Association; *U.S. Private*, pg. 50

HOLLAND AMERICA LINE—Cruise Line—Carnival Corporation; *U.S. Public*, pg. 306

HOLLAND AMERICA LINE-WESTOURS—Transportation and Tours—Carnival Corporation; *U.S. Public*, pg. 306

HOLLAND AMERICA LINE - WESTOURS INC—NONE—Holland America Line Westours; *U.S. Public*, pg. 306

HOLLAND HOUSE—Drink Mixes—Cadbury Beverages; *Int'l*, pg. 248

HOLLAND HOUSE—Cocktail Mixer—Cadbury Beverages North America; *Int'l*, pg. 248

HOLLAND HOUSE—Cocktail Mixers—Cadbury Schweppes p.l.c.; *Int'l*, pg. 247

HOLLAND MEDIA GROEP RTL4,5 & VERONICA—Luxembourg Broadcasting—CLT-UFA; *Int'l*, pg. 561

HOLLAND MEDIA HOUSE—Netherlands Production Company—CLT-UFA; *Int'l*, pg. 561

HOLLAND RUSK—Toast—Nabisco Inc.; *U.S. Public*, pg. 1355

HOLLAND SEMINAR—Newspaper—Shivers Trading & Operating Co.; *U.S. Private*, pg. 994

HOLLAND'S—Pie—Northern Foods plc; *Int'l*, pg. 967

HOLLEY—Automotive Prods.—Coltec Industries Inc.; *U.S. Public*, pg. 401

HOLLINGTON—Chairs—Herman Miller, Inc.; *U.S. Public*, pg. 1111

HOLLOW LEGIONS—Game—Monarch Avalon, Inc.; *U.S. Public*, pg. 1123

HOLLOWSHAFT—Vertical Hollow Shaft Motors—U.S. Electrical Motor Division; *U.S. Public*, pg. 573

HOLLY—Sugar—Holly Sugar Corporation; *U.S. Public*, pg. 872

HOLLY FARMS—Fresh Poultry—Louis Kemp Seafood Co.; *U.S. Public*, pg. 1652

HOLLY HILL & DESIGN—Lumber, Plywood & Fiberboard—Georgia-Pacific Corporation; *U.S. Public*, pg. 735

HOLLY HOBBIE—NONE—American Greetings Corporation; *U.S. Public*, pg. 77

HOLLY HOBBIE—Greeting Cards, Stationery—American Greetings U.S. Greeting Card Division; *U.S. Public*, pg. 78

HOLLY PAK—Further-processed poultry items—Louis Kemp Seafood Co.; *U.S. Public*, pg. 1652

HOLLY RIDGE FARMS—Meats—Thorn Apple Valley, Inc.; *U.S. Public*, pg. 1602

HOLLY SUGAR CORPORATION—NONE—Imperial Holly Corporation; *U.S. Public*, pg. 872

HOLLY'S BISTROS—Full Service Restaurants—Holly's Inc.; *U.S. Private*, pg. 535

HOLLY'S BY GOLLY—Full Service Restaurants—Holly's Inc.; *U.S. Private*, pg. 535

HOLLY'S LANDINGS—Full Service Restaurants—Holly's Inc.; *U.S. Private*, pg. 535

HOLLYMATIC—Food Processing Machinery—Hollymatic Corporation; *U.S. Private*, pg. 535

HOLLYTEX OF CALIFORNIA—Carpeting—Hollytex Carpet Mills, Inc.; *U.S. Private*, pg. 535

HOLLYWOOD—Cigarettes—B.A.T Industries P.L.C.; *Int'l*, pg. 110

Brand Name Index

HOLLYWOOD—A Line of Premium Healthy Oils & Other Specialty Products—The Hain Food Group Inc.; *U.S. Public*, pg. 774

HOLLYWOOD—Gum—Kraft Jacobs Suchard; *U.S. Public*, pg. 1290

HOLLYWOOD—Diet Bread—Metz Baking Company (WI); *U.S. Private*, pg. 1022

HOLLYWOOD—Chewing Gum—Philip Morris Companies Inc.; *U.S. Public*, pg. 1287

HOLLYWOOD HIPPO—Greeting Cards—American Greetings Corporation; *U.S. Public*, pg. 77

HOLLYWOOD PARK—Race Course—Hollywood Park, Inc.; *U.S. Public*, pg. 830

HOLLYWOOD PARK CASINO—Card Club—Hollywood Park, Inc.; *U.S. Public*, pg. 830

HOLLYWOOD PICTURES—Motion Picture Production Company—The Walt Disney Company; *U.S. Public*, pg. 511

THE HOLLYWOOD REPORTER—Magazine; Books on Movies; Directories—BPI Communications Inc.; *Int'l*, pg. 1446

HOLMATRO—Rescue Equipment—Holmatro, Inc.; *Int'l*, pg. 632

HOLMATRO—Rescue Equipment—Holmatro Industrial & Rescue Equipment; *Int'l*, pg. 632

HOLMATRO FLOW STOPPERS—Sealing Equipment—Holmatro Industrial & Rescue Equipment; *Int'l*, pg. 632

HOLMATRO GLASSCUTTER—Glasscutter—Holmatro Industrial & Rescue Equipment; *Int'l*, pg. 632

HOLMATRO PERSONAL POWER RESCUE SYSTEMS—Rescue Systems—Holmatro Industrial & Rescue Equipment; *Int'l*, pg. 632

HOLMATRO POWER WEDGE—Hydraulic Wedge Jack—Holmatro Industrial & Rescue Equipment; *Int'l*, pg. 632

HOLMATRO SECUNET—Airbag Cover, Rescue Equipment—Holmatro Industrial & Rescue Equipment; *Int'l*, pg. 632

HOLMATRO WHISPER SERIES—Low Noise Level Petrol Pumps—Holmatro Industrial & Rescue Equipment; *Int'l*, pg. 632

HOLMBERG—Electronics—Thomas & Betts Electronics Division; *U.S. Public*, pg. 1597

HOLMBERG D—Subminiature & Cardedge Connectors—Thomas & Betts Corporation; *U.S. Public*, pg. 1597

HOLMES—Sea Food Prods.—George Weston Limited; *Int'l*, pg. 1494

HOLMES COMPUTECT 2000 COMMMAND CENTER—User-Friendly Alarm—Holmes Protection Group, Inc.; *U.S. Public*, pg. 1649

HOLMES LIFENET IN-VEHICLE—User-Friendly Alarm—Holmes Protection Group, Inc.; *U.S. Public*, pg. 1649

HOLNAM—Portland, Masonry & White Cements—Holnam Inc. (West Division); *Int'l*, pg. 628

HOLO—Cereals—Bestfoods; *U.S. Public*, pg. 223

HOLO-FLITE—Indirect Heat Exchangers—Svedala Pumps & Process; *Int'l*, pg. 1325

HOLOGON T—Camera Lense—Carl Zeiss; *Int'l*, pg. 1522

HOLOMAGNETICS—Non-Forgable Magnetics—Control Module, Inc.; *U.S. Private*, pg. 271

HOLONETICS—Machine Readable Hologram For Identification—Control Module, Inc.; *U.S. Private*, pg. 271

HOLOSIGHT—Gun Sight—Bushnell Corporation; *U.S. Private*, pg. 1191

HOLSTED—Stemware & Barware—Dansk International Designs Ltd.; *U.S. Public*, pg. 261

HOLSUM—Bread—Interstate Brands Corporation; *U.S. Public*, pg. 909

HOLSUM—Bread, Buns, Croutons & Sweet Goods—Metz Baking Company; *U.S. Private*, pg. 1022

HOLSUM—Bread, Buns, Croutons, Sweet Goods—Metz Baking Company (WI); *U.S. Private*, pg. 1022

HOLSUM—Foods—Ventura Foods; *U.S. Private*, pg. 508

HOLTON—Musical Instruments & Accessories—G. Leblanc Corporation; *U.S. Private*, pg. 656

HOLZ HER—Electrical Power Tools—Karl M. Reich Maschinenfabrik GmbH; *Int'l*, pg. 1101

HOMASOTE—Easy Ply Roof Deck Building Board—Homasote Company; *U.S. Public*, pg. 831

HOMASOTE 4-WAY—Floor Deck Multiple Building Board—Homasote Company; *U.S. Public*, pg. 831

HOMASOTE SUPER 440—Building Board—Homasote Company; *U.S. Public*, pg. 831

HOME—Home Decorating Magazine—Hachette Filipacchi Magazines Inc.; *Int'l*, pg. 794

HOME—Premium—The Lion Brewery, Inc.; *U.S. Public*, pg. 1000

HOME—Beers & Ale—Scottish & Newcastle plc; *Int'l*, pg. 1211

HOME ACCENTS TODAY—Merchandising & Fashion Magazine for the Home Accent & Gift Industries—Reed Elsevier Business Information; *Int'l*, pg. 1095

HOME & GARDEN SAVINGS CLUB—Home & Garden Goods & Services—Encore Marketing International, Inc.; *U.S. Public*, pg. 580

HOME & OFFICE—Business Products—Union Camp Corporation; *U.S. Public*, pg. 1665

HOME & PERSONAL CARE—NONE—Lever Brothers West Indies Ltd.; *Int'l*, pg. 1437

HOME BASICS—NONE—White Consolidated Industries, Inc.; *Int'l*, pg. 439

HOME BOX OFFICE—Pay Television Service—Home Box Office, Inc.; *U.S. Public*, pg. 1612

HOME BRANDS—Preserves, Jelly & Peanut Butter—ConAgra, Inc.; *U.S. Public*, pg. 425

HOME BUYERS—Savings Account With Discounts for TSB Home Buyers—The Troy Savings Bank; *U.S. Private*, pg. 1106

HOME COOKIN'—Soup—Campbell Soup Company; *U.S. Public*, pg. 298

HOME COOKING—Culinary Magazine—House of White Birches, Inc.; *U.S. Private*, pg. 542

HOME DECORATOR—Paint—Sherwin-Williams Consumer Brands Division; *U.S. Public*, pg. 1466

HOME DEPOT—Home Improvement Prods.—The Home Depot, Inc.; *U.S. Public*, pg. 831

HOME FASHIONS—Business Publication Magazine—Fairchild Publications; *U.S. Public*, pg. 513

HOME FURNISHING DAILY—Business Publication—Fairchild Publications; *U.S. Public*, pg. 513

HOME GOODS—Off-Price Home Fashions—The TJX Companies, Inc.; *U.S. Public*, pg. 1556

HOME GYM & FITNESS—Magazine—Century Publishing Company; *U.S. Private*, pg. 226

HOME IDEAS—Home Fashion Stores—Montgomery Ward & Co., Inc.; *U.S. Private*, pg. 758

HOME IMPROVEMENT MARKET—Magazine Serving Home Improvement Retailers—Reed Elsevier Business Information; *Int'l*, pg. 1095

HOME JUICE—Juice—Home Juice Co.; *U.S. Private*, pg. 537

HOME MANAGEMENT HELPER—Computer Programming for TV—Sony Electronics; *Int'l*, pg. 1281

HOME MINDER—Home Security System—Thomson Consumer Electronics Inc.; *Int'l*, pg. 1383

HOME OF THE NEVER EMPTY COFFEE POT—Restaurant—IHOP Corp.; *U.S. Public*, pg. 862

HOME OFFICE COMPUTING—Computer Publication Directed To Small Business Owners; Monthly—Scholastic Inc.; *U.S. Public*, pg. 1440

HOME PC—Magazine—CMP Media, Inc.; *U.S. Public*, pg. 279

HOME PRIDE—Bakery Products—Goodman Fielder Limited; *Int'l*, pg. 555

HOME PRIDE—Bread & Rolls—Ralston Purina Company; *U.S. Public*, pg. 1359

HOME PRO—NONE—L & L Nursery Supply, Inc.; *U.S. Private*, pg. 638

HOME SHOPPING NETWORK—TV Program—Home Shopping Network, Inc.; *U.S. Public*, pg. 1685

HOME SHOWCASE—Decorative Accessories—Home Showcase Products; *U.S. Private*, pg. 1101

HOME STYLE—NONE—Goodman Fielder Limited; *Int'l*, pg. 555

HOME STYLE—Frozen Potatoes—Ore-Ida Foods, Inc.; *U.S. Public*, pg. 805

HOME STYLE—NONE—Quality Bakers New Zealand Ltd.; *Int'l*, pg. 556

HOME STYLER—Paint—Sherwin-Williams Consumer Brands Division; *U.S. Public*, pg. 1466

HOME STYLES—Furniture—Ameriwood Industries International Inc.; *U.S. Public*, pg. 98

HOME TEXTILES TODAY—Newspaper for the Marketing/Merchandising/Retailing of Home Textile Product—Reed Elsevier Business Information; *Int'l*, pg. 1095

HOME THEATER—Magazine—Freedom Communication Inc.; *U.S. Private*, pg. 425

HOME TOWN TREES—Tree Planting Program—IGA, Inc. (Independent Grocers Alliance); *U.S. Private*, pg. 555

HOME VIDEO STORE—Wireless Cable TV Systems—People's Choice TV Corp.; *U.S. Public*, pg. 1274

HOMEBIZ—Home Business Insurance—Utica Mutual Insurance Company; *U.S. Private*, pg. 1129

HOMEBUYER'S MORTGAGE—NONE—Washington Homes, Inc.; *U.S. Public*, pg. 1741

HOMEBUYER'S PREFERRED—Radon Detection Program—Landauer, Inc.; *U.S. Public*, pg. 977

HOMECHOICE—Automated Peritoneal Dialysis System—Baxter International Inc.; *U.S. Public*, pg. 196

HOMECREDIT EQUITY LINE—Home Financing—Bank of the Hudson; *U.S. Public*, pg. 1319

HOMECREST—Aluminum Roofing—Alcoa Building Products, Inc.; *U.S. Public*, pg. 61

HOMEFOLKS—Food Products—Allen Canning Company; *U.S. Private*, pg. 36

HOMEGUARD SECURITY SYSTEMS—Monitored Home & Business Security—Puget Sound Energy, Inc.; *U.S. Public*, pg. 1342

HOMELAND—Hard Salami—Hormel Foods Corp.; *U.S. Public*, pg. 840

HOMELIFE—NONE—Sears, Roebuck and Co.; *U.S. Public*, pg. 1452

HOMELINE—Aerosols—Pegasus International Corporation; *U.S. Private*, pg. 1046

HOMELINE—Circuit Breakers—Square D Company; *Int'l*, pg. 1208

HOMELITE—Walk-Behind & Hand-Held Power Products—Deere & Company; *U.S. Public*, pg. 491

HOMEMADE BRAND—Ice Cream—United Dairy Farmers, Inc.; *U.S. Private*, pg. 1121

HOMEMAID—Liquid Molasses—Crompton & Knowles Ingredient Technology Corp.; *U.S. Public*, pg. 459

HOMEMATE—Wireless Convenience Products—The Lamson & Sessions Co.; *U.S. Public*, pg. 976

HOMEPUMP ECLIPSE—Infusion Pump for the Delivery of Intermittent Antibiotics—Hillenbrand Industries, Inc.; *U.S. Public*, pg. 828

HOMES & GARDENS—Home Interest Magazine—IPC Magazines Limited; *Int'l*, pg. 651

HOMES OF MERIT—Mobile Homes & Real Estate Investors—Homes of Merit Inc.; *U.S. Private*, pg. 537

HOMESHIELD—Building Accessories—Nichols-Homeshield; *U.S. Public*, pg. 1350

HOMESTAR—Insurance Product—Eagle Star; *Int'l*, pg. 110

THE HOMESTEAD—Hotel—The Homestead L.C.; *U.S. Private*, pg. 247

HOMESTEAD—Door Systems—Pease Industries, Inc.; *U.S. Private*, pg. 845

HOMESTYLE—Gravy—H.J. Heinz Company; *U.S. Public*, pg. 805

HOMESTYLE—NONE—Maplehurst Farms, Inc.; *U.S. Public*, pg. 490

HOMESTYLE BAKED FILLETS—NONE—National Sea Products Limited; *Int'l*, pg. 909

HOMESTYLE BURGER—Hamburger Sandwiches—International Dairy Queen, Inc.; *U.S. Public*, pg. 220

HOMESTYLE BURGERS—Hamburger Patties—Harker's Distribution, Inc.; *U.S. Private*, pg. 502

HOMESTYLE ENTREE—Stir Frys, Sweet & Sour, Stroganoff—Harker's Distribution, Inc.; *U.S. Private*, pg. 502

HOMESTYLE SEASONED SALT—Seasoning—McCormick/Schilling; *U.S. Public*, pg. 1066

HOMETOWN—Bread & Rolls—Flowers Industries, Inc.; *U.S. Public*, pg. 656

HOMETOWN—Shutters, Lumber & Wood Products—Georgia-Pacific Corporation; *U.S. Public*, pg. 735

HOMETOWN BUFFET—Buffet Restaurants—Buffets, Inc.; *U.S. Public*, pg. 267

HOMETOWN BUFFET—Restaurants—Summit Family Restaurants, Inc.; *U.S. Public*, pg. 278

HOMETOWN PROUD—IGA Image Advertising Program—IGA, Inc. (Independent Grocers Alliance); *U.S. Private*, pg. 555

HOMEWATCH—Security Products—The Lamson & Sessions Co.; *U.S. Public*, pg. 976

HOMEWIRE—Residential And Commercial Electrical Wire—Southwire Company; *U.S. Private*, pg. 1019

HOMEWOOD SUITES—Hotels—Promus Hotel Corporation; *U.S. Public*, pg. 1335

HOMEWORKS—Desk Top (Which Fits Over Two Twin-Drawer Filing Cabinets)—Rubbermaid Incorporated; *U.S. Public*, pg. 1411

HOMEWORKS—Breadband Communications—Zenith Electronics Corp.; *U.S. Public*, pg. 1790

HOMEWORTHY—Furniture—Silentnight Holdings Plc; *Int'l*, pg. 1249

HOMEX-300—Concrete Joint Filler—Homasote Company; *U.S. Public*, pg. 831

HOMINY FEED—Flours & Cereals—ADM Milling Co.; *U.S. Public*, pg. 128

HOMY—Car—Nissan Motor Co., Ltd.; *Int'l*, pg. 943

HON—Office Furniture—The HON Co.; *U.S. Public*, pg. 772

HON—Office Furniture—HON Industries Inc.; *U.S. Public*, pg. 772

HONCHO—Herbicide—Monsanto Company; *U.S. Public*, pg. 1124

HONDA—Power Products & Parts—American Honda Motor Co., Inc.; *Int'l*, pg. 634

HONDA—Automobile—American Honda Motor Co., Inc. Automobile Sales Division; *Int'l*, pg. 634

HONDA—Motorcycles, All Terrain Vehicles, Motorscooters—American Honda Motor Co., Inc. Motorcycle Division; *Int'l*, pg. 634

HONDA—Autos, Motorcycles, Power Products—Honda Motor Co., Ltd.; *Int'l*, pg. 634

HONDA—Auto—Loeber Motors, Inc.; *U.S. Private*, pg. 672

HONDA EAST—NONE—Beechmont Investments Inc.; *U.S. Private*, pg. 129

HONDA EXPRESS—Motorcycle—American Honda Motor Co., Inc. Motorcycle Division; *Int'l*, pg. 634

HONDA ODYSSEY—Automobile—Honda Motor Co., Ltd.; *Int'l*, pg. 634

HONDALINE—Motorcycle Accessories—American Honda Motor Co., Inc. Motorcycle Division; *Int'l*, pg. 634

HONDALINE HAWKS—Motorcycle Helmets—American Honda Motor Co., Inc. Motorcycle Division; *Int'l*, pg. 634

HONDAMATIC—Motorcycle—American Honda Motor Co., Inc. Motorcycle Division; *Int'l*, pg. 634

HONDURAN BUNDLES—Premium Cigars—Consolidated Cigar Corporation; *U.S. Private*, pg. 690

HONEST—Scotch Snuff—Conwood Company L.P.; *U.S. Private*, pg. 272

HONEY AMBER—Premium Beer—The Lion Brewery, Inc.; *U.S. Public*, pg. 1000

HONEY BEAR—Poultry Items—Louis Kemp Seafood Co.; *U.S. Public*, pg. 1652

HONEY BEAR—Poultry Items—Tyson Foods, Inc.; *U.S. Public*, pg. 1652

HONEY BUNCHES OF OATS—Breakfast Cereal—Kraft Foods, Inc.; *U.S. Public*, pg. 1287

HONEY COLLECTION—Accessories—Honey Fashions Ltd.; *U.S. Private*, pg. 537

HONEY CRUNCH RICE BRAN—Topping—The Quaker Oats Company; *U.S. Public*, pg. 1347

HONEY CRUNCHERS—Snack Food—Nabisco Inc.; *U.S. Public*, pg. 1355

HONEY FROSTED WHEATIES—Cereal—General Mills, Inc.; *U.S. Public*, pg. 717

HONEY GRAHAMS—Crackers—Keebler Company; *U.S. Public*, pg. 657

HONEY LOVE TEDDY BEARS—Greeting Cards—American Greetings Corporation; *U.S. Public*, pg. 77

HONEY MAID—Graham Crackers—Nabisco Inc.; *U.S. Public*, pg. 1355

HONEY MAID—Cinnamon & Honey Graham Crackers—RJR Nabisco Holdings Corp.; *U.S. Public*, pg. 1354

HONEY NUT CHEERIOS—Cereal—General Mills, Inc.; *U.S. Public*, pg. 717

HONEY NUT CLUSTERS—Cereal—General Mills, Inc.; *U.S. Public*, pg. 717

HONEY NUT TOASTY O'S—Cereal—Malt-O-Meal Company; *U.S. Private*, pg. 699

HONEY STUNG—Further-processed poultry items—Louis Kemp Seafood Co.; *U.S. Public*, pg. 1652

HONEY STUNG—Frozen Poultry—Tyson Foods, Inc.; *U.S. Public*, pg. 1652

HONEYBEAR BOOKS—Books—Unisystems, Inc.; *U.S. Private*, pg. 1120

HONEYBRAN—Bread—Roman Meal Company; *U.S. Private*, pg. 942

HONEYCOMB—Breakfast Cereal—Kraft Foods, Inc.; *U.S. Public*, pg. 1287

HONEYCOMB 10—Textured Thermally Sealed-Edge Border Wiper—The Texwipe Co., Inc.; *U.S. Private*, pg. 1079

HONEYSOY—Food Product—Honeymead Products Co.; *U.S. Private*, pg. 533

HONEYSUCKLE WHITE—Premium Turkey—Cargill; *U.S. Private*, pg. 210

HONEYWELL—Controls & Air Cleaners—Excelsior Manufacturing & Supply Corp.; *U.S. Private*, pg. 387

HONEYWELL—Controls—The Habegger Corporation; *U.S. Private*, pg. 492

HONEYWELL—NONE—Honeywell Limited; *U.S. Public*, pg. 835

HONGKONGBANK—Mktg. Name of The Hongkong and Shanghai Banking Corporation Limited—The Hongkong and Shanghai Banking Corporation Limited (HongkongBank); *Int'l*, pg. 583

HONICA—Accordions—Hohner/HSS Inc.; *U.S. Private*, pg. 533

HONIG—Pasta, Soups, Sauces & Baking Mixes—CSM N.V.; *Int'l*, pg. 243

HONOR—Office Furniture—HON Industries Inc.; *U.S. Public*, pg. 772

HONOR CRAFT—Cookware—Regal Ware, Inc.; *U.S. Private*, pg. 917

HONOR ROLL—Pencils—Dixon Ticonderoga Company; *U.S. Public*, pg. 514

HONORED GUEST—NONE—Marriott International, Inc.; *U.S. Public*, pg. 1047

HONY TAB—Tabletting Agent for Pharmaceutical & Nutritional Tablets—Crompton & Knowles Ingredient Technology Corp.; *U.S. Public*, pg. 459

HOOK-A-WEIGH—Crane Scale—Harnischfeger Industries, Inc.; *U.S. Public*, pg. 788

HOOK & LADDER—Texas Style Chili—Skyline Chili, Inc.; *U.S. Public*, pg. 1475

HOOK EM'S—Storage Hooks—Bulldog VSI; *U.S. Public*, pg. 1176

HOOK-FLEX—Waistband Closures—North & Judd; *U.S. Public*, pg. 804

HOOKER—Anchors—Rule Industries, Inc.; *U.S. Public*, pg. 950

HOOKER—Sprinkler Head Fitting—Victaulic Company of America; *U.S. Private*, pg. 1138

HOOKER COMPETITION HEADERS—Performance Exhaust Systems—Hooker Industries; *U.S. Private*, pg. 538

HOOKER SUPER COMPETITION HEADERS—Performance Exhaust Systems—Hooker Industries; *U.S. Private*, pg. 538

HOOKIT SBS—Automotive Refinishing Pads—3M; *U.S. Public*, pg. 1604

HOOP-DE-DOOS—Embroidery Hoops—Wm. E. Wright Limited Partnership; *U.S. Private*, pg. 1192

HOOV-R-LINE—Plumbing Supplies—Fortune Brands, Inc.; *U.S. Public*, pg. 674

HOOV-R-LINE—NONE—MasterBrand Industries, Inc.; *U.S. Public*, pg. 675

HOOV-R-LINE—NONE—Moen Incorporated; *U.S. Public*, pg. 675

HOOVER—Household Appliances—Candy S.p.A.; *Int'l*, pg. 259

HOOVER—Floor Care Products—Maytag Corporation; *U.S. Public*, pg. 1064

HOPCAID—Liquid Plant Food—Mapco Inc.; *U.S. Public*, pg. 1042

HOPE—Steel & Aluminum Custom Windows—Hope's Architectural Products Inc.; *U.S. Private*, pg. 538

HOPE EDUCATION—Educational Stationery—Fine Art Developments plc; *Int'l*, pg. 485

HOPPER—Printing Paper—Georgia-Pacific Corporation; *U.S. Public*, pg. 735

HOPPE'S—Gun Care Products—Hoppe's A Brunswick Company; *U.S. Public*, pg. 266

HOPTO—Hydraulic Excavators—Avis Industrial Corporation; *U.S. Private*, pg. 102

HORACE MANN—Insuring America's Educational Community—Horace Mann Educators Corporation; *U.S. Public*, pg. 835

THE HORCHOW COLLECTION—Catalogue—Harcourt General, Inc.; *U.S. Public*, pg. 782

HORIZON—Term Life Insurance—American United Life Insurance Company; *U.S. Private*, pg. 64

HORIZON—Spa—Coleman Spas, Inc.; *U.S. Private*, pg. 691

HORIZON—Hose—The Goodyear Tire & Rubber Company; *U.S. Public*, pg. 752

HORIZON—NONE—Life Technologies, Inc.; *U.S. Public*, pg. 504

HORIZON—Software—Litton Industries, Inc.; *U.S. Public*, pg. 1002

HORIZON—Hospitality Communications System, Call Management System—Lucent Technologies Inc.; *U.S. Public*, pg. 1017

HORIZON—Real Estate Holdings—MCO Properties Inc.; *U.S. Public*, pg. 1062

HORIZON—Carpets & Rugs—Mohawk Industries, Inc.; *U.S. Public*, pg. 1121

HORIZON—Marine Radios—Standard Communications Corp.; *Int'l*, pg. 841

HORIZON—Machinery/Graphic—Standard Duplicating Machines Corp.; *U.S. Private*, pg. 1031

HORIZON—Routing Systems—Tektronix-Video & Networking Div., Grass Valley Products; *U.S. Public*, pg. 1567

HORIZON—Access Control Systems—Thorn Security Group, Ltd.; *Int'l*, pg. 1386

HORIZON—NONE—Western Atlas Logging Services; *U.S. Public*, pg. 1757

HORIZON AIR—Air Transportation—Horizon Air Industries; *U.S. Public*, pg. 35

HORIZON BLUE—Fluorescent Color—Day-Glo Color Corp.; *U.S. Public*, pg. 1357

HORIZON COLLECTION—Aluminum Siding—Alcoa Building Products, Inc.; *U.S. Public*, pg. 61

HORIZON LITE—Skylight—O'Keeffe's, Inc.; *U.S. Private*, pg. 813

HORIZON 9000WS—Catheterization Measuring System—Mennen Medical Ltd.; *Int'l*, pg. 858

HORIZON SHANGLE—Asphalt Roofing—CertainTeed Corporation; *Int'l*, pg. 1170

HORIZON XL—Patient Monitoring System—Mennen Medical Ltd.; *Int'l*, pg. 858

HORIZONS—Patient Monitor—Mennen Medical Inc.; *Int'l*, pg. 858

HORIZONS MATH—Home School Curriculum—Alpha Omega Publications; *U.S. Private*, pg. 168

HORIZONTAL PLATE FILTER—NONE—Bird Machine Company; *U.S. Public*, pg. 166

HORIZONTAL TRANSFER—NONE—EcoScience Corporation; *U.S. Public*, pg. 563

HORLICKS—Malted Food & Hot Chocolate Drinks—SmithKline Beecham Corporation; *Int'l*, pg. 1264

HORLICKS—Nutritional Healthcare—SmithKline Beecham plc; *Int'l*, pg. 1264

HORLUCKS—Premium Ice Cream—Darigold, Inc.; *U.S. Private*, pg. 311

HORMEL—Food Products—Hormel Foods Corp.; *U.S. Public*, pg. 840

HORMEL—Food Preparations—Hormel Foodservice Division; *U.S. Public*, pg. 840

HORNADY—Bullets—Hornady Manufacturing Company; *U.S. Private*, pg. 539

HORNER RAUSCH—Optical Retail Stores—Horner Rausch Optical Company East, Inc.; *U.S. Private*, pg. 540

HORNET—Operating Room & Surgery Decision Support System—Allegiant Physician Services; *U.S. Public*, pg. 45

HORNET—Canister Vacuum—Hoover Company; *U.S. Public*, pg. 1065

HORNET—Operating Room Surgery Decision Support System—Surgical Information Systems; *U.S. Public*, pg. 45

HORNITOS—Tequila—Domecq Importers Inc.; *Int'l*, pg. 63

HORSE AND HOUND—Equestrian Magazine—IPC Magazines Limited; *Int'l*, pg. 651

HORSE & PONY—Equestrian Magazine—EMAP Pursuit Publishing; *Int'l*, pg. 451

HORSE EXCHANGE—Equestrian Magazine—IPC Magazines Limited; *Int'l*, pg. 651

HORSE MAGAZINE—Equestrian Magazine—IPC Magazines Limited; *Int'l*, pg. 651

HORSE & RIDER—Periodical—Cowles Enthusiast Media, Inc.; *U.S. Private*, pg. 281

HORSE SHO-GLO—Horse Feed—Manna Pro Corporation; *U.S. Private*, pg. 700

HORSEHEAD—Tires—Bridgestone/Firestone, Inc.; *Int'l*, pg. 213

HORSEMAN'S CHOICE—Livestock Equipment—Behlen Mfg. Co.; *U.S. Private*, pg. 130

HORSEPOWER—Handy Clamp—American Tool Companies, Inc.; *U.S. Private*, pg. 63

HORTON AUTOMATICS—Automatic Door Products—Overhead Door Corporation; *U.S. Private*, pg. 822

HORZU—Magazine—Axel Springer Verlag AG; *Int'l*, pg. 102

HOSANNA! MUSIC—NONE—Integrity Incorporated; *U.S. Public*, pg. 886

HOSE KING—Hose Reels—Ames Company; *U.S. Public*, pg. 1683

HOSE'N GO GREEN UP—Fertilizer—The Chas. H. Lilly Co.; *U.S. Private*, pg. 667

HOSE'N GO MOSS OUT—Fertilizer—The Chas. H. Lilly Co.; *U.S. Private*, pg. 667

HOSE'N GO WEED & FEED—Lawn Food—The Chas. H. Lilly Co.; *U.S. Private*, pg. 667

HOSIERY & UNDERWEAR—Trade Periodical—Advantar Communications; *U.S. Private*, pg. 22

HOSKYNS—NONE—CAP Gemini S.A.; *Int'l*, pg. 263

HOSOKAWA MICRON—Powder Process Equipment—Hosokawa Micron International Inc.; *Int'l*, pg. 635

HOSPITAL HELP—Hospital Indemnity Insurance—Commercial Travelers Mutual Insurance Company; *U.S. Private*, pg. 258

HOSPITAL SYSTEMS—NONE—Allied Healthcare Products, Inc.; *U.S. Public*, pg. 48

HOSPITALIANO—(Slogan)—Olive Garden Italian Restaurants; *U.S. Public*, pg. 484

HOSPITALITY—Mixes—Gilster Mary Lee Corp.; *U.S. Private*, pg. 455

HOSPITALITY PRODUCT NEWS—Trade Periodical—Advantar Communications; *U.S. Private*, pg. 22

HOSPITEX—Surgical Masks & Caps, Gowns, Binders & Bandages—Allegiance Healthcare Corp.; *U.S. Public*, pg. 44

HOST INTERNATIONAL—Airport Food, Beverage & Concessionaire—Marriott International, Inc.; *U.S. Public*, pg. 1047

HOST MONITOR FACILITY—Software Which Monitors Network—Computer Network Technology Corporation; *U.S. Public*, pg. 421

HOSTAFLON—Fluoropolymers—Hoechst Aktiengesellschaft; *Int'l*, pg. 624

HOSTAFORM—Polyacetal Resin—Hoechst Aktiengesellschaft; *Int'l*, pg. 624

HOSTALEN—Polymers—Hoechst Aktiengesellschaft; *Int'l*, pg. 624

HOSTALEN PP—Polypropylene—Hoechst Aktiengesellschaft; *Int'l*, pg. 624

HOSTALIT—Polyvinylchloride—Hoechst Aktiengesellschaft; *Int'l*, pg. 624

HOSTAPERM—Organic Pigments—Hoechst Aktiengesellschaft; *Int'l*, pg. 624

HOSTAPHAN—Polyester Film—Hoechst Aktiengesellschaft; *Int'l*, pg. 624

HOSTAPUR SAS—Secondary Alkanesulfonate—Hoechst Aktiengesellschaft; *Int'l*, pg. 624

HOSTAQUICK—Herbicide—Hoechst Aktiengesellschaft; *Int'l*, pg. 624

HOSTATHION—Insecticide—Hoechst Aktiengesellschaft; *Int'l*, pg. 624

HOSTESS—Hams—Armour Swift Eckrich; *U.S. Public*, pg. 426

HOSTESS—Snack Cakes—Interstate Brands Corporation; *U.S. Public*, pg. 909

HOSTESS—Snack Cakes & Pies—Ralston Purina Company; *U.S. Public*, pg. 1359

HOSTESS—Baked Goods—George Weston Limited; *Int'l*, pg. 1494

HOSTMARK—Periodical Newsletter (Travel & Touring)—American Automobile Association; *U.S. Private*, pg. 50

HOT & CREAMY WHEAT CEREAL—Hot Cereal—The Quaker Oats Company; *U.S. Public*, pg. 1347

HOT BITES—Frozen Chicken Nuggets—ConAgra Frozen Food Company; *U.S. Public*, pg. 427

HOT BOND—Thermal-Bonded Plastic Tubing—NewAge Industries Inc.; *U.S. Private*, pg. 796

HOT BOND—Thermal-Bonded Plastic Tubing—Newage Industries Inc., Plastics Technology Group; *U.S. Private*, pg. 796

HOT BOX—Diesel Engine Compartment Heater—Stewart-Warner South Wind Corp.; *Int'l*, pg. 127

HOT CHA CHA—Salsa Sauce—Allied Old English, Inc.; *U.S. Private*, pg. 39

HOT COLES—Junior Swimwear—Cole of California; *U.S. Public*, pg. 148

HOT COUNTRY FORMAT—Hit-Oriented Music Programming—Westwood One, Inc.; *U.S. Public*, pg. 1763

HOT CYCLE—Ride-on Toys—Empire of Carolina, Inc.; *U.S. Public*, pg. 579

HOT-DOG PRESS—Biweekly General Interest Men's Magazine—Kodansha Ltd.; *Int'l*, pg. 742

HOT DOGGER—Electric Hot Dog Cooker—National Presto Industries, Inc.; *U.S. Public*, pg. 1159

HOT DOGGIES—NONE—Star-Kist Foods, Inc.; *U.S. Public*, pg. 806

HOT HAM N CHEESE—Sandwich—Hardee's Food Systems, Inc.; *U.S. Public*, pg. 278

HOT HATS—Sandwiches—Straw Hat Cooperative Corp.; *U.S. Private*, pg. 1046

HOT KEYS—Electronic Toys—Tyco Toys, Inc.; *U.S. Public*, pg. 1058

HOT KNOTS—Soft Pretzels—J & J Snack Foods Corporation; *U.S. Public*, pg. 916

HOT LINER—Pens—The Gillette Company; *U.S. Public*, pg. 743

HOT LIXX GUITAR—Electronic Toys—Tyco Toys, Inc.; *U.S. Public*, pg. 1058

HOT-N-BUTTERY—Waffles—The Pillsbury Company; *Int'l*, pg. 411

HOT 'N KOLDHANDLE CUPS—Paper Cups—The Mead Corporation; *U.S. Public*, pg. 1074

HOT'N SPICY—Fried Chicken—ConAgra Frozen Food Company; *U.S. Public*, pg. 427

THE HOT ONE—Portable Electric Unit—Cadet Manufacturing Company; *U.S. Private*, pg. 198

THE HOT ONE—Shave Cream—The Gillette Company; *U.S. Public*, pg. 743

HOT-RAGEOUS—Sausages—GoodMark Foods, Inc.; *U.S. Public*, pg. 751

HOT ROD—Hot Dog Grill—American Wyott Corporation; *U.S. Private*, pg. 1193

HOT ROD—Magazine—Petersen Publishing Company, L.L.C.; *U.S. Private*, pg. 856

HOT SAM—Pretzels—Mrs. Fields' Original Cookies, Inc.; *U.S. Private*, pg. 688

HOT SHIFT—Transmission—Snow-Nabstedt Power Transmissions; *U.S. Private*, pg. 36

HOT SHOT—Tennis Racquet—Head USA, Inc.; *U.S. Private*, pg. 514

HOT SHOT—Seasoning—McCormick/Schilling; *U.S. Public*, pg. 1066

HOT SHOT—Hot Beverage Makers—Sunbeam Household Products; *U.S. Public*, pg. 1533

HOT SHOT—Aluminum Beach Chair—Telescope Casual Furniture, Inc.; *U.S. Private*, pg. 1074

HOT SPA—Whirlpool Hot Spa—Pollenex; *U.S. Public*, pg. 1391

HOT SPOT MINITUB—Spas—Watkins Manufacturing Corp./Hot Spring Portable Spas; *U.S. Public*, pg. 1054

HOT SPOTZ—Hi-Temp Insulation—The Zippertubing Co.; *U.S. Private*, pg. 1207

HOT SPRING CLASSIC—Portable Spa Model—Watkins Manufacturing Corp./Hot Spring Portable Spas; *U.S. Public*, pg. 1054

HOT SPRING GRANDEE—Portable Spa Model—Watkins Manufacturing Corp./Hot Spring Portable Spas; *U.S. Public*, pg. 1054

HOT SPRING JETSETTER—Portable Spa Model—Watkins Manufacturing Corp./Hot Spring Portable Spas; *U.S. Public*, pg. 1054

HOT SPRING PRODIGY—Portable Spa Model—Watkins Manufacturing Corp./Hot Spring Portable Spas; *U.S. Public*, pg. 1054

HOT SPRING SOVEIRGN—Portable Spa Model—Watkins Manufacturing Corp./Hot Spring Portable Spas; *U.S. Public*, pg. 1054

HOT SPRINGS VILLAGE—Recreational & Retirement Communities—Cooper Communities, Inc.; *U.S. Private*, pg. 273

HOT STUFF—Gas Fish Cooker—W.C. Bradley Co.; *U.S. Private*, pg. 164

HOT SURFACE IGNITION—Furnace Controls for Heating—White-Rodgers Div., Emerson Electric Co.; *U.S. Public*, pg. 573

HOT TAMALES—Candy—Just Born, Inc.; *U.S. Private*, pg. 602

HOT TOOLS—NONE—Helen of Troy Corporation; *U.S. Public*, pg. 807

HOT TYPE—Column—Chicago Reader, Inc.; *U.S. Private*, pg. 235

HOT WATER CIRCULATOR—Pump—Little Giant Pump Company; *U.S. Public*, pg. 1566

HOT WHEAT CEREAL—NONE—Malt-O-Meal Company; *U.S. Public*, pg. 699

HOT WHEELS—Toy Vehicles & Accessories—Mattel, Inc.; *U.S. Public*, pg. 1057

HOT WINGS—Further-processed Poultry Items—Louis Kemp Seafood Co.; *U.S. Public*, pg. 1652

HOT WINGS—Menu Item—Kentucky Fried Chicken Corporation (KFC); *U.S. Public*, pg. 1636

HOT WINGS—Frozen Poultry—Tyson Foods, Inc.; *U.S. Public*, pg. 1652

HOT WIRE—DSL Systems—Paradyne; *U.S. Private*, pg. 838

HOT-Z—Golf Bags—The Arnold Palmer Golf Company; *U.S. Public*, pg. 132

HOTEL & MOTEL MANAGEMENT—Trade Periodical—Advantar Communications; *U.S. Private*, pg. 22

HOTEL & RESTAURANT BLEND—Coffee—New England Coffee Company; *U.S. Private*, pg. 792

HOTELEPHONE—Telephone—Comdial Corporation; *U.S. Public*, pg. 407

HOTELIA—Hotels for Senior Citizens—Accor S.A.; *Int'l*, pg. 20

HOTELS—Magazine Providing Information for Professionals in Hotel Industries—Reed Elsevier Business Information; *Int'l*, pg. 1095

HOTLINE—Demisting Vehicle Rear Windows—Pilkington Australasia Limited; *Int'l*, pg. 1057

HOTPO—Powdery Beverage—Otsuka Pharmaceutical Co., Ltd.; *Int'l*, pg. 1013

HOTPOINT—Major Appliances—G.E. Appliances; *U.S. Public*, pg. 710

HOTPOINT—Washing machines, dryers, freezers & dishwashers—The General Electric Company, p.l.c.; *Int'l*, pg. 543

HOTSHOT—Hardware—The Stanley Works; *U.S. Public*, pg. 1508

HOTSHOT—Automatic Telephone Dialer—Zoom Telephonics, Inc.; *U.S. Public*, pg. 1794

HOTSPOT—Coffee Warmer—Salton/Maxim Housewares, Inc.; *U.S. Public*, pg. 1430

HOTSPOT—NONE—UtiliCorp United Inc.; *U.S. Public*, pg. 1700

HOTSPUR—Herbicide—The Dow Chemical Company; *U.S. Public*, pg. 522

HOTSTUFF—Supplements—National Health Products; *U.S. Private*, pg. 784

HOTSY—Cleaning Equip.—The Hotsy Corporation; *U.S. Private*, pg. 500

HOTZ—Smoked Link Sausage with Jalapeno Peppers—Bob Evans Farms, Inc.; *U.S. Public*, pg. 596

HOTZ—Smoked Link Sausage with Jalepenos—Bob Evans Farms, Inc. Sausage Division; *U.S. Public*, pg. 596

HOUDINI—Playpen—Evenflo Company, Inc.; *U.S. Private*, pg. 629

HOUDINI—Play Yard—Spalding & Evenflo Companies, Inc.; *U.S. Private*, pg. 629

HOUGHTO-SAFE—Fire Resistant Fluids—Houghton International Inc.; *U.S. Private*, pg. 541

HOUGHTON MIFFLIN—Publishing—Houghton Mifflin Company; *U.S. Public*, pg. 841

HOUILLERS—Extraction Transformation of Coal—Houilleres de Bassin du Centre et du Midi; *Int'l*, pg. 280

HOULIHAN'S OLD PLACE—Restaurants—Houlihan's Restaurant Group; *U.S. Public*, pg. 841

HOUND DOG—Pet Foods—Ag Processing Inc., A Cooperative; *U.S. Private*, pg. 26

HOUR GLASSES—Optician Services—AVC/Nu-Vision, Inc.; *U.S. Public*, pg. 9

HOUSE & GARDEN—NONE—The Conde Nast Publications Inc.; *U.S. Private*, pg. 20

HOUSE BEAUTIFUL—Magazine—The Hearst Corporation; *U.S. Private*, pg. 515

HOUSE BEAUTIFUL—Magazine—Hearst Magazines Division; *U.S. Private*, pg. 516

HOUSE BEAUTIFUL—Magazine—The National Magazine Company Ltd.; *U.S. Private*, pg. 518

HOUSE CALL—Telemarketing—Kaufman and Broad Home Corporation; *U.S. Public*, pg. 944

HOUSE OF A MILLION SCREWS—Hardware—Service Supply Co. Inc. of Indiana; *U.S. Private*, pg. 987

HOUSE OF BIANCHI—Wedding Attire—House of Bianchi, Inc.; *U.S. Private*, pg. 541

THE HOUSE OF BLUES RADIO HOUR—Rock Programming—Westwood One, Inc.; *U.S. Public*, pg. 1763

HOUSE OF FABRICS—Fabric & Craft Store—House of Fabrics, Inc.; *U.S. Public*, pg. 842

HOUSE OF LORDS—Pipe Tobacco—Lane Limited; *Int'l*, pg. 1129

THE HOUSE OF MAYFAIR—Wallcoverings—Forbo Holding SA; *Int'l*, pg. 496

HOUSE OF NAPKINS—Party Goods—American Greetings U.S. Greeting Card Division; *U.S. Public*, pg. 78

HOUSE OF STUART—Whisky—Barton Incorporated; *U.S. Public*, pg. 300

HOUSE OF STUART SCOTCH—NONE—Barton Brands, Ltd.; *U.S. Public*, pg. 300

HOUSE OF TIME-DOTLINE—Calendars—Renaissance Publishing Co., Inc.; *Int'l*, pg. 185

HOUSE OF TSANG—Seasoning Oils, Marinades & Sauces—Hormel Foods Corp.; *U.S. Public*, pg. 840

HOUSE SAVER—Paint—Mautz Paint Co.; *U.S. Private*, pg. 715

HOUSECALL—Retail Services such as Appliance Repair, CO Detection, Home Security—Consumers Energy; *U.S. Public*, pg. 280

HOUSTON BUSINESS JOURNAL—Business Journal—Business First of New York, Inc.; *U.S. Private*, pg. 19

HOUSTON CHRONICLE—Newspaper—The Hearst Corporation; *U.S. Private*, pg. 515

HOUSTON HALO—Cervical Immobilization—Camp Healthcare; *Int'l*, pg. 1425

HOVERSPEED—Ferry Operator—Sea Containers Ltd.; *Int'l*, pg. 1213

HOVIS—Bread, Flour—Ranks Hovis McDougall Limited; *Int'l*, pg. 1395

HOVOGLAS—Glass Filter Materials—Hollingsworth & Vose Co.; *U.S. Private*, pg. 534

HOVOSEAL—Gasket Materials—Hollingsworth & Vose Co.; *U.S. Private*, pg. 534

HOVOSORB—Battery Separator—Hollingsworth & Vose Co.; *U.S. Private*, pg. 534

HOVOTEX—Non Woven Materials—Hollingsworth & Vose Co.; *U.S. Private*, pg. 534

HOW—Magazine—F & W Publications, Inc.; *U.S. Private*, pg. 388

HOWARD—Organs & Pianos—Baldwin Piano & Organ Company; *U.S. Public*, pg. 169

HOWARD—Carpets—Salem Carpet Mills, Inc.; *U.S. Public*, pg. 1464

HOWARD—Farm Machinery—Thrige Agro A/S; *Int'l*, pg. 1386

HOWARD JOHNSON FRANCHISE SYSTEM, INC.—Hotel Chain—HFS, Incorporated; *U.S. Public*, pg. 321

HOWARD JOHNSON'S RESTAURANTS—NONE—Bickford's Family Restaurants; *U.S. Public*, pg. 545

HOWARD LINEN—Writing, Text & Cover Paper—Fox River Paper Company; *U.S. Private*, pg. 422

HOWARD MILLER—Clocks—Howard Miller; *U.S. Private*, pg. 747

HOWARD WOLF—Women's Apparel—Howard B. Wolf, Inc.; *U.S. Public*, pg. 1774

HOYLE—Playing Cards—Brown & Bigelow, Inc.; *U.S. Private*, pg. 172

HOYO DE MONTERREY—Cigar—Villazon Company Inc.; *U.S. Private*, pg. 1140

HRB—Baler—Harris Waste Mgmt. Group, Inc.; *Int'l*, pg. 473

HYDROMET—Chemical Process to Recycle Depleted Uranium—Starmet Corporation; *U.S. Public*, pg. 1511

HTG—NONE—Solitec Wafer Processing, Inc.; *U.S. Private*, pg. 1013

HUB CITY—Enclosed Gear Drives Mounted Bearings—Hub City, Inc.; *U.S. Private*, pg. 1371

HUBBA BUBBA—Chunk Bubble Gum—Amurol Confections Co.; *U.S. Public*, pg. 1781

HUBBA BUBBA—Bubble Gum—Wrigley Canada Inc.; *U.S. Public*, pg. 1781

HUBBA BUBBA ORIGINAL BUBBLE GUM SODA—Soda—Select Canfield; *U.S. Private*, pg. 982

HUBBARD—Television Broadcasting Stations—Hubbard Broadcasting, Inc.; *U.S. Private*, pg. 543

HUBBARD FARMS—Poultry—Hubbard Farms, Inc.; *U.S. Public*, pg. 1092

HUBBARD FARMS—Poultry—Hubbard Farms, Inc.; *Int'l*, pg. 1114

HUBBARD MILLING—Livestock Feed & Pet Food—Hubbard Feeds Inc.; *Int'l*, pg. 1116

HUBBELL—Wiring Devices—Bryant Electric Supply Company, Inc.; *U.S. Private*, pg. 177

HUBER—Beer—Joseph Huber Brewing Co., Inc.; *U.S. Private*, pg. 545

HUBER BOCK—Beer—Joseph Huber Brewing Co., Inc.; *U.S. Private*, pg. 545

HUBNAIL—NONE—Royal Rubber & Manufacturing Co.; *U.S. Private*, pg. 949

HYBRITUBE—NONE—Life Technologies, Inc.; *U.S. Public*, pg. 504

HUCK-CUNCIT—NONE—Thiokol Corporation; *U.S. Public*, pg. 1596

HUCK-SPIN—NONE—Thiokol Corporation; *U.S. Public*, pg. 1596

HUCKBOLTZ—NONE—Huck International, Inc.; *U.S. Public*, pg. 1597

HUCKCOMP—NONE—Thiokol Corporation; *U.S. Public*, pg. 1596

HUDEPOHL—Beer—Hudepohl-Schoenling Brewing Company; *U.S. Private*, pg. 545

HUDSON—Facial Tissue, Bath Tissue, Paper Napkins & Towels—Georgia-Pacific Corporation; *U.S. Public*, pg. 735

HUDSON—NONE—Hudson, RCI; *U.S. Private*, pg. 546

HUDSON & MIDDLETON LTD—Chinaware—Ebeling & Reuss Company; *U.S. Private*, pg. 358

HUDSON BAY MILLING COMPANY—Bread, Buns & Croutons—Metz Baking Company; *U.S. Private*, pg. 1022

HUDSON BAY MILLING COMPANY—Bread, Buns, Croutons—Metz Baking Company (WI); *U.S. Private*, pg. 1022

HUDSON RIVER TRADERS—NONE—Tandy Brands Accessories, Inc.; *U.S. Public*, pg. 1560

HUDSON VITAMINS—Vitamins & Over The Counter Drugs—Nature's Bounty Inc.; *U.S. Public*, pg. 1166

HUDY DELIGHT—Beer—Hudepohl-Schoenling Brewing Company; *U.S. Private*, pg. 545

HUE—Legwear—Kayser-Roth Corporation, Inc.; *Int'l*, pg. 576

HUE—Socks/Hosiery—The Leslie Fay Companies, Inc.; *U.S. Public*, pg. 989

HUEBSCH—Commercial Washers, Dryers, Stack Dryers, Washer-Extractors—Raytheon Appliances; *U.S. Public*, pg. 1366

HUESO—Sugar Confectionery—Cadbury Schweppes p.l.c.; *Int'l*, pg. 247

HUFF-N-PUFF—Gas Turbine Air Filter System—Donaldson Company, Inc.; *U.S. Public*, pg. 517

HUFFMAN KOOS—Home Furnishings Store—Huffman Koos; *U.S. Private*, pg. 546

HUFFY—Bicycles—Huffy Corporation; *U.S. Public*, pg. 846

HUFFY SLAM JAM—Sports Equipment—Huffy Corporation; *U.S. Public*, pg. 846

HUFFY SPORTS—Sports Related Equipment—Huffy Corporation; *U.S. Public*, pg. 846

HUFFY SPORTS—NONE—Huffy Sports Company; *U.S. Public*, pg. 846

HUGGER—Fitted Shirts & Sportswear—Gant; *U.S. Public*, pg. 1291

HUGGIES—Disposable Diapers & Baby Wipes—Kimberly-Clark Corporation; *U.S. Public*, pg. 958

HUGGIES PULL-UPS—Disposable Training Pants—Kimberly-Clark Corporation; *U.S. Public*, pg. 958

HUGGIES ULTRATRIM—Diapers—Kimberly-Clark Corporation; *U.S. Public*, pg. 958

HUGGY TUB—Bath Tub—Century Products Co.; *U.S. Private*, pg. 226

HUGO—Men's Fashions—Hugo Boss AG; *Int'l*, pg. 637

HULA HOOP—Exercise Hoop—Mattel, Inc.; *U.S. Public*, pg. 1057

HULA HOOP—Exercise Hoop—Mattel Power Wheels; *U.S. Public*, pg. 1058

HULA HOOP—Toy—Wham-O, Inc.; *U.S. Private*, pg. 1170

HULLINSUL—Glass Fiber Board—Johns Manville Corporation; *U.S. Public*, pg. 927

HULS/AMERICA—Sheet—Ryan Herco Products Corp.; *U.S. Private*, pg. 953

HULSTKAMP—Schnapps—Eckes AG; *Int'l*, pg. 432

HUMALOG—NONE—Eli Lilly and Company; *U.S. Public*, pg. 992

HUMANA HEALTH CARE PLANS—Prepaid Health Plan & Indemnity Insurance—Humana Inc.; *U.S. Public*, pg. 847

HUMATE-P—Antihemophilic Factor (Human) Pasteurized—Centeon, L.L.C.; *Int'l*, pg. 626

HUMATROPE—Somatropin of Recombinant DNA Origin, Lilly—Eli Lilly and Company; *U.S. Public*, pg. 992

HUMATROPE—DNA Growth Hormone—Eli Lilly Italia, S.p.A.; *U.S. Public*, pg. 994

HUMBROL—Plastic Model Kits—Borden, Inc.; *U.S. Private*, pg. 157

HUMEGON—Menopausal Gonadotrophin—Akzo Nobel N.V.; *Int'l*, pg. 42

HUMEGON—Pharmaceutical—Organon Inc.; *Int'l*, pg. 48

HUMES—Pre-Cast Concrete Pipes & Concrete Products—CSR Limited; *Int'l*, pg. 245

HUMI-TECH I.E.B.—Polymer system—The Dow Chemical Company; *U.S. Public*, pg. 522

HUMIBID—NONE—Medeva PLC; *Int'l*, pg. 852

HUMIDISPRAY—Humidifier—Lennox International Inc.; *U.S. Private*, pg. 659

HUMIDIWHEEL—Humidifier—Lennox International Inc.; *U.S. Private*, pg. 659

HUMISEAL—Conformal Coatings—Chase Corporation; *U.S. Public*, pg. 337

HUMISEAL—Insulation—Humiseal Div.; *U.S. Public*, pg. 337

HUMITENN—Test Equipment—Tenney Environmental; *U.S. Public*, pg. 1076

HUMITEX—Chart—The Foxboro Company; *Int'l*, pg. 1243

HUMMER—Civilian Version of HMMWV—AM General Corporation; *U.S. Private*, pg. 922

HUMMER—High Gluten—Cargill Flour Div.; *U.S. Private*, pg. 210

HUMMER—NONE—Stryker Corporation; *U.S. Public*, pg. 1525

HUMMINBIRD—NONE—Techsonic Industries, Inc.; *U.S. Public*, pg. 1570

HUMPHREY—Air Cylinders—Humphrey Products Company; *U.S. Private*, pg. 547

HUMPRHEY THE DINOSAUR—Children's Hamper—Rubbermaid Incorporated; *U.S. Public*, pg. 1411

HUMPTY DUMPTY—Potato Chips—Borden, Inc.; *U.S. Private*, pg. 157

HUMPTY DUMPTY—Canned Salmon—Peter Pan Seafoods, Inc.; *Int'l*, pg. 928

HUMPTY DUMPTY'S—Magazine for Children—Benjamin Franklin Literary & Medical Society, Inc.; *U.S. Private*, pg. 133

HUMULIN—Human Insulin of Recombinant DNA Origin, Lilly—Eli Lilly and Company; *U.S. Public*, pg. 992

HUMULIN—DNA Insulin—Eli Lilly Italia, S.p.A.; *U.S. Public*, pg. 994

HUMULIN L—Human Insulin of Recombinant DNA Origin, Zinc Suspension, Lilly—Eli Lilly and Company; *U.S. Public*, pg. 992

Brand Name Index

HUMULIN N—NPH Human Insulin of Recombinant DNA Origin, Isophane Suspension, Lilly—Eli Lilly and Company; *U.S. Public*, pg. 992

HUMULIN R—Regular Human Insulin of Recombinant DNA Origin, Lilly—Eli Lilly and Company; *U.S. Public*, pg. 992

HUMULIN 70/30—70% Human Insulin Isophane Suspension & 30% Human Insulin Injection of Reco—Eli Lilly and Company; *U.S. Public*, pg. 992

HUMULIN U—Extended Human Insulin of Recombinant DNA Origin, Zinc Suspension, Lilly—Eli Lilly and Company; *U.S. Public*, pg. 992

HUMVEE—HMMWV Vehicle—AM General Corporation; *U.S. Private*, pg. 922

HUNGRY HIPPOS—Game—Milton Bradley Company; *U.S. Public*, pg. 797

HUNGRY JACK—Pancakes/Syrup—Grand Metropolitan Plc; *Int'l*, pg. 408

HUNGRY JACK—Frozen Pancakes & Pancake Mix; Instant Potatoes; Prepared Dough & Syrup—The Pillsbury Company; *Int'l*, pg. 411

HUNGRYMAN—NONE—Swanson; *U.S. Public*, pg. 299

HUNT—Artist Pens—Hunt Corporation; *U.S. Public*, pg. 848

HUNT & BROADHURST—Stationery—Fine Art Developments plc; *Int'l*, pg. 485

HUNT CLUB—Apparel—JC Penney Company, Inc.; *U.S. Public*, pg. 916

HUNT CLUB OAK—Lumber & Wood Products—Georgia-Pacific Corporation; *U.S. Public*, pg. 735

HUNTCO STEEL, INC.—NONE—Huntco Inc.; *U.S. Public*, pg. 849

HUNTER—NONE—ETEX; *Int'l*, pg. 430

HUNTER—Waterproof Footwear—The Gates Rubber Company Ltd.; *Int'l*, pg. 1397

HUNTER—Engineers—Hunter Engineering Co., Inc.; *Int'l*, pg. 474

HUNTER—Sail Boats—Hunter Marine Corporation; *U.S. Private*, pg. 549

HUNTER—Unmanned Reconnaisance Aircraft/Short Range—Israel Aircraft Industries Ltd.; *Int'l*, pg. 689

HUNTER—Meat Products—John Morrell & Co.; *U.S. Public*, pg. 1479

HUNTER—GPS Sensor Antenna—Rockwell International Corporation; *U.S. Public*, pg. 1397

HUNTER—Dairy Products—Ruddick Corporation; *U.S. Public*, pg. 1412

HUNTER ADVERTISING—NONE—Ralston Purina Company; *U.S. Public*, pg. 1359

HUNTER DOUGLAS—Two-Inch Aluminum Blinds—Hunter Douglas, Inc.; *Int'l*, pg. 639

HUNTER DOUGLAS CELEBRITY BLINDS—Aluminum Horizontal Blinds with .006 ga. Slat—Hunter Douglas, Inc.; *Int'l*, pg. 639

HUNTER DOUGLAS DECOR BLINDS—Aluminum Horizontal Blinds—Hunter Douglas, Inc.; *Int'l*, pg. 639

HUNTER DOUGLAS EASY GLIDE PLEATED SHADES—Clutch Mechanism for Pleated Shades—Hunter Douglas, Inc.; *Int'l*, pg. 639

HUNTER DOUGLAS PERMALIGN VERTICAL TRACK SYSTEM—Window Track that Keeps Vanes Perfectly Aligned at any Angle—Hunter Douglas, Inc.; *Int'l*, pg. 639

HUNTER DOUGLAS TWI-NIGHTER—Two-Inch Aluminum Blinds for Extra Light Control—Hunter Douglas, Inc.; *Int'l*, pg. 639

HUNTER DOUGLAS VERTICAL BLINDS—Trouble-Free Track with Posi-Tilt System to Keep Vane Perfectly Aligned—Hunter Douglas, Inc.; *Int'l*, pg. 639

HUNTER DOUGLAS VERTICAL SPECIALTY SYSTEMS—System Specifically Deisgned to Accomodate Odd-Shaped Windows—Hunter Douglas, Inc.; *Int'l*, pg. 639

HUNTER DOUGLAS WINDOW SHADES—Roller Shades on a Clutch System—Hunter Douglas, Inc.; *Int'l*, pg. 639

HUNTER'S CHOICE—Dog Food—The Jim Dandy Co., Inc.; *Int'l*, pg. 918

HUNTERS CHOICE—Dog Foods—Alpo Pet Foods, Inc.; *Int'l*, pg. 917

HUNTER'S CHOICE—NONE—Nestle USA; *Int'l*, pg. 916

HUNTING—Magazine—Petersen Publishing Company, L.L.C.; *U.S. Private*, pg. 856

HUNTINGTON—Manufactured Homes—Champion Enterprises, Inc.; *U.S. Public*, pg. 332

HUNTINGTON—Commercial Bank—Huntington National Bank; *U.S. Public*, pg. 850

HUNTLEY & PALMERS—Biscuits—Danone Group; *Int'l*, pg. 379

HUNTLEY OF YORK—Apparel—Cross Creek Apparel, Inc.; *U.S. Public*, pg. 1413

HUNTLY & GUNN—Gin—Distillers Corporation S.A.; *Int'l*, pg. 1129

HUNTS—Pudding, Tomato Sauce, Ketchup—ConAgra, Inc.; *U.S. Public*, pg. 425

HUNT'S—Ketchup & Tomato Products—Hunt-Wesson, Inc.; *U.S. Public*, pg. 428

HURD—Locks & Keys—Avis Industrial Corporation; *U.S. Private*, pg. 102

HURG—NONE—Elcor Corporation; *U.S. Public*, pg. 567

HURLBUT GENTLEMAN DESIGN—Specialty Papers—The Mead Corporation; *U.S. Public*, pg. 1074

HURLETRON—Automated Control Systems—Altair Corporation; *U.S. Private*, pg. 46

HURON—Quick Connectors—Bundy North America; *Int'l*, pg. 1340

HURON DAILY TRIBUNE—Newspaper—The Hearst Corporation; *U.S. Private*, pg. 515

HURRICAINE—Topical Anesthetics-Liquid Gel & Aerosol—Beutlich, L.P.; *U.S. Private*, pg. 141

HURRICANE—Motorcycle—American Honda Motor Co., Inc. Motorcycle Division; *Int'l*, pg. 634

HURRICANE—Loaders—K-Tron International, Inc.; *U.S. Public*, pg. 938

HURRICANE—NONE—SEEQ Technology Inc.; *U.S. Public*, pg. 1417

HURRICLEAN—Steam Cleaning Gun—Oakite Products, Inc.; *Int'l*, pg. 861

HURRISEAL—Dentin Desensitizer—Beutlich, L.P.; *U.S. Private*, pg. 141

HURST—Power Transmission—Echlin Inc.; *U.S. Public*, pg. 560

HURST—Motors—Emerson Electric Co.; *U.S. Public*, pg. 572

HURST JAWS OF LIFE—Rescue System—IDEX Corporation; *U.S. Public*, pg. 862

HURTY-PECK—Flavor Products—Universal Foods Corporation; *U.S. Public*, pg. 1695

HUSER—Vinegar—Burns, Philp & Company Limited; *Int'l*, pg. 236

HUSH—Valve Trim—Copes-Vulcan Inc.; *U.S. Private*, pg. 274

HUSH—Fire Engine—Federal Signal Corporation; *U.S. Public*, pg. 616

HUSH—Smoke Alarms—Fyrnetics, Inc.; *Int'l*, pg. 1499

HUSH DUCT—Air Conditioning Insulation—Carter Holt Harvey Limited; *Int'l*, pg. 904

HUSH PUPPIES—Shoes—Wolverine World Wide, Inc.; *U.S. Public*, pg. 1775

HUSH PUPPIES SHOES—Shoe Stores—Wolverine World Wide, Inc.; *U.S. Public*, pg. 1775

HUSH-STEP—Vinyl to Carpet Mats—Pawling Corporation; *U.S. Private*, pg. 844

HUSHALON—Acoustical Felt—American Felt & Filter; *U.S. Private*, pg. 54

HUSHED POWER—Demolition Tools—Chicago Pneumatic Tool Company; *Int'l*, pg. 96

HUSKEE—Power Equip.—Tractor Supply Co.; *U.S. Public*, pg. 1627

HUSKER HARVEST DAYS—Trade Show—Farm Progress Publications; *U.S. Public*, pg. 513

HUSKY—Standard Heavy Duty Crane Trolley—Ederer Inc.; *U.S. Private*, pg. 363

HUSKY—Air Powered Double Diaphragm Pump—Graco Inc.; *U.S. Public*, pg. 756

HUSKY—Hardware—The Shelburne Corporation; *U.S. Private*, pg. 991

HUSKY—Paper Products—Weyerhaeuser Company; *U.S. Public*, pg. 1764

HUSKY HY-BULK—Printing Papers—Weyerhaeuser Company; *U.S. Public*, pg. 1764

HUSKY OFFSET—Printing Papers—Weyerhaeuser Company; *U.S. Public*, pg. 1764

HUSKY XEROCOPY D.P.—Reprographic Papers—Weyerhaeuser Company; *U.S. Public*, pg. 1764

HUSKY XEROCOPY II—Reprographic Papers—Weyerhaeuser Company; *U.S. Public*, pg. 1764

HUSKY-BRONCO—Wheelbarrows & Shovels—Ames Company; *U.S. Public*, pg. 1683

HUSQVARNA—Household Appliances—Electrolux, AB; *Int'l*, pg. 438

HUSQVARNA—Forest & Garden—Husqvarna Forest & Garden Products; *Int'l*, pg. 440

HUSQVARNA—Sewing Machines—VWS, Inc.; *Int'l*, pg. 440

HUSQVARNA—Chainsaws—White Consolidated Industries, Inc.; *Int'l*, pg. 439

HUSQVARNA EMBROIDERY CUSTOMIZING SYSTEM—NONE—VWS, Inc.; *Int'l*, pg. 440

HUSQVARNA EMBROIDERY—NONE—VWS, Inc.; *Int'l*, pg. 440

HUSSEY—Seating—Hussey Seating Company; *U.S. Private*, pg. 550

HUSSMETIC—Refrigerating & Condensing Units—Hussmann Corp.; *U.S. Public*, pg. 1766

HUSTLER—Grounds Equipment—Excel Industries, Inc.; *U.S. Private*, pg. 387

HUSTLER—Vertical/Foam/Fill/Seal Machines—Package Machinery Co.; *U.S. Private*, pg. 832

HUSTLER—Tote Handling System—SI Handling Systems, Inc.; *U.S. Public*, pg. 1418

HUSTLER—Gas Pizza Oven—Vulcan-Hart Corp.; *U.S. Public*, pg. 1322

HUTCH—Athletic Equipment—Hutch Sports USA, Inc.; *U.S. Public*, pg. 1354

HUTCH—Supensions, Sliding Subframes & Custom Steel Castings—Hutchens Industries Inc.; *U.S. Private*, pg. 550

HUTH—Bending & Expanding Equipment—IPC-International Parts Corp.; *U.S. Public*, pg. 1766

HUTSCHEN REUTHER—China—WMF/USA; *U.S. Private*, pg. 1144

HUTTENKASE—Softcream Cheese—Danone Group; *Int'l*, pg. 379

HUVA-CUP—Hydraulic Packings—John Crane Mechanical Seals; *Int'l*, pg. 1339

HUYCK—Fabric Forming—BTR plc; *Int'l*, pg. 124

HY-GAIN—Antennas—Telex Communications, Inc.; *U.S. Private*, pg. 1074

HY-PRINT—Labels—Avery Dennison Corporation Label Group; *U.S. Public*, pg. 153

HY-Q—Sluice Gates—Rodney Hunt Company; *U.S. Private*, pg. 549

HY Q—Custom Media & Delivery Systems—HyClone Laboratories Inc.; *Int'l*, pg. 1037

HY Q BOVINE INSULIN—Bovine Insulin—HyClone Laboratories Inc.; *Int'l*, pg. 1037

HY Q BOVINE TRANSFERRIN—Bovine Transferrin—HyClone Laboratories Inc.; *Int'l*, pg. 1037

HY Q-CCM—Serum-free Media Optimized for Hybridomas, Human Fibroblasts & Insect Cells—HyClone Laboratories Inc.; *Int'l*, pg. 1037

HY Q CELL CULTURE—Media, Salts & Reagents—HyClone Laboratories Inc.; *Int'l*, pg. 1037

HY Q LONG R3IGF-I—Insulin Substitute for Cell Culture—HyClone Laboratories Inc.; *Int'l*, pg. 1037

HY-QUAD—Antenna—Telex Communications, Inc.; *U.S. Private*, pg. 1074

HY-RA 49—NONE—Carpenter Technology Corporation; *U.S. Public*, pg. 307

HY-RAM—Hydraulic Mounted Breaker—Allied Construction Products, Inc.; *U.S. Public*, pg. 1339

HY-SAT—NONE—Carpenter Technology Corporation; *U.S. Public*, pg. 307

HY SHIELD—Flat-Roof Waterproofing Prod.—The Braas Group; *Int'l*, pg. 1091

HY SHIELD—Roofing Membrane—Haartz-Mason, Inc.; *U.S. Public*, pg. 1358

HY-SYNC—Motors, Gear Motors & Motor Controls—Bodine Electric Company; *U.S. Private*, pg. 154

HY TONE—Pharmaceutical—Dermik Laboratories, Inc.; *Int'l*, pg. 1110

HY-TOWER—Antenna—Telex Communications, Inc.; *U.S. Private*, pg. 1074

HY TRAK—Rough Terrain Forklift-Straight Mast—OmniQuip International, Inc.; *U.S. Private*, pg. 500

HYAMAT—Fully Automatic Pressure Boosting—KSB Aktiengesellschaft; *Int'l*, pg. 721

HYAMINE 1622—Topical Biocide—Lonza Inc.; *Int'l*, pg. 67

HYATT—Bearings—General Motors Corporation; *U.S. Public*, pg. 718

HYATT—Hotels—Hyatt Hotels Corporation; *U.S. Private*, pg. 551

HYATT DIAMOND CARD—Advanced Levels of Frequent Stay Programs—Hyatt Hotels Corporation; *U.S. Private*, pg. 551

HYATT EXPRESS—Small Meeting Service—Hyatt Hotels Corporation; *U.S. Private*, pg. 551

HYATT GOLD PASSPORT—Frequent Stay Program—Hyatt Hotels Corporation; *U.S. Private*, pg. 551

HYATT LAKE TAHOE—Resort & Casino—Hyatt Regency Lake Tahoe Resort & Casino; *U.S. Private*, pg. 551

HYATT PLATINUM CARD—Advanced Levels of Frequent Stay Program—Hyatt Hotels Corporation; *U.S. Private*, pg. 551

HYBON—Glass Fibers—PPG Industries, Inc.; *U.S. Public*, pg. 1245

HYBOND—Contact Adhesive—Pierce & Stevens Corp.; *U.S. Private*, pg. 1019

HYBOND—Contact Cement—Pratt & Lambert United, Inc.; *U.S. Public*, pg. 1466

HYBRI-DOT—NONE—Life Technologies, Inc.; *U.S. Public*, pg. 504

HYBRI-SLOT—NONE—Life Technologies, Inc.; *U.S. Public*, pg. 504

HYBRID RECORDINGS—Recorded Music—Ogden Corporation; *U.S. Public*, pg. 1213

HYBRID THERMAL TREATMENT SYSTEM (HITS)—Incineration Technology—International Technology Corporation; *U.S. Public*, pg. 907

HYBRID-2—Ball Point Pen—Pentel of America, Ltd.; *Int'l*, pg. 1035

HYBRIDUR—Acrylic-Urethane Polymers—Air Products and Chemicals, Inc.; *U.S. Public*, pg. 30

HYCALOG—Diamond Bits—Camco International Inc.; *U.S. Public*, pg. 297

HYCOE—Wire Turning, Suction Couch or Breast Roll Cover—Harnischfeger Industries, Inc.; *U.S. Public*, pg. 788

HYCOE II—Wire Turning, Suction Couch Or Breast Roll—Beloit Corporation; *U.S. Public*, pg. 789

HYCOOL—Wafer Cooling System—Varian Associates, Inc.; *U.S. Public*, pg. 1710

HYDE—Footwear—Hyde Athletic Industries, Inc.; *U.S. Public*, pg. 851

HYDE—Industrial Hand & Machine Tools, Knives—Hyde Manufacturing Co.; *U.S. Private*, pg. 551

HYDE CLOTHES, LTD.—Apparel—Bayer Clothing Group; *U.S. Private*, pg. 124

HYDE PARK—Oxford Shirt—Lands' End, Inc.; *U.S. Public*, pg. 977

HYDE PARK—Health & Beauty Aid Prods.—Super D Drug Stores; *U.S. Private*, pg. 642

HYDENSE—Stearates—Mallinckrodt Inc.; *U.S. Public*, pg. 1039

HYDENSEL—Release Coating—Wausau-Mosinee Paper Corporation; *U.S. Public*, pg. 1747

HYDERBENE—Tablets/Liquid Capsules for Symptoms of Mental Deterioration—Sandoz Pharmaceuticals Corp.; *Int'l*, pg. 974

HYDERGINE—Pharmaceutical—Novartis AG; *Int'l*, pg. 971

HYDEX 100—Carbohydrate for use as Humectants, Sweeteners, Vicosity Improvers—Lonza Inc.; *Int'l*, pg. 67

HYDRA—Integrated Circuit, Chipset—LSI Logic Corp.; *U.S. Public*, pg. 971

HYDRA—Remotely Operated Vehicle—Oceaneering International, Inc.; *U.S. Public*, pg. 1211

HYDRA-BLAST—Downhole Cleaning Service—Halliburton Energy Services; *U.S. Public*, pg. 776

HYDRA-BORER—Travel Carrier—Case Corporation; *U.S. Public*, pg. 311

HYDRA-CAT—Proportioning Pumps—Graco Inc.; *U.S. Public*, pg. 756

HYDRA-CLEAN—High Pressure Washers—Graco Inc.; *U.S. Public*, pg. 756

HYDRA DIOR—Skin Care Products—Christian Dior Perfumes Inc.; *Int'l*, pg. 781

HYDRA-FLEX—Vibratory Conveyor—TCC Industries; *U.S. Public*, pg. 1554

HYDRA GATE—Valves—United States Pipe & Foundry Company, Inc.; *U.S. Public*, pg. 1736

HYDRA-GAUGE—Dynamoters—M&W; *U.S. Public*, pg. 35

HYDRA JAR—Drilling Jar—Wilson Industries Inc.; *U.S. Private*, pg. 1181

HYDRA-LITE—Deadweight Testers—U.S. Gauge; *U.S. Public*, pg. 100

HYDRA-MATIC—Transmissions—General Motors Corporation; *U.S. Public*, pg. 718

HYDRA-MATIC TRANSMISSIONS—NONE—GM Powertrain Group; *U.S. Public*, pg. 719

HYDRA-MOLE—High-Performance Tools—The Stanley Works; *U.S. Public*, pg. 1508

HYDRA-POISE—Autopsy Table with Hydraulic Height Adjustment—The Jewett Refrigerator Co., Inc.; *U.S. Public*, pg. 952

HYDRA 70—NONE—BEI Defense Systems Company; *U.S. Public*, pg. 160

HYDRA-SPORTS—Fiberglass Boats—Outboard Marine Corporation; *U.S. Private*, pg. 478

HYDRA-SPRAY—Airless Spray Painting Equipment—Graco Inc.; *U.S. Public*, pg. 756

HYDRA SWITCH 3000—Solar Powered Stank Alone Switch Stand—L.B. Foster Company; *U.S. Public*, pg. 675

HYDRA-TRAK—Hydraulic Retarder Mechanisms—General Railway Signal Corp.; *Int'l*, pg. 1194

HYDRA-SET—NONE—Del Mar Avionics; *U.S. Private*, pg. 321

HYDRACARE—Body Oil—Stanhome Inc.; *U.S. Public*, pg. 1508

HYDRACHEK—Leveler Lip Support Systems—Rite-Hite Corporation; *U.S. Private*, pg. 933

HYDRASAN—Hydrants—Josam Company; *U.S. Private*, pg. 600

HYDRASPUN—Nonwoven Fabrics—The Dexter Corporation; *U.S. Public*, pg. 504

HYDRASPUN FR—Specialty Paper—The Dexter Corporation; *U.S. Public*, pg. 504

HYDRAULAN—Brake Fluid—BASF AG; *Int'l*, pg. 103

HYDRAULICS & PNEUMATICS—Periodical—Penton Publishing, Inc.; *U.S. Public*, pg. 1306

HYDRAVER—Chemical Reagant—Hach Company; *U.S. Public*, pg. 773

HYDRAWAY—Soil Drainage Mats—Monsanto Company; *U.S. Public*, pg. 1124

HYDREA—Cancer Therapy Product—Bristol-Myers Squibb Company; *U.S. Public*, pg. 253

HYDREA—Antineoplstic Agent for treatment of Cancer—Bristol-Myers Squibb U.S. Pharmaceutical Group; *U.S. Public*, pg. 255

HYDREFINER—Water Softening & Purification Equipment—RainSoft Water Treatment Systems; *U.S. Private*, pg. 78

HYDRIL—Mfr. of Oilfield Equip.—Hydril Company; *U.S. Private*, pg. 551

HYDRO-AIRE—Thermal Processing Systems—Fuller Company; *Int'l*, pg. 475

HYDRO-ARC—Electric Arc Furnaces—Whiting Corporation; *U.S. Public*, pg. 1173

HYDRO-AX—Feller Bunchers—Blount International, Inc.; *U.S. Public*, pg. 237

HYDRO BLAZE—Paint—Mautz Paint Co.; *U.S. Private*, pg. 715

HYDRO-BONDER—Cementing Prod.—Weatherford Enterra Incorporated; *U.S. Public*, pg. 1749

HYDRO-BOOST—Hydraulic Brake Booster—AlliedSignal Inc.; *U.S. Public*, pg. 49

HYDRO CONDUIT—Pre-Cast Concrete Pipes & Concrete Products—CSR Limited; *Int'l*, pg. 245

HYDRO DIURIL—Hydrochlorothiazide—Merck & Co., Inc.; *U.S. Public*, pg. 1090

HYDRO GEL ADVANCED MOISTURIZER—Skincare Product—The Procter & Gamble Company; *U.S. Public*, pg. 1330

HYDRO-LIFT—Full Closure Core Catcher—Baker Hughes INTEQ; *U.S. Public*, pg. 166

HYDRO MULCH—Mulch Fibers—Leucadia Inc. Manufacturing Division; *U.S. Public*, pg. 990

HYDRO 100—NONE—Vulcan Chemicals; *U.S. Public*, pg. 1725

HYDRO-POSTURE—Mattress—Therapedic Associates, Inc.; *U.S. Private*, pg. 1079

HYDRO-POWER—Household Clothes Washing Machines—General Electric Canada Inc.; *U.S. Public*, pg. 713

HYDRO-REZ—NONE—Lawter International, Inc.; *U.S. Public*, pg. 980

HYDRO-SHUR—Waterproofing Coatings—Devoe Paint; *Int'l*, pg. 663

HYDRO-SHUR—Elastomeric Waterproofing Coating—Grow Group, Inc.; *Int'l*, pg. 663

HYDRO-SHUR—Waterproofing Coatings—ICI Paints; *Int'l*, pg. 664

HYDRO-STACK—Hydraulic Valves & Manifold—The Oilgear Company; *U.S. Public*, pg. 1215

HYDRO STAK & DESIGN—Containers Made from Wax Coated Corrugated Paperboard—Georgia-Pacific Corporation; *U.S. Public*, pg. 735

HYDRO-TITE—Baseboard Expansion Joint—Slant/Fin Corporation; *U.S. Private*, pg. 1005

HYDRO TREATED—Oil-Based Lubricants—Petro-Canada; *Int'l*, pg. 1041

HYDRO-VAC—Small Vacuum—Advance Machine Company; *Int'l*, pg. 932

HYDROCAL—Plaster—USG Corporation; *U.S. Public*, pg. 1660

HYDROCARE—Contact Lens Care Product—Allergan, Inc.; *U.S. Public*, pg. 46

HYDROCET—Pain Reduction Product—Carnrick Laboratories, Inc.; *U.S. Private*, pg. 436

HYDROCIL INSTANT—Pharmaceutical Products—Solvay Pharmaceuticals, Inc.; *Int'l*, pg. 1278

HYDROCLEANER—Cleaning System—Electrovert; *Int'l*, pg. 328

HYDROCOL—Sterile Hydrocolloid Wound Dressing—Dow Hickam Pharmaceuticals Inc.; *U.S. Public*, pg. 1143

HYDROCONE—Crushers—Svedala Industries Inc.; *Int'l*, pg. 1325

HYDROCRETE—High Strength Castable—A.P. Green Industries, Inc.; *U.S. Public*, pg. 761

HYDRODARCO—Activated Carbons—American Norit Co. Inc.; *Int'l*, pg. 958

HYDRODERM—Elastomeric Coatings in the Hydro-Shur Family—Devoe Paint; *Int'l*, pg. 663

HYDRODERM—Elastomeric Coatings—ICI Paints; *Int'l*, pg. 664

HYDRODRY—Small Vacuum—Advance Machine Company; *Int'l*, pg. 932

HYDROFIL—Apparel Yarns—AlliedSignal Inc.; *U.S. Public*, pg. 49

HYDROFLEX—NONE—AGA Gas, Inc.; *Int'l*, pg. 13

HYDROFLEX—Elastomeric Coatings in the Hydro-Shur Family—Devoe Paint; *Int'l*, pg. 663

HYDROFLEX—Waterborne Film Lalination Adhesive—H.B. Fuller Company; *U.S. Public*, pg. 645

HYDROFLEX—Elastomeric Coatings—ICI Paints; *Int'l*, pg. 664

HYDROFORM—Metal Forming Presses—Verson Division; *U.S. Public*, pg. 48

HYDROGEM—NONE—Lawter International, Inc.; *U.S. Public*, pg. 980

HYDROGRATE—Stoker—Detroit Stoker Co.; *U.S. Public*, pg. 1679

HYDROJECT 3000—NONE—The Toro Company; *U.S. Public*, pg. 1623

HYDROLASTIC—Elastomeric Coatings in the Hydro-Shur Family—Devoe Paint; *Int'l*, pg. 663

HYDROLECTRIC—Electric Lift Trucks—Hydrolectric Lift Trucks Inc.; *U.S. Public*, pg. 61

HYDROLOG—NONE—Western Atlas Logging Services; *U.S. Public*, pg. 1757

HYDROLYSER—NONE—Cordis, a Johnson & Johnson Company; *U.S. Public*, pg. 928

HYDROMARC—Soft Contact Lenses—Vistakon Johnson & Johnson Vision Products, Inc.; *U.S. Public*, pg. 929

HYDROMATIC—Pumps—Aurora Pump; *U.S. Public*, pg. 726

HYDRON—Textile Dye—Hoechst Aktiengesellschaft; *Int'l*, pg. 624

HYDRONEAL—Gas Generators—Engelhard Corporation; *U.S. Public*, pg. 582

HYDROPATCH—Elastomeric Coatings in the Hydro-Shur Family—Devoe Paint; *Int'l*, pg. 663

HYDROPATCH—Elastomeric Coatings—ICI Paints; *Int'l*, pg. 664

HYDROPLAS—Water Borne Coating—Red Spot Paint & Varnish Co.; *U.S. Private*, pg. 915

HYDROPLASTIC—Elastomeric Coatings—ICI Paints; *Int'l*, pg. 664

HYDROPLASTIC—Elastomeric Coatings in the Hydro-Shur Family—Devoe Paint; *Int'l*, pg. 663

HYDROPRIME—Elastomeric Coatings—ICI Paints; *Int'l*, pg. 664

HYDROPRIME-WB—Elastomeric Coatings in the Hydro-Shur Family—Devoe Paint; *Int'l*, pg. 663

HYDROSEALER—Elastomeric Coatings in the Hydro-Shur Family—Devoe Paint; *Int'l*, pg. 663

HYDROSEALER—Elastomeric Coatings—ICI Paints; *Int'l*, pg. 664

HYDROSEALER-WB—Elastomeric Coatings in the Hydro-Shur Family—Devoe Paint; *Int'l*, pg. 663

Brand Name Index

Brand Name Index

HYDROSET—Control—Svedala Industries Inc.; *Int'l*, pg. 1325
HYDROSLIDE—Knee Board—Mattel, Inc.; *U.S. Public*, pg. 1057
HYDROSLIDE—Knee Board—Mattel Power Wheels; *U.S. Public*, pg. 1058
HYDROSMOOTH—Marine Transmissions—Regal-Beloit Corporation; *U.S. Public*, pg. 1370
HYDROSOAK—Contact Lens Solution—Novartis; *Int'l*, pg. 972
HYDROSONICS—Surgical Instruments—Alcon Laboratories, Inc.; *Int'l*, pg. 916
HYDROSTAR—Motors—KYB Corporation of America; *Int'l*, pg. 727
HYDROSTATIC DRIVE—Transmission System—Baker Material Handling Corp.; *Int'l*, pg. 810
HYDROSTRIKE—Game—Pressman Toy Corp.; *U.S. Private*, pg. 882
HYDROSWAGE—Tool for Installation of Tubing in Heat Exchangers—Haskel International, Inc.; *U.S. Public*, pg. 798
HYDROTAINER—Water-Resistant Paperboard Boxes—Georgia-Pacific Corporation; *U.S. Public*, pg. 735
HYDROTECH—Boat Shoe—The Timberland Company; *U.S. Public*, pg. 1609
HYDROVANE—Rotary Compressors—ComPair LeRoi; *Int'l*, pg. 1242
HYDROX—Cookies—Keebler Company; *U.S. Public*, pg. 657
HYDROX—Cookies—Sunshine Biscuits, Inc.; *U.S. Private*, pg. 434
HYDROX—Cookies—Sunshine Biscuits, Inc.; *U.S. Public*, pg. 657
HYDROZON—Water Treatment Process—Carus Corporation; *U.S. Private*, pg. 217
HYDURA PRODUCTS—Hydraulic Equipment—The Oilgear Company; *U.S. Public*, pg. 1215
HYFLEX—Computor Controlled Flexible Production Machinery—Kingsbury Corporation; *U.S. Private*, pg. 621
HYFLEX—Insulation Tubing & Electrical Spring Connectors—3M; *U.S. Public*, pg. 1604
HYGEIA—Milk, Orange Juice, Ice Cream—Hygeia Dairy Co.; *U.S. Private*, pg. 552
HYGENE—Water Purifier of Silver-Activated Carbon Particles—Ionics, Incorporated; *U.S. Public*, pg. 912
HYGRADE—Processed Meats—Hygrade Food Products Corporation; *U.S. Public*, pg. 1433
HYGRADE—Meat Products—Sara Lee Corporation; *U.S. Public*, pg. 1432
HYGRADE—Automotive Products—Standard Motor Products Inc.; *U.S. Public*, pg. 1503
HYGROMIX—Hygromycin B, Elanco—Eli Lilly and Company; *U.S. Public*, pg. 992
HYGROMULL—Soil Improvers—BASF AG; *Int'l*, pg. 103
HYGROTON—Pharmaceuticals—Rhone-Poulenc Rorer - U.S.; *Int'l*, pg. 1110
HYLARTIN—Veterinary—Pharmacia & Upjohn Adria Laboratories; *Int'l*, pg. 1049
HYLITER S—High Bay Industrial—Guth Lighting Company; *Int'l*, pg. 821
HYLON—Nylon-type Rope—The American Group; *U.S. Public*, pg. 56
HYLOREL—Tablets (Guanadrel Sulfate)—Medeva Pharmaceuticals; *Int'l*, pg. 852
HYLOZENE—Rubber Separator Film—Industrial Coatings Group, Inc.; *U.S. Private*, pg. 434
HYMOR—High Strength Castable Refractories—Plibrico Co.; *U.S. Private*, pg. 872
HYMOSA—Vitamins & Food Supplements—Hanson PLC; *Int'l*, pg. 592
HYNAUTIC—NONE—Morse Controls; *U.S. Public*, pg. 857
HYPAK—Prefillable Syringes—Becton Dickinson & Company; *U.S. Public*, pg. 199
HYPAK—Hydraulic Seal—James Walker & Co. Limited; *U.S. Public*, pg. 1485
HYPALON—Synthetic Rubber—Du Pont (E.I. Du Pont De Nemours & Co.); *U.S. Public*, pg. 530
HYPER STEAM—Convection Steamer—Groen, A Dover Industries Co.; *U.S. Public*, pg. 521
HYPERCAD 54, WHERE ARE YOU?—Role Playing—Monarch Avalon, Inc.; *U.S. Public*, pg. 1123
HYPERCHANNEL—High Speed Data Communications—Network Systems Corporation; *U.S. Public*, pg. 1522

HYPERCHANNEL-DX—High Speed Data Communications—Network Systems Corporation; *U.S. Public*, pg. 1522
HYPERCHANNEL-50—High Speed Data Communications—Network Systems Corporation; *U.S. Public*, pg. 1522
HYPERCOLOR—Apparel & Accessories—The Generra Company; *U.S. Private*, pg. 446
HYPERFEED—High-Speed Data Feed—PC Quote, Inc.; *U.S. Public*, pg. 1240
HYPERGAM + CF—NONE—Nabi; *U.S. Public*, pg. 1148
HYPERGLIDE—Bicycle Parts—Shimano Inc.; *Int'l*, pg. 1232
HYPERHELP—Computer Product—International Business Machines Corporation; *U.S. Public*, pg. 895
HYPERMARKETS—Supermarkets—B & W Stormarknader AB; *Int'l*, pg. 708
HYPERMART—Superstore—The Daiei, Inc.; *Int'l*, pg. 364
HYPERSCRAM—Emergency Release Scrubber—ATMI, Inc.; *U.S. Public*, pg. 12
HYPERSTAT—Diazoxide, USP Injection—Key Pharmaceuticals; *U.S. Public*, pg. 1438
HYPERTAC—NONE—Hypertronics Corporation; *Int'l*, pg. 1268
HYPERWISE—Computer Product—International Business Machines Corporation; *U.S. Public*, pg. 895
HYPO-GEN—Hypochlorite Generator—Capital Controls Company Inc.; *Int'l*, pg. 1226
HYPOFLEX—Metal Tubing—Superior Tube Company; *U.S. Private*, pg. 1056
HYPOFORS—Reinforced Polyester Polyamide—Akzo Nobel N.V.; *Int'l*, pg. 42
HYPOL—Polyurethane Prepolymer—Hampshire Chemical Corp.; *U.S. Private*, pg. 498
HYPONEX—Plant Care—Hyponex Corporation; *U.S. Public*, pg. 1447
HYPONEX—Organic Products—The Scotts Company; *U.S. Public*, pg. 1446
HYPORET—Disposable Syringe, Lilly—Eli Lilly and Company; *U.S. Public*, pg. 992
HYPRESS—Steel Suitable for Pressing—British Steel Plc; *Int'l*, pg. 220
HYPRO—Pumps—Hypro Corporation; *U.S. Public*, pg. 1767
HYPRO—Agricultural & Industrial Pipe Lines—Lear Siegler Diversified Holdings Corp.; *U.S. Private*, pg. 655
HYPRO—NONE—WICOR, Inc.; *U.S. Public*, pg. 1767
HYRATE—Gunning Plastic Refractories—Plibrico Co.; *U.S. Private*, pg. 872
HYSEAL—Foam-in-Place Gasketing—The Dexter Corporation; *U.S. Public*, pg. 504
HYSKON—Pharmaceutical—Pharmacia & Upjohn Adria Laboratories; *Int'l*, pg. 1049
HYSLIK—Polyester Base Coated Magnet Wire—Rea Magnet Wire Company, Inc.; *U.S. Private*, pg. 913
HYSOL—Coating Powders, Composites, Films/Foams, Formulated Liquids, Primers, Inks—The Dexter Corporation; *U.S. Public*, pg. 504
HYSRON—Anticancer Agents & Hormones—Kyowa Hakko Kogyo Company, Ltd.; *Int'l*, pg. 778
HYSTAR—Carbohydrates for use as Humectants, Sweeteners, Viscosity Improvers—Lonza Inc.; *Int'l*, pg. 67
HYSTER—Forklift Trucks & Related Service Parts—NACCO Industries, Inc.; *U.S. Public*, pg. 1149
HYSTEROSCOPY REDIKIT—Surgical Preparatory Kit—The Cooper Companies, Inc.; *U.S. Public*, pg. 442
HYTEC—Work Holding Equipment—SPX Corporation; *U.S. Public*, pg. 1420
HYTEMCO—Resistance Alloy—Driver-Harris Company; *U.S. Public*, pg. 530
HYTHERM—Dyes for Plastics—Morton International Inc.; *U.S. Public*, pg. 1135
HYTONE—Pharmaceuticals—Rhone-Poulenc Rorer - U.S.; *Int'l*, pg. 1110
HYTONE & DESIGN—School & Office Products & Stationery—The Mead Corporation; *U.S. Public*, pg. 1074
HYTREL—Polyester & Thermoplastic Elastomer—Du Pont (E.I. Du Pont De Nemours & Co.); *U.S. Public*, pg. 530

HYTREX—Cartridge Filters—Osmonics, Inc.; *U.S. Public*, pg. 1233
HYTREX II—Cartridge Filters—Osmonics, Inc.; *U.S. Public*, pg. 1233
HYTRIN—Terazosin—Abbott Laboratories; *U.S. Public*, pg. 12
HYTROL—Anti Skid for Aircraft—Hydro-Aire; *U.S. Public*, pg. 457
HYTROL CONVEYORS—Conveyors—Hy-Tek Material Handling, Inc.; *U.S. Private*, pg. 550
HYUNDAI—Electronics America, Ltd; Corporate Series—Hyundai Electronics America; *Int'l*, pg. 641
HYVAR—Herbicide—Du Pont (E.I. Du Pont De Nemours & Co.); *U.S. Public*, pg. 530
HYVEX—High Temperature Resin Compounds—Ferro Corporation; *U.S. Public*, pg. 618
HYVOL—Separators & Filters—Ferguson International, Inc.; *U.S. Private*, pg. 401
HYZEEN—Hydrzine Solution—BetzDearborn Inc.; *U.S. Public*, pg. 226
HYZOD—Extruded Polycarbonates—DSM Sheffield Plastics; *Int'l*, pg. 354

I

IAA—Computer System—International Business Machines Corporation; *U.S. Public*, pg. 895
IAS—NONE—SunGard Data Systems Inc.; *U.S. Public*, pg. 1534
I/A SERIES—Applications, Systems & Services For Intelligent Automation—The Foxboro Company; *Int'l*, pg. 1243
I AM LOVED—Jewelry—Helzberg's Diamond Shops, Inc.; *U.S. Public*, pg. 220
IBC—NONE—Cadbury Beverages; *Int'l*, pg. 248
I.B.C.—Root Beer & Creme Soda—Dr Pepper/Seven Up No. America; *Int'l*, pg. 248
I.B. DIFFUSION—Women's Clothing—I.B. Diffusion, LP; *U.S. Private*, pg. 553
IBM—Industrial Strength PC's—Associated Process Controls; *U.S. Private*, pg. 92
IBM—Business Systems—International Business Machines Corporation; *U.S. Public*, pg. 895
IBMLINK—Business Products—International Business Machines Corporation; *U.S. Public*, pg. 895
IBM NETWORKING PRODUCTS—Network Products—Moss Telecommunications Services; *U.S. Private*, pg. 763
IBM THINK PAD—Personal Portable Computer—International Business Machines Corporation; *U.S. Public*, pg. 895
IBS—Seat Belt System—Starcraft Corporation; *U.S. Public*, pg. 1510
IBSS—Integrated Broadband Services Switch—DSC Communications Corporation; *U.S. Public*, pg. 475
I-BEAM—NONE—Berg Electronics; *U.S. Public*, pg. 212
I/C—Engine Line—Briggs & Stratton Corporation; *U.S. Public*, pg. 252
ICA—Chain of Supermarkets—Hakon Gruppen AS; *Int'l*, pg. 643
ICA—Ionized Calcium Analyzer—Radiometer A/S; *Int'l*, pg. 1083
ICAMS—Indus. Central Atmosphere Monitoring System—The Perkin-Elmer Corporation; *U.S. Public*, pg. 1279
ICAP—NONE—Thermo Jarrell Ash Corporation; *U.S. Public*, pg. 1594
ICB DUR T-58—Toluene Di Isociante—CYDSA S.A.; *Int'l*, pg. 246
ICC—Computer Software—Attachmate; *U.S. Private*, pg. 98
ICC—Intelligent Communications Connector—GenRad, Inc.; *U.S. Public*, pg. 731
ICC/UNIMAIL—Computer Software—Attachmate; *U.S. Private*, pg. 98
ICE—Electronic Instrument—Intel Corporation; *U.S. Public*, pg. 886
I.C.E.—Information Conversion Express-Fast Data Transmission Device—Saztec International, Inc.; *U.S. Public*, pg. 1435
ICEL—Electronic Instrument—Intel Corporation; *U.S. Public*, pg. 886
ICG—Extruded Film & Treated Textiles—Industrial Coatings Group, Inc.; *U.S. Private*, pg. 434
I.C. GOLDEN LAGER—Beer—Pittsburgh Brewing Company; *U.S. Private*, pg. 619

I.C. LIGHT—Beer—Pittsburgh Brewing Company; *U.S. Private*, pg. 619

ICOM—Computer Software—Attachmate; *U.S. Private*, pg. 98

IC-PAK—Anion Column & Concentration Insert, Cation Column & Guard Column Kit—Millipore Corporation; *U.S. Public*, pg. 1112

ICS—Reagents & Apparatus—Beckman Instruments, Inc.; *U.S. Public*, pg. 199

ICS—Concrete Cutting Systems—Blount International, Inc.; *U.S. Public*, pg. 237

ICS—Electronic Instrument—Intel Corporation; *U.S. Public*, pg. 886

I.C. WINTERS—Apparel—Fred Meyer Stores; *U.S. Public*, pg. 1103

I CAN'T BELIEVE IT'S NOT BUTTER—Butter-Substitute Margarine—Chesebrough-Pond's; *Int'l*, pg. 1436

I CAN'T BELIEVE IT'S NOT BUTTER—NONE—Van den Bergh Foods Company; *Int'l*, pg. 1436

I CAN'T BELIEVE IT'S NOT YOGURT—Yogurt Shops—Yogen Fruz Worldwide Inc.; *Int'l*, pg. 1520

ID—Business Publication—Bill Communications, Inc.; *Int'l*, pg. 1446

IDA—Ink Dispersion Analyzer—Kevlin Corporation; *U.S. Public*, pg. 953

IDBP—Electronic Instrument—Intel Corporation; *U.S. Public*, pg. 886

IDB 2000—Electronic Catalogue—Bell & Howell Holdings; *U.S. Public*, pg. 201

ID/BAR—Bar Code Creating & Imaging System—Imaging Technologies Corp.; *U.S. Public*, pg. 870

IDIS—Electronic Instrument—Intel Corporation; *U.S. Public*, pg. 886

IDM-INTERNATIONAL DESIGNS FOR MEN—Sports Outerwear—Fox-Knapp; *U.S. Private*, pg. 860

IDNX—Multiservice Bandwidth Manager—Network Equipment Technologies, Inc.; *U.S. Public*, pg. 1168

IDS—NONE—American Express Company; *U.S. Public*, pg. 73

IDS—Communications Systems—Executone Information Systems, Inc.; *U.S. Public*, pg. 599

IDSR INDICATOR FUSE—Powr Gard Fuse—Littelfuse, Inc.; *U.S. Public*, pg. 1001

IDX750—NONE—The Titan Corporation; *U.S. Public*, pg. 1618

IDXTEND R—The First Relational Solution To Scale The IDN—IDX Systems Corporation; *U.S. Public*, pg. 854

IDX3000—NONE—The Titan Corporation; *U.S. Public*, pg. 1618

ID ZONE—Electrophoresis Control Reagents—Beckman Instruments, Inc.; *U.S. Public*, pg. 199

I-DEAS—Software for Mechanical Design & Mfg.—Structural Dynamics Research Corp.; *U.S. Public*, pg. 1525

I-DEAS ABAQUS DATA TRANSLATOR—NONE—Structural Dynamics Research Corp.; *U.S. Public*, pg. 1525

I-DEAS ADVANCED FEM—NONE—Structural Dynamics Research Corp.; *U.S. Public*, pg. 1525

I-DEAS ADVANCED POST PROCESSING—NONE—Structural Dynamics Research Corp.; *U.S. Public*, pg. 1525

I-DEAS ANASYS DATA TRANSLATOR—NONE—Structural Dynamics Research Corp.; *U.S. Public*, pg. 1525

I-DEAS BEAM MODELING—NONE—Structural Dynamics Research Corp.; *U.S. Public*, pg. 1525

I-DEAS BI-DIRECTIONAL EDA INTERFACE—NONE—Structural Dynamics Research Corp.; *U.S. Public*, pg. 1525

I-DEAS CADAM DATA TRANSLATOR—NONE—Structural Dynamics Research Corp.; *U.S. Public*, pg. 1525

I-DEAS CATIA DATA TRANSLATOR—NONE—Structural Dynamics Research Corp.; *U.S. Public*, pg. 1525

I-DEAS CORRELATION—NONE—Structural Dynamics Research Corp.; *U.S. Public*, pg. 1525

I-DEAS COSMIC NASTRAN DATA TRANSLATOR—NONE—Structural Dynamics Research Corp.; *U.S. Public*, pg. 1525

I-DEAS DATA ACQUISITION—NONE—Structural Dynamics Research Corp.; *U.S. Public*, pg. 1525

I-DEAS DATA READER: MSC/NASTRAN—NONE—Structural Dynamics Research Corp.; *U.S. Public*, pg. 1525

I-DEAS DATA TRANSLATORS—NONE—Structural Dynamics Research Corp.; *U.S. Public*, pg. 1525

I-DEAS DESIGN ANALYSIS—NONE—Structural Dynamics Research Corp.; *U.S. Public*, pg. 1525

I-DEAS DESIGN OPTIMIZATION—NONE—Structural Dynamics Research Corp.; *U.S. Public*, pg. 1525

I-DEAS DRAFTING—NONE—Structural Dynamics Research Corp.; *U.S. Public*, pg. 1525

I-DEAS DRAFTING IGES DATA TRANSLATOR—NONE—Structural Dynamics Research Corp.; *U.S. Public*, pg. 1525

I-DEAS DRAFTING SYMBOLS CATALOG—NONE—Structural Dynamics Research Corp.; *U.S. Public*, pg. 1525

I-DEAS DXF DATA TRANSLATOR—NONE—Structural Dynamics Research Corp.; *U.S. Public*, pg. 1525

I-DEAS EXPERIMENTAL DYNAMICS—NONE—Structural Dynamics Research Corp.; *U.S. Public*, pg. 1525

I-DEAS EXTENDED FINITE ELEMENT MODELING—NONE—Structural Dynamics Research Corp.; *U.S. Public*, pg. 1525

I-DEAS FATIGUE—NONE—Structural Dynamics Research Corp.; *U.S. Public*, pg. 1525

I-DEAS FEM—NONE—Structural Dynamics Research Corp.; *U.S. Public*, pg. 1525

I-DEAS FEM & ANALYSIS—NONE—Structural Dynamics Research Corp.; *U.S. Public*, pg. 1525

I-DEAS FINITE ELEMENT MODELING—NONE—Structural Dynamics Research Corp.; *U.S. Public*, pg. 1525

I-DEAS FINITE ELEMENT MODELING AND ANALYSIS—NONE—Structural Dynamics Research Corp.; *U.S. Public*, pg. 1525

I-DEAS FOR TEST CORRELATION—NONE—Structural Dynamics Research Corp.; *U.S. Public*, pg. 1525

I-DEAS GENERATIVE MACHINING—NONE—Structural Dynamics Research Corp.; *U.S. Public*, pg. 1525

I-DEAS GNC—NONE—Structural Dynamics Research Corp.; *U.S. Public*, pg. 1525

I-DEAS GNC G-POST—NONE—Structural Dynamics Research Corp.; *U.S. Public*, pg. 1525

I-DEAS GNC MULTI-AXIS—NONE—Structural Dynamics Research Corp.; *U.S. Public*, pg. 1525

I-DEAS HARMONIC POST PROCESSING—NONE—Structural Dynamics Research Corp.; *U.S. Public*, pg. 1525

I-DEAS LAMINATE COMPOSITES—NONE—Structural Dynamics Research Corp.; *U.S. Public*, pg. 1525

I-DEAS MASTER ASSEMBLY—NONE—Structural Dynamics Research Corp.; *U.S. Public*, pg. 1525

I-DEAS MASTER MODELER—NONE—Structural Dynamics Research Corp.; *U.S. Public*, pg. 1525

I-DEAS MASTER SERIES—NONE—Structural Dynamics Research Corp.; *U.S. Public*, pg. 1525

I-DEAS MASTER SURFACING—NONE—Structural Dynamics Research Corp.; *U.S. Public*, pg. 1525

I-DEAS MATERIAL DATA CATALOG - INFODEX—NONE—Structural Dynamics Research Corp.; *U.S. Public*, pg. 1525

I-DEAS MATERIAL DATA CATALOG - PLASTICS—NONE—Structural Dynamics Research Corp.; *U.S. Public*, pg. 1525

I-DEAS MATERIAL DATA SYSTEM—NONE—Structural Dynamics Research Corp.; *U.S. Public*, pg. 1525

I-DEAS MECHANISM DESIGN—NONE—Structural Dynamics Research Corp.; *U.S. Public*, pg. 1525

I-DEAS MODAL—NONE—Structural Dynamics Research Corp.; *U.S. Public*, pg. 1525

I-DEAS MODAL ANALYSIS AUTOMATION—NONE—Structural Dynamics Research Corp.; *U.S. Public*, pg. 1525

I-DEAS MODEL RESPONSE—NONE—Structural Dynamics Research Corp.; *U.S. Public*, pg. 1525

I-DEAS MODEL SOLUTION—NONE—Structural Dynamics Research Corp.; *U.S. Public*, pg. 1525

I-DEAS MODEL SOLUTION LINEAR—NONE—Structural Dynamics Research Corp.; *U.S. Public*, pg. 1525

I-DEAS MODEL SOLUTION NONLINEAR—NONE—Structural Dynamics Research Corp.; *U.S. Public*, pg. 1525

I-DEAS MOLD ANALYSIS—NONE—Structural Dynamics Research Corp.; *U.S. Public*, pg. 1525

I-DEAS MOLD BASE CATALOG—NONE—Structural Dynamics Research Corp.; *U.S. Public*, pg. 1525

I-DEAS MOLD BASE DATA BASE—NONE—Structural Dynamics Research Corp.; *U.S. Public*, pg. 1525

I-DEAS MOLD COOLING—NONE—Structural Dynamics Research Corp.; *U.S. Public*, pg. 1525

I-DEAS MOLD FILLING—NONE—Structural Dynamics Research Corp.; *U.S. Public*, pg. 1525

I-DEAS MSC NASTRAN DATA TRANSLATOR—NONE—Structural Dynamics Research Corp.; *U.S. Public*, pg. 1525

I-DEAS MULTI-AXIS MIGRATION—NONE—Structural Dynamics Research Corp.; *U.S. Public*, pg. 1525

I-DEAS NC MIGRATION—NONE—Structural Dynamics Research Corp.; *U.S. Public*, pg. 1525

I-DEAS OPEN DATA—NONE—Structural Dynamics Research Corp.; *U.S. Public*, pg. 1525

I-DEAS OPEN LANGUAGE—NONE—Structural Dynamics Research Corp.; *U.S. Public*, pg. 1525

I-DEAS OPEN LINK—NONE—Structural Dynamics Research Corp.; *U.S. Public*, pg. 1525

I-DEAS OPTIMIZATION—NONE—Structural Dynamics Research Corp.; *U.S. Public*, pg. 1525

I-DEAS ORDER TRACKING—NONE—Structural Dynamics Research Corp.; *U.S. Public*, pg. 1525

I-DEAS PCB DATA TRANSLATOR—NONE—Structural Dynamics Research Corp.; *U.S. Public*, pg. 1525

I-DEAS PEARL—NONE—Structural Dynamics Research Corp.; *U.S. Public*, pg. 1525

I-DEAS PLASTICS ANALYSIS—NONE—Structural Dynamics Research Corp.; *U.S. Public*, pg. 1525

I-DEAS PLASTICS PROCESSING—NONE—Structural Dynamics Research Corp.; *U.S. Public*, pg. 1525

I-DEAS POST WRITER—NONE—Structural Dynamics Research Corp.; *U.S. Public*, pg. 1525

I-DEAS PROCESS SIMULATION—NONE—Structural Dynamics Research Corp.; *U.S. Public*, pg. 1525

I-DEAS PUBLISHING PACKAGE—NONE—Structural Dynamics Research Corp.; *U.S. Public*, pg. 1525

I-DEAS RAPID PROTOTYPING DATA TRANSLATOR—NONE—Structural Dynamics Research Corp.; *U.S. Public*, pg. 1525

I-DEAS SET DATA TRANSLATOR—NONE—Structural Dynamics Research Corp.; *U.S. Public*, pg. 1525

I-DEAS SHEET METAL DESIGN—NONE—Structural Dynamics Research Corp.; *U.S. Public*, pg. 1525

I-DEAS SIGNAL ANALYSIS—NONE—Structural Dynamics Research Corp.; *U.S. Public*, pg. 1525

I-DEAS SIGNAL PROCESSING BASE—NONE—Structural Dynamics Research Corp.; *U.S. Public*, pg. 1525

I-DEAS SIMULATION ADVISOR—NONE—Structural Dynamics Research Corp.; *U.S. Public*, pg. 1525

Brand Name Index

Brand Name Index

I-DEAS SMART VIEW—NONE—Structural Dynamics Research Corp.; *U.S. Public*, pg. 1525

I-DEAS SOLID LINK—NONE—Structural Dynamics Research Corp.; *U.S. Public*, pg. 1525

I-DEAS STANDARD MEASUREMENTS—NONE—Structural Dynamics Research Corp.; *U.S. Public*, pg. 1525

I-DEAS STANDARD PARTS CATALOG—NONE—Structural Dynamics Research Corp.; *U.S. Public*, pg. 1525

I-DEAS STANDARD POST PROCESSING—NONE—Structural Dynamics Research Corp.; *U.S. Public*, pg. 1525

I-DEAS STRUCTURAL MODIFICATION—NONE—Structural Dynamics Research Corp.; *U.S. Public*, pg. 1525

I-DEAS SYSTEM DYNAMICS ANALYSIS—NONE—Structural Dynamics Research Corp.; *U.S. Public*, pg. 1525

I-DEAS TEAM DATA MANAGER—NONE—Structural Dynamics Research Corp.; *U.S. Public*, pg. 1525

I-DEAS TEAM DESIGN—NONE—Structural Dynamics Research Corp.; *U.S. Public*, pg. 1525

I-DEAS TEAM ENGINEERING—NONE—Structural Dynamics Research Corp.; *U.S. Public*, pg. 1525

I-DEAS TEAM NC—NONE—Structural Dynamics Research Corp.; *U.S. Public*, pg. 1525

I-DEAS TEST—NONE—Structural Dynamics Research Corp.; *U.S. Public*, pg. 1525

I-DEAS TEST ANALYSIS INTERCONNECT KIT—NONE—Structural Dynamics Research Corp.; *U.S. Public*, pg. 1525

I-DEAS TEST AND MEASUREMENT—NONE—Structural Dynamics Research Corp.; *U.S. Public*, pg. 1525

I-DEAS TEST DATA ANALYSIS—NONE—Structural Dynamics Research Corp.; *U.S. Public*, pg. 1525

I-DEAS TEST DATA DISPLAY—NONE—Structural Dynamics Research Corp.; *U.S. Public*, pg. 1525

I-DEAS THERMOPLASTIC MOLDING—NONE—Structural Dynamics Research Corp.; *U.S. Public*, pg. 1525

I-DEAS THERMOSET MOLDING—NONE—Structural Dynamics Research Corp.; *U.S. Public*, pg. 1525

I-DEAS 3D IGES DATA TRANSLATOR—NONE—Structural Dynamics Research Corp.; *U.S. Public*, pg. 1525

I-DEAS TMG—NONE—Structural Dynamics Research Corp.; *U.S. Public*, pg. 1525

I-DEAS TMG COMPLETE—NONE—Structural Dynamics Research Corp.; *U.S. Public*, pg. 1525

I-DEAS TOLERANCE ANALYSIS—NONE—Structural Dynamics Research Corp.; *U.S. Public*, pg. 1525

I-DEAS VDA DATA TRANSLATOR—NONE—Structural Dynamics Research Corp.; *U.S. Public*, pg. 1525

I-DEAS VDA-FS DATA TRANSLATOR—NONE—Structural Dynamics Research Corp.; *U.S. Public*, pg. 1525

I-DEAS VEW AND MARKUP—NONE—Structural Dynamics Research Corp.; *U.S. Public*, pg. 1525

I-DEAS WARP AND SHRINK—NONE—Structural Dynamics Research Corp.; *U.S. Public*, pg. 1525

I-DEAS WELD LOCATOR—NONE—Structural Dynamics Research Corp.; *U.S. Public*, pg. 1525

I-DEAS WIRE EDM—NONE—Structural Dynamics Research Corp.; *U.S. Public*, pg. 1525

IE AIR—Mini Clean Room Process—Intelligent Systems Corp.; *U.S. Public*, pg. 888

I.E.C.—Generators—Baylor Company; *Int'l*, pg. 1134

IEC—Israel Electric Corporation—The Israel Electric Corporation Ltd.; *Int'l*, pg. 690

IEE—Display Makers—Industrial Electronic Engineers, Inc.; *U.S. Private*, pg. 561

I.E.S.—Energy Recovery Products—Thomas & Betts Reznor Division; *U.S. Public*, pg. 1598

IFA—Farm Supplies & Feeds—Intermountain Farmers Association; *U.S. Private*, pg. 568

IFC—Filter Cartridges—American Felt & Filter; *U.S. Private*, pg. 54

IFD—Incipient Fire Detection—Environment/One Corporation; *U.S. Public*, pg. 586

IFEX—Anti-Cancer Agent—Bristol-Myers Squibb Company; *U.S. Public*, pg. 253

IFEX—Pharmaceutical Used in Treatment of Several Types of Cancer—Bristol-Myers Squibb U.S. Pharmaceutical Group; *U.S. Public*, pg. 255

IFG—Inorganic Fiber Gasketing—Garlock Sealing Technologies; *U.S. Public*, pg. 402

IFMAC—Process Control System—Eastman Kodak Company; *U.S. Public*, pg. 550

IFPS/PLUS—Decision Support System—Comshare, Incorporated; *U.S. Public*, pg. 425

I-FLEX—Non-Strand Mount Amplifier for European Mkt.—C-COR Electronics, Inc.; *U.S. Public*, pg. 272

IGA—National Brands—Bozzuto's Inc.; *U.S. Public*, pg. 249

IGA—Retail Grocery—Covington Foods, Inc.; *U.S. Private*, pg. 280

IGA—Controlled Label Brand for Grocery Items—IGA, Inc. (Independent Grocers Alliance); *U.S. Private*, pg. 555

IGA—NONE—Richfood Holdings, Inc.; *U.S. Public*, pg. 1388

IG-LO—Refrigerants—Valvoline Company; *U.S. Public*, pg. 139

IHCP—Steel Bar Products—LaSalle Steel Company; *U.S. Public*, pg. 1181

IHOP—Pancake House—International House of Pancakes, Inc.; *U.S. Public*, pg. 862

IIN—Business Product—International Business Machines Corporation; *U.S. Public*, pg. 895

IIOP—NONE—Tricord Systems, Inc.; *U.S. Public*, pg. 1637

ITT AUTOMOTIVE SWF—Wipers and Motors—ITT Industries, Inc.; *U.S. Public*, pg. 859

IKOS VOYAGER—VHDL Software & Hardware Simulators—IKOS Systems, Inc.; *U.S. Public*, pg. 864

I-KNIFE—Surgical Instruments—Alcon Laboratories, Inc.; *Int'l*, pg. 916

ILBX—Electronic Instrument—Intel Corporation; *U.S. Public*, pg. 886

ILE—Business Product—International Business Machines Corporation; *U.S. Public*, pg. 895

IL-4 RECEPTOR—Immunological Therapeutic—Immunex Corporation; *U.S. Public*, pg. 871

IL-1 RECEPTOR—Immunological Therapeutic—Immunex Corporation; *U.S. Public*, pg. 871

ILS—Navigation Equipment—Wilcox Electric, Inc.; *Int'l*, pg. 1384

ILS/400—COmputer System—International Business Machines Corporation; *U.S. Public*, pg. 895

I-L-X B12 CAPLETS—Iron Supplement for Nutritional & Iron Deficiency Anemias—Bradley Pharmaceuticals; *U.S. Public*, pg. 249

I-L-X B12 CAPLETS—Iron Supplement for Nutritional & Iron Deficiency Anemias—Doak Dermatologics; *U.S. Public*, pg. 250

I-L-X B12 ELIXIR—Iron Supplement for Nutritional & Iron Deficiency Anemias—Bradley Pharmaceuticals; *U.S. Public*, pg. 249

I-L-X B12 ELIXIR—Iron Supplement for Nutritional & Iron Deficiency Anemias—Doak Dermatologics; *U.S. Public*, pg. 250

I-L-X B12 SUGAR FREE ELIXIR—Iron Supplement for Nutritional & Iron Deficiency Anemias—Bradley Pharmaceuticals; *U.S. Public*, pg. 249

I-L-X B12 SUGAR FREE ELIXIR—Iron Supplement for Nutritional & Iron Deficiency Anemias—Doak Dermatologics; *U.S. Public*, pg. 250

I-L-X ELIXIR—Iron Supplement for Nutritional & Iron Deficiency Anemias—Bradley Pharmaceuticals; *U.S. Public*, pg. 249

I-L-X ELIXIR—Iron Supplement for Nutritional & Iron Deficiency Anemias—Doak Dermatologics; *U.S. Public*, pg. 250

I-LIMITER—Current Limiting Circuit Breakers—Square D Company; *Int'l*, pg. 1208

I-LINE—Incandescent Lamps—General Electric Canada Inc.; *U.S. Public*, pg. 713

I-LINE—Panelboards, Busways—Square D Company; *Int'l*, pg. 1208

IM—Intramuscular Needles & Syringes—Becton Dickinson & Company; *U.S. Public*, pg. 199

IM—Electronic Instrument—Intel Corporation; *U.S. Public*, pg. 886

I.M.A.—Liquid Metal Joining Equip.—Fisher Gauge Limited; *Int'l*, pg. 491

IMF-IMS MANAGEMENT FACILITIES—Series of Performance Moniters that Manage Current IMS Activity—Boole & Babbage, Inc.; *U.S. Public*, pg. 244

IMI—Metals, Engineering Prods., Valves, Compressed Air Equip., Drinks—IMI Plc; *Int'l*, pg. 646

IMMX—Electronic Instrument—Intel Corporation; *U.S. Public*, pg. 886

IMO—Food Dressings—The Earthgrains Company; *U.S. Public*, pg. 547

IMO PUMP—NONE—IMO Pump; *U.S. Public*, pg. 857

IMO PUMPS—Screw Pumps—IMO Industries Inc.; *U.S. Public*, pg. 856

IMPS—Industry Media Publishing System for Magazine Publishers—Global Turnkey Systems Inc.; *U.S. Private*, pg. 457

IMS—Computer Support Furniture—Howe Furniture Corporation; *U.S. Public*, pg. 543

IMS—NONE—Lam Research Corporation; *U.S. Public*, pg. 975

IMS CS/2—Computer System—International Business Machines Corporation; *U.S. Public*, pg. 895

IMS CLIENT SERVER/2—Computer System—International Business Machines Corporation; *U.S. Public*, pg. 895

IMS/ESA—Computer System—International Business Machines Corporation; *U.S. Public*, pg. 895

IMS ONLINE—Document Management Systems, Electronic Imaging—Lanier Worldwide Inc.; *U.S. Public*, pg. 791

IMSYN—Optoelectronic Processors—Essex Corporation; *U.S. Public*, pg. 593

IMT—Micrographic Equipment—Eastman Kodak Company; *U.S. Public*, pg. 550

IMT-50—Micrographic Equipment—Eastman Kodak Company; *U.S. Public*, pg. 550

IMTN—Telecommunications Switching Equipment—DSC Communications Corporation; *U.S. Public*, pg. 475

IMT-100—Micrographic Equipment—Eastman Kodak Company; *U.S. Public*, pg. 550

IMT-150—Micrographic Equipment—Eastman Kodak Company; *U.S. Public*, pg. 550

IMT-300—Micrographic Equipment—Eastman Kodak Company; *U.S. Public*, pg. 550

IMT-200—Micrographic Equipment—Eastman Kodak Company; *U.S. Public*, pg. 550

IMT-250—Micrographic Equipment—Eastman Kodak Company; *U.S. Public*, pg. 550

IMX—Diagnostic Products—Abbott Laboratories; *U.S. Public*, pg. 12

IMX—Business Telephone System—Inter-Tel, Incorporated; *U.S. Public*, pg. 888

I-MAG—NONE—IMO Pump; *U.S. Public*, pg. 857

INA—Insurance—Cigna Corp.; *U.S. Public*, pg. 356

INA—Installation for Lighting, Heating, Steam Generating & Cooking—Sime Darby Berhad; *Int'l*, pg. 1249

INC—Magazine—The Goldhirsh Group; *U.S. Private*, pg. 461

INCA—Architecture for Next-Generation Mixed Language Solutions—Cadence Design Systems, Inc.; *U.S. Public*, pg. 290

INC 500—NONE—The Goldhirsh Group; *U.S. Private*, pg. 461

INC TECHNOLOGY—NONE—The Goldhirsh Group; *U.S. Private*, pg. 461

INMF—Computer Software & Hardware Prod. for Integrated Local Area Mngmt.—Datapoint Corporation; *Int'l*, pg. 384

INTRX—High Tech Outpatient Service—Continental Health Affiliates, Inc.; *U.S. Public*, pg. 440

INX—Computer Hardware & Software Prods. for Local Area Network Admin.—Datapoint Corporation; *Int'l*, pg. 384

INX—High Strength Low Alloy Steels—Inland Steel Industries, Inc.; *U.S. Public*, pg. 879

INX-PC—Computer Software & Hardware Prod. for Integrated Local Area Networks—Datapoint Corporation; *Int'l*, pg. 384

INX-32—Intelligent Network Executive Computer Software Prod.—Datapoint Corporation; *Int'l*, pg. 384

IOBAN—Antimicrobial Incise Drapes, Patient Isolation Systems—3M; *U.S. Public*, pg. 1604

I/O EXPRESS—Disk Caching Software—Executive Software; *U.S. Private*, pg. 388

IOFIXT T-M—Salt—Morton Salt; *U.S. Public*, pg. 1135

I/O-JET PLUS—Database Publishing and Electronic Printing—Group 1 Software, Inc.; *U.S. Public*, pg. 417

IOSP—Electronic Instrument—Intel Corporation; *U.S. Public*, pg. 886

IOX—IOT Equipped UHF TV Transmitter—Comark Communications, Inc.; *Int'l*, pg. 1383

I-125 SEEDS—NONE—Amersham Corporation; *Int'l*, pg. 992

IPA—Pale Ale—Labatt U.S.A.; *Int'l*, pg. 679

IPC POWER RESISTORS—High Power Electrical Resistors—Halma p.l.c.; *Int'l*, pg. 589

IPC RESISTORS—High Power Electrical Resistors—Halma p.l.c.; *Int'l*, pg. 589

IPDS—Electronic Instrument—Intel Corporation; *U.S. Public*, pg. 886

IPDS—Computer Product—International Business Machines Corporation; *U.S. Public*, pg. 895

IPI—Brake Parts—Echlin Inc.; *U.S. Public*, pg. 560

IPOL—Poliovirus Vaccine, Inactivated—Connaught Laboratories, Inc.; *Int'l*, pg. 1109

IPSC—Electronic Instrument—Intel Corporation; *U.S. Public*, pg. 886

I/PEX—Instruments—Masoneilan North American Operations; *U.S. Public*, pg. 528

I.Q.—NONE—SunGard Data Systems Inc.; *U.S. Public*, pg. 1534

IQ ACCESS—Data Retrieval & Transfer Software—IQ Software Corporation; *U.S. Public*, pg. 858

IQF SPECIALTY PRODUCTS—Hash Browns (Loose), Diner Slices, Quick Cook Hash Browns—Lamb-Weston, Inc.; *U.S. Public*, pg. 427

IQ/LIVE WEB—Facility for Corporate Information over World Wide Web—IQ Software Corporation; *U.S. Public*, pg. 858

IQ/OBJECTS—Object Based Client/Server Query & Reporting Tools—IQ Software Corporation; *U.S. Public*, pg. 858

IQ SERIES—Computed Tomography—Picker International, Inc.; *Int'l*, pg. 545

IQ/SMART SERVER—Three Tier Architecture Implementation—IQ Software Corporation; *U.S. Public*, pg. 858

IQ2000—PM Window Software—IRD Mechanalysis, Inc. (U.S.A.); *U.S. Public*, pg. 789

IQ/VISION—Multidimensional Analysis Tool—IQ Software Corporation; *U.S. Public*, pg. 858

IQZOOM—Camera Equipment—Asahi Optical Co., Ltd.; *Int'l*, pg. 85

IRC BUDGET BLEND—Pipe Tobaccos—Consolidated Cigar Corporation; *U.S. Private*, pg. 690

IRC-100—Programmable Infrared Receiver—Retzlaff Incorporated; *U.S. Private*, pg. 925

IRD—Vibration Meters, Analyzers—IRD Mechanalysis, Inc. (U.S.A.); *U.S. Public*, pg. 789

IRL—Interactive Reader Language—Intermec Technologies Corporation; *U.S. Public*, pg. 1699

IR LINK—On-Line Inspection Systems—Galileo Corp.; *U.S. Public*, pg. 698

IRMA—Computer Software—Attachmate; *U.S. Private*, pg. 98

IRMA LAN—Computer Software—Attachmate; *U.S. Private*, pg. 98

IRMA WORKSTATION FOR DOS—Computer Software—Attachmate; *U.S. Private*, pg. 98

IRMA WORKSTATION FOR MACINTOSH—Computer Software—Attachmate; *U.S. Private*, pg. 98

IRMA WORKSTATION FOR WINDOWS—Computer Software—Attachmate; *U.S. Private*, pg. 98

IRMK—Electronic Instrument—Intel Corporation; *U.S. Public*, pg. 886

IRMX—Electronic Instrument—Intel Corporation; *U.S. Public*, pg. 886

IRS 19—Immunologic Products—Kali-Chemie Aktiengesellschaft; *Int'l*, pg. 1278

ISA PROCESS—Copper Refining Process—M.I.M. Holdings Ltd.; *Int'l*, pg. 827

ISBC—Electronic Instrument—Intel Corporation; *U.S. Public*, pg. 886

ISBX—Electronic Instrument—Intel Corporation; *U.S. Public*, pg. 886

ISC—Wines—Canandaigua Wine Company, Inc.; *U.S. Public*, pg. 300

ISCA—Computer Software—Attachmate; *U.S. Private*, pg. 98

ISDM—Electronic Instrument—Intel Corporation; *U.S. Public*, pg. 886

ISDN PC ADAPTER—Terminal Adapter—Hayes Microcomputer Products, Inc.; *U.S. Public*, pg. 801

ISDN SYSTEM ADAPTER—Terminal Adapter—Hayes Microcomputer Products, Inc.; *U.S. Public*, pg. 801

ISDNX—Internetworking Product—Network Equipment Technologies, Inc.; *U.S. Public*, pg. 1168

ISE—Electronics—National Semiconductor Corporation; *U.S. Public*, pg. 1159

ISMIS—Intelligent Shock Mitigation & Isolation System—Enidine Incorporated; *U.S. Private*, pg. 377

ISMO—Pharmaceutical Products—Wyeth-Ayerst Laboratories, Inc.; *U.S. Public*, pg. 80

ISN—NONE—Information Systems & Network Corporation; *U.S. Private*, pg. 561

ISO-CEPTIC—Relieves the Pain of Bedsores & Burns—Bethurum Research & Development, Inc.; *U.S. Private*, pg. 141

ISO-DAC—Isolator D/A Converter—Analog Devices, Inc.; *U.S. Public*, pg. 107

ISO-FORM—Crowns, Temporary Bicuspid Crowns—3M; *U.S. Public*, pg. 1604

ISO-OHM—Dielectric Coatings & Films—Ferro Corporation; *U.S. Public*, pg. 618

ISO-SET—Isotope Modules—Beckman Instruments, Inc.; *U.S. Public*, pg. 199

ISO-TEC—Communications Systems—Executone Information Systems, Inc.; *U.S. Public*, pg. 599

ISO-TIP—Soldering Iron, Cordless—Wahl Clipper Corp.; *U.S. Private*, pg. 1146

ISO-Z—High Density Zircon—A.P. Green Industries, Inc.; *U.S. Public*, pg. 761

ISS—Building Maintenance Hygiene Services—ISS-International Service System A/S; *Int'l*, pg. 656

ISSC—Computer Product—International Business Machines Corporation; *U.S. Public*, pg. 895

ISXM—Electronic Instrument—Intel Corporation; *U.S. Public*, pg. 886

ISYS—NONE—EcoScience Corporation; *U.S. Public*, pg. 563

I SERIES—InterBold ATM Product Line—Diebold, Incorporated; *U.S. Public*, pg. 506

I SKI—Sunglasses—Outlook Eyewear Company; *U.S. Public*, pg. 195

I-SPEAR—Surgical Sponges—Alcon Laboratories, Inc.; *Int'l*, pg. 916

ITA GROUP—Full Service Travel Incentive—ITA Group Inc.; *U.S. Private*, pg. 555

ITAM—Furnaces—Itam Tech Italimplianti, Inc.; *Int'l*, pg. 655

ITC—Graphic Art Supplies—Esselte AB; *Int'l*, pg. 459

ITC—Industrial Training Programs—ITC Learning Corp.; *U.S. Public*, pg. 859

ITD—Ion Trap Detector—Finnigan Corporation; *U.S. Public*, pg. 1591

I-T-E—Circuit Breakers, Electrical Distribution & Circuit Protection Product Line—Siemens Energy & Automation Inc.; *Int'l*, pg. 1245

I.T.S.—NONE—Interactive Telecard Services, Inc. (ITS); *U.S. Private*, pg. 566

IT SERVICE VISION—Business Solution IT Service Delivery—SAS Institute Inc.; *U.S. Private*, pg. 966

ITT AUTOMOTIVE TEVES—Brake Systems—ITT Industries, Inc.; *U.S. Public*, pg. 859

ITT HARTFORD—NONE—The Hartford Financial Services Group Inc.; *U.S. Public*, pg. 794

ITT SHERATON CLUBMILES—NONE—American Express Company; *U.S. Public*, pg. 73

ITW WOODWORTH—Metal Working Tools & Equipment—ITW Woodworth; *U.S. Public*, pg. 867

I30 (INFINITI)—Automobile—Nissan Motor Corporation in U.S.A.; *Int'l*, pg. 945

I2ICE—Electronic Instrument—Intel Corporation; *U.S. Public*, pg. 886

IV-D—Software for Technology Training, Computer-Aided Instruction—Computer Sciences Corporation; *U.S. Public*, pg. 422

IV SOLUTION—Solution for Piggyback System—Otsuka Pharmaceutical Co., Ltd.; *Int'l*, pg. 1013

I.V. START PAK—I.V. Start Kit—Becton Dickinson & Company; *U.S. Public*, pg. 199

IVUS—Ultrasound System—Diasonics Ultra Sound, Inc.; *Int'l*, pg. 644

IVX-500—Voice Mail Messaging System—Inter-Tel, Incorporated; *U.S. Public*, pg. 888

IW—Grinding Machines—Litton Industries, Inc.; *U.S. Public*, pg. 1002

I W HARPER GOLD MEDAL—NONE—Guinness Plc; *Int'l*, pg. 412

I W HARPER PRESIDENT S RESERVE—NONE—Guinness Plc; *Int'l*, pg. 412

I W HARPER TWELVE YEAR OLD—NONE—Guinness Plc; *Int'l*, pg. 412

IXF—File Transfer Software—Tandem Computers Inc.; *U.S. Public*, pg. 417

IXL—Cabinets, Wall Systems & Hutches—IXL Cabinets; *U.S. Public*, pg. 1634

IXL—Conserves—J.M. Smucker Company; *U.S. Public*, pg. 1480

IXL—Kitchen & Vanity Cabinets—Triangle Pacific Corporation; *U.S. Public*, pg. 1634

IX WORKS—NONE—Wind River Systems, Inc.; *U.S. Public*, pg. 1770

INTERCOM—Computer Software—Attachmate; *U.S. Private*, pg. 98

IRMAX—Computer Software—Attachmate; *U.S. Private*, pg. 98

IAMS—Pet Food—Iams Company; *U.S. Private*, pg. 556

IAMS LESS ACTIVE—Pet Food—Iams Company; *U.S. Private*, pg. 556

IBERIA—Rice, Beans, Corn Oil—Bestfoods; *U.S. Public*, pg. 223

IBERNA—Household Appliances—Candy S.p.A.; *Int'l*, pg. 259

IBEX—Computerized Research Services—The Mead Corporation; *U.S. Public*, pg. 1074

IBID—Electronic, PC-Based Whiteboards—Microtouch Systems, Inc.; *U.S. Public*, pg. 1108

IBIS—Economy Hotels—Accor S.A.; *Int'l*, pg. 20

IBIS—NONE—Carpenter Technology Corporation; *U.S. Public*, pg. 307

IBIS—Mortadella—I.B.I.S.-S.p.A.; *Int'l*, pg. 642

IBIZ—Car Wax—Pegasus International Corporation; *U.S. Private*, pg. 1046

IBIZA—Broadloom—Couristan Inc.; *U.S. Private*, pg. 279

IBUPRIN—Ibuprofen Based Analgesic—Thompson Medical Company, Inc.; *U.S. Private*, pg. 1083

IBUTAB—Pain Reliever—Zee Medical, Inc.; *U.S. Public*, pg. 1073

IBUTOP—Topical Analgesic—Akzo Nobel N.V.; *Int'l*, pg. 42

ICE BLUE—Men's Toiletries—SmithKline Beecham plc; *Int'l*, pg. 1264

ICE BREAKER—Ice Scrapers & Snowbrushes—Latshaw Enterprises, Inc.; *U.S. Public*, pg. 979

ICE CHILLER—High Pressure Receiver, Recirculation Package, Surge Drum—Baltimore Aircoil Company; *U.S. Private*, pg. 68

ICE CREAM PARLOR—Electric Ice Cream Maker—Waring Products; *U.S. Public*, pg. 286

ICE DESIGNS—NONE—Rubbermaid Incorporated; *U.S. Public*, pg. 1411

ICE-LOGIC—Ice Thickness Controller—Baltimore Aircoil Company; *U.S. Private*, pg. 68

ICE MELTER—Snow & Ice Melter Pellets—Hydro/Kirby Agri Service, Inc.; *U.S. Private*, pg. 552

ICE MINT—Foot Cream—Westwood-Squibb Pharmaceuticals Inc.; *U.S. Public*, pg. 255

ICE MOUNTAIN—Mineral Water—Nestle S.A.; *Int'l*, pg. 915

ICE MOUNTAIN—Mineral Water—The Perrier Group of America; *Int'l*, pg. 919

ICE-O-MATIC—Electric Ice Crusher—The Rival Company; *U.S. Public*, pg. 1391

ICE-O-MATIC—Icemaking Equipment—Welbilt Corporation; *Int'l*, pg. 188

ICE-OFF—Auto Products—CRC Industries, Inc.; *U.S. Private*, pg. 138

ICE 101—Liqueur—White Rock Distilleries Inc.; *U.S. Private*, pg. 1173

ICE SCULPTURES—Decorative Ice Molds—Carlisle Food Service Products; *U.S. Public*, pg. 305

ICEBERG—Calcined Kaolin—Burgess Pigment Co.; *U.S. Private*, pg. 182

ICEBREAKER—Canned Iced Coffee—Nestle S.A.; *Int'l*, pg. 915

ICECAP—NONE—Nestle USA; *Int'l*, pg. 916

ICECHASER—Ice Melting Compound—Consolidated Coatings Corp.; *U.S. Public*, pg. 1357

ICECREAMNOW—Frozen Dessert Maker—National Presto Industries, Inc.; *U.S. Public*, pg. 1159

ICEE—Semi-Frozen Carbonated Beverage—J & J Snack Foods Corporation; *U.S. Public*, pg. 916

ICEHOUSE—Beer—Miller Brewing Company; *U.S. Public*, pg. 1289

ICEHOUSE—Beer—Philip Morris Companies Inc.; *U.S. Public*, pg. 1287

ICELAND—Grocery Stores—Iceland Group plc; *Int'l*, pg. 658

ICELAND—Frozen Seafood—Iceland Seafood Corporation; *U.S. Private*, pg. 556

ICELANDAIR—International Air Transportation—IceLandAir; *Int'l*, pg. 658

ICELANDIC—Frozen Seafood—Coldwater Seafood Corporation; *U.S. Private*, pg. 251

ICEMATIC—Automatic Ice Making Equipment—Scotsman Industries, Inc.; *U.S. Public*, pg. 1444

ICESTOP—Coils to Prevent Ice Build-Up on Roofs—Raychem Corporation; *U.S. Public*, pg. 1362

ICHIBAN KAJU—Wine—Sapporo Breweries Ltd.; *Int'l*, pg. 1193

ICHIBAN SHIBORI PREMIUM—Beer—Kirin Brewery Co., Ltd.; *Int'l*, pg. 735

ICI—Women's Fragrance—Coty Inc.; *Int'l*, pg. 185

ICICLE—Seafood—Icicle Seafoods, Inc.; *U.S. Private*, pg. 556

ICING—NONE—Claire's Stores Inc.; *U.S. Public*, pg. 381

ICON—Men's Hair Care—Matrix Essentials, Inc.; *U.S. Public*, pg. 254

ICONE—Treatment—Christian Dior Perfumes Inc.; *Int'l*, pg. 781

ICONSIM—NONE—Berg Electronics; *U.S. Public*, pg. 212

ICOPAL—Roofing Felt; Asphalt Shingles—Icopal a/s; *Int'l*, pg. 658

ICUT—Ground Engaging Tools-Teeth, Tips & Adaptors—Intertractor Zweigniederlassung der Wirtgen GmbH; *Int'l*, pg. 1511

ICY CAPE—Sea Foods—Wards Cove Packing Company; *U.S. Private*, pg. 1149

ICY HOT—Analgesic—The Procter & Gamble Company; *U.S. Public*, pg. 1330

ICY HOT CREAM—Topical Analgesic—Chattem, Inc., Consumer Products Division; *U.S. Public*, pg. 341

ICY POINT—Canned—Ocean Beauty Seafoods, Inc.; *U.S. Private*, pg. 810

IDAHO NATURALLY—Dehydrated Potatoes, Frozen Hash Browns, Slices & Dices—Magic Valley Foods, Inc.; *U.S. Private*, pg. 695

IDAHO SUPREME—Fresh & Processed Potatoes—Idaho Supreme Company; *U.S. Private*, pg. 557

IDAHOAN—Dehydrated Potatoes—Idahoan Foods; *U.S. Private*, pg. 557

IDARAC—Neuro-Muscular—SmithKline Beecham Research Limited; *Int'l*, pg. 1266

THE IDEA GENERATOR PLUS—Software to Develop & Evaluate Ideas—Experience In Software, Inc.; *U.S. Private*, pg. 388

IDEAL—Combines—AGCO Corporation; *U.S. Public*, pg. 28

IDEAL—Tape—American Biltrite Inc.; *U.S. Public*, pg. 68

IDEAL—Boilers & Radiators—Caradon Plc; *Int'l*, pg. 266

IDEAL—Office Products—Esselte AB; *Int'l*, pg. 459

IDEAL—Stainless Steel Flanges—Ideal Forging Corporation; *U.S. Private*, pg. 557

IDEAL—Dairy Products—Nestle S.A.; *Int'l*, pg. 915

IDEAL—Baking Products; Colors, Extracts, Emulsions, Concentrates, Jams & Jellies—Purity Products Inc.; *U.S. Private*, pg. 896

IDEAL—Canned Vegetables—RJR Nabisco Holdings Corp.; *U.S. Public*, pg. 1354

IDEAL—Chocolate & Peanut Imported Danish Cookies—RJR Nabisco Holdings Corp.; *U.S. Public*, pg. 1354

IDEAL—Window & Floor Squeegees—W.J. & Dennis Co.; *U.S. Private*, pg. 1144

IDEAL—Printing Papers—Westvaco Corporation; *U.S. Public*, pg. 1762

IDEAL BY SAN GIORGIO—Pasta—Hershey Pasta and Grocery Group; *U.S. Public*, pg. 812

IDEAL DAIRY—Milk & Dairy Products—Q.U.F. Industries Ltd.; *Int'l*, pg. 1074

IDEAL HOME—Home Interest Magazine—IPC Magazines Limited; *Int'l*, pg. 651

IDEAL NURSERY—Dolls—Tyco Toys, Inc.; *U.S. Public*, pg. 1058

IDEAL SCHOOL SUPPLY CO—Educational Materials—Creative Publications; *U.S. Private*, pg. 288

IDEAL-STANDARD—Plumbing Products—American Standard Inc.; *U.S. Public*, pg. 91

IDEALARC—Welder—The Lincoln Electric Company; *U.S. Public*, pg. 996

IDEAS TO GROW WITH—Agricultural Chemicals—Wilbur-Ellis Company & Connell Brothers Company; *U.S. Private*, pg. 1175

IDEM—Paper—Arjo Wiggins Appleton plc; *Int'l*, pg. 567

IDEM SUPERFAX—Fax Paper—Arjo Wiggins Appleton plc; *Int'l*, pg. 567

IDENTI-CODE—Formula Identification Code, Lilly—Eli Lilly and Company; *U.S. Public*, pg. 992

IDENTI-DOSE—Unit Dose Medication, Lilly—Eli Lilly and Company; *U.S. Public*, pg. 992

IDENTI PROM—NONE—Xicor, Inc.; *U.S. Public*, pg. 1785

IDENTICAM—Automatic Identification Systems—IDenticard Systems, Inc.; *U.S. Private*, pg. 557

IDENTICARD—Security Identification Systems—IDenticard Systems, Inc.; *U.S. Private*, pg. 557

IDENTIPASS—Access Control System—IDenticard Systems, Inc.; *U.S. Private*, pg. 557

IDENTITY—Outerwear—American Marketing Industries, Inc.; *U.S. Private*, pg. 58

IDENTIWRAP—Contiuous Wrapped Edge on ID Cards—IDenticard Systems, Inc.; *U.S. Private*, pg. 557

IDO—Sanitary Porcelain—Metra Corporation; *Int'l*, pg. 862

IDO—Bathroom Ceramics—Sanitec Ltd. Oy; *Int'l*, pg. 863

IDO TONICUM—Tonic—Novo Nordisk A/S; *Int'l*, pg. 987

IDOFORM—Lactic Acid Bacteria—Novo Nordisk A/S; *Int'l*, pg. 987

IDOLOBA—Natural Remedy, Ginkgo Biloba Extract—Novo Nordisk A/S; *Int'l*, pg. 987

IDOTYL—Analgesic—Novo Nordisk A/S; *Int'l*, pg. 987

IFNOTE—Letter-Size & Laptop PC's—Oki Electric Industry Company, Ltd.; *Int'l*, pg. 999

IFO—Sanitary Porlelain—Metra Corporation; *Int'l*, pg. 862

IFO—Bathroom Ceramics—Sanitec Ltd. Oy; *Int'l*, pg. 863

IG LO—Automotive Refrigerants—Ashland, Inc.; *U.S. Public*, pg. 138

IGGY 5 IN 1—Beverage Cooler—Igloo Products Corporation; *U.S. Public*, pg. 265

IGGY 4 IN 1—Beverage Cooler—Igloo Products Corporation; *U.S. Public*, pg. 265

IGLOO—Grocery Stroes—Iceland Group plc; *Int'l*, pg. 658

IGLOO—Ice Chest—Igloo Products Corporation; *U.S. Public*, pg. 265

IGLOO ICE—Beverage Cooler—Igloo Products Corporation; *U.S. Public*, pg. 265

IGNIS—Major Appliances—Whirlpool Corporation; *U.S. Public*, pg. 1764

IIMAK—NONE—PAXAR Corporation; *U.S. Public*, pg. 1266

IKEA—Housewares & Furniture—Ikea North America, Inc.; *Int'l*, pg. 660

IKEGAMI—Electronics—Ikegami Electronics (U.S.A.), Inc.; *Int'l*, pg. 660

IKMISOU SOFA—Lounge Seating—Vecta; *U.S. Private*, pg. 1038

IKMISOU TABLE—NONE—Vecta; *U.S. Private*, pg. 1038

IL POGGIONE—Wine—Paterno Imports Limited; *U.S. Private*, pg. 843

IL PRIMO—Sausages & Cheese—Armour Swift Eckrich; *U.S. Public*, pg. 426

ILCO—Key Blanks, Padlocks—Ilco Unican Corp.; *Int'l*, pg. 1432

ILCO—Locks—Unican Security Systems Ltd.; *Int'l*, pg. 1432

ILEODRESS—Ostomy Care Products—Bristol-Myers Squibb Company; *U.S. Public*, pg. 253

ILETIN II—Purified Insulin Injection, Lilly—Eli Lilly and Company; *U.S. Public*, pg. 992

ILFO-SPEED—Photographic Paper—Novartis; *Int'l*, pg. 972

ILFOCHROME 100—Colour Reversal Film—Novartis; *Int'l*, pg. 972

ILFOCOLOR 100 & 400—Colour Negative Film—Novartis; *Int'l*, pg. 972

ILFORD XP1—Black & White Film—Novartis; *Int'l*, pg. 972

ILISE STEVENS—Women's Dresses—Kellwood Company; *U.S. Public*, pg. 948

ILLAWARRA MERCURY—NONE—John Fairfax Holdings Limited; *Int'l*, pg. 477

ILLEGAL LENGTHS—Mascara—Maybelline, Inc.; *Int'l*, pg. 819

ILLINOIS—Locks—The Eastern Company; *U.S. Public*, pg. 548

ILLINOIS BRONZE—Spray Paints—Sherwin-Williams Diversified Brands, Inc.; *U.S. Public*, pg. 1466

ILLINOIS CAPACITATOR—NONE—Milgray Electronics, Inc.; *U.S. Public*, pg. 205

ILLINOIS GEAR—Custom Gears & Track Wheels—Foote-Jones/Illinois Gear; *U.S. Public*, pg. 1370

ILLINOIS MANUFACTURERS DIRECTORY—Directory—Manufacturers' News, Inc.; *U.S. Private*, pg. 700

ILLINOIS SERVICES DIRECTORY—Directory—Manufacturers' News, Inc.; *U.S. Private*, pg. 700

ILLOXAN—Agrochemicals—Hoechst Aktiengesellschaft; *Int'l*, pg. 624

ILLUMINATED BOOKS AND MANUSCRIPTS—Computer Product—International Business Machines Corporation; *U.S. Public*, pg. 895

ILLUMINATED DIRECTORY—System to Create & Update Illuminated Directories—Kroy Inc.; *U.S. Public*, pg. 1339

ILLUMINATOR—NONE—Donnelly Corporation; *U.S. Public*, pg. 519

THE ILLUMINATOR—NONE—Life Technologies, Inc.; *U.S. Public*, pg. 504

ILLUSION—Foundation—Elizabeth Arden Company; *Int'l*, pg. 1435

ILLUSION—Paneling—Weyerhaeuser Forest Products Company; *U.S. Public*, pg. 1764

ILLUSION—Zipper—YKK (U.S.A.); *Int'l*, pg. 1515

ILLUSIONS—Decorative Faucets—The Chicago Faucet Co.; *U.S. Private*, pg. 234

ILLVA DI SARONNO—Rabarbaro Zucca Liquor & Artic Vodka—Armando Testa S.p.A; *Int'l*, pg. 1377

ILOSONE—Erythromycin Estolate, Dista—Eli Lilly and Company; *U.S. Public*, pg. 992

ILOSONE CHEWABLE—Erythromycin Estolate, Dista—Eli Lilly and Company; *U.S. Public*, pg. 992

ILOSONE LIQUID 125—Erythromycin Estolate, Dista—Eli Lilly and Company; *U.S. Public*, pg. 992

ILOSONE LIQUID 250—Erythromycin Estolate, Dista—Eli Lilly and Company; *U.S. Public*, pg. 992

ILOSONE READY-MIXED DROPS—Erythromycin Estolate, Dista—Eli Lilly and Company; *U.S. Public*, pg. 992

ILOSONE 125—Erythromycin Estolate, Dista—Eli Lilly and Company; *U.S. Public*, pg. 992

ILOTYCIN—Erythromycin, Dista—Eli Lilly and Company; *U.S. Public*, pg. 992

ILOTYCIN GLUCEPTATE, I.V.—Erythromycin Gluceptate, Dista—Eli Lilly and Company; *U.S. Public*, pg. 992

ILSCO—Electrical Connector—Ilsco; *U.S. Private*, pg. 558

IMACILLIN—Antibiotic—Astra AB; *Int'l*, pg. 93

IMAGCLEAR—Resolution Medical Mammography Scanner—DBA Systems, Inc.; *U.S. Public*, pg. 472

IMAGE—Automated Test Equipment—AAI/ACL Technologies; *U.S. Public*, pg. 1679

IMAGE—Floor Coverings—Domco Inc.; *Int'l*, pg. 415

IMAGE—Synthetic Gut Racquet String—Ektelon; *U.S. Private*, pg. 884

IMAGE—Coated Paper—Georgia-Pacific Corporation; *U.S. Public*, pg. 735

IMAGE—NONE—Image Entertainment, Inc.; *U.S. Public*, pg. 870

IMAGE—Entrance & Anti-Fatigue—Ludlow Composites Corporation; *U.S. Private*, pg. 680

IMAGE—Game—Monarch Avalon, Inc.; *U.S. Public*, pg. 1123

IMAGE—Computer-generated Visual Systems—Raytheon Systems Co.; *U.S. Public*, pg. 1364

IMAGE—NONE—Regal Ware, Inc.; *U.S. Private*, pg. 917

IMAGE ASSISTANT—Image Editing Software—Caere Corporation; *U.S. Public*, pg. 291

IMAGE BOND INTEGRITY—In-Store Bar Code Shelf Label and Signage Production System—Diagraph Corporation; *U.S. Private*, pg. 330

IMAGE BOOKS—Book Imprint—Bertelsmann AG; *Int'l*, pg. 189

IMAGE BUILDER—Stationery Supplies—H.C. Miller Company; *U.S. Private*, pg. 747

IMAGE CARD—Laser Printer Controller—Imaging Technologies Corp.; *U.S. Public*, pg. 870

IMAGE COPY PLUS—IMS Database Utility—BMC Software, Inc.; *U.S. Public*, pg. 162

IMAGE FLOW—Imagine Media—Labelon Corporation; *U.S. Private*, pg. 641

IMAGE FONT—Digital Typefaces for Laser Printing—Imaging Technologies Corp.; *U.S. Public*, pg. 870

IMAGE GUARD—Microfilm Process Monitoring Service—Eastman Kodak Company; *U.S. Public*, pg. 550

IMAGE HANDLER—Information Handling/Retrieval Equipment—Eastman Kodak Company; *U.S. Public*, pg. 550

IMAGE LOOK—Autofocus System—Telex Communications, Inc.; *U.S. Private*, pg. 1074

IMAGE MAGIC—NONE—Eastman Kodak Company; *U.S. Public*, pg. 550

IMAGE-MAKER—Plastic Binding System—General Binding Corporation; *U.S. Public*, pg. 707

IMAGE NET—Printer Sharing System—Imaging Technologies Corp.; *U.S. Public*, pg. 870

IMAGE OF SAINTS—Votive Candles—Will & Baumer Incorporated; *U.S. Private*, pg. 1176

IMAGE 1—Produces Laminated Custom-Cover Folders or Counter Cards—Varitronic Systems, Inc.; *U.S. Public*, pg. 250

IMAGE SCRIPT—Desktop Publishing Software—Imaging Technologies Corp.; *U.S. Public*, pg. 870

IMAGE SEARCH CONTROLLER—Document Management Products—Bell & Howell Holdings; *U.S. Public*, pg. 201

IMAGE WRITER—Dot Matrix Printer—Apple Computer, Inc.; *U.S. Public*, pg. 121

IMAGECAPTURE—Microfilm—Eastman Kodak Company; *U.S. Public*, pg. 550

IMAGEKEEPER—NONE—Kronos Incorporated; *U.S. Public*, pg. 967

IMAGELINK—Microfilm, Software, Micrographic Equipment—Eastman Kodak Company; *U.S. Public*, pg. 550

IMAGELITE—Film—Eastman Kodak Company; *U.S. Public*, pg. 550

IMAGELITE—Fiber Optic Illuminator—Stocker & Yale, Inc.; *U.S. Public*, pg. 1518

IMAGEMAKER PLUS—Signmaker Film—Fasson Films; *U.S. Public*, pg. 153

IMAGEMARK—Envelopes—Westvaco Corporation; *U.S. Public*, pg. 1762

IMAGEMASTER—Video Cassettes—Eastman Kodak Company; *U.S. Public*, pg. 550

IMAGEMATE—Photographic Paper & Chemicals for Micrographics Applications—Eastman Kodak Company; *U.S. Public*, pg. 550

IMAGEPLUS—Computer Product—International Business Machines Corporation; *U.S. Public*, pg. 895

IMAGEPRO—LCD Projector—Dukane Corporation; *U.S. Private*, pg. 345

IMAGERY SERIES—Ultra Premium Limited Production Wines—Glen Ellen Winery; *U.S. Private*, pg. 455

IMAGES—Costume Jewelry—American Greetings Corporation; *U.S. Public*, pg. 77

IMAGES—Glazed Ceramic Tile—Porcelanite, Inc.; *Int'l*, pg. 573

IMAGESOURCE—Copiers—Danka Office Imaging; *U.S. Public*, pg. 551

IMAGESTAR—Microfilm Readers, Reader-Printers—Eastman Kodak Company; *U.S. Public*, pg. 550

IMAGEWATCH—NONE—Eastman Kodak Company; *U.S. Public*, pg. 550

IMAGEXPRESS—Software—CSC Financial Services Group; *U.S. Public*, pg. 422

IMAGIMAKER SERIES—NONE—Broderbund Software, Inc.; *U.S. Public*, pg. 258

IMAGINATION MADE POSSIBLE—Computer Product—International Business Machines Corporation; *U.S. Public*, pg. 895

IMAGINATIONS—Particleboard—Georgia-Pacific Corporation; *U.S. Public*, pg. 735

IMAGINE 128—Product Name—Number Nine Visual Technology; *U.S. Public*, pg. 1206

IMAGING INSIGHTS—Publications in the Field of Diagnostic Imaging—Mallinckrodt Inc.; *U.S. Public*, pg. 1039

IMAGIX—NONE—Polaroid Corporation; *U.S. Public*, pg. 1313

IMAGOTORE—Still Store System—Chyron Corp.; *Int'l*, pg. 1372

IMARI—Fragrance—Avon Products, Inc.; *U.S. Public*, pg. 155

IMATION—NONE—Taylor Impression, Inc.; *U.S. Private*, pg. 1070

IMATRA STEEL—NONE—Metra Corporation; *Int'l*, pg. 862

IMATRACH—Medico-Surgical Tubes & Medico-Surgical Tube Appliances—Mallinckrodt Inc.; *U.S. Public*, pg. 1039

IMAX—NONE—Imax Corporation; *Int'l*, pg. 661

IMAX DOME—NONE—Imax Corporation; *Int'l*, pg. 661

IMAX HD—NONE—Imax Corporation; *Int'l*, pg. 661

IMAX MAGIC CARPET—NONE—Imax Corporation; *Int'l*, pg. 661

IMAX RIDEFILM—NONE—Imax Corporation; *Int'l*, pg. 661

IMAX SIMULATOR RIDE—NONE—Imax Corporation; *Int'l*, pg. 661

IMAX 3D—NONE—Imax Corporation; *Int'l*, pg. 661

IMDOC—Item Processing—SLM Holding Corp.; *U.S. Public*, pg. 1419

IMDUR—Nitrate Preparation Used for Angina Pectoris—Astra AB; *Int'l*, pg. 93

IMDUR—Oral Nitrate Drug for Treatment of Angina Pectoris—Schering-Plough Corporation; *U.S. Public*, pg. 1438

IMEDEEN—Dietary Supplement—Novo Nordisk A/S; *Int'l*, pg. 987

IMEX II—NONE—SunGard Data Systems Inc.; *U.S. Public*, pg. 1534

IMICURE—Epoxy Curatives—Air Products and Chemicals, Inc.; *U.S. Public*, pg. 30

IMIDEZE—Aromatic Polyimide—Phelps Dodge Magnet Wire Co.; *U.S. Public*, pg. 1286

IMIGRAN—Drug to Treat Migraine Headaches—Glaxo Wellcome plc; *Int'l*, pg. 552

IMITATION BACON BITS—NONE—The Quaker Oats Company; *U.S. Public*, pg. 1347

IMITATION CHEESE—NONE—The Quaker Oats Company; *U.S. Public*, pg. 1347

IMITATION HAM BITS—NONE—The Quaker Oats Company; *U.S. Public*, pg. 1347

IMITREX—Anti-Migraine—Glaxo Wellcome Inc.; *Int'l*, pg. 552

IMMAC—Depilatories & Body Care—Reckitt & Colman plc; *Int'l*, pg. 1089

IMMEDIATE RESPONSE CLAIMS SERVICE—Progressive Toll-Free, 24 Hour Claims Reporting Service—The Progressive Corporation; *U.S. Public*, pg. 1334

IMMERSIBLE-CX—Ultrafilter Unit—Millipore Corporation; *U.S. Public*, pg. 1112

IMMOBILON—Membrane Filter—Millipore Corporation; *U.S. Public*, pg. 1112

IMMUNAGE—Skin Care—Elizabeth Arden Company; *Int'l*, pg. 1435

IMMUNEX CRP—Latex Slide Test—Wampole Laboratories; *U.S. Public*, pg. 310

IMMUNOCARD—Rapid, Color Change Tests for Infectious Disease—Meridian Diagnostics, Inc.; *U.S. Public*, pg. 1094

IMMUNOCOUNT—Reagents—Ortho Clinical Diagnostic Systems Inc.; *U.S. Public*, pg. 929

IMMUNODETECTION—Technology to Perform Immunoassays in a Flow-Thru Column Format—PerSeptive Biosystems, Inc.; *U.S. Public*, pg. 1279

IMMUNODYNE—Membranes—Pall Corporation; *U.S. Public*, pg. 1253

IMMUNOFIT—Computer Program—Beckman Instruments, Inc.; *U.S. Public*, pg. 199

IMMUNOPHENOTYPING—Reagents—Ortho Clinical Diagnostic Systems Inc.; *U.S. Public*, pg. 929

IMODIUM—Pharmaceutical—Janssen Pharmaceutica, Inc.; *U.S. Public*, pg. 928

IMODIUM—Antidiarrheal Agent—Johnson & Johnson; *U.S. Public*, pg. 927

IMODIUM—Proprietary Drugs—McNeil Consumer Products Company; *U.S. Public*, pg. 928

IMODIUM A-D—Antidiarrheal Agent—Johnson & Johnson; *U.S. Public*, pg. 927

IMOGAM RABIES—Rabies Immune Globulin-Human—Connaught Laboratories, Inc.; *Int'l*, pg. 1109

IMOSAKUKUN—Chocolate Snacks—Meiji Seika Kaisha, Ltd.; *Int'l*, pg. 855

IMOVAX RABIES—Rabies Vaccine—Connaught Laboratories, Inc.; *Int'l*, pg. 1109

IMOVAX RABIES ID—Rabies Vaccine-Pre-Exposure—Connaught Laboratories, Inc.; *Int'l*, pg. 1109

IMPAC—Standard Conveyor Controllers—Dorner Manufacturing Corp.; *U.S. Private*, pg. 340

IMPACT—Educational Services—Alcon Laboratories, Inc.; *U.S. Public*, pg. 916

IMPACT—NONE—Baldwin Technology Company, Inc.; *U.S. Public*, pg. 169

IMPACT—Insecticides: Ant & Roach Bait Stations—The Clorox Company; *U.S. Public*, pg. 386

IMPACT—Business Telephone System—Comdial Corporation; *U.S. Public*, pg. 407

IMPACT—Service Mark for Care Unit Program Manuals—Comprehensive Care Corporation; *U.S. Public*, pg. 419

IMPACT—Machine Warewashing Detergent—Ecolab Inc.; *U.S. Public*, pg. 562

IMPACT—Display Merchandise for Supermarkets—Hussmann Corp.; *U.S. Public*, pg. 1766

IMPACT—Industrial Laser System—Lumonics Inc.; *Int'l*, pg. 1314

IMPACT—NONE—Minerallac Co.; *U.S. Private*, pg. 750

IMPACT—Promotional Supermarket Sampling & Demonstrations—News America Marketing; *Int'l*, pg. 925

IMPACT—Tube Feeding—Novartis Nutrition Corporation; *Int'l*, pg. 974

IMPACT BY HICKOK—NONE—Tandy Brands Accessories, Inc.; *U.S. Public*, pg. 1560

IMPACT MACHINING—Controlled Flow Techniques in Cold Forming—Verson Division; *U.S. Public*, pg. 48

IMPACT PLUS—Co-operative Advertising Program—Eastman Kodak Company; *U.S. Public*, pg. 550

IMPACT RUBELLA—Rubella Anitbody Detector—Wampole Laboratories; *U.S. Public*, pg. 310

IMPACT TILE—Rubber Tiles—Dodge Regupol, Inc.; *U.S. Private*, pg. 337

IMPACTMASTER—Crusher—Svedala Industries-Universal Engineering; *Int'l*, pg. 1326

IMPACTMASTER II—Crusher—Svedala Industries-Universal Engineering; *Int'l*, pg. 1326

IMPACTOR—Indoor Illuminated Sign Series—American Sign & Marketing Services, Inc.; *U.S. Public*, pg. 1309

IMPACTWALL 3000—Hurricane Impact Aluminium Systems—Arch Aluminium & Glass L.C.; *U.S. Public*, pg. 79

IMPACTWRITER—Business Product—International Business Machines Corporation; *U.S. Public*, pg. 895

IMPAK—Printed Graphic Art—Weyerhaeuser Company; *U.S. Public*, pg. 1764

IMPAQ—Real Time Enterprise Wide Infomation Distribution System—Quintus Corporation; *U.S. Private*, pg. 901

Brand Name Index

IMPCO—Carburetors, Regulators, Fuel Lock-Offs, Adapters, FuelControl Processors,—IMPCO AirSensors Technologies; *U.S. Public*, pg. 34

IMPCO—Pulp Processing Machinery—Silver-Weibull; *U.S. Public*, pg. 705

IMPEDE—Disposable Fabric—Lakeland Industries, Inc.; *U.S. Public*, pg. 975

IMPERIAL—Felt—American Felt & Filter; *U.S. Private*, pg. 54

IMPERIAL—NONE—Barton Brands, Ltd.; *U.S. Public*, pg. 300

IMPERIAL—Blended Whiskey—Barton Incorporated; *U.S. Public*, pg. 300

IMPERIAL—Sporting Goods—Brunswick Bowling & Billiards Corp.; *U.S. Public*, pg. 265

IMPERIAL—Margarine/Spread—Chesebrough-Pond's; *Int'l*, pg. 1436

IMPERIAL—Yo-Yo—Duncan Toys Company; *U.S. Private*, pg. 409

IMPERIAL—Gasoline—Exxon Corporation; *U.S. Public*, pg. 601

IMPERIAL—Clothing Separates for Men—Haggar Corporation; *U.S. Public*, pg. 774

IMPERIAL—Tobacco Products—Hanson PLC; *Int'l*, pg. 592

IMPERIAL—Hats—HATCO, Inc.; *U.S. Private*, pg. 510

IMPERIAL—Recreational Vehicle—Holiday Rambler; *U.S. Public*, pg. 1123

IMPERIAL—Cutlery—Imperial Schrade Corp.; *U.S. Private*, pg. 559

IMPERIAL—Aluminum Sliding Windows—International Aluminum Corporation; *U.S. Public*, pg. 894

IMPERIAL—Margarine—Lever Brothers Co.; *Int'l*, pg. 1435

IMPERIAL—Cooking Utensils—Regal Ware, Inc.; *U.S. Private*, pg. 917

IMPERIAL—Van Conversions—Starcraft Corporation; *U.S. Public*, pg. 1510

IMPERIAL—Diamond Coated Abrasives, Automotive Glaze—3M; *U.S. Public*, pg. 1604

IMPERIAL—Margarine—Unilever Plc; *Int'l*, pg. 1433

IMPERIAL & DESIGN—NONE—Regal Ware, Inc.; *U.S. Private*, pg. 917

IMPERIAL CHERRIES—Candy—Brach & Brock Confections Inc.; *U.S. Private*, pg. 163

IMPERIAL COMFORT—Mattress & Box Spring Sets—Kingsdown, Inc.; *U.S. Private*, pg. 622

IMPERIAL DIAMOND—Cookware—Regal Ware, Inc.; *U.S. Private*, pg. 917

IMPERIAL EASTMAN—Hose, Fittings, Couplings—Mark IV Industries Inc.; *U.S. Public*, pg. 1044

IMPERIAL FALCON—Tires—Bridgestone/Firestone, Inc.; *Int'l*, pg. 213

IMPERIAL GARDENS—Food Products—Rymer Foods Inc.; *U.S. Public*, pg. 1414

IMPERIAL GOLD—Paint—ICI Paints; *Int'l*, pg. 664

IMPERIAL HOLLY—Sugar—Imperial Holly Corporation; *U.S. Public*, pg. 872

IMPERIAL LEATHER—Soap & Toiletries—Cussons (U.K.) LTD.; *Int'l*, pg. 1024

IMPERIAL MEATS—NONE—Sara Lee Corporation; *U.S. Public*, pg. 1432

IMPERIAL SAMPAN—Food Products—Rymer Foods Inc.; *U.S. Public*, pg. 1414

IMPERIAL SUGAR COMPANY—NONE—Imperial Holly Corporation; *U.S. Public*, pg. 872

IMPERIAL TOUCH—Paint—ICI Paints; *Int'l*, pg. 664

IMPERIAL VELOUR—Broadloom—Couristan Inc.; *U.S. Private*, pg. 279

IMPERON—Textile Dye for Textile Printing—Hoechst Aktiengesellschaft; *Int'l*, pg. 624

IMPERSONATIONS—Greeting Cards—American Greetings Corporation; *U.S. Public*, pg. 77

IMPERVEX—Latex Gloss Enamel—Benjamin Moore & Co.; *U.S. Private*, pg. 133

IMPERVO—Solvent Enamels & Varnishes—Benjamin Moore & Co.; *U.S. Private*, pg. 133

IMPET—Liquid-Crystal Polyester—Hoechst Aktiengesellschaft; *Int'l*, pg. 624

IMPINGER—Conveyor Ovens—Lincoln Foodservice Products, Inc.; *Int'l*, pg. 188

IMPINJAIR—Liquid-Solids Separation Equipment—Komline-Sanderson Engineering Corp.; *U.S. Private*, pg. 631

IMPLEX—Acrylic Plastic—Rohm and Haas Company; *U.S. Public*, pg. 1403

IMPO—Perfume—Coop Switzerland; *Int'l*, pg. 329

IMPORT—Device—Medtronic, Inc.; *U.S. Public*, pg. 1082

IMPORT FOR SERVERS—NONE—BMC Software, Inc.; *U.S. Public*, pg. 162

IMPRENAL—Liquid Resin—Raschig GmbH; *U.S. Private*, pg. 827

IMPRESS—In-Mold Coating for Plastic—Ferro Corporation; *U.S. Public*, pg. 618

IMPRESS—Page Description Language—QMS, Inc.; *U.S. Public*, pg. 1346

IMPRESS—Shower Gel—SBS Products, Inc.; *U.S. Private*, pg. 955

IMPRESSIONS—Magazine—Miller Freeman Inc.; *Int'l*, pg. 1443

IMPRESSIONS—Premium Wiring Devices—Pass & Seymour/Legrand; *Int'l*, pg. 806

IMPRESSIONS—Envelopes—Westvaco Corporation; *U.S. Public*, pg. 1762

IMPREZA—Automobile—Subaru of America, Inc.; *Int'l*, pg. 523

IMPRINT—Dental Impression Material—3M; *U.S. Public*, pg. 1604

IMPROMPTU—NONE—Cognos Corp.; *Int'l*, pg. 306

IMPROMPTU—Shelf-Stable Entrees—Kraft Foods, Inc.; *U.S. Public*, pg. 1287

IMPROV—Seating—Haworth, Inc.; *U.S. Private*, pg. 511

IMPROVE YOUR COURSE FISHING—Fishing Magazine—EMAP Pursuit Publishing; *Int'l*, pg. 451

IMPROVE YOUR SEA ANGLING—Fishing Magazine—EMAP Pursuit Publishing; *Int'l*, pg. 451

IMPROVED DRUG ENTITIES—Patented Drug Development—KV Pharmaceutical Company; *U.S. Public*, pg. 941

IMPROVED LIVING—Women's Fashions & Home Furnishings Merchandise—Blair Corporation; *U.S. Public*, pg. 236

IMPROVEMENTS—Do it Yourself Home Improvement Catalog—Hanover Direct, Inc.; *U.S. Public*, pg. 782

IMPULSE—Source Tagging—Checkpoint Systems Inc.; *U.S. Public*, pg. 343

IMPULSE—Mall Stores—Circuit City Stores, Inc.; *U.S. Public*, pg. 374

IMPULSE—NONE—Insignia Systems, Inc.; *U.S. Public*, pg. 881

IMPULSE—Cordless Power Nailing System—Paslode; *U.S. Public*, pg. 867

IMPULSE—Camera—Polaroid Corporation; *U.S. Public*, pg. 1313

IMPULSE—Communication Equipment—Uniden America Corporation; *Int'l*, pg. 1433

IMPULSE "DEVOTION"—Body Spray Fragrances—Chesebrough-Pond's USA Co.; *Int'l*, pg. 1435

IMPULSE BODY SPRAY "SO HOT"—Body Spray Fragrance—Chesebrough-Pond's USA Co.; *Int'l*, pg. 1435

IMPULSE IM-250—Airless Cordless Nailer—Illinois Tool Works Inc.; *U.S. Public*, pg. 865

IMPULSE 7000—Cable TV Addressable Set-Top Converters—Broadband Networks Group; *U.S. Public*, pg. 716

IMUDON—Immunologic Products—Kali-Chemie Aktiengesellschaft; *Int'l*, pg. 1278

IMUGARD—Transfusion Products—Terumo Medical Corporation; *Int'l*, pg. 1376

IMURAN—Prescription Arthritis Treatment—Glaxo Wellcome PLC; *Int'l*, pg. 553

IMURESP—NONE—Pfizer Inc.; *U.S. Public*, pg. 1281

IMUS IN THE MORNING—Talk Radio Program—Westwood One Entertainment; *U.S. Public*, pg. 1763

IMUS IN THE MORNING—Talk Show—Westwood One, Inc.; *U.S. Public*, pg. 1763

IMUTABS—Vitamins—Health Products Corporation; *U.S. Private*, pg. 514

IN CONCERT—Rock Music Radio Program—Westwood One Entertainment; *U.S. Public*, pg. 1763

IN CONCERT—Rock Show—Westwood One, Inc.; *U.S. Public*, pg. 1763

IN CONTROL—Hosiery & Related Apparel—Mayer/Berkshire Corporation; *U.S. Private*, pg. 717

IN CONTROL—Girdles—Warner's; *U.S. Public*, pg. 1738

IN FOCUS SYSTEMS—NONE—In Focus Systems, Inc.; *U.S. Public*, pg. 873

IN HOUSE—Newsletter—The Mead Corporation; *U.S. Public*, pg. 1074

IN PLANT REPRODUCTIONS & ELECTRONIC PUBLISHING—Magazine—North American Publishing Company; *U.S. Private*, pg. 803

IN SHORT—Women's Clothing—Niches, Inc.; *U.S. Public*, pg. 1181

IN SIGHT IT MUST BE RIGHT—Restaurants—Consolidated Products, Inc.; *U.S. Public*, pg. 436

IN SIGHT IT MUST BE RIGHT—Restaurants—Steak 'n Shake, Inc.; *U.S. Public*, pg. 437

IN-SINK-ERATOR—Private Label Appliances—Emerson Electric Co.; *U.S. Public*, pg. 572

IN-SITE—Subcutaneous Infusion System—Inamed Corporation; *U.S. Public*, pg. 873

IN-SOURCE—Electronic CVD Units—Applied Materials, Inc.; *U.S. Public*, pg. 123

IN THE 1ST DEGREE—NONE—Broderbund Software, Inc.; *U.S. Public*, pg. 258

IN THE GARDEN BY FRANK'S—NONE—General Host Corporation; *U.S. Public*, pg. 715

IN THE MARKETPLACE—News Program—Westwood One, Inc.; *U.S. Public*, pg. 1763

IN THE WIND—Magazine—Paisano Publications, Inc.; *U.S. Private*, pg. 834

IN THE ZONE—Music Radio Program—Westwood One Entertainment; *U.S. Public*, pg. 1763

IN THE ZONE—Alternative Rock Program—Westwood One, Inc.; *U.S. Public*, pg. 1763

IN TOUCH—Greeting Cards—American Greetings Corporation; *U.S. Public*, pg. 77

IN VISION—GVI Laser Application Scr ting Tool—InterVoice, Inc.; *U.S. Public*, pg. 910

INACOMP—Computer Centers—Inacom Corp.; *U.S. Public*, pg. 873

INAMEL—Enamelling Steel—Inland Steel Industries, Inc.; *U.S. Public*, pg. 879

INAMORI JEWELRY—Gemstone Who esale—Kyocera International, Inc.; *Int'l*, pg. 775

INAPSINE—Pharmaceutical—Janssen Pharmaceutica, Inc.; *U.S. Public*, pg. 928

INBOARD—Electronic Instrument—Intel Corporation; *U.S. Public*, pg. 886

INCENTIVE—Business Publication—Bill Communications, Inc.; *Int'l*, pg. 1446

INCHEQUE—Internal Steam Indicator Sheets—3M; *U.S. Public*, pg. 1604

INCINOMITE—Indus. Heating Equip.—Midco International Inc.; *U.S. Private*, pg. 744

INCITE—Multi-Media Products—InteCom; *Int'l*, pg. 794

INCO—Nickel Alloys—Inco Alloys International, Inc.; *Int'l*, pg. 672

INCO—Electro Nickel—Inco Limited; *Int'l*, pg. 672

INCO—Nickel Pellets—International Nickel, Inc.; *Int'l*, pg. 672

INCO R-ROUNDS—Electrolytic Nickel—International Nickel, Inc.; *Int'l*, pg. 672

INCO S-ROUNDS—Electrolytic Nickel—International Nickel, Inc.; *Int'l*, pg. 672

INCO UTILITY—Nickel Shot—International Nickel, Inc.; *Int'l*, pg. 672

INCO-WELD—Welding Electrodes—Inco Alloys International, Inc.; *Int'l*, pg. 672

INCOCLAD—Clad Metal Alloys—Inco Limited; *Int'l*, pg. 672

INCOGNITO—Perfume—Cover Girl Cosmetics; *U.S. Public*, pg. 1330

INCOLOY—Nickel-Iron-Chromium Alloys—Inco Alloys International, Inc.; *Int'l*, pg. 672

INCOLOY—Alloy—Inco Limited; *Int'l*, pg. 672

INCOMBUSTIBLE MICROLITE—Insulation—Johns Manville Corporation; *U.S. Public*, pg. 927

INCOMET—Nickel—Inco Limited; *Int'l*, pg. 672

INCONEL—Nickel-Chromium-Iron Alloys—Inco Alloys International, Inc.; *Int'l*, pg. 672

INCONEL—Alloy—Inco Limited; *Int'l*, pg. 672

INCONTINENCE—Men's Incontinent Brief/Women's Incontinent Panty—Camp Healthcare; *Int'l*, pg. 1425

INCOR—NONE—Dale Industries Inc.; *U.S. Private*, pg. 308

INCORP—Computerized Research Services—The Mead Corporation; *U.S. Public*, pg. 1074

INCOS—Mass Spectrometer—Finnigan Corporation; *U.S. Public*, pg. 1591

INCOTE—Powder Coatings for Glass Reinforced Plastic Substrates—Morton International Inc.; *U.S. Public*, pg. 1134

INCREDIBLE CRASH DUMMIES—Action Figures—Tyco Toys, Inc.; *U.S. Public*, pg. 1058

INCREDIBLE UNIVERSE—Consumer Electronics & Computer Stores—Tandy Corporation; *U.S. Public*, pg. 1560

INCREMENTAL POWER—Amplification System—Altec Lansing Corp.; *U.S. Private*, pg. 479

INCRON—NONE—Lawter International, Inc.; *U.S. Public*, pg. 980

INCUT—Free-Machining Steels—Inland Steel Industries, Inc.; *U.S. Public*, pg. 879

INCUTEMP—Medical Skin Temperature Sensors—Mallinckrodt Inc.; *U.S. Public*, pg. 1039

INCUTROL—Temperature Regulator—Hach Company; *U.S. Public*, pg. 773

INDALEX—Aluminum—Caradon Plc; *Int'l*, pg. 266

INDANTHREN—Dyes—BASF AG; *Int'l*, pg. 103

INDANTHREN—Textile—Hoechst Aktiengesellschaft; *Int'l*, pg. 624

INDAR—Agricultural Fungicide—Rohm and Haas Company; *U.S. Public*, pg. 1403

INDENTRON—Hardness Tester—NewAge Industries Inc.; *U.S. Private*, pg. 796

INDENTRON—Hardness Tester—Newage Industries Inc., Testing Instruments Group; *U.S. Private*, pg. 796

INDEO—Software Technology—Intel Corporation; *U.S. Public*, pg. 886

INDEPENDENCE—NONE—Amerimark Inc.; *U.S. Public*, pg. 1237

INDEPENDENCE—Bond Paper—The Mead Corporation; *U.S. Public*, pg. 1074

INDEPENDENCE SERIES—Business Product—International Business Machines Corporation; *U.S. Public*, pg. 895

INDEPENDENCE SHANGLE—NONE—CertainTeed Corporation; *Int'l*, pg. 1170

INDEPENDENT STYLE—Women's Designer Separates—Paul Harris Stores, Inc.; *U.S. Public*, pg. 792

INDERAL—Pharmaceutical—Zeneca Group Plc; *Int'l*, pg. 1524

INDERAL FAMILY—Propranolol - Treatment Of Hypertension & Angina, Prevents Migraines—American Home Products Corporation; *U.S. Public*, pg. 79

INDERAL LA—Beta Blocking Agent—Wyeth-Ayerst Laboratories, Inc.; *U.S. Public*, pg. 80

INDERIDE LA—Antihypertensive Agent—Wyeth-Ayerst Laboratories, Inc.; *U.S. Public*, pg. 80

INDESIT—NONE—Merloni Elettrodomestici S.P.A.; *Int'l*, pg. 860

INDEX—Industrial Excimer—Lumonics Inc.; *Int'l*, pg. 1314

INDEXICON—Automated Indexing Software for Personal Computers—Innovex, Inc.; *U.S. Public*, pg. 880

INDEXOMATIC—NONE—Gilman; *Int'l*, pg. 1389

INDEXTRON—Cathode Ray Tubes for Color Video Projectors & TV—Sony Electronics; *Int'l*, pg. 1281

INDI-PEP—Hot Sauce—Trappey's Fine Foods, Inc.; *U.S. Private*, pg. 105

INDIA—Sharpening Stones—Norton Company; *Int'l*, pg. 1173

INDIA PALE ALE—Beer—Genesee Corporation; *U.S. Public*, pg. 728

INDIAGE—Enzyme for Textile Industry—Cultor Ltd.; *Int'l*, pg. 349

INDIAN BRAND—Corn Chips—Borden, Inc.; *U.S. Private*, pg. 157

INDIAN HEAD—Corn Meal—Wilkins-Rogers Incorporated; *U.S. Private*, pg. 1176

INDIAN RIVER GOLD—NONE—EcoScience Corporation; *U.S. Public*, pg. 563

INDIAN SUMMER—Juice, Vinegar, Cider & Applesauce—Nakano Foods Inc.; *Int'l*, pg. 883

INDIAN TRAIL—Food Prods.—Dean Pickle & Specialty Products Co.; *U.S. Public*, pg. 490

INDIANA MANUFACTURERS DIRECTORY—Directory—Manufacturers' News, Inc.; *U.S. Private*, pg. 700

INDICATOR—Toothbrushes—Oral-B Laboratories; *U.S. Public*, pg. 743

INDICATORS—NONE—Philips Automotive Electronics; *Int'l*, pg. 1054

INDIGLO—Lighted Watch—Timex Corporation; *U.S. Private*, pg. 1088

INDIGO HILLS—NONE—E. & J. Gallo Winery; *U.S. Private*, pg. 438

INDIUM IN III—Cisternography Agent—Amersham Healthcare; *Int'l*, pg. 992

INDO-PERSIAN—Rugs—Couristan Inc.; *U.S. Private*, pg. 279

INDOCIN—Indomethacin—Merck & Co., Inc.; *U.S. Public*, pg. 1090

INDOOR GARDEN COLLECTION—NONE—Celebrity Incorporated; *U.S. Public*, pg. 319

INDOPOL—Polybutenes—Amoco Chemicals; *U.S. Public*, pg. 102

INDOPOL—Butylene Polymers—Amoco Corporation; *U.S. Public*, pg. 101

INDOSOL—Cellulose Fibers—Clariant International Ltd.; *Int'l*, pg. 624

INDOSOL SF—Cellulose Dyes—Novartis AG; *Int'l*, pg. 971

INDOX—Ethylene Oxide Gas Indicator Tape—3M; *U.S. Public*, pg. 1604

INDUCLOR—Calcium Hypochlorite Granules—PPG Industries, Inc.; *U.S. Public*, pg. 1245

INDUCTION ELECTROLOG—NONE—Western Atlas Logging Services; *U.S. Public*, pg. 1757

INDUCTION POWER LADLE—Induction Heated Steel Ladle—Inductotherm Corp.; *U.S. Private*, pg. 560

INDUCTO—Induction Heating & Melting Furnaces & Access.—Inductotherm Corp.; *U.S. Private*, pg. 560

INDUCTO-FLEX—Coil Insulation—Inductotherm Corp.; *U.S. Private*, pg. 560

INDUCTO-POUR—Automatic Metal Pouring System for Foundries—Inductotherm Corp.; *U.S. Private*, pg. 560

INDUCTOBACK—Refractories for Induction Furnaces—Inductotherm Corp.; *U.S. Private*, pg. 560

INDUCTOCAST—Refractories for Induction Furnaces—Inductotherm Corp.; *U.S. Private*, pg. 560

INDUCTOGROG—Refractories for Induction Furnaces—Inductotherm Corp.; *U.S. Private*, pg. 560

INDUCTOMAG—Refractories for Induction Furnaces—Inductotherm Corp.; *U.S. Private*, pg. 560

INDUCTOPAK—Refractories for Induction Furnaces—Inductotherm Corp.; *U.S. Private*, pg. 560

INDUCTORAM—Refractories for Induction Furnaces—Inductotherm Corp.; *U.S. Private*, pg. 560

INDUCTOSEAL—Refractories for Induction Furnaces—Inductotherm Corp.; *U.S. Private*, pg. 560

INDUCTOSIL—Refractories for Induction Furnaces—Inductotherm Corp.; *U.S. Private*, pg. 560

INDUCTOSYN—NONE—Farrand Controls; *U.S. Private*, pg. 951

INDUCTOSYN—Transducers & Electronics—Ruhle Companies, Inc.; *U.S. Private*, pg. 950

INDUCTRON—Solid State Power Supply—Tocco, Inc.; *U.S. Public*, pg. 1259

INDULIN—Lignin Chemicals—Westvaco Corporation; *U.S. Public*, pg. 1762

INDUPLAST—NONE—ETEX; *Int'l*, pg. 430

INDURA—Catheter for Drug Pump—Medtronic, Inc.; *U.S. Public*, pg. 1082

INDUSTRAPANEL—Particleboard—Georgia-Pacific Corporation; *U.S. Public*, pg. 735

INDUSTRAVAC—Indus. Vacuum Cleaner—The Spencer Turbine Co.; *U.S. Private*, pg. 1025

INDUSTRELEK—Advisory Service on Electrotechnological Based Solutions in Industry—Eskom; *Int'l*, pg. 459

INDUSTREX—Pattern Glass—AFG Industries, Inc.; *Int'l*, pg. 84

INDUSTREX—X-ray Film, Paper, Chemicals, Processing Equipment—Eastman Kodak Company; *U.S. Public*, pg. 550

INDUSTRIAL ADHESIVES—Adhesives—Burmah Castrol plc; *Int'l*, pg. 234

INDUSTRIAL BOAT & TRAILER RIB—Tires—Bridgestone/Firestone, Inc.; *Int'l*, pg. 213

INDUSTRIAL CONTROLSTATION—NONE—Nematron Corp.; *U.S. Private*, pg. 791

INDUSTRIAL DISTRIBUTION—Magazine for Professionals in General-Line & Specialized Distribution Firms—Reed Elsevier Business Information; *Int'l*, pg. 1095

INDUSTRIAL ENCODER DIVISION—Encoders—BEI Sensors and Systems Company; *U.S. Public*, pg. 160

INDUSTRIAL INTERFACES—NONE—Molex Incorporated; *U.S. Public*, pg. 1121

INDUSTRIAL MAINTENANCE & PLANT OPERATION—News Magazine—Reed Elsevier Business Information; *Int'l*, pg. 1095

INDUSTRIAL PAINT & POWDER—Magazine Focusing on Paint & Powder Coating Technologies—Reed Elsevier Business Information; *Int'l*, pg. 1095

INDUSTRIAL PRO—Custom Design Material Handling Products—Cannon Equipment; *Int'l*, pg. 646

INDUSTRIAL PRODUCT BULLETIN—Trade Publication—Gordon Publications, Inc.; *Int'l*, pg. 1096

INDUSTRIAL PRODUCT BULLETIN—New-Product Tabloid for the Processing & Metalworking Industries—Reed Elsevier Business Information; *Int'l*, pg. 1095

INDUSTRIAL SAFETY & HYGIENE NEWS—Tabloid Publication Directed to Heavy Industry for Safety Professionals—Reed Elsevier Business Information; *Int'l*, pg. 1095

INDUSTRIAL SPECIAL—Tires—Bridgestone/Firestone, Inc.; *Int'l*, pg. 213

INDUSTRIAL STRENGTH SPAGHETTI SAUCE—Spaghetti Sauce—Newman's Own, Inc.; *U.S. Private*, pg. 797

INDUSTRIAL WERKSTATION—NONE—Nematron Corp.; *U.S. Private*, pg. 791

INDUSTRIELLE DE TUILES—Clay Roofing Tiles—Poliet; *Int'l*, pg. 1177

INDUSTRY WEEK—Periodical—Penton Publishing, Inc.; *U.S. Public*, pg. 1306

INDY—Eyewear—Aearo Company; *U.S. Private*, pg. 23

INDY—NONE—Juno Lighting, Inc.; *U.S. Public*, pg. 935

INDY 500—Long-Wear Soling Compound—The Goodyear Tire & Rubber Company; *U.S. Public*, pg. 752

INEBPATCH 90—Patching Compound—DAP Inc.; *Int'l*, pg. 1486

INERGEN—Clean Extinguishing Agent—Ansul Incorporated; *U.S. Public*, pg. 1648

INERTIA DYNAMICS—Drives & Motion Control Group House Mark—Rockwell International Corporation; *U.S. Public*, pg. 1397

INESTRUM—Nutritional Aid to Dairy Reproductivity—DuCoa L.P.; *U.S. Private*, pg. 301

INFACT—NONE—SunGard Data Systems Inc.; *U.S. Public*, pg. 1534

INFANRIX—NONE—SmithKline Beecham Corporation; *Int'l*, pg. 1264

INFANT STAR—Ventilator—Nellcor Puritan Bennett Incorporated; *U.S. Public*, pg. 1039

INFANTRY—CPR Training Manikins—Vital Signs, Inc.; *U.S. Public*, pg. 1723

INFASURF—Lung Surfactant—Forest Laboratories, Inc.; *U.S. Public*, pg. 670

INFERGEN—NONE—Amgen Inc.; *U.S. Public*, pg. 100

INFI 90—Distributed Control System—Bailey Controls Company; *Int'l*, pg. 654

INFINITE BLESSINGS—Greeting Cards—American Greetings Corporation; *U.S. Public*, pg. 77

INFINITI—NONE—Cordis, a Johnson & Johnson Company; *U.S. Public*, pg. 928

INFINITI—Auto—Loeber Motors, Inc.; *U.S. Private*, pg. 672

INFINITI—Automobile—Nissan Motor Corporation in U.S.A.; *Int'l*, pg. 945

INFINITI Q45—Car—Nissan Motor Co., Ltd.; *Int'l*, pg. 943

INFINITIF—Women's Fragrance—Coty Inc.; *Int'l*, pg. 185

INFINITY—Loud Speakers—Harman International Industries, Inc.; *U.S. Public*, pg. 787

INFINITY—Fragrance—Jean Philippe Fragrances, Inc.; *U.S. Public*, pg. 924

Brand Name Index

INFINITY—Cameras—Olympus Optical Co., Ltd.; *Int'l*, pg. 1004

INFINITY—Premium Standard & Economy Recycled Grade Single Part Stock Computer Paper—Shade/Allied, Inc.; *U.S. Public*, pg. 89

INFINITY—Ambulatory Care Management Software—US SerVis; *U.S. Public*, pg. 1687

INFINITY—Printing Ink—Van Son Holland Ink Corp. of America; *U.S. Private*, pg. 1133

INFINITY CAMERAS—35mm Cameras—Olympus America Inc.; *Int'l*, pg. 1005

INFINITY 90—Open System Computer System—Encore Computer Corporation; *U.S. Public*, pg. 580

INFINITY R/T—Real Time Computer System—Encore Computer Corporation; *U.S. Public*, pg. 580

INFINITY S/P—Computer System—Encore Computer Corporation; *U.S. Public*, pg. 580

INFINITY TWIST—Dust Mops—Golden Star Inc.; *U.S. Private*, pg. 460

INFLIGHT DUTY FREE SHOPS—On-Board Duty Free Shops (Airlines)—Duty Free International, Inc.; *Int'l*, pg. 103

INFLUENCE—Floor Coverings—Domco Inc.; *Int'l*, pg. 415

INFLUENCE GLOSS—Coated Paper—Champion International Corp.; *U.S. Public*, pg. 333

INFLUENCE GRAVURE—Coated Paper—Champion International Corp.; *U.S. Public*, pg. 333

INFLUENCE MATTE—Coated Paper—Champion International Corp.; *U.S. Public*, pg. 333

INFO—Business Correspondence Paper—The Mead Corporation; *U.S. Public*, pg. 1074

INFO-LINK—Software Program for Computer Output Microfilmers—Eastman Kodak Company; *U.S. Public*, pg. 550

INFO-LINK—Magazine—Reed Business Information Pty. Limited; *Int'l*, pg. 1094

INFO-LINK HOSPITALITY—Magazine—Reed Business Information Pty. Limited; *Int'l*, pg. 1094

INFO-LINK SE ASIA—Magazine—Reed Business Information Pty. Limited; *Int'l*, pg. 1094

INFO-LINK THE BOOK—Directory—Reed Business Information Pty. Limited; *Int'l*, pg. 1094

INFO-LINK THE BOOK CD—Directory—Reed Business Information Pty. Limited; *Int'l*, pg. 1094

INFO/MDR—Telecommunications Management System—Moscom Corporation; *U.S. Public*, pg. 1136

INFO-TEL—Product Information Service to Customers—Eastman Kodak Company; *U.S. Public*, pg. 550

INFO 24—Enhanced Services Software—Tandem Computers Inc.; *U.S. Public*, pg. 417

INFOBASE—Enhancement Services—Acxiom Corporation; *U.S. Public*, pg. 18

INFOCAPTURE—Microfilm—Eastman Kodak Company; *U.S. Public*, pg. 550

INFOCIPHER—Data Receiver for Personal Computers—Satellite Data Networks; *U.S. Public*, pg. 716

INFOCOM—Story-Telling Games—Activision; *U.S. Public*, pg. 17

INFOCOM—Digital Information Exchange System—Dictaphone Corp.; *U.S. Private*, pg. 1045

INFOCRAFTER—Computer Product—International Business Machines Corporation; *U.S. Public*, pg. 895

INFOEXPLORER—Computer Product—International Business Machines Corporation; *U.S. Public*, pg. 895

INFOGRAMES ENTERTAINMENT—NONE—CLT-UFA; *Int'l*, pg. 561

INFOIMAGE—Imaging System—Unisys Corporation; *U.S. Public*, pg. 1671

INFOLINK—Health Information—Hooper Holmes Corporation; *U.S. Public*, pg. 835

INFOMAIL—Messaging Software for Voice & Fax Mail—Digital Sound Corporation; *U.S. Public*, pg. 508

INFOMAIL EXPRESS—Messaging Software for Voice, Fax & E-Mail—Digital Sound Corporation; *U.S. Public*, pg. 508

INFOMAIL EXPRESS 2.1—Messaging Software for Voice, Fax & E-Mail with Web Access to all Messages—Digital Sound Corporation; *U.S. Public*, pg. 508

INFOMASTER—Information Service—AT&T Strategy & New Service Innovations; *U.S. Public*, pg. 11

INFOMEDIA—Luxembourg—CLT-UFA; *Int'l*, pg. 561

INFORMATION & TECHNOLOGY TRANSFER DATABASE—Full-Text Documents Retrieval Covering Multi-Discipline Topics & Subjects—International Research & Evaluation; *U.S. Private*, pg. 571

INFORMATION ASSISTANT—Computer Product—International Business Machines Corporation; *U.S. Public*, pg. 895

INFORMATION PLEASE ALMANACS—Reference Work—INSO Corporation; *U.S. Public*, pg. 882

INFORMATION RETRIEVAL SYMBOL—Computer Product—International Business Machines Corporation; *U.S. Public*, pg. 895

INFORMATION WAREHOUSE—Computer Product—International Business Machines Corporation; *U.S. Public*, pg. 895

INFORMATIONWEEK—Magazine—CMP Media, Inc.; *U.S. Public*, pg. 279

INFORMATIQUES—Magazine—CMP Media, Inc.; *U.S. Public*, pg. 279

THE INFORMER—Service Indicator—Donaldson Company, Inc.; *U.S. Public*, pg. 517

INFORMIX—Company Name—Informix Software; *U.S. Public*, pg. 876

INFORMIX-DYNAMIC SCALABLE ARCHITECTURE—Database Architecture—Informix Software; *U.S. Public*, pg. 876

INFORMIX-4GL—Fourth Generation Programming Language—Informix Software; *U.S. Public*, pg. 876

INFORMIX-NEW ERA—Graphical, Object-Oriented Development Environmental—Informix Software; *U.S. Public*, pg. 876

INFORMIX-ONLINE—OLTP Server—Informix Software; *U.S. Public*, pg. 876

INFORMIX-ONLINE DYNAMIC SERVER—Database Server—Informix Software; *U.S. Public*, pg. 876

INFORMIX-VIEW POINT—Software—Informix Software; *U.S. Public*, pg. 876

INFORMIX-VIEW POINT PRO—Software—Informix Software; *U.S. Public*, pg. 876

INFORUM—Technology Mart—AMC, Inc.; *U.S. Private*, pg. 6

INFOSCAN—Syndication Market Research—Information Resources, Inc.; *U.S. Public*, pg. 875

INFOSTAR—Communications Systems—Executone Information Systems, Inc.; *U.S. Public*, pg. 599

INFOTEX—Voice Processing Application—Octel Messaging Division; *U.S. Public*, pg. 1017

INFOTRAINER—Computer Product—International Business Machines Corporation; *U.S. Public*, pg. 895

INFOWAY—Electronic Pipeline Service—Tandem Computers Inc.; *U.S. Public*, pg. 417

INFOWINDOW—Computer Product—International Business Machines Corporation; *U.S. Public*, pg. 895

INFRA-REZ—Low Intensity Infra-red Heater—Thomas & Betts Reznor Division; *U.S. Public*, pg. 1598

INFRA-SPARGE—NONE—O.I. Corporation; *U.S. Public*, pg. 1208

INFRA-REDIATOR—Heater—Fisher Scientific Company; *U.S. Private*, pg. 658

INFRABAND—Infrared Bandpass Filters—Optical Coating Laboratory, Inc.; *U.S. Public*, pg. 1227

INFRADURA—Welding Lenses—Uvex Safety, Inc.; *Int'l*, pg. 132

INFRALARM—Infrared Intrusion Alarm—Barnes Engineering; *U.S. Public*, pg. 542

INFRANOR—Flood Light Fixtures—Sterner Lighting Systems Incorporated; *U.S. Private*, pg. 1042

INFRASCOPE—Thermal Micro Image—Barnes Engineering; *U.S. Public*, pg. 542

INFRASONICS—NONE—Nellcor Puritan Bennett Incorporated; *U.S. Public*, pg. 1039

INFRINGEMENT STUDY ICED BLENDED—NONE—Koo Koo Roo, Inc.; *U.S. Public*, pg. 966

INFUMORPH—Intravenous Preservative-free Morphine Sulfate Sterile Solution—Wyeth-Ayerst Laboratories, Inc.; *U.S. Public*, pg. 80

INFURNOX—Low Emission Burner Technology—John Zink Co.; *U.S. Private*, pg. 628

INFUSABLE—Disposable Pressure Infusor—Vital Signs, Inc.; *U.S. Public*, pg. 1723

INFUSE-A-CATH—NONE—Pfizer Inc.; *U.S. Public*, pg. 1281

INFUSE-A-PORT—NONE—Pfizer Inc.; *U.S. Public*, pg. 1281

INFUSIUM 23—Professional Hair Care Products—Bristol-Myers Squibb Company; *U.S. Public*, pg. 253

INGERSOLL—Lawn & Garden Tractors, Front Cut Mowers & Loader-Backhoe Tractors—Ingersoll Equipment Co., Inc.; *Int'l*, pg. 1129

INGERSOLL-DRESSER—Pumps—Dresser Industries, Inc.; *U.S. Public*, pg. 528

INGERSOLL-DRESSER PUMPS—NONE—Ingersoll-Rand Company; *U.S. Public*, pg. 876

INGERSOLL INTERNATIONAL—Custom Built Machine Tools & Complete Manufacturing Systems—Ingersoll International Inc.; *U.S. Private*, pg. 562

INGERSOLL-RAND—Pumps—Ingersoll-Dresser Pump Company; *U.S. Public*, pg. 529

INGERSOLL-RAND—Tools & Hoists—Tool & Hoist Division; *U.S. Public*, pg. 877

INGLENOOK—Wine—Canandaigua Wine Company Div.; *U.S. Public*, pg. 300

INGLES—Grocery Stores—Ingles Markets, Incorporated; *U.S. Public*, pg. 878

INGLIS—Major Appliances—Whirlpool Corporation; *U.S. Public*, pg. 1764

INGRAHAM—Clocks & Timers—Toastmaster, Inc.; *U.S. Public*, pg. 1619

INGRAM ALLIANCE—NONE—Ingram Micro Inc.; *U.S. Public*, pg. 878

INGRAM MICRO—Distributor of Microcomputer Products—Ingram Micro Inc.; *U.S. Public*, pg. 878

INGRID—Plastic Houseware & Horticulture Prods.—Ingrid Division of Lawnware; *U.S. Private*, pg. 654

INHALER COUNTER—Plastic Dial on Inhaler—The West Company, Incorporated; *U.S. Public*, pg. 1755

INHIBACE—Ace-Inhibitor, Antihypertensive—Roche Holding Ltd.; *Int'l*, pg. 1119

INHIBISOL SPRAY—Solvent Spray Cleaner—Wechco, Inc.; *U.S. Private*, pg. 1158

INHIBISOL SPRAY—Solvent Spray Cleaner—West Chemical Products, Inc.; *U.S. Private*, pg. 1158

INITARD—Product for Diabetes Care—Novo Nordisk A/S; *Int'l*, pg. 987

INITIALS—Catalog Sales of Personalized Gift Items Incl. Sterling, Leather & Apparel—Artistic Greetings, Inc.; *U.S. Public*, pg. 136

INJECT-ACRE BURNER—Forced Draft Industrial 881

INJECTA COLOR SYSTEM—Liquid Colorant for Plastic—Morton Automotive Coatings; *U.S. Public*, pg. 1135

INJECTED METAL ASSEMBLY—Liquid Metal Joining Equipment—Fisher Gauge Limited; *Int'l*, pg. 491

INK WELL—Printing Center—International Center for Entrepreneurial Development, Inc.; *U.S. Private*, pg. 568

INKA—Presswood Pallets—Inka Paletten GmbH; *Int'l*, pg. 678

INKJET PRINTER—Proprietary Software—Signtech USA, Ltd.; *U.S. Private*, pg. 999

INKLINGS—Stickers—Highlights for Children Inc.; *U.S. Private*, pg. 528

INKOGNITO—NONE—Polaroid Corporation; *U.S. Public*, pg. 1313

INKOVAR—Hydrocarbon Resin—Hercules Incorporated; *U.S. Public*, pg. 809

INKSOURCE FLUIDS—NONE—Videojet Systems International, Inc.; *Int'l*, pg. 545

INLAND AA & RA—Special Steels—Inland Steel Industries, Inc.; *U.S. Public*, pg. 879

INLAND VALLEY—Potato Products—Universal Foods Corporation; *U.S. Public*, pg. 1695

INLINER—Mixers—Lightnin Mixers; *U.S. Public*, pg. 726

INMARSAT—Satellite Communications—COMSAT Corporation; *U.S. Public*, pg. 424

INMETCO—NONE—Independent Metals; *U.S. Private*, pg. 559

INN MAID—Egg Noodles—Lancaster Colony Corporation; *U.S. Public*, pg. 976

INN MAID—Noodles—T. Marzetti Company; *U.S. Public*, pg. 977

INN TOUCH—Telephone System for Lodging & Hospitality Markets—Comdial Corporation; *U.S. Public*, pg. 407

INNER-SEAL—Oriented Strand Board—Louisiana Pacific Corporation; *U.S. Public*, pg. 1015

INNERSEAL—Weatherstripping—W.J. & Dennis Co.; *U.S. Private*, pg. 1144

INNERSHIELD—Electrode—The Lincoln Electric Company; *U.S. Public*, pg. 996

INNERVISION—Video Production—InnerVision Studios Inc.; *U.S. Public*, pg. 114

INNERVISION—Endoscope—Medtronic, Inc.; *U.S. Public*, pg. 1082

INNO—Department Stores—GIB Group; *Int'l*, pg. 532

INNOCENCE—Toiletries—International Cosmetics Co., Ltd.; *Int'l*, pg. 684

INNOVA—Ion Laser—Coherent, Inc.; *U.S. Public*, pg. 395

INNOVA—Incontinence Treatment System—EMPI, Inc.; *U.S. Public*, pg. 545

INNOVA—Biological Shakers—New Brunswick Scientific Co., Inc.; *U.S. Public*, pg. 1169

INNOVAR—Pharmaceutical—Janssen Pharmaceutica, Inc.; *U.S. Public*, pg. 928

INNOVATION—Automatic IC Loader & Unloader— Reliability Incorporated; *U.S. Public*, pg. 1373

INNOVATION NOT IMITATION—Beloit Corporation—Beloit Corporation; *U.S. Public*, pg. 789

INNOVATOR—NONE—Lennox International Inc.; *U.S. Private*, pg. 659

INNOVATOR—Tumble Grinder, Tub Grinder— Portec, Inc.-Construction Equipment Div.; *U.S. Public*, pg. 1318

INOCOR I.V.—NONE—Eastman Kodak Company; *U.S. Public*, pg. 550

INOCULAN FOR WINDOWS NT, NETWARE— Anti-Virus Software—Cheyenne; *U.S. Public*, pg. 420

INOCUPAC—Standardizing System, Inoculum— 3M; *U.S. Public*, pg. 1604

INOVAIR—Slider Suspension With Axles—Reyco Industries, Inc.; *U.S. Private*, pg. 926

INOVAN—Cardiovascular Agents—Kyowa Hakko Kogyo Company, Ltd.; *Int'l*, pg. 778

INOVATM—Advanced PVD System—Novellus Systems, Inc.; *U.S. Public*, pg. 1204

INPAKIT—Bags—American Packaging Corporation; *U.S. Private*, pg. 60

INPOWER—NONE—Integral Systems, Inc.; *Int'l*, pg. 242

INPUT—Airborne Pulse Electromagnetic Prospecting Device—Barringer Technologies Inc.; *U.S. Public*, pg. 191

INQUISITIVE—Report Writing Software—Cognos Inc.; *Int'l*, pg. 305

INRAD—NONE—Medtronic, Inc.; *U.S. Public*, pg. 1082

INSALL/BURSTEIN II—Constrained Condylar Knee—Bristol-Myers Squibb Company; *U.S. Public*, pg. 253

INSBRUCK—Shoes, Slippers & Moccasins— Wigwam Mills, Inc.; *U.S. Private*, pg. 1175

INSCEPTOR—Sputter-coated film—Material Sciences Corporation; *U.S. Public*, pg. 1056

INSECT-XPRESS—Serum-Free Media— BioWhittaker, Inc.; *U.S. Public*, pg. 297

INSECTAPE—Insecticidal Strips—Hercon Environmental Corporation; *U.S. Public*, pg. 802

INSERTA—Perecutaneous Catheter Introducer Trays—Vital Signs, Inc.; *U.S. Public*, pg. 1723

INSERTAMATE—Two-Station Mail Inserter—Pitney Bowes Inc.; *U.S. Public*, pg. 1303

INSESSION3270—Computer Software— Attachmate; *U.S. Public*, pg. 98

INSIDE EDGE—Ski Outerwear—Pacific Trail Inc.; *U.S. Private*, pg. 673

INSIDE SPORTS—Magazine—Century Publishing Company; *U.S. Private*, pg. 226

INSIDE THE NFL—Sports Radio Program— Westwood One Entertainment; *U.S. Public*, pg. 1763

INSIDE THE NFL—Sports Program—Westwood One, Inc.; *U.S. Public*, pg. 1763

INSIDE TRACK—NONE—Market Facts, Inc.; *U.S. Public*, pg. 1046

INSIDERS—Premier Shopping Club—Damark International, Inc.; *U.S. Public*, pg. 478

INSIGHT—DNA Probe Test—IG Laboratories, Inc.; *U.S. Public*, pg. 733

INSIGHT—Guides—Simon & Schuster; *U.S. Private*, pg. 777

INSIGHT—Inventory Management System (Computerized)—Spring Arbor Distributors; *U.S. Private*, pg. 563

INSIGHT/AM—Software—Alpha Microsystems; *U.S. Public*, pg. 57

INSIGHTS—Greeting Cards—American Greetings Corporation; *U.S. Public*, pg. 77

INSIGHTS—Greeting Cards—American Greetings U.S. Greeting Card Division; *U.S. Public*, pg. 78

INSIGNIA—Decorator Faucets—T & S Brass & Bronze Works, Inc.; *U.S. Private*, pg. 1061

INSIGNIA POPS—NONE—Insignia Systems, Inc.; *U.S. Public*, pg. 881

INSITE—Software for Site Location & Market Analysis—CACI International Inc; *U.S. Public*, pg. 272

INSITE—Electronic Instrument—Intel Corporation; *U.S. Public*, pg. 886

INSITE VENDING LOCK SYSTEM—Electronic Key for Pay Telephone Coin Box Collection— Hillenbrand Industries, Inc.; *U.S. Public*, pg. 828

INSITUCUTTER—Remote-Controlled Pipe Cutter— Enviroq; *U.S. Public*, pg. 881

INSITUFORM—Trenchless Pipe Reconstruction— Enviroq; *U.S. Public*, pg. 881

INSITUPIPE—Jointless Pipe—Enviroq; *U.S. Public*, pg. 881

INSITUTUBE—Watertight Tubing—Enviroq; *U.S. Public*, pg. 881

INSLEY—Backhoes—Avis Industrial Corporation; *U.S. Private*, pg. 102

INSLEY—Hydraulic Excavators—Badger Equipment Co.; *U.S. Private*, pg. 102

INSOL-U-25—Agricultural Urea Formaldehyde Concentrate—Georgia-Pacific Corporation; *U.S. Public*, pg. 735

INSOURCE—Corporate Computerized Tax Accounting System—Computer Language Research, Inc.; *U.S. Public*, pg. 421

INSOURCE—Tube Feeding—Novartis Nutrition Corporation; *Int'l*, pg. 974

INSPECT—Debugging Software—Tandem Computers Inc.; *U.S. Public*, pg. 417

INSPECTOR—Illuminated Hand Held Inspection Magnifier—Stocker & Yale, Inc.; *U.S. Public*, pg. 1518

INSPECTOR IV—Tape Evalutator Cleaner— Anacomp Magnetics, Inc.; *U.S. Public*, pg. 107

INSPIRATION—Printing Paper—Westvaco Corporation; *U.S. Public*, pg. 1762

INSPIRATIONAL—Greeting Cards—Gibson Greetings, Inc.; *U.S. Public*, pg. 742

INST-A-MATIC—Metal Bed Frames—Dresher, Inc.; *U.S. Public*, pg. 986

INSTA BLS 2—2% Bisacrylamide Solution— Scientific Imaging Systems; *U.S. Public*, pg. 550

INSTA-BOND—Specialty Adhesives for Orthodontics—Lee Pharmaceuticals; *U.S. Public*, pg. 984

INSTA-DRIVE—Computer Equipment—Emulex Corporation; *U.S. Public*, pg. 579

INSTA-FLUOR—Xylene-Based Cocktail—Packard Instrument Co., Inc.; *U.S. Private*, pg. 833

INSTA FOCUS—Binoculars—Bushnell Corporation; *U.S. Private*, pg. 1191

INSTA-GEL XF—Pseudocumene-Based Cocktail— Packard Instrument Co., Inc.; *U.S. Private*, pg. 833

INSTA-GLUCOSE—Prescription Drug—ICN Pharmaceuticals, Inc.; *U.S. Public*, pg. 853

INSTA H2OOP—Sports Equipment—Huffy Corporation; *U.S. Public*, pg. 846

INSTA - HUT—Splicing Tents—Klein Tools Inc.; *U.S. Private*, pg. 625

INSTA-LOK—Cleaning Pad Holders—3M; *U.S. Public*, pg. 1604

INSTA-PREP—Alcohol Prep Pads—Medline Industries, Inc.; *U.S. Private*, pg. 728

INSTA-RAMP—Do-it-Yourself Ramp Kits for 2x8 or 2x12 Boards—Universal Industrial Products Co.; *U.S. Public*, pg. 1677

INSTA-SEAL—Poly-Urethane Foam Insulation & Sealing—Insta-Foam Products, Inc.; *U.S. Private*, pg. 412

INSTACARE—Contact Lens One-Step Cleaning & Disinfection Product—Novartis; *Int'l*, pg. 972

INSTACOUNT—Instrument Inventory Mngmt. System—Aesculap, Inc.; *Int'l*, pg. 29

INSTAFAX—Photograohic Processing Chemicals— Eastman Kodak Company; *U.S. Public*, pg. 550

INSTAFLEX—House Installation System for Water—Georg Fischer Ltd.; *Int'l*, pg. 488

INSTAFOCUS—Binoculars—Bausch & Lomb Incorporated; *U.S. Public*, pg. 194

INSTAGRAPHIC—Cameras, Film & Video Imaging Accessories—Eastman Kodak Company; *U.S. Public*, pg. 550

INSTAJET—Nozzle—Flow International Corporation; *U.S. Public*, pg. 656

INSTALAB—Furniture—Kewaunee Scientific Corporation; *U.S. Public*, pg. 953

INSTAMATCH—Butane Utility Lighter—Duraflame, Inc.; *U.S. Private*, pg. 348

INSTAMATIC—Gas Ovens, Roll-In Rack Convection Ovens—Cres-Cor; *U.S. Private*, pg. 288

INSTAMATIC—Cameras, Projectors, Accessories, Microfilming Apparatus, Film, Chemicals— Eastman Kodak Company; *U.S. Public*, pg. 550

INSTANT ACCESS—Lease Card Application Center—Trans Leasing International Inc.; *U.S. Public*, pg. 1628

INSTANT BEAUTY—NONE—Bristol-Myers Squibb Company; *U.S. Public*, pg. 253

INSTANT BOND—Glue—Elixir Industries; *U.S. Private*, pg. 371

INSTANT CASH—NONE—Norwest Corporation; *U.S. Public*, pg. 1201

INSTANT CHEF—Charcoal Hardwood Briquets— Embers Charcoal Company, Inc.; *U.S. Private*, pg. 373

INSTANT COUPON MACHINE—At-Shelf Electronic Couponing—News America Marketing; *Int'l*, pg. 925

INSTANT DISCOUNT—Stamp Frequency C-Stores—Carlson Retail Marketing; *U.S. Private*, pg. 212

INSTANT LITE—Charcoal Hardwood Briquets— Embers Charcoal Company, Inc.; *U.S. Private*, pg. 373

INSTANT LUNCH—Soup—Maruchan Inc.; *U.S. Private*, pg. 710

INSTANT MAIL MANAGER—Communications Software—AT&T Strategy & New Service Innovations; *U.S. Public*, pg. 11

INSTANT MAILER—Envelopes—Westvaco Corporation; *U.S. Public*, pg. 1762

INSTANT NFDM—Chef's Helper-Institutional Size & Industrial Dehydrated Products—North Central AMPI, Inc.; *U.S. Private*, pg. 804

INSTANT OIL CHANGE—Quick Lube Outlets— Ashland, Inc.; *U.S. Public*, pg. 138

INSTANT POST BREAKFAST—Cereal—Kraft Foods, Inc.; *U.S. Public*, pg. 1287

INSTANT PROTEIN—Nutritional Products— Shaklee Corporation; *U.S. Public*, pg. 1518

INSTANT QUAKER OATMEAL—Instant Oatmeal—The Quaker Oats Company; *U.S. Public*, pg. 1347

INSTANT SCRATCHES—NONE—Tattersalls; *Int'l*, pg. 1357

INSTANT SLIMMER BY FLEXEES—Control Garments—True Form Intimate Apparel; *U.S. Private*, pg. 697

INSTANT WHIP—Hair Lightener—Clairol, Inc.; *U.S. Public*, pg. 254

INSTANTLOK—Adhesive—Unilever Plc; *Int'l*, pg. 1433

INSTAPAGE 19—Bisacrylamide Solution— Scientific Imaging Systems; *U.S. Public*, pg. 550

INSTAPAK—Foam-in-Place Packaging Systems— Sealed Air Corporation; *U.S. Public*, pg. 1450

INSTAPUMP—Athletic Shoe—Reebok International Ltd.; *U.S. Public*, pg. 1369

INSTAPURE—Water Filter & Air Filter—Teledyne Water Pik; *U.S. Public*, pg. 44

INSTATECH—Camera—Eastman Kodak Company; *U.S. Public*, pg. 550

INSTATHANE—NONE—Dennis Chemical Co., Inc.; *U.S. Private*, pg. 324

INSTATHERM—Glass Vessel Heating System—Ace Glass Incorporated; *U.S. Private*, pg. 12

INSTAVISION—Binoculars—Bushnell Corporation; *U.S. Private*, pg. 1191

INSTEEMATIC—Cleaning Solution—Clayton Industries Co.; *U.S. Private*, pg. 245

INSTINCT—NONE—Cordis, a Johnson & Johnson Company; *U.S. Public*, pg. 928

INSTINET ANALYTICS—Real-Time & Historical Trade Decision Support—Instinet Corporation; *Int'l*, pg. 1106

THE INSTINET REAL-TIME NETWORK—Instinet's Global Equities Trading System—Instinet Corporation; *Int'l*, pg. 1106

INSTINET'S ORDER MANAGEMENT SYSTEM—Enter, Manage, & Trade Lists of Orders—Instinet Corporation; *Int'l*, pg. 1106

INSTITUTIONAL DISTRIBUTION—Magazine of Interest to Foodservice Managers—ID Magazine; *Int'l*, pg. 1446

INSTRACRYL—Acrylamide Gel—Eastman Kodak Company; *U.S. Public*, pg. 550

INSTROMARK—Instrument Labeling—TimeMed Labeling Systems, Inc.; *U.S. Private*, pg. 1087

INSTRUCTIONAL FAIR—Educational Materials—Creative Publications; *U.S. Private*, pg. 288

INSTRUCTOR—Filmstrip Projector—Telex Communications, Inc.; *U.S. Private*, pg. 1074

INSTRUCTOR MAGAZINE—For Tchrs. & Admin. K-8: Curriculum Enrichment; Current Issues In Education—Scholastic Inc.; *U.S. Public*, pg. 1440

INSTRUCTPLUS—Authorized Training Classes—GE Capital/IT Solutions; *U.S. Public*, pg. 711

INSTRUMENTATION & AUTOMATION NEWS—Product News Tabloid—Reed Elsevier Business Information; *Int'l*, pg. 1095

INSUJECT—Insulin Injection System—Novo Nordisk A/S; *Int'l*, pg. 987

INSUL-AID—Vapor Barrier Paint—ICI Paints; *Int'l*, pg. 664

INSUL-BASE—Roof Insulation—Johns Manville Corporation; *U.S. Public*, pg. 927

INSUL-BLAZE—Paint—ICI Paints; *Int'l*, pg. 664

INSUL-DRAIN—Insulation/Drainage Board—Owens Corning/Foamular; *U.S. Public*, pg. 1237

INSUL-DRI—Hot Melt Matrix—H.B. Fuller Company; *U.S. Public*, pg. 686

INSUL-LOCK—Rubber Products—Rubatex Corporation; *U.S. Private*, pg. 56

INSUL-QUICK—Glass Fiber Insulation—Owens Corning; *U.S. Public*, pg. 1236

INSUL-SAFE—Fiberglass Insulation For Blown-In Application—CertainTeed Corporation; *Int'l*, pg. 1170

INSUL SAFE III—NONE—CertainTeed Corporation; *Int'l*, pg. 1170

INSUL-SHEET—Rubber Products—Rubatex Corporation; *U.S. Private*, pg. 56

INSUL-SHIELD—Insulation Board—Johns Manville Corporation; *U.S. Public*, pg. 927

INSUL-TAPE—Rubber Products—Rubatex Corporation; *U.S. Private*, pg. 56

INSUL-THIN—Microporous Board Insulation—Johns Manville Corporation; *U.S. Public*, pg. 927

INSUL-TILE—Insulated Lay-in Panels for Suspended Ceilings—Owens Corning; *U.S. Public*, pg. 1236

INSUL-TUBE—Rubber Products—Rubatex Corporation; *U.S. Private*, pg. 56

INSUL-VENT—Attic Ventilating System—Owens Corning; *U.S. Public*, pg. 1236

INSUL-PANEL—Insulating Boards for Building Walls—Owens Corning; *U.S. Public*, pg. 1236

INSULATARD—Product for Diabetes Care—Novo Nordisk A/S; *Int'l*, pg. 987

INSULCORE—Flame Resistant Paper—The Mead Corporation; *U.S. Public*, pg. 1074

INSULEDGE—Multiple Glazing Window Units—PPG Industries, Inc.; *U.S. Public*, pg. 1245

INSULEK—Insulating Components—International Electronic Research Corp.; *U.S. Public*, pg. 286

INSULJEL—Silicone Coating Material for Waterproofing Porcelain Electrical Insulators—General Electric Canada Inc.; *U.S. Public*, pg. 713

INSULKOTE—Weather Protective Coatings—Johns Manville Corporation; *U.S. Public*, pg. 927

INSULMAT—NONE—Essex Specialty Products; *U.S. Public*, pg. 523

INSULOK—Cable Fixing Tie System—Bowthorpe plc; *Int'l*, pg. 207

INSULPINK—Extruded Polystyrene Basement Wall Insulation—Owens Corning; *U.S. Public*, pg. 1236

INSULPINK—Basement Wall Insulation System—Owens Corning/Foamular; *U.S. Public*, pg. 1237

INSULSTACK—Fireplaces—HON Industries Inc.; *U.S. Public*, pg. 772

INSULSTRUC—Thermoset Polyester Molding Compound—Industrial Dielectrics, Inc.; *U.S. Private*, pg. 560

INSULTITE—Heat Shrinkable Cable Splice—3M; *U.S. Public*, pg. 1604

INSULUBE—Insulating Components—International Electronic Research Corp.; *U.S. Public*, pg. 286

INSURANCE & TECHNOLOGY—Magazine—Miller Freeman Inc.; *Int'l*, pg. 1443

INSURANCE APPLICATION ARCHITECTURE—Computer Product—International Business Machines Corporation; *U.S. Public*, pg. 895

INSURANCE PAD—Heat Shield—Mill-Rose Company; *U.S. Private*, pg. 746

INSURANCE PRODUCTS—NONE—CUC International, Inc.; *U.S. Public*, pg. 320

INSUREPOINT—Web Site—Atlantic Mutual Companies; *U.S. Public*, pg. 95

INSWOOL—Ceramic Fiber—A.P. Green Industries, Inc.; *U.S. Public*, pg. 761

INSYTE—Intravenous Catheter Placement Unit with Vialon—Becton Dickinson & Company; *U.S. Public*, pg. 199

INSYTE-A—Arterial Catheter with Vialon—Becton Dickinson & Company; *U.S. Public*, pg. 199

INSYTE-W—Intravenous Catheter Placement Unit with Vialon—Becton Dickinson & Company; *U.S. Public*, pg. 199

INTACT—Tissue Heart Valves—Medtronic, Inc.; *U.S. Public*, pg. 1082

INTAGLIO—Watches—Tiffany & Co.; *U.S. Public*, pg. 1608

INTAL CAPSULES—Cromolyn Sodium for Inhalation, USP—Medeva Pharmaceuticals; *Int'l*, pg. 852

INTAL INHALER—Cromolyn Sodium Inhalation Aerosol—Medeva Pharmaceuticals; *Int'l*, pg. 852

INTAL NEBULIZER SOLUTION—Cromolyn Sodium Inhalation Solution, USP—Medeva Pharmaceuticals; *Int'l*, pg. 852

INTALOX—Chemical Tower Packing—Norton Company; *Int'l*, pg. 1173

INTAS—NONE—SunGard Data Systems Inc.; *U.S. Public*, pg. 1534

INTCHLOR—Coatings—International Paint Co., Inc.; *Int'l*, pg. 338

INTECOM E—Communications Platform—InteCom; *Int'l*, pg. 794

INTEGRA—Automobile—American Honda Motor Co., Inc.; *Int'l*, pg. 634

INTEGRA—Automobile—American Honda Motor Co., Inc. Automobile Sales Division; *Int'l*, pg. 634

INTEGRA—Acura Automobile—American Honda Motor Co., Inc. Motorcycle Division; *Int'l*, pg. 634

INTEGRAL—NONE—Integral Systems, Inc.; *Int'l*, pg. 242

INTEGRAL—Automated Workstation to Perform Rapid Immunoassays—PerSeptive Biosystems, Inc.; *U.S. Public*, pg. 1279

INTEGRAL BLADE—Stabilizer—Baker Hughes INTEQ; *U.S. Public*, pg. 166

INTEGRATED BANKING APPLICATIONS—Primary Software Product—Hogan Systems, Inc.; *U.S. Public*, pg. 422

INTEGRATED ELECTRONIC OFFICE—Office Automation Computer System—Datapoint Corporation; *Int'l*, pg. 384

INTEGRATED LANGUAGE ENVIRONMENT—Computer Product—International Business Machines Corporation; *U.S. Public*, pg. 895

THE INTEGRATED REASONING SHELL—Computer System—International Business Machines Corporation; *U.S. Public*, pg. 895

INTEGRATED SOLUTION—Clean Room Systems—Daw Technologies, Inc.; *U.S. Public*, pg. 489

INTEGRATED SYSTEMS SOLUTIONS—Computer Product—International Business Machines Corporation; *U.S. Public*, pg. 895

INTEGRATING PLATFORM—Computer Product—International Business Machines Corporation; *U.S. Public*, pg. 895

INTEGRATOR—Photo Typesetters—AGFA EPS Division; *Int'l*, pg. 172

INTEGRATOR—Guided Vehicles—Litton Industries, Inc.; *U.S. Public*, pg. 1002

INTEGRITE—Skin Care—Coty Inc.; *Int'l*, pg. 185

INTEGRITEST-E—Automatic Filter Measurement Device—Millipore Corporation; *U.S. Public*, pg. 1112

INTEGRITY—Computer System—Tandem Computers Inc.; *U.S. Public*, pg. 417

INTEGRITY MUTUAL INSURANCE—Insurance Company—Integrity Mutual Insurance Company; *U.S. Public*, pg. 566

INTEGRITY S2—Computer System—Tandem Computers Inc.; *U.S. Public*, pg. 417

INTEGRITY SERIES UNIVERSAL LIFE—Universal Life Insurance—Pan-American Life Insurance Company; *U.S. Private*, pg. 836

INTEGRITY SERIES WHOLE LIFE—Whole Life Insurance—Pan-American Life Insurance Company; *U.S. Private*, pg. 836

INTEGRON—Two-layer Surgical Glove—Becton Dickinson & Company; *U.S. Public*, pg. 199

INTEK—Information Technology Services—John H. Harland Company; *U.S. Public*, pg. 785

INTEL—Electronic Instrument—Intel Corporation; *U.S. Public*, pg. 886

INTELAN—LAN Internetworking—InteCom; *Int'l*, pg. 794

INTELBOS—Electronic Instrument—Intel Corporation; *U.S. Public*, pg. 886

INTELDX2—Microprocessor—Intel Corporation; *U.S. Public*, pg. 886

INTELEK—Sensors—Delphi Energy & Engine Management Systems; *U.S. Public*, pg. 719

INTELEVISION—Electronic Instrument—Intel Corporation; *U.S. Public*, pg. 886

INTELIGENT IDENTIFIER—Electronic Instrument—Intel Corporation; *U.S. Public*, pg. 886

INTELIGENT PROGRAMMING—Electronic Instrument—Intel Corporation; *U.S. Public*, pg. 886

INTELINK—Intermodule Communication Network—Millipore Corporation; *U.S. Public*, pg. 1112

INTELL-IGNITION—Ignition System—White-Rodgers Div., Emerson Electric Co.; *U.S. Public*, pg. 573

INTELLEC—Electronic Instrument—Intel Corporation; *U.S. Public*, pg. 886

INTELLI★MAX—Call-Processing System—Intellicall, Inc.; *U.S. Public*, pg. 887

INTELLI★SERV—Non-Coin Pay Phone System—Intellicall, Inc.; *U.S. Public*, pg. 887

INTELLI★STAR—Hardware, Software & Services—Intellicall, Inc.; *U.S. Public*, pg. 887

INTELLI WATCH—Suite of Management Tools for Lotus Notes—Candle Corporation; *U.S. Private*, pg. 204

INTELLICODE—Access Security System—The Genie Company; *U.S. Private*, pg. 823

INTELLIDRIVE—Control System—The Raymond Corporation; *Int'l*, pg. 123

INTELLIDRIVE 2—Control System—The Raymond Corporation; *Int'l*, pg. 123

INTELLIFINDER—Reference Work—INSO Corporation; *U.S. Public*, pg. 882

INTELLIFONT—Proprietary Typeface Data System—AGFA EPS Division; *Int'l*, pg. 172

INTELLIGENT ADDRESS CORRECTION—Microcomputer Software for Canadian Mailers—Group 1 Software, Inc.; *U.S. Public*, pg. 417

THE INTELLIGENT CHOICE—Insurance—The Guardian Life Insurance Company of America; *U.S. Private*, pg. 486

INTELLIGENT NETWORK—Integrated Local Area Network Computer System—Datapoint Corporation; *Int'l*, pg. 384

INTELLIGENT NETWORK EXECUTIVE—Computer Software & Hardware Prods. for Integrated Local Area Networks—Datapoint Corporation; *Int'l*, pg. 384

INTELLIGENT NETWORK MANAGEMENT FACILTY—Computer Software & Hardware Prod. for Local Area Network Admin.—Datapoint Corporation; *Int'l*, pg. 384

INTELLIGENT NETWORK TOOLKIT—Computer Hardware & Software Prods. for Local Area Network Admin.—Datapoint Corporation; *Int'l*, pg. 384

INTELLIGENT PRINTER DATA STREAM—Computer Product—International Business Machines Corporation; *U.S. Public*, pg. 895

INTELLIGENT QUERY(IQ)—Query & Report Writing Software—IQ Software Corporation; *U.S. Public*, pg. 858

INTELLIGENT UNIVERSE—Telecommunications Apparatus & Equip.—Northern Telecom Limited; *Int'l*, pg. 968

THE INTELLIGENT WINDOW—Glass Panes—PPG Industries, Inc.; *U.S. Public*, pg. 1245

INTELLIGRAPHICS INTERNATIONAL—NONE—Analytical Surveys, Inc.; *U.S. Public*, pg. 110

INTELLIGUIDE—Wire Guidance—The Raymond Corporation; *Int'l*, pg. 123

INTELLINET—Communications Facility—Cerner Corporation; *U.S. Public*, pg. 331

INTELLINK—Electronic Instrument—Intel Corporation; *U.S. Public*, pg. 886

INTELLIPLACE—Industrial Products—The Black & Decker Corporation; *U.S. Public*, pg. 233

INTELLISCOPE—Information Management Tools—INSO Corporation; *U.S. Public*, pg. 882

INTELLISENSE—Dishwasher—Maytag Corporation; *U.S. Public*, pg. 1064

INTELLISERT—Industrial Products—The Black & Decker Corporation; *U.S. Public*, pg. 233

INTELLISPEED—Speed Control—The Raymond Corporation; *Int'l*, pg. 123

INTELLISYS—Security Systems (MULTI-NET, PHOTO NET, ENTRY NET, ALERT NET)—Diebold, Incorporated; *U.S. Public*, pg. 506

INTELLITAG—Electronic Identification Device—Amtech Corporation; *U.S. Public*, pg. 105

INTELLITOUCH—Oven Control—The Blodgett Oven Co., Inc.; *U.S. Public*, pg. 1064

INTELLITOUCH—Surface Wave Touchscreen—Elo TouchSystems, Inc.; *U.S. Public*, pg. 1362

INTELSAT—Satellite Communications—COMSAT Corporation; *U.S. Public*, pg. 424

INTENNA—Cordless Telephone—Cobra Electronics Corporation; *U.S. Public*, pg. 391

INTENSE PROTEIN—Conditioner—Clairol, Inc.; *U.S. Public*, pg. 254

INTENSIFLEX—Printing Ink for Paper Products—Georgia-Pacific Corporation; *U.S. Public*, pg. 735

INTENSITRON—Spectral Line Emitting Lamps—The Perkin-Elmer Corporation; *U.S. Public*, pg. 1279

INTENSIVE MIXER—Machinery—Kobelco Stewart Bolling, Inc.; *Int'l*, pg. 740

INTENSIVE TASK SEATING—Industrail Multi Task Seating—Cramer Inc.; *U.S. Private*, pg. 285

INTENSIVE USE SEATING—24 Hour Use Seating—Domore Corporation; *U.S. Private*, pg. 339

INTEQ—Premium Television Receiver—Zenith Electronics Corp.; *U.S. Public*, pg. 1790

INTER CHANGE—Indoor Illuminated Sign Series—American Sign & Marketing Services, Inc.; *U.S. Public*, pg. 1309

INTER-FEAR-ON-MAGIC—Cold Sores & Fever Blisters Disappear in Days—Bethurum Research & Development, Inc.; *U.S. Private*, pg. 141

INTER-LOC—Siding—Weyerhaeuser Forest Products Company; *U.S. Public*, pg. 1764

INTER-TEL.NET—Internet/Intranet IP Gateway Telecommunications Network—Inter-Tel, Incorporated; *U.S. Public*, pg. 888

INTER-CHEM—NONE—International Chemical Company; *U.S. Private*, pg. 568

INTERACK-30—Conveyor System—Interlake Material Handling Div.; *U.S. Public*, pg. 893

INTERACT—Joysticks, Game Controllers, Speakers & Accessories—Recoton Corporation; *U.S. Public*, pg. 1369

INTERACT—Conditioning Systems—Reliability Incorporated; *U.S. Public*, pg. 1373

INTERACT II—Training Simulator—Scientific Software-Intercomp, Inc.; *U.S. Public*, pg. 1443

INTERACT UPS—Battery Backup—Best Power; *U.S. Private*, pg. 140

INTERACTIVE AGE—Newspaper—CMP Media, Inc.; *U.S. Public*, pg. 279

INTERACTIVE PC LINK—Micro to Mainframe Link—Dun & Bradstreet Software Services; *Int'l*, pg. 532

INTERACTIVE SERVICES—On-Line Membership to Shopping, Travel, Auto & Dining Services—CUC International, Inc.; *U.S. Public*, pg. 320

INTERACTIVE VOICE RESPONSE—NONE—Market Facts, Inc.; *U.S. Public*, pg. 1046

INTERAM—Mat Mount Material, Automotive, Wood Stoves, Heat Absorbing/Expanding Mats—3M; *U.S. Public*, pg. 1604

INTERAX—NONE—Pfizer Inc.; *U.S. Public*, pg. 1281

INTERBIO—NONE—InterBio Inc.; *U.S. Private*, pg. 566

INTERBOLD—Diebold/IBM Corporation Joint Venture—Diebold, Incorporated; *U.S. Public*, pg. 506

INTERBOND—Coatings—International Paint Co., Inc.; *Int'l*, pg. 338

INTERBRIDGE—Apple Talk Network Bridge—Hayes Microcomputer Products, Inc.; *U.S. Public*, pg. 801

INTERCAP—Passive Components—International Components Corporation; *U.S. Private*, pg. 569

INTERCAR—Driers, Organometallic-Based—Akzo Nobel N.V.; *Int'l*, pg. 42

INTERCARE—Coatings—International Paint Co., Inc.; *Int'l*, pg. 338

INTERCAT—Feline Interferon Agent—Toray Industries, Inc.; *Int'l*, pg. 1399

INTERCEED—Absorbable Adhesion Barrier—Johnson & Johnson Medical, Inc.; *U.S. Public*, pg. 928

INTERCELL—Raised Flooring—Interface Inc.; *U.S. Public*, pg. 889

INTERCEPT—Insecticide—Roussel Corporation; *Int'l*, pg. 625

INTERCEPTOR—Motorcycle—American Honda Motor Co., Inc. Motorcycle Division; *Int'l*, pg. 634

INTERCEPTOR—Antiparasitic—Ciba Specialty Chemicals; *Int'l*, pg. 291

INTERCEPTOR—NONE—Dynatech Corporation; *U.S. Public*, pg. 539

INTERCEPTOR—Racquetball Eyewear—Ektelon; *U.S. Private*, pg. 884

INTERCEPTOR—Electronic Siren/Radio Amplifier—Federal Signal Corporation, Signal Div.; *U.S. Public*, pg. 616

INTERCEPTOR—Toxic Chemical Protection Fabric—Lakeland Industries, Inc.; *U.S. Public*, pg. 975

INTERCEPTOR—Bug Shield—Lund International Holdings, Inc.; *U.S. Public*, pg. 1020

INTERCEPTOR—Heartworm Preventative Medicine for Dogs—Novartis; *Int'l*, pg. 972

INTERCLENE—Coatings—International Paint Co., Inc.; *Int'l*, pg. 338

INTERCOMP WIRE & CABLE—NONE—Communication Cable, Inc.; *U.S. Public*, pg. 968

INTER-CONTINENTAL—Hotels—Inter-Continental Hotels & Resorts Corporation; *Int'l*, pg. 1178

INTERCRAFT—Frames, Albums—Intercraft Company; *U.S. Public*, pg. 1177

INTERCRAFT—Picture Frames—Newell Co.; *U.S. Public*, pg. 1176

INTERDENS—Wood Preservative—BASF AG; *Int'l*, pg. 103

INTERDIAL—Predictive Dialer—InterVoice, Inc.; *U.S. Public*, pg. 910

INTERDIGITAL—Manufacturing the Future of Communications—InterDigital Communications Corp.; *U.S. Public*, pg. 889

INTERFACE—Floor Coverings—Interface Flooring Systems Inc.; *U.S. Public*, pg. 889

INTERFOAM—Specialty Chemicals—Akzo Nobel Inc.; *Int'l*, pg. 47

INTERFORM—Application Generator Environment—InterVoice, Inc.; *U.S. Public*, pg. 910

INTERGARD—Epoxy—International Paint Co., Inc.; *Int'l*, pg. 338

INTERGARD KNITTED—Collagen Coated Knitted Polyester Vascular Prosthesis—Datascope Corp.; *U.S. Public*, pg. 487

INTERGARD WOVEN—Collagen Coated Woven Polyester Vascular Prosthesis—Datascope Corp.; *U.S. Public*, pg. 487

INTERGRAPH—Graphic Workstations & Software—Intergraph Corporation; *U.S. Public*, pg. 890

INTERIM ACCOUNTING PROFESSIONALS—Accounting Support Staffing—Interim Services Inc.; *U.S. Public*, pg. 892

INTERIM ATTORNEYS—Attorney Staffing Services—Interim Services Inc.; *U.S. Public*, pg. 892

INTERIM CARE MANAGEMENT—Total Care Management Services—Interim Services Inc.; *U.S. Public*, pg. 892

INTERIM COURT REPORTING—Court Reporting Staffing Services—Interim Services Inc.; *U.S. Public*, pg. 892

INTERIM HEALTHCARE—Home Care & Staffing Service—Interim Services Inc.; *U.S. Public*, pg. 892

INTERIM HOME SOLUTIONS—IV Therapy/Management Services—Interim Services Inc.; *U.S. Public*, pg. 892

INTERIM HUMAN RESOURCES PROFESSIONALS—Human Resources Staffing Services—Interim Services Inc.; *U.S. Public*, pg. 892

INTERIM IN-TOUCH—Two-Way Voice Monitoring/Communication System Services—Interim Services Inc.; *U.S. Public*, pg. 892

INTERIM LEGAL PROFESSIONALS—Legal Support Staffing-Temp/Perm—Interim Services Inc.; *U.S. Public*, pg. 892

INTERIM MESSENGER SERVICES—Messenger Staffing Services—Interim Services Inc.; *U.S. Public*, pg. 892

INTERIM ON-PREMISE—On-Site Staffing Management—Interim Services Inc.; *U.S. Public*, pg. 892

INTERIM PERSONNEL—Placement Services—Interim Services Inc.; *U.S. Public*, pg. 892

INTERIM PHYSICIANS—Locum Tenens—Interim Services Inc.; *U.S. Public*, pg. 892

INTERIM SEARCH SOLUTIONS—Staff Search Services—Interim Services Inc.; *U.S. Public*, pg. 892

INTERIM SERVICES—Temporary/Perm Staffing Services—Interim Services Inc.; *U.S. Public*, pg. 892

INTERIM STAFFING—Temporary Staffing Services—Interim Services Inc.; *U.S. Public*, pg. 892

INTERIM TECHNOLOGY—Technology Staffing Services—Interim Services Inc.; *U.S. Public*, pg. 892

INTERIM THERAPY SERVICES—Therapy Staffing Services—Interim Services Inc.; *U.S. Public*, pg. 892

INTERIOR DESIGN—Magazine for Designers of Office, Commercial & Residential Interiors—Reed Elsevier Business Information; *Int'l*, pg. 1095

INTERIOR SPACE PLANNERS—Space Planners & Interior Designers—The W.B. Wood Company; *U.S. Private*, pg. 1186

INTERIORS—Magazine—BPI Communications Inc.; *Int'l*, pg. 1446

INTERLAC—Coatings—International Paint Co., Inc.; *Int'l*, pg. 338

INTERLEUKIN-6—Blood Cell Growth Factor—Genetics Institute, Inc.; *U.S. Public*, pg. 79

INTERLEUKIN-3—Blood Cell Growth Factor—Genetics Institute, Inc.; *U.S. Public*, pg. 79

INTERLINK—Computer Hardware & Software—Beckman Instruments, Inc.; *U.S. Public*, pg. 199

INTERLOCHEN—Knit Shirt—Lands' End, Inc.; *U.S. Public*, pg. 977

INTERLOCK—Rifle Bullet—Hornady Manufacturing Company; *U.S. Private*, pg. 539

INTERLOK—Rubber Tile—Pawling Corporation; *U.S. Private*, pg. 844

INTERLUDE—Mattresses—Flexsteel Industries, Inc.; *U.S. Public*, pg. 653

INTERLUDES—NONE—Integrity Incorporated; *U.S. Public*, pg. 886

INTERLUX—Yacht Finishes—Courtaulds Coatings Inc.; *Int'l*, pg. 338

INTERLUX—Enamel—International Paint Co., Inc.; *Int'l*, pg. 338

INTERMEC—Bar Code Readers & Peripheral Products—Intermec Technologies Corporation; *U.S. Public*, pg. 1699

INTERMODAL—Piggyback Rail Service—Conrail, Inc.; *U.S. Public*, pg. 431

INTERNATIONAL—Manufactured Homes—Clayton Homes, Inc.; *U.S. Public*, pg. 382

INTERNATIONAL—Marine Coatings—Courtaulds Coatings Inc.; *Int'l*, pg. 338

INTERNATIONAL—Aluminum Sliding Doors & Windows—International Aluminum Corporation; *U.S. Public*, pg. 894

INTERNATIONAL—Trucks—Navistar International Corporation; *U.S. Public*, pg. 1167

INTERNATIONAL—NONE—Navistar International Transportation Corp.; *U.S. Public*, pg. 1167

INTERNATIONAL—Furniture—Schnadig Corporation; *U.S. Private*, pg. 971

INTERNATIONAL—Travel Irons—Sunbeam Household Products; *U.S. Public*, pg. 1533

INTERNATIONAL CHRISTMAS—Christmas Items—Syratech Corporation; *U.S. Private*, pg. 1060

INTERNATIONAL CIRCULATION DISTRIBUTORS—Magazine Distribution—The Hearst Corporation; *U.S. Private*, pg. 515

INTERNATIONAL COFFEES—Various Flavors Regular & Sugar Free Instant Coffee—Kraft Foods, Inc.; *U.S. Public*, pg. 1287

INTERNATIONAL CONSTRUCTION—Publication for Construction Industry—Intertec Publishing; *U.S. Public*, pg. 1327

INTERNATIONAL CORRECT SPELL—Software—Houghton Mifflin Company; *U.S. Public*, pg. 841

INTERNATIONAL CORRECTSPELL—Proofing Tool—INSO Corporation; *U.S. Public*, pg. 882

INTERNATIONAL DELIGHT—Gourmet Non-Dairy Coffee Creamer in Various Flavors—The Morning Star Group; *U.S. Public*, pg. 1527

INTERNATIONAL DOCUMENT SERVICE—International Document Delivery—DHL Worldwide Express; *U.S. Private*, pg. 301

INTERNATIONAL 800 SERVICE—International Toll Free Calling—Teleglobe, Inc.; *Int'l*, pg. 1373

INTERNATIONAL ELECTRONIC THESAURUS—Reference Work—INSO Corporation; *U.S. Public*, pg. 882

INTERNATIONAL ENERGY SAVER—Evaporative Cooling & Energy Recovery Equipment—Thomas & Betts Corporation; *U.S. Public*, pg. 1597

INTERNATIONAL ENTREE—Line of Frozen Entrees—Armour Swift Eckrich; *U.S. Public*, pg. 426

THE INTERNATIONAL EXECUTIVE—Journal—John Wiley & Sons, Inc.; *U.S. Public*, pg. 1768

INTERNATIONAL EXPRESS—NONE—Express Newspapers plc; *Int'l*, pg. 1443

INTERNATIONAL EXPRESSFREIGHT SERVICE—Shipments Above 150603

INTERNATIONAL FREEFONE 0800—International Toll-Free Service—British Telecommunications plc; *Int'l*, pg. 222

INTERNATIONAL HOUSE OF PANCAKES—Restaurants—IHOP Corp.; *U.S. Public*, pg. 862

INTERNATIONAL HYPHENATOR—Proofing Tool—INSO Corporation; *U.S. Public*, pg. 882

INTERNATIONAL LASER SYSTEMS—Lasers—Litton Industries, Inc.; *U.S. Public*, pg. 1002

INTERNATIONAL LITERARY MARKET PLACE—International Directory for Publishing Industry—R.R. Bowker; *Int'l*, pg. 1096

INTERNATIONAL MALE—Catalog Containing Unique Men's Apparel—Hanover Direct, Inc.; *U.S. Public*, pg. 782

INTERNATIONAL MALE—Men's Clothing—Hanover Direct Pennsylvania, Inc.; *U.S. Public*, pg. 782

INTERNATIONAL MANAGERS EDITION—FBO Information—Intertec Publishing; *U.S. Public*, pg. 1327

INTERNATIONAL MUSIC & MEDIA CONFERENCE—Marketing Information Services—BPI Communications Inc.; *Int'l*, pg. 1446

INTERNATIONAL PAIN AND IMPLANTS—Device/Apparatus—Medtronic, Inc.; *U.S. Public*, pg. 1082

INTERNATIONAL PRIORITY SERVICE—Shipments Below 150603

INTERNATIONAL PROOFREADER—Proofing Tool—INSO Corporation; *U.S. Public*, pg. 882

INTERNATIONAL RAILWAY JOURNAL—Monthly Magazine—Simmons-Boardman Publishing Corp.; *U.S. Private*, pg. 1000

INTERNATIONAL SILVER—NONE—Carvel Hall; *U.S. Private*, pg. 1061

INTERNATIONAL SILVER COMPANY—Flatware, Holloware, Giftware—Syratech Corporation; *U.S. Private*, pg. 1060

INTERNATIONAL TABLES—Furniture—Schnadig Corporation; *U.S. Private*, pg. 971

INTERNATIONAL TIMBER—Wood Imports—Meyer International PLC; *Int'l*, pg. 864

INTERNATIONAL TYPEFACE CORPORATION—Graphic Art Supplies—Esselte AB; *Int'l*, pg. 459

INTERNET—NONE—EMAP Business Communications Division; *Int'l*, pg. 451

INTERNET ADVISORY GROUP—Provides Help with Internet Research, Training & Web Site Development—Find/SVP, Inc.; *U.S. Public*, pg. 623

INTERNET OFFICE LP—Low Profile UPS System—Trippe Mfg. Co.; *U.S. Private*, pg. 1104

INTERPLAK—Dental Products—Bausch & Lomb Incorporated; *U.S. Public*, pg. 194

INTERPLAK—Dental Products—Conair Corporation; *U.S. Private*, pg. 261

INTERPLAK PLUS—Dental Equipment—Bausch & Lomb Incorporated; *U.S. Public*, pg. 194

INTERPLAK VOYAGER—Dental Equipment—Bausch & Lomb Incorporated; *U.S. Public*, pg. 194

INTERPON—Powder Coatings—Courtaulds Coatings Inc.; *Int'l*, pg. 338

INTERPON—Powder—International Paint Co., Inc.; *Int'l*, pg. 338

INTERPRETATIONS—Area Rugs—Couristan Inc.; *U.S. Private*, pg. 279

INTERPRIME—Coatings—International Paint Co., Inc.; *Int'l*, pg. 338

INTERPROBE—Periodontal Diagnostic Equipment—Bausch & Lomb Incorporated; *U.S. Public*, pg. 194

INTERROYAL—Steel Storage Products—Deluxe Storage Systems, Inc.; *U.S. Private*, pg. 323

INTERSCIENCE—Books—John Wiley & Sons, Inc.; *U.S. Public*, pg. 1768

INTERSECT—Conditioning Systems—Reliability Incorporated; *U.S. Public*, pg. 1373

INTERSEPT—Antimicrobial—AAF-International; *U.S. Private*, pg. 3

INTERSEPT—Antimicrobal Agent—Interface Inc.; *U.S. Public*, pg. 889

INTERSEPT—Blood Filter—Medtronic, Inc.; *U.S. Public*, pg. 1082

INTERSEPT—Small-Volume Industrial Electrostatic Precipitator—United McGill Corp.; *U.S. Private*, pg. 1122

INTERSMOOTH—Coatings—International Paint Co., Inc.; *Int'l*, pg. 338

INTERSORT—Conditioning Systems—Reliability Incorporated; *U.S. Public*, pg. 1373

INTERSPEED—Coatings—International Paint Co., Inc.; *Int'l*, pg. 338

INTERSTAB—Plastic Stabilizers—Akzo Nobel N.V.; *Int'l*, pg. 42

INTERSTATE—Motorcycle—American Honda Motor Co., Inc. Motorcycle Division; *Int'l*, pg. 634

INTERSTATE ELECTRONICS—NONE—Figgie International Inc.; *U.S. Public*, pg. 622

INTERSTATER—Gang Hwy. Mowers—Alamo Group, Inc.; *U.S. Public*, pg. 35

INTERTHANE—Polyurethanes—International Paint Co., Inc.; *Int'l*, pg. 338

INTERTHERM—NONE—Nordyne Inc.; *U.S. Public*, pg. 1193

INTERTUF—Coatings—International Paint Co., Inc.; *Int'l*, pg. 338

INTERURBAN—Tire & Tubes—Bridgestone/Firestone, Inc.; *Int'l*, pg. 213

INTERURBAN SUPER TRACTION—Tires—Bridgestone/Firestone, Inc.; *Int'l*, pg. 213

INTERVAL INTERNATIONAL—Time Share Exchange—CUC International, Inc.; *U.S. Public*, pg. 320

INTERVENTIONAL MEDICAL—NONE—Medtronic, Inc.; *U.S. Public*, pg. 1082

INTERVENTIONAL VASCULAR—NONE—Medtronic, Inc.; *U.S. Public*, pg. 1082

INTERVET—Vaccines—Akzo Nobel Inc.; *Int'l*, pg. 47

INTERVINUX—Coatings—International Paint Co., Inc.; *Int'l*, pg. 338

INTERVOX—Audible Device—International Components Corporation; *U.S. Private*, pg. 569

INTERWAVE VR—NONE—UB Networks; *Int'l*, pg. 924

INTERWOVEN—Socks—Kayser-Roth Corporation, Inc.; *U.S. Public*, pg. 576

INTERZINC—Zinc Silicates—International Paint Co., Inc.; *Int'l*, pg. 338

INTIMA—I.V. Catheter Placement Unit—Becton Dickinson & Company; *U.S. Public*, pg. 199

INTIMA CHERRY—Intimate Apparel—VF Corporation; *U.S. Public*, pg. 1702

INTIMATE—NONE—Jean Philippe Fragrances, Inc.; *U.S. Public*, pg. 924

INTIMATE AFTERTHOUGHTS—Greeting Cards—American Greetings Corporation; *U.S. Public*, pg. 77

INTIMATE ATTITUDES—Women's Undergarments—National Corset Supply House; *U.S. Private*, pg. 781

INTOUCH—Shower Heads and Hand-Held Showers, Shower Valves, Shower Accessories—Interbath, Inc.; *U.S. Private*, pg. 566

INTOUCH ORGANIZATION—Shower Organization—Interbath, Inc.; *U.S. Private*, pg. 566

INTRA-AORTIC BALLOON PUMPS—Pumps—Datascope Corp.; *U.S. Public*, pg. 487

INTRA-GARD—Multi-Cell Conduit Designed for System Flexibility & Economy—The Lamson & Sessions Co.; *U.S. Public*, pg. 976

INTRA NET—Communications Facility—Cerner Corporation; *U.S. Public*, pg. 331

INTRA-OP—Autotransfusion System—C.R. Bard, Inc.; *U.S. Public*, pg. 189

INTRA TRAC II—Intranasal Vaccine (Canine & Feline)—Schering-Plough Corporation; *U.S. Public*, pg. 1438

INTRA-SHIELD—Electronic Components—General Instrument Corporation; *U.S. Public*, pg. 716

INTRADER—NONE—SunGard Data Systems Inc.; *U.S. Public*, pg. 1534

INTRALIPID—Fat Emulsion—Otsuka Pharmaceutical Co., Ltd.; *Int'l*, pg. 1013

INTRALIPID—NONE—Pharmacia & Upjohn, Inc.; *Int'l*, pg. 1047

INTRALOX—All Plastic, Modular Construction Conveyor Belting—Intralox, Inc.; *U.S. Private*, pg. 643

INTRALOX—Plastic Conveyor Belting—The Laitram Corporation; *U.S. Private*, pg. 643

INTRAN—Scuff-Proof Uppers—International Seaway Trading Corporation; *U.S. Private*, pg. 572

INTRAN—Intrauterine Catheter—Utah Medical Products, Inc.; *U.S. Public*, pg. 1700

INTRANITE—Scuff-Proof Soles—International Seaway Trading Corporation; *U.S. Private*, pg. 572

INTRASPOT—Closed Circuit Televison Equipment—Vicon Industries, Inc.; *U.S. Public*, pg. 1719

INTRAVANCE—Timing Devices—Ambac International Corp.; *U.S. Private*, pg. 48

INTRAVIEW—NONE—SunGard Data Systems Inc.; *U.S. Public*, pg. 1534

INTREPID—Photo Typesetters—AGFA EPS Division; *Int'l*, pg. 172

INTRIGUE—Vinyl Tile—Congoleum Corporation; *U.S. Public*, pg. 69

INTRIGUE—Women's Footwear—International Seaway Trading Corporation; *U.S. Private*, pg. 572

INTRO—Car Care Products—Meristem plc; *Int'l*, pg. 858

INTRON A—Alpha Interferon—Schering-Plough Corporation; *U.S. Public*, pg. 1438

INTROSPECTS—Greeting Cards & Posters—American Greetings Corporation; *U.S. Public*, pg. 77

INTROSPECTS—Greeting Cards—American Greetings U.S. Greeting Card Division; *U.S. Public*, pg. 78

INTRUDER—Motorcycle—American Suzuki Motor Corporation; *Int'l*, pg. 1323

INTUMEX—Fire-Protection Products—DSM Chemie Linz GmbH; *Int'l*, pg. 356

INVACARE—Home Health Care & Respiratory Products for Health Care Professionals—Invacare Corporation; *U.S. Public*, pg. 911

INVEN-TEL—Precision Level Gauge—Robertshaw Tennessee; *Int'l*, pg. 1243

INVENT—Canopy Hood System—The Blodgett Oven Co., Inc.; *U.S. Public*, pg. 1064

INVENTIONS—Leisure Time Game—Monarch Avalon, Inc.; *U.S. Public*, pg. 1123

INVER HOUSE SCOTCH—NONE—Barton Brands, Ltd.; *U.S. Public*, pg. 300

INVERNESS—Ear Piercing Systems—Inverness Corp.; *U.S. Private*, pg. 574

INVERSESKETCHER—Design Analysis Software—Harnischfeger Industries, Inc.; *U.S. Public*, pg. 788

INVERSOL—Inverse Solubility Lubricants—Ferro Corporation; *U.S. Public*, pg. 618

INVERTEC—Power Source—The Lincoln Electric Company; *U.S. Public*, pg. 996

INVERTOR-DUTY—Adjustable Speed Drive Motors—Magnetek Motors & Generators; *U.S. Public*, pg. 1037

INVERTOSE—Corn Syrups & Natural Sweeteners—Bestfoods; *U.S. Public*, pg. 223

INVEST ONE—Investment Accounting for Bank Commingled Funds & Mutual Funds—SunGard Data Systems Inc.; *U.S. Public*, pg. 1534

INVEST 3000—Computer System—SEI Investments; *U.S. Public*, pg. 1417

INVESTAR—Mutual Fund System—SunGard Data Systems Inc.; *U.S. Public*, pg. 1534

INVESTIGATOR—Electrophoresis Instrumentation—ESA, Inc.; *U.S. Private*, pg. 354

INVESTING FOR YOUR FAMILY—NONE—American Express Company; *U.S. Public*, pg. 73

INVESTMENT—Castings—Hitchiner Manufacturing Company, Inc.; *U.S. Private*, pg. 531

INVESTMENT REWARDS—NONE—American Express Company; *U.S. Public*, pg. 73

INVICTA—Tires—The Goodyear Tire & Rubber Company; *U.S. Public*, pg. 752

INVINCIBLE—Fly Line—Gladding Braided Products LLC; *U.S. Private*, pg. 291

INVINCIBLE—Steel Office Furniture—Invincible Office Furniture; *U.S. Private*, pg. 575

INVIRASE—HIV Protease Inhibitor—Roche Holding Ltd.; *Int'l*, pg. 1119

INVIRO BRAND—Adhesives—DAP Inc.; *Int'l*, pg. 1486

INVISA—Completely in the Canol Hearing Aid—Beltone Electronics Corporation; *U.S. Private*, pg. 132

INVISIBANDS—Strip Eyelashes—American International Industries; *U.S. Private*, pg. 57

THE INVISIBLE CONCEALER—Blemish Concealer—Cover Girl Cosmetics; *U.S. Public*, pg. 1330

THE INVISIBLE FILTER—Cigarette Filter—Venturi Inc.; *U.S. Private*, pg. 1136

THE INVISIBLE SALESMAN—Plastic Film—Reynolds Metals Company; *U.S. Public*, pg. 1385

INVISIFOCALS—Bifocal Eyeglassses—AVC/Nu-Vision, Inc.; *U.S. Private*, pg. 9

INVISIGLASS—Visual Displays Coatings—Optical Coating Laboratory, Inc.; *U.S. Public*, pg. 1227

INVISION—In House & Remote IBM-Based Healthcare Info. System—Shared Medical Systems Corporation; *U.S. Public*, pg. 1463

INVITATION—Almonds—Blue Diamond Growers; *U.S. Private*, pg. 152

INVITATION—Floor Coverings—Domco Inc.; *Int'l*, pg. 415

INVITE—Color Cosmetics—Coty Inc.; *Int'l*, pg. 185

INZO—Skin Cream-Wound Care—Medline Industries, Inc.; *U.S. Private*, pg. 728

IOBIO—Bacteria, Slime and Algae Control—Baltimore Aircoil Company; *U.S. Private*, pg. 68

IODEX—NONE—Lee Pharmaceuticals; *U.S. Public*, pg. 984

IODEX—Pharmaceuticals—Medtech Inc.; *U.S. Private*, pg. 728

IODEX-P—Ointment—Medtech Inc.; *U.S. Private*, pg. 728

IODOSAN—NONE—SmithKline Beecham Corporation; *Int'l*, pg. 1264

IODOSAN—Coughs, Colds & Influenza Product—SmithKline Beecham plc; *Int'l*, pg. 1264

IODOSORB—Wound Care Medication—Perstorp Pharma Ltd. Wound Care Division; *Int'l*, pg. 1037

IOLAB—NONE—Johnson & Johnson; *U.S. Public*, pg. 927

IOMEGA—NONE—Texas Instruments Incorporated; *U.S. Public*, pg. 1585

IOMEGA LASERSAFE M0600 FOR WORKSTATION—600MB Rewritable Magneto Optical Subsystem for Workstations—Iomega Corporation; *U.S. Public*, pg. 912

ION BOND—Physical Vapor Deposition Process—Andal Corp.; *U.S. Public*, pg. 111

ION SPORT—Sunglasses—Outlook Eyewear Company; *U.S. Private*, pg. 195

IONAC—Ion Exchange Resins—Sybron Chemicals Inc.; *U.S. Public*, pg. 73

IONAMIN—Capsules (Phentermine Resin)—Medeva Pharmaceuticals; *Int'l*, pg. 852

IONAX—Pharmaceutical Products—Galderma Laboratories, Inc.; *Int'l*, pg. 819

ION-EX—Cartridge C Column—Millipore Corporation; *U.S. Public*, pg. 1112

IONGUARD—Ion Implantation System—Spire Corporation; *U.S. Public*, pg. 1499

IONGUARD 3000—Ion Implantation System—Spire Corporation; *U.S. Public*, pg. 1499

IONICRON—Water Conditioning Units for Domestic Use—Ionics, Incorporated; *U.S. Public*, pg. 912

IONICS LOGO—ED Equipment & Analytical Instruments—Ionics, Incorporated; *U.S. Public*, pg. 912

IONIL—Pharmaceutical Products—Galderma Laboratories, Inc.; *Int'l*, pg. 819

IONIL PLUS—Pharmaceutical Products—Galderma Laboratories, Inc.; *Int'l*, pg. 819

IONIL T—Pharmaceutical Products—Galderma Laboratories, Inc.; *Int'l*, pg. 819

IONIL T PLUS—Pharmaceutical Products—Galderma Laboratories, Inc.; *Int'l*, pg. 819

IONPAC—Chromatography Columns—Dionex Corporation; *U.S. Public*, pg. 510

IONSCAN—Analytical Instrument for Drug & Explosive Detection—Barringer Technologies Inc.; *U.S. Public*, pg. 191

IONSEP—Chromatography Reagents—Dionex Corporation; *U.S. Public*, pg. 510

IOPIDINE 1%—Apraclonidine Ophthalmic Solution—Alcon Laboratories, Inc.; *Int'l*, pg. 916

IOWA GOLD—Smoked Meats—BeefAmerica Operating Co., Inc.; *U.S. Private*, pg. 130

IOWA MANUFACTURERS REGISTER—Register—Manufacturers' News, Inc.; *U.S. Private*, pg. 700

IOWA PAINT—Paint—Iowa Paint Mfg. Company, Inc.; *U.S. Private*, pg. 575

IOWA TESTS OF BASIC SKILLS—School Testing System—Houghton Mifflin Company; *U.S. Public*, pg. 841

IOWARE—NONE—Adaptec, Inc.; *U.S. Public*, pg. 19

IOX—Digital PBXs—Oki Electric Industry Company, Ltd.; *Int'l*, pg. 999

IPERMONDO—NONE—GS Societa Generale Supermercati; *Int'l*, pg. 186

IPERSTORE—NONE—GS Societa Generale Supermercati; *Int'l*, pg. 186

IPRAGAZ—Liquid Propane Gas—SHV Holdings N.V.; *Int'l*, pg. 1154

IPSATOL—Cough Formula; Pediatric Antitussive/Expectorant—Bradley Pharmaceuticals; *U.S. Public*, pg. 249

IPSATOL—Cough Formula; Pediatric Antitussive/Expectorant—Doak Dermatologics; *U.S. Public*, pg. 250

IQ-LINK—Computer Systems—Sequent Computer Systems, Inc.; *U.S. Public*, pg. 1459

IQ SERIES—Controllers for Electric Motors—Rockwell International Corporation; *U.S. Public*, pg. 1397

IQZOOM—35 Millimeter Camera with Motorized Zoom Lens—Pentax Corporation; *Int'l*, pg. 85

IRADICAV—Fluoride Prods.—Johnson & Johnson Consumer Products; *U.S. Public*, pg. 928

IRAUTO—Engine System—Echlin Inc.; *U.S. Public*, pg. 560

IRCON—Iron Supplement—Bradley Pharmaceuticals; *U.S. Public*, pg. 249

IRCON—Iron Supplement—Doak Dermatologics; *U.S. Public*, pg. 250

IRCON-FA—Iron Supplement with Folic Acid—Bradley Pharmaceuticals; *U.S. Public*, pg. 249

IRCON-FA—Iron Supplement with Folic Acid—Doak Dermatologics; *U.S. Public*, pg. 250

IRELAND—Coffee & Tea—Ireland Coffee Tea, Inc.; *U.S. Public*, pg. 351

IRGANOX L57—Additive for Lubricants—Novartis; *Int'l*, pg. 972

IRGAROL—Algicide—Ciba Specialty Chemicals; *Int'l*, pg. 291

IRGAZIN—Pigments—Ciba Specialty Chemicals; *Int'l*, pg. 291

IRGAZIN—Pigments—Novartis; *Int'l*, pg. 972

IRIS—Food & Non-Food Products—Smart & Final; *Int'l*, pg. 563

IRIS 100—X-Ray Image Intensifying Systems for Medical Purposes—Varian Associates, Inc.; *U.S. Public*, pg. 1710

IRISH MIST—Liquor—Hiram Walker; *Int'l*, pg. 63

IRISH MIST LIQUEUR—Spirit—Allied Domecq PLC; *Int'l*, pg. 62

IRISH MIST LIQUEUR—NONE—Cantrell & Cochrane Group; *Int'l*, pg. 63

IRISH SETTER—Outdoor Sport Boots—Red Wing Shoe Co., Inc.; *U.S. Private*, pg. 915

IRISH SPRING—Soap—Colgate-Palmolive Company; *U.S. Public*, pg. 397

IRIX—Nuclear Medicine—Picker International, Inc.; *Int'l*, pg. 545

IRLON D-70—NONE—Lawter International, Inc.; *U.S. Public*, pg. 980

IRLON G-73—NONE—Lawter International, Inc.; *U.S. Public*, pg. 980

IRLON 66'—NONE—Lawter International, Inc.; *U.S. Public*, pg. 980

IRMAKEY/3270—Computer Software—Attachmate; *U.S. Private*, pg. 98

IRMALINK—Computer Software—Attachmate; *U.S. Private*, pg. 98

IRMA SHORELL'S FORMULA FOR CLEANSING—Cosmetics—Irma Shorell, Inc.; *U.S. Private*, pg. 1101

IRMA3—Computer Software—Attachmate; *U.S. Private*, pg. 98

IRMAPRINT—Computer Software—Attachmate; *U.S. Private*, pg. 98

IRMAREMOTE—Computer Software—Attachmate; *U.S. Private*, pg. 98

IRMATRAC—Computer Hardware—Attachmate; *U.S. Private*, pg. 98

IROGEL—Use with Metallo-Organic Thixotropic Agents—The Lubrizol Corporation; *U.S. Public*, pg. 1016

IRON CITY—Beer—Pittsburgh Brewing Company; *U.S. Private*, pg. 619

IRON CITY DARK—Beer—Pittsburgh Brewing Company; *U.S. Private*, pg. 619

IRON GLIDE—Ironing Board Cover—Magla Products; *U.S. Private*, pg. 695

IRON HORSE—Sawhorse—Hirsh Company; *U.S. Public*, pg. 963

IRON IKE—Industrial Chemical—Hercules Chemical Co., Inc.; *U.S. Private*, pg. 523

IRON KE-MIN—Fertilizer—Georgia-Pacific Corporation; *U.S. Public*, pg. 735

IRON KIDS—Bread; Health & Fitness Program—The Earthgrains Company; *U.S. Public*, pg. 547

IRON RICH MATERIAL—NONE—Horsehead Resource Development Company, Inc.; *U.S. Private*, pg. 540

IRON-TUFF—Sub-Zero Clothing—Refrigiwear, Inc.; *U.S. Private*, pg. 917

IRONCLAD—Industrial Coatings—Benjamin Moore & Co.; *U.S. Private*, pg. 133

IRONEX—Chemical reagent—ESA, Inc.; *U.S. Private*, pg. 354

IRONMAN TRIATHLON—Licensee—Timex Corporation; *U.S. Private*, pg. 1088

Brand Name Index

IRONMASTER—Irons—Sunbeam Household Products; *U.S. Public*, pg. 1533

IRONSIDE—Lumber—Georgia-Pacific Corporation; *U.S. Public*, pg. 735

IRONSMITH—Metal-Working Tools—Tractor Supply Co.; *U.S. Public*, pg. 1627

IRONTEX—Iron-On Tapes—EZ International; *U.S. Private*, pg. 1192

IRONTONE—Chelated Iron—Dexol; *U.S. Public*, pg. 1390

IROX—Solar Control Glass—Schott Glaswerke; *Int'l*, pg. 1523

IRRAFLEX—Cable—Rockbestos-Suprenant Cable Corp.; *U.S. Private*, pg. 938

IRRAVIN—Wire—Rockbestos-Suprenant Cable Corp.; *U.S. Private*, pg. 938

IRRIGATION SPECIAL—Tires—Bridgestone/Firestone, Inc.; *Int'l*, pg. 213

IRRITROL—Irrigation—James Hardie Industries Ltd.; *Int'l*, pg. 596

IRTRAN—Infrared Transmitting Materials & Optics—Eastman Kodak Company; *U.S. Public*, pg. 550

IRVINE PARK—Men's Apparel—Blair Corporation; *U.S. Public*, pg. 236

IRVINES—NONE—Quality Bakers New Zealand Ltd.; *Int'l*, pg. 556

IRWIN—Woodboring & Cutting Tools—American Tool Companies, Inc.; *U.S. Public*, pg. 63

ISALY—Frozen Novelty Ice Cream Products—Empire of Carolina, Inc.; *U.S. Public*, pg. 579

ISALY KLONDIKE—Frozen Novelty Ice Cream Products—Empire of Carolina, Inc.; *U.S. Public*, pg. 579

ISAMILL—Fine Grinding Technology—M.I.M. Holdings Ltd.; *Int'l*, pg. 827

ISASMELT—Efficient Smelting Technology—M.I.M. Holdings Ltd.; *Int'l*, pg. 827

ISENBECK—Dark—Warsteiner Importers Agency; *Int'l*, pg. 1486

ISEPACIN—Aminoglycoside Antibiotic—Schering-Plough Corporation; *U.S. Public*, pg. 1438

ISIFIT—Gas Lift Column for Office Chairs—Suspa Compart AG; *Int'l*, pg. 1322

ISIS—Baby Products—Cannon Rubber Ltd.; *Int'l*, pg. 261

ISIS—Infrared & Microwave Intrusion System—Litton Industries, Inc.; *U.S. Public*, pg. 1002

ISLAND—Outdoor Leisure Furniture—Cox Wood Preserving Co.; *U.S. Private*, pg. 283

ISLAND—Records—Philips Electronics N.V.; *Int'l*, pg. 1051

ISLAND—Records & Cassettes—Polygram Records, Inc.; *Int'l*, pg. 1052

ISLAND BOOKS—NONE—Dell Publishing; *Int'l*, pg. 191

ISLAND GUAVA—Hawaiian Guava Juice Drink—Ocean Spray Cranberries, Inc.; *U.S. Private*, pg. 811

ISMELIN—NONE—Novartis Pharmaceuticals; *Int'l*, pg. 973

ISMO—Angina Drug—American Home Products Corporation; *U.S. Public*, pg. 79

ISMO—Cardiac Drug—Boehringer Mannheim GmbH; *Int'l*, pg. 331

ISMOTIC—Isosorbide Solution—Alcon Laboratories, Inc.; *Int'l*, pg. 916

ISOBAR—Surge Suppressors—Trippe Mfg. Co.; *U.S. Private*, pg. 1104

ISOBIND—Isocyanate Binders—The Dow Chemical Company; *U.S. Public*, pg. 522

ISOC—Integrated System of Care—PHP Healthcare Corporation; *U.S. Public*, pg. 1241

ISOCAL—Adult Vitamins—Bristol-Myers Squibb Company; *U.S. Public*, pg. 253

ISOCAL—GR227X Mini-Calibration Service—GenRad, Inc.; *U.S. Public*, pg. 731

ISOCAL HCN—Liquid Diet for Tube Feeding—Mead Johnson Nutritional Group; *U.S. Public*, pg. 254

ISOCEF—Ceftibuten, Antibiotic—Recordati Industria Chimica e Farmaceutica S.p.A.; *Int'l*, pg. 1090

ISOCHECK—Control Serum—Beckman Instruments, Inc.; *U.S. Public*, pg. 199

ISOCIL—NONE—Lonza Inc.; *U.S. Public*, pg. 67

ISOCORE—Coaxial Cable—Rogers Corporation; *U.S. Public*, pg. 1402

ISOCULT—In-Office Diagnostic Culturing System—Beckman Instruments, Inc.; *U.S. Public*, pg. 199

ISOCURE—Foundry Binder—Ashland, Inc.; *U.S. Public*, pg. 138

ISOCUT—Cutting Fluid—Buehler, Limited; *U.S. Public*, pg. 574

ISODINE GARGLE—Pharmaceuticals—Meiji Seika Kaisha, Ltd.; *Int'l*, pg. 855

ISODINE SOLUTION—Veterinary Medicines & Germicides—Meiji Seika Kaisha, Ltd.; *Int'l*, pg. 855

ISOFAX—Fax Machine Surge Suppressor—Trippe Mfg. Co.; *U.S. Private*, pg. 1104

ISOFLO—Naso-Gastric Feeding Tube—Quest Medical, Inc.; *U.S. Public*, pg. 1352

ISO-FLOW—NONE—Petro Chem Development Company; *U.S. Private*, pg. 858

ISOLATOR—Switches—Kearney Company; *U.S. Public*, pg. 444

ISOLENE—Liquid Polyisoprene Rubber Polymer—Hardman Division of Harcros Chemicals, Inc.; *Int'l*, pg. 598

ISOLEX—EMI/RFI Coating—Morton International Inc.; *U.S. Public*, pg. 1135

ISOLEX 300—Magnetic Cell Separator System—Baxter International Inc.; *U.S. Public*, pg. 196

ISOLITE—Unsaturated Polyesters—Schenectady International, Inc.; *U.S. Private*, pg. 969

ISOLOG—Inspection—Tuboscope Incorporated; *U.S. Public*, pg. 1643

ISOMAP—NONE—Landmark Graphics Corporation; *U.S. Public*, pg. 776

ISOMAX—NONE—Acos Villares S.A.; *Int'l*, pg. 23

ISOMAX—Magnetic Recording Media—Eastman Kodak Company; *U.S. Public*, pg. 550

ISOMELT—Polyurethane Coating—Schenectady International, Inc.; *U.S. Private*, pg. 969

ISOMID—Insulating Varnishes—Schenectady International, Inc.; *U.S. Private*, pg. 969

ISOMIL—Infant Formula—Abbott Laboratories; *U.S. Public*, pg. 12

ISOMIL—Soy Infant Feeding—Ross Products; *U.S. Public*, pg. 13

ISOMOD—Stimulator—Medtronic, Inc.; *U.S. Public*, pg. 1082

ISONA D—Antioxidant to Protect Beer from Dissolved Oxygen & from Head Space Air—Royal Gist-Brocades N.V.; *Int'l*, pg. 1142

ISONATE—Urethanes—The Dow Chemical Company; *U.S. Public*, pg. 522

ISONEL—Insulating Varnishes—Schenectady International, Inc.; *U.S. Private*, pg. 969

ISONOL—Polyols—The Dow Chemical Company; *U.S. Public*, pg. 522

ISONOX—Antioxidant—Schenectady International, Inc.; *U.S. Private*, pg. 969

ISOPACS—Capacitors—Semtech Corporation; *U.S. Public*, pg. 1456

ISOPLAST—Thermoplastic Engineering Resin—The Dow Chemical Company; *U.S. Public*, pg. 522

ISOPLUS—Nutrional Supplements—Eastman Kodak Company; *U.S. Public*, pg. 550

ISOPOXY—High Bond Strength; Recommended for Hermetic Units—Schenectady International, Inc.; *U.S. Private*, pg. 969

ISOPREP—Recirculating Iso-Electric Focusing Apparatus—Ionics, Incorporated; *U.S. Public*, pg. 912

ISOPTIN—Pharmaceuticals—Knoll Pharmaceutical Company; *Int'l*, pg. 105

ISOPTIN SR—Pharmaceuticals—Knoll Pharmaceutical Company; *Int'l*, pg. 105

ISOPTO ALKALINE—Hydroxypropl Dav. Methylcellulose—Alcon Laboratories, Inc.; *Int'l*, pg. 916

ISOPTO ATROPINE—Atropine Sulfate—Alcon Laboratories, Inc.; *Int'l*, pg. 916

ISOPTO CARBACHOL—Carbachol—Alcon Laboratories, Inc.; *Int'l*, pg. 916

ISOPTO CARPINE—Pilocarpine Hydrochloride—Alcon Laboratories, Inc.; *Int'l*, pg. 916

ISOPTO CETAMIDE—Sulfacetamide Sodium—Alcon Laboratories, Inc.; *Int'l*, pg. 916

ISOPTO CETAPRED—Sulfacetamide Sodium/Prednisolone Acetate—Alcon Laboratories, Inc.; *Int'l*, pg. 916

ISOPTO ESERINE—Physostigmine Salicylate—Alcon Laboratories, Inc.; *Int'l*, pg. 916

ISOPTO FRIN—Phenylephrine Hydrochloride—Alcon Laboratories, Inc.; *Int'l*, pg. 916

ISOPTO HOMATROPINE—Homatropine Hydrobromide—Alcon Laboratories, Inc.; *Int'l*, pg. 916

ISOPTO HYOSCINE—Scopolamine Hydrobromide—Alcon Laboratories, Inc.; *Int'l*, pg. 916

ISOPTO P-ES—Pilocarpine Hydrochloride 2%—Alcon Laboratories, Inc.; *Int'l*, pg. 916

ISOPTO PLAIN—Hydroxypropyl Methylcellulose—Alcon Laboratories, Inc.; *Int'l*, pg. 916

ISOPTO TEARS—Hydroxypropyl Methylcellulose—Alcon Laboratories, Inc.; *Int'l*, pg. 916

ISORDIL—Angina Drug—American Home Products Corporation; *U.S. Public*, pg. 79

ISOSET—Emulsion Urethane Adhesives—Ashland, Inc.; *U.S. Public*, pg. 138

ISOSTAR—Isotonic Drink—Novartis AG; *Int'l*, pg. 971

ISOSTAT MICROBIAL SYSTEM—Blood Culture System—Wampole Laboratories; *U.S. Public*, pg. 310

ISOTEC—Filters & Filter Sets—Quest Medical, Inc.; *U.S. Public*, pg. 1352

ISOTEMP—Temperature Control Apparatus—Fisher Scientific Company; *U.S. Private*, pg. 658

ISOTONER—Gloves, Slippers & Knitted Accessories—Sara Lee Corporation; *U.S. Public*, pg. 1432

ISOTONER—Slippers, Gloves, Knits, Socks & Umbrellas—Totes/Isotoner, Inc.; *U.S. Public*, pg. 1433

ISOVUE—Nonionic Imaging Agent—Bristol-Myers Squibb Company; *U.S. Public*, pg. 253

ISOVUE-M—Nonionic Imaging Agent—Bristol-Myers Squibb Company; *U.S. Public*, pg. 253

ISOWELD—Solderable Esterimides—Schenectady International, Inc.; *U.S. Private*, pg. 969

ISRAEL DIAMOND AND PRECIOUS STONES—News Magazine—Reed Elsevier Business Information; *Int'l*, pg. 1095

ISSIMA—Skincare—Guerlain, Inc.; *Int'l*, pg. 780

ISUZU AMIGO—Mini SOV—American Isuzu Motors Inc.; *Int'l*, pg. 692

ISUZU OASIS—Commpact Mini-Van—American Isuzu Motors Inc.; *Int'l*, pg. 692

ISUZU PICKUP—Compact Pickup Truck—American Isuzu Motors Inc.; *Int'l*, pg. 692

ISUZU RODEO—Two Wheel & Four-Wheel Drive Utility Vehicle—American Isuzu Motors Inc.; *Int'l*, pg. 692

ISUZU TROOPER—Four-Wheel Drive Utility Vehicle—American Isuzu Motors Inc.; *int'l*, pg. 692

IT FITS, IT FITS!—Hosiery & Related Apparel—Mayer/Berkshire Corporation; *U.S. Private*, pg. 717

IT'S YOUR BUSINESS—TV Weekly Debate/Discussion Program—Nation's Business; *U.S. Private*, pg. 788

ITALIAN COLLECTION BY TREADEASY—Shoes—P.W. Minor & Son, Inc.; *U.S. Private*, pg. 751

ITALIAN KITCHEN—Wine Vinegar—Star Fine Foods, Inc.; *U.S. Private*, pg. 1034

ITALIAN MARKET—Italian Food Products—The Pillsbury Company; *Int'l*, pg. 411

ITALIAN SWISS COLONY—Dessert Wines—The Beverage Source, Inc.; *U.S. Public*, pg. 591

ITALIANA LUCE—Contemporary Lighting Fixtures—IL International Inc.; *U.S. Public*, pg. 855

ITALSEI—Prosciutto—I.B.I.S.-S.p.A.; *Int'l*, pg. 642

ITAPSA—Brake Block—Echlin Inc.; *U.S. Public*, pg. 560

ITASCA—Motor Homes—Winnebago Industries, Inc.; *U.S. Public*, pg. 1772

ITCH-B-GONE—Relieves Animals of Itching—Bethurum Research & Development, Inc.; *U.S. Private*, pg. 141

ITEK—Optical & Photographic Equipment—Litton Industries, Inc.; *U.S. Public*, pg. 1002

ITEK—Optical Systems & Components—Raytheon Optical Systems; *U.S. Public*, pg. 1364

ITEK GRAPHIX—Pre-Press, Press, Post-Press Equipment & Supplies—A.B. Dick Company; *U.S. Private*, pg. 791

ITEMATIC—Less Than Full Case Order Selection System—SI Handling Systems, Inc.; *U.S. Public*, pg. 1418

ITEMS—Database Management System—International Technology Corporation; *U.S. Public*, pg. 907

ITOKIN BLOUSE—Women's Apparel—International Cosmetics Co., Ltd.; *Int'l*, pg. 684

ITRAC—Undercarriage Components-Track Links, Track Shoes, Idlers, Sprockets, etc.—Intertractor Zweigniederlassung der Wirtgen GmbH; *Int'l*, pg. 1511

ITREL—Pulse Generator—Medtronic, Inc.; *U.S. Public*, pg. 1082

ITREL EZ—Stimulator—Medtronic, Inc.; *U.S. Public*, pg. 1082

ITREL 3—Stimulator—Medtronic, Inc.; *U.S. Public*, pg. 1082

ITREL II—Stimulator—Medtronic, Inc.; *U.S. Public*, pg. 1082

ITRIZOLE—NONE—Johnson & Johnson; *U.S. Public*, pg. 927

IT'S A SONY GROWING S DESIGN—Most Products—Sony Electronics; *Int'l*, pg. 1281

IT'S ABOUT GAMES—Buys & Sells Used & New Video Games—Grow Biz International, Inc.; *U.S. Public*, pg. 767

IT'S BLISS—U.K. Young Women's Magazine—EMAP Elan; *Int'l*, pg. 451

IT'S ORGANIC NATURALLY—Hair Products—Dena Corporation; *U.S. Private*, pg. 324

ITS PAQUETTE—Large Size Sportswear—Byer California; *U.S. Private*, pg. 191

IT'S REALLY SOMETHING—Bras—Warner's; *U.S. Public*, pg. 1738

IT'S REYNOLDS SURE SEAL OR BUST—Plastic Bags—Reynolds Metals Company; *U.S. Public*, pg. 1385

IT'S THAT SIMPLE—NONE—The Stop & Shop Companies, Inc.; *Int'l*, pg. 750

IT'S THE EXPERIENCE—Recruiting & Advertising Package—RE/MAX International, Inc.; *U.S. Private*, pg. 912

ITS WORLD—Trade Periodical—Advanstar Communications; *U.S. Private*, pg. 22

IT'S YOUR BUSINESS—Catalog Sales of Personalized Business Accessories—Artistic Greetings, Inc.; *U.S. Public*, pg. 136

IUCREDI BAR—Bar Code Labeling—Peak Technologies Group, Inc.; *Int'l*, pg. 890

IVARAN LINES—NONE—A/S Ivaran Rederi; *Int'l*, pg. 696

IVAREST—Poison Ivy Cream—Blistex, Inc.; *U.S. Private*, pg. 149

IVECO—Truck—Fiat Auto SpA; *Int'l*, pg. 480

IVECO—Trucks & Parts—Iveco France S.A.; *Int'l*, pg. 696

IVECO—Diesel Trucks Euro-Line—Iveco Trucks Of North America Inc.; *Int'l*, pg. 484

IVECO—Truck Parts—Iveco-Unic S.A.; *Int'l*, pg. 484

IVECO FORD—Truck—Iveco-Ford Truck Ltd.; *Int'l*, pg. 484

IVEX—Filter Unit—Millipore Corporation; *U.S. Public*, pg. 1112

IVIS—Electronic Video Imaging Systems—IDenticard Systems, Inc.; *U.S. Private*, pg. 557

IVOMEC—Ivermectin Veterinary Antiparasitic Preparation—Merck & Co., Inc.; *U.S. Public*, pg. 1090

IVOMEC—Animal Health Pharmaceuticals—Merial Ltd.; *U.S. Public*, pg. 1092

IVOMEC—Animal Health Pharmaceuticals—Merial Ltd.; *Int'l*, pg. 1109

IVOMEC INJECTION FOR SWINE—NONE—Merial Ltd.; *U.S. Public*, pg. 1092

IVOMEC INJECTION FOR SWINE—NONE—Merial Ltd.; *Int'l*, pg. 1109

IVOMEC PLUS—NONE—Merial Ltd.; *U.S. Public*, pg. 1092

IVOMEC PLUS—NONE—Merial Ltd.; *Int'l*, pg. 1109

IVOMEC PREMIX FOR SWINE—NONE—Merial Ltd.; *U.S. Public*, pg. 1092

IVOMEC PREMIX FOR SWINE—NONE—Merial Ltd.; *Int'l*, pg. 1109

IVOMEC SR BOLUS—Animal Health Pharmaceuticals—Merial Ltd.; *U.S. Public*, pg. 1092

IVOMEC SR BOLUS—Animal Health Pharmaceuticals—Merial Ltd.; *Int'l*, pg. 1109

IVOMEC POUR-ON—Animal Health Pharmaceuticals—Merial Ltd.; *U.S. Public*, pg. 1092

IVOMEC POUR-ON—Animal Health Pharmaceuticals—Merial Ltd.; *Int'l*, pg. 1109

IVORY—Detergent, Soap, Conditioner, Shampoo—The Procter & Gamble Company; *U.S. Public*, pg. 1330

IVORY LIQUID—Dishwashing Detergent—The Procter & Gamble Company; *U.S. Public*, pg. 1330

IVORY SNOW—Laundry Products—The Procter & Gamble Company; *U.S. Public*, pg. 1330

IVY—Office Management Systems—Alcon Laboratories, Inc.; *Int'l*, pg. 916

IVY—NONE—Kellwood Company; *U.S. Public*, pg. 948

IVY—Book Publishing—Random House, Inc.; *U.S. Private*, pg. 20

IVY ADDITIONS—NONE—Kellwood Company; *U.S. Public*, pg. 948

IVY CREW—NONE—Tandy Brands Accessories, Inc.; *U.S. Public*, pg. 1560

IVY HILL—Slacks—Master Industries Corp.; *U.S. Private*, pg. 713

IVY IMPRESSIONS—NONE—Kellwood Company; *U.S. Public*, pg. 948

IVY WORKS—NONE—Kellwood Company; *U.S. Public*, pg. 948

IVYWEAR—NONE—Kellwood Company; *U.S. Public*, pg. 948

IZOD LACOSTE—Sportswear—Izod; *U.S. Public*, pg. 1292

J

J. A. JONES APPLIED RESEARCH CO.—Research & Development Company—J.A. Jones, Inc.; *Int'l*, pg. 633

J. A. JONES CONSTRUCTION CO.—Construction Company-General Contractor—J.A. Jones, Inc.; *Int'l*, pg. 633

JAM—Joint Analyzed Makeup Tubular Service Tool—Weatherford Enterra Incorporated; *U.S. Public*, pg. 1749

J&B EDWARDIAN—NONE—J&B Scotland; *Int'l*, pg. 410

J&B RARE—Spirits—Gilbeys of Ireland; *Int'l*, pg. 409

J & B RARE—Scotch Whiskey—Grand Metropolitan Plc; *Int'l*, pg. 408

J & B RARE—Rare Scotch Whiskey—IDV North America; *Int'l*, pg. 411

J & B RARE—NONE—International Distillers Caribbean; *Int'l*, pg. 410

J&B RARE—NONE—Justerini & Brooks Ltd.; *Int'l*, pg. 409

J & B RARE—NONE—Societe Pour la Vente des Produits Cinzano SA; *Int'l*, pg. 410

J&B RESERVE—NONE—Justerini & Brooks Ltd.; *Int'l*, pg. 409

J & B RESERVE—NONE—Societe Pour la Vente des Produits Cinzano SA; *Int'l*, pg. 410

J&B RESERVE 15 YEAR OLD—NONE—J&B Scotland; *Int'l*, pg. 410

J&B SCOTCH WHISKY—Whisky—Dateo Import S.P.A.; *Int'l*, pg. 385

J & B SELECT—Scotch Whisky—Grand Metropolitan Plc; *Int'l*, pg. 408

J & B SELECT—Matured Oak Casks—IDV North America; *Int'l*, pg. 411

J&B SELECT—NONE—Justerini & Brooks Ltd.; *Int'l*, pg. 409

J&B ULTIMA—NONE—Justerini & Brooks Ltd.; *Int'l*, pg. 409

J&B VICTORIAN—NONE—J&B Scotland; *Int'l*, pg. 410

J&H MARSH & MCLENNAN—Insurance Broking Services—Marsh & McLennan Companies, Inc.; *U.S. Public*, pg. 1048

J & H WILSON SELECTION—SP No.1, Top Mill No.1, Medicated 99, Kensington - Snuffs—Imperial Tobacco Group, Ltd.; *Int'l*, pg. 666

J & L FIBER SYSTEMS—Refiner Plates & Screen Baskets—Beloit Corporation; *U.S. Public*, pg. 789

J & M—Shoes—Genesco Inc.; *U.S. Public*, pg. 728

J & M—Shoes—Johnston & Murphy Co.; *U.S. Public*, pg. 728

J&M—Refrigeration-Free Halal Meals—My Own Meals, Inc.; *U.S. Private*, pg. 770

J & P COATS—Home Sewing Thread—Coats & Clark Inc.; *Int'l*, pg. 300

J & T—Diesel Engine Distributor—Johnson & Towers, Inc.; *U.S. Private*, pg. 590

JB—Hot Sauces, Mustard, Pickles, Olives—Bestfoods; *U.S. Public*, pg. 223

J B & S LEES—NONE—Glynwed International PLC; *Int'l*, pg. 554

JBL—NONE—Harman Consumer Group; *U.S. Public*, pg. 787

JBL—Loud Speakers—Harman International Industries, Inc.; *U.S. Public*, pg. 787

J.B. ROBINSON—Retail Jewelers—J.B. Robinson Jewelers, Inc.; *Int'l*, pg. 1248

J.B. WINBERIE—Restaurant—Select Restaurants, Inc.; *U.S. Public*, pg. 982

J. BLAST—Abrasives—IMI Plc; *Int'l*, pg. 646

JB'S RESTAURANTS—Restaurants—Summit Family Restaurants, Inc.; *U.S. Public*, pg. 278

J.C. BRADFORD & CO.—NONE—J.C. Bradford & Co.; *U.S. Private*, pg. 163

JCI—Computer Services—JCI Data Processing, Inc.; *U.S. Private*, pg. 577

JCK—Magazine for Jewelers—Reed Elsevier Business Information; *Int'l*, pg. 1095

JCK JAPAN—Japanese Language News Publication for Japanese Retail Jewelers—Reed Elsevier Business Information; *Int'l*, pg. 1095

JCK'S HIGH-VOLUME JEWELER—Publication for Executives in High-Volume Jewelery Industry—Reed Elsevier Business Information; *Int'l*, pg. 1095

JCK'S VISTA JOYERA—Bilingual Magazine for Retail Jewelers—Reed Elsevier Business Information; *Int'l*, pg. 1095

J. C. PENNEY—Department Stores—JC Penney Company, Inc.; *U.S. Public*, pg. 916

J. CHUCKLES—Women's Apparel—A&E Stores, Inc.; *U.S. Private*, pg. 1

JDS—Jaguar Diagnostic System—GenRad, Inc.; *U.S. Public*, pg. 731

J.E. PREMIER SERIES—Cooling Tower—Baltimore Aircoil Company; *U.S. Private*, pg. 68

J.E.T.—Instruments—BF Goodrich Avionic Systems, Inc.; *U.S. Public*, pg. 751

J11—Processor Option—GenRad, Inc.; *U.S. Public*, pg. 731

JFG—Coffee—Reily Foods & Co.; *U.S. Private*, pg. 919

JGA 502—Conventional Liquid Air Spray Gun—Illinois Tool Works Inc.; *U.S. Public*, pg. 865

J.G. HOOK—Apparel for Boys—Hampton Industries, Inc.; *U.S. Public*, pg. 779

J. G. HOOK—Men's Tailored Clothing—Hartmarx Corporation; *U.S. Public*, pg. 795

J.G. HOOK—NONE—Holt Hosiery Mills, Inc.; *U.S. Private*, pg. 536

JG HOOK—NONE—J.G. Hook, Inc.; *U.S. Private*, pg. 538

JG HOOK COLLECTION—NONE—J.G. Hook, Inc.; *U.S. Private*, pg. 538

J-GRIPPER—Seamless Cotton Heat Glove-Nitrile J—Jomac, Inc.; *U.S. Private*, pg. 595

J.J. COCHRAN BOYS—Clothing—Hampton Industries, Inc.; *U.S. Public*, pg. 779

JJ FLATS—Crispy, Unleavened Bread with Various Flavored Coatings—Bestfoods; *U.S. Public*, pg. 223

J. JILL—Mail Order Women's Apparel—DM Management Company; *U.S. Public*, pg. 473

JK—Quartz Piezoelectric Crystals—CTS Corporation; *U.S. Public*, pg. 285

J. K. LASSER TAX INSTITUTE—Guides—Simon & Schuster; *U.S. Private*, pg. 777

J.L. COLEBROOK—NONE—G-III Apparel Group, Ltd.; *U.S. Public*, pg. 690

JLGLIFT—Aerial Work Platforms—JLG Industries, Inc.; *U.S. Public*, pg. 918

JLG SIZZOR—Aerial Work Platform—JLG Industries, Inc.; *U.S. Public*, pg. 918

JMF—Men's Cologne—Stanhome Inc.; *U.S. Public*, pg. 1508

J.M. NEY—Electronic Components & Materials—Ney Dental International; *Int'l*, pg. 388

JMP SOFTWARE—Interactive Statistical Data Discovery and Experimentation Package—SAS Institute Inc.; *U.S. Private*, pg. 966

J.M. SMUCKERS—NONE—J.M. Smucker Company; *U.S. Public*, pg. 1480

J. MOREAU—Chablis, Blanc & Rouge; Varietal Wines—Frederick Wildman & Sons Ltd.; *U.S. Private*, pg. 1176

J. MURPHY—Shoes—Johnston & Murphy Co.; *U.S. Public*, pg. 728

JOI—Soft Drinks—Central de Cervejas, S.A.; *Int'l*, pg. 279

JP—NONE—JP Foodservice, Inc.; *U.S. Public*, pg. 918

J.P.A.—Junior Putters of America—Professional Putters Association; *U.S. Private*, pg. 896

JP BLUE—NONE—JP Foodservice, Inc.; *U.S. Public*, pg. 918

JP CONNECTION—NONE—JP Foodservice, Inc.; *U.S. Public*, pg. 918

JP DIRECTADVANTAGE—NONE—JP Foodservice, Inc.; *U.S. Public*, pg. 918

JP EXPRESS REBATE—NONE—JP Foodservice, Inc.; *U.S. Public*, pg. 918

JP FOODNEWS—NONE—JP Foodservice, Inc.; *U.S. Public*, pg. 918

JP FOODSERVICE, INC.—NONE—JP Foodservice, Inc.; *U.S. Public*, pg. 918

JP FOODSERVICE, INC. CATTLEMAN'S CHOICE—NONE—JP Foodservice, Inc.; *U.S. Public*, pg. 918

JP FOODSERVICE, INC. SERVICE MAKES A DIFFERENCE—NONE—JP Foodservice, Inc.; *U.S. Public*, pg. 918

JP GOLD—NONE—JP Foodservice, Inc.; *U.S. Public*, pg. 918

JP POWER—NONE—JP Foodservice, Inc.; *U.S. Public*, pg. 918

JP POWER BY JP FOODSERVICE—NONE—JP Foodservice, Inc.; *U.S. Public*, pg. 918

JP RED—NONE—JP Foodservice, Inc.; *U.S. Public*, pg. 918

JP 390C—Brush Cutter—Hoffco/Comet Industries, Inc.; *U.S. Private*, pg. 532

JP 390F—Brush Cutter—Hoffco/Comet Industries, Inc.; *U.S. Private*, pg. 532

JP 260C—Brush Cutter—Hoffco/Comet Industries, Inc.; *U.S. Private*, pg. 532

JP 220F—Brush Cutter—Hoffco/Comet Industries, Inc.; *U.S. Private*, pg. 532

J. RIGGINGS—Men's Apparel—Edison Brothers Stores, Inc.; *U.S. Public*, pg. 563

J. ROGET—Wines—Canandaigua Wine Company, Inc.; *U.S. Public*, pg. 300

J. SCHOENEMAN—Tailored Clothing—Bidermann International S.A.; *Int'l*, pg. 194

J-16—Asphalt Sealer—Maintenance, Inc.; *Int'l*, pg. 1068

JT FAX 9600—Fax Server—Hayes Microcomputer Products, Inc.; *U.S. Public*, pg. 801

JT15D—Aircraft Engine—Pratt & Whitney Canada Inc.; *U.S. Public*, pg. 1690

JT21—Staple Gun—Arrow Fastener Co., Inc.; *U.S. Private*, pg. 85

J-TECH—NONE—Milgray Electronics, Inc.; *U.S. Public*, pg. 205

J30—Automobile—Nissan Motor Corporation in U.S.A.; *Int'l*, pg. 945

J.W.—Food Products—Rykoff-Sexton, Inc.; *U.S. Public*, pg. 918

JW DUNDEE'S HONEY BROWN LAGER—Beer—Genesee Corporation; *U.S. Public*, pg. 728

JW LOGO—Audio Cassettes, Computer Programs, Books—John Wiley & Sons, Inc.; *U.S. Public*, pg. 1768

JW'S BY JOHN WEITZ—Men's Slacks—Glen Oaks Industries, Inc.; *U.S. Private*, pg. 456

J-WALK—Rooftop Walkway System—Johns Manville Corporation; *U.S. Public*, pg. 927

J-WOOD—Kitchen & Bathroom Cabinets—Electrolux, AB; *Int'l*, pg. 438

JABSCO—Pumps—ITT Jabsco; *U.S. Public*, pg. 860

JABSCO—Pumps—Ryan Herco Products Corp.; *U.S. Private*, pg. 953

JACK—Hand Saws—American Tool Companies, Inc.; *U.S. Private*, pg. 63

JACK—Canned Coffee—Sapporo Breweries Ltd.; *Int'l*, pg. 1193

JACK AND JILL—Magazine for Children—Benjamin Franklin Literary & Medical Society, Inc.; *U.S. Private*, pg. 133

JACK & JILL—Retail Grocery Stores—Nash Finch Company; *U.S. Public*, pg. 1151

JACK AND THE BEANSTALK—Canned Food—Agripac Inc.; *U.S. Private*, pg. 26

JACK BAKER'S LOBSTER SHANTY—Restaurants—Chefs International, Inc.; *U.S. Public*, pg. 343

JACK DANIEL CHARCOAL BRIQUETS—Premium Charcoal Briquet Made with Jack Daniel's Barrel Wood—Hickory Specialties, Inc.; *U.S. Public*, pg. 596

JACK DANIEL'S TENNESSEE WHISKEY—Whiskey—Brown-Forman Beverages Worldwide; *U.S. Public*, pg. 261

JACK DANIEL'S—Tennessee Whiskey, Country Cocktails—Brown-Forman Corporation; *U.S. Public*, pg. 261

JACK DANIEL'S & COLA—NONE—Brown-Forman Beverages Worldwide; *U.S. Public*, pg. 261

JACK DANIEL'S COUNTRY COCKTAILS—Cooler-Type Cocktails—Brown-Forman Beverages Worldwide; *U.S. Public*, pg. 261

JACK DANIEL'S COUNTRY COCKTAILS—Whiskey—Jack Daniels Distillery; *U.S. Public*, pg. 261

JACK DANIEL'S MASTER DISTILLER—Whiskey—Brown-Forman Beverages Worldwide; *U.S. Public*, pg. 261

JACK DANIEL'S OAK-AGED BEERS—NONE—Brown-Forman Beverages Worldwide; *U.S. Public*, pg. 261

JACK DANIEL'S SINGLE BARREL—Whiskey—Brown-Forman Beverages Worldwide; *U.S. Public*, pg. 261

JACK DANIEL'S TENNESSEE—Whiskey—Jack Daniels Distillery; *U.S. Public*, pg. 261

JACK FROST—Pure Cane Sugar—Refined Sugars, Inc.; *Int'l*, pg. 699

JACK IN THE BOX—Restaurants—Foodmaker, Inc.; *U.S. Public*, pg. 661

JACK NICKLAUS—Apparel—Hartmarx Corporation; *U.S. Public*, pg. 795

JACK NICKLAUS—Golf Equipment—MacGregor Golf Company; *Int'l*, pg. 72

JACK NICKLAUS SIGNATURE—Apparel—MacGregor Golf Company; *Int'l*, pg. 72

JACK RABBIT—Dry Beans, Peas & Lentils—ConAgra, Inc.; *U.S. Public*, pg. 425

JACK WOLFSKIN—Tents, Backpacks, Outdoor Clothing & Accessories—Johnson Worldwide Associates, Inc.; *U.S. Public*, pg. 932

JACK'S—Frozen Pizza—Kraft Foods Inc.; *U.S. Public*, pg. 1288

JACKS—Boys Shoes—Jumping Jacks; *U.S. Private*, pg. 767

JACK'S—Frozen Pizza—Philip Morris Companies Inc.; *U.S. Public*, pg. 1287

JACK'S—Cookies—President Baking Company; *Int'l*, pg. 1069

JACKSON—Medicated Cough Drops—Cadbury Schweppes p.l.c.; *Int'l*, pg. 247

JACKSON—Lawn & Garden Tools—Huffy Corporation; *U.S. Public*, pg. 846

JACKSON—Restaurant Equipment—Jackson MSC; *U.S. Private*, pg. 579

JACKSON—Buffs—Jason Incorporated; *U.S. Public*, pg. 923

JACKSON—Wheelbarrows—True Temper Hardware Company; *U.S. Public*, pg. 846

JACKSON & PERKINS—Nurserymen—Jackson & Perkins; *Int'l*, pg. 1518

JACKSON & CHURCH—HVAC Equipment—Donlee Technologies Inc.; *U.S. Private*, pg. 339

THE JACKSON CITIZEN PATRIOT—Newspaper—Booth Newspapers, Inc.; *U.S. Private*, pg. 157

JACKSON HOLE—Ski Resort—Jackson Hole Ski Resort; *U.S. Private*, pg. 579

JACKSON-PRATT—Suction Drains, Reservoirs & Associated Connectors for Wound Drainage—Allegiance Healthcare Corp.; *U.S. Public*, pg. 44

JACKSON'S—Cookies—President Baking Company; *Int'l*, pg. 1069

JACKSONVILLE BUSINESS JOURNAL—Business Journal—Business First of New York, Inc.; *U.S. Private*, pg. 19

JACKY—Refrigerated Products—Nestle S.A.; *Int'l*, pg. 915

JACLYN—Purses & Handbags—Jaclyn, Inc.; *U.S. Public*, pg. 920

JACMAR—Restaurant Food—Jacmar Companies, Inc.; *U.S. Private*, pg. 580

JACO—Hose Fittings—Ryan Herco Products Corp.; *U.S. Private*, pg. 953

JACOB BEST PREMIUM LIGHT—Beer—Pabst Brewing Co.; *U.S. Private*, pg. 954

JACOB'S—Biscuits & Coffee—Irish Biscuits; *Int'l*, pg. 688

JACOBS—Portable Drill Chucks—Danaher Tool Group; *U.S. Public*, pg. 480

JACOB'S—Biscuits, Crackers—Danone Group; *Int'l*, pg. 379

JACOBS—Registered Trademark Name—Jacobs Vehicle Equipment Company; *U.S. Public*, pg. 481

JACOBS—Coffee—Kraft Jacobs Suchard AG; *U.S. Public*, pg. 1288

JACOB'S CREEK—Dry Red Wine—Groupe Pernod Ricard; *Int'l*, pg. 566

JACOBS CREEK WINES—Wine—Austin Nichols & Co. Inc.; *Int'l*, pg. 566

JAY JACOBS—Clothing Stores—Jay Jacobs, Inc.; *U.S. Public*, pg. 922

JACOB'S WELL—NONE—Fortune Brands, Inc.; *U.S. Public*, pg. 674

JACOBSDAL ESTATE—Wine—Distillers Corporation S.A.; *Int'l*, pg. 1129

JACOBSON—Stores—Jacobson Stores Inc.; *U.S. Public*, pg. 922

JACQMOTTE—Coffee Product—Sara Lee Corporation; *U.S. Public*, pg. 1432

JACQUE BONET—Brandy—Canandaigua Wine Company Div.; *U.S. Public*, pg. 300

JACQUE BONET—Wines—Canandaigua Wine Company, Inc.; *U.S. Public*, pg. 300

JACQUERT—Champagne—Paterno Imports Limited; *U.S. Private*, pg. 843

JACQUES BONET—Sparkling Wines—The Beverage Source, Inc.; *U.S. Public*, pg. 591

JACQUES BONET BRANDY—NONE—Barton Brands, Ltd.; *U.S. Public*, pg. 300

JACQUES DEPAGNEUX—Beaujolais Wines—Frederick Wildman & Sons Ltd.; *U.S. Private*, pg. 1176

JACQUES ESTEREL—Perfume Line—Stanhome Inc.; *U.S. Public*, pg. 1508

JACQUES MORET—Women's Apparel—Jacques Moret, Inc.; *U.S. Private*, pg. 580

JACQUES MORET KIDS—Children's Apparel—Jacques Moret, Inc.; *U.S. Private*, pg. 580

JACQUES VABRE—Coffee—Kraft Jacobs Suchard; *U.S. Public*, pg. 1290

JACQUET—Bread—Groupe Limagrain; *Int'l*, pg. 566

JACQUIN—Liquors & Cordials—Charles Jacquin et Cie, Inc.; *U.S. Private*, pg. 580

JACTO—Fresh Yeast—Royal Gist-Brocades N.V.; *Int'l*, pg. 1142

JACUZZI—Pump & Water Systems—Jacuzzi Bros., Jacuzzi, Inc.; *U.S. Public*, pg. 1684

JAEGER—NONE—Coats Viyella plc; *Int'l*, pg. 299

JAEGER—Bread, Buns, Sweet Goods—Metz Baking Company (WI); *U.S. Private*, pg. 1022

JAEGER-LE COULTRE—Watches—Jaeger-Le Coultre; *Int'l*, pg. 697

JAEGER-LE COULTRE—Fine Watches—Swiss Prestige, Inc.; *Int'l*, pg. 697

JAFAESTER—Fatty Acid Esters—Pronova Oleochemicals a.s.; *Int'l*, pg. 961

JAFFELIN—Burgundy Wine—Remy Amerique Inc.; *Int'l*, pg. 1102

JAG—Womens Contemporary Swim & Beachwear—Beach Patrol Inc.; *U.S. Private*, pg. 125

JAGUAR—NONE—IMO Pump; *U.S. Public*, pg. 857

JAGUAR—Luxury Vehicles—Jaguar Cars; *U.S. Public*, pg. 664

JAGUAR—Automobiles—Jaguar Cars Limited; *U.S. Public*, pg. 666

JAGUAR—Binocular—Swift Instruments, Inc.; *U.S. Private*, pg. 1058

JAGUAR 64—Home Video Game System—JTS Corporation; *U.S. Public*, pg. 919

JAGUAR TEXT & COVER—Printing Papers—Weyerhaeuser Company; *U.S. Public*, pg. 1764

JAHN BRACKET—Forming Hardware—Dayton Superior Corporation; *U.S. Private*, pg. 931

JAKE BRAKE—Retarders—Jacobs Vehicle Equipment Company; *U.S. Public*, pg. 481

JAKE'S DIET COLA—Diet Cola—Pepsi-Cola Company; *U.S. Public*, pg. 1277

JAKE'S JOKES—Joke Cards—Mattel Games/Puzzles; *U.S. Public*, pg. 1058

JAKSON—Bath Products—CHF Industries, Inc.; *U.S. Private*, pg. 1094

JAKSON—Shower Curtains—Jakson-A CHF Company; *U.S. Private*, pg. 1094

JALLATTE—NONE—ETEX; *Int'l*, pg. 430

JALLATTE AB—NONE—ETEX; *Int'l*, pg. 430

JAMAICA ALMOND FUDGE—NONE—Baskin-Robbins Canada; *Int'l*, pg. 63

JAMB-JACK—Fasteners—Pease Industries, Inc.; *U.S. Private*, pg. 845

JAMBOL—Plant Protectives—DSM Chemie Linz GmbH; *Int'l*, pg. 356

JAMBOREE—Motor Home—Fleetwood Enterprises, Inc.; *U.S. Public*, pg. 650

JAMBOREE—Fruit Juice—Nestle Chocolate & Confection; *Int'l*, pg. 917

JAMCO—NONE—North America Foods; *U.S. Public*, pg. 901

JAMES B. FAIRCHILD—Menswear—Tandy Brands Accessories, Inc.; *U.S. Public*, pg. 1560

JAMES DISCOVERS MATH—NONE—Broderbund Software, Inc.; *U.S. Public*, pg. 258

JAMES K. POLK—Motel—JRN, Inc.; *U.S. Private*, pg. 578

JAMES RIVER—NONE—The Smithfield Companies, Inc.; *U.S. Public*, pg. 1479

JAMES RIVER BRAND—Canned Meat & Meat Entrees—Bunker Hill Foods Inc.; *U.S. Private*, pg. 219

JAMES SEEMAN STUDIOS—Wallcoverings—Borden, Inc.; *U.S. Private*, pg. 157

JAMESON—Chocolate—Cadbury Schweppes p.l.c.; *Int'l*, pg. 247

JAMESON—Irish Whiskey—Groupe Pernod Ricard; *Int'l*, pg. 566

JAMESON—Irish Whiskey—The House of Seagram; *Int'l*, pg. 1217

JAMESON—Irish Whiskey—The Seagram Company Ltd.; *Int'l*, pg. 1214

JAMESON CELL—Flotation Cell Technology—M.I.M. Holdings Ltd.; *Int'l*, pg. 827

JAMESON IRISH WHISKY—NONE—Austin Nichols & Co. Inc.; *Int'l*, pg. 566

JAMESTOWN—Aluminum Siding—Reynolds Metals Company; *U.S. Public*, pg. 1385

JAMESTOWN—Paper for Office & Personal Copiers—Union Camp Corporation; *U.S. Public*, pg. 1665

JAMESTOWN BRAND—Meat Products—The Smithfield Packing Co., Inc.; *U.S. Public*, pg. 1479

JAMIE—Yarn—Lion Brand Yarn Co.; *U.S. Private*, pg. 669

JAMIS—Job Cost Accounting & Management Information System—Maxwell Technologies, Inc.; *U.S. Public*, pg. 1061

JAMSHIDI—Biopsy Needles—Allegiance Healthcare Corp.; *U.S. Public*, pg. 44

JAMY—Barley Tea Bags—Meiji Seika Kaisha, Ltd.; *Int'l*, pg. 855

JAN III SOBIESKI—Cigarettes—B.A.T Industries P.L.C.; *Int'l*, pg. 110

JANDY VALES—NONE—Teledyne Laars/Jandy Products; *U.S. Public*, pg. 43

JANE—NONE—Estee Lauder Companies Inc.; *U.S. Public*, pg. 594

JANE PARKER—Doughnuts & Cakes—The Great Atlantic & Pacific Tea Company, Inc.; *Int'l*, pg. 1375

JANEIRO—Fruit Drink—Groupe Pernod Ricard; *Int'l*, pg. 566

JANE'S COMBAT SIMULATIONS—Military/Flight Simulation—Electronic Arts; *U.S. Public*, pg. 569

JANESVILLE—Fiber Insulation—Janesville Products; *U.S. Public*, pg. 924

JANESVILLE—Automotive Insulation—Jason Incorporated; *U.S. Public*, pg. 923

JANET DAVIS—Frozen Poultry—Louis Kemp Seafood Co.; *U.S. Public*, pg. 1652

JANET DAVIS—Frozen Poultry—Tyson Foods, Inc.; *U.S. Public*, pg. 1652

JANET LEE—NONE—Albertson's, Inc.; *U.S. Public*, pg. 38

JANET THOMAS BOOKS—Books—Thomas Nelson Inc.; *U.S. Public*, pg. 1167

JANITOR-IN-A-DRUM—Cleaner—The Dow Chemical Company; *U.S. Public*, pg. 522

JANLYNN—Needlecraft—Janlynn Corporation; *U.S. Private*, pg. 582

JANNEAU—Armagnac—Seagram Chateau & Estate Wines Co.; *Int'l*, pg. 1215

JANSEN—Beer—Central de Cervejas, S.A.; *Int'l*, pg. 279

JANSPORT—Daypacks—VF Corporation; *U.S. Public*, pg. 1702

JANSPORT, INC.—Backpacks—JanSport; *U.S. Public*, pg. 1702

JANSSEN—NONE—Johnson & Johnson; *U.S. Public*, pg. 927

JANTZEN—Swimwear, Activewear & Sweaters for Women—Jantzen; *U.S. Public*, pg. 1702

JANTZEN—Clothing—Kosugi Sangyo Co., Ltd.; *Int'l*, pg. 759

JANTZEN—Swimsuits; Sportswear—VF Corporation; *U.S. Public*, pg. 1702

JANUS—Elevator Controls & Saftey Systems—Halma p.l.c.; *Int'l*, pg. 589

JAPAN AIRLINES—Airlines—Japan Airlines American Region; *Int'l*, pg. 700

JAR KING—Hydraulic Drilling Jar—Baker Hughes INTEQ; *U.S. Public*, pg. 166

JARCAL—Food Grade Calcium Chloride—Jarchem Industries, Inc.; *U.S. Private*, pg. 582

JARDINAY—Gold Jewelry—Michael Anthony Jewelers, Inc.; *U.S. Public*, pg. 1103

JARMAN—Shoes—Genesco Inc.; *U.S. Public*, pg. 728

JARRAH—Flavoured Instant Coffee—Novartis AG; *Int'l*, pg. 971

JARVIS—Casters & Wheels—Standex International Corporation; *U.S. Public*, pg. 1505

JASON—Binoculars—Bushnell Corporation; *U.S. Private*, pg. 1191

JASON—Spotting Scopes—Bushnell Corporation; *U.S. Private*, pg. 1191

JASON—Automotive Trim, Finishing Products & Power Generation Products—Jason Incorporated; *U.S. Public*, pg. 923

JASPER NEWS-BOY—Newspaper—The Hearst Corporation; *U.S. Private*, pg. 515

JAUS—Baked Snacks—Borden, Inc.; *U.S. Private*, pg. 157

JAVA COAST—Coffee Shop Outlet—Yogen Fruz Worldwide Inc.; *Int'l*, pg. 1520

JAVELAN—Software Program—Barrister Information Systems Corporation; *U.S. Public*, pg. 192

JAVELIN—Biological Insecticide—Novartis AG; *Int'l*, pg. 971

JAVELIN—Boats—Outboard Marine Corporation; *U.S. Private*, pg. 478

JAVELIN—Closed Circuit TV Systems—Pittway Corporation; *U.S. Public*, pg. 1305

JAVELIN—Insecticide—Sandoz Agro, Inc.; *Int'l*, pg. 974

JAVELIN WEB—Coated Web Offset Gloss—Champion International Corp.; *U.S. Public*, pg. 333

JAVEX—Liquid Bleach—Colgate-Palmolive Company; *U.S. Public*, pg. 397

JAW-BLOCKER—NONE—Ballard Medical Products; *U.S. Public*, pg. 171

JAX—Cheese Twists—Bachman Company; *U.S. Private*, pg. 109

JAX—Beer—Pearl Brewing Company; *U.S. Private*, pg. 954

JAY—Seating & Positioning Systems—Sunrise Medical, Inc.; *U.S. Public*, pg. 1535

JAY SERIES—Recreational Vehicle—Jayco Inc.; *U.S. Public*, pg. 583

JAYCAPS—Tamper Evident Containers—Carter Holt Harvey Limited; *U.S. Public*, pg. 904

JAYCO—Recreational Vehicle—Jayco Inc.; *U.S. Private*, pg. 583

JAYCO VANS—Van Conversion—Jayco Inc.; *U.S. Private*, pg. 583

JAYHAWK BOXES—Corrugated Boxes—Lawrence Paper Company; *U.S. Private*, pg. 654

JAYMAR—Men's Apparel—Hartmarx Corporation; *U.S. Public*, pg. 795

JAYMAR/SANSABELT—Slack Shop—Trans-Apparel Group; *U.S. Public*, pg. 796

JAYS—Potato Chips—Jays Foods LLC; *U.S. Private*, pg. 584

JAZZ—Paper & Plastic Cups, Plates & Containers—Sweetheart Cup Company Inc.; *U.S. Public*, pg. 1058

JAZZ DOG FOOD—Pet Foods—Doane Products Co., Branded Sales Div.; *U.S. Private*, pg. 337

JAZZ KIDS—Girls Clothing—Chorus Line Corporation; *U.S. Private*, pg. 238

JAZZ SPORT—Junior Sportswear—Chorus Line Corporation; *U.S. Private*, pg. 238

JAZZERCISE—Exercise Program—Jazzercise, Inc.; *U.S. Private*, pg. 584

JAZZERTOGS—Dancewear—Jazzercise, Inc.; *U.S. Private*, pg. 584

JAZZING—NONE—Bristol-Myers Squibb Company; *U.S. Public*, pg. 253

JAZZING—Hair Coloring—Clairol, Inc.; *U.S. Public*, pg. 254

JAZZY—Power Wheelchair—Pride Health Care, Inc.; *U.S. Private*, pg. 883

JAZZY JEWELERY AND ACCESSORIES—Kits for Pre-Teen Personal Expression—Binney & Smith Ltd.; *U.S. Private*, pg. 496

JE-VAX—Japanese Encephalitis Vaccine—Connaught Laboratories, Inc.; *Int'l*, pg. 1109

JEAN ARNOU—Ladies & Childrens Clothes—Arnotts plc; *Int'l*, pg. 81

JEAN DANFLOU—Brandies & Cordials—Marie Brizard Wines & Spirits USA; *U.S. Private*, pg. 702

JEAN LA FOOTE'S CINNAMON CRUNCH—Presweetened Cereal—The Quaker Oats Company; *U.S. Public*, pg. 1347

JEAN NICOLE—NONE—Petrie Retail, Inc.; *U.S. Private*, pg. 858

JEAN PHILIPPE—Fragrances—Jean Philippe Fragrances, Inc.; *U.S. Public*, pg. 924

JEANERATION—Jeanswear—Sao Paulo Alpargatas S.A.; *Int'l*, pg. 1193

JEANIE—ATM—Fifth Third Bancorp; *U.S. Public*, pg. 621

JEANMARIE—NONE—Blyth Industries; *U.S. Public*, pg. 239

JEANNE GATINEAU—Fragrance—Revlon, Inc.; *U.S. Private*, pg. 689

JEANS WEST—Young Men's Apparel—Edison Brothers Stores, Inc.; *U.S. Public*, pg. 563

JECTAIR—Air Movers—Coppus Murray Group, Tuthill Corporation; *U.S. Private*, pg. 1110

JEEP—On & Off Road Vehicles—Jeep; *U.S. Public*, pg. 353

JEEP CHEROKEE—Sport Utility Vehicle—Chrysler Corporation; *U.S. Public*, pg. 352

JEEP COMANCHE—Truck—Jeep; *U.S. Public*, pg. 353

JEEP GRAND—Wagoneer—Jeep; *U.S. Public*, pg. 353

JEEP GRAND CHEROKEE—Sport Utility—Chrysler Corporation; *U.S. Public*, pg. 352

JEEP GRAND CHEROKEE LAREDO—Sport Utility Vehicle—Chrysler Corporation; *U.S. Public*, pg. 352

JEEP WRANGLER—Sport Utility—Chrysler Corporation; *U.S. Public*, pg. 352

JEEP WRANGLER—Truck—Jeep; *U.S. Public*, pg. 353

JEFFERSON PILOT FINANCIAL—Covers all Companies That are Within The Jefferson-Pilot Corporation—Jefferson-Pilot Corporation; *U.S. Public*, pg. 925

JEFFERIES GROUP—Security Brokers—Jefferies Group, Inc.; *U.S. Public*, pg. 924

JEFFERS—Inductors—Vishay Intertechnology, Inc.; *U.S. Public*, pg. 1721

JEFFERSON—Transformers—MagneTek, Inc.; *U.S. Public*, pg. 1037

JEFFERSON COUNTY—Pork Products—Farmland Foods, Inc.; *U.S. Private*, pg. 396

JEFFERSON-PLUS—Transformers—MagneTek, Inc.; *U.S. Public*, pg. 1037

JEFFERSONIAN II—Pre-Finished Laminate—Bruce Hardwood Floors; *U.S. Public*, pg. 1634

JEFFS—Vegetables—Northern Foods plc; *Int'l*, pg. 967

JEKAL—Casein Glues—PKL Verpackungssysteme GmbH; *Int'l*, pg. 1020

JEKEL VINEYARDS—California Wines—Brown-Forman Beverages Worldwide; *U.S. Public*, pg. 261

JEKEL VINEYARDS—California Wines—Brown-Forman Corporation; *U.S. Public*, pg. 261

JEL-FLUX—Plumbing Chemical—Hercules Chemical Co., Inc.; *U.S. Private*, pg. 523

JELCO—I.V. Catheters—Johnson & Johnson Medical, Inc.; *U.S. Public*, pg. 928

JELL-O—Gelatin, Pudding, Pie Filling, Frozen Deserts, Fruit Bars & Cheese Cake Mix—Kraft Foods, Inc.; *U.S. Public*, pg. 1287

Brand Name Index

JELL-O—Desserts—Philip Morris Companies Inc.; *U.S. Public*, pg. 1287

JELL-O AMERICANA—Golden Egg Custard, Rice & Tapioca Pudding Mixes—Kraft Foods, Inc.; *U.S. Public*, pg. 1287

JELL-O CITRUS SNOWBURST—Frozen Novelty—Kraft Foods, Inc.; *U.S. Public*, pg. 1287

JELL-O GELATIN POPS—Bars—Kraft Foods, Inc.; *U.S. Public*, pg. 1287

JELL-O PUDDING POPS—Bars—Kraft Foods, Inc.; *U.S. Public*, pg. 1287

JELL-O RICH & LUSCIOUS—Mousse—Kraft Foods, Inc.; *U.S. Public*, pg. 1287

JEM—Jet Engine Monitor—Howell Instruments Inc.; *U.S. Private*, pg. 543

JEM KOTE—Liquid Laminated Cards—Sillcocks Plastics, Inc.; *U.S. Private*, pg. 63

JENAER GLAS—Glassware—Schott Glaswerke; *Int'l*, pg. 1523

JENEST-28—Pharmaceutical—Organon Inc.; *Int'l*, pg. 48

JENGA—Game—Milton Bradley Company; *U.S. Public*, pg. 797

JENKINS—Whiskey, Liqueurs, Brandy, Rum, Gin—Jenkins Spirits Corp. Ltd.; *U.S. Private*, pg. 585

JENN-AIR—Appliances—Jenn-Air; *U.S. Public*, pg. 1064

JENN-AIR—NONE—Maytag Cleveland Cooking Products; *U.S. Public*, pg. 1064

JENN-AIR—Ranges, Dishwashers, Microwave Ovens, Disposers & Refrigerators—Maytag Corporation; *U.S. Public*, pg. 1064

JENN-AIR—Refrigerators—Maytag Galesburg Refrigeration Products; *U.S. Public*, pg. 1064

JENNFAN—Commercial, Industrial, Restaurant & Institutional Ventilation Products—AAF McQuay, Inc.; *U.S. Private*, pg. 2

JENNIE-O—Turkey Products—Hormel Foods Corp.; *U.S. Public*, pg. 840

JENNIFER CONVERTIBLES—Sofabeds—Jennifer Convertibles Inc.; *U.S. Public*, pg. 926

JENNY A LITTLE LOVEABLE WITH DESIGN—Greeting Cards, Note Paper & Envelopes, Invits. & Anncmnts., Thank U Notes—American Greetings Corporation; *U.S. Public*, pg. 77

JENNY CRAIG—Weight Loss Centers—Jenny Craig, Inc.; *U.S. Public*, pg. 926

JENNY WITH DESIGN—Calendars & Greeting Cards—American Greetings Corporation; *U.S. Public*, pg. 77

JENNY'S CUISINE—NONE—Jenny Craig, Inc.; *U.S. Public*, pg. 926

JENO'S—Pizza—Pillsbury Co.; *Int'l*, pg. 411

JENOS—Frozen Pizza—Grand Metropolitan Plc; *Int'l*, pg. 408

JENO'S—Frozen Pizza & Pizza Snacks—The Pillsbury Company; *Int'l*, pg. 411

JENSEN—Tools—Mail Media Companies; *U.S. Public*, pg. 1509

JENSEN—Loudspeakers—Recoton Auto Corporation; *U.S. Public*, pg. 1369

JENSEN—Automotive Speakers, Subwoofers, Amplifiers, CD Changers—Recoton Corporation; *U.S. Public*, pg. 1369

JERGEN BODY SHAMPOO—Body Shampoo—Kao Corporation of America (DE); *Int'l*, pg. 717

JERGENS—Face Cream, Bath Prods., Soap—The Andrew Jergens Company; *Int'l*, pg. 717

JERGENS ADVANCED THERAPY—Hand & Body Lotion—The Andrew Jergens Company; *Int'l*, pg. 717

JERGENS LOTION—Hand Lotion—Kao Corporation of America (DE); *Int'l*, pg. 717

JERGENS SOAP—Soap—Kao Corporation of America (DE); *Int'l*, pg. 717

JERI BATH—Pharmaceuticals—Rhone-Poulenc Rorer - U.S.; *Int'l*, pg. 1110

JERKY TREATS—Pet Food—H.J. Heinz Company; *U.S. Public*, pg. 805

JERKY TREATS—NONE—Star-Kist Foods, Inc.; *U.S. Public*, pg. 806

JERO—Non-Alcoholic Drink Mixes—Red Wings Inc.; *Int'l*, pg. 1398

JEROME—NONE—Arizona Instrument Corporation; *U.S. Public*, pg. 129

JEROME'S—Food Service Turkey—Jerome Foods Inc.; *U.S. Private*, pg. 586

JERR DAN—Vehicle Retrievers—Durakon Industries, Inc.; *U.S. Public*, pg. 537

JERROLD—Electronic Components—General Instrument Corporation; *U.S. Public*, pg. 716

JERROLD STAR-LOK—Electronic Components—General Instrument Corporation; *U.S. Public*, pg. 716

JERRY JUG—Ice Chest—Igloo Products Corporation; *U.S. Public*, pg. 265

JERRY'S—24 Hr. Family Restaurant—BR Associates, Inc.; *U.S. Private*, pg. 107

JERUM—Summer-Only Hotels—Aritmos AB; *Int'l*, pg. 1072

JERUSALEM BIBLE—Book Imprint—Bertelsmann AG; *Int'l*, pg. 189

JERVIS WEBB—NONE—Key Handling Systems, Inc.; *U.S. Private*, pg. 618

JERZEE—NONE—Diehl Inc.; *U.S. Private*, pg. 332

JERZEES—Activewear—Russell Corp., Jerzees Div.; *U.S. Public*, pg. 1413

JERZEES—Knit Athletic Wear—Russell Corporation; *U.S. Public*, pg. 1413

JESSUP—Door—LDI, Ltd.; *U.S. Private*, pg. 639

JESTER—Cigarette Tobacco—Lane Limited; *Int'l*, pg. 1129

JESTERS—Studio Greeting Cards—American Greetings U.S. Greeting Card Division; *U.S. Public*, pg. 78

JESUS CHRIST SUPERSTAR—Musical—Really Useful Holdings Limited; *Int'l*, pg. 1089

JET—Magazine—Johnson Publishing Company, Inc.; *U.S. Private*, pg. 591

JET BACK—Sporting Goods—Brunswick Bowling & Billiards Corp.; *U.S. Public*, pg. 265

JET-CLEAN—Glassware Washer—Fisher Scientific Company; *U.S. Public*, pg. 658

JET-CLEAN—Jet Pulse Type Separator—The Spencer Turbine Co.; *U.S. Private*, pg. 1025

JET COAT—Premium Coated Ink Jet Paper for Color Ink Jet Printers—Shade/Allied, Inc.; *U.S. Public*, pg. 89

JET DRY—Rinse Agent for Automatic Dishwashers—Benckiser Consumer Products Inc.; *U.S. Public*, pg. 185

JET-FLECS—NONE—Molex Incorporated; *U.S. Public*, pg. 1121

JET-FLOW—Channel Furnace Inductor—Ajax Magnethermic Corp.; *Int'l*, pg. 113

JET FLOW—Sporting Goods—Brunswick Bowling & Billiards Corp.; *U.S. Public*, pg. 265

JET-GLO—Coating—Pratt & Lambert United, Inc.; *U.S. Public*, pg. 1466

JET-LH—Electrode—The Lincoln Electric Company; *U.S. Public*, pg. 996

JET LINE—Writing Instruments—Dixon Ticonderoga Company; *U.S. Public*, pg. 514

JET-LITE—Closed Back Shovels—UnionTools, Inc.; *U.S. Public*, pg. 17

JET-MELT—Hot Melt Adhesive Cartridges—3M; *U.S. Public*, pg. 1604

JET MIST—NONE—New England Stone Industries, Inc.; *U.S. Private*, pg. 793

JET MIX—Vortex Type Gas Burner—NAO, Inc.; *U.S. Private*, pg. 771

JET-PAK—Spray System—Sherwin-Williams Diversified Brands, Inc.; *U.S. Public*, pg. 1466

JET POINT—Bit Tip—American Tool Companies, Inc.; *U.S. Public*, pg. 63

JET POUCH—Air Courier Pouch & Envelopes—Uniflex, Inc.; *U.S. Public*, pg. 1665

JET PRINTING—Uncoated for Offset—Great Northern Paper, Inc.; *U.S. Public*, pg. 248

JET-RODDER—Water Sewer Cleaner—Vactor Mfg. Inc.; *U.S. Public*, pg. 617

JET SET—Hair Dryers—Sunbeam Household Products; *U.S. Public*, pg. 1533

JET SETTER—Faucet—The Black & Decker Corporation; *U.S. Public*, pg. 233

JET SKI—Water Sport Vehicle—Kawasaki Motors Corp., U.S.A.; *Int'l*, pg. 725

JET STREAM—Vehicle Warning Light—Federal Signal Corporation; *U.S. Public*, pg. 616

JET-TECH—Inkjet Paper—Gilbert Paper; *U.S. Public*, pg. 1074

JET-TECH RECYCLED—Recycled Inkjet Paper—Gilbert Paper; *U.S. Public*, pg. 1074

JET TORCH—Solio Brass Torches—BernzOmatic; *U.S. Public*, pg. 1177

JETBLADE—Gloss Coated Two Side Offset & Rotogravure—Great Northern Paper, Inc.; *U.S. Public*, pg. 248

JETCAL—Analyzer—Howell Instruments Inc.; *U.S. Private*, pg. 543

JETEX—NONE—AGA Gas, Inc.; *Int'l*, pg. 13

JETGLAS—Gas, Electric & Oil Powered Heaters—Bradford-White Corporation; *U.S. Private*, pg. 164

JETLINK—Commuter Partners with Regional Jets—Northwest Airlines, Inc.; *U.S. Public*, pg. 1200

JETREADER—Sheet-fed Scanner—Xerox Imaging Systems, Inc.; *U.S. Public*, pg. 1785

JETSCRIPT—Printer Enhancement—QMS, Inc.; *U.S. Public*, pg. 1346

JETSEAL—Seal designed for the JetStar Plunger—Belden & Blake Corporation; *U.S. Private*, pg. 1078

JETSERVE FOR NETWARE—Backup Solution for Large Novell Superservers—Cheyenne; *U.S. Public*, pg. 420

JETSONIC—Vehicle Warning Light/Loudspeaker—Federal Signal Corporation; *U.S. Public*, pg. 616

JETSTAR—Encoding System—Bell & Howell Holdings; *U.S. Public*, pg. 201

JETSTAR—Aerospace Manufacturing—Lockheed Aeronautical Systems Company; *U.S. Public*, pg. 1007

JETSTREAM—Civil Aircraft—British Aerospace p.l.c.; *Int'l*, pg. 217

JETVAC—Wet/Dry Shop Vacuum—Philips Electronics N.V.; *Int'l*, pg. 1051

JETWELD—Electrode—The Lincoln Electric Company; *U.S. Public*, pg. 996

JEUMONT SCHNEIDER PUMPS—Pumps—Ingersoll-Dresser Pump Company; *U.S. Public*, pg. 529

JEUMONT-SCHNEIDER PUMPS—NONE—Ingersoll-Rand Company; *U.S. Public*, pg. 876

JEVITY—Medical Nutrional Tube-Feeding Product—Abbott Laboratories; *U.S. Public*, pg. 12

JEWEL—Aquariums, Terrariums & Lab Equipment—American Educational Products; *U.S. Public*, pg. 71

JEWEL—Food Stores—Jewel-Osco; *U.S. Public*, pg. 93

JEWEL—Arrhythmia Management Device—Medtronic, Inc.; *U.S. Public*, pg. 1082

JEWEL CD—Arrhythmia Management Device—Medtronic, Inc.; *U.S. Public*, pg. 1082

JEWEL PCD—Implantable Defibrillator—Medtronic, Inc.; *U.S. Public*, pg. 1082

JEWEL PLUS—Implantable Cardioverter Defibrillator—Medtronic, Inc.; *U.S. Public*, pg. 1082

JEWELL—Electrical Instruments—The Jewell Electrical Instruments Co.; *U.S. Private*, pg. 36

JEWSON—Builders Merchants—Meyer International PLC; *Int'l*, pg. 864

JEX—Analgesic—Reckitt & Colman plc; *Int'l*, pg. 1089

JEYES TOILET CARE—NONE—Kiwi Brands Pty. Ltd.; *U.S. Public*, pg. 1434

JHERI REDDING—Hair Care Line—Conair Corporation; *U.S. Private*, pg. 261

JHIRMACK—Hair Care Products—Playtex Products Inc.; *U.S. Public*, pg. 1310

JHIRMACK E.F.A.—Hair Products—Playtex Beauty Care, Inc.; *U.S. Public*, pg. 1311

JHIRMACK EXTRA HOLD—Pump & Aerosol Hair Products—Playtex Beauty Care, Inc.; *U.S. Public*, pg. 1311

JHIRMACK FABULOUSLY CLEAN—Hair Products—Playtex Beauty Care, Inc.; *U.S. Public*, pg. 1311

JHIRMACK FREEZE—Styling Product—Playtex Beauty Care, Inc.; *U.S. Public*, pg. 1311

JHIRMACK GELAVE—Hair Products—Playtex Beauty Care, Inc.; *U.S. Public*, pg. 1311

JHIRMACK GENTLE HOLD—Pump & Aerosol Hair Products—Playtex Beauty Care, Inc.; *U.S. Public*, pg. 1311

JHIRMACK LITE—Hair Products—Playtex Beauty Care, Inc.; *U.S. Public*, pg. 1311

JHIRMACK MOISTUREPHLEX—Conditioner—Playtex Beauty Care, Inc.; *U.S. Public*, pg. 1311

JHIRMACK MOUSSE—Hair Product—Playtex Beauty Care, Inc.; *U.S. Public*, pg. 1311

JHIRMACK NUTRI-BODY—Hair Products—Playtex Beauty Care, Inc.; *U.S. Public*, pg. 1311

JHIRMACK PLUS 2 IN 1—Hair Products—Playtex Beauty Care, Inc.; *U.S. Public*, pg. 1311

JHIRMACK POWER MIST HAIR SPRAY—Hair Product—Playtex Beauty Care, Inc.; *U.S. Public*, pg. 1311

JHIRMACK SHINE—Hair Products—Playtex Beauty Care, Inc.; *U.S. Public*, pg. 1311

JHIRMACK SILVER—Hair ProductS—Playtex Beauty Care, Inc.; *U.S. Public*, pg. 1311

JHIRMACK SPRITZ—Hair Product—Playtex Beauty Care, Inc.; *U.S. Public*, pg. 1311

JHIRMACK STYLING GEL—Hair Product—Playtex Beauty Care, Inc.; *U.S. Public*, pg. 1311

JHIRMACK ULTIMATE HOLD—Pump & Aerosol Hair Products—Playtex Beauty Care, Inc.; *U.S. Public*, pg. 1311

JIF—Peanut Butter—The Procter & Gamble Company; *U.S. Public*, pg. 1330

JIF-E MART—Service Marks—Piggly Wiggly Co.; *U.S. Public*, pg. 653

JIFFEE-JOINT—Drain Outlet Connection—Josam Company; *U.S. Private*, pg. 600

JIFFEE-SET—Hub Connection—Josam Company; *U.S. Private*, pg. 600

JIFFIES—Precooked Sausage in a Pancake—Jones Dairy Farm; *U.S. Private*, pg. 596

JIFFLOX—Converter Dolly—Todco; *U.S. Private*, pg. 823

JIFFY—Toothache Drops—Block Drug Company, Inc.; *U.S. Public*, pg. 236

JIFFY—Prepared Frozen Foods—ConAgra Frozen Food Company; *U.S. Public*, pg. 427

JIFFY—Prepared Frozen Foods—ConAgra Frozen Foods; *U.S. Public*, pg. 427

JIFFY—Yarn—Lion Brand Yarn Co.; *U.S. Private*, pg. 669

JIFFY—Steel Fastener One Hole Strap—Minerallac Co.; *U.S. Private*, pg. 750

JIFFY—Padded Mailers—Sealed Air Corporation; *U.S. Public*, pg. 1450

JIFFY COVER—Plastic Drop Cloth—Flex-O-Glass, Inc.; *U.S. Private*, pg. 412

JIFFY-COVER—Drop Cloths—Warp Brothers; *U.S. Private*, pg. 412

JIFFY DRY—Enamel & Stain—Jones Blair Company; *U.S. Private*, pg. 596

JIFFY-GRO—Garden Products—Jiffy Products of America, Inc.; *Int'l*, pg. 706

JIFFY KIT—Automotive Products—Standard Motor Products Inc.; *U.S. Public*, pg. 1503

JIFFY LUBE—Oil Change Facilities—Jiffy Lube International, Inc.; *U.S. Public*, pg. 1272

JIFFY MIRACLE PEAT—Garden Products—Jiffy Products of America, Inc.; *Int'l*, pg. 706

JIFFY-MIX—Garden Products—Jiffy Products of America, Inc.; *Int'l*, pg. 706

JIFFY POP—Popcorn—International Home Foods Inc.; *U.S. Private*, pg. 526

JIFFY-POTS—Garden Products—Jiffy Products of America, Inc.; *Int'l*, pg. 706

JIFFY PREP—Paint Condition—Jones Blair Company; *U.S. Private*, pg. 596

JIFFY-7—Garden Products—Jiffy Products of America, Inc.; *Int'l*, pg. 706

JIFFY-7 GREENHOUSE—Garden Products—Jiffy Products of America, Inc.; *Int'l*, pg. 706

JIFFY-STRIPS—Garden Products—Jiffy Products of America, Inc.; *Int'l*, pg. 706

JIFFYLITE—Bubble Cushioned Mailers—Sealed Air Corporation; *U.S. Public*, pg. 1450

JIGGER—NONE—Bacardi-Martini Belgium; *U.S. Private*, pg. 109

JIL SANDER—Fragrance, Sun Care & Color Cosmetics—Lancaster Group Worldwide; *Int'l*, pg. 185

JIM BEAM—Bourbon Whiskey—Fortune Brands, Inc.; *U.S. Public*, pg. 674

THE JIM BOHANNON SHOW—Talk Radio Program—Westwood One Entertainment; *U.S. Public*, pg. 1763

THE JIM BOHANNON SHOW—Late-Night Programming—Westwood One, Inc.; *U.S. Public*, pg. 1763

JIM DANDY—Dog Foods—Alpo Pet Foods, Inc.; *Int'l*, pg. 917

JIM DANDY—NONE—Nestle USA; *Int'l*, pg. 916

JIM DANDY—Snack—The Pillsbury Company; *Int'l*, pg. 411

JIM DANDY COMPLETE DOG RATION—Dog Food—The Jim Dandy Co., Inc.; *Int'l*, pg. 918

JIM DANDY HUNKS O'CHUNX—Dog Foods—The Jim Dandy Co., Inc.; *Int'l*, pg. 918

JIMMI—Seasonings, Spices—Bestfoods; *U.S. Public*, pg. 223

JIMMY DEAN—Sausage—Sara Lee Corporation; *U.S. Public*, pg. 1432

JIMMY DEAN BACON—NONE—Jimmy Dean Foods; *U.S. Public*, pg. 1433

JIMMY DEAN CHICKEN BISCUITS—Biscuit Sandwich—Jimmy Dean Foods; *U.S. Public*, pg. 1433

JIMMY DEAN FLAP STICKS—Sausage & Pancake on a Stick—Jimmy Dean Foods; *U.S. Public*, pg. 1433

JIMMY DEAN MINI HOTDOGS—NONE—Jimmy Dean Foods; *U.S. Public*, pg. 1433

JIMMY DEAN SAUSAGE—Fresh Breakfast Sausage-Rolls, Links & Patties—Jimmy Dean Foods; *U.S. Public*, pg. 1433

JIMMY DEAN SAUSAGE BISCUITS—Biscuit Sandwich—Jimmy Dean Foods; *U.S. Public*, pg. 1433

JIMMY DEAN STEAK BISCUITS—Biscuit Sandwich—Jimmy Dean Foods; *U.S. Public*, pg. 1433

JIMTEN—NONE—ETEX; *Int'l*, pg. 430

JISTEL—Telecommunications—Jeumont-Schneider Trenformeteurs; *Int'l*, pg. 706

JISTRAL—Microcomputers—Jeumont-Schneider Trenformeteurs; *Int'l*, pg. 706

JIT—Auto Industry Service—Conrail, Inc.; *U.S. Public*, pg. 431

JITNEY JUNGLE—SUPERMARKET—Jitney-Jungle Stores of America, Inc.; *U.S. Private*, pg. 588

JJUST JJUICY—Aseptic Fruit Juices—Johanna Foods Inc.; *U.S. Private*, pg. 589

JO-ANN FABRIC & CRAFTS—Retail Stores Selling Fabric, Crafts & Notions—Fabri-Centers of America, Inc.; *U.S. Public*, pg. 609

JOAN & DAVID—Shoes, Boots & Accessories—Joan & David Helpern, Inc.; *U.S. Private*, pg. 521

JOAN LESLIE SPORTSWEAR—Women's Clothing—The Leslie Fay Companies, Inc.; *U.S. Public*, pg. 989

JOAN OF ARC—Canned Bean—Grand Metropolitan Plc; *Int'l*, pg. 408

JOAN OF ARC—Canned Vegetables & Beans—The Pillsbury Company; *Int'l*, pg. 411

JOAN VASS, U.S.A.—Apparel—Heritage Sportswear; *U.S. Public*, pg. 1472

JOAN VASS U.S.A.—Women's Knit Apparel—Signal Apparel Company, Inc.; *U.S. Public*, pg. 1472

JOAO PIRES—NONE—Lancers; *Int'l*, pg. 411

JOB HANDLERS—4500 Series Tools—Red Devil Inc.; *U.S. Private*, pg. 915

JOB PRO—Lighting Tools & Heaters—The Canadian Coleman Co., Ltd.; *U.S. Private*, pg. 691

JOB RATED—NONE—The Wooster Brush Company; *U.S. Private*, pg. 1188

JOB SITE BRAND—Adhesives, Caulks & Grouts Product Logo—Miracle Adhesives; *U.S. Public*, pg. 1466

JOB SITE BRAND—Adhesive—Pratt & Lambert United, Inc.; *U.S. Public*, pg. 1466

JOBBER—Herbicides—Agrolinz Melamin GmbH; *Int'l*, pg. 356

JOBBER—Plant Protectives—DSM Chemie Linz GmbH; *Int'l*, pg. 356

JOBBER FL.—Herbicides—Agrolinz Melamin GmbH; *Int'l*, pg. 356

JOBBER PLUS—Herbicides—Agrolinz Melamin GmbH; *Int'l*, pg. 356

JOBE'S—Plant Care Products—Weatherly Consumer Products; *U.S. Public*, pg. 1682

JOBOX—Construction Site Storage Boxes—Delta Consolidated Industries, Inc. (Co. Headquarters); *U.S. Public*, pg. 481

JOBROZO—Table Salt—Akzo Nobel N.V.; *Int'l*, pg. 42

JOBSITE—Construction Site Storage Boxes—Delta Consolidated Industries, Inc. (Co. Headquarters); *U.S. Public*, pg. 481

JOCKEY—Cheese—Danone Group; *Int'l*, pg. 379

JOCKEY—Underwear, Hosiery, Sportswear & Sleepwear—Jockey International, Inc.; *U.S. Private*, pg. 588

JOCKEY—Socks—Sara Lee Sock Company; *U.S. Public*, pg. 1434

JOCKEY FOR HER—Underwear & Sleepwear—Jockey International, Inc.; *U.S. Private*, pg. 588

JOCKEY SLEEPWEAR—Sleepwear—Host Apparel, Inc.; *U.S. Private*, pg. 540

JOCO—Steam Specialties—The Johnson Corporation; *U.S. Private*, pg. 591

JOE BOXER WATCHES—Licensee—Timex Corporation; *U.S. Private*, pg. 1088

JOE FROM BELOW—Stuffed Toy Figures; Canisters; Towels; T-Shirts—American Greetings Corporation; *U.S. Public*, pg. 77

JOERNS—Nursing Home Beds & Furniture—Sunrise Medical, Inc.; *U.S. Public*, pg. 1535

JOE'S CRAB SHACK—Restaurant Chain—Landry's Seafood Restaurants Inc.; *U.S. Public*, pg. 977

JOFCO—Wood Office Furniture—Jofco Inc.; *U.S. Private*, pg. 588

JOGMATE PROTEIN—Protein Dietary Supplement—Otsuka Pharmaceutical Co., Ltd.; *Int'l*, pg. 1013

JOHANNA—Milk Products—Labatt Brewing Company Limited; *Int'l*, pg. 679

JOHANNISQUELL—Mineralized Water—Apollinaris & Schweppes Gmbh & Co.; *Int'l*, pg. 78

JOHN ALEXANDER—Men's Apparel—Hartmarx Corporation; *U.S. Public*, pg. 795

JOHN BEGG BLUE CAP—Scotch—Shieffelin Somerset Co.; *Int'l*, pg. 412

JOHN BEGG DELUXE—12-Year Old Scotch—Shieffelin Somerset Co.; *Int'l*, pg. 412

JOHN BLAIR—Men's Apparel—Blair Corporation; *U.S. Public*, pg. 236

JOHN CARAGE AMBOR LAGOR—Lagor—Scottish & Newcastle Importers Co.; *Int'l*, pg. 1212

JOHN COURAGE—Ale—Foster's Brewing Group Limited; *Int'l*, pg. 500

JOHN COURAGE—Beer—Philip Morris Companies Inc.; *U.S. Public*, pg. 1287

JOHN CRANE—Packings, Gaskets & Seals—John Crane Mechanical Seals; *U.S. Public*, pg. 1339

JOHN CRANE—NONE—TI Group plc; *Int'l*, pg. 1337

JOHN DEERE—Boots—Florsheim Group Inc.; *U.S. Public*, pg. 656

JOHN DEERE—Products—Deere & Company; *U.S. Public*, pg. 491

JOHN EBEN—Men's Shoes—E.J. Footwear Corp.; *U.S. Public*, pg. 1684

JOHN HANCOCK FINANCIAL SERVICES—Corporate ID—John Hancock Mutual Life Insurance Company; *U.S. Private*, pg. 589

JOHN HARVEY—Sherry—Allied Domecq PLC; *Int'l*, pg. 62

JOHN HASSALL—Special Cold Forged Products & Fasteners—John Hassall, Inc.; *U.S. Private*, pg. 509

JOHN HENRY—Plug Tobacco—Brown & Williamson Tobacco Corp.; *Int'l*, pg. 111

JOHN HENRY—Men's Wear—The Manhattan Shirt Co.; *U.S. Public*, pg. 1429

JOHN HENRY—Clothing—Salant Corporation; *U.S. Public*, pg. 1429

JOHN LOBB—Footwear—Hermes International; *Int'l*, pg. 617

JOHN MENZIES RETAIL—Clothing Store Retailer—John Menzies plc; *Int'l*, pg. 707

JOHN MENZIES WHOLESALE—News & Magazine Distributor—John Menzies plc; *Int'l*, pg. 707

JOHN MOIR—Dessert Mixes—CSM N.V.; *Int'l*, pg. 243

JOHN MORRELL—Meat Products—John Morrell & Co.; *U.S. Public*, pg. 1479

THE JOHN P. SCRIPPS NEWSPAPERS—Operating Name—The E.W. Scripps Company; *U.S. Public*, pg. 1447

JOHN PEEL LTD.—Apparel—Bayer Clothing Group; *U.S. Private*, pg. 124

JOHN PLAYER—Cigarettes—Hanson PLC; *Int'l*, pg. 592

JOHN PLAYER—King Size Light Filter Cigarettes—Imperial Tobacco Group, Ltd.; *Int'l*, pg. 666

JOHN PLAYER SPECIAL—Cigarettes—B.A.T Industries P.L.C.; *Int'l*, pg. 110

JOHN PLAYER SPECIALS—NONE—Malaysian Tobacco Co./B.A.T. Indust.; *Int'l*, pg. 111

JOHN ROLFE—Pipe Tobacco—Lane Limited; *Int'l*, pg. 1129

JOHN SMITH'S—Yorkshire Bitter—Foster's Brewing Group Limited; *Int'l*, pg. 500

JOHN TAMS GROUP—Fine China—Ebeling & Reuss Company; *U.S. Private*, pg. 358
JOHN WEITZ—Apparel—Bayer Clothing Group; *U.S. Private*, pg. 124
JOHN WEITZ—Sleepwear—Host Apparel, Inc.; *U.S. Private*, pg. 540
JOHN ZINK—Air Quality Control Systems—John Zink Co.; *U.S. Private*, pg. 628
JOHNI BOLT—Industrial Chemical—Hercules Chemical Co., Inc.; *U.S. Private*, pg. 523
JOHNI-RING—Plumbing Chemical—Hercules Chemical Co., Inc.; *U.S. Private*, pg. 523
JOHNNIE WALKER BLACK—Twelve Year Old Scotch—Schieffelin & Somerset Co.; *Int'l*, pg. 412
JOHNNIE WALKER BLACK LABEL—NONE—Guinness Plc; *Int'l*, pg. 412
JOHNNIE WALKER BLACK LABEL—12 Year Old Scotch—Shieffelin Somerset Co.; *Int'l*, pg. 412
JOHNNIE WALKER BLUE LABEL—NONE—Guinness Plc; *Int'l*, pg. 412
JOHNNIE WALKER PREMIER—NONE—Guinness Plc; *Int'l*, pg. 412
JOHNNIE WALKER RED—Scotch—Shieffelin Somerset Co.; *Int'l*, pg. 412
JOHNNIE WALKER RED LABEL—NONE—Guinness Plc; *Int'l*, pg. 412
JOHNNIE WALKER RED LABEL—Scotch—Schieffelin & Somerset Co.; *Int'l*, pg. 412
JOHNNIE WALKER SWING—NONE—Guinness Plc; *Int'l*, pg. 412
JOHNNIE WALKER SWING—Scotch—Schieffelin & Somerset Co.; *Int'l*, pg. 412
JOHNNIE WALKER SWING—Scotch—Shieffelin Somerset Co.; *Int'l*, pg. 412
JOHNNY CARSON—Men's Apparel—Hartmarx Corporation; *U.S. Public*, pg. 795
JOHNNY CARSON—Apparel—Intercontinental Branded Apparel; *U.S. Public*, pg. 796
JOHNNY CARSON—Apparel—Johnny Carson Apparel, Inc.; *U.S. Public*, pg. 796
JOHNNY JUMP-UP—Exerciser—Evenflo Company, Inc.; *U.S. Private*, pg. 629
JOHNNY QUEST—Action Figures—Galoob Toys, Inc.; *U.S. Public*, pg. 698
JOHNNY WEISSMULLER SWIMMING POOLS—Swimming Pool—Delair Group, L.L.C.; *U.S. Private*, pg. 47
JOHNSON—Furnace & Air Conditioning—Excelsior Manufacturing & Supply Corp.; *U.S. Private*, pg. 387
JOHNSON—Micromotors—Johnson Electric Holdings Limited; *Int'l*, pg. 712
JOHNSON—Reels & Rods—Johnson Worldwide Associates, Inc.; *U.S. Public*, pg. 932
JOHNSON—Outboard Boat Motors, Parts & Accessories, Electric Fishing Motors—Outboard Marine Corporation; *U.S. Private*, pg. 478
JOHNSON & JOHNSON—Hygienic Products, Pharmaceuticals & Medical Equipment—Johnson & Johnson; *U.S. Public*, pg. 927
JOHNSON & JOHNSON—Dental Floss—Johnson & Johnson Consumer Products; *U.S. Public*, pg. 928
JOHNSON & JOHNSON—Baby Products—Johnson & Johnson Limited; *U.S. Public*, pg. 930
JOHNSON BROTHERS—China—Waterford Crystal, Inc.; *Int'l*, pg. 1487
JOHNSON BROTHERS—Tableware—Waterford Wedgwood UK Plc; *Int'l*, pg. 1487
JOHNSON CONTROLS—Vehicle Seating—Johnson Controls, Inc.; *U.S. Public*, pg. 932
JOHNSON LURES—Spoons & Softbody Plastics—Johnson Worldwide Associates, Inc.; *U.S. Public*, pg. 932
JOHNSON NUT—Nut Meats—Metz Baking Company (WI); *U.S. Public*, pg. 1022
JOHNSON READY MIX—Ready Mix Concrete—LeGrand Johnson Construction Co.; *U.S. Private*, pg. 591
JOHNSON'S—NONE—Johnson & Johnson; *U.S. Public*, pg. 927
JOHNSONIAN—Men's Shoes—E.J. Footwear Corp.; *U.S. Public*, pg. 1684
JOHNSON'S BABY CONDITIONER—Hair Conditioner, Oil, Powder Talc & Shampoo—Johnson & Johnson Consumer Products; *U.S. Public*, pg. 928

JOHNSON'S BABY LOTION—Skin Lotion—Johnson & Johnson Consumer Products; *U.S. Public*, pg. 928
JOHNSON'S BABY OIL—Baby Oil—Johnson & Johnson Consumer Products; *U.S. Public*, pg. 928
JOHNSON'S BABY POWDER—Baby Powder—Johnson & Johnson Consumer Products; *U.S. Public*, pg. 928
JOHNSON'S BABY SHAMPOO—Baby Shampoo—Johnson & Johnson Consumer Products; *U.S. Public*, pg. 928
JOHNSON'S BABY SUNBLOCK—Baby Sunblock—Johnson & Johnson Consumer Products; *U.S. Public*, pg. 928
JOHNSON'S BABY WASH CLOTHS—Wipes—Johnson & Johnson Consumer Products; *U.S. Public*, pg. 928
JOHNSON'S BATHTIME BUDDIES—Children's Bath Products—Johnson & Johnson Consumer Products; *U.S. Public*, pg. 928
JOHNSON'S DIAPER RASH RELIEF—Diaper Rash Medication—Johnson & Johnson Consumer Products; *U.S. Public*, pg. 928
JOHNSON'S FOOT SOAP—Foot Soap—Combe Incorporated; *U.S. Private*, pg. 257
JOHNSON'S NO MORE TANGLES—Detangler Spray—Johnson & Johnson Consumer Products; *U.S. Public*, pg. 928
JOHNSON'S SWABS—Cotton Swabs—Johnson & Johnson Consumer Products; *U.S. Public*, pg. 928
JOHNSONVILLE—Mfr. Sausage—Johnsonville Foods, Inc.; *U.S. Private*, pg. 595
JOHNSTON & MURPHY—Footwear—Genesco Inc.; *U.S. Public*, pg. 728
JOHNSTON & MURPHY—Shoes—Johnston & Murphy Co.; *U.S. Public*, pg. 728
JOINTMASTER—Expansion Joints—Pawling Corporation; *U.S. Private*, pg. 844
JOJOBA FARMS—Hair Care Product—Carme' Cosmeceutical Sciences, Inc.; *U.S. Private*, pg. 213
JOKERS WILD—Casino—Boyd Gaming Corporation; *U.S. Public*, pg. 249
JOKISCH—Soups & Ready Meals—GrandMet Foods GmbH; *Int'l*, pg. 409
JOLENE—Shoes—Tober Industries, Inc.; *U.S. Private*, pg. 1089
JOLIPEL—Premium Woven Fabrics—Girmes GmbH; *Int'l*, pg. 552
JOLLY GOOD—Soft Drinks—Krier Foods, Inc.; *U.S. Private*, pg. 636
JOLLY HOLLYDAYS—Greeting Cards—American Greetings Corporation; *U.S. Public*, pg. 77
JOLLY RANCHER—Candy—Huhtamaki Oy; *Int'l*, pg. 638
JOLT—Cola—Global Beverage Co.; *U.S. Private*, pg. 457
JON DONAIRE—Frozen Cheesecakes, Moussecakes & Ice Cream Cakes—Presto Food Products, Inc.; *U.S. Public*, pg. 1527
JON-E—Pocket Hand-Warmers—Blount International, Inc.; *U.S. Public*, pg. 237
JON-E—Hand Warmer—Orbex Inc.; *U.S. Public*, pg. 238
JON GNAGY—Art Sets—Martin/F. Weber Company; *U.S. Private*, pg. 710
JON LAWRENCE—Women's Sportswear—Catherines Stores Corporation; *U.S. Public*, pg. 317
JONATHAN STEWART—NONE—Tandy Brands Accessories, Inc.; *U.S. Public*, pg. 1560
JONCHEM—Chemicals—Westvaco Corporation; *U.S. Public*, pg. 1762
JONES—Stock Preparation—Beloit Corporation; *U.S. Public*, pg. 789
JONES—Drugs & Food Supplements—Jones Medical Industries Inc.; *U.S. Public*, pg. 933
JONES & CO—"Dressy Casual Sportswear—Jones Apparel Group, Inc.; *U.S. Public*, pg. 933
JONES CAPITAL CORP.—Holding Company—J.A. Jones, Inc.; *Int'l*, pg. 633
JONES DAIRY FARM—Bacon, Sausage, Hams, Canadian Bacon & Liver Sausage—Jones Dairy Farm; *U.S. Private*, pg. 596
HERFF JONES—Scholastic-Related Graduation Products—Herff Jones Inc.; *U.S. Private*, pg. 523

JONES JEANS—Denin & Cotton Based Jeans Collection—Jones Apparel Group, Inc.; *U.S. Public*, pg. 933
JONES MANAGEMENT SERVICES COMPANY—Management & Operations Co.—J.A. Jones, Inc.; *Int'l*, pg. 633
JONES NEW YORK—Career Sportwear—Jones Apparel Group, Inc.; *U.S. Public*, pg. 933
JONES NEWYORK COUNTRY—Classic Country Styled Casual Sportswear—Jones Apparel Group, Inc.; *U.S. Public*, pg. 933
JONES NEWYORK SPORT—Casual Sportswear—Jones Apparel Group, Inc.; *U.S. Public*, pg. 933
JONES WEAR—NONE—Jones Apparel Group, Inc.; *U.S. Public*, pg. 933
JONES YAVVEL—Direct Delivery of News & Magazines—John Menzies plc; *Int'l*, pg. 707
JONNY CAT—Cat Litter—First Brands Corporation; *U.S. Public*, pg. 626
JONREZ—Specialty Chemicals—Westvaco Corporation; *U.S. Public*, pg. 1762
JONSERED—Garden Equipment—Electrolux, AB; *Int'l*, pg. 438
JONSERED—Forestry Cranes—Partek Corporation; *Int'l*, pg. 1024
JOOP!—Fragrance—Lancaster Group Worldwide; *Int'l*, pg. 185
JORAN—Drill Bits—American Tool Companies, Inc.; *U.S. Private*, pg. 63
JORDACHE—Apparel—Jordache Enterprises, Inc.; *U.S. Private*, pg. 597
JORDACHE LOOKS—Fragrance—Jean Philippe Fragrances, Inc.; *U.S. Public*, pg. 924
JORDAPON—Surfactant for Manufacturer of Soap & Detergent—PPG Industries, Inc.; *U.S. Public*, pg. 1245
JORDON COMMERICAL REFRIGERATOR—Commerical Freezers & Refrigerators—Jordon Commercial Refrigerator Co.; *U.S. Private*, pg. 599
JORDON SCIENTIFIC—Temperature Controlled Equipment, Laboratory & Blood Bank Equipment—Jordon Commercial Refrigerator Co.; *U.S. Private*, pg. 599
JOSE CUERVO—Tequila—Grand Metropolitan Plc; *Int'l*, pg. 408
JOSE CUERVO—Tequilas—Heublein, Inc.; *Int'l*, pg. 410
JOSE CUERVO—NONE—International Distillers Caribbean; *Int'l*, pg. 410
JOSE EBER'S SECRET HAIR—Hair Care Product—Advantage Life Products, Inc.; *U.S. Public*, pg. 22
JOSEPH ABBOUD—Footwear—Florsheim Group Inc.; *U.S. Public*, pg. 656
JOSEPH & THE AMAZING TECHNICOLOR DREAMCOAT—Musical—Really Useful Holdings Limited; *Int'l*, pg. 1089
JOSHUA'S CHRISTIAN STORES—Retail Christian Oriented Books, Music, Gifts—Tandycrafts, Inc.; *U.S. Public*, pg. 1561
JOSTENS—Motivation & Recognition Prods., Class Rings & Graduation Prods.—Jostens; *U.S. Public*, pg. 934
JOTTER—Writing Instruments & Desk Sets—Gillette Co.-Parker Pen USA; *U.S. Public*, pg. 745
JOUCOMATIC—Air Controls—Ascolectric Limited; *U.S. Public*, pg. 575
JOUCOMATIC—Pneumatic & General-Purpose Solenoid Valves—Emerson Electric Co.; *U.S. Public*, pg. 572
JOURGENSEN—Ewe Marking Harness—Nasco Modesto; *U.S. Private*, pg. 446
JOURNAL FUR DIE FRAU—Magazine—Axel Springer Verlag AG; *Int'l*, pg. 102
JOURNAL MANAGER PLUS—CICS Data Recovery Product—BMC Software, Inc.; *U.S. Public*, pg. 162
JOURNAL OF COMMERCE—NONE—The Economist Group Limited.; *Int'l*, pg. 1026
JOURNAL OF COMMERCE—International Business Daily Newspaper—Journal of Commerce, Inc.; *Int'l*, pg. 1026
JOURNEY CURRICULUM—NONE—La Petite Academy Inc.; *U.S. Private*, pg. 640
JOURNEYMAN—Wheeled Luggage Items—Andiamo, Inc.; *U.S. Private*, pg. 73
JOURNEYMAN—NONE—The Wooster Brush Company; *U.S. Private*, pg. 1188

JOURNEYS—Footwear—Genesco Inc.; *U.S. Public*, pg. 728

JOVAN MUSK—Men's Fragrance—Coty Inc.; *Int'l*, pg. 185

JOVE—NONE—Berkley Publishing Corp.; *Int'l*, pg. 1027

JOY—Junior Fashions—Deb Shops, Inc.; *U.S. Public*, pg. 491

JOY—Air Compressors—Gardner Denver Machinery Inc.; *U.S. Public*, pg. 703

JOY—Bathroom Tissue—Kimberly-Clark Corporation; *U.S. Public*, pg. 958

JOY—Detergent—The Procter & Gamble Company; *U.S. Public*, pg. 1330

JOY ENERGY SYSTEMS INC.—Incineration Systems—Joy Mining Machinery; *U.S. Public*, pg. 789

JOY RIDE—Infant Car Seat & Carrier—Evenflo Company, Inc.; *U.S. Private*, pg. 629

JOY RIDER—Tractor Seats—Fleischer Manufacturing, Inc.; *U.S. Private*, pg. 410

JOY TOY—Toys—Strombecker Corporation; *U.S. Private*, pg. 1047

JOYCE INTERNATIONAL—Office Furniture & Products; Mfg. & Distr.—Joyce International, Inc.; *U.S. Private*, pg. 602

JOZO—Table Salt—Akzo Nobel N.V.; *Int'l*, pg. 42

JR. FOOD STORE—Convenience Stores—E-Z Serve Convenience Stores, Inc.; *U.S. Public*, pg. 540

JR. FOOD STORE—Convenience Stores—E-Z Serve Corp.; *U.S. Public*, pg. 540

JUBILEE—Packaging Ribbon—American Greetings Corporation; *U.S. Public*, pg. 77

JUBILEE—Stout—Bass PLC; *Int'l*, pg. 169

JUBILEE—Tires—Bridgestone/Firestone, Inc.; *Int'l*, pg. 213

JUBILEE—Cameras—Eastman Kodak Company; *U.S. Public*, pg. 550

JUBILEE—Hardboard Paneling—Georgia-Pacific Corporation; *U.S. Public*, pg. 735

JUBILEE—Furniture Polish—S.C. Johnson & Son, Inc.; *U.S. Private*, pg. 592

JUBILEE—NONE—N.V. Johnson Wax Belgium S.A.; *U.S. Private*, pg. 593

JUDSON-ATKINSON CANDIES—Candies—Judson-Atkinson Candies, Inc.; *U.S. Private*, pg. 602

JUICE—Junior Swimwear—Cole of California; *U.S. Public*, pg. 148

JUICE JAM—NONE—Ocean Spray Cranberries, Inc.; *U.S. Private*, pg. 811

JUICE-O-MAT—Juicer—The Rival Company; *U.S. Public*, pg. 1391

JUICE STIX—Frozen Novelties—Borden, Inc.; *U.S. Private*, pg. 157

JUICE-UPS—Juice Drink—Veryfine Products, Inc.; *U.S. Private*, pg. 1137

JUICE WORKS—Juice Bar—TCBY Enterprises Inc.; *U.S. Public*, pg. 1553

JUICEFULS—Filled Hard Candy with Juice Added—Ragold, Inc.; *Int'l*, pg. 1084

JUICEFULS—Gummies—Ragold, Inc.; *Int'l*, pg. 1084

JUICEMAN—Juice Extractors—Salton/Maxim Housewares, Inc.; *U.S. Public*, pg. 1430

JUICY FRUIT—Chewing Gum—Wrigley Canada Inc.; *U.S. Public*, pg. 1781

JUICY FRUIT—Gum—Wm. Wrigley Jr. Company; *U.S. Public*, pg. 1781

JUICY JUICE—Juice Product—Nestle Chocolate & Confection; *Int'l*, pg. 917

JUICY JUICE—Fruit Beverage—Nestle S.A.; *Int'l*, pg. 915

JUICYS AMBI-PUR—NONE—Kiwi Brands Pty. Ltd.; *U.S. Public*, pg. 1434

JUKE BOX CHOCOLATES—Boxed Chocolates—Borden, Inc.; *U.S. Private*, pg. 157

JUKI—Sewing Machines & Printers—Juki Corporation; *Int'l*, pg. 716

JULIAN MESSNER—Books—Simon & Schuster; *U.S. Private*, pg. 777

JULIUS SUPREME—Soft Drinks—Orange Julius of America; *U.S. Public*, pg. 220

JUMBO—Dry Soup Mixes & Boullion—Borden, Inc.; *U.S. Private*, pg. 157

JUMBO—Soft Drink—Double-Cola Co.-USA; *U.S. Private*, pg. 341

JUMBO—Cereal Assortment in 25 Single-Serving Packages—Kellogg Company; *U.S. Public*, pg. 947

JUMBO BAR—Harrow-Rigid Tooth—Midwest Industries, Inc.; *U.S. Private*, pg. 744

JUMBO GRILLER—Hot Dogs—Hatfield Quality Meats; *U.S. Private*, pg. 510

JUMBO HOT SPOT—Carafe/Casserole Warmer—Salton/Maxim Housewares, Inc.; *U.S. Public*, pg. 1430

JUMBO INSTA-MARKER—Marking Pens—Diagraph Corporation; *U.S. Private*, pg. 330

JUMBO JET—NONE—Western Atlas Logging Services; *U.S. Public*, pg. 1757

JUMBO JIFFY-GRO—Garden Products—Jiffy Products of America, Inc.; *Int'l*, pg. 706

JUMBO 160 M—Intermediate Dry Mounting/Laminating Press—Seal Products Incorporated; *U.S. Public*, pg. 849

JUMBO VACS—Large Capacity Industrial Vacs—Breuer/Tornado; *U.S. Private*, pg. 167

JUMP—Magazine—Weider Publications, Inc.; *U.S. Private*, pg. 1159

JUMPER CABLE—Jolt Cola & Rum Drink—Global Beverage Co.; *U.S. Private*, pg. 457

JUMPIN' MONKEYS—Game—Pressman Toy Corp.; *U.S. Private*, pg. 882

JUMPING-JACKS—Children's Shoes—Jumping Jacks; *U.S. Private*, pg. 767

JUNCTION XPRESS—Vectorless Test Technique for Opens on SMD's—GenRad, Inc.; *U.S. Public*, pg. 731

JUNEAU EMPIRE—Newspaper—Shivers Trading & Operating Co.; *U.S. Private*, pg. 994

JUNGLE GARDENIA—Tuvache-Fragrance for Women—Yardley of London, Inc.; *Int'l*, pg. 819

JUNGLE JOLLIES—Fruit Candy—R.L. Albert & Son, Inc.; *U.S. Private*, pg. 32

JUNGLE JUICE—Interior Plant Products—Security Lawn & Garden Co.; *U.S. Private*, pg. 397

JUNGLE JUNCTION—Greeting Cards—American Greetings Corporation; *U.S. Public*, pg. 77

JUNGLE TOUGH PALLETS—Custom Designed Pallets to Suit Customer Needs—Seaman Timber Company, Inc.; *U.S. Private*, pg. 979

JUNIOR—Tricycle—Roadmaster/Brunswick; *U.S. Public*, pg. 265

JUNIOR DISPROL—Analgesic—Reckitt & Colman plc; *Int'l*, pg. 1089

JUNIOR JUICE—Boxed Juice—McCain Citrus Inc.; *Int'l*, pg. 850

JUNIOR LEMSIP—Cold Relief—Reckitt & Colman plc; *Int'l*, pg. 1089

JUNIOR MINTS—Chocolate/Caramel Candies—Tootsie Roll Industries, Inc.; *U.S. Public*, pg. 1621

JUNIOR PUTTERS OF AMERICA—Trade Name in Conjunction with Putt-Putts Junior Putting Program—Putt Putt Golf Courses of America, Inc.; *U.S. Public*, pg. 896

JUNKBOTS—Action Figures—Tyco Toys, Inc.; *U.S. Public*, pg. 1058

JUNKER—Industrial Furnaces—Otto Junker GmbH Lammersdorf; *Int'l*, pg. 1014

JUNKERS—Heating and Hot Water Equipments—Robert Bosch GmbH; *Int'l*, pg. 203

JUNO—NONE—Electrolux, AB; *Int'l*, pg. 438

JUNO—Lighting Fixtures—Juno Lighting, Inc.; *U.S. Public*, pg. 935

JUNO DOWN-LITES—Lighting Fixture—Juno Lighting, Inc.; *U.S. Public*, pg. 935

JUNO TRAC-MASTER—Trac Lighting Fixtures—Juno Lighting, Inc.; *U.S. Public*, pg. 935

JUPILER—Lager—Interbrew S.A.; *Int'l*, pg. 679

JUPITER MISSION 1999—Microcomputer Game—Monarch Avalon, Inc.; *U.S. Public*, pg. 1123

JURASSIC PARK—Toys—Hasbro; *U.S. Public*, pg. 797

JURASSIC PARK—Kenner Products—Hasbro, Inc.; *U.S. Public*, pg. 797

JURGEN LANGBEIN—Soups & Ready Meals—GrandMet Foods GmbH; *Int'l*, pg. 409

JURIS-CLASSEUR—Loose Leaf—Editions du Juris-Classeur; *Int'l*, pg. 1095

JURIS DATA—Database—Editions du Juris-Classeur; *Int'l*, pg. 1095

JURISOFT DIRECTCONNECT—Software—The Mead Corporation; *U.S. Public*, pg. 1074

JURUBATECH—Specialty Service Tools—SPX Corporation; *U.S. Public*, pg. 1420

JUS-ROL—Frozen & Chilled Pastry & Frozen Potato Products—GrandMet Foods UK; *Int'l*, pg. 408

JUSCOAT—NONE—Pfizer Inc.; *U.S. Public*, pg. 1281

JUST—Detergent That Dissolves Grease Stains Without Excessive Suds—Kao Corporation; *Int'l*, pg. 717

JUST BETWEEN US—Mail Order—Miles Kimball Company; *U.S. Private*, pg. 745

JUST 5—NONE—Combe Incorporated; *U.S. Private*, pg. 257

JUST FOR COPIES—Opaquing Fluid—The Gillette Company; *U.S. Public*, pg. 743

JUST FOR FEET—NONE—Just For Feet, Inc.; *U.S. Public*, pg. 935

JUST FOR FORMS—Correction Fluid—The Gillette Company; *U.S. Public*, pg. 743

JUST-FOR-KIDS—NONE—Integrity Incorporated; *U.S. Public*, pg. 886

JUST FOR ME—Children's Hair Products—Pro-Line Corporation; *U.S. Private*, pg. 887

JUST FOR MEN BRUSH-IN COLOR GEL—Male Hair Dye—Combe Incorporated; *U.S. Private*, pg. 257

JUST FOR MEN SHAMPOO-IN HAIRCOLOR—Male Hair Dye—Combe Incorporated; *U.S. Private*, pg. 257

JUST FOR THE HEALTH OF IT—NONE—Koo Koo Roo, Inc.; *U.S. Public*, pg. 966

JUST FOR YOU—Hosiery & Related Apparel—Mayer/Berkshire Corporation; *U.S. Private*, pg. 717

JUST HOW I FEEL—Line of Greeting Cards—Hallmark Cards, Inc.; *U.S. Private*, pg. 495

JUST-IN-CASE—First Aid Kits—Sentinel Consumer Products, Inc.; *U.S. Private*, pg. 984

JUST JUICE—Fruit Juice—Ranks Hovis McDougall Limited; *Int'l*, pg. 1395

JUST KIDDIN'—Greeting Cards—Fine Art Developments plc; *Int'l*, pg. 485

JUST MY SIZE—Hosiery—L'eggs Products, Inc.; *U.S. Public*, pg. 1434

JUST MY STYLECARPET—NONE—Peerless Carpet Corporation; *U.S. Public*, pg. 1032

JUST ONE BITE—Rat & Mouse Bait—Security Lawn & Garden Co.; *U.S. Private*, pg. 397

JUST PIKT—Processed Fruit Products—Fresh Juice Company; *U.S. Private*, pg. 427

JUST RIGHT WITH FIBER NUGGETS—Whole Wheat, Corn, Rice & Oat Cereal with High-Fiber Nuggets—Kellogg Company; *U.S. Public*, pg. 947

JUST RIGHT WITH RAISINS DATES & NUTS—Whole Wheat, Corn Rice & Oat Cereal with Raisins, Dates & Nuts—Kellogg Company; *U.S. Public*, pg. 947

JUST 17—U.K. Young Women's Magazine—EMAP Elan; *Int'l*, pg. 451

JUST WHISTLE—Twin Blade Self-Adjusting Razor—The Gillette Company; *U.S. Public*, pg. 743

JUST YOUR FIT—Bras—Warner's; *U.S. Public*, pg. 1738

JUSTIN—Boots—Justin Boot Company; *U.S. Public*, pg. 937

JUSTIN—Footwear—Justin Industries, Inc.; *U.S. Public*, pg. 936

JUSTIN JUNIORS—Boots—Justin Boot Company; *U.S. Public*, pg. 937

JUSTIN LACE R'S—Shoes—Justin Boot Company; *U.S. Public*, pg. 937

JUSTRITE—Safety Containers—Federal Signal Corporation; *U.S. Public*, pg. 616

JUSTRITE—Industrial Safety Products—Justrite Manufacturing Company; *U.S. Public*, pg. 617

JUSTUS—Log Homes—Lindal Cedar Homes, Inc.; *U.S. Public*, pg. 998

JUSTY—Automobile Produced by Subaru—Fuji Heavy Industries, Ltd.; *Int'l*, pg. 522

JUSTY—Auotmobile—Subaru of America, Inc.; *Int'l*, pg. 523

JUTLAND—Game—Monarch Avalon, Inc.; *U.S. Public*, pg. 1123

JUVEL—Vitamin Supplement—SmithKline Beecham plc; *Int'l*, pg. 1264

JVIEW—Board—LSI Logic Corp.; *U.S. Public*, pg. 971

K

K—Footwear—Clarks International; *Int'l*, pg. 296

K—Metalcutting & Mining Tools—Kennametal Inc.; *U.S. Public*, pg. 950

Brand Name Index

K—Liquor—Matthew Clark Brands; *Int'l*, pg. 848

KAI GUAVA—Fruit—C. Brewer & Company, Limited; *U.S. Private*, pg. 190

KAM—Affinity Separation Products—Eastman Kodak Company; *U.S. Public*, pg. 550

KAO DATA CARTRIDGES—Diskettes—Kao Infosystems Company (MA); *Int'l*, pg. 717

KAO DATS—Diskettes—Kao Infosystems Company (MA); *Int'l*, pg. 717

KAO DISKETTE MAILERS—Diskettes—Kao Infosystems Company (MA); *Int'l*, pg. 717

KAP—Kids Are People Savings Accounts—The Troy Savings Bank; *U.S. Private*, pg. 1106

KAR—Photographic Resist, Developer & Thinner—Eastman Kodak Company; *U.S. Public*, pg. 550

KAS—Potato Chips—Borden, Inc.; *U.S. Private*, pg. 157

K & B—Vault Closures—3M; *U.S. Public*, pg. 1604

K & M—Silver Plating—Kirk & Matz Ltd.; *U.S. Private*, pg. 623

KB & COMPANY—Shoes—Fred Meyer Stores; *U.S. Public*, pg. 1103

KB BRAND—NONE—Blue Grass Quality Meats; *U.S. Private*, pg. 152

KBI—Aluminum Master Alloys—KB Alloys, Inc.; *U.S. Private*, pg. 249

KB JARDIN—Perfume—Rhone-Poulenc S.A.; *Int'l*, pg. 1108

K-BLAZER—Food Products—Kraft Food Ingredients Corp.; *U.S. Public*, pg. 1288

K C—Baking Powder—Hulman & Company; *U.S. Private*, pg. 547

KCLI—Stock Symbol—Kansas City Life Insurance Co.; *U.S. Public*, pg. 942

K.C. MASTERPIECE—Barbecue Sauce—The Clorox Company; *U.S. Public*, pg. 386

KCP 1000—Kinetic Cavity Preparation System—American Dental Technologies; *U.S. Public*, pg. 70

KCP 2000—Kinetic Cavity Preparation System—American Dental Technologies; *U.S. Public*, pg. 70

KC 1000—Gas Fired Water Heater-Boiler Line—Aerco International Inc.; *U.S. Private*, pg. 23

K-CHITOS—Potato Chips—Borden, Inc.; *U.S. Private*, pg. 157

K-CHROME—Photographic Film—Eastman Kodak Company; *U.S. Public*, pg. 550

K-COLOR—Photographic Film—Eastman Kodak Company; *U.S. Public*, pg. 550

K-D—Truck Lighting & Mirrors—K-D Lamp Company; *U.S. Private*, pg. 603

KDP—Generators—Dresser-Rand Sales; *U.S. Public*, pg. 529

KDS AMERICA—Electronic Components—Interface Electronics Corporation; *U.S. Private*, pg. 567

K-D TOOLS—Automotive Specialty & Hand Tools—Danaher Tool Group; *U.S. Public*, pg. 480

K-DUR—Potassium Chloride—Key Pharmaceuticals; *U.S. Public*, pg. 1438

K-DUR—Sustained-Release Potassium Supplement—Schering-Plough Corporation; *U.S. Public*, pg. 1438

KEBR—Photographic Resist—Eastman Kodak Company; *U.S. Public*, pg. 550

KEL-F—Thermoplastic Polymer—3M; *U.S. Public*, pg. 1604

KF—Coffee Maker—Regal Ware, Inc.; *U.S. Private*, pg. 917

KF—Valves—Watts Industries, Inc.; *U.S. Public*, pg. 1746

KF—Plumbing Supplies; Floor Protective Hardware—Waxman Industries, Inc.; *U.S. Public*, pg. 1748

KF & DESIGN—Cookware—Regal Ware, Inc.; *U.S. Private*, pg. 917

KFC—Restaurants—Kentucky Fried Chicken Corporation (KFC); *U.S. Public*, pg. 1636

KFYR-AG SHOW—Stock & Equipment Show—Meyer Broadcasting Company; *U.S. Private*, pg. 739

KFYR-Radio—Radio Station—Meyer Broadcasting Company; *U.S. Private*, pg. 739

KFYR-TV—Television Station—Meyer Broadcasting Company; *U.S. Private*, pg. 739

K-FAST—Installation Tooling for Aerospace & Commercial Fasteners—KTI; *U.S. Public*, pg. 939

K-FLEX—Cable, Galvanized & Stainless Steel & Resin for Terminations—Loos & Co., Inc.; *U.S. Private*, pg. 675

K4300—Thermal Transfer & Direct Thermal Printer—Kroy Inc.; *U.S. Public*, pg. 1339

K4200—Thermal Transfer & Direct Thermal Printer—Kroy Inc.; *U.S. Public*, pg. 1339

KG 5.5—Loudspeaker Systems—Klipsch, Inc.; *U.S. Private*, pg. 626

KG 4.5—Loudspeaker Systems—Klipsch, Inc.; *U.S. Private*, pg. 626

KGNC AM/FM—Radio—Shivers Trading & Operating Co.; *U.S. Private*, pg. 994

KG1.5—Loudspeaker Systems—Klipsch, Inc.; *U.S. Private*, pg. 626

KG3.5—Loudspeaker Systems—Klipsch, Inc.; *U.S. Private*, pg. 626

KG2.5—Loudspeaker Systems—Klipsch, Inc.; *U.S. Private*, pg. 626

KHA SUPER PINION CUTTER—High-Speed Steel Cutter—Kobe Steel, Ltd.; *Int'l*, pg. 740

KHG-7—Vitamin—Health Products Corporation; *U.S. Private*, pg. 514

KI-1000—Processor of Digitalized Medical Images—Konica Corporation; *Int'l*, pg. 748

KI-500—Processor of Digitalized Medical Images—Konica Corporation; *Int'l*, pg. 748

KJV—King James Version—American Bible Society; *U.S. Private*, pg. 51

KK—Electronic Components—Molex Incorporated; *U.S. Public*, pg. 1121

KK 2000—Kitchen Cabinets—Kitchen Kompact, Inc.; *U.S. Private*, pg. 624

KL—Fragrance for Women—Elizabeth Arden Company; *Int'l*, pg. 1435

KLA 5000—NONE—KLA Tencor Corporation; *U.S. Public*, pg. 939

KLA 2551—NONE—KLA Tencor Corporation; *U.S. Public*, pg. 939

KLA 2111—NONE—KLA Tencor Corporation; *U.S. Public*, pg. 939

KLA 2100—NONE—KLA Tencor Corporation; *U.S. Public*, pg. 939

KLA 2110—NONE—KLA Tencor Corporation; *U.S. Public*, pg. 939

KLA 2130—NONE—KLA Tencor Corporation; *U.S. Public*, pg. 939

KLA 2131—NONE—KLA Tencor Corporation; *U.S. Public*, pg. 939

KLA 2608—NONE—KLA Tencor Corporation; *U.S. Public*, pg. 939

KLA 2000—NONE—KLA Tencor Corporation; *U.S. Public*, pg. 939

KLIM—Whole Milk Powder—Borden, Inc.; *U.S. Private*, pg. 157

KLIT-FM—Radio Station - Los Angeles, CA—Golden West Broadcasters; *U.S. Private*, pg. 461

KLLM—Transport Services—KLLM Transport Services, Inc.; *U.S. Public*, pg. 939

KLM—International Airline—KLM Royal Dutch Airlines; *Int'l*, pg. 719

KLM—Airlines—KLM Royal Dutch Airlines; *Int'l*, pg. 719

KLM ROYAL DUTCH AIRLINES—Airlines—KLM Royal Dutch Airlines; *Int'l*, pg. 719

KLM-UK—Regional Brand Name-Europe—Air UK Ltd.; *Int'l*, pg. 38

KL-990—Marine Products—Rule Industries, Inc.; *U.S. Public*, pg. 950

KLS—Lubricating Specialists—Kaibab Industries; *U.S. Private*, pg. 605

KLS SERIES—Compact Laser System—Lasag AG; *Int'l*, pg. 1161

"K" LINE—NONE—"K" Line (Kawasaki Kisen Kaisha, Ltd.); *Int'l*, pg. 717

K-LOR—Potassium Supplement—Abbott Laboratories; *U.S. Public*, pg. 12

K LUBE—Oils & Greases—Mallet & Co.; *U.S. Private*, pg. 698

K-LUX—Decorator & Lighting Panels—ICI Acrylics Inc.; *Int'l*, pg. 663

K-LYTE—Potassium Supplement—Bristol-Myers Squibb Company; *U.S. Public*, pg. 253

K-LYTE—Tablets for Treatment of Potassium Deficiency—Bristol-Myers Squibb U.S. Pharmaceutical Group; *U.S. Public*, pg. 255

K-LYTE/CL—Potassium Chloride Supplement—Bristol-Myers Squibb U.S. Pharmaceutical Group; *U.S. Public*, pg. 255

KM—Metalcutting Tools—Kennametal Inc.; *U.S. Public*, pg. 950

KM—Chemicals—Kerr-McGee Chemical Corp.; *U.S. Public*, pg. 952

KMBC-TV—Broadcasting—The Hearst Corporation; *U.S. Private*, pg. 515

K M BY KRIZIA—Men's Apparel—Hartmarx Corporation; *U.S. Public*, pg. 795

KMER—Photographic Resist—Eastman Kodak Company; *U.S. Public*, pg. 550

KMOT AGR INTERNATION—Stock & Equipment Show—Meyer Broadcasting Company; *U.S. Private*, pg. 739

KMOT-TV—Television Station—Meyer Broadcasting Company; *U.S. Private*, pg. 739

KMPC-AM—Radio Station - Los Angeles, CA—Golden West Broadcasters; *U.S. Private*, pg. 461

KMXR—Photographic Resist—Eastman Kodak Company; *U.S. Public*, pg. 550

K-MAG—Magnetic Flowmeter—Bailey, Fischer & Porter Company; *Int'l*, pg. 449

K-MAX—External Lift Heicopter—Kaman Corporation; *U.S. Public*, pg. 941

K-MAX—Rotary Control Valve—Leslie Controls, Inc.; *U.S. Public*, pg. 1746

K-MILL—Milling Cutters—Kennametal Inc.; *U.S. Public*, pg. 950

K-MILL—Milling Tool—Smith International, Inc.; *U.S. Public*, pg. 1478

KNA—Sodium Potassium Analyzer—Radiometer A/S; *Int'l*, pg. 1083

KN SOLUTION—Carbohydrate-electrolyte Solution—Otsuka Pharmaceutical Co., Ltd.; *Int'l*, pg. 1013

KNZ—De-Icing Salt—Akzo Nobel N.V.; *Int'l*, pg. 42

K-NORM—Extended-Release Capsules (Potassium Chloride, USP)—Medeva Pharmaceuticals; *Int'l*, pg. 852

KOA-KAMPGROUNDS—Campgrounds—Kampgrounds of America, Inc.; *U.S. Private*, pg. 603

KOM—Microfilming Machines & Accessories—Eastman Kodak Company; *U.S. Public*, pg. 550

KOR—Photographic Resist Products—Eastman Kodak Company; *U.S. Public*, pg. 550

K180K82—Personal Labeling Systems—Kroy Inc.; *U.S. Public*, pg. 1339

K100E—Trucks—Kenworth Truck Company; *U.S. Public*, pg. 1246

KP—Snacks—United Biscuits (Holdings) Plc; *Int'l*, pg. 1442

KP—Snacks—United Biscuits (UK) Limited; *Int'l*, pg. 1442

KPL—Photosensitive Lacquer—Eastman Kodak Company; *U.S. Public*, pg. 550

KPLZ-FM—Radio Station - Seattle, WA—Golden West Broadcasters; *U.S. Private*, pg. 461

KPS—Knowledge Based Services—R.A. Jones & Co. Inc.; *U.S. Private*, pg. 597

K-PAC—Waste Handling Equipment—Krause Plow Corp.; *U.S. Private*, pg. 635

K PRIME—Chromatography Systems—Amicon, Inc.; *U.S. Public*, pg. 1113

KQCD-TV—Television Station—Meyer Broadcasting Company; *U.S. Private*, pg. 739

KRBS—Materials Distribution System For Radios—Multi-Ad Services, Incorporated; *U.S. Private*, pg. 766

K-RESIN—Styrene Butadiene Copolymers—Phillips Petroleum Company; *U.S. Public*, pg. 1290

K-S—Liquid-Solids Separation Equipment—Komline-Sanderson Engineering Corp.; *U.S. Private*, pg. 631

KSB—Pumps & Valves—KSB Aktiengesellschaft; *Int'l*, pg. 721

KSF—Impact Breaker—Svedala Industries Inc.; *Int'l*, pg. 1325

KS-4—Castables—A.P. Green Industries, Inc.; *U.S. Public*, pg. 761

KSTP—TV Station—KSTP-TV; *U.S. Private*, pg. 544

K-SEAL—Reclosable Poly Bag—KCL Corporation; *U.S. Private*, pg. 603

K SERIES—NONE—NEC Electronics Inc.; *Int'l*, pg. 900

K-SERVIPLAN—NONE—Coop Switzerland; *Int'l*, pg. 329

K-SWISS—Athletic Wear-T-Shirts, Caps, Socks etc.—K-Swiss Inc.; *U.S. Public*, pg. 937

K.T. MCKENZIE—Private Label—Jerell, Inc.; *U.S. Private*, pg. 586

KTP/532—NONE—Laserscope Surgical Systems; *U.S. Public*, pg. 979

KTP/YAG—NONE—Laserscope Surgical Systems; *U.S. Public*, pg. 979

K-TAB—Potassium Supplement—Abbott Laboratories; *U.S. Public*, pg. 12

K-TEL—Music & Non-Music Production—K-Tel International, Inc.; *U.S. Public*, pg. 937

K-TRON SODER—Soder-Feeder—K-Tron International, Inc.; *U.S. Public*, pg. 938

K-II—Photographic Film—Eastman Kodak Company; *U.S. Public*, pg. 550

K2—Skis, Snowboards—K2 Inc.; *U.S. Public*, pg. 940

K2—Silicone Compound—Marson/Creative Fastener, Inc.; *U.S. Private*, pg. 708

K2—Catheter—Medtronic, Inc.; *U.S. Public*, pg. 1082

K-2—Premier Motor Home Chassis—Spartan Motors, Inc.; *U.S. Public*, pg. 1495

K-2-8—Electronic Learning Aid—Tiger Electronics, Inc.; *U.S. Private*, pg. 1086

K2 OUTDOOR—Backpacks & Hydration Systems—K2 Inc.; *U.S. Public*, pg. 940

K2R—Spot Lifter—Spontex, Inc.; *Int'l*, pg. 1409

K2 ROFLEX—Mountain Bicycles—K2 Inc.; *U.S. Public*, pg. 940

K225—On-Line Labeler—Kroy Inc.; *U.S. Public*, pg. 1339

KUMV-TV—Television Station—Meyer Broadcasting Company; *U.S. Private*, pg. 739

KVI-AM—Radio Station - Seattle, WA—Golden West Broadcasters; *U.S. Private*, pg. 461

KVLY-TV—Television Station—Meyer Broadcasting Company; *U.S. Private*, pg. 739

KVP—Parchment—Fort James Corporation; *U.S. Public*, pg. 670

KV/24—Once-Daily Dosing for Tablets or Capsules—KV Pharmaceutical Company; *U.S. Public*, pg. 941

K-VENIENCE—Closet & Kitchen Fixtures—Knape & Vogt Mfg. Co.; *U.S. Public*, pg. 963

K-W—NONE—Carpenter Technology Corporation; *U.S. Public*, pg. 307

KWA—NONE—Siemens AG; *Int'l*, pg. 1244

KWW—Filler Clay—Engelhard Corporation; *U.S. Public*, pg. 582

K-WOOD—Kitchen Cabinets—Kitchen Kompact, Inc.; *U.S. Private*, pg. 624

KXL—Long-Life Panel Finishes—Varco-Pruden Buildings; *U.S. Public*, pg. 1677

KX-99—Super Duty Firebrick—A.P. Green Industries, Inc.; *U.S. Public*, pg. 761

KYB—Shock Absorbers—KYB Corporation of America; *Int'l*, pg. 727

KYB—NONE—Kayaba Industry Co., Ltd.; *Int'l*, pg. 727

K-Y BRAND LONG LASTING LUBRICANT—NONE—Ortho-McNeil Pharmaceutical Corporation; *U.S. Public*, pg. 929

K-Y BRAND LUBRICATING JELLY—NONE—Ortho-McNeil Pharmaceutical Corporation; *U.S. Public*, pg. 929

K-Y JELLY—Lubricant—Johnson & Johnson Consumer Products; *U.S. Public*, pg. 928

KYS—Berry Baskets—The Chinet Co.; *Int'l*, pg. 1146

KYS FILLER—Flats for Eggs—The Chinet Co.; *Int'l*, pg. 1146

KYS-PAK—Containers for Apples—The Chinet Co.; *Int'l*, pg. 1146

KYYY-FM—Radio Station—Meyer Broadcasting Company; *U.S. Private*, pg. 739

KZK LIMITED—Woven & Knit Garments—Niches, Inc.; *U.S. Public*, pg. 1181

K. ZILDJIAN—Cymbals—Avedis Zildjian Company; *U.S. Public*, pg. 1206

KAANAPALI BEACH—Resorts—Amfac, Inc.; *U.S. Private*, pg. 577

KABOODLES—Egg Noodles—Foulds Inc.; *U.S. Private*, pg. 421

KABOOM—Teen Clothes—Buster Brown Apparel, Inc.; *U.S. Private*, pg. 189

KABOOM—Cereal—General Mills, Inc.; *U.S. Public*, pg. 717

KADE WE—Department Store—Hertie Waren-und Kaufhaus GmbH; *Int'l*, pg. 724

KADEL—Polyketone High Temperature Engineering Resins—Amoco Chemicals; *U.S. Public*, pg. 102

KADEL—High-Tech Polymer—Amoco Corporation; *U.S. Public*, pg. 101

KADENZA—Digital Picture Processor, Video—Tektronix-Video & Networking Div., Grass Valley Products; *U.S. Public*, pg. 1567

KADIAN—Pharmaceutical—Zeneca Group Plc; *Int'l*, pg. 1524

KADIZID—Cadmium Process—LeaRonal, Inc.; *U.S. Public*, pg. 982

KADOX ZINC OXIDE—NONE—Zinc Corporation of America; *U.S. Private*, pg. 540

KADUR—Taptite—Kamax-G.B. DuPont L.P.; *U.S. Private*, pg. 606

KADUS—Hairdressing Products—Wella Group; *Int'l*, pg. 1489

KAEPA—Athletic Footwear—Kaepa Inc.; *U.S. Private*, pg. 604

KAHLUA—Liqueur—Allied Domecq PLC; *Int'l*, pg. 62

KAHLUA—NONE—Allied Domecq Spirits & Wine (UK) Ltd.; *Int'l*, pg. 63

KAHLUA—Liqueur—Hiram Walker; *Int'l*, pg. 63

KAHN'S—Packaged Meats & Processed Meat Products—Hillshire Farm & Kahn's; *U.S. Public*, pg. 1433

KAHN'S—Meat Products—Sara Lee Corporation; *U.S. Public*, pg. 1432

KAISER—Beer—Cervejarias Kaiser Brasil Ltda.; *Int'l*, pg. 279

KAISER—Cement Products—Hanson PLC; *Int'l*, pg. 592

KAISER—Cement—Kaiser Cement Corporation; *Int'l*, pg. 593

KAISER BOCK—Bock Beer—Cervejarias Kaiser Brasil Ltda.; *Int'l*, pg. 279

KAISER GOLD—Extra Beer—Cervejarias Kaiser Brasil Ltda.; *Int'l*, pg. 279

KAISER SUMMER DRAFT—Draft Beer—Cervejarias Kaiser Brasil Ltda.; *Int'l*, pg. 279

KAISER'S—Grocery Store—Tengelmann Warenhandelsgesellschaft; *Int'l*, pg. 1375

KAKE MATE—Cake Emulsifier—Mallet & Co.; *U.S. Private*, pg. 698

KAL EQUIP—Automotive Test Equipment—Actron Manufacturing Company; *U.S. Private*, pg. 16

KAL-FOIL—Gum Paper Labels—Kal Grafx; *U.S. Private*, pg. 387

KAL-GUM—Gum Paper Labels—Kal Grafx; *U.S. Private*, pg. 387

KAL KAN—Pet Foods—Mars, Incorporated; *U.S. Private*, pg. 707

KAL-NAMEL—Gum Paper Labels—Kal Grafx; *U.S. Private*, pg. 387

KALAMAZOO—NONE—Research Environmental Industries, Inc.; *U.S. Private*, pg. 924

THE KALAMAZOO GAZETTE—Newspaper—Booth Newspapers, Inc.; *U.S. Private*, pg. 157

KALAR—Crosslinked Butyl Rubber—Hardman Division of Harcros Chemicals, Inc.; *Int'l*, pg. 598

KALCO—Gum Paper Labels—Kal Grafx; *U.S. Private*, pg. 387

KALEIDA—Multimedia Computer Systems—Apple Computer, Inc.; *U.S. Public*, pg. 121

KALEIDOCOLORS—Hair Products—Bristol-Myers Squibb Company; *U.S. Public*, pg. 253

KALEIDOSCOPE—Office Furniture—HON Industries Inc.; *U.S. Public*, pg. 772

KALEIDOSCOPE—Digital Effects System—Tektronix-Video & Networking Div., Grass Valley Products; *U.S. Public*, pg. 1567

KALENE—Elastomeric Compounds—Hardman Division of Harcros Chemicals, Inc.; *Int'l*, pg. 598

KALEX—Two-Part Polyurethane Elastomers—Hardman Division of Harcros Chemicals, Inc.; *Int'l*, pg. 598

KALIA—Laundry Additive—Benckiser Consumer Products Inc.; *Int'l*, pg. 185

KALIBER—Non-Alcoholic Brew—Guinness Import Company; *Int'l*, pg. 412

KALIBER—NONE—Guinness Plc; *Int'l*, pg. 412

KALIBER SIN—NONE—Guinness Plc; *Int'l*, pg. 412

KALIFORNIAKOLORS—Spray Paint—Sherwin-Williams Diversified Brands, Inc.; *U.S. Public*, pg. 1466

KALIUM DURULES—Potassium Supplement—Astra AB; *Int'l*, pg. 93

KALKHOFF—Cycle—Derby International Corporation S.A.; *Int'l*, pg. 394

KALLOTEX—NONE—Fred B. Johnston Company, Inc.; *U.S. Private*, pg. 595

KALMBACH—Book & Magazine Publishing—Kalmbach Publishing Co.; *U.S. Private*, pg. 606

KALOYANNIS OUZO—NONE—Metaxa Greece; *Int'l*, pg. 410

KALREZ—Perfluoroelastomer—Du Pont (E.I. Du Pont De Nemours & Co.); *U.S. Public*, pg. 530

KALTRON—Polyurethane Foam, Solvents and Refrigerants, Aerosols—Kali-Chemie Aktiengesellschaft; *Int'l*, pg. 1278

KALZANA D—Calcium Supplement—SmithKline Beecham plc; *Int'l*, pg. 1264

KAMAKAZI—Cocktail—Montebello Brands Inc.; *U.S. Private*, pg. 758

KAMASOL GREEN—Liquid Fertilizer—BASF AG; *Int'l*, pg. 103

KAMAX—Klub—Kamax-G.B. DuPont L.P.; *U.S. Private*, pg. 606

KAMAX—Plastic Additives—Rohm and Haas Company; *U.S. Public*, pg. 1403

KAMCHATKA—Vodka—Fortune Brands, Inc.; *U.S. Public*, pg. 674

KAMEWA—Marine Engineering-Propulsion Systems—Vickers PLC; *Int'l*, pg. 1466

KAMIK—Footwear—Genfoot Inc.; *Int'l*, pg. 549

KAMINSKY—Fashion Dress Trousers & Shorts—H. R. Kaminsky & Sons, Inc.; *U.S. Private*, pg. 606

KAMLOK—Fittings—Ryan Herco Products Corp.; *U.S. Private*, pg. 953

KAMORA—Cordial—Fortune Brands, Inc.; *U.S. Public*, pg. 674

KAMORAN—Actaplanin, Elanco—Eli Lilly and Company; *U.S. Public*, pg. 992

KAMWELD—Plastic Welders—Ryan Herco Products Corp.; *U.S. Private*, pg. 953

KAMYNEX—Kanamycin Sulfate—Royal Gist-Brocades N.V.; *Int'l*, pg. 1142

KAN TONG FRIED RICE—NONE—Uncle Ben's, Inc.; *U.S. Private*, pg. 707

KANAMASTIN—Veterinary Medicines—Meiji Seika Kaisha, Ltd.; *Int'l*, pg. 855

KANAMYCIN—Veterinary Medicines & Antibiotics—Meiji Seika Kaisha, Ltd.; *Int'l*, pg. 855

KANE COUNTY (IL) MARKETING DIRECTORY—Directory—Manufacturers' News, Inc.; *U.S. Private*, pg. 700

KANE KRAFT—Woven Fabrics for Casual Furniture—Tyco International Ltd.; *U.S. Public*, pg. 1647

KANEKRAFT—Paper Yarn Fabric—Ludlow Corporation; *U.S. Public*, pg. 1651

KANENDOMYCIN—Antibiotics—Meiji Seika Kaisha, Ltd.; *Int'l*, pg. 855

KANGA ROCKA ROO—Carrier—Century Products Co.; *U.S. Private*, pg. 226

KANGABACK—Urethane Cushion—Textile Rubber & Chemical Company; *U.S. Private*, pg. 1079

KANGAROO—Enteral Feeding Systems & Access Devices—American Home Products Corporation; *U.S. Public*, pg. 79

KANGAROO—Lawn & Leaf Bag Cart—Ames Company; *U.S. Public*, pg. 1683

KANGAROO—Mens' & Boys' Underwear—Fruit of the Loom, Inc.; *U.S. Public*, pg. 685

KANGAROO—Health Care Products—Sherwood-Davis & Geck; *U.S. Public*, pg. 80

KANIGEN—Nickel Plated Products—Electro-Coatings, Inc.; *U.S. Private*, pg. 368

KANIS & GUNNICK—Coffee—Sara Lee Corporation; *U.S. Public*, pg. 1432

KANKA—Mouth Sore Medication—Blistex, Inc.; *U.S. Private*, pg. 149

KANPAI—Camera Responding To Voice Commands—Konica Corporation; *Int'l*, pg. 748

KANSA—Newspaper Inserters—Baldwin Technology Company, Inc.; *U.S. Public*, pg. 169

KANSAS CITY BUSINESS JOURNAL—Business Journal—Business First of New York, Inc.; *U.S. Private*, pg. 19

KANSAS CITY CHIEFS—Football Club—Kansas City Chiefs Football Club, Inc.; *U.S. Private*, pg. 607

KANSAS CITY STAR—Newspaper—The Kansas City Star Company; *U.S. Public*, pg. 964

KANSAS FARMER—NONE—Farm Progress Publications; *U.S. Public*, pg. 513

KANSAS JACK—Collision Damage Repair Systems—Hein-Werner Corporation; *U.S. Public*, pg. 805

KANSAS MANUFACTURERS REGISTER—Register—Manufacturers' News, Inc.; *U.S. Private*, pg. 700

KANT-SLIP—Pressure Sensitive Labels—The Standard Register Company; *U.S. Public*, pg. 1505

KANTERBRAU—Beer—Danone Group; *Int'l*, pg. 379

KANTREX—Gastrointestinal Antibiotic—Bristol-Myers Squibb Company; *U.S. Public*, pg. 253

KANVET—Banners & Pennants—Chicago Show Printing Co.; *U.S. Private*, pg. 235

KAO 5.25" DISKETTES—Diskettes—Kao Infosystems Company (MA); *Int'l*, pg. 717

KAO LECTROLYTE—NONE—Pharmacia & Upjohn; *Int'l*, pg. 1048

KAO 3.5" DISKETTES—Diskettes—Kao Infosystems Company (MA); *Int'l*, pg. 717

KAOCRETE—NONE—Thermal Ceramics Inc.; *Int'l*, pg. 894

KAOLA GOLD—Fats & Oils—Van den Bergh Foods Company; *Int'l*, pg. 1436

KAOLITE—NONE—Thermal Ceramics Inc.; *Int'l*, pg. 894

KAOMEL—Fats & Oils—Van den Bergh Foods Company; *Int'l*, pg. 1436

KAOPECTATE—Pharmaceutical Products—Pharmacia & Upjohn; *Int'l*, pg. 1048

KAOWOOL—NONE—Thermal Ceramics Inc.; *Int'l*, pg. 894

KAPLAN—NONE—Kaplan Educational Centers Ltd.; *U.S. Public*, pg. 1743

KAPLAN EDUCATIONAL SERVICES—Test Preparation—The Washington Post Company; *U.S. Public*, pg. 1742

KAPTON—Plastics—AlliedSignal Inc.; *U.S. Public*, pg. 49

KAPTON—Polyimide Film—Du Pont (E.I. Du Pont De Nemours & Co.); *U.S. Public*, pg. 530

KAR 'N HOME—Perc Kits—The Metal Ware Corp.; *U.S. Private*, pg. 734

KAR-TOTE—Tow Dolly—Automatic Equipment Mfg. Co.; *U.S. Private*, pg. 101

KARAMIK—Floor Coverings—Domco Inc.; *Int'l*, pg. 415

KARASTAN—Rugs and Carpets—Fieldcrest Cannon, Inc.; *U.S. Public*, pg. 1296

KARASTAN—Carpets—Karastan; *U.S. Public*, pg. 1121

KARASTAN—Carpets & Rugs—Mohawk Industries, Inc.; *U.S. Public*, pg. 1121

KARBONOFF—Cleaning Solution—Clayton Industries Co.; *U.S. Private*, pg. 245

KARD-KARRIER—Envelopes—Tension Envelope Corp.; *U.S. Private*, pg. 1077

KARD-O-PAK—Bags—American Packaging Corporation; *U.S. Private*, pg. 60

KARELIA FILTER—NONE—Karelia Tobacco Company Inc.; *Int'l*, pg. 724

KARELIA LIGHTS—NONE—Karelia Tobacco Company Inc.; *Int'l*, pg. 724

KARELIA LIGHTS 100's—NONE—Karelia Tobacco Company Inc.; *Int'l*, pg. 724

KARELIA MEDIUM—NONE—Karelia Tobacco Company Inc.; *Int'l*, pg. 724

KARELIA SLIMS—NONE—Karelia Tobacco Company Inc.; *Int'l*, pg. 724

KARELIA ULTRA LOW 25's—NONE—Karelia Tobacco Company Inc.; *Int'l*, pg. 724

KARGES BY HAND—Wood Furniture—The Karges Furniture Company Inc.; *U.S. Private*, pg. 607

KARIN—Stemware—Dansk International Designs Ltd.; *U.S. Public*, pg. 261

KARINZIA—Feminine Personal Care—Reckitt & Colman plc; *Int'l*, pg. 1089

KARISMA—Polyester Artifical Flowers—Celebrity Incorporated; *U.S. Public*, pg. 319

KARL BRAND—Corn Snacks—Meiji Seika Kaisha, Ltd.; *Int'l*, pg. 855

KARL LAGERFELD—Men's Tailored Clothing—Hartmarx Corporation; *U.S. Public*, pg. 795

KARL MARX VODKA—Spirits—Leonard Kreusch, Inc.; *U.S. Private*, pg. 635

KARL VON STETTER—German Wine—M.S. Walker, Inc.; *U.S. Private*, pg. 1147

KARLEX—Polycarbonate Compounds—Ferro Corporation; *U.S. Public*, pg. 618

KARMA COLLECTION—Metal Casegoods—CorryHiebert Corporation; *U.S. Public*, pg. 772

KARMEX—Herbicide—Du Pont (E.I. Du Pont De Nemours & Co.); *U.S. Public*, pg. 530

KARO—Syrups—Best Foods; *U.S. Public*, pg. 224

KARO—Syrups—Bestfoods; *U.S. Public*, pg. 223

KAROLTON—Envelopes—Kimberly-Clark Corporation; *U.S. Public*, pg. 958

KARPEN—Furniture—Schnadig Corporation; *U.S. Private*, pg. 971

KARP'S—Bakery Ingredients—CSM N.V.; *Int'l*, pg. 243

KARRY—Self-Service Wholesale Stores—SHV Holdings N.V.; *Int'l*, pg. 1154

KARRY-ALL—Platform with Enclosed Storage—The Knapheide Mfg. Co.; *U.S. Private*, pg. 626

KARUIZAWA—Spirits—Mercian Corporation; *Int'l*, pg. 858

KARVAN CEVITAM—Rosehip Syrup—CSM N.V.; *Int'l*, pg. 243

KARVOL—NONE—Boots Healthcare International; *Int'l*, pg. 202

KARY KART—Luggage Cart System—American Locker Group, Inc.; *U.S. Public*, pg. 85

KARYOMAX—NONE—Life Technologies, Inc.; *U.S. Public*, pg. 504

KASCO—Knives & Blades—Bairnco Corporation; *U.S. Public*, pg. 165

KASHIMAR—Rugs & Broadloom—Couristan Inc.; *U.S. Private*, pg. 279

KASIL—Potassium Silicates—PQ Corporation; *U.S. Private*, pg. 827

KASOF—NONE—Lee Pharmaceuticals; *U.S. Public*, pg. 984

KASOF—Laxative Tablet—Roberts Pharmaceutical Corporation; *U.S. Public*, pg. 1393

KASSER—Wines—Canandaigua Wine Company, Inc.; *U.S. Public*, pg. 300

KASSER—Vodka—Laird & Company; *U.S. Private*, pg. 642

KASSERS '51' BLEND—Gin—Laird & Company; *U.S. Private*, pg. 642

KAST-O-LITE—Castables—A.P. Green Industries, Inc.; *U.S. Public*, pg. 761

KASTITE—Refractory—CFB Industries, Inc.; *U.S. Private*, pg. 194

KASTITE—Refractory—Chicago Fire Brick Co.; *U.S. Private*, pg. 194

KASTLE SYSTEMS—Office Building Security Systems—Kastle Systems LLC; *U.S. Private*, pg. 608

KATANA—Motorcycle—American Suzuki Motor Corporation; *Int'l*, pg. 1323

KATFISH PICKINS—Dry Cat Food—Ralston Purina Company; *U.S. Public*, pg. 1359

KATHABAR—Dehumidifiers & Humidity Pumps—Kathabar Incorporated; *U.S. Private*, pg. 609

KATHARINE GIBBS—Office Skills Training Schools—Katharine Gibbs School, Inc.; *U.S. Private*, pg. 209

KATHERINE BISHOP—Apparel—Fred Meyer Stores; *U.S. Public*, pg. 1103

KATHIE LEE—NONE—Kellwood Company; *U.S. Public*, pg. 948

KATHON—Biocide—Rohm and Haas Company; *U.S. Public*, pg. 1403

KATHY LEE—Women's Jewelry—Swank, Inc.; *U.S. Public*, pg. 1543

KATHY WHITE—Women's Sportswear—Catherines Stores Corporation; *U.S. Public*, pg. 317

KATIES—NONE—Coles Myer Ltd.; *Int'l*, pg. 306

KATIN—Surf Apparel—K2 Inc.; *U.S. Public*, pg. 940

KATIVO—Powder Coatings—H.B. Fuller Company; *U.S. Public*, pg. 686

KATO—Kato Engineering House Mark—Rockwell International Corporation; *U.S. Public*, pg. 1397

KATOLIGHT—Engine Generators—McDonald Equipment Co.; *U.S. Private*, pg. 721

KATRIN—Tissue Paper—Metsa-Serla Corporation; *Int'l*, pg. 863

KATU TELEVISION—NONE—Fisher Broadcasting Inc.; *U.S. Public*, pg. 648

KATY—Industrial Products—Katy Industries, Inc.; *U.S. Public*, pg. 944

KATZ AMERICAN TELEVISION—Television Advertising Representitive Service—Katz Media Group, Inc.; *U.S. Public*, pg. 335

KATZ CONTINENTAL TELEVISION—Television Advertising Representitive Service—Katz Media Group, Inc.; *U.S. Public*, pg. 335

KATZ HISPANIC RADIO SALES—Radio Advertising Representitive Service—Katz Media Group, Inc.; *U.S. Public*, pg. 335

KATZ NATIONAL TELEVISION—Television Advertising Representative Service—Katz Media Group, Inc.; *U.S. Public*, pg. 335

KATZ RADIO—Radio Advertising Representitive Service—Katz Media Group, Inc.; *U.S. Public*, pg. 335

KAUAI COFFEE—Estate-Grown Roasted Coffee—Alexander & Baldwin, Inc.; *U.S. Public*, pg. 39

KAUFMAN & BROAD—Homebuilding—Kaufman and Broad Home Corporation; *U.S. Public*, pg. 944

KAUFMANN'S—Department Stores—The May Department Stores Company; *U.S. Public*, pg. 1063

KAUKAUNA—Cheese—Bel/Kaukauna USA; *U.S. Private*, pg. 130

KAVA—Instant Coffee—Borden, Inc.; *U.S. Private*, pg. 157

KAVEPENIN—Antibiotic—Astra AB; *Int'l*, pg. 93

KAWASAKI—Carbon Pipe & Steel Products—Thomas Pipe & Steel, Inc.; *U.S. Private*, pg. 508

KAWASAKI MOUNTAIN BIKES—Recreation Vehicles—Kawasaki Motors Corp., U.S.A.; *Int'l*, pg. 725

KAY—Jewelers—Sterling Jewelers, Inc.; *Int'l*, pg. 1248

KAYACELON E—Disperse Dies—Nippon Kayaku Co. Ltd.; *Int'l*, pg. 934

KAYACELON REACT—Reactive Dies—Nippon Kayaku Co. Ltd.; *Int'l*, pg. 934

KAYACRYL—Caustic Dies—Nippon Kayaku Co. Ltd.; *Int'l*, pg. 934

KAYAFECT—Direct Dyes for Papers—Nippon Kayaku Co. Ltd.; *Int'l*, pg. 934

KAYAHARD—Epoxy Resins Curing Agents—Nippon Kayaku Co. Ltd.; *Int'l*, pg. 934

KAYALON POLYESTER—Disperse Dyes—Nippon Kayaku Co. Ltd.; *Int'l*, pg. 934

KAYAMITE—Emulsion Explosives—Nippon Kayaku Co. Ltd.; *Int'l*, pg. 934

KAYARAD—Specialty Acrylates—Nippon Kayaku Co. Ltd.; *Int'l*, pg. 934

KAYARUS—Direct Dies—Nippon Kayaku Co. Ltd.; *Int'l*, pg. 934

KAYASET—Plastic, Resin Colors—Nippon Kayaku Co. Ltd.; *Int'l*, pg. 934

KAYCEL—Non-Woven Material—Kimberly-Clark Corporation; *U.S. Public*, pg. 958

KAYDRY—Wipers—Kimberly-Clark Corporation; *U.S. Public*, pg. 958

KAYEM—Processed Meats—Kayem Foods, Inc.; *U.S. Private*, pg. 610

KAYNAR—Aerospace Fasteners—KTI; *U.S. Public*, pg. 939

KAYO—Hot Chocolate—Superior Coffee and Foods; *U.S. Public*, pg. 1434

KAYOL—White Mineral Oil—Witco Corporation; *U.S. Public*, pg. 1773

KAYON—Door Covering—Clark Door Co., Inc.; *U.S. Private*, pg. 242

KAYSENS—Desserts—Grand Metropolitan Plc; *Int'l*, pg. 408

KAYSTRIP—Cleaning Products—Clayton Industries Co.; *U.S. Private*, pg. 245

KAYWOODIE—Smoking Pipes & Related Products—S.M. Frank & Co., Inc.; *U.S. Private*, pg. 423

KAZ DYNAMIST—Vaporizer—Kaz, Inc.; *U.S. Private*, pg. 610

KAZ SAFEGUARD—Vaporizer—Kaz, Inc.; *U.S. Private*, pg. 610

KE-MIN—Material for Supplying Trace Minerals to Plants—Georgia-Pacific Corporation; *U.S. Public*, pg. 735

KE-MUL—Asphalt Emulsifier—Georgia-Pacific Corporation; *U.S. Public*, pg. 735

KEANE CONTROLS—Control Systems, Valves & Regulators—Circle Seal Controls, Inc.; *U.S. Public*, pg. 1746

KEARNALEX—Inhibitor-Contact Aid—Kearney Company; *U.S. Public*, pg. 444

KEARNEY & TRECKER—NONE—Giddings & Lewis Automation Technology; *Int'l*, pg. 1389

KEARNOIL—Hydraulic Oil—Kearney Company; *U.S. Public*, pg. 444

KED ESSENTIALS—Women's Casual Footwear—The Stride Rite Corporation; *U.S. Public*, pg. 1524

KED'S—Men's, Women's, Children's Casual Footwear—The Stride Rite Corporation; *U.S. Public*, pg. 1524

KEDS—Footwear—The Keds Corporation; *U.S. Public*, pg. 1525

KEDS APPAREL—NONE—Signal Apparel Company, Inc.; *U.S. Public*, pg. 1472

KEE KLAMPS—Specialised Fittings—BTR plc; *Int'l*, pg. 124

KEEBLER CONES—Ice Cream Cones—Keebler Company; *U.S. Public*, pg. 657

KEEBLER RICERS SNACK CHIPS—Snack Food—Keebler Company; *U.S. Public*, pg. 657

KEEBLER TOASTED—Crackers—Keebler Company; *U.S. Public*, pg. 657

KEELER—Ophthalmic Instruments—Halma p.l.c.; *Int'l*, pg. 589

KEEN—NONE—Nestle USA; *Int'l*, pg. 916

KEEN EDGE—Business Paper—Moore Corporation Limited; *Int'l*, pg. 888

KEEP 'EM BLOOMIN'—Interior Plant Prods.—Security Lawn & Garden Co.; *U.S. Private*, pg. 397

KEEP/SAFE—Safe—Sentry Group; *U.S. Private*, pg. 984

KEEP-TITE!—Specialty Fasteners—R&B, Inc.; *U.S. Public*, pg. 1354

KEEPBOX—Household Storage Containers—Myers Industries, Inc.; *U.S. Public*, pg. 1143

KEEPIN' TABS—Stationery Products—The Mead Corporation; *U.S. Public*, pg. 1074

KEEPS—Bowl Cleaner—Willert Home Products, Inc.; *U.S. Private*, pg. 1177

KEEPSAFER—NONE—Linear Corporation; *U.S. Public*, pg. 1193

KEEPSAKE—NONE—Commemorative Brands, Inc.; *U.S. Private*, pg. 258

KEEPSAKE—Children's Shoes—E.J. Footwear Corp.; *U.S. Public*, pg. 1684

KEFLET—Cephalexin, Dista—Eli Lilly and Company; *U.S. Public*, pg. 992

KEFLEX—Cephalexin, Dista—Eli Lilly and Company; *U.S. Public*, pg. 992

KEFLIN—Cephalothin Sodium, Lilly—Eli Lilly and Company; *U.S. Public*, pg. 992

KEFLIN, NEUTRAL—Cephalothin Sodium, Lilly—Eli Lilly and Company; *U.S. Public*, pg. 992

KEFORAL—Cephalexin—Eli Lilly Italia, S.p.A.; *U.S. Public*, pg. 994

KEFRANE—NONE—Johnson & Johnson; *U.S. Public*, pg. 927

KEFTAB—Cephalexin Hydrochloride, Dista—Eli Lilly and Company; *U.S. Public*, pg. 992

KEFUROX—Cefuroxime, Lilly—Eli Lilly and Company; *U.S. Public*, pg. 992

KEFZOL—Cefazolin Sodium, Lilly—Eli Lilly and Company; *U.S. Public*, pg. 992

KEIJE—Cabinet Organizers—Clairson International Corp.; *U.S. Public*, pg. 575

KEIL—Chemicals, Lubricants, Additives—Ferro Corporation; *U.S. Public*, pg. 618

KEIL—Padlocks, Key Machines—Ilco Unican Corp.; *Int'l*, pg. 1432

KEIL—Padlocks, Key Machines—Unican Security Systems Ltd.; *Int'l*, pg. 1432

KEILLER—Specialty Products—Nestle Chocolate & Confection; *Int'l*, pg. 917

KEILLER—Marmalade—Ranks Hovis McDougall Limited; *Int'l*, pg. 1395

KEIPER RECARO—Automobile Parts & Seats—Recaro North America, Inc.; *U.S. Private*, pg. 914

KEITH HIGHLANDERS—Shoes—Geo. E. Keith Company; *U.S. Private*, pg. 611

KEL-LITE XANTHAN GUM—Shortening Replacement Blends—The NutraSweet Kelco Company; *U.S. Public*, pg. 1125

KELACID—Alginic Acid—The NutraSweet Kelco Company; *U.S. Public*, pg. 1125

KELATIN—D-Penicillamine Free Amino Acid—Royal Gist-Brocades N.V.; *Int'l*, pg. 1142

KELBURON—Polypropylene Compounds—DSM N.V.; *Int'l*, pg. 352

KELCOGEL—Gellan Gum—The NutraSweet Kelco Company; *U.S. Public*, pg. 1125

KELCOLOID—Propylene Glycol Alginate—The NutraSweet Kelco Company; *U.S. Public*, pg. 1125

KELCOSOL—Sodium Alginate—The NutraSweet Kelco Company; *U.S. Public*, pg. 1125

KELEMATA—Eye Care System—Orlane, Inc.; *Int'l*, pg. 1011

KELER—NONE—Guinness Plc; *Int'l*, pg. 412

KELEX—Chelating Agents—Witco Corporation; *U.S. Public*, pg. 1773

KELFIZINA—Chemotherapeutics—Kyowa Hakko Kogyo Company, Ltd.; *Int'l*, pg. 778

KELGIN—Sodium Alginate—The NutraSweet Kelco Company; *U.S. Public*, pg. 1125

KELGUM—Xanthan Gum Blend—The NutraSweet Kelco Company; *U.S. Public*, pg. 1125

KELKLAVE—Autoclave Gloves—Jomac, Inc.; *U.S. Private*, pg. 595

KELLER—Business Schools—DeVry Institutes; *U.S. Public*, pg. 503

KELLER—Business School—Keller Graduate School of Management; *U.S. Public*, pg. 504

KELLER—Household Furniture—The Keller Manufacturing Co., Inc.; *U.S. Private*, pg. 612

KELLER-DORIAN—Print Rolls—Standex International Corporation; *U.S. Public*, pg. 1505

KELLER-GEISTER—Wine—Canandaigua Wine Company, Inc.; *U.S. Public*, pg. 300

KELLER-SOFT—Regulatory Software—J.J. Keller & Associates, Inc.; *U.S. Private*, pg. 612

KELLING KERNEL FRESH—Inst./ Food Service—Fairmont Snack Group, Inc.; *U.S. Private*, pg. 392

KELLOGG—Reciprocating Compressors—ComPair LeRoi; *Int'l*, pg. 1242

KELLOGG—Air Dryers—ComPair LeRoi; *Int'l*, pg. 1242

KELLOGG—Kiln Furniture—Ferro Corporation; *U.S. Public*, pg. 618

KELLOGG TEMPTATIONS—Breakfast Cereal—Kellogg Company; *U.S. Public*, pg. 947

KELLOGG'S—Breakfast Cereals—Kellogg Company of Great Britain Ltd.; *U.S. Public*, pg. 947

KELLOGG'S BRAN FLAKES—Wheat Bran Flakes Cereal—Kellogg Company; *U.S. Public*, pg. 947

KELLOGG'S CINNAMON MINI BUNS—Ready-Sweetened Corn & Whole Oats Cereal with Real Cinnamon—Kellogg Company; *U.S. Public*, pg. 947

KELLOGG'S CORN FLAKES—Corn Flakes Cereal—Kellogg Company; *U.S. Public*, pg. 947

KELLOGG'S CORN FLAKES CRUMBS—Corn Flake Crumbs—Kellogg Company; *U.S. Public*, pg. 947

KELLOGG'S FROSTED BRAN—Lighty Frosted Flakes of Whole Wheat & Wheat Bran Plus Corn—Kellogg Company; *U.S. Public*, pg. 947

KELLOGG'S FROSTED FLAKES—Frosted Flakes of Corn Cereal—Kellogg Company; *U.S. Public*, pg. 947

KELLOGG'S JUST RIGHT—Whole Wheat, Rice & Oat Cereal—Kellogg Company; *U.S. Public*, pg. 947

KELLOGG'S LOW-FAT GRANOLA—Granola with Raisins—Kellogg Company; *U.S. Public*, pg. 947

KELLOGG'S LOW-SODIUM PACK—Low-Sodium Cereals in Eight Single-Serving Packages—Kellogg Company; *U.S. Public*, pg. 947

KELLOGG'S RAISIN BRAN—Wheat Bran Flake Cereal with Raisins—Kellogg Company; *U.S. Public*, pg. 947

KELLTRIDE—Furnace Refractory—Ferro Corporation; *U.S. Public*, pg. 618

KELLUNDITE—Alumina Porous Shapes—Ferro Corporation; *U.S. Public*, pg. 618

KELLY—Office Chair—Vecta; *U.S. Private*, pg. 1038

KELLY ASSISTED LIVING—Home Care Services Program—Kelly Services, Inc.; *U.S. Public*, pg. 949

KELLY KDM—Tire—The Kelly-Springfield Tire Company; *U.S. Public*, pg. 753

KELLY KDT—Tire—The Kelly-Springfield Tire Company; *U.S. Public*, pg. 753

KELLY KSR—Tire—The Kelly-Springfield Tire Company; *U.S. Public*, pg. 753

KELLY SPRINGFIELD—Tires—The Kelly-Springfield Tire Company; *U.S. Public*, pg. 753

KELMAR—Potassium Alginate—The NutraSweet Kelco Company; *U.S. Public*, pg. 1125

KELON—Mallet Instruments—Ludwig Industries; *U.S. Public*, pg. 1514

KELPROX—Thermoplastic Elastometers—DSM N.V.; *Int'l*, pg. 352

KELRINAL—Chemically Modified Rubber—DSM N.V.; *Int'l*, pg. 352

KELSET—Sodium Alginate—The NutraSweet Kelco Company; *U.S. Public*, pg. 1125

KELSEY-HAYES—Automotive Components—LucasVarity Inc.; *Int'l*, pg. 820

KELSEY HAYES—NONE—LucasVarity plc; *Int'l*, pg. 819

KELTAN—Rubber—DSM N.V.; *Int'l*, pg. 352

KELTAN TP—Thermoplastic Rubber—DSM N.V.; *Int'l*, pg. 352

KELTGEN—Seeds—The Dow Chemical Company; *U.S. Public*, pg. 522

KELTONE—Sodium Alginate—The NutraSweet Kelco Company; *U.S. Public*, pg. 1125

KELTOSE—Ammonium Calcium Alginate—The NutraSweet Kelco Company; *U.S. Public*, pg. 1125

KELTROL T—Xanthan Gum—The NutraSweet Kelco Company; *U.S. Public*, pg. 1125

KELTY—Backpacks, Sleeping Bags & Tents—American Recreation Products, Inc.; *U.S. Public*, pg. 948

KELTY—NONE—Kellwood Company; *U.S. Public*, pg. 948

KELVINATOR—Household Appliances—Candy S.p.A.; *Int'l*, pg. 259

KELVINATOR—Commercial Refrigeration—Electrolux, AB; *Int'l*, pg. 438

KELVINATOR—Major Appliances—Email Limited; *Int'l*, pg. 450

KELVINATOR—Appliances—Frigidaire Home Products; *Int'l*, pg. 439

KELVINATOR—Major Appliances—White Consolidated Industries, Inc.; *Int'l*, pg. 439

KELVINATOR APPLIANCE—Mfr. of Refrigerator-Freezers, Laundry Products, Electric Ranges—Kelvinator Appliances; *Int'l*, pg. 440

KELVINATOR SCIENTIFIC—Commercial Refrigeration—White Consolidated Industries, Inc.; *Int'l*, pg. 439

KELVIS—Sodium Alginate—The NutraSweet Kelco Company; *U.S. Public*, pg. 1125

KELWELD—Welding Gloves—Jomac, Inc.; *U.S. Private*, pg. 595

KELZAN—Xanthan Gum—The NutraSweet Kelco Company; *U.S. Public*, pg. 1125

KELZAN AR—Xanthan Gum with Altered Rheology & Alkali Resistance—The NutraSweet Kelco Company; *U.S. Public*, pg. 1125

KELZAN S—Dispersible Xanthan Gum—The NutraSweet Kelco Company; *U.S. Public*, pg. 1125

KEM—Paints & Coatings—The Sherwin-Williams Company; *U.S. Public*, pg. 1465

KEM O DRY—Solvent—Detrex Corporation; *U.S. Public*, pg. 501

KEM-TONE—Paint—The Sherwin-Williams Company; *U.S. Public*, pg. 1465

KEMADRIN—Prescription Parkinson's Disease Treatment—Glaxo Wellcome PLC; *Int'l*, pg. 553

KEMAX—Treated Cones, Cores & Tubes—Sonoco Products Company; *U.S. Public*, pg. 1485

KEMDEX—Denture Cleaning Preparations—SmithKline Beecham plc; *Int'l*, pg. 1264

KEMESTER—Fatty & Non-Fatty Esters—Witco Corporation; *U.S. Public*, pg. 1773

KEMGO—Compounds—Markem Corporation; *U.S. Private*, pg. 704

KEMI ART—White Top Kraftliner—Metsa-Serla Corporation; *Int'l*, pg. 863

KEMID—Polyetherimide Film for Electrical Applications—Norton Performance Plastics; *Int'l*, pg. 1174

KEMANINE—Fatty Armines & Quaternaire—Witco Corporation; *U.S. Public*, pg. 1773

KEMLEX—Specialty Resin Compounds—Ferro Corporation; *U.S. Public*, pg. 618

KEMMERER—Carbonated Beverages—Select Beverages, Inc.; *U.S. Private*, pg. 982

KEMPENAAR—Pre-baked Products—Meneba N.V.; *Int'l*, pg. 555

KEMPER—Kitchen & Bathroom Cabinets—Electrolux, AB; *Int'l*, pg. 438

KEMPER—Cabinets—White Consolidated Industries, Inc.; *Int'l*, pg. 439

KEMPER FUNDS—Mutual Funds & 401K Products—Zurich Kemper Investments, Inc.; *Int'l*, pg. 1530

KEMPORE—Specialty Chemical—Uniroyal Chemical Company, Inc.; *U.S. Public*, pg. 460

KEMRESIN—Epoxy Resin Worktop—Kewaunee Scientific Corporation; *U.S. Public*, pg. 953

KEMROCK—NONE—Kewaunee Scientific Corporation; *U.S. Public*, pg. 953

KEMSHIELD—NONE—Kewaunee Scientific Corporation; *U.S. Public*, pg. 953

KEMSTREME—Glycerine USP—Witco Corporation; *U.S. Public*, pg. 1773

KEN GUARD—Briefs/Urologicals—The Kendall Company; *U.S. Public*, pg. 1647

KEN-L RATION—Dog Food—H.J. Heinz Company; *U.S. Public*, pg. 805

KEN-L RATION—NONE—Star-Kist Foods Inc.; *U.S. Public*, pg. 805

KEN-L RATION DOG FOOD—Dog Food—The Quaker Oats Company; *U.S. Public*, pg. 1347

KEN-L RATION MOIST 'N BEEFY—Dog Food—The Quaker Oats Company; *U.S. Public*, pg. 1347

KEN-L RATION 100% NATURAL TREATS—Dog Treats—The Quaker Oats Company; *U.S. Public*, pg. 1347

KEN-L RATION PUPPERONIS—Dog Food Snack—H.J. Heinz Company; *U.S. Public*, pg. 805

KEN SEAL—Resilient Seated Wedge Gate Valve—Grinnell Corporation; *U.S. Public*, pg. 1651

KEN-SEAL—Resilient Seated Valve—Kennedy Valve; *U.S. Private*, pg. 725

KEN-TOOL—NONE—Summit Tool Company; *U.S. Private*, pg. 1050

KEN-L RATION TENDER CHOPS—Semi-Moist Dog Food—H.J. Heinz Company; *U.S. Public*, pg. 805

KENAI PENINSULA CLARION—Newspaper—Shivers Trading & Operating Co.; *U.S. Private*, pg. 994

KENALOG—Dermatological Therapy—Bristol-Myers Squibb Company; *U.S. Public*, pg. 253

KENALOG—Topical Steroid—Westwood-Squibb Pharmaceuticals Inc.; *U.S. Public*, pg. 255

KENBORE—Boring Bars—Kennametal Inc.; *U.S. Public*, pg. 950

KENCLAW—Drilling System—Kennametal Inc.; *U.S. Public*, pg. 950

KENCO—Truck & Van Accessories—Kenco; *U.S. Public*, pg. 1769

KENCOVE—1/8" & .080" Vinyl Wall Base—Kentile Operting Co.; *U.S. Private*, pg. 615

KENDALL ATHLETIC—NONE—Futuro Inc.; *Int'l*, pg. 182

KENDEX—Metalcutting Tools—Kennametal Inc.; *U.S. Public*, pg. 950

KENERGA—Weapon Systems—Allied Research Corporation; *U.S. Public*, pg. 48

KENFACE—Crushed Cemented Carbide—Kennametal Inc.; *U.S. Public*, pg. 950

KENGARD—Wear Parts—Kennametal Inc.; *U.S. Public*, pg. 950

KENLOC—Metalcutting Tools—Kennametal Inc.; *U.S. Public*, pg. 950

KENMORE—NONE—Sears, Roebuck and Co.; *U.S. Public*, pg. 1452

KENNAMETAL—Carbide Metals, Tools—Kennametal Inc.; *U.S. Public*, pg. 950

KENNEDY—Tool Boxes, Chests, Cabinets—Kennedy Manufacturing Company; *U.S. Private*, pg. 614

KENNEDY—Tape Drives—Shugart Corporation; *U.S. Private*, pg. 997

KENNEDY L.A.D.—Orthopedic Augmentation Device—3M; *U.S. Public*, pg. 1604

KENNEDY'S—Scotch Whiskey—M.S. Walker, Inc.; *U.S. Private*, pg. 1147

KENNEDY'S CANADIAN—Whiskey—M.S. Walker, Inc.; *U.S. Private*, pg. 1147

KENNEL KRUNCHER—Pet Foods—Ag Processing Inc., A Cooperative; *U.S. Private*, pg. 26

KENNER—NONE—MB Espana, S.A.; *U.S. Public*, pg. 798

KENNER PRODUCTS—NONE—Hasbro, Inc.; *U.S. Public*, pg. 797

KENNERTIUM—Tungsten Alloy—Kennametal Inc.; *U.S. Public*, pg. 950

KENNETH COLE—Designer Footwear & Accessories—Kenneth Cole Productions; *U.S. Public*, pg. 951

KENNETH COLE—Men's Jewelry—Swank, Inc.; *U.S. Public*, pg. 1543

KENNETT—Book Cloth—Industrial Coatings Group, Inc.; *U.S. Private*, pg. 434

KENNY CLASSICS—Dresses—Donnkenny, Inc.; *U.S. Public*, pg. 519

KENO—NONE—Tattersalls; *Int'l*, pg. 1357

KENSINGTON—NONE—ACCO Brands, Inc.; *U.S. Public*, pg. 674

KENSINGTON—Computer Accessories—ACCO World Corporation; *U.S. Public*, pg. 674

KENSINGTON—Computer Accessories—Fortune Brands, Inc.; *U.S. Public*, pg. 674

KENSINGTON—Wood Case Goods—Helikon Furniture Co., Inc.; *U.S. Private*, pg. 520

KENSITAS CLUB—NONE—Gallaher Tobacco Ltd.; *Int'l*, pg. 539

KENT—Cigarettes—B.A.T Industries P.L.C.; *Int'l*, pg. 110

KENT—Commercial Cleaning Equipment—Electrolux, AB; *Int'l*, pg. 438

KENT—Steel Molds—Gougler Industries, Inc.; *U.S. Private*, pg. 466

KENT—Livestock Feed—Kent Feeds Inc.; *U.S. Private*, pg. 1134

KENT—Cigarettes—Loews Corporation; *U.S. Public*, pg. 1010

KENT—Cigarette—Lorillard Tobacco Company; *U.S. Public*, pg. 1011

KENT—NONE—Malaysian Tobacco Co./B.A.T. Indust.; *Int'l*, pg. 111

KENT—Juice—McCain Foods Limited; *Int'l*, pg. 850

KENT—Commercial & Industrial Floor Care Prods.—National Union Electric Corp.; *Int'l*, pg. 440

KENT—Commercial Floor Care Equipment—White Consolidated Industries, Inc.; *Int'l*, pg. 439

THE KENT COMPANY—Vaccuum Cleaners & Industrial Floor Machines—The Kent Company; *Int'l*, pg. 440

KENT GOLDEN LIGHTS—Cigarettes—Loews Corporation; *U.S. Public*, pg. 1010

KENT-MOORE—Service Tools & Equipment—SPX Corporation; *U.S. Public*, pg. 1420

KENT OLD BROWN—Bitter Ale—Carlton & United Breweries Ltd.; *Int'l*, pg. 500

KENT OLD BROWN—Ale—Foster's Brewing Group Limited; *Int'l*, pg. 500

KENT III—Cigarettes—Loews Corporation; *U.S. Public*, pg. 1010

KENTACEF—Cefatrizine—Bristol-Myers Squibb Company; *U.S. Public*, pg. 253

KENTROL—Inserts For Metalcutting Tools—Kennametal Inc.; *U.S. Public*, pg. 950

KENTUCKY—Twist Tobaccos—Conwood Company L.P.; *U.S. Private*, pg. 272

KENTUCKY—Insurance Company—South Carolina Insurance Company; *U.S. Public*, pg. 1453

KENTUCKY CONNECTOR—Electrical Connector—Ilsco; *U.S. Private*, pg. 558

KENTUCKY FRIED CHICKEN—Chicken Restaurant Chain—JRN, Inc.; *U.S. Private*, pg. 578

KENTUCKY FRIED CHICKEN—Chicken Restaurant Chain—PepsiCo, Inc.; *U.S. Public*, pg. 1276

KENTUCKY GENTLEMAN—Bourbon & Whiskey—Barton Incorporated; *U.S. Public*, pg. 300

KENTUCKY GENTLEMAN-BLEND—NONE—Barton Brands, Ltd.; *U.S. Public*, pg. 300

KENTUCKY GENTLEMAN BOURBON—NONE—Barton Brands, Ltd.; *U.S. Public*, pg. 300

KENTUCKY KING—Twist Tobacco—Conwood Company L.P.; *U.S. Private*, pg. 272

KENTUCKY MANUFACTURERS REGISTER—Register—Manufacturers' News, Inc.; *U.S. Private*, pg. 700

KENTUCKY NUGGETS—Menu Item—Kentucky Fried Chicken Corporation (KFC); *U.S. Public*, pg. 1636

THE KENTUCKY POST—Newspaper—The E.W. Scripps Company; *U.S. Public*, pg. 1447

KENTUCKY PRAIRIE FARMER—NONE—Farm Progress Publications; *U.S. Public*, pg. 513

KENTUCKY'S TAVERN—NONE—Barton Brands, Ltd.; *U.S. Public*, pg. 300

KENWOOD—Car Stereo, Home, Audio, Video Communications—Kenwood USA; *Int'l*, pg. 730

KENWOOD THERAPEUTIC LIQUID—Vitamin/Mineral Supplement for Children & Adults with Poor Diet—Bradley Pharmaceuticals; *U.S. Public*, pg. 249

KENWOOD THERAPEUTIC LIQUID—Vitamin/Mineral Supplement for Children & Adults with Poor Diet—Doak Dermatologics; *U.S. Public*, pg. 250

KENWORTH—T-Shirt—Holoubek Inc.; *U.S. Private*, pg. 536

KENWORTH—Trucks—Paccar Inc.; *U.S. Public*, pg. 1246

KENYA—Doll—Tyco Toys, Inc.; *U.S. Public*, pg. 1058

KEOPS—NONE—Johnson & Johnson; *U.S. Public*, pg. 927

KEP-DRI—Leather Waterproofing Systems—Henkel Corporation; *Int'l*, pg. 610

KEP-TITE—Emulsion Leather Finish—Henkel Corporation; *Int'l*, pg. 610

KEPECO—Water Miscible Leather Finishes—Henkel Corporation; *Int'l*, pg. 610

KEPOLAC—Lacquer Leather Finishes—Henkel Corporation; *Int'l*, pg. 610

KEPOS PLUS—NONE—OMRON Systems, Inc.; *Int'l*, pg. 1005

KEPROM—Electronic Instrument—Intel Corporation; *U.S. Public*, pg. 886

KERAGENICS—Hair Care Products—American International Industries; *U.S. Private*, pg. 57

KERALYT GEL—Salicylic Acid Gel—Westwood-Squibb Pharmaceuticals Inc.; *U.S. Public*, pg. 255

KERAMAG—Sanitary Porcelain—Metra Corporation; *Int'l*, pg. 862

KERAMAG—Bathroom Ceramics—Sanitec Ltd. Oy; *Int'l*, pg. 863

KERANAP—Boards—Kerlane; *Int'l*, pg. 1176

KERANATOR—Cosmetics & Hair Preparation—Clairol, Inc.; *U.S. Public*, pg. 254

KERASILK-LIQUID LINE—NONE—Goldwell Cosmetics (USA) Inc.; *Int'l*, pg. 718

KERASTASE—Hair Care—L'Oreal S.A.; *Int'l*, pg. 818

KERB—Agri. Herbicide—Rohm and Haas Company; *U.S. Public*, pg. 1403

KERBER KIDS—Greeting Cards—American Greetings Corporation; *U.S. Public*, pg. 77

KERBOOM—Lead Core Fly Line—Cortland Line Co., Inc.; *U.S. Private*, pg. 277

KERFEX—Plant Protectives—DSM Chemie Linz GmbH; *Int'l*, pg. 356

KERFUL—Cleaning Solution—Clayton Industries Co.; *U.S. Private*, pg. 245

KERI JUG—Ice Chest—Igloo Products Corporation; *U.S. Public*, pg. 265

KERI LOTION—Moisturizer—Bristol-Myers Squibb Company; *U.S. Public*, pg. 253

KERIMID—High Performance Polymer—Novartis; *Int'l*, pg. 972

KERITE—Insulated Wire—The Kerite Company; *U.S. Public*, pg. 844

KERLANE—Blankets, Bulk—Kerlane; *Int'l*, pg. 1176

KERLIDEX—Beta-Blocker for Hypertension—L'Oreal S.A.; *Int'l*, pg. 818

KERLITE—Cleaning Solution—Clayton Industries Co.; *U.S. Private*, pg. 245

KERLIX—Bandages—The Kendall Company; *U.S. Public*, pg. 1647

KERLONE—Beta-Blocker for Hypertension—L'Oreal S.A.; *Int'l*, pg. 818

KERLONE—Pharmaceutical—Monsanto Company; *U.S. Public*, pg. 1124

KERLONE—Hypertension Treatment—Searle & Co.; *U.S. Public*, pg. 1125

KERMEED—Cleaning Products—Clayton Industries Co.; *U.S. Private*, pg. 245

KERMID—Thermostable Resins—Rhone-Poulenc S.A.; *Int'l*, pg. 1108

KERN—Food Products—Kern Industries; *U.S. Private*, pg. 616

KERN'S—Bakery—Kern's Bakeries, Incorporated; *U.S. Public*, pg. 547

KERN'S—Fruit Juices—Nestle S.A.; *Int'l*, pg. 915

KERNEL—Hot Water Storage—IMI Plc; *Int'l*, pg. 646

KERO—Corn Syrup—Refinerias de Maiz S.A.I.C.F.; *U.S. Public*, pg. 448

KEROPUR—Plant Protectives—DSM Chemie Linz GmbH; *Int'l*, pg. 356

KERPLUNK—Lead Core Fishing Line—Cortland Line Co.; *U.S. Private*, pg. 277

KERPLUNK—Games—Tyco Toys, Inc.; *U.S. Public*, pg. 1058

KERR—Home Canning Products—Alltrista Corporation; *U.S. Public*, pg. 56

KERR—Glass Jars, Crowns, Food Products—Kerr Group, Inc.; *U.S. Public*, pg. 952

KERR—Dental Related Products—Sybron International Corporation; *U.S. Public*, pg. 1544

KERR-MCGEE—Petroleum Products & Chemicals—Kerr-McGee Corporation; *U.S. Public*, pg. 952

KERRANG!—U.K. Entertainment Magazine—EMAP Metro; *Int'l*, pg. 451

KERRICK KLEANERS—Cleaning Solution—Clayton Industries Co.; *U.S. Private*, pg. 245

KERRY—Ultrasonic Cleaning & Welding Equipment—Halma p.l.c.; *Int'l*, pg. 589

KERRY FOODS CHINATOWN—Duckling Products—Kerry Group PLC; *Int'l*, pg. 731

KERRYKREME—CREAMING AGENTS—Kerry Group PLC; *Int'l*, pg. 731

KERRYMAID—Butter & Dairy Spreads—Kerry Group PLC; *Int'l*, pg. 731

KERRYSPRING MINERAL WATER—Minteral Water—Kerry Group PLC; *Int'l*, pg. 731

KERSHAW—NONE—New England Stone Industries, Inc.; *U.S. Private*, pg. 793

KERVRANS SILICA—Dietary Supplements—Novo Nordisk A/S; *Int'l*, pg. 987

KESET—High Security Locks—National Cabinet Lock, Inc.; *U.S. Private*, pg. 270

KESET—Locks—Valhi, Inc.; *U.S. Private*, pg. 270

KESHET—Woodfree Two Side Coated, Mat & Glossy; One Side Coat—American Israeli Paper Mills Ltd.; *Int'l*, pg. 74

KESSCO—Surfactant-Esters—Stepan Company; *U.S. Public*, pg. 1514

KESSLER—American Blended Whiskey—Fortune Brands, Inc.; *U.S. Public*, pg. 674

KESTER—Solder—Litton Industries, Inc.; *U.S. Public*, pg. 1002

KESTREL—Ion Implanter—Genus Inc.; *U.S. Public*, pg. 732

KESTREL—Lager Beer—Scottish & Newcastle plc; *Int'l*, pg. 1211

KESTREL—Binoculars—Swift Instruments, Inc.; *U.S. Private*, pg. 1058

KETASET—Veterinary Pharmaceuticals—American Home Products Corporation; *U.S. Public*, pg. 79

KETCH—Purse—Lands' End, Inc.; *U.S. Public*, pg. 977

KETJENBLACK—Electroconductive Carbon Black—Akzo Nobel N.V.; *Int'l*, pg. 42

KETJENCAT—Catalysts for the Petroleum Refining Industry—Akzo Nobel N.V.; *Int'l*, pg. 42

KETJENFINE—Catalysts for the Petroleum Refining Industry—Akzo Nobel N.V.; *Int'l*, pg. 42

KETJENFLEX—Fungicides—Akzo Nobel N.V.; *Int'l*, pg. 42

KETJENSOL—Wine Cleaning Agents—Akzo Nobel N.V.; *Int'l*, pg. 42

KETRON—Polyether Etherketone Shapes—DSM Engineering Plastic Products; *Int'l*, pg. 354

KETTLE CLEANERS PLUS—Heavy Duty & Delicate Surface Scrubbers—Stanhome Inc.; *U.S. Public*, pg. 1508

KETTMEIR—Table Wine—Paterno Imports Limited; *U.S. Private*, pg. 843

KEVEX-RAY—X-Ray Spectrometer—Kevex Instruments; *U.S. Public*, pg. 1594

KEVLAR—Fiberglass Material—Du Pont (E.I. Du Pont De Nemours & Co.); *U.S. Public*, pg. 530

KEVLAR—Aramid Fiber—Tyco International Ltd.; *U.S. Public*, pg. 1647

KEVLIN MICROWAVE—Microwave—Kevlin Corporation; *U.S. Public*, pg. 953

KEVORKIAN COLLECTOR—Gynecological Device—The Cooper Companies, Inc.; *U.S. Public*, pg. 442

KEVOR-CURETTE—Gynecological Device—The Cooper Companies, Inc.; *U.S. Public*, pg. 442

KEWPIE—Greeting Cards—American Greetings U.S. Greeting Card Division; *U.S. Public*, pg. 78

KEX—Tire Repair—Kex Products, Inc.; *U.S. Private*, pg. 138

KEY—Men's Clothing—Key Industries, Inc.; *U.S. Private*, pg. 618

KEY-BOND—Pretreatment Coatings—D.A. Stuart Company; *U.S. Private*, pg. 1048

KEY-CHEM—Liquid & Powder Cleaners—D.A. Stuart Company; *U.S. Private*, pg. 1048

KEY IMPERIAL—Men's Clothing—Key Industries, Inc.; *U.S. Private*, pg. 618

KEY INDEX ANNUITY—NONE—Keyport Life Insurance Company; *U.S. Private*, pg. 666

KEY KASUALS—Casual Wear—Key Industries, Inc.; *U.S. Private*, pg. 618

KEY-MATE—Ultra Miniature Aluminum Flashlights—Streamlight Inc.; *U.S. Private*, pg. 1047

KEY-MEM—Effects Memory System—Tektronix-Video & Networking Div., Grass Valley Products; *U.S. Public*, pg. 1567

KEY-MIX—Liquid & Powder Cleaners—D.A. Stuart Company; *U.S. Private*, pg. 1048

KEY NOTES—Design Footwear—J. Baker, Inc.; *U.S. Public*, pg. 167

KEY REST—Computer Keyboard Holders—Hunt Corporation; *U.S. Public*, pg. 848

KEY SELECT—NONE—Keyport Life Insurance Company; *U.S. Private*, pg. 666

KEY-TAINERS—Key Holders—DHP Limited Partnership; *U.S. Private*, pg. 302

KEY TRONIC—Computer Keyboards & Input Devices—Key Tronic Corporation; *U.S. Public*, pg. 953

KEYANNUITY—NONE—Keyport Life Insurance Company; *U.S. Private*, pg. 666

KEYBOARD—Magazine—Miller Freeman Inc.; *Int'l*, pg. 1443

KEYBOARD KORDS—Computer Cords—Whitney Blake Company of Vermont, Inc.; *U.S. Private*, pg. 148

KEYBOARD WETSWAB—Presaturated Cleaning Swab—The Texwipe Co., Inc.; *U.S. Private*, pg. 1079

KEYBONUS 100—NONE—Keyport Life Insurance Company; *U.S. Private*, pg. 666

KEYDECK—Wire Mesh—Keystone Steel & Wire Co.; *U.S. Public*, pg. 955

KEYFLEX—NONE—Keyport Life Insurance Company; *U.S. Private*, pg. 666

KEYGROWTH—NONE—Keyport Life Insurance Company; *U.S. Private*, pg. 666

KEYKODE—Machine-Readable Numbers—Eastman Kodak Company; *U.S. Public*, pg. 550

KEYLIFE—NONE—Keyport Life Insurance Company; *U.S. Private*, pg. 666

KEYLINE—NONE—Keyport Life Insurance Company; *U.S. Private*, pg. 666

KEYLINE—Netting & Hardware Cloth—Keystone Steel & Wire Co.; *U.S. Public*, pg. 955

KEYMESH—Stucco Netting—Keystone Steel & Wire Co.; *U.S. Public*, pg. 955

KEYNOTE—Door Chimes—The Lamson & Sessions Co.; *U.S. Public*, pg. 976

KEYPLAN—NONE—Keyport Life Insurance Company; *U.S. Private*, pg. 666

KEYPLUS—Adjunct Unit for Key Telephone Systems—Lucent Technologies Inc.; *U.S. Public*, pg. 1017

KEYPLUS 20—Electronic Key Telephone System—Lucent Technologies Inc.; *U.S. Public*, pg. 1017

KEYPORT ADVISOR—NONE—Keyport Life Insurance Company; *U.S. Private*, pg. 666

KEYPORT LOGO—NONE—Keyport Life Insurance Company; *U.S. Private*, pg. 666

KEYSAVER—NONE—Keyport Life Insurance Company; *U.S. Private*, pg. 666

KEYSGONE?—Service Products—R&B, Inc.; *U.S. Public*, pg. 1354

KEYSOURCE—NONE—Keyport Life Insurance Company; *U.S. Private*, pg. 666

KEYSTONE—Cabinetry—Aristokraft, Inc.; *U.S. Public*, pg. 675

KEYSTONE—Poster—Champion International Corp.; *U.S. Public*, pg. 333

KEYSTONE—NONE—Commemorative Brands, Inc.; *U.S. Private*, pg. 258

KEYSTONE—NONE—Concord Camera Corporation; *U.S. Public*, pg. 429

KEYSTONE—Beer—Adolph Coors Company; *U.S. Public*, pg. 445

KEYSTONE—Machine Bolt Expansion—Gunnebo Fastening Corp.; *U.S. Private*, pg. 488

KEYSTONE—Flow Control Products—Keystone International, Inc.; *U.S. Public*, pg. 1650

KEYSTONE—Pressure Sensitive Tapes—M & C Specialties Company; *U.S. Private*, pg. 684

KEYSTONE—Filters/Media—Met-Pro Corporation; *U.S. Public*, pg. 1100

KEYSTONE—NONE—Ralcorp Holdings Inc.; *U.S. Public*, pg. 1359

KEYSTONE CASUALS—NONE—Key Industries, Inc.; *U.S. Private*, pg. 618

KEYSTONE COFFEE—Coffee—Mr. Wright's Amazing Coffee Factory; *U.S. Private*, pg. 765

KEYSTONE DRY—Beer—Adolph Coors Company; *U.S. Public*, pg. 445

KEYSTONE ICE—Beer—Adolph Coors Company; *U.S. Public*, pg. 445

KEYSTONE LIGHT—Low-Calorie Beer—Adolph Coors Company; *U.S. Public*, pg. 445

KEYSTONE II—Cabinetry—Aristokraft, Inc.; *U.S. Public*, pg. 675

KEYVALUE—NONE—Keyport Life Insurance Company; *U.S. Private*, pg. 666

KEYVANTAGE—NONE—Keyport Life Insurance Company; *U.S. Private*, pg. 666

KEZIZ—Pressure Sintered Compositions—Kennametal Inc.; *U.S. Public*, pg. 950

KHAZANA—Women's Clothing—Niches, Inc.; *U.S. Public*, pg. 1181

KIARA—Thermally Bonded Fabric—Chicopee Inc.; *Int'l*, pg. 113

KIBBLE—Variety Mix Dog Food—H.J. Heinz Co. of Canada Ltd.; *U.S. Public*, pg. 806

KIBBLES & CHEEZY CHEWS—Soft-Dry Dog Food—Ralston Purina Company; *U.S. Public*, pg. 1359

KIBBLES & CHUNKS—Dog Food—Ralston Purina Company; *U.S. Public*, pg. 1359

KIBBLES 'N BITS—Dog Food—H.J. Heinz Company; *U.S. Public*, pg. 805

KIBBLES 'N BITS—NONE—Star-Kist Foods Inc.; *U.S. Public*, pg. 805

KIBBLES' N BITS—Dry & Semi-Moist Dog Food—Star-Kist Foods, Inc.; *U.S. Public*, pg. 806

KIBBLES 'N BITS LEAN—Dog Food—H.J. Heinz Company; *U.S. Public*, pg. 805

KIBON—Ice Cream—Philip Morris Companies Inc.; *U.S. Public*, pg. 1287

KIBUN GOLD—Frozen Entrees, Seafood, Beef & Chicken—Hosho America Inc.; *Int'l*, pg. 733

KICKAPOO—Soft Drink—The Monarch Company, Inc.; *U.S. Private*, pg. 756

KICKS—Hosiery & Related Apparel—Mayer/Berkshire Corporation; *U.S. Private*, pg. 717

KICNET—Telemarketing Services—Eastman Kodak Company; *U.S. Public*, pg. 550

KID BUILDERS—Gymnastic Playground Equipment—Rubbermaid Incorporated; *U.S. Public*, pg. 1411

KID CARE—Childrens Toiletries—Tsumura International; *Int'l*, pg. 1426

KID-CORDER—Tape Recorder—Thomson Consumer Electronics Inc.; *Int'l*, pg. 1383

KID CUISINE—Dinners, Frozen Breakfasts—ConAgra Frozen Food Company; *U.S. Public*, pg. 427

KID CUISINE—Frozen Dinners—ConAgra, Inc.; *U.S. Public*, pg. 425

KID KART—Pediatric Chairs—Sunrise Medical, Inc.; *U.S. Public*, pg. 1535

KID PIX—NONE—Broderbund Software, Inc.; *U.S. Public*, pg. 258

KID PIX STUDIO—NONE—Broderbund Software, Inc.; *U.S. Public*, pg. 258

KID STUFF—Premoistened Towelettes—Reynolds Metals Company; *U.S. Public*, pg. 1385

KID-TOUGH—Junior Wheel Goods—Roadmaster/Brunswick; *U.S. Public*, pg. 265

KIDDICRAFT—Plastic Toys—Fisher-Price, Inc.; *U.S. Public*, pg. 1058

KIDDIE CAMPER—Portable Play Yard—Evenflo Company, Inc.; *U.S. Private*, pg. 629

KIDDIE KIT—Children's Hair Products—Pro-Line Corporation; *U.S. Private*, pg. 887

KIDDIGEM—Jewelry—Uncas Manufacturing Company; *U.S. Private*, pg. 1116

KIDDY CABBY—Children's Tricycle—Hedstrom Corporation; *U.S. Private*, pg. 526

Brand Name Index

KIDMIN—Amino Acid Solution for Kidney Failure—Otsuka Pharmaceutical Co., Ltd.; *Int'l*, pg. 1013

KIDPROOF—Jeans—Healthtex; *U.S. Public*, pg. 1702

KIDRON—Refrigerated Truck Bodies—Transportation Technologies, Inc.; *U.S. Private*, pg. 1097

KIDS—Cameras—Eastman Kodak Company; *U.S. Public*, pg. 550

KIDS CHOICE—NONE—KinderCare Learning Centers, Inc.; *U.S. Public*, pg. 961

KIDS CLUB—Children's Meals, Activities—Burger King Corporation; *Int'l*, pg. 411

KID'S CLUD HOUSE—Soft Playground Equipment—Stainless Incorporated; *U.S. Private*, pg. 1029

KIDS FOOT LOCKER—Children's Athletic Footwear & Apparel—Woolworth Corporation; *U.S. Public*, pg. 1777

KIDS INFUSION PUMP—Provide Intravenous Fluid & Drug Therapies for Neonatal Infants & Children—Medex Inc.; *U.S. Public*, pg. 689

KID'S KITCHEN—Microwavable Entrees—Hormel Foods Corp.; *U.S. Public*, pg. 840

KIDS KLASSICS—Videos—Remco Toys; *U.S. Public*, pg. 923

KIDS MART—Promotionaly Prices Brand-Name Infants' & Children's Apparel—Woolworth Corporation; *U.S. Public*, pg. 1777

KIDS MART—Infants' & Children's Apparel—F.W. Woolworth Co.; *U.S. Public*, pg. 1777

KIDS "R" US—Children's Clothing & Accesories—Kids "R" Us; *U.S. Public*, pg. 1626

KIDS "R" US—Retail Children's Apparel Stores—Toys "R" Us, Inc.; *U.S. Public*, pg. 1626

KIDS STORE—Children's Apparel Stores—Montgomery Ward & Co., Inc.; *U.S. Private*, pg. 758

KIDS TO COLLEGE—Higher Education Encouragement—SLM Holding Corp.; *U.S. Public*, pg. 1419

KIDSONGS—Video Cassettes—Tyco Toys, Inc.; *U.S. Public*, pg. 1058

KIDSSCAPE—Wall Designs & Borders, Self-Adhesive Vinyl Coverings for Children's Rooms—Rubbermaid Incorporated; *U.S. Public*, pg. 1411

KIDSWORLD—Superstore Encompassing All 3 "R" Us Concepts Under 1 Roof—Toys "R" Us, Inc.; *U.S. Public*, pg. 1626

KIDTRONICS—Toy—Fisher-Price, Inc.; *U.S. Public*, pg. 1058

KIDZ—Bubble Baths, Bubble Gum & Grape Bubble Gum Fragrance—Benjamin Ansehl Company; *U.S. Private*, pg. 75

KIDZELS—Pretzels—Bachman Company; *U.S. Private*, pg. 109

KIJAFA—Sparkling Wine—Austin Nichols & Co. Inc.; *Int'l*, pg. 566

KIK-STEP—Step-Stool—Cramer Inc.; *U.S. Private*, pg. 285

KIKKOMAN—Soy Sauce, Teriyaki Sauce & Stir-Fry Sauce—Kikkoman International, Inc.; *Int'l*, pg. 733

KILGORE—NONE—Kilgore Operations; *U.S. Public*, pg. 47

KILGOUR FRENCH & STANBURY—Clothing—Genesco Inc.; *U.S. Public*, pg. 728

KILGOUR FRENCH & STANBURY—Men's Tailored Clothing—Hartmarx Corporation; *U.S. Public*, pg. 795

KILIAN—Bearings—The Torrington Co.; *U.S. Public*, pg. 877

KILKENNY—NONE—Guinness Plc; *Int'l*, pg. 412

KILL-KO—Rodenticides—Rigo/Black Leaf; *U.S. Public*, pg. 1390

KILLER KANE—Herbicide Applicator/Cartridges—Security Lawn & Garden Co.; *U.S. Private*, pg. 397

KILLIAN'S HONEY ALE—Specialty Beer—Adolph Coors Company; *U.S. Public*, pg. 445

KILLIAN'S IRISH RED—Super Premium Beer—Adolph Coors Company; *U.S. Public*, pg. 445

KILO PAK ENGINES—Marine Engines—Reagan Equipment Company, Inc.; *U.S. Private*, pg. 913

KILOSEIS—Seismic Data Processing System—Litton Industries, Inc.; *U.S. Public*, pg. 1002

KILOSTREAM—Digital Private Circuit—British Telecommunications plc; *Int'l*, pg. 222

KILOVAC—Division—Communications Instruments Inc.; *U.S. Private*, pg. 259

KILOVOLT STAC—Semi-Conductor Devices—Semtech Corporation; *U.S. Public*, pg. 1456

KILOWATT KILLER—Motor—Franklin Electric Co., Inc.; *U.S. Public*, pg. 679

KILPATRICK'S—Bakery Products—The Earthgrains Company; *U.S. Public*, pg. 547

KILSTAIN—Stain Killer—Devoe Paint; *Int'l*, pg. 663

KILSTAIN—Stain Killer—ICI Paints; *Int'l*, pg. 664

KILSTAIN-WB—Waterborne Primer-Sealer—Devoe Paint; *Int'l*, pg. 663

KILSTAIN WB—Waterborne Primer-Sealer—ICI Paints; *Int'l*, pg. 664

KIM—Cigarettes—B.A.T Industries P.L.C.; *Int'l*, pg. 110

KIM—Children's Dresses—Seibel & Stern Corp.; *U.S. Private*, pg. 981

KIMBALL—Retail Supplies—Esselte AB; *Int'l*, pg. 459

KIMBALL—Trade Name—Esselte Meto Kimball Systems; *Int'l*, pg. 460

KIMBALL—Pianos, Office Furniture—Kimball International, Inc.; *U.S. Public*, pg. 956

KIMBALL—Esselte Meto—Meto, USA; *Int'l*, pg. 460

KIMBALL CLEAN HARBORS TECHNOLOGY—Incineration of Hazardous Wastes—Clean Harbors, Inc.; *U.S. Public*, pg. 383

KIMBERLY-CLARK—Indus. Wipers, Disp. Garments, Washroom Prod., SurgicalGowns, Drapes, Packs—Kimberly-Clark Corporation; *U.S. Public*, pg. 958

KIMBERTON—Carpet—Lees Carpets; *U.S. Public*, pg. 268

KIMBI/KIMBIES—Disposable Diapers—Kimberly-Clark Corporation; *U.S. Public*, pg. 958

KIMCEL—Industrial Wipers—Kimberly-Clark Corporation; *U.S. Public*, pg. 958

KIMCO MAGNETICS—Brushless Motors/Actuators—BEI Sensors and Systems Company; *U.S. Public*, pg. 160

KIMDRI/KIMDRY—Industrial Wipers—Kimberly-Clark Corporation; *U.S. Public*, pg. 958

KIMDURA—Synthetic Paper—Kimberly-Clark Corporation; *U.S. Public*, pg. 958

KIMGUARD—Sterilization Wrap, Surgical Accessories & Disposable Garments—Kimberly-Clark Corporation; *U.S. Public*, pg. 958

KIMKLEEN TAG—Tag that Offers Clean Release from Backing Paper—Meto, USA; *Int'l*, pg. 460

KIMLARK—Disposable Wipes & Towels—Kimberly-Clark Corporation; *U.S. Public*, pg. 958

KIMLON—Disposable Bed Linens, Hospital Products—Kimberly-Clark Corporation; *U.S. Public*, pg. 958

KIMMARK—Disposable Wipes & Towels—Kimberly-Clark Corporation; *U.S. Public*, pg. 958

KIMNET—Industrial Wipers—Kimberly-Clark Corporation; *U.S. Public*, pg. 958

KIMNOFF—Vodka & Gin—M.S. Walker, Inc.; *U.S. Private*, pg. 1147

KIMPAK—Interior Packaging—Kimberly-Clark Corporation; *U.S. Public*, pg. 958

KIMS—Information Handling & Retreival Systems—Eastman Kodak Company; *U.S. Public*, pg. 550

KIMTEX—Disposable Wipes & Towels—Kimberly-Clark Corporation; *U.S. Public*, pg. 958

KIMTOWELS—Wipers—Kimberly-Clark Corporation; *U.S. Public*, pg. 958

KIMTUFF—Disposable Wipes & Towels—Kimberly-Clark Corporation; *U.S. Public*, pg. 958

KIMWEAR—Protective Garment Wear—Kimberly-Clark Corporation; *U.S. Public*, pg. 958

KIMWIPES—Towels—Kimberly-Clark Corporation; *U.S. Public*, pg. 958

KINATECHNICS—Assembly Equipment—Marshall Industries; *U.S. Public*, pg. 1051

KIND TO COLOR—Permanent—Clairol, Inc.; *U.S. Public*, pg. 254

KIND TO HAIR—Permanent—Clairol, Inc.; *U.S. Public*, pg. 254

KINDEL—Furniture—Kindel Furniture Company; *U.S. Private*, pg. 620

KINDER—Chocolate Candy for Children—Ferrero; *Int'l*, pg. 480

KINDER—Chocolate Candy for Children—Ferrero U.S.A., Inc.; *Int'l*, pg. 480

KINDER-CARE—Learning Centers—KinderCare Learning Centers, Inc.; *U.S. Public*, pg. 961

KINDERCARE AT WORK—NONE—KinderCare Learning Centers, Inc.; *U.S. Public*, pg. 961

KINDERMINS—Vitamins for Infants & Children—Herbalife International of America, Inc.; *U.S. Public*, pg. 809

KINDNESS—Heated Rollers—Bristol-Myers Squibb Company; *U.S. Public*, pg. 253

KINDNESS—Conditioner, Hairsetters & Quartz Dryer for Curly Hair—Clairol, Inc.; *U.S. Public*, pg. 254

KINDORF—Metal Framing System—Thomas & Betts Corporation; *U.S. Public*, pg. 1597

KINEL—Molding Powders—Rhone-Poulenc S.A.; *Int'l*, pg. 1108

KINEMATIC—NONE—Pfizer Inc.; *U.S. Public*, pg. 1281

KINEMAX—Glass Polishing Material—Ferro Corporation; *U.S. Public*, pg. 618

KINEMAX—NONE—Pfizer Inc.; *U.S. Public*, pg. 1281

KINEMOX—NONE—Howmedica, Inc.; *U.S. Public*, pg. 1282

KINERET—Kosher Frozen Foods for Today's Convenience—The Hain Food Group Inc.; *U.S. Public*, pg. 774

KINETIC EXPANSION SYSTEM—Outerwear for Men & Boys—I. Spiewak & Sons, Inc.; *U.S. Private*, pg. 1025

KINETIC QCL—Kinetic Endotoxin Test—BioWhittaker, Inc.; *U.S. Public*, pg. 297

KINETIC WEDGE—Motion Enhancing Orthotic System—The Langer Biomechanics Group, Inc.; *U.S. Public*, pg. 978

KINETICS—Furniture—Carter Holt Harvey Limited; *U.S. Public*, pg. 904

KINETICS—Office Furniture and Seating—Haworth, Inc.; *U.S. Private*, pg. 1151

KINEVAC—Diagnostics—Bristol-Myers Squibb Company; *U.S. Public*, pg. 253

KING—NONE—British-American Tobacco (Germany) GmbH; *Int'l*, pg. 111

KING—Sporting Goods—Brunswick Bowling & Billiards Corp.; *U.S. Public*, pg. 265

KING—Peppermints—CSM N.V.; *Int'l*, pg. 243

KING—NONE—King Milling Company; *U.S. Private*, pg. 621

KING—Wood/Coal—Martin Industries, Inc. (AL); *U.S. Private*, pg. 709

KING AIR CURTAINS—NONE—King Company; *U.S. Public*, pg. 1676

KING & PRINCE—Processed Sea Foods—King & Prince Seafood Company; *U.S. Private*, pg. 620

KING COBRA—Malt Liquor—Anheuser-Busch Companies, Inc.; *U.S. Public*, pg. 113

KING COBRA—Golf Clubs—Cobra Golf Incorporated; *U.S. Public*, pg. 675

KING COBRA—NONE—Fortune Brands, Inc.; *U.S. Public*, pg. 674

KING COBRA—Band Saw Blades—Sandvik/Milford Corporation; *Int'l*, pg. 1185

KING COBRA MALLET—NONE—Fortune Brands, Inc.; *U.S. Public*, pg. 674

KING COBRA MALLET PUTTERS—NONE—Cobra Golf Incorporated; *U.S. Public*, pg. 675

KING COBRA TI—NONE—Cobra Golf Incorporated; *U.S. Public*, pg. 675

KING COBRA TI—NONE—Fortune Brands, Inc.; *U.S. Public*, pg. 674

KING COBRA II—NONE—Fortune Brands, Inc.; *U.S. Public*, pg. 674

KING COTTON—Wine—Adams Wine Co.; *U.S. Private*, pg. 17

KING CUTTER—PDC Bits—Baker Hughes INTEQ; *U.S. Public*, pg. 166

KING EDWARD—Cigar—Swisher International Group, Inc.; *U.S. Public*, pg. 1543

KING EDWARD CORONETS—Cigars—Imperial Tobacco Group, Ltd.; *Int'l*, pg. 666

KING FEATURES—Syndicate—The Hearst Corporation; *U.S. Private*, pg. 515

KING INSTRUMENTS—Rotameters—Ryan Herco Products Corp.; *U.S. Private*, pg. 953

KING KOIL—Bedding—Blue Bell/King Koil, Inc.; *U.S. Private*, pg. 150

KING KOIL BEDQUARTERS—Retail Gallery—King Koil Licensing Company Inc.; *U.S. Private*, pg. 621

KING KULLEN—Grocery Stores—King Kullen Grocery Co., Inc.; *U.S. Private*, pg. 621

KING KUTS—Dog Food—The Quaker Oats Company; *U.S. Public*, pg. 1347

KING LEO—Candy—Standard Candy Co., Inc.; *U.S. Private*, pg. 1030

KING LOUIE—Shirts, Jackets & Caps—King Louie International; *U.S. Private*, pg. 621

KING NATIONAL—Industrial Heating—King Company; *U.S. Public*, pg. 1676

KING-O-PEDIC—Mattresses—Kingsdown, Inc.; *U.S. Private*, pg. 622

KING OF BEERS—Slogan—Anheuser-Busch Companies, Inc.; *U.S. Public*, pg. 113

KING OF STEAKS—Meat—Stock Yards Packing Co., Inc.; *U.S. Private*, pg. 1043

KING OF THE ROAD—5th Wheel & Travel Trailers—Chief Industries, Inc.; *U.S. Private*, pg. 236

KING PUMP SHROUD—Configuration—Graco Inc.; *U.S. Public*, pg. 756

KING QUAD—Motorcycle—American Suzuki Motor Corporation; *Int'l*, pg. 1323

KING REFRIGERATED AIR—NONE—King Company; *U.S. Public*, pg. 1676

KING-SEELEY—Appliance Controls—Eaton Corporation; *U.S. Public*, pg. 555

KING-SEELEY—Appliance Controls—Eaton Corporation Automotive Controls Division; *U.S. Public*, pg. 557

KING SIX—NONE—Fortune Brands, Inc.; *U.S. Public*, pg. 674

KING SIX—NONE—Gallaher Tobacco Ltd.; *Int'l*, pg. 539

KING SIZE—Permanent Marker—Sanford Corporation; *U.S. Public*, pg. 1178

KING SOLOMON'S—Kosher Wines—Warner Vineyards; *U.S. Private*, pg. 1151

KING SOOPERS—Mexican Food Products—Wilson Products Co.; *U.S. Private*, pg. 1181

KING VITAMAN—Cereal—The Quaker Oats Company; *U.S. Public*, pg. 1347

KING WILLIAM—Meat Wrap—Wausau-Mosinee Paper Corporation; *U.S. Public*, pg. 1747

KING-MEC—NONE—Fortune Brands, Inc.; *U.S. Public*, pg. 674

KING'S—Edible Dried Beans—Trinidad/Benham Corp.; *U.S. Private*, pg. 1103

KINGSDOWN TUFF GRIP—Mattress Handles—Kingsdown, Inc.; *U.S. Private*, pg. 622

KINGFISHER—Wallcoverings—Forbo Holding SA; *Int'l*, pg. 496

KINGMAKER—Diplomacy Game—Monarch Avalon, Inc.; *U.S. Public*, pg. 1123

KINGS CROWN—Scotch—Montebello Brands Inc.; *U.S. Private*, pg. 758

KINGSBURY—Metal Cutting, Assembly Machines & Vertical Turning Systems—Kingsbury Corporation; *U.S. Private*, pg. 621

KINGSDOWN INC—Mattress & Box Springs—Kingsdown, Inc.; *U.S. Private*, pg. 622

KINGSDOWN POSTURE—Sleeping Sofa Mattress—Kingsdown, Inc.; *U.S. Private*, pg. 622

KINGSFORD—Charcoal Briquets & Lighter Fluid—The Clorox Company; *U.S. Public*, pg. 386

KINGSFORD—Charcoal Briquets—The Kingsford Products Company; *U.S. Public*, pg. 387

KINGSFORD'S—Corn Starch—Best Foods; *U.S. Public*, pg. 224

KINGSLON—NONE—Mauney Hosiery Mills, Inc.; *U.S. Private*, pg. 715

KINGSMILL—Resort & Conference Center—Anheuser-Busch Companies, Inc.; *U.S. Public*, pg. 113

KINGSPORT—Rum—Marie Brizard Wines & Spirits USA; *U.S. Private*, pg. 702

KINGSTON—General Merchandise, Dry Groceries, Frozen Foods—Topco Associates, Inc.; *U.S. Private*, pg. 1091

KINGSWOOD—Manufactured Homes—Champion Enterprises, Inc.; *U.S. Public*, pg. 332

KINGTREAD—Workboots—Kaufman Footwear; *Int'l*, pg. 725

KINIDIN DURULES—Antiarrhythmic—Astra AB; *Int'l*, pg. 93

KINNEY—Family Shoe Stores—Kinney Shoe Corporation; *U.S. Public*, pg. 1777

KINNEY—Family Shoe Stores—Woolworth Corporation; *U.S. Public*, pg. 1777

KINSMAN—Round Bale Feeders & Movers—Fleischer Manufacturing, Inc.; *U.S. Private*, pg. 410

KINZBACH—Valves—Weatherford Enterra Incorporated; *U.S. Public*, pg. 1749

KIPLINGER TAX CUT—Tax Preparation Software—H & R Block, Inc.; *U.S. Public*, pg. 770

KIPP—Lubrication Equipment—IDEX Corporation; *U.S. Public*, pg. 862

KIRBY—Vacuum Cleaner—Berkshire Hathaway Inc.; *U.S. Public*, pg. 217

KIRBY—Vacuum Cleaners—The Scott Fetzer Company; *U.S. Public*, pg. 217

KIRBY KOALA—Greeting Cards—Gibson Greetings, Inc.; *U.S. Public*, pg. 742

KIRI-MAIKKI—Additive for Grass Feeds—Cultor Ltd.; *Int'l*, pg. 349

KIRIN BEER—Beer—Kirin USA, Inc.; *Int'l*, pg. 736

KIRK BELLE AUBERGE—Flatware—Lenox Brands; *U.S. Public*, pg. 261

KIRK & BLUM—Dust & Fume Control Systems—The Kirk & Blum Mfg. Co.; *U.S. Private*, pg. 623

KIRK STIEFF—Silver & Pewter—Brown-Forman Corporation; *U.S. Public*, pg. 261

KIRK-STIEFF—Sterling Silver Flatware—Lenox Brands; *U.S. Public*, pg. 261

KIRK STIEFF—Silver, Gold, Pewter & Giftware—Lenox Brands; *U.S. Public*, pg. 261

KIRK STIEFF—Pewter, Sterling, Stainless Flatware—Lenox, Incorporated; *U.S. Public*, pg. 261

KIRKLAND & ROSE—Bakery Ingredients—CSM N.V.; *Int'l*, pg. 243

KIRKMAN—Soap Products—Colgate-Palmolive Company; *U.S. Public*, pg. 397

KIRK'S—Soap—The Procter & Gamble Company; *U.S. Public*, pg. 1330

KIRSBERRY—Fruit Wine—Danisco Distillers; *Int'l*, pg. 378

KIRSCH—Drapery Hardware & Custom Window Coverings—Kirsch; *U.S. Public*, pg. 1176

KISS—Laser Printer—QMS, Inc.; *U.S. Public*, pg. 1346

KISS COOL—Candy—Kraft Jacobs Suchard; *U.S. Public*, pg. 1290

KIST—Jams, Juices—Bestfoods; *U.S. Public*, pg. 223

KIST—Soft Drink—The Monarch Company, Inc.; *U.S. Private*, pg. 756

KIT—Automotive Products—Northern Labs, Inc.; *U.S. Private*, pg. 805

KIT & KABOODLE—Greeting Cards, Stationery & Party Goods—American Greetings Corporation; *U.S. Public*, pg. 77

KIT KAT—Candy—Hershey Chocolate U.S.A.; *U.S. Public*, pg. 812

KIT KAT—Wafer Bar—Hershey Foods Corporation; *U.S. Public*, pg. 811

KIT KAT—Candy Bar—Nestle-Rowntree Ltd.; *Int'l*, pg. 921

KIT 'N KABOODLE—Cat Food—Ralston Purina Company; *U.S. Public*, pg. 1359

KITANO—Seasonings, Spices—Bestfoods; *U.S. Public*, pg. 223

KITASAMYCIN—Macrolide Antibiotic—Asahi Chemical Industry Co., Ltd.; *Int'l*, pg. 83

KITCHEN & HOME—Upscale Kitchen & Home Products Catalog—Hanover Direct, Inc.; *U.S. Public*, pg. 782

KITCHEN & BATH BUSINESS—Magazine—Miller Freeman Inc.; *Int'l*, pg. 1443

KITCHEN BOUQUET—Browning & Seasoning Sauce & Gravy Aid—The Clorox Company; *U.S. Public*, pg. 386

KITCHEN BOUQUET—Browning Agent & Flavor Enhancer—The Kingsford Products Company; *U.S. Public*, pg. 387

KITCHEN CENTER—Food Preparation Appliance—Sunbeam Household Products; *U.S. Public*, pg. 1533

KITCHEN CHARM—Waxed Paper—Marcal Paper Mills, Inc.; *U.S. Private*, pg. 701

KITCHEN CLASSICS—Kitchen Tools—Ekco Housewares, Inc.; *U.S. Public*, pg. 566

KITCHEN COMPANION—Radios—Thomson Consumer Electronics Inc.; *Int'l*, pg. 1383

KITCHEN COOKS—Teakwood Accessories—Dansk International Designs Ltd.; *U.S. Public*, pg. 261

KITCHEN DEL SOL—NONE—The Smithfield Companies, Inc.; *U.S. Public*, pg. 1479

KITCHEN FACTORY—Cookware—Regal Ware, Inc.; *U.S. Private*, pg. 917

KITCHEN FAIR—Cookware—Regal Ware, Inc.; *U.S. Private*, pg. 917

KITCHEN GEM—Food Products—Rykoff-Sexton, Inc.; *U.S. Public*, pg. 918

KITCHEN HANDSOAP—Liquid Soap—Yardley of London, Inc.; *Int'l*, pg. 819

THE KITCHEN HELPER—Waxed Paper—Reynolds Metals Company; *U.S. Public*, pg. 1385

KITCHEN KETTLE—Multi-Cooker—National Presto Industries, Inc.; *U.S. Public*, pg. 1159

KITCHEN KING—Peanut Butter—J.M. Smucker Company; *U.S. Public*, pg. 1480

KITCHEN NUTRITION—Cookware, Education Services—Regal Ware, Inc.; *U.S. Private*, pg. 917

KITCHEN PLACE—Housewares—Lechters, Inc.; *U.S. Public*, pg. 983

KITCHEN PRIDE—Cookware—Regal Ware, Inc.; *U.S. Private*, pg. 917

KITCHEN PRO—Collection—Regal Ware, Inc.; *U.S. Private*, pg. 917

KITCHEN TREAT—Prepared Frozen Foods—ConAgra Frozen Food Company; *U.S. Public*, pg. 427

KITCHEN TREAT—Prepared Frozen Foods—ConAgra Frozen Foods; *U.S. Public*, pg. 427

KITCHENAID—Major Appliances—Whirlpool Corporation; *U.S. Public*, pg. 1764

KITCHENEER—Meat & Salad Grinder—The Rival Company; *U.S. Public*, pg. 1391

KITCHENS BEST—Cooking Wines—Gibson Wine Company; *U.S. Private*, pg. 452

KITE—Cigarette Tobacco—Brown & Williamson Tobacco Corp.; *Int'l*, pg. 111

KITEC—PVC Pipe—James Hardie Industries Ltd.; *Int'l*, pg. 596

KITEKAT—Petfood—Mars Petfoods (UNISABI); *U.S. Private*, pg. 707

KITTEN—NONE—Kiwi Brands Pty. Ltd.; *U.S. Public*, pg. 1434

KITTEN—Auto Care—Sara Lee Corporation; *U.S. Public*, pg. 1432

KITTEN CHOW—Cat Food—Ralston Purina Company; *U.S. Public*, pg. 1359

KITTY—Pet Food—Allied Foods, Inc.; *U.S. Private*, pg. 39

KITTY CLOVER—Potato Chips—Borden, Inc.; *U.S. Private*, pg. 157

KITTY CREAM—Pet Foods—Ag Processing Inc., A Cooperative; *U.S. Private*, pg. 26

KITTY IN THE GRASS—Gift Wrap Paper—American Greetings Corporation; *U.S. Public*, pg. 77

KITTY KITTY KITTENS—Plush—Tyco Toys, Inc.; *U.S. Public*, pg. 1058

KITTY LITTER MAXX—Cat Box Filler—Golden Cat Corporation; *U.S. Public*, pg. 1360

KITTY LITTER MAXX SCOOP—Scooping Cat Box Filler—Golden Cat Corporation; *U.S. Public*, pg. 1360

KITTYHAWK—Fluff Pulp—Weyerhaeuser Company; *U.S. Public*, pg. 1764

KIWI—Shoe Polish—Kiwi Brands; *U.S. Public*, pg. 1433

KIWI—NONE—Kiwi Brands Pty. Ltd.; *U.S. Public*, pg. 1434

KIWI—Shoe Care Products—Sara Lee Corporation; *U.S. Public*, pg. 1432

KIWI/PELI—Furniture Care—Sara Lee Corporation; *U.S. Public*, pg. 1432

KIX—Cereal—General Mills, Inc.; *U.S. Public*, pg. 717

KLACID—Macrolide Anti-Infective—Abbott Laboratories; *U.S. Public*, pg. 12

KLAFS—NONE—Klafs Saunabau GmbH & Co. KG Medizinische Technik; *Int'l*, pg. 736

KLAJSE—Ladies Separates—Arnotts plc; *Int'l*, pg. 81

KLAMATH DOOR—Door—Jeld-Wen, Inc.; *U.S. Private*, pg. 585

KLAMP-FLANGE—Metal Coupling Hardware—Varian Associates, Inc.; *U.S. Public*, pg. 1710

KLARAID—Oily Waste Treatment—BetzDearborn Inc.; *U.S. Public*, pg. 226

KLASS—Facia Concealed Gutter Systems—Carter Holt Harvey Limited; *U.S. Public*, pg. 904

KLASSIC KARDS—Greeting Cards—American Greetings Corporation; *U.S. Public*, pg. 77

KLAXON—Automobile Horns—Fiamm S.p.A.; *Int'l*, pg. 480

KLAXON SIGNALS—Sound Equipment & Air Movement Products—Halma p.l.c.; *Int'l*, pg. 589

KLAY—Laundry Powder Soaps—Nuevo Federal S.A.; *Int'l*, pg. 990

KLEAN-GREEN—Solvents, Removers, Thinners, Protectors & Cleaners—W.M. Barr & Co., Inc.; *U.S. Private*, pg. 117

KLEAN'N SHINE—Furniture Cleaner—S.C. Johnson & Son, Inc.; *U.S. Private*, pg. 592

KLEAN-STRIP—Solvents, Removers, Thinners, Protectors, Cleaners & Fuels—W.M. Barr & Co., Inc.; *U.S. Private*, pg. 117

KLEAR—Floor Polish—S.C. Johnson & Son, Inc.; *U.S. Private*, pg. 592

KLEBCIL—Pharmaceutical Prods.—SmithKline Beecham Laboratories; *Int'l*, pg. 1264

KLEBFIX—Wet-Gummed Tapes and Taping Rolls—PKL Verpackungssysteme GmbH; *Int'l*, pg. 1020

KLEEN-AIRE—Air Filters—Tecumseh Products Co. Engine & Transmission Group; *U.S. Public*, pg. 1566

KLEEN & DRY—Treated Cleaning Cloth—The Texwipe Co.; *U.S. Private*, pg. 1079

KLEEN BEBE—Disposable Diapers—Kimberly-Clark Corporation; *U.S. Public*, pg. 958

KLEEN-CHANGE—Filter Assembly—Pall Corporation; *U.S. Public*, pg. 1253

KLEEN EARTH—Recycled Shears & Rulers—Acme United Corporation; *U.S. Public*, pg. 17

KLEEN-GARD—Grease Filter—Research Products Corporation; *U.S. Private*, pg. 924

KLEEN KITTY—Cat Litter—Superior Brands, Inc.; *Int'l*, pg. 917

KLEEN-KOIL—Cleaning Products—Clayton Industries Co.; *U.S. Private*, pg. 245

KLEEN KUTLETTER HEADS—Clean Perforations Continuous Letter Heads—Hano Document Printers, Inc.; *U.S. Public*, pg. 1686

KLEEN SEAL—Electrical Resistance Heated Wire—Reynolds Metals Company; *U.S. Public*, pg. 1385

KLEENATRON—Cleanouts—Josam Company; *U.S. Private*, pg. 600

KLEENCUT—Scissors & Shears—Acme United Corporation; *U.S. Public*, pg. 17

KLEENER—Cabin Air Filter—Champion Laboratories, Inc.; *U.S. Private*, pg. 1113

KLEENEX—Facial & Bathroom Tissue, Disposable Household Towels, Disposable Diapers—Kimberly-Clark Corporation; *U.S. Public*, pg. 958

KLEENEX CLUB—Facial Tissue—Kimberly-Clark Corporation; *U.S. Public*, pg. 958

KLEENEX PREMIUM—Bathroom Tissues—Kimberly-Clark Corporation; *U.S. Public*, pg. 958

KLEENGUARD—Disposable Garments—Kimberly-Clark Corporation; *U.S. Public*, pg. 958

KLEENITE—Denture Cleaner—Richardson-Vicks, Inc. Personal Care Products Div.; *U.S. Private*, pg. 1331

KLEENKUT—Emulsion Soluble Oils—D.A. Stuart Company; *U.S. Private*, pg. 1048

KLEENODENSE—Concrete Densifier—Akzo Nobel N.V.; *Int'l*, pg. 42

KLEENOL—Spot Remover—Ronson Corporation; *U.S. Public*, pg. 1405

KLEENOPLAST—Concrete Retardant/Plasticiser—Akzo Nobel N.V.; *Int'l*, pg. 42

KLEENOPOR—Frost Resistance Formulation—Akzo Nobel N.V.; *Int'l*, pg. 42

KLEENOTARD—Concrete Retardant Formulation—Akzo Nobel N.V.; *Int'l*, pg. 42

KLEENOTONE—Pigments for Concrete—Akzo Nobel N.V.; *Int'l*, pg. 42

KLEENSEAL—Sealed & Gasketed Troffers—Guth Lighting Company; *Int'l*, pg. 821

KLEENSEAL—Portable Lubrication System—Lincoln Industrial; *U.S. Public*, pg. 1273

KLEENTEK—Electrostatic Fluid—United Air Specialists, Inc.; *U.S. Public*, pg. 382

KLEENUPS—Wipers—Kimberly-Clark Corporation; *U.S. Public*, pg. 958

KLEER-VU—Custom Products—Kleer-Vu Plastics Corp.; *U.S. Public*, pg. 962

KLEERMOUNT—Biological Supplies—Carolina Biological Supply Co.; *U.S. Private*, pg. 213

KLEIN—Electrician Tools—Bryant Electric Supply Company, Inc.; *U.S. Private*, pg. 177

KLEIN—Hand Tools—Klein Tools Inc.; *U.S. Private*, pg. 625

KLEIN-BENFIELD—Conduit Benders—Klein Tools Inc.; *U.S. Private*, pg. 625

KLEIN-FLEX—Fish Tape—Klein Tools Inc.; *U.S. Private*, pg. 625

KLEIN-KORD—Occupational Belting—Klein Tools Inc.; *U.S. Private*, pg. 625

KLEIN-LITE—Non-Metallic Fish Tapes—Klein Tools Inc.; *U.S. Private*, pg. 625

KLEIN-LOK—Locking Pliers & Snap Hooks—Klein Tools Inc.; *U.S. Private*, pg. 625

KLEMM—NONE—Ingersoll-Rand Company; *U.S. Public*, pg. 876

KLENK'S EPOXY—Tub & Tile Finish—Zynolyte Products Company; *Int'l*, pg. 663

KLENK'S AQUA TECH—Tub & Tile Finish—Zynolyte Products Company; *Int'l*, pg. 663

KLENZ-GLIDE—Conveyor Sanitizer & Lubricant—Ecolab Inc.; *U.S. Public*, pg. 562

KLENZADE—Sanitizing Product—Ecolab Inc.; *U.S. Public*, pg. 562

KLEPO/STABYLIA—Rubber Products—Weatherford Enterra Incorporated; *U.S. Public*, pg. 1749

KLER—NONE—The Hartstone Group PLC; *Int'l*, pg. 599

KLERZYME—Pectinases Used for Clarificaiton of Fruit Juices—Royal Gist-Brocades N.V.; *Int'l*, pg. 1142

KLIK—Hand & Power Riveters—Marson/Creative Fastener, Inc.; *U.S. Private*, pg. 708

KLIK-ER—Hand Riveter—Marson/Creative Fastener, Inc.; *U.S. Private*, pg. 708

KLIK-FAST—Blind Rivets—Marson/Creative Fastener, Inc.; *U.S. Private*, pg. 708

KLIK-LOK—Plastic Rivets—Marson/Creative Fastener, Inc.; *U.S. Private*, pg. 708

KLINA—Flame System & Accessories—Beckman Instruments, Inc.; *U.S. Private*, pg. 199

KLING—Furniture—Ethan Allen, Inc.; *U.S. Public*, pg. 595

KLIOGEST—Product for Gynaecological Use—Novo Nordisk A/S; *Int'l*, pg. 987

KLIPDRIFT—Brandy—Distillers Corporation S.A.; *Int'l*, pg. 1129

KLIPRING—Retaining Ring—Waldes Truarc/Industrial Retaining Ring; *U.S. Public*, pg. 1632

KLIPSCHORN—Loudspeaker Systems—Klipsch, Inc.; *U.S. Private*, pg. 626

KLOBER—Seating—Carter Holt Harvey Limited; *U.S. Public*, pg. 904

KLONDIKE—Frozen Ice Cream Bar—CLR Corporation; *U.S. Public*, pg. 579

KLONDIKE—Battery Booster Cables—General Cable Corporation; *Int'l*, pg. 1486

KLONOPIN—Anticonvulsant Agent—Hoffmann-La Roche Inc.; *Int'l*, pg. 1120

KLONOPIN—Anticonvulsant—Roche Holding Ltd.; *Int'l*, pg. 1119

KLOPMAN—Apparel Fabrics—Burlington Industries, Inc.; *U.S. Public*, pg. 268

KLOPMAN—Fabrics—Dominion Textile Inc.; *Int'l*, pg. 415

KLORANE—Botanical Shampoo—Bristol-Myers Squibb Company; *U.S. Public*, pg. 253

KLORO—Plasticizers—Ferro Corporation; *U.S. Public*, pg. 618

KLORO-CHEK—Chlorinated Paraffins—Ferro Corporation; *U.S. Public*, pg. 618

KLORVESS—Prevention & Treatment of Potassium Depletion—Sandoz Pharmaceuticals Corp.; *Int'l*, pg. 974

KLOTRIX—Potassium-Chloride Supplement—Bristol-Myers Squibb Company; *U.S. Public*, pg. 253

KLOTRIX—Potassium-Chloride Supplement—Bristol-Myers Squibb U.S. Pharmaceutical Group; *U.S. Public*, pg. 255

KLOZURE—Buttons—Eagle Button Co., Inc.; *U.S. Private*, pg. 354

KLOZURE—Oil Seals—Garlock Sealing Technologies; *U.S. Public*, pg. 402

KLUBERLUBRICATION—Specialty Lubricant & Grease—Freudenberg & Company; *Int'l*, pg. 505

KLUCEL—Hydroxypropylcellulose—Hercules Incorporated; *U.S. Public*, pg. 809

KLUTCH—Denture Adhesive Powder—Lee Pharmaceuticals; *U.S. Public*, pg. 984

KMART—NONE—Coles Myer Ltd.; *Int'l*, pg. 306

KMART—Chain Stores—Kmart Corporation; *U.S. Public*, pg. 963

THE KNACK—Razor—The Gillette Company; *U.S. Public*, pg. 743

KNACK & BACK—Chilled Dough Products—GrandMet Foods GmbH; *Int'l*, pg. 409

KNAP KAP—Pickup Cap—The Knapheide Mfg. Co.; *U.S. Private*, pg. 626

KNAP-PACK—Storage Compartment—The Knapheide Mfg. Co.; *U.S. Private*, pg. 626

KNAPHOIST—Hydraulic Hoist—The Knapheide Mfg. Co.; *U.S. Private*, pg. 626

KNAPP—Shoes—Knapp Shoes Inc.; *U.S. Private*, pg. 401

KNAPP MONARCH—Heaters—Frigid Products, Inc.; *U.S. Private*, pg. 883

KNAUSS—Dried Beef—E.W. Knauss & Son, Inc.; *U.S. Private*, pg. 626

KNEADER—Continuous Compounding Machine for Thermoplastics, Thermosets & Food—Buss (America) Inc.; *Int'l*, pg. 490

KNEEWELL—Centrifuge—Beckman Instruments, Inc.; *U.S. Private*, pg. 199

KNEIP—Meat Products—John Morrell & Co.; *U.S. Public*, pg. 1479

KNET—TCP/IP Network Software—N Base Communications; *U.S. Public*, pg. 1027

KNIFE COLLECTION—Cutlery—Imperial Schrade Corp.; *U.S. Private*, pg. 559

KNIFE-EDGE—Small End Roll Conveyors Designed to TransportSmall Products—Flomaster Div.; *U.S. Public*, pg. 1318

THE KNIGHT—Lambskin & Thermal Stretch Glove—Horace Small Apparel Company; *Int'l*, pg. 635

KNIGHT-WARE—Chemical Equipment—Koch Engineering Company, Inc.; *U.S. Private*, pg. 628

KNIGHTS INN—Hotel Chain—HFS, Incorporated; *U.S. Public*, pg. 321

KNIGHTS OF THE AIR—Game—Monarch Avalon, Inc.; *U.S. Public*, pg. 1123

KNIGHTSBRIDGE—Random Slate—Porcelanite, Inc.; *Int'l*, pg. 573

KNIGHTSTAR—Respiratory Support System—Nellcor Puritan Bennett Incorporated; *U.S. Public*, pg. 1039

KNIT MATES—Interchangeable Knitting System—Wm. E. Wright Limited Partnership; *U.S. Private*, pg. 1192

KNITMAKERS—Knitwear—Beldoch Industries; *U.S. Public*, pg. 519

KNITMASTER—Kit Containing Different Sizes Knitting Needles in Plastic—Wm. E. Wright Limited Partnership; *U.S. Private*, pg. 1192

THE KNITTING COLLECTION—Adult Continuity Books—Golden Books Family Entertainment Inc.; *U.S. Public*, pg. 749

KNITTING WORLD—Crafts Magazine—House of White Birches, Inc.; *U.S. Private*, pg. 542

KNOB CREEK—Furniture—Ethan Allen, Inc.; *U.S. Public*, pg. 595

KNOB CREEK—Small Batch Bourbon—Fortune Brands, Inc.; *U.S. Public*, pg. 674

KNOBBY—Reamer Cutter—Smith International, Inc.; *U.S. Public*, pg. 1478

KNOCABOUTS—Luggage—Hartmann Luggage & Leather Goods Group; *U.S. Public*, pg. 261

KNOCK OUT—Weed & Grasskiller—The Chas. H. Lilly Co.; *U.S. Private*, pg. 667

KNOCKABOUTS—Women's Apparel—Pendleton Woolen Mills, Inc.; *U.S. Private*, pg. 848

KNOCKANDO—Single Malt Whisky—Grand Metropolitan Plc; *Int'l*, pg. 408

KNOCKANDO—NONE—Societe Pour la Vente des Produits Cinzano SA; *Int'l*, pg. 410

KNOCKANDO SINGLE MALT—Single Malt Scotch—IDV North America; *Int'l*, pg. 411

KNOCKANDO SINGLE MALT—NONE—Justerini & Brooks Ltd.; *Int'l*, pg. 409

KNOLL WAUBY CLESTRA HAUSERMAN—Steel Wall Panel—Clestra Hauserman, Inc.; *Int'l*, pg. 569

KNOOR—Seasoning—Cadbury Nigeria PLC; *Int'l*, pg. 248

KNOPF—Book Imprint—Random House, Inc.; *U.S. Private*, pg. 20

KNORR—Dehydrated Soups, Sauces & Bouillons—Best Foods; *U.S. Public*, pg. 224

KNORR—Soups, Bouillons, Sauces, Mealmakers, Seasonings, Spices, Potato Products—Bestfoods; *U.S. Public*, pg. 223

KNORR—Soups, Sauces, Meal Makers—CPC Foods (Ireland) Ltd.; *U.S. Public*, pg. 225

KNORR—Bouillons, Soups, Condiments,Dishes & Mashed Potatoes—Refinerias de Maiz S.A.I.C.F.; *U.S. Public*, pg. 448

KNORR-BREMSE—Railroad Brakes, Power Devices, Foundry Products—Knorr-Bremse AG; *Int'l*, pg. 738

KNOT BAG—Plastic Grocery Sacks—Sonoco Products Company; *U.S. Public*, pg. 1485

KNOTT'S BERRY FARM—Amusement Park—Knott's Berry Farm; *U.S. Private*, pg. 627

KNOW MORE DIET—Diet Program—Jazzercise, Inc.; *U.S. Private*, pg. 584

KNOW THE LAND AND THE PEOPLE—Educational & Entertainment Services—Eastman Kodak Company; *U.S. Public*, pg. 550

KNOWLEDGE DIRECTOR—Computer Product—International Business Machines Corporation; *U.S. Public*, pg. 895

KNOWLEDGE MINING CENTER—Computer Product—International Business Machines Corporation; *U.S. Public*, pg. 895

KNOWLEDGE-STATION—Online Environment for Moving Between Applications, Queries & Batch Jobs—Computer Associates International, Inc.; *U.S. Public*, pg. 420

KNOWLEDGEFLOW-CINS—Correpondence Management—Information & Engineering Technology; *U.S. Private*, pg. 351

KNOWLEDGETOOL—Computer Product—International Business Machines Corporation; *U.S. Public*, pg. 895

KNOXVILLE NEWS-SENTINEL—Newspaper—Knoxville News-Sentinel Company; *U.S. Public*, pg. 1448

KNOX—Gelatin—Thomas J. Lipton Company; *Int'l*, pg. 1435

KNOX—Porcelain—Porcelain Products; *U.S. Public*, pg. 308

KNOX—Gelatin—Unilever Plc; *Int'l*, pg. 1433

KNOXALL—Shovels & Scoops—Ames Company; *U.S. Public*, pg. 1683

THE KNOXVILLE NEWS-SENTINEL—Newspaper—The E.W. Scripps Company; *U.S. Public*, pg. 1447

KNUDSEN—Cultured Dairy Products—Kraft Foods Inc.; *U.S. Public*, pg. 1288

KNUDSON—Ice Cream & Cultured Dairy Products—Philip Morris Companies Inc.; *U.S. Public*, pg. 1287

KO-REC-COPY—Correction Paper—Ko-Rec-Type; *U.S. Private*, pg. 117

KO-REC-KOTE—Copying Film—Ko-Rec-Type; *U.S. Private*, pg. 117

KO-REC-T'BLE—Ribbons—Ko-Rec-Type; *U.S. Private*, pg. 117

KO-REC-TYPE—Correction Paper—Ko-Rec-Type; *U.S. Private*, pg. 117

KOAGARI—Tatami Mat—The Dow Chemical Company; *U.S. Public*, pg. 522

KOAL-KING—Industrial Machinery—Pennsylvania Crusher Corp.; *U.S. Private*, pg. 850

KOALA COLLECTION—Indoor/Outdoor Wood Furniture Collection—Telescope Casual Furniture, Inc.; *U.S. Private*, pg. 1074

KOALA YUMMIES—Bite-Sized Cookies—Lotte U.S.A., Inc.; *Int'l*, pg. 819

KOATE—Biological—Bayer AG; *Int'l*, pg. 171

KOBELCO—Hydraulic Excavators—Kobe Steel, Ltd.; *Int'l*, pg. 740

KOBENHAVN—Stainless Steel Flatware—Dansk International Designs Ltd.; *U.S. Public*, pg. 261

KOBENSTYLE—Enameled Cookware—Dansk International Designs Ltd.; *U.S. Public*, pg. 261

KOBOLD—Vacuum Cleaner—Vorwerk & Co.; *Int'l*, pg. 1480

KOCH'S GOLDEN ANNIVERSARY—Beer—Genesee Corporation; *U.S. Public*, pg. 728

KOCH'S GOLDEN ANNIVERSARY LIGHT—Beer—Genesee Corporation; *U.S. Public*, pg. 728

KOCHWOCHE—Magazine—Axel Springer Verlag AG; *Int'l*, pg. 102

KOCIDE—NONE—Griffin Corporation; *U.S. Private*, pg. 480

KOCOLENE—Fuel—Kocolene Oil Corp.; *U.S. Private*, pg. 629

KODABLITZ—Flash Lighting Apparatus—Eastman Kodak Company; *U.S. Public*, pg. 550

KODABOND—Copolyester—Eastman Kodak Company; *U.S. Public*, pg. 550

KODABROME—Photo Paper—Eastman Kodak Company; *U.S. Public*, pg. 550

KODABROMIDE—Photo Paper—Eastman Kodak Company; *U.S. Public*, pg. 550

KODACARE—Blood Analysis Chemicals & Equipment—Eastman Kodak Company; *U.S. Public*, pg. 550

KODACEL—Plastic Sheeting—Eastman Kodak Company; *U.S. Public*, pg. 550

KODACHROME—Color Photo Film, Prints & Transparancies Enlargement Processing Service—Eastman Kodak Company; *U.S. Public*, pg. 550

KODACHROME-X—Color Photographic Film—Eastman Kodak Company; *U.S. Public*, pg. 550

KODACOLOR—Color Photo Film & Prints—Eastman Kodak Company; *U.S. Public*, pg. 550

KODACOLOR VR—Photographic Film—Eastman Kodak Company; *U.S. Public*, pg. 550

KODACOLOR-X—Color Photographic Film—Eastman Kodak Company; *U.S. Public*, pg. 550

KODACRAFT—Photo Developing Equipment—Eastman Kodak Company; *U.S. Public*, pg. 550

KODAFIX—Photo Fixer—Eastman Kodak Company; *U.S. Public*, pg. 550

KODAFLAT—Adhesive—Eastman Kodak Company; *U.S. Public*, pg. 550

KODAFLEX—Plasticizers & Radiographic Film—Eastman Kodak Company; *U.S. Public*, pg. 550

KODAGRAPH—Industrial Photo Film, Paper, Chemicals—Eastman Kodak Company; *U.S. Public*, pg. 550

KODAIRE—Synthetic Fiber Materials—Eastman Kodak Company; *U.S. Public*, pg. 550

KODAK—Products & Services—Eastman Kodak Company; *U.S. Public*, pg. 550

KODAK—Photography Equipment—N.V. Kodak S.A.; *U.S. Public*, pg. 554

KODAK APPROVAL—Digital Color Proofing System—Eastman Kodak Company; *U.S. Public*, pg. 550

KODAK BEACON—Enlargers—Eastman Kodak Company; *U.S. Public*, pg. 550

KODAK BISNET—Business Assistance Network & Software—Eastman Kodak Company; *U.S. Public*, pg. 550

KODAK CAMEO EX—35 mm Camera—Kodak Korea Ltd.; *U.S. Public*, pg. 555

KODAK CEREBRAL MANAGER—Software Programs—Eastman Kodak Company; *U.S. Public*, pg. 550

KODAK DIAPORAMA—Projector Dissolve Units, Cases—Eastman Kodak Company; *U.S. Public*, pg. 550

KODAK EKTACHROME ELITE—Film—Kodak Korea Ltd.; *U.S. Public*, pg. 555

KODAK EXPRESS—Photofinishing Quality Control Services—Eastman Kodak Company; *U.S. Public*, pg. 550

KODAK GOLD III—Film—Kodak Korea Ltd.; *U.S. Public*, pg. 555

KODAK MEDLINK—Business Assistance Network & Software—Eastman Kodak Company; *U.S. Public*, pg. 550

KODAK PHOTOJOY CAMERA—Single Use Camera—Kodak Korea Ltd.; *U.S. Public*, pg. 555

KODAK PREVIEW—Computer Network, Terminals—Eastman Kodak Company; *U.S. Public*, pg. 550

KODAK SIGNATURE—Color Proofing Material, Apparatus, Chemicals—Eastman Kodak Company; *U.S. Public*, pg. 550

KODAK SUPER CLEAR—Film—Kodak Korea Ltd.; *U.S. Public*, pg. 555

KODAK ULTRALINE—Graphic Arts Film; Chemicals—Eastman Kodak Company; *U.S. Public*, pg. 550

KODAKERY—Newspaper—Eastman Kodak Company; *U.S. Public*, pg. 550

KODALINE—Photo Film & Paper—Eastman Kodak Company; *U.S. Public*, pg. 550

KODALITE—Flash Lighting Equipment, Photographic Film—Eastman Kodak Company; *U.S. Public*, pg. 550

KODALITH—Photo Film, Chemicals, Developer & Fixer, Paper, Processing Equipment—Eastman Kodak Company; *U.S. Public*, pg. 550

KODALK—Balanced Alkali for Use in Developers & Other Solutions—Eastman Kodak Company; *U.S. Public*, pg. 550

KODALUX—Flash Unit—Eastman Kodak Company; *U.S. Public*, pg. 550

KODAMATIC—Processing Apparatus, Film, Instant Cameras, Flash—Eastman Kodak Company; *U.S. Public*, pg. 550

KODAPAK—Polyester Bottle Polymer & Synthetic Resins—Eastman Kodak Company; *U.S. Public*, pg. 550

KODAR—Copolyester Plastics, Photographic Lenses & Synthetic Resins—Eastman Kodak Company; *U.S. Public*, pg. 550

KODARAMA—Display—Eastman Kodak Company; *U.S. Public*, pg. 550

KODASCAN—Photofinishing Equipment—Eastman Kodak Company; *U.S. Public*, pg. 550

KODASE—Industrial Enzymes—Eastman Kodak Company; *U.S. Public*, pg. 550

KODASLIDE—Slide Projectors, Viewers, Filing Containers—Eastman Kodak Company; *U.S. Public*, pg. 550

KODASTAR—Photographic Film, Chemicals—Eastman Kodak Company; *U.S. Public*, pg. 550

KODATROL—Blood Analyzer Chemicals—Eastman Kodak Company; *U.S. Public*, pg. 550

KODAVISION—Video Products—Eastman Kodak Company; *U.S. Public*, pg. 550

KODAVUE—Electrophoresis Visualization Kit—Eastman Kodak Company; *U.S. Public*, pg. 550

KODEL—Staple Fiber & Synthetic Yarn—Eastman Kodak Company; *U.S. Public*, pg. 550

KODESTAR—Barcode Readers—Eastman Kodak Company; *U.S. Public*, pg. 550

KODET—Camera Lenses—Eastman Kodak Company; *U.S. Public*, pg. 550

KODEWORD—Darkroom Audio Cassettes—Eastman Kodak Company; *U.S. Public*, pg. 550

KODIAK—Cordless Tools—The Black & Decker Corporation; *U.S. Public*, pg. 233

KODIAK—Moist Smokeless Tobacco—Conwood Company L.P.; *U.S. Private*, pg. 272

KODIAK—Trucks—General Motors Corporation; *U.S. Public*, pg. 718

KODOFILL—Synthetic Fiber Materials—Eastman Kodak Company; *U.S. Public*, pg. 550

KODOMO—Children's Shoes—Bangkok Athletic Co., Ltd.; *Int'l*, pg. 146

KODOSOFF—Synthetic Fiber Materials—Eastman Kodak Company; *U.S. Public*, pg. 550

KOGENATE—Pharmaceutical—Bayer Corporation/Pharmaceutical Division; *Int'l*, pg. 173

KOH COLPOTOMIZER—Gynecological Device—The Cooper Companies, Inc.; *U.S. Public*, pg. 442

KOH CUP—Gynecological Device—The Cooper Companies, Inc.; *U.S. Public*, pg. 442

KOH-I-LAR—High Quality Polymer Drawing Leads—Koh-I-Noor, Inc.; *U.S. Private*, pg. 629

KOHL'S—Food Store—The Great Atlantic & Pacific Tea Company, Inc.; *Int'l*, pg. 1375

KOHL'S—Retail Department Stores—Kohl's Corporation; *U.S. Public*, pg. 965

KOHL'S—Grocery Store—Tengelmann Warenhandelsgesellschaft; *Int'l*, pg. 1375

KOHLANGAZ—NONE—Glynwed International PLC; *Int'l*, pg. 554

KOHLER—Plumbing Fixtures, Engines & Generators—Kohler Company; *U.S. Private*, pg. 630

KOHLER—Dairy Mixes—Michael Foods, Inc.; *U.S. Public*, pg. 1103

KOHLER—Chocolate & Confectionery—Nestle S.A.; *Int'l*, pg. 915

KOHLER—Plumbing Fixtures—W.A. Roosevelt Co.; *U.S. Private*, pg. 943

KOHLER—Generators—Valley Detroit Diesel Allison; *U.S. Private*, pg. 1132

KOHLER PLUMBING—Toilets, Bathtubs—The Gage Company; *U.S. Private*, pg. 437

KOHL'S—Food Stores—Kohl's Food Stores; *Int'l*, pg. 1375

Brand Name Index

KOILED KORDS—Retractile Cords—Whitney Blake Company of Vermont, Inc.; *U.S. Private*, pg. 148

KOKACHIN—Restaurant Services—Omni Hotels; *U.S. Private*, pg. 1065

KOKANEE—Beer—Labatt Brewing Company Limited; *Int'l*, pg. 679

KOKEN—Barber Shop & Beauty Shop Equipment—Koken Mfg. Co. Inc.; *Int'l*, pg. 1349

KOKO BLANCO—Coconut Drink—Yoo Hoo Chocolate Beverage Corp.; *Int'l*, pg. 567

KOKOMO—Photographic Printers, Filter Accessories—Eastman Kodak Company; *U.S. Public*, pg. 550

KOKOSRINGLI—Coconut Ring—Coop Switzerland; *Int'l*, pg. 329

KOLBERG—NONE—Portec, Inc.-Construction Equipment Div.; *U.S. Public*, pg. 1318

KOLBY—Stemware & Barware—Dansk International Designs Ltd.; *U.S. Public*, pg. 261

KOLD-DRAFT—Ice Making Equipment—Uniflow Manufacturing Co.; *U.S. Private*, pg. 1117

KOLD N KLOSE—Sheath Repair Systems—Thomas & Betts Corporation; *U.S. Public*, pg. 1597

KOLD PAK—Test Equipment—Tenney Environmental; *U.S. Private*, pg. 1076

KOLD-DRAFT—Ice Cube Maker, Flaker & Crusher, Ice Bins—Kold Draft; *U.S. Private*, pg. 1117

KOLD-HOLD—Hold Over Plates For Frozen Foods & Perishables—Tranter, Inc.; *U.S. Public*, pg. 521

KOLESTON—Hair Care Products—Wella Group; *Int'l*, pg. 1489

KOLESTRAL—Hair Care Products—The Wella Corporation; *Int'l*, pg. 1489

KOLLMORGEN—Specialty Motors, Intercon Systems, Color & Lighting Products—Kollmorgen Corporation; *U.S. Public*, pg. 965

KOLO—SANITARY PORLELAIN—Metra Corporation; *Int'l*, pg. 862

KOLOR-BAK—Hair Care Products—Benjamin Ansehl Company; *U.S. Private*, pg. 75

KOLORKINS—Cameras & Stuffed Soys—Eastman Kodak Company; *U.S. Public*, pg. 550

KOLPAK—Walk-in Coolers & Freezers—The Manitowoc Company, Inc.; *U.S. Public*, pg. 1040

KOLVAC—Zinc & Uitc Tablets—Alva/Amco Pharmacal Companies, Inc.; *U.S. Private*, pg. 47

KOLYUM—Liquid Potassuim Gluconate and Potassium Chloride—Medeva Pharmaceuticals; *Int'l*, pg. 852

KOM-80—Microfilming Machines & Accessories—Eastman Kodak Company; *U.S. Public*, pg. 550

KOM-85—Microfilming Machines & Accessories—Eastman Kodak Company; *U.S. Public*, pg. 550

KOM-90—Microfilming Machines & Accessories—Eastman Kodak Company; *U.S. Public*, pg. 550

KOMATSU—Earth Moving & Demolition Equipment—Kimmins Corp.; *U.S. Public*, pg. 960

KOMATSU—NONE—Komatsu America Industries Corp.; *Int'l*, pg. 744

KOMATSU—Heavy Duty Construction Equipment—Komatsu America International Company; *Int'l*, pg. 744

KOMAX—Mixers—Ryan Herco Products Corp.; *U.S. Private*, pg. 953

KOMBAT GEAR—NONE—L.A. Gear, Inc.; *U.S. Public*, pg. 969

KOMBI—Underwear & Socks—Kombi, Ltd.; *U.S. Private*, pg. 631

KOMO TV—NONE—Fisher Broadcasting Inc.; *U.S. Public*, pg. 648

KOMPASS—Economic Information—Kompass International Neuenschwander SA; *Int'l*, pg. 745

KOMPOSITION—Anti-Fouling Paints & Coatings—Rule Industries, Inc.; *U.S. Public*, pg. 950

KOMPRESS—Liquid-Solids Separation Equipment—Komline-Sanderson Engineering Corp.; *U.S. Private*, pg. 631

KOMSTAR—Microimage Processors & Lenses—Eastman Kodak Company; *U.S. Public*, pg. 550

KONA GOLD—Hawaiian Spiny & Slipper Lobstertails—Mitsui Foods, Inc.; *Int'l*, pg. 879

KONDAR—Acrylic Automotive Coating Composition—PPG Industries, Inc.; *U.S. Public*, pg. 1245

KONDENSOMAT—Steam Trap—GESTRA GmbH; *Int'l*, pg. 549

KONDUCTOMET—Conductive Mounting Compound—Buehler, Limited; *U.S. Public*, pg. 574

KONE—NONE—Kone Corporation; *Int'l*, pg. 746

KONEPAC—Air Cleaner—Donaldson Company, Inc.; *U.S. Public*, pg. 517

KONICA—Plain Paper Copiers, Digital Printers, Duplicators & Multifunction Products—Konica Business Machines USA, Inc.; *Int'l*, pg. 748

KONICA—Cameras—Konica Corporation; *Int'l*, pg. 748

KONICA—Films—Konica Imaging USA, Inc.; *Int'l*, pg. 749

KONICA COLOR SUPER X9—Color Films—Konica Corporation; *Int'l*, pg. 748

KONICA COLOR SUPER X9400—Color Film—Konica Corporation; *Int'l*, pg. 748

KONICA COLOR X9-V3200—High Speed Color Film—Konica Corporation; *Int'l*, pg. 748

KONICA COLOR 7—Copier—Konica Corporation; *Int'l*, pg. 748

KONICA MEDICAL SUPER RAPID SYSTEM—High Speed MedicalFilm Processing—Konica Corporation; *Int'l*, pg. 748

KONICA XR—Floppy Disk—Konica Corporation; *Int'l*, pg. 748

KONICAL—Ultracentrifuge Tubes—Beckman Instruments, Inc.; *U.S. Public*, pg. 199

KONINGSGIST—Fresh Yeast—Royal Gist-Brocades N.V.; *Int'l*, pg. 1142

KONINKLIJKE LUCHTVAART MAATSCHAPPY—Airlines—KLM Royal Dutch Airlines; *Int'l*, pg. 719

KONITE—Sodium Hydrosulphite—Akzo Nobel N.V.; *Int'l*, pg. 42

KONKA—NONE—Semi-Tech Corporation; *Int'l*, pg. 1220

KONMAR—Groceries—Vendex International N.V.; *Int'l*, pg. 1462

KONSENSUS—Color Proofing—Konica Imaging USA, Inc.; *Int'l*, pg. 749

KONSENSUS II—Color Printing Machinery—Konica Corporation; *Int'l*, pg. 748

KONSUM—Supermarkets—KF/Konsum Coop Group; *Int'l*, pg. 718

KONTROL-FLO—Deep Lane Pallet Flow—Jarke Corporation; *U.S. Private*, pg. 583

KOO-KOO-ROO—NONE—Koo Koo Roo, Inc.; *U.S. Public*, pg. 966

KOO KOO ROO GOOD FOR YOO—NONE—Koo Koo Roo, Inc.; *U.S. Public*, pg. 966

KOO KOO ROO ORIGINAL FLAME-BROLED CHICKEN—NONE—Koo Koo Roo, Inc.; *U.S. Public*, pg. 966

KOOGALABA SHAMPOO—Botanical Shampoo—Health Products Corporation; *U.S. Private*, pg. 514

KOOKY CAKES—Cake Decorations—McCormick/Schilling; *U.S. Public*, pg. 1066

KOOL—Cigarettes—B.A.T Industries P.L.C.; *Int'l*, pg. 110

KOOL—Cigarettes—Brown & Williamson Tobacco Corp.; *Int'l*, pg. 111

KOOL-AID—Soft Drink Mixes & Frozen Desserts—Kraft Foods, Inc.; *U.S. Public*, pg. 1287

KOOL-AID—Powdered Beverages—Philip Morris Companies Inc.; *U.S. Public*, pg. 1287

KOOL-AID KOOL-POPS—Frozen Dessert—Kraft Foods, Inc.; *U.S. Public*, pg. 1287

KOOL-AID KOOLERS—Fruit Drinks—Kraft Foods, Inc.; *U.S. Public*, pg. 1287

KOOL FOOT—Foot Prod.—Blistex, Inc.; *U.S. Private*, pg. 149

KOOL-LITE—Spark Ignition System—Harper-Wyman Co.; *U.S. Public*, pg. 1209

KOOL MADE—Thermo Electric Cooler/Warmer—Igloo Products Corporation; *U.S. Public*, pg. 265

KOOL MATE—Thermoelectric Cooler/Warmer—Igloo Products Corporation; *U.S. Public*, pg. 265

KOOL'N KLEEN—NONE—Medline Industries, Inc.; *U.S. Private*, pg. 728

KOOL-PAK—Resistance Film—Caddock Electronics, Inc.; *U.S. Private*, pg. 198

KOOL REST—Ice Chest—Igloo Products Corporation; *U.S. Public*, pg. 265

KOOL SHADES—Youth Electronics—Alaron Inc.; *U.S. Private*, pg. 31

KOOL-TAB—Resistance Film—Caddock Electronics, Inc.; *U.S. Private*, pg. 198

KOOL-TOUCH COVERS—Food Service Inset Covers—The Vollrath Company, L.L.C.; *U.S. Private*, pg. 1143

KOOL-TOUCH LADLES—Coated S.S. Ladles—The Vollrath Company, L.L.C.; *U.S. Private*, pg. 1143

KOOLGAS—Automatic Defrost System—Hussmann Corp.; *U.S. Public*, pg. 1766

KOOLVUE BRONZE—Float Glass—AFG Industries, Inc.; *Int'l*, pg. 84

KOOSH BALL—Toy—OddzOn Products, Inc.; *U.S. Public*, pg. 797

KOP—Hand Dishwashing Detergent—Benckiser Consumer Products Inc.; *Int'l*, pg. 185

KOPI-SPOT—Business Forms—Master Craft Corp.; *Int'l*, pg. 267

KOPI-SPRED—Statement Analysis System—Master Craft Corp.; *Int'l*, pg. 267

KOPY KLEAR OPAKE—NONE—Fraser Papers, Inc.; *U.S. Public*, pg. 434

KORANTIN—Corrosion Inhibitors—BASF AG; *Int'l*, pg. 103

KORBEL—Brandy—Brown-Forman Beverages Worldwide; *U.S. Public*, pg. 261

KORBEL—California Champagnes & Brandies—Brown-Forman Corporation; *U.S. Public*, pg. 261

KORBEL CALIFORNIA—Champagnes & Brandy—Brown-Forman Beverages Worldwide; *U.S. Public*, pg. 261

KORBX—Computers & Computer Programs—Lucent Technologies Inc.; *U.S. Public*, pg. 1017

KORDITE—Disposable Cups & Dishes—Mobil Oil Corporation; *U.S. Public*, pg. 1118

KOREA T—Swine Feed—Manna Pro Corporation; *U.S. Private*, pg. 700

KORET—Women's Leather Accessories & Handbags—Koret Pierre Cardin; *U.S. Private*, pg. 632

KORET OF CALIFORNIA—Women's Apparel—Koret of California, Inc.; *U.S. Private*, pg. 632

KORFUND DYNAMICS—Shock & Vibration—Aeroflex Incorporated; *U.S. Public*, pg. 23

KORINA—Plywood, Veneer & Lumber—Georgia-Pacific Corporation; *U.S. Public*, pg. 735

KORK-EASE—Footwear—Cherokee Inc.; *U.S. Public*, pg. 345

KORKTEX—Cork Cellulose Combination—Bontex; *U.S. Public*, pg. 734

KORKTEX—Cork Particle Product—Georgia-Bonded Fibers, Inc.; *U.S. Public*, pg. 734

KORKY—Rubber Specialties—Lavelle Industries Inc.; *U.S. Private*, pg. 653

KORLOK—Adhesive—Unilever Plc; *Int'l*, pg. 1433

KORODY-COLYER DIESEL ENGINE PARTS—Engine Parts—CR Services; *Int'l*, pg. 1157

KOROFLEX—Elastomeric Aircraft Primer—DeSoto Inc.; *U.S. Public*, pg. 956

KOROLITE—Primers & Topcoats (Polyester) for SMC—DeSoto Inc.; *U.S. Public*, pg. 956

KOROPON—Epoxy Primers for Aircraft—DeSoto Inc.; *U.S. Public*, pg. 956

KORTON—Fluoropolymer Films—Norton Performance Plastics; *Int'l*, pg. 1174

KORVEX—Heat Shrinkable Fluoropolymer Tubing—Norton Performance Plastics; *Int'l*, pg. 1174

KOSCUISZKOWY—Pickles—Dean Pickle & Specialty Products Co.; *U.S. Public*, pg. 490

KOSETTER—Molasses—Danisco Sugar; *Int'l*, pg. 378

KOSHER KING—Food Products—National Foods Inc.; *U.S. Public*, pg. 429

KOSLA—Laundry Additive—Benckiser Consumer Products Inc.; *Int'l*, pg. 185

KOSS—Stereophones, Audio/Video Equipment—Koss Corporation; *U.S. Public*, pg. 966

KOST-KUT—Chemicals—Westvaco Corporation; *U.S. Public*, pg. 1762

KOSUGI—Clothing—Kosugi Sangyo Co., Ltd.; *Int'l*, pg. 759

KOTEX—Feminine Napkins, Tampons, Sanitary Belts—Kimberly-Clark Corporation; *U.S. Public*, pg. 958

KOTEX—NONE—Tambrands Inc.; *U.S. Public*, pg. 1331

KOTEX LIBERTE—Feminine Pads—Kimberly-Clark Corporation; *U.S. Private*, pg. 958

KOTRON—RF Level Switches & Transmitters—Magnetrol International; *U.S. Private*, pg. 696

KOU KOU LE—NONE—Koo Koo Roo, Inc.; *U.S. Public*, pg. 966

KOULUNAKKI—Child's Snack—Cultor Ltd.; *Int'l*, pg. 349

KOURT KIDS—Children's Shoes—E.J. Footwear Corp.; *U.S. Public*, pg. 1684

KOU'S—Wholesale Club—The Daiei, Inc.; *Int'l*, pg. 364

KOVA—Urinalysis System—Hycor Biomedical, Inc.; *U.S. Public*, pg. 851

KOVAR—NONE—Carpenter Technology Corporation; *U.S. Public*, pg. 307

KOWALITY—Sausages, Hams & Luncheon Meats—Kowalski Sausage Co., Inc.; *U.S. Private*, pg. 634

KOWALSKI—Sausages, Hams & Luncheon Meats—Kowalski Sausage Co., Inc.; *U.S. Private*, pg. 634

KOWET—Chemical—Warner-Jenkinson Co.; *U.S. Public*, pg. 1696

KOWTOWLS—Paper Towels—Fort James Corporation; *U.S. Public*, pg. 670

KOZAK—Cigarettes—B.A.T Industries P.L.C.; *Int'l*, pg. 110

KOZY KITTEN—NONE—Star-Kist Foods Inc.; *U.S. Public*, pg. 805

KOZY KITTEN—Canned—Star-Kist Foods, Inc.; *U.S. Public*, pg. 806

KRACKEL—Chocolate Bar—Hershey Chocolate U.S.A.; *U.S. Public*, pg. 812

KRACKEL—Chocolate Bar—Hershey Foods Corporation; *U.S. Public*, pg. 811

KRAFBRITE—Clay-Coated Preprint Linerboard—Riverwood International Corporation; *U.S. Public*, pg. 1391

KRAFKOTE—Paperboard—Johns Manville Corporation; *U.S. Public*, pg. 927

KRAFT—NONE—Alliant Foodservice, Inc.; *U.S. Private*, pg. 244

KRAFT—Cheese and Cheese Powders—Kraft Food Ingredients Corp.; *U.S. Public*, pg. 1288

KRAFT—Processed, Packaged Foods—Kraft Foods Inc.; *U.S. Public*, pg. 1288

KRAFT—(Cheese)—Morinaga Milk Industry Co., Ltd.; *Int'l*, pg. 895

KRAFT—Jams, Jellies, Preserves, & Mayonnaise—Philip Morris Companies Inc.; *U.S. Public*, pg. 1287

KRAFT FREE—NONE—Alliant Foodservice, Inc.; *U.S. Private*, pg. 244

KRAFT FREE SINGLES—Fat-Free Sliced Cheese Product—Kraft Foods, Inc.; *U.S. Public*, pg. 1287

KRAFT KING—Home Improvement—Fred Meyer Stores; *U.S. Public*, pg. 1103

KRAFT LABEL—Foods—Alliant Foodservice; *U.S. Private*, pg. 244

KRAFT LIGHT SINGLES—Low-Calorie Cheese Slices—Kraft Foods Inc.; *U.S. Public*, pg. 1288

KRAFT MACARONI & CHEESE DINNER—Instant Pasta Dinner—Kraft Foods Inc.; *U.S. Public*, pg. 1288

KRAFT SINGLES—Cheese Product—Kraft Foods, Inc.; *U.S. Public*, pg. 1287

KRAFT SQUEEZABLE MAYONNAISE—Mayonnaise—Kraft Foods Inc.; *U.S. Public*, pg. 1288

KRAFT THICK 'N SPICY—NONE—Alliant Foodservice, Inc.; *U.S. Private*, pg. 244

KRAFTPAK—Folding Carton Stock—Westvaco Corporation; *U.S. Public*, pg. 1762

KRAK-STIK—Water Sealant—La-Co Industries Markal Company; *U.S. Public*, pg. 640

KRAKUS—Imported Polish Ham—Atalanta Corporation; *U.S. Private*, pg. 93

KRANBERI VODKA—NONE—Barton Brands, Ltd.; *U.S. Public*, pg. 300

KRANK2O—Caffeinated Water—Global Beverage Co.; *U.S. Private*, pg. 457

KRASDALE—Grocery Products—Krasdale Foods Inc.; *U.S. Public*, pg. 635

KRATON—Elastomers—Shell Oil Company; *Int'l*, pg. 1136

KRAUSE'S—NONE—Krause's Furniture Inc.; *U.S. Public*, pg. 967

KRAUSE'S—Upholstered Furniture—Krause's Sofa Factory; *U.S. Public*, pg. 967

KRAUSE'S SOFA FACTORY—NONE—Krause's Furniture Inc.; *U.S. Public*, pg. 967

KRAUSE'S SOFAS—NONE—Krause's Furniture Inc.; *U.S. Public*, pg. 967

KRAUSZER'S—Convenience Stores—National Food Stores, Inc.; *U.S. Private*, pg. 783

KRAZY GLUE—Cyanoacrylate Adhesive—Krazy Glue Inc.; *U.S. Private*, pg. 158

KRE-MEL—Desserts, Baking Aids—Bestfoods; *U.S. Public*, pg. 223

KREDEX—NONE—SmithKline Beecham Corporation; *Int'l*, pg. 1264

KREDEX—Cardiopulmonary Drug—SmithKline Beecham plc; *Int'l*, pg. 1264

KREGAN—Insecticide—The Dow Chemical Company; *U.S. Public*, pg. 522

KREM-TOP—Coffee Creams—Nestle S.A.; *Int'l*, pg. 915

KREMA—Candy—Kraft Jacobs Suchard; *U.S. Public*, pg. 1290

KREMCO—Well Service Rigs—National-Oilwell/Dreco; *U.S. Public*, pg. 1158

KREMLIN—War Game—Monarch Avalon, Inc.; *U.S. Public*, pg. 1123

KRENITE—Brush Control Agents—Du Pont (E.I. Du Pont De Nemours & Co.); *U.S. Public*, pg. 530

KRENTENBROODCREME TULBA—Bread Improver—Royal Gist-Brocades N.V.; *Int'l*, pg. 1142

KREON—Digestive Preparation—Solvay S.A.; *Int'l*, pg. 1277

KRESGE—Chain Stores in Canada—Kmart Corporation; *U.S. Public*, pg. 963

KRETSCHMAR—Meat Products—John Morrell & Co.; *U.S. Public*, pg. 1479

KRETSCHMER—Wheat Germ—The Quaker Oats Company; *U.S. Public*, pg. 1347

KREY FOODS—Meat Products—John Morrell & Co.; *U.S. Public*, pg. 1479

KRISP KREEM—Cookies—Keebler Company; *U.S. Public*, pg. 657

KRISPY—Crackers—Keebler Company; *U.S. Public*, pg. 657

KRISPY—Crackers—Sunshine Biscuits, Inc.; *U.S. Private*, pg. 434

KRISPY—Crackers—Sunshine Biscuits, Inc.; *U.S. Public*, pg. 657

KRISTALEX—Hydrocarbon Resin—Hercules Incorporated; *U.S. Public*, pg. 809

KRISTALINE—Interior Wall and Countertop Tile—Monarch Tile, Inc.; *U.S. Private*, pg. 287

KRISWELL—Pipe Tobaccos—Consolidated Cigar Corporation; *U.S. Public*, pg. 690

KROELER—Furniture—Schottenstein Stores Corporation; *U.S. Private*, pg. 972

THE KROGER CO.—Supermarkets—The Kroger Co.; *U.S. Public*, pg. 967

KROMALON—Enhanced Polymer Resins—Lyondell Petrochemical Company; *U.S. Public*, pg. 1022

KROMAPLAST—Blended Dry Colorants for Plastics—Ampacet Corporation; *U.S. Private*, pg. 67

KROMEKOTE—Recycled One & Two Sided Cover, Enamel (C2S Offset), Folding Bd., Litho—Champion International Corp.; *U.S. Public*, pg. 333

KROMMENIE—Floor Coverings—Forbo Holding SA; *Int'l*, pg. 496

KROMOS—Converting Papers—Kimberly-Clark Corporation; *U.S. Public*, pg. 958

KRON CHOCOLATIER—Chocolates—Boyer Candy Company Inc.; *U.S. Private*, pg. 162

KRONE—Cigarettes—B.A.T Industries P.L.C.; *Int'l*, pg. 110

KRONENBOURG—Beer—Danone Group; *Int'l*, pg. 379

KRONENBOURG 1664—Bitter Ale—Foster's Brewing Group Limited; *Int'l*, pg. 500

KRONOS—NONE—Kronos Incorporated; *U.S. Public*, pg. 967

KROSSALIN—Ice Cream Ingredient—Royal Gist-Brocades N.V.; *Int'l*, pg. 1142

KROSSI—Grain Based Feed Range for Milk Cows—Cultor Ltd.; *Int'l*, pg. 349

KROUPANA—Sueded Upholstery Leather—Wolverine World Wide, Inc.; *U.S. Public*, pg. 1775

KROVAR—Herbicide—Du Pont (E.I. Du Pont De Nemours & Co.); *U.S. Public*, pg. 530

KROWN-REGAL—Ball Bearing Pillow Blocks—McGill Manufacturing Company, Inc.; *U.S. Public*, pg. 573

KROY—Lettering & Sign Systems—Kroy Inc.; *U.S. Public*, pg. 1339

KROY—Label Equipments & Supplies—Pubco Corporation; *U.S. Public*, pg. 1339

KROY K2000—Portable Barcode Printer—Kroy Inc.; *U.S. Public*, pg. 1339

KRRRRISP KRAUT—Sauerkraut Products—Great Lakes Kraut Co.; *U.S. Private*, pg. 887

KRUEGER—Beer & Ale—Falstaff Brewing Corporation; *U.S. Private*, pg. 955

KRUG—Champagne—Remy Amerique Inc.; *Int'l*, pg. 1102

KRUGER—NONE—Kruger Inc.; *Int'l*, pg. 761

KRUMBHAAR—NONE—Lawter International, Inc.; *U.S. Public*, pg. 980

KRUNCHERS—Potato Chips—Clover Club Foods, Inc.; *U.S. Private*, pg. 456

KRUNCHIES—Peanut Butter Candy Puffs—Nestle Chocolate & Confection; *Int'l*, pg. 917

KRUPS—NONE—Moulinex S.A.; *Int'l*, pg. 896

KRUSE—Auction Services—Kruse International; *U.S. Private*, pg. 636

KRUZITE—Castables—A.P. Green Industries, Inc.; *U.S. Public*, pg. 761

KRUZITE-70—High Alumina Brick—A.P. Green Industries, Inc.; *U.S. Public*, pg. 761

KRYLINER—Marking System—Sherwin-Williams Diversified Brands, Inc.; *U.S. Public*, pg. 1466

KRYLON—Hardware & Industrial Aerosols—Pegasus International Corporation; *U.S. Private*, pg. 1046

KRYLON—Aerosol—The Sherwin-Williams Company; *U.S. Public*, pg. 1465

KRYLON—Interior & Exterior Enamel—Sherwin-Williams Diversified Brands, Inc.; *U.S. Public*, pg. 1466

KRYOCIDE—Chemical—Elf Atochem North America, Inc.; *Int'l*, pg. 445

KRYPTON GAS GENERATOR—Ventilation Studies—Amersham Healthcare; *Int'l*, pg. 992

KRYSTAL—Fast Food Restaurants—Krystal Company; *U.S. Private*, pg. 636

KRYSTAL KEYS—Wall & Floor Accent Pieces—Monarch Tile, Inc.; *U.S. Private*, pg. 287

KRYSTAL KLEAR—Envelopes—Westvaco Corporation; *U.S. Public*, pg. 1762

KRYSTAL-KOTE—Varnish—Lilly Industries, Inc.; *U.S. Public*, pg. 994

KRYSTALKLEAR—Tempered Glass—AFG Industries, Inc.; *Int'l*, pg. 84

KRYSTALTITE—Film—AlliedSignal Inc.; *U.S. Public*, pg. 49

KRYSTAR—Fructose—Tate & Lyle PLC; *Int'l*, pg. 1356

KRYTOX—Fluorinated Oil—Du Pont (E.I. Du Pont De Nemours & Co.); *U.S. Public*, pg. 530

KU-ZYME—NONE—Schwarz Pharma Inc.; *Int'l*, pg. 1211

KUBOTA—Tractors—Kubota Tractor Corp.; *Int'l*, pg. 762

KUCHEN-BETZ—Baked Sweet Snacks—Borden, Inc.; *U.S. Private*, pg. 157

KUDOS—Chocolate Covered Granola Bars—Mars, Incorporated; *U.S. Private*, pg. 707

KUDOS SNACK—NONE—M&M/Mars; *U.S. Private*, pg. 707

KUDROX—NONE—Schwarz Pharma Inc.; *Int'l*, pg. 1211

KUKIDENT—Denture Care—Reckitt & Colman plc; *Int'l*, pg. 1089

KUKUI—Jams & Jellies—C. Brewer & Company, Limited; *U.S. Private*, pg. 190

KULLASTRI—Women's Apparel—International Cosmetics Co., Ltd.; *Int'l*, pg. 684

KUMAGAI—Construction Machinery & Equip.—Kumagai Gumi Co., Ltd.; *Int'l*, pg. 763

KUNER—Food—Faribault Foods Inc.; *U.S. Private*, pg. 393

KUNER-EMPSON—Canned Vegetables—Kuner-Empson Company; *U.S. Private*, pg. 393

KUNTO—Rye Fiber Bomb—Cultor Ltd.; *Int'l*, pg. 349

KUPLER—Electrical Connector—Ilsco; *U.S. Private*, pg. 558

KUPPENHEIMER—Men's Apparel—Hartmarx Corporation; *U.S. Public*, pg. 795

KURALON—Polyvinyl Alcohol Fiber—Kuraray Co., Ltd.; *Int'l*, pg. 764

KURFEES—Paint—Progress Paint Mfg. Co.; *U.S. Private*, pg. 890

KURLASH—Eye Care Products—The Cook Bates Division; *Int'l*, pg. 815

KURMARK—Cigarettes—B.A.T Industries P.L.C.; *Int'l*, pg. 110

KURON—Weed & Brush Killer—The Dow Chemical Company; *U.S. Public*, pg. 522

KURT CHECK—SPC Measurements Computer Gaging System—Kurt Manufacturing Co. Inc.; *U.S. Private*, pg. 637

KURTA DIGITIZERS—NONE—Mutoh America Inc.; *Int'l*, pg. 897

KURTIS MSD—Meconium Suction Device—Vital Signs, Inc.; *U.S. Public*, pg. 1723

KURZ-KASCH—Plastics Processing & Technology—Kurz-Kasch, Inc.; *U.S. Private*, pg. 637

KUSHION KRAFT—Cellulose Wadding—Sealed Air Corporation; *U.S. Public*, pg. 1450

KUSTOM KING—Advertising Specialties & Business Gifts—The W.E. Bassett Company; *U.S. Private*, pg. 122

KUT—Cutting Fluids—Quaker Chemical Corporation; *U.S. Public*, pg. 1346

KUT-GUARD—Cut Resistant Gloves & Apparel—Eastco Industrial Safety Corp.; *U.S. Public*, pg. 548

KUTAPRESSIN—NONE—Schwarz Pharma Inc.; *Int'l*, pg. 1211

KUTRASE—NONE—Schwarz Pharma Inc.; *Int'l*, pg. 1211

KUTZIT—Paint Remover Liquid—The Savogran Company; *U.S. Public*, pg. 968

KWAN LOONG—NONE—Tiger Medicals Ltd.; *Int'l*, pg. 603

KWATTA—Chocolate Spread—Campbell Soup Company; *U.S. Public*, pg. 298

KWIC—Computerized Research Services—The Mead Corporation; *U.S. Public*, pg. 1074

KWIC NEWS—Publication—The Mead Corporation; *U.S. Public*, pg. 1074

KWIK—Nickel Cadium Batteries & Charger—Eastman Kodak Company; *U.S. Public*, pg. 550

KWIK—Release Hinges—Hartwell Corporation; *U.S. Private*, pg. 1168

KWIK BITS—Screwdriver Bits—Greenlee Textron; *U.S. Public*, pg. 1589

KWIK-BOLT—Anchors—Hilti Inc.; *Int'l*, pg. 620

KWIK CLAMP—Nylon Double Bond Hose Clamp—NewAge Industries Inc.; *U.S. Private*, pg. 796

KWIK CLAMPS—Plastic Clamps—Newage Industries Inc., Plastics Technology Group; *U.S. Private*, pg. 796

KWIK CYCLE—Crimper—Greenlee Textron; *U.S. Public*, pg. 1589

KWIK-DRAW—Solder—Kester Solder; *U.S. Public*, pg. 1003

KWIK-DRAW—Solder—Litton Industries, Inc.; *U.S. Public*, pg. 1002

KWIK-KOPY—Instant Printing Centers—International Center for Entrepreneurial Development, Inc.; *U.S. Private*, pg. 568

KWIK-LOK—Clamps—Standun, Inc.; *U.S. Private*, pg. 1032

KWIK PANTRY—Convenienvce Store—FFP Marketing Company, Inc.; *U.S. Public*, pg. 604

KWIK-SEAL—Caulk—DAP Inc.; *Int'l*, pg. 1486

KWIK SLITTER—Stripper—Greenlee Textron; *U.S. Public*, pg. 1589

KWIK STEPPER—Bits—Greenlee Textron; *U.S. Public*, pg. 1589

KWIK STRIPPER—Wire Stripper—Greenlee Textron; *U.S. Public*, pg. 1589

KWIK-TIP—Tooth Equipment for Earthmoving Buckets—Esco Corporation; *U.S. Private*, pg. 382

KWIK-TOG—Anchors—Hilti Inc.; *Int'l*, pg. 620

KWIKEE—Plastic Masking Products—Marson/Creative Fastener, Inc.; *U.S. Private*, pg. 708

KWIKEE KOLOR—Product Illustration System—Multi-Ad Services, Incorporated; *U.S. Private*, pg. 766

KWIKEE RECAS—Coop Information System—Multi-Ad Services, Incorporated; *U.S. Private*, pg. 766

KWIKEE SYSTEMS—Product Illustration System—Multi-Ad Services, Incorporated; *U.S. Private*, pg. 766

KWIKEEZE—Paint/Brush Cleaner—The Savogran Company; *U.S. Private*, pg. 968

KWIKHEAT—Soldering Irons—Litton Industries, Inc.; *U.S. Public*, pg. 1002

KWIKLOK—Clamps—Eagle Electric Mfg. Co., Inc.; *U.S. Private*, pg. 354

KWIKSET—Residential Door Hardware—The Black & Decker Corporation; *U.S. Public*, pg. 233

KWIKSET—Locksets—Kwikset Corporation; *U.S. Public*, pg. 233

KWIKURE—Glasteel Repair System—Pfaudler, Inc.; *U.S. Public*, pg. 1393

KYLE—Distribution Switchgear—Cooper Industries, Inc.; *U.S. Public*, pg. 442

KYLIAN—Beer—Heineken N.V.; *Int'l*, pg. 608

KYMENE—Synthetic Resin—Hercules Incorporated; *U.S. Public*, pg. 809

KYNAR—High Performance Plastics—Elf Atochem North America, Inc.; *Int'l*, pg. 445

KYNAR 500—Based Architectural Coatings—Elf Atochem North America, Inc.; *Int'l*, pg. 445

KYOCERA—Electronic Systems—Kyocera International, Inc.; *Int'l*, pg. 775

KYON—Metalcutting Tool Inserts—Kennametal Inc.; *U.S. Public*, pg. 950

KYSFOAM—Hinged Lid Containers—The Chinet Co.; *Int'l*, pg. 1146

KYSOR/WARREN—Refrigerator Display Equipment—Kysor/Warren; *U.S. Public*, pg. 1445

KYTRIL—NONE—SmithKline Beecham Corporation; *Int'l*, pg. 1264

KYTRIL—Gastrointestinal Drug—SmithKline Beecham plc; *Int'l*, pg. 1264

L

LA-CO LOC ANAEROBIC—Pipe Thread Sealant with Teflon—La-Co Industries Markal Company; *U.S. Private*, pg. 640

LA GEAR—Activewear—L.A. Gear, Inc.; *U.S. Public*, pg. 969

LA LIGHTS—Children—L.A. Gear, Inc.; *U.S. Public*, pg. 969

L. A. LOOKS—Styling Products & Hair Care Items—Dep Corporation; *U.S. Public*, pg. 500

L.A. MEX—NONE—Checkers Drive-In Restaurants, Inc.; *U.S. Public*, pg. 342

LAN/WAN EXCHANGE—Internetworking Product—Network Equipment Technologies, Inc.; *U.S. Public*, pg. 1168

LA RESTAURANTE—Tortilla Chips—Snyder Berlin; *U.S. Private*, pg. 887

LA TECH—Athletic—L.A. Gear, Inc.; *U.S. Public*, pg. 969

L & L—A Unique Dairy Spread—Morinaga Milk Industry Co., Ltd.; *Int'l*, pg. 895

L&M—Cigarettes—Liggett Group Inc.; *U.S. Public*, pg. 259

L & M—Cigarettes—Philip Morris Companies Inc.; *U.S. Public*, pg. 1287

L & N—NONE—Ruby Tuesday, Inc.; *U.S. Public*, pg. 1411

L & P—Bed Springs—Leggett & Platt, Incorporated; *U.S. Public*, pg. 985

L & R—Ultrasonic & Mechanical Cleaning Machines & Solutions—L&R Manufacturing Co.; *U.S. Private*, pg. 638

L&S—Bearings, Oil Seals, Motor Mounts—L & S Bearing Co.; *U.S. Public*, pg. 970

L-B-C—Lead Barrier Compound (Lead Paint Encapsulant)—California Products Corp.; *U.S. Private*, pg. 201

LBMGR—Computer Programs & Related Documentation—Beckman Instruments, Inc.; *U.S. Public*, pg. 199

LB SERIES—Line Printers—Dataproducts Corporation; *Int'l*, pg. 620

LB SERIES FUND, INC.—Variable Product Fund—Lutheran Brotherhood; *U.S. Private*, pg. 681

L-BAG—Packaging Material—Grace Packaging; *U.S. Public*, pg. 755

LC GC—Trade Periodical—Advanstar Communications; *U.S. Private*, pg. 22

LC GC INTERNATIONAL—Trade Periodical—Advanstar Communications; *U.S. Private*, pg. 22

LCA—Ammonia-iCi Process—KTI Group B.V.; *Int'l*, pg. 837

LCA—Logic Cell Array—Xilinx, Inc.; *U.S. Public*, pg. 1786

LCAD—Liquid Crystal Active Drive—Three-Five Systems; *U.S. Public*, pg. 1604

L.C. GERMAIN—Cutlery & Flatware—Lifetime Hoan Corp.; *U.S. Public*, pg. 992

LCID—Liquid Crystal Intense Display—Three-Five Systems; *U.S. Public*, pg. 1604

LCN CLOSERS—NONE—Ingersoll-Rand Company; *U.S. Public*, pg. 876

LCOS—Liquid Crystal On Silicon—Three-Five Systems; *U.S. Public*, pg. 1604

LCP—Ink Jet Systems—Marsh Company; *U.S. Private*, pg. 707

LC-PAD—Railroad Roller Bearing Adapter Mounts—Lord Corporation; *U.S. Private*, pg. 675

LC-PARTIGEN KITS—Immunodiffusion Reagents—Dade Behring Inc.; *U.S. Private*, pg. 110

LCS TOTAL KNEE SYSTEM—Orthopedic Product—DePuy, Inc.; *Int'l*, pg. 331

LC-65—Contact Lens Care Product—Allergan, Inc.; *U.S. Public*, pg. 46

LCV'S—NONE—Vauxhall; *U.S. Public*, pg. 724

LDA—Fuel Additive—The Lubrizol Corporation; *U.S. Public*, pg. 1016

LDD—NONE—Laserscope Surgical Systems; *U.S. Public*, pg. 979

LDF—Low Density Film—The Dow Chemical Company; *U.S. Public*, pg. 522

L D O—Lubricants—Amoco Corporation; *U.S. Public*, pg. 101

LDO MOTOR OIL—Motor Oil—Amoco Oil Company; *U.S. Public*, pg. 102

LDS—Software—LSI Logic Corp.; *U.S. Public*, pg. 971

LDS—Surgical Staplers—U.S. Surgical Corp.; *U.S. Public*, pg. 1687

LDS & LDM—Local Data Sets and Local Data Modem—Gandalf Technologies Inc.; *Int'l*, pg. 540

LDS 1—Software—LSI Logic Corp.; *U.S. Public*, pg. 971

LDS-2—Surgical Staplers—U.S. Surgical Corp.; *U.S. Public*, pg. 1687

LD 300—Tread Rubber Stock—Bridgestone/Firestone, Inc.; *Int'l*, pg. 213

LD 12—Universal Laser Detector—David White, L.L.C.; *U.S. Public*, pg. 1765

LD 12—Universal Laser Detector—David White, L.L.C.; *U.S. Private*, pg. 1765

LD-21—Laser Detector—David White, L.L.C.; *U.S. Public*, pg. 1765

LD-21—Laser Detector—David White, L.L.C.; *U.S. Private*, pg. 1765

L/E—Women's Golf Clubs—Square Two Golf Incorporated; *U.S. Public*, pg. 1501

L.E.S.S.—Intimate Apparel—Lily of France, Inc.; *U.S. Private*, pg. 140

L.E.X.—Texturized Fiber Glass Yarns for Cloth Manufacturing Applications—PPG Industries, Inc.; *U.S. Public*, pg. 1245

LF—Electronic Fuses—Littelfuse, Inc.; *U.S. Public*, pg. 1001

LFE—Display & Control Instruments—LFE Instruments; *U.S. Public*, pg. 482

LFH—NONE—Molex Incorporated; *U.S. Public*, pg. 1121

LF-P—Powdered Infant Formula—Morinaga Milk Industry Co., Ltd.; *Int'l*, pg. 895

LG—NONE—Bon Ton Foods, Inc.; *U.S. Private*, pg. 65

LG—Corn Seeds—Groupe Limagrain; *Int'l*, pg. 566

LGS LIGHT GUIDE SYSTEM—Family of Fiber-Optic Cable Management Products—The Lamson & Sessions Co.; *U.S. Public*, pg. 976

LGX—Fiber Optic Distributing System, Fiber Optic Distributing Frame—Lucent Technologies Inc.; *U.S. Public*, pg. 1017

LHR—Reflective Glass—PPG Industries, Inc.; *U.S. Public*, pg. 1245

LIL—Laboratories Interface Language—Beckman Instruments, Inc.; *U.S. Public*, pg. 199

LIMS 2000—Laboratory Information Mngmt. System—The Perkin-Elmer Corporation; *U.S. Public*, pg. 1279

LIX REAGENTS—Solvent Extraction Reagents—Henkel Corporation; *Int'l*, pg. 610

L L & E—Oil & Gas Exploration & Development Company—The Louisiana Land and Exploration Company; *U.S. Public*, pg. 269

L. L. BEAN—Sporting Specialties—L.L. Bean, Inc.; *U.S. Private*, pg. 639

LL 100—Laser Carpenters Level—David White, L.L.C.; *U.S. Public*, pg. 1765

LL 100—Laser Carpenters Level—David White, L.L.C.; *U.S. Private*, pg. 1765

LL 200—Laser Carpenters Level—David White, L.L.C.; *U.S. Public*, pg. 1765

LL 200—Laser Carpenters Level—David White, L.L.C.; *U.S. Private*, pg. 1765

L/M—Fertilizer—The Chas. H. Lilly Co.; *U.S. Private*, pg. 667

LMF—Survival Knife—Fiskars-Gerber; *Int'l*, pg. 492

L.M.I.—Pumps—Ryan Herco Products Corp.; *U.S. Private*, pg. 953

LMMP—Learjet Maintenance Management Program—Executive Jet Aviation, Inc.; *U.S. Private*, pg. 388

LM SERIES—Line Matrix Printers—Dataproducts Corporation; *Int'l*, pg. 620

LMX—NONE—Raychem Corporation; *U.S. Public*, pg. 1362

LNC—Lincoln National Corporation—Lincoln National Corporation; *U.S. Public*, pg. 997

LNDA—NONE—Pico Products, Inc.; *U.S. Public*, pg. 1294

LNRM—Lincoln National Risk Management—Lincoln National Corporation; *U.S. Public*, pg. 997

LN 700—Computer Control System—Honeywell, Inc.; *U.S. Public*, pg. 834

L.NET—Software—CACI International Inc; *U.S. Public*, pg. 272

L.O.C.—Liquid Organic Cleaner—Amway Corporation; *U.S. Private*, pg. 69

LODB—Valves—Masoneilan North American Operations; *U.S. Public*, pg. 528

L'OFFICE—Product Discriptor—Kaufman and Broad Home Corporation; *U.S. Public*, pg. 944

LP—Polymer—Morton International Inc.; *U.S. Public*, pg. 1134

LP—Liquid Polysulfide—Morton International Inc.; *U.S. Public*, pg. 1135

LPC—Logo/Name—Lincoln Property Company; *U.S. Private*, pg. 668

LPC 1—ASIC Microprocessor Chips—Imaging Technologies Corp.; *U.S. Public*, pg. 870

LP/GAS—Trade Periodical—Advanstar Communications; *U.S. Private*, pg. 22

LPH—Germicidal Detergent—Calgon Vestal Laboratories; *U.S. Public*, pg. 1515

LPRACT—Well Completion Concept Using Horizontal Drilling Technology—Nowsco Well Service Inc.; *Int'l*, pg. 990

LPZ—Adjustable Angle Conveyor—Dorner Manufacturing Corp.; *U.S. Private*, pg. 340

LP-3015—Laser Printer—Konica Corporation; *Int'l*, pg. 748

LP-3110—Laser Printer—Konica Corporation; *Int'l*, pg. 748

LQ-870—Dot Matrix Printer—Epson America Inc.; *Int'l*, pg. 1219

LQ-1170—Dot Matrix Printer—Epson America Inc.; *Int'l*, pg. 1219

LQ-570+—Dot Matrix Printer—Epson America Inc.; *Int'l*, pg. 1219

LQ-1070+—Dot Matrix Printer—Epson America Inc.; *Int'l*, pg. 1219

LQ-2550—Dot Matrix Printer—Epson America Inc.; *Int'l*, pg. 1219

LRC—Electronic Connectors, Adapters & Accessories—Thomas & Betts Corporation; *U.S. Public*, pg. 1597

LR-100—Electronic Support System—Amecom Div.; *U.S. Public*, pg. 1002

LRS—Process Application—Genus Inc.; *U.S. Public*, pg. 732

L ROTHSCHILD—Women's Wear—Lilli Ann Corporation; *U.S. Private*, pg. 582

L S AYRES—Department Stores—The May Department Stores Company; *U.S. Public*, pg. 1063

LSD—Steam Cleaning Detergent—Oakite Products, Inc.; *Int'l*, pg. 861

LS-8000—Hand Held Laser Scanner—Symbol Technologies, Inc.; *U.S. Public*, pg. 1546

LSF—Transparent Polyvinyl Chloride Film—Reynolds Metals Company; *U.S. Public*, pg. 1385

L-S 50 WATER SOLUBLE—Antibiotic—Pharmacia & Upjohn; *Int'l*, pg. 1048

LSI LOGIC LOGO DESIGN—Corporate Logo—LSI Logic Corp.; *U.S. Public*, pg. 971

LS-1—NONE—Brown & Sharpe Manufacturing Company; *U.S. Public*, pg. 260

LS SERIES—Underground Cable & Line Locators—Heath Consultants Incorporated; *U.S. Private*, pg. 518

LS-7000 II—Hand Held Laser Scanner—Symbol Technologies, Inc.; *U.S. Public*, pg. 1546

LS-6500—Fixed Mount Scanner—Symbol Technologies, Inc.; *U.S. Public*, pg. 1546

L.S. STUDIO—Shoes—Brown Group, Inc.; *U.S. Public*, pg. 262

L.S. STUDIO—Shoes—Brown Shoe Company; *U.S. Public*, pg. 262

LST—Lightweight Pocket Knives—Fiskars-Gerber; *Int'l*, pg. 492

LS-3100/4001—Fixed Mount Scanners—Symbol Technologies, Inc.; *U.S. Public*, pg. 1546

L SERIES—Wireless Microphones—Shure Brothers Incorporated; *U.S. Private*, pg. 997

LT—NONE—Linear Technology Corp.; *U.S. Public*, pg. 1000

LT—Heavy Van—Volkswagen AG; *Int'l*, pg. 1473

LTA—Transparent Glass & Plastic Laminate for Vehicle Window Applications—PPG Industries, Inc.; *U.S. Public*, pg. 1245

LTA/SECURITECT—Glass & Plastic Vehicle Window Laminate—PPG Industries, Inc.; *U.S. Public*, pg. 1245

LTC—NONE—Linear Technology Corp.; *U.S. Public*, pg. 1000

LTD—Beauty Salon Furniture—Belvedere Company; *U.S. Private*, pg. 1008

LTD—Lumber Transfer and Distribution Service—Conrail, Inc.; *U.S. Public*, pg. 431

LTD GRAPHITE—Fly Reel—Cortland Line Co., Inc.; *U.S. Private*, pg. 277

LTE 5000—Notebook Computer—COMPAQ Computer Corporation; *U.S. Public*, pg. 417

LT PIVERT—Perfume—Rhone-Poulenc S.A.; *Int'l*, pg. 1108

LTS—Liquid Treatment System—Isolyser Company, Inc.; *U.S. Public*, pg. 914

LTV—Diversified Company Engaged in Steel—The LTV Corporation; *U.S. Public*, pg. 971

LTX—Comapny Name—LTX Corporation; *U.S. Public*, pg. 972

L-TEC—Welding Machines—Esab AB; *Int'l*, pg. 281

L-289—Unmanned Airborne Surveillance Systems—Bombardier Inc.; *Int'l*, pg. 199

LU BISCUITS—Biscuits—Great Brands of Europe; *Int'l*, pg. 381

LUS—Life Underwriting System—Lincoln National Corporation; *U.S. Public*, pg. 997

LVS-4500—Direct Access Storage Devices (Unix & NT)—Amdahl Corporation; *Int'l*, pg. 527

LVT—Light Valves—Eastman Kodak Company; *U.S. Public*, pg. 550

LW PRIVATE RESERVE—Juliennes, Shoestrings, Thin Cuts, Regular Cuts, Steak House Fries—Lamb-Weston, Inc.; *U.S. Public*, pg. 427

LX—Luggage—American Tourister, Inc.; *U.S. Public*, pg. 1430

LXN—Multi-User Microcomputer—Tandem Computers Inc.; *U.S. Public*, pg. 417

LXT FAMILY—Disk Drives—Maxtor Corporation; *Int'l*, pg. 641

LX-300—Dot Matrix Printer—Epson America Inc.; *Int'l*, pg. 1219

LXX—Tires—Bridgestone/Firestone, Inc.; *Int'l*, pg. 213

LXX MACH 1—Tires—Bridgestone/Firestone, Inc.; *Int'l*, pg. 213

LYM-TECH—Clean Room Wipes—John R. Lyman Company; *U.S. Private*, pg. 683

LYS—Facial Tissue, Bathroom Tissue, Cocktail & Table Napkins—Kimberly-Clark Corporation; *U.S. Public*, pg. 958

LYT-ALL—Paint—Pratt & Lambert United, Inc.; *U.S. Public*, pg. 1466

LZ—Lubricating Additives—The Lubrizol Corporation; *U.S. Public*, pg. 1016

LZR 1200 SERIES—Laser Printers—Dataproducts Corporation; *Int'l*, pg. 620

LZR 2600 SERIES—Laser Printers—Dataproducts Corporation; *Int'l*, pg. 620

LATIN TRADE—Magazine Publication—Freedom Communication Inc.; *U.S. Private*, pg. 425

LA BONNE CUISINE—French Women's Interest Magazine—EMAP France; *Int'l*, pg. 451

LA CASA—Salsa—Ventre Packing Company, Inc.; *U.S. Private*, pg. 1135

LA CHEDDA—Cheese Sauce—Land O'Lakes, Inc.; *U.S. Private*, pg. 645

LA CHOY—Oriental Foods—ConAgra, Inc.; *U.S. Public*, pg. 425

LA CHOY—Oriental Foods—Hunt-Wesson, Inc.; *U.S. Public*, pg. 428

LA CHOY FROZEN FOODS—Frozen Entrees—ConAgra Frozen Food Company; *U.S. Public*, pg. 427

LA CIDRAIE—Cider—Groupe Pernod Ricard; *Int'l*, pg. 566

LA COCINA DE MCCORMICK—Seasonings & Sauces—McCormick/Schilling; *U.S. Public*, pg. 1066

LA COCINERA—Frozen Ready Meals—Danone Group; *Int'l*, pg. 379

LA COCINA—MexicanFoods—FTI Foodtech International Inc.; *Int'l*, pg. 476

LA CORONAS—Domestic Cigars—Consolidated Cigar Corporation; *U.S. Public*, pg. 399

LA COUPE—Hair Products—Playtex Beauty Care, Inc.; *U.S. Public*, pg. 1311

LA CROSS—Manicuring Implement & Other Beauty Accessories—Del Laboratories, Inc.; *U.S. Public*, pg. 494

LA DIFFERENCE—Brassieres—Lilyette Brassiere Co.; *U.S. Private*, pg. 697

LA DIVA—Domestic Grated Cheese & Whey Blend—Suprema Specialties, Inc.; *U.S. Public*, pg. 1541

LA DOOR—Interior French Doors—Wing Industries, Inc.; *U.S. Private*, pg. 1183

LA DUCHESSE—Eau de Vie—Groupe Pernod Ricard; *Int'l*, pg. 566

LA FAMIGLIA DI ROBERT MONDAVI—NONE—Robert Mondavi Winery, Inc.; *U.S. Public*, pg. 1393

LA FAMILIA—Pasta—Danone Group; *Int'l*, pg. 379

LA FAMOSA—Juices & Nectars—Borden, Inc.; *U.S. Private*, pg. 157

LA FAMOUS—Chilis, Dips, Sauces & Spices—Borden, Inc.; *U.S. Private*, pg. 157

LA FAMOUS—Tortilla Chips—Clover Club Foods, Inc.; *U.S. Private*, pg. 469

LA FEMME—Women's Apparel—International Cosmetics Co., Ltd.; *Int'l*, pg. 684

LA FINA—Salt—CYDSA S.A.; *Int'l*, pg. 246

LA-FLORA—Italian Dressing—Conway Import Co. Inc.; *U.S. Private*, pg. 272

LA FRANCE BRIGHTENER—NONE—The Dial Corporation; *U.S. Public*, pg. 505

LA INA—Sherry—Allied Domecq PLC; *Int'l*, pg. 62

LA INA—Sherry—Domecq Importers Inc.; *Int'l*, pg. 63

L.A. INTIMATES—NONE—Kellwood Company; *U.S. Public*, pg. 948

LA ITALIA—Italian Specialty Meats—Gallo/Galileo Salame; *U.S. Public*, pg. 1433

LA LECHERA—NONE—Nestle USA; *Int'l*, pg. 916

LA-LED—Steel Bar Products—LaSalle Steel Company; *U.S. Public*, pg. 1181

LA MACHINE—Food Processors—Regal Ware, Inc.; *U.S. Private*, pg. 917

LA MARINIERE—Sea Foods—Purdel, Cooperative Agro-Alimentaire; *Int'l*, pg. 1073

LA MARTINIQUE SALAD DRESSINGS—Salad Dressings—Reily Foods Company; *U.S. Private*, pg. 919

LA MODE—Sewing Kits—Carlyle Industries, Inc.; *U.S. Public*, pg. 1187

LA MONTE—Safety Paper—Georgia-Pacific Corporation; *U.S. Public*, pg. 735

LA MOTTE ESTATE—Wine—Distillers Corporation S.A.; *Int'l*, pg. 1129

LA NOUVELLE REVUE DU SON—French Sound Magazine—EMAP France; *Int'l*, pg. 451

LA OFICINA—Periodical—Penton Publishing, Inc.; *U.S. Public*, pg. 1306

LA PECHE ET LES POISSONS—French Outdoor Pursuits Magazine—EMAP France; *Int'l*, pg. 451

LA PERLA—Perfume—International Cosmetics Co., Ltd.; *Int'l*, pg. 684

Brand Name Index

LA PETITE ACADEMY—NONE—La Petite Academy Inc.; *U.S. Private*, pg. 640

LA PINA—Flour—General Mills, Inc.; *U.S. Public*, pg. 717

LA PREFERIDA—Ethnic Foods—La Preferida, Inc.; *U.S. Private*, pg. 640

LA PRIMERA—Sausages—Armour Swift Eckrich; *U.S. Public*, pg. 426

LA QUINTA INNS—Hotels—La Quinta Inns, Inc.; *U.S. Public*, pg. 972

LA RESTAURANTE—Chips & Salsa—Curtice Burns Foods; *U.S. Private*, pg. 887

LA REVUE NAT. DE LA CHASSE—French Outdoor Magazine—EMAP France; *Int'l*, pg. 451

LA ROSA—Biscuits—Nestle S.A.; *Int'l*, pg. 915

LA ROSSA—Beer—Labatt U.S.A.; *Int'l*, pg. 679

LA SALLE - THE BANK THAT WORKS—NONE—LaSalle National Bank; *Int'l*, pg. 10

LA SCALA—Loudspeaker Systems—Klipsch, Inc.; *U.S. Private*, pg. 626

LA SHAPEUR—Foundations—The Strouse, Adler Company; *U.S. Private*, pg. 1047

LA SORCIER—NONE—Avon Products Co., Ltd.; *U.S. Public*, pg. 156

LA SUPREMA—Tortilla Chips & Salsa—Curtice Burns Foods; *U.S. Private*, pg. 887

LA TOUR—Side Chair—Vecta; *U.S. Private*, pg. 1038

LA VICTORIA—Salsa & Sauces—La Victoria Foods, Inc.; *U.S. Private*, pg. 641

LA VOSGIENNE—Candy—Kraft Jacobs Suchard; *U.S. Public*, pg. 1290

LA VOSGIENNE—NONE—Philip Morris Companies Inc.; *U.S. Public*, pg. 1287

LA YOGURT—Refrigerated Yogurt—Johanna Foods Inc.; *U.S. Private*, pg. 589

LA YOGURT—Yogurt—Labatt Brewing Company Limited; *Int'l*, pg. 679

LA-Z-BOY—NONE—La-Z-Boy Incorporated; *U.S. Public*, pg. 972

LA-Z-REST—Rocker Recliner—La-Z-Boy Incorporated; *U.S. Public*, pg. 972

LA-Z-ROCKER—Swivel Rocker—La-Z-Boy Incorporated; *U.S. Public*, pg. 972

LA-Z-SLEEPER—Sofa Bed—La-Z-Boy Incorporated; *U.S. Public*, pg. 972

LA-Z-SOFA—Couch—La-Z-Boy Incorporated; *U.S. Public*, pg. 972

LA-Z-TOUCH—Massage Recliner—La-Z-Boy Incorporated; *U.S. Public*, pg. 972

LAAGLAND—Precision Machinery—Hunter Douglas N.V.; *Int'l*, pg. 639

LAARS LX HEATERS—NONE—Teledyne Laars/Jandy Products; *U.S. Public*, pg. 43

LAB FLO—Lab Faucets & Fittings—T & S Brass & Bronze Works, Inc.; *U.S. Private*, pg. 1061

LAB MANAGER—Computer Programs & Related Documentation—Beckman Instruments, Inc.; *U.S. Public*, pg. 199

LAB NEWS—Magazine—Reed Business Information Pty. Limited; *Int'l*, pg. 1094

LAB SEAL—Reclosable Specimen Bag w/ Pocket—KCL Corporation; *U.S. Private*, pg. 603

LAB-LARM—Alarm—Fisher Scientific Company; *U.S. Private*, pg. 658

LAB-PAC—Set of Analytical Reagents—Fisher Scientific Company; *U.S. Private*, pg. 658

LABARGE—Electronic Communications Equipment—LaBarge, Inc.; *U.S. Public*, pg. 973

LABATT BLEUE—Beer—La Brasserie Labatt Limitee; *Int'l*, pg. 679

LABATT BLEUE DRY—Beer—La Brasserie Labatt Limitee; *Int'l*, pg. 679

LABATT BLEUE LEGERE—Lager—La Brasserie Labatt Limitee; *Int'l*, pg. 679

LABATT BLUE—Beer—London Brewery; *Int'l*, pg. 679

LABATT BLUE LIGHT—Beer—London Brewery; *Int'l*, pg. 679

LABATT CELTIQUE—Beer—La Brasserie Labatt Limitee; *Int'l*, pg. 679

LABATT EXTRA DRY—Beer—La Brasserie Labatt Limitee; *Int'l*, pg. 679

LABATT EXTRA DRY—Beer—London Brewery; *Int'l*, pg. 679

LABATT 50—Beer—La Brasserie Labatt Limitee; *Int'l*, pg. 679

LABATT 50—Beer—London Brewery; *Int'l*, pg. 679

LABATT 50 LEGERE—Lager—La Brasserie Labatt Limitee; *Int'l*, pg. 679

LABATT 5—Beer—La Brasserie Labatt Limitee; *Int'l*, pg. 679

LABATT GENUINE DRAFT—Beer—London Brewery; *Int'l*, pg. 679

LABATT ICE BEER—Beer—La Brasserie Labatt Limitee; *Int'l*, pg. 679

LABATT ICE BEER—Beer—London Brewery; *Int'l*, pg. 679

JOHN LABATT CLASSIC—Beer—Labatt Brewing Company Limited; *Int'l*, pg. 679

JOHN LABATT CLASSIC LIGHT—Beer—Labatt Brewing Company Limited; *Int'l*, pg. 679

LABATT LITE—Beer—London Brewery; *Int'l*, pg. 679

LABATT MAXIMUM ICE—Beer—La Brasserie Labatt Limitee; *Int'l*, pg. 679

LABATT MAXIMUM ICE—Beer—London Brewery; *Int'l*, pg. 679

LABATT'S—Beer—Labatt Brewing Company Limited; *Int'l*, pg. 679

LABATT'S BLUE LIGHT—Beer—Labatt Brewing Company Limited; *Int'l*, pg. 679

LABATT'S 50—Ale—Labatt Brewing Company Limited; *Int'l*, pg. 679

LABATT'S LITE—Beer—Labatt Brewing Company Limited; *Int'l*, pg. 679

LABATT TWIST—Beer—La Brasserie Labatt Limitee; *Int'l*, pg. 679

LABATT VELVET CREAM PORTER—NONE—La Brasserie Labatt Limitee; *Int'l*, pg. 679

LABATT WILDCAT—Beer—La Brasserie Labatt Limitee; *Int'l*, pg. 679

LABATT WILDCAT—Beer—London Brewery; *Int'l*, pg. 679

LABATT WILDCAT DRY—Beer—La Brasserie Labatt Limitee; *Int'l*, pg. 679

LABATT WILDCAT LIGHT—Beer—La Brasserie Labatt Limitee; *Int'l*, pg. 679

LABATT WILDCAT LIGHT—Beer—London Brewery; *Int'l*, pg. 679

LABATT WILDCAT MOUNTAIN ALE—Ale—London Brewery; *Int'l*, pg. 679

LABATT WILDCAT STRONG—Beer—La Brasserie Labatt Limitee; *Int'l*, pg. 679

LABATT WILDCAT STRONG—Beer—London Brewery; *Int'l*, pg. 679

LABATT'S BLUE—Beer—Labatt U.S.A.; *Int'l*, pg. 679

LABATT'S BLUE LIGHT—Beer—Labatt U.S.A.; *Int'l*, pg. 679

LABATT'S 50 ALE—Ale—Labatt U.S.A.; *Int'l*, pg. 679

LABEL-AIRE—Automatic Labeling Equip.—Label-Aire Inc.; *U.S. Private*, pg. 641

LABEL DIRECTOR—Label Design Bar Code Software—Esselte Meto Kimball Systems; *Int'l*, pg. 460

LABEL DIRECTOR—Label Design & Database Software for Thermal Printers—Meto, USA; *Int'l*, pg. 460

LABEL PEN—Computer Software Marker—Sanford Corporation; *U.S. Public*, pg. 1178

LABEL PRINTING PLUS—Database Publishing and Electronic Printing—Group 1 Software, Inc.; *U.S. Public*, pg. 417

LABELFLEX—Polystyrene—Plastic Suppliers, Inc.; *U.S. Private*, pg. 871

LABELFLEX—Biaxially Oriented Polystyrene Plastic Label Film—Plastic Suppliers Inc.; *U.S. Private*, pg. 871

LABELGARD—Address Label & Packing List Attachment & Protection Tapes & Dispensers—3M; *U.S. Public*, pg. 1604

LABELIZER—Printing System—W.H. Brady Co.; *U.S. Public*, pg. 250

LABELLA'S—NONE—Galaxy Food Company; *U.S. Public*, pg. 697

LABELLO—NONE—Beiersdorf S.A.; *Int'l*, pg. 183

LABELPRO—NONE—Avery Dennison Corporation; *U.S. Public*, pg. 152

LABEL'R—Portable Labeling System—Kroy Inc.; *U.S. Public*, pg. 1339

LABET HERITAGE MERLOT/CABERNET—French Wine—Laird & Company; *U.S. Private*, pg. 642

LABET POULLY FUISSE—French Wine—Laird & Company; *U.S. Private*, pg. 642

LABET SAUVIGNON BLANC—French Wine—Laird & Company; *U.S. Private*, pg. 642

LABLEADER—Analytical Standard Materials—Eastman Kodak Company; *U.S. Public*, pg. 550

LABLYTE—Automated & Semi-Automated Clinical Chemistry Analyzers & Reagents—Beckman Instruments, Inc.; *U.S. Public*, pg. 199

LABMASTER—Filtration System—Serfilco, Ltd.; *U.S. Private*, pg. 985

LABMASTER II—Film Processor—Houston Fearless 76 Inc.; *U.S. Private*, pg. 542

LABOR SAVER—Coatings—Rust-Oleum Corporation; *U.S. Public*, pg. 1358

LABORATORY EQUIPMENT—Tabloid Featuring New Products for Scientists, Chemists & R&D Managers—Reed Elsevier Business Information; *Int'l*, pg. 1095

LABOTECH—NONE—BioChem Pharma Inc.; *Int'l*, pg. 196

LABRADOR—Spring Water—Danone Group; *Int'l*, pg. 379

LABRI-SEAL—Bearing Protectors—John Crane Mechanical Seals; *Int'l*, pg. 1339

LABSCO—Laboratory Supply Company—Laboratory Supply Company, Inc.; *U.S. Private*, pg. 641

LABTAP—Laboratory Fixtures—Bradley Corporation; *U.S. Private*, pg. 164

LABTRON—NONE—Graham-Field Health Products, Inc.; *U.S. Public*, pg. 757

LABWAVE 9000—NONE—CEM Corporation; *U.S. Public*, pg. 277

LAC-HYDRIN—Dermatological Therapy—Bristol-Myers Squibb Company; *U.S. Public*, pg. 253

LAC-HYDRIN FIVE—Dry Skin Care—Westwood-Squibb Pharmaceuticals Inc.; *U.S. Public*, pg. 255

LAC-TOL—NONE—Ballard Medical Products; *U.S. Public*, pg. 171

L'ACCOMMODEUR—Magazine—Quebecor Inc.; *Int'l*, pg. 1075

LACELON—Decorative Ribbon—3M; *U.S. Public*, pg. 1604

LACEYS—Ballerina Shoes—Oomphies, Inc.; *U.S. Private*, pg. 817

LACO—Pure, Imported Olive Oil—Pompeiian, Inc.; *U.S. Private*, pg. 875

LACOSTE—Men's Apparel—International Cosmetics Co., Ltd.; *Int'l*, pg. 684

LACPRODAN 60, 70, 80—Bio-Product—Kali-Chemie Aktiengesellschaft; *Int'l*, pg. 1278

LACRISERT—Hydroxypropyk Cellulose—Merck & Co., Inc.; *U.S. Public*, pg. 1090

LACROIX—Soups, Pates, Sauces—Campbell Soup Company; *U.S. Public*, pg. 298

LACSLATE—Insulation Board—The Dow Chemical Company; *U.S. Public*, pg. 522

LACTACYD—NONE—SmithKline Beecham Corporation; *Int'l*, pg. 1264

LACTAID—Milk Digestant—McNeil Consumer Products Company; *U.S. Public*, pg. 928

LACTAID—Milk—Q.U.F. Industries Ltd.; *Int'l*, pg. 1074

LACTALINS—Pharmaceuticals—Health Products Corporation; *U.S. Private*, pg. 514

LACTAN—Bakers' Sundries—Royal Gist-Brocades N.V.; *Int'l*, pg. 1142

LACTANIA—Milk Products—Labatt Brewing Company Limited; *Int'l*, pg. 679

LACTEC SERIES—Carbohydrate-electrolyte Solution—Otsuka Pharmaceutical Co., Ltd.; *Int'l*, pg. 1013

LACTEL—Dairy Products—Compagnie Laitiere BESNIER; *Int'l*, pg. 322

LACTICOL—Specialty Algin Blends—The NutraSweet Kelco Company; *U.S. Public*, pg. 1125

LACTO-PREP—Dairy Feed—Manna Pro Corporation; *U.S. Private*, pg. 700

LACTOFREE—Lactose-Free Infant Formula—Mead Johnson Nutritional Group; *U.S. Public*, pg. 254

LACTOGEN—Infant Foods & Dietetic Products—Nestle S.A.; *Int'l*, pg. 915

LACTOGEST—Digestive Aid—Thompson Medical Company, Inc.; *U.S. Private*, pg. 1083

LACTOMER—Surgical Staples—U.S. Surgical Corp.; *U.S. Public*, pg. 1687

LACTRASE—NONE—Schwarz Pharma Inc.; *Int'l*, pg. 1211

LACTRAY—Display Tray—The Dow Chemical Company; *U.S. Public*, pg. 522

LACY LUXURIES—Bras, Panties—Olga Div.; *U.S. Public*, pg. 1738

LACY TEXTURES—Bras, Panties—Olga Div.; *U.S. Public*, pg. 1738

LADALROD—Aluminum and Aluminum Alloy Rod—Reynolds Metals Company; *U.S. Public*, pg. 1385

LADD TRANSPORTATION—Trucking—Ladd Furniture, Inc.; *U.S. Public*, pg. 974

LADDER PLATFORMS—NONE—Bronto Skylift Oy AB; *U.S. Public*, pg. 617

LADDIE—Pencils—Dixon Ticonderoga Company; *U.S. Public*, pg. 514

LADIES' GEMS—NONE—Callaway Golf Company; *U.S. Public*, pg. 294

LADIES' HOME JOURNAL—Magazine—Ladies' Home Journal; *U.S. Public*, pg. 1094

LADIES' HOME JOURNAL—Magazine—Meredith Corporation; *U.S. Public*, pg. 1094

LADIES ONLY—Work & Garden Gloves—Boss Manufacturing Company; *U.S. Public*, pg. 1142

LADLE-KAST—Refractory—CFB Industries, Inc.; *U.S. Private*, pg. 194

LADLE-KAST—Refractory—Chicago Fire Brick Co.; *U.S. Private*, pg. 194

LADY—NONE—Jotun A/S; *Int'l*, pg. 714

LADY ASTER—Specialty Frozen Foods—Louis Kemp Seafood Co.; *U.S. Public*, pg. 1652

LADY BEN—Clocks—Westclox; *U.S. Private*, pg. 445

LADY BLAIR—Women's Apparel—Blair Corporation; *U.S. Public*, pg. 236

LADY BORDEN—Ice Cream—Borden, Inc.; *U.S. Private*, pg. 157

LADY BORDEN EXCELLENCE—Ice Cream—Borden, Inc.; *U.S. Private*, pg. 157

LADY BRAUN ELEGANCE—Electric Shaver—Braun, North America; *U.S. Public*, pg. 743

LADY BRAUN STYLE—Electric Shaver—Braun, North America; *U.S. Public*, pg. 743

LADY CAROLYN—Drinks—Home Juice Co.; *U.S. Private*, pg. 537

LADY CATHERINE—Hairbrush—Stanhome Inc.; *U.S. Public*, pg. 1508

LADY COBRA—Golf Clubs—Cobra Golf Incorporated; *U.S. Public*, pg. 675

LADY ESTHER—Facial Cream & Powder—Menley & James Laboratories, Inc.; *U.S. Public*, pg. 1086

LADY FOOT LOCKER—Women's Athletic Footwear & Apparel Stores—Kinney Shoe Corporation; *U.S. Public*, pg. 1777

LADY FOOT LOCKER—Women's Athletic Footwear & Apparel—Woolworth Corporation; *U.S. Public*, pg. 1777

LADY FOOT LOCKER CASUALS—Women's Casual Apparel—Woolworth Corporation; *U.S. Public*, pg. 1777

LADY HARDWICK—Clothing—Hardwick Clothes Inc.; *U.S. Private*, pg. 502

LADY KING COBRA—NONE—Fortune Brands, Inc.; *U.S. Public*, pg. 674

LADY LASER—Golf Equipment—RAM Golf Corporation; *U.S. Private*, pg. 908

LADY LEE—NONE—Eagle Food Centers, Inc.; *U.S. Public*, pg. 547

LADY PEPPERELL—Bed & Bath Accessories—WestPoint Stevens Inc.; *U.S. Public*, pg. 1762

LADY PLUS—Larger-Sized Women's Apparel Stores—Woolworth Corporation; *U.S. Public*, pg. 1777

LADY POWER ROLL-ON—Clear Anti-Perspirants—Chesebrough-Pond's USA Co.; *Int'l*, pg. 1435

LADY POWER STICK—Anti-Perspirant—Chesebrough-Pond's USA Co.; *Int'l*, pg. 1435

LADY REMINGTON—Electric Shavers—Remington Products Company, L.L.C.; *U.S. Private*, pg. 921

LADY SANSABELT—Slacks, Skirts, Shorts, Culottes & Blouses—Trans-Apparel Group; *U.S. Public*, pg. 796

LADY SEYMOUR—Housewares—Lear Siegler Diversified Holdings Corp.; *U.S. Private*, pg. 655

LADY SPEED DRY—Roll-On Anti-Perspirant—The Mennen Company; *U.S. Public*, pg. 397

LADY SPEED SMOOTH-ON—Anti-Perspirant—The Mennen Company; *U.S. Public*, pg. 397

LADY SPEED STICK—Anti-Perspirant—The Mennen Company; *U.S. Public*, pg. 397

LADY STETSON—Fragrance—Coty Inc.; *Int'l*, pg. 185

LADY SUPREME—Hosiery & Related Apparel—Mayer/Berkshire Corporation; *U.S. Private*, pg. 717

LADY WAHL—Shaver—Wahl Clipper Corp.; *U.S. Private*, pg. 1146

LADYBIRD—NONE—Coats Viyella plc; *Int'l*, pg. 299

LADYBUG—Gift Wrap—American Greetings Corporation; *U.S. Public*, pg. 77

LADYCARE—Vitamins & Minerals—Novo Nordisk A/S; *Int'l*, pg. 987

LADY'S CHOICE—Peanut Butters, Margarines, Pastas, Desserts, Baking Aids, Beverages—Bestfoods; *U.S. Public*, pg. 223

LADY'S CHOICE—Antiperspirant Deodorants—Carter-Wallace, Inc.; *U.S. Public*, pg. 309

LAFARGE—Cement, Concrete & Related Products—Lafarge Corporation; *Int'l*, pg. 788

LAFF LINES—Greeting Cards—American Greetings Corporation; *U.S. Public*, pg. 77

LAFF LINES—Greeting Cards—American Greetings U.S. Greeting Card Division; *U.S. Public*, pg. 78

LAFFY TAFFY—Candy—Nestle USA; *Int'l*, pg. 916

LAFORRE—Cosmetics—International Cosmetics Co., Ltd.; *Int'l*, pg. 684

LAGAVULIN—NONE—Guinness Plc; *Int'l*, pg. 412

LAGERFELD—Fragrance for Men—Elizabeth Arden Company; *Int'l*, pg. 1435

LAGERFELD PHOTO—Fragrance for Men—Elizabeth Arden Company; *Int'l*, pg. 1435

LAGO—Cross Court Training Shoe—K-Swiss Inc.; *U.S. Public*, pg. 937

LAGONDA—Auto—Aston Martin Lagonda of North America, Inc.; *U.S. Public*, pg. 664

LAGOON—Chocolates—Huhtamaki Oy; *Int'l*, pg. 638

LAGUNA—Boat—Sea Ray; *U.S. Public*, pg. 266

LAIDLAW—Contract Transportation—Laidlaw Transit, Inc; *Int'l*, pg. 259

L'AIGLON—Gifts, Belts, Leather Accessories—Swank, Inc.; *U.S. Public*, pg. 1543

L'AIMANT—Fragrance—Coty Inc.; *Int'l*, pg. 185

L'AIR DU TEMPS—Women's Fragrance—Accecones Ricci U.S.A., Inc.; *Int'l*, pg. 445

LAIRD'S—Vodka & Gin—Laird & Company; *U.S. Private*, pg. 642

LAIRD'S APPLEJACK—Brandy—Laird & Company; *U.S. Private*, pg. 642

LAIRD'S BOTTLED IN BOND APPLE BRANDY—Apple Brandy—Laird & Company; *U.S. Private*, pg. 642

LAIRD'S RARE OLD BRANDY—Brandy—Laird & Company; *U.S. Private*, pg. 642

LAIT GUIGOZ—Infant Food—Nestle S.A.; *Int'l*, pg. 915

LAITRAM MACHINERY—Shrimp Processing Machinery—The Laitram Corporation; *U.S. Private*, pg. 643

LAKE COUNTRY—Wine—Canandaigua Wine Co.; *U.S. Public*, pg. 300

LAKE COUNTY (IL) BUSINESS DIRECTORY—Directory—Manufacturers' News, Inc.; *U.S. Private*, pg. 700

LAKE FOREST EXTERIORS—Kynar Coated Cedar-Look Siding & Accessories—Alcoa Building Products, Inc.; *U.S. Public*, pg. 61

LAKE MATE—Cutlery—Buck Knives, Inc.; *U.S. Private*, pg. 177

LAKE NIAGARA—Wine & Grape Juice—Widmer's Wine Cellars, Inc.; *U.S. Public*, pg. 300

LAKE PLACID GROVES—Citrus Groves & Packers—Consolidated-Tomoka Land Co.; *U.S. Public*, pg. 437

LAKE PLACID ICE SKATES—Ice Skates—Roller Derby Skate Corp.; *U.S. Private*, pg. 941

LAKELAND—Nurseries Sales—Hanover Direct Pennsylvania, Inc.; *U.S. Public*, pg. 782

LAKEROL—Pastilles—Huhtamaki Oy; *Int'l*, pg. 638

LAKESIDE—House Mark—The Dow Chemical Company; *U.S. Public*, pg. 522

LAKESIDE—NONE—Lakeside Foods, Inc.; *U.S. Private*, pg. 643

LAKEWOOD—Converting Paper—Boise Cascade Corporation; *U.S. Public*, pg. 242

LAKEWOOD—Power Transmission—Echlin Inc.; *U.S. Public*, pg. 560

LAKOLENE—FD&C Lake—Warner-Jenkinson Co.; *U.S. Public*, pg. 1696

LAKRISAL—NONE—Huhtamaki Oy; *Int'l*, pg. 638

LALIQUE—Crystal, Perfume, Leather Accessories, & Jewelry—Lalique North America; *Int'l*, pg. 797

LAM—Lighting—JJI Lighting Group Inc.; *Int'l*, pg. 821

LAM—NONE—Lam Research Corporation; *U.S. Public*, pg. 975

LAMA—Lamb Feed—Manna Pro Corporation; *U.S. Private*, pg. 700

LAMAL—Packaging Adhesive—Morton International Inc.; *U.S. Public*, pg. 1135

LAMALITE—Laminated Sheets of Aluminum—Reynolds Metals Company; *U.S. Public*, pg. 1385

LAMB—Electric Motors—AMETEK, Inc.; *U.S. Public*, pg. 99

LAMB—Europe—Enterprises International Inc.; *U.S. Private*, pg. 377

LAMB—North America—Enterprises International Inc.; *U.S. Private*, pg. 377

LAMB—Machine Tools—Litton Industries, Inc.; *U.S. Public*, pg. 1002

LAMB'S NAVY RUM—NONE—Allied Domecq Spirits & Wine (UK) Ltd.; *Int'l*, pg. 63

LAMB'S SEASONED—NONE—Lamb-Weston, Inc.; *U.S. Public*, pg. 427

LAMBDA—NONE—Brown & Sharpe Manufacturing Company; *U.S. Public*, pg. 260

LAMBDA—Power Supply Products—Lambda Electronics Inc.; *Int'l*, pg. 1241

LAMBDA—Lube-Free Roller Chain—U.S. Tsubaki, Inc.; *Int'l*, pg. 1425

LAMBDA FASTRACK—Computer Programmable IEEE-488 Power Systems—Lambda Electronics Inc.; *Int'l*, pg. 1241

LAMBDACARD—Din, VME-type power supplies—Lambda Electronics Inc.; *Int'l*, pg. 1241

LAMBERT & BUTLER—Cigarettes—Hanson PLC; *Int'l*, pg. 592

LAMBERT & BUTLER—100s King Size Low Tar Filter Cigarettes—Imperial Tobacco Group, Ltd.; *Int'l*, pg. 666

LAMBERT KAY—Pet Products—Carter-Wallace, Inc.; *U.S. Public*, pg. 309

LAMBERTS—Vitamins & Minerals—Novo Nordisk A/S; *Int'l*, pg. 987

LAMBI—Tissue Paper—Metsa-Serla Corporation; *Int'l*, pg. 863

LAMBORGHINI DIABLO—Car—Chrysler Corporation; *U.S. Public*, pg. 352

LAMB'S CRISPYCOAT—Shoestrings, Thin Cuts, Regular Cuts, CrissCut Fries—Lamb-Weston, Inc.; *U.S. Public*, pg. 427

LAMB'S NATURAL—Thin Cut, Regular Cut, CrissCuts, Wedges, Munchstrips, Munchskins—Lamb-Weston, Inc.; *U.S. Public*, pg. 427

LAMBS NAVY RUM—Spirit—Allied Domecq PLC; *Int'l*, pg. 62

LAMB'S PALE GOLD RUM—Rum—Allied Domecq PLC; *Int'l*, pg. 62

LAMB'S RANCH RECIPE—Wedge Cuts—Lamb-Weston, Inc.; *U.S. Public*, pg. 427

LAMB'S SOUTHERN STYLE RECIPE—Wedge Cuts, Tater Babies—Lamb-Weston, Inc.; *U.S. Public*, pg. 427

LAMB'S STEALTH FRIES—Shoestrings, Thin Cuts, Regular Cuts, Oven Shoestrings, CrissCut Fries—Lamb-Weston, Inc.; *U.S. Public*, pg. 427

LAMB'S SUPREME—Hi-Fries, Shoestrings, Thin Cuts, Regular Cuts, Steak House Fries—Lamb-Weston, Inc.; *U.S. Public*, pg. 427

LAMB'S SUPREME MASHED POTATOES—Original, Lightly Seasoned, Seasoned, Seasoned with Chives—Lamb-Weston, Inc.; *U.S. Public*, pg. 427

LAMCHORD—Composite Wood—Weyerhaeuser Forest Products Company; *U.S. Public*, pg. 1764

LAMDEK—Fiber-Optic Connectors & Equipment—Eastman Kodak Company; *U.S. Public*, pg. 550

LAMI-BOARD—Laminated Hardboard—Georgia-Pacific Corporation; *U.S. Public*, pg. 735

L'AMI DES JARDINS—French Gardening Magazine—EMAP France; *Int'l*, pg. 451

LAMI-FLOOR—Laminated Hardboard Flooring—Georgia-Pacific Corporation; *U.S. Public*, pg. 735

LAMICTAL—Anti-Epileptic—Glaxo Wellcome PLC; *Int'l*, pg. 553

LAMIGLASS—Flat Glass—PPG Industries, Inc.; *U.S. Public*, pg. 1245

Brand Name Index

LAMILUX—Corrugated Carton Stock—Georgia-Pacific Corporation; *U.S. Public*, pg. 735

LAMINA—NONE—Anchor Lamina Inc.; *Int'l*, pg. 75

LAMINAR HL—Wet Lamination Dry Film Photo Resists—Morton International Inc.; *U.S. Public*, pg. 1134

LAMINAR X500—Aerospace Coating—The Dexter Corporation; *U.S. Public*, pg. 504

LAMINEER—Processed Lumber—Weyerhaeuser Forest Products Company; *U.S. Public*, pg. 1764

LAMIN8—Solventless Film Laminating Adhesive—H.B. Fuller Company; *U.S. Public*, pg. 686

LAMISIL—Oral & Topical Anti-Fungal Compound—Novartis AG; *Int'l*, pg. 971

LAMISIL—Anti-Fungal—Sandoz Pharmaceuticals Corp.; *Int'l*, pg. 974

LAMISOY—Food Product—Honeymead Products Co.; *U.S. Private*, pg. 537

LAMISTAT—Anti-Static Work Surface—IAC Industries; *U.S. Private*, pg. 553

LAMOT LAGER—Lager—Bass PLC; *Int'l*, pg. 169

LAMOT PILS—Lager—Bass PLC; *Int'l*, pg. 169

LAMP POST PIZZA—Restaurants—Lamp Post Franchise Corporation; *U.S. Private*, pg. 644

LAMPENIER—Lightning—RetailNet B.V.; *Int'l*, pg. 750

LAMPRENE—NONE—Novartis Pharmaceuticals; *Int'l*, pg. 973

LAMPREP—Flexible Wood Block Mat—Baltek Corporation; *U.S. Public*, pg. 171

LAMSON HOME PRODUCTS—Consumer Products—The Lamson & Sessions Co.; *U.S. Public*, pg. 976

LAMSTATION—NONE—Lam Research Corporation; *U.S. Public*, pg. 975

LAN—Magazine—Miller Freeman Inc.; *Int'l*, pg. 1443

LAN CHILE—Airlines—LanChile Airlines; *U.S. Private*, pg. 645

LAN DISTANCE—Computer System—International Business Machines Corporation; *U.S. Public*, pg. 895

LAN MAGAZINE—NONE—EMAP Business Communications Division; *Int'l*, pg. 451

LAN MANAGEMENT TOOLS—Computer Hardware & Software Prods. for Local Area Network Admin.—Datapoint Corporation; *Int'l*, pg. 384

LAN-O-SHEEN—Fine Fabric Cleaner—Lan-O-Sheen, Inc.; *U.S. Private*, pg. 645

LAN-O-SOFT—Soft Water Soap Prod.—Lan-O-Sheen, Inc.; *U.S. Private*, pg. 645

LAN-O-WIPE—Hard Surface Cleaner—Lan-O-Sheen, Inc.; *U.S. Private*, pg. 645

LAN-PAC—LAN Power Source—Reliability Incorporated; *U.S. Public*, pg. 1373

LAN*TMS—Router—General Datacomm Industries, Inc.; *U.S. Public*, pg. 708

LAN/WAN OPTIMIZER—Internetworking Data Compressors—Telco Systems, Inc.; *U.S. Public*, pg. 1568

LAN-RINGER—Stretch Packaging Systems—Lantech Inc.; *U.S. Private*, pg. 650

LAN-WRAPPER—Stretch Wrapping Systems—Lantech Inc.; *U.S. Private*, pg. 650

LANABIOTIC—Triple Antibiotic Creme—Combe Incorporated; *U.S. Private*, pg. 257

LANACANE—Cream Medication—Combe Incorporated; *U.S. Private*, pg. 257

LANACORT—Hydrocortisone Preparation—Combe Incorporated; *U.S. Private*, pg. 257

LANAI—Lumber & Wood Products—Georgia-Pacific Corporation; *U.S. Public*, pg. 735

LANASET—Dyeing System for Wool—Ciba Specialty Chemicals; *Int'l*, pg. 291

LANASET—Dyeing System for Wool—Novartis; *Int'l*, pg. 972

LANASYN—Wool—Clariant International Ltd.; *Int'l*, pg. 624

LANCASHIRE DAIRIES—Whole Milk—Lancashire Dairies Ltd.; *Int'l*, pg. 798

LANCASTER—Glass—Lancaster Glass Corporation; *U.S. Public*, pg. 977

LANCASTER—Fragrance, Skin Care, Sun Care & Color Cosmetics—Lancaster Group Worldwide; *Int'l*, pg. 185

LANCASTER—Bond Paper—The Mead Corporation; *U.S. Public*, pg. 1074

LANCASTER—Chewing Tobacco—Swisher International Group, Inc.; *U.S. Public*, pg. 1543

LANCASTER BRAND—Fresh, Frozen, Smoked Meats & Prepared Dinners—American Stores Company; *U.S. Public*, pg. 92

LANCASTER FOODS INC.—Wholesale Distributorship—Guest Services, Inc.; *U.S. Private*, pg. 486

LANCE—Remanufactured Auto Replacement Parts—Arrow Automotive Industries, Inc.; *U.S. Public*, pg. 133

LANCE—Packaged Food Prods.—Lance, Inc.; *U.S. Public*, pg. 977

LANCE—NONE—Oshkosh Truck Corporation; *U.S. Public*, pg. 1233

LANCELOT—Mold Inhibitor—Mallet & Co.; *U.S. Private*, pg. 698

LANCELOT—Pen—Pentel of America, Ltd.; *Int'l*, pg. 1035

LANCER 2000—Modular Power Base Wheelchair—Everest & Jennings, Inc.; *U.S. Public*, pg. 758

LANCERS—Wine—Grand Metropolitan Plc; *Int'l*, pg. 408

LANCERS—NONE—Lancers; *Int'l*, pg. 411

LANCERS WINE—Wine—Heublein Inc.; *Int'l*, pg. 410

LANCERS WINES—Wines—Heublein, Inc.; *Int'l*, pg. 410

LANCHEM—Coatings—Akzo Nobel Inc.; *Int'l*, pg. 47

LANCIA—Automobile—Fiat Auto SpA; *Int'l*, pg. 480

LANCOME—Cosmetics—Cosmair, Inc.; *Int'l*, pg. 818

LANCOME—NONE—L'Oreal Parfumerie; *Int'l*, pg. 819

LANCOME—Toiletries, Cosmetics—L'Oreal S.A.; *Int'l*, pg. 818

LANCONNECTIONS—Computer Equipment—Black Box Corporation of PA; *U.S. Public*, pg. 235

LAND CRUISER—Trucks & Buses—Toyota Motor Corporation; *Int'l*, pg. 1411

LAND CRUISER—Sport Utility—Toyota Motor Sales, U.S.A., Inc.; *Int'l*, pg. 1412

LAND FILL—Tires—Bridgestone/Firestone, Inc.; *Int'l*, pg. 213

LAND-N-LAKES—Mens Apparel—Gordon & Ferguson of Delaware, Inc.; *U.S. Private*, pg. 465

LAND O LAKES—Food & Agricultural Supply Prods.—Land O'Lakes, Inc.; *U.S. Private*, pg. 645

LAND-O-SUN—Dairy Products—Land-O-Sun Dairies, Inc.; *U.S. Private*, pg. 646

LAND PRIDE—Implements for Tractors up to 65 hp.—Great Plains Manufacturing, Inc.; *U.S. Private*, pg. 475

LAND ROVER—4WD Vehicle—British Aerospace p.l.c.; *Int'l*, pg. 217

LAND ROVER NINETY—4WD Vehicle—British Aerospace p.l.c.; *Int'l*, pg. 217

LAND ROVER ONE TEN—4WD Vehicle—British Aerospace p.l.c.; *Int'l*, pg. 217

LAND ROVER OWNER INTERNATIONAL—Magazine—EMAP Nationals; *Int'l*, pg. 451

LANDCOMMANDER—Disk Chisel—Brillion Iron Works, Inc.; *U.S. Public*, pg. 933

LANDER—Toiletries—Lander Co., Inc.; *U.S. Private*, pg. 647

LANDINI—Tractors—AGCO Corporation; *U.S. Public*, pg. 28

LANDIS—Grinding Machines—Landis; *U.S. Public*, pg. 1699

LANDIS—Cylindrical Grinding Machines—Litton Industries, Inc.; *U.S. Public*, pg. 1002

LANDMARK—Midline Catheters—Johnson & Johnson Medical, Inc.; *U.S. Public*, pg. 928

LANDMARK—Lighting Fixtures—Kaufel Group Ltd.; *Int'l*, pg. 724

LANDMARK—Temperature Systems—Land Instruments International Ltd.; *Int'l*, pg. 798

LANDMARK—NONE—Landmark Graphics Corporation; *U.S. Public*, pg. 776

LANDMARK—Beer—Minnesota Brewing Company; *U.S. Public*, pg. 1115

LANDMARK BANCORP—NONE—California State Bank-La Habra; *U.S. Public*, pg. 294

LANDMARK BANK—NONE—California State Bank-La Habra; *U.S. Public*, pg. 294

LANDMARK GEODATA WORKS—NONE—Landmark Graphics Corporation; *U.S. Public*, pg. 776

LANDMARK OPAQUE—Uncoated Printing & Writing Paper—Georgia-Pacific Corporation; *U.S. Public*, pg. 735

LANDMARK SHINGLE—Asphalt Roofing—CertainTeed Corporation; *Int'l*, pg. 1170

LANDMARK SYSTEMS—Software Developer—Landmark Systems Corporation; *U.S. Private*, pg. 649

LANDMASTER—Herbicide—Monsanto Company; *U.S. Public*, pg. 1124

LANDP—Computer System—International Business Machines Corporation; *U.S. Public*, pg. 895

LANDRY'S SEAFOOD HOUSE—Restaurant Chain—Landry's Seafood Restaurants Inc.; *U.S. Public*, pg. 977

LANDS' END—Logo—Lands' End, Inc.; *U.S. Public*, pg. 977

LANDS' END DIRECT MERCHANTS—Logo—Lands' End, Inc.; *U.S. Public*, pg. 977

LANDS' END LIGHTHOUSE—Logo—Lands' End, Inc.; *U.S. Public*, pg. 977

LANDS' END NOT QUITE PERFECT STORE—Store—Lands' End, Inc.; *U.S. Public*, pg. 977

LANDS' END OUTLET—Logo—Lands' End, Inc.; *U.S. Public*, pg. 977

LANDSCAN—Infrared Linescan Systems—Land Instruments International Ltd.; *Int'l*, pg. 798

LANDSCAPE MANAGEMENT—Trade Periodical—Advanstar Communications; *U.S. Private*, pg. 22

LANDSLIDE—D.E. Filter with Ring-Lok Access—Jacuzzi Bros, Jacuzzi, Inc.; *U.S. Public*, pg. 1684

LANDSMAN—Tillage Equip.—Krause Plow Corp.; *U.S. Private*, pg. 635

LANDSWEAVE—Sportshirts—Lands' End, Inc.; *U.S. Public*, pg. 977

LANE—Hardware—The Black & Decker Corporation; *U.S. Public*, pg. 233

LANE—Furniture—Furniture Brands International Inc.; *U.S. Public*, pg. 688

LANE AVENUE—Show Cases—Columbus Show Case Company; *U.S. Private*, pg. 257

LANE BRYANT—Women's Specialty Apparel Stores—Lane Bryant; *U.S. Public*, pg. 995

LANEX—Intensifying Screens—Eastman Kodak Company; *U.S. Public*, pg. 550

LANEXPRESS—For Remote PC Users Acessing a Corporate LAN—Microcom; *U.S. Public*, pg. 417

LANGE—Hockey Equipment—Bauer Sports Inc.; *U.S. Public*, pg. 1184

LANGIS—Cocktail Mix/Bouillon—Lever Brothers Co.; *Int'l*, pg. 1435

LANGIS—Cocktail Mix/Bouillon—Unilever Plc; *Int'l*, pg. 1433

LANGUAGE ENVIRONMENT—Computer Product—International Business Machines Corporation; *U.S. Public*, pg. 895

LANGUAGE MASTER—Electronic Dictionary, Thesaurus & Phonetic Speller—Franklin Electronic Publishers, Inc.; *U.S. Public*, pg. 679

LANGUAGE MASTER 4000—Electronic Dictionary—Franklin Electronic Publishers, Inc.; *U.S. Public*, pg. 679

LANGURU—Network Analyzer & Monitoring Services—Network Associates, Inc.; *U.S. Public*, pg. 1168

LANIER DIGITAL LOGGER—NONE—Lanier Worldwide Inc.; *U.S. Public*, pg. 791

LANIER LINK—Facsimile Network Server—Lanier Worldwide Inc.; *U.S. Public*, pg. 791

LANIER 6000 SERIES—Copying Systems—Lanier Worldwide Inc.; *U.S. Public*, pg. 791

LANIERFAX—Facsimile Unit—Lanier Worldwide Inc.; *U.S. Public*, pg. 791

LANITOP—Glycoside—Boehringer Mannheim GmbH; *Int'l*, pg. 331

LANJARON—Mineral Water—Danone Group; *Int'l*, pg. 379

LANKYD—Alkyd Resins—Akzo Nobel N.V.; *Int'l*, pg. 42

LANLINE—Remote Access—Gandalf Technologies Inc.; *Int'l*, pg. 540

LANMARK—NONE—Sulcus Computer Corp.; *U.S. Public*, pg. 1527

LANNATE—Insecticides—Du Pont (E.I. Du Pont De Nemours & Co.); *U.S. Public*, pg. 530

LANOLIN PLUS—Hair Care & Skin Care Products—Hazel Bishop International; *U.S. Private*, pg. 514

LANOLINE—Skin Care Product—Glaxo Wellcome PLC; *Int'l*, pg. 553

LANOSAN—Dermal Function Bath Lotion—Wella Group; *Int'l*, pg. 1489

LANOXICAPS—Prescription Cardiac Stimulant—Glaxo Wellcome PLC; *Int'l*, pg. 553

LANOXIN—Prescription Cardiac Stimulant—Glaxo Wellcome PLC; *Int'l*, pg. 553

LANPAK—Local Area Netowrk Manager for Novell, 3COM & IBM Networks—Computer Associates International, Inc.; *U.S. Public*, pg. 420

LANSBURY HOTELS—Hotels—Whitbread PLC; *Int'l*, pg. 1498

LANSDOWNE—Weather Instrument—Swift Instruments, Inc.; *U.S. Private*, pg. 1058

LANSTAR—Local Data Communications Equip.—Northern Telecom Limited; *Int'l*, pg. 968

LANSTEP—Network Operating System—Hayes Microcomputer Products, Inc.; *U.S. Public*, pg. 801

LANSTREAMER—Computer Product—International Business Machines Corporation; *U.S. Public*, pg. 895

LANTASTIC—Local Area Network—Artisoft, Inc.; *U.S. Public*, pg. 136

LANTEK/LANTEK PRO XL—Category 5 Cable Tester—Wavetek Corporation; *U.S. Private*, pg. 1154

LANVAL—NONE—L'Oreal Parfumerie; *Int'l*, pg. 819

LANVIN—Men's Tailored Clothing—Hartmarx Corporation; *U.S. Public*, pg. 795

LANVIN—Perfumes—L'Oreal S.A.; *Int'l*, pg. 818

LANVIN LUNETTES—European Eyewear—Logo of the Americas; *Int'l*, pg. 462

LANVIN STUDIO—Men's Tailored Clothing—Hartmarx Corporation; *U.S. Public*, pg. 795

LANZ—Respiratory Therapy Care & Inhalation Therapy Products—Mallinckrodt Inc.; *U.S. Public*, pg. 1039

LANZ OF SALZBURG—Sleepwear—Lanz, Inc.; *U.S. Private*, pg. 650

LANZ ORGINALS—Dresses—Lanz, Inc.; *U.S. Private*, pg. 650

LANZA—Laundry Detergent—Benckiser Consumer Products Inc.; *Int'l*, pg. 185

LAPAROVAC—NONE—Laserscope Surgical Systems; *U.S. Public*, pg. 979

LAPEYRE—Industrial Joinery—Poliet; *Int'l*, pg. 1177

LAPEYRE STAIR—Alternating Tread Stair—The Laitram Corporation; *U.S. Private*, pg. 643

LAPHROAIG ISLAY MALT SCOTCH WHISKEY—Spirit—Allied Domecq PLC; *Int'l*, pg. 62

LAPHROAIG SINGLE MALT SCOTCH—Scotch—Hiram Walker; *Int'l*, pg. 63

LAPIEQUI CHANTE—Candies—Danone Group; *Int'l*, pg. 379

LAPORA—Jewelry—Litton Industries, Inc.; *U.S. Public*, pg. 1002

LAPPO LUMBER—NONE—Wickes Inc.; *U.S. Public*, pg. 1391

LAPRA-TY—Suture Clip—Ethicon, Inc.; *U.S. Public*, pg. 928

LAPRO—Slab Saw—Buehler, Limited; *U.S. Public*, pg. 574

LAPROSTAT—NONE—Laserscope Surgical Systems; *U.S. Public*, pg. 979

LAPTRAN—Fungicide—The Dow Chemical Company; *U.S. Public*, pg. 522

LARAMIE—Sunglasses—Bausch & Lomb Incorporated; *U.S. Public*, pg. 194

LARCH-LAP—Garden Fences—Newmond PLC; *Int'l*, pg. 924

L'ARCHE—Highway Restaurants—Accor S.A.; *Int'l*, pg. 20

LAREDO—Film Cleaning Equipment—Eastman Kodak Company; *U.S. Public*, pg. 550

LAREDO—Boots—Genesco Inc.; *U.S. Public*, pg. 728

LAREDO MORNING TIMES—Newspaper—The Hearst Corporation; *U.S. Private*, pg. 515

LARENSTAN—Area Rug—Couristan Inc.; *U.S. Private*, pg. 279

LARGE ANIMAL PHARMACEUTICALS—NONE—Schering-Plough Animal Health; *U.S. Public*, pg. 1438

LARGE LUXURY CARS—NONE—Ford Motor Co. of Canada Ltd; *U.S. Public*, pg. 666

LARGO—Rattan Furniture—Avon Workshop Ficks Reed; *U.S. Private*, pg. 102

LARGO—Car—Nissan Motor Co., Ltd.; *Int'l*, pg. 943

LARIAM—Antimalarial—Roche Holding Ltd.; *Int'l*, pg. 1119

LARIAT—NONE—Ballard Medical Products; *U.S. Public*, pg. 171

LARIAT—Herbicide—Monsanto Company; *U.S. Public*, pg. 1124

THE LARIAT—Meat Hanging Rope—Outdoor Technologies Group; *U.S. Private*, pg. 822

LARIL—NONE—Lati Industria Termoplastici S.p.A.; *Int'l*, pg. 804

LARIN—Chocolate Candy—The Quaker Oats Company; *U.S. Public*, pg. 1347

LARK—Cigarettes—Liggett Group Inc.; *U.S. Public*, pg. 259

LARK—3 & 4 Wheeled Scooters—Ortho-Kinetics, Inc.; *U.S. Private*, pg. 820

LARK—Cigarettes—Philip Morris Companies Inc.; *U.S. Public*, pg. 1287

LARK—Luggage—Samsonite Corporation; *U.S. Public*, pg. 1430

LARKIN—Refrigeration Products—Heatcraft, Inc.-Refrigeration Products Division; *U.S. Private*, pg. 659

LARKWOOD FARMS—Poultry—ConAgra Poultry Co.; *U.S. Public*, pg. 427

LA ROCHE—NONE—L'Oreal Parfumerie; *Int'l*, pg. 819

LAROCHE AUX FEES—Refrigerated Products—Nestle S.A.; *Int'l*, pg. 915

LAROSTAT—Antistatic Agent for use in Synthetic Fibers, Fiberglass & Plastics—PPG Industries, Inc.; *U.S. Public*, pg. 1245

LAROTID—Pharmaceutical Prods.—SmithKline Beecham Laboratories; *Int'l*, pg. 1264

LARRY KING LIVE—Talk Radio Program—Westwood One Entertainment; *U.S. Public*, pg. 1763

LARRY KING LIVE—Talk Show—Westwood One, Inc.; *U.S. Public*, pg. 1763

LARRY KING SUPER SPECIALS—Talk Radio Specials—Westwood One Entertainment; *U.S. Public*, pg. 1763

LARRY KING SUPER SPECIALS—Talk Show—Westwood One, Inc.; *U.S. Public*, pg. 1763

LARRY MAHAN—NONE—Genesco Inc.; *U.S. Public*, pg. 728

LARRY'S—Old Fashioned Ice Cream—Bresler's Industries, Inc.; *Int'l*, pg. 1520

LARRY STUART—Shoes—Brown Group, Inc.; *U.S. Public*, pg. 262

LARRY STUART—Shoes—Brown Shoe Company; *U.S. Public*, pg. 262

LARSEN—Canned & Frozen Vegatables—Dean Foods Company; *U.S. Public*, pg. 489

LARSON—Fiberglass Boats—Genmar Holdings, Inc.; *U.S. Private*, pg. 447

LARTON—NONE—Lati Industria Termoplastici S.p.A.; *Int'l*, pg. 804

LARVADEX—Fly Control—Ciba Specialty Chemicals; *Int'l*, pg. 291

LARVADEX—Fly Control—Novartis; *Int'l*, pg. 972

LARZAC—Military Turbofan Engine—SNECMA - Societe Nationale d'Etude et de Construction de Moteurs d'Aviation; *Int'l*, pg. 1165

LAS CABRILLAS—Premium Cigars—Consolidated Cigar Corporation; *U.S. Private*, pg. 690

LAS VEGAS SUN—Newspaper—Las Vegas Sun; *U.S. Private*, pg. 652

LASALLE—NONE—Cross Huller; *Int'l*, pg. 1389

LASCCO—Smoked & Cured Fish—Los Angeles Smoking & Curing Company; *U.S. Private*, pg. 810

LASCO—Rubber Footwear—International Seaway Trading Corporation; *U.S. Private*, pg. 572

LASCO—Pipe Fittings, Bath Fixtures, Tubs & Showers—Lasco Bathware; *U.S. Private*, pg. 1397

LASCO STEAM—Steam Showers & Tub/ Showers—Lasco Bathware; *Int'l*, pg. 1397

LASCOAT—Bathware Product Material—Lasco Bathware; *Int'l*, pg. 1397

LASCOLITE—Fiberglass Building Panels—Lasco Bathware; *Int'l*, pg. 1397

LASER—NONE—Hansberger Precision Golf Inc.; *U.S. Private*, pg. 499

LASER—Monorail Tractor—Harnischfeger Industries, Inc.; *U.S. Public*, pg. 788

LASER—Cutlery—McPherson's Limited; *Int'l*, pg. 852

LASER—Golf Clubs & Balls—RAM Golf Corporation; *U.S. Private*, pg. 908

LASER—Consumer Turf Machinery—Ransomes Plc; *Int'l*, pg. 1087

LASER BOND—Facesheet Material Resisting Abrasion & Bonds Toner to Documents—Esselte Meto Kimball Systems; *Int'l*, pg. 460

LASER CHRP—Coagulation & Hemastatic Resection of the Prostate—Surgical Laser Technologies, Inc.; *U.S. Public*, pg. 1542

LASER CHALLENGE—Toy—Toymax International Inc.; *U.S. Public*, pg. 1626

LASER CLASS FAX-L770—Fax Machine—Canon U.S.A., Inc.; *Int'l*, pg. 262

LASER-FLEX—Tracheal Tube—Mallinckrodt Inc.; *U.S. Public*, pg. 1039

LASER FLEX AND DESIGN—Tracheal Tubes—Mallinckrodt Inc.; *U.S. Public*, pg. 1039

LASER IMAGE—Desk Top Printers—Imaging Technologies Corp.; *U.S. Public*, pg. 870

LASER-LX—Printer—Tandem Computers Inc.; *U.S. Public*, pg. 417

LASER LINE—Laser Gases, Equipment & Services—AGA Ges.m.b.H.; *Int'l*, pg. 13

LASER LINK—Tag & Label Imprinting Service Bureau—Esselte Meto Kimball Systems; *Int'l*, pg. 460

LASER-LINK SERVICE BUREAU—48 hour Laser Printer Network—Meto, USA; *Int'l*, pg. 460

LASER MARKSMAN—Laser Transmitters & Detectors for Use with Weapon Simulators & Targets—Litton Industries, Inc.; *U.S. Public*, pg. 1002

LASER 1—Character Print Bands—Aspen Imaging International, Inc.; *U.S. Public*, pg. 1339

LASER PLANE—Construction Laser Equip.—Spectra-Physics Laserplane Inc.; *U.S. Public*, pg. 1594

LASER-PLATE—NONE—Fred B. Johnston Company, Inc.; *U.S. Private*, pg. 595

LASER POWER + PLUS—Beam Delivery & Diagnostic Products—Laser Power Corporation; *U.S. Private*, pg. 652

LASER SENTRY—Laser Particulate Sensor—Elliott Company; *U.S. Private*, pg. 373

LASER SPEED—Paper for Copying, Printing & Duplicating—Georgia-Pacific Corporation; *U.S. Public*, pg. 735

LASER SYSTEMS—Mfr. of Military & Comml. Laser Systems, Rangefinders & Radiometers—Laser Systems; *U.S. Public*, pg. 1002

LASER III—Wheelchair—Medline Industries, Inc.; *U.S. Private*, pg. 728

LASER-TWIST—Writing Instrument—Union Pen Company; *U.S. Private*, pg. 1119

LASER WRITER—Laser Printer—Apple Computer, Inc.; *U.S. Public*, pg. 121

LA SERAINE JURIDIQUE—Weekly Publication—Editions du Juris-Classeur; *Int'l*, pg. 1095

LASERCAT—Laser Disc Based Information Workstation—CCI/Triad Automotive; *U.S. Private*, pg. 193

LASERCHART—Custom Reporting Module—Nellcor Puritan Bennett Incorporated; *U.S. Public*, pg. 1039

LASERCHECK 2811—Symbol Verifier—Symbol Technologies, Inc.; *U.S. Public*, pg. 1546

LASERKEY—Communication Products—Arkwright, Inc; *U.S. Private*, pg. 994

LASERLINE CONTINUOUS FORM—Laser Printers—Printronix, Inc.; *U.S. Public*, pg. 1329

LASERLUGE—Snow Sleds—Quality Special Products; *Int'l*, pg. 1075

LASERMARK—Marking Systems—Lumonics Inc.; *Int'l*, pg. 1314

LASERNET—Photo/Laser Sensor—Namco Controls Corporation; *U.S. Public*, pg. 482

LASERPACK—ID Badges—IDenticard Systems, Inc.; *U.S. Private*, pg. 557

LASERQUEST—Library Patron Access System Software—GRC International, Inc.; *U.S. Public*, pg. 695

LASERS & OPTRONICS—New-Product Tabloid Serving the Lasers & Electro-Optics Market—Reed Elsevier Business Information; *Int'l*, pg. 1095

LASER'S EDGE—Computer Wheel Aligner—Bee Line Company; *U.S. Private*, pg. 129

LASERSAFE (650 MB)—Optical—Iomega Corporation; *U.S. Public*, pg. 912

LASERSCOPE—NONE—Laserscope Surgical Systems; *U.S. Public*, pg. 979

LASERSCRIBE—Lasers—Excel Technology, Inc.; *U.S. Public*, pg. 599

LASERSITE—NONE—PolyMedica Industries, Inc.; *U.S. Public*, pg. 1315

LASERSOLUTION—NONE—Avenor, Inc.; *Int'l*, pg. 101

LASERSPEED—Process Monitor—TSI Incorporated; *U.S. Public*, pg. 1559

LASERTAB—Label—W.H. Brady Co.; *U.S. Public*, pg. 250

LASERTEKLM—Coated Polyester—Tekra Corporation; *U.S. Private*, pg. 1073

LASERTEX—Cold Rolled Steel—Cockerill Sambre; *Int'l*, pg. 301

LASERTHERMIA—NONE—Surgical Laser Technologies, Inc.; *U.S. Public*, pg. 1542

LASERTOOL—Laser Punch Press—Strippit, Inc.; *U.S. Public*, pg. 862

LASERTRAIN II—Laser Gun Simulators & Targets—Litton Industries, Inc.; *U.S. Public*, pg. 1002

LASETTA—Craft Kits—National Spinning Co., Inc.; *U.S. Private*, pg. 786

LASHLITES—Strip Eyelashes—American International Industries; *U.S. Private*, pg. 57

LASIX—Cardiac—Hoechst Marion Roussel, Inc.; *Int'l*, pg. 624

LASIX—Treatment of Edema & Hypertension—Hoechst Marion Roussel North America; *Int'l*, pg. 625

LASSA—Tires—Sabanci Holding A.S.; *Int'l*, pg. 1167

LASSALE—NONE—Seiko Corporation; *Int'l*, pg. 1218

LASSALE—Watches—SEIKO Corporation of America; *Int'l*, pg. 1218

LASSIE—Grocery Products—Sara Lee Corporation; *U.S. Public*, pg. 1432

LASSIE JANE—Pickles—Dean Pickles & Specialty Products; *U.S. Public*, pg. 490

LASSO—Herbicide—The Agricultural Group, Monsanto Company; *U.S. Public*, pg. 1125

LASSO—Herbicide—Monsanto Company; *U.S. Public*, pg. 1124

LAST ARMOR—Armor System for Military Vehicles—Foster-Miller, Inc.; *U.S. Private*, pg. 421

THE LAST HURRAH—Restaurant, Tavern & Hotel—Omni Hotels; *U.S. Private*, pg. 1065

LAST NIGHT ON LARRY KING LIVE—Talk Radio Feature—Westwood One Entertainment; *U.S. Public*, pg. 1763

LAST NIGHT ON LARRY KING LIVE—Highlight Version of Larry King Live—Westwood One, Inc.; *U.S. Public*, pg. 1763

LAST NIGHT ON TONIGHT WITH JAY LENO—Talk Radio Program—Westwood One Entertainment; *U.S. Public*, pg. 1763

LAST NIGHT ON TONIGHT WITH JAY LENO—Entertainment Programming—Westwood One, Inc.; *U.S. Public*, pg. 1763

LASTANE—NONE—Lati Industria Termoplastici S.p.A.; *Int'l*, pg. 804

LASTEK—Crack/Joint Sealants—Maintenance, Inc.; *Int'l*, pg. 1068

LASTET—Antineoplastic Agents—Nippon Kayaku Co. Ltd.; *Int'l*, pg. 934

LASTIGLAS—Steel Lined Containers—Enerfab Inc.; *U.S. Private*, pg. 376

LASTILAC—NONE—Lati Industria Termoplastici S.p.A.; *Int'l*, pg. 804

LASTING IMPRESSIONS—NONE—Anchor Glass Container Corporation; *Int'l*, pg. 327

LASTING MEMORIES—Ceramic Plates—American Greetings Corporation; *U.S. Public*, pg. 77

LASTING PERFORMANCE—Mascara—Cover Girl Cosmetics; *U.S. Public*, pg. 1330

LASTING PRIDE—Scoopable Cat Litter—Oil-Dri Corporation of America; *U.S. Public*, pg. 1214

LASTOFLEX—Elastomeric Laminated Bearings—Lord Corporation; *U.S. Private*, pg. 675

LASTOFLEX BEARINGS—Bearings—Lord Corporation, Mechanical Products Division; *U.S. Private*, pg. 676

LASTOSPHERE—Shock Absorbing Access.—Lord Corporation; *U.S. Private*, pg. 675

LASULF—NONE—Lati Industria Termoplastici S.p.A.; *Int'l*, pg. 804

LATAMID 6—NONE—Lati Industria Termoplastici S.p.A.; *Int'l*, pg. 804

LATAMID 66—NONE—Lati Industria Termoplastici S.p.A.; *Int'l*, pg. 804

LATAN—NONE—Lati Industria Termoplastici S.p.A.; *Int'l*, pg. 804

LATCH-LOCK—Bin Door—CTB International Corp.; *U.S. Public*, pg. 284

LATCH-N-LOK—NONE—Berg Electronics; *U.S. Public*, pg. 212

THE LATE LATE RADIO SHOW WITH TOM SNYDER—Entertainment-Oriented Talk Programming—Westwood One, Inc.; *U.S. Public*, pg. 1763

LATE SHOW WITH DAVID LETTERMAN TOP TEN—Previous Evening's Top Ten List Featured—Westwood One, Inc.; *U.S. Public*, pg. 1763

LATENE—NONE—Lati Industria Termoplastici S.p.A.; *Int'l*, pg. 804

LATER—NONE—Lati Industria Termoplastici S.p.A.; *Int'l*, pg. 804

LATERAL FILES—Free Standing Storage System—Haworth, Inc.; *U.S. Private*, pg. 511

LATH-ART—Wall Hangings—Austin Productions, Inc.; *U.S. Private*, pg. 100

LATHANOL—Surfactant—Stepan Company; *U.S. Public*, pg. 1514

LATHURN—Soap Dispenser—American Specialties Inc.; *U.S. Private*, pg. 62

LATHURSHELF—Soap Dispenser—American Specialties Inc.; *U.S. Private*, pg. 62

LATHURVALV—Soap Dispenser—American Specialties Inc.; *U.S. Private*, pg. 62

LATILON—NONE—Lati Industria Termoplastici S.p.A.; *Int'l*, pg. 804

LATROLET—Fittings—Bonney Forge Corporation; *U.S. Private*, pg. 156

LATTA—Margarine—Van den Bergh Foods Company; *Int'l*, pg. 1436

LATTECCINO—Powdered Latte & Cappuccino Mix—Superior Coffee and Foods; *U.S. Public*, pg. 1434

LAUB M'—Abrasion Resistant Steel—Laubeck Corporation/Cross; *U.S. Private*, pg. 652

LAUDA—Circulators—Brinkmann Instruments, Inc.; *U.S. Private*, pg. 169

LAUDERHILL LEASING—Leasing Co.—Ed Morse Automotive Group; *U.S. Private*, pg. 763

LAUDERS—Imported Scotch Whisky—Barton Incorporated; *U.S. Public*, pg. 300

LAUDER'S SCOTCH—NONE—Barton Brands, Ltd.; *U.S. Public*, pg. 300

LAUGHTER—Teen Fragrances—Yardley of London, Inc.; *Int'l*, pg. 819

LAUKE PARNICIL—NONE—Wacoal Corporation; *Int'l*, pg. 1484

LAUNCHTRAC—Product Launch Information—Pharmaceutical Marketing Services Inc.; *U.S. Public*, pg. 1284

LAUNDRY BRAIN—Laundry Products & Dispenser—Ecolab Inc.; *U.S. Public*, pg. 562

LAURA—High Speed Color Printer—Datametrics Corporation; *U.S. Public*, pg. 487

LAURA ASHLEY—Clothing—Laura Ashley Holdings Plc; *Int'l*, pg. 804

LAURA ASHLEY—Women's Clothing & Accessories—Laura Ashley (USA) Inc.; *Int'l*, pg. 804

LAURA ASHLEY MOTHER & CHILD—Clothing—Laura Ashley Holdings Plc; *Int'l*, pg. 804

LAURA CLAYTON—Uniforms—Angelica Corporation; *U.S. Public*, pg. 113

LAURA JEFFRIES—NONE—G-III Apparel Group, Ltd.; *U.S. Public*, pg. 690

LAURA LYNN—Store Brand—Ingles Markets, Incorporated; *U.S. Public*, pg. 878

LAURA SCOTT—NONE—Sears, Roebuck and Co.; *U.S. Public*, pg. 1452

LAURA SCUDDER'S—Snacks, All Natural Peanut Butter—Borden, Inc.; *U.S. Private*, pg. 157

LAURA SCUDDER'S—Potato Chips & Peanut Butter—J.M. Smucker Company; *U.S. Public*, pg. 1480

LAUREL—Greeting Cards; Wrapping Paper & Ribbon—American Greetings Corporation; *U.S. Public*, pg. 77

LAUREL—Greeting Cards, Stationery—American Greetings U.S. Greeting Card Division; *U.S. Public*, pg. 78

LAUREL—NONE—Dell Publishing; *Int'l*, pg. 191

LAUREL—Car—Nissan Motor Co., Ltd.; *Int'l*, pg. 943

LAUREL STRIP—Pre-Finished Strip—Bruce Hardwood Floors; *U.S. Public*, pg. 1634

LAUREN BY RALPH LAUREN—Fragrance—Cosmair, Inc., Ralph Lauren Fragrance Division; *Int'l*, pg. 818

LAURENT PERRIER CHAMPAGNE—Champagne—Dateo Import S.P.A.; *Int'l*, pg. 385

LAURENT-PERRIER CHAMPAGNE—Champagne—Heublein Inc.; *Int'l*, pg. 410

LAURENTIS—Espresso—Superior Coffee and Foods; *U.S. Public*, pg. 1434

LAURIDIT—Nonionics—Akzo Nobel N.V.; *Int'l*, pg. 42

LAURIER—Sanitary Napkins—Kao Corporation; *Int'l*, pg. 717

LAUROX, LAURYDOL—Di-Acyl Peroxide—Akzo Nobel N.V.; *Int'l*, pg. 42

L'AUTO JOURNAL—French Auto Magazine—EMAP France; *Int'l*, pg. 451

LAVA—Soap—The Procter & Gamble Company; *U.S. Public*, pg. 1330

LAVA BOOTIES—Thermal Heated Slippers—R.G. Barry Corporation; *U.S. Public*, pg. 192

LAVA-LITE—Lamps—Lava World International/Haggerty Enterprises, Inc.; *U.S. Private*, pg. 653

LAVABUNS—Thermal Heated Stadium Seat Cushions—R.G. Barry Corporation; *U.S. Public*, pg. 192

LAVACUATOR—Medico-Surgical Tubes & Medico-Surgical Tube Appliances—Mallinckrodt Inc.; *U.S. Public*, pg. 1039

LAVALOC—Carrier Locking Device—Josam Company; *U.S. Private*, pg. 600

LAVAPAC—Thermal Heating Pads—R.G. Barry Corporation; *U.S. Public*, pg. 192

LAVAX—Paint Enamels, Varnishes & Ready-Mixed Paints—PPG Industries, Inc.; *U.S. Public*, pg. 1245

LAVENDER—Women's Fragrance Products—Yardley of London, Inc.; *Int'l*, pg. 819

LAVENDER SACHET—Fabric Softener—Reckitt & Colman Inc.; *Int'l*, pg. 1090

LAVONA—Dermal Function Bath Lotion—Wella Group; *Int'l*, pg. 1489

LAVORIS—Mouthwash Products—Dep Corporation; *U.S. Public*, pg. 500

LAW ON DISC—CD-ROM Product—The Mead Corporation; *U.S. Public*, pg. 1074

LAW TECHNOLOGY ADVENT NEWS—NONE—New York Law Journal; *Int'l*, pg. 956

LAWDESK—Publication—Lawyers Cooperative Publishing Co.; *U.S. Public*, pg. 1602

LAWN-BOY—Outdoor Power Equip. for Lawn & Garden—Lawn-Boy Inc.; *U.S. Public*, pg. 1624

LAWN-BOY—Lawn Care Products—The Toro Company; *U.S. Public*, pg. 1623

LAWN CHIEF—Lawnmowers, Tillers, Riders—TruServ Corporation; *U.S. Private*, pg. 1108

LAWN DOCTOR—Lawn Care—Lawn Doctor Inc.; *U.S. Private*, pg. 653

LAWN GENIE—Irrigation—James Hardie Industries Ltd.; *Int'l*, pg. 596

LAWN RAKER—Outdoor Products—The Black & Decker Corporation; *U.S. Public*, pg. 233

LAWN RESTORE—Garden Prods.—Ringer Corporation; *U.S. Public*, pg. 1390

LAWNCRAFTER—Lawn & Garden Equipment—Kay Home Products, Inc.; *U.S. Public*, pg. 1258

LAWNFLITE—Power Mowers—MTD Products, Inc.; *U.S. Private*, pg. 688

LAWNTURF—Artificial Turf Made of Polyvinylidene Chloride Filament, etc.—Asahi Chemical Industry Co., Ltd.; *Int'l*, pg. 83

LAWRENCE—Metal Products—Lawrence Metal Products, Inc.; *U.S. Private*, pg. 654

LAWRENCE BRAND—Lead Shot—Taracorp, Inc.; *U.S. Public*, pg. 1068

LAWRENCE LIQUORS—Liqueur—White Rock Distilleries Inc.; *U.S. Private*, pg. 1173

LAWRENCE LTD.—Men's & Young Men's Dress Slacks, Shorts & Suits—H. R. Kaminsky & Sons, Inc.; *U.S. Private*, pg. 606

LAWRENCE TECHNOLOGY—Electric Cable—Camco International Inc.; *U.S. Public*, pg. 297

LAWRY'S—Seasoned Salt & Dry Mixes—Lawry's Foods, Inc.; *Int'l*, pg. 1435

LAWRY'S—Restaurants—Lawry's Restaurants, Inc.; *U.S. Private*, pg. 654

LAWSON—Paper Cutters—Baum USA; *Int'l*, pg. 1293

LAWSON—Gas, Electric & Oil Powered Heaters—Bradford-White Corporation; *U.S. Private*, pg. 164

LAWSON INSIGHT—Brandname of Lawson's New Business Management Software Products—Lawson Software; *U.S. Private*, pg. 654

LAWTER—NONE—Lawter International, Inc.; *U.S. Public*, pg. 980

LAWTOMATION—NONE—Sulcus Computer Corp.; *U.S. Public*, pg. 1527

LAWYERS COOPERATIVE PUBLISHING—NONE—Lawyers Cooperative Publishing Co.; *U.S. Public*, pg. 1602

LAWYERS PROTECTOR PLAN—Insurance Package Program—Poe & Brown, Inc.; *U.S. Public*, pg. 1312

LAXOBERAL—Laxative—Boehringer Ingelheim GmbH; *Int'l*, pg. 199

LAY-IN-LUG—Grounding Connector for Bushings/Terminators—O-Z/Gedney Co.; *U.S. Public*, pg. 727

LAY'S "THREE LITTLE PIGS"—NONE—Lay's Fine Foods; *U.S. Private*, pg. 655

LAYCO—Herbs & Spices—Burns, Philp & Company Limited; *Int'l*, pg. 236

LAYEZEE—Mattresses, Bedroom Furniture—Silentnight Holdings Plc; *Int'l*, pg. 1249

LAYFLAT—Flat Reinforced PVC Tubing—Newage Industries Inc., Plastics Technology Group; *U.S. Private*, pg. 796

LAYNE & BOWLER—Pumps—Aurora Pump; *U.S. Public*, pg. 726

LAYONS—Natural Wood Veneer Tape & Jointed Rolls—Carter Holt Harvey Limited; *U.S. Public*, pg. 904

LAYOUT PACK—Wide Shingled Bacon—Hormel Foods Corp.; *U.S. Public*, pg. 840

LAY'S—Potato Chips—Frito-Lay Company; *U.S. Public*, pg. 1277

LAYSA—Acoustic Absorbers—Freudenberg & Company; *Int'l*, pg. 505

LAYSAPLAN—Acoustic Absorbers—Freudenberg & Company; *Int'l*, pg. 505

LAZARD BROS.—Investment Banking—Pearson plc; *Int'l*, pg. 1025

LAZARE DIAMOND JEWELRY—18K & Platinum Jewelry—Lazare Kaplan Intl., Inc.; *U.S. Public*, pg. 981

LAZARE DIAMONDS—Polished Diamonds—Lazare Kaplan Intl., Inc.; *U.S. Public*, pg. 981

LAZARUS—Department Stores—Federated Department Stores, Inc.; *U.S. Public*, pg. 617

LAZER WIZARD—Printing of Money Orders & Other Negotiable Instruments—FFP Marketing Company, Inc.; *U.S. Public*, pg. 604

LAZERMARK—Model of Bolt Action Rifle—Weatherby, Inc.; *U.S. Private*, pg. 1155

LAZY IKE—Fishing Lines—EBSCO Industries, Inc.; *U.S. Private*, pg. 358

LAZY MAPLE BACON—Bacon—Armour Swift Eckrich; *U.S. Public*, pg. 426

LAZZARONI—NONE—Nestle USA; *Int'l*, pg. 916

LE BISQUIT—Kosher Foods—Rokeach Food Distributing Inc.; *U.S. Private*, pg. 940

LE BOEUF JARDINIER—Restaurants—Accor S.A.; *Int'l*, pg. 20

LE BONHEUR ESTATE—Wine—Distillers Corporation S.A.; *Int'l*, pg. 1129

LE BOUTON—Buttons—Carlyle Industries, Inc.; *U.S. Public*, pg. 1187

LE CAFE—Coffee—Kraft Foods, Inc.; *U.S. Public*, pg. 1287

LE CHASSEUR FRANCAIS—French Outdoor Magazine—EMAP France; *Int'l*, pg. 451

LE CHEF—Food Processors—Sunbeam Household Products; *U.S. Public*, pg. 1533

LE CHIC—Buttons & Buckles—Carlyle Industries, Inc.; *U.S. Public*, pg. 1187

LE CONFISEUR—French Truffles—Nestle Chocolate & Confection; *Int'l*, pg. 917

LE CONFISEUR—French Truffles—Nestle S.A.; *Int'l*, pg. 915

LE COQ SPORTIF—Shoes—Brown Group, Inc.; *U.S. Public*, pg. 262

LE COQ SPORTIF—Women's Shoes & Apparel—Excelsior Inc.; *U.S. Public*, pg. 387

LE CRAYON GLACE—Cosmetics—Cosmair, Inc.; *Int'l*, pg. 818

LE CYCLE—French Cycling Magazine—EMAP France; *Int'l*, pg. 451

LE DOMAINE CHAMPAGNE—Wine—Canandaigua Wine Company Div.; *U.S. Public*, pg. 300

LE FLEURIER—Low Fat Spread—Unigate PLC; *Int'l*, pg. 1433

LE GOURMET—White Rice—Producers Rice Mill Inc.; *U.S. Public*, pg. 888

LE GOUT—Foodservice Products—Bestfoods; *U.S. Public*, pg. 223

LE GOUT—Soup, Sauces & Bases—CPC Foodservice Group; *U.S. Public*, pg. 224

LE JOURNAL DE MONTREAL—Newspaper—Quebecor Inc.; *Int'l*, pg. 1075

LE JOURNAL DE QUEBEC—Newspaper—Quebecor Inc.; *Int'l*, pg. 1075

LE LUNDI—Magazine—Quebecor Inc.; *Int'l*, pg. 1075

LE MANS—Luggage—American Tourister, Inc.; *U.S. Public*, pg. 1430

LE MENU—Frozen Foods—Campbell Soup Company Ltd.; *U.S. Public*, pg. 299

LE PEEP—Restaurants—Le Peep's Grill Inc.; *U.S. Private*, pg. 655

LE PIAT D'OR—Wine—Carillon Importers, Ltd.; *Int'l*, pg. 409

LE PIAT D'OR—NONE—International Distillers Caribbean; *Int'l*, pg. 410

LE PIAT D'OR—NONE—IDV France; *Int'l*, pg. 410

LE SHUTTLE—Transport Through Eurotunnel—The Eurotunnel Group; *Int'l*, pg. 466

LE SYSTEME—Premium Skin Care Regime—Dep Corporation; *U.S. Public*, pg. 500

LE TONG—Plastic Serving Tongs—The Vollrath Company, L.L.C.; *U.S. Private*, pg. 1143

LEA & PERRINS—Sauces—Danone Group; *Int'l*, pg. 379

LEA & PERRINS—Sauces—Lea & Perrins, Inc.; *Int'l*, pg. 380

LEA INDUSTRIES—Furniture—Ladd Furniture, Inc.; *U.S. Public*, pg. 974

LEAD—NONE—Koo Koo Roo, Inc.; *U.S. Public*, pg. 966

LEAD-GASKET—Specialty Nails—Maze Nails; *U.S. Private*, pg. 718

LEAD PACK—X-Ray Film Pack—Eastman Kodak Company; *U.S. Public*, pg. 776

LEADER—High Quality Aluminum Storm Windows—Binning's Building Products, Inc.; *U.S. Public*, pg. 67

LEADER—Envelopes—Georgia-Pacific Corporation; *U.S. Public*, pg. 735

LEADER—Electrical Test Equipment—Leader Instruments Corporation; *U.S. Private*, pg. 655

LEADER DRUGSTORES—NONE—Cardinal Health Inc.; *U.S. Public*, pg. 304

THE LEADER IN DIGITAL AUDIO—Digital Audio Equipment—Sony Electronics; *Int'l*, pg. 1281

THE LEADER IN DISPERSED DATA PROCESSING—Slogan—Datapoint Corporation; *Int'l*, pg. 384

LEADER OFFICE FURNITURE—Metal Filing Cabinets, Desks & Combination Cabinets—Steelworks, Inc. Dover Division; *U.S. Private*, pg. 1039

LEADERSHIP—Magazine—Christianity Today, Inc.; *U.S. Private*, pg. 238

LEADING LADY—Bath Tissue, Paper Towels & Napkins—Georgia-Pacific Corporation; *U.S. Public*, pg. 735

LEADING THE LEADERS—Advanced Management Training—RE/MAX International, Inc.; *U.S. Private*, pg. 912

LEADTRAK—Test Kit—Hach Company; *U.S. Public*, pg. 773

LEAF RIVER 90—Wood Pulp—Georgia-Pacific Corporation; *U.S. Public*, pg. 735

LEAFBUSTER—NONE—The Black & Decker Corporation; *U.S. Public*, pg. 233

LEAK SEALER—Liquid Spray Caulk—Jelmar Company; *U.S. Private*, pg. 585

LEAKPROOF—Foundation Coating Products—Monsey-Bakor; *U.S. Private*, pg. 757

LEAKTEK—Water Audits & Meter Testing—Heath Consultants Incorporated; *U.S. Private*, pg. 518

LEAN CREAM—Food Products—Land O'Lakes, Inc.; *U.S. Private*, pg. 645

LEAN CUISINE—Frozen Foods—Nestle S.A.; *Int'l*, pg. 915

LEAN OLE—NONE—Don Miguel Mexican Foods, Inc.; *U.S. Private*, pg. 339

LEANER WEINER—Food Products—Oscar Mayer Foods Corp.; *U.S. Public*, pg. 1288

LEANING TOWER—NONE—Quality Bakers New Zealand Ltd.; *Int'l*, pg. 556

LEAP GEAR—Athletic—L.A. Gear, Inc.; *U.S. Public*, pg. 969

LEAPFROG—VHDL Simulator—Cadence Design Systems, Inc.; *U.S. Public*, pg. 290

LEARJET MODEL 31 A—6-8 Seat Light Business Jet—Bombardier, Learjet Inc.; *Int'l*, pg. 200

LEARJET—Business Aircraft—Bombardier Inc.; *Int'l*, pg. 199

LEARJET—Jet Aircraft—Bombardier, Learjet Inc.; *Int'l*, pg. 200

LEARJET MODEL 60—6-8 Seat Mid-Size Business Jet with Walk-Around Cabin—Bombardier, Learjet Inc.; *Int'l*, pg. 200

LEARJET MODEL 35 A—6-8 Seat Light Business Jet—Bombardier, Learjet Inc.; *Int'l*, pg. 200

LEARJET MODEL 36 A—6-8 Seat Light Business Jet—Bombardier, Learjet Inc.; *Int'l*, pg. 200

LEARN NOT TO BURN—Firesafety Education—National Fire Protection Association; *U.S. Private*, pg. 782

LEARN THE ART OF MAGIC—NONE—Broderbund Software, Inc.; *U.S. Public*, pg. 258

LEARNING ADVANTAGE LIBRARY 1—NONE—Broderbund Software, Inc.; *U.S. Public*, pg. 258

LEARNING ADVANTAGE LIBRARY 2—NONE—Broderbund Software, Inc.; *U.S. Public*, pg. 258

THE LEARNING CHANNEL—Cable Network Channel—Discovery Networks, Inc.; *U.S. Private*, pg. 334

LEARNING CORPORATION OF AMERICA (LCA)—Film & Video—Coronet/MTI; *U.S. Private*, pg. 863

LEARNING INTERNATIONAL—Business Training & Consulting Services—Learning International; *U.S. Public*, pg. 1617

LEARNSTAR—NONE—The Titan Corporation; *U.S. Public*, pg. 1618

LEASECARD—Pre-Approved Credit Program for Efficient Provision of Equipment—Trans Leasing International Inc.; *U.S. Public*, pg. 1628

LEASEMAP—NONE—Landmark Graphics Corporation; *U.S. Public*, pg. 770

LEATHERHIT—Agent for Surface Treatment Materials of Artificial Leather—Dainichiseika Colour & Chemicals Mfg. Co., Ltd.; *Int'l*, pg. 369

LEATHERNECK—Sulphate Paper—Georgia-Pacific Corporation; *U.S. Public*, pg. 735

LEATHEROID—Agent for Surface Treatment Materials of Artificial Leather—Dainichiseika Colour & Chemicals Mfg. Co., Ltd.; *Int'l*, pg. 369

LEBANITE—Hardboard—Georgia-Pacific Corporation; *U.S. Public*, pg. 735

LEBEAU VITRES D'AUTOS—Retail ARG Sales—TCG International Inc.; *Int'l*, pg. 1336

LEBILLS—NONE—Tandy Brands Accessories, Inc.; *U.S. Public*, pg. 1560

LEBLANC (PARIS)—Musical Instruments—G. Leblanc Corporation; *U.S. Private*, pg. 656

LEBOW—Load Cells, Torque Sensors, Strain Gauge Instrumentation—Eaton Corporation; *U.S. Public*, pg. 555

LECH—Lightweight Aggregates—Scancem AB; *Int'l*, pg. 1198

LECHTERS—Housewares—Lechters, Inc.; *U.S. Public*, pg. 983

LECLAIRE PLANK—Pre-Finished Laminate—Bruce Hardwood Floors; *U.S. Public*, pg. 1634

LECLIC—NONE—Concord Camera Corporation; *U.S. Public*, pg. 429

L'ECLUSE—Wine Bars—Accor S.A.; *Int'l*, pg. 20

LECTADE—Animal Health Product—SmithKline Beecham plc; *Int'l*, pg. 1264

LECTRA-CON—Conductants—Schlegel Corporation; *Int'l*, pg. 1255

LECTRA-LIFT—Power Recliner—La-Z-Boy Incorporated; *U.S. Public*, pg. 972

LECTRA-LOUNGER—Power Recliner—La-Z-Boy Incorporated; *U.S. Public*, pg. 972

LECTRA SHIELD—Flexible Packaging—Westvaco Corporation; *U.S. Public*, pg. 1762

LECTRAFLEX—Cells—Bryant Grinder Corp.; *U.S. Private*, pg. 461

LECTRAFORM—Grinder—Bryant Grinder Corp.; *U.S. Private*, pg. 461

LECTRALINE—Grinder—Bryant Grinder Corp.; *U.S. Private*, pg. 461

LECTRIC SHAVE—Pre-Electric Shave Lotion—SmithKline Beecham plc; *Int'l*, pg. 1264

LECTRIFY—Hair Products—Dena Corporation; *U.S. Private*, pg. 324

LECTRO-CAM—Grinder—Bryant Grinder Corp.; *U.S. Private*, pg. 461

LECTRO-LOK—Box Springs—Leggett & Platt, Incorporated; *U.S. Public*, pg. 985

LECTRO-PADS—Medical ECG Electrolyte Pad—Burdick, Inc.; *U.S. Private*, pg. 181

LECTRO-SONIC—Medical Transmission Gel—Burdick, Inc.; *U.S. Private*, pg. 181

LECTROCAT—One-Component, Cathodic Electrocoating System—DeSoto Inc.; *U.S. Public*, pg. 956

LECTRODRYER—Equipment for Drying Air, Gases & Liquids—Lectrodryer Div., Ajax Magnethermic Corp.; *Int'l*, pg. 113

LECTROLITE—Fabrics—Herculite Products, Inc.; *U.S. Public*, pg. 802

LECTROLITE COMFORT—Fabrics—Herculite Products, Inc.; *U.S. Public*, pg. 802

LECTROPON—Anodic Electrocoating System—DeSoto Inc.; *U.S. Public*, pg. 956

LECTURSPHERE—Container—Fisher Scientific Company; *U.S. Private*, pg. 658

LEDLOY—Free-Machining Steels—Inland Steel Industries, Inc.; *U.S. Public*, pg. 879

LEDLOY AX—Free-Machining Steels—Inland Steel Industries, Inc.; *U.S. Public*, pg. 879

LEDU—Lamps—Luxo A/S; *Int'l*, pg. 821

LEE—Filter Prods.—Champion Laboratories, Inc.; *U.S. Private*, pg. 1113

LEE—Men's Apparel—Mass Market Division; *U.S. Public*, pg. 1702

LEE—Men's Hats—Stetson Hat Co.; *U.S. Private*, pg. 510

LEE—Jeanswear—VF Corporation; *U.S. Public*, pg. 1702

LEE BONDED RETAINER—Fiberglass Strands & Self-Curing Composite for Orthodontics—Lee Pharmaceuticals; *U.S. Public*, pg. 984

LEE CHEK—NONE—Lee Company; *U.S. Private*, pg. 657

LEE COMPANY—Mfr. of Miniature Hydraulic Inserts—Lee Company; *U.S. Private*, pg. 657

LEE COOPER EYEWEAR—Eyewear—Logo of the Americas; *Int'l*, pg. 462

LEE DAVID LTD.—NONE—The Dress Barn, Inc.; *U.S. Public*, pg. 528

LEE ENDO-FILL—Silicone Root Canal Sealant—Lee Pharmaceuticals; *U.S. Public*, pg. 984

LEE EUROPE—Apparel—Mass Market Division; *U.S. Public*, pg. 1702

LEE-FISCHER—Ceramic Reinforced Plastic Brackets—Lee Pharmaceuticals; *U.S. Public*, pg. 984

LEE HECHT HARRISON—Outplacement Services—Adecco Employment Services; *Int'l*, pg. 24

LEE HIGH FASHION NAIL TIP KIT—Glamour Length Glue-on Nail Tips—Lee Pharmaceuticals; *U.S. Public*, pg. 984

LEE INSTA-BOND—NONE—Lee Pharmaceuticals; *U.S. Public*, pg. 984

LEE JET—NONE—Lee Company; *U.S. Private*, pg. 657

LEE MYLES—Transmissions—Lee Myles Associates Corporation; *U.S. Private*, pg. 657

LEE NAILS—Brush-on Acrylic Product for Lengthening & Mending Fingernails—Lee Pharmaceuticals; *U.S. Public*, pg. 984

LEE NATURAL NAIL CARE COLLECTION—Nail Care—Lee Pharmaceuticals; *U.S. Public*, pg. 984

LEE ORTHO PRIME—Orthodontic Bonding Material—Lee Pharmaceuticals; *U.S. Public*, pg. 984

LEE PLUG—NONE—Lee Company; *U.S. Private*, pg. 657

LEE PRESS-ON-NAILS—False Nails—Lee Pharmaceuticals; *U.S. Public*, pg. 984

LEE READY SPLINT—Fiberglass Splint & Adhesive Used in Tooth Stabilization—Lee Pharmaceuticals; *U.S. Public*, pg. 984

LEE SPORT—NONE—Nutmeg Mills Inc.; *U.S. Public*, pg. 1702

LEE SPORT—Decorated Knitwear—VF Corporation; *U.S. Public*, pg. 1702

LEE VS. GRANT—War Game—Monarch Avalon, Inc.; *U.S. Public*, pg. 1123

LEE WHITE WIRE—Tooth-Colored Orthodontic Wire—Lee Pharmaceuticals; *U.S. Public*, pg. 984

LEECO—Natural & Finger Jointed Timber—Carter Holt Harvey Limited; *U.S. Public*, pg. 904

LEED'S INDEX OPTION ALERT—Financial Fax Newsletter—KCI Communications, Inc; *U.S. Private*, pg. 784

LEEDSHILL-HERKENHOFF INC—Engineering Consulting—ASCG, Inc.; *U.S. Private*, pg. 80

LEEP—Medical Apparatus—The Cooper Companies, Inc.; *U.S. Public*, pg. 442

LEEP ELECTRODE—Uterus Surgical Instruments—The Cooper Companies, Inc.; *U.S. Public*, pg. 442

LEEP REDIKIT—Surgical Preparatory Kits—The Cooper Companies, Inc.; *U.S. Public*, pg. 442

LEEP SYSTEM 6000—Loop Electrosurgical Excision Equipment—The Cooper Companies, Inc.; *U.S. Public*, pg. 442

LEEP VAC—Smoke Evacuator Equipment—The Cooper Companies, Inc.; *U.S. Public*, pg. 442

LEERDAMMER—Cheese—Koninklijke BolsWessanen nv; *Int'l*, pg. 750

LEES—NONE—Burlington Industries, Inc.; *U.S. Public*, pg. 268

LEES CARPETS—Carpets—Burlington Industries, Inc.; *U.S. Public*, pg. 268

LEE'S FAMOUS RECIPE—Chicken Outlets—Shoney's, Inc.; *U.S. Public*, pg. 1467

LEE'S FAMOUS RECIPE COUNTRY CHICKEN—Chicken—Lee's Famous Recipe Restaurant; *U.S. Private*, pg. 906

LEES FOR LIFE—NONE—Burlington Industries, Inc.; *U.S. Public*, pg. 268

LEEWARD—Cruise Ship—Norwegian Cruise Line; *U.S. Private*, pg. 808

LEFFE—Abbey Beer—Interbrew S.A.; *Int'l*, pg. 679

LEFFE—Beer—Labatt U.S.A.; *Int'l*, pg. 679

LEFRANC—Building Paints for Exterior & Interior (Retail Uses)—Akzo Nobel N.V.; *Int'l*, pg. 42

LEG LOOKS BY BURLINGTON—Hosiery—Kayser-Roth Corporation, Inc.; *Int'l*, pg. 576

LEG MATE—Razors—American Safety Razor Company; *U.S. Public*, pg. 597

LEGACY—Surgical Instrument—Alcon Laboratories, Inc.; *Int'l*, pg. 916

LEGACY—Whole Life Insurance—American United Life Insurance Company; *U.S. Private*, pg. 64

LEGACY—Binoculars—Bausch & Lomb Incorporated; *U.S. Public*, pg. 194

LEGACY—Decorative Faucet—The Chicago Faucet Co.; *U.S. Private*, pg. 234

LEGACY—Motion Picture Series—Eastman Kodak Company; *U.S. Public*, pg. 550

LEGACY—1900 Film Stocking Program—Fasson Films; *U.S. Public*, pg. 153

LEGACY—Automobile Produced by Subaru—Fuji Heavy Industries, Ltd.; *Int'l*, pg. 522

LEGACY—Upright Vacuum Cleaner—Hoover Company; *U.S. Public*, pg. 1065

LEGACY—Printing Papers—International Paper Company; *U.S. Public*, pg. 901

LEGACY—Small Center Cartoner—R.A. Jones & Co. Inc.; *U.S. Private*, pg. 597

LEGACY—Vitatron Pacemaker—Medtronic, Inc.; *U.S. Public*, pg. 1082

LEGACY—Hosiery—Sara Lee Corporation; *U.S. Public*, pg. 1432

LEGACY—Nominal 4"4 Flat-To-Flat Lt. Duty Floor & Wall Tile W/ 12 Accent "Dot" Tile—United States Ceramic Tile Co.; *U.S. Private*, pg. 1124

LEGACY II—Vitatron Pacemaker—Medtronic, Inc.; *U.S. Public*, pg. 1082

LEGAL TOOLBOX—Software Product—The Mead Corporation; *U.S. Public*, pg. 1074

LEGART—Hosiery—Coop Switzerland; *Int'l*, pg. 329

LEGATO LINEAR—Amps/Audio Receivers—Sony Electronics; *Int'l*, pg. 1281

LEGATO NETWORKER—NONE—Legato Systems, Inc.; *U.S. Public*, pg. 984

LEGATRIN PM—For Sleeplessness & Pain—Columbia Laboratories, Inc.; *U.S. Public*, pg. 405

LEGEND—Automobile—American Honda Motor Co., Inc. Automobile Sales Division; *Int'l*, pg. 634

LEGEND—Cameras—Eastman Kodak Company; *U.S. Public*, pg. 550

LEGEND—Sail Boats—Hunter Marine Corporation; *U.S. Private*, pg. 549

LEGEND—Beverage Cooler—Igloo Products Corporation; *U.S. Public*, pg. 265

LEGEND—Pacemaker—Medtronic, Inc.; *U.S. Public*, pg. 1082

LEGEND—Home Health Care Scooter—Pride Health Care, Inc.; *U.S. Private*, pg. 883

LEGEND—Goggles—U.S. Safety; *U.S. Private*, pg. 1125

LEGEND—Security Hardware Products—Waxman Industries, Inc.; *U.S. Public*, pg. 1748

LEGEND OF LOVE—Cologne Mist—Stanhome Inc.; *U.S. Public*, pg. 1508

LEGEND OF THE SEAS—Ship—Royal Caribbean Cruises Ltd.; *U.S. Public*, pg. 1410

LEGEND PLUS—Pacemaker—Medtronic, Inc.; *U.S. Public*, pg. 1082

LEGEND ST—Pacemaker—Medtronic, Inc.; *U.S. Public*, pg. 1082

LEGEND II—Pacemakers—Medtronic, Inc.; *U.S. Public*, pg. 1082

LEGENDRY—Printing Paper—Georgia-Pacific Corporation; *U.S. Public*, pg. 735

LEGENDS OF THE LOST REALM—Computer Game—Monarch Avalon, Inc.; *U.S. Public*, pg. 1123

LEGER DE SAINT MORET—Cream Cheese—Bongrain S.A.; *Int'l*, pg. 201

LEGER DE TARTARE—Cream Cheese—Bongrain S.A.; *Int'l*, pg. 201

LEGG—NONE—Chloride Group PLC; *Int'l*, pg. 287

LEGG MASONVALUE TRUST—Equity Mutual Fund—Legg Mason, Inc.; *U.S. Public*, pg. 984

L'EGGS—Hosiery—L'eggs Products, Inc.; *U.S. Public*, pg. 1434

L'EGGS—Women's Hosiery—Sara Lee Corporation; *U.S. Public*, pg. 1432

L'EGGS RELIANCE—Hosiery—L'eggs Products, Inc.; *U.S. Public*, pg. 1434

LEGI-SLATE—On-Line Information—The Washington Post Company; *U.S. Public*, pg. 1742

LEGIA—Ammunition—Herstal S.A.; *Int'l*, pg. 617

LEGIONELLA IFA—Test Systems—Wampole Laboratories; *U.S. Public*, pg. 310

LEGITRONIC—Electronic Label Printer—Weber Marking Systems, Inc.; *U.S. Private*, pg. 1157

LEGO—Children's Building Sets—LEGO Systems, Inc.; *Int'l*, pg. 805

LEGO CONNECTOR—Newsletter—LEGO Systems, Inc.; *Int'l*, pg. 805

LEGO IMAGINATION CENTER—Entertainment Services/Exhibits—LEGO Systems, Inc.; *Int'l*, pg. 805

LEGO MANIAC—Slogan—LEGO Systems, Inc.; *Int'l*, pg. 805

LEGO SYSTEM—Children's Building Sets—LEGO Systems, Inc.; *Int'l*, pg. 805

LEGOLAND—Theme Parks/Entertainment—LEGO Systems, Inc.; *Int'l*, pg. 805

LEGRAND—Low-Voltage Fittings & Accessories—LeGrand S.A.; *Int'l*, pg. 805

LEGRAND GROUP—Financial Information Providers—Success Development International; *U.S. Private*, pg. 1048

LEHIGH—Safety Shoes—E.J. Footwear Corp.; *U.S. Public*, pg. 1684

LEHIGH—Milk Products—Labatt Brewing Company Limited; *Int'l*, pg. 679

LEHIGH—Portland & Masonry Cements—Lehigh Portland Cement Company; *Int'l*, pg. 605

LEHIGH—Transmission Towers—Thomas & Betts Corporation; *U.S. Public*, pg. 1597

LEHIGH VALLEY—Block—Glen-Gery Corporation; *Int'l*, pg. 658

LEI EXTRAS—NONE—Lowrance Electronics, Inc.; *U.S. Public*, pg. 1015

LEIBINGER/FISHER RM ZD—NONE—Pfizer Inc.; *U.S. Public*, pg. 1281

LEICA CM 1900—Cryostat—Leica Inc.; *Int'l*, pg. 806

LEICA DM RXA—Automated Microscope—Leica Inc.; *Int'l*, pg. 806

LEICA DM IRB—Inverted Research Microscope—Leica Inc.; *Int'l*, pg. 806

LEICA DM LS—Clinical Lab Microscope—Leica Inc.; *Int'l*, pg. 806

LEICA G27—Stereomicroscope—Leica Inc.; *Int'l*, pg. 806

LEICA G26E—Steromicroscope—Leica Inc.; *Int'l*, pg. 806

LEICA GALEN—Microscope—Leica Inc.; *Int'l*, pg. 806

LEICA GZ4—Stereomicroscope—Leica Inc.; *Int'l*, pg. 806

LEICA INS 1000—Wafer Inspection Station—Leica Inc.; *Int'l*, pg. 806

LEICA INS2000—Wafer Inspection Station—Leica Inc.; *Int'l*, pg. 806

LEICA MEF4—Metallograph—Leica Inc.; *Int'l*, pg. 806

LEICA M55—Stereomicroscope—Leica Inc.; *Int'l*, pg. 806

LEICA M212—Steromicroscope—Leica Inc.; *Int'l*, pg. 806

LEICA MZ8—Stereomicroscope—Leica Inc.; *Int'l*, pg. 806

LEICA MZ6—Stereomicroscope—Leica Inc.; *Int'l*, pg. 806

LEICA Q550IW—Image Analysis System—Leica Inc.; *Int'l*, pg. 806

LEICA RM 2155—Rotary Microphone—Leica Inc.; *Int'l*, pg. 806

LEICA RM 2145—Rotary Microtome—Leica Inc.; *Int'l*, pg. 806

LEICA RM 2135—Rotary Microtome—Leica Inc.; *Int'l*, pg. 806

LEICA STRATALAB—Microscope—Leica Inc.; *Int'l*, pg. 806

LEICA TCSNT—Confocal Microscope—Leica Inc.; *Int'l*, pg. 806

LEICA TP 1050—Tissue Processor—Leica Inc.; *Int'l*, pg. 806

LEICA 2165—NONE—Leica Inc.; *Int'l*, pg. 806

LEICHT & CROSS—Extruded Bread—Danone Group; *Int'l*, pg. 379

LEICHTUNG WORKSHOPS—Woodworking & Hobby Catalog—Hanover Direct, Inc.; *U.S. Public*, pg. 782

LEINENKUGEL'S MAPLE BROWN LAGER—Lager—Jacob Leinenkugel Brewing Co.; *U.S. Public*, pg. 1289

LEINENKUGEL—Premium Beer—Jacob Leinenkugel Brewing Co.; *U.S. Public*, pg. 1289

LEINENKUGEL'S—Beer—Philip Morris Companies Inc.; *U.S. Public*, pg. 1287

LEINER DAVIS GELATIN—Gelatin—Goodman Fielder Limited; *Int'l*, pg. 555

LEISI—Refrigerated Pastry for Home Baking—Nestle S.A.; *Int'l*, pg. 915

LEISURE—NONE—Glynwed International PLC; *Int'l*, pg. 554

LEISURE—Active Adult, Retirement, Family & Recreational Communities—Leisure Technology, Inc.; *U.S. Private*, pg. 659

LEISURE LIFE—Greeting Cards—American Greetings U.S. Greeting Card Division; *U.S. Public*, pg. 78

LEKTRIFEED—Control System—Gardner Abrasives; *U.S. Public*, pg. 1699

LEKTRO—Duplicating Papers—Avenor, Inc.; *Int'l*, pg. 101

LEMANIC—Packages & Printing Machines—Bobst S.A.; *Int'l*, pg. 198

LEMANS—Tires—Bridgestone/Firestone, Inc.; *Int'l*, pg. 213

LEMBEY—Sparkling Wine—Domecq Importers Inc.; *Int'l*, pg. 63

LEMOCIN—Pharmaceutical—Novartis AG; *Int'l*, pg. 971

LEMON COOLERS—Cookies—Sunshine Biscuits, Inc.; *U.S. Private*, pg. 434

LEMON COOLERS—Cookies—Sunshine Biscuits, Inc.; *U.S. Public*, pg. 657

LEMON FRESH COMET—Liquid Chlorine Bleach—The Procter & Gamble Company; *U.S. Public*, pg. 1330

LEMON HART RUM—Rum—Allied Domecq PLC; *Int'l*, pg. 62

LEMON HERB GARNI—Seasoning—McCormick & Company, Incorporated; *U.S. Public*, pg. 1066

LEMON LOTION HAND CLEANER—Industrial Chemical—Hercules Chemical Co., Inc.; *U.S. Private*, pg. 523

LEMON MIST—Herb Tea—Celestial Seasonings; *U.S. Public*, pg. 319

LEMON POWER—All Purpose Cleaner—Blue Cross Laboratories; *U.S. Private*, pg. 152

LEMON UP—Shampoo & Creme Rinse—The Gillette Company; *U.S. Public*, pg. 743

LEMON ZINGER—Herb Tea—Celestial Seasonings; *U.S. Public*, pg. 319

LEMSIP—Cold Relief—Reckitt & Colman plc; *Int'l*, pg. 1089

LEND ME A TENOR—Musical—Really Useful Holdings Limited; *Int'l*, pg. 1089

LENDER'S—Bagels—Kellogg Company; *U.S. Public*, pg. 947

LENDER'S—Bagels—Lender's Bagel Bakery; *U.S. Public*, pg. 1288

LENDER'S BAGELETTES—Small Bagels—Lender's Bagel Bakery; *U.S. Public*, pg. 1288

LENI—Tissue Paper—Metsa-Serla Corporation; *Int'l*, pg. 863

LENOR—NONE—Procter & Gamble Espana S.A.; *U.S. Public*, pg. 1332

LENOTRE—Gastronomic Catering & Restaurants—Accor S.A.; *Int'l*, pg. 20

LENOX—Saw Blades—American Saw & Mfg. Company; *U.S. Public*, pg. 61

LENOX—China, Crystal & Collections Products—Brown-Forman Corporation; *U.S. Public*, pg. 261

LENOX—China Dinnerware, Crystal Stemware And Gifts—Lenox Brands; *U.S. Public*, pg. 261

LENOX—Chinaware—Lenox, Incorporated; *U.S. Public*, pg. 261

LENOX CHINA—NONE—Lenox, Incorporated; *U.S. Public*, pg. 261

LENOX CHINASTONE—Casual Dinnerware—Lenox Brands; *U.S. Public*, pg. 261

LENOX CLASSICS—Sterling Silver Flatware—Lenox Brands; *U.S. Public*, pg. 261

LENOX COLLECTIONS—Collectibles—Lenox, Incorporated; *U.S. Public*, pg. 261

LENOX CRYSTAL—NONE—Lenox, Incorporated; *U.S. Public*, pg. 261

LENOX KIRK-STIEFF COLLECTION—Stainless Steel Flatware, Sterling Silver Flatware, Pewter gifts—Lenox Brands; *U.S. Public*, pg. 261

LENOX/KIRK STIEFF SILVER—NONE—Lenox, Incorporated; *U.S. Public*, pg. 261

LENS FRESH—Contact Lens Care Product—Allergan, Inc.; *U.S. Public*, pg. 46

LENS-GLIDE—Surgical Instrument—Alcon Laboratories, Inc.; *Int'l*, pg. 916

LENS PLUS—Contact Lens Care Product—Allergan, Inc.; *U.S. Public*, pg. 46

LENSED COURT SPEC—Racquetball Eyewear—Ektelon; *U.S. Public*, pg. 884

LENSGARD—Clear Protective Coating for Polycarbonate—Morton Automotive Coatings; *U.S. Public*, pg. 1135

LENTACOL—Plant Protectives—DSM Chemie Linz GmbH; *Int'l*, pg. 356

LENTAGRAN KOMBI—Herbicides—Agrolinz Melamin GmbH; *Int'l*, pg. 356

LENTAGRAN—Herbicides—Agrolinz Melamin GmbH; *Int'l*, pg. 356

LENTAGRAN—Plant Protectives—DSM Chemie Linz GmbH; *Int'l*, pg. 356

LENTAGRAN PLUS—Herbicides—Agrolinz Melamin GmbH; *Int'l*, pg. 356

LENTAGRAN WP—Herbicides—Agrolinz Melamin GmbH; *Int'l*, pg. 356

LENTARON—Selective Aromatase Inhibitor—Novartis; *Int'l*, pg. 972

LENTAZIN—Plant Protectives—DSM Chemie Linz GmbH; *Int'l*, pg. 356

LENTE ILETIN—Insulin Zinc Suspension, Lilly—Eli Lilly and Company; *U.S. Public*, pg. 992

LENTE ILETIN II—Purified Insulin Zinc Suspension, Lilly—Eli Lilly and Company; *U.S. Public*, pg. 992

LENTEBOK—NONE—Grolsch N.V.; *Int'l*, pg. 559

LENTEMUL—Plant Protectives—DSM Chemie Linz GmbH; *Int'l*, pg. 356

LENTREK—Insecticide—The Dow Chemical Company; *U.S. Public*, pg. 522

LEONA—Nylon 66 Filament—Asahi Chemical Industry Co., Ltd.; *Int'l*, pg. 83

LEONARDINI—Wine—Leonard Kreusch, Inc.; *U.S. Private*, pg. 635

LEOPARD—Car—Nissan Motor Co., Ltd.; *Int'l*, pg. 943

LEOPARD—Spotting Scope—Swift Instruments, Inc.; *U.S. Private*, pg. 1058

LEPAGE'S—Adhesives—LePage's, Inc.; *U.S. Private*, pg. 598

LEPAGE'S—Adhesives—Unilever Plc; *Int'l*, pg. 1433

LEPETIT—Dairy Products—Compagnie Laitiere BESNIER; *Int'l*, pg. 322

LEPETIT—House Mark—The Dow Chemical Company; *U.S. Public*, pg. 522

LEPTAVOID H—Cattle & Swine Vaccine—Mallinckrodt Inc.; *U.S. Public*, pg. 1039

LEPTYNE—Turpentine Substitute—PPG Industries, Inc.; *U.S. Public*, pg. 1245

LEROI—NONE—ComPair LeRoi; *Int'l*, pg. 1242

LES IDEES DE MA MAISON—Magazine—Quebecor Inc.; *Int'l*, pg. 1075

LES METEORITES—Cosmetics—Guerlain, Inc.; *U.S. Public*, pg. 780

LES-SONIC—Valves & Regulators—Leslie Controls, Inc.; *U.S. Public*, pg. 1746

LESA—Linear Electrohydraulic Servo Actuators—Vickers Actuator Products; *U.S. Public*, pg. 24

LESABRE—Automobile—Buick Motor Div. General Motors Corp.; *U.S. Public*, pg. 720

LESCAL—Dairy Products—Quality Chekd Dairies, Inc.; *U.S. Private*, pg. 898

LESCALLOY M50 VIM-VAR—Vacuum Melted High Strength Alloy Steel—Latrobe Steel Company; *U.S. Public*, pg. 1617

LESCALLOY 300 M VAC-ARC—Vacuum Melted High Strength Alloy Steel—Latrobe Steel Company; *U.S. Public*, pg. 1617

LESCHEN—Wire Rope—Wire Rope Corporation of America, Inc.; *U.S. Private*, pg. 1184

LESCO—NONE—Lesco, Inc.; *U.S. Public*, pg. 989

LESCO A-6—Cold Work Die Steel—Latrobe Steel Company; *U.S. Public*, pg. 1617

LESCO BRAKE DIE—Cold Work Die Steel—Latrobe Steel Company; *U.S. Public*, pg. 1617

LESCO S-7—Shock Resisting Die Steel—Latrobe Steel Company; *U.S. Public*, pg. 1617

LESCOFFIER—Microwave Ovens—Litton Industries, Inc.; *U.S. Public*, pg. 1002

LESCOL—Cholesterol Reduction—Sandoz Pharmaceuticals Corp.; *Int'l*, pg. 974

LESIEUR—Dressings—Bestfoods; *U.S. Public*, pg. 223

LESLIE—Salt—Cargill; *U.S. Private*, pg. 210

LESLIE—Sodium Chloride-Common Salt-All Types—Cargill Salt; *U.S. Private*, pg. 210

LESLIE—Valves—Watts Industries, Inc.; *U.S. Public*, pg. 1746

LESLIE FAY DRESS—Women's Clothing—The Leslie Fay Companies, Inc.; *U.S. Public*, pg. 989

LESLIE FAY SPORTSWEAR—Women's Clothing—The Leslie Fay Companies, Inc.; *U.S. Public*, pg. 989

LESLIE RAVEN—Eyeglass Frames—AVC/Nu-Vision, Inc.; *U.S. Private*, pg. 9

LESONAL—Automotive, Aircraft & Aerospace Ind. Coatings & Refinishes—Akzo Nobel N.V.; *Int'l*, pg. 42

LESS—Bread & Rolls—Lepage Bakery, Inc.; *U.S. Private*, pg. 660

LESS—Diet Bread—Metz Baking Company; *U.S. Private*, pg. 1022

LESS—Diet Bread—Metz Baking Company (WI); *U.S. Private*, pg. 1022

LESS BREAD—Variety Bread—Stroehmann Bakeries, L.C.; *Int'l*, pg. 1495

LESS ROLLS—Variety Bread—Stroehmann Bakeries, L.C.; *Int'l*, pg. 1495

LESTER B. KNIGHT—Management Consultants—Lester B. Knight & Associates, Inc.; *U.S. Private*, pg. 626

LESTOIL—Heavy Duty Cleaner—The Clorox Company; *U.S. Public*, pg. 386

LET-GO—Penetrating Oil—Sherwin-Williams Diversified Brands, Inc.; *U.S. Public*, pg. 1466

LETOURNEAU—Handling Equipment & Londers—Le Tourneau, Inc.; *U.S. Public*, pg. 1410

LETRASET—Graphic Art Supplies—Esselte AB; *Int'l*, pg. 459

LET'S GO FISHING—Game—Pressman Toy Corp.; *U.S. Private*, pg. 882

LET'S MAKE A DEAL—Game Show—Dick Clark Productions, Inc.; *U.S. Public*, pg. 382

LET'S PLAY DOLLS—Play Dolls—Alexander Doll Company, Inc.; *U.S. Private*, pg. 33

LETTER OF CREDIT SYSTEM (LCS)—NONE—American Management Systems, Inc.; *U.S. Public*, pg. 86

LETTER OPENER—Five Styles—Pacific Handy Cutter, Inc.; *U.S. Private*, pg. 831

LETTERFLEX—Printing Plate System—Polyfibron Technologies Corp.; *U.S. Private*, pg. 875

LETTUCE ENTERTAIN YOU—Restaurants & Night Clubs—Lettuce Entertain You Enterprises, Inc.; *U.S. Private*, pg. 661

LEUCOMAX—Blood Cell Growth Factor—Genetics Institute, Inc.; *U.S. Public*, pg. 79

LEUCOMAX—Blood-cell Growth Factor—Novartis AG; *Int'l*, pg. 971

LEUCOMYCIN—Macrolide Antibiotic—Asahi Chemical Industry Co., Ltd.; *Int'l*, pg. 83

LEUCOPHOR—NONE—Clariant International Ltd.; *Int'l*, pg. 624

LEUCOPURE—Additives—Clariant International Ltd.; *Int'l*, pg. 624

LEUCOSORB—NONE—Pall Corporation; *U.S. Public*, pg. 1253

LEUCOVORIN CALCIUM—Pharmaceutical Product—Glaxo Wellcome PLC; *Int'l*, pg. 553

LEUKERAN—Prescription Leukemia Treatment—Glaxo Wellcome PLC; *Int'l*, pg. 553

LEUKINE—Oncology Therapy—American Home Products Corporation; *U.S. Public*, pg. 79

LEUKINE—GM-CSF (Colony Stimulating Factor)—Immunex Corporation; *U.S. Public*, pg. 871

LEUKOCELL—NONE—Pfizer Inc.; *U.S. Public*, pg. 1281

LEUKOCELL—Vaccine for Preventing Feline Leukemia—SmithKline Beecham Corporation; *Int'l*, pg. 1264

LEUKOCELL 2—Animal Vaccine—SmithKline Beecham plc; *Int'l*, pg. 1264

LEUKOGUARD-6—NONE—Pall Corporation; *U.S. Public*, pg. 1253

LEUKOPHOR—Pre-Treatment Chemicals—Clariant International Ltd.; *Int'l*, pg. 624

LEUKOPLAST—Adhesive Tape—Beiersdorf Group; *Int'l*, pg. 182

LEUKORIT—Skittle Balls—Raschig GmbH; *U.S. Private*, pg. 827

LEUNASE—Anticancer Agents—Kyowa Hakko Kogyo Company, Ltd.; *Int'l*, pg. 778

LEUPOLD—Sports Optics—Leupold & Stevens, Inc.; *U.S. Private*, pg. 662

LEUSTATIN—NONE—Johnson & Johnson; *U.S. Public*, pg. 927

LEV-O-MATIC—Liquid Level Controller—Barber Industries Inc.; *Int'l*, pg. 164

LEVAFIX—Reactive Dyes—Bayer AG; *Int'l*, pg. 171

LEVALLOY—Tin Alloy—Belmont Metals, Inc.; *U.S. Private*, pg. 132

LEVATOL—NONE—Schwarz Pharma Inc.; *Int'l*, pg. 1211

LEVBID—NONE—Schwarz Pharma Inc.; *Int'l*, pg. 1211

LEVEL-BEST—Floor Leveler & Spackling Compound)—The Savogran Company; *U.S. Private*, pg. 968

LEVEL 5 OBJECT—Export System Object-Oriented System for Microsoft Windows—Information Builders; *U.S. Private*, pg. 561

LEVEL GAUGE CLEANER—Holding Tank Probe Cleaner—Thetford Corporation; *U.S. Private*, pg. 352

LEVEL MASTER—Refrigeration Control—Sporlan Valve Company; *U.S. Private*, pg. 1026

LEVEL PLUS—Liquid Level Sensors—MTS Systems Corporation; *U.S. Public*, pg. 1028

LEVEL SITE—NONE—Barksdale, Inc.; *U.S. Public*, pg. 457

LEVELEZE—Drains—Josam Company; *U.S. Private*, pg. 600

LEVELMATIC—Liquid Controllers—Leslie Controls, Inc.; *U.S. Public*, pg. 1746

LEVELOC—Positioning Screw—Josam Company; *U.S. Private*, pg. 600

LEVELTONE—Resinated-Pigment Finish For Leather—Henkel Corporation; *Int'l*, pg. 610

LEVER—Metalworking Machinery—Lever Mfg. Corp.; *U.S. Private*, pg. 1081

LEVER MANUFACTURING—Slitting & Binding Machines—Thermwell Products Co., Inc.; *U.S. Private*, pg. 1081

LEVER 2000—Soap—Lever Brothers Co.; *Int'l*, pg. 1435

LEVERWHEEL—Switches—Cherry Electrical Products Corporation; *U.S. Public*, pg. 346

LEVI GARRETT—Scotch Snuff, Plug & Loose Leaf Chewing Tobacco—Conwood Company L.P.; *U.S. Private*, pg. 272

LEVIATHAN—Conical Refiner—Harnischfeger Industries, Inc.; *U.S. Public*, pg. 788

LEVIN-LITE—Leavening Agent—Monsanto Company; *U.S. Public*, pg. 1124

LEVIN-LITE—Bakery Leavening Agent—Solutia Inc.; *U.S. Public*, pg. 1483

LEVI'S BRAND—Jeans, Men's, Women's, Children Clothing & Accessories—Levi Strauss & Co.; *U.S. Private*, pg. 662

LEVITON—Structured Cabling System—Moss Telecommunications Services; *U.S. Private*, pg. 763

LEVL-FLO—Screen—Svedala Industries Inc.; *Int'l*, pg. 1325

LEVOLOR—Fabric Window Shades—Newell Co.; *U.S. Public*, pg. 1176

LEVOTHROID—Thyroid Product, U.S. Rights Only—Forest Laboratories, Inc.; *U.S. Public*, pg. 670

LEVOTHROID—Pharmaceuticals—Rhone-Poulenc Rorer - U.S.; *Int'l*, pg. 1110

LEVOXYL—Thyroid Hormone—Jones Medical Industries Inc.; *U.S. Public*, pg. 933

LEVSIN—NONE—Schwarz Pharma Inc.; *Int'l*, pg. 1211

LEVSINEX—NONE—Schwarz Pharma Inc.; *Int'l*, pg. 1211

LEVURE MENAGERE CAPPA—Fresh Yeast—Royal Gist-Brocades N.V.; *Int'l*, pg. 1142

LEVURE LA PARISIENNE—Fresh Yeast—Royal Gist-Brocades N.V.; *Int'l*, pg. 1142

LEVURE PROUVY—Fresh Yeast—Royal Gist-Brocades N.V.; *Int'l*, pg. 1142

LEVURE ROYALE—Fresh Yeast—Royal Gist-Brocades N.V.; *Int'l*, pg. 1142

LEVY'S—Specialty Baked Goods, Breads—Bestfoods; *U.S. Public*, pg. 223

LEVYS—Bread—CPC Baking Business; *U.S. Public*, pg. 224

LEWATIT—Specialty Resins—Bayer AG; *Int'l*, pg. 171

LEWIS—NONE—Automation Control; *Int'l*, pg. 1389

LEWIS—Aircraft Instrumention—Coltec Industries Inc.; *U.S. Public*, pg. 401

LEWIS—Electonic Components—Lewis Engineering Company; *U.S. Public*, pg. 402

LEWIS—Family Shoe Stores—F.W. Woolworth Co.; *U.S. Public*, pg. 1777

LEWIS FRIMEL—Sleepwear—Donnkenny, Inc.; *U.S. Public*, pg. 519

LEWISOL—Synthetic Resin—Hercules Incorporated; *U.S. Public*, pg. 809

LEX-A-DEX—Workstation Flipcards—The Mead Corporation; *U.S. Public*, pg. 1074

LEX AUTOCENTRES—Car Servicing for All Makes—Lex Service PLC; *Int'l*, pg. 806

LEX-C—Polycarbonate Crossing Signals—General Railway Signal Corp.; *Int'l*, pg. 1194

LEX COMMERCIALS—Truck Retailing—Lex Service PLC; *Int'l*, pg. 806

LEX HARVEY—Fork Truck Leasing—Lex Service PLC; *Int'l*, pg. 806

LEX MULTIPART—Parts Distribution—Lex Service PLC; *Int'l*, pg. 806

LEX RETAIL GROUP—Car Retailing—Lex Service PLC; *Int'l*, pg. 806

LEX TRANSFLEET—Truck Contract Lease—Lex Service PLC; *Int'l*, pg. 806

LEX VEHICLE LEASING—Car Leasing—Lex Service PLC; *Int'l*, pg. 806

LEXAN—Synthetic Resinous Compositions Useful in Molding Applications—General Electric Canada Inc.; *U.S. Public*, pg. 713

LEXAN—Plastic Bottled Water & Beverage Containers—General Electric Company; *U.S. Public*, pg. 709

LEXCITE—Computer-Assisted Research Services—The Mead Corporation; *U.S. Public*, pg. 1074

LEXCODE—Software Product—The Mead Corporation; *U.S. Public*, pg. 1074

LEXDOC—Document Retrieval Feature—The Mead Corporation; *U.S. Public*, pg. 1074

LEXFILE—Software for Full Text Storage & Retrieval—The Mead Corporation; *U.S. Public*, pg. 1074

LEXFORM—Software Product—The Mead Corporation; *U.S. Public*, pg. 1074

LEXGARD—Laminated Window Glazing—General Electric Canada Inc.; *U.S. Public*, pg. 713

LEXICON—Digital Audio Processing Equipment—Harman International Industries, Inc.; *U.S. Public*, pg. 787

LEXIMAGE—Computerized Research Services—The Mead Corporation; *U.S. Public*, pg. 1074

LEXINGTON—Bath Accessories—Baldwin Hardware Corporation; *U.S. Public*, pg. 1053

LEXINGTON—Weather Instrument—Swift Instruments, Inc.; *U.S. Private*, pg. 1058

LEXINGTON—Ash Tray—Willert Home Products, Inc.; *U.S. Private*, pg. 1177

LEXINOR—Antibiotic—Astra AB; *Int'l*, pg. 93

LEXIS GRAPHITE RTS—Racquetball Racquet—Ektelon; *U.S. Private*, pg. 884

LEXONE—Herbicide—Du Pont (E.I. Du Pont De Nemours & Co.); *U.S. Public*, pg. 530

LEXOTANIL—Tranquilizer—Roche Holding Ltd.; *Int'l*, pg. 1119

LEXPAT—Computerized Research Services—The Mead Corporation; *U.S. Public*, pg. 1074

LEXSEARCH—Computer Program for Performing Computer Assisted Research—The Mead Corporation; *U.S. Public*, pg. 1074

LEXSEE—Computerized Research Services—The Mead Corporation; *U.S. Public*, pg. 1074

LEXSTAT—Computer-Assisted Research Services—The Mead Corporation; *U.S. Public*, pg. 1074

LEXSUCO—Roofing Components—BMCA Insulation Products, Inc.; *U.S. Private*, pg. 433

LEXTRACK—Computerized Research Services—The Mead Corporation; *U.S. Public*, pg. 1074

LEXTRAN—Database Retrieval Feature—The Mead Corporation; *U.S. Public*, pg. 1074

LEXUS—Automobile—Toyota Motor Corporation; *Int'l*, pg. 1411

LEXUS—Luxury Automobile—Toyota Motor Sales, U.S.A., Inc.; *Int'l*, pg. 1412

LEYKAM—NONE—American Israeli Paper Mills Ltd.; *Int'l*, pg. 74

LEYLAND DAF—British Built Trucks & Vans—DAF Trucks N.V.; *U.S. Public*, pg. 1247

L'FILM FRANCAIS—French Film Magazine—EMAP France; *Int'l*, pg. 451

LHERMITE—High Speed Punches for Graphic Arts Industry—James Burn Intl.; *U.S. Public*, pg. 1506

L'HEURE BLEU—Fragrance—Guerlain S.A.; *Int'l*, pg. 780

LI'L ROUGHNECK—Children's Product Line—Rubbermaid Incorporated; *U.S. Public*, pg. 1411

LIABEL—Knit Products—Sara Lee Corporation; *U.S. Public*, pg. 1432

LIAISON—Publication—The Mead Corporation; *U.S. Public*, pg. 1074

LIAR'S MAZE—Family Game—Mattel Games/Puzzles; *U.S. Public*, pg. 1058

LIBBY—Foods—Seneca Foods Corporation; *U.S. Public*, pg. 1456

LIBBY'S—Culinary Products—Nestle S.A.; *Int'l*, pg. 915

LIBBY'S—Food Products—Nestle USA; *Int'l*, pg. 916

LIBBY'S ASIAN FAVORITES—NONE—Nestle USA; *Int'l*, pg. 916

LIBBY'S JUICE BLAST—NONE—Nestle USA; *Int'l*, pg. 916

LIBBY'S JUICY JUICE—NONE—Nestle USA; *Int'l*, pg. 916

LIBBY'S KERNS—NONE—Nestle USA; *Int'l*, pg. 916

LIBBY'S KOALA—NONE—Nestle USA; *Int'l*, pg. 916

LIBBY'S MORNING CLASSICS—NONE—Nestle USA; *Int'l*, pg. 916

LIBBY'S SPREADABLES—NONE—Nestle USA; *Int'l*, pg. 916

LIBBY'S WACKY SACKS—NONE—Nestle USA; *Int'l*, pg. 916

LIBBY'S ZING—NONE—Nestle USA; *Int'l*, pg. 916

LIBERA E BELLA—Hair Shampoos—SmithKline Beecham plc; *Int'l*, pg. 1264

LIBERATOR—Equity Release Mortgage Plans—Derbyshire Building Society; *Int'l*, pg. 394

LIBERTY—Inclined Platform Lift—Access Industries; *U.S. Private*, pg. 11

LIBERTY—Ag Chemical—AgrEvo USA Company; *Int'l*, pg. 1203

LIBERTY—Paint & Animation Software—Chyron Corp.; *Int'l*, pg. 1372

LIBERTY—Computer Hardware—Evans & Sutherland Computer Corporation; *U.S. Public*, pg. 595

LIBERTY—Filing System—Fellowes Manufacturing Co.; *U.S. Public*, pg. 400

LIBERTY—Sugar-Free Hard Candy—Ferrero; *Int'l*, pg. 480

LIBERTY—Banking Software—Jack Henry & Associates, Inc.; *U.S. Public*, pg. 808

LIBERTY—Cast Iron Oil Boiler—Slant/Fin Corporation; *U.S. Private*, pg. 1005

LIBERTY—Propane Torch—Sycamore Plant; *U.S. Public*, pg. 444

LIBERTY—Electrostimulation Device to Treat Female Urinary Incontinence—Utah Medical Products, Inc.; *U.S. Public*, pg. 1700

LIBERTY—Body Sprays—Winstar Global Products, Inc.; *U.S. Public*, pg. 1772

LIBERTY BELL—NONE—Bachmann Industries, Inc.; *U.S. Private*, pg. 109

LIBERTY BELLS—Sporting Goods—Brunswick Bowling & Billiards Corp.; *U.S. Public*, pg. 265

LIBERTY COAT—Porcelain Enamel Frits—Ferro Corporation; *U.S. Public*, pg. 618

LIBERTY ELITE SERIES—Vinyl Siding & Accessories—Alcoa Building Products, Inc.; *U.S. Public*, pg. 61

LIBERTY HOUSE—Retail—Amfac, Inc.; *U.S. Private*, pg. 577

LIBERTY KLAD—Aluminum & Wood Patio Doors & Windows—Binning's Building Products, Inc.; *U.S. Public*, pg. 67

LIBERTY OF LONDON—Fabric Retailers—Liberty PLC; *Int'l*, pg. 807

LIBERTY OF LONDON—Clothing—Salant Corporation; *U.S. Public*, pg. 1429

LIBERTY 1000—Valve Regulated Batteries—C&D Charter Power Systems; *U.S. Public*, pg. 271

LIBERTY 2000—Reduced-Maintenance Valve-Regulated Batteries—C&D Charter Power Systems; *U.S. Public*, pg. 271

LIBERTY WEB—Commercial Printing Papers—International Paper Company; *U.S. Public*, pg. 901

LIBRA—Electrical Wire & Cable for Communications Uses & Applications—Lucent Technologies Inc.; *U.S. Public*, pg. 1017

LIBRARY EFFICIENCY—NONE—Life Technologies, Inc.; *U.S. Public*, pg. 504

LIBRARY JOURNAL—Magazine for Librarians in Public, Academic & Special Libraries—Reed Elsevier Business Information; *Int'l*, pg. 1095

LIBRARY MANAGER—Electronic Instrument—Intel Corporation; *U.S. Public*, pg. 886

LIBRARY READER—Computer Product—International Business Machines Corporation; *U.S. Public*, pg. 895

LIBRAX—Bromide—Roche Holding Ltd.; *Int'l*, pg. 1119

LICENSE-TITE!—License Plate Fasteners—R&B, Inc.; *U.S. Public*, pg. 1354

LICKIN' LIZARDS—Game—Tyco Toys, Inc.; *U.S. Public*, pg. 1058

LICON—Snap Action Switches—ITW Switches; *U.S. Public*, pg. 867

LICRON—Microwave Oven Power Supplies—Litton Industries, Inc.; *U.S. Public*, pg. 1002

LID WIPES SPF—Sterile Preservative-Free Cleansing Pad for Eyelid Margins—Akorn, Inc.; *U.S. Public*, pg. 34

LIDA-MANTLE-HC CREAM 1/2%—Pharmaceutical—Bayer Corporation/Pharmaceutical Division; *Int'l*, pg. 173

LIDANO—Potato Products—Bestfoods; *U.S. Public*, pg. 223

LIDDLE GRIDDLE—Mini-Griddle—National Presto Industries, Inc.; *U.S. Public*, pg. 1159

LIDER—Cigarettes—Philip Morris Companies Inc.; *U.S. Public*, pg. 1287

LIDEX—Fluocinonide—Syntex; *Int'l*, pg. 1120

LIDIE—NONE—Kimberly-Clark Corporation; *U.S. Public*, pg. 958

LIDO—Herbicides—Agrolinz Melamin GmbH; *Int'l*, pg. 356

LIDO—Cookies—Culinar Inc.; *Int'l*, pg. 348

LIDO—Plant Protectives—DSM Chemie Linz GmbH; *Int'l*, pg. 356

LIDO FLUSSIG—Herbicides—Agrolinz Melamin GmbH; *Int'l*, pg. 356

LIDOPEN AUTO-INJECTOR—Lidocaine for Self-Administrator—Meridian Medical Technology, Inc.; *U.S. Public*, pg. 1095

LIDOSPORIN—Otic Solution—Glaxo Wellcome PLC; *Int'l*, pg. 553

LIDSYSTEM—Local Injection & Detection System—Siecor Corporation; *U.S. Public*, pg. 449

LIDSYSTEM—Local Injection & Detection System—Siecor Corporation; *Int'l*, pg. 1245

LIEBERMAN'S—Loose Leaf Chewing Tobacco—Conwood Company L.P.; *U.S. Private*, pg. 272

LIEBERT—Computer Power Systems—Emerson Electric Co.; *U.S. Public*, pg. 572

LIEBHERR—Construction Machinery/Refrigerators/Machine & Aircraft Tools/Mining Equip.—Liebherr-International AG; *Int'l*, pg. 807

LIEBOTSCHONER—Cream Ale—The Lion Brewery, Inc.; *U.S. Public*, pg. 1000

LIF-O-GEN—Filled Disposable Oxygen Cylinders—Allied Healthcare Products, Inc.; *U.S. Public*, pg. 48

LIFA—Helly Hansen Brand—Helly-Hansen A/S; *Int'l*, pg. 1010

LIFA—Polypropylene Bodywear—Helly-Hansen (US), Inc.; *Int'l*, pg. 1010

LIFE—Retail Uniform Store Services—Angelica Corporation; *U.S. Public*, pg. 113

LIFE—Watches—Citizen Watch Co. of America, Inc.; *Int'l*, pg. 294

LIFE—Game—Milton Bradley Company; *U.S. Public*, pg. 797

LIFE—Cereal—The Quaker Oats Company; *U.S. Public*, pg. 1347

LIFE—Magazine—Time Warner Inc.; *U.S. Public*, pg. 1610

LIFE AS WE KNOW IT—Greeting Cards—Gibson Greetings, Inc.; *U.S. Public*, pg. 742

LIFE-COMM—Software—CSC Financial Services Group; *U.S. Public*, pg. 422

LIFE/FORM—Replicas & Medical Procedure Simulators—Nasco; *U.S. Private*, pg. 446

LIFE/FORM—Anatomical Replicas—Nasco Modesto; *U.S. Private*, pg. 446

LIFE GUARD—Rules & Tapes—The Stanley Works; *U.S. Public*, pg. 1508

LIFE GUARD—NONE—Xentek, Inc.; *Int'l*, pg. 1349

LIFE JACKET—Laminating Film—General Binding Corporation; *U.S. Public*, pg. 707

LIFE JUST GOT BETTER—Slogan—Guarantee Life Insurance Co.; *U.S. Public*, pg. 768

LIFE LENS—Opthalmic Lenses—AVC/Nu-Vision, Inc.; *U.S. Private*, pg. 9

LIFE-LITE—Pavement Markers—Thomas & Betts/Amerace; *U.S. Public*, pg. 1598

LIFE-PORT—NONE—Pfizer Inc.; *U.S. Public*, pg. 1281

LIFE SAVERS—Candy—Hershey Foods Corporation; *U.S. Public*, pg. 811

LIFE SAVERS—Candies—Nabisco Inc.; *U.S. Public*, pg. 1355

LIFE/70—Software—CSC Financial Services Group; *U.S. Public*, pg. 422

LIFE-SPAN—Anti-Embolism Stockings—Alba-Waldensian Health Products Div.; *U.S. Public*, pg. 36

LIFE-SPAN—Health Products—Alba-Waldensian, Inc.; *U.S. Public*, pg. 35

LIFE STRIDE—Shoes—Brown Group, Inc.; *U.S. Public*, pg. 262

LIFE STRIDE—Shoes—Brown Shoe Company; *U.S. Public*, pg. 262

LIFE SUPPORT PRODUCTS—NONE—Allied Healthcare Products, Inc.; *U.S. Public*, pg. 48

LIFE TECHNOLOGIES—NONE—Life Technologies, Inc.; *U.S. Public*, pg. 504

LIFEBUOY—Bar Soap—Lever Brothers Co.; *Int'l*, pg. 1435

LIFEBUOY—Soap—Unilever Plc; *Int'l*, pg. 1433

LIFECARE—I.V. Equipment—Abbott Laboratories; *U.S. Public*, pg. 12

LIFECHEM—Laboratory Services—Fresenius Medical Care (North America); *Int'l*, pg. 505

LIFECOTE 2000—Nonstick Cookware—Regal Ware, Inc.; *U.S. Private*, pg. 917

LIFEGARD—Personal Distress Service—Allen Telecom Inc.; *U.S. Public*, pg. 45

LIFEGARD—Personal Emergency Response System—Interactive Technologies, Inc.; *U.S. Public*, pg. 888

LIFEGARD—Cartridge Filter—Millipore Corporation; *U.S. Public*, pg. 1112

LIFEGUARD—Trailer—Dorsey Trailers, Inc.; *U.S. Public*, pg. 520

LIFEGUIDE—Brochures Regarding Clinical Chemistry—Beckman Instruments, Inc.; *U.S. Public*, pg. 199

LIFELINE—Trademark Name For GFI Plug—Andis Company; *U.S. Private*, pg. 73

LIFELINE—Cable TV Status Monitoring Systems—Broadband Networks Group; *U.S. Public*, pg. 716

LIFELINE—Link to the Laboratory—Fresenius Medical Care (North America); *Int'l*, pg. 505

LIFELINE—PC-Based Laboratory Data Management System—Fresenius Medical Care (North America); *Int'l*, pg. 505

LIFELINE—Personal Electronic Emergency Response System—Lifeline Systems, Inc.; *U.S. Public*, pg. 992

LIFELINE—Traffic Paint—Linear Dynamics Inc.; *U.S. Private*, pg. 668

LIFELINE—LS Cables—Tamaqua Cable Products Corp.; *Int'l*, pg. 417

LIFELINER—Shelf Liner—Warp Brothers; *U.S. Private*, pg. 412

LIFELINK—Chemical Dependency Program—PacifiCare Health Systems, Inc.; *U.S. Public*, pg. 1250

LIFEMASTER—Paint—ICI Paints; *Int'l*, pg. 664

LIFEMASTER-PRO—Paint—ICI Paints; *Int'l*, pg. 664

LIFEMASTER 2000—No-Voc Paint—ICI Paints; *Int'l*, pg. 664

LIFEPAC—Home School Curriculum—Alpha Omega Publications; *U.S. Private*, pg. 168

LIFEPAK—Defibrillator/monitors—Physio-Control Corporation; *U.S. Public*, pg. 1294

LIFEPATCH—ECG Electrodes—Physio-Control Corporation; *U.S. Public*, pg. 1294

LIFESAVER—Communications System—Executone Information Systems, Inc.; *U.S. Public*, pg. 599

LIFESAVER—Smoke Alarms—Fyrnetics, Inc.; *Int'l*, pg. 1499

LIFESAVER—NONE—Hudson, RCI; *U.S. Private*, pg. 546

LIFESAVERS—Roll Candy—Planters Company; *U.S. Public*, pg. 1355

LIFESAVERS—Friut Flavored Candies—RJR Nabisco Holdings Corp.; *U.S. Public*, pg. 1354

LIFESAVERS GUMMI SAVERS—Candy—Planters Company; *U.S. Public*, pg. 1355

LIFESAVERS PUNCH SODA—Soft Drink—Planters Company; *U.S. Public*, pg. 1355

LIFESCAN—NONE—Johnson & Johnson; *U.S. Public*, pg. 927

LIFESERVER—Field-Erected Municipal Wastewater Treatment Plant—U.S. Filter/Davis Water & Waste Industries, Inc.; *U.S. Public*, pg. 1682

LIFESPAN—Strap & Tee Hinges—The Stanley Works; *U.S. Public*, pg. 1508

LIFESTYES—Carpet—Lees Carpets; *U.S. Public*, pg. 268

LIFESTYLE—Employee Wellness Program—Beloit Corporation; *U.S. Public*, pg. 789

LIFESTYLE—Music Systems—Bose Corporation; *U.S. Private*, pg. 160

LIFESTYLE—Manufacturer Photo Prints for Professionals—Eastman Kodak Company; *U.S. Public*, pg. 550

LIFESTYLES—Condoms—Pacific Dunlop Limited; *Int'l*, pg. 1021

LIFESTYLE HEART PROGRAM—NONE—Oxford Health Plans Inc.; *U.S. Public*, pg. 1238

LIFESTYLE PROTECTION SERIES—Accident and Sickness Insurance—Colonial Companies, Inc.; *U.S. Public*, pg. 1699

Brand Name Index

LIFESTYLES—Custom-Made Curtains & Draperies—Robertson Factories, Inc.; *U.S. Private*, pg. 936

LIFETIME—NONE—FMC Corp., Lithium Division; *U.S. Public*, pg. 605

LIFETIME—Cable—The Hearst Corporation; *U.S. Private*, pg. 515

LIFETIME—Control Valves—Leslie Controls, Inc.; *U.S. Public*, pg. 1746

LIFETIME—Wiring Devices—Pass & Seymour/Legrand; *Int'l*, pg. 806

LIFETIME—Brand Caulk—Red Devil Inc.; *U.S. Private*, pg. 915

LIFETIME—Clothes Brush—Stanhome Inc.; *U.S. Public*, pg. 1508

LIFETIME LEARNING—Educational Programs—Communications International (NY); *U.S. Private*, pg. 259

LIFETIME LEDGER—Bond Paper—The Mead Corporation; *U.S. Public*, pg. 1074

LIFETIME PLUS—Electrical Extension Cords, Spark Plug Wire Sets—General Cable Corporation; *Int'l*, pg. 1486

LIFETIME POSTS—Round Creosoted Fence Posts Various Sizes & Lengths—Seaman Timber Company, Inc.; *U.S. Private*, pg. 979

LIFEWOOD—Treated Lumber—Weyerhaeuser Company; *U.S. Public*, pg. 1764

LIFEWOOD—Treated Lumber—Weyerhaeuser Forest Products Company; *U.S. Public*, pg. 1764

LIFEWORKS—Consultation & Referral Service—Work/Family Directions; *U.S. Private*, pg. 1188

LIFT—Liquid In-Furrow Inoculant—LiphaTech, Inc.; *Int'l*, pg. 812

LIFT'N TOSS—Wastebaskets—Rubbermaid Incorporated; *U.S. Public*, pg. 1411

LIFT-A-LOFT—Aerial Work Platforms—Hy-Tek Material Handling, Inc.; *U.S. Private*, pg. 550

LIFT-PAK—Passenger Bridge Power Cable Storage & Retrieval Device—Jervis B. Webb Company; *U.S. Private*, pg. 1156

LIFTABOUT—Hoists & Cranes—Shepard Niles, Inc.; *U.S. Private*, pg. 992

LIFTECO—Truck-Mounted Access Platform—Simon Engineering plc; *Int'l*, pg. 1251

LIFTER—Hand Cleaner—La-Co Industries Markal Company; *U.S. Private*, pg. 640

LIFTERS—Gas Charged Lift Supports—AP North American Aftermarket Division; *U.S. Private*, pg. 230

LIFTKLEEN—Automatic Parts Cleaner—Graymills Corp.; *U.S. Private*, pg. 473

LIFTMASTER—Automatic Garage Door Opener—The Chamberlain Group, Inc.; *U.S. Private*, pg. 344

LIFTMASTER—Gas Pumps—Halliburton Energy Services; *U.S. Public*, pg. 776

LIFTPAK—AC & DC Motor Generator Sets & Drivers for Elevators—Rockwell International Corporation; *U.S. Public*, pg. 1397

LIGAPAK—Dispensing Reel/Ligature—Ethicon, Inc.; *U.S. Public*, pg. 928

LIGHT—Pizza—Tombstone Pizza Corporation; *U.S. Public*, pg. 1288

LIGHT-A-MATIC—Photo Sensitive Control—Eagle Electric Mfg. Co., Inc.; *U.S. Private*, pg. 354

LIGHT 'N EASY—Aluminum Beach Chairs—Telescope Casual Furniture, Inc.; *U.S. Private*, pg. 1074

LIGHT & FRESH BALSAM—Shampoo—Alberto-Culver Company; *U.S. Public*, pg. 37

LIGHT & LEAN—Meat Products—Hormel Foods Corp.; *U.S. Public*, pg. 840

LIGHT BLEND—Salad Dressing—Cains Foods, L.P.; *U.S. Private*, pg. 199

LIGHT CRUST—Flour—Cargill; *U.S. Private*, pg. 210

LIGHT CRUST—Family Flour & Mixes—Cargill Flour Div.; *U.S. Private*, pg. 210

LIGHT EFFECTS—Haircolor—Bristol-Myers Squibb Company; *U.S. Public*, pg. 253

LIGHT 'EM UPS—Small Toy Vehicles with Head & Tail Lights—Empire of Carolina, Inc.; *U.S. Public*, pg. 579

LIGHT ESKIMO PIE—Reduced Calorie Ice Cream—Eskimo Pie Corporation; *U.S. Public*, pg. 592

LIGHT FANTASTIC—Salad Dressing—Nalleys Fine Foods; *U.S. Private*, pg. 887

LIGHT FANTASTICS—Entree Items—Harker's Distribution, Inc.; *U.S. Private*, pg. 502

LIGHT FORCE—Fiber Optic Cable; Fiber OPtic Connections; Fiber OPtic Cable Assemblies—Lucent Technologies Inc.; *U.S. Public*, pg. 1017

LIGHT GEAR—Athletic—L.A. Gear, Inc.; *U.S. Public*, pg. 969

LIGHT GUARD—Pulse Oximetry Sensor Disposable Bandages—Datascope Corp.; *U.S. Public*, pg. 487

LIGHT HEARTED—Salad Dressing—Cains Foods, L.P.; *U.S. Private*, pg. 199

LIGHT-LEAD—Lead-Polyethylene Shielding—Reactor Experiments, Inc.; *U.S. Public*, pg. 1594

LIGHT MAGNUM—Enhanced Velocity Ammunition—Hornady Manufacturing Company; *U.S. Private*, pg. 539

LIGHT N' DELIGHTFUL—Entrees—Eat N Park Restaurants; *U.S. Private*, pg. 358

LIGHT'N EASY—Household Product—The Black & Decker Corporation; *U.S. Public*, pg. 233

LIGHT 'N FLUFFY—Macaroni Prods—Delmonico Foods; *U.S. Public*, pg. 812

LIGHT 'N FLUFFY—Noodles—Hershey Foods Corporation; *U.S. Public*, pg. 811

LIGHT 'N FLUFFY—Noodles—Hershey Pasta and Grocery Group; *U.S. Public*, pg. 812

LIGHT 'N LIVELY—Yogurt & Cottage Cheese—Kraft Foods Inc.; *U.S. Public*, pg. 1288

LIGHT N' LIVELY—Ice Milk & Cultured Dairy Products—Philip Morris Companies Inc.; *U.S. Public*, pg. 1287

LIGHT N NATURAL—Variety Bread—Stroehmann Bakeries, L.C.; *Int'l*, pg. 1495

LIGHT 'N TASTY—Frozen Poultry—Tyson Foods, Inc.; *U.S. Public*, pg. 1652

LIGHT STROKES PROFESSIONAL NAIL ARTISTRY—Nail Care System—Zotos International; *Int'l*, pg. 1236

LIGHT TONIGHT—Microwaveable Fish Fillets—National Sea Products Limited; *Int'l*, pg. 909

LIGHT TOUCH—Electronic Computer Control System—Applied Materials, Inc.; *U.S. Public*, pg. 123

LIGHT WATER—Aqueous Film Forming Foam Fire Extinguishing Agent & Products—3M; *U.S. Public*, pg. 1604

LIGHT-WRYTER—Transfer Paper—UVP, Inc.; *U.S. Private*, pg. 1115

LIGHTDAYS—Pantiliners—Kimberly-Clark Corporation; *U.S. Public*, pg. 958

LIGHTFOOT—Refrigeration Equipment—Lonrho plc; *Int'l*, pg. 817

LIGHTGARD—Fiber Optic Asset Protection System—Interactive Technologies, Inc.; *U.S. Public*, pg. 888

LIGHTHOUSE—Luggage—Lands' End, Inc.; *U.S. Public*, pg. 977

LIGHTHOUSE—Software—Tandem Computers Inc.; *U.S. Public*, pg. 417

LIGHTHOUSE KEEPER—Software—Tandem Computers Inc.; *U.S. Public*, pg. 417

LIGHTING DIMENSIONS—Publication for Lighting Professionals—Intertec Publishing; *U.S. Public*, pg. 1327

LIGHTING PRODUCTS—NONE—RAYOVAC Corporation; *U.S. Public*, pg. 912

LIGHTLINES MINI AND MICRO BLINDS—Aluminium Horizontal Blinds With Maximum Light Control—Hunter Douglas, Inc.; *Int'l*, pg. 639

LIGHTLINK—Optical Data Transmission System—Datapoint Corporation; *Int'l*, pg. 384

LIGHTLOK—NONE—Berg Electronics; *U.S. Public*, pg. 212

LIGHTNIN—Mixers & Aerators—Lightnin Mixers; *U.S. Public*, pg. 726

LIGHTNING—35' and 42' Sport Boats—Fountain Powerboat Industries, Inc.; *U.S. Public*, pg. 678

LIGHTNING ROD—Rod—Outdoor Technologies Group; *U.S. Private*, pg. 822

LIGHTOLIER—Lighting Fixtures—The Genlyte Group Incorporated; *U.S. Public*, pg. 729

LIGHTOLIER CONTROLS—Lighting Controls—The Genlyte Group Incorporated; *U.S. Public*, pg. 729

LIGHTPACK—Lightwave Cable, Lightguide—Lucent Technologies Inc.; *U.S. Public*, pg. 1017

LIGHTRAX—Fiber Optic Raceway System—TII Industries, Inc.; *U.S. Public*, pg. 1556

LIGHTS AND SOUNDS OF CHRISTMAS—Musical Item—Mr. Christmas Inc.; *U.S. Private*, pg. 765

LIGHTSABER—Laser Etching Process On Our Floptical Media—Iomega Corporation; *U.S. Public*, pg. 912

LIGHTSHIP—Light Beer—Boston Beer Company; *U.S. Public*, pg. 246

LIGHTSPEED—Color Layout Systems—Du Pont (E.I. Du Pont De Nemours & Co.); *U.S. Public*, pg. 530

LIGHTSTREAM—NONE—GTE Internetworking; *U.S. Public*, pg. 696

LIGHTSTYLE—Pleated Shades—Kirsch; *U.S. Public*, pg. 1176

LIGHTSTYLE—Low Calorie Drink—Ocean Spray Cranberries, Inc.; *U.S. Private*, pg. 811

LIGHTWADES—Boots—E.J. Footwear Corp.; *U.S. Public*, pg. 1684

LIGHTWRITER—Yag Marking Systems—Lumonics Inc.; *Int'l*, pg. 1314

LIGNO—LWC—K & P Leykam Austria; *Int'l*, pg. 757

LIGNOBOND—NONE—Avenor, Inc.; *Int'l*, pg. 101

LIGNOSITE—Cement Dispersing Agent—Georgia-Pacific Corporation; *U.S. Public*, pg. 735

LIGURIA—Meat Products—John Morrell & Co.; *U.S. Public*, pg. 1479

LIK-M-AID—NONE—Nestle USA; *Int'l*, pg. 916

LIKE—Soft Drink—Dr. Pepper Co.; *Int'l*, pg. 248

LIKE MAGIC—NONE—Cleaning Solutions Group/Cello; *U.S. Public*, pg. 1466

LIKE-NU—Brake Parts—Echlin Inc.; *U.S. Public*, pg. 560

LIKE ONLY YESTERDAY—Historical Events News Programming—Westwood One, Inc.; *U.S. Public*, pg. 1763

LIKWIDURN—Soap Dispenser—American Specialties Inc.; *U.S. Private*, pg. 62

LIKWIDVALV—Soap Dispenser—American Specialties Inc.; *U.S. Private*, pg. 62

LIL BRUTES—Small Toy Vehicles—Empire of Carolina, Inc.; *U.S. Public*, pg. 579

LI'L BUTTERBALL—Turkey—Armour Swift Eckrich; *U.S. Public*, pg. 426

LI'L CRITTERS—Boxed Chocolates—Borden, Inc.; *U.S. Private*, pg. 157

LIL' EXTRAS—Household Paper Goods—Orchids Paper Products Co.; *U.S. Private*, pg. 819

L'IL FISHER—Power Fishing System—Greenlee Textron; *U.S. Public*, pg. 1589

LIL HOE—Tiller/Cultivator Plus & Big Li'l Hoe & Attachments—Hoffco/Comet Industries, Inc.; *U.S. Private*, pg. 532

LIL' LABEL'R PLUS—Portable Labeling System—Kroy Inc.; *U.S. Public*, pg. 1339

LIL-LETS—Feminine Hygiene Product—Smith & Nephew PLC; *Int'l*, pg. 1263

LI'L MISS DRESS UP—Doll—Mattel, Inc.; *U.S. Public*, pg. 1057

LI'L MISS MAKEUP—Doll—Mattel, Inc.; *U.S. Public*, pg. 1057

LI'L PRO—Children's Chairs—Clarin; *U.S. Private*, pg. 242

LI'L SCHOLAR—Children's Chairs—Clarin; *U.S. Private*, pg. 242

LI'L SHAVER—Greeting Cards & Stationery—American Greetings Corporation; *U.S. Public*, pg. 77

LIL SHAVER—Sno-Kone Machine—Gold Medal Products Co.; *U.S. Private*, pg. 459

LI'L STICK—Sticky Fly Trap—Security Lawn & Garden Co.; *U.S. Private*, pg. 397

LI'L TROLLS—Children's Footwear—International Seaway Trading Corporation; *U.S. Private*, pg. 729

LILA PAUSE—Chocolate Bar—Kraft Jacobs Suchard AG; *U.S. Public*, pg. 1288

LILIANTE FRANCE—NONE—Beiersdorf S.A.; *Int'l*, pg. 183

LILLI ANN—Women's Apparel—Lilli Ann Corporation; *U.S. Private*, pg. 582

LILLIAN AUGUST—NONE—Drexel Heritage Furnishings Inc.; *U.S. Private*, pg. 432

LILLIAN VERNON—Mail Order House—Lillian Vernon Corporation; *U.S. Public*, pg. 1716

LILLISTON—Farm Equipment—Allied Products Corporation; *U.S. Public*, pg. 48

LILLY/MILLER—Flower, Vegetable, & Grass Seed—The Chas. H. Lilly Co.; *U.S. Private*, pg. 667

LILLY/MILLER CHEMICALS—Insecticides, Herbicides, Pesticides—The Chas. H. Lilly Co.; *U.S. Private*, pg. 667

LILLY'S KIDS—Children's Catalog—Lillian Vernon Corporation; *U.S. Public*, pg. 1716

LILLY'S KITCHEN—Kitchen Catalog—Lillian Vernon Corporation; *U.S. Public*, pg. 1716

LILT—Home Permanent—Dep Corporation; *U.S. Public*, pg. 500

LILY—NONE—Kimberly-Clark Corporation; *U.S. Public*, pg. 958

LILY OF FRANCE—Bras—Bestform Foundations, Inc.; *U.S. Private*, pg. 140

LILY'S/CRICKET'S—Restaurants—Houlihan's Restaurant Group; *U.S. Public*, pg. 841

LILYETTE—Brassieres—Lilyette Brassiere Co.; *U.S. Private*, pg. 697

LILYETTE MINIMIZER—Brassieres—Lilyette Brassiere Co.; *U.S. Public*, pg. 697

LIMA MAC—Generators—Marathon Electric Manufacturing Corp.; *U.S. Public*, pg. 1371

LIMA SER—Generators—Marathon Electric Manufacturing Corp.; *U.S. Public*, pg. 1371

LIMB-LOPPER—Hydraulic Pruners, Chain Saws—Greenlee Textron; *U.S. Public*, pg. 1589

LIME-A-WAY—Hardsurface Cleaner—Benckiser Consumer Products Inc.; *Int'l*, pg. 185

LIMELIGHT—Watches—Swatch Watch U.S.A.; *Int'l*, pg. 1161

LIMIT—Growth Regulator for Turf—The Agricultural Group, Monsanto Company; *U.S. Public*, pg. 1125

LIMITED—Syringes—Merit Medical Systems, Inc.; *U.S. Public*, pg. 1096

LIMITED EDITION—NONE—Wechsler Coffee Corp.; *U.S. Private*, pg. 1158

LIMITED SERVICE SPARE—Tires—Bridgestone/Firestone, Inc.; *Int'l*, pg. 213

THE LIMITED—Clothing Stores—The Limited, Inc.; *U.S. Public*, pg. 995

LIMITRACE—Heating Cable—O-Z/Gedney, Nelson Firestop Products; *U.S. Public*, pg. 726

LIMOUSINE AND CHAUFFEURED TRANSPORTATION—NONE—Bobit Publishing Company; *U.S. Private*, pg. 154

LIMZUL—Laundry Powder Soap—Nuevo Federal S.A.; *Int'l*, pg. 990

LIN PULSE—NONE—AGA Gas, Inc.; *Int'l*, pg. 13

LINACOUSTIC—Fiberglass Duct Liner—Johns Manville Corporation; *U.S. Public*, pg. 927

LINAGRAPH—Photo Papers, Film & Chemicals—Eastman Kodak Company; *U.S. Public*, pg. 550

LINALOG—Pipeline Inspection—Tuboscope Incorporated; *U.S. Public*, pg. 1643

LINASCAN—Weld Line Inspection—Tuboscope Incorporated; *U.S. Public*, pg. 1643

LINATEX—Lined Equipment—Harrisons & Crosfield plc; *Int'l*, pg. 598

LINATEX—Abrasion Resistant Rubber Linings—Linatex Corporation of America; *Int'l*, pg. 599

LINATHANE—Abrasion Resistant Polyurethane—Linatex Corporation of America; *Int'l*, pg. 599

LINATONE—Animal Food Supplement—Carter-Wallace, Inc.; *U.S. Public*, pg. 309

LINATRON—Radiographic Apparatus—Varian Associates, Inc.; *U.S. Public*, pg. 1710

LINC—Computer Software System—Unisys Corporation; *U.S. Public*, pg. 1671

LINC-FILL—Feature—The Lincoln Electric Company; *U.S. Public*, pg. 996

LINC-PACK—Welder—The Lincoln Electric Company; *U.S. Public*, pg. 996

LINC-THAW—Accessory—The Lincoln Electric Company; *U.S. Public*, pg. 996

LINCGUARD—Motor—The Lincoln Electric Company; *U.S. Public*, pg. 996

LINCOCIN—Antibiotic—Pharmacia & Upjohn; *Int'l*, pg. 1048

LINCOLN—Apple Products—Knouse Foods Inc.; *U.S. Private*, pg. 627

LINCOLN—Lubrication Equipment—Lincoln Industrial; *U.S. Public*, pg. 1273

LINCOLN—Fruit Juices, Natural Juices, Juice Cocktails, Juice Drinks—Sundor Brands Inc.; *U.S. Public*, pg. 1331

LINCOLN—Conveyor Ovens, Kitchenware & Food Preparation Equipment—Welbilt Corporation; *Int'l*, pg. 188

LINCOLN BENEFIT LIFE—Annuities & Savings—The Allstate Corporation; *U.S. Public*, pg. 55

LINCOLN CONTINENTAL—Car—Ford Motor Company; *U.S. Public*, pg. 661

LINCOLN ELECTRIC—Welding Machines—Welsco Inc.; *U.S. Public*, pg. 1161

LINCOLN LIFE—Various Insurance & Financial Planning Services—Lincoln National Corporation; *U.S. Public*, pg. 997

LINCOLN LIFE DIRECTOR—Pension Product—Lincoln National Corporation; *U.S. Public*, pg. 997

LINCOLN-LITE—Electrode—The Lincoln Electric Company; *U.S. Public*, pg. 996

LINCOLN MARK VIII—Car—Ford Motor Company; *U.S. Public*, pg. 661

LINCOLN NATIONAL—Various Insurance & Financial Planning Services—Lincoln National Corporation; *U.S. Public*, pg. 997

LINCOLN NATIONAL REINSURANCE MEDICAL RESOURCE—Reinsurance Newsletter—Lincoln National Corporation; *U.S. Public*, pg. 997

LINCOLN NAVIGATOR—Truck—Ford Motor Company; *U.S. Public*, pg. 661

LINCOLN SILHOUETTE DESIGN—Various Insurance & Financial Planning Services—Lincoln National Corporation; *U.S. Public*, pg. 997

LINCOLN TOWN CAR—Car—Ford Motor Company; *U.S. Public*, pg. 661

LINCOLNDUCTOR—Cable—The Lincoln Electric Company; *U.S. Public*, pg. 996

LINCOLNWELD—Electrode—The Lincoln Electric Company; *U.S. Public*, pg. 996

LINCOMIX—Antibiotic Feed Additive—Pharmacia & Upjohn; *Int'l*, pg. 1048

LINCONDITIONER—Accessory—The Lincoln Electric Company; *U.S. Public*, pg. 996

LINCONDITIONING—Service—The Lincoln Electric Company; *U.S. Public*, pg. 996

LINCONTROL—Accessory—The Lincoln Electric Company; *U.S. Public*, pg. 996

LINCORE—Electrode—The Lincoln Electric Company; *U.S. Public*, pg. 996

LINCWELDER—Welder—The Lincoln Electric Company; *U.S. Public*, pg. 996

LINDAL—Pre-Cut Cedar Homes & Sunrooms—Lindal Cedar Homes, Inc.; *U.S. Public*, pg. 998

LINDEMANS WINES—Wine—Southcorp Holdings Ltd.; *Int'l*, pg. 1287

LINDEN PRESS—Books—Simon & Schuster; *U.S. Private*, pg. 777

LINDOYA—Mineral Water—Nestle S.A.; *Int'l*, pg. 915

LINDSAY GLEN—Varietal Wines—The Beverage Source, Inc.; *U.S. Public*, pg. 591

LINDSY SCOTT—Moderate Misses Sportswear—Jerell, Inc.; *U.S. Private*, pg. 586

LINDURE—Ferritic Nitrocarburizing Process—Lindberg Corporation; *U.S. Public*, pg. 999

LINE-A-BED—Truck Liners—Lancaster Colony Corporation; *U.S. Public*, pg. 976

LINE-ALLS—NONE—Medline Industries, Inc.; *U.S. Private*, pg. 728

LINE LAZER—Striper—Graco Inc.; *U.S. Public*, pg. 756

LINE-O-GRAPH—Industrial Newsletter—Eastman Kodak Company; *U.S. Public*, pg. 550

LINE POST—High Voltage Porcelain Insulators—Lapp Insulator Company; *U.S. Private*, pg. 473

LINE-RUPTER—Circuit Interrupter for Line and Cable Switching—S & C Electric Company; *U.S. Public*, pg. 954

LINE-UP—Service Products—R&B, Inc.; *U.S. Public*, pg. 1354

LINE-R—Line Conditioners—American Power Conversion Corporation; *U.S. Public*, pg. 89

LINEA—Dinnerware—Dansk International Designs Ltd.; *U.S. Public*, pg. 261

LINEA—Margarine—FIMA-Productos Alimentares, Lda; *Int'l*, pg. 471

LINEAGE—Converter Plant, Battery Plant, Battery Reserve AC System, Power System—Lucent Technologies Inc.; *U.S. Public*, pg. 1017

LINEAR—Sporting Goods—Brunswick Bowling & Billiards Corp.; *U.S. Public*, pg. 265

LINEAR—Hot Melt Coated Reinforcement Tapes & Strings—H.B. Fuller Company; *U.S. Public*, pg. 686

LINEAR FILM—Polyethline, Stretch Film—Atlantis Plastic, Inc.; *U.S. Public*, pg. 145

LINEAR GRAPHITE—Rod—Outdoor Technologies Group; *U.S. Private*, pg. 822

LINEAR MOTOR—Subfractional Horse Power Stepper Motor—Haydon Switch & Instrument, Inc.; *U.S. Private*, pg. 513

LINEAR TECHNOLOGY CORPORATION—NONE—Linear Technology Corp.; *U.S. Public*, pg. 1000

LINEBACKER—Power Fail Transfer Units—Porta Systems Corp.; *U.S. Public*, pg. 1317

LINEBERRY—Cutters & Router Bits—Vermont American Tool Corp.; *U.S. Public*, pg. 575

LINEGARD—Powder Coatings for Piplines—Ferro Corporation; *U.S. Public*, pg. 618

LINEGUARD—Control Equipment—Henkel Surface Technologies; *U.S. Public*, pg. 610

LINEMELT—Line Frequency Channel Furnace Induction Melting Systems—Inductotherm Corp.; *U.S. Public*, pg. 560

LINEN-SET—Offset Printable Book Cloth—Industrial Coatings Group, Inc.; *U.S. Private*, pg. 434

LINEN SOFT—Napkins—Fort James Corporation; *U.S. Public*, pg. 670

LINENS 'N THINGS—Linens & Household Items—Linens 'n Things, Inc.; *U.S. Private*, pg. 668

LINENSERVE—Paper Napkins—Georgia-Pacific Corporation; *U.S. Public*, pg. 735

LINEONE—Socks—Ridgeview, Inc.; *U.S. Private*, pg. 930

LINER PILOT CENTRALIZER—Centralizer—Weatherford Enterra Incorporated; *U.S. Public*, pg. 1749

LINESCAN—X-Ray System—EG & G Astrophysics; *U.S. Public*, pg. 543

LINESCAN—Specialty X-Ray Equipment—EG & G, Inc.; *U.S. Public*, pg. 542

LINESS—Servicing—SLM Holding Corp.; *U.S. Public*, pg. 1419

LINEWORKS—Eyeliners—Maybelline, Inc.; *Int'l*, pg. 819

LINGEN'S BLOND—Beer—Heineken N.V.; *Int'l*, pg. 608

LINGERIE FOR LEGS—NONE—Victoria's Secret Stores; *U.S. Public*, pg. 995

LINGOTS—Chocolates—Nestle Chocolate & Confection; *Int'l*, pg. 917

LINGOTS—Candy—Nestle S.A.; *Int'l*, pg. 915

LINIE N—Hair Care Products—Wella Group; *Int'l*, pg. 1489

LINK—Packetized Voice Subsystem—Ascom Timeplex; *Int'l*, pg. 86

THE LINK—Retail Consumer Electronics Stores—Dixons Group plc; *Int'l*, pg. 413

LINK—Fully Integrated Computer-Based Natural Gas Pipeline Information System—Duke Energy International, L.L.C.; *U.S. Public*, pg. 534

LINK—Online Retrieval—The Mead Corporation; *U.S. Public*, pg. 1074

LINK ADAPTER—High Speed Data Communications—Network Systems Corporation; *U.S. Public*, pg. 1522

LINK BELT—Power Transmission Products; Bearings, Chains, Speed Reducers—Rexnord Corporation; *Int'l*, pg. 127

LINK 5000—Analog & Digital Displays for, Depth, Wind & Speed Information—Datamarine International, Inc.; *U.S. Public*, pg. 486

LINK-LETTERS—Greeting Cards—American Greetings Corporation; *U.S. Public*, pg. 77

LINK LOCK—Fasteners—Southtec, Inc.; *U.S. Private*, pg. 1015

LINK/1—Facilities Management System—Ascom Timeplex; *Int'l*, pg. 86

LINK/100—Digital Networking Switch—Ascom Timeplex; *Int'l*, pg. 86

LINK-TAYLOR—Household Furniture—Lexington Furniture Industries; *U.S. Private*, pg. 432

LINK/2—Data/Voice Network Exchange—Ascom Timeplex; *Int'l*, pg. 86

LINK 2000—Battery Monitor & Inverter Remote Control—Valley Forge Corporation; *U.S. Public*, pg. 1705

LINK/VIEW—Network Mgt. System—Ascom Timeplex; *Int'l*, pg. 86

LINKABIT—Communication Apparatus—The Titan Corporation; *U.S. Public*, pg. 1618

LINKLINE—Enhanced Public Switched Telephone Network Service—British Telecommunications plc; *Int'l*, pg. 222

LINKLORD—Software—Computer Network Technology Corporation; *U.S. Public*, pg. 421

Brand Name Index

LINKSALE—Loan Sales—SLM Holding Corp.; *U.S. Public*, pg. 1419

LINKSPORT—Clothing—The Austad Company; *U.S. Public*, pg. 782

LINKTENN—Computer Software Interface—Tenney Environmental; *U.S. Private*, pg. 1076

LINKTUF—Agricultural Film—The Dow Chemical Company; *U.S. Public*, pg. 522

LINKWARE—NONE—UB Networks; *Int'l*, pg. 924

LINKWARE CONTACT—Networking Software—Tandem Computers Inc.; *U.S. Public*, pg. 417

LINKWAY—Computer Product—International Business Machines Corporation; *U.S. Public*, pg. 895

LINNIPHAN—Coldseal Coated Laminates—PKL Verpackungssysteme GmbH; *Int'l*, pg. 1020

LINOCOLOR—Color System—Linotype-Hell Company; *Int'l*, pg. 604

LINOFIX—Resins Binders—Raschig GmbH; *U.S. Private*, pg. 827

LINOMIDE—NONE—Pharmacia & Upjohn, Inc.; *Int'l*, pg. 1047

LINOPLAST—Resin Binders—Raschig GmbH; *U.S. Private*, pg. 827

LINOTRONIC 530—Laser Imagesetter—Linotype-Hell Company; *Int'l*, pg. 604

LINOTRONIC 330—Laser Imagesetter—Linotype-Hell Company; *Int'l*, pg. 604

LINOTRONIC 230—Laser Imagesetter—Linotype-Hell Company; *Int'l*, pg. 604

LINQ—Direct Access Information—The Mead Corporation; *U.S. Public*, pg. 1074

LINTEK—Radar Cross Section Measurement—Aeroflex Incorporated; *U.S. Public*, pg. 23

LINUSIT—Stomach/Indigestion Remedy—SmithKline Beecham plc; *Int'l*, pg. 1264

LINZER—Print Applicators—Linzer Products Corp.; *U.S. Private*, pg. 669

LIOFOL—Laminating Adhesives—Henkel Corporation; *Int'l*, pg. 610

LION—Jellied Sweets—Cadbury Schweppes p.l.c.; *Int'l*, pg. 247

LION—Embroidered Emblems & Caps—Lion Brothers Company, Inc.; *U.S. Private*, pg. 669

LION BAR—Chocolate Bar—Nestle-Rowntree Ltd.; *Int'l*, pg. 921

LION BRAND—Yarn—Lion Brand Yarn Co.; *U.S. Private*, pg. 669

LION BREWERY ROOT BEER—Soft Drink—The Lion Brewery, Inc.; *U.S. Public*, pg. 1000

LIONCELLE—Jointing—James Walker & Co. Limited; *Int'l*, pg. 1485

LIONEL—Model Electric Trains—Lionel LLC; *U.S. Private*, pg. 669

LIONELLA—Artificial Leather—Forbo Holding SA; *Int'l*, pg. 496

LIONHEART—NONE—Eastman Kodak Company; *U.S. Public*, pg. 550

LIONITE—Hardboard Paneling—Georgia-Pacific Corporation; *U.S. Public*, pg. 735

LIONITE/LIONBLAST—Aluminum Oxide—Treibacher Schleifmittel Corp.; *U.S. Private*, pg. 1099

LIONSHEAD—Deluxe Pilsner Beer—The Lion Brewery, Inc.; *U.S. Public*, pg. 1000

LIORESAL—Pharmaceutical—Novartis; *Int'l*, pg. 972

LIORESAL—NONE—Novartis Pharmaceuticals; *Int'l*, pg. 973

LIP—Fine fabric Wash—Benckiser Consumer Products Inc.; *Int'l*, pg. 185

LIP GLOSS—NONE—Urban Outfitters, Inc.; *U.S. Public*, pg. 1700

LIPE—Clutches—Echlin Inc.; *U.S. Public*, pg. 560

LIPISORB—Enteral Nutritional for Patients with Fat Malabsorption—Mead Johnson Nutritional Group; *U.S. Public*, pg. 254

LIPITOR—Atorvastatin—Pfizer Inc.; *U.S. Public*, pg. 1281

LIPO-BOND—Activated Fiber Supplement—Herbalife International of America, Inc.; *U.S. Public*, pg. 809

LIPO-TEARS—Lubricating Eye Drops—The Cooper Companies, Inc.; *U.S. Public*, pg. 442

LIPOCLOR—Chlorinated Natural Fats—Caffaro S.p.A.; *Int'l*, pg. 248

LIPOFECTACE—NONE—Life Technologies, Inc.; *U.S. Public*, pg. 504

LIPOFECTAMINE—NONE—Life Technologies, Inc.; *U.S. Public*, pg. 504

LIPOFECTIN—NONE—Life Technologies, Inc.; *U.S. Public*, pg. 504

LIPOMAX—NONE—Life Technologies, Inc.; *U.S. Public*, pg. 504

LIPOMAX—Lipase for the Break Down of Fats—Royal Gist-Brocades N.V.; *Int'l*, pg. 1142

LIPOMUL—NONE—Lee Pharmaceuticals; *U.S. Public*, pg. 984

LIPOSORB—Exteral Nutritional—Bristol-Myers Squibb Company; *U.S. Public*, pg. 253

LIPOSTAT—Cardiovascular Product—Bristol-Myers Squibb Company; *U.S. Public*, pg. 253

LIPPINCOTT & MARGULIES—Corporate Identity & Image Management Consultants—Marsh & McLennan Companies, Inc.; *U.S. Public*, pg. 1048

LIPSCOMB FEEDS—Formula Feeds For Animals-US—Ag Processing Inc., A Cooperative; *U.S. Private*, pg. 26

LIPTON—Tea—Deutsche Unilever Gmbh; *Int'l*, pg. 1436

LIPTON—Tea—FIMA-Productos Alimentares, Lda; *Int'l*, pg. 471

LIPTON—Tea—Lever Brothers Co.; *Int'l*, pg. 1435

LIPTON—Ready-to-Drink Teas—Thomas J. Lipton Company; *Int'l*, pg. 1435

LIPTON—Regular Tea Bags—Thomas J. Lipton Company; *Int'l*, pg. 1435

LIPTON—Tea—Unilever Plc; *Int'l*, pg. 1433

LIPTON RECIPE SECRETS—NONE—Thomas J. Lipton Company; *Int'l*, pg. 1435

LIPTOUICE—Iced Tea—Apollinaris & Schweppes Gmbh & Co.; *Int'l*, pg. 78

LIQ-QA-PAC—Kit for Checking Spectrophotometer Accuracy—Beckman Instruments, Inc.; *U.S. Public*, pg. 199

LIQRENE—Chemicals—Westvaco Corporation; *U.S. Public*, pg. 1762

LIQRO—Chemicals—Westvaco Corporation; *U.S. Public*, pg. 1762

LIQUA-LIME—Liquid Limestone—Security Lawn & Garden Co.; *U.S. Private*, pg. 397

LIQUA-SULFUR—Liquid Sulfur—Security Lawn & Garden Co.; *U.S. Private*, pg. 397

LIQUEMIN—Anticoagulant—Roche Holding Ltd.; *Int'l*, pg. 1119

LIQUETTE—Taste-Free Liquid Suspensions—KV Pharmaceutical Company; *U.S. Public*, pg. 941

LIQUI-BOX—Molded Containers—Liqui-Box Corporation; *U.S. Public*, pg. 1000

LIQUI-CHAR—Liquid Charcoal—Jones Medical Industries Inc.; *U.S. Public*, pg. 933

LIQUI-COR—Medical ECG Electrolyte Liquid—Burdick, Inc.; *U.S. Private*, pg. 181

LIQUI-DET—Liquid Detergent—Oakite Products, Inc.; *Int'l*, pg. 861

LIQUI/DRY—Dual Chamber Prefill Syringe—Becton Dickinson & Company; *U.S. Public*, pg. 199

LIQUI/JECTOR—Liquid/Gas Coalescer—Osmonics, Inc.; *U.S. Public*, pg. 1233

LIQUI-LEA—Nutritional Products—Shaklee Corporation; *Int'l*, pg. 1518

LIQUI-MOVER—Condensate Handling Systems (Positive Displacement Pumps)—The Johnson Corporation; *U.S. Private*, pg. 591

LIQUIBROM—Water Treatment—Great Lakes Chemical Corporation; *U.S. Public*, pg. 760

LIQUID ALUMINUM AND POURED PAINT DESIGN—Paints Containing Aluminuous Metal Pigment—Reynolds Metals Company; *U.S. Public*, pg. 1385

LIQUID ASSURE—Presoak Detarnisher—Ecolab Inc.; *U.S. Public*, pg. 562

LIQUID BOLD-3—Liquid Laundry Product—The Procter & Gamble Company; *U.S. Public*, pg. 1330

LIQUID CRYSTAL—Car Wax—Turtle Wax, Inc.; *U.S. Private*, pg. 1110

LIQUID DIAL—NONE—The Dial Corporation; *U.S. Public*, pg. 505

LIQUID DIAL FOR KIDS—NONE—The Dial Corporation; *U.S. Public*, pg. 505

LIQUID EMBROIDERY—Ball Point Pen Decorating Craft—Tri-Chem, Inc.; *U.S. Private*, pg. 1100

LIQUID GLYCERIN COMPLEXION SOAP—Complexion Soap—Yardley of London, Inc.; *Int'l*, pg. 819

LIQUID-L—Laundry Concentrate—Shaklee Corporation; *Int'l*, pg. 1518

LIQUID LITE—Liquid Paraffin & Beeswax—Will & Baumer Incorporated; *U.S. Private*, pg. 1176

LIQUID NAILS—Adhesives—ICI Paints; *Int'l*, pg. 664

LIQUID NEUTROGENA—Liquid Cleanser—Neutrogena Corporation; *U.S. Public*, pg. 928

LIQUID PAPER—Correction Fluids & Typewriter Correction Film—The Gillette Company; *U.S. Public*, pg. 743

LIQUID-PLUMR—Drain Opener—The Clorox Company; *U.S. Public*, pg. 386

LIQUID POLI-GRIP—Denture Adhesive—Block Drug Company, Inc.; *U.S. Public*, pg. 236

LIQUID POLIBAR—Colon X-Ray Oral Contrast Medium—E-Z-Em, Inc.; *U.S. Public*, pg. 540

LIQUID S—Multi-Purpose Cleaner—Ecolab Inc.; *U.S. Public*, pg. 562

LIQUID SAFEGUARD—Liquid Hand Soap—The Procter & Gamble Company; *U.S. Public*, pg. 1330

LIQUID-STAT—Liquid Enzyme Reagents—Beckman Instruments, Inc.; *U.S. Public*, pg. 199

LIQUID TEX—Setting Lotion—Revlon-Realistic Professional Products, Inc.; *U.S. Private*, pg. 690

LIQUID UNIT DOSE—Foil Container—Reynolds Metals Company; *U.S. Public*, pg. 1385

LIQUID WRENCH—Lubricant & Penetrant-Radiator Specialty Company; *U.S. Private*, pg. 906

LIQUIDATOR—Small Vacuum—Advance Machine Company; *Int'l*, pg. 932

LIQUIDEMON—Steam Cleaning Solvent—Clayton Industries Co.; *U.S. Private*, pg. 245

LIQUIDOW—Calcium Chloride—The Dow Chemical Company; *U.S. Public*, pg. 522

LIQUIDTIGHT—Electrical Connectors—Thomas & Betts Corporation; *U.S. Public*, pg. 1597

LIQUIFILM—Sterile Ophthalmic Solution—Allergan, Inc.; *U.S. Public*, pg. 46

LIQUIMAT—Pharmaceutical Products—Galderma Laboratories, Inc.; *Int'l*, pg. 819

LIQUIMENT—Chemicals for the Construction Industry—DSM Chemie Linz GmbH; *Int'l*, pg. 356

LIQUIMMUNE—Immunoassay Control—Medical Analysis Systems Inc.; *U.S. Private*, pg. 727

LIQUIPAR—Cosmetic Preservatives—International Specialty Products, Inc.; *U.S. Public*, pg. 858

LIQUIPLEX—Bulk Liquid Storage Containers—Longview Fibre Company; *U.S. Public*, pg. 1013

LIQUIPRIN—Children's Analgesic—Menley & James Laboratories, Inc.; *U.S. Public*, pg. 1086

LIQUITEX—Fine Art Materials—Binney & Smith Ltd.; *U.S. Private*, pg. 496

LIQUITEX—Artist Supplies—Hallmark Cards, Inc.; *U.S. Private*, pg. 495

LIQUITOTE—Transportable Plastic, Steel & Aluminum Containers-55 to 550 Gallon Cap.—Hoover Group; *U.S. Private*, pg. 538

LIQUORE—Cordial—Marie Brizard Wines & Spirits USA; *U.S. Private*, pg. 702

LIQUORLAND—NONE—Coles Myer Ltd.; *Int'l*, pg. 306

LISA—Magazine—Burda Holding GmbH & Co., KG; *Int'l*, pg. 233

LISA—Strapdown AHRS—Litton Industries, Inc.; *U.S. Public*, pg. 1002

LISA L—NONE—Urban Outfitters, Inc.; *U.S. Public*, pg. 1700

LISE J.—NONE—The Dress Barn, Inc.; *U.S. Public*, pg. 528

LIST CONVERSION PLUS—Mailing Efficiency—Group 1 Software, Inc.; *U.S. Public*, pg. 417

LISTER PETTER DIESELS—Diesel Engines—Lister-Petter Ltd.; *Int'l*, pg. 125

LISTEREX—Dermatological Products—Warner-Lambert Company; *U.S. Public*, pg. 1738

LISTERINE—Mouthwash—Warner-Lambert Company; *U.S. Public*, pg. 1738

LISTERINE—Mouthwash—Warner-Lambert K.K.; *U.S. Public*, pg. 1739

LISTERINE—Antiseptic Mouthwash—Warner-Lambert Consumer Healthcare; *U.S. Public*, pg. 1739

LISTERMINT—Mouthwash—Warner-Lambert Company; *U.S. Public*, pg. 1738

LISTERMINT—Mouthwash—Warner-Lambert Consumer Healthcare; *U.S. Public*, pg. 1739

LISTO—All Purpose Cleaner—The Dow Chemical Company; *U.S. Public*, pg. 522

LISTOMATIC—Photocopying Apparatus—Eastman Kodak Company; *U.S. Public*, pg. 550

LITAMIN—NONE—Procter & Gamble Espana S.A.; *U.S. Public*, pg. 1332

LITCOM—Facsimile Transmitters—Litton Industries, Inc.; *U.S. Public*, pg. 1002

LITE—Salt—Morton Salt; *U.S. Public*, pg. 1135

LITE—Soda Ash—Rhone-Poulenc Basic Chemicals Co.; *Int'l*, pg. 1110

LITE ACE—Trucks & Buses—Toyota Motor Corporation; *Int'l*, pg. 1411

LITE BAKERY—No Chloresterol Low Fat Bakery Goods—Galaxy Food Company; *U.S. Public*, pg. 697

LITE BOX—Lantern—Streamlight Inc.; *U.S. Private*, pg. 1047

LITE BRITE—Game—Milton Bradley Company; *U.S. Public*, pg. 797

LITE DELIGHTS—Foundations—The Strouse, Adler Company; *U.S. Private*, pg. 1047

LITE DIET SKINNY WAIST—Foundations—The Strouse, Adler Company; *U.S. Private*, pg. 1047

LITE-GARD—Plastic Film—Reynolds Metals Company; *U.S. Public*, pg. 1385

LITE JACKET—Cathotic Protection—Alltrista Corporation; *U.S. Public*, pg. 56

LITE-LINE—Milk, Cottage Cheese, Sour Cream & Yogurt—Borden, Inc.; *U.S. Private*, pg. 157

LITE MITE—Circular Flourescent Illuminator—Stocker & Yale, Inc.; *U.S. Public*, pg. 1518

LITE-MIX—Gypsum Plaster—Georgia-Pacific Corporation; *U.S. Public*, pg. 735

LITE 'N' CRISPY—Menu Item—PepsiCo, Inc.; *U.S. Public*, pg. 1276

LITE 'N EASY—Vodka, Gin & Whiskey—M.S. Walker, Inc.; *U.S. Private*, pg. 1147

LITE "N" LESS—NONE—Galaxy Food Company; *U.S. Public*, pg. 697

LITE N' NATURAL—Wax—Bruce Hardwood Floors; *U.S. Public*, pg. 1634

THE LITE ONE—Surgical Mask—Kimberly-Clark Tecnol; *U.S. Public*, pg. 959

LITE SITE—Riflescopes—Bushnell Corporation; *U.S. Private*, pg. 1191

LITE SNACKS—Rice Cakes—The Quaker Oats Company; *U.S. Public*, pg. 1347

LITE TAMER—Photochromic Lenses for Eyeglasses—AVC/Nu-Vision, Inc.; *U.S. Private*, pg. 9

LITE TIME—Dairy Products—Quality Chekd Dairies, Inc.; *U.S. Private*, pg. 898

LITE-UP—Lightsticks—View-Master, Inc.; *U.S. Public*, pg. 1058

LITE WAY—Top Soil, Potting Soil, Organic Peat & Manure—Premier Brands, Inc.; *Int'l*, pg. 1068

LITE-N-AIRE—Airmover—Swartwout Industries; *Int'l*, pg. 1398

LITE-PAC—Trays—Master Craft Corp.; *Int'l*, pg. 267

LITE-R-LINE—Advertising Specialties—The Cook Bates Division; *Int'l*, pg. 815

LITECOTE—Kaolin Pigment—Engelhard Corporation; *U.S. Public*, pg. 582

LITEDRIVE—Hard Disk Subsystems—Ameriquest Technologies; *U.S. Public*, pg. 96

LITEFILBLOCK—Foam Block for Lightweight Fill—The Dow Chemical Company; *U.S. Public*, pg. 522

LITEGUARD—Plastic Fluorescent Tube Shield—Newage Industries Inc., Plastics Technology Group; *U.S. Private*, pg. 796

LITERARY GUILD—Book Club—Doubleday Direct; *Int'l*, pg. 191

LITERARY MARKET PLACE—Directory for Professionals in the Publishing Industry—R.R. Bowker; *Int'l*, pg. 1096

LITESPAN—Digital Telephone Equipment—DSC Communications Corporation; *U.S. Public*, pg. 475

LITESTAK—Statue Indicator—Federal Signal Corporation, Signal Div.; *U.S. Public*, pg. 616

LITH-X—Dry Powder—Ansul Incorporated; *U.S. Public*, pg. 1648

LITHCHIPS—Lithium Carbonate Granules—FMC Corp., Lithium Division; *U.S. Public*, pg. 605

LITHIUM BALATA—Golf Equipment—RAM Golf Corporation; *U.S. Private*, pg. 908

LITHIUM +—Batteries—Eveready Battery Co.; *U.S. Public*, pg. 1360

LITHKYD—NONE—Lawter International, Inc.; *U.S. Public*, pg. 980

LITHO-COR—Containers—Westvaco Corporation; *U.S. Public*, pg. 1762

LITHO LITE KOTE—Paper—Boise Cascade Corporation; *U.S. Public*, pg. 242

LITHOBRITE—Paperboard Containers—Westvaco Corporation; *U.S. Public*, pg. 1762

LITHOCRAFT—Print Paper, Book Paper, Cover & Writing Paper—Georgia-Pacific Corporation; *U.S. Public*, pg. 735

LITHOCROME ANTIQUING RELEASE—NONE—L.M. Scofield Company; *U.S. Private*, pg. 976

LITHOCROME CHEMICAL STAIN—NONE—L.M. Scofield Company; *U.S. Private*, pg. 976

LITHOCROME COLOR HARDENER—NONE—L.M. Scofield Company; *U.S. Private*, pg. 976

LITHOCROME COLORSTONE—NONE—L.M. Scofield Company; *U.S. Private*, pg. 976

LITHOCROME COLORWAX—Color Wax—L.M. Scofield Company; *U.S. Private*, pg. 976

LITHOKING—Single-Width, Web Offset Press—Publishers Equipment Corporation; *U.S. Public*, pg. 1341

LITHONIA—Fluorescent & HID Fixtures—Bryant Electric Supply Company, Inc.; *U.S. Private*, pg. 177

LITHONIA LIGHTING—Lighting Fixtures—National Service Industries, Inc.; *U.S. Public*, pg. 1160

LITHOREX—Coloring Agent for Offset Printing Ink—Dainichiseika Colour & Chemicals Mfg. Co., Ltd.; *Int'l*, pg. 369

LITHOSCAPE—Drainings System—L.M. Scofield Company; *U.S. Private*, pg. 976

LITHOSPAR—Feldspathic Sand—FMC Corp., Lithium Division; *U.S. Public*, pg. 605

LITHOTEX—Form Liners for Texturing Concrete—L.M. Scofield Company; *U.S. Public*, pg. 976

LITHPIRIN—Lithium Acetylsalicylate—FMC Corp., Lithium Division; *U.S. Public*, pg. 605

LITHRONE—Sheet-Fed Press—Komori America Corporation; *Int'l*, pg. 745

LITHROPLATE—NONE—Fred B. Johnston Company, Inc.; *U.S. Private*, pg. 595

LITTELFUSE—NONE—Littelfuse, Inc.; *U.S. Public*, pg. 1001

LITTELITES—Indicator Lights—Littelfuse, Inc.; *U.S. Public*, pg. 1001

LITTERGUARD—NONE—Pfizer Inc.; *U.S. Public*, pg. 1281

LITTERGUARD—Animal Vaccine—SmithKline Beecham plc; *Int'l*, pg. 1264

LITTERLESS—Lunch Kit Eliminates Foil—Rubbermaid Incorporated; *U.S. Public*, pg. 1411

LITTLE BEAR ORGANIC FOODS—Snack Foods—Westbrae Natural, Inc.; *U.S. Public*, pg. 774

LITTLE BITS—Semisweet Chocolate Chips—Nestle Chocolate & Confection; *Int'l*, pg. 917

LITTLE, BROWN—Publishers—Little, Brown & Co.; *U.S. Public*, pg. 1612

LITTLE BROWN—Book Publisher—Time Warner Inc.; *U.S. Public*, pg. 1610

LITTLE CAPEZIO—Girls' Shoes—Jumping Jacks; *U.S. Private*, pg. 767

LITTLE CHAMP—Precision Pliers—Channellock, Inc.; *U.S. Private*, pg. 229

LITTLE DEBBIE—Snack Cakes—McKee Foods Corporation; *U.S. Private*, pg. 723

LITTLE DEVILS—Fix Resistor Carbon Components—Ohmite Manufacturing Company; *U.S. Private*, pg. 813

LITTLE FOLK SHOP—Brand Name Infants' & Children's Apparel—Woolworth Corporation; *U.S. Public*, pg. 1777

LITTLE FOLK SHOP—Brand Name Infants' & Children's Apparel—F.W. Woolworth Co.; *U.S. Public*, pg. 1777

LITTLE FOLKS—Furniture—Simmons Juvenile Products Co., Inc.; *U.S. Private*, pg. 1001

LITTLE GENERAL—Pressure Switch—Barksdale, Inc.; *U.S. Private*, pg. 457

LITTLE GIANT WATER WIZARD—Pump—Little Giant Pump Company; *U.S. Public*, pg. 1566

LITTLE GOLDEN BOOK—Series of Children's Story Books—Golden Books Publishing; *U.S. Public*, pg. 749

LITTLE GOLDEN BOOKS—NONE—Golden Books Family Entertainment Inc.; *U.S. Public*, pg. 749

LITTLE GUY—1200 Watt Compact Dryer—Clairol, Inc.; *U.S. Public*, pg. 254

A LITTLE JAZZ—Styling Aid With Temporary Color—Clairol, Inc.; *U.S. Public*, pg. 254

LITTLE JOHN—Skid-Steer Loader—JLG Industries, Inc.; *U.S. Public*, pg. 918

LITTLE JOHN GIN—NONE--Star Industries Inc.; *U.S. Private*, pg. 1034

LITTLE KICKER—Bender—Greenlee Textron; *U.S. Public*, pg. 1589

LITTLE KOOL REST—Beverage Cooler—Igloo Products Corporation; *U.S. Public*, pg. 265

LITTLE LADY PIZZA—Pizza—Little Lady Foods, Inc.; *U.S. Private*, pg. 671

LITTLE L'EGGS—Girls' Slippers—L'eggs Products, Inc.; *U.S. Public*, pg. 1434

LITTLE L'EGGS—Hosiery—Sara Lee Corporation; *U.S. Public*, pg. 1432

LITTLE LOVEABLES AND DESIGN—Bed & Bath Linens; Toys; Clothing & Sleepwear—American Greetings Corporation; *U.S. Public*, pg. 77

LITTLE LOVEABLES CHARACTERS—Greeting Type Note Cards—American Greetings Corporation; *U.S. Public*, pg. 77

LITTLE ME—Children's Clothing—S. Schwab Company; *U.S. Private*, pg. 974

THE LITTLE MERMAID—Dolls—Tyco Toys, Inc.; *U.S. Public*, pg. 1058

LITTLE MISS VICKY—Greeting Cards—American Greetings Corporation; *U.S. Public*, pg. 77

LITTLE ONES—Pediatric Ostomy Products—Bristol-Myers Squibb Company; *U.S. Public*, pg. 253

LITTLE PANCHO—Tortillas, Chilis, Dips, Sauces & Spices—Borden, Inc.; *U.S. Private*, pg. 157

LITTLE PEOPLE—Little Play Figures—Fisher-Price, Inc.; *U.S. Public*, pg. 1058

LITTLE PEOPLE, BIG BOOKS—Juvenile Book Series—Time-Life, Inc.; *U.S. Public*, pg. 1613

LITTLE PIG—Barbeque Sauce—Clements Foods Co.; *U.S. Private*, pg. 245

LITTLE PLAYMATE—Ice Chest—Igloo Products Corporation; *U.S. Public*, pg. 265

LITTLE POISON—NONE—Callaway Golf Company; *U.S. Public*, pg. 294

LITTLE POLLY—Greeting Cards—American Greetings Corporation; *U.S. Public*, pg. 77

LITTLE PRETTY—Doll—Mattel, Inc.; *U.S. Public*, pg. 1057

LITTLE PRO—Food Processor—Cuisinart Inc.; *U.S. Private*, pg. 261

LITTLE RED WAGON—Wagons—M&W; *U.S. Public*, pg. 35

LITTLE RHINE BEAR LIEBFRAUMILCH—German Wine—Laird & Company; *U.S. Private*, pg. 642

A LITTLE SEXY—Fragrance—Parfums De Coeur Ltd.; *U.S. Private*, pg. 839

LITTLE SIMON—Paperback Books—Simon & Schuster; *U.S. Private*, pg. 777

LITTLE SIZZLERS—Pork Sausage—Hormel Foods Corp.; *U.S. Public*, pg. 840

LITTLE STAR—Todler and Children's Sportswear & Dresses—Seibel & Stern Corp.; *U.S. Private*, pg. 981

LITTLE STEPS—Preschool Line—Steven Manufacturing Co.; *U.S. Private*, pg. 1042

LITTLE SWITZERLAND—NONE—Little Switzerland, Inc.; *U.S. Public*, pg. 1001

LITTLE TIKES—Play Center—The Little Tikes Company; *U.S. Public*, pg. 1411

LITTLE TIKES—Line of Toys—Rubbermaid Incorporated; *U.S. Public*, pg. 1411

LITTLE TRAVELERS—Facial Tissue—Kimberly-Clark Corporation; *U.S. Public*, pg. 958

LITTLE TWIRL—Mini Curling Iron—Clairol, Inc.; *U.S. Public*, pg. 254

LITTLE WHACKER—Insect Control—Bushwhacker Associates, Inc.; *U.S. Private*, pg. 141

LITTLE WOMEN JOURNALS—Play Dolls Based on L.A. Alcot Novel—Alexander Doll Company, Inc.; *U.S. Private*, pg. 33

LITTLEFOOT—Footwear—Cherokee Inc.; *U.S. Public*, pg. 345

LITTLEGEM—Reusable Fittings—Aeroquip Corporation; *U.S. Public*, pg. 24

LITTLEST PET SHOP—Playskool Preschool & Infant Toys—Hasbro, Inc.; *U.S. Public*, pg. 797

LITTLETON—Coin Collections—Littleton Coin Inc.; *U.S. Private*, pg. 671

LITTMANN—Stethoscopes, Anesthescope, ECG Mounts, Mounters, Trimmer, Gel-pads—3M; *U.S. Public*, pg. 1604

LITTON COMPUTER SERVICES—Services—Litton Industries, Inc.; *U.S. Public*, pg. 1002

LIV-IN-ROOM—Upholstered Furniture—The Berkline Corporation; *U.S. Private*, pg. 432

LIVE FOR LIFE—NONE—Johnson & Johnson; *U.S. Public*, pg. 927

LIVE FOR THE MOMENT—NONE—Polaroid Corporation; *U.S. Public*, pg. 1313

LIVE HOME VIDEO—Home Video Entertainment—LIVE Entertainment Inc.; *U.S. Private*, pg. 671

LIVE N' KICKING—NONE—BBC Magazines; *Int'l*, pg. 114

LIVE THE LEGEND—Riverboat Cruise Trips—American Classic Voyagers Company; *U.S. Private*, pg. 380

LIVE WIRE—Women's Sports Apparel & Footwear—F.W. Woolworth Co.; *U.S. Public*, pg. 1777

LIVELY SET—Hair Setting Lotion—Revlon-Realistic Professional Products, Inc.; *U.S. Private*, pg. 690

LIVEWIRE—Catheter—St. Jude Medical, Inc.; *U.S. Public*, pg. 1427

LIVIA—Pension Insurance & Savings—Nordbanken AB; *Int'l*, pg. 957

LIVIAL—NONE—Akzo Nobel N.V.; *Int'l*, pg. 42

LIVING—Gloves—Playtex Products Corp.; *U.S. Public*, pg. 1311

LIVING COLOR—TV Receivers—Thomson Consumer Electronics Inc.; *Int'l*, pg. 1383

LIVING COLORS—Hair Coloring Products—Kao Corporation; *Int'l*, pg. 717

LIVING FIT—Magazine—Weider Publications, Inc.; *U.S. Private*, pg. 1159

LIVING WORDS—Greeting Cards—American Greetings Corporation; *U.S. Public*, pg. 77

LIVING WORDS—Greeting Cards—American Greetings U.S. Greeting Card Division; *U.S. Public*, pg. 78

LIVINGSTON CELLARS—Wine—E. & J. Gallo Winery; *U.S. Private*, pg. 438

LIVINGSTON HIRE—NONE—Brammer plc; *Int'l*, pg. 212

LIVITAMIN—Pharmaceutical Prods.—SmithKline Beecham Laboratories; *Int'l*, pg. 1264

LIVITAMIN—Treatment of Anemia—SmithKline Beecham plc; *Int'l*, pg. 1264

LIVOSTIN—NONE—Johnson & Johnson; *U.S. Public*, pg. 927

LIVRE DE POCHE—Books—Lagardere Groupe North America; *Int'l*, pg. 794

LIZ—NONE—Brown & Sharpe Manufacturing Company; *U.S. Public*, pg. 260

LIZ—Women's Apparel—Liz Claiborne, Inc.; *U.S. Public*, pg. 1005

LIZ & CO.—Women's Apparel—Liz Claiborne, Inc.; *U.S. Public*, pg. 1005

LIZ AND ME—Women's Sportswear—Catherines Stores Corporation; *U.S. Public*, pg. 317

LIZ CLAIBORNE—Cosmetics—Liz Claiborne Cosmetics, Inc.; *U.S. Public*, pg. 1006

LIZ CLAIBORNE—Women's Apparel—Liz Claiborne, Inc.; *U.S. Public*, pg. 1005

LIZ CLAIBORNE—Sunglasses & Readers—Outlook Eyewear Company; *U.S. Public*, pg. 195

LIZ CLAIBORNE—Hosiery—Sara Lee Corporation; *U.S. Public*, pg. 1432

LIZ CLAIBORNE COLLECTION—Optical Quality Sunglasses—Outlook Eyewear Company; *U.S. Public*, pg. 195

LIZANO—Mayonnaise & Sauces—Bestfoods; *U.S. Public*, pg. 223

LIZSPORT—Women's Apparel—Liz Claiborne, Inc.; *U.S. Public*, pg. 1005

LIZWEAR—Women's Apparel—Liz Claiborne, Inc.; *U.S. Public*, pg. 1005

LJUNGSTROM—Heat Recovery Equipment—ABB Air Preheater Inc.; *Int'l*, pg. 3

LJUNGSTROM—Rotary Air Preheaters—ABB Inc.; *Int'l*, pg. 3

LLOYD—Test & Calibration Instruments—AMETEK, Inc.; *U.S. Public*, pg. 99

LLOYDAIRE—HVAC—Eljer Plumbingware; *U.S. Public*, pg. 1794

LO-ABRADE—Castables—A.P. Green Industries, Inc.; *U.S. Public*, pg. 761

LO-BACK—Electrodes—Staodyn Inc.; *U.S. Public*, pg. 1509

LO-BOY—Compressor—Binks Sames Corporation; *U.S. Public*, pg. 229

LO-CAP—Computer Cable—General Cable Corporation; *Int'l*, pg. 1486

LO-FLO—Regulators—American Meter Company; *Int'l*, pg. 1149

LO GO—Low Calorie Chocolate Bar—Huhtamaki Oy; *Int'l*, pg. 638

LO JACK—Device for Recovering Stolen Vehicles—LoJack Corporation; *U.S. Public*, pg. 1012

LO LIGHT—Low Calorie Chocolate Bar—Huhtamaki Oy; *Int'l*, pg. 638

LO-LOSS—Flow Meters—Badger Meter, Inc.; *U.S. Public*, pg. 164

LO/OVRAL—Norgestrel - Monophasic Oral Contraceptive—American Home Products Corporation; *U.S. Public*, pg. 79

LO/OVRAL—Oral Contraceptive—Wyeth-Ayerst Laboratories, Inc.; *U.S. Public*, pg. 80

LO-PRO—Tracheal Tube—Mallinckrodt Inc.; *U.S. Public*, pg. 1039

LO-RIDER—Scissor Lift—Simon Engineering plc; *Int'l*, pg. 1251

LO-TOW—Material Handling Systems—SI Handling Systems, Inc.; *U.S. Public*, pg. 1418

LO-VEL—Flatting Agents for Industrial Arts Applications—PPG Industries, Inc.; *U.S. Public*, pg. 1245

LO-VIT—Ceramic Body Modifier—Ferro Corporation; *U.S. Public*, pg. 618

LOAD COMMANDER—Concrete Mixers—T.L. Smith Machine; *U.S. Private*, pg. 1009

LOAD/DB—NONE—BMC Software, Inc.; *U.S. Public*, pg. 162

LOAD KING—NONE—CMI Corporation; *U.S. Public*, pg. 278

LOAD-LEVELER—Stabilizing Unit—Monroe Auto Equipment Co.; *U.S. Public*, pg. 1577

LOAD MASTER—Shock Absorbers—Bridgestone/Firestone, Inc.; *Int'l*, pg. 213

LOAD PRO—Pipe Handler—JLG Industries, Inc.; *U.S. Public*, pg. 918

LOAD-SPAN—NONE—Oshkosh Truck Corporation; *U.S. Public*, pg. 1233

LOADBUSTER—Portable Loadbreak Tool—S & C Electric Company; *U.S. Private*, pg. 954

LOADBUSTER DISCONNECT—Disconnect Switch—S & C Electric Company; *U.S. Private*, pg. 954

LOADED—Music & Lifestyle Magazine—IPC Magazines Limited; *Int'l*, pg. 651

LOADER-DOZER—Tires—Bridgestone/Firestone, Inc.; *Int'l*, pg. 213

LOADLEVELER—Computer Product—International Business Machines Corporation; *U.S. Public*, pg. 895

LOADMASTER—Pallet Wrap—AEP Industries, Inc.; *U.S. Public*, pg. 4

LOADMASTER—Palletwrap Film—Borden, Inc.; *U.S. Private*, pg. 157

LOADPLUS/EP FOR IMS—NONE—BMC Software, Inc.; *U.S. Public*, pg. 162

LOADPLUS FOR DB2—DB2 Database Utility—BMC Software, Inc.; *U.S. Public*, pg. 162

LOADPLUS FOR IMS—NONE—BMC Software, Inc.; *U.S. Public*, pg. 162

LOAFERS—NONE—Tandy Brands Accessories, Inc.; *U.S. Public*, pg. 1560

LOAN PROCESSOR—Software—Bankers Systems Incorporated; *U.S. Private*, pg. 114

LOAN QUICK—Unsecured Installment Loan—Fifth Third Bancorp; *U.S. Public*, pg. 621

LOANDA—Herbal Soap—Carme' Cosmeceutical Sciences, Inc.; *U.S. Private*, pg. 213

LOBE-AIRE—Positive Displacement Blower—The Spencer Turbine Co.; *U.S. Private*, pg. 1025

LOBO—Men's Apparel—Pendleton Woolen Mills, Inc.; *U.S. Private*, pg. 848

LOBSTER DELIGHTS—Surimi Analog Items—Louis Kemp Seafood Co.; *U.S. Public*, pg. 1652

LOBSTER DELIGHTS—Imitation Lobster—Louis Kemp Seafood Company; *U.S. Public*, pg. 1652

LOBSTER SHANTY—Restaurants—Chefs International, Inc.; *U.S. Public*, pg. 343

LOC-FIT—Electrical Terminals—Litton Industries, Inc.; *U.S. Public*, pg. 1002

LOC-WEL—Locking Fasteners-Nuts, Bolts, Screws—SPS Technologies, Inc.; *U.S. Public*, pg. 1419

LOCAL—NONE—Lawter International, Inc.; *U.S. Public*, pg. 980

LOCAL AREA MARKETING—NONE—HongKong Bank of Canada; *Int'l*, pg. 583

LOCAL COPY PLUS—IMS Data Communications Enhancement—BMC Software, Inc.; *U.S. Public*, pg. 162

LOCALITE—Industrial Machine-Tool Lights—Fostoria Industries, Inc.; *U.S. Private*, pg. 421

LOCARNO—Cross Court Shoe—K-Swiss Inc.; *U.S. Public*, pg. 937

LOCATE IN SCOTLAND—NONE—Scottish Enterprise; *Int'l*, pg. 1212

LOCATIONONE—NONE—UtiliCorp United Inc.; *U.S. Public*, pg. 1700

LOCATOR—Emergency Response Capabilities Data Base—Ecology and Environment, Inc.; *U.S. Public*, pg. 562

LOCERYL—Antifungal—Roche Holding Ltd.; *Int'l*, pg. 1119

LOCH DHU—Single Malt Whiskey—Schieffelin & Somerset Co.; *Int'l*, pg. 412

LOCHNAGAR HIGHLAND—Malt Whisky—Shieffelin Somerset Co.; *Int'l*, pg. 412

LOCK-GRIP—Reinforced Tape for Packaging Uses—Georgia-Pacific Corporation; *U.S. Public*, pg. 735

LOCK'N ROLL—Flexible Stylers—Bristol-Myers Squibb Company; *U.S. Public*, pg. 253

LOCK-N-SEAL—Dipstick & Tube Combination; Blowout Proof & Leak Proof—Moeller Products Co., Inc.; *U.S. Private*, pg. 755

LOCK N' SHOP—NONE—Countrywide Home Loans Inc.; *U.S. Public*, pg. 452

LOCK-O-SEAL—Fastener Seal—Seal Group; *U.S. Public*, pg. 1262

LOCK-ON—Insecticide—The Dow Chemical Company; *U.S. Public*, pg. 522

LOCK-SPAN—Light Duty Shelving—Lear Siegler Diversified Holdings Corp.; *U.S. Private*, pg. 655

LOCK-TITE—Anchored Flooring—Robbins, Inc.; *U.S. Private*, pg. 934

LOCK 'UP—Garbage Bags (Europe Only)—The Dow Chemical Company; *U.S. Public*, pg. 522

LOCKER MATES—Beauty & Bath Accessories—Paris Presents; *U.S. Private*, pg. 839

LOCKETS—Candy—Mars, Incorporated; *U.S. Private*, pg. 707

LOCKETS—Liquid Center Cough Tablet—Mars, Incorporated; *U.S. Private*, pg. 707

LOCKETTE—Hair Rollers—Wilhold Inc.; *U.S. Public*, pg. 78

LOCKJOINT—Flexible Manhole Sleeves—The Chardon Rubber Co.; *U.S. Private*, pg. 229

LOCKWELL—Release Pins—Hartwell Corporation; *U.S. Private*, pg. 1168

LOCKWELL—Hair Care Products—The Wella Corporation; *Int'l*, pg. 1489

LOCKWOOD—Farm Equipments—Agromac International, Inc.; *U.S. Private*, pg. 27

LOCKWOOD—Building Products—Email Limited; *Int'l*, pg. 450

LOCOLOC—Oval & Stop Sleeves, Cable Assembly Kit, Hand, Manual Bench & Power Swagers—Loos & Co., Inc.; *U.S. Private*, pg. 675

LOCOMOTIVA—Tarpaulins—Sao Paulo Alpargatas S.A.; *Int'l*, pg. 1193

LOCTITE—Adhesives & Sealants—Loctite Corp. North American Group; *Int'l*, pg. 611

LOCTITE CHIPBONDER—Adhesive—Loctite Corporation; *Int'l*, pg. 611

LOCTITE PNEUMATIC/HYDRAULIC SEAL—Pneumatic Hydraulic Seal—Loctite Corporation; *Int'l*, pg. 611

LOCTITE SPEEDBONDER—Adhesive—Loctite Corporation; *Int'l*, pg. 611

LODERUNNER—High-Load Press Roll Cover—Harnischfeger Industries, Inc.; *U.S. Public*, pg. 788

LODESTAR—Microfilm Reader & Printer—Eastman Kodak Company; *U.S. Public*, pg. 550

LODESTAR—Children's Hardcover Books—Penguin Putnam Inc.; *Int'l*, pg. 1027

LODGEMATE—NONE—Sulcus Computer Corp.; *U.S. Public*, pg. 1527

LODGING HOSPITALITY—Periodical—Penton Publishing, Inc.; *U.S. Public*, pg. 1306

LODGISTIX—NONE—Sulcus Computer Corp.; *U.S. Public*, pg. 1527

LODI—Retread Equipment—Admiral Heintz, Inc.; *U.S. Public*, pg. 1143

LODINE—Etodolac - Treatment Of Osteoarthritis And Pain—American Home Products Corporation; *U.S. Public*, pg. 79

LODINE—Anti-Arthritic Drug—Wyeth-Ayerst Laboratories, Inc.; *U.S. Public*, pg. 80

LODTRAK—Solid State Devices for Protecting Electric Motors—General Electric Canada Inc.; *U.S. Public*, pg. 713

LOEB—NONE—Provigo Inc.; *Int'l*, pg. 1072

LOEWS—Hotels & Motels—Loews Hotels; *U.S. Public*, pg. 1011

LOEWS HOTELS—Hotels—Loews Corporation; *U.S. Public*, pg. 1010

LOEWS THEATRES—NONE—Loews Theatre Management Corp.; *Int'l*, pg. 1282

LOFENALAC—Infant Formula—Mead Johnson Nutritional Group; *U.S. Public*, pg. 254

L'OFFICIEL DU CYCLE—French Cycling Magazine—EMAP France; *Int'l*, pg. 451

LOFRIC—Hydrophilic Drainage Catheter—Astra AB; *Int'l*, pg. 93

LOFT—Panel Products—Weyerhaeuser Company; *U.S. Public*, pg. 1764

LOFT—Low Odor Formaldehyde Treatment—Weyerhaeuser Forest Products Company; *U.S. Public*, pg. 1764

LOFTEEZ—Activewear—Fruit of the Loom, Inc.; *U.S. Public*, pg. 685

LOFTYL—Buflomedil—Abbott Laboratories; *U.S. Public*, pg. 12

LOG CABIN—Syrup—Kraft Foods, Inc.; *U.S. Public*, pg. 1287

LOG CABIN—Syrups—Philip Morris Companies Inc.; *U.S. Public*, pg. 1287

LOG CABIN DEMOCRAT—Newspaper—Shivers Trading & Operating Co.; *U.S. Private*, pg. 994

LOG HOME FOAM—Gasketing Material for Log Homes—Norton Performance Plastics; *Int'l*, pg. 1174

LOG MASTER—Waterproof Boots & Shoes—International Seaway Trading Corporation; *U.S. Private*, pg. 572

LOG 911—Newsletter—Eastman Kodak Company; *U.S. Public*, pg. 550

LOGAN—Paper—The Mead Corporation; *U.S. Public*, pg. 1074

LOGE—Photographic Equip.—LogEtronics Corporation; *U.S. Public*, pg. 6

LOGE-ON-LINE—On-Line Processing Systems—LogEtronics Corporation; *U.S. Public*, pg. 6

LOGELINE—Rapid Access Processors (Graphic Arts)—LogEtronics Corporation; *U.S. Public*, pg. 6

LOGETEK—Rapid Access Processors (Graphic Arts)—LogEtronics Corporation; *U.S. Public*, pg. 6

LOGIC AC—AC Motor Speed Controls—B & B Motor & Control Corporation; *U.S. Private*, pg. 105

LOGIC CELL ARRAYS—Xilinx Devices—Xilinx, Inc.; *U.S. Public*, pg. 1786

LOGIC DEVICES—NONE—Milgray Electronics, Inc.; *U.S. Public*, pg. 205

LOGIC INTEGRATOR—Software—LSI Logic Corp.; *U.S. Public*, pg. 971

LOGIC II—DC Motor Controls—B & B Motor & Control Corporation; *U.S. Private*, pg. 105

LOGICAL JOURNEY OF THE ZOOMBINIS—NONE—Broderbund Software, Inc.; *U.S. Public*, pg. 258

LOGICIAN—Medical Care Management Software—US SerVis; *U.S. Public*, pg. 1687

LOGICON—Computers & Electronic Systems & Services—Logicon, Inc.; *U.S. Public*, pg. 1198

LOGICS—NONE—Bristol-Myers Squibb Company; *U.S. Public*, pg. 253

LOGICS—Hair Color & Hair Care—Clairol, Inc.; *U.S. Public*, pg. 254

LOGICS—Hair Color—Matrix Essentials, Inc.; *U.S. Public*, pg. 254

LOGILITY PLANNING SOLUTIONS—Software System—American Software, Inc.; *U.S. Public*, pg. 91

LOGIS—Logistic Information System—Air Express International Corporation; *U.S. Public*, pg. 30

LOGISTICS MANAGEMENT—Magazine Covering Logistics, Transportation & Distribution of Materials—Reed Elsevier Business Information; *Int'l*, pg. 1095

LOGITENN—Test Equipment—Tenney Environmental; *U.S. Private*, pg. 1076

LOGLIFT—Forestry Cranes—Partek Corporation; *Int'l*, pg. 1024

LOGLINK—Data Parser Software—GenRad, Inc.; *U.S. Public*, pg. 731

LOGMATE—NONE—GenRad, Inc.; *U.S. Public*, pg. 731

LOGMAX—NONE—BMC Software, Inc.; *U.S. Public*, pg. 162

LOGO—Mechanical Pencil—Sanford Corporation; *U.S. Public*, pg. 1178

LOGO ATHLETIC—Licensed Sport Apparel—Tultex Corporation; *U.S. Public*, pg. 1644

LOGO IV—Mechanical Pencil—Sanford Corporation; *U.S. Public*, pg. 1178

LOGO PARIS—European Eyewear—Logo of the Americas; *Int'l*, pg. 462

LOGO PIC—Framed Reproductions—Voyager Emblems, Inc.; *U.S. Public*, pg. 1143

LOGO 7—Licensed Sports Apparel—Tultex Corporation; *U.S. Public*, pg. 1644

LOGO III—Mechanical Pencil—Sanford Corporation; *U.S. Public*, pg. 1178

LOGO II—Mechanical Pencil—Sanford Corporation; *U.S. Public*, pg. 1178

LOGRAN—wEED cONTROL—Novartis; *Int'l*, pg. 972

LOGROCK—Tires—Bridgestone/Firestone, Inc.; *Int'l*, pg. 213

LOGSTAR—NONE—Western Atlas Logging Services; *U.S. Public*, pg. 1757

LOHMANS—Specialty Glass Vegetables—Seneca Foods Corporation; *U.S. Public*, pg. 1456

LOIS—Jewelry—Uncas Manufacturing Company; *U.S. Private*, pg. 1116

LOK-ALL—Locker—American Locker Group, Inc.; *U.S. Public*, pg. 85

LOK-ALL—Locker—American Locker Security Systems, Inc.; *U.S. Public*, pg. 86

LOK/BOLT—Sleeve Anchor—Powers Fastening, Inc.; *U.S. Private*, pg. 878

LOK-COLLET—Collet—Becton Dickinson & Co., Massachusetts Div.; *U.S. Public*, pg. 199

LOK-DOWEL—Dowel Pin—Driv-Lok, Inc.; *U.S. Private*, pg. 343

LOK-FAST, SEMIFLEX, WEBLOK—Boxspring Components—Leggett & Platt, Incorporated; *U.S. Public*, pg. 985

LOK-IN—Post Hardware—Hall Sign, Inc.; *U.S. Private*, pg. 495

LOK-LINE—Poultry Netting—CF & I Steel, L.P.; *U.S. Public*, pg. 1230

LOK-RING—Restrained Joint Pipe—American Cast Iron Pipe Co.; *U.S. Private*, pg. 51

LOLLI-POP—Sporting Goods—Brunswick Bowling & Billiards Corp.; *U.S. Public*, pg. 265

LOLLI-PUPS—Doggie Donuts, People Crackers, Say Cheese—Pet Life Foods, Inc.; *U.S. Private*, pg. 856

LOLLY POPS—Children's Shoes—E.J. Footwear Corp.; *U.S. Private*, pg. 1684

LOLON—Hardware—Loos & Co., Inc.; *U.S. Private*, pg. 675

LOMA LINDA—NONE—Worthington Foods Inc.; *U.S. Public*, pg. 1780

LOMBARDINI—Diesel Engines—McDonald Equipment Co.; *U.S. Private*, pg. 721

LOMBARDY—Watches—Baume Mercier, Inc.; *U.S. Private*, pg. 124

LOMEXIN—Fenticonazole, Antimicotic—Recordati Industria Chimica e Farmaceutica S.p.A.; *Int'l*, pg. 1090

LOMINUT—Pastry Ingredient—Royal Gist-Brocades N.V.; *Int'l*, pg. 1142

LOMOD—Engineered Plastics—General Electric Company; *U.S. Public*, pg. 709

LOMOTIL—Pharmaceutical—Monsanto Company; *U.S. Public*, pg. 1124

LOMOTIL—Anti-Diarrheal—Searle & Co.; *U.S. Public*, pg. 1125

LOMOTIL—Pharmaceutical Products—Searle Laboratories; *U.S. Public*, pg. 1125

LONALEVE—Tarpaulins—Sao Paulo Alpargatas S.A.; *Int'l*, pg. 1193

LONDON—Bricks—Hanson PLC; *Int'l*, pg. 592

LONDON—Records—Philips Electronics N.V.; *Int'l*, pg. 1051

LONDON—Records & Cassettes—Polygram Records, Inc.; *Int'l*, pg. 1052

LONDON BLITZ—Microcomputer Game—Monarch Avalon, Inc.; *U.S. Public*, pg. 1123

LONDON FOG—Headwear—AJD; *U.S. Private*, pg. 510

LONDON FOG—NONE—London Fog Industries, Inc.; *U.S. Private*, pg. 673

LONDON FOG—NONE—Tandy Brands Accessories, Inc.; *U.S. Public*, pg. 1560

LONDON PORTRAIT—Country Pursuits & Property—IPC Magazines Limited; *Int'l*, pg. 651

LONDON PRIDE—Ale—Fuller, Smith & Turner Plc; *Int'l*, pg. 529

LONDON PUB—Imported Food Products—World Finer Foods, Inc.; *U.S. Private*, pg. 1190

LONDON TOWER—Gin—Charles Jacquin et Cie, Inc.; *U.S. Private*, pg. 580

LONE STAR—Carbon Pipe & Steel Products—Thomas Pipe & Steel, Inc.; *U.S. Private*, pg. 508

LONE STAR STEEL—Pipe & Tube—Lone Star Steel Company; *U.S. Public*, pg. 1012

LONESTAR—Cement, Concrete—Lone Star Industries, Inc.; *U.S. Public*, pg. 1012

LONESTAR—Van Conversions—Starcraft Corporation; *U.S. Public*, pg. 1510

LONEY'S—Dehydrated Soups and Bases—Culinar Inc.; *Int'l*, pg. 348

LONG—Heat Exchange Products, Air-Conditioner Evaporators—Echlin Inc.; *U.S. Public*, pg. 560

LONG & SILKY—Conditioning Lotion—Clairol, Inc.; *U.S. Public*, pg. 254

LONG GONE BANLON—Men's Sportswear Apparel—Garan, Incorporated; *U.S. Public*, pg. 703

THE LONG ISLAND RAIL ROAD—Commuter Rail Service—MTA Long Island Rail Road; *U.S. Private*, pg. 739

LONG JOHN—Antenna—Telex Communications, Inc.; *U.S. Private*, pg. 1074

LONG JOHN SILVER'S—Fast Food Seafood Restaurants—BR Associates, Inc.; *U.S. Private*, pg. 107

LONG JOHN SILVER'S—Seafood Restaurant—Long John Silver's, Inc.; *U.S. Private*, pg. 674

LONG JOHN'S WRAPS—Food Product—Long John Silver's, Inc.; *U.S. Private*, pg. 674

LONG LIFE—Pet Supplies—The Hartz Mountain Corp.; *U.S. Private*, pg. 508

LONG LIFE—Roof Coating Products—Monsey-Bakor; *U.S. Private*, pg. 757

LONG-LIFE MICROCHANNEL PLATES—Longer Lifetime Microchannel Plate—Galileo Corp.; *U.S. Public*, pg. 698

LONG LIFE PRINTS—Photographic Paper—Konica Corporation; *Int'l*, pg. 748

LONG-MASK—Masking Tape—3M; *U.S. Public*, pg. 1604

LONG 'N LUSH—Mascara—Cover Girl Cosmetics; *U.S. Public*, pg. 1330

LONG RIDGE—Lumber & Wood Products—Georgia-Pacific Corporation; *U.S. Public*, pg. 735

LONG SHOT—Aluminum Beach Chaise—Telescope Casual Furniture, Inc.; *U.S. Private*, pg. 1074

LONG WEARING—Nail Polish, Makeup, Lipstick—Maybelline, Inc.; *Int'l*, pg. 819

LONGBEACH PLANK—Pre-Finished Laminate—Bruce Hardwood Floors; *U.S. Public*, pg. 1634

LONGEST DAY—War Game—Monarch Avalon, Inc.; *U.S. Public*, pg. 1123

LONGFELLA—Cosmetics—Naturistics; *U.S. Public*, pg. 494

LONGHAULER—Tires—Bridgestone/Firestone, Inc.; *Int'l*, pg. 213

LONGHORN—Cement—Kaiser Cement Corporation; *Int'l*, pg. 593

LONGING—Women's Fragrance—Coty Inc.; *Int'l*, pg. 185

LONGLIFE—NONE—Huhtamaki Oy; *Int'l*, pg. 638

LONGMAN—Study Aids—Pearson plc; *Int'l*, pg. 1025

LONGMONT—Fresh Turkey Products—ConAgra, Inc.; *U.S. Public*, pg. 425

LONGMONT GOLDEN SUPREME—Turkey Products—Longmont Foods; *U.S. Public*, pg. 426

LONGMONT LITE SUPREME—Turkey Products—Longmont Foods; *U.S. Public*, pg. 426

LONGMONT SUPREME—Turkey Products—Longmont Foods; *U.S. Public*, pg. 426

LONGS—NONE—Longs Drug Stores Corporation; *U.S. Public*, pg. 1013

Brand Name Index

LONGWOOD DIVISION—NONE—Allyn & Bacon; *U.S. Private*, pg. 778

LONIL—Tarpaulins—Sao Paulo Alpargatas S.A.; *Int'l*, pg. 1193

LONPAR—Herbicide—The Dow Chemical Company; *U.S. Public*, pg. 522

LONTREL—Herbicide—The Dow Chemical Company; *U.S. Public*, pg. 522

LONTRYX—Herbicide—The Dow Chemical Company; *U.S. Public*, pg. 522

LONZA—Graphite—Alusuisse-Lonza Holding Ltd.; *Int'l*, pg. 66

LONZABAC-4—Biocide for Germicidal Application—Lonza Inc.; *Int'l*, pg. 67

LONZABAC-12—Biocide for Germicidal Application—Lonza Inc.; *Int'l*, pg. 67

LONZAINE—Amphoteric Surfactant—Lonza Inc.; *Int'l*, pg. 67

LONZEST143-S—Skin Emollient—Lonza Inc.; *Int'l*, pg. 67

LOOK—Candy—Annabelle Candy Company, Inc.; *U.S. Private*, pg. 75

THE LOOK—Beauty Products—DeMert & Dougherty, Inc.; *U.S. Private*, pg. 323

LOOK!—Sidview Mirror Glass—R&B, Inc.; *U.S. Public*, pg. 1354

LOOK ALIKE—Key Blanks—Ilco Unican Corp.; *Int'l*, pg. 1432

LOOK ALIKE—Key Blanks—Unican Security Systems Ltd.; *Int'l*, pg. 1432

LOOK OF BUTTERMILK—Hair Care Products—Clairol, Inc.; *U.S. Public*, pg. 254

LOOK OF NATURE—Setting Gel—The Gillette Company; *U.S. Public*, pg. 743

LOOK SEE—Lens Cleaner—Stanhome Inc.; *U.S. Public*, pg. 1508

LOOK WHAT'S IN STORE—Video Program—National Video, Inc.; *U.S. Public*, pg. 1755

LOOK-O-LOOK—Candies—Van Melle N.V.; *Int'l*, pg. 1450

LOOKEL—Throat Spray & Nasal Spray Line—Shiseido Company Ltd.; *Int'l*, pg. 1235

LOOKS—U.K. Young Women's Magazine—EMAP Elan; *Int'l*, pg. 451

LOOMIS FARGO—49% Owned Armored Cars—Borg-Warner Security Corporation; *U.S. Public*, pg. 245

LOOMSPHERE—Maintains Exact & Constant Environment Around Looms (Textile)—Luwa Bahnson, Inc.; *U.S. Private*, pg. 682

LOONEY TUNES—Children's Meals—Tyson Foods, Inc.; *U.S. Public*, pg. 1652

LOOS ENDS—Hardware—Loos & Co., Inc.; *U.S. Private*, pg. 675

LOOSLAY—Plastic Impregnated Cables—Loos & Co., Inc.; *U.S. Private*, pg. 675

LOPERAMIDE—Prescription Drug—ICN Pharmaceuticals, Inc.; *U.S. Public*, pg. 853

LOPID—Lipid Regulator—Warner-Lambert Company; *U.S. Public*, pg. 1738

LOPRESSOR—Blood Pressure Medication—Ciba Specialty Chemicals; *Int'l*, pg. 291

LOPRESSOR—Antihypertensive—Novartis; *Int'l*, pg. 972

LOPRESSOR/LOPRESSOR HCT—NONE—Novartis Pharmaceuticals; *Int'l*, pg. 973

LOPRODYNE—Membrane—Pall Corporation; *U.S. Public*, pg. 1253

LORABID—Loracarbef, Lilly—Eli Lilly and Company; *U.S. Public*, pg. 992

LORAD—NONE—LORAD Corporation; *U.S. Public*, pg. 1595

LORADS—Laser Transmitter & Laser Target Designator—Litton Industries, Inc.; *U.S. Public*, pg. 1002

LORAIN—Mill Liners—Johnstown Corporation; *U.S. Private*, pg. 595

LORAIN—NONE—RELTEC Corporation; *U.S. Private*, pg. 921

LORAIN & P&H—Rough Terrain & Truck Mobile Cranes—Terex Corporation; *U.S. Public*, pg. 1581

LORAN—Digital Chart Navigation System.—Datamarine International, Inc.; *U.S. Public*, pg. 486

LORCET PLUS—Pharmaceutical—Forest Laboratories, Inc.; *U.S. Public*, pg. 670

LORD & MAYFAIR AND DESIGN—Toiletries for Hotel/Motel Distibution; Including Chower Caps & Sewing Kits—Marietta Corporation; *U.S. Private*, pg. 702

LORD & TAYLOR—Department Stores—The May Department Stores Company; *U.S. Public*, pg. 1063

LORD ASTER—Specialty Frozen Foods—Louis Kemp Seafood Co.; *U.S. Public*, pg. 1652

LORD CALVERT—Canadian Whiskey—Fortune Brands, Inc.; *U.S. Public*, pg. 674

LORD SANDWICH—Food—Coop Switzerland; *Int'l*, pg. 329

LORD WEST—Formal Wear for Men—West Mill Clothes, Inc.; *U.S. Private*, pg. 1163

LORDS OF CREATION—Role Playing Game—Monarch Avalon, Inc.; *U.S. Public*, pg. 1123

L'OREAL—Hair Preparations & Cosmetics—Cosmair, Inc.; *Int'l*, pg. 818

L'OREAL—Cosmetics—L'Oreal S.A.; *Int'l*, pg. 818

LORELCO—Anti-hyperlipidemic—Otsuka Pharmaceutical Co., Ltd.; *Int'l*, pg. 1013

LORESTAT—Tolrestat, Diabetic Neuropathy—Recordati Industria Chimica e Farmaceutica S.p.A.; *Int'l*, pg. 1090

LORIA—Surface Analyzer—Ashland, Inc.; *U.S. Public*, pg. 138

LORILLARD—Cigarette Company—Loews Corporation; *U.S. Public*, pg. 1010

LORIMERS—Ale—Vaux Group Plc; *Int'l*, pg. 1453

L'ORMARINS ESTATE—Wine—Distillers Corporation S.A.; *Int'l*, pg. 1129

LORNA DOONE—Shortbread—Nabisco Inc.; *U.S. Public*, pg. 1355

LORNA DOONE—Shortbread—RJR Nabisco Holdings Corp.; *U.S. Public*, pg. 1354

LOROX—Herbicide—Du Pont (E.I. Du Pont De Nemours & Co.); *U.S. Public*, pg. 530

LOROXIDE—Pharmaceuticals—Rhone-Poulenc Rorer - U.S.; *Int'l*, pg. 1110

LORRAINE—Lingerie—O'Bryan Brothers Inc.; *U.S. Private*, pg. 810

LORSBAN—Insecticide—The Dow Chemical Company; *U.S. Public*, pg. 522

LORUS BRANDS—NONE—Seiko Corporation; *Int'l*, pg. 1218

LOS ANDES—Skis—Mizuno Corporation; *Int'l*, pg. 884

LOS ANGELES RAIDERS—Football Team—Oakland Raiders; *U.S. Private*, pg. 809

LOS HERMANOS—Vineyards—Wine World Estates Company; *Int'l*, pg. 917

LOSALT—Corrosion Inhibitors—BetzDearborn Inc.; *U.S. Public*, pg. 226

LOSE IT—Girdles—AGP Industrial Corporation; *Int'l*, pg. 14

LOSEC—Gastrointestinal Agent—Astra AB; *Int'l*, pg. 93

LOSILPHOS—Ferrophosphorus Briquettes—Solutia Inc.; *U.S. Public*, pg. 1483

LOSONE—Ventilators—Broan Mfg. Co., Inc.; *U.S. Public*, pg. 1193

LOST ACRES—Preserves & Jellies—J.M. Smucker Company; *U.S. Public*, pg. 1480

LOST RIVER—NONE—Kellwood Company; *U.S. Public*, pg. 948

LOSTOKER—Stoker—Detroit Stoker Co.; *U.S. Private*, pg. 1679

A LOT OF BANK FOR YOUR MONEY—NONE—Magna Group, Inc.; *U.S. Public*, pg. 1037

LOTENSIN—Blood Pressure Medication—Ciba Specialty Chemicals; *Int'l*, pg. 291

LOTENSIN—ACE-Inhibitor for Hypertension—Novartis; *Int'l*, pg. 972

LOTENSIN/LOTENSIN HCT—NONE—Novartis Pharmaceuticals; *Int'l*, pg. 973

LOTHROP, LEE & SHEPARD—Books—The Hearst Corporation; *U.S. Private*, pg. 515

LOTHROP, LEE & SHEPARD—Juvenile Books—William Morrow & Co., Inc.; *U.S. Private*, pg. 515

LOTREL—NONE—Novartis Pharmaceuticals; *Int'l*, pg. 973

LOTRIMIN AF—Anti-Fungal Agent—Schering-Plough Healthcare Products Inc.; *U.S. Public*, pg. 1438

LOTRIMIN AF—Athlete's Foot Antifungal—Schering-Plough Corporation; *U.S. Public*, pg. 1438

LOTRISONE—Antifungal/Anti-Inflammatory Cream—Schering-Plough Corporation; *U.S. Public*, pg. 1438

LOTTE—Department Stores—Lotte Shopping Co. Ltd.; *Int'l*, pg. 819

LOTUS—Carpet—Columbus Mills, Inc.; *U.S. Private*, pg. 256

LOTUS—NONE—Fort James Corporation; *U.S. Public*, pg. 670

LOTUS—Automobiles—Lotus Cars USA, Inc.; *Int'l*, pg. 1071

LOTUS—Computer Software—Lotus Development Corporation; *U.S. Public*, pg. 896

LOTUS—NONE—Regal Ware, Inc.; *U.S. Private*, pg. 917

LOU—Intimate Apparel—VF Corporation; *U.S. Public*, pg. 1702

LOU ANA—Vegetable Oils—Lou Ana Foods, Inc.; *Int'l*, pg. 879

LOU LOU—Fragrance—Cosmair, Inc., Ralph Lauren Fragrance Division; *Int'l*, pg. 818

LOUD 'N CLEAR—Zinc Air Hearing Aid Batteries—RAYOVAC Corporation; *U.S. Private*, pg. 912

LOUDEN—Cranes, Stackers & Monorial Systems—Acco Chain & Lifting Products; *Int'l*, pg. 473

LOUGINES—Watches—SMH Swiss Corporation for Micro Electronics & Watchmaking Indus. Ltd.; *Int'l*, pg. 1160

LOUIE LOOP—Roofing Fastener—Powers Fastening, Inc.; *U.S. Private*, pg. 878

LOUIS ALLIS—Motors—MagneTek, Inc.; *U.S. Public*, pg. 1037

LOUIS DREYFUS NATURAL GAS—Oil—Louis Dreyfus Natural Gas Corp.; *U.S. Private*, pg. 342

LOUIS JOONE—Women's Apparel—International Cosmetics Co., Ltd.; *Int'l*, pg. 684

LOUIS KEMP—Surimi Analog Items—Louis Kemp Seafood Co.; *U.S. Public*, pg. 1652

LOUIS KEMP—Seafood Products—Philip Morris Companies Inc.; *U.S. Public*, pg. 1287

LOUIS LATOUR—Wine—Pacific Wine Co.; *U.S. Private*, pg. 843

LOUIS RICH—Luncheon Meats, Franks & Fresh Turkey Cuts & Products—Kraft Foods, Inc.; *U.S. Public*, pg. 1287

LOUIS RICH—Turkey Products—Kraft Foods Inc.; *U.S. Public*, pg. 1288

LOUIS RICH—Food Products—Oscar Mayer Foods Corp.; *U.S. Public*, pg. 1288

LOUIS RICH—Turkey Cuts, Luncheon Meats & Other Meat Products—Philip Morris Companies Inc.; *U.S. Public*, pg. 1287

LOUIS ROEDERER—Wine—Pacific Wine Co.; *U.S. Private*, pg. 843

LOUIS ROEDERER—Champagne—Paterno Imports Limited; *U.S. Private*, pg. 843

LOUIS SHERRY—Ice Cream (New York)—Borden, Inc.; *U.S. Private*, pg. 157

LOUIS SHERRY—Ice Cream—Labatt Brewing Company Limited; *Int'l*, pg. 679

LOUIS TRAUTH DAIRY, INC.—Dairy Products—Trauth Dairy Inc.; *U.S. Private*, pg. 1098

LOUIS XIV—Brandy—Distillers Corporation S.A.; *Int'l*, pg. 1129

LOUISE'S—Pasta Products—Labatt Brewing Company Limited; *Int'l*, pg. 679

LOUISIANA—Hot Sauce—Bruce Foods Corp.; *U.S. Private*, pg. 175

LOUISIANA—Hot Sauce—Trappey's Fine Foods, Inc.; *U.S. Private*, pg. 105

LOUISIANA DOWNS—Thoroughbred Race Track—Louisiana Downs; *U.S. Private*, pg. 319

LOUISIANA GOLD—Hot Sauce—Bruce Foods Corp.; *U.S. Private*, pg. 175

LOUISIANA MANUFACTURERS REGISTER—Register—Manufacturers' News, Inc.; *U.S. Private*, pg. 700

LOUISVILLE—Hockey Sticks—Hillerich & Bradsby Co.; *U.S. Private*, pg. 530

LOUISVILLE LADDER—Fiberglass, Aluminum, Wood & Steel Ladders—Emerson Electric Co.; *U.S. Public*, pg. 572

LOUISVILLE SLUGGER—Sporting Goods—Hillerich & Bradsby Co.; *U.S. Private*, pg. 530

LOURNAY—Skin Care Prod.—Colgate-Palmolive Company; *U.S. Public*, pg. 397

LOUVERBORD—Hardboard—Georgia-Pacific Corporation; *U.S. Public*, pg. 735

LOUVRE KING—Jalousie Windows—International Aluminum Corporation; *U.S. Public*, pg. 894

LOVE—Temperature Control—Dwyer Instruments Inc.; *U.S. Private*, pg. 350

LOVE—Shipping Containers—Love Packaging Group; *U.S. Private*, pg. 677

LOVE NOTES—Fragrance for Women—Yardley of London, Inc.; *Int'l*, pg. 819

LOVE TALK—NONE—American Greetings Corporation; *U.S. Public*, pg. 77

LOVE THEME—Greeting Cards—American Greetings Corporation; *U.S. Public*, pg. 77

LOVEJOY—Power Transmission—Lovejoy Inc.; *U.S. Private*, pg. 677

LOVEJOY-ROSTA—Power Transmission—Lovejoy Inc.; *U.S. Private*, pg. 677

LOVEJOY'S—College Guides—Simon & Schuster; *U.S. Private*, pg. 777

LOVELINE—Advice/Talk Radio Program—Westwood One Entertainment; *U.S. Public*, pg. 1763

LOVELINE—Advice & General Interest Programming—Westwood One, Inc.; *U.S. Public*, pg. 1763

LOVESWEPT—Book Publishing—Bertelsmann AG; *Int'l*, pg. 189

LOVING CARE—Haircolor—Bristol-Myers Squibb Company; *U.S. Public*, pg. 253

LOVING COUPLES—Greeting Cards, Gift Wrap Paper & Ceramic Plates—American Greetings Corporation; *U.S. Public*, pg. 77

LOVING HANDS—Latex Gloves—Magla Products; *U.S. Public*, pg. 695

LOVOC—Low VOC Coatings for Plastic—Morton Automotive Coatings; *U.S. Public*, pg. 1135

LOW AIR LEAF—Chassis Suspension—Peterbilt Motors Co.; *U.S. Public*, pg. 1247

LOW BOY—Tires—Bridgestone/Firestone, Inc.; *Int'l*, pg. 213

LOW BOY—Paper Napkins—Georgia-Pacific Corporation; *U.S. Public*, pg. 735

LOW-FAT & FAST—NONE—Cowles Enthusiast Media, Inc.; *U.S. Private*, pg. 281

LOW LOW—Butter & Dairy Spreads—Kerry Group PLC; *Int'l*, pg. 731

LOW MARK—Paper, Cones & Tubes Made from Paper—Sonoco Products Company; *U.S. Public*, pg. 1485

LOW POROSITY WOVEN—Woven Polyester Vascular Prosthesis—Datascope Corp.; *U.S. Public*, pg. 487

LOW SUGAR—Reduced-Sugar Fruit Spreads—J.M. Smucker Company; *U.S. Public*, pg. 1480

LOW-T GRAY—Float Glass—AFG Industries, Inc.; *Int'l*, pg. 84

LOW-HEAD—Screen—Svedala Industries Inc.; *Int'l*, pg. 1325

LOW-LINE—Ventilators—Swartwout Industries; *Int'l*, pg. 1398

LOWARA—European Water Pumps—Goulds Pumps, Incorporated; *U.S. Public*, pg. 860

LOWE—Boats—Outboard Marine Corporation; *U.S. Private*, pg. 478

LOWENBRAU—Lowenbrau Dark Special—Miller Brewing Company; *U.S. Public*, pg. 1289

LOWENBRAU—Beer—Philip Morris Companies Inc.; *U.S. Public*, pg. 1287

LOWENER TOOLS—Service Tools—SPX Corporation; *U.S. Public*, pg. 1420

LOWERATOR—Self Leveling Dispenser—American Wyott Corporation; *U.S. Private*, pg. 1193

LOWE'S THEATERS—Motion Picture Theaters—Sony Pictures Studios; *Int'l*, pg. 1283

LOWILA CAKE—Soap-Free Skin Cleanser—Westwood-Squibb Pharmaceuticals Inc.; *U.S. Public*, pg. 255

LOWRANCE—Liquid Crystal Graphs—Lowrance Electronics, Inc.; *U.S. Public*, pg. 1015

LOWRANCE AVIONICS—NONE—Lowrance Electronics, Inc.; *U.S. Public*, pg. 1015

LOX—Adhesive Cement—Bridgestone/Firestone, Inc.; *Int'l*, pg. 213

LOXITE—Adhesive Cement—Bridgestone/Firestone, Inc.; *Int'l*, pg. 213

LOYALTYLOOP—National Direct-Marketing Venture—Provident Financial Group, Inc.; *U.S. Public*, pg. 1338

LOZOL—Pharmaceuticals—Rhone-Poulenc Rorer - U.S.; *Int'l*, pg. 1110

L'PHOTOGRAPHE—French Photography Magazine—EMAP France; *Int'l*, pg. 451

LU—Biscuits—Danone Group; *Int'l*, pg. 379

LU—Cookies—Mother's Cake & Cookie Co.; *U.S. Private*, pg. 1022

LU✱SEE—NONE—Cordis, a Johnson & Johnson Company; *U.S. Public*, pg. 928

LUB-E—NONE—Ace Hardware Corporation; *U.S. Private*, pg. 12

LUBAFAX—Prescription Drug—Glaxo Wellcome PLC; *Int'l*, pg. 553

LUBBOCK AVALANCHE JOURNAL—Newspaper—Shivers Trading & Operating Co.; *U.S. Private*, pg. 994

LUBE-BOOSTER—Water Based Lubricity Additive—Ferro Corporation; *U.S. Public*, pg. 618

LUBE-GUARD THREAD COMPOUND—Pipe Thread Lubricant—Weatherford Enterra Incorporated; *U.S. Public*, pg. 1749

LUBE-MYND-R—Differential Pressure Indicators—Pall Corporation; *U.S. Public*, pg. 1253

LUBE-SEAL THREAD COMPOUND—Pipe Thread Lubricant—Weatherford Enterra Incorporated; *U.S. Public*, pg. 1749

LUBECON—Lubricating Oils & Greases-Automated Equipment—LubeCon Systems, Inc.; *U.S. Private*, pg. 679

LUBECRAFT—Centralized Series Progressive Lubrication Systems—LubeCon Systems, Inc.; *U.S. Private*, pg. 679

LUBEN—Specialty Adhesives & Scrims—Alpha Associates, Inc.; *U.S. Private*, pg. 44

LUBER-FINER—Heavy-Duty Filters—Champion Laboratories, Inc.; *U.S. Private*, pg. 1113

LUBRACAL—Calcium Stearate-Based Aque—Witco Corporation; *U.S. Public*, pg. 1773

LUBREX—Inside Tire Mold Lubricant—Harwick Standard Distribution Corporation; *U.S. Private*, pg. 509

LUBRI-FLUID—Lubricating Oil—Universal Cooperatives, Inc.; *U.S. Private*, pg. 1127

LUBRICOAT—Hyaluronic Acid—Ethicon, Inc.; *U.S. Public*, pg. 928

LUBRIDERM—Dermatological Products—Warner-Lambert Company; *U.S. Public*, pg. 1738

LUBRIDERM—Skin Lotions—Warner-Lambert Consumer Healthcare; *U.S. Public*, pg. 1739

LUBRIKUHL—Synthetic Refrigeration Lubricants—The Lubrizol Corporation; *U.S. Public*, pg. 1016

LUBRIMATE—Special Grade of Carbon/Graphite Seal Material for Severe Service—The Johnson Corporation; *U.S. Private*, pg. 591

LUBRIN—Inserts; Personal Lubricating Inserts for Use in Vaginal Dryness—Bradley Pharmaceuticals; *U.S. Public*, pg. 249

LUBRIN—Inserts; Personal Lubricating Inserts for Use in Vaginal Dryness—Doak Dermatologics; *U.S. Public*, pg. 250

LUBRIPLATE—Lubricants—Lubriplate Div. of Fiske Bros. Refining Co.; *U.S. Private*, pg. 409

LUBRIQUIP—Lubrication Equipment—IDEX Corporation; *U.S. Public*, pg. 862

LUBRISOFT—Packing Rings—Leslie Controls, Inc.; *U.S. Public*, pg. 1746

LUBRITAB—Natural Lubricant—Penford Corp.; *U.S. Public*, pg. 1269

LUBRITAN—Leather Chemical—Rohm and Haas Company; *U.S. Public*, pg. 1403

LUBRIZOL—Lubricating Additives—The Lubrizol Corporation; *U.S. Public*, pg. 1016

LUBY'S CAFETERIAS—Cafeterias—Luby's Cafeterias, Inc.; *U.S. Public*, pg. 1017

LUCALEN—Ethylene Copolymers—BASF AG; *Int'l*, pg. 103

LUCALOX—Electric Descharge Lamps—General Electric Canada Inc.; *U.S. Public*, pg. 713

LUCARELLI—NONE—Tandy Brands Accessories, Inc.; *U.S. Public*, pg. 1560

LUCAS—Alternators, Headlights—Fiat Auto SpA; *Int'l*, pg. 480

LUCAS—Boring, Drilling & Milling Machines—Litton Industries, Inc.; *U.S. Public*, pg. 1002

LUCAS—Aerospace, Automotive, Industrial & Agricultural Products—Lucas Industries Inc.; *Int'l*, pg. 820

LUCAS—NONE—LucasVarity plc; *Int'l*, pg. 819

LUCAS—Luggage—Monarch Luggage Co. Inc.; *U.S. Private*, pg. 757

LUCAS DECROLON—Acrylic Spray Enamel—Sherwin-Williams Coatings Division; *U.S. Public*, pg. 1466

LUCAS QUICK 'N EASY—Spray Enamel—Sherwin-Williams Coatings Division; *U.S. Public*, pg. 1466

LUCAS RUST BEATER—Acrylic Spray Enamel—Sherwin-Williams Coatings Division; *U.S. Public*, pg. 1466

LUCCA—Italian Food Products—Don Miguel Mexican Foods, Inc.; *U.S. Private*, pg. 339

LUCENT—Cordless Phone—Lucent Technologies Inc.; *U.S. Public*, pg. 1017

LUCERNE—Dairy Products & Eggs—Safeway Inc.; *U.S. Public*, pg. 1426

LUCIDENE—Graphic Arts Polymers—Morton International Inc.; *U.S. Public*, pg. 1135

LUCIDOL—Di-acyl Peroxides, Aromatic—Akzo Nobel N.V.; *Int'l*, pg. 42

LUCIDOL—Organic Peroxides—Elf Atochem North America, Inc.; *Int'l*, pg. 445

LUCIEN DESCHAUX—Wines—Leonard Kreusch, Inc.; *U.S. Private*, pg. 635

LUCIEN LELONG PARFUMS—Fragrances—E.T. Browne Drug Co., Inc.; *U.S. Private*, pg. 175

LUCILLE'S COUNTRY DINNER HOUSE—Restaurants—Houlihan's Restaurant Group; *U.S. Public*, pg. 841

LUCINO—Car—Nissan Motor Co., Ltd.; *Int'l*, pg. 943

LUCITE—Cast Acrylic Sheet—Du Pont (E.I. Du Pont De Nemours & Co.); *U.S. Public*, pg. 530

LUCITE L—Cast Acrylic Sheet—ICI Acrylics Inc.; *Int'l*, pg. 663

LUCITE SAR II—Cast Acrylic Sheet—ICI Acrylics Inc.; *Int'l*, pg. 663

LUCITE XL—Cast Acrylic Sheet—ICI Acrylics Inc.; *Int'l*, pg. 663

LUCK PLUS—Card Game—Mattel Games/Puzzles; *U.S. Public*, pg. 1058

LUCK'S INC.—Canned Beans—International Home Foods Inc.; *U.S. Private*, pg. 526

LUCKY—Supermarkets—Lucky Stores Northern California Division; *U.S. Public*, pg. 93

LUCKY—Children's Books—Scholastic Inc.; *U.S. Public*, pg. 1440

LUCKY CHARMS—Cereal—General Mills, Inc.; *U.S. Public*, pg. 717

LUCKY DOG—Dog Food—Ralston Purina Company; *U.S. Public*, pg. 1359

LUCKY DRAFT—Beer—General Brewing Company; *U.S. Private*, pg. 954

LUCKY DUTCH—NONE—Griffin Manufacturing Co.; *U.S. Private*, pg. 481

LUCKY EGGS—Candy, Surprise Toy, Easter Decoration—Ferrero; *Int'l*, pg. 480

LUCKY KENTUCKY—Hair Care Products—Palm Beach Beauty Products Co.; *U.S. Private*, pg. 834

LUCKY LAGER—Beer—General Brewing Company; *U.S. Private*, pg. 954

LUCKY LAGER—Lager—La Brasserie Labatt Limitee; *Int'l*, pg. 679

LUCKY LEAF—Apple Products—Knouse Foods Inc.; *U.S. Private*, pg. 627

LUCKY STICK CHOCOLATE—Chocolate Products—Meiji Seika Kaisha, Ltd.; *Int'l*, pg. 855

LUCKY STRIKE—Cigarettes—B.A.T Industries P.L.C.; *Int'l*, pg. 110

LUCKY STRIKE—NONE—British-American Tobacco (Germany) GmbH; *Int'l*, pg. 111

LUCKY STRIKE—Cigarettes—Brown & Williamson Tobacco Corp.; *Int'l*, pg. 111

LUCKY STRIKE—NONE—Malaysian Tobacco Co./B.A.T. Indust.; *Int'l*, pg. 111

LUCKY STRIKE—NONE—SEITA, Societe Nationale D'Exploitation Industrielle des Tabacs et des Allumettes; *Int'l*, pg. 1219

LUCKY STRONG—NONE—La Brasserie Labatt Limitee; *Int'l*, pg. 679

LUCKY WHIP—Topping—Lever Brothers Co.; *Int'l*, pg. 1435

LUCKY WHIP—Topping—Unilever Plc; *Int'l*, pg. 1433

LUCOBIT—Polyethylene/Bitumen—BASF AG; *Int'l*, pg. 103

LUCOZADE—Sparkling Glucose Drinks—SmithKline Beecham Corporation; *Int'l*, pg. 1264

LUCOZADE—Nutritional Healthcare—SmithKline Beecham plc; *Int'l*, pg. 1264

LUDEN'S—Throat Drops—Hershey Chocolate U.S.A.; *U.S. Public*, pg. 812

LUDEN'S—Throat Drops—Hershey Foods Corporation; *U.S. Public*, pg. 811

Brand Name Index

LUDEN'S—Cough Drops—Luden's Inc.; *U.S. Public*, pg. 812

LUDEN'S ELITE—Cordial Cherries—Luden's Inc.; *U.S. Public*, pg. 812

LUDEN'S THROAT DROPS—Cough/Throat Drops—Luden's Inc.; *U.S. Public*, pg. 812

LUDIOMIL—Antidepressant—Ciba Specialty Chemicals; *Int'l*, pg. 291

LUDIOMIL—Antidepressant—Novartis; *Int'l*, pg. 972

LUDOX—Colloidal Silica—Du Pont (E.I. Du Pont De Nemours & Co.); *U.S. Public*, pg. 530

LUDWIG—Drums & Precussion Instruments—Ludwig Industries; *U.S. Public*, pg. 1514

LUDWIG—Drums & Tuned Percussion—The Selmer Co., Inc.; *U.S. Public*, pg. 1514

LUDWIG TIMPANI—Hi Volume Snare Drums—Ludwig Industries; *U.S. Public*, pg. 1514

LUFKIN—Tape Measures and Rules—Cooper Hand Tools; *U.S. Public*, pg. 444

LUFKIN—Measuring Tapes & Rules—Cooper Industries, Inc.; *U.S. Public*, pg. 442

LUFKIN—Biopsy Needles—E-Z-Em, Inc.; *U.S. Public*, pg. 540

LUFKIN—Oil Field & Industrial Equip.—Lufkin Industries, Inc.; *U.S. Public*, pg. 1019

LUFKIN INTERNATIONAL ULTRA-CLEAN—NONE—Regal Ware, Inc.; *U.S. Private*, pg. 917

LUFTWAFFE—War Game—Monarch Avalon, Inc.; *U.S. Public*, pg. 1123

LUFYLLIN—Broncho Spasms—Wallace Laboratories; *U.S. Public*, pg. 310

LUG MASTER—Fasteners—R&B, Inc.; *U.S. Public*, pg. 1354

LUG TRAC—Tire Treads—Bandag, Incorporated; *U.S. Public*, pg. 177

LUGALVAN—Specialty Chemicals for the Electroplating Industry—BASF AG; *Int'l*, pg. 103

LUGGAGE GALLERY—Fine Luggage, Attaches, & Portfolios in Vinyls & Leather—Seward Inc.; *U.S. Private*, pg. 988

LUGZ—Casual Shoes—Jack Schwartz Shoes, Inc.; *U.S. Private*, pg. 974

LUHR—NONE—Pfizer Inc.; *U.S. Public*, pg. 1281

LUIGI'S—Ices—J & J Snack Foods Corporation; *U.S. Public*, pg. 916

LUKENS STEEL—Plate Steels—Lukens Inc.; *U.S. Public*, pg. 1019

LULL—Rough Terrain Forklift-Variable Reach—OmniQuip International, Inc.; *U.S. Private*, pg. 500

LULLABYE—Juvenile Furniture—Spalding & Evenflo Companies, Inc.; *U.S. Private*, pg. 629

LUM-EX—Computer Software Feature—Beckman Instruments, Inc.; *U.S. Public*, pg. 199

LUMA VI—Lighting Controls—Pass & Seymour/Legrand; *Int'l*, pg. 806

LUMA 2—Super Premium Flashlight With Emergency Lithium Backup System—RAYOVAC Corporation; *U.S. Private*, pg. 912

LUMACLAD—Flashlight Reflectors—Eastman Kodak Company; *U.S. Public*, pg. 550

LUMADEX—Fetal Lung Maturity Test—Beckman Instruments, Inc.; *U.S. Public*, pg. 199

LUMAFAST—Enzyme for Detergent Industry—Cultor Ltd.; *Int'l*, pg. 349

LUMAGLOW—Industrial Luminaires—General Electric Canada Inc.; *U.S. Public*, pg. 713

LUMARK—Indoor & Outdoor Lighting—Cooper Industries, Inc.; *U.S. Public*, pg. 442

LUMASPEC—Dimmers & Fan Speed Controls—Pass & Seymour/Legrand; *Int'l*, pg. 806

LUMATHREAD—Standard Handle w/ Attached Metal End—Flo-Pac Corporation; *U.S. Private*, pg. 414

LUMBER—Crayons—Dixon Ticonderoga Company; *U.S. Public*, pg. 514

LUMBER LOCK—All-Weather Construciton Adhesive—Miracle Adhesives; *U.S. Public*, pg. 1466

LUMBER LOCK—Sealant—Pratt & Lambert United, Inc.; *U.S. Public*, pg. 1466

LUMBERJACK—Baked Goods—Grocers Baking Co.; *U.S. Private*, pg. 482

LUMEC—Decorative Commercial Outdoor Lighting—Thomas Industries Inc.; *U.S. Public*, pg. 1598

LUMEC-SCHREDER—Roadway Lighting—Thomas Industries Inc.; *U.S. Public*, pg. 1598

LUMENIZED—Lenses—Eastman Kodak Company; *U.S. Public*, pg. 550

LUMENX—NONE—LumenX Company; *U.S. Public*, pg. 56

LUMIERE—NONE—Eastman Kodak Company; *U.S. Public*, pg. 550

LUMILINE—Electric Lamps & Fittings—General Electric Canada Inc.; *U.S. Public*, pg. 713

LUMIN—Uterine Manipulation Tool—Utah Medical Products, Inc.; *U.S. Public*, pg. 1700

LUMINA—Automobile—Chevrolet Motor Div. General Motors Corp.; *U.S. Public*, pg. 720

LUMINA—Passenger Car—General Motors Corporation; *U.S. Public*, pg. 718

LUMINA MINIVAN—Minivan—Chevrolet Motor Div. General Motors Corp.; *U.S. Public*, pg. 720

LUMINESS—Vinyl Windows and Doors—Owens Corning; *U.S. Public*, pg. 1236

LUMINESSE—Lipstick—Cover Girl Cosmetics; *U.S. Public*, pg. 1330

LUMINESSE SATIN FINISH EYE LINER—Eye pencils—Cover Girl Cosmetics; *U.S. Public*, pg. 1330

LUMINETTE PRIVACY SHEERS—Soft Vertical Fabric Vanes Between Sheer Fabric Facings—Hunter Douglas, Inc.; *Int'l*, pg. 639

LUMINEX—Collection—Regal Ware, Inc.; *U.S. Private*, pg. 917

LUMINIZE—Hair Conditioner & Colourant—Bristol-Myers Squibb Company; *U.S. Public*, pg. 253

LUMIRROR—Polyester Film—Toray Industries, Inc.; *Int'l*, pg. 1399

LUMITEX—Veneer, Plywood & Lumber Faced or Backed with Metal—Georgia-Pacific Corporation; *U.S. Public*, pg. 735

LUMITEX—Athletic—L.A. Gear, Inc.; *U.S. Public*, pg. 969

LUMNITE—Calcium Aluminate Cement—Lehigh Portland Cement Company; *Int'l*, pg. 605

LUNA—Full Glue Installed Sheet Vinyl Flooring—Mannington Resilient Floors; *U.S. Private*, pg. 700

LUNA—Margarine—Sabanci Holding A.S.; *Int'l*, pg. 1167

LUNA MYSTIQUE—NONE—Chesebrough-Pond's USA Co.; *Int'l*, pg. 1435

LUNA PIER—Imprintable Sportsware—Broder Bros. Co.; *U.S. Private*, pg. 170

LUNAR—Interior Wall and Countertop—Monarch Tile, Inc.; *U.S. Public*, pg. 287

LUNCH AND MORE—NONE—Swanson; *U.S. Public*, pg. 299

LUNCH BREAK—NONE—Rubbermaid Incorporated; *U.S. Public*, pg. 1411

LUNCH GARDEN—Restaurants—GIB Group; *Int'l*, pg. 532

LUNCHABLES—Packaged Lunches—Philip Morris Companies Inc.; *U.S. Public*, pg. 1287

LUNCHEON VOUCHERS—Meal Vouchers—Accor S.A.; *Int'l*, pg. 20

LUNCHLUGGER—Insulated Food Container—The Thermos Company; *Int'l*, pg. 938

LUNCHMATE—Ice Chest—Igloo Products Corporation; *U.S. Public*, pg. 265

LUND—Aluminum Boats—Genmar Holdings, Inc.; *U.S. Private*, pg. 447

LUND SUNVISOR—Sunvisor for Trucks & Vans—Lund International Holdings, Inc.; *U.S. Public*, pg. 1020

LUNDIA—Filing & Storage Shelving Systems—Lundia Div. of MII, Inc.; *U.S. Private*, pg. 680

LUNEBEST—Yogurt—Nestle S.A.; *Int'l*, pg. 915

LUNELLE—Soft Contact Lens—Essilor International Compagnie Generale d'Optique; *Int'l*, pg. 462

LUNSTEAD—Office Furiture and Seating—Haworth, Inc.; *U.S. Public*, pg. 511

LUNT—Silverplate, Tableware & Pewter Tableware—Rogers, Lunt & Bowlen Co.; *U.S. Private*, pg. 939

LUNT STERLING—Sterling Silver Tableware—Rogers, Lunt & Bowlen Co.; *U.S. Private*, pg. 939

LUPOLEN—Polyethylenes of High & Low Density—BASF AG; *Int'l*, pg. 103

LUPOS—NONE—ETEX; *Int'l*, pg. 430

LUPRANAT—Polyurethane Basic Prods.—BASF AG; *Int'l*, pg. 103

LUPRANOL—Polyetherols—BASF AG; *Int'l*, pg. 103

LUPRON—Leuprolide—Abbott Laboratories; *U.S. Public*, pg. 12

LURE FLY—Fly Paper—Security Lawn & Garden Co.; *U.S. Private*, pg. 397

LURE FLY—Sticky Fly Ribbons—Security Lawn & Garden Co.; *U.S. Private*, pg. 397

LURE-N'-KILL—Insecticide—Hercon Environmental Corporation; *U.S. Public*, pg. 802

LURE TAPE—Control Release Dispensers—Hercon Environmental Corporation; *U.S. Public*, pg. 802

LURIA'S—Jewelry Stores—L. Luria & Son, Inc.; *U.S. Public*, pg. 1020

LURPAK—Butter—MD Foods; *Int'l*, pg. 826

LUSAC—Brake Parts—Echlin Inc.; *U.S. Public*, pg. 560

LUSH LIPS—Cosmetics—Naturistics; *U.S. Public*, pg. 494

LUSKEYS ROPER—Boot and Hats—Luskeys Western Stores, Inc.; *U.S. Private*, pg. 681

LUSO—Water—Central de Cervejas, S.A.; *Int'l*, pg. 279

LUSTAIR HAIR SPRAY—NONE—Shiseido Company Ltd.; *Int'l*, pg. 1235

LUSTER—Glazed ceramic wall tile—Precision Die & Engineering; *U.S. Public*, pg. 1322

LUSTERSOY—Food Product—Honeymead Products Co.; *U.S. Private*, pg. 537

LUSTERTONE—Cabinet Sink—Elkay Manufacturing Company; *U.S. Private*, pg. 372

LUSTRA—Plastic Cutlery—Amcel Corp.; *U.S. Private*, pg. 48

LUSTRA—Gift Wrapping—Mobil Land Development Corporation; *U.S. Public*, pg. 1118

LUSTRA-BUFF—General Scrubbing & Buffing Rotary Brush—Flo-Pac Corporation; *U.S. Private*, pg. 414

LUSTRA COLORS—Hair Coloring Preparations—The Gillette Company; *U.S. Public*, pg. 743

LUSTRA-CURL—Hair Permanent Kits—The Gillette Company; *U.S. Public*, pg. 743

LUSTRA SWEEP—Fine Sweeping Dust Brush w/ Self Flagging Plastic—Flo-Pac Corporation; *U.S. Public*, pg. 414

LUSTRA-ZYME—Sculpturing Glaze, Creme Relaxer, Protein Conditioner & Creme Shampoo—The Gillette Company; *U.S. Public*, pg. 743

LUSTRALITE—Overlay Paper—The Mead Corporation; *U.S. Public*, pg. 1074

LUSTRAN—Thermoplastics—Monsanto Company; *U.S. Public*, pg. 1124

LUSTRAN—Extrusion & Molding Resin—Solutia Inc.; *U.S. Public*, pg. 1483

LUSTRASILK—Hair Care Preparations—The Gillette Company; *U.S. Public*, pg. 743

LUSTRE BY FLEXEES—Control Garments—True Form Intimate Apparel; *U.S. Private*, pg. 697

LUSTRE GLO—Film Laminated Paperboard—Hazen Paper Company; *U.S. Private*, pg. 514

LUSTRE KING—Sporting Goods—Brunswick Bowling & Billiards Corp.; *U.S. Public*, pg. 265

LUSTRE-KING—Sporting Equipment—Brunswick Bowling & Billiards Corp.; *U.S. Public*, pg. 265

LUSTRE LANE—Greeting Cards—American Greetings Corporation; *U.S. Public*, pg. 77

LUSTRE LAST—Tarnish Preventive Silver Polish—Stanhome Inc.; *U.S. Public*, pg. 1508

LUSTRE-LUXE—Photo Paper Suface—Eastman Kodak Company; *U.S. Public*, pg. 550

LUSTRE-PHOS—Dentifrice Abrasive—Solutia Inc.; *U.S. Public*, pg. 1483

LUSTRE ZINC—Bright Zinc Plated Finish—E.H. Titchener & Company; *U.S. Private*, pg. 1089

LUSTRECAL—Decals—American Decal & Mfg. Co.; *U.S. Private*, pg. 53

LUSTRO—Printing Papers—S.D. Warren Co.; *Int'l*, pg. 1193

LUSTROLITO—Printing Papers—Kimberly-Clark Corporation; *U.S. Public*, pg. 958

LUSTROX—Glass Polishing Composition—Ferro Corporation; *U.S. Public*, pg. 618

LUTALYSE—Gynecological Preparation—Pharmacia & Upjohn; *Int'l*, pg. 1048

LUTECE—Four-Star French Restaurant Recently Trademarked for Potential Licensing—Ark Restaurants Corp.; *U.S. Public*, pg. 129

LUTENSIT—Ionic Surfactants—BASF AG; *Int'l*, pg. 103

LUTENSOL—Non-Ionic Surfactants—BASF AG; *Int'l*, pg. 103

LUTER'S—Processed Meats—Smithfield Foods, Inc.; *U.S. Public*, pg. 1479

LUTERS—Meat Products—The Smithfield Packing Co., Inc.; *U.S. Public*, pg. 1479

LUTHERAN BROTHERHOOD—Insurance—Lutheran Brotherhood; *U.S. Private*, pg. 681

LUTHERAN TRUST—Property - Casualty Insurer—Lutheran Brotherhood; *U.S. Private*, pg. 681

LUTICIN—Hare Care Products—Wella Group; *Int'l*, pg. 1489

LUTRABOND—Polyester Non-Wovens for Roof Covers—Freudenberg & Company; *Int'l*, pg. 505

LUTRADUR—Polyester Non-Woven—Freudenberg & Company; *Int'l*, pg. 505

LUTRAVIL—Mfr. of Spun-Bonded Wovens—Freudenberg & Company; *Int'l*, pg. 505

LUTRON—Chemicals for the Printed Circuit Board Industry—BASF AG; *Int'l*, pg. 103

LUTROPUR—Chemicals for the Printed Circuit Board Industry—BASF AG; *Int'l*, pg. 103

LUTZ—Pumps—Ryan Herco Products Corp.; *U.S. Private*, pg. 953

LUV—Manufactured Homes—Clayton Homes, Inc.; *U.S. Public*, pg. 382

LUV STUFF—Greeting Cards—American Greetings Corporation; *U.S. Public*, pg. 77

LUVIPOL—Wooden Doors External & Internal—Vicente Puig Oliver S.A.; *Int'l*, pg. 1001

LUVS—Diapers—The Procter & Gamble Company; *U.S. Public*, pg. 1330

LUX—Floor Care Products—Electrolux, AB; *Int'l*, pg. 438

LUX—Bar Soap & Dishwashing Liquid—Lever Brothers Co.; *Int'l*, pg. 1435

LUX—Soap & Dishwashing Liquid—Unilever Plc; *Int'l*, pg. 1433

LUX STEEL—NONE—The Lux Co., Inc.; *U.S. Public*, pg. 388

LUXAFLEX—Window Covering Product—Hunter Douglas N.V.; *Int'l*, pg. 639

LUXAIRE—Residential Air Conditioners & Furnaces—Unitary Products Group; *U.S. Public*, pg. 1788

LUXAIRE—Air Freshener—Willert Home Products, Inc.; *U.S. Private*, pg. 1177

LUXALON—Architectural Product—Hunter Douglas N.V.; *Int'l*, pg. 639

LUXER—Non-Woven Fabric of Synthetic Filament—Asahi Chemical Industry Co., Ltd.; *Int'l*, pg. 83

LUXIVA—Skin Care Cosmetics—Merle Norman Cosmetics, Inc.; *U.S. Private*, pg. 733

LUXO—Lighting Systems—Luxo A/S; *Int'l*, pg. 821

LUXOR—Audio Visual Material Storage Cabinets—Luxor; *U.S. Private*, pg. 359

LUXOR—Motor Home—Winnebago Industries, Inc.; *U.S. Public*, pg. 1772

LUXOTTICA—NONE—Luxottica Group S.p.A.; *Int'l*, pg. 822

LUXRI FOLD—Disposable Paper Products—Wisconsin Tissue Mills, Inc.; *U.S. Public*, pg. 347

LUXSTAR—Laser Welding System—Lumonics Inc.; *Int'l*, pg. 1314

LUXURY—Pasta—Borden, Inc.; *U.S. Private*, pg. 157

LUXURY—Pasta Products—Borden Italian Foods; *U.S. Private*, pg. 158

THE LUXURY COLLECTION—NONE—ITT Sheraton Corporation; *U.S. Public*, pg. 1512

LUXURY COMFORT—Mattress—The Spring Air Company; *U.S. Private*, pg. 1027

LUXURY MATTE—Lipstick—Elizabeth Arden Company; *Int'l*, pg. 1435

LUXXUS TONNEAU COVER—Cover for Bed of Pick-Up—Lund International Holdings, Inc.; *U.S. Public*, pg. 1020

LUZERN—Women's Cross Court Shoe—K-Swiss Inc.; *U.S. Public*, pg. 937

LUZIANNE—Tea & Coffee—William B. Reily & Co., Inc.; *U.S. Private*, pg. 919

LUZIANNE CAJUN CREOLE FOODS—Packaged Dinners—Reily Foods Company; *U.S. Private*, pg. 919

LUZIANNE CAJUN PURE COFFEE—Coffee—Reily Foods Company; *U.S. Private*, pg. 919

LUZIANNE CREOLE SEASONING—Dry Seasoning & Paste—Reily Foods Company; *U.S. Private*, pg. 919

LUZIANNE DECAF TEA—Tea—Reily Foods Company; *U.S. Private*, pg. 919

LUZIANNE PREMIUM BLEND—Coffee & Chicory—Reily Foods Company; *U.S. Private*, pg. 919

LUZIANNE TEA—Tea—Reily Foods Company; *U.S. Private*, pg. 919

LUZIANNE WHITE LABEL—Coffee—Reily Foods Company; *U.S. Private*, pg. 919

LUZZATI—NONE—Alliant Foodservice, Inc.; *U.S. Private*, pg. 244

LVPLUS III—A Universal Life Insurance Product—The Life Insurance Co. of Virginia; *U.S. Public*, pg. 712

LYCRA—Spandex Fiber—Du Pont (E.I. Du Pont De Nemours & Co.); *U.S. Public*, pg. 530

LYDIAN—Supports Enhanced & Prepaid Calling, Prepaid Wireless & Toll-Free Services—Precision Systems, Inc.; *U.S. Public*, pg. 1321

LYLE & SCOTT—Knitwear & Leisurewear—Courtaulds Textiles Plc; *Int'l*, pg. 339

LYMAN—Company Name & Logo—Lyman Products Corporation; *U.S. Private*, pg. 683

LYMEVAX—Veterinary Pharmaceuticals—American Home Products Corporation; *U.S. Public*, pg. 79

LYMPHA PRESS—Lymphadema Pump—Camp Healthcare; *Int'l*, pg. 1425

LYNKS—Seeds—The Dow Chemical Company; *U.S. Public*, pg. 522

LYNN WILSON'S—Mexican Food Products—Wilson Products Co.; *U.S. Private*, pg. 1181

LYNTONE—Belts, Suspenders & Small Leather Accessories—Gem-Dandy, Inc.; *U.S. Private*, pg. 442

LYNX—Snowmobiles—Bombardier Inc.; *Int'l*, pg. 199

LYNX—Portable Video Game System—JTS Corporation; *U.S. Public*, pg. 919

LYNX—Golf Clubs—Lynx Golf, Inc.; *U.S. Private*, pg. 684

LYNX OPAQUE—Printing Paper—Weyerhaeuser Company; *U.S. Public*, pg. 1764

LYNX OPAQUE-LASER GUARANTEED—Electronic Publishing Papers—Weyerhaeuser Company; *U.S. Public*, pg. 1764

LYNX2—CVD Process Module—Genus Inc.; *U.S. Public*, pg. 732

LYOFOAM—Non-Medicated Wound Dressing—Ionics, Incorporated; *U.S. Public*, pg. 912

LYOGEN—Dyeing Chemicals—Clariant International Ltd.; *Int'l*, pg. 624

LYON—Storage Products—Lyon Metal Products, Inc.; *U.S. Private*, pg. 638

LYONS—Family Restaurants—Lyon's Restaurants, Inc.; *U.S. Private*, pg. 684

LYONS—Speedometer Seals—Peco Mfg. Co., Inc.; *U.S. Private*, pg. 846

LYOPHILIZED CYTOXAN—Alkylating Agent for Cancerous Malignancies—Bristol-Myers Squibb U.S. Pharmaceutical Group; *U.S. Public*, pg. 255

LYPRO—lab & Pilot Freeze Dryers—Hull Corporation; *U.S. Private*, pg. 547

LYRICA—Chinaware—The Homer Laughlin China Company; *U.S. Private*, pg. 653

LYSMINA—Medicinal Cosmetic—Kali-Chemie Aktiengesellschaft; *Int'l*, pg. 1278

LYSODASE—NONE—Enzon, Inc.; *U.S. Public*, pg. 587

LYSODREN—Cancer Therapy Product—Bristol-Myers Squibb Company; *U.S. Public*, pg. 253

LYSODREN—Andrenal Cytotoxic Agent to Treat Inoperable Cortical Carcinoma—Bristol-Myers Squibb U.S. Pharmaceutical Group; *U.S. Public*, pg. 255

LYSOL—Disinfectant—Reckitt & Colman Inc.; *Int'l*, pg. 1090

LYSOL—Disinfectants—Reckitt & Colman plc; *Int'l*, pg. 1089

LYTE-FIT—Orthotics Made From Carbon Graphite—The Langer Biomechanics Group, Inc.; *U.S. Public*, pg. 978

LYTECASTER—Recessed Lighting—Lightolier Division; *U.S. Public*, pg. 730

LYTEPRO—HID Wallprisms—Stonco Genlyte; *U.S. Public*, pg. 730

LYTESPAN—Track Lighting—Lightolier Division; *U.S. Public*, pg. 730

LYTOR—Tall Oil Rosin—Georgia-Pacific Corporation; *U.S. Public*, pg. 735

LYTRON—Plastic Pigments—Morton International Inc.; *U.S. Public*, pg. 1135

LYXASAN—Endoxylanase Chicken Feed Additive for Improving the Digestibility of Wheat—Royal Gist-Brocades N.V.; *Int'l*, pg. 1142

M

MA—Gold Jewelry—Michael Anthony Jewelers, Inc.; *U.S. Public*, pg. 1103

M.A. ELECTRIC & HYDRAULIC TIMERS—Timers—Weather Tec Corporation; *U.S. Private*, pg. 1155

M.A.B.—Paint—M.A. Bruder & Sons, Incorporated; *U.S. Private*, pg. 175

MABC—Automatic Boost Control System—Officine A. Maserati S.p.A.; *Int'l*, pg. 482

MAC—NONE—CEM Corporation; *U.S. Public*, pg. 277

MAC—Antiseptic Throat Lozenges—SmithKline Beecham plc; *Int'l*, pg. 1264

M/A-COM—Semicondutors & Related Devices—M/A-Com, Inc. Components Group; *U.S. Public*, pg. 8

MAG SS—Spark Plug Wire Sets—General Cable Corporation; *Int'l*, pg. 1486

MAS-51—Mechanical Adjustable Speed Drives—Rockwell International Corporation; *U.S. Public*, pg. 1397

MAS 7000—NONE—CEM Corporation; *U.S. Public*, pg. 277

MA-200—Ceramic Wall Tile Adhesive—Pratt & Lambert United, Inc.; *U.S. Public*, pg. 1466

M & B DPA—Light Mild Beer—Bass PLC; *Int'l*, pg. 169

M & B MILD—Dark Mild Beer—Bass PLC; *Int'l*, pg. 169

M & F—Enamel—The Valspar Corp. Protective Coatings Div.; *U.S. Public*, pg. 1707

M & M'S—Confectionary—Mars Confectionery; *U.S. Private*, pg. 707

M & M'S—Candy—Mars, Incorporated; *U.S. Private*, pg. 707

M&M'S BRAND—NONE—M&M/Mars; *U.S. Private*, pg. 707

MB—NONE—MB Espana, S.A.; *U.S. Public*, pg. 798

MBG METAL GAS—Burner—Hauck Mfg. Co.; *U.S. Private*, pg. 510

MBG MICRON DIAMOND—Grinding Diamond—G.E. Superabrasives; *U.S. Public*, pg. 711

MBIX—Operating System—Barrister Information Systems Corporation; *U.S. Public*, pg. 192

MBOS—Operating System—Barrister Information Systems Corporation; *U.S. Public*, pg. 192

MBS DIAMOND—Saw Diamond—G.E. Superabrasives; *U.S. Public*, pg. 711

MBT—Broth Products—Borden, Inc.; *U.S. Private*, pg. 157

MBTC—Model-Based Temperature Control—Silicon Valley Group, Inc.; *U.S. Public*, pg. 1474

MC—Polyamide Shapes & Parts—DSM Engineering Plastic Products; *Int'l*, pg. 354

MC—Mechanical Lubricator—Portec Inc., Railway Maintenance Products Div.; *U.S. Public*, pg. 1318

MCA TV—Television Programs—Universal Studios TV; *Int'l*, pg. 1215

MC 860—Processor—Mercury Computer Systems, Inc.; *U.S. Private*, pg. 732

MC1813—J Axis Horizontal Machining Center—Makino Inc.; *Int'l*, pg. 831

MC86—Horizontal Machining Center—Makino Inc.; *Int'l*, pg. 831

MC1510—Horizontal Machining Center—Makino Inc.; *Int'l*, pg. 831

MC1513—Horizontal Machining Center—Makino Inc.; *Int'l*, pg. 831

MCI—Long Distance Data Services—Moss Telecommunications Services; *U.S. Private*, pg. 763

MCI CALL USA—Overseas Telephone Access to USA—MCI International Inc.; *U.S. Public*, pg. 1024

MCI CARD—Telephone Calling Card—MCI International Inc.; *U.S. Public*, pg. 1024

Brand Name Index

MCI FAX—Facsimile Service—MCI International Inc.; *U.S. Public*, pg. 1024

MCI MAIL—Electronic Messaging Service—MCI International Inc.; *U.S. Public*, pg. 1024

MCL—Horizontal Earth Drill—McLaughlin Manufacturing Company; *U.S. Private*, pg. 724

MCM-PAK—Reagent Kits—Beckman Instruments, Inc.; *U.S. Public*, pg. 199

MCMRE—Systemss of equipment to Receive, Sort & Process Recyclables—COUNTEC Recycling Systems Division; *U.S. Public*, pg. 1318

MCN, AMERICAN JOURNAL OF MATERNAL/ CHILD NURSING—Magazine—American Journal of Nursing Company; *Int'l*, pg. 1513

MCO—Community Development—MAXXAM Property Company; *U.S. Public*, pg. 1062

MC108—Horizontal Machining Center—Makino Inc.; *Int'l*, pg. 831

MC1 TEMPATROL—NONE—Scotsman Industries, Inc.; *U.S. Public*, pg. 1444

MCP—Pectin for Making Jams & Jellies—Firmenich; *Int'l*, pg. 486

MCPP—Weedkilling Compound—Riverdale Chemical Co.; *U.S. Private*, pg. 934

MCR SERIES—Voltage Regulator—Best Power; *U.S. Private*, pg. 140

MC RAIL—NONE—Pfizer Inc.; *U.S. Public*, pg. 1281

MCS—Photo Typesetter—AGFA EPS Division; *Int'l*, pg. 172

MCS—Electronic Instrument—Intel Corporation; *U.S. Public*, pg. 886

MCS POWERVIEW—Photo Typesetters—AGFA EPS Division; *Int'l*, pg. 172

MC1710—Horizontal Machining Center—Makino Inc.; *Int'l*, pg. 831

MC65—Horizontal Machining Center—Makino Inc.; *Int'l*, pg. 831

MCT—Temperature Controllers for Hot Wire Plastics Film Sealers—Reynolds Metals Company; *U.S. Public*, pg. 1385

MCT OIL—Dietary Fat Supplement—Mead Johnson Nutritional Group; *U.S. Public*, pg. 254

MC-3—Rail Wiping Bar—Portec Inc., Railway Maintenance Products Div.; *U.S. Public*, pg. 1318

MC1210—Horizontal Machining Center—Makino Inc.; *Int'l*, pg. 831

MC1213—Horizontal Machining Center—Makino Inc.; *Int'l*, pg. 831

MC2210—Horizontal Machining Center—Makino Inc.; *Int'l*, pg. 831

MC2—Laminates—Glasteel Industrial Laminates; *U.S. Private*, pg. 45

MCW—Creme Moisturizer & Conditioner for Hair—The Gillette Company; *U.S. Public*, pg. 743

MCX—Golf Clubs—MacGregor Golf Company; *Int'l*, pg. 72

M/CHANNEL—Computer Software—Attachmate; *U.S. Private*, pg. 98

M/COAX—Computer Software—Attachmate; *U.S. Private*, pg. 98

M. CHAPOUTIER—Wine—Paterno Imports Limited; *U.S. Private*, pg. 843

MD—Stock Preparation—Beloit Corporation; *U.S. Public*, pg. 789

M D—Bathroom Tissue, Toilet Seat Covers & Dispensers—Georgia-Pacific Corporation; *U.S. Public*, pg. 735

MDA 180—Integrated Hemostasis Testing System—Akzo Nobel N.V.; *Int'l*, pg. 42

MD & DESIGN—Tissue Seat Covers & Dispensers—Georgia-Pacific Corporation; *U.S. Public*, pg. 735

MDE—Software—LSI Logic Corp.; *U.S. Public*, pg. 971

MD-80—Airliner—McDonnell Aircraft & Missile Systems Div.; *U.S. Public*, pg. 241

MD-11—Airliner—McDonnell Aircraft & Missile Systems Div.; *U.S. Public*, pg. 241

MDF—Multiple-Domain Feature Computer Product—Amdahl Corporation; *Int'l*, pg. 527

MD-500—Business Helicopter—McDonnell Aircraft & Missile Systems Div.; *U.S. Public*, pg. 241

MD 500E—Helicopter—Boeing Helicopter Division; *U.S. Public*, pg. 241

MD 530F—Helicopter—Boeing Helicopter Division; *U.S. Public*, pg. 241

MD 520N—Helicopter—Boeing Helicopter Division; *U.S. Public*, pg. 241

MD-GASTROVIEW—X-Ray Contrast Medium for Radiographic Examination—Mallinckrodt Inc.; *U.S. Public*, pg. 1039

MDLINK—Physician Link—Cerner Corporation; *U.S. Public*, pg. 331

MD-91—Propfan Airliner—McDonnell Aircraft & Missile Systems Div.; *U.S. Public*, pg. 241

MDP—Manual Direct Projection Microform Reader—Dukane Corporation; *U.S. Private*, pg. 345

MDR-5000—Digital Microwave Radio—Alcatel Telecom; *Int'l*, pg. 55

MDR-4000—Digital Microwave Radio—Alcatel Telecom; *Int'l*, pg. 55

MDR-7000—Digital Microwave Radio—Alcatel Telecom; *Int'l*, pg. 55

MDR-6000—Digital Microwave Radio—Alcatel Telecom; *Int'l*, pg. 55

MDS—Memory Disc Systems—SpeedFan International, Inc.; *U.S. Public*, pg. 1497

MDSS—Multi-Dimensional Switching Automatic—Packard Instrument Co., Inc.; *U.S. Private*, pg. 833

MDS 2000—NONE—CEM Corporation; *U.S. Public*, pg. 277

MD-76—X-Ray Contrast Medium for Intravascular Use—Mallinckrodt Inc.; *U.S. Public*, pg. 1039

MD 600N—Helicopter—Boeing Helicopter Division; *U.S. Public*, pg. 241

MD-60—X-Ray Contrast Medium for Intravascular Use—Mallinckrodt Inc.; *U.S. Public*, pg. 1039

MD 20/20—Wine—The Wine Group; *U.S. Private*, pg. 1182

MD-VAC—Poultry Biologic—Salsbury Laboratories, Inc.; *Int'l*, pg. 1277

MD-VAC—Poultry Biologic—Solvay Animal Health, Inc.; *Int'l*, pg. 1277

MD-VAC—Poultry Biologic—Solvay S.A.; *Int'l*, pg. 1277

MDX—Telephone System—Inter-Tel, Incorporated; *U.S. Public*, pg. 888

MDX—Business Helicopter—McDonnell Aircraft & Missile Systems Div.; *U.S. Public*, pg. 241

MEA—Mechanized Electronic Assembly—Universal Instruments Corporation; *U.S. Public*, pg. 522

MEF—Moldable Polyethylene Foam—Asahi Chemical Industry Co., Ltd.; *Int'l*, pg. 83

MEPC—NONE—MEPC American Properties; *U.S. Private*, pg. 686

MES 1000—NONE—CEM Corporation; *U.S. Public*, pg. 277

META—Pacemaker—St. Jude Medical, Inc.; *U.S. Public*, pg. 1427

M8.2E/L—Fitness Software Package for Home Exercise—Premark International, Inc.; *U.S. Public*, pg. 1321

M 88—Military Turbofan Engine—SNECMA - Societe Nationale d'Etude et de Construction de Moteurs d'Aviation; *Int'l*, pg. 1165

MFA—Farm Supplies, Agricultural Services—MFA Incorporated; *U.S. Private*, pg. 686

MFA OIL—Gasoline, Oils & Greases & Propane Gas—MFA Oil Company; *U.S. Private*, pg. 687

MFB—Conveyor Belting—Fenner Drives; *U.S. Private*, pg. 400

MFG—Concrete Forms, Custom Products—Molded Fiber Glass Co.; *U.S. Private*, pg. 756

MFI CONNECT—NONE—Market Facts, Inc.; *U.S. Public*, pg. 1046

MF-MILLIPORE—Filter—Millipore Corporation; *U.S. Public*, pg. 1112

MF(1687

MFP—NONE—Western Atlas Logging Services; *U.S. Public*, pg. 1757

MF TRINICON—Color Video Cameras—Sony Electronics; *Int'l*, pg. 1281

M 53—Military Turbofan Engine—SNECMA - Societe Nationale d'Etude et de Construction de Moteurs d'Aviation; *Int'l*, pg. 1165

M4—Opthamalic Lenses—American Optical Corporation; *U.S. Private*, pg. 60

M4 HILNDEX—Opthamalic Lenses—American Optical Corporation; *U.S. Private*, pg. 60

M400—NONE—Pfizer Inc.; *U.S. Public*, pg. 1281

M-14—Magnetic Tape Recorders—Eastman Kodak Company; *U.S. Public*, pg. 550

MG—Carpet Care—Kiwi Brands Pty. Ltd.; *U.S. Public*, pg. 1434

MGA—Feed Additive—Pharmacia & Upjohn; *Int'l*, pg. 1048

MG-BAC—Poultry Biologic—Solvay S.A.; *Int'l*, pg. 1277

MG-BAC BIOLOGIC—Poultry Biologic—Solvay Animal Health, Inc.; *Int'l*, pg. 1277

MG-BAC BIOLOGIC—Poultry Biologic—Salsbury Laboratories, Inc.; *Int'l*, pg. 1277

MG400—Managed Care Management Software—US SerVis; *U.S. Public*, pg. 1687

MGK—Pesticides—McLaughlin Gormley King Company; *U.S. Private*, pg. 723

MGM—Spring-Loaded Safety Brake Activators—TBG Management S.A.M.; *Int'l*, pg. 1335

MGM BRAKES—Heavy Duty Truck & Bus Spring Brake Actuators—Indian Head Industries Inc.; *U.S. Private*, pg. 559

MGM GRAND—Logo & Related Characters—MGM Grand, Inc.; *U.S. Public*, pg. 1026

MGM GRAND HOTEL—Logo & Related—MGM Grand, Inc.; *U.S. Public*, pg. 1026

MGR—Shock Resisting Die Steel—Latrobe Steel Company; *U.S. Public*, pg. 1617

MGS 10/20—Gamma Counter—Beckman Instruments, Inc.; *U.S. Public*, pg. 199

MGTS—CCS7 Network Diagnostic Tool—Tekelec; *U.S. Public*, pg. 1566

MG II—Precoat Total Knee System—Bristol-Myers Squibb Company; *U.S. Public*, pg. 253

M.G. VALLEJO—Wine—Glen Ellen Winery; *U.S. Private*, pg. 455

MHA—Methionine Hydroxy Analog—The Agricultural Group, Monsanto Company; *U.S. Public*, pg. 1125

M.H.M.—NONE—Kellwood Company; *U.S. Public*, pg. 948

MHT—Magnesium Hydroxide—The Dow Chemical Company; *U.S. Public*, pg. 522

MHX—Message Handling Software—Tandem Computers Inc.; *U.S. Public*, pg. 417

MI ABRAMS MAIN BATTLE TANK—NONE—General Dynamics Corporation; *U.S. Public*, pg. 708

MIC BOWEL MANAGEMENT KIT—NONE—Medical Innovations Corp.; *U.S. Public*, pg. 171

MIC GASTROSTOMY TUBE—Medical Tube—Medical Innovations Corp.; *U.S. Public*, pg. 171

MIC JEJUNAL TUBE—Medical Tube—Medical Innovations Corp.; *U.S. Public*, pg. 171

MIC JEJUNOSTOMY TUBE—Medical Tube—Medical Innovations Corp.; *U.S. Public*, pg. 171

MIC-KEY SKIN LEVEL GASTROSTOMY FEEDING KIT—Pediatric Feeding Tube—Ballard Medical Products; *U.S. Public*, pg. 171

MIC-PEG—Feeding Tube—Ballard Medical Products; *U.S. Public*, pg. 171

MIC PEG—Catheter—Medical Innovations Corp.; *U.S. Public*, pg. 171

MIC TRANSGASTRIC JEJUNAL TUBE—Feeding Tube—Ballard Medical Products; *U.S. Public*, pg. 171

MIC TRANSGASTRIC JEJUNAL TUBE—Feeding Tube—Medical Innovations Corp.; *U.S. Public*, pg. 171

MIL—Minimum Induced Loss Agitatiors—Svedala Pumps & Process; *Int'l*, pg. 1325

MIL-C—NONE—Molex Incorporated; *U.S. Public*, pg. 1121

MI 951—Series PC Keyboard Wedge—Metrologic Instruments, Inc.; *U.S. Public*, pg. 1102

MIQ—Mineral Insulated Heating Cables—Thermon Manufacturing Company; *U.S. Private*, pg. 1080

MI-TIQUE—Antiquing Solutions—Hubbard Hall Inc.; *U.S. Private*, pg. 544

MJB—Coffee—Nestle S.A.; *Int'l*, pg. 915

MJB—Coffee—Nestle USA; *Int'l*, pg. 916

MKC—Enzymes—Solvay S.A.; *Int'l*, pg. 1277

MK ELECTRIC—Electrical Accessories—Caradon Plc; *Int'l*, pg. 266

MKM MULTICOORDINATE MANIPULATOR—Computer Assisted Guidance for Surgical Microscopes—Carl Zeiss; *Int'l*, pg. 1522

ML CAMPBELL—Paints—Pratt & Lambert United, Inc.; *U.S. Public*, pg. 1466

ML-80—Prefinished Industrial Panels—Weyerhaeuser Forest Products Company; *U.S. Public*, pg. 1764

MLS—Navigational Equipment—Wilcox Electric, Inc.; *Int'l*, pg. 1384

MLS-6—PARTNER Family Proprietary 6-Button Telephone—Lucent Technologies Inc.; *U.S. Public*, pg. 1017

MLS-12—PARTNER Family 12-Button Proprietary Telephone—Lucent Technologies Inc.; *U.S. Public*, pg. 1017

MLS-12D—PARTNER Family 12-Button Proprietary Display Telephone—Lucent Technologies Inc.; *U.S. Public*, pg. 1017

MLT—Medico-Surgical Tubes—Mallinckrodt Inc.; *U.S. Public*, pg. 1039

MLX-16DP—Telephones—Lucent Technologies Inc.; *U.S. Public*, pg. 1017

MLX-10—Electronic Key Telephone System—Lucent Technologies Inc.; *U.S. Public*, pg. 1017

MLX-10D—Electronic Key Telephone System—Lucent Technologies Inc.; *U.S. Public*, pg. 1017

MLX-10DP—Telephones—Lucent Technologies Inc.; *U.S. Public*, pg. 1017

MLX-28D—Electronic Key Telephone System—Lucent Technologies Inc.; *U.S. Public*, pg. 1017

MLX-20L—Electronic Key Telephone System—Lucent Technologies Inc.; *U.S. Public*, pg. 1017

M LASTIC TAPE—Cohesive Tape—Mueller Sports Medicine, Inc.; *U.S. Private*, pg. 766

MM—Inks & Thinner—Markem Corporation; *U.S. Private*, pg. 704

MM—Mountain Master MH Chassis—Spartan Motors, Inc.; *U.S. Public*, pg. 1495

MMAC-PLUS SMARTSWITCH—NONE—Cabletron Systems, Inc.; *U.S. Public*, pg. 288

M M BY KRIZIA—Women's Wear—Hartmarx Corporation; *U.S. Public*, pg. 795

MMC—German Broadcasting—CLT-UFA; *Int'l*, pg. 561

MMFG—Pultrusions—Ryan Herco Products Corp.; *U.S. Private*, pg. 953

MMI—Chain Link Fence Manufacturing—MMI Products, Inc.; *U.S. Private*, pg. 687

MMI PRO SET—Cement Ad Mixture—MMI Products, Inc.; *U.S. Private*, pg. 687

M. M. MADES—Processed Meat—Labatt Brewing Company Limited; *Int'l*, pg. 679

MMP—Media Management Program Kit—Anacomp Magnetics, Inc.; *U.S. Public*, pg. 119

MMR 16 + 35—Motorized Microform Reader—Dukane Corporation; *U.S. Private*, pg. 345

M-M-R II—Measles, Mumps & Rubella Virus Vaccine—Merck & Co., Inc.; *U.S. Public*, pg. 1090

MMS—Circuit Tester—Teradyne, Inc.; *U.S. Public*, pg. 1580

MNP FASTENER—NONE—MNP Corp.; *U.S. Private*, pg. 687

MNS—Management Network Services—NDC Tokyo Representative Office; *U.S. Public*, pg. 1156

MNSD—Desuperheaters—Copes-Vulcan Inc.; *U.S. Private*, pg. 274

M 9 BAYONET/FIELD KNIFE—Cutlery—Buck Knives, Inc.; *U.S. Private*, pg. 177

MOD 300—Distributed Control Systems—ABB Industrial Systems, Inc.; *Int'l*, pg. 4

MODCA—Computer System—International Business Machines Corporation; *U.S. Public*, pg. 895

MOE—Metal on Elastomer—Elastomeric Technologies, Inc.; *U.S. Public*, pg. 1598

MO-MAX—Tool Bits—Greenfield Industries; *U.S. Public*, pg. 950

M.O.S.—Prescription Drug—ICN Pharmaceuticals, Inc.; *U.S. Public*, pg. 853

M-1000—Digital PBX System—TIE/Communications, Inc.; *U.S. Private*, pg. 1085

MP—NONE—U.S. Surgical Corp.; *U.S. Public*, pg. 1687

MPC—Moldable Phenolic Composite—Rogers Corporation; *U.S. Public*, pg. 1402

MPC MICROTRONIC—Grinding Machines—Landis; *U.S. Public*, pg. 1699

MPD—Shrinkable Film—Grace Packaging; *U.S. Public*, pg. 755

MPE I—Miniature Plugger Enginer, 5-Channel—Rockwell International Corporation; *U.S. Public*, pg. 1397

MPE II—Miniature Plugger Engine, 10-Channel—Rockwell International Corporation; *U.S. Public*, pg. 1397

MPIC—Mobile Phase Ion Chromatography Columns—Dionex Corporation; *U.S. Public*, pg. 510

MP LOCKS—Manipulation-Proof Combination Locks—Sargent & Greenleaf, Inc.; *U.S. Private*, pg. 965

MP 159—Metal Alloy—SPS Technologies, Inc.; *U.S. Public*, pg. 1419

MPS—NONE—Stryker Corporation; *U.S. Public*, pg. 1525

MPS—NONE—Xicor, Inc.; *U.S. Public*, pg. 1785

MPSI—Software—MPSI Systems Inc.; *U.S. Public*, pg. 1027

MP6100—Machine Controller—Gaston County Dyeing Machine Co.; *U.S. Private*, pg. 441

MP 35 N—Metal Alloy—SPS Technologies, Inc.; *U.S. Public*, pg. 1419

MPII—Photographic Films & Chemicals—Eastman Kodak Company; *U.S. Public*, pg. 550

MP 200—Electric Apparatus for Perming & Conditioning—Revlon-Realistic Professional Products, Inc.; *U.S. Public*, pg. 690

MPV—Mini Van—Mazda Motor of America, Inc.; *Int'l*, pg. 849

MPV'S—NONE—Vauxhall; *U.S. Public*, pg. 724

MPX 32—Real Time Operating System—Encore Computer Corporation; *U.S. Public*, pg. 580

MPZ—Engine Assembly Lube; Synthetic Oils—D.A. Stuart Company; *U.S. Private*, pg. 1048

M-PARTIGEN KITS—Immunodiffusion Reagents—Dade Behring Inc.; *U.S. Public*, pg. 110

M-PEDE—Pesticides—Mycogen Corporation; *U.S. Public*, pg. 1142

M-PERIL—Bioinsecticide—Mycogen Corporation; *U.S. Public*, pg. 1142

MPULSE—Surveillance System—IRD Mechanalysis, Inc. (U.S.A.); *U.S. Public*, pg. 789

M-PYROL—Solvent—International Specialty Products, Inc.; *U.S. Public*, pg. 858

MQSERIES—Computer Systems—International Business Machines Corporation; *U.S. Public*, pg. 895

MQ VIEW—Centralized Management for Server—Apertus Technologies Incorporated; *U.S. Public*, pg. 119

M-QUAT—Surfactant—PPG Industries, Inc.; *U.S. Public*, pg. 1245

MR—Sales Consultants—Management Recruiters International, Inc.; *U.S. Public*, pg. 277

MRC—Bearings—MRC Bearings; *Int'l*, pg. 1157

MRE—Ready-to-Eat Meals—Star Food Processing, Inc.; *U.S. Private*, pg. 1034

MRI—Sales Consultants—Management Recruiters International, Inc.; *U.S. Public*, pg. 277

MRNET—Medical Records—Cerner Corporation; *U.S. Public*, pg. 331

MRO—Industrial Coatings & Chemicals—Seymour of Sycamore, Inc.; *U.S. Private*, pg. 988

MR, THE QUARTERLY MAGAZINE OF MAGNETIC RESONANCE—Magazine—Miller Freeman Inc.; *Int'l*, pg. 1443

MR II—Car—Toyota Motor Sales, U.S.A., Inc.; *Int'l*, pg. 1412

MRV—Marathon Running Vitamin—Health Products Corporation; *U.S. Private*, pg. 514

M/REMOTE—Computer Software—Attachmate; *U.S. Private*, pg. 98

M ROY—Pumps—Milton Roy Company; *U.S. Public*, pg. 1534

M.S.—Locks—Adams Rite Manufacturing Co.; *U.S. Private*, pg. 17

MS—Magazine—MacDonald Communications; *U.S. Private*, pg. 691

MSA/AUER—Safety Equipment—MSA Nederland B.V.; *U.S. Public*, pg. 1115

MSA/AUER—Gas Detection Equipment—MSA Nederland B.V.; *U.S. Public*, pg. 1115

MSC/CAL—PC Based Products for Graphical Modeling—The Macneal-Schwendler Corp.; *U.S. Public*, pg. 1030

MSC/DYNA—Program Used to Solve Highly Nonlinear, Transient Dynamic Problems—The Macneal-Schwendler Corp.; *U.S. Public*, pg. 1030

MSC/EMAS—Electromagnetic Analysis System—The Macneal-Schwendler Corp.; *U.S. Public*, pg. 1030

MSC/MOD—PC Based Products for Structural, Thermal & Electromagnetic Analysis—The Macneal-Schwendler Corp.; *U.S. Public*, pg. 1030

MSC/NASTRAN—Program-Solution Structural Analysis Problems Using Finite Element Method—The Macneal-Schwendler Corp.; *U.S. Public*, pg. 1030

MSC/PAL 2—PC Based Products for Structural, Thermal, Electromagnetic Analysis—The Macneal-Schwendler Corp.; *U.S. Public*, pg. 1030

MSC/PROBE—Analysis Program for Detailed Stress Calculations—The Macneal-Schwendler Corp.; *U.S. Public*, pg. 1030

MSC/XL—Interactive Modeling & Results Interpretation Tool—The Macneal-Schwendler Corp.; *U.S. Public*, pg. 1030

MS-CUBE—Gas Analysis Units—Balzers; *Int'l*, pg. 997

MS-DOS—Compatible Computers—Data General Corporation; *U.S. Public*, pg. 485

MS-DOS—Computer Operating System—Microsoft Corporation; *U.S. Public*, pg. 1107

MS 800—In-Counter Laser Scanner—Metrologic Instruments, Inc.; *U.S. Public*, pg. 1102

MS 860 MINI SLOT—Laser Bar Code Scanner—Metrologic Instruments, Inc.; *U.S. Public*, pg. 1102

MSF—Transparent Polyvinyl Chloride Stretch Film—Reynolds Metals Company; *U.S. Public*, pg. 1385

M. S. HERSHEY—Boxed Chocolates—Hershey Chocolate U.S.A.; *U.S. Public*, pg. 812

MSM—Multi-Shaft Batch Mixers—Premier Mill Corp.; *U.S. Private*, pg. 881

MSM & DESIGN—Repair & Manufacture of Machinery—Georgia-Pacific Corporation; *U.S. Public*, pg. 735

MS MEDS—Pharmacy Information Systems—Cerner Corporation; *U.S. Public*, pg. 331

MS 981 SCANGLOVE—Laser Scanner—Metrologic Instruments, Inc.; *U.S. Public*, pg. 1102

MS 900 SERIES—Handheld Laser Scanner—Metrologic Instruments, Inc.; *U.S. Public*, pg. 1102

MS 921—Laser Scanning Engine—Metrologic Instruments, Inc.; *U.S. Public*, pg. 1102

MSP—Heat-Shrinkable, Transparent Polyvinyl Chloride Film—Reynolds Metals Company; *U.S. Public*, pg. 1385

MSP PLUS—High Speed Color Photographic Printer—AGFA Division of Bayer Corporation; *Int'l*, pg. 172

M.S. PLUS—Latch/Lock Combination—Adams Rite Manufacturing Co.; *U.S. Private*, pg. 17

MS/RV—Mobile Storage Retrieval Vehicle—Jervis B. Webb Company; *U.S. Private*, pg. 1156

M.S. RACING—NONE—LDI, Ltd.; *U.S. Private*, pg. 639

MSS II—Modular Drawer Cabinets—Lyon Metal Products, Inc.; *U.S. Private*, pg. 638

MS SCRIPT—Outpatient Pharmacy Information System—Cerner Corporation; *U.S. Public*, pg. 331

MS 700—Projection Scanner—Metrologic Instruments, Inc.; *U.S. Public*, pg. 1102

MS 60—Electromyograph—Vickers PLC; *Int'l*, pg. 1466

MST—Electronics—National Semiconductor Corporation; *U.S. Public*, pg. 1159

MSTA—Mumps Skin Test Antigen, USP—Connaught Laboratories, Inc.; *Int'l*, pg. 1109

MS 2—Telecommunication Protected Entrance Terminal—3M; *U.S. Public*, pg. 1604

MSW—Automotive Equipment & Parts, Power Tech.—Triple A Specialty Company; *U.S. Private*, pg. 1103

M.S. WALKER—Premium Scotch—M.S. Walker, Inc.; *U.S. Private*, pg. 1147

M SCREEN—Stock Preparation—Beloit Corporation; *U.S. Public*, pg. 789

M SERIES—Serial Dot—Dataproducts Corporation; *Int'l*, pg. 620

M-SERIES—Molding Compounds—The Geon Company; *U.S. Public*, pg. 733

M 77—Bolt Action Rifles—Sturm, Ruger & Co., Inc.; *U.S. Public*, pg. 1526

M6—French Broadcasting—CLT-UFA; *Int'l*, pg. 561

M STORES—Department Stores—Socanav Inc.; *Int'l*, pg. 1272

MTA LONG ISLAND RAIL ROAD—NONE—MTA Long Island Rail Road; *U.S. Private*, pg. 739

MTC—Japanese Food—Mutual Trading Co., Inc.; *U.S. Public*, pg. 770

MTD STEELS—Heat-Treated Steels Designed for Mold, Tool 7 Die Applications—Lukens Steel Company; *U.S. Public*, pg. 1020

MT5 PLUS—Dry Mount Tissue—Seal Products Incorporated; *U.S. Public*, pg. 849

MTI—Film & Video—Coronet/MTI; *U.S. Private*, pg. 863

MTI 1000 FOTONIC SENSOR—Measuring System—Mechanical Technology Inc.; *U.S. Public*, pg. 1077

MTI 2000 FOTONIC SENSOR—Measuring System—Mechanical Technology Inc.; *U.S. Public*, pg. 1077

MT-95K2—8-32 Channel Recorder—Astro-Med, Inc.; *U.S. Public*, pg. 141

MT-95000—8-16 Channel Recorder—Astro-Med, Inc.; *U.S. Public*, pg. 141

MTR390—Helicopter Engine—Rolls-Royce Military Aero Engines Ltd.; *Int'l*, pg. 1127

MTS—Electrohydraulic Test Systems—MTS Systems Corporation; *U.S. Public*, pg. 1028

MT-13—Toluene Di Isociante—CYDSA S.A.; *Int'l*, pg. 246

MT TOURNEY—Golf Clubs—MacGregor Golf Company; *Int'l*, pg. 72

MTU—NONE—Daimler-Benz Aktiengesellschaft; *Int'l*, pg. 366

MTV—Cable TV Network—Viacom Inc.; *U.S. Private*, pg. 775

MTV RADIO NETWORK—Rock Music Entertainment Radio Program—Westwood One Entertainment; *U.S. Public*, pg. 1763

MTV RADIO NETWORK—Rock Programming—Westwood One, Inc.; *U.S. Public*, pg. 1763

M TAPE—All Cotton Sports Tape—Mueller Sports Medicine, Inc.; *U.S. Private*, pg. 766

M3—Opthamalic Lenses—American Optical Corporation; *U.S. Private*, pg. 60

M3—Sedan—BMW (US) Holding Corporation; *Int'l*, pg. 177

M3 HILNDEX—Opthamalic Lenses—American Optical Corporation; *U.S. Private*, pg. 60

M2—Case Tumbler—Hornady Manufacturing Company; *U.S. Private*, pg. 539

MU—Music Universe On-Line—Bam Media; *U.S. Private*, pg. 113

MU—Sports Utility Vehicles—Isuzu Motors Limited; *Int'l*, pg. 692

MU-SE—Slenium Injection (Equine & Bovine)—Schering-Plough Corporation; *U.S. Public*, pg. 1438

MU-STRIP—Radiative & Receiving Antennas—Ball Corporation; *U.S. Public*, pg. 170

MV.BASE—Database Software for Windows NT & Windows 95—General Automation, Inc.; *U.S. Public*, pg. 706

MV.ENTERPRISE—Database Software for Unix—General Automation, Inc.; *U.S. Public*, pg. 706

MV HORIZON—NONE—Celebrity Cruises, Inc.; *U.S. Public*, pg. 1410

MV MANAGER for DB2—Online Performance Management Package & Reporting Tool—Boole & Babbage, Inc.; *U.S. Public*, pg. 244

MV MERIDIAN—NONE—Celebrity Cruises, Inc.; *U.S. Public*, pg. 1410

MVP—Self-Closing Faucets—The Chicago Faucet Co.; *U.S. Private*, pg. 234

MVP—Sports Card Pages—Command Plastic Corporation; *U.S. Private*, pg. 257

MVP—Automatic Voice Delivery System—Dictaphone Corp.; *U.S. Private*, pg. 1045

MVP—Telephone Voice Messaging Systems—Glenayre Technologies, Inc.; *U.S. Public*, pg. 746

MVP—Bioinsecticide—Mycogen Corporation; *U.S. Public*, pg. 1142

MVP—Plastic Containers & Lids—Reynolds Metals Company; *U.S. Public*, pg. 1385

MVS—Syrgical Equipment—Alcon Laboratories, Inc.; *Int'l*, pg. 916

MVS—Conveyor Belting—Fenner Drives; *U.S. Private*, pg. 400

MVS/DFP—Computer System—International Business Machines Corporation; *U.S. Public*, pg. 895

MVS/ESA—Computer System—International Business Machines Corporation; *U.S. Public*, pg. 895

MVSRJS—Computer System—International Business Machines Corporation; *U.S. Public*, pg. 895

MVS/SP—Computer System—International Business Machines Corporation; *U.S. Public*, pg. 895

MVS/XA—Computer System—International Business Machines Corporation; *U.S. Public*, pg. 895

M/VISION—Materials Software System—MacNeal-Schwendler Corp.; *U.S. Public*, pg. 1031

MW—Wood Windows, Flush & Louvered Doors—Hanson PLC; *Int'l*, pg. 592

MW DESIGN—Closures, Particularly For Cosmetic, Toiletries and Pharmaceutical Products—The West Company, Incorporated; *U.S. Public*, pg. 1755

M.W. KELLOGG—Engineering Services—The M.W. Kellogg Company; *U.S. Public*, pg. 528

MWAVE—Computer System—International Business Machines Corporation; *U.S. Public*, pg. 895

M WRAP—Foam Underwrap—Mueller Sports Medicine, Inc.; *U.S. Private*, pg. 766

MX—NONE—Molex Incorporated; *U.S. Public*, pg. 1121

MX-50—Electronic Components—Molex Incorporated; *U.S. Public*, pg. 1121

MX-5 MINTA—Car—Mazda Motor of America, Inc.; *Int'l*, pg. 849

MX-PLUS—NONE—Molex Incorporated; *U.S. Public*, pg. 1121

MXSITE—Polyethylene Resins—Eastman Chemical Company; *U.S. Public*, pg. 550

MX-6—Car—Mazda Motor of America, Inc.; *Int'l*, pg. 849

MXSTEN—Plastics Polymer—Eastman Chemical Company; *U.S. Public*, pg. 550

MXT FAMILY SERIES 7000—Disk Drives—Maxtor Corporation; *Int'l*, pg. 641

MX-3—Car—Mazda Motor of America, Inc.; *Int'l*, pg. 849

MX2—Blood Gas Monitor/Sensor—Medtronic, Inc.; *U.S. Public*, pg. 1082

MXII—NONE—Molex Incorporated; *U.S. Public*, pg. 1121

MA'ARIV—Major Israeli Daily Newspaper—The Israel Land Development Co., Ltd.; *Int'l*, pg. 691

MA'ARIV LANOAR—Weekly Teenage Magazine—The Israel Land Development Co., Ltd.; *Int'l*, pg. 691

MA BROWN—Pickles—Dean Foods Company; *U.S. Public*, pg. 489

MAACO—Body Shops—Maaco Enterprises Inc.; *U.S. Private*, pg. 689

MAALOX—Antacid—Novartis; *Int'l*, pg. 972

MAALOX—Antacid—Rhone-Poulenc Rorer - U.S.; *Int'l*, pg. 1110

MAALOX PLUS—Antacid—Novartis; *Int'l*, pg. 972

MAALOX PLUS—Antacid—Rhone-Poulenc Rorer - U.S.; *Int'l*, pg. 1110

MAALOX TC—Antacid—Rhone-Poulenc Rorer - U.S.; *Int'l*, pg. 1110

MAALOX TC—Antacid—Novartis; *Int'l*, pg. 972

MABADOFU—Seasoning Mix For Tofu—Ajinomoto Company Inc.; *Int'l*, pg. 40

MABLEX ABS—Polycarbonate Blend—The Dow Chemical Company; *U.S. Public*, pg. 522

MABOR—Tires—Continental AG; *Int'l*, pg. 327

MAC—Access Control System—CASI-RUSCO Inc.; *U.S. Private*, pg. 218

MAC—NONE—Estee Lauder Companies Inc.; *U.S. Public*, pg. 594

MAC—Mechanic Tools—Mechanics Tool Div.; *U.S. Public*, pg. 1509

MAC FRUGALS BARGAINS CLOSEOUTS—Retail Store—Mac Frugal's Bargains Close-Outs Inc.; *U.S. Public*, pg. 437

MAC JACK—Mobile Car Jack—Portec Inc., Railway Maintenance Products Div.; *U.S. Public*, pg. 1318

MAC OPAQUE TEXT—Paper—Georgia-Pacific Corporation; *U.S. Public*, pg. 735

MAC-PAK—Valves & Fittings—A.Y. McDonald Industries, Inc.; *U.S. Private*, pg. 721

MAC SCRAMBLE EEZ—Prepared Egg Product—McAnally Enterprises, Inc.; *U.S. Private*, pg. 718

MAC TOOLS—Automotive Tools—The Stanley Works; *U.S. Public*, pg. 1508

MAC II—NONE—Berg Electronics; *U.S. Public*, pg. 212

THE MACALLAN—Single Malt Scotch—The Highland Distilleries Company plc; *Int'l*, pg. 619

MACANUDO—Cigars—General Cigar Company, Inc.; *U.S. Public*, pg. 708

MACARDLE S ALE—NONE—Guinness Plc; *Int'l*, pg. 412

MACASSAR—Men's Toiletries—Wella Group; *Int'l*, pg. 1489

MACAUDIO—Auto Sound Accessories—Recoton Corporation; *U.S. Public*, pg. 1369

MACBASIC—Measurement & Control Software—Analog Devices, Inc.; *U.S. Public*, pg. 107

MACCABEES—Life & Health Insurance—Royal Financial Services Inc.; *Int'l*, pg. 1130

MACCO—Adhesives, Caulks, Sealants—ICI Paints; *Int'l*, pg. 664

MACDERMID—Specialty Chemicals—MacDermid Incorporated; *U.S. Public*, pg. 1029

MACDONALD SELECT—Cigarettes-Canada—R.J. Reynolds Tobacco Intl., Inc.; *U.S. Public*, pg. 1355

MACDONALD SPECIAL—Cigarettes-Canada—R.J. Reynolds Tobacco Intl., Inc.; *U.S. Public*, pg. 1355

MACE—Teflon Flow Control Components—Osmonics, Inc.; *U.S. Public*, pg. 1233

MACFISHERIES—Fish Products—The Albert Fisher Group PLC; *Int'l*, pg. 491

MACGOLD—Precision Hot Rolled Steel Bar—Quanex Corporation; *U.S. Public*, pg. 1349

MACGREGOR—Youth Baseball—Sport Supply Group, Inc.; *U.S. Public*, pg. 1499

MACH 5—Lubricant—Petroliam Nasional Berhad (Petronas); *Int'l*, pg. 1046

MACH-MATE—Building Block System—Setco; *U.S. Private*, pg. 987

MACH II—Valves—Barksdale, Inc.; *U.S. Public*, pg. 457

MACH 6—Universal Indexable Drill—Rogers Tool Works, Inc.; *U.S. Public*, pg. 950

MACHETE—Herbicide—The Agricultural Group, Monsanto Company; *U.S. Public*, pg. 1125

MACHETE—Herbicide—Monsanto Company; *U.S. Public*, pg. 1124

MACHINE DESIGN—Periodical—Penton Publishing, Inc.; *U.S. Public*, pg. 1306

MACHINE MATED—Business Forms—The Standard Register Company; *U.S. Public*, pg. 1505

MACHINECLAD—Stains for Machine Application—Devoe Paint; *Int'l*, pg. 663

MACHINECLAD—Stains for Machine Application—ICI Paints; *Int'l*, pg. 664

MACHINEGUARD—Protection Program—National Video, Inc.; *U.S. Public*, pg. 1755

MACHINING FUNDAMENTALS—Textbook Covering Techniques of Machining & Shaping Modern Metals—Goodheart-Willcox Publisher; *U.S. Private*, pg. 464

MACHLETT—X-Ray Tubes—Varian Associates, Inc.; *U.S. Public*, pg. 1710

MACHO—NONE—The Black & Decker Corporation; *U.S. Public*, pg. 233

MACHO NACHO'S—NONE—Del Taco, Inc.; *U.S. Private*, pg. 321

MACIEIRA—Brandy—The Seagram Company Ltd.; *Int'l*, pg. 1214

MACIMAGE—Graphics Sofware For The Macintosh—Xerox Imaging Systems, Inc.; *U.S. Public*, pg. 1785

MACINTOSH—Personal Computer—Apple Computer, Inc.; *U.S. Public*, pg. 121

MACINTOSH BOURBON APPLE—Specialty Drink—Montebello Brands Inc.; *U.S. Private*, pg. 758

MACINTOSH PERFORMA—Personal Computer—Apple Computer, Inc.; *U.S. Public*, pg. 121

MACINTOSH PLUS—Personal Computer—Apple Computer, Inc.; *U.S. Public*, pg. 121

MACINTOSH POWER BOOK—Personal Computer—Apple Computer, Inc.; *U.S. Public*, pg. 121

MACINTOSH QUADRA—Personal Computer—Apple Computer, Inc.; *U.S. Public*, pg. 121

MACINTOSH SE—Personal Computer—Apple Computer, Inc.; *U.S. Public*, pg. 121

MACINTOSH SE/30—Personal Computer—Apple Computer, Inc.; *U.S. Public*, pg. 121

MACINTOSH II—Personal Computer—Apple Computer, Inc.; *U.S. Public*, pg. 121

MACIRMA—Computer Software—Attachmate; *U.S. Private*, pg. 98

MACIRMALAN—Computer Software—Attachmate; *U.S. Private*, pg. 98

MACKINAW MILLING CO—Baked Goods—Grocers Baking Co.; *U.S. Private*, pg. 482
MACLACHIANS—Scotch Whiskey—John Gross & Co.; *U.S. Private*, pg. 483
MACLEANS—Whisky—Distillers Corporation S.A.; *Int'l*, pg. 1129
MACLEANS—Toothpaste—SmithKline Beecham Corporation; *Int'l*, pg. 1264
MACLEANS—Oral Care—SmithKline Beecham plc; *Int'l*, pg. 1264
MACLOCK—Fasteners—Maclean-Fogg Co.; *U.S. Private*, pg. 692
MACMILLAN—Publishing—Macmillan Publishing USA; *U.S. Private*, pg. 777
MACOL—Surfactants—PPG Industries, Inc.; *U.S. Public*, pg. 1245
MACON-LUGNY LES CHARMES—White Burgundy—Seagram Chateau & Estate Wines Co.; *Int'l*, pg. 1215
MACPLANE—NONE—Berg Electronics; *U.S. Public*, pg. 212
MACPLAY—Entertainment Software for Macintosh Computers—Interplay Productions, Inc.; *U.S. Private*, pg. 572
MACPLUS—Cold Finished Steel Bar—Quanex Corporation; *U.S. Public*, pg. 1349
MACREADYS—NONE—Glynwed International PLC; *Int'l*, pg. 554
MACRO ASSEMBLER/2—Computer System—International Business Machines Corporation; *U.S. Public*, pg. 895
MACROBERTSON—Chocolates—Cadbury Schweppes p.l.c.; *Int'l*, pg. 247
MACROBID—Urinary Tract Antibacterial—Procter & Gamble Pharmaceuticals, Inc.; *U.S. Public*, pg. 1331
MACROBLADE—Roller Skates—Rollerblade, Inc.; *U.S. Private*, pg. 941
MACROBORE—Liquid Chromatograph Equipment—PPG Industries, Inc.; *U.S. Public*, pg. 1245
MACROBUS—NONE—NEC Electronics Inc.; *Int'l*, pg. 900
MACRODANTIN—Urinary Tract Antibacterial—Procter & Gamble Pharmaceuticals, Inc.; *U.S. Public*, pg. 1331
MACRODEX—Pharmaceutical—Pharmacia & Upjohn Adria Laboratories; *Int'l*, pg. 1049
MACROLYTE—Conductive Adhesive Polymer—Conmed Corporation; *U.S. Public*, pg. 431
MACROMELT—Hot Melt Adhesives—Henkel Corporation; *Int'l*, pg. 610
MACROMET—Rockwell-Type Hardness Tester—Buehler, Limited; *U.S. Public*, pg. 574
MACROMETER—Surveying Equipment—Litton Industries, Inc.; *U.S. Public*, pg. 1002
MACROMETRY—GPS Survey Services—Litton Industries, Inc.; *U.S. Public*, pg. 1002
MACROMETRY II—GPS Survey Receiver—Litton Industries, Inc.; *U.S. Public*, pg. 1002
MACROPLAST—Polyurethane Adhesives—Henkel Corporation; *Int'l*, pg. 610
MAC'S—Automotive Chemicals—Valvoline Company; *U.S. Public*, pg. 139
MACS-PAC—Monitoring Systems—Atlas Copco AB; *Int'l*, pg. 95
MACS II—Modular Administrative Communications System—Dukane Corporation; *U.S. Private*, pg. 345
MACSTEEL—Hot Rolled Steel Bar Producer—Quanex Corporation; *U.S. Public*, pg. 1349
MACSYM—Measurement & Control System—Analog Devices, Inc.; *U.S. Public*, pg. 107
MACTAC—Self-Adhesive Papers—MACtac Morgan Adhesive Company; *U.S. Public*, pg. 210
MACTAVISH FURNITURE INDUSTRIES—Furniture Manufacturing Division—Aaron Rents, Inc.; *U.S. Public*, pg. 12
MACTOPAS—Computer Graphics Software—Lucent Technologies Inc.; *U.S. Public*, pg. 1017
MACVECTOR—Macintosh Protein & DNA Sequence Analysis Program—Scientific Imaging Systems; *U.S. Public*, pg. 550
MACWRITE PRO—Computer Software—Claris Corporation; *U.S. Public*, pg. 121
MACY'S—Department Store—Federated Department Stores, Inc.; *U.S. Public*, pg. 617
MAD MAGAZINE—Book & Magazine Publishing Imprint—DC Comics, Inc.; *U.S. Public*, pg. 1614
MADAM—NONE—Cruspi S.A.; *Int'l*, pg. 348

MADAME ALEXANDER—Collectible Dolls—Alexander Doll Company, Inc.; *U.S. Private*, pg. 33
MADAME OLGA PREDICTS—Greeting Cards—American Greetings Corporation; *U.S. Public*, pg. 77
MADAME TUSSAUD'S—Entertainment—Pearson plc; *Int'l*, pg. 1025
MADE SIMPLE BOOKS—Book Imprint—Bertelsmann AG; *Int'l*, pg. 189
MADEIRA—Glassware—Indiana Glass Company; *U.S. Public*, pg. 976
MADEIRA—Writing Paper & Envelopes—The Mead Corporation; *U.S. Public*, pg. 1074
MADEMOISELLE—Salon Dryers—Belvedere Company; *U.S. Private*, pg. 1008
MADEMOISELLE—Magazine—The Conde Nast Publications Inc.; *U.S. Private*, pg. 20
MADEMOISELLE RICCI—Women's Fragrance—Accecones Ricci U.S.A., Inc.; *Int'l*, pg. 445
MADERITE—Paper—The Mead Corporation; *U.S. Public*, pg. 1074
MADI—Audio Router—Chyron Corp.; *Int'l*, pg. 1372
MADISON CABLE NETWORK—Cable TV—Madison Newspapers, Inc.; *U.S. Public*, pg. 984
MADISON PLANK—Pre-Finished Strip—Bruce Hardwood Floors; *U.S. Public*, pg. 1634
MADLIBS—Game Books—Price Stern Sloan Inc.; *Int'l*, pg. 1215
MADOPAR—Parkinson's Syndrome Medication—Roche Holding Ltd.; *Int'l*, pg. 1119
MADSHUS—Cross Country Skis—K2 Inc.; *U.S. Public*, pg. 940
MADSOUNDS—NONE—Motown Record Company, J.P.; *Int'l*, pg. 1052
MADYE'S—Slippers—R.G. Barry Corporation; *U.S. Public*, pg. 192
MAES—Beer—Danone Group; *Int'l*, pg. 379
MAESTRANI SWISS CHOCOLATE BARS—Chocolate Bars—The Promotion in Motion Companies; *U.S. Private*, pg. 890
MAESTRO—Automobile—British Aerospace p.l.c.; *Int'l*, pg. 217
MAESTRO—NONE—Brown & Sharpe Manufacturing Company; *U.S. Public*, pg. 260
MAESTRO—Oven Paper—The Dow Chemical Company; *U.S. Public*, pg. 522
MAESTRO—Wood Windows & Doors—International Aluminum Corporation; *U.S. Public*, pg. 894
MAESTRO—Telephone Products—Northern Telecom; *Int'l*, pg. 969
MAESTRO COLORS—Paint & Colors for Paint—PPG Industries, Inc.; *U.S. Public*, pg. 1245
MAESTRO TOUCH TONE—Telephone Handsets—BCE Inc.; *Int'l*, pg. 114
MAFILL—Filled Polypropylene—The Dow Chemical Company; *U.S. Public*, pg. 522
MAFLEX—Polystyrene Resins—The Dow Chemical Company; *U.S. Public*, pg. 522
MAFLOC—Synthetic Organic Polymeric Flocculants—PPG Industries, Inc.; *U.S. Public*, pg. 1245
MAFO—Surfactants—PPG Industries, Inc.; *U.S. Public*, pg. 1245
MAG—Automobile Antennas—Fiamm S.p.A.; *Int'l*, pg. 480
MAG DRIVER—Changeable Tip Screwdriver with Handle Storage—Lyman Products Corporation; *U.S. Private*, pg. 683
MAG-LINK—Control Measurement—Brooks Instrument; *U.S. Public*, pg. 574
MAG-LITE—Synthetic Cut Racquet String—Ektelon; *U.S. Private*, pg. 884
MAG 7000—Control Measurement—Brooks Instrument; *U.S. Public*, pg. 574
MAG-X—Magnetic Flowmeter—Bailey, Fischer & Porter Company; *Int'l*, pg. 449
MAGA-SEEN—Office Supplies—JM Company; *U.S. Private*, pg. 577
MAGAZINE & BOOKSELLER—Magazine—North American Publishing Company; *U.S. Public*, pg. 803
MAGEE—Picture Frames—Tandycrafts, Inc.; *U.S. Public*, pg. 1561
MAGELLAN—Petroleum & Natural Gas—Magellan Petroleum Corporation; *U.S. Public*, pg. 1036
MAGELLAN—NONE—Northern Telecom Limited; *Int'l*, pg. 968

MAGELLAN—Remote Operated Vehicle—Oceaneering International, Inc.; *U.S. Public*, pg. 1211
MAGELLAN SL—360 Degree Scanner—PSC Inc.; *U.S. Public*, pg. 1245
MAGGI—Culinary Products—Nestle S.A.; *Int'l*, pg. 915
MAGGI—Bouillon Cubes, Soup Mixes, Seasonings—Nestle USA; *Int'l*, pg. 916
MAGGIE BARNES—Women's Sportswear—Catherines Stores Corporation; *U.S. Public*, pg. 317
MAGGIE LAWRENCE-STEFANO—Women's Apparel—Charming Shoppes, Inc.; *U.S. Public*, pg. 335
MAGI DIRECT—Computer & Data Processing Services—Database America Companies; *U.S. Private*, pg. 312
MAGI-TUNE FM—Radio—Clarion Corporation of America; *Int'l*, pg. 296
MAGIC—Flashers—Eagle Electric Mfg. Co., Inc.; *U.S. Private*, pg. 354
MAGIC—Binding Posts—Fellowes Manufacturing Co.; *U.S. Private*, pg. 400
MAGIC—Aerosol Cleaner—Magic American Corporation; *U.S. Private*, pg. 695
MAGIC—Women's Fragrance—Marilyn Miglin, L.P.; *U.S. Private*, pg. 745
MAGIC—Baking Powder—RJR Nabisco Holdings Corp.; *U.S. Public*, pg. 1354
MAGIC—Christmas Ornaments & Items—Syratech Corporation; *U.S. Private*, pg. 1060
MAGIC—Matte-Finish Transparent Tape, PSA—3M; *U.S. Public*, pg. 1604
MAGIC BOTTLE BABY—Dolls—Tyco Toys, Inc.; *U.S. Public*, pg. 1058
MAGIC BRAIN & DESIGN—TV Receivers—Thomson Consumer Electronics Inc.; *Int'l*, pg. 1383
MAGIC CHEF—Appliances—Jenn-Air; *U.S. Public*, pg. 1064
MAGIC CHEF—NONE—Maytag Cleveland Cooking Products; *U.S. Public*, pg. 1064
MAGIC-CHEF—Micro. Ovens, Ranges, Dehumidifiers, Washer/Dryers, Dishwashers & Refrig.—Maytag Corporation; *U.S. Public*, pg. 1064
MAGIC CHEF—Refrigerators—Maytag Galesburg Refrigeration Products; *U.S. Public*, pg. 1064
MAGIC CIRCLE STEERING—Floating Eccentric Gear Linkage Between Steer Wheel Ring Mounts—Baker Material Handling Corp.; *Int'l*, pg. 810
MAGIC COPIER—Activity Toy—Tyco Toys, Inc.; *U.S. Public*, pg. 1058
MAGIC DOOR—Door Operating Equipment—The Stanley Works; *U.S. Public*, pg. 1508
MAGIC 8 BALL—Game—Tyco Toys, Inc.; *U.S. Public*, pg. 1058
MAGIC FEEDING BABY—Doll—Tyco Toys, Inc.; *U.S. Public*, pg. 1058
MAGIC FLASHER—Outlet Winker—Eagle Electric Mfg. Co., Inc.; *U.S. Private*, pg. 354
MAGIC HEAT—Heat Reclaimers & Coal Heaters—Flint Manufacturing Co.; *U.S. Private*, pg. 413
MAGIC HOSTESS—Slow Cooker—The Rival Company; *U.S. Public*, pg. 1391
MAGIC JOHNSON THEATRES—NONE—Loews Theatre Management Corp.; *Int'l*, pg. 1282
MAGIC KOTE—Form Release Chemical—Symons Corporation; *U.S. Private*, pg. 932
MAGIC LADY—Fashionable Women's Underwear—AGP Industrial Corporation; *Int'l*, pg. 14
MAGIC LANTERN—Air Fresheners—Stanhome Inc.; *U.S. Public*, pg. 1508
MAGIC LINK—Electronic Pocket Organizer—Sony Electronics; *Int'l*, pg. 1281
MAGIC MAKER—Toy—Toymax International Inc.; *U.S. Public*, pg. 1626
MAGIC MOMENTS—Prepared Desserts—Borden, Inc.; *U.S. Private*, pg. 157
MAGIC MOOD—Dinner Candles & Cartridge Candles—Will & Baumer Incorporated; *U.S. Private*, pg. 1176
MAGIC MUSHROOM—Air Freshener—Reckitt & Colman Inc.; *Int'l*, pg. 1090
MAGIC NURSERY—Dolls—Mattel, Inc.; *U.S. Public*, pg. 1057

MAGIC PAPER—Business Product—International Business Machines Corporation; *U.S. Public*, pg. 895

MAGIC REALM—Fantasy Game—Monarch Avalon, Inc.; *U.S. Public*, pg. 1123

MAGIC ROCKS—Toy—RPM, Inc.; *U.S. Public*, pg. 1356

MAGIC SHELL—Ice Cream Coating—J.M. Smucker Company; *U.S. Public*, pg. 1480

MAGIC SHIELD—No-Wax Floors—Stanhome Inc.; *U.S. Public*, pg. 1508

MAGIC SLATE—Children's Toy—Golden Books Family Entertainment Inc.; *U.S. Public*, pg. 749

MAGIC STRETCH—Stretch Fabrics—Haggar Corporation; *U.S. Public*, pg. 774

MAGIC: THE GATHERING—Card Game—Wizards of the Coast; *U.S. Private*, pg. 1185

MAGIC VALLEY—Instant Potatoes, Potato Flakes—Magic Valley Foods, Inc.; *U.S. Private*, pg. 695

MAGIC WALLSTENT—NONE—Pfizer Inc.; *U.S. Public*, pg. 1281

MAGICAL SPEEDY—NONE—Pfizer Inc.; *U.S. Public*, pg. 1281

MAGICAM—Video Equipment—National Video, Inc.; *U.S. Public*, pg. 1755

MAGICBLOCK—Control Block for ORION RO—Osmonics, Inc.; *U.S. Public*, pg. 1233

MAGICFIT—Window Shades—Newell Co.; *U.S. Public*, pg. 1176

MAGICHEM—Water Treatment Chemical—RainSoft Water Treatment Systems; *U.S. Private*, pg. 78

MAGICLEAN FOAM—Removes Cooking Grime From Kitchen Surfaces With Foaming Action—Kao Corporation; *Int'l*, pg. 717

MAGICOLOR—Paint—The Valspar Corporation; *U.S. Public*, pg. 1707

MAGICSILK—Polyester Artificial Flowers—Celebrity Incorporated; *U.S. Public*, pg. 319

MAGICTRONIC—NONE—Liuski International, Inc.; *U.S. Public*, pg. 1005

MAGLAFOM—Sponges & Cleansing Pad—Magla Products; *U.S. Private*, pg. 695

MAGLINER—Dockboards, 2 & 4 Wheel Trucks—Magline, Inc.; *U.S. Private*, pg. 695

MAGNA—Motorcycle—American Honda Motor Co., Inc. Motorcycle Division; *Int'l*, pg. 634

MAGNA—NONE—Magna Group, Inc.; *U.S. Public*, pg. 1037

MAGNA—Automotive Parts—Magna International Inc.; *Int'l*, pg. 829

MAGNA—Cigarettes—RJR Nabisco Holdings Corp.; *U.S. Public*, pg. 1354

MAGNA—Full Flavor 85's & 80's Box, Lights 85's Cigarettes—R.J. Reynolds Tobacco Company; *U.S. Public*, pg. 1355

MAGNA—Screwdriver Bits—Vermont American Tool Corp.; *U.S. Public*, pg. 575

MAGNA DOODLE—Games—Tyco Toys, Inc.; *U.S. Public*, pg. 1058

MAGNA FORCE—Air Compressors—Coleman Powermate Compressors; *U.S. Private*, pg. 691

MAGNA FRAME—Projection Image Enlargement—Telex Communications, Inc.; *U.S. Private*, pg. 1074

MAGNA FX—Cannulated Screw Fixation System—Bristol-Myers Squibb Company; *U.S. Public*, pg. 253

MAGNA LIF—Cleaning Equipment—Man-Gill Chemical Company; *U.S. Private*, pg. 699

MAGNA LITE—Lamps—Lava World International/ Haggerty Enterprises, Inc.; *U.S. Private*, pg. 653

MAGNA MAX—Generators—Marathon Electric Manufacturing Corp.; *U.S. Public*, pg. 1371

MAGNA ONE—Generators—Marathon Electric Manufacturing Corp.; *U.S. Public*, pg. 1371

MAGNA PLUS—Generators—Marathon Electric Manufacturing Corp.; *U.S. Public*, pg. 1371

MAGNA-SEP—NONE—Life Technologies, Inc.; *U.S. Public*, pg. 504

MAGNA-TECTOR—NONE—Western Atlas Logging Services; *U.S. Public*, pg. 1757

MAGNA-TITE—NONE—Thiokol Corporation; *U.S. Public*, pg. 1596

MAGNA TOP-FLITE—Golf Ball—Spalding Sports Worldwide; *U.S. Private*, pg. 630

MAGNA II—Vitamins—Nature's Bounty Inc.; *U.S. Public*, pg. 1166

MAGNABAR—Magnetized Holders for Knives & Tools—Magnagrip; *U.S. Private*, pg. 142

MAGNACOLOR—Television Picture Tubes—Philips Consumer Electronics; *Int'l*, pg. 1054

MAGNADOR—Masking Fragrances—Crompton & Knowles Ingredient Technology Corp.; *U.S. Public*, pg. 459

MAGNAFICHE—Microfilm Readers—Eastman Kodak Company; *U.S. Public*, pg. 550

MAGNAFLEX—Exterior Can Coating—The Dexter Corporation; *U.S. Public*, pg. 666

MAGNAFLEX—Flexible Machining Equip.—Liberty Precision Industries; *U.S. Private*, pg. 666

MAGNAGLO—Fluorescent Magnetic Particle Testing—ITW Magnaflux; *U.S. Public*, pg. 866

MAGNAGRIP—Kitchen Tool Rack, & Magnetized Soap Holder—Magnagrip; *U.S. Private*, pg. 142

MAGNALATCH—Magnet Latching Solenoid Valve—Skinner Valve Division; *U.S. Public*, pg. 1260

MAGNALERT—Magnetic Drive Pump—Flowserve Corporation; *U.S. Public*, pg. 658

MAGNALITE—Cookware—General Housewares Corp.; *U.S. Public*, pg. 715

MAGNALITE CLASSIC—Cookware—General Housewares Corp.; *U.S. Public*, pg. 715

MAGNALITE COMMERCIAL—Cookware—General Housewares Corp.; *U.S. Public*, pg. 715

MAGNALITE PROFESSIONAL—Cookware—General Housewares Corp.; *U.S. Public*, pg. 715

MAGNALITE PROFESSIONAL STAINLESS STEEL—Cookware—General Housewares Corp.; *U.S. Public*, pg. 715

MAGNAPAK—Magnetostrictive Ultrasonic Equipment—Branson Ultrasonics Corp. - Precision Cleaning Div.; *U.S. Public*, pg. 574

MAGNAPEX—Commerical Vaccum Press—Seal Products Incorporated; *U.S. Public*, pg. 849

MAGNAPLAY—Magnetic Puzzles—Life-Like Products, Inc.; *U.S. Private*, pg. 666

MAGNAPRINT—Microfilm Readers & Printers—Eastman Kodak Company; *U.S. Public*, pg. 550

MAGNAPRINT35—Color Printer Service—Eastman Kodak Company; *U.S. Public*, pg. 550

MAGNARAIL—NONE—Pfizer Inc.; *U.S. Public*, pg. 1281

MAGNASHARP—Cutlery—General Housewares Corp.; *U.S. Public*, pg. 715

MAGNASHIELD PLUS—Durable Magnetic Stripe Transaction Cards—Schlumberger Malco Inc.; *Int'l*, pg. 1206

MAGNASIV—Cracking Catalyst—Engelhard Corporation; *U.S. Public*, pg. 582

MAGNASYNC—Communications Logging Equipment—J & R Film / Moviola Digital Co.; *U.S. Private*, pg. 576

MAGNAT—Car Speakers & Amplifiers—Recoton Corporation; *U.S. Public*, pg. 1369

MAGNATECH—Cutlery—General Housewares Corp.; *U.S. Public*, pg. 715

MAGNAVALVE—Ventilator—Swartwout Industries; *Int'l*, pg. 1398

MAGNAVISION—Oversized Motion Picture Screen—Iwerks Entertainment; *U.S. Public*, pg. 915

MAGNAVOX—Video/TV & Audio Prods.—Philips Electronics North America Corporation; *Int'l*, pg. 1053

MAGNAVOX—Cable TV, Radio—Philips Electronics N.V.; *Int'l*, pg. 1051

MAGNE-BOOST—Pumps—March Manufacturing Inc.; *U.S. Private*, pg. 702

MAGNE-FLEX—Vibratoy Conveyors—TCC Industries; *U.S. Public*, pg. 1554

MAGNEATO—Stationery Products—The Mead Corporation; *U.S. Public*, pg. 1074

MAGNEDRAFT—Machinery—Hollingsworth Saco Lowell Corporation, Inc.; *U.S. Private*, pg. 535

MAGNEFLEX—Magnetically Opoerated Between Glass Blinds—Hunter Douglas, Inc.; *Int'l*, pg. 639

MAGNEHELIC—Pressure Gage—Dwyer Instruments Inc.; *U.S. Private*, pg. 350

MAGNEQUENCH—Cordless Driver/Drill—Pentair, Inc.; *U.S. Public*, pg. 1273

MAGNET—Truck & Van Accessories—Kenco; *U.S. Public*, pg. 1769

MAGNETECTOR—Magnetic Switches—General Electric Canada Inc.; *U.S. Public*, pg. 713

MAGNETEK—Electrical Equip.—MagneTek, Inc.; *U.S. Public*, pg. 1037

MAGNETI MARELLI—Motors—Fiat Auto SpA; *Int'l*, pg. 480

MAGNETIC CIRCUIT BREAKERS—NONE—Philips Automotive Electronics; *Int'l*, pg. 1054

MAGNETIC DATA, INC—Flying Disc—Magnetics Data Inc.; *U.S. Private*, pg. 695

MAGNETIC METALS—Metal Fabricators—Magnetic Metals Corp.; *U.S. Private*, pg. 560

MAGNETIC SUSPENSION MELTING SYSTEM—Containerless Levitation Melting Process—Inductotherm Corp.; *U.S. Private*, pg. 560

MAGNETICS—Electronic Components—Spang & Company; *U.S. Private*, pg. 1020

MAGNETIL—Electrical Steel—Cockerill Sambre; *Int'l*, pg. 301

MAGNETORQUE—Motors, Brakes, Speed Controls—Harnischfeger Industries, Inc.; *U.S. Public*, pg. 788

MAGNI-SINO—Rugs—Couristan Inc.; *U.S. Private*, pg. 279

MAGNITE—Electrical Steel Sheet—British Steel Plc; *Int'l*, pg. 220

MAGNIVIEW 840—True Color Computer Data Projector—Dukane Corporation; *U.S. Private*, pg. 345

MAGNIVIEW 800—Data Projector—Dukane Corporation; *U.S. Private*, pg. 345

MAGNIVIEW 807—Data Projector; International Model—Dukane Corporation; *U.S. Private*, pg. 345

MAGNIVIEW 860—Data Projector—Dukane Corporation; *U.S. Private*, pg. 345

MAGNIVIEW 822—Data Projector—Dukane Corporation; *U.S. Private*, pg. 345

MAGNIVIEW SERIES—LCD Computer Data Projection Panels—Dukane Corporation; *U.S. Private*, pg. 345

MAGNO—Woodfree Coated Papers—K & P Leykam Austria; *Int'l*, pg. 757

MAGNOLIA BRAND—Sweetened Condensed Filled Dairy Blend—Borden, Inc.; *U.S. Private*, pg. 157

MAGNOPLAN—Film Faced Plywood for Concrete Formwork—Westag & Getalit AG; *Int'l*, pg. 1491

MAGNUM—Automotive—Allen Telecom, Inc.; *U.S. Public*, pg. 45

MAGNUM—Fire Truck—Ansul Incorporated; *U.S. Public*, pg. 1648

MAGNUM—Dozer Cutting Edges—Bucyrus Blades Inc.; *U.S. Public*, pg. 383

MAGNUM—Terminal Strips—Bussmann Division; *U.S. Public*, pg. 443

MAGNUM—Condoms—Carter-Wallace, Inc.; *U.S. Public*, pg. 309

MAGNUM—2 Wheel Drive Tractors—Case Corporation; *U.S. Public*, pg. 311

MAGNUM—Hot Mix asphalt Equipment—Cedarapids, Inc.; *U.S. Public*, pg. 1365

MAGNUM—Terminal Strips—Cooper Industries, Inc.; *U.S. Public*, pg. 442

MAGNUM—Truck Boxes—Delta Consolidated Industries, Inc. (Co. Headquarters); *U.S. Public*, pg. 481

MAGNUM—Racquetball String & Weightlifting Glove—Ektelon; *U.S. Private*, pg. 884

MAGNUM—Pool & Spa Pump Featuring Ring-Lok Access—Jacuzzi Bros., Jacuzzi, Inc.; *U.S. Public*, pg. 1684

MAGNUM—Gun & Cable—The Lincoln Electric Company; *U.S. Public*, pg. 996

MAGNUM—Price Marking Gun—Meto, USA; *Int'l*, pg. 460

MAGNUM—Malt Liquor—Miller Brewing Company; *U.S. Public*, pg. 1289

MAGNUM—Terminal Tractors—Partek Corporation; *Int'l*, pg. 1024

MAGNUM—Malt Liquor—Philip Morris Companies Inc.; *U.S. Public*, pg. 1287

MAGNUM—NONE—Porcelanite, Inc.; *Int'l*, pg. 573

MAGNUM—Controller Board & Bar Code Printers—QMS, Inc.; *U.S. Public*, pg. 1346

MAGNUM—Tractors—Tenneco Inc.; *U.S. Public*, pg. 1577

MAGNUM ABS—Resin—The Dow Chemical Company; *U.S. Public*, pg. 522

MAGNUM ALERT—Control Panels—Napco Security Systems, Inc.; *U.S. Public*, pg. 1151

MAGNUM BY DELTA—Truck Boxes—Delta Consolidated Industries, Inc. (Co. Headquarters); *U.S. Public*, pg. 481

MAGNUM FIRE ALERT—Fire Alarm Panels—Napco Security Systems, Inc.; *U.S. Public*, pg. 1151

MAGNUM GRAPHITE RTS—Racquetball Racquet—Ektelon; *U.S. Private*, pg. 884

MAGNUM MEIER—NONE—Pfizer Inc.; *U.S. Public*, pg. 1281

MAGNUM SERIES—Seating for Office & Highway Equipment—Seats Incorporated; *U.S. Private*, pg. 410

MAGNUM 44—Permanent Marker—Sanford Corporation; *U.S. Public*, pg. 1178

MAGPAD—Magnetic Cutter Clamp Pad—3M; *U.S. Public*, pg. 1604

MAGTECH—Industrial Brushless DC Motors—Axsys Technologies, Inc.; *U.S. Public*, pg. 157

MAHATMA—Rice—Riviana Foods Inc.; *U.S. Public*, pg. 1392

MAHLER OIL SOAP—Cleaner—Blue Cross Laboratories; *U.S. Private*, pg. 152

MAHONEY'S—NONE—Quality Bakers New Zealand Ltd.; *Int'l*, pg. 556

MAHOU—Beer—Danone Group; *Int'l*, pg. 379

MAICRO—Thermosetting Powder Coatings—DSM N.V.; *Int'l*, pg. 352

MAID-O-MIST—Heating Specialties—Maid-O-Mist; *U.S. Private*, pg. 1053

MAIDENFORM—Brassieres, Women's Undergarments & Daywear—Maidenform Worldwide; *U.S. Private*, pg. 697

MAIL-AWAY—Mailing Materials—Intertape Polymer Group; *Int'l*, pg. 685

MAIL CANADA—Mailing Efficiency for Canada—Group 1 Software, Inc.; *U.S. Public*, pg. 417

MAIL MONITOR—NONE—Market Facts, Inc.; *U.S. Public*, pg. 1046

MAIL POUCH—Chewing Tobacco—Swisher International Group, Inc.; *U.S. Public*, pg. 1543

MAIL POUCH COUNTRY BLEND—Chewing Tobacco—Swisher International Group, Inc.; *U.S. Public*, pg. 1543

MAIL PRODUCTION SERVICES—Full Lettershop Services—Metromail Corporation; *U.S. Public*, pg. 1102

MAIL-WELL—Correspondence & Mailing Envelopes—Georgia-Pacific Corporation; *U.S. Public*, pg. 735

MAILBAG—Software—The Mead Corporation; *U.S. Public*, pg. 1074

MAILBOX COLLECTION—Stationary Products—The Mead Corporation; *U.S. Public*, pg. 1074

MAILBOX VALUES—Shared Advertising Mail Packets—ADVO, Inc.; *U.S. Public*, pg. 23

MAILBOX VALUES WRAP—Shared Advertising Mail Packet—ADVO, Inc.; *U.S. Public*, pg. 23

MAILGRAM—Message Services—New Valley Corporation; *U.S. Public*, pg. 1173

MAILGRAM—Message Services—Western Union Financial Services, Inc.; *U.S. Public*, pg. 631

MAILLE—Condiments—Danone Group; *Int'l*, pg. 379

MAILLE—Mustards—Lea & Perrins, Inc.; *Int'l*, pg. 380

MAILMOBILE—Vehicle—Bell & Howell Holdings; *U.S. Public*, pg. 201

MAILSTAR—Inserter—Bell & Howell Holdings; *U.S. Public*, pg. 201

MAILSTREAM PLUS—Mailing Efficiency—Group 1 Software, Inc.; *U.S. Public*, pg. 417

MAIN STREAM—NONE—Tri-Clover Inc.; *Int'l*, pg. 1379

MAIN STREET—Vinyl Siding—CertainTeed Corporation; *Int'l*, pg. 1170

MAIN/TRACKER—Maintenance Management System—System Software Associates, Inc.; *U.S. Public*, pg. 1552

MAIN-LINE—Line Frequency Coreless Furnace Induction Melting Systems—Inductotherm Corp.; *U.S. Private*, pg. 560

MAINE FAMILIE IND ICH—Magazine—Burda Holding GmbH & Co., KG; *Int'l*, pg. 233

MAINE GUIDE—Guiding Catheter—Medtronic, Inc.; *U.S. Public*, pg. 1082

MAINELITE—Coated Groundwood—Champion International Corp.; *U.S. Public*, pg. 333

MAINEWEB—Coated Groundwood—Champion International Corp.; *U.S. Public*, pg. 333

MAINFRAME COMMUNICATION ASSISTANT—Computer System—International Business Machines Corporation; *U.S. Public*, pg. 895

MAINGATE—Two-Way Communication to Utility Company Over Cable, Satellite, RF Networks—Scientific-Atlanta, Inc.; *U.S. Public*, pg. 1443

MAINLIGHTER—Electric Discharge Lamp—General Electric Canada Inc.; *U.S. Public*, pg. 713

MAINLINER—Hose—HBD Industries, Inc.; *U.S. Private*, pg. 489

MAINLINER—Sewer Cleaner—Roto-Rooter; *U.S. Public*, pg. 344

MAINSITE—Onsite Staffing for Equipment Repairs—GE Capital/IT Solutions; *U.S. Public*, pg. 711

MAINSTAY—The MacKay-Shields MainStay Family of Funds—New York Life Insurance Company; *U.S. Private*, pg. 794

MAINSTAY—NONE—Pfizer Inc.; *U.S. Public*, pg. 1281

MAINSTAY—Dog Food—Ralston Purina Company; *U.S. Public*, pg. 1359

MAINSTREAM COUNTRY FORMAT—24-Hour Satellite Delivered Music Format—Westwood One, Inc.; *U.S. Public*, pg. 1763

MAINTENANCE CHOICE—Catalog Services for Parts—J.A. Sexauer, Inc.; *U.S. Private*, pg. 352

MAINTENANCE EXPRESS—Provide Repair Services for Telecommunications Switching Systems for Others—Lucent Technologies Inc.; *U.S. Public*, pg. 1017

MAINVIEW—Structure for Systems Management & Automation—Boole & Babbage, Inc.; *U.S. Public*, pg. 244

MAISON DEUTZ—Wine—Wine World Estates Company; *Int'l*, pg. 917

MAISON DU CAFE—Coffee Products—Sara Lee Corporation; *U.S. Public*, pg. 1432

MAISON EN FRANCE—French Women's Interest Magazine—EMAP France; *Int'l*, pg. 451

MAISON THORIN—Fine Burgundies—Racke USA; *Int'l*, pg. 1083

MAIZENA—Corn & Other Starches, Desserts, Baking Aids—Bestfoods; *U.S. Public*, pg. 223

MAIZENA—Corn Starch—Refinerias de Maiz S.A.I.C.F.; *U.S. Public*, pg. 448

MAIZENA EXPRESS—Sauce Binders—Bestfoods; *U.S. Public*, pg. 223

MAIZETOS—Tortilla Chips—Golden Flake Snack Foods, Inc.; *U.S. Public*, pg. 750

MAJAC—Powder Processing Machinery—Hosokawa Micron International Inc.; *Int'l*, pg. 635

MAJAC—Air Classifier, Jet Mill—Hosokawa Micron Powder Systems; *Int'l*, pg. 636

MAJALA—Desserts, Baking Aids—Bestfoods; *U.S. Public*, pg. 223

MAJESTIC—Vinyl Tile—Congoleum Corporation; *U.S. Public*, pg. 69

MAJESTIC—Conical Refiner—Harnischfeger Industries, Inc.; *U.S. Public*, pg. 788

MAJESTIC II—Vacuum Cleaner—HMI Industries; *U.S. Public*, pg. 771

MAJESTY OF SEAS—Ships—Royal Caribbean Cruises Ltd.; *U.S. Public*, pg. 1410

MAJIK MARKET—Convenience Stores—E-Z Serve Convenience Stores, Inc.; *U.S. Public*, pg. 540

MAJIK MARKET—Convenience Stores—E-Z Serve Corp.; *U.S. Public*, pg. 540

MAJOR—Fuels—Burmah Castrol plc; *Int'l*, pg. 234

MAJOR ACCENT—Quick Reference Marker—Sanford Corporation; *U.S. Public*, pg. 1178

MAJOR COLLEGE BASKETBALL—Sports Program—Westwood One, Inc.; *U.S. Public*, pg. 1763

MAJOR COLLEGE FOOTBALL—Sports Program—Westwood One, Inc.; *U.S. Public*, pg. 1763

MAJOR LEAGUE BASEBALL—Men's Apparel—Garan, Incorporated; *U.S. Public*, pg. 703

MAJOR PETERS—Bloody Mary Mix & Non-Alcoholic Drink Mixes—Red Wings Inc.; *Int'l*, pg. 1398

MAJORCA—Broadloom—Couristan Inc.; *U.S. Private*, pg. 279

MAJORICA—Organic Man-Made Pearls—Majorica Jewelry Ltd.; *U.S. Private*, pg. 697

MAJORSTEA GIN—NONE—Star Industries Inc.; *U.S. Private*, pg. 1034

MAJORSTEA VODKA—NONE—Star Industries Inc.; *U.S. Private*, pg. 1034

MAJORX—Prescription Drug Plan—PCS Health Systems, Inc.; *U.S. Public*, pg. 993

MAKE A FRIEND FOR LIFE—NONE—The Vermont Teddy Bear Company, Inc.; *U.S. Public*, pg. 1716

MAKE-A-WISH—Ice Cream Bars—Integrated Brands Inc.; *U.S. Public*, pg. 883

MAKE IT COUNT FOR YOU—Plastic Caps—The West Company, Incorporated; *U.S. Public*, pg. 1755

MAKE UP AIR—Coml. & Indus. Heating Equip.—Midco International Inc.; *U.S. Private*, pg. 744

MAKER'S MARK—Spirit—Allied Domecq PLC; *Int'l*, pg. 62

MAKER'S MARK—Bourbon—Hiram Walker; *Int'l*, pg. 63

MAKER'S MARK—Bourbon—Maker's Mark Distillery, Inc.; *Int'l*, pg. 63

MAKEUPMATE—Cosmetic Products—Cover Girl Cosmetics; *U.S. Public*, pg. 1330

MAKI—Rodenticides—LiphaTech, Inc.; *Int'l*, pg. 812

MAKIN CAJUN—Sauces, Spices & Dinner Mixes—Ridg's Finer Foods; *U.S. Public*, pg. 1288

MAKING LIFE A LITTLE EASIER—NONE—Western Resources, Inc.; *U.S. Public*, pg. 1759

MAKING STRATEGY WORK—Maximizing Value Of Human Capital To Achieve Competitive Advantage—Watson Wyatt Worldwide; *U.S. Private*, pg. 1154

MAKING TRAVEL LESS PRIMITIVE—NONE—American Tourister, Inc.; *U.S. Public*, pg. 1430

MAKITA—Electric Power Tools—Makita Corporation; *Int'l*, pg. 831

MAKO—Hi-Pressure Breathing Air Systems & Components—CompAir Mako; *Int'l*, pg. 1242

MAKO—Asbestos Vacuum System—Kimmins Corp.; *U.S. Public*, pg. 960

MAKON—NONE—Stepan Company; *U.S. Public*, pg. 1514

MAKRO—Self-Service Wholesale Stores—SHV Holdings N.V.; *Int'l*, pg. 1154

MAKROBLEND—Plastic Fiber—Bayer AG; *Int'l*, pg. 171

MAKROLON—Polycarbonate—Bayer AG; *Int'l*, pg. 171

MAKROLON—Plastic Prods.—Rohm GmbH; *Int'l*, pg. 1454

MALABAR—Gum—Kraft Jacobs Suchard; *U.S. Public*, pg. 1290

MALAGA—Broadloom—Couristan Inc.; *U.S. Private*, pg. 279

MALE FACTOR 1000—Herbal Formula with Swiss Oats—Herbalife International of America, Inc.; *U.S. Public*, pg. 809

MALEV HUNGARIAN AIRLINES—Airline—Malev Hungarian Airlines, Plc.; *Int'l*, pg. 833

MALIBU—Safety Eyewear—Aearo Company; *U.S. Private*, pg. 23

MALIBU—Watches—Baume Mercier, Inc.; *U.S. Private*, pg. 124

MALIBU—Tobacco—Brown & Williamson Tobacco Corp.; *Int'l*, pg. 111

MALIBU—NONE—Gio. Buton S.p.a.; *Int'l*, pg. 409

MALIBU—Car—Chevrolet Motor Div. General Motors Corp.; *U.S. Public*, pg. 720

MALIBU—Spirits—Gilbeys of Ireland; *Int'l*, pg. 409

MALIBU—Pens & Pen & Pencil Sets—The Gillette Company; *U.S. Public*, pg. 743

MALIBU—Wine & Spirits—Grand Metropolitan Plc; *Int'l*, pg. 408

MALIBU—Coconut Flavored Rum—IDV North America; *Int'l*, pg. 411

MALIBU—Low Voltage Outdoor Lighting—Intermatic Inc.; *U.S. Private*, pg. 567

MALIBU—NONE—International Distillers Caribbean; *Int'l*, pg. 410

MALIBU—NONE—Societe Pour la Vente des Produits Cinzano SA; *Int'l*, pg. 410

MALIBU—NONE—Tegner & Son AB; *Int'l*, pg. 412

MALIBU—Caribbean White Rum with Coconut—Twelve Islands Shipping Company; *Int'l*, pg. 409

MALIBU MIRAGE—Aircraft—The New Piper Aircraft, Inc.; *U.S. Private*, pg. 794

MALIBU MUSK—Fragrance—Parfums De Coeur Ltd.; *U.S. Private*, pg. 839

MALILE—Desserts, Baking Aids—Bestfoods; *U.S. Public*, pg. 223

MALLARD—Travel Trailer—Fleetwood Enterprises, Inc.; *U.S. Public*, pg. 650

MALLIAC ARMAGNAC—Spirit—Allied Domecq PLC; *Int'l*, pg. 62

MALLINCKRODT—Pharmaceutical Logo—Mallinckrodt Inc.; *U.S. Public*, pg. 1039

MALLINCKRODT MEDICAL & DESIGN—Drug Intermediates—Mallinckrodt Inc.; *U.S. Public*, pg. 1039

MALLINCKRODT METHADONE MANAGMENT—Computer Hardware & Software for Managing Addiction Therapy—Mallinckrodt Inc.; *U.S. Public*, pg. 1039

MALLINCKRODT WASTE DISPOSAL SERVICE—Waste Disposal-Specifically Laboratory Chemicals—Mallinckrodt Inc.; *U.S. Public*, pg. 1039

MALLO CUP—Confectionery—Boyer Candy Company Inc.; *U.S. Private*, pg. 162

MALLOMARS—Chocolate Cakes—Nabisco Inc.; *U.S. Public*, pg. 1354

MALLOMARS—Marshmallow Cakes—RJR Nabisco Holdings Corp.; *U.S. Public*, pg. 1354

MALLORY—NONE—Duracell International Inc.; *U.S. Public*, pg. 743

MALLORY—Men's Hats—Stetson Hat Co.; *U.S. Private*, pg. 510

MALONE SKATEBOARDS—Skateboards—Roller Derby Skate Corp.; *U.S. Private*, pg. 941

MALPOTANE—Vitamin—Health Products Corporation; *U.S. Private*, pg. 514

MALT-O-MEAL—Hot Wheat Cereal, Puffed Wheat, Puffed Rice Cereals—Malt-O-Meal Company; *U.S. Private*, pg. 699

MALT-O-MEAL—Hot Wheat Cereal, Puffed Wheat & Puffed Rice Cereals—Malt-O-Meal Company; *U.S. Private*, pg. 699

MALTA—Windows & Patio Doors—Malta Div.-Tomkins Industries, Inc.; *Int'l*, pg. 1398

MALTA GUINNESS—NONE—Guinness Plc; *Int'l*, pg. 412

MALTA HOLIDAYS (UK) LTD—Inclusive Tour Operator—Air Malta Co. Ltd.; *Int'l*, pg. 37

MALTA SWEET—Sugar Confectionary—Cadbury Nigeria PLC; *Int'l*, pg. 248

MALTEX—Hot Cereal—International Home Foods Inc.; *U.S. Private*, pg. 526

MALTLAGE—Dairy Feed—Labatt Brewing Company Limited; *Int'l*, pg. 679

MALTLAGE—Dairy Feed—Miracle Feeds Inc.; *U.S. Private*, pg. 432

MALTON—Bacon & Ham Products—Unigate PLC; *Int'l*, pg. 1433

MALTSUPEX—Laxative—Wallace Laboratories; *U.S. Public*, pg. 310

MALUBE—Industrial Synthetic Lubricant Additive—PPG Industries, Inc.; *U.S. Public*, pg. 1245

MALVERN WATER—Seltzer Water—Cadbury Schweppes p.l.c.; *Int'l*, pg. 247

MALVO—Dairy Products—Crowley Foods, Inc.; *Int'l*, pg. 752

MAMA BEAR'S COLD CARE—Herb Tea—Celestial Seasonings; *U.S. Public*, pg. 319

MAMA TISH—Ices—J & J Snack Foods Corporation; *U.S. Public*, pg. 916

MAMACITA—Tortilla Chips—Clover Club Foods, Inc.; *U.S. Private*, pg. 469

MAMBA SOFT—Fruit Chews—Storck U.S.A., L.P.; *Int'l*, pg. 1304

MAMMA ILARDO'S—Restaurant Chain—Mamma Ilardo's Corp.; *U.S. Private*, pg. 699

MAMMI—Draperi—Procter & Gamble Venezuela, C.A.; *U.S. Public*, pg. 1332

MAMMOMAT—Mammography Imaging System—Siemens Corporation; *Int'l*, pg. 1245

MAMMOTEST—X-Ray Equipment—Fischer Imaging Corporation; *U.S. Public*, pg. 647

MAMMOTH—Air Conditioners—Nortek, Inc.; *U.S. Public*, pg. 1192

MAMMOTH CAVE—Twist Tobacco—Conwood Company L.P.; *U.S. Private*, pg. 272

MAMMOVISION—X-Ray Equipment—Fischer Imaging Corporation; *U.S. Public*, pg. 647

MAN & SEXTANT DESIGN—GPS Surveying Equipment—Litton Industries, Inc.; *U.S. Public*, pg. 1002

MAN & SUN DESIGN—Nautical & Navigation Instruments—Litton Industries, Inc.; *U.S. Public*, pg. 1002

MAN-MATE—Powered Servo-Control Manipulator Systems—General Electric Canada Inc.; *U.S. Public*, pg. 713

MAN-O-WAR—Horse Feeds—Manna Pro Corporation; *U.S. Private*, pg. 700

MAN SIZE—Facial Tissue—Kimberly-Clark Corporation; *U.S. Public*, pg. 958

MAN-U-SERT—Manual Assembly System—Universal Instruments Corporation; *U.S. Public*, pg. 522

MANAGE—Industrial Turf Growth—Monsanto Company; *U.S. Public*, pg. 1124

MANAGE BY FACT NOT BY QUESS—NONE—SunGard Data Systems Inc.; *U.S. Public*, pg. 1534

MANAGE 2000—Computer Hardware & Software—Automatic Data Processing, Inc.; *U.S. Public*, pg. 150

MANAGED ACCESS—Prescription Drug Plan—PCS Health Systems, Inc.; *U.S. Public*, pg. 993

MANAGED CARE—NONE—Dermik Laboratories, Inc.; *Int'l*, pg. 1110

MANAGED HEALTHCARE—Trade Periodical—Advanstar Communications; *U.S. Private*, pg. 22

MANAGEMENT SERIES—Stationery Products—The Mead Corporation; *U.S. Public*, pg. 1074

MANAGEWARE—Software—International Business Machines Corporation; *U.S. Public*, pg. 895

MANAGING OFFICE TECHNOLOGY—Periodical—Penton Publishing, Inc.; *U.S. Public*, pg. 1306

MANCHESTER PLANK—Pre-Finished Strip—Bruce Hardwood Floors; *U.S. Public*, pg. 1634

MANDALAY—White Rice—Producers Rice Mill Inc.; *U.S. Private*, pg. 888

MANDARIN MAGIC—Mandarin Orange Juice Drink—Ocean Spray Cranberries, Inc.; *U.S. Private*, pg. 811

MANDARIN ORANGE SLICE—Beverage—Pepsi-Cola Company; *U.S. Public*, pg. 1277

MANDARIN ORANGE SPICE—Herb Tea—Celestial Seasonings; *U.S. Public*, pg. 319

MANDARINE NAPOLEON—NONE—Barton Brands, Ltd.; *U.S. Public*, pg. 300

MANDELAMINE—UTI—Warner-Chilcott Laboratories, Inc.; *Int'l*, pg. 436

MANCHESTER GUARDIAN—Weekly Newspaper—Manchester Guardian; *Int'l*, pg. 577

MANDOKEF—Cephamandol—Eli Lilly Italia, S.p.A.; *U.S. Public*, pg. 994

MANDOL—Cefamandole Nafate, Lilly—Eli Lilly and Company; *U.S. Public*, pg. 992

MANDRIELLE-MELLOT—Red Wine—Banfi Vintners; *U.S. Private*, pg. 113

MANETAN—Liquid Polyurethane Waterproof Membranes—The Dow Chemical Company; *U.S. Public*, pg. 522

MANGJET—Electrode—The Lincoln Electric Company; *U.S. Public*, pg. 996

MAGNUM—Hand-held Labeling Tool—Esselte Meto Kimball Systems; *Int'l*, pg. 460

MANGO MANGO—Mango Hawaiian Guava Juice Drink—Ocean Spray Cranberries, Inc.; *U.S. Private*, pg. 811

MANGUSTA A129—Helicopter—Agusta Aerospace Corporation; *Int'l*, pg. 32

MANHANDLER—Self-Propelled Access Platform—Simon Engineering plc; *Int'l*, pg. 1251

MANHANDLER—Jeans—The Spencer Group Inc.; *U.S. Private*, pg. 1025

MANHATTAN—Bath Accessories—Baldwin Hardware Corporation; *U.S. Public*, pg. 1053

MANHATTAN—Beloit Manhattan—Beloit Corporation; *U.S. Public*, pg. 789

MANHATTAN—Records—Capitol Records, Inc.; *Int'l*, pg. 428

MANHATTAN—General Elastomeric Roll Cover & Roll Hardness Tester—Harnischfeger Industries, Inc.; *U.S. Public*, pg. 788

MANHATTAN—Men's Wear—The Manhattan Shirt Co.; *U.S. Public*, pg. 1429

MANHATTAN—Clothing—Salant Corporation; *U.S. Public*, pg. 1429

MANHATTAN—NONE—Tandy Brands Accessories, Inc.; *U.S. Public*, pg. 1560

THE MANHATTAN COLLECTION—Honeycomb Shades Featuring Sleek New Headrail & Woven Fabrics—Hunter Douglas, Inc.; *Int'l*, pg. 639

MANHATTAN SMP—NONE—AST Research Inc.; *Int'l*, pg. 1181

MANIFEST—Fine Printing—Eastern Fine Paper; *U.S. Private*, pg. 357

MANIFLEX—NONE—Carpenter Technology Corporation; *U.S. Public*, pg. 307

MANIFOLD—Fluid Path Administration—Merit Medical Systems, Inc.; *U.S. Public*, pg. 1096

MANISCHEWITZ—Wine—Canandaigua Wine Company, Inc.; *U.S. Public*, pg. 300

MANISCHEWITZ—Kosher Foods—The B. Manischewitz Company; *U.S. Private*, pg. 699

MANITEX—Cranes—The Manitowoc Company, Inc.; *U.S. Public*, pg. 1040

MANITOU—Mtn. Bike Suspension Fork—LDI, Ltd.; *U.S. Private*, pg. 639

MANITOU—Fork Lift Trucks—Manitou BF; *Int'l*, pg. 834

MANITOWOC—Cranes—The Manitowoc Company, Inc.; *U.S. Public*, pg. 1040

MANITOWOC—Cranes, Ice Cubers—The Manitowoc Company, Inc.; *U.S. Public*, pg. 1040

MANITOWOC—Ice Machine—Manitowoc Ice, Inc.; *U.S. Public*, pg. 1041

MANN & HUMMEL—NONE—Filterwerk Mann & Hummel GmbH; *Int'l*, pg. 484

MANN-FILTER—NONE—Filterwerk Mann & Hummel GmbH; *Int'l*, pg. 484

MANNA-ELITE—Horse Feed—Manna Pro Corporation; *U.S. Private*, pg. 700

MANNA-MATE—Dairy Feed—Manna Pro Corporation; *U.S. Private*, pg. 700

MANNA-PRO—Dairy Feed—Manna Pro Corporation; *U.S. Private*, pg. 700

MANNEQUIN DELICE—Light Fromages—Nestle S.A.; *Int'l*, pg. 915

MANNINGTON—Company Logo—Mannington Mills, Inc.; *U.S. Private*, pg. 700

MANNINGTON—NONE—Porcelanite, Inc.; *Int'l*, pg. 573

MANNINGTON BRONZE—Sheet Vinyl Floor Covering—Mannington Mills, Inc.; *U.S. Private*, pg. 700

MANINNGTON CLASSIC—Full Glue Installed Sheet Vinyl Flooring—Mannington Resilient Floors; *U.S. Private*, pg. 700

MANNINGTON GOLD—Sheet Vinyl Floor Covering—Mannington Mills, Inc.; *U.S. Private*, pg. 700

MANNINGTON SILVER—Sheet Vinyl Floor Covering—Mannington Mills, Inc.; *U.S. Private*, pg. 700

MANNINGTON STERLING—Perimeter Installed Sheet Vinyl Flooring—Mannington Resilient Floors; *U.S. Private*, pg. 700

MANOR—Bakery Products—The Earthgrains Company; *U.S. Private*, pg. 547

MANOR HALL—Interior Wall & Woodwork, Liquid & Paste Paints, Primer, Enamels, Varnishes—PPG Industries, Inc.; *U.S. Public*, pg. 1245

MANOR HOUSES—Restaurants & Catering—Scottish & Newcastle plc; *Int'l*, pg. 1211

MANOR WALK—NONE—Porcelanite, Inc.; *Int'l*, pg. 573

MANPOWER—Temporary Help Services—Manpower Inc.; *U.S. Public*, pg. 1042

MANSAVER—Mechanical Grabs—Acco Chain & Lifting Products; *Int'l*, pg. 473

MANSIL—Granulated Silico-Manganese—Elkem ASA; *Int'l*, pg. 446

MANSION—Furniture Polish—Reckitt & Colman plc; *Int'l*, pg. 1089

MANSION HOUSE—Paint—Pratt & Lambert United, Inc.; *U.S. Public*, pg. 1466

MANTA—Silkworm Enhancement Additive—Novartis AG; *Int'l*, pg. 971

MANTADIL CREAM—Antipruritic Cream—Glaxo Wellcome PLC; *Int'l*, pg. 553

MANTARAY—Horns with Extremely Accurate Coverage—Altec Lansing Corp.; *U.S. Private*, pg. 479

MANTIS—Reinforcing Bar Chairs—Smorgon A.R.C.; *Int'l*, pg. 1269

MANUCOL—Sodium Alginate—The NutraSweet Kelco Company; *U.S. Public*, pg. 1125

MANUCOL ESTER—Propylene Glycol Alginates—The NutraSweet Kelco Company; *U.S. Public*, pg. 1125

MANUELITA—Toilet Soaps—Nuevo Federal S.A.; *Int'l*, pg. 990

Brand Name Index

MANUFACTURERS PROTECTOR PLAN—NONE—Poe & Brown, Inc.; *U.S. Public*, pg. 1312

MANUFACTURING MARKETPLACE—Manufacturing-Sector Information Resource on the World Wide Web—Reed Elsevier Business Information; *Int'l*, pg. 1095

MANUFACTURING SYSTEMS—Management Magazine Focused on Information Technology—Reed Elsevier Business Information; *Int'l*, pg. 1095

MANUGEL—Sodium Alginate—The NutraSweet Kelco Company; *U.S. Public*, pg. 1125

MANVER—Chemical Reagant—Hach Company; *U.S. Public*, pg. 773

MANVILLE GOLDEN PINE—Plywood & Lumber—Riverwood International Corporation; *U.S. Public*, pg. 1391

MANWICH—Sloppy Joe Sandwich—ConAgra, Inc.; *U.S. Public*, pg. 425

MANWICH—Sloppy Joe Sauce—Hunt-Wesson, Inc.; *U.S. Public*, pg. 428

MANY FACES—Cosmetic Brushes—American International Industries; *U.S. Private*, pg. 57

MANZATE—Fungicides—Du Pont (E.I. Du Pont De Nemours & Co.); *U.S. Public*, pg. 530

MANZEL—Lubrication Equipment—IDEX Corporation; *U.S. Public*, pg. 862

MAP—Angioplasty Kit—Merit Medical Systems, Inc.; *U.S. Public*, pg. 1096

MAP BASIC—Programming Language to Extend Functionality of Mapinfo Professional—MapInfo Corp.; *U.S. Public*, pg. 1042

MAP-MASTER—Software—Borland International, Inc.; *U.S. Public*, pg. 246

MAP-NET—Electronic Instrument—Intel Corporation; *U.S. Public*, pg. 886

MAP-PAK—Pocket Portfolio Folder For Maps—American Automobile Association; *U.S. Private*, pg. 50

MAP X—Used To Embed Mapping Functionality into New/ Existing Applications—MapInfo Corp.; *U.S. Public*, pg. 1042

MAPAX—Modified Atmosphere Packaging—AGA Ges.m.b.H.; *Int'l*, pg. 13

MAPEG—Surfactants—PPG Industries, Inc.; *U.S. Public*, pg. 1245

MAPHOS—Surfactants—PPG Industries, Inc.; *U.S. Public*, pg. 1245

MAPICS—Computer Product—International Business Machines Corporation; *U.S. Public*, pg. 895

MAPICS—NONE—Marcam Solutions, Inc.; *U.S. Public*, pg. 1042

MAPINFO PROALIGN—Territory Management Solution for Sales & Marketing Applications—MapInfo Corp.; *U.S. Public*, pg. 1042

MAPINFO PROFESSIONAL—Desktop Mapping Software—MapInfo Corp.; *U.S. Public*, pg. 1042

MAPLE LEAF—Food Prods.—Maple Leaf Foods Inc.; *Int'l*, pg. 841

MAPLE PORTER—Beer—The F.X. Matt Brewing Co.; *U.S. Private*, pg. 714

MAPLE RICH—Syrup—ConAgra, Inc.; *U.S. Public*, pg. 425

MAPLE RIVER—Pork Products—Farmland Foods, Inc.; *U.S. Private*, pg. 396

MAPLEHURST FARMS—NONE—Maplehurst Farms, Inc.; *U.S. Public*, pg. 490

MAPLEINE—Extract—McCormick/Schilling; *U.S. Public*, pg. 1066

MAPP—MasterCard Automated Point-of-Sale Program—Mastercard International, Inc.; *U.S. Private*, pg. 714

MAPP GAS—Fuel Gas—The BOC Group Inc. (Delaware); *Int'l*, pg. 121

MAPPER—Computer Software System—Unisys Corporation; *U.S. Public*, pg. 1671

MAPXSITE—Used by Developers to Embed "Dealer Location" Capabilities on the Web—MapInfo Corp.; *U.S. Public*, pg. 1042

MAPXTREME—Web Application Server Enables Access & Development of mapping on Internet—MapInfo Corp.; *U.S. Public*, pg. 1042

MAR-FLEX—Conventional Bellows-Type Expansion Joints; Mechanical Couplings—Marquette Coppersmithing Co., Inc.; *U.S. Private*, pg. 706

MAR-GLASS—Body Filler—Marson/Creative Fastener, Inc.; *U.S. Private*, pg. 708

MAR-HYDE—Touch-Up Lacquer, Vinyl Color—Mar-Hyde Corporation; *U.S. Public*, pg. 1357

MAR LODGE—Malt Whisky—Marie Brizard Wines & Spirits USA; *U.S. Private*, pg. 702

MAR-HYDE—Auto Finishing Products—RPM, Inc.; *U.S. Public*, pg. 1356

MARA INTIMATES—Women's Undergarments—National Corset Supply House; *U.S. Private*, pg. 781

MARABOU—Milk Chocolate Roll—Hershey Chocolate U.S.A.; *U.S. Public*, pg. 812

MARABOU—Milk Chocolate Roll—Hershey Foods Corporation; *U.S. Public*, pg. 811

MARABOU MINT CRISP—Chocolate Roll—Hershey Chocolate U.S.A.; *U.S. Public*, pg. 812

MARABOU MINT CRISP—Chocolate Roll—Hershey Foods Corporation; *U.S. Public*, pg. 811

MARAMIC—Marking Compounds—Markem Corporation; *U.S. Private*, pg. 704

MARATHERM—Heating & Cooling Products—International Comfort Products Corp.; *U.S. Public*, pg. 898

MARATHON—Saw Blades—American Tool Companies, Inc.; *U.S. Private*, pg. 63

MARATHON—Luggage—American Tourister, Inc.; *U.S. Public*, pg. 1430

MARATHON—Hinges—Amerock Corporation; *U.S. Public*, pg. 1177

MARATHON—Inlaid Sheet Vinyl Flooring—Congoleum Corporation; *U.S. Public*, pg. 69

MARATHON—Mascara & Eye Liner—Cover Girl Cosmetics; *U.S. Public*, pg. 1330

MARATHON—Towels, Tissue—Fort James Corporation; *U.S. Public*, pg. 670

MARATHON—Sensors for Heat Treatment & Boiler Controls—Halma p.l.c.; *Int'l*, pg. 589

MARATHON—Machinery—Hollingsworth Saco Lowell Corporation, Inc.; *U.S. Private*, pg. 535

MARATHON—Cryogenic Pumps for High Vacuum Systems—Intermagnetics General Corporation; *U.S. Public*, pg. 893

MARATHON—Tradename—Marathon Ashland Petroleum LLC; *U.S. Public*, pg. 139

MARATHON—Candy—Mars, Incorporated; *U.S. Private*, pg. 707

MARATHON—Architectural & Marine Paints & Wood Stains—PPG Industries, Inc.; *U.S. Public*, pg. 1245

MARATHON—Water Heater—Rheem Water Heater; *Int'l*, pg. 1022

MARATHON—Buses—Sabanci Holding A.S.; *Int'l*, pg. 1167

MARATHON ELECTRIC—Electric Motors and Generators—Regal-Beloit Corporation; *U.S. Public*, pg. 1370

MARAUDER—Athletic Apparel—Bike Athletic Co.; *U.S. Private*, pg. 143

MARAUDER—Sporting Goods—Brunswick Bowling & Billiards Corp.; *U.S. Private*, pg. 265

MARBIG-REXEL—NONE—Fortune Brands, Inc.; *U.S. Public*, pg. 674

MARBLESQUE—Ceramic Wall Tile—Monarch Tile, Inc.; *U.S. Private*, pg. 287

MARBLEX—Wet-End Roll Cover—Harnischfeger Industries, Inc.; *U.S. Public*, pg. 788

MARBLIEZED—Vinyl Composition Tile—Kentile Operting Co.; *U.S. Private*, pg. 615

MARBRO—Lamps—Masco Corporation; *U.S. Public*, pg. 1052

MARCAD—Diversity Wireless Microphone Receiver—Shure Brothers Incorporated; *U.S. Private*, pg. 997

MARCAINE/SENSORCAINE—Local Anesthetic—Astra AB; *Int'l*, pg. 185

MARCAL—Household Paper Prods.—Marcal Paper Mills, Inc.; *U.S. Private*, pg. 701

MARCASSOU—NONE—Sara Lee Corporation; *U.S. Public*, pg. 1432

MARCH—Pumps—March Manufacturing Inc.; *U.S. Private*, pg. 702

MARCH—Car—Nissan Motor Co., Ltd.; *Int'l*, pg. 943

MARCH—Pumps—Ryan Herco Products Corp.; *U.S. Private*, pg. 953

MARCH MADNESS—Sports—Monarch Avalon, Inc.; *U.S. Public*, pg. 1123

MARCHESI DI GRESY—Wine—Paterno Imports Limited; *U.S. Private*, pg. 843

MARCHON—NONE—Marchon Eyewear; *U.S. Private*, pg. 702

MARCILLA—Coffee—Sara Lee Corporation; *U.S. Public*, pg. 1432

MARCO—Marine Machinery—Marine Construction & Design Co.; *U.S. Private*, pg. 703

MARCO—Navigation System for the Blind & the Visually Impaired—Telesensory Corporation; *U.S. Private*, pg. 1074

MARCO FELLUGA—Wine—Paterno Imports Limited; *U.S. Private*, pg. 843

MARCOLIO—NONE—Marchon Eyewear; *U.S. Private*, pg. 702

MARCON COATINGS—Reflective & Low-Emmissivity Coatings for Building Glass.—Apogee Enterprises, Inc.; *U.S. Public*, pg. 120

MARCONNECT—Door-to-Door LCL & Ocean—Danzas Corporation; *Int'l*, pg. 382

MARCORE—Pumps—Ryan Herco Products Corp.; *U.S. Private*, pg. 953

MARCUS—NONE—The Eurotunnel Group; *Int'l*, pg. 466

MARCUS JAMES—Wines—Canandaigua Wine Company, Inc.; *U.S. Public*, pg. 300

MARCY—Matte—Appleton Papers Inc.; *Int'l*, pg. 567

MARCY—Fitness Products—Escalade Sports; *U.S. Public*, pg. 591

MARDEN—Crystals—CTS Corporation; *U.S. Public*, pg. 285

MARDI GRAS—Broadloom—Couristan Inc.; *U.S. Private*, pg. 279

MARDI GRAS—Liquor Stores & Lounges—Flanigan's Enterprises, Inc.; *U.S. Public*, pg. 648

MARDI GRAS—Plastic Laminates—Georgia-Pacific Corporation; *U.S. Public*, pg. 735

MARDI GRAS—Cookware Coffee Maker—Regal Ware, Inc.; *U.S. Private*, pg. 917

MAREGA HOLBAR BIANCO—Italian Wine—Laird & Company; *U.S. Private*, pg. 642

MAREGA HOLBAR ROSSO—Italian Wine—Laird & Company; *U.S. Private*, pg. 642

MAREGA PINOT BIANCO—Italian Wine—Laird & Company; *U.S. Private*, pg. 642

MAREGA PINOT GRIGIO—Italian Wine—Laird & Company; *U.S. Private*, pg. 642

MAREGA TOCAI—Italian Wine—Laird & Company; *U.S. Private*, pg. 642

MAREMONT—Auto Parts—Arvin Industries, Inc.; *U.S. Public*, pg. 136

MAREMONT—Shock Absorbers & Exhaust Systems—Maremont Exhaust Systems Product Division; *U.S. Public*, pg. 137

MARFAID—Valve—Hays Fluid Controls-Division of Romac Industries; *U.S. Private*, pg. 942

MARFAK—Chassis Lubricant—Texaco Inc.; *U.S. Public*, pg. 1582

MARGARD—Synthetic Resins, Plastics (Sheet Form), Plates, Foils, Blocks, Filaments—General Electric Canada Inc.; *U.S. Public*, pg. 713

MARGARET ASTOR—Color Cosmetics & Skin Care—Coty Inc.; *Int'l*, pg. 185

MARGATE—NONE—Marriott International, Inc.; *U.S. Public*, pg. 1047

MARI-NET—Extruded Plastic Net—Nalle Plastics Inc.; *U.S. Private*, pg. 773

MARIACHI—NewYork Area—Azteca Foods, Incorporated; *U.S. Private*, pg. 104

MARIACRON—Brandy—Eckes AG; *Int'l*, pg. 432

MARIACRON PREMIUM—Brandy—Eckes AG; *Int'l*, pg. 432

MARIANNE—NONE—Petrie Retail, Inc.; *U.S. Private*, pg. 858

MARIBO—Seeds for Sugar Beets, Fodder Beets, Sunflowers & Peas—Danisco Seed; *Int'l*, pg. 378

MARIE—Ready-to-Serve-Dishes—Danone Group; *Int'l*, pg. 379

MARIE BRIZARD—Cordials—Marie Brizard Wines & Spirits USA; *U.S. Private*, pg. 702

MARIE CLAIRE—NONE—The Hartstone Group PLC; *Int'l*, pg. 599

MARIE CLAIRE—Magazine—The Hearst Corporation; *U.S. Private*, pg. 515

MARIE CLAIRE—Magazine—Hearst Magazines Division; *U.S. Private*, pg. 516

MARIE CLAIRE—Fashion & Beauty Magazine—IPC Magazines Limited; *Int'l*, pg. 651

MARIE CLAIRE HEALTH & BEAUTY—Fashion & Beauty Magazine—IPC Magazines Limited; *Int'l*, pg. 651

MARIE'S SALAD DRESSINGS—Salad Dressings—Campbell Soup Company; *U.S. Public*, pg. 298

MARIGOLD—Sporting Goods—Brunswick Bowling & Billiards Corp.; *U.S. Public*, pg. 265

MARIGOLD—Household & Industrial Gloves—London International Group plc; *Int'l*, pg. 815

MARIGOLD/KEMP—Dairy Products—Koninklijke BolsWessanen nv; *Int'l*, pg. 750

MARINA—Bathroom Tissue—Consumer Products Business; *U.S. Public*, pg. 671

MARINA—Tissue—Fort James Corporation; *U.S. Public*, pg. 670

MARINALOY—NONE—Carpenter Technology Corporation; *U.S. Public*, pg. 307

MARINCO—Marine & Industry Wiring Devices—Valley Forge Corporation; *U.S. Public*, pg. 1705

MARINE—Coolers—The Canadian Coleman Co., Ltd.; *U.S. Private*, pg. 691

MARINE FRESH—Toiletries—International Cosmetics Co., Ltd.; *Int'l*, pg. 684

MARINE HARVEST—Salmon—Booker PLC; *Int'l*, pg. 202

MARINE HOTEL—Resort Hotels—Accor S.A.; *Int'l*, pg. 20

MARINE LOG—Monthly Magazine—Simmons-Boardman Publishing Corp.; *U.S. Private*, pg. 1000

MARINE-TITE!—Marine Fastener Installation Kits—R&B, Inc.; *U.S. Public*, pg. 1354

MARINE TRAVELIFT—Marine Mobile Boat Hoists—Marine Travelift, Inc.; *U.S. Private*, pg. 703

MARINE WORLD AFRICA USA—Nonprofit Theme Park—Marine World Africa USA; *U.S. Private*, pg. 703

MARINEFAX—Marine Weather Chart Recorders—Alden Electronics, Inc.; *U.S. Private*, pg. 872

MARINER—Sporting Goods—Brunswick Bowling & Billiards Corp.; *U.S. Public*, pg. 265

MARINER—Outboard Motors—Brunswick Corporation; *U.S. Public*, pg. 265

MARINER—Men's Apparel—International Cosmetics Co., Ltd.; *Int'l*, pg. 684

MARINER—Marine Forklift—Marine Travelift, Inc.; *U.S. Private*, pg. 703

MARINER'S—Skin Lotion—The Gillette Company; *U.S. Public*, pg. 743

MARINERS COVE—Clam Chowder—Curtice Burns Foods; *U.S. Private*, pg. 887

MARINETRAC—Drapery Hardware—Kirsch; *U.S. Public*, pg. 1176

MARINR—Catheter—Medtronic, Inc.; *U.S. Public*, pg. 1082

MARIO PIAMONTI—Hosiery for Women—Grupo Synkro, S.A. de C.V.; *Int'l*, pg. 576

MARION LADEWIG—Sporting Goods—Brunswick Bowling & Billiards Corp.; *U.S. Public*, pg. 265

MARIS—Ladies & Children's Wear—Kosugi Sangyo Co., Ltd.; *Int'l*, pg. 759

MARISA CHRISTINA—Knit Sweaters—Marisa Christina Inc.; *U.S. Public*, pg. 1044

MARITEK 21—Mapping Camera—Raytheon Optical Systems; *U.S. Public*, pg. 1364

MARITHE & FRANCOIS GIRBAUD—Jeanswear—VF Corporation; *U.S. Public*, pg. 1702

MARITZ—Motivation & Training Programs—Maritz Inc.; *U.S. Private*, pg. 703

MARK—House Mark—The Dow Chemical Company; *U.S. Public*, pg. 522

MARK—Epoxy Resin Catalysts—Witco Corporation; *U.S. Public*, pg. 1773

MARK ALEXANDER—NONE—Tandy Brands Accessories, Inc.; *U.S. Public*, pg. 1560

MARK ANDY—NONE—Mark Andy, Inc.; *U.S. Public*, pg. 521

MARK CROSS—Accessories—Sara Lee Corporation; *U.S. Public*, pg. 1432

MARK V—Extruder—Davis Standard Corporation; *U.S. Public*, pg. 459

MARK V—Lead Core Tolling Line—Gladding Braided Products LLC; *U.S. Private*, pg. 291

MARK V—Coated Paper—The Mead Corporation; *U.S. Public*, pg. 1074

MARK HUGHES COLLECTIONS—Skin Care Regimens for Women & Men—Herbalife International of America, Inc.; *U.S. Public*, pg. 809

MARK JEFFREY—Footwear—J. Baker, Inc.; *U.S. Public*, pg. 167

MARK LEVINSON—Electronic Components—Harman International Industries, Inc.; *U.S. Public*, pg. 787

MARK OF A PRO—Athletic Equipmemt & Sporting Goods—Rawlings Sporting Goods Company; *U.S. Public*, pg. 1361

THE MARK OF A WINNER—NONE—Stuart Entertainment Inc.; *U.S. Public*, pg. 1526

MARK I—High Gloss Paper—The Mead Corporation; *U.S. Public*, pg. 1074

MARK I AUTO-INJECTOR—Sequential Injection Package—Meridian Medical Technology, Inc.; *U.S. Public*, pg. 1095

MARK P TRIM—Dev Trim—Leslie Controls, Inc.; *U.S. Public*, pg. 1746

MARK SCOT COLLECTION—Golf Apparel—Tommy Armour Golf; *U.S. Public*, pg. 1683

MARK VI—Extruder—Davis Standard Corporation; *U.S. Public*, pg. 459

MARK X—Bowling Ball—Brunswick Bowling & Billiards Corp.; *U.S. Public*, pg. 265

MARK III—NONE—Bird Machine Company; *U.S. Public*, pg. 166

MARK III—Rotary Embossing Machines—Eastern Engraving; *U.S. Public*, pg. 1506

MARK III—Computer Time-Sharing Services & Data Processing Services—General Electric Canada Inc.; *U.S. Public*, pg. 713

MARK III—Centrifuge—Ketema, Inc.; *U.S. Private*, pg. 604

MARK III SERIES AIR FEED—Automatic Tension Control & Tension Indicators—P/A Industries, Inc.; *U.S. Private*, pg. 825

MARK III VANS—Luxury Vans—Mark III Industries; *U.S. Private*, pg. 704

MARK TIME—Timers & Timing Devices—M.H. Rhodes, Inc.; *U.S. Public*, pg. 927

MARK II—NONE—Regal Ware, Inc.; *U.S. Private*, pg. 917

MARK II—Automobile—Toyota Motor Corporation; *Int'l*, pg. 1411

MARK II-DONUT ROBOT—Bakery Equipment—Belshaw Brothers, Inc.; *Int'l*, pg. 188

MARK-X—Marking Pens—Diagraph Corporation; *U.S. Private*, pg. 330

MARKER CHANNEL—NONE—Medtronic, Inc.; *U.S. Public*, pg. 1082

MARKET∗AMERICA—Market Information & Analysis System—CACI International Inc; *U.S. Public*, pg. 272

MARKET BASKET—Canned Vegetables—Bush Brothers & Company; *U.S. Private*, pg. 189

MARKET∗MASTER—Direct Marketing Software—CACI International Inc; *U.S. Public*, pg. 272

MARKET REPORTS—Price Valuation Guides—Intertec Publishing; *U.S. Public*, pg. 1327

MARKET STATISTICS—Demographic Data & Market Analysis—Bill Communications, Inc.; *Int'l*, pg. 1046

MARKET UMBRELLAS—Wood & Aluminum Outdoor Furniture—Telescope Casual Furniture, Inc.; *U.S. Private*, pg. 1074

MARKETEST 2000—Market Research Products—Market Facts, Inc.; *U.S. Public*, pg. 1046

MARKETING COMPUTERS—Advertisers & Agencies Magazine—BPI Communications Inc.; *Int'l*, pg. 1446

MARKETING PROFESSIONAL'S INFOCENTER—Microcomputer Product—Group 1 Software, Inc.; *U.S. Public*, pg. 417

MARKETMATCH—The Pre-Opening Match—Instinet Corporation; *Int'l*, pg. 1106

MARKETOTE—Grocery Bags—Tenneco Packaging, Consumer Products Group; *U.S. Public*, pg. 1579

MARKETSMART—Real Time & Delayed Market Data—PC Quote, Inc.; *U.S. Public*, pg. 1240

MARKINGS—Gift Products—Thomas Nelson Inc.; *U.S. Public*, pg. 1167

MARKITE—Variable Resistors, Potentiometers, Thermistors—Litton Industries, Inc.; *U.S. Public*, pg. 1002

MARKLAD—Insulators—Litton Industries, Inc.; *U.S. Public*, pg. 1002

MARKLINK—Distributed Data Processing Terminals & Services—General Electric Canada Inc.; *U.S. Public*, pg. 713

MARKS-FITZGERALD—NONE—Rhodes, Inc.; *U.S. Public*, pg. 805

MARKSMAN—Computerized Cooling Water Treatment Monitoring & Control Systems—Calgon Corporation; *Int'l*, pg. 455

MARKSMAN—Herbicides—Novartis AG; *Int'l*, pg. 971

MARKSMAN—Beverage Carriers & Packaging Machine—Riverwood International Corporation; *U.S. Public*, pg. 1391

MARKSMAN—Herbicide—Sandoz Agro, Inc.; *Int'l*, pg. 974

MARKSMAN SHOOTING/TRAP SHOOTING—Videogame—Sega of America Inc.; *Int'l*, pg. 1218

MARKSTAT—Antistatic Agents—Witco Corporation; *U.S. Public*, pg. 1773

MARLBORO—Cigarettes—Philip Morris Companies Inc.; *U.S. Public*, pg. 1287

MARLBORO—Cigarettes—Philip Morris U.S.A.; *U.S. Public*, pg. 1289

MARLBORO LIGHTS—Cigarettes—Philip Morris Companies Inc.; *U.S. Public*, pg. 1287

MARLBORO LIGHTS 100'S—Cigarettes—Philip Morris Companies Inc.; *U.S. Public*, pg. 1287

MARLBORO LIGHTS 25'S—Cigarettes—Philip Morris Companies Inc.; *U.S. Public*, pg. 1287

MARLBORO MENTHOL—Cigarettes—Philip Morris Companies Inc.; *U.S. Public*, pg. 1287

MARLBORO 100'S—Cigarettes—Philip Morris Companies Inc.; *U.S. Public*, pg. 1287

MARLBORO 25'S—Cigarettes—Philip Morris Companies Inc.; *U.S. Public*, pg. 1287

MARLETTE—Manufactured Housing—Schult Homes Corporation; *U.S. Public*, pg. 1442

MARLETTE (MI) LEADER—Newspaper—The Hearst Corporation; *U.S. Private*, pg. 515

MARLEX—Polyolefins—Phillips Petroleum Company; *U.S. Public*, pg. 1290

MARLEY—Roof Tiles, Flooring, Plastic Products—Marley PLC; *Int'l*, pg. 843

MARLEY COOLING TOWER—Water Cooling Towers—The Marley Cooling Tower Co.; *U.S. Public*, pg. 1676

MARLIN—Binoculars—Swift Instruments, Inc.; *U.S. Private*, pg. 1058

MARLITE—DBA Name—Marlite; *U.S. Private*, pg. 705

MARLOID—Specialty Algin Blends—The NutraSweet Kelco Company; *U.S. Public*, pg. 1125

MARMALADE—Cutlery & Flatware—Lifetime Hoan Corp.; *U.S. Public*, pg. 992

MARMITE—Yeast Spread—Bestfoods; *U.S. Public*, pg. 223

MARMITE—Spread—CPC Foods (Ireland) Ltd.; *U.S. Public*, pg. 225

MARMOLEUM—Linoleum—Forbo Holding SA; *Int'l*, pg. 496

MARNOT FILMS—Hardcoated Polyester & Polycarbonate—Tekra Corporation; *U.S. Private*, pg. 1073

MAROMI—Sweet Condiment—Ajinomoto Company Inc.; *Int'l*, pg. 40

MARONE CINZANO—NONE—Gio. Buton S.p.a.; *Int'l*, pg. 409

MARQUEE—Health & Beauty Aids—Fleming Companies, Inc.; *U.S. Public*, pg. 652

MARQUEE 8000—CRT Projector—Electrohome Ltd.; *Int'l*, pg. 438

MARQUEE 9000—CRT Projector—Electrohome Ltd.; *Int'l*, pg. 438

MARQUES DE RISCAL—Spanish Wine—Schieffelin & Somerset Co.; *Int'l*, pg. 412

MARQUES DEL PUERTO—Spanish Wines—Marie Brizard Wines & Spirits USA; *U.S. Private*, pg. 702

MARQUESA LANA—Fabrics—Amoco Corporation; *U.S. Public*, pg. 101

MARQUIS—Ceramic Wall Tile—Monarch Tile, Inc.; *U.S. Private*, pg. 287

MARQUIS—Crystal—Waterford Crystal, Inc.; *Int'l*, pg. 1487

MARQUIS—Crystal—Waterford Wedgwood Plc; *Int'l*, pg. 1487

MARQUIS—Hand Cut Crystal—Waterford Wedgwood UK Plc; *Int'l*, pg. 1487

MARQUIS DE MONTESQIOU—Armagnac—Groupe Pernod Ricard; *Int'l*, pg. 566

MARQUIS DE MONTESQIOU—Armagnac—Austin Nichols & Co. Inc.; *Int'l*, pg. 566

THE MARQUIS LINE—NONE—Overholtzer Church Furniture, Inc.; *U.S. Private*, pg. 823

MARQUIS WHO'S WHO—Biographical Reference Books—Marquis Who's Who; *Int'l*, pg. 1096

MARRAKESH—Broadloom—Couristan Inc.; *U.S. Private*, pg. 279

MARRAKESH EXPRESS—Couscous—Hormel Foods Corp.; *U.S. Public*, pg. 840

MARRIAGE PARTNERSHIP—Magazine—Christianity Today, Inc.; *U.S. Private*, pg. 238

MARRIOTT—Hotel Chain—Marriott Hotels, Resorts, and Suites; *U.S. Public*, pg. 1048

MARRIOTT HOTELS AND RESORTS—Hotel Chain—Marriott International, Inc.; *U.S. Public*, pg. 1047

MARRIOTT SUITE—Hotel Chain—Marriott International, Inc.; *U.S. Public*, pg. 1047

MARS—Magnetic Tape Recorders—Eastman Kodak Company; *U.S. Public*, pg. 550

MARS—Confectionary—Mars Confectionery; *U.S. Private*, pg. 707

MARS—Turbine Products—Solar Turbines Incorporated; *U.S. Public*, pg. 316

MARS BRAND—NONE—M&M/Mars; *U.S. Private*, pg. 707

MARSALA FLORIO—NONE—Societe Pour la Vente des Produits Cinzano SA; *Int'l*, pg. 410

MARSH—Stencil Machines—Marsh Company; *U.S. Private*, pg. 707

MARSH—Supermarkets—Marsh Supermarkets, Inc.; *U.S. Public*, pg. 1049

MARSH INSTRUMENTS—Pressure & Temp. Gauges—Desco Corporation; *U.S. Private*, pg. 326

MARSH MELLOW—Fabric Reinforced Rubber Springs—Bridgestone/Firestone, Inc.; *Int'l*, pg. 213

MARSH PRODUCTS—Sewer Pipe—Premarc Corporation; *U.S. Private*, pg. 881

MARSHALL ERDMAN—Design, Enrng., & Construction of Medical Bldgs.—Marshall Erdman and Associates, Inc.; *U.S. Private*, pg. 380

MARSHALL FIELD'S—Department Stores—Marshall Field; *U.S. Public*, pg. 489

MARSHALLAN—BBQ Grills—Kay Home Products, Inc.; *U.S. Public*, pg. 1258

MARSHALLS—Retail Stores—Marshalls, Inc.; *U.S. Public*, pg. 1557

MARSHFIELD DOORS—Architectural Doors—Weyerhaeuser Forest Products Company; *U.S. Public*, pg. 1764

MARSHMALLOW MATEY'S—Frosted Oat Cereal with Marshmallow Bits—Malt-O-Meal Company; *U.S. Private*, pg. 699

MARSTERS—Incubator—Becton Dickinson Primary Care Diagnostics; *U.S. Public*, pg. 199

MARSTON—Heat Exchangers, Anodes, Tanks—IMI Plc; *Int'l*, pg. 646

MART—Telecommunications Retailer—Gordon Publications, Inc.; *Int'l*, pg. 1096

MARTA TECHNOLOGIES—Emissions Testing—Allen Telecom, Inc.; *U.S. Public*, pg. 45

MARTEL—Canned Seafood—Atalanta Corporation; *U.S. Private*, pg. 93

MARTELL—Cognac—Joseph E. Seagram & Sons, Inc.; *Int'l*, pg. 1215

MARTEST 21—Type of Hard Plastic—Virco Mfg. Corporation; *U.S. Public*, pg. 1721

MARTEX—Bed & Bath Accessories—WestPoint Stevens Inc.; *U.S. Public*, pg. 1762

MARTHA WHITE—Baking Mixes—Grand Metropolitan Plc; *Int'l*, pg. 408

MARTIN—Sprockets & Gears—Bryant Electric Supply Company, Inc.; *U.S. Private*, pg. 177

MARTIN—Musical Instruments—G. Leblanc Corporation; *U.S. Public*, pg. 656

MARTIN—Gas Space Heaters—Martin Industries, Inc. (AL); *U.S. Private*, pg. 709

MARTIN—Universal Design—Martin Universal Design, Inc.; *U.S. Private*, pg. 709

MARTIN—Gasoline—J.D. Streett & Co., Inc.; *U.S. Private*, pg. 1047

MARTIN BRIGHT STEELS—Metal Products—Email Limited; *Int'l*, pg. 450

MARTIN-BROWER—Fast Food Distribution—Dalgety Plc; *Int'l*, pg. 376

MARTIN FINGER SHIELD GARAGE DOORS—Garage Doors Which Help Prevent Severed Fingers In Door Section Joints—Martin Door Mfg., Inc.; *U.S. Private*, pg. 708

MARTIN LAWRENCE FRAME SHOPS—Retail Operations—Martin Lawrence Limited Editions, Inc.; *U.S. Private*, pg. 709

MARTIN LAWRENCE GALLERIES—Art Publisher & Retailer—Martin Lawrence Limited Editions, Inc.; *U.S. Private*, pg. 709

MARTIN LAWRENCE MODERN—Art Publisher & Retailer—Martin Lawrence Limited Editions, Inc.; *U.S. Private*, pg. 709

MARTIN LAWRENCE MUSEUM SHOPS—Retail Operations—Martin Lawrence Limited Editions, Inc.; *U.S. Private*, pg. 709

MARTIN-SENOUR—Paints & Coatings—The Sherwin-Williams Company; *U.S. Public*, pg. 1465

MARTINEZ PORTS—Wine—Allied Domecq PLC; *Int'l*, pg. 62

MARTINI—NONE—Bacardi-Martini Belgium; *U.S. Private*, pg. 109

MARTINI & ROSSI—China Martini Liquor—Armando Testa S.p.A; *Int'l*, pg. 1377

MARTINI & ROSSI ASTI SPUMANTE—Sparkling Wine—Bacardi-Martini, USA, Inc.; *U.S. Private*, pg. 109

MARTINI & ROSSI BIANCO—Vermouth—Bacardi-Martini, USA, Inc.; *U.S. Private*, pg. 109

MARTINI & ROSSI EXTRA DRY—Vermouth—Bacardi-Martini, USA, Inc.; *U.S. Private*, pg. 109

MARTINI & ROSSI ROSSO—Vermouth—Bacardi-Martini, USA, Inc.; *U.S. Private*, pg. 109

MARTINS—Fruit Juices & Juice Drinks-Shelf Stable—Sundor Brands Inc.; *U.S. Private*, pg. 1331

MARTINSITE—High Strength Steel—Inland Steel Industries, Inc.; *U.S. Public*, pg. 879

MARTINSON—Coffee—Tetley USA Inc.; *Int'l*, pg. 1377

MARTINSON RICH & SINGLE COFFEE BAGS—Single Serving Coffee Portions—Tetley USA Inc.; *Int'l*, pg. 1377

MARTONAIR—Pneumatic Valves & Cylinders—IMI Plc; *Int'l*, pg. 646

MARTOS-10—Carbohydrate Solution—Otsuka Pharmaceutical Co., Ltd.; *Int'l*, pg. 1013

MARUHA—NONE—Maruha Corporation; *Int'l*, pg. 845

MARVA—Book & Printing Papers—Westvaco Corporation; *U.S. Public*, pg. 1762

MARVAL—Turkey & Cooked Turkey Products—Rocco Inc.; *U.S. Private*, pg. 937

MARVAL—Further Processed & Cooked Products—Rocco Quality Foods; *U.S. Private*, pg. 937

MARVAL—Turkey & Turkey Products—Shady Brook Farms; *U.S. Private*, pg. 937

MARVALOY—Acrylic modified styrene—Marval Industries, Inc.; *U.S. Private*, pg. 710

MARVEER—Polishes—Kiwi Brands Pty. Ltd.; *U.S. Public*, pg. 1434

MARVEL—NONE—Cordis, a Johnson & Johnson Company; *U.S. Public*, pg. 928

MARVEL—Office Furniture—Masco Corporation; *U.S. Public*, pg. 1052

MARVELLA—Jewelry—Richton International Corporation; *U.S. Public*, pg. 1389

MARVELO—Several Products—Koninklijke Ahold NV; *Int'l*, pg. 749

MARVELON—NONE—Akzo Nobel N.V.; *Int'l*, pg. 42

MARVELOUS MIDDLE—Mattresses—Restonic Mattress Corporation; *U.S. Private*, pg. 925

MARVIN WOOD DOORS—NONE—Marvin Lumber & Cedar Company; *U.S. Private*, pg. 710

MARVIN WOOD WINDOWS—NONE—Marvin Lumber & Cedar Company; *U.S. Private*, pg. 710

MARVL—Distance Measuring Equipment—The Titan Corporation; *U.S. Public*, pg. 1618

MARVOLINN—NONE—Kiwi Brands Pty. Ltd.; *U.S. Public*, pg. 1434

MARVYLAN—Polyvinyl Chloride—DSM N.V.; *Int'l*, pg. 352

MARY ELLEN—Preserves & Jellies—J.M. Smucker Company; *U.S. Public*, pg. 1480

MARY JANE—Taffy—New England Confectionery Co.; *U.S. Private*, pg. 1113

MARY JANE—Candy—Stark Candy Company; *U.S. Private*, pg. 1113

MARY KAY—Cosmetics & Toiletries—Mary Kay, Inc.; *U.S. Private*, pg. 711

MARY KITCHEN—Food Products—Hormel Foods Corp.; *U.S. Public*, pg. 840

THE MARY MATALIN SHOW—Talk Program—Westwood One, Inc.; *U.S. Public*, pg. 1763

MARYLAND / D.C. MANUFACTURERS DIRECTORY—Directory—Manufacturers' News, Inc.; *U.S. Private*, pg. 700

MARYLAND CHIEF—Processed Food—Hanover Foods Corporation; *U.S. Private*, pg. 499

MARZETTI—Salad Dressings, Chip Dips, Dairy Snacks & Desserts—Lancaster Colony Corporation; *U.S. Public*, pg. 976

MARZETTI—Salad Dressings—T. Marzetti Company; *U.S. Public*, pg. 977

MASA HARINA—Tortilla Flour Mix—The Quaker Oats Company; *U.S. Public*, pg. 1347

MASA TRIGO—Mix For Making Tortillas—The Quaker Oats Company; *U.S. Public*, pg. 1347

MASERATI—Perfume—International Cosmetics Co., Ltd.; *Int'l*, pg. 684

MASERATI—Automobiles—Maserati Automobiles, Incorporated; *U.S. Private*, pg. 482

MASERATI—Automobile—Officine A. Maserati S.p.A.; *Int'l*, pg. 482

MASH'S—Processed Meats—Smithfield Foods, Inc.; *U.S. Public*, pg. 1479

MASI—Wine—Paterno Imports Limited; *U.S. Private*, pg. 843

MASIL—Silicone Fluid & Emulsions for Food, Industrial, Manufacturing Applications—PPG Industries, Inc.; *U.S. Public*, pg. 1245

MASK MATE—Paper Dispenser—Marson/Creative Fastener, Inc.; *U.S. Private*, pg. 708

MASKVIEW—Computer Program, Software—Lucent Technologies Inc.; *U.S. Public*, pg. 1017

MASLIP—Synthetic Lubricants & Additives—PPG Industries, Inc.; *U.S. Public*, pg. 1245

MASON—Men's & Women's Shoes—Mason Shoe Mfg. Co.; *U.S. Private*, pg. 712

MASON—Candlelamps—Standex International Corporation; *U.S. Public*, pg. 1505

MASON—Candy—World Trade & Marketing, LTD.; *U.S. Public*, pg. 1621

MASON DOTS—Candy—Tootsie Roll Industries, Inc.; *U.S. Public*, pg. 1621

MASON STREET FUNDS—Mutual Funds—Northwestern Mutual Life Insurance Co.; *U.S. Private*, pg. 807

MASON'S—Soft Drink—The Monarch Company, Inc.; *U.S. Private*, pg. 756

MASON'S IRONSTONE—Tableware, Lightingware & Giftware—Waterford Wedgwood UK Plc; *Int'l*, pg. 1487

MASONEILAN—Control Valves & Activators—Dresser Industries, Inc.; *U.S. Public*, pg. 528

MASONITE—Laminated Panels—International Paper Company; *U.S. Public*, pg. 901

MASQUERADER—Sofa Sleepers—Flexsteel Industries, Inc.; *U.S. Public*, pg. 653

MASS—NONE—Life Technologies, Inc.; *U.S. Public*, pg. 504

MASSAGE ACTION—Hand Held & Wall Mounted Showers—Alsons Corporation; *U.S. Public*, pg. 1053

MASSAGE MASTER—2-Speed Massager—Wahl Clipper Corp.; *U.S. Private*, pg. 1146

MASSE—Breast Cream—Ortho-McNeil Pharmaceutical Corporation; *U.S. Public*, pg. 929

MASSENGILL—Feminine Hygiene Prods.—SmithKline Beecham Consumer Healthcare, U.S.; *Int'l*, pg. 1264

MASSENGILL—Feminine Hygiene Products—SmithKline Beecham Corporation; *Int'l*, pg. 1264

MASSENGILL—Feminine Hygiene Prods.—SmithKline Beecham plc; *Int'l*, pg. 1264

MASSEY FERGUSON—Tractors—AGCO Corporation; *U.S. Public*, pg. 28

MASSIMO—Food Products—Rykoff-Sexton, Inc.; *U.S. Public*, pg. 918

MASSLINN—Cleaning Cloths, Sports Towels, Shop Towels, Nonwoven Roll Goods—Chicopee Inc.; *Int'l*, pg. 113

MASSON—Vineyards—Canandaigua Wine Co.; *U.S. Public*, pg. 300

MASSTECH—Speed Sensors, Tachometers—TransTechnology Corporation; *U.S. Public*, pg. 1632

MASSWEIGH—En Masse Gravimetric Feeder—Vibra Screw Inc.; *U.S. Private*, pg. 1138

MAST MICROWAVE—Microwave—Kevlin Corporation; *U.S. Public*, pg. 953

MASTER—Clipper—Andis Company; *U.S. Private*, pg. 73

MASTER—NONE—Brown & Sharpe Manufacturing Company; *U.S. Public*, pg. 260

MASTER—NONE—Commemorative Brands, Inc.; *U.S. Private*, pg. 258

MASTER—Locks, Doorlocks & Padlocks—Fortune Brands, Inc.; *U.S. Public*, pg. 674

MASTER—NONE—MasterBrand Industries, Inc.; *U.S. Public*, pg. 675

MASTER—Bread—Metz Baking Company; *U.S. Private*, pg. 1022

MASTER—Mechanical Group House Mark—Rockwell International Corporation; *U.S. Public*, pg. 1397

MASTER-BILT—Coolers & Freezers—Standex International Corporation; *U.S. Public*, pg. 1505

MASTER BLEND—Formula Feeds For Animals-Canada—Ag Processing Inc., A Cooperative; *U.S. Private*, pg. 26

MASTER BLEND—Ground Coffee—Kraft Foods, Inc.; *U.S. Public*, pg. 1287

MASTER CHEF—Specialty Oils, Pepperocini—Purity Products Inc.; *U.S. Private*, pg. 896

MASTER CHOICE—Food Products—The Great Atlantic & Pacific Tea Company, Inc.; *Int'l*, pg. 1375

MASTER CONTROL—Chain Saw Feature—Stihl Inc.; *Int'l*, pg. 1301

MASTER CONTROL 2000—Data Acquisition System—Logica Plc; *Int'l*, pg. 814

MASTER COTE—Interior/Exterior Paint—Buten, Division of Duron; *U.S. Private*, pg. 349

MASTER DELIVERY SERIES—Microcomputer Software for Canadian Mailers—Group 1 Software, Inc.; *U.S. Public*, pg. 417

MASTER DISTRIBUTORS—NONE—Master International Corp.; *U.S. Private*, pg. 713

MASTER-FLEX—Latex Saturated Enamel—Appleton Papers Inc.; *Int'l*, pg. 567

MASTER FOLD—Dispoable Paper Products—Wisconsin Tissue Mills, Inc.; *U.S. Public*, pg. 347

MASTER FORCE—Air Compressors—Coleman Powermate Compressors; *U.S. Private*, pg. 691

MASTER-GUARD—Int./Ext. Acrylic Latex Paint—Devoe Paint; *Int'l*, pg. 663

MASTER HEALTH—NONE—Blue Cross and Blue Shield of Massachusetts; *U.S. Private*, pg. 151

MASTER HEAT GUN—Flameless Heat Gun—Master Appliance Corp.; *U.S. Private*, pg. 713

MASTER KEY—Locking Devices—Best Access Systems; *U.S. Public*, pg. 223

MASTER LOCK—Locks, Doorlocks & Padlocks—Fortune Brands, Inc.; *U.S. Public*, pg. 674

MASTER LOCK—NONE—Master Lock Company; *U.S. Public*, pg. 675

MASTER LOCK—Key & Combination Padlocks, Locker Locks, Chain & Cable Locks, Door Locks—MasterBrand Industries, Inc.; *U.S. Public*, pg. 675

MASTER MEDICAL—NONE—Blue Cross and Blue Shield of Massachusetts; *U.S. Private*, pg. 151

MASTER-MITE—Heat Gun—Master Appliance Corp.; *U.S. Private*, pg. 713

MASTER MIX & DESIGN—Livestock & Poultry Feeds, Dogs, Etc—Ag Processing Inc., A Cooperative; *U.S. Private*, pg. 26

MASTER MIX FEEDS—Formula Feeds For Animal-US—Ag Processing Inc., A Cooperative; *U.S. Private*, pg. 26

THE MASTER PALETTE—Color System—ICI Paints; *Int'l*, pg. 664

MASTER PIECES—Personal Check Products—John H. Harland Company; *U.S. Public*, pg. 785

MASTER-PRO—Enamel, Paint—Pratt & Lambert United, Inc.; *U.S. Public*, pg. 1466

MASTER SERIES—Drawer Slides—Amerock Corporation; *U.S. Public*, pg. 1177

MASTER SERIES—Power Tools—The Black & Decker Corporation; *U.S. Public*, pg. 233

MASTER SLAB—NONE—CertainTeed Corporation; *Int'l*, pg. 1170

MASTER TENNA—TV Antenna—Thomson Consumer Electronics Inc.; *Int'l*, pg. 1383

MASTER TROWELS—Cement Finishing Equipment—East Moline Metal Products Company; *U.S. Private*, pg. 357

MASTER VAC—Power Brake Units—AlliedSignal Inc.; *U.S. Public*, pg. 49

MASTER-GUARD—Int./Ext. Acrylic Latex Paint—ICI Paints; *Int'l*, pg. 664

MASTER'S CHOICE—Dog Treats—Superior Brands, Inc.; *Int'l*, pg. 917

MASTERCARD BUSINESSCARD—Corporate Card—Mastercard International, Inc.; *U.S. Private*, pg. 714

MASTERCARD CARD—Credit Card—Mastercard International, Inc.; *U.S. Private*, pg. 714

MASTERCARD/CIRRUS ATM NETWORK—ATM Network—Mastercard International, Inc.; *U.S. Private*, pg. 714

MASTERCARD DEBIT—Debit Card Program—Mastercard International, Inc.; *U.S. Private*, pg. 714

MASTERCARD TRAVELERS CHEQUES—Travelers Cheque—Mastercard International, Inc.; *U.S. Private*, pg. 714

MASTERCARE—Automotive Service—Bridgestone/Firestone Inc. Retail Operations; *Int'l*, pg. 213

MASTERCARE—Automotive Repair Services—Bridgestone/Firestone, Inc.; *Int'l*, pg. 213

MASTERCARE—Provider of After Sale Service—Dixons Group plc; *Int'l*, pg. 413

MASTERCOLOR—Color & Additive Concentrates for Plastics—Ampacet Corporation; *U.S. Private*, pg. 67

MASTERCOM—Electronic Imaging System—Mastercard International, Inc.; *U.S. Private*, pg. 714

MASTERCOPY—Copy Paper—Georgia-Pacific Corporation; *U.S. Public*, pg. 735

MASTERCOTE—Chemical—Warner-Jenkinson Co.; *U.S. Public*, pg. 1696

MASTERCOUNT—NONE—Master International Corp.; *U.S. Private*, pg. 713

MASTERCRAFT—Furniture—Baker Knapp & Tubbs Inc.; *U.S. Private*, pg. 630

MASTERCRAFT—Water Ski Boats—The Coleman Company, Inc.; *U.S. Private*, pg. 690

MASTERCRAFT—Tires—The Cooper Tire Company; *U.S. Public*, pg. 445

MASTERCRAFT—Furniture—Mastercraft Furniture Corp.; *U.S. Private*, pg. 714

MASTERCRAFT—Entry Handles—Triangle Brass Manufacturing; *U.S. Private*, pg. 1101

MASTERCUTS—Family Hair Salon—Regis Corporation; *U.S. Public*, pg. 1373

MASTERFLEX—Pumps—Ryan Herco Products Corp.; *U.S. Public*, pg. 953

MASTERFLOR—Floor Coverings—Domco Inc.; *Int'l*, pg. 415

MASTERFLOW—Heat Blower—Master Appliance Corp.; *U.S. Private*, pg. 713

MASTERFLOW—Grouts—Master Builders Inc.; *Int'l*, pg. 1465

MASTERGUILD—Housewares—Stanley Roberts, Inc.; *U.S. Private*, pg. 936

MASTERLAB SYSTEM—Computer Aided Chemistry Robotics System—The Perkin-Elmer Corporation; *U.S. Public*, pg. 1279

MASTERLAN—NONE—UB Networks; *Int'l*, pg. 924

MASTERLAN FT—NONE—UB Networks; *Int'l*, pg. 924

MASTERLINE—Broad Band Amplifiers—Blonder-Tongue Laboratories, Inc.; *U.S. Public*, pg. 237

MASTERLINE—Paint—Pratt & Lambert United, Inc.; *U.S. Public*, pg. 1466

MASTERMAILER—Inserter—Bell & Howell Holdings; *U.S. Public*, pg. 201

MASTERMARK—Doors—Simpson Door Company; *U.S. Private*, pg. 1003

MASTERMET—Polishing Suspension—Buehler, Limited; *U.S. Public*, pg. 574

MASTERMIND—Engine Analyzer—Bridgestone/Firestone, Inc.; *Int'l*, pg. 213

MASTERMIND—Game—Pressman Toy Corp.; *U.S. Private*, pg. 882

MASTERMIND—Modular Accessory System for Valve Actuators—Worcester Controls Corp.; *Int'l*, pg. 128

MASTERMIX—Mixing Room—Binks Sames Corporation; *U.S. Public*, pg. 229

MASTERPEAK—Satellite Tracking Sequence fro Home Satellite TV Receiver/Descrambler—Satellite Data Networks; *U.S. Public*, pg. 716

MASTERPIECE—Ophthalmic Lenses & Blanks—American Optical Corporation; *U.S. Private*, pg. 60

MASTERPIECE—Coating Products—Columbia Paint & Coatings; *U.S. Private*, pg. 256

MASTERPIECE—Accounting Software—Computer Associates International, Inc.; *U.S. Public*, pg. 420

MASTERPIECE—Paint—Graham Paint and Varnish Company; *U.S. Private*, pg. 468

MASTERPIECE—Infrared Heaters—Martin Industries, Inc. (AL); *U.S. Private*, pg. 709

MASTERPIECE—Low Lustre Latex Wall & Trim Paint—Perry & Derrick Co.; *U.S. Private*, pg. 854

MASTERPIECE:EDI OPTION—A Facility that Electronically Transmits/Receives Transactions—Computer Associates International, Inc.; *U.S. Public*, pg. 420

MASTERPIECE 500 T-X—Commercial Dry Mounting/Laminating Press—Seal Products Incorporated; *U.S. Public*, pg. 849

MASTERPIECE GRO—Graphics Production Software with CA-General Ledger Interface—Computer Associates International, Inc.; *U.S. Public*, pg. 420

MASTERPIECES—Chocolate—New England Confectionery Co.; *U.S. Private*, pg. 1113

MASTERPIECES OF THE WORLD—Retail—Martin Lawrence Limited Editions, Inc.; *U.S. Private*, pg. 709

MASTERPLATE—Dry Shake Surface Hardeners for Concrete—Master Builders Inc.; *Int'l*, pg. 1465

MASTERQUERY—Inquiry & Reporting System for Access to Data in Masterpiece Applications—Computer Associates International, Inc.; *U.S. Public*, pg. 420

MASTERS—Department Stores—Masters, Inc.; *U.S. Private*, pg. 714

MASTERS COLLECTION—Domestic Cigars—Consolidated Cigar Corporation; *U.S. Private*, pg. 690

MASTERS GOLF TOURNAMENT—Sports Program—Westwood One, Inc.; *U.S. Public*, pg. 1763

MASTERS SERIES—Mechanical Heart Valve—St. Jude Medical, Inc.; *U.S. Public*, pg. 1427

MASTER'S TOUCH—Fresh Produce—DNAP Holding Corp.; *Int'l*, pg. 454

MASTERSCAN—Graphic Screens—Novartis; *Int'l*, pg. 972

MASTERSOURCE FOR INGREDIENTS—CD-ROM Product Providing a Range of Ingredient & Related Information—Reed Elsevier Business Information; *Int'l*, pg. 1095

MASTERTEK—Feed Additive—Tate & Lyle PLC; *Int'l*, pg. 1356

MASTERTEX—Polishing Cloth—Buehler, Limited; *U.S. Public*, pg. 574

MASTERTHERM—Conveyor Ovens—The Blodgett Oven Co., Inc.; *U.S. Public*, pg. 1064

MASTERTIME—NONE—Master International Corp.; *U.S. Private*, pg. 713

MASTERTONE—Paint—Graham Paint and Varnish Company; *U.S. Private*, pg. 468

MASTERVISION—Customized Masterpiece Information Delivery—Computer Associates International, Inc.; *U.S. Public*, pg. 420

MASTERWORKS—Record Label—Sony Corporation; *Int'l*, pg. 1280

MASTERWORKS—Direct Vent Gas Fireplaces—Temco Fireplace Products, Inc.; *U.S. Public*, pg. 1576

MASTERWORKS 280—NONE—Temtex Industries Inc.; *U.S. Public*, pg. 1575

MASTERY—Learning System Video Tapes & Guide Books—3M; *U.S. Public*, pg. 1604

MASTREX—Styrene-Maleic Anhydride Copolymer—The Dow Chemical Company; *U.S. Public*, pg. 522

MASURY—Paints—Masury Paint; *U.S. Public*, pg. 1707

MASURY—Paint—The Valspar Corporation; *U.S. Public*, pg. 1707

MAT-KONTROL—NONE—Blaw-Knox Construction Equipment Corporation; *U.S. Public*, pg. 877

MAT NITRO—Farm Equip—Miller-St. Nazianz, Inc.; *U.S. Private*, pg. 748

MATACAN BUNDLES—Premium Cigars—Consolidated Cigar Corporation; *U.S. Private*, pg. 690

MATADOR—Small Vacuum—Advance Machine Company; *Int'l*, pg. 932

MATADOR—Giftwrap—Fine Art Developments plc; *Int'l*, pg. 485

METAL FILL—Feature—The Lincoln Electric Company; *U.S. Public*, pg. 996

MATBRO—Telescopic Handlers—Powerscreen International Plc; *Int'l*, pg. 1066

MATCH—Football Magazine—EMAP Pursuit Publishing; *Int'l*, pg. 451

MATCH—Racquetball Racquet—Head USA, Inc.; *U.S. Private*, pg. 514

MATCH BIG SHOTS—Football Magazine—EMAP Pursuit Publishing; *Int'l*, pg. 451

MATCH-BLOMATIC—Foundry Mold Making Machine—Pettibone Corporation; *U.S. Private*, pg. 859

MATCH LIGHT—Instant Lighting Charcoal Briquets—The Clorox Company; *U.S. Public*, pg. 386

MATCH LIGHT—Instant Lighting Charcoal-Briquets—The Kingsford Products Company; *U.S. Public*, pg. 387

MATCH MAKERS—Plumbing Products—The Black & Decker Corporation; *U.S. Public*, pg. 233

MATCH MATE—Spectromonitor—Milton Roy Company; *U.S. Public*, pg. 1534

MATCH OF THE DAY—NONE—BBC Magazines; *Int'l*, pg. 114

MATCHBLOWATICS—NONE—Beardsley & Piper, L.L.C.; *U.S. Private*, pg. 859

MATCHBOX—Cars—Tyco Toys, Inc.; *U.S. Public*, pg. 1058

MATCHLESS—Extruded Neopren Tubing & Cord—Minor Rubber Co., Inc.; *U.S. Private*, pg. 751

MATCHLESS—Barbecue Grill—National Presto Industries, Inc.; *U.S. Public*, pg. 1159

MATCHMAKER—Mail Inserting Machine—Bell & Howell Holdings; *U.S. Public*, pg. 201

MATCHMAKER—Power Transmission Belting—The Goodyear Tire & Rubber Company; *U.S. Public*, pg. 752

MATCHMAKERS—Confections—Nestle-Rowntree Ltd.; *Int'l*, pg. 921

MATCHMATE—Packaging Sytems—Sanderson Plumbing Products Inc.; *U.S. Private*, pg. 964

MATCHMATE PLUS—Hydraulic Hose—Aeroquip Corporation; *U.S. Public*, pg. 24

MATCOTE—Pit Liner—International Paint Co., Inc.; *Int'l*, pg. 338

MATCOTE PROCESS—Flake Glass Linings—International Paint Co., Inc.; *Int'l*, pg. 338

MATE PERFECT—Motor Parts/Part Sets—Groschopp, Inc.; *Int'l*, pg. 559

MATEOUS—Wines—Canandaigua Wine Company, Inc.; *U.S. Public*, pg. 300

MATERIAL HANDLING ENGINEERING—Periodical—Penton Publishing, Inc.; *U.S. Public*, pg. 1306

MATERIAL HANDLING PRODUCT NEWS—New-Product Tabloid Covering Materials Handling—Reed Elsevier Business Information; *Int'l*, pg. 1095

MATERNALINK—NONE—Matria Healthcare, Inc.; *U.S. Public*, pg. 1057

MATERNITY—Women's Apparel—International Cosmetics Co., Ltd.; *Int'l*, pg. 684

MATEUS—Corn & Other Starches & Jams—Bestfoods; *U.S. Public*, pg. 223

MATEY—NONE—Kiwi Brands Pty. Ltd.; *U.S. Public*, pg. 1434

MATH SAFARI—Electronic Learning Aid—Educational Insights, Inc.; *U.S. Public*, pg. 565

MATH WORKSHOP—NONE—Broderbund Software, Inc.; *U.S. Public*, pg. 258

MATHDOC—Document Delivery Service—American Mathematical Society, Inc.; *U.S. Private*, pg. 59

MATHEMATICA JOURNAL—Magazine—Miller Freeman Inc.; *Int'l*, pg. 1443

MATHER—Sealing devices—Federal-Mogul Corporation; *U.S. Public*, pg. 615

MATHERS—Brand-name Family Shoe Stores—Woolworth Corporation; *U.S. Public*, pg. 1777

MATHEW BROWN—Ales—Scottish & Newcastle plc; *Int'l*, pg. 1211

MATHEY TISSOT—Liscensed Name Brand Watch—Jan Bell Marketing Inc.; *U.S. Public*, pg. 207

MATHSCI—Database—American Mathematical Society, Inc.; *U.S. Private*, pg. 59

MATHSCINET—Online Database—American Mathematical Society, Inc.; *U.S. Private*, pg. 59

MATILDA BAY BITTER—Bitter Ale—Carlton & United Breweries Ltd.; *Int'l*, pg. 500

MATINEE—Cigarettes—Imasco Limited; *Int'l*, pg. 112

MATINESSE—Nylon—BASF Corporation Fiber Products Division; *Int'l*, pg. 105

MATO—Belt Fasteners—Clipper Belt Lacer Company; *U.S. Private*, pg. 413

MATO MATO—Ketchup—Philip Morris Companies Inc.; *U.S. Public*, pg. 1287

MATREX—Chromatography Media—Amicon, Inc.; *U.S. Public*, pg. 1113

MATRIGON—Herbicide—The Dow Chemical Company; *U.S. Public*, pg. 522

MATRIX—Information Management—Adra Systems, Inc.; *U.S. Private*, pg. 18

MATRIX—Broadloom—Couristan Inc.; *U.S. Private*, pg. 279

MATRIX—Raised Access Floor Systems—Daw Technologies, Inc.; *U.S. Public*, pg. 489

MATRIX—Hair Care Prods.—Matrix Essentials, Inc.; *U.S. Public*, pg. 254

MATRIX—Bond Paper & Stationery Products—The Mead Corporation; *U.S. Public*, pg. 1074

MATRIX—Electronic Lighting Controls—Thomas Industries Inc.; *U.S. Public*, pg. 1598

MATRIX—Light Control System—Thomas Lighting-C&I Indoor Divison; *U.S. Public*, pg. 1599

MATRIX—Faceshield—U.S. Safety; *U.S. Public*, pg. 1125

MATRIX 88—Closed-Circuit Television Equipment—Vicon Industries, Inc.; *U.S. Public*, pg. 1719

MATRIX 44—Closed-Circuit Television Equipment—Vicon Industries, Inc.; *U.S. Public*, pg. 1719

MATRIX IV—Steel Electronic Cabinet—Zero Corporation; *U.S. Public*, pg. 1791

MATRIX 96—Direct Beta Counter—Packard Instrument Co., Inc.; *U.S. Private*, pg. 833

MATRIX 7—Cookware & Design—Regal Ware, Inc.; *U.S. Private*, pg. 917

MATRIX SOUND—HiFi Sound in TV—Sony Electronics; *Int'l*, pg. 1281

MATRIX-UPS—Uninterruptible Power Supplies—American Power Conversion Corporation; *U.S. Public*, pg. 89

MATROCOLOR—Color Proofing—Castcraft Industries, Inc.; *U.S. Private*, pg. 219

MATROTYPE—Linecasting Matrices—Castcraft Industries, Inc.; *U.S. Private*, pg. 219

MATSON—Ocean Transportation—Alexander & Baldwin, Inc.; *U.S. Public*, pg. 39

MATSON—Freight Service in the Pacific—Matson Navigation Company, Inc.; *U.S. Public*, pg. 39

MATSTICK—Adhesive—International Paint Co., Inc.; *Int'l*, pg. 338

MATSTOP—NONE—Blaw-Knox Construction Equipment Corporation; *U.S. Public*, pg. 877

MATSUI—Label Brand—Dixons Group plc; *Int'l*, pg. 413

MATTCH—Bioinsecticide—Mycogen Corporation; *U.S. Public*, pg. 1142

MATTE—Interior Wall and Countertop—Monarch Tile, Inc.; *U.S. Public*, pg. 287

MATTE GLAZE—Glazed Ceramic Wall Tile—Florida Tile Industries, Inc.; *U.S. Public*, pg. 1322

MATTE GLAZE—Nominal 4" Matte Glazed Wall Tile for Use on Walls & Lt. Duty Bath Floors—United States Ceramic Tile Co.; *U.S. Private*, pg. 1124

MATTE PLUS—Interior Walls & Floors—Monarch Tile, Inc.; *U.S. Private*, pg. 287

MATTEL—Toys—Mattel Espana, S.A.; *U.S. Public*, pg. 1059

MATTEL GAMES—Games—Mattel, Inc.; *U.S. Public*, pg. 1057

MATTEL PRESCHOOL—Toys—Mattel, Inc.; *U.S. Public*, pg. 1057

MATTERHORN—Asphalt Shingles—Atlas Roofing Corp.; *U.S. Private*, pg. 96

MATTERHORN—NONE—Porcelanite, Inc.; *Int'l*, pg. 573

MATTISON—Surface Grinder—Mattison Technologies, Inc.; *U.S. Private*, pg. 714

MATTRIX—Stimulator—Medtronic, Inc.; *U.S. Public*, pg. 1082

MATT'S—Premium & Light—The F.X. Matt Brewing Co.; *U.S. Private*, pg. 714

MATURE CARE—NONE—Pioneer Life Insurance Co. of Illinois; *U.S. Public*, pg. 434

MATURE WISDOM—Products for the Mature Audience—Hanover Direct Pennsylvania, Inc.; *U.S. Public*, pg. 782

MATZINGER—Pet Foods—Nestle S.A.; *Int'l*, pg. 915

MAUI—Schnapps—White Rock Distilleries Inc.; *U.S. Private*, pg. 1173

MAUI BRAND—Washed Raw Sugar—Alexander & Baldwin, Inc.; *U.S. Public*, pg. 39

MAUNA KEA—Coffee—C. Brewer & Company, Limited; *U.S. Private*, pg. 190

MAUNA LA'I—Tropical Fruit Drinks—Ocean Spray Cranberries, Inc.; *U.S. Private*, pg. 811

MAUNA LOA—Macadamia Nuts—C. Brewer & Company, Limited; *U.S. Private*, pg. 190

MAUNA LOA—Macadamia Nuts & Macadamia Nut Confections—Mauna Loa Macadamia Nut Corporation; *U.S. Private*, pg. 190

MAUNA LOA ORCHIDS, LTD.—Hawaiian Exotic/Tropical Flowers—Flowers of Hawaii; *U.S. Private*, pg. 415

MAURI—Food Preparations—Burns, Philp & Company Limited; *Int'l*, pg. 236

MAURICE—Imported Food Products—World Finer Foods, Inc.; *U.S. Private*, pg. 1190

MAUTZ—Paint—Mautz Paint Co.; *U.S. Private*, pg. 715

MAVADISC—NONE—Bird Machine Company; *U.S. Public*, pg. 166

MAVERICK—Beef Pattie Melt—Harker's Distribution, Inc.; *U.S. Private*, pg. 502

MAVERICK—Cigarette—Lorillard Tobacco Company; *U.S. Public*, pg. 1011

MAVERICK—Jeanswear—VF Corporation; *U.S. Public*, pg. 1702

MAVERICK SERIES MONEY CLIPS—NONE—Camillus Cutlery Co.; *U.S. Private*, pg. 203

MAVERIK—Convenience Stores—Maverik Country Stores, Inc.; *U.S. Private*, pg. 715

MAVICA—Magnetic Video Camera—Sony Electronics; *Int'l*, pg. 1281

MAVICARD—Magnetic Card—Sony Electronics; *Int'l*, pg. 1281

MAVIGRAPH—Printer for Camera with Magnetic Recording Disc—Sony Electronics; *Int'l*, pg. 1281

MAVIPAK—Magnetic Camera—Sony Electronics; *Int'l*, pg. 1281

MAVRIK—Insecticide—Novartis AG; *Int'l*, pg. 971

MAVRIK AQUAFLOW—Insecticide—Sandoz Agro, Inc.; *Int'l*, pg. 974

MAX—Aeromedical Helicopter—Agusta Aerospace Corporation; *Int'l*, pg. 32

MAX—NONE—Altera Corporation; *U.S. Public*, pg. 59

MAX—CPE Systems—Electronic Tele-Communications, Inc.; *U.S. Public*, pg. 570

MAX—Cigarettes—Loews Corporation; *U.S. Public*, pg. 1010

MAX—Cigarette—Lorillard Tobacco Company; *U.S. Public*, pg. 1011

MAX-A-FORM—Concrete Forming System—Symons Corporation; *U.S. Private*, pg. 932

MAX-AIR—Air Adjustable Shock—Monroe Auto Equipment Co.; *U.S. Public*, pg. 1577

MAX-AMINE—Gas Treating Technology—BetzDearborn Inc.; *U.S. Public*, pg. 226

MAX & ERMA'S—Restaurants—Max & Erma's Restaurants; *U.S. Public*, pg. 1060

MAX-E-GLAS—Swimming Pool Pumps—Sta-Rite Water Systems; *U.S. Public*, pg. 1767

MAX EFFICIENCY—NONE—Life Technologies, Inc.; *U.S. Public*, pg. 504

MAX FACTOR—Cosmetics—The Procter & Gamble Company; *U.S. Public*, pg. 1330

MAX FACTOR—Cosmetics—Procter & Gamble Venezuela, C.A.; *U.S. Public*, pg. 1332

MAX FACTOR COSMETICS—NONE—Procter & Gamble Cosmetics Co.; *U.S. Public*, pg. 1330

MAX-50—Moisture Analyzer—Arizona Instrument Corporation; *U.S. Public*, pg. 129

MAX 5—Whole House Electronic—Trion, Inc.; *U.S. Public*, pg. 1639

MAX 5000—NONE—Altera Corporation; *U.S. Public*, pg. 59

MAX IV, 32—Modular Application Executive Operating System—Modcomp; *U.S. Public*, pg. 283

MAX GON—Coal Car—Thrall Car Mfg. Co.; *U.S. Private*, pg. 344

MAX KLEIN—Plastic Houseware & Horticulture Prods.—Ingrid Division of Lawnware; *U.S. Private*, pg. 654

MAX 9000—NONE—Altera Corporation; *U.S. Public*, pg. 59

MAX-1—Distributed Control Systems—Honeywell, Inc.; *U.S. Public*, pg. 834

MAX 1000-MOISTURE ANALYZER—NONE—Arizona Instrument Corporation; *U.S. Public*, pg. 129

MAX+PLUS—NONE—Altera Corporation; *U.S. Public*, pg. 59

MAX+PLUS II—NONE—Altera Corporation; *U.S. Public*, pg. 59

MAX POWER—Car Magazine—EMAP Nationals; *Int'l*, pg. 451

MAX-PRO—Oilfield Filters—Pall Corporation; *U.S. Public*, pg. 1253

MAX 7000—NONE—Altera Corporation; *U.S. Public*, pg. 59

MAX-TRAK—Electronic Interconnection Components—SAE Engineering, Inc.; *U.S. Private*, pg. 955

MAX 2000-MOISTURE ANALYZER—NONE—Arizona Instrument Corporation; *U.S. Public*, pg. 129

MAXALIQ—Amyloglucosidase for the Conversion of Glucose into Alcohol—Royal Gist-Brocades N.V.; *Int'l*, pg. 1142

MAXAQUIN—Anti-Infective—Monsanto Company; *U.S. Public*, pg. 1124

MAXAROME—Natural Flavour—Royal Gist-Brocades N.V.; *Int'l*, pg. 1142

MAXAVOR—Baker's Yeast Extract—Royal Gist-Brocades N.V.; *Int'l*, pg. 1142

MAXAZYME—Glucose Isomerase for the Continuous Production of High Fructose Syrups—Royal Gist-Brocades N.V.; *Int'l*, pg. 1142

MAXBOND—Adhesives—TEC Incorporated; *U.S. Public*, pg. 687

MAXCESS (R) BUSINESS SERVICES—Dedicated & Switched-Access Commercial Services—Frontier Communications Services; *U.S. Public*, pg. 684

MAXCHANGER—Heat Exchangers—Tranter, Inc.; *U.S. Public*, pg. 521

MAXECON—Hose—HBD Industries, Inc.; *U.S. Private*, pg. 489

MAXELL—Audio & Video Magnetic Recording Tapes; Floppy Disks; Batteries—Maxell Corp. Of America; *Int'l*, pg. 621

MAXFLIGHT—De-Icing & Anti-Icing Fluid—Octagon Process Inc.; *U.S. Private*, pg. 811

MAXI—Chain of Superstore Supermarkets—Hakon Gruppen AS; *Int'l*, pg. 643

MAXI—Controller—Rain Bird Sprinklers Manufacturing Corp.; *U.S. Private*, pg. 907

MAXI-BUNDLE—Fiber Optic Cable—Siecor Corporation; *U.S. Public*, pg. 449

MAXI-BUNDLE—Fiber Optic Cable—Siecor Corporation; *Int'l*, pg. 1245

MAXI-DRIVER—Orthopedic Surgery Instrumentation—3M; *U.S. Public*, pg. 1604

MAXI-FLEX & VAC—Medico-Surgical Tubes & Medico-Surgical Tube Appliances—Mallinckrodt Inc.; *U.S. Public*, pg. 1039

MAXI FUSE—Auto Fuses—Littelfuse, Inc.; *U.S. Public*, pg. 1001

MAXI-LIFT—Tilting Device For Concrete Walls—Richmond Screw Anchor Company; *U.S. Private*, pg. 932

MAXI-LINER—Paint Striping Truck—Linear Dynamics Inc.; *U.S. Private*, pg. 668

MAXI-LOK—Chuck Assembly—Buehler, Limited; *U.S. Public*, pg. 574

MAXI-MAIL—Mailing Efficiency System—Group 1 Software, Inc.; *U.S. Public*, pg. 417

MAXI-MISER—Fluorescent Lamp Ballasts-Fluorescent Lamps—General Electric Canada Inc.; *U.S. Public*, pg. 713

MAXI-PAC—Actuator—Duff-Norton; *U.S. Public*, pg. 406

MAXI-PRO 435—4 Wheel Sprayer—Hahn Equipment Co.; *U.S. Public*, pg. 1624

MAXI-ROM—Electronics—National Semiconductor Corporation; *U.S. Public*, pg. 1159

MAXI SNEAKER—Line Layer—Case Corporation; *U.S. Public*, pg. 311

MAXI SWING—Lathes—WCI Machine Tools & Systems; *Int'l*, pg. 440

MAXI-THERM—Single Patient Use Hyper-Hypothermia Blankets—Cincinnati Sub-Zero Products, Inc.; *U.S. Private*, pg. 240

MAXIBAN—Animal Health—Elanco Animal Health; *U.S. Public*, pg. 993

MAXIBAN—Narasin & Nicarbazine, Elanco—Eli Lilly and Company; *U.S. Public*, pg. 992

MAXIBAND—V-Belts—HBD Industries, Inc.; *U.S. Private*, pg. 489

MAXIBRAKE—Brake Parts—Echlin Inc.; *U.S. Public*, pg. 560

MAXICHIP—Ceramic Microwave Capacitors—AVX Corporation; *Int'l*, pg. 775

MAXIDEX—Dexamethasone Suspension & Ointment—Alcon Laboratories, Inc.; *Int'l*, pg. 916

MAXIFRUIT—Cookies—Culinar Inc.; *Int'l*, pg. 348

MAXIGATOR—Irrigation Equipment Lateral Move—Reinke Manufacturing Co., Inc.; *U.S. Private*, pg. 920

MAXIGRIND—Materials Reduction Grinder—Rexworks Inc.; *U.S. Private*, pg. 926

MAXILACT—Dairy Enzyme to Hydrolize the Lactose in Milk & Whey—Royal Gist-Brocades N.V.; *Int'l*, pg. 1142

MAXIM—Heat Exchange System—Ashland, Inc.; *U.S. Public*, pg. 138

MAXIM—Indus. Silencers—Beaird Industries, Inc.; *U.S. Public*, pg. 1639

MAXIM—Coffee—Kraft Foods, Inc.; *U.S. Public*, pg. 1287

MAXIM—Graphic Arts Rapid Access Processors—LogEtronics Corporation; *U.S. Public*, pg. 6

MAXIM—Freeze-Dried Coffee—Philip Morris Companies Inc.; *U.S. Public*, pg. 1287

MAXIM—Food Products—Rykoff-Sexton, Inc.; *U.S. Public*, pg. 918

MAXIM—Manual Wheelchair—Theradyne Corporation; *U.S. Private*, pg. 637

MAXIM-ALL—Multi-Vitamin Mineral—Nature's Bounty Inc.; *U.S. Public*, pg. 1166

MAXIM EVAPORATORS—Sea Water Desalinators—Beaird Industries, Inc.; *U.S. Public*, pg. 1639

MAXIM*GP—NONE—Zygo Corporation; *U.S. Public*, pg. 1795

MARY MAXIM—Yarn, Needlework & Crafts—Mary Maxim, Inc.; *U.S. Private*, pg. 716

MAXIMA—Luggage—American Tourister, Inc.; *U.S. Public*, pg. 1430

MAXIMA—Oxygenator—Medtronic, Inc.; *U.S. Public*, pg. 1082

MAXIMA—MP&G Accelerator—Sigma Designs, Inc.; *U.S. Public*, pg. 1472

MAXIMA—Longest Battery Life in Industry—Staodyn Inc.; *U.S. Public*, pg. 1509

MAXIMA-NISSAN—Automobile—Nissan Motor Corporation in U.S.A.; *Int'l*, pg. 945

MAXIMA PLUS—Oxygenator—Medtronic, Inc.; *U.S. Public*, pg. 1082

MAXIMA II—Oxygenator—Medtronic, Inc.; *U.S. Public*, pg. 1082

MAXIMET—Grinding & Polishing System—Buehler, Limited; *U.S. Public*, pg. 574

MAXIMI$ER—Radio Audience Measurement Software System for Radio Stations—The Arbitron Company; *U.S. Public*, pg. 331

MAXIMILIAN—NONE—Gio. Buton S.p.a.; *Int'l*, pg. 409

MAXIMUM PLUS—Interior & Exterior Paints—PPG Industries, Inc.; *U.S. Public*, pg. 1245

MAXIMIZER—Solid Bowl Scroll Centrifuge—Alfa Laval Separation Inc.; *Int'l*, pg. 1378

MAXIMIZER—Electronic Components—General Instrument Corporation; *U.S. Public*, pg. 716

MAXIMIZER—Golf Club—Mizuno Corporation; *Int'l*, pg. 884

MAXIMIZER—Road Machinery-Asphalt Distributor—Rosco Manufacturing Co.; *U.S. Private*, pg. 944

MAXIMO ADVANTAGE—CMMS—PSDI; *U.S. Private*, pg. 828

MAXIMO ENTERPRISE—CMMS—PSDI; *U.S. Private*, pg. 828

MAXIMO WORKGROUP—CMMS—PSDI; *U.S. Private*, pg. 828

MAXIMUM—Anti-Glare CRT Filter—Optical Coating Laboratory, Inc.; *U.S. Public*, pg. 1227

MAXIMUM—Paint—PPG Industries, Inc.; *U.S. Public*, pg. 1245

MAXIMUM—Lead-Free Gasolines—Petro-Canada; *Int'l*, pg. 1041

MAXIMUM—Catheter—St. Jude Medical, Inc.; *U.S. Public*, pg. 1427

MAXIMUM PLUS—Anti-Glare CRT Filter—Optical Coating Laboratory, Inc.; *U.S. Public*, pg. 1227

MAXIMUM SECURITY PLUS—Latches & Locks—Adams Rite Manufacturing Co.; *U.S. Private*, pg. 17

MAXIMUM STRENGTH OFF!—Insect Repellent—S.C. Johnson & Son, Inc.; *U.S. Private*, pg. 592

MAXIMUM STRENGTH PEPTO-BISMOL—Stomach Remedy—The Procter & Gamble Company; *U.S. Public*, pg. 1330

MAXIMUM STRENGTH TYLENOL SINUS MEDICATION—Proprietary Drugs—McNeil Consumer Products Company; *U.S. Public*, pg. 928

MAXIMUM TREATMENT—Conditioner—Revlon-Realistic Professional Products, Inc.; *U.S. Private*, pg. 690

MAXIN—NONE—AGA Gas, Inc.; *Int'l*, pg. 13

MAXINVERT—Yeast Invertase for the Confectionary Industry—Royal Gist-Brocades N.V.; *Int'l*, pg. 1142

MAXION—Tractors—AGCO Corporation; *U.S. Public*, pg. 28

MAXION—Automotive Products—Iochpe-Maxion S.A.; *Int'l*, pg. 688

MAXION INDUSTRIAL—Farm Machinery—Iochpe-Maxion S.A.; *Int'l*, pg. 688

MAXIPEDIC—Mattress—Simmons Company; *Int'l*, pg. 686

MAXIPOWER—V-Belts—HBD Industries, Inc.; *U.S. Private*, pg. 489

MAXIPRES—Machinery—National Machinery; *U.S. Private*, pg. 785

MAXIPULSE—Seismic Exploration Services—Litton Industries, Inc.; *U.S. Public*, pg. 1002

MAXIREN—Chymosin-Containing Rennet for Cheese Making—Royal Gist-Brocades N.V.; *Int'l*, pg. 1142

MAXIS—Typesetting Terminals & Computers—Eastman Kodak Company; *U.S. Public*, pg. 550

MAXITAP—System for Production of Monoclonal Antibodies—Bausch & Lomb Incorporated; *U.S. Public*, pg. 194

MAXITHINS—Feminine Napkins—The Tranzonic Companies; *U.S. Public*, pg. 1632

MAXITOL—Protective Agent & Softener for Wool—Dexter Chemical Corp.; *U.S. Private*, pg. 329

MAXITROL—Dexamethasone Suspension & Ointment—Alcon Laboratories, Inc.; *Int'l*, pg. 916

MAXITROL—Pressure Regulator Valves—Maxitrol Co.; *U.S. Private*, pg. 716

MAXIVATE LOTION—Topical Steroid—Westwood-Squibb Pharmaceuticals Inc.; *U.S. Public*, pg. 255

MAXIVATE OINTMENT—Topical Steroid—Westwood-Squibb Pharmaceuticals Inc.; *U.S. Public*, pg. 255

MAXIVENT—Bursting Discs—IMI Plc; *Int'l*, pg. 646

MAXIVENT—Anti-Asthma Drug—Roberts Pharmaceutical Corporation; *U.S. Public*, pg. 1393

MAXLIMS—Computerized Laboratory Information Systems—Maxwell Technologies, Inc.; *U.S. Public*, pg. 1061

MAXNET—Distributed System—Modcomp; *U.S. Public*, pg. 283

MAXOLON—Gastrointestinal Drug—SmithKline Beecham plc; *Int'l*, pg. 1264

MAXON—Mfr. Industrial Gas & Oil—Maxon Corporation; *U.S. Private*, pg. 716

MAXOPTIX RXT-800HS DRIVE—Disk Drives—Maxtor Corporation; *Int'l*, pg. 641

MAXOPTIX TAHITI FAMILY—Disk Drives—Maxtor Corporation; *Int'l*, pg. 641

MAXPAC—System—Medtronic, Inc.; *U.S. Public*, pg. 1082

MAXPAC—Industrial Process Monitoring & Control System—Modcomp; *U.S. Public*, pg. 283

MAXPAK—Variable Speed Motor Drives—Rockwell International Corporation; *U.S. Public*, pg. 1397

MAXPLUS—Business Telephone—Comdial Corporation; *U.S. Public*, pg. 407

MAXPLUS—NONE—MTS Systems Corporation; *U.S. Public*, pg. 1028

MAXPLUS II—Telephone—Comdial Corporation; *U.S. Public*, pg. 407

MAXSAVER—Market Rate Interest Savings—Fifth Third Bancorp; *U.S. Public*, pg. 621

MAXSHEAR—In-Line Dispersers—Premier Mill Corp.; *U.S. Private*, pg. 881

MAXSPAN—Vinyl Soffit—CertainTeed Corporation; *Int'l*, pg. 1170

MAXSTAR—Welding & Cutting Equip.—Miller Electric Manufacturing Co.; *U.S. Public*, pg. 867

MAXTALK—Interface Module—Tandem Computers Inc.; *U.S. Public*, pg. 1488

MAXTALK—NONE—UB Networks; *Int'l*, pg. 924

MAXTECH—Industrial Paints—Premier Coatings, Inc.; *Int'l*, pg. 1488

MAXTEMP—Through Hardened Cutting Edges—Bucyrus Blades Inc.; *U.S. Private*, pg. 383

MAXUM—Fiberglass Boats—Brunswick Corporation; *U.S. Public*, pg. 265

MAXUM—Exterior & Interior Coatings—Premier Coatings, Inc.; *Int'l*, pg. 1488

MAXUM—Concentric Reducers—Rockwell International Corporation; *U.S. Public*, pg. 1397

MAXUM—Printer—Videojet Systems International, Inc.; *Int'l*, pg. 545

MAXVUE—Visual Simulator System—CAE Inc.; *Int'l*, pg. 237

MAXWELL—Coffee—Kraft Jacobs Suchard; *U.S. Public*, pg. 1290

MAXWELL HOUSE—Coffee—Kraft Foods, Inc.; *U.S. Public*, pg. 1287

MAXWELL HOUSE—Instant & Ground Coffee—Philip Morris Companies Inc.; *U.S. Public*, pg. 1287

MAXWELL HOUSE FILTER PACKS—Coffee—Kraft Foods, Inc.; *U.S. Public*, pg. 1287

MAXWELL HOUSE PRIVATE COLLECTION—Gourmet Ground Coffee—Kraft Foods, Inc.; *U.S. Public*, pg. 1287

MAXWELL HOUSE SANKA—Decaffeinated Coffee—Kraft Foods, Inc.; *U.S. Public*, pg. 1287

MAXWELL-PHILLIP—Restaurant Equip.—Sterno, Inc.; *U.S. Public*, pg. 397

MAXX—Flow Controller—Interbath, Inc.; *U.S. Private*, pg. 566

MAXX—Special Lager Beer—Pabst Brewing Co./Tumwater; *U.S. Private*, pg. 954

MAXX GRIP—Putty Knives, Scrapers—Hyde Manufacturing Co.; *U.S. Private*, pg. 551

MAXXI—Foods, Non-Foods, General Merchandise—Topco Associates, Inc.; *U.S. Private*, pg. 1091

MAXXIM—Hose—The Goodyear Tire & Rubber Company; *U.S. Public*, pg. 752

MAXXON—Cushion Foam—Bontex; *U.S. Public*, pg. 734

MAXXUM—Two-Wheel-Drive Tractors, 70-100 HP—Case Corporation; *U.S. Public*, pg. 311

MAXXUM—Pencils—Dixon Ticonderoga Company; *U.S. Public*, pg. 514

MAXXUUM—Camera—Minolta Corporation; *Int'l*, pg. 869

MAXZIDE—Diuretic—American Home Products Corporation; *U.S. Public*, pg. 79

MAXZIDE—Anti-Hypertensive Licensed to Lederle—Mylan Laboratories, Inc.; *U.S. Public*, pg. 1143

MAXZIDE 25—Anti-Hypertensive Licensed to Lederle—Mylan Laboratories, Inc.; *U.S. Public*, pg. 1143

MAY & CHRISTE—Ballasts, Transformers—MagneTek, Inc.; *U.S. Public*, pg. 1037

MAYCO—NONE—MultiQuip, Inc.; *Int'l*, pg. 695

MAYDAY—Portable Handheld CB Radios—Kraco Enterprises, Inc.; *U.S. Private*, pg. 634

MAYER—Hosiery & Related Apparel—Mayer/Berkshire Corporation; *U.S. Private*, pg. 717

MAYFAIR—Supermarkets—Arden Group, Inc.; *U.S. Public*, pg. 128

MAYFAIR—Vinyl & Paper Wallcoverings—Forbo Holding SA; *Int'l*, pg. 496

MAYFAIR—NONE—Fortune Brands, Inc.; *U.S. Public*, pg. 674

MAYFAIR—NONE—Gallaher Tobacco Ltd.; *Int'l*, pg. 539

MAYFIELD—Milk & Ice Cream—Dean Foods Company; *U.S. Public*, pg. 489

MAYFRAN—Steel Belt Conveyors—Mayfran International, Inc.; *Int'l*, pg. 1397

MAYNARDS—Jellied Sweets—Cadbury Schweppes p.l.c.; *Int'l*, pg. 247

MAYPO—Hot Cereal—International Home Foods Inc.; *U.S. Private*, pg. 526

MAYROSE—Processed Meats—Armour Swift Eckrich; *U.S. Public*, pg. 426

MAYTAG—NONE—Maytag Cleveland Cooking Products; *U.S. Public*, pg. 1064

MAYTAG—Microwave Ovens, Ranges, Dishwashers, Refrigerators & Washers & Dryers—Maytag Corporation; *U.S. Public*, pg. 1064

MAYTAG—Refrigerators—Maytag Galesburg Refrigeration Products; *U.S. Public*, pg. 1064

MAYTAG AIRCRAFT—NONE—Mercury Air Group Inc.; *U.S. Public*, pg. 1092

MAYTRIX—Chart Paper—Ludlow Corporation; *U.S. Public*, pg. 1651

MAZAMIDE—Surfactants—PPG Industries, Inc.; *U.S. Public*, pg. 1245

MAZAWAX—Surfactants—PPG Industries, Inc.; *U.S. Public*, pg. 1245

MAZAWET—Surfactants—PPG Industries, Inc.; *U.S. Public*, pg. 1245

MAZCLEAN—Concentrated Liquid Detergent for Industrial Cleaning Applications—PPG Industries, Inc.; *U.S. Public*, pg. 1245

MAZDA—Electric Lamps—General Electric Canada Inc.; *U.S. Public*, pg. 713

MAZDA—Automobiles and Trucks—Mazda Motor of America, Inc.; *Int'l*, pg. 849

MAZDA—Batteries—Ralston Purina Company; *U.S. Public*, pg. 1359

MAZDA—Autos & Parts—Transnational Motors Inc.; *U.S. Private*, pg. 1097

MAZDA ANFINI MS-8—NONE—Mazda Motor Corporation; *Int'l*, pg. 849

MAZDA AUTOZAM AZ—NONE—Mazda Motor Corporation; *Int'l*, pg. 849

MAZDA AUTOZAM CAROL—NONE—Mazda Motor Corporation; *Int'l*, pg. 849

MAZDA AUTOZAM CLEF SEDAN—NONE—Mazda Motor Corporation; *Int'l*, pg. 849

MAZDA AUTOZAM SCRUM—Micro-Mini Van & Truck—Mazda Motor Corporation; *Int'l*, pg. 849

MAZDA B SERIES—Pickup—Mazda Motor Corporation; *Int'l*, pg. 849

MAZDA CAPELLA CARGO—Van—Mazda Motor Corporation; *Int'l*, pg. 849

MAZDA E SERIES—Bongo, Bongo Brawny, Pickup/Van/Wagon/Coach—Mazda Motor Corporation; *Int'l*, pg. 849

MAZDA EUNOS COSMO—Coupe—Mazda Motor Corporation; *Int'l*, pg. 849

MAZDA MPV—Minivan—Mazda Motor Corporation; *Int'l*, pg. 849

MAZDA MX-5 ROADSTER—Eunos Roadster—Mazda Motor Corporation; *Int'l*, pg. 849

MAZDA MX-6 COUPE—NONE—Mazda Motor Corporation; *Int'l*, pg. 849

MAZDA MX-3 COUPE—Eunos Presso, Autozam AZ-3—Mazda Motor Corporation; *Int'l*, pg. 849

MAZDA NAVAJO SPORTS UTILITY—NONE—Mazda Motor Corporation; *Int'l*, pg. 849

MADZA 929—Sedan/Hardtop—Mazda Motor Corporation; *Int'l*, pg. 849

MAZDA 121 SEDAN—NONE—Mazda Motor Corporation; *Int'l*, pg. 849

MAZDA PROCEED MARVIE—Sport Utility—Mazda Motor Corporation; *Int'l*, pg. 849

MAZDA RX-7-COUPE—Anfini RX-7—Mazda Motor Corporation; *Int'l*, pg. 849

MAZDA 626-CAPELLA—Sedan/Hatchback/Coupe/Van/Wagon—Mazda Motor Corporation; *Int'l*, pg. 849

MAZDA T SERIES-BUS—Parkway—Mazda Motor Corporation; *Int'l*, pg. 849

MAZDA T SERIES-TITAN—Truck—Mazda Motor Corporation; *Int'l*, pg. 849

MAZDA 323-FAMILIA—Hatchback/Sedan/Wagon/Cabriolet—Mazda Motor Corporation; *Int'l*, pg. 849

MAZDA XEDOS 6 SEDAN—NONE—Mazda Motor Corporation; *Int'l*, pg. 849

MAZE—Specialty Nails—Maze Nails; *U.S. Private*, pg. 718

MAZE & MAYFLOWER—Nominal 4″ Dapple Glazed Tile Avail. w/Decorative Inserts in Blue or Brown—United States Ceramic Tile Co.; *U.S. Private*, pg. 1124

MAZEEN—Surfactants—PPG Industries, Inc.; *U.S. Public*, pg. 1245

MAZEMADE—Specialty Nails—Maze Nails; *U.S. Private*, pg. 718

MAZENATE—Amine Salts Surfactants—PPG Industries, Inc.; *U.S. Public*, pg. 1245

MAZIDE—Pesticide—PPG Industries, Inc.; *U.S. Public*, pg. 1245

MAZOL—Surfactants—PPG Industries, Inc.; *U.S. Public*, pg. 1245

MAZOLA—Corn Oil, Margarine, Regular, Diet & Unsalted—Best Foods; *U.S. Public*, pg. 224

MAZOLA—Corn Oil & Margarine, Mayonnaise,—Bestfoods; *U.S. Public*, pg. 223

MAZOLA—Corn Oil—CPC Foods (Ireland) Ltd.; *U.S. Public*, pg. 225

MAZOLA—Corn Oil—CPC Foodservice Group; *U.S. Public*, pg. 224

MAZOLA—Corn Oil & Mayonnaise—Refinerias de Maiz S.A.I.C.F.; *U.S. Public*, pg. 448

MAZOLA NO STICK—Aerosol Cooking Aid—Best Foods; *U.S. Public*, pg. 224

MAZON—Surfactants—PPG Industries, Inc.; *U.S. Public*, pg. 1245

MAZOX—Surfactants—PPG Industries, Inc.; *U.S. Public*, pg. 1245

MAZSPERSE—Organic Dispersant Chemicals for Water Treatment Applications—PPG Industries, Inc.; *U.S. Public*, pg. 1245

MAZTREAT—Antiscalant Surfactants—PPG Industries, Inc.; *U.S. Public*, pg. 1245

MAZTROL—Oil Field Treating Chemicals, Pour Point Depressants, Corrosion Inhibitors—PPG Industries, Inc.; *U.S. Public*, pg. 1245

MAZU—Surfactants—PPG Industries, Inc.; *U.S. Public*, pg. 1245

MAZVAP—Evaporator Antiscalant Chemicals for Multiple Effect Evaporators—PPG Industries, Inc.; *U.S. Public*, pg. 1245

MAZZETTI GRAPPA FRUITTI, ROSE, GEMME—Grappa—Laird & Company; *U.S. Private*, pg. 642

MAZZONI—Wine—Paterno Imports Limited; *U.S. Private*, pg. 843

MCARTHUR—Milk—Dean Foods Company; *U.S. Public*, pg. 489

MCBEE—One-Write Bookeeping Systems & Business Forms—McBee Systems, Inc.; *U.S. Private*, pg. 718

MCBRIAR SPORTSWEAR—NONE—Nutmeg Mills Inc.; *U.S. Public*, pg. 1702

MCCAIN—Juices—McCain Citrus Inc.; *Int'l*, pg. 850

MCCAIN—Foods—McCain Foods Inc.; *Int'l*, pg. 850

MCCAIN—Juice, Vegetables & Frozen Potato Products—McCain Foods Limited; *Int'l*, pg. 850

MCCAIN ZIPPINI—Juice Boxes—McCain Citrus Inc.; *Int'l*, pg. 850

MCCALL—Reach-in Refrigerator & Freezers—The Manitowoc Company, Inc.; *U.S. Public*, pg. 1040

McCALLS—Vodka—Montebello Brands Inc.; *U.S. Private*, pg. 758

McCALLS CANADIAN—Whiskey—Montebello Brands Inc.; *U.S. Private*, pg. 758

MCCANN'S—Irish Oatmeal Cookies—RCB Baking Company; *U.S. Public*, pg. 1354

MCCARTY FARMS—Chicken Products—Tyson Foods, Inc.; *U.S. Public*, pg. 1652

MCCARVEY—Coffee—Superior Coffee and Foods; *U.S. Public*, pg. 1434

MCCAW—Cellular Communications—AT&T Wireless Services; *U.S. Public*, pg. 11

MCCAW TELEANSWER—Paging Service Provider—AT&T Wireless Services; *U.S. Public*, pg. 11

MCCAW TELEPAGE—Paging Service Provider—AT&T Wireless Services; *U.S. Public*, pg. 11

MCCHICKEN—Chicken Sandwich—McDonald's Corporation; *U.S. Public*, pg. 1068

MCCLAREN—Tires & Tubes—Bridgestone/Firestone, Inc.; *Int'l*, pg. 213

MCCLATCHY—Newspapers—McClatchy Newspapers Inc.; *U.S. Public*, pg. 1065

MCCLOSKEY—Paint—The Valspar Corporation; *U.S. Public*, pg. 1707

MCCOLLS—Dairy Produts—Crystal Cream & Butter Company; *U.S. Private*, pg. 294

MCCOLL'S—Scotch Whiskey—John Gross & Co.; *U.S. Private*, pg. 483

MCCOLLS SCOTCH—NONE—Star Industries Inc.; *U.S. Private*, pg. 1034

MCCORMICK—Spices, Extracts—McCormick & Company, Incorporated; *U.S. Public*, pg. 1066

MCCORMICK—Distilled Spirits—McCormick Distilling Co.; *U.S. Private*, pg. 720

MCCORMICK COLLECTION—Sauce Mixes & Seasonings—McCormick/Schilling; *U.S. Public*, pg. 1066

MCCORMICK PLACE ON THE LAKE—Restaurant—The Levy Organization; *U.S. Private*, pg. 664

MCCORMICK-SCHILLING—Spices, Extracts, Seasonings—McCormick/Schilling; *U.S. Public*, pg. 1066

MCCORMICKS—Cookies—Culinar Inc.; *Int'l*, pg. 348

MCCORMICK'S GOODY—Confectionery—Culinar Inc.; *Int'l*, pg. 348

MCCOURT—Labels—McCourt Label Co.; *U.S. Private*, pg. 720

MCCRARY—Saw Blades—Vermont American Tool Corp.; *U.S. Public*, pg. 575

MCCULLOUGH—Well-Logging & Perforating Services—Litton Industries, Inc.; *U.S. Public*, pg. 1002

MCCULLOUGH—NONE—Western Atlas Logging Services; *U.S. Public*, pg. 1757

MCDONALDLAND—Playground—McDonald's Corporation; *U.S. Public*, pg. 1068

MCDONALD'S—Pure Maple Syrup—Borden, Inc.; *U.S. Private*, pg. 157

MCDONALD'S—Fast Food—McDonald's Hamburgers Limited; *U.S. Public*, pg. 1069

MCDONALD'S HAMBURGERS—Sandwich—McDonald's Corporation; *U.S. Public*, pg. 1068

MCDONNELLL & MILLER—Boiler Controls & Flow Switches—ITT Fluid Handling; *U.S. Public*, pg. 860

MCDOUGAL LITTELL & COMPANY—Textbook Pubishers—McDougal/Littell; *U.S. Public*, pg. 841

MCDOUGALL'S—Specialty Foods—Ranks Hovis McDougall Limited; *Int'l*, pg. 1395

MCEWAN'S—Ales—Scottish & Newcastle plc; *Int'l*, pg. 1211

MCEWANS EXPORT—Ale—Scottish & Newcastle Importers Co.; *Int'l*, pg. 1212

MCEWANS SCOTCH—Ale—Scottish & Newcastle Importers Co.; *Int'l*, pg. 1212

MCGRAW-EDISON—Indoor & Outdoor Lighting & Industrial Electrical Equipment—Cooper Industries, Inc.; *U.S. Public*, pg. 442

MCGRAW-HILL—Publisher—The McGraw-Hill Companies; *U.S. Public*, pg. 1069

McGREGOR—Headwear—AJD; *U.S. Private*, pg. 510

MCGREGOR—NONE—M. Fine & Sons Manufacturing Co., Inc.; *U.S. Private*, pg. 405

MCGREGOR—Slacks, Jeans, Shorts—The Spencer Group Inc.; *U.S. Private*, pg. 1025

MCGUFFEY'S—Restaurants—McGuffey's Restaurants, Inc.; *U.S. Private*, pg. 721

MCGUIRE—Door Levelers/Seals/Shelters; Traffic Doors—Overhead Door Corporation; *U.S. Private*, pg. 822

MCGUIRES—Cream Liqueur—NWS Inc.; *U.S. Private*, pg. 772

MCHENRY COUNTY (IL) BUSINESS DIRECTORY—Directory—Manufacturers' News, Inc.; *U.S. Private*, pg. 700

MCILHENNY FARMS—Pepper Sauce—McIlhenny Company; *U.S. Private*, pg. 722

MCKEE—Snacks—McKee Foods Corporation; *U.S. Private*, pg. 723

MCKENZIE—NONE—Berg Electronics; *U.S. Public*, pg. 212

MCKENZIE TOWABLES—Towable Recreational Vehicles—Monaco Coach Corporation; *U.S. Public*, pg. 1123

MCKENZIE'S—Frozen Vegetables & Fruit—Curtice Burns Foods; *U.S. Private*, pg. 887

MCKENZIE'S—Frozen Food—Southern Frozen Foods; *U.S. Private*, pg. 887

MCKESSON—Examining & Operatory Equipment—Getinge/Castle Inc.; *Int'l*, pg. 551

MCKESSON—Proprietary Drugs—McKesson U.S. Health Care; *U.S. Public*, pg. 1073

MCKIDS—Children's Clothing—McDonald's Corporation; *U.S. Public*, pg. 1068

MCKINNEY—Door Hinges—Essex Industries, Inc.; *Int'l*, pg. 18

MCKINNEY/PARKER—Washroom Accessories—Essex Industries, Inc.; *Int'l*, pg. 18

MCLARENS—Pickles & Relishes—International Multifoods Corporation; *U.S. Public*, pg. 900

McLARENS—Pickels & Condiments—Robin Hood Multifoods Inc.; *U.S. Public*, pg. 901

MCLEAN DELUXE—91% Fat Free Hamburger Sandwich—McDonald's Corporation; *U.S. Public*, pg. 1068

MCMAHON—Snaps & Swivels—Outdoor Technologies Group; *U.S. Private*, pg. 822

MCMILLIN—Fried Pies & Pecan Pies—The Pillsbury Company; *Int'l*, pg. 18

MCNAUGHTON CANADIAN—Canadian Whiskey—United Distillers USA, Inc.; *Int'l*, pg. 412

MCNEIL—NONE—Johnson & Johnson; *U.S. Public*, pg. 927

MCNESS—Feed Premix & Household Products—Furst-McNess Company; *U.S. Private*, pg. 432

MCOS—Operating System—Mercury Computer Systems, Inc.; *U.S. Private*, pg. 732

MCPHILBEN—Indoor & Outdoor Lighting Fixtures—Thomas Industries Inc.; *U.S. Public*, pg. 1598

MCPHILBEN—Lighting—Thomas Lighting-C&I Indoor Divison; *U.S. Public*, pg. 1599

MCQUAY—Commercial Air Conditioning & Heating—AAF McQuay, Inc.; *U.S. Private*, pg. 2

MCQUAY AIR CONDITIONING—HVAC Products—McQuay International; *U.S. Private*, pg. 3

MCQUICK'S OILUBE, INC.—Fast Lube Centers—Quaker State Corporation; *U.S. Public*, pg. 1348

MCRAE'S—Department Stores—McRae's, Inc.; *U.S. Public*, pg. 1333

MCRAE'S—Department Store—Proffitt's, Inc.; *U.S. Public*, pg. 1333

MCTUFF 1, 2, 3—Die Blocks—McInnes Steel Company; *U.S. Private*, pg. 722

MCVITIE'S BISCUITS—Biscuits—United Biscuits (Holdings) Plc; *Int'l*, pg. 1442

MCVITIES—Biscuits—United Biscuits (UK) Limited; *Int'l*, pg. 1442

MDII SERIES—Newest Generation of Compact Hematology Analyzers—Beckman Coulter; *U.S. Public*, pg. 199

ME & MY CAT—Moist Cat Food—H.J. Heinz Co. of Canada Ltd.; *U.S. Public*, pg. 806

ME DESIGN—Electric Decorative Lighting Sets & Parts—General Cable Corporation; *Int'l*, pg. 1486

ME N YOU—Children's Clothing—S. Schwab Company; *U.S. Private*, pg. 974

ME-2—Loungewear—Miss Elaine Inc.; *U.S. Private*, pg. 752

ME-2—Hardness Tester—Newage Industries Inc., Testing Instruments Group; *U.S. Private*, pg. 796

ME-Z—Hardness Tester—NewAge Industries Inc.; *U.S. Private*, pg. 796

MEAD—Corporate Signature—The Mead Corporation; *U.S. Public*, pg. 1074

MEAD—Retail Displays—Mead Packaging; *U.S. Public*, pg. 1074

MEAD—Office Supplies—Mead School & Office Products; *U.S. Public*, pg. 1074

MEAD DATA CENTRAL—Computerized Research Services—The Mead Corporation; *U.S. Public*, pg. 1074

MEAD FORM-L BOARD—Paperboard—The Mead Corporation; *U.S. Public*, pg. 1074

MEAD GRAD—Stationery Items—The Mead Corporation; *U.S. Public*, pg. 1074

MEAD HARMONY—Recycled Paper—The Mead Corporation; *U.S. Public*, pg. 1074

MEAD KOLUMN KASE—Shipping Container—The Mead Corporation; *U.S. Public*, pg. 1074

MEAD MARK 1—High Gloss Paper—The Mead Corporation; *U.S. Public*, pg. 1074

MEAD OFFSET ENAMEL—Coated Offset Printing Paper—The Mead Corporation; *U.S. Public*, pg. 1074

MEAD OPAS—Carbonless Paper—The Mead Corporation; *U.S. Public*, pg. 1074

MEAD OPAS—Carbonless Paper & Coating Agents for Paper; Consulting Service—The Mead Corporation; *U.S. Public*, pg. 1074

MEAD PAN-L BOARD—Paperboard—The Mead Corporation; *U.S. Public*, pg. 1074

MEAD POLAR-CORR—Corrugated Board & Cartons—The Mead Corporation; *U.S. Public*, pg. 1074

MEAD WEB ENAMEL—Printing Paper—The Mead Corporation; *U.S. Public*, pg. 1074

MEADNET—Computerized Research Services—The Mead Corporation; *U.S. Public*, pg. 1074

MEADOMATIC—Containers—The Mead Corporation; *U.S. Public*, pg. 1074

MEADOW BLEND—Soap-Free Liquid Cleanser & Soap Bar—Shaklee Corporation; *Int'l*, pg. 1518

MEADOW CREEK—Manufactured Homes—Champion Enterprises, Inc.; *U.S. Public*, pg. 332

MEADOW GOLD—Dairy Products, Fruit Drinks & Ice Cream Novelties—Borden, Inc.; *U.S. Private*, pg. 157

MEADOW GOLD—NONE—Medical Meadow Gold Dairies, Inc.; *U.S. Public*, pg. 1016

MEADOW LEA—Margarine—Goodman Fielder Limited; *Int'l*, pg. 555

MEADOWCRAFT—Metal Household Furniture—Meadowcraft, Inc.; *U.S. Private*, pg. 725

MEAL-IN-ONE—Microwave Ovens—Litton Industries, Inc.; *U.S. Public*, pg. 1002

MEAL-TIME—Feeding System or Feeder—CTB International Corp.; *U.S. Public*, pg. 284

MEALMASTER FEEDKAR—Cage Feeder—CTB International Corp.; *U.S. Public*, pg. 284

MEAN GREENS—Collard Greens—Kentucky Fried Chicken Corporation (KFC); *U.S. Public*, pg. 1636

MEAN MACHINES SEGA—Games Magazine—EMAP Images; *Int'l*, pg. 451

MEAN STREAK—Waterproof Marking Pen—Sanford Corporation; *U.S. Public*, pg. 1178

MEARS—Heating Controls—Eaton Corporation; *U.S. Public*, pg. 555

MEARS—Heating Controls—Eaton Corporation Automotive Controls Division; *U.S. Public*, pg. 557

THE MEASURABLE DIFFERENCE—Gages—Moore Products Co.; *U.S. Public*, pg. 1128

MEASURE—Software Tool—Tandem Computers Inc.; *U.S. Public*, pg. 417

MEASURE MASTER—Two Piece Orifice Meters—Perry Equipment Corporation; *U.S. Private*, pg. 855

MEASURE MAX—NONE—Giddings & Lewis Sheffield Measurement Systems; *Int'l*, pg. 1389

MEASURE MISER—Portion Control Serving Spoons—Carlisle Food Service Products; *U.S. Public*, pg. 305

MEASUROMETER II—Precise Industrial Monitors—Analogic Corporation; *U.S. Public*, pg. 109

MEATY BONE—Dog Biscuits—H.J. Heinz Company; *U.S. Public*, pg. 805

MEATY BONE—Dog Biscuits—Star-Kist Foods Inc.; *U.S. Public*, pg. 805

MEATY BONES—NONE—Star-Kist Foods, Inc.; *U.S. Public*, pg. 806

MEBENDAZOLE—Anthelmintics—Kyowa Hakko Kogyo Company, Ltd.; *Int'l*, pg. 778

MEBES III—Electron Beam Lithography System Mask Writing—Etec Systems, Inc.; *U.S. Public*, pg. 594

MEBICINA—Tobramycin—Eli Lilly Italia, S.p.A.; *U.S. Public*, pg. 994

MECAFRANCE—Valves—IMI Plc; *Int'l*, pg. 646

MECANIPLAST—Automobile Antennas—Fiamm S.p.A.; *Int'l*, pg. 480

MECAR—Weapon Systems—Allied Research Corporation; *U.S. Public*, pg. 48

MECHANALYSIS—Vibration Analysis Systems—IRD Mechanalysis, Inc. (U.S.A.); *U.S. Public*, pg. 789

MECHANIC TO MECHANIC—Educational Services—American Suzuki Motor Corporation; *Int'l*, pg. 1323

MECHANICA—Mechanical Pencils—Pentel of America, Ltd.; *Int'l*, pg. 1035

MECHANICAL-T—Bolted Branch Outlet—Victaulic Company of America; *U.S. Private*, pg. 1138

MECO—Outdoor Access—Meco Corporation; *U.S. Private*, pg. 726

MECO BELTS—NONE—Joy Mining Machinery; *U.S. Public*, pg. 790

MED-LEMON—Coughs, Colds & Influenza Product—SmithKline Beecham plc; *Int'l*, pg. 1264

MED-PAK—Medical Supply Division—Uniflex, Inc.; *U.S. Public*, pg. 1665

MED-TOX—Medical Toxicity Analysis Program—Ecology and Environment, Inc.; *U.S. Public*, pg. 562

MEDA'S—Highway Restaurants—Accor S.A.; *Int'l*, pg. 20

MEDADI—Diamond Knife Sharpener Compound—Buehler, Limited; *U.S. Public*, pg. 574

MEDAGLIA D'ORO—Expresso—Tetley USA Inc.; *Int'l*, pg. 1377

MEDAL OF HONOR—Pipe Tobacco & Cigars—Lane Limited; *Int'l*, pg. 1129

MEDALIST—Contact Lens—Bausch & Lomb Incorporated; *U.S. Public*, pg. 194

MEDALIST—Abrasive—Carborundum Abrasives North America; *Int'l*, pg. 1174

MEDALIST—Sheet Vinyl Flooring—Congoleum Corporation; *U.S. Public*, pg. 69

MEDALIST—Photographic Paper, Cameras & Projectors—Eastman Kodak Company; *U.S. Public*, pg. 550

MEDALIST SST—Wiring Devices—Pass & Seymour/Legrand; *Int'l*, pg. 806

MEDALLION—Enamels—Colony Paints; *U.S. Public*, pg. 1707

MEDALLION—Car Seat—Evenflo Company, Inc.; *U.S. Private*, pg. 629

MEDALLION—Ranges, Refrigerators, Dishwashers, Clothes Washers & Dryers—General Electric Canada Inc.; *U.S. Public*, pg. 713

MEDALLION—Drapery Hardware-Window Blinds—Kirsch; *U.S. Public*, pg. 1176

MEDALLION—Syringes—Merit Medical Systems, Inc.; *U.S. Public*, pg. 1096

MEDALLION—Air Conditioners—Nordyne Inc.; *U.S. Public*, pg. 1193

MEDALLION—Air Conditioners—Nortek, Inc.; *U.S. Public*, pg. 1192

MEDALLION—Quiet Lockers—Penco Products; *U.S. Private*, pg. 848

MEDALLION CONSTRUCTION—NONE—Timberline Software Corporation; *U.S. Public*, pg. 1609

MEDALLION QUALITY FEEDS—Horse Feed—Southern States Cooperative, Inc.; *U.S. Private*, pg. 1017

MEDCHECK—Bill Review & Reimbursement Provider—CorVel Corporation; *U.S. Public*, pg. 451

MEDCO—Containment Services—MEDCO Containment Services, Inc.; *U.S. Public*, pg. 1091

MEDCREST—Textile Division—Medline Industries, Inc.; *U.S. Private*, pg. 728

MEDEC COMMUNICATIONS—Communication Services—Medical Economics Company Inc.; *U.S. Public*, pg. 1601

MEDEC DENTAL COMMUNICATIONS—Dental Publications—Medical Economics Company Inc.; *U.S. Public*, pg. 1601

MEDEI—Cuisine—Ventre Packing Company, Inc.; *U.S. Private*, pg. 1135

MEDELEC—Neuro-Diagnostic Equipment—Vickers PLC; *Int'l*, pg. 1466

MEDEMYCIN—Antibiotics—Meiji Seika Kaisha, Ltd.; *Int'l*, pg. 855

MEDERIA—Mobile Home—Wick Bldg. Systems Inc. Manufactured Homes Div.; *U.S. Private*, pg. 1174

MEDEX—NONE—Blue Cross and Blue Shield of Massachusetts; *U.S. Private*, pg. 151

MEDFORD'S—Meat Products—Hatfield Quality Meats; *U.S. Private*, pg. 510

MEDGRAPHICS—Testing System—Medical Graphics Corp.; *U.S. Public*, pg. 1080

MEDI-CAN—Designer Inspired, OSHA Compliant: Steel Step Cans—United Receptical, Inc.; *U.S. Private*, pg. 1123

MEDI CLEAN—Medicated Pet Shampoo—Carter-Wallace, Inc.; *U.S. Public*, pg. 309

MEDI-COIL—Mattress—Therapedic Associates, Inc.; *U.S. Private*, pg. 1079

MEDI-GUARD—Dietary supplements—American Stores Company; *U.S. Public*, pg. 92

MEDI QUIK—First Aid Products—Mentholatum Company; *Int'l*, pg. 1126

MEDI SCOPASTE BANDAGE—NONE—Graham-Field Health Products, Inc.; *U.S. Public*, pg. 757

MEDI-TYPE—TPE Tubing For Use in Medical Applications & Manufacturing—The West Company, Incorporated; *U.S. Public*, pg. 1755

MEDI-VAC—Medical Suction Collection Containers & Associated Attachments—Allegiance Healthcare Corp.; *U.S. Public*, pg. 44

MEDI-AID—Wound Dressing Products—PolyMedica Industries, Inc.; *U.S. Public*, pg. 1315

MEDIA ASSURANCES—NONE—CLT-UFA; *Int'l*, pg. 561

MEDIA BOX—NONE—Posso S.A.; *Int'l*, pg. 1064

MEDIA MATE—Computer Products—Esselte Corporation; *Int'l*, pg. 459

MEDIA MAX—Large Group Conferencing Systems—VTEL Corporation; *U.S. Public*, pg. 1703

MEDIA PLAY—Pre-recorded Audio & Video Tapes, CD's, Books, Software, & Greeting Cards—Musicland Group Inc.; *U.S. Public*, pg. 1142

MEDIA PROFESSIONAL—Radio Audience Measurement Software—The Arbitron Company; *U.S. Public*, pg. 331

MEDIAEXPRESS—Image Display System—Proxima Corporation; *U.S. Public*, pg. 1339

MEDIAKING—Single-Width, Web Offset Press—Publishers Equipment Corporation; *U.S. Public*, pg. 1341

MEDIAMATE—multimedia Speaker—Bose Corporation; *U.S. Private*, pg. 160

MEDIAPATH—Voice Operating System Running Under Microsoft Windows—Mitel Corporation; *Int'l*, pg. 870

MEDIAWEEK—Advertisers & Agencies Magazine—BPI Communications Inc.; *Int'l*, pg. 1446

MEDIBASE—Physician List Management—Pharmaceutical Marketing Services Inc.; *U.S. Public*, pg. 1284

MEDIC-5—Emergency Monitoring System—Burdick, Inc.; *U.S. Private*, pg. 181

MEDICAL—Hair Care—Palm Beach Beauty Products Co.; *U.S. Private*, pg. 834

MEDICAL ASSURANCE—Provider of Liability Insurance to Physicians, Hospitals & Dentists—Medical Assurance, Inc.; *U.S. Public*, pg. 1079

MEDICAL BLUE—Patient Care Products—The Vollrath Company, L.L.C.; *U.S. Private*, pg. 1143

MEDICAL CARE PRODUCTS—Patient-Care, Product News Publication—Reed Elsevier Business Information; *Int'l*, pg. 1095

MEDICAL DESIGN TECHNOLOGY—Tabloid Supplying Information About New Products, Services & Applications—Reed Elsevier Business Information; *Int'l*, pg. 1095

MEDICAL DEVICE TECHNOLOGY—Trade Periodical—Advanstar Communicåtions; *U.S. Private*, pg. 22

MEDICAL ECONOMICS—Magazine—Medical Economics Company Inc.; *U.S. Public*, pg. 1601

MEDICAL ECONOMICS FOR SURGEONS—Medical Publication—Medical Economics Company Inc.; *U.S. Public*, pg. 1601

MEDICAL IMAGING & MONITORING—Magazine—Reed Business Information Pty. Limited; *Int'l*, pg. 1094

MEDICAL IMAGING SYSTEMS—Sale of X-Ray & Medical Imaging Equipment—Halma p.l.c.; *Int'l*, pg. 589

MEDICAL INNOVATIONS CORPORATION—NONE—Ballard Medical Products; *U.S. Public*, pg. 171

MEDICAL LABORATORY OBSERVOR—Medical Publication—Medical Economics Company Inc.; *U.S. Public*, pg. 1601

MEDICAL-PAK I.V.—Laminates of Aluminum Foil & Plastic Film & Pouches—Reynolds Metals Company; *U.S. Public*, pg. 1385

MEDICAL UPDATE—Newsletter—Benjamin Franklin Literary & Medical Society, Inc.; *U.S. Private*, pg. 133

MEDICALODGE—Health Care Facility—Medicalodges, Inc.; *U.S. Private*, pg. 728

MEDICARB—Carbon Artificial Joint Surfaces—BTR plc; *Int'l*, pg. 124

MEDICATED FLOWLINE MEI GUI HUA—Hair Growth Tonic—Shiseido Company Ltd.; *Int'l*, pg. 1235

THE MEDICINE SHOPPE—NONE—Cardinal Health Inc.; *U.S. Public*, pg. 304

THE MEDICINE SHOPPE—Professional Pharmacies—Medicine Shoppe International, Inc.; *U.S. Public*, pg. 304

MEDICIPS—Tubes for Hospital & Laboratory Services—KM-Europa Metal Aktiengesellschaft; *Int'l*, pg. 719

MEDICO—Smoking Pipes & Related Products—S.M. Frank & Co., Inc.; *U.S. Private*, pg. 423

MEDICYL—NONE—AGA Gas, Inc.; *Int'l*, pg. 13

MEDIGUARD—NONE—Rentokil Initial plc; *Int'l*, pg. 1285

MEDIHALER—Inhalers, Prescription Drug—3M; *U.S. Public*, pg. 1604

MEDILITE—Homecare—AGA Ges.m.b.H.; *Int'l*, pg. 13

MEDIMAT—Electrolytic Apparatus for Treating Liquid Protein Solutions—Ionics, Incorporated; *U.S. Public*, pg. 912

MEDIMEDIA PUBLICATIONS—Pre-Recorded Tape Cassettes—John Wiley & Sons, Inc.; *U.S. Public*, pg. 1768

MEDIMIST—Nebulizer—CAIRE, Inc.; *U.S. Private*, pg. 751

MEDIAONE—Multiple Systems Cable TV—MediaOne; *U.S. Public*, pg. 1688

MEDIPAD—NONE—Elan Corporation Plc; *Int'l*, pg. 435

MEDIPLAST—Salicylic Acid Plaster—Beiersdorf, Inc.; *Int'l*, pg. 182

MEDIPORE—Dressing Cover—3M; *U.S. Public*, pg. 1604

MEDIQ—Healthcare Services—MEDIQ Incorporated; *U.S. Public*, pg. 1081

MEDIQ/PRN—NONE—MEDIQ Incorporated; *U.S. Public*, pg. 1081

MEDIS—Computerized Research Services—The Mead Corporation; *U.S. Public*, pg. 1074

MEDISCOPE—NONE—Market Facts, Inc.; *U.S. Public*, pg. 1046

MEDISTRAINTS—Restraints—Medline Industries, Inc.; *U.S. Private*, pg. 728

MEDITE—Reconstituted Wood Panels—Valhi, Inc.; *U.S. Private*, pg. 270

MEDITRON—Electro-Surgical Devices—BEI Medical Systems Company; *U.S. Private*, pg. 106

MEDIWALK—Homecare—AGA Ges.m.b.H.; *Int'l*, pg. 13

MEDIX-VISITRAY—Card Indexers—Carstens Inc.; *U.S. Private*, pg. 216

MEDLINE—Health Care Prods.—Medline Industries, Inc.; *U.S. Private*, pg. 728

MEDLINK—Business Assistance Network & Software—Eastman Kodak Company; *U.S. Public*, pg. 550

MEDLINK—(Sub-acute services)—National Health Care Affiliates, Inc.; *U.S. Private*, pg. 784

MEDNET—Internal Medicine—Cerner Corporation; *U.S. Public*, pg. 331

MEDREC II—Medical Chart Management System—Lanier Worldwide Inc.; *U.S. Public*, pg. 791

MEDSTATION—NONE—Cardinal Health Inc.; *U.S. Public*, pg. 304

MEDSTONE STS LITHOTRIPTER—Stop Gap Technology for Treatment of Kidney Stones—Medstone International, Inc.; *U.S. Public*, pg. 1082

MEDTRONIC—Model & Logo—Medtronic, Inc.; *U.S. Public*, pg. 1082

MEDTRONIC CARDIOVASCULAR ALLIANCE—Marketing Program—Medtronic, Inc.; *U.S. Public*, pg. 1082

MEDTRONIC FIRST ALLIANCE—NONE—Medtronic, Inc.; *U.S. Public*, pg. 1082

MEDTRONIC HALL—Prosthetic Heart Valve—Medtronic, Inc.; *U.S. Public*, pg. 1082

MEDTRONIC NEURO—Logo—Medtronic, Inc.; *U.S. Public*, pg. 1082

MEDTRONIC PREFERRED ALLIANCE—NONE—Medtronic, Inc.; *U.S. Public*, pg. 1082

MEDTRONIC PULSE—Publication—Medtronic, Inc.; *U.S. Public*, pg. 1082

MEDUSA—Cement—Medusa Corporation; *U.S. Public*, pg. 1084

MEDWEAVE—Bedspread—Medline Industries, Inc.; *U.S. Private*, pg. 728

MEDWIRE—Medical Wire—Sigmund Cohn Corp.; *U.S. Private*, pg. 250

MEDWORD—Medical Transcription—Lanier Worldwide Inc.; *U.S. Public*, pg. 791

MEE TU—Chinese Condiments—Allied Old English, Inc.; *U.S. Private*, pg. 39

MEERENDAL ESTATE—Wine—Distillers Corporation S.A.; *Int'l*, pg. 1129

MEERLUST ESTATE—Wine—Distillers Corporation S.A.; *Int'l*, pg. 1129

MEESTER—Meat Products—Koninklijke Ahold NV; *Int'l*, pg. 749

MEET ME—Paging Infrastructure Equipment System—Glenayre Technologies, Inc.; *U.S. Public*, pg. 746

MEETING NEWS—Newspaper—Miller Freeman Inc.; *Int'l*, pg. 1443

MEFIAG—Filtration Systems—Met-Pro Corporation; *U.S. Public*, pg. 1100

MEFOREX—CFC Substitutes—Montedison S.p.A.; *Int'l*, pg. 324

MEFOXIN—Cefoxitin—Merck & Co., Inc.; *U.S. Public*, pg. 1090

MEFOXIN—Pharmaceutical—Merck Human Health Division (U.S. Human Health); *U.S. Public*, pg. 1091

MEG-O-METER—Assembly—Millipore Corporation; *U.S. Public*, pg. 1112

MEGA—Hockey Equipment—Bauer Sports Inc.; *U.S. Public*, pg. 1184

MEGA—Library—The Mead Corporation; *U.S. Public*, pg. 1074

MEGA—Medical Electronic Gas Alarms System—Nellcor Puritan Bennett Incorporated; *U.S. Public*, pg. 1039

MEGA—Dry Groceries & Frozen Foods—Topco Associates, Inc.; *U.S. Private*, pg. 1091

MEGA BITE—Instrument—U.S. Surgical Corp.; *U.S. Public*, pg. 1687

MEGA BOND ELUT—Large Volume Solid Phase Extraction Columns—Varian Associates, Inc.; *U.S. Public*, pg. 1710

MEGA BUMP FLOAM—Toys—Mattel, Inc.; *U.S. Public*, pg. 1057

THE MEGA CARTRIDGES—Videogames—Sega of America Inc.; *Int'l*, pg. 1218

MEGA DEAL—NONE—Nomura Securities International, Inc.; *Int'l*, pg. 956

MEGA FUSE—Auto Fuse—Littelfuse, Inc.; *U.S. Public*, pg. 1001

MEGA-HEALTH 75—Vitamin—Health Products Corporation; *U.S. Private*, pg. 514

MEGA PURE—Glass Still—Barnstead/Thermolyne Corporation; *U.S. Public*, pg. 1545

MEGA STRESS CAPSULES & TABLETS—B-Complex with 500 mg. Vitamin C—Weider Nutrition Intl.; *U.S. Private*, pg. 1159

MEGA TR—Tires—The Hercules Tire & Rubber Company; *U.S. Private*, pg. 523

MEGA-LASER—Printing Ink—Van Son Holland Ink Corp. of America; *U.S. Private*, pg. 1133

MEGABAR—NONE—Ryan's Family Steak Houses, Inc.; *U.S. Public*, pg. 1413

MEGABLOC—Low-Pressure Centrifugal Pumps in Close-Coupled Design—KSB Aktiengesellschaft; *Int'l*, pg. 721

MEGACAST—Castables—A.P. Green Industries, Inc.; *U.S. Public*, pg. 761

MEGACE—Anti-Cancer Agent—Bristol-Myers Squibb Company; *U.S. Public*, pg. 253

MEGACE—Progestational Product—Bristol-Myers Squibb U.S. Pharmaceutical Group; *U.S. Public*, pg. 255

MEGACENTER—Computer Recovery Disaster Center—SunGard Data Systems Inc.; *U.S. Public*, pg. 1534

MEGACHASSIS—Electronic Instrument—Intel Corporation; *U.S. Public*, pg. 886

MEGADAC—Multi-Channel Electronics—Bowthorpe plc; *Int'l*, pg. 207

MEGAELEKTRA—NONE—Grupo Elektra S.A. de C.V.; *Int'l*, pg. 573

MEGAFLEX—NONE—Gates Europe; *Int'l*, pg. 1396

MEGAHUB—High Capacity Telecommunications Switching System—DSC Communications Corporation; *U.S. Public*, pg. 475

MEGALAC RUMEN BYPASS FAT—Animal Nutrition Supplement—Church & Dwight Co., Inc.; *U.S. Public*, pg. 355

MEGALOC 1—Plumbing Chemical—Hercules Chemical Co., Inc.; *U.S. Private*, pg. 523

MEGAMELON—Melon Fruit Drink—Ocean Spray Cranberries, Inc.; *U.S. Private*, pg. 811

MEGAMARKET—SUPERMARKET—Jitney-Jungle Stores of America, Inc.; *U.S. Private*, pg. 588

MEGAMISER—Carbottom Furnace—Lindberg, A General Signal Company; *U.S. Public*, pg. 727

MEGANORM—Low-Pressure Centrifugal Pumps—KSB Aktiengesellschaft; *Int'l*, pg. 721

MEGAPLUS—Image Sensing Cameras—Eastman Kodak Company; *U.S. Public*, pg. 550

MEGARAD—Polycarbonate Resins—The Dow Chemical Company; *U.S. Public*, pg. 522

MEGAS—Cotton—American Safety Razor Company; *U.S. Private*, pg. 597

MEGASORB—Industrial & Laboratory Vacuum Pumps—Varian Associates, Inc.; *U.S. Public*, pg. 1710

MEGASOURCE—Viewer—Eastman Kodak Company; *U.S. Public*, pg. 550

MEGASPINAL—NONE—Gates Europe; *Int'l*, pg. 1396

MEGASTREAM—High Capacity Digital Private Circuit—British Telecommunications plc; *Int'l*, pg. 222

MEGASYS—Total Gas Management Systems for the Electronic Industry—Air Products and Chemicals, Inc.; *U.S. Public*, pg. 30

MEGASYS—Hydraulic Hoses & Couplings—The Gates Rubber Company; *Int'l*, pg. 1396

MEGATHERM—Thermal Storage—Precision Parts Corp.; *U.S. Private*, pg. 879

MEGAVIEW—Integrated Network Management Architecture—General Datacomm Industries, Inc.; *U.S. Public*, pg. 708

MEGGAGEWAY—Electronic Data Interchange Software—Tandem Computers Inc.; *U.S. Public*, pg. 417

MEGGER—Electrical Insulation Testers—Avo International; *U.S. Private*, pg. 9

MEGGER—Electrial Test & Measuring Instrument—AVO International; *Int'l*, pg. 1335

MEGGRAB—Software for Imaging Sensing Cameras—Eastman Kodak Company; *U.S. Public*, pg. 550

MEGULASTIK—Rubber/Metal Technical Goods—Freudenberg & Company; *Int'l*, pg. 505

MEICELIN—Injectable Cephalosporins—Bristol-Myers Squibb Company; *U.S. Public*, pg. 253

MEIER & FRANK—Department Stores—The May Department Stores Company; *U.S. Public*, pg. 1063

MEIFLASH—Edible Fungus Cultivation Activator—Meiji Seika Kaisha, Ltd.; *Int'l*, pg. 855

MEIJER—Department Stores—Meijer, Inc.; *U.S. Private*, pg. 729

MEIJI McVITIES—Digestive Biscuits—Meiji Seika Kaisha, Ltd.; *Int'l*, pg. 855

MEILINK—NONE—Fire King International, Inc.; *U.S. Private*, pg. 406

MEIN SCHONER GARTEN—Magazine—Burda Holding GmbH & Co., KG; *Int'l*, pg. 233

MEINKNACKE—Snack Foods—Meiji Seika Kaisha, Ltd.; *Int'l*, pg. 855

MEIPAC—Collagen Wound Dressing—Meiji Seika Kaisha, Ltd.; *Int'l*, pg. 855

MEIRICH—Veterinary Medicines—Meiji Seika Kaisha, Ltd.; *Int'l*, pg. 855

MEISTER BRAU—Beer—Miller Brewing Company; *U.S. Public*, pg. 1289

MEISTER BRAU—Beer—Philip Morris Companies Inc.; *U.S. Public*, pg. 1287

MEISTERCHEF—Processed Meats—Kayem Foods, Inc.; *U.S. Private*, pg. 610

MEJORAL—NONE—SmithKline Beecham Corporation; *Int'l*, pg. 1264

MEKAN-I-KLOTH—Paper Towels—Georgia-Pacific Corporation; *U.S. Public*, pg. 735

MEL-FRY—Fats & Oils—Van den Bergh Foods Company; *Int'l*, pg. 1436

MEL-TROL—NONE—Carpenter Technology Corporation; *U.S. Public*, pg. 307

MELANEX—Topical Solution—Neutrogena Corporation; *U.S. Public*, pg. 928

MELANNCO INTERNATIONAL—Silverware—Syratech Corporation; *U.S. Private*, pg. 1060

MELATONIN P.M.—Melatonin—Celestial Seasonings; *U.S. Public*, pg. 319

MELBOURNE BITTER—Bitter Ale—Carlton & United Breweries Ltd.; *Int'l*, pg. 500

MELBOURNE BITTER—Bitter Ale—Foster's Brewing Group Limited; *Int'l*, pg. 500

MELCOR II—Decorative Laminates—Pioneer Plastics Corporation; *U.S. Public*, pg. 867

MELDIN—Plastics—Furon Co.; *U.S. Public*, pg. 689

MELDIN—Polyimide Material—Furon Company; *U.S. Public*, pg. 688

MELE—Jewel Boxes—Mele Manufacturing Co., Inc.; *U.S. Private*, pg. 730

MELETTI ANISETTE AND SAMBUCA—Liqueur—Paterno Imports Limited; *U.S. Public*, pg. 843

MELFIAT 105—Pharmaceutical Products—Solvay Pharmaceuticals, Inc.; *Int'l*, pg. 1278

MELHI—Thermoplastic Resin—Hercules Incorporated; *U.S. Public*, pg. 809

MELIA—NONE—Sol Melia; *Int'l*, pg. 1277

MELIA COMFORT—NONE—Sol Melia; *Int'l*, pg. 1277

MELINEX—Polyester—Plastic Suppliers, Inc.; *U.S. Private*, pg. 871

MELINI—Wine—Frederick Wildman & Sons Ltd.; *U.S. Private*, pg. 1176

MELIO—Chemicals—Clariant International Ltd.; *Int'l*, pg. 624

MELISSA—Women's Clothing & Accessories—Jerell, Inc.; *U.S. Private*, pg. 586

MELISSA PETITES—Petite Dresses—Jerell, Inc.; *U.S. Private*, pg. 586

MELITTA—Coffee Maker—Melitta Unternehmensgruppe Bentz KG; *Int'l*, pg. 856

MELITTA—Coffee, Coffeemakers & Coffee Filters—Melitta U.S.A., Inc.; *Int'l*, pg. 857

MELLARIL—Tablets/Oral Solution for Psychotic Disorders—Sandoz Pharmaceuticals Corp.; *Int'l*, pg. 974

MELLERIL—Pharmaceutical—Novartis AG; *Int'l*, pg. 971

MELLIN—Baby Foods—Danone Group; *Int'l*, pg. 379

MELLO—Vegetable Oil—Mallet & Co.; *U.S. Private*, pg. 698

MELLO—Frozen Yogurt—MelloButtercup Ice Cream Inc.; *U.S. Private*, pg. 730

MELLO GOLD—Vegetable Oil—Mallet & Co.; *U.S. Private*, pg. 698

MELLO MINT—Peppermint Patties—Hershey Chocolate U.S.A.; *U.S. Public*, pg. 812

MELLO MINT—Chocolate Covered Peppermint Patties—Hershey Foods Corporation; *U.S. Public*, pg. 811

MELLO YELLO—Regular & Diet Soft Drink—The Coca-Cola Company; *U.S. Public*, pg. 392

MELLOBUTTERCUP—Ice Cream—MelloButtercup Ice Cream Inc.; *U.S. Private*, pg. 730

MELLOCHROME—Dull Coated Bristol-Cover—Appleton Papers Inc.; *Int'l*, pg. 1159

MELLOW MINT—Herb Tea—Celestial Seasonings; *U.S. Public*, pg. 319

MELLOW ROAST—Coffee—Kraft Foods, Inc.; *U.S. Public*, pg. 1287

MELLOW ROAST—Coffee—Philip Morris Companies Inc.; *U.S. Public*, pg. 1287

MELLOW VIRGINIA—NONE—Fortune Brands, Inc.; *U.S. Public*, pg. 674

MELLOW VIRGINIA—Pipe Tobacco—Gallaher Tobacco Ltd.; *Int'l*, pg. 539

MELLOW YELLOW—Soft Drink—The Coca-Cola Bottling Co. of New York, Inc.; *U.S. Public*, pg. 393

MELODY—Women's Apparel—International Cosmetics Co., Ltd.; *Int'l*, pg. 684

MELODY FARMS—Dairy Products—Melody Foods, Inc.; *U.S. Private*, pg. 730

MELODY MAKER—Music & Lifestyle Magazine—IPC Magazines Limited; *Int'l*, pg. 651

MELROSE—NONE—Kellwood Company; *U.S. Public*, pg. 948

MELT-MANAGER—Built-In Computer—Inductotherm Corp.; *U.S. Private*, pg. 560

MELTATOX—Crop Protection Agent—BASF AG; *Int'l*, pg. 103

MELTMINDER—Computer Control & Maintenance System—Inductotherm Corp.; *U.S. Private*, pg. 560

MELTONIAN—Shoe Polish—Kiwi Brands; *U.S. Public*, pg. 1433

MELTONIAN—Shoe Care Products—Sara Lee Corporation; *U.S. Public*, pg. 1432

MELTYKISS—Chocolate—Meiji Seika Kaisha, Ltd.; *Int'l*, pg. 855

MEMBERS ONLY—Outerwear—Members Only By Europe Craft; *U.S. Public*, pg. 129

MEMBERS ONLY BRAND FURNITURE—RTA Furniture—Ameriwood Industries International Inc.; *U.S. Public*, pg. 98

MEMBERSHIP—For Mail Order Sales in the Field—American Automobile Association; *U.S. Private*, pg. 50

MEMBERSHIP HAS ITS PRIVILEGES—Special Range of Services for Card Members—American Express Company; *U.S. Public*, pg. 73

MEMBERSHIP MILES—NONE—American Express Company; *U.S. Public*, pg. 73

MEMBERSHIP REWARDS—NONE—American Express Company; *U.S. Public*, pg. 73

MEMBRALOX—Ceramic Membrance Filters—Aluminum Company of America; *U.S. Public*, pg. 60

MEMBRANE EX—Pacemaker Lead—St. Jude Medical, Inc.; *U.S. Public*, pg. 1427

MEMBRELLE—Microporous Membranes for Medical Laboratory Electrophoresis Applications—PPG Industries, Inc.; *U.S. Public*, pg. 1245

MEMCO—Elevator Controls & Saftey Systems—Halma p.l.c.; *Int'l*, pg. 589

MEMOIRE CHERIE—Fragrance—Elizabeth Arden Company; *Int'l*, pg. 1435

MEMORASE—Eprom Erasing—UVP, Inc.; *U.S. Private*, pg. 1115

MEMORIES—Magazine—Lagardere Groupe North America; *Int'l*, pg. 794

MEMORY—Candy—Brach & Brock Confections Inc.; *U.S. Private*, pg. 163

MEMORY—Tickets, Tags, Labels, Credit Cards—Litton Industries, Inc.; *U.S. Public*, pg. 1002

MEMORY ARC—Pattern Control—Rain Bird Sprinklers Manufacturing Corp.; *U.S. Private*, pg. 907

MEMORY BANK—Wallets & Clutch Bags—Eastman Kodak Company; *U.S. Public*, pg. 550

MEMORY CHANNEL—Computer Memory System—Encore Computer Corporation; *U.S. Public*, pg. 580

MEMORY CLOTH—Fabric - Patient apparel—Medline Industries, Inc.; *U.S. Private*, pg. 728

MEMORY LANE—Retail Card & Gift Store Services—American Greetings Corporation; *U.S. Public*, pg. 77

MEMORY MATCH—Games—Colorforms; *U.S. Public*, pg. 1625

MEMORY-PAC—Program Modules—Beckman Instruments, Inc.; *U.S. Public*, pg. 199

MEMORYMASTER—Software Tools—Gatefield Corporation; *U.S. Public*, pg. 703

MEMORYMATIC—Microwave Ovens—Litton Industries, Inc.; *U.S. Public*, pg. 1002

MEMORYTRACE—Monitor—Medtronic, Inc.; *U.S. Public*, pg. 1082

MEMPHIS—NONE—Jean Philippe Fragrances, Inc.; *U.S. Public*, pg. 924

MEMPHIS 10—NONE—Callaway Golf Company; *U.S. Public*, pg. 294

MEMSCAN—Closed-Circuit Television Equipment—Vicon Industries, Inc.; *U.S. Public*, pg. 1719

MEMSEP—Cartridge—Millipore Corporation; *U.S. Public*, pg. 1112

MEMTREX—Pleated Membrane Cartridge Filters—Osmonics, Inc.; *U.S. Public*, pg. 1233

MEMTREX PC—Filter Cartridge—Osmonics, Inc.; *U.S. Public*, pg. 1233

MEN AMERICA—Men's Clothing—Hanover Direct Pennsylvania, Inc.; *U.S. Public*, pg. 782

MEN'S CHOICE—Hair spray—Bristol-Myers Squibb Company; *U.S. Public*, pg. 253

MEN'S HEALTH—Magazine—Rodale Press, Inc.; *U.S. Private*, pg. 939

MENARDI-CRISWELL—Industrial Filter Bags—Hosokawa Micron International Inc.; *Int'l*, pg. 635

MENASCO—Aircraft Landing Gear & Flight Controls—Coltec Industries Inc.; *U.S. Public*, pg. 401

MENCEVAX—NONE—SmithKline Beecham Corporation; *Int'l*, pg. 1264

MENCEVAX—Vaccine—SmithKline Beecham plc; *Int'l*, pg. 1264

MENEST—Pharmaceutical Products—SmithKline Beecham Corporation; *Int'l*, pg. 1264

MENEST—Pharmaceutical Prods.—SmithKline Beecham Laboratories; *Int'l*, pg. 1264

MENNEN—NONE—Colgate-Palmolive S.A.I.C.; *U.S. Public*, pg. 399

MENNEN—Various Toiletry & Shaving Prods.—The Mennen Company; *U.S. Public*, pg. 397

MENOMUNE—Meningococcal Vaccine—Connaught Laboratories, Inc.; *Int'l*, pg. 1109

MENOPREM—NONE—Wyeth Australia Pty. Ltd.; *U.S. Public*, pg. 82

MEN'S CONFIDENTIAL—Newsletter—Rodale Press, Inc.; *U.S. Private*, pg. 939

MEN'S FITNESS—Magazine—Weider Publications, Inc.; *U.S. Private*, pg. 1159

MENSAJERA—Prepaid Calling Cards—Fone America, Inc.; *U.S. Public*, pg. 661

MENTADENT—Toothpaste—Chesebrough-Pond's USA Co.; *Int'l*, pg. 1435

MENTADENT—Toothpaste—Unilever Plc; *Int'l*, pg. 1433

MENTHOL H & R—Aromen Chemical—Haarmann & Reimer Corp.; *Int'l*, pg. 173

MENTHOLATUM—Deep Heating Rub, Lip Balm & Ointment—Mentholatum Company; *Int'l*, pg. 1126

MENTHOLATUM—Deep Heating Lotions & Rubs—Rohto Pharmaceutical Co.; *Int'l*, pg. 1126

MENTO FACTOR—Computer Services—Science Management Corporation; *U.S. Public*, pg. 1717

MENTOR—Condoms—Carter-Wallace, Inc.; *U.S. Public*, pg. 309

MENTOR—Hardware & Software for Video & Test Signal Control—Chyron Corp.; *Int'l*, pg. 1372

MENTOR—Database Software—General Automation, Inc.; *U.S. Public*, pg. 706

MENTOR—Health Care Products—Mentor Corporation; *U.S. Public*, pg. 1086

MENTOR PLUS—Condoms—Carter-Wallace, Inc.; *U.S. Public*, pg. 309

MENTOS—Candies—Van Melle N.V.; *Int'l*, pg. 1450

MENTOS—Candy Mints—Van Melle USA, Inc.; *Int'l*, pg. 1451

MENTOS CANDY—Candy—Warner-Lambert K.K.; *U.S. Public*, pg. 1739

MENU MAKER—Food Products—Rymer Foods Inc.; *U.S. Public*, pg. 1414

MENUMASTER—Microwave Ovens—Litton Industries, Inc.; *U.S. Public*, pg. 1002

MEOW MIX—Cat Food—Ralston Purina Company; *U.S. Public*, pg. 1359

MEPPS SPINNERS—Recreational Fishing Lures—Sheldons' Inc.; *U.S. Public*, pg. 992

MEPTIN—Bronchodilator—Otsuka Pharmaceutical Co., Ltd.; *Int'l*, pg. 1013

MERAKLON—Polypropylene Yarn & Staple—Montedison S.p.A.; *Int'l*, pg. 324

MERCANTILE BANK—Logo—Mercantile Bancorporation Inc.; *U.S. Public*, pg. 1087

MERCEDES BENZ—Automobiles—Daimler-Benz Aktiengesellschaft; *Int'l*, pg. 366

MERCEDES-BENZ—Automobiles—Lantzsch-Andreas Enterprises, Inc.; *U.S. Private*, pg. 650

MERCEDES BENZ—Auto—Loeber Motors, Inc.; *U.S. Private*, pg. 672

MERCEDES-BENZ—Passenger Cars—Mercedes-Benz of North America, Inc.; *Int'l*, pg. 368

MERCER MANAGEMENT CONSULTING, INC.—Management Services—Marsh & McLennan Companies, Inc.; *U.S. Public*, pg. 1048

MERCHANDISER—Hand-held Labeling Tool—Esselte Meto Kimball Systems; *Int'l*, pg. 460

MERCHANDISER—Price Marking Gun—Meto, USA; *Int'l*, pg. 460

MERCHANTS HOME DELIVERY SERVICE—NONE—NFC plc; *Int'l*, pg. 901

MERCHANTS OF VENUS—Strategy Game—Monarch Avalon, Inc.; *U.S. Public*, pg. 1123

MERCIAN BRANDY X.O.—Brandy—Mercian Corporation; *Int'l*, pg. 858

MERCIER—NONE—LVMH Moet Hennessy Louis Vuitton; *Int'l*, pg. 779

MERCILON—Ultra-Low Estrogen Pill—Akzo Nobel N.V.; *Int'l*, pg. 42

MERCKENS—Chocolate Products—Grace Cocoa/ Ambrosia Chocolate; *U.S. Public*, pg. 128

MERCO—Food Warming Equipment—Welbilt Corporation; *Int'l*, pg. 188

MERCO CENTRIFUGE—NONE—Dorr-Oliver Incorporated; *Int'l*, pg. 839

MERCOID—Controls—Dwyer Instruments Inc.; *U.S. Private*, pg. 350

MERCOID—Switches—Dwyer Instruments Inc.; *U.S. Private*, pg. 350

MERCRUISER—Stern Drives & Inboards—Brunswick Corporation; *U.S. Public*, pg. 265

MERCRUISER—Stern Drives in Board Engines—Mercury Marine; *U.S. Public*, pg. 265

MERCURE—Hotel—Accor S.A.; *Int'l*, pg. 20

MERCURY—Outboard Motors—Brunswick Corporation; *U.S. Public*, pg. 265

MERCURY—Reinforced Vinyl Banner Material—Industrial Coatings Group, Inc.; *U.S. Private*, pg. 434

MERCURY—Records—Philips Electronics N.V.; *Int'l*, pg. 1051

MERCURY—Records & Cassettes—Polygram Records, Inc.; *Int'l*, pg. 1052

MERCURY AIR CARGO—NONE—Mercury Air Group Inc.; *U.S. Public*, pg. 1092

MERCURY AIR CENTERS—NONE—Mercury Air Group Inc.; *U.S. Public*, pg. 1092

MERCURY CENTER—Electronic Information—San Jose Mercury News; *U.S. Public*, pg. 964

MERCURY GRAND MARQUIS—Car—Ford Motor Company; *U.S. Public*, pg. 661

MERCURY MOUNTAINEER—Truck—Ford Motor Company; *U.S. Public*, pg. 661

MERCURY MYSTIQUE—Automobile—Ford Motor Company; *U.S. Public*, pg. 661

MERCURY SABLE—Car—Ford Motor Company; *U.S. Public*, pg. 661

MERCURY TRACER—Car—Ford Motor Company; *U.S. Public*, pg. 661

MERCURY VILLAGER—Mini-Van—Ford Motor Company; *U.S. Public*, pg. 661

MERCUVER—Chemical Reagant—Hach Company; *U.S. Public*, pg. 773

MEREDIAN—Electrodes—Honeywell, Inc.; *U.S. Public*, pg. 834

MEREDITH CABLE, INC.—NONE—Meredith Corporation; *U.S. Public*, pg. 1094

MEREDITH PRESS—NONE—Meredith Corporation; *U.S. Public*, pg. 1094

MEREDITH PUBLISHING SERVICES—Custom Publishing—Meredith Corporation; *U.S. Public*, pg. 1094

MEREDITH VIDEO PUBLISHING—Video Production—Meredith Corporation; *U.S. Public*, pg. 1094

MERGE/PURGE ONLINE—Mailing Efficiency—Group 1 Software, Inc.; *U.S. Public*, pg. 417

MERGE/PURGE PLUS—Mailing Efficiency—Group 1 Software, Inc.; *U.S. Public*, pg. 417

MERGENT—Comprehensive Securities Solutions—Utimaco Safeware, Inc.; *Int'l*, pg. 1444

MERIAM—Pressure Measuring Instruments—The Scott Fetzer Company; *U.S. Public*, pg. 217

MERICO—Bakery Products—The Earthgrains Company; *U.S. Public*, pg. 547

MERIDIA—Appetite Suppressant—Knoll Pharmaceutical Company; *Int'l*, pg. 105

MERIDIAN—Office Communication Systems—BCE Inc.; *Int'l*, pg. 114

MERIDIAN—NONE—CertainTeed Corporation; *Int'l*, pg. 1170

MERIDIAN—Wine—Nestle S.A.; *Int'l*, pg. 915

MERIDIAN—Coffee—Starbucks Coffee Company; *U.S. Public*, pg. 1510

MERIDIAN—Level-Transit—David White, L.L.C.; *U.S. Public*, pg. 1765

MERIDIAN—Level-Transit—David White, L.L.C.; *U.S. Private*, pg. 1765

MERIDIAN—Vineyards—Wine World Estates Company; *Int'l*, pg. 917

MERIDIAN CAMPUS—Real Estate Service—Weyerhaeuser Company; *U.S. Public*, pg. 1764

MERIDIAN 1—Integrated Voice/Data Communications System—Northern Telecom; *Int'l*, pg. 969

Brand Name Index

MERIDIAN 1—Information Mngmt. System—Northern Telecom Limited; *Int'l*, pg. 968

MERIDIAN STONE—Pre-Finished Laminate—Bruce Hardwood Floors; *U.S. Public*, pg. 1634

MERIDIEN—Hotels—Meridian Hotels, Inc.; *Int'l*, pg. 556

MERIFLUOR—Fluorescence-Based Immunoassays for Infectious Disease—Meridian Diagnostics, Inc.; *U.S. Public*, pg. 1094

MERILAC—Milk Replacer—Novartis Nutrition Corporation; *Int'l*, pg. 974

MERILLAT—Wood Kitchen Cabinetry—Masco Corporation; *U.S. Public*, pg. 1052

MERIMIX—Custard Dessert Mix—Novartis Nutrition Corporation; *Int'l*, pg. 974

MERINOS—NONE—Merinos; *Int'l*, pg. 858

MERIT—Shoes—E.J. Footwear Corp.; *U.S. Public*, pg. 1684

MERIT—Tires—The Hercules Tire & Rubber Company; *U.S. Private*, pg. 523

MERIT—Cigarettes—Philip Morris Companies Inc.; *U.S. Public*, pg. 1287

MERIT—Cigarettes—Philip Morris U.S.A.; *U.S. Public*, pg. 1289

MERIT CONTROL SYRINGE—Control Syringe—Merit Medical Systems, Inc.; *U.S. Public*, pg. 1096

MERIT INTELLISYSTEM INFLATION SYSTEM—Syringe for Balloon Angioplasty—Merit Medical Systems, Inc.; *U.S. Public*, pg. 1096

MERIT MANIFOLD—Fluid Path Administration—Merit Medical Systems, Inc.; *U.S. Public*, pg. 1096

MERIT MEDICAL CCS CONTROL SYRINGE—Syringe—Merit Medical Systems, Inc.; *U.S. Public*, pg. 1096

MERIT MENTHOL—Cigarettes—Philip Morris Companies Inc.; *U.S. Public*, pg. 1287

MERIT 100'S—Cigarettes—Philip Morris Companies Inc.; *U.S. Public*, pg. 1287

MERIT 100'S ULTRA LIGHTS—Cigarettes—Philip Morris Companies Inc.; *U.S. Public*, pg. 1287

MERIT 100'S ULTRA LIGHTS MENTHOL—Cigarettes—Philip Morris Companies Inc.; *U.S. Public*, pg. 1287

MERIT PLUS—Voluntary Advertising; Private Label—f. Dohmen Company; *U.S. Private*, pg. 338

MERIT ULTRA LIGHTS—Cigarettes—Philip Morris Companies Inc.; *U.S. Public*, pg. 1287

MERIT ULTRA LIGHTS MENTHOL—Cigarettes—Philip Morris Companies Inc.; *U.S. Public*, pg. 1287

MERIT VALU—NONE—Provident Financial Group, Inc.; *U.S. Public*, pg. 1338

MERITA—Bread—Interstate Brands Corporation; *U.S. Public*, pg. 909

MERITEC—Rapid Agglutination Tests for Infectious Disease—Meridian Diagnostics, Inc.; *U.S. Public*, pg. 1094

MERITENE—Oral Supplement—Novartis Nutrition Corporation; *Int'l*, pg. 974

MERIWETHER'S PIGTAIL—Twist Tobacco—Conwood Company L.P.; *U.S. Private*, pg. 272

MERKUR—Compasses—Litton Industries, Inc.; *U.S. Public*, pg. 1002

MERLE NORMAN—Cosmetics—Merle Norman Cosmetics, Inc.; *U.S. Private*, pg. 733

MERLIN—Automobile—British Aerospace p.l.c.; *Int'l*, pg. 217

MERLIN—Communications System, Electronic Key Telephone System, Cordless Telephone—Lucent Technologies Inc.; *U.S. Public*, pg. 1017

MERLIN—Electronic Lettering System—Varitronic Systems, Inc.; *U.S. Public*, pg. 250

MERLIN EXPRESS—Presentation Lettering System—Varitronic Systems, Inc.; *U.S. Public*, pg. 250

MERLIN EXPRESS ELITE—Thermal Lettering System—Varitronic Systems, Inc.; *U.S. Public*, pg. 250

MERLIN EXPRESS XT—Lettering System—Varitronic Systems, Inc.; *U.S. Public*, pg. 250

MERLIN GELIN—Electrical & Industrial Control—Schneider S.A.; *Int'l*, pg. 1207

MERLIN LEGENDS—Communications System, Electronic Key Telephone System—Lucent Technologies Inc.; *U.S. Public*, pg. 1017

MERLIN MAIL—Voice Messaging System—Lucent Technologies Inc.; *U.S. Public*, pg. 1017

MERLIN PFC—Integrated Telephone, Facsimile Machine—Lucent Technologies Inc.; *U.S. Public*, pg. 1017

MERLINO—Pasta Products—Borden Italian Foods; *U.S. Private*, pg. 158

MERLINO'S—Pasta—Borden, Inc.; *U.S. Private*, pg. 157

MERLINO'S—Macaroni—Merlino's Macaroni, Inc.; *U.S. Private*, pg. 158

MERMAID—Food Service Equip.—Zero Corporation; *U.S. Public*, pg. 1791

MERONA—Sport Shoes—Schwartz & Benjamin, Inc.; *U.S. Private*, pg. 974

MERPOL—Surfactant—Du Pont (E.I. Du Pont De Nemours & Co.); *U.S. Public*, pg. 530

MERREM/MERONEM—Pharmaceutical—Zeneca Group Plc; *Int'l*, pg. 1524

MERRI-OATS—Cereal—The Quaker Oats Company; *U.S. Public*, pg. 1347

MERRIAM WEBSTER—Books & Software—Encyclopaedia Britannica, Inc.; *U.S. Private*, pg. 375

MERRIAM-WEBSTER—Reference Books—Merriam-Webster, Inc.; *U.S. Private*, pg. 375

MERRIES—Disposable Diapers—Kao Corporation; *Int'l*, pg. 717

MERRIGOLD PRESS—NONE—Golden Books Family Entertainment Inc.; *U.S. Public*, pg. 749

MERRILL LYNCH, PIERCE, FENNER & SMITH, INC.—Investment Services—Merrill Lynch, Pierce, Fenner & Smith, Inc.; *U.S. Public*, pg. 1098

MERRILD—Coffee—Sara Lee Corporation; *U.S. Public*, pg. 1432

MERRILL BROTHERS—Clamps, Forgings—York Plant; *U.S. Public*, pg. 444

MERRILL LYNCH—Investment Service—Merrill Lynch & Co., Inc.; *U.S. Public*, pg. 1097

MERRILLLINK—Portable Printing Device—Merrill Corporation; *U.S. Public*, pg. 1097

MERRY—Brooms & Waxers—Foam Pro Manufacturing; *U.S. Private*, pg. 415

MERRY LAND APARTMENT COMMUNITIES—Apartment Company—Merry Land & Investment Company, Inc.; *U.S. Public*, pg. 1098

MERRY MAIDS—Maid Service—Duskin Co., Ltd.; *Int'l*, pg. 422

MERRY MAIDS—Maid Service—The ServiceMaster Company; *U.S. Public*, pg. 1461

MERRY MINT—Patient Care Utensils—The Vollrath Company, L.L.C.; *U.S. Private*, pg. 1143

MERRY RIDER—Toys—Processed Plastic Company; *U.S. Private*, pg. 888

MERRYDOWN—Cider—Gilbeys of Ireland; *Int'l*, pg. 409

MERSENE—Denture Cleaner—Colgate-Palmolive Company; *U.S. Public*, pg. 397

MERSILENE—Polyester Fiber Suture/Mesh/Strip—Ethicon, Inc.; *U.S. Public*, pg. 928

MERTECT—Thiabendazole Plant Fungicide—Merck & Co., Inc.; *U.S. Public*, pg. 1090

MERTIK—Gas Valves, Temperature Controls—Maxitrol Co.; *U.S. Private*, pg. 716

MERVA—Computer Product—International Business Machines Corporation; *U.S. Public*, pg. 895

MERVYN'S—Department Store—Mervyn's California; *U.S. Public*, pg. 489

MESA—Dinnerware, Stemware & Flatware—Dansk International Designs Ltd.; *U.S. Public*, pg. 261

MESA—Film Handling Equipment—Eastman Kodak Company; *U.S. Public*, pg. 550

MESANTOIN—Control of Grand Mal, Focal, Jacksonian & Psychomotor Seisures—Sandoz Pharmaceuticals Corp.; *Int'l*, pg. 974

MESMERIZE FOR MEN—Men's Cologne—Avon Products, Inc.; *U.S. Public*, pg. 155

MESNEX—Pharmeceutical Used in Conjuction with Ifex—Bristol-Myers Squibb U.S. Pharmaceutical Group; *U.S. Public*, pg. 255

MESOLID—Pharmaceutical—Novartis AG; *Int'l*, pg. 971

MESOTEX—Needle Bonded Carpets—Forbo Holding SA; *Int'l*, pg. 496

MESSAGE PROCESSING SYSTEM (MPS)—NONE—American Management Systems, Inc.; *U.S. Public*, pg. 86

MESSAGEFAX—Facsimile Equipment—Litton Industries, Inc.; *U.S. Public*, pg. 1002

MESSAGEMAKER—NONE—Life Technologies, Inc.; *U.S. Public*, pg. 504

MESSENGER—Funeral Supplies—Renaissance Publishing Co., Inc.; *Int'l*, pg. 185

MESSINA—Beer—Heineken N.V.; *Int'l*, pg. 608

MESSMA-KELCH—Tool Presetters—The Wickman Corp.; *U.S. Private*, pg. 1175

MESTINON—Prescription Drug—ICN Pharmaceuticals, Inc.; *U.S. Public*, pg. 853

MESURA—Sweeteners, Health Foods—Danone Group; *Int'l*, pg. 379

MESURFLO—Controls—Hays Fluid Controls-Division of Romac Industries; *U.S. Private*, pg. 942

MET—Company Name—Metropolitan Life Insurance Co.; *U.S. Private*, pg. 737

MET-FLO—Cold Forming Taps—Regal-Beloit Corporation; *U.S. Public*, pg. 1370

MET-KUP—Mounting Mold—Buehler, Limited; *U.S. Public*, pg. 574

MET-L-KYL—Dry Powder—Ansul Incorporated; *U.S. Public*, pg. 1648

MET-L-X—Dry Chemical Agent—Ansul Incorporated; *U.S. Public*, pg. 1648

META—Metaldehyde—Alusuisse-Lonza Holding Ltd.; *Int'l*, pg. 66

META—Hair Products—Dena Corporation; *U.S. Private*, pg. 324

META—Healthcare Uniforms—Whiteswan/Meta; *U.S. Private*, pg. 342

META HENNA—Creme—Meta International, Inc.; *U.S. Private*, pg. 324

META 1 STEP—Hair Products—Dena Corporation; *U.S. Private*, pg. 324

META/PARA CRESOL BLENDS—NONE—Sasol Alpha Olefins; *Int'l*, pg. 1196

META/PARA CRESOL BLENDS—NONE—Sasol Chemicals Europe Limited; *Int'l*, pg. 1196

METAB—Tablets—Fisher Scientific Company; *U.S. Private*, pg. 658

METABOLIC FORMULAS—Infant Formulas—Bristol-Myers Squibb Company; *U.S. Public*, pg. 253

METACURE—Metal-Based Catalysts—Air Products and Chemicals, Inc.; *U.S. Public*, pg. 30

METADI—Diamond Polishing Compound—Buehler, Limited; *U.S. Public*, pg. 574

METAFLEX—Spiral-Wound Gaskets—James Walker & Co. Limited; *Int'l*, pg. 1485

METAL—Cologne for Women—Paco Rabanne Compar; *Int'l*, pg. 1073

METAL-CAL—NONE—Fred B. Johnston Company, Inc.; *U.S. Private*, pg. 595

METAL CENTER NEWS—Metal-Service Magazine—Reed Elsevier Business Information; *Int'l*, pg. 1095

METAL CLAD—Blankets, Shrouds—Johns Manville Corporation; *U.S. Public*, pg. 927

METAL DEVILS—Metal Film Fix Resistors—Ohmite Manufacturing Company; *U.S. Private*, pg. 813

METAL-FLO III—Hydroforming Process—H & H Tube & Manufacturing Co.; *U.S. Private*, pg. 489

METAL GUARD—Corrosion Inhibitors & Rust Preventatives—Hubbard Hall Inc.; *U.S. Private*, pg. 544

METAL HEAT TREATING—Periodical—Penton Publishing, Inc.; *U.S. Public*, pg. 1306

METAL LUBRICANTS—NONE—Fuchs Lubricants, Midlantic Div.; *Int'l*, pg. 518

METAL MENDER—Solder—Litton Industries, Inc.; *U.S. Public*, pg. 1002

METAL MOLDER—Toy—Toymax International Inc.; *U.S. Public*, pg. 1626

METAL REMOVAL—Carbide Tools—Greenfield Industries Inc.; *U.S. Public*, pg. 950

METAL ROLLER—Rolling Ball Pen—Stationery Products Division; *U.S. Public*, pg. 744

METAL SAVER—Coatings—Rust-Oleum Corporation; *U.S. Public*, pg. 1358

METAL SIGNATURE—Water Analysis Services—The Dow Chemical Company; *U.S. Public*, pg. 522

METAL WORK!—Service Products—R&B, Inc.; *U.S. Public*, pg. 1354

METALASTIC—Expansion Joint Cover—BMCA Insulation Products, Inc.; *U.S. Private*, pg. 433

METALASTIK—Rubber to Metal Bondings—BTR plc; *Int'l*, pg. 124

METALBESTOS—HVAC—Eljer Plumbingware; *U.S. Public*, pg. 1794

METALEAF—Aluminum Paint—PPG Industries, Inc.; *U.S. Public*, pg. 1245

METALEX—Corrective Conditioner—Clairol, Inc.; *U.S. Public*, pg. 254

METALFRIO—Household Appliances—BS Continental S.A. Utilidades Domesticas; *Int'l*, pg. 123

METALHIDE—Liquid & Paste Paints—PPG Industries, Inc.; *U.S. Public*, pg. 1245

METALITE—Coated Abrasives—Norton Company; *Int'l*, pg. 1173

METALLAN—Convolute & Spiral Tubes—Sonoco Products Company; *U.S. Public*, pg. 1485

METALLEX—Laminated Engravable Plastic—New Hermes Incorporated; *U.S. Private*, pg. 793

METALOPLAST—PFTE Bearings for High Load Applications—Norton Performance Plastics; *Int'l*, pg. 1174

METALTRACE—Test Kit—Hach Company; *U.S. Public*, pg. 773

METALUM—Polishing Compound—Ferro Corporation; *U.S. Public*, pg. 618

METALUX—Fluorescent Lighting—Cooper Industries, Inc.; *U.S. Public*, pg. 442

METALWORKING—Magazine—Reed Business Information Pty. Limited; *Int'l*, pg. 1094

METALWORKING DIGEST—Oil & Gas Technology—Gordon Publications, Inc.; *Int'l*, pg. 1096

METALWORKING DIGEST—"New Technology" Publication for Engineers & Managers—Reed Elsevier Business Information; *Int'l*, pg. 1095

METALYN—Fatty Acid Ester—Hercules Incorporated; *U.S. Public*, pg. 809

METAMUCIL—Laxative—The Procter & Gamble Company; *U.S. Public*, pg. 1330

METANETICS—Digital Image Processing Technology—Telxon Corporation; *U.S. Public*, pg. 1573

METAPREL—Inhalation Aerosol Bronchodilator/Syrup/Tablets for Asthma, Bronchitis—Sandoz Pharmaceuticals Corp.; *Int'l*, pg. 974

METASTRON—Strontium 89 Chloride-Injection—Amersham Corporation; *Int'l*, pg. 992

METASUITE FAMILY OF PRODUCTS—NONE—BMC Software, Inc.; *U.S. Public*, pg. 162

METASYS—Buildng Automation Systems—Johnson Controls, Inc.; *U.S. Public*, pg. 932

METASYS—Facility Management Control Systems—Johnson Controls, Inc., Controls Group; *U.S. Public*, pg. 932

METATOOL—Computer Program Software—Lucent Technologies Inc.; *U.S. Public*, pg. 1017

METAXA—Brandy—Grand Metropolitan Plc; *Int'l*, pg. 408

METAXA—NONE—Metaxa Distilleries; *Int'l*, pg. 410

METAXA—NONE—Societe Pour la Vente des Produits Cinzano SA; *Int'l*, pg. 410

METAXA BRANDY 5 STAR—NONE—Carillon Importers, Ltd.; *Int'l*, pg. 409

METAXA BRANDY GRAND FINE—NONE—Carillon Importers, Ltd.; *Int'l*, pg. 409

METAXA BRANDY 7 STAR—NONE—Carillon Importers, Ltd.; *Int'l*, pg. 409

METAXA OUZO—NONE—Carillon Importers, Ltd.; *Int'l*, pg. 409

METAZENE—Odorless Odor Counteractant Additive—Surco Products, Inc.; *U.S. Private*, pg. 1056

METCLOTH—Polishing Cloth—Buehler, Limited; *U.S. Public*, pg. 574

METCO—Thick-Film Thermal Spray Coatings—The Perkin-Elmer Corporation; *U.S. Public*, pg. 1279

METCOLITE—Paricled Bulk Grit—The Perkin-Elmer Corporation; *U.S. Public*, pg. 1279

METCOLITE—Abrasive Grits—Sulzer Metco (Westbury) Inc.; *Int'l*, pg. 1307

METCOLOY—Nickel-Chromium & Chromium Alloy Wires—The Perkin-Elmer Corporation; *U.S. Public*, pg. 1279

METCOSEAL—Metal Surface Paints & Thinners—The Perkin-Elmer Corporation; *U.S. Public*, pg. 1279

METCUT—Indexable Tooling—Greenfield Industries Inc.; *U.S. Public*, pg. 950

METEOR—Sporting Goods—Brunswick Bowling & Billiards Corp.; *U.S. Public*, pg. 265

METER MISER—Lighting Fixtures—Graybar Electric Company, Inc.; *U.S. Private*, pg. 472

METER RELEASE—Controlled Release Technology for Tablets & Capsules—KV Pharmaceutical Company; *U.S. Public*, pg. 941

METER SPRAGUE—Gas Meters & Regulators—Schlumberger Industries; *U.S. Public*, pg. 1439

METERMASTER—Electronics—Arrow/Schweber Electronics; *U.S. Public*, pg. 134

METEXCHANGE—Chemical reagent—ESA, Inc.; *U.S. Private*, pg. 354

METFIT—Pipe Connectors—Raychem Corporation; *U.S. Public*, pg. 1362

METFORMINE—NONE—ICN Pharmaceuticals, Inc.; *U.S. Public*, pg. 853

METGARD—Corrosion Inhibitor—The Dow Chemical Company; *U.S. Public*, pg. 522

METGLAS—Amorphous Metal—AlliedSignal Inc.; *U.S. Public*, pg. 49

METGLAS—Amorphorus Alloys—AlliedSignal Inc., Engineered Materials; *U.S. Public*, pg. 51

METHADOSE—NONE—Mallinckrodt Inc.; *U.S. Public*, pg. 1039

METHASAN—Rubber Processing Chemical—Solutia Inc.; *U.S. Public*, pg. 1483

METHELON—Photo Developing Agent—Eastman Kodak Company; *U.S. Public*, pg. 550

METHERGINE—Injection/Tablets for Postpartum Hemmorrhage Control—Sandoz Pharmaceuticals Corp.; *Int'l*, pg. 974

METHIONINE—Amino Acids—Nippon Kayaku Co. Ltd.; *Int'l*, pg. 934

METHOCEL—Cellulose Ether—The Dow Chemical Company; *U.S. Public*, pg. 522

METHODE—Electronics—Methode Electronics Inc.; *U.S. Public*, pg. 1101

METL-PLAS—Insert Moldings—Capsonic Group, Inc.; *U.S. Private*, pg. 207

METLIFE—Company Name—Metropolitan Life Insurance Co.; *U.S. Private*, pg. 737

METO—Price Marking—Esselte AB; *Int'l*, pg. 459

METO—Company Trade Name—Esselte Meto Kimball Systems; *Int'l*, pg. 460

METO—Esselte Meto Brandname—Meto, USA; *Int'l*, pg. 460

METOPIRONE—NONE—Novartis Pharmaceuticals; *Int'l*, pg. 973

METOXILITE—Semi-Conductor Devices—Semtech Corporation; *U.S. Public*, pg. 1456

METPOLISH—Polishing Compound—Buehler, Limited; *U.S. Public*, pg. 574

METRA—Commuter Rail Transportation—Metra Commuter Rail; *U.S. Private*, pg. 919

METRAFLO—Filter Bags—American Felt & Filter; *U.S. Private*, pg. 54

METRAL—NONE—Berg Electronics; *U.S. Public*, pg. 212

METRI-PACK—Electrical Connections—Delphi Packard Electric Systems; *U.S. Public*, pg. 719

METRI-TORO—High Grade Metic Fastening Systems—Lawson Products, Inc.; *U.S. Public*, pg. 980

METRI-12—High Grade Metric Fastening Systems—Lawson Products, Inc.; *U.S. Public*, pg. 980

METRIC—Tire—The Kelly-Springfield Tire Company; *U.S. Public*, pg. 753

METRIC CONSTRUCTORS, INC.—Construction Company-General Contractors—J.A. Jones, Inc.; *U.S. Public*, pg. 633

METRICEL—Filtration Products—Gelman Sciences, Inc.; *U.S. Public*, pg. 1253

METRIS—Gas Meters—Schlumberger Industries; *U.S. Public*, pg. 1439

METRISITE—Transducers—Gould Instrument Systems, Inc.; *U.S. Public*, pg. 1592

METRO—NONE—Bobit Publishing Company; *U.S. Private*, pg. 154

METRO—Medicare—Everest & Jennings, Inc.; *U.S. Public*, pg. 758

METRO—City Transit Bus—The Flxible Corp.; *U.S. Private*, pg. 444

METRO—Sunglasses—Goody Products, Inc.; *U.S. Public*, pg. 1177

METRO—Distribution Company—SHV Holdings N.V.; *Int'l*, pg. 1154

METRO BRICK—Face, Paving & Common Bricks—Bristile Clay Tiles, Ltd.; *Int'l*, pg. 216

METRO CAP—Post Hardware—Hall Sign, Inc.; *U.S. Private*, pg. 495

METRO COMMUNITY NEWS—Newspaper—Rama Group of Companies; *U.S. Private*, pg. 908

METRO ONE—Cellular Service—AT&T Wireless Services; *U.S. Public*, pg. 11

METRO-PUCK COMIC NETWORK—NONE—Metropolitan Sunday Newspapers, Inc.; *U.S. Private*, pg. 739

METRO-PUCK COMICS NETWORK—Sunday Comics National Advertising Sales—Metro-Puck Comics Network; *U.S. Private*, pg. 739

METROBASE +—Database Management System—Metromail Corporation; *U.S. Public*, pg. 1102

METROCENTER—NONE—SunGard Data Systems Inc.; *U.S. Public*, pg. 1534

METRODIN HP—Highly Purified Follicle Stimulating Hormone—Ares-Serono S.A.; *Int'l*, pg. 80

METROGEL—Pharmaceutical Products—Galderma Laboratories, Inc.; *Int'l*, pg. 819

METROHM—Data Acquisition—Bowthorpe plc; *Int'l*, pg. 207

METROHM—Titrators—Brinkmann Instruments, Inc.; *U.S. Private*, pg. 169

METROMAIL—Marketing & Mail Services—Metromail Corporation; *U.S. Public*, pg. 1102

METRON ELECTRONIC PIPETTE—Microprocessor controlled automated pipetting system—Medical Laboratory Automation, Inc.; *U.S. Private*, pg. 727

METRON PLUS ELECTRONIC PIPETTE—Microprocessor controlled automated pipetting system—Medical Laboratory Automation, Inc.; *U.S. Private*, pg. 727

METRONET—Consumer Information Verification—Metromail Corporation; *U.S. Public*, pg. 1102

METROPOLIS—NONE—A.T. Cross Co.; *U.S. Public*, pg. 460

METROPOLIS—NONE—Helen of Troy Corporation; *U.S. Public*, pg. 807

METROPOLITAN—Floor Tile—American Biltrite Inc.; *U.S. Public*, pg. 68

METROPOLITAN—Toaster—The Black & Decker Corporation; *U.S. Public*, pg. 233

METROPOLITAN—Furniture—Carter Holt Harvey Limited; *U.S. Public*, pg. 904

METROPOLITAN—Vinyl Tile—Congoleum Corporation; *U.S. Public*, pg. 69

METROPOLITAN—Cutlery—General Housewares Corp.; *U.S. Public*, pg. 715

METROPOLITAN—Company Name—Metropolitan Life Insurance Co.; *U.S. Private*, pg. 737

METROPOLITAN—Coffee—Superior Coffee and Foods; *U.S. Public*, pg. 1434

METROPOLITAN—Fire Hydrants—United States Pipe & Foundry Company, Inc.; *U.S. Public*, pg. 1736

METROPOLITAN HOME—Home Decorating Magazine—Hachette Filipacchi Magazines Inc.; *Int'l*, pg. 794

METROPOLITAN HOME—Magazine—Meredith Corporation; *U.S. Public*, pg. 1094

METROPOLITAN VIEW—NONE—Bloomingdale's; *U.S. Public*, pg. 617

METROSEAL—Valve Resilient Seat—United States Pipe & Foundry Company, Inc.; *U.S. Public*, pg. 1736

METSO—Sodium Metasilicates—PQ Corporation; *U.S. Private*, pg. 827

METSPLICE—Abrasive Belt Joint—Buehler, Limited; *U.S. Public*, pg. 574

METTE MUNK—Frozen Bakery Products—Danisco Foods; *Int'l*, pg. 378

METTLER—Precision Balances & Scales—Mettler-Toledo, Inc.; *U.S. Private*, pg. 4

METTLER TOLEDO—NONE—Mettler-Toledo Inc.; *U.S. Private*, pg. 4

MEVACOR—Lovastatin—Merck & Co., Inc.; *U.S. Public*, pg. 1090

MEVACOR—Pharmaceutical—Merck Human Health Division (U.S. Human Health); *U.S. Public*, pg. 1091

MEVATRON—Radiation Therapy System—Siemens Corporation; *Int'l*, pg. 1245

MEXAFORM—Pharmaceutical—Novartis; *Int'l*, pg. 972

MEXENE—Chili Powder & Beans—Bruce Foods Corp.; *U.S. Private*, pg. 175

MEXI-MIX—Food Service—Tyson Foods, Inc.; *U.S. Public*, pg. 1652

MEXI-PEP—Hot Sauce—Trappey's Fine Foods, Inc.; *U.S. Private*, pg. 105

Brand Name Index

MEXI ROLLS—Filled, Fried Burrito-Like Product—Taco John's International, Inc.; *U.S. Private*, pg. 1066
MEXICALI—Snack Foods—Wyandot Inc.; *U.S. Private*, pg. 1193
MEXICAN BUNDLES—Premium Cigars—Consolidated Cigar Corporation; *U.S. Private*, pg. 690
MEXICAN CHEF—Chilis & Seasonings—Snack America; *U.S. Private*, pg. 1010
MEXICAN HOLIDAY—Mexican Food Products—Don Miguel Mexican Foods, Inc.; *U.S. Private*, pg. 339
MEXICAN ORIGINAL—Mexican Food Items—Louis Kemp Seafood Co.; *U.S. Public*, pg. 1652
MEXICAN ORIGINAL—Mexican Food Items—Tyson Foods, Inc.; *U.S. Public*, pg. 1652
MEXICAN STYLE—Frozen Pizza—Tombstone Pizza Corporation; *U.S. Public*, pg. 1288
MEXICANA AIRLINES—International & Commercial Airline—Mexicana Airlines; *Int'l*, pg. 332
MEXICANA JOES—Seasoning—McCormick & Company, Incorporated; *U.S. Public*, pg. 1066
MEXITIL—Treatment of Cardiac Arhythmias—Boehringer Ingelheim GmbH; *Int'l*, pg. 199
MEXITIL—Anti-Arhythmic—Boehringer Ingelheim Pharmaceuticals, Inc.; *Int'l*, pg. 199
MEXSANA—Medicated Powder—Schering-Plough Healthcare Products Inc.; *U.S. Public*, pg. 1438
MEYER—Forest Products—Meyer International PLC; *Int'l*, pg. 864
MEYER—Steel Poles—Thomas & Betts Corporation; *U.S. Public*, pg. 1597
MEYER TREASURE CHEST—Jewelry Stores—Meyer Jewelers; *U.S. Private*, pg. 739
MEZLIN—Pharmaceutical—Bayer Corporation/Pharmaceutical Division; *Int'l*, pg. 173
MEZZER—Field Strength Meters—PTS Electronics Corporation; *U.S. Private*, pg. 828
MGM—NONE—Metro-Goldwyn-Mayer Inc.; *U.S. Public*, pg. 1101
MIACALCIC—Pharmaceutical—Novartis AG; *Int'l*, pg. 971
MIAMI CHILL—Cosmetics—Maybelline, Inc.; *Int'l*, pg. 819
MIAMI HERALD—Newspaper—The Miami Herald; *U.S. Public*, pg. 964
MIAMI MISS—Bicycles, Scooters—Hedstrom Corporation; *U.S. Private*, pg. 526
MIAMI SEAQUARIUM—Marine Aquatic Park—Wometco Enterprises, Inc.; *U.S. Private*, pg. 1186
MIAMI SUBS—Restaurants—Miami Subs Corporation; *U.S. Public*, pg. 1103
MIAMI SUBS GRILL—NONE—Miami Subs Corporation; *U.S. Public*, pg. 1103
MIATA—Automobile—Mazda Motor of America, Inc.; *Int'l*, pg. 849
MIC TECHNOLOGY—Microelectronic Interconnect Products—Aeroflex Incorporated; *U.S. Public*, pg. 23
MICH—Beer—Anheuser-Busch Companies, Inc.; *U.S. Public*, pg. 113
MICHAEL ANTHONY—Gold Jewelry—Michael Anthony Jewelers, Inc.; *U.S. Public*, pg. 1103
MICHAEL MORGAN—Apparel—Fred Meyer Stores; *U.S. Public*, pg. 1103
MICHAEL RECYCLE—Aluminum Cans & Aluminum Foil—Reynolds Metals Company; *U.S. Public*, pg. 1385
MICHAEL SHEA'S BLACK & TAN—Beer—Genesee Corporation; *U.S. Public*, pg. 728
MICHAEL SHEA'S BLONDE LAGER—Beer—Genesee Corporation; *U.S. Public*, pg. 728
MICHAEL SHEA'S IRISH AMBER—Beer—Genesee Corporation; *U.S. Public*, pg. 728
MICHAEL'S—Real Estate Developer—Michael's Development Company; *U.S. Private*, pg. 740
MICHAELOK—Spray Dried Flavors—David Michael & Co. Inc.; *U.S. Private*, pg. 740
MICHCO—Universal Lawnmower Replacement Blades & Parts—Universal Industrial Products Co.; *U.S. Public*, pg. 1677
MICHEL LYNCH—Bordeaux—Seagram Chateau & Estate Wines Co.; *Int'l*, pg. 1215
MICHEL PICARD FRENCH WINES—NONE—Brown-Forman Beverages Worldwide; *U.S. Public*, pg. 261
MICHELIN—Tires—Michelin Americas Small Tires (MAST); *Int'l*, pg. 322

MICHELIN—Tires—Michelin North America; *Int'l*, pg. 322
MICHELIN—Tires—Midwest Tire & Muffler, Inc.; *U.S. Private*, pg. 745
MICHELIN PASSENGER, LIGHT TRUCK, TRUCK, O.T.R.—NONE—Michelin North America (Canada) Inc.; *Int'l*, pg. 322
MICHELINI—Spagetti Sauces—Ventre Packing Company, Inc.; *U.S. Private*, pg. 1135
MICHELOB—Beer—Anheuser-Busch Companies, Inc.; *U.S. Public*, pg. 113
MICHELOB CLASSIC DARK—Dark Beer—Anheuser-Busch Companies, Inc.; *U.S. Public*, pg. 113
MICHELOB DRY—Beer—Anheuser-Busch Companies, Inc.; *U.S. Public*, pg. 113
MICHELOB GOLDEN DRAFT—Beer—Anheuser-Busch Companies, Inc.; *U.S. Public*, pg. 113
MICHELOB GOLDEN DRAFT LIGHT—Beer—Anheuser-Busch Companies, Inc.; *U.S. Public*, pg. 113
MICHELOB LIGHT—Beer—Anheuser-Busch Companies, Inc.; *U.S. Public*, pg. 113
MICHIGAN—Wheel Loaders—Euclid Hitachi; *Int'l*, pg. 622
MICHIGAN BELL—Telephone Company—Ameritech; *U.S. Public*, pg. 97
MICHIGAN BULB—Garden Stock by Mail—Michigan Bulb Company; *U.S. Private*, pg. 421
MICHIGAN FARMER—Farm Publication-15 Issues/Year—Farm Progress Publications; *U.S. Public*, pg. 513
MICHIGAN PROPELLERS—Boat Propellers—Michigan Wheel Corporation; *U.S. Private*, pg. 741
MICHIGAN WHEEL CORPORATION—Marine Propulsion Systems—Michigan Wheel Corporation; *U.S. Private*, pg. 741
MICHIGAN 77—Engine Bearings—Glacier Vandervell, Inc.; *Int'l*, pg. 1334
MICHTEX—Stabilizer—David Michael & Co. Inc.; *U.S. Private*, pg. 740
MICKELOTTI—NONE—Mizuno Corporation; *Int'l*, pg. 884
MICKEY—Snack Cakes—Interstate Brands Corporation; *U.S. Public*, pg. 909
MICKEY & PALS—Childrens' Adhesive Bandages—American White Cross; *U.S. Public*, pg. 694
MICKEY MOUSE—Boys & Girls Underwear—Heyman Corporation; *U.S. Private*, pg. 524
MICO—Brakes—Mico Inc.; *U.S. Private*, pg. 741
MICOFLEX—Baking Enamel—The Dexter Corporation; *U.S. Public*, pg. 504
MICOLON—Waterborne Nonstick Coating—The Dexter Corporation; *U.S. Public*, pg. 504
MICON—Computer-based Process Control Systems—Powell Industries, Inc.; *U.S. Public*, pg. 1319
MICOR—Physiological Recording & Reporting Systems—Siemens Corporation; *Int'l*, pg. 1245
MICROBOARD—Wood Composite Panel—Weyerhaeuser Company; *U.S. Public*, pg. 1764
MICOTHANE—Polyurethane Coating—The Dexter Corporation; *U.S. Public*, pg. 504
MICOTHANE ONE—Polyurethane Coating—The Dexter Corporation; *U.S. Public*, pg. 504
MICOTIL—Animal Health—Elanco Animal Health; *U.S. Public*, pg. 993
MICOTIL—Tilmicosin, Elanco—Eli Lilly and Company; *U.S. Public*, pg. 992
MICRAININ—Combination Tranquilizer/Analgesic—Wallace Laboratories; *U.S. Public*, pg. 310
MICRASCAN—Step-and-Scan Lithography System—Silicon Valley Group, Inc.; *U.S. Public*, pg. 1474
MICREFINER—Water Softening & Purification Equipment—RainSoft Water Treatment Systems; *U.S. Private*, pg. 78
MICRHOGAM RH (D)—Immune Globulin—Ortho Clinical Diagnostic Systems Inc.; *U.S. Public*, pg. 929
MICRICON—Micro Based Control—Research, Incorporated; *U.S. Public*, pg. 1382
MICRIHOST PC—Control Supervision Software—Research, Incorporated; *U.S. Public*, pg. 1382
MICRISTAR—Digital Controller/Programmer—Research, Incorporated; *U.S. Public*, pg. 1382
MICRO—Saw Chain—Stihl Inc.; *Int'l*, pg. 1301

MICRO A—Desktop Mainframe—Unisys Corporation; *U.S. Public*, pg. 1671
MICRO ACOUSTILOG—NONE—Western Atlas Logging Services; *U.S. Public*, pg. 1757
MICRO/ADD/STAT—NONE—Laserscope Surgical Systems; *U.S. Public*, pg. 979
MICRO-AIRE—FG Duct Board—Johns Manville Corporation; *U.S. Public*, pg. 927
MICRO-AT—Source Transfer Control Switch—S & C Electric Company; *U.S. Private*, pg. 954
MICRO BIRD—Spinner—Rain Bird Sprinklers Manufacturing Corp.; *U.S. Private*, pg. 907
MICRO-BLADES—Blades—Becton Dickinson & Co., Massachusetts Div.; *U.S. Public*, pg. 199
MICRO BRAID—Braided Monofilament—Cortland Line Co., Inc.; *U.S. Private*, pg. 277
MICRO-C—NONE—Molex Incorporated; *U.S. Public*, pg. 1121
MICRO CHANNEL—Computer Product—International Business Machines Corporation; *U.S. Public*, pg. 895
MICRO-CHEK—Antimicrobial Agent for PVC—Ferro Corporation; *U.S. Public*, pg. 618
MICRO-CHEK—Product Code Verifier—Matthews International Corp.; *U.S. Public*, pg. 1059
MICRO-COM—Two-way FM Radios—Relm Communications, Inc.; *U.S. Public*, pg. 1376
MICRO-COMPARE—Cost Analysis Service—Eastman Kodak Company; *U.S. Public*, pg. 550
MICRO COPY—Document Management Products—Bell & Howell Holdings; *U.S. Public*, pg. 201
MICRO-DAC—Electronics—National Semiconductor Corporation; *U.S. Public*, pg. 1159
MICRO-DCI—Electronic Panelboard Instruments—Bailey, Fischer & Porter Company; *Int'l*, pg. 449
MICRO-DIP—Miniature Printed Circuit Board Switch—Transico Incorporated; *U.S. Public*, pg. 1630
MICRO-DOSE—Security X-Ray Inspection Equipment—American Science & Engineering, Inc.; *U.S. Public*, pg. 90
MICRO ELITE—Hearing Aids—Dahlberg, Inc.; *U.S. Public*, pg. 194
MICRO-FIBER—Bulk, Felt, Web, Mat—Johns Manville Corporation; *U.S. Public*, pg. 927
MICRO-FILE—Microfilm—Eastman Kodak Company; *U.S. Public*, pg. 550
MICRO-FINE—Plywood—Georgia-Pacific Corporation; *U.S. Public*, pg. 735
MICRO-FIT 3.0—NONE—Molex Incorporated; *U.S. Public*, pg. 1121
MICRO FOG—Lubricators for Compressed Air Systems—IMI Plc; *Int'l*, pg. 646
MICRO-FREEZE—Plastic Wrap—Reynolds Metals Company; *U.S. Public*, pg. 1385
MICRO-GARD—Microscope Drapes—Bristol-Myers Squibb Company; *U.S. Public*, pg. 253
MICRO-GEM—Sapphire Knives & Blades—Becton Dickinson & Co., Massachusetts Div.; *U.S. Public*, pg. 199
MICRO JEWEL—Implantable Cardioverter Defibrillator—Medtronic, Inc.; *U.S. Public*, pg. 1082
MICRO-K—NONE—American Home Products Corporation; *U.S. Public*, pg. 79
MICRO-K—Potassium Replacement Therapy—Wyeth-Ayerst Laboratories, Inc.; *U.S. Public*, pg. 80
MICRO LED—World's Smallest SMD CBI—Dialight Corporation; *Int'l*, pg. 1130
MICRO LINEAR—Electronic Components—Interface Electronics Corporation; *U.S. Private*, pg. 567
MICRO-LOK—Fiberglass Pipe Insulation—Johns Manville Corporation; *U.S. Public*, pg. 927
MICRO MACHINES—Vehicles—Galoob Toys, Inc.; *U.S. Public*, pg. 698
MICRO MAGAZINES—Pocket-Size Periodicals—American Media, Inc.; *U.S. Public*, pg. 87
MICRO-MAGNETIC SYSTEMS—NONE—Sentry Technology Corp.; *U.S. Public*, pg. 1458
MICRO MASTER—Lab Microscopes—Fisher Scientific Company; *U.S. Private*, pg. 658
MICRO-MELT—NONE—Carpenter Technology Corporation; *U.S. Public*, pg. 307
MICRO/MINI-LAB—Microscale Apparatus—Ace Glass Incorporated; *U.S. Private*, pg. 12
MICRO MINIX—Small Cardiac Pacemaker—Medtronic, Inc.; *U.S. Public*, pg. 1082

MICRO MIST—NONE—Hudson, RCI; *U.S. Private*, pg. 546

MICRO MOTION—Direct Mass Flow Measurement for Fluids—Emerson Electric Co.; *U.S. Public*, pg. 572

MICRO NETWORKS—Data Conversion Components, Oscillators, Signal Processing Circuits—Micro Networks Corp.; *U.S. Private*, pg. 969

MICRO 100—Clean Room Latex Gloves—Phoenix Medical Technology, Inc.; *U.S. Public*, pg. 1292

MICRO-ORGANIZER—Microfiche Storage Trays—Eastman Kodak Company; *U.S. Public*, pg. 550

MICRO-PACK—Electrical/Electronic Connections—Delphi Packard Electric Systems; *U.S. Public*, pg. 719

MICRO-PAK—Microfilm Jackets—Eastman Kodak Company; *U.S. Public*, pg. 550

MICRO-PAK—Capsules—IGI, Inc.; *U.S. Public*, pg. 855

MICRO-PHASE—Liquid Detergent for Industrial Cleaning Applications—PPG Industries, Inc.; *U.S. Public*, pg. 1245

MICRO-POINT—Surgical Needles—Ethicon, Inc.; *U.S. Public*, pg. 928

MICRO POWER SYSTEMS—NONE—Milgray Electronics, Inc.; *U.S. Public*, pg. 205

MICRO-PRECISION—Assembly & Gaging Machines—Micromatic Textron; *U.S. Public*, pg. 1589

MICRO-REDI—Disposable Container—Reynolds Metals Company; *U.S. Public*, pg. 1385

MICRO-REL—Circuits & Logo—Medtronic, Inc.; *U.S. Public*, pg. 1082

MICRO RELEASE—Controlled Micro Release Technology—KV Pharmaceutical Company; *U.S. Public*, pg. 941

MICRO-SCAN—Microprocessor Control & Monitoring System—Inductotherm Corp.; *U.S. Private*, pg. 560

MICRO SCREEN—Electric Shaver—Remington Products Company, L.L.C.; *U.S. Private*, pg. 921

MICRO SCREEN ELITE—Electric Shaver—Remington Products Company, L.L.C.; *U.S. Private*, pg. 921

MICRO SERIES—Encoders, Itek Encoders—Litton Industries, Inc.; *U.S. Public*, pg. 1002

MICRO SERIES & DESIGN—Encoders—Litton Industries, Inc.; *U.S. Public*, pg. 1002

MICRO-SHARPS—Blades—Becton Dickinson & Co., Massachusetts Div.; *U.S. Public*, pg. 199

MICRO-SIPE—Tread Process—Bandag, Incorporated; *U.S. Public*, pg. 177

MICRO SPHERE—Electrostatic Lubricating—Ball Corporation; *U.S. Public*, pg. 170

MICRO SPOT & DESIGN—Information Gathering & Recording—The Mead Corporation; *U.S. Public*, pg. 1074

MICRO-STEP—Surfactant-Agricultural Emulsion—Stepan Company; *U.S. Public*, pg. 1514

MICRO-TEC—Bearing Protector Seal—Garlock Sealing Technologies; *U.S. Public*, pg. 402

MICRO-TEMP—Food Thermometers—Litton Industries, Inc.; *U.S. Public*, pg. 1002

MICRO-THIN—Microfilm Jackets—Eastman Kodak Company; *U.S. Public*, pg. 550

MICRO-TIMER—Microwave Oven Timer Control—Litton Industries, Inc.; *U.S. Public*, pg. 1002

MICRO-TOUCH—Latex Medical & Surgical Gloves—Johnson & Johnson Medical, Inc.; *U.S. Public*, pg. 928

MICRO-TRI-BEAM—NONE—Berg Electronics; *U.S. Public*, pg. 212

MICRO-UNITOME—Disposable Knife—Becton Dickinson & Co., Massachusetts Div.; *U.S. Public*, pg. 199

MICRO-VISUAL—Computer Programs Recorded on Magnetic Disks, Electronic Circuit Boards—Bell & Howell Holdings; *U.S. Public*, pg. 201

MICRO-ENDO—Diagnostic & Corrective Products for the Spine—Sofamor Danek Group, Inc.; *U.S. Public*, pg. 1482

MICRO-GO-ROUND—Automatic Food Rotater for Microwave Ovens—Nordic Ware; *U.S. Private*, pg. 806

MICROBAN—Antimicrobial Agent Used in Vinyl Gloves—Phoenix Medical Technology, Inc.; *U.S. Public*, pg. 1292

MICROBAN—Insecticide, Germicide, Fungicide & Odorant—Surco Products, Inc.; *U.S. Private*, pg. 1056

MICROBE MASTERS—NONE—InterBio Inc.; *U.S. Private*, pg. 566

MICROBEAM—NONE—Laserscope Surgical Systems; *U.S. Public*, pg. 979

MICROBIOLOGY AUSTRALIA—Magazine—Reed Business Information Pty. Limited; *Int'l*, pg. 1094

MICROBLACK—Trinitron Picture Tube—Sony Electronics; *Int'l*, pg. 1281

MICROBLOCK—NONE—Elkem ASA; *Int'l*, pg. 446

MICROBOARD—Composite Panel—Weyerhaeuser Forest Products Company; *U.S. Public*, pg. 1764

MICROBORE—NONE—DeVlieg-Bullard Inc.; *U.S. Public*, pg. 502

MICROBROILER—Vitreous Materials—Litton Industries, Inc.; *U.S. Public*, pg. 1002

MICROBROWNER—Microwave Oven Cookware—Litton Industries, Inc.; *U.S. Public*, pg. 1002

MICROBUS—Electronics—National Semiconductor Corporation; *U.S. Public*, pg. 1159

MICROCAB—Carborne Control System—Union Switch & Signal Inc.; *Int'l*, pg. 77

MICROCAM—Microscope Instant Camera—Polaroid Corporation; *U.S. Public*, pg. 1313

MICROCAPS—ATC Parallel Plate (Single Layer) Ceramic Capacitors for DC to 50 GHz—American Technical Ceramics Corp.; *U.S. Public*, pg. 93

MICROCASSETTE—Tape Recorders—Olympus America Inc.; *Int'l*, pg. 1005

MICROCHEM—Water Mngmt. Control Equip.—The Dexter Corporation; *U.S. Public*, pg. 504

MICROCHEM—Integrated Product Line of Automated Water Treatment Feed & Control Equip.—Diversey Water Technologies, Inc.; *U.S. Public*, pg. 1150

MICROCHRON—Microprocessor Timer—General Railway Signal Corp.; *Int'l*, pg. 1194

MICROCLOTH—Polishing Cloth—Buehler, Limited; *U.S. Public*, pg. 574

MICROCOM BRIDGE—NONE—Microcom; *U.S. Public*, pg. 417

MICROCOM ROUTERS—NONE—Microcom; *U.S. Public*, pg. 417

MICROCON—Microconcentrators—Amicon, Inc.; *U.S. Public*, pg. 1113

MICROCONSOLE—Test System Controller—MTS Systems Corporation; *U.S. Public*, pg. 1028

MICROCORE—Thermal Heated Products—R.G. Barry Corporation; *U.S. Public*, pg. 192

MICROCORR—Custom E-Flute Folding Cartons—Calumet Carton Company; *U.S. Private*, pg. 201

MICROCOUSTIC—High Frequency Precision Cleaning—Branson Ultrasonics Corp. - Precision Cleaning Div.; *U.S. Public*, pg. 574

MICROCUT—Machining Coolants—Quaker Chemical Corporation; *U.S. Public*, pg. 1346

MICRODEX—Wet Laminate Adhesive—The Dexter Corporation; *U.S. Public*, pg. 504

MICRODIAL—Rotor Parts—Litton Industries, Inc.; *U.S. Public*, pg. 1002

MICRODISK—NONE—Micropolis Corporation; *U.S. Private*, pg. 742

MICRODOL-X—Photo Developer & Replenisher—Eastman Kodak Company; *U.S. Public*, pg. 550

MICRODON—Non-Woven Air Filter—Freudenberg & Company; *Int'l*, pg. 505

MICRODON—Nonadherent Burn Sheeting & Surgical Dressings—3M; *U.S. Public*, pg. 1604

MICRODOT—Inserts for Commercial & Aerospace Industries—KTI; *U.S. Public*, pg. 939

MICRODUSTER OS—Safe to the Environment Compressed Gas Duster—The Texwipe Co., Inc.; *U.S. Private*, pg. 1079

MICRODYNE—Satellite TV Systems—Microdyne Corporation; *U.S. Public*, pg. 1105

MICROEDGE—Photographic Films & Processing Chemicals—Eastman Kodak Company; *U.S. Public*, pg. 550

MICROETCH—Ion Milling—Veeco Instruments, Inc.; *U.S. Public*, pg. 1711

MICROFAX—PC Facsimile Card—Xerox Imaging Systems, Inc.; *U.S. Public*, pg. 1785

MICROFEED—Metal Grinding Machines—Litton Industries, Inc.; *U.S. Public*, pg. 1002

MICROFINE—Particleboard—Georgia-Pacific Corporation; *U.S. Public*, pg. 735

MICROFINER—Water Softening & Purification Equipment—RainSoft Water Treatment Systems; *U.S. Private*, pg. 78

MICROFLAT—Lapping Machines—Micromatic Textron; *U.S. Public*, pg. 1589

MICROFLEX—Microcellular Foam Systems—The Dow Chemical Company; *U.S. Public*, pg. 522

MICROFLEX—Miniature Condensor Microphones—Shure Brothers Incorporated; *U.S. Private*, pg. 997

MICROFLITE—Microprocessor-based Trainer/Simulators—Raytheon Systems Co.; *U.S. Public*, pg. 1364

MICROFLO PROCESS—Paints—PPG Industries, Inc.; *U.S. Public*, pg. 1245

MICROFOAM—Surfactant-Nonionil—Stepan Company; *U.S. Public*, pg. 1514

MICROFOAM—Foam Backing Stretchy Surgical Tape—3M; *U.S. Public*, pg. 1604

MICROFOIL—Metallic Balloons—Continental American Corp.; *U.S. Private*, pg. 267

MICROFOIL—Insulating Tape—Johns Manville Corporation; *U.S. Public*, pg. 927

MICROFOILER—Insulating Material—AMETEK, Inc.; *U.S. Public*, pg. 99

MICROFORM—Copper & Copper Alloy Rolled Sheet & Strip—Austral Bronze Crane Copper Limited; *Int'l*, pg. 340

MICROFORM—Precision CNC Lathe—Taylor Hobson Pneumo; *Int'l*, pg. 1087

MICROFOX—Fiber-Optic Telecom Signal Converter—Telco Systems, Inc.; *U.S. Public*, pg. 1568

MICROFRAGRANCE—Encapsulated Fragrances—3M; *U.S. Public*, pg. 1604

MICROFREEZ—Plastic Bags—The Dow Chemical Company; *U.S. Public*, pg. 522

MICROFUGE—Centrifuge—Beckman Instruments, Inc.; *U.S. Public*, pg. 199

MICROFUSE—Electronic Fuses—Littelfuse, Inc.; *U.S. Public*, pg. 1001

MICROGATOR—Microwave-Based Reusable Tag Designed to Protect Soft Goods—Sensormatic Electronics Corporation; *U.S. Public*, pg. 1457

MICROGLIDE—Air Bearing Systems—Anorad Corporation; *U.S. Private*, pg. 75

MICROGRAV—Part Per Billion Gas Mixture—Scott Specialty Gases; *U.S. Private*, pg. 977

MICROGRIND—Grinding Coolants—Quaker Chemical Corporation; *U.S. Public*, pg. 1346

MICROGUARD II—Electronic Controller—Amot Controls Corporation; *U.S. Public*, pg. 1405

MICROHELPERS—Microwave Access.—Ekco Housewares, Inc.; *U.S. Public*, pg. 566

MICROHONE—Honing Process Machines & Tooling—Micromatic Textron; *U.S. Public*, pg. 1589

MICROLAB—Laboratory Instrument For Precision Fluid Handling—Hamilton Co., Inc.; *U.S. Private*, pg. 497

MICROLACER—Belt Fasteners—Clipper Belt Lacer Company; *U.S. Private*, pg. 413

MICROLASER—NONE—Texas Instruments Incorporated; *U.S. Public*, pg. 1585

MICROLAX—NONE—Pharmacia & Upjohn, Inc.; *Int'l*, pg. 1047

MICROLINE—Dot Matrix Printers—Oki Electric Industry Company, Ltd.; *Int'l*, pg. 999

MICROLINE—Dot Matrix Printers—Okidata Group; *Int'l*, pg. 1000

MICROLINE—Fine Wire Insulating System—Royle Systems Group; *U.S. Private*, pg. 949

MICROLINER—Marker—Dixon Ticonderoga Company; *U.S. Public*, pg. 514

MICROLINK—Outboard—American Suzuki Motor Corporation; *Int'l*, pg. 1323

MICROLINK—NONE—Chemfab Corporation; *U.S. Public*, pg. 344

MICROLINK—Digital Data Transmission Service—SBC Communications Inc.; *U.S. Public*, pg. 1415

MICROLINK/2—Data/Voice Network Exchange—Ascom Timeplex; *Int'l*, pg. 86

MICROLITE—AA Blankets & Uncured Phenolic—Johns Manville Corporation; *U.S. Public*, pg. 927

MICROLITE—Coated Abrasives—Norton Company; *Int'l*, pg. 1173

MICROLITE—Lighting Control Systems—Pittway Corporation; *U.S. Public*, pg. 1305

MICROLITER—Fitted Stainless Steel Plunger Syringes—Hamilton Co., Inc.; *U.S. Private*, pg. 497

MICROLITH—Fiberglass Mat—Johns Manville Corporation; *U.S. Public*, pg. 927

MICROLLAM—NONE—TJ International, Inc.; *U.S. Public*, pg. 1556

MICROLOCK—Small, Non-Electronic Clamps which Adhere to Jewelry to Deter Shoplifting—Sensormatic Electronics Corporation; *U.S. Public*, pg. 1457

MICROLOK—Vital Interlocking Control System—Union Switch & Signal Inc.; *Int'l*, pg. 77

MICROLOY—Rivetless Conveyor Chain—Jervis B. Webb Company; *U.S. Private*, pg. 1156

MICROMAGIC—Microwave Potato Products—J.R. Simplot Company; *U.S. Private*, pg. 1002

MICROMAGIC PIZZA MILANO—Microwavable Pizza—J.R. Simplot Company; *U.S. Private*, pg. 1002

MICROMAINFRAME—Electronic Instrument—Intel Corporation; *U.S. Public*, pg. 886

MICROMATE—Microwave Shelf/Range Hood—Broan Mfg. Co., Inc.; *U.S. Public*, pg. 1193

MICROMATE—SMD Fixturing System—GenRad, Inc.; *U.S. Public*, pg. 731

MICROMATE 196—Simultaneous 96-Well Harvester—Packard Instrument Co., Inc.; *U.S. Private*, pg. 833

MICROMATIC—Audio-Visual Equip.—Dukane Corporation; *U.S. Private*, pg. 345

MICROMATIC—Honing Machines & Tooling—Micromatic Textron; *U.S. Public*, pg. 1589

MICROMATIC—Surface Finishing Equip. & Tools—Textron Inc.; *U.S. Public*, pg. 1588

MICROMAX—NONE—Elkem ASA; *Int'l*, pg. 446

MICROMAX—Process Mngmt. Center—Honeywell, Inc.; *U.S. Public*, pg. 834

MICROMAX—World's Smallest EAS System for Protection of Soft Goods—Sensormatic Electronics Corporation; *U.S. Public*, pg. 1457

MICROMAX—Microwaveable Plastic Containers—Tenneco Specialty Products; *U.S. Public*, pg. 1579

MICROMAX—TV Receivers—Zenith Electronics Corp.; *U.S. Public*, pg. 1790

MICROMET—Micro-Hardness Tester—Buehler, Limited; *U.S. Public*, pg. 574

MICROMET—Resistance Film—Caddock Electronics, Inc.; *U.S. Private*, pg. 198

MICROMIST—Mist Sprayers—Automatic Equipment Mfg. Co.; *U.S. Private*, pg. 101

MICROMITE—Machine Controller—Gaston County Dyeing Machine Co.; *U.S. Private*, pg. 441

MICROMITE—Indicator Calibrator—Thermo Electric Co., Inc.; *U.S. Private*, pg. 1080

MICROMITE—NONE—Uniroyal Chemical Company, Inc.; *U.S. Public*, pg. 460

MICROMOLD—Abrasives—Micromatic Textron; *U.S. Public*, pg. 1589

MICRON—Dacron Trolling Line—Cortland Line Co., Inc.; *U.S. Private*, pg. 277

MICRON—Powder Processing Systems—Hosokawa Micron International Inc.; *Int'l*, pg. 635

MICRON—NONE—Mikropul Environmental Systems Div.; *Int'l*, pg. 636

MICRON—Binoculars—Swift Instruments, Inc.; *U.S. Private*, pg. 1058

MICRON AIR JET SIEVE—NONE—Hosokawa Micron Powder Systems; *Int'l*, pg. 636

MICRON CAROTID PATCH—Knitted Polyester Vascular Patch—Datascope Corp.; *U.S. Public*, pg. 487

MICRON KNITTED—Knitted Polyester Vascular Prosthesis—Datascope Corp.; *U.S. Public*, pg. 487

MICRONAIR—Air Filters—Freudenberg Nonwovens; *Int'l*, pg. 505

MICRONAL—Polishing Agent for CR-39 Hard Resin Lenses—Ferro Corporation; *U.S. Public*, pg. 618

MICRONASE—Prescription Anti-Diabetes Agent—Pharmacia & Upjohn; *Int'l*, pg. 1048

MICRONET—Data Entry System—Landmark Systems Inc.; *U.S. Private*, pg. 649

MICRONICS—NONE—Milgray Electronics, Inc.; *U.S. Public*, pg. 205

MICRONOR—Tablets—Ortho-McNeil Pharmaceutical Corporation; *U.S. Public*, pg. 929

MICRONOVA—Microcomputers—Data General Corporation; *U.S. Public*, pg. 485

MICRONOX—Resistance Film—Caddock Electronics, Inc.; *U.S. Private*, pg. 198

MICRONSPOT—NONE—Laserscope Surgical Systems; *U.S. Public*, pg. 979

MICRONTA—Test Instruments—RadioShack; *U.S. Public*, pg. 1560

MICRONY—Pacemaker—St. Jude Medical, Inc.; *U.S. Public*, pg. 1427

MICROPAK—Chromatographic Columns—Varian Associates, Inc.; *U.S. Public*, pg. 1710

MICROPAX—NONE—Berg Electronics; *U.S. Public*, pg. 212

MICROPIG—Laboratory Animals—Bausch & Lomb Incorporated; *U.S. Public*, pg. 194

MICROPIX—Cathode Ray Tube—Litton Industries, Inc.; *U.S. Public*, pg. 1002

MICROPLEX—Multiplex Communications—Vindicator Technologies; *U.S. Private*, pg. 1141

MICROPLEXER—Statistical Multiplexer—Ascom Timeplex; *Int'l*, pg. 86

MICROPOLIS—NONE—Micropolis Corporation; *U.S. Private*, pg. 742

MICROPOLIS—NONE—Milgray Electronics, Inc.; *U.S. Public*, pg. 205

MICROPOLISH—Aluminized Polishing Compound—Buehler, Limited; *U.S. Public*, pg. 574

MICROPORE—Surgical Tape, Microporous, First Aid Tape—3M; *U.S. Public*, pg. 1604

MICROPOT—Potentiometers—Litton Industries, Inc.; *U.S. Public*, pg. 1002

MICROPRINT—Rotary Hot Melt Adhesive Applications—Graco Inc.; *U.S. Public*, pg. 756

MICROPRO—Microbial Products—InterBio Inc.; *U.S. Private*, pg. 566

MICROPROBE—Miniature Combination Electrode—Fisher Scientific Company; *U.S. Private*, pg. 658

MICROPUMP—Pumps—IDEX Corporation; *U.S. Public*, pg. 862

MICROPUMP—Pumps—Ryan Herco Products Corp.; *U.S. Private*, pg. 953

MICROROLLER—Pens—Dixon Ticonderoga Company; *U.S. Public*, pg. 514

MICROS—Point-of-Sale Systems—Micros Systems Inc.; *U.S. Public*, pg. 1106

MICROSENTINELUX—Cross-Platform Hardware Key for Open-Systems & UNIX Applications—Rainbow Technologies, Inc.; *U.S. Public*, pg. 1359

MICROSEP—NONE—Chemfab Corporation; *U.S. Public*, pg. 344

MICROSIZE—Diamond Abrasive Reaming Machines & Tooling—Micromatic Textron; *U.S. Public*, pg. 1589

MICROSIZE—Surface Finishing Equip. & Tools—Textron Inc.; *U.S. Public*, pg. 1588

MICROSMOOTH—Surgical Instruments—Alcon Laboratories, Inc.; *Int'l*, pg. 916

MICROSOFT—Computer Software—Microsoft Corporation; *U.S. Public*, pg. 1107

MICROSOFT SYSTEMS JOURNAL—Magazine—Miller Freeman Inc.; *Int'l*, pg. 1443

MICROSPC—Controls Software—Micromatic Textron; *U.S. Public*, pg. 1589

MICROSPEC—Digital Control System—The Foxboro Company; *Int'l*, pg. 1243

MICROSPHERE—Metal Sheet Lubricant—Alltrista Corporation; *U.S. Public*, pg. 56

MICROSPONGE—Teardrop Sterile Sponge—Alcon Laboratories, Inc.; *Int'l*, pg. 916

MICROSPOT—Electronics—Coop Switzerland; *Int'l*, pg. 329

MICROSTAR—Microfilm Readers—Eastman Kodak Company; *U.S. Public*, pg. 550

MICROSTAR—Microscope—Leica, Inc.; *Int'l*, pg. 806

MICROSTAT—Ultra Sonic Nabulizer—CAIRE, Inc.; *U.S. Public*, pg. 751

MICROSTAT—Environmental Filter System—The Kent Company; *Int'l*, pg. 440

MICROSTAT—NONE—Laserscope Surgical Systems; *U.S. Public*, pg. 979

MICROSURGICAL INSTRUMENTS—Surgical Instruments—Alcon Laboratories, Inc.; *Int'l*, pg. 916

MICROTAINER—Blood Collection Device—Becton Dickinson & Company; *U.S. Public*, pg. 199

MICROTECH—Security Systems—Pittway Corporation; *U.S. Public*, pg. 1305

MICROTECTOR—Micromanometer—Dwyer Instruments Inc.; *U.S. Private*, pg. 350

MICROTEK—Duct Free Range Hood System—Broan Mfg. Co., Inc.; *U.S. Public*, pg. 1193

MICROTEL—NONE—Magnetrol International; *U.S. Private*, pg. 696

MICROTENN—Microprocessor Programmer—Tenney Environmental; *U.S. Private*, pg. 1076

MICROTESTER—Conditioning Systems—Reliability Incorporated; *U.S. Public*, pg. 1373

MICROTEX—Slip Resistant Plastics—Uniflex, Inc.; *U.S. Public*, pg. 1665

MICROTHENE—Powdered Polyolefin Resins—Millennium Petrochemicals, Inc.; *Int'l*, pg. 594

MICROTHERM—Thermometer—Cooper Instrument Corp.; *U.S. Private*, pg. 274

MICROTIMES—Computer Publication—Bam Media; *U.S. Private*, pg. 113

MICROTOUCH—Touch Screens for Computer Terminals—Microtouch Systems, Inc.; *U.S. Public*, pg. 1108

MICROTOUCH—NONE—Milgray Electronics, Inc.; *U.S. Public*, pg. 205

MICROTRAC—Disposable Razor—The Gillette Company; *U.S. Public*, pg. 743

MICROTRAC—Particle Size Analyzer—Honeywell, Inc.; *U.S. Public*, pg. 834

MICROTRAC—Drives—MagneTek, Inc.; *U.S. Public*, pg. 1037

MICROTRACKER LP—GPS Mobile Computing Products—Rockwell International Corporation; *U.S. Public*, pg. 1397

MICROTRAK—Culture Confimation Tests & Direct Specimen Tests—Syntex; *Int'l*, pg. 1120

MICROTRAK 7000—Laser Displacement System—Mechanical Technology Inc.; *U.S. Public*, pg. 1077

MICROTRANS—NONE—SunGard Data Systems Inc.; *U.S. Public*, pg. 1534

MICROTRAX—Electronic Coded Track Circuit—Union Switch & Signal Inc.; *Int'l*, pg. 77

MICROTRON—Cooker Magnetron—Litton Industries, Inc.; *U.S. Public*, pg. 1002

MICROTRONIC—Electrical Control Apparatus for Grinding Machines—Litton Industries, Inc.; *U.S. Public*, pg. 1002

MICROTRUST—Accounting System for Bank Trust Departments—SunGard Data Systems Inc.; *U.S. Public*, pg. 1534

MICROTUBE—Tubecub—Beckman Instruments, Inc.; *U.S. Public*, pg. 199

MICROTURBO—Gas Turbines for Aircraft & Helicopters—Labinal SA; *Int'l*, pg. 785

MICROVEL—Paper, Vellums & Film—Dietzgen Corporation; *U.S. Private*, pg. 332

MICROVEL—Double Velour Graft—Meadox Medicals, Inc.; *U.S. Public*, pg. 247

MICROVENT—Contact Lenses—40 Fort Eye Associates; *U.S. Private*, pg. 420

MICROVENT—Fabrics—Herculite Products, Inc.; *U.S. Public*, pg. 802

MICROVENT SOFT—Fabrics—Herculite Products, Inc.; *U.S. Public*, pg. 802

MICROVER—Remotely Operated Vehicle—Benthos, Inc.; *U.S. Public*, pg. 212

MICROVIDEO SYSTEM—Television Microscope System—Circon Corporation; *U.S. Public*, pg. 373

MICROVISION—Film—Du Pont (E.I. Du Pont De Nemours & Co.); *U.S. Public*, pg. 530

MICROVISION BORESCOPES—Industrial Borescopes—Galileo Corp.; *U.S. Public*, pg. 698

MICROWAVES & RF—Periodical—Penton Publishing, Inc.; *U.S. Public*, pg. 1306

MICROWELL ELISA—Test System—Ortho Clinical Diagnostic Systems Inc.; *U.S. Public*, pg. 929

MICROWIRE—Electronics—National Semiconductor Corporation; *U.S. Public*, pg. 1159

MICROWORKS—NONE—Cambridge Soundworks, Inc.; *U.S. Private*, pg. 202

MICROWORKS BY HENRY KLOSS—NONE—Cambridge Soundworks, Inc.; *U.S. Private*, pg. 202

MICROX—Instant Imaging System—Bell & Howell Holdings; *U.S. Public*, pg. 201

Brand Name Index

MICROZOL—Lubricating Additives—The Lubrizol Corporation; *U.S. Public*, pg. 1016

MICROZONE—Electrophoresis Analyzer—Beckman Instruments, Inc.; *U.S. Public*, pg. 199

MICROZOOM—Microscope—Leica, Inc.; *Int'l*, pg. 806

MID-SOUTH FARMER—Farm Publication-12 Issues/Year—Farm Progress Publications; *U.S. Public*, pg. 513

MIDAMOR—Amiloride Hydrochloride—Merck & Co., Inc.; *U.S. Public*, pg. 1090

MIDAS—Machinery Interactive Display & Analysis—GenRad, Inc.; *U.S. Public*, pg. 731

MIDAS—Foam Bath—SmithKline Beecham plc; *Int'l*, pg. 1264

MIDAS INTERNATIONAL—Auto Service Franchises—Midas-International Corp.; *U.S. Public*, pg. 1766

MIDCON CORPORATION—Natural Gas Transmission—Occidental Petroleum Corporation; *U.S. Public*, pg. 1210

MIDDELVLEI ESTATE—Wine—Distillers Corporation S.A.; *Int'l*, pg. 1129

MIDDLEBY MARSHALL—Conveyor Cooking Equipment—The Middleby Corporation; *U.S. Public*, pg. 1109

MIDDLETON AEROSPACE—NONE—Magellan Aerospace Corporation; *Int'l*, pg. 829

MIDDLETON PLACE—Prefinished Wall Paneling—Georgia-Pacific Corporation; *U.S. Public*, pg. 735

MIDEAST—Aluminum—Caradon Plc; *Int'l*, pg. 266

MIDI—NONE—Vauxhall; *U.S. Public*, pg. 724

MIDI FUSE—Auto Fuses—Littelfuse, Inc.; *U.S. Public*, pg. 1001

MIDICONTROL—Programmable Controllers—B & R Industrial Automation; *U.S. Private*, pg. 105

MIDLAND—Heavy Duty Brake Parts—Echlin Inc.; *U.S. Public*, pg. 560

MIDLAND DAILY NEWS—Newspaper—The Hearst Corporation; *U.S. Private*, pg. 515

MIDLAND REPORTER-TELEGRAM—Newspaper—The Hearst Corporation; *U.S. Private*, pg. 515

MIDLAND STEEL PRODUCTS—NONE—Iochpe-Maxion S.A.; *Int'l*, pg. 688

MIDNIGHT—Fragrances—Charles of the Ritz Group Ltd.; *U.S. Private*, pg. 689

MIDNIGHT GREY—NONE—New England Stone Industries, Inc.; *U.S. Private*, pg. 793

MIDNITE BUFFET—Late Night Food Service—Eat N Park Restaurants; *U.S. Private*, pg. 358

MIDNITE SUN—Dairy Products—Eskimo Pie Corporation; *U.S. Public*, pg. 592

MIDO—Watches—SMH Swiss Corporation for Micro Electronics & Watchmaking Indus. Ltd.; *Int'l*, pg. 1160

MIDOL 200—NONE—SmithKline Beecham Research Limited; *Int'l*, pg. 1266

MIDORI—Melon Liqueur—Suntory International Corp.; *Int'l*, pg. 1321

MIDORI—Liqueur—Suntory Ltd.; *Int'l*, pg. 1321

MIDRAN—Proteinase Inhibitor—Novo Nordisk A/S; *Int'l*, pg. 987

MIDRIN—Headache Pharmaceutical Product—Carnrick Laboratories, Inc.; *U.S. Private*, pg. 436

MIDSOUTH—Ice Mfg.-Packaged Ice—Spencer Companies Inc.; *U.S. Private*, pg. 1024

MIDST—System Development Tool—Dun & Bradstreet Software Services; *Int'l*, pg. 532

MIDTEX—Division—Communications Instruments Inc.; *U.S. Private*, pg. 259

MIDWARE—Software—International Business Machines Corporation; *U.S. Public*, pg. 895

MIDWAY—War Game—Monarch Avalon, Inc.; *U.S. Public*, pg. 1123

MIDWAY—Arcade Games—WMS Industries Inc.; *U.S. Public*, pg. 1727

MIDWAY COUTURE—Hair Care Products—The Wella Corporation; *Int'l*, pg. 1489

MIDWEST—Sight Flow Indicators—Dwyer Instruments Inc.; *U.S. Private*, pg. 350

MIDWEST EXPRESS—Airline Service—Kimberly-Clark Corporation; *U.S. Public*, pg. 958

MIDWEST EXPRESS—The Best Care in The Air—Midwest Express Airlines, Inc.; *U.S. Public*, pg. 1111

MIDWEST EXPRESS AIRLINES—Scheduled Commercial Airline—Midwest Express Holdings, Inc.; *U.S. Public*, pg. 1111

MIDWEST EXPRESS CONNECTION—Midwest Express along with Point-to-Point Service—Midwest Express Holdings, Inc.; *U.S. Public*, pg. 1111

MIDWEST LAMINATING—Countertops—Patrick Industries Inc.; *U.S. Public*, pg. 1264

MIDWEST LIVING—Magazine—Meredith Corporation; *U.S. Public*, pg. 1094

MIDWEST MIX—Dairy Mixes—Michael Foods, Inc.; *U.S. Public*, pg. 1103

MIDWEST PRODUCTS, INC.—NONE—Huntco Inc.; *U.S. Public*, pg. 849

MIDWEST REAL ESTATE NEWS—Real Estate Tabloid for Midwest—Intertec Publishing; *U.S. Public*, pg. 1327

MIDWEST REAL ESTATE NEWS—Monthly Publication—Intertec Publishing; *U.S. Public*, pg. 1328

MIDWEST VISION CENTERS—Optical Retail—Midwest Vision Centers; *U.S. Private*, pg. 745

MIELE—NONE—Miele Appliances, Inc.; *Int'l*, pg. 865

MIETHER—Bearing Prods.—Miether Bearing Products, Inc.; *U.S. Private*, pg. 33

MIGHTI-SCRUBB—Liquid Hand Soap—Georgia-Pacific Corporation; *U.S. Public*, pg. 735

MIGHTY—Automotive Parts—Mighty Distributing System; *U.S. Private*, pg. 745

MIGHTY CLEAR!—Replacement Parts—R&B, Inc.; *U.S. Public*, pg. 1354

MIGHTY DOG—Dog Food—Nestle S.A.; *Int'l*, pg. 915

MIGHTY DUCKS—Hockey Team—The Mighty Ducks of Anaheim; *U.S. Public*, pg. 513

MIGHTY FLOW!—Air Intake, Carburetor Preheater & Defroster Duct Hoses—R&B, Inc.; *U.S. Public*, pg. 1354

MIGHTY LIFT!—Trunk, Hood, & Hatchback Lift Supports—R&B, Inc.; *U.S. Public*, pg. 1354

MIGHTY LITES—NONE—Camillus Cutlery Co.; *U.S. Private*, pg. 203

MIGHTY-MAC—NONE—M. Fine & Sons Manufacturing Co., Inc.; *U.S. Private*, pg. 405

MIGHTY MAC—Small Automatic Injection Molding Press—Hull Corporation; *U.S. Private*, pg. 547

MIGHTY MAID—Small Vacuum—Advance Machine Company; *U.S. Private*, pg. 932

MIGHTY MALTS—Malted Milk Balls—New England Confectionery Co.; *U.S. Private*, pg. 1113

MIGHTY MATE—Effluent Sump Pump—Zoeller Co.; *U.S. Private*, pg. 1207

MIGHTY MAX—2 Wheel Drive Truck—Mitsubishi Motor Sales of America, Inc.; *Int'l*, pg. 875

MIGHTY MINT—Peppermint Patty—Borden, Inc.; *U.S. Private*, pg. 157

MIGHTY MITE—Vacuum Cleaner—The Eureka Company; *Int'l*, pg. 440

MIGHTY MOLE—Rotary Compaction Boring Machine—McLaughlin Manufacturing Company; *U.S. Private*, pg. 724

MIGHTY MOUSER—Fishing System—Greenlee Textron; *U.S. Public*, pg. 1589

MIGHTY OAK—Cutlery—Imperial Schrade Corp.; *U.S. Private*, pg. 559

MIGHTY SOFT—Softener—Eastman Kodak Company; *U.S. Public*, pg. 550

MIGHTY-SONIC HORN—Safety Horns—Falcon Safety Products Inc.; *U.S. Private*, pg. 392

MIGHTY TONKA—Scale-Model Steel Cars & Trucks—Tonka Corporation; *U.S. Public*, pg. 797

MIGHTYPLATE—Roofing Products Line—Texas Refinery Corp.; *U.S. Private*, pg. 1078

MIGHTYPLY—Cold Applied Roofing Membrane—Texas Refinery Corp.; *U.S. Private*, pg. 1078

MIGITS—Miniature Integrated GPS/INS Tactical System—Rockwell International Corporation; *U.S. Public*, pg. 1397

MIGRAL—Prescription Drug—Glaxo Wellcome PLC; *U.S. Public*, pg. 553

MIGRALEVE—NONE—Pfizer Inc.; *U.S. Public*, pg. 1281

MIGRATE 'N' GROW—Business Product—International Business Machines Corporation; *U.S. Public*, pg. 895

MIJI LIF—Cleaning Equipment—Man-Gill Chemical Company; *U.S. Private*, pg. 699

MIKAEL YORK—NONE—Tandy Brands Accessories, Inc.; *U.S. Public*, pg. 1560

MIKASA—Compaction Equipment—MultiQuip, Inc.; *Int'l*, pg. 695

MIKE ALBERT—Automobile Leasing—Mike Albert Leasing, Inc.; *U.S. Private*, pg. 32

MIKE & IKE—Candy—Just Born, Inc.; *U.S. Private*, pg. 602

MIKE CONSUMER PRODUCTS—NONE—Barbour Thread, Inc.; *Int'l*, pg. 618

MIKE ROSE FOODS—Food Mfr. & Supplier—Shoney's, Inc.; *U.S. Public*, pg. 1467

MIKELAN—Beta Blocker—Otsuka Pharmaceutical Co., Ltd.; *Int'l*, pg. 1013

MIKELAN EYE DROPS—Beta-Blocker Ophthalmic Solution—Otsuka Pharmaceutical Co., Ltd.; *Int'l*, pg. 1013

MIKELAN LA—Sustained-Release Beta Blocker—Otsuka Pharmaceutical Co., Ltd.; *Int'l*, pg. 1013

MIKO—Lounge Seating—Vecta; *U.S. Private*, pg. 1038

MIKOHN CLASSICS—Games—Mikohn Gaming Corporation; *U.S. Public*, pg. 1111

MIKOHNVISION—Graphic Displays—Mikohn Gaming Corporation; *U.S. Public*, pg. 1111

MIKRO—Hammer and Screen Mill—Hosokawa Micron Powder Systems; *Int'l*, pg. 636

MIKRO ACM—Powder Processing Systems—Hosokawa Micron International Inc.; *Int'l*, pg. 635

MIKRO ACM—NONE—Mikropul Environmental Systems Div.; *Int'l*, pg. 636

MIKRO-ACM—NONE—Hosokawa Micron Powder Systems; *Int'l*, pg. 636

MIKRO-ACM CX—NONE—Hosokawa Micron Powder Systems; *Int'l*, pg. 636

MIKRO-AIRLOCK—NONE—Hosokawa Micron Powder Systems; *Int'l*, pg. 636

MIKRO-ATOMIZER—NONE—Hosokawa Micron Powder Systems; *Int'l*, pg. 636

MIKRO-BAC—Germicidal Detergent—Ecolab Inc.; *U.S. Public*, pg. 562

MIKRO-BANTAM—NONE—Hosokawa Micron Powder Systems; *Int'l*, pg. 636

MIKRO-CHLOR—Germicidal Detergent—Ecolab Inc.; *U.S. Public*, pg. 562

MIKRO-KLENE—Germicidal Detergent—Ecolab Inc.; *U.S. Public*, pg. 562

MIKRO-PULVERIZER—NONE—Hosokawa Micron Powder Systems; *Int'l*, pg. 636

MIKRO-SAMPLMILL—NONE—Hosokawa Micron Powder Systems; *Int'l*, pg. 636

MIKRO-SPRAY—Detergent/Sanitizer Dispenser—Ecolab Inc.; *U.S. Public*, pg. 562

MIKRON—Machinery & Tools—Mikron Holding AG; *Int'l*, pg. 866

MIKROPUL—Air Pollution Contol Systems—Hosokawa Micron International Inc.; *Int'l*, pg. 635

MIKROQUAT—Germicidal Detergent—Ecolab Inc.; *U.S. Public*, pg. 562

MIKUNI—Carburetors—Mikuni Corporation; *Int'l*, pg. 867

MIL—NONE—James Hardie Industries Ltd.; *Int'l*, pg. 596

MIL-CARBS—Washers—Wrought Washer Mfg., Inc.; *U.S. Private*, pg. 1192

MIL-FAB—Prototype Parts—The Budd Company; *Int'l*, pg. 1388

MIL/PAC—High Density Military Power Supplies—Abbott Electronics, Inc.; *U.S. Private*, pg. 9

MILDEW CHECK—Mildewcidal/Algicidal House Wash—PPG Industries, Inc.; *U.S. Public*, pg. 1245

MILDU-BAN—Mildew Preventative—Surco Products, Inc.; *U.S. Private*, pg. 1056

MILEMAKER—Computerized Mileage System—Rand McNally & Company; *U.S. Private*, pg. 908

MILEMASTER—Pens—Dixon Ticonderoga Company; *U.S. Public*, pg. 514

MILES—Polycarbonate—Plastic Suppliers, Inc.; *U.S. Private*, pg. 871

MILES ABOVE—NONE—Northwest Airlines, Inc.; *U.S. Public*, pg. 1200

MILES KIMBALL—Mail Order—Miles Kimball Company; *U.S. Private*, pg. 745

MILES NERVINE—Sedative—Bayer AG; *Int'l*, pg. 171

MILES NERVINE—Sedative—Bayer Corporation/Consumer Care Division; *Int'l*, pg. 173

MILESTONE—Building System—Pascoe Building Systems, Inc.; *U.S. Private*, pg. 842

MILEX—Milk Powder—MD Foods; *Int'l*, pg. 826

MILFORD—Chinaware—The Homer Laughlin China Company; *U.S. Private*, pg. 653

MILFORD—Saw Blades—Sandvik/Milford Corporation; *Int'l*, pg. 1185

MILITARY BOOK CLUB—NONE—Doubleday Direct; *Int'l*, pg. 191

MILITARY HISTORY—Periodical—Cowles Enthusiast Media, Inc.; *U.S. Private*, pg. 281

MILK & HONEY VACATIONS—NONE—El Al Israel Airlines, Ltd.; *Int'l*, pg. 435

MILK-BONE—Brand Flavor Dog Snacks, Dog Treats—Nabisco Inc.; *U.S. Public*, pg. 1355

MILK BONE—Pet Snacks—RJR Nabisco Holdings Corp.; *U.S. Public*, pg. 1354

MILK DUDS—Candy—Huhtamaki Oy; *Int'l*, pg. 638

MILK MATE—NONE—Borden Foods Canada; *U.S. Private*, pg. 159

MILK MATE—Dairy Feed Milk Replacer—Manna Pro Corporation; *U.S. Private*, pg. 700

MILK N HONEY—Hair Care Line—Conair Corporation; *U.S. Private*, pg. 261

MILK PLUS 6—Hair Conditioner, Shampoo—Revlon-Realistic Professional Products, Inc.; *U.S. Private*, pg. 690

MILKA—Chocolate—Kraft Jacobs Suchard; *U.S. Public*, pg. 1290

MILKA—Chocolate—Kraft Jacobs Suchard AG; *U.S. Public*, pg. 1288

MILKINOL—NONE—Schwarz Pharma Inc.; *Int'l*, pg. 1211

MILKMAID—Dairy Products—Nestle S.A.; *Int'l*, pg. 915

MILKRITE MILKING MACHINE—Milking Machine—Carter Holt Harvey Limited; *U.S. Public*, pg. 904

MILKSLICE—Chilled Dessert—Ferrero; *Int'l*, pg. 480

MILKY WAY—Candy—Mars, Incorporated; *U.S. Private*, pg. 707

MILKY WAY DARK—Candy Bar—Mars, Incorporated; *U.S. Private*, pg. 707

MILKY WAY II—Lesser Calorie Candy Bar—Mars, Incorporated; *U.S. Private*, pg. 707

MILKYWAY BRAND—NONE—M&M/Mars; *U.S. Private*, pg. 707

MILL CREEK—Hair & Skin Care Products—Carme' Cosmeceutical Sciences, Inc.; *U.S. Private*, pg. 213

MILL EL—Military Electroluminescent Display—Industrial Electronic Engineers, Inc.; *U.S. Private*, pg. 561

MILLBRITE—End Sealer—ISK BioSciences; *Int'l*, pg. 689

MILLBRITE—Interior Walls and Countertops—Monarch Tile, Inc.; *U.S. Private*, pg. 287

MILLBROOK—Bread—Interstate Brands Corporation; *U.S. Public*, pg. 909

MILLCRAFT—Machine Wood Products—Meyer International PLC; *Int'l*, pg. 864

MILLENIA—Car—Mazda Motor of America, Inc.; *Int'l*, pg. 849

MILLENIUM—Main Frame Computer—Amdahl Corporation; *Int'l*, pg. 527

MILLENIUM—Skin Care—Elizabeth Arden Company; *Int'l*, pg. 1435

MILLENNIUM—NONE—Everest & Jennings, Inc.; *U.S. Public*, pg. 758

MILLENNIUM—Designer Chair Line—Harter; *U.S. Private*, pg. 581

MILLENNIM BANKING—Call Center & Branch Automation System—Broadway & Seymour, Inc.; *U.S. Public*, pg. 258

MILLENNIUM 8000—High Density Rack—Hayes Microcomputer Products, Inc.; *U.S. Public*, pg. 801

MILLENNIUM FYI—Real-Time Memorandum System—Dun & Bradstreet Software Services; *Int'l*, pg. 532

MILLENNIUM MANAGEMENT REPORT WRITER—Report Writer Software—Dun & Bradstreet Software Services; *Int'l*, pg. 532

MILLENNIUM SYSTEMS DEVELOPMENT TOOL—System Development Software—Dun & Bradstreet Software Services; *Int'l*, pg. 532

MILLENNIUM VIEWPRINT—Report Writing Software—Dun & Bradstreet Software Services; *Int'l*, pg. 532

MILLER—Fluid Mixing, Metering Equipment—IDEX Corporation; *U.S. Public*, pg. 862

MILLER—NONE—Nordyne Inc.; *U.S. Public*, pg. 1193

MILLER BREWING—T-Shirts & Sweatshirts—Holoubek Inc.; *U.S. Private*, pg. 536

MILLER CLEAR—Beer—Miller Brewing Company; *U.S. Public*, pg. 1289

MILLER ELECTRIC—Welding Machines & Accessories—Welsco Inc.; *U.S. Private*, pg. 1161

MILLER EQUIPMENT—Safety Equipment—WGM Safety Corporation; *Int'l*, pg. 462

MILLER FUNDRAISING—Gifts & Greeting Cards—Fine Art Developments plc; *Int'l*, pg. 485

MILLER/GALANTE—Unicompartmental Knee System—Bristol-Myers Squibb Company; *U.S. Public*, pg. 253

MILLER GENUINE DRAFT—Beer—Miller Brewing Company; *U.S. Public*, pg. 1289

MILLER GENUINE DRAFT—Beer—Philip Morris Companies Inc.; *U.S. Public*, pg. 1287

MILLER GENUINE DRAFT LIGHT—Beer—Miller Brewing Company; *U.S. Public*, pg. 1289

MILLER HIGH LIFE—Beer—Miller Brewing Company; *U.S. Public*, pg. 1289

MILLER HIGH LIFE—Beer—Philip Morris Companies Inc.; *U.S. Public*, pg. 1287

MILLER HYDRO—Case Packers—Lynch Machinery, Inc.; *U.S. Public*, pg. 1022

MILLER LEGEND—Welding & Cutting Equip.—Miller Electric Manufacturing Co.; *U.S. Public*, pg. 867

MILLER LITE—Beer—Miller Brewing Company; *U.S. Public*, pg. 1289

MILLER LITE—Beer—Philip Morris Companies Inc.; *U.S. Public*, pg. 1287

MILLER LITE ICE—Beer—Philip Morris Companies Inc.; *U.S. Public*, pg. 1287

MILLER PRO—Farm Equipment—Miller-St. Nazianz, Inc.; *U.S. Private*, pg. 748

MILLER RESERVE—Beer—Philip Morris Companies Inc.; *U.S. Public*, pg. 1287

MILLER/ROSASKA—Crystal Stemware & Giftware—Reed & Barton Corporation; *U.S. Private*, pg. 916

MILLER/SHANDWICK—NONE—Shandwick International Plc; *Int'l*, pg. 1226

MILLER SPECIAL TOOLS—Service Tools—SPX Corporation; *U.S. Public*, pg. 1420

MILLER-WOHL—NONE—Petrie Retail, Inc.; *U.S. Private*, pg. 858

MILLERS AND ROBIRCH—Pork and Savoury Products—Kerry Group PLC; *Int'l*, pg. 731

MILLERS FALLS—Cutting Tools—Rule Industries, Inc.; *U.S. Public*, pg. 950

MILLEX—Filter Unit—Millipore Corporation; *U.S. Public*, pg. 1112

MILLI-GRID—NONE—Molex Incorporated; *U.S. Public*, pg. 1121

MILLI-Q—Water System—Millipore Corporation; *U.S. Public*, pg. 1112

MILLI-RO—Water System—Millipore Corporation; *U.S. Public*, pg. 1112

MILLICELL—Culture Plate Insert—Millipore Corporation; *U.S. Public*, pg. 1112

MILLIDISK—Cartridge Filter—Millipore Corporation; *U.S. Public*, pg. 1112

MILLIFLEX—Test System—Millipore Corporation; *U.S. Public*, pg. 1112

MILLIGARD—Cartridge Filter—Millipore Corporation; *U.S. Public*, pg. 1112

MILLIKEN—Textiles & Chemicals—Milliken & Company; *U.S. Private*, pg. 748

MILLILAB—Automated Sample Preparation Products—Millipore Corporation; *U.S. Public*, pg. 1112

MILLIMETER—Monthly Magazine—Intertec Publishing; *U.S. Public*, pg. 1327

MILLING ROAD—Furniture—Baker Knapp & Tubbs Inc.; *U.S. Private*, pg. 630

MILLIONAIRE—After Shave & Cologne—The Mennen Company; *U.S. Public*, pg. 397

MILLIONAIRE MAKER—NONE—Harrah's Entertainment, Inc.; *U.S. Public*, pg. 790

MILLIONAIRE SUCCESS SYSTEM—Financial Information Program—Success Development International; *U.S. Private*, pg. 1048

MILLIONAIRE TRAINING WORKSHOP—Financial Information Services—Success Development International; *U.S. Private*, pg. 1048

MILLIONAIRES—Candy—Pangburn Candy Company; *U.S. Private*, pg. 836

MILLIPAK—Filter—Millipore Corporation; *U.S. Public*, pg. 1112

MILLISCOPE—Newsletter—Millipore Corporation; *U.S. Public*, pg. 1112

MILLISEP—Filter Module—Millipore Corporation; *U.S. Public*, pg. 1112

MILLISROL—Nitroglycerin Solution for Injection—Nippon Kayaku Co. Ltd.; *Int'l*, pg. 934

MILLISTAK—Filter Unit—Millipore Corporation; *U.S. Public*, pg. 1112

MILLITE—Dry Fog—Devoe Paint; *Int'l*, pg. 663

MILLITE—Dry Fog—ICI Paints; *Int'l*, pg. 664

MILLITITER—Filtration System—Millipore Corporation; *U.S. Public*, pg. 1112

MILLMASTER—Milling Technology—Smith International, Inc.; *U.S. Public*, pg. 1478

MILLPLANK—Prefinished Wall Paneling—Georgia-Pacific Corporation; *U.S. Public*, pg. 735

MILLS—Jewelers—Reeds Jewelers, Inc.; *U.S. Public*, pg. 1370

MILLS—Boilers—H.B. Smith Co., Inc.; *U.S. Private*, pg. 1008

MILLSTONE—Interior Wall and Countertop—Monarch Tile, Inc.; *U.S. Private*, pg. 287

MILLWAY—Industrial Process Instrumentation Equipment & Automation Sys.—Valmet Corporation; *Int'l*, pg. 1447

MILLWOOD—Whiskey Cream—Groupe Pernod Ricard; *Int'l*, pg. 566

MILNAV—Land Navigation System—Kearfott Guidance & Navigation Corp.; *U.S. Private*, pg. 93

MILNE FEEDS—Stock Feed—Peters & Brownes Foods Ltd.; *Int'l*, pg. 1040

MILNOT—Canned Milk—The Milnot Company; *U.S. Private*, pg. 749

MILO—Chocolate Drink—Nestle S.A.; *Int'l*, pg. 915

MILO—NONE—Nestle USA; *Int'l*, pg. 916

MILO—Otsuka Beverage - Nestle's Product—Otsuka Pharmaceutical Co., Ltd.; *Int'l*, pg. 1013

MILPAK—NONE—Solid State Devices, Inc.; *U.S. Private*, pg. 1012

MILROYAL—Pumps—Milton Roy Company; *U.S. Public*, pg. 1534

MILTON—Baby Bottle Steralizer—Permark International (Pty.) Ltd.; *Int'l*, pg. 1036

MILTON—NONE—Procter & Gamble Espana S.A.; *U.S. Public*, pg. 1332

MILTON BRADLEY—Games—Hasbro, Inc.; *U.S. Public*, pg. 797

MILTON J WERSHOW—Auctioneers, Liquidators, Appraisers & Realtors—Wershow-Ash-Lewis; *U.S. Private*, pg. 1162

MILTONDUFF MALT WHISKEY—Spirit—Allied Domecq PLC; *Int'l*, pg. 62

MILTOWN—Tranquilizer—Wallace Laboratories; *U.S. Public*, pg. 310

MILTOX—Cupio-Organic Fungicides—Novartis AG; *Int'l*, pg. 971

MILUMIL—NONE—Milupa S.A.; *Int'l*, pg. 991

MILUZ—Building Paints for Exterior, Interior, Prof. & Retail Uses—Akzo Nobel N.V.; *Int'l*, pg. 42

MILWAUKEE—Electric Power Tools & Access.—Essex Industries; *Int'l*, pg. 18

MILWAUKEE BUCKS—Professional Basketball—Milwaukee Bucks, Inc.; *U.S. Private*, pg. 749

MILWAUKEE'S BEST—Beer—Philip Morris Companies Inc.; *U.S. Public*, pg. 1287

MILWAUKEE'S BEST—Beer—Miller Brewing Company; *U.S. Public*, pg. 1289

MIMIC—Low Risk Insecticide—Rohm and Haas Company; *U.S. Public*, pg. 1403

MIN-E—Steel Fastener One Hole Straps/Conduit Hangers—Minerallac Co.; *U.S. Private*, pg. 750

MIN-I-PHASE—Bus Duct for Electrical Distribution Systems—General Electric Canada Inc.; *U.S. Public*, pg. 713

MIN-K—Flexible, Molded Metal Encased—Johns Manville Corporation; *U.S. Public*, pg. 927

MIN-R—X-ray Films & Screens—Eastman Kodak Company; *U.S. Public*, pg. 550

MIN-U-GEL AR—A-Gel-HVM—Engelhard Corp.-Quincy Operations; *U.S. Public*, pg. 582

MIN-U-GEL CW—Industrial Chemical-A-Gel-HVM—Engelhard Corp.-Quincy Operations; *U.S. Public*, pg. 582

MIN-U-GEL FG—Industrial Chemical-A-Gel-HVM—Engelhard Corp.-Quincy Operations; *U.S. Public*, pg. 582

MIN-U-GEL 400—Industrial Chemical-A-Gel-HVM—Engelhard Corp.-Quincy Operations; *U.S. Public*, pg. 582

MIN-U-GEL LF—Industrial Chemical-A-Gel-HVM—Engelhard Corp.-Quincy Operations; *U.S. Public*, pg. 582

MIN-U-GEL MB—Industrial Chemical-A-Gel-HVM—Engelhard Corp.-Quincy Operations; *U.S. Public*, pg. 582

MIN-U-GEL 100—Industrial Chemical-A-Gel-HVM—Engelhard Corp.-Quincy Operations; *U.S. Public*, pg. 582

MIN-U-GEL PC—Industrial Chemical-A-Gel-HVM—Engelhard Corp.-Quincy Operations; *U.S. Public*, pg. 582

MIN-U-GEL 200—Industrial Chemical-A-Gel-HVM—Engelhard Corp.-Quincy Operations; *U.S. Public*, pg. 582

MIN-U GEL AA SPECIAL—Industrial Chemical-A-Gel-HVM—Engelhard Corp.-Quincy Operations; *U.S. Public*, pg. 582

MINA GEAR—Power Transmission Equipment—Regal-Beloit Corporation; *U.S. Public*, pg. 1370

MINARD'S—Liniment—SmithKline Beecham plc; *Int'l*, pg. 1264

MINATE VENTILATION—Pacemaker—St. Jude Medical, Inc.; *U.S. Public*, pg. 1427

MINAXI—Gamma System—Packard Instrument Co., Inc.; *U.S. Private*, pg. 833

MINDEL—High-Tech Polymer—Amoco Corporation; *U.S. Public*, pg. 101

MINDEL RESINS—High Temperature Engineering Resins—Amoco Chemicals; *U.S. Public*, pg. 102

MINDS—Maxwell Integrators of Networked Distributed Solutions—Maxwell Technologies, Inc.; *U.S. Public*, pg. 1061

MINDSCAPE—Developers & Publishers of Multimedia Products—Pearson plc; *Int'l*, pg. 1025

MINE—Biweekly General Interest Women's Magazine—Kodansha Ltd.; *Int'l*, pg. 742

MINE—Safety & Health Equip.—Mine Safety Appliances Co.; *U.S. Public*, pg. 1114

MINELMA—Margarine—Vandemoortele N.V.; *Int'l*, pg. 1451

MINERAL WATER—Shampoo & Rinse—Shiseido Company Ltd.; *Int'l*, pg. 1235

MINERALIGHT—Short Wave Lamps—UVP, Inc.; *U.S. Private*, pg. 1115

MINERALITE—Sporting Goods—Brunswick Bowling & Billiards Corp.; *U.S. Public*, pg. 265

MINERALLAC—Company Name Conduit Hanger—Minerallac Co.; *U.S. Private*, pg. 750

MINERALOX—Stone & Mineral Polish—Ferro Corporation; *U.S. Public*, pg. 618

MINERE—Mineral Water—Nestle S.A.; *Int'l*, pg. 915

MINGAY'S RETAILS GUIDE DIRECTORY—NONE—Reed Business Information Pty. Limited; *Int'l*, pg. 1094

MINI—Subcompact Car—British Aerospace p.l.c.; *Int'l*, pg. 217

MINI-ALERT—Horns & Strobes—System Sensor Division; *U.S. Public*, pg. 1306

MINI-AXID—NONE—Molex Incorporated; *U.S. Public*, pg. 1121

MINI BERTHA—Games—Mikohn Gaming Corporation; *U.S. Public*, pg. 1111

MINI-BLADES—Blades—Becton Dickinson & Co., Massachusetts Div.; *U.S. Public*, pg. 199

MINI BUCK—Cutlery—Buck Knives, Inc.; *U.S. Private*, pg. 177

MINI-BUNDLE CABLE—Fiber Optic Cable—Siecor Corporation; *U.S. Public*, pg. 449

MINI-BUNDLE CABLE—Fiber Optic Cable—Siecor Corporation; *Int'l*, pg. 1245

MINI-CAM—NONE—Molex Incorporated; *U.S. Public*, pg. 1121

MINI-CART—Smaller Automatic Guided Vehicles—Jervis B. Webb Company; *U.S. Private*, pg. 1156

MINI-CARTRAC—Material Handling System—SI Handling Systems, Inc.; *U.S. Public*, pg. 1418

MINI-CATH—Winged Infusion Set—Becton Dickinson & Company; *U.S. Public*, pg. 199

MINI-CHECK—Locker—American Locker Group, Inc.; *U.S. Public*, pg. 85

MINI-CHECK—Small Item Locker—American Locker Security Systems, Inc.; *U.S. Public*, pg. 86

MINI CHILL—Ice Cream Maker—Salton/Maxim Housewares, Inc.; *U.S. Public*, pg. 1430

MINI CHIPS—Semi-Sweet Chocolate—Hershey Chocolate U.S.A.; *U.S. Public*, pg. 812

MINI CHIPS—Semi-Sweet Chocolate—Hershey Foods Corporation; *U.S. Public*, pg. 811

MINI CHUNKS—Pet Food—Iams Company; *U.S. Private*, pg. 556

MINI-COM—Two-way FM Radios—Relm Communications, Inc.; *U.S. Public*, pg. 1376

MINI-COMPACTA—Shock-Proof Faeces Lifting Plant—KSB Aktiengesellschaft; *Int'l*, pg. 721

MINI-CURE—Vulcanizing System—Royle Systems Group; *U.S. Private*, pg. 949

MINI DIAMOND—Jewelry—Helzberg's Diamond Shops, Inc.; *U.S. Public*, pg. 220

MINI-DIP—Miniature Printed Circuit Board Switch—Transico Incorporated; *U.S. Public*, pg. 1630

MINI-DRIVER—Surgical Instrument—3M; *U.S. Public*, pg. 1604

MINI 8—Videocassette Recorders, Cameras, Cassettes—Sony Electronics; *Int'l*, pg. 1281

MINI-FILE—Scientific Glassware for Laboratory Use—Wheaton Inc.; *Int'l*, pg. 67

MINI-FIT—NONE—Molex Incorporated; *U.S. Public*, pg. 1121

MINI-FIT, BMI—NONE—Molex Incorporated; *U.S. Public*, pg. 1121

MINI-FIT, JR.—NONE—Molex Incorporated; *U.S. Public*, pg. 1121

MINI-FIT, TPA—NONE—Molex Incorporated; *U.S. Public*, pg. 1121

MINI FLEX-VENT—Oil Ring Part—Hastings Manufacturing Company; *U.S. Public*, pg. 798

MINI-14—Semi-Automatic Rifles—Sturm, Ruger & Co., Inc.; *U.S. Public*, pg. 1526

MINI FUSE—Auto fuse—Littelfuse, Inc.; *U.S. Public*, pg. 1001

MINI-GAMULIN-RH—Immune Globulin Human—Centeon, L.L.C.; *Int'l*, pg. 626

MINI-GASKLEEN III—Filter Assembly—Pall Corporation; *U.S. Public*, pg. 1253

MINI-GEN—Signal Generators—Synchro-Start Products, Inc.; *U.S. Private*, pg. 627

MINI-GRAPH—Card Duplicator—Weber Marking Systems, Inc.; *U.S. Private*, pg. 1157

MINI-GUN—Hot Air Convection Heater—Raychem Corporation; *U.S. Public*, pg. 1362

MINI-HEEL—Coreless Holding Furnaces—Inductotherm Corp.; *U.S. Private*, pg. 560

MINI KING—Bilge Pump—Attwood Corporation; *U.S. Private*, pg. 1038

MINI-LINK—Calibration Software—O.I. Corporation; *U.S. Public*, pg. 1208

MINI-MAC—GPS Survey Receiver—Litton Industries, Inc.; *U.S. Public*, pg. 1002

MINI-MACH—Small Indexable Tooling Drill—Rogers Tool Works, Inc.; *U.S. Public*, pg. 950

MINI-MAG—Magnetic Flowmeters—Bailey, Fischer & Porter Company; *Int'l*, pg. 449

MINI-MARK—Small Character Ink Jet—Marsh Company; *U.S. Private*, pg. 707

MINI MART—Convenience Store—Mini Mart, Inc.; *U.S. Public*, pg. 967

MINI-MATIC II—Automatic Sound Filmstrip Viewer—Dukane Corporation; *U.S. Private*, pg. 345

MINI-MISER—Brew Basket—Regal Ware, Inc.; *U.S. Private*, pg. 917

MINI-MIST—Purse Size Fragrance Dispensers—Risdon Corporation; *U.S. Public*, pg. 463

MINI-MITE—Cordless, Small MultiPro—Dremel; *U.S. Public*, pg. 574

MINI MITE—Cordless Vacuum Cleaner—The Eureka Company; *Int'l*, pg. 440

MINI-MIZER—Electronic/Pneumatic Interface—Humphrey Products Company; *U.S. Private*, pg. 547

MINI-MODULE—Storage Racks—Jarke Corporation; *U.S. Private*, pg. 583

MINI-MONO—Computer Equipment—Emulex Corporation; *U.S. Public*, pg. 579

MINI-MULE—Spare Tire Holders—Selas Corporation of America; *U.S. Public*, pg. 1454

MINI-MYTE—Electric Air Valves—Humphrey Products Company; *U.S. Private*, pg. 547

MINI-NET—Data Communications Network—O.I. Corporation; *U.S. Public*, pg. 1208

MINI 90—Compact Control System—Bailey Controls Company; *Int'l*, pg. 654

MINI-PAC—Actuator—Duff-Norton; *U.S. Public*, pg. 406

MINI-PAL—Servo Accelerometer—AlliedSignal Commercial Avionics Systems; *U.S. Public*, pg. 50

MINI PAW—Sprinklers—Rain Bird Sprinklers Manufacturing Corp.; *U.S. Private*, pg. 907

MINI-PIK—Crane—Harnischfeger Industries, Inc.; *U.S. Public*, pg. 788

MINI-PISTON—Switches—Barksdale, Inc.; *U.S. Public*, pg. 457

MINI-PLUG—Electric Line Cords—General Cable Corporation; *U.S. Public*, pg. 1486

MINI POLY-Q—Plastic Scintillation Vials—Beckman Instruments, Inc.; *U.S. Public*, pg. 199

MINI PV—NONE—Berg Electronics; *U.S. Public*, pg. 212

MINI-Q—Fasteners—Southtec, Inc.; *U.S. Private*, pg. 1015

MINI-QUICK—Household Clothes Washing Machines—General Electric Canada Inc.; *U.S. Public*, pg. 713

MINI-RUPTER—Interrupter Switch—S & C Electric Company; *U.S. Private*, pg. 954

MINI SNEAKER—Cable Plow—Case Corporation; *U.S. Public*, pg. 311

MINI-SPORTS—Tires—Bridgestone/Firestone, Inc.; *Int'l*, pg. 213

MINI-SUN CHAISES—Aluminum Beach Chairs—Telescope Casual Furniture, Inc.; *U.S. Private*, pg. 1074

MINI-T-PAK—Hydraulic Packings—John Crane Mechanical Seals; *Int'l*, pg. 1339

MINI THIRTY—Rifle—Sturm, Ruger & Co., Inc.; *U.S. Public*, pg. 1526

MINI TORK—Valves—Masoneilan North American Operations; *U.S. Public*, pg. 528

MINI TOWNSEND—Gynecological Device—The Cooper Companies, Inc.; *U.S. Public*, pg. 442

MINI-TRAIL—Motorcycle—American Honda Motor Co., Inc. Motorcycle Division; *Int'l*, pg. 634

MINI TRIEVER—Small Vacuum—Advance Machine Company; *Int'l*, pg. 932

MINI-ULTRAGASKLEEN—NONE—Pall Corporation; *U.S. Public*, pg. 1253

MINI-WASH—Washing Machines—General Electric Canada Inc.; *U.S. Public*, pg. 713

MINI-JUMP—NONE—Berg Electronics; *U.S. Public*, pg. 212

MINICAMS—Airmonitoring Product—O.I. Corporation; *U.S. Public*, pg. 1208

MINICARD—Photo Film, Chemicals Data Handling Equipment—Eastman Kodak Company; *U.S. Public*, pg. 550

MINICO—Polymer Thick Film Matls.—Emerson & Cuming Specialty Polymers; *Int'l*, pg. 1435

MINICOLORMASTER—Film Processor—Houston Fearless 76 Inc.; *U.S. Private*, pg. 542

MINICOM—Emergency Vehicle Warning Siren—Federal Signal Corporation; *U.S. Public*, pg. 616

MINICON—Microconcentrators—Amicon, Inc.; *U.S. Public*, pg. 1113

MINICONTROL—Programmable Controllers—B & R Industrial Automation; *U.S. Private*, pg. 105

MINIDAC—Miniature Converters—Analog Devices, Inc.; *U.S. Public*, pg. 107

MINIFOLD—Filtration Manifolds—Schleicher & Schuell, Inc.; *Int'l*, pg. 1206

MINIFORM—Paper Products—Georgia-Pacific Corporation; *U.S. Public*, pg. 735

MINIGRAPH—Recorders—Dwyer Instruments Inc.; *U.S. Private*, pg. 350

MINIHELIC—Differential Pressure Gage—Dwyer Instruments Inc.; *U.S. Private*, pg. 350

MINIJAMMER—Blowers—AMETEK, Inc.; *U.S. Public*, pg. 99

MINIJUMP—NONE—Berg Electronics; *U.S. Public*, pg. 212

MINIKIN—TV Receivers—Thomson Consumer Electronics Inc.; *Int'l*, pg. 1383

MINILABMASTER—Film Processor—Houston Fearless 76 Inc.; *U.S. Private*, pg. 542

MINILINK/1—T1 Facilities Management System—Ascom Timeplex; *Int'l*, pg. 86

MINILINK/2—Data/Voice Network Exchange—Ascom Timeplex; *Int'l*, pg. 86

MINILOG—NONE—Western Atlas Logging Services; *U.S. Public*, pg. 1757

Brand Name Index

Brand Name Index

MINILUNG—Artificial Respiratory Apparatus—Nellcor Puritan Bennett Incorporated; *U.S. Public*, pg. 1039
MINIMASTER—FLowmeter—Dwyer Instruments Inc.; *U.S. Private*, pg. 350
MINIMATE—Plastic Grocery Sacks—Sonoco Products Company; *U.S. Public*, pg. 1485
MINIMAX—Swimming Pool Heater—Essef Corporation; *U.S. Public*, pg. 592
MINIMAX—Oxygenator—Medtronic, Inc.; *U.S. Public*, pg. 1082
MINIMAX PLUS—Oxygenator—Medtronic, Inc.; *U.S. Public*, pg. 1082
MINIMED—Intravenous Infusion Device—Siemens Corporation; *Int'l*, pg. 1245
MINIMET—Automatic Polisher/Grinder—Buehler, Limited; *U.S. Public*, pg. 574
MINIMITE—Digital Thermometer—Thermo Electric Co., Inc.; *U.S. Private*, pg. 1080
MINIPAC—Escape Seat—McDonnell Aircraft & Missile Systems Div.; *U.S. Public*, pg. 241
MINIPIG—Laboratory Animals—Bausch & Lomb Incorporated; *U.S. Public*, pg. 194
MINIPORTRAIT—Passport Camera—Polaroid Corporation; *U.S. Public*, pg. 1313
MINIPRESS—Prazosin—Pfizer Inc.; *U.S. Public*, pg. 1281
MINIPRESS XL—Prazosin GITS—Pfizer Inc.; *U.S. Public*, pg. 1281
MINIPULSE—Portable Programmable Polarity Switching Unit—Scientific Imaging Systems; *U.S. Public*, pg. 550
MINIQUICK 5X10 T—Pocket Telescope—Carl Zeiss; *Int'l*, pg. 1522
MINIRISC—Semiconductor Device—LSI Logic Corp.; *U.S. Public*, pg. 971
MINIROVER—Remotely Operated Vehicle—Benthos, Inc.; *U.S. Public*, pg. 212
MINISCAN—Cabinet X-Ray Inspection System—EG & G Astrophysics; *U.S. Public*, pg. 543
MINISCAN—Specialty X-Ray Equipment—EG & G, Inc.; *U.S. Public*, pg. 542
MINISCAN—Access Control System—Federal APD, Inc.; *U.S. Public*, pg. 616
MINISCREEN—NONE—Market Facts, Inc.; *U.S. Public*, pg. 1046
MINISEAL—Crimp Splices—Raychem Corporation; *U.S. Public*, pg. 1362
MINISERT—NONE—Berg Electronics; *U.S. Public*, pg. 212
MINISITE—Instrument—U.S. Surgical Corp.; *U.S. Public*, pg. 1687
MINISKIIP—Power Semiconductors for Printed Circuit Boards—Semikron International, GmbH & Co. KG; *Int'l*, pg. 1220
MINISTAC—Semi-Conductor Devices—Semtech Corporation; *U.S. Public*, pg. 1456
MINISTIC—Semi-Conductor Devices—Semtech Corporation; *U.S. Public*, pg. 1456
MINIT-RUB—Analgesic Balm—Bristol-Myers Squibb Company; *U.S. Public*, pg. 253
MINITAC—NONE—Hypertronics Corporation; *Int'l*, pg. 1268
MINITAN—Ultrafiltration System—Millipore Corporation; *U.S. Public*, pg. 1112
MINITEK—NONE—Berg Electronics; *U.S. Public*, pg. 212
MINITMAN—Food Stores—Spencer Companies Inc.; *U.S. Private*, pg. 1024
MINITRAN—Prescription Drug—3M; *U.S. Public*, pg. 1604
MINITREE—Cantilever Rack—Jarke Corporation; *U.S. Private*, pg. 583
MINITRIM—Plywood, Wood, Hardboard, Wood Fiber & Plastic Products—Georgia-Pacific Corporation; *U.S. Public*, pg. 735
MINITRON—Small Vacuum—Advance Machine Company; *Int'l*, pg. 932
MINIVANS—NONE—Ford Motor Co. of Canada Ltd; *U.S. Public*, pg. 666
MINIVATOR—Lift Devices—Sunrise Medical, Inc.; *U.S. Public*, pg. 1535
MINIVITIN—Slimming Drink—Novartis AG; *Int'l*, pg. 971
MINIX—Pacemaker—Medtronic, Inc.; *U.S. Public*, pg. 1082
MINIX ST—Pacemaker—Medtronic, Inc.; *U.S. Public*, pg. 1082
MINK DIFFERENCE—Hair Styling Preparations—The Gillette Company; *U.S. Public*, pg. 743

MINLON—Engineering Thermoplastic—Du Pont (E.I. Du Pont De Nemours & Co.); *U.S. Public*, pg. 530
MINN KOTA—Electric Fishing Motors, Power Equipment & Accessories—Johnson Worldwide Associates, Inc.; *U.S. Public*, pg. 932
MINNA—Women's Apparel—International Cosmetics Co., Ltd.; *Int'l*, pg. 684
MINNEGASCO—NONE—NorAm Energy Corp.; *U.S. Public*, pg. 843
MINNESOTA MANUFACTURERS REGISTER—Register—Manufacturers' News, Inc.; *U.S. Private*, pg. 700
MINNESOTA POWER—Electric Utility—Minnesota Power; *U.S. Public*, pg. 1116
MINNESOTA RUBBER—Molded Rubber Parts—Quadion Corporation; *U.S. Private*, pg. 898
MINNIE—Motor Home—Winnebago Industries, Inc.; *U.S. Public*, pg. 1772
MINNIE WINNIE—Motor Homes—Winnebago Industries, Inc.; *U.S. Public*, pg. 1772
MINOCIN—Anti-Infective—American Home Products Corporation; *U.S. Public*, pg. 79
MINOLTA—Cameras, Copiers, Fax Machines, Laser Printers,Doc. Imaging,Indus. Instru.—Minolta Singapore (Pte.) Ltd.; *Int'l*, pg. 869
MINOMYCIN—NONE—Wyeth Australia Pty. Ltd.; *U.S. Public*, pg. 82
MINOR—Rubber—Minor Rubber Co., Inc.; *U.S. Private*, pg. 751
MINOR'S—NONE—Nestle USA; *Int'l*, pg. 916
MINOS—Surgical Drill—3M; *U.S. Public*, pg. 1604
MINOX—Thermocouple—The Foxboro Company; *Int'l*, pg. 1243
MINIPLEX—Telephone Line Digital Multiplexer—Raychem Corporation; *U.S. Public*, pg. 1362
MINSERT—NONE—Berg Electronics; *U.S. Public*, pg. 212
MINSTREL—Digest-Size Paperbacks for Young Readers—Pocket Books; *U.S. Private*, pg. 777
MINT*A*BURST—Mint Flavor Gum—Adams U.S.A.; *U.S. Public*, pg. 1739
MINT CONDITION—Car Care Products—Amway Corporation; *U.S. Private*, pg. 69
MINT CRISP—Candy—Huhtamaki Oy; *Int'l*, pg. 638
MINT MAGIC—Herb Tea—Celestial Seasonings; *U.S. Public*, pg. 319
MINT PRINT—Custom Stamp—Sanford Corporation; *U.S. Public*, pg. 1178
MINTAKA FILMS B.V.—Theatrical Distribution (Netherlands)—Metromedia International Group, Inc.; *U.S. Public*, pg. 1102
MINT'EES—Almonds—Blue Diamond Growers; *U.S. Private*, pg. 152
MINTEX—Brake Friction Materials—BBA Friction LTD.; *Int'l*, pg. 112
MINTLETS—Candy—Brach & Brock Confections Inc.; *U.S. Private*, pg. 163
MINTON—Bone China Dinnerware & Giftware—Royal Doulton USA Inc.; *Int'l*, pg. 1135
MINTSYSTEM—Market Intelligence Tracking System—Advertising Checking Bureau Incorporated; *U.S. Private*, pg. 23
MINUET—Pacemaker—Medtronic, Inc.; *U.S. Public*, pg. 1082
MINULET—NONE—Wyeth Australia Pty. Ltd.; *U.S. Public*, pg. 82
MINUS 50 SUIT—Cold Weather Clothing—Refrigiwear, Inc.; *U.S. Private*, pg. 917
MINUTE—Brand Tapioca—Kraft Foods, Inc.; *U.S. Public*, pg. 1287
MINUTE—Rice & Packaged Dinners—Philip Morris Companies Inc.; *U.S. Public*, pg. 1287
MINUTE CLASSIC—Long Grain Rice in a Pouch—Kraft Foods, Inc.; *U.S. Public*, pg. 1287
MINUTE MAID—Regular & Diet Flavored Soda—The Coca-Cola Company; *U.S. Public*, pg. 392
MINUTE MAID—Fruit Juices, Ades & Punch—The Minute Maid Company; *U.S. Public*, pg. 392
MINUTE MAID FRUIT JUICEE—Frozen Confection—Good Humor/Breyers Ice Cream; *Int'l*, pg. 1435
MINUTE MAID PREMIUM CHOICE—Orange Juice—The Minute Maid Company; *U.S. Public*, pg. 392
MINUTE MAN BRAND—NONE—Colonial Beef Co.; *U.S. Private*, pg. 253
MINUTE MARK—Traffic Paint—Linear Dynamics Inc.; *U.S. Private*, pg. 668

MINUTE MEND—Epoxy Stick—CRC Industries, Inc.; *U.S. Private*, pg. 138
MINUTE MENU—Hamburgers, Steaks, Meatballs—DeVault Foods; *U.S. Private*, pg. 329
MINUTE RICE—Rice Mix—Kraft Foods, Inc.; *U.S. Public*, pg. 1287
MINUTE WAX—Car Wax—Turtle Wax, Inc.; *U.S. Private*, pg. 1110
MINUTEMAN—Hardware & Housewares—Distribution America; *U.S. Private*, pg. 335
MINUTEMAN—A 100 Mile Plus High-Pressure Natural Gas Delivery System—Duke Energy International, L.L.C.; *U.S. Public*, pg. 534
MINUTEMAN—Cleaning Products—Minuteman International, Inc.; *Int'l*, pg. 587
MINUTEMAN—Driveway Sealer Products—Monsey-Bakor; *U.S. Private*, pg. 757
MINUTEMAN—Service Mark—Sentry Insurance, A Mutual Company; *U.S. Public*, pg. 984
MINUTEMARKER—Construction Laser Equip.—Spectra-Physics Laserplane Inc.; *U.S. Public*, pg. 1594
MINWAX—Wood Finishing Products—Minwax Company Div.; *U.S. Public*, pg. 1466
MINX—Multimedia Networking & videoconferencing System—Datapoint Corporation; *Int'l*, pg. 384
MINXFER—Network Screen Transfer System—Datapoint Corporation; *Int'l*, pg. 384
MIOKAMYCIN—Antibiotics—Meiji Seika Kaisha, Ltd.; *Int'l*, pg. 855
MIOSTAT—Intraocular Carbachol—Alcon Laboratories, Inc.; *Int'l*, pg. 916
MIPCO—Electrical Connector—Thomas & Betts/Amerace; *U.S. Public*, pg. 1598
MIPCO—Power Connectors—Thomas & Betts Corporation; *U.S. Public*, pg. 1597
MIPOLAM—Vinyl Tile—Huls America Inc.; *Int'l*, pg. 1455
MIPRODAN—Milk Proteins—MD Foods; *Int'l*, pg. 826
MIR—Soap Product—Lever Brothers Co.; *Int'l*, pg. 1435
MIR—Soap Prod.—Unilever Plc; *Int'l*, pg. 1433
MIR-O-CRON—Coatings for Mirror Backing—PPG Industries, Inc.; *U.S. Public*, pg. 1245
MIRA—Showers—Caradon Plc; *Int'l*, pg. 266
MIRA—Sapphire Laser—Coherent, Inc.; *U.S. Public*, pg. 395
MIRA—NONE—Harlequin Enterprises Ltd.; *Int'l*, pg. 1402
MIRA-COIL—Continuous Coil Springs & Constructions—Leggett & Platt, Incorporated; *U.S. Public*, pg. 985
MIRA-FOAM—Polyurethane Foam Cushions & Pads—Leggett & Platt, Incorporated; *U.S. Public*, pg. 985
MIRA-GLOS—Gloss Coating—Morton International Inc.; *U.S. Public*, pg. 1135
MIRABEL—Frozen Seafood Products—Fishery Products International Ltd.; *Int'l*, pg. 492
MIRABELLA—NONE—Hachette Filipacchi Magazines Inc.; *Int'l*, pg. 794
MIRACABLE—Motion Transmitting Remote Control Assys—Teleflex Incorporated; *U.S. Public*, pg. 1569
MIRACID—Plant Food & Soil Acidifier—Scott's Miracle-Gro Products, Inc.; *U.S. Public*, pg. 1447
MIRACLE—Compressed Air Sprayers & Shears—Ames Company; *U.S. Public*, pg. 1683
MIRACLE—Monofilament Fishing Line—Cortland Line Co., Inc.; *U.S. Private*, pg. 277
MIRACLE—Adhesives, Caulks & Grouts Product Logo—Miracle Adhesives; *U.S. Public*, pg. 1466
MIRACLE—Auto Painting & Body Repair—Multiple Allied Services, Inc.; *U.S. Private*, pg. 767
MIRACLE BRA—Lingerie—Victoria's Secret Stores; *U.S. Public*, pg. 194
MIRACLE-EAR—Hearing Aids—Dahlberg, Inc.; *U.S. Public*, pg. 194
MIRACLE-GARDEN-CAVE—NONE—Scott's Miracle-Gro Products, Inc.; *U.S. Public*, pg. 1447
MIRACLE-GRO—All Purpose Plant Food—Scott's Miracle-Gro Products, Inc.; *U.S. Public*, pg. 1447
MIRACLE HITCH—Dragline Bucket Accessory—Harnischfeger Industries, Inc.; *U.S. Public*, pg. 788

MIRACLE LIME—Masonry Construction Type S Lime—Corson Lime Company; *U.S. Public*, pg. 1685

MIRACLE LIME—Crushed Limestone—United States Lime & Minerals; *U.S. Public*, pg. 1684

MIRACLE WHIP—NONE—Alliant Foodservice, Inc.; *U.S. Private*, pg. 244

MIRACLE WHIP—Salad Dressing—Kraft Foods Inc.; *U.S. Public*, pg. 1288

MIRACLE WHIP—Salad Dressing—Philip Morris Companies Inc.; *U.S. Public*, pg. 1287

MIRACLE WHITE—Laundry Detergent Booster—Kiwi Brands; *U.S. Public*, pg. 1433

MIRACLEAR—Clear Film Label—Kal Grafx; *U.S. Private*, pg. 387

MIRACODE—Microfilm Indexing Equipment—Eastman Kodak Company; *U.S. Public*, pg. 550

MIRACOLI—Pasta Dinners—Philip Morris Companies Inc.; *U.S. Public*, pg. 1287

MIRACRYL—Display Trays-Mirrored—Carlisle Food Service Products; *U.S. Public*, pg. 305

MIRADA—16g Racquet String—Ektelon; *U.S. Private*, pg. 884

MIRADA—Eye Protection—U.S. Safety; *U.S. Private*, pg. 1125

MIRADA GRAPHITE RTS—Racquetball Racquet—Ektelon; *U.S. Private*, pg. 884

MIRADAPT—Dental Restorative—Johnson & Johnson Consumer Products; *U.S. Public*, pg. 928

MIRADO—Pencils—Empire Berol U.S.A.; *U.S. Public*, pg. 1178

MIRADO—Woodcase Pencil—Sanford Corporation; *U.S. Public*, pg. 1178

MIRADON—Anisindione—Key Pharmaceuticals; *U.S. Public*, pg. 1438

MIRAFIORE—Wine—Paterno Imports Limited; *U.S. Private*, pg. 843

MIRAFLEX—Glass Fiber Used in Insulation—Owens Corning; *U.S. Public*, pg. 1236

MIRAFLEX—NONE—Owens-Corning Canada; *U.S. Public*, pg. 1237

MIRAFLON—Fluorocarbon rubber—Asahi Chemical Industry Co., Ltd.; *Int'l*, pg. 83

MIRAFLOW—Contact Lens Solution—Novartis; *Int'l*, pg. 972

MIRAGE—NONE—Avery Dennison Corporation; *U.S. Public*, pg. 152

MIRAGE—Proximity Card Reader—Checkpoint Systems Inc.; *U.S. Public*, pg. 343

MIRAGE—Hearing Aids—Dahlberg, Inc.; *U.S. Public*, pg. 194

MIRAGE—Multi-role Aircraft—Dassault Aviation Group; *Int'l*, pg. 383

MIRAGE—NONE—Mirage Resorts Incorporated; *U.S. Public*, pg. 1116

MIRAGE—Automobile—Mitsubishi Motor Sales of America, Inc.; *Int'l*, pg. 875

MIRAGE—Bottled Water Cooler—Sunroc Corporation; *U.S. Private*, pg. 1053

MIRAGLAZE—NONE—Lawter International, Inc.; *U.S. Public*, pg. 980

MIRAI—35 Millimeter SLR Camera—Ricoh Corporation; *Int'l*, pg. 1114

MIRALUG—Work Shoes—E.J. Footwear Corp.; *U.S. Public*, pg. 1684

MIRAMAX—Motion Picture Production Company—The Walt Disney Company; *U.S. Public*, pg. 511

MIRAMAX—Polishing Compound for Mirrors—Ferro Corporation; *U.S. Public*, pg. 618

MIRAMAX—NONE—Miramax Films, Inc.; *U.S. Public*, pg. 514

MIRAMAX CAFE—NONE—Miramax Films, Inc.; *U.S. Public*, pg. 514

MIRARI—NONE—Luxottica Group S.p.A.; *Int'l*, pg. 822

MIRASEPT—Contact Lens Care Solutions—Alcon Laboratories, Inc.; *Int'l*, pg. 916

MIRASEPT—Contact Lens Solution—Novartis; *Int'l*, pg. 972

MIRASEPT—Hydrogen Peroxide Disinfecting System—Wesley-Jessen; *U.S. Private*, pg. 111

MIRASEPT LENS & CUP HOLDER—NONE—Alcon Laboratories, Inc.; *Int'l*, pg. 916

MIRASEPT STEP 1—Disinfecting Solution—Alcon Laboratories, Inc.; *Int'l*, pg. 916

MIRASEPT STEP 2—Multidose Rinsing & Neutralizing Solution—Alcon Laboratories, Inc.; *Int'l*, pg. 916

MIRATEL—Broadcasting Equip.—Ball Corporation; *U.S. Public*, pg. 170

MIRATRADE INTERNATIONAL—Dairy Feed—Miracle Feeds Inc.; *U.S. Private*, pg. 432

MIRAVISTA—Shake Shingles—Owens Corning; *U.S. Public*, pg. 1236

MIRCO—Wrapped Gum Rubber Tubing—Minor Rubber Co., Inc.; *U.S. Private*, pg. 751

MIRDAC—Analysis Monitor—IRD Mechanalysis, Inc. (U.S.A.); *U.S. Public*, pg. 789

MIRITAN—Tantalum Capacitors—AVX Corporation; *Int'l*, pg. 775

MIROGARD—Anti-Reflective Glass—Deutsche Spezialglas AG; *Int'l*, pg. 1523

MIROLITE—Oral Hygiene Aids—John O. Butler Co.; *Int'l*, pg. 1320

MIROMET—Polishing Compound—Buehler, Limited; *U.S. Public*, pg. 574

MIRREX—NONE—Lawter International, Inc.; *U.S. Public*, pg. 980

MIRRITE—NONE—Lawter International, Inc.; *U.S. Public*, pg. 980

MIRRO—Cookware, Bakeware, Pressure Cookers—Mirro Company; *U.S. Public*, pg. 1177

MIRRO—Cookware—Newell Co.; *U.S. Public*, pg. 1176

MIRROCELL—RF Coverage Solutions—Ortel Corporation; *U.S. Public*, pg. 1232

MIRROLAC—All Purpose Enamel—Devoe Paint; *Int'l*, pg. 663

MIRROLAC—All Purpose Enamel—ICI Paints; *Int'l*, pg. 664

MIRROLAC-WB—Waterborne Enamel—Devoe Paint; *Int'l*, pg. 663

MIRROLAC WB—Waterborne Enamel—ICI Paints; *Int'l*, pg. 664

MIRROR FINISH—Abrasive—Carborundum Abrasives North America; *Int'l*, pg. 1174

MIRROR GO LIGHTLY—Lighted Makeup Mirror—Windmere-Durable Holdings; *U.S. Public*, pg. 1771

MIRROR, MIRROR—Portable Lighted Mirror—Clairol, Inc.; *U.S. Public*, pg. 254

MIRRORBLACK—Trinitron Screen—Sony Electronics; *Int'l*, pg. 1281

MISER—Geophysical Data Processing Services—Litton Industries, Inc.; *U.S. Public*, pg. 1002

MISER—Ball Valve—Worcester Controls Corp.; *Int'l*, pg. 128

MISIA JUANA—Cachapa Mix—International Multifoods Corporation; *U.S. Public*, pg. 900

MISON—Shielding Gas—AGA AB; *Int'l*, pg. 12

MISON—NONE—AGA Gas, Inc.; *Int'l*, pg. 13

MISON—Shielding Gases—AGA Ges.m.b.H.; *Int'l*, pg. 13

MISS CAPEZIO—Girls & Teen Shoes—Jumping Jacks; *U.S. Private*, pg. 767

MISS CLAIROL—Haircolor—Bristol-Myers Squibb Company; *U.S. Public*, pg. 253

MISS COUNTY FAIR—Turkey—Jerome Foods Inc.; *U.S. Private*, pg. 586

MISS DIOR—Women's Fragrence—Christian Dior Perfumes Inc.; *Int'l*, pg. 781

MISS ELAINE—Women's Sleepwear—Miss Elaine Inc.; *U.S. Private*, pg. 752

MISS ELLIETTE OF CALIFORNIA—Missy Social Occasion—Vivian & Elliette, Inc.; *U.S. Private*, pg. 1142

MISS ELLIETTE WOMAN—Plus Size Social Occasion—Vivian & Elliette, Inc.; *U.S. Private*, pg. 1142

MISS GOLDY—Fresh Chicken—Sanderson Farms, Inc.; *U.S. Public*, pg. 1430

MISS LEE PRESS-ON NAILS—Smaller Size False Fingernails—Lee Pharmaceuticals; *U.S. Public*, pg. 984

MISS PENDLETON—Women's Apparel—Pendleton Woolen Mills, Inc.; *U.S. Private*, pg. 848

MISS RAQUET—Heavy Knit Athletic Socks—Wigwam Mills, Inc.; *U.S. Private*, pg. 1175

MISS SOPHISTICATES—Women's Apparel—Pendleton Woolen Mills, Inc.; *U.S. Private*, pg. 848

MISS SPORTY—Color Cosmetics—Coty Inc.; *Int'l*, pg. 185

MISS WISCONSIN—Cheese—Armour Food Company; *U.S. Public*, pg. 427

MISSILE-AIR—Latch, Sealed—Hartwell Corporation; *U.S. Private*, pg. 1168

MISSION—Pasta—The Quaker Oats Company; *U.S. Public*, pg. 1347

MISSISSIPPI BARBECUE SAUCE—Barbecue Sause—The Fremont Co.; *U.S. Private*, pg. 426

MISSISSIPPI JAMBALAYA—Riverboat Cruise Trips—American Classic Voyagers Company; *U.S. Private*, pg. 380

MISSISSIPPI MANUFACTURERS REGISTER—Register—Manufacturers' News, Inc.; *U.S. Private*, pg. 700

MISSISSIPPI MUD—Ice Cream Novelties—Borden, Inc.; *U.S. Public*, pg. 157

MISSISSIPPI QUEEN—Riverboat—American Classic Voyagers Company; *U.S. Private*, pg. 380

MISSOURI MANUFACTURERS REGISTER—Register—Manufacturers' News, Inc.; *U.S. Private*, pg. 700

MISSOURI RED—NONE—New England Stone Industries, Inc.; *U.S. Private*, pg. 793

MISSOURI RURALIST—Farm Publication 15-Issues/Year—Farm Progress Publications; *U.S. Public*, pg. 513

MIST & DRY 24—Hair Setters—Sunbeam Household Products; *U.S. Public*, pg. 1533

MIST ASSIST—NONE—Ballard Medical Products; *U.S. Public*, pg. 171

MIST COAT—Primer—Jones Blair Company; *U.S. Private*, pg. 596

MIST-MASTER—High-Load Knitted-Mesh Mist Eliminator—Beco Engineering Company; *U.S. Private*, pg. 129

MIST-O-MATIC—Seed Treatment—The Dow Chemical Company; *U.S. Public*, pg. 522

MIST-STICK—Curling Irons—Sunbeam Household Products; *U.S. Public*, pg. 1533

MIST-STRACTOR—Reverse-Flow Depth Coalescer—Osmonics, Inc.; *U.S. Public*, pg. 1233

MISTAKE OUT—Correction Fluid—The Gillette Company; *U.S. Public*, pg. 743

MR. CUT-RATE—Convenience Stores—FFP Marketing Company, Inc.; *U.S. Public*, pg. 604

MISTER DONUT—Donut Shop Chain—Allied Domecq PLC; *Int'l*, pg. 62

MISTER DONUT—DONUTS—Dunkin' Donuts Incorporated; *Int'l*, pg. 63

MISTER DONUT—Doughnut Shop—Duskin Co., Ltd.; *Int'l*, pg. 422

MISTER DONUT—Doughnuts—Mister Donut of America, Inc.; *Int'l*, pg. 63

MISTER SALTY—Pretzels—Nabisco Inc.; *U.S. Public*, pg. 1355

MISTER TWISTER—Soft Plastic Fishing Lures, Recreational Fishing Lures—Sheldons' Inc.; *U.S. Private*, pg. 992

MISTIC—Soft Drink—Grant-Lydick Beverage Co.; *U.S. Private*, pg. 470

MISTIC—Premium Beverages—Triarc Companies, Inc.; *U.S. Public*, pg. 1634

MISTIFIER—Sprayer Hair Brush—Goody Products, Inc.; *U.S. Public*, pg. 1177

MISTLETOE—Food & Related Paper Products—Butler Wholesale Products, Inc.; *U.S. Private*, pg. 190

MISTRAL—NONE—Brown & Sharpe Manufacturing Company; *U.S. Public*, pg. 260

MISTRAL—Car—Nissan Motor Co., Ltd.; *Int'l*, pg. 943

MISTRAL—Fragrance Sprays, Deodorants, Talcum Powder—SmithKline Beecham plc; *Int'l*, pg. 1264

MISTRAL SP—NONE—Brown & Sharpe Manufacturing Company; *U.S. Public*, pg. 260

MISTURA FINA—Cigarettes—Philip Morris Companies Inc.; *U.S. Public*, pg. 1287

MISTY—Cigarettes—Brown & Williamson Tobacco Corp.; *Int'l*, pg. 111

MITA—Photographic Equipment—Mita Copystar America Inc.; *Int'l*, pg. 870

MITA—Copying Machine—Mita Industrial Company, Ltd.; *Int'l*, pg. 870

MITAC—Agricultural Chemical—AgrEvo USA Company; *Int'l*, pg. 1203

MITCHELL—Buttonfeeders & Related Products—AMF Reece Incorporated; *U.S. Private*, pg. 7

MITCHELL—Reels & Rods—Johnson Worldwide Associates, Inc.; *U.S. Public*, pg. 932

MITCHELL DESIGNS—Wallcovering—Borden, Inc.; *U.S. Private*, pg. 157

MITCHELL INTERNATIONAL—Computer & Business Services—Mitchell International; *U.S. Public*, pg. 1601

MITE-Y-PIN—NONE—Molex Incorporated; *U.S. Public*, pg. 1121

MITEK—Truss Manufacturing Equipment—MiTek, Inc.; *Int'l*, pg. 1106

MITEK 2000—Truss Engineering Software—MiTek, Inc.; *Int'l*, pg. 1106

MITEL DATACOM—Telecommunication Prods.—Mitel, Inc.; *Int'l*, pg. 870

MITEL PERSONAL ASSISTANT—Computer Attached Telephone & Software Applications—Mitel Corporation; *Int'l*, pg. 870

MITER-AL-BRAZE—Aluminum Brazing Alloy—Belmont Metals, Inc.; *U.S. Private*, pg. 132

MITEX—Membrane Disc Filter—Millipore Corporation; *U.S. Public*, pg. 1112

MITHRACIN—Pharmaceutical—Bayer Corporation/Pharmaceutical Division; *Int'l*, pg. 173

MITIA—Mexican Food Products—Wilson Products Co.; *U.S. Private*, pg. 1181

MITRAFLEX—Wound Dressing Products—PolyMedica Industries, Inc.; *U.S. Public*, pg. 1315

MITRE—Athletic Shoes—Genesco Inc.; *U.S. Public*, pg. 728

MITRE SPORTS—Sports Equipment & Accessories—Mitre Sports (U.S.); *Int'l*, pg. 1036

MITSUBA-TV—Audio-Spurs, Electronics—Luskin's, Inc.; *U.S. Private*, pg. 681

MITSUBISHI—Electronic Components—Interface Electronics Corporation; *U.S. Public*, pg. 567

MITSUBISHI—NONE—Milgray Electronics, Inc.; *U.S. Public*, pg. 205

MITSUBISHI FUSO—Trucks—Mitsubishi Fuso Truck of America, Inc.; *Int'l*, pg. 875

MITSUKAN—General Food Condiments—Nakano Vinegar Co., Ltd.; *Int'l*, pg. 904

MITY-LITE—Furniture—Mity-Lite, Inc.; *U.S. Public*, pg. 1118

MITY-MITE—Regulator—Grove Valve & Regulator Company; *U.S. Private*, pg. 484

MIVAC—Microwave Vacuum Driers—Aeroglide Corporation; *U.S. Private*, pg. 24

MIVACRON—Muscle Relaxant—Glaxo Wellcome PLC; *Int'l*, pg. 553

MIVIDA—Surgical, Medical, Dental & Vetinary Instruments & Apparatus—Sime Darby Berhad; *Int'l*, pg. 1249

MIX-ALL—Feed Grinder—Gehl Company; *U.S. Public*, pg. 704

MIX-FINDER—Mixers & Mixer Controls—Sunbeam Household Products; *U.S. Public*, pg. 1533

MIX SELF—Women's Apparel—International Cosmetics Co., Ltd.; *Int'l*, pg. 684

MIX-O-MATIC—Portable Mixer—The Rival Company; *U.S. Public*, pg. 1391

MIXCO—Agitators—Lightnin Mixers; *U.S. Public*, pg. 726

MIXED GRILL—Dinners—Bakers Square Restaurants; *U.S. Public*, pg. 1719

MIXER/AGITATOR—NONE—Blaw-Knox Construction Equipment Corporation; *U.S. Public*, pg. 877

MIXER & DESIGN—Sporting Goods—Brunswick Bowling & Billiards Corp.; *U.S. Public*, pg. 265

MIXEVAN—Vanilla—David Michael & Co. Inc.; *U.S. Private*, pg. 740

MIXEX—Plate Heat Exchangers—Tranter, Inc.; *U.S. Public*, pg. 521

MIXMASTER—Food Mixers—Sunbeam Household Products; *U.S. Public*, pg. 1533

MIXTARD 30/70—Product for Diabetes Care—Novo Nordisk A/S; *Int'l*, pg. 987

MIXTRUDER—Mixer—Littleford Day Inc.; *U.S. Private*, pg. 671

MIXTURE NO. 79—Pipe Tobaccos—Consolidated Cigar Corporation; *U.S. Private*, pg. 690

MIXTURE 79—Pipe Tobacco—Consolidated Cigar Corp.; *U.S. Private*, pg. 690

MIYAKO—Japanese Food—Mutual Trading Co., Inc.; *U.S. Private*, pg. 770

MIZER—Vent Damper & Automatic System for Furnaces & Boilers—Johnson Controls, Inc., Controls Group; *U.S. Public*, pg. 932

MIZUNO—Footwear, Equipment & Apparel for Baseball/Softball, Running, Volleyball—Mizuno USA, Inc.; *Int'l*, pg. 885

MIZUNO—Footwear, Clothing & Accesories—Sao Paulo Alpargatas S.A.; *Int'l*, pg. 1193

MIZUNO PRO—Golf Clubs—Mizuno Corporation; *Int'l*, pg. 884

MIZUNOPRO WD—Golf Clubs—Mizuno Corporation; *Int'l*, pg. 884

MIZZ—Young Women's Interest Magazine—IPC Magazines Limited; *Int'l*, pg. 651

MIZZOU—Castables—A.P. Green Industries, Inc.; *U.S. Public*, pg. 761

M'LADY BRUHN—Ladies Wear—Dick Bruhn Incorporated; *U.S. Private*, pg. 175

MOBIC—Antirheumatic Drug—Boehringer Ingelheim GmbH; *Int'l*, pg. 199

MOBIL—Mining & Minerals—Mobil Mining & Minerals Company; *U.S. Public*, pg. 1118

MOBIL—Petroleum Prods.—Mobil Oil Corporation; *U.S. Public*, pg. 1118

MOBIL 1—Motor Oil—Mobil Oil Corporation; *U.S. Public*, pg. 1118

MOBIL SUPER—Motor Oil—Mobil Oil Corporation; *U.S. Public*, pg. 1118

MOBIL SWEEPERS—Street Sweeper—Athey Products Corporation; *U.S. Public*, pg. 142

MOBILCRAFT—Cabinet Doors—Patrick Industries Inc.; *U.S. Public*, pg. 1264

MOBILE BAY TOWING—NONE—Hvide Marine Incorporated; *U.S. Public*, pg. 851

MOBILE ELECTRONICS RETAILER—NONE—Bobit Publishing Company; *U.S. Private*, pg. 154

MOBILE MODULAR—Relocatable Modular Offices—McGrath RentCorp; *U.S. Public*, pg. 1069

MOBILE OFFICE & COMPUTING—Magazine—Freedom Communication Inc.; *U.S. Private*, pg. 425

MOBILE PHONES—All Brands—C.M.C. SA; *Int'l*, pg. 792

MOBILE RADIO TECHNOLOGY—News and Technical Articles—Intertec Publishing; *U.S. Public*, pg. 1327

MOBILE SEARCH—Mobile Security X-ray System—American Science & Engineering, Inc.; *U.S. Public*, pg. 90

MOBILE-2000—NONE—American Management Systems, Inc.; *U.S. Public*, pg. 86

MOBILEMANAGER—PC Workstation—Rubbermaid Incorporated; *U.S. Public*, pg. 1411

MOBILEMAX DESKRUNNERREADER WRITER—NONE—Maxtor Corporation; *Int'l*, pg. 641

MOBILEMAX FLASH MEMORY CARDS—NONE—Maxtor Corporation; *Int'l*, pg. 641

MOBILEMAX HARD DRIVES—NONE—Maxtor Corporation; *Int'l*, pg. 641

MOBILFOAM—Meat Trays, Egg Cartons, Produce Trays—Tenneco Packaging, Consumer Products Group; *U.S. Public*, pg. 1579

MOBILMATIC—Small Vacuum—Advance Machine Company; *Int'l*, pg. 932

MOBILRAP—Pallet Stretch Films—Tenneco Packaging, Consumer Products Group; *U.S. Public*, pg. 1579

MOBILTUFF—Trash Bags—Tenneco Packaging, Consumer Products Group; *U.S. Public*, pg. 1579

MOBILWARE—Disposable Dinnerware—Tenneco Packaging, Consumer Products Group; *U.S. Public*, pg. 1579

MOBIMATE—NONE—Molex Incorporated; *U.S. Public*, pg. 1121

MOBINSUL—Home Insulations—Johns Manville Corporation; *U.S. Public*, pg. 927

MOBIRA—Mobile Telephone—Nokia Sourcing, Inc.; *Int'l*, pg. 953

MOBITEX—Mobile Data Communication—Telefonaktiebolaget LM Ericsson; *Int'l*, pg. 1363

MOCAP—Ethoprop Insecticide—Rhone-Poulenc S.A.; *Int'l*, pg. 1108

MOCCONA—Food Service Coffee & Beverage Systems—Sara Lee Corporation; *U.S. Public*, pg. 1432

MOCHA COOLER—Canned Iced Coffee—Nestle S.A.; *Int'l*, pg. 915

MOCHA MIX—Refrigerated Non-Dairy Creamer & Frozen Dessert—Presto Food Products, Inc.; *U.S. Public*, pg. 1527

MOCON—Company Name—Modern Controls, Inc.; *U.S. Public*, pg. 1120

MOD-CAL—Portable Solid-State Calibrator—AMETEK, Inc.; *U.S. Public*, pg. 99

MOD LINE—Material Handling Equipment—C.R. Daniels, Inc.; *U.S. Private*, pg. 310

MOD-U-LEX—Insulated Communication Cables & Apparatus—General Cable Corporation; *Int'l*, pg. 1486

MOD-U-LINE—Electric Discharge Lamp—General Electric Canada Inc.; *U.S. Public*, pg. 713

MOD-U-TORQUE—Drive—Harnischfeger Industries, Inc.; *U.S. Public*, pg. 788

MODACS—Modular Data Acquisition & Control System—Modcomp; *U.S. Public*, pg. 283

MODACUR—Cure Promoter for Coatings—Monsanto Company; *U.S. Public*, pg. 1124

MODAFLOW—Resin Modifier—Monsanto Company; *U.S. Public*, pg. 1124

MODAR—Furniture—Knape & Vogt Mfg. Co.; *U.S. Public*, pg. 963

MODBUS—Communication Network—Schneider Automation, Inc.; *Int'l*, pg. 1208

MODCOMP—Modular Computer System—Modcomp; *U.S. Public*, pg. 283

MODDUS/PRIMO—Plant Growth Regulator—Novartis; *Int'l*, pg. 972

MODE—Magazine—Freedom Communication Inc.; *U.S. Private*, pg. 425

MODE CRAFT—Fashions—Burlington Coat Factory Warehouse Corporation; *U.S. Public*, pg. 268

MODEL B—Wall Screen—Da-Lite Screen Company, Inc.; *U.S. Private*, pg. 306

MODEL 840—Flatbed Scanner—Xerox Imaging Systems, Inc.; *U.S. Public*, pg. 1785

MODEL 840 I—Flatbed Scanner—Xerox Imaging Systems, Inc.; *U.S. Public*, pg. 1785

MODEL 830—Flatbed Scanner—Xerox Imaging Systems, Inc.; *U.S. Public*, pg. 1785

MODEL ELEVEN—NONE—Cambridge Soundworks, Inc.; *U.S. Private*, pg. 202

MODEL F—Trucks & Buses—Toyota Motor Corporation; *Int'l*, pg. 1411

MODEL G-90 BARRIER GATE—High Speed Barrier Gate—Federal APD, Inc.; *U.S. Public*, pg. 616

MODEL H—Stringing Machine—Ektelon; *U.S. Private*, pg. 884

MODEL MASTER—Car Paints—The Testor Corporation; *U.S. Public*, pg. 1358

MODEL MASTER FS—Paints—The Testor Corporation; *U.S. Public*, pg. 1358

MODEL MASTERS—Ps Paints—The Testor Corporation; *U.S. Public*, pg. 1358

MODEL 930 ARGON LASER—Medical Instrument—Coherent, Inc.; *U.S. Public*, pg. 395

MODEL 920 ARGON LASER—Medical Instrument—Coherent, Inc.; *U.S. Public*, pg. 395

MODEL 90—Lab Dispersers, High Speed Dispersers—Premier Mill Corp.; *U.S. Private*, pg. 881

MODEL 92—Ganged Test Module—Bodine Assembly and Test Systems; *U.S. Private*, pg. 154

MODEL 1—Database Marketing—Group 1 Software, Inc.; *U.S. Public*, pg. 417

MODEL R2175—Military Test System—Xebec Corporation; *U.S. Private*, pg. 1194

MODEL RAILROADER—Magazine—Kalmbach Publishing Co.; *U.S. Public*, pg. 606

MODEL RETAILER—Magazine—Kalmbach Publishing Co.; *U.S. Public*, pg. 606

MODEL 730—Flatbed Scanner—Xerox Imaging Systems, Inc.; *U.S. Public*, pg. 1785

MODEL SEVENTEEN—NONE—Cambridge Soundworks, Inc.; *U.S. Private*, pg. 202

MODEL 76—Walking Beam Assembly and Test Machine—Bodine Assembly and Test Systems; *U.S. Private*, pg. 154

MODEL SIX—NONE—Cambridge Soundworks, Inc.; *U.S. Private*, pg. 202

MODEL 64—In-line carrousel—Bodine Assembly and Test Systems; *U.S. Private*, pg. 154

MODEL 66—Security X-ray System—American Science & Engineering, Inc.; *U.S. Public*, pg. 90

MODEL STAR—Valves—The Wm. Powell Company; *U.S. Private*, pg. 877

MODEL TEN-A—NONE—Cambridge Soundworks, Inc.; *U.S. Private*, pg. 202

MODEL 300C—Piston—Schweizer Aircraft Corporation; *U.S. Private*, pg. 975

MODEL 300 CB—NONE—Schweizer Aircraft Corporation; *U.S. Private*, pg. 975

MODEL 330—Turbine—Schweizer Aircraft Corporation; *U.S. Private*, pg. 975

MODEL TWELVE—NONE—Cambridge Soundworks, Inc.; *U.S. Private*, pg. 202

MODEL 7000—Ink Jet Base—Videojet Systems International, Inc.; *Int'l*, pg. 545

MODELO ESPECIAL—Mexican Beer—Barton Beers, Ltd.; *U.S. Public*, pg. 300

MODELS COAT—Coverups—Swirl, II LTD; *U.S. Private*, pg. 1059

MODERN AUTOMOTIVE MECHANICS—Textbook Covering Theory & Service of Late-Model, High-Technology Cars—Goodheart-Willcox Publisher; *U.S. Private*, pg. 464

MODERN BULK TRANSPORTER—Coverage of Bulk Industry—Intertec Publishing; *U.S. Public*, pg. 1327

MODERN CABINETMAKING—Text Covering a Variety of Cabinetmaking & Woodworking Techniques—Goodheart-Willcox Publisher; *U.S. Private*, pg. 464

MODERN CARPENTRY—Textbook Covering the Basics of Building Materials & Methods—Goodheart-Willcox Publisher; *U.S. Private*, pg. 464

MODERN CIRRICULUM PRESS—Publishers—Simon & Schuster; *U.S. Private*, pg. 777

MODERN HEALTHCARE—Magazine—Crain Communications, Inc.; *U.S. Private*, pg. 284

MODERN LIBRARY—Classic Books—Random House; *U.S. Private*, pg. 21

MODERN LIBRARY—Book Imprint—Random House, Inc.; *U.S. Private*, pg. 20

MODERN LINE—Garden Tools—MTD Products, Inc.; *U.S. Private*, pg. 688

MODERN MACHINE SHOP—Business to Business Magazine—Gardner Publications, Inc.; *U.S. Private*, pg. 440

MODERN MASONRY—Textbook Covering Methods of Laying Brick, Block & Stone—Goodheart-Willcox Publisher; *U.S. Private*, pg. 464

MODERN MASTERPIECES—Massive Style Entry Handles—Triangle Brass Manufacturing; *U.S. Private*, pg. 1101

MODERN MATERIALS HANDLING—Magazine for Managers/Engineers who Handle Materials & Inventories—Reed Elsevier Business Information; *Int'l*, pg. 1095

MODERN MEDICINE—Travel Periodical—Advanstar Communications; *U.S. Private*, pg. 22

MODERN PUBLISHING—Publishing—Unisystems, Inc.; *U.S. Private*, pg. 1120

MODERN REFRIGERATION AND AIR CONDITIONING—Text Covering Fundamentals of Refrigeration & Air Conditioning—Goodheart-Willcox Publisher; *U.S. Private*, pg. 464

MODERN RESIDENTIAL WIRING—Textbook Covering Many Aspects of Residential Wiring—Goodheart-Willcox Publisher; *U.S. Private*, pg. 464

MODERN TIRE DEALER—Business Publication—Bill Communications, Inc.; *Int'l*, pg. 1446

MODERN WELDING—Textbook Covering All Aspects of Welding Technology—Goodheart-Willcox Publisher; *U.S. Private*, pg. 464

MODERN WOODMEN OF AMERICA—Life Insurance—Modern Woodmen of America; *U.S. Private*, pg. 755

MODERNA/DER SCHUH—Family Shoe Stores—Woolworth Corporation; *U.S. Public*, pg. 1777

MODERNFOLD—Partitions—Modernfold, Inc.; *U.S. Private*, pg. 755

MODERNSCREEN—Fireplace Access.—Byers Portland Willamette; *U.S. Private*, pg. 191

MODES & TRAVAUX—French Women's Interests Magazine—EMAP France; *Int'l*, pg. 451

MODESS—Sanitary Napkins—Johnson & Johnson; *U.S. Public*, pg. 927

MODESS—Feminine Napkins—Personal Products Co.; *U.S. Public*, pg. 929

MODI SHIELD—Flat-Roof Waterproofing Prod.—The Braas Group; *Int'l*, pg. 1091

MODICON—Programmable Controller—Schneider Automation, Inc.; *Int'l*, pg. 1208

MODICON 28—28 Tablets—Ortho-McNeil Pharmaceutical Corporation; *U.S. Public*, pg. 929

MODICON 21—21 Tablets—Ortho-McNeil Pharmaceutical Corporation; *U.S. Public*, pg. 929

MODIFAST—Weight-Reducing Food Products—Novartis AG; *Int'l*, pg. 971

MODIFIED DIAMOND DESIGN—Medico-Surgical Tubing Appliances—Mallinckrodt Inc.; *U.S. Public*, pg. 1039

MODIP—Cardiovascular Pharmaceutical—Astra AB; *Int'l*, pg. 93

MODLOK—Plybent Wood Chair—Sauder Manufacturing Corporation; *U.S. Private*, pg. 967

MODOWN—Bifenon Herbicide—Rhone-Poulenc S.A.; *Int'l*, pg. 1108

MODSIM II—Software—CACI International Inc; *U.S. Public*, pg. 272

MODU-DENSE—Conveying Systems—Fuller Company; *U.S. Private*, pg. 475

MODUALL—Modular Construction Paper Machine—Harnischfeger Industries, Inc.; *U.S. Public*, pg. 788

MODUBAR—Foundations—Restonic Mattress Corporation; *U.S. Private*, pg. 925

MODUCAL—Dietary Carbohydrate—Mead Johnson Nutritional Group; *U.S. Public*, pg. 254

MODUCOIL—Spring Assemblies for Furniture—Leggett & Platt, Incorporated; *U.S. Public*, pg. 985

MODULAR—Musical Instrument Stands—Ludwig Industries; *U.S. Public*, pg. 1514

MODULAR AUSTIN MOORE HIP—Artificial Hip—Bristol-Myers Squibb Company; *U.S. Public*, pg. 253

MODULAR CONTROLLER—Control Products—Bailey, Fischer & Porter Company; *Int'l*, pg. 449

MODULAR DESIGN ENVIRONMENT—Software—LSI Logic Corp.; *U.S. Public*, pg. 971

MODULAR FLEX—Flexible Circut—Advanced Circuit Technology; *U.S. Private*, pg. 21

MODULAR LUBE—Centralized Lubrication Equipment for Industry—Lincoln Industrial; *U.S. Public*, pg. 1273

MODULAR ONE—Automatic Filling Equipment—Liqui-Box Corporation; *U.S. Public*, pg. 1000

MODULATION OPTICS—Company Name—Slant/Fin Corporation; *U.S. Private*, pg. 1005

MODULE-AIRE—Ventilator—Swartwout Industries; *Int'l*, pg. 1398

MODULEFLOR—Floor Coverings—Domco Inc.; *Int'l*, pg. 415

MODULEMATE—NONE—Berg Electronics; *U.S. Public*, pg. 212

MODULEVEL—Level Controllers—Magnetrol International; *U.S. Private*, pg. 696

MODULEX—Industrial Signage—LEGO Systems, Inc.; *Int'l*, pg. 805

MODULINE—Chromatographic Columns—Amicon, Inc.; *U.S. Public*, pg. 1113

MODULINE—Concentric Shaft Gearmotors & Reducers—Nuttall Gear Corporation; *U.S. Private*, pg. 809

MODULINE—Storage Systems—Plastic Reel Corp. of America; *U.S. Private*, pg. 871

MODULINK—Mobile Microphone Cordset System—Shure Brothers Incorporated; *U.S. Private*, pg. 997

MODULINK—Floor Boxes—Walker Systems, Inc.; *U.S. Private*, pg. 1184

MODULUS—Sporting Goods—The Black & Decker Corporation; *U.S. Public*, pg. 233

MODULUS EV40—NONE—The Black & Decker Corporation; *U.S. Public*, pg. 233

MODUPAC—Enclosure—Analogic Corporation; *U.S. Public*, pg. 109

MODUPULSE—Closed-Circuit Television Equipment—Vicon Industries, Inc.; *U.S. Public*, pg. 1719

MODURETIC—Amiloride Hydrochloride with Hydrochlorothiazide—Merck & Co., Inc.; *U.S. Public*, pg. 1090

MODUTENS—Postoperative Electrical Pain Control Device—Bristol-Myers Squibb Company; *U.S. Public*, pg. 253

MOE-AIR—Painting Outfit—Binks Sames Corporation; *U.S. Public*, pg. 229

MOEN—Faucets & Plumbing Supplies—Fortune Brands, Inc.; *U.S. Public*, pg. 674

MOEN—Kitchen & Bath Faucets & Sikns, Shower Valves & Related Accessories—MasterBrand Industries, Inc.; *U.S. Public*, pg. 675

MOEN—Plumbing Supplies—Moen Incorporated; *U.S. Public*, pg. 675

MOET AND CHANDON—NONE—LVMH Moet Hennessy Louis Vuitton; *Int'l*, pg. 779

MOET & CHANDON—Champagnes—Schieffelin & Somerset Co.; *Int'l*, pg. 1000

MOGEN DAVID—Wine—The Wine Group; *U.S. Private*, pg. 1182

MOGENSEN SIZER—Screen—Royer Industries, Inc.; *Int'l*, pg. 1066

MOHAWK—Cordials, Schnapps, Brandy, Rum, Bourbon, Gin & Vodka—Marie Brizard Wines & Spirits USA; *U.S. Private*, pg. 702

MOHAWK—Carpets & Rugs—Mohawk Industries, Inc.; *U.S. Public*, pg. 1121

MOHAWK—Wood Care Products—RPM, Inc.; *U.S. Public*, pg. 1356

MOHAWK—Rotary Cutters—United Farm Tools, Inc.; *U.S. Private*, pg. 1122

MOHAWK ARTEMIS—Premium Textured Uncoated Text and Cover—Mohawk Paper Mills, Inc.; *U.S. Private*, pg. 755

MOHAWK BRAND—Tires—Yokohama Tire Corporation; *Int'l*, pg. 1521

MOHAWK 50/10—Recycled Coated Paper with Post Consumer Waste—Mohawk Paper Mills, Inc.; *U.S. Private*, pg. 755

MOHAWK INNOVATION II—Premium Matte-Coated Paper—Mohawk Paper Mills, Inc.; *U.S. Private*, pg. 755

MOHAWK IRISH LINEN—Recycled & Virgin Premium Textured Uncoated Text & Cover—Mohawk Paper Mills, Inc.; *U.S. Private*, pg. 755

MOHAWK NAVAJO COVER—Premium Non-Textured Uncoated Cover—Mohawk Paper Mills, Inc.; *U.S. Private*, pg. 755

MOHAWK OPAQUE—Recycled Covered & Uncoated Text—Mohawk Paper Mills, Inc.; *U.S. Private*, pg. 755

MOHAWK SATIN—Recycled & Virgin Non-Textured Text & Cover Uncoated—Mohawk Paper Mills, Inc.; *U.S. Private*, pg. 755

MOHAWK SUPERFINE—Premium Non-Textured Uncoated—Mohawk Paper Mills, Inc.; *U.S. Private*, pg. 755

MOHAWK TICONDEROGA—Premium Textured Uncoated Text and Cover—Mohawk Paper Mills, Inc.; *U.S. Private*, pg. 755

MOHAWK TOMOHAWK—Recycled & Virgin Premium Textured Uncoated Text & Cover—Mohawk Paper Mills, Inc.; *U.S. Private*, pg. 755

MOHAWK ULTRAFELT—Premium Textured Uncoated Text and Cover Uncoatee—Mohawk Paper Mills, Inc.; *U.S. Private*, pg. 755

MOHAWK UNCOATED SELECTIONS—Ravenna Cover, Golden Star, Natural Parchment, Imported, Uncoated Papers—Mohawk Paper Mills, Inc.; *U.S. Private*, pg. 755

MOHAWK VELLUM—Recycled & Virgin Non-Textured Text & Cover Uncoated—Mohawk Paper Mills, Inc.; *U.S. Private*, pg. 755

MOHITE—Fire Brick—CFB Industries, Inc.; *U.S. Private*, pg. 194

MOHITE—Fire Brick—Chicago Fire Brick Co.; *U.S. Private*, pg. 194

MOIST 'N RICH—Moisturizing Skin Care—Freeman Cosmetic Corp.; *U.S. Private*, pg. 426

MOIST & MEATY—Dog Food—Ralston Purina Company; *U.S. Public*, pg. 1359

MOIST 'N BEEFY—Dog Food—H.J. Heinz Company; *U.S. Public*, pg. 805

MOISTCURE—Hair Treatment Preparation—Revlon-Realistic Professional Products, Inc.; *U.S. Private*, pg. 690

MOISTEX—Hair Care—Palm Beach Beauty Products Co.; *U.S. Private*, pg. 834

MOISTOP—Concrete Underlay—Carter Holt Harvey Limited; *U.S. Public*, pg. 904

MOISTRITE—Bond Paper—The Mead Corporation; *U.S. Public*, pg. 1074

MOISTURE CURL—Steam Hairsetter—Remington Products Company, L.L.C.; *U.S. Private*, pg. 921

MOISTURE LOVER—NONE—Clairol, Inc.; *U.S. Public*, pg. 254

MOISTURE MASTER—Pipes—Aquapore Moisture Systems, Inc.; *Int'l*, pg. 1066

MOISTURE 35—Cosmetics—Irma Shorell, Inc.; *U.S. Private*, pg. 1101

MOISTURE WHIP—Makeup & Lipstick—Maybelline, Inc.; *Int'l*, pg. 819

MOISTUREL—Skin Care Product—Bristol-Myers Squibb Company; *U.S. Public*, pg. 253

MOISTUREL—Dryskin Care Aids & Sensitive Skin Cleanser; Cream & Lotion—Westwood-Squibb Pharmaceuticals Inc.; *U.S. Public*, pg. 255

MOISTUREWEAR—Liquid, Cream, Powder, Blush & Concealer—Cover Girl Cosmetics; *U.S. Public*, pg. 1330

MOISTURIZING LIQUID DIAL—NONE—The Dial Corporation; *U.S. Public*, pg. 505

MOJAVE—All-Terrain Vehicle—Kawasaki Motors Corp., U.S.A.; *Int'l*, pg. 725

MOJAVE—Seasonings, Peppers, Corn Husks—McCormick/Schilling; *U.S. Public*, pg. 1066

MOJAVE—Socks & Knitted Headwear—Wigwam Mills, Inc.; *U.S. Private*, pg. 1175

MOJAZZ—Records—Motown Record Company, J.P.; *Int'l*, pg. 1052

MOJO—U.K. Entertainment Magazine—EMAP Metro; *Int'l*, pg. 451

MOKA PLC—Cereal—Nestle S.A.; *Int'l*, pg. 915

MOKON—Circulating Temp. Controls—Protective Closures Co., Inc.; *U.S. Public*, pg. 1045

MOL-CREE—NONE—Wacoal Corporation; *Int'l*, pg. 1484

MOLA-TAB—TablettingAgent for Pharmaceutical & Nutritional Tablets—Crompton & Knowles Ingredient Technology Corp.; *U.S. Public*, pg. 459

MOLAINE—Yarn—Lion Brand Yarn Co.; *U.S. Private*, pg. 669

MOLCUT—Membrane Filter—Millipore Corporation; *U.S. Public*, pg. 1112

MOLD-TECH—Mold Engravings—Standex International Corporation; *U.S. Public*, pg. 1505

MOLDATHERM—Lightweight Ceramic Fiber Insulation—Lindberg, A General Signal Company; *U.S. Public*, pg. 727

MOLDCAST—Outdoor Lighting Fixtures—Prescolite Moldcast Lighting Company; *U.S. Public*, pg. 1684

MOLDED TOPLINER—Faced Headliner—Johns Manville Corporation; *U.S. Public*, pg. 927

MOLDEX—Paint—Swire Pacific Limited; *Int'l*, pg. 1328

MOLDMATE—Couplers—Parker Hannifin Corp., Quick Coupling Div.; *U.S. Public*, pg. 1260

MOLE ELIMINATOR—Mole Trap—Security Lawn & Garden Co.; *U.S. Private*, pg. 397

MOLE MAP—Directional Mapping System—McLaughlin Manufacturing Company; *U.S. Private*, pg. 724

THE MOLE—Automated Storage Systems—Litton Industries, Inc.; *U.S. Public*, pg. 1002

MOLENBERG—NONE—Quality Bakers New Zealand Ltd.; *Int'l*, pg. 556

MOLENBERG—Whole Grain Bread—Quality Bakers of America Cooperative, Inc.; *U.S. Private*, pg. 898

MOLETTO CABERNET—Italian Wine—Laird & Company; *U.S. Private*, pg. 642

MOLETTO CHARDONNAY—Italian Wine—Laird & Company; *U.S. Private*, pg. 642

MOLETTO COLMELLO BIANCO—Italian Wine—Laird & Company; *U.S. Private*, pg. 642

MOLETTO COLMELLO BIANCO BARRIQUE—Italian Wine—Laird & Company; *U.S. Private*, pg. 642

MOLETTO COLMELLO ROSSO BARRIQUE—Italian Wine—Laird & Company; *U.S. Private*, pg. 642

MOLETTO COLMETTO ROSSO—Italian Wine—Laird & Company; *U.S. Private*, pg. 642

MOLETTO MERLOT—Italian Wine—Laird & Company; *U.S. Private*, pg. 642

MOLETTO PINOT GRIGIO—Italian Wine—Laird & Company; *U.S. Private*, pg. 642

MOLETTO PROSECCO—Italian Wine—Laird & Company; *U.S. Private*, pg. 642

MOLEX—Electronic Components—Molex Incorporated; *U.S. Public*, pg. 1121

MOLEX-ETC—NONE—Molex Incorporated; *U.S. Public*, pg. 1121

MOLIFT—Storage & Retrieval Equipment—Litton Industries, Inc.; *U.S. Public*, pg. 1002

MOLLAN—Materials for Plastics—DSM Chemie Linz GmbH; *Int'l*, pg. 356

MOLLEY MALLOY—Career & Evening Wear Missy Clothing—Chorus Line Corporation; *U.S. Private*, pg. 238

MOLLY—Wall Anchors, Self-Drilling Screws & Other Mechanical Fasteners—The Black & Decker Corporation; *U.S. Public*, pg. 233

MOLLY MCBUTTER—Food Seasoning—Alberto-Culver Company; *U.S. Public*, pg. 37

MOLOL—Petrolalums—Witco Corporation; *U.S. Public*, pg. 1773

MOLSON—Beer—Foster's Brewing Group Limited; *Int'l*, pg. 500

MOLSON—Canadian Beer & Ale—The Molson Companies Limited; *Int'l*, pg. 887

MOLSON—Beer—Philip Morris Companies Inc.; *U.S. Public*, pg. 1287

MOLSON ICE—Beer—Miller Brewing Company; *U.S. Public*, pg. 1289

MOLSON ICE—Beer—Philip Morris Companies Inc.; *U.S. Public*, pg. 1287

MOLTEX—Diapers—VP-Schickedanz AG; *U.S. Public*, pg. 1333

MOLTO SMALTO—Perfume—International Cosmetics Co., Ltd.; *Int'l*, pg. 684

MOLYCORP—Miners & Processors—Molycorp, Inc.; *U.S. Public*, pg. 1698

MOLYDAG—Lubricants—Acheson Colloids Company; *U.S. Private*, pg. 12

MOLYKOTE—Specialty Lubricants—Dow Corning Corporation; *U.S. Public*, pg. 523

MOLYLUBE—Oil Lubricant—Bel-Ray Company, Inc.; *U.S. Private*, pg. 130

MOLYVER—Chemical Reagant—Hach Company; *U.S. Public*, pg. 773

MOM HOT—Epidermis Agents—Nippon Kayaku Co. Ltd.; *Int'l*, pg. 934

MOM N POP'S BUFFET & BAKERY—Restaurant—WSMP, Inc.; *U.S. Public*, pg. 1729

MOM N' POPS COUNTRY BISCUITS—Food Products—WSMP, Inc.; *U.S. Public*, pg. 1729

MOM N' POPS COUNTRY HAM—Food Prod.—WSMP, Inc.; *U.S. Public*, pg. 1729

MOM TAPE—Epidermis Agents—Nippon Kayaku Co. Ltd.; *Int'l*, pg. 934

MOMENTS—Pet Foods—Nestle S.A.; *Int'l*, pg. 915

MOMENTS OF INSPIRATION—Greeting Cards—American Greetings Corporation; *U.S. Public*, pg. 77

MOMENTUM—NONE—Whitehall-Robins Healthcare; *U.S. Public*, pg. 80

MOMI-MOMI—Massage Chairs—Matsushita Electric Works, Ltd.; *Int'l*, pg. 847

MOMMESSIN—Wines French—Marie Brizard Wines & Spirits USA; *U.S. Private*, pg. 702

MOMMY'S HAVING A BABY—Doll—Tyco Toys, Inc.; *U.S. Public*, pg. 1058

MOM'S—Margarine—Lever Brothers Co.; *Int'l*, pg. 1435

MOM'S—Margarine—Unilever Plc; *Int'l*, pg. 1433

MOM'S CHOICE—NONE—Idaho Supreme Company; *U.S. Private*, pg. 557

MOM'S HOME STYLE FUDGE—Fudge Making Machine—Gold Medal Products Co.; *U.S. Private*, pg. 459

MON-A-THERM—Temperature Monitoring Systems—Mallinckrodt Inc.; *U.S. Public*, pg. 1039

MON CHERI—Chocolates—Ferrero; *Int'l*, pg. 480

MON CHERI—Fine Chocolate—Ferrero U.S.A., Inc.; *Int'l*, pg. 480

MON IMAGE—Beauty & Bath Accessories—Paris Presents; *U.S. Private*, pg. 839

MONA—Pasta Prods.—Bernardi Italian Foods; *U.S. Private*, pg. 1182

MONA—Nail Care Products—Revlon-Realistic Professional Products, Inc.; *U.S. Private*, pg. 690

MONACO—Motorhomes—Monaco Coach Corporation; *U.S. Public*, pg. 1123

MONARCH—Sporting Goods—Brunswick Bowling & Billiards Corp.; *U.S. Public*, pg. 265

MONARCH—Manufactured Homes—Champion Enterprises, Inc.; *U.S. Public*, pg. 332

MONARCH—Faceshields—The Fibre-Metal Products Company; *U.S. Private*, pg. 402

MONARCH—Cooking Oil, Margarine & Spread—Lever Brothers Co.; *Int'l*, pg. 1435

MONARCH—Slings—Macwhyte Co.; *U.S. Private*, pg. 68

MONARCH—Portable Digital Inflation Device—Merit Medical Systems, Inc.; *U.S. Public*, pg. 1096

MONARCH—Luggage—Monarch Luggage Co. Inc.; *U.S. Private*, pg. 757

MONARCH—Machine Tools—The Monarch Machine Tool Company; *U.S. Public*, pg. 1123

MONARCH—NONE—PAXAR Corporation; *U.S. Public*, pg. 1266

MONARCH—Test Preparation—Simon & Schuster; *U.S. Private*, pg. 777

MONARCH—Cooking Oil, Margarine & Spread—Unilever Plc; *Int'l*, pg. 1433

MONARCH OF SEAS—Ships—Royal Caribbean Cruises Ltd.; *U.S. Public*, pg. 1410

MONARCH WARE—Metal Fabrication—Monarch Ware, Inc.; *U.S. Private*, pg. 735

MONARK—Bicycles & Stationary Bikes—Aritmos AB; *Int'l*, pg. 1072

MONARK—Pumps—Graco Inc.; *U.S. Public*, pg. 756

MONARK—Egg Prods.—Monark Egg Corporation; *U.S. Public*, pg. 1104

MONASPOR—Antibiotic—Novartis; *Int'l*, pg. 972

MONASTERY—Cordials—NWS Inc.; *U.S. Private*, pg. 772

MONCHEL—Face & Body Bar Soap—The Procter & Gamble Company; *U.S. Public*, pg. 1330

MONCRISTO—NONE—Tabacalera, S.A.; *Int'l*, pg. 1345

MONDAMIN FIX—Sauce Binders—Bestfoods; *U.S. Public*, pg. 223

MONDAVI—NONE—Robert Mondavi Winery, Inc.; *U.S. Public*, pg. 1393

MONDER—Pasta—Borden, Inc.; *U.S. Private*, pg. 157

MONDO—Beauty Salon Furniture—Belvedere Company; *U.S. Private*, pg. 1008

MONDO DI MARCO—Clothing—Genesco Inc.; *U.S. Public*, pg. 728

MONDORO—Wines—Canandaigua Wine Company, Inc.; *U.S. Public*, pg. 300

MONEL—Nickel-Copper Alloys—Inco Alloys International, Inc.; *Int'l*, pg. 672

MONEL—Alloy—Inco Limited; *Int'l*, pg. 672

MONET—Ceramic Wall Tile—Monarch Tile, Inc.; *U.S. Private*, pg. 287

MONET—Costume Jewelry—Monet Jewelers; *U.S. Private*, pg. 757

MONEX—Leverage, Option, Financial & Cash Purchases—Monex Deposit Co.; *U.S. Private*, pg. 757

MONEY—Magazine—Time Warner Inc.; *U.S. Public*, pg. 1610

MONEY CLIP KNIFE—Money Clip with Knife—Fiskars-Gerber; *Int'l*, pg. 492

MONEY MANAGEMENT—Magazine—Reed Business Information Pty. Limited; *Int'l*, pg. 1094

MONEY MONITOR—PC Home Banking—Downey Savings & Loan Association, F.A.; *U.S. Public*, pg. 526

MONEYGRAM—Wire Transfer System—First Data Corporation; *U.S. Public*, pg. 631

MONEYMAKER—ATM—Affiliated Computer Services, Inc.; *U.S. Public*, pg. 27

MONEYMARKET II—Securities Trading & Back-Office System for Banks—SunGard Data Systems Inc.; *U.S. Public*, pg. 1534

MONEYMAX—Portfolio Management System—SunGard Data Systems Inc.; *U.S. Public*, pg. 1534

MONEYMOVER—24 Hour Teller—NBD Bank (Indiana); *U.S. Public*, pg. 628

MONEYSAVER—Checking/Savings Accounts—NBD Bank (Indiana); *U.S. Public*, pg. 628

MONEYTIME—Bonusing Games—Mikohn Gaming Corporation; *U.S. Public*, pg. 1111

MONFORT—Fresh & Frozen Meat Products—ConAgra, Inc.; *U.S. Public*, pg. 425

MONGOL—Woodcase Pencil—Sanford Corporation; *U.S. Public*, pg. 1178

MONGOLIAN FIRE—Food Seasoning—Hormel Foods Corp.; *U.S. Public*, pg. 840

MONGOOSE—Bicycles & Parts—Brunswick Corporation; *U.S. Public*, pg. 265

MONICA—Segmentation Capability Classification System—CACI International Inc; *U.S. Public*, pg. 272

MONICA—Rice—International Multifoods Corporation; *U.S. Public*, pg. 900

MONICA—NONE—LPC Industrias Alimenticias S.A.; *Int'l*, pg. 380

MONIER—Cement Roof Tiles—CSR Limited; *Int'l*, pg. 245

MONIER—Roof Tile—Monier Inc.; *Int'l*, pg. 1091

MONILER—Toilet Soaps—Procter & Gamble Venezuela, C.A.; *U.S. Public*, pg. 1332

MONISTAT—Topical Antifungal—Johnson & Johnson; *U.S. Public*, pg. 927

MONISTAT-DERM—Cream—Ortho-McNeil Pharmaceutical Corporation; *U.S. Public*, pg. 929

MONISTAT DUAL-PAK—NONE—Ortho-McNeil Pharmaceutical Corporation; *U.S. Public*, pg. 929

MONISTAT I.V.—Pharmaceutical—Janssen Pharmaceutica, Inc.; *U.S. Public*, pg. 928

MONISTAT 7—Vaginal Suppositories—Ortho-McNeil Pharmaceutical Corporation; *U.S. Public*, pg. 929

MONISTAT 7—Vaginal Cream—Ortho-McNeil Pharmaceutical Corporation; *U.S. Public*, pg. 929

MONISTAT 3—Vaginal Suppositories—Ortho-McNeil Pharmaceutical Corporation; *U.S. Public*, pg. 929

MONISTAT 3 DUALPAK—NONE—Ortho-McNeil Pharmaceutical Corporation; *U.S. Public*, pg. 929

MONITEMP—Patient Temperature Monitor—Cincinnati Sub-Zero Products, Inc.; *U.S. Private*, pg. 240

MONITOR—Insecticide—Bayer AG; *Int'l*, pg. 171

MONITOR—NONE—Brown & Sharpe Manufacturing Company; *U.S. Public*, pg. 260

MONITOR—Microfilm Readers & Motion Picture Cameras—Eastman Kodak Company; *U.S. Public*, pg. 550

MONITOR—Prefinished Wall Paneling—Georgia-Pacific Corporation; *U.S. Public*, pg. 735

MONITOR—Electronic Iron—Sunbeam Household Products; *U.S. Public*, pg. 1533

MONITOR LABS—Environmental Monitoring Instruments—Bowthorpe plc; *Int'l*, pg. 207

MONITORMARK—Product Exposure Indicators—3M; *U.S. Public*, pg. 1604

MONITRACE—Computerized Monitoring System for Heat Trace—Raychem Corporation; *U.S. Public*, pg. 1362

MONITRIX—Monitoring Software—Cheyenne; *U.S. Public*, pg. 420

MONITRON—Electric Boiler—Slant/Fin Corporation; *U.S. Private*, pg. 1005

MONK'S—Felt—American Felt & Filter; *U.S. Private*, pg. 54

MONMORE—NONE—Glynwed International PLC; *Int'l*, pg. 554

MONO—Pumps—Dresser Industries, Inc.; *U.S. Public*, pg. 528

MONO-COAT—Acrylic Shingle Paint—GAF Premium Products, Inc.; *U.S. Private*, pg. 433

MONO GAS—Gas Generator—Seco Warwick Corporation; *U.S. Private*, pg. 980

MONO-GESIC—NONE—Schwarz Pharma Inc.; *Int'l*, pg. 1211

MONO-LATEX—Latex Infectious Mononucleosis Slide Test—Wampole Laboratories; *U.S. Public*, pg. 310

MONO-LUBE—Tire Releasant—Chem-Trend Incorporated; *Int'l*, pg. 235

MONO P—Biotechnology—Pharmacia & Upjohn Adria Laboratories; *Int'l*, pg. 1049

MONO PAC—Coating—Pratt & Lambert United, Inc.; *U.S. Public*, pg. 1466

MONO-PLUS—Immunosorbent Assay for Mono—Wampole Laboratories; *U.S. Public*, pg. 310

MONO Q—Biotechnology—Pharmacia & Upjohn Adria Laboratories; *Int'l*, pg. 1049

MONO S—Biotechnology—Pharmacia & Upjohn Adria Laboratories; *Int'l*, pg. 1049

MONO TEST—Slide Test for Mono—Wampole Laboratories; *U.S. Public*, pg. 310

MONO-VACC—Tuberculin Test—Connaught Laboratories, Inc.; *Int'l*, pg. 1109

MONO-WELD—Heavy Duty Fin & Tube Radiator Construction—Young Radiator Company; *U.S. Private*, pg. 1201

MONO-GESIC—Pharmaceutical Products—Schwarz Pharma Manufacturing, Inc.; *Int'l*, pg. 1211

MONO-GLASS—Capacitors—Philips Components; *Int'l*, pg. 1054

MONO-KAP—Capacitors—Philips Components; *Int'l*, pg. 1054

MONO-PAK—Capacitors—Philips Components; *Int'l*, pg. 1054

MONOBEADS—Biotechnology—Pharmacia & Upjohn Adria Laboratories; *Int'l*, pg. 1049

MONOBOX—Electrical Cranes & Hoists—American Crane & Equipment Corp.; *U.S. Private*, pg. 52

MONOCAST—Polyamide Shapes & Parts—DSM Engineering Plastic Products; *Int'l*, pg. 354

MONOCET—Food Emulsifier—Eastman Kodak Company; *U.S. Public*, pg. 550

MONOCID—NONE—SmithKline Beecham Corporation; *Int'l*, pg. 1264

MONOCID—Anti-Infective—SmithKline Beecham plc; *Int'l*, pg. 1264

MONOCLATE-P FACTOR VIII:C—Pasteurized, Monoclonal Antibody Purified Antihemophilic Factor (Human)—Centeon, L.L.C.; *Int'l*, pg. 626

MONOCRYL—Suture—Ethicon, Inc.; *U.S. Public*, pg. 928

MONOCRYL—NONE—Johnson & Johnson; *U.S. Public*, pg. 927

MONODEX—Rotary Switches—Oak Grigsby; *U.S. Public*, pg. 1209

MONOFIRE—Tile Setters—Ferro Corporation; *U.S. Public*, pg. 618

MONOFLEX—Intraocular Lenses—Alcon Laboratories, Inc.; *Int'l*, pg. 916

MONOFRAX—Refractory—The Carborundum Corporation; *Int'l*, pg. 1173

MONOGRAM—Vinyl Siding—CertainTeed Corporation; *Int'l*, pg. 1170

MONOGRAM—Major Appliances—G.E. Appliances; *U.S. Public*, pg. 710

MONOGRAM—NONE—Pfizer Inc.; *U.S. Public*, pg. 1281

MONOGRAM—Model Kits—Revell-Monogram Inc.; *U.S. Private*, pg. 926

MONOGRAM BLEND—Gin—Laird & Company; *U.S. Private*, pg. 642

MONOJECT—Needles And Syringes, Procedure Trays And Blood Collection Tubes—American Home Products Corporation; *U.S. Public*, pg. 79

MONOJECT—Health Care Products—Sherwood-Davis & Geck; *U.S. Public*, pg. 80

MONOKET—NONE—Schwarz Pharma Inc.; *Int'l*, pg. 1211

MONOKORE—Cable—Loos & Co., Inc.; *U.S. Private*, pg. 675

MONOKOTE—Fireproofing—Grace Construction Products; *U.S. Public*, pg. 755

MONOKOTE—Fireproofing Materials—W.R. Grace & Co.; *U.S. Public*, pg. 754

MONOLEX—Wheel Rims—Georg Fischer Ltd.; *Int'l*, pg. 488

MONONINE—Coagulation Factor IX (Human) Monoclonal Antibody Purified—Centeon, L.L.C.; *Int'l*, pg. 626

MONOPHASE S—Pseudocumene-Based Cocktail—Packard Instrument Co., Inc.; *U.S. Private*, pg. 833

MONOPLEX—Artificial Eyes—American Optical Corporation; *U.S. Private*, pg. 60

MONOPLEX—Monomeric Plasticizers—The C.P. Hall Company; *U.S. Private*, pg. 495

MONOPOLY—Board Game—Parker Brothers; *U.S. Public*, pg. 797

MONOPOXY—Single Component Epoxy Compound—Hardman Division of Harcros Chemicals, Inc.; *Int'l*, pg. 598

MONOPRIL—Cardiovascular Therapy Product—Bristol-Myers Squibb Company; *U.S. Public*, pg. 253

MONOPRIL—ACE Inhibitor for treatment of Hypertension—Bristol-Myers Squibb U.S. Pharmaceutical Group; *U.S. Public*, pg. 255

MONOPTY—Urological Instrument—C.R. Bard, Inc.; *U.S. Public*, pg. 189

MONOSET—Headphone—Telex Communications, Inc.; *U.S. Private*, pg. 1074

MONOSOF—Sutures—U.S. Surgical Corp.; *U.S. Public*, pg. 1687

MONOSPOT/MONOLERT—Rapid Tests for Detecting Infectious Mononucleosis—Meridian Diagnostics, Inc.; *U.S. Public*, pg. 1094

MONOSTRESS—High Performance Light Weight Steel Drum—Van Leer Containers, Inc.; *Int'l*, pg. 1146

MONOTARD—Product for Diabetes Care—Novo Nordisk A/S; *Int'l*, pg. 987

MONOTEC—X-Ray Cassettes—Spectronics Corporation; *U.S. Private*, pg. 1024

MONOTUBE—NONE—Pfizer Inc.; *U.S. Public*, pg. 1281

MONOVER—Chemical Reagant—Hach Company; *U.S. Public*, pg. 773

MONOXOR—Measuring Instrument—Bacharach Inc.; *U.S. Private*, pg. 109

MONOZOOM—Microscope—Leica, Inc.; *Int'l*, pg. 806

MONRO-MAGNUM 60—Shock Absorbers—Monroe Auto Equipment Co.; *U.S. Public*, pg. 1577

MONRO-MATIC—Shock Absorbers—Monroe Auto Equipment Co.; *U.S. Public*, pg. 1577

MONRO-MATIC PLUS—Shock Absorbers—Monroe Auto Equipment Co.; *U.S. Public*, pg. 1577

MONROVIA—Whlse. Grower of Ornamental Nursery Stock—Monrovia Nursery Co.; *U.S. Private*, pg. 757

MONSIEUR MUFFLER—Mufflers, Brakes, Shock Absorbers, Front-End Parts & Tires—TCG International Inc.; *Int'l*, pg. 1336

MONSIEUR ROCHAS—Men's Toiletries—Wella Group; *Int'l*, pg. 1489

MONSOON—Women's Fragrance—Coty Inc.; *Int'l*, pg. 185

MONSTER—NONE—Noble Roman's Inc.; *U.S. Public*, pg. 1187

MONT BLANC—NONE—Porcelanite, Inc.; *Int'l*, pg. 573

MONT BLOIS ESTATE—Wine—Distillers Corporation S.A.; *Int'l*, pg. 1129

MONT DORE—Spring Water—Danone Group; *Int'l*, pg. 379

MONTAG—Stationery Products—The Mead Corporation; *U.S. Public*, pg. 1074

MONTAGNARD—Cheese—BG SAS; *Int'l*, pg. 201

MONTAGNES MAGAZINE—French Outdoor Pursuits Magazine—EMAP France; *Int'l*, pg. 451

MONTAGUT—Men's Apparel—International Cosmetics Co., Ltd.; *Int'l*, pg. 684

MONTANA—Perfume—Clarins; *Int'l*, pg. 295

MONTANA—NONE—Fiskars Oy AB; *Int'l*, pg. 492

MONTANA COVER—Cover Stock—FiberMark Inc.; *U.S. Public*, pg. 620

MONTCLAIR—Cigarettes—Brown & Williamson Tobacco Corp.; *Int'l*, pg. 111

MONTCLAIR—Mineral Water—Nestle S.A.; *Int'l*, pg. 915

MONTCO—Private Label Grocery, Perishables & Frozen Items—Fleming Companies, Inc.; *U.S. Public*, pg. 652

MONTE—Apparel—Angelica Corporation; *U.S. Public*, pg. 113

MONTE ALBAN MEZCAL—NONE—Barton Brands, Ltd.; *U.S. Public*, pg. 300

MONTE ALBAN MEZCAL CON GUSANO—Mezcal—Barton Incorporated; *U.S. Public*, pg. 300

MONTE CARLO—Luggage—American Tourister, Inc.; *U.S. Public*, pg. 1430

MONTE CARLO—Automobile—General Motors Corporation; *U.S. Public*, pg. 718

MONTE CARLO—NONE—Radica USA Limited; *U.S. Public*, pg. 906

MONTE CARLO—Cigarettes-Middle East—R.J. Reynolds Tobacco Intl., Inc.; *U.S. Public*, pg. 1355

MONTE-CARLO—NONE—Supreme International Corp.; *U.S. Public*, pg. 1542

MONTE SALINE BARDOLINO—Wine—Paterno Imports Limited; *U.S. Private*, pg. 843

MONTEBAN—Animal Health—Elanco Animal Health; *U.S. Public*, pg. 993

MONTEBAN—Narasin, Elanco—Eli Lilly and Company; *U.S. Public*, pg. 992

MONTEBELLO BLOODY MARIA—Bloody Mary Mix—Montebello Brands Inc.; *U.S. Private*, pg. 758

MONTEBELLO NUTS & BERRIES—Creme Liqueur—Montebello Brands Inc.; *U.S. Private*, pg. 758

MONTEBELLO ORIGINAL ICED COFFEE—Cocktail—Montebello Brands Inc.; *U.S. Private*, pg. 758

MONTEBELLO ORIGINAL KIR—Cocktail—Montebello Brands Inc.; *U.S. Private*, pg. 758

MONTEBELLO ORIGINAL LONG ISLAND ICED TEA—Cocktail—Montebello Brands Inc.; *U.S. Private*, pg. 758

MONTECRISTO—Cigars—Rothmans UK Holdings Limited; *Int'l*, pg. 1129

MONTECRUZ—Cigars—Lane Limited; *Int'l*, pg. 1129

MONTEGO—Confections—Nestle-Rowntree Ltd.; *Int'l*, pg. 921

MONTEIL PARIS—Fragrance, Skin Care & Color Cosmetics—Lancaster Group Worldwide; *Int'l*, pg. 185

MONTEMPS—Packaged Cake & Pancake Mix—Kao Corporation; *Int'l*, pg. 717

MONTEREY—Area Rugs—American Rug Craftsmen; *U.S. Public*, pg. 1121

MONTEREY—Luggage—American Tourister, Inc.; *U.S. Public*, pg. 1430

MONTEREY—Mushrooms—Amfac, Inc.; *U.S. Private*, pg. 577

MONTEREY—Magazine Paper—Fort James Corporation; *U.S. Public*, pg. 670

MONTEREY—Mexican Restaurants—Monterey's Acquisition Corp.; *U.S. Private*, pg. 758

MONTEREY—Air Cooled Pckg Terminal—Slant/Fin Corporation; *U.S. Private*, pg. 1005

MONTEREY CLUB—Sports Outerwear—Fox-Knapp; *U.S. Private*, pg. 860

MONTEREY PLANK—Pre-Finished Laminate—Bruce Hardwood Floors; *U.S. Public*, pg. 1634

MONTEREY'S TEX MEX CAFE—Family, Sitdown Mexican Food Restaurant—ShowBiz Pizza Time, Inc.; *U.S. Public*, pg. 1468

MONTEREZ—Specialty Product—Allied Domecq PLC; *Int'l*, pg. 62

MONTERO—Automobile—Mitsubishi Motor Sales of America, Inc.; *Int'l*, pg. 875

MONTERRA—Super Premium Wines—Delicato Vineyards; *U.S. Private*, pg. 322

MONTEVINA—Winery—Sutter Home Winery, Inc.; *U.S. Private*, pg. 1057

MONTEZUMA—Tequila—Barton Incorporated; *U.S. Public*, pg. 300

MONTEZUMA TEQUILA—NONE—Barton Brands, Ltd.; *U.S. Public*, pg. 300

MONTEZUMA TRIPLE SEC—NONE—Barton Brands, Ltd.; *U.S. Public*, pg. 300

MONTGOMERY—NONE—Kone Corporation; *Int'l*, pg. 746

MONTGOMERY—Printing Paper—Weyerhaeuser Company; *U.S. Public*, pg. 1764

MONTGOMERY WARD—Department Store—Montgomery Ward & Co., Inc.; *U.S. Private*, pg. 758

MONTGOMERY WARDS OPTICAL—Eyewear—Cole National Corporation; *U.S. Public*, pg. 396

MONTICELLO—Pre-Finished Strip—Bruce Hardwood Floors; *U.S. Public*, pg. 1634

MONTICELLO—Bed & Bath Products—Fieldcrest Cannon, Inc.; *U.S. Public*, pg. 1296

MONTICELLO—NONE—Fortune Brands, Inc.; *U.S. Public*, pg. 674

MONTICELLO—Bath Accessories—Melard Manufacturing Corporation; *U.S. Private*, pg. 729

MONTMARTRE—Chocolate Cakes—Meiji Seika Kaisha, Ltd.; *Int'l*, pg. 855

MONTRACHER—Goat Cheese—Bongrain Cheese USA; *Int'l*, pg. 201

MONY AMERICA—Tradename—The Mutual Life Insurance Company of New York; *U.S. Private*, pg. 769

MONY, MUTUAL OF NEW YORK—Tradename—The Mutual Life Insurance Company of New York; *U.S. Private*, pg. 769

MOOD MAGIC—Dimmer Socket—Eagle Electric Mfg. Co., Inc.; *U.S. Private*, pg. 354

MOOD MASTER—Dimmer Controls—The Lamson & Sessions Co.; *U.S. Public*, pg. 976

MOOD MENDER—Blend with B Vitamins—Celestial Seasonings; *U.S. Public*, pg. 319

MOOG—Automotive Replacement Parts—Moog Automotive, Inc.; *U.S. Public*, pg. 443

MOOG—Servocontrols—Moog Incorporated; *U.S. Public*, pg. 1127

MOON BEACH GRILLE—NONE—Harrah's Entertainment, Inc.; *U.S. Public*, pg. 790

MOON PALACE—Imported Food Products—World Finer Foods, Inc.; *U.S. Private*, pg. 1190

MOONCREST—Desk Accessories—Smith McDonald Corp.; *U.S. Public*, pg. 1009

MOONLIGHT OAK—Paneling—Georgia-Pacific Corporation; *U.S. Public*, pg. 735

MOONLIGHT TOBACCO COMPANY—Premium Tobacco Products—RJR Tobacco Company, Inc.; *U.S. Public*, pg. 1355

MOONSHADOW—Wood & Wood Fiber Products—Georgia-Pacific Corporation; *U.S. Public*, pg. 735

MOONSHINE—Interior Plant Prods.—Security Lawn & Garden Co.; *U.S. Private*, pg. 397

MOONVISOR—Lighted Sunvisor—Lund International Holdings, Inc.; *U.S. Public*, pg. 1020

MOORCRAFT—Professional Coatings—Benjamin Moore & Co.; *U.S. Private*, pg. 133

MOORE—Generic Drugs & Medical Supplies—Moore Medical Corp.; *U.S. Public*, pg. 1128

MOORE—Machine Tool & Measuring Machines—The Producto Machine Co.; *U.S. Private*, pg. 889

MOORE AUTOSIZE—Automatic Sizing System—Moore Tool Company, Inc.; *U.S. Private*, pg. 889

MOORE BUSINESS COMMUNICATION SERVICES—Project Management of Variable-Imaged Mailings—Moore Document Solutions; *Int'l*, pg. 890

MOORE CLEAN PRINT—Carbonless Paper—Moore Document Solutions; *Int'l*, pg. 890

MOOREGUARD—Document Security Feature—Moore Document Solutions; *Int'l*, pg. 890

MOORE'S—Potato Chips, Snack Foods—Borden, Inc.; *U.S. Private*, pg. 157

MOORE'S RED LEAF—Twist Tobaccos—Conwood Company L.P.; *U.S. Private*, pg. 272

MOORGARD—Latex House Paint—Benjamin Moore & Co.; *U.S. Private*, pg. 133

MOORGLO—Latex House Paint—Benjamin Moore & Co.; *U.S. Private*, pg. 133

MOORMAN—Food & Kindred Prods.—Moorman's Inc.; *U.S. Private*, pg. 760

MOORWOOD—Exterior Stains—Benjamin Moore & Co.; *U.S. Private*, pg. 133

MOOSEHEAD—Lager—Bass PLC; *Int'l*, pg. 169

MOOSEHEAD—Canadian Beer—Guinness Import Company; *Int'l*, pg. 412

MOOSEHEAD—Beer—Whitbread PLC; *Int'l*, pg. 1498

MOOSEHEAD LIGHT—Canadian Beer—Guinness Import Company; *Int'l*, pg. 412

MOOSMANN—Musical Instruments—G. Leblanc Corporation; *U.S. Private*, pg. 656

MOP & GLO—Floor Cleaner—Reckitt & Colman Inc.; *Int'l*, pg. 1090

MOP & SHINE—Floor Polish—Blue Cross Laboratories; *U.S. Private*, pg. 152

MOPLEFAN—Polypropylene Film—Montedison S.p.A.; *Int'l*, pg. 324

MOPLEN—Polypropylene Resin—Montedison S.p.A.; *Int'l*, pg. 324

MOPRAL—Gastrointestinal Drug—Astra AB; *Int'l*, pg. 93

MOPROD—Ignition & Fuel System Parts—Echlin Inc.; *U.S. Public*, pg. 560

MOR-AD—Industrial Adhesive—Morton International Inc.; *U.S. Public*, pg. 1135

MOR-FLO—Polymer emulsion—Morton International Inc.; *U.S. Public*, pg. 1135

MOR-FLOAMERICAN—Water Heaters—Southcorp Holdings Ltd.; *U.S. Public*, pg. 1287

MOR-GLO—Polymer emulsion—Morton International Inc.; *U.S. Public*, pg. 1135

MORAMATIC—Liquifeeder—Feed Service Corp.; *U.S. Private*, pg. 399

MORANOL—Liquifeeder—Feed Service Corp.; *U.S. Private*, pg. 399

MORCROP—Fertilizer—The Chas. H. Lilly Co.; *U.S. Public*, pg. 667

MORE!—U.K. Young Women's Magazine—EMAP Elan; *Int'l*, pg. 451

MORE—Cigarettes—RJR Nabisco Holdings Corp.; *U.S. Public*, pg. 1354

MORE—120's Filter & Menthol, Lts. 100-Box, Menthol Box, Lts.120's Menthol & Reg.—R.J. Reynolds Tobacco Company; *U.S. Public*, pg. 1355

MORE—Cigarettes—R.J. Reynolds Tobacco Intl., Inc.; *U.S. Public*, pg. 1355

MORE FOR LESS—Seasonings—McCormick/Schilling; *U.S. Public*, pg. 1066

MORE 4—Combo Food & Drug—Erickson's Diversified Corp.; *U.S. Private*, pg. 381

MORE INTIMATES—NONE—Kellwood Company; *U.S. Public*, pg. 948

MORE JAZZ—Large Size & Maternity Clothing—Chorus Line Corporation; *U.S. Private*, pg. 238

MORE 1/2—Concentrated Dishwashing Liquid—Kao Corporation; *Int'l*, pg. 717

MORE THAN HEALTHCARE, HUMANCARE—NONE—Oxford Health Plans Inc.; *U.S. Public*, pg. 1238

MORE THAN MEDICARE, HUMANCARE—NONE—Oxford Health Plans Inc.; *U.S. Public*, pg. 1238

MOREA—Liquifeed—Feed Service Corp.; *U.S. Private*, pg. 399

MOREL—Commercial Turf Machinery—Ransomes Plc; *Int'l*, pg. 1087

MORETTI—Beer—Heineken N.V.; *Int'l*, pg. 608

MORETTI—Beer—Labatt U.S.A.; *Int'l*, pg. 679

MOREY BOOGIE—Body Boards—Mattel, Inc.; *U.S. Public*, pg. 1057

MOREY BOOGIE—Body Boards—Mattel Power Wheels; *U.S. Public*, pg. 1058

MOREZ—Polymer emulsion—Morton International Inc.; *U.S. Public*, pg. 1135

MORFAST—Industrial Liquid Dyes—Morton International Inc.; *U.S. Public*, pg. 1134

MORFLEX—Couplings—Emerson Power Transmission Corporation; *U.S. Public*, pg. 573

MORFRUIT—Glace (Candied Fruit)—Paradise, Inc.; *U.S. Private*, pg. 1256

MORGAN—Wood Doors—Morgan Products Ltd.; *U.S. Public*, pg. 1132

MORGAN—Digital PBX System—TIE/Communications, Inc.; *U.S. Private*, pg. 1085

MORI-NU—Tofu—Morinaga Milk Industry Co., Ltd.; *Int'l*, pg. 895

MORIMER—PVC Coated Products on Non-Wovens—Bontex; *U.S. Public*, pg. 734

MORIMER—PVC Expanded on Fabric—Georgia-Bonded Fibers, Inc.; *U.S. Public*, pg. 734

MORINAGA—Milk—Morinaga Milk Industry Co., Ltd.; *Int'l*, pg. 895

MORLITE—X-Ray Film—Eastman Kodak Company; *U.S. Public*, pg. 550

MORLITE—Lighting—JJI Lighting Group Inc.; *Int'l*, pg. 821

MORNING FRESH—Washing Up Liquid—Cussons (U.K.) LTD.; *Int'l*, pg. 1024

MORNING STAR—Pleasure Boats—Mitsubishi Heavy Industries Ltd.; *Int'l*, pg. 873

MORNING THUNDER—Tea—Celestial Seasonings; *U.S. Public*, pg. 319

MORNINGSIDE—Lumber & Wood Products—Georgia-Pacific Corporation; *U.S. Public*, pg. 735

MORNINGSTAR FARMS—NONE—Worthington Foods Inc.; *U.S. Public*, pg. 1780

MOROKOSHIMURA—Snack Foods—Meiji Seika Kaisha, Ltd.; *Int'l*, pg. 855

MORPAC—Margarine Machines—Lynch Machinery, Inc.; *U.S. Public*, pg. 1022

MORPAC—Semi-Conductor Devices—Semtech Corporation; *U.S. Public*, pg. 1456

MORPHEE PLUS—Nasal CPAP Generator—Nellcor Puritan Bennett Incorporated; *U.S. Public*, pg. 1039

MORPHY RICHARDS—Household Appliances—The Glen Dimplex Group; *Int'l*, pg. 553

MORPRIME—Organosol Dispersions—Morton International Inc.; *U.S. Public*, pg. 1135

MORRIS HELI-GROOVE—Spiral Grooved Tubing For Conveying Plastic Pellets—Morris Coupling Co.; *U.S. Private*, pg. 762

MORRISON & SCHIFF—Food Products—National Foods Inc.; *U.S. Public*, pg. 429

MORRISON FRESH COOKING—NONE—Morrison Restaurants, Inc.; *U.S. Public*, pg. 1134

MORRISON'S CAFETERIAS—NONE—Morrison Restaurants, Inc.; *U.S. Public*, pg. 1134

MORROW—Adult Books—William Morrow & Co., Inc.; *U.S. Private*, pg. 515

MORROW ADULT BOOKS—Books—The Hearst Corporation; *U.S. Private*, pg. 515

MORROW JUNIOR BOOKS—Books—The Hearst Corporation; *U.S. Private*, pg. 515

MORROW JUNIOR BOOKS—Juvenile Books—William Morrow & Co., Inc.; *U.S. Private*, pg. 515

MORSE CONTROLS—Sliding Cable Controls—IMO Industries Inc.; *U.S. Public*, pg. 856

MORSE MANIFOLD—NONE—Pfizer Inc.; *U.S. Public*, pg. 1281

MORTAL KOMBAT—Interactive Entertainment Software—Acclaim Entertainment, Inc.; *U.S. Public*, pg. 15

MORTAR & PESTLE DESIGN—Radiopharmaceuticals for Diagnostic Imaging Purposes—Mallinckrodt Inc.; *U.S. Public*, pg. 1039

MORTARA ELI 100/STM—Continuous 12 Lead ST Segment Monitor—Datascope Corp.; *U.S. Public*, pg. 487

MORTEIN—Pest Control—Reckitt & Colman plc; *Int'l*, pg. 1089

MORTEX—Coating—Essex Specialty Products; *U.S. Public*, pg. 523

MORTGAGE EXPERT—NONE—Countrywide Home Loans Inc.; *U.S. Public*, pg. 452

MORTGAGE MONEY MOVER—NONE—Countrywide Home Loans Inc.; *U.S. Public*, pg. 452

MORTHANE—Specialty Chemical Resin—Morton International Inc.; *U.S. Public*, pg. 1135

MORTITE—Weather Stripping—Essex Specialty Products; *U.S. Public*, pg. 523

MORTITE—Consumer Products—Thermwell Products Co., Inc.; *U.S. Private*, pg. 1081

MORTON—Frozen Foods—ConAgra Frozen Food Company; *U.S. Public*, pg. 427

MORTON—Frozen Dinners—ConAgra, Inc.; *U.S. Public*, pg. 425

MORTON—Table Salt—Morton International Inc.; *U.S. Public*, pg. 1134

MORTON GARLIC SALT—Salt—Morton Salt; *U.S. Public*, pg. 1135

MORTON HOUSE—NONE—Castleberry/Snow's Brands Inc.; *U.S. Private*, pg. 219

MORTON HOUSE—Canned Meat Products—ConAgra Frozen Food Company; *U.S. Public*, pg. 427

MORTON HOUSE—Canned Meat Products—ConAgra Frozen Foods; *U.S. Public*, pg. 427

MORTON HOUSE BRAND—Canned Meat & Meat Entrees—Bunker Hill Foods Inc.; *U.S. Private*, pg. 219

MORTON SEASONED SALT—Salt—Morton Salt; *U.S. Public*, pg. 1135

MORTON SYSTEM SAVER PELLETS—Salt—Morton Salt; *U.S. Public*, pg. 1135

MORTON THIOKOL—Thermal Barrier Compound—Morton International Inc.; *U.S. Public*, pg. 1135

MORWET—Wetting & Dispensing Agents—Witco Corporation; *U.S. Public*, pg. 1773

MOSAIC—LMR Antenna—Allen Telecom Inc.; *U.S. Public*, pg. 45

MOSAIC—Thermally Stable/PDC Bits—Baker Hughes INTEQ; *U.S. Public*, pg. 166

MOSAIC—Dinnerware—Dansk International Designs Ltd.; *U.S. Private*, pg. 261

MOSAIC—Prosthetic Heart Valve—Medtronic, Inc.; *U.S. Public*, pg. 1082

MOSAIC OA—Applications Software for Banking—Olsy North America Inc.; *Int'l*, pg. 1002

MOSCO—Callus & Corn Remover & Foot Relaxer Gel—Medtech Inc.; *U.S. Private*, pg. 728

MOSCOM—NONE—Moscom Corporation; *U.S. Public*, pg. 1136

MOSEL TECHNOLOGY—NONE—Milgray Electronics, Inc.; *U.S. Public*, pg. 205

MOSEY'S—Meat Products—John Morrell & Co.; *U.S. Public*, pg. 1479

MOSFIT—Parameter Extraction Software—Keithley Instruments, Inc.; *U.S. Public*, pg. 946

MOSLER—Security Products—Mosler Inc.; *U.S. Private*, pg. 763

MOSLEY—Baler—Harris Waste Mgmt. Group, Inc.; *Int'l*, pg. 473

MOSS BROS—NONE—Moss Bros Group PLC; *Int'l*, pg. 895

MOSS MASTER—Moss Controller—Security Lawn & Garden Co.; *U.S. Private*, pg. 397

THE MOST SOLID FEEL IN GOLF—NONE—Callaway Golf Company; *U.S. Public*, pg. 294

MOSTLY MEN—Male Toiletries—The Body Shop International; *Int'l*, pg. 199

MOTARJEME—Catheters—Mallinckrodt Inc.; *U.S. Public*, pg. 1039

MOTCH—Vertical & Horizontal Turning Machines; FMS, FMC & Special Machines—Motch Corporation; *Int'l*, pg. 1128

MOTCH VNC—Vertical & Horizontal Numerically Controlled Chuckers—Motch Corporation; *Int'l*, pg. 1128

MOTCH VNP—Vertical Numerically Programmed High Production Chuckers—Motch Corporation; *Int'l*, pg. 1128

MOTCH VTC—Vertical Turning Centers—Motch Corporation; *Int'l*, pg. 1128

MOTEL 6—Motel—Motel 6 Operating L.P.; *Int'l*, pg. 21

MOTEL 6—American Budget Hotels—Accor S.A.; *Int'l*, pg. 20

MOTHER & HEALTH—U.K. Parenting Magazine—EMAP Elan; *Int'l*, pg. 451

MOTHER EARTH—Magazine Publishers—Mother Earth News; *U.S. Private*, pg. 1056

MOTHER EARTH—NONE—Sussex Publishers, Inc.; *U.S. Private*, pg. 1056

MOTHER GOLDSTEIN—Wine—Adams Wine Co.; *U.S. Private*, pg. 17

MOTHER TRUCKER—Antennas—Telex Communications, Inc.; *U.S. Private*, pg. 1074

MOTHER'S—Breads—Metz Baking Company; *U.S. Private*, pg. 1022

MOTHERS—Breads—Metz Baking Company (WI); *U.S. Private*, pg. 1022

MOTHER'S—Cookies & Crackers—President Baking-Louisville; *U.S. Public*, pg. 1069

MOTHER'S—Cereal, Rice Cakes—The Quaker Oats Company; *U.S. Public*, pg. 1347

MOTHERS—Kosher Foods—Rokeach Food Distributing Inc.; *U.S. Private*, pg. 940

MOTHER'S CHOICE—Baby & Toddler Personal Care Products—The Cook Bates Division; *Int'l*, pg. 815

MOTHER'S CHOICE—Margarine—Goodman Fielder Limited; *Int'l*, pg. 555

MOTHER'S COOKIES—Cookies—Mother's Cake & Cookie Co.; *U.S. Private*, pg. 1022

MOTHER'S OATS—Cereals—The Quaker Oats Company; *U.S. Public*, pg. 1347

MOTHERS PRIDE—Bread—Ranks Hovis McDougall Limited; *Int'l*, pg. 1395

MOTHER'S SPECIAL—Dietary Supplement for Nursing Mothers—SmithKline Beecham plc; *Int'l*, pg. 1264

MOTHERS TOUCH—Breast Feeding Pumps & Accessories—Hollister Medical Systems Division; *U.S. Private*, pg. 535

MOTHER'S WHOLE WHEAT—Hot Cereal—The Quaker Oats Company; *U.S. Public*, pg. 1347

MOTIF—Permanent Gel Colorant—Bristol-Myers Squibb Company; *U.S. Public*, pg. 253

MOTILIUM—NONE—Johnson & Johnson; *U.S. Public*, pg. 927

MOTION MASTER—Seat-Based Motion Simulation—Iwerks Entertainment; *U.S. Public*, pg. 915

MOTION-MODULAR—Modular Seating—La-Z-Boy Incorporated; *U.S. Public*, pg. 972

MOTION PICTURE GUIDE—24-Volume Encyclopedia—CineBooks, Inc.; *Int'l*, pg. 925

MOTION PLUS—Motion Control Servomotors—MTS Systems Corporation; *U.S. Public*, pg. 1028

MOTIONMATE—Robots—Schrader Bellows Division; *U.S. Public*, pg. 1261

MOTO DRIVE—Mechanical Adjustable Speed Drives—Rockwell International Corporation; *U.S. Public*, pg. 1397

MOTO MIRROR—Heavy Truck Mirrors—Echlin Inc.; *U.S. Public*, pg. 560

MOTO-MASSAGE—Moving Hydrotherapy Jet—Watkins Manufacturing Corp./Hot Spring Portable Spas; *U.S. Public*, pg. 1054

MOTOFEN—Anti-Diarrheal—Carnrick Laboratories, Inc.; *U.S. Private*, pg. 436

MOTOMETER—Automotive Instrumentation—Robert Bosch GmbH; *Int'l*, pg. 203

MOTOR AGE—Technical Publication for Domestic & Import Automotive Service Industr—Reed Elsevier Business Information; *Int'l*, pg. 1095

MOTOR BIT—High Speed Bits—Reed Tool Company; *U.S. Public*, pg. 298

MOTOR BOATING & SAILING—Magazine—Motor Boating & Sailing; *U.S. Private*, pg. 517

MOTOR BOATING & SAILING—Magazine—The Hearst Corporation; *U.S. Private*, pg. 515

MOTOR BOATING & SAILING—Magazine—Hearst Magazines Division; *U.S. Private*, pg. 516

MOTOR BOOKS—Books—The Hearst Corporation; *U.S. Private*, pg. 515

MOTOR CRASH ESTIMATING GUIDE—Books—The Hearst Corporation; *U.S. Private*, pg. 515

MOTOR CUSHION—Engine Viabration Damper—Arvin Industries, Inc.; *U.S. Public*, pg. 136

MOTOR CYCLE NEWS—Magazine—EMAP Nationals; *Int'l*, pg. 451

MOTOR KING—Batteries—Bridgestone/Firestone, Inc.; *Int'l*, pg. 213

MOTOR MAGAZINE—Magazine—The Hearst Corporation; *U.S. Private*, pg. 515

MOTOR MASTER—Transportation Replacement Parts—Zeller Corp.; *U.S. Public*, pg. 1204

MOTOR-MEDIC—Oil Additive—Radiator Specialty Company; *U.S. Private*, pg. 906

MOTOR PROFESSIONAL—Manuals—The Hearst Corporation; *U.S. Private*, pg. 515

MOTOR TREND—Magazine—Petersen Publishing Company, L.L.C.; *U.S. Private*, pg. 856

MOTORBOAT AND YACHTING—Yachting Magazine—IPC Magazines Limited; *Int'l*, pg. 651

MOTORCITY—Playset—Tyco Toys, Inc.; *U.S. Public*, pg. 1058

MOTORCRAFT—Car Parts & Access.—Ford Motor Company; *U.S. Public*, pg. 661

MOTORCYCLIST—Magazine—Petersen Publishing Company, L.L.C.; *U.S. Private*, pg. 856

MOTORDOR—Exhaust Fans—Broan Mfg. Co., Inc.; *U.S. Public*, pg. 1193

MOTORGUARD—3 Phase Motor Protectors—Amprobe Instrument; *U.S. Public*, pg. 1676

MOTORGUIDE—Electric Trolling Motor—Brunswick Corporation; *U.S. Public*, pg. 265

MOTORGUIDE—Electric Trolling Motors—Zebco; *U.S. Public*, pg. 265

MOTORMATIC—Cameras & Microfilm Readers—Eastman Kodak Company; *U.S. Public*, pg. 550

MOTOROLA—Electronics—Motorola, Inc.; *U.S. Public*, pg. 1136

MOTORSTAR—Insurance Product—Eagle Star; *Int'l*, pg. 110

MOTOWN—Records—Motown Record Company, J.P.; *Int'l*, pg. 1052

MOTRIN—Analgesic—Pharmacia & Upjohn; *Int'l*, pg. 1048

MOTRIN IB—Analgesic—Pharmacia & Upjohn; *Int'l*, pg. 1048

MOTT'S—Apple Juice, Applesauce—Cadbury Schweppes p.l.c.; *Int'l*, pg. 247

MOTT'S—Fruit Juices—Cadbury Beverages; *Int'l*, pg. 248

MOTT'S—Apple Juice & Apple Sauces—Cadbury Beverages North America; *Int'l*, pg. 248

MOULBIE—Mixed Flours—Grands Moulins de Paris S.A.; *Int'l*, pg. 556

MOULENEX—NONE—Moulinex S.A.; *Int'l*, pg. 896

MOUNDS—Candy Bar—Hershey Chocolate U.S.A.; *U.S. Public*, pg. 812

MOUNDS—Candy Bar—Hershey Foods Corporation; *U.S. Public*, pg. 811

MOUNT ELIZABETH—Hospital—Parkway Holdings Limited; *Int'l*, pg. 1023

MT. HOOD—Hardboard—Georgia-Pacific Corporation; *U.S. Public*, pg. 735

MOUNT MIRACLE—Stuffed Toy Figures; Canisters; Towels; T-Shirts—American Greetings Corporation; *U.S. Public*, pg. 77

MOUNT ROYAL LIGHT—Liquor—The House of Seagram; *Int'l*, pg. 1217

MT. STIRLING—Foodservice Items—Performance Food Group Company; *U.S. Public*, pg. 1278

MOUNT VERNON—Hardwood Doors—Georgia-Pacific Corporation; *U.S. Public*, pg. 735

MOUNTAIN BAR—Chocolate Coated Fondant Center—Brown & Haley; *U.S. Private*, pg. 173

MOUNTAIN BERRY ALE—Beer—The F.X. Matt Brewing Company; *U.S. Private*, pg. 714

MOUNTAIN BIKE—Magazine—Rodale Press, Inc.; *U.S. Private*, pg. 939

Brand Name Index

MOUNTAIN BIKE RIDER—Sports Magazine—IPC Magazines Limited; *Int'l*, pg. 651

MOUNTAIN BLACKBERRY—Sparkling Mineral Water—Clearly Canadian Beverage Corp.; *Int'l*, pg. 297

MOUNTAIN DAIRY—Dairy Products—Smith's Food & Drug Centers, Inc.; *U.S. Public*, pg. 1103

MOUNTAIN DEW—Soft Drink—Pepsi-Cola Company; *U.S. Public*, pg. 1277

MOUNTAIN DEW—Citrus Drink—PepsiCo, Inc.; *U.S. Public*, pg. 1276

MOUNTAIN DEW SPORT—Sports Drink—Pepsi-Cola Company; *U.S. Public*, pg. 1277

MOUNTAIN FRESH DIAL BAR SOAP—NONE—The Dial Corporation; *U.S. Public*, pg. 505

MOUNTAIN HERBERY—Hair Care Products—Carme' Cosmeceutical Sciences, Inc.; *U.S. Private*, pg. 213

MOUNTAIN HIGH—Yogurt—Borden, Inc.; *U.S. Private*, pg. 157

MOUNTAIN HOUSE—Freeze Dried Food Prods.—Oregon Freeze Dry, Inc.; *U.S. Private*, pg. 819

MOUNTAIN LEAF—Pipe Tobacco—Lane Limited; *Int'l*, pg. 1129

MOUNTAIN LION—Men's, Women's & Children's Clothes—Garan, Incorporated; *U.S. Public*, pg. 703

MOUNTAIN MAGIC—Western Bark & Cedar—MWCA; *U.S. Public*, pg. 804

MOUNTAIN MUG—Stainless Steel—The Canadian Coleman Co., Ltd.; *U.S. Private*, pg. 691

MOUNTAIN TOP—Frozen Unbaked Pies—Lancaster Colony Corporation; *U.S. Public*, pg. 976

MOUNTAIN TOP—Frozen Pies—T. Marzetti Company; *U.S. Public*, pg. 977

MOUNTAIN VALLEY WATER—Bottled Water—Mountain Valley Spring Company; *U.S. Private*, pg. 963

MOUNTBATTEN—Pipe Tobacco—Lane Limited; *Int'l*, pg. 1129

MOUNTFIELD—Consumer Turf Machinery—Ransomes Plc; *Int'l*, pg. 1087

MOUQUIN—French Brandy—Boulevard Distillers and Importers Inc.; *Int'l*, pg. 567

MOUSE BLASTER—Game—Tyco Toys, Inc.; *U.S. Public*, pg. 1058

MOUSEMAN—Ergonomic Computer Mouse—Logitech International SA; *Int'l*, pg. 815

MOUSETRAP—Game—Hasbro, Inc.; *U.S. Public*, pg. 797

MOUSETRAP—Game—Milton Bradley Company; *U.S. Public*, pg. 797

MOUSSEPOEDER CHIPO—Pastry Ingredient—Royal Gist-Brocades N.V.; *Int'l*, pg. 1142

MOUSSEPOEDER DIFRI—Pastry Ingredient—Royal Gist-Brocades N.V.; *Int'l*, pg. 1142

MOUSSY—Non-Alcoholic Beer—Labatt Brewing Company Limited; *Int'l*, pg. 679

MOUSSY—Non-Alcoholic Malt Beverage—White Rock Products Corp.; *U.S. Private*, pg. 1173

MOUSTACHE—Men's Toiletries—Wella Group; *Int'l*, pg. 1489

MOUTON-CADET WINES—NONE—Heublein, Inc.; *Int'l*, pg. 410

MOVABLE WALLS—Movable Steel Walls—Steelcase Inc.; *U.S. Private*, pg. 1038

MOVADO—Watches, Leather Goods and Accessories—Movado Group, Inc.; *U.S. Public*, pg. 1140

MOVE—850 cc Semi-Cab Over—Daihatsu Motor Corporation, Ltd.; *Int'l*, pg. 364

MOVE FOR DB2—NONE—BMC Software, Inc.; *U.S. Public*, pg. 162

MOVEFORWARD—Mailing Efficiency—Group 1 Software, Inc.; *U.S. Public*, pg. 417

MOVER—Split-type Expansion Joint—Victaulic Company of America; *U.S. Private*, pg. 1138

MOVI—High-Pressure Centrifugal Pump—KSB Aktiengesellschaft; *Int'l*, pg. 721

MOVICHROM—High-Pressure In-Line Pumps—KSB Aktiengesellschaft; *Int'l*, pg. 721

THE MOVIE CHANNEL—Pay Television—Showtime Networks Inc.; *U.S. Private*, pg. 779

THE MOVIE CHANNEL—Pay Cable—Viacom Inc.; *U.S. Private*, pg. 775

MOVIE EXPRESS—Video Rental Program—National Video, Inc.; *U.S. Public*, pg. 1755

MOVIE PAK—Gift Coupon Package—National Video, Inc.; *U.S. Public*, pg. 1755

MOVIE SIX-PAK—VIdeo Rental Program—National Video, Inc.; *U.S. Public*, pg. 1755

MOVIE STAR—Ladies Loungewear, Daywear & Sleepwear—Movie Star, Inc.; *U.S. Public*, pg. 1140

MOVIE TIC*IT—Discount Program—National Video, Inc.; *U.S. Public*, pg. 1755

MOVIEBUFF—T-Shirt Program—National Video, Inc.; *U.S. Public*, pg. 1755

MOVIEBUY—Discount Program—National Video, Inc.; *U.S. Public*, pg. 1755

MOVIEDECK—Motion Picture Projectors—Eastman Kodak Company; *U.S. Public*, pg. 550

MOVIEGUARD—Protection Program—National Video, Inc.; *U.S. Public*, pg. 1755

MOVIEMATE—Rental Video Players—National Video, Inc.; *U.S. Public*, pg. 1755

MOVIEMATE FUN-PAK—Video Player Rental—National Video, Inc.; *U.S. Public*, pg. 1755

MOVIEMATE TWIN-PAK—Rental Video Players—National Video, Inc.; *U.S. Public*, pg. 1755

MOVIEQUIK—Video Film Rental Service—The Southland Corporation; *Int'l*, pg. 693

MOVIEWORKS—NONE—Cambridge Soundworks, Inc.; *U.S. Private*, pg. 202

MOVINCOOL—Industrial Spot Air Conditioners—Denso Sales California; *Int'l*, pg. 1412

MOVINCOOL—Portable Spot Cooling Equipment—Denso Sales California; *Int'l*, pg. 1412

MOVING MACHINE—FAX Transmitted Real Estate Listings—ERA Real Estate; *U.S. Public*, pg. 321

MOVING PICTURES INTERNATIONAL—Monthly Magazine for Product Buyers & Sellers in Film/TV Industry—Reed Elsevier Business Information; *Int'l*, pg. 1095

MOVIOLA—Film Editing Equipment—J & R Film / Moviola Digital Co.; *U.S. Private*, pg. 576

MOWE—Egg Pasta Products—CSM N.V.; *Int'l*, pg. 243

MOX-TAPE—Self Adhering Silicone Rubber Tape—Moxness Products, Inc.; *U.S. Public*, pg. 124

MOX-TOUCHKEYS—Silicone Touchpads for Electronic Devices—Moxness Products, Inc.; *U.S. Public*, pg. 124

MOXEES—Women's Duty Shoes—Jumping Jacks; *U.S. Private*, pg. 767

MOXIE—Ethnic Hair Care Products—Johnson Products Co., Inc.; *U.S. Public*, pg. 915

MOXIE—Soft Drink—The Monarch Company, Inc.; *U.S. Private*, pg. 756

MOYGASHEL—Woven Linen Blend Fabric—Lamont Holdings Plc; *Int'l*, pg. 797

MOYNO—Progressing Cavity Pumps—Robbins & Myers, Inc.; *U.S. Public*, pg. 1393

MOZZARELLA CRISPS—Finger Food—Harker's Distribution, Inc.; *U.S. Private*, pg. 502

MOZZARELLA'S—Restaurants—Ruby Tuesday, Inc.; *U.S. Public*, pg. 1411

MR. & MRS. T—Drink Mixes—Cadbury Beverages; *Int'l*, pg. 248

MR. & MRS. " T "—Cocktail Mixers—Cadbury Beverages North America; *Int'l*, pg. 248

MR. AND MRS. " T "—Drink Mixes—Cadbury Schweppes p.l.c.; *Int'l*, pg. 247

MR. AUTOMATIC—Coffee—Tetley USA Inc.; *Int'l*, pg. 1377

MR. BARCO—Professional Apparel—Barco of California; *U.S. Private*, pg. 115

MR. BIG—Paper Towels, Bath Tissue & Napkins—Georgia-Pacific Corporation; *U.S. Public*, pg. 735

MR. BIG—Chocolate Bar—George Weston Limited; *Int'l*, pg. 1494

MR. BLUE—Toilet Bowl Cleaner—Reynolds Metals Company; *U.S. Public*, pg. 1385

MR. BOGGS—Stuffed Toy Figures; Canisters; Towels; T-Shirts—American Greetings Corporation; *U.S. Public*, pg. 77

MR. BOSTON—NONE—Barton Brands, Ltd.; *U.S. Public*, pg. 300

MR. BRAKESHOE—NONE—Connecticut Drive Shaft, Inc.; *U.S. Private*, pg. 263

MR. BUBBLES—Toy—Strombecker Corporation; *U.S. Private*, pg. 1047

MR. CHEF—Rubber Mats—The Akro Corporation; *U.S. Public*, pg. 399

MR. CLEAN—Household Cleaner—The Procter & Gamble Company; *U.S. Public*, pg. 1330

MR. CLEAN BATHROOM—Liquid Bathroom Cleaner—The Procter & Gamble Company; *U.S. Public*, pg. 1330

MR. COFFEE—Coffee Makers, Filters & Accessories—Signature Brands USA, Inc.; *U.S. Public*, pg. 1472

MR. DODDLER—Watercolor Non-Toxic Markers—Dri Mark Products, Inc.; *U.S. Private*, pg. 342

MR. FIX—Do-It-Yourself Auto Repair & Care Prods—Marson/Creative Fastener, Inc.; *U.S. Private*, pg. 708

MR. FREEZE—Candy—Huhtamaki Oy; *Int'l*, pg. 638

MR. GASKET—Engine System Parts—Echlin Inc.; *U.S. Public*, pg. 560

MR. GATTI'S—Pizza Franchise—Mr. Gatti's, Inc.; *U.S. Private*, pg. 639

MR. GOODBAR—Chocolate Bar—Hershey Chocolate U.S.A.; *U.S. Public*, pg. 812

MR HARRY—NONE—Moss Bros Group PLC; *Int'l*, pg. 895

MR. HERO—Franchised Restaurant System—Restaurant Developers Corp.; *U.S. Private*, pg. 925

MR. HOST—Ham—Armour Swift Eckrich; *U.S. Public*, pg. 426

MR. INSIDE—Carpet-to Vinyl Mats & Matting—The Akro Corporation; *U.S. Public*, pg. 399

MR. JOHN—Liquid Automatic Bowl Cleaner—Blue Cross Laboratories; *U.S. Private*, pg. 152

MR. JUMBO—Household Paper Goods—Orchids Paper Products Co.; *U.S. Private*, pg. 819

MR. KIPLING—Cakes—Ranks Hovis McDougall Limited; *Int'l*, pg. 1395

MR. KITZEL—Pickle Prods.—Vienna Sausage Mfg. Co.; *U.S. Private*, pg. 1139

MR. LOKUT—Socks—Wigwam Mills, Inc.; *U.S. Private*, pg. 1175

MR. MAC'S—Concrete, Metal & Wood Repair—Macklanburg-Duncan Co.; *U.S. Private*, pg. 692

MR. MISTY—Dessert—American Dairy Queen Corporation; *U.S. Public*, pg. 220

MR. MISTY—Slush-type Drink—International Dairy Queen, Inc.; *U.S. Public*, pg. 220

MR. MISTY KISS—Frozen Novelty—International Dairy Queen, Inc.; *U.S. Public*, pg. 220

MR. MUSCLE—Oven Cleaner—Bristol-Myers Squibb Company; *U.S. Public*, pg. 253

MR. MUSTACHE—Men's Mustache & Beard Grooming Equipment—The Cook Bates Division; *Int'l*, pg. 815

MR. PHILLY—Franchised Restaurant System—Restaurant Developers Corp.; *U.S. Private*, pg. 925

MR. PHIPPS—Pretzel Chips—Nabisco Inc.; *U.S. Public*, pg. 1355

MR. PHIPPS—Pretzel Chips—RJR Nabisco Holdings Corp.; *U.S. Public*, pg. 1354

MR. PHIPPS TATER CRISPS—Potato Crisps—Nabisco Inc.; *U.S. Public*, pg. 1355

MR. PIBB—Regular & Diet Sodas—The Coca-Cola Company; *U.S. Public*, pg. 392

MR. POTATO HEAD—Toy—Hasbro, Inc.; *U.S. Public*, pg. 797

MR. PROPER—NONE—Procter & Gamble Espana S.A.; *U.S. Public*, pg. 1332

MR. PURE—Juice—Home Juice Co.; *U.S. Private*, pg. 537

MR. QUICK/INSTANT LITE—Premium Charcoal Briquets Instant Lighting—Hickory Specialties, Inc.; *U.S. Public*, pg. 596

MR. RATCHET—Tools—Latshaw Enterprises, Inc.; *U.S. Public*, pg. 979

MR. RIB—Rib Shaped Boneless Pork Patties—Harker's Distribution, Inc.; *U.S. Private*, pg. 502

MR. ROOTER—Sewer & Draincleaning Businesses—The Dwyer Group, Inc.; *U.S. Public*, pg. 537

MR. SCRAPER—Carpet-to-Vinyl Mats & Matting—The Akro Corporation; *U.S. Public*, pg. 399

MR. SERVICE—Accessories—The Hercules Tire & Rubber Company; *U.S. Private*, pg. 523

MR. SHARPY—Pencil Sharpener—Sunbeam Household Products; *U.S. Public*, pg. 1533

MR SHEEN—Furniture Polish—Reckitt & Colman plc; *Int'l*, pg. 1089

MR. SILK SHINE—NONE—Celebrity Incorporated; *U.S. Public*, pg. 319

MR. SKETCH—Scented Watercolor Markers—Sanford Corporation; *U.S. Public*, pg. 1178

MR. SPRAY—Paint—Plasti-Kote Company Inc.; *U.S. Private*, pg. 870

MR. SPUD—Instant Potatoes, Potato Flakes—Magic Valley Foods, Inc.; *U.S. Private*, pg. 695

MR. TRANSMISSION—Transmission Repair & Service Centers—Moran Industries, Inc.; *U.S. Private*, pg. 760

MR. TURKEY—Turkey Prods.—Bil Mar Foods, Inc.; *U.S. Public*, pg. 1433

MR. TURKEY—Meat Product—Sara Lee Corporation; *U.S. Public*, pg. 1432

MR. TWISTER—Soft Pretzels—J & J Snack Foods Corporation; *U.S. Public*, pg. 916

MRS—Steel Plate—Inland Steel Industries, Inc.; *U.S. Public*, pg. 879

MRS. ALISON'S—Cookies—Mrs. Alison's Cookie Company; *U.S. Private*, pg. 765

MRS ALISON'S—Crackers & Pretzels—Mrs. Alison's Cookie Company; *U.S. Private*, pg. 765

MRS. BAIRD'S—Bakery—Mrs. Baird's Bakeries, Inc.; *U.S. Private*, pg. 765

MRS. BAKER'S ORIGINAL RECIPE—NONE—Blyth Industries; *U.S. Public*, pg. 239

MRS. BUTTERWORTH'S—Syrup, Pancake & Waffle Mixes—Chesebrough-Pond's; *Int'l*, pg. 1436

MRS. BUTTERWORTHS—Pancake Mix & Syrup—Van den Bergh Foods Company; *Int'l*, pg. 1436

MRS. BUTTERWORTH'S LITE—Syrup—Chesebrough-Pond's; *Int'l*, pg. 1436

MRS. CRUTCHFIELD'S—Muffin Mix—Wilkins-Rogers Incorporated; *U.S. Private*, pg. 1176

MRS. CUBBISON'S—Poultry Dressings & Salad Croutons—Mrs. Cubbison's Foods, Inc.; *U.S. Public*, pg. 909

MRS. CUBBISON'S STUFFING MIX & CROUTONS—Stuffing Mix & Croutons—Interstate Brands Corporation; *U.S. Public*, pg. 909

MRS. DASH—Salt Alternative—Alberto-Culver Canada, Inc.; *U.S. Public*, pg. 38

MRS. DASH—Food Seasoning—Alberto-Culver Company; *U.S. Public*, pg. 37

MRS. DIFILLIPPO'S—Meatballs—DeVault Foods; *U.S. Private*, pg. 329

MRS. FANNING'S—Bread 'n Butter Pickles—GFA Brands, Inc.; *U.S. Private*, pg. 435

MRS. FIELDS'—Cookies—Mrs. Fields' Original Cookies, Inc.; *U.S. Private*, pg. 688

MRS. FILBERT'S—Margarine/Spread/Salad Dressing/Mayonnaise—Chesebrough-Pond's; *Int'l*, pg. 1436

MRS. FRESHLEY'S—Snack Cakes—Flowers Industries, Inc.; *U.S. Public*, pg. 656

MRS. FRIDAYS—Fish—Fishking Processors, Inc.; *Int'l*, pg. 940

MRS. GILES COUNTRY KITCHENS—Deli Products—Bob Evans Farms, Inc. Restaurant Division; *U.S. Public*, pg. 596

MRS. GILES COUNTRY KITCHENS—Refrigerated Salads—Mrs. Giles Country Kitchens, Inc.; *U.S. Public*, pg. 596

MRS. GRASS—Soups & Dry Mixes—Borden, Inc.; *U.S. Private*, pg. 157

MRS. GRASS—Pasta Products—Borden Italian Foods; *U.S. Public*, pg. 158

MRS. GRIMES—Food—Faribault Foods Inc.; *U.S. Private*, pg. 393

MRS. IHRIES—NONE—Bon Ton Foods, Inc.; *U.S. Private*, pg. 65

MRS. KARL'S—Bread—Interstate Brands Corporation; *U.S. Public*, pg. 909

MRS. LEVY'S DELI—Restaurant—The Levy Organization; *U.S. Private*, pg. 664

MRS. PATERSON'S AUSSIE PIE—Meat-Filled pastries—Hormel Foods Corp.; *U.S. Public*, pg. 840

MRS. PAULS—Frozen Seafood & Vegetables—Campbell Soup Company; *U.S. Public*, pg. 298

MRS. SMITH'S—Frozen Pies—Flowers Industries, Inc.; *U.S. Public*, pg. 656

MRS. STOVER'S CANDIES—Candy—Russell Stover Candies, Inc.; *U.S. Public*, pg. 953

MRS. WEISS—Noodles—Hershey Pasta and Grocery Group; *U.S. Public*, pg. 812

MRS. WHEATLEY'S—Cookies—Mother's Cake & Cookie Co.; *U.S. Private*, pg. 1022

MRS. WINNER'S—Chicken & Biscuit Restaurants—Mrs. Winner's Chicken & Biscuit Restaurants; *U.S. Private*, pg. 766

MRS. WRIGHTS—Bakery Products—Safeway Inc.; *U.S. Public*, pg. 1426

MRS. MCGREGORS—Margarine—Goodman Fielder Limited; *Int'l*, pg. 555

MS. SKINNY WAIST—Foundations—The Strouse, Adler Company; *U.S. Private*, pg. 1047

MSICs—Mixed Signal Interated Circuits—Silicon Systems, Inc.; *U.S. Public*, pg. 1585

MUCAMOX—Antibiotic—SmithKline Beecham Research Limited; *Int'l*, pg. 1266

MUCHMORE—Standard Grade Controlled Label Prods.—IGA, Inc. (Independent Grocers Alliance); *U.S. Private*, pg. 555

MUCOMYST—Respiratory Pharmaceutical—Astra AB; *Int'l*, pg. 93

MUCOMYST—NONE—Bristol-Myers Squibb Company; *U.S. Public*, pg. 253

MUCOSIL—Dey Brand Acetylcysteine Solution USP—Dey Laboratories Inc.; *Int'l*, pg. 812

MUCOSOLVAN—Mucolytics—Boehringer Ingelheim GmbH; *Int'l*, pg. 199

MUCOSTA TABLETS—Anti-Ulcer Agent—Otsuka Pharmaceutical Co., Ltd.; *Int'l*, pg. 1013

MUCRET—Mucolic Agent—Astra AB; *Int'l*, pg. 93

MUD CAT—Auger Dredge—Ellicott Machine Corporation International; *U.S. Private*, pg. 372

MUD HOG—NONE—Fluidrive Inc.; *U.S. Private*, pg. 415

MUD-HOG—Pumps—ITT A-C Pump/ITT Marlow; *U.S. Public*, pg. 860

MUDD MASK—Facial Mask—Chattem, Inc.; *U.S. Public*, pg. 341

MUDD MASK—Deep Cleansing Treatment—Chattem, Inc., Consumer Products Division; *U.S. Public*, pg. 341

MUDMASTER—Rotary Drilling Rigs—The George E. Failing Company; *U.S. Private*, pg. 153

MUDPICK—Hydraulic Cleaning Action—Reed Tool Company; *U.S. Public*, pg. 298

MUELLER—Office Furniture and Seating—Haworth, Inc.; *U.S. Private*, pg. 511

MUELLER—Fire Hydrants, Valves & Fittings—Tyco International Ltd.; *U.S. Public*, pg. 1647

MUELLER GUARD—Protective Dental Guard—Mueller Sports Medicine, Inc.; *U.S. Private*, pg. 766

MUELLER MATIC—Automatic Washing System—Paul Mueller Company; *U.S. Public*, pg. 1141

MUELLER'S—Pasta—Best Foods; *U.S. Public*, pg. 224

MUELLERGESIC—Mild Analgesic Ointment—Mueller Sports Medicine, Inc.; *U.S. Private*, pg. 766

MUELLERKOLD—Instant Ice Pack—Mueller Sports Medicine, Inc.; *U.S. Private*, pg. 766

MUELLER'S—Pasta Products—Bestfoods; *U.S. Public*, pg. 223

MUELLERTAPE—Sports Tape—Mueller Sports Medicine, Inc.; *U.S. Private*, pg. 766

MUESCO—Valves—Watts Industries, Inc.; *U.S. Public*, pg. 1746

MUESLIX CRISPY BLEND—Whole Grain Barley, Brown Rice, Wheat & Oats with Raisins, Dates & Almonds—Kellogg Company; *U.S. Public*, pg. 947

MUESLIX GOLDEN CRUNCH—Crunchy Blend of Whole Wheat, Barley, Oats, Corn & Rice with Apples/Almonds—Kellogg Company; *U.S. Public*, pg. 947

MUFFLINGS—Children's Clothing—S. Schwab Company; *U.S. Private*, pg. 974

MUG ROOT BEER—Soft Drink—Pepsi-Cola Company; *U.S. Public*, pg. 1277

MUG ROOT BEER—Soft Drink-Root Beer—PepsiCo, Inc.; *U.S. Public*, pg. 1276

MUIRFIELD—Golf Clubs—MacGregor Golf Company; *Int'l*, pg. 72

MUKLUKS—Slipper Sox—Reliable Knitting Works; *U.S. Private*, pg. 920

MUL-T-CON MLM-TM—Air Traffic Control—Israel Aircraft Industries Ltd.; *Int'l*, pg. 689

MUL-TEA—NONE—Regal Ware, Inc.; *U.S. Private*, pg. 917

MULBERRY—Books—The Hearst Corporation; *U.S. Private*, pg. 515

MULBERRY BOOKS—Juvenile Paperback Books—William Morrow & Co., Inc.; *U.S. Private*, pg. 515

MULCO—NONE—Sico Inc.; *Int'l*, pg. 1239

MULE—Utility Vehicle—Kawasaki Motors Corp., U.S.A.; *Int'l*, pg. 725

MULE-KICK—Cleaners—J.A. Sexauer, Inc.; *U.S. Private*, pg. 352

MULT-AU-MATIC—Chucking Machine—WCI Machine Tools & Systems; *Int'l*, pg. 440

MULT-O—Machinery & Complete Binding Systems—Standex International Corporation; *U.S. Public*, pg. 1505

MULT-O-LOOSE—Loose Leaf Metals—James Burn Intl.; *U.S. Public*, pg. 1506

MULTEC—Gasoline Fuel Injectors—Delphi Energy & Engine Management Systems; *U.S. Public*, pg. 719

MULTEEJET—Spray Nozzle—Spraying Systems Co.; *U.S. Private*, pg. 1026

MULTI-AD CREATOR—Ad-Layout Software—Multi-Ad Services, Incorporated; *U.S. Private*, pg. 766

MULTI-AD SEARCH—Image Indexing Software—Multi-Ad Services, Incorporated; *U.S. Private*, pg. 766

MULTI-ALERT—Horns & Strobes—System Sensor Division; *U.S. Public*, pg. 1306

MULTI-AMP—Electrical Test & Measuring Instrument—AVO International; *Int'l*, pg. 1335

MULTI-ARC—Retaining Ring—Waldes Truarc/Industrial Retaining Ring; *U.S. Public*, pg. 1632

MULTI-BAG—Filter Vessels—American Felt & Filter; *U.S. Private*, pg. 54

MULTI-CABLE TRANSIT—Fire Stop Device—O-Z/Gedney, Nelson Firestop Products; *U.S. Public*, pg. 726

MULTI-CLEAN—NONE—Minuteman International, Inc.; *Int'l*, pg. 587

MULTI-COOKER—Frypans—Sunbeam Household Products; *U.S. Public*, pg. 1533

MULTI D—Stock Preparation—Beloit Corporation; *U.S. Public*, pg. 789

MULTI-DISC—Centrifuge Accessories—Beckman Instruments, Inc.; *U.S. Public*, pg. 199

MULTI-DONOR—Cellular Repeater Application—Allen Telecom Inc.; *U.S. Public*, pg. 45

MULTI DRUM-VAC—Dust Filter For the Textile Industry—Luwa Bahnson, Inc.; *U.S. Private*, pg. 682

MULTI-FLO—Adapter—Becton Dickinson & Company; *U.S. Public*, pg. 199

MULTI FLUTE CHAMBER-SINK—Solid Carbide Combination Chamber Countersink—National Twist Drill Div.; *U.S. Public*, pg. 1370

MULTI FLUTE CHAMFER-SINK—Solid Carbide Combination Chamfer Countersink—Regal-Beloit Corporation; *U.S. Public*, pg. 1370

MULTI-FUEL—Stove—The Canadian Coleman Co., Ltd.; *U.S. Private*, pg. 691

MULTI-GARD—Multi Cell Conduit System—The Lamson & Sessions Co.; *U.S. Public*, pg. 976

MULTI GRAIN CHEERIOS—Cereal—General Mills, Inc.; *U.S. Public*, pg. 717

MULTI-GRIP—Primer—Jones Blair Company; *U.S. Private*, pg. 596

MULTI-HOP—Cellular Repeater Application—Allen Telecom Inc.; *U.S. Public*, pg. 45

MULTI HUB—Intelligent Wiring Center—N Base Communications; *U.S. Public*, pg. 1027

MULTI KE-MIN—Fertilizer—Georgia-Pacific Corporation; *U.S. Public*, pg. 735

MULTI-LUBE—Penetrant Spray Lubricant—Ronson Corporation; *U.S. Public*, pg. 1405

MULTI-MAC—Multi Plunger Transfer Encapsulation Press, All Electric—Hull Corporation; *U.S. Private*, pg. 547

MULTI-MATIC—Bakery Equipment—Belshaw Brothers, Inc.; *Int'l*, pg. 188

MULTI-METALS—Carbide Products—Vermont American Tool Corp.; *U.S. Public*, pg. 575

MULTI-MICRO-VENTURI—High-Efficieny Venturi Scrubber—Beco Engineering Company; *U.S. Private*, pg. 129

MULTI-MODULE—Dip Inserter—Universal Instruments Corporation; *U.S. Public*, pg. 522

MULTI-NET—Trunked Radio—E.F. Johnson Radio Systems; *U.S. Public*, pg. 1630

MULTI/PAK—Hydronic Baseboard—Slant/Fin Corporation; *U.S. Public*, pg. 1005

MULTI-PLUG—Fire Stop Device—O-Z/Gedney, Nelson Firestop Products; *U.S. Public*, pg. 726

MULTI-POWER—Electrical Wire & Cable—General Cable Corporation; *Int'l*, pg. 1486

MULTI-PRIAS—Multi-Detector Gamma Counter—Packard Instrument Co., Inc.; *U.S. Private*, pg. 833

Brand Name Index

MULTI-PRO 418—4 Wheel Sprayer, Spreader, Utility Truck & Arefier—Hahn Equipment Co.; *U.S. Public*, pg. 1624

MULTI-PURPOSE—Primer—Jones Blair Company; *U.S. Private*, pg. 596

MULTI-RANGE—Test Equipment—Tenney Environmental; *U.S. Private*, pg. 1076

MULTI-SET—Drop In Anchors—ITW Ramset/Red Head; *U.S. Public*, pg. 867

MULTI-SLIDE—Machinery—The U.S. Baird Corporation; *U.S. Private*, pg. 1124

MULTI SPACED MULTI MATIC—Bakery Equipment—Belshaw Brothers, Inc.; *Int'l*, pg. 188

MULTI-STAGE—NONE—Harris Calorific Co.; *U.S. Public*, pg. 996

MULTI SWAGE—Electronic Parts—Bead Industries Inc.; *U.S. Private*, pg. 126

MULTI-TABS—Vitamins & Minerals—Novo Nordisk A/S; *Int'l*, pg. 987

MULTI-TEST CMI—Skin Test Antigen for Cellular Hypersensitivity—Connaught Laboratories, Inc.; *Int'l*, pg. 1109

MULTI-TRACIN & DESIGN—Material for Supplying Trace Minerals to Trees—Georgia-Pacific Corporation; *U.S. Public*, pg. 735

MULTI-VAPOR—Electric Discharge Lamp—General Electric Canada Inc.; *U.S. Public*, pg. 713

MULTI-VENT—Laminar Flow Panels—Anemostat Products; *U.S. Public*, pg. 286

MULTIBLES AT HOME—Direct Marketing—Jerell, Inc.; *U.S. Private*, pg. 586

MULTIBUS—Electronic Instrument—Intel Corporation; *U.S. Public*, pg. 886

MULTICARD—Shared Cost Mail Survey—NFO Research, Inc.; *U.S. Public*, pg. 1146

MULTICHANNEL—NONE—Adaptec, Inc.; *U.S. Public*, pg. 19

MULTICHANNEL—Electronic Instrument—Intel Corporation; *U.S. Public*, pg. 886

MULTICHANNEL NEWS—Weekly Newspaper for Professionals in Cable TV & Telecommunication Industry—Reed Elsevier Business Information; *Int'l*, pg. 1095

MULTICHANNEL NEWS INTERNATIONAL—International Tabloid Providing News for Telecommunications Executives—Reed Elsevier Business Information; *Int'l*, pg. 1095

MULTICIDE—Pesticides—McLaughlin Gormley King Company; *U.S. Private*, pg. 723

MULTICONTRAST HS—Black & White Photographic—AGFA Division of Bayer Corporation; *Int'l*, pg. 172

MULTICONTROL—Programmable Controllers—B & R Industrial Automation; *U.S. Private*, pg. 105

MULTICUENTA POPULAR—Checking Account With Savings & a Reserve Credit Line—Banco Popular de Puerto Rico; *U.S. Public*, pg. 175

MULTICUT—Coated Abrasives—3M; *U.S. Public*, pg. 1604

MULTIDEX—Rotary Switches—Oak Grigsby; *U.S. Public*, pg. 1209

MULTIDISC—Stock Preparation—Beloit Corporation; *U.S. Public*, pg. 789

MULTIDISK 150—NONE—Iomega Corporation; *U.S. Public*, pg. 912

MULTIFIBER—Particleboard—Georgia-Pacific Corporation; *U.S. Public*, pg. 735

MULTIFILL—Butane—Ronson Corporation; *U.S. Public*, pg. 1405

MULTIFILTER—Cigarettes—Philip Morris Companies Inc.; *U.S. Public*, pg. 1287

MULTIFIRE—Conductor Paste—Ferro Corporation; *U.S. Public*, pg. 618

MULTIFIRE—Instrument—U.S. Surgical Corp.; *U.S. Public*, pg. 1687

MULTIFIRE ENDO GIA—Stapler—U.S. Surgical Corp.; *U.S. Public*, pg. 1687

MULTIFIRE ENDO HERNIA—Stapler—U.S. Surgical Corp.; *U.S. Public*, pg. 1687

MULTIFIRE GIA—Stapler—U.S. Surgical Corp.; *U.S. Public*, pg. 1687

MULTIFIRE GRAFTAC-S—Surgical Staplers—U.S. Surgical Corp.; *U.S. Public*, pg. 1687

MULTIFIRE PREMIUM—Stapler—U.S. Surgical Corp.; *U.S. Public*, pg. 1687

MULTIFIRE VERSATACK—Stapler—U.S. Surgical Corp.; *U.S. Public*, pg. 1687

MULTIFLEX—Intraocular Lenses—Alcon Laboratories, Inc.; *Int'l*, pg. 916

MULTIFLEX—Brushes—The Carbide/Graphite Group, Inc.; *U.S. Public*, pg. 304

MULTIFLO—Feed Delivery System or Conveying System—CTB International Corp.; *U.S. Public*, pg. 284

MULTIFLOW—Resin Modifier—Solutia Inc.; *U.S. Public*, pg. 1483

MULTIFLUOR—Halogenated Hydrocarbon Fluids—Air Products and Chemicals, Inc.; *U.S. Public*, pg. 30

MULTIFOODS—NONE—North America Foods; *U.S. Public*, pg. 901

MULTIFUND—Variable Annuity Product—Lincoln National Corporation; *U.S. Public*, pg. 997

MULTIGESIC—Analgesic Tablets—Alva/Amco Pharmacal Companies, Inc.; *U.S. Private*, pg. 47

MULTIGUARD—Motor—The Lincoln Electric Company; *U.S. Public*, pg. 996

MULTIKWIK—Plastic WC Fan Connectors—Marley PLC; *Int'l*, pg. 843

MULTILAN—Local Area Network Connectivity Products—Tandem Computers Inc.; *U.S. Public*, pg. 417

MULTILIFT—Demountable Equipment—Partek Corporation; *Int'l*, pg. 1024

MULTILINK—Data Communications Software—Datapoint Corporation; *Int'l*, pg. 384

MULTIMASTER—Multiple Processor Scheme For Industrial Computers—Pro-Log Corporation; *U.S. Private*, pg. 887

MULTIMATE ADVANTAGE II—Software—Borland International, Inc.; *U.S. Public*, pg. 246

MULTIMATE ADVANTAGE 3.6—Software—Borland International, Inc.; *U.S. Public*, pg. 246

MULTIMATE 3.3 SERIES—Software—Borland International, Inc.; *U.S. Public*, pg. 246

MULTIMEDIA CONNECTION—NONE—Adaptec, Inc.; *U.S. Public*, pg. 19

MULTIMEDIA ENGINE—NONE—Adaptec, Inc.; *U.S. Public*, pg. 19

MULTIMEDIA INFORMATION NETWORK EXCHANGE—Multimedia Networking & Videoconferencing System—Datapoint Corporation; *Int'l*, pg. 384

MULTIMEDIA PRESENTATION MANAGER/2—Computer System—International Business Machines Corporation; *U.S. Public*, pg. 895

MULTIMODE ETF—Tri-Axis & Crossbar Feed-Electronic—Verson Division; *U.S. Public*, pg. 48

MULTIMODULE—Electronic Instrument—Intel Corporation; *U.S. Public*, pg. 886

MULTIMOUNT—Dry Mounting Adhesive—Seal Products Incorporated; *U.S. Public*, pg. 849

MULTINEX—Three Gas, Respiration Gas Monitor—Datascope Corp.; *U.S. Public*, pg. 487

MULTINEX ID—Three Gas, Respiration Gas Monitor that Identifies Gas Characteristics—Datascope Corp.; *U.S. Public*, pg. 487

MULTINEX PLUS—Five Gas, Respiration Bench Monitor—Datascope Corp.; *U.S. Public*, pg. 487

MULTIPHASE—Metal Alloy—SPS Technologies, Inc.; *U.S. Public*, pg. 1419

MULTIPLATE—Flat & Laminated Glass—PPG Industries, Inc.; *U.S. Public*, pg. 1245

MULTIPLE TRANSFER PRESS—Presses—The U.S. Baird Corporation; *U.S. Private*, pg. 1124

MULTIPLEX—Multi-hardener Alloy—KB Alloys, Inc.; *U.S. Private*, pg. 249

MULTIPOINT—NONE—Texas Instruments Incorporated; *U.S. Public*, pg. 1585

MULTIPOLAR—Bipolar Cup for Use in Hip Replacements—Bristol-Myers Squibb Company; *U.S. Public*, pg. 253

MULTIPORT—IV Tubing Set—Quest Medical, Inc.; *U.S. Public*, pg. 1352

MULTIPRIME—Paint Primers—PPG Industries, Inc.; *U.S. Public*, pg. 1245

MULTIPRO-TOOL—Electric Tools—Dremel; *U.S. Public*, pg. 574

MULTIPULL—Collision Correction-Automotive—Bee Line Company; *U.S. Private*, pg. 129

MULTISCAN—NONE—Brown & Sharpe Manufacturing Company; *U.S. Public*, pg. 260

MULTISCRIPTOR—Multi-Channel Cardiac & Circulation Recorder—PPG Industries, Inc.; *U.S. Public*, pg. 1245

MULTISOFT—Paper Napkins—Georgia-Pacific Corporation; *U.S. Public*, pg. 735

MULTISPARK—Ignition Distributors—Mallory, Inc.; *U.S. Private*, pg. 698

MULTISTATE TRANSMISSIONS—Transmission Repair & Service Centers—Moran Industries, Inc.; *U.S. Private*, pg. 760

MULTISTEP—Vinyl Coverings—Forbo Holding SA; *Int'l*, pg. 496

MULTISTIX—Reagent Strips—Bayer Corporation/Consumer Care Division; *Int'l*, pg. 173

MULTITERM—Data Communications Software—Datapoint Corporation; *Int'l*, pg. 384

MULTITUBE/SPIRAL-FLOW—Tubular Heat Exchanger—Paul Mueller Company; *U.S. Public*, pg. 1141

MULTIVENT—Air Distribution Equipment—Dynamics Corporation of America; *U.S. Public*, pg. 286

MULTIVISION—France Broadcasting—CLT-UFA; *Int'l*, pg. 561

MULTIWALL—High Pressure Layered Vessel—Struthers Wells Corp.; *U.S. Private*, pg. 1048

MULTIWAX—Microcrystalline Waxes—Witco Corporation; *U.S. Public*, pg. 1773

MUM—Deodorant—Bristol-Myers Squibb Company; *U.S. Public*, pg. 253

MUM FOR MEN—NONE—Bristol-Myers Squibb Company; *U.S. Public*, pg. 253

MUM 21—NONE—Bristol-Myers Squibb Company; *U.S. Public*, pg. 253

MUMM VSOP COGNAC—Cognac—The Seagram Company Ltd.; *Int'l*, pg. 1214

MUNCH—Candy—Mars, Incorporated; *U.S. Private*, pg. 707

MUNCHERS STEALTH NATURAL CUT FRIES—Shoestrings, Thin Cuts, Regular Cuts—Lamb-Weston, Inc.; *U.S. Public*, pg. 427

MUNCHETTES—Containers with Easy-Lift Tabs—Rubbermaid Incorporated; *U.S. Public*, pg. 1411

MUNCHIE CUP—Finger Food Containers—Sweetheart Cup Company Inc.; *U.S. Private*, pg. 1058

MUNCHKIN PUNCH—Non-Carbonated Drink—Dunkin' Donuts Incorporated; *Int'l*, pg. 63

MUNCHKINS—Bite-Size Donuts—Dunkin' Donuts Incorporated; *Int'l*, pg. 63

MUNCHMATES—Snack Foods—Wyandot Inc.; *U.S. Private*, pg. 1193

MUNCHOS—Potato Chips—Frito-Lay Company; *U.S. Public*, pg. 1277

MUNCHRIGHTS—Snack Foods—Wyandot Inc.; *U.S. Private*, pg. 1193

MUNDIAL—Knives & Cutlery—Zivi S.A. Cutelaria; *Int'l*, pg. 1529

MUNISING LP—Clean Room Paper—Kimberly-Clark Corporation; *U.S. Public*, pg. 958

MUNSINGWEAR—Underwear & Activewear—Fruit of the Loom, Inc.; *U.S. Public*, pg. 685

MUNSINGWEAR—Men's Sportswear & Underwear—PremiumWear, Inc.; *U.S. Public*, pg. 1323

MURATA—NONE—Milgray Electronics, Inc.; *U.S. Public*, pg. 205

MURATTI AMBASSADOR—Cigarettes—Philip Morris Companies Inc.; *U.S. Public*, pg. 1287

MURCO—Petroleum Products in the United Kingdom—Murphy Oil Corporation; *U.S. Public*, pg. 1141

MURESCO—Ceiling Paint—Benjamin Moore & Co.; *U.S. Private*, pg. 133

MUREX—Welding Equipment—Esab AB; *Int'l*, pg. 281

MURFOTOX—Insecticide—The Dow Chemical Company; *U.S. Public*, pg. 522

MURIEL PIPE TOBACCO CIGARS—Domestic Cigars—Consolidated Cigar Corporation; *U.S. Private*, pg. 690

MURIEL SWEET LITTLE CIGARS—Domestic Cigars—Consolidated Cigar Corporation; *U.S. Private*, pg. 690

MURIELS—Domestic Cigars—Consolidated Cigar Corporation; *U.S. Private*, pg. 690

MURINE—Eye Drops & Ear Drops—Abbott Laboratories; *U.S. Public*, pg. 12

MURO—Ophthalmic Solution—Bausch & Lomb Incorporated; *U.S. Public*, pg. 194

MURPHY-MILLER—Office Furniture—HON Industries Inc.; *U.S. Public*, pg. 772

MURPHY OIL—Soap—Colgate-Palmolive Co., Institutional Products Div.; *U.S. Public*, pg. 397

MURPHY-SELECT MARKET—Food Markets—C & K Market, Inc.; *U.S. Private*, pg. 191

MURPHYS—Potato Chips & Nuts—Borden, Inc.; *U.S. Private*, pg. 157

MURPHY'S—Irish Stout—Whitbread PLC; *Int'l*, pg. 1498

MURPHY'S IRISH STOUT—Beer—Heineken USA Inc.; *Int'l*, pg. 608

MURPHY'S IRISH AMBER—NONE—Heineken USA Inc.; *Int'l*, pg. 608

MURPHY'S IRISH STOUT—Irish Stout—Heineken N.V.; *Int'l*, pg. 608

MURPHY'S OIL SOAP—Household Cleaner—Colgate-Palmolive Company; *U.S. Public*, pg. 397

MURPHY'S OIL SOAP—Soap—Murphy-Phoenix Co.; *U.S. Public*, pg. 397

MURRAY—Bicycles—The Murray Ohio Mfg. Co.; *Int'l*, pg. 1397

MURRAY—Lawn Mowers—The Murray Ohio Mfg. Co.; *Int'l*, pg. 1397

MURRAY—Cookies—President Baking Company; *Int'l*, pg. 1069

MURRAY—Turbines—Tuthill Corporation; *U.S. Private*, pg. 1110

MURRAY PHX—Baling Press—Continental Eagle Corporation; *U.S. Private*, pg. 267

MURRY'S—Meat Products—Murry's, Inc.; *U.S. Private*, pg. 768

MUSCALM—CNS Agents—Nippon Kayaku Co. Ltd.; *Int'l*, pg. 934

MUSCLE—NONE—N.V. Johnson Wax Belgium S.A.; *U.S. Private*, pg. 593

MUSCLE & FITNESS—Magazine—Weider Publications, Inc.; *U.S. Private*, pg. 1159

MUSCLE CREME—Pharmaceuticals—Health Products Corporation; *U.S. Private*, pg. 514

MUSEUM OF THE MOVING IMAGE—Museum—British Film Institute; *Int'l*, pg. 219

MUSHROOM N' SWISS—Hamburger Sandwich—Hardee's Food Systems, Inc.; *U.S. Public*, pg. 278

MUSIC & MEDIA—Magazine in Amsterdam; Directories—BPI Communications Inc.; *Int'l*, pg. 1446

THE MUSIC AND VIDEO CLUB—Music & Video Store—Kingfisher plc; *Int'l*, pg. 733

THE MUSIC DISC—NONE—Image Entertainment, Inc.; *U.S. Public*, pg. 870

MUSIC GO ROUND—Buys, Sells, Trades & Consigns Used & New Musical Instruments & Equipment—Grow Biz International, Inc.; *U.S. Public*, pg. 767

MUSIC OF THE RIVERS—Riverboat Cruise Trips—American Classic Voyagers Company; *U.S. Private*, pg. 380

MUSIC PLUS—Satellite Delivered Services—Muzak Limited Partnership; *U.S. Private*, pg. 222

MUSIC SALES—Music Publishing—Music Sales Corporation; *U.S. Private*, pg. 768

MUSIC SEQUENCER—Electronic Product for Music Compostion—Yamaha Corporation; *Int'l*, pg. 1515

MUSIC SHUTTLE—Portable Car Stereo—Sony Electronics; *Int'l*, pg. 1281

MUSIC UNIVERSE—On-Line Music—Bam Media; *U.S. Public*, pg. 113

MUSIC VIDEO CONFERENCE AWARDS—Business Information Services—BPI Communications Inc.; *Int'l*, pg. 1446

MUSICAL ORNAMENT—Christmas Ornament—Stanhome Inc.; *U.S. Public*, pg. 1508

MUSICAL TOILETTE PLUS—Musical Toilet Trainer & Step Stool—Cosco, Inc.; *U.S. Private*, pg. 277

MUSICIAN—Magazine—BPI Communications Inc.; *Int'l*, pg. 1446

MUSICLAND—Pre-Recorded Audio & Video Tapes, Blank Tapes & Accessories—Musicland Group Inc.; *U.S. Public*, pg. 1142

MUSICWAYS, INC.—Music Publishing (Television)—Metromedia International Group, Inc.; *U.S. Public*, pg. 1102

MUSK DUST—Plastic Bags—The Dow Chemical Company; *U.S. Public*, pg. 522

MUSKEGON—Machinery—AE Goetze-North America; *Int'l*, pg. 1334

THE MUSKEGON CHRONICLE—Newspaper—Booth Newspapers, Inc.; *U.S. Private*, pg. 157

MUSKIN—Swimming Pools—Muskin Leisure Products, Inc.; *U.S. Private*, pg. 768

MUSKOL—Insect Repellents—Schering-Plough Corporation; *U.S. Public*, pg. 1438

MUSKOL—Insect Repellent—Schering-Plough Healthcare Products Inc.; *U.S. Public*, pg. 1438

MUSKY MASTER—Braided Fishing Line—Cortland Line Co., Inc.; *U.S. Private*, pg. 277

MUSSELMANS—Apple Products—Knouse Foods Inc.; *U.S. Private*, pg. 627

MUSSER—Vibes, Marimbas, Xylos—Ludwig Industries; *U.S. Public*, pg. 1514

MUSSER—Seeds—Novartis AG; *Int'l*, pg. 971

MUSSER—Tuned Percussion—The Selmer Co., Inc.; *U.S. Public*, pg. 1514

MUSSO—Passenger car—Ssangyong Business Group; *Int'l*, pg. 1291

MUSTANG—Wheelbarrows—Ames Company; *U.S. Public*, pg. 1683

MUSTANG—Office Supplies—Dixon Ticonderoga Company; *U.S. Public*, pg. 514

MUSTANG—Insecticide—FMC Corp., Agricultural Products Group; *U.S. Public*, pg. 605

MUSTANG—Car—Ford Motor Company; *U.S. Public*, pg. 661

MUSTANG—Loaders—Mustang Manufacturing Company, Inc.; *U.S. Public*, pg. 704

MUSTANG—Engines, Tractors & Material Handling Equipment—Mustang Tractor & Equip. Co.; *U.S. Private*, pg. 704

MUSTANG—Beer—Pittsburgh Brewing Company; *U.S. Private*, pg. 619

MUSTER—Herbicide—Du Pont (E.I. Du Pont De Nemours & Co.); *U.S. Public*, pg. 530

MUTAMYCIN—Anti-Cancer Agent—Bristol-Myers Squibb Company; *U.S. Public*, pg. 253

MUTAMYCIN—Antibiotic for the Treatment of Adenocarcinomas—Bristol-Myers Squibb U.S. Pharmaceutical Group; *U.S. Public*, pg. 255

MUTOH PLOTTERS & SIGN CUTTERS—NONE—Mutoh America Inc.; *U.S. Public*, pg. 897

MUTUAL ASSURANCE—Provider of Liability Insurance to Physicians, Hospitals & Dentists—Medical Assurance, Inc.; *U.S. Public*, pg. 1079

MUTUAL NEWS—Newscasts & Updates—Westwood One, Inc.; *U.S. Public*, pg. 1763

MUTUAL OF OMAHA—Accident & Health Insurance—Mutual of Omaha Insurance Company; *U.S. Private*, pg. 769

MUTZIG—Beer—Heineken N.V.; *Int'l*, pg. 608

MUZAK—Satellite Delivered Instrumental Music—Muzak Limited Partnership; *U.S. Private*, pg. 222

MUZAK DISH NETWORK FOR BUSINESS—NONE—Muzak Limited Partnership; *U.S. Private*, pg. 222

MUZIK—Music & Lifestyle Magazine—IPC Magazines Limited; *Int'l*, pg. 651

MXOPEN SYSTEM—NONE—Honeywell-Measurex Corporation; *U.S. Public*, pg. 833

MXOPEN WEB INSPECTION SYSTEM—NONE—Honeywell-Measurex Corporation; *U.S. Public*, pg. 833

MXOPEN X-VIEW OPERATOR SYSTEM—NONE—Honeywell-Measurex Corporation; *U.S. Public*, pg. 833

MY BUDDY—Tool Boxes—The Disston Co.; *U.S. Public*, pg. 950

MY BUDDY—Candy Bars—Tom's Foods, Inc.; *U.S. Private*, pg. 1090

MY FAVORITE PASTA—Pasta & Sauce—My Own Meals, Inc.; *U.S. Private*, pg. 770

MY FIRST—Crayons, Markers—Dixon Ticonderoga Company; *U.S. Public*, pg. 514

MY FIRST BED—Toddler Bed—Evenflo Company, Inc.; *U.S. Private*, pg. 629

MY FIRST BUDDYS—Toy Vehicles—Empire of Carolina, Inc.; *U.S. Public*, pg. 579

MY FIRST CAMERA—Cameras—Eastman Kodak Company; *U.S. Public*, pg. 550

MY FIRST COLGATE—Children's Toothbrush—Colgate-Palmolive Company; *U.S. Public*, pg. 397

MY FIRST UNO—Card Game—Mattel Games/ Puzzles; *U.S. Public*, pg. 1058

MY HERO—Videogame—Sega of America Inc.; *Int'l*, pg. 1218

MY ISLANDS—Women's Cologne—The Gillette Company; *U.S. Public*, pg. 743

MY KIND OF CHICKEN—Chicken Brownrice & Veggies—My Own Meals, Inc.; *U.S. Private*, pg. 770

MY KIND OF MEAL—Various Components—My Own Meals, Inc.; *U.S. Private*, pg. 770

MY LIFE—Home Series—Toyota Motor Corporation; *Int'l*, pg. 1411

MY MEAT BALLS & SHELLS—Meatballs & Macaroni Shells—My Own Meals, Inc.; *U.S. Private*, pg. 770

MY MICHELLE—Girls & Juniors Sportswear & Dresses—Fritzi of California Manufacturing Corp.; *U.S. Private*, pg. 429

MY OWN KITCHEN—Play Kitchen—Fisher-Price, Inc.; *U.S. Public*, pg. 1058

MY OWN MEAL—Refrigeration-Free Kosher Meals—My Own Meals, Inc.; *U.S. Private*, pg. 770

MY SONGMAKER—Toytronics—Alaron Inc.; *U.S. Private*, pg. 31

MY-T-FINE—Pudding & Pie Fillings—Nabisco Inc.; *U.S. Public*, pg. 1355

MY-T-FINE—Puddings—RJR Nabisco Holdings Corp.; *U.S. Public*, pg. 1354

MY TURKEY MEATBALLS—Turkey Meatballs, Noodles & Veggies—My Own Meals, Inc.; *U.S. Private*, pg. 770

MY VERY FIRST ART STUDIO—NONE—Broderbund Software, Inc.; *U.S. Public*, pg. 258

MY VERY FIRST SOFTWARE—NONE—Broderbund Software, Inc.; *U.S. Public*, pg. 258

MY VERY FIRST STORYBOOK—NONE—Broderbund Software, Inc.; *U.S. Public*, pg. 258

MY-TE-FINE—Food Products—Fred Meyer Stores; *U.S. Public*, pg. 1103

MYAD—Self Stick Labels—Chicago Show Printing Co.; *U.S. Private*, pg. 235

MYAMBUTOL—Anti-Infective—American Home Products Corporation; *U.S. Public*, pg. 79

MYCELEX-G—Pharmaceutical—Bayer Corporation/Pharmaceutical Division; *Int'l*, pg. 173

MYCELEX-7—Pharmaceutical—Bayer Corporation/ Consumer Care Division; *Int'l*, pg. 173

MYCIGUENT—NONE—Lee Pharmaceuticals; *U.S. Public*, pg. 984

MYCIL—NONE—Boots Healthcare International; *Int'l*, pg. 202

MYCILLIN SOL—Veterinary Medicines—Meiji Seika Kaisha, Ltd.; *Int'l*, pg. 855

MYCITRACIN—Antibiotic Ointment—Pharmacia & Upjohn; *Int'l*, pg. 1048

MYCO-LOCK—Mold Inhibitor—DuCoa L.P.; *U.S. Private*, pg. 301

MYCOBUTIN—NONE—Pharmacia & Upjohn, Inc.; *Int'l*, pg. 1047

MYCODEX—NONE—Pfizer Inc.; *U.S. Public*, pg. 1281

MYCODEX—Animal Parasiticide—SmithKline Beecham plc; *Int'l*, pg. 1264

MYCOGEN—Brand Planting Seeds—Mycogen Corporation; *U.S. Public*, pg. 1142

MYCOGEN—Planting Seeds—Mycogen Seeds; *U.S. Public*, pg. 1142

MYCOLASE—Fungal Amylase for the Production of High Maltose Containing Syrups—Royal Gist-Brocades N.V.; *Int'l*, pg. 1142

MYCOLOG-II—Topical Antifungal—Westwood-Squibb Pharmaceuticals Inc.; *U.S. Public*, pg. 255

MYCOLOG II—Skin Care Product—Bristol-Myers Squibb Company; *U.S. Public*, pg. 253

MYCONOS—Broadloom—Couristan Inc.; *U.S. Private*, pg. 279

MYCOPLASMA PNEUMONIA—IFA Test System—Wampole Laboratories; *U.S. Public*, pg. 310

MYCOSPOR—Pharmaceutical, Cardiovascular—Bayer AG; *Int'l*, pg. 171

MYCOSTATIN—Dermatological Therapy Product—Bristol-Myers Squibb Company; *U.S. Public*, pg. 253

MYCOSTATIN—Antifungal Antibiotic used for Treatment of Vulvovaginal Candidiasis—Bristol-Myers Squibb U.S. Pharmaceutical Group; *U.S. Public*, pg. 255

MYCOSTATIN—Topical Antifungal—Westwood-Squibb Pharmaceuticals Inc.; *U.S. Public*, pg. 255

MYCOTECT—NONE—Life Technologies, Inc.; *U.S. Public*, pg. 504

MYCRO—Distributed Control Systems—Moore Products Co.; *U.S. Public*, pg. 1128

MYCRO ADVANTAGE—Industrial Instrumentation—Moore Products Co.; *U.S. Public*, pg. 1128

Brand Name Index

MYCRO APACS—Process Controller—Moore Products Co.; *U.S. Public*, pg. 1128

MYCRO XTC—Industrial Instrumentation—Moore Products Co.; *U.S. Public*, pg. 1128

MYDFRIN—Phenylephrine HC1—Alcon Laboratories, Inc.; *Int'l*, pg. 916

MYDRIACYL—Tropicamide—Alcon Laboratories, Inc.; *Int'l*, pg. 916

MYELOSCAN—Chemical-Namely, Iogulamide for Use as a Myelographic Agent—Mallinckrodt Inc.; *U.S. Public*, pg. 1039

MYER GRACEBROS—NONE—Coles Myer Ltd.; *Int'l*, pg. 306

MYER'S GOLDEN RICH—Jamaican Rum—The Seagram Company Ltd.; *Int'l*, pg. 1214

MYER'S ORIGINAL DARK—Jamaican Rum—The Seagram Company Ltd.; *Int'l*, pg. 1214

MYER'S PLATINUM WHITE—Jamaican Rum—The Seagram Company Ltd.; *Int'l*, pg. 1214

MYERS—Processed Frozen Entrees & Soups—Hanover Foods Corporation; *U.S. Private*, pg. 499

MYERS—Pumps & Water Systems—F.E. Myers; *U.S. Public*, pg. 1273

MYERS—Pot Pies, Entrees & Croquettes—Myers Foods Company; *U.S. Private*, pg. 499

MYERS'S ORIGINAL—Dark Rum—The House of Seagram; *Int'l*, pg. 1217

MYKROX—Metolazone Tablets—Medeva Pharmaceuticals; *Int'l*, pg. 852

MYLANTA II—Antacid—Johnson & Johnson; *U.S. Public*, pg. 927

MYLAR—Polyester Film—Du Pont (E.I. Du Pont De Nemours & Co.); *U.S. Public*, pg. 530

MYLERAN—Leukemia Treatment—Glaxo Wellcome PLC; *Int'l*, pg. 553

MYNTHON—Pastilles—Huhtamaki Oy; *Int'l*, pg. 638

MYO MANAGER—Cardioplegia Delivery System—Gish Biomedical, Inc.; *U.S. Public*, pg. 745

MYOCARE—Neuromuscular Stimulation System—3M; *U.S. Public*, pg. 1604

MYOFLEX—Analgesic—Rhone-Poulenc Rorer - U.S.; *Int'l*, pg. 1110

MYOKO—Personal Care Prods.—The Gillette Company; *U.S. Public*, pg. 743

MYOSCINT—Cardiac Imaging Agent—Centocor, Inc.; *U.S. Public*, pg. 323

MYOVIEW—Kit for Tc 99m Exametazime—Amersham Corporation; *Int'l*, pg. 992

MYPLABIN—Macrolide Antibiotic—Asahi Chemical Industry Co., Ltd.; *Int'l*, pg. 83

MYRIADE—Hose—The Goodyear Tire & Rubber Company; *U.S. Public*, pg. 752

MYROXIM—Anti-depressant—Solvay S.A.; *Int'l*, pg. 1277

MYRRH—Records—Word, Incorporated; *U.S. Public*, pg. 704

MYRTLE—Office Furniture & Seating—Haworth, Inc.; *U.S. Private*, pg. 511

MYSOLINE—Anticonvulsion Agent—Wyeth-Ayerst Laboratories, Inc.; *U.S. Public*, pg. 80

MYSON—Heating Products—Blue Circle Industries PLC; *Int'l*, pg. 197

MYST—NONE—Broderbund Software, Inc.; *U.S. Public*, pg. 258

MYSTERIES OF THE UNKNOWN—Book Series—Time-Life, Inc.; *U.S. Public*, pg. 1613

MYSTERIOUS PRESS—Books—Warner Books, Inc.; *U.S. Public*, pg. 1614

MYSTERY GUILD BOOK CLUB—NONE—Doubleday Direct; *Int'l*, pg. 191

MYSTERY JACKPOT—Bonusing System—Mikohn Gaming Corporation; *U.S. Public*, pg. 1111

MYSTIC—Women's Fragrance—Marilyn Miglin, L.P.; *U.S. Private*, pg. 745

MYSTIC—Mint Sandwich Cookies—Nabisco Inc.; *U.S. Public*, pg. 1355

MYSTIC—NONE—Pfizer Inc.; *U.S. Public*, pg. 1281

MYSTIC—Mint Sandwich Cookies—RJR Nabisco Holdings Corp.; *U.S. Public*, pg. 1354

MYSTIC—Printing Paper—Westvaco Corporation; *U.S. Public*, pg. 1762

MYSTIQUE—Laid Offset, Writing & Cover—Champion International Corp.; *U.S. Public*, pg. 333

MYSTO-GRIP—Felt—American Felt & Filter; *U.S. Private*, pg. 54

MYVACET—Acetylated Monoglycerides—Eastman Kodak Company; *U.S. Public*, pg. 550

MYVAPLEX—Food-Grade Monoglycerides—Eastman Kodak Company; *U.S. Public*, pg. 550

MYVATEX—Food Emulsifiers Containing Monoglycerides—Eastman Kodak Company; *U.S. Public*, pg. 550

MYVATEX TL—Tablet Lubricant—Eastman Kodak Company; *U.S. Public*, pg. 550

MYVEROL—Monoglycerides—Eastman Kodak Company; *U.S. Public*, pg. 550

N

N—Athletic Shoes & Apparel—New Balance Athletic Shoe, Inc.; *U.S. Private*, pg. 792

NABI—NONE—Nabi; *U.S. Public*, pg. 1148

NA-CHURS—Liquid Fertilizer—Na-Churs Plant Food Company; *U.S. Private*, pg. 1096

NA-CHURS DOUBLE OK—Liquid Potassium—Na-Churs Plant Food Company; *U.S. Private*, pg. 1096

NAFE—National Association for Female Executives—The National Association for Female Executives, Inc.; *U.S. Private*, pg. 691

NAIS—Mew's Worldwide Brand Name—Aromat Corporation; *Int'l*, pg. 847

NA 100—Surgical Needle/Drilling Laser—Lasag AG; *Int'l*, pg. 1161

NAPA—Distribution Centers—Genuine Parts Company; *U.S. Public*, pg. 732

NAPA ECHLIN—Electrical & Fuel System Parts—Echlin Inc.; *U.S. Public*, pg. 560

NAPA UNITED—Brake Parts—Echlin Inc.; *U.S. Public*, pg. 560

NAR—National Auto Research Guides—The Hearst Corporation; *U.S. Private*, pg. 515

NASCO—NONE—Nasco Industries Inc.; *U.S. Private*, pg. 774

NAS SERIES—Clear Acrylic Copolymersfor Injection Molding—Nova Chemicals, Inc.; *Int'l*, pg. 971

NATO—War Game—Monarch Avalon, Inc.; *U.S. Public*, pg. 1123

NA 301—Surgical Needle/Drilling Laser—Lasag AG; *Int'l*, pg. 1161

NA-X—Dry Powder—Ansul Incorporated; *U.S. Public*, pg. 1648

NB—Athletic Shoes & Apparel—New Balance Athletic Shoe, Inc.; *U.S. Private*, pg. 792

NBA—Sportsgame-Computer—Monarch Avalon, Inc.; *U.S. Public*, pg. 1123

NBA JAM EXTREME—Interactive Entertainment Software—Acclaim Entertainment, Inc.; *U.S. Public*, pg. 15

NBC—Broadcast Stations—National Broadcasting Co., Inc.; *U.S. Public*, pg. 712

NBC EXTRA—In-Depth News Coverage—Westwood One, Inc.; *U.S. Public*, pg. 1763

NBC RADIO NETWORK—24-Hour News Network—Westwood One, Inc.; *U.S. Public*, pg. 1763

NBF—Trampolines—Hedstrom Corporation; *U.S. Private*, pg. 526

NBF TRAMPOLINES—All Sizes Trampolines, Body Building & Exercise Equipment—N.B.F. Bollinger Industries; *U.S. Public*, pg. 243

NB JACKETS—Document Management Products—Bell & Howell Holdings; *U.S. Public*, pg. 201

NBO STORES—NONE—Gerald Group Inc.; *U.S. Private*, pg. 448

NC—Nitrocellulose—Schleicher & Schuell, Inc.; *Int'l*, pg. 1206

NCAA PACKAGE—Sports Programming—Westwood One, Inc.; *U.S. Public*, pg. 1763

NCAP—Liquid Crystal Displays—Raychem Corporation; *U.S. Public*, pg. 1362

NCCI—NONE—CUC International, Inc.; *U.S. Public*, pg. 320

N.C.F.R. HOMASOTE—U/L Rated Board—Homasote Company; *U.S. Public*, pg. 831

NC50 EXPRESS—Motorcycle—American Honda Motor Co., Inc. Motorcycle Division; *Int'l*, pg. 634

NCG—Respiratory Therapy Equipment—Allied Healthcare Products, Inc.; *U.S. Public*, pg. 48

NCI—Furniture—Nemschoff Chairs, Inc.; *U.S. Private*, pg. 791

NCP—Nylon Rod Winding—Gudebrod, Inc.; *U.S. Private*, pg. 486

NCR—Computer Systems—NCR Corporation; *U.S. Public*, pg. 1146

NCR COOPERATION—Software—NCR Corporation; *U.S. Public*, pg. 1146

NCR OPEN NETWORKING ENVIRONMENT—Data Communications—NCR Corporation; *U.S. Public*, pg. 1146

NCR PAPER—Paper—Appleton Papers Inc.; *Int'l*, pg. 567

NCR PAPER* BRAND—Carbonless Paper—Appleton Papers Inc.; *Int'l*, pg. 567

NCR SYSTEM 3000—Computers—NCR Corporation; *U.S. Public*, pg. 1146

NCR TOWER—Supermicrocomputers—NCR Corporation; *U.S. Public*, pg. 1146

NCT—Protective & Decorative Motor Vehiicle Coatings—PPG Industries, Inc.; *U.S. Public*, pg. 1245

N-CAT—Continuous Non-Invasive Blood Pressure Monitor—Nellcor Puritan Bennett Incorporated; *U.S. Public*, pg. 1039

ND—Automotive, Motorcycle, Small Engine Spark Plugs-Domestic & Import—Denso Sales California; *Int'l*, pg. 1412

ND CC—Tires—Bridgestone/Firestone, Inc.; *Int'l*, pg. 213

ND DUPLEX—Tires—Bridgestone/Firestone, Inc.; *Int'l*, pg. 213

NDNA—Crithidia Luciliae Autoimmune Test System—Wampole Laboratories; *U.S. Public*, pg. 310

NDS—Next-Day Delivery Service—Danzas Corporation; *Int'l*, pg. 382

NDT—NONE—Western Atlas Logging Services; *Int'l*, pg. 1757

NDX—Computer System—Tandem Computers Inc.; *U.S. Public*, pg. 417

NEBS—NONE—New England Business Service, Inc.; *U.S. Public*, pg. 1170

NEC—NONE—Milgray Electronics, Inc.; *U.S. Public*, pg. 205

NEC—International 9—NEC Corporation; *Int'l*, pg. 899

NEC—NONE—NEC Electronics Inc.; *Int'l*, pg. 900

NEC ELECTRONICS—Electronic Components-Interface Electronics Corporation; *U.S. Private*, pg. 567

NE NERINA—Cereal Mix—Bestfoods; *U.S. Public*, pg. 223

NEPS—Polystyrene Expandable Beads—Asahi Chemical Industry Co., Ltd.; *Int'l*, pg. 83

NER DATA PRODUCTS—Computer Printer Supplies—Hargro Enterprises, Inc.; *U.S. Private*, pg. 502

N.E.T.—Window "Racing" Nets—Lund International Holdings, Inc.; *U.S. Public*, pg. 1020

NETS—Banking Software—NDC Tokyo Representative Office; *U.S. Public*, pg. 1156

NFB—Phosphoric Acids for Aluminum Brightening—Monsanto Company; *U.S. Public*, pg. 1124

NFL & 30 NFL TEAMS—Insignia—National Football League Properties, Inc.; *U.S. Private*, pg. 783

NFL FOOTBALL—Sports Radio Program—Westwood One Entertainment; *U.S. Public*, pg. 1763

NFL FOOTBALL—Sports Programming—Westwood One, Inc.; *U.S. Public*, pg. 1763

NFL FOOTBALL SUNDAY AFTERNOON DOUBLE HEADER—Sports Radio Program—Westwood One Entertainment; *U.S. Public*, pg. 1763

NFL GUARDIAN—Sports Mouth Guards—Brimms Inc.; *U.S. Private*, pg. 169

NFL PREVIEW—Sports Programming—Westwood One, Inc.; *U.S. Public*, pg. 1763

NFL QUARTERBACK CLUB' 96—Interactive Entertainment Software—Acclaim Entertainment, Inc.; *U.S. Public*, pg. 15

NFL WARM-UP—Sports Radio Program—Westwood One Entertainment; *U.S. Public*, pg. 1763

NFL WARM UP—Sports Program—Westwood One, Inc.; *U.S. Public*, pg. 1763

NFO—Fastest Possible Delivery—Danzas Corporation; *Int'l*, pg. 382

NFO/ASI TARGETED COPY TESTING—Advertising Testing Among Targeted Samples of Consumers—NFO Research, Inc.; *U.S. Public*, pg. 1146

NFO HEALTHMED—Serving Healthcare & Pharmaceutical Marketers—NFO Research, Inc.; *U.S. Public*, pg. 1146

THE NFO HISPANIC PANEL—Prescreened Hispanic Households for Consumer Surveys—NFO Research, Inc.; *U.S. Public*, pg. 1146

THE NFO PANEL—450,000 Prescreened US Households Used for Consumer Surveys—NFO Research, Inc.; *U.S. Public*, pg. 1146

THE NFO SMARTSYSTEM—Data Management System—NFO Research, Inc.; *U.S. Public*, pg. 1146

NFO TRAVELS AMERICA—Syndicated Pleasure Travel Monitor—NFO Research, Inc.; *U.S. Public*, pg. 1146

NFX—NONE—ECI Telecom Ltd.; *Int'l*, pg. 643

N 50—SLR Camera—Nikon Inc.; *Int'l*, pg. 931

N-FLOAT—Sludge Flotation-Thickening System—U.S. Filter/Davis Water & Waste Industries, Inc.; *U.S. Public*, pg. 1682

N-FLOW—Solvent Delivery System & Components—Beckman Instruments, Inc.; *U.S. Public*, pg. 199

NG & SF—Fresh Yeast—Royal Gist-Brocades N.V.; *Int'l*, pg. 1142

NGP—NONE—Western Atlas Logging Services; *U.S. Public*, pg. 1757

NHBB—NONE—New Hampshire Ball Bearings, Inc.; *Int'l*, pg. 868

NHI 810—Computerized Engraving—New Hermes Incorporated; *U.S. Private*, pg. 793

NHI 1219—Computerized Engraving—New Hermes Incorporated; *U.S. Private*, pg. 793

NHL STANLEY CUP FINALS—Sports Radio Program—Westwood One Entertainment; *U.S. Public*, pg. 1763

NHL STANLEY CUP FINALS—All Star Game Programming—Westwood One, Inc.; *U.S. Public*, pg. 1763

NHT—Loudspeakers—Recoton Auto Corporation; *U.S. Public*, pg. 1369

NHT (NOW HEAR THIS)—Loudspeakers—NHT; *U.S. Public*, pg. 1369

NHT(NOW HEAR THIS)—Home Speakers—Recoton Corporation; *U.S. Public*, pg. 1369

NIFDA—Multi-Lines—Kesterson Food Company, Inc.; *U.S. Private*, pg. 616

NIM—NONE—GenRad, Inc.; *U.S. Public*, pg. 731

NIN-RX—Ninhydrin Reagents—Beckman Instruments, Inc.; *U.S. Public*, pg. 199

NIU—Network Interface Unit—Tandem Computers Inc.; *U.S. Public*, pg. 417

NIU—NONE—UB Networks; *Int'l*, pg. 924

NIV CHILDREN'S BIBLE—Illustrated Children's Bible—The Zondervan Corporation; *Int'l*, pg. 927

NIV PULPIT BIBLE—New International Version Pulpit Bible—The Zondervan Corporation; *Int'l*, pg. 927

NIV STUDY BIBLE—New International Version Study Bible—The Zondervan Corporation; *Int'l*, pg. 927

NIX—Head Lice Medicated Shampoo—Warner-Lambert Consumer Healthcare; *U.S. Public*, pg. 1739

NIZN—Nickel-Zinc Alloy—Thomas Steel Strip Corp.; *Int'l*, pg. 756

NIZN-COTE—Electroplated Colded Rolled Steel Strip—Thomas Steel Strip Corp.; *Int'l*, pg. 756

NJ101.5—FM Broadcasting Station—Press Communications, LLC; *U.S. Private*, pg. 882

NLX—Computer—Tandem Computers Inc.; *U.S. Public*, pg. 417

NMB—Bearings, Fanmotors—Minebea Co., Ltd.; *Int'l*, pg. 867

NMC—Peritoneal Dialysis Solutions, Supplies & Bloodlines—Fresenius Medical Care (North America); *Int'l*, pg. 505

NMP—Solvent—International Specialty Products, Inc.; *U.S. Public*, pg. 858

N MAC—Measurement & Control Software—Analog Devices, Inc.; *U.S. Public*, pg. 107

N 90 S—NONE—Nikon Inc.; *Int'l*, pg. 931

NOBO—Cookies—Campbell Soup Company; *U.S. Public*, pg. 298

NOSL—Computer Programming Language Software Component—Datapoint Corporation; *Int'l*, pg. 384

N1—Golf Equipment—Nicklaus Golf Company, L.C.; *U.S. Private*, pg. 799

NP—Honeycomb Material—Hexcel Corporation; *U.S. Public*, pg. 824

NPB—NONE—Nellcor Puritan Bennett Incorporated; *U.S. Public*, pg. 1039

NPD—Paint & Paint Sundries Retailers/Distributors—PRO Group, Inc.; *U.S. Private*, pg. 887

NPG—Glycol Chemicals—Eastman Chemical Company; *U.S. Public*, pg. 550

NPG—Glycol Chemicals—Eastman Kodak Company; *U.S. Public*, pg. 550

NPH ILETIN—Isophane Insulin Suspension, Lilly—Eli Lilly and Company; *U.S. Public*, pg. 992

NPH ILETIN II—Isophane Purified Insulin Suspension, Lilly—Eli Lilly and Company; *U.S. Public*, pg. 992

NPPF—NONE—First DataBank; *U.S. Private*, pg. 515

NPR—Commercial Truck—American Isuzu Motors Inc.; *Int'l*, pg. 692

NPR—Fastening System—The Black & Decker Corporation; *U.S. Public*, pg. 233

NPR-E&I—Commerical Truck—American Isuzu Motors Inc.; *Int'l*, pg. 692

NPS Q/A—Photographic Printer/Processor—Konica Corporation; *Int'l*, pg. 748

NP77—Rubber Products—Rubatex Corporation; *U.S. Private*, pg. 56

NP-27—Athlete's Foot Treatment—Thompson Medical Company, Inc.; *U.S. Private*, pg. 1083

N.P.W.—Boys' Wear—Farah Incorporated; *U.S. Public*, pg. 612

NQS/MVS—Computer System—International Business Machines Corporation; *U.S. Public*, pg. 895

NR—Electrode—The Lincoln Electric Company; *U.S. Public*, pg. 996

NRG—Pure Guarana Tablets—Herbalife International of America, Inc.; *U.S. Public*, pg. 809

NRG—Guarana Tea—Herbalife International of America, Inc.; *U.S. Public*, pg. 809

NRM—Livestock Feed—Goodman Fielder Limited; *Int'l*, pg. 555

NR. SICHER—Construction Chemical Products for the Specialized Construction Trade—Heidelberger Zement A.G.; *Int'l*, pg. 605

NSA—NONE—National Safety Associates; *U.S. Private*, pg. 786

NSC—Mfr. of High-Speed Data Communications Systems—Network Systems Corporation; *U.S. Public*, pg. 1522

NSF—NONE—LucasVarity plc; *Int'l*, pg. 819

NSIM—Hardware Simulator—IKOS Systems, Inc.; *U.S. Public*, pg. 864

NSK—Measuring Tools—Fred V. Fowler Company, Inc.; *U.S. Private*, pg. 422

NSR—German Broadcasting—CLT-UFA; *Int'l*, pg. 561

N SERIES—Nuclear Safety Related Miniature Recorder—Westronics, Inc.; *U.S. Public*, pg. 1593

N-SERVE—Nitrogen Stabilizers—The Dow Chemical Company; *U.S. Public*, pg. 522

N-SERVE—NONE—The Dow Chemical Company; *U.S. Public*, pg. 522

N 70—NONE—Nikon Inc.; *Int'l*, pg. 931

N 70 SLR—NONE—Nikon Inc.; *Int'l*, pg. 931

N66—Membrane Filters—Pall Corporation; *U.S. Public*, pg. 1253

N SPHEROGEL—Chromatography Columns & Column Packing Materials—Beckman Instruments, Inc.; *U.S. Public*, pg. 199

NT STUDIO—Travel Periodical—Advanstar Communications; *U.S. Private*, pg. 22

NTW—NONE—Sears, Roebuck and Co.; *U.S. Public*, pg. 1452

NTX 2000—Computer Systems—Sequent Computer Systems, Inc.; *U.S. Public*, pg. 1459

NTRAK—Test Kit—Hach Company; *U.S. Public*, pg. 773

NU50 MI URBAN EXPRESS—Motorcycle—American Honda Motor Co., Inc. Motorcycle Division; *Int'l*, pg. 634

NUVA-SIL—Ultra-Violet Silicones—Loctite Corporation; *Int'l*, pg. 611

NV HOMES—NONE—NVR, Inc.; *U.S. Public*, pg. 1148

NVR MORTGAGE—NONE—NVR, Inc.; *U.S. Public*, pg. 1148

NVR SETTLEMENT—NONE—NVR, Inc.; *U.S. Public*, pg. 1148

NVS MIRRORS—Automatic-Dimming Rearview Mirrors for Motor Vehicles—Gentex Corporation; *U.S. Public*, pg. 731

NVX ACTIVE SYSTEMS—Noise Control—Lord Corporation, Mechanical Products Division; *U.S. Private*, pg. 676

NVIEW DIAMOND—DLP Projector—nVIEW Corporation; *U.S. Public*, pg. 1206

NW BRAND—Lumber—Weyerhaeuser Company; *U.S. Public*, pg. 1764

NWAYS—Computer System—International Business Machines Corporation; *U.S. Public*, pg. 895

NX—Motorcycle—American Honda Motor Co., Inc. Motorcycle Division; *Int'l*, pg. 634

NY NY—Stainless Steel Roll Top Schaffer—The Vollrath Company, L.L.C.; *U.S. Private*, pg. 1143

NYPM—National Yellow Pages Monitor Division—NFO Research, Inc.; *U.S. Public*, pg. 1146

NYK LINE—NONE—Nippon Yusen K.K.; *Int'l*, pg. 941

NORWALK NATURAL GAS FUELING SYSTEMS—NONE—Norwalk Co., Inc.; *U.S. Private*, pg. 807

NORWALK COMPRESSORS—NONE—Norwalk Co., Inc.; *U.S. Private*, pg. 807

NAB—Packs—Nabisco Inc.; *U.S. Public*, pg. 1355

NABCO—Flags, Pennants & Banners—National Banner Company, Inc.; *U.S. Private*, pg. 780

NABISCO SHREDDED WHEAT CEREAL—Cereal—Nabisco Inc.; *U.S. Public*, pg. 1355

NACCO—Indigo Dye—Buffalo Color Corporation; *U.S. Private*, pg. 178

NACCONOL—Sulfonate—Stepan Company; *U.S. Public*, pg. 1514

NACHIPS—Tortilla Chips—The Pillsbury Company; *Int'l*, pg. 411

NACHOS—Snacks—Gold Medal Products Co.; *U.S. Private*, pg. 459

NACO—Windows—James Hardie Industries Ltd.; *Int'l*, pg. 596

NACRYLIC—Resin—Unilever Plc; *Int'l*, pg. 1433

NACS—NONE—Life Technologies, Inc.; *U.S. Public*, pg. 504

NACTON—Peptic Ulcer Products—SmithKline Beecham plc; *Int'l*, pg. 1264

NACTRAN—Herbicide—The Dow Chemical Company; *U.S. Public*, pg. 522

NADINE—Formals—S.A.S.I. Corporation; *U.S. Private*, pg. 955

NADIS—Customer Information File Management—Group 1 Software, Inc.; *U.S. Public*, pg. 417

NADY—Wireless Microphones, Video Camera Accessories, Infrared Headset System.—Nady Systems, Inc.; *U.S. Private*, pg. 773

NADY—El. Guitar & Bass Amplifiers & Motorcycle Elect Accessories.—Nady Systems, Inc.; *U.S. Private*, pg. 773

NAFCIL—Infectious Disease Therapy—Bristol-Myers Squibb Company; *U.S. Public*, pg. 253

NAFION—Perfluorosulfoniz Membrane—Du Pont (E.I. Du Pont De Nemours & Co.); *U.S. Public*, pg. 530

NAFTIN—Topical Antifungal Cream—Allergan, Inc.; *U.S. Public*, pg. 46

NAGEL—Office Machinery—Standard Duplicating Machines Corp.; *U.S. Private*, pg. 1031

NAHEMA—Fragrance—Guerlain S.A.; *Int'l*, pg. 780

NAIL EATERS—BITS—Greenlee Textron; *U.S. Public*, pg. 1589

NAIL LOCK—General Construction Adhesive—Miracle Adhesives; *U.S. Public*, pg. 1466

NAIL WORKS—NONE—Clairol, Inc.; *U.S. Public*, pg. 254

NAILMASTER—Hammers—The Stanley Works; *U.S. Public*, pg. 1508

NAILS—NONE—Bobit Publishing Company; *U.S. Private*, pg. 154

NAILS, NAILS, NAILS—Pharmaceuticals—Health Products Corporation; *U.S. Private*, pg. 514

NAILSLICKS—Polish—Cover Girl Cosmetics; *U.S. Public*, pg. 1330

NAIR—Depilatory—Carter Products, Canada; *U.S. Public*, pg. 310

NAIR—Depilatory—Carter-Wallace, Inc.; *U.S. Public*, pg. 309

NAIRN—Vinyl Linoleum—Forbo Holding SA; *Int'l*, pg. 496

NAKAJIMA PRO MODEL—Golf Clubs—Mizuno Corporation; *Int'l*, pg. 884

NAKAYOSHI—Monthly Japanese Comic Magazine—Kodansha Ltd.; *Int'l*, pg. 742

NAKS-PAK—Pouches of Popcorn—Gold Medal Products Co.; *U.S. Private*, pg. 459

NAKS POP—Bars of Coconut Oil—Gold Medal Products Co.; *U.S. Private*, pg. 459

NALAN—Water Repellents—Du Pont (E.I. Du Pont De Nemours & Co.); *U.S. Public*, pg. 530

NALDECON—Nasal-Congestion Remedy—Bristol-Myers Squibb Company; *U.S. Public*, pg. 253

NALFON—Fenoprofen Calcium, Dista—Eli Lilly and Company; *U.S. Public*, pg. 992

NALGENE—Plastic Labware, Blowers—Nalge Company; *U.S. Public*, pg. 1545

NALGENE—Tanks—Ryan Herco Products Corp.; *U.S. Private*, pg. 953

NALGENE—Plastic Labware—Sybron International Corporation; *U.S. Public*, pg. 1544

NALKEN—Fertilizers—Kyowa Hakko Kogyo Company, Ltd.; *Int'l*, pg. 778

NALKYLENE—Detergent Alkylate—Condea Vista Company; *Int'l*, pg. 325

NALLEY'S—Dressings, Mayonnaise, Canned Foods, Syrup, Pickles, Dip, Condiments, Snack—Nalleys Fine Foods; *U.S. Private*, pg. 887

NALLPEN—Pharmaceutical Prods.—SmithKline Beecham Laboratories; *Int'l*, pg. 1264

NALLPEN—Pharmaceutical—SmithKline Beecham plc; *Int'l*, pg. 1264

NALTEX—Extruded Plastic Net—Nalle Plastics Inc.; *U.S. Private*, pg. 773

NAMCO—Furniture—Email Limited; *Int'l*, pg. 450

NAMCO—Solenoids/Switches—Namco Controls Corporation; *U.S. Public*, pg. 482

NAN—Infant Foods & Dietetic Products—Nestle S.A.; *Int'l*, pg. 915

NANCE'S—Mustard Sauce—Nance's Food Products, Inc.; *U.S. Public*, pg. 1347

NANCY LOPEZ—Footwear—E.J. Footwear Corp.; *U.S. Public*, pg. 1684

NANIK—Wood Window Coverings—Wausau Metals, Nanik Division; *U.S. Public*, pg. 1500

NANO PURE—Deionization System—Barnstead/Thermolyne Corporation; *U.S. Public*, pg. 1545

NANO2—Electronic Fuse—Littelfuse, Inc.; *U.S. Public*, pg. 1001

NANOCHEM—Synthetic Resin—Hercules Incorporated; *U.S. Public*, pg. 809

NANOFORM—Ultra Precision CNC Lathe—Taylor Hobson Pneumo; *Int'l*, pg. 1087

NANOFUSE—Electronic Fuses—Littelfuse, Inc.; *U.S. Public*, pg. 1001

NANOLINE MODEL 50-2—Linewidth Measuring Systems—Nanometrics Incorporated; *U.S. Public*, pg. 1151

NANOSPEC/AFT 8000—Automated Film Thickness Measurement System—Nanometrics Incorporated; *U.S. Public*, pg. 1151

NANOSPEC/AFT 8300—Automated Film Thickness Measurement System—Nanometrics Incorporated; *U.S. Public*, pg. 1151

NANOSPEC/AFT 4150—Film Thickness Measurement Systems—Nanometrics Incorporated; *U.S. Public*, pg. 1151

NANOSPEC/AFT 5500—Automated Film Thickness Measurement System for FPD's—Nanometrics Incorporated; *U.S. Public*, pg. 1151

NANOSPEC/AFT 2100—Thin Film Thickness Measurement System—Nanometrics Incorporated; *U.S. Public*, pg. 1151

NANOSTRIP—Electronic Chemical—Laporte plc; *Int'l*, pg. 801

NAP-GARD—Pipe Coatings—Herberts-O'Brien Inc.; *Int'l*, pg. 626

NAP-LAM—Laminating Film—General Binding Corporation; *U.S. Public*, pg. 707

NAP ROLL—Toddler Blanket With Attached Pillow—Polar Fleece—Dakotah, Inc.; *U.S. Public*, pg. 477

NAPA MARINE PARTS—Engine Parts—Echlin Inc.; *U.S. Public*, pg. 560

NAPA POWER EQUIPMENT PARTS—NONE—Echlin Inc.; *U.S. Public*, pg. 560

NAPA RIDGE—Wine—Wine World Estates; *Int'l*, pg. 917

NAPA VALLEY BANK—NONE—Westamerica Bancorporation; *U.S. Public*, pg. 1756

NAPCO—Electroplating Equip.—NAPCO, Inc.; *U.S. Public*, pg. 1592

NAPCO INTERNATIONAL INC.—International Marketing Company—Venturian Corp.; *U.S. Public*, pg. 1716

NAPHCON—Naphazoline HC1—Alcon Laboratories, Inc.; *Int'l*, pg. 916

NAPHCON-A—Naphazoline HCl-Pheniramine Maleate—Alcon Laboratories, Inc.; *Int'l*, pg. 916

NAPHCON FORTE—Naphazoline Hydrochloride—Alcon Laboratories, Inc.; *Int'l*, pg. 916

NAPHTHA—Lanterns & Stoves—The Canadian Coleman Co., Ltd.; *U.S. Private*, pg. 691

NAPIER—Jewelry—The Napier Co.; *U.S. Private*, pg. 774

NAPLES DAILY NEWS—Newspaper—The E.W. Scripps Company; *U.S. Public*, pg. 1447

NAPOLEON—Game—Monarch Avalon, Inc.; *U.S. Public*, pg. 1123

NAPOLEON'S BATTLES—War Game—Monarch Avalon, Inc.; *U.S. Public*, pg. 1123

NAPOLINA—Corn Oil & Other Oils, Soups, Seasonings, Spices, Pastas, Tomato Sauces—Bestfoods; *U.S. Public*, pg. 223

NAPOLINA—Pasta, Pasta Sauces, Tomatoes, Pizzeria—CPC Foods (Ireland) Ltd.; *U.S. Public*, pg. 225

NAPRELAN—Anti-Inflammatory Drug—American Home Products Corporation; *U.S. Public*, pg. 79

NAPRELAN—NONE—Elan Corporation Plc; *Int'l*, pg. 435

NAPROSYN—Naproxen, Antirheumatic—Recordati Industria Chimica e Farmaceutica S.p.A.; *Int'l*, pg. 1090

NAPROSYN—Nonsteroidal Antirheumatic Drug—Roche Holding Ltd.; *Int'l*, pg. 1119

NAPROSYN—Naproxen—Syntex; *Int'l*, pg. 1120

NAQUA—Trichlormethiazide—Key Pharmaceuticals; *U.S. Public*, pg. 1438

NAQUA-MATIC—Slurry Solution Car—General Electric Capital Railcar Services; *U.S. Public*, pg. 712

NARCO—Avionics—Telonic Berkeley, Inc.; *U.S. Private*, pg. 1074

NARDALERT—Personal Radiation(RF) Monitor—L3 Communications Narda-Microwave Div.; *U.S. Private*, pg. 638

NARDI BRUNELLO—Italian Wine—Laird & Company; *U.S. Private*, pg. 642

NARDI ROSSO DE MONTALCINO—Italian Wine—Laird & Company; *U.S. Private*, pg. 642

NARRAGANSETT—Beer & Ale—Falstaff Brewing Corporation; *U.S. Private*, pg. 955

NARRO-SIDE—Fiber-Cement Siding—GAF Premium Products, Inc.; *U.S. Private*, pg. 433

NARROW BAND DESIGN—Abrasive Wheels or Disks—Litton Industries, Inc.; *U.S. Public*, pg. 1002

NARUMI BONE CHINA—Tableware Made of Bone China—Narumi China Corporation; *Int'l*, pg. 906

NASALCROM—Nasal Solution (Cromolyn Sodium Nasal Solution, USP)—Medeva Pharmaceuticals; *Int'l*, pg. 852

NASALIDE—Flunisolide—Syntex; *Int'l*, pg. 1120

NASBA—RNA-HIV-1 Assay System—Akzo Nobel N.V.; *Int'l*, pg. 42

NASBA-QR—NONE—Akzo Nobel N.V.; *Int'l*, pg. 42

NASCO—Education & Farm Supplies—Nasco Modesto; *U.S. Private*, pg. 446

NASCO-GUARD—Preserved Specimens—Nasco Modesto; *U.S. Private*, pg. 446

NASCOBAL—NONE—Schwarz Pharma Inc.; *Int'l*, pg. 1211

NASHUA—Computer Disc Packs, Photocopy Machines, Toner, Paper—Nashua Corporation; *U.S. Public*, pg. 1152

NASHUA—Mobile & Sectional Homes—Nashua Homes of Idaho Inc.; *U.S. Private*, pg. 774

NASHUATEC—Office Equipment—Gestetner Corporation; *Int'l*, pg. 1115

NASHUATEC—Office Equipment—Gestetner Holdings PLC; *Int'l*, pg. 1114

NASHVILLE—Photo Typesetters—AGFA EPS Division; *Int'l*, pg. 172

NASOYA—Tofu & Condiments—Vitasoy (U.S.A.) Inc.; *Int'l*, pg. 1469

NASSAU—Safety Eyewear—Aearo Company; *U.S. Private*, pg. 23

NASSAU—Sporting Goods—Brunswick Bowling & Billiards Corp.; *U.S. Public*, pg. 265

NASSAU ROYALE—Liqueur—Bacardi-Martini, USA, Inc.; *U.S. Private*, pg. 109

NASSCO—Shipbuilding & Repair, Construction of Offshore Modules—National Steel & Shipbuilding Company; *U.S. Private*, pg. 787

NASTRO AZZURRO—Beer—Danone Group; *Int'l*, pg. 379

NATACYN—Natamycin—Alcon Laboratories, Inc.; *Int'l*, pg. 916

NATALINA—Pizza—Crestar Food Products, Inc.; *U.S. Public*, pg. 805

NATALINS—Prenatal Vitamin Supplement—Bristol-Myers Squibb Company; *U.S. Public*, pg. 253

NATALINS—Vitamin & Mineral Supplement for Pregnant or Lactating Women—Bristol-Myers Squibb U.S. Pharmaceutical Group; *U.S. Public*, pg. 255

NATALINS RX—Vitamin & Mineral Supplement for use During Pregnancy & Lactation—Bristol-Myers Squibb U.S. Pharmaceutical Group; *U.S. Public*, pg. 255

NATCO—Generators—Dresser-Rand Sales; *U.S. Public*, pg. 529

NATHAN'S—Meat Products—John Morrell & Co.; *U.S. Public*, pg. 1479

NATHAN'S FAMOUS—Hot Dog Restaurants—Nathan's Famous Inc.; *U.S. Public*, pg. 1152

NATION'S BUSINESS—Magazine—Nation's Business; *U.S. Private*, pg. 788

NATIONAL—Blank Books—Dennison Stationery Products Company; *U.S. Public*, pg. 153

NATIONAL—Sealing devices—Federal-Mogul Corporation; *U.S. Public*, pg. 615

NATIONAL—Office Furniture—Kimball International, Inc.; *U.S. Public*, pg. 956

NATIONAL—Electric & Electronic Prods.—Matsushita Electric Industrial Co., Ltd.; *Int'l*, pg. 846

NATIONAL—Electrical Products—Matsushita Electric Works, Ltd.; *Int'l*, pg. 847

NATIONAL—Bread & Buns—Metz Baking Company; *U.S. Private*, pg. 1022

NATIONAL—Bread, Buns—Metz Baking Company (WI); *U.S. Private*, pg. 1022

NATIONAL—Textbooks—NTC/Contemporary Publishing Group; *U.S. Public*, pg. 1635

NATIONAL—Arrowroot Biscuits—Nabisco Inc.; *U.S. Public*, pg. 1355

NATIONAL—Poultry Bands—National Band & Tag Co.; *U.S. Private*, pg. 780

NATIONAL—Live Stock & Meat—National Cattlemen's Beef Association; *U.S. Private*, pg. 780

NATIONAL ACME—NONE—DeVlieg-Bullard Inc.; *U.S. Public*, pg. 502

THE NATIONAL ANTHEM—Electronics—National Semiconductor Corporation; *U.S. Public*, pg. 1159

NATIONAL ARROW-ROOT—Biscuits—RJR Nabisco Holdings Corp.; *U.S. Public*, pg. 1354

NATIONAL BANK BOND—Bond Paper—Georgia-Pacific Corporation; *U.S. Public*, pg. 735

NATIONAL BARREL HORSE ASSN.—Association—Shivers Trading & Operating Co.; *U.S. Private*, pg. 994

NATIONAL BENEFIT—Insurance—Travelers Group; *U.S. Public*, pg. 1632

NATIONAL BRANDS—Foods-Non Foods—Alliant Foodservice; *U.S. Private*, pg. 244

NATIONAL BUSINESS EMPLOYMENT WEEKLY—Weekly Publication—Dow Jones & Company, Inc.; *U.S. Public*, pg. 524

NATIONAL BUSINESS SYSTEMS—Credit Card & Credit Related Services—NBS Technologies, Inc.; *Int'l*, pg. 898

NATIONAL CAR RENTAL—Car Rental—National Car Rental System, Inc.; *U.S. Public*, pg. 1379

NATIONAL CHAMPION—Dairy Prods.—Land O'Lakes, Inc.; *U.S. Private*, pg. 646

NATIONAL CHAMPIONSHIP OF SLOTS—NONE—Harrah's Entertainment, Inc.; *U.S. Public*, pg. 790

NATIONAL DATA—Computer Service—National Data Corporation; *U.S. Public*, pg. 1155

NATIONAL DELI—Meat Products—National Foods Inc.; *U.S. Public*, pg. 429

NATIONAL DEPOSIT LIFE—Insurance Company—Protective Life Corporation; *U.S. Public*, pg. 1336

NATIONAL ELECTRICAL CODE—Fire Prevention—National Fire Protection Association; *U.S. Private*, pg. 782

NATIONAL ELECTRONICS—Electronics—Richardson Electronics, Ltd.; *U.S. Public*, pg. 1387

NATIONAL ENQUIRER—Newspaper—American Media, Inc.; *U.S. Public*, pg. 87

NATIONAL FILM THEATRE—Cinemas—British Film Institute; *Int'l*, pg. 219

NATIONAL FIRE CODES—Fire Prevention—National Fire Protection Association; *U.S. Private*, pg. 782

NATIONAL FIRE HOSE—Fire Hose—Snap-Tite, Inc.; *U.S. Private*, pg. 1010

NATIONAL FLOOD CHECK—Insurance Service—Weyerhaeuser Company; *U.S. Public*, pg. 1764

NATIONAL FOOTBALL LEAGUE—Men's Apparel—Garan, Incorporated; *U.S. Public*, pg. 703

NATIONAL GEOGRAPHIC—Magazine—National Geographic Society; *U.S. Private*, pg. 783

NATIONAL GOLD—Tin Surface Treatment—National Twist Drill Div.; *U.S. Public*, pg. 1370

NATIONAL GOLD—Tin Surface Treatment—Regal-Beloit Corporation; *U.S. Public*, pg. 1370

NATIONAL HOG FARMER—Publication on Hog Industry—Intertec Publishing; *U.S. Public*, pg. 1327

NATIONAL JEWELER—Magazine—Miller Freeman Inc.; *Int'l*, pg. 1443

NATIONAL LABORATORIES—Professional Product Line—Eastman Kodak Company; *U.S. Public*, pg. 550

THE NATIONAL LAW JOURNAL—NONE—New York Law Journal; *Int'l*, pg. 956

NATIONAL LIFE OF VERMONT—Insurance Company—National Life Insurance Company; *U.S. Private*, pg. 785

NATIONAL LINEN SVC.—Linen Supply—National Service Industries, Inc.; *U.S. Public*, pg. 1160

NATIONAL MAGAZINE CO., LTD.—Magazines—The Hearst Corporation; *U.S. Private*, pg. 515

NATIONAL MORTGAGE MARKET DATABASE—Software—CACI International Inc; *U.S. Public*, pg. 272

NATIONAL PRETZELS—NONE—Anderson Bakery Co., Inc.; *U.S. Private*, pg. 65

NATIONAL REAL ESTATE INVESTOR—Commercial Real Estate Magazine—Intertec Publishing; *U.S. Public*, pg. 1327

NATIONAL REAL ESTATE INVESTOR (NREI)—Monthly Publication—Intertec Publishing; *U.S. Public*, pg. 1328

NATIONAL REAL ESTATE INVESTOR SOURCEBOOK DIRECTORY—Annual Publication—Intertec Publishing; *U.S. Public*, pg. 1328

NATIONAL SHOWCASE—NONE—Market Facts, Inc.; *U.S. Public*, pg. 1046

NATIONAL TELEPHONE CENTER—NONE—Market Facts, Inc.; *U.S. Public*, pg. 1046

NATIONAL TILDEN/INTERRENT—Car Rental Marketing Umbrellas—National Car Rental System, Inc.; *U.S. Public*, pg. 1379

NATIONAL TWIST DRILL—Metal Cutting Tools—National Twist Drill Div.; *U.S. Public*, pg. 1370

NATIONAL VAN LINES—Household Goods Carrier—National Van Lines, Inc.; *U.S. Private*, pg. 788

NATIONAL WAX—Coatings—Burmah Castrol plc; *Int'l*, pg. 234

NATIONAL/INTERRENT—Car Rental Marketing Umbrellas—National Car Rental System, Inc.; *U.S. Public*, pg. 1379

NATIONALE—Fresh Yeast—Royal Gist-Brocades N.V.; *Int'l*, pg. 1142

NATIONALEASE—Truck Leasing System—National Truck Leasing System; *U.S. Private*, pg. 787

NATIONWIDE—Homes—Nationwide Homes, Inc.; *U.S. Private*, pg. 788

NATIONWIDE—Insurance Holding Co.—Nationwide Mutual Insurance Co.; *U.S. Private*, pg. 789

NATIONWIDE MUTUAL INSURANCE—Insurance Services—Nationwide Insurance Enterprise; *U.S. Private*, pg. 788

NATIVA—Infant Foods & Dietetic Products—Nestle S.A.; *Int'l*, pg. 915

NATRECOR BNP—NONE—Scios Inc.; *U.S. Public*, pg. 1444

NATRENE—Sweetener—Bayer AG; *Int'l*, pg. 171

NATRETS—Caustic Soda—Akzo Nobel N.V.; *Int'l*, pg. 42

NATROSOL—Hydroxyethylcellulose—Hercules Incorporated; *U.S. Public*, pg. 809

NATROSOL FPS—Water-Soluble Polymer Suspension—Hercules Incorporated; *U.S. Public*, pg. 809

NATSYN—Polyisoprene Rubber—The Goodyear Tire & Rubber Company; *U.S. Public*, pg. 752

NATUAL—Cholesterol Extracted Butter & Cheese—Entremont S.A.; *Int'l*, pg. 458

NATUPHOS—Phosphorusless Phosphorus Source to Spare the Environment—Royal Gist-Brocades N.V.; *Int'l*, pg. 1142

NATUPINK—Yeast-Based Natural Pigment for Salmon, Trout & Shrimp—Royal Gist-Brocades N.V.; *Int'l*, pg. 1142

NATUR—Soil Release/Absorbant Finish—Guilford Mills, Inc.; *U.S. Public*, pg. 768

NATUR PLUS—Polyester Fabric—Guilford Mills, Inc.; *U.S. Public*, pg. 768

NATURA—Craft Kits—Caron International; *U.S. Private*, pg. 786

NATURA—Organic Beef—Coop Switzerland; *Int'l*, pg. 329

NATURA—Glazed Floor Tile—Florida Tile Industries, Inc.; *U.S. Public*, pg. 1322

NATURA—Yarn—National Spinning Co., Inc.; *U.S. Private*, pg. 786

NATURA—Fruit Juice—Nestle S.A.; *Int'l*, pg. 915

NATURA—Paints—Sime Darby Berhad; *Int'l*, pg. 1249

NATURAL—4th Generation Language—Software AG; *Int'l*, pg. 1276

NATURAL ENERGY-PERM—NONE—Goldwell Cosmetics (USA) Inc.; *Int'l*, pg. 718

NATURAL ESTERS AND ALCOHOLS—NONE—Haltermann AG; *Int'l*, pg. 590

NATURAL HISTORY PRESS—Book Imprint—Bertelsmann AG; *Int'l*, pg. 189

NATURAL HONEY—Hair Curling Lotion & Neutralizer—Revlon-Realistic Professional Products, Inc.; *U.S. Private*, pg. 690

NATURAL IMPRESSIONS—Personal Care Products—Shaklee Corporation; *Int'l*, pg. 1518

NATURAL ISSUE—NONE—Supreme International Corp.; *U.S. Public*, pg. 1542

NATURAL LIGHT—Beer—Anheuser-Busch Companies, Inc.; *U.S. Public*, pg. 113

NATURAL PILSNER—Beer—Anheuser-Busch Companies, Inc.; *U.S. Public*, pg. 113

THE NATURAL RESOURCE—Natural Colors—Warner-Jenkinson Co.; *U.S. Public*, pg. 1696

NATURAL RESOURCE—NONE—Alliant Foodservice, Inc.; *U.S. Private*, pg. 244

NATURAL RESOURCES—Boys & Young Men's Jeans & Pants—Master Industries Corp.; *U.S. Private*, pg. 713

NATURAL SELECT—Dairy Products—Alta-Dena Certified Dairy; *Int'l*, pg. 201

NATURAL SELECT ORGANICS—Organic Dairy Products—Alta-Dena Certified Dairy; *Int'l*, pg. 201

NATURAL SMOOTHIE—Foundations—The Strouse, Adler Company; *U.S. Private*, pg. 1047

NATURAL SPRINGS—Bottled Water—Beverage Canners International Corp.; *U.S. Private*, pg. 106

NATURAL SUN—Citrus Products—Internut; *U.S. Private*, pg. 915

NATURAL TOUCH—NONE—Worthington Foods Inc.; *U.S. Public*, pg. 1780

NATURAL TOUCH/ELEGANCE COLORED LENSES—NONE—Pilkington Barnes Hind (PBH); *U.S. Private*, pg. 111

NATURALAMB—Male Contraceptive—Carter-Wallace, Inc.; *U.S. Public*, pg. 309

NATURALIZER—Shoe Stores—Brown Group, Inc.; *U.S. Public*, pg. 262

NATURALIZER—Shoes—Brown Group, Inc.; *U.S. Public*, pg. 262

NATURALIZER—Shoes—Brown Shoe Company; *U.S. Public*, pg. 262

NATURALIZER—Shoes—Brown Shoe Co. of Canada Ltd.; *U.S. Public*, pg. 262

NATURALLY BLONDE—Shampoo-In-Toner Kit & Quick Lightener Kit—Clairol, Inc.; *U.S. Public*, pg. 254

NATURALLY GOOD—Frozen Fruit—Curtice Burns Foods; *U.S. Private*, pg. 887

NATURALLY NORTHWEST—NONE—Pacific Foods, Inc.; *U.S. Private*, pg. 831

NATURALLY UNTAMED—Themed Merchandise—Ogden Corporation; *U.S. Public*, pg. 1213

NATURALLY YOURS—No Fat Sour Cream—The Morning Star Group; *U.S. Public*, pg. 1527

THE NATURALS BY COMARE—NONE—Comare Products; *U.S. Public*, pg. 1771

NATURALSPORT—Shoes—Brown Group, Inc.; *U.S. Public*, pg. 262

NATURALSPORT—Shoe—Brown Shoe Company; *U.S. Public*, pg. 262

NATURALWEAR—Breast Forms & Other Masectomy Prods.—Camp Healthcare; *Int'l*, pg. 1425

NATURALYTE—Bicarbonate Concentrate For Single Patient Systems—Fresenius Medical Care (North America); *Int'l*, pg. 505

NATURE BRIGHT—Household/Laundry Brightener—Shaklee Corporation; *Int'l*, pg. 1518

NATURE GLO HICKORY WOOD SMOKING CHIPS—Premium Barbecue Smoking Chips—Hickory Specialties, Inc.; *U.S. Public*, pg. 596

NATURE GLO JACK DANIEL BARREL CHIPS—Premium Barbecue Smoking Chips—Hickory Specialties, Inc.; *U.S. Public*, pg. 596

NATURE GLO MESQUITE 50—Premium Charcoal Briquets & Mesquite Wood Briquet—Hickory Specialties, Inc.; *U.S. Public*, pg. 596

NATURE GLO MESQUITE WOOD SMOKING CHIPS—Premium Barbecue Smoking Chips—Hickory Specialties, Inc.; *U.S. Public*, pg. 596

NATURE GUARD—Cellulose Insulation—Louisiana Pacific Corporation; *U.S. Public*, pg. 1015

NATURE MADE—Vitamin Supplements—Otsuka Pharmaceutical Co., Ltd.; *Int'l*, pg. 1013

NATURE MADE—Vitamins & Food Supplements—Pharmavite Corp.; *U.S. Private*, pg. 860

NATURE PLUS—NONE—Porcelanite, Inc.; *Int'l*, pg. 573

NATURE'S BEST—Vitamins & Minerals—Novo Nordisk A/S; *Int'l*, pg. 987

NATURE SAVER—Office Products—Genuine Parts Company; *U.S. Public*, pg. 732

NATURE SCENT—Organic Fan Freshener—Surco Products, Inc.; *U.S. Private*, pg. 1056

NATURE SEAL—NONE—EcoScience Corporation; *U.S. Public*, pg. 563

NATURE SHOWER—Personal Care Products—Amway Corporation; *U.S. Private*, pg. 69

NATURE TONES—Natural Flavorings—Kerry Group PLC; *Int'l*, pg. 731

NATURE VALLEY GRANOLA—Cereal—General Mills, Inc.; *U.S. Public*, pg. 717

NATURE VALLEY GRANOLA BARS—Snacks—General Mills, Inc.; *U.S. Public*, pg. 717

NATURE VALLEY GRANOLA BARS—NONE—Snacks Unlimited Division; *U.S. Public*, pg. 718

NATURE'S ACCENTS BODY SCRUBS—NONE—The Dial Corporation; *U.S. Public*, pg. 505

NATURE'S ACCENTS BODY WASHES—NONE—The Dial Corporation; *U.S. Public*, pg. 505

NATURE'S ACCENTS BUBBLE BATHS—NONE—The Dial Corporation; *U.S. Public*, pg. 505

NATURE'S ACCENTS CANDLES—NONE—The Dial Corporation; *U.S. Public*, pg. 505

NATURE'S ACCENTS GLYCERIN BAR SOAPS—NONE—The Dial Corporation; *U.S. Public*, pg. 505

NATURE'S ACCENTS LOTIONS—NONE—The Dial Corporation; *U.S. Public*, pg. 505

NATUREGARD—Planting Seeds—Mycogen Corporation; *U.S. Public*, pg. 1142

NATUREGARD—Planting Seeds—Mycogen Seeds; *U.S. Public*, pg. 1142

NATURELLA—Candies—Ferrero U.S.A., Inc.; *Int'l*, pg. 480

NATURE'S BOUNTY—Natural Vitamins & Cosmetics—Nature's Bounty Inc.; *U.S. Public*, pg. 1166

NATURE'S COURSE—Pet Food—Ralston Purina Company; *U.S. Public*, pg. 1359

NATURES FAMILY—Natural Skin Care Products—Dep Corporation; *U.S. Public*, pg. 500

NATURE'S FLAVORS—Soft Drink—R.J. Corr Naturals, Inc.; *U.S. Private*, pg. 276

NATURE'S GATE—Cosmetics—Levlad, Inc.; *U.S. Private*, pg. 663

NATURES HARVEST—Bread—Metz Baking Company; *U.S. Private*, pg. 1022

NATURES HARVEST—Bread—Metz Baking Company (WI); *U.S. Private*, pg. 1022

NATURES OWN—Apple Juice—Brooklyn Bottling Co. of Milton, NY; *U.S. Private*, pg. 171

NATURE'S OWN—Bread & Rolls—Flowers Industries, Inc.; *U.S. Public*, pg. 656

NATURE'S PORTRAITS—Greeting Cards—American Greetings Corporation; *U.S. Public*, pg. 77

NATURE'S RECIPE—NONE—Star-Kist Foods Inc.; *U.S. Public*, pg. 805

NATURE'S SEAL—Waterless Cookware—Nature's Sunshine Products, Inc.; *U.S. Public*, pg. 1166

NATURE'S SEASONS—Salt—Morton Salt; *U.S. Public*, pg. 1135

NATURE'S SUNSHINE—Health Products—Nature's Sunshine Products, Inc.; *U.S. Public*, pg. 1166

NATURESQU—NONE—Avon Products Co., Ltd.; *U.S. Public*, pg. 156

NATUSAN—NONE—Johnson & Johnson; *U.S. Public*, pg. 927

NATUVIT—Fiber Products—Novo Nordisk A/S; *Int'l*, pg. 987

NAUGAFORM—Thermoformable Coated Fabric—Uniroyal Technology Corporation; *U.S. Public*, pg. 1670

NAUGALUBE—Petroleum Additive—Uniroyal Chemical Company, Inc.; *U.S. Public*, pg. 460

NAUGARD—Antioxidant & Polymerization Inhibitors—Uniroyal Chemical Company, Inc.; *U.S. Public*, pg. 460

NAUGHTY NELLIES—Greeting Cards—American Greetings Corporation; *U.S. Public*, pg. 77

NAUTA—NONE—Hosokawa Micron Powder Systems; *Int'l*, pg. 636

NAUTIC LIGHT—Beer—UNICER-Uniao Cervejeira, S.A.; *Int'l*, pg. 1432

NAUTICA—NONE—Genesco Inc.; *U.S. Public*, pg. 728

NAUTICA—Men's Suits—Oxford Industries, Inc.; *U.S. Public*, pg. 1239

NAUTICA WATCHES—Licensee—Timex Corporation; *U.S. Private*, pg. 1088

NAUTILUS—Range Hoods, Ventilating Fans, Bathroom Heaters, Bathroom Cabinets—Broan Mfg. Co., Inc.; *U.S. Public*, pg. 1193

NAUTILUS—Sports Gum—Clark Gum Company; *U.S. Private*, pg. 243

NAUTILUS—Physical Fitness Equipment—Delta Woodside Industries, Inc.; *U.S. Public*, pg. 497

NAUTILUS—Sports-Drink—Dr. Pepper Co.; *Int'l*, pg. 248

NAUTILUS—Swimming Pool Accessories—Essef Corporation; *U.S. Public*, pg. 592

NAUTILUS—Exercise Machines & Video Tapes—Nautilus International; *U.S. Public*, pg. 498

NAUTIQUE EXCEL—Power Boat—Correct Craft, Inc.; *U.S. Private*, pg. 276

NAUTIQUE EXCEL OPEN BOW—Power Boat—Correct Craft, Inc.; *U.S. Private*, pg. 276

NAUTIQUE SUPERSPORT—Power Boat—Correct Craft, Inc.; *U.S. Private*, pg. 276

NAUZELIN—Gastrointestinal Agent—Kyowa Hakko Kogyo Company, Ltd.; *Int'l*, pg. 778

NAVAJO—Polymer R.V. Pickup Caps—Gem Top Mfg., Inc.; *U.S. Private*, pg. 443

NAVAJO—Automobile—Mazda Motor of America, Inc.; *Int'l*, pg. 849

NAVAL—Flush Valves—Sloan Valve Company; *U.S. Private*, pg. 1006

NAVAL WAR—War Game—Monarch Avalon, Inc.; *U.S. Public*, pg. 1123

NAVANE—Thiothixene—Pfizer Inc.; *U.S. Public*, pg. 1281

NAVCARD LP—GPS Mobile Computing Products—Rockwell International Corporation; *U.S. Public*, pg. 1397

NAVCORE—Satellite Navigation & Positioning Equipment—Rockwell International Corporation; *U.S. Public*, pg. 1397

NAVCORE V—Global Positioning System Receiver Engine—Rockwell International Corporation; *U.S. Public*, pg. 1397

NAVI-DRILL—Downhole Motor—Baker Hughes INTEQ; *U.S. Public*, pg. 166

NAVI-TRAK—MWD—Baker Hughes INTEQ; *U.S. Public*, pg. 166

NAVICOMP—Nautical & Navigational Instruments—Litton Industries, Inc.; *U.S. Public*, pg. 1002

NAVIGAT—Nautical & Navigational Instruments—Litton Industries, Inc.; *U.S. Public*, pg. 1002

NAVIGATION BY BOATWORKS—Sports Outerwear—Fox-Knapp; *U.S. Private*, pg. 860

NAVIGATOR—Guidance Systems—Automatic Equipment Mfg. Co.; *U.S. Private*, pg. 101

NAVIGATOR—NONE—Automation Control; *Int'l*, pg. 1389

NAVIGATOR—Neuro-Diagnostic Instrumentation—Bio-Logic Systems Corp.; *U.S. Public*, pg. 230

NAVIGATOR—Recreation Vehicle—Holiday Rambler; *U.S. Public*, pg. 1123

NAVIGATOR 600—Tire—The Kelly-Springfield Tire Company; *U.S. Public*, pg. 753

NAVIGLOBE—Wire Data Recievers—Litton Industries, Inc.; *U.S. Public*, pg. 1002

NAVISTAR—Sextants—Litton Industries, Inc.; *U.S. Public*, pg. 1002

NAVOBAN—Antiemetic—Novartis AG; *Int'l*, pg. 971

NAVY—Perfume—Cover Girl Cosmetics; *U.S. Public*, pg. 1330

NAVY—Fragrance—The Procter & Gamble Company; *U.S. Public*, pg. 1330

NAVY SWEET—Dry Snuff—Swisher International Group, Inc.; *U.S. Private*, pg. 1543

NAXCEL—Antibiotic—Pharmacia & Upjohn; *Int'l*, pg. 1048

NAYA SPRING WATER—Bottled Water—Grant-Lydick Beverage Co.; *U.S. Private*, pg. 470

NAZARETH BOOKS—Book Imprint—Bertelsmann AG; *Int'l*, pg. 189

NAZDAR—Screen Printing Inks—Burmah Castrol plc; *Int'l*, pg. 234

NCR BLACK PRINT—Standard Grade Multipart Carbonless Stock Computer Paper—Shade/Allied, Inc.; *U.S. Public*, pg. 89

NEAPCO—Constant Velocity Joints—Neapco, Inc.; *U.S. Private*, pg. 1113

NEAR EAST—Flavored Rice & Grain Mixes—Golden Grain Company; *U.S. Public*, pg. 1348

NEAR PERFECT—Pajamas—Lands' End, Inc.; *U.S. Public*, pg. 977

NEARLYWED PARTY—NONE—Welcome Wagon-Intl., Inc.; *U.S. Public*, pg. 321

NEARNET—NONE—GTE Internetworking; *U.S. Public*, pg. 696

NEAT GARDS—Disposable Plastic Aprons—Handgards Inc.; *U.S. Private*, pg. 499

NEAT N' EASY WINDOW GARDEN—Garden Products—Jiffy Products of America, Inc.; *Int'l*, pg. 706

NEAT SHEET—Notebooks—The Mead Corporation; *U.S. Public*, pg. 1074

NEATBOOK—Stationary Products, Notebooks—The Mead Corporation; *U.S. Public*, pg. 1074

NEATFORM—Paper Napkins—Georgia-Pacific Corporation; *U.S. Public*, pg. 735

NEBAR—Jointing—James Walker & Co. Limited; *Int'l*, pg. 1485

NEBCIN—Tobramycin Sulfate, Lilly—Eli Lilly and Company; *U.S. Public*, pg. 992

NEBRASKA BEEF—Boxed Beef—BeefAmerica Operating Co., Inc.; *U.S. Private*, pg. 130

NEBRASKA BOXED BEEF—Boxed Beef—BeefAmerica Operating Co., Inc.; *U.S. Private*, pg. 130

NEBRASKA FARMER—Monthly Farm Publication—Farm Progress Publications; *U.S. Public*, pg. 513

NEBRASKA MANUFACTURERS REGISTER—Register—Manufacturers' News, Inc.; *U.S. Private*, pg. 700

NECCO—Candy Buttons & Wafers—New England Confectionery Co.; *U.S. Private*, pg. 1113

NECTARA—NONE—Metaxa Distilleries; *Int'l*, pg. 410

NED DAY GRIP—Sporting Goods—Brunswick Bowling & Billiards Corp.; *U.S. Public*, pg. 265

NEDAL—Architectural Product—Hunter Douglas N.V.; *Int'l*, pg. 639

NEDOX—Synergistic Coating Process—General Magnaplate Corporation; *U.S. Public*, pg. 717

NEEDLELESS ACCESS—Pharmaceutical Container Closures—The West Company, Incorporated; *U.S. Public*, pg. 1755

NEEDLEMASTER—Kit Containing Differnt Size Knitting Needles—Wm. E. Wright Limited Partnership; *U.S. Private*, pg. 1192

NEENAH—Paper—Kimberly-Clark Corporation; *U.S. Public*, pg. 958

NEENAH—Construction & Industrial Castings—Neenah Foundry Company; *U.S. Private*, pg. 790

NEET—Manual Warewashing Product—Ecolab Inc.; *U.S. Public*, pg. 562

NEET—Hair Remover—Premier, Inc.; *U.S. Private*, pg. 647

NEET—Hair Removing Creme—Reckitt & Colman Inc.; *Int'l*, pg. 1090

NEET—Depilatories—Reckitt & Colman plc; *Int'l*, pg. 1089

NEF DELTA 124—Low Energy, Pre-Fabricated Housing—Hochtief AG; *Int'l*, pg. 623

NEFF—NONE—Neff (UK) Limited; *Int'l*, pg. 912

NEFFICIENCY—NONE—Neff (UK) Limited; *Int'l*, pg. 912

NEG'ATOR—Constant Force Spring—AMETEK, Inc.; *U.S. Public*, pg. 99

NEGI—NONE—Mizuno Corporation; *Int'l*, pg. 884

NEGRA MODELO—Mexican Beer—Barton Beers, Ltd.; *U.S. Public*, pg. 300

NEHI—Soft Drink—Triarc Companies, Inc.; *U.S. Public*, pg. 1634

NEIGHBORHOOD MAILBOX VALUES—Shared Advertising Mail Packets—ADVO, Inc.; *U.S. Public*, pg. 23

NEIGHBORHOOD THEATRES—Motion Picture Theaters—Cineplex Odeon Corporation; *Int'l*, pg. 292

NEIL FABER MEDIA—Marketing & Media Consulting—Neil Faber Media Inc.; *U.S. Private*, pg. 390

NEIL MARTIN—NONE—Tandy Brands Accessories, Inc.; *U.S. Public*, pg. 1560

NEILSON—Dairy Confection—George Weston Limited; *Int'l*, pg. 1494

NEJICON—Deformed Steel Bars—Kobe Steel, Ltd.; *Int'l*, pg. 740

NEK-SEAM—Composite Cans With Tapered Ends—Sonoco Products Company; *U.S. Public*, pg. 1485

NEKAL—Alkyl Naphtalene Sulphonate—BASF AG; *Int'l*, pg. 103

NEKOOSA—Papers—Georgia-Pacific Corporation; *U.S. Public*, pg. 735

NEKOOSA COMMUNICATION PAPERS—Bond, Duplicator, Ledger, Offset & Manifold—Georgia-Pacific Corporation; *U.S. Public*, pg. 735

NEKOOSA LASER 1000—Paper for Copying, Printing & Duplicating—Georgia-Pacific Corporation; *U.S. Public*, pg. 735

NEKOOSA 90—Bleached Kraft Wood Pulp—Georgia-Pacific Corporation; *U.S. Public*, pg. 735

NEKOOSA PAPERS & DESIGN—Bond, Ledger, Mimeo & Duplicating Paper—Georgia-Pacific Corporation; *U.S. Public*, pg. 735

NEKOOSA WOOD WIND—Offset, Offset Cover, Text & Cover Papers—Georgia-Pacific Corporation; *U.S. Public*, pg. 735

NELCON—Heating Cable—O-Z/Gedney, Nelson Firestop Products; *U.S. Public*, pg. 726

NELDISC—Butterfly Valve—Neles-Jamesburv Corp.; *Int'l*, pg. 1428

NELEX—Heating Cable—O-Z/Gedney, Nelson Firestop Products; *U.S. Public*, pg. 726

NELIA—Fresh Pasta—Borden, Inc.; *U.S. Private*, pg. 157

NELLCOR—NONE—Nellcor Puritan Bennett Incorporated; *U.S. Public*, pg. 1039

NELLCOR N-1500—Anesthetic Agent Analyzer—Nellcor Puritan Bennett Incorporated; *U.S. Public*, pg. 1039

NELLCOR N-40—HandheldPulse Oximeter—Nellcor Puritan Bennett Incorporated; *U.S. Public*, pg. 1039

NELLCOR N-400—Fetal Oximeter—Nellcor Puritan Bennett Incorporated; *U.S. Public*, pg. 1039

NELLCOR N-100—Pulse Oximeter—Nellcor Puritan Bennett Incorporated; *U.S. Public*, pg. 1039

NELLCOR N-180—Pulse Oximeter—Nellcor Puritan Bennett Incorporated; *U.S. Public*, pg. 1039

NELLCOR N-1000—Multi-Function Monitor—Nellcor Puritan Bennett Incorporated; *U.S. Public*, pg. 1039

NELLCOR N-75—Handheld Capnograph/Pulse Oximeter—Nellcor Puritan Bennett Incorporated; *U.S. Public*, pg. 1039

NELLCOR N-10—Pulse Oximeter—Nellcor Puritan Bennett Incorporated; *U.S. Public*, pg. 1039

NELLCOR N-30—Pocket-size Pulse Oximeter—Nellcor Puritan Bennett Incorporated; *U.S. Public*, pg. 1039

NELLCOR N-20—Portable Handheld Oximeter—Nellcor Puritan Bennett Incorporated; *U.S. Public*, pg. 1039

NELLCOR N-2500—Anesthesia Safety Monitor—Nellcor Puritan Bennett Incorporated; *U.S. Public*, pg. 1039

NELLCOR N-200—Pulse Oximeter—Nellcor Puritan Bennett Incorporated; *U.S. Public*, pg. 1039

NELLCOR PURITAN BENNETT—NONE—Nellcor Puritan Bennett Incorporated; *U.S. Public*, pg. 1039

NELLCOR SYMPHONY N-3000—Pulse Oximeter with Oxismart & Alarm Management Technology—Nellcor Puritan Bennett Incorporated; *U.S. Public*, pg. 1039

NELLCOR SYMPHONY N-3100—Noninvasive Blood Pressure Monitor—Nellcor Puritan Bennett Incorporated; *U.S. Public*, pg. 1039

NELOVA—Oral Contraceptives—Warner-Chilcott Laboratories, Inc.; *Int'l*, pg. 436

NELPON—Herbicide—The Dow Chemical Company; *U.S. Public*, pg. 522

NELSCOPE—Diagnostic Device—Neles-Jamesbury Corp.; *Int'l*, pg. 1428

NELSON CLK—Fire Stop Caulk—O-Z/Gedney, Nelson Firestop Products; *U.S. Public*, pg. 726

NELSON CMP—Fire Stop Compound—O-Z/Gedney, Nelson Firestop Products; *U.S. Public*, pg. 726

NELSON CTG—Firestop Coating—O-Z/Gedney, Nelson Firestop Products; *U.S. Public*, pg. 726

NELSON PCS—Pipe Choke System—O-Z/Gedney, Nelson Firestop Products; *U.S. Public*, pg. 726

NELSON PLW—Fire Stop Pillows—O-Z/Gedney, Nelson Firestop Products; *U.S. Public*, pg. 726

NELSON'S—Investment Managemnt Information—Primedia Inc.; *U.S. Public*, pg. 1327

NELTAPE—Pressure-sensitive Adhesive Tapes & Films-Graphic Arts & Electrical—Dielectric Polymers, Inc.; *U.S. Public*, pg. 1258

NELVEK—Herbicide—The Dow Chemical Company; *U.S. Public*, pg. 522

NEMA—Electrical Enclosures—Crenlo, Inc.; *U.S. Private*, pg. 288

NEMATRON—Industrial Computer—Nematron Corp.; *U.S. Private*, pg. 791

NEMEF—Hardware—The Black & Decker Corporation; *U.S. Public*, pg. 233

NEMEX—Pyrantel Pamoate—Pfizer Inc.; *U.S. Public*, pg. 1281

NEMIC-LAMBDA—NONE—Nemic-Lambda KK; *Int'l*, pg. 1242

NEMO—Progressing Cavity Pumps—Netzsch Incorporated; *U.S. Private*, pg. 792

NEMONIX PLUS—Ordering Capability—Cerner Corporation; *U.S. Public*, pg. 331

NEMSCHOFF—Furniture—Nemschoff Chairs, Inc.; *U.S. Private*, pg. 791

NENUCO—Baby Care Products—Reckitt & Colman plc; *Int'l*, pg. 1089

NEO-CALCLUCON—Syrup for Dietary Supplement Where Calcium Deficiency Exists—Sandoz Pharmaceuticals Corp.; *Int'l*, pg. 974

NEO-FAT—Fatty Acid—Akzo Nobel N.V.; *Int'l*, pg. 42

NEO-GILURYTMAL—Cardiovascular Preparations—Kali-Chemie Aktiengesellschaft; *Int'l*, pg. 1278

NEO-PRO—Enzyme Hydrolyzed Fish Digest—DuCoa L.P.; *U.S. Private*, pg. 301

NEO RES—Polyurethane Resin Dispersions—ICI Polyurethanes Group; *Int'l*, pg. 664

NEO-TERRAMYCIN—Oxytetracycline Neomycin—Pfizer Inc.; *U.S. Public*, pg. 1281

NEO-VISION—TV Picture Tubes—Thomson Consumer Electronics Inc.; *Int'l*, pg. 1383

NEO-X—Mechanical Pencil Lead—The Pilot Pen Corp. of America; *Int'l*, pg. 1057

NEOAV DISPLAYS—Active Matrix Liquid Crystal Displays for Jet Aircraft—Rogerson Aircraft Corporation; *U.S. Private*, pg. 940

NEOBEE—Organic Chemicals—Stepan Company; *U.S. Public*, pg. 1514

NEOBOR—5 Mol Borax—U.S. Borax Inc.; *Int'l*, pg. 1119

NEOCID—Pest Control—Reckitt & Colman plc; *Int'l*, pg. 1089

NEOCITRAN—Pharmaceutical—Novartis AG; *Int'l*, pg. 971

NEOCLASSIC—Designer Chair Line—Harter; *U.S. Private*, pg. 581

NEOCRYL—Acrylic Resins & Emulsions—ICI Polyurethanes Group; *Int'l*, pg. 664

NEOFAB—NONE—Flexfab Horizons International, Inc.; *U.S. Private*, pg. 412

NEOFLEX—Ducting—HBD Industries, Inc.; *U.S. Private*, pg. 489

NEOGAM—Treatment for Staph A & Epi Infections—Nabi; *U.S. Public*, pg. 1148

NEOGEL—Unsaturated Styrenized Polyester Resins—DSM N.V.; *Int'l*, pg. 352

NEOHELIOPAN—Sunscreen—Haarmann & Reimer Corp.; *Int'l*, pg. 173

NEOLAMIN—Vitamin Preparation—Nippon Kayaku Co. Ltd.; *Int'l*, pg. 934

NEOLITE—Shoe Prods.—The Goodyear Tire & Rubber Company; *U.S. Public*, pg. 752

NEOLOID—Castor Oil; Laxative—Bradley Pharmaceuticals; *U.S. Public*, pg. 249

NEOLOID—Castor Oil; Laxative—Doak Dermatologics; *U.S. Public*, pg. 250

NEOLUS—Hypodermic Needles—Terumo Medical Corporation; *Int'l*, pg. 1376

NEOLYN—Synthetic Resin—Hercules Incorporated; *U.S. Public*, pg. 809

NEON—Automobile—Chrysler Corporation; *U.S. Public*, pg. 352

NEON—Business Order & Inventory Status Services—Georgia-Pacific Corporation; *U.S. Public*, pg. 735

NEON—NONE—Kiwi Brands Pty. Ltd.; *U.S. Public*, pg. 1434

NEON BABY—Adjustable-Height Headrest Soft Carriet—Cosco, Inc.; *U.S. Private*, pg. 277

NEON BEACH TUBE BUBBLE GUM—Tube Bubble Gum—Amurol Confections Co.; *U.S. Public*, pg. 1781

NEON BUBBLE STRIPS—Bubble Gum—Amurol Confections Co.; *U.S. Public*, pg. 1781

NEON LITES—Roller Ball Pens—Sanford Corporation; *U.S. Public*, pg. 1178

NEON RED—Fluorescent Color—Day-Glo Color Corp.; *U.S. Public*, pg. 1357

NEONATAL "Y" TRACH CARE—Catheter—Ballard Medical Products; *U.S. Public*, pg. 171

NEONISIDINA—Analgetic—Boehringer Ingelheim Italia S.p.A.; *Int'l*, pg. 199

NEONS—Safety Eyewear—Aearo Company; *U.S. Private*, pg. 23

NEOPERIDOL—Central Nervous System Agents—Kyowa Hakko Kogyo Company, Ltd.; *Int'l*, pg. 778

NEOPHAN—Spectacle Lens Blanks—Deutsche Spezialglas AG; *Int'l*, pg. 1523

NEOPHOS—Automatic Dishwashing Detergent—Benckiser Consumer Products Inc.; *Int'l*, pg. 185

NEOPON—Alkyl Sulfate—Witco Corporation; *U.S. Public*, pg. 1773

NEOPYOPREN—Antibiotic—SmithKline Beecham plc; *Int'l*, pg. 1264

NEOSAN—Veterinary Specialties—SmithKline Beecham plc; *Int'l*, pg. 1264

NEOSCAN—Gallium Ga67 Citrate Tumor Imaging—Amersham Healthcare; *Int'l*, pg. 992

NEOSPORIN—Antibiotic—Glaxo Wellcome PLC; *Int'l*, pg. 553

NEOSPORIN—Topical Antibiotic—Warner-Lambert Consumer Healthcare; *U.S. Public*, pg. 1739

NEOSPORIN MAXIMUM STRENGTH—Antibiotic—Glaxo Wellcome PLC; *Int'l*, pg. 553

NEOTHERM—Furnace Observation Glass—Deutsche Spezialglas AG; *Int'l*, pg. 1523

NEOTIGASON—Dermatology Pharmaceutical—Roche Holding Ltd.; *Int'l*, pg. 1119

NEOXIL—Unsaturated Styrenized Resins—DSM N.V.; *Int'l*, pg. 352

NEPCO—Wrapping Paper—Georgia-Pacific Corporation; *U.S. Public*, pg. 735

NEPOREX—Insecticide—Novartis; *Int'l*, pg. 972

NEPTUNE—Bottled Water—Hinckley & Schmitt, Inc.; *Int'l*, pg. 1322

NEPTUNE—Electric Boat Motors, Power Equipment & Accessories—Johnson Worldwide Associates, Inc.; *U.S. Public*, pg. 932

NERA—Economic Consulting Services—Marsh & McLennan Companies, Inc.; *U.S. Public*, pg. 1048

NEREUS—Miniature Solenoid Valve—Humphrey Products Company; *U.S. Private*, pg. 547

NERF—Toys—Hasbro; *U.S. Public*, pg. 797

NERF—NONE—Hasbro, Inc.; *U.S. Public*, pg. 797

NERVAL—Cosmetics—Henkel KGaA; *Int'l*, pg. 609

NESA—Electrically Conductive Coated Glass—PPG Industries, Inc.; *U.S. Public*, pg. 1245

NESACAINE—Local Anesthetic—Astra AB; *Int'l*, pg. 93

NESACAINE—Pharmaceutical Products—Astra USA, Inc.; *Int'l*, pg. 93

NESATRON—Electrically Conductive Glass—PPG Industries, Inc.; *U.S. Public*, pg. 1245

NESBITT—HVAC Equipment—Mestek, Inc.; *U.S. Public*, pg. 1099

NESBITT'S—Soft Drink—The Monarch Company, Inc.; *U.S. Private*, pg. 756

NESCAFE—Instant Coffee—Nestle S.A.; *Int'l*, pg. 915

NESCAFE—Instant Coffee—Nestle USA; *Int'l*, pg. 916

NESCAFE CLASSICO—NONE—Nestle USA; *Int'l*, pg. 916

NESCAFE COFFEE CANS—Canned Coffee Beverages—Otsuka Pharmaceutical Co., Ltd.; *Int'l*, pg. 1013

NESCAFE MOUNTAIN BLEND—NONE—Nestle USA; *Int'l*, pg. 916

NESCAFE SUNRISE—NONE—Nestle USA; *Int'l*, pg. 916

NESCAO—Chocolate Drinks—Nestle S.A.; *Int'l*, pg. 915

NESCAU—Instant Chocolate Drink—Nestle S.A.; *Int'l*, pg. 915

NESCO—Electric Roaster/Ovens—The Metal Ware Corp.; *U.S. Private*, pg. 734

NESCO—Giftware—Stanhome Inc.; *U.S. Public*, pg. 1508

NESCORE—Instant Coffee—Nestle S.A.; *Int'l*, pg. 915

NESPRAY—Dairy Products—Nestle S.A.; *Int'l*, pg. 915

NESPRESSO—Instant Coffee—Nestle USA; *Int'l*, pg. 916

NESQUICK—Chocolate Drinks—Nestle S.A.; *Int'l*, pg. 915

NESSEN—Lighting—JJI Lighting Group Inc.; *Int'l*, pg. 821

NESTAFLEX—Portable Conveyors—AXIA Incorporated; *U.S. Private*, pg. 103

NESTAINER—Stackable Storage Racks—AXIA Incorporated; *U.S. Private*, pg. 103

NESTEA—NONE—The Coca-Cola Company; *U.S. Public*, pg. 392

NESTEA—Instant Tea—Nestle S.A.; *Int'l*, pg. 915

NESTEA—Tea—Nestle USA; *Int'l*, pg. 916

NESTEA HERITAGE—NONE—Nestle USA; *Int'l*, pg. 916

NESTEA ICE TEASERS—NONE—Nestle USA; *Int'l*, pg. 916

NESTEA ICED TEA—Iced Tea—The Coca-Cola Bottling Co. of New York, Inc.; *U.S. Public*, pg. 393

NESTEA NUEVO TEA—NONE—Nestle USA; *Int'l*, pg. 916

NESTEA SUNTEA—NONE—Nestle USA; *Int'l*, pg. 916

NESTIER—Plastic Containers for Shipping & Storage—Buckhorn Inc.; *U.S. Public*, pg. 1143

NESTIER—Plastic Containers—Myers Industries, Inc.; *U.S. Public*, pg. 1143

NESTLE—Milk Chocolate Bar—Nestle Chocolate & Confection; *Int'l*, pg. 917

NESTLE—Chocolate & Confectionery—Nestle S.A.; *Int'l*, pg. 915

NESTLE—NONE—Nestle USA; *Int'l*, pg. 916

NESTLE—Sasso Olive Oil & Berni Salad Dressing—Armando Testa S.p.A.; *Int'l*, pg. 1377

NESTLE-BEICH—Fund Raising Candies—Kathryn Beich, Inc.; *Int'l*, pg. 917

Brand Name Index

NESTLE CRUNCH—Milk Chocolate Bar with Crisped Rice—Nestle Chocolate & Confection; *Int'l*, pg. 917

NESTLE CRUNCH BARS—Ice Cream Bars—Nestle Ice Cream Co.; *Int'l*, pg. 918

NESTLE EUROPEAN STYLE HOT CHOCOLATE—Hot Chocolate—Nestle S.A.; *Int'l*, pg. 915

NESTLE FOODSERVICES—NONE—Nestle USA; *Int'l*, pg. 916

NESTLE FORMULA SERIES—Nestle's Products—Otsuka Pharmaceutical Co., Ltd.; *Int'l*, pg. 1013

NESTLE MORSELS—Flavored Candy Morsels for Baking—Nestle Chocolate & Confection; *Int'l*, pg. 917

NESTLE $100,000 BAR—Chocolate Bar—Nestle Chocolate & Confection; *Int'l*, pg. 917

NESTLE QUIK—Chocolate, Strawberry Milk Additive—Nestle Chocolate & Confection; *Int'l*, pg. 917

NESTLE SUPERIOR QUALITY—Milk Chocolate with Almonds Bar—Nestle Chocolate & Confection; *Int'l*, pg. 917

NESTLE SWEET SUCCESS—Powdered Diet Drinks—Nestle S.A.; *Int'l*, pg. 915

NESTLE TOLL HOUSE MORSELS—Chocolate Chips—Nestle Chocolate & Confection; *Int'l*, pg. 917

NESTUM—Infant Foods & Dietetic Products—Nestle S.A.; *Int'l*, pg. 915

NESTUM—NONE—Nestle USA; *Int'l*, pg. 916

NESTYLE—Containers—Sealright Company, Inc.; *U.S. Public*, pg. 1451

NET—NONE—Excite, Inc.; *U.S. Public*, pg. 599

NET/AVAIL—MVS Host-Based: Collects & Reports on Network Communications Activities—Boole & Babbage, Inc.; *U.S. Public*, pg. 244

NET/COMMAND—Powerful, User-Customizable Turnkey Operations & Fault Management System—Boole & Babbage, Inc.; *U.S. Public*, pg. 244

NET MARKET—NONE—CUC International, Inc.; *U.S. Public*, pg. 320

NET/ONE—Network Management System—Tandem Computers Inc.; *U.S. Public*, pg. 417

NET/ONE—Network System, Map/One, Access/One—UB Networks; *Int'l*, pg. 924

NET SECURE—Software—Exabyte Corporation; *U.S. Public*, pg. 597

NET 25—High Performance Packet Switching and Frame RElay Network Systems—Telematics Inc.; *Int'l*, pg. 643

NETA—Building Products—Email Limited; *Int'l*, pg. 450

NETADVICE—NONE—UB Networks; *Int'l*, pg. 924

NETARCHITECT—Trademark—Zitel Corporation; *U.S. Public*, pg. 1793

NETARRAY—NONE—Ciprico, Inc.; *U.S. Public*, pg. 370

NETASSISTANT—Networking Software—Tandem Computers Inc.; *U.S. Public*, pg. 417

NETASSISTANT—NONE—UB Networks; *Int'l*, pg. 924

NETBATCH—Job Management System—Tandem Computers Inc.; *U.S. Public*, pg. 417

NETCARE—Janitorial Maintainance Pproducts—Network Services Company; *U.S. Private*, pg. 791

NETCENTER—Computer System—International Business Machines Corporation; *U.S. Public*, pg. 895

NETCON—Network Management Systems—General Datacomm Industries, Inc.; *U.S. Public*, pg. 708

NETDETECT—Network Line Monitor & Protocol Analyzer—Tandem Computers Inc.; *U.S. Public*, pg. 417

NETDETECT—NONE—UB Networks; *Int'l*, pg. 924

NETDIRECTOR—Network Management System—Tandem Computers Inc.; *U.S. Public*, pg. 417

NETDIRECTOR—NONE—UB Networks; *Int'l*, pg. 924

NETDOOR—Computer System—International Business Machines Corporation; *U.S. Public*, pg. 895

NETEX—High Speed Data Communications Software—Network Systems Corporation; *U.S. Public*, pg. 1522

NETGUIDE—Magazine—CMP Media, Inc.; *U.S. Public*, pg. 279

NETMARK—Ultrasonic Locator—Dukane Corporation; *U.S. Private*, pg. 345

NETMAXER—NONE—BMC Software, Inc.; *U.S. Public*, pg. 162

NETMAXER/CICS—NONE—BMC Software, Inc.; *U.S. Public*, pg. 162

NETOBJECT—NONE—CACI International Inc; *U.S. Public*, pg. 272

NETPARTNER—Computer Program, Software & Netwrok Management System—Lucent Technologies Inc.; *U.S. Public*, pg. 1017

NETREVIEW—Computer System—International Business Machines Corporation; *U.S. Public*, pg. 895

NETROMYCIN—Antibiotic—Schering-Plough Corporation; *U.S. Public*, pg. 1438

NETSENTINEL—Protects Software Running on LAN's -Software Security Device—Rainbow Technologies, Inc.; *U.S. Public*, pg. 1359

NETSHARE—Staffed MRI Service—Mobile Technology Inc.; *U.S. Private*, pg. 754

NETSTAR—Performance Monitoring System—ADC Telecommunications, Inc.; *U.S. Public*, pg. 4

NETSWITCH—Vocal Net Server Platform—Inter-Tel, Incorporated; *U.S. Public*, pg. 888

NETTUNE PRO—NONE—BMC Software, Inc.; *U.S. Public*, pg. 162

NETVAULT—Computer Programs for Data Backup & Recovery—Lucent Technologies Inc.; *U.S. Public*, pg. 1017

NETVIEW—Computer System—International Business Machines Corporation; *U.S. Public*, pg. 895

NETWARE—Network Operating System Software—Novell, Inc.; *U.S. Public*, pg. 1203

NETWORK—Wall Systems—Daw Technologies, Inc.; *U.S. Public*, pg. 489

NETWORK—NONE—EMAP Business Communications Division; *Int'l*, pg. 451

NETWORK ALIGNMENT CO.—Logo—Reinalt-Thomas Corp.; *U.S. Private*, pg. 919

NETWORK COMPUTING—Magazine—CMP Media, Inc.; *U.S. Public*, pg. 279

THE NETWORK DIALTONE—NONE—UB Networks; *Int'l*, pg. 924

NETWORK GENERAL—NONE—Network Associates, Inc.; *U.S. Public*, pg. 1168

NETWORK PROBLEM AND CHANGE APPLICATION—Network Management Software—International Business Machines Corporation; *U.S. Public*, pg. 895

NETWORK STORAGE MADE SIMPLE—NONE—Tricord Systems, Inc.; *U.S. Public*, pg. 1637

NETWORK SYSTEMS—Mfr. of Data Communications Systems—Network Systems Corporation; *U.S. Public*, pg. 1522

THE NETWORK—Advertising & Sales of Journals—Business First of New York, Inc.; *U.S. Private*, pg. 19

NETWORK II.5—Simulation Modeling Language—CACI International Inc; *U.S. Public*, pg. 272

NETWORK UPS—Battery Backup—Best Power; *U.S. Private*, pg. 140

NETWORK WEEK—NONE—EMAP Business Communications Division; *Int'l*, pg. 451

NETWORX—NONE—The HON Co.; *U.S. Public*, pg. 772

NEU-TECH—Uncoated Paper—The Mead Corporation; *U.S. Public*, pg. 1074

NEU-TRI—Solvent—The Dow Chemical Company; *U.S. Public*, pg. 522

NEU-UP—G-CSF Derivative—Kyowa Hakko Kogyo Company, Ltd.; *Int'l*, pg. 778

NEUMANN—Electronics—Sennheiser Electronic Corp.; *U.S. Private*, pg. 984

NEUMASKS—Masking Fragrances—Crompton & Knowles Ingredient Technology Corp.; *U.S. Public*, pg. 459

NEUMEGA—Platelet Growth Factor—American Home Products Corporation; *U.S. Public*, pg. 79

NEUPHOR—Sizing Agent—Hercules Incorporated; *U.S. Public*, pg. 809

NEUPOGEN—Recombinant Granulocyte Colony Stimulating Factor—Amgen Inc.; *U.S. Public*, pg. 100

NEUPOGEN—Growth Factor G-CSF—Roche Holding Ltd.; *Int'l*, pg. 1119

NEUPREX (rBPI)—Drug for Infectious Diseases, Arthritis & Cancerous Tumors—XOMA Corporation; *U.S. Public*, pg. 1786

NEURAL CONNECTION—Neural Network Modeling Software—SPSS Inc.; *U.S. Public*, pg. 1420

NEUROBASAL—NONE—Life Technologies, Inc.; *U.S. Public*, pg. 504

NEUROMET—Neurosciences—SmithKline Beecham plc; *Int'l*, pg. 1264

NEUTECH 100% COTTON—Cotton Fiber Paper—Gilbert Paper; *U.S. Public*, pg. 1074

NEUTECH 25% COTTON—Cotton Fiber Paper—Gilbert Paper; *U.S. Public*, pg. 1074

NEUTRA RINSE 40—Post-Plate Rinse—LeaRonal, Inc.; *U.S. Public*, pg. 982

NEUTRAFILM—Inhibitor—BetzDearborn Inc.; *U.S. Public*, pg. 226

NEUTRAL—Specialty Detergent—Sara Lee Corporation; *U.S. Public*, pg. 1432

NEUTRALON—Brown Surgical Gloves—Johnson & Johnson Medical, Inc.; *U.S. Public*, pg. 928

NEUTRAMEEN—Neutralizing Amine—BetzDearborn Inc.; *U.S. Public*, pg. 226

NEUTREXIN—An Alternative Therapy for Treatment of Mederate-to-Sever PCP—U.S. Bioscience, Inc.; *U.S. Public*, pg. 1681

NEUTRO ROBERTS—Toiletries—SmithKline Beecham plc; *Int'l*, pg. 1264

NEUTROGENA ACNE CLEANSING FORMULA SOAP—Acne Soap—Neutrogena Corporation; *U.S. Public*, pg. 928

NEUTROGENA ACNE DRYING GEL—Gel—Neutrogena Corporation; *U.S. Public*, pg. 928

NEUTROGENA ACNE MASK—Skin Mask—Neutrogena Corporation; *U.S. Public*, pg. 928

NEUTROGENA ANTISEPTIC CLEANSER—Skin Cleanser—Neutrogena Corporation; *U.S. Public*, pg. 928

NEUTROGENA ANTISEPTIC PADS—Cleansing Pads—Neutrogena Corporation; *U.S. Public*, pg. 928

NEUTROGENA BABY CLEANSING FORMULA SOAP—Soap for Babies—Neutrogena Corporation; *U.S. Public*, pg. 928

NEUTROGENA BODY LOTION—Body Lotion—Neutrogena Corporation; *U.S. Public*, pg. 928

NEUTROGENA BODY OIL—Body Oil—Neutrogena Corporation; *U.S. Public*, pg. 928

NEUTROGENA CLEANSING BAR—Soap for Acne-Prone Skin—Neutrogena Corporation; *U.S. Public*, pg. 928

NEUTROGENA CLEANSING LOTION—Liquid Cleanser—Neutrogena Corporation; *U.S. Public*, pg. 928

NEUTROGENA CLEANSING WASH—Skin Cleanser—Neutrogena Corporation; *U.S. Public*, pg. 928

NEUTROGENA CLEAR PORE TREATMENT—NONE—Neutrogena Corporation; *U.S. Public*, pg. 928

NEUTROGENA CONDITIONER—Conditioner—Neutrogena Corporation; *U.S. Public*, pg. 928

NEUTROGENA DRY SKIN FORMULA SOAP—Soap for Dry Skin—Neutrogena Corporation; *U.S. Public*, pg. 928

NEUTROGENA EYE-MAKEUP REMOVER GEL—Makeup Remover—Neutrogena Corporation; *U.S. Public*, pg. 928

NEUTROGENA FRESH FOAMING CLEANSER—NONE—Neutrogena Corporation; *U.S. Public*, pg. 928

NEUTROGENA HEATSAFE—Hair Protectant from Blow Drying—Neutrogena Corporation; *U.S. Public*, pg. 928

NEUTROGENA HEALTHY SCALP SHAMPOO—Shampoo—Neutrogena Corporation; *U.S. Public*, pg. 928

NEUTROGENA INTENSIFIED DAY CREAM—Facial Moisturizer—Neutrogena Corporation; *U.S. Public*, pg. 928

NEUTROGENA INTENSIFIED EYE CREAM—Eye Cream—Neutrogena Corporation; *U.S. Public*, pg. 928

NEUTROGENA LIGHT NIGHT CREAM—Facial Cream—Neutrogena Corporation; *U.S. Public*, pg. 928

NEUTROGENA LIP MOISTURIZER—Lip Moisturizer—Neutrogena Corporation; *U.S. Public*, pg. 928

NEUTROGENA MOISTURE—Facial Moisturizer—Neutrogena Corporation; *U.S. Public*, pg. 928

NEUTROGENA MOISTURE SPF 15—Moisturizer for Sun-Protection—Neutrogena Corporation; *U.S. Public*, pg. 928

NEUTROGENA NATURAL SESAME BODY OIL—Body Oil—Neutrogena Corporation; *U.S. Public*, pg. 928

NEUTROGENA NON-DRYING CLEANSING LOTION—Cleansing Lotion—Neutrogena Corporation; *U.S. Public*, pg. 928

NEUTROGENA NORWEGIAN FORMULA—Hand Cream & Emulsion—Neutrogena Corporation; *U.S. Public*, pg. 928

NEUTROGENA OIL-FREE ACNE WASH—Skin Cleaner—Neutrogena Corporation; *U.S. Public*, pg. 928

NEUTROGENA ON-THE-SPOT ACNE TREATMENT—Acne Medicine—Neutrogena Corporation; *U.S. Public*, pg. 928

NEUTROGENA ORIGINAL FORMULA SOAP—Soap—Neutrogena Corporation; *U.S. Public*, pg. 928

NEUTROGENA RAINBATH—Shower & Bath Gel—Neutrogena Corporation; *U.S. Public*, pg. 928

NEUTROGENA SHAMPOO—Shampoo—Neutrogena Corporation; *U.S. Public*, pg. 928

NEUTROGENA SOLID SOAP SHAMPOO—Shampoo—Neutrogena Corporation; *U.S. Public*, pg. 928

NEUTROGENA SUNBLOCK—Sunblock—Neutrogena Corporation; *U.S. Public*, pg. 928

NEUTROGENA TONER—Facial Toner—Neutrogena Corporation; *U.S. Public*, pg. 928

NEUTRONYX—Surfactant-Nonionic—Stepan Company; *U.S. Public*, pg. 1514

NEUTROSORB—NONE—Carpenter Technology Corporation; *U.S. Public*, pg. 307

NEUTROSORB PLUS—NONE—Carpenter Technology Corporation; *U.S. Public*, pg. 307

NEUTROVAC—Static Eliminator Dust Collector—Simco; *U.S. Public*, pg. 865

NEUVE—Moisturizing Cleanser—Shiseido Company Ltd.; *Int'l*, pg. 1235

NEVADA—Ice Cream—Borden, Inc.; *U.S. Private*, pg. 157

NEVADA—Networked Voice & Data—Mitel Corporation; *Int'l*, pg. 870

NEVADA ARMIGER—Premises Wiring Products—Thomas & Betts Corporation; *U.S. Public*, pg. 1597

NEVADA EPITOME—Premises Wiring Products—Thomas & Betts Corporation; *U.S. Public*, pg. 1597

NEVADA WESTERN—Premises Wiring Products—Thomas & Betts Corporation; *U.S. Public*, pg. 1597

NEVERSTIK—Coated Release Papers—Eastern Fine Paper; *U.S. Private*, pg. 357

NEW—NONE—Martin Universal Design, Inc.; *U.S. Private*, pg. 709

NEW AGAIN—Automotive Body Repair System—3M; *U.S. Public*, pg. 1604

NEW AGE BOOKS—Book Publishing—Bertelsmann AG; *Int'l*, pg. 189

NEW BALANCE—Athletic Shoes & Apparel—New Balance Athletic Shoe, Inc.; *U.S. Private*, pg. 792

THE NEW BOOK OF KNOWLEDGE—Encyclopedia—Grolier Inc.; *Int'l*, pg. 794

NEW BRITAIN—Machine Tools—Litton Industries, Inc.; *U.S. Public*, pg. 1002

NEW BRITAIN MACHINE—NONE—DeVlieg-Bullard Inc.; *U.S. Public*, pg. 502

NEW BRITAIN MACHINE—Multiple Spindle—The Machine Tool Group; *U.S. Public*, pg. 503

NEW CASTLE—Vinyl Window—CertainTeed Corporation; *Int'l*, pg. 1170

NEW CENTURY—Tension Tent—Anchor Industries Inc.; *U.S. Private*, pg. 71

NEW CHAMPION GUIDE GRIP—Tires—Bridgestone/Firestone, Inc.; *Int'l*, pg. 213

NEW CHOICES FOR THE BEST YEARS—Magazine—The Reader's Digest Association, Inc.; *U.S. Public*, pg. 1367

NEW CLOTHING COMPANY—NONE—Kellwood Company; *U.S. Public*, pg. 948

NEW CONCEPT—Personal Care Products—Shaklee Corporation; *Int'l*, pg. 1518

NEW DAWN—FDS Spray—Alberto-Culver Canada, Inc.; *U.S. Private*, pg. 38

NEW DIMENSION—Cotton Blend Shirt for Comfort & Ease of Movement—Horace Small Apparel Company; *Int'l*, pg. 635

NEW DIMENSION—Reloading Dies—Hornady Manufacturing Company; *U.S. Private*, pg. 539

NEW DIMENSION—Glass for Use in Windows & Doors—Reynolds Metals Company; *U.S. Public*, pg. 1385

NEW DIRECTION—Weight Loss Program—Ross Products; *U.S. Public*, pg. 13

NEW DIRECTIONS—Slatwall—RHC/Spacemaster Corporation; *U.S. Private*, pg. 904

NEW ENGLAND CABLE NEWS—Cable—The Hearst Corporation; *U.S. Private*, pg. 515

NEW ENGLAND CAMP AND SUPPLY—Camping Equipment—Sport Supply Group, Inc.; *U.S. Public*, pg. 1499

THE NEW ENGLAND—Insurance & Financial Services—The New England; *U.S. Private*, pg. 737

NEW EQUIPMENT DIGEST—Periodical—Penton Publishing, Inc.; *Int'l*, pg. 1306

NEW ERA—Vitamins & Food Supplements—Hanson PLC; *Int'l*, pg. 592

NEW ERA—Machinery—Hollingsworth Saco Lowell Corporation, Inc.; *U.S. Private*, pg. 535

NEW ERA—Fabrics—Thomaston Mills, Inc.; *U.S. Public*, pg. 1599

NEW EXPERIENCE IV—Mattresses—Kingsdown, Inc.; *U.S. Private*, pg. 622

NEW EXPERIENCE VI—Mattresses—Kingsdown, Inc.; *U.S. Private*, pg. 622

NEW FREEDOM—Feminine Pads & Pantiliners—Kimberly-Clark Corporation; *U.S. Public*, pg. 958

NEW GENERATION—Floor Tile—American Biltrite Inc.; *U.S. Public*, pg. 68

NEW GENERATION—Homes—Centex Corporation; *U.S. Public*, pg. 322

NEW GENERATION—Washable Wool Blend Shirts & Trousers—Horace Small Apparel Company; *Int'l*, pg. 635

NEW GENERATION II—Versatile Outerwear—Horace Small Apparel Company; *Int'l*, pg. 635

NEW GOLD CD—Oldies Programming—Westwood One, Inc.; *U.S. Public*, pg. 1763

NEW GOLD ON CD—Adult Contemporary Radio Program—Westwood One Entertainment; *U.S. Public*, pg. 1763

THE NEW HAMPSHIRE—Insurance Group—New Hampshire Insurance Group; *U.S. Public*, pg. 84

NEW HERRINGBONE—Laminated Parquet—Robbins, Inc.; *U.S. Private*, pg. 934

NEW HOLLAND—Semi-Soft Cheese—BC-USA; *Int'l*, pg. 201

NEW HOLLAND—Semi-Soft Cheese—Bongrain Cheese USA; *Int'l*, pg. 201

NEW HOLLAND—Combines, Hay & Forage—New Holland Ltd.; *Int'l*, pg. 484

NEW HOME—Sewing Machines—Janome Sewing Machine Co., Ltd.; *Int'l*, pg. 699

NEW HOMEBUYER'S TITLE—NONE—Washington Homes, Inc.; *U.S. Public*, pg. 1741

NEW IMAGE—Gelatin Desserts & Pudding—Enzopac, Inc.; *U.S. Private*, pg. 379

NEW IMAGE—Greeting Cards—Fine Art Developments plc; *Int'l*, pg. 485

NEW IRRIGATION SPECIAL—Tires—Bridgestone/Firestone, Inc.; *Int'l*, pg. 213

NEW JAMESTOWN—Rugs—Couristan Inc.; *U.S. Private*, pg. 279

NEW JEFFERSONIAN—Laminated Parquet—Robbins, Inc.; *U.S. Private*, pg. 934

NEW JERSEY MANUFACTURERS REGISTER—Register—Manufacturers' News, Inc.; *U.S. Private*, pg. 700

A NEW KIND OF AUDIO COMPANY—NONE—Cambridge Soundworks, Inc.; *U.S. Private*, pg. 202

A NEW KIND OF HEALTHY—NONE—Time Inc. Health; *U.S. Public*, pg. 1613

NEW LEADER—Truck-Mounted Agricultural Fertilizer & Lime Spreaders—Highway Equipment Company; *U.S. Private*, pg. 529

NEW LEASH ON LIFE—Greeting Cards—American Greetings Corporation; *U.S. Public*, pg. 77

NEW MAN—Men's Apparel—International Cosmetics Co., Ltd.; *Int'l*, pg. 684

NEW MEXICO MANUFACTURERS REGISTER—Register—Manufacturers' News, Inc.; *U.S. Private*, pg. 700

NEW MILL—Pasta—Borden, Inc.; *U.S. Private*, pg. 157

NEW MULTI S—Distribution Panelboards—Matsushita Electric Works, Ltd.; *Int'l*, pg. 847

NEW MUSICAL EXPRESS—Music & Lifestyle Magazine—IPC Magazines Limited; *Int'l*, pg. 651

NEW ORLEANS—Bath Accessories—Baldwin Hardware Corporation; *U.S. Public*, pg. 1053

NEW ORLEANS PUBLIC SERVICE—Ulitilty Distributors—Entergy New Orleans, Inc.; *U.S. Public*, pg. 586

NEW POWER IMPLEMENT—Tires—Bridgestone/Firestone, Inc.; *Int'l*, pg. 213

NEW PROCESS—Baking Co.—Metz Baking Co.; *U.S. Private*, pg. 1022

NEW PRODUCT NEWS—Magazine—BPI Communications Inc.; *Int'l*, pg. 1446

NEW RIB TRACTOR—Tires—Bridgestone/Firestone, Inc.; *Int'l*, pg. 213

NEW SCIENTIST—Magazine—Reed Business Information Pty. Limited; *Int'l*, pg. 1094

NEW SKIN—Pharmaceuticals—Medtech Inc.; *U.S. Private*, pg. 728

NEW STANDARD—Encyclopedia—Ferguson Publishing Company; *U.S. Private*, pg. 401

NEW STEEL—Magazine Covering Primary Metals Industry—Reed Elsevier Business Information; *Int'l*, pg. 1095

NEW TRADITIONS—Frozen Meats for Microwave—Hormel Foods Corp.; *U.S. Public*, pg. 840

NEW VUES—Soft Color Conrtact Lenses—Novartis; *Int'l*, pg. 972

NEW WAVE—Dermal Function Bath Lotion—Wella Group; *Int'l*, pg. 1489

A NEW WAY OF THINKING—NONE—GenRad, Inc.; *U.S. Public*, pg. 731

NEW WOMAN—U.K. Women's Magazine—EMAP Elan; *Int'l*, pg. 451

NEW WOMAN—Magazine—Rodale Press, Inc.; *U.S. Private*, pg. 939

NEW WORLD—Strategy Game—Monarch Avalon, Inc.; *U.S. Public*, pg. 1123

NEW WORLD ENTERTAINMENT—Motion Picture & Television Production—New World Entertainment, Inc.; *Int'l*, pg. 926

NEW YORK—Cameras—Eastman Kodak Company; *U.S. Public*, pg. 550

NEW YORK—Frozen Bread—T. Marzetti Company; *U.S. Public*, pg. 977

NEW YORK CITY OFF TRACK BETTING—Horse-racing—New York City Off-Track Betting Corp.; *U.S. Private*, pg. 794

NEW YORK DELI—Potato Chips—Borden, Inc.; *U.S. Private*, pg. 157

NEW YORK DELI—Potato Chips—Wise Foods, Inc.; *U.S. Private*, pg. 157

NEW YORK DIAMONDS—Magazine Focusing on Worldwide Trade & Manufacturing of Diamonds—Reed Elsevier Business Information; *Int'l*, pg. 1095

NEW YORK FABRICS & CRAFTS—Retail Stores Selling Fabric, Notions & Crafts—Fabri-Centers of America, Inc.; *U.S. Public*, pg. 609

NEW YORK FARM SHOW—Trade Show 50% Owned by Farm Progress—Farm Progress Publications; *U.S. Public*, pg. 513

NEW YORK FROZEN FOODS—Partially Baked Frozen Bread—Lancaster Colony Corporation; *U.S. Public*, pg. 976

NEW YORK LAW JOURNAL—Legal Newspaper—New York Law Journal; *Int'l*, pg. 956

N.Y. LUG CO.—Clothing—Jack Schwartz Shoes, Inc.; *U.S. Private*, pg. 974

NEW YORK MAGAZINE—Magazine—New York Magazine; *U.S. Public*, pg. 1328

NEW YORK POST—Newspaper—The New York Post; *Int'l*, pg. 927

NEW YORK STYLE—Bagel Chips, Bite Size Bagel Chips & Pita Chips—RJR Nabisco Holdings Corp.; *U.S. Public*, pg. 1354

NEW YORK STYLE BAGEL CHIPS—Bagel Chips—Nabisco Inc.; *U.S. Public*, pg. 1355

THE NEW YORK TIMES—Newspaper—The New York Times; *U.S. Public*, pg. 1174

THE NEW YORK TIMES—Newspaper—The New York Times Company; *U.S. Public*, pg. 1173

Brand Name Index

Brand Name Index

NEW YORK VENTURE FUND—Mutual Fund—Davis Selected Advisors, L.P.; *U.S. Private*, pg. 315

THE NEW YORKER—Magazine—The New Yorker Magazine; *U.S. Private*, pg. 795

NEW ZEALAND HAIR PARADISE DRAGON TREE—Shampoo—Redmond Products, Inc.; *U.S. Public*, pg. 254

NEW ZEALAND HAIR PARADISE GOLDEN SEAL ROOT—Conditioner—Redmond Products, Inc.; *U.S. Public*, pg. 254

NEWAY—Suspension Systems—Lear Siegler Diversified Holdings Corp.; *U.S. Private*, pg. 655

NEWAY—Air & Mechanical Suspension Systems—Neway Anchorlok International Inc.; *U.S. Private*, pg. 796

NEWAY AIRRIDE—Air Suspension System—Neway Anchorlok International Inc.; *U.S. Private*, pg. 796

NEWBORN BABY BUBBLES—Doll—Tyco Toys, Inc.; *U.S. Public*, pg. 1058

NEWBORN BABY CHECKUP—Doll—Hasbro; *U.S. Public*, pg. 797

NEWBURY HOUSE—English as a Second Language Textbooks—Heinle & Heinle Publishers, Inc.; *U.S. Public*, pg. 1600

NEWCASTLE—Ales—Scottish & Newcastle plc; *Int'l*, pg. 1211

NEWCASTLE BROWN—Ale—Scottish & Newcastle Importers Co.; *Int'l*, pg. 1212

THE NEWCASTLE HERALD—NONE—John Fairfax Holdings Limited; *Int'l*, pg. 477

NEWCOR—Electrical Steel Sheet—British Steel Plc; *Int'l*, pg. 220

NEWELL—All Product Lines—Newell Co.; *U.S. Public*, pg. 1176

NEWFLEX—Spiral Reinforced PVC Suction Hose—NewAge Industries Inc.; *U.S. Private*, pg. 796

NEWFLEX—Spiral Reinforced PVC Tubing—Newage Industries Inc., Plastics Technology Group; *U.S. Private*, pg. 796

NEWHOUSE GROUP—Desks, Tables, Cabinets & Credenzas—Herman Miller, Inc.; *U.S. Public*, pg. 1111

NEWLOC—Plastic Push-to-Connect Fittings—NewAge Industries Inc.; *U.S. Private*, pg. 796

NEWLOC—Push-to-Connect Plastic Fittings—Newage Industries Inc., Plastics Technology Group; *U.S. Private*, pg. 796

NEWLY WEDS—Bread & Batter Seasonings, English Muffins, Spices and Ice Cream Cake Roll—Newly Weds Foods Inc.; *U.S. Private*, pg. 796

NEWMAN—Watchman's Clocks—Detex Corporation; *U.S. Private*, pg. 327

NEWMAN-TIPPER—NONE—Glynwed International PLC; *Int'l*, pg. 554

NEWMAN'S OWN—Food Products—Newman's Own, Inc.; *U.S. Private*, pg. 797

NEWMENU—Spices, Meat Analogue Proudcts—Vitasoy (U.S.A.) Inc.; *Int'l*, pg. 1469

NEWPORT—Cigarettes—Loews Corporation; *U.S. Public*, pg. 1010

NEWPORT—Cigarette—Lorillard Tobacco Company; *U.S. Public*, pg. 1011

NEWPORT—Liquors & Cordials—Marie Brizard Wines & Spirits USA; *U.S. Private*, pg. 702

NEWPORT—Ceramic Wall Tile—Monarch Tile, Inc.; *U.S. Private*, pg. 287

NEWPORT—Digital Instruments—Newport Electronics, Inc.; *U.S. Private*, pg. 816

NEWPORT NEWS—Women's Clothing Catalog—Newport News, Inc.; *U.S. Public*, pg. 1499

NEWPORT NEWS—Moderate Women's Apparel—Spiegel, Inc.; *U.S. Public*, pg. 1498

NEWPORT RED—Cigarette—Lorillard Tobacco Company; *U.S. Public*, pg. 1011

NEWPORT STRIPES—Cigarettes—Loews Corporation; *U.S. Public*, pg. 1010

NEWS BRIEF—Publication—The Mead Corporation; *U.S. Public*, pg. 1074

NEWS 90—Plastic Strapping Machine—Illinois Tool Works Inc.; *U.S. Public*, pg. 865

NEWS PLUS—Computer Assisted Research Services—The Mead Corporation; *U.S. Public*, pg. 1074

NEWSKING—Single-Width, Web Offset Press—Publishers Equipment Corporation; *U.S. Public*, pg. 1341

NEWSTALK 93.6—German Broadcasting—CLT-UFA; *Int'l*, pg. 561

NEWSWEEK—Magazine—Newsweek, Inc.; *U.S. Public*, pg. 1743

NEWSWEEK—Magazine—The Washington Post Company; *U.S. Public*, pg. 1742

NEWTAN KANSAN—Newspaper—Shivers Trading & Operating Co.; *U.S. Private*, pg. 994

NEWTEX—Natural Latex Rubber Tubing—NewAge Industries Inc.; *U.S. Private*, pg. 796

NEWTEX—Natural Latex Rubber Tubing—Newage Industries Inc., Plastics Technology Group; *U.S. Private*, pg. 796

NEWTON—Pen-Based Computer—Apple Computer, Inc.; *U.S. Public*, pg. 121

NEWTONS—Cookies—Nabisco Inc.; *U.S. Public*, pg. 1355

NEWTONS—Fruit Chewy Cookies—RJR Nabisco Holdings Corp.; *U.S. Public*, pg. 1354

NEWVIEW—Analytical Reporting Tool—SPSS Inc.; *U.S. Public*, pg. 1420

NEWVIEW 100—NONE—Zygo Corporation; *U.S. Public*, pg. 1795

NEXON—High Strength High Impact Packaging Materials—Nexus Plastics, Inc.; *U.S. Private*, pg. 797

NEXT—Software—Apple Computer, Inc.; *U.S. Public*, pg. 121

NEXT CENTURY—NONE—Franklin Electronic Publishers, Inc.; *U.S. Public*, pg. 679

NEXT FLIGHT OUT—Delivery Service—Trans World Airlines, Inc.; *U.S. Public*, pg. 1629

NEXT GENERATION—Copy Paper, Writing Paper, Offset Paper & Cover Paper—Georgia-Pacific Corporation; *U.S. Public*, pg. 735

NEXT STEP—Carseat—Century Products Co.; *U.S. Private*, pg. 226

NEXT STEP—Toddler Formula—Mead Johnson Nutritional Group; *U.S. Public*, pg. 254

NEXT WAVE—Stationery Products—The Mead Corporation; *U.S. Public*, pg. 1074

NEXTEL—NONE—Nextel Communications; *U.S. Public*, pg. 1180

NEXTEL—Ceramic Fiber High Temperature Fabrics—3M; *U.S. Public*, pg. 1604

NEXUS—Car Seat—Century Products Co.; *U.S. Private*, pg. 226

NEXUS—NONE—James Hardie Industries Ltd.; *Int'l*, pg. 596

NEZERIL—Nose Drops—Astra AB; *Int'l*, pg. 93

NEZO—Table Salt—Akzo Nobel N.V.; *Int'l*, pg. 42

NI-SPAN—Alloy—Inco Limited; *Int'l*, pg. 672

NIAGARA—Spray Starch & Sizing—Best Foods; *U.S. Public*, pg. 224

NIAGARA—Laundry Starches, Tints & Dyes—Bestfoods; *U.S. Public*, pg. 223

NIAGARA—NONE—Consolidated Papers, Inc.; *U.S. Public*, pg. 436

NIAGARA—Photographic Printers—Eastman Kodak Company; *U.S. Public*, pg. 550

NIAGARA—Filters—Ketema, Inc.; *U.S. Private*, pg. 604

NIAGARA MOHAWK—Public Utility—Niagara Mohawk Power Corporation; *U.S. Public*, pg. 1181

NIAGARA NO-FROST—Air Coolers—Niagara Blower Company; *U.S. Private*, pg. 798

NIAGESTIN—Gynaecological Product used for Endometrial & Mammary Cancer—Novo Nordisk A/S; *Int'l*, pg. 987

NIAL—NONE—Carpenter Technology Corporation; *U.S. Public*, pg. 307

NIARD—Pipe Cleaner—Roto-Rooter; *U.S. Public*, pg. 344

NIBCO—Brand of Glass Swabs—Summit Plastic Solutions, Inc.; *U.S. Private*, pg. 1050

NIBOND—Refractory Material—Ferro Corporation; *U.S. Public*, pg. 618

NIBROC—Towels—Fort James Corporation; *U.S. Public*, pg. 670

NIBS—Candy—Hershey Chocolate U.S.A.; *U.S. Public*, pg. 812

NIBS—Candy—Hershey Foods Corporation; *U.S. Public*, pg. 811

NICALON—Semiconductor Protective Coatings—Dow Corning Corporation; *U.S. Public*, pg. 523

NICARB—Coccidiosis Control—Merck & Co., Inc.; *U.S. Public*, pg. 1090

N'ICE—Cough Lozenges & Cough Throat Spray—SmithKline Beecham Consumer Healthcare, U.S.; *Int'l*, pg. 1264

N'ICE—NONE—SmithKline Beecham Corporation; *Int'l*, pg. 1264

N'ICE—Coughs, Colds & Influenza Product—SmithKline Beecham plc; *Int'l*, pg. 1264

NICE 'N CLEAN—Moist Towelettes, Baby Wipes, Eye Makeup & Nail Polish Remover—Nice-Pak Products, Inc.; *U.S. Private*, pg. 798

NICE 'N EASY—Haircolor—Bristol-Myers Squibb Company; *U.S. Public*, pg. 253

NICE 'N EASY—Hair Coloring—Clairol, Inc.; *U.S. Public*, pg. 254

NICE 'N SOFT—Bathroom Tissue—Consumer Products Business; *U.S. Public*, pg. 671

NICE 'N SOFT—Tissue—Fort James Corporation; *U.S. Public*, pg. 670

NICE N' THICK—Hair Care—Palm Beach Beauty Products Co.; *U.S. Private*, pg. 834

NICE PRINT SYSTEM—Color Film Processing System—Konica Corporation; *Int'l*, pg. 748

NICE-TOUCH 2—NONE—Nikon Inc.; *Int'l*, pg. 931

NICHOLAS—Breeding Stock for Turkeys—Arbor Acres Farm, Inc.; *Int'l*, pg. 202

NICHOLSON—Files and Saws—Cooper Hand Tools; *U.S. Public*, pg. 444

NICHOLSON—Files, Rasps & Saws—Cooper Industries, Inc.; *U.S. Public*, pg. 442

NICHOLSON—Valves—Watts Industries, Inc.; *U.S. Public*, pg. 1746

NICHOLSON'S LONDON DRY GIN—Spirit—Allied Domecq PLC; *Int'l*, pg. 62

NICHROME—Nicr Resistance Alloys—Driver-Harris Company; *U.S. Public*, pg. 530

NICKEL-NU—Metal Cleaner—Litton Industries, Inc.; *U.S. Public*, pg. 1002

NICKELL ENTERPRISES—Drawer Sides—Patrick Industries, Inc.; *U.S. Public*, pg. 1264

NICKELODEON—Cable TV Network—Viacom Inc.; *U.S. Public*, pg. 775

NICKELPLAST—Rehabilitation Product—Alimed, Inc.; *U.S. Private*, pg. 34

NICKELVAC—NONE—Allvac; *U.S. Public*, pg. 43

NICKERSON—Corn Seeds—Groupe Limagrain; *Int'l*, pg. 566

NICKLAUS—Golf Equipment—Nicklaus Golf Company, L.C.; *U.S. Private*, pg. 799

NICKLES—NONE—Alfred Nickles Bakery, Inc.; *U.S. Private*, pg. 799

NICK'S DISCOUNT SUPERMARKET—Grocery Store—Farm Fresh, Inc.; *U.S. Public*, pg. 1388

NICLOCIDE TABLETS—Pharmaceutical—Bayer Corporation/Pharmaceutical Division; *Int'l*, pg. 173

NICOBID—Pharmaceuticals—Rhone-Poulenc Rorer - U.S.; *Int'l*, pg. 1110

NICODERM—Nicotine Transdermal System—Hoechst Marion Roussel North America; *Int'l*, pg. 625

NICODERM CQ—Transdermal System—SmithKline Beecham Consumer Healthcare, U.S.; *Int'l*, pg. 1264

NICODERM CQ—Smoking Cessation Patch—SmithKline Beecham Corporation; *Int'l*, pg. 1264

NICOLAR—Pharmaceuticals—Rhone-Poulenc Rorer - U.S.; *Int'l*, pg. 1110

NICOLAS—Wine—Remy Amerique Inc.; *Int'l*, pg. 1102

NICOLE—Stemware & Barware—Dansk International Designs Ltd.; *U.S. Public*, pg. 261

NICOLE MILLER—Boyswear Clothing—Hartmarx Corporation; *U.S. Public*, pg. 795

NICOLE SUMMERS—Mail Order Women's Apparel—DM Management Company; *U.S. Public*, pg. 473

NICOLL—NONE—ETEX; *Int'l*, pg. 430

NICOLL ASIA LIMITED—NONE—ETEX; *Int'l*, pg. 430

NICOLL ETERPLAST—NONE—ETEX; *Int'l*, pg. 430

NICOLSON'S BEST BITTER—Wine—Allied Domecq PLC; *Int'l*, pg. 62

NICORETTE—NONE—Pharmacia & Upjohn, Inc.; *Int'l*, pg. 1047

NICORETTE—Smoking Cessation—SmithKline Beecham Consumer Healthcare, U.S.; *Int'l*, pg. 1264

NICORETTE—NONE—SmithKline Beecham Corporation; *Int'l*, pg. 1264

NICOSEAL—NONE—Carpenter Technology Corporation; *U.S. Public*, pg. 307

NICOSTAN—Tin-Nickel Process—LeaRonal, Inc.; *U.S. Public*, pg. 982

NICOTEMP—Nickel Process—LeaRonal, Inc.; *U.S. Public*, pg. 982

NICOTROL—Smoking Cessation Patch—McNeil Consumer Products Company; *U.S. Public*, pg. 928

NICOTROL—NONE—Pharmacia & Upjohn, Inc.; *Int'l*, pg. 1047

NICROBRAZ—High-temp Service Brazing Alloys—Wall Colmonoy Corp.; *U.S. Private*, pg. 1148

NICROCRAFT—Aircraft Exhaust Systems—Wall Colmonoy Corp.; *U.S. Private*, pg. 1148

NIDO—Dairy Products—Nestle S.A.; *Int'l*, pg. 915

NIDO—NONE—Nestle USA; *Int'l*, pg. 916

NIEDIECK BRILLIANT—Velvet & Corduroy—Girmes GmbH; *Int'l*, pg. 552

NIEHOFF—Electrical & Fuel System Parts—Echlin Inc.; *U.S. Public*, pg. 560

NIELSEN—Picture Framing Products—Esselte AB; *Int'l*, pg. 459

NIFAXSHARE—Automated Fax Server—Mitek Systems, Inc.; *U.S. Public*, pg. 1117

NIFEREX—NONE—Schwarz Pharma Inc.; *Int'l*, pg. 1211

NIFEREX—Pharmaceutical Products—Schwarz Pharma Manufacturing, Inc.; *Int'l*, pg. 1211

NIFEREX-PN—NONE—Schwarz Pharma Inc.; *Int'l*, pg. 1211

NIFEREX-PN FORTE—NONE—Schwarz Pharma Inc.; *Int'l*, pg. 1211

NIGEL'S—Men's Tailored Clothing—Pincus Bros., Inc.; *U.S. Private*, pg. 865

NIGHT AND DAY—Awnings—Sao Paulo Alpargatas S.A.; *Int'l*, pg. 1193

NIGHT & DAY INTIMATES—Intimate Apparel—Hanover Direct Pennsylvania, Inc.; *U.S. Public*, pg. 782

NIGHT-FIGHTER—Emergency Vehicle Spot-Flood Light—Federal Signal Corporation, Signal Div.; *U.S. Public*, pg. 616

NIGHT LIFE—Shoes—Brown Group, Inc.; *U.S. Public*, pg. 262

NIGHT LIFE—Shoes—Brown Shoe Company; *U.S. Public*, pg. 262

NIGHT MUSK—Fragrance—Parfums De Coeur Ltd.; *U.S. Private*, pg. 839

NIGHT NURSE—NONE—SmithKline Beecham Corporation; *Int'l*, pg. 1264

NIGHT NURSE—Coughs, Colds & Influenza Product—SmithKline Beecham plc; *Int'l*, pg. 1264

NIGHT WATCH 5—Searchlight, 5 Cell—Bright Star Industries, Inc.; *U.S. Public*, pg. 1341

NIGHTHAWK—Spotting Scope Series—Swift Instruments, Inc.; *U.S. Private*, pg. 1058

NIGHTINGALE-CONANT—Pre-Recorded Self Improvement Audio & Video Tapes—Nightingale-Conant Corp.; *U.S. Private*, pg. 799

NIGHTLACE—Sleepwear—Olga Div.; *U.S. Public*, pg. 1738

NIGHTSCAN—Combination Lighting—The Will-Burt Company; *U.S. Private*, pg. 1177

NIGHTSCAN CHIEF—Telescoping Mast for Emergency Lighting—The Will-Burt Company; *U.S. Private*, pg. 1177

NIGHTSIGHT—Flashlights—The Canadian Coleman Co., Ltd.; *U.S. Private*, pg. 691

NIGHTSIGHT—Coolers—The Canadian Coleman Co., Ltd.; *U.S. Private*, pg. 691

NIGHTSIGHT—NONE—Texas Instruments Incorporated; *U.S. Public*, pg. 1585

NIGHTWEAR BY VAN HEUSEN—Sleepwear—Host Apparel, Inc.; *U.S. Private*, pg. 540

NIGHTY—Women's Apparel—International Cosmetics Co., Ltd.; *Int'l*, pg. 684

NIK-NAKS—Snacks—Borden, Inc.; *U.S. Private*, pg. 157

NIKAL PC3—Nickel Process—LeaRonal, Inc.; *U.S. Public*, pg. 982

NIKE—Shoes, Apparel & Bags—Nike, Inc.; *U.S. Public*, pg. 1184

NIKE—Sportswear—Nike (U.K.) Limited; *U.S. Public*, pg. 1184

NIKE SWIM—NONE—Jantzen; *U.S. Public*, pg. 1702

NIKKEI—Abbreviation Of Company Name—Nihon Keizai Shimbun, Inc.; *Int'l*, pg. 929

NIKKOR—Auto Focus Lenses—Nikon Inc.; *Int'l*, pg. 931

NIKON—Cameras—Nikon Inc.; *Int'l*, pg. 931

NIKONOS—Underwater Cameras—Nikon Inc.; *Int'l*, pg. 931

NIKONOS RS—Underwater Camera—Nikon Inc.; *Int'l*, pg. 931

NIKOS—Fragrance—Lancaster Group Worldwide; *Int'l*, pg. 185

NILFISK—Vacuum Cleaners—Nilfisk A/S; *Int'l*, pg. 932

NILLA—Nilla Wafers—Nabisco Inc.; *U.S. Public*, pg. 1355

NILLA WAFERS—Vanilla Flavored Cookies—RJR Nabisco Holdings Corp.; *U.S. Public*, pg. 1354

NILO—Nickel-Iron Alloys—Inco Alloys International, Inc.; *Int'l*, pg. 672

NILO—Alloy Series—Inco Limited; *Int'l*, pg. 672

NILSON—Four Slide Machines—The A.H. Nilson Machine Co.; *U.S. Private*, pg. 1124

NILSON—Four Slide Machine—The U.S. Baird Corporation; *U.S. Private*, pg. 1124

NILSTAIN—NONE—Carpenter Technology Corporation; *U.S. Public*, pg. 307

NIMARK—NONE—Carpenter Technology Corporation; *U.S. Public*, pg. 307

NIMBLE—Bread—Ranks Hovis McDougall Limited; *Int'l*, pg. 1395

NIMBUS 50—Recycled Printing & Writing Papers—The Sorg Paper Co.; *U.S. Public*, pg. 1747

NIMOCAST—Alloy Series—Inco Limited; *Int'l*, pg. 672

NIMONIC—Heat-Resisting Alloys—Inco Alloys International, Inc.; *Int'l*, pg. 672

NIMONIC—Alloy Series—Inco Limited; *Int'l*, pg. 672

NIMOTOP—Anti Organic Brain Syndrome Drug—Bayer AG; *Int'l*, pg. 171

NIMOTOP—Pharmaceutical—Bayer Corporation/Pharmaceutical Division; *Int'l*, pg. 173

NIMROD—Pipe Lighters—Consolidated Cigar Corp.; *U.S. Public*, pg. 690

NIMROD—Long Range Laser Guided Tactical Missile—Israel Aircraft Industries Ltd.; *Int'l*, pg. 689

NINA—Women's Fragrance—Accecones Ricci U.S.A., Inc.; *Int'l*, pg. 445

NINAS—Cigars—SEITA, Societe Nationale D'Exploitation Industrielle des Tabacs et des Allumettes; *Int'l*, pg. 1219

NINATE—Sulfonate—Stepan Company; *U.S. Public*, pg. 1514

903—Specimen Collection Paper—Schleicher & Schuell, Inc.; *Int'l*, pg. 1206

9 & CO—Women's Shoes & Accessories—Nine West Group, Inc.; *U.S. Public*, pg. 1185

986 TOUR—Golf Clubs—Tommy Armour Golf; *U.S. Public*, pg. 1683

9FX—Product Name—Number Nine Visual Technology; *U.S. Public*, pg. 1206

9FX MOTION—Product Name—Number Nine Visual Technology; *U.S. Public*, pg. 1206

9FX Reality—Product Name—Number Nine Visual Technology; *U.S. Public*, pg. 1206

9FX VISION—Product Name—Number Nine Visual Technology; *U.S. Public*, pg. 1206

944—Pavement Markers—Thomas & Betts/Amerace; *U.S. Public*, pg. 1598

900 SERIES—Optical Encoder—Oak Grigsby; *U.S. Public*, pg. 1209

9 LIVES—Cat Food—H.J. Heinz Company; *U.S. Public*, pg. 805

9-LIVES—Cat Food—H.J. Heinz Co. of Canada Ltd.; *U.S. Public*, pg. 806

9-LIVES—Canned Cat Food—Star-Kist Foods, Inc.; *U.S. Public*, pg. 806

9 LIVES CAT NIPPERS—Cat Treats—H.J. Heinz Company; *U.S. Public*, pg. 805

9-LIVES FINICKY BITS—Cat Food—Star-Kist Foods Inc.; *U.S. Public*, pg. 805

9 LIVES LEAN MATURE—Cat Food—H.J. Heinz Company; *U.S. Public*, pg. 805

9 LIVES PLUS—Cat Food—H.J. Heinz Company; *U.S. Public*, pg. 805

9-LIVES MATURE—Soft/Moist Cat Food—Star-Kist Foods, Inc.; *U.S. Public*, pg. 806

9-1-1—First Aid Sprays & Creams—S.C. Johnson & Son, Inc.; *U.S. Private*, pg. 592

911 SERIES—Fire Apparatus Seating—Seats Incorporated; *U.S. Private*, pg. 410

9.6V TURBO—Radio Control—Tyco Toys, Inc.; *U.S. Public*, pg. 1058

9000 SERIES—Serial Dot Matrix Printers—Dataproducts Corporation; *Int'l*, pg. 620

928—Young Men's Suited Separates—Oxford Industries, Inc.; *U.S. Public*, pg. 1239

929—Car—Mazda Motor of America, Inc.; *Int'l*, pg. 849

9 WEST—Women's Shoes & Accessories—Nine West Group, Inc.; *U.S. Public*, pg. 1185

9076 SP1—Computer System—International Business Machines Corporation; *U.S. Public*, pg. 895

9076 SP2—Computer System—International Business Machines Corporation; *U.S. Public*, pg. 895

NINES—Cosmetics—Revlon, Inc.; *U.S. Private*, pg. 689

19—Young Women's Interest Magazine—IPC Magazines Limited; *Int'l*, pg. 651

1900 TR—Liquid Scintillation Analyzer—Packard Instrument Co., Inc.; *U.S. Private*, pg. 833

90'S CHAIR SERIES—Task, Tool And Guest Seating—United Chair, Inc.; *U.S. Private*, pg. 512

90'S COUNTRY—Country Music Radio Program—Westwood One Entertainment; *U.S. Public*, pg. 1763

90S COUNTRY—Country Star Profile Programming—Westwood One, Inc.; *U.S. Public*, pg. 1763

NINETY-EIGHT—Automobile—Oldsmobile Div. General Motors Corp.; *U.S. Public*, pg. 720

9800 SERIES PRINTER—Printer—Monarch Marking Systems; *U.S. Public*, pg. 1266

95 SERIES—Heavy Duty Trucks—DAF Trucks N.V.; *U.S. Public*, pg. 1247

9400 SERIES PRINTER—Printer—Monarch Marking Systems; *U.S. Public*, pg. 1266

99-AD—High Alumina Brick—A.P. Green Industries, Inc.; *U.S. Public*, pg. 761

99 BANANAS—NONE—Barton Brands, Ltd.; *U.S. Public*, pg. 300

9910—Print Server—Prepress Solutions, Inc.; *U.S. Private*, pg. 882

9920—Color Trapping Workstation—Prepress Solutions, Inc.; *U.S. Private*, pg. 882

90 PARK—Women's Jewelry—Swank, Inc.; *U.S. Public*, pg. 1543

90-75—Water Conserving Metering Faucet—Bradley Corporation; *U.S. Private*, pg. 164

90Xi—NONE—Zebra Technologies Corporation; *U.S. Public*, pg. 1790

NINJA—Motorcycle—Kawasaki Motors Corp., U.S.A.; *Int'l*, pg. 725

NINJA—Fragrance—Parfums De Coeur Ltd.; *U.S. Private*, pg. 839

THE NINJA—Videogame—Sega of America Inc.; *Int'l*, pg. 1218

NINO CERRUTI—Apparel—Intercontinental Branded Apparel; *U.S. Public*, pg. 796

NINO CERRUTI—Clothing—Salant Corporation; *U.S. Public*, pg. 1429

NINO CERRUTI RUE ROYALE—Men's Apparel—Hartmarx Corporation; *U.S. Public*, pg. 795

NINOL—Organic Chemicals—Stepan Company; *U.S. Public*, pg. 1514

NINOX—Surfactant-Amides—Stepan Company; *U.S. Public*, pg. 1514

NINTENDO—Home Video Entertainment System—Konami Corporation of America Inc.; *Int'l*, pg. 746

NINTENDO—Video Games—Nintendo Company, Ltd.; *Int'l*, pg. 932

NINTENDO ENTERTAINMENT SYSTEM—Videogame Hardware System—Nintendo of America; *Int'l*, pg. 932

NINTENDO MAGAZINE SYSTEM—Games Magazine—EMAP Images; *Int'l*, pg. 451

NINTENDO 64—Videogame Hardware System—Nintendo of America; *Int'l*, pg. 932

NIOBE—NONE—Adaptec, Inc.; *U.S. Public*, pg. 19

NIOBOND—Anodes—IMI Plc; *Int'l*, pg. 646

NIOMAX—Superconductor—IMI Plc; *Int'l*, pg. 646

NIPOL—Agricultural Emlsifier—Stepan Company; *U.S. Public*, pg. 1514

NIPLOET—Fittings—Bonney Forge Corporation; *U.S. Private*, pg. 156

NIPPON—Carbon Pipe & Steel Products—Thomas Pipe & Steel, Inc.; *U.S. Private*, pg. 508

NIPS—NONE—Nestle USA; *Int'l*, pg. 916

NIPS—Cheddar Cheese Snack Crackers—RJR Nabisco Holdings Corp.; *U.S. Public*, pg. 1354

NIPURE—NONE—Carpenter Technology Corporation; *U.S. Public*, pg. 307

Brand Name Index

NIREZ—Polyterpene & Terpene Phenol Resins—Arizona Chemical Div.; *U.S. Public*, pg. 901

NIRF—Markers & Inks—Eastman Chemical Company; *U.S. Public*, pg. 550

NIRON—NONE—Carpenter Technology Corporation; *U.S. Public*, pg. 307

NISHIKI—Cycle—Derby International Corporation S.A.; *Int'l*, pg. 394

NISSAN—Auto—Loeber Motors, Inc.; *U.S. Private*, pg. 672

NISSAN—Cars & Trucks—Nissan Motor Corporation in U.S.A.; *Int'l*, pg. 945

NISTRIA—Meat Products—Koninklijke Ahold NV; *Int'l*, pg. 749

NITE-BEAM—Lamps—Eagle Electric Mfg. Co., Inc.; *U.S. Public*, pg. 354

NITE-EYES—Road Lights—Unity Manufacturing Co.; *U.S. Public*, pg. 1126

NITE LITER—Indoor Night Lights—Guth Lighting Company; *Int'l*, pg. 821

NITELIGHTER—Photoelectric Controls & Time Switches—Fisher Pierce Division; *U.S. Public*, pg. 1250

NITELINE—Paint—Linear Dynamics Inc.; *U.S. Private*, pg. 668

NITEX—Nylon Fabric Monofilament—Tetko, Inc.; *U.S. Private*, pg. 1078

NITINOL—Orthodontic Archwires—3M; *U.S. Public*, pg. 1604

NITRAGIN—Inoculants—LiphaTech, Inc.; *Int'l*, pg. 812

NITRAGIN GOLD—Pre-Inoculant for Alfalfa or Clover—LiphaTech, Inc.; *Int'l*, pg. 812

NITRAMONCAL—Fertilizers—DSM Chemie Linz GmbH; *Int'l*, pg. 356

NITRAVER—Chemical Reagant—Hach Company; *U.S. Public*, pg. 773

NITRENE—Fatty Diethanol Amides—Henkel Corporation; *Int'l*, pg. 610

NITREX—NONE—Carpenter Technology Corporation; *U.S. Public*, pg. 307

NITRICLEAN 2000—Top Quality Cleanroom NitrileGloves—Phoenix Medical Technology, Inc.; *U.S. Public*, pg. 1292

NITRIVER—Chemical Reagant—Hach Company; *U.S. Public*, pg. 773

NITRO—NONE—Everest & Jennings, Inc.; *U.S. Public*, pg. 758

NITRO—Golf Balls—Prince Golf International; *U.S. Private*, pg. 884

NITRO-BID—Cardiovascular Preparation—Hoechst Marion Roussel North America; *Int'l*, pg. 625

NITRO-DUR—Transdermal Infusion System—Key Pharmaceuticals; *U.S. Public*, pg. 1438

NITRO-DUR—Transdermal Nitroglycerin Patches for Treatment of Angina—Schering-Plough Corporation; *U.S. Public*, pg. 1438

NITRO PRIME—NONE—AGA Gas, Inc.; *Int'l*, pg. 13

NITRODERM TTS—Patch for the Treatment of Angina Pectoris—Novartis; *Int'l*, pg. 972

NITRODISC—Anti-Anginal—Roberts Pharmaceutical Corporation; *U.S. Public*, pg. 1393

NITRODISC—Treatment Of Angina Pectoris—Searle & Co.; *U.S. Public*, pg. 1125

NITRODISC—Pharmaceutical Products—Searle Laboratories; *U.S. Public*, pg. 1125

NITROFLEX—NONE—AGA Gas, Inc.; *Int'l*, pg. 13

NITROGLYN—Extended Release Nitroglycerin Capsules; For the Prevention of Angina—Bradley Pharmaceuticals; *U.S. Public*, pg. 249

NITROGLYN—Extended Release Nitroglycerin; For the Prevention of Angina—Doak Dermatologics; *U.S. Public*, pg. 250

NITROGLYN—Sustained Release Capsules—Key Pharmaceuticals; *U.S. Public*, pg. 1438

NITROL—Pharmaceuticals—Rhone-Poulenc Rorer - U.S.; *Int'l*, pg. 1110

NITROLINGUAL SPRAY—Pharmaceuticals—Rhone-Poulenc Rorer - U.S.; *Int'l*, pg. 1110

NITRONEAL—Gas Generators—Engelhard Corporation; *U.S. Public*, pg. 582

NITROPHOSKA—Complex Fertilizer—BASF AG; *Int'l*, pg. 103

NITROPHOSKA PERFECT—All Purpose Complex Fertilizer—BASF AG; *Int'l*, pg. 103

NITROPHYL—Cellular Rubber—Rogers Corporation; *U.S. Public*, pg. 1402

NITROSEAL—NONE—Victor Products; *U.S. Public*, pg. 480

NITROSPAN—Pharmaceuticals—Rhone-Poulenc Rorer - U.S.; *Int'l*, pg. 1110

NIVEA—Toiletries—Beiersdorf Group; *Int'l*, pg. 182

NIVEA—Skin Care Products—Beiersdorf, Inc.; *Int'l*, pg. 182

NIVEA—NONE—Beiersdorf S.A.; *Int'l*, pg. 183

NIVEA—Skin Care Products—Smith & Nephew PLC; *Int'l*, pg. 1263

NIVEA SUN—Moisturizing Protective Products—Beiersdorf, Inc.; *Int'l*, pg. 182

NIVEA VISAGE—Facial Cream & Lotion—Beiersdorf, Inc.; *Int'l*, pg. 182

NIVEA VISAGE—Skincare Product—Smith & Nephew PLC; *Int'l*, pg. 1263

NIX—Prescription Pediculicide—Glaxo Wellcome PLC; *Int'l*, pg. 553

NIZAX—Nizatedine—Eli Lilly Italia, S.p.A.; *U.S. Public*, pg. 994

NIZORAL—Pharmaceutical—Janssen Pharmaceutica, Inc.; *U.S. Public*, pg. 928

NIZORAL—Systemic Antifungal—Johnson & Johnson; *U.S. Public*, pg. 927

NIZORAL CREAM—Pharmaceutical—Janssen Pharmaceutica, Inc.; *U.S. Public*, pg. 928

NIZORAL SHAMPOO—Pharmaceutical—Janssen Pharmaceutica, Inc.; *U.S. Public*, pg. 928

NIZOSTAR—Concentrated Lactic Acid Bacterial Cultures for Dairy Products—Royal Gist-Brocades N.V.; *Int'l*, pg. 1142

NO-CAF—Decaffeinated Cola—Select Canfield; *U.S. Private*, pg. 982

NO-CHAT—Extremely Dense Boring Bars—Rogers Tool Works, Inc.; *U.S. Public*, pg. 950

NO-COST VIDEO—NONE—Alliance Semiconductor Corp.; *U.S. Public*, pg. 47

NO DOZ—Keep Alert Tablets—Bristol-Myers Squibb Company; *U.S. Public*, pg. 253

NO DRIP—Tape—Essex Specialty Products; *U.S. Public*, pg. 523

NO EXAGGERATION—Bras—Warner's; *U.S. Public*, pg. 1738

NO FADE—Men's & Women's Shirts—C.R. Anthony Company; *U.S. Private*, pg. 1029

NO FAULT PERSONALIZING SYSTEMS—Pressure Sensitive Plates & Patches for Identification of Personal Items—Kingsley Machine Co.; *U.S. Public*, pg. 866

NO-HOE—Garden Mulch—Flex-O-Glass, Inc.; *U.S. Private*, pg. 412

NO-HOE—Plastic Garden Mulch—Warp Brothers; *U.S. Private*, pg. 412

NO LIK—Envelopes—The Mead Corporation; *U.S. Public*, pg. 1074

NO-MAR—Set Screw—PIC Design; *U.S. Private*, pg. 864

NO-MOIST—Bill Straps—Brandt, Inc.; *Int'l*, pg. 387

NO MORE—First Aid Products—Johnson & Johnson; *U.S. Public*, pg. 927

NO-NECK—NONE—Callaway Golf Company; *U.S. Public*, pg. 294

NO NONSENSE—Women's Undergarments—AGP Industrial Corporation; *Int'l*, pg. 14

NO NONSENSE—Pantyhose & Socks—Kayser-Roth Corporation, Inc.; *Int'l*, pg. 576

NO NONSENSE SOFT SOCKS—Socks—Kayser-Roth Corporation, Inc.; *Int'l*, pg. 576

NO-PROBLEM—Personal Binding System—General Binding Corporation; *U.S. Public*, pg. 707

NO PROBLEM—Mascara—Maybelline, Inc.; *Int'l*, pg. 819

THE "NO PROBLEM" PEOPLE—Used With & As a Part of Auto Insurance Logo—Auto-Owners Insurance; *U.S. Private*, pg. 100

NO RULES—Stationary Products—The Mead Corporation; *U.S. Public*, pg. 1074

NO-SAG—Furniture Springs—Lear Siegler Diversified Holdings Corp.; *U.S. Private*, pg. 655

NO-SAG—Automobile Seating Systems—Leggett & Platt, Incorporated; *U.S. Public*, pg. 985

NO-SHA—Cleansing Conditioner for Hair—The Gillette Company; *U.S. Public*, pg. 743

NO SHOCK—Antistatic Nylon Fiber—Monsanto Company; *U.S. Public*, pg. 1124

NO-SLIDE—Timing Belts—PIC Design; *U.S. Private*, pg. 864

NO-SLIP—Positioning Belts—PIC Design; *U.S. Private*, pg. 864

THE NO-SMOKING CAR—Car For Non-Smokers—Thrifty Rent-a-Car System, Inc.; *U.S. Public*, pg. 354

NO SPUT—Solder Fluxes—Litton Industries, Inc.; *U.S. Public*, pg. 1002

NO STOPPING THE TOPPING SUNDAE BAR—All-You-Can-Eat Sundae Bar—Ponderosa Steakhouse; *U.S. Private*, pg. 736

NO SWEAT—Deodorant—Revlon, Inc.; *U.S. Private*, pg. 689

NO-TARM—Cloths Bags—The Dow Chemical Company; *U.S. Public*, pg. 522

NO TARN EC—Post Treatment for Brass & Copper—LeaRonal, Inc.; *U.S. Public*, pg. 982

NO TARN S—Post Treatment for Brass & Copper—LeaRonal, Inc.; *U.S. Public*, pg. 982

NO-TOX—Oil Lubricant—Bel-Ray Company, Inc.; *U.S. Private*, pg. 130

NO TRANSFER—Scientific Glassware for Laboratory Use—Wheaton Inc.; *Int'l*, pg. 67

NO YOLKS—Egg Noodle Substitute—Foulds Inc.; *U.S. Private*, pg. 421

NOAH'S ARK—Low-Moisture Foods—Vacu-Dry Company; *U.S. Public*, pg. 1704

NOALOX—Anti-Oxidant—Ideal Industries, Inc.; *U.S. Public*, pg. 557

NOBEL—NONE—Tabacalera, S.A.; *Int'l*, pg. 1345

NOBILITY—Authentic Chinese Dimsum—Mitsui Foods, Inc.; *U.S. Public*, pg. 879

NOBLE ROMAN'S—Pizza Restaurants—Noble Roman's Inc.; *U.S. Public*, pg. 1187

NOBLES—Floor Maintenance Equipment—Castex Incorporated; *U.S. Public*, pg. 1577

NOBLES SPIN KLEEN—Parts Washing—Nobles Mfg. Inc.; *U.S. Private*, pg. 800

NOBLES TURBO DRYER—Parts Dryer—Nobles Mfg. Inc.; *U.S. Private*, pg. 800

NOBLET—Musical Instruments—G. Leblanc Corporation; *U.S. Private*, pg. 656

NOBLEX—Television, Audio, Video & Microwave Oven—Noblex Argentina S.A.C. e I.; *Int'l*, pg. 951

NOBLIA—Watches—Citizen Watch Co. of America, Inc.; *Int'l*, pg. 294

NOBODY COVERS YOU BETTER—Roofing Services—Bridgestone/Firestone, Inc.; *Int'l*, pg. 213

NOBODY DOES BREAKFAST LIKE IHOP DOES BREAKFAST—Restaurant—IHOP Corp.; *U.S. Public*, pg. 862

NOBRE—Packaged Meat—Sara Lee Corporation; *U.S. Public*, pg. 1432

NOCILLA—Chocolate Spread—Danone Group; *Int'l*, pg. 379

NOCOL—Bentonite Carbon Blend—AMCOL International Corp.; *U.S. Public*, pg. 63

NOCONA—Boot—Justin Industries, Inc.; *U.S. Public*, pg. 936

NODDY—NONE—BBC Magazines; *Int'l*, pg. 114

NODESTAR—Software—Alpha Microsystems; *U.S. Public*, pg. 57

NODILON—Automation, Programmable Logic Controllers—Schneider S.A.; *Int'l*, pg. 1207

NODOR—Dartboards—Sportcraft Ltd.; *U.S. Private*, pg. 1026

NOGA—Bulky Paper for Book Printing by Letter-Press or Offset—American Israeli Paper Mills Ltd.; *Int'l*, pg. 74

NOGGY—Chocolate Jewels—Ferrero; *Int'l*, pg. 480

NOGGY—Chocolate Jewels—Ferrero U.S.A., Inc.; *Int'l*, pg. 480

NOGUCHI—Table—Herman Miller, Inc.; *U.S. Public*, pg. 1111

NOILLY PRAT VERMOUTH—Liquor—Brown-Forman Beverages Worldwide; *U.S. Public*, pg. 261

NOILLY PRAT VERMOUTHS—Wines—Brown-Forman Corporation; *U.S. Public*, pg. 261

NOISEGARD—Hearing Protectors—The Fibre-Metal Products Company; *U.S. Private*, pg. 402

NOJO—Infant Bedding—Noel Joanna, Inc.; *U.S. Public*, pg. 465

NOKIA—Monitor—Oy Nokia Ab/Nokia Group; *Int'l*, pg. 951

NOKIA—Mobile Telephone—Nokia Sourcing, Inc.; *Int'l*, pg. 953

NOKIA DX200—Digital Exchange—Oy Nokia Ab/Nokia Group; *Int'l*, pg. 951

NOKIA MEDIAMASTER 95005—Multi Media Terminal—Oy Nokia Ab/Nokia Group; *Int'l*, pg. 951

NOKIA PRIMESITE—Base Station—Oy Nokia Ab/ Nokia Group; *Int'l*, pg. 951

NOKIA 2110—Mobile Phone for the GSM Cellular System—Oy Nokia Ab/Nokia Group; *Int'l*, pg. 951

NOKIA 2120—Mobile Phone for the U.S. Digital TDMA Standard)—Oy Nokia Ab/Nokia Group; *Int'l*, pg. 951

NOLAHIST—Antihistamine—Carnrick Laboratories, Inc.; *U.S. Private*, pg. 436

NOLAMINE—Time-Released Cold Tablets— Carnrick Laboratories, Inc.; *U.S. Private*, pg. 436

NOLAN—Polycarbonate Helmets for Motorcyclists—Opticos S.r.l.; *Int'l*, pg. 1007

NOLAN RYAN FOR MEN—NONE—Bollinger Industries Inc.; *U.S. Public*, pg. 243

NOLEX LA—Decongestant-Head & Lung— Carnrick Laboratories, Inc.; *U.S. Private*, pg. 436

NOLVADEX—Pharmaceutical—Zeneca Group Plc; *Int'l*, pg. 1524

NOMA-INTERNATIONAL—Christmas Tree Light Sets & Decorations—Noma-International, Inc.; *Int'l*, pg. 955

NOMAD—Cordless Telephones—Lucent Technologies Inc.; *U.S. Public*, pg. 1017

NOMAD—Floor Matting Material—3M; *U.S. Public*, pg. 1604

NOMAFOAM—O.E.M. Applicatoins for Closed-Cell Polythelene Foam—Nomaco, Inc.; *U.S. Private*, pg. 801

NOMAPAK—Packaging Applications for Closed-Cell Polythelene Foam—Nomaco, Inc.; *U.S. Private*, pg. 801

NOMATIL—Electrical Steel—Cockerill Sambre; *Int'l*, pg. 301

NOMEX—Aramid—Du Pont (E.I. Du Pont De Nemours & Co.); *U.S. Public*, pg. 530

NOMIS—Processed Vegetables—Furman Foods, Inc.; *U.S. Private*, pg. 431

NOMURA DIRECT—NONE—Nomura Securities International, Inc.; *Int'l*, pg. 956

NON-GRO—Silicon Carbide Tile—Ferro Corporation; *U.S. Public*, pg. 618

NON SCENTS—Hand Cleaner & Odor Eliminator—Wisconsin Pharmacal Co., Inc.; *U.S. Private*, pg. 1185

NON-TRANSFERABLE UNDERCOVER—Labels—Avery Dennison Corporation Label Group; *U.S. Public*, pg. 153

NONAQ—Grease—Fisher Scientific Company; *U.S. Private*, pg. 658

NONCORSIN—Cooling Brines—Akzo Nobel N.V.; *Int'l*, pg. 42

NONE-SUCH—Mince Meat—Borden, Inc.; *U.S. Private*, pg. 157

NONIUS—X-Ray Diffraction—Delft Instruments N.V.; *Int'l*, pg. 388

NONONSENSE—Writing Instruments—Sheaffer Inc.; *Int'l*, pg. 542

NONSTOP—Fault Tolerant Computing System—Tandem Computers Inc.; *U.S. Public*, pg. 417

NONSTOP KERNEL—Operating System—Tandem Computers Inc.; *U.S. Public*, pg. 417

NONSTOP-UX—Operating System—Tandem Computers Inc.; *U.S. Public*, pg. 417

NONSTOP V PLUS—I/O Business—Tandem Computers Inc.; *U.S. Public*, pg. 417

NOODLE KIDOODLE—Retail Toy Store—Noodle Kidoodle Inc.; *U.S. Public*, pg. 1188

NOODLE LOOP—NONE—Royal Rubber & Manufacturing Co.; *U.S. Private*, pg. 949

NOODLE RONI—Noodle Side Dish Mix—Golden Grain Company; *U.S. Public*, pg. 1348

NOODLE-RONI—Noodles—The Quaker Oats Company; *U.S. Public*, pg. 1347

NOPON—Plant Protectives—DSM Chemie Linz GmbH; *Int'l*, pg. 356

NOPRI—Franchised Supermarkets—GIB Group; *Int'l*, pg. 532

NOR-PARTIGEN KITS—Immunodiffusion Reagents—Dade Behring Inc.; *U.S. Private*, pg. 110

NORA—Rubber Flooring & Soling—Freudenberg & Company; *Int'l*, pg. 505

NORAFLOR—Spun-Bonded Flooring for Carpets—Freudenberg & Company; *Int'l*, pg. 505

NORALASTIC—Acoustic Flooring—Freudenberg & Company; *Int'l*, pg. 505

NORALEN—Elastic Roof Cover Material—Freudenberg & Company; *Int'l*, pg. 505

NORALIDE—Bearings, Heat Engine Components, Mechanical Seal Rings& Cutting Tools—Norton Company; *Int'l*, pg. 1173

NORAMCO—NONE—Johnson & Johnson; *U.S. Public*, pg. 927

NORAMENT—Special Designed Floors—Freudenberg & Company; *Int'l*, pg. 505

NORAMID—Flooring Material—Freudenberg & Company; *Int'l*, pg. 505

NORAND—Computing Systems—Norand Mobile Systems Div.; *U.S. Public*, pg. 1699

NORAPLAN—Flooring Material—Freudenberg & Company; *Int'l*, pg. 505

NORATLANTIC—Marine Clothing—Goldbergs Marine Distributors; *U.S. Public*, pg. 1756

NORBA—Waste Handling Systems—Partek Corporation; *Int'l*, pg. 1024

NORBEST—Turkeys & turkey products—Norbest, Inc.; *U.S. Private*, pg. 801

NORBOND—Adhesive—Demco Inc.; *U.S. Private*, pg. 323

NORCURON—Muscle Relaxant—Akzo Nobel N.V.; *Int'l*, pg. 42

NORCURON—Pharmaceutical—Organon Inc.; *Int'l*, pg. 48

NORD—Photographic Package Printers—Photo Control Corporation; *U.S. Public*, pg. 1292

NORD DOOR—Door—Jeld-Wen, Inc.; *U.S. Private*, pg. 585

NORDBANKEN KAPITALFORVALTNING—NONE—Nordbanken AB; *Int'l*, pg. 957

NORDBERG—Con-agg Crushing Equipment—Cleveland Brothers Equipment Co., Inc.; *U.S. Private*, pg. 245

NORDBERG—Track Maintenance Machinery—Nordco, Inc.; *U.S. Public*, pg. 1209

NORDDEUTSCHENACHRICHTEN—Newspaper—Burda Holding GmbH & Co., KG; *Int'l*, pg. 233

NORDEL—Hydrocarbon—Du Pont (E.I. Du Pont De Nemours & Co.); *U.S. Public*, pg. 530

NORDETTE—NONE—American Home Products Corporation; *U.S. Public*, pg. 79

NORDETTE—NONE—Wyeth Australia Pty. Ltd.; *U.S. Public*, pg. 82

NORDETTE—Oral Contraceptive—Wyeth-Ayerst Laboratories, Inc.; *U.S. Public*, pg. 80

NORDIC ADVANTAGE—NONE—CML Group, Inc.; *U.S. Public*, pg. 279

NORDIC ADVANTAGE—Clothing, Personal Care Products—NordicTrack, Inc.; *U.S. Public*, pg. 279

NORDIC EMPRESS—Ships—Royal Caribbean Cruises Ltd.; *U.S. Public*, pg. 1410

NORDIC MIST—Flavored Sparkling Water—The Coca-Cola Company; *U.S. Public*, pg. 392

NORDIC TRACK—Cross Country Ski Simulator—NordicTrack, Inc.; *U.S. Public*, pg. 279

NORDIC WARE—Cookware & Bakeware—Nordic Ware; *U.S. Private*, pg. 806

NORDIC WARE—NONE—Northland Aluminum Products, Inc.; *U.S. Private*, pg. 805

NORDICTRACK—Exercise Machine—CML Group, Inc.; *U.S. Public*, pg. 279

NORDIMMUN—Haematology Product—Novo Nordisk A/S; *Int'l*, pg. 987

NORDITROPIN—Product for Growth Hormone Deficiency—Novo Nordisk A/S; *Int'l*, pg. 987

NORDLYS—Non-Woven Textiles—Dominion Textile Inc.; *Int'l*, pg. 415

NORDSON—Equipment to apply Liquid and Powder Coatings, Thermoplastic Adhesive—Nordson Corporation; *U.S. Public*, pg. 1188

NORDSTEN—Farm Machinery—Thrige Agro A/S; *Int'l*, pg. 1386,

NORDX/CDT—Cabling Systems—Moss Telecommunications Services; *U.S. Private*, pg. 763

NORELCO—Personal Care & Domestic Appliances—Philips Electronics North America Corporation; *Int'l*, pg. 1053

NORELCO—Men's Razors—Philips Electronics N.V.; *Int'l*, pg. 1051

NOREO—Windows—Jeld-Wen, Inc.; *U.S. Private*, pg. 585

NORETHIN—Oral Contraceptive—Monsanto Company; *U.S. Public*, pg. 1124

NORETHIN—Oral Contraceptive—Roberts Pharmaceutical Corporation; *U.S. Public*, pg. 1393

NOREX—Butyl Coating Foam Extrusion—Norton Performance Plastics; *Int'l*, pg. 1174

NORFLEX—Orphenardrine Citrate—3M; *U.S. Public*, pg. 1604

NORFORMS—Feminine Deodorant Vaginal Suppositories—C. B. Fleet Co., Inc.; *U.S. Private*, pg. 410

NORGANIC—Water System—Millipore Corporation; *U.S. Public*, pg. 1112

NORGE—Washer & Dryers—Maytag Corporation; *U.S. Public*, pg. 1064

NORGE—Socks & Knitted Headwear—Wigwam Mills, Inc.; *U.S. Private*, pg. 1175

NORGESIC—Orphenardrine Citrate—3M; *U.S. Public*, pg. 1604

NORGESIC FORTE—Orphenardrine Citrate—3M; *U.S. Public*, pg. 1604

NORGLIDE—High Load Bearings—Norton Performance Plastics; *Int'l*, pg. 1174

NORGREN—Filters, Regulators, Lubricators, Valves & Flow Rate & Pressur—IMI Plc; *Int'l*, pg. 646

NORI—Globe Valves—KSB Aktiengesellschaft; *Int'l*, pg. 721

NORIT—Activated Carbons—American Norit Co. Inc.; *Int'l*, pg. 958

NORIT—Gen. Carbon Name—NORIT N.V.; *Int'l*, pg. 958

NORLANTIC—Marine Clothing—E & B Marine Incorporated; *U.S. Public*, pg. 1756

NORLANTIC—Boats—Goldbergs Marine Distributors; *U.S. Public*, pg. 1756

NORLETT—Garden Equipment—Electrolux, AB; *Int'l*, pg. 438

NORLITE—Paper Used to Make Newspapers—Georgia-Pacific Corporation; *U.S. Public*, pg. 735

NORM-O-TEMP—Hyperthermia Equipment—Cincinnati Sub-Zero Products, Inc.; *U.S. Private*, pg. 240

NORMALATE—Pharmaceutical Prods.—Alva/ Amco Pharmacal Companies, Inc.; *U.S. Private*, pg. 47

NORMAN—Electronic Flash Equipment—Photo Control Corporation; *U.S. Public*, pg. 1292

NORMAN LEVY—Auctioneers—Norman Levy Associates, Inc.; *U.S. Private*, pg. 664

NORMANDY—Musical Instruments—G. Leblanc Corporation; *U.S. Private*, pg. 656

NORMAX—NONE—Medeva PLC; *Int'l*, pg. 852

NORMAX—Bonded Abrasives—Norton Company; *Int'l*, pg. 1173

NORMAX—Laxative—SmithKline Beecham plc; *Int'l*, pg. 1264

NORMIFLO—Heparin—American Home Products Corporation; *U.S. Public*, pg. 79

NORMIFLO—Pharmaceutical Products—Wyeth-Ayerst Laboratories, Inc.; *U.S. Public*, pg. 80

NORMISON—NONE—Wyeth Australia Pty. Ltd.; *U.S. Public*, pg. 82

NORMLCERA-PLUS—Tissue Culture Sera—Nabi; *U.S. Public*, pg. 1148

NORMODYNE—Labetalol Hydrochloride—Key Pharmaceuticals; *U.S. Public*, pg. 1438

NORMODYNE—Antihypertensive Cardiovascular Product—Schering-Plough Corporation; *U.S. Public*, pg. 1438

NORMOPLEGIA—Normothermic Cardioplegia Catheter—Baxter Research Medical, Inc.; *U.S. Public*, pg. 196

NORMOUNT—Foam Plastic Sealant—Norton Performance Plastics; *Int'l*, pg. 1174

NORMOZIDE—Labetalol HCL/ Hydrochlorothiazide—Key Pharmaceuticals; *U.S. Public*, pg. 1438

NOROC—Boron Carbide & Silicon Carbide Armoe—Norton Company; *Int'l*, pg. 1173

NOROXIN—Norfloxacin—Merck & Co., Inc.; *U.S. Public*, pg. 1090

NOROXIN—Pharmaceutical—Merck Human Health Division (U.S. Human Health); *U.S. Public*, pg. 1091

NOROXIN—Antibiotic for Treatment of Prostatitis—Roberts Pharmaceutical Corporation; *U.S. Public*, pg. 1393

NORPACE—Pharmaceutical—Monsanto Company; *U.S. Public*, pg. 1124

NORPACE—Anti-Arrhythmic—Searle & Co.; *U.S. Public*, pg. 1125

NORPACE—Pharmaceutical Products—Searle Laboratories; *U.S. Public*, pg. 1125

NORPACE CR—Pharmaceutical Products—Searle Laboratories; *U.S. Public*, pg. 1125

NORPLANT DTC—Contraceptive Implant—Wyeth-Ayerst Laboratories, Inc.; *U.S. Public*, pg. 80

NORPOL—Unsaturated Polyester Resin—Jotun A/S; *Int'l*, pg. 714

NORPRENE—Plastic Tubing for Higher Heats—Norton Performance Plastics; *Int'l*, pg. 1174

NORPROLAC—Prolactin-Lowering Agent—Novartis AG; *Int'l*, pg. 971

NORR—Stemware & Barware—Dansk International Designs Ltd.; *U.S. Public*, pg. 261

NORRELL—Temporary Help Service—Norrell Corporation; *U.S. Public*, pg. 1192

NORRIS—Manufactured Homes—Clayton Homes, Inc.; *U.S. Public*, pg. 382

NORRIS—Milk Dispenser—Stevens-Lee Company; *U.S. Private*, pg. 1042

NORSEAL—Sealing Compounds—Norton Performance Plastics; *Int'l*, pg. 1174

NORSEMAN—Traction Tires—Pirelli Armstrong Tire Corporation; *Int'l*, pg. 1058

NORSTAR—Communications System—Northern Telecom; *Int'l*, pg. 969

NORSTAR—Telecommunications—Northern Telecom Limited; *Int'l*, pg. 968

NORTEL—NONE—Northern Telecom Limited; *Int'l*, pg. 968

NORTELL—NONE—TIE/Communications, Inc.; *U.S. Private*, pg. 1085

NORTH AMERICA—Syndicate—The Hearst Corporation; *U.S. Private*, pg. 515

NORTH AMERICAN OUTDOOR—NONE—CUC International, Inc.; *U.S. Public*, pg. 320

NORTH AMERICAN PRODUCTS—Carbide Cutting Tools for Woodworking, Non-Ferrous Metal—North American Products Corp.; *U.S. Private*, pg. 803

NORTH AMERICAN VENTURES—Holding Co.—Butler International, Inc.; *U.S. Public*, pg. 270

NORTH ATLANTIC TRADING CO—Clothing—E & B Marine Incorporated; *U.S. Public*, pg. 1756

NORTH ATLANTIC TRADING CO—Clothing—Goldbergs Marine Distributors; *U.S. Public*, pg. 1756

NORTH BAY—Produce—Cherry Central Cooperative; *U.S. Private*, pg. 233

NORTH BAY OUTFITTERS—Better Mens Sweaters—Winona Knitting Mills, Inc.; *U.S. Public*, pg. 779

NORTH BEACH DELI—NONE—Harrah's Entertainment, Inc.; *U.S. Public*, pg. 790

NORTH BROS. CO.—Insulation—National Service Industries, Inc.; *U.S. Public*, pg. 1160

NORTH CAPE—Fish Sticks & Portions—Frionor U.S.A. Inc.; *Int'l*, pg. 516

NORTH CAROLINA MANUFACTURERS REGISTER—Register—Manufacturers' News, Inc.; *U.S. Private*, pg. 700

NORTH CAROLINA POWER—Electric Utility—Virginia Electric and Power Company; *U.S. Public*, pg. 516

NORTH COAST CELLARS—Varietal Wines—The Beverage Source, Inc.; *U.S. Public*, pg. 591

NORTH DAKOTA MANUFACTURERSREGISTER—Register—Manufacturers' News, Inc.; *U.S. Private*, pg. 700

NORTH EASTERN—Bitter/Ale—Bass PLC; *Int'l*, pg. 169

NORTH END CLASSICS—Spaghetti/Pizza Sauce—Cains Foods, L.P.; *U.S. Private*, pg. 199

NORTH HILLS—NONE—Stadelman Fruit L.L.C.; *U.S. Private*, pg. 1028

NORTH LIGHT ART SCHOOL—Home Study—F & W Publications, Inc.; *U.S. Private*, pg. 388

NORTH LIGHT BOOK CLUB—Book Club—F & W Publications, Inc.; *U.S. Private*, pg. 388

NORTH LIGHT BOOKS—Book Publishers—F & W Publications, Inc.; *U.S. Private*, pg. 388

NORTH POLE PRODUCTS—Christmas Decorations—Wellington Home Products; *U.S. Private*, pg. 1161

NORTH STAR—Compass—The Sherrill Corp.; *U.S. Private*, pg. 298

NORTH STAR—Carbon Pipe & Steel Products—Thomas Pipe & Steel, Inc.; *U.S. Private*, pg. 508

NORTH STAR LANTERN—Back Packs, Duffle Bags, Air Mattresses—The Canadian Coleman Co., Ltd.; *U.S. Private*, pg. 691

NORTHBROOK LIFE—Life Insurance & Savings—The Allstate Corporation; *U.S. Public*, pg. 55

NORTHBROOK PROPERTY & CASUALTY—Commerce Insurance—The Allstate Corporation; *U.S. Public*, pg. 55

NORTHCOTE WEB ENAMEL—Printing Paper—The Mead Corporation; *U.S. Public*, pg. 1074

NORTHEAST COPY—Multi-Purpose Bond—Lindenmeyr Munroe; *U.S. Private*, pg. 224

NORTHERN—Tissue, Towel, Napkin—Fort James Corporation; *U.S. Public*, pg. 670

NORTHERN—Gear Pumps—McNally Industries, Inc.; *U.S. Private*, pg. 724

NORTHERN BRIGHTS—Text Cover-Bright Lights—Badger Paper Mills, Inc.; *U.S. Public*, pg. 165

NORTHERN COMPUTERS—Card Key Access—American Trading and Production Corporation; *U.S. Private*, pg. 63

NORTHERN ELECTRIC CO.—Automatic Blankets—Sunbeam Corporation; *U.S. Public*, pg. 1533

NORTHERN ENGINEERING—Cranes—Crane Manufacturing; *U.S. Private*, pg. 286

NORTHERN ISLES—NONE—Kellwood Company; *U.S. Public*, pg. 948

NORTHERN LIGHT—Canadian Whisky—Barton Incorporated; *U.S. Public*, pg. 300

NORTHERN LIGHT—Security & High Vandalism Lighting Equip.—Sterner Lighting Systems Incorporated; *U.S. Public*, pg. 1042

NORTHERN LIGHT CANADIAN—NONE—Barton Brands, Ltd.; *U.S. Public*, pg. 300

NORTHERN LIGHTS—Broadloom—Couristan Inc.; *U.S. Private*, pg. 279

NORTHERN REFLECTIONS—Outdoor Sportswear for Women—Woolworth Corporation; *U.S. Public*, pg. 1777

NORTHERN REFLECTIONS—Women's Leisurewear—F.W. Woolworth Co.; *U.S. Public*, pg. 1777

NORTHERN RUBBER—Rubber Components—Tomkins PLC; *Int'l*, pg. 1395

NORTHERN SATELLITE—Satellite Antenna Systems Ranging in Size from 0.85 Meters to 2.4 Meters—SierraCom; *U.S. Private*, pg. 999

NORTHERN STAR—Vinyl Siding—ABT Building Products Corporation; *Int'l*, pg. 20

NORTHERN STAR—NONE—Harrah's Entertainment, Inc.; *U.S. Public*, pg. 790

NORTHERN STATES—Electric & Gas Utility Services—Northern States Power Company; *U.S. Public*, pg. 1195

NORTHERN TRUST—Bank—Northern Trust Corporation; *U.S. Public*, pg. 1195

NORTHERN TRUST BANK—Bank—The Northern Trust Company; *U.S. Public*, pg. 1197

NORTHERN TURF & LANDSCAPE PRESS—NONE—Intertec Publishing; *U.S. Public*, pg. 1328

NORTHERN TURF MANAGEMENT—NONE—Farm Press; *U.S. Public*, pg. 1328

NORTHLAKE OUTDOOR FOOTWEAR—Hunting & Hiking Boots—Georgia/Durango Boot Company; *U.S. Public*, pg. 1684

NORTHLAND—Electric Motors—The Scott Fetzer Company; *U.S. Public*, pg. 217

NORTHLAND—Publishing—Justin Industries, Inc.; *U.S. Public*, pg. 936

NORTHLAND—100% Juice Products & Fresh Cranberries—Northland Cranberries, Inc.; *U.S. Public*, pg. 1197

NORTHLAND QUEEN—Imported Food Products—World Finer Foods, Inc.; *U.S. Private*, pg. 1190

NORTHRUP KING—Seeds—Northrup King Co.; *Int'l*, pg. 974

NORTHRUP KING—Seeds—Novartis AG; *Int'l*, pg. 971

NORTHSTAR SYSTEM—Powertrain—Cadillac Motor Car Division; *U.S. Public*, pg. 720

NORTHSTONE—Alcoholic Beverage—Miller Brewing Company; *U.S. Public*, pg. 1289

NORTHWEST FABRICS—Retailer—ConAgra, Inc.; *U.S. Public*, pg. 425

NORTHWEST HOME—Home—Fred Meyer Stores; *U.S. Public*, pg. 1103

NORTHWEST LANDING—Real Estate Services—Weyerhaeuser Company; *U.S. Public*, pg. 1764

NORTHWESTERN MUTUAL—Life Insurance, Disability Income Insurance, Annuities—Northwestern Mutual Life Insurance Co.; *U.S. Private*, pg. 807

NORTHWOODS—Wood Accessories—Dansk International Designs Ltd.; *U.S. Public*, pg. 261

NORTHWOODS—Syrup—Dean Pickles & Specialty Products; *U.S. Public*, pg. 490

NORTON—Grinding Wheels & Sharpening Stones—Norton Company; *Int'l*, pg. 1173

NORTON—Tubing—Ryan Herco Products Corp.; *U.S. Public*, pg. 953

NORTON CONSTRUCTION PRODUCTS—Diamond Core Drill Bits—Norton Company; *Int'l*, pg. 1173

NORTON SG—Abrasive Products—Norton Company; *Int'l*, pg. 1173

NORTRAK—Steerable Downhole Motor—Baker Hughes INTEQ; *U.S. Public*, pg. 166

NORTRAK—Steerable Drilling System—Norton Company; *Int'l*, pg. 1173

NORTRON SC—Agricultural Chemical—AgrEvo USA Company; *Int'l*, pg. 1203

NORVAL—Cover Stock—FiberMark Inc.; *U.S. Public*, pg. 620

NORVAL—Treatment of Depression—SmithKline Beecham plc; *Int'l*, pg. 1264

NORVASC—Amlodipine—Pfizer Inc.; *U.S. Public*, pg. 1281

NORWALK FURNITURE—Residential Upholstered Furniture—Norwalk Furniture Corporation; *U.S. Private*, pg. 807

NORWAY—Cruise Ship—Norwegian Cruise Line; *U.S. Private*, pg. 808

NORWAY—Flat Head Elevator Bolts—Screw Conveyor Corp.; *U.S. Private*, pg. 977

NORWEGIAN CROWN—Cruise Ship—Norwegian Cruise Line; *U.S. Private*, pg. 808

NORWEGIAN CRUISE LINE—Cruise Line—Norwegian Cruise Line; *U.S. Private*, pg. 808

NORWEGIAN DREAM—Cruise Ship—Norwegian Cruise Line; *U.S. Private*, pg. 808

NORWEGIAN DYNASTY—Cruise Ship—Norwegian Cruise Line; *U.S. Private*, pg. 808

NORWEGIAN MAJESTY—Cruise Ship—Norwegian Cruise Line; *U.S. Private*, pg. 808

NORWEGIAN SEA—Cruise Ship—Norwegian Cruise Line; *U.S. Private*, pg. 808

NORWEGIAN STAR—Cruise Ship—Norwegian Cruise Line; *U.S. Private*, pg. 808

NORWELL—TFE Ground Water Monitoring Components—Norton Performance Plastics; *Int'l*, pg. 1174

NORWEST—NONE—Norwest Corporation; *U.S. Public*, pg. 1201

NORWEST—Financial Services—Norwest Financial, Inc.; *U.S. Public*, pg. 1202

NORWESTERN—Deli Turkey—Jerome Foods Inc.; *U.S. Private*, pg. 586

NORWICH—Aspirin—Chattem, Inc., Consumer Products Division; *U.S. Public*, pg. 341

NORWICH—Aspirin—The Procter & Gamble Company; *U.S. Public*, pg. 1330

NORYL—Thermoplastic Resins Based on Polyphenylene Oxide not having Ion Exchange—General Electric Canada Inc.; *U.S. Public*, pg. 713

NORYL—Engineered Plastics—General Electric Company; *U.S. Public*, pg. 709

NORYL GTX—Engineered Plastics—General Electric Company; *U.S. Public*, pg. 709

NORZON—Bonded & Coated Abrasives—Norton Company; *Int'l*, pg. 1173

NOSE BETTER—Nasal Spray—Lee Pharmaceuticals; *U.S. Public*, pg. 984

NOSTER—Off-Highway Power Transmission Products—Regal-Beloit Corporation; *U.S. Public*, pg. 1370

NOT-A-KNOT—Leaders—Outdoor Technologies Group; *U.S. Private*, pg. 822

NOT A STITCH ON—Bras—Warner's; *U.S. Public*, pg. 1738

NOT-A-STRAP-ON—Bras—Warner's; *U.S. Public*, pg. 1738

NOT ALL THAT—Bras—Warner's; *U.S. Public*, pg. 1738

NOT SO SLOPPY JOE—Sloppy Joe Sauce—Hormel Foods Corp.; *U.S. Public*, pg. 840

NOTAR—Anti-Torque System—Boeing Helicopter Division; *U.S. Public*, pg. 241

NOTAR—Helicopter—McDonnell Aircraft & Missile Systems Div.; *U.S. Public*, pg. 241

NOTE STIX—Self-Adhesive Notes—Moore Corporation Limited; *Int'l*, pg. 888

NOTE STIX—Repositional Business Forms—Moore Document Solutions; *Int'l*, pg. 890

NOTEBOOK GAMES—Game—Tyco Toys, Inc.; *U.S. Public*, pg. 1058

NOTES—NONE—Lotus Development Corporation; *U.S. Public*, pg. 896

NOTEWORTHY—NONE—Noteworthy Industries Inc.; *U.S. Private*, pg. 808

NOTIFIER—Alarms—Fire Lite Alarms, Inc./Notifier Co.; *U.S. Public*, pg. 1306

NOTIFIER—Commerical Fire Alarm Systems—Pittway Corporation; *U.S. Public*, pg. 1305

NOTRE DAME FOOTBALL—Sports Radio Program—Westwood One Entertainment; *U.S. Public*, pg. 1763

NOTRE DAME FOOTBALL—Sports Programming—Westwood One, Inc.; *U.S. Public*, pg. 1763

NOURACID—Fatty Acids, Vegetable Oil derived—Akzo Nobel N.V.; *Int'l*, pg. 42

NOURICHE—Cosmetics—Charles of the Ritz Group Ltd.; *U.S. Private*, pg. 689

NOURY—Azo Compounds—Akzo Nobel N.V.; *Int'l*, pg. 42

NOURY-DRY—Driers, Organometallic-Based—Akzo Nobel N.V.; *Int'l*, pg. 42

NOURYSET—Comonomers—Akzo Nobel N.V.; *Int'l*, pg. 42

NOUS DEUX—French Women's Interests Magazine—EMAP France; *Int'l*, pg. 451

NOUVEAU—Cookware—Princess House, Inc.; *U.S. Public*, pg. 399

NOVA—Sporting Goods—Brunswick Bowling & Billiards Corp.; *U.S. Public*, pg. 265

NOVA—Computer Systems—Data General Corporation; *U.S. Public*, pg. 485

NOVA—Kitchen Tools and Accesories—Ekco Housewares, Inc.; *U.S. Public*, pg. 566

NOVA—NONE—Eljer Plumbingware; *U.S. Public*, pg. 1794

NOVA—Pens for Specialty Advertising—Golden Books Family Entertainment Inc.; *U.S. Public*, pg. 749

NOVA—NONE—Rohm and Haas Company; *U.S. Public*, pg. 1403

NOVA—Side Chair—Vecta; *U.S. Private*, pg. 1038

NOVA-BOND—Insulator Pads—Leggett & Platt, Incorporated; *U.S. Public*, pg. 985

NOVA CARPETS—Carpet—World Carpets, Inc.; *U.S. Private*, pg. 1190

NOVA CONTROLS—DC Motor Speed Controls—B & B Motor & Control Corporation; *U.S. Private*, pg. 105

NOVA-LOF—Insulator Pads—Leggett & Platt, Incorporated; *U.S. Public*, pg. 985

NOVA-PAC—Valve Bag—McNeel International Corp.; *U.S. Private*, pg. 724

NOVA-PAK—C18, CN, Phenyl Column & Cartridge & Packing Family—Millipore Corporation; *U.S. Public*, pg. 1112

NOVA 2070—Semiconductor Product—Morton International Inc.; *U.S. Public*, pg. 1134

NOVACEL—Adhesive Plastic—Chargeurs; *Int'l*, pg. 280

NOVACLAD—Adhesiveless Laminate—Sheldahl, Inc.; *U.S. Public*, pg. 1465

NOVACOR—Left Ventricular Assist System—Baxter International Inc.; *U.S. Public*, pg. 196

NOVACRON—Furniture Coating Composition—PPG Industries, Inc.; *U.S. Public*, pg. 1245

NOVAERA—Femine Pads—Kimberly-Clark Corporation; *U.S. Public*, pg. 958

NOVAFIRE PROTECTION CO—Fire Protection System—Robert Gibb & Sons, Inc.; *U.S. Private*, pg. 451

NOVAFLEX—Flexible Circuits Made From Novaclad—Sheldahl, Inc.; *U.S. Public*, pg. 1465

NOVAFLO—Liquid Size Agent Used in Papermaking—Georgia-Pacific Corporation; *U.S. Public*, pg. 735

NOVAHISTINE—Cough/Cold Medicine—Hoechst Marion Roussel North America; *Int'l*, pg. 625

NOVAHISTINE—Cough/Cold Products—SmithKline Beecham Consumer Healthcare, U.S.; *Int'l*, pg. 1264

NOVALGIN—Pain/Fever—Hoechst Marion Roussel, Inc.; *Int'l*, pg. 624

NOVALON—Intravenous Catheter Placement Unit—Becton Dickinson & Company; *U.S. Public*, pg. 199

NOVALUX—Color Coated Paperboard—Hazen Paper Company; *U.S. Private*, pg. 514

NOVALUZID—Gastrointestinal Drug—Astra AB; *Int'l*, pg. 93

NOVALYZER—Sensors—ATMI, Inc.; *U.S. Public*, pg. 12

NOVAMEDIA—NONE—Newspapers First; *U.S. Public*, pg. 964

NOVAMOS—Materials & Delivery Systems—ATMI, Inc.; *U.S. Public*, pg. 12

NOVANTRONE—Oncology Therapy—American Home Products Corporation; *U.S. Public*, pg. 79

NOVANTRONE—NONE—Wyeth Australia Pty. Ltd.; *U.S. Public*, pg. 82

NOVAPREP—Liquid Chromatography Apparatus—PPG Industries, Inc.; *U.S. Public*, pg. 1245

NOVAPURE—Dry Chemical Scrubber—ATMI, Inc.; *U.S. Public*, pg. 12

NOVARA—REI Bicycles & Apparel—Recreational Equipment, Inc.; *U.S. Private*, pg. 914

NOVASET—Foundry Binder—Ashland, Inc.; *U.S. Public*, pg. 138

NOVASIL—Flow Agent for Feeds—DuCoa L.P.; *U.S. Private*, pg. 301

NOVASIZE—Tall Oil Rosin Size—Georgia-Pacific Corporation; *U.S. Public*, pg. 735

NOVASOFT—Intraocular Lenses—Alcon Laboratories, Inc.; *Int'l*, pg. 916

NOVASOME—Microencapsulation—IGI, Inc.; *U.S. Public*, pg. 855

NOVASOURCE—Gas Delivery—ATMI, Inc.; *U.S. Public*, pg. 12

NOVASPERSE—Rosin Size—Georgia-Pacific Corporation; *U.S. Public*, pg. 735

NOVATRANS—Pressure Transducers Monitor the Cardiovascular System—Medex Inc.; *U.S. Public*, pg. 689

NOVATRON—Cast Polyurethane Shapes—DSM Engineering Plastic Products; *Int'l*, pg. 354

NOVAWELD—Solvent—Genova Products, Inc.; *U.S. Private*, pg. 447

NOVEL—Biodegradeable Nonionics—Condea Vista Company; *Int'l*, pg. 325

NOVEL & SHORT STORY WRITER'S MARKET—Market Book—F & W Publications, Inc.; *U.S. Private*, pg. 388

NOVEL PLASMINOGEN ACTIVATOR—Thrombolytic Agent—Genetics Institute, Inc.; *U.S. Public*, pg. 79

NOVELL—Computer Software & Hardware—Novell, Inc.; *U.S. Public*, pg. 1203

NOVELLUS—Semiconductors—Novellus Systems, Inc.; *U.S. Public*, pg. 1204

NOVICOLOR—Cushioned Vinyl Floor Coverings—Forbo Holding SA; *Int'l*, pg. 496

NOVILON—Cushioned Vinyl Floor Coverings—Forbo Holding SA; *Int'l*, pg. 496

NOVILUX—Cushion Vinyl Floorcoverings—Forbo Holding SA; *Int'l*, pg. 496

NOVIOL—Safety Lens—American Optical Corporation; *U.S. Public*, pg. 60

NOVOBORD—Particleboard—Georgia-Pacific Corporation; *U.S. Public*, pg. 735

NOVOCELL—Wood Pulp—Avenor, Inc.; *Int'l*, pg. 101

NOVOCOLL—Adhesive—Pratt & Lambert United, Inc.; *U.S. Public*, pg. 1466

NOVOCORE—Boards & Doors Formed of Wood Particles—Georgia-Pacific Corporation; *U.S. Public*, pg. 735

NOVOCS—Ground Water Remediation—EG & G Environmental, Inc.; *U.S. Public*, pg. 543

NOVODECK—Wood Panels—Georgia-Pacific Corporation; *U.S. Public*, pg. 735

NOVODOR—Doors—Georgia-Pacific Corporation; *U.S. Public*, pg. 735

NOVODOR—Biological Product for Control of Colorado Beetle Larvae—Novo Nordisk A/S; *Int'l*, pg. 987

NOVOFLOR—Flooring—Georgia-Pacific Corporation; *U.S. Public*, pg. 735

NOVOFOLD—Wood Products—Georgia-Pacific Corporation; *U.S. Public*, pg. 735

NOVOGAS—Liquid Propane Gas—SHV Holdings N.V.; *Int'l*, pg. 1154

NOVOGRAIN—Lumber, Wood & Wood Fiber Products—Georgia-Pacific Corporation; *U.S. Public*, pg. 735

NOVOLEN—Propylene Homo & Copolymers—BASF AG; *Int'l*, pg. 103

NOVOLET—Insulin Injection System—Novo Nordisk A/S; *Int'l*, pg. 987

NOVOLITE—Door Cores—Georgia-Pacific Corporation; *U.S. Public*, pg. 735

NOVOOPEN—Insulin Injection System—Novo Nordisk A/S; *Int'l*, pg. 987

NOVOPERM—Organic Pigment—Hoechst Aktiengesellschaft; *Int'l*, pg. 624

NOVOPLAY—Wood, Particleboard, Wood Chips & Wood Fiber—Georgia-Pacific Corporation; *U.S. Public*, pg. 735

NOVOPLY—Particleboard—Georgia-Pacific Corporation; *U.S. Public*, pg. 735

NOVOSHELF—Particleboard—Georgia-Pacific Corporation; *U.S. Public*, pg. 735

NOVOSTEP—Steps Used in the Construction of Stairs—Georgia-Pacific Corporation; *U.S. Public*, pg. 735

NOVOSTRAND—Oriented Strand Board & Flooring—Georgia-Pacific Corporation; *U.S. Public*, pg. 735

NOVOTEL—Hotels—Accor S.A.; *Int'l*, pg. 20

NOVOTEX—Plywood, Paneling, Siding, Roofing & Acoustical Tile—Georgia-Pacific Corporation; *U.S. Public*, pg. 735

NOVOTILE—Composition Board—Georgia-Pacific Corporation; *U.S. Public*, pg. 735

NOVOTOUR—Travel Agency—Accor S.A.; *Int'l*, pg. 20

NOVOWALL—Wall Panels—Georgia-Pacific Corporation; *U.S. Public*, pg. 735

NOVOWELD—Plywood, Siding, Roofing & Flooring—Georgia-Pacific Corporation; *U.S. Public*, pg. 735

NOVOWOOD—Particle Board—Georgia-Pacific Corporation; *U.S. Public*, pg. 735

NOVOZYM—Enzymes for Protoplast Preparation—Novo Nordisk A/S; *Int'l*, pg. 987

NOVRAMS—NONE—Xicor, Inc.; *U.S. Public*, pg. 1785

NOVUS—Polymers—BetzDearborn Inc.; *U.S. Public*, pg. 226

NOVUS FINANCIAL CORPORATION—Consumer Loans—Dean Witter, Discover & Co.; *U.S. Public*, pg. 1132

NOVUS NETWORK—Financial Services—Dean Witter, Discover & Co.; *U.S. Public*, pg. 1132

NOVUS OMNI—Multi-Wavelength Photocoagulation—Coherent, Inc.; *U.S. Public*, pg. 395

NOVUS 2000—Laser Photocoagulator—Coherent, Inc.; *U.S. Public*, pg. 395

NOW—Women's Weekly Magazine—IPC Magazines Limited; *Int'l*, pg. 651

NOW—Cigarettes—Reemtsma Cigarettenfabriken GmbH, Hamburg; *Int'l*, pg. 1100

NOW—Filter, Box, Menthol, 100's-Filter, Menthol, Box Cigarettes—R.J. Reynolds Tobacco Company; *U.S. Public*, pg. 1355

NOW—Spray Paint—Sherwin-Williams Diversified Brands, Inc.; *U.S. Public*, pg. 1466

NOW AND LATER—Candy—Nabisco Inc.; *U.S. Public*, pg. 1355

NOW AND LATER—Fruit Flavored Candies—RJR Nabisco Holdings Corp.; *U.S. Public*, pg. 1354

NOW & LATER SPLITSTIX—Candy—Planters Company; *U.S. Public*, pg. 1355

NOWA—Cosmetics—Henkel KGaA; *Int'l*, pg. 609

NOWAVE—Winder—Beloit Corporation; *U.S. Public*, pg. 789

NOWCAM—Coiled Tubing & Nitrogen Services—Camco International Inc.; *U.S. Public*, pg. 297

NOX-RUST—Rust Proofing Protection—Daubert Industries, Inc.; *U.S. Private*, pg. 313

NOXFISH—Fish Toxicant—Roussel Corporation; *Int'l*, pg. 625

NOXFISH—Fish Toxicant—Roussel UCLAF S.A.; *Int'l*, pg. 626

NOXON—Metal Polish—Reckitt & Colman Inc.; *Int'l*, pg. 1090

NOXZEMA—Skin Care Products—The Procter & Gamble Company; *U.S. Public*, pg. 1330

NOZ-L-MIX—Burner—Selas Corporation of America; *U.S. Public*, pg. 1454

NTUNE—Computer System—International Business Machines Corporation; *U.S. Public*, pg. 895

Brand Name Index

Brand Name Index

NTUNEMON—Computer System—International Business Machines Corporation; *U.S. Public*, pg. 895

NTUNENCP—Computer System—International Business Machines Corporation; *U.S. Public*, pg. 895

NU-BLOCK—Preformed Refractory Shapes—Norton Company; *Int'l*, pg. 1173

NU-BOND—Kiln Furniture—Ferro Corporation; *U.S. Public*, pg. 618

NU BROOM—Carpet Sweeper—Bissell Inc.; *U.S. Private*, pg. 145

NU-COR—Carbon Pipe & Steel Products—Thomas Pipe & Steel, Inc.; *U.S. Private*, pg. 508

NU GAUZE—General-Use Sponges—Johnson & Johnson Medical, Inc.; *U.S. Public*, pg. 928

NU HUE—Spray Enamel—Sherwin-Williams Diversified Brands, Inc.; *U.S. Public*, pg. 1466

NU-HY—Grain Buckets—Screw Conveyor Corp.; *U.S. Private*, pg. 977

NU KLAD—Protective Surfacing—Ameron Concrete & Steel Pipe Group; *U.S. Public*, pg. 99

NU-KLAD—Protective Surfacing—Ameron International Corporation; *U.S. Public*, pg. 98

NU-PAREIL—Timed Release Agents for Pharmaceutical Capsules—Crompton & Knowles Ingredient Technology Corp.; *U.S. Public*, pg. 459

NU PASTELS—Pastels—Sanford Corporation; *U.S. Public*, pg. 1178

NU-PIPE—Process for Non-Destructive Reconstruction of Sewers, Tunnels & Pipelines—Enviroq; *U.S. Public*, pg. 881

NU-POWER—Engine Treatment—Radiator Specialty Company; *U.S. Public*, pg. 906

NU-SALT—Salt Substitute—Cumberland Packing Corp.; *U.S. Private*, pg. 295

NU-SITE—Needleless Injection System—Medex Inc.; *U.S. Public*, pg. 689

NU-STONE—Thermoset Polyester Molding Compound—Industrial Dielectrics, Inc.; *U.S. Private*, pg. 560

NU SYSTEM CUISINE—Calorie Controlled Entrees—Nutri/System Inc.; *U.S. Private*, pg. 859

NU-TAB—Tabletting Agent for Pharmaceutical & Nutritional Tablets—Crompton & Knowles Ingredient Technology Corp.; *U.S. Public*, pg. 459

NU-TRISH A/B—NONE—Chr. Hansen, Inc.; *Int'l*, pg. 288

NU-WAY—Swing Plow—Long MFG. NC, Inc.; *U.S. Private*, pg. 674

NU-WAY OIL—Convenience Stores—FFP Marketing Company, Inc.; *U.S. Public*, pg. 604

NU-LETH-R—Adv. Specialties—Winthrop-Atkins Co., Inc.; *U.S. Private*, pg. 1183

NUARAMID—Fiber Gloves-Aramid—Eastco Industrial Safety Corp.; *U.S. Public*, pg. 548

NUBBIES—Golf Shoes—The Austad Company; *U.S. Public*, pg. 782

NUBE—Toilet Soap—Nuevo Federal S.A.; *Int'l*, pg. 990

NUBLEND—NONE—Dynamics Corporation of America; *U.S. Public*, pg. 286

NUCA—Globe Valves—KSB Aktiengesellschaft; *Int'l*, pg. 721

NUCEL—Wood Pulp—Westvaco Corporation; *U.S. Public*, pg. 1762

NUCERITE—Metal Composite—Pfaudler, Inc.; *U.S. Public*, pg. 1393

NUCHAR—Carbons & Carbonaceous Materials—Westvaco Corporation; *U.S. Public*, pg. 1762

NUCLAY—Kaolin for use in The Paper Industry—Engelhard Corporation; *U.S. Public*, pg. 582

NUCLEAR—Specialty Detergent—Sara Lee Corporation; *U.S. Public*, pg. 1432

NUCLETRON—Radiotherapy—Delft Instruments N.V.; *Int'l*, pg. 388

NUCLEUS—Central Dictation System—Dictaphone Corp.; *U.S. Public*, pg. 1045

NUCLEUS STOCK AUDIT—Software—Peak Technologies Group, Inc.; *Int'l*, pg. 890

NUCOA—Margarine—GFA Brands, Inc.; *U.S. Private*, pg. 435

NUCOFED—Cough & Cold Medicine—Roberts Pharmaceutical Corporation; *U.S. Public*, pg. 1393

NUCOFED—Pharmaceutical Prods.—SmithKline Beecham Laboratories; *Int'l*, pg. 1264

NUCOFED—Decongestant—SmithKline Beecham plc; *Int'l*, pg. 1264

NUCOR BEARING PRODUCTS—Precision Bearings & Other Steel Machined Products—Nucor Corporation; *U.S. Public*, pg. 1205

NUCOR BUILDING SYSTEMS—Pre-Engineered Steel Building Systems—Nucor Corporation; *U.S. Public*, pg. 1205

NUCOR COLD FINISHED BAR—Steel Cold Finished Bars—Nucor Corporation; *U.S. Public*, pg. 1205

NUCOR FASTENERS—Steel Industrial Fasteners—Nucor Corporation; *U.S. Public*, pg. 1205

NUCOR GRINDING BALLS—Steel Grinding Media—Nucor Corporation; *U.S. Public*, pg. 1205

NUCOR STEEL—Hot Rolled Steel Bar, Sheet, Structural Products—Nucor Corporation; *U.S. Public*, pg. 1205

NUCORE—Framing System—Kawneer Company; *U.S. Public*, pg. 60

NUDIT—Facial Hair Bleach & Remover—Medtech Inc.; *U.S. Private*, pg. 728

NUEVO MUNDO—Spanish Language Weekly—San Jose Mercury News; *U.S. Public*, pg. 964

NUFILMS—Residue Control Agent—Miller Chemical & Fertilizer Corp.; *U.S. Private*, pg. 33

NUFORM—Condoms—Durex Consumer Products; *Int'l*, pg. 815

NUGGET—Valves—IMI Plc; *Int'l*, pg. 646

THE NUGGET—Casino With Bar & Restaurant Services—Jackpot Enterprises, Inc.; *U.S. Public*, pg. 920

NUGGET—NONE—Lady Baltimore Foods, Inc.; *U.S. Public*, pg. 975

NUGGET—Shoe Care—Reckitt & Colman plc; *Int'l*, pg. 1089

NUGLASS—Nylon Cam-Op & Pin Lug Couplings—NewAge Industries Inc.; *U.S. Private*, pg. 796

NUGRAPE—Soft Drink—The Monarch Company, Inc.; *U.S. Private*, pg. 756

NUGRAPH—Clay-Graphite Crucibles—Ferro Corporation; *U.S. Public*, pg. 618

NUJOY—Candy—Standard Candy Co., Inc.; *U.S. Private*, pg. 1030

NUK—Pacifiers, Nursers & Accessories—Gerber Products Company; *Int'l*, pg. 973

NULACIN—Peptic Ulcer Products—SmithKline Beecham plc; *Int'l*, pg. 1264

NULINE—Imaging System—Nuarc Company, Inc.; *U.S. Public*, pg. 808

NULL & ASSOCIATES—NONE—Bromar Inc.; *U.S. Private*, pg. 171

NULLMATIC—Industrial Instrumentation—Moore Products Co.; *U.S. Public*, pg. 1128

NULOFOND—DryFondant Sugar—Crompton & Knowles Ingredient Technology Corp.; *U.S. Public*, pg. 459

NULOMOLINE—Standardized Invert Sugar—Crompton & Knowles Ingredient Technology Corp.; *U.S. Public*, pg. 459

NUMA-Q—Computer System—Sequent Computer Systems, Inc.; *U.S. Public*, pg. 1459

NO. 883—NONE—Carpenter Technology Corporation; *U.S. Public*, pg. 307

NO. 11 SPECIAL—NONE—Carpenter Technology Corporation; *U.S. Public*, pg. 307

NO. 484—NONE—Carpenter Technology Corporation; *U.S. Public*, pg. 307

NUMBER NINE—Company Name—Number Nine Visual Technology; *U.S. Public*, pg. 1206

NO. 1 JR—NONE—Carpenter Technology Corporation; *U.S. Public*, pg. 307

NO. 7—Waxes, Washes & Specialty Products—Armor All Products Group; *U.S. Public*, pg. 387

NO. 610—NONE—Carpenter Technology Corporation; *U.S. Public*, pg. 307

NO.375 GARAGE DOOR OPENER—Garage Door Opener—Wayne Dalton of Sterling; *U.S. Private*, pg. 1155

NUMEAT—NONE—Northwestern Meats Inc.; *U.S. Private*, pg. 807

NUMERI CENTER—NONE—Automation Control; *Int'l*, pg. 1389

NUMERIS—Integrated Systems Digital Network—France Telecom; *Int'l*, pg. 503

NUMERO VERT—Toll Free Calling—France Telecom; *Int'l*, pg. 503

NUMITRON—Electron Tubes—Thomson Consumer Electronics Inc.; *Int'l*, pg. 1383

NUNN-BUSH—Shoes—Weyco Group, Inc.; *U.S. Public*, pg. 1763

NUNUS—Apparel—Fred Meyer Stores; *U.S. Public*, pg. 1103

NUPRIN—Analgesic—Bristol-Myers Squibb Company; *U.S. Public*, pg. 253

NUPRO—Prophy Paste—Johnson & Johnson; *U.S. Public*, pg. 927

NUPRO—Prophylaxis Paste, Fluorides—Johnson & Johnson Consumer Products; *U.S. Public*, pg. 928

NUR HIER—Baked Sweet Snacks—Borden, Inc.; *U.S. Private*, pg. 157

NURELLE—Insecticide—The Dow Chemical Company; *U.S. Public*, pg. 522

NURISH—Animal Fiber Ingredients—Ralston Purina Company; *U.S. Public*, pg. 1359

NUROFEN—NONE—Boots Healthcare International; *Int'l*, pg. 202

NUROLON—Nylon Suture—Ethicon, Inc.; *U.S. Public*, pg. 928

NUROMAX—Muscle Relaxant—Glaxo Wellcome PLC; *Int'l*, pg. 553

NURSE MATES—NONE—Kellwood Company; *U.S. Public*, pg. 948

NURSE 'N EASY—Women's Undergarments—AGP Industrial Corporation; *Int'l*, pg. 14

NURSECOM—Communications System—Executone Information Systems, Inc.; *U.S. Public*, pg. 599

NURSEMATES—Footwear—Morse Shoe, Inc.; *U.S. Public*, pg. 168

NURSERY PRO—Material Handling Equipment for Nursery Industry—Cannon Equipment; *Int'l*, pg. 646

NURSETALK—Communications System—Executone Information Systems, Inc.; *U.S. Public*, pg. 599

NURSETTE—Disposable Glass Bottle Service for Hospital Feedings—Mead Johnson Nutritional Group; *U.S. Public*, pg. 254

NURSING OPPORTUNITIES—Medical Publication—Medical Economics Company Inc.; *U.S. Public*, pg. 1601

NURSING RESEARCH—Magazine—American Journal of Nursing Company; *Int'l*, pg. 1513

NURSOY—Soy-Based Infant Formula—Wyeth-Ayerst Laboratories, Inc.; *U.S. Public*, pg. 80

NURTURA—Skin Care Products—Avon Products, Inc.; *U.S. Public*, pg. 155

NUSCHELBERGER—Baked Sweet Snacks—Borden, Inc.; *U.S. Private*, pg. 157

NUSYN-NOXFISH—Fish Toxicants—Roussel UCLAF S.A.; *Int'l*, pg. 626

NUT & HONEY CRUNCH—Flakes of Corn Coated with Nuts & Real Honey—Kellogg Company; *U.S. Public*, pg. 947

NUT & HONEY CRUNCH O'S—Whole Grain Oat Cereal with Honey & Almonds—Kellogg Company; *U.S. Public*, pg. 947

NUTAPER—Paper & Plastic Cones—Sonoco Products Company; *U.S. Public*, pg. 1485

NUTCRACKER SWEET—Black Tea—Celestial Seasonings; *U.S. Public*, pg. 319

NUTEC—NONE—Lawter International, Inc.; *U.S. Public*, pg. 980

NUTELLA—Confections & Hazelnut Spread—Ferrero; *Int'l*, pg. 480

NUTELLA—Hazelnut Spread—Ferrero U.S.A., Inc.; *Int'l*, pg. 480

NUTMEG—Decorated Knitwear—VF Corporation; *U.S. Public*, pg. 1702

NUTMEG MILLS—Clothing—Nutmeg Mills Inc.; *U.S. Public*, pg. 1702

NUTONE—Exhaust Fans—NuTone, Inc.; *Int'l*, pg. 1499

NUTOP—Vinyl Board Cover—OCE-U.S.A.; *Int'l*, pg. 994

NUTRA—Vitamins—SmithKline Beecham plc; *Int'l*, pg. 1264

NUTRA CARE—Hair Care Prods.—CCA Industries, Inc.; *U.S. Public*, pg. 276

NUTRA-E—Skin Care Products—Pharmavite Corp.; *U.S. Private*, pg. 860

NUTRA-SOOTHE—Medicine Bath—Brimms Inc.; *U.S. Private*, pg. 169

NUTRACORT—Pharmaceutical Products—Galderma Laboratories, Inc.; *Int'l*, pg. 819

NUTRADERM—Pharmaceutical Products—Galderma Laboratories, Inc.; *Int'l*, pg. 819

NUTRADIET—Diet Canned Foods—Tri Valley Growers; *U.S. Private*, pg. 1101

NUTRAMENT—Energy Food—Bristol-Myers Squibb Company; *U.S. Public*, pg. 253

NUTRAMENT—Nutritional Drink—Mead Johnson Nutritional Group; *U.S. Public*, pg. 254

NUTRAMIGEN—Infant Formulas—Bristol-Myers Squibb Company; *U.S. Public*, pg. 253

NUTRAMIGEN—Hypoallergenic Powdered Protein Formula—Mead Johnson Nutritional Group; *U.S. Public*, pg. 254

NUTRAPLUS—Pharmaceutical Products—Galderma Laboratories, Inc.; *Int'l*, pg. 819

NUTRASWEET—Low-Calorie Sweetener—Monsanto Company; *U.S. Public*, pg. 1124

NUTRASWEET—Low Calorie Sweetener—The NutraSweet Company; *U.S. Public*, pg. 1125

NUTRASWEET SPOONFUL—Table-Top Sweetener—The NutraSweet Company; *U.S. Public*, pg. 1125

NUTRADERM BATH OIL—Bath Oil—Galderma Laboratories, Inc.; *Int'l*, pg. 819

NUTRENA—Feeds—Cargill; *U.S. Private*, pg. 210

NUTRENA—Feeds—Cargill Animal Nutrition Div.; *U.S. Private*, pg. 210

NUTREND—Dietetic Products—Nestle S.A.; *Int'l*, pg. 915

NUTREX—Vinegar—Coop Switzerland; *Int'l*, pg. 329

NUTRI-BRAN—Bread—Roman Meal Company; *U.S. Private*, pg. 942

NUTRI/DATA—Computer Weight Analysis—Nutri/System Inc.; *U.S. Private*, pg. 859

NUTRI-GRAIN—Wheat, Nuggets & Raisin Bran—Kellogg Company; *U.S. Public*, pg. 947

NUTRI-GRAIN BARS—Blueberry, Strawberry, Peach, Cherry & Apple   Grain & Cereal Bars—Kellogg Company; *U.S. Public*, pg. 947

NUTRI-GRAIN FROZEN WAFFLES—Waffles—Kellogg Company; *U.S. Public*, pg. 947

NUTRI-HAIR—Multi-Vitamin—Nature's Bounty Inc.; *U.S. Public*, pg. 1166

NUTRI MEGA—Vitamins—Nature's Bounty Inc.; *U.S. Public*, pg. 1166

NUTRI/SYSTEM—Weight Loss Program—Nutri/System Inc.; *U.S. Private*, pg. 859

NUTRIBASICS—Feed Premixes—DuCoa L.P.; *U.S. Private*, pg. 301

NUTRIENE—Tocotrienols—Eastman Chemical Company; *U.S. Public*, pg. 550

NUTRIFOS—Food Ingredient—Solutia Inc.; *U.S. Public*, pg. 1483

NUTRILAC—Bio-Products—Kali-Chemie Aktiengesellschaft; *Int'l*, pg. 1278

NUTRILEAF—Fertilizer—Miller Chemical & Fertilizer Corp.; *U.S. Private*, pg. 33

NUTRILITE—Vitamin & Mineral Supplements—Amway Corporation; *U.S. Private*, pg. 69

NUTRIMETICS—Direct Selling (Cosmetics)—Sara Lee Corporation; *U.S. Public*, pg. 1432

NUTRIMIX—Nutritional Containers—Abbott Laboratories; *U.S. Public*, pg. 12

NUTRIPLAZ—for Baby Pig Diets—DuCoa L.P.; *U.S. Private*, pg. 301

NUTRITIONIST IV—NONE—First DataBank; *U.S. Private*, pg. 515

NUTROPIN—Somatropin (DNA Origin) for Injection, Human Growth Hormone—Genentech, Inc.; *Int'l*, pg. 1120

NUTSHELL NEWS—Magazine—Kalmbach Publishing Co.; *U.S. Private*, pg. 606

NUTTER BUTTER—Cookie—Nabisco Inc.; *U.S. Public*, pg. 1355

NUTTER BUTTER—Peanut Butter Flavored Cookies—RJR Nabisco Holdings Corp.; *U.S. Public*, pg. 1354

NUTZELS—Pretzels—Bachman Company; *U.S. Private*, pg. 109

NUVAC—Instant Vacuum System—Nuarc Company, Inc.; *U.S. Private*, pg. 808

NUVEL—Surfacing Material—Formica Corporation; *Int'l*, pg. 129

NUVIS 125 I—Compact Camera—Nikon Inc.; *Int'l*, pg. 931

NUVIS 75 I—Compact camera—Nikon Inc.; *Int'l*, pg. 931

NUVISION—Optometry & Opticianary Service—AVC/Nu-Vision, Inc.; *U.S. Private*, pg. 9

NUVO COSMETICS—Direct Selling Cosmetics—Sara Lee Corporation; *U.S. Public*, pg. 1432

NUWAVE—Patented Waveform—Staodyn Inc.; *U.S. Public*, pg. 1509

NUWAY—Utility Trailers—Martin Industries, Inc. (AL); *U.S. Private*, pg. 709

NY-TROUS+—Gas Mixture—Nellcor Puritan Bennett Incorporated; *U.S. Public*, pg. 1039

NY-WHITE—Yarn Lubricants—Henkel Corporation; *Int'l*, pg. 610

NYACOL—Inorganic Colloids—PQ Corporation; *U.S. Private*, pg. 827

NYAFAT—Shortening—Rokeach Food Distributing Inc.; *U.S. Private*, pg. 940

NYBEX—Polyamide Compounds—Ferro Corporation; *U.S. Public*, pg. 618

NYBORG—Industrial Laundry Equipment—Electrolux, AB; *Int'l*, pg. 438

NYBRAD—Abrasive Monfilament—Glassmaster Company; *U.S. Public*, pg. 745

NYCOA—Nylon Engineered Resins, Copolymers & Compounds—Nyltech North America Inc.; *Int'l*, pg. 482

NYE-CARB—Metal Coatings—Electro-Coatings, Inc.; *U.S. Private*, pg. 368

NYE-KOTE—Metal Coatings—Electro-Coatings, Inc.; *U.S. Private*, pg. 368

NYGREN DAHLY—Paper Drills—Baum USA; *Int'l*, pg. 1293

NYLA-K—Ball Bearing Pillow Blocks—McGill Manufacturing Company, Inc.; *U.S. Public*, pg. 573

NYLAFLO—Filtration Products—Gelman Sciences, Inc.; *U.S. Public*, pg. 1253

NYLAFLOW—Synthetic Polymeric Tubing—DSM Engineering Plastic Products; *Int'l*, pg. 354

NYLAIR—Hose—HBD Industries, Inc.; *U.S. Private*, pg. 489

NYLASINT—Pressed & Sintered Polymeric Articles—DSM Engineering Plastic Products; *Int'l*, pg. 354

NYLASORB—Filtration Products—Gelman Sciences, Inc.; *U.S. Public*, pg. 1253

NYLATCH—Plastic Fasteners—Hartwell Corporation; *U.S. Private*, pg. 1168

NYLATRON—Polymeric Molding Resins, Shapes & Parts—DSM Engineering Plastic Products; *Int'l*, pg. 354

NYLEX—NONE—Cordis, a Johnson & Johnson Company; *U.S. Public*, pg. 928

NYLEZE/NYLEZE 155—Modified Polyurethane with Polyamide Overcoat—Phelps Dodge Magnet Wire Co.; *U.S. Public*, pg. 1286

NYLIFE—Brand Name for Investment & Registered Products—New York Life Insurance Company; *U.S. Private*, pg. 794

NYLO-GRIT—Abrasive Rotary Brush for Scrubbing & Stripping—Flo-Pac Corporation; *U.S. Private*, pg. 414

NYLOBRADE—Braid Reinforced PVC Tubing—NewAge Industries Inc.; *U.S. Private*, pg. 796

NYLOBRADE—Reinforced PVC Hose—Newage Industries Inc., Plastics Technology Group; *U.S. Private*, pg. 796

NYLOCK—Belting—HBD Industries, Inc.; *U.S. Private*, pg. 489

NYLOGARD—Mens Rain Wear—Rainfair, Inc.; *U.S. Private*, pg. 907

NYLOPAK—Plastic Film—The Dow Chemical Company; *U.S. Public*, pg. 522

NYLOPRESS—Filter—American Felt & Filter; *U.S. Private*, pg. 54

NYLOSAN—Wool—Clariant International Ltd.; *Int'l*, pg. 624

NYLOSEAL—Mens Rain Wear—Rainfair, Inc.; *U.S. Private*, pg. 907

NYLOTUBE-11—Nylon-11 Tubing—NewAge Industries Inc.; *U.S. Private*, pg. 796

NYLOTUBE-11—Nylon 11 Tubing—Newage Industries Inc., Plastics Technology Group; *U.S. Private*, pg. 796

NYLOX—Adhesive Composition for Nylon—Hardman Division of Harcros Chemicals, Inc.; *Int'l*, pg. 598

NYPEL—Engineering Plastic—AlliedSignal Inc.; *Int'l*, pg. 49

NYPOL—NONE—Lawter International, Inc.; *U.S. Public*, pg. 980

NYQUIL—Cold Remedy—The Procter & Gamble Company; *U.S. Public*, pg. 1330

NYQUIL—Colds Medication Liquid—Richardson-Vicks, Inc., Health Care Products; *U.S. Public*, pg. 1331

NYQUIL LIQUICAPS—Cold Remedy—Richardson-Vicks, Inc., Health Care Products; *U.S. Public*, pg. 1331

NYSOL—Polyurethane Insulated Magnet Wire—Rea Magnet Wire Company, Inc.; *U.S. Private*, pg. 913

NYSTAR—ENG Testing System—Nicolet Analytical; *U.S. Public*, pg. 1593

NYSTROM—Maps, Glopes & Multimedia—Herff Jones Inc.; *U.S. Private*, pg. 523

NUSYN-NOXFISH—Fish Toxicant—Roussel Corporation; *Int'l*, pg. 625

NYTOL—Sleeping Tablets—Block Drug Company, Inc.; *U.S. Public*, pg. 236

NYTOL—Sleep Aid—Stafford-Miller Limited; *U.S. Public*, pg. 237

NYTRAN—Transfer Media—Schleicher & Schuell, Inc.; *Int'l*, pg. 1206

NYTRON—Inductors—Vishay Intertechnology, Inc., *U.S. Public*, pg. 1721

O

OA—Olympic Airways—Olympic Airways; *Int'l*, pg. 1004

OA COMFORT—Luninaires for Offices—Matsushita Electric Works, Ltd.; *Int'l*, pg. 847

OAG CARGO GUIDE—NONE—OAG; *Int'l*, pg. 1097

OAG DESKTOP FLIGHT GUIDES—North American & Worldwide Editions—OAG; *Int'l*, pg. 1097

OAG ELECTRONIC EDITION TRAVEL SERVICE—NONE—OAG; *Int'l*, pg. 1097

OAG FLIGHTDISK—North American and Worldwide Editions—OAG; *Int'l*, pg. 1097

OAG POCKET FLIGHT GUIDES—North & Latin American, Caribbean, Asia/Pacific, Europe—OAG; *Int'l*, pg. 1097

O&K—Rhombus with the Letters O & K Inside—O&K Orenstein & Koppel Aktiengesellschaft; *Int'l*, pg. 516

O&K TRIPOWER SYSTEM—NONE—O&K Orenstein & Koppel Aktiengesellschaft; *Int'l*, pg. 516

OB—Sanitary Tampons—Johnson & Johnson; *U.S. Public*, pg. 927

O.B.—Tampons—Personal Products Co.; *U.S. Public*, pg. 929

OB—NONE—Tambrands Inc.; *U.S. Public*, pg. 1331

OBI—Hardware & Bldg. Supply Stores in France—GIB Group; *Int'l*, pg. 532

O/B MILL—Micromedia Mill—Premier Mill Corp.; *U.S. Private*, pg. 881

OBS!—Hypermarket—KF/Konsum Coop Group; *Int'l*, pg. 718

OBS! INTERIOR—Specialty Stores—KF/Konsum Coop Group; *Int'l*, pg. 718

O'BAO—Toiletries—L'Oreal S.A.; *Int'l*, pg. 818

OCE—Office Systems, Inc.—OCE USA, Inc.; *Int'l*, pg. 994

OCE—Copiers, Printers, Blotters & Supplies—Oce-van der Grinten N.V.; *Int'l*, pg. 993

OCE-BRUNING—Bruning—OCE USA, Inc.; *Int'l*, pg. 994

OCF—Opern Clinical Foundation Fata Repository—Cerner Corporation; *U.S. Public*, pg. 331

OCI—Oxygen Concentration Indicator—Nellcor Puritan Bennett Incorporated; *U.S. Public*, pg. 1039

OCR PLUS—Optical Character Recognition Software—Xerox Imaging Systems, Inc.; *U.S. Public*, pg. 1785

O!CASSIONS—Year Round Gift Catalog—The Popcorn Factory; *U.S. Private*, pg. 421

O-CEDAR—Handle Goods—Bristol-Myers Squibb Company; *U.S. Public*, pg. 253

ODC—Drilling Fluid Base Oil—Condea Vista Company; *Int'l*, pg. 325

O.D.E.—NONE—Australian Oil & Gas Corporation Limited; *Int'l*, pg. 101

ODE—In the Canal Hearing Aid—Beltone Electronics Corporation; *U.S. Private*, pg. 132

ODL—Lightwave Data Link, TRansmitter & Receiver—Lucent Technologies Inc.; *U.S. Public*, pg. 1017

O.E.I.—Business forms—Office Electronics, Inc.; *U.S. Private*, pg. 812

OEM—NONE—RAYOVAC Corporation; *U.S. Private*, pg. 912

OEM MAGAZINE—Magazine—CMP Media, Inc.; *U.S. Public*, pg. 279

OEM MEDICAL—Repiratory Care—Rusch; *U.S. Public*, pg. 1569

OE 1—Optical Encoder—Oak Grigsby; *U.S. Public*, pg. 1209

O E PLUS—Yarn—National Spinning Co., Inc.; *U.S. Private*, pg. 786

OE 2—Optical Encoder—Oak Grigsby; *U.S. Public*, pg. 1209

O4—Contact Lens Material—Bausch & Lomb Incorporated; *U.S. Public*, pg. 194

OG&E ELECTRIC SERVICES—Registered Tradename—OGE Energy Corp.; *U.S. Public*, pg. 1207

OGG—Office Chairs—Steelcase Wood Div.; *U.S. Private*, pg. 1038

O-GAMMA—Natural Interferon Gamma—Otsuka Pharmaceutical Co., Ltd.; *Int'l*, pg. 1013

OH-58D—Kiowa Warrior Attack Single Engine—Bell Helicopter Textron; *U.S. Public*, pg. 1588

OHM RANGEN—Resistor Selection Box—Ohmite Manufacturing Company; *U.S. Private*, pg. 813

OHSE—Foods—Farmland Foods, Inc.; *U.S. Private*, pg. 396

OIF—Natural Interferon-Alpha Preparation—Otsuka Pharmaceutical Co., Ltd.; *Int'l*, pg. 1013

O.I. NET—Window Sweep—O.I. Corporation; *U.S. Public*, pg. 1208

OK—Fuses—Eagle Electric Mfg. Co., Inc.; *U.S. Private*, pg. 354

OK COOP—Gas Stations & Convenience Stores—Coop Switzerland; *Int'l*, pg. 329

OKI PHONE 800/900—Cellular Phones—Oki Electric Industry Company, Ltd.; *Int'l*, pg. 999

OKI PHONES—Cellular & Portable Phones & Access.—Oki Telecom Group; *Int'l*, pg. 1000

OK KHAKI—Men's Slacks & Shorts—Tropical Sportswear International; *U.S. Private*, pg. 1105

O.K. STRIPS—Sterilization Products—Propper Manufacturing Co., Inc.; *U.S. Private*, pg. 891

OKT—NONE—Johnson & Johnson; *U.S. Public*, pg. 927

O-KE-DOKE—Cheese Popcorn—Jays Foods LLC; *U.S. Private*, pg. 584

OL—Non-Impact LED Printers—Oki Electric Industry Company, Ltd.; *Int'l*, pg. 999

O L FASTENERS—Non Standard Fasteners—Service Supply Co. Inc. of Indiana; *U.S. Private*, pg. 987

OL LED—Page Printers—Okidata Group; *Int'l*, pg. 1000

OLS—NONE—O&K Orenstein & Koppel Aktiengesellschaft; *Int'l*, pg. 516

OMA—Optical Multichannel Analyzer—EG & G Instruments Applied Research; *U.S. Public*, pg. 543

OMF—Open Management Foundation Data Repository—Cerner Corporation; *U.S. Public*, pg. 331

OM5—OfficeMates5—Management Recruiters International, Inc.; *U.S. Public*, pg. 277

OMR—Filter Coalescer—American Felt & Filter; *U.S. Private*, pg. 54

OM SYSTEM—35mm SLR Camera System—Olympus America Inc.; *Int'l*, pg. 1005

OMYA—Calcium Carbonates—Pluess-Staufer AG; *Int'l*, pg. 1061

O-MAG—Metallic Reloading Press—Lyman Products Corporation; *U.S. Private*, pg. 683

O'MALIA—Food Markets—O'Malia Food Markets Inc.; *U.S. Private*, pg. 816

ONCE—Electronic Instrument—Intel Corporation; *U.S. Public*, pg. 886

O.N.E.—Nutrition Oriented Dog Food—Ralston Purina Company; *U.S. Public*, pg. 1359

ONG—Natural Gas Public Utility—ONEOK Inc.; *U.S. Public*, pg. 1226

O12—Children's Clothing—Benetton U.S.A. Corporation; *Int'l*, pg. 186

OPC—Computer System—International Business Machines Corporation; *U.S. Public*, pg. 895

O.P.C.—Okosheath Protective Covering—The Okonite Company; *U.S. Private*, pg. 813

OPD—Telephone Transmission & Data Handling Equipment—NORDX/CDT; *U.S. Public*, pg. 287

OPI—Well Stimulation Pumps—Gardner Denver Machinery Inc.; *U.S. Public*, pg. 703

OPS—Operational Performance Systems Software for Retail Store Improvements—MPSI Systems Inc.; *U.S. Public*, pg. 1027

OPSR—Photo Imageable Solder Mask—LeaRonal, Inc.; *U.S. Public*, pg. 982

OPT—Medical Services—Medtronic, Inc.; *U.S. Public*, pg. 1082

OPT OPTIMAL RACING THERAPY—NONE—Medtronic, Inc.; *U.S. Public*, pg. 1082

ORC—Copper—Inco Limited; *Int'l*, pg. 672

O.R. ONLY—Textile Products For OR - Skin Cream, Gloves—Medline Industries, Inc.; *U.S. Private*, pg. 728

OS-59—Dielectric Heat Transfer Fluid—Monsanto Company; *U.S. Public*, pg. 1124

OS-59—Dielectric Heat Transfer Fluid—Solutia Inc.; *U.S. Public*, pg. 1483

OS/400—Computer System—International Business Machines Corporation; *U.S. Public*, pg. 895

OSI—Wood Office Furniture—GF Office Furniture Ltd.; *U.S. Private*, pg. 434

OSM—Oxygen Saturation Meter—Radiometer A/S; *Int'l*, pg. 1083

OSO—Iron Oxide Pigment—Hitox Corporation of America; *U.S. Public*, pg. 829

OS-124—High Temperature Industrial Functional Fluid—Solutia Inc.; *U.S. Public*, pg. 1483

OS/2—Computer System—International Business Machines Corporation; *U.S. Public*, pg. 895

OS/2 CRASH PROTECTION—Computer System—International Business Machines Corporation; *U.S. Public*, pg. 895

OS/2 DEVELOPER—Magazine—Miller Freeman Inc.; *Int'l*, pg. 1443

OS/2 MAGAZINE—Magazine—Miller Freeman Inc.; *Int'l*, pg. 1443

OS/2 32—Computer System—International Business Machines Corporation; *U.S. Public*, pg. 895

OS/2 WARP—Computer Operating System—International Business Machines Corporation; *U.S. Public*, pg. 895

O.S. WALKER—Magnetic Chucks, Lift Magnets & Instruments—O.S. Walker Co. Inc.; *U.S. Private*, pg. 1147

O/SHIP—NONE—Keyport Life Insurance Company; *U.S. Private*, pg. 666

OTC—Service Tools & Equipment—SPX Corporation; *U.S. Public*, pg. 1420

OTP—Electronic Instrument—Intel Corporation; *U.S. Public*, pg. 886

OTT—Salad Dressings & Barbeque Sauces—Ott Food Products; *U.S. Private*, pg. 821

O3—Contact Lens Material—Bausch & Lomb Incorporated; *U.S. Public*, pg. 194

O-TITE!—O-rings—R&B, Inc.; *U.S. Public*, pg. 1354

O2—NONE—Silicon Graphics, Inc.; *U.S. Public*, pg. 1473

OXI—Pulse Oximeter—Radiometer A/S; *Int'l*, pg. 1083

OZP—Quiet Zone Propeller; 3-Bladed—McCauley Propeller Systems; *U.S. Public*, pg. 1589

OAK—Electronic Component—Oak Industries Inc.; *U.S. Public*, pg. 1209

OAK—Home Series—Toyota Motor Corporation; *Int'l*, pg. 1411

THE OAK BROOK COLLECTION—NONE—Ace Hardware Corporation; *U.S. Private*, pg. 12

OAK CREST—Mobile Home—Kit Manufacturing Company; *U.S. Public*, pg. 962

OAK GROVE—Lumber & Wood Products—Georgia-Pacific Corporation; *U.S. Public*, pg. 735

OAK LEAF—Lumber & Wood Products—Georgia-Pacific Corporation; *U.S. Public*, pg. 735

OAKLOK—Plybent Wood Chair—Sauder Manufacturing Corporation; *U.S. Private*, pg. 967

OAKMONT—Pre-Finished Strip—Bruce Hardwood Floors; *U.S. Public*, pg. 1634

OAKMONT FEATURE STRIP—Pre-Finished Strip—Bruce Hardwood Floors; *U.S. Public*, pg. 1634

OAKRIGDE—Roofing Shingles which Give a Shadow Effect—Owens Corning; *U.S. Public*, pg. 1236

OAKTREE—Men's Apparel—Edison Brothers Stores, Inc.; *U.S. Public*, pg. 563

OAKWOOD HOMES—Mobile Homes—Oakwood Homes Corporation; *U.S. Public*, pg. 1209

OASIS—Soft Drinks—Cadbury Schweppes p.l.c.; *Int'l*, pg. 247

OASIS—Family Tent—The Canadian Coleman Co., Ltd.; *U.S. Private*, pg. 691

OASIS—NONE—Ecolab Inc.; *U.S. Public*, pg. 562

OASIS—Mineral Water—Nestle S.A.; *Int'l*, pg. 915

OASIS—Electric Water Coolers & Dehumidifiers—Oasis Corp.; *U.S. Private*, pg. 810

OASIS—Mineral Water—The Perrier Group of America; *Int'l*, pg. 919

OASYS—Orbit Analysis System—Integral Systems, Inc.; *U.S. Public*, pg. 883

OAT BRAN—Cereal—The Quaker Oats Company; *U.S. Public*, pg. 1347

OAT THINS—Crackers—Nabisco Inc.; *U.S. Public*, pg. 1355

OAT THINS—Snack Crackers—RJR Nabisco Holdings Corp.; *U.S. Public*, pg. 1354

OATMEAL CRISP—Cereal—General Mills, Inc.; *U.S. Public*, pg. 717

OATMEAL CRISP ALMOND—Cereal—General Mills, Inc.; *U.S. Public*, pg. 717

OATMEAL CRISP RAISIN—Cereal—General Mills, Inc.; *U.S. Public*, pg. 717

OATMEAL CRUNCH—Ready-to-Eat Cereal—The Quaker Oats Company; *U.S. Public*, pg. 1347

OATMEAL GOODNESS—Bread—Ralston Purina Company; *U.S. Public*, pg. 1359

THE OATMEAL SOAP—Soap—Yardley of London, Inc.; *Int'l*, pg. 819

OATS 'N FIBER—Cereal—GFA Brands, Inc.; *U.S. Private*, pg. 435

OBAN—NONE—Guinness Plc; *Int'l*, pg. 412

OBERMEYER—NONE—Sport Obermeyer Ltd., USA; *U.S. Private*, pg. 1026

OBJECT—NONE—Brown & Sharpe Manufacturing Company; *U.S. Public*, pg. 260

OBJECT CORE—NONE—American Management Systems, Inc.; *U.S. Public*, pg. 86

OBJECT.MGR—NONE—CACI International Inc; *U.S. Public*, pg. 272

OBJECTSTAR—Applications Development Software Product—Amdahl Corporation; *Int'l*, pg. 527

OBLIO SAMBUCAS—NONE—Brown-Forman Beverages Worldwide; *U.S. Public*, pg. 261

O'BOISE—Snack Foods—The O'Boise Corporation; *U.S. Private*, pg. 810

O'BRIEN—Water Skis—The Coleman Company, Inc.; *U.S. Private*, pg. 690

O'BRIEN POWDER COATINGS—Thermoset Powder Coatings—Herberts-O'Brien Inc.; *Int'l*, pg. 626

OBSERVER—Binoculars—Swift Instruments, Inc.; *U.S. Private*, pg. 1058

THE OBSERVER—NONE—HomeTown Communications Network, Inc.; *U.S. Private*, pg. 537

OBSESSION—Women's Fragrance Products—Calvin Klein Cosmetics Company; *Int'l*, pg. 1435

OBSESSION FOR MEN—Men's Fragrance Products—Calvin Klein Cosmetics Company; *Int'l*, pg. 1435

OBSTGARTEN—Yogurt—Danone Group; *Int'l*, pg. 379

OBTURA—Root Canal Delivery System—Bristol-Myers Squibb Company; *U.S. Public*, pg. 253

OBUS—Backrest—Camp Healthcare; *Int'l*, pg. 1425

OCCIDENTAL CHEMICAL CORPORATION—Chemicals—Occidental Petroleum Corporation; *U.S. Public*, pg. 1210

OCCIDENTAL OIL & GAS CORPORATION—Oil & Gas—Occidental Petroleum Corporation; *U.S. Public*, pg. 1210

OCCUPATIONAL HAZARDS—Periodical—Penton Publishing, Inc.; *U.S. Public*, pg. 1306

OCEAN—Valves—Watts Industries, Inc.; *U.S. Public*, pg. 1746

OCEAN BEAUTY—Salmon—Ocean Beauty Seafoods, Inc.; *U.S. Private*, pg. 810

OCEAN EXPLORER—Remote Operated Vehicle—Oceaneering International, Inc.; *U.S. Public*, pg. 1211

OCEAN HARVEST—NONE—Castleberry/Snow's Brands Inc.; *U.S. Private*, pg. 219

OCEAN KAYAK—Sit-On-Top KayaKs—Johnson Worldwide Associates, Inc.; *U.S. Public*, pg. 932

OCEAN MASTER—Fish & Seafood Items—Louis Kemp Seafood Co.; *U.S. Public*, pg. 1652

OCEAN MATE—Cutlery—Buck Knives, Inc.; *U.S. Private*, pg. 177

OCEAN PRINCE—Canned Seafood—Crown Prince, Inc. (CA); *U.S. Private*, pg. 293

OCEAN PRIZE—Food Products—Rymer Foods Inc.; *U.S. Public*, pg. 1414

OCEAN SPRAY—Jellied Cranberry Sauce, Fresh Cranberries, Fruit Juice Beverages—Ocean Spray Cranberries, Inc.; *U.S. Private*, pg. 811

OCEAN SPRAY FRUIT WAVES—Hard Candy—Adams U.S.A.; *U.S. Public*, pg. 1739

OCEANA—Marine Life Stadium—Cedar Fair, L.P.; *U.S. Public*, pg. 319

OCEANA—NONE—Cedar Point; *U.S. Public*, pg. 319

OCEANIC—Binoculars—Swift Instruments, Inc.; *U.S. Private*, pg. 1058

OCEANICS—Self Contained, Complete Salt Water Environments—American Educational Products; *U.S. Public*, pg. 71

OCEANMASTER—Marine Crane—Weatherford Enterra Incorporated; *U.S. Public*, pg. 1749

OCEANS OF FUN—Waterpark—Cedar Fair, L.P.; *U.S. Public*, pg. 319

OCEANTEACH LTD.—Survey Company—ASCG, Inc.; *U.S. Public*, pg. 80

OCEANWAY—Seafood—King & Prince Seafood Corporation; *U.S. Private*, pg. 620

O'CEDAR—Furniture Polishes—Reckitt & Colman plc; *Int'l*, pg. 1089

OCELOT—Athletic Shoe—Avia; *U.S. Private*, pg. 62

OCHSNER 200 WOVEN—Woven Polyester Vascular Prosthesis—Datascope Corp.; *U.S. Public*, pg. 487

OCKLEY—Bricks—Blue Circle Industries PLC; *Int'l*, pg. 197

OCOMA—Frozen Food—Louis Kemp Seafood Co.; *U.S. Public*, pg. 1652

OCOMA—Frozen Food—Tyson Foods, Inc.; *U.S. Public*, pg. 1652

OCONEE—NONE—New England Stone Industries, Inc.; *U.S. Private*, pg. 793

OCTABRITE—Acid Cleaners—Octagon Process Inc.; *U.S. Private*, pg. 811

OCTACAT—Fluid Cracking Catalysts—W.R. Grace & Co.; *U.S. Public*, pg. 754

OCTAFILM—Filming Amine—BetzDearborn Inc.; *U.S. Public*, pg. 226

OCTAFINING—Aromatics Isomerization Process to Produce Paraxylene—Engelhard Corporation; *U.S. Public*, pg. 582

OCTAFLO—Aircraft De-Icing Fluid—Octagon Process Inc.; *U.S. Private*, pg. 811

OCTAGEN—NONE—Lawter International, Inc.; *U.S. Public*, pg. 980

OCTAGON—Detergent—Colgate-Palmolive Company; *U.S. Public*, pg. 397

OCTAGON FORTY BELOW—Aircraft Anti-Icing Fluid—Octagon Process Inc.; *U.S. Private*, pg. 811

OCTAKLEEN—Cleaners—Octagon Process Inc.; *U.S. Private*, pg. 811

OCTAMELT—Runway De-Icing Fluid—Octagon Process Inc.; *U.S. Private*, pg. 811

OCTANE—NONE—Silicon Graphics, Inc.; *U.S. Public*, pg. 1473

OCTANE 104 PLUS—NONE—Gold Eagle Company; *U.S. Private*, pg. 459

OCTASTRIP—Paint Strippers—Octagon Process Inc.; *U.S. Private*, pg. 811

OCTEL ANA MESSAGING SOFTWARE—Software Package—Octel Messaging Division; *U.S. Public*, pg. 1017

OCTEL ARIA FAX PROCESSING—Adds Fax Processing Capability to Octel Message Servers—Octel Messaging Division; *U.S. Public*, pg. 1017

OCTEL OVERTURE PC—Message Server—Octel Messaging Division; *U.S. Public*, pg. 1017

OCTEL OVERTURE PC—PC-Based Voice Processing Product—Octel Messaging Division; *U.S. Public*, pg. 1017

OCTEL OVERTURE 300—Voice Processing System Message Server—Octel Messaging Division; *U.S. Public*, pg. 1017

OCTEL OVERTURE 350—Voice Processing Message Server—Octel Messaging Division; *U.S. Public*, pg. 1017

OCTEL OVERTURE 200—Voice Processing System Message Server—Octel Messaging Division; *U.S. Public*, pg. 1017

OCTEL OVERTURE 250—Voice Processing System Message Server—Octel Messaging Division; *U.S. Public*, pg. 1017

OCTEL SERENADE FAX PROCESSING—Provide Fax Processing Cabability for Octel Products—Octel Messaging Division; *U.S. Public*, pg. 1017

OCTEL SERENADE MESSAGING SOFTWARE—Supports Octel 200 & 300 Message Servers—Octel Messaging Division; *U.S. Public*, pg. 1017

OCTISIV—Cracking Catalyst—Engelhard Corporation; *U.S. Public*, pg. 582

OCTO FREINS ET SILENCIEUX—Brakes—TCG International Inc.; *Int'l*, pg. 1336

OCTOATE—NONE—Lawter International, Inc.; *U.S. Public*, pg. 980

OCTOBER FILMS—NONE—October Films, Inc.; *Int'l*, pg. 1216

OCTOIL—Lubricating Oils—Octagon Process Inc.; *U.S. Private*, pg. 811

OCTREOSCAN—Tumor Imaging Agent—Mallinckrodt Inc.; *U.S. Public*, pg. 1039

OCTREOSCAN—Diagnostic Radiopharmaceuticals—Mallinckrodt Inc.; *U.S. Public*, pg. 1039

OCU CAPS—Antioxident Vitamin Supplement—Akorn, Inc.; *U.S. Public*, pg. 34

OCU CLEAR—Eye Drops—Schering-Plough Healthcare Products Inc.; *U.S. Public*, pg. 1438

OCU-LUBE—Eye Ointment—Bausch & Lomb Incorporated; *U.S. Public*, pg. 194

OCUCLEAR—Opthalmic Drops for Relief of Eye Irritation—Schering-Plough Corporation; *U.S. Public*, pg. 1438

OCUFEN—Drug for Pupil Dilation—Allergan, Inc.; *U.S. Public*, pg. 46

OCUFLOX—Ophthalmic Solution—Allergan, Inc.; *U.S. Public*, pg. 46

OCUHIST—NONE—Pfizer Inc.; *U.S. Public*, pg. 1281

OCULEARN—Computer Systems—Alcon Laboratories, Inc.; *Int'l*, pg. 916

OCULUS—Side Chair—Vecta; *U.S. Private*, pg. 1038

OCUPRESS—Glaucoma Treatment—Otsuka Pharmaceutical Co., Ltd.; *Int'l*, pg. 1013

OCUSCAN—Digital Biometric Ultrasound Equipment—Alcon Laboratories, Inc.; *Int'l*, pg. 916

OCUSERT—Ocular Therapeutic System—Alza Corporation; *U.S. Public*, pg. 62

OCUTOME—Surgical System—Alcon Laboratories, Inc.; *Int'l*, pg. 916

O'DARBY—NONE—R & A Bailey & Co.; *Int'l*, pg. 409

ODAS—Data Acquisition Service—Halliburton Energy Services; *U.S. Public*, pg. 776

ODDS 'N+ ENDS—Paint—Plasti-Kote Company Inc.; *U.S. Private*, pg. 870

ODEL—NONE—Jotun A/S; *Int'l*, pg. 714

ODELYS—Skincare for Sensitive & Weakened Skin—Guerlain, Inc.; *Int'l*, pg. 780

ODEN-NO-MOTO—Japanese Stew Base—Meiji Seika Kaisha, Ltd.; *Int'l*, pg. 855

ODEX—NONE—Colgate-Palmolive S.A.I.C.; *U.S. Public*, pg. 399

ODIN—Stainless Steel Flatware—Dansk International Designs Ltd.; *U.S. Public*, pg. 261

ODIN—Oki Digital Information Networks—Oki Electric Industry Company, Ltd.; *Int'l*, pg. 999

ODOL—NONE—SmithKline Beecham Corporation; *Int'l*, pg. 1264

ODOL—Oral Care—SmithKline Beecham plc; *Int'l*, pg. 1264

ODOMASTER—Odor Control System—Surco Products, Inc.; *U.S. Private*, pg. 1056

ODOPHUS—Removes Phosphorus & Improves Solids Conditioning in Sewage Treatment Facil—U.S. Filter/Davis Water & Waste Industries, Inc.; *U.S. Public*, pg. 1682

ODOR-AIRE—Air Freshener—Willert Home Products, Inc.; *U.S. Private*, pg. 1177

ODOR EATERS—Footcare Products—Combe Incorporated; *U.S. Private*, pg. 257

ODOROX—NONE—AGA Gas, Inc.; *Int'l*, pg. 13

O'DOUL'S—Non-Alcoholic Beer—Anheuser-Busch Companies, Inc.; *U.S. Public*, pg. 113

ODYSSEY—Van—American Honda Motor Co., Inc.; *Int'l*, pg. 634

ODYSSEY—Specialty Vehicle—American Honda Motor Co., Inc. Motorcycle Division; *Int'l*, pg. 634

ODYSSEY—Nuclear Medicine—Picker International, Inc.; *Int'l*, pg. 545

OFF!—Insect Repellent—S.C. Johnson & Son, Inc.; *U.S. Public*, pg. 592

OFF—Repellent—S.C. Johnson & Son, Limited; *U.S. Private*, pg. 593

THE OFF-BEAT—News Programming—Westwood One, Inc.; *U.S. Public*, pg. 1763

OFF 5TH—Outlet Store—Saks Fifth Avenue; *U.S. Public*, pg. 1429

OFF-HAND—Cleaning Towels—The Gillette Company; *U.S. Public*, pg. 743

OFF! SKINTASTIC—Repellents—S.C. Johnson & Son, Inc.; *U.S. Private*, pg. 592

OFF THE RECORD—Rock Music Radio Program—Westwood One Entertainment; *U.S. Public*, pg. 1763

OFF THE RECORD—Rock Programming—Westwood One, Inc.; *U.S. Public*, pg. 1763

OFF-EZY—Wart Remover—Del Pharmaceuticals, Inc.; *U.S. Public*, pg. 494

OFF-PEAK—Electric Thermal Storage Equipment—Fostoria Industries, Inc.; *U.S. Private*, pg. 421

OFFERLIGHTS—Votive Candles—Will & Baumer Incorporated; *U.S. Private*, pg. 1176

OFFICE—Multi-faceted Office Applications Software—Microsoft Corporation; *U.S. Public*, pg. 1107

OFFICE ACCESS—E-Mail Software—AT&T Strategy & New Service Innovations; *U.S. Public*, pg. 11

OFFICE & SHOP—Home Series—Toyota Motor Corporation; *Int'l*, pg. 1411

THE OFFICE BY STANLEY—Home Office Furniture—Stanley Furniture Co. Inc.; *U.S. Public*, pg. 1508

THE OFFICE MACHINE—Slogan—Datapoint Corporation; *Int'l*, pg. 384

OFFICE PARTNERS—File Cabinets—HON Industries Inc.; *U.S. Public*, pg. 772

OFFICE POWER—Electrical Surge Suppressors, Extennsion Cords, Outlet Strips & Phone Acces—General Cable Corporation; *Int'l*, pg. 1486

OFFICECAM—Office Video Camera—Circon Corporation; *U.S. Public*, pg. 373

OFFICEMAX—Office Supply Retail Stores—OfficeMax; *U.S. Public*, pg. 1212

OFFICEMAX ONLINE—Cyberspace Retailing Concept Online Service; Buy Products off Home Computer—OfficeMax; *U.S. Public*, pg. 1212

OFFICETEAM—Specialized Temporary Administrative Support Staffing—Robert Half International Inc.; *U.S. Public*, pg. 774

OFFICEVISION—Computer System—International Business Machines Corporation; *U.S. Public*, pg. 895

OFFICEVISION/400—Computer System—International Business Machines Corporation; *U.S. Public*, pg. 895

OFFICEVISION/MVS—Computer System—International Business Machines Corporation; *U.S. Public*, pg. 895

OFFICEVISION/2—Computer System—International Business Machines Corporation; *U.S. Public*, pg. 895

OFFICEVISION/VM—Computer System—International Business Machines Corporation; *U.S. Public*, pg. 895

OFFICEWORKS—NONE—Coles Myer Ltd.; *Int'l*, pg. 306

OFFICEWORKS—NONE—Rubbermaid Incorporated; *U.S. Public*, pg. 1411

OFFICIAL—Stationery Products—The Mead Corporation; *U.S. Public*, pg. 1074

OFFICIAL AIRLINE GUIDE—Travel Publications—OAG; *Int'l*, pg. 1097

THE OFFICIAL BLUE BOOK OF UNITED STATES COINS—Dealer Buying Guide—Golden Books Publishing; *U.S. Public*, pg. 749

OFFICIAL BOARD MARKETS—Newsletter—Advantar Communications; *U.S. Private*, pg. 22

OFFICIAL CONTAINER DIRECTORY—Trade Directory—Advantar Communications; *U.S. Private*, pg. 22

OFFICIAL EXPORT GUIDE—Magazine—North American Publishing Company; *U.S. Private*, pg. 803

OFFICIAL MUSEUM DIRECTORY—Museum Reference—National Register Publishing; *Int'l*, pg. 1096

THE OFFICIAL RED BOOK OF UNITED STATES COINS—Coin Collecting Handbook—Golden Books Publishing; *U.S. Public*, pg. 749

OFFLEY—NONE—Bacardi-Martini Belgium; *U.S. Private*, pg. 109

OFFSET LITHOGRAPHIC TECHNOLOGY—Textbook Covering Methods Used in the Graphic Arts Industry—Goodheart-Willcox Publisher; *U.S. Private*, pg. 464

OFFSET SOLUTION—NONE—Avenor, Inc.; *Int'l*, pg. 101

OGEN—Estropipate—Abbott Laboratories; *U.S. Public*, pg. 12

OH BOY—Syrup—Dean Pickles & Specialty Products; *U.S. Public*, pg. 490

OH BOY—Frozen Specialties—Oh Boy Corporation; *U.S. Private*, pg. 812

OH HENRY!—Chocolate Bar—Hershey Foods Corporation; *U.S. Public*, pg. 811

OH HENRY—Candy Bar—Nestle Chocolate & Confection; *Int'l*, pg. 917

OH HENRY!—Candy Bar—Nestle S.A.; *Int'l*, pg. 915

OH HENRY—Candy Bar—Nestle USA; *Int'l*, pg. 916

OHAUS—Line of Laboratory Balances—Novartis; *Int'l*, pg. 972

OHIO BLUE TIP—Matches—Diamond Brands, Inc.; *U.S. Private*, pg. 330

OHIO FARMER—Farm Publication-15 Issues/Year—Farm Progress Publications; *U.S. Public*, pg. 513

OHIO MANUFACTURERS DIRECTORY—Directory—Manufacturers' News, Inc.; *U.S. Private*, pg. 700

OHMTEK—Resistors/Potentiometers—Vishay Intertechnology, Inc.; *U.S. Public*, pg. 1721

OH'S—Bran Cereal—The Quaker Oats Company; *U.S. Public*, pg. 1347

OHSE—Foods—Ohse Foods Inc.; *U.S. Private*, pg. 396

OIL BASE SHIELDZ—Pre-Wallcovering Primer—Wm. Zinsser & Co., Inc.; *U.S. Public*, pg. 1358

OIL BLEO—Antineoplastic Agents—Nippon Kayaku Co. Ltd.; *Int'l*, pg. 934

OIL DRAULIC—Elevators—Dover Corporation; *U.S. Public*, pg. 520

OIL DRI—All-Purpose Oil & Grease Absorbent—Oil-Dri Corporation of America; *U.S. Public*, pg. 1214

OIL-DRI LITE—Oil & Grease Absorbent (Synthetic)—Oil-Dri Corporation of America; *U.S. Public*, pg. 1214

OIL FOIL—Filter Bags—American Felt & Filter; *U.S. Private*, pg. 54

OIL-GLO—Fluorescent Additive—Spectronics Corporation; *U.S. Private*, pg. 1024

OIL-HARD—NONE—Carpenter Technology Corporation; *U.S. Public*, pg. 307

OIL OF OLAY—Skin Care Products—Permark International (Pty.) Ltd.; *Int'l*, pg. 1036

OIL OF OLAY—Skin Cream—The Procter & Gamble Company; *U.S. Public*, pg. 1330

OIL OF OLAY RENEWAL CREAM—Facial Cream—The Procter & Gamble Company; *U.S. Public*, pg. 1330

OIL-TITE!—Oil Drain Plugs & Gaskets—R&B, Inc.; *U.S. Public*, pg. 1354

OIL-TOUGH—NONE—Carpenter Technology Corporation; *U.S. Public*, pg. 307

OIL-WEAR—NONE—Carpenter Technology Corporation; *U.S. Public*, pg. 307

OILDAG—Lubricants—Acheson Colloids Company; *U.S. Private*, pg. 12

OILDRAULIC—Hydraulic Passenger & Freight Elevators—Dover Elevator Systems, Inc.; *U.S. Public*, pg. 521

OILDRAULIC—Automotive Lifts—Rotary Lift; *U.S. Public*, pg. 521

OILDYNE—Miniature Hydraulic Components—Commercial Intertech Corp.; *U.S. Public*, pg. 411

OILDYNE—Medium & High Pressure Compact Power Units, Pumps, Motors, Cylinders, Valve—Oildyne; *U.S. Public*, pg. 411

OILFOS—Viscosity Control for Oil Well Drilling Muds—Solutia Inc.; *U.S. Public*, pg. 1483

OILGEAR—Hydraulic Systems & Components—The Oilgear Company; *U.S. Public*, pg. 1215

OILOMATIC SAW CHAIN—Saw Chain—Stihl Inc.; *Int'l*, pg. 1301

OILY SKIN FORMULA SOAP—Soap for Oily Skin—Neutrogena Corporation; *U.S. Public*, pg. 928

OILZUM—Motor Oils—Dryden Oil of New England; *Int'l*, pg. 235

OIME—Drilling Mud Pumps & Equipment—Parker Drilling Company; *U.S. Public*, pg. 1259

OKA—NONE—Agropur; *Int'l*, pg. 31

O'KEEFE—Beer—Foster's Brewing Group Limited; *Int'l*, pg. 500

OKIFAX—Facsimiles—Oki Electric Industry Company, Ltd.; *Int'l*, pg. 999

OKITAC 2300—Banking Systems—Oki Electric Industry Company, Ltd.; *Int'l*, pg. 999

OKITEL—Modems—Okidata Group; *Int'l*, pg. 1000

OKLAHOMA—Newspaper Publishing & Broadcasting—Oklahoma Publishing Company; *U.S. Private*, pg. 813

OKLAHOMA CITY TIMES—Daily Newspaper—The Daily & Sunday Oklahoman; *U.S. Private*, pg. 813

OKLAHOMA FARM SHOW—Trade Show—Farm Progress Publications; *U.S. Public*, pg. 513

OKLAHOMA FARMER-STOCKMAN—Monthly Farm Publication—Farm Progress Publications; *U.S. Public*, pg. 513

OKLAHOMA MANUFACTURERS REGISTER—Register—Manufacturers' News, Inc.; *U.S. Private*, pg. 700

OKLAHOMA NATURAL GAS COMPANY—Natural Gas Public Utility—ONEOK Inc.; *U.S. Public*, pg. 1226

OKOBON—Moisture Resistant Cable Finish—The Okonite Company; *U.S. Private*, pg. 813

OKOCAL—Paper Insulated Cable—The Okonite Company; *U.S. Private*, pg. 813

OKOCLAD—Welded Smooth Sheath Type MC Cable—The Okonite Company; *U.S. Private*, pg. 813

OKOCLEAR TP—Non-Halogenated Low Smoke Thermoplastic Cable Jackets—The Okonite Company; *U.S. Private*, pg. 813

OKOCLEAR TS—Non-Halogenated Low Smoke Thermoset Jackets—The Okonite Company; *U.S. Private*, pg. 813

OKOCORD—Rubber Insulated, Reinforced Jacketed, Mold Cured Portable, Flexible Jacket—The Okonite Company; *U.S. Private*, pg. 813

OKOGUARD—Power Cables—The Okonite Company; *U.S. Private*, pg. 813

OKOLAST—Tree Wire with Brake Lining Armor & Braid Covering—The Okonite Company; *U.S. Private*, pg. 813

OKOLON—Vulcanized Chlorosulfonated Polyethylene Insulation and/or Jacket Compound—The Okonite Company; *U.S. Private*, pg. 813

OKOLOY—Corrosion Resistant Lead Alloy Coated for Copper Conductor—The Okonite Company; *U.S. Private*, pg. 813

OKONEX—High Voltage Butyl Rubber Insulated Cables—The Okonite Company; *U.S. Private*, pg. 813

OKONITE FMR—Power & Control Cables—The Okonite Company; *U.S. Private*, pg. 813

OKOTEMP TPR—Thermoplastic Rubber Jackets—The Okonite Company; *U.S. Private*, pg. 813

OKOTHERM—Heat Resistant Silicone Rubber Base Insulation—The Okonite Company; *U.S. Private*, pg. 813

OKOVOX—Electrical Cable & Insulating Material—The Okonite Company; *U.S. Private*, pg. 813

OKOWELD—Protective, Electric, Insulating, Moisture-Sealing, Weather Proofing Tape—The Okonite Company; *U.S. Private*, pg. 813

OKOZEL—Flame & Radiation Resistant Insulating & Jacketing Compound—The Okonite Company; *U.S. Private*, pg. 813

OKRAY'S—Frozen Potato Products—J.R. Simplot Company; *U.S. Private*, pg. 1002

OL' SAVANNAH—Prefinished Wall Paneling—Georgia-Pacific Corporation; *U.S. Public*, pg. 735

OLA—Laundry Soap—Colgate-Palmolive Company; *U.S. Public*, pg. 397

OLAPON—Shampoo—Wella Group; *Int'l*, pg. 1489

OLAY—Cream & Lotion—Richardson-Vicks, Inc. Personal Care Products Div.; *U.S. Public*, pg. 1331

OLAY BATH BAR—Soap—The Procter & Gamble Company; *U.S. Public*, pg. 1330

OLD AMERICAN—Frozen Food—Tyson Foods, Inc.; *U.S. Public*, pg. 1652

OLD ANNAPOLIS—Giftware—Lenox Brands; *U.S. Public*, pg. 261

OLD ARMY—Cap & Ball Revolver—Sturm, Ruger & Co., Inc.; *U.S. Public*, pg. 1526

OLD BAY—Seasoning—McCormick & Company, Incorporated; *U.S. Public*, pg. 1066

OLD BAY—Seafood Line—McCormick/Schilling; *U.S. Public*, pg. 1066

OLD BLUE—Jean Treatment—Malco Products, Inc.; *U.S. Private*, pg. 698

OLD BROOKVILLE BLANC de BLANCS—Sparkling Wine—Banfi Vintners; *U.S. Private*, pg. 113

OLD BROOKVILLE CHARDONNEY—Wine—Banfi Vintners; *U.S. Private*, pg. 113

OLD CHICAGO—Beer—Joseph Huber Brewing Co.; *U.S. Private*, pg. 545

OLD CHICAGO—Pasta, Pizza & Beer—Rock Bottom Restaurants; *U.S. Public*, pg. 1396

OLD COUNCIL TREE—Bond Paper—Kimberly-Clark Corporation; *U.S. Public*, pg. 958

OLD COUNTRY BUFFET—Buffet Restaurants—Buffets, Inc.; *U.S. Public*, pg. 267

OLD CRAFTSMAN—Wood Products—Georgia-Pacific Corporation; *U.S. Public*, pg. 735

OLD DUTCH—Food Products—Old Dutch Foods, Inc.; *U.S. Private*, pg. 814

OLD DUTCH—Beer—Pittsburgh Brewing Company; *U.S. Private*, pg. 619

OLD DUTCH—Salad Dressing—Reily Foods Company; *U.S. Private*, pg. 919

OLD EL PASO—Mexican Foods—Grand Metropolitan Plc; *Int'l*, pg. 408

OLD EL PASO—Mexican Food Products, Canned & Frozen—The Pillsbury Company; *Int'l*, pg. 411

OLD ENGLISH—Photo Typesetters—AGFA EPS Division; *Int'l*, pg. 172

OLD ENGLISH—Processed Cheese—Alliant Foodservice, Inc.; *U.S. Private*, pg. 244

OLD ENGLISH—Furniture Polish—Reckitt & Colman Inc.; *Int'l*, pg. 1090

OLD ENGLISH—Furniture Polish—Reckitt & Colman plc; *Int'l*, pg. 1089

OLD FAITHFUL—Pedestal Sump Pump—Zoeller Co.; *U.S. Public*, pg. 1207

THE OLD FARMER'S ALMANAC—Annual Almanac—Yankee Publishing Incorporated; *U.S. Private*, pg. 1195

OLD FASHIONED & QUICK—Hot Cereal—The Quaker Oats Company; *U.S. Public*, pg. 1347

OLD FASHIONED GINGER SNAPS—Cookies—Nabisco Inc.; *U.S. Public*, pg. 1355

OLD FITZGERALD—Bourbon—Shieffelin Somerset Co.; *Int'l*, pg. 412

OLD FITZGERALD—Bourbon—United Distillers USA, Inc.; *Int'l*, pg. 412

OLD FORESTER KENTUCKY—Bourbon—Brown-Forman Beverages Worldwide; *U.S. Public*, pg. 261

OLD FORESTER KENTUCKY STRAIGHT—Bourbon Whisky—Brown-Forman Corporation; *U.S. Public*, pg. 261

OLD GERMAN—Beer—Pittsburgh Brewing Company; *U.S. Private*, pg. 619

OLD GOLD—Cigarettes—Loews Corporation; *U.S. Public*, pg. 1010

OLD GOLD & OLD GOLD LIGHTS 100s—Cigarettes—Lorillard Tobacco Company; *U.S. Public*, pg. 1011

OLD GOLD BRAND—Seeds—L.L. Olds Seed Company; *U.S. Private*, pg. 814

OLD GRAND-DAD—Bourbon Whiskey—Fortune Brands, Inc.; *U.S. Public*, pg. 674

OLD HICKORY—Knives—Servotronics, Inc.; *U.S. Public*, pg. 1462

OLD HOLBORN—NONE—Fortune Brands, Inc.; *U.S. Public*, pg. 674

OLD HOLBORN—Roll-Your-Own Cigarettes—Gallaher Tobacco Ltd.; *Int'l*, pg. 539

OLD HOME—Bread—Metz Baking Company; *U.S. Private*, pg. 1022

OLD HOMESTEAD—Cutlery & Flatware—Lifetime Hoan Corp.; *U.S. Public*, pg. 992

OLD IRONSIDES—Writing Paper—The Mead Corporation; *U.S. Public*, pg. 1074

OLD JOE—Twist Tobacco—Conwood Company L.P.; *U.S. Private*, pg. 272

OLD LONDON—Specialty Baked Goods, Breads—Bestfoods; *U.S. Public*, pg. 223

OLD MASTER—NONE—Dunhill Scotch Whisky Sales Limited; *Int'l*, pg. 409

OLD MCCALL—Bourbon—Montebello Brands Inc.; *U.S. Private*, pg. 758

OLD MILL—Dairy Products—Crowley Foods, Inc.; *Int'l*, pg. 752

OLD MILL—Oatmeal—International Multifoods Corporation; *U.S. Public*, pg. 900

OLD MILL—Oats—Robin Hood Multifoods Inc.; *U.S. Public*, pg. 901

OLD MILWAUKEE—Beer & Non-Alcoholic Beer—The Stroh Brewery Company; *U.S. Private*, pg. 1047

OLD MILWAUKEE LIGHT—Beer—The Stroh Brewery Company; *U.S. Private*, pg. 1047

OLD MILWAUKEE N.A.—Non-Alcoholic Beer—The Stroh Brewery Company; *U.S. Private*, pg. 1047

OLD NEW ENGLAND—Egg Nog—M.S. Walker, Inc.; *U.S. Private*, pg. 1147

OLD PAL—Pet Supplies: Chains & Retention Devices—Ekco Group, Inc.; *U.S. Public*, pg. 566

OLD PARR ELIZABETHAN—NONE—Guinness Plc; *Int'l*, pg. 412

OLD PARR SUPERIOR—NONE—Guinness Plc; *Int'l*, pg. 412

OLD PARR TRIBUTE—NONE—Guinness Plc; *Int'l*, pg. 412

OLD PLANTATION—Molasses—Dean Pickles & Specialty Products; *U.S. Public*, pg. 490

OLD PLANTATION—Seasonings—A.C. Legg Packing Company, Inc.; *U.S. Private*, pg. 658

OLD PRO—Professional Applicators—Sherwin-Williams Coatings Division; *U.S. Public*, pg. 1466

OLD QUAKER—Paint—The Sherwin-Williams Company; *U.S. Public*, pg. 1465

OLD SAN FRANCISCO STYLE—Sour Dough & Cinnamon Bread Snacks—Granny Goose Foods, Inc.; *U.S. Private*, pg. 469

OLD SAVANNAH—Food Service Prods.—Savannah Foods & Industries, Inc.; *U.S. Public*, pg. 872

OLD SEA DOG—Rum—Peerless Importers, Inc.; *U.S. Private*, pg. 847

OLD SECURITY—Bond Paper—The Mead Corporation; *U.S. Public*, pg. 1074

OLD SMOKEHOUSE STEAK SAUCE PLUS—Sauce—Hormel Foods Corp.; *U.S. Public*, pg. 840

OLD SMUGGLER SCOTCH—Scotch—Hiram Walker; *Int'l*, pg. 63

OLD SMUGGLER SCOTCH WHISKY—Spirit—Allied Domecq PLC; *Int'l*, pg. 62

OLD SOUTH—Line of OJ & Fresh Citrus—Lykes Brothers Inc.; *U.S. Private*, pg. 682

OLD SOUTH—Log Rolls—Standard Candy Co., Inc.; *U.S. Private*, pg. 1030

OLD SPICE—Fragrances—The Procter & Gamble Company; *U.S. Public*, pg. 1330

OLD TAYLOR—Twist Tobacco—Conwood Company L.P.; *U.S. Private*, pg. 272

OLD TIME—Foods—Roundy's, Inc.; *U.S. Private*, pg. 948

OLD TIME—Corn Meal—Wilkins-Rogers Incorporated; *U.S. Private*, pg. 1176

OLD TIME BODY & AGE—Flavoring—David Michael & Co. Inc.; *U.S. Private*, pg. 740

OLD TIME CROCHET PATTERNS & DESIGNS—Crafts Magazine—House of White Birches, Inc.; *U.S. Private*, pg. 542

OLD TIMER—Cutlery—Imperial Schrade Corp.; *U.S. Private*, pg. 559

OLD TIMER KNIVES—Pocket & Hunting Knives with Delrin Handles—Imperial Schrade Corp.; *U.S. Private*, pg. 559

OLD TOOTH—Former Name of Kent Old Brown—Foster's Brewing Group Limited; *Int'l*, pg. 500

OLD TOWN—Meat Products—Gwaltney of Smithfield, Ltd.; *U.S. Public*, pg. 1479

OLD TOWN—Canoes & Kayaks—Johnson Worldwide Associates, Inc.; *U.S. Public*, pg. 932

OLD TOWN OVEN STUFFS—Microwaveable Deli Sandwich—The Quaker Oats Company; *U.S. Public*, pg. 1347

OLD TYME—Syrups—Bestfoods; *U.S. Public*, pg. 223

OLD VIENNA—Lager Beer—Foster's Brewing Group Limited; *Int'l*, pg. 500

OLD VILLAGE SHOP—Gifts—Hanover Direct Pennsylvania, Inc.; *U.S. Public*, pg. 782

OLD WISCONSIN—Sausage & Cheese—Carl Buddig & Company; *U.S. Private*, pg. 178

OLD WORLD—Sausages—Armour Swift Eckrich; *U.S. Public*, pg. 426

OLDBRIDGE—Wood, Lumber & Wood Fiber Products—Georgia-Pacific Corporation; *U.S. Public*, pg. 735

OLDE DUTCH—Vinyl Siding & Accessories—Alcoa Building Products, Inc.; *U.S. Public*, pg. 61

OLDE ENGLISH 800+ MALT LIQUOR—Malt Liquor—Pabst Brewing Co.; *U.S. Private*, pg. 954

OLDE FASHIONED RECIPE—Ice Cream—Borden, Inc.; *U.S. Private*, pg. 157

OLDE FROTHINGSLOSH—Ale—Pittsburgh Brewing Company; *U.S. Private*, pg. 619

OLDE MASTER—Wood Cleaner—Stanhome Inc.; *U.S. Public*, pg. 1508

OLDE NEW ENGLAND—Brownies—President Baking Company; *Int'l*, pg. 1069

OLDE SMITHFIELD—Meat Products—Gwaltney of Smithfield, Ltd.; *U.S. Public*, pg. 1479

OLDE WORLD GOURMET GUMMY BEARS—Candy—Brach & Brock Confections Inc.; *U.S. Private*, pg. 163

OLDELFT—Radiodiagnosis, Radiotherapy Planning, Robotic Vision—Delft Instruments N.V.; *Int'l*, pg. 388

THE OLDIES CHANNEL FORMAT—24-Hour satellite Delivered Music Format—Westwood One, Inc.; *U.S. Public*, pg. 1763

OLDS BRAND—Seeds—L.L. Olds Seed Company; *U.S. Private*, pg. 814

OLDSMOBILE—Cars—General Motors Corporation; *U.S. Public*, pg. 718

OLDTOWNE—Prefinished Wall Paneling—Georgia-Pacific Corporation; *U.S. Public*, pg. 735

OLE CAROLINA—Meats—Thorn Apple Valley, Inc.; *U.S. Public*, pg. 1602

OLEFIL—Grade of Poly-Propylene—Amoco Chemicals; *U.S. Public*, pg. 102

OLEG CASSINI—Emery Boards, Clippers, Scissors, Tweezers, Gift Sets—The Cook Bates Division; *Int'l*, pg. 815

OLETRON—Extruded Shapes & Parts—DSM Engineering Plastic Products; *Int'l*, pg. 354

OLEX—NONE—Pacific Dunlop Limited; *Int'l*, pg. 1021

OLGA—Intimate Apparel—Warnaco Inc.; *U.S. Public*, pg. 1738

OLGA-BRIGHTS—Bras, Panties—Olga Div.; *U.S. Public*, pg. 1738

OLGALACE—Bras, Panties, Shapewear—Olga Div.; *U.S. Public*, pg. 1738

OLICARD—Cardiovascular Preparations—Kali-Chemie Aktiengesellschaft; *Int'l*, pg. 1278

OLIFANT GENEVER—Spirit—Allied Domecq PLC; *Int'l*, pg. 62

OLIN—Skis—K2 Inc.; *U.S. Public*, pg. 940

OLIN—Chemicals—Olin Corporation; *U.S. Public*, pg. 1218

THE OLIVE GARDEN—Restaurant Chain—Darden Restaurants, Inc.; *U.S. Public*, pg. 483

OLIVER—Interactive Analysis & Debugging for CICS with Strong pl/1 Support—Compuware Corporation; *U.S. Public*, pg. 423

OLIVER—NONE—Luxottica Group S.p.A.; *Int'l*, pg. 822

OLIVER MACLEOD—Chimneys & Fireplaces—Security Chimneys International Ltd.; *Int'l*, pg. 1217

OLIVER NELSON—Books—Thomas Nelson Inc.; *U.S. Public*, pg. 1167

OLIVERI—Stainless Steel Kitchen Sink Units—Carter Holt Harvey Limited; *U.S. Public*, pg. 904

OLIVER'S GREENHOUSE COLLECTION—NONE—Celebrity Incorporated; *U.S. Public*, pg. 319

OLIVETTI—Business Management—Olivetti Management of America, Inc.; *Int'l*, pg. 1002

OLIVIER LEFLAIVE—Burgundy—Frederick Wildman & Sons Ltd.; *U.S. Private*, pg. 1176

OLSON'S EUROPE—Deluxe & Superior First Class Tours To Europe—Noel Olson Group; *U.S. Private*, pg. 800

OLSTEN HEALTH SERVICES—Health Care Services—Olsten Corporation; *U.S. Public*, pg. 1220

OLSTEN KIMBERLY QUALITYCARE—Health Care Services—Olsten Corporation; *U.S. Public*, pg. 1220

OLSTEN STAFFING SERVICES—Temporary Help Services—Olsten Corporation; *U.S. Public*, pg. 1220

OLYMPIA—Beer—Pabst Brewing Co.; *U.S. Private*, pg. 954

OLYMPIA—Beer—Pabst Brewing Co./Tumwater; *U.S. Private*, pg. 954

OLYMPIA GOLD—Beer—Pabst Brewing Co.; *U.S. Private*, pg. 954

OLYMPIA GOLD—Beer—Pabst Brewing Co./Tumwater; *U.S. Private*, pg. 954

OLYMPIA LIGHT—Beer—Pabst Brewing Co.; *U.S. Private*, pg. 954

OLYMPIA STELLAFLEX—NONE—Windmoeller & Hoelscher; *Int'l*, pg. 1510

OLYMPIAN—Sunglasses—Bausch & Lomb Incorporated; *U.S. Public*, pg. 194

OLYMPIAN—Filters, Regulators, Lubricators, Valves & Flow Rate & Pressu—IMI Plc; *Int'l*, pg. 646

OLYMPIC—Wood Stains & Architectural Coatings—PPG Industries, Inc.; *U.S. Public*, pg. 1245

OLYMPIC D-2—Cold Work Die Steel—Latrobe Steel Company; *U.S. Public*, pg. 1617

OLYMPIC-LOK—Structural Blind Rivets—Allfast Fastening Systems, Inc.; *U.S. Private*, pg. 37

OLYMPIC OVERCOAT—Wood Stains—PPG Industries, Inc.; *U.S. Public*, pg. 1245

OLYMPIC WEATHERSCREEN—Wood Stains & Paints—PPG Industries, Inc.; *U.S. Public*, pg. 1245

OLYMPUS—Medical & Clinical Instruments, 35mm Cameras—Olympus America Inc.; *Int'l*, pg. 1005

OLYMPUS—Cameras, Microscopes, Endoscopes—Olympus Optical Co., Ltd.; *Int'l*, pg. 1004

OLYMPUS 593—Commercial Jet Engine—SNECMA - Societe Nationale d'Etude et de Construction de Moteurs d'Aviation; *Int'l*, pg. 1165

OLYMPUS INFINITY STYLUS ZOOM—Compact Camera—Olympus America Inc.; *Int'l*, pg. 1005

OMAHA STEAKS—Steaks—Omaha Steaks; *U.S. Private*, pg. 815

OMAHA STEAKS INTERNATIONAL—Steaks—Omaha Steaks; *U.S. Private*, pg. 815

OMCAR—California Restaurants—Controladora Comercial Mexicana, S.A. de C.V.; *Int'l*, pg. 328

OMCAR—Photo Typesetters—AGFA EPS Division; *Int'l*, pg. 172

OMEGA—Service Station Services—Amoco Corporation; *U.S. Public*, pg. 101

OMEGA—Dry Chemical Feeders—BIF; *U.S. Public*, pg. 726

OMEGA—Athletic Tape—Bike Athletic Co.; *U.S. Private*, pg. 143

OMEGA—NONE—Brown & Sharpe Manufacturing Company; *U.S. Public*, pg. 260

OMEGA—Vinegar—Burns, Philp & Company Limited; *Int'l*, pg. 236

OMEGA—Power Steering Components—Cooper Industries, Inc.; *U.S. Public*, pg. 442

OMEGA—Electronic Components—General Instrument Corporation; *U.S. Public*, pg. 716

OMEGA—Dog & Cat Food—Harrisons & Crosfield plc; *Int'l*, pg. 598

OMEGA—Polyethylene Banner Material—Industrial Coatings Group, Inc.; *U.S. Private*, pg. 434

OMEGA—Premium Bellows-Type Expansion Joints; Shaft & Mechanical Couplings—Marquette Coppersmithing Co., Inc.; *U.S. Private*, pg. 706

OMEGA—Oxygen Concentrator—Nellcor Puritan Bennett Incorporated; *U.S. Public*, pg. 1039

OMEGA—Fire Fighting Equip.—Premier Farnell; *Int'l*, pg. 1068

Brand Name Index

OMEGA—Watches—SMH Swiss Corporation for Micro Electronics & Watchmaking Indus. Ltd.; *Int'l*, pg. 1160

OMEGA—Architectural Downlighting—Thomas Industries Inc.; *U.S. Public*, pg. 1598

OMEGA—NONE—Vauxhall; *U.S. Public*, pg. 724

OMEGA—Electronic Controls—Weather Tec Corporation; *U.S. Private*, pg. 1155

OMEGA82C194—NONE—Trident Microsystems, Inc.; *U.S. Public*, pg. 1637

OMEGA82C128—NONE—Trident Microsystems, Inc.; *U.S. Public*, pg. 1637

OMEGA82C7226—NONE—Trident Microsystems, Inc.; *U.S. Public*, pg. 1637

OMEGA82C365—NONE—Trident Microsystems, Inc.; *U.S. Public*, pg. 1637

OMEGA82C28—NONE—Trident Microsystems, Inc.; *U.S. Public*, pg. 1637

OMEGA82C094—NONE—Trident Microsystems, Inc.; *U.S. Public*, pg. 1637

OMEGA 4—Analogue Addressable Fire Parel—JSB Electrical PLC; *Int'l*, pg. 453

OMEGA RX—NONE—Cardinal Health Inc.; *U.S. Public*, pg. 304

OMEGALARM—Security System—Radionics, Inc.; *U.S. Public*, pg. 501

OMEGALINK—Security System—Radionics, Inc.; *U.S. Public*, pg. 501

OMEGAMON—Performance Monitor for MVS, CICS, DB2, IMS, SMS & VFAM—Candle Corporation; *U.S. Private*, pg. 204

OMEGAPAK—Adjustable Frequency Controllers—Square D Company; *Int'l*, pg. 1208

OMEPRAL—Gastrointestinal Drug—Astra AB; *Int'l*, pg. 93

OMIDERM—Wound & Burn Dressings in Various Sizes—Bradley Pharmaceuticals; *U.S. Public*, pg. 249

OMIDERM—Wound & Burn Dressings in Various Sizes—Doak Dermatologics; *U.S. Public*, pg. 250

OMITE—Insecticide—Uniroyal Chemical Company, Inc.; *U.S. Public*, pg. 460

OMNI—Opthamalic Lenses—American Optical Corporation; *U.S. Private*, pg. 60

OMNI—On-Line Service—General Media International Inc.; *U.S. Private*, pg. 444

OMNI—Hotel—Omni Hotels; *U.S. Private*, pg. 1065

THE OMNI—Leasing Coliseum Facilities—Omni Hotels; *U.S. Private*, pg. 1065

OMNI—Science Magazine—Omni Publications International Ltd.; *U.S. Private*, pg. 444

OMNI—NONE—Rubbermaid Incorporated; *U.S. Public*, pg. 1411

OMNI—Transaction Systems—VeriFone, Inc.; *U.S. Public*, pg. 815

OMNI-AIR—Respirator—Aearo Company; *U.S. Private*, pg. 23

OMNI-BLOK—Fuse Block—Littelfuse, Inc.; *U.S. Public*, pg. 1001

OMNI-DX—Extended Wear Contact Lens, Gas Permeable—40 Fort Eye Associates; *U.S. Private*, pg. 420

OMNI EXPRESS—Planning & Organization of Meetings for Businesses and Other Organizations—Omni Hotels; *U.S. Private*, pg. 1065

OMNI-FILL—Paint Filling System—Sherwin-Williams Diversified Brands, Inc.; *U.S. Public*, pg. 1466

OMNI-FLO—Eye/Face Wash—Haws Drinking Faucet Co.; *U.S. Private*, pg. 512

OMNI GS—NONE—SunGard Data Systems Inc.; *U.S. Public*, pg. 1534

OMNI GRAPHITE RTS—Racquetball Racquet—Ektelon; *U.S. Private*, pg. 884

OMNI INTERNATIONAL—Rental of Commercial Space in a Planned Community—Omni Hotels; *U.S. Private*, pg. 1065

OMNI-LENS—Contact Lenses—40 Fort Eye Associates; *U.S. Private*, pg. 420

OMNI-LOC—Mast Angle Adjustment—Allen Telecom Inc.; *U.S. Public*, pg. 45

OMNI-ONE—Employment Agency—General Employment Enterprises, Inc.; *U.S. Public*, pg. 714

OMNI-PAK—Paint Filling System—Sherwin-Williams Diversified Brands, Inc.; *U.S. Public*, pg. 1466

OMNI PAY—NONE—SunGard Data Systems Inc.; *U.S. Public*, pg. 1534

OMNI-PETTE—Scientific Glassware for Laboratory Use—Wheaton Inc.; *Int'l*, pg. 67

OMNI PLAN—NONE—SunGard Data Systems Inc.; *U.S. Public*, pg. 1534

OMNI-PURPOSE—Loudspeaker Mounting Bracket—Atlas/Soundolier; *U.S. Private*, pg. 64

OMNI-RUPTER—Interrupter Switch—S & C Electric Company; *U.S. Private*, pg. 954

OMNI SENSOR—Intelligent Smoke Detector—System Sensor Division; *U.S. Public*, pg. 1306

OMNI-SPENSE—Scientific Glassware for Laboratory Use—Wheaton Inc.; *Int'l*, pg. 67

OMNI-STAR—Respirator—Aearo Company; *U.S. Private*, pg. 23

OMNI-TRADE—NONE—Taylor Impression, Inc.; *U.S. Private*, pg. 1070

OMNI-VIAL—Scientific Glassware for Laboratory Use—Wheaton Inc.; *Int'l*, pg. 67

OMNI VUFORE—Smart, Screen-Based Telephone—VeriFone, Inc.; *U.S. Public*, pg. 815

OMNIA—Perimeter Installed Sheet Vinyl Flooring—Mannington Resilient Floors; *U.S. Private*, pg. 700

OMNIBAC—Backing for Carpeting—Interface Inc.; *U.S. Public*, pg. 889

OMNIBASIC—Software—Alpha Microsystems; *U.S. Public*, pg. 57

OMNIBOX—Worm Reducers—The Falk Corporation; *U.S. Public*, pg. 1534

OMNICARE GERIATRIC PHARMACEUTICAL CARE GUIDELINES—Proprietary Drug Formulary Designed for the Elderly—Omnicare, Inc.; *U.S. Public*, pg. 815

OMNICHARGER—Table Top Chargers—Sanyo Energy (U.S.A.) Corporation; *Int'l*, pg. 1191

OMNICON SERIES—X-Ray—Picker International, Inc.; *Int'l*, pg. 545

OMNICROM—Graphic Art Supplies—Esselte AB; *Int'l*, pg. 459

OMNIDERM—Wound Care Medication—Perstorp Pharma Ltd. Wound Care Division; *Int'l*, pg. 1037

OMNIFILTER—Filters—Nellcor Puritan Bennett Incorporated; *U.S. Public*, pg. 1039

OMNIFIT—Valves & Connectors for Scientific Instruments—Halma p.l.c.; *Int'l*, pg. 589

OMNIFIT—Anaerobic Adhesives—Henkel Corporation; *Int'l*, pg. 610

OMNIFIT—Chemicals—Henkel KGaA; *Int'l*, pg. 609

OMNIFIT—NONE—Stryker Corporation; *U.S. Public*, pg. 1525

OMNIFLEX—NONE—Stryker Corporation; *U.S. Public*, pg. 1525

OMNIFLIGHT—Trnademark—Omniflight, Inc.; *U.S. Private*, pg. 816

OMNIFLO—Reflowsoldering System—Electrovert; *Int'l*, pg. 328

OMNIGAM—Treatment for Staphylococcal & Enteroccoci—Nabi; *U.S. Public*, pg. 1148

OMNIGRID—NONE—Molex Incorporated; *U.S. Public*, pg. 1121

OMNIGUARD—NONE—Axent Technologies; *U.S. Public*, pg. 157

OMNIGUARD/DEFENDER—NONE—Axent Technologies; *U.S. Public*, pg. 157

OMNIGUARD/ENTERPRISE ACCESS CONTROL—NONE—Axent Technologies; *U.S. Public*, pg. 157

OMNIGUARD/ENTERPRISE RESOURCE MANAGER—NONE—Axent Technologies; *U.S. Public*, pg. 157

OMNIGUARD/ENTERPRISE SECURITY MANAGER (ESM)—NONE—Axent Technologies; *U.S. Public*, pg. 157

OMNIGUARD/INTRUDER ALERT (ITA)—NONE—Axent Technologies; *U.S. Public*, pg. 157

OMNIGUARD/POWERVPN—NONE—Axent Technologies; *U.S. Public*, pg. 157

OMNIGUARD/UNIX PRIVILEGE MANAGER—NONE—Axent Technologies; *U.S. Public*, pg. 157

OMNIHOST—Client/Server Networking Software—VeriFone, Inc.; *U.S. Public*, pg. 815

OMNIKONE—NONE—Western Atlas Logging Services; *U.S. Public*, pg. 1757

OMNILINE—Systems—WCI Machine Tools & Systems; *Int'l*, pg. 440

OMNILINK—Computer Services—Omni Hotels; *U.S. Private*, pg. 1065

OMNIMET—Image Analyzer—Buehler, Limited; *U.S. Public*, pg. 574

OMNIMIL—Machinery Centers—WCI Machine Tools & Systems; *Int'l*, pg. 440

OMNIPAC—Chromatography Columns—Dionex Corporation; *U.S. Public*, pg. 510

OMNIPACK—Video Batteries—Sanyo Energy (U.S.A.) Corporation; *Int'l*, pg. 1191

OMNIPAGE—Document Scanner Software—Caere Corporation; *U.S. Public*, pg. 291

OMNIPATH—PC/LAN to Mainframe—AMATI Communications Corp.; *U.S. Public*, pg. 1585

OMNIPLACE—SMC Placement System—Universal Instruments Corporation; *U.S. Public*, pg. 522

OMNIPLANE—Film Changer—Medrad, Inc.; *Int'l*, pg. 1204

OMNIPRO—UPS System—Trippe Mfg. Co.; *U.S. Private*, pg. 1104

OMNIPULSE—Seismic Survey Air Gun—Bolt Technology Corporation; *U.S. Public*, pg. 244

OMNIPULSE—Monitoring Equipment—Lucent Technologies Inc.; *U.S. Public*, pg. 1017

OMNISCAN—Document Scanner—Caere Corporation; *U.S. Public*, pg. 291

OMNISCAN—NONE—Eastman Kodak Company; *U.S. Public*, pg. 550

OMNISCAN—Closed-Circuit Television Equipment—Vicon Industries, Inc.; *U.S. Public*, pg. 1719

OMNISCRRED—NONE—Blaw-Knox Construction Equipment Corporation; *U.S. Public*, pg. 877

OMNISEAL—Spring Energized Seals—Furon Company; *U.S. Public*, pg. 688

OMNISMART PNP SERIES—UPS Systems—Trippe Mfg. Co.; *U.S. Private*, pg. 1104

OMNITRACS—NONE—QUALCOMM; *U.S. Public*, pg. 1348

OMNITRUST—Accounting Products for Bank Trust Departments—SunGard Data Systems Inc.; *U.S. Public*, pg. 1534

OMNIVISION—Dome-shaped Motion Picture Screen—Iwerks Entertainment; *U.S. Public*, pg. 915

OMO—Detergents—Lever S.A.; *Int'l*, pg. 1438

OMO—Detergent—Unilever Plc; *Int'l*, pg. 1433

OMRON—Retail System Terminals & Payment System Terminals—OMRON Systems, Inc.; *Int'l*, pg. 1005

ON CAMPUS—NONE—Life Technologies, Inc.; *U.S. Public*, pg. 504

ON-COR-FROZEN FOODS—Frozen Foods—On-Cor Frozen Foods Inc.; *U.S. Private*, pg. 817

ON CUE—Pre-Recorded Audio & Video Tapes, Blank Tapes & Accessories—Musicland Group Inc.; *U.S. Public*, pg. 1142

ON DEMAND—Medical Vacuum & Compressed Air Systems—Squire-Cogswell Company; *U.S. Private*, pg. 1027

ON-GLASS—Glass-Mount Antennas—Allen Telecom Inc.; *U.S. Public*, pg. 45

ON MY WAY—Infant Car Seat—Evenflo Company, Inc.; *U.S. Public*, pg. 629

ON-POINT—NONE—Medtronic, Inc.; *U.S. Public*, pg. 1082

ON THE BORDER—Full Service, Casual Mexican Restaurant—Brinker International, Inc.; *U.S. Public*, pg. 253

ON THE EDGE—Modern Rock Programming—Westwood One, Inc.; *U.S. Public*, pg. 1763

ON THE GARDEN LINE WITH JERRY BAKER—Talk Radio Program—Westwood One Entertainment; *U.S. Public*, pg. 1763

ON THE GARDEN LINE WITH JERRY BAKER—Gardening Tips Programming—Westwood One, Inc.; *U.S. Public*, pg. 1763

ON THE MOVE—NONE—Northwest Airlines, Inc.; *U.S. Public*, pg. 1200

ON THE RADIO—Music Radio Program/ Rhythm Base Program—Westwood One Entertainment; *U.S. Public*, pg. 1763

ON THE RADIO—Rock N' Roll Programming—Westwood One, Inc.; *U.S. Public*, pg. 1763

ON TOP—Non-Dairy Topping—Rich Products Corp.; *U.S. Private*, pg. 928

ON YOUR OWN—Greeting Cards—American Greetings Corporation; *U.S. Public*, pg. 77

ONAMER—Organic Chemicals—Stepan Company; *U.S. Public*, pg. 1514

ONAN—Generating Equip.—Onan Corporation; *U.S. Public*, pg. 468

ONAN BT—Bypass Transfer Switch—Onan Corporation; *U.S. Public*, pg. 468

ONAN ISPS—Paralleling Systems—Onan Corporation; *U.S. Public*, pg. 468

ONAN OSPS—Paralleling Systems—Onan Corporation; *U.S. Public*, pg. 468

ONAN OT III—Transfer Switches—Onan Corporation; *U.S. Public*, pg. 468

ONAN QUIETSITE—Generators—Onan Corporation; *U.S. Public*, pg. 468

ONAN SEA SUX—Generators—Onan Corporation; *U.S. Public*, pg. 468

ONAN SSPS—Paralleling System—Onan Corporation; *U.S. Public*, pg. 468

ONCASPAR—NONE—Enzon, Inc.; *U.S. Public*, pg. 587

ONCE—Hand Cleanser for Use Without Water—Hardman Division of Harcros Chemicals, Inc.; *Int'l*, pg. 598

ONCE-A-DAY—Twenty-Four Hour Odor Counteractant—Surco Products, Inc.; *U.S. Private*, pg. 1056

ONCE UPON A CHILD—Buys, Sells, Trades & Consigns Used & New Children's Clothes & Toys—Grow Biz International, Inc.; *U.S. Public*, pg. 767

ONCE UPON A TIME ... (SVSC)—Childrens Pre-Recorded Video Cassettes—Sony Electronics; *Int'l*, pg. 1281

ONCO—Coffee—Philip Morris Companies Inc.; *U.S. Public*, pg. 1287

ONCORAD—Cancer Radioisotopic Therapy Products—Cytogen Corporation; *U.S. Public*, pg. 471

ONCORE SYSTEM—High-Capacity Switching Hub—3Com Corporation; *U.S. Public*, pg. 1604

ONCOSCINT—Cancer Diagnostic Imaging Products—Cytogen Corporation; *U.S. Public*, pg. 471

ONCOVIN—Vincristine Sulfate, Lilly—Eli Lilly and Company; *U.S. Public*, pg. 992

ONDAFLEX—NONE—Pfizer Inc.; *U.S. Public*, pg. 1281

ONDINE—Showers, Fixture Fittings—Interbath, Inc.; *U.S. Private*, pg. 566

ONE-A-DAY—Vitamins—Bayer AG; *Int'l*, pg. 171

ONE-A-DAY—NONE—Bayer Corporation; *Int'l*, pg. 172

ONE-A-DAY—Vitamin Products—Bayer Corporation/Consumer Care Division; *Int'l*, pg. 173

ONE A NIGHT—Beverage—Otsuka Pharmaceutical Co., Ltd.; *Int'l*, pg. 1013

ONE ACCOUNT—Checking Account Package—Fifth Third Bancorp; *U.S. Public*, pg. 621

ONE ACCOUNT ADVANTAGE—NONE—Fifth Third Bancorp; *U.S. Public*, pg. 621

ONE ACCOUNT GOLD—Checking Account Package—Fifth Third Bancorp; *U.S. Public*, pg. 621

ONE ACCOUNT PLUS—Checking Account Package—Fifth Third Bancorp; *U.S. Public*, pg. 621

ONE-ALL—Herbicide—Ishihara Sangyo Kaisha, Ltd.; *Int'l*, pg. 689

THE ONE AND ONLY—Logo—Sony Electronics; *Int'l*, pg. 1281

ONE-CAL—Soft Drinks—Ranks Hovis McDougall Limited; *Int'l*, pg. 1395

1-800—Children's Wear—Master Industries Corp.; *U.S. Private*, pg. 713

1 800 AUTO PRO—Toll-Free 24 Hour Insurance Shopping Service—The Progressive Corporation; *U.S. Public*, pg. 1334

1-800-CALL-HOME—Hotels—Promus Hotel Corporation; *U.S. Public*, pg. 1335

1-800-GO FEDEX—NONE—FDX Corporation; *U.S. Public*, pg. 603

180SX—Car—Nissan Motor Co., Ltd.; *Int'l*, pg. 943

1-FITS-ALL—Ballpoint Refill—Eversharp Pen Co.; *U.S. Private*, pg. 386

ONE FOR THE ROAD—1200 Watt Compact Dryer—Clairol, Inc.; *U.S. Public*, pg. 254

ONE HOUR MOTO PHOTO—Retail Film Processing—Moto Photo, Inc.; *U.S. Public*, pg. 1136

140Xi—NONE—Zebra Technologies Corporation; *U.S. Public*, pg. 1790

104.6 RTL—German Broadcasting—CLT-UFA; *Int'l*, pg. 561

100 GRAND BAR—Candy Bar—Nestle S.A.; *Int'l*, pg. 915

101—Fragrances—Halston Enterprises, Inc.; *U.S. Private*, pg. 690

101 GT—Conveyor-Based System—American Science & Engineering, Inc.; *U.S. Public*, pg. 90

101 Z—Stationary Conveyor-Based System—American Science & Engineering, Inc.; *U.S. Public*, pg. 90

101 ZZ—Stationary Conveyor-Based System—American Science & Engineering, Inc.; *U.S. Public*, pg. 90

100% NATURAL CEREAL—Cereals—The Quaker Oats Company; *U.S. Public*, pg. 1347

100 PIPERS—Scotch—The Seagram Company Ltd.; *Int'l*, pg. 1214

ONE HUNDRED PLUS—Hammers & Screwdrivers—The Stanley Works; *U.S. Public*, pg. 1508

100-S—NONE—Lawter International, Inc.; *U.S. Public*, pg. 980

100 SERIES CELL COUNTERS—Chemistry Analyzer—BioChem ImmunoSystems, Inc.; *Int'l*, pg. 196

170Xi—NONE—Zebra Technologies Corporation; *U.S. Public*, pg. 1790

1 MINUTE DIET BY FLEXEES—Control Garments—True Form Intimate Apparel; *U.S. Private*, pg. 697

ONE PRICE—NONE—One Price Clothing Stores, Inc.; *U.S. Public*, pg. 1225

1 PRICE TIRE STORES—Tire Store Services—Bridgestone/Firestone, Inc.; *Int'l*, pg. 213

1SO-Z—High Density Zircon Tile—A.P. Green Industries, Inc.; *U.S. Public*, pg. 761

ONE SHOT—Case Tumbler—Hornady Manufacturing Company; *U.S. Private*, pg. 539

ONE SHOT—NONE—Pfizer Inc.; *U.S. Public*, pg. 1281

ONE SHOT—Animal Vaccine—SmithKline Beecham plc; *Int'l*, pg. 1264

ONE-SHOT—Automatically Compresses a Single Xydex Filtration Device—Whatman Inc.; *Int'l*, pg. 1498

ONE STAR—Food Products—Rykoff-Sexton, Inc.; *U.S. Public*, pg. 918

ONE-STEP—Rust Converter Primer Sealer—Mar-Hyde Corporation; *U.S. Public*, pg. 1357

ONE STEP—Floor Care & Homecare Products—Penn Champ; *U.S. Public*, pg. 145

ONE STEP—Car Seat—Spalding & Evenflo Companies, Inc.; *U.S. Private*, pg. 629

ONE STEP AT A TIME—Smoking Withdrawal System—Teledyne Water Pik; *U.S. Public*, pg. 44

ONE-STEP RELAY—Package with Peelable Foil—Ethicon, Inc.; *U.S. Public*, pg. 928

ONE STEP 600—Camera—Polaroid Corporation; *U.S. Public*, pg. 1313

ONE STEP TALKING CAMERA—Instant Camera with Sound Recording Capabilities—Polaroid Corporation; *U.S. Public*, pg. 1313

THE ONE STOP MOVIE SHOP—Video Rental Store—National Video, Inc.; *U.S. Public*, pg. 1755

1000 AX—ATM Switching System—Alcatel Telecom; *Int'l*, pg. 55

1001—Household Cleaners—Cussons (U.K.) LTD.; *Int'l*, pg. 1024

1047 RTL—Swedeish Broadcasting—CLT-UFA; *Int'l*, pg. 561

1100/1200 SERIES—Tables—Howe Furniture Corporation; *U.S. Private*, pg. 543

1000 SERIES—Desks—GF Office Furniture; *U.S. Private*, pg. 435

1000 SPRINGS—Rainbow Trout—Clear Springs Foods, Inc.; *U.S. Private*, pg. 245

ONE TIME—Sterile Trays—Acme United Corporation; *U.S. Public*, pg. 17

ONE TOUCH—Hair Removal Products—Inverness Corp.; *U.S. Private*, pg. 574

ONE TOUCH—NONE—Johnson & Johnson; *U.S. Public*, pg. 927

ONE TOUCH—Blood Glucose Monitoring Prods.—LifeScan, Inc.; *U.S. Public*, pg. 928

ONE TOUCH—Barbeque Kettle—Weber-Stephen Products Co.; *U.S. Private*, pg. 1157

ONE TOUCH BASIC—Blood Glucose Monitoring Prod.—LifeScan, Inc.; *U.S. Public*, pg. 928

ONE TOUCH HOSPITAL SYSTEM—Blood Glucose Monitoring Prod.—LifeScan, Inc.; *U.S. Public*, pg. 928

ONE TOUCH PROFILE—Blood Glucose Monitoring Prod.—LifeScan, Inc.; *U.S. Public*, pg. 928

ONE TOUCH 2—Blood Glucose Monitoring Prod.—LifeScan, Inc.; *U.S. Public*, pg. 928

ONE TRAC—Inexpensive Copy/Fax Control for Commercial Applications—Equitrac Corporation; *U.S. Public*, pg. 590

1-12—Fragrances—Halston Enterprises, Inc.; *U.S. Private*, pg. 690

ONE UP—Golf Gloves—The Grandoe Corp.; *U.S. Private*, pg. 469

ONE WORLD—Configurd Network Computing—J.D. Edwards & Company; *U.S. Private*, pg. 365

ONE-WRAP—Straps—Velcro Industries N.V.; *Int'l*, pg. 1462

ONE WRAP—NONE—Velcro USA Inc.; *Int'l*, pg. 1462

ONE WRITE PLUS—NONE—New England Business Service, Inc.; *U.S. Public*, pg. 1170

ONECIDE—Herbicide—Ishihara Sangyo Kaisha, Ltd.; *Int'l*, pg. 689

ONEIDA—Photographic Printers—Eastman Kodak Company; *U.S. Public*, pg. 550

ONEIDA—Metal & Jewelry Cleaners—Malco Products, Inc.; *U.S. Private*, pg. 698

ONEIDA—Silverware—Oneida Ltd.; *U.S. Public*, pg. 1225

ONESHOT—Stencil Roller—Diagraph Corporation; *U.S. Private*, pg. 330

ONESIES—One-Piece Underwear—Gerber Products Company; *Int'l*, pg. 973

ONESTEP—Software—Wall Data Incorporated; *U.S. Public*, pg. 1734

ONETIME—Spackling Compound, Glazing Compound—Red Devil Inc.; *U.S. Private*, pg. 915

ONEVISION—Steel Industry Enterprise Automation System—Computer Task Group, Inc. (CTG); *U.S. Public*, pg. 423

ONEVOICE—Interactive Voice Response System—InterVoice, Inc.; *U.S. Public*, pg. 910

ONION CRISPS—Finger Food—Harker's Distribution, Inc.; *U.S. Private*, pg. 502

ONION RINGERS—Frozen Vegetables—Ore-Ida Foods, Inc.; *U.S. Public*, pg. 805

ONIX—Beer—Central de Cervejas, S.A.; *Int'l*, pg. 279

ONLINE APPRAISAL & STATISTICAL INFORMATION SYSTEM—NONE—American Management Systems, Inc.; *U.S. Public*, pg. 86

ONLINE INFORMATION NETWORK—National Directories—American Business Information, Inc.; *U.S. Public*, pg. 69

ONLINE SYSTEM CONCENTRATOR—Intelligent Switching Hub And Related Products—3Com Corporation; *U.S. Public*, pg. 1604

ONLY ONE—NONE—Ariel Corporation; *U.S. Private*, pg. 81

ONSERTER—SMC Placement System—Universal Instruments Corporation; *U.S. Public*, pg. 522

ONSITE TECHNOLOGY—Environmental Clean up of Soil—Parker Drilling Company; *U.S. Public*, pg. 1259

ONTARGET—NONE—Market Facts, Inc.; *U.S. Public*, pg. 1046

ONWA—NONE—Semi-Tech Corporation; *Int'l*, pg. 1220

ONYX—Cigars—Lane Limited; *Int'l*, pg. 1129

ONYX—Saturating Paper—The Mead Corporation; *U.S. Public*, pg. 1074

ONYX—Noninvasive Ventilator—Nellcor Puritan Bennett Incorporated; *U.S. Public*, pg. 1039

ONYX—Adult Mass Market Paperback Books—Penguin Putnam Inc.; *Int'l*, pg. 1027

ONYX—Printing Plate—3M; *U.S. Public*, pg. 1604

ONYX—Centrex, Key Systems—TIE/Communications, Inc.; *U.S. Private*, pg. 1085

ONYX PLUS—Noninvasive Ventilator—Nellcor Puritan Bennett Incorporated; *U.S. Public*, pg. 1039

ONYX2—NONE—Silicon Graphics, Inc.; *U.S. Public*, pg. 1473

ONYXIDE—Biocidal—Stepan Company; *U.S. Public*, pg. 1514

OOMPH!—At Home Leisure Footwear—Oomphies, Inc.; *U.S. Private*, pg. 817

Brand Name Index

OOMPHIES—Women Slippers—Oomphies, Inc.; *U.S. Private,* pg. 817

OOPSIE DAISY DOLL—Dolls—Tyco Toys, Inc.; *U.S. Public,* pg. 1058

OP-TACH—Digital Optical Tachometers—Amprobe Instrument; *U.S. Public,* pg. 1676

OPAL—X-Ray Tubes—Litton Industries, Inc.; *U.S. Public,* pg. 1002

OPAL—Insect Screening—New York Wire Co.; *U.S. Private,* pg. 795

OPAL—Paint—Swire Pacific Limited; *Int'l,* pg. 1328

OPAL—Dental Porcelain System—3M; *U.S. Public,* pg. 1604

OPAL NERA—Spirit—Allied Domecq PLC; *Int'l,* pg. 62

OPAL NERA—Premium Liqueur—Hiram Walker; *Int'l,* pg. 63

OPALURE—Photo Film—Eastman Kodak Company; *U.S. Public,* pg. 550

OPAS—Coating Materials & Carbonless Paper—The Mead Corporation; *U.S. Public,* pg. 1074

OPAVIA—Biscuits—Danone Group; *Int'l,* pg. 379

OPEL—Passenger Cars—General Motors Corporation; *U.S. Public,* pg. 718

OPEL—Automobile—OPEL Nederland B.V.; *U.S. Public,* pg. 723

OPEL—Automobile—Opel Norge AS; *U.S. Public,* pg. 723

OPEN—Software—Wang Laboratories, Inc.; *U.S. Public,* pg. 1737

OPEN-ALL—Can Openers—Sunbeam Household Products; *U.S. Public,* pg. 1533

OPEN COUNTRY—Campware—The Metal Ware Corp.; *U.S. Private,* pg. 734

OPEN FFS—NONE—American Management Systems, Inc.; *U.S. Public,* pg. 86

OPEN FIRE—War Game—Monarch Avalon, Inc.; *U.S. Public,* pg. 1123

OPEN ME FIRST—Camera, Film, Accessories—Eastman Kodak Company; *U.S. Public,* pg. 550

OPEN NET—Electronic Instrument—Intel Corporation; *U.S. Public,* pg. 886

OPEN PIT—Barbecue Sauce—Campbell Soup Company; *U.S. Public,* pg. 298

OPEN SYSTEMS TODAY—Newspaper—CMP Media, Inc.; *U.S. Public,* pg. 279

OPEN WHEEL—Magazine—General Media International Inc.; *U.S. Private,* pg. 444

OPEN WORLD—Telecommunications Apparatus & Equip.—Northern Telecom Limited; *Int'l,* pg. 968

OPENCAD DESIGN SYSTEM—NONE—NEC Electronics Inc.; *Int'l,* pg. 900

OPENEDITION—Computer Product—International Business Machines Corporation; *U.S. Public,* pg. 895

OPENELT—Advanced Image Exploitation Software—DBA Systems, Inc.; *U.S. Public,* pg. 472

OPENHUB—Program for Third-Party Network Product Vendors—3Com Corporation; *U.S. Public,* pg. 1604

OPENS XPRESS—Test Technique to Identify Opens to the Specific Pin onConnectors & Sockets—GenRad, Inc.; *U.S. Public,* pg. 731

OPENSERVER 400—Computer Software—Vertel; *U.S. Public,* pg. 1717

OPENWORKS—NONE—Landmark Graphics Corporation; *U.S. Public,* pg. 776

OPERA—In the Canal Hearing Aid—Beltone Electronics Corporation; *U.S. Private,* pg. 132

OPERA—Folding Table—Vecta; *U.S. Private,* pg. 1038

OPERA BEAM SEATING—Lounge Seating—Vecta; *U.S. Private,* pg. 1038

OPERATING SYSTEM/400—Computer System—International Business Machines Corporation; *U.S. Public,* pg. 895

OPERATING SYSTEM SECURITY—NONE—Check Point Software Technologies Ltd.; *U.S. Public,* pg. 342

OPERATING SYSTEM/2—Computer System—International Business Machines Corporation; *U.S. Public,* pg. 895

OPERATION—Game—Milton Bradley Company; *U.S. Public,* pg. 797

OPERATION BET SMART—NONE—Harrah's Entertainment, Inc.; *U.S. Public,* pg. 790

OPERATION SUCCESS—Food Service—Tyson Foods, Inc.; *U.S. Public,* pg. 1652

OPERATIONAL ASSISTANT—Computer System—International Business Machines Corporation; *U.S. Public,* pg. 895

OPERTUNE FOR DB2—NONE—BMC Software, Inc.; *U.S. Public,* pg. 162

OPERTUNE FOR HP-UX AND SOLARIS—NONE—BMC Software, Inc.; *U.S. Public,* pg. 162

OPERTUNE FOR MOSERIES—NONE—BMC Software, Inc.; *U.S. Public,* pg. 162

OPERTUNE FOR NCP—NONE—BMC Software, Inc.; *U.S. Public,* pg. 162

OPEX—Racquetball Racquet—Ektelon; *U.S. Private,* pg. 884

OPEX—Specialty Chemical—Uniroyal Chemical Company, Inc.; *U.S. Public,* pg. 460

OPHTHALAS—Surgical Lasers, Equipment & Accessories—Alcon Laboratories, Inc.; *Int'l,* pg. 916

OPHTHALMOLOGY TIMES—Trade Periodical—Advanstar Communications; *U.S. Private,* pg. 22

OPHTHASAN—Spectacle Lens Blanks—Deutsche Spezialglas AG; *Int'l,* pg. 1523

OPHTHASCAN—Diagnostic & Biometric Ultrasound Equipment—Alcon Laboratories, Inc.; *Int'l,* pg. 916

OPINIONGRAM—Message Services—New Valley Corporation; *U.S. Public,* pg. 1173

OPINIONGRAM—Message Services—Western Union Financial Services, Inc.; *U.S. Public,* pg. 631

OPPANOL—Polyisobutene—BASF AG; *Int'l,* pg. 103

OPPTIMUM—Metallized Polypropylene Film—Borden, Inc.; *U.S. Public,* pg. 157

OPT TINT—Custom Ophthalmic Lens Tint—Sterling Vision, Inc.; *U.S. Public,* pg. 1516

OPTA 5—NONE—Cordis, a Johnson & Johnson Company; *U.S. Public,* pg. 928

OPTAFORM—Hairdressing Product—Wella Group; *Int'l,* pg. 1489

OPTAMINT—Flavors—Haarmann & Reimer Corp.; *Int'l,* pg. 173

OPTANE SP 98—Unleaded Gasoline—Elf Aquitane; *Int'l,* pg. 444

OPTANE SP 95—Unleaded Gasoline—Elf Aquitane; *Int'l,* pg. 444

OPTAROME—Flavor—Haarmann & Reimer Corp.; *Int'l,* pg. 173

OPTAS—NONE—SunGard Data Systems Inc.; *U.S. Public,* pg. 1534

OPTE-PAK—Pallets—Menasha Corporation; *U.S. Private,* pg. 731

OPTECH—Fiber-Optic Line—Vicon Industries, Inc.; *U.S. Public,* pg. 1719

OPTECHSP—Dental Porcelain—Customedix Corporation; *U.S. Private,* pg. 298

OPTEMP—Sterile, Disposable Cautery—Alcon Laboratories, Inc.; *Int'l,* pg. 916

OPTI—NONE—Coats Viyella plc; *Int'l,* pg. 299

OPTI—NONE—GenRad, Inc.; *U.S. Public,* pg. 731

OPTI-CLEAN—Lens Cleaner—Nestle S.A.; *Int'l,* pg. 915

OPTI CLEAN DAILY CLEANER—Contact Lens Cleaning Solution—Alcon Laboratories, Inc.; *Int'l,* pg. 916

OPTI CLEAN II DAILY CLEANER FOR SENSITIVE EYES—Cleaning Solution without Thimerosol—Alcon Laboratories, Inc.; *Int'l,* pg. 916

OPTI-DIAMOND C-METRIC—Metric Taps—Greenfield Industries; *U.S. Public,* pg. 950

OPTI-FLUOR O—Environmentally Safe Cocktail for Counting Organic Samples—Packard Instrument Co., Inc.; *U.S. Private,* pg. 833

OPTI FONTS—Alphabet Lettering for Macintosh & IBM—Castcraft Industries, Inc.; *U.S. Private,* pg. 219

OPTI FREE—Rinsing, Disinfecting, Storage Solution—Alcon Laboratories, Inc.; *Int'l,* pg. 916

OPTI FREE—Enzymatic Cleaner—Alcon Laboratories, Inc.; *Int'l,* pg. 916

OPTI FREE—Daily Cleaner—Alcon Laboratories, Inc.; *Int'l,* pg. 916

OPTI FREE—Rewetting Drops—Alcon Laboratories, Inc.; *Int'l,* pg. 916

OPTI-MATE—Calf Milk Replacer—Manna Pro Corporation; *U.S. Private,* pg. 700

OPTI-MEM—NONE—Life Technologies, Inc.; *U.S. Public,* pg. 504

OPTI-METRIC—Metric Taps—Greenfield Industries; *U.S. Public,* pg. 950

OPTI-ONE—Multipurpose Solution—Alcon Laboratories, Inc.; *Int'l,* pg. 916

OPTI-ONE—Rewetting Drops—Alcon Laboratories, Inc.; *Int'l,* pg. 916

OPTI-PORT—Apparatus, Swivel Connectors & Parts for Medical—Mallinckrodt Inc.; *U.S. Public,* pg. 1039

OPTI-POUCH—NONE—Uniflex, Inc.; *U.S. Public,* pg. 1665

OPTI PURE—Sterile Saline Solution for Soft Contact Lenses—Alcon Laboratories, Inc.; *Int'l,* pg. 916

OPTI-RAY—Sunglasses—Goody Products, Inc.; *U.S. Public,* pg. 1177

OPTI-SOAK—Contact Lens Care Solution—Alcon Laboratories, Inc.; *Int'l,* pg. 916

OPTI SOFT—Sterile Solution for use with Soft Contact Lenses—Alcon Laboratories, Inc.; *Int'l,* pg. 916

OPTI-SPARK—Ignition—Delphi Energy & Engine Management Systems; *U.S. Public,* pg. 719

OPTI TEARS—Soothing Drops for use with Daily & Extended Wear Contact Lenses—Alcon Laboratories, Inc.; *Int'l,* pg. 916

OPTI TWIST—Fiber-Copper Cable—Siecor Corporation; *U.S. Public,* pg. 449

OPTI TWIST—Fiber-Copper Cable—Siecor Corporation; *Int'l,* pg. 1245

OPTI ZYME—Weekly Enzyme Cleaner for Soft Contact Lenses—Alcon Laboratories, Inc.; *Int'l,* pg. 916

OPTIBASIC—NONE—Nematron Corp.; *U.S. Private,* pg. 791

OPTIBIND—Supported Membrane—Schleicher & Schuell, Inc.; *Int'l,* pg. 1206

OPTIC-GARD—Fiber-Optic Corrugated Conduit (PVC)—The Lamson & Sessions Co.; *U.S. Public,* pg. 976

OPTIC-GARD PE—Fiber-Optic Corrugated Conduit (Polyethylene)—The Lamson & Sessions Co.; *U.S. Public,* pg. 976

OPTIC LITE—Fiber-Optic Insulators—The Ohio Brass Co.; *U.S. Public,* pg. 845

OPTIC RULE—Micro-Measuring System—Slant/Fin Corporation; *U.S. Private,* pg. 1005

OPTICAL CONCLUSIONS—Puzzle Game—Mattel Games/Puzzles; *U.S. Public,* pg. 1058

OPTICAL RESOLVER—Optical Encoder—BEI Sensors and Systems Company; *U.S. Public,* pg. 160

OPTICATH—Blood Oxygen Monitoring System—Abbott Laboratories; *U.S. Public,* pg. 12

OPTICELL—System for In Vitro Bioprocessing—Bausch & Lomb Incorporated; *U.S. Public,* pg. 194

OPTICHEM 132—Flourescent Dye for Water Leak Testing—PPG Industries, Inc.; *U.S. Public,* pg. 1245

OPTICHROME—NONE—Elcor Corporation; *U.S. Public,* pg. 567

OPTICHROME—NONE—Lawter International, Inc.; *U.S. Public,* pg. 980

OPTICITE—Label Film—The Dow Chemical Company; *U.S. Public,* pg. 522

OPTICLEAR—Containers—Owens-Illinois, Inc.; *U.S. Public,* pg. 1238

OPTICLUDE—Orthoptic Eye Patch—3M; *U.S. Public,* pg. 1604

OPTICMIC—Hand Microphone/Bar Code Reader—Dictaphone Corp.; *U.S. Private,* pg. 1045

OPTICOM—Priority Traffic Control Systems For Emergency & Transit Vehicles—3M; *U.S. Public,* pg. 1604

OPTICS PLUS—Thin-film Cleaner For CRTs & Fine Optics—Optical Coating Laboratory, Inc.; *U.S. Public,* pg. 1227

OPTIDURA—Scratch Resistant Coating—Uvex Safety, Inc.; *Int'l,* pg. 132

OPTIFAST—Clinical Slimming Agent—Novartis AG; *Int'l,* pg. 971

OPTIFIX—Dyeing Chemicals—Clariant International Ltd.; *Int'l,* pg. 624

OPTIFLEX—Retention & Drainage Aids—BetzDearborn Inc.; *U.S. Public,* pg. 226

OPTIFLEX—Flexible Machining Equip.—Liberty Precision Industries; *U.S. Private,* pg. 666

OPTIFLEX—Somidobove, Elanco—Eli Lilly and Company; *U.S. Public*, pg. 992

OPTIFLEX—Cable—Medtronic, Inc.; *U.S. Public*, pg. 1082

OPTIFLO—Cartridge Dust Collector—AAF-International; *U.S. Private*, pg. 3

OPTIGARD—Fiber Optic Coatings—Dow Corning Corporation; *U.S. Public*, pg. 523

OPTIGUARD—Quality Control Program—Eastman Kodak Company; *U.S. Public*, pg. 550

OPTILAN—Wool Processing Consulting Service—Novartis AG; *Int'l*, pg. 971

OPTILITE—Lenses—U.S. Safety; *U.S. Private*, pg. 1125

OPTIM—Glycerine—The Dow Chemical Company; *U.S. Public*, pg. 522

OPTIMA—Credit Card Services—American Express Company; *U.S. Public*, pg. 73

OPTIMA—Thermal Facsimile Papers—Appleton Papers Inc.; *Int'l*, pg. 567

OPTIMA—Tinted Contact Lenses—Bausch & Lomb Incorporated; *U.S. Public*, pg. 194

OPTIMA—Ultracentrifuge—Beckman Instruments, Inc.; *U.S. Public*, pg. 199

OPTIMA—Weightlifting Glove—Ektelon; *U.S. Private*, pg. 884

OPTIMA—Thermoplastic Adhesive—H.B. Fuller Company; *U.S. Public*, pg. 686

OPTIMA—Poly-cotton Cover Material—Industrial Coatings Group, Inc.; *U.S. Private*, pg. 434

OPTIMA—Electronic Flush Valves, Faucets, Dispensers, Dryers—Sloan Valve Company; *U.S. Private*, pg. 1006

OPTIMA—Petroleum Products—Sun Company, Inc.; *U.S. Public*, pg. 1530

OPTIMA—NONE—Western Atlas Logging Services; *U.S. Public*, pg. 1757

OPTIMA 96 + FAX 96—Modem & Fax—Hayes Microcomputer Products, Inc.; *U.S. Public*, pg. 801

OPTIMA 144—Modem—Hayes Microcomputer Products, Inc.; *U.S. Public*, pg. 801

OPTIMA 144 + FAX 144—Modem & Fax—Hayes Microcomputer Products, Inc.; *U.S. Public*, pg. 801

OPTIMA 144 + FAX 144 POCKET EDITION—Modem & Fax—Hayes Microcomputer Products, Inc.; *U.S. Public*, pg. 801

OPTIMA PLUS—Battery Operated Flush Valves—Sloan Valve Company; *U.S. Private*, pg. 1006

OPTIMA RECOVER—Fax Paper—Arjo Wiggins Appleton plc; *Int'l*, pg. 567

OPTIMA SERIES—Anti Glare Filter—Optical Coating Laboratory, Inc.; *U.S. Public*, pg. 1227

OPTIMA TRUE GRACE CARD—NONE—American Express Company; *U.S. Public*, pg. 73

OPTIMA 24 + FAX 96—Modem & Fax—Hayes Microcomputer Products, Inc.; *U.S. Public*, pg. 801

OPTIMAB—NONE—Life Technologies, Inc.; *U.S. Public*, pg. 504

OPTIMAIR—Respirators—Kimmins Corp.; *U.S. Public*, pg. 960

OPTIMELT—Low Temperature Application Hot Melt—H.B. Fuller Company; *U.S. Public*, pg. 686

OPTIMIL—Dairy Feeds—Manna Pro Corporation; *U.S. Private*, pg. 700

OPTIMIN—Proteinated Trace Minerals—DuCoa L.P.; *U.S. Private*, pg. 301

OPTIMIX—Typesetting & Composing Terminals—Eastman Kodak Company; *U.S. Public*, pg. 550

OPTIMIZED IDLE—NONE—Detroit Diesel Corp.; *U.S. Private*, pg. 850

OPTIMIZER—Coal & Multi Fuels—The Bethlehem Corporation; *U.S. Public*, pg. 225

OPTIMO—Cigars—Swisher International Group, Inc.; *U.S. Public*, pg. 1543

OPTIMOUNT—NONE—Boston Gear; *U.S. Public*, pg. 857

OPTIMUM—Hair Care Prods.—Soft Sheen Products, Inc.; *U.S. Private*, pg. 1012

OPTIMUS—Hi-Fi Stereo Equipment—RadioShack; *U.S. Public*, pg. 1560

OPTIMUS—Audio/Video Equipment—Tandy Corporation; *U.S. Public*, pg. 1560

OPTION—Mens Hair Color—Bristol-Myers Squibb Company; *U.S. Public*, pg. 253

OPTION—Hair Coloring Product—Clairol, Inc.; *U.S. Public*, pg. 254

OPTION FIT—Custom Design Services for Truck Bodies—The Knapheide Mfg. Co.; *U.S. Private*, pg. 626

OPTION IV—Plaques—Tropar Mfg. Co., Inc.; *U.S. Private*, pg. 1105

OPTION ONE—Systems Furniture—Carter Holt Harvey Limited; *U.S. Public*, pg. 904

OPTIONS—Outdoor Sign Programs—American Sign & Marketing Services, Inc.; *U.S. Public*, pg. 1309

OPTIONS—Total System Approach for Marketing Cremation Products—Hillenbrand Industries, Inc.; *U.S. Public*, pg. 828

OPTIONS—Fashion & Beauty Magazine—IPC Magazines Limited; *Int'l*, pg. 651

OPTIONS—Instant Chocolate-Flavored Drinks—Novartis AG; *Int'l*, pg. 971

OPTIPRANOLOL—Galucoma Drug—Bausch & Lomb Incorporated; *U.S. Public*, pg. 194

OPTIPROBE—Meter Probe—Radix Corporation; *U.S. Private*, pg. 906

OPTIQUE—Optical—D.O.C. Optics Corporation; *U.S. Private*, pg. 305

OPTIRAY—Ioversol—Mallinckrodt Inc.; *U.S. Public*, pg. 1039

OPTISAL—Cellulose Fibers—Clariant International Ltd.; *Int'l*, pg. 624

OPTISPERSE—Alkaline Cleaning Compounds—BetzDearborn Inc.; *U.S. Public*, pg. 226

OPTISTAR—Microimage Terminals and Datawriters—Eastman Kodak Company; *U.S. Public*, pg. 550

OPTIVE—NONE—SunGard Data Systems Inc.; *U.S. Public*, pg. 1534

OPTIWHITE—Calcined Kaolin—Burgess Pigment Co.; *U.S. Private*, pg. 182

OPTIWHITE P—Calcined Kaolin—Burgess Pigment Co.; *U.S. Private*, pg. 182

OPTIWORLD—Optical Centers—Lenscrafters; *Int'l*, pg. 822

OPTIWRITER—Microfilm—Eastman Kodak Company; *U.S. Public*, pg. 550

OPTIX—Blinds—Wausau Metals, Nanik Division; *U.S. Public*, pg. 1500

OPTIXX—Rigid Rear Projection Screen—Da-Lite Screen Company, Inc.; *U.S. Private*, pg. 306

OPTO-PAK—NONE—Gems Sensors; *U.S. Public*, pg. 481

OPTOFORM—Contact Lens Lathe—Taylor Hobson Pneumo; *Int'l*, pg. 1087

OPTOMATE—ATE Vision System—GenRad, Inc.; *U.S. Public*, pg. 731

OPTOMETRISTS PROTECTOR PLAN—Insurance Package Program—Poe & Brown, Inc.; *U.S. Public*, pg. 1312

OPTOPIPE—Light Pipe—Dialight Corporation; *Int'l*, pg. 1130

OPTREX—NONE—Boots Healthcare International; *Int'l*, pg. 202

OPTREX AMERICA—NONE—Interface Electronics Corporation; *U.S. Private*, pg. 567

OPTUM—Thermoplastic Polymer Resin—Ferro Corporation; *U.S. Public*, pg. 618

OPTYL—Designer Eyewear—Optimaxx International; *U.S. Private*, pg. 818

OPULENCE—Floor Coverings—Domco Inc.; *Int'l*, pg. 415

OPUS—Catheter/Stylet—Medtronic, Inc.; *U.S. Public*, pg. 1082

OPUS—NONE—Robert Mondavi Winery, Inc.; *U.S. Public*, pg. 1393

OPUS ONE—NONE—Robert Mondavi Winery, Inc.; *U.S. Public*, pg. 1393

ORABASE—Lip Healer—Colgate Oral Pharmaceutical; *U.S. Public*, pg. 397

ORACIN—Throat Lozenges—Richardson-Vicks, Inc., Health Care Products; *U.S. Public*, pg. 1331

ORACLE—Microfilmers & Reader Printers—Eastman Kodak Company; *U.S. Public*, pg. 550

ORAFIX—Denture Adhesive—Advanced Polymer Systems; *U.S. Public*, pg. 22

ORAGRAFIN—Calcium Granules & Sodium Capsules—Bristol-Myers Squibb Company; *U.S. Public*, pg. 253

ORAHESIVE—Oral Bandage—Bristol-Myers Squibb Company; *U.S. Public*, pg. 253

ORAJEL—For Toothache Pain—Del Pharmaceuticals, Inc.; *U.S. Public*, pg. 494

ORAJEL COVERMED TINTED—Cold Sore Medicine—Del Pharmaceuticals, Inc.; *U.S. Public*, pg. 494

ORAJEL DENTURE—Denture Prod.—Del Pharmaceuticals, Inc.; *U.S. Public*, pg. 494

ORAJEL MOUTH-AID—For Canker Sores—Del Pharmaceuticals, Inc.; *U.S. Public*, pg. 494

ORAJEL PERIOSEPTIC ANTISEPTIC LIQUID—NONE—Del Pharmaceuticals, Inc.; *U.S. Public*, pg. 494

ORAL-B—Toothbrush—The Gillette Company; *U.S. Public*, pg. 743

ORAL-B—Dental Care Products—Oral-B Laboratories; *U.S. Public*, pg. 743

ORALAN—Absorbing Glass—Deutsche Spezialglas AG; *Int'l*, pg. 1523

ORALITE—Anti Dehydration Prod.—SmithKline Beecham plc; *Int'l*, pg. 1264

ORALIUM—Dental Bands—Engelhard Corporation; *U.S. Public*, pg. 582

ORANGE COUNTY REGISTER—Newspaper—The Orange County Register; *U.S. Public*, pg. 425

ORANGE CRUSH—Soft Drink—The Procter & Gamble Company; *U.S. Public*, pg. 1330

ORANGE CRUSHER—Metallic Reloading Press—Lyman Products Corporation; *U.S. Private*, pg. 683

ORANGE DRIVER—Cocktail Mix—Montebello Brands Inc.; *U.S. Private*, pg. 758

ORANGE-GO—Urethane Belts—Fenner Drives; *U.S. Private*, pg. 400

ORANGE JULIUS—Orange Flavored Drink—Orange Julius of America; *U.S. Public*, pg. 220

ORANGE MIRACLE—All Purpose Spot & Stain Remover—Stanhome Inc.; *U.S. Public*, pg. 1508

ORANGE PEELER—Muffler—Arvin Industries, Inc.; *U.S. Public*, pg. 136

ORANGE RIM—Abrasive Disc—Gardner Abrasives; *U.S. Public*, pg. 1699

ORANGE SPICE TEA—Tea—Celestial Seasonings; *U.S. Public*, pg. 319

ORANGE ZINGER—Herb Tea—Celestial Seasonings; *U.S. Public*, pg. 319

ORANGINA—Carbonated Orange Drink—Groupe Pernod Ricard; *Int'l*, pg. 566

ORANGINA—Sparkling Citrus Beverage—Austin Nichols & Co. Inc.; *Int'l*, pg. 566

ORASPOR—Antibiotic—Ciba Specialty Chemicals; *Int'l*, pg. 291

ORASPOR—Antibiotic—Novartis; *Int'l*, pg. 972

ORBAN—Broadcast Processors—Harman International Industries, Inc.; *U.S. Public*, pg. 787

ORBENIN—Mastitis Preparation—SmithKline Beecham Corporation; *Int'l*, pg. 1264

ORBENIN—Animal Antibacterial—SmithKline Beecham plc; *Int'l*, pg. 1264

ORBENIN—Antibiotic—SmithKline Beecham Research Limited; *Int'l*, pg. 1266

ORBEX—Bar-Buoys, Flyboxes—Blount, Inc. Sporting Equipment Group; *U.S. Public*, pg. 238

ORBI-TRAK—Carton Feed, Small & Large Center Cartoners—R.A. Jones & Co. Inc.; *U.S. Private*, pg. 597

ORBIS—Measuring Equipment—British Steel Plc; *Int'l*, pg. 220

ORBITAL—Sporting Goods—Brunswick Bowling & Billiards Corp.; *U.S. Public*, pg. 265

ORBITER 6000—Rotary Filler—Liqui-Box Corporation; *U.S. Public*, pg. 1000

ORCHARD—Decorative Overlays—Borden, Inc.; *U.S. Private*, pg. 157

ORCHARD—Fruit Drinks—Nestle S.A.; *Int'l*, pg. 915

ORCHARD BOY—Food Products—National Fruit Product Company; *U.S. Public*, pg. 783

ORCHARD COUNTY—Canned Fruit—Cherry Central Cooperative; *U.S. Private*, pg. 233

ORCHARD MEDLEY—Dinnerware—Princess House, Inc.; *U.S. Public*, pg. 399

ORCHARD PARK—Drink Mixes—Park Foods L.P.; *U.S. Private*, pg. 839

ORCHARD PEACH—Sparkling Mineral Water—Clearly Canadian Beverage Corp.; *Int'l*, pg. 297

ORCHARD SUPPLY HARDWARE—NONE—Sears, Roebuck and Co.; *U.S. Public*, pg. 1452

ORCHID PLUS—Fertilizer—Sun Bulb Company, Inc.; *U.S. Private*, pg. 1050

Brand Name Index

ORCHIDS EXOTICA—Interior Plant Prods.—Security Lawn & Garden Co.; *U.S. Private*, pg. 397

ORCO-PD—Precurved Tread Rubber—Oliver Rubber Co.; *U.S. Public*, pg. 1504

ORCOHESION—Repair Material—Oliver Rubber Co.; *U.S. Public*, pg. 1504

ORDER ASSIST—Product Ordering System—John H. Harland Company; *U.S. Public*, pg. 785

ORDER-MATIC—Printed Order Form—Eastman Kodak Company; *U.S. Public*, pg. 550

ORDER OF MERIT—Canadian Whiskey—United Distillers USA, Inc.; *Int'l*, pg. 412

ORDER PROCESSING ACTIVITY MANAGER—Software—Brock International Inc.; *U.S. Public*, pg. 258

ORDERMATIC—Full Case Order Selection System—SI Handling Systems, Inc.; *U.S. Public*, pg. 1418

ORE-IDA—Potato Products—H.J. Heinz Company; *U.S. Public*, pg. 805

ORE-IDA SPECIALTY PRODUCTS—Frozen Snacks, Paste & Sandwiches—H.J. Heinz Company; *U.S. Public*, pg. 805

OREGON—Saw Chain, Bars & Sprockets—Blount International, Inc.; *U.S. Public*, pg. 237

OREGON—NONE—Illinois Auto Electric Co.; *U.S. Private*, pg. 557

OREGON FARMS—Frozen Desserts—Flowers Industries, Inc.; *U.S. Public*, pg. 656

OREGON FARMS—Food Products—Labatt Brewing Company Limited; *Int'l*, pg. 679

OREMET—Titanium—Oregon Metallurgical Corporation; *U.S. Public*, pg. 43

ORENDA—NONE—Magellan Aerospace Corporation; *Int'l*, pg. 829

OREO—Cookies—Nabisco Inc.; *U.S. Public*, pg. 1355

OREO—Cookies—RJR Nabisco Holdings Corp.; *U.S. Public*, pg. 1354

OREO CHOCOLATE CONES—Chocolate Cones—Nabisco Inc.; *U.S. Public*, pg. 1355

ORETON METHYL—Prescription Drug—ICN Pharmaceuticals, Inc.; *U.S. Public*, pg. 853

OREX DEGRADABLES—Hot Water Soluble Polymer—Isolyser Company, Inc.; *U.S. Public*, pg. 914

OREXIN—NONE—Lee Pharmaceuticals; *U.S. Public*, pg. 984

OREXIN—High Potency Chewable Vitamin—Roberts Pharmaceutical Corporation; *U.S. Public*, pg. 1393

ORG PLUS—NONE—Broderbund Software, Inc.; *U.S. Public*, pg. 258

ORGANEX-Q—Cartridge Filter—Millipore Corporation; *U.S. Public*, pg. 1112

ORGANIC GARDENING—Magazine—Rodale Press, Inc.; *U.S. Private*, pg. 939

ORGANIDIN—Expectorant—Wallace Laboratories; *U.S. Public*, pg. 310

ORGANIZER PLUS—Luggage—American Tourister, Inc.; *U.S. Public*, pg. 1430

THE ORGANIZER—School Supplies—The Mead Corporation; *U.S. Public*, pg. 1074

THE ORGANIZER II—Luggage—American Tourister, Inc.; *U.S. Public*, pg. 1430

ORGANOKROME—Protective Coatings for Metals—PPG Industries, Inc.; *U.S. Public*, pg. 1245

ORGANON—Ethical Pharmaceuticals, Tests—Akzo Nobel Inc.; *Int'l*, pg. 47

ORGAREX—Office Products—Esselte AB; *Int'l*, pg. 459

ORGATRON—Organs—The Wurlitzer Company; *U.S. Public*, pg. 169

ORI-FLOWRATOR—Flowrator—Bailey, Fischer & Porter Company; *Int'l*, pg. 449

ORIENT—NONE—Brown & Sharpe Manufacturing Company; *U.S. Public*, pg. 260

ORIENT—Coal—Freeman Energy Corporation; *U.S. Public*, pg. 709

ORIENT-EXPRESS HOTELS—Hotels—Sea Containers Ltd.; *Int'l*, pg. 1213

ORIENT XPRESS—Test Technique to Catch Misoriented Components on SMT's—GenRad, Inc.; *U.S. Public*, pg. 731

ORIENTAL CHEF—Salad Dressings—Q & B Foods, Inc.; *Int'l*, pg. 1074

ORIGA—Wood Pulp & Printing Paper—Westvaco Corporation; *U.S. Public*, pg. 1762

ORIGIN—Games Relating to Action & Fantasy Role-Playing—Electronic Arts; *U.S. Public*, pg. 569

ORIGIN—Vitamins—Nature's Bounty Inc.; *U.S. Public*, pg. 1166

ORIGIN200—NONE—Silicon Graphics, Inc.; *U.S. Public*, pg. 1473

ORIGIN2000—NONE—Silicon Graphics, Inc.; *U.S. Public*, pg. 1473

ORIGINAL ALE 6—Beer—Asahi Breweries Ltd.; *Int'l*, pg. 83

THE ORIGINAL COLORADO LAVA ROCK—Briquette for Outdoor Gas Grills—MWCA; *U.S. Public*, pg. 804

ORIGINAL COORS—Premium Beer—Adolph Coors Company; *U.S. Public*, pg. 445

ORIGINAL DELUXE—Fruit Cakes—Collin Street Bakery; *U.S. Private*, pg. 252

ORIGINAL KINGSDOWN—Mattress & Box Spring Sets—Kingsdown, Inc.; *U.S. Private*, pg. 622

ORIGINAL MEMORY—Game—Milton Bradley Company; *U.S. Public*, pg. 797

THE ORIGINAL MIX-IN—Ice Cream—Integrated Brands Inc.; *U.S. Public*, pg. 883

ORIGINAL RECIPE CHICKEN—Menu Item—Kentucky Fried Chicken Corporation (KFC); *U.S. Public*, pg. 1636

ORIGINAL YOPLAIT—Yogurt—Yoplait USA; *U.S. Public*, pg. 718

ORIGINS—Skin Care Product—Estee Lauder Companies Inc.; *U.S. Public*, pg. 594

ORIMETEM—Pharmaceutical—Novartis; *Int'l*, pg. 972

ORIMUNE—Vaccine—American Home Products Corporation; *U.S. Public*, pg. 79

ORINOCO—Shower Squeegee—Interbath, Inc.; *U.S. Private*, pg. 566

ORIOLE—Pencils—Dixon Ticonderoga Company; *U.S. Public*, pg. 514

ORIOLE LINEN & DESIGN—Printing & Writing Paper—Georgia-Pacific Corporation; *U.S. Public*, pg. 735

ORION—Valve—Badger Meter, Inc.; *U.S. Public*, pg. 164

ORION—Enamel Coated Printing Paper—Consolidated Papers, Inc.; *U.S. Public*, pg. 436

ORION—Floor Coverings—Domco Inc.; *Int'l*, pg. 415

ORION—NONE—Giddings & Lewis Automation Technology; *Int'l*, pg. 1389

ORION—NONE—Laserscope Surgical Systems; *U.S. Public*, pg. 979

ORION—Reverse Osmosis—Osmonics, Inc.; *U.S. Public*, pg. 1233

ORION—Book Imprint—Random House, Inc.; *U.S. Private*, pg. 20

ORION—Orion Fixation System—Sofamor Danek Group, Inc.; *U.S. Public*, pg. 1482

ORION—O/U Shotgun—Weatherby, Inc.; *U.S. Private*, pg. 1155

ORION I—NONE—Weatherby, Inc.; *U.S. Private*, pg. 1155

ORION III—NONE—Weatherby, Inc.; *U.S. Private*, pg. 1155

ORION II—NONE—Weatherby, Inc.; *U.S. Private*, pg. 1155

ORKIN—Termite Control Services—Orkin Exterminating Co., Inc.; *U.S. Public*, pg. 1404

ORKIN—Pest Control, Lawn Care & Plantscaping—Rollins, Inc.; *U.S. Public*, pg. 1404

ORLANDO BUSINESS JOURNAL—Business Journal—Business First of New York, Inc.; *U.S. Private*, pg. 19

THE ORLANDO SENTINEL—Newspaper—Orlando Sentinel Communications; *U.S. Public*, pg. 1636

THE ORLANDO SENTINEL—Daily Newspaper—Tribune Company; *U.S. Public*, pg. 1635

ORLANE—Complete Line of Cosmetics, Skin Care, Color and Fragrances—Orlane, Inc.; *Int'l*, pg. 1011

ORLEANS—Canned Seafood Products—Borden, Inc.; *U.S. Private*, pg. 157

ORLEANS—NONE—Tandy Brands Accessories, Inc.; *U.S. Public*, pg. 1560

ORLEY MEYER—Cranes—The Manitowoc Company, Inc.; *U.S. Public*, pg. 1040

ORLON—Acrylic Fiber—Du Pont (E.I. Du Pont De Nemours & Co.); *U.S. Public*, pg. 530

ORMCO—Orthodontic Supplies—Sybron International Corporation; *U.S. Public*, pg. 1544

ORMET—Conductive Inks—Kester Solder; *U.S. Public*, pg. 1003

ORMEX—Materials—Essilor International Compagnie Generale d'Optique; *Int'l*, pg. 462

ORMIL—Materials—Essilor International Compagnie Generale d'Optique; *Int'l*, pg. 462

ORNADE—NONE—SmithKline Beecham Corporation; *Int'l*, pg. 1264

ORNADE—Allergy/Cough/Cold Product—SmithKline Beecham plc; *Int'l*, pg. 1264

ORNEX—Cold Medication Caplet—Menley & James Laboratories, Inc.; *U.S. Public*, pg. 1086

ORNEX—Analgesic—SmithKline Beecham Research Limited; *Int'l*, pg. 1266

OROCLAD—Chemicals for Electro Plating—Technic Incorporated; *U.S. Private*, pg. 1071

OROMERSE—Chemicals For Electro Plating—Technic Incorporated; *U.S. Private*, pg. 1071

ORONAMIN-C DRINK—Beverage—Otsuka Pharmaceutical Co., Ltd.; *Int'l*, pg. 1013

ORONINE-H OINTMENT—Dermal Preparation—Otsuka Pharmaceutical Co., Ltd.; *Int'l*, pg. 1013

ORONITE—Fuel & Lubricant Additives—Chevron Corporation; *U.S. Public*, pg. 347

ORONITE ALKANE—Detergent Alkylate—Chevron Chemical Co.; *U.S. Public*, pg. 348

ORONITE ALKANE—Detergent Alkylate—Chevron Corporation; *U.S. Public*, pg. 347

OROPON—Leather Chemical—Rohm and Haas Company; *U.S. Public*, pg. 1403

OROPON—Enzymes—Rohm GmbH; *Int'l*, pg. 1454

OROS—Osmotic Therapeutic System—Alza Corporation; *U.S. Public*, pg. 62

OROSENE—Chemicals for Electro Plating—Technic Incorporated; *U.S. Private*, pg. 1071

OROTEMP—Chemicals for Electro Plating—Technic Incorporated; *U.S. Private*, pg. 1071

OROTHERM—Chemicals for Electro Plating—Technic Incorporated; *U.S. Private*, pg. 1071

OROVITE—Vitamin & Tonic—SmithKline Beecham plc; *Int'l*, pg. 1264

OROWEAT—Bread—Bestfoods; *U.S. Public*, pg. 223

ORR—Felts—The Orr Felt Company; *U.S. Private*, pg. 820

ORSOPHENGESIC—Muscle Relaxant—Pharmaceutical Resources; *U.S. Public*, pg. 1285

ORSOPHENGESIC FORTE—Muscle Relaxant—Pharmaceutical Resources; *U.S. Public*, pg. 1285

ORTAC—Hose—The Goodyear Tire & Rubber Company; *U.S. Public*, pg. 752

ORTEGA—Mexican Foods—Nestle S.A.; *Int'l*, pg. 915

ORTEGA—Taco Shells & Seasonings—Nestle USA; *Int'l*, pg. 916

ORTEGA—Mexican Foods—RJR Nabisco Holdings Corp.; *U.S. Public*, pg. 1354

ORTH—Bakery Ingredients—CSM N.V.; *Int'l*, pg. 243

ORTHO—Brain Thromboplastin—Ortho Clinical Diagnostic Systems Inc.; *U.S. Public*, pg. 929

ORTHO—Diaphragms—Ortho-McNeil Pharmaceutical Corporation; *U.S. Public*, pg. 929

ORTHO—Measured-Dose Applicator—Ortho-McNeil Pharmaceutical Corporation; *U.S. Public*, pg. 929

ORTHO—Universal Introducer—Ortho-McNeil Pharmaceutical Corporation; *U.S. Public*, pg. 929

ORTHO ALL-FLEX—Arching Spring Diaphragm—Ortho-McNeil Pharmaceutical Corporation; *U.S. Public*, pg. 929

ORTHO-BIOTIC—Specialty Patient Line of Recliners, Rockers & Positioning Chairs—Lumex Medical Products; *U.S. Public*, pg. 758

ORTHO CEPT—Oral Contraceptive—Akzo Nobel N.V.; *Int'l*, pg. 42

ORTHO CEPT—Contraceptive—Johnson & Johnson; *U.S. Public*, pg. 927

ORTHO-CEPT TABLETS—Desogestrel/Ethinyl Estradiol—Ortho-McNeil Pharmaceutical Corporation; *U.S. Public*, pg. 929

ORTHO CLONE—Contraceptive—Johnson & Johnson; *U.S. Public*, pg. 927

ORTHO COIL SPRING DIAPHRAGM—NONE—Ortho-McNeil Pharmaceutical Corporation; *U.S. Public*, pg. 929

Brand Name Index

ORTHO-CRESOL—NONE—Sasol Alpha Olefins; *Int'l*, pg. 1196

ORTHO-CRESOL—NONE—Sasol Chemicals Europe Limited; *Int'l*, pg. 1196

ORTHO CYCLEN—Contraceptive—Johnson & Johnson; *U.S. Public*, pg. 927

ORTHO-CYCLEN TABLETS—Norgestimate/ Ethinyl Estradiol—Ortho-McNeil Pharmaceutical Corporation; *U.S. Public*, pg. 929

ORTHO DIENESTROL CREAM—NONE—Ortho-McNeil Pharmaceutical Corporation; *U.S. Public*, pg. 929

ORTHO DIMERKLONE—NONE—Ortho Clinical Diagnostic Systems Inc.; *U.S. Public*, pg. 929

ORTHO-EST—.625 & 1.25 Estropipate Tablets—Ortho-McNeil Pharmaceutical Corporation; *U.S. Public*, pg. 929

ORTHO FITTING RINGS—NONE—Ortho-McNeil Pharmaceutical Corporation; *U.S. Public*, pg. 929

ORTHO-NOVUM—Oral Contraceptives—Johnson & Johnson; *U.S. Public*, pg. 927

ORTHO-NOVUM—Tablets—Ortho-McNeil Pharmaceutical Corporation; *U.S. Public*, pg. 929

ORTHO-NOVUM—1/35 21 Tablets—Ortho-McNeil Pharmaceutical Corporation; *U.S. Public*, pg. 929

ORTHO-NOVUM—1/35 28 Tablets—Ortho-McNeil Pharmaceutical Corporation; *U.S. Public*, pg. 929

ORTHO-NOVUM—1/50 21 Tablets—Ortho-McNeil Pharmaceutical Corporation; *U.S. Public*, pg. 929

ORTHO-NOVUM—1/50 28 Tablets—Ortho-McNeil Pharmaceutical Corporation; *U.S. Public*, pg. 929

ORTHO-NOVUM—7/7/7 21 Tablets—Ortho-McNeil Pharmaceutical Corporation; *U.S. Public*, pg. 929

ORTHO-NOVUM—7/7/7 28 Tablets—Ortho-McNeil Pharmaceutical Corporation; *U.S. Public*, pg. 929

ORTHO-NOVUM—10/11 21 Tablets—Ortho-McNeil Pharmaceutical Corporation; *U.S. Public*, pg. 929

ORTHO-NOVUM—10/11 28 Tablets—Ortho-McNeil Pharmaceutical Corporation; *U.S. Public*, pg. 929

ORTHO TRI-CYCLEN TABLETS—Norgestimate/ Ethinyl Estradiol—Ortho-McNeil Pharmaceutical Corporation; *U.S. Public*, pg. 929

ORTHO TRICYCLEN—Contraceptive—Johnson & Johnson; *U.S. Public*, pg. 927

ORTHO-WHITE—Flat Spring Diaphragm—Ortho-McNeil Pharmaceutical Corporation; *U.S. Public*, pg. 929

ORTHOARTS—Drape Sheets for Surgery—Kimberly-Clark Corporation; *U.S. Public*, pg. 958

ORTHOFIX—Bone Fixation Devices—Orthofix International N.V.; *Int'l*, pg. 1011

ORTHOFUSER—Post Operative Blood Salvage Device—Gish Biomedical, Inc.; *U.S. Public*, pg. 745

ORTHOTONIC—Mattresses—Restonic Mattress Corporation; *U.S. Private*, pg. 925

ORTHOXICOL—NONE—Lee Pharmaceuticals; *U.S. Public*, pg. 984

ORTHPANTOMOGRAPH—Panoramic Dental Imaging System—Instrumentarium Imaging, Inc.; *U.S. Private*, pg. 565

ORUDIS—Anti-Inflammatory Drug—American Home Products Corporation; *U.S. Public*, pg. 79

ORUDIS—Nonsteroidal Antiinflammatory/Analgesic Agent—Wyeth-Ayerst Laboratories, Inc.; *U.S. Public*, pg. 80

ORUDIS KT—NONE—American Home Products Corporation; *U.S. Public*, pg. 79

ORUDIS KT—Analgesic—Whitehall-Robins Healthcare; *U.S. Public*, pg. 80

ORUVAIL—Anti-Inflammatory Drug—American Home Products Corporation; *U.S. Public*, pg. 79

ORVAC—NONE—PAXAR Corporation; *U.S. Public*, pg. 1266

ORVILLE REDENBACHER—Popcorn—ConAgra, Inc.; *U.S. Public*, pg. 425

ORVILLE REDENBACHER—Gourmet Popping Corn & Oil—Hunt-Wesson, Inc.; *U.S. Public*, pg. 428

ORVIS—Fishing Gear, Sporting Goods & Sportswear—The Orvis Company, Inc.; *U.S. Private*, pg. 820

ORYZA—Rice—CSM N.V.; *Int'l*, pg. 243

ORYZEMATE—Agricultural Chemicals—Meiji Seika Kaisha, Ltd.; *Int'l*, pg. 855

OS-CAL—Calcuim Supplement—SmithKline Beecham Consumer Healthcare, U.S.; *Int'l*, pg. 1264

OSAR—NONE—FileNet Corporation; *U.S. Public*, pg. 622

OSBORN—Brushes—Jason Incorporated; *U.S. Public*, pg. 923

OSBORN—Industrial Brushes—Osborn Manufacturing; *U.S. Public*, pg. 924

OSCAR—Bone Cement Removal System—Orthofix International N.V.; *Int'l*, pg. 1011

OSCAR DE LA RENTA—Men's Suits—Oxford Industries, Inc.; *U.S. Public*, pg. 1239

OSCAR DE LA RENTA—Jewelry—Richton International Corporation; *U.S. Public*, pg. 1389

OSCAR MAYER—Bacon, Sausage, Ham, Luncheon Meats, Wieners & Turkey Products—Kraft Foods, Inc.; *U.S. Public*, pg. 1287

OSCAR MAYER—Hot Dogs, Bacon, & Sliced Meats—Kraft Foods Inc.; *U.S. Public*, pg. 1288

OSCAR MAYER—Meats—Philip Morris Companies Inc.; *U.S. Public*, pg. 1287

OSCAR MAYER INGREDIENTS—Seasonings—Kraft Food Ingredients Corp.; *U.S. Public*, pg. 1288

OSCAR MAYER LUNCHABLES—Lunch Combos—Kraft Foods, Inc.; *U.S. Public*, pg. 1287

OSCIL—NONE—Nordyne Inc.; *U.S. Public*, pg. 1193

OSCILLAMET—Abrasive Cutter—Buehler, Limited; *U.S. Public*, pg. 574

OSCILLATING MOTOR—Subfractional Horse Power Stepper Motor—Haydon Switch & Instrument, Inc.; *U.S. Private*, pg. 513

OSCIPLATE—Calciner—Harrop Industries, Inc.; *U.S. Private*, pg. 506

OSCO—Drug Stores—Jewel-Osco; *U.S. Public*, pg. 93

OSCO DRUG—Drug Stores—American Drug Stores Inc.; *U.S. Public*, pg. 93

OSCOREL—Inflammation & Tissue Repair—SmithKline Beecham plc; *Int'l*, pg. 1264

THE OSGOOD FILE—News Program—Westwood One, Inc.; *U.S. Public*, pg. 1763

OSHKOSH—Clothing—OshKosh B'Gosh, Inc.; *U.S. Public*, pg. 1232

OSHKOSH—Trucks—Oshkosh Truck Corporation; *U.S. Public*, pg. 1233

OSHKOSH B'GOSH—Hosiery, Underwear & Layette—Heyman Corporation; *U.S. Private*, pg. 524

OSHKOSH B'GOSH—Clothing—OshKosh B'Gosh, Inc.; *U.S. Public*, pg. 1232

OSHKOSH KIDS—Eyewear—Logo of the Americas; *Int'l*, pg. 462

OSHKOSH MENSWEAR—Clothing—OshKosh B'Gosh, Inc.; *U.S. Public*, pg. 1232

OSHKOSH MIXERS—NONE—3ummit Performance Dist. Inc.; *U.S. Public*, pg. 1233

OSKAR PLUS—Food Processor—Sunbeam Household Products; *U.S. Public*, pg. 1533

OSMAN—Household Textiles—Tootal Group plc; *Int'l*, pg. 300

OSMIROID—Calligraphy Pens—Hunt Corporation; *U.S. Public*, pg. 848

OSMO—RO Machines, Sepralators & Housings—Osmonics, Inc.; *U.S. Public*, pg. 1233

OSMO ORION—Compact Reverse Osmosis Unit—Osmonics, Inc.; *U.S. Public*, pg. 1233

OSMOGLYN—50% Glycerin—Alcon Laboratories, Inc.; *Int'l*, pg. 916

OSMOLITE—Isotonic Liquid Nutritional—Abbott Laboratories; *U.S. Public*, pg. 12

OSMONICS—NONE—Osmonics, Inc.; *U.S. Public*, pg. 1233

OSMOPLASTIC—Wood Preservative—Osmose Wood Preserving, Inc.; *U.S. Private*, pg. 821

OSMOSE—Treated Lumber—Holbrook Lumber Company; *U.S. Private*, pg. 533

OSMOSE—Lumber & Supplies—Osmose Wood Preserving, Inc.; *U.S. Private*, pg. 821

OSMOSE—Wood preservative—Osmose Wood Preserving, Inc.; *U.S. Private*, pg. 821

OSMOSE K-33—Wood Preservative—Osmose Wood Preserving, Inc.; *U.S. Private*, pg. 821

OSMOSTILL—Multiple & Single-Effect Stills, Pure Steam Generators—Osmonics, Inc.; *U.S. Public*, pg. 1233

OSNA CU58—Free Cutting Copper for Welding Mozzles, Torch Tips—KM-Europa Metal Aktiengesellschaft; *Int'l*, pg. 719

OSNALINE—Tube Bundles & Accessories for Meteoring & Control Systems—KM-Europa Metal Aktiengesellschaft; *Int'l*, pg. 719

OSRAM—NONE—Siemens AG; *Int'l*, pg. 1244

OSTEO-MESH—Mandibular Tray—Bristol-Myers Squibb Company; *U.S. Public*, pg. 253

OSTEONICS—NONE—Stryker Corporation; *U.S. Public*, pg. 1525

OSTEOSCAN HDP—Radioactive Diagnostic Kit—Mallinckrodt Inc.; *U.S. Public*, pg. 1039

OSTER—Appliances, Personal Care Products—Sunbeam Corporation; *U.S. Public*, pg. 1533

OSTERIZER—Blender—Sunbeam Household Products; *U.S. Public*, pg. 1533

OSTMANN—Herbs & Spices—Burns, Philp & Company Limited; *Int'l*, pg. 236

O'SULLIVAN—Plastic Products—O'Sullivan Corporation; *U.S. Public*, pg. 1234

OSWOS—Services—Halliburton Energy Services; *U.S. Public*, pg. 776

OTAMAH—Cigarettes—B.A.T Industries P.L.C.; *Int'l*, pg. 110

OTAN—Gas Pipeline Valves—IMI Plc; *Int'l*, pg. 646

OTARI—Audio Tape Recorders—Otari Corporation; *Int'l*, pg. 1013

OTARI—Audio Tape Recorders—Otari, Inc.; *Int'l*, pg. 1013

OTEK-OTEK—NONE—American Israeli Paper Mills Ltd.; *Int'l*, pg. 74

OTHELLO—Game—Pressman Toy Corp.; *U.S. Private*, pg. 882

OTIC-DOME—Pharmaceutical—Bayer Corporation/ Pharmaceutical Division; *Int'l*, pg. 173

OTIS—Elevator—Otis Elevator Company; *U.S. Public*, pg. 1690

OTIS—Elevators—United Technologies Corporation; *U.S. Public*, pg. 1689

OTOMAX—Ointment (Canine & Feline)—Schering-Plough Corporation; *U.S. Public*, pg. 1438

OTOMIZE—Pharmaceutical—Stafford-Miller Limited; *U.S. Public*, pg. 237

OTOMODACHI—Monthly Japanese Children's Magazine—Kodansha Ltd.; *Int'l*, pg. 742

OTSEIN—Household Appliances—Candy S.p.A.; *Int'l*, pg. 259

OTSUKA CEZ INJECTION-MC—Cephem Antibiotic Intravenous Infusion—Otsuka Pharmaceutical Co., Ltd.; *Int'l*, pg. 1013

OTSUKA MV INJECTION—Multivitamin Preparation—Otsuka Pharmaceutical Co., Ltd.; *Int'l*, pg. 1013

OTTASEPT—Fungicides, Biocides for Cosmetics, Soaps—Ferro Corporation; *U.S. Public*, pg. 618

OTTAWA—Terminal Tractors—Partek Corporation; *Int'l*, pg. 1024

OTTO REICHELT—Supermarkets—SHV Holdings N.V.; *Int'l*, pg. 1154

OUCH—Bubble gum—Amurol Confections Co.; *U.S. Public*, pg. 1781

OUCH KIT—First Aid Kits—Sentinel Consumer Products, Inc.; *U.S. Private*, pg. 984

OUCH-PREVENTION—Plumbing Products—The Black & Decker Corporation; *U.S. Public*, pg. 233

OUD BRUIN—NONE—Grolsch N.V.; *Int'l*, pg. 559

OUDE MEESTER—Brandy—Distillers Corporation S.A.; *Int'l*, pg. 1129

OUR BABY—Women's Special Interest Magazine—IPC Magazines Limited; *Int'l*, pg. 651

OUR BETR FRY—Shortening—Ventura Foods LLC; *U.S. Public*, pg. 879

OUR CLASSIC—Food Products—Oscar Mayer Foods Corp.; *U.S. Public*, pg. 1288

OUR COMPLIMENTS—NONE—The Oshawa Group Limited; *Int'l*, pg. 1012

OUR DELUXE—Food Products—Oscar Mayer Foods Corp.; *U.S. Public*, pg. 1288

OUR FAMILY—Food Products—Nash Finch Company; *U.S. Public*, pg. 1151

OUR FAMILY FOODS—Retail Grocery Store—Nash Finch Company; *U.S. Public*, pg. 1151

Brand Name Index

OUR FAMILY'S OPINION/NUESTRA FAMILIA OPINA—Hispanic Research Panel—NFO Research, Inc.; *U.S. Public*, pg. 1146

OUR GANG—Boyswear—Healthtex; *U.S. Public*, pg. 1702

OUR GIRL—Girlswear—Healthtex; *U.S. Public*, pg. 1702

OUR OWN—Tea—The Great Atlantic & Pacific Tea Company, Inc.; *Int'l*, pg. 1375

OUR PREMIUM—Food Products—Oscar Mayer Foods Corp.; *U.S. Public*, pg. 1288

OUR QUALITY SHINES THROUGH—Aluminum Paste, Products & Alloys—Reynolds Metals Company; *U.S. Public*, pg. 1385

OUR SUNDAY VISITOR—Publr. Religious Books & Matls.—Our Sunday Visitor, Inc.; *U.S. Private*, pg. 821

OUT IN FRONT—Recruiting & Advertising Package—RE/MAX International, Inc.; *U.S. Private*, pg. 912

OUT OF ORDER—Rock Music Radio Program—Westwood One Entertainment; *U.S. Public*, pg. 1763

OUT OF ORDER—Alternative Rock Show—Westwood One, Inc.; *U.S. Public*, pg. 1763

OUT RUN—Videogames—Sega of America Inc.; *Int'l*, pg. 1218

OUT-THINK—Slogan—Datapoint Corporation; *Int'l*, pg. 384

OUTBACK—NONE—Imperial Schrade Corp.; *U.S. Private*, pg. 559

OUTBACK—Sport Utility Wagon—Subaru of America, Inc.; *Int'l*, pg. 523

OUTBACK STEAKHOUSE—NONE—Outback Steakhouse Inc.; *U.S. Public*, pg. 1235

OUTBOARD MARINE CORP.—Mfg. of Boats & Marine Products—OMC Milwaukee; *U.S. Private*, pg. 478

OUTBURST—Family Picture Game—Golden Books Family Entertainment Inc.; *U.S. Public*, pg. 749

THE OUTDOOR—NONE—Cambridge Soundworks, Inc.; *U.S. Private*, pg. 202

OUTDOOR BIBLE SERIES—Book Imprint—Bertelsmann AG; *Int'l*, pg. 189

OUTDOOR LIFE—Magazine—Times Mirror Magazines, Inc.; *U.S. Public*, pg. 1616

OUTDOOR LIGHTING SOLUTIONS—Dusk to Dawn Specialty—APS; *U.S. Public*, pg. 1297

OUTDOOR PARCEL POST—Parcel Locker—American Locker Group, Inc.; *U.S. Public*, pg. 85

OUTDOOR RETAILER—Magazine—Miller Freeman Inc.; *Int'l*, pg. 1443

OUTDOOR SURVIVAL—Game—Monarch Avalon, Inc.; *U.S. Public*, pg. 1123

OUTDOORSMAN—Sunglasses—Bausch & Lomb Incorporated; *U.S. Public*, pg. 194

OUTDOORSMAN—Men's Apparel—Pendleton Woolen Mills, Inc.; *U.S. Private*, pg. 848

OUTDORABLES—Casual Footwear—Daniel Green Co.; *U.S. Private*, pg. 477

OUTERS—Gun Card Prods.—Blount, Inc. Sporting Equipment Group; *U.S. Public*, pg. 238

OUTERS—Gun Care, Traps & Targets—Blount International, Inc.; *U.S. Public*, pg. 237

OUTERSHIELD—Electrode—The Lincoln Electric Company; *U.S. Public*, pg. 996

OUTFITTERS—NONE—Sport Mart, Inc.; *U.S. Public*, pg. 1499

OUTLANDER—Women's Clothing—The Leslie Fay Companies, Inc.; *U.S. Public*, pg. 989

OUTLAW—Radio Control—Tyco Toys, Inc.; *U.S. Public*, pg. 1058

OUTLET RETAILER—Supplement to Shopping Center World—Intertec Publishing; *U.S. Public*, pg. 1327

OUTLET RETAILER—Monthly Publ.—Intertec Publishing; *U.S. Public*, pg. 1328

OUTLINER II—Hair Trimmer—Andis Company; *U.S. Private*, pg. 73

OUTLOOK—Magnetic Resonance Imaging—Picker International, Inc.; *Int'l*, pg. 545

OUTRIDER—Sidewall Fusion Equipment—T.D. Williamson, Inc.; *U.S. Private*, pg. 1179

OUTRIGGER—Lumber & Wood Products—Georgia-Pacific Corporation; *U.S. Public*, pg. 735

OUZO BY METAXA—NONE—Metaxa Distilleries; *Int'l*, pg. 410

OUZO BY METAXA—NONE—Societe Pour la Vente des Produits Cinzano SA; *Int'l*, pg. 410

OUZO NAFTAKI—NONE—Metaxa Distilleries; *Int'l*, pg. 410

OUZO 12—NONE—Carillon Importers, Ltd.; *Int'l*, pg. 409

OUZO 12—NONE—Metaxa Distilleries; *Int'l*, pg. 410

OVABAN—Progestogen Tablets (Canine & Feline)—Schering-Plough Corporation; *U.S. Public*, pg. 1438

OVAL FACETTE—Barware—Dansk International Designs Ltd.; *U.S. Public*, pg. 261

OVAL KOSTER PEARSON-BLUE DIAMOND—Religious Calendars—Renaissance Publishing Co., Inc.; *Int'l*, pg. 185

OVALOK—Lock Nuts—RB&W Corporation; *U.S. Public*, pg. 1259

OVALS & ARROWS—NONE—Carpenter Technology Corporation; *U.S. Public*, pg. 307

OVALSTRAPPING—U.S. & Canada—Enterprises International Inc.; *U.S. Private*, pg. 377

OVALTINE—Instant Drink—Novartis AG; *Int'l*, pg. 971

OVALTINE—Nutritional Drinks—Novartis Nutrition Corporation; *Int'l*, pg. 971

OVAMED—NONE—BEI Medical Systems Company; *U.S. Private*, pg. 106

OVATION—Eyeglass Frames—AVC/Nu-Vision, Inc.; *U.S. Private*, pg. 9

OVATION—Carseat—Century Products Co.; *U.S. Private*, pg. 226

OVATION—Chocolate Covered Sticks—Hershey Foods Corporation; *U.S. Public*, pg. 811

OVCON—Ovulation Control Product—Bristol-Myers Squibb Company; *U.S. Public*, pg. 253

OVCON-50—Oral Contraceptive—Bristol-Myers Squibb U.S. Pharmaceutical Group; *U.S. Public*, pg. 255

OVCON-35—Oral Contraceptive—Bristol-Myers Squibb U.S. Pharmaceutical Group; *U.S. Public*, pg. 255

OVALITE—Enamel Undercoat Paint for Interiors—PPG Industries, Inc.; *U.S. Public*, pg. 1245

OVEN CLASSIC—Poultry Items—Louis Kemp Seafood Co.; *U.S. Public*, pg. 1652

OVEN CLASSIC—Poultry Items—Tyson Foods, Inc.; *U.S. Public*, pg. 1652

OVEN EASY—Foodservice Frozen Items—Louis Kemp Seafood Co.; *U.S. Public*, pg. 1652

OVEN EXPRESS—Further-processed Poultry Items—Louis Kemp Seafood Co.; *U.S. Public*, pg. 1652

OVEN EXPRESS—Frozen Food—Tyson Foods, Inc.; *U.S. Public*, pg. 1652

OVEN FRY—Coating—Kraft Foods, Inc.; *U.S. Public*, pg. 1287

OVEN FRY—Coatings—Philip Morris Companies Inc.; *U.S. Public*, pg. 1287

OVEN STUFFERS—Roasters—Perdue Farms Incorporated; *U.S. Private*, pg. 852

OVENFRESH—Baked Goods—Grocers Baking Co.; *U.S. Private*, pg. 482

OVENWARE—Trays—The Chinet Co.; *Int'l*, pg. 1146

OVER-N-UNDER—Gravity-Flow, Overhead Transfer Conveyors—Jervis B. Webb Company; *U.S. Private*, pg. 1156

OVERBROOK—Egg Nog—M.S. Walker, Inc.; *U.S. Private*, pg. 1147

OVERCOAT—House Paint—PPG Industries, Inc.; *U.S. Public*, pg. 1245

OVERHEAD—Door Products—Overhead Door Corporation; *U.S. Private*, pg. 822

OVERHEAD DOOR—Garage Door Opener—The Genie Company; *U.S. Private*, pg. 823

OVERHILL—NONE—Huntco Inc.; *U.S. Public*, pg. 849

OVERHOLTZER—Church Furniture—Overholtzer Church Furniture, Inc.; *U.S. Private*, pg. 823

OVERNIGHT BOX—For Larger Items—FDX Corporation; *U.S. Public*, pg. 603

THE OVERNIGHT BUSINESS TRAVELER—Luggage—Hartmann Luggage & Leather Goods Group; *U.S. Public*, pg. 261

OVERNIGHT LETTER—For Correspondence—FDX Corporation; *U.S. Public*, pg. 603

OVERNIGHT TUBE—For Items not to be Folded—FDX Corporation; *U.S. Public*, pg. 603

OVERSTOLZ—Cigarettes-Germany—R.J. Reynolds Tobacco Intl., Inc.; *U.S. Public*, pg. 1355

OVERTOP—Headliner—Monsanto Company; *U.S. Public*, pg. 1124

OVERTURE—Variable Life Insurance—Ameritas Life Insurance Corp.; *U.S. Private*, pg. 65

OVERTURE—Kitchen Cabinets—Georgia-Pacific Corporation; *U.S. Public*, pg. 735

OVERTURE 8—ADSL/DMT Modem—AMATI Communications Corp.; *U.S. Public*, pg. 1585

OVERUM—Agricultural Implements—Electrolux, AB; *Int'l*, pg. 438

OVOLINE—Low-Calorie Drink—Novartis AG; *Int'l*, pg. 971

OVONIC—Nickel Metal Hydride Batteries—Energy Conversion Devices, Inc.; *U.S. Public*, pg. 581

OVRAL—NONE—American Home Products Corporation; *U.S. Public*, pg. 79

OVRETTE—NONE—American Home Products Corporation; *U.S. Public*, pg. 79

OVUKIT—Human Fertility Products—Quidel Corporation; *U.S. Public*, pg. 1352

OVUQUICK—Human Fertility Products—Quidel Corporation; *U.S. Public*, pg. 1352

OWEN HEALTHCARE—Hospital Pharmacy Management Services—Owen Health Care, Inc.; *U.S. Public*, pg. 304

OWEN KING PRINTERS—Printer—McPherson's Limited; *Int'l*, pg. 852

OWENS COUNTRY SAUSAGE—Sausage Products—Bob Evans Farms, Inc.; *U.S. Public*, pg. 596

OWENS COUNTRY SAUSAGE—Sausage & Other Products—Bob Evans Farms, Inc. Restaurant Division; *U.S. Public*, pg. 596

OWEN'S COUNTRY SAUSAGE—Sausage—Owens Country Sausage, Inc.; *U.S. Public*, pg. 596

OWENS FAMILY RESTAURANTS—Family Restaurants—Bob Evans Farms, Inc.; *U.S. Public*, pg. 596

OWENS FAMILY RESTAURANTS—Family Restaurants—Bob Evans Farms, Inc. Restaurant Division; *U.S. Public*, pg. 596

OWEN'S SPRING CREEK—Farm Brand—Owens Country Sausage, Inc.; *U.S. Public*, pg. 596

OWL CLUB—Casino—Jackpot Enterprises, Inc.; *U.S. Public*, pg. 920

OWNER OPERATOR—Business Magazine for Independent Truckers & Small Fleet Owners/Operators—Reed Elsevier Business Information; *Int'l*, pg. 1095

OX-TRAN—Measures Levels of Oxygen Transmission Through Barrier Materials—Modern Controls, Inc.; *U.S. Public*, pg. 1120

OXAL-95-R—Refractory—CFB Industries, Inc.; *U.S. Private*, pg. 194

OXAL-95-R—Refractory—Chicago Fire Brick Co.; *U.S. Private*, pg. 194

OXBOARD—Oriented Strand Board—Potlatch Corporation; *U.S. Public*, pg. 1318

OXFORD—Pickles, Relishes excluding Fruit Relishes, Peppers, Olives & Mayonnaise—Cains Foods, L.P.; *U.S. Private*, pg. 199

OXFORD—Storage Prods.—Esselte AB; *Int'l*, pg. 459

OXFORD—Filing Supplies, Binders, Report Covers, Desk Accessories—Esselte Corporation; *Int'l*, pg. 459

OXFORD—Hardwood Doors—Georgia-Pacific Corporation; *U.S. Public*, pg. 735

OXFORD—Puzzles—Milton Bradley Company; *U.S. Public*, pg. 797

OXFORD—Biscuits—United Biscuits (Holdings) Plc; *Int'l*, pg. 1442

OXFORD CUSTOM BLEND—Mayonnaise—Cains Foods, L.P.; *U.S. Private*, pg. 199

OXFORD LOGO—NONE—Oxford Health Plans Inc.; *U.S. Public*, pg. 1238

OXFORD SHIRTINGS—Men's Shirts—Oxford Industries, Inc.; *U.S. Public*, pg. 1239

OXFORD WEAVE DESIGN—Bond & Writing Paper—The Mead Corporation; *U.S. Public*, pg. 1074

OXI-ARC—Archive—Nellcor Puritan Bennett Incorporated; *U.S. Public*, pg. 1039

OXI-CHEK—Antioxidants, High Purity Solid With Low Toxicity—Ferro Corporation; *U.S. Public*, pg. 618

OXI-DISK—Data Disk—Nellcor Puritan Bennett Incorporated; *U.S. Public*, pg. 1039

OXI-GLAZE—Rubber Stopper for Bottles—The West Company, Incorporated; *U.S. Public*, pg. 1755

OXI-TABS—Antioxidants—Novo Nordisk A/S; *Int'l*, pg. 987

OXIBAND—Adhesive Oxygen Transducer—Nellcor Puritan Bennett Incorporated; *U.S. Public*, pg. 1039

OXICHIP—Circuit—Nellcor Puritan Bennett Incorporated; *U.S. Public*, pg. 1039

OXICLIQ—Sensor—Nellcor Puritan Bennett Incorporated; *U.S. Public*, pg. 1039

OXIFLOW—Multichannel Recorder to Screen Sleep Breathing Disorders—Nellcor Puritan Bennett Incorporated; *U.S. Public*, pg. 1039

OXIFREE—Ultraviolet Disinfection System—Capital Controls Company Inc.; *Int'l*, pg. 1226

OXIGARD—NONE—Pharmacia & Upjohn, Inc.; *Int'l*, pg. 1047

OXIMETRIX—Blood Oxygen Monitoring Equipment—Abbott Laboratories; *U.S. Public*, pg. 12

OXINET—Pulse Oximetry Network—Nellcor Puritan Bennett Incorporated; *U.S. Public*, pg. 1039

OXIQUIP—Home Respiratory Care Products—Allied Healthcare Products, Inc.; *U.S. Public*, pg. 48

OXISENSOR—Adhesive Sensor—Nellcor Puritan Bennett Incorporated; *U.S. Public*, pg. 1039

OXISENSOR II—Adhesive Sensor—Nellcor Puritan Bennett Incorporated; *U.S. Public*, pg. 1039

OXISMART—Advanced Signal Processing & Alarm Management Technology—Nellcor Puritan Bennett Incorporated; *U.S. Public*, pg. 1039

OXITRACE—Oxident Analyzer—Capital Controls Company Inc.; *Int'l*, pg. 1226

OXIVENT—Bronchodilator—Boehringer Ingelheim GmbH; *Int'l*, pg. 199

OXMOOR HOUSE—Books—Southern Progress Corporation; *U.S. Public*, pg. 1612

OXO—Kitchen Tools—General Housewares Corp.; *U.S. Public*, pg. 715

OXPRO OR—Technology for Recycling Mixed Office Wastepaper—Air Products and Chemicals, Inc.; *U.S. Public*, pg. 30

OXSOL—Non-Ozone Depleting Solvents—Occidental Chemical Corporation; *U.S. Public*, pg. 1210

OXSORALEN—Prescription Drug—ICN Pharmaceuticals, Inc.; *U.S. Public*, pg. 853

OXSORALEN-ULTRA—Prescription Drug—ICN Pharmaceuticals, Inc.; *U.S. Public*, pg. 853

OXY—Acne Treatment—SmithKline Beecham Corporation; *Int'l*, pg. 1264

OXY—Topical/Skincare—SmithKline Beecham plc; *Int'l*, pg. 1264

OXY BALANCE—Acne Medication—SmithKline Beecham Consumer Healthcare, U.S.; *Int'l*, pg. 1264

OXY CLEAN—Medicated Cleanser, Pads, Scrub & Soap—SmithKline Beecham Consumer Healthcare, U.S.; *Int'l*, pg. 1264

OXY-GARD—Hydrogen Peroxide-Based Teat Dip—Ecolab Inc.; *U.S. Public*, pg. 562

OXY-GLASS—NONE—AGA Gas, Inc.; *Int'l*, pg. 13

OXY RESIDON'T—Facial Cleanser—SmithKline Beecham Corporation; *Int'l*, pg. 1264

OXY-TEC—Cheical Type Acid Cleaner/Conditioner for Concrete, Mortar, Brass & Bronze—Calgon Vestal Laboratories; *U.S. Public*, pg. 1515

OXYCAT—Exhaust Purifiers for Gas & Diesel Engines; Catalytic Converters; Catalysts—Met-Pro Corp. Systems Division; *U.S. Public*, pg. 1100

OXYCAT—Catalysts, Purifiers & Catalytic Converters—Met-Pro Corporation; *U.S. Public*, pg. 1100

OXYCLAR—Hydrogen Peroxide—Montedison S.p.A.; *Int'l*, pg. 324

OXYCOIL—NONE—Chad Therapeutics; *U.S. Public*, pg. 332

OXYDOL—Laundry Product—The Procter & Gamble Company; *U.S. Public*, pg. 1330

OXYESTER—Monomer & Coating Resin—Veba AG; *Int'l*, pg. 1454

OXYGEN—Snowboards & In-Line Skates—Amer Group Ltd.; *Int'l*, pg. 72

OXYGEN PLUS—Water Soluable Fertilizer—Ringer Corporation; *U.S. Public*, pg. 1390

OXYLENE—Fireproof Timber—Meyer International PLC; *Int'l*, pg. 864

OXYLITE—NONE—Chad Therapeutics; *U.S. Public*, pg. 332

OXYMATIC—NONE—Chad Therapeutics; *U.S. Public*, pg. 332

OXYMIZER—NONE—Chad Therapeutics; *U.S. Public*, pg. 332

OXYPHAN—Membrane for the Supply of Oxygen to Blood during Open Heart Surgery—Akzo Nobel N.V.; *Int'l*, pg. 42

OXYPRIME—NONE—AGA Gas, Inc.; *Int'l*, pg. 13

OXYSEPT—Neutralizing Tablets—Allergan, Inc.; *U.S. Public*, pg. 46

OYLTITE-STIK—Sealant—La-Co Industries Markal Company; *U.S. Private*, pg. 640

OYSTERETTES—Soup & Oyster Crackers—Nabisco Inc.; *U.S. Public*, pg. 1355

OYSTERETTES—Soup & Oyster Crackers—RJR Nabisco Holdings Corp.; *U.S. Public*, pg. 1354

OZADISC—Magnetic-Optical Data Storage—Hoechst Aktiengesellschaft; *Int'l*, pg. 624

OZARK FAMILY RECIPE—Poultry Items—Tyson Foods, Inc.; *U.S. Public*, pg. 1652

OZARK FRY—Frozen Poultry—Louis Kemp Seafood Co.; *U.S. Public*, pg. 1652

OZARK FRY—Poultry Items—Tyson Foods, Inc.; *U.S. Public*, pg. 1652

OZARKA—Mineral Water—Nestle S.A.; *Int'l*, pg. 915

OZARKA—Bottled Water—The Perrier Group of America; *Int'l*, pg. 919

OZATEC—Dry Film Resist—Hoechst Aktiengesellschaft; *Int'l*, pg. 624

OZEKI-SAKE—Rice Wine—Ozeki Corporation; *Int'l*, pg. 1019

OZONE RESEARCH & EQUIPMENT CORPORATION—Ozonators—Osmonics, Inc.; *U.S. Public*, pg. 1233

OZOTHIN—Bronchial Decongestant—SmithKline Beecham plc; *Int'l*, pg. 1264

OZPAC—NONE—CPAC, Inc.; *U.S. Public*, pg. 282

OZZY ENZYME—Bioremediating Parts Washer Enzymes—Intelligent Systems Corp.; *U.S. Public*, pg. 888

P

P—Brakes—Rockwell International Corporation; *U.S. Public*, pg. 1397

P.A. BERGNER & CO.—General Store—Carson Pirie Scott & Co.; *U.S. Public*, pg. 309

P-A-C—NONE—Lee Pharmaceuticals; *U.S. Public*, pg. 984

PACX—Private Automatic Computer Exchange—Gandalf Technologies Inc.; *Int'l*, pg. 540

PAF—Power Assisted Fuse—G & W Electric Co.; *U.S. Private*, pg. 433

PAL—Business Product—International Business Machines Corporation; *U.S. Public*, pg. 895

PAM CONSTRUCTION—NONE—Professional Apartment Management, Inc.; *U.S. Private*, pg. 889

PAM DEVELOPMENT INC.—NONE—Professional Apartment Management, Inc.; *U.S. Private*, pg. 889

PAM INC.—NONE—Professional Apartment Management, Inc.; *U.S. Private*, pg. 889

P A R—Reflector Light Bulb—Duro-Test Corporation; *U.S. Public*, pg. 349

P A REGNAULT—Protective Paints, Varnishes, Lacquers—Sime Darby Berhad; *Int'l*, pg. 1249

PA 2000—Tires—Bridgestone/Firestone, Inc.; *Int'l*, pg. 213

P/ACE—High Performance Capillary Electrophoresis System—Beckman Instruments, Inc.; *U.S. Public*, pg. 199

P & C—Power & Communications—The Lamson & Sessions Co.; *U.S. Public*, pg. 976

P & C—Food Products—P & C Food Markets, Inc.; *U.S. Public*, pg. 1270

P & C FLEX—Corrugated Flexible Conduit—The Lamson & Sessions Co.; *U.S. Public*, pg. 976

P&C FOODS—Supermarkets—The Penn Traffic Company; *U.S. Public*, pg. 1270

P & D—Automotive Beauty Products—W.M. Barr & Co., Inc.; *U.S. Private*, pg. 117

P&H—Cranes, Hoists, Shovels, Etc.—Harnischfeger Industries, Inc.; *U.S. Public*, pg. 788

P & L—Varnishes, Enamel, Etc.—Pratt & Lambert United, Inc.; *U.S. Public*, pg. 1466

P & R—Pasta—Hershey Foods Corporation; *U.S. Public*, pg. 811

P & R—Pasta—Hershey Pasta and Grocery Group; *U.S. Public*, pg. 812

P&T PAD—Control Disc—Vicon Industries, Inc.; *U.S. Public*, pg. 1719

PB—NONE—Nellcor Puritan Bennett Incorporated; *U.S. Public*, pg. 1039

PBC—Console Copier—Pitney Bowes Inc.; *U.S. Public*, pg. 1303

PBDM—Laminated Wood Beams—Weyerhaeuser Company; *U.S. Public*, pg. 1764

PBDM—Laminated Wood Beams—Weyerhaeuser Forest Products Company; *U.S. Public*, pg. 1764

PBDS—Delivery of Medical Procedure Kits to Customer Via Truck or Van—Allegiance Healthcare Corp.; *U.S. Public*, pg. 44

PBM—Men's Apparel—Pincus Bros., Inc.; *U.S. Private*, pg. 865

PBM WOMEN—Women's Apparel—Pincus Bros., Inc.; *U.S. Private*, pg. 865

PB-MAX—NONE—Life Technologies, Inc.; *U.S. Public*, pg. 504

P.B. MAX—Peanut Butter Candy—Mars, Incorporated; *U.S. Private*, pg. 707

PB MAX BRAND—NONE—M&M/Mars; *U.S. Private*, pg. 707

PB-NC—Plastic-baked Nitrocellulose—Schleicher & Schuell, Inc.; *Int'l*, pg. 1206

PBO-8—Brand of Insecticide Synergist—Prentiss Incorporated; *U.S. Private*, pg. 882

PB PURITAN BENNETT WE'RE IN IT FOR LIFE—NONE—Nellcor Puritan Bennett Incorporated; *U.S. Public*, pg. 1039

PBS—Prebound Periodicals—The American Companies, Inc.; *U.S. Private*, pg. 52

PBS—Bypass Equipment—Medtronic, Inc.; *U.S. Public*, pg. 1082

PBS-4100—Portable Balancing System—Mechanical Technology Inc.; *U.S. Public*, pg. 1077

PBS-4100R—Portable Balancing System—Mechanical Technology Inc.; *U.S. Public*, pg. 1077

PBZ—NONE—Novartis Pharmaceuticals; *Int'l*, pg. 973

PBZ-SR—NONE—Novartis Pharmaceuticals; *Int'l*, pg. 973

P C—Combination Binder Notebook & Calculator—The Mead Corporation; *U.S. Public*, pg. 1074

PC/AIM—Automatic Inventory Management Systems/PC's—Jervis B. Webb Company; *U.S. Private*, pg. 1156

PC BUBBLE—Electronic Instrument—Intel Corporation; *U.S. Public*, pg. 886

PCC II CONTROLLER—Multi-Loop Controller for Process/Combustion Control—Preferred Utilities Manufacturing Corp.; *U.S. Private*, pg. 881

PCC-2000 SYSTEM—Data Aquisition System with Active Custom Graphics—Preferred Utilities Manufacturing Corp.; *U.S. Private*, pg. 881

PC/CHIP—NONE—Chips and Technologies, Inc.; *U.S. Public*, pg. 349

PCD—Device—Medtronic, Inc.; *U.S. Public*, pg. 1082

PC/DACS FOR DOS & WINDOWS—Client/Workstation Access Control—Utimaco Safeware, Inc.; *Int'l*, pg. 1444

PC/DACS FOR OS/2—Workstation & Server Access Control—Utimaco Safeware, Inc.; *Int'l*, pg. 1444

PCE—Erythromycin Particles in Tablets—Abbott Laboratories; *U.S. Public*, pg. 12

PCFORMAT—File Formatting System—Tandem Computers Inc.; *U.S. Public*, pg. 417

PC/4—Hand-Held Labeling System—TimeMed Labeling Systems, Inc.; *U.S. Private*, pg. 1087

PC GAMES—Computer Games Magazine—EMAP Images; *Int'l*, pg. 451

PC GLOBE MAPS 'N' FACTS—NONE—Broderbund Software, Inc.; *U.S. Public*, pg. 258

PC GRAPHICS & VIDEO—Trade Periodical—Advanstar Communications; *U.S. Private*, pg. 22

PCI—Natural Polymer for Inhibiting Corrosion—Georgia-Pacific Corporation; *U.S. Public*, pg. 735

Brand Name Index

PCI INTERNATIONAL—Stationery Items & Binder Fixtures—The Mead Corporation; *U.S. Public*, pg. 1074

PCI SCSI MASTER—NONE—Adaptec, Inc.; *U.S. Public*, pg. 19

PC IMAGE—Image/Graphics Software—Xerox Imaging Systems, Inc.; *U.S. Public*, pg. 1785

PC-INTELLIGENT NETWORK—Intelligent Network Executive Computer Software Prod.—Datapoint Corporation; *Int'l*, pg. 384

PC-INTERFACE—Connects PCs to Unix Systems Providing File & Resource Sharing—Platinum Solutions; *U.S. Public*, pg. 1309

PCJR—Computer—International Business Machines Corporation; *U.S. Public*, pg. 895

PCMX—Antimicrobials—Ferro Corporation; *U.S. Public*, pg. 618

PC MARKETPLACE—NONE—EMAP Business Communications Division; *Int'l*, pg. 451

PC-MET—Manual Printed Circuit Board Accessory—Buehler, Limited; *U.S. Public*, pg. 574

PC MINLINK—Micro-to-Mini Link Software—Dun & Bradstreet Software Services; *Int'l*, pg. 532

PC-MOTION—Computer Software for a Multimedia Presentation System—The Titan Corporation; *U.S. Public*, pg. 1618

PCN GOLD—Photographic Film—Eastman Kodak Company; *U.S. Public*, pg. 550

PCN HEALTH NETWORK—Practice Management Software—Physician Computer Network, Inc.; *U.S. Public*, pg. 1293

PCN MCARE—Full Risk Managed Care Application—Physician Computer Network, Inc.; *U.S. Public*, pg. 1293

PCN MENDS ICF—Practice Management Software—Physician Computer Network, Inc.; *U.S. Public*, pg. 1293

PCNS—Personal Computer Network Services—Datapoint Corporation; *Int'l*, pg. 384

PC-9 TURBO TRAINERS—Civilian Aviation—Oerlikon-Buhrle Holding AG; *Int'l*, pg. 996

PC-123—Hair Culture Solution to Assist in Pressing & Curling Hair—The Gillette Company; *U.S. Public*, pg. 743

PCPI—Corporate Name—Imaging Technologies Corp.; *U.S. Public*, pg. 870

PC PRIME—Needle—Ethicon, Inc.; *U.S. Public*, pg. 928

PC QUOTE 6.0—Real Time Professional Market Data—PC Quote, Inc.; *U.S. Public*, pg. 1240

PCR—Power Control Rooms—Powell Industries, Inc.; *U.S. Public*, pg. 1319

PCRADIO—Computer Product—International Business Machines Corporation; *U.S. Public*, pg. 895

PC READER—Bar Code Scanning System—Caere Corporation; *U.S. Public*, pg. 291

PC REVIEW—Computer Magazine—EMAP Images; *Int'l*, pg. 451

PCSC (PET CARE SAVINGS CLUB)—Pet Goods & Services—Encore Marketing International, Inc.; *U.S. Public*, pg. 580

PCS FINANCIAL SERVICES—Real Estate Accounting Software—MCRB Service Bureau, Inc.; *U.S. Private*, pg. 686

PC SCANNER—Bar Code Scanning System—Caere Corporation; *U.S. Public*, pg. 291

PC-7 TURBO TRAINERS—Civilian Aviation—Oerlikon-Buhrle Holding AG; *Int'l*, pg. 996

PC SIMSCRIPT II.5—Programming Computer Simulation Language System—CACI International Inc.; *U.S. Public*, pg. 272

PC-6300—Personal Computers—AT&T Corporation; *U.S. Public*, pg. 10

PC/SOLUTION—Modular IBM-PC Compatible Computer—Imaging Technologies Corp.; *U.S. Public*, pg. 870

PCT—Photographic Paper, Film, Apparatus & Chemicals—Eastman Kodak Company; *U.S. Public*, pg. 550

PC-1344—Oil Defoamer—Monsanto Company; *U.S. Public*, pg. 1124

PC-1344—Oil DeFoamer—Solutia Inc.; *U.S. Public*, pg. 1483

PC-12—Corporate Commuter—Oerlikon-Buhrle Holding AG; *Int'l*, pg. 996

PC-1244—Oil Defoamer—Monsanto Company; *U.S. Public*, pg. 1124

PC-1244—Oil DeFoamer—Solutia Inc.; *U.S. Public*, pg. 1483

PC-2000—Computer Perming Device—Revlon-Realistic Professional Products, Inc.; *U.S. Private*, pg. 690

PC USER—NONE—EMAP Business Communications Division; *Int'l*, pg. 451

PCVAULT—Computer Programs that Provide Backup, Archive & Recovery for PCs—Lucent Technologies Inc.; *U.S. Public*, pg. 1017

PC VIEW+—NONE—Trident Microsystems, Inc.; *U.S. Public*, pg. 1637

PC VOICEWRITER—Digital Dictation—Lanier Worldwide Inc.; *U.S. Public*, pg. 791

PC WORLD—Reatil Consumer Electronics Stores—Dixons Group plc; *Int'l*, pg. 413

PC/XT—Computer—International Business Machines Corporation; *U.S. Public*, pg. 895

PCX II—Cavity Back Golf Clubs For Men & Women—Square Two Golf Incorporated; *U.S. Public*, pg. 1501

PC XSIGHT—X Window Server for PCs running MS-Dos—Platinum Solutions; *U.S. Public*, pg. 1309

PC-XWARE—Software—Network Computing Devices, Inc.; *U.S. Public*, pg. 1168

P/COMPOSITE—Application-Specific Finite Element Analysis Software—MacNeal-Schwendler Corp.; *U.S. Public*, pg. 1031

P/CONCEPT ANALYSIS—Application-Specific Finite Element Analysis Software—MacNeal-Schwendler Corp.; *U.S. Public*, pg. 1031

PD—Pressure Diazo Equipment & Supplies—OCE-U.S.A.; *Int'l*, pg. 994

P.D.—Parker Diagonistic Series—Parker Hannifin Corp., Quick Coupling Div.; *U.S. Public*, pg. 1260

PD—Non-invasive Cardiac Device—Zoll Medical Corporation; *U.S. Private*, pg. 1207

PD ACTIVATOR—Pressure Diazo Developer—OCE-U.S.A.; *Int'l*, pg. 994

PDC—NONE—Polaroid Corporation; *U.S. Public*, pg. 1313

PD CHEM—Test for Peritoneal Dialysis Patients—Fresenius Medical Care (North America); *Int'l*, pg. 505

PDI—Liquid Color & Dispersion Additives for Plastics—Ferro Corporation; *U.S. Public*, pg. 618

PDI—Disposable Medical Products—Nice-Pak Products, Inc.; *U.S. Private*, pg. 798

PDK-100—NONE—Western Atlas Logging Services; *U.S. Public*, pg. 1757

PDL—Paste Solder—Litton Industries, Inc.; *U.S. Public*, pg. 1002

PD PLUS—Blowers—MD Pneumatics; *U.S. Private*, pg. 1111

PDQ MANAGEMENT SYSTEM—NONE—SunGard Data Systems Inc.; *U.S. Public*, pg. 1534

PDQ MILK FLAVORING—Treat Drink Served Hot or Cold—Novartis Nutrition Corporation; *Int'l*, pg. 974

P.D.R.P.—Rust Preventive Lubricant—Sherwin-Williams Diversified Brands, Inc.; *U.S. Public*, pg. 1466

PDS—Polydioxanone Suture—Ethicon, Inc.; *U.S. Public*, pg. 928

PDX—Portland Intl. Airport—Port of Portland; *U.S. Private*, pg. 876

PE—Pilocarpine Hydrochloride/Epinephrine Bitartrate—Alcon Laboratories, Inc.; *Int'l*, pg. 916

P.E./DEL MAR—Door Hardware—Watsco, Inc.; *U.S. Public*, pg. 1745

PEI—Motorcycle—American Suzuki Motor Corporation; *Int'l*, pg. 1323

PEM—Fasteners—Penn Engineering & Manufacturing Corp.; *U.S. Public*, pg. 1269

PEP—Interactive Touch Display—Industrial Electronic Engineers, Inc.; *U.S. Private*, pg. 561

P85—9 mm Pistol—Sturm, Ruger & Co., Inc.; *U.S. Public*, pg. 1526

P84—Packaging Machine System—Printpac-UEB Case Group; *U.S. Public*, pg. 905

PF—Heat Transfer Products—Modine Manufacturing Company; *U.S. Public*, pg. 1121

PFA-GASKLEEN III—Filter Assembly—Pall Corporation; *U.S. Public*, pg. 1253

PFA-ULTRAGASKLEEN—NONE—Pall Corporation; *U.S. Public*, pg. 1253

PFC—Patio Furniture Cleaner—Jelmar Company; *U.S. Private*, pg. 585

P.F.C.—NONE—Johnson & Johnson; *U.S. Public*, pg. 927

PF FLYERS—Footwear—Hyde Athletic Industries, Inc.; *U.S. Public*, pg. 851

PF 4—Diagnostic Products—Abbott Laboratories; *U.S. Public*, pg. 12

PF 95 DUCT LINER ADHESIVE—Adhesive—Pratt & Lambert United, Inc.; *U.S. Public*, pg. 1466

PFV—Wire Rope—Macwhyte Co.; *U.S. Private*, pg. 68

PFX—Application Software for Print File Transfer—Network Systems Corporation; *U.S. Public*, pg. 1522

PFASTBAC—NONE—Life Technologies, Inc.; *U.S. Public*, pg. 504

P/FATIGUE—Application-Specific Finite Element Analysis Software—MacNeal-Schwendler Corp.; *U.S. Public*, pg. 1031

P/FEA—Application Specific Finite Element Analysis Software—MacNeal-Schwendler Corp.; *U.S. Public*, pg. 1031

P-50—Dental Ceramic—3M; *U.S. Public*, pg. 1604

P/FLOTRAN—Application-Specific Finite Element Analysis Software—MacNeal-Schwendler Corp.; *U.S. Public*, pg. 1031

P-45—Polyethylene & PVC Insulated 1000 V Multiple Conductor Control Cable—The Okonite Company; *U.S. Private*, pg. 813

PG—Coated Abrasive Flap Wheels—3M; *U.S. Public*, pg. 1604

PGA TOUR—Clothing—RAM Golf Corporation; *U.S. Private*, pg. 908

PGH—Clay Bricks—CSR Limited; *Int'l*, pg. 245

PGL—Valves & Fittings—Pegler-Hattersley Plc; *Int'l*, pg. 1395

P-GLYCOCHEK C219—Multidrug Resistance Test—Centocor, Inc.; *U.S. Public*, pg. 323

PH BALANCER—Shampoo & Conditioner—Clairol, Inc.; *U.S. Public*, pg. 254

PHF-VAX—Vaccine (Equine & Bovine)—Schering-Plough Corporation; *U.S. Public*, pg. 1438

PHI—pH Meters—Beckman Instruments, Inc.; *U.S. Public*, pg. 199

PH/ORP—Conductivity, Dissolved Oxygen & Residual Chlorine Analyzer—Rosemount Analytical, Uniloc Div.; *U.S. Public*, pg. 574

PIA—Pakistan Intl. Airlines—Pakistan International Airlines Corporation; *Int'l*, pg. 1022

PIC—Reagent & Reagent Sampler Kit—Millipore Corporation; *U.S. Public*, pg. 1112

PIC-100—Programmable Infrared Remote Controller—Retzlaff Incorporated; *U.S. Private*, pg. 925

PIX—Color Imaging Retouching & Manipulation System—AGFA Division of Bayer Corporation; *Int'l*, pg. 172

PIX—Photo Typesetter—AGFA EPS Division; *Int'l*, pg. 172

P.J. SPARKLES—Doll—Mattel, Inc.; *U.S. Public*, pg. 1057

PJAC SYSTEM—Air Cleaner—Donaldson Company, Inc.; *U.S. Public*, pg. 517

P. J. KENNEDY & SON'S OFFICIAL CATHOLIC DIRECTORY—Official Reference Register—National Register Publishing; *U.S. Public*, pg. 1096

P.J. LANE—Sleepwear—Lanz, Inc.; *U.S. Private*, pg. 650

PKWF—Printing Ink Oils—Haltermann AG; *Int'l*, pg. 590

PL—Fluorescents—Philips Electronics N.V.; *Int'l*, pg. 1051

PLC—Programmable Logic Controllers—Rockwell International Corporation; *U.S. Public*, pg. 1397

PLDTEST PLUS—Software—Data I/O Corporation; *U.S. Public*, pg. 486

PL50—Platelet Filter—Pall Corporation; *U.S. Public*, pg. 1253

PLGR+—Portable GPS—Rockwell International Corporation; *U.S. Public*, pg. 1397

PLGR+GLS—Gun/laying GPS—Rockwell International Corporation; *U.S. Public*, pg. 1397

PLGR+96—Portable GPS—Rockwell International Corporation; *U.S. Public*, pg. 1397

PLJ—Lemon Juice—SmithKline Beecham plc; *Int'l*, pg. 1264

PLM—Planetary Mixers—Premier Mill Corp.; *U.S. Private*, pg. 881

PLM AZUR—Resort Hotels—Accor S.A.; *Int'l*, pg. 20

PLM RENT-A-VAULT—Portable Storage Units—PLM International, Inc.; *U.S. Public*, pg. 1241

PL100—Platelet Filter—Pall Corporation; *U.S. Public*, pg. 1253

PLX—NONE—Plantronics Inc.; *U.S. Public*, pg. 1308

PM—Shock Absorber Series—Enidine Incorporated; *U.S. Private*, pg. 377

PMC—Electro-Pneumatic Controllers—Leslie Controls, Inc.; *U.S. Public*, pg. 1746

PMC INDUSTRIES—Gages, Instruments, Machinery, Tools & Sub-contract Graphic Instrumentation—PMC Industries Inc.; *U.S. Private*, pg. 827

PMF—Porous Metal Fiber Filter—Pall Corporation; *U.S. Public*, pg. 1253

PM GROUP LIFE INSURANCE COMPANY—Group Employee Benefits—Pacific Life Insurance Company; *U.S. Private*, pg. 831

PMI—Balers—AGCO Corporation; *U.S. Public*, pg. 28

PMI—NONE—Brown & Sharpe Manufacturing Company; *U.S. Public*, pg. 260

PML SECURITIES CO.—Broker/Dealer—Provident Mutual Life Insurance Co.; *U.S. Private*, pg. 891

PMM—NONE—Brown & Sharpe Manufacturing Company; *U.S. Public*, pg. 260

PMM—Porous Metal Membrane Filter—Pall Corporation; *U.S. Public*, pg. 1253

PM/PLUS—End Mills—Greenfield Industries; *U.S. Public*, pg. 950

PMR—Manually Operated Resuscitator—Nellcor Puritan Bennett Incorporated; *U.S. Public*, pg. 1039

PM REALTY ADVISORS, INC.—Real Estate Advisory Service—Pacific Life Insurance Company; *U.S. Private*, pg. 831

PMS—Pump Managing System—O&K Orenstein & Koppel Aktiengesellschaft; *Int'l*, pg. 516

PM SYSTEMS ELECTRIC BLANKETS—Low EMF Electric Blankets—Sunbeam Household Products; *U.S. Public*, pg. 1533

PMT—Photographic Materials & Chemicals—Eastman Kodak Company; *U.S. Public*, pg. 550

PMUX—Multiplexer—Beckman Instruments, Inc.; *U.S. Public*, pg. 199

P/MECHANISM—Application-Specific Finite Element Analysis Software—MacNeal-Schwendler Corp.; *U.S. Public*, pg. 1031

PNC FINANCIAL CORP—Bank Holding Company—PNC Bank Corp.; *U.S. Public*, pg. 1242

PNF—Synthetic Rubber—Bridgestone/Firestone, Inc.; *Int'l*, pg. 213

PNI—Data Courier—Bell & Howell Holdings; *U.S. Public*, pg. 201

POL-NU—Wood Utility Pole Preservative—ISK BioSciences; *Int'l*, pg. 689

PO MILLENNIUM—Purchasing Information System—Dun & Bradstreet Software Services; *Int'l*, pg. 532

P.O.P.—Refrigerated Drawers—American Wyott Corporation; *U.S. Private*, pg. 1193

POP—Rivets—The Black & Decker Corporation; *U.S. Public*, pg. 233

POP NUT—Fastening Systems—The Black & Decker Corporation; *U.S. Public*, pg. 233

POR EQUAL—Pre Permanent Conditioning for Extra Resistant Hair—The Gillette Company; *U.S. Public*, pg. 743

POS—In-House PC Based Physicians Billng System—Shared Medical Systems Corporation; *U.S. Public*, pg. 1463

POS/EM—Point-of-Sale Exception Monitoring System—Sensormatic Electronics Corporation; *U.S. Public*, pg. 1457

P.O.V.—Magazine Publication—Freedom Communication Inc.; *U.S. Public*, pg. 425

P.P.A.—Professional Putters Association—Professional Putters Association; *U.S. Private*, pg. 896

PPDM—Product & Process Document Management Software—Tandem Computers Inc.; *U.S. Public*, pg. 417

PPI—NONE—Pacesetter Corporation; *U.S. Private*, pg. 830

PPI, INC—NONE—Pacesetter Corporation; *U.S. Private*, pg. 830

PPINICI—Pulsed Positive Ion/Negative Ion Chemical Ionization—Finnigan Corporation; *U.S. Public*, pg. 1591

PPM—All-Terrain Mobile Cranes & Telesceptic Container Handlers—Terex Corporation; *U.S. Public*, pg. 1581

PPO—Synthetic Thermoplastic Resinous Material, for Molding & Forming of Devices—General Electric Canada Inc.; *U.S. Public*, pg. 713

PPT—Soft TissueSupplement—The Langer Biomechanics Group, Inc.; *U.S. Public*, pg. 978

P PRIME—Needle—Ethicon, Inc.; *U.S. Public*, pg. 928

PPROEX—NONE—Life Technologies, Inc.; *U.S. Public*, pg. 504

PQ—Alkali Silicates—PQ Corporation; *U.S. Private*, pg. 827

PQ NETWORK—NONE—UtiliCorp United Inc.; *U.S. Public*, pg. 1700

PQS—Quality Designator for Thermal Printers & Media—Eastman Kodak Company; *U.S. Public*, pg. 550

PQ SERIES—Computed Tomography—Picker International, Inc.; *Int'l*, pg. 545

P.R.—NONE—Boots Healthcare International; *Int'l*, pg. 202

PRC—Computer Programming Services—The Black & Decker Corporation; *U.S. Public*, pg. 233

PRC ENGINEERING SYSTEMS, INC.—Computer Programming Services—The Black & Decker Corporation; *U.S. Public*, pg. 233

PRC ENVIRONMENTAL MANAGEMENT, INC.—Computer Programming Services—The Black & Decker Corporation; *U.S. Public*, pg. 233

PRC OF AMERICA—Audio & Video Products—Plastic Reel Corp. of America; *U.S. Private*, pg. 871

PRC PUBLIC SECTOR, INC.—Computer Programming Services—The Black & Decker Corporation; *U.S. Public*, pg. 233

PRC REALTY SYSTEMS, INC.—Computer Programming Services—The Black & Decker Corporation; *U.S. Public*, pg. 233

PRP—Progressive Resistance Padding—Bike Athletic Co.; *U.S. Private*, pg. 143

PRP—"Polymeric Reverse Phase"-HPLC Column Packings—Hamilton Co., Inc.; *U.S. Private*, pg. 497

PRS—NONE—CPAC, Inc.; *U.S. Public*, pg. 282

PRSCO—NONE—Philadelphia Reserve Supply Company; *U.S. Private*, pg. 861

PR/SM—Computer System—International Business Machines Corporation; *U.S. Public*, pg. 895

PRS PORTFOLIO REALIGNMENT SYSTEM—NONE—SunGard Data Systems Inc.; *U.S. Public*, pg. 1534

PR-VAC—NONE—Pfizer Inc.; *U.S. Public*, pg. 1281

PS—Color Plates—Konica Corporation; *Int'l*, pg. 748

PS—Corporate Business Forms—The Standard Register Company; *U.S. Public*, pg. 1505

PSA STAT—NONE—Bard Diagnostic Sciences; *U.S. Public*, pg. 189

P.S.B.—W. Germany—Key Handling Systems, Inc.; *U.S. Private*, pg. 618

P.S. CHIMNEY—HVAC—Eljer Plumbingware; *U.S. Public*, pg. 1794

PSE—Premier Systems Engineering Grp.—Premier Mill Corp.; *U.S. Private*, pg. 881

PSF—Computer Product—International Business Machines Corporation; *U.S. Public*, pg. 895

PSF/6000—Computer Product—International Business Machines Corporation; *U.S. Public*, pg. 895

PSI—Aerospace Bearings—Rexnord Corporation; *Int'l*, pg. 127

PSI FACTOR: CHRONICLES OF THE PARANORMAL—Paranormal Research News Program—Westwood One, Inc.; *U.S. Public*, pg. 1763

PSINET—Computer Product—International Business Machines Corporation; *U.S. Public*, pg. 895

PSJET—Printer Enhancement—QMS, Inc.; *U.S. Public*, pg. 1346

PSL—Performance Specified Linerboard—Gaylord Container Corporation; *U.S. Public*, pg. 704

PSL—Computer Product—International Business Machines Corporation; *U.S. Public*, pg. 895

PSL EXPLORER—Computer Product—International Business Machines Corporation; *U.S. Public*, pg. 895

PS MAIL—Electronic Mail Software—Tandem Computers Inc.; *U.S. Public*, pg. 417

PS MEDICAL—Devices—Medtronic, Inc.; *U.S. Public*, pg. 1082

PS/NOTE—Computer Product—International Business Machines Corporation; *U.S. Public*, pg. 895

PS/1—Desktop Products—International Business Machines Corporation; *U.S. Public*, pg. 895

PS/1 CLUB—Computer Product—International Business Machines Corporation; *U.S. Public*, pg. 895

PS PRIME—Needle—Ethicon, Inc.; *U.S. Public*, pg. 928

PSS—Filters—Pall Corporation; *U.S. Public*, pg. 1253

P.S. SUPER—Refractory—CFB Industries, Inc.; *U.S. Private*, pg. 194

P.S. SUPER—Refractory—Chicago Fire Brick Co.; *U.S. Private*, pg. 194

P.S.T.—Towels—Marcal Paper Mills, Inc.; *U.S. Private*, pg. 701

PST—Pressure Vessels—Pressed Steel Tank Co., Inc.; *U.S. Private*, pg. 882

PS TEXT—Text Editing & Formatting Software—Tandem Computers Inc.; *U.S. Public*, pg. 417

PS/2—Desktop Product—International Business Machines Corporation; *U.S. Public*, pg. 895

PS/VALUEPOINT—Computer Product—International Business Machines Corporation; *U.S. Public*, pg. 895

PSX—Workstations—Tandem Computers Inc.; *U.S. Public*, pg. 417

PSY—Portland Ship Yard—Port of Portland; *U.S. Private*, pg. 876

PS 22—Closure Liner Sealings Materials—Tekni-Plex, Inc.; *U.S. Private*, pg. 1073

P7—Electric Ranges—General Electric Canada Inc.; *U.S. Public*, pg. 713

P7 AND DESIGN—Electric Ranges—General Electric Canada Inc.; *U.S. Public*, pg. 713

PT—Closures—White Cap, Inc.; *Int'l*, pg. 1207

PTC—NONE—Parametric Technology Corporation; *U.S. Public*, pg. 1257

PTCFUSES—Electronic Resettable Fuse—Littelfuse, Inc.; *U.S. Public*, pg. 1001

PTC-PRO-E—Mechanical CAD Software—Onyx Technologies Ltd.; *Int'l*, pg. 1007

THE PT DISTRIBUTOR—Periodical—Penton Publishing, Inc.; *U.S. Public*, pg. 1306

PTL—Specialty Nails—Maze Nails; *U.S. Private*, pg. 718

PTS—Television & Electronic Circuit Boards—PTS Electronics Corporation; *U.S. Private*, pg. 828

PT6—Aircraft Engine—Pratt & Whitney Canada Inc.; *U.S. Public*, pg. 1690

PTX—Catalytic Exhaust Gas Purifier—Engelhard Corporation; *U.S. Public*, pg. 582

PTX—Operating Systems—Sequent Computer Systems, Inc.; *U.S. Public*, pg. 1459

P/THERMAL—Application-Specific Finite Element Analysis Software—MacNeal-Schwendler Corp.; *U.S. Public*, pg. 1031

P-30—Polyethylene & PVC Insulated Conductor Control Cable—The Okonite Company; *U.S. Private*, pg. 813

P3/ADVANCED FEA—Application-Specific Finite Element Analysis Software—MacNeal-Schwendler Corp.; *U.S. Public*, pg. 1031

P3/ANIMATION—Application-Specific Finite Element Analysis Software—MacNeal-Schwendler Corp.; *U.S. Public*, pg. 1031

P3/CFD—Application-Specific Finite Element Analysis Software—MacNeal-Schwendler Corp.; *U.S. Public*, pg. 1031

P-300—PVC Substitute for Printing—Transilwrap Company, Inc.; *U.S. Private*, pg. 1097

P-26 RED EDGE—Interfacings—Specialty Textile Products; *U.S. Private*, pg. 1023

P2CMOS—Electronics—National Semiconductor Corporation; *U.S. Public*, pg. 1159

P2P—Computer Product—International Business Machines Corporation; *U.S. Public*, pg. 895

P-U-L-S-E—Water Cooling System Monitors—Ashland, Inc.; *U.S. Public*, pg. 138

PV—Dryer—Beloit Corporation; *U.S. Public*, pg. 789

PV—NONE—Berg Electronics; *U.S. Public*, pg. 212

PVC—Plumbing Chemical; Plastic Pipe Cement—Hercules Chemical Co., Inc.; *U.S. Private*, pg. 523

PV4 MASTER—Shock Absorbers—Bridgestone/Firestone, Inc.; *Int'l*, pg. 213

P.V.M.—High Protein Meal-Replacement—SmithKline Beecham plc; *Int'l*, pg. 1264

PVO—Price Volume Optimzer Software for Retail PetroleumPricing Decisions—MPSI Systems Inc.; *U.S. Public*, pg. 1027

PVT-EXPERT—NONE—Western Atlas Logging Services; *U.S. Public*, pg. 1757

P-V TUSSIN SYRUP—Pharmaceutical Products—Solvay Pharmaceuticals, Inc.; *Int'l*, pg. 1278

P-V TUSSIN TABLETS—Pharmecutical Products—Solvay Pharmaceuticals, Inc.; *Int'l*, pg. 1278

PWB ANCHOR—Metal Products—Email Limited; *Int'l*, pg. 450

PW500—Aircraft Engine—Pratt & Whitney Canada Inc.; *U.S. Public*, pg. 1690

PW901A—Aircraft Engine—Pratt & Whitney Canada Inc.; *U.S. Public*, pg. 1690

PW100—Aircraft Engine—Pratt & Whitney Canada Inc.; *U.S. Public*, pg. 1690

PWP—Personal Word Processor—Smith Corona Corp.; *U.S. Public*, pg. 1007

PW300—Aircraft Engine—Pratt & Whitney Canada Inc.; *U.S. Public*, pg. 1690

PW200—Aircraft Engine—Pratt & Whitney Canada Inc.; *U.S. Public*, pg. 1690

PW2—PERSONAL COMPUTERS—Unisys Corporation; *U.S. Public*, pg. 1671

P/X—Project Mngmt. Software—PSDI; *U.S. Private*, pg. 828

PX—Overnight Parcel Delivery—Transnet Ltd.; *Int'l*, pg. 1417

PXMTOOLS—Computer Program, Software—Lucent Technologies Inc.; *U.S. Public*, pg. 1017

PX2—Motor Oil—Petroliam Nasional Berhad (Petronas); *Int'l*, pg. 1046

PYP—Radioactive Diagnostic Preparations—Mallinckrodt Inc.; *U.S. Public*, pg. 1039

PENTAX—NONE—Pentax Canada Inc.; *Int'l*, pg. 85

PA DUTCH—Sausages—Hatfield Quality Meats; *U.S. Private*, pg. 510

PA-QEL—Bicomponent Acrylic Fibers—Solutia Inc.; *U.S. Public*, pg. 1483

PAARLAN—Herbicide—The Dow Chemical Company; *U.S. Public*, pg. 522

PAAS—Easter Egg Decorating Kits & Children's Halloween Activity & Make-Up Kits—Schering-Plough Corporation; *U.S. Public*, pg. 1438

PAAS—Easter Egg Colors, Halloween Make-Up—Schering-Plough Healthcare Products Inc.; *U.S. Public*, pg. 1438

PABST BLUE RIBBON—Beer—Pabst Brewing Co.; *U.S. Private*, pg. 954

PABST EXTRA LIGHT & LIGHT—Beer—Pabst Brewing Co.; *U.S. Private*, pg. 954

PABST GENUINE DRAFT—Beer—Pabst Brewing Co.; *U.S. Private*, pg. 954

PABST GENUINE DRAFT LIGHT—Light Beer—Pabst Brewing Co.; *U.S. Private*, pg. 954

PAC—Socks & Knitted Headwear—Wigwam Mills, Inc.; *U.S. Private*, pg. 1175

PAC-A-DAP—Module Control—Litton Industries, Inc.; *U.S. Public*, pg. 1002

PAC-CLAD—Kynar 500 Coated Steel & Aluminum—Petersen Aluminum Corporation; *U.S. Private*, pg. 856

PAC-FAB—Swimming Pool Accessories—Essef Corporation; *U.S. Public*, pg. 592

PAC RITE—Packing & Canning Equipment—EcoScience Produce Systems Corp.; *U.S. Public*, pg. 563

PACIII ROLLAWAY—Electronic Precipitators—Trion, Inc.; *U.S. Public*, pg. 1639

PACAL—NONE—Paper Calmenson & Co.; *U.S. Private*, pg. 837

PACAL BLADES—NONE—Paper Calmenson & Co.; *U.S. Private*, pg. 837

PACDOG—NONE—BMC Software, Inc.; *U.S. Public*, pg. 162

PACE—NONE—Ace Hardware Corporation; *U.S. Private*, pg. 12

PACE—Mexican Sauces—Campbell Soup Company; *U.S. Public*, pg. 298

PACE—Pool Product—Olin Corporation; *U.S. Public*, pg. 1218

PACE—Suburban Transit System—Pace; *U.S. Private*, pg. 919

PACE ARROW—Motor Home—Fleetwood Enterprises, Inc.; *U.S. Public*, pg. 650

PACE/32—Process Control Software—Modcomp; *U.S. Public*, pg. 283

PACE WIPES—Disposable Paper Wipers—Georgia-Pacific Corporation; *U.S. Public*, pg. 735

PACEMAKER—Small Vacuum—Advance Machine Company; *Int'l*, pg. 932

PACEMAKER—Integral Quench Furnace—Lindberg, A General Signal Company; *U.S. Public*, pg. 727

PACEMAKER—Motors—Louis Allis Company; *U.S. Private*, pg. 677

PACEMAKER/STARLITE—Sink—Elkay Manufacturing Company; *U.S. Private*, pg. 372

PACEMARK—Dot Matrix Printers—Oki Electric Industry Company, Ltd.; *Int'l*, pg. 999

PACEMARK—Dot Matrix Printers—Okidata Group; *Int'l*, pg. 1000

PACEMASTER—Crusher—Svedala Industries-Universal Engineering; *Int'l*, pg. 1326

PACENE—High Density Plastic Bag Products—T C Manufacturing Company, Inc.; *U.S. Private*, pg. 1062

PACER—NONE—Ace Hardware Corporation; *U.S. Private*, pg. 12

PACER—Solid State Power Supply 1kz to 10khz—Ajax Magnethermic Corp.; *Int'l*, pg. 113

PACER—Lift Truck—The Raymond Corporation; *Int'l*, pg. 123

PACER—Plastic Film—Reynolds Metals Company; *U.S. Public*, pg. 1385

PACER—Pump for Agriculture, Marine, Irrigation, Petrochem—Serfilco, Ltd.; *U.S. Private*, pg. 985

PACER ROLLER SKATES—Roller Skates—Roller Derby Skate Corp.; *U.S. Private*, pg. 941

PACESETTER—Sporting Goods—Brunswick Bowling & Billiards Corp.; *U.S. Public*, pg. 265

PACESETTER—Platform Model—The Knapheide Mfg. Co.; *U.S. Private*, pg. 626

PACESETTER—NONE—Pacesetter Corporation; *U.S. Private*, pg. 830

PACESETTER PLUS—Computerized Chemical Feed & Monitoring System—BetzDearborn Inc.; *U.S. Public*, pg. 226

PACESETTER-X—Platform Model—The Knapheide Mfg. Co.; *U.S. Private*, pg. 626

PACHYDYNE—Solid State Power Supply 200hz to 10khz—Ajax Magnethermic Corp.; *Int'l*, pg. 113

PACIFIC—Alcohol Free—Groupe Pernod Ricard; *Int'l*, pg. 566

PACIFIC—Pumps—Ingersoll-Dresser Pump Company; *U.S. Public*, pg. 529

PACIFIC—NONE—Ingersoll-Rand Company; *U.S. Public*, pg. 876

PACIFIC—Molasses & Animal Nutrition—Tate & Lyle PLC; *Int'l*, pg. 1356

PACIFIC BELL—Communications Services—Pacific Bell; *U.S. Public*, pg. 1416

PACIFIC BELL TELEPHONE DIRECTORIES—Telephone Directories—Pacific Bell; *U.S. Public*, pg. 1416

PACIFIC BUSINESS NEWS—Business News Publication—Business First of New York, Inc.; *U.S. Private*, pg. 19

PACIFIC CENTURY—NONE—Pacific Century Financial Corporation; *U.S. Public*, pg. 1248

PACIFIC CENTURY BANK—NONE—Pacific Century Financial Corporation; *U.S. Public*, pg. 1248

PACIFIC CENTURY INVESTMENT SERVICES—NONE—Pacific Century Financial Corporation; *U.S. Public*, pg. 1248

PACIFIC CENTURY LEASING—NONE—Pacific Century Financial Corporation; *U.S. Public*, pg. 1248

PACIFIC COAST—Motorcycle—American Honda Motor Co., Inc. Motorcycle Division; *Int'l*, pg. 634

PACIFIC JADE—Food Products—Rykoff-Sexton, Inc.; *U.S. Public*, pg. 918

PACIFIC LIFE INSURANCE CO—Financial Services Companies—Pacific Life Insurance Company; *U.S. Private*, pg. 831

PACIFIC MEZZANINE INVESTORS—Junior Capital Mgmt. Firm—Pacific Life Insurance Company; *U.S. Private*, pg. 831

PACIFIC MUTUAL DISTRIBUTORS, INC.—Broker-Dealer Services—Pacific Life Insurance Company; *U.S. Private*, pg. 831

PACIFIC RIDGE PALE ALE—Specialty Beer—Anheuser-Busch Companies, Inc.; *U.S. Public*, pg. 113

PACIFIC RIM BONSAI COLLECTION—Educational Services—Weyerhaeuser Company; *U.S. Public*, pg. 1764

PACIFIC SILVERCLOTH—Fabric (Protects Silver From Tarnishing)—Springs Industries, Inc.; *U.S. Public*, pg. 1499

PACIFIC TRADING CO.—Adult & Kids Outerwear—Pacific Trail Inc.; *U.S. Private*, pg. 673

PACIFIC TRAIL—Adult & Kids Outerwear—Pacific Trail Inc.; *U.S. Private*, pg. 673

PACIFIC WIETZ—Seal—Flowserve Corporation; *U.S. Public*, pg. 658

PACIFIC WIETZ SEALS—Seals—BW/IP International, Inc.; *U.S. Public*, pg. 658

PACIFICO—Mexican Beer—Barton Beers, Ltd.; *U.S. Public*, pg. 300

PACIFICORP—Electric Utility—Utah Power & Light; *U.S. Public*, pg. 1251

PACIS—NONE—BioChem Pharma Inc.; *Int'l*, pg. 196

PACK IT—Computer-Aided Laboratory-Packaging & Waste Management Program—International Technology Corporation; *U.S. Public*, pg. 907

PACK-STOCK—Sidetracking Tools—Smith International, Inc.; *U.S. Public*, pg. 1478

PACKAGE PRINTING & CONVERTING—Magazine—North American Publishing Company; *U.S. Private*, pg. 803

PACKAGED POWER—Encapsulated Power Supplies—Computer Products, Inc.; *U.S. Public*, pg. 422

PACKAGING—Industrial Magazine—Reed Business Information Pty. Limited; *Int'l*, pg. 1094

PACKAGING DIGEST—Magazine—Reed Elsevier Business Information; *Int'l*, pg. 1095

PACKARD—Photo Typesetters—AGFA EPS Division; *Int'l*, pg. 172

PACKERLAND PACKING CO—Boned Beef Product—Packerland Packing Co.; *U.S. Private*, pg. 833

PACKET BRAND—Salt & Pepper—Diamond Crystal Specialty Foods, Inc.; *U.S. Private*, pg. 330

PACKET CONTROL FACILITY—Security Feature for Enterprise Networks—Network Systems Corporation; *U.S. Public*, pg. 1522

PACKETRON—Pouch Making Machine—Pneumatic Scale Corporation; *U.S. Private*, pg. 118

PACKTECH—Packaging Machinery—Gessner/Miller Corporation; *U.S. Private*, pg. 435

PACO—Refractories—North State Pyrophyllite; *U.S. Private*, pg. 924

PACO RABANNE—NONE—Compar; *Int'l*, pg. 1073

PACO-RABANNE—Perfume—International Cosmetics Co., Ltd.; *Int'l*, pg. 684

PACO RABANNE—Cologne for Men—Paco Rabanne Compar; *Int'l*, pg. 1073

PACOL—White Mineral Oil—Witco Corporation; *U.S. Public*, pg. 1773

PACO'S—Independent Pizza/Taco Restaurant—BR Associates, Inc.; *U.S. Private*, pg. 107

PACQUIN—NONE—Pfizer Inc.; *U.S. Public*, pg. 1281

PACRITE—NONE—EcoScience Corporation; *U.S. Public*, pg. 563

PACTRA—Paint—The Testor Corporation; *U.S. Public*, pg. 1358

PACTROL—Electronic Controls—IMI Plc; *Int'l*, pg. 646

PACXNET—Data Networking Switches—Gandalf Technologies Inc.; *Int'l*, pg. 540

PAD/DOCK—Box—Rubbermaid Incorporated; *U.S. Public*, pg. 1411

PAD-GRAB III—Two Piece Pad Holder—Flo-Pac Corporation; *U.S. Private*, pg. 414

PADDOCK—Trade Contractors—Paddock Pool Construction Co., Inc.; *U.S. Private*, pg. 833

PADDOCK PUBLICATIONS—Publishers—Paddock Publications, Inc.; *U.S. Private*, pg. 833

PADFLEX—Pad Transfor Printers—Autoroll Machine Co., LLC; *U.S. Private*, pg. 101

PADMISER SWITCHES—Low Profile, Padmounted Load Break Switches—G & W Electric Co.; *U.S. Private*, pg. 433

PAFF—Sewing Machines—Pfaff American Sales Corp.; *Int'l*, pg. 1046

PAGE—Page Draglines—Harnischfeger Industries, Inc.; *U.S. Public*, pg. 788

PAGE-MATIC—Lubrication System—Harnischfeger Industries, Inc.; *U.S. Public*, pg. 788

PAGE-TEC—Graphic Arts Line Films—Eastman Kodak Company; *U.S. Public*, pg. 550

PAGEANT—Insecticide—The Dow Chemical Company; *U.S. Public*, pg. 522

PAGEANT—Motion Picture Projectors—Eastman Kodak Company; *U.S. Public*, pg. 550

PAGEANTRY—Offset & Cover—Champion International Corp.; *U.S. Public*, pg. 333

PAGECHIP—NONE—Adaptec, Inc.; *U.S. Public*, pg. 19

PAGEKEEPER—Text & File Retrieval Software—Caere Corporation; *U.S. Public*, pg. 291

PAGEKOM—Paging & Intercom System—Atlas/Soundolier; *U.S. Private*, pg. 64

PAGEMAIL—Voice Messaging and Answering Pager Services—Paging Network, Inc.; *U.S. Public*, pg. 1252

PAGEMAIL BOX—Voice Messaging & Answering Pager Services—Paging Network, Inc.; *U.S. Public*, pg. 1252

PAGEMANAGER—Software—Eastman Kodak Company; *U.S. Public*, pg. 550

PAGENET—NONE—Paging Network, Inc.; *U.S. Public*, pg. 1252

PAGEX SYSTEMS—Computer & Data Processing Services—Database America Companies; *U.S. Private*, pg. 312

PAGI-SET—Phototypesetting Film—Eastman Kodak Company; *U.S. Public*, pg. 550

PAIC CITRON—Dishwashing Liquids—Colgate-Palmolive Company; *U.S. Public*, pg. 397

PAIN COURANT VITEX—Bakery Ingredients—Royal Gist-Brocades N.V.; *Int'l*, pg. 1142

PAIN SPECIAL VITEX—Bakery Ingredients—Royal Gist-Brocades N.V.; *Int'l*, pg. 1142

PAINAID—Pain Tablets—Zee Medical, Inc.; *U.S. Public*, pg. 1073

PAINALAY—Antiseptic & Anesthetic—Medtech Inc.; *U.S. Private*, pg. 728

PAINE FURNITURE—Retail Home Furnishings—Paine Furniture Co.; *U.S. Private*, pg. 834

PAINT USA—Haw & Paint Sunary—Bloch/New England, Inc.; *U.S. Private*, pg. 149

PAINT WITH WATER—Children's Activity—Golden Books Family Entertainment Inc.; *U.S. Public*, pg. 749

PAINTED DESERT—Color Glassware & Giftware—World Tableware, Inc.; *Int'l*, pg. 1056

PAINTER'S TEAM—Maintenance Painting Equipment—Graco Inc.; *U.S. Public*, pg. 756

THE PAINTIN' PLACE—NONE—Ace Hardware Corporation; *U.S. Public*, pg. 12

PAIOL—Retail Store—SHV Holdings N.V.; *Int'l*, pg. 1154

PAIR-PAK II—Surgical Sutures & Needles—Alcon Laboratories, Inc.; *Int'l*, pg. 916

PAIRGAIN—NONE—PairGain Technologies Inc.; *U.S. Public*, pg. 1253

PAIRGAIN LOGO—NONE—PairGain Technologies Inc.; *U.S. Public*, pg. 1253

PAIRSPAN—High Capacity Telecommunications Switching System—DSC Communications Corporation; *U.S. Public*, pg. 475

PAK-A-POTTI—Portable Toilets—Thetford Corporation; *U.S. Private*, pg. 352

PAK-A-ROBE—Sport & Leisure Blanket—Faribault Woolen Mill Co.; *U.S. Private*, pg. 394

PAK-LINE—Custom Industrial Packaging—Homasote Company; *U.S. Public*, pg. 831

PAK-LOK—Corrugated Container—Georgia-Pacific Corporation; *U.S. Public*, pg. 735

PAK-MASTER—NONE—SASIB Packaging North America; *Int'l*, pg. 1194

PAK 'N SAVE—Retail Discount Food Stores—Safeway Inc.; *U.S. Public*, pg. 1426

PAK-WIPES—Disposable Paper Wipers—Georgia-Pacific Corporation; *U.S. Public*, pg. 735

PAKLON—Film Backing for Various Industrial Tapes—3M; *U.S. Public*, pg. 1604

PAKSCAN—Specialty X-Ray—EG & G, Inc.; *U.S. Public*, pg. 542

PAKUNIL—Cellulose & Non-Cellulose-Based Prods. & Blends—Akzo Nobel N.V.; *Int'l*, pg. 42

PAL—Razor Blades—American Safety Razor Company; *U.S. Private*, pg. 597

PAL—Fishing Implements—The Cook Bates Division; *Int'l*, pg. 815

PAL—NONE—Landmark Graphics Corporation; *U.S. Public*, pg. 776

PAL 5—Personal Safety Systems—Detex Corporation; *U.S. Private*, pg. 327

PAL III—Personal Safety Systems—Detex Corporation; *U.S. Private*, pg. 327

PALACIO—Photo Typesetters—AGFA EPS Division; *Int'l*, pg. 172

PALAGONIA BREAD—Bread—J.M.P. Bakery Co., Inc.; *U.S. Private*, pg. 578

PALAIS ROYAL—NONE—Stage Stores, Inc.; *U.S. Private*, pg. 1028

PALASTOR—Palletizer Conveyor—Litton Industries, Inc.; *U.S. Public*, pg. 1002

PALASWEET—Liquid Sweeteners—Tate & Lyle PLC; *Int'l*, pg. 1356

PALAVALE—Anti-Mycotic—Otsuka Pharmaceutical Co., Ltd.; *Int'l*, pg. 1013

PALAWAN—Plywood—Georgia-Pacific Corporation; *U.S. Public*, pg. 735

PALCO—Lumber—The Pacific Lumber Company; *U.S. Public*, pg. 1062

PALCORE—Multilayer Process—Parlex Corporation; *U.S. Public*, pg. 1264

PALE ALE—Premium Beer—The Lion Brewery, Inc.; *U.S. Public*, pg. 1000

PALE ALE—Beer—The F.X. Matt Brewing Co.; *U.S. Private*, pg. 714

PALETTE—Silverware—Oneida Ltd.; *U.S. Public*, pg. 1225

PALETTE—Computer Image Recorder—Polaroid Corporation; *U.S. Public*, pg. 1313

PALETTE DESIGN—Stationary—The Mead Corporation; *U.S. Public*, pg. 1074

PALETTE LETTERS—Stationary—The Mead Corporation; *U.S. Public*, pg. 1074

PALFLEX—Adhesives Material—Parlex Corporation; *U.S. Public*, pg. 1264

PALGARD—Epoxy Coating—Pratt & Lambert United, Inc.; *U.S. Public*, pg. 1466

PALINTEST—Reagents & Equipment for Analysis of Water & Pollutants—Halma p.l.c.; *Int'l*, pg. 589

PALISADE—Straight, Rigid Metal Batten & Trim—Georgia-Pacific Corporation; *U.S. Public*, pg. 735

PALL—Filters—Pall Corporation; *U.S. Public*, pg. 1253

PALL MALL—Cigarettes—B.A.T Industries P.L.C.; *Int'l*, pg. 110

PALL MALL—NONE—British-American Tobacco (Germany) GmbH; *Int'l*, pg. 111

PALL MALL—Cigarettes—Brown & Williamson Tobacco Corp.; *Int'l*, pg. 111

PALL MALL—NONE—SEITA, Societe Nationale D'Exploitation Industrielle des Tabacs et des Allumettes; *Int'l*, pg. 1219

PALLABAR—Chemicals for Electro Plating—Technic Incorporated; *U.S. Private*, pg. 1071

PALLADURE 100—Bright High Purity Palladium Deposits—LeaRonal, Inc.; *U.S. Public*, pg. 982

PALLAMERSE—Chemicals for Electro Plating—Technic Incorporated; *U.S. Private*, pg. 1071

PALLAMET 75—Bright High Purity Palladium Nickel Alloy—LeaRonal, Inc.; *U.S. Public*, pg. 982

PALLASPEED—Chemicals for Electro Plating—Technic Incorporated; *U.S. Private*, pg. 1071

PALLATECH—Electroplating Solution—Lucent Technologies Inc.; *U.S. Public*, pg. 1017

PALLCELL—Filters—Pall Corporation; *U.S. Public*, pg. 1253

PALLET PRO—Forklift—JLG Industries, Inc.; *U.S. Public*, pg. 918

PALLET SEARCH—Security X-ray System for Searching Pallets—American Science & Engineering, Inc.; *U.S. Public*, pg. 90

PALLETILER—Work Handling—WCI Machine Tools & Systems; *Int'l*, pg. 440

PALLETITE—Adhesive—H.B. Fuller Company; *U.S. Public*, pg. 686

PALLETIZATION PLUS—Mailing Efficiency—Group 1 Software, Inc.; *U.S. Public*, pg. 417

PALLETIZER—Work Handling—WCI Machine Tools & Systems; *Int'l*, pg. 440

PALLSCOPE—Fluid Analysis Service—Pall Corporation; *U.S. Public*, pg. 1253

PALLSORB—Filters—Pall Corporation; *U.S. Public*, pg. 1253

PALLTAARB—Multi-Layer Thermal Acoustic Insulation—Pall Corporation; *U.S. Public*, pg. 1253

PALLTHERM—Temperature Actuated Valve—Pall Corporation; *U.S. Public*, pg. 1253

PALLTRONIC—Integrity Test Kit—Pall Corporation; *U.S. Public*, pg. 1253

PALM BEACH—Bath Accessories—Baldwin Hardware Corporation; *U.S. Public*, pg. 1053

PALM VALLEY—Residential Community—Suncor Development Company; *U.S. Public*, pg. 1298

PALMAZ—NONE—Johnson & Johnson; *U.S. Public*, pg. 927

PALMAZ-SCHATZ—NONE—Johnson & Johnson; *U.S. Public*, pg. 927

PALMER—Equipment for Detecting Underground Water Leaks—Halma p.l.c.; *Int'l*, pg. 589

PALMER—Aircraft Couplings—IMI Plc; *Int'l*, pg. 646

PALMERS COCOA BUTTER—Lotion—E.T. Browne Drug Co., Inc.; *U.S. Private*, pg. 175

PALMER'S SKIN SUCCESS & HAIR SUCCESS—Creams, Shampoos, Conditioners—E.T. Browne Drug Co., Inc.; *U.S. Private*, pg. 175

PALMOLIVE—NONE—Colgate-Palmolive; *U.S. Public*, pg. 398

PALMOLIVE—Dishwashing Liquid & Bath Soap—Colgate-Palmolive Company; *U.S. Public*, pg. 397

PALMOLIVE—Soap & Bath Products—Colgate-Palmolive Ltd.; *U.S. Public*, pg. 398

PALMOLIVE—NONE—Colgate-Palmolive S.A.I.C.; *U.S. Public*, pg. 399

PALMOLIVE AUTOMATIC—Dishwasher Liquid—Colgate-Palmolive Company; *U.S. Public*, pg. 397

PALMOLIVE BEAUTY BAR—Bar Soap—Colgate-Palmolive Company; *U.S. Public*, pg. 397

PALMOLIVE BRUSHLESS SHAVE CREAM—Shaving Cream—Colgate-Palmolive Company; *U.S. Public*, pg. 397

PALMOLIVE GOLD—Soap—Colgate-Palmolive Company; *U.S. Public*, pg. 397

PALMOLIVE LATHER SHAVING CREAM—Shaving Cream—Colgate-Palmolive Company; *U.S. Public*, pg. 397

PALOMA PICASSO—Fragrance—Cosmair, Inc., Ralph Lauren Fragrance Division; *Int'l*, pg. 818

PALOMA PICASSO—NONE—Villeroy & Boch AG; *Int'l*, pg. 1468

PALOMA PICCASSO—NONE—L'Oreal Parfumerie; *Int'l*, pg. 819

PALOMAR—Area Rugs—Couristan Inc.; *U.S. Private*, pg. 279

PALOMAR—Hardboard—Georgia-Pacific Corporation; *U.S. Public*, pg. 735

PALS—Business Product—International Business Machines Corporation; *U.S. Public*, pg. 895

PALTIER—Pallet Rack—Lyon Metal Products, Inc.; *U.S. Private*, pg. 638

PALUSOL—Fireboards—BASF AG; *Int'l*, pg. 103

PAM—Cooking Spray—International Home Foods Inc.; *U.S. Private*, pg. 526

PAM-PAM—Fruit Juice—Groupe Pernod Ricard; *Int'l*, pg. 566

PAM UNDIES—Ladies Apparel—Movie Star, Inc.; *U.S. Public*, pg. 1140

PAMAK—Tall Oil Fatty Acid—Hercules Incorporated; *U.S. Public*, pg. 809

PAMELOR—Antidepressant—Novartis AG; *Int'l*, pg. 971

PAMELOR—Capsules/Oral Solution for Relief of Depression—Sandoz Pharmaceuticals Corp.; *Int'l*, pg. 974

PAMGAS—Liquid Propane Gas—SHV Holdings N.V.; *Int'l*, pg. 1154

PAMIDA—General Merchandise Department Stores—Pamida Holdings Corporation; *U.S. Public*, pg. 1255

PAMINE—Anticholinergic/Antispasmatic—Bradley Pharmaceuticals; *U.S. Public*, pg. 249

PAMINE—Tablets; Anticholinergic/Antispasmatic—Doak Dermatologics; *U.S. Public*, pg. 250

PAMOLYN—Fatty Acid—Hercules Incorporated; *U.S. Public*, pg. 809

PAMPAS—NONE—Quality Bakers Australia Ltd.; *Int'l*, pg. 555

PAMPAS PASTRY—Pastry—Goodman Fielder Limited; *Int'l*, pg. 555

PAMPERO ESPECIAL—NONE—Guinness Plc; *Int'l*, pg. 412

PAMPERS—Diapers—The Procter & Gamble Company; *U.S. Public*, pg. 1330

PAMPERS—Diapers—Procter & Gamble (Health & Beauty Care) Limited; *U.S. Public*, pg. 1332

PAMPERS TRAINERS—Disposable Diapers—The Procter & Gamble Company; *U.S. Public*, pg. 1330

PAMPERS ULTRA DRY THIN—Diapers—The Procter & Gamble Company; *U.S. Public*, pg. 1330

PAMPRIN—Menstrual Relief Line—Chattem, Inc.; *U.S. Public*, pg. 341

PAMPRIN—Menstrual Product—Chattem, Inc., Consumer Products Division; *U.S. Public*, pg. 341

PAMPRYL—Fruit Juice—Groupe Pernod Ricard; *Int'l*, pg. 566

PAN—Sport Wear—Bangkok Athletic Co., Ltd.; *Int'l*, pg. 146

PAN-AL—Aluminum Soffit—Reynolds Metals Company; *U.S. Public*, pg. 1385

PAN AMERICAN—Seed—Ball Horticultural Company; *U.S. Private*, pg. 112

PAN COATING VITEX—Greasing Product—Royal Gist-Brocades N.V.; *Int'l*, pg. 1142

PAN ENTERAL—Medical Food & Supplements for Tube Feeding—Otsuka Pharmaceutical Co., Ltd.; *Int'l*, pg. 1013

PAN MASTER—Alkaline Detergent for Bakery Pan Washing—Ecolab Inc.; *U.S. Public*, pg. 562

PAN-O-LITE—Bakery Leavening Agent—Solutia Inc.; *U.S. Public*, pg. 1483

PAN ONE—NONE—Noble Roman's Inc.; *U.S. Public*, pg. 1187

PAN PAL—Non-Stick Pan Coating—Blue Cross Laboratories; *U.S. Private*, pg. 152

PAN YAN—Pickles—Nestle-Rowntree Ltd.; *Int'l*, pg. 921

PANA-FLEXI—Flexible Plastic Conduits—Matsushita Electric Works, Ltd.; *Int'l*, pg. 847

PANA-VUE—Slides & Viewers—View-Master, Inc.; *U.S. Public*, pg. 1058

PANACEF—Cefaclor—Eli Lilly Italia, S.p.A.; *U.S. Public*, pg. 994

PANACH—Shandy—Heineken N.V.; *Int'l*, pg. 608

PANACORAN—High-Frequency Therapeutic Device—Matsushita Electric Works, Ltd.; *Int'l*, pg. 847

PANACUR—Vermifuge—Hoechst Aktiengesellschaft; *Int'l*, pg. 624

PANADEINE—NONE—SmithKline Beecham Corporation; *Int'l*, pg. 1264

PANADOL—NONE—SmithKline Beecham Corporation; *Int'l*, pg. 1264

PANADOL—NONE—SmithKline Beecham Research Limited; *Int'l*, pg. 1266

PANADOL COLD AND FLU—NONE—SmithKline Beecham Corporation; *Int'l*, pg. 1264

PANAFIL—Pharmaceutical Products—Rystan Company, Inc.; *U.S. Private*, pg. 436

PANAFLEX—Flexible on Premise Sign Faces—3M; *U.S. Public*, pg. 1604

PANALANE—Hydrogenated Polybutenes—Amoco Chemicals; *U.S. Public*, pg. 102

PANALARM—System Monitoring Device—AMETEK, Inc.; *U.S. Public*, pg. 99

PANALARM—Monitoring Systems—Panalarm Products, Ametek, Inc.; *U.S. Public*, pg. 100

PANALURE—Photographic Paper—Eastman Kodak Company; *U.S. Public*, pg. 550

PANAMA—Cigars—Hanson PLC; *Int'l*, pg. 592

PANAMA—Cigars—Imperial Tobacco Group, Ltd.; *Int'l*, pg. 666

PANAPAP—Epidermis Agents—Nippon Kayaku Co. Ltd.; *Int'l*, pg. 934

PANASOL—Solvent—Amoco Corporation; *U.S. Public*, pg. 101

PANASONIC—Radios, Television, Appliances, Auto Products, VCR Products—Matsushita Electric Corporation of America; *Int'l*, pg. 847

PANASONIC—Radios, T.V.'s, Appliances; Auto Prods.,Indus. Electronics—Matsushita Electric Industrial Co., Ltd.; *Int'l*, pg. 846

PANASONIC—Commercial & Industrial Electronic Products—Panasonic Industrial Co.; *Int'l*, pg. 847

PANATOMIC-X—Photo Film—Eastman Kodak Company; *U.S. Public*, pg. 550

PANAX—NONE—Chemfab Corporation; *U.S. Public*, pg. 344

PANCAKE—Dry Gum Label Papers & Business Forms—Brown-Bridge; *U.S. Public*, pg. 1022

PANCAKE MOTOR—Subfractional Horse Power Stepper Motor—Haydon Switch & Instrument, Inc.; *U.S. Private*, pg. 513

PANCAKE PEOPLE—Toy Design—IHOP Corp.; *U.S. Public*, pg. 862

PANCETTERIA LAVORAZIONE PARMA—Pancette—I.B.I.S.-S.p.A.; *Int'l*, pg. 642

PANCHO'S MEXICAN BUFFET—Buffet-Style Restaurants Serving Mexican Food—Pancho's Mexican Buffet, Inc.; *U.S. Public*, pg. 1255

PANCREASE—Capsules—Ortho-McNeil Pharmaceutical Corporation; *U.S. Public*, pg. 929

PANDAC—Suture Management Program—Owens & Minor Inc.; *U.S. Public*, pg. 1236

PANDALINK—Integrated Intra-European Service—Air Express International Corporation; *U.S. Public*, pg. 30

PANDANDY—Warewashing Detergent—Ecolab Inc.; *U.S. Public*, pg. 562

PANEL-15—Prefinished Siding—Weyerhaeuser Forest Products Company; *U.S. Public*, pg. 1764

PANEL LOCK—Panel Adhesive—Miracle Adhesives; *U.S. Public*, pg. 1466

PANEL-LOK—Envelopes—Tension Envelope Corp.; *U.S. Private*, pg. 1077

PANEL MAGIC—Aerosol Cleaner—Magic American Corporation; *U.S. Public*, pg. 695

PANEL PLY—Natural Veneered Decorative Panel—Carter Holt Harvey Limited; *U.S. Public*, pg. 904

PANEL TAPE—Natural Wood Veneer Edge Tape—Carter Holt Harvey Limited; *U.S. Public*, pg. 904

PANEL-TEST—NONE—GenRad, Inc.; *U.S. Public*, pg. 731

PANEL VAR—Wood Paneling Coating Systems—Akzo Nobel Coatings Inc. (KY); *Int'l*, pg. 47

PANEL WELD—Panel Adhesive—DAP Inc.; *Int'l*, pg. 1486

PANELBILD—Wood Panels for Floors, Roofs & Walls—Georgia-Pacific Corporation; *U.S. Public*, pg. 735

PANELBILD SYSTEMS—Building Components Such as Roof & Wall Panels—Georgia-Pacific Corporation; *U.S. Public*, pg. 735

PANELCLAD—Fibre Cement Building Boards—James Hardie Industries Ltd.; *Int'l*, pg. 596

PANELCOIL—Heat Exchangers—Tranter, Inc.; *U.S. Public*, pg. 521

PANELDRAIN—Roofing & Siding—Wheeling Corrugating Co.; *U.S. Public*, pg. 1727

PANELINE—Wood Arch Panel—Howard Manufacturing; *U.S. Private*, pg. 477

PANELINE—Panic Push Device for Entrances—Kawneer Company; *U.S. Public*, pg. 60

PANELMAX—Industrial Operator Interface Products—Rockwell International Corporation; *U.S. Public*, pg. 1397

PANELWARE—Modular Man-Machine Interface—B & R Industrial Automation; *U.S. Private*, pg. 105

PANEMUL—Greasing Product—Royal Gist-Brocades N.V.; *Int'l*, pg. 1142

PANFIBRE—Medium Density Fiberboard—Uniboard Canada Inc.; *Int'l*, pg. 1431

PANFOCUS—Electron Gun—Sony Electronics; *Int'l*, pg. 1281

PANFOIL—Decorative Paper Overlay—Uniboard Canada Inc.; *Int'l*, pg. 1431

PANIC GUARD—Futt-Time Emergency Exit with Security—Kawneer Company; *U.S. Public*, pg. 60

PANIMYCIN—Antibiotics—Meiji Seika Kaisha, Ltd.; *Int'l*, pg. 855

PANKREOFLAT—Gastrointestional Preparations—Kali-Chemie Aktiengesellschaft; *Int'l*, pg. 1278

PANKREON—Gastrointestinal Preparations—Kali-Chemie Aktiengesellschaft; *Int'l*, pg. 1278

PANNI—Imported Food Products—World Finer Foods, Inc.; *U.S. Private*, pg. 1190

PANODAN—Food Emulsifier—Danisco Ingredients USA, Inc.; *Int'l*, pg. 378

PANOFINA—Bakery & Confectionery Products—Coop Switzerland; *Int'l*, pg. 329

PANOL—Greasing Product—Royal Gist-Brocades N.V.; *Int'l*, pg. 1142

PANOPLY—Base/Cap Sheets—Herbert Malarkey Roofing Company; *U.S. Private*, pg. 698

PANORAMA—Satellite Programming Package—Satellite Data Networks; *U.S. Public*, pg. 716

PANOREX—Colorectol Cancer Therapeutic—Centocor, Inc.; *U.S. Public*, pg. 323

PANPAS—Ready Rolled Puff Pastry Sheets—The Quaker Oats Company; *U.S. Public*, pg. 1347

PANRICO—Bread/Donuts—Allied Domecq PLC; *Int'l*, pg. 62

PANSIRON—Gastroenteric Drug—Rohto Pharmaceutical Co.; *Int'l*, pg. 1126

PANTAK—Specialty X-Ray Equipment—EG & G, Inc.; *U.S. Public*, pg. 542

PANTENE—Hair Care Products—Permark International (Pty.) Ltd.; *Int'l*, pg. 1036

PANTENE—Hair Care Products—The Procter & Gamble Company; *U.S. Public*, pg. 1330

PANTENE—NONE—Procter & Gamble Espana S.A.; *U.S. Public*, pg. 1332

PANTENE PRO-V STYLING PRODUCTS—Hair Care Products—The Procter & Gamble Company; *U.S. Public*, pg. 1330

PANTHEON—Distribution Automation System—American Meter Company; *Int'l*, pg. 1149

PANTHEON—Books—Pantheon Books, Inc.; *U.S. Private*, pg. 21

PANTHEON—Book Imprint—Random House, Inc.; *U.S. Private*, pg. 20

PANTHER—Instant Firing Torch Gun—BernzOmatic; *U.S. Public*, pg. 1177

PANTHER—NONE—Eastman Kodak Company; *U.S. Public*, pg. 550

PANTHER—Catheter Systems—Medtronic, Inc.; *U.S. Public*, pg. 1082

PANTHER—Home & Small Business Communication Systems—Mitel Corporation; *Int'l*, pg. 870

PANTHER—Spotting Scopes—Swift Instruments, Inc.; *U.S. Private*, pg. 1058

PANTHER CREEK—Bentonite—AMCOL International Corp.; *U.S. Public*, pg. 63

PANTHER FAMILY—Disk Drives—Maxtor Corporation; *Int'l*, pg. 641

PANTI THERMIC—Hosiery for Women—Grupo Synkro, S.A. de C.V.; *Int'l*, pg. 576

PANTONE—Graphic Arts Supplies—Esselte AB; *Int'l*, pg. 459

PANTOPAQUE—Radiography Contrast Medium—Eastman Kodak Company; *U.S. Public*, pg. 550

PANTRAK KITS—Clinical Chemistry Reagents—Dade Behring Inc.; *U.S. Private*, pg. 110

PANTRI RESERVE—Low-Moisture Foods—Vacu-Dry Company; *U.S. Public*, pg. 1704

THE PANTRY—NONE—The Pantry, Inc.; *U.S. Private*, pg. 837

PANVAL—Melamine—Uniboard Canada Inc.; *Int'l*, pg. 1431

PANXTROL—Binder—Raschig GmbH; *U.S. Private*, pg. 827

PANZANI—Pasta—Danone Group; *Int'l*, pg. 379

PANZER—Globe & Gate Valves—KSB Aktiengesellschaft; *Int'l*, pg. 721

PAOLI—Chairs and Desks—Paoli, Inc.; *U.S. Private*, pg. 837

PAOLO CORDERO BAROLO—Wine—Wine World Estates Company; *Int'l*, pg. 917

PAP PLUS—Air Package Centrifugal Compressors—Elliott Company; *U.S. Private*, pg. 373

PAPA DASH—Low-Salt Seasoning—Alberto-Culver Company; *U.S. Public*, pg. 37

PAPA GINO'S—Pizza Restaurant Chain—Papa Gino's Inc.; *U.S. Private*, pg. 837

PAPA LYNN—Mexican Food Products—Wilson Products Co.; *U.S. Private*, pg. 1181

PAPA VINO'S—Restaurant—Quality Dining Inc.; *U.S. Public*, pg. 1349

PAPALLAM—Parallel Strand Lumber—Trus Joist MacMillan; *Int'l*, pg. 829

PAPALLAM—Parallel Strand Lumber—Trus Joist MacMillan; *U.S. Public*, pg. 1556

PAPA'S PIROSHKI—Frozen Sandwiches—Ore-Ida Foods, Inc.; *U.S. Public*, pg. 805

PAPAYA—Hair Care Line—Freeman Cosmetic Corp.; *U.S. Private*, pg. 426

PAPAYA EASE—NONE—Dena Corporation; *U.S. Private*, pg. 324

PAPER CONNECTION—Roll-Paper Distribution Network—Conrail, Inc.; *U.S. Public*, pg. 431

PAPER, FILM & FOIL CONVERTER—Industry News—Intertec Publishing; *U.S. Public*, pg. 1327

PAPER HOSTESS—Paper Prods.—American Greetings U.S. Greeting Card Division; *U.S. Public*, pg. 78

PAPER-LIKE INTERFACE—Computer Product—International Business Machines Corporation; *U.S. Public*, pg. 895

PAPER MAID—Cups, Wrap—Fort James Corporation; *U.S. Public*, pg. 670

PAPER MATE—Ball Point Pens, Fountain Pens, Pencils & Refills—The Gillette Company; *U.S. Public*, pg. 743

PAPER MATE FLAIR—Pens—Stationery Products Division; *U.S. Public*, pg. 744

PAPER PLUS—Retail Stores—Ikon Office Solutions, Inc.; *U.S. Public*, pg. 862

PAPER RITER—Fine-Line Felt Tip Pen—La-Co Industries Markal Company; *U.S. Private*, pg. 640

PAPER ROUTE & DESIGN—Greeting Cards—American Greetings Corporation; *U.S. Public*, pg. 77

THE PAPER ROUTE—Greeting Cards—American Greetings Corporation; *U.S. Public*, pg. 77

PAPER SCRAPER—(Wallcovering Removal Tool)—Wm. Zinsser & Co., Inc.; *U.S. Public*, pg. 1358

THE PAPER SHOP—Retail Stores—The Ailing & Cory Company; *U.S. Public*, pg. 1666

THE PAPER WORKS COLLECTION—Prefinished Wall Paneling—Georgia-Pacific Corporation; *U.S. Public*, pg. 735

PAPERAD—Pigment—Reynolds Metals Company; *U.S. Public*, pg. 1385

PAPERBOARD KNOWLEDGE—Conducting Seminars & Training Programs in the Paperboard Technology—The Mead Corporation; *U.S. Public*, pg. 1074

PAPERBOARD PACKAGING—Trade Periodical—Advanstar Communications; *U.S. Private*, pg. 22

PAPERCLUB—Paper—PaperDirect, Inc.; *U.S. Public*, pg. 498

PAPERCREME—Fingertip Moistener—The Gillette Company; *U.S. Public*, pg. 743

PAPERFRAMES—Paper—PaperDirect, Inc.; *U.S. Public*, pg. 498

PAPERKIT—Paper—PaperDirect, Inc.; *U.S. Public*, pg. 498

PAPERMATCH—Plastic Compounds—A. Schulman, Inc.; *U.S. Public*, pg. 1441

PAPERTIGER—Wallcovering Removal Tool—Wm. Zinsser & Co., Inc.; *U.S. Public*, pg. 1358

PAPERTREE—Retail Gift Shops—Fine Art Developments plc; *Int'l*, pg. 485

PAPI—Urethane Products—The Dow Chemical Company; *U.S. Public*, pg. 522

PAPO LINO—Pizza—Crestar Food Products, Inc.; *U.S. Public*, pg. 805

PAPOOSE—Small Vacuum—Advance Machine Company; *Int'l*, pg. 932

PAPPAGALLO—Women's Shoes—Nine West Group, Inc.; *U.S. Public*, pg. 1185

PAPPALO'S—Frozen Pizza—The Pillsbury Company; *Int'l*, pg. 411

PAPRUS—Formed Fiber Plates—The Chinet Co.; *Int'l*, pg. 1146

PAQUETTE—Misses Sportswear—Byer California; *U.S. Private*, pg. 191

PAQUETTE TOO—Misses Dresses—Byer California; *U.S. Private*, pg. 191

PAR—Chemistry Controls—Medical Analysis Systems Inc.; *U.S. Private*, pg. 727

PAR—Patient Activated Reservoir Device—Medtronic, Inc.; *U.S. Public*, pg. 1082

PAR—Computer Products—PAR Technology Corporation; *U.S. Public*, pg. 1256

PAR—Paints—Sime Darby Berhad; *Int'l*, pg. 1249

PAR EX—Professional Quality Golf Course Fertilizer Mixes—IMC Agribusiness; *U.S. Public*, pg. 856

PAR EX—Golf Greens Product—The Vigoro Corporation; *U.S. Public*, pg. 856

PAR EXCELLENCE—Parboil Rice—Producers Rice Mill Inc.; *U.S. Private*, pg. 888

PAR-I-TY—Control Measurement—Brooks Instrument; *U.S. Public*, pg. 574

PARA-FLEX—Elastomeric Couplings—Rockwell International Corporation; *U.S. Public*, pg. 1397

PARA-FLOOR—Polyurethane Reinforced Alkyd Interior & Exterior Floor Enamel—Paragon Paint & Varnish Corp.; *U.S. Private*, pg. 838

PARA-FLUTE—Type of Flute Design on Drill—National Twist Drill Div.; *U.S. Public*, pg. 1370

PARABELLUM—Folding Knife—Fiskars-Gerber; *Int'l*, pg. 492

PARABIS—Resin Intermediate—The Dow Chemical Company; *U.S. Public*, pg. 522

PARABOLIC—Mining Teeth & Adapters—GH Hensley Industries, Inc.; *U.S. Private*, pg. 439

PARABOLT—Fastening Systems—The Black & Decker Corporation; *U.S. Public*, pg. 233

PARAC—Adhesive Powder—Georgia-Pacific Corporation; *U.S. Public*, pg. 735

PARACOL—Emulsions—Hercules Incorporated; *U.S. Public*, pg. 809

PARACORD—Men's Shoes—E.J. Footwear Corp.; *U.S. Public*, pg. 1684

PARACRIL—High Performance Polymers—Uniroyal Chemical Company, Inc.; *U.S. Public*, pg. 460

PARACRYLIC LATEX HOUSE PAINT—One Coat Exterior Acrylic Latex House Paint—Paragon Paint & Varnish Corp.; *U.S. Private*, pg. 838

PARACRYLIC LATEX HOUSE & TRIM GLOSS—One Coat Exterior Acrylic Latex House & Trim Gloss—Paragon Paint & Varnish Corp.; *U.S. Private*, pg. 838

PARACUBE—Lighting Diffusers—American Louver Co.; *U.S. Private*, pg. 58

PARADE—Textile Floorcoverings—Forbo Holding SA; *Int'l*, pg. 496

PARADE—Product Line—GSC Enterprises, Inc.; *U.S. Private*, pg. 436

PARADE—Publishers—Parade Publications Inc.; *U.S. Private*, pg. 20

PARADE—Hair Colouring—Wella Group; *Int'l*, pg. 1489

PARADE NET—On-Line Publishers—Parade Publications Inc.; *U.S. Private*, pg. 20

PARADIGM—Office Furniture—Steelcase Wood Div.; *U.S. Private*, pg. 1038

PARADISE—Glace (Candied Fruit)—Paradise, Inc.; *U.S. Public*, pg. 1256

PARADISE MOUNTAIN—Coffee—Sapporo Breweries Ltd.; *Int'l*, pg. 1193

PARADISUS—NONE—Sol Melia; *Int'l*, pg. 1277

PARADOX—Software—Borland International, Inc.; *U.S. Public*, pg. 246

PARADOX PRESS—Book & Magazine Publishing Imprint—DC Comics, Inc.; *U.S. Public*, pg. 1614

PARADRYL WITH EPHEDRINE—Cough Expectorant—Novo Nordisk A/S; *Int'l*, pg. 987

PARAFLEX CAPLETS—NONE—Ortho-McNeil Pharmaceutical Corporation; *U.S. Public*, pg. 929

PARAFLOOD—HID General Purpose Flood—Stonco Genlyte; *U.S. Public*, pg. 730

PARAFLOW—Plate Heat Exchanger—APV Crepaco, Inc.; *Int'l*, pg. 1240

PARAGARO T. 380A—NONE—Ortho-McNeil Pharmaceutical Corporation; *U.S. Public*, pg. 929

PARAGON—Bath Accessories—Baldwin Hardware Corporation; *U.S. Public*, pg. 1053

PARAGON—Electrophoresis System—Beckman Instruments, Inc.; *U.S. Public*, pg. 199

PARAGON—NONE—GenRad, Inc.; *U.S. Public*, pg. 731

PARAGON—NONE—Pitney Bowes Inc.; *U.S. Public*, pg. 1303

PARAGON—NONE—Shandwick International Plc; *Int'l*, pg. 1226

PARAGON—Posterior Spinal System—Sofamor Danek Group, Inc.; *U.S. Public*, pg. 1482

PARAGON READY MIXED ALUMINUM—Interior & Exterior High Leaf Paint—Paragon Paint & Varnish Corp.; *U.S. Private*, pg. 838

PARAGON SATIN FINISH VARNISJ—Polyurethane Reinforced Intrerior/Exterior—Paragon Paint & Varnish Corp.; *U.S. Private*, pg. 838

PARAGON URETHANE CLEAR COATING—Interior & Exterior High Gloss & Satin Finish Coating—Paragon Paint & Varnish Corp.; *U.S. Private*, pg. 838

PARAGON WAX—Coatings—Burmah Castrol plc; *Int'l*, pg. 234

PARAGRAPH—Neuromuscular Blockade Inhibitor—Vital Signs, Inc.; *U.S. Public*, pg. 1723

PARALAC—Liquid Mirror Alkyd Quick Dry High Gloss Enamel—Paragon Paint & Varnish Corp.; *U.S. Private*, pg. 838

PARELEX CLINTEMPS—Temporary Staffing Services—PAREXEL International Corporation; *U.S. Public*, pg. 1257

PARALLAM—Parallel Strand Lumber—TJ International, Inc.; *U.S. Public*, pg. 1556

PARALLEL ARRAY SYNTHESIS—NONE—Life Technologies, Inc.; *U.S. Public*, pg. 504

PARALLEL DIAMOND—Stainless Steel Flatware—Dansk International Designs Ltd.; *U.S. Public*, pg. 261

PARALLEX—Broadloom—Couristan Inc.; *U.S. Private*, pg. 279

PARALOID—Plastic Additive—Rohm and Haas Company; *U.S. Public*, pg. 1403

PARALUX—Enamel White Alkyd—Paragon Paint & Varnish Corp.; *U.S. Private*, pg. 838

PARAMAX—Automated Chemistry Analyzer System—Baxter International Inc.; *U.S. Public*, pg. 196

PARAMAX—Inflammation & Tissue Repair—SmithKline Beecham plc; *Int'l*, pg. 1264

PARAMED—Analgesic—SmithKline Beecham plc; *Int'l*, pg. 1264

PARAMETIC TECHNOLOGY CORPORATION—NONE—Parametric Technology Corporation; *U.S. Public*, pg. 1257

PARAMONT—Cigarettes—Reemtsma Cigarettenfabriken GmbH, Hamburg; *Int'l*, pg. 1100

PARAMOUNT—Broilers—Cargill; *U.S. Private*, pg. 210

PARAMOUNT—Pickles—Dean Pickle & Specialty Products Co.; *U.S. Public*, pg. 490

PARAMOUNT FARMS—NONE—Roll International Corporation; *U.S. Private*, pg. 941

PARAMOUNT FITNESS CENTER—Multi-Station Weight Training for up to 2 People—Paramount Fitness Corp.; *U.S. Private*, pg. 838

PARAMOUNT FTX—Multi-Station Weight Training for 4-6 People—Paramount Fitness Corp.; *U.S. Private*, pg. 838

PARAMOUNT PICTURES—Motion Pictures—Paramount Pictures Corporation; *U.S. Private*, pg. 776

PARAMOUNT'S GREAT AMERICA—Theme Park—Paramount Parks; *U.S. Private*, pg. 776

PARAMOUNT'S KINGS DOMINION—Theme Park—Paramount Parks; *U.S. Private*, pg. 776

PARAMOUNT'S KINGS ISLAND—Theme Park—Paramount Parks; *U.S. Private*, pg. 776

PARAPAK—Collection, Preservation & Transport for Human Specimen—Meridian Diagnostics, Inc.; *U.S. Public*, pg. 1094

PARAPLATIN—Anti-Cancer Agent—Bristol-Myers Squibb Company; *U.S. Public*, pg. 253

PARAPLATIN—Platinum Compound—Bristol-Myers Squibb U.S. Pharmaceutical Group; *U.S. Public*, pg. 255

PARAPLEX—Polymeric Plasticizers—The C.P. Hall Company; *U.S. Private*, pg. 495

PARAPON PORTE DSC CAPLETS—NONE—Ortho-McNeil Pharmaceutical Corporation; *U.S. Public*, pg. 929

PARASEAL—Waterproofing—RPM, Inc.; *U.S. Public*, pg. 1356

PARASTIM—Single-Use Sensor for Blockade Assessment—Vital Signs, Inc.; *U.S. Public*, pg. 1723

PARATECT FLEX—Morantel Tartrate—Pfizer Inc.; *U.S. Public*, pg. 1281

PARATONE—Paints—Sime Darby Berhad; *Int'l*, pg. 1249

PARATRON—Testing Service—Litton Industries, Inc.; *U.S. Public*, pg. 1002

PARATROOPER—Game—Monarch Avalon, Inc.; *U.S. Public*, pg. 1123

PARAWEDGE—Lighting Diffusers—American Louver Co.; *U.S. Private*, pg. 58

PARBAK—Backup Sealing Rings—Seal Group; *U.S. Public*, pg. 1262

PARC—Ammonia Process—KTI Group B.V.; *Int'l*, pg. 837

PARCELMATIC—Automatic Parcel Weighing System—Pitney Bowes Inc.; *U.S. Public*, pg. 1303

PARCHEESI—Game—Milton Bradley Company; *U.S. Public*, pg. 797

PARCHTEX—Printing Papers—The Sorg Paper Co.; *U.S. Public*, pg. 1747

PARCO—Hydraulic Pumps, Rig Equipment—Parker Drilling Company; *U.S. Public*, pg. 1259

PARCO-LINK—Mats—Pawling Corporation; *U.S. Private*, pg. 844

PARDNERS—Western Apparel—Sheplers, Inc.; *U.S. Private*, pg. 993

PARENTROVITE—High Potency Vitamin Products—SmithKline Beecham plc; *Int'l*, pg. 1264

PARENTS—U.K. Parenting Magazine—EMAP Elan; *Int'l*, pg. 451

PARENTS MAGAZINE—Magazine—Gruner + Jahr USA Publishing, Inc.; *Int'l*, pg. 190

PARENTS MAGAZINE—Magazine—Parents Magazine; *Int'l*, pg. 191

PARENTS MAGAZINE CHILD DEVELOPEMENT TOYS—Toys—Gruner + Jahr USA Publishing, Inc.; *Int'l*, pg. 190

PARENTS MAGAZINE READ ALOUD BOOK CLUB—Children's Book Club—Gruner + Jahr USA Publishing, Inc.; *Int'l*, pg. 190

PAREPECTOLIN—Pharmaceuticals—Rhone-Poulenc Rorer - U.S.; *Int'l*, pg. 1110

PAREX—Corn Razors—American Safety Razor Company; *U.S. Private*, pg. 597

PARFLEX—Hose—Parker Hannifin Corporation; *U.S. Public*, pg. 1259

PARFUMS SCHIAPARELLI—Fragrances Imported From Paris—Del Laboratories, Inc.; *U.S. Public*, pg. 494

PARGO'S—Casual Restaurant & Bar—Shoney's, Inc.; *U.S. Public*, pg. 1467

PARIO CLEANERS—Metalworking Chemical—Henkel Surface Technologies; *Int'l*, pg. 610

PARIOLENE—Metalworking Chemical—Henkel Surface Technologies; *Int'l*, pg. 610

PARIS SPLENDOR—Colored Handle Flatware—Lifetime Hoan Corp.; *U.S. Public*, pg. 992

PARISH—Frames, Side Rails, Cradles, Crossmembers & Support Arms—Dana Corporation; *U.S. Public*, pg. 479

PARISIAN—Baked Goods—Parisian Bakeries; *U.S. Public*, pg. 909

PARISIAN—Specialty Department Stores—Parisian, Inc.; *U.S. Public*, pg. 1333

PARISIAN—Sour Dough Bakers—San Francisco French Bread Company; *U.S. Public*, pg. 909

PARK—Heat Treating Supplies—Heat Bath Park Metallurgical Products; *U.S. Private*, pg. 518

PARK AVE—Bath Accessories—Melard Manufacturing Corporation; *U.S. Private*, pg. 729

PARK AVENUE—Photo Typesetters—AGFA EPS Division; *Int'l*, pg. 172

PARK AVENUE—Luggage—American Tourister, Inc.; *U.S. Public*, pg. 1430

PARK AVENUE—Formals, Stationary, Boxes—Dillard, A ResourceNet International Company; *U.S. Public*, pg. 901

PARK AVENUE—Coffee—Park Foods L.P.; *U.S. Private*, pg. 839

PARK AVENUE—Candy Bars—Tom's Foods, Inc.; *U.S. Private*, pg. 1090

PARK AVENUE—Disposable Paper Products—Wisconsin Tissue Mills, Inc.; *U.S. Public*, pg. 347

PARK AVENUE ULTRA—NONE—Wisconsin Tissue Mills, Inc.; *U.S. Public*, pg. 347

PARK CAKES—Cakes & Sandwiches—Northern Foods plc; *Int'l*, pg. 967

PARK HYATT—Small European Style Hotels—Hyatt Hotels Corporation; *U.S. Private*, pg. 551

PARK-O-MATIC—Access Control For Parking Areas—CASI-RUSCO Inc.; *U.S. Private*, pg. 218

PARK REGENCY—Coffee—Park Foods L.P.; *U.S. Private*, pg. 839

PARK RIVER—Manufactured Homes—Champion Enterprises, Inc.; *U.S. Public*, pg. 332

PARK STREET—Executive Dress Shirts—UniFirst Corporation; *U.S. Public*, pg. 1665

PARKAY—NONE—Alliant Foodservice, Inc.; *U.S. Private*, pg. 244

PARKAY—Margarine—Kraft Foods Inc.; *U.S. Public*, pg. 1288

PARKAY—Margarine—Nabisco Inc.; *U.S. Public*, pg. 1355

PARKE-DAVIS—Ethical Pharmaceuticals—Parke-Davis Group; *U.S. Public*, pg. 1739

PARKE-DAVIS—Pharmaceuticals—Warner-Lambert Company; *U.S. Public*, pg. 1738

PARKER—Writing Instruments & Accessories—Gillette Co.-Parker Pen USA; *U.S. Public*, pg. 745

PARKER—Pens—The Gillette Company; *U.S. Public*, pg. 743

PARKER—NONE—MB Espana, S.A.; *U.S. Public*, pg. 798

PARKER BROTHERS—Games—Hasbro, Inc.; *U.S. Public*, pg. 797

PARKER-HALE—Firearms—Cortland Line Co., Inc.; *U.S. Private*, pg. 277

PARKER HANNIFIN—Couplers—Parker Hannifin Corp., Quick Coupling Div.; *U.S. Public*, pg. 1260

PARKER HOUSE—Hotel—Omni Hotels; *U.S. Private*, pg. 1065

PARKER-KALON—Mechanical Fastening Systems—The Black & Decker Corporation; *U.S. Public*, pg. 233

PARKER 1/2 RUNNER—Garden Beans—Green Seed Co.; *U.S. Private*, pg. 477

PARKER ROLLER DOORS—Garage Doors—Carter Holt Harvey Limited; *U.S. Public*, pg. 904

PARKER 75—Writing Instruments—Gillette Co.-Parker Pen USA; *U.S. Public*, pg. 745

PARKER SWEEPER—NONE—Minuteman International, Inc.; *Int'l*, pg. 587

PARKERS' LIGHTHOUSE—Seafood & Beer Restaurants—Select Restaurants, Inc.; *U.S. Private*, pg. 982

PARKINSON COWAN—Household Appliances—Electrolux, AB; *Int'l*, pg. 438

PARKMASTER—Institutional Mower—The Toro Company; *U.S. Public*, pg. 1623

PARKRIDGE—Manufactured Homes—Champion Enterprises, Inc.; *U.S. Public*, pg. 332

PARKSIDE—Wood & Lumber Products—Georgia-Pacific Corporation; *U.S. Public*, pg. 735

PARKUT—Square Cross Section, Lathe Cut Seals—Seal Group; *U.S. Public*, pg. 1262

PARKWAY—Hospital—Parkway Holdings Limited; *Int'l*, pg. 1023

PARLIAMENT—Cigarettes—Philip Morris U.S.A.; *U.S. Public*, pg. 1289

PARLIAMENT LIGHTS—Cigarettes—Philip Morris Companies Inc.; *U.S. Public*, pg. 1287

PARLIAMENT LIGHTS 100'S—Cigarettes—Philip Morris Companies Inc.; *U.S. Public*, pg. 1287

PARLODEL—Pharmaceutical—Novartis AG; *Int'l*, pg. 971

PARLODEL—Tabs/Tablets/Capsules—Sandoz Pharmaceuticals Corp.; *Int'l*, pg. 974

PARMA—Table Wines—The Beverage Source, Inc.; *U.S. Public*, pg. 591

PARMA—NONE—Principal Marques Meat Co.; *Int'l*, pg. 841

PARMA BRAND—Prosciutti Ham—Hormel Foods Corp.; *U.S. Public*, pg. 840

PARMAMEC—Pre-Sliced Meat—I.B.I.S.-S.p.A.; *Int'l*, pg. 642

PARMAN—Petroleum Products; Convenience Stores—The Parman Corporation; *U.S. Private*, pg. 840

PAROC—Fireproof Rock Wool Insulation—Partek Corporation; *Int'l*, pg. 1024

PAROL—Mineral Oils—Penreco; *U.S. Public*, pg. 1273

PAROZONE—Bleach—Cadbury Nigeria PLC; *Int'l*, pg. 248

PARRY'S—Air Freshener—Sara Lee Corporation; *U.S. Public*, pg. 1432

PARRYS—Air Fresheners & Insecticides—Kiwi Brands Pty. Ltd.; *U.S. Public*, pg. 1434

PARSEC—Antenna for Radios & TV—Recoton Corporation; *U.S. Public*, pg. 1369

PARSONS—Paper—Parsons Paper Div. of NVF Co.; *U.S. Private*, pg. 772

PARSONS—NONE—SASIB Packaging North America; *Int'l*, pg. 1194

PARSYSTEM—Software—ScanTron Corporation; *U.S. Public*, pg. 786

PARTAGAS—Cigars—General Cigar Company, Inc.; *U.S. Public*, pg. 708

PARTAGER—French Table Wine—Canandaigua Wine Co.; *U.S. Public*, pg. 300

PARTECH—Hydraulic Pumps, Rig Equipment—Parker Drilling Company; *U.S. Public*, pg. 1259

PARTEK—Locates Cracks on Porous Bodies—ITW Magnaflux; *U.S. Public*, pg. 866

PARTHENON—Serviced Apartment Hotels—Accor S.A.; *Int'l*, pg. 20

PARTICIPATING PROVIDER OPTION—Preferred Provider Network—Blue Cross & Blue Shield of Illinois; *U.S. Private*, pg. 151

PARTICON—Scraped Surface Heat Exchanger—Groen, A Dover Industries Co.; *U.S. Public*, pg. 521

PARTILOK—Screening Vehicle—Ferro Corporation; *U.S. Public*, pg. 618

PARTISANS—War Game—Monarch Avalon, Inc.; *U.S. Public*, pg. 1123

PARTITIONER—Chromatography Apparatus—Fisher Scientific Company; *U.S. Private*, pg. 658

PARTMOBILE—Service & Transport Vertical—Jarke Corporation; *U.S. Private*, pg. 583

PARTNER—Garden Equipment—Electrolux, AB; *Int'l*, pg. 438

PARTNER—Communications System, Electronic Key Telephone System—Lucent Technologies Inc.; *U.S. Public*, pg. 1017

PARTNER—Industrial Cutting Saws—White Consolidated Industries, Inc.; *Int'l*, pg. 439

PARTNER MAIL—Voice Messaging System—Lucent Technologies Inc.; *U.S. Public*, pg. 1017

PARTNER MAIL VS—Voice Messaging System—Lucent Technologies Inc.; *U.S. Public*, pg. 1017

PARTNER II—Communications System, Electronic Key Telephone System—Lucent Technologies Inc.; *U.S. Public*, pg. 1017

PARTNERS IN PROGRESS—Life Insurance—Old American Insurance Co.; *U.S. Public*, pg. 943

PARTNERSHIP—NONE—Howmedica, Inc.; *U.S. Public*, pg. 1282

PARTNERSHIP—NONE—Pfizer Inc.; *U.S. Public*, pg. 1281

PARTNERSHIPPING—Graphic Art Services—Weyerhaeuser Company; *U.S. Public*, pg. 1764

PARTRIDGE—Meat Products—John Morrell & Co.; *U.S. Public*, pg. 1479

PARTS AMERICA—NONE—Sears, Roebuck and Co.; *U.S. Public*, pg. 1452

PARTS PLUS—Motor Oils & Transmission Fluid, Chemicals—A.P.S.; *U.S. Public*, pg. 10

PARTS PLUS—New Automobile Replacement Parts—A.P.S.; *U.S. Public*, pg. 10

PARTS POSSE—After Market Parts—Utility Trailer Manufacturing Co.; *U.S. Private*, pg. 1130

PARTSMASTER—NONE—Plews/Edelmann; *Int'l*, pg. 1396

PARTSVISION—Electronic Parts Catalog—The Reynolds and Reynolds Company; *U.S. Public*, pg. 1384

PARTY—Tents—Anchor Industries Inc.; *U.S. Private*, pg. 71

PARTY CAKE—Dessert—General Mills, Inc.; *U.S. Public*, pg. 717

PARTY CLUB—Snacks & Soft Drinks—P & C Food Markets, Inc.; *U.S. Public*, pg. 1270

PARTY FROSTING—Dessert—General Mills, Inc.; *U.S. Public*, pg. 717

PARTY ISLAND—NONE—Harrah's Entertainment, Inc.; *U.S. Public*, pg. 790

PARTY MAID—Party Goods—American Greetings U.S. Greeting Card Division; *U.S. Public*, pg. 78

PARTY NOGG—Imitation Egg Nog Drink—Diehl Inc.; *U.S. Private*, pg. 332

PARTY PAC—Mixes—Gilster Mary Lee Corp.; *U.S. Private*, pg. 455

PARTY SOURCE—Magazine—Miller Freeman Inc.; *Int'l*, pg. 1443

PARTY TREAT—Juice Drinks—Certified Grocers of California; *U.S. Private*, pg. 226

PARTYFLASH—Instant Cameras—Eastman Kodak Company; *U.S. Public*, pg. 550

PARTYLINE PAK—Party Identifiers—TII Industries, Inc.; *U.S. Public*, pg. 1556

PARTYLITE GIFTS—NONE—Blyth Industries; *U.S. Public*, pg. 239

PARTYSTAR—Instant Cameras—Eastman Kodak Company; *U.S. Public*, pg. 550

PARTYTIME—Instant Cameras—Eastman Kodak Company; *U.S. Public*, pg. 550

PASADO—NONE—JP Foodservice, Inc.; *U.S. Public*, pg. 918

PASADO AUTHENTIC MEXICAN CUISINE—NONE—JP Foodservice, Inc.; *U.S. Public*, pg. 918

PASAN—Bread Improvers—Royal Gist-Brocades N.V.; *Int'l*, pg. 1142

PASCAL COMPILER/2—Computer System—International Business Machines Corporation; *U.S. Public*, pg. 895

PASCALL—Licorice, Toffee & Other Sweets—Cadbury Schweppes p.l.c.; *Int'l*, pg. 247

PASCO—Breads & Cakes—Shikishima Baking Co., Ltd.; *Int'l*, pg. 1231

PASCON 1000—Color Finish System—Pascoe Building Systems, Inc.; *U.S. Private*, pg. 842

PASEO—Automobile—Toyota Motor Sales, U.S.A., Inc.; *Int'l*, pg. 1412

PASER III—Abrasive Jet Cutting System—Flow International Corporation; *U.S. Public*, pg. 656

PASETOCIN—Antibiotics—Kyowa Hakko Kogyo Company, Ltd.; *Int'l*, pg. 778

PASPAT—Pediatric Pharmaceutical—BYK Gulden, S.A. de C.V.; *Int'l*, pg. 66

PASPERTASE—Gastrointestinal Preparations—Kali-Chemie Aktiengesellschaft; *Int'l*, pg. 1278

PASPERTIN—Gastrointestinal Prepartions—Kali-Chemie Aktiengesellschaft; *Int'l*, pg. 1278

PASQUALE'S—Pizza & Pasta—Labatt Brewing Company Limited; *Int'l*, pg. 679

PASS—Positioning Analysis & Segmentation Summary—BASES Worldwide; *U.S. Private*, pg. 120

PASS—Cathodic Protection—Corrpro Companies, Inc.; *U.S. Public*, pg. 451

PASS KEY—Automotive Anti-Theft—Delco Electronics Corporation; *U.S. Public*, pg. 720

PASS-THRU—Board Handling—Universal Instruments Corporation; *U.S. Public*, pg. 522

PASSAGE—Sail Boats—Hunter Marine Corporation; *U.S. Private*, pg. 549

PASSAGE—Motor Homes—Winnebago Industries, Inc.; *U.S. Public*, pg. 1772

PASSAGE WAY—Telecommunications Interface Between a Telephone & a Personal Computer—Lucent Technologies Inc.; *U.S. Public*, pg. 1017

PASSAGER—Endovascular Graft—Meadox Medicals, Inc.; *U.S. Public*, pg. 247

PASSAT—Automobile—Volkswagen AG; *Int'l*, pg. 1473

PASSAT VARIANT—Station Wagon—Volkswagen AG; *Int'l*, pg. 1473

PASSION—Perfume—Unilever Plc; *Int'l*, pg. 1433

PASSIVE EXTREME PRESSURE—Metal Working Fluid—The Lubrizol Corporation; *U.S. Public*, pg. 1016

PASSIVE PLUS—Pacemaker Lead—St. Jude Medical, Inc.; *U.S. Public*, pg. 1427

PASSPORT—Portable/Bedside Vital Signs Monitor With 5 Lead ECG or Large EL Display—Datascope Corp.; *U.S. Public*, pg. 487

PASSPORT—Integrated LAN/WAN Management—Gandalf Technologies Inc.; *Int'l*, pg. 540

PASSPORT—Scotch—The House of Seagram; *Int'l*, pg. 1217

PASSPORT—Debit Card—NBD Bank (Indiana); *U.S. Public*, pg. 628

PASSPORT—NONE—Northern Telecom Limited; *Int'l*, pg. 968

PASSPORT—Hand-held Computer—Radix Corporation; *U.S. Private*, pg. 906

PASSPORT—Scotch—The Seagram Company Ltd.; *Int'l*, pg. 1214

PASSPORT BREAKFAST—Menu Item—IHOP Corp.; *U.S. Public*, pg. 862

PASSPORT DFIB—Portable Defibrillator with Hands-Free Electrodes or Reusable Paddles—Datascope Corp.; *U.S. Public*, pg. 487

PASSPORT PLUS—Card Reader—Federal APD, Inc.; *U.S. Public*, pg. 616

PASSWORD—Game—Milton Bradley Company; *U.S. Public*, pg. 797

PASTA—Women's Leisure Wear—Paul Harris Stores, Inc.; *U.S. Public*, pg. 792

PASTA FRESCA—Pasta Cart—Mamma Ilardo's Corp.; *U.S. Private*, pg. 699

PASTA GALA—Pasta—Coop Switzerland; *Int'l*, pg. 329

PASTA PERFECT—Frozen Pasta & Vegetable Blends—Norpac Foods, Inc.; *U.S. Private*, pg. 802

PASTA PRIMA—Italian Seasoning Mix—McCormick/Schilling; *U.S. Public*, pg. 1066

PASTA SELECT—Canned Pasta—Faribault Foods Inc.; *U.S. Private*, pg. 393

PASTAPAZAZZ—Wheat Based Pellet Snack—Bachman Company; *U.S. Private*, pg. 109

PASTENE FOODS—Wines—The Pastene Companies Ltd.; *U.S. Private*, pg. 842

PASTILLE FRIEZE—Broadloom—Couristan Inc.; *U.S. Private*, pg. 279

PASTIS 51—Anis—Groupe Pernod Ricard; *Int'l*, pg. 566

PASTRY KING—Flour—ADM Milling Co.; *U.S. Public*, pg. 128

PASTRY PRIDE—Frozen Non-Dairy Topping—Presto Food Products, Inc.; *U.S. Public*, pg. 1527

PASYS—Pacemaker—Medtronic, Inc.; *U.S. Public*, pg. 1082

PASYS ST—Pacemaker—Medtronic, Inc.; *U.S. Public*, pg. 1082

PATAGONIA—Outdoor Clothing—Lost Arrow Corporation; *U.S. Private*, pg. 676

PATAK'S—Authentic Ethnic Foods—Hormel Foods Corp.; *U.S. Public*, pg. 840

PATCH KITS FOR PEOPLE—NONE—PolyMedica Industries, Inc.; *U.S. Public*, pg. 1315

PATCHMATE—Data Products—ADC Telecommunications, Inc.; *U.S. Public*, pg. 4

PATCRAFT MILLS—Patcraft Carpets—Patcraft Commercial Carpet; *U.S. Private*, pg. 900

PATE—Gasoline & Oil—Exxon Corporation; *U.S. Public*, pg. 601

PATERSON—Gear Motors—Regal-Beloit Corporation; *U.S. Public*, pg. 1370

PATH—Steps(Used by StrategyWare)—Fair, Isaac and Company, Inc.; *U.S. Public*, pg. 609

PATH—Programmable Analog Test Head—GenRad, Inc.; *U.S. Public*, pg. 731

PATH—PC-Fascimile Interface—Pitney Bowes Inc.; *U.S. Public*, pg. 1303

PATH-LINE II—Cable Driven Live Roller Conveyor—Unex Conveying Systems, Inc.; *U.S. Private*, pg. 1117

PATHFINDER—Pet Foods—Ag Processing Inc., A Cooperative; *U.S. Private*, pg. 26

PATHFINDER—Herbicide—The Dow Chemical Company; *U.S. Public*, pg. 522

PATHFINDER—Cookie & Pastry Flour—King Milling Company; *U.S. Private*, pg. 621

PATHFINDER—Marking Systems—Monarch Marking Systems; *U.S. Public*, pg. 1266

PATHFINDER—Evoked Potential Testing System—Nicolet Analytical; *U.S. Public*, pg. 1593

PATHFINDER—Sport-Utility Vehicle—Nissan Motor Corporation in U.S.A.; *Int'l*, pg. 945

PATHFINDER ADS—Basic Automated Guided Vehicle Systems for Manufacturing & Warehouse—Pathfinder Div.; *U.S. Public*, pg. 1318

PATHFINDER II—Electronic Wire Guidance System—Pathfinder Div.; *U.S. Public*, pg. 1318

PATHMAKER—COBOL Application Generator—Tandem Computers Inc.; *U.S. Public*, pg. 417

PATHMASTER—Route Guidance & Information System—Rockwell International Corporation; *U.S. Public*, pg. 1397

PATHNET—Laboratory Information System—Cerner Corporation; *U.S. Public*, pg. 331

PATHOZONE—Cefoperazone—Pfizer Inc.; *U.S. Public*, pg. 1281

PATHVU—NONE—Compuware Corporation; *U.S. Public*, pg. 423

PATHWAY—Blood Gas Control Material—Beckman Instruments, Inc.; *U.S. Public*, pg. 199

PATIENT CARE—Medical Publication—Medical Economics Company Inc.; *U.S. Public*, pg. 1601

PATIENT CARE INC.—Home Health Agency—Patient Care, Inc.; *U.S. Public*, pg. 344

PATIENT HOME DIRECT—Home Care Program—Medline Industries, Inc.; *U.S. Private*, pg. 728

PATIENT LINK—Record Retention—Universal Standard Healthcare, Inc.; *U.S. Public*, pg. 1697

PATIENT TEST RESULTS—Automated System to Deliver Test Results—National Health Enhancement Systems, Inc.; *U.S. Public*, pg. 1157

PATIENTFACTS—NONE—Market Facts, Inc.; *U.S. Public*, pg. 1046

PATIENTLINK—NONE—American Management Systems, Inc.; *U.S. Public*, pg. 86

PATINA—NONE—S.D. Warren Co.; *Int'l*, pg. 1193

PATIO—Frozen Foods—ConAgra Frozen Food Company; *U.S. Public*, pg. 427

PATIO—Frozen Mexican Foods—ConAgra, Inc.; *U.S. Public*, pg. 425

PATIO HAULER—Recreational Vehicle—Kit Manufacturing Company; *U.S. Public*, pg. 962

PATIO-MATE—NONE—Kay Home Products, Inc.; *U.S. Public*, pg. 1258

PATLON—Fabrics—Amoco Corporation; *U.S. Public*, pg. 101

PATORAN—Crop Protection Agent—BASF AG; *Int'l*, pg. 103

PATRAN—Software—MacNeal-Schwendler Corp.; *U.S. Public*, pg. 1031

PATRAN 3—Next Generation Engineering Analysis Software—MacNeal-Schwendler Corp.; *U.S. Public*, pg. 1031

PATRICIAN—Plywood—Georgia-Pacific Corporation; *U.S. Public*, pg. 735

PATRICK CUDAHY—Bacon, Hams, Sausage—Patrick Cudahy Inc.; *U.S. Public*, pg. 1479

PATRICK CUDAHY—Processed Meats—Smithfield Foods, Inc.; *U.S. Public*, pg. 1479

PATRICK THERMOFORMING—Molded Products-Fiberglass/Plastic—Patrick Industries Inc.; *U.S. Public*, pg. 1264

PATRIOT—Dog Food, Animal Feed For Horses, Cats & Rabbits , Domestic Animal Feed—Ag Processing Inc., A Cooperative; *U.S. Private*, pg. 26

PATRIOT—8″ Beaded Aluminum Siding—Alcoa Building Products, Inc.; *U.S. Public*, pg. 61

PATRIOT—HIGH RESOLUTION COLOR MONITORS—Aydin Corporation; *U.S. Public*, pg. 158

PATRIOT—Missile—Raytheon Company; *U.S. Public*, pg. 1364

PATRIOT—Chemical Applicator—Tyler Industries; *U.S. Private*, pg. 1112

PATRIOT POOLS & ACCESSORIES—Swimming Pools, Decks, Patios, Vacuum Poles—Delair Group, L.L.C.; *U.S. Private*, pg. 47

PATROL—Application Management—BMC Software, Inc.; *U.S. Public*, pg. 162

PATROL MANAGEMENT SUITE—NONE—BMC Software, Inc.; *U.S. Public*, pg. 162

PATRON—Industrial Vegetation Control and Brush Control—Riverdale Chemical Co.; *U.S. Private*, pg. 934

PATTERN A—NONE—Elcor Corporation; *U.S. Public*, pg. 567

PATTERN 62—Pattern Glass—AFG Industries, Inc.; *Int'l*, pg. 84

PATTERNCLAD—Glass—PPG Industries, Inc.; *U.S. Public*, pg. 1245

PATTERNLITE—Glass Panels—PPG Industries, Inc.; *U.S. Public*, pg. 1245

PATTERNS—Styling Line—Bristol-Myers Squibb Company; *U.S. Public*, pg. 253

PATTERNS—Styling Aids—Clairol, Inc.; *U.S. Public*, pg. 254

PATTI—Purge & Trap Total Interface—O.I. Corporation; *U.S. Public*, pg. 1208

PATTI JEAN—Frozen Poultry—Louis Kemp Seafood Co.; *U.S. Public*, pg. 1652

PATTI JEAN—Frozen Food—Tyson Foods, Inc.; *U.S. Public*, pg. 1652

PATTIE CAKES—Greeting Cards, Stationery & Party Goods—American Greetings Corporation; *U.S. Public*, pg. 77

PATTON—Fans & Heaters—The Rival Company; *U.S. Public*, pg. 1391

PATTON'S BEST—War Game—Monarch Avalon, Inc.; *U.S. Public*, pg. 1123

PATUXENT FARMS—NONE—JP Foodservice, Inc.; *U.S. Public*, pg. 918

PAUL FABRICATIONS—NONE—Glynwed International PLC; *Int'l*, pg. 554

PAUL J. BARNETT—Cheese—Churny Company Inc.; *U.S. Public*, pg. 1288

PAUL JABOULET AINE—Rhone Wines—Frederick Wildman & Sons Ltd.; *U.S. Private*, pg. 1176

PAUL MASSON—Full Line of Premium California Wines—Canandaigua Wine Co.; *U.S. Public*, pg. 300

PAUL MICHEL—Designer Line Optical Frames—Sterling Vision, Inc.; *U.S. Public*, pg. 1516

PAUL RUNYAN—NONE—Callaway Golf Company; *U.S. Public*, pg. 294

PAUL STUART—Retail Store—Paul Stuart, Inc.; *U.S. Private*, pg. 844

PAULINS—Crackers—Culinar Inc.; *Int'l*, pg. 348

PAULK—Peanut Inverter—United Farm Tools, Mohawk; *U.S. Private*, pg. 1122

PAULS—Animal Feed—Harrisons & Crosfield plc; *Int'l*, pg. 598

PAULS—Dairy Products & Milks Including Flavored Milk—Q.U.F. Industries Ltd.; *Int'l*, pg. 1074

PAULY—Natural & Process Cheeses—Beatrice Cheese Co.; *U.S. Public*, pg. 426

PAULY—Prepared Desserts—ConAgra, Inc.; *U.S. Public*, pg. 425

PAVABID—Cardiovascular Preparation—Hoechst Marion Roussel North America; *Int'l*, pg. 625

PAVANA—Skin Moisturizer—Stanhome Inc.; *U.S. Public*, pg. 1508

PAVANNE—Jewelry—Richton International Corporation; *U.S. Public*, pg. 1389

PAVE COMMANDER—Concrete Mixers—T.L. Smith Machine; *U.S. Private*, pg. 1009

PAVESAFE—Rubber Flooring—Dodge Regupol, Inc.; *U.S. Private*, pg. 337

PAVEY—Envelopes—Pavey Envelope & Tag Corp.; *U.S. Public*, pg. 1038

PAVIBLOC—Industrial Floorcoverings—Forbo Holding SA; *Int'l*, pg. 496

PAVILIONS—Supermarkets—The Vons Companies, Inc.; *U.S. Public*, pg. 1426

PAVULON—Pharmaceutical—Organon Inc.; *Int'l*, pg. 48

PAW PAW—Juice & Vinegar—Nakano Foods Inc.; *Int'l*, pg. 883

PAX—Lawn & Garden Fertilizer—Pax Company; *U.S. Private*, pg. 1207

PAX SNOW & ICE MELTER—Snow & Ice Melter—Pax Company; *U.S. Private*, pg. 1207

PAX WILD BIRD SEED—Wild Bird Seeds—Pax Company; *U.S. Private*, pg. 1207

PAXALL—Packaging Machinery—SASIB Packaging North America; *Int'l*, pg. 1194

PAXAR—NONE—PAXAR Corporation; *U.S. Public*, pg. 1266

PAXENE—Cancer Agent—IVAX Corporation; *U.S. Public*, pg. 914

PAXIL—NONE—SmithKline Beecham Corporation; *Int'l*, pg. 1264

PAXIL/SEROXAT—Neurosciences—SmithKline Beecham plc; *Int'l*, pg. 1264

PAXMAN—Diesels—The General Electric Company, p.l.c.; *Int'l*, pg. 543

PAXO—Specialty Foods & Cooking—Ranks Hovis McDougall Limited; *Int'l*, pg. 1395

PAXON—High-Density Polyethylene—AlliedSignal Inc.; *U.S. Public*, pg. 49

PAXUS—Software—CSC Financial Services Group; *U.S. Public*, pg. 422

PAY-FOR-PERFORMANCE—NONE—Catalina Marketing Corporation; *U.S. Public*, pg. 314

PAYARA—Corn Flour—International Multifoods Corporation; *U.S. Public*, pg. 900

PAYBACK—Database Retrieval Feature—The Mead Corporation; *U.S. Public*, pg. 1074

PAYBACK—Insurance Policy—Sentry Insurance, A Mutual Company; *U.S. Private*, pg. 984

PAYCO PRIVATE LINES—Soybeans—Interstate Payco Seed Company; *U.S. Private*, pg. 573

PAYCODE—NONE—Stuart Entertainment Inc.; *U.S. Public*, pg. 1526

PAYDAY—Candy Bar—Huhtamaki Oy; *Int'l*, pg. 638

PAYDIRT—Game—Monarch Avalon, Inc.; *U.S. Public*, pg. 1123

PAYEN—Automotive Gaskets—T & N Plc; *Int'l*, pg. 1334

PAYHALF—Womens, Mens & Kids Apparel—A&E Stores, Inc.; *U.S. Private*, pg. 1

PAYLEAN—Ractopamine, Elanco—Eli Lilly and Company; *U.S. Public*, pg. 992

PAYLINER—Vacuum-Formed Containers—Hedwin Corporation; *Int'l*, pg. 1278

PAYLINK—Payroll Software—Paychex, Inc.; *U.S. Public*, pg. 1267

PAYLOAD—NONE—Delta Consolidated Industries, Inc. (Co. Headquarters); *U.S. Public*, pg. 481

PAYLOAD PLUS—Truck Storage Boxes—Delta Consolidated Industries, Inc. (Co. Headquarters); *U.S. Public*, pg. 481

PAYMASTER—Automatic Slack Adjusters—Rockwell International Corporation; *U.S. Public*, pg. 1397

PAYNE—Heating & Air Conditioning Equipment—Carrier Corp.; *U.S. Public*, pg. 1690

PAYNE—Air Conditioning & Heating—Carrier Corporation; *U.S. Public*, pg. 1689

PAYNE—Air Conditioners—The Climatic Corp.; *U.S. Private*, pg. 246

PAYNE STEWART—Golf Wear—Pincus Bros., Inc.; *U.S. Private*, pg. 865

PAYNOCIL—Analgesic—SmithKline Beecham plc; *Int'l*, pg. 1264

PAYSON—Casters & Wheels—Payson Casters, Inc.; *U.S. Private*, pg. 844

PAZAZZ—Sheer Color Wash, Mousse, Gel—Clairol, Inc.; *U.S. Public*, pg. 254

PAZO—Ointment—Bristol-Myers Squibb Company; *U.S. Public*, pg. 253

PAZZAZZ—Cameras—Eastman Kodak Company; *U.S. Public*, pg. 550

PEA BEU—Pest Control—Reckitt & Colman plc; *Int'l*, pg. 1089

PEABODY—COAL—Hanson PLC; *Int'l*, pg. 592

PEACE OF MIND—Service—Luskin's, Inc.; *U.S. Private*, pg. 681

PEACE OF MIND—Life Insurance—Old American Insurance Co.; *U.S. Public*, pg. 943

PEACH—Sweet Snuff—Conwood Company L.P.; *U.S. Private*, pg. 272

PEACH & HONEY—Cocktail—Montebello Brands Inc.; *U.S. Private*, pg. 758

PEACH BELLINI—Shampoo/Conditioner—Zotos International; *Int'l*, pg. 1236

PEACHEY—Loose Leaf Chewing Tobacco—Conwood Company L.P.; *U.S. Private*, pg. 272

PEACHTREE—NONE—The Smithfield Companies, Inc.; *U.S. Public*, pg. 1479

PEACHTREE FIZZ—Spirits—Mercian Corporation; *Int'l*, pg. 858

PEACOCK—Watercolors—Binney & Smith Inc.; *U.S. Public*, pg. 496

PEACOCK PRESS—Book Publishing—Bertelsmann AG; *Int'l*, pg. 189

PEAK—Investment Plans—Derbyshire Building Society; *Int'l*, pg. 394

PEAK—Anti-Freeze—Old World Industries, Inc.; *U.S. Public*, pg. 814

THE PEAK ADVANTAGE—Flexible Bar Code Application System—Peak Technologies Group, Inc.; *Int'l*, pg. 890

PEAK COOKQUIK—Dehydrated Edible Beans—Trinidad/Benham Corp.; *U.S. Private*, pg. 1103

PEAK FLOW—Catheter—Medtronic, Inc.; *U.S. Public*, pg. 1082

PEAK FREANS—Cookie Biscuits, Mktg. in U.S.—RJR Nabisco Holdings Corp.; *U.S. Public*, pg. 1354

PEAK 1—NONE—The Canadian Coleman Co., Ltd.; *U.S. Private*, pg. 691

PEAK 1—Backpacking Gear—The Coleman Company, Inc.; *U.S. Private*, pg. 690

PEAK PERFORMANCE—Personal Care Accessories—Foot Locker; *U.S. Public*, pg. 1777

PEAK POWER—Car Audio Products—Gold Peak Industries (Holdings) Limited; *Int'l*, pg. 537

PEAK SCREEN SHAPER—Screen Translator—Peak Technologies Group, Inc.; *Int'l*, pg. 890

PEAKFIT—Automated Peak-Fitting Software—SPSS Inc.; *U.S. Public*, pg. 1420

PEAKLITE—Translucent Fibreglass Reinforced Plastic Skylights—Sequentia Inc.; *U.S. Private*, pg. 985

PEAKLITE II—Sleeping Bags—The Canadian Coleman Co., Ltd.; *U.S. Private*, pg. 691

PEAKPRO—Chromatography Analysis Software—Beckman Instruments, Inc.; *U.S. Public*, pg. 199

PEAKSET—Hardware—Chips and Technologies, Inc.; *U.S. Public*, pg. 349

PEANUT BUSTER PARFAIT—Dessert—International Dairy Queen, Inc.; *U.S. Public*, pg. 220

PEANUT BUTTER CUP—Candy—Boyer Candy Company Inc.; *U.S. Private*, pg. 162

PEANUT BUTTER LOG—Candy Bars—Tom's Foods, Inc.; *U.S. Private*, pg. 1090

PEANUT BUTTER SNICKERS—Candy Bar—Mars, Incorporated; *U.S. Private*, pg. 707

PEANUT GALLERY—Pocket Knives—Camillus Cutlery Co.; *U.S. Private*, pg. 203

PEANUT PAK—Corrugated Container—Georgia-Pacific Corporation; *U.S. Public*, pg. 735

PEANUT PATCH—Boiled Peanuts—Dean Pickles & Specialty Products; *U.S. Public*, pg. 490

PEANUT ROLL—Candy Bars—Tom's Foods, Inc.; *U.S. Private*, pg. 1090

THE PEANUT SHOP—NONE—The Smithfield Companies, Inc.; *U.S. Public*, pg. 1479

PEANUTS—Clothing—Salant Corporation; *U.S. Public*, pg. 1429

PEARL—HPS Outdoor Bracket—Guth Lighting Company; *Int'l*, pg. 821

PEARL—Filmless Direct Imaging Technology—Presstek, Inc.; *U.S. Public*, pg. 1324

PEARL DROPS—Toothpaste—Carter Products, Canada; *U.S. Public*, pg. 310

PEARL DROPS—Tooth Polish—Carter-Wallace, Inc.; *U.S. Public*, pg. 309

PEARL DROPS BAKING SODA WHITENING TOOTHPASTE—Toothpaste—Carter-Wallace, Inc.; *U.S. Public*, pg. 309

PEARL-GLO—Pearlescent Pigments—International Specialty Products, Inc.; *U.S. Public*, pg. 858

PEARL-KOTE—Clay-Coated Folding Boxboard—Riverwood International Corporation; *U.S. Public*, pg. 1391

PEARL LIGHT—Beer—Pearl Brewing Company; *U.S. Private*, pg. 954

PEARL PREMIUM—Beer—Pearl Brewing Company; *U.S. Private*, pg. 954

PEARLCORDER—Microcassette Recorders, Dictators & Transcribers—Olympus America Inc.; *Int'l*, pg. 1005

PEARLCORDER—Micro-Cassette Tape Recorder—Olympus Optical Co., Ltd.; *Int'l*, pg. 1004

PEARLE EXPRESS—One Hour Service Optical Stores—Pearle Vision Express; *U.S. Public*, pg. 397

PEARLE EYE & TECH—Corrective Lenses—Pearle Inc.; *U.S. Public*, pg. 396

PEARLE EYELAB EXPRESS—Eye Examination and Corrective Lenses—Pearle Inc.; *U.S. Public*, pg. 396

PEARLE VISION—Eyecare Products & Services—Pearle Vision, Inc.; *U.S. Public*, pg. 397

PEARLE VISION CENTER—Corrective Lenses—Pearle Inc.; *U.S. Public*, pg. 396

PEARLE VISION EXPRESS—Corrective Lenses—Pearle Inc.; *U.S. Public*, pg. 396

PEARS—Soap, Bath Prods.—Chesebrough-Pond's USA Co.; *Int'l*, pg. 1435

PEARS PERSONAL PLEASURES—Bath Products—Chesebrough-Pond's USA Co.; *Int'l*, pg. 1435

PEARSON—Furniture—Furniture Brands International Inc.; *U.S. Public*, pg. 688

PEARSON—Candy—Nestle Chocolate & Confection; *Int'l*, pg. 917

PEARSON—Candy—Nestle S.A.; *Int'l*, pg. 915

PEARSON INTERNATIONAL—Publishers—Pearson plc; *Int'l*, pg. 1025

PEARSON NEW ENTERTAINMENT—Magazine & Videos—Pearson plc; *Int'l*, pg. 1025

PEARSON TELEVISION—NONE—Pearson plc; *Int'l*, pg. 1025

PEAUDOUCE—NONE—Kimberly-Clark Corporation; *U.S. Public*, pg. 958

PEAVEY—Complete Line of Musical Amplification & Sound Reinforcement—Peavey Electronics Corp.; *U.S. Private*, pg. 845

PEBAX—Elastameric—Elf Atochem North America, Inc.; *Int'l*, pg. 445

PEBBLECREEK RESORT—Active Adult Community In Phoenix—Robson Communities; *U.S. Private*, pg. 937

PEBBLES—Breakfast Cereal—Kraft Foods, Inc.; *U.S. Public*, pg. 1287

PEBOC—Chemical/Pharmaceutical Intermediates—Eastman Chemical Company; *U.S. Public*, pg. 550

PEBS—Blanket Insulation—Johns Manville Corporation; *U.S. Public*, pg. 927

PECAN PLACE—Prefinished Wall Paneling—Georgia-Pacific Corporation; *U.S. Public*, pg. 735

PECAN SANDIES—Cookies—Keebler Company; *U.S. Public*, pg. 657

PECAN SUPREME—Cookies—Nabisco Inc.; *U.S. Public*, pg. 1355

PECAN SUPREME—Cookies—RJR Nabisco Holdings Corp.; *U.S. Public*, pg. 1354

PECAN TWIRLS—Bakery Goods—The Pillsbury Company; *Int'l*, pg. 411

PECAP—Polyester Fabric Monofilament—Tetko, Inc.; *U.S. Private*, pg. 1078

PECHE PRATIQUE—French Outdoor Pursuits Magazine—EMAP France; *Int'l*, pg. 451

PECO—NONE—Perry Equipment Corporation; *U.S. Private*, pg. 855

PECO PAK—Memory Disc Pack—Peco Mfg. Co., Inc.; *U.S. Private*, pg. 846

PECTIN—NONE—Firmenich; *Int'l*, pg. 486

PEDAL-UP!—Replacement Parts—R&B, Inc.; *U.S. Public*, pg. 1354

PEDCAP—Closure Systems—Raychem Corporation; *U.S. Public*, pg. 1362

PEDESTAL BOOM—Stationary Mounted Breaker System—Allied Construction Products, Inc.; *U.S. Public*, pg. 1339

PEDESTALS—NONE—USG Corporation; *U.S. Public*, pg. 1660

PEDI-CAP—Disposable End-Tidal Carbon Dioxide Detector—Nellcor Puritan Bennett Incorporated; *U.S. Public*, pg. 1039

PEDI CHECK—NONE—Nellcor Puritan Bennett Incorporated; *U.S. Public*, pg. 1039

PEDI-FOAM—Slippers—Medline Industries, Inc.; *U.S. Private*, pg. 728

PEDIACARE—Cough/Cold Preparations—Johnson & Johnson; *U.S. Public*, pg. 927

PEDIACARE—Proprietary Drugs—McNeil Consumer Products Company; *U.S. Public*, pg. 928

PEDIALYTE—Electrolyte Maintenance Solution—Abbott Laboratories; *U.S. Public*, pg. 12

PEDIALYTE—Oral Electrolyte Solution—Ross Products; *U.S. Public*, pg. 13

PEDIAPRED—Oral Liquid (Prednisolone Sodium Phosphate, USP)—Medeva Pharmaceuticals; *Int'l*, pg. 852

PEDIASURE—Infant & Medical Nutritional—Abbott Laboratories; *U.S. Public*, pg. 12

PEDIATRIC FORMULA 44—Children's Cough Medicine—The Procter & Gamble Company; *U.S. Public*, pg. 1330

PEDIATRIC IAB—Pediatric Intra-Aortic Balloon—Datascope Corp.; *U.S. Public*, pg. 487

PEDIAZOLE—Erythromycin Ethylsuccinate & Sulfisoxazole Acetyl—Abbott Laboratories; *U.S. Public*, pg. 12

PEDIBLUE—Resuscitators—Vital Signs, Inc.; *U.S. Public*, pg. 1723

PEDIGREE—Meat Dogfood—Kal Kan Foods, Inc.; *U.S. Private*, pg. 707

PEDIGREE PAL—Petfood—Mars Petfoods (UNISABI); *U.S. Private*, pg. 707

PEDIOTIC—Optical Pharmaceutical—Glaxo Wellcome PLC; *Int'l*, pg. 553

PEDRO DOMECQ—Wine—Domecq Importers Inc.; *Int'l*, pg. 63

PEDVAX HIB—Haemophilus b Conjugate Vaccine—Merck & Co., Inc.; *U.S. Public*, pg. 1090

PEE-CHEE—Paper & Folders—The Mead Corporation; *U.S. Public*, pg. 1074

PEEDEE DOSE—NONE—PolyMedica Industries, Inc.; *U.S. Public*, pg. 1315

PEEK-A-BOO ACTIVITY TUNNEL—NONE—Rubbermaid Incorporated; *U.S. Public*, pg. 1411

PEEK A TOE—Children's Clothing—S. Schwab Company; *U.S. Private*, pg. 974

PEEL & PEEK—Pressure Sensitive Lamination with Hidden Printing—Zimmer Custom-Made Packaging Co.; *U.S. Private*, pg. 802

PEEK FREANS—Biscuits—Danone Group; *Int'l*, pg. 379

PEEL ON—Pressure Sensitive Labels—Menasha Corp., Printed Systems Div.; *U.S. Private*, pg. 731

PEEL & SEEL—Envelopes—Kimberly-Clark Corporation; *U.S. Public*, pg. 958

PEEPS/BUNNIES—Candy—Just Born, Inc.; *U.S. Private*, pg. 602

PEERASOL—Aerosol Container—Peerless Tube Company; *U.S. Public*, pg. 1269

PEERCRAFT—Porch & Floor Alkyd Enamel—Paragon Paint & Varnish Corp.; *U.S. Private*, pg. 838

PEERCRAFT 480—Latex Interior Sand Finish White—Paragon Paint & Varnish Corp.; *U.S. Private*, pg. 838

PEERLESS—Golf Equipment—The Arnold Palmer Golf Company; *U.S. Public*, pg. 632

PEERLESS—Do-It-Yourself Faucet—Delta Faucet Corporation; *U.S. Public*, pg. 1053

PEERLESS—Reamers—Greenfield Industries; *U.S. Public*, pg. 950

PEERLESS—Manual & Electric Chain Hoists; Crane Component & Package Systems—Harrington Hoists, Inc.; *U.S. Private*, pg. 504

PEERLESS—Pump—TBG Services, Inc.; *Int'l*, pg. 1335

PEERLESS—Drive Train Components—Tecumseh Products Co. Engine & Transmission Group; *U.S. Public*, pg. 1566

PEERLESS—Machinery—Wisconsin Automated Machinery Corp.; *U.S. Private*, pg. 1184

PEERLESS CARPET—Broadloom Carpets—Peerless Carpet Corporation; *Int'l*, pg. 1032

PEERLESS ENSEMBLE—Commercial Carpets—Peerless Carpet Corporation; *Int'l*, pg. 1032

PEERLESS INTERNATIONAL CARPET—NONE—Peerless Carpet Corporation; *Int'l*, pg. 1032

PEERLESS LATEX HOUSE PAINT—Exterior House Paint—Paragon Paint & Varnish Corp.; *U.S. Private*, pg. 838

PEERLESS RAM—Shovels & Wheelbarrows—Ames Company; *U.S. Public*, pg. 1683

PEERLUX ALKYD SEMI-GLOSS—Semi Gloss—Paragon Paint & Varnish Corp.; *U.S. Private*, pg. 838

PEERLUX BEST HIDE—Latex Flat White—Paragon Paint & Varnish Corp.; *U.S. Private*, pg. 838

PEERLUX DEEP COLOR—Latex Semi-Gloss—Paragon Paint & Varnish Corp.; *U.S. Private*, pg. 838

PEERLUX 800—Latex Eggshell Enamel White—Paragon Paint & Varnish Corp.; *U.S. Private*, pg. 838

PEERLUX LATEX TRIM PAINT—Exterior Trim Paint—Paragon Paint & Varnish Corp.; *U.S. Private*, pg. 838

PEERLUX NE00 SERIES—Latex Velet Flat Enamel—Paragon Paint & Varnish Corp.; *U.S. Private*, pg. 838

PEERLUX PERMAWHITE—Latex Gloss Enamel—Paragon Paint & Varnish Corp.; *U.S. Private*, pg. 838

PEERLUX POOL & FLOOR—Latex, Pool, Patio & Floor Paint—Paragon Paint & Varnish Corp.; *U.S. Private*, pg. 838

PEERLUX SV00 SERIES—Latex Semi-Gloss—Paragon Paint & Varnish Corp.; *U.S. Private*, pg. 838

PEERLUX TRIM PAINT—Exterior Alkyd Trim Paint—Paragon Paint & Varnish Corp.; *U.S. Private*, pg. 838

PEERLUX VL00 SERIES—Latex Flat—Paragon Paint & Varnish Corp.; *U.S. Private*, pg. 838

PEG EM'S—Storage Hooks—Bulldog VSI; *U.S. Public*, pg. 1176

PEG-RITE—Accounting System—Master Craft Corp.; *Int'l*, pg. 267

PEG-RITE III—Accounting System—Master Craft Corp.; *Int'l*, pg. 267

PEGASUS—Vitality Plan Tabs—Alva/Amco Pharmacal Companies, Inc.; *U.S. Private*, pg. 47

PEGASUS—Electronic Identification Device—Amtech Corporation; *U.S. Public*, pg. 105

PEGASUS—Military Engine—Rolls-Royce Military Aero Engines Ltd.; *Int'l*, pg. 1127

PEGLER-SUNVIC—Heating & Appliance Controls—Tomkins PLC; *Int'l*, pg. 1395

PEGOSPERSE—Emulsifier—Lonza Inc.; *Int'l*, pg. 67

PEIR—Performance Evaluation & Information Reduction—The Foxboro Company; *Int'l*, pg. 1243

PIERRE CARDIN—NONE—Koret Pierre Cardin; *U.S. Private*, pg. 632

PEKAMELT—Holtmelt Coated Laminates—PKL Verpackungssysteme GmbH; *Int'l*, pg. 1020

PEKONI—Pig Feed—Cultor Ltd.; *Int'l*, pg. 349

PEL-UNITE—Pellet Binder—Oil-Dri Corporation of America; *U.S. Public*, pg. 1214

PELADOW—Calcium Chloride—The Dow Chemical Company; *U.S. Public*, pg. 522

PELAMAG—Metallurgical Granules—The Dow Chemical Company; *U.S. Public*, pg. 522

PELANGI—Paints—Sime Darby Berhad; *Int'l*, pg. 1249

PELASPAN MOLD-A-PAC—Packing Products—The Dow Chemical Company; *U.S. Public*, pg. 522

PELASPAN-PAC—Plastic Loose Fill—The Dow Chemical Company; *U.S. Public*, pg. 522

PELBOX 10455—High Resolution Recorder—ECRM; *U.S. Private*, pg. 353

PELBOX 3000—High Resolution Recorders—ECRM; *U.S. Private*, pg. 353

PELBOX 12455—High Resolution Recorders—ECRM; *U.S. Private*, pg. 353

PELFORTH—Beer—Heineken N.V.; *Int'l*, pg. 608

PELICAN—Street Sweepers—Elgin Sweeper Company; *U.S. Public*, pg. 617

PELICAN—Beer—Heineken N.V.; *Int'l*, pg. 608

PELICAN PREMIER—Street Sweepers—Elgin Sweeper Company; *U.S. Public*, pg. 617

PELINOC—A Pellet Inoculant for Small, Medium & Large Seeded Legumes—LiphaTech, Inc.; *Int'l*, pg. 812

PELION—NONE—Porcelanite, Inc.; *Int'l*, pg. 573

PELLA—Doors, Skylights, Sunrooms, Windows—Pella Corporation; *U.S. Private*, pg. 848

PELLACOL—Plant Protectives—DSM Chemie Linz GmbH; *Int'l*, pg. 356

PELLER ESTATES—Wine—Andres Wines Ltd.; *Int'l*, pg. 75

PELLET SYSTEM—Ansul-Plus—Aladdin Synergetics, Inc.; *U.S. Private*, pg. 31

PELLET VENT—Chimney Pipe for Pellet Stoves—Simpson Dura-Vent Co., Inc.; *U.S. Public*, pg. 1474

PELLETHANE TPU—Elastomers—The Dow Chemical Company; *U.S. Public*, pg. 522

PELLICON—Cassette System—Millipore Corporation; *U.S. Public*, pg. 1112

PELLON—Non-Woven Company—Freudenberg & Company; *Int'l*, pg. 505

PELLON—Consumer Products—Freudenberg Nonwovens; *Int'l*, pg. 505

PELOPONNESE—Olive Oil, Olives, Vinegar, Herbs & Spices—Hormel Foods Corp.; *U.S. Public*, pg. 840

PELOPONNESIAN WAR—War Game—Monarch Avalon, Inc.; *U.S. Public*, pg. 1123

PELOUZE—Commercial Scales—Signature Brands USA, Inc.; *U.S. Public*, pg. 1472

PELS—Caustic Soda—PPG Industries, Inc.; *U.S. Public*, pg. 1245

PELTOR—Hearing Protection—Aearo Company; *U.S. Private*, pg. 23

PEMAGRAPHICS—Permanent Artist Color Markers—Dri Mark Products, Inc.; *U.S. Private*, pg. 342

PEMCO—Casters & Wheels—Standex International Corporation; *U.S. Public*, pg. 1505

PEMFLEX—Self-Locking Fastener—Penn Engineering & Manufacturing Corp.; *U.S. Public*, pg. 1269

PEMHEX—Self-Locking Fastener—Penn Engineering & Manufacturing Corp.; *U.S. Public*, pg. 1269

PEMILASTON—NONE—Bristol-Myers Squibb Company; *U.S. Public*, pg. 253

PEMMICAN—Meat Snacks—GoodMark Foods, Inc.; *U.S. Public*, pg. 751

PEMSERT—Flush Fastener—Penn Engineering & Manufacturing Corp.; *U.S. Public*, pg. 1269

PEMSERTER—Press—Penn Engineering & Manufacturing Corp.; *U.S. Public*, pg. 1269

PEN & INK—Correction Fluid—The Gillette Company; *U.S. Public*, pg. 743

PEN*KEY—Computing System—Norand Mobile Systems Div.; *U.S. Public*, pg. 1699

PEN-O-PREP—(Penetrating Sealer)—The Valspar Corp. Protective Coatings Div.; *U.S. Public*, pg. 1707

PEN PRO—Automotive Test Equipment—Actron Manufacturing Company; *U.S. Private*, pg. 16

PEN-RAY—UV Light Sources—UVP, Inc.; *U.S. Private*, pg. 1115

Brand Name Index

PENAFIEL—Mineral Water—Cadbury Schweppes p.l.c.; *Int'l*, pg. 247

PENAFIEL—Mineral Water & Fruit-Flavored Drinks—Wisdom Imports Sales Co. Inc.; *Int'l*, pg. 679

PENAIR—Aircraft Cleaner—Wechco, Inc.; *U.S. Private*, pg. 1158

PENAIR—Military & Aerospace Aircraft Cleaners—West Chemical Products, Inc.; *U.S. Private*, pg. 1158

PENAL WARE—Stainless Steel Plumbing Fixtures—Acorn Engineering Company; *U.S. Private*, pg. 14

PENALJO—Footwear—Brown Group, Inc.; *U.S. Public*, pg. 262

PENALJO—Shoes—Brown Shoe Company; *U.S. Public*, pg. 262

PENAMOX—Antibiotic—SmithKline Beecham plc; *Int'l*, pg. 1264

PENARROYA—Lead—Imetal; *Int'l*, pg. 661

PENATEN—NONE—Johnson & Johnson; *U.S. Public*, pg. 927

PENBRITIN—NONE—SmithKline Beecham Corporation; *Int'l*, pg. 1264

PENBRITIN—Anti-Infective—SmithKline Beecham plc; *Int'l*, pg. 1264

PENBRITIN—Antibiotic—SmithKline Beecham Research Limited; *Int'l*, pg. 1266

PENCILETTE—Electrosurgery Pencil—Conmed Corporation; *U.S. Public*, pg. 431

PENCILIER—Mechanical Pencil—The Pilot Pen Corp. of America; *Int'l*, pg. 1057

PENDAFLEX—Suspension Filing Systems—Esselte AB; *Int'l*, pg. 459

PENDAFLEX—Hanging File Folders—Esselte Corporation; *Int'l*, pg. 459

PENESOLVE—Felt & Wire Cleaners for Pulp & Paper Industry—West Chemical Products, Inc.; *U.S. Private*, pg. 1158

PENETECK—Mineral Oils—Penreco; *U.S. Public*, pg. 1273

PENETRANT—Cleaner—Oakite Products, Inc.; *Int'l*, pg. 861

PENETRATOR—Antenna—Telex Communications, Inc.; *U.S. Private*, pg. 1074

PENETROL—Oil/Alkyd Paint Conditioner—The Flood Company; *U.S. Private*, pg. 414

PENFOLDS—Wines—Southcorp Holdings Ltd.; *Int'l*, pg. 1287

PENGLOBE—Anti-Biotic, Ampicillin Preparation—Astra AB; *Int'l*, pg. 93

PENGLOSS—Coating Binder—Penford Corp.; *U.S. Public*, pg. 1269

PENGUIN—Books—Pearson plc; *Int'l*, pg. 1025

PENGUIN—Adult Paperback Books—Penguin Putnam Inc.; *Int'l*, pg. 1027

PENGUIN—Freezer Wrap Marker—Sanford Corporation; *U.S. Public*, pg. 1178

PENGUIN'S—Frozen Yogurt—Penguin's Industries; *Int'l*, pg. 201

PENICILLIN G—Sodium & Potassium Infectious Disease Therapy—Bristol-Myers Squibb Company; *U.S. Public*, pg. 253

PENICYLINDERS—Tubes—Fisher Scientific Company; *U.S. Private*, pg. 658

PENINSULA TABLE—NONE—Rubbermaid Incorporated; *U.S. Public*, pg. 1411

PENIT—Polymer Paint Pen—Sanford Corporation; *U.S. Public*, pg. 1178

PENMUL—Heavy Duty Emulsion Cleaner—Wechco, Inc.; *U.S. Private*, pg. 1158

PENN—Entire Brand Name for Refrigeration & Temperature Control Line—Johnson Controls, Inc., Controls Group; *U.S. Public*, pg. 932

PENN—Tennis Balls—Penn Racquet Sports; *U.S. Public*, pg. 706

PENN BOND—Embroidery—The Penn Companies; *U.S. Private*, pg. 849

PENNBROIDERY—Heat Seal Applied Logos—The Penn Companies; *U.S. Private*, pg. 849

PENN DRAKE PETROSUL—Petroleum Sulfonates—Penreco; *U.S. Public*, pg. 1273

PENN DUTCH—Noodles—Borden Foods Co.; *U.S. Private*, pg. 158

PENN ENGINEERING—NONE—Penn Engineering & Manufacturing Corp.; *U.S. Public*, pg. 1269

PENN FARMS—Ice Cream—Kemps Foods, Inc.; *Int'l*, pg. 752

PENN FARMS—Novelties—Kemps Foods, Inc.; *Int'l*, pg. 752

PENN SEAL—Identification Products—The Penn Companies; *U.S. Private*, pg. 849

PENN TEXT—Fabric Print Emblem—The Penn Companies; *U.S. Private*, pg. 849

PENN ULTRA-BLUE—Racquetball Balls—Penn Racquet Sports; *U.S. Public*, pg. 706

PENNANT—Business Product—International Business Machines Corporation; *U.S. Public*, pg. 895

PENNANT—Glace (Candied Fruit)—Paradise, Inc.; *U.S. Public*, pg. 1256

PENNANT—NONE—Portland Food Products Company; *U.S. Private*, pg. 876

PENNANT—Frozen Dough—Van den Bergh Foods Company; *Int'l*, pg. 1436

PENNANT RACE—Sports Game—Monarch Avalon, Inc.; *U.S. Public*, pg. 1123

PENNANT SYSTEMS—Business Product—International Business Machines Corporation; *U.S. Public*, pg. 895

PENNLON—Plastics—Furon Co.; *U.S. Public*, pg. 689

PENNRAY—Billiard Equipment & Supplies—WICO; *U.S. Private*, pg. 1144

PENNSYLVANIA BLUE SHIELD—Health Care Coverage—Highmark Inc.; *U.S. Private*, pg. 528

PENNSYLVANIA BRADFORD HAMMERMILL—Industrial Machinery—Pennsylvania Crusher Corp.; *U.S. Private*, pg. 850

PENNSYLVANIA DUTCH—Egg Noodle Products—Borden, Inc.; *U.S. Private*, pg. 157

PENNSYLVANIA DUTCH—Pasta Products—Borden Italian Foods; *U.S. Private*, pg. 158

PENNSYLVANIA DUTCH—Egg Nog—Charles Jacquin et Cie, Inc.; *U.S. Private*, pg. 580

PENNSYLVANIA FARMER—Farm Publication-15 Issues/Year—Farm Progress Publications; *U.S. Public*, pg. 513

PENNSYLVANIA HOUSE—Furniture—Ladd Furniture, Inc.; *U.S. Public*, pg. 974

PENNSYLVANIA MANUFACTURERS REGISTER—Register—Manufacturers' News, Inc.; *U.S. Private*, pg. 700

PENNSYLVANIA REVERSIBLE IMPACTOR—Industrial Machinery—Pennsylvania Crusher Corp.; *U.S. Private*, pg. 850

PENNSYLVANIA'S BEST—Hard Pretzels—Bachman Company; *U.S. Private*, pg. 109

PENNTECHNIC—Industrial Machinery—Pennsylvania Crusher Corp.; *U.S. Private*, pg. 850

PENNTROWEL—Coatings—Elf Atochem North America, Inc.; *Int'l*, pg. 445

PENNY & GILES—NONE—Bowthorpe plc; *Int'l*, pg. 207

PENNY CURTISS—Bakeries—The Penn Traffic Company; *U.S. Public*, pg. 1270

PENNY FROM HEAVEN—Stuffed Toy Figures; Canisters; Towels; T-Shirts—American Greetings Corporation; *U.S. Public*, pg. 77

THE PENNY PINCHERS—Budget-Priced Nail Tips, Nail Glue, Nail Charms & Full Press-on Nails—Lee Pharmaceuticals; *U.S. Public*, pg. 984

PENNYSAVER—Newspaper—The Gazette Company; *U.S. Private*, pg. 442

PENNZOIL—Oil Products—Pennzoil Company; *U.S. Public*, pg. 1272

PENNZOIL MOTOR OIL—Motor Oil—Pennzoil Products Co.; *U.S. Public*, pg. 1272

PENPLUS—Potato Starch—Penford Corp.; *U.S. Public*, pg. 1269

PENRECO—Petrolatums—Penreco; *U.S. Public*, pg. 1273

PENRIGHT!—NONE—AST Research Inc.; *Int'l*, pg. 1181

PENRIL DATACOMM—Data Communications Equipment—Hayes Corporation, Regional Office; *U.S. Public*, pg. 801

PENROSE—Meat Snacks—GoodMark Foods, Inc.; *U.S. Private*, pg. 751

PENSION SOLUTIONS INC—Pension Plans & Admin.—MSI Insurance Companies; *U.S. Private*, pg. 688

PENSIONS & INVESTMENTS—Newspaper—Crain Communications, Inc.; *U.S. Private*, pg. 284

PENSTAR—Electronic Anesthesia Machine—BTR plc; *Int'l*, pg. 124

PENSUPREME—Ice Cream, Milk & Related Dairy Products—Kemps Foods, Inc.; *Int'l*, pg. 752

PENTA FLEX—Exterior Flat Paint—Benjamin Moore & Co.; *U.S. Private*, pg. 133

PENTA-LATCH—Tamper Resistant Door Latching Mechanism—S & C Electric Company; *U.S. Private*, pg. 954

PENTAC—Insecticides—Novartis AG; *Int'l*, pg. 971

PENTAC—Miticide—Sandoz Agro, Inc.; *Int'l*, pg. 974

PENTACLEAR—Rigid Plastic Film—Klockner-Werke AG; *Int'l*, pg. 736

PENTADUR—Rigid Plastic Films—Klockner-Werke AG; *Int'l*, pg. 736

PENTAFOOD—Plastic Food Wrap—Klockner-Werke AG; *Int'l*, pg. 736

PENTAFORM—Plastic Films—Klockner-Werke AG; *Int'l*, pg. 736

PENTAL—Rosin Ester—Hercules Incorporated; *U.S. Public*, pg. 809

PENTALAN—Rigid Plastic Film—Klockner-Werke AG; *Int'l*, pg. 736

PENTALYN—Synthetic Resin—Hercules Incorporated; *U.S. Public*, pg. 809

PENTAMED—Plastic Packaging for Medical Devices—Klockner-Werke AG; *Int'l*, pg. 736

PENTAPHARM—Pharmaceutical Pkgng.—Klockner-Werke AG; *Int'l*, pg. 736

PENTAPRINT—Rigid PVC Film—Klockner-Werke AG; *Int'l*, pg. 736

PENTASOUND—Transparent Plastic Film for Recording Discs—Klockner-Werke AG; *Int'l*, pg. 736

PENTATHERM—Low Smoke Films—Klockner-Werke AG; *Int'l*, pg. 736

PENTAX—Camera Equipment—Asahi Optical Co., Ltd.; *Int'l*, pg. 85

PENTAX—Photo Optical—Pentax Corporation; *Int'l*, pg. 85

PENTAX—Endoscopy Equipment—Pentax Precision Instrument Corp.; *Int'l*, pg. 85

PENTEL R.S.V.P.—Ball Point Pen—Pentel of America, Ltd.; *Int'l*, pg. 1035

PENTENE-1—NONE—Sasol Alpha Olefins; *Int'l*, pg. 1196

PENTHOUSE—Magazine—General Media International Inc.; *U.S. Private*, pg. 444

PENTHOUSE LETTERS—Magazine—General Media International Inc.; *U.S. Private*, pg. 444

PENTHOUSE SKI WEAR—Ski Wear—Reliable Knitting Works; *U.S. Private*, pg. 920

PENTIUM—Microprocessor—Intel Corporation; *U.S. Public*, pg. 886

PENTO—Men's Hair Products—SmithKline Beecham plc; *Int'l*, pg. 1264

PENTON—Magazines—Pittway Corporation; *U.S. Public*, pg. 1305

PENTON EXECUTIVE NETWORK—Periodical—Penton Publishing, Inc.; *U.S. Public*, pg. 1306

PENTONE—Chemicals & Allied Products—West Penetone Corporation; *U.S. Private*, pg. 1158

PENTOTHAL—Thiopental Sodium—Abbott Laboratories; *U.S. Public*, pg. 12

PENTRA-BOND—Dental Bondings—Customedix Corporation; *U.S. Private*, pg. 298

PENTRA-FIL—Dental Fillings—Customedix Corporation; *U.S. Private*, pg. 298

PENTREX—Rosin Esters—Hercules Incorporated; *U.S. Public*, pg. 809

PENTRITOL—Pharmaceuticals—Rhone-Poulenc Rorer - U.S.; *Int'l*, pg. 1110

PENTRON—Automotive Test Equipment—Actron Manufacturing Company; *U.S. Private*, pg. 16

PENTROOF—Motorcycle—American Honda Motor Co., Inc. Motorcycle Division; *Int'l*, pg. 634

PEONY—Interior Walls—Monarch Tile, Inc.; *U.S. Private*, pg. 287

PEOPLE—Magazine—Time Warner Inc.; *U.S. Public*, pg. 1610

PEOPLE MANAGEMENT RESOURCES—Series Of Benchmarking/Best Practices Handbooks—Watson Wyatt Worldwide; *U.S. Private*, pg. 1154

PEOPLE PLEDGED TO EXCELLENCE—NONE—Harrah's Entertainment, Inc.; *U.S. Public*, pg. 790

THE PEOPLE—NONE—Mirror Group plc; *Int'l*, pg. 869

PEOPLE'S CHOICE TV—Wireless Cable TV System—People's Choice TV Corp.; *U.S. Public*, pg. 1274

PEOX—Polymer—The Dow Chemical Company; *U.S. Public*, pg. 522

PEP-BACK—Stimulant Tabs—Alva/Amco Pharmacal Companies, Inc.; *U.S. Private*, pg. 47

PEP BOYS-MANNY, MOE & JACK—Auto Accessories—The Pep Boys-Manny, Moe & Jack; *U.S. Public*, pg. 1276

PEP SET—Foundry Resin—Ashland, Inc.; *U.S. Public*, pg. 138

PEPCID—Famotidine—Merck & Co., Inc.; *U.S. Public*, pg. 1090

PEPCID—Pharmaceutical—Merck Human Health Division (U.S. Human Health); *U.S. Public*, pg. 1091

PEPCO—NONE—Ballard Medical Products; *U.S. Public*, pg. 171

PEPCO—NONE—Potomac Electric Power Company; *U.S. Public*, pg. 1318

PEPE LOPEZ—Tequila—Brown-Forman Beverages Worldwide; *U.S. Public*, pg. 261

PEPE LOPEZ—Tequila—Brown-Forman Corporation; *U.S. Public*, pg. 261

PEPE'S—Pizza—Crestar Food Products, Inc.; *U.S. Public*, pg. 805

PEPITOS—Tortilla Chips—Borden, Inc.; *U.S. Private*, pg. 157

PEPLOMYCIN—Antineoplastic Agents—Nippon Kayaku Co. Ltd.; *Int'l*, pg. 934

PEPPERIDGE FARM—Food Products—Campbell Soup Company; *U.S. Public*, pg. 298

PEPPERIDGE FARM—Baked Goods—Campbell Soup Company Ltd.; *U.S. Public*, pg. 299

PEPPERIDGE FARM—Fresh & Frozen Bakery & Food Products—Pepperidge Farm, Incorporated; *U.S. Public*, pg. 299

PEPPERIDGE FARM AMERICAN COLLECTION—Premium Cookies—Pepperidge Farm, Incorporated; *U.S. Public*, pg. 299

PEPPERIDGE FARM AMERICAN COLLECTION DESSERTS—Frozen Microwavable Desserts—Pepperidge Farm, Incorporated; *U.S. Public*, pg. 299

PEPPERMILL—Prepasted Vinyl Coated Strippable Wallcovering—York Wallcoverings Inc.; *U.S. Private*, pg. 1196

PEPPERMILL GRIND—Black Pepper—McCormick & Company, Incorporated; *U.S. Public*, pg. 1066

PEPPERMINT—Herb Tea—Celestial Seasonings; *U.S. Public*, pg. 319

PEPPERONI GRILL—Restaurant & Bar—Eateries, Inc.; *U.S. Public*, pg. 555

PEPSI—Soft Drink—Buffalo Rock Company; *U.S. Private*, pg. 179

PEPSI—Soft Drink—PepsiCo, Inc.; *U.S. Public*, pg. 1276

PEPSI—Soft Drink—Pepsi-Co. International; *U.S. Public*, pg. 1277

PEPSI-COLA—Soft Drink—Pepsi-Cola Company; *U.S. Public*, pg. 1277

PEPSI-FREE—Caffeine-Free Cola—Pepsi-Cola Company; *U.S. Public*, pg. 1277

PEPSI MAX—Sugar-Free Soft Drink—PepsiCo. Australia Pty. Ltd.; *U.S. Public*, pg. 1277

PEPSODENT—Toothpaste, Toothbrushes—Chesebrough-Pond's USA Co.; *Int'l*, pg. 1435

PEPSODENT WITH BAKING SODA—Toothpaste—Chesebrough-Pond's USA Co.; *Int'l*, pg. 1435

PEPTEIN 2000—Hydrolyzed Animal Protein—Hormel Foods Corp.; *U.S. Public*, pg. 840

PEPTI-FER—Cleaner for Ion-Exchange Resin—Ionics, Incorporated; *U.S. Public*, pg. 912

PEPTO-BISMOL—Stomach Remedy—The Procter & Gamble Company; *U.S. Public*, pg. 1330

PEPTO-BISMOL—NONE—Procter & Gamble Venezuela, C.A.; *U.S. Public*, pg. 1332

PER-LYTE—Neckwear Interlinings—Specialty Textile Products; *U.S. Private*, pg. 1023

PER-SON-ALL—Checking System—Master Craft Corp.; *Int'l*, pg. 267

PERAL—Bonding Agent—Raschig GmbH; *U.S. Private*, pg. 827

PERAMA—Marine Engine—Varity Perkins; *Int'l*, pg. 820

PERC—Protective & Decorative Coatings—Ferro Corporation; *U.S. Public*, pg. 618

PERC—Salt Free Seasonings—Tone Brothers Inc.; *Int'l*, pg. 237

PERCEPTIONS—Hair Spray, Freezing Spray, Shampoo, Conditioner & Spray Gel—DeMert & Dougherty, Inc.; *U.S. Private*, pg. 323

PERCHLORACAP—NONE—Mallinckrodt Inc.; *U.S. Public*, pg. 1039

PERCOGESIC—Analgesic—The Procter & Gamble Company; *U.S. Public*, pg. 1330

PERCOLL—Biotechnology—Pharmacia & Upjohn Adria Laboratories; *Int'l*, pg. 1049

PERCOR—Intra-Aortic Balloon; Percutaneous Introducer for Intra-Aortic Balloon—Datascope Corp.; *U.S. Public*, pg. 487

PERCUCUT—Biopsy Needles—E-Z-Em, Inc.; *U.S. Public*, pg. 540

PERCUGUIDE—Lesion Marking System—E-Z-Em, Inc.; *U.S. Public*, pg. 540

PERCUPASS—Tunneling Tool—Medtronic, Inc.; *U.S. Public*, pg. 1082

PERCUPASS II—Tunneling Tool—Medtronic, Inc.; *U.S. Public*, pg. 1082

PERCUPUMP—Remote Control Injection of Contrast Media—E-Z-Em, Inc.; *U.S. Public*, pg. 540

PERCUSET—Standardized Interventional Procedure Trays—E-Z-Em, Inc.; *U.S. Public*, pg. 540

PERCUVAC—Self-Aspirating Biopsy Needle—E-Z-Em, Inc.; *U.S. Public*, pg. 540

PERDIEM—Laxative—Novartis; *Int'l*, pg. 972

PERDIEM—Laxative—Rhone-Poulenc Rorer - U.S.; *Int'l*, pg. 1110

PERDEIM PLAIN—Laxative—Novartis; *Int'l*, pg. 972

PERDIEM PLAIN—Laxative—Rhone-Poulenc Rorer - U.S.; *Int'l*, pg. 1110

PERDUE—Poultry—Perdue Farms Incorporated; *U.S. Private*, pg. 852

PERDUE DONE IT!—Fully Cooked Poultry Food Line—Perdue Farms Incorporated; *U.S. Private*, pg. 852

PERE MAGLOIRE—Calvados—Paterno Imports Limited; *U.S. Private*, pg. 843

PEREGAL—Textile Auxiliary Chemicals—International Specialty Products, Inc.; *U.S. Public*, pg. 858

PERF4—ERISA Reporting & Performance Measurement—SunGard Data Systems Inc.; *U.S. Public*, pg. 1534

PERFECT SURFACES—NONE—Evans & Sutherland Computer Corporation; *U.S. Public*, pg. 595

PERFAN—Cardiovascular Stimulant—Hoechst Marion Roussel North America; *Int'l*, pg. 625

PERFDESK—Business Product—International Business Machines Corporation; *U.S. Public*, pg. 895

PERFECOPY—Paper—Georgia-Pacific Corporation; *U.S. Public*, pg. 735

PERFECPROOF—Heat Seal Coated Film—Perfecseal Company; *U.S. Public*, pg. 210

PERFECRAFT—Heat Seal Coated Paper—Perfecseal Company; *U.S. Public*, pg. 210

PERFECSEAL—Medical Packaging Products—Perfecseal Company; *U.S. Public*, pg. 210

PERFECT—Barbed Wire—CF & I Steel, L.P.; *U.S. Public*, pg. 1230

PERFECT—Penny Loafers—Lands' End, Inc.; *U.S. Public*, pg. 977

PERFECT—Haircare Appliances—Sunbeam Household Products; *U.S. Public*, pg. 1533

PERFECT BAKE—Cookware—Lechters, Inc.; *U.S. Public*, pg. 983

PERFECT BALANCE—Treatment—Marilyn Miglin, L.P.; *U.S. Private*, pg. 745

PERFECT BALANCE—Blend of Regular & Decaffeinated Coffee—Nestle S.A.; *Int'l*, pg. 915

PERFECT BLEND—Eye Pencils—Cover Girl Cosmetics; *U.S. Public*, pg. 1330

PERFECT CIRCLE—Piston Rings, Pistons, Piston Pins, Camshafts, Cylinder Sleeves, Valve Seals—Dana Corporation; *U.S. Public*, pg. 479

PERFECT CIRCLE—Chassis Parts—Dana Corporation; *U.S. Public*, pg. 479

PERFECT CLIMATE COMFORT CENTER—Climate Control—Honeywell Inc.; *U.S. Public*, pg. 833

PERFECT CONTROL—Hair Care Products—The Wella Corporation; *Int'l*, pg. 1489

PERFECT CONTROL—Perm Products—Wella Group; *Int'l*, pg. 1489

PERFECT-IT—Foam Glaze & Pads—3M; *U.S. Public*, pg. 1604

PERFECT MAIL—NONE—CACI International Inc; *U.S. Public*, pg. 272

PERFECT NIGHT—Mattress & Foundation—Serta, Inc.; *U.S. Private*, pg. 985

PERFECT PROFIT PROGRAM—NONE—Automobile Protection Corporation-APCO; *U.S. Public*, pg. 150

PERFECT SCENTS—Potpourri—M. Kamenstein, Inc.; *U.S. Private*, pg. 606

PERFECT SILHOUETTE—NONE—Victoria's Secret Stores; *U.S. Public*, pg. 995

PERFECT SLEEPER—Mattress & Foundation—Serta, Inc.; *U.S. Private*, pg. 985

PERFECT VALVE—Ceramic Cartridge Valve—Speakman Company; *U.S. Private*, pg. 1021

PERFECTION—Industrial Products—Email Limited; *Int'l*, pg. 450

PERFECTION—Microwavable Pasta Products—Hershey Foods Corporation; *U.S. Public*, pg. 811

PERFECTION—Baby Shoes—Jumping Jacks; *U.S. Private*, pg. 767

PERFECTION—Paints—Masury Paint; *U.S. Public*, pg. 1707

PERFECTION—Office & Stationery Products—Perfecseal Company; *U.S. Public*, pg. 210

PERFECTION—Frozen Baking Products—Perfection Bakeries Inc.; *U.S. Private*, pg. 852

PERFECTION—Gas & Oil Room Heaters & Wall Furnaces—Perfection-Schwank Inc.; *U.S. Private*, pg. 853

PERFECTION—Frozen Foods—Seneca Foods Corporation; *U.S. Public*, pg. 1456

PERFECTION/SCHWANK INFRA-RED—Gas Infra-Red Heaters—Perfection-Schwank Inc.; *U.S. Private*, pg. 853

PERFECTOFFICE—Computer Software—Corel Corporation; *Int'l*, pg. 331

PERFEKTHION—Crop Protection Agent—BASF AG; *Int'l*, pg. 103

PERFELOPE—Continuous Envelopes—Georgia-Pacific Corporation; *U.S. Public*, pg. 735

PERFI-CLEAN—Bathroom & Kitchen Cleaner—Stanhome Inc.; *U.S. Public*, pg. 1508

PERFICURE—Tire Repair—Kex Products, Inc.; *U.S. Private*, pg. 138

PERFICUT—Printing, Converting, Specialty & Wrapping—Georgia-Pacific Corporation; *U.S. Public*, pg. 735

PERFIX—Computer Programs for Linear Accelerators—Varian Associates, Inc.; *U.S. Public*, pg. 1710

PERFLAN—Herbicide—The Dow Chemical Company; *U.S. Public*, pg. 522

PERFO—Synthetic Chamois Leathers—Akzo Nobel N.V.; *Int'l*, pg. 42

PERFO-ROUND—Perforated Panels—Georgia-Pacific Corporation; *U.S. Public*, pg. 735

PERFO-SQUARE—Perforated Panels—Georgia-Pacific Corporation; *U.S. Public*, pg. 735

PERFORM—Bleaching Absorbent—Oil-Dri Corporation of America; *U.S. Public*, pg. 1214

PERFORM—Hair Products—SmithKline Beecham plc; *Int'l*, pg. 1264

PERFORM—Dance/Drill Team—Tighe Industries, Inc.; *U.S. Private*, pg. 1086

PERFORMA—Floor Coverings—Domco Inc.; *Int'l*, pg. 415

PERFORMAGRAPHICS I, II, III—Printing on Corrugated—Boise Cascade Corporation; *U.S. Public*, pg. 242

PERFORMANCE—Hosiery & Related Apparel—Mayer/Berkshire Corporation; *U.S. Private*, pg. 717

PERFORMANCE—Video Game Accessories—Recoton Corporation; *U.S. Public*, pg. 1369

PERFORMANCE BIKES—Magazine—EMAP Nationals; *Int'l*, pg. 451

PERFORMANCE CAR—Magazine—EMAP Nationals; *Int'l*, pg. 451

THE PERFORMANCE CYCLE—Consulting Tool Utilized for Organizational Diagnosis & Re-design—Franklin Covey; *U.S. Public*, pg. 679

PERFORMANCE LINE—Fitness Equipment—Paramount Fitness Corp.; *U.S. Private*, pg. 838

PERFORMANCE-MATCHED—Computer Aided Design Bearing—General Bearing Corp.; *U.S. Public*, pg. 706

PERFORMANCE MONITORS—Quality Control Test—Beckman Instruments, Inc.; *U.S. Public*, pg. 199

Brand Name Index

PERFORMANCE PAC—Electrodes—Beckman Instruments, Inc.; *U.S. Public*, pg. 199

PERFORMANCE PANS—Premium Quality Bakeware—Wilton Industries, Inc.; *U.S. Private*, pg. 1181

PERFORMANCE PLUS—Saw Blades—American Tool Companies, Inc.; *U.S. Private*, pg. 63

PERFORMANCE PLUS—Learning System—National Real Estate Services, Inc.; *Int'l*, pg. 909

PERFORMANCE PLUS—Joist—TJ International, Inc.; *U.S. Public*, pg. 1556

PERFORMANCE PLUS—Corrugated Container—Union Camp Corporation; *U.S. Public*, pg. 1665

PERFORMANCE POLY—Tires—Bridgestone/Firestone, Inc.; *Int'l*, pg. 213

PERFORMANCE RATED—Apparel Wear Warranty—Guilford Mills, Inc.; *U.S. Public*, pg. 768

PERFORMANCE SERIES—Electronic Label Printing Software—Diagraph Corporation; *U.S. Private*, pg. 330

PERFORMANCE SPORTS SYSTEMS—Sporting Goods—Nixdorff Krein Industries Inc.; *U.S. Private*, pg. 799

PERFORMANCE YOU CAN COUNT ON—Dispensing of Natural Gas Via a Pipeline & Transit Dist. of Electricity—Orange and Rockland Utilities, Inc.; *U.S. Public*, pg. 1229

PERFORMANCEEDGE—Business Product—International Business Machines Corporation; *U.S. Public*, pg. 895

PERFORMAPAK I, II, IV, V—Corrugated—Boise Cascade Corporation; *U.S. Public*, pg. 242

PERFORMAX—Printers—Datasouth Computer Corporation; *U.S. Public*, pg. 267

PERFORMAX—Filter—Pall Corporation; *U.S. Public*, pg. 1253

PERFORMER—Manifolds—Edelbrock Corp.; *U.S. Public*, pg. 563

PERFORMER—Racquetball Glove—Ektelon; *U.S. Private*, pg. 884

PERFORMER—Vending Service Body—Hackney and Sons, Inc.; *U.S. Private*, pg. 1097

PERFORMER LINK—Timing Chains—Edelbrock Corp.; *U.S. Public*, pg. 563

PERFORMIK—Automatic Developing System—Konica Corporation; *Int'l*, pg. 748

PERFOWOOD—Perforated Hardboard—Georgia-Pacific Corporation; *U.S. Public*, pg. 735

PERFUSION CHROMATOGRAPHY—Patented Process & Media to Separate Biomolecules Very Quickly—PerSeptive Biosystems, Inc.; *U.S. Public*, pg. 1279

PERGOPAK—Paper Industry Chemicals—Alusuisse-Lonza Holding Ltd.; *Int'l*, pg. 66

PERI-COLACE—NONE—Bristol-Myers Squibb Company; *U.S. Public*, pg. 253

PERI-COLACE—Laxative—Roberts Pharmaceutical Corporation; *U.S. Public*, pg. 1393

PERI-PRO—Automatic X-Ray Film Processor—Air Techniques, Inc.; *U.S. Private*, pg. 28

PERI-COLACE—Laxative with Stool Softener—Bristol-Myers Squibb U.S. Pharmaceutical Group; *U.S. Public*, pg. 255

PERICOM SEMICONDUCTOR—NONE—Interface Electronics Corporation; *U.S. Private*, pg. 567

PERIDENTAL—Oral Hygiene Aid—John O. Butler Co.; *Int'l*, pg. 1320

PERIDEX—Dental Oral Rinse—The Procter & Gamble Company; *U.S. Public*, pg. 1330

PERIDIN-C—Dietary Supplement—Beutlich, L.P.; *U.S. Private*, pg. 141

PERIDUR—Organic Binders for Coal Agglomeration—Akzo Nobel N.V.; *Int'l*, pg. 42

PERIGEE BOOKS—NONE—Berkley Publishing Corp.; *Int'l*, pg. 1027

PERIGORD PRESS—Book Publishing—Bertelsmann AG; *Int'l*, pg. 189

PERIMATE—Plastic Foam Insulation—The Dow Chemical Company; *U.S. Public*, pg. 522

PERIMETER—Mosquito Pesticides—Roussel UCLAF S.A.; *Int'l*, pg. 626

PERIMETERS—Merchandising Wall System—Marlite; *U.S. Private*, pg. 705

PERIO PIC—Toothpick—John O. Butler Co.; *Int'l*, pg. 1320

PERIOD LIVING—U.K. Home Decorating Magazine—EMAP Elan; *Int'l*, pg. 451

PERIODICAL PUBLISHERS' SERVICE BUREAU—Subscriptions—The Hearst Corporation; *U.S. Private*, pg. 515

PERIPHERAL—Auto Sound Accessories—Recoton Corporation; *U.S. Public*, pg. 1369

PERIPORT—NONE—Pfizer Inc.; *U.S. Public*, pg. 1281

PERITRATE—Pharmaceutical Products—Warner-Lambert Company; *U.S. Public*, pg. 1738

PERK—Solvents—Detrex Corporation; *U.S. Public*, pg. 501

PERK-UPS—Greeting Cards, Stationery & Party Goods—American Greetings Corporation; *U.S. Public*, pg. 77

PERKACIT—Polymer Process Chemical—Akzo Nobel N.V.; *Int'l*, pg. 42

PERKADOX—Di-Acyl Peroxides, Aromatic—Akzo Nobel N.V.; *Int'l*, pg. 42

PERKALINK 900—Antireversion Agent for Rubbers—Akzo Nobel N.V.; *Int'l*, pg. 42

PERKARE—Dry Cleaning Solvent—PPG Industries, Inc.; *U.S. Public*, pg. 1245

PERKIN-ELMER—Analytical Instruments & Surface Technology Systems—The Perkin-Elmer Corporation; *U.S. Public*, pg. 1279

PERKINS—Diesel Engines—LucasVarity Inc.; *Int'l*, pg. 820

PERKINS—NONE—LucasVarity plc; *Int'l*, pg. 819

PERKINS—Family Restaurants—Perkins Family Restaurants; *U.S. Private*, pg. 925

PERKINS—Converting & Finishing Machinery & Systems—Standex International Corporation; *U.S. Public*, pg. 1505

PERKINS—Engines—Varity Perkins; *Int'l*, pg. 820

PERKINS BAKERY—NONE—Perkins Family Restaurants; *U.S. Private*, pg. 925

PERKINS ENGINES—Diesel Engines—Valley Detroit Diesel Allison; *U.S. Private*, pg. 1132

PERKINS EXPRESS AND BAKERY—NONE—Perkins Family Restaurants; *U.S. Private*, pg. 925

PERKINS FAMILY RESTAURANT—NONE—Perkins Family Restaurants; *U.S. Private*, pg. 925

PERKINS FAMILY RESTAURANT AND BAKERY—NONE—Perkins Family Restaurants; *U.S. Private*, pg. 925

PERKS—NONE—Countrywide Home Loans Inc.; *U.S. Public*, pg. 452

PERKY PADS—Stationery & Note Pads—American Greetings Corporation; *U.S. Public*, pg. 77

PERL GLASS—Hair Care Product—Wella Group; *Int'l*, pg. 1489

PERLAC—Animal Feed-Mix—Kali-Chemie Aktiengesellschaft; *Int'l*, pg. 1278

PERLATIM—Petrolaliums—Witco Corporation; *U.S. Public*, pg. 1773

PERLE DE BRILLET LIQUEUR—NONE—Carillon Importers, Ltd.; *Int'l*, pg. 409

PERLON—Monofilament Fishing Line—Bayer AG; *Int'l*, pg. 171

PEERLUX VL30 SERIES—Latex Ceiling Paint—Paragon Paint & Varnish Corp.; *U.S. Private*, pg. 838

PERM-A-CLOR—Solvents—Detrex Corporation; *U.S. Public*, pg. 501

PERM-A-KLEEN—Solvents—Detrex Corporation; *U.S. Public*, pg. 501

PERM-COTE—Rust Proofing Compound—Detrex Corporation; *U.S. Public*, pg. 501

PERM LIFE—Permanent-Hair Maintenance Products—Revlon-Realistic Professional Products, Inc.; *U.S. Private*, pg. 690

PERM-REPAIR—Product for Damaged Hair—Pro-Line Corporation; *U.S. Private*, pg. 887

PERM-RUFF—Granulated Grip on PVC Gloves—Jomac, Inc.; *U.S. Private*, pg. 595

PERM-AID—Hair Treatment—Hask Toiletries; *U.S. Private*, pg. 509

PERMA—Storage Products—ACCO World Corporation; *U.S. Public*, pg. 674

PERMA—Slant Cultures—Fisher Scientific Company; *U.S. Private*, pg. 658

PERMA BOND—Super Glue—DAP Inc.; *Int'l*, pg. 1486

PERMA BOND—Footwear—E.J. Footwear Corp.; *U.S. Public*, pg. 1684

PERMA CAST—Biological Supplies—Carolina Biological Supply Co.; *U.S. Private*, pg. 213

PERMA-CLAD—Coatings—The Sherwin-Williams Company; *U.S. Public*, pg. 1465

PERMA-DRILL—Packers—Halliburton Energy Services; *U.S. Public*, pg. 776

PERMA-EZE—Furniture Seat and Back Springs—Leggett & Platt, Incorporated; *U.S. Public*, pg. 985

PERMA-50—Drilling Mud Additive—Georgia-Pacific Corporation; *U.S. Public*, pg. 735

PERMA-FIX PROCESS—NONE—Perma-Fix Environmental Services, Inc.; *U.S. Public*, pg. 1279

PERMA-FLEX STRAW—Plastic Straws—Sweetheart Cup Company Inc.; *U.S. Private*, pg. 1058

PERMA GARD—Welded Wire Fabric—Gilbert & Bennett Manufacturing Company; *U.S. Private*, pg. 453

PERMA-GRIP—Denture Adhesive—Lee Pharmaceuticals; *U.S. Public*, pg. 984

PERMA GRIP—Mattress—Therapedic Associates, Inc.; *U.S. Private*, pg. 1079

PERMA-HAND—Silk Suture—Ethicon, Inc.; *U.S. Public*, pg. 928

PERMA-LACH—Packers—Halliburton Energy Services; *U.S. Public*, pg. 776

PERMA-LOK—Anaerobic Adhesive/Sealants—Permabond International; *Int'l*, pg. 1435

PERMA-MOLD—Release Agent—Chem-Trend Incorporated; *Int'l*, pg. 235

PERMA/MOUNT—Adhesive Mounting Cards—Falcon Safety Products Inc.; *U.S. Private*, pg. 392

PERMA-PAK—Low-Moisture Foods—Vacu-Dry Company; *U.S. Public*, pg. 1704

PERMA-PEL—Feed Binder—Georgia-Pacific Corporation; *U.S. Public*, pg. 735

PERMA-PIPE—Pre-Fabricated Insulated Pipe—MFRI Inc.; *U.S. Public*, pg. 1026

PERMA PLATE—Zinc Plating Process—Attwood Corporation; *U.S. Private*, pg. 1038

PERMA PRODUCTS—NONE—ACCO Brands, Inc.; *U.S. Public*, pg. 674

PERMA PRODUCTS—Corrugated Storage Products—Fortune Brands, Inc.; *U.S. Public*, pg. 674

PERMA PURE—Gas Dryers for Gas Handling & Analysis—Halma p.l.c.; *Int'l*, pg. 589

PERMA-SEAL—Polyvinyl Chloride Jacket—General Cable Corporation; *Int'l*, pg. 1486

PERMA-SEAL—NONE—Molex Incorporated; *U.S. Public*, pg. 1121

PERMA-SEAL—Corrosion & Resistant Coating—Powers Fastening, Inc.; *U.S. Private*, pg. 878

PERMA-SERIES—Packers—Halliburton Energy Services; *U.S. Public*, pg. 776

PERMA SPHERE—Novel Dosage Form—KV Pharmaceutical Company; *U.S. Public*, pg. 941

PERMA STABIL—Encapsulated Oil—Firmenich; *Int'l*, pg. 486

PERMA-THINZ—Well Drilling, Mud Additives—Georgia-Pacific Corporation; *U.S. Public*, pg. 735

PERMA-TREAT—Pressure-Treated Lumber—Coastal Lumber Company; *U.S. Private*, pg. 248

PERMA-TUBE—Golf Bags—Ajay Leisure Products, Inc.; *U.S. Public*, pg. 34

PERMA-WHITE—Bathroom Wall & Ceiling Paint—Wm. Zinsser & Co., Inc.; *U.S. Public*, pg. 1358

PERMA WOOD—Raidiata Pine Treated Timber—Carter Holt Harvey Limited; *U.S. Public*, pg. 904

PERMA-WOOD—Polyethyle-Wood-Like Stats—United Receptical, Inc.; *U.S. Private*, pg. 1123

PERMA-FUSION—Vitamin Hair Treatment—Hask Toiletries; *U.S. Private*, pg. 509

PERMA-LEAF—Aluminum Pigment Paste—Reynolds Metals Company; *U.S. Public*, pg. 1385

PERMABOND—Cyanocrylate Adhesives—Permabond International; *Int'l*, pg. 1435

PERMACEL—Industrial Tapes—Permacel; *Int'l*, pg. 950

PERMACELL—Cathodic Protection—Corrpro Companies, Inc.; *U.S. Public*, pg. 451

PERMACHROME—TV Tube Mechanisms—Thomson Consumer Electronics Inc.; *Int'l*, pg. 1383

PERMACOLOR—Carpet Warranties—Amoco Corporation; *U.S. Public*, pg. 101

PERMACOUPLE—Heat-Shrinkable Tube Couplings—Raychem Corporation; *U.S. Public*, pg. 1362

PERMADIE—Die Blocks—McInnes Steel Company; *U.S. Private*, pg. 722

PERMADIZED—Bonded Rubber Seals—Hutchenson Seal Corporation; *U.S. Private*, pg. 550

PERMAFLEX—Soft Flexible Wear Contact Lens—The Cooper Companies, Inc.; *U.S. Public*, pg. 442

PERMAFLEX—Cloth Covered Hardsided Luggage—Lark Luggage Company, Inc.; *U.S. Public*, pg. 1430

PERMAFLEX NATURALS—Flexible-Wear Soft Contact Lens—The Cooper Companies, Inc.; *U.S. Public*, pg. 442

PERMAFLEX THIN—Flexible-Wear Soft Contact Lens—The Cooper Companies, Inc.; *U.S. Public*, pg. 442

PERMAFLEX UV NATURALS—Flexible-Wear Soft Contact Lens—The Cooper Companies, Inc.; *U.S. Public*, pg. 442

PERMAFLUOR E—Pseudocumene-Based Cocktail—Packard Instrument Co., Inc.; *U.S. Private*, pg. 833

PERMAFLUOR V—Toluene-Based Cocktail—Packard Instrument Co., Inc.; *U.S. Private*, pg. 833

PERMAFUSE—Fusion-Bonded Epoxy Coating for Valves—United States Pipe & Foundry Company, Inc.; *U.S. Public*, pg. 1736

PERMAG—Magnetic Materials—The Dexter Corporation; *U.S. Public*, pg. 504

PERMAGARD—Lumber & Wood Products—Georgia-Pacific Corporation; *U.S. Public*, pg. 735

PERMAGLAS—Water Heaters, Industrial Dry Storage—A.O. Smith Corporation; *U.S. Public*, pg. 1476

PERMAGRAPHIC—Photo Typesetters—AGFA EPS Division; *Int'l*, pg. 172

PERMAGRID—Wet Deck Surface—Baltimore Aircoil Company; *U.S. Private*, pg. 68

PERMAGRID—Ceramic Tile Fill—Justin Industries, Inc.; *U.S. Public*, pg. 936

PERMAGRIP—Roofing Insulation—BMCA Insulation Products, Inc.; *U.S. Private*, pg. 433

PERMALATOR, PLASTEEL, FLEXNET—Bedding Insulators—Leggett & Platt, Incorporated; *U.S. Public*, pg. 985

PERMALBA—Art Materials—Martin/F. Weber Company; *U.S. Private*, pg. 710

PERMALENS—Flexible-Wear Soft Contact Lens—The Cooper Companies, Inc.; *U.S. Public*, pg. 442

PERMALENS—Stylized Soft Flexible Wear Contaxct Lens—The Cooper Companies, Inc.; *U.S. Public*, pg. 442

PERMALENS APHAKIC—Soft, Specialty Wear Contact Lens—The Cooper Companies, Inc.; *U.S. Public*, pg. 442

PERMALENS THERAPEUTIC—Soft, Specialty Wear Contact Lens—The Cooper Companies, Inc.; *U.S. Public*, pg. 442

PERMALENS XL—Flexible-Wear Soft Contact Lens—The Cooper Companies, Inc.; *U.S. Public*, pg. 442

PERMALINE—Electrical Wire & Cable—General Cable Corporation; *Int'l*, pg. 1486

PERMALITE—Optical Lens—American Optical Corporation; *U.S. Public*, pg. 60

PERMALITE—Perlite Roof Insulation Prods.—BMCA Insulation Products, Inc.; *U.S. Private*, pg. 433

PERMALITE—Cooling Towers—Baltimore Aircoil Company; *U.S. Private*, pg. 68

PERMALITE—Cooling Towers—Justin Industries, Inc.; *U.S. Public*, pg. 936

PERMALITE—Luggage—Lark Luggage Company, Inc.; *U.S. Public*, pg. 1430

PERMALIZE—Paint—Pratt & Lambert United, Inc.; *U.S. Public*, pg. 1466

PERMALOK—Tool Holders—Rogers Tool Works, Inc.; *U.S. Public*, pg. 950

PERMALUBE—Motor Oil—Amoco Corporation; *U.S. Public*, pg. 101

PERMALUM—Architectural Product—Hunter Douglas N.V.; *Int'l*, pg. 639

PERMALUME—NONE—Pfizer Inc.; *U.S. Public*, pg. 1281

PERMALYN—Synthetic Resin—Hercules Incorporated; *U.S. Public*, pg. 809

PERMAMATIC—Luggage—Lark Luggage Company, Inc.; *U.S. Public*, pg. 1430

PERMANENT WAVE INSURANCE—Permanent Enhancer—Redmond Products, Inc.; *U.S. Public*, pg. 254

PERMANENTE—Cement—Kaiser Cement Corporation; *Int'l*, pg. 593

PERMANITE—NONE—The Flexitallic Group, Inc.; *U.S. Private*, pg. 413

PERMANITE—Mortar—Koch Engineering Company, Inc.; *U.S. Private*, pg. 628

PERMANIZER PLUS—Wood-Treating Coating—PPG Industries, Inc.; *U.S. Public*, pg. 1245

PERMANODE—Cathodic Protection—Corrpro Companies, Inc.; *U.S. Public*, pg. 451

PERMANONE—Insecticide—Roussel Corporation; *Int'l*, pg. 625

PERMAPANNEL—Exterior House Cladding—Carter Holt Harvey Limited; *U.S. Public*, pg. 904

PERMAPOL—Specialty Polymers—Courtaulds Aerospace; *Int'l*, pg. 339

PERMARAD—Anode Lead Wire—Raychem Corporation; *U.S. Public*, pg. 1362

PERMAROOF—Roof Coating—RPM, Inc.; *U.S. Public*, pg. 1356

PERMAS—Weights—Fisher Scientific Company; *U.S. Private*, pg. 658

PERMASCALE—Flat Film—Dietzgen Corporation; *U.S. Private*, pg. 332

PERMASEAL—Plug Valve—DEZurik; *U.S. Public*, pg. 726

PERMASHIELD—Insulated Wire—The Kerite Company; *U.S. Public*, pg. 844

PERMASOLE—Men's Shoes—E.J. Footwear Corp.; *U.S. Public*, pg. 1684

PERMASTAT—Film Support—Eastman Kodak Company; *U.S. Public*, pg. 550

PERMATEX—Photo Processing Chemicals—Eastman Kodak Company; *U.S. Public*, pg. 550

PERMATEX—Super Weatherstrip Adhesive—Loctite Corp. North American Group; *Int'l*, pg. 611

PERMATHENE—Hair Care Prods.—CCA Industries, Inc.; *U.S. Public*, pg. 276

PERMATILE—Polyurethane High Gloss Paint—Buten, Division of Duron; *U.S. Private*, pg. 349

PERMATOX 10-S—Industrial Wood Preservative—ISK BioSciences; *Int'l*, pg. 689

PERMATRAK—Tools—American Machine & Tool Company, Inc.; *U.S. Private*, pg. 58

PERMATRAN-W—Device that Determines Water Transmission Rates thru Barrier Materials—Modern Controls, Inc.; *U.S. Public*, pg. 1120

PERMATREAT—Conversion Coating for Metals—BetzDearborn Inc.; *U.S. Public*, pg. 226

PERMAVIVE TECHNICARE—Hair Color—Cosmair, Inc.; *Int'l*, pg. 818

PERMAX—NONE—Elan Corporation Plc; *Int'l*, pg. 435

PERMAX—NONE—Eli Lilly and Company; *U.S. Public*, pg. 992

PERMABASE—Bedplate—Goulds Pumps, Incorporated; *U.S. Public*, pg. 860

PERMESSENTIALS—Hair Care Products—DeMert & Dougherty, Inc.; *U.S. Private*, pg. 323

PERMILAN—Plant Protectives—DSM Chemie Linz GmbH; *Int'l*, pg. 356

PERMIX—Herbicide—The Dow Chemical Company; *U.S. Public*, pg. 522

PERMIXON—Treatment of Prostatic Disorders—SmithKline Beecham plc; *Int'l*, pg. 1264

PERMOUNT—Mounting Medium—Fisher Scientific Company; *U.S. Private*, pg. 658

PERMUTIT—Water Treatment Equip.—U.S. Filter/Permutit; *U.S. Public*, pg. 1682

PERMYL—Ultraviolet Absorber—Ferro Corporation; *U.S. Public*, pg. 618

PERNOD—Anis—Groupe Pernod Ricard; *Int'l*, pg. 566

PERNOX—Acne Cleanser & Shampoo for Oily Hair—Westwood-Squibb Pharmaceuticals Inc.; *U.S. Public*, pg. 255

PERNYZOL—Metronidazole Gel—Recordati Industria Chimica e Farmaceutica S.p.A.; *Int'l*, pg. 1090

PERONI—Italian Beer—Barton Beers, Ltd.; *U.S. Public*, pg. 300

PERONI—Italian Beer—Barton Incorporated; *U.S. Public*, pg. 300

PERONI—Beer—Danone Group; *Int'l*, pg. 379

PEROX—Dyes for Plastics—Morton International Inc.; *U.S. Public*, pg. 1135

PEROX-SERV—NONE—Vulcan Chemicals; *U.S. Public*, pg. 1725

PEROXYL—First Aid Rinse—Colgate Oral Pharmaceutical; *U.S. Public*, pg. 397

PERRIER—Mineral Water—Eckes AG; *Int'l*, pg. 432

PERRIER—Mineral Water—Nestle S.A.; *Int'l*, pg. 915

PERRIER—Mineral Water—The Perrier Group of America; *Int'l*, pg. 919

PERRIER JOUET—Wine—Pacific Wine Co.; *U.S. Private*, pg. 843

PERRIER-JOUET—Champagne—Seagram Chateau & Estate Wines Co.; *Int'l*, pg. 1215

PERRIER-JOVET—Champagnes—Joseph E. Seagram & Sons, Inc.; *Int'l*, pg. 1215

PERRINE—Fly Boxes—Blount International, Inc.; *U.S. Public*, pg. 237

PERRINE—Fly Boxes—Orbex Inc.; *U.S. Public*, pg. 238

PERRY & DERRICK—Paint—Perry & Derrick Co.; *U.S. Private*, pg. 854

PERRY ELLIS—Men's Apparel—Genesco Inc.; *U.S. Public*, pg. 728

PERRY ELLIS—Men's Tailored Clothing—Hartmarx Corporation; *U.S. Public*, pg. 795

PERRY ELLIS—Sleepwear—Host Apparel, Inc.; *U.S. Public*, pg. 540

PERRY ELLIS—Men's Wear—The Manhattan Shirt Co.; *U.S. Public*, pg. 1429

PERRY ELLIS—NONE—Members Only By Europe Craft; *U.S. Public*, pg. 129

PERRY ELLIS—Fragrances—Parlux Fragrances Inc.; *U.S. Public*, pg. 1264

PERRY ELLIS—Clothing—Salant Corporation; *U.S. Public*, pg. 1429

PERRY ELLIS—Formalwear For Men—West Mill Clothes, Inc.; *U.S. Private*, pg. 1163

PERRY ELLIS AMERICA—Men's Apparel—Genesco Inc.; *U.S. Public*, pg. 728

PERRY ELLIS HOSIERY—Hosiery—Arrow Shirt Company; *Int'l*, pg. 194

PERRY ELLIS PORTFOLIO—Men's Apparel—Genesco Inc.; *U.S. Public*, pg. 728

PERRY ELLIS PORTFOLIO—Men's Tailored Clothing—Hartmarx Corporation; *U.S. Public*, pg. 795

FRED PERRY—Athletic Shoes—Etonic Tretorn; *U.S. Private*, pg. 629

PERRY'S—Ice Cream—Perry's Ice Cream Co., Inc.; *U.S. Private*, pg. 855

PERSANTINE—Platelet-Aggregation Inhibitor—Boehringer Ingelheim GmbH; *Int'l*, pg. 199

PERSANTINE—Cardiac Drug—Boehringer Ingelheim Pharmaceuticals, Inc.; *Int'l*, pg. 199

PERSEC—Chemical—Vulcan Chemicals; *U.S. Public*, pg. 1725

PERSIA—Interior Walls & Floors—Monarch Tile, Inc.; *U.S. Private*, pg. 287

PERSIL—Wash Powder—Henkel KGaA; *Int'l*, pg. 609

PERSIL LIQUID—Washing Product—Unilever Plc; *Int'l*, pg. 1433

PERSON TO PERSON—Business Product—International Business Machines Corporation; *U.S. Public*, pg. 895

PERSON TO PERSON/2—Business Product—International Business Machines Corporation; *U.S. Public*, pg. 895

PERSONA-PHONE—Personal Listening Device—Telex Communications, Inc.; *U.S. Private*, pg. 1074

PERSONAL—Chromatograph—Beckman Instruments, Inc.; *U.S. Public*, pg. 199

PERSONAL—Computer Products—Imaging Technologies Corp.; *U.S. Public*, pg. 870

PERSONAL—Women's Clothing—The Leslie Fay Companies, Inc.; *U.S. Public*, pg. 989

PERSONAL CMM—NONE—Brown & Sharpe Manufacturing Company; *U.S. Public*, pg. 260

PERSONAL CARD—NONE—American Express Service Europe Ltd.; *U.S. Public*, pg. 74

PERSONAL CHOICE—Men's Apparel—Blair Corporation; *U.S. Public*, pg. 236

PERSONAL CHOICE—Health, Beauty & Food—Fred Meyer Stores; *U.S. Public*, pg. 1103

PERSONAL CHOICE—Health & Beauty—Fred Meyer Stores; *U.S. Public*, pg. 1103

Brand Name Index

PERSONAL CHOICE PROGRAM—Weight Loss Program—Weight Watchers International, Inc.; *U.S. Public*, pg. 806

PERSONAL COMPUTER AT—Computer—International Business Machines Corporation; *U.S. Public*, pg. 895

PERSONAL COMPUTER NETWORK SERVICES—Local Area Network Integration Hardware & Software for MS-DOS PCs—Datapoint Corporation; *Int'l*, pg. 384

PERSONAL COMPUTER XT—Computer—International Business Machines Corporation; *U.S. Public*, pg. 895

PERSONAL DECISION SERIES—Business Product—International Business Machines Corporation; *U.S. Public*, pg. 895

PERSONAL FINANCE—Financial Newsletter—KCI Communications, Inc; *U.S. Private*, pg. 784

PERSONAL INTELLIGENT COMMUNICATOR—Electronic Pocket Organizer—Panasonic Consumer Electric Co.; *Int'l*, pg. 847

PERSONAL LAB—NONE—BioChem Pharma Inc.; *Int'l*, pg. 196

PERSONAL MEDICAL MANAGEMENT—HMO Product—Qual-Med, Inc.; *U.S. Public*, pg. 678

PERSONAL NIU—Network Interface Unit—Tandem Computers Inc.; *U.S. Public*, pg. 417

PERSONAL POST OFFICE—NONE—Pitney Bowes Inc.; *U.S. Public*, pg. 1303

PERSONAL PROTECTOR—A Package Policy that Covers Auto, Home, Boat & Recreational Vehicles—Peerless Insurance Company; *Int'l*, pg. 648

PERSONAL SAFETY SIREN—NONE—Remington Products Company, L.L.C.; *U.S. Private*, pg. 921

PERSONAL SCIENCE LABORATORY—Computer Product—International Business Machines Corporation; *U.S. Public*, pg. 895

PERSONAL SECURITY—Computer Product—International Business Machines Corporation; *U.S. Public*, pg. 895

PERSONAL SHOWERS—Hand Held & Wall Mounted Showers—Alsons Corporation; *U.S. Public*, pg. 1053

PERSONAL SYSTEM/1—Computer—International Business Machines Corporation; *U.S. Public*, pg. 895

PERSONAL SYSTEM/2—Computer—International Business Machines Corporation; *U.S. Public*, pg. 895

PERSONAL TOUCH—Catalog Sales of Personalized Paper & Gift Items—Artistic Greetings, Inc.; *U.S. Public*, pg. 136

PERSONAL TOUCH—Shaving System—Warner-Lambert Company; *U.S. Public*, pg. 1738

PERSONAL TOUCH—Woman's Permanent Razor—Warner-Lambert Shaving Products Group; *U.S. Public*, pg. 1739

PERSONALITY FONTS—NONE—Broderbund Software, Inc.; *U.S. Public*, pg. 258

PERSONALIZED LEARNING SERIES—Business Product—International Business Machines Corporation; *U.S. Public*, pg. 895

PERSONALIZED PROFILE—Characteristics Assessment—Nutri/System Inc.; *U.S. Private*, pg. 859

PERSONATOR—Microcomputer Software for US Mailers—Group 1 Software, Inc.; *U.S. Public*, pg. 417

PERSONNA—Shavers—American Safety Razor Company; *U.S. Private*, pg. 597

PERSONNELLE—Cosmetics; Home, Health, & Beauty Products—The Jean Coutu Group (PJC) Inc.; *Int'l*, pg. 340

PERSPEX CP—Cell Cast Acylic in Colors, Textures & Shapes—ICI Acrylics Inc.; *Int'l*, pg. 663

PERSYST—Computer Equipment—Emulex Corporation; *U.S. Public*, pg. 579

PERT—Shampoo—The Procter & Gamble Company; *U.S. Public*, pg. 1330

PERT FOR KIDS—Shampoo—The Procter & Gamble Company; *U.S. Public*, pg. 1330

PERT PLUS—Combination Shampoo & Conditioner—The Procter & Gamble Company; *U.S. Public*, pg. 1330

PERT PLUS EXTRA—Shampoo—The Procter & Gamble Company; *U.S. Public*, pg. 1330

PERTOFRANE—Pharmaceuticals—Rhone-Poulenc Rorer - U.S.; *Int'l*, pg. 1110

PERTUSSIN—Cough Treatment—SmithKline Beecham plc; *Int'l*, pg. 1264

PERUGINA—Chocolate—Nestle USA; *Int'l*, pg. 916

PERUGINA—Chocolates—Perugina Brands of America; *Int'l*, pg. 917

PERUGINA BACI—NONE—Nestle USA; *Int'l*, pg. 916

PERUGINA CHOCOLATE & CONFECTIONS—Candy—Nestle Chocolate & Confection; *Int'l*, pg. 917

PERUGINA GIANDUIA—NONE—Nestle USA; *Int'l*, pg. 916

PERUGINA ORE LIETE—NONE—Nestle USA; *Int'l*, pg. 916

PERUNA—Tonic & Tablets—Benjamin Ansehl Company; *U.S. Private*, pg. 75

PESCA ALTO MAR—Brazilian Lobstertails—Mitsui Foods, Inc.; *Int'l*, pg. 879

PESCALASE—Filtering Aid for Fish Processing—Royal Gist-Brocades N.V.; *Int'l*, pg. 1142

PESCHEL—Voltage Regulator & Variable Transformer—Hipotronics, Inc.; *U.S. Public*, pg. 844

PEST CONTROL—Trade Periodical—Advanstar Communications; *U.S. Private*, pg. 22

PEST DUCT—Armored Polyethylene Duct—Tamaqua Cable Products Corp.; *Int'l*, pg. 417

PESTA—Pickles—Dean Foods Company; *U.S. Public*, pg. 489

PESTA—Food Products—Dean Pickle & Specialty Products Co.; *U.S. Public*, pg. 490

PET—Ice Cream & Dairy Prods.—Land-O-Sun Dairies, Inc.; *U.S. Private*, pg. 646

PET—Evaporated Milk—The Pillsbury Company; *Int'l*, pg. 411

PET CLUB—Pet Products—Topco Associates, Inc.; *U.S. Private*, pg. 1091

PET LIFE—Dog & Cat Food, Biscuits & Treats—Pet Life Foods, Inc.; *U.S. Private*, pg. 856

PET LIGHT PREMIUM—Ice Milk—The Pillsbury Company; *Int'l*, pg. 411

PET PRODUCT MARKETING—Pet Trade Magazine—EMAP Pursuit Publishing; *Int'l*, pg. 451

PET RITZ—Frozen Dessert Foods—The Pillsbury Company; *Int'l*, pg. 411

PET RITZ HOMEMADE STYLE—Pie Crusts—The Pillsbury Company; *Int'l*, pg. 411

PET-TABS—Feed Additives—SmithKline Beecham Corporation; *Int'l*, pg. 1264

PET-TABS—Animal Health Product—SmithKline Beecham plc; *Int'l*, pg. 1264

PET TREATS—Dog & Cat Snacks—Nestle S.A.; *Int'l*, pg. 915

PETAL FRESH—Skin Care—Levlad, Inc.; *U.S. Private*, pg. 663

PETBOOK—Travel Guide Book For Persons Traveling With Pets—American Automobile Association; *U.S. Private*, pg. 50

PETCO—Fishing and Rental Tools—Weatherford U.S., Inc.; *U.S. Public*, pg. 1749

PETE'S BEST—NONE—Stadelman Fruit L.L.C.; *U.S. Private*, pg. 1028

PETE'S WICKED MAPLE PORTER—Sweet Maple Aroma & Roasted Malt—Pete's Brewing Company; *U.S. Public*, pg. 1280

PETE'S WICKED MULTI GRAIN—Blend of Oats, Rye, Wheat & Barley Witha Copper Color and subtle Sweetness—Pete's Brewing Company; *U.S. Public*, pg. 1280

PETER—Chocolate & Confectionery—Nestle S.A.; *Int'l*, pg. 915

PETER DOMINIC—Off-License Liquor Stores—Whitbread PLC; *Int'l*, pg. 1498

PETER ECKRICH—Deli Meats—ConAgra, Inc.; *U.S. Public*, pg. 425

PETER ENGLAND—Clothing—Cliftex; *U.S. Public*, pg. 1777

PETER ENGLAND—Sportswear—The Richman Brothers Co.; *U.S. Public*, pg. 1777

PETER JACKSON—Cigarettes—Philip Morris Companies Inc.; *U.S. Public*, pg. 1287

PETER PAK—Shrink Film & Systems—Paper Enterprises, Inc.; *U.S. Private*, pg. 837

PETER PAN—Peanut Butter—ConAgra, Inc.; *U.S. Public*, pg. 425

PETER PAN—Peanut Butter—Hunt-Wesson, Inc.; *U.S. Public*, pg. 428

PETER PAN—Bus Lines—Peter Pan Bus Lines, Inc.; *U.S. Private*, pg. 856

PETER PAN—Canned Salmon—Peter Pan Seafoods, Inc.; *Int'l*, pg. 928

PETER PAN SEAFOODS—Frozen Products—Peter Pan Seafoods, Inc.; *Int'l*, pg. 928

PETER PIPER—Pickles—Dean Foods Company; *U.S. Public*, pg. 489

PETER PIPER—Pickles—Dean Pickle & Specialty Products Co.; *U.S. Public*, pg. 490

PETER STUYVESANT—Cigarettes—Rothmans UK Holdings Limited; *Int'l*, pg. 1129

PETERBILT—Trucks & Tractors—Great Lakes Peterbilt, GMC; *U.S. Private*, pg. 475

PETERBILT—Trucks—Paccar Inc.; *U.S. Public*, pg. 1246

PETERBILT—Logo—Peterbilt Motors Co.; *U.S. Public*, pg. 1247

PETERS—Ice Cream Products—Peters & Brownes Foods Ltd.; *Int'l*, pg. 1040

PETERS—Ammunition—Remington Arms Company, Inc.; *U.S. Private*, pg. 921

PETER'S BROC—NONE—Nestle USA; *Int'l*, pg. 916

PETER'S BROKEN ORINOCO—NONE—Nestle USA; *Int'l*, pg. 916

PETER'S BURGUNDY—NONE—Nestle USA; *Int'l*, pg. 916

PETER'S CHATHAM—NONE—Nestle USA; *Int'l*, pg. 916

PETER'S CHOCOLATE—Candy—Nestle Chocolate & Confection; *Int'l*, pg. 917

PETER'S COMMANDER—NONE—Nestle USA; *Int'l*, pg. 916

PETER'S CREMA—NONE—Nestle USA; *Int'l*, pg. 916

PETER'S GIBRALTAR—NONE—Nestle USA; *Int'l*, pg. 916

PETER'S GLENMERE—NONE—Nestle USA; *Int'l*, pg. 916

PETER'S HAMILTON—NONE—Nestle USA; *Int'l*, pg. 916

PETER'S HERITAGE—NONE—Nestle USA; *Int'l*, pg. 916

PETER'S JEWEL—NONE—Nestle USA; *Int'l*, pg. 916

PETER'S MADISON—NONE—Nestle USA; *Int'l*, pg. 916

PETER'S MASTERPIECE—NONE—Nestle USA; *Int'l*, pg. 916

PETER'S MONOGRAM—NONE—Nestle USA; *Int'l*, pg. 916

PETER'S MONTEREY—NONE—Nestle USA; *Int'l*, pg. 916

PETER'S NEWPORT—NONE—Nestle USA; *Int'l*, pg. 916

PETER'S NO. 23—NONE—Nestle USA; *Int'l*, pg. 916

PETER'S PHOENIX—NONE—Nestle USA; *Int'l*, pg. 916

PETER'S RED GLO—NONE—Nestle USA; *Int'l*, pg. 916

PETER'S SUPERFINE—NONE—Nestle USA; *Int'l*, pg. 916

PETER'S ULTRA—NONE—Nestle USA; *Int'l*, pg. 916

PETER'S VIKING—NONE—Nestle USA; *Int'l*, pg. 916

PETER'S ZENDA—NONE—Nestle USA; *Int'l*, pg. 916

PETERSON'S—Retail/Gift/Premium—Fairmont Snack Group, Inc.; *U.S. Private*, pg. 392

PETE'S WICKED ALE—Specialty Beer—Pete's Brewing Company; *U.S. Public*, pg. 1280

PETE'S WICKED AMBER ALE—Formally Known as Pete's Wicked Red—Pete's Brewing Company; *U.S. Public*, pg. 1280

PETE'S WICKED BOHEMIAN PILSNER—Golden Brew w/ Spicy Czech Saaz Hops—Pete's Brewing Company; *U.S. Public*, pg. 1280

PETE'S WICKED HONEY WHEAT—A Touch Of Honey Enchances The Depth Of The Beer—Pete's Brewing Company; *U.S. Public*, pg. 1280

PETE'S WICKED OKTOBERFEST—NONE—Pete's Brewing Company; *U.S. Public*, pg. 1280

PETE'S WICKED PALE ALE—Color and Initially Sweet Yet Spicy With a Lingering Bitter Finish—Pete's Brewing Company; *U.S. Public*, pg. 1280

PETE'S WICKED SPRINGFEST—NONE—Pete's Brewing Company; *U.S. Public*, pg. 1280

PETE'S WICKED STRAWBERRY BLONDE—NONE—Pete's Brewing Company; *U.S. Public*, pg. 1280

PETE'S WICKED SUMMER BREW—NONE—Pete's Brewing Company; *U.S. Public*, pg. 1280

PETE'S WICKED WINTER BREW—NONE—Pete's Brewing Company; *U.S. Public*, pg. 1280

PETEX—Monofilament Polyester-Textile Printing—Tetko, Inc.; *U.S. Private*, pg. 1078

PETIT ASSORT—Chocolate—Meiji Seika Kaisha, Ltd.; *Int'l*, pg. 855

PETIT BABINA—Baby Food—Morinaga Milk Industry Co., Ltd.; *Int'l*, pg. 895

PETIT CHERI—Baby Care Products—Sara Lee Corporation; *U.S. Public*, pg. 1432

PETIT CHOSE—Cheese—BG SAS; *Int'l*, pg. 201

PETIT-POINT CLASSICS—Area Rugs—Couristan Inc.; *U.S. Private*, pg. 279

PETITBON'S AMERICAN GRILL & BAR—Restaurant—Guest Services, Inc.; *U.S. Private*, pg. 486

PETITE—In the Canal Hearing Aid—Beltone Electronics Corporation; *U.S. Private*, pg. 132

PETITE—French Sparkling Liqueur—Schieffelin & Somerset Co.; *Int'l*, pg. 412

PETITE PLUS—In-The-Canal Hearing Aid—Beltone Electronics Corporation; *U.S. Private*, pg. 132

PETITES BY MISS ELLIETTE—Petite Social Occasion—Vivian & Elliette, Inc.; *U.S. Private*, pg. 1142

PETRA—Engineering Plastic—AlliedSignal Inc.; *U.S. Public*, pg. 49

PETREX—Synthetic Resin—Hercules Incorporated; *U.S. Public*, pg. 809

PETRI BRAVO—Table Wines—The Beverage Source, Inc.; *U.S. Public*, pg. 591

PETRI-PAD—Unit—Millipore Corporation; *U.S. Public*, pg. 1112

PETRIE—NONE—Petrie Retail, Inc.; *U.S. Private*, pg. 858

PETRIFILM—Microbiological Pour Plate—3M; *U.S. Public*, pg. 1604

PETRO—Anionic Surfactants—DeSoto Inc.; *U.S. Public*, pg. 956

PETRO—Dispersants—Witco Corporation; *U.S. Public*, pg. 1773

PETRO BELT—Gasoline Skimmer—Ferguson International, Inc.; *U.S. Private*, pg. 401

PETRO-CANADA—Gasolines—Petro-Canada; *Int'l*, pg. 1041

PETRO-PASS—Truck Fueling Facilities—Petro-Canada; *Int'l*, pg. 1041

PETRO-REZ—NONE—Lawter International, Inc.; *U.S. Public*, pg. 980

PETRO-TECH—NONE—Western Atlas Logging Services; *U.S. Public*, pg. 1757

PETRO-THIN—Petrographic Polishing & Grinding Device—Buehler, Limited; *U.S. Public*, pg. 574

PETRO-CHEM—NONE—Petro Chem Development Company; *U.S. Private*, pg. 858

PETROCLEAN—Technology for the On-Site Bioremediation of Soil & Groundwater—CILCORP Inc.; *U.S. Public*, pg. 367

PETROCOUNT IMS—Control Measurement—Brooks Instrument; *U.S. Public*, pg. 574

PETRODYNE PRODUCTS—Petrochemical & Oilfield Equipment—The Oilgear Company; *U.S. Public*, pg. 1215

PETROFLO—Petroleum Process Additives—BetzDearborn Inc.; *U.S. Public*, pg. 226

PETROGAS—Liquid Propane Gas Dist.—Energy West Inc.; *U.S. Public*, pg. 581

PETROL-MIZER—Ball Valve-Petroleum—Worcester Controls Corp.; *Int'l*, pg. 128

PETROLAM—NONE—Chemfab Corporation; *U.S. Public*, pg. 344

PETROMAT—Paving Reinforcement Fabric—Amoco Chemicals; *U.S. Public*, pg. 102

PETROMEEN—Product Inhibitor—BetzDearborn Inc.; *U.S. Public*, pg. 226

PETRONET—Conveyance of Petroleum Products—Transnet Ltd.; *Int'l*, pg. 1417

PETRONOR—Oil & Gas Distribution—Repsol S.A.; *Int'l*, pg. 1104

PETROPOLIS—Mineral Water—Nestle S.A.; *Int'l*, pg. 915

PETROSORB—Filter Cartridge—Pall Corporation; *U.S. Public*, pg. 1253

PETROTHENE—High, Low & Linear Density Polyethylene Resins—Millennium Petrochemicals, Inc.; *Int'l*, pg. 594

PETROTHENE XL—Cross-Linkable Polyethylene Resins—Millennium Petrochemicals, Inc.; *Int'l*, pg. 594

PETROTITE—Underground Tank Testing System—Heath Consultants Incorporated; *U.S. Private*, pg. 518

PETROTRACE—Downhole Heater—Raychem Corporation; *U.S. Public*, pg. 1362

PETROWET—Surfactants—Du Pont (E.I. Du Pont De Nemours & Co.); *U.S. Public*, pg. 530

PETROWORKS—NONE—Landmark Graphics Corporation; *U.S. Public*, pg. 776

PETS FOR PEOPLE—NONE—Ralston Purina Company; *U.S. Public*, pg. 1359

PETTIBONE KRANE—Hydraulic Cranes and Parts—Pettibone Corporation; *U.S. Private*, pg. 859

PETTIBONE MERCURY—Fork Lift and Tow Tractors & Parts—Pettibone Corporation; *U.S. Private*, pg. 859

PETTIBONE MICHIGAN—Extendable Forklifts—Pettibone Corporation; *U.S. Private*, pg. 859

PETTIJOHN'S—Rolled Wheat—The Quaker Oats Company; *U.S. Public*, pg. 1347

PETTIT—Marine Coatings—RPM, Inc.; *U.S. Public*, pg. 1356

PEUGEOT—Automobile—Peugeot Motors of America Inc.; *Int'l*, pg. 1020

PEUGEOT—Automobile—Peugeot S.A.; *Int'l*, pg. 1020

PEVELY—Dairy Products—Pevely Dairy Company; *U.S. Private*, pg. 879

PEWTER OAK—Wood & Lumber Products—Georgia-Pacific Corporation; *U.S. Public*, pg. 735

PEXALYN—Synthetic Resin—Hercules Incorporated; *U.S. Public*, pg. 809

PEXITE—Wood Rosin—Hercules Incorporated; *U.S. Public*, pg. 809

PEXOL—Rosin Size—Hercules Incorporated; *U.S. Public*, pg. 809

PEYTON'S—Meat Products—John Morrell & Co.; *U.S. Public*, pg. 1479

PEZ—NONE—Cruspi S.A.; *Int'l*, pg. 348

THE PFABULOUS PFAUCET WITH THE PFUNNY NAME—Faucets—The Black & Decker Corporation; *U.S. Public*, pg. 233

PFAFF—NONE—Semi-Tech Corporation; *Int'l*, pg. 1220

PFANNI—Potato Products—Bestfoods; *U.S. Public*, pg. 223

PFAUDLER—Glass Lined Reactor Vessels—Robbins & Myers, Inc.; *U.S. Public*, pg. 1393

PFEIFFER—Salad Dressings—Lancaster Colony Corporation; *U.S. Public*, pg. 976

PFEIFFER—Salad Dressings—T. Marzetti Company; *U.S. Public*, pg. 977

PFINODAL—Copper/Nickel/Tin Strip—AMETEK, Inc.; *U.S. Public*, pg. 99

PFOREVER PFAUCET—NONE—The Black & Decker Corporation; *U.S. Public*, pg. 233

PFREQUENT PFAUCET—Plumbing Products—The Black & Decker Corporation; *U.S. Public*, pg. 233

PH.D—Hair Care System—The Wella Corporation; *Int'l*, pg. 1489

PHACO-EMULSIFIER—Surgical Equipment—Alcon Laboratories, Inc.; *U.S. Public*, pg. 916

PHACOFLEX—Intraocular Lens—Allergan, Inc.; *U.S. Public*, pg. 46

PHACOPLUS SENSORY V—Surgical Instrument—Allergan, Inc.; *U.S. Public*, pg. 46

PHADE—Age Spot Fading Gel—Alva/Amco Pharmacal Companies, Inc.; *U.S. Private*, pg. 47

PHADEBACT—Diagnostic—Pharmacia & Upjohn Adria Laboratories; *Int'l*, pg. 1049

PHADEBAS—Diagnostic—Pharmacia & Upjohn Adria Laboratories; *Int'l*, pg. 1049

PHADEBAS RAST—Diagnostic—Pharmacia & Upjohn Adria Laboratories; *Int'l*, pg. 1049

PHADEZYM—Diagnostic—Pharmacia & Upjohn Adria Laboratories; *Int'l*, pg. 1049

PHADEZYM PRIST—Diagnostic—Pharmacia & Upjohn Adria Laboratories; *Int'l*, pg. 1049

PHALAROPE—Nature Guides—Simon & Schuster; *U.S. Private*, pg. 777

PHALCON—Early Warning System—Israel Aircraft Industries Ltd.; *Int'l*, pg. 689

PHANTOM—Chart—The Foxboro Company; *Int'l*, pg. 1243

THE PHANTOM OF THE OPERA—Musical—Really Useful Holdings Limited; *Int'l*, pg. 1089

PHANTOMS—QCtor X-ray, Therapy, OT & Water—Capintec Inc.; *U.S. Private*, pg. 205

PHAR-MOR—Drug Stores—Phar-Mor, Inc.; *U.S. Public*, pg. 1284

PHARM—NONE—Seaway Food Town, Inc.; *U.S. Public*, pg. 1452

PHARM SCREEN—Hand held, On-Site Drug Testing—PharmChem Laboratories, Inc.; *U.S. Public*, pg. 1285

PHARMACEUTICAL EXECUTIVE—Trade Periodical—Advanstar Communications; *U.S. Private*, pg. 22

PHARMACEUTICAL PROCESSING—Publication for Engineers & Managers—Reed Elsevier Business Information; *Int'l*, pg. 1095

PHARMACEUTICAL TECHNOLOGY—Trade Periodical—Advanstar Communications; *U.S. Private*, pg. 22

PHARMACEUTICAL TECHNOLOGY EUROPE—Trade Periodical—Advanstar Communications; *U.S. Private*, pg. 22

PHARMACIA CAP SYSTEM—NONE—Pharmacia & Upjohn, Inc.; *Int'l*, pg. 1047

PHARMACY TRADE—Magazine—Reed Business Information Pty. Limited; *Int'l*, pg. 1094

PHARMALGEN—Allergenic Extract—Pharmacia & Upjohn Adria Laboratories; *Int'l*, pg. 1049

PHARMALYTE—Biotechnology—Pharmacia & Upjohn Adria Laboratories; *Int'l*, pg. 1049

PHARMAPRIX—Drugstore—Imasco Limited; *Int'l*, pg. 112

PHARMAQUIK—Aluminum Foil Laminates—Reynolds Metals Company; *U.S. Public*, pg. 1385

PHARMASORB—Activated Attapulgite for use in Medicines & Pharmaceuticals—Engelhard Corporation; *U.S. Public*, pg. 582

PHARMCHEK—Sweat Patch Device for Drug Testing—PharmChem Laboratories, Inc.; *U.S. Public*, pg. 1285

PHARMHOUSE—NONE—PharmHouse, Inc.; *U.S. Public*, pg. 1285

PHARMNET—Pharmacy Information System—Cerner Corporation; *U.S. Public*, pg. 331

PHAROS—Actuators—Flowserve Corporation; *U.S. Public*, pg. 658

PHAS—Cosmetics—L'Oreal S.A.; *Int'l*, pg. 818

PHASE ALPHA—Sheet Molding Compound Resins System—Ashland, Inc.; *U.S. Public*, pg. 138

PHASE EIGHT—Closed-Circuit Television Equipment—Vicon Industries, Inc.; *U.S. Public*, pg. 1719

PHASE ENGINE—NONE—Adaptec, Inc.; *U.S. Public*, pg. 19

PHASE EPSILON—System for Molding Automotive Body Panels—Ashland, Inc.; *U.S. Public*, pg. 138

PHASE II—NONE—Excelled Sheepskin & Leather Coat Corporation; *U.S. Private*, pg. 387

PHASE LINEAR—Loudspeakers—Recoton Auto Corporation; *U.S. Public*, pg. 1369

PHASE SHIFT—Machine Capable of Washing Multi-Sized Pharmaceutical Containers—The West Company, Incorporated; *U.S. Public*, pg. 1755

PHASE 3—NONE—SunGard Data Systems Inc.; *U.S. Public*, pg. 1534

PHASELINEAR—Automotive Amplifiers—Recoton Corporation; *U.S. Public*, pg. 1369

PHASER—Power Control—Research, Incorporated; *U.S. Public*, pg. 1382

PHASES—Multi-Use High Chair—Evenflo Company, Inc.; *U.S. Private*, pg. 629

PHAZER—Actuator—Flowserve Corporation; *U.S. Public*, pg. 658

PHAZER—Rod—Outdoor Technologies Group; *U.S. Private*, pg. 822

PHEASANT—Socks & Knitted Headwear—Wigwam Mills, Inc.; *U.S. Private*, pg. 1175

PHEASANT HOLLOW—Varietal Wines—Gibson Wine Company; *U.S. Private*, pg. 452

PHENAZINE—Agricultural Chemicals—Meiji Seika Kaisha, Ltd.; *Int'l*, pg. 855

PHENERGAN—NONE—American Home Products Corporation; *U.S. Public*, pg. 79

Brand Name Index

PHENERGAN—Cough, Cold, Allergy Medication—Wyeth-Ayerst Laboratories, Inc.; *U.S. Public*, pg. 80

PHENOL—NONE—Sasol Alpha Olefins; *Int'l*, pg. 1196

PHENOL—NONE—Sasol Chemicals Europe Limited; *Int'l*, pg. 1196

PHENOLINE—Protective Coatings—Carboline Co.; *U.S. Public*, pg. 1357

PHENOLITE—Laminated Plastic—NVF Company; *U.S. Private*, pg. 772

PHENOWELD—Phenolic Adhesive—Hardman Division of Harcros Chemicals, Inc.; *Int'l*, pg. 598

PHENSIC—Analgesic—SmithKline Beecham Corporation; *Int'l*, pg. 1264

PHENSIC—Analgesic—SmithKline Beecham plc; *Int'l*, pg. 1264

PHEONIX—NONE—Molex Incorporated; *U.S. Public*, pg. 1121

PHEROMONE—Women's Fragrance—Marilyn Miglin, L.P.; *U.S. Private*, pg. 745

PHEROMONE FOR MEN—Men's Fragrance—Marilyn Miglin, L.P.; *U.S. Private*, pg. 745

PHERROVET—Veterinary Medicine—Cultor Ltd.; *Int'l*, pg. 349

PHIL-JO—Polyethylene Film—Industrial Coatings Group, Inc.; *U.S. Private*, pg. 434

PHILADELPHIA—Carpets—Shaw Industries, Inc.; *U.S. Public*, pg. 1464

PHILADELPHIA BRAND—NONE—Alliant Foodservice, Inc.; *U.S. Private*, pg. 244

PHILADELPHIA BRAND—Cream Cheese—Kraft Foods Inc.; *U.S. Public*, pg. 1288

PHILADELPHIA BRAND—Cream Cheese—Philip Morris Companies Inc.; *U.S. Public*, pg. 1287

PHILADELPHIA INQUIRER—Newspaper—The Philadelphia Inquirer; *U.S. Public*, pg. 964

PHILADELPHIA PHILLIES—Professional Baseball—The Phillies-A Limited Partnership; *U.S. Private*, pg. 861

PHILCO—Audio-Video Products—Philips Consumer Electronics; *Int'l*, pg. 1054

PHILCO—Electronics—Philips Electronics N.V.; *Int'l*, pg. 1051

PHILEAS—Men's Fragrance—Accecones Ricci U.S.A., Inc.; *Int'l*, pg. 445

PHILEAS FOGG—Snacks—United Biscuits (Holdings) Plc; *Int'l*, pg. 1442

PHILEAS FOGG—Snacks—United Biscuits (UK) Limited; *Int'l*, pg. 1442

PHILIP MORRIS—Cigarettes—Philip Morris Companies Inc.; *U.S. Public*, pg. 1287

PHILIP MORRIS COMMANDER—Cigarettes—Philip Morris Companies Inc.; *U.S. Public*, pg. 1287

PHILIP MORRIS LIGHT AMERICAN—Cigarettes—Philip Morris Companies Inc.; *U.S. Public*, pg. 1287

PHILIP MORRIS SUPER LIGHTS—Cigarettes—Philip Morris Companies Inc.; *U.S. Public*, pg. 1287

PHILIPPE DESHOULIERES—Limoges Porcelain & Ovenware—Lalique North America; *Int'l*, pg. 797

PHILIPPE MATIGNON—Hosiery—Sara Lee Corporation; *U.S. Public*, pg. 1432

PHILIPPONNAT—Champagner—Eckes AG; *Int'l*, pg. 432

PHILIPPONNAT—Champagne—Marie Brizard Wines & Spirits USA; *U.S. Private*, pg. 702

PHILIPS—Export Products—Philips do Brasil-Walita Div.; *Int'l*, pg. 1055

PHILIPS—Lamps—Philips Electronics North America Corporation; *Int'l*, pg. 1053

PHILIPS—Lighting Products, Electronic Products—Philips Electronics N.V.; *Int'l*, pg. 1051

PHILIPS—Lighting—Philips Lighting; *Int'l*, pg. 1055

PHILIPS—Dictation Systems & Recorders—Philips Speech Processing; *Int'l*, pg. 1055

PHILIPS—Records & Cassettes—Polygram Records, Inc.; *Int'l*, pg. 1052

PHILIPS CD-i—Software—Philips Electronics North America Corporation; *Int'l*, pg. 1053

PHILIPS CLASSICS—Record Label—Philips Electronics N.V.; *Int'l*, pg. 1051

PHILIPS LIGHTING—Incandescent & Fluorescent Lighting—Bryant Electric Supply Company, Inc.; *U.S. Private*, pg. 177

PHILIPS MILK OF MAGNESIA—NONE—SmithKline Beecham Research Limited; *Int'l*, pg. 1266

PHILLIPINE AIRLINES—National Airline of the Phillipines—Philippine Airlines, Inc.; *Int'l*, pg. 1051

PHILLIPS—Processed Food—Hanover Foods Corporation; *U.S. Private*, pg. 499

PHILLIPS—Art Auctioneers—Phillips Fine Art Auctioneers; *U.S. Private*, pg. 861

PHILLIPS—Fastening System—Rule Industries, Inc.; *U.S. Public*, pg. 950

PHILLIPS AIRE—Heating & Ventilation Equipment—Mestek, Inc.; *U.S. Public*, pg. 1099

PHILLIPS MILK OF MAGNESIA—NONE—SmithKline Beecham Corporation; *Int'l*, pg. 1264

PHILLIPS OLD ENGLISH ALCOHOLIC CORDIALS—Spirit—Allied Domecq PLC; *Int'l*, pg. 62

PHILLIPS 66—Gasoline, Lubricants, Chemicals & Plastics—Phillips Petroleum Company; *U.S. Public*, pg. 1290

PHILLIPSBURG—Inserter—Bell & Howell Holdings; *U.S. Public*, pg. 201

PHILMAC—NONE—Glynwed International PLC; *Int'l*, pg. 554

PHILOMEL BOOKS—Books—The Putnam & Grosset Group; *Int'l*, pg. 1027

PHILTERKOL—Anthracite—Reading Anthracite Co.; *U.S. Private*, pg. 913

PHINEAS & CARNEGIES—Restaurants—Houlihan's Restaurant Group; *U.S. Public*, pg. 841

PHISODERM—Facial Cleanser—Chattem, Inc.; *U.S. Public*, pg. 341

PHISODERM—Facial Cleanser—Chattem, Inc., Consumer Products Division; *U.S. Public*, pg. 341

PHOCUS—Diagnostic—Pharmacia & Upjohn Adria Laboratories; *Int'l*, pg. 1049

PHODIS—Digistal Photogrammetry—Carl Zeiss; *Int'l*, pg. 1522

PHODIS ST—Digital Stereomodel Generator & Evaluator—Carl Zeiss; *Int'l*, pg. 1522

PHOENIX—Combustion Scrubber—ATMI, Inc.; *U.S. Public*, pg. 12

PHOENIX—Herbicides—Agrolinz Melamin GmbH; *Int'l*, pg. 356

PHOENIX—Clothing—Genesco Inc.; *U.S. Public*, pg. 728

PHOENIX—System—Harnischfeger Industries, Inc.; *U.S. Public*, pg. 788

PHOENIX—NONE—Oshkosh Truck Corporation; *U.S. Public*, pg. 1233

PHOENIX—Pacemaker—St. Jude Medical, Inc.; *U.S. Public*, pg. 1427

PHOENIX EDGE—Eye Protection—U.S. Safety; *U.S. Private*, pg. 1125

PHOENIX GLOVE 2000—Top Quality Vinyl Cleanroom Glove—Phoenix Medical Technology, Inc.; *U.S. Public*, pg. 1292

PHOENIX GRILL—Gas Grills—Whitin Roberts Co.; *U.S. Private*, pg. 309

PHOENIX I—Eye Protection—U.S. Safety; *U.S. Private*, pg. 1125

PHOENIX STRATEGIC MAINTENANCE INITIATIVE (SMI)—NONE—American Management Systems, Inc.; *U.S. Public*, pg. 86

PHOENIX SYSTEMS—NONE—Harman Consumer Group; *U.S. Public*, pg. 787

PHOENIX III—Fire Safe High-Performance Valves—Fisher Controls International, Inc.; *U.S. Public*, pg. 573

PHOENIX II—Eye Protection—U.S. Safety; *U.S. Private*, pg. 1125

PHOENIX VIRTUAL CHIPS—Synthesizable Cores for Peripheral Interconnect Implementations—Phoenix Technologies Ltd.; *U.S. Public*, pg. 1292

PHOENIXBIOS—Basic Input Output System for Desktop PCs, Portable PCs & PC Servers—Phoenix Technologies Ltd.; *U.S. Public*, pg. 1292

PHOENIXPICO—System Software for Information Appliances—Phoenix Technologies Ltd.; *U.S. Public*, pg. 1292

PHONE DISC—Phone Book on CD-ROM—British Telecommunications plc; *Int'l*, pg. 222

PHONE FICHE—Directory—Bell & Howell Holdings; *U.S. Public*, pg. 201

PHONE SAFE—Telephone Enclosures—The Lamson & Sessions Co.; *U.S. Public*, pg. 976

PHONECOMMUNICATOR—Business Product—International Business Machines Corporation; *U.S. Public*, pg. 895

PHONEFUNDS—NONE—American Express Company; *U.S. Public*, pg. 73

PHONELINK—Modem Communication—Nellcor Puritan Bennett Incorporated; *U.S. Public*, pg. 1039

PHONEMAIL—Voice Processing System—Siemens Corporation; *Int'l*, pg. 1245

PHONEMATE—Telephone Answering Machines—Casio Phone-Mate, Inc.; *Int'l*, pg. 274

PHONEVISION—Pay-Per-View Radio & TV Systems—Zenith Electronics Corp.; *U.S. Public*, pg. 1790

PHONOCARD—Debit Card System—Landis & Staefa, Inc.; *Int'l*, pg. 800

PHORWITE—Optical Brighteners—Bayer AG; *Int'l*, pg. 171

PHOS-CHEK—Fire Retardant—Monsanto Company; *U.S. Public*, pg. 1124

PHOS-CHEK—Fire Retardant—Solutia Inc.; *U.S. Public*, pg. 1483

PHOSGARD—Metal Finishing Agents—BetzDearborn Inc.; *U.S. Public*, pg. 226

PHOSPHO-SODA—Proprietary Medicine—C. B. Fleet Co., Inc.; *U.S. Private*, pg. 410

PHOSVER—Chemical Reagant—Hach Company; *U.S. Public*, pg. 773

PHOTO ANSWERS—U.K. Photography Magazine—EMAP Apex; *Int'l*, pg. 451

PHOTO CLING—Imagine Media—Labelon Corporation; *U.S. Private*, pg. 641

PHOTO DISTRICT NEWS—Magazine Photography Market—BPI Communications Inc.; *Int'l*, pg. 1446

PHOTO-FLO—Photo Wetting Agent—Eastman Kodak Company; *U.S. Public*, pg. 550

PHOTO FRIENDS—Greeting Cards—American Greetings Corporation; *U.S. Public*, pg. 77

PHOTO GRAPHIC—Computer Product—International Business Machines Corporation; *U.S. Public*, pg. 895

PHOTO MARKER—Photographic Paper—Pinnacle Coating & Converting, Inc.; *U.S. Private*, pg. 866

PHOTO MOUNT—Adhesives, Aerosol—3M; *U.S. Public*, pg. 1604

PHOTO STRESS—Stress Analysis—Vishay Intertechnology, Inc.; *U.S. Public*, pg. 1721

PHOTO TECHNIQUE—Special Interest Magazine—IPC Magazines Limited; *Int'l*, pg. 651

PHOTO TECHNOLOGY—Textbook Covering Basci Through Advanced Procedures of Photography—Goodheart-Willcox Publisher; *U.S. Private*, pg. 464

PHOTO TYPOSITOR—Headline Typesetter—GraphLine Inc.; *U.S. Private*, pg. 471

PHOTO WALLET ENVELOPES—Envelopes—Tension Envelope Corp.; *U.S. Private*, pg. 1077

PHOTOBLOT—NONE—Life Technologies, Inc.; *U.S. Public*, pg. 504

PHOTOCAP—Solar Cell Encapsulant Film—Springborn Testing & Research, Inc.; *U.S. Private*, pg. 1027

PHOTOCELL—NONE—Avenor, Inc.; *Int'l*, pg. 101

PHOTOFLURE—Photo Film—Eastman Kodak Company; *U.S. Public*, pg. 550

PHOTOGARD—Photo Protective Coating—3M; *U.S. Public*, pg. 1604

PHOTOGENE—NONE—Life Technologies, Inc.; *U.S. Public*, pg. 504

PHOTOGLAZE—UV/EB Cure Coating—Lord Corporation; *U.S. Public*, pg. 675

PHOTOGRAPHER'S MARKET—Market Book—F & W Publications, Inc.; *U.S. Private*, pg. 388

PHOTOGRAPHIC—Magazine—Petersen Publishing Company, L.L.C.; *U.S. Private*, pg. 856

PHOTOHELIC—Pressure Gage-Switch—Dwyer Instruments Inc.; *U.S. Private*, pg. 350

PHOTOLIFE—Batteries—Eastman Kodak Company; *U.S. Public*, pg. 550

PHOTOMOTION—Computer Product—International Business Machines Corporation; *U.S. Public*, pg. 895

PHOTON—Laser Transmitters & Optical Nodes—Thomas & Betts Corporation; *U.S. Public*, pg. 1597

PHOTOPHONE—Film Recording Equipment—Thomson Consumer Electronics Inc.; *Int'l*, pg. 1383

PHOTOPLAS—Ultra-violet Curable Coating—Red Spot Paint & Varnish Co.; *U.S. Private*, pg. 915

PHOTOPLAST—Photo Plates—Eastman Kodak Company; *U.S. Public*, pg. 550

PHOTORENDER—NONE—Evans & Sutherland Computer Corporation; *U.S. Public*, pg. 595

PHOTOSOL—Photochromic Lens Blanks—Deutsche Spezialglas AG; *Int'l*, pg. 1523

PHOTOSOL—Organic Dyes for Paints, Inks & Plastics—PPG Industries, Inc.; *U.S. Public*, pg. 1245

PHOTOSOLAR—Photochromic Lens Blanks—Deutsche Spezialglas AG; *Int'l*, pg. 1523

PHOTOSTAR—Automatic Camera System—Leica, Inc.; *Int'l*, pg. 806

PHOTOSWITCH—Photoelectric Controls & Sensors—Rockwell International Corporation; *U.S. Public*, pg. 1397

PHOTOZOOM—Microscope—Leica, Inc.; *Int'l*, pg. 806

PHREEDOM—Cooling Water Chemicals for Acid Elimination & Water Conservation—Calgon Corporation; *Int'l*, pg. 455

PHRENILIN—Headache Tablets—Carnrick Laboratories, Inc.; *U.S. Private*, pg. 436

PHRENILIN FORTE—Headache Capsules—Carnrick Laboratories, Inc.; *U.S. Private*, pg. 436

PHRESH 3.5—Skin Cleansing Liquid—3M; *U.S. Public*, pg. 1604

PHYNYLTROPE—Mydriotic Ophthalmic Solution—The Cooper Companies, Inc.; *U.S. Public*, pg. 442

PHYSICAL—Milk—Q.U.F. Industries Ltd.; *Int'l*, pg. 1074

PHYSICAL SKIM—Milk—Q.U.F. Industries Ltd.; *Int'l*, pg. 1074

THE PHYSICIAN COMPANY—NONE—Coastal Physician Group, Inc.; *U.S. Public*, pg. 391

PHYSICIAN PLANS—NONE—Poe & Brown, Inc.; *U.S. Public*, pg. 1312

PHYSICIANS—Weight Loss Centers—Physicians Weight Loss Centers, Inc.; *U.S. Private*, pg. 864

PHYSICIAN'S DESK REF. FOR NON-PRESCRIPTION DRUGS—Medical Publication—Medical Economics Company Inc.; *U.S. Public*, pg. 1601

PHYSICIAN'S DESK REFERENCE—Medical Publication—Medical Economics Company Inc.; *U.S. Public*, pg. 1601

PHYSICIAN'S DESK REFERENCE FOR OPTHALMOLOGY—Medical Publication—Medical Economics Company Inc.; *U.S. Public*, pg. 1601

PHYSICIAN'S MANAGEMENT—Trade Periodical—Advanstar Communications; *U.S. Private*, pg. 22

PHYSICIANS PROTECTOR PLAN—Insurance Package Program—Poe & Brown, Inc.; *U.S. Public*, pg. 1312

PHYSIO-STIM—Bone Growth Stimulator System—Orthofix Inc.; *Int'l*, pg. 1011

PHYSIO-STIM—Bone Growth Stimulator—Orthofix International N.V.; *Int'l*, pg. 1011

PHYTA CLONE—Cultures—Fisher Scientific Company; *U.S. Private*, pg. 658

PHYTAGAR—NONE—Life Technologies, Inc.; *U.S. Public*, pg. 504

PHYTION—NONE—Life Technologies, Inc.; *U.S. Public*, pg. 504

PHYXIS—NONE—Cardinal Health Inc.; *U.S. Public*, pg. 304

PIAGET—Watches & Jewelry—Movado Group, Inc.; *U.S. Public*, pg. 1140

PIANORAMICK—Paint—Progress Paint Mfg. Co.; *U.S. Private*, pg. 890

PIANOSOFT—Pre-Recorded Disks—Yamaha Corporation; *Int'l*, pg. 1515

PIAS—Cosmetics—International Cosmetics Co., Ltd.; *Int'l*, pg. 684

PIASTEN—Chocolates—Cadbury Schweppes p.l.c.; *Int'l*, pg. 247

PIAT BEAUJOLAIS—NONE—IDV France; *Int'l*, pg. 410

PIAT D'OR—Wine—Grand Metropolitan Plc; *Int'l*, pg. 408

PIAT D'OR WINES—ROUGE & BLANC—Carillon Importers, Ltd.; *Int'l*, pg. 409

PIAT PERE & FILS—Wines—Piat Pere & Fils; *Int'l*, pg. 410

PIAT RESERVE—NONE—Piat Pere & Fils; *Int'l*, pg. 410

PIAT VARIETALS—NONE—IDV France; *Int'l*, pg. 410

PIC—Precision Industrial Components—PIC Design; *U.S. Private*, pg. 864

PIC 'N PAY—Shoe Stores—Pic'n Pay Stores, Inc.; *U.S. Private*, pg. 864

PIC-FLOW—Skate Wheel-Pallet Flow—Jarke Corporation; *U.S. Private*, pg. 583

PIC 'N' SAVE—Retail Store—Mac Frugal's Bargains Close-Outs Inc.; *U.S. Public*, pg. 437

PIC 77—Icing Powders—Mallet & Co.; *U.S. Private*, pg. 698

PIC STIX—Aluminum Framing Elements—PIC Design; *U.S. Private*, pg. 864

PICANTE SPORTSWEAR—Sport Sandals—Deckers Outdoor Corporation; *U.S. Public*, pg. 491

PICASSO—Perfumes—L'Oreal S.A.; *Int'l*, pg. 818

PICCANTASE—Lipase-Esterase for Cheese Flavor—Royal Gist-Brocades N.V.; *Int'l*, pg. 1142

PICCHIO—Lamps—Luxo A/S; *Int'l*, pg. 821

PICCO—Hydrocarbon Resin—Hercules Incorporated; *U.S. Public*, pg. 809

PICCODIENE—Hydrocarbon Resin—Hercules Incorporated; *U.S. Public*, pg. 809

PICCOFYN—Hydrocarbon Resin—Hercules Incorporated; *U.S. Public*, pg. 809

PICCOLASTIC—Hydrocarbon Resin—Hercules Incorporated; *U.S. Public*, pg. 809

PICCOLYTE—Hydrocarbon Resin—Hercules Incorporated; *U.S. Public*, pg. 809

PICCOMER—Hydrocarbon Resin—Hercules Incorporated; *U.S. Public*, pg. 809

PICCONOL—Resin Emulsions—Hercules Incorporated; *U.S. Public*, pg. 809

PICCOPALE—Hydrocarbon Resin—Hercules Incorporated; *U.S. Public*, pg. 809

PICCOTAC—Hydrocarbon Resin—Hercules Incorporated; *U.S. Public*, pg. 809

PICCOTEX—Hydrocarbon Resin—Hercules Incorporated; *U.S. Public*, pg. 809

PICCOTONER—Hydrocarbon Resin—Hercules Incorporated; *U.S. Public*, pg. 809

PICCOVAR—Hydrocarbon Resin—Hercules Incorporated; *U.S. Public*, pg. 809

PICK MATE—Paperless Picking—Interlake Material Handling Div.; *U.S. Public*, pg. 893

PICK-ME-UP—Bouquet—FTD, Inc./Florists Transworld Delivery, Inc.; *U.S. Private*, pg. 389

PICK 'N SAVE—Warehouse Food Stores—Roundy's, Inc.; *U.S. Private*, pg. 948

PICK O' THE GROVE—Nuts—John B. Sanfilippo & Son, Inc.; *U.S. Public*, pg. 1431

PICK OF THE PROFESSIONALS—Cliche—Andis Company; *U.S. Private*, pg. 73

PICK OF THE STICK—Frankfurters—Alpine Packing Company; *U.S. Private*, pg. 45

PICK PICKERING LAMINATES—NONE—Pickering Inc.; *U.S. Private*, pg. 864

PICK UPS—Single Serve Snacks—Borden, Inc.; *U.S. Private*, pg. 157

PICKER—Medical Equip.—The General Electric Company, p.l.c.; *Int'l*, pg. 543

PICKERCHEST—X-Ray—Picker International, Inc.; *Int'l*, pg. 545

PICKWICK—Beer & Ale—Falstaff Brewing Corporation; *U.S. Private*, pg. 955

PICKWICK—Tea—Sara Lee Corporation; *U.S. Public*, pg. 1432

PICKWICK—Tea—Superior Coffee and Foods; *U.S. Public*, pg. 1434

PICNIC—Juice—McCain Foods Limited; *Int'l*, pg. 850

PICO-FLUOR 15—Pseudocumene-Based Cocktail—Packard Instrument Co., Inc.; *U.S. Private*, pg. 833

PICO-FLUOR 40—Pseudocumene-Based Cocktail—Packard Instrument Co., Inc.; *U.S. Private*, pg. 833

PICO FUSE—Fuses—Littelfuse, Inc.; *U.S. Public*, pg. 1001

PICO HANG-IN VIAL—6.5ml Liquid Scintillation Counting Vial—Packard Instrument Co., Inc.; *U.S. Private*, pg. 833

PICO-PRO VIAL—4ml Vial—Packard Instrument Co., Inc.; *U.S. Private*, pg. 833

PICO TAG—Amino Acid Analysis System, Method, Column, Eluents, Chem. Pkg. & Diluent—Millipore Corporation; *U.S. Public*, pg. 1112

PICOFLEX—NONE—Molex Incorporated; *U.S. Public*, pg. 1121

PICOPORE—Ion-Permeable Membranes—Ionics, Incorporated; *U.S. Public*, pg. 912

PICTIONARY—Adult Game—Golden Books Family Entertainment Inc.; *U.S. Public*, pg. 749

PICTSWEET—Frozen Vegetables—United Foods, Inc.; *U.S. Public*, pg. 1677

PICTURE THIS HOME! KITCHEN—Software for the Kitchen—Autodesk, Inc.; *U.S. Public*, pg. 148

PIDILAT—Cardiovascular Preparations—Kali-Chemie Aktiengesellschaft; *Int'l*, pg. 1278

PIE PIPER—Cheesecakes & Quiche—Vienna Sausage Mfg. Co.; *U.S. Private*, pg. 1139

PIEDMONT CHERRY—Prefinished Wall Paneling—Georgia-Pacific Corporation; *U.S. Public*, pg. 735

PIEDRA—Vinyl Composition Tile—Kentile Operting Co.; *U.S. Private*, pg. 615

PIELS—Beer—The Stroh Brewery Company; *U.S. Private*, pg. 1047

PIELS LIGHT—Beer—The Stroh Brewery Company; *U.S. Private*, pg. 1047

PIEMONTELLO—Wine—Allied Domecq PLC; *Int'l*, pg. 62

PIENI PYOREA—Round Crisp Bread—Cultor Ltd.; *Int'l*, pg. 349

PIEPSER—Wristwatch-Pager—SMH Swiss Corporation for Micro Electronics & Watchmaking Indus. Ltd.; *Int'l*, pg. 1160

PIER 1—Retail Housefurnishings & Imports Stores—Pier 1 Imports, Inc.; *U.S. Public*, pg. 1295

PIERCE—Aerosol Penetrant—La-Co Industries Markal Company; *U.S. Private*, pg. 640

PIERCE—Fire & Emergency Trucks—Oshkosh Truck Corporation; *U.S. Public*, pg. 1233

PIERCE-ALL—Machine Tool—The Producto Machine Co.; *U.S. Private*, pg. 889

PIERCE GOVERNORS—Automatic Chokes—The Pierce Co., Inc.; *U.S. Private*, pg. 102

PIERRE BALMAIR—Watches—SMH Swiss Corporation for Micro Electronics & Watchmaking Indus. Ltd.; *Int'l*, pg. 1160

PIERRE CARDIN—Clothing—Beldoch Industries; *U.S. Public*, pg. 519

PIERRE CARDIN—Liscensed Name Brand Watch—Jan Bell Marketing Inc.; *U.S. Public*, pg. 207

PIERRE CARDIN—Men's Tailored Clothing—Hartmarx Corporation; *U.S. Public*, pg. 795

PIERRE CARDIN—Gifts, Leather Accessories, Belts, Jewelry—Swank, Inc.; *U.S. Public*, pg. 1543

PIERRE CARDIN—Fragrance—Tsumura International; *Int'l*, pg. 1426

PIERRE CARDIN—Formal Wear for Men—West Mill Clothes, Inc.; *U.S. Private*, pg. 1163

PIERRE CARDIN INSATIABLE—Men's Fragrance—Tsumura International; *Int'l*, pg. 1426

PIERRE CARDIN SPORTIF—Men's Fragrance—Tsumura International; *Int'l*, pg. 1426

PIERRE FABRE—Cosmetics—Pierre Fabre S.A.; *Int'l*, pg. 1056

PIERSON OUTFITTERS—Adult Outerwear—Pacific Trail Inc.; *U.S. Private*, pg. 673

PIETRAFITTA CHIANTI—Italian Wine—Laird & Company; *U.S. Private*, pg. 642

PIETRAFITTA VERNACCIA—Italian Wine—Laird & Company; *U.S. Private*, pg. 642

PIETRAFITTA VERNACCIA BORGHETTO—Italian Wine—Laird & Company; *U.S. Private*, pg. 642

PIETRAFITTA VERNACCIA LA COSTA—Italian Wine—Laird & Company; *U.S. Private*, pg. 642

PIETRAFITTA VIN SANTO—Italian Wine—Laird & Company; *U.S. Private*, pg. 642

PIEZAS PLASTICAS—NONE—ETEX; *Int'l*, pg. 430

PIEZO BALANCE—Particle Monitor—TSI Incorporated; *U.S. Public*, pg. 1559

PIEZO CRYSTAL—Communications Crystals, Oscillators & Filters—Premier Metal Products Co.; *U.S. Private*, pg. 881

PIG'S EYE—Beer—Minnesota Brewing Company; *U.S. Public*, pg. 1115

PIGGLY WIGGLY—Grocery Store Chain—Bruno's Inc.; *U.S. Public*, pg. 265

PIGGLY WIGGLY—Food Prods.—Piggly Wiggly Co.; *U.S. Public*, pg. 653

PIGGLY WIGGLY—Supermarket—Piggly Wiggly Co.; *U.S. Public*, pg. 653

PIGGLY WIGGLY—Retail Supermarket—Schultz Sav-O Stores, Inc.; *U.S. Public*, pg. 1442

PIGGY PACKER—Intermodal Material Hnadling Equipment—MI-Jack Products, Inc.; *U.S. Private*, pg. 740

PIGGYBACK—Labels—Avery Dennison Corporation; *U.S. Public*, pg. 152

PIGGYBACK—Stabilizer—Baker Hughes INTEQ; *U.S. Public*, pg. 166

PIGGYBACK—Tire Treads—Bandag, Incorporated; *U.S. Public*, pg. 177

PIGGYBACK—Luggage—Lark Luggage Company, Inc.; *U.S. Public*, pg. 1430

PIGGYBACK SYSTEM—V Solution 100ml, 50m—Otsuka Pharmaceutical Co., Ltd.; *Int'l*, pg. 1013

PIK-A-NUT—Automotive Fasteners—Champ/Pik-A-Nut Service Line; *U.S. Public*, pg. 1503

PIK-A-NUT—Automotive Fasteners—Standard Motor Products Inc.; *U.S. Public*, pg. 1503

PIK-NIK—Snack Foods—Tri Valley Growers; *U.S. Private*, pg. 1101

PIK POCKET—Subgingival Delivery System—Teledyne Water Pik; *U.S. Public*, pg. 44

PIKE ATTACKER—Marine Products; Boats & Canoes—Sea Nymph Inc.; *U.S. Private*, pg. 478

PIKEMAN GIN—NONE—Barton Brands, Ltd.; *U.S. Public*, pg. 300

PIKNIK—Flavored Milk—Morinaga Milk Industry Co., Ltd.; *Int'l*, pg. 895

PILE DRIVER—Piston Pumps—Lincoln Industrial; *U.S. Public*, pg. 1273

PILE DRIVER III—High-Pressure Material Dispensing Pumps—Lincoln Industrial; *U.S. Public*, pg. 1273

PILGRIM—Cable Tray Systems—Thomas & Betts Corporation; *U.S. Public*, pg. 1597

PILGRIM'S PRIDE—Poultry & Poultry Products—Pilgrim's Pride Corporation; *U.S. Public*, pg. 1296

PILKINGTONS TILES—Tiles—BTR plc; *Int'l*, pg. 124

PILLARROCK—Canned—Ocean Beauty Seafoods, Inc.; *U.S. Private*, pg. 810

PILLIGUARD—Pinkeye-I Trivalent Vaccine (Equine & Bovine)—Schering-Plough Corporation; *U.S. Public*, pg. 1438

PILLIOD—Furniture—Ladd Furniture, Inc.; *U.S. Public*, pg. 974

PILLOWBACKS—Shoes—P.W. Minor & Son, Inc.; *U.S. Private*, pg. 751

PILLSBURY—Chilled Dough Products—GrandMet Foods GmbH; *Int'l*, pg. 409

PILLSBURY—Baking Mixes, Frosting, Flour, Gravy, Instant Breakfast,Potatoes, Pizza—The Pillsbury Company; *Int'l*, pg. 411

PILO PORT—Control Port—Halliburton Energy Services; *U.S. Public*, pg. 776

PILOPINE HS GEL—Pilocarpine Hydrochloride—Alcon Laboratories, Inc.; *Int'l*, pg. 916

PILOT—Specialty Vehicle—American Honda Motor Co., Inc. Motorcycle Division; *Int'l*, pg. 634

PILOT—NONE—Pilot Corporation; *U.S. Private*, pg. 865

PILOT-POINT—Accessories—The Black & Decker Corporation; *U.S. Public*, pg. 233

PILOT TRAVEL CENTERS—NONE—Pilot Corporation; *U.S. Private*, pg. 865

PILOT'S CHOICE—Clear Acrylic Sheet—Uniroyal Technology Corporation; *U.S. Public*, pg. 1670

PILSNER URQUELL—Czechoslovakian Beer—Guinness Import Company; *Int'l*, pg. 412

PILT—Wood Preservative Coating Composition—PPG Industries, Inc.; *U.S. Public*, pg. 1245

PIM—Hosiery—Sara Lee Corporation; *U.S. Public*, pg. 1432

PIMAC—Tracks Pipeline Informaion Software—Scientific Software-Intercomp, Inc.; *U.S. Public*, pg. 1443

PIMIC—Metal Ion Control Services—The Dow Chemical Company; *U.S. Public*, pg. 522

PIMM'S SPECIALTY—Liqueur—Shieffelin Somerset Co.; *Int'l*, pg. 412

PIMMS NO ONE—NONE—Guinness Plc; *Int'l*, pg. 412

PIN BAR—Electronic Connectors—Lear Siegler Diversified Holdings Corp.; *U.S. Private*, pg. 655

PIN BRINELL—Hardness Tester—NewAge Industries Inc.; *U.S. Private*, pg. 796

PIN BRINELL—Hardness Tester—Newage Industries Inc., Testing Instruments Group; *U.S. Private*, pg. 796

PIN DOT—Slating & Positioning—Invacare Corporation; *U.S. Public*, pg. 911

PIN FINDER—Sporting Goods—Brunswick Bowling & Billiards Corp.; *U.S. Public*, pg. 265

PIN LIFE—Sporting Goods—Brunswick Bowling & Billiards Corp.; *U.S. Public*, pg. 265

PIN MONEY—Pickles & Pickle Relishes—Cains Foods, L.P.; *U.S. Private*, pg. 199

PIN-ON—Marking Systems—Monarch Marking Systems; *U.S. Public*, pg. 1266

THE PIN—Dowel Pins—Saunders Brothers; *U.S. Private*, pg. 968

PINATA—Mexican Food Products—Don Miguel Mexican Foods, Inc.; *U.S. Private*, pg. 339

PINCHLESS—Loose Leaf Notebooks—The Mead Corporation; *U.S. Public*, pg. 1074

PINE CREST—Sports Outerwear—Fox-Knapp; *U.S. Private*, pg. 860

PINE FOREST—All Purpose Cleaner—Blue Cross Laboratories; *U.S. Private*, pg. 152

PINE MAGIC—Cleaner—The Dow Chemical Company; *U.S. Public*, pg. 522

PINE O CLEEN—Surface Care—Reckitt & Colman plc; *Int'l*, pg. 1089

PINE PLUS—Paintable & Stainable Moulding—ABT Building Products Corporation; *Int'l*, pg. 20

PINE POWER—Disinfectant Cleaner—The Dow Chemical Company; *U.S. Public*, pg. 522

PINE POWER—Household Cleaner—DowBrands, L.P.; *U.S. Public*, pg. 523

PINE-SOL—Liquid Cleaner & Spray Cleaner—The Clorox Company; *U.S. Public*, pg. 386

PINEHURST—Offset Smooth & Vellum Uncoated Paper—Champion International Corp.; *U.S. Public*, pg. 333

PINELINER—Containerboards—International Paper Company; *U.S. Public*, pg. 901

PINERIDGE—External Cladding—James Hardie Industries Ltd.; *Int'l*, pg. 596

PINES BROOK VINTNERS—Spirits—Leonard Kreusch, Inc.; *U.S. Private*, pg. 635

PING—Golf Equip.—Karsten Manufacturing Corporation; *U.S. Private*, pg. 608

PING PONG—NONE—Escalade Sports; *U.S. Public*, pg. 591

PINGO DOCE/FEIRA NOVA—Chain Stores-Portugal—Koninklijke Ahold NV; *Int'l*, pg. 749

PINGU—NONE—BBC Magazines; *Int'l*, pg. 114

PINK PEARL—Eraser Products—Sanford Corporation; *U.S. Public*, pg. 1178

PINK PET—Eraser Products—Sanford Corporation; *U.S. Public*, pg. 1178

PINKCORE—Extruded Polystyrene Insulation and Connector Ties—Owens Corning; *U.S. Public*, pg. 1236

PINKERTON—Security Services—Pinkerton's Inc.; *U.S. Public*, pg. 1296

PINKHAM LUMBER & DESIGN—Lumber, Wood Lath & Timbers—Georgia-Pacific Corporation; *U.S. Public*, pg. 735

PINKPLUS—Glass Fiber Residential Insulation—Owens Corning; *U.S. Public*, pg. 1236

PINKPLUS—NONE—Owens-Corning Canada; *U.S. Public*, pg. 1237

PINKSEAL—Polyurethane Foam Sealant—Owens Corning; *U.S. Public*, pg. 1236

PINKWRAP—Housewrap—Owens Corning; *U.S. Public*, pg. 1236

PINNACLE—Asphalt Laminated Fiber Glass Roof Shingle—Atlas Roofing Corp.; *U.S. Private*, pg. 96

PINNACLE—Food Preparations—Burns, Philp & Company Limited; *Int'l*, pg. 236

PINNACLE—Telecommunications Software—Lucent Technologies Inc.; *U.S. Public*, pg. 1017

PINNACLE—NONE—Pinnacle Brands, Inc.; *U.S. Private*, pg. 866

PINNACLE DISTANCE—Golf Balls—Acushnet Company; *U.S. Public*, pg. 675

PINNACLE DISTANCE—NONE—Titleist & Foot-Joy Worldwide; *U.S. Public*, pg. 675

PINNACLE DISTANCE EXTREME—Golf Balls—Fortune Brands, Inc.; *U.S. Public*, pg. 674

PINNACLE EQUALIZER—NONE—Fortune Brands, Inc.; *U.S. Public*, pg. 674

PINORUBIN—Antineoplastic Agents—Nippon Kayaku Co. Ltd.; *Int'l*, pg. 934

PINOT CHARDONNAY—NONE—Gio. Buton S.p.a.; *Int'l*, pg. 409

PINOT NOIR—Women's Clothing—Niches, Inc.; *U.S. Public*, pg. 1181

PINOT-CHARDONNAY CINZANO—NONE—Societe Pour la Vente des Produits Cinzano SA; *Int'l*, pg. 410

PINPOINT—Guided Probe—GenRad, Inc.; *U.S. Public*, pg. 731

PINSETTER—NONE—Molex Incorporated; *U.S. Public*, pg. 1121

PINTASOL—Pigment Preparation—Clariant International Ltd.; *Int'l*, pg. 624

PINTO—Wheelbarrows—Ames Company; *U.S. Public*, pg. 1683

PINTO POP—Popcorn Machine—Gold Medal Products Co.; *U.S. Private*, pg. 459

PINWHEEL CAKES—Cakes—Nabisco Inc.; *U.S. Public*, pg. 1355

PINWHEELS—Chocolate & Marshmellow Cakes—RJR Nabisco Holdings Corp.; *U.S. Public*, pg. 1354

PIO CESARE—Wine—Paterno Imports Limited; *U.S. Private*, pg. 843

PIONEER—NONE—Amerimark Inc.; *U.S. Public*, pg. 1237

PIONEER—Unmanned Reconnaissance Aircraft—Israel Aircraft Industries Ltd.; *Int'l*, pg. 689

PIONEER—Couplers—Parker Hannifin Corp., Quick Coupling Div.; *U.S. Public*, pg. 1260

PIONEER—Peptide Synthesizer Instrument System—PerSeptive Biosystems, Inc.; *U.S. Public*, pg. 1279

PIONEER—Audio, Video, Car Electronics Products And Others—Pioneer Electronic Corporation; *Int'l*, pg. 1057

PIONEER—Car Stereo & Home Audio & Video—Pioneer Electronics (USA) Inc.; *Int'l*, pg. 1058

PIONEER—Seed & Microbial Products—Pioneer Hi-Bred International, Inc.; *U.S. Public*, pg. 1298

PIONEER—Electronic Components—Pioneer-Standard Electronics, Inc.; *U.S. Public*, pg. 1300

PIONEER—NONE—Portec, Inc.-Construction Equipment Div.; *U.S. Public*, pg. 1318

PIONEER—Sugar—Savannah Foods & Industries, Inc.; *U.S. Public*, pg. 872

PIONEER ELECTRONICS—Consumer Electronic Equipment—Hamburg Brothers; *U.S. Private*, pg. 497

PIONEER LIFE—Life Insurance—Pioneer Life Insurance Co. of Illinois; *U.S. Public*, pg. 434

PIONEER PUMPS—Pumps—Gusher Pumps, Inc.; *U.S. Private*, pg. 488

PIONEER QUADRAMATIC—Paper Towels—Georgia-Pacific Corporation; *U.S. Public*, pg. 735

PIONEER 2100—Super Buffer—Pioneer/Eclipse Corp.; *Int'l*, pg. 71

PIONEX—Decorative Laminates—Pioneer Plastics Corporation; *U.S. Private*, pg. 867

PIONITE—Decorative Laminates—Pioneer Plastics Corporation; *U.S. Private*, pg. 867

PIONJAR—Fuel-Powered Drills—Atlas Copco AB; *Int'l*, pg. 95

PIOS MANUFACTURING—Manufacturing Software—Dun & Bradstreet Software Services; *Int'l*, pg. 488

PIPE EXPLORER—Invented Membrane to Deploy Sensors to Survey Radiations Contaminants—Science & Engineering Associates; *U.S. Private*, pg. 975

PIPE GUARD—Extruded Plastic Net—Nalle Plastics Inc.; *U.S. Private*, pg. 773

PIPE MATE—Pipe Tobaccos—Consolidated Cigar Corporation; *U.S. Public*, pg. 690

PIPE PRODUCTS—NONE—Ford Meter Box Company; *U.S. Private*, pg. 418

PIPELASER 1550—Visible Beam—David White, L.L.C.; *U.S. Public*, pg. 1765

PIPELASER 1550—Visible Beam—David White, L.L.C.; *U.S. Private*, pg. 1765

PIPELINE MONITOR—Software—Scientific Software-Intercomp, Inc.; *U.S. Public*, pg. 1443

PIPER—Personal, Training, Utility & Business Aircraft—The New Piper Aircraft, Inc.; *U.S. Private*, pg. 794

PIPER HEIDSIECK—Champagne—Remy Amerique Inc.; *Int'l*, pg. 1102

PIPETITE-STIK—Pipe Thread Compound—La-Co Industries Markal Company; *U.S. Private*, pg. 640

PIPING DESIGN DIVISION—Consultants to Power & Process Piping Users—Marquette Coppersmithing Co., Inc.; *U.S. Private*, pg. 706

PIPIX—Cathode Ray Tubes—Litton Industries, Inc.; *U.S. Public*, pg. 1002

PIPRACIL—Anti-Infective—American Home Products Corporation; *U.S. Public*, pg. 79

PIPRON—Fungicide—The Dow Chemical Company; *U.S. Public*, pg. 522

PIPS—Greeting Cards—American Greetings Corporation; *U.S. Public*, pg. 77

PIRANHA—Saw Blades—The Black & Decker Corporation; *U.S. Public*, pg. 233

PIRANHA—High-Pressure Synthetic Hose—DSM Engineering Plastic Products; *Int'l*, pg. 354

PIRANHA—Milling Tool—Smith International, Inc.; *U.S. Public*, pg. 1478

PIRANHA PRO—NONE—The Black & Decker Corporation; *U.S. Public*, pg. 233

PIRANHA ULTRA—Saw Blades—The Black & Decker Corporation; *U.S. Public*, pg. 233

PIRATES KEG GOURMET SODAS—Colas—Global Beverage Co.; *U.S. Private*, pg. 457

PIRELLI—Passenger, Farm, Light Truck, Motorcycle Tires—Pirelli Armstrong Tire Corporation; *Int'l*, pg. 1058

PIRELLI ARMSTRONG—Tires & Rubber—Pirelli Armstrong Tire Corporation; *Int'l*, pg. 1058

PIRITON—Pharmaceutical—Stafford-Miller Limited; *U.S. Public*, pg. 237

PIRKKA—Groceries and Daily Goods—Kesko Ltd.; *Int'l*, pg. 732

PISANG AMBON—Liqueur—Bols Royal Distilleries; *Int'l*, pg. 751

PISCES—Stimulator—Medtronic, Inc.; *U.S. Public*, pg. 1082

PISCES DELTA—NONE—Medtronic, Inc.; *U.S. Public*, pg. 1082

PISCES-QUAD—Stimulator—Medtronic, Inc.; *U.S. Public*, pg. 1082

PISCES-QUAD PLUS—Lead—Medtronic, Inc.; *U.S. Public*, pg. 1082

PISCES-QUINTA—Lead—Medtronic, Inc.; *U.S. Public*, pg. 1082

PISCES-SELECTRX—Stimulator—Medtronic, Inc.; *U.S. Public*, pg. 1082

PISCES-SIGMA—Lead—Medtronic, Inc.; *U.S. Public*, pg. 1082

PISTOL—Locker—American Locker Group, Inc.; *U.S. Public*, pg. 85

PIT & QUARRY—Trade Periodical—Advanstar Communications; *U.S. Private*, pg. 22

PITCH'R PAK—Dessert Toppings—Borden, Inc.; *U.S. Private*, pg. 157

PITCO FRIALATOR—Fryer—Pitco Frialator Inc.; *U.S. Public*, pg. 1065

PITMO—Dc Motors—Penn Engineering & Manufacturing Corp.; *U.S. Public*, pg. 1269

PITRALON—After-Shave & Men's Toiletries—SmithKline Beecham plc; *Int'l*, pg. 1264

PITT-CHAR—Fire-Retardant Building Material Coating—PPG Industries, Inc.; *U.S. Public*, pg. 1245

PITT-CRYL—Acrylic Paints—PPG Industries, Inc.; *U.S. Public*, pg. 1245

PITT-DES MOINES, INC.—Diversified Engineering & Construction; Carbon Steel Products—Pitt-Des Moines, Inc.; *U.S. Public*, pg. 1304

PITT-FLEX—Elastomeric Exterior Masonry Coating—PPG Industries, Inc.; *U.S. Public*, pg. 1245

PITT-GLAZE—Coatings, Solvents & Thermosettable Components for Coating Manufacture—PPG Industries, Inc.; *U.S. Public*, pg. 1245

PITT-GUARD—Heavy-Duty Maintenance Coating—PPG Industries, Inc.; *U.S. Public*, pg. 1245

PITT-THERM—Corrosion Protective Coating—PPG Industries, Inc.; *U.S. Public*, pg. 1245

PITTABS—Water Treatment Chemicals—PPG Industries, Inc.; *U.S. Public*, pg. 1245

PITTCHLOR—Hypochlorite—PPG Industries, Inc.; *U.S. Public*, pg. 1245

PITTEX—Abrasive-Containing Plastic Filaments—PPG Industries, Inc.; *U.S. Public*, pg. 1245

PITTHANE—Urethane Coatings—PPG Industries, Inc.; *U.S. Public*, pg. 1245

PITTMAN—DC Motors—Penn Engineering & Manufacturing Corp.; *U.S. Public*, pg. 1269

PITTSBURG MORNING SUN—Newspaper—Shivers Trading & Operating Co.; *U.S. Private*, pg. 994

PITTSBURGH—Paints, Coatings, Primers, Enamels, Lacquers, Shellacs, Stains, Varnishes—PPG Industries, Inc.; *U.S. Public*, pg. 1245

PITTSBURGH NATIONAL BANK—Banking & Banking Services—PNC Bank, N.A.; *U.S. Public*, pg. 1243

PITTSBURGH POST-GAZETTE—Newspaper—Blade Communications, Inc.; *U.S. Private*, pg. 147

PITTSBURGH TUBE—Steel Tubing—Pittsburgh Tube Co.; *U.S. Private*, pg. 867

PITTSTON COAL—Underground Mining—The Pittston Company; *U.S. Public*, pg. 1305

PITTSTON MINERALS—Underground Mining—The Pittston Company; *U.S. Public*, pg. 1305

PIVOT—Computer Programs—Lucent Technologies Inc.; *U.S. Public*, pg. 1017

PIX—Crop Protection Agent—BASF AG; *Int'l*, pg. 103

PIX—Magazine for the Photography Market—BPI Communications Inc.; *Int'l*, pg. 1446

PIXIE—Miniature Carnations—Denver Wholesale Florists Company; *U.S. Private*, pg. 326

PIXY STIX—Candy—Nestle USA; *Int'l*, pg. 916

PIZ BUIN—Sunscreen—Johnson & Johnson; *U.S. Public*, pg. 927

PIZAZZ—Liquor Stores & Lounges—Flanigan's Enterprises, Inc.; *U.S. Public*, pg. 648

PIZZA DEL ARTE—Italian Restaurants—Accor S.A.; *Int'l*, pg. 20

PIZZA HAVEN—Pizza Restaurants—Pizza Haven Inc.; *U.S. Private*, pg. 868

PIZZA HUT—Pizza Restaurant & Delivery—NPC International, Inc.; *U.S. Public*, pg. 1146

PIZZA HUT—Specialty Restaurants—Pizza Hut, Inc.; *U.S. Public*, pg. 1636

PIZZA HUT—Restaurant—Whitbread PLC; *Int'l*, pg. 1498

PIZZA HUT RESTAURANTS—NONE—Lundy Enterprises, Inc.; *U.S. Private*, pg. 681

PIZZA INN—NONE—Pizza Inn, Inc.; *U.S. Public*, pg. 1307

PIZZA-MATE—Shredded Cheese Substitute Products—Borden, Inc.; *U.S. Private*, pg. 157

PIZZA! PIZZA!—Pizza—Little Caesar Enterprises, Inc.; *U.S. Private*, pg. 671

PIZZA PIZZAZZ—Eat in/Drive Through Restaurant—Domino's Pizza Inc.; *U.S. Private*, pg. 339

PIZZA PRESTO—NONE—Crestar Food Products, Inc.; *U.S. Public*, pg. 805

PIZZA QUICK—Sauces, Toppings, Crust Mix—Chesebrough-Pond's; *Int'l*, pg. 1436

PIZZA QUICK—Sauces, Toppings, Crust Mix—Ragu Foods, Inc.; *Int'l*, pg. 1436

PIZZA SOLO—NONE—Crestar Food Products, Inc.; *U.S. Public*, pg. 805

PIZZA SUPERIORE—Pizza Flour—International Multifoods Corporation; *U.S. Public*, pg. 900

PIZZA VITA—Pizza—Little Lady Foods, Inc.; *U.S. Private*, pg. 671

PIZZAPI—Pizza—Cara Operations Limited; *Int'l*, pg. 266

PIZZARIAS—Snack Food—The O'Boise Corporation; *U.S. Private*, pg. 810

PIZZAZZ—Interior Walls—Monarch Tile, Inc.; *U.S. Private*, pg. 287

PIZZERIA UNO—Original Deep Dish Pizza—Uno Restaurant Corporation; *U.S. Public*, pg. 1698

THE PLACE—Children's Clothing Stores—The Children's Place Retail Stores, Inc.; *U.S. Private*, pg. 237

PLACE-RITE—Repositionable Adhesive—Fasson Films; *U.S. Public*, pg. 153

PLACENTA PLUS—Hair Care—Palm Beach Beauty Products Co.; *U.S. Private*, pg. 834

PLACES—Wood & Metal Casegoods, Freestanding & Open Office Furniture—Haworth, Inc.; *U.S. Private*, pg. 511

PLACIDO—Premium Wines—Banfi Vintners; *U.S. Private*, pg. 113

PALCO-LOC—Finger-jointed Lumber—The Pacific Lumber Company; *U.S. Public*, pg. 1062

PLACTIDIL—Pharmaceutical—Novartis AG; *Int'l*, pg. 971

PLAIN ROLLER—Tires—Bridgestone/Firestone, Inc.; *Int'l*, pg. 213

PLAIN TALK—Insurance Policy—Sentry Insurance, A Mutual Company; *U.S. Private*, pg. 984

PLAIN TREAD LOADER DOZER—Tires—Bridgestone/Firestone, Inc.; *Int'l*, pg. 213

PLAIN TREAD LOADER DOZER UNDERGROUND MINING SERV.—Tires—Bridgestone/Firestone, Inc.; *Int'l*, pg. 213

PLAINLOCK—Pipe Couplings—Victaulic Company of America; *U.S. Private*, pg. 1138

PLAINS—Muzzle Loading Pistol—Lyman Products Corporation; *U.S. Private*, pg. 683

PLAINSMAN—Asphalt Shingles—Atlas Roofing Corp.; *U.S. Private*, pg. 96

PLAINSMAN—NONE—Ganin Tire Co., Inc.; *U.S. Private*, pg. 439

PLAINVIEW DAILY HERALD—Newspaper—The Hearst Corporation; *U.S. Private*, pg. 515

PLAKFINDER—Oral Hygiene Aids—John O. Butler Co.; *Int'l*, pg. 1320

PLAN BUILDER—Computer Product—International Business Machines Corporation; *U.S. Public*, pg. 895

PLAN ONE—Accounting System—SunGard Data Systems Inc.; *U.S. Public*, pg. 1534

PLANAR—Toughened Safety Glass Assemblies—Pilkington Australasia Limited; *Int'l*, pg. 1057

PLANAR T—Camera Lense—Carl Zeiss; *Int'l*, pg. 1522

PLANAT—Cognac—Marie Brizard Wines & Spirits USA; *U.S. Private*, pg. 702

PLAND—Stainlees Steel Sinks—Lonrho plc; *Int'l*, pg. 817

PLANET EARTH—Skateboards—K2 Inc.; *U.S. Public*, pg. 940

PLANET POWER—Planetary Reducers—U.S. Electrical Motor Division; *U.S. Public*, pg. 573

PLANETA—Printing Presses—VEB Polygraph Druckmachinenwerk Planeta Radebeul; *Int'l*, pg. 1445

PLANETOR—Hardware Products—Rule Industries, Inc.; *U.S. Public*, pg. 950

PLANK-TONE—Prefinished Plywood—Georgia-Pacific Corporation; *U.S. Public*, pg. 735

PLANKTEX—Plywood—Georgia-Pacific Corporation; *U.S. Public*, pg. 735

PLANKWELD—Lumber & Wood Construction Material—Georgia-Pacific Corporation; *U.S. Public*, pg. 735

PLANNING DYNAMICS—NONE—JP Foodservice, Inc.; *U.S. Public*, pg. 918

PLANO—Tackle & Tool Boxes & Cosmetic Organizers—Plano Molding Co.; *U.S. Private*, pg. 869

PLANOFORM—Ultra Precision Flycutting Machine—Taylor Hobson Pneumo; *Int'l*, pg. 1087

PLANS DE MAISONS DU QUEBEC—Magazine—Quebecor Inc.; *Int'l*, pg. 1075

PLANT ENGINEERING—Magazine for Engineering Professionals Handling Operations of Facilities—Reed Elsevier Business Information; *Int'l*, pg. 1095

PLANT FLOOR SERIES—Business Product—International Business Machines Corporation; *U.S. Public*, pg. 895

PLANTS, SITES & PARKS—Magazine & Directories—BPI Communications Inc.; *Int'l*, pg. 1446

PLANT SYSTEM 80—Rational Plant Growing—Stora Kopparbergs Bergslags AB; *Int'l*, pg. 1302

PLANTA—Margarine—FIMA-Productos Alimentares, Lda; *Int'l*, pg. 471

PLANTATION—Molasses—Allied Old English, Inc.; *U.S. Private*, pg. 39

PLANTATION—Poultry & Poultry Products—Plantation Foods Inc.; *U.S. Private*, pg. 869

PLANTATION—Brownies—President Baking Company; *Int'l*, pg. 1069

PLANTATION—Vinyl Siding—Reynolds Metals Company; *U.S. Public*, pg. 1385

PLANTATION FENCE—5" Round Posts; Domed 1/2" Round Rails—Seaman Timber Company, Inc.; *U.S. Private*, pg. 979

PLANTATION PATTERNS—Metal Household Furniture—Meadowcraft, Inc.; *U.S. Private*, pg. 725

PLANTERS—Nuts—Hershey Foods Corporation; *U.S. Public*, pg. 811

PLANTERS—Nuts & Snacks—Nabisco Inc.; *U.S. Public*, pg. 1355

PLANTERS—Nuts, Candies & Snacks—Planters Company; *U.S. Public*, pg. 1355

PLANTERS—Nuts & Snacks—RJR Nabisco Holdings Corp.; *U.S. Public*, pg. 1354

PLANTLINE—Magazine—Reed Business Information Pty. Limited; *Int'l*, pg. 1094

PLANTMOBILE—Mobile Classroom Equipment for the Growth and Study of Plants—American Educational Products; *U.S. Public*, pg. 71

PLANTO—Rapidly Biodegradeable Lubricants—Fuchs Petrolub AG Oel + Chemie; *Int'l*, pg. 517

PLANTRONICS MIRAGE—Telephone Headset—Plantronics Inc.; *U.S. Public*, pg. 1308

PLANTRONICS STARSET—Telephone Headset—Plantronics Inc.; *U.S. Public*, pg. 1308

PLANTRONICS SUPRA—Telephone Headset—Plantronics Inc.; *U.S. Public*, pg. 1308

PLANTWORKS—Business Product—International Business Machines Corporation; *U.S. Public*, pg. 895

PLAQUE REMOVER—Dental Tool—The Gillette Company; *U.S. Public*, pg. 743

PLAS-AMINO—Amino Acid Solution—Otsuka Pharmaceutical Co., Ltd.; *Int'l*, pg. 1013

PLAS-CHEK—Plasticizers—Ferro Corporation; *U.S. Public*, pg. 618

PLAS-T-COTE—Sealant—Elixir Industries; *U.S. Private*, pg. 371

PLAS-TOP—Closures—Owens-Illinois, Inc.; *U.S. Public*, pg. 1238

PLAS-TOP—Closure for Composite Cans—Sonoco Products Company; *U.S. Public*, pg. 1485

PLASBESTOS—Automotive Brake System—Echlin Inc.; *U.S. Public*, pg. 560

PLASCOLUME—Lighting Fixtures—Guth Lighting Company; *Int'l*, pg. 821

PLASDONE—Povidone—International Specialty Products, Inc.; *U.S. Public*, pg. 858

PLASITE—Anti-Corrosion Products—RPM, Inc.; *U.S. Public*, pg. 1356

PLASMA—Baseball Shoes—Mizuno Corporation; *Int'l*, pg. 884

PLASMA PLEX—Plasma Protein Fraction (Human) 5% Solution Heat Treated—Centeon, L.L.C.; *Int'l*, pg. 626

PLASMA QUAD—Inorganic Mass Spectrometer—Kevex X-Ray; *U.S. Public*, pg. 1594

PLASMA QUAD—Inorganic Mass Spectrometer—VG Instruments plc; *U.S. Public*, pg. 1595

PLASMADIZE—Composite Coating Technology—General Magnaplate Corporation; *U.S. Public*, pg. 717

PLASMADOT—Gas Discharge Displays—Cherry Electrical Products Corporation; *U.S. Public*, pg. 346

PLASMALUX—Gas Discharge Displays—Cherry Electrical Products Corporation; *U.S. Public*, pg. 346

PLASMAPHAN—Plasmapheresis—Akzo Nobel N.V.; *Int'l*, pg. 42

PLASMATEIN—NONE—Alpha Therapeutic Corp.; *Int'l*, pg. 558

PLASMOCHIN—Tropical Medicine for Treatment of Malaria—Bayer AG; *Int'l*, pg. 171

PLAST-O-MAT—Shelf Liner, Floor Runner—Flex-O-Glass, Inc.; *U.S. Private*, pg. 412

PLAST-O-MAT—Shelf Liner & Floor Runner—Warp Brothers; *U.S. Private*, pg. 412

PLAST-O-MATIC—Valves—Ryan Herco Products Corp.; *U.S. Private*, pg. 953

THE PLASTAG LINE—Plastic Specialties—Plastag Corporation; *U.S. Private*, pg. 870

PLASTECH/RMI-P—Plastic Products—Rotonics Manufacturing Inc.; *U.S. Public*, pg. 1406

PLASTECH/RMI-T—Plastic Products—Rotonics Manufacturing Inc.; *U.S. Public*, pg. 1406

PLASTHALL—Plasticizers—The C.P. Hall Company; *U.S. Private*, pg. 495

PLASTI-FAST—Thread Rolling Screws for Plastic—Parker Kalon; *U.S. Public*, pg. 233

PLASTI GLASS—Window Material—Warp Brothers; *U.S. Private*, pg. 412

PLASTI-LINE—Signs & Advertising Displays—Plasti-Line, Inc.; *U.S. Public*, pg. 1308

PLASTI-PAK—Packaged Greeting Cards—American Greetings Corporation; *U.S. Public*, pg. 77

PLASTI-PANE—Window Material—Warp Brothers; *U.S. Public*, pg. 412

PLASTI-SHIELD—Containers—Owens-Illinois, Inc.; *U.S. Public*, pg. 1238

PLASTIC CANVAS WORLD—Craft Magazine—House of White Birches, Inc.; *U.S. Private*, pg. 542

PLASTIC-KIT—Mounting Compound—Buehler, Limited; *U.S. Public*, pg. 574

PLASTIC PACK—Backing Material—Svedala Industries Inc.; *Int'l*, pg. 1325

PLASTIC PLUS—NONE—Bowmar Instrument Corporation; *U.S. Public*, pg. 248

PLASTIC SEAL—Plumbing Chemical—Hercules Chemical Co., Inc.; *U.S. Private*, pg. 523

PLASTICELL—NONE—Avenor, Inc.; *Int'l*, pg. 101

PLASTICRETE—Concrete Products—Plasticrete Block & Supply Corp.; *U.S. Private*, pg. 871

PLASTICS NEWS—Newspaper—Crain Communications, Inc.; *U.S. Private*, pg. 284

PLASTICS TECHNOLOGY—Business Publication—Bill Communications, Inc.; *Int'l*, pg. 1446

PLASTICVILLE, USA—NONE—Bachmann Industries, Inc.; *U.S. Private*, pg. 109

PLASTIFAST—Fastening System—The Black & Decker Corporation; *U.S. Public*, pg. 233

PLASTIFORM—Bonded Magnets—The Arnold Engineering Company; *U.S. Public*, pg. 1420

PLASTIMENT—Admixture, Retarding Densifier—Sika Corporation; *Int'l*, pg. 1249

PLASTIN—Binder—Raschig GmbH; *U.S. Private*, pg. 827

PLASTINET—NONE—Applied Extrusion Technologies, Inc.; *U.S. Public*, pg. 122

PLASTIPAD—Reuseable Hyper-Hypothermia Blankets—Cincinnati Sub-Zero Products, Inc.; *U.S. Private*, pg. 240

PLASTIPAK—Hypodermic Syringes—Becton Dickinson & Company; *U.S. Public*, pg. 199

PLASTIPRINT—Binding Preparation for Paints—Signtech USA, Ltd.; *U.S. Private*, pg. 999

PLASTIROLL—Ink Rolls—Markem Corporation; *U.S. Private*, pg. 704

PLASTITE—Bolts & Screws—Continental/Midland, Inc.; *U.S. Private*, pg. 268

PLASTIX—Reflective Traffic Marking Materials—Linear Dynamics Inc.; *U.S. Private*, pg. 668

PLASTO JOINT STIK FAST—Pipe Thread Compound—La-Co Industries Markal Company; *U.S. Private*, pg. 640

PLASTOCRETE—Admixture, Strength-Producer—Sika Corporation; *Int'l*, pg. 1249

PLASTONE—Processing Aids—Harwick Standard Distribution Corporation; *U.S. Private*, pg. 509

PLASTRAK—Feed Shelves—The Mead Corporation; *U.S. Public*, pg. 1074

PLASTUSA—Tape Backing Material—Industrial Coatings Group, Inc.; *U.S. Private*, pg. 434

PLASTYLE—Containers—Sealright Company, Inc.; *U.S. Public*, pg. 1451

PLASVATA—Thrombolytic Agent—Asahi Chemical Industry Co., Ltd.; *Int'l*, pg. 83

PLATA—NONE—Carillon Importers, Ltd.; *Int'l*, pg. 409

PLATAMID—Textile Adhesives—Elf Atochem North America, Inc.; *Int'l*, pg. 445

PLATE—Canned Meat Products—Campbell Soup Company; *U.S. Public*, pg. 298

PLATE WELD—Dental Aid/Device (Denture)—Menley & James Laboratories, Inc.; *U.S. Public*, pg. 1086

PLATECOIL—Industrial Plate Type Heat Exchangers—Tranter, Inc.; *U.S. Public*, pg. 521

PLATFORM—Platform Mattress—Kingsdown, Inc.; *U.S. Private*, pg. 622

PLATFORM PLUS—Special Platrform with Qualofil—Kingsdown, Inc.; *U.S. Private*, pg. 622

PLATINOL—Anti-Cancer Agent—Bristol-Myers Squibb Company; *U.S. Public*, pg. 253

PLATINOL—Pharmaceutical Used to Treat Tumors—Bristol-Myers Squibb U.S. Pharmaceutical Group; *U.S. Public*, pg. 255

PLATINUM—Premium Body Fillers—Marson/Creative Fastener, Inc.; *U.S. Private*, pg. 708

PLATINUM CARD—Charge Card Services—American Express Company; *U.S. Public*, pg. 73

PLATINUM ONE ACCOUNT—Market Rate Interest Bearing Checking—Fifth Third Bancorp; *U.S. Public*, pg. 621

PLATINUM-PLUS—Blades—The Gillette Company; *U.S. Public*, pg. 743

PLATOON—War Game—Monarch Avalon, Inc.; *U.S. Public*, pg. 1123

PLAX—NONE—Johnson & Johnson; *U.S. Public*, pg. 927

PLAX—NONE—Pfizer Inc.; *U.S. Public*, pg. 1281

PLAY DOH—NONE—MB Espana, S.A.; *U.S. Public*, pg. 798

PLAY-FACES—Sculpted Toy Pillows—Play by Play Toys & Novelties, Inc.; *U.S. Public*, pg. 1309

PLAY IT AGAIN SPORTS—Buys, Sells, Trades & Consigns Used & New Sporting Equipment—Grow Biz International, Inc.; *U.S. Public*, pg. 767

PLAY SYSTEMS—NONE—Stainless Incorporated; *U.S. Private*, pg. 1029

PLAY TIME—Swimming Pool Paint—California Products Corp.; *U.S. Private*, pg. 201

PLAYBACK—NONE—Compuware Corporation; *U.S. Public*, pg. 423

PLAYBACK—Wood Frame Side Chair, ai Collection—Vecta; *U.S. Private*, pg. 1038

PLAYBOY—Magazine, Products & Video—Playboy Enterprises, Inc.; *U.S. Public*, pg. 1309

PLAYDAYS—NONE—BBC Magazines; *Int'l*, pg. 114

PLAYER MEDIUM NAVY CUT—Flake Pipe Tobacco—Imperial Tobacco Group, Ltd.; *Int'l*, pg. 666

PLAYER'S—Cigarettes—Imasco Limited; *Int'l*, pg. 112

PLAYERS—Cigarettes—Philip Morris Companies Inc.; *U.S. Public*, pg. 1287

PLAYERS—Apparel—Phillips-Van Heusen Corporation; *U.S. Public*, pg. 1291

PLAYERS LIGHTS 25'S—Cigarettes—Philip Morris Companies Inc.; *U.S. Public*, pg. 1287

PLAYERS LIGHTS 25'S MENTHOL—Cigarettes—Philip Morris Companies Inc.; *U.S. Public*, pg. 1287

PLAYERS LIGHTS 25'S 100'S—Cigarettes—Philip Morris Companies Inc.; *U.S. Public*, pg. 1287

PLAYERS LIGHTS 25'S 100'S MENTHOL—Cigarettes—Philip Morris Companies Inc.; *U.S. Public*, pg. 1287

PLAYERS MEDIUM NAVY CUT—Cigarettes—Imperial Tobacco Group, Ltd.; *Int'l*, pg. 666

PLAYERS MENTHOL—Cigarettes—Philip Morris Companies Inc.; *U.S. Public*, pg. 1287

PLAYERS NAVY-CUT MEDIUM—Cigarettes—Philip Morris Companies Inc.; *U.S. Public*, pg. 1287

PLAYERS 100'S—Cigarettes—Philip Morris Companies Inc.; *U.S. Public*, pg. 1287

PLAYERS 100'S MENTHOL—Cigarettes—Philip Morris Companies Inc.; *U.S. Public*, pg. 1287

PLAYGYMS—Swing Sets—Flexible Flyer Toys; *U.S. Private*, pg. 412

PLAYLAND BOOKS—Books—The Putnam & Grosset Group; *Int'l*, pg. 1027

PLAYMASTER—Pre-School—Roadmaster/Brunswick; *U.S. Public*, pg. 265

PLAYMASTER BILLIARDS—Billiard Products—AMF Bowling Worldwide; *U.S. Private*, pg. 6

PLAYMATE—Products—Playboy Enterprises, Inc.; *U.S. Public*, pg. 1309

PLAYMATE PLUS—Ice Chest—Igloo Products Corporation; *U.S. Private*, pg. 265

PLAYMATES TEENAGE MUTANT NINJA TURTLE—Action Figures—Playmates Toys Inc.; *Int'l*, pg. 1060

THE PLAYROOM—NONE—Broderbund Software, Inc.; *U.S. Public*, pg. 258

PLAYSKOOL—Preschool & Infant Toys—Hasbro, Inc.; *U.S. Public*, pg. 797

PLAYSKOOL—NONE—MB Espana, S.A.; *U.S. Public*, pg. 798

PLAYSTATION—Videogame Hardware System—Sony Electronics; *Int'l*, pg. 1281

PLAYTEX—Rubber Gloves, Tampons—Playtex Products Corp.; *U.S. Public*, pg. 1311

PLAYTEX—Tampons, Baby Feeding Systems, Rubber Gloves—Playtex Products Inc.; *U.S. Public*, pg. 1310

PLAYTEX—Intimate Apparel—Sara Lee Corporation; *U.S. Public*, pg. 1432

PLAYTEX—NONE—Tambrands Inc.; *U.S. Public*, pg. 1331

PLAYTEX SECRETS—NONE—Playtex Apparel, Inc.; *U.S. Public*, pg. 1433

PLAZA—Cigarettes—B.A.T Industries P.L.C.; *Int'l*, pg. 110

PLAZA CARPETS—Carpet—World Carpets, Inc.; *U.S. Private*, pg. 1190

PLAZA LAS GLORIAS—Hotels—Grupo Sidek, S.A. de C.V.; *Int'l*, pg. 576

PLAZA III—Restaurants—Houlihan's Restaurant Group; *U.S. Public*, pg. 841

PLAZCRAFT—Air Plasma Cutting Torches—Dovatech, Ltd.; *U.S. Public*, pg. 520

PLEASER—Instant Camera—Eastman Kodak Company; *U.S. Public*, pg. 550

PLEASURE CHEST OF STEAKS—Meats—Stock Yards Packing Co., Inc.; *U.S. Private*, pg. 1043

PLEATLOC—Filter Media—Donaldson Company, Inc.; *U.S. Public*, pg. 517

PLEDGE—Furniture Polish—S.C. Johnson & Son, Inc.; *U.S. Private*, pg. 592

PLEDGE—Furniture Polish—S.C. Johnson & Son, Limited; *U.S. Private*, pg. 593

PLEDGE—NONE—N.V. Johnson Wax Belgium S.A.; *U.S. Private*, pg. 593

PLEDGE DUSTER—Furniture Care—S.C. Johnson & Son, Inc.; *U.S. Private*, pg. 592

PLEDGE HOUSEHOLD CLEANER—Cleaners—S.C. Johnson & Son, Inc.; *U.S. Private*, pg. 592

PLEDGE WOOD CLEANER—Furniture Care—S.C. Johnson & Son, Inc.; *U.S. Private*, pg. 592

PLEIADES—Cigars—SEITA, Societe Nationale D'Exploitation Industrielle des Tabacs et des Allumettes; *Int'l*, pg. 1219

PLENDIL—Cardiovascular Agent, Calcium Antagonist—Astra AB; *Int'l*, pg. 93

PLENDIL—Felodipine—Merck & Co., Inc.; *U.S. Public*, pg. 1090

PLENITUDE—Skin Care—L'Oreal S.A.; *Int'l*, pg. 818

PLENITUDE PERFECTED—Self-Tanning Lotion—Cosmair, Inc.; *Int'l*, pg. 818

PLENUM-GARD—Plenum & Riser Fiber-Optic Conduit—The Lamson & Sessions Co.; *U.S. Public*, pg. 976

PLENUM PRESS—NONE—Plenum Publishing Corporation; *U.S. Public*, pg. 1311

PLENUM-PULSE—Dust Collector—Fuller Company; *Int'l*, pg. 475

PLETAAL—Anti-Platelet Agent—Otsuka Pharmaceutical Co., Ltd.; *Int'l*, pg. 1013

PLEUGER—Pumps—Ingersoll-Dresser Pump Company; *U.S. Public*, pg. 529

PLEUGER—NONE—Ingersoll-Rand Company; *U.S. Public*, pg. 876

PLEURA-GARD—Chest Drainage Device—Conmed Corporation; *U.S. Public*, pg. 431

PLEWS TOOLS—NONE—Plews/Edelmann; *Int'l*, pg. 1396

PLEX—Reagents—Millipore Corporation; *U.S. Public*, pg. 1112

PLEXAR—Adhesive—DSM N.V.; *Int'l*, pg. 352

PLEXAR—Extrudable Adhesive Resins—Millennium Petrochemicals, Inc.; *Int'l*, pg. 594

PLEXAR—Communications System—SBC Communications Inc.; *U.S. Public*, pg. 1415

PLEXI TRACK—Synthetic Running Track System—California Products Corp.; *U.S. Private*, pg. 201

PLEXICOURT—Tennis Court System—California Products Corp.; *U.S. Private*, pg. 201

PLEXICUSHION—Tennis Court Sub-Surface—California Products Corp.; *U.S. Private*, pg. 201

PLEXIGLAS—Plastic Sheet, Molding Powders—Rohm and Haas Company; *U.S. Public*, pg. 1403

PLEXIGLAS—Plastic Prods.—Rohm GmbH; *Int'l*, pg. 1454

PLEXIGUM—Plastic Prods.—Rohm GmbH; *Int'l*, pg. 1454

PLEXIMID—Plastic Prods.—Rohm GmbH; *Int'l*, pg. 1454

PLEXIPAVE—Tennis Court System—California Products Corp.; *U.S. Private*, pg. 201

PLEXISOL—Plastic Prods.—Rohm GmbH; *Int'l*, pg. 1454

PLEXTOL—Plastic Prods.—Rohm GmbH; *Int'l*, pg. 1454

PLIAGEL—Cleaning Solution—Alcon Laboratories, Inc.; *Int'l*, pg. 916

PLIAGEL—Cleaning Solution—Wesley-Jessen; *U.S. Private*, pg. 111

PLIBRICO—Plastic Refractories—Plibrico Co.; *U.S. Private*, pg. 872

PLICAST—Castable Refractories—Plibrico Co.; *U.S. Private*, pg. 872

PLIGUN—Gun Mix Refractories—Plibrico Co.; *U.S. Private*, pg. 872

PLIO-MAGIC—Plastic Film Cases & Reels—Plastic Reel Corp. of America; *U.S. Public*, pg. 871

PLIOBOND—Adhesives for Roofing—Ashland, Inc.; *U.S. Public*, pg. 138

PLIOCORD—Styrene Butadiene/Vinylpyridine Latices—The Goodyear Tire & Rubber Company; *U.S. Public*, pg. 752

PLIOFLEX—Styrene/Butadiene Rubber—The Goodyear Tire & Rubber Company; *U.S. Public*, pg. 752

PLIOGRIP II—Structural Adhesive—Ashland, Inc.; *U.S. Public*, pg. 138

PLIOLITE—Latex & Resins—The Goodyear Tire & Rubber Company; *U.S. Public*, pg. 752

PLION—Monofilament—Cortland Line Co., Inc.; *U.S. Private*, pg. 277

PLIOTONE—Resin—The Goodyear Tire & Rubber Company; *U.S. Public*, pg. 752

PLIOVIC—Polyvinyl Chloride Resin—The Goodyear Tire & Rubber Company; *U.S. Public*, pg. 752

PLIOWAY—Resin—The Goodyear Tire & Rubber Company; *U.S. Public*, pg. 752

PLIRAM—Ram Mix Refractories—Plibrico Co.; *U.S. Private*, pg. 872

PLITT THEATRES—Motion Picture Theaters—Cineplex Odeon Corporation; *Int'l*, pg. 292

PLOT 10—Computer Graphics Software—Tektronix, Inc.; *U.S. Public*, pg. 1567

PLOUGH TILE—NONE—Alfa Laval Separation Inc.; *Int'l*, pg. 1378

PLOUGHSHARE—Dryer—Littleford Day Inc.; *U.S. Private*, pg. 671

PLOUGHSHARE—Mixer—Littleford Day Inc.; *U.S. Private*, pg. 671

PLOVER—Binocular—Swift Instruments, Inc.; *U.S. Private*, pg. 1058

PLOW—Tires—Bridgestone/Firestone, Inc.; *Int'l*, pg. 213

PLOW BOY—Corn & Cane Syrup—Whitfield Foods, Inc.; *U.S. Private*, pg. 1173

POLYPUR—Plastic Compounds—A. Schulman, Inc.; *U.S. Public*, pg. 1441

PLUG 'N' GO—Business Product—International Business Machines Corporation; *U.S. Public*, pg. 895

PLUG-A-BUBBLE—Electronic Instrument—Intel Corporation; *U.S. Public*, pg. 886

PLUGIN DATAMATION—World Wide Web Navigator & On-Line Resource Center for IT Executives—Reed Elsevier Business Information; *Int'l*, pg. 1095

PLUM CREEK—Lumber & Plywood—Plum Creek Timber Co., L.P.; *U.S. Public*, pg. 1311

PLUMB—Hammers and Axes—Cooper Hand Tools; *U.S. Public*, pg. 444

PLUMB—Hammers, Axes & Hatchets—Cooper Industries, Inc.; *U.S. Public*, pg. 442

PLUMB—NONE—Cooper Tools; *U.S. Public*, pg. 444

PLUMBCRAFT—Plumbing Supplies—Waxman Industries, Inc.; *U.S. Public*, pg. 1748

PLUMBERS CAULK—Plumbing Chemical—Hercules Chemical Co., Inc.; *U.S. Private*, pg. 523

PLUMBERS GREASE—Plumbing Chemical—Hercules Chemical Co., Inc.; *U.S. Private*, pg. 523

PLUMBICON—Camera Tubes—Philips Components; *Int'l*, pg. 1054

PLUMBKING—Plumbing Supplies—Waxman Industries, Inc.; *U.S. Public*, pg. 1748

PLUMBLINE—Plumbing Supplies—Waxman Industries, Inc.; *U.S. Public*, pg. 1748

PLUMBSET—Putty—La-Co Industries Markal Company; *U.S. Private*, pg. 640

PLUME & MERIDIAN—Adult Paperback Books—Penguin Putnam Inc.; *Int'l*, pg. 1027

PLUMPS—Moist Towelettes—Reynolds Metals Company; *U.S. Public*, pg. 1385

PLUMS—Less Expensive Sweaters—Winona Knits; *U.S. Private*, pg. 1183

PLURAFAC—Non-Ionic Surfactants—BASF AG; *Int'l*, pg. 103

PLURIOL—Non-Ionic Surfactants—BASF AG; *Int'l*, pg. 103

PLURONIC—Non-Ionic Surfactants—BASF AG; *Int'l*, pg. 103

PLUS—Kitchen Tools—General Housewares Corp.; *U.S. Public*, pg. 715

PLUS—Grocery Store—Tengelmann Warenhandelsgesellschaft; *Int'l*, pg. 1375

PLUS + S—Liquid Fertilizer—Na-Churs Plant Food Company; *U.S. Private*, pg. 1096

PLUS A—Thin Wall Non-Metallic Conduit—The Lamson & Sessions Co.; *U.S. Public*, pg. 976

PLUS CHEM—Chemical Reagents—Beckman Instruments, Inc.; *U.S. Public*, pg. 199

PLUS 80—Non-Metallic Schedule 80 Conduit—The Lamson & Sessions Co.; *U.S. Public*, pg. 976

PLUS-FIFTY—Dry Chemical Agent—Ansul Incorporated; *U.S. Public*, pg. 1648

PLUS-FORMA—Dietary Supplement—SmithKline Beecham plc; *Int'l*, pg. 1264

PLUS 40—Non-Metallic Schedule 40 Conduit—The Lamson & Sessions Co.; *U.S. Public*, pg. 976

PLUS LATCH—Pre-Catch Latch—Hartwell Corporation; *U.S. Private*, pg. 1168

PLUS+MARK—Greeting Cards; Gift Wrap & Ribbon—American Greetings Corporation; *U.S. Public*, pg. 77

+MEDIC—Physician Information System—Medic Computer Systems, Inc.; *Int'l*, pg. 870

PLUS ONE—Clinical Nutrition—Novo Nordisk A/S; *Int'l*, pg. 987

PLUS PLATINUM—Razor Blades—Warner-Lambert Company; *U.S. Public*, pg. 1738

PLUS 3—Joint Compound—USG Corporation; *U.S. Public*, pg. 1660

PLUS+WHITE—NONE—CCA Industries, Inc.; *U.S. Public*, pg. 276

PLUS-X—Photographic Film—Eastman Kodak Company; *U.S. Public*, pg. 550

PLUSBUS—NONE—UB Networks; *Int'l*, pg. 924

PLUSH PIPPIN—Pies—Nabisco Inc.; *U.S. Public*, pg. 1355

PLUSH PIPPIN PIES—Creme, Fruit, Meringue & Specialty Pies—RJR Nabisco Holdings Corp.; *U.S. Public*, pg. 1354

PLUSPOINT—Publicity Agency—RetailNet B.V.; *Int'l*, pg. 750

PLUTIN LA—Tin Lead Process—LeaRonal, Inc.; *U.S. Private*, pg. 982

PLUTIN II—Bright Tin-Lead Plating Process—LeaRonal, Inc.; *U.S. Public*, pg. 982

PLY FRAME—Plywood Panels—Georgia-Pacific Corporation; *U.S. Public*, pg. 735

PLY-VENEER—Paneling—Weyerhaeuser Forest Products Company; *U.S. Public*, pg. 1764

PLYARC—Arc & Fireproofing Tape—Plymouth Rubber Company, Inc.; *U.S. Public*, pg. 1311

PLYBRAID—Copper Sheilding Braid—Plymouth Rubber Company, Inc.; *U.S. Public*, pg. 1311

PLYCAST—Epoxy Kit—Plymouth Rubber Company, Inc.; *U.S. Public*, pg. 1311

PLYCOM—Plywood Patch Compound—ISK BioSciences; *Int'l*, pg. 689

PLYDUCT—Duct Tape—Plymouth Rubber Company, Inc.; *U.S. Public*, pg. 1311

PLYFLEX—L.V. Splice Kit—Plymouth Rubber Company, Inc.; *U.S. Public*, pg. 1311

PLYFOLD—Plybent Wood Chair—Sauder Manufacturing Corporation; *U.S. Private*, pg. 967

PLYGLAS—Glass Cloth Tape—Plymouth Rubber Company, Inc.; *U.S. Public*, pg. 1311

PLYGLASS—Plywood With Reinforced Plastic—Molded Fiber Glass Companies; *U.S. Private*, pg. 755

PLYGUARD—Low Pressure Laminates—Pickering Inc.; *U.S. Private*, pg. 864

PLYJOINT—Cable Splice Kit—Plymouth Rubber Company, Inc.; *U.S. Public*, pg. 1311

PLYLOK—Chair Plybent Wood—Sauder Manufacturing Corporation; *U.S. Private*, pg. 967

PLYLON—Conveyor Belting—The Goodyear Tire & Rubber Company; *U.S. Public*, pg. 752

PLYMARK—Wire Markers—Plymouth Rubber Company, Inc.; *U.S. Public*, pg. 1311

PLYMASTER—Machinery—Hollingsworth Saco Lowell Corporation, Inc.; *U.S. Private*, pg. 535
PLYMOUTH—Locomotives—Plymouth Industries, Inc.; *U.S. Private*, pg. 873
PLYMOUTH ACCLAIM—Car—Chrysler Corporation; *U.S. Public*, pg. 352
PLYMOUTH COLT—Car—Chrysler Corporation; *U.S. Public*, pg. 352
PLYMOUTH COLT VISTA—Station Wagon—Chrysler Corporation; *U.S. Public*, pg. 352
PLYMOUTH FARMS—Chunk Natural Cheeses—Sargento Foods Inc.; *U.S. Private*, pg. 966
PLYMOUTH GRAND VOYAGER—Minivan—Chrysler Corporation; *U.S. Public*, pg. 352
PLYMOUTH LASER—Car—Chrysler Corporation; *U.S. Public*, pg. 352
PLYMOUTH PRIDE—Turkeys—Norbest, Inc.; *U.S. Private*, pg. 801
PLYMOUTH RELIANT—Car—Chrysler Corporation; *U.S. Public*, pg. 352
PLYMOUTH SUNDANCE—Car—Chrysler Corporation; *U.S. Public*, pg. 352
PLYMOUTH VOYAGER—Minivan—Chrysler Corporation; *U.S. Public*, pg. 352
PLYSAFE—H.V. Insulating Tape w/Liner—Plymouth Rubber Company, Inc.; *U.S. Public*, pg. 1311
PLYSEAL—Industrial Plywood End Seal—ISK BioSciences; *Int'l*, pg. 689
PLYSEAL—Mastics—Plymouth Rubber Company, Inc.; *U.S. Public*, pg. 1311
PLYSHIELD—Shielding Tape—Plymouth Rubber Company, Inc.; *U.S. Public*, pg. 1311
PLYSIL—Silicone Rubber Tape—Plymouth Rubber Company, Inc.; *U.S. Public*, pg. 1311
PLYSTRAP—Copper Ground Strap—Plymouth Rubber Company, Inc.; *U.S. Public*, pg. 1311
PLYTERM—Cable Termination Kits—Plymouth Rubber Company, Inc.; *U.S. Public*, pg. 1311
PLYTRAX—Laminates—Norton Performance Plastics; *Int'l*, pg. 1174
PLYVOLT—H.V. Insulating Tape w/Liner—Plymouth Rubber Company, Inc.; *U.S. Public*, pg. 1311
PLYWALL—Method for Fabricating High Pressure Processing Vessels—Nooter Corporation; *U.S. Private*, pg. 801
PLYWRAP—Pipewrap Tape—Plymouth Rubber Company, Inc.; *U.S. Public*, pg. 1311
PMPLUS—NONE—GenRad, Inc.; *U.S. Public*, pg. 731
PNEU PAC—Swine Vaccine—Schering-Plough Corporation; *U.S. Public*, pg. 1438
PNEUFLEX—Equipment & Treads—Oliver Rubber Co.; *U.S. Public*, pg. 1504
PNEUMACAPPER—Capping Machine—Pneumatic Scale Corporation; *U.S. Private*, pg. 118
PNEUMACLEAN—Air Cleaning Machine—Pneumatic Scale Corporation; *U.S. Private*, pg. 118
PNEUMAFLOW—Liquid Filler—Pneumatic Scale Corporation; *U.S. Private*, pg. 118
PNEUMATRON—Weighing Machine—Pneumatic Scale Corporation; *U.S. Private*, pg. 118
PNEUMET—Mounting Press—Buehler, Limited; *U.S. Public*, pg. 574
PNEUMOVAX—Pneumoccal Vaccine Polyvalent—Merck & Co., Inc.; *U.S. Public*, pg. 1090
PNU-IMUNE 23—Vaccine—American Home Products Corporation; *U.S. Public*, pg. 79
POAST—Crop Protection Agent—BASF AG; *Int'l*, pg. 103
POCAHONTAS—Foodservice Items—Performance Food Group Company; *U.S. Public*, pg. 1278
POCAN—Plastic—Bayer AG; *Int'l*, pg. 171
POCARI—Beverage—Otsuka Pharmaceutical Co., Ltd.; *Int'l*, pg. 1013
POCARI STEVIA—Beverage—Otsuka Pharmaceutical Co., Ltd.; *Int'l*, pg. 1013
POCKET ACCENT—Quick Reference Marker—Sanford Corporation; *U.S. Public*, pg. 1178
POCKET BOOKS—Mass Market Paperback Books—Pocket Books; *U.S. Public*, pg. 777
POCKET BOOKS—Paperback Books—Simon & Schuster; *U.S. Private*, pg. 777
POCKET BOOKS HARDCOVERS—Cloth Bound Books—Pocket Books; *U.S. Private*, pg. 777
POCKET BOOKS TRADE PAPERBACKS—Trade-Sized Paperback Publications—Pocket Books; *U.S. Private*, pg. 777

POCKET COFFEE—Chocolate-Filled with Liquid Coffee—Ferrero; *Int'l*, pg. 480
POCKET COFFEE—Chocolate Filled With Liquid Coffee—Ferrero U.S.A., Inc.; *Int'l*, pg. 480
POCKET-MATE—Ultra Miniature Aluminum Flashlights—Streamlight Inc.; *U.S. Private*, pg. 1047
POCKET-PAIR—Ultra Miniature Aluminum Flashlights—Streamlight Inc.; *U.S. Private*, pg. 1047
POCKET SECRETARY—Micro Cassette Recorder—Lanier Worldwide Inc.; *U.S. Public*, pg. 791
POCKET SIMON—Game—Milton Bradley Company; *U.S. Public*, pg. 797
POCKETFOLD—NONE—Wisconsin Tissue Mills, Inc.; *U.S. Private*, pg. 347
POCKETOOLS—Toy—Toymax International Inc.; *U.S. Public*, pg. 1626
POCKETS—Children's Magazine—The Upper Room; *U.S. Private*, pg. 1129
POCKETS FULL OF POSIES—Greeting Cards—American Greetings Corporation; *U.S. Public*, pg. 77
POCLAIN—Excavators—Case Corporation; *U.S. Public*, pg. 311
POCONO—Photographic Printer/Processors—Eastman Kodak Company; *U.S. Public*, pg. 550
POCONO—Fiber-Cement Siding—GAF Premium Products, Inc.; *U.S. Public*, pg. 433
POCONO RASPBERRY—Premium Beer—The Lion Brewery, Inc.; *U.S. Public*, pg. 1000
PODOSIL—Silicone Gel for Preparation of Medical or Surgical Treatments or Appliance—General Electric Canada Inc.; *U.S. Public*, pg. 713
POET—Software—International Business Machines Corporation; *U.S. Public*, pg. 895
POET II—Instrument for Measurement of Anasthetic Agents—Criticare Systems, Inc.; *U.S. Public*, pg. 459
POET'S MARKET—Market Book—F & W Publications, Inc.; *U.S. Private*, pg. 388
POGGIO ALL'ORO BRUNNELLO—Single Vineyard—Castello Banfi Srl.; *U.S. Private*, pg. 113
POGO—Pump—Binks Sames Corporation; *U.S. Public*, pg. 229
POGO—NONE—Landmark Graphics Corporation; *U.S. Public*, pg. 776
POGON—Adult & Young Transporter Type Wheelchairs—Theradyne Corporation; *U.S. Private*, pg. 637
POINT—Pharmacy Order Integrating—Cerner Corporation; *U.S. Public*, pg. 331
POINT AMBER CLASSIC—Beer—Barton Beers, Ltd.; *U.S. Public*, pg. 300
POINT BOCK—Beer—Barton Beers, Ltd.; *U.S. Public*, pg. 300
POINT MAPLE WHEAT—Beer—Barton Beers, Ltd.; *U.S. Public*, pg. 300
POINT OF CARE—Blood Screening-Heart Attacks—EG & G, Inc.; *U.S. Public*, pg. 542
POINT OF VIEW—Magazine—Ethicon, Inc.; *U.S. Public*, pg. 928
POINT P—Building & Home Improvement Product Wholesaling—Poliet; *Int'l*, pg. 1177
POINT PALE ALE—Beer—Barton Beers, Ltd.; *U.S. Public*, pg. 300
POINT PRO—Needle Re-Capper—Medtronic, Inc.; *U.S. Public*, pg. 1082
POINT SPECIAL—Lager—Barton Beers, Ltd.; *U.S. Public*, pg. 300
POINT VIEW—Processed Vegetables—Furman Foods, Inc.; *U.S. Private*, pg. 43
POINT WINTER SPICE—Beer—Barton Beers, Ltd.; *U.S. Public*, pg. 300
POINTER—Unmanned Air Vehicle—Aerovironment, Inc.; *U.S. Private*, pg. 25
POINTER—Dog Food—Bush Brothers & Company; *U.S. Private*, pg. 189
POINTER CHECKER PLUS—IMS Database Utility—BMC Software, Inc.; *U.S. Public*, pg. 162
POINTS WEST—NONE—Tandy Brands Accessories, Inc.; *U.S. Public*, pg. 1560
POISE—Feminine Guards—Kimberly-Clark Corporation; *U.S. Public*, pg. 958
POISON—Perfume—Christian Dior Perfumes Inc.; *Int'l*, pg. 781
POKENO—Game—The United States Playing Card Company; *U.S. Private*, pg. 1125

POL ROGER—Champagne—Frederick Wildman & Sons Ltd.; *U.S. Private*, pg. 1176
POLA-SCREEN—Polarizing Screen—Eastman Kodak Company; *U.S. Public*, pg. 550
POLACHROME—35mm Color Transparency Film—Polaroid Corporation; *U.S. Public*, pg. 1313
POLACID—Disinfectants—Akzo Nobel N.V.; *Int'l*, pg. 42
POLACOAT—Rigid Rear Projection Screen—Da-Lite Screen Company, Inc.; *U.S. Private*, pg. 306
POLACOLOR—Print Film—Polaroid Corporation; *U.S. Public*, pg. 1313
POLACURE 740M—Curing Agent—Polaroid Corporation; *U.S. Public*, pg. 1313
POLAGRAPH—High Contrast Transparency Film—Polaroid Corporation; *U.S. Public*, pg. 1313
POLAIRE—Wine—Sapporo Breweries Ltd.; *Int'l*, pg. 1193
POLAND SPRING—Mineral Water—The Perrier Group of America; *Int'l*, pg. 919
POLAND SPRING—Bottled Water—Poland Spring Corporation; *Int'l*, pg. 919
POLAND SPRINGS—Mineral Water—Nestle S.A.; *Int'l*, pg. 915
POLAND SPRINGS—Liqueur—White Rock Distilleries Inc.; *U.S. Private*, pg. 1173
POLANE—Paints & Coatings—The Sherwin-Williams Company; *U.S. Public*, pg. 1465
POLANER—Fruit Preservatives—International Home Foods Inc.; *U.S. Private*, pg. 526
POLAPRINTER—Slide Printer—Polaroid Corporation; *U.S. Public*, pg. 1313
POLAPROOF—Anti-Counterfeiting Material—Polaroid Corporation; *U.S. Public*, pg. 1313
POLAR—Soft Drink—Polar Beverages; *U.S. Private*, pg. 873
POLAR—Stainless Steel Hospital & Restaurant Utensils—Polar Ware Company; *U.S. Private*, pg. 873
POLAR BEAR—Delivery Body or Trailer Styles—Hackney and Sons, Inc.; *U.S. Private*, pg. 1097
POLAR BOOTS—Slipper Boots—Reliable Knitting Works; *U.S. Private*, pg. 920
POLAR BRAND—Candles—Will & Baumer Incorporated; *U.S. Private*, pg. 1176
POLAR COLLECTION—Crystal Animals—Dansk International Designs Ltd.; *U.S. Public*, pg. 261
POLAR-CORR—Corrugated Board & Cartons—The Mead Corporation; *U.S. Public*, pg. 1074
POLAR GRIP—Tires—Bridgestone/Firestone, Inc.; *Int'l*, pg. 213
POLAR JAC/VEST—Apparel—American Honda Motor Co., Inc.; *Int'l*, pg. 634
POLAR KING—Men's Clothing—Key Industries, Inc.; *U.S. Private*, pg. 618
POLAR PETE—Slush Machine—Gold Medal Products Co.; *U.S. Private*, pg. 459
POLAR POWER—Electrical Extension Cords—General Cable Corporation; *Int'l*, pg. 1486
POLAR TRANSPORT—Tires—Bridgestone/Firestone, Inc.; *Int'l*, pg. 213
POLARAMINE—Expectorant Repetabs, Syrup & Tablets—Schering-Plough Corporation; *U.S. Public*, pg. 1438
POLARCUP—Disposable Paper Dishes & Food Packaging—Huhtamaki Oy; *Int'l*, pg. 638
POLARGUARD—Fiberglass Insulated Door—Todco; *U.S. Private*, pg. 823
POLARIS—Enamel Printing Paper—Consolidated Papers, Inc.; *U.S. Public*, pg. 436
POLARIS—Aircraft Leasing—General Electric Capital Aviation Services; *U.S. Public*, pg. 712
POLARIS—Growth Regulator for Sugarcane—Monsanto Company; *U.S. Public*, pg. 1124
POLARIS—Magnetic Resonance—Picker International, Inc.; *Int'l*, pg. 545
POLARIS—All-Terrain Vehicles, Snowmobiles & Personal Watercraft—Polaris Industries, Inc.; *U.S. Public*, pg. 1313
POLARIS—Water Heaters—Southcorp Holdings Ltd.; *Int'l*, pg. 1287
POLAROGRAPH—Voltammetric Analyzer—Sargent-Welch Scientific Company; *U.S. Public*, pg. 1704
POLAROID—Instant Cameras, Film, Sunglasses & Lenses, Sheet Polarizers, Videocassettes—Polaroid Corporation; *U.S. Public*, pg. 1313
POLAROID MACRO—NONE—Polaroid Corporation; *U.S. Public*, pg. 1313

POLAROID MAKE-A-MEMORY—NONE—Polaroid Corporation; *U.S. Public*, pg. 1313

POLAROID MAKE-A-PRINT—NONE—Polaroid Corporation; *U.S. Public*, pg. 1313

POLAROID PHOTOPAD—NONE—Polaroid Corporation; *U.S. Public*, pg. 1313

POLARSTAR—Compact Economical Refrigerator—The Jewett Refrigerator Co., Inc.; *U.S. Private*, pg. 952

POLARSTAR—Lab Refrigerators & Freezers-Economy Line—Ruslander & Sons, Inc.; *U.S. Private*, pg. 952

POLARVAN—Refrigerated Truck Body & Slip In For Pickup Trucks—Kidron Inc.; *U.S. Private*, pg. 619

POLATHANE XPE SYSTEM—Prepolymers & Curing Agents—Polaroid Corporation; *U.S. Public*, pg. 1313

POLAVIEW—NONE—Polaroid Corporation; *U.S. Public*, pg. 1313

POLECTRON—Emulsion Copolymers—International Specialty Products, Inc.; *U.S. Public*, pg. 858

POLI-GRIP—Denture Adhesive Cream—Block Drug Company, Inc.; *U.S. Public*, pg. 236

POLI-GRIP—Denture Creme—Stafford-Miller Limited; *U.S. Public*, pg. 237

POLICE—NONE—Bobit Publishing Company; *U.S. Private*, pg. 154

POLICE BLOTTA—Computer Game—Monarch Avalon, Inc.; *U.S. Public*, pg. 1123

POLICEFAX—Non-Impact, Ultra-High Speed Digital Printers—Litton Industries, Inc.; *U.S. Public*, pg. 1002

POLIDENT—Denture Cleanser Powder & Tablets—Block Drug Company, Inc.; *U.S. Public*, pg. 236

POLIFIX—Resins—Raschig GmbH; *U.S. Private*, pg. 827

POLIGEN—Polyethylene Waxes, Polyethylene Wax Oxidates, Montan Ester Waxes—BASF AG; *Int'l*, pg. 103

POLIMET—Abrasive Disc Grinder/Polisher—Buehler, Limited; *U.S. Private*, pg. 574

POLINAT—Resins—Raschig GmbH; *U.S. Private*, pg. 827

POLIO SABIN—NONE—SmithKline Beecham Corporation; *Int'l*, pg. 1264

POLIO SABIN—Vaccine—SmithKline Beecham plc; *Int'l*, pg. 1264

POLIO SABIN—Vaccine—SmithKline Beecham Research Limited; *Int'l*, pg. 1266

POLIPLEX—PVC—James Hardie Industries Ltd.; *Int'l*, pg. 596

POLISHMASTER—Waxer/Polishers—The Chamberlain Group, Inc.; *U.S. Private*, pg. 344

POLITICAL CODING SYSTEM—Database Marketing System—Group 1 Software, Inc.; *U.S. Public*, pg. 417

POLITICS IN AMERICA—Biennial Book Profiling Members Congress—The Times Publishing Co.; *U.S. Private*, pg. 1087

POLITOL—Chemicals—Westvaco Corporation; *U.S. Public*, pg. 1762

POLIVE—Cotton Dressing & Tissues—Polive/Tricosteril; *U.S. Public*, pg. 673

POLIVEX—Hygiene Products—Polive/Tricosteril; *U.S. Public*, pg. 673

POLK—Loudspeaker Systems—Polk Audio, Inc.; *U.S. Public*, pg. 1315

POLLAGEN—Treatment of Hay Fever—SmithKline Beecham plc; *Int'l*, pg. 1264

POLLEN-TECTOR—Paper Bags—Georgia-Pacific Corporation; *U.S. Public*, pg. 735

POLLENEX—Showerheads, Massagers—The Rival Company; *U.S. Public*, pg. 1391

POLLINEX—NONE—SmithKline Beecham Corporation; *Int'l*, pg. 1264

POLLINEX—Allergy/Cough/Cold Product—SmithKline Beecham plc; *Int'l*, pg. 1264

POLLUTION ENGINEERING—Magazine for Environmental Professionals—Reed Elsevier Business Information; *Int'l*, pg. 1095

POLLY—Rice Flour—Bestfoods; *U.S. Public*, pg. 223

POLLY-O—Cheeses—Kraft Foods Inc.; *U.S. Public*, pg. 1288

POLLY-O—Cheese—Philip Morris Companies Inc.; *U.S. Public*, pg. 1287

POLLY-O—Dairy Products—Pollio Dairy Products; *U.S. Public*, pg. 1288

POLLY PEP—Bread Emulsifiers—Mallet & Co.; *U.S. Private*, pg. 698

POLLY POCKET—Fashion Dolls—Mattel, Inc.; *U.S. Public*, pg. 1057

POLO—Fragrance for Men—Cosmair, Inc., Ralph Lauren Fragrance Division; *U.S. Public*, pg. 818

POLO—Candies—Nestle-Rowntree Ltd.; *Int'l*, pg. 921

POLO—Automobile—Volkswagen AG; *Int'l*, pg. 1473

POLO BY RALPH LAUREN—Boy's Shirts & Sportswear—Oxford Industries, Inc.; *U.S. Public*, pg. 1239

POLO FOR BOYS—Boyswear—Oxford Industries, Inc.; *U.S. Public*, pg. 1239

POLO/PEGASUS—Insect Control for Cotton, Fruit, Vegetables & Ornamentals—Novartis; *Int'l*, pg. 972

POLO/RALPH LAUREN—Clothing, Fragrances, & Home Furnishings—Polo/Ralph Lauren Corporation; *U.S. Private*, pg. 874

POLO UNIVERSITY CLUB—Men's Tailored Clothing—Hartmarx Corporation; *U.S. Public*, pg. 795

POLO UNIVERSITY CLUB BY RALPH LAUREN—Clothing—Genesco Inc.; *U.S. Public*, pg. 728

POLOCAINE—Pharmaceutical Products—Astra USA, Inc.; *Int'l*, pg. 93

POLORIS—Poultice—Block Drug Company, Inc.; *U.S. Public*, pg. 236

POLSTER BOY—Upholstery Cleaning Machine—Vorwerk & Co.; *Int'l*, pg. 1480

POLVAC—Treatment of Hay Fever—SmithKline Beecham plc; *Int'l*, pg. 1264

POLVICUCAR—Pastry Ingredient—Royal Gist-Brocades N.V.; *Int'l*, pg. 1142

POLY—NONE—Regal Ware, Inc.; *U.S. Private*, pg. 917

POLY BAC—Fabrics—Amoco Corporation; *U.S. Public*, pg. 101

POLY BAG—Polyetherene Bags—Cadillac Products, Inc.; *U.S. Private*, pg. 198

POLY-BOND—Non-Woven Textiles—Dominion Textile Inc.; *Int'l*, pg. 415

POLY-BOND—Weatherstripping—Schlegel Corporation; *Int'l*, pg. 128

POLY-BRAID—Package Conveying Machinery—Alvey Systems, Inc; *U.S. Private*, pg. 47

POLY CS—Surgical Staplers—U.S. Surgical Corp.; *U.S. Public*, pg. 1687

POLY CHAIN GT—Synchronous Belt—The Gates Rubber Company; *Int'l*, pg. 1396

POLY-CHEK—Additives for Polymers—Ferro Corporation; *U.S. Public*, pg. 618

POLY-COVER—Plastic Sheeting—Flex-O-Glass, Inc.; *U.S. Private*, pg. 412

POLY-COVER—Polyethylene Sheeting—Warp Brothers; *U.S. Private*, pg. 412

POLY CUT—Trimmer Cutting Attachment—Stihl Inc.; *Int'l*, pg. 1301

POLY DRIP—NONE—Regal Ware, Inc.; *U.S. Private*, pg. 917

POLY-ENA—Extractable Nuclear Antibodies—Wampole Laboratories; *U.S. Public*, pg. 310

POLY-EPOXY—Paint, Enamel—Pratt & Lambert United, Inc.; *U.S. Private*, pg. 1466

POLY-FLOC—Coagulant Aid—BetzDearborn Inc.; *U.S. Public*, pg. 226

POLY-FLOWLINES—Double Containment—Ryan Herco Products Corp.; *U.S. Private*, pg. 953

POLY-FLUOR—General-Purpose Cocktail for Aqueous & Organic Samples—Packard Instrument Co., Inc.; *U.S. Private*, pg. 833

POLY GIA—Surgical Staplers—U.S. Surgical Corp.; *U.S. Public*, pg. 1687

POLY GLASS—Well Water Reservoir Vessel—Essef Corporation; *U.S. Public*, pg. 592

POLY-GLO—Paint—Pratt & Lambert United, Inc.; *U.S. Public*, pg. 1466

POLY HOT POT—Beverage Warmer—Regal Ware, Inc.; *U.S. Private*, pg. 917

POLY-INSULATED—Rail Joints—Portec Inc., Railway Maintenance Products Div.; *U.S. Public*, pg. 1318

POLY-KLEAR—Envelopes—Westvaco Corporation; *U.S. Public*, pg. 1762

POLY MAID—Plastic Bags—Brawny Plastics West; *U.S. Private*, pg. 166

POLY MAN—Rope—Outdoor Technologies Group; *U.S. Private*, pg. 822

POLY-MARK—Photo Polymer Printing Plates—Markem Corporation; *U.S. Private*, pg. 704

POLY-MAX—Fine-Line Polymer Leads—Koh-I-Noor, Inc.; *U.S. Private*, pg. 629

POLY-MELT—Insulated Wire—General Electric Canada Inc.; *U.S. Public*, pg. 713

POLY-N—Ammoniated Poly Phosphate Solution—PCS Nitrogen; *Int'l*, pg. 1064

POLY-PAC—Promotional Kit for Papers—Eastman Kodak Company; *U.S. Public*, pg. 550

POLY-PALE—Resin—Hercules Incorporated; *U.S. Public*, pg. 809

POLY-PANE—Storm Window Kit—Warp Brothers; *U.S. Private*, pg. 412

POLY-PANEL—NONE—Fred B. Johnston Company, Inc.; *U.S. Private*, pg. 595

POLY PERK—Coffee Makers—Regal Ware, Inc.; *U.S. Private*, pg. 917

POLY-PLATE—NONE—Fred B. Johnston Company, Inc.; *U.S. Private*, pg. 595

POLY PLATE—Fiberglass Reinforced Plastic Traffic Control Sign Blanks—Sequentia Inc.; *U.S. Private*, pg. 985

POLY-PRIDE—Plastic Bags—Brawny Plastics West; *U.S. Private*, pg. 166

POLY-PRIME—Body Filler—Marson/Creative Fastener, Inc.; *U.S. Private*, pg. 708

POLY PROFILE—Polyethylene Organizing Products—ATAPCO Office Products Group; *U.S. Private*, pg. 64

POLY-Q—Vial—Beckman Instruments, Inc.; *U.S. Public*, pg. 199

POLY RICH—Non-Dairy Creamer—Rich Products Corp.; *U.S. Private*, pg. 928

POLY-SCIENTIFIC—Slip Ring Assemblies—Litton Industries, Inc.; *U.S. Public*, pg. 1002

POLY-SEAL—Cone Line Closure—Poly-Seal Corporation; *U.S. Private*, pg. 875

POLY SLICK—Release Paper—Fort James Corporation; *U.S. Public*, pg. 670

POLY-SOFT—X-Ray Film Packet—Eastman Kodak Company; *U.S. Public*, pg. 550

POLY SURGICLIP—Clip Appliers—U.S. Surgical Corp.; *U.S. Public*, pg. 1687

POLY-TAB—Pull-Tab Induction Liner System—Poly-Seal Corporation; *U.S. Private*, pg. 875

POLY-THERM—Polyurethane Pipe—MFRI Inc.; *U.S. Public*, pg. 1026

POLY THREAD—Fiberglass Reinforced Plastic Piping—A.O. Smith Corporation; *U.S. Public*, pg. 1476

POLY TISSUE—Disposable Paper Products—Wisconsin Tissue Mills, Inc.; *U.S. Public*, pg. 347

POLY-TOGGLE—Screw Anchor—Powers Fastening, Inc.; *U.S. Private*, pg. 878

POLY-TONER—Photo Toner—Eastman Kodak Company; *U.S. Public*, pg. 550

POLY TUFF—Livestock Equipment—Behlen Mfg. Co.; *U.S. Private*, pg. 130

POLY-VI-FLOR—11 Essential Vitamins Plus Fluoride—Mead Johnson Nutritional Group; *U.S. Public*, pg. 254

POLY-VI-FLOR WITH IRON—11 Essential Vitamins Plus Fluoride & Iron—Mead Johnson Nutritional Group; *U.S. Public*, pg. 254

POLY-VI-SOL—10 Essential Vitamins for Infants & Children—Mead Johnson Nutritional Group; *U.S. Public*, pg. 254

POLY WITH PARROT & REGAL CROWN DESIGN—NONE—Regal Ware, Inc.; *U.S. Private*, pg. 917

POLY-XL—Jacket Compound—Electron Beam Technologies; *U.S. Private*, pg. 370

POLY-VI-SOL—Children's Vitamin—Bristol-Myers Squibb Company; *U.S. Public*, pg. 253

POLYALDO—Emulsifier—Lonza Inc.; *Int'l*, pg. 67

POLYARMOR BELT—PVK Belt—Mayfran International, Inc.; *Int'l*, pg. 1397

POLYBAC—Carpet Backing—Amoco Chemicals; *U.S. Public*, pg. 102

POLYBASE—Polyester—Plastic Suppliers, Inc.; *U.S. Private*, pg. 871

POLYBASE—Polyester Lay-Out Base—Plastic Suppliers Inc.; *U.S. Private*, pg. 871

POLYBATCH—Plastic Compounds—A. Schulman, Inc.; *U.S. Public*, pg. 1441

POLYBAU—NONE—Carbo Plc; *Int'l*, pg. 268

POLYBINDER—Textile Binder—Morton International Inc.; *U.S. Public*, pg. 1135

Brand Name Index

POLYBLAK—Plastic Compounds—A. Schulman, Inc.; *U.S. Public*, pg. 1441

POLYBOARD—NONE—Applied Extrusion Technologies, Inc.; *U.S. Public*, pg. 122

POLYBOND—Chemically-Modified Polyolefin—Uniroyal Chemical Company, Inc.; *U.S. Public*, pg. 460

POLYBRANE—Roofing & Waterproofing Systems—Polymer Plastics Corporation; *U.S. Private*, pg. 875

POLYBUFFER—Biotechnology—Pharmacia & Upjohn Adria Laboratories; *Int'l*, pg. 1049

POLYCAP—Air Cellular Cushioning Material—Sealed Air Corporation; *U.S. Public*, pg. 1450

POLYCAST—Type of Centrifugal Casting—Sandusky International Inc.; *U.S. Private*, pg. 964

POLYCAST—Acrylic Sheet, Rods & Tubes—Uniroyal Technology Corporation; *U.S. Public*, pg. 1670

POLYCAT—Catalysts—Air Products and Chemicals, Inc.; *U.S. Public*, pg. 30

POLYCERAGUARD—Spray Booth Grate Coatings—BetzDearborn Inc.; *U.S. Public*, pg. 226

POLYCHROM—Solid State Detectors for Liquid Analysis—Varian Associates, Inc.; *U.S. Public*, pg. 1710

POLYCILLIN—Synthetic Penicillin—Bristol-Myers Squibb Company; *U.S. Public*, pg. 253

POLYCIZER—Plasticizer—Harwick Standard Distribution Corporation; *U.S. Private*, pg. 509

POLYCLAD—Protective Coatings—Carboline Co.; *U.S. Public*, pg. 1357

POLYCLAR—Clarifier & Stabilizer—International Specialty Products, Inc.; *U.S. Public*, pg. 858

POLYCLEAN—Plastic Compounds—A. Schulman, Inc.; *U.S. Public*, pg. 1441

POLYCLENS—Lens Cleaner—Nestle S.A.; *Int'l*, pg. 915

POLYCLUTCH—Coatings, Paints, Enamels, Primers & Thinners—PPG Industries, Inc.; *U.S. Public*, pg. 1245

POLYCOLD—NONE—Polycold Systems International, Inc.; *U.S. Public*, pg. 894

POLYCONTRAST—Photo Paper & Filters—Eastman Kodak Company; *U.S. Public*, pg. 550

POLYCOOL—Film Cooling—Battenfeld Gloucester Engineering Inc.; *U.S. Private*, pg. 123

POLYCOP—Anti-Fouling Paints & Coatings—Rule Industries, Inc.; *U.S. Public*, pg. 950

POLYCOR—Gel Coats—Cook Composites & Polymers Inc.; *Int'l*, pg. 1409

POLYCOR—NONE—Synergistics Industries Limited; *U.S. Public*, pg. 734

POLYCORE COMPOSITES—Constrained layer composite materials—Material Sciences Corporation; *U.S. Public*, pg. 1056

POLYCRON—Paint—PPG Industries, Inc.; *U.S. Public*, pg. 1245

POLYCUT—Coated Abrasive With Grinding Aid Additives—3M; *U.S. Public*, pg. 1604

POLYDISK—Disc Filter/Saveall—Harnischfeger Industries, Inc.; *U.S. Public*, pg. 788

POLYDOL—Photo Developer & Replenisher—Eastman Kodak Company; *U.S. Public*, pg. 550

POLYDOR—Records—Philips Electronics N.V.; *Int'l*, pg. 1051

POLYDOR—Records & Cassettes—Polygram Records, Inc.; *Int'l*, pg. 1052

POLYDROX—NONE—DSM N.V.; *Int'l*, pg. 352

POLYFIBER—Photographic Paper—Eastman Kodak Company; *U.S. Public*, pg. 550

POLYFIBRON—Printing Blankets—Polyfibron Technologies Corp.; *U.S. Private*, pg. 875

POLYFIL—Sewing Thread—Tootal Group plc; *Int'l*, pg. 300

POLYFILL—Seat Material—Worcester Controls Corp.; *Int'l*, pg. 128

POLYFLAM—Plastic Compounds—A. Schulman, Inc.; *U.S. Public*, pg. 1441

POLYFLEX—Polyurethane Based Compositions—The Dow Chemical Company; *U.S. Public*, pg. 522

POLYFLEX—House Paint—Jones Blair Company; *U.S. Private*, pg. 596

POLYFLEX—Hose—Parker Hannifin Corporation; *U.S. Public*, pg. 1259

POLYFLEX—Polystyrene—Plastic Suppliers, Inc.; *U.S. Public*, pg. 871

POLYFLEX—Biaxially Oriented Polystyrene Plastic Sheet—Plastic Suppliers Inc.; *U.S. Private*, pg. 871

POLYFON—Lignosulfonates—Westvaco Corporation; *U.S. Public*, pg. 1762

POLYGARD—Polymeric Sealing Paste—Ferro Corporation; *U.S. Public*, pg. 618

POLYGARD—Cartridge Filter—Millipore Corporation; *U.S. Public*, pg. 1112

POLYGARDE—NONE—Raychem Corporation; *U.S. Public*, pg. 1362

POLYGEL—Shock Absorbing Silicone Elastomer—Wacker Silicones Corporation; *Int'l*, pg. 625

POLYGLAZE—Mirror Coating—Carolina Mirror Company; *U.S. Public*, pg. 214

POLYGLIDE—NONE—Lawter International, Inc.; *U.S. Public*, pg. 980

POLYGON—Transformers—MagneTek, Inc.; *U.S. Public*, pg. 1037

POLYGRADE—Degradable Masterbatches for Plastics—Ampacet Corporation; *U.S. Private*, pg. 67

POLYGRAM—Discs & Records—Philips Electronics N.V.; *Int'l*, pg. 1051

POLYGRAM—Record, Cassettes & Videos—Polygram Records, Inc.; *Int'l*, pg. 1052

POLYGRAM MUSIC VIDEO—Video Production—Philips Electronics N.V.; *Int'l*, pg. 1051

POLYGUN—Hot-Melt Adhesive Applicator Guns & Accessories—3M; *U.S. Public*, pg. 1604

POLYGYR—Analog Electronic Controls—Landis & Staefa, Inc.; *Int'l*, pg. 800

POLYHESIVE—NONE—Pfizer Inc.; *U.S. Public*, pg. 1281

POLYLECTRIC—NONE—Regal Ware, Inc.; *U.S. Private*, pg. 917

POLYLINED—Pipe—United States Pipe & Foundry Company, Inc.; *U.S. Public*, pg. 1736

POLYLOCK—File—Fellowes Manufacturing Co.; *U.S. Private*, pg. 400

POLYLOK—NONE—Material Sciences Corporation; *U.S. Public*, pg. 1056

POLYLON—Mens Rain Wear—Rainfair, Inc.; *U.S. Private*, pg. 907

POLYMAIL—Plastic Mailers—Poly Pak America, Inc.; *U.S. Public*, pg. 875

POLYMAN—Plastic Compounds—A. Schulman, Inc.; *U.S. Public*, pg. 1441

POLYMAR—Injection (plastic) Molding Operation—Serfilco, Ltd.; *U.S. Private*, pg. 985

POLYMATIC—Presensitized Litho Plates, Processing Chemicals & Little Plate Processors—Eastman Kodak Company; *U.S. Public*, pg. 550

POLYMATIC—Trimmer Head—Stihl Inc.; *Int'l*, pg. 1301

POLYMATRIX—Components for Heat Tracing—Raychem Corporation; *U.S. Public*, pg. 1362

POLYMAX—Photographic Paper; Chemicals; Filters; Processing Apparatus—Eastman Kodak Company; *U.S. Public*, pg. 550

POLYMEG—Specialty Chemicals—Great Lakes Chemical Corporation; *U.S. Public*, pg. 760

POLYMENT—Products for Concrete Maintenance—Heidelberger Zement A.G.; *Int'l*, pg. 605

POLYMER COMPOUNDS—Structural Epoxy Products—Polymer Plastics Corporation; *U.S. Private*, pg. 875

POLYMER TOWER—Corrosion Resistant—AEC, Inc.; *U.S. Public*, pg. 500

POLYMERIC TRANSPORT SYSTEMS—Cosmetics & Toiletries—Advanced Polymer Systems; *U.S. Public*, pg. 22

POLYMET—Plastic Filled Sintered Metal—DSM Engineering Plastic Products; *Int'l*, pg. 354

POLYMIN—Process Chemicals & Colorants—BASF AG; *Int'l*, pg. 103

POLYMIST—Waxes—AlliedSignal Inc.; *U.S. Public*, pg. 49

POLYMIST-F—Fluropolymer—AlliedSignal Inc.; *U.S. Public*, pg. 49

POLYMIZER—Solid Bowl Scroll Centrifuge—Alfa Laval Separation Inc.; *Int'l*, pg. 1378

POLYMOX—Synthetic Penicillin—Bristol-Myers Squibb Company; *U.S. Public*, pg. 253

POLYMYXIN B SULFATE—Pharmaceutical Product—Glaxo Wellcome PLC; *Int'l*, pg. 553

POLYNESIAN—Sauces—Allied Old English, Inc.; *U.S. Private*, pg. 39

POLYNODIC—Inhibitor—BetzDearborn Inc.; *U.S. Public*, pg. 226

POLYPAC—Containers—Fisher Scientific Company; *U.S. Public*, pg. 658

POLYPACE—Composite Polymer Insulators—Lapp Insulator Company; *U.S. Private*, pg. 473

POLYPAK—Hydraulic Packing—Seal Group; *U.S. Public*, pg. 1262

POLYPENCO—Shaped Synthetic Resins—DSM Engineering Plastic Products; *Int'l*, pg. 354

POLYPLASDONE—Tablet Disintegrant—International Specialty Products, Inc.; *U.S. Public*, pg. 858

POLYPRED—Sterile Ophthalmic Solution—Allergan, Inc.; *U.S. Public*, pg. 46

POLYPRINT—Photographic Paper—Eastman Kodak Company; *U.S. Public*, pg. 550

POLYPURE—Filtration Products—Gelman Sciences, Inc.; *U.S. Public*, pg. 1253

POLYQUAT—Organic Chemicals—Stepan Company; *U.S. Public*, pg. 1514

POLYRAD—Insulated Electrical Wire & Cable—BICC Brand-Rex; *Int'l*, pg. 120

POLYRAD—Rosin Amine-Ethylene Oxide Adducts—Hercules Incorporated; *U.S. Public*, pg. 809

POLYRAM—Crop Protection Agent—BASF AG; *Int'l*, pg. 103

POLYSEAL—Electric Motors—General Electric Canada Inc.; *U.S. Public*, pg. 713

POLYSEAL—Plastic Film—Industrial Coatings Group, Inc.; *U.S. Public*, pg. 434

POLYSEAL—High Abrasion Resistant Rod or Piston Seal—Macrotech Plyseal, Inc.; *U.S. Private*, pg. 693

POLYSHELL—Car Polish—Turtle Wax, Inc.; *U.S. Private*, pg. 1110

POLYSORB—Replacement Insoles—Kimberly-Clark Corporation; *U.S. Public*, pg. 958

POLYSORB—Sutures—U.S. Surgical Corp.; *U.S. Public*, pg. 1687

POLYSPORIN—Ophthalmic Antibiotic—Glaxo Wellcome PLC; *Int'l*, pg. 553

POLYSTAL—Advanced Composite—Bayer AG; *Int'l*, pg. 171

POLYSTAT—Plastic Compounds—A. Schulman, Inc.; *U.S. Public*, pg. 1441

POLYSTAY—Antioxidant—The Goodyear Tire & Rubber Company; *U.S. Public*, pg. 752

POLYSTEP—Surfactants-Emulsion Polymerization—Stepan Company; *U.S. Public*, pg. 1514

POLYSTOP—Coatings—Akzo Nobel Inc.; *Int'l*, pg. 47

POLYSTRIP—Industrial Paint Stripper & Industrial Chemicals—PPG Industries, Inc.; *U.S. Public*, pg. 1245

POLYSWITCH—Circuit Protection Devices—Raychem Corporation; *U.S. Public*, pg. 1362

POLYTAL—Talc for Plastics—Whittaker, Clark & Daniels, Inc.; *U.S. Private*, pg. 1174

POLYTARD—Cement Grinding Aid—Westvaco Corporation; *U.S. Public*, pg. 1762

POLYTEC—Polyurethane Roll Cover for General Paper Machine Applications—Harnischfeger Industries, Inc.; *U.S. Public*, pg. 788

POLYTHANE—Pipelining for aggressive/corrosive sewage—United States Pipe & Foundry Company; *U.S. Public*, pg. 1736

POLYTRANS—Color Proofing Film—Eastman Kodak Company; *U.S. Public*, pg. 550

POLYTREND—Industrial Colorant—Veba AG; *Int'l*, pg. 1454

POLYTRIM—Sterile Ophthalmic Solution—Allergan, Inc.; *U.S. Public*, pg. 46

POLYTRIM—Anti-Infective—Glaxo Wellcome PLC; *Int'l*, pg. 553

POLYTROP—Seating—GF Office Furniture; *U.S. Private*, pg. 435

POLYTROPE—Plastic Compounds—A. Schulman, Inc.; *U.S. Public*, pg. 1441

POLYTWIST—Limited Rotation Electrical Rotary Joint—Litton Industries, Inc.; *U.S. Public*, pg. 1002

POLYVEL—Heavy Weight Drafting Vellums—OCE-U.S.A.; *Int'l*, pg. 994

POLYVIN—Plastic Compounds—A. Schulman, Inc.; *U.S. Public*, pg. 1441

POLYWELD—Circuit Boards—Litton Industries, Inc.; *U.S. Public*, pg. 1002

POLYWET—Dispersant—Uniroyal Chemical Company, Inc.; *U.S. Public*, pg. 460

POLYWEVE—Langston Woven Polypropylene Bags—Langston Companies; *U.S. Private*, pg. 650

POM POM—Ribbon Bows for Gift Wrapping—American Greetings Corporation; *U.S. Public*, pg. 77

POM POMS—Chocolate/Caramel Candies—Tootsie Roll Industries, Inc.; *U.S. Public*, pg. 1621

POM STAMPER—Pre-Inked Stamps—Sanford Corporation; *U.S. Public*, pg. 1178

POMMERY—NONE—LVMH Moet Hennessy Louis Vuitton; *Int'l*, pg. 779

POMMERY—Spirits—Mercian Corporation; *Int'l*, · pg. 858

POMODORISSIMO—Jellies, Jams & Other Spreads; Tomato Sauces & Catsup—Bestfoods; *U.S. Public*, pg. 223

POMPEIAN—Virgin Olive Oil—Pompeiian, Inc.; *U.S. Private*, pg. 875

POND'S—Nourishing Moisturizer Lotion & Cream—Chesebrough-Pond's USA Co.; *Int'l*, pg. 1435

POND'S—Nourishing Moisturizer With Sunscreen (SPF 15)—Chesebrough-Pond's USA Co.; *Int'l*, pg. 1435

POND'S—Overnight Nourishing Complex Cream—Chesebrough-Pond's USA Co.; *Int'l*, pg. 1435

POND'S—Revitalizing Eye Gel—Chesebrough-Pond's USA Co.; *Int'l*, pg. 1435

POND'S DRAMATIC RESULTS—Skin Smoothing Capsules—Chesebrough-Pond's USA Co.; *Int'l*, pg. 1435

PONDEROSA—Animal Feed—ConAgra, Inc.; *U.S. Public*, pg. 425

PONDEROSA—Shoes—E.J. Footwear Corp.; *U.S. Public*, pg. 1684

PONDMASTER—Aquatic Herbicide—Monsanto Company; *U.S. Public*, pg. 1124

POND'S—Facial Cleansers & Moisturizers—Chesebrough-Pond's USA Co.; *Int'l*, pg. 1435

PONN HOSE—Fire Hose—Snap-Tite, Inc.; *U.S. Private*, pg. 1010

PONSTAN—Analgesic, Anti-Inflammatory & Anti-Pyretic—Parke-Davis & Company, Limited; *U.S. Public*, pg. 1739

PONSTEL—Pharmaceutical Products—Warner-Lambert Company; *U.S. Public*, pg. 1738

PONT MEYER—Builder Forest Products In Holland & Germany—Meyer International PLC; *Int'l*, pg. 864

PONTE—Pasta—Danone Group; *Int'l*, pg. 379

PONTIAC—Cars—General Motors Corporation; *U.S. Public*, pg. 718

PONTINS—Holiday Villages—Scottish & Newcastle plc; *Int'l*, pg. 1211

PONY—Shovels & Wheelbarrows—Ames Company; *U.S. Public*, pg. 1683

PONY—Mixer—Littleford Day Inc.; *U.S. Private*, pg. 671

PONY—Athletic Bags, Socks, Apparel—Pony U.S.A.; *Int'l*, pg. 1036

PONY EXPRESS—Transportation Services—Borg-Warner Security Corporation; *U.S. Public*, pg. 245

PONY EXPRESS—Casino—Jackpot Enterprises, Inc.; *U.S. Public*, pg. 920

PONY EXPRESS—Courier Service—Pony Express Delivery Services, Inc.; *U.S. Public*, pg. 245

PONY EXPRESS—Home Security—Wells Fargo Alarm Services, Inc.; *U.S. Public*, pg. 246

PONY VIAL—Miniature Scintillation Vial—Packard Instrument Co., Inc.; *U.S. Private*, pg. 833

PONYWRAPS—Ponytail Holders—Wilhold Inc.; *U.S. Public*, pg. 78

POOL-DASD—Centralized Control of Data Set Placement—Boole & Babbage, Inc.; *U.S. Public*, pg. 244

POOL GENE—Swimming Pool/Water Purifier Using Silver/Carbon Filter—Ionics, Incorporated; *U.S. Public*, pg. 912

POOL SHIELD—Swimming Pool Finish—Pratt & Lambert United, Inc.; *U.S. Public*, pg. 1466

POOLED SCREENING CELLS—Reagent Red Blood Cells—Ortho Clinical Diagnostic Systems Inc.; *U.S. Public*, pg. 929

THE POOLS—NONE—Tattersalls; *Int'l*, pg. 1357

POP-A-LOT—Popcorn Machine—Gold Medal Products Co.; *U.S. Private*, pg. 459

POP-A-WAY—Sprinklers—Rain Bird Sprinklers Manufacturing Corp.; *U.S. Private*, pg. 907

POP-ALL—Fats & Oils—Van den Bergh Foods Company; *Int'l*, pg. 1436

POP DELUXE—Ready-to-Eat Popcorn—Keebler Company; *U.S. Public*, pg. 657

POP-DOWN—Four Slice Toaster—Merco/Savory Inc.; *Int'l*, pg. 189

POP EASEL—Easel—Colad Group Inc.; *U.S. Private*, pg. 250

POP-ICE—Frozen Confection—The Jel Sert Co.; *U.S. Private*, pg. 585

POP-OFF—Needles—U.S. Surgical Corp.; *U.S. Public*, pg. 1687

POP-OUT PLANT STARTER—Garden Product—Jiffy Products of America, Inc.; *Int'l*, pg. 706

POP QUOTES—Rock Programming—Westwood One, Inc.; *U.S. Public*, pg. 1763

POP SECRET—Microwave Popcorn—General Mills, Inc.; *U.S. Public*, pg. 717

POP SECRET MICROWAVE POPCORN—NONE—Snacks Unlimited Division; *U.S. Public*, pg. 718

POP SUPER—Comact Camera With Built-In Motor & Flash—Konica Corporation; *Int'l*, pg. 748

POP-TARTS—Frosted and/or Filled Toaster Pastries—Kellogg Company; *U.S. Public*, pg. 947

POP-TARTS CRUNCH—Cereal—Kellogg Company; *U.S. Public*, pg. 947

POP-TARTS MINI—Snack Food—Kellogg Company; *U.S. Public*, pg. 947

POP TOP—Seasoning—McCormick/Schilling; *U.S. Public*, pg. 1066

POP-TOP—Soda Can Pop Opener—Pacific Handy Cutter, Inc.; *U.S. Private*, pg. 831

POP TOPS—Ladies Apparel—Movie Star, Inc.; *U.S. Public*, pg. 1140

POP UP—Boxes Containing Tissue or Nonwoven Products—Kimberly-Clark Corporation; *U.S. Public*, pg. 958

THE POPCORN FACTORY—Popcorn—The Popcorn Factory; *U.S. Private*, pg. 421

POPCORN'S—Liquor Stores & Lounges—Flanigan's Enterprises, Inc.; *U.S. Public*, pg. 648

POPCORNNOW—Corn Popper—National Presto Industries, Inc.; *U.S. Public*, pg. 1159

POPE—NONE—Belden Inc.; *U.S. Public*, pg. 200

POPEE—Bathroom Tissue, Paper Napkins, Paper Towels—Kimberly-Clark Corporation; *U.S. Public*, pg. 958

POPEIL—Automatic Pasta Maker—Ronco Inventions, LLC; *U.S. Private*, pg. 943

POPEIL PRODUCTS—Pasta Machines—Salton/Maxim Housewares, Inc.; *U.S. Public*, pg. 1430

POPEYE—Bubble Gum—Amurol Confections Co.; *U.S. Public*, pg. 1781

POPEYE—Popcorn—Curtice Burns Foods; *U.S. Private*, pg. 887

POPEYE—Cereal—The Quaker Oats Company; *U.S. Public*, pg. 1347

POPEYE LEAF SPINACH—Food Products—Allen Canning Company; *U.S. Private*, pg. 36

POPEYE'S CHICKEN & BISCUITS—Fast Food Restaurant Specializing in Fried Chicken—AFC Enterprises; *U.S. Public*, pg. 5

POPEYE'S CHICKEN & BISCUITS—NONE—Popeye's Chicken & Biscuits; *U.S. Private*, pg. 5

POPINI—Office Seating—United Chair, Inc.; *U.S. Private*, pg. 512

POPLITE—Hot Air Corn Popper—National Presto Industries, Inc.; *U.S. Public*, pg. 1159

POPMATIC—Fastening System—The Black & Decker Corporation; *U.S. Public*, pg. 233

POPORON—Chocolate Snacks—Meiji Seika Kaisha, Ltd.; *Int'l*, pg. 855

POPOV—Vodka—Grand Metropolitan Plc; *Int'l*, pg. 408

POPOV VODKA—Vodka—Heublein, Inc.; *Int'l*, pg. 410

POPOV VODKA—NONE—International Distillers Caribbean; *Int'l*, pg. 410

POPPIES—Restaurant—Omni Hotels; *U.S. Private*, pg. 1065

POPPIN TOPPIN—Popcorn Toppin—Ventura Foods; *U.S. Private*, pg. 508

POPPY—Sleepwear—Lanz, Inc.; *U.S. Public*, pg. 650

POPPYCOCK—Snack Product—Novartis Nutrition Corporation; *Int'l*, pg. 974

POPS RITE—Popcorn—Comstock Michigan Fruit; *U.S. Private*, pg. 887

POPS-RITE—Popcorn—Curtice Burns Foods; *U.S. Private*, pg. 887

POPSICLE BRAND—Ice Pops—Good Humor/Breyers Ice Cream; *Int'l*, pg. 1435

POPSY—Children's Toothpaste—SmithKline Beecham plc; *Int'l*, pg. 1264

POPTOP—Transplantable Detector Capsule for High-Purity Germanium Detectors—EG & G Ortec *U.S. Public*, pg. 543

POPULAR CLASSICS—Car Magazine—EMAP Nationals; *Int'l*, pg. 451

POPULAR MAGAZINES—Crossword Puzzle, Wordgames, Astrology Magazines—Hachette Filipacchi Magazines Inc.; *Int'l*, pg. 794

POPULAR MECHANICS—Magazine—The Hearst Corporation; *U.S. Private*, pg. 515

POPULAR MECHANICS—Magazine—Hearst Magazines Division; *U.S. Private*, pg. 516

POPULAR MECHANICS—Magazine—Popular Mechanics; *U.S. Private*, pg. 517

POPULAR PHOTOGRAPHY—Photography Magazine—Hachette Filipacchi Magazines Inc.; *Int'l*, pg. 794

POPULAR PLUS—Account that Combines Fin. Rels. w/Banco Popular in a Statement of Account—Banco Popular de Puerto Rico; *U.S. Public*, pg. 175

POPULAR SCIENCE—Magazine—Times Mirror Magazines, Inc.; *U.S. Public*, pg. 1616

POPULAR SERVICES—Catalog Mail Order—J. Crew Group, Inc.; *U.S. Private*, pg. 1078

POPULAR WOODWORKING—Magazine—F & W Publications, Inc.; *U.S. Private*, pg. 388

POPWEAVER—Caramel Corn, Microwave, Poly Bags—Weaver Popcorn Company, Inc.; *U.S. Private*, pg. 1156

POR LARRANAGA—Premium Cigars—Consolidated Cigar Corporation; *U.S. Private*, pg. 690

PORAPAK—Spherical Silica GC Packing—Millipore Corporation; *U.S. Public*, pg. 1112

PORASIL—BLC Bulk Packing—Millipore Corporation; *U.S. Public*, pg. 1112

PORCELANA—Skin Care Products—Dep Corporation; *U.S. Public*, pg. 500

PORCELANITE—NONE—Porcelanite, Inc.; *Int'l*, pg. 573

PORCH & FLOOR—Enamel—Jones Blair Company; *U.S. Private*, pg. 596

PORCH EMAMEL—Paints—Sherwin-Williams Consumer Brands Division; *U.S. Public*, pg. 1466

PORCHER—Plumbing Products—American Standard Inc.; *U.S. Public*, pg. 91

PORCUPINE—Indirect Dryer & Processor—The Bethlehem Corporation; *U.S. Public*, pg. 225

PORETICS—Polycarbonate Membrane Filters—Osmonics, Inc.; *U.S. Public*, pg. 1233

PORK FARMS—Meat Prods.—Northern Foods plc; *Int'l*, pg. 967

PORON—Microcellular Polyurethane Material—Rogers Corporation; *U.S. Public*, pg. 1402

POROS—Perfusion Chromatography Media & Columns—PerSeptive Biosystems, Inc.; *U.S. Public*, pg. 1279

POROSIT—Swelling Binder—Raschig GmbH; *U.S. Private*, pg. 827

POROSZYME—Immobilized Enzyme Cartridges for Rapid Digestion of Biomolecules—PerSeptive Biosystems, Inc.; *U.S. Public*, pg. 1279

POROWRAP—Specialty Paper—Kimberly-Clark Corporation; *U.S. Public*, pg. 958

POROX—Vitrified Silica Medium-Density Grinding Media—Ferro Corporation; *U.S. Public*, pg. 618

PORSCHE—Automobiles—Lantzsch-Andreas Enterprises, Inc.; *U.S. Private*, pg. 650

PORSCHE—Cars, Parts, Access. & Clothing—Porsche Cars North America, Inc.; *Int'l*, pg. 1063

PORSCHE DESIGN—Ophthalmic & Sunglasses—Optimaxx International; *U.S. Private*, pg. 818

PORSGRUND—Sanitary Porlelain—Metra Corporation; *Int'l*, pg. 862

PORSGRUND—Bathroom Ceramics—Sanitec Ltd. Oy; *Int'l*, pg. 863

PORT-A-ANALYST—Electronic Component—PTS Electronics Corporation; *U.S. Private*, pg. 828

PORT-A-PET—Plastic Case—International Container Systems; *Int'l*, pg. 685

PORT-A-PUNCH—Business Product—International Business Machines Corporation; *U.S. Public*, pg. 895

PORT-A-TUNER—Electronic Component—PTS Electronics Corporation; *U.S. Public*, pg. 828

PORT-AIRE—Filtration Cases—Coppus Murray Group, Tuthill Corporation; *U.S. Private*, pg. 1110

PORT CANAVERAL TOWING—NONE—Hvide Marine Incorporated; *U.S. Public*, pg. 851

PORT CLYDE—Sea Food Products—George Weston Limited; *Int'l*, pg. 1494

PORT EVERGLADES TOWING—NONE—Hvide Marine Incorporated; *U.S. Public*, pg. 851

PORTA-CATH—Infusion Device—Pharmacia & Upjohn Adria Laboratories; *Int'l*, pg. 1049

PORTA-FID—Flame Ionization Gas Leak Detector—Heath Consultants Incorporated; *U.S. Private*, pg. 518

PORTA-FLOW—Medical Equipment—The Cooper Companies, Inc.; *U.S. Public*, pg. 442

PORTA-PIG—Radionuclide Carrier—Reactor Experiments, Inc.; *U.S. Public*, pg. 1594

PORTA POTTI—Portable Toilets—Thetford Corporation; *U.S. Private*, pg. 615

PORTA SYSTEMS—Telephone & Telegraph Apparatus—Porta Systems Corp.; *U.S. Public*, pg. 1317

PORTA-THREAD—Portable Threader—Greenlee Textron; *U.S. Public*, pg. 1589

PORTA-TOOL—Service Tools—SPX Corporation; *U.S. Public*, pg. 1420

PORTA-TRUNK—Fume Exhauster—Donaldson Company, Inc.; *U.S. Public*, pg. 517

PORTACOUNT—Respirator Fit Tester—TSI Incorporated; *U.S. Public*, pg. 1559

PORTAGE—Tires—Bridgestone/Firestone, Inc.; *Int'l*, pg. 213

PORTAGEN—Food Fat/Lactose Dietary Powder—Mead Johnson Nutritional Group; *U.S. Public*, pg. 254

PORTAIR—Ventilating Fans—Coppus Murray Group, Tuthill Corporation; *U.S. Private*, pg. 1110

PORTALAB—Portable Turbidimeter—Hach Company; *U.S. Public*, pg. 773

PORTALIT—Decorative Laminate Faced Doors & Frames—Westag & Getalit AG; *Int'l*, pg. 1491

PORTALLOY—Steel Alloy—Webster Industries Inc.; *U.S. Public*, pg. 1157

PORTAMEDIC—Healthcare Services & Health Information—Hooper Holmes Corporation; *U.S. Public*, pg. 835

PORTAMET—Portable Electrolytic Polisher—Buehler, Limited; *U.S. Public*, pg. 574

PORTAPOWER—Lightweight Canister Cleaner—Hoover Company; *U.S. Public*, pg. 1065

PORTAPRO—Handheld Data Capturing—Cerner Corporation; *U.S. Public*, pg. 331

PORTAPURE—Small Dialyses Unit—Osmonics, Inc.; *U.S. Public*, pg. 1233

PORTASOUND—Portable Electronic Keyboard—Yamaha Corporation of America; *Int'l*, pg. 1516

PORTATONE—Portable Electronic Keyboard—Yamaha Corporation of America; *Int'l*, pg. 1516

PORTEC-BOND—NONE—Portec Inc., Railway Maintenance Products Div.; *U.S. Public*, pg. 1318

PORTER INTERNATIONAL—High Performance Coatings—Courtaulds Coatings Inc.; *Int'l*, pg. 338

PORTER PAINTS—Architectural Coatings—Courtaulds Coatings Inc.; *Int'l*, pg. 338

PORTEX—Athletic Apparel—Bike Athletic Co.; *U.S. Private*, pg. 143

THE PORTFOLIO—Computer—JTS Corporation; *U.S. Public*, pg. 919

PORTFOLIO BRAND FURNITURE—RTA Furniture—Ameriwood Industries International Inc.; *U.S. Public*, pg. 98

THE PORTFOLIO COLLECTION—Stoneware—The Pfaltzgraff Co.; *U.S. Private*, pg. 860

PORTFOLIO RELIEF—Loan Servicing—SLM Holding Corp.; *U.S. Public*, pg. 1419

PORTILLA II—Vinyl Composition Tile—Kentile Operating Co.; *U.S. Private*, pg. 615

PORTION POUR—Portion Control Serving Container—Carlisle Food Service Products; *U.S. Public*, pg. 305

PORTLAND GLASS FIRESCREEN—Glass Firescreen & Firescreen Enclosure—Byers Portland Willamette; *U.S. Private*, pg. 191

PORTMAN RECRUITMENT—NONE—Rentokil Initial plc; *Int'l*, pg. 1285

PORTMASTER—Computer Product—International Business Machines Corporation; *U.S. Public*, pg. 895

PORTNET—Port Support Services—Transnet Ltd.; *Int'l*, pg. 1417

PORTOBELLO—Yacht Club—The Levy Organization; *U.S. Private*, pg. 664

PORTOFINO—Broadloom—Couristan Inc.; *U.S. Private*, pg. 279

PORTOFINO—Designer Line Optical Frames—Sterling Vision, Inc.; *U.S. Public*, pg. 1516

PORTRA—Accessory Lenses—Eastman Kodak Company; *U.S. Public*, pg. 550

PORTRAITS BY NORTHERN ISLES—NONE—Kellwood Company; *U.S. Public*, pg. 948

PORTRALURE—Photo Paper—Eastman Kodak Company; *U.S. Public*, pg. 550

PORTSMOUTH—Wall Paneling—Georgia-Pacific Corporation; *U.S. Public*, pg. 735

PORTSS—Loan Servicing Software—SLM Holding Corp.; *U.S. Public*, pg. 1419

PORZYME—Multienzyme Increases Nutritive Value of Pig Feeds—Cultor Ltd.; *Int'l*, pg. 349

POS-I-CHEK—Envelopes—Georgia-Pacific Corporation; *U.S. Public*, pg. 735

POS-I-PHASE—Diversity Wireless System—Telex Communications, Inc.; *U.S. Private*, pg. 1074

POS ONE SYSTEM STAT—Camera/Processor—GraphLine Inc.; *U.S. Private*, pg. 471

POS-Z-SPREADER—Family of Spreading Devices—Beloit Lenox, Div.; *U.S. Public*, pg. 789

POS-Z SPREADER—Slitter Spreader Roll—Harnischfeger Industries, Inc.; *U.S. Public*, pg. 788

POSCOLOR—Color Camera/Processor—GraphLine Inc.; *U.S. Private*, pg. 471

POSEIDON PRESS—Paperback Books—Simon & Schuster; *U.S. Public*, pg. 777

POSI-FLEX—Soles for Shoes—E.J. Footwear Corp.; *U.S. Public*, pg. 1684

POSI-FLO—Swimming Pool & Spa Filters—Sta-Rite Water Systems; *U.S. Public*, pg. 1767

POSI-SEAL—High Performance Butterfly Valves—Associated Process Controls; *U.S. Private*, pg. 92

POSI-TRACK—Linear Capstan—Royle Systems Group; *U.S. Private*, pg. 949

POSIDYNE—Filters—Pall Corporation; *U.S. Public*, pg. 1253

POSIFLO—Feed Flow Control—CTB International Corp.; *U.S. Public*, pg. 284

POSIGRIP—NONE—Connector Manufacturing Company; *U.S. Private*, pg. 264

POSISTOR—NONE—Murata Manufacturing Co., Ltd.; *Int'l*, pg. 897

POSITANO—Broadloom—Couristan Inc.; *U.S. Private*, pg. 279

POSITECT—Enclosed Distribution Cutout—S & C Electric Company; *U.S. Private*, pg. 954

POSITIONING YOUR PRACTICE FOR SUCCESS—NONE—U.S. Surgical Corp.; *U.S. Public*, pg. 1687

POSITIVE REACTION—Conditioner—Clairol, Inc.; *U.S. Public*, pg. 254

POSITRIM—System For Weight Control—Amway Corporation; *U.S. Private*, pg. 69

POSITROL—Universal Fuse Link—S & C Electric Company; *U.S. Private*, pg. 954

POSSO—NONE—Posso S.A.; *Int'l*, pg. 1064

POST—Cereals—Kraft Foods, Inc.; *U.S. Public*, pg. 1287

POST—Cereals—Philip Morris Companies Inc.; *U.S. Public*, pg. 1287

POST FRUIT & FIBRE—Whole Wheat & Bran Cereal—Kraft Foods, Inc.; *U.S. Public*, pg. 1287

POST FRUITY PEBBLES—Cereal—Kraft Foods, Inc.; *U.S. Public*, pg. 1287

POST GLOVER—High Power Electrical Resistors—Halma p.l.c.; *Int'l*, pg. 589

POST GRAPE-NUTS—Brand Cereal—Kraft Foods, Inc.; *U.S. Public*, pg. 1287

POST HONEY NUT CRUNCH RAISIN BRAN—Cereal—Kraft Foods, Inc.; *U.S. Public*, pg. 1287

POST HONEYCOMB BRAND—Crunchy Sweetened Corn & Oat Cereal—Kraft Foods, Inc.; *U.S. Public*, pg. 1287

POST HORIZON TRAIL MIX—Cereal—Kraft Foods, Inc.; *U.S. Public*, pg. 1287

POST-IT—Reusable Adhesive-Coated Note Pads, Reminder Note Tapes—3M; *U.S. Public*, pg. 1604

POST-L-PACK—Book Mailer—Stone Container Corporation; *U.S. Public*, pg. 1520

POST-L-SLANT PACK—Book Mailer—Stone Container Corporation; *U.S. Public*, pg. 1520

POST NATURAL RAISIN BRAN—Cereal—Kraft Foods, Inc.; *U.S. Public*, pg. 1287

POST RAISIN BRAN—Breakfast Cereal—Kraft Foods, Inc.; *U.S. Public*, pg. 1287

POST SUPER GOLDEN CRISP—Cereal—Kraft Foods, Inc.; *U.S. Public*, pg. 1287

POST-TENS—Cereal—Kraft Foods, Inc.; *U.S. Public*, pg. 1287

POST TOOL—Woodworking Equip.—Trend-Lines Inc.; *U.S. Public*, pg. 1099

POSTAGE BY PHONE—Meter Resetting System—Pitney Bowes Inc.; *U.S. Public*, pg. 1303

POSTAGE SAVER—CD mail Pouch—Calumet Carton Company; *U.S. Private*, pg. 201

POSTAL KODER—Font Cartridge for Ink-Jet Printers—Eastman Kodak Company; *U.S. Public*, pg. 550

POSTAL MARKER—Permanent Marker—Sanford Corporation; *U.S. Public*, pg. 1178

POSTBANKEN—Retail Banking—Nordbanken AB; *Int'l*, pg. 957

POSTER PRINTER—Enlarges Originals to Poster Size—Varitronic Systems, Inc.; *U.S. Public*, pg. 250

POSTER-BINDER—Check Writing System—Master Craft Corp.; *Int'l*, pg. 267

POSTERGRIP—Front-Loading Frames—Marketing Displays International; *U.S. Private*, pg. 705

POSTICOMM—Data Processing & Communication Apparatus—The Titan Corporation; *U.S. Public*, pg. 1618

POSTNET BARCODING PLUS—Mailing Efficiency—Group 1 Software, Inc.; *U.S. Public*, pg. 417

POSTPERFECT—NONE—Pitney Bowes Inc.; *U.S. Public*, pg. 1303

POSTPRO—Electronic Remittance Posting Software—CIS Technologies, Inc.; *U.S. Public*, pg. 1155

POSTSAVER—Microcomputer Software for US Mailers—Group 1 Software, Inc.; *U.S. Public*, pg. 417

POSTSCRIPT—Language Interpreter System—Adobe Systems Incorporated; *U.S. Public*, pg. 20

POSTSCRIPT LANGUAGE DISCS—Computer discs for Macintosh and IBM—Castcraft Industries, Inc.; *U.S. Public*, pg. 219

POSTSTACK—NONE—Landmark Graphics Corporation; *U.S. Public*, pg. 776

POSTUM—Instant Imitation Coffee, Instant Grain Beverage—Kraft Foods, Inc.; *U.S. Public*, pg. 1287

POSTUM—Instant Cereal Beverage—Philip Morris Companies Inc.; *U.S. Public*, pg. 1287

POSTURE BOND—Sleep Products—King Koil Licensing Company Inc.; *U.S. Private*, pg. 621

POSTURE CENTER—Mattress—The Spring Air Company; *U.S. Private*, pg. 1027

POSTURE CONTROL—Mattress—Therapedic Associates, Inc.; *U.S. Private*, pg. 1079

POSTURE CUSHION—Mattress—The Spring Air Company; *U.S. Private*, pg. 1027

POSTURE PRO—Wheelchair Seating System—Lumex Medical Products; *U.S. Public*, pg. 758

POSTUREPEDIC—Bedding—Sealy Corporation; *U.S. Public*, pg. 978

POSZFLO—Stock Preparation—Beloit Corporation; *U.S. Public*, pg. 789

POT NOODLE—Instant Hot Snack Business—Bestfoods; *U.S. Public*, pg. 223

POT-O-PLENTY—NONE—Regal Ware, Inc.; *U.S. Private*, pg. 917

POT OF GOLD—Boxed Chocolates—Hershey Foods Corporation; *U.S. Public*, pg. 811

POT SCRUBBER—Household Dishwashers—General Electric Canada Inc.; *U.S. Public*, pg. 713

POTABLE AQUA—Water Purification Tablet—Wisconsin Pharmacal Co., Inc.; *U.S. Private*, pg. 1185

POTACOL-R—Carbohydrate-electrolyte Solution—Otsuka Pharmaceutical Co., Ltd.; *Int'l*, pg. 1013

POTATO BUDS—Dehydrated Potatoes—General Mills, Inc.; *U.S. Public*, pg. 717

POTATO OLE'S—Potato Round, Seasoned—Taco John's International, Inc.; *U.S. Private*, pg. 1066

POTATO SHAKERS—Seasonings—General Mills, Inc.; *U.S. Public*, pg. 717

POTATO TOPPERS—Seasoning Mix—McCormick/Schilling; *U.S. Public*, pg. 1066

POTENT—Pump—Little Giant Pump Company; *U.S. Public*, pg. 1566

POTENTIALS IN MARKETING—Business Publication—Bill Communications, Inc.; *Int'l*, pg. 1446

POTI—Desserts, Baking Aids—Bestfoods; *U.S. Public*, pg. 223

POTOCKY NEEDLE—Retractable Needle—The Cooper Companies, Inc.; *U.S. Public*, pg. 442

POTOMAC—Wood & Lumber Products—Georgia-Pacific Corporation; *U.S. Public*, pg. 735

POTOMAC SPIRTI—Cruise & Dining Ship, Excursions/Sightseeing Trips—Spirit Cruises, Inc.; *Int'l*, pg. 1274

POTOWMACK LANDING—Restaurant—Guest Services, Inc.; *U.S. Private*, pg. 486

POTPOURRI-CROCK—NONE—The Rival Company; *U.S. Public*, pg. 1391

POTTER'S CHOICE—Glazed Ceramic Wall Tile—Florida Tile Industries, Inc.; *U.S. Public*, pg. 1322

POTTER'S TOUCH—Glazed Ceramic Wall Tile—Florida Tile Industries, Inc.; *U.S. Public*, pg. 1322

POTTER'S TOUCH—Glazed ceramic wall tile—Precision Die & Engineering, Inc.; *U.S. Public*, pg. 1322

POTTERTON—Heating Products—Blue Circle Industries PLC; *Int'l*, pg. 197

THE POTTERY BARN—Retail Contemporary Lifestyle Merchandise, Mail Order & Retail—Williams-Sonoma, Inc.; *U.S. Public*, pg. 1770

POTTY FRESH—Portable Toilet Concentrate—Surco Products, Inc.; *U.S. Private*, pg. 1056

POU—NONE—Martin Universal Design, Inc.; *U.S. Private*, pg. 709

POUCH KING—Pouch Machine—R.A. Jones & Co. Inc.; *U.S. Private*, pg. 597

POUDRE BRONZEE—Cosmetics—Cosmair, Inc.; *Int'l*, pg. 818

POUFLEX—NONE—Martin Universal Design, Inc.; *U.S. Private*, pg. 709

POULAIN—Chocolates—Cadbury Schweppes p.l.c.; *Int'l*, pg. 247

POULAN—Chain Saws & Lawn Mowers—Frigidaire Home Products-Specialty Power Equipment; *Int'l*, pg. 440

POULAN—Lawn & Garden Products—White Consolidated Industries, Inc.; *Int'l*, pg. 439

POULAN/WEED EATER—Garden Equipment—Electrolux, AB; *Int'l*, pg. 438

POULTRY PRO—Material Handling Equipment for Poultry Industry—Cannon Equipment; *Int'l*, pg. 646

POUNCE—Insecticide—FMC Corp., Agricultural Products Group; *U.S. Public*, pg. 605

POUNCE—Cat Treats—H.J. Heinz Company; *U.S. Public*, pg. 805

POUNCE—Cat Treats—The Quaker Oats Company; *U.S. Public*, pg. 1347

POUNCE—NONE—Star-Kist Foods Inc.; *U.S. Public*, pg. 805

POUND PUPPIES—Plush & Plastic Animals—Galoob Toys, Inc.; *U.S. Public*, pg. 698

POUNDO YAM—Yams—Cadbury Nigeria PLC; *Int'l*, pg. 248

POUR-A-QUICHE—Frozen Quiche Filling—Flowers Industries, Inc.; *U.S. Public*, pg. 656

POUR FREE—Container—Carlisle Food Service Products; *U.S. Public*, pg. 305

POUR MATIC—Plate Pourer—New Brunswick Scientific Co., Inc.; *U.S. Public*, pg. 1169

POUR RITE—Container—Carlisle Food Service Products; *U.S. Public*, pg. 305

POUR-O-MATIC—Coffee Brewer—Bunn-O-Matic Corporation; *U.S. Private*, pg. 180

POUSSE CONTROLEE VITEX—Bakery Ingredient—Royal Gist-Brocades N.V.; *Int'l*, pg. 1142

POW WOW—Snack Foods—Wyandot Inc.; *U.S. Private*, pg. 1193

POWAR—NONE—Landmark Graphics Corporation; *U.S. Public*, pg. 776

POWDER—Publications & Productions—For Better Living, Inc.; *U.S. Private*, pg. 417

POWDER/BULK SOLIDS—New-Product Tabloid—Reed Elsevier Business Information; *Int'l*, pg. 1095

POWDER KEG—Germicidal Detergent—Calgon Vestal Laboratories; *U.S. Public*, pg. 1515

POWDER ROOM—Toilet Paper—Georgia-Pacific Corporation; *U.S. Public*, pg. 735

POWDERTECH—Ferrites—PowderTech Corporation; *Int'l*, pg. 878

POWDURN—Soap Dispenser—American Specialties Inc.; *U.S. Private*, pg. 62

POWELL—Valves—The Wm. Powell Company; *U.S. Private*, pg. 877

POWER & FREE—Conveyors—Rapid Industries, Inc.; *U.S. Private*, pg. 910

POWER ARCHITECTURE—Computer Product—International Business Machines Corporation; *U.S. Public*, pg. 895

POWER BACK-UP—Standby Generators—International Research & Evaluation; *U.S. Private*, pg. 571

POWER BASE—DBMS Software for IBM & Wang PC's—Compuware Corporation; *U.S. Public*, pg. 423

THE POWER BASE—Wire Circuitry System—Haworth, Inc.; *U.S. Private*, pg. 511

POWER BEAM—Rodless Cylinder—Ascolectric Limited; *U.S. Public*, pg. 575

POWER BLOC—NONE—Thermal Ceramics Inc.; *Int'l*, pg. 894

POWER BOX—Asphalt Pavers—Gehl Company; *U.S. Public*, pg. 704

POWER BREEZE—Blower/Dryer—Sunbeam Household Products; *U.S. Public*, pg. 1533

POWER BRUSH—Small Vacuum—Advance Machine Company; *Int'l*, pg. 932

POWER CELL—Electronic Ignition Power Booster—Mallory, Inc.; *U.S. Private*, pg. 698

POWER CHAMBER—Motorcycle—American Honda Motor Co., Inc. Motorcycle Division; *Int'l*, pg. 634

POWER CHANGERS—Car—Tyco Toys, Inc.; *U.S. Public*, pg. 1058

POWER CHARGER—Non-Invasive Cardiac Device—Zoll Medical Corporation; *U.S. Private*, pg. 1207

POWER CIRCLE—Graphite Shafted Irons Featuring Oversize Cavity Design—Square Two Golf Incorporated; *U.S. Public*, pg. 1501

POWER COM—Network Power Management System—Sparton Corporation; *U.S. Public*, pg. 1496

POWER COMMANDER—Power Shift Transmissions & Electronic Control Systems—Twin Disc, Incorporated; *U.S. Public*, pg. 1646

POWER COOL—NONE—Detroit Diesel Corp.; *U.S. Private*, pg. 850

POWER CUSHION—Coil Springs—Arvin Industries, Inc.; *U.S. Public*, pg. 136

POWER CUSTOM—Tires—Bridgestone/Firestone, Inc.; *Int'l*, pg. 213

POWER CUT—Marching Drums—Ludwig Industries; *U.S. Public*, pg. 1514

POWER DECK—Communications Workstation—V-Band Corporation; *U.S. Public*, pg. 1701

POWER DESIGNER—Application Development Software—Cognos Inc.; *Int'l*, pg. 305

POWER-DET—Cleaning Compound—Oakite Products, Inc.; *Int'l*, pg. 861

POWER DOT—Distribution Panel Load Centres—General Electric Canada Inc.; *U.S. Public*, pg. 713

POWER DRIVE—Tires—Bridgestone/Firestone, Inc.; *Int'l*, pg. 213

POWER DRIVE—Power Driven Fasteners—Bulldog VSI; *U.S. Public*, pg. 1176

POWER DRIVE—Vacuum Cleaner Feature—Hoover Company; *U.S. Public*, pg. 1065

POWER DRIVE—Headphones, Microphones, Car Speakers & Automotive Accessories—Recoton Corporation; *U.S. Public*, pg. 1369

POWER DRIVERS—Toy Vehicles—Empire of Carolina, Inc.; *U.S. Public*, pg. 579

POWER FALCON—Tires—Bridgestone/Firestone, Inc.; *Int'l*, pg. 213

POWER FINDER—Circuit Tracer—Greenlee Textron; *U.S. Public*, pg. 1589

POWER FLO—Pneumatic Pump—Graco Inc.; *U.S. Public*, pg. 756

POWER FLOW—Industrial Chemical—Hercules Chemical Co., Inc.; *U.S. Private*, pg. 523

POWER GRIP—Fillet Knives—Fiskars-Gerber; *Int'l*, pg. 492

POWER GRIP—NONE—Gates Europe; *Int'l*, pg. 1396

POWER GROOM—Cordless/Rechargeable Beard & Mustache Trimmer—Andis Company; *U.S. Private*, pg. 73

POWER GROOVE—Fluorescent Lamps—General Electric Canada Inc.; *U.S. Public*, pg. 713

POWER GT4—Computer Product—International Business Machines Corporation; *U.S. Public*, pg. 895

POWER GT4E—Computer Product—International Business Machines Corporation; *U.S. Public*, pg. 895

POWER GT4i—Computer Product—International Business Machines Corporation; *U.S. Public*, pg. 895

POWER GT4X—Computer Product—International Business Machines Corporation; *U.S. Public*, pg. 895

POWER GT4XI—Computer Product—International Business Machines Corporation; *U.S. Public*, pg. 895

POWER GT1—Computer Product—International Business Machines Corporation; *U.S. Public*, pg. 895

POWER GT3—Computer Product—International Business Machines Corporation; *U.S. Public*, pg. 895

POWER GT3I—Computer Product—International Business Machines Corporation; *U.S. Public*, pg. 895

POWER GTO—Computer Product—International Business Machines Corporation; *U.S. Public*, pg. 895

POWER GUARD—NONE—Xentek, Inc.; *Int'l*, pg. 1349

POWER GUARD/GARD—NONE—Detroit Diesel Corp.; *U.S. Private*, pg. 850

POWER GUIDE—Electrical Guide—Dranetz-BMI; *U.S. Private*, pg. 1144

POWER HOUSE—Lantern, Stove—The Canadian Coleman Co., Ltd.; *U.S. Private*, pg. 691

POWER HOUSE—NONE—Cognos Corp.; *Int'l*, pg. 306

POWER HOUSE—Application Development Software—Cognos Inc.; *Int'l*, pg. 305

POWER IMPLEMENT—Tires—Bridgestone/Firestone, Inc.; *Int'l*, pg. 213

POWER IMPLEMENT NON DIRECTIONAL—Tires—Bridgestone/Firestone, Inc.; *Int'l*, pg. 213

THE POWER IS IN THE PAPER—Coated Paper & Sensitized Film—The Mead Corporation; *U.S. Public*, pg. 1074

POWER KIDS BREAD—Bread—Quality Bakers of America Cooperative, Inc.; *U.S. Private*, pg. 898

POWER KING—Tractors & Equip.—HCC Inc.; *U.S. Private*, pg. 490

THE POWER LINE—Telemarketing Services—Publishers Clearing House; *U.S. Private*, pg. 893

POWER LOG—NONE—Thermal Ceramics Inc.; *Int'l*, pg. 894

POWER-LUBE—Plunger Lubricant—Chem-Trend Incorporated; *Int'l*, pg. 235

POWER-LUG—Tires—Bridgestone/Firestone, Inc.; *Int'l*, pg. 213

POWER-LUG DEEP TREAD—Tires—Bridgestone/Firestone, Inc.; *Int'l*, pg. 213

POWER LUG DEEP TREAD HRC—Tires—Bridgestone/Firestone, Inc.; *Int'l*, pg. 213

POWER MACINTOSH 8500—Mutlimedia Computer—Apple Computer, Inc.; *U.S. Public*, pg. 121

POWER MARK—Tire—The Kelly-Springfield Tire Company; *U.S. Public*, pg. 753

POWER MARK RADIAL—Tire—The Kelly-Springfield Tire Company; *U.S. Public*, pg. 753

POWER MARKER—Permanent Marker—Sanford Corporation; *U.S. Public*, pg. 1178

POWER MASTER—PMDC Motors—Groschopp, Inc.; *Int'l*, pg. 559

POWER MASTER—Piston Pumps—Lincoln Industrial; *U.S. Public*, pg. 1273

POWER MASTER—Amplifier—Shure Brothers Incorporated; *U.S. Private*, pg. 997

POWER MASTER III—Piston, Pneumatic Pumps—Lincoln Industrial; *U.S. Public*, pg. 1273

POWER MATCH—High Pressure Hydraulic Systems—Vickers, Incorporated; *U.S. Public*, pg. 24

POWER MINDER—Two-Speed Heat Pump—Lennox International Inc.; *U.S. Private*, pg. 659

POWER MITES—Toy—Toymax International Inc.; *U.S. Public*, pg. 1626

POWER MIZER—Cast Centrifugal Blower—The Spencer Turbine Co.; *U.S. Private*, pg. 1025

POWER MOLD—NONE—Applied Extrusion Technologies, Inc.; *U.S. Public*, pg. 122

POWER-OHM—NONE—Spectrol Electronics Corporation; *U.S. Private*, pg. 351

POWER-ONE—Logo—Power-One, Inc.; *U.S. Private*, pg. 878

POWER-ONE ISO LOGO—Logo—Power-One, Inc.; *U.S. Private*, pg. 878

POWER PACK—Accessory—Carefree of Colorado; *U.S. Public*, pg. 217

POWER PACK—High Current Electrical Connections—Delphi Packard Electric Systems; *U.S. Public*, pg. 719

POWER PACKER—OEM Hydraulic Systems—Applied Power Inc.; *U.S. Public*, pg. 124

POWER PAL—Portable Air Power Source—Campbell Hausfeld Division of Scott Fetzer; *U.S. Public*, pg. 217

POWER PAL—Conditioning Styling Mist for Blow Drying—Clairol, Inc.; *U.S. Public*, pg. 254

POWER PAR—Halogen Light—Duro-Test Corporation; *U.S. Private*, pg. 349

POWERPC 601—Computer Product—International Business Machines Corporation; *U.S. Public*, pg. 895

POWER PEELER—Electric Vegetable Peeler—Premark International, Inc.; *U.S. Public*, pg. 1321

POWER PIERCE—Can Openers—Sunbeam Household Products; *U.S. Public*, pg. 1533

POWER PLATFORM PPI—Electrical Technology—Dranetz-BMI; *U.S. Private*, pg. 1144

POWER PLAY—NONE—Cognos Corp.; *Int'l*, pg. 306

POWER PLAY—Application Development Software—Cognos Inc.; *Int'l*, pg. 305

POWER PLUS—Engine System Parts—Echlin Inc.; *U.S. Public*, pg. 560

POWER PLUS—V-Belts—HBD Industries, Inc.; *U.S. Private*, pg. 489

POWER PLUS—Hand Mixers—Sunbeam Household Products; *U.S. Public*, pg. 1533

POWER POINT—Electric Batteries & Chargers—General Electric Canada Inc.; *U.S. Public*, pg. 713

POWER POLE—Rod—Outdoor Technologies Group; *U.S. Private*, pg. 822

POWER-PRIME—Electrodeposition Coating—PPG Industries, Inc.; *U.S. Public*, pg. 1245

POWER PRO—Mixer—The Black & Decker Corporation; *U.S. Public*, pg. 233

POWER PUREE'N RICER—Accessory—Sunbeam Household Products; *U.S. Public*, pg. 1533

POWER QUALITY CHAT—NONE—UtiliCorp United Inc.; *U.S. Public*, pg. 1700

POWER RIB—Tires—Bridgestone/Firestone, Inc.; *Int'l*, pg. 213

POWER ROLLER-STRETCH—Film Delivery Systems—Lantech Inc.; *U.S. Private*, pg. 650

POWER SAVER—Two-Speed Air Conditioner—Lennox International Inc.; *U.S. Private*, pg. 659

POWER-SEAL—Clamp—TransTechnology Corporation; *U.S. Public*, pg. 1632

POWER SELECT—NONE—Detroit Diesel Corp.; *U.S. Private*, pg. 850

POWER SENTRY—TV Receivers—Zenith Electronics Corp.; *U.S. Public*, pg. 1790

POWER SERVICE PARTS—NONE—Detroit Diesel Corp.; *U.S. Private*, pg. 850

POWER SHOT—Batteries—Bright Star Industries, Inc.; *U.S. Public*, pg. 1341

POWER SHOWER—Showerhead—Pollenex; *U.S. Public*, pg. 1391

POWER SOUND—Tape Players—General Electric Canada Inc.; *U.S. Public*, pg. 713

POWER STAR—Bipolar Scissors—Ethicon, Inc.; *U.S. Public*, pg. 928

POWER STATION—Unix-Based Proprietary System—May & Speh, Inc.; *U.S. Public*, pg. 1063

POWER STATION—A/V Stereo Component—Shure Brothers Incorporated; *U.S. Private*, pg. 997

POWER STEMMER—Blast Hole Stemming Device—Arnold Machinery Company; *U.S. Private*, pg. 84

POWER STICK—Deodorant/Anti-Perspirants—Chesebrough-Pond's USA Co.; *Int'l*, pg. 1435

POWER STROKE—Motorcycle Oils—D.A. Stuart Company; *U.S. Private*, pg. 1048

POWER SURE—Industrial Products—Email Limited; *Int'l*, pg. 450

POWER SWING—Power Unit That Raises People Up and Down the Outside of a Building—Safway Steel Products Inc.; *Int'l*, pg. 1389

POWER SYSTEMS—NONE—Fiskars Oy AB; *Int'l*, pg. 492

POWER TEAM—Computer Team—International Business Machines Corporation; *U.S. Public*, pg. 895

POWER TEAM—Hydraulic Tools—SPX Corporation; *U.S. Public*, pg. 1420

POWER TEAM AND LOGO—NONE—Detroit Diesel Corp.; *U.S. Private*, pg. 850

POWER TECH—Auto. Equip.—Triple A Specialty Company; *U.S. Private*, pg. 1103

POWER TEMPEST—Small Vacuum—Advance Machine Company; *Int'l*, pg. 932

POWER TEST—Petroleum Products—Getty Petroleum Marketing Inc.; *U.S. Public*, pg. 740

POWER-THRU—Conveyor—Lantech Inc.; *U.S. Private*, pg. 650

POWER TO PERSUADE—Sensitized Film—The Mead Corporation; *U.S. Public*, pg. 1074

THE POWER TO WIN—Computerized Research Services—The Mead Corporation; *U.S. Public*, pg. 1074

POWER-TORQUE—Workshop Make-Up/Break-Out Machine—Baker Hughes INTEQ; *U.S. Public*, pg. 166

POWER TRAC—NONE—Detroit Diesel Corp.; *U.S. Private*, pg. 850

POWER TRAK—Non-Metallic Surface Wiring System—The Lamson & Sessions Co.; *U.S. Public*, pg. 976

POWER TRANSMISSION DESIGN—Periodical—Penton Publishing, Inc.; *U.S. Public*, pg. 1306

POWER TROF II—Swarf Conveyors—Mayfran International, Inc.; *Int'l*, pg. 1397

POWER2 ARCHITECTURE—Computer Product—International Business Machines Corporation; *U.S. Public*, pg. 895

POWER VISUALIZATION SYSTEM—Computer Product—International Business Machines Corporation; *U.S. Public*, pg. 895

POWER WHEELS—Battery-Operated Ride-Ons—Mattel, Inc.; *U.S. Public*, pg. 1057

POWER WHEELS—Battery-Operated Ride-Ons—Mattel Power Wheels; *U.S. Public*, pg. 1058

POWER WORKOUT—Athletic Shoes—Reebok International Ltd.; *U.S. Public*, pg. 1369

POWER ZONE—Industrial Products—Email Limited; *Int'l*, pg. 450

POWER-LOCK—Keyley Shaft-to-Hub Locking Device—U.S. Tsubaki, Inc.; *Int'l*, pg. 1425

POWER-STRETCH—Film Delivery System—Lantech Inc.; *U.S. Private*, pg. 650

POWERADE—Sports Drink—The Coca-Cola Company; *U.S. Public*, pg. 392

POWERAKE—Lawn Thatcher—F. D. Kees Power Equipment; *U.S. Private*, pg. 1195

POWERBAND DIGITAI—Telephone Service—AirTouch Cellular - Western Region; *U.S. Public*, pg. 34

POWERBASE—Concentrator—National Presto Industries, Inc.; *U.S. Public*, pg. 1159

POWERBILT—Golf Clubs—Hillerich & Bradsby Co.; *U.S. Private*, pg. 530

POWERBLOCK—Modular Electrical Control—Osmonics, Inc.; *U.S. Public*, pg. 1233

POWERBOLT—Electronic Dead Bolt—Weiser Inc.; *U.S. Public*, pg. 1055

POWERBOLT—Electronic Keyless Entry System—Weiser Lock; *U.S. Public*, pg. 1053

POWERBOND—NONE—Solid State Devices, Inc.; *U.S. Public*, pg. 1012

POWERBOSS—Industrial/Commercial Sweepers & Scrubbers—AAR Corp.; *U.S. Public*, pg. 1

POWERBRAILLE—Electronically Alterable Computer Controlled Braille Displays—Telesensory Corporation; *U.S. Private*, pg. 1074

POWERBUS—NONE—Tricord Systems, Inc.; *U.S. Public*, pg. 1637

POWERCACHE—Energy Storage Device—Maxwell Technologies, Inc.; *U.S. Public*, pg. 1061

POWERCELL—Uninterruptible Power Supplies—American Power Conversion Corporation; *U.S. Public*, pg. 89

POWERCHART—Graphics Monitor System—Cerner Corporation; *U.S. Public*, pg. 331

POWERCHUTE—Network Shutdown Software—American Power Conversion Corporation; *U.S. Public*, pg. 89

POWERCOMMAND—Generating/Paralleling Equip.—Onan Corporation; *U.S. Public*, pg. 468

POWERCRAFT—NONE—Plews/Edelmann; *Int'l*, pg. 1396

POWERCRISP—Microwave Bacon Cooker—National Presto Industries, Inc.; *U.S. Public*, pg. 1159

POWERCRON—Electrodeposition Coatings—PPG Industries, Inc.; *U.S. Public*, pg. 1245

POWERCUP—Concentrator—National Presto Industries, Inc.; *U.S. Public*, pg. 1159

POWERDOCTOR—Tracks & Diagnoses Power Quality—American Power Conversion Corporation; *U.S. Public*, pg. 89

POWERDRIVER—Power Tools—The Black & Decker Corporation; *U.S. Public*, pg. 233

POWERED SUBWOOFER—NONE—Cambridge Soundworks, Inc.; *U.S. Private*, pg. 202

POWEREXEC—NONE—AST Research Inc.; *Int'l*, pg. 1181

POWERFILE—Power Tools—The Black & Decker Corporation; *U.S. Public*, pg. 233

POWERFLEX—Upgradable ISA—Advanced Logic Research, Inc.; *U.S. Public*, pg. 703

POWERFLEX—Solid State Power Supply 200hz to 600hz—Ajax Magnethermic Corp.; *Int'l*, pg. 113

POWERFLEX—Capacitor Controls—Fisher Pierce Division; *U.S. Public*, pg. 1250

POWERFLEX—Fiberglass Handle Tools—UnionTools, Inc.; *U.S. Public*, pg. 17

POWERFLEX FLYER—NONE—Advanced Logic Research, Inc.; *U.S. Public*, pg. 703

POWERFLEX 19—Wire Rope—Broderick & Bascom Rope Co.; *U.S. Private*, pg. 68

POWERFLIGHT—NONE—Blaw-Knox Construction Equipment Corporation; *U.S. Public*, pg. 877

POWERFLOAT—NONE—Gilman; *Int'l*, pg. 1389

POWERFLOOD—Outdoor Floodlighting Equipment—General Electric Canada Inc.; *U.S. Public*, pg. 713

POWERFLOW—NONE—Fastenal Company; *U.S. Public*, pg. 614

POWERFONE—NONE—Nextel Communications; *U.S. Public*, pg. 1180

POWERFRAME—NONE—Tricord Systems, Inc.; *U.S. Public*, pg. 1637

POWERGARD—Plastic Film—Reynolds Metals Company; *U.S. Public*, pg. 1385

POWERGEN—Software—Symbol Technologies, Portable Systems Division; *U.S. Public*, pg. 1546

POWERGLAS—Sports Equipment—Huffy Corporation; *U.S. Public*, pg. 846

POWERHOOK—Extruded Hook—YKK (U.S.A.); *Int'l*, pg. 1515

POWERKEY—Encryption/Decryption Hardware & Software—Scientific-Atlanta, Inc.; *U.S. Public*, pg. 1443

POWERLAM—Laminated Crossarms & Power Pole for Utility Industry—Willamette Industries, Inc.; *U.S. Public*, pg. 1769

POWERLINE—NONE—Chloride Group PLC; *Int'l*, pg. 287

POWERLINE—Plunger Pumps—Hypro Corporation; *U.S. Public*, pg. 1767

POWERLINE CARRIER COMPONENTS—Line Carrier—Leviton Mfg. Co., Inc.; *U.S. Private*, pg. 663

POWERLITE—Chipset—LSI Logic Corp.; *U.S. Public*, pg. 971

POWERLOCK—Tape Rules—The Stanley Works; *U.S. Public*, pg. 1508

POWERLOGIC—PLC'S—Square D Company; *Int'l*, pg. 1208

POWERLOK—Bolts & Screws—Continental/Midland, Inc.; *U.S. Private*, pg. 268

POWERLUBE—General Purpose Lubricants—CRC Industries, Inc.; *U.S. Private*, pg. 138

POWERMAST—Stacker Crane—Harnischfeger Industries, Inc.; *U.S. Public*, pg. 788

POWERMASTER—Panelboards, Switchboards & Busway—Challenger Electrical Equipment Corp.; *U.S. Public*, pg. 558

POWERMASTER—NONE—D.C. Taylor Co.; *U.S. Private*, pg. 1070

POWERMAT—NONE—CertainTeed Corporation; *Int'l*, pg. 1170

POWERMATE—NONE—Berg Electronics; *U.S. Public*, pg. 212

POWERMATE—Lighting Tools & Heaters—The Canadian Coleman Co., Ltd.; *U.S. Private*, pg. 691

POWERMATE—Electric Generators—The Coleman Company, Inc.; *U.S. Private*, pg. 690

POWERMATE—Overhead Projector with Electric Outlets—Da-Lite Screen Company, Inc.; *U.S. Private*, pg. 306

POWERMATIC—NONE—DeVlieg-Bullard Inc.; *U.S. Public*, pg. 502

POWERMATIC—Power Nozzle for Vacuum Cleaner—Hoover Company; *U.S. Public*, pg. 1065

POWERMATIC—Woodworking & Metalworking Machine Tools—Powermatic; *U.S. Public*, pg. 502

POWERMAX—Commercial Wet/Dry Vacuum Cleaner—Hoover Company; *U.S. Public*, pg. 1065

POWERMET—Abrasive Cutter—Buehler, Limited; *U.S. Public*, pg. 574

POWERMISER—Air Conditioners—Nordyne Inc.; *U.S. Public*, pg. 1193

POWERMON—UPS Software—Best Power; *U.S. Private*, pg. 140

POWERMOW—Lawn Mower—F. D. Kees Power Equipment; *U.S. Private*, pg. 1195

POWERNET—Software for Network Power Management—American Power Conversion Corporation; *U.S. Public*, pg. 89

POWEROHM—Resistor Paste—Ferro Corporation; *U.S. Public*, pg. 618

POWEROPEN—Computer Product—International Business Machines Corporation; *U.S. Public*, pg. 895

POWERPARALLEL—Computer Product—International Business Machines Corporation; *U.S. Public*, pg. 895

POWERPC—Computer Product—International Business Machines Corporation; *U.S. Public*, pg. 895

POWERPC ARCHITECTURE—Computer Product—International Business Machines Corporation; *U.S. Public*, pg. 895

POWERPC 603—Computer Product—International Business Machines Corporation; *U.S. Public*, pg. 895

POWERPICK—Customer Retail Access Electric Program—Orange and Rockland Utilities, Inc.; *U.S. Public*, pg. 1229

POWERPLUG—Lawn Plugger-Aerator—F. D. Kees Power Equipment; *U.S. Private*, pg. 1195

POWERPOINT—Ball Point Pens & Refills—The Gillette Company; *U.S. Public*, pg. 743

POWERPOP—Microwave Multi-Popper—National Presto Industries, Inc.; *U.S. Public*, pg. 1159

POWERPRESS—Pipe Clamps—American Tool Companies, Inc.; *U.S. Private*, pg. 63

POWERPRO—Multiprocessor—Advanced Logic Research, Inc.; *U.S. Public*, pg. 703

POWERPRO—Photo Typesetters—AGFA EPS Division; *Int'l*, pg. 172

POWERRAC—Cylinder Actuator—DEZurik; *U.S. Public*, pg. 726

POWERRING—Technology for Enhanced Reliability & Fault-Tolerancefor Token Ring Ntwks—3Com Corporation; *U.S. Public*, pg. 1604

POWERS—Glass Containers Inspection Equipment—The Black & Decker Corporation; *U.S. Public*, pg. 233

POWERSAFE—Recombination Lead Acid Batteries for Telecommunications—Chloride Industrial Batteries Ltd.; *Int'l*, pg. 125

POWERSCREEN—NONE—Powerscreen International Plc; *Int'l*, pg. 1066

POWERSENTRY—NONE—Tricord Systems, Inc.; *U.S. Public*, pg. 1637

POWERSERVER—Computer Product—International Business Machines Corporation; *U.S. Public*, pg. 895

POWERSHIELD—Uninterruptible Power Supplies—American Power Conversion Corporation; *U.S. Public*, pg. 89

POWERSHIELD—Chemical Additives for Gasoline—The Lubrizol Corporation; *U.S. Public*, pg. 1016

POWERSHOT—NONE—The Black & Decker Corporation; *U.S. Public*, pg. 233

POWERSHRED—Office Shredders—Fellowes Manufacturing Co.; *U.S. Private*, pg. 400

POWERSIL—Electrical Insulator Coating—Wacker Silicones Corporation; *Int'l*, pg. 625

POWERSLEEVE—Connectors—Raychem Corporation; *U.S. Public*, pg. 1362

POWERSLEUTH—UPS Software—Best Power; *U.S. Private*, pg. 140

POWERSLICE—Lawn Aerator—F. D. Kees Power Equipment; *U.S. Private*, pg. 1195

POWERSOFT—Development Tool Software—Sybase, Inc.; *U.S. Public*, pg. 1544

POWERSOURCE—NONE—The Black & Decker Corporation; *U.S. Public*, pg. 233

POWERSTAR—Woodworking Machine Tool—Powermatic; *U.S. Public*, pg. 502

POWERSTAR BURNER SYSTEM—Asphalt Hot Mix Burner System—Hauck Mfg. Co.; *U.S. Private*, pg. 510

POWERSTATION—Computer Product—International Business Machines Corporation; *U.S. Public*, pg. 895

POWERSTEEL—Wire Rope—Broderick & Bascom Rope Co.; *U.S. Private*, pg. 68

POWERSTEEL PLUS—Wire Rope—Broderick & Bascom Rope Co.; *U.S. Private*, pg. 68

POWERTACTS—Contacts—Raychem Corporation; *U.S. Public*, pg. 1362

POWERTEC—AC-DC Power Supplies—Astec America Inc.; *Int'l*, pg. 93

POWERTEK—Dynamometers—MTS Systems Corporation; *U.S. Public*, pg. 1028

POWERTITE—Receptacles and Plugs—Appleton Electric Co.; *U.S. Public*, pg. 572

POWERTOOL—Power Analysis Software—IKOS Systems, Inc.; *U.S. Public*, pg. 864

POWERTRACK—NONE—Gilman; *Int'l*, pg. 1389

POWERTWIST—Fluorescent Lamp—Duro-Test Corporation; *U.S. Private*, pg. 349

POWERTWIST-V—Belts—Fenner Drives; *U.S. Private*, pg. 400

POWERVEISA—NONE—Advanced Logic Research, Inc.; *U.S. Public*, pg. 703

POWERVIEW—Binoculars—Bushnell Corporation; *U.S. Private*, pg. 1191

POWERWAND—Small Vacuum—Advance Machine Company; *Int'l*, pg. 932

POWERWARE—Uninterruptible Power Supplies—Exide Electronics Group, Inc.; *Int'l*, pg. 126

POWERWORKS—Spa Powerlimit—Coleman Spas, Inc.; *U.S. Private*, pg. 691

POWL-VAC—Vacuum Circuit Breaker—Powell Industries, Inc.; *U.S. Public*, pg. 1319

POWR/BRACKET—Pole Mountable, Pre-Wired Lighting Assembly with Dependent Luminaire—General Electric Canada Inc.; *U.S. Public*, pg. 713

POWR-CENTER—Extension Cords—General Cable Corporation; *U.S. Public*, pg. 1486

POWR-FOAM—Television Transmission Cable—General Cable Corporation; *Int'l*, pg. 1486

POWR-PAK—Generators—Avis Industrial Corporation; *U.S. Private*, pg. 102

POWRARM—Workholding Tool—Wilton Corporation; *U.S. Public*, pg. 1181

POWREACTOR—Regulators—Grove Valve & Regulator Company; *U.S. Private*, pg. 484

POWRPAK—Generators & Electric Plants—Winpower Inc.; *U.S. Private*, pg. 350

POWERSILK—Nylon—BASF Corporation Fiber Products Division; *Int'l*, pg. 105

POWRWORKER—NONE—Clark Material Handling Company; *U.S. Private*, pg. 243

POXINE—Poultry Biologic—Salsbury Laboratories, Inc.; *Int'l*, pg. 1277

POXINE—Poultry Biologic—Solvay Animal Health, Inc.; *Int'l*, pg. 1277

POXINE—Poultry Biologic—Solvay S.A.; *Int'l*, pg. 1277

POZIDRIV—Fastening System—Rule Industries, Inc.; *U.S. Public*, pg. 950

POZZI—Windows—Jeld-Wen, Inc.; *U.S. Private*, pg. 585

POZZI-GINORI—Sanitary Porlelain—Metra Corporation; *Int'l*, pg. 862

POZZI-GINORI—Bathroom Ceramics—Sanitec Ltd. Oy; *Int'l*, pg. 863

POZZOLITH—Chemical Admixtures for Concrete & Mortar—Master Builders Inc.; *Int'l*, pg. 1465

POZZOLITH—Concrete Admixtures—Novartis AG; *Int'l*, pg. 971

POZZUTEC 20—Admixture for Placing Concrete in Cold Weather—Master Builders Inc.; *Int'l*, pg. 1465

PRACT—Computer Research Services—The Mead Corporation; *U.S. Public*, pg. 1074

PRACTICAL BOAT PLANNER—Yachting Magazine—IPC Magazines Limited; *Int'l*, pg. 651

PRACTICAL CLASSICS—Car Magazine—EMAP Nationals; *Int'l*, pg. 451

PRACTICAL FISHKEEPING—Pet Magazine—EMAP Pursuit Publishing; *Int'l*, pg. 451

PRACTICAL GARDENING—U.K. Gardening Magazine—EMAP Apex; *Int'l*, pg. 451

PRACTICAL HORSEMAN—Periodical—Cowles Enthusiast Media, Inc.; *U.S. Private*, pg. 281

PRACTICAL PARENTING—Women's Special Interest Magazine—IPC Magazines Limited; *Int'l*, pg. 651

PRACTICAL PARENTING—Magazine—Reed Business Information Pty. Limited; *Int'l*, pg. 1094

PRACTICAL PHOTOGRAPHY—U.K. Photography Magazine—EMAP Apex; *Int'l*, pg. 451

PRADO—Plant Protectivesns—DSM Chemie Linz GmbH; *Int'l*, pg. 356

PRADO WP—Herbicides—Agrolinz Melamin GmbH; *Int'l*, pg. 356

PRAGUE POWDER—Cure—Griffith Laboratories Worldwide, Inc.; *U.S. Private*, pg. 481

PRAIRIE FARMER—Farm Publication—Farm Progress Publications; *U.S. Public*, pg. 513

PRAIRIE FARMS—Food Products—Prairie Farms Dairy, Inc.; *U.S. Private*, pg. 878

PRAIRIE JOY—Car—Nissan Motor Co., Ltd.; *Int'l*, pg. 943

PRAIRIE MAID—Cereal—Lever Brothers Co.; *Int'l*, pg. 1435

PRAIRIE MAID—Cereal—Unilever Plc; *Int'l*, pg. 1433

PRAIRIE MARKET—Retail Grocery Stores—Nash Finch Company; *U.S. Public*, pg. 1151

PRAISE—NONE—Avon Products Co., Ltd.; *U.S. Public*, pg. 156

PRAISE—Dog Food—Ralston Purina Company; *U.S. Public*, pg. 1359

PRAISE AEROBICS—NONE—Integrity Incorporated; *U.S. Public*, pg. 886

PRAMACE—Cardiovascular Pharmaceutical—Astra AB; *Int'l*, pg. 93

PRAMEX—Pesticide-Insectide—Roussel Corporation; *Int'l*, pg. 625

PRAMEX—Pesticide/Insecticide—Roussel UCLAF S.A.; *Int'l*, pg. 626

PRANG—Art Matls., Watercolors, Crayons—Dixon Ticonderoga Company; *U.S. Public*, pg. 514

PRATT & LAMBERT—Paints—Pratt & Lambert United, Inc.; *U.S. Public*, pg. 1466

PRATT & WHITNEY—Aircraft Engines—United Technologies Corporation; *U.S. Public*, pg. 1689

PRATT-READ—Hardware & Tools—Pratt-Read Corporation; *U.S. Private*, pg. 879

PRATTS—Patent Liquid Dryer—Pratt & Lambert United, Inc.; *U.S. Public*, pg. 1466

PRATTY & LAMBERT—Paints & Coatings—The Sherwin-Williams Company; *U.S. Public*, pg. 1465

PRAVACHOL—Cholesterol-Lowering Drug—Bristol-Myers Squibb International; *U.S. Public*, pg. 254

PRAVACOL—Reductase Inhibitor—Bristol-Myers Squibb Company; *U.S. Public*, pg. 253

Brand Name Index

PRAXAIR—Industrial Gas—Praxair Inc.; *U.S. Public*, pg. 1319

PRE/AFT—Shave Lotion—Parks Products, Inc.; *U.S. Private*, pg. 840

PRE-BASES—Early Concept Screening—BASES Worldwide; *U.S. Private*, pg. 120

PRE-BYPASS PLUS—Blood Filter—Pall Corporation; *U.S. Public*, pg. 1253

PRE/SEIS—Seismic Data Processing Equipment—Litton Industries, Inc.; *U.S. Public*, pg. 1002

PRE-SUN—Sunscreen—Bristol-Myers Squibb Company; *U.S. Public*, pg. 253

PREACHING TODAY—Audio Cassette—Christianity Today, Inc.; *U.S. Private*, pg. 238

PREAM—Powdered Non-Dairy Creamer—Rich Products Corp.; *U.S. Private*, pg. 840

PRECEPT—Racquetball Eyewear—Ektelon; *U.S. Private*, pg. 884

PRECI-JET—Needle-Less Insulin Injection System—HMI Industries; *U.S. Public*, pg. 771

PRECIOUS—Italian Cheese—Sorrento Cheese Company, Inc.; *Int'l*, pg. 323

PRECIOUS—Children's Disposable Diapers—The Tranzonic Companies; *U.S. Public*, pg. 1632

PRECIOUS—Baby Diapers—Tranzonic Personal Care Division; *U.S. Public*, pg. 1632

PRECIOUS MOMENTS—Cologne Spray—Stanhome Inc.; *U.S. Public*, pg. 1508

PRECIPITRON—Electronic Collectors—The Howden Fan Co.; *U.S. Private*, pg. 543

PRECIS—Sizing Agent—Hercules Incorporated; *U.S. Public*, pg. 767

PRECISE—Cleaner & Disinfectant—The Dow Chemical Company; *U.S. Public*, pg. 522

PRECISE—Conditioning Relaxer—Johnson Products Co., Inc.; *U.S. Public*, pg. 915

PRECISE—Stainless Steel Orthodontic Brackets—Lee Pharmaceuticals; *U.S. Public*, pg. 984

PRECISE—Software—Olsten Corporation; *U.S. Public*, pg. 1220

PRECISE—Skin Stapler—3M; *U.S. Public*, pg. 1604

PRECISE HCG—Pregnancy Test—Becton Dickinson & Company; *U.S. Public*, pg. 199

PRECISION—Floppy Discs—Anacomp, Inc.; *U.S. Public*, pg. 106

PRECISION—Office Furniture—Carter Holt Harvey Limited; *U.S. Public*, pg. 904

PRECISION—Boiler—Precision Parts Corp.; *U.S. Private*, pg. 879

PRECISION—Twist Drills—Precision Twist Drill Co.; *Int'l*, pg. 1185

PRECISION AIR FEED—Air Feed—P/A Industries, Inc.; *U.S. Private*, pg. 825

PRECISION ESTIMATING—NONE—Timberline Software Corporation; *U.S. Public*, pg. 1609

PRECISION/KTO—Ergonomic Freestanding & Desking Systems—Jami, Inc.; *U.S. Private*, pg. 581

PRECISION LINE—Photo Film, Plates—Eastman Kodak Company; *U.S. Public*, pg. 550

PRECISION-LITE—Photographic & Reprographic Films & Paper—Eastman Kodak Company; *U.S. Public*, pg. 550

PRECISION MONOLITHICS—Analog & Data Conversion Integrated Circuits—Analog Devices; *U.S. Public*, pg. 108

PRECISION I—Fly Rods & Leaders—Cortland Line Co., Inc.; *U.S. Private*, pg. 277

PRECISION PIPE—Sewer Pipe—Premarc Corporation; *U.S. Private*, pg. 881

PRECISION PLASMIDS—NONE—Life Technologies, Inc.; *U.S. Public*, pg. 504

PRECISION STUDIOS—Ceramic Transfers—Waterford Wedgwood UK Plc; *Int'l*, pg. 1487

PRECISION SYSTEMS & SPACE DIVISION—Encoders & Servos—BEI Sensors and Systems Company; *U.S. Public*, pg. 160

PRECISION TUNE—Automobile Tune-Up Service—Precision Tune Autocare; *U.S. Public*, pg. 1321

PRECISION UV SOFT DISPOSABLE CONTACT LENSES—NONE—Pilkington Barnes Hind (PBH); *U.S. Private*, pg. 111

PRECIUM—Precious Metal Alloy—Handy & Harman; *U.S. Public*, pg. 780

PRECOMP—Premenstrual Tablets—Zee Medical, Inc.; *U.S. Public*, pg. 1073

PRECON—Conduitized Conductors—Reynolds Metals Company; *U.S. Public*, pg. 1385

PRECOR—Exercise Equip.—Precor, Inc.; *U.S. Public*, pg. 1322

PRECOR—Fitness Equipment—Premark International, Inc.; *U.S. Public*, pg. 1321

PRED FORTE—Sterile Ophthalmic Solution—Allergan, Inc.; *U.S. Public*, pg. 46

PRED G—Sterile Ophthalmic Solutions—Allergan, Inc.; *U.S. Public*, pg. 46

PREDATOR—Foam Insulation Dispenser—Binks Sames Corporation; *U.S. Public*, pg. 229

PREDATOR—NONE—Cordis, a Johnson & Johnson Company; *U.S. Public*, pg. 928

PREDATOR—Laser Printers—Diagraph Corporation; *U.S. Private*, pg. 330

PREDATOR I & II—Hoodshield—Lund International Holdings, Inc.; *U.S. Public*, pg. 1020

PREDEC—Gypsum Paneling—Georgia-Pacific Corporation; *U.S. Public*, pg. 735

PREDENT—NONE—SmithKline Beecham Research Limited; *Int'l*, pg. 1266

PREDICT—Reliability Prediction Software—Harnischfeger Industries, Inc.; *U.S. Public*, pg. 788

PREDICTOR—OTC Pregnancy Test—Akzo Nobel N.V.; *Int'l*, pg. 42

PREDITOR/2—Source Code Editor for Programmers Working in OS/2—Compuware Corporation; *U.S. Public*, pg. 423

PREDMYCIN—Sterile Ophthalmic Solution—Allergan, Inc.; *U.S. Public*, pg. 46

PREDNICEN-M—Pharmacuetical Products—Schwarz Pharma Manufacturing, Inc.; *Int'l*, pg. 1211

PREEN—Garden Prod.—Lebanon Seaboard Corporation; *U.S. Private*, pg. 656

PREEN 'N GREEN—Garden Prod.—Lebanon Seaboard Corporation; *U.S. Private*, pg. 656

PREET 33—Automotive Paint Primers—PPG Industries, Inc.; *U.S. Public*, pg. 1245

PREFERENCE—Contact Lenses—The Cooper Companies, Inc.; *U.S. Public*, pg. 442

PREFERENCE—Hair Color—Cosmair, Inc.; *Int'l*, pg. 818

PREFERENCE—Credit Card—Credit Mutuel; *Int'l*, pg. 344

PREFERENCE—Bathtub Wall Kit—Plaskolite Inc.; *U.S. Private*, pg. 870

PREFERENCE DESIGN—Paper & Plastic Cups, Plates & Containers—Sweetheart Cup Company Inc.; *U.S. Private*, pg. 1058

PREFERRED—Coupled Hose Assemblies—Echlin Inc.; *U.S. Public*, pg. 560

PREFERRED ADVISOR—NONE—Keyport Life Insurance Company; *U.S. Private*, pg. 666

PREFERRED BUYERS' CLUB—NONE—Damark International, Inc.; *U.S. Public*, pg. 478

PREFERRED CARE—Specialty Patient Recliners—Lumex Medical Products; *U.S. Public*, pg. 758

PREFERRED CARE-USA—Health Insurance—Blue Cross and Blue Shield Association; *U.S. Private*, pg. 151

PREFERRED ENGINEERING—Nuclear Services—Preferred Utilities Manufacturing Corp.; *U.S. Private*, pg. 881

PREFERRED INSTRUMENTS—Combustion Controls—Preferred Instruments; *U.S. Private*, pg. 881

PREFERRED INSTRUMENTS—Combustion Controls—Preferred Utilities Manufacturing Corp.; *U.S. Private*, pg. 881

PREFERRED STOCK—Men's Fragrance—Coty Inc.; *Int'l*, pg. 185

PREFERRED STOCK BY MAGNALITE—Cookware—General Housewares Corp.; *U.S. Public*, pg. 715

PREFERRED TRAVELLER—Travel Publication—Encore Marketing International, Inc.; *U.S. Public*, pg. 580

PREFINISHED—Manufacturing Process for Pre-Finished Mouldings—ABT Building Products Corporation; *Int'l*, pg. 20

PREFIX RESOLUTION PLUS—IMS Database Utility—BMC Software, Inc.; *U.S. Public*, pg. 162

PREFLEX FOR SENSITIVE EYES—Sterile Cleaning Solution for Soft Contact Lenses—Alcon Laboratories; *U.S. Public*, pg. 916

PREFLOW GF—Filtration Products—Gelman Sciences, Inc.; *U.S. Public*, pg. 1253

PREFORMERS—Potato Products—J.R. Simplot Company; *U.S. Private*, pg. 1002

PREGESTIMIL—Infant Formulas—Bristol-Myers Squibb Company; *U.S. Public*, pg. 253

PREGESTIMIL—Hypoallergenic Infant Formula—Mead Johnson Nutritional Group; *U.S. Public*, pg. 254

PREGNANCY & BIRTH—U.K. Parenting Magazine—EMAP Elan; *Int'l*, pg. 451

PREGNAVITE FORTE F—Vitamin/Mineral Supplement—SmithKline Beecham plc; *Int'l*, pg. 1264

PREGNYL—Pharmaceutical—Organon Inc.; *Int'l*, pg. 48

PREGO—Spaghetti Sauce—Campbell Soup Company; *U.S. Public*, pg. 298

PREGO—Food Products—Campbell Soup Company Ltd.; *U.S. Public*, pg. 299

PREHISTORIC PETS—Children's Rubber Stampers—Mattel Games/Puzzles; *U.S. Public*, pg. 1058

PRELETE—Defluxer—The Dow Chemical Company; *U.S. Public*, pg. 522

PRELL—Shampoo—The Procter & Gamble Company; *U.S. Public*, pg. 1330

PRELONE—Liquid Steroid—Muro Pharmaceutical, Inc.; *U.S. Private*, pg. 767

PRELUDE—Automobile—American Honda Motor Co., Inc. Automobile Sales Division; *Int'l*, pg. 634

PRELUDE—Doors—Morgan Products Ltd.; *U.S. Public*, pg. 1132

PRELUDE—Ergonomic Seating—Trendway Corporation; *U.S. Private*, pg. 1099

PREM-LASS—Liquid Feed—Feed Service Corp.; *U.S. Private*, pg. 399

PREMABRAZE—Brazing Alloy—Handy & Harman; *U.S. Public*, pg. 780

PREMALOY—Silver Contact Material—Handy & Harman; *U.S. Public*, pg. 780

PREMARIN—Conjugated Estrogens - Prevention Of Osteoporosis—American Home Products Corporation; *U.S. Public*, pg. 79

PREMARIN—NONE—Wyeth Australia Pty. Ltd.; *U.S. Public*, pg. 82

PREMARIN DTC—Estrogen—Wyeth-Ayerst Laboratories, Inc.; *U.S. Public*, pg. 80

PREMDOR—Interior Wood Door—Premdor Inc.; *Int'l*, pg. 1066

PREMIER—Diesel Fuel—Amoco Corporation; *U.S. Public*, pg. 101

PREMIER—Photo Paper & Printer Accessories—Eastman Kodak Company; *U.S. Public*, pg. 550

PREMIER—NONE—Escalade Sports; *U.S. Public*, pg. 591

PREMIER—Lightweight Wheelchair—Everest & Jennings, Inc.; *U.S. Public*, pg. 758

PREMIER—Writing Instruments & Desk Sets—Gillette Co.-Parker Pen USA; *U.S. Public*, pg. 745

PREMIER—Graphic Products—The Goodyear Tire & Rubber Company; *U.S. Public*, pg. 752

PREMIER—Semi-Automatic Fillers—Liqui-Box Corporation; *U.S. Public*, pg. 1000

PREMIER—Enzyme Immunoassays for Infectious Disease Diagnosis—Meridian Diagnostics, Inc.; *U.S. Public*, pg. 1094

PREMIER—Roof Coating Products—Monsey-Bakor; *U.S. Private*, pg. 757

PREMIER—High End Car Stereo Systems—Pioneer Electronics (USA) Inc.; *Int'l*, pg. 1058

PREMIER—Coatings—Premier Coatings, Inc.; *Int'l*, pg. 1488

PREMIER—Electronic Cabinets, Cases & Accessories; Trimline Enclosures—Premier Metal Products Company; *U.S. Public*, pg. 881

PREMIER—Locksmiths' Work, Safes & Cash Boxes—Sime Darby Berhad; *Int'l*, pg. 1249

PREMIER—Rotary Mower Engines—Tecumseh Products Co. Engine & Transmission Group; *U.S. Public*, pg. 1566

PREMIER—Lighting Fixtures—Thomas Industries, Consumer Lighting Division; *U.S. Public*, pg. 1599

PREMIER—Lighting Fixtures—Thomas Industries Inc.; *U.S. Public*, pg. 1598

PREMIER—Faucets—Waxman Industries, Inc.; *U.S. Public*, pg. 1748

PREMIER—Professional Beauty Products—Windmere-Durable Holdings; *U.S. Public*, pg. 1771

PREMIER & PRO MIX—Peat Moss—Premier CDN Enterprises Ltd.; *Int'l*, pg. 1067

PREMIER COLLECT—Collection Program—I.C. System, Inc.; *U.S. Private*, pg. 553

PREMIER COLLECTION—Photo Typesetters—AGFA EPS Division; *Int'l*, pg. 172

PREMIER DAIRIES—NONE—Avenmore Waterford Foods plc; *Int'l*, pg. 102

PREMIER DINING—Discount Dining for Members at Participating Restaurants—CUC International, Inc.; *U.S. Public*, pg. 320

PREMIER FORMS PROCESSOR—Automated Forms Processor—Mitek Systems, Inc.; *U.S. Public*, pg. 1117

THE PREMIER NAME IN CASINO ENTERTAINMENT—NONE—Harrah's Entertainment, Inc.; *U.S. Public*, pg. 790

PREMIER I—Airplane—Raytheon Aircraft Company; *U.S. Public*, pg. 1365

PREMIER-PAK—Cartridge for Use in Blood Analyzer—Mallinckrodt Inc.; *U.S. Public*, pg. 1039

PREMIER RED—Abrasive—Carborundum Abrasives North America; *Int'l*, pg. 1174

PREMIER SMALL PACKAGE SERVICE—Vacation Packaging—America West Airlines, Inc.; *U.S. Public*, pg. 67

PREMIER TECH—Peat Moss—Premier CDN Enterprises Ltd.; *Int'l*, pg. 1067

PREMIER 5220 & 5210—LAN Bridges—Gandalf Technologies Inc.; *Int'l*, pg. 540

PREMIERE—Sporting Goods—Brunswick Bowling & Billiards Corp.; *U.S. Public*, pg. 265

PREMIERE—U.K. Entertainment Magazine—EMAP Metro; *Int'l*, pg. 451

PREMIERE—Cookware—Premark International, Inc.; *U.S. Public*, pg. 1321

PREMIERE EDITIONS—Ladies Apparel—Hanover Direct Pennsylvania, Inc.; *U.S. Public*, pg. 782

PREMIERE FRAGRANCES—Body Sprays & Fragrances—Tristar Corp.; *U.S. Public*, pg. 1640

PREMIERE PROVIDER SM—High-Level Disability with Guaranteed Long-Term Care Benefit at Age 65—Colonial Companies, Inc.; *U.S. Public*, pg. 1699

PREMIOR—Chocolate Confectionery—Thorntons PLC; *Int'l*, pg. 1386

PREMIS—Electronic Claims Management Software—CIS Technologies, Inc.; *U.S. Public*, pg. 1155

PREMISE—Office Furniture & Systems—Haworth, Inc.; *U.S. Private*, pg. 511

PREMISYS—NONE—Premisys Communications, Inc.; *U.S. Public*, pg. 1323

PREMIUM—Potatoes—Chiquita Brands International, Inc.; *U.S. Public*, pg. 349

PREMIUM—Adding Machine Paper—Georgia-Pacific Corporation; *U.S. Public*, pg. 735

PREMIUM—Rope—Macwhyte Co.; *U.S. Private*, pg. 68

PREMIUM—Crackers—Nabisco Inc.; *U.S. Public*, pg. 1355

PREMIUM—Saltine Crackers—RJR Nabisco Holdings Corp.; *U.S. Public*, pg. 1354

PREMIUM—Surgical Staplers & Laparoscopic Instruments—U.S. Surgical Corp.; *U.S. Public*, pg. 1687

PREMIUM ARCHITECTURAL SERIES—1/8" Commercial Vinyl Composition Tile—Kentile Operting Co.; *U.S. Private*, pg. 615

PREMIUM CEEA—Stapler—U.S. Surgical Corp.; *U.S. Public*, pg. 1687

PREMIUM CANADIAN—Brandy—Laird & Company; *U.S. Private*, pg. 642

THE PREMIUM CHOICE—NONE—Elcor Corporation; *U.S. Public*, pg. 567

PREMIUM COLONY—Varietal Wines—The Beverage Source, Inc.; *U.S. Public*, pg. 591

PREMIUM CROSS BAR XM—Tires—Bridgestone/Firestone, Inc.; *Int'l*, pg. 213

PREMIUM DURALITE—NONE—Monier Inc.; *Int'l*, pg. 1091

PREMIUM ESD—Tires—Bridgestone/Firestone, Inc.; *Int'l*, pg. 213

PREMIUM E2—Motor Oil—Coastal Refining & Marketing; *U.S. Public*, pg. 390

PREMIUM GOLD—NONE—Champion Ignition Products; *U.S. Public*, pg. 442

PREMIUM MULTIFIRE TA—Stapler—U.S. Surgical Corp.; *U.S. Public*, pg. 1687

PREMIUM PLUS CEEA—Stapler—U.S. Surgical Corp.; *U.S. Public*, pg. 1687

PREMIUM POLY CS—Stapler—U.S. Surgical Corp.; *U.S. Public*, pg. 1687

PREMIUM POLYSORB* 55—DLU—U.S. Surgical Corp.; *U.S. Public*, pg. 1687

PREMIUM RECIPE—Food Service Item—Performance Food Group Company; *U.S. Public*, pg. 1278

PREMIUM SURGICLIP—Automatic Clip Applier—U.S. Surgical Corp.; *U.S. Public*, pg. 1687

PREMIUM TRACTION HEAVY DUTY—Tires—Bridgestone/Firestone, Inc.; *Int'l*, pg. 213

PREMIX—Foundry Sand Additives—Hill & Griffith Company; *U.S. Private*, pg. 529

PREMMIA—NONE—AST Research Inc.; *Int'l*, pg. 1181

PREMONDE ALPINE LACE—Low Fat & Low Sodium Cheese—Alpine Lace Brands, Inc.; *U.S. Private*, pg. 646

PREMPHASE—Hormone Replacement Therapy—American Home Products Corporation; *U.S. Public*, pg. 79

PREMPRO—Hormone Replacement Therapy—American Home Products Corporation; *U.S. Public*, pg. 79

PREMSYN PMS—Pre-Menstrual Syndrome Products—Chattem, Inc.; *U.S. Public*, pg. 341

PREMSYN PMS—PMS Product—Chattem, Inc., Consumer Products Division; *U.S. Public*, pg. 341

PRENATAL—Baby Clothes—RetailNet B.V.; *Int'l*, pg. 750

PRENSES—Buses—Sabanci Holding A.S.; *Int'l*, pg. 1167

PRENTICE—Log Loaders, Feller Buncher & Harvesters—Blount International, Inc.; *U.S. Public*, pg. 237

PRENTICE-HALL—Publishers—Simon & Schuster; *U.S. Private*, pg. 777

PRENTOX—Insecticide—Prentiss Incorporated; *U.S. Private*, pg. 882

PREP—Outboard—American Suzuki Motor Corporation; *Int'l*, pg. 1323

PREP—Shave Lotion—Parks Products, Inc.; *U.S. Private*, pg. 840

PREP-AIR—NONE—Schrader Bellows Division; *U.S. Public*, pg. 1261

PREP-MASTER—Finishing Prep. Station—Binks Sames Corporation; *U.S. Public*, pg. 229

PREP TEAM—Automotive Refinishing/Reconditioning Products—3M; *U.S. Public*, pg. 1604

PREP 3000—Preparative Chromatography System—Millipore Corporation; *U.S. Public*, pg. 1112

PREP-TOWLS—Paper Towels—Bay West Paper Corp. Towel & Tissue Div.; *U.S. Public*, pg. 1747

PREPAC—NONE—Life Technologies, Inc.; *U.S. Public*, pg. 504

PREPARATION H—Hemorrhoidal Treatment - Ointment, Suppositories, And Cream—American Home Products Corporation; *U.S. Public*, pg. 79

PREPARATION H—Hemorrhoid Treatment-Ointment, Suppositories & Cream—Whitehall-Robins Healthcare; *U.S. Public*, pg. 80

PREPARE—Razors—Shiseido Company Ltd.; *Int'l*, pg. 1235

PREPARED FOODS—Magazine for Companies in the High-Value-Added Food & Beverage Industry—Reed Elsevier Business Information; *Int'l*, pg. 1095

PREPJET—Kinetic Cavity Preperation System—American Dental Technologies; *U.S. Public*, pg. 70

PREPLINK—NONE—CEM Corporation; *U.S. Public*, pg. 277

PREPPAK—Silica Cartridge—Millipore Corporation; *U.S. Public*, pg. 1112

PREPULSID—NONE—Johnson & Johnson; *U.S. Public*, pg. 927

PRESARIO—Personal Computer—COMPAQ Computer Corporation; *U.S. Public*, pg. 417

PRESCO DYNES—Safety Systems-Hydraulic & Pneumatic Emergency Shutdown Systems—Barber Industries Inc.; *Int'l*, pg. 164

PRESCO PILOT—Pressure Pilot—Barber Industries Inc.; *Int'l*, pg. 164

PRESCO SWITCHES—Pressure Switches—Barber Industries Inc.; *Int'l*, pg. 164

PRESCO TEES—Tees—Barber Industries Inc.; *Int'l*, pg. 164

PRESCOLITE—Lighting Fixtures—Prescolite Moldcast Lighting Company; *U.S. Public*, pg. 1684

PRESCORE SERVICE—NONE—Fair, Isaac and Company, Inc.; *U.S. Public*, pg. 609

PRESCRIBED CARE—Prescription & Over-the-Counter Drugs—Almay, Inc.; *U.S. Private*, pg. 689

PRESCRIPTION DIET—Dietary Animal Food—Hill's Pet Nutrition; *U.S. Public*, pg. 397

PRESCRIPTION IV—Hair Preparation Product—Clairol, Inc.; *U.S. Public*, pg. 254

PRESCRIPTION PHARMACEUTICALS—NONE—Wyeth Australia Pty. Ltd.; *U.S. Public*, pg. 82

PRESCRIPTION SOLUTIONS—Pharmacies—PacifiCare Health Systems, Inc.; *U.S. Public*, pg. 1250

PRESCRIPTION WHEELS—Crane Wheels—Harnischfeger Industries, Inc.; *U.S. Public*, pg. 788

PRESCRIPTIVES—Treatment & Cosmetic Products—Estee Lauder Companies Inc.; *U.S. Public*, pg. 594

PRESEA—Car—Nissan Motor Co., Ltd.; *Int'l*, pg. 943

PRESEASON—Athletic Shoes—Reebok International Ltd.; *U.S. Public*, pg. 1369

PRESENTATION MANAGER—Software—International Business Machines Corporation; *U.S. Public*, pg. 895

PRESENTATION PACK—Software—Borland International, Inc.; *U.S. Public*, pg. 246

PRESENTATIONS—Business Publications—Bill Communications, Inc.; *Int'l*, pg. 1446

PRESENTATIONS—Glassware—Indiana Glass Company; *U.S. Public*, pg. 976

THE PRESERVATION PRESS—Books—John Wiley & Sons, Inc.; *U.S. Public*, pg. 1768

PRESIDE—Herbicide—The Dow Chemical Company; *U.S. Public*, pg. 522

PRESIDENT—Dairy Products—Compagnie Laitiere BESNIER; *Int'l*, pg. 322

PRESIDENT—Pumps—Graco Inc.; *U.S. Public*, pg. 756

PRESIDENT—Car—Nissan Motor Co., Ltd.; *Int'l*, pg. 943

PRESIDENT—Communication Equipment—Uniden America Corporation; *Int'l*, pg. 1433

PRESIDENT—Ash Trays—Willert Home Products, Inc.; *U.S. Private*, pg. 1177

PRESIDENT XD—Golf Clubs—Mizuno Corporation; *Int'l*, pg. 884

PRESIDENTE—Spirit—Allied Domecq PLC; *Int'l*, pg. 62

PRESIDENTE—Brandy—Domecq Importers Inc.; *Int'l*, pg. 63

PRESIDENTS PRIDE—Meat & Cheese Products—Bar-S Foods Co.; *U.S. Private*, pg. 114

PRESMET—Powder Metal Components—The Presmet Corp.; *U.S. Private*, pg. 882

PRESOMEN—Hormone Preparations—Kali-Chemie Aktiengesellschaft; *Int'l*, pg. 1278

PRESPONSE—Veterinary Pharmaceuticals—American Home Products Corporation; *U.S. Public*, pg. 79

THE PRESS—Industry News—Intertec Publishing; *U.S. Public*, pg. 1327

PRESS AND CLOSE—NONE—Uniflex, Inc.; *U.S. Public*, pg. 1665

PRESS CLUB BLEND—Whiskey—Laird & Company; *U.S. Private*, pg. 642

PRESS CLUB DE FRANCE—Press Club—Accor S.A.; *Int'l*, pg. 20

PRESS-GUARD—Type One Pressboard Coated & Embossed—FiberMark Inc.; *U.S. Public*, pg. 620

PRESS-IN-PLACE—Caulking Compound; Window Glazing—3M; *U.S. Public*, pg. 1604

PRESS MASTER—Press Roll Cover—Harnischfeger Industries, Inc.; *U.S. Public*, pg. 788

PRESS MATE—Make-Ready Pressboard—FiberMark Inc.; *U.S. Public*, pg. 620

PRESS 'N SAND—Adhesive-Backed Abrasive Forms & Devices—3M; *U.S. Public*, pg. 1604

PRESS'N SEAL—Reclosable Poly Bag—KCL Corporation; *U.S. Private*, pg. 603

PRESS-ON—Optical Lenses—3M; *U.S. Public*, pg. 1604

PRESS ON-TWIST OFF—Closures—White Cap, Inc.; *Int'l*, pg. 1207

PRESS PRO—Washing Solutions for Treating Printing Presses—The Mead Corporation; *U.S. Public*, pg. 1074

PRESS QUEEN—Ironing Board Covers—Magla Products; *U.S. Private*, pg. 695

PRESSDATE—Customer Service—Westvaco Corporation; *U.S. Public*, pg. 1762

PRESSDUCTOR—Load Cells—ABB AB; *Int'l*, pg. 7

PRESSEAL—Self-Sealing Corrugated Paper Boxes—Georgia-Pacific Corporation; *U.S. Public*, pg. 735

PRESSFIT—Schedule Five Pipe Joining System—Victaulic Company of America; *U.S. Private*, pg. 1138

PRESSIT-SEALIT—Envelopes—The Mead Corporation; *U.S. Public*, pg. 1074

PRESSMAN—Toys & Games—Pressman Toy Corp.; *U.S. Private*, pg. 882

PRESSMASTER OFFSET 1671

PRESSMASTER II—Dewatering Press—Beloit Corporation; *U.S. Public*, pg. 789

PRESSMOBILE—Positioning Table—Jarke Corporation; *U.S. Private*, pg. 583

PRESSPAK—Make Ready for Printing Presses—FiberMark Inc.; *U.S. Private*, pg. 550

PRESSSTOCK—Paper & Printing Supply Store Services—The Mead Corporation; *U.S. Public*, pg. 1074

PRESSTAPE—Film Splicer & Tapes—Eastman Kodak Company; *U.S. Public*, pg. 550

PRESSURA—Hospital Applications—TSI Incorporated; *U.S. Public*, pg. 1559

PRESSURAID 6—Pressure Differential Covered Hopper Car—ACF Industries, Inc.; *U.S. Private*, pg. 556

PRESSURE CORING—In-Situ Coring System—Baker Hughes INTEQ; *U.S. Public*, pg. 166

PRESSURE CUFFS—Reusable/Disposable Non-Invasive Blood Pressure Cuffs—Datascope Corp.; *U.S. Public*, pg. 487

PRESSURE GRAVITY FILLER—Liquid Filling—U.S. Bottlers Machinery Co.; *U.S. Private*, pg. 1124

PRESSURE PAK—Dispensing System (Food Products)—Liqui-Box Corporation; *U.S. Public*, pg. 1000

PRESSURE-TEMP—Floor Coverings—Domco Inc.; *Int'l*, pg. 415

PRESSUREGUARD—Dynamic Turning Mattress—Span-America Medical Systems Inc.; *U.S. Public*, pg. 1495

PREST-O-MATIC—Automatic Doors—Clark Door Co., Inc.; *U.S. Private*, pg. 242

PRESTA LIGHT—Carbonated Low-Calorie Fruit Juice—Apollinaris & Schweppes Gmbh & Co.; *Int'l*, pg. 78

PRESTCOLD—Compressors—Copeland Corporation Ltd.; *U.S. Public*, pg. 576

PRESTIGE—Stereo Equipment—Audiovox Corporation; *U.S. Public*, pg. 147

PRESTIGE—Cellular Phones—Audiovox Corporation; *U.S. Public*, pg. 147

PRESTIGE—Fragrances & Toiletries—Charles of the Ritz Group Ltd.; *U.S. Private*, pg. 689

PRESTIGE—Sheet Vinyl Flooring—Congoleum Corporation; *U.S. Public*, pg. 69

PRESTIGE—Residential Roofing Shingles—Domtar Inc.; *Int'l*, pg. 416

PRESTIGE—Photographic Paper—Eastman Kodak Company; *U.S. Public*, pg. 550

PRESTIGE—MRI System—Elscint Ltd.; *Int'l*, pg. 450

PRESTIGE—Liquid Bonding Agent for Orthodontics—Lee Pharmaceuticals; *U.S. Public*, pg. 984

PRESTIGE—Ski Rope—Outdoor Technologies Group; *U.S. Private*, pg. 822

PRESTIGE—Wood Office Furniture—Tab Products Co.; *U.S. Public*, pg. 1559

PRESTIGE—Office Products—Union Camp Corporation; *U.S. Public*, pg. 1665

PRESTIGE—Nominal 4" & Hexagon w/Textured Surface for Wall & Light-Duty Bath Floors—United States Ceramic Tile Co.; *U.S. Private*, pg. 1124

PRESTIGE—Solid Brass Product—Weiser Inc.; *U.S. Public*, pg. 1055

PRESTIGE—Brass Door Hardware—Weiser Lock; *U.S. Public*, pg. 1053

PRESTIGE FRAGRANCE & COSMETICS—Discount Retail Cosmetic Stores—The Cosmetic Center Inc.; *U.S. Private*, pg. 689

THE PRESTIGE LINE—Cushions—Wellington Home Products; *U.S. Private*, pg. 1161

PRESTIGE PLAN—Checking Account Package—Standard Bank Investment Corporation Limited; *Int'l*, pg. 1293

PRESTIGE PLUS—Dental Filling Composite Resin—Lee Pharmaceuticals; *U.S. Public*, pg. 984

PRESTIGE SECURITY—Stereo Equipment—Audiovox Corporation; *U.S. Public*, pg. 147

PRESTIQUE—Premium Laminated Fiberglass Asphalt Shingles—Elcor Corporation; *U.S. Public*, pg. 567

PRESTIS—Midibus—Sabanci Holding A.S.; *Int'l*, pg. 1167

PRESTIS—Italian Seasonings—Tone Brothers Inc.; *Int'l*, pg. 237

PRESTISSIMO—Pasta—Sanwa Foods, Inc.; *U.S. Public*, pg. 299

PRESTO—NONE—Carpenter Technology Corporation; *U.S. Public*, pg. 307

PRESTO—Dry Color Mill Coloring Leather—Henkel Corporation; *Int'l*, pg. 610

PRESTO—Housemark/Service Mark—National Presto Industries, Inc.; *U.S. Public*, pg. 1159

PRESTO—Plastic Film & Bags, Cotton Swabs, Moist Towelettes—Reynolds Metals Company; *U.S. Public*, pg. 1385

PRESTO—Retail Stores—Safeway PLC; *Int'l*, pg. 1169

PRESTO FOOD STORES—Grocery Stores with SS Gasoline—Presto Food Stores, Inc.; *U.S. Private*, pg. 882

PRESTO LOCK—Fascia & Flashing System—Johns Manville Corporation; *U.S. Public*, pg. 927

PRESTO-PAK—Lubrication Pump—Graco Inc.; *U.S. Public*, pg. 756

PRESTO PRIDE—Housemark—National Presto Industries, Inc.; *U.S. Public*, pg. 1159

PRESTO!—ATM's & EFTS Operations—Publix Supermarkets Inc.; *U.S. Private*, pg. 893

PRESTOBURGER/2—Hamburger Cooker—National Presto Industries, Inc.; *U.S. Public*, pg. 1159

PRESTOCAL—Decals—American Decal & Mfg. Co.; *U.S. Private*, pg. 53

PRESTOFILM—Decals—American Decal & Mfg. Co.; *U.S. Private*, pg. 53

PRESTONE—NONE—AlliedSignal, Automotive Aftermarket; *U.S. Public*, pg. 51

PRESUICK—Procedual Kits—Customedix Corporation; *U.S. Private*, pg. 298

PRESUR-PAK—Breathing Apparatus—Scott Aviation; *U.S. Public*, pg. 622

PRETIS—Italian Seasonings—Tone Brothers Inc.; *Int'l*, pg. 237

PRETTY LITE DIET SKINNYWAIST—Foundations—The Strouse, Adler Company; *U.S. Private*, pg. 1047

PRETTY NEAT—Personal Organizers—Goody Products, Inc.; *U.S. Public*, pg. 1177

PRETTY POLLY—Hosiery—Sara Lee Corporation; *U.S. Public*, pg. 1432

PRETTY POWER—Hair Dryer—Clairol, Inc.; *U.S. Public*, pg. 254

PRETTY QUICK—Fast Heating Curling Irons/Brush—Andis Company; *U.S. Private*, pg. 73

PRETZEL NUTS—NONE—Galaxy Food Company; *U.S. Public*, pg. 697

PRETZEL TIME—Pretzels—Mrs. Fields' Original Cookies, Inc.; *U.S. Public*, pg. 688

PRETZEL TIME—Pretzels—Pretzel Time Inc.; *U.S. Private*, pg. 688

PREVAIL—Thermoplastic Resin—The Dow Chemical Company; *U.S. Public*, pg. 522

PREVENT—Toothbrushes—Johnson & Johnson; *U.S. Public*, pg. 927

PREVENT—Toothbrush—Johnson & Johnson Consumer Products; *U.S. Public*, pg. 928

PREVENT—Hair Care Product—Palm Beach Beauty Products Co.; *U.S. Private*, pg. 834

PREVENTION—Magazine—Rodale Press, Inc.; *U.S. Private*, pg. 939

PREVIA—Van—Toyota Motor Sales, U.S.A., Inc.; *Int'l*, pg. 1412

PREVIEW—Customized Pay Per View Listing Guides Distributed Monthly by Cable Systems—TV Host Inc.; *U.S. Private*, pg. 1066

PREVISE—Analysis Services—Halliburton Energy Services; *U.S. Public*, pg. 776

PRIAMA—Candy Bar—Mars, Incorporated; *U.S. Private*, pg. 707

PRICE ACCEPTANCE—Service to Identify Optimum Price Point—BASES Worldwide; *U.S. Private*, pg. 120

PRICE ALERT—NONE—First DataBank; *U.S. Private*, pg. 515

PRICE ALERT-PC—NONE—First DataBank; *U.S. Private*, pg. 515

PRICE CHOPPER—Supermarket—Price Chopper Operating Co., Inc.; *U.S. Private*, pg. 463

PRICE MARQUEE MERCHANDISING SYSTEM—Retail Signage System—Meto, USA; *Int'l*, pg. 460

PRICE PFISTER—Plumbing Products—The Black & Decker Corporation; *U.S. Public*, pg. 233

PRICE PROBE—NONE—First DataBank; *U.S. Private*, pg. 515

PRICE SAVER—Grocery & Perishable Products—Shurfine International, Inc.; *U.S. Private*, pg. 997

PRICE/VALUE BRAND—Cigarettes—Liggett Group Inc.; *U.S. Public*, pg. 259

PRICE WATERHOUSE LLP—Accounting & Auditing, Tax, Management Consulting—Price Waterhouse L.L.P. - U.S.; *U.S. Private*, pg. 883

PRICEBUSTER—Designation Applies to our Tour Prod., per our Discretion of High Value—General Tours Inc.; *U.S. Private*, pg. 445

PRICECUTTER FOOD WAREHOUSE—Food Club—Harp's Food Stores, Inc.; *U.S. Private*, pg. 504

PRICEDYNAMICS—NONE—Market Facts, Inc.; *U.S. Public*, pg. 1046

PRICE'S—Milk—Dean Foods Company; *U.S. Public*, pg. 489

PRIDE—Canned Vegetables—Faribault Foods Inc.; *U.S. Private*, pg. 393

PRIDE—Corn Seeds—Groupe Limagrain; *Int'l*, pg. 566

PRIDE—Fluridone, Elanco—Eli Lilly and Company; *U.S. Public*, pg. 992

PRIDE—Household Appliances; Toys—Pride Products, Inc.; *U.S. Private*, pg. 883

PRIDE—Potato, Fruit & Vegetable Products—J.R. Simplot Company; *U.S. Private*, pg. 1002

PRIDE MASTERCRAFT—Paint Sundries Products—PRO Group, Inc.; *U.S. Private*, pg. 887

PRIDE O' THE FARM—Cookies, Muffins, Health Baked Goods—J & J Snack Foods Corporation; *U.S. Public*, pg. 916

PRIDE OF ALASKA—Seafood Products—UniSea Foods, Inc.; *U.S. Private*, pg. 940

PRIDE OF AMERICA—Vodka & Gin—Montebello Brands Inc.; *U.S. Private*, pg. 758

PRIDE OF THE FARM—Livestock Equipment—Hawkeye Steel Products, Inc.; *U.S. Private*, pg. 511

PRIEMERE CUVEE—Sparkling Wine—Domecq Importers Inc.; *Int'l*, pg. 63

PRIGNITZER ZEITUNG—Newspaper—Burda Holding GmbH & Co., KG; *Int'l*, pg. 233

PRILCO—NONE—Sico Inc.; *Int'l*, pg. 1239

PRILOSEC—Ulcer Drug, U.S. Only—Merck & Co., Inc.; *U.S. Public*, pg. 1090

PRIMA—Gynecological Device—The Cooper Companies, Inc.; *U.S. Public*, pg. 442

PRIMA—Kitchen Tools—General Housewares Corp.; *U.S. Public*, pg. 715

PRIMA—Marine Engine—Varity Perkins; *Int'l*, pg. 820

PRIMA PORTA—Sausages—Hatfield Quality Meats; *U.S. Private*, pg. 510

PRIMA SERIES—Gynecological Device—The Cooper Companies, Inc.; *U.S. Public*, pg. 442

PRIMA SPORT—Socks—Kayser-Roth Corporation, Inc.; *U.S. Public*, pg. 576

PRIMACOR—Adhesive Polymer—The Dow Chemical Company; *U.S. Public*, pg. 522

PRIMAFAST—Enzyme for Textile Industry—Cultor Ltd.; *Int'l*, pg. 349

PRIMAGAZ—Liquid Propane Gas—SHV Holdings N.V.; *Int'l*, pg. 1154

PRIMAKAP—Roof Membranes—Johns Manville Corporation; *U.S. Public*, pg. 927

PRIMALOFT—Synthetic Down—Albany International Corp.; *U.S. Public*, pg. 36

PRIMANATURAL—Socks—Kayser-Roth Corporation, Inc.; *Int'l*, pg. 576

PRIMAPLY—Roof Membranes—Johns Manville Corporation; *U.S. Public*, pg. 927

PRIMARIO—Pouch Tomato Products—Furman Foods, Inc.; *U.S. Private*, pg. 431

PRIMARK—Retail Supplies—Esselte AB; *Int'l*, pg. 459

PRIMARK—Price Marking System—Esselte Meto Kimball Systems; *Int'l*, pg. 460

PRIMARK—Thermal Printers Price Making Hand Tool—Meto, USA; *Int'l*, pg. 460

PRIMAS—Motor Oil—Petroliam Nasional Berhad (Petronas); *Int'l*, pg. 1046

PRIMATENE—Epinephrine Inhaler And Tablets—American Home Products Corporation; *U.S. Public*, pg. 79

PRIMATENE—Epinephrine Inhaler & Epherene/Quaifenesen Tablets—Whitehall-Robins Healthcare; *U.S. Public*, pg. 80

PRIMATIC—Hot Water Storage—IMI Plc; *Int'l*, pg. 646

PRIMAVERA—Food Products—Rykoff-Sexton, Inc.; *U.S. Public*, pg. 918

PRIMAX—NONE—Avery Dennison Corporation; *U.S. Public*, pg. 152

PRIMAX—White Label Film—Fasson Films; *U.S. Public*, pg. 153

PRIMAXIN—Imipenem & Cilastatin—Merck & Co., Inc.; *U.S. Public*, pg. 1090

PRIMAXIN—Pharmaceutical—Merck Human Health Division (U.S. Human Health); *U.S. Public*, pg. 1091

PRIME—Cigarettes—Brown & Williamson Tobacco Corp.; *Int'l*, pg. 111

PRIME—Poultry—Maple Leaf Foods Inc.; *Int'l*, pg. 841

PRIME—Computers & Software—Parametric Technology Corporation; *U.S. Public*, pg. 1257

PRIME—Fresh Mushrooms—Quincy Corp.; *U.S. Public*, pg. 1545

PRIME ANGLE—Slotted Angle System—Unistrut Corporation; *U.S. Public*, pg. 1651

PRIME CATCH—Canned Tuna—Star-Kist Foods Inc.; *U.S. Public*, pg. 805

PRIME-COAT—Alkyd Shop/Field Primer—Devoe Paint; *Int'l*, pg. 663

PRIME FRY—Liquid Frying Fat—Mallet & Co.; *U.S. Private*, pg. 698

PRIME HEALTH & FITNESS—Magazine—Weider Publications, Inc.; *U.S. Private*, pg. 1159

PRIME LINE—Electrical & Fuel System Parts—Echlin Inc.; *U.S. Public*, pg. 560

PRIME-MD—NONE—Pfizer Inc.; *U.S. Public*, pg. 1281

PRIME-1-TIME—All Purpose Primer—Evans Adhesive Corp.; *U.S. Private*, pg. 384

PRIME OPTION—Credit Card—Dean Witter, Discover & Co.; *U.S. Public*, pg. 1132

PRIME PARTS—Cut up Poultry Parts—Perdue Farms Incorporated; *U.S. Private*, pg. 852

PRIME-SHINE—NONE—EcoScience Corporation; *U.S. Public*, pg. 563

PRIME SIRLOIN—Steak & Seafood Restaurants—WSMP, Inc.; *U.S. Public*, pg. 1729

PRIME SIRLOIN BUFFET BAKERY & STEAKS—Restaurants—WSMP, Inc.; *U.S. Public*, pg. 1729

PRIME TIME—Filters & Filter Sets—Quest Medical, Inc.; *U.S. Public*, pg. 1352

PRIME VOICE—Advanced Compression & Switching—Network Equipment Technologies, Inc.; *U.S. Public*, pg. 1168

PRIMEBASE—Printing Paper—The Mead Corporation; *U.S. Public*, pg. 1074

PRIMECOAT—Alkyd Shop/Field Primer—ICI Paints; *Int'l*, pg. 664

PRIMELINE—Labeler—Avery Dennison Corporation; *U.S. Public*, pg. 152

PRIMELINE—Hose—The Goodyear Tire & Rubber Company; *U.S. Public*, pg. 752

PRIMELINE—Induction Generators—Marathon Electric Manufacturing Corp.; *U.S. Public*, pg. 1371

PRIMEMOULD—Primed Mouldings—ABT Building Products Corporation; *Int'l*, pg. 20

PRIMENE—Primary Amine—Rohm and Haas Company; *U.S. Public*, pg. 1403

PRIMERA—Car—Nissan Motor Co., Ltd.; *Int'l*, pg. 943

PRIMERA—Indoor-Outdoor Aluminum Casual Furniture—Telescope Casual Furniture, Inc.; *U.S. Private*, pg. 1074

PRIMERBA—Seasonings, Spices—Bestfoods; *U.S. Public*, pg. 223

PRIMERRO—Pizza—Little Lady Foods, Inc.; *U.S. Private*, pg. 671

PRIMEX—Private Communications Package—British Telecommunications plc; *Int'l*, pg. 222

PRIMO—(Baby Toys/6 to 24 Months)—LEGO Systems, Inc.; *Int'l*, pg. 805

PRIMO—Italian Foods—The Pillsbury Company; *Int'l*, pg. 411

PRIMO DEL REY—Premium Cigars—Consolidated Cigar Corporation; *U.S. Public*, pg. 690

PRIMO-SEAL—Lumber & Wood Products—Georgia-Pacific Corporation; *U.S. Public*, pg. 735

PRIMO!—Fragrance—Parfums De Coeur Ltd.; *U.S. Private*, pg. 839

PRIMOR—Sulfadimethoxine/Ormetoprim—Pfizer Inc.; *U.S. Public*, pg. 1281

PRIMOR—Animal Antibacterial—SmithKline Beecham plc; *Int'l*, pg. 1264

PRIMUCELL FIP—Animal Vaccine—SmithKline Beecham plc; *Int'l*, pg. 1264

PRIMUCELL FIP—NONE—Pfizer Inc.; *U.S. Public*, pg. 1281

PRIMUS—Beer—Heineken N.V.; *Int'l*, pg. 608

PRINCE—Pasta & Spaghetti Sauce—Borden, Inc.; *U.S. Private*, pg. 157

PRINCE—Pasta Products—Borden Italian Foods; *U.S. Private*, pg. 158

PRINCE—NONE—British-American Tobacco (Germany) GmbH; *Int'l*, pg. 111

PRINCE—Biscuits—Danone Group; *Int'l*, pg. 379

PRINCE—Air-Powered Pumps—Graco Inc.; *U.S. Public*, pg. 756

PRINCE—Tennis Equipment—Prince Sports Group Inc.; *U.S. Private*, pg. 884

PRINCE DENMARK—Cigarettes—B.A.T Industries P.L.C.; *Int'l*, pg. 110

PRINCE HUBERT DE POLIGNAC—Cognac—Eckes AG; *Int'l*, pg. 432

PRINCE NOIR—Chocolate Truffles—Nestle S.A.; *Int'l*, pg. 915

PRINCE OF PERSIA CD COLLECTION—NONE—Broderbund Software, Inc.; *U.S. Public*, pg. 258

PRINCE ST.—Broadloom—Interface Inc.; *U.S. Public*, pg. 889

PRINCECRAFT—Boats—Outboard Marine Corporation; *U.S. Private*, pg. 478

PRINCELLA—NONE—Allen Canning Company; *U.S. Private*, pg. 36

PRINCESA—Knit Products—Sara Lee Corporation; *U.S. Public*, pg. 1432

PRINCESS—Vacuum Cleaner—HMI Industries; *U.S. Public*, pg. 771

PRINCESS—Telephone—Lucent Technologies Inc.; *U.S. Public*, pg. 1017

PRINCESS—Aerobic Shoe—Reebok International Ltd.; *U.S. Public*, pg. 1369

PRINCESS—Aluminum Cookware—Regal Ware, Inc.; *U.S. Private*, pg. 917

PRINCESS BED—Toddler Bed—Evenflo Company, Inc.; *U.S. Private*, pg. 629

PRINCESS CRUISES—Ocean Cruises—Princess Cruise Lines; *Int'l*, pg. 1035

PRINCESS HERITAGE—Full Line of Fine Hand Blown Crystal Stemware & Decorative Accessories—Princess House, Inc.; *U.S. Public*, pg. 399

PRINCESS HOTELS INTERNATIONAL—Hotel Chain—Princess Hotels International Inc.; *Int'l*, pg. 818

PRINCESS HOUSE PETS—24% Full Lead Crystal Pets—Princess House, Inc.; *U.S. Public*, pg. 399

PRINCETON—University Press—Princeton University Press; *U.S. Public*, pg. 885

PRINCETON CLUB—NONE—The Dress Barn, Inc.; *U.S. Public*, pg. 528

PRINCETON GALLERY—Consumer Durables—Brown-Forman Corporation; *U.S. Public*, pg. 261

PRINCETON GALLERY—Collectibles—Lenox, Incorporated; *U.S. Public*, pg. 261

PRINCETON PLANK—Solid 3-4-5" Plank-Beveled—Robbins, Inc.; *U.S. Private*, pg. 934

THE PRINCIPAL—Mutual Life Insurance—The Principal Financial Group; *U.S. Private*, pg. 885

THE PRINCIPAL—Second Reference to Principal Mutual Life Insurance Co.—Principal Mutual Life Insurance Co.; *U.S. Private*, pg. 886

PRINCIPEN/POLYCILLIN N—Infectious Disease Therapy—Bristol-Myers Squibb Company; *U.S. Public*, pg. 253

PRINCIPESSA GAVI—Wine—Banfi Vintners; *U.S. Private*, pg. 113

PRINCIPESSA GAVI—NONE—Castello Banfi Srl.; *U.S. Private*, pg. 113

THE PRINCIPLE-CENTERED CHANGE PROCESS—A Rigorous Methodology for Organizational Change Management—Franklin Covey; *U.S. Public*, pg. 679

PRINGLE'S—Potato Chips—The Procter & Gamble Company; *U.S. Public*, pg. 1330

PRINIVIL—Lisinopril—Merck & Co., Inc.; *U.S. Public*, pg. 1090

PRINIVIL—Pharmaceutical—Merck Human Health Division (U.S. Human Health); *U.S. Public*, pg. 1091

PRINT EASY—Envelopes—The Mead Corporation; *U.S. Public*, pg. 1074

PRINT LOG—Tracks Output to Digital Network Devices—Equitrac Corporation; *U.S. Public*, pg. 590

PRINT SERVICES FACILITY—Computer Product—International Business Machines Corporation; *U.S. Public*, pg. 895

THE PRINT SHOP—NONE—Broderbund Software, Inc.; *U.S. Public*, pg. 258

THE PRINT SHOP DELUXE III—NONE—Broderbund Software, Inc.; *U.S. Public*, pg. 258

THE PRINT SHOP ENSEMBLE III—NONE—Broderbund Software, Inc.; *U.S. Public*, pg. 258

THE PRINT SHOP PHOTO FOLIO'S PREMIUM COLLECTION—NONE—Broderbund Software, Inc.; *U.S. Public*, pg. 258

PRINTAC—Imagine Media—Labelon Corporation; *U.S. Private*, pg. 641

PRINTBRITE—Coated Linerboard—Westvaco Corporation; *U.S. Public*, pg. 1762

PRINTCARDS—Magazine—North American Publishing Company; *U.S. Private*, pg. 803

PRINTCOM—Program—Eastman Kodak Company; *U.S. Public*, pg. 550

PRINTED CIRCUIT DESIGN—Magazine—Miller Freeman Inc.; *Int'l*, pg. 1443

PRINTED CIRCUIT FABRICATION—Magazine—Miller Freeman Inc.; *Int'l*, pg. 1443

PRINTELLE—Yarn—Lion Brand Yarn Co.; *U.S. Private*, pg. 669

PRINTER SYSTEMS—NONE—Genicom Corporation; *U.S. Public*, pg. 729

PRINTER'S PLUS—System Software Products—Compuware Corporation; *U.S. Public*, pg. 423

PRINTGUARD-UV—Laminating Film—Seal Products Incorporated; *U.S. Public*, pg. 849

THE PRINTING HOUSE—NONE—Printing House, Inc.; *U.S. Private*, pg. 886

PRINTING IMPRESSIONS—Magazine—North American Publishing Company; *U.S. Private*, pg. 803

PRINTIQUES—Photo Seminars—Eastman Kodak Company; *U.S. Public*, pg. 550

PRINTITE—Envelope Printing Service—Westvaco Corporation; *U.S. Public*, pg. 1762

PRINTKOTE—Bleached Paperboard—Westvaco Corporation; *U.S. Public*, pg. 1762

PRINTKOTE COVER—Bristol Printing Paper—Westvaco Corporation; *U.S. Public*, pg. 1762

PRINTKOTE EAGLE—Coated Paperboard—Westvaco Corporation; *U.S. Public*, pg. 1762

PRINTKOTE HI-GLOSS—Coated Paperboard—Westvaco Corporation; *U.S. Public*, pg. 1762

PRINTKRAFT—Linerboard—Westvaco Corporation; *U.S. Public*, pg. 1762

PRINTLINK—Connectivity Product—QMS, Inc.; *U.S. Public*, pg. 1346

PRINTMANAGER—Computer Product—International Business Machines Corporation; *U.S. Public*, pg. 895

PRINTOSOL—Printing Ink Oils—Haltermann AG; *Int'l*, pg. 590

PRINTRONIX—Computer Printers—Printronix, Inc.; *U.S. Public*, pg. 1329

PRINTS PLUS—Art, Picture Frames & Decor—CPI Corp.; *U.S. Public*, pg. 283

PRINTSTAR—Bar Code Printers: Dot Matrix & Thermal—CiMatrix L.L.C.; *U.S. Public*, pg. 1395

PRINZIDE—Lisinopril-Hydrochlorothiazide—Merck & Co., Inc.; *U.S. Public*, pg. 1090

PRIORITE—Skincare Products—Dana Perfumes Corp.; *U.S. Private*, pg. 922

PRIORITIES—Personal Information Management Magazine—Franklin Covey; *U.S. Public*, pg. 679

PRIORITY CLUB—Hotel Membership Club—Holiday Inn Worldwide; *Int'l*, pg. 170

PRIORITY LINE—Products—Despatch Industries; *U.S. Private*, pg. 327

PRIORITY 1—Overnight Packaging Ssrvice—FDX Corporation; *U.S. Public*, pg. 603

PRIORITYCARE—Preventive Maintenance Program—Roto-Rooter; *U.S. Public*, pg. 344

PRISCILLA—Cooking Utensils—Vollrath-Kewaunee Plant; *U.S. Private*, pg. 1143

PRISCOLINE—NONE—Novartis Pharmaceuticals; *Int'l*, pg. 973

PRISM—Pressure Swing Absorption & Membrane Systems—Air Products and Chemicals, Inc.; *U.S. Public*, pg. 30

PRISM—Multidimensional Modeling, Analysis & Reporting—Comshare, Incorporated; *U.S. Public*, pg. 425

PRISM—Barware—Dansk International Designs Ltd.; *U.S. Public*, pg. 261

PRISM—SMD Circuit Board Indicators—Dialight Corporation; *Int'l*, pg. 1130

PRISM—Electronic Previewing System—Eastman Kodak Company; *U.S. Public*, pg. 550

PRISM—NONE—KLA Tencor Corporation; *U.S. Public*, pg. 939

PRISM—Instant Adhesives—Loctite Corporation; *Int'l*, pg. 611

PRISM—Software System Designed for the Process Manufacturing Industries—Marcam Solutions, Inc.; *U.S. Public*, pg. 1042

PRISM—Cellulose-Base Paper—The Mead Corporation; *U.S. Public*, pg. 1074

PRISM—Separator Systems—Monsanto Company; *U.S. Public*, pg. 1124

PRISM—Advanced MOCVD—Novellus Systems, Inc.; *U.S. Public*, pg. 1204

PRISM—Nuclear Medicine—Picker International, Inc.; *Int'l*, pg. 545

PRISM—Sanitation Services & Supplies—Prism Integrated Sanitation Management, Inc.; *U.S. Private*, pg. 592

PRISM—NONE—Western Atlas Logging Services; *U.S. Public*, pg. 1757

PRISM—Video Inspection Service—T.D. Williamson, Inc.; *U.S. Private*, pg. 1179

PRISM QM—Software System for Inventory Management—Marcam Solutions, Inc.; *U.S. Public*, pg. 1042

PRISMA—Opto-Electronics Products—Scientific-Atlanta, Inc.; *U.S. Public*, pg. 1443

PRISMACOLOR—Art Markers & Color Pencils—Empire Berol U.S.A.; *U.S. Public*, pg. 1178

PRISMACOLOR—Art Materials—Sanford Corporation; *U.S. Public*, pg. 1178

PRISMO RX2—Module—Kerlane; *Int'l*, pg. 1176

PRISMOSEAL—Crack Sealants & Equipment—Linear Dynamics Inc.; *U.S. Private*, pg. 668

PRIST—Fuel Additive, Cleaning Preparations & Polishing Compounds—PPG Industries, Inc.; *U.S. Public*, pg. 1245

PRIST—Diagnostic—Pharmacia & Upjohn Adria Laboratories; *Int'l*, pg. 1049

PRISTINE—Chinaware—The Homer Laughlin China Company; *U.S. Private*, pg. 653

PRIVACY GUARD—Provides Access to Credit Bureau, Motor Vehicle & Social Security Records—CUC International, Inc.; *U.S. Public*, pg. 320

PRIVATE—Mini System—Pioneer Electronic Corporation; *Int'l*, pg. 1057

PRIVATE ESTATES—Mausoleums—Cold Spring Granite Company; *U.S. Private*, pg. 250

PRIVATE EYE—Video Security Monitoring Systems—Go-Video, Inc.; *U.S. Public*, pg. 748

PRIVATE ISSUE—Credit Card—NOVUS Services, Inc.; *U.S. Public*, pg. 1132

PRIVATE LABEL—Ice Cream—FieldBrook Farms, Inc.; *U.S. Private*, pg. 403

PRIVATE LABEL—NONE—Supreme International Corp.; *U.S. Public*, pg. 1542

PRIVATE LABEL—Foods—Ventura Foods; *U.S. Private*, pg. 508

PRIVATE LABEL—Tires—Yokohama Tire Corporation; *Int'l*, pg. 1521

PRIVATE LABELING—Fertilizer—Hydro/Kirby Agri Service, Inc.; *U.S. Private*, pg. 552

PRIVATE PRO—Golf Training Aids—Ajay Leisure Products, Inc.; *U.S. Public*, pg. 34

PRIVATE RESERVE—NONE—Lamb-Weston, Inc.; *U.S. Public*, pg. 427

PRIVATE STOCK—Cigarettes—Brown & Williamson Tobacco Corp.; *Int'l*, pg. 111

PRIVATE STOCK—Bourbon Whiskey—Laird & Company; *U.S. Private*, pg. 642

PRIVIET—Vodka—PepsiCo, Inc.; *U.S. Public*, pg. 1276

PRIVIET VODKA—NONE—Carillon Importers, Ltd.; *Int'l*, pg. 409

PRIVILEGE—MRI System—Elscint Ltd.; *Int'l*, pg. 450

PRIZE—Pet Foods—Certified Grocers of California; *U.S. Private*, pg. 226

PRIZE—Yogurt—Unigate PLC; *Int'l*, pg. 1433

PRIZE TAKER—NONE—Griffin Manufacturing Co.; *U.S. Private*, pg. 481

PRO—Shock Absorber Series—Enidine Incorporated; *U.S. Private*, pg. 377

PRO—NONE—TJ International, Inc.; *U.S. Public*, pg. 1556

PRO-AIRE—Blower/Dryers—Sunbeam Household Products; *U.S. Public*, pg. 1533

PRO AM—Pencil—Pentel of America, Ltd.; *Int'l*, pg. 1035

PRO-ARM—Motorcycle—American Honda Motor Co., Inc. Motorcycle Division; *Int'l*, pg. 634

PRO-BANTHINE—Treatment Of Peptic Ulcer—Searle & Co.; *U.S. Public*, pg. 1125

PRO-BANTHINE—Pharmaceutical Products—Searle Laboratories; *U.S. Public*, pg. 1125

PRO BOND DISPLAY MOUNT—Pressure-Sensitive Board—Seal Products Incorporated; *U.S. Public*, pg. 849

PRO BOOST—Automotive Battery Booster Cables—General Cable Corporation; *Int'l*, pg. 1486

PRO-CHEF—Work Table—John Boos & Company; *U.S. Private*, pg. 156

THE PRO CIRCUIT—Racquetball Shoes—Ektelon; *U.S. Private*, pg. 884

PRO CLASSIC—Golf Carts—Ajay Leisure Products, Inc.; *U.S. Public*, pg. 34

PRO-COAT—Pet Shampoo—Carter-Wallace, Inc.; *U.S. Public*, pg. 309

PRO COTE—Interior/Exterior Paint—Buten, Division of Duron; *U.S. Private*, pg. 349

PRO-COTE—Soy Protein Product—Ralston Purina Company; *U.S. Public*, pg. 1359

PRO CU—Profiles & Hollow Conductors—KM-Europa Metal Aktiengesellschaft; *Int'l*, pg. 719

PRO CUISINE—Collection—Regal Ware, Inc.; *U.S. Private*, pg. 917

PRO CURL—Professional Beauty Products—Windmere-Durable Holdings; *U.S. Public*, pg. 1771

PRO CUSTOM—Sporting Goods—Brunswick Bowling & Billiards Corp.; *U.S. Public*, pg. 265

PRO-CUT—Plasma Cutter—The Lincoln Electric Company; *U.S. Public*, pg. 996

PRO-DOPE—Industrial Chemical—Hercules Chemical Co., Inc.; *U.S. Private*, pg. 523

PRO ENERGY—Pet Food—Cargill Animal Nutrition Div.; *U.S. Private*, pg. 210

PRO/ENGINEER—Software Products—Parametric Technology Corporation; *U.S. Public*, pg. 1257

PRO-EX—Wrap for Coextruded Products Division—AEP Industries, Inc.; *U.S. Public*, pg. 4

PRO15—Othamalic Lenses—American Optical Corporation; *U.S. Private*, pg. 60

PRO-FILLED—Flats & Pots—Premier Brands, Inc.; *Int'l*, pg. 1068

PRO-FIT—Vinyl Ventilated & Nonventilated Soffit—Alcoa Building Products, Inc.; *U.S. Public*, pg. 61

PRO-FIT—Jackets & Caps—King Louie International; *U.S. Private*, pg. 621

PRO-FIT—Muffler—Walker Manufacturing Co.; *U.S. Public*, pg. 1578

PRO 500—Athletic Shoes—E.J. Footwear Corp.; *U.S. Public*, pg. 1684

PRO FLO—Air Cleaners—Edelbrock Corp.; *U.S. Public*, pg. 563

PRO FOAM—Polyurethane Foam—Ohio Sealants Inc.; *Int'l*, pg. 802

PRO-FORCE—Air Compressors—Coleman Powermate Compressors; *U.S. Private*, pg. 691

PRO-IV—Software 4th Generation Language—McDonnell Aircraft & Missile Systems Div.; *U.S. Public*, pg. 241

PRO4000—Electrostatic Airspray Guns—Graco Inc.; *U.S. Public*, pg. 756

PRO-GAMES—Promotional World Games—Eastman Kodak Company; *U.S. Public*, pg. 550

PRO-GENESIS—Sterilization Control System—Environmental Tectonics Corporation (ETC); *U.S. Public*, pg. 587

PRO-GIBB—Gibberellic Acid—Abbott Laboratories; *U.S. Public*, pg. 12

PRO GOLF—Sports Game—Monarch Avalon, Inc.; *U.S. Public*, pg. 1123

PRO-GRADE—Contractor Grade Roof Coatings & Cements—Monsey-Bakor; *U.S. Private*, pg. 757

PRO GRADE & DESIGN—Electrical Extension Cords—General Cable Corporation; *Int'l*, pg. 1486

PRO-GRIP—Cookware—Regal Ware, Inc.; *U.S. Private*, pg. 917

PRO-GROOM—Pet Coat Spray—Carter-Wallace, Inc.; *U.S. Public*, pg. 309

PRO-GUARD—Two & Three Way Recovery Systems & Retractable Lifelines—Klein Tools Inc.; *U.S. Private*, pg. 625

PRO-GUIDE—Hunting Knives—Fiskars-Gerber; *Int'l*, pg. 492

PRO GUN 1000—Hair Dryer—Clairol, Inc.; *U.S. Public*, pg. 254

PRO HARDWARE—Hardware, Building Supplies Distributors/Retailers—PRO Group, Inc.; *U.S. Private*, pg. 887

PRO-HIDE PLUS—Paints—Pratt & Lambert United, Inc.; *U.S. Public*, pg. 1466

PRO-HONDA—Motorcycle Accessories—American Honda Motor Co., Inc. Motorcycle Division; *Int'l*, pg. 634

PRO INFUSION CATHETER—Catheter—E-Z-Em, Inc.; *U.S. Public*, pg. 540

PRO-JECTOR—Reloading Press—Hornady Manufacturing Company; *U.S. Private*, pg. 539

PRO-KEDS—Men's, Boys' Footwear—The Stride Rite Corporation; *U.S. Public*, pg. 1524

PRO:LEAN—Swine Feeds—Agway, Inc.; *U.S. Private*, pg. 27

PRO-LEAN—Dedicated Electronic Fuel Management System for Heavy-Duty Diesel Engines—Synchro-Start Products, Inc.; *U.S. Private*, pg. 627

PRO-LECIN—Nutritional Products—Shaklee Corporation; *Int'l*, pg. 1518

PRO-LIFT—Hydraulic Elevator—Access Industries; *U.S. Private*, pg. 11

PRO-LINE—Photo Accessories—Kleer-Vu Plastics Corp.; *U.S. Public*, pg. 962

PRO LINE—Hearing Aid Batteries—RAYOVAC Corporation; *U.S. Private*, pg. 912

PRO-LINER—Refrigerated Display Case Liner—Solutia Inc.; *U.S. Public*, pg. 1483

PRO-LINK—Motorcycle—American Honda Motor Co., Inc. Motorcycle Division; *Int'l*, pg. 634

PRO LITE—Athletic Equipment—Bike Athletic Co.; *U.S. Private*, pg. 143

PRO LOCK SIDING—Self-Aligning Hidden Nail System—ABT Building Products Corporation; *Int'l*, pg. 20

PRO-LOG—Microprocessor Systems & Software—Pro-Log Corporation; *U.S. Public*, pg. 887

PRO-LOK—Tile—Pawling Corporation; *U.S. Private*, pg. 844

PRO-MAK—Liquid Tar Emulsion Resurfacer—Elastic Materials, Inc.; *U.S. Private*, pg. 367

PRO MAKER—Golf Equipment—RAM Golf Corporation; *U.S. Private*, pg. 908

PRO MARK—Protective Apparel—Stihl Inc.; *Int'l*, pg. 1301

PRO MASTER—Power Console & Speaker System—Shure Brothers Incorporated; *U.S. Private*, pg. 997

PRO-MAX—Tennis Rackets—Mizuno Corporation; *Int'l*, pg. 884

PRO/MECHANICA—NONE—Parametric Technology Corporation; *U.S. Public*, pg. 1257

PRO-MIX—Soilless Mixes—Premier Brands, Inc.; *Int'l*, pg. 1068

PRO 900—Athletic Shoes—E.J. Footwear Corp.; *U.S. Public*, pg. 1684

PRO-90—Vinyl Vent and Non-Vent Soffit—Alcoa Building Products, Inc.; *U.S. Public*, pg. 61

PRO-1—Roaring Resier Process—ABT Building Products Corporation; *Int'l*, pg. 20

PRO I—Headset—Telex Communications, Inc.; *U.S. Private*, pg. 1074

PRO OXYGENE—Hair Care—Palm Beach Beauty Products Co.; *U.S. Private*, pg. 834

PRO PARTS—NONE—Detroit Diesel Corp.; *U.S. Private*, pg. 850

PRO PASSPORT—Program—Eastman Kodak Company; *U.S. Public*, pg. 550

PRO PENN—Racquetball Balls—Penn Racquet Sports; *U.S. Public*, pg. 706

PRO PENN—Tennis Balls—Penn Racquet Sports; *U.S. Public*, pg. 706

PRO-PEP—Energy Booster Tablets—Alva/Amco Pharmacal Companies, Inc.; *U.S. Private*, pg. 47

PRO PERM—Hair Care Prods.—CCA Industries, Inc.; *U.S. Public*, pg. 276

PRO PLAN—Premium Cat & Dog Foods—Ralston Purina Company; *U.S. Public*, pg. 1359

PRO PLUS—Sport Bag—Ektelon; *U.S. Private*, pg. 884

PRO POINT SCREWS—Self Tapping Sheetmetal Screws—Duro Dyne Corporation; *U.S. Private*, pg. 349

PRO-PORT—Access Door—Hercules Chemical Co., Inc.; *U.S. Private*, pg. 523

PRO POXY—Plumbing Chemical—Hercules Chemical Co., Inc.; *U.S. Private*, pg. 523

PRO-POXY 20—Plumbing Chemical—Hercules Chemical Co., Inc.; *U.S. Private*, pg. 523

PRO PREP—Scrapers & Blades for Scrapers (8)—Pacific Handy Cutter, Inc.; *U.S. Private*, pg. 831

PRO-PRINT—Synthetic Paper for Printing—Transilwrap Company, Inc.; *U.S. Private*, pg. 1097

PRO PUP—Puppy Food—The Jim Dandy Co., Inc.; *Int'l*, pg. 918

PRO RATER PLUS—Rating Software to Calculate Insurance Rates for Customers—The Progressive Corporation; *U.S. Public*, pg. 1334

PRO-SEAL—Sealants—Courtaulds Aerospace; *Int'l*, pg. 339

PRO-SEAL—Natural Polypropylene Pipe, Valves & Fittings—George Fischer Sloane, Inc.; *Int'l*, pg. 430

PRO-SELECT—Vinyl VENT and NON-VENT Soffit—Alcoa Building Products, Inc.; *U.S. Public*, pg. 61

PRO-SELECT—Power Tool Accessories Designed for Professionals—The Disston Co.; *U.S. Public*, pg. 950

PRO SENTRY—LAN Monitoring Tool—Bytex Corporation; *U.S. Public*, pg. 1522

PRO SERIES—NONE—Harris Calorific Co.; *U.S. Public*, pg. 996

PRO SERIES—Padlock—Master Lock Company; *U.S. Public*, pg. 675

PRO SET—Athletic Footwear—E.J. Footwear Corp.; *U.S. Public*, pg. 1684

PRO/SHIELD—Disposable, High Comfort, Low Cost Garments—Kappler Safety Group, Inc.; *U.S. Private*, pg. 607

PRO16—Opthamalic Lenses—American Optical Corporation; *U.S. Private*, pg. 60

PRO-SPEC—Single & Multi-Viscosity Oils—Texas Refinery Corp.; *U.S. Private*, pg. 1078

PRO SPORTSTER—Bowling Shoes—E.J. Footwear Corp.; *U.S. Public*, pg. 1684

PRO-STAT—Electronic Setback Thermostat—Harper-Wyman Co.; *U.S. Public*, pg. 1209

PRO-STICK—Curler/Stylers—Sunbeam Household Products; *U.S. Public*, pg. 1533

PRO STRIP—Paper Collation System for Strip Nails—Paslode; *U.S. Public*, pg. 867

PRO-SWEEP—Rugged Push Brooms for Heavy Duty Usage—Felton Brush Inc.; *U.S. Private*, pg. 400

PRO-TALK—Publication—Eastman Kodak Company; *U.S. Public*, pg. 550

PRO-TEC—Silicone Surgical Glove—Inamed Corporation; *U.S. Public*, pg. 873

PRO-TEC—Pulmonary Filter—Pall Corporation; *U.S. Public*, pg. 1253

PRO-TEC—Filter—Pall Corporation; *U.S. Public*, pg. 1253

PRO TECH—Electronic Imaging Papers—Fort James Corporation; *U.S. Public*, pg. 670

PRO TECH—Security Documents—Hano Document Printers, Inc.; *U.S. Public*, pg. 1686

PRO-TECH PLUS—Vinyl Ventilated & Nonventilated Soffit—Alcoa Building Products, Inc.; *U.S. Public*, pg. 61

PRO TECTA—Truck Bed Liners—Lancaster Colony Corporation; *U.S. Public*, pg. 976

PRO-TEK—NONE—Eastman Kodak Company; *U.S. Public*, pg. 550

PRO-TEK—Impact Protection For Walls, Floors, & Doors—Pawling Corporation; *U.S. Private*, pg. 844

PRO TOUCH—Professional Beauty Products—Windmere-Durable Holdings; *U.S. Public*, pg. 1771

PRO-TRAC—Tires—Cragar Industries, Inc.; *U.S. Public*, pg. 456

PRO-TREAT—Bulk, Dry Fungicide/Molybdenum Soybeen Seed Treatment—LiphaTech, Inc.; *Int'l*, pg. 812

PRO-TREAT L—Liquid Fungicide/Molybdenum Seed Treatment—LiphaTech, Inc.; *Int'l*, pg. 812

PRO-TREAT 3—Inoculant/Thirman/Fungicide Soybeen Seed Treatment—LiphaTech, Inc.; *Int'l*, pg. 812

PRO-TUFT—Olefin—Bemis Company, Inc.; *U.S. Public*, pg. 210

PRO UNDERWRITING—Process of Risk Selection Guidelines—Lincoln National Corporation; *U.S. Public*, pg. 997

PRO VAL—Semi Professional Applicators—Sherwin-Williams Coatings Division; *U.S. Public*, pg. 1466

PRO VIDIA—NONE—Trident Microsystems, Inc.; *U.S. Public*, pg. 1637

PRO VIDIA9685—NONE—Trident Microsystems, Inc.; *U.S. Public*, pg. 1637

PRO VIDIA9683—NONE—Trident Microsystems, Inc.; *U.S. Public*, pg. 1637

PRO VIDIA9682—NONE—Trident Microsystems, Inc.; *U.S. Public*, pg. 1637

PRO-VISTA—Office Automation Software System—Datapoint Corporation; *Int'l*, pg. 384

PRO WALL 3—Bathtub Wall Kit—Plaskolite Inc.; *U.S. Private*, pg. 870

PRO WATCH—Product Series—Faraday, Inc.; *Int'l*, pg. 1246

PRO WONDER—Camcorders—Thomson Consumer Electronics Inc.; *Int'l*, pg. 1383

PRO-WRESTLING—Videogame—Sega of America Inc.; *Int'l*, pg. 1218

PRO-LAWN—NONE—Lesco, Inc.; *U.S. Public*, pg. 989

PRO'S CHOICE—Interior Paint—Buten, Division of Duron; *U.S. Private*, pg. 349

PROACT—Solvent—The Dow Chemical Company; *U.S. Public*, pg. 522

PROACT—Industrial Enzymes—Eastman Kodak Company; *U.S. Public*, pg. 550

PROAID—NONE—Akrochem Corporation; *U.S. Private*, pg. 30

PROAMATINE—Pharmaceutical to Raise Blood Pressure—Roberts Pharmaceutical Corporation; *U.S. Public*, pg. 1393

PROANA MABS—Mabs monitoring system—HyClone Laboratories Inc.; *Int'l*, pg. 1037

PROASIC—Family Name—Gatefield Corporation; *U.S. Public*, pg. 703

PROAUSA—Engine System Parts—Echlin Inc.; *U.S. Public*, pg. 560

PROBAK—Blades—The Gillette Company; *U.S. Public*, pg. 743

PROBAK JR.—Blades—The Gillette Company; *U.S. Public*, pg. 743

PROBE—Network Analyze System—Datapoint Corporation; *Int'l*, pg. 384

PROBE—Herbicide—Novartis AG; *Int'l*, pg. 971

PROBE—Sample Processing Workstation—Packard Instrument Co., Inc.; *U.S. Private*, pg. 833

PROBEC—NONE—Lee Pharmaceuticals; *U.S. Public*, pg. 984

PROBEC-T—High Potency Vitamin Tablet—Roberts Pharmaceutical Corporation; *U.S. Public*, pg. 1393

PROBUMAGE—Advanced Liquid Photo Resist for Printed Circuit Board Production—Novartis; *Int'l*, pg. 972

PROBIOCIN—Microbial Inoculant Products—Pioneer Hi-Bred International, Inc.; *U.S. Public*, pg. 1298

PROBIOS—Microbial Inoculant Products—Pioneer Hi-Bred International, Inc.; *U.S. Public*, pg. 1298

PROBLOCK—Fire Resistant Fabric—ATHOL Corporation; *U.S. Private*, pg. 94

PROBOND—Mounting Adhesive Sheets—Seal Products Incorporated; *U.S. Public*, pg. 849

PROBRANCH—Computer Product—International Business Machines Corporation; *U.S. Public*, pg. 895

PROBUG—Software—SBE, Inc.; *U.S. Public*, pg. 1416

PROCAN SR—Medication for Irregular Heartbeat—Warner-Lambert Company; *U.S. Public*, pg. 1738

PROCARDIA—Nifedipine—Pfizer Inc.; *U.S. Public*, pg. 1281

PROCARDIA XL—Nifedipine GITS—Pfizer Inc.; *U.S. Public*, pg. 1281

PROCARE—Automotive Service—BP Oil Co.; *Int'l*, pg. 220

PROCARE—Crane Maintenance—Harnischfeger Industries, Inc.; *U.S. Public*, pg. 788

PROCARE—Extended Warranty Protection—Zenith Electronics Corp.; *U.S. Public*, pg. 1790

PROCARE 4000—Healthcare Facility Communication System—Dukane Corporation; *U.S. Private*, pg. 345

PROCARE 6000—Health Facility Comm. System—Dukane Corporation; *U.S. Private*, pg. 345

PROCARE 60—NONE—Dukane Corporation; *U.S. Private*, pg. 345

PROCARE 2000—Health Care Facility Communications System—Dukane Corporation; *U.S. Private*, pg. 345

PROCEDURE BASED DELIVERY SYSTEM—Medical Consulting Services Recommending Surgery Supplies & Products—Allegiance Healthcare Corp.; *U.S. Public*, pg. 44

PROCEDURES—NONE—Brown & Sharpe Manufacturing Company; *U.S. Public*, pg. 260

PROCEED—Electronic Components—Harman International Industries, Inc.; *U.S. Public*, pg. 787

PROCELL—NONE—Duracell International Inc.; *U.S. Public*, pg. 743

PROCENTEX—Surface Care—Reckitt & Colman plc; *U.S. Public*, pg. 1089

PROCESS ANALYSIS NAVIGATION SYSTEM—Computer Product—International Business Machines Corporation; *U.S. Public*, pg. 895

PROCESS CONTROL STATION—Control Product—Bailey, Fischer & Porter Company; *Int'l*, pg. 449

PROCESS FOR RECOVERING CYANIDE SOLUTIONS—NONE—Coeur D'Alene Mines Corporation; *U.S. Public*, pg. 394

PROCESS PLATE—Coated Paper—The Mead Corporation; *U.S. Public*, pg. 1074

PROCESS 2000—NONE—Bird Machine Company; *U.S. Public*, pg. 166

PROCESSES OF MANUFACTURING—Textbook Providing Comprehensive Instruction in Manufacturing Processes—Goodheart-Willcox Publisher; *U.S. Private*, pg. 464

PROCESSKING—Single-Width Web Offset Press—Publishers Equipment Corporation; *U.S. Public*, pg. 1341

PROCESSMASTER—Computer Product—International Business Machines Corporation; *U.S. Public*, pg. 895

PROCESSOR—Batch Filtration System—Whatman Inc.; *Int'l*, pg. 1498

PROCESSOR RESOURCE/SYSTEMS MANAGER—Computer Product—International Business Machines Corporation; *U.S. Public*, pg. 895

PROCESS & CONTROL ENGINEERING PACE—Industrial Magazine—Reed Business Information Pty. Limited; *Int'l*, pg. 1094

PROCHEM—H-Series Agitators—Robbins & Myers, Inc.; *U.S. Public*, pg. 1393

PROCION—Router Control Software & Audio/Video Monitoring—Chyron Corp.; *Int'l*, pg. 1372

PROCON—Carbonator Pumps—Standex International Corporation; *U.S. Public*, pg. 1505

PROCORE—Family Name—Gatefield Corporation; *U.S. Public*, pg. 703

PROCORT—NONE—Lee Pharmaceuticals; *U.S. Public*, pg. 984

PROCOTE—Nonstick Cookware—Regal Ware, Inc.; *U.S. Private*, pg. 917

PROCRAFT—Fishing Boats—Brunswick Corporation; *U.S. Public*, pg. 265

PROCRIT—NONE—Johnson & Johnson; *U.S. Public*, pg. 927

PROCTASE-P—Anti Inflammatory Enzyme—Meiji Seika Kaisha, Ltd.; *Int'l*, pg. 855

PROCTOCORT—Pharmaceutical Products—Solvay Pharmaceuticals, Inc.; *Int'l*, pg. 1278

PROCTOCREAM—Pharmaceutical—Stafford-Miller Limited; *U.S. Public*, pg. 237

PROCTOCREAM—NONE—Schwarz Pharma Inc.; *Int'l*, pg. 1211

PROCTOFOAM-HC—NONE—Schwarz Pharma Inc.; *Int'l*, pg. 1211

PROCTOR-SILEX—Small Appliances—Hamilton Beach/Proctor-Silex, Inc.; *U.S. Public*, pg. 1149

PROCTOR-SILEX—Toasters, Coffeemakers, Irons & Other Portable Electric Appliances—NACCO Industries, Inc.; *U.S. Public*, pg. 1149

PROCTOSEDYL—Anti-Hemorrhoidal—SmithKline Beecham Research Limited; *U.S. Public*, pg. 1266

PROCUREMENT DESKTOP (PDT)—NONE—American Management Systems, Inc.; *U.S. Public*, pg. 86

PRODAG—Lubricants—Acheson Colloids Company; *U.S. Private*, pg. 12

PRODATE—Plant Protectives—DSM Chemie Linz GmbH; *Int'l*, pg. 356

PRODENT—Toothpaste—Sara Lee Corporation; *U.S. Public*, pg. 1432

PRODERM—OTC Topical Wound Spray for Chronic Ulcers—Dow Hickam Pharmaceuticals Inc.; *U.S. Public*, pg. 1143

PRODIGY 21—Wall Hung Boiler—Slant/Fin Corporation; *U.S. Private*, pg. 1005

PRODRIVE—Disk Drive—Quantum Corporation; *U.S. Public*, pg. 1350

PRODRIVE SERIES—Disk Drives—Quantum Corporation; *U.S. Public*, pg. 1350

PRODRIVER—NONE—Detroit Diesel Corp.; *U.S. Private*, pg. 850

PRODUCE PARTNERS—Toppings & Complements—McCormick & Company, Incorporated; *U.S. Public*, pg. 1066

PRODUCE PARTNERS—Seasoning Mixes, Soups, Dips—McCormick/Schilling; *U.S. Public*, pg. 1066

PRODUCE PRODUCTS—Seasoning Powders—Nestle S.A.; *Int'l*, pg. 915

PRODUCER—MP&G Encoder—Sigma Designs, Inc.; *U.S. Public*, pg. 1472

PRODUCER—Wood Director Chair—Telescope Casual Furniture, Inc.; *U.S. Private*, pg. 1074

THE PRODUCER—Video Switchers, Color Processors, Enhancers & Stabilizers—Recoton Corporation; *U.S. Public*, pg. 1369

THE PRODUCER'S MASTERGUIDE—Directories—BPI Communications Inc.; *Int'l*, pg. 1446

PRODUCT DESIGN AND DEVELOPMENT—Product News Tabloid for Design Engineers & Engineering Management—Reed Elsevier Business Information; *Int'l*, pg. 1095

PRODUCT 19—Flakes of Toasted Corn, Oats, Wheat & Rice Cereal with Iron & Zinc—Kellogg Company; *U.S. Public*, pg. 947

PRODUCT QUEST—NONE—Market Facts, Inc.; *U.S. Public*, pg. 1046

PRODUCTION—Aluminum Oxide-Coated Abrasives—3M; *U.S. Public*, pg. 1604

PRODUCTION ENTERPRISES—Door Hardware—Watsco, Inc.; *U.S. Public*, pg. 1745

PRODUCTION MASTER—Crusher Jaws—Esco Corporation; *U.S. Private*, pg. 382

PRODUCTION WOOD—NONE—MEG; *U.S. Private*, pg. 686

PRODUCTIVITY EDGE—Information Technology & Services—The Black & Decker Corporation; *U.S. Public*, pg. 233

PRODUCTIVITY PARTNERS—NONE—Nellcor Puritan Bennett Incorporated; *U.S. Public*, pg. 1039

PRODUCTMANAGER—Computer Product—International Business Machines Corporation; *U.S. Public*, pg. 895

PRODUCTO—Machine Tools & Tooling Components—The Producto Machine Co.; *U.S. Private*, pg. 889

PRODUCTOLITH—Enamel Printing Paper—Consolidated Papers, Inc.; *U.S. Public*, pg. 436

PRODUCTPAC—Computer Product—International Business Machines Corporation; *U.S. Public*, pg. 895

PRODUCTS FINISHING—Business to Business Magazine—Gardner Publications, Inc.; *U.S. Private*, pg. 440

PROFAX—Polypropylene Resins—Montedison S.p.A.; *Int'l*, pg. 324

PROFEEL—Component TV—Sony Electronics; *Int'l*, pg. 1281

PROFEEL PRO TRINITRON—Television—Sony Corporation; *Int'l*, pg. 1280

PROFENAL—Suprofen Non-Steroidal Anti-Inflammatory Drug—Alcon Laboratories, Inc.; *Int'l*, pg. 916

PROFESSIONAL—Finishing Powder, Mascara & Eye Lining Pencils—Cover Girl Cosmetics; *U.S. Public*, pg. 1330

PROFESSIONAL—Cutlery—Imperial Schrade Corp.; *U.S. Private*, pg. 559

PROFESSIONAL—Institutional Equipment—The Toro Company; *U.S. Public*, pg. 1623

PROFESSIONAL BUILDER—New-Residential Construction Magazine for Builders—Reed Elsevier Business Information; *Int'l*, pg. 1095

PROFESSIONAL BUILDER'S HOME PLAN DATABASE CD-ROM—Source of Information for Builders, Architects, Designers & Consumers—Reed Elsevier Business Information; *Int'l*, pg. 1095

PROFESSIONAL COLLECTION—Photo Prints for Professionals—Eastman Kodak Company; *U.S. Public*, pg. 550

PROFESSIONAL EDITOR—Software—International Business Machines Corporation; *U.S. Public*, pg. 895

PROFESSIONAL FILHO—Soccer Shoes—Mizuno Corporation; *Int'l*, pg. 884

PROFESSIONAL FORMULA—Dog Food—The Jim Dandy Co., Inc.; *Int'l*, pg. 918

PROFESSIONAL FORMULA—Dog Food—Manna Pro Corporation; *U.S. Private*, pg. 700

PROFESSIONAL OFFICE DESIGN—Magazine—North American Publishing Company; *U.S. Private*, pg. 803

PROFESSIONAL ONE—Hair Care Products—DeMert & Dougherty, Inc.; *U.S. Private*, pg. 323

PROFESSIONAL PFRANCHISE CLUB—NONE—The Black & Decker Corporation; *U.S. Public*, pg. 233

PROFESSIONAL PLUS—NONE—Rubbermaid Incorporated; *U.S. Public*, pg. 1411

PROFESSIONAL PROTECTOR PLAN—Insurance Package Program—Poe & Brown, Inc.; *U.S. Public*, pg. 1312

PROFESSIONAL PUTTERS ASSOCIATION—Trade Name in Conjunction with Putt-Putts Tournament Program—Putt Putt Golf Courses of America, Inc.; *U.S. Private*, pg. 896

PROFESSIONAL REMODELER—Source of Industry Information for Remodelers, Buyers & Specifiers—Reed Elsevier Business Information; *Int'l*, pg. 1095

PROFESSIONAL SERVICES—Customized Support—AT&T Strategy & New Service Innovations; *U.S. Public*, pg. 11

PROFESSIONAL STRENGTH RAID—Insecticide—S.C. Johnson & Son, Inc.; *U.S. Private*, pg. 592

THE PROFESSIONALS—Brand Name for Hospitals to Distribute Health Reference Information—National Health Enhancement Systems, Inc.; *U.S. Public*, pg. 1157

THE PROFESSIONALS' CHOICE—Roofing Shingles & Mineral Surfaced Roll Roofing—Georgia-Pacific Corporation; *U.S. Public*, pg. 735

PROFESSOR VIDEO—Video Tapes—Blockbuster Entertainment Group; *U.S. Private*, pg. 775

PROFESSOR WILEY—Children's Game Books—John Wiley & Sons, Inc.; *U.S. Public*, pg. 1768

PROFICARE—Hair Care Products—Wella Group; *Int'l*, pg. 1489

PROFIL—Lens—Essilor International Compagnie Generale d'Optique; *Int'l*, pg. 462

PROFILE—In the Ear Hearing Aid—Beltone Electronics Corporation; *U.S. Private*, pg. 132

PROFILE—NONE—Brown & Sharpe Manufacturing Company; *U.S. Public*, pg. 260

PROFILE—Car Mats—Cannon Rubber Ltd.; *Int'l*, pg. 261

PROFILE—Test System—GenRad, Inc.; *U.S. Public*, pg. 731

PROFILE—Pens & Pen & Pencil Sets—The Gillette Company; *U.S. Public*, pg. 743

PROFILE—Feminine Pads—Kimberly-Clark Corporation; *U.S. Public*, pg. 958

PROFILE—NONE—Landmark Graphics Corporation; *U.S. Public*, pg. 776

PROFILE—Cutlery—Oneida Ltd.; *U.S. Public*, pg. 1225

PROFILE—NONE—Pall Corporation; *U.S. Public*, pg. 1253

PROFILE AMERICA—Market Profile System—CACI International Inc; *U.S. Public*, pg. 272

PROFILE BAG FILTER—Beta Rated Bag Filter—Pall Corporation; *U.S. Public*, pg. 1253

PROFILE COLLECTION—Teakwood—Dansk International Designs Ltd.; *U.S. Public*, pg. 261

PROFILE GALLERY—NONE—American Greetings Corporation; *U.S. Public*, pg. 77

PROFILE II—Filters—Pall Corporation; *U.S. Public*, pg. 1253

PROFILE II PLUS—Positively Charged Polypropylene Filter—Pall Corporation; *U.S. Public*, pg. 1253

PROFILER—Plastic Film Measurement Gauge—Modern Controls, Inc.; *U.S. Public*, pg. 1120

PROFILES—Curved Bakery Show Cases—Columbus Show Case Company; *U.S. Private*, pg. 257

PROFILES CLASSIQUE—Curved European Bakery Show Cases—Columbus Show Case Company; *U.S. Private*, pg. 257

PROFILNINE—NONE—Alpha Therapeutic Corp.; *Int'l*, pg. 558

PROFIMAT—Automatic Turret Winder for Tissue, Tower, Nonwovens—Beloit Lenox, Div.; *U.S. Public*, pg. 789

PROFIT STRIP—Packaging Configuration for Batteries—Eastman Kodak Company; *U.S. Public*, pg. 550

PROFITT'S INC.—Department Store—Proffitt's, Inc.; *U.S. Public*, pg. 1333

PROFORCE—Motor Oil & Lubricants—J.D. Streett & Co., Inc.; *U.S. Private*, pg. 1047

PROFORM—NONE—Amerimark Inc.; *U.S. Public*, pg. 1237

PROFORM—Fire Resistant Fabric—ATHOL Corporation; *U.S. Private*, pg. 94

PROFS—Software—International Business Machines Corporation; *U.S. Public*, pg. 895

PROGAINE—NONE—Pharmacia & Upjohn; *Int'l*, pg. 1048

PROGESTASERT—Intrauterine Progesterone Contraceptive System—Alza Corporation; *U.S. Public*, pg. 62

PROGLIDE—Cookware—Regal Ware, Inc.; *U.S. Private*, pg. 917

PROGLYDE—Glycol Diether—The Dow Chemical Company; *U.S. Public*, pg. 522

PROGRAF—Pharmaceutical Preparations—Fujisawa U.S.A. Inc.; *Int'l*, pg. 525

PROGRAM COMMANDER—Electronic Components—General Instrument Corporation; *U.S. Public*, pg. 716

PROGRAM XPLORER—NONE—GenRad, Inc.; *U.S. Public*, pg. 731

PROGRAMATOR—NONE—CAP Gemini S.A.; *Int'l*, pg. 263

PROGRASS—Specialty Chemical—AgrEvo USA Company; *Int'l*, pg. 1203

PROGRESS—Garden Equipment, Floor Care Products—Electrolux, AB; *Int'l*, pg. 438

PROGRESS—NONE—Zanussi Italia S.p.A.; *Int'l*, pg. 442

PROGRESS INDUSTRIAL—Paint—Progress Paint Mfg. Co.; *U.S. Private*, pg. 890

PROGRESS NOTES—Magazine—Nellcor Puritan Bennett Incorporated; *U.S. Public*, pg. 1039

PROGRESSIVE FARMER—Monthly Magazine—Southern Progress Corporation; *U.S. Public*, pg. 1612

PROGRESSIVE FARMER—Magazine—Time Warner Inc.; *U.S. Public*, pg. 1610

PROGRESSO—Italian Foods/Soups—Grand Metropolitan Plc; *Int'l*, pg. 408

PROGRESSO—Italian Ready-to-Eat Soups—The Pillsbury Company; *Int'l*, pg. 411

PROGRESSO HEALTHY CLASSICS—Soup—The Pillsbury Company; *Int'l*, pg. 411

PROGRESSO TO GO—Low Calorie Shelf-Stable Meals—The Pillsbury Company; *Int'l*, pg. 411

PROHEAT—Heat Gun—Master Appliance Corp.; *U.S. Private*, pg. 713

PROHIBIT—Haemophilus B Conjugate Vaccine—Connaught Laboratories, Inc.; *Int'l*, pg. 1109

PROHIBIT—Face Masks—Medline Industries, Inc.; *U.S. Private*, pg. 728

PROJECT ASSISTANT—Computer Product—International Business Machines Corporation; *U.S. Public*, pg. 895

PROJECT KICKSTART—Software to Plan & Develop Projects—Experience In Software, Inc.; *U.S. Private*, pg. 388

PROJECT-O-STAND—Projector Tables—Da-Lite Screen Company, Inc.; *U.S. Private*, pg. 306

PROJECT 70—NONE—Carpenter Technology Corporation; *U.S. Public*, pg. 307

PROJECT STARSHIP—Family of High Performance Computer Prods.—Datapoint Corporation; *Int'l*, pg. 384

PROJECT 21—NONE—Harrah's Entertainment, Inc.; *U.S. Public*, pg. 790

PROJECTOR PLUS—Projector/Viewer—Telex Communications, Inc.; *U.S. Private*, pg. 1074

PROJIDEN—NONE—Procter & Gamble Espana S.A.; *U.S. Public*, pg. 1332

PROLACTIN—Diagnostic Products—Abbott Laboratories; *U.S. Public*, pg. 12

PROLAK—Fish Meal Analog for Dairy Cattle Industry—H.J. Baker & Bro., Inc.; *U.S. Private*, pg. 112

PROLAM—Preferred Industrial Panels—Weyerhaeuser Forest Products Company; *U.S. Public*, pg. 1764

PROLASTIN—Emphysema Drug—Bayer AG; *Int'l*, pg. 171

PROLASTIN—Alpha, Proteinase Inhibitor-Human—Bayer Corporation/Consumer Care Division; *Int'l*, pg. 173

PROLENE—Polypropylene Suture, Mesh—Ethicon, Inc.; *U.S. Public*, pg. 928

PROLINE—Power Tools—The Black & Decker Corporation; *U.S. Public*, pg. 233

PROLINE—Roofing Shingles, and Mineral Surface Rolls—Georgia-Pacific Corporation; *U.S. Public*, pg. 735

PROLINE—Paints—Sherwin-Williams Consumer Brands Division; *U.S. Public*, pg. 1466

PROLINE—DAT Tape Solutions—Tecmar Technologies, Inc.; *Int'l*, pg. 1361

PROLINE 15—Asphalt Saturated Felt—Georgia-Pacific Corporation; *U.S. Public*, pg. 735

PROLINE PREMIUM—Paints—Sherwin-Williams Consumer Brands Division; *U.S. Public*, pg. 1466

PROLINE SHADOW 30—Roofing Shingles—Georgia-Pacific Corporation; *U.S. Public*, pg. 735

PROLINE SHADOW 35—Roofing Shingles—Georgia-Pacific Corporation; *U.S. Public*, pg. 735

PROLINE 30—Asphalt Saturated Felt—Georgia-Pacific Corporation; *U.S. Public*, pg. 735

PROLINER—Refrigerated Produce Display Case Liner—Monsanto Company; *U.S. Public*, pg. 1124

PROLINESERIES 5—Line Matrix Printers—Printronix, Inc.; *U.S. Public*, pg. 1329

PROLITE—Polypropylene Tubing—NewAge Industries Inc.; *U.S. Private*, pg. 796

PROLITE—Polypropylene Tubing—Newage Industries Inc., Plastics Technology Group; *U.S. Private*, pg. 796

PROLIXIN—Central Nervous System Therapy—Bristol-Myers Squibb Company; *U.S. Public*, pg. 253

PROLOG—Digital Communications Recording System—Dictaphone Corp.; *U.S. Private*, pg. 1045

PROLOG—NONE—Western Atlas Logging Services; *U.S. Public*, pg. 1757

PROLOGUE—Microphones & Circuitry—Shure Brothers Incorporated; *U.S. Private*, pg. 997

PROLOPRIM—Prescription Anti-Infective—Glaxo Wellcome PLC; *Int'l*, pg. 553

PROM—Home Permanent, Hand Lotion & Shampoo—The Gillette Company; *U.S. Public*, pg. 743

PROMALIN—Plant Growth Regulator—Abbott Laboratories; *U.S. Public*, pg. 12

PROMANAGER—NONE—Detroit Diesel Corp.; *U.S. Private*, pg. 850

PROMAR—Coatings—The Sherwin-Williams Company; *U.S. Public*, pg. 1465

PROMARK—Pet Foods—Doane Products Co., Branded Sales Div.; *U.S. Private*, pg. 337

PROMASTER—Pocket Knives—Camillus Cutlery Co.; *U.S. Private*, pg. 203

PROMAT—NONE—ETEX; *Int'l*, pg. 430

PROMEON—Polymers, Hydrogels—Medtronic, Inc.; *U.S. Public*, pg. 1082

PROMINENCE—Roofing Shingles—Owens Corning; *U.S. Public*, pg. 1236

PROMINENT—Pumps—Ryan Herco Products Corp.; *U.S. Private*, pg. 953

PROMINJECT—Medical—Pharmacia & Upjohn Adria Laboratories; *Int'l*, pg. 1049

PROMISE—Toothpaste—Block Drug Company, Inc.; *U.S. Public*, pg. 236

PROMISE—Margarine/Spread—Chesebrough-Pond's; *Int'l*, pg. 1436

PROMISE—Margarine—Unilever Plc; *Int'l*, pg. 1433

PROMISE EXTRA LIGHT—Margarine/Spread—Chesebrough-Pond's; *Int'l*, pg. 1436

PROMISE ULTRA FAT-FREE—Margarine—Chesebrough-Pond's; *Int'l*, pg. 1436

PROMISE ULTRA FAT FREE—NONE—Van den Bergh Foods Company; *Int'l*, pg. 1436

PROMIT—Medical—Pharmacia & Upjohn Adria Laboratories; *Int'l*, pg. 1049

PROMLINK—Software—Data I/O Corporation; *U.S. Public*, pg. 486

PROMOD—Protein Supplement—Abbott Laboratories; *U.S. Public*, pg. 12

PROMODELER—Plastic Model Kits & Modeling Accessories—Revell-Monogram Inc.; *U.S. Private*, pg. 926

PROMONIX—Process Chromatography—Millipore Corporation; *U.S. Public*, pg. 1112

PROMOTION-ED-4D—NONE—Alliance Semiconductor Corp.; *U.S. Public*, pg. 47

PROMOTION WATCH—Promotion Security & Accountability Services—Valassis Communications, Inc.; *U.S. Public*, pg. 1704

PROMOTIONAL-PLUS—Retroreflective Polyester Film—Fasson Films; *U.S. Public*, pg. 153

PROMOTOR—Hair Dryer & Hair Clipper—Andis Company; *U.S. Private*, pg. 73

PROMPT—Electronic Instrument—Intel Corporation; *U.S. Public*, pg. 886

PROMPT—Inoculation System—3M; *U.S. Public*, pg. 1604

PROMUS—NONE—Harrah's Entertainment, Inc.; *U.S. Public*, pg. 790

PROMUS—Catering—KF/Konsum Coop Group; *Int'l*, pg. 718

PROMUS—Hotels—Promus Hotel Corporation; *U.S. Public*, pg. 1335

PROMWARE—Electronic Instrument—Intel Corporation; *U.S. Public*, pg. 886

PRONE—Gummed Label Paper—Perfecseal Company; *U.S. Public*, pg. 210

PRONE STANDER—Standing Techniques Chairs—Ortho-Kinetics, Inc.; *U.S. Private*, pg. 820

PRONEA 6 I—Advanced Photo System SLR Camera—Nikon Inc.; *Int'l*, pg. 931

PRONET—Order Communications System—Cerner Corporation; *U.S. Public*, pg. 331

PRONG-LOCK—Retaining Ring—Waldes Truarc/Industrial Retaining Ring; *U.S. Public*, pg. 1632

PRONIC—Network Circuitry—Zenith Electronics Corp.; *U.S. Public*, pg. 1790

PRONTO—Food Drinks—Cadbury Nigeria PLC; *Int'l*, pg. 248

PRONTO—For Lice Infestation—Del Pharmaceuticals, Inc.; *U.S. Public*, pg. 494

PRONTO—Digital Thermometer—Thermo Electric Co., Inc.; *U.S. Private*, pg. 1080

PRONTO—Cyanoacrylate Adhesives—3M; *U.S. Public*, pg. 1604

PRONTO PUP MIX—Coating Mix for Hot Dogs—Gold Medal Products Co.; *U.S. Private*, pg. 459

PRONTOSIL—Anaesthetic—Bayer AG; *Int'l*, pg. 171

PRONTOW—Automatic Guided Vehicles, Towing—Jervis B. Webb Company; *U.S. Private*, pg. 1156

PROOF—Heavy-Duty Chlorinated Detergent with Metal Protecting Properties—Ecolab Inc.; *U.S. Public*, pg. 562

PROOF-ER—Liquid Level Switch—Magnetrol International; *U.S. Private*, pg. 696

THE PROOF'S IN THE POWER—Disinfectant & Cleaner—The Dow Chemical Company; *U.S. Public*, pg. 522

PROP—Pre-Shave—The Mennen Company; *U.S. Public*, pg. 397

PROP-TITE!—Fasteners—R&B, Inc.; *U.S. Public*, pg. 1354

PROP-MASTER—Drivelines—Rockwell International Corporation; *U.S. Public*, pg. 1397

PROPA PH—Acne Medication—Del Pharmaceuticals, Inc.; *U.S. Public*, pg. 494

PROPAC—Gun Mixes—North State Pyrophyllite; *U.S. Private*, pg. 924

PROPADERM—Agent for Epidermis—Kyowa Hakko Kogyo Company, Ltd.; *Int'l*, pg. 778

PROPAGE—Laser Bond, Singles & Labels—Moore Document Solutions; *Int'l*, pg. 890

PROPAGEST—Decongestant—Carnrick Laboratories, Inc.; *U.S. Private*, pg. 436

PROPAK—Fish Meal Analog for Broiler Industry—H.J. Baker & Bro., Inc.; *U.S. Private*, pg. 112

PROPANE—Lanterns & Stoves—The Canadian Coleman Co., Ltd.; *U.S. Private*, pg. 691

PROPAQ—Vital Signs Monitor—Protocol Systems, Inc.; *U.S. Public*, pg. 1336

PROPARTNERS—NONE—Eli Lilly and Company; *U.S. Public*, pg. 992

PROPE—Engineering Resins—The Dow Chemical Company; *U.S. Public*, pg. 522

PROPECIA—Hair Restorative Product—Merck & Co., Inc.; *U.S. Public*, pg. 1090

PROPER CHAIR—Chairs—Herman Miller, Inc.; *U.S. Public*, pg. 1111

PROPERT'S—Shoe Polish—Kiwi Brands; *U.S. Public*, pg. 1433

PROPERTY MANAGEMENT GOLD—NONE—Timberline Software Corporation; *U.S. Public*, pg. 1609

PROPET—Hair Clipper—Andis Company; *U.S. Private*, pg. 73

PROPEX—NONE—AGA Gas, Inc.; *Int'l*, pg. 13

PROPEX—Fabric—Amoco Chemicals; *U.S. Public*, pg. 102

PROPEX—Fabrics—Amoco Corporation; *U.S. Public*, pg. 101

PROPEX SILT STOP—Geotextile—Amoco Chemicals; *U.S. Public*, pg. 102

PROPHECY—Software Used for Color Proofing Systems—Eastman Kodak Company; *U.S. Public*, pg. 550

PROPHECY—NONE—Kellwood Company; *U.S. Public*, pg. 948

PROPHYLLIN—Pharmaceutical Products—Rystan Company, Inc.; *U.S. Private*, pg. 436

PROPILE—Thermal Pile—Helly-Hansen (US), Inc.; *Int'l*, pg. 1010

PROPIMAX—Air Moving Devices—EG & G Rotron; *U.S. Public*, pg. 543

PROPINE—Anti-Glaucome—Allergan, Inc.; *U.S. Public*, pg. 46

PROPIREY—Biorented Polypropilene Film—CYDSA S.A.; *Int'l*, pg. 246

PROPLEX—Pharmaceutical Prod.—Baxter-Hyland; *U.S. Public*, pg. 196

PROPLUS—Soy Proteins—Ralston Purina Company; *U.S. Public*, pg. 1359

PROPMAN—HF Propagation Software—Rockwell International Corporation; *U.S. Public*, pg. 1397

PROPOGLASS—Polypropylene Cam-Op & Pin Lug Couplings—NewAge Industries Inc.; *U.S. Private*, pg. 796

PROPOMEEN—Specialty Chemicals—Akzo Nobel Inc.; *Int'l*, pg. 47

PROPONITE—Packaging Film—Borden, Inc.; *U.S. Private*, pg. 157

PROPORTIONEERS—Metering Pumps—BIF; *U.S. Public*, pg. 726

PROPPER—Surgical, Hospital & Laboratory Supplies—Propper Manufacturing Co., Inc.; *U.S. Private*, pg. 891

PROPRANOLOL HCl—Generic Drug—American Home Products Corporation; *U.S. Public*, pg. 79

PROPRINT—Preprinted Linerboard—Georgia-Pacific Corporation; *U.S. Public*, pg. 735

PROPRINTER—Computer Printer—International Business Machines Corporation; *U.S. Public*, pg. 895

PROPULSID—NONE—Johnson & Johnson; *U.S. Public*, pg. 927

PROP2Q ENCORE—Vital Signs Monitor—Protocol Systems, Inc.; *U.S. Public*, pg. 1336

PROQUANTUM—Diagnostic Products—Abbott Laboratories; *U.S. Public*, pg. 12

PRORECO—Marine Rubber Caulk—Courtaulds Aerospace; *Int'l*, pg. 339

PRO'S CHOICE—Roof Coating & Cements—The Gibson-Homans Company; *U.S. Private*, pg. 451

PROSCAN—TV Receivers—Thomson Consumer Electronics Inc.; *Int'l*, pg. 1383

PROSCAR—Finasteride—Merck & Co., Inc.; *U.S. Public*, pg. 1090

PROSCAR—Pharmaceutical—Merck Human Health Division (U.S. Human Health); *U.S. Public*, pg. 1091

PROSEAL—Environmental Splice Kit—Master Appliance Corp.; *U.S. Private*, pg. 713

PROSEAL—Roofing Shingles with Sealants—Owens Corning; *U.S. Public*, pg. 1236

PROSEAL—Professional Vaccum Presses—Seal Products Incorporated; *U.S. Public*, pg. 849

PROSELECT—Network Circuitry—Zenith Electronics Corp.; *U.S. Public*, pg. 1790

PROSERIES—Tackle Box Line—Rubbermaid Incorporated; *U.S. Public*, pg. 1411

PROSET—Photo Typesetter—AGFA EPS Division; *Int'l*, pg. 172

PROSHARE—Personal Conferencing Products—Intel Corporation; *U.S. Public*, pg. 886

PROSHIELD—Corneal Collagen Shield—Alcon Laboratories, Inc.; *Int'l*, pg. 916

PROSHIELD—Corrosion Control Agents—BetzDearborn Inc.; *U.S. Public*, pg. 226

PROSHUWA—Bath Additive—Shiseido Company Ltd.; *Int'l*, pg. 1235

PROSNIP—Snips—American Tool Companies, Inc.; *U.S. Private*, pg. 63

PROSOBEE—Infant Formulas—Bristol-Myers Squibb Company; *U.S. Public*, pg. 253

PROSOBEE—Milk-Free Soy Formula for Infants—Mead Johnson Nutritional Group; *U.S. Public*, pg. 254

PROSOFT—NONE—J.M. Process Systems Inc.; *U.S. Private*, pg. 577

PROSOM—Sleep Medication—Abbott Laboratories; *U.S. Public*, pg. 12

PROSORT—Microcomputer Software for US Mailers—Group 1 Software, Inc.; *U.S. Public*, pg. 417

PROSPARK—Spark Plug Wire Sets—General Cable Corporation; *Int'l*, pg. 1486

PROSPEC—Industrial Safety Eyewear—Uvex Safety, Inc.; *Int'l*, pg. 132

PROSPECT PLUS—Artificial Intelligence Modeling System—I.C. System, Inc.; *U.S. Private*, pg. 553

PROSSER—Portable Submersible Dewatering Pumps—Barnes Pumps, Inc.; *U.S. Public*, pg. 457

PROSTA FINK—Treatment of Bladder Weakness—SmithKline Beecham plc; *Int'l*, pg. 1264

PROSTAK—Filtration Module & Filtration System—Millipore Corporation; *U.S. Public*, pg. 1112

PROSTAR—Specialty Chemical—AgrEvo USA Company; *Int'l*, pg. 1203

PROSTAR—Photo Processing Apparatus & Chemicals—Eastman Kodak Company; *U.S. Public*, pg. 550

PROSTAR—Cutlery—Lifetime Hoan Corp.; *U.S. Public*, pg. 992

PROSTASCINT—Cancer Diagnostic Imaging Product—Cytogen Corporation; *U.S. Public*, pg. 471

PROSTATE—Blend with Saw Palmetto—Celestial Seasonings; *U.S. Public*, pg. 319

PROSTATE S.P.—Herbal Supplement—Celestial Seasonings; *U.S. Public*, pg. 319

PROSTHODENT—Dental Resin/Filler—Lee Pharmaceuticals; *U.S. Public*, pg. 984

PROSTHODENT VL-2—Dental Composite Material—Lee Pharmaceuticals; *U.S. Public*, pg. 984

PROSTRIPE—Self-Adhesive Auto Body Side, Wheel & Door Moldings for Refinishing Trade—Spartan International Inc.; *U.S. Private*, pg. 1020

PROSYSTEM—1/2″ Hardboard Siding—ABT Building Products Corporation; *Int'l*, pg. 20

PROTEAN—NONE—Marcam Solutions, Inc.; *U.S. Public*, pg. 1042

PROTEC—Roll Cover—Beloit Corporation; *U.S. Public*, pg. 789

PROTECH—NONE—Regal Ware, Inc.; *U.S. Private*, pg. 917

PROTECH—Closed Circuit Television Equipment—Vicon Industries, Inc.; *U.S. Public*, pg. 1719

PROTECRITE—Protective Films—American Biltrite Inc.; *U.S. Public*, pg. 68

PROTECT—Gel Toothpaste—John O. Butler Co.; *Int'l*, pg. 1320

PROTECT—Dental Products—The Dow Chemical Company; *U.S. Public*, pg. 522

PROTECT-A-GLAZE—Synthetic Resin, Plastics, Plates, Fluids, Blocks, Filaments, Rods, Tubes—General Electric Canada Inc.; *U.S. Public*, pg. 713

PROTECT-O-GUARD—Lawn Equipment—Bridgestone/Firestone, Inc.; *Int'l*, pg. 213

PROTECT-YOUR-CARDS—Credit Card Registration Service—Encore Marketing International, Inc.; *U.S. Public*, pg. 580

PROTECTA LITE—Line Protectors—The Ohio Brass Co.; *U.S. Public*, pg. 845

PROTECTAFILM—Microfilming Service—Eastman Kodak Company; *U.S. Public*, pg. 550

THE PROTECTING HAND—Insurance—Woodmen Accident & Life Co.; *U.S. Private*, pg. 1187

PROTECTION PLUS—Soaps—Medline Industries, Inc.; *U.S. Private*, pg. 728

PROTECTIV—NONE—Johnson & Johnson; *U.S. Public*, pg. 927

PROTECTIV—I.V. Catheter Safety System—Johnson & Johnson Medical, Inc.; *U.S. Public*, pg. 928

PROTECTIVE BENEFITS COMMUNICATIONS—Insurance Services—Protective Life Corporation; *U.S. Public*, pg. 1336

PROTECTIVE EQUITY SERVICES—Insurance Services—Protective Life Corporation; *U.S. Public*, pg. 1336

PROTECTIVE FINANCIAL CORPORATION—Insurance Company—Protective Life Corporation; *U.S. Public*, pg. 1336

PROTECTIVE LIFE CORPORATION—Insurance Company—Protective Life Corporation; *U.S. Public*, pg. 1336

PROTECTIVE LIFE INSURANCE COMPANY—Insurance Company—Protective Life Corporation; *U.S. Public*, pg. 1336

PROTECTIVES—Cosmetics—Almay, Inc.; *U.S. Private*, pg. 689

PROTECTNET—Data Line Protection—American Power Conversion Corporation; *U.S. Public*, pg. 89

PROTECTO—Gun Cases—Hoppe's A Brunswick Company; *U.S. Public*, pg. 266

PROTECTO—Pit & Fissure Sealer/Dental Restorative—Lee Pharmaceuticals; *U.S. Public*, pg. 984

PROTECTO—Resin Coating—Litton Industries, Inc.; *U.S. Public*, pg. 1002

PROTECTON—Vitamin & Tonic—SmithKline Beecham plc; *Int'l*, pg. 1264

PROTECTOR—Cartridge Cleaner—Anacomp Magnetics, Inc.; *U.S. Public*, pg. 107

PROTECTOR—Laminator—General Binding Corporation; *U.S. Public*, pg. 707

PROTECTOR—Crash, Fire & Rescue Vehicles—Simon Engineering plc; *Int'l*, pg. 1251

PROTECTOR—Fire Protection Equipment—Snap-Tite, Inc.; *U.S. Public*, pg. 1010

PROTECTOR PACKS—Voltage & Surge Protection—Porta Systems Corp.; *U.S. Public*, pg. 1317

THE PROTECTOR—Rustproofing—The Protector Corporation; *U.S. Private*, pg. 891

PROTECTOR II—Rail Lubricators—Portec Inc., Railway Maintenance Products Div.; *U.S. Public*, pg. 1318

PROTEGE—Car—Mazda Motor of America, Inc.; *Int'l*, pg. 849

PROTEGRA—NONE—Whitehall-Robins Healthcare; *U.S. Public*, pg. 80

PROTEIN-PAK—Gel Filtration Column & Ion Exchange Column—Millipore Corporation; *U.S. Public*, pg. 1112

PROTEIN 29—Conditioning Hair Grooms—The Mennen Company; *U.S. Public*, pg. 397

PROTEIN 21—Shampoo & Hair Spray—The Mennen Company; *U.S. Public*, pg. 397

PROTEIN 85—Vegetal High Protein Food—Meiji Seika Kaisha, Ltd.; *Int'l*, pg. 855

PROTEK—Teat Dip—H.B. Fuller Company; *U.S. Public*, pg. 686

PROTEKWOOD—Panels of Laminated Construction—Georgia-Pacific Corporation; *U.S. Public*, pg. 735

PROTENATE—Plasma Protein Fraction (Human)—Baxter-Hyland; *U.S. Public*, pg. 196

PROTERRA & DESIGN—NONE—Marietta Corporation; *U.S. Private*, pg. 702

PROTEX—Bath Soap—Colgate-Palmolive Company; *U.S. Public*, pg. 397

PROTEX-RAY—Disposable Cassette Covers—Uniflex, Inc.; *U.S. Public*, pg. 1665

PROTHIL—Hormone Preparations—Kali-Chemie Aktiengesellschaft; *Int'l*, pg. 1278

PROTIMETER—Moisture Measuring Instruments—Bowthorpe plc; *Int'l*, pg. 1018

PROTINA—Hair Treatment Preparation—Revlon-Realistic Professional Products, Inc.; *U.S. Private*, pg. 690

PROTO—Tool Line—The Stanley Works; *U.S. Public*, pg. 1508

PROTOCOL—Refrigeration System—Hussmann Corp.; *U.S. Public*, pg. 1766

PROTOCOL CORDLESS—Telemetry Monitoring System—Protocol Systems, Inc.; *U.S. Public*, pg. 1336

PRODODYNE—Test Equipment—3M; *U.S. Public*, pg. 1604

PROTOSLO—Biological Supplies—Carolina Biological Supply Co.; *U.S. Private*, pg. 213

PROTOSTAT—Tablets—Ortho-McNeil Pharmaceutical Corporation; *U.S. Public*, pg. 929

PROTOTRAK—Prototype CNC—Southwestern Industries, Inc.; *U.S. Private*, pg. 1019

PROTOUCH—Gynecological Device—The Cooper Companies, Inc.; *U.S. Public*, pg. 442

PROTRAC—Track Drafting Machines—OCE-U.S.A.; *Int'l*, pg. 994

PROTRAC II—Track Drafting Machines—OCE-U.S.A.; *Int'l*, pg. 994

PROTRAK—Profitability Analysis—John H. Harland Company; *U.S. Public*, pg. 785

PROTROPIN—Somatrem for Injection, Human Growth Hormone—Genentech, Inc.; *Int'l*, pg. 1120

PROTURF—Urethane Gym Floors—Southwest Recreational Industries Inc.; *U.S. Private*, pg. 1018

PROUD PAWS—Pet Foods—Ag Processing Inc., A Cooperative; *U.S. Private*, pg. 26

PROUD PET—Cat Food—Triple F, Inc.; *U.S. Private*, pg. 1104

PROVATI—NONE—Crestar Food Products, Inc.; *U.S. Public*, pg. 805

PROVEN BRANDS—Line of Quality Paint & Related Products—PRO Group, Inc.; *U.S. Private*, pg. 887

PROVEN MARKETING GROUP—Cabinet Hardware Distributors/Retailers—PRO Group, Inc.; *U.S. Private*, pg. 887

PROVENCE—Dinnerware—Dansk International Designs Ltd.; *U.S. Public*, pg. 261

PROVENTIL—Asthma Products—Schering-Plough Corporation; *U.S. Public*, pg. 1438

PROVERA—Progestational Agent—Pharmacia & Upjohn; *Int'l*, pg. 1048

PROVIDE—Protein Hair Care System—Stanhome Inc.; *U.S. Public*, pg. 1508

PROVIDENT—Bank—The Provident Bank; *U.S. Public*, pg. 1338

PROVIDENT MUTUAL—Life Insurance—Provident Mutual Life Insurance Co.; *U.S. Private*, pg. 891

PROVIDENTMUTUAL LIFE AND ANNUITY—Annuities—Provident Mutual Life Insurance Co.; *U.S. Private*, pg. 891

PROVIGO—NONE—Provigo Inc.; *Int'l*, pg. 1072

PROVINCETOWN—Lumber & Wood Products—Georgia-Pacific Corporation; *U.S. Public*, pg. 735

PROVINCIA—Cheese—Churny Company Inc.; *U.S. Public*, pg. 1288

PROVISC—Viscoelastic Solution—Alcon Laboratories, Inc.; *Int'l*, pg. 916

PROVISION—Industrial Safety Eyewear—Uvex Safety, Inc.; *Int'l*, pg. 132

PROVISIONS—NONE—Ralston Purina Company; *U.S. Public*, pg. 1359

PROVOX—Distributed Control Systems—Associated Process Controls; *U.S. Private*, pg. 92

PROVOX—Instrumentation—Monsanto Company; *U.S. Public*, pg. 1124

PROWARE—NONE—Sulcus Computer Corp.; *U.S. Public*, pg. 1527

PROWL—Herbicide—American Home Products Corporation; *U.S. Public*, pg. 79

PROWLER—Travel Trailer—Fleetwood Enterprises, Inc.; *U.S. Public*, pg. 650

PROWRAP—Housewrap—ABT Building Products Corporation; *Int'l*, pg. 20

PROXABRUSH—Oral Hygiene Aid—John O. Butler Co.; *Int'l*, pg. 1320

PROXAPIC—Oral Hygiene Aids—John O. Butler Co.; *Int'l*, pg. 1320

PROXCOTE—Color Coated Paper & Paperboard—Hazen Paper Company; *U.S. Private*, pg. 514

PROXI-STRIP—Skin Closure—Ethicon, Inc.; *U.S. Public*, pg. 928

PROXIMA OVATION—LCD Panel—Proxima Corporation; *U.S. Public*, pg. 1339

PROXIMA OVATION +—LCD Panel—Proxima Corporation; *U.S. Public*, pg. 1339

PROXIMITY—Level Control, Valve Position Indicator—Dwyer Instruments Inc.; *U.S. Private*, pg. 350

PROXIMITY—NONE—Northern Telecom Limited; *Int'l*, pg. 968

PROXOL 80SP—Specialty Chemical—AgrEvo USA Company; *Int'l*, pg. 1203

PROXPRESS—Household Product—The Black & Decker Corporation; *U.S. Public*, pg. 233

PROZAC—Fluoxetine Hydrochloride, Dista—Eli Lilly and Company; *U.S. Public*, pg. 992

PROZAC—Fluoxetine—Eli Lilly Italia, S.p.A.; *U.S. Public*, pg. 994

PROZI-SOIR—NONE—Alimentation Couche Tard Inc.; *Int'l*, pg. 57

PRUDENCE BRAND—Canned Meat & Meat Entrees—Bunker Hill Foods Inc.; *U.S. Private*, pg. 219

PRUFCOAT—Industrial Coating—Grow Group, Inc.; *Int'l*, pg. 663

PRUFCOAT—Industrial Coating—ICI Paints; *Int'l*, pg. 664

PRUNZ—Dietary Supplement Tablets—Alva/Amco Pharmacal Companies, Inc.; *U.S. Private*, pg. 47

PRUV—Lubricant—Penford Corp.; *U.S. Public*, pg. 1269

PRYCA—Groceries—Carrefour; *Int'l*, pg. 272

PRYFON—Termiticide—Bayer AG; *Int'l*, pg. 171

PRYM—Buttons—Prym-Dritz Corporation; *Int'l*, pg. 1499

PSORCON—Pharmaceutical—Dermik Laboratories, Inc.; *Int'l*, pg. 1110

PSORCON C OINT—Topical Cortico Steroid—Dermik Laboratories, Inc.; *Int'l*, pg. 1110

PSORIGEL—Pharmaceutical Products—Galderma Laboratories, Inc.; *Int'l*, pg. 819

PSSSSSST—Spray Shampoo—Clairol, Inc.; *U.S. Public*, pg. 254

PSYCHOLOGY TODAY—Magazine Publishers—Psychology Today; *U.S. Private*, pg. 1056

PSYCHOLOGY TODAY—NONE—Sussex Publishers, Inc.; *U.S. Private*, pg. 1056

PSYCHRO-NOMIC—Evaporative Cooling System—Baltimore Aircoil Company; *U.S. Private*, pg. 68

PUB PET—Beer Containers—Carter Holt Harvey Limited; *U.S. Public*, pg. 904

PUBLIC NETWORK EUROPE—NONE—The Economist Group Limited; *Int'l*, pg. 1026

PUBLIC STORAGE—Self-Storage Facilities—Public Storage, Inc.; *U.S. Public*, pg. 1340

PUBLISHERS CLEARING HOUSE—Magazine Subscriptions by Mail—Publishers Clearing House; *U.S. Private*, pg. 893

PUBLISHERS' INTERNATIONAL MARKETING SERVICES—Publishers' Services—The Hearst Corporation; *U.S. Private*, pg. 515

PUBLISHERS MATTE—Printing Paper—The Mead Corporation; *U.S. Public*, pg. 1074

PUBLISHERS THINBULK—Coated Printing Paper—The Mead Corporation; *U.S. Public*, pg. 1074

PUBLISHERS WEEKLY—Magazine of the Book Publishing Industry—Reed Elsevier Business Information; *Int'l*, pg. 1095

PUBLISHING TECHNOLOGY—Magazine—North American Publishing Company; *U.S. Private*, pg. 803

PUBLIX—Grocery & Non-Foods—Publix Supermarkets Inc.; *U.S. Private*, pg. 893

PUBLIX PREMIER—Yogurt—Publix Supermarkets Inc.; *U.S. Private*, pg. 893

PUBLIX PREMIUM—Ice Cream Items—Publix Supermarkets Inc.; *U.S. Private*, pg. 893

PUCK—Cheese—MD Foods; *Int'l*, pg. 826

PUCKER HUSTLE—Sweet & Sour Candies—Brach & Brock Confections Inc.; *U.S. Private*, pg. 163

PUDDING PLUS—Ready to Eat Puddings—Dean Foods Company; *U.S. Public*, pg. 489

PUDDING ROLL UPS—NONE—Snacks Unlimited Division; *U.S. Public*, pg. 718

PUEBLO—Barbed Wire—CF & I Steel, L.P.; *U.S. Public*, pg. 1230

PUEBLO SUPERMARKETS—Conventional Supermarkets—Pueblo Xtra International, Inc.; *U.S. Private*, pg. 894

PUERTO RICO—Dominican Republic—Caribe Express; *U.S. Private*, pg. 211

PUFF KIDS—Soft Toys—Fisher-Price, Inc.; *U.S. Public*, pg. 1058

PUFFED RICE—Breakfast Cereal—The Quaker Oats Company; *U.S. Public*, pg. 1347

PUFFED WHEAT—Breakfast Cereal—The Quaker Oats Company; *U.S. Public*, pg. 1347

PUFFED WHEAT & RICE—Cereal—Malt-O-Meal Company; *U.S. Private*, pg. 699

PUFFIN—Children's Paperback Books—Penguin Putnam Inc.; *Int'l*, pg. 1027

PUFFS—Facial Tissue—The Procter & Gamble Company; *U.S. Public*, pg. 1330

PUFFS FREE—Facial Tissue—The Procter & Gamble Company; *U.S. Public*, pg. 1330

PUFFS PLUS—Unscented, Lotion Impregnated Tissue—The Procter & Gamble Company; *U.S. Public*, pg. 1330

PUFFY—Soft Vinyl Seats—Sanderson Plumbing Products Inc.; *U.S. Private*, pg. 964

PUGET—Sulfite Wood Pulp—Georgia-Pacific Corporation; *U.S. Public*, pg. 735

PUGET FREE—Pulp—Georgia-Pacific Corporation; *U.S. Public*, pg. 735

PUGET SOUND BUSINESS JOURNAL—Business Journal—Business First of New York, Inc.; *U.S. Private*, pg. 19

PUGETSOL—Alcohol for Use as an Industrial Solvent—Georgia-Pacific Corporation; *U.S. Public*, pg. 735

PUIFORCAT—China & Silver—Baccarat (Cie des Cristalleries); *Int'l*, pg. 132

PUIFORCAT—China & Silver Sold Retail Only—Baccarat, Inc.; *Int'l*, pg. 132

PUIFORCAT—Silversmith—Hermes International; *Int'l*, pg. 617

PUIFORCAT—Silver & Limoges Porcelain—Lalique North America; *Int'l*, pg. 797

PULGARD—Tilmicosin, Elanco—Eli Lilly and Company; *U.S. Public*, pg. 992

PULL-N-SOAP—Pulling Lubricant—Greenlee Textron; *U.S. Public*, pg. 1589

PULL-OPE—Envelopes—Tension Envelope Corp.; *U.S. Private*, pg. 1077

PULL-PAC—Products in the Electronics & Communications Industry—General Cable Corporation; *Int'l*, pg. 1486

PULL-UPS—Training Pants—Kimberly-Clark Corporation; *U.S. Public*, pg. 958

PULLMAN—Chick Boxes & Egg Cases—Inland Container Corporation; *U.S. Public*, pg. 1575

PULMAN/SOFITEL—Intl. Luxury Hotels—Accor S.A.; *Int'l*, pg. 1119

PULMICORT—Inhalant Based on Cortisone Compounds—Astra AB; *Int'l*, pg. 93

PULMOCARE—Liquid Nutritional—Abbott Laboratories; *U.S. Public*, pg. 12

PULMOTIL—Animal Health—Elanco Animal Health; *U.S. Public*, pg. 993

PULMOZYME—Dormase Alfa Inhalation Solution, DNase—Genentech, Inc.; *Int'l*, pg. 1120

PULMOZYME—Recombinant Human DNase—Roche Holding Ltd.; *Int'l*, pg. 1119

PULP & PAPER—Magazine—Miller Freeman Inc.; *Int'l*, pg. 1443

PULP & PAPER INTERNATIONAL—Magazine—Miller Freeman Inc.; *Int'l*, pg. 1443

PULPETTER—Fodder—Danisco Sugar; *Int'l*, pg. 378

PULPMASTER—Stock Preparation—Beloit Corporation; *U.S. Public*, pg. 789

PULSAFEEDER—Pumps—IDEX Corporation; *U.S. Public*, pg. 862

PULSAIR—Positioner—Worcester Controls Corp.; *Int'l*, pg. 128

PULSAN—Fungicide—Novartis AG; *Int'l*, pg. 971

PULSAR—Computerized Relay Test Equipment—AVO International; *Int'l*, pg. 1335

PULSAR—Customer-Resident Computer Publishing System—R.R. Donnelley & Sons Company; *U.S. Public*, pg. 517

PULSAR—Car—Nissan Motor Co., Ltd.; *Int'l*, pg. 943

PULSAR—NONE—Seiko Corporation; *Int'l*, pg. 1218

PULSAR—Watches—SEIKO Corporation of America; *Int'l*, pg. 1218

PULSAR VALVE—Digital Electro-Hydraulic Valve—Applied Power Inc.; *U.S. Public*, pg. 124

PULSCALE—Digital Read-out Equip.—Futaba Corporation; *Int'l*, pg. 531

PULSE—Engineering Polymers—The Dow Chemical Company; *U.S. Public*, pg. 522

PULSE—Gas Furnace—Lennox International Inc.; *U.S. Private*, pg. 659

PULSE PLUS—Oven Control—The Blodgett Oven Co., Inc.; *U.S. Public*, pg. 1064

PULSE POWER—Power Source—The Lincoln Electric Company; *U.S. Public*, pg. 996

PULSE SHIELD—Inverter Motor-Duty Magnet Wire—Rea Magnet Wire Company, Inc.; *U.S. Private*, pg. 913

PULSE SPRAY—Pulsed Infusion System—E-Z-Em, Inc.; *U.S. Public*, pg. 540

PULSEMASTER—Dental Laser—American Dental Technologies; *U.S. Public*, pg. 70

PULSESURVEY—Software—ScanTron Corporation; *U.S. Public*, pg. 786

PULVI-MULCHER—Seedbed Preparation Tool—Brillion Iron Works, Inc.; *U.S. Public*, pg. 933

PULVINET—Agricultural Disinfectant—The Dow Chemical Company; *U.S. Public*, pg. 522

PULVULES—Filled Gelatin Capsules, Lilly—Eli Lilly and Company; *U.S. Public*, pg. 992

PUMA—Ag Chemical—AgrEvo USA Company; *Int'l*, pg. 1203

PUMA—Herbicide—Hoechst Aktiengesellschaft; *Int'l*, pg. 624

PUMA—Athletic Shoes—Puma North America; *Int'l*, pg. 1072

PUMICE LOTION HAND CLEANER—Industrial Chemical—Hercules Chemical Co., Inc.; *U.S. Private*, pg. 523

THE PUMP—Athletic Shoes—Reebok International Ltd.; *U.S. Public*, pg. 1369

PUMP-COLORIMETER—On-Line Process Monitor—Hach Company; *U.S. Public*, pg. 773

PUMP ROOM—Restaurant—Omni Hotels; *U.S. Private*, pg. 1065

PUMP 24—Card Activated Gas Pump—CENEX, Inc.; *U.S. Private*, pg. 221

PUMP 24—Automated Fuel Service—Cenex/Land O'Lakes, Inc.; *U.S. Private*, pg. 222

PUMPFLEX—Hose—HBD Industries, Inc.; *U.S. Private*, pg. 489

PUNA—Papayas—Amfac, Inc.; *U.S. Private*, pg. 577

PUNCH—Detergent—Colgate-Palmolive Company; *U.S. Public*, pg. 397

PUNCH—Cigar—Villazon Company Inc.; *U.S. Private*, pg. 1140

PUNCH-N-FRUITY—Non-carbonated Drink—White Rock Products Corp.; *U.S. Private*, pg. 1173

PUNCHLINE—Hanging Cord Built Into Standing Ream of Certaflex—CertainTeed Corporation; *Int'l*, pg. 1170

PUNCTILIOUS—Ethyl Alcohol—Millennium Petrochemicals, Inc.; *Int'l*, pg. 594

PUNCTURE SEAL—Seals & Inflates Tires—Radiator Specialty Company; *U.S. Private*, pg. 906

PUNNY BUSINESS—Greeting Cards—American Greetings Corporation; *U.S. Public*, pg. 77

PUNT E MES—Aperitif—Carillon Importers, Ltd.; *Int'l*, pg. 409

PUNTO—Van—Fiat Auto Ireland Ltd.; *Int'l*, pg. 481

PUP-PERONI—Dog Treats—H.J. Heinz Company; *U.S. Public*, pg. 805

PUP-PERONI—Dog Treats—The Quaker Oats Company; *U.S. Public*, pg. 1347

PUPPERONI—NONE—Star-Kist Foods Inc.; *U.S. Public*, pg. 805

PUPPIZZAS—NONE—Star-Kist Foods, Inc.; *U.S. Public*, pg. 806

PUPPY CHOW—Dog Food—Ralston Purina Company; *U.S. Public*, pg. 1359

PUPPY LOVE—Dog Food—The Jim Dandy Co., Inc.; *Int'l*, pg. 918

PUPPY LOVES—Greeting Cards, Stationery & Party Goods—American Greetings Corporation; *U.S. Public*, pg. 77

PUR-FLO—Natural PVDF Pipe, Valves & Fittings—George Fischer Sloane, Inc.; *Int'l*, pg. 430

PURA—Release Agent—Chem-Trend Incorporated; *Int'l*, pg. 235

PURAC—Lactic Acid and Derivatives—CSM N.V.; *Int'l*, pg. 243

PURAFECT—Enzymes for Detergent Industry—Cultor Ltd.; *Int'l*, pg. 349

PURCHASE PROTECTION—Service Enhancements for Cardmembers—American Express Company; *U.S. Public*, pg. 73

PURCHASING—Magazine for Purchasing Professionals in all Businesses & Industries—Reed Elsevier Business Information; *Int'l*, pg. 1095

PURCHASING CARD—NONE—American Express Company; *U.S. Public*, pg. 73

PURCOAT—Elastomeric Stoppers For Pharmaceutical Containers & Vials—The West Company, Incorporated; *U.S. Public*, pg. 1755

PURE AIR99—Water Filter—Pollenex; *U.S. Public*, pg. 1391

PURE & SIMPLE—Skin Cream & Lotion—SmithKline Beecham plc; *Int'l*, pg. 1264

PURE BEESWAX—Beeswax—Will & Baumer Incorporated; *U.S. Private*, pg. 1176

PURE CARE—Makeup & Skin Care Products—Avon Products, Inc.; *U.S. Public*, pg. 155

PURE CARE—Cosmetics—International Cosmetics Co., Ltd.; *Int'l*, pg. 684

PURE DRIP—Coffeemakers—Melitta U.S.A., Inc.; *Int'l*, pg. 857

PURE-FLO—Bleaching Clay—Oil-Dri Corporation of America; *U.S. Public*, pg. 1214

PURE-FLO—Starch—Unilever Plc; *Int'l*, pg. 1433

PURE GOLD—Syrup—Dean Pickles & Specialty Products; *U.S. Public*, pg. 490

PURE PACK—Packaging—Tiedemanns - Joh.H.Andresen ANS; *Int'l*, pg. 1389

PURE-PAK—Packaging Machinery—Elopak, Inc.; *Int'l*, pg. 1390

PURE SHINE—Shampoo, Conditioner, Etc.—Hask Toiletries; *U.S. Private*, pg. 509

PURE SILK—NONE—Pfizer Inc.; *U.S. Public*, pg. 1281

PURE SLUMBER—Pillows—Medline Industries, Inc.; *U.S. Private*, pg. 728

PURE WATER99—Water Filter—Pollenex; *U.S. Public*, pg. 1391

PURE WHITE—Hair Preparation—Clairol, Inc.; *U.S. Public*, pg. 254

PURE-PAK—Packaging—Southcorp Holdings Ltd.; *Int'l*, pg. 1287

PUREBEAM—NONE—The Titan Corporation; *U.S. Public*, pg. 1618

PUREBRIGHT—Kills Bacteria on Food Packaging Surfaces—Maxwell Technologies, Inc.; *U.S. Public*, pg. 1061

PUREGAS—Meter Panels & Air Dryers—American Financial Group; *U.S. Public*, pg. 83

PUREGOLD—Beer—Asahi Breweries Ltd.; *Int'l*, pg. 83

PUREGON—Recombinant Gonadotrophin FSH—Akzo Nobel N.V.; *Int'l*, pg. 42

PURELIN—Facial & Bathroom Tissue, Paper Towels—Georgia-Pacific Corporation; *U.S. Public*, pg. 735

PURELINE—Teflon Lined Dual Wall Tubing—Bunnell Plastics Division; *U.S. Public*, pg. 689

PURELOC—Compression Fittings Of TEFLON—NewAge Industries Inc.; *U.S. Private*, pg. 796

PURELOC—Injection Molded Teflon Fittings—Newage Industries Inc., Plastics Technology Group; *U.S. Private*, pg. 796

PURELY FRUIT—Allfruit Spread—J.M. Smucker Company; *U.S. Public*, pg. 1480

PURELY PACIFIC—Bottled Water—Darigold, Inc.; *U.S. Private*, pg. 311

PURENESS—Skin Care—Shiseido Cosmetics (America) Ltd.; *Int'l*, pg. 1235

PUREX—Swimming Pool Products—Essef Corporation; *U.S. Public*, pg. 592

PUREX DRY BLEACH—NONE—The Dial Corporation; *U.S. Public*, pg. 505

PUREX RINSE 'N SOFT FABRIC SOFTENER SHEETS—NONE—The Dial Corporation; *U.S. Public*, pg. 505

PUREX RINSE 'N SOFT LIQUID FABRIC SOFTENER PLUS—NONE—The Dial Corporation; *U.S. Public*, pg. 505

PUREX STA PUF CONCENTRATED LIQUID FABRIC SOFTENER—NONE—The Dial Corporation; *U.S. Public*, pg. 505

PUREX-TRITION—Swimming Pool Products—Essef Corporation; *U.S. Public*, pg. 592

PURFLUX—Automotive Oil Filters—Labinal SA; *Int'l*, pg. 785

PURGEMASTER—Flowmeter—Bailey, Fischer & Porter Company; *Int'l*, pg. 449

PURI-CLEAR—Air Purifier—Slant/Fin Corporation; *U.S. Private*, pg. 1005

PURIFAX—Sludge Stabilization System—BIF; *U.S. Public*, pg. 726

PURIFIRE—Atmosphere Systems—Air Products and Chemicals, Inc.; *U.S. Public*, pg. 30

PURIFLOC—Flocculant—The Dow Chemical Company; *U.S. Public*, pg. 522

PURIGARD—Cartridge Filter—Millipore Corporation; *U.S. Public*, pg. 1112

PURINA BISCUITS—Dog Biscuits—Ralston Purina Company; *U.S. Public*, pg. 1359

PURINA CHOW—Animal Feeds—Purina Mills, Inc.; *U.S. Private*, pg. 895

PURINA ONE—Dog Food—Ralston Purina Company; *U.S. Public*, pg. 1359

PURINA PREMIUM—Cat Food—Ralston Purina Company; *U.S. Public*, pg. 1359

PURINETHOL—Leukemia Treatment—Glaxo Wellcome PLC; *Int'l*, pg. 553

PURITAN—Canned Meats—Lever Brothers Co.; *Int'l*, pg. 1435

PURITAN—NONE—Nellcor Puritan Bennett Incorporated; *U.S. Public*, pg. 1039

PURITAN—Oil—The Procter & Gamble Company; *U.S. Public*, pg. 1330

PURITAN—Canned Meats—Unilever Plc; *Int'l*, pg. 1433

PURITAN BENNETT—NONE—Nellcor Puritan Bennett Incorporated; *U.S. Public*, pg. 1039

PURITAN/CHURCHILL—Consumer & Industrial Cleaners & Specialty Chemical Compounds—Puritan/Churchill Chemical Company; *U.S. Private*, pg. 895

PURITAN'S PRIDE—Natural Vitamins & Cosmetics—Nature's Bounty Inc.; *U.S. Public*, pg. 1166

PURITAP—Drinking Water Systems—Arrowhead Mountain Spring Water Company; *Int'l*, pg. 919

PURITY—Salt & Salt Products—Akzo Nobel Inc.; *Int'l*, pg. 47

PURITY—Spirit—Allied Domecq PLC; *Int'l*, pg. 62

PURITY—Absorbent Cotton—Kimberly-Clark Corporation; *U.S. Public*, pg. 958

PURITY—Soup Bases, Dressings, Mayonnaise, Toppings, Olive Oil—Purity Products Inc.; *U.S. Private*, pg. 896

PURITY CEREAL—NONE—Robin Hood Multifoods Inc.; *U.S. Public*, pg. 901

PURITY MILK—Milk—Purity Dairies Inc.; *U.S. Private*, pg. 895

PURLITE—Sunflower Oil—Bestfoods; *U.S. Public*, pg. 223

PUROLATOR—Filter Products—Mark IV Automotive Canada Inc.; *U.S. Public*, pg. 1045

PUROLATOR—Auto & Other Filters—Mark IV Industries Inc.; *U.S. Public*, pg. 1044

PURPAX—Oil Free Air Compressors—Squire-Cogswell Company; *U.S. Private*, pg. 1027

PURPOSE—Dual-Treatment Moisturizer—Johnson & Johnson; *U.S. Public*, pg. 927

PURPOSE—Dual Treatment Moisturizer with SPF 12—Ortho-McNeil Pharmaceutical Corporation; *U.S. Public*, pg. 929

PURR—Canned Cat Food—Star-Kist Foods Inc.; *U.S. Public*, pg. 805

PURRFECT—Pet Food—Dalgety Plc; *Int'l*, pg. 376

PURSOUP—Vacumn-Packed Soup—Danone Group; *Int'l*, pg. 379

PURSTRING—Surgical Staplers—U.S. Surgical Corp.; *U.S. Public*, pg. 1687

PURSUE—Disinfectant Products—Amway Corporation; *U.S. Private*, pg. 69

PURSUIT—Herbicide—American Home Products Corporation; *U.S. Public*, pg. 79

PURSUIT—Infra-red Combat Survival Game For Outdoor And Indoor Play—Daisy Manufacturing Company, Inc.; *U.S. Private*, pg. 308

PURSUIT—Class A Motor Home—Georgie Boy Manufacturing, Inc.; *U.S. Public*, pg. 388

PURSUIT SECURITY—Stereo Equipment—Audiovox Corporation; *U.S. Public*, pg. 147

PURTREX—Depth Cartridge Filters—Osmonics, Inc.; *U.S. Public*, pg. 1233

PUSH-BUTTON—Portable Boat Horn—Falcon Safety Products Inc.; *U.S. Private*, pg. 392

PUSH N' MOLE—Pipe Pusher—McLaughlin Manufacturing Company; *U.S. Private*, pg. 724

PUSH'N RIDE—Walker—Rubbermaid Incorporated; *U.S. Public*, pg. 1411

PUSH-PAL—Push Back Carts—Jarke Corporation; *U.S. Private*, pg. 583

PUSH POP LOLLIPOPS—Candy—The Topps Company, Inc.; *U.S. Public*, pg. 1621

PUSH-UPS—Ice Cream—Nestle USA; *Int'l*, pg. 916

PUSHAROUND—Hand Trucks—B & P Manufacturing; *U.S. Private*, pg. 105

PUSHER—Oil Recovery Polymer, Caustic Soda Beads, Sodium Bromide Solution—The Dow Chemical Company; *U.S. Public*, pg. 522

PUSHPOT—NONE—Xicor, Inc.; *U.S. Public*, pg. 1785

PUSHWHEEL—Switches—Cherry Electrical Products Corporation; *U.S. Public*, pg. 346

PUSS'N BOOTS—Cat Food—H.J. Heinz Company; *U.S. Public*, pg. 805

PUTICRAPE—Snacks—Meiji Seika Kaisha, Ltd.; *Int'l*, pg. 855

PUTNAM—End Mills—Greenfield Industries Inc.; *U.S. Public*, pg. 950

PUTNAM—Investment Management Services—Marsh & McLennan Companies, Inc.; *U.S. Public*, pg. 1048

PUTNAM BERKLEY—NONE—Pearson plc; *Int'l*, pg. 1025

PUTT N'PAR—Socks & Knitted Headwear—Wigwam Mills, Inc.; *U.S. Private*, pg. 1175

PUTT-PUTT—Intl. Franchised Miniature Golf Course, Gameroom, Recreational Facilities—Putt Putt Golf Courses of America, Inc.; *U.S. Private*, pg. 896

PUTT-PUTT GOLF—Golf Course—Putt Putt Golf Courses of America, Inc.; *U.S. Private*, pg. 896

PUTT-PUTT PAUL—Clown Figure used for Promotions—Putt Putt Golf Courses of America, Inc.; *U.S. Private*, pg. 896

PUTT TO WIN—NONE—Infinicom; *U.S. Private*, pg. 561

PUZZLE MANIA—Puzzle Books—Highlights for Children; *U.S. Private*, pg. 528

PY-CO-PAY SOFTEX—Toothbrushes—Block Drug Company, Inc.; *U.S. Public*, pg. 236

PY.CO.TWIN—Interdental Brush—Block Drug Company, Inc.; *U.S. Public*, pg. 236

PY-O-MY—Mixes—Gilster Mary Lee Corp.; *U.S. Private*, pg. 455

PY-RAN—Food Leavening Agent—Monsanto Company; *U.S. Public*, pg. 1124

PYCOPAY—Toothbrushes & Tooth Powder—Block Drug Company, Inc.; *U.S. Public*, pg. 236

PYNEBOARD—Particleboard—CSR Limited; *Int'l*, pg. 245

PYOPEN—Pharmaceutical Prods.—SmithKline Beecham Laboratories; *Int'l*, pg. 1264

PYOPEN—Pharmaceutical—SmithKline Beecham plc; *Int'l*, pg. 1264

PYRACUBE—Industrial Products—Email Limited; *Int'l*, pg. 450

PYRAD—High Temperature, Fire Resistant Wire—Champlain Cable Corp.; *Int'l*, pg. 637

PYRALIN—Coatings For Microelectronics—Du Pont (E.I. Du Pont De Nemours & Co.); *U.S. Public*, pg. 530

PYRALUX—Flexible Printed Circuit Systems—Du Pont (E.I. Du Pont De Nemours & Co.); *U.S. Public*, pg. 530

PYRAMID—Veterinary Pharmaceuticals—American Home Products Corporation; *U.S. Public*, pg. 79

PYRAMID—Cage Layer System or Cages—CTB International Corp.; *U.S. Public*, pg. 284

PYRAMID—Cigarette Paper—Kimberly-Clark Corporation; *U.S. Public*, pg. 958

PYRAMID—Cigarettes—Liggett Group Inc.; *U.S. Public*, pg. 259

PYRAMID LIFE—Insurance—The Pyramid Life Insurance Co.; *U.S. Public*, pg. 1694

PYRAMID NORTHERN—Mouldings—Pyramid Mouldings; *Int'l*, pg. 1335

PYRAMIN—Crop Protection Agent—BASF AG; *Int'l*, pg. 103

PYRAMIS—ECG Management System—Burdick, Inc.; *U.S. Private*, pg. 181

PYRAN—Fire-Resisting Glass—Schott Glaswerke; *Int'l*, pg. 1523

PYRENONE—Insecticide—Roussel Corporation; *Int'l*, pg. 625

PYREX—Glassware—Corning Incorporated; *U.S. Public*, pg. 448

PYRIDIUM—UTI—Warner-Chilcott Laboratories, Inc.; *Int'l*, pg. 436

PYRO-CHEK—Flame Retardant Additives—Ferro Corporation; *U.S. Public*, pg. 618

PYRO LANCE—Temperature Measuring Device—Alnor Instrument Company; *U.S. Public*, pg. 1559

PYRO PANL—UL-25 Fire Retardant Panels—Sequentia Inc.; *U.S. Private*, pg. 985

PYROCIDE—Pesticides—McLaughlin Gormley King Company; *U.S. Public*, pg. 723

PYROCON—Temperature Measuring Device—Alnor Instrument Company; *U.S. Public*, pg. 1559

PYROCRETE—Fireproofing—Carboline Co.; *U.S. Public*, pg. 1357

PYROFLEX—Tank Linings—Koch Engineering Company, Inc.; *U.S. Private*, pg. 628

PYROFUZE—Fuse Wire—Sigmund Cohn Corp.; *U.S. Private*, pg. 250

PYROGARD—Ultrafiltration Cartridge—Millipore Corporation; *U.S. Public*, pg. 1112

PYROGENT—Gel Clot LAL Test—BioWhittaker, Inc.; *U.S. Public*, pg. 297

PYROIL—Automotive Additives—Ashland, Inc.; *U.S. Public*, pg. 138

PYROIL—Automotive Products—Valvoline Company; *U.S. Public*, pg. 139

PYROJECTOR—Relief Unit—Swartwout Industries; *Int'l*, pg. 1398

PYROLON—Fire Retardant Disposable Garments—Lakeland Industries, Inc.; *U.S. Public*, pg. 975

PYROMARK—High Temperature Paint—Tempil Inc.; *U.S. Private*, pg. 90

PYROMATIC—Temperature Device—Alnor Instrument Company; *U.S. Public*, pg. 1559

PYROMET—NONE—Carpenter Technology Corporation; *U.S. Public*, pg. 307

PYRON—Herbicides—Agrolinz Melamin GmbH; *Int'l*, pg. 356

PYRONAP—Felts—Kerlane; *Int'l*, pg. 1176

PYRONYL—Synergized Pyrethum Products—Prentiss Incorporated; *U.S. Private*, pg. 882

PYROPEL—Heat-Resistant Polymers—Albany International Corp.; *U.S. Public*, pg. 36

PYROPREG—High Temperature Glass Fabric—Ferro Corporation; *U.S. Public*, pg. 618

PYROPURE—Water Purification Systems—Paul Mueller Company; *U.S. Public*, pg. 1141

PYROTEX—Reinforced plastic—Universal Composites-U.S.C.; *U.S. Private*, pg. 1126

PYROTOOL—NONE—Carpenter Technology Corporation; *U.S. Public*, pg. 307

PYROTOUGH—NONE—Carpenter Technology Corporation; *U.S. Public*, pg. 307

PYROVATEX—Flame Retardant—Ciba Specialty Chemicals; *Int'l*, pg. 291

PYROVENT—Heat & Smoke vent—Wasco Products, Inc.; *U.S. Private*, pg. 1152

PYROWEAR—NONE—Carpenter Technology Corporation; *U.S. Public*, pg. 307

PYROX—Appliances—Southcorp Holdings Ltd.; *Int'l*, pg. 1287

PYRROXATE—NONE—Lee Pharmaceuticals; *U.S. Public*, pg. 984

PYSEAL—Sealing Cement—Fisher Scientific Company; *U.S. Private*, pg. 658

Q

Q—U.K. Entertainment Magazine—EMAP Metro; *Int'l*, pg. 451

Q.A.—Heavy Duty Bulk Rack—Interlake Material Handling Div.; *U.S. Public*, pg. 893

QA/DIRECTOR—NONE—Compuware Corporation; *U.S. Public*, pg. 423

QA PRODUCTS—Bakery Ingredients—CSM N.V.; *Int'l*, pg. 243

QBC—Malaria Test Kit—Becton Dickinson & Company; *U.S. Public*, pg. 199

QBC—Hematology Chemistry System—Becton Dickinson Primary Care Diagnostics; *U.S. Public*, pg. 199

Q-B II—Well Drilling Mud Thinner—Georgia-Pacific Corporation; *U.S. Public*, pg. 735

Q BALL—Ball Valve—Neles-Jamesbury Corp.; *Int'l*, pg. 1428

Q-BROXIN—Well Drilling Mud Thinner—Georgia-Pacific Corporation; *U.S. Public*, pg. 735

QCA—Chemistry Analyzer—Becton Dickinson Primary Care Diagnostics; *U.S. Public*, pg. 199

QC BRITISH SHERRY—British Sherry—Matthew Clark Brands; *Int'l*, pg. 848

QCC—Conduit—Electron Beam Technologies; *U.S. Private*, pg. 370

QCD—Quick Connect/Disconnect Valve System—Liqui-Box Corporation; *U.S. Public*, pg. 1000

QCF—Photographic Film—Eastman Kodak Company; *U.S. Public*, pg. 550

QCF7—Photographic Film—Eastman Kodak Company; *U.S. Public*, pg. 550

QC-HEPATITIS—Multi-Level Control Sera—Nabi; *U.S. Public*, pg. 1148

QC-HIV—HIV-1 Multi-Level Control Sera—Nabi; *U.S. Public*, pg. 1148

QCL-4000—Chromogenic Endotoxin Test—BioWhittaker, Inc.; *U.S. Public*, pg. 297

QCP—Graphic Arts Paper—Eastman Kodak Company; *U.S. Public*, pg. 550

Q CAGE—Globe Valve—Neles-Jamesbury Corp.; *Int'l*, pg. 1428

Q-CEL—Hollow Microspheres—PQ Corporation; *U.S. Public*, pg. 827

QD—Pulleys—Electron Corp.; *U.S. Private*, pg. 370

QDF—Photographic Film—Eastman Kodak Company; *U.S. Public*, pg. 550

QDF7—Photographic Film—Eastman Kodak Company; *U.S. Public*, pg. 550

QDM—Photographic Film—Eastman Kodak Company; *U.S. Public*, pg. 550

QDM7—Photographic Film—Eastman Kodak Company; *U.S. Public*, pg. 550

QEA—Sodium & Potassium Electrolyte Analyzer—Becton Dickinson Primary Care Diagnostics; *U.S. Public*, pg. 199

QEMM—Quarterdeck Expanded Memory Manager—Quarterdeck Corp.; *U.S. Public*, pg. 1350

QEST—Polybutylene Piping Systems—Eljer Plumbingware; *U.S. Public*, pg. 1794

QESTPEX—NONE—Eljer Plumbingware; *U.S. Public*, pg. 1794

Q.F.C.—Food Centers—Quality Food Centers, Inc.; *U.S. Public*, pg. 1349

QF-50—NONE—Molex Incorporated; *U.S. Public*, pg. 1121

QFS—Coagulation Analyzer—Becton Dickinson Primary Care Diagnostics; *U.S. Public*, pg. 199

Q-FELT—High Temperature Insulation—Johns Manville Corporation; *U.S. Public*, pg. 927

Q-FIBER—High Temperature Insulation—Johns Manville Corporation; *U.S. Public*, pg. 927

Q-FLEX—Servo Accelerometer—AlliedSignal Commercial Avionics Systems; *U.S. Public*, pg. 50

Q45 INFINITI—Luxury Sedan—Nissan Motor Corporation in U.S.A.; *Int'l*, pg. 945

Q-GUARD—Insulation Jacketing—Chemfab Corporation; *U.S. Public*, pg. 344

QHA/5—Hematology Analyzer—Becton Dickinson Primary Care Diagnostics; *U.S. Public*, pg. 199

QHA/7—Hematology Analyzer—Becton Dickinson Primary Care Diagnostics; *U.S. Public*, pg. 199

QHA/3—Hematology Analyzer—Becton Dickinson Primary Care Diagnostics; *U.S. Public*, pg. 199

QI ANALYST—Statistical Process Control (SPC)—SPSS Inc.; *U.S. Public*, pg. 1420

QIC IONCHROM ANALYZER—Analytical Instrument—Dionex Corporation; *U.S. Public*, pg. 510

QIK-FLECS—NONE—Molex Incorporated; *U.S. Public*, pg. 1121

QIML—Quick Sim to IKOS Mixed-Level Accelerator—IKOS Systems, Inc.; *U.S. Public*, pg. 864

QIXL—Quick Sim to IKOS Accelerator—IKOS Systems, Inc.; *U.S. Public*, pg. 864

Q-LAB—Process Monitoring System—Eastman Kodak Company; *U.S. Public*, pg. 550

Q LEVEL—One-Brightener System—LeaRonal, Inc.; *U.S. Public*, pg. 982

Q/LIGHT—Metallic Cans—Reynolds Metals Company; *U.S. Public*, pg. 1385

Q LOGO—Logo—Quest Medical, Inc.; *U.S. Public*, pg. 1352

Q-LON—Weather Seal—Schlegel Corporation; *Int'l*, pg. 128

Q-LOOP—NONE—QST Industries, Inc.; *U.S. Private*, pg. 897

Q LUBE—Fast Lubes—Quaker State Corporation; *U.S. Public*, pg. 1348

QMAP—Risk Management & Reporting Software—Medical Assurance, Inc.; *U.S. Public*, pg. 1079

QMF—Computer Product—International Business Machines Corporation; *U.S. Public*, pg. 895

QMR—NONE—First DataBank; *U.S. Private*, pg. 515

QMR PLASTICS—Molded Plastic Parts—Quadion Corporation; *U.S. Private*, pg. 898

QMS—Print Systems—QMS, Inc.; *U.S. Public*, pg. 1346

QMS—NONE—Seradyn, Inc.; *Int'l*, pg. 871

QMS COLORSCRIPT—Thermal Color Printer—QMS, Inc.; *U.S. Public*, pg. 1346

QMS CROWN—Printer Multi-Tasking Operating System—QMS, Inc.; *U.S. Public*, pg. 1346

QMS ESP—Emulation Sensing Processor Technology—QMS, Inc.; *U.S. Public*, pg. 1346

QMS HAMMERHEAD—Laser Printer—QMS, Inc.; *U.S. Public*, pg. 1346

QMS LASERGRAFIX—Laser Printer—QMS, Inc.; *U.S. Public*, pg. 1346

QMS-PS—Laser Printer—QMS, Inc.; *U.S. Public*, pg. 1346

QMS WRITER—Printer—QMS, Inc.; *U.S. Public*, pg. 1346

Q-MARK—Lasers—Excel Technology, Inc.; *U.S. Public*, pg. 599

Q MARK—NONE—Marley Electric Heating Company; *U.S. Public*, pg. 1676

Q-PIPE—Heat Recovery Equipment—ABB Air Preheater Inc.; *Int'l*, pg. 3

Q-PIPE—Air Preheaters—ABB Inc.; *Int'l*, pg. 3

QPLACE—Placement System—Cadence Design Systems, Inc.; *U.S. Public*, pg. 290

Q-PLUS—Extended Service Brakes—Rockwell International Corporation; *U.S. Public*, pg. 1397

QRK—Turntables—Broadcast Electronics, Inc.; *U.S. Private*, pg. 531

QS1500—Theft Prevention System—Checkpoint Systems Inc.; *U.S. Public*, pg. 343

QS 4000—Theft Prevention System—Checkpoint Systems Inc.; *U.S. Public*, pg. 343

QS90—Blood Sampler Syringe—Radiometer A/S; *Int'l*, pg. 1083

QS1600—Theft Prevention System—Checkpoint Systems Inc.; *U.S. Public*, pg. 343

QST—Magazine—American Radio Relay League; *U.S. Private*, pg. 60

QS 3000—Theft Prevention System—Checkpoint Systems Inc.; *U.S. Public*, pg. 343

QS2000—Electronic Retail Theft Prevention System—Checkpoint Systems Inc.; *U.S. Public*, pg. 343

Q SCAN—X-Ray Inspection System Used to Detect Foreign Contaminants in Containers—PAR Technology Corporation; *U.S. Public*, pg. 1256

QTEKPLOT—Software—QMS, Inc.; *U.S. Public*, pg. 1346

QTROFF—Software—QMS, Inc.; *U.S. Public*, pg. 1346

Q TEST—Materials Test System—MTS Systems Corporation; *U.S. Public*, pg. 1028

Q TEST STREP—Betahemolytic Group A Strep Diagnostic Kit—Becton Dickinson Primary Care Diagnostics; *U.S. Public*, pg. 199

Q-TIPS—Cotton Swabs, Cotton Balls, Cosmetic Applicators—Chesebrough-Pond's USA Co.; *Int'l*, pg. 1435

Q-TRACK—Indoor Air Quality Monitor—TSI Incorporated; *U.S. Public*, pg. 1559

Q-TRACKER—Ultrasonic—Badger Meter, Inc.; *U.S. Public*, pg. 164

Q TRIM—Ball, Segment & Globe Valve—Neles-Jamesbury Corp.; *Int'l*, pg. 1428

QX4 (INFINITI)—Sports Utility Vehicle—Nissan Motor Corporation in U.S.A.; *Int'l*, pg. 945

QUENCH—Soft Drink—The Monarch Company, Inc.; *U.S. Private*, pg. 756

QANTAS—NONE—Qantas Airways Ltd.; *Int'l*, pg. 1074

QANTAS—Airlines—Qantas Airways Ltd.; *Int'l*, pg. 1075

QANTAS HOLIDAYS—NONE—Qantas Airways Ltd.; *Int'l*, pg. 1074

QIX—Quick Insert Exchange—Watts Fluidair; *Int'l*, pg. 1243

QMANAGER IMS—NONE—BMC Software, Inc.; *U.S. Public*, pg. 162

QMANAGER IMS EP—NONE—BMC Software, Inc.; *U.S. Public*, pg. 162

QO—Circuit Breakers—Square D Company; *Int'l*, pg. 1208

QRAM—NONE—Alliance Semiconductor Corp.; *U.S. Public*, pg. 47

QST—NONE—QST Industries, Inc.; *U.S. Private*, pg. 897

QSTAR IV—Mattress—Medline Industries, Inc.; *U.S. Private*, pg. 728

QTRACS—NONE—QUALCOMM; *U.S. Public*, pg. 1348

QUACAST—Lubricants for the Casting of Ferrous & Non-ferrous Metals—Quaker Chemical Corporation; *U.S. Public*, pg. 1346

QUACKERS—Baby Exerciser—Evenflo Company, Inc.; *U.S. Private*, pg. 629

QUACKERS—Crackers—RJR Nabisco Holdings Corp.; *U.S. Public*, pg. 1354

QUAD—Magnetic Resonance Systems (MRI)—Fonar Corporation; *U.S. Public*, pg. 661

QUAD-BOND—Shipping Containers—Weyerhaeuser Company; *U.S. Public*, pg. 1764

QUAD NECK—NONE—Reynolds Metals Co.-Can Division Headquarters; *U.S. Public*, pg. 1386

QUAD-PLUS—NONE—Spectrol Electronics Corporation; *U.S. Private*, pg. 351

QUAD POWER—NONE—Gates Europe; *Int'l*, pg. 1396

QUAD-SPEED—Control—Harnischfeger Industries, Inc.; *U.S. Public*, pg. 788

QUADCADER—NONE—ECI Telecom Ltd.; *Int'l*, pg. 643

QUADCO—Mechanical Controls—Adams Rite Manufacturing Co.; *U.S. Private*, pg. 17

QUADEX—Photo Typesetters—AGFA EPS Division; *Int'l*, pg. 172

QUADEX IQ—Photo Typesetter—AGFA EPS Division; *Int'l*, pg. 172

QUADLOG—Safety System—Moore Products Co.; *U.S. Public*, pg. 1128

QUADMAX—Online Electronic Retailing Concept—OfficeMax; *U.S. Public*, pg. 1212

QUADRA—Tires—Bridgestone/Firestone, Inc.; *Int'l*, pg. 213

QUADRA—Portfolio—The Mead Corporation; *U.S. Public*, pg. 1074

QUADRA PRESS—Filters—Flowserve Corporation; *U.S. Public*, pg. 658

QUADRA XT2—Tires—Bridgestone/Firestone, Inc.; *Int'l*, pg. 213

QUADRA-POWR—Actuator—Neles-Jamesbury Corp.; *Int'l*, pg. 1428

QUADRAFLEX—Vacuum Cleaner Agitator—Hoover Company; *U.S. Public*, pg. 1065

QUADRAFLEX—Continuous Gas Monitoring System—Scott Aviation; *U.S. Public*, pg. 622

QUADRAFUEL—Multi-Fuel Burner—Cedarapids, Inc.; *U.S. Public*, pg. 1365

QUADRAMATIC—Drive System Having Two or More Synchronous Motors Coupled Through Clutches—General Electric Canada Inc.; *U.S. Public*, pg. 713

QUADRAMATIC—Centrifuge—Western States Machine Company; *U.S. Private*, pg. 1168

QUADRAMET—Bone Pain Palliation—Cytogen Corporation; *U.S. Public*, pg. 471

QUADRANT—In State of Washington—Weyerhaeuser Company; *U.S. Public*, pg. 1764

QUADRAPAK—NONE—Allied Diagnostic Imaging Resources, Inc.; *U.S. Public*, pg. 282

QUADRASTAT—Mechanical Controls—Adams Rite Manufacturing Co.; *U.S. Private*, pg. 17

QUADRATAG—Detection System—3M; *U.S. Public*, pg. 1604

QUADRAWALL—Corrugated Board—Boise Cascade Corporation; *U.S. Public*, pg. 242

QUADREX—Self-Propelled Aerial Work Platform—Mayville Engineering Co., Inc.; *U.S. Private*, pg. 718

QUADRILOK—Tooth Equipment for Earthmoving Buckets—Esco Corporation; *U.S. Private*, pg. 382

QUADRIVE—Shaft Mounted Drive—The Falk Corporation; *U.S. Public*, pg. 1534

QUADRO—Gas Pump—Dresser Industries Wayne Division; *U.S. Public*, pg. 528

QUADROBLOC, PERGABLOC, BLOCPAC—Carton Packaging Systems For Fresh Liquid Food Products—PKL Verpackungssysteme GmbH; *Int'l*, pg. 1020

QUADRUNNER—Motorcycle—American Suzuki Motor Corporation; *Int'l*, pg. 1323

QUADSPORT—Motorcycle—American Suzuki Motor Corporation; *Int'l*, pg. 1323

QUADSTAR—SMT Equipment—Quad Systems Corporation; *U.S. Private*, pg. 898

QUADTRAC—Tractor—Case Corporation; *U.S. Public*, pg. 311

QUAIL HOLLOW—Leisure & Outer Wear—Duck Head Apparel; *U.S. Public*, pg. 498

QUAKE—Cereal—The Quaker Oats Company; *U.S. Public*, pg. 1347

QUAKER—Tray Tables, Screen House & Patio Enclosures—Kay Home Products, Inc.; *U.S. Public*, pg. 1258

QUAKER—Ready-to-Eat Cereals, Puffed Wheat & Puffed Rice, Oatmeal—The Quaker Oats Company; *U.S. Public*, pg. 1347

QUAKER CHEWY—Granola Bars—The Quaker Oats Company; *U.S. Public*, pg. 1347

QUAKER ENRICHED CORN MEAL—Corn Meal—The Quaker Oats Company; *U.S. Public*, pg. 1347

QUAKER ENRICHED WHITE HOMINY GRITS—Grits—The Quaker Oats Company; *U.S. Public*, pg. 1347

QUAKER ENRICHED WHITE HOMINY QUICK GRITS—Grits—The Quaker Oats Company; *U.S. Public*, pg. 1347

QUAKER EXTRA—Instant Oatmeal—The Quaker Oats Company; *U.S. Public*, pg. 1347

QUAKER INSTANT GRITS—Grits—The Quaker Oats Company; *U.S. Public*, pg. 1347

QUAKER MAID—Kitchen & Bathroom Cabinets—Electrolux, AB; *Int'l*, pg. 438

QUAKER OAT BRAN—Ready-to-Eat Cereal—The Quaker Oats Company; *U.S. Public*, pg. 1347

QUAKER OAT SQUARES—Oat Cereal—The Quaker Oats Company; *U.S. Public*, pg. 1347

QUAKER OATMEAL—Cereal—The Quaker Oats Company; *U.S. Public*, pg. 1347

QUAKER OATS—Oats—The Quaker Oats Company; *U.S. Public*, pg. 1347

QUAKER QUAKEROL—Rolling Lubricants—Quaker Chemical Corporation; *U.S. Public*, pg. 1346

QUAKER QUASOL—Metal Cleaners—Quaker Chemical Corporation; *U.S. Public*, pg. 1346

QUAKER RICE CAKES—Rice Cakes—The Quaker Oats Company; *U.S. Public*, pg. 1347

QUAKER SCOTCH BRAND PEARLED BARLEY—Barley—The Quaker Oats Company; *U.S. Public*, pg. 1347

QUAKER STATE—Automotive Products—Quaker State Corporation; *U.S. Public*, pg. 1348

QUAKER STATE MINIT-LUBE, INC.—Fast Lubes—Quaker State Corporation; *U.S. Public*, pg. 1348

QUAKOTE—Dry Film Lubricant—Quaker Chemical Corporation; *U.S. Public*, pg. 1346

QUAL-O-RIMETER—Gas Monitor—Selas Corporation of America; *U.S. Public*, pg. 1454

QUALATEX—Latex Balloons—Continental American Corp.; *U.S. Private*, pg. 267

QUALATEX—Extruded Gum Rubber Tubing & Cord—Minor Rubber Co., Inc.; *U.S. Private*, pg. 751

QUALAWASH—Tank Trailer & Container Washing Service—Chemical Leaman Corporation; *U.S. Private*, pg. 233

QUALCOMM—NONE—QUALCOMM; *U.S. Public*, pg. 1348

QUALCRAFT—Diagnostic Imaging Accessories—Alimed, Inc.; *U.S. Private*, pg. 34

QUALEX—Photofinishing—Qualex Inc.; *U.S. Public*, pg. 551

QUALFORM—Insulated Electrical Wires & Cables—General Cable Corporation; *Int'l*, pg. 1486

QUALHEIM—NONE—Dynamics Corporation of America; *U.S. Public*, pg. 286

QUALHEIM—Commercial Food Service Appliances—Qualheim, Inc.; *U.S. Public*, pg. 286

QUALHEIM BY WARING—Commercial Food Service Equipment—Waring Products; *U.S. Public*, pg. 286

QUALI-FRY—NONE—Alliant Foodservice, Inc.; *U.S. Private*, pg. 244

QUALICHECK—Blood Gas Controls—Radiometer America Inc.; *Int'l*, pg. 1083

QUALIDATE—Dating System, Medical Laboratory Supplies—3M; *U.S. Public*, pg. 1604

QUALIFIED PRODUCTS INTERNATIONAL—Textile Sewing Supplies—Union Special Corp.; *Int'l*, pg. 716

QUALIFLEX—Innersole Material—Texon Materials Inc.; *U.S. Private*, pg. 1079

QUALINEX—One-Piece Ostomy Pouches—Bristol-Myers Squibb Company; *U.S. Public*, pg. 253

QUALIPOINTU.S. PrivateQRP—Radio Broadcast Rating Services—CRN International, Inc.; , pg. 197

QUALITAS—Sanitary Ware—Blue Circle Industries PLC; *Int'l*, pg. 197

QUALITATE—Patent Spring Wheat Flour—Cargill Flour Div.; *U.S. Private*, pg. 210

QUALITE—Cosmetics—Kao Corporation; *Int'l*, pg. 717

QUALITEC—Quality Program Development—Raytheon Engineers & Constructors International, Inc.; *U.S. Public*, pg. 1366

QUALITY—Lighting—JJI Lighting Group Inc.; *Int'l*, pg. 821

QUALITY—Magazine for Quality Assurance Manufacturing Professionals—Reed Elsevier Business Information; *Int'l*, pg. 1095

QUALITY BAKERS EUROPE—Bread & Baked Goods—Goodman Fielder Limited; *Int'l*, pg. 555

QUALITY CARE—NONE—Cleaning Solutions Group/Cello; *U.S. Public*, pg. 1466

QUALITY CARE—Household Spray Cleaners—Sherwin-Williams Diversified Brands, Inc.; *U.S. Public*, pg. 1466

QUALITY CHEKD—Dairy Foods—Quality Chekd Dairies, Inc.; *U.S. Private*, pg. 898

QUALITY CHOICE—Grocery Products—Shurfine International, Inc.; *U.S. Private*, pg. 997

QUALITY CLASSIC SELECTION—Spring & Sparkling Water Products—The Southland Corporation; *Int'l*, pg. 693

QUALITY COVER—Cover Paper—Fox River Paper Company; *U.S. Private*, pg. 422

QUALITY FARE—Food Products—Domgroup Ltd.; *Int'l*, pg. 631

QUALITY FARM & FLEET STORES—Retail Stores—Quality Stores Inc.; *U.S. Private*, pg. 899

THE QUALITY GOES IN BEFORE THE NAME GOES ON—Zenith Products—Zenith Electronics Corp.; *U.S. Public*, pg. 1790

QUALITY HOMES BY DESIGN—Custom Homes—Toll Brothers, Inc.; *U.S. Public*, pg. 1620

QUALITY INNS—Main Stay Suites (Extended Stay Hotels)—Choice Hotels International, Inc.; *U.S. Public*, pg. 351

QUALITY MARKETS—Retail Food Outlets—The Penn Traffic Company; *U.S. Public*, pg. 1270

QUALITY MICRO SYSTEMS—Print Systems—QMS, Inc.; *U.S. Public*, pg. 1346

QUALITY PAK—Packaged Fasteners—Bulldog VSI; *U.S. Public*, pg. 1176

QUALITY-PAK—Industrial Plastic Containers—Ropak Corporation; *Int'l*, pg. 811

QUALITY PAPERBACK BOOK CLUB—Club—Time Warner Inc.; *U.S. Public*, pg. 1610

QUALITY ST.—Chocolates & Confections—Nestle-Rowntree Ltd.; *Int'l*, pg. 921

QUALITY STAR—Grocery & Perishable Products—Shurfine International, Inc.; *U.S. Private*, pg. 997

QUALITY STREET—NONE—Nestle USA; *Int'l*, pg. 916

QUALITY SUITES—Main Stay Suites (Extended Stay Hotels)—Choice Hotels International, Inc.; *U.S. Public*, pg. 351

QUALITY TAPE—Media—Tecmar Technologies, Inc.; *Int'l*, pg. 1361

QUALLA—Hair Care—Palm Beach Beauty Products Co.; *U.S. Private*, pg. 834

QUALMED PLANS FOR HEALTH—HMO Products—Qual-Med, Inc.; *U.S. Public*, pg. 678

QUALNET—Telecommunications Services—Lucent Technologies Inc.; *U.S. Public*, pg. 1017

QUALPETH—Electric Cables—General Cable Corporation; *Int'l*, pg. 1486

QUALY—NONE—Sadia Group; *Int'l*, pg. 1168

QUANTA—Digital Panel Meter—Newport Electronics, Inc.; *U.S. Private*, pg. 816

QUANTAWASH—Diagnostic Products—Abbott Laboratories; *U.S. Public*, pg. 12

QUANTEL—Market Research—Madison Newspapers, Inc.; *U.S. Public*, pg. 984

QUANTIM SYSTEMS—Lateral Files—GF Office Furniture; *U.S. Private*, pg. 435

QUANTITATIVE FIBRINOGEN—Reagents—Ortho Clinical Diagnostic Systems Inc.; *U.S. Public*, pg. 929

QUANTO—Fabric Softener—Benckiser Consumer Products Inc.; *Int'l*, pg. 185

QUANTOPHOS—Liquid Acid Phosphatase Control—Beckman Instruments, Inc.; *U.S. Public*, pg. 199

QUANTOX—Non-Contact Oxide-Monitoring System—Keithley Instruments, Inc.; *U.S. Public*, pg. 946

QUANTREX-ULTRASONIC—Cleaning System—L&R Manufacturing Co.; *U.S. Private*, pg. 638

QUANTUM—Analyzer—Abbott Laboratories; *U.S. Public*, pg. 12

QUANTUM—Contact Lens & Hearing Aid—Bausch & Lomb Incorporated; *U.S. Public*, pg. 194

QUANTUM—Engine Line—Briggs & Stratton Corporation; *U.S. Public*, pg. 252

QUANTUM—Fresh & Saltwater Fishing Equipment—Brunswick Corporation; *U.S. Public*, pg. 265

QUANTUM—Racquetball Eyewear—Ektelon; *U.S. Private*, pg. 884

QUANTUM—Hair Products—Helene Curtis Industries, Inc.; *Int'l*, pg. 1434

QUANTUM—Electrical Enclosures—Killark Electric Manufacturing Co.; *U.S. Public*, pg. 844

QUANTUM—NONE—Eli Lilly and Company; *U.S. Public*, pg. 992

QUANTUM—NONE—Oshkosh Truck Corporation; *U.S. Public*, pg. 1233

QUANTUM—Fishing Tackle—Zebco; *U.S. Public*, pg. 265

QUANTUM GONDOLA—NONE—MEG; *U.S. Private*, pg. 686

QUANTUM OUTERWEAR SYSTEM—Three Jackets in One to Achieve Ultimate Layering Protection—Horace Small Apparel Company; *Int'l*, pg. 635

QUANTUM PLUS—Carpet Tile—Interface Inc.; *U.S. Public*, pg. 889

QUANTUM PLUS—Prescription Drug Plan—PCS Health Systems, Inc.; *U.S. Public*, pg. 993

QUANTUM PRESS—Book Imprint—Bertelsmann AG; *Int'l*, pg. 189

QUANTUM TSI—Customer-Programmable Microcomputer CPU/Switching System—Vicon Industries, Inc.; *U.S. Public*, pg. 1719

QUANTUM II—Analyzer—Abbott Laboratories; *U.S. Public*, pg. 12

QUANTUM II—Contact Lens—Bausch & Lomb Incorporated; *U.S. Public*, pg. 194

QUANTUMATIC—Analyzer—Abbott Laboratories; *U.S. Public*, pg. 12

QUANTUS GRAPHITE RTS—Racquetball Racquet—Ektelon; *U.S. Private*, pg. 884

QUARITE—Acrylic Particle Filled Sheet—Aristech Chemical Corporation; *Int'l*, pg. 872

QUARITE PLUS—Composite Laminate Sheet—Aristech Chemical Corporation; *Int'l*, pg. 872

QUARK—Monthly Japanese Science Magazine—Kodansha Ltd.; *Int'l*, pg. 742

QUARKEXPRESS—Desktop Publishing Program—Quark Inc.; *U.S. Private*, pg. 900

QUARTER HORSE NEWS—Magazine—Shivers Trading & Operating Co.; *U.S. Private*, pg. 994

QUARTER POUNDER—Sandwich—McDonald's Corporation; *U.S. Public*, pg. 1068

QUARTERMASTER—Garage Building—Behlen Mfg. Co.; *U.S. Private*, pg. 130

QUARTET—Printing Paper—Georgia-Pacific Corporation; *U.S. Public*, pg. 735

QUARTET—Videogame—Sega of America Inc.; *Int'l*, pg. 1218

QUARTZ +—Electronic Direct Current Meters—Hobbs Corporation; *Int'l*, pg. 127

QUARTZEL—Quartz Fiber—Saint-Gobain Advanced Materials Corporation; *Int'l*, pg. 1173

QUARTZLINE—Incandescent Lamps—General Electric Canada Inc.; *U.S. Public*, pg. 713

QUARTZLITE—Weatherproof Floodlights for Halogen Lamps—Appleton Electric Co.; *U.S. Public*, pg. 572

QUASAR—Televisions—The Climatic Corp.; *U.S. Private*, pg. 246

QUASAR—TV, VCR, Microwave Ovens, Camcorders, Fax Machines—Matsushita Electric Corporation of America; *Int'l*, pg. 847

QUASAR—Televisions, Microwave Ovens, Audio Systems—Matsushita Electric Industrial Co., Ltd.; *Int'l*, pg. 846

QUATREFOIL DESIGN—NONE—Regal Ware, Inc.; *U.S. Private*, pg. 917

QUATRENE—Quaternary Ammonium Derivative—Henkel Corporation; *Int'l*, pg. 610

QUATREX—Electronic Grade Resins—The Dow Chemical Company; *U.S. Public*, pg. 522

QUATRO PRO—Computer Software—Corel Corporation; *Int'l*, pg. 331

QUATTRO—Spreadsheet Software—Borland International, Inc.; *U.S. Public*, pg. 246

QUATTRO—Power Tools—The Black & Decker Corporation; *U.S. Public*, pg. 233

QUATURN—Cartridge—The Chicago Faucet Co.; *U.S. Private*, pg. 234

QUAZAR—Racquetball Racquet—Ektelon; *U.S. Private*, pg. 884

QUBE—Modular FRL's—Watts Fluidair; *Int'l*, pg. 1243

QUE BUENO—Mexican Food—Nestle S.A.; *Int'l*, pg. 915

QUE BUENO!—Mexican Food Products—Nestle USA; *Int'l*, pg. 916

QUEBEC—Analytical Instrument—Leica, Inc.; *Int'l*, pg. 806

QUEBON—Fluid Milk & Ice Cream—Agropur; *Int'l*, pg. 31

QUEEN—Sporting Goods—Brunswick Bowling & Billiards Corp.; *U.S. Public*, pg. 265

QUEEN—Knives—Servotronics, Inc.; *U.S. Public*, pg. 1462

QUEEN ANNE—Chocolate Covered Cherries & Thin Mints—Hershey Chocolate U.S.A.; *U.S. Public*, pg. 812

QUEEN ANNE—Thin Mints—Hershey Foods Corporation; *U.S. Public*, pg. 811

QUEEN ANNE—NONE—Portland Food Products Company; *U.S. Private*, pg. 876

QUEEN ANNE—Scotch—The Seagram Company Ltd.; *Int'l*, pg. 1214

QUEEN ANNE'S BEST—Chocolates—Hershey Chocolate U.S.A.; *U.S. Public*, pg. 812

QUEEN ANNE'S BEST—Chocolates—Hershey Foods Corporation; *U.S. Public*, pg. 811

QUEEN KRISTINA—Canned Hams—M.H. Greenebaum, Inc.; *U.S. Private*, pg. 477

QUEEN OF MY HEARTS—Chocolate—Brown & Haley; *U.S. Private*, pg. 173

QUEEN'S CHOICE—Hard Ice Cream—International Dairy Queen, Inc.; *U.S. Public*, pg. 220

QUEENS PROPERTIES, INC.—Real Estate Development—J.A. Jones, Inc.; *Int'l*, pg. 633

QUEENSDOWN—Mattresses—Kingsdown, Inc.; *U.S. Private*, pg. 622

QUEER CREEK—Sharpening Stones—Norton Company; *Int'l*, pg. 1173

QUELL—Fire & Safety Equipment—James Hardie Industries Ltd.; *Int'l*, pg. 596

QUENCH GUM—Sports Gum—Mueller Sports Medicine, Inc.; *U.S. Private*, pg. 766

QUENCH SOFT DRINKS—Soft Drinks—Q.U.F. Industries Ltd.; *Int'l*, pg. 1074

QUENCHER—Cosmetics—Del Laboratories, Inc.; *U.S. Public*, pg. 494

QUENCHETTE—Wine Cooler—Labatt Brewing Company Limited; *Int'l*, pg. 679

QUENTY—Cosmetics—Bayer AG; *Int'l*, pg. 171

QUEQUEMINUT—Pastry Ingredient—Royal Gist-Brocades N.V.; *Int'l*, pg. 1142

QUEST—Exercise Tolerance Testing System—Burdick, Inc.; *U.S. Private*, pg. 181

QUEST—NONE—Everest & Jennings, Inc.; *U.S. Public*, pg. 758

QUEST—Text & Cover Paper—Fox River Paper Company; *U.S. Private*, pg. 422

QUEST—Racquetball Racquet—Head USA, Inc.; *U.S. Private*, pg. 514

QUEST—NONE—Integrity Incorporated; *U.S. Public*, pg. 886

QUEST—Electronic Instrument—Intel Corporation; *U.S. Public*, pg. 886

QUEST—Tents, Backpacks, Luggage & Other Related Products—Jinwoong Inc.; *Int'l*, pg. 706

QUEST—Van—Nissan Motor Corporation in U.S.A.; *Int'l*, pg. 945

QUEST—Prime Time Filter, Self-Priming, Air-Eliminating Filter for IV Tubing—Quest Medical, Inc.; *U.S. Public*, pg. 1352

QUEST FOR THE IDEAL MATE—Game—Monarch Avalon, Inc.; *U.S. Public*, pg. 1123

QUESTEX—Chelating Chemicals—Rhone-Poulenc Basic Chemicals Co.; *Int'l*, pg. 1110

QUESTRA—NONE—The Black & Decker Corporation; *U.S. Public*, pg. 233

QUESTRAN—Cardiovascular Pharmaceutical—Astra AB; *Int'l*, pg. 93

QUESTRAN—Cholesterol Reducing Agent—Bristol-Myers Squibb Company; *U.S. Public*, pg. 253

QUESTRAN—Pharmaceutical Product for Lowering of Elevated Serum Cholestrol Levels—Bristol-Myers Squibb U.S. Pharmaceutical Group; *U.S. Public*, pg. 255

QUESTRON—Children's Books & Cassettes—Price Stern Sloan Inc.; *Int'l*, pg. 1215

QUEX—Electronic Instrument—Intel Corporation; *U.S. Public*, pg. 886

QUIBRON—Treatment for Asthma & Bronchitis—Bristol-Myers Squibb Company; *U.S. Public*, pg. 253

QUIBRON—Oral Bronchodilators—Bristol-Myers Squibb U.S. Pharmaceutical Group; *U.S. Public*, pg. 255

QUIBRON PLUS—Oral Bronchodilators—Bristol-Myers Squibb U.S. Pharmaceutical Group; *U.S. Public*, pg. 255

QUIBRON-SR—Oral Bronchodilators—Bristol-Myers Squibb U.S. Pharmaceutical Group; *U.S. Public*, pg. 255

QUIBRON-T—Oral Bronchodilators—Bristol-Myers Squibb U.S. Pharmaceutical Group; *U.S. Public*, pg. 255

QUIBRON-300—Oral Bronchodilators—Bristol-Myers Squibb U.S. Pharmaceutical Group; *U.S. Public*, pg. 255

QUICK—Fecal Cleanser—Dow Hickam Pharmaceuticals Inc.; *U.S. Public*, pg. 1143

QUICK—Hamburger Restaurants—GIB Group; *Int'l*, pg. 532

QUICK—Chocolate Drinks—Nestle S.A.; *Int'l*, pg. 915

QUICK-ALIGN—Letter & Number Labels—W.H. Brady Co.; *U.S. Public*, pg. 250

QUICK & EASY CRAFTS—NDafts Magazine—House of White Birches, Inc.; *U.S. Private*, pg. 542

QUICK & EASY QUILTING—Crafts Magazine—House of White Birches, Inc.; *U.S. Private*, pg. 542

QUICK-AS-A-WINK—Sewer & Draincleaning Businesses—The Dwyer Group; *U.S. Public*, pg. 537

QUICK ASSETS—Cash Management Service with Free Check Writing—The Quick & Reilly Group Inc.; *U.S. Public*, pg. 650

QUICK ASSETS—Cash Management Account Service—Quick & Reilly, Inc.; *U.S. Public*, pg. 650

QUICK BLOT—Kit to Purify/Immobilize mRNA—Schleicher & Schuell, Inc.; *Int'l*, pg. 1206

QUICK BOND—Panel & Foam Adhesive—Ohio Sealants Inc.; *Int'l*, pg. 802

QUICK BOND—Toughened Acrylic Adhesive—Permabond International; *Int'l*, pg. 1435

QUICK CASH—Money Services—New Valley Corporation; *U.S. Public*, pg. 1173

QUICK CASH—Money Services—Western Union Financial Services, Inc.; *U.S. Public*, pg. 631

QUICK CHANGE—Modular Dressing Table/Storage Cubes—Cosco, Inc.; *U.S. Private*, pg. 277

QUICK-CHANGE—Paper Pad Easel—Da-Lite Screen Company, Inc.; *U.S. Private*, pg. 306

QUICK-CHANGE CELL—Radioisotope Detector System—Beckman Instruments, Inc.; *U.S. Public*, pg. 199

QUICK CHECK—Bar Code Verifiers—PSC Inc.; *U.S. Public*, pg. 1245

QUICK CHEF—Microwave Cookware—Regal Ware, Inc.; *U.S. Private*, pg. 917

QUICK CLAIM—Patient Transaction Slip for M.D. & DDS—Safeguard Business Systems, Inc.; *U.S. Private*, pg. 960

QUICK CLASSICS—Refrigerated Sauces & Marinades—McCormick & Company, Incorporated; *U.S. Public*, pg. 1066

QUICK/CLICK—Plastic Boxes—Pass & Seymour/Legrand; *Int'l*, pg. 806

QUICK COLLECT—Money Services—New Valley Corporation; *U.S. Public*, pg. 1173

QUICK COLLECT—Money Services—Western Union Financial Services, Inc.; *U.S. Public*, pg. 631

QUICK CONNECT—Plant Ties—Security Lawn & Garden Co.; *U.S. Private*, pg. 397

QUICK CONTROL—Weight Loss Program—Weight Watchers International, Inc.; *U.S. Public*, pg. 806

QUICK DELIGHT—Microwaveable Soups and Entrees—Stegner Food Products Co.; *U.S. Private*, pg. 1039

QUICK-DRAW—Card Case—Hugo Bosca Co., Inc.; *U.S. Private*, pg. 160

QUICK DRAW—Punch Driver—Greenlee Textron; *U.S. Public*, pg. 1589

QUICK DRAW—Hot Melt Drawing Compound—The Lubrizol Corporation; *U.S. Public*, pg. 1016

QUICK DRAW—Plastic Trash Bags—Reynolds Metals Company; *U.S. Public*, pg. 1385

QUICK DRY—Undercoater—Jones Blair Company; *U.S. Private*, pg. 596

QUICK EDGE TRIM—Vinyl U Shaped Push On Trim—The Standard Products Company; *U.S. Public*, pg. 1504

QUICK EGG CUSTARD—Dessert Mix—Novartis Nutrition Corporation; *Int'l*, pg. 974

QUICK ELASTIC—Starches—A.E. Staley Manufacturing Co.; *Int'l*, pg. 1356

QUICK/ENTRY—Process for Entering Cable into Plastic Boxes—Pass & Seymour/Legrand; *Int'l*, pg. 806

QUICK-FINISH—Photographic Processing Chemicals—Eastman Kodak Company; *U.S. Public*, pg. 550

QUICK-FIT—Laboratory Equipment Accessory—Galileo Corp.; *U.S. Public*, pg. 698

QUICK FIT SYRINGE DISPOSABLES—For Computer Tomography and MR—Medrad, Inc.; *Int'l*, pg. 1204

QUICK GEL SUPER GLUE—Adhesive—Loctite Corporation; *Int'l*, pg. 611

QUICK-GRIP—Clamping Products—American Tool Companies, Inc.; *U.S. Private*, pg. 63

QUICK HEAT—Instant Heat Hair Setter—Windmere-Durable Holdings; *U.S. Public*, pg. 1771

QUICK HOOK—Luggage—Lark Luggage Company, Inc.; *U.S. Public*, pg. 1430

QUICK LOCK—Fasteners—Southtec, Inc.; *U.S. Private*, pg. 1015

QUICK MEAN—32 Item line of Sandwiches—Hormel Foods Corp.; *U.S. Public*, pg. 840

QUICK MOUNT INSTALLATION—Mounting Service Bodies—The Knapheide Mfg. Co.; *U.S. Private*, pg. 626

QUICK'N CRISPY—Oven Prepared French Fries—J.R. Simplot Company; *U.S. Private*, pg. 1002

QUICK'N EASY—Furniture Assembly System—Bush Industries Inc.; *U.S. Public*, pg. 270

QUICK-N-EASY—Ready To Use Ceiling Texture—USG Corporation; *U.S. Public*, pg. 1660

QUICK 'N' EASY CROCHETING—Adult Continuity Books—Golden Books Family Entertainment Inc.; *U.S. Public*, pg. 749

QUICK N GENTLE—Eye Makeup Remover—American International Industries; *U.S. Private*, pg. 57

QUICK 'N HEARTY—Microwaveable Oatmeal—The Quaker Oats Company; *U.S. Public*, pg. 1347

QUICK-OPE—Envelopes—Tension Envelope Corp.; *U.S. Private*, pg. 1077

QUICK PEARLED BARLEY—Barley—The Quaker Oats Company; *U.S. Public*, pg. 1347

QUICK PICK—NONE—U.S. Surgical Corp.; *U.S. Public*, pg. 1687

QUICK-PULSE PROGRAMMING—Electronic Instrument—Intel Corporation; *U.S. Public*, pg. 886

QUICK-REP—NONE—Ballard Medical Products; *U.S. Public*, pg. 171

QUICK RISE—Yeast—Universal Foods Corporation; *U.S. Public*, pg. 1695

QUICK SCAN—Recorders—Dwyer Instruments Inc.; *U.S. Private*, pg. 350

QUICK SCAN—Handheld Laser Scanner—PSC Inc.; *U.S. Public*, pg. 1245

QUICK SCREEN—Radon Detectors—Landauer, Inc.; *U.S. Public*, pg. 977

QUICK-SEAL—Centrifuge Tubes—Beckman Instruments, Inc.; *U.S. Public*, pg. 199

QUICK-SEAL—Pressure Sensitive Tape—Georgia-Pacific Corporation; *U.S. Public*, pg. 735

QUICK SEAL—Fasteners—R&B, Inc.; *U.S. Public*, pg. 1354

QUICK SEAL—Plastic Bags—Reynolds Metals Company; *U.S. Public*, pg. 1385

QUICK-SEAL—Test Plugs—Tuthill Pump; *U.S. Private*, pg. 1111

QUICK-SET—Dies, Gages, Adjustable Reamers—Greenfield Industries; *U.S. Public*, pg. 950

QUICK-SET—Adjustable Oscillating Sprinkler—L.R. Nelson Corporation; *U.S. Private*, pg. 790

QUICK-SPRAY—Blockout Inks & Adhesives—Diagraph Corporation; *U.S. Private*, pg. 330

QUICK START—Diesel Starting Unit—Sycamore Plant; *U.S. Public*, pg. 444

QUICK STATION—NONE—QST Industries, Inc.; *U.S. Private*, pg. 897

QUICK STICK—NONE—National Sea Products Limited; *Int'l*, pg. 909

QUICK STOP—Chain Brake System—Stihl Inc.; *Int'l*, pg. 1301

QUICK TAN—Cosmetics—Palm Beach Beauty Products Co.; *U.S. Private*, pg. 834

QUICK TEEJET—Spray Nozzle—Spraying Systems Co.; *U.S. Private*, pg. 1026

QUICK 10—Auto Service Center—Investors Management Corp.; *U.S. Private*, pg. 574

QUICK THROTTLE—Magazine—Paisano Publications, Inc.; *U.S. Private*, pg. 834

QUICK TRASH—Garbage Bag Holder—Pacific Handy Cutter, Inc.; *U.S. Private*, pg. 831

QUICK TRIM—NONE—The Black & Decker Corporation; *U.S. Public*, pg. 233

QUICK-TURN—Retail Building Supply Store Services—Georgia-Pacific Corporation; *U.S. Public*, pg. 735

QUICK-TURN—Financial Information Program—Success Development International; *U.S. Private*, pg. 1048

QUICK-TURN TOTAL PANELING PROGRAM—Retail Building Supply Store Services—Georgia-Pacific Corporation; *U.S. Public*, pg. 735

QUICK-TWIST—Brushes—Mill-Rose Company; *U.S. Private*, pg. 746

QUICK VIEW PLUS—Information Management Tools—INSO Corporation; *U.S. Public*, pg. 882

QUICK VUE—Infectious Disease Products—Quidel Corporation; *U.S. Public*, pg. 1352

QUICK WAY—On-Line Investment Service—The Quick & Reilly Group Inc.; *U.S. Public*, pg. 650

QUICK WHIP—Topping—Lever Brothers Co.; *Int'l*, pg. 1435

QUICK WHIP—Topping—Unilever Plc; *Int'l*, pg. 1433

QUICK WORK-FACTOR—Manufacturing Analysis System—Science Management Corporation; *U.S. Public*, pg. 1717

QUICKARGILE—Facial Skin Care Products—SmithKline Beecham plc; *Int'l*, pg. 1264

QUICKBID—NONE—CACI International Inc; *U.S. Public*, pg. 272

QUICKCAM—Digital Video Camera—Connectix Corporation; *U.S. Private*, pg. 264

QUICKEDI—Computer Product—International Business Machines Corporation; *U.S. Public*, pg. 895

QUICKER CLICKER—Pencils—Pentel of America, Ltd.; *Int'l*, pg. 1035

QUICKETT—Dry Gum Business Forms—Brown-Bridge; *U.S. Public*, pg. 1022

QUICKFINISH—Power Tools—The Black & Decker Corporation; *U.S. Public*, pg. 233

QUICKFIT—Scientific Product-Glass—J. Bibby & Sons Plc; *Int'l*, pg. 152

QUICKFLASH—Radial Artery Catheter—Arrow International, Inc.; *U.S. Public*, pg. 135

QUICKGEN—Software—Symbol Technologies, Portable Systems Division; *U.S. Public*, pg. 1546

QUICKIE—NONE—Berg Electronics; *U.S. Public*, pg. 212

QUICKIE—Manual & Power Wheelchairs—Sunrise Medical, Inc.; *U.S. Public*, pg. 1535

QUICKIES—Make-Up Remover Pads—SmithKline Beecham plc; *Int'l*, pg. 1264

QUICKJET—Nozzles—Spraying Systems Co.; *U.S. Private*, pg. 1026

QUICKLIGHTS—Recessed Lighting Products—Thomas Industries Inc.; *U.S. Public*, pg. 1598

QUICKLUB—Industrial Lubrication Equipment—Lincoln Industrial; *U.S. Public*, pg. 1273

QUICKMODEL—Software—Alias Wavefront; *U.S. Public*, pg. 1474

QUICKPRINT PRODUCTS—Publication for Buyers at Small Commercial & Franchise Quick-Printers—Reed Elsevier Business Information; *Int'l*, pg. 1095

QUICKREADER—Reader Interface Barcode to Computer—McRae Industries, Inc.; *U.S. Public*, pg. 1073

QUICKSAND—Gum—Fleer-Skybox International Inc.; *U.S. Public*, pg. 1052

QUICKSET—Industrial Products—Email Limited; *Int'l*, pg. 450

QUICKSET—Jam Thickener—Tate & Lyle PLC; *Int'l*, pg. 1356

QUICKSHADE—Software Providing Simplified View of the Surface of a Design—Alias Wavefront; *U.S. Public*, pg. 1474

QUICKSILVER—BB's—Daisy Manufacturing Company, Inc.; *U.S. Private*, pg. 308

QUICKSILVER—Pens—The Gillette Company; *U.S. Public*, pg. 743

QUICKSILVER—Full Glue Installed Sheet Vinyl Flooring—Mannington Resilient Floors; *U.S. Private*, pg. 700

QUICKSILVER—Marine Parts & Accessories—Mercury Marine; *U.S. Public*, pg. 265

QUICKSIM—NONE—GenRad, Inc.; *U.S. Public*, pg. 731

QUICKSNAP—Connector—Lucent Technologies Inc.; *U.S. Public*, pg. 1017

QUICKSON—Printing Ink—Van Son Holland Ink Corp. of America; *U.S. Private*, pg. 1133

QUICKSOURCE—Telephone Information Service—SBC Communications Inc.; *U.S. Public*, pg. 1415

QUICKSTART FOR DATA ENTRY—NONE—American Management Systems, Inc.; *U.S. Public*, pg. 86

QUICKSTART FOR MVS—NONE—BMC Software, Inc.; *U.S. Public*, pg. 162

QUICKSTROKES—Handprint Character Recognition API—Mitek Systems, Inc.; *U.S. Public*, pg. 1117

QUICKTEST—NONE—GenRad, Inc.; *U.S. Public*, pg. 731

QUICKTITE—High Performance Super Glue—Loctite Corp. North American Group; *Int'l*, pg. 611

QUICKVOICE—Satellite Communications Modem—The Titan Corporation; *U.S. Public*, pg. 1618

QUICKWAY PLUS—On-Line Software—Quick & Reilly, Inc.; *U.S. Public*, pg. 650

QUICKWRITER—Business System—International Business Machines Corporation; *U.S. Public*, pg. 895

QUIDDITY—Open Architecture, On-Line Relational Marketing Database—May & Speh, Inc.; *U.S. Public*, pg. 1063

QUIET—Business Product—International Business Machines Corporation; *U.S. Public*, pg. 895

QUIET-LATCH—Stake Rack Connector—The Knapheide Mfg. Co.; *U.S. Private*, pg. 626

QUIET MOMENTS—Greeting Cards—American Greetings Corporation; *U.S. Public*, pg. 77

THE QUIET ONE—Surface Planer—Powermatic; *U.S. Public*, pg. 502

QUIET/SLIDE—Baseboard Radiation—Edwards Engineering Corporation; *U.S. Private*, pg. 365

QUIET THOUGHTS—Greeting Cards & Stationery—American Greetings Corporation; *U.S. Public*, pg. 77

QUIET THOUGHTS—Greeting Cards—American Greetings U.S. Greeting Card Division; *U.S. Public*, pg. 78

QUIET TIP—Ear Plugs—Aearo Company; *U.S. Private*, pg. 23

QUIET TOUCH—Hairpainting—Bristol-Myers Squibb Company; *U.S. Public*, pg. 253

QUIET TOUCH—Hair Coloring—Clairol, Inc.; *U.S. Public*, pg. 254

QUIETLY CHAMOMILE—Herbal Tea Bags—Thomas J. Lipton Company; *Int'l*, pg. 1435

QUIETUNK—Elevator Hoistway Cable/Chain—BIW Cable Systems, Inc.; *Int'l*, pg. 417

QUIETWRITER—Business Product—International Business Machines Corporation; *U.S. Public*, pg. 895

QUIETZONE—Glass Fiber Insulation Used for Sound Control—Owens Corning; *U.S. Public*, pg. 1236

QUIK—Powdered Chocolate Mix—Nestle USA; *Int'l*, pg. 916

QUIK-CALC—ATC Multilayer Capacitor Calculator Disk—American Technical Ceramics Corp.; *U.S. Public*, pg. 93

QUIK-CHEK—Plastic Grocer Sack—Sonoco Products Company; *U.S. Public*, pg. 1485

QUIK-CLEAN—Nonstick Broiler Pan—Ekco Housewares, Inc.; *U.S. Public*, pg. 566

QUIK-COMM—Electronic Business Communication Services—General Electric Canada Inc.; *U.S. Public*, pg. 713

QUIK DROP—Video Return System—Blockbuster Entertainment Group; *U.S. Private*, pg. 775

QUIK-FIX—Emergency Denture Repair—Brimms Inc.; *U.S. Private*, pg. 169

QUIK FLEX—Mortar—TEC Incorporated; *U.S. Public*, pg. 687

QUIK-GO—Urethane Belts—Fenner Drives; *U.S. Private*, pg. 400

QUIK-HOOK—Drapery Hooks—Kirsch; *U.S. Public*, pg. 1176

QUIK JON—Sewage Removal System—Zoeller Co.; *U.S. Private*, pg. 1207

QUIK-LOK—Wiring Terminals—Eagle Electric Mfg. Co., Inc.; *U.S. Private*, pg. 354

QUIK-LOK CORD—NONE—Milwaukee Electric Tool Corp.; *Int'l*, pg. 96

QUIK-LOOK—Difibrillation Paddles—Physio-Control Corporation; *U.S. Public*, pg. 1294

QUIK-MATE—Plastic Grocer Sack—Sonoco Products Company; *U.S. Public*, pg. 1485

QUIK-PACE—External Transchest Pacing Electrodes—Physio-Control Corporation; *U.S. Public*, pg. 1294

QUIK-PEP—Pharmaceutical Products—Thompson Medical Company, Inc.; *U.S. Private*, pg. 1083

QUIK PICK 48 HOUR SHIPMENT SYSTEM—48 Hour Shipment of Selected ATC Products—American Technical Ceramics Corp.; *U.S. Public*, pg. 93

QUIK-SEPT—Disinfecting System for Contact Lenses—Bausch & Lomb Incorporated; *U.S. Public*, pg. 194

QUIK SHIP—Expedited Delivery Service—John H. Harland Company; *U.S. Public*, pg. 785

QUIK-STIK—Laminating Agent on Core Surface—Sonoco Products Company; *U.S. Public*, pg. 1485

QUIK TIER—Boltless Structural Pallet Rack—Jarke Corporation; *U.S. Private*, pg. 583

QUIK-TO-FIX—NONE—Gorges/Quik-To-Fix Foods; *U.S. Private*, pg. 465

QUIK-PICK—Repair Part Kits—J.A. Sexauer, Inc.; *U.S. Private*, pg. 352

QUIKLOK—Fastening Device—Telsmith, Inc.; *U.S. Public*, pg. 141

QUIKLOOK—Electronics—National Semiconductor Corporation; *U.S. Public*, pg. 1159

QUIKSTIK—Pressure Sensitive Tapes—Gould Packaging, Inc.; *U.S. Public*, pg. 466

QUIKTREE—Cantilever Rack—Jarke Corporation; *U.S. Private*, pg. 583

QUIKTRIP—Convenience Stores—QuikTrip Corporation; *U.S. Private*, pg. 901

QUIKUT—Knives—Douglas/Quikut; *U.S. Public*, pg. 217

QUIKUT—Premium Cutlery—The Scott Fetzer Company; *U.S. Public*, pg. 217

QUIKWASH—Diagnostic Products—Abbott Laboratories; *U.S. Public*, pg. 12

QUIKWRAP—Pressure Sensitive Tapes—Gould Packaging, Inc.; *U.S. Public*, pg. 466

QUILITE—Blanket—Johns Manville Corporation; *U.S. Public*, pg. 927

QUILL—Books—The Hearst Corporation; *U.S. Private*, pg. 515

QUILL PAPERBACKS—Trade Paperback Books—William Morrow & Co., Inc.; *U.S. Private*, pg. 515

QUILLY—Greeting Cards—American Greetings Corporation; *U.S. Public*, pg. 77

QUILONIUM-R—Psychotrophic—SmithKline Beecham Research Limited; *Int'l*, pg. 1266

QUILT RAP—Sandwich Wrap—Fort James Corporation; *U.S. Public*, pg. 670

QUILT WORLD—Crafts Publications—House of White Birches, Inc.; *U.S. Private*, pg. 542

QUILTED CRYSTAL—Glass Jar Design—Alltrista Corporation; *U.S. Public*, pg. 56

QUILTED CRYSTAL—Glassware—Ball Corporation; *U.S. Public*, pg. 170

QUILTED NORTHERN—Bathroom Tissue—Consumer Products Business; *U.S. Public*, pg. 671

QUILTER'S TREASURY—NONE—House of White Birches, Inc.; *U.S. Private*, pg. 542

QUILTOG—Cold Weather Clothing—Refrigiwear, Inc.; *U.S. Private*, pg. 917

QUINCY—Air Compressors—Coltec Industries Inc.; *U.S. Public*, pg. 401

QUINCY FARMS—Fresh Mushrooms—Quincy Corp.; *U.S. Public*, pg. 1545

QUINCY'S FAMILY STEAKHOUSE—Restaurant Chain—Advantica Restaurant Group, Inc.; *U.S. Public*, pg. 22

QUINIDEX—Cardiovascular Drug—American Home Products Corporation; *U.S. Public*, pg. 79

QUINIDEX—Antiarrhythmic Agent—Wyeth-Ayerst Laboratories, Inc.; *U.S. Public*, pg. 80

QUINLAN—Pretzels—Quinlan Pretzel Co., Inc.; *U.S. Private*, pg. 158

QUINLAN—Pretzels—Wise Foods, Inc.; *U.S. Private*, pg. 157

QUINODIS—Antibacterial—Roche Holding Ltd.; *Int'l*, pg. 1119

QUINORA—Quinidine, Sulfate Tablets—Key Pharmaceuticals; *U.S. Public*, pg. 1438

QUINSANA—Foot Care Powders—The Mennen Company; *U.S. Public*, pg. 397

QUINTA DA CORTE—NONE—Delaforce Sons & Ca Vinhos Lda.; *Int'l*, pg. 409

QUINTET—Warewash Products & Related Dispensing Equipment—Puritan/Churchill Chemical Company; *U.S. Private*, pg. 895

QUINTOLUBRIC—Fire-Resistant & Specialty Hydraulic Fluids—Quaker Chemical Corporation; *U.S. Public*, pg. 1346

QUINTON—Treadmills And Other Fitness Equipment—American Home Products Corporation; *U.S. Public*, pg. 79

QUINTON HAZELL—Clutches, Transmission Parts, Steering & Suspension System Components—Echlin Inc.; *U.S. Public*, pg. 560

QUINTRON—Paging Infrastructure Equipment System—Glenayre Technologies, Inc.; *U.S. Public*, pg. 746

QUINTS DOLLS—Dolls—Tyco Toys, Inc.; *U.S. Public*, pg. 1058

QUINTUS—Hydraulic Presses—ABB AB; *Int'l*, pg. 7

QUISP—Cereal—The Quaker Oats Company; *U.S. Public*, pg. 1347

QUITEQUIET—Telecommunications Products—Lucent Technologies Inc.; *U.S. Public*, pg. 1017

QUIXPENSER—Hard Ice Cream Dispenser—A & S Tribal Industries; *U.S. Private*, pg. 1

QUOIZEL, INC—Manufacturer of Lamps & Lighting Fixtures—Quoizel Inc.; *U.S. Private*, pg. 901

QUORUM—Perfume—International Cosmetics Co., Ltd.; *Int'l*, pg. 684

QUORUM—Teleconferencing Equipment—Lucent Technologies Inc.; *U.S. Public*, pg. 1017

QUORUM-PUIG—Men's Cologne—Paco Rabanne Compar; *Int'l*, pg. 1073

QUOTA—Weight Control—The Quaker Oats Company; *U.S. Public*, pg. 1347

QUOTE FINDER—Stock Quote Service—The Mead Corporation; *U.S. Public*, pg. 1074

QUOTE SAVER—Stock Quote Service—The Mead Corporation; *U.S. Public*, pg. 1074

QUOTECHECK—Quotation Checking Feature—The Mead Corporation; *U.S. Public*, pg. 1074

QUOTESOCKETS—NONE—PC Quote, Inc.; *U.S. Public*, pg. 1240

QUOTESOCKETS—Development Tool—PC Quote, Inc.; *U.S. Public*, pg. 1240

QURON—Herbicide—The Dow Chemical Company; *U.S. Public*, pg. 522

QWENE—Pickling Aids & Associated Metal Surface Conditioners—Quaker Chemical Corporation; *U.S. Public*, pg. 1346

QWERL—Rolling Adjuncts & Metal Surface Conditioners—Quaker Chemical Corporation; *U.S. Public*, pg. 1346

QWIK-GARD—Ground Fault Interrupters—Square D Company; *Int'l*, pg. 1208

QWIK SINK—Tapered Leader—Outdoor Technologies Group; *U.S. Private*, pg. 822

R

R—Equipment—Halliburton Energy Services; *U.S. Public*, pg. 776

R.A. BRIGGS—Broadwoven Fabrics—R.A. Briggs & Co.; *U.S. Private*, pg. 536

RACF—Computer Product—International Business Machines Corporation; *U.S. Public*, pg. 895

RAF SYSTEM—Lounge Seating—Vecta; *U.S. Private*, pg. 1038

RAM CARD—PCMCIA Cards—Epson America Inc.; *Int'l*, pg. 1219

RAP—Seismographic Data Analysis—Litton Industries, Inc.; *U.S. Public*, pg. 1002

RAR—Photo Film—Eastman Kodak Company; *U.S. Public*, pg. 550

RASL—Computer Programming Language Software Component—Datapoint Corporation; *Int'l*, pg. 384

R & F—Pasta—Borden, Inc.; *U.S. Private*, pg. 157

R & F ALLOY WIRE—Wire—Pegasus International Corporation; *U.S. Private*, pg. 1046

R & R—Investment Casting Materials—Dentsply International Inc.; *U.S. Public*, pg. 498

R & R—Fragrances—Halston Enterprises, Inc.; *U.S. Private*, pg. 536

R & S STRAUSS—Auto Parts & Service Stores—Strauss Discount Auto; *U.S. Private*, pg. 1046

RB—Boilers & Heaters—Babcock & Wilcox Co.; *U.S. Public*, pg. 1068

RB-50—Sunglasses—Bausch & Lomb Incorporated; *U.S. Public*, pg. 194

RB-48 SWEEPER—Road Machinery—Rosco Manufacturing Co.; *U.S. Private*, pg. 944

RB199—Military Engine—Rolls-Royce Military Aero Engines Ltd.; *Int'l*, pg. 1127

R-BOARD—Residential Polyiso foam Insulation—Atlas Roofing Corp.; *U.S. Private*, pg. 96

RCA—Major Appliances—G.E. Appliances; *U.S. Public*, pg. 710

RCA—Electronic Products—General Electric Company; *U.S. Public*, pg. 709

RCA DIGITAL SATELLITE SYSTEM (DSS)—Satellite for Television Service—Thomson Consumer Electronics Inc.; *Int'l*, pg. 1383

RCA RECORDS—Records—Bertelsmann AG; *Int'l*, pg. 189

RCBS—Reloading Equipment—Blount, Inc. Sporting Equipment Group; *U.S. Public*, pg. 238

RCBS—Reloading Equipment for Guns—Blount International, Inc.; *U.S. Public*, pg. 237

R/C BANDIT—Radio Control—Tyco Toys, Inc.; *U.S. Public*, pg. 1058

RC COLA—Soft Drink—Triarc Companies, Inc.; *U.S. Public*, pg. 1634

R. C. COOPER'S—Deli-Style Restaurant—Wall Street Deli, Inc.; *U.S. Public*, pg. 1734

R/C FAST TRAXX—Radio Control—Tyco Toys, Inc.; *U.S. Public*, pg. 1058

RC 50—Red Cell Filter—Pall Corporation; *U.S. Public*, pg. 1253

RC 400—Leukocyte Removal Filter—Pall Corporation; *U.S. Public*, pg. 1253

RCH 90—NONE—Callaway Golf Company; *U.S. Public*, pg. 294

RCI—Poke-Thru—Walker Systems, Inc.; *U.S. Private*, pg. 1184

RCITRAVEL—Travel Agency—Resort Condominiums International; *U.S. Public*, pg. 322

RCITRAVEL PLUS—Exit Sales Program—Resort Condominiums International; *U.S. Public*, pg. 322

RCM-100—Radial Compression Module—Millipore Corporation; *U.S. Public*, pg. 1112

RC 100—Red Cell Filter—Pall Corporation; *U.S. Public*, pg. 1253

RCPC—Royal China & Porcelain Companies Giftware—The Royal China & Porcelain Companies Inc.; *U.S. Private*, pg. 948

RC PRINT DRYER—RC Print Dry System—Falcon Safety Products Inc.; *U.S. Private*, pg. 392

RCR—Retroactive Claim Reprocessing—Health Management Systems, Inc.; *U.S. Public*, pg. 802

RCR RADIO COMMUNICATIONS REPORT—Newspaper—Crain Communications, Inc.; *U.S. Private*, pg. 284

RCII—Photographic Paper—Eastman Kodak Company; *U.S. Public*, pg. 550

R/C WILD THING—Radio Control—Tyco Toys, Inc.; *U.S. Public*, pg. 1058

R-CHANGE ACCUM—NONE—BMC Software, Inc.; *U.S. Public*, pg. 162

R-D—Root Destroyer—Hercules Chemical Co., Inc.; *U.S. Private*, pg. 523

RDC PROCESS—Pulping Machines—Beloit Corporation; *U.S. Public*, pg. 789

R.D.D.—Ruminal Delivery Device, Elanco—Eli Lilly and Company; *U.S. Public*, pg. 992

RDF—Remote Duplicate Database Facility—Tandem Computers Inc.; *U.S. Public*, pg. 417

RD-4A—Digital Microwave Radio System—Northern Telecom Limited; *Int'l*, pg. 968

RDH—Pulping System—Beloit Corporation; *U.S. Public*, pg. 789

RDI—Refrigeration Systems—The Manitowoc Company, Inc.; *U.S. Public*, pg. 1040

RDP—Rust Preventive—Chem-Trend Incorporated; *Int'l*, pg. 235

RDS—Rader Disk Screen—Beloit Corporation; *U.S. Public*, pg. 789

R.D.S.—NONE—Carpenter Technology Corporation; *U.S. Public*, pg. 307

RDS—Remote Device Support for Extending Distance Between IBM Host & Peripherals—Network Systems Corporation; *U.S. Public*, pg. 1522

RD-6A—Digital Microwave Radio System—Northern Telecom Limited; *Int'l*, pg. 968

RD305—Inspecting, Reconditioning & Restoring Turbine Engines—Teleflex Incorporated; *U.S. Public*, pg. 1569

RE—Electric Motors—Reuland Electric Company; *U.S. Private*, pg. 925

REA CONSTRUCTION COMPANY—Construction Company-Roadbuilders—J.A. Jones, Inc.; *Int'l*, pg. 633

REA MAGNET WIRE—Overall Product Description—Rea Magnet Wire Company, Inc.; *U.S. Private*, pg. 913

R-E-A 70—Liquid Electrostatic Gun—Illinois Tool Works Inc.; *U.S. Public*, pg. 865

REI—Registered DBA—Recreational Equipment, Inc.; *U.S. Private*, pg. 914

REI Coop—Registered DBA—Recreational Equipment, Inc.; *U.S. Private*, pg. 914

REM—NONE—Pfizer Inc.; *U.S. Public*, pg. 1281

REX—Meat & Cheese Products—Bar-S Foods Co.; *U.S. Private*, pg. 114

REX—Desserts, Baking Aids—Bestfoods; *U.S. Public*, pg. 223

REX—Mechanical Power Equipment—Rexnord Corporation; *Int'l*, pg. 127

REZ—Interior/Exterior Wood & Masonry Stains & Sealer—PPG Industries, Inc.; *U.S. Public*, pg. 1245

R-F—Pasta Products—Ravarino & Freschi, Inc.; *U.S. Private*, pg. 158

RF—Non-asbestos on-road brakes—Universal Composites-U.S.C.; *U.S. Private*, pg. 1126

RF ABLATR—Catheter—Medtronic, Inc.; *U.S. Public*, pg. 1082

RFD LATEX—Barn Paint—Jones Blair Company; *U.S. Private*, pg. 596

RF DESIGN—Publication on Radio Frequency—Intertec Publishing; *U.S. Public*, pg. 1327

RF DESIGN—Monthly Publications—Intertec Publishing; *U.S. Public*, pg. 1328

RF GAIN—Electronics—Richardson Electronics, Ltd.; *U.S. Public*, pg. 1387

RFI—Interference Filters—Del Global Technologies; *U.S. Public*, pg. 493

RF MARINR—Electrophysiology Catheter—Medtronic, Inc.; *U.S. Public*, pg. 1082

RFVC—Radial Four Valve Combustion Chamber—American Honda Motor Co., Inc. Motorcycle Division; *Int'l*, pg. 634

RFX—Lightweight Nonwoven Fabric—Amoco Chemicals; *U.S. Public*, pg. 102

R-5—Skis—Mizuno Corporation; *Int'l*, pg. 884

R/FLEX—Flexible Laminate Material—Rogers Corporation; *U.S. Public*, pg. 1402

RG—Lecithins—Central Soya Company, Inc., *Int'l*, pg. 324

RG—Insulators—Lapp Insulator Company; *U.S. Private*, pg. 473

R-GEN—Pharmaceutical Products—Galderma Laboratories, Inc.; *Int'l*, pg. 819

R-GUARD—Wallboard—Georgia-Pacific Corporation; *U.S. Public*, pg. 735

RHC—Store Fixtures—RHC/Spacemaster Corporation; *U.S. Public*, pg. 904

RHF—Rheumatoid Factor Reagent Kit—Beckman Instruments, Inc.; *U.S. Public*, pg. 199

RH-HR—Typing Reagents—Ortho Clinical Diagnostic Systems Inc.; *U.S. Public*, pg. 929

RHI CONSULTING—Information Technology Staffing—Robert Half International Inc.; *U.S. Public*, pg. 774

RHI MANAGEMENT RESOURCES—Senior-Level Project-Based Financial Staffing—Robert Half International Inc.; *U.S. Public*, pg. 774

RIP—Raster Image Processor—Linotype-Hell Company; *Int'l*, pg. 604

RIS LITE—Athletic Equipment—Bike Athletic Co.; *U.S. Private*, pg. 143

RIT—Tints, Dyes & Fabric Treatments—Bestfoods; *U.S. Public*, pg. 223

R.J. COLT—Footwear—Jimlar Corporation; *U.S. Private*, pg. 587

RJ-100—Styrene-Allyl Alcohol Resin—Solutia Inc.; *U.S. Public*, pg. 1483

RJ-101—Styrene-Allyl Alcohol Resins—Monsanto Company; *U.S. Public*, pg. 1124

RJ-101—Styrene-Allyl Alcohol Resin—Solutia Inc.; *U.S. Public*, pg. 1483

RJR NABISCO—Tradename—RJR Nabisco Holdings Corp.; *U.S. Public*, pg. 1354

R. JOHNS—NONE—Commemorative Brands, Inc.; *U.S. Private*, pg. 258

R.J.'s GINSENG—Beer—R.J. Corr Naturals, Inc.; *U.S. Private*, pg. 276

RKG—Automotive Parts—Cinch Connector Division; *Int'l*, pg. 786

RKL—Pinch Valves—Robbins & Myers, Inc.; *U.S. Public*, pg. 1393

RKO CENTURY WARNER THEATRES—Motion Picture Theaters—Cineplex Odeon Corporation; *Int'l*, pg. 292

R-KIVE—Filing System—Fellowes Manufacturing Co.; *U.S. Private*, pg. 400

RL—Automobile—American Honda Motor Co., Inc.; *Int'l*, pg. 634

R.L. POLK & CO—Marketing Services Motor Vehicle Statistics & Publishers of Directories—R.L. Polk & Co.; *U.S. Private*, pg. 874

RLX—Fan—CTB International Corp.; *U.S. Public*, pg. 284

R-LINE—Equipment—Halliburton Energy Services; *U.S. Public*, pg. 776

RMAC—NONE—Lindsay Manufacturing Company; *U.S. Public*, pg. 999

RMC—Aluminum & Aluminum Alloy Ingots & Extrusions—Reynolds Metals Company; *U.S. Public*, pg. 1385

RMF—Computer Product—International Business Machines Corporation; *U.S. Public*, pg. 895

RMI—Heating Cable—Raychem Corporation; *U.S. Public*, pg. 1362

RMI—Plastic Products—Rotonics Manufacturing Inc.; *U.S. Public*, pg. 1406

RMI-C—Plastic Products—Rotonics Manufacturing Inc.; *U.S. Public*, pg. 1406

RMI-D—Plastic Products—Rotonics Manufacturing Inc.; *U.S. Public*, pg. 1406

RMI-F—Plastic Products—Rotonics Manufacturing Inc.; *U.S. Public*, pg. 1406

RMI-I—Plastic Products—Rotonics Manufacturing Inc.; *U.S. Public*, pg. 1406

RMI-W—Plastic Products—Rotonics Manufacturing Inc.; *U.S. Public*, pg. 1406

RMS—Computer Operating System—Datapoint Corporation; *Int'l*, pg. 384

RMVA—Remote Mechanical Valve Actuator Systems—Teleflex Incorporated; *U.S. Public*, pg. 1569

RMX/80—Electronic Instrument—Intel Corporation; *U.S. Public*, pg. 886

RMONITOR—Computer Product—International Business Machines Corporation; *U.S. Public*, pg. 895

RN MAGAZINE—Medical Publication—Medical Economics Company Inc.; *U.S. Public*, pg. 1601

ROB—Gourmet Markets—GIB Group; *Int'l*, pg. 532

ROC—Computer Timesharing Services—Litton Industries, Inc.; *U.S. Public*, pg. 1002

ROC—Adult Mass Market Paperback Books—Penguin Putnam Inc.; *Int'l*, pg. 1027

ROC—NONE—SunGard Data Systems Inc.; *U.S. Public*, pg. 1534

ROC-R—Rocking Piston Pump—Gast Mfg. Corp.; *U.S. Private*, pg. 440

ROHSI—Rogers High Speed Interconnections—Rogers Corporation; *U.S. Public*, pg. 1402

RO99—NONE—CertainTeed Corporation; *Int'l*, pg. 1170

RO2800—Low Dielectric Constant Circuit Material—Rogers Corporation; *U.S. Public*, pg. 1402

RO2500—Low Dielectric Constant Flexible Circuit Material—Rogers Corporation; *U.S. Public*, pg. 1402

R1 MINIMA—Cigarettes—Reemtsma Cigarettenfabriken GmbH, Hamburg; *Int'l*, pg. 1100

RP—All Aluminum Grease Filters—Research Products Corporation; *U.S. Private*, pg. 924

RP & C—Cylinders—Conbraco Industries Inc.; *U.S. Private*, pg. 261

RPC—Simulator Software for Vehicle Test Systems—MTS Systems Corporation; *U.S. Public*, pg. 1028

RPEZ-KLEEN—Filter—Research Products Corporation; *U.S. Private*, pg. 924

R P F—NONE—U.S. Surgical Corp.; *U.S. Public*, pg. 1687

RPG/400—Computer Product—International Business Machines Corporation; *U.S. Public*, pg. 895

RPM—Release Agent—Chem-Trend Incorporated; *Int'l*, pg. 235

RPM—Motor Oils—Chevron Corporation; *U.S. Public*, pg. 347

RPM—Real-Time Process Monitor Technology for Analysis & Monitoring—PerSeptive Biosystems, Inc.; *U.S. Public*, pg. 1279

RPM III—DC Motors—Rockwell International Corporation; *U.S. Public*, pg. 1397

RPR—NONE—Kiwi Brands Pty. Ltd.; *U.S. Public*, pg. 1434

RPS—Waters 600 Gradient Module—Millipore Corporation; *U.S. Public*, pg. 1112

RPT—Reinforced Paper Tape—H.B. Fuller Company; *U.S. Public*, pg. 686

R-PRIDE—Flexible non-asbestos woven clutch facing liner—Universal Composites-U.S.C.; *U.S. Private*, pg. 1126

RQT 501/601/701—Steel Plates, Sections, Bars—British Steel Plc; *Int'l*, pg. 220

R-RESOURCE MAXIMIZER—NONE—BMC Software, Inc.; *U.S. Public*, pg. 162

R-RO—Electrolytic Nickel—Inco Limited; *Int'l*, pg. 672

RS—Vertical Pressurized Media Mill—Premier Mill Corp.; *U.S. Private*, pg. 881

RS/DISCOVER—Software Packages—GTE Internetworking; *U.S. Public*, pg. 696

RS/EXPLORE—Software Packages—GTE Internetworking; *U.S. Public*, pg. 696

RS/1—Software Package—GTE Internetworking; *U.S. Public*, pg. 696

RS-1000 MIXER—Crude Oil Mixing Nozzle—Matrix Service Company; *U.S. Public*, pg. 1057

RS/PROBE—Software—GTE Internetworking; *U.S. Public*, pg. 696

RS/QCA—Software—GTE Internetworking; *U.S. Public*, pg. 696

RS/SERIES—NONE—GTE Internetworking; *U.S. Public*, pg. 696

RS/6000—Computer Product—International Business Machines Corporation; *U.S. Public*, pg. 895

RSV ANTIGEN ELISA—Test—Ortho Clinical Diagnostic Systems Inc.; *U.S. Public*, pg. 929

RSVP—NONE—Beckett Papers; *U.S. Public*, pg. 903

RSVP—Floor Coverings—Domco Inc.; *Int'l*, pg. 415

RSVP—Raised Surface Variable Printing—The Standard Register Company; *U.S. Public*, pg. 1505

R-SERIES MICROLITE—Duct Insulation—Johns Manville Corporation; *U.S. Public*, pg. 927

R-7—Skis—Mizuno Corporation; *Int'l*, pg. 884

RT—Computer—International Business Machines Corporation; *U.S. Public*, pg. 895

RT—Coffee—William B. Reily & Co., Inc.; *U.S. Private*, pg. 919

RTA—Transit Authority—Regional Transportation Authority (RTA); *U.S. Private*, pg. 918

RTB—Registered Test Bar—Beloit Corporation; *U.S. Public*, pg. 789

RTC SOFT START—Soft Start Motor Control—Reuland Electric Company; *U.S. Private*, pg. 925

RT/DUROID—Microwave Laminate—Rogers Corporation; *U.S. Public*, pg. 1402

RTE—Power & Distribution Transformers & Components, Switches & Switchgear—Cooper Industries, Inc.; *U.S. Public*, pg. 442

RTEC—NONE—RELTEC Corporation; *U.S. Private*, pg. 921

RTI—Measurement & Control Module—Analog Devices, Inc.; *U.S. Public*, pg. 107

R.T. JUNIOR (PRESSED)—Twist Tobacco—Conwood Company L.P.; *U.S. Private*, pg. 272

RTL TELE LETZEBURG—Luxembourg Broadcasting—CLT-UFA; *Int'l*, pg. 561

RTL COUNTRY 1035—U.K. Broadcasting & CLT-UFA Intl.—CLT-UFA; *Int'l*, pg. 561

RTL9—French Broadcasting—CLT-UFA; *Int'l*, pg. 561

RTL RADIO—German Radio Station Die Grossten Oldies—CLT-UFA; *Int'l*, pg. 561

RTL RADIO LETZEBURG—Luxembourg Broadcasting—CLT-UFA; *Int'l*, pg. 561

RTL TVI—TV Broadcasting for Belgium—CLT-UFA; *Int'l*, pg. 561

RTL TELEVISION—German T.V. Station—CLT-UFA; *Int'l*, pg. 561

RTL2—French Broadcasting—CLT-UFA; *Int'l*, pg. 561

RTL2—German Broadcasting—CLT-UFA; *Int'l*, pg. 561

RTM322—Helicopter Engine—Rolls-Royce Military Aero Engines Ltd.; *Int'l*, pg. 1127

RTOC—NONE—SunGard Data Systems Inc.; *U.S. Public*, pg. 1534

RTP—Data Aquisition & Control System—Computer Products, Inc.; *U.S. Public*, pg. 422

RT PC—Computer—International Business Machines Corporation; *U.S. Public*, pg. 895

RT PERSONAL COMPUTER—Computer—International Business Machines Corporation; *U.S. Public*, pg. 895

RTS TRANSPORT—Sport Bag—Ektelon; *U.S. Private*, pg. 884

RTW—Carbide Cutting Tools—Rogers Tool Works, Inc.; *U.S. Public*, pg. 950

R204 MICRO FINE SUPERBALL—Pens—Pentel of America, Ltd.; *Int'l*, pg. 1035

R206 SUPERBALL—Pens—Pentel of America, Ltd.; *Int'l*, pg. 1035

RUPI—Electronic Instrument—Intel Corporation; *U.S. Public*, pg. 886

RUV—Radiation Curcable Coatings—Akzo Nobel Coatings Inc. (KY); *Int'l*, pg. 47

R.V.—Windows & Doors—Creation Windows of Indiana, Inc.; *U.S. Private*, pg. 287

R.V.—NONE—Urban Outfitters, Inc.; *U.S. Public*, pg. 1700

RV DEPOT—RV Sales & Service—Cruise America, Inc.; *U.S. Private*, pg. 178

RVG MICRON DIAMOND—Grinding Diamond—G.E. Superabrasives; *U.S. Public*, pg. 711

R.V.I.—Custom Seating—Flexsteel Industries, Inc.; *U.S. Public*, pg. 653

RV/MARINE TOILET TISSUE—Economic 1-Ply Toilet Tissue—Thetford Corporation; *U.S. Private*, pg. 352

RVP SERIES 9000—Rapid Vertical Thermal Processor—Silicon Valley Group, Inc.; *U.S. Public*, pg. 1474

THE R.W. KNUDSEN FAMILY—Fruit and Vegetable Juices—J.M. Smucker Company; *U.S. Public*, pg. 1480

RX—Engineering Thermoset Material—Rogers Corporation; *U.S. Public*, pg. 1402

THE RX PLACE—Deep Discount Drug Stores—Woolworth Corporation; *U.S. Public*, pg. 1777

RX-7—Car—Mazda Motor of America, Inc.; *Int'l*, pg. 849

RX TRIAGE—NONE—First DataBank; *U.S. Private*, pg. 515

RYO TOBACCOS—Cigarette Rolling Tobacco—Consolidated Cigar Corporation; *U.S. Private*, pg. 690

RDI—Terminal Blocks—Thomas & Betts Corporation; *U.S. Public*, pg. 1597

RAADVAD—NONE—Fiskars Oy AB; *Int'l*, pg. 492

RAB2IT—NONE—NEC Electronics Inc.; *Int'l*, pg. 900

RABARBARO ZUCCA APERITIF—NONE—Societe Pour la Vente des Produits Cinzano SA; *Int'l*, pg. 410

RABBIT HEAD DESIGN—Products—Playboy Enterprises, Inc.; *U.S. Public*, pg. 1309

RACAL—NONE—The Racal Corporation; *Int'l*, pg. 1082

RACAL—NONE—Racal Electronics Plc; *Int'l*, pg. 1082

RACE—Office Furniture System—Haworth, Inc.; *U.S. Public*, pg. 511

RACER TED—NONE—The Vermont Teddy Bear Company, Inc.; *U.S. Public*, pg. 1716

RACERBACK—Cabfairing—Lund International Holdings, Inc.; *U.S. Public*, pg. 1020

RACETRAC—Suture Packaging—U.S. Surgical Corp.; *U.S. Public*, pg. 1687

RACINE SECO—Radial Piston Pumps—Robert Bosch Fluid Power Corporation; *Int'l*, pg. 204

RACING GEAR—Oil—D.A. Stuart Company; *U.S. Private*, pg. 1048

RACING STAR—Athletic Shoes—Mizuno Corporation; *Int'l*, pg. 884

RACK-N-ROLL—Mobile Racks—Cres-Cor; *U.S. Private*, pg. 288

RACON-11—Refrigerant Gases—Essex Chemical Corporation; *U.S. Public*, pg. 523

RACON-502—Refrigerant Gases—Essex Chemical Corporation; *U.S. Public*, pg. 523

RACON-12—Refrigerant Gases—Essex Chemical Corporation; *U.S. Public*, pg. 523

RACON-22—Refrigerant Gases—Essex Chemical Corporation; *U.S. Public*, pg. 523

RACOR—Specialty Trackwork Products—ABC Rail Products Corp.; *U.S. Public*, pg. 2

RACQUET CLUB—Slacks & Sportswear—Trans-Apparel Group; *U.S. Public*, pg. 796

RACQUET CLUB/WIMBLEDON COLLECTION—Men's Apparel—Hartmarx Corporation; *U.S. Public*, pg. 795

RACQUETBALL/SQUASH/BADMINTON—Ektelon—Prince Sports Group Inc.; *U.S. Private*, pg. 884

RACQUETBALLER—Racquetball Glove—Ektelon; *U.S. Private*, pg. 884

RAD DOG—Stationary Items-Notebooks—The Mead Corporation; *U.S. Public*, pg. 1074

RAD-FREE—Non-isotropic Detection Kits—Schleicher & Schuell, Inc.; *Int'l*, pg. 1206

RAD-GLO—Flourescent Pigment—RPM, Inc.; *U.S. Public*, pg. 1356

RADARFAX—Facsimile—Litton Industries, Inc.; *U.S. Public*, pg. 1002

RADCAM—Medical Instrument/Computer—Capintec Inc.; *U.S. Private*, pg. 205

RADCLIFFE—NONE—Kellwood Company; *U.S. Public*, pg. 948

RADEL—Polyarylsulfone High Temperature Engineering Resins—Amoco Chemicals; *U.S. Public*, pg. 102

RADEL—Polyaryl Sulfane Resins—Amoco Corporation; *U.S. Public*, pg. 101

RADER—Rader Companies—Beloit Corporation; *U.S. Public*, pg. 789

RADER-FLO—Pulpwood Chippers—Beloit Corporation; *U.S. Public*, pg. 789

RADERFLEX—Rader—Beloit Corporation; *U.S. Public*, pg. 789

RADEX—Pine Timber—CSR Limited; *Int'l*, pg. 245

RADIA-TIZED—X-Ray Film—Eastman Kodak Company; *U.S. Public*, pg. 550

RADIAL—Atletic Footwear—Head USA, Inc.; *U.S. Private*, pg. 514

RADIAL ATX—Tires—Bridgestone/Firestone, Inc.; *Int'l*, pg. 213

RADIAL ALL TRACTION FWD—Tires—Bridgestone/Firestone, Inc.; *Int'l*, pg. 213

RADIAL ALL TRACTION 23—Tires—Bridgestone/Firestone, Inc.; *Int'l*, pg. 213

RADIAL V—Tires—Bridgestone/Firestone, Inc.; *Int'l*, pg. 213

RADIAL 500—Athletic Footwear—Head USA, Inc.; *U.S. Private*, pg. 514

RADIAL GRAPHITE—Rod—Outdoor Technologies Group; *U.S. Private*, pg. 822

RADIAL MASTER—Shock Absorbers—Bridgestone/Firestone, Inc.; *Int'l*, pg. 213

RADIAL-MATIC—Shock Absorbers—Monroe Auto Equipment Co.; *U.S. Public*, pg. 1577

RADIAL-PAK—Radial Compression Cartridge—Millipore Corporation; *U.S. Public*, pg. 1112

RADIAL POWER GUN—Assembly Tool—Waldes Truarc/Industrial Retaining Ring; *U.S. Public*, pg. 1632

RADIAL TAPER PIPE TAP—Taper Pipe Tap for Cast Iron—National Twist Drill Div.; *U.S. Public*, pg. 1370

RADIAL TAPER PIPE TAP—Type of Taper Pipe Tap for Cast Iron—Regal-Beloit Corporation; *U.S. Public*, pg. 1370

RADIALSEAL—Air Filter—Donaldson Company, Inc.; *U.S. Public*, pg. 517

RADIANCE—Bormat Furnace—Air Techniques, Inc.; *U.S. Private*, pg. 28

RADIANCE—Photographic Color Paper—Eastman Kodak Company; *U.S. Public*, pg. 550

RADIANCE—Writing Paper & Bond Paper—The Mead Corporation; *U.S. Public*, pg. 1074

RADIANCE—Vitamins—Nature's Bounty Inc.; *U.S. Public*, pg. 1166

RADIANT GLO—Hair Care Products & Cosmetics—Palm Beach Beauty Products Co.; *U.S. Private*, pg. 834

RADIANTE—All Purpose Cleaner—The Dow Chemical Company; *U.S. Public*, pg. 522

RADIANTLINE—Papers for Decorative Laminates—The Mead Corporation; *U.S. Public*, pg. 1074

RADIANTLY RED—Hair Coloring—Clairol, Inc.; *U.S. Public*, pg. 254

RADIAX—Slotted Coaxial Cable—Andrew Corporation; *U.S. Public*, pg. 112

RADICA GAMES—NONE—Radica USA Limited; *U.S. Private*, pg. 906

RADICAL BLAST—Beverage—Baskin-Robbins Incorporated; *Int'l*, pg. 63

RADIFOCUS—Guidewires—Terumo Medical Corporation; *Int'l*, pg. 1376

RADINYL—Hypoxic Tumor Cell Radiosensitizers—Roberts Pharmaceutical Corporation; *U.S. Public*, pg. 1393

RADIO CITY CHRISTMAS SPECTACULAR—NONE—Radio City Productions; *Int'l*, pg. 873

RADIO CITY ROCKETTES—Dance Team—Radio City Productions; *Int'l*, pg. 873

RADIO CITY SPRING SPECTACULAR—NONE—Radio City Productions; *Int'l*, pg. 873

RADIO CONTACT—Belgium Broadcasting—CLT-UFA; *Int'l*, pg. 561

RADIO GIRL—Perfume—Benjamin Ansehl Company; *U.S. Private*, pg. 75

RADIO QUARTERLY—Local Market Report—The
    Arbitron Company; *U.S. Public*, pg. 331
RADIO ROUGH—Hats—Bailey Hats; *U.S. Private*,
    pg. 155
RADIO TIMES—NONE—BBC Magazines; *Int'l*,
    pg. 114
RADIOLINK—RF Communication—Nellcor Puritan
    Bennett Incorporated; *U.S. Public*, pg. 1039
RADIOLUCENT—Laparoscopic Instruments—U.S.
    Surgical Corp.; *U.S. Public*, pg. 1687
RADION—Detergent—Lever Brothers Co.; *Int'l*,
    pg. 1435
RADION—Washing Powder—Unilever Plc; *Int'l*,
    pg. 1433
RADIONICS—Security System—Radionics, Inc.;
    U.S. Public, pg. 501
RADIOSHACK—NONE—Tandy Corporation; *U.S.
    Public*, pg. 1560
RADIOTROL—NONE—Boston Gear; *U.S. Public*,
    pg. 857
RADISSON HOTELS—Hotels—Carlson
    Companies, Inc.; *U.S. Private*, pg. 211
RADISSON HOTELS. INTL. WORLDWIDE—
    Logo—Radisson Hotel Corporation; *U.S.
    Private*, pg. 212
RADIUS ACCELERATOR 16—Computer
    Equipment—Radius Inc.; *U.S. Public*, pg. 1358
RADIUS ACCELERATOR 25—Computer
    Equipment—Radius Inc.; *U.S. Public*, pg. 1358
RADIUS COLOR DISPLAY—Computer Display
    Terminal—Radius Inc.; *U.S. Public*, pg. 1358
RADIUS DIRECTCOLOR—Computer Display
    Terminal—Radius Inc.; *U.S. Public*, pg. 1358
RADIUS DYNAMIC DESKTOP—Computer Display
    Terminal—Radius Inc.; *U.S. Public*, pg. 1358
RADIUS FULL PAGE DISPLAY—Compact Display
    System—Radius Inc.; *U.S. Public*, pg. 1358
RADIUS GS/C INTERFACE—Computer
    Equipment—Radius Inc.; *U.S. Public*, pg. 1358
RADIUS ONE—Desk Accessories—Smith
    McDonald Corp.; *U.S. Private*, pg. 1009
RADIUS PIVOT DISPLAY—Compact Display
    System—Radius Inc.; *U.S. Public*, pg. 1358
RADIUS PRECISIONCOLOR CALIBRATOR—
    Computer Visual System—Radius Inc.; *U.S.
    Public*, pg. 1358
RADIUS QUICKCAD GRAPHICS ENGINE—
    Computer Graphics System—Radius Inc.; *U.S.
    Public*, pg. 1358
RADIUS QUICKCOLOR GRAPHICS ENGINE—
    Computer Graphics System—Radius Inc.; *U.S.
    Public*, pg. 1358
RADIUS THEATRICS—Computer Equipment—
    Radius Inc.; *U.S. Public*, pg. 1358
RADIUS TWO—Desk Accessories—Smith
    McDonald Corp.; *U.S. Private*, pg. 1009
RADIUS TWO PAGE DISPLAY/19—Compact
    Display System—Radius Inc.; *U.S. Public*,
    pg. 1358
RADIUS TWO PAGE DISPLAY/21—Compact
    Display System—Radius Inc.; *U.S. Public*,
    pg. 1358
RADIUSWARE—Computer Equipment—Radius
    Inc.; *U.S. Public*, pg. 1358
RADIX—Wire—Radix Wire Company; *U.S. Private*,
    pg. 907
RADMARK—Materials Handling Equipment—Beloit
    Corporation; *U.S. Public*, pg. 789
RADNET—Radiology Information System—Cerner
    Corporation; *U.S. Public*, pg. 331
RADO—Watches—SMH Swiss Corporation for
    Micro Electronics & Watchmaking Indus. Ltd.;
    Int'l, pg. 1160
RADOX—NONE—Kiwi Brands Pty. Ltd.; *U.S.
    Public*, pg. 1434
RADOX—Body Care—Sara Lee Corporation; *U.S.
    Public*, pg. 1432
RADPRO—NONE—Landauer, Inc.; *U.S. Public*,
    pg. 977
RADTRAK—Radon Detectors—Landauer, Inc.;
    U.S. Public, pg. 977
RAFALE—Fully Multipurpose Combat Aircraft—
    Dassault Aviation Group; *Int'l*, pg. 383
RAFFLES—Cigarettes—Philip Morris Companies
    Inc.; *U.S. Public*, pg. 1287
RAFHAN—Corn Oil & Other Oils, Corn & Other
    Starches—Bestfoods; *U.S. Public*, pg. 223
RAFT-R-MATE—Extruded Polystyrene Attic Rafter
    Vents—Owens Corning; *U.S. Public*, pg. 1236

RAG-ON-A-ROLL—Disposable Wipes & Towels—
    Kimberly-Clark Corporation; *U.S. Public*,
    pg. 958
THR RAG SHOP—NONE—Rag Shops, Inc.; *U.S.
    Public*, pg. 1358
RAGA MUFFINS—Muffin Mix—Wilkins-Rogers
    Incorporated; *U.S. Private*, pg. 1176
RAGAZZIS—Restaurant—Investors Management
    Corp.; *U.S. Private*, pg. 574
RAGE—Card Game—Mattel Games/Puzzles; *U.S.
    Public*, pg. 1058
RAGLANS—Unisex Casual Apparel—F.W.
    Woolworth Co.; *U.S. Public*, pg. 1777
RAGLANS/WILLOW RIDGE—Unisex Casual
    Apparel—Woolworth Corporation; *U.S. Public*,
    pg. 1777
RAGTRADER—Magazine—Reed Business
    Information Pty. Limited; *Int'l*, pg. 1094
RAGTRADER FASHION DIRECTORY—NONE—
    Reed Business Information Pty. Limited; *Int'l*,
    pg. 1094
RAGU—Spaghetti Sauces & Meat Toppings—
    Chesebrough-Pond's; *Int'l*, pg. 1436
RAGU—Spaghetti Sauces & Meat Toppings—Ragu
    Foods, Inc.; *Int'l*, pg. 1436
RAGU—Pasta Sauce—Van den Bergh Foods
    Company; *Int'l*, pg. 1436
RAID—Insecticides—S.C. Johnson & Son, Inc.;
    U.S. Public, pg. 592
RAID—Insecticide—S.C. Johnson & Son, Limited;
    U.S. Private, pg. 593
RAID MAX—Insecticide—S.C. Johnson & Son,
    Inc.; *U.S. Private*, pg. 592
RAID ON ST. NAZAIR—War Game—Monarch
    Avalon, Inc.; *U.S. Public*, pg. 1123
RAID ROACH CONTROLLER—Roach Bait
    Units—S.C. Johnson & Son, Inc.; *U.S. Private*,
    pg. 592
RAIDER—Sporting Goods—Brunswick Bowling &
    Billiards Corp.; *U.S. Public*, pg. 265
RAIDER—NONE—Griffin Manufacturing Co.; *U.S.
    Private*, pg. 481
RAIDION—NONE—Micropolis Corporation; *U.S.
    Private*, pg. 742
RAIL—U.K. Railways Magazine—EMAP Apex; *Int'l*,
    pg. 451
RAIL BARON—Game—Monarch Avalon, Inc.; *U.S.
    Public*, pg. 1123
RAIL EASY—Stair System—Morgan Products Ltd.;
    U.S. Public, pg. 1132
RAIL ROAD MILLS—Dry Snuff—Swisher
    International Group, Inc.; *U.S. Public*, pg. 1543
RAIL TRANSPORT—Tires—Bridgestone/
    Firestone, Inc.; *Int'l*, pg. 213
RAILROAD PROTECTOR PLAN—NONE—Poe &
    Brown, Inc.; *U.S. Public*, pg. 1312
RAILROADER—Enclosed Vans Designed for
    Highway & Railway Usage—Norfolk Southern
    Corporation; *U.S. Public*, pg. 1190
RAILWAY AGE—Monthly Magazine—Simmons-
    Boardman Publishing Corp.; *U.S. Private*,
    pg. 1000
RAILWAY MAGAZINE—Special Interest
    Magazine—IPC Magazines Limited; *Int'l*,
    pg. 651
RAILWAY TRACK & STRUCTURES—Monthly
    Magazine—Simmons-Boardman Publishing
    Corp.; *U.S. Private*, pg. 1000
RAIN—Pattern Glass—AFG Industries, Inc.; *Int'l*,
    pg. 84
RAIN BAG—Emitter—Rain Bird Sprinklers
    Manufacturing Corp.; *U.S. Private*, pg. 907
RAIN BARREL—Fabric Softener—S.C. Johnson &
    Son, Inc.; *U.S. Private*, pg. 592
RAIN BIRD—Sprinklers—Rain Bird Sprinklers
    Manufacturing Corp.; *U.S. Private*, pg. 907
RAIN CLOX—Timer—Rain Bird Sprinklers
    Manufacturing Corp.; *U.S. Private*, pg. 907
RAIN DATE—Water Timers—L.R. Nelson
    Corporation; *U.S. Private*, pg. 790
RAIN DIAL—Irrigation—James Hardie Industries
    Ltd.; *Int'l*, pg. 596
RAIN GUN—Sprinklers—Rain Bird Sprinklers
    Manufacturing Corp.; *U.S. Private*, pg. 907
RAIN KING—Sprinkler—Aircap Industries Corp.;
    U.S. Private, pg. 688
RAIN-RUN—Plastic Splash Guards—Reynolds
    Metals Company; *U.S. Public*, pg. 1385
RAIN TAPE—Drip Tubing—Rain Bird Sprinklers
    Manufacturing Corp.; *U.S. Private*, pg. 907

RAIN-X—Glass Treatment—Blue Coral/Slick 50;
    U.S. Public, pg. 1348
RAINBATH MOISTURIZING BODY MIST—
    NONE—Neutrogena Corporation; *U.S. Public*,
    pg. 928
RAINBATH SKIN-SMOOTHING POWDER—Body
    Powder—Neutrogena Corporation; *U.S. Public*,
    pg. 928
RAINBATH SPLASH—After-Bath Splash—
    Neutrogena Corporation; *U.S. Public*, pg. 928
RAINBATH SPRAY-ON DRY OIL—NONE—
    Neutrogena Corporation; *U.S. Public*, pg. 928
RAINBLO—NONE—Huhtamaki Oy; *Int'l*, pg. 638
RAINBO—Service Station Services—Amoco
    Corporation; *U.S. Public*, pg. 101
RAINBO—Pickles—Dean Foods Company; *U.S.
    Public*, pg. 489
RAINBO—Pickles—Dean Pickle & Specialty
    Products Co.; *U.S. Public*, pg. 490
RAINBO—Bakery Products—The Earthgrains
    Company; *U.S. Public*, pg. 547
RAINBOW—Sweet Snuffs—Conwood Company
    L.P.; *U.S. Private*, pg. 272
RAINBOW—Parchment—Eastern Fine Paper; *U.S.
    Private*, pg. 357
RAINBOW—Private Label Grocery, Perishables &
    Frozen Items—Fleming Companies, Inc.; *U.S.
    Public*, pg. 652
RAINBOW—Paper Tablets—The Mead
    Corporation; *U.S. Public*, pg. 1074
RAINBOW—Home Furnishing Rentals—Rainbow
    Rentals, Inc.; *U.S. Public*, pg. 907
RAINBOW—Vacuum Cleaner—Rexair, Inc.; *U.S.
    Public*, pg. 1684
RAINBOW—Color Video Magnifier—Telesensory
    Corporation; *U.S. Private*, pg. 1074
RAINBOW APPAREL DISTRIBUTION—Apparel
    Chain Stores—Rainbow Apparel Distribution
    Center; *U.S. Private*, pg. 907
RAINBOW CHIPS DELUXE—Cookies—Keebler
    Company; *U.S. Public*, pg. 657
RAINBOW POWER HUMIDIFIER—Furnace
    Humidifier—Maid-O-Mist; *U.S. Private*, pg. 1053
RAINBOW SPIRITS—Gin, Vodka, Rum & Triple
    Sec—Marie Brizard Wines & Spirits USA; *U.S.
    Private*, pg. 702
RAINBOW WATER—Bottled Water—Hinckley &
    Schmitt, Inc.; *Int'l*, pg. 1322
RAINDANCE—Car Waxes, Washes & Polishes—
    Armor All Products Group; *U.S. Public*, pg. 387
RAINDROP—Nebulizers & Nebulizer Masks—
    Nellcor Puritan Bennett Incorporated; *U.S.
    Public*, pg. 1039
RAINERI—Pasta—Borden, Inc.; *U.S. Private*,
    pg. 157
RAINFAIR—Rainwear & Coated Fabrics—Rainfair,
    Inc.; *U.S. Private*, pg. 907
RAINGO—Gutter & Down Spouts—Genova
    Products, Inc.; *U.S. Private*, pg. 447
RAINHA—Athletic Footwear—Sao Paulo
    Alpargatas S.A.; *Int'l*, pg. 1193
RAINLOCK—Roofing—Reynolds Metals Company;
    U.S. Public, pg. 1385
RAINMAKERS—Shower Head & Hand Held
    Shower—Interbath, Inc.; *U.S. Private*, pg. 566
RAINMATIC—Electronic Water Timers—L.R.
    Nelson Corporation; *U.S. Private*, pg. 790
RAINMISER—Water Saving Nozzle—L.R. Nelson
    Corporation; *U.S. Private*, pg. 790
RAINPULSE—Impulse Sprinklers—L.R. Nelson
    Corporation; *U.S. Private*, pg. 790
RAINSHOWER—Oscillating Sprinklers—L.R.
    Nelson Corporation; *U.S. Private*, pg. 790
RAINSILK—Personal Care Products—Shaklee
    Corporation; *Int'l*, pg. 1518
RAINSPRAY—Irrigation—James Hardie Industries
    Ltd.; *Int'l*, pg. 596
RAINSWIRL—Whirling Sprinklers—L.R. Nelson
    Corporation; *U.S. Private*, pg. 790
RAINTRAIN—Traveling Sprinklers—L.R. Nelson
    Corporation; *U.S. Private*, pg. 790
RAISED PROFILE—NONE—Elcor Corporation;
    U.S. Public, pg. 567
RAISIN LIFE—Cereal—The Quaker Oats
    Company; *U.S. Public*, pg. 1347
RAISIN MATE—Raisin Juice Concentrate
    Replacement—David Michael & Co. Inc.; *U.S.
    Private*, pg. 740
RAISIN NUT BRAN—Cereal—General Mills, Inc.;
    U.S. Public, pg. 717

RAISIN SQUARES—Raisin-Filled Whole Wheat Biscuits—Kellogg Company; *U.S. Public*, pg. 947

RAISINETS—Candy—Nestle Chocolate & Confection; *Int'l*, pg. 917

RAISINETS—Candy—Nestle USA; *Int'l*, pg. 916

RAISING KIDS IN THE 90'S—Practical Parenting Tips New Program—Westwood One, Inc.; *U.S. Public*, pg. 1763

RAISON—Cider—Groupe Pernod Ricard; *Int'l*, pg. 566

RAJAH—Indian Foods—Danone Group; *Int'l*, pg. 379

RAK—Crop Protection Agent—BASF AG; *Int'l*, pg. 103

RAK 5 + 6—Crop Protection Agent—BASF AG; *Int'l*, pg. 103

RAK 1 PLUS—Crop Protection Agent—BASF AG; *Int'l*, pg. 103

RAK 2—Crop Protection Agent—BASF AG; *Int'l*, pg. 103

RAKE-O-VAC—Turf Rake & Vacuum—The Toro Company; *U.S. Public*, pg. 1623

RALEIGH—Cigarettes—Brown & Williamson Tobacco Corp.; *Int'l*, pg. 111

RALEIGH—Cycles—Derby International Corporation S.A.; *Int'l*, pg. 394

RALEIGH EXTRA—Cigarettes—Brown & Williamson Tobacco Corp.; *Int'l*, pg. 111

RALGEX—Topical/Skincare—SmithKline Beecham plc; *Int'l*, pg. 1264

RALLO—NONE—Banfi Vintners; *U.S. Private*, pg. 113

RALLY—Luggage—American Tourister, Inc.; *U.S. Public*, pg. 1430

RALLY—Car Waxes, Washes & Polishes—Armor All Products Group; *U.S. Public*, pg. 387

RALLY—Garden Equipment—Electrolux, AB; *Int'l*, pg. 438

RALLY—Lawn & Garden Equipment—Frigidaire Home Products; *Int'l*, pg. 439

RALLY—Motorcycle Boots—Georgia/Durango Boot Company; *U.S. Public*, pg. 1684

RALLY—Pens—The Gillette Company; *U.S. Public*, pg. 743

RALLY—Balloon, Hot Air Sport—Raven Industries, Inc.; *U.S. Public*, pg. 1361

RALLY—Fungicide—Rohm and Haas Company; *U.S. Public*, pg. 1403

RALLY—Lawn & Garden Products—White Consolidated Industries, Inc.; *Int'l*, pg. 439

RALLY CHECKMATE—Sporting Goods—Brunswick Bowling & Billiards Corp.; *U.S. Public*, pg. 265

RALLY PEPPERMATE—Sporting Goods—Brunswick Bowling & Billiards Corp.; *U.S. Public*, pg. 265

RALLY PINTO—Sporting Equipment—Brunswick Bowling & Billiards Corp.; *U.S. Public*, pg. 265

RALOX—Antioxidants—Raschig GmbH; *U.S. Private*, pg. 827

RALPH & KACOO'S—Seafood Restaurants—Piccadilly Cafeterias, Inc.; *U.S. Public*, pg. 1294

RALPH LAUREN—Women's Wear—Arrow Shirt Company; *Int'l*, pg. 194

RALPH LAUREN—Fragrances—Cosmair, Inc.; *Int'l*, pg. 818

RALPH LAUREN—NONE—L'Oreal Parfumerie; *Int'l*, pg. 819

RALPH LAUREN—Casualwear—Sao Paulo Alpargatas S.A.; *Int'l*, pg. 1193

RALPH'S—Grocery Stores—Ralphs Grocery Company; *U.S. Private*, pg. 1202

RALSTON—NONE—Ralcorp Holdings Inc.; *U.S. Public*, pg. 1359

RALU-PAC—Structured Mass Transfer Packings—Raschig GmbH; *U.S. Private*, pg. 827

RALUFLEX—Special Emulsion With Rubber Addition for Surface Treatment & Repair—Raschig GmbH; *U.S. Private*, pg. 827

RALUFORM—Coating Materials & Hardners—Raschig GmbH; *U.S. Private*, pg. 827

RALULAC—Chemicals for Paint & Varnish—Raschig GmbH; *U.S. Private*, pg. 827

RALUMIX—Lustourous Carbon Former—Raschig GmbH; *U.S. Private*, pg. 827

RALUPAST—Core Oils, Parting Agents & Core Adhesives—Raschig GmbH; *U.S. Private*, pg. 827

RALUPOL—Moulding Compound—Raschig GmbH; *U.S. Private*, pg. 827

RALUSET—Sodium Silicate Binder—Raschig GmbH; *U.S. Private*, pg. 827

RAM—Scoops—Ames Company; *U.S. Public*, pg. 1683

RAM—Mixer Reducer—The Falk Corporation; *U.S. Public*, pg. 1534

RAM—NONE—Hansberger Precision Golf Inc.; *U.S. Private*, pg. 499

RAM—Golf Clubs & Balls—RAM Golf Corporation; *U.S. Private*, pg. 908

RAM DOUBLER—Software Utility—Connectix Corporation; *U.S. Private*, pg. 264

RAM 11/22—Power Line Modems—Data Control Systems; *U.S. Public*, pg. 420

RAM GOLF—Golf Equipment—RAM Golf Corporation; *U.S. Private*, pg. 908

RAM-LINE—Synthetic Stocks—Blount, Inc. Sporting Equipment Group; *U.S. Public*, pg. 238

RAM-LINE—Gun Stocks, Gun-Care Accessories—Blount International, Inc.; *U.S. Public*, pg. 237

RAM TOUR—Golf Equipment—RAM Golf Corporation; *U.S. Private*, pg. 908

RAMA—Margarine—Deutsche Unilever Gmbh; *Int'l*, pg. 1436

RAMACE—Cardiovascular Pharmaceutical—Astra AB; *Int'l*, pg. 93

RAMADA EXPRESS—Hotels—Aztar Corporation; *U.S. Public*, pg. 158

RAMADA FRANCHISE SYSTEMS, INC.—Hotel Chain—HFS, Incorporated; *U.S. Public*, pg. 321

RAMAPET/INDOPET—Bottle Resin—Indo Rama Synthetics P.T.; *Int'l*, pg. 673

RAMBAR—Dryer—Beloit Corporation; *U.S. Public*, pg. 789

RAMDISK/ALX—Solid State Mass Memory SubSystem—Zitel Corporation; *U.S. Public*, pg. 1793

RAMDISK/MLX—Solid State Mass Memory Subsystem—Zitel Corporation; *U.S. Public*, pg. 1793

RAMEN PRIDE—Oriental Noodles—Sanwa Foods, Inc.; *U.S. Public*, pg. 299

RAMEN SOUP—Oriental Noodles/Cup—Sanwa Foods, Inc.; *U.S. Public*, pg. 299

RAMEN SUPREME—Noodle Soup—Maruchan Inc.; *U.S. Private*, pg. 710

RAMON ALLONES—Cigars—General Cigar Company, Inc.; *U.S. Public*, pg. 758

RAMON ALONES—Cigars—Rothmans UK Holdings Limited; *Int'l*, pg. 1129

RAMROD—Herbicide—The Agricultural Group, Monsanto Company; *U.S. Public*, pg. 1125

RAMROD—Herbicide—Monsanto Company; *U.S. Public*, pg. 1124

RAM'S HORN—Twist Tobacco—Conwood Company L.P.; *U.S. Private*, pg. 272

RAMSES—Condoms—Durex Consumer Products; *Int'l*, pg. 815

RAMSES—Latex Condoms—London International Group plc; *Int'l*, pg. 815

RAMTOUR—NONE—Hansberger Precision Golf Inc.; *U.S. Private*, pg. 499

RANCH FRIES—Snacks—Borden, Inc.; *U.S. Private*, pg. 157

RANCH-PLY—Plywood—Georgia-Pacific Corporation; *U.S. Public*, pg. 735

RANCH STYLE—Beans—International Home Foods Inc.; *U.S. Private*, pg. 526

RANCH TONE—Stain—Mautz Paint Co.; *U.S. Private*, pg. 715

RANCHERO—Wood Stain—Jones Blair Company; *U.S. Private*, pg. 596

RANCHER'S CHOICE—Salad Dressing—Alliant Foodservice, Inc.; *U.S. Private*, pg. 244

RANCHGUARD—Metal Fencing, Barbed Wire, Metal Roofing & Siding, & Baling Twine—Georgia-Pacific Corporation; *U.S. Public*, pg. 735

RANCHMASTER—Livestock Equipment—Behlen Mfg. Co.; *U.S. Private*, pg. 130

RANCHWOOD STAIN—Stain—Mautz Paint Co.; *U.S. Private*, pg. 715

RANCO—Automatic Control Device—Ranco Inc.; *Int'l*, pg. 1243

RANDA—Cancer Drug—Nippon Kayaku Co. Ltd.; *Int'l*, pg. 934

RANDMARK—Educational Maps & Globes—Rand McNally & Company; *U.S. Private*, pg. 908

RANDOM HOUSE—Books—Random House, Inc.; *U.S. Private*, pg. 20

RANDY RIVER—Men's Casual Apparel—Woolworth Corporation; *U.S. Public*, pg. 1777

RANDY RIVER—Footwear & Men's Clothing—F.W. Woolworth Co.; *U.S. Public*, pg. 1777

RANEY—Catalysts—W.R. Grace & Co.; *U.S. Public*, pg. 754

RANG—Sugar Candies—CSM N.V.; *Int'l*, pg. 243

RANGAIRE—Lighting Fixtures, Range Hoods—Rangaire Inc.; *U.S. Public*, pg. 1193

THE RANGE—NONE—Harrah's Entertainment, Inc.; *U.S. Public*, pg. 790

RANGE BRAND WRANGLERS—Meat Products; Bacon—Hormel Foods Corp.; *U.S. Public*, pg. 840

RANGE-FINDER—Sporting Goods—Brunswick Bowling & Billiards Corp.; *U.S. Public*, pg. 265

RANGE ROVER—4WD Vehicle—British Aerospace p.l.c.; *Int'l*, pg. 217

RANGE ROVER—Automobiles—Lantzsch-Andreas Enterprises, Inc.; *U.S. Private*, pg. 650

RANGEMASTER—Kitchen Range Hoods—Aubrey Manufacturing Company; *U.S. Public*, pg. 1193

RANGER—NONE—Alberta Energy Company, Ltd.; *Int'l*, pg. 48

RANGER—Power Tools—The Black & Decker Corporation; *U.S. Public*, pg. 233

RANGER—Cutlery—Buck Knives, Inc.; *U.S. Private*, pg. 177

RANGER—Truck—Ford Motor Company; *U.S. Public*, pg. 661

RANGER—Fiberglass Bass Boats And Offshore Fishing Boats—Genmar Holdings, Inc.; *U.S. Private*, pg. 447

RANGER—Wood Stain—Jones Blair Company; *U.S. Private*, pg. 596

RANGER—Unmanned Air Vehicle System—Oerlikon-Contraves AG; *Int'l*, pg. 998

RANGER—Truck-Mounted Access Platform—Simon Engineering plc; *Int'l*, pg. 1251

RANGER—Electrical Spring Connectors—3M; *U.S. Public*, pg. 1604

RANGER F-SERIES—NONE—Ford Motor Co. of Canada Ltd; *U.S. Public*, pg. 666

RANGER M—Upgradable Notebook—Advanced Logic Research, Inc.; *U.S. Public*, pg. 703

RANGER QCT—Rotary Control Valve—Cashco, Inc.; *U.S. Private*, pg. 218

RANGER II—Power Electronic Charging System—C&D Charter Power Systems; *U.S. Public*, pg. 271

RANGING—Range Finders, Rangematic Optical Viewing & Measuring Devices—Bushnell Corporation; *U.S. Private*, pg. 1191

RANKPNEUMO—Machining Systems Division—Taylor Hobson Pneumo; *Int'l*, pg. 1087

RANSOMES—Turf Equipment—Ransomes-Cushman-Ryan; *Int'l*, pg. 1088

RANSOMES—Commercial Turf Machinery—Ransomes Plc; *Int'l*, pg. 1088

RANTEX—Personal Hygiene Towelette—The Clinipad Corporation; *U.S. Private*, pg. 246

RAP—Random Acquisition Program—GenRad, Inc.; *U.S. Public*, pg. 731

RAP-A-MAT—Container Forming & Sealing Equipment—Stone Container Corporation; *U.S. Public*, pg. 1520

RAP-I-FORM—Metal Products—Kaibab Industries; *U.S. Private*, pg. 605

RAPALA—Fishing Lures—Normark Corporation; *U.S. Private*, pg. 802

RAPHA—Psychiatric Programs—Intelligent Systems Corp.; *U.S. Public*, pg. 888

RAPHAEL—Costume Jewelry—Artra Group Incorporated; *U.S. Public*, pg. 136

RAPI-DRIV—Screwdriver With Rotating Blade—Klein Tools Inc.; *U.S. Private*, pg. 625

RAPI TEX—Research Biochemicals—Dade Behring Inc.; *U.S. Private*, pg. 110

RAPICOM—Facsimile Equipment—Ricoh Corporation; *Int'l*, pg. 1114

RAPID—Replacement Parts, Repair Assemblies & Components Kit—Beckman Instruments, Inc.; *U.S. Public*, pg. 199

RAPID—NONE—KLA Tencor Corporation; *U.S. Public*, pg. 939

RAPID-ADE—Rabbit Feeds—Manna Pro Corporation; *U.S. Private*, pg. 700

RAPID AMERICAN—Retail Chain Stores—McCrory Corporation; *U.S. Private*, pg. 720

RAPID ARC—High Speed Welding—AGA Ges.m.b.H.; *Int'l*, pg. 13

Brand Name Index

RAPID BLUE—Enzyme Stains—Eastman Kodak Company; *U.S. Public*, pg. 550

RAPID CHANGER—Mini Jukebox-12" Optical Storage System—Philip Laser Magnetic Storage; *Int'l*, pg. 1054

RAPID FLEX—Conveyors—Rapid Industries, Inc.; *U.S. Private*, pg. 910

RAPID FREEZE—NONE—Scotsman Industries, Inc.; *U.S. Public*, pg. 1444

RAPID MELT—High Speed Welding—AGA Ges.m.b.H.; *Int'l*, pg. 13

RAPID PROCESSING—High Speed Welding—AGA Ges.m.b.H.; *Int'l*, pg. 13

RAPID RISE—Yeast—Fleischmann's Yeast; *Int'l*, pg. 237

RAPID-ROLL—Overhead Doors—Albany International Corp.; *U.S. Public*, pg. 36

RAPID SCAN—Software—AlliedSignal Commercial Avionics Systems; *U.S. Public*, pg. 50

RAPID WIPER—Cleaning Cloth—Spontex, Inc.; *Int'l*, pg. 1409

RAPIDASE—Amylase for Baking Desizing Processes—Royal Gist-Brocades N.V.; *Int'l*, pg. 1142

RAPIDCOST—NONE—Manufacturers Technologies, Inc.; *U.S. Private*, pg. 701

RAPIDEAL—Trade Offer & Execution Tool with on-the-Spot Cash Incentives—Gelco Information Network, Inc.; *U.S. Private*, pg. 442

RAPIDESIGN—Templates—Empire Berol U.S.A.; *U.S. Public*, pg. 1178

RAPIDEX—Reactive Hot Melt Adhesive—H.B. Fuller Company; *U.S. Public*, pg. 686

RAPIDFILE—Software—Borland International, Inc.; *U.S. Public*, pg. 246

RAPIDFIRE—Heating System for Aluminum, Non-Ferrous Metals—Air Products and Chemicals, Inc.; *U.S. Public*, pg. 30

RAPIDO-EZE—Pen Cleaning Solution—Koh-I-Noor, Inc.; *U.S. Private*, pg. 629

RAPIDO 400—X-Ray—Picker International, Inc.; *Int'l*, pg. 545

RAPIDOGRAPH—Technical Pens, Drawing Inks & Drawing Materials—Koh-I-Noor, Inc.; *U.S. Private*, pg. 629

RAPIDOMATIC—Automatic Fine-Line Drawing Pencils—Koh-I-Noor, Inc.; *U.S. Private*, pg. 629

RAPIDOPLOT—Plotter Supplies, Plotter Ink—Koh-I-Noor, Inc.; *U.S. Private*, pg. 629

RAPIDPAY—Direct Mail Trade Offer & Execution with Instant Cash Incentives—Gelco Information Network, Inc.; *U.S. Private*, pg. 442

RAPIDRAFT—Trade Payment Management Service with Immediate Settlement Authority—Gelco Information Network, Inc.; *U.S. Private*, pg. 442

RAPIDTEST-STREP—Latex Strep A Test—Beckman Instruments, Inc.; *U.S. Public*, pg. 199

RAPIDTRAK—Rodless Cylinders—Warner Electric Industrial Products Division; *U.S. Public*, pg. 480

RAPIDYNE—Disinfectant/Germicide—West Chemical Products, Inc.; *U.S. Private*, pg. 1158

RAPIER—Guided Missile—British Aerospace p.l.c.; *Int'l*, pg. 217

RAPIER—Envelope, Converting Paper—Champion International Corp.; *U.S. Public*, pg. 333

RAPIFAX—Facsimile Equipment—Ricoh Corporation; *Int'l*, pg. 1114

RAPIGNOST—Urine Test Strips—Dade Behring Inc.; *U.S. Private*, pg. 110

RAPIMAT—Urinalysis Analyzer—Dade Behring Inc.; *U.S. Private*, pg. 110

RAPISTAN—Material Handling Systems—Lear Siegler Diversified Holdings Corp.; *U.S. Private*, pg. 655

RAPOX—Solid Resins—Raschig GmbH; *U.S. Private*, pg. 827

RAPPORT—NONE—Northern Telecom Limited; *Int'l*, pg. 968

RAPTOR—NONE—Cedar Point; *U.S. Public*, pg. 319

RARE EDITIONS—Dresses—Star Children's Dress Company, Inc.; *U.S. Private*, pg. 1034

RARE GOLD—Women's Global Fragrance—Avon Products, Inc.; *U.S. Public*, pg. 155

RASCAL—Sporting Goods—Brunswick Bowling & Billiards Corp.; *U.S. Public*, pg. 265

RASHEEN—Car—Nissan Motor Co., Ltd.; *Int'l*, pg. 943

RASPBERRY PATCH—Herb Tea—Celestial Seasonings; *U.S. Public*, pg. 319

RASTYROL—Lustrous Carbon Fibre—Raschig GmbH; *U.S. Private*, pg. 827

RATCH-LATCH—Packers—Halliburton Energy Services; *U.S. Public*, pg. 776

RATCH TECH—Alternate Lacing System—Jack Schwartz Shoes, Inc.; *U.S. Private*, pg. 974

RATCHET-PRO—Floor Boxes—Walker Systems, Inc.; *U.S. Private*, pg. 1184

RATE-CHEK—Motion Dampeners—Hartwell Corporation; *U.S. Private*, pg. 1168

RATE MASTER—Flow Meter—Dwyer Instruments Inc.; *U.S. Private*, pg. 350

RATE-MATE—Envelopes—Westvaco Corporation; *U.S. Public*, pg. 1762

RATH BLACKHAWK—Meat Products—John Morrell & Co.; *U.S. Public*, pg. 1479

RATIO—Technical Data & Graphs—Beckman Instruments, Inc.; *U.S. Public*, pg. 199

RATIO—Turbidimeter-Laboratory & On-Line—Hach Company; *U.S. Public*, pg. 773

RATIONAL SURFACE DESIGN—Technique for Creating Synthetic Surface to Which Target Biomolecules Bind—PerSeptive Biosystems, Inc.; *U.S. Public*, pg. 1279

RATIOSCOPE—Industrial Instrument—Capintec Inc.; *U.S. Private*, pg. 205

RATOALARM—Flowmeters—Bailey, Fischer & Porter Company; *Int'l*, pg. 449

RATOSIGHT—Flowmeter—Bailey, Fischer & Porter Company; *Int'l*, pg. 449

RATTLERS BRAND—Fabrics—Thomaston Mills, Inc.; *U.S. Private*, pg. 1599

RAUCH—Christmas Ornaments & Novelties—Rauch Industries, Inc.; *U.S. Private*, pg. 1061

RAUCH INDUSTRIES—Christmas Ornaments & Items—Syratech Corporation; *U.S. Private*, pg. 1060

RAVARINO & FRESCHI—Pasta Products—Borden Italian Foods; *U.S. Private*, pg. 158

RAVARINO & FRESCHI—Pasta—Borden, Inc.; *U.S. Private*, pg. 157

RAVE—Hairspray, Styling Aids, Shampoos, Conditioners, Perms—Chesebrough-Pond's USA Co.; *Int'l*, pg. 1435

RAVE—Deep Moisturizing Conditioner—Chesebrough-Pond's USA Co.; *Int'l*, pg. 1435

RAVE—Heat Styling Mist—Chesebrough-Pond's USA Co.; *Int'l*, pg. 1435

RAVE—Spray Gel—Chesebrough-Pond's USA Co.; *Int'l*, pg. 1435

RAVE—Whipped Styling Gel—Chesebrough-Pond's USA Co.; *Int'l*, pg. 1435

RAVE—NONE—Petrie Retail, Inc.; *U.S. Private*, pg. 858

RAVE MICROSPRAY—Hairspray—Chesebrough-Pond's USA Co.; *Int'l*, pg. 1435

RAVELGEN—Vitamin & Tonic—SmithKline Beecham plc; *Int'l*, pg. 1264

RAVEN—Valve Trim—Copes-Vulcan Inc.; *U.S. Private*, pg. 274

RAVEN—Sportswear—Raven Industries, Inc.; *U.S. Public*, pg. 1361

RAVEN—Skiwear—Raven Industries Sportswear Div.; *U.S. Public*, pg. 1361

RAVEN—Tanks—Ryan Herco Products Corp.; *U.S. Private*, pg. 953

RAVENLOFT—Books & Games—TSR, Inc.; *U.S. Private*, pg. 1185

RAVINIA FESTIVAL DINING—Food Service—The Levy Organization; *U.S. Private*, pg. 664

RAVISSANT BY BRIDAL ORIGINALS—Bridal Gowns—S.A.S.I. Corporation; *U.S. Private*, pg. 955

RAW—U.K. Entertainment Magazine—EMAP Metro; *Int'l*, pg. 451

RAW SILK—Fragrance—Parfums De Coeur Ltd.; *U.S. Private*, pg. 839

RAWL-BOLT—Expansion Anchor—Powers Fastening, Inc.; *U.S. Private*, pg. 878

RAWL-STUD—Wedge Anchor—Powers Fastening, Inc.; *U.S. Private*, pg. 878

RAWLDRILL—Masonry Drills—Powers Fastening, Inc.; *U.S. Private*, pg. 878

RAWLINGS—Athletic Equipment & Sporting Goods—Rawlings Sporting Goods Company; *U.S. Public*, pg. 1361

RAWLITE—Roofing Fastener—Powers Fastening, Inc.; *U.S. Private*, pg. 878

RAWLPLUG—Fixings—Newmond PLC; *Int'l*, pg. 924

RAWLPLUG—Fiber Screw Anchors—Powers Fastening, Inc.; *U.S. Private*, pg. 878

RAWLY—Hollow Wall Anchor—Powers Fastening, Inc.; *U.S. Private*, pg. 878

RAWN—Tools—Audits & Surveys Worldwide; *U.S. Public*, pg. 147

RAX—Restaurants—Rax Restaurants; *U.S. Private*, pg. 911

RAY-BAN—Sunglasses—Bausch & Lomb Incorporated; *U.S. Public*, pg. 194

RAY-BAN LARGE METAL—Sunglasses—Bausch & Lomb Incorporated; *U.S. Public*, pg. 194

RAY BAN WAYFARER—Sunglasses—Bausch & Lomb Incorporated; *U.S. Public*, pg. 194

RAY-DATA—Warehouse Computer Program—The Raymond Corporation; *Int'l*, pg. 123

RAY-FLEX—Press-Size Roll Cover—Harnischfeger Industries, Inc.; *U.S. Public*, pg. 788

RAY FLOYD—Footwear—E.J. Footwear Corp.; *U.S. Public*, pg. 1684

RAY-GUIDE—Wire Guidance—The Raymond Corporation; *Int'l*, pg. 123

RAY-JET—Fabric Filter Dust Collector—ABB Inc.; *Int'l*, pg. 3

RAY SPORTS—Sports Radio Network—Ray Communications, Inc.; *U.S. Private*, pg. 911

RAYATEN—Insulation Products—Raychem Corporation; *U.S. Public*, pg. 1362

RAYBESTOS—Brake Parts—Echlin Inc.; *U.S. Public*, pg. 560

RAYBESTOS—Automotive Friction Material—Raytech Corporation; *U.S. Public*, pg. 1363

RAYBESTOS—Aftermarket distribution of clutch liners—Universal Composites-U.S.C.; *U.S. Private*, pg. 1126

RAYBURN—NONE—Glynwed International PLC; *Int'l*, pg. 554

RAYCHEM—NONE—Raychem Corporation; *U.S. Public*, pg. 1362

RAYCRON—Radiation-Hardenable Coatings—PPG Industries, Inc.; *U.S. Public*, pg. 1245

RAYDEL—Microwave Transmissive Composite—Chemfab Corporation; *U.S. Public*, pg. 344

RAYLENE—Oil Lubricant—Bel-Ray Company, Inc.; *U.S. Private*, pg. 130

RAYLOC—Automotive Products—Genuine Parts Company; *U.S. Public*, pg. 732

RAYMOND—Rotary Hazardous Material Incinerators—ABB Inc.; *Int'l*, pg. 3

RAYMOND JAMES FINANCIAL—Investment & Financial Planning Services—Raymond James Financial, Inc.; *U.S. Public*, pg. 923

RAYNOR—Overhead Doors & Door Operators—Raynor Garage Doors; *U.S. Private*, pg. 912

RAYOSCOPE—Radiographic Films—Eastman Kodak Company; *U.S. Public*, pg. 550

RAYOTUBE—Radiation Thermometer—Honeywell, Inc.; *U.S. Public*, pg. 834

RAYPAK—Pool & Spa Heaters—Rheem Manufacturing Co.; *Int'l*, pg. 1022

RAYPARTS—Computerized Parts Ordering System—The Raymond Corporation; *Int'l*, pg. 123

RAY'S FOOD PLACE—Food Markets—C & K Market, Inc.; *U.S. Private*, pg. 191

RAY'S FOOD WAREHOUSE—Food Markets—C & K Market, Inc.; *U.S. Private*, pg. 191

RAY'S PRICE LESS FOODS—Food Markets—C & K Market, Inc.; *U.S. Private*, pg. 191

RAY'S SHOP SMART FOOD WAREHOUSE—Food Markets—C & K Market, Inc.; *U.S. Private*, pg. 191

RAYSEAL—Flameless Gas Repair Sleeve—Raychem Corporation; *U.S. Public*, pg. 1362

RAYSIL—Ladies' Wear—Tootal Group plc; *Int'l*, pg. 300

RAYSULATE—Electrical Insulation Systems—Raychem Corporation; *U.S. Public*, pg. 1362

RAYTHEON—Semiconductors & Electronic Equipment—Raytheon Company; *U.S. Public*, pg. 1364

RAYTREX—Liquid Dispersion—Eastman Kodak Company; *U.S. Public*, pg. 550

RAYVOLVE—Splice Kits—Raychem Corporation; *U.S. Public*, pg. 1362

RAZ—Eye Protection—U.S. Safety; *U.S. Private*, pg. 1125

RAZOR-BACK—Farm & Garden Tools—UnionTools, Inc.; *U.S. Public*, pg. 17

RAZOR POINT—Marker Pen—The Pilot Pen Corp. of America; *Int'l*, pg. 1057

RAZZAMATAZZ—Hosiery—Sara Lee Corporation; *U.S. Public*, pg. 1432

RAZZLES—Candy Products—Fleer-Skybox International Inc.; *U.S. Public*, pg. 1052

RE-CIRK-IT—Pushbutton Circuit Protectors—Eaton Corporation-Heinemann Products, Commercial Controls Division; *U.S. Public*, pg. 557

RE-COMM—Printing Paper—Georgia-Pacific Corporation; *U.S. Public*, pg. 735

RE/FLEX—Inspiratory Filter—Nellcor Puritan Bennett Incorporated; *U.S. Public*, pg. 1039

RE/MAX—Tradename—RE/MAX International, Inc.; *U.S. Private*, pg. 912

RE/MAX-100% Commission Concept—Recruitment—RE/MAX International, Inc.; *U.S. Private*, pg. 912

RE-MI—Foodservice Products—Borden, Inc.; *U.S. Private*, pg. 157

RE-NEW-COAT—Masonry Coating—Devoe Paint; *Int'l*, pg. 663

RE-NEW-COAT—Masonry Coating—ICI Paints; *Int'l*, pg. 664

RE-RUN—Printing Paper—Georgia-Pacific Corporation; *U.S. Public*, pg. 735

RE-TRAK—Hose Retractor—Binks Sames Corporation; *U.S. Public*, pg. 229

RE-UNION—Men's Sportswear—Seattle Pacific Industries, Inc.; *U.S. Private*, pg. 980

RE-USE-A-SEAL—Envelopes—Westvaco Corporation; *U.S. Public*, pg. 1762

REACH—Toothbrush—Johnson & Johnson; *U.S. Public*, pg. 927

REACH—Toothbrush—Johnson & Johnson Consumer Products; *U.S. Public*, pg. 928

REACH-FORK—Scissors Mechanism—The Raymond Corporation; *Int'l*, pg. 123

REACT—Electronic Temp. Control—The Chicago Faucet Co.; *U.S. Public*, pg. 234

REACT—NONE—Life Technologies, Inc.; *U.S. Public*, pg. 504

REACT—Publishers—Parade Publications Inc.; *U.S. Private*, pg. 20

REACTINE—Cetirizine—Pfizer Inc.; *U.S. Public*, pg. 1281

REACTOMER—Acrylic Monomers—Morton International Inc.; *U.S. Public*, pg. 1135

READ—Canned Prepared Salads—Owatonna Canning Company; *U.S. Public*, pg. 349

READ-O-MATIC—Water Meter Register—Badger Meter, Inc.; *U.S. Public*, pg. 164

READACRIT—Centrifuge—Becton Dickinson Primary Care Diagnostics; *U.S. Public*, pg. 199

READER—Newspaper—Chicago Reader, Inc.; *U.S. Private*, pg. 235

READER'S DIGEST—Magazine—The Reader's Digest Association, Inc.; *U.S. Public*, pg. 1367

READI-ACCESS—On Line Tracking System of Newspaper & Circulation Advertising—Advertising Checking Bureau Incorporated; *U.S. Private*, pg. 23

READI-CAT—Oral Contrast Medium for CT Scans—E-Z-Em, Inc.; *U.S. Public*, pg. 540

READI-PENCILS—Cartridge Pencils—The Mead Corporation; *U.S. Public*, pg. 1074

READI-REEL—Electrode—The Lincoln Electric Company; *U.S. Public*, pg. 996

READI-STAIN—Biological Supplies—Carolina Biological Supply Co.; *U.S. Private*, pg. 213

READINESS SET GO—Home School Curriculum—Alpha Omega Publications; *U.S. Private*, pg. 168

READING—Densitometers—Eastman Kodak Company; *U.S. Public*, pg. 550

THE READING ADVANTEDGE—OCR Software for Blind & Print-Disabled—Xerox Imaging Systems, Inc.; *U.S. Public*, pg. 1785

THE READING EDGE—Reading Machine for Blind & Print-Disabled—Xerox Imaging Systems, Inc.; *U.S. Public*, pg. 1785

READING GALAXY—NONE—Broderbund Software, Inc.; *U.S. Public*, pg. 258

READING ON MY OWN BOOKS—Book Imprint—Bertelsmann AG; *Int'l*, pg. 189

READING SERVICE BODY—Body Works—Reading Body Works, Inc.; *U.S. Private*, pg. 913

READING STAKE BODY—Body Works—Reading Body Works, Inc.; *U.S. Private*, pg. 913

READIVAC—Vacuum Cleaner—Douglas/Quikut; *U.S. Public*, pg. 217

READY-BEAD—Corner Bead—Georgia-Pacific Corporation; *U.S. Public*, pg. 735

READY-BOX—Electrially Heated Boxes for Temperature Maintenance—Mallinckrodt Inc.; *U.S. Public*, pg. 1039

READY CAP—Solid Scintillation Medium—Beckman Instruments, Inc.; *U.S. Public*, pg. 199

READY CAP—Pick-Up Cap—Reading Body Works, Inc.; *U.S. Public*, pg. 913

READY CARE—Oral Care Device—Ballard Medical Products; *U.S. Public*, pg. 171

READY FILTER—Filter Material—Beckman Instruments, Inc.; *U.S. Public*, pg. 199

READY FLOW III—Liquid Scintillation Cocktail—Beckman Instruments, Inc.; *U.S. Public*, pg. 199

READY-FOCUS—3 Zone Fixed Focus Video Camera Lens—Sony Electronics; *Int'l*, pg. 1281

READY GEL—Liquid Scintillation Cocktail—Beckman Instruments, Inc.; *U.S. Public*, pg. 199

READY-LABEL—NONE—Life Technologies, Inc.; *U.S. Public*, pg. 504

READY-LOAD—NONE—Life Technologies, Inc.; *U.S. Public*, pg. 504

READY MICRO—Liquid Scintillation Cocktail—Beckman Instruments, Inc.; *U.S. Public*, pg. 199

READY-MOUNT—Transparency Mounts—Eastman Kodak Company; *U.S. Public*, pg. 550

READY-NIN—Amino Acid Detection Kit—Beckman Instruments, Inc.; *U.S. Public*, pg. 199

READY ORGANIC—Liquid Scintillation Cocktail—Beckman Instruments, Inc.; *U.S. Public*, pg. 199

READY-PACK II—Radiographic Film Pack—Eastman Kodak Company; *U.S. Public*, pg. 550

READY PROTEIN +—Liquid Scintillation Cocktail—Beckman Instruments, Inc.; *U.S. Public*, pg. 199

READY SAFE—Liquid Scintillation Cocktail—Beckman Instruments, Inc.; *U.S. Public*, pg. 199

READY SET—Hair Products—Dena Corporation; *U.S. Private*, pg. 324

READY-SOLV—Scintillation Solution—Beckman Instruments, Inc.; *U.S. Public*, pg. 199

READY VALUE—Liquid Scintillation Cocktail—Beckman Instruments, Inc.; *U.S. Public*, pg. 199

READY WALL—Steel Wall Panel—Clestra Hauserman; *Int'l*, pg. 569

READYKEY—Access Control System—Radionics, Inc.; *U.S. Public*, pg. 501

READYLOAD—Photographic Film Packaging Configurations—Eastman Kodak Company; *U.S. Public*, pg. 550

READYMATIC—Slide Projectors, Viewers, Chargers Processing Apparatus, Chemicals—Eastman Kodak Company; *U.S. Public*, pg. 550

READYMIX—Pre-Mixed Concrete—CSR Limited; *Int'l*, pg. 245

READYPRINT—Photocopy Apparatus—Eastman Kodak Company; *U.S. Public*, pg. 550

READYROLL—Decorative Borders—Forbo Holding SA; *Int'l*, pg. 496

REAGENT RED BLOOD CELLS—Blood Cells—Ortho Clinical Diagnostic Systems Inc.; *U.S. Public*, pg. 929

REAL—Peanut Butter—ConAgra, Inc.; *U.S. Public*, pg. 425

REAL COOKIN' FOOD—3-Minute Ice Cream Maker & Real Cookin' Tastybake Oven—Tyco Toys, Inc.; *U.S. Public*, pg. 1058

REAL CRAW—Fish Attractant—EBSCO Industries, Inc.; *U.S. Public*, pg. 358

REAL CREAM—Non-Dairy Aerosol Whipped Topping—Broughton Foods Company; *U.S. Public*, pg. 259

THE REAL CURL—Promotional Material for Hazir Care Products—The Gillette Company; *U.S. Public*, pg. 743

REAL ESTATE HOTLINE—Interactive Marketing & Listing Solution for the Real Estate Industry—Brite Voice Systems, Inc.; *U.S. Public*, pg. 257

REAL ESTATE SERVICE—Franchise Operation—Meredith Corporation; *U.S. Public*, pg. 1094

THE REAL ESTATE SUPER STARS—Recruiting and Advertising Package—RE/MAX International, Inc.; *U.S. Private*, pg. 912

REAL LEAN DELUXE—Low Fat Hamburger—Hardee's Food Systems, Inc.; *U.S. Public*, pg. 278

REAL MCCOY—Bras—Warner's; *U.S. Public*, pg. 1738

REAL NAIL—NONE—Juno Lighting, Inc.; *U.S. Public*, pg. 935

REAL-NAIL BAR HANGER—Installation Component for Lighting Fixture—Juno Lighting, Inc.; *U.S. Public*, pg. 935

REAL/IX—Real-Time UNIX O/S—Modcomp; *U.S. Public*, pg. 283

REAL OBJECTS—NONE—Cognos Corp.; *Int'l*, pg. 306

THE REAL PRINTERS—Printing Franchise—American Speedy Printing Centers, Inc.; *U.S. Private*, pg. 62

REAL THRILLS—Amusement Park—Cedar Fair, L.P.; *U.S. Public*, pg. 319

REAL-TIME—Product (RTP) Sub-Systems—Computer Products, Inc.; *U.S. Public*, pg. 422

REAL-TIME—Digital Mini-Computers—Modcomp; *U.S. Public*, pg. 283

REAL-TIME RASTERIZATION—Technology—QMS, Inc.; *U.S. Public*, pg. 1346

REAL-TUFF—Plumbing Chemical—Hercules Chemical Co., Inc.; *U.S. Private*, pg. 523

REAL-WOOD—Exterior Wood Preservative—Star Bronze Company; *U.S. Private*, pg. 1034

THE REAL YELLOW PAGES—Business Telephone Directory—BellSouth Corporation; *U.S. Public*, pg. 207

REALEMON—NONE—Borden Foods Canada; *U.S. Private*, pg. 159

REALEMON—NONE—Borden Foods Co.; *U.S. Private*, pg. 158

REALEMON—Lemon Juice—Borden, Inc.; *U.S. Private*, pg. 157

REALIME—Lime Juice—Borden, Inc.; *U.S. Private*, pg. 157

REALISTIC—Electronic Equipment—RadioShack; *U.S. Public*, pg. 1560

REALITIES—Greeting Cards—American Greetings Corporation; *U.S. Public*, pg. 77

REALITIES—Dress Shoes—Oomphies, Inc.; *U.S. Private*, pg. 817

REALLY NATURALS—Fruit Snacks—Farley Candy Company; *U.S. Private*, pg. 397

REALTIME—Laboratory Control Serum—Beckman Instruments, Inc.; *U.S. Public*, pg. 199

REALTY MANAGEMENT SERVICES (PRIVATE) LIMITED—Real Estate Management—Singapore Land Limited; *Int'l*, pg. 1252

REALVIEW—Large Screen Display System—Curtis Mathes Holding Corp.; *U.S. Public*, pg. 1057

REAM-A-MATIC—Condenser Tube Cleaner—Goodway Technologies Corporation; *U.S. Private*, pg. 464

REAM-EZE—Solid Carbide Reamer—National Twist Drill Div.; *U.S. Public*, pg. 1370

REAM-EZE—Solid Carbide Reamer—Regal-Beloit Corporation; *U.S. Public*, pg. 1370

REAMES—Frozen Specialty Noodles, Pastas, & Breaded Specialty Items—Lancaster Colony Corporation; *U.S. Public*, pg. 976

REAMES—Egg Noodles—T. Marzetti Company; *U.S. Public*, pg. 977

REAMES—Egg Noodles—Reames Foods Inc.; *U.S. Public*, pg. 977

REATTA—Luxury Car—General Motors Corporation; *U.S. Public*, pg. 718

REAX—Chemical Preparation & Lignin Products—Westvaco Corporation; *U.S. Public*, pg. 1762

RED BULL—Malt Liquor Beer—The Stroh Brewery Company; *U.S. Private*, pg. 1047

REBEL—Street Bike—American Honda Motor Co., Inc.; *Int'l*, pg. 634

REBEL—Motorcycle—American Honda Motor Co., Inc. Motorcycle Division; *Int'l*, pg. 634

REBEL—Fishing Lures—EBSCO Industries, Inc.; *U.S. Private*, pg. 358

REBEL—Motorcycle—Honda Motor Co., Ltd.; *Int'l*, pg. 634

REBEL YELL—NONE—Guinness Plc; *Int'l*, pg. 412

REBEL YELL—Bourbon—Shieffelin Somerset Co.; *Int'l*, pg. 412

REBEL YELL—Bourbon—United Distillers USA, Inc.; *Int'l*, pg. 412

Brand Name Index

REBIF—Recombinant Interferon Beta—Ares-Serono S.A.; *Int'l*, pg. 80

REBOUND—Clear Vinyl—Fasson Films; *U.S. Public*, pg. 153

REBUS—Business Product—International Business Machines Corporation; *U.S. Public*, pg. 895

REC OIL—Products for Separating Soluble Oils From Wastewaters—BetzDearborn Inc.; *U.S. Public*, pg. 226

REC-TECH—Tennis Court Color Surfacing—Maintenance, Inc.; *Int'l*, pg. 1068

RECAP—Prescription Drug Plan—PCS Health Systems, Inc.; *U.S. Public*, pg. 993

RECARDO ERRANTE—Voice Mail Service—Fone America, Inc.; *U.S. Public*, pg. 661

RECARO—Seats Brandnames—Recaro North America, Inc.; *U.S. Private*, pg. 914

RECAT—Catalyst Oxidizer—ATMI, Inc.; *U.S. Public*, pg. 12

RECHARGACELL—Ni-CD Batteries—Sanyo Energy (U.S.A.) Corporation; *Int'l*, pg. 1191

RECHARGE—Electrolyte Added Beverage—J.M. Smucker Company; *U.S. Public*, pg. 1480

RECHARGEABLE ALKALINE—NONE—RAYOVAC Corporation; *U.S. Private*, pg. 912

RECIPE—Dog Food—H.J. Heinz Company; *U.S. Public*, pg. 805

RECIPE—NONE—Star-Kist Foods Inc.; *U.S. Public*, pg. 805

RECIPROGRATE—Stoker—Detroit Stoker Co.; *U.S. Public*, pg. 1679

RECLAIM—Herbicide—The Dow Chemical Company; *U.S. Public*, pg. 522

RECLAMIZER—Locker Refurbish—Steiner Co., Inc.; *U.S. Private*, pg. 1039

RECLINA-REST—Reclining Chair—La-Z-Boy Incorporated; *U.S. Public*, pg. 972

RECLINA-ROCKER—Chair—La-Z-Boy Incorporated; *U.S. Public*, pg. 972

RECLINA-WAY—Wall Recliner—La-Z-Boy Incorporated; *U.S. Public*, pg. 972

RECOGEN—Vapor Recovery/Power Generation—Edwards Engineering Corporation; *U.S. Private*, pg. 365

RECOIL—Wire Thread Insert Systems for Automotive, Industrial, & Aerospace Markets—KTI; *U.S. Public*, pg. 939

RECOLLECTIONS—Greeting Cards—American Greetings Corporation; *U.S. Public*, pg. 77

RECOLLECTIONS—Rattan Furniture—Avon Workshop Ficks Reed; *U.S. Private*, pg. 102

RECOMBIGEN HIV-1 EIA—Test System—Ortho Clinical Diagnostic Systems Inc.; *U.S. Public*, pg. 929

RECOMBINATE—Recombinant Clotting Factor For Hemophiliacs—Baxter International Inc.; *U.S. Public*, pg. 196

RECOMBINATE—Blood Clotting Protein—Genetics Institute, Inc.; *U.S. Public*, pg. 79

RECOMBIVAX HB—Hepatitis B Vaccine-Recombinant—Merck & Co., Inc.; *U.S. Public*, pg. 1090

RECOMBIVAX-HB—Vaccine for Human Use—Merck Human Health Division (U.S. Human Health); *U.S. Public*, pg. 1091

RECOMBULIN—NONE—Life Technologies, Inc.; *U.S. Public*, pg. 504

RECON—Ovens—Foster Refrigerator Corporation; *U.S. Private*, pg. 421

RECON + PLUS—Reconstitutors—Foster Refrigerator Corporation; *U.S. Private*, pg. 421

RECOP—Fungicide—Novartis AG; *Int'l*, pg. 971

RECORD—Private Brand Paper—The Cincinnati Cordage & Paper Company; *U.S. Private*, pg. 239

RECORD—NONE—Everest & Jennings, Inc.; *U.S. Public*, pg. 758

THE RECORD—Newspaper—Quebecor Inc.; *Int'l*, pg. 1075

RECORD—Dry Pasta—Ranks Hovis McDougall Limited; *Int'l*, pg. 1395

RECORD EXPRESS 1000/2000—Report Management System—Dictaphone Corp.; *U.S. Private*, pg. 1045

RECORD EXPRESS 770—Medical Transcription System—Dictaphone Corp.; *U.S. Private*, pg. 1045

RECORD GUARD—Reinforcement Strips for Punched Records—Carstens Inc.; *U.S. Private*, pg. 216

RECORD TOWN—Retail Music Store—Trans World Entertainment Corporation; *U.S. Public*, pg. 1629

RECORDAK—Microfilming Equipment, Films, Papers & Chemicals & Check Endorsers—Eastman Kodak Company; *U.S. Public*, pg. 550

RECORDALL—Water Meter—Badger Meter, Inc.; *U.S. Public*, pg. 164

RECORDLINK—NONE—American Management Systems, Inc.; *U.S. Public*, pg. 86

RECORDOSE—Medical Instrument—Capintec Inc.; *U.S. Private*, pg. 205

RECORDPLATE—Business Forms—Moore Corporation Limited; *Int'l*, pg. 888

RECORMON & EPOGIN—Protein of the Production of Red Blood Cells—Genetics Institute, Inc.; *Int'l*, pg. 79

RECOTON—Electronic Accessories—Recoton Corporation; *U.S. Public*, pg. 1369

RECOVER—Recycled Papers—Appleton Papers Inc.; *Int'l*, pg. 567

RECOVER—Recycled Carbonless Paper—Arjo Wiggins Appleton plc; *Int'l*, pg. 567

RECOVERPLUS FOR DB2—NONE—BMC Software, Inc.; *U.S. Public*, pg. 162

RECOVERY MANAGER FOR DB2—NONE—BMC Software, Inc.; *U.S. Public*, pg. 162

RECOVERY MANAGER FOR IMS—NONE—BMC Software, Inc.; *U.S. Public*, pg. 162

RECOVERY PLUS—Disaster Response Service—Diebold, Incorporated; *U.S. Public*, pg. 506

RECOVERY PLUS—Collections Program—I.C. System, Inc.; *U.S. Private*, pg. 553

RECOVERY PLUS FOR CICS/VSAM—NONE—BMC Software, Inc.; *U.S. Public*, pg. 162

RECOVERY PLUS FOR IMS—NONE—BMC Software, Inc.; *U.S. Public*, pg. 162

RECOVERY SOLUTIONS THROUGH PARTNERSHIP—NONE—SunGard Data Systems Inc.; *U.S. Public*, pg. 1534

RECREATIONAL TENNIS & BAGS—NONE—Prince Sports Group Inc.; *U.S. Private*, pg. 884

RECTOID—Pharmaceutical—Pharmacia & Upjohn Adria Laboratories; *Int'l*, pg. 1049

RECYCLE ONE—Refuse Collection Truck—Dempster Equipment; *U.S. Public*, pg. 1089

RECYCLED LYNX OPAQUE—Printing Papers—Weyerhaeuser Company; *U.S. Public*, pg. 1764

RECYCLEGRAM—Newsletter—Nellcor Puritan Bennett Incorporated; *U.S. Public*, pg. 1039

RECYCLER BRAND MOWER—Mulching Mower—The Toro Company; *U.S. Public*, pg. 1623

RED APPLE—Supermarkets—Associated Grocers, Inc.; *U.S. Private*, pg. 90

RED APPLE—Grocery Stores—Red Apple Companies; *U.S. Private*, pg. 914

RED APPLE—Food & Variety Stores—Red Apple, Inc.; *U.S. Private*, pg. 915

RED BAND—Liquorice Candies—CSM N.V.; *Int'l*, pg. 243

RED BAND—Abrasive Disc—Gardner Abrasives; *U.S. Public*, pg. 1699

RED BAND—Flour—General Mills, Inc.; *U.S. Public*, pg. 717

RED BAND ON AMPULES—Mark Comprises a RED Band Encircling the Bulb of an Ampul—The West Company, Incorporated; *U.S. Public*, pg. 1755

RED BARON—Frozen Pizza—Schwan's Sales Enterprises; *U.S. Private*, pg. 974

THE RED BARON—Fishing Tools & Services—Smith International, Inc.; *U.S. Public*, pg. 1478

RED BARON DRILL-PAX—Drilling Tool With Diamonds—Smith International, Inc.; *U.S. Public*, pg. 1478

RED BARON PRIVATE RECIPE—Frozen Pizza—Schwan's Sales Enterprises; *U.S. Private*, pg. 974

RED BARRICADES—War Game—Monarch Avalon, Inc.; *U.S. Public*, pg. 1123

RED BRAND—Fence—Keystone Consolidated Industries, Inc.; *U.S. Public*, pg. 955

RED BRAND—Fence, Nails, Baler Wire, Electric Fence Wire & Confinement Panels—Keystone Steel & Wire Co.; *U.S. Public*, pg. 955

RED CARPET DELIVERY—Service—Luskin's, Inc.; *U.S. Private*, pg. 681

RED CHEEK—Apple Juice—Cadbury Beverages; *Int'l*, pg. 248

RED CHEEK—Apple Juice—Cadbury Beverages North America; *Int'l*, pg. 248

RED CIRCLE—Coffee—The Great Atlantic & Pacific Tea Company, Inc.; *Int'l*, pg. 1375

RED COON—Plug Chewing Tobacco—Conwood Company L.P.; *U.S. Private*, pg. 272

RED-COTE—Oral Hygiene Aids—John O. Butler Co.; *Int'l*, pg. 1320

RED CROSS—Pasta—Borden, Inc.; *U.S. Private*, pg. 157

RED CROSS—Table Salt—Cargill Salt Inc.; *Int'l*, pg. 48

RED CROSS—Processed Vegetables—Furman Foods, Inc.; *U.S. Private*, pg. 431

RED CROSS—Toothache Drops—Mentholatum Company; *Int'l*, pg. 1126

RED CROWN—Sporting Goods—Brunswick Bowling & Billiards Corp.; *U.S. Public*, pg. 265

RED DEVIL—Paints, Clear Finishes & Wood Stains—The Thompson's Company; *U.S. Public*, pg. 1466

RED DEVIL BUFFALO STYLE—Cayenne Pepper—Trappey's Fine Foods, Inc.; *U.S. Private*, pg. 105

RED DEVIL ORIGINAL—Cayenne Pepper—Trappey's Fine Foods, Inc.; *U.S. Private*, pg. 105

RED DIAMOND—Convenience Stores—E-Z Serve Corp.; *U.S. Public*, pg. 540

RED DIAMOND TRUST—Convenience Stores—E-Z Serve Convenience Stores, Inc.; *U.S. Public*, pg. 540

RED DOG—Beer—Miller Brewing Company; *U.S. Public*, pg. 1289

RED DOOR—Fragrance for Women—Elizabeth Arden Company; *Int'l*, pg. 1435

RED DOT—Monitoring Electrodes, ECG—3M; *U.S. Public*, pg. 1604

RED DOT TANDEM ALIGNER—Truck & Trailer Tandem Aligner—Bee Line Company; *U.S. Private*, pg. 129

RED-EYE—Industrial Instrument—Capintec Inc.; *U.S. Private*, pg. 205

RED FOX—Loose Leaf Chewing Tobacco—Conwood Company L.P.; *U.S. Private*, pg. 272

RWD-GO—Urethane Belts—Fenner Drives; *U.S. Private*, pg. 400

RED GOAT—Commercial Waste Disposers—General Slicing/Red Goat Disposers; *U.S. Public*, pg. 1506

RED GOAT—Waste Disposers—Standex International Corporation; *U.S. Public*, pg. 1505

RED-HARD—NONE—Carpenter Technology Corporation; *U.S. Public*, pg. 307

RED HAT—Solenoid Valves—Ascolectric Limited; *U.S. Public*, pg. 575

RED-HAT—Solenoid & Air Operated Valves & Accessories—Automatic Switch Co.; *U.S. Public*, pg. 573

RED HAT II—Solenoid Valves—Ascolectric Limited; *U.S. Public*, pg. 575

RED HEAD—Anchors—ITW Ramset/Red Head; *U.S. Public*, pg. 867

RED HEART—Spirit—Allied Domecq PLC; *Int'l*, pg. 62

RED HEART—Yarn Hand Knitting—Coats & Clark Inc.; *Int'l*, pg. 300

RED HILL—Corn & Cane Syrup—Whitfield Foods, Inc.; *U.S. Private*, pg. 1173

RED HOT SPECIAL SITUATIONS—Financial Fax Newsletter—KCI Communications, Inc; *U.S. Private*, pg. 784

RED HOTS WITH DESIGN—Greeting Cards—American Greetings Corporation; *U.S. Public*, pg. 77

RED JACKET—Water & Petroleum Submersible Pumps & Leak Detection Equipment—Marley Pump; *U.S. Public*, pg. 1676

RED JUICE—Plug Tobacco—Brown & Williamson Tobacco Corp.; *Int'l*, pg. 111

RED KAP—Occupational Apparel—VF Corporation; *U.S. Public*, pg. 1702

RED LABEL—Coffee—Reily Foods Company; *U.S. Private*, pg. 919

RED LOBSTER—Restaurant Chain—Darden Restaurants, Inc.; *U.S. Public*, pg. 483

RED LOBSTER—Seafood Restaurants—Red Lobster USA; *U.S. Public*, pg. 484

RED RIDERS—Advertising Slogan—American Honda Motor Co., Inc. Motorcycle Division; *Int'l*, pg. 634

RED RIM—Abrasive Discs—Gardner Abrasives; *U.S. Public*, pg. 1699

RED-RIM—Abrasive Tools, Wheels & Discs—Litton Industries, Inc.; *U.S. Public*, pg. 1002

RED RIVER CEREAL—NONE—Robin Hood Multifoods Inc.; *U.S. Public*, pg. 901

RED ROCKERS—Aluminum Roller Rocker Arms—Edelbrock Corp.; *U.S. Public*, pg. 563

RED ROOF INN—Motels—Red Roof Inns, Inc.; *U.S. Public*, pg. 1369

RED ROOSTER—Cheese—Churny Company Inc.; *U.S. Public*, pg. 1288

RED ROOSTER—NONE—Coles Myer Ltd.; *Int'l*, pg. 306

RED ROOSTER 21—Wine—Adams Wine Co.; *U.S. Private*, pg. 17

RED ROVER JUNIOR SPORTSWEAR—NONE—Niches, Inc.; *U.S. Private*, pg. 1181

RED RYDER—Shock Absorbers & Gas Shock Absorbers—Arvin Industries, Inc.; *U.S. Public*, pg. 136

RED SEAL—Snacks—Borden, Inc.; *U.S. Private*, pg. 157

RED SEAL—Potato Chips & Corn Chips—Metz Baking Company (WI); *U.S. Private*, pg. 1022

RED SEAL—Color Products—Universal Foods Corporation; *U.S. Public*, pg. 1695

RED SEAL—Trolleys—Jervis B. Webb Company; *U.S. Private*, pg. 1156

RED SEAL GUARD—Anti-Contaminant Seals—Jervis B. Webb Company; *U.S. Private*, pg. 1156

RED SEAL SPECTRABLEND CLEAR—Chemical—Warner-Jenkinson Co.; *U.S. Public*, pg. 1696

RED SEAL SPECTRACOAT—Dispersions—Warner-Jenkinson Co.; *U.S. Public*, pg. 1696

RED SEAL SPECTRASPRAY—Chemical—Warner-Jenkinson Co.; *U.S. Public*, pg. 1696

RED670—NONE—Life Technologies, Inc.; *U.S. Public*, pg. 504

RED613—NONE—Life Technologies, Inc.; *U.S. Public*, pg. 504

RED STAR—Putty Knives, Scrapers—Hyde Manufacturing Co.; *U.S. Private*, pg. 551

RED STAR—Yeast—Universal Foods Corporation; *U.S. Public*, pg. 1695

RED STREAK—Industrial Products—Brown-Bridge; *U.S. Public*, pg. 1022

RED STREAK—Adhesive Coated Paper & Cloth—Kimberly-Clark Corporation; *U.S. Public*, pg. 958

RED STRIPE—NONE—Guinness Plc; *Int'l*, pg. 412

RED THREAD II—Fiberglass Reinforced Plastic Piping—A.O. Smith Corporation; *U.S. Public*, pg. 1476

RED TOP—Posts—Keystone Consolidated Industries, Inc.; *U.S. Public*, pg. 955

RED TOP—Fence Posts—Keystone Steel & Wire Co.; *U.S. Public*, pg. 955

RED-TOUGH—NONE—Carpenter Technology Corporation; *U.S. Public*, pg. 307

RED TULIP—Chocolates—Cadbury Schweppes p.l.c.; *Int'l*, pg. 247

RED-WEAR—NONE—Carpenter Technology Corporation; *U.S. Public*, pg. 307

RED, WHITE & BLUE—Mens' Clothing—Key Industries, Inc.; *U.S. Private*, pg. 618

RED WING—Work & Sport Shoes, Boots—Red Wing Shoe Co., Inc.; *U.S. Private*, pg. 915

RED WOLF—Alcoholic Beverage—Anheuser-Busch Companies, Inc.; *U.S. Public*, pg. 113

RED ZINGER—Herb Tea—Celestial Seasonings; *U.S. Public*, pg. 319

REDA—Electric Submersible Pumping Systems—Camco International Inc.; *U.S. Public*, pg. 297

REDBACK BITTER—Bitter Ale—Carlton & United Breweries Ltd.; *Int'l*, pg. 500

REDBOOK—Magazine—The Hearst Corporation; *U.S. Private*, pg. 515

REDBOOK—Magazine—Hearst Magazines Division; *U.S. Private*, pg. 516

REDBOOK—Magazine—Redbook; *U.S. Private*, pg. 517

REDCO—Republic Electric & Devel. Co.—Jetronic Industries, Inc.; *U.S. Public*, pg. 926

REDCO—Food Slicer—Lincoln Foodservice Products, Inc.; *U.S. Public*, pg. 188

REDDI-SEALER—Apparatus for Crimping Lids on Aluminum Foil Containers—Reynolds Metals Company; *U.S. Public*, pg. 1385

REDDI WHIP—Prepared Whipped Cream—ConAgra, Inc.; *U.S. Public*, pg. 425

REDDI-WIP—Aerosol, Real & Non-Dairy—Beatrice Cheese Co.; *U.S. Public*, pg. 426

REDDING RECORD SEARCHLIGHT—J.P. Scripps Newspaper Group Dailies—The E.W. Scripps Company; *U.S. Public*, pg. 1447

REDDY—Sauces—Vandemoortele N.V.; *Int'l*, pg. 1451

REDEEM—Herbicide—The Dow Chemical Company; *U.S. Public*, pg. 522

REDEFINING PRINTING—Business Product—International Business Machines Corporation; *U.S. Public*, pg. 895

REDENBUDDER'S—Microwave Popcorn—Hunt-Wesson, Inc.; *U.S. Public*, pg. 428

REDGLO—Liquid Vitamin Supplement—Farnam Companies, Inc.; *U.S. Private*, pg. 396

REDHAWK—Double-Action Revolvers—Sturm, Ruger & Co., Inc.; *U.S. Public*, pg. 1526

REDI—NONE—ETEX; *Int'l*, pg. 430

REDI—Spray—Graco Inc.; *U.S. Public*, pg. 756

REDI-BIT—Carbide Bits—ITW Ramset/Red Head; *U.S. Public*, pg. 867

REDI-CAP—Scientific Glassware for Laboratory Use—Wheaton Inc.; *Int'l*, pg. 67

REDI-CHEM—NONE—Allied Diagnostic Imaging Resources, Inc.; *U.S. Public*, pg. 282

REDI-CHEM—Epoxy Anchoring System—ITW Ramset/Red Head; *U.S. Public*, pg. 867

REDI-CUTS—Plywood, Lumber, Particleboard & Hardboard—Georgia-Pacific Corporation; *U.S. Public*, pg. 735

REDI-DRILL—Power Tools—ITW Ramset/Red Head; *U.S. Public*, pg. 867

REDI-DRIVE—Pin & Wire Loop Installation System—ITW Ramset/Red Head; *U.S. Public*, pg. 867

REDI-FIT—Powder Actuated Pins & Loads—ITW Ramset/Red Head; *U.S. Public*, pg. 867

REDY-FLOW—Horizontal Form, Fill, & Seal Machinery—G.D. Packaging Machinery Inc.; *Int'l*, pg. 531

REDI-HIT—Nail Drive Anchors—ITW Ramset/Red Head; *U.S. Public*, pg. 867

REDI-HOOK—Drapery Hooks—Kirsch; *U.S. Public*, pg. 1176

REDI I—NONE—Names for Dames, Inc.; *U.S. Private*, pg. 773

REDI LITE—Electric Trouble Lights & Portable Lights—General Cable Corporation; *Int'l*, pg. 1486

REDI-PAK—Baler Wire—CF & I Steel, L.P.; *U.S. Public*, pg. 1230

REDI-PAN—Foil Pans—Reynolds Metals Company; *U.S. Public*, pg. 1385

REDI PIERCE—Self Piercing Fasteners—Maclean-Fogg Co.; *U.S. Private*, pg. 692

REDI-PLUG—Electrical Connectors & Adaptors—Zenith Electronics Corp.; *U.S. Public*, pg. 1790

REDI-SERVE—Thermoformed Microwavable Trays—American National Can Company; *Int'l*, pg. 1029

REDI VIAL—Dual-Compartment Vial, Lilly—Eli Lilly and Company; *U.S. Public*, pg. 992

REDI-HANDLE—Foil Pans—Reynolds Metals Company; *U.S. Public*, pg. 1385

REDI/PLATE—Plates—Fisher Scientific Company; *U.S. Private*, pg. 658

REDICOTE—Specialty Chemicals—Akzo Nobel Inc.; *Int'l*, pg. 47

REDICOTE—Asphalt Emulsifiers—Akzo Nobel N.V.; *Int'l*, pg. 42

REDINGTON—Packaging Machinery—G.D. Packaging Machinery Inc.; *Int'l*, pg. 531

REDIREAD—Computer Software Feature—Beckman Instruments, Inc.; *U.S. Public*, pg. 199

REDISCAN—Computer Software Feature—Beckman Instruments, Inc.; *U.S. Public*, pg. 199

REDLER—En Masse Conveyors—Svedala Bulk Materials Handling Engineered Products; *Int'l*, pg. 1326

REDLINE—Specialty Gas Equipment—AGA Ges.m.b.H.; *Int'l*, pg. 13

REDLINE—Hand Portable & Wheeled Fire Extinguishers—Ansul Incorporated; *U.S. Public*, pg. 1648

REDLINE—Product Family for Transportation Market—DSP Technology Inc.; *U.S. Public*, pg. 475

REDLINE—Racquet Strings—Head USA, Inc.; *U.S. Private*, pg. 514

REDLINE—NONE—Life Technologies, Inc.; *U.S. Public*, pg. 504

REDLINE—NONE—Morse Controls; *U.S. Public*, pg. 857

REDLINE ACAP—Combustion Analysis System—DSP Technology Inc.; *U.S. Public*, pg. 475

REDLINE ADAPT—Dynamometer Control & Test System—DSP Technology Inc.; *U.S. Public*, pg. 475

REDLINE ASSIST—Remote ISDN Service System—DSP Technology Inc.; *U.S. Public*, pg. 475

REDPATH—Sugars—Tate & Lyle PLC; *Int'l*, pg. 1356

REDRING—Water heaters, showers, hand dryers—The General Electric Company, p.l.c.; *Int'l*, pg. 543

REDROPE—Filing Pockets—Smead Manufacturing Company; *U.S. Public*, pg. 1006

REDUCE—Saves I/O Time & DASD Space for DL/1 & DB2 by Compressing Databases—Boole & Babbage, Inc.; *U.S. Public*, pg. 244

REDUCTROL 30—Cable—Rockbestos-Supranant Cable Corp.; *U.S. Private*, pg. 938

REDCUTROL 20—Cable—Rockbestos-Supranant Cable Corp.; *U.S. Private*, pg. 938

REDUX—Appetite Suppressant—Wyeth-Ayerst Laboratories, Inc.; *U.S. Public*, pg. 80

REDWOOD—Moist Snuff Smokeless Tobacco—Swisher International Group, Inc.; *U.S. Public*, pg. 1543

REEBOK—NONE—Reebok International Ltd.; *U.S. Public*, pg. 1369

REEBOK BRAND—Athletic Footwear & Apparel—Reebok International Ltd.; *U.S. Public*, pg. 1369

REEBOK CLASSIC—Golf Competition—Reebok International Ltd.; *U.S. Public*, pg. 1369

REEBOK GOLF—Golf Program—Reebok International Ltd.; *U.S. Public*, pg. 1369

REECE—Specialized Machinery—AMF Reece Incorporated; *U.S. Private*, pg. 7

REED—Rock Bits—Camco International Inc.; *U.S. Public*, pg. 297

REED—Injection Molding Machines—Package Machinery Co.; *U.S. Private*, pg. 832

REED—Tools—Reed Tool Company; *U.S. Public*, pg. 298

REED—Tools—Ryan Herco Products Corp.; *U.S. Private*, pg. 953

REED & BARTON—Flatware & Holloware—Reed & Barton Corporation; *U.S. Private*, pg. 916

REED HARD CANDY—Roll Hard Candy—Amurol Confections Co.; *U.S. Public*, pg. 1781

REED PRENTICE—Injection Molding Machines—Package Machinery Co.; *U.S. Private*, pg. 832

REED ST. JAMES—Sleepwear—Host Apparel, Inc.; *U.S. Private*, pg. 540

REED ST. JAMES—Menswear—Tandy Brands Accessories, Inc.; *U.S. Public*, pg. 1560

REED'S SWEETS—NONE—Amurol Confections Co.; *U.S. Public*, pg. 1781

REEDLITE—Heavy Metal Free Color Concentrate Product Line—Reedspectrum; *Int'l*, pg. 624

REEDS—Jewelers—Reeds Jewelers, Inc.; *U.S. Public*, pg. 1370

REEDSPECTRUM—Color & Additive Concentrates for Thermoplastics—Reedspectrum; *Int'l*, pg. 624

REEL A CORD—Electrical Cord Set & Reel—General Cable Corporation; *Int'l*, pg. 1486

THE REEL LEADER—Reels—Hannay Reels; *U.S. Private*, pg. 499

REEL-PAK—Reels—Plastic Reel Corp. of America; *U.S. Private*, pg. 871

REEL PEOPLE—Publication—Eastman Kodak Company; *U.S. Public*, pg. 550

REELITES—Power Source for Movable/Portable Equipment—Appleton Electric Co.; *U.S. Public*, pg. 572

REELMASTER—Institutional Mower—The Toro Company; *U.S. Public*, pg. 1623

REESE'S—Peanut Butter & Crunchy Cups, Peanut Butter Chips And Peanut Butter Eggs—Hershey Chocolate U.S.A.; *U.S. Public*, pg. 812

REESE'S CRUNCHY COOKIE CUPS—Confection—Hershey Chocolate U.S.A.; *U.S. Public*, pg. 812

Brand Name Index

REESE'S CRUNCHY PEANUT BUTTER CUPS—Candy—Hershey Foods Corporation; *U.S. Public*, pg. 811

REESE'S MINIATURES—Candy—Hershey Foods Corporation; *U.S. Public*, pg. 811

REESE'S PEANUT BUTTER CHIPS—Candy Chips—Hershey Foods Corporation; *U.S. Public*, pg. 811

REESE'S PEANUT BUTTER CUPS—Candy—Hershey Foods Corporation; *U.S. Public*, pg. 811

REESES PEANUT BUTTER PUFFS—Cereal—General Mills, Inc.; *U.S. Public*, pg. 717

REESE'S PIECES—Candy—Hershey Chocolate U.S.A.; *U.S. Public*, pg. 812

REESE'S PIECES—Candy—Hershey Foods Corporation; *U.S. Public*, pg. 811

REEVAIR—Polyurethane Coated Fabrics—Reeves International; *U.S. Private*, pg. 507

REEVECOTE—Specialty Coated Fabrics—Reeves International; *U.S. Private*, pg. 507

REEVES—Lampholders—IMI Plc; *Int'l*, pg. 646

REEVES—Speed Varying Power Transmission Devices House Mark—Rockwell International Corporation; *U.S. Public*, pg. 1397

REEVETECH—Barrier & Containment Coated Fabrics—Reeves International; *U.S. Private*, pg. 507

REFAX—Recycled Plastic Materials—Montedison S.p.A.; *Int'l*, pg. 324

REFCON—Calcium Aluminate Cement—Lehigh Portland Cement Company; *Int'l*, pg. 605

REFERENCE FUELS—NONE—Haltermann AG; *Int'l*, pg. 590

REFIL-A-LITE—Lighter—Ronson Corporation; *U.S. Public*, pg. 1405

REFINE—Herbicide—Du Pont (E.I. Du Pont De Nemours & Co.); *U.S. Public*, pg. 530

REFLAB—Chemistry Reagents—Medical Analysis Systems Inc.; *U.S. Private*, pg. 727

REFLECT—NONE—Wisconsin Pharmacal Co., Inc.; *U.S. Private*, pg. 1185

REFLECTION—Church Worship Bulletins—Warner Press, Inc.; *U.S. Private*, pg. 1150

REFLECTIONS—Luggage—American Tourister, Inc.; *U.S. Public*, pg. 1430

REFLECTIONS—Juvenile Bedding Products—CHF Industries, Inc.; *U.S. Private*, pg. 1094

REFLECTIONS—Decorative Faucets—The Chicago Faucet Co.; *U.S. Private*, pg. 234

REFLECTIONS—Enamel Printing Paper—Consolidated Papers, Inc.; *U.S. Public*, pg. 436

REFLECTIONS—Cameras—Eastman Kodak Company; *U.S. Public*, pg. 550

REFLECTIONS—Greeting Cards—Fine Art Developments plc; *Int'l*, pg. 485

REFLECTIONS—Indirect Lighting—Guth Lighting Company; *Int'l*, pg. 821

REFLECTIONS—Mass Merchandise Brassieres—Lilyette Brassiere Co.; *U.S. Private*, pg. 697

REFLECTIONS—Mirrors & Accessories—Quoizel Inc.; *U.S. Private*, pg. 901

REFLECTIONS—Nonstick Interior & Exterior—Regal Ware, Inc.; *U.S. Private*, pg. 917

REFLECTIONS II—Luggage—American Tourister, Inc.; *U.S. Public*, pg. 1430

REFLECTO-LITE—Retroreflective Sheeting, Molded Plastic Reflectors, Adhesive—3M; *U.S. Public*, pg. 1604

REFLEX—Motorcycle—American Honda Motor Co., Inc. Motorcycle Division; *Int'l*, pg. 634

REFLEX—Outdoor Products—The Black & Decker Corporation; *U.S. Public*, pg. 233

REFLEX SM—To Reinsure Flexible Spending Accounts—Colonial Life & Accident Insurance Co.; *U.S. Private*, pg. 1699

REFLEXITE—Reflective Cable—Loos & Co., Inc.; *U.S. Private*, pg. 675

REFRAC-T-BACK—NONE—ESAB Welding & Cutting Products; *Int'l*, pg. 281

REFRACTIVEHORIZONS—Educational & Consulting Services—Alcon Laboratories, Inc.; *Int'l*, pg. 916

REFRAX—Refractory—The Carborundum Corporation; *Int'l*, pg. 1173

REFRESH—Lubricant Ophthalmic Solution—Allergan, Inc.; *U.S. Public*, pg. 46

REFRESHENAIR—Room Freshener—Surco Products, Inc.; *U.S. Private*, pg. 1056

REFRESHER—Paper Cups—Westvaco Corporation; *U.S. Public*, pg. 1762

REFRESHERS—Juice Drinks—Ocean Spray Cranberries, Inc.; *U.S. Private*, pg. 811

REFRIGERATED TRANSPORTER—Trucking Trade Magazine—Intertec Publishing; *U.S. Public*, pg. 1327

REFRIGEWEAR—Insulated Clothing—Crouch Supply Company, Inc.; *U.S. Private*, pg. 291

REG-CHECK—Service for Checking Federal Regulations—The Dow Chemical Company; *U.S. Public*, pg. 522

REG-U-LINER—Control Valves—Schlumberger Industries; *U.S. Public*, pg. 1439

REGAL—Sporting Goods—Brunswick Bowling & Billiards Corp.; *U.S. Public*, pg. 265

REGAL—Automobile—Buick Motor Div. General Motors Corp.; *U.S. Public*, pg. 720

REGAL—Roses—Denver Wholesale Florists Company; *U.S. Private*, pg. 326

REGAL—Beer—General Brewing Company; *U.S. Private*, pg. 954

REGAL—Luxury Car—General Motors Corporation; *U.S. Public*, pg. 718

REGAL—Dry Dog Food—H.J. Heinz Co. of Canada Ltd.; *U.S. Public*, pg. 806

REGAL—King Size Mild Filter Cigarettes—Imperial Tobacco Group, Ltd.; *Int'l*, pg. 666

REGAL—Engine Lathes—Makino Inc.; *Int'l*, pg. 831

REGAL—Pleasure Boat Name—Regal Marine Industries Inc.; *U.S. Private*, pg. 917

REGAL—Cookware, Coffee Makers, Portable Electrics, Accessories—Regal Ware, Inc.; *U.S. Private*, pg. 917

REGAL—Memorials—Rock of Ages Corporation; *U.S. Public*, pg. 1396

REGAL—Plybent Wood Chair—Sauder Manufacturing Corporation; *U.S. Private*, pg. 967

REGAL—For Abrasives, Ceramic Aluminum Oxide—3M; *U.S. Public*, pg. 1604

REGAL AQUA PEARL—Interior Latex Enamel—Benjamin Moore & Co.; *U.S. Private*, pg. 133

REGAL AQUA VELVET—Interior Latex Enamel—Benjamin Moore & Co.; *U.S. Private*, pg. 133

REGAL AQUAGLO—Interior Latex Enamel—Benjamin Moore & Co.; *U.S. Private*, pg. 133

REGAL BRAU—Beer—Joseph Huber Brewing Co., Inc.; *U.S. Private*, pg. 545

REGAL BURGER—Prepared Meat Product—American Foodservice Corp.; *U.S. Private*, pg. 54

REGAL CROWN—Canned Hams—M.H. Greenebaum, Inc.; *U.S. Private*, pg. 477

REGAL CURES—Cure—Griffith Laboratories Worldwide, Inc.; *U.S. Private*, pg. 481

REGAL FOODS—Prepared Poultry Products—Armour Swift Eckrich; *U.S. Public*, pg. 426

REGAL GOLD—Titanium Nitride Coating—Regal-Beloit Corporation; *U.S. Public*, pg. 1370

REGAL KING SIZE—Cigarettes—Hanson PLC; *Int'l*, pg. 592

REGAL-LINE—Off Highway Power Transmission Products—Regal-Beloit Corporation; *U.S. Public*, pg. 1370

REGAL PREMIUM—Precision Cutting Tools; Gage Product & Standard Taps—Regal-Beloit Corporation; *U.S. Public*, pg. 1370

REGAL RAPID ROUTER—5 & 10 Degree Routers—Regal-Beloit Corporation; *U.S. Public*, pg. 1370

REGAL-SERV—Plastic Containers—Tenneco Specialty Products; *U.S. Public*, pg. 1579

REGAL 2000—Stainless Steel Cookware—Regal Ware, Inc.; *U.S. Private*, pg. 917

REGAL WALL SATIN—Interior Latex Flat Finish—Benjamin Moore & Co.; *U.S. Private*, pg. 133

REGALBRITE—Floor Coverings—Domco Inc.; *Int'l*, pg. 415

REGALE—NONE—Mauney Hosiery Mills, Inc.; *U.S. Private*, pg. 715

REGALFLOR—Floor Coverings—Domco Inc.; *Int'l*, pg. 415

REGALITE—Resin Bond Cloth Coated-Abrasive Belt—3M; *U.S. Public*, pg. 1604

REGALLOY—Ceramic Aluminum Oxide—3M; *U.S. Public*, pg. 1604

REGALREZ—Resin—Hercules Incorporated; *U.S. Public*, pg. 809

REGARD—Furniture Polish—S.C. Johnson & Son, Inc.; *U.S. Private*, pg. 592

REGARD—Nonwoven Fabrics—Kimberly-Clark Corporation; *U.S. Public*, pg. 958

REGARD—Plastic Film—Reynolds Metals Company; *U.S. Public*, pg. 1385

REGATTA—Game—Monarch Avalon, Inc.; *U.S. Public*, pg. 1123

REGATTA—Interior Wall and Countertop—Monarch Tile, Inc.; *U.S. Private*, pg. 287

REGENAIR—Blower—Gast Mfg. Corp.; *U.S. Private*, pg. 440

REGENCY—Tires—Bridgestone/Firestone, Inc.; *Int'l*, pg. 213

REGENCY—Wall & House Paint—Devoe Paint; *Int'l*, pg. 663

REGENCY—Sanitary Maintenance Supplies—Dillard, A ResourceNet International Company; *U.S. Public*, pg. 901

REGENCY—Wall & House Paint—ICI Paints; *Int'l*, pg. 664

REGENCY—Boxed Papeteries, Paper & Envelopes—The Mead Corporation; *U.S. Public*, pg. 1074

REGENCY—Bibles—Thomas Nelson Inc.; *U.S. Public*, pg. 1167

REGENCY—Pacemaker—St. Jude Medical, Inc.; *U.S. Public*, pg. 1427

REGENCY—Griddles & Broilers—Wolf Range Co.; *U.S. Public*, pg. 1322

REGENCY CHOCOLATE COLLECTION—High Quality Chocolate Coating—Grace Cocoa/Ambrosia Chocolate; *U.S. Public*, pg. 128

REGENCY CLUB—Executive Level, Special Service Floors—Hyatt Hotels Corporation; *U.S. Private*, pg. 551

REGENCY DUAL CUT—High Grade Cutting Tools—Lawson Products, Inc.; *U.S. Public*, pg. 980

REGENCY 30—Tires—Bridgestone/Firestone, Inc.; *Int'l*, pg. 213

REGENESIS—Recycled Paper Business Forms—Moore Corporation Limited; *Int'l*, pg. 888

REGENESIS—Recycled Forms & Computer Paper—Moore Document Solutions; *Int'l*, pg. 890

REGENEVER—Chemical Reagant—Hach Company; *U.S. Public*, pg. 773

REGENT—Photocopy Apparatus—Eastman Kodak Company; *U.S. Public*, pg. 550

REGENT—Intruder Alarm—JSB Electrical PLC; *Int'l*, pg. 453

REGENT—Enamel Finish Steel Receptacles & Smokers' Urns with Perma-Wood Slats—United Receptical, Inc.; *U.S. Private*, pg. 1123

REGENT—Plumbing Products—Waxman Industries, Inc.; *U.S. Public*, pg. 1748

REGENT BIOGEL—Powder-Free Surgical Gloves—London International Group plc; *Int'l*, pg. 815

REGENT COLLECTION—Office Furniture—The HON Co.; *U.S. Public*, pg. 772

REGENT GALLERY—Housewares—Lechters, Inc.; *U.S. Public*, pg. 983

REGENT INTERNATIONAL—NONE—Four Seasons Hotels Inc.; *Int'l*, pg. 502

REGENT SEA—Cruise Ship—Regency Cruises Inc.; *U.S. Private*, pg. 918

REGENT SHEFFIELD—Cutlery—McPherson's Limited; *Int'l*, pg. 852

REGENT STAR—Cruise Ship—Regency Cruises Inc.; *U.S. Private*, pg. 918

REGENT SUN—Cruise Ship—Regency Cruises Inc.; *U.S. Private*, pg. 918

REGINA—Cooking Wines & Vinegars—Nabisco Inc.; *U.S. Public*, pg. 1355

REGINA—Floor Care—Philips Electronics North America Corporation; *Int'l*, pg. 1053

REGINA—Wine Vinegar—RJR Nabisco Holdings Corp.; *U.S. Public*, pg. 1354

REGINE'S—Fragrance—Jean Philippe Fragrances, Inc.; *U.S. Public*, pg. 924

REGIO—Bathroom Tissue—Copamex Industrias S.A. de C.V.; *Int'l*, pg. 330

REGIONS—NONE—Regions Financial Corporation; *U.S. Public*, pg. 1371

REGIONSBANK—NONE—Regions Financial Corporation; *U.S. Public*, pg. 1371

REGIS HAIRSTYLISTS—Full-Service Upscale Beauty Salon—Regis Corporation; *U.S. Public*, pg. 1373

REGIS ROYAL—Scotch Whiskey—John Gross & Co.; *U.S. Private*, pg. 483

THE REGISTER GUARD—Newspaper—Guard Publishing Company; *U.S. Private*, pg. 485

THE REGISTER—Electric Fan Forced Wall Heater—Cadet Manufacturing Company; *U.S. Private*, pg. 198

REGISTERED PREMIUM RIB—Tire—The Kelly-Springfield Tire Company; *U.S. Public*, pg. 753

REGISTRATOR—Platens—The Standard Register Company; *U.S. Public*, pg. 1505

REGISTRY—Door Systems—Pease Industries, Inc.; *U.S. Private*, pg. 845

REGISTRY HOTELS & RESORTS—A 20-Year Old Four-Star/Four-Diamond Brand Reknowned for Quality Services—Carnival Hotels & Casinos; *U.S. Public*, pg. 1265

REGITINE—NONE—Novartis Pharmaceuticals; *Int'l*, pg. 973

REGLAN—Oncology Therapy—American Home Products Corporation; *U.S. Public*, pg. 79

REGO—Fitness Shoe—K-Swiss Inc.; *U.S. Public*, pg. 937

REGONOL—Pharmaceutical—Organon Inc.; *Int'l*, pg. 48

REGULAR ILETIN—Purified Insulin Injection, Lilly—Eli Lilly and Company; *U.S. Public*, pg. 992

REGUPOL—Rubber Products—Dodge Regupol, Inc.; *U.S. Private*, pg. 337

REHAB WORKS, INC.—NONE—Continental Medical Systems, Inc.; *U.S. Public*, pg. 839

REHABILITY—NONE—American Rehability Services, Inc.; *U.S. Public*, pg. 1257

REHEARSAL ROOM—Restaurant—The Levy Organization; *U.S. Private*, pg. 664

THE REICH STUFF—Role Playing—Monarch Avalon, Inc.; *U.S. Public*, pg. 1123

REIMASSAS—Pasta Products—Nestle S.A.; *Int'l*, pg. 915

REINITAS—Cigars—SEITA, Societe Nationale D'Exploitation Industrielle des Tabacs et des Allumettes; *Int'l*, pg. 1219

REINKE—Irrigation Systems—Reinke Manufacturing Co., Inc.; *U.S. Private*, pg. 920

REINKE—45 Ft. Truck Trailers—Reinke Manufacturing Co., Inc.; *U.S. Private*, pg. 920

REINSHAGEN—Cable & Wiring Systems—General Motors Corporation; *U.S. Public*, pg. 718

REINSTEIN—NONE—Quality Bakers New Zealand Ltd.; *Int'l*, pg. 556

REINSURANCE REPORTER—Magazine Containing Insurance/Reinsurance Articles—Lincoln National Corporation; *U.S. Public*, pg. 997

REITER'S—Milk & Ice Cream—Dean Foods Company; *U.S. Public*, pg. 489

REITER'S SIGNATURE—Premium Ice Cream—Dean Foods Company; *U.S. Public*, pg. 489

REJUVIA—Vitamine E Skin Care Products—Del Laboratories, Inc.; *U.S. Private*, pg. 494

REL-REZ—Polymers—Akzo Nobel Coatings Inc. (KY); *Int'l*, pg. 47

REL-SHIELD—Pre-Engineered Bldg. Coating Systems—Akzo Nobel Coatings Inc. (KY); *Int'l*, pg. 47

REL-TRON EMI/RFI—Electronis Shield Coatings—Akzo Nobel Coatings Inc. (KY); *Int'l*, pg. 47

REL-VAR—Catalyzed Wood Finishes—Akzo Nobel Coatings Inc. (KY); *Int'l*, pg. 47

REL-VOC—Office Machinery & Equipment Coating—Akzo Nobel Coatings Inc. (KY); *Int'l*, pg. 47

RELAFEN—Pharmaceutical—SmithKline Beecham Corporation; *Int'l*, pg. 1264

RELATE—Relational Database—I.C. System, Inc.; *U.S. Private*, pg. 553

RELAX—Trade Periodical—Advanstar Communications; *U.S. Private*, pg. 22

RELAX WATER—Lotion & Moisturizer—Shiseido Company Ltd.; *Int'l*, pg. 1235

RELAY—Suture Delivery System & Package—Ethicon, Inc.; *U.S. Public*, pg. 928

RELAY—Furniture—Herman Miller, Inc.; *U.S. Public*, pg. 1111

RELAYMASTER—NONE—Master International Corp.; *U.S. Private*, pg. 713

RELDAN—Insecticides—The Dow Chemical Company; *U.S. Public*, pg. 522

RELEASE—Growth Regulator—Abbott Laboratories; *U.S. Public*, pg. 12

RELEASE—Recreational Products—The Black & Decker Corporation; *U.S. Public*, pg. 233

RELIABILITY—NONE—Milgray Electronics, Inc.; *U.S. Public*, pg. 205

RELIABILT—NONE—Detroit Diesel Corp.; *U.S. Private*, pg. 850

RELIABLE—Cleaning Chemicals for Janitorial Use—The Mead Corporation; *U.S. Public*, pg. 1074

RELIABLE ELECTRIC—NONE—RELTEC Corporation; *U.S. Private*, pg. 921

RELIALAB—Test Equipment—Tenney Environmental; *U.S. Private*, pg. 1076

RELIANCE—Watches—Croton Watch Company & Nationwide Time; *U.S. Private*, pg. 291

RELIANCE—Vinyl Siding—Owens Corning; *U.S. Public*, pg. 1236

RELIANCE—Electrical Components—Reliance Electric Company; *U.S. Public*, pg. 1398

RELIANCE ELECTRIC—Electric Motor Drives—Rockwell Automation; *U.S. Public*, pg. 1397

RELIANCE-UNIVERSAL—Industrial Coatings—Akzo Nobel Inc.; *Int'l*, pg. 47

RELIANT—Microfilming Machine & Accessories—Eastman Kodak Company; *U.S. Public*, pg. 550

RELIANT—Cast Iron Gas Boiler—Slant/Fin Corporation; *U.S. Private*, pg. 1005

RELIAVAC—Closed Wound Suction Device—Davol Inc.; *U.S. Public*, pg. 189

RELIC—NONE—Fossil Inc.; *U.S. Private*, pg. 420

RELIEF—Disposable Diapers for Adults—Kao Corporation; *Int'l*, pg. 717

RELIFEX—NONE—SmithKline Beecham Corporation; *Int'l*, pg. 1264

RELIFEX—Inflammation & Tissue Repair—SmithKline Beecham plc; *Int'l*, pg. 1264

RELIFEX—Anti-Inflammatory—SmithKline Beecham Research Limited; *Int'l*, pg. 1266

RELIFLEX—NONE—Berg Electronics; *U.S. Public*, pg. 212

RELIMATE—NONE—Berg Electronics; *U.S. Public*, pg. 212

RELIPRESS—NONE—Berg Electronics; *U.S. Public*, pg. 212

RELM PLUS—Two Way FM Radios—Relm Communications, Inc.; *U.S. Public*, pg. 1376

RELSKA VODKA—NONE—Heublein, Inc.; *Int'l*, pg. 410

RELTEC—NONE—RELTEC Corporation; *U.S. Private*, pg. 921

RELUBE—Waste Lube Oil Rerefining—KTI Group B.V.; *Int'l*, pg. 837

RELVIRON—Kitchen Cabinet Environmental Coatings—Akzo Nobel Coatings Inc. (KY); *Int'l*, pg. 47

RELY—Ag Chemical—AgrEvo USA Company; *Int'l*, pg. 1203

RELY—Manual Warewashing Product—Ecolab Inc.; *U.S. Public*, pg. 562

REMAC—Thumb-Crotch Patch on Glove—Jomac, Inc.; *U.S. Private*, pg. 624

REMAZOL—Dyes for Cellulose Fibres—Hoechst Aktiengesellschaft; *Int'l*, pg. 624

REMBRANDT—Tooth Paste & Whitener—Den-Mat Corporation; *U.S. Private*, pg. 324

REMBRANDT—Stereo & Television antennas—Recoton Corporation; *U.S. Public*, pg. 1369

REMCO—TV & Stereo Rental—Remco America, Inc.; *Int'l*, pg. 1385

REMCO—Toys—Remco Toys; *U.S. Public*, pg. 923

REMCO BABY—Baby Accessories—Remco Toys; *U.S. Public*, pg. 923

REMEGEL—Antacid—Warner-Lambert Company; *U.S. Public*, pg. 1738

REMEMBER—Bicomponent Acrylic Fiber—Monsanto Company; *U.S. Public*, pg. 1124

REMEMBER—Bicomponent Acrylic Fibers—Solutia Inc.; *U.S. Public*, pg. 1483

REMERON—Antidepressant—Akzo Nobel N.V.; *Int'l*, pg. 42

REMGRIT—Abrasive Tools—Rule Industries, Inc.; *U.S. Public*, pg. 950

REMINGTON—Tires—Dunlop Tire Corporation; *Int'l*, pg. 1317

REMINGTON—Firearms, Ammunition, Traps—Remington Arms Company, Inc.; *U.S. Private*, pg. 921

REMINGTON—Electric Shavers—Remington Products Company, L.L.C.; *U.S. Private*, pg. 921

REMINGTON LAMPS—Lamps—Adelphia Lamp & Shade Inc.; *U.S. Private*, pg. 17

REMINISCENCE—Greeting Cards—American Greetings Corporation; *U.S. Public*, pg. 77

REMODELINE—Sectional Showers & Tub/Showers—Lasco Bathware; *Int'l*, pg. 1397

REMOTAIRE—Food Service Equipment—United Service Equipment Company; *U.S. Public*, pg. 1507

REMOTE COMMANDER—Remote Control—Sony Electronics; *Int'l*, pg. 1281

REMOTE CONTROL/2—NONE—Compuware Corporation; *U.S. Public*, pg. 423

REMOTE DATA INTERFACE—NONE—Detroit Diesel Corp.; *U.S. Private*, pg. 850

REMOTE PARAMETER CONTROL—Simulator Software for Vehicle Test Systems—MTS Systems Corporation; *U.S. Public*, pg. 1028

REMOTE SENTRY—Environmental Remediation Services—Van Waters & Rogers; *Int'l*, pg. 1147

REMOTESCAN—2-Way Outdoor Warning Siren Status Monitor & Control System—Federal Signal Corporation, Signal Div.; *U.S. Public*, pg. 616

REMSTAR CHOICE—Nasal CPAP System—Respironics, Inc.; *U.S. Public*, pg. 1383

REMY MARTIN—Spirits—Mercian Corporation; *Int'l*, pg. 858

REMY MARTIN—Wines & Spirits—Remy Amerique Inc.; *Int'l*, pg. 1102

REN-O-SAL—Poultry Pharmaceutic—Salsbury Laboratories, Inc.; *Int'l*, pg. 1277

REN-SHAPE—Epoxy Plastics—CIBA Specialty Chemicals; *Int'l*, pg. 291

REN-WELD—Adhesives—CIBA Specialty Chemicals; *Int'l*, pg. 291

RENA ROWAN FOR SAVILLE—Career Sportswear—Jones Apparel Group, Inc.; *U.S. Public*, pg. 933

RENAISSANCE—Keratometer Equipment & Accessories—Alcon Laboratories, Inc.; *Int'l*, pg. 916

RENAISSANCE—NONE—Alliant Foodservice, Inc.; *U.S. Private*, pg. 244

RENAISSANCE—Decorative Faucet—The Chicago Faucet Co.; *U.S. Private*, pg. 234

RENAISSANCE—Prefinished Wall Paneling—Georgia-Pacific Corporation; *U.S. Public*, pg. 735

RENAISSANCE—Office Supplies—JM Company; *U.S. Private*, pg. 577

RENAISSANCE—Interior Floor Tile—Monarch Tile, Inc.; *U.S. Private*, pg. 287

RENAISSANCE—Spirometry System—Nellcor Puritan Bennett Incorporated; *U.S. Public*, pg. 1039

RENAISSANCE BANKING—Banking Service for Seniors—First National Bank of Chicago; *U.S. Public*, pg. 627

RENAISSANCE BILLIARDS—Billiard Products—AMF Bowling Worldwide; *U.S. Private*, pg. 6

RENAISSANCE CS—Client/Server Enterprise Resource Planning System—Ross Systems, Inc.; *U.S. Public*, pg. 1406

THE RENAISSANCE OF ITALIAN TASTE—NONE—JP Foodservice, Inc.; *U.S. Public*, pg. 918

RENATO RATTI—Wine—Paterno Imports Limited; *U.S. Private*, pg. 843

RENAULT—Automobiles—Renault USA; *Int'l*, pg. 1102

RENAULT—Automobile—Renault V.I.; *Int'l*, pg. 1102

RENE FURTHERER—Cosmetics—Pierre Fabre S.A.; *Int'l*, pg. 1056

RENE GARRAUD—Skin Cosmetics—Wella Group; *Int'l*, pg. 1489

RENEGADE—Eye Protection—U.S. Safety; *U.S. Private*, pg. 1125

RENEW—Plastic & Other Products—Chelsea Industries, Inc.; *U.S. Private*, pg. 231

RENEW—NONE—FMC Corp., Lithium Division; *U.S. Public*, pg. 605

RENEW—Repair & Rebuild Service—The Falk Corporation; *U.S. Public*, pg. 1534

RENEW—System Electronics—MTS Systems Corporation; *U.S. Public*, pg. 1028

RENEWAL—Rechargeable Alkaline Batteries & Chargers—RAYOVAC Corporation; *U.S. Private*, pg. 912

RENGASIL—Antirheumatic—Novartis; *Int'l*, pg. 972

RENISHAW—Generic—Renishaw plc; *Int'l*, pg. 1103

Brand Name Index

RENNER DAVIS—Hand-Crafted Stationery & Giftware—Golden Books Family Entertainment Inc.; *U.S. Public*, pg. 749

RENOCAST—Mold Release Agents—Fuchs Petrolub AG Oel + Chemie; *Int'l*, pg. 517

RENOCLEAN—Industrial Detergents & Degreasers—Fuchs Petrolub AG Oel + Chemie; *Int'l*, pg. 517

RENOGRAFIN—Diagnostics—Bristol-Myers Squibb Company; *U.S. Public*, pg. 253

RENOLD GEARBOXES—Custom Made Gear Reducers for Industry—Renold, Inc.; *Int'l*, pg. 1104

RENOLIT—Greases—Fuchs Petrolub AG Oel + Chemie; *Int'l*, pg. 517

RENOVA—Cream 0.05%—Ortho-McNeil Pharmaceutical Corporation; *U.S. Public*, pg. 929

RENOVATE—Software—CACI International Inc; *U.S. Public*, pg. 272

RENOVATION BRICOLAGE—Magazine—Quebecor Inc.; *Int'l*, pg. 1075

RENOVATOR—Windows with Vinyl Frames—Reynolds Metals Company; *U.S. Public*, pg. 1385

RENOVER—Magazine—Quebecor Inc.; *Int'l*, pg. 1075

RENPRESS—Antihypertensive—Novartis AG; *Int'l*, pg. 971

RENTALEASE—Rental & Leasing of Data Processing Equipment—General Electric Canada Inc.; *U.S. Public*, pg. 713

RENU—Contact Lens Cleaning Solution—Bausch & Lomb Incorporated; *U.S. Public*, pg. 194

RENUZIT—Solid & Aerosol Air Freshener—Bristol-Myers Squibb Company; *U.S. Public*, pg. 253

RENUZIT ADJUSTABLE—NONE—The Dial Corporation; *U.S. Public*, pg. 505

RENUZIT AEROSOL—NONE—The Dial Corporation; *U.S. Public*, pg. 505

RENUZIT AROMASENSE CANDLES—NONE—The Dial Corporation; *U.S. Public*, pg. 505

RENUZIT CARPET & ROOM DEODORIZER—NONE—The Dial Corporation; *U.S. Public*, pg. 505

RENUZIT CRYSTAL ACSCENT CANDLES—NONE—The Dial Corporation; *U.S. Public*, pg. 505

RENUZIT ELECTRIC—NONE—The Dial Corporation; *U.S. Public*, pg. 505

RENUZIT FRESHELL—Solid Air Freshener—Bristol-Myers Squibb Company; *U.S. Public*, pg. 253

RENUZIT ROOMMATE—NONE—The Dial Corporation; *U.S. Public*, pg. 505

RENUZIT ROOMMATE DECORATORS—NONE—The Dial Corporation; *U.S. Public*, pg. 505

REOMAR—Photo Lenses—Eastman Kodak Company; *U.S. Public*, pg. 550

REOPRO—Treatment For Blood Clot Formation—Centocor, Inc.; *U.S. Public*, pg. 323

REOPRO—NONE—Eli Lilly and Company; *U.S. Public*, pg. 992

REORG PLUS FOR DB2—DB2 Database Utility—BMC Software, Inc.; *U.S. Public*, pg. 162

REORG PLUS FOR VSE—VSE Database Utility—BMC Software, Inc.; *U.S. Public*, pg. 162

REPCO—NONE—Pacific Dunlop Limited; *Int'l*, pg. 1021

THE REPEATER—Shovels—UnionTools, Inc.; *U.S. Public*, pg. 17

REPEL—Hydophobic & Breathable Membrane—Gelman Sciences, Inc.; *U.S. Public*, pg. 1253

REPEL—Insect Repellent—Wisconsin Pharmacal Co., Inc.; *U.S. Private*, pg. 1185

REPETE—Recycled Polyester Resin—The Goodyear Tire & Rubber Company; *U.S. Public*, pg. 752

REPIPET—Glass Volumetric Dispensing Devices—Packard Instrument Co., Inc.; *U.S. Private*, pg. 833

REPISURE—Animal Vaccine—SmithKline Beecham plc; *Int'l*, pg. 1264

REPLACE IT—Replacement Parts—R&B, Inc.; *U.S. Public*, pg. 1354

REPLACEMENTS—China & Crystal—Replacements, Ltd.; *U.S. Private*, pg. 923

REPLENA—High Calorie Nutritional—Abbott Laboratories; *U.S. Public*, pg. 12

REPLENISH—Fertilizer—Rose Acre Farms; *U.S. Private*, pg. 944

REPLENS—Vaginal Moisturizer—Columbia Laboratories, Inc.; *U.S. Public*, pg. 405

REPLENS—Vaginal Moisturizer—Warner-Lambert Consumer Healthcare; *U.S. Public*, pg. 1739

REPLI-KEY—Key Blanks—Ilco Unican Corp.; *Int'l*, pg. 1432

REPLICA—Film—Konica Imaging USA, Inc.; *Int'l*, pg. 749

REPLICOPY—Xerographic—Dillard, A ResourceNet International Company; *U.S. Public*, pg. 901

REPLIFAX—Fax Paper—Dillard, A ResourceNet International Company; *U.S. Public*, pg. 901

REPLIFORM—Computer Paper—Dillard, A ResourceNet International Company; *U.S. Public*, pg. 901

REPLOGLE—World Globes & Sundials—Replogle Globes, Inc.; *U.S. Private*, pg. 923

REPON—Self-Service Wholesale Stores—SHV Holdings N.V.; *Int'l*, pg. 1154

REPORT CONSOLIDATION SYSTEM—Mailing Efficiency System—Group 1 Software, Inc.; *U.S. Public*, pg. 417

REPORTER—Document Management Products—Bell & Howell Holdings; *U.S. Public*, pg. 201

REPORTING ASSISTANT—Computer Product—International Business Machines Corporation; *U.S. Public*, pg. 895

REPOSITORY MANAGER—Computer Product—International Business Machines Corporation; *U.S. Public*, pg. 895

REPOSITORY MANAGER/400—Computer Product—International Business Machines Corporation; *U.S. Public*, pg. 895

REPOSITORY MANAGER/MVS—Computer Product—International Business Machines Corporation; *U.S. Public*, pg. 895

REPOXIT—Industrial Floorcoverings—Forbo Holding SA; *Int'l*, pg. 496

REPP LTD. BIG & TALL—NONE—Edison Brothers Stores, Inc.; *U.S. Public*, pg. 563

REPRISE—High Recycled Content Products Lines—FiberMark Inc.; *U.S. Public*, pg. 620

REPSOL—Oil & Natural Gas Distribution—Repsol S.A.; *Int'l*, pg. 1104

REPUBLIC—Gas, Electric & Oil Powered Heaters—Bradford-White Corporation; *U.S. Private*, pg. 164

REPUBLIC MOLDING—NONE—Ingrid Division of Lawnware; *U.S. Private*, pg. 654

REPUBLIC OF ROME—Strategy Game—Monarch Avalon, Inc.; *U.S. Public*, pg. 1123

REPUBLICA DOMINICANA—Premium Cigars—Consolidated Cigar Corporation; *U.S. Private*, pg. 690

REPUTATION—Food Products—National Fruit Product Company; *U.S. Private*, pg. 783

REQUEST—Computer Programs—Lucent Technologies Inc.; *U.S. Public*, pg. 1017

REQUEST—Entertainment Magazine—Musicland Group Inc.; *U.S. Public*, pg. 1142

REQUISITION BOND—Printing & Writing Paper—Georgia-Pacific Corporation; *U.S. Public*, pg. 735

RES-FELT—Roofing Felt—Georgia-Pacific Corporation; *U.S. Public*, pg. 735

RES-Q—On-Site Ion Exchange Resin Cleaning—BetzDearborn; *U.S. Public*, pg. 226

RESAMINE—Agent for Polyurethane Resins—Dainichiseika Colour & Chemicals Mfg. Co., Ltd.; *Int'l*, pg. 369

RESAN—Sinks & Basins of Polycarbonate—Forbo Holding SA; *Int'l*, pg. 496

RESCAMUNE—NONE—Pfizer Inc.; *U.S. Public*, pg. 1281

RESCH'S DRAUGHT—Ale—Carlton & United Breweries Ltd.; *Int'l*, pg. 500

RESCH'S PILSENER—Pilsener Ale—Carlton & United Breweries Ltd.; *Int'l*, pg. 500

RESCH'S REAL—Ale—Carlton & United Breweries Ltd.; *Int'l*, pg. 500

RESCH'S—Draught Beer—Foster's Brewing Group Limited; *Int'l*, pg. 500

RESCO—Refractories—Resco Products, Inc.; *U.S. Private*, pg. 924

RESCUE—Soap-Filled Abrasive Pad—3M; *U.S. Public*, pg. 1604

RESEARCH & DEVELOPMENT—Magazine for Professionals in Applied Research & Development—Reed Elsevier Business Information; *Int'l*, pg. 1095

RESEARCH CONTROL—Precision Control Valves—Badger Meter, Inc.; *U.S. Public*, pg. 164

THE RESEARCH GROUP—Research Services—Medical Economics Company Inc.; *U.S. Public*, pg. 1601

RESELLER MANAGEMENT—Magazine—The Washington Post Company; *U.S. Public*, pg. 1742

RESHEF—Woodfree for Continuous Forms—American Israeli Paper Mills Ltd.; *Int'l*, pg. 74

RESHEF PAZ—Recycled for Continuous Forms—American Israeli Paper Mills Ltd.; *Int'l*, pg. 74

RESHEF PAZ SPECIAL—NONE—American Israeli Paper Mills Ltd.; *Int'l*, pg. 74

RESHEF P.C.—NONE—American Israeli Paper Mills Ltd.; *Int'l*, pg. 74

RESHEF SPECIAL—NONE—American Israeli Paper Mills Ltd.; *Int'l*, pg. 74

RESI—Frying Fat—Vandemoortele N.V.; *Int'l*, pg. 1451

RESI-BOND—Resin Used in the Manufacture of Paper & Paperboard—Georgia-Pacific Corporation; *U.S. Public*, pg. 735

RESI-CAST—Foundry Binder Resins—Georgia-Pacific Corporation; *U.S. Public*, pg. 735

RESI-CHEM—Concrete Curing Chemical—Symons Corporation; *U.S. Private*, pg. 932

RESI-FLAKE—Foundry Resins—Georgia-Pacific Corporation; *U.S. Public*, pg. 735

RESI-GROW—Liquid Fertilizer—Georgia-Pacific Corporation; *U.S. Public*, pg. 735

RESI-LAM—Resin Adhesive—Georgia-Pacific Corporation; *U.S. Public*, pg. 735

RESI-LAT—Plywood Adhesive—Georgia-Pacific Corporation; *U.S. Public*, pg. 735

RESI-MAT—Resins Used as a Binder—Georgia-Pacific Corporation; *U.S. Public*, pg. 735

RESI-MIX—Plywood Adhesive—Georgia-Pacific Corporation; *U.S. Public*, pg. 735

RESI-OL—Polyol—Georgia-Pacific Corporation; *U.S. Public*, pg. 735

RESI-PATCH—Plywood Patching Compound—Georgia-Pacific Corporation; *U.S. Public*, pg. 735

RESI-PLY—Concrete Forming System—Symons Corporation; *U.S. Private*, pg. 932

RESI-SET—Foundry Resins—Georgia-Pacific Corporation; *U.S. Public*, pg. 735

RESI-SHELL—Foundry Binder Resins—Georgia-Pacific Corporation; *U.S. Public*, pg. 735

RESI-STRAN—Resins for Use in the Manufacture of Oriented Strand Board—Georgia-Pacific Corporation; *U.S. Public*, pg. 735

RESI-VAT—Chemicals for Treatment of Wood Bolts—Georgia-Pacific Corporation; *U.S. Public*, pg. 735

RESIBOND—Resin—Koch Engineering Company, Inc.; *U.S. Private*, pg. 628

RESIDENCE INN BY MARRIOTT—Hotel Chain—Marriott International, Inc.; *U.S. Public*, pg. 1047

RESIDENTIAL HOUSING—Textbook with Expanded Information on the Principles of Design—Goodheart-Willcox Publisher; *U.S. Private*, pg. 464

RESIDUR—Beadings—KSB Aktiengesellschaft; *Int'l*, pg. 721

RESIFIX- NOPINOL—Cold Setting Furan & Phenolic Resins—Raschig GmbH; *U.S. Private*, pg. 827

RESILIENCE—Hosiery—Hanes Hosiery, Inc.; *U.S. Public*, pg. 1434

RESILOCORK—Cork Products—Dodge Regupol, Inc.; *U.S. Private*, pg. 337

RESIMENE—Amino Crosslinker Resins—Monsanto Company; *U.S. Public*, pg. 1124

RESIMENE—Melamine & Urea Formadehyde—Solutia Inc.; *U.S. Public*, pg. 1483

RESIMENE 3520—Hexamethoxy Methyl Melamine—Solutia Inc.; *U.S. Public*, pg. 1483

RESIN-FIVE—Solder—Litton Industries, Inc.; *U.S. Public*, pg. 1002

RESINCORE I—Phenolic Resin Particle Board—Rodman Industries; *U.S. Private*, pg. 402

RESINCORE III—Urea Resin Particle Board—Rodman Industries; *U.S. Private*, pg. 402

RESINEX—Hydrocarbon Resins—Harwick Standard Distribution Corporation; *U.S. Private*, pg. 509

Brand Name Index

RESINGARD PELLETS—Water Softener Salt—Cargill Salt Inc.; *Int'l*, pg. 48

RESINITE—Food Packaging Film—AEP Industries, Inc.; *U.S. Public*, pg. 4

RESINITE—Packaging Film—Borden, Inc.; *U.S. Private*, pg. 157

RESINITE—Resin Over Glue Bonded Coated Abrasives—3M; *U.S. Public*, pg. 1604

RESINOL—Liquid Components For Rigid Polyurethane Foams—DSM N.V.; *Int'l*, pg. 352

RESINOL—Sports Spray—Mentholatum Company; *Int'l*, pg. 1126

RESINTER—International Hotel Reservations—Accor S.A.; *Int'l*, pg. 20

RESINTITE—Lumber—Roseburg Forest Products Co.; *U.S. Private*, pg. 905

RESIPLAST—Indus. Resins—Raschig GmbH; *U.S. Private*, pg. 827

RESISTAT—Fiber Collection—BASF Corporation Fiber Products Division; *Int'l*, pg. 105

RESISTIC—Powder—Alloy Technology International Inc.; *U.S. Private*, pg. 42

RESISTO—Photo Paper—Eastman Kodak Company; *U.S. Public*, pg. 550

RESISTOL—Hats—HATCO, Inc.; *U.S. Private*, pg. 510

RESISTOVAR—Catalyzed Varnish Finish—Lilly Industries, Inc.; *U.S. Public*, pg. 994

RESIWELD—Epoxy Adhesives—H.B. Fuller Company; *U.S. Public*, pg. 686

RESOCHIN—Tropical Medicine for Treatment of Malaria—Bayer AG; *Int'l*, pg. 171

RESOFLOOR—Laminate Floorcoverings—Forbo Holding SA; *Int'l*, pg. 496

RESOLUTE—Paper—Kimberly-Clark Corporation; *U.S. Public*, pg. 958

RESOLVE—Herbicide—American Home Products Corporation; *U.S. Public*, pg. 79

RESOLVE—Silica Column, Cartridge & Packing—Millipore Corporation; *U.S. Public*, pg. 1112

RESOLVE—Carpet Cleaner—Reckitt & Colman Inc.; *Int'l*, pg. 1090

RESOLVE—Carpet Care—Reckitt & Colman plc; *Int'l*, pg. 1089

RESOLVE—NONE—SmithKline Beecham Corporation; *Int'l*, pg. 1264

RESOLVE—Analgesic—SmithKline Beecham plc; *Int'l*, pg. 1264

RESOLVE PANELS A, B & C—Reagent Red Blood Cells—Ortho Clinical Diagnostic Systems Inc.; *U.S. Public*, pg. 929

RESOLVE PLUS—Provides Online , Realtime Information on MVS Systems Status—Boole & Babbage, Inc.; *U.S. Public*, pg. 244

RESOMER—Polymer—Boehringer Ingelheim GmbH; *Int'l*, pg. 199

RESOPAL—Laminates for Furniture & Interior Decorating—Forbo Holding SA; *Int'l*, pg. 496

RESOPALAN—Edge-banding Material—Forbo Holding SA; *Int'l*, pg. 496

RESOPALIT—Coated Chipboard—Forbo Holding SA; *Int'l*, pg. 496

RESOPLAN—Facade Panels—Forbo Holding SA; *Int'l*, pg. 496

RESORSABOND—Resin Adhesive—Georgia-Pacific Corporation; *U.S. Public*, pg. 735

RESORT CRUISING—On-Shore Resort Facilities—Costa Cruise Lines, N.V.; *U.S. Private*, pg. 278

RESORTLINK 2000—Software & Hardware Integration Products—Resort Condominiums International; *U.S. Public*, pg. 322

RESOURCE—Magazine—General Media International Inc.; *U.S. Private*, pg. 444

RESOURCE—Writing Paper—The Mead Corporation; *U.S. Public*, pg. 1074

RESOURCE—Oral Supplement—Novartis Nutrition Corporation; *Int'l*, pg. 974

RESOURCE CHAIN VOYAGER—Software System—American Software, Inc.; *U.S. Public*, pg. 91

RESOURCE MANAGEMENT SYSTEM—Computer Operating System—Datapoint Corporation; *Int'l*, pg. 384

RESOURCE MEASUREMENT FACILITY—Business Product—International Business Machines Corporation; *U.S. Public*, pg. 895

RESPIGAM—Respiratory Syncytial Virus Immune Globulin Intravenous (Human)—MedImmune, Inc.; *U.S. Public*, pg. 1108

RESPIRAL—Medicated Lozenges—Cadbury Schweppes p.l.c.; *Int'l*, pg. 247

RESPIRATORY CARE—Inhalation Therapy Equipment & Services—Hudson, RCI; *U.S. Private*, pg. 546

RESPISURE/STELLAMUNE—NONE—Pfizer Inc.; *U.S. Public*, pg. 1281

RESPONDER—Hazmat Worldwide Leader in Protective Clothing—Kappler Safety Group, Inc.; *U.S. Private*, pg. 607

RESPONDER—Nurse Call Communications System—Rauland-Borg Corporation; *U.S. Private*, pg. 911

RESPONDER PLUS—Softer, Stronger, High-Viz Garment for the Hazmat Market—Kappler Safety Group, Inc.; *U.S. Private*, pg. 607

RESPONSE TV—Trade Periodical—Advanstar Communications; *U.S. Public*, pg. 22

RESPONSEPAK—Fiber Drums for the Disposal of Hazardous Waste—Sonoco Products Company; *U.S. Public*, pg. 1485

RESPONSES PHOTO—French Photo Magazine—EMAP France; *Int'l*, pg. 451

RESPONSES VIDEO—French Video Magazine—EMAP France; *Int'l*, pg. 451

REST ASSURED—Mattress Pads—Kimberly-Clark Corporation; *U.S. Public*, pg. 958

RESTAGER—Restage Established Brands Sales Forecasting—BASES Worldwide; *U.S. Private*, pg. 120

RESTAURANT BUSINESS—Business Publication—Bill Communications, Inc.; *Int'l*, pg. 1446

RESTAURANT HOSPITALITY—Periodical—Penton Publishing, Inc.; *U.S. Public*, pg. 1306

RESTAURANTS & INSTITUTIONS—Publication for Owners/Operators of Restaurants & Foodservice Institutions—Reed Elsevier Business Information; *Int'l*, pg. 1095

RESTAURANTS & INSTITUTIONS MARKETPLACE—Tabloid Containing New Products & Promotions for the Foodservice Field—Reed Elsevier Business Information; *Int'l*, pg. 1095

RESTCUE CC DYNAMIC AIR THERAPY—Unit for the Treatment of Pressure Ulcers—Hillenbrand Industries, Inc.; *U.S. Public*, pg. 828

RESTEK—Lab Bench Top Material—Fisher Scientific Company; *U.S. Private*, pg. 658

RESTOBOND—Dentin-Enamel Bonding Agent—Lee Pharmaceuticals; *U.S. Public*, pg. 984

RESTODENT—Dental Filling Resin—Lee Pharmaceuticals; *U.S. Public*, pg. 984

RESTOLUX SP-2—Light-Cured Anterior Dental Restorative—Lee Pharmaceuticals; *U.S. Public*, pg. 984

RESTOLUX SP-4—Light-Cured Dental Composite—Lee Pharmaceuticals; *U.S. Public*, pg. 984

RESTON—Foam Pads, Self Adhesive—3M; *U.S. Public*, pg. 1604

RESTON—Heel & Elbow Protectors—3M; *U.S. Public*, pg. 1604

RESTORATION—NONE—CertainTeed Corporation; *Int'l*, pg. 1170

RESTORATION—NONE—Stryker Corporation; *U.S. Public*, pg. 1525

RESTORATION COLLECTION—Vinyl Siding—CertainTeed Corporation; *Int'l*, pg. 1170

RESTORATION SERIES THREE—NONE—CertainTeed Corporation; *Int'l*, pg. 1170

RESTORATIVE CARE SERIES—NONE—Continental Medical Systems, Inc.; *U.S. Public*, pg. 839

RESTORE—All-Natural Fertilizer—Ringer Corporation; *U.S. Public*, pg. 1390

RESTORIA—Hair Darkening Products—SmithKline Beecham plc; *Int'l*, pg. 1264

RESTORIL—Pharmaceutical—Novartis AG; *Int'l*, pg. 971

RESTORIL—Short-Term Treatment of Insomnia—Sandoz Pharmaceuticals Corp.; *Int'l*, pg. 974

RESULTANTE—Treatment Line—Christian Dior Perfumes Inc.; *Int'l*, pg. 781

RESULTS PUBLISHING, INC.—Financial Information Publication—Success Development International; *U.S. Private*, pg. 1048

RESUME—Stimulator, Lead—Medtronic, Inc.; *U.S. Public*, pg. 1082

RESUME TL—Stimulator, Lead—Medtronic, Inc.; *U.S. Public*, pg. 1082

RESUME II—Electrode—Medtronic, Inc.; *U.S. Public*, pg. 1082

RESYN—Resin—Unilever Plc; *Int'l*, pg. 1433

RETAIL DIRECT—Audience Measurement & Qualitative Information Software System Media—The Arbitron Company; *U.S. Public*, pg. 331

RETAIL PLANNING SYSTEM—Software for Retail Capital and Operational Decisions—MPSI Systems Inc.; *U.S. Public*, pg. 1221

RETAIL SERVICES GROUP—Direct Marketing Services to the Retail Industry—Metromail Corporation; *U.S. Public*, pg. 1102

RETAIL STORE IMAGE—Image Magazine—Intertec Publishing; *U.S. Public*, pg. 1327

RETAIL STORE IMAGE—6X Publication—Intertec Publishing; *U.S. Public*, pg. 1328

RETAIN—Computer Product—International Business Machines Corporation; *U.S. Public*, pg. 895

RETARDINE—Dye Assistant—Henkel Corporation; *Int'l*, pg. 610

RETARDO—Fire Retardant & Rustinhibitive Paint—Benjamin Moore & Co.; *U.S. Private*, pg. 133

RETEN—Synthetic Water-Soluble Polymer—Hercules Incorporated; *U.S. Public*, pg. 809

RETIFLEX—Polypropylene Asbestos Substitute—Montedison S.p.A.; *Int'l*, pg. 324

RETIN-A—Dermatological Product—Johnson & Johnson; *U.S. Public*, pg. 927

RETIN-A—Cream—Ortho-McNeil Pharmaceutical Corporation; *U.S. Public*, pg. 929

RETIN-A—Cream .025%—Ortho-McNeil Pharmaceutical Corporation; *U.S. Public*, pg. 929

RETIN-A—Cream .1%—Ortho-McNeil Pharmaceutical Corporation; *U.S. Public*, pg. 929

RETIN-A—.05%—Ortho-McNeil Pharmaceutical Corporation; *U.S. Public*, pg. 929

RETIN-A CREAM—.025% & PURPOSE Dual Treatment—Ortho-McNeil Pharmaceutical Corporation; *U.S. Public*, pg. 929

RETIN-A CREAM—.1% & PURPOSE—Ortho-McNeil Pharmaceutical Corporation; *U.S. Public*, pg. 929

RETIN-A CREAM—.025% & PURPOSE Dual Treatment—Ortho-McNeil Pharmaceutical Corporation; *U.S. Public*, pg. 929

RETIN-A GEL—NONE—Ortho-McNeil Pharmaceutical Corporation; *U.S. Public*, pg. 929

RETIN-A GEL—.025%—Ortho-McNeil Pharmaceutical Corporation; *U.S. Public*, pg. 929

RETIN-A GEL—.01%—Ortho-McNeil Pharmaceutical Corporation; *U.S. Public*, pg. 929

RETIN-A GEL—.01% & PURPOSE Dual Treatment—Ortho-McNeil Pharmaceutical Corporation; *U.S. Public*, pg. 929

RETIN-A LIQUID—.05%—Ortho-McNeil Pharmaceutical Corporation; *U.S. Public*, pg. 929

RETIN-A REGIMEN KIT—NONE—Ortho-McNeil Pharmaceutical Corporation; *U.S. Public*, pg. 929

RETINA—Camera & Accessories—Eastman Kodak Company; *U.S. Public*, pg. 550

RETINETTE—Camera—Eastman Kodak Company; *U.S. Public*, pg. 550

RETIREMENT ADVISORS, INC.—Magazine—The Hearst Corporation; *U.S. Private*, pg. 515

RETIX—Computer Software—Vertel; *U.S. Public*, pg. 1717

RETNAR—Microfilming Apparatus—Eastman Kodak Company; *U.S. Public*, pg. 550

RETRACT-O-TAPE—Surgical Tape—Quest Medical, Inc.; *U.S. Public*, pg. 1352

RETRIEVALWARE—Suite of Information Retrival Software Products Using APRP—Excalibur Technologies Corporation; *U.S. Public*, pg. 598

RETRIEVALWARE IMAGE SERVERS—Provides Tools for Developing Applications—Excalibur Technologies Corporation; *U.S. Public*, pg. 598

RETRIEVALWARE PROFILING SERVER—High Performance System for Filtering Newswires, Electronic Mail Messages—Excalibur Technologies Corporation; *U.S. Public*, pg. 598

RETRIEVALWARE SDK—Software Developer's Kit—Excalibur Technologies Corporation; *U.S. Public*, pg. 598

Brand Name Index

RETRIEVALWARE TEXT SERVERS—Servers Built Upon an Open & Extensible Pipeline of Processing Modules—Excalibur Technologies Corporation; *U.S. Public*, pg. 598

RETRIEVALWARE WEB SERVER—Component Solution that Interfaces with any http Server—Excalibur Technologies Corporation; *U.S. Public*, pg. 598

RETRIEVE IT—Recycling Systems for Leftover Readi-Mix—Portec, Inc.-Construction Equipment Div.; *U.S. Public*, pg. 1318

RETRIEVER—Small Vacuum—Advance Machine Company; *Int'l*, pg. 932

RETRIEVER—Storage/Retrieval Machine—Jervis B. Webb Company; *U.S. Public*, pg. 1156

THE RETRO SHOW—Adult Contemporary Radio Program—Westwood One Entertainment; *U.S. Public*, pg. 1763

THE RETRO SHOW—70's Hits Programming—Westwood One, Inc.; *U.S. Public*, pg. 1763

RETRO SPECS—Sunglasses—Goody Products, Inc.; *U.S. Public*, pg. 1177

RETROCLAD—Field Repair Pipeline Coatings—Raychem Corporation; *U.S. Public*, pg. 1362

RETROFIT—NONE—Compuware Corporation; *U.S. Public*, pg. 423

RETROPLEGIA—Catheter—Baxter Research Medical, Inc.; *U.S. Public*, pg. 196

RETROVIR—Anti-HIV Drug—Glaxo Wellcome PLC; *Int'l*, pg. 553

RETSCH—Grinders—Brinkmann Instruments, Inc.; *U.S. Private*, pg. 169

RETURN-AIR—Centrifigual Atomizing Humidification Equipment—Herrmidifier Co., Inc.; *U.S. Public*, pg. 1639

REUNA—Women's Walking Shoe—K-Swiss Inc.; *U.S. Public*, pg. 937

REUNION PLANK—Pre-Finished Laminate—Bruce Hardwood Floors; *U.S. Public*, pg. 1634

REUOMINOX—Amine Oxides—Witco Corporation; *U.S. Public*, pg. 1773

REUOTERIC—Amphoterics—Witco Corporation; *U.S. Public*, pg. 1773

REUTER SOLLAMI ROTARY VANE ACTUATOR—Rotary Vane Actuator—Reuter Manufacturing Inc.; *U.S. Public*, pg. 1383

REV-GUARD—X-Ray Tube Rotational Monitors—Litton Industries, Inc.; *U.S. Public*, pg. 1002

REVCO—Refrigerators & Freezers—Revco Scientific; *U.S. Public*, pg. 727

REVEAL—Clear Labling Film—Fasson Films; *U.S. Public*, pg. 153

REVEAL—Leak Detection System—UVP, Inc.; *U.S. Private*, pg. 1115

REVELATION—Bras, Girdles—Goddess Bra Company; *U.S. Private*, pg. 458

REVELATIONS—Shoes—Brown Group, Inc.; *U.S. Public*, pg. 262

REVELL—Model Kits & Die-Cast Vehicles—Revell-Monogram Inc.; *U.S. Private*, pg. 926

REVELL-MONOGRAM—Model Kits—Binney & Smith Ltd.; *U.S. Private*, pg. 496

REVERE—Coated Printing Paper—The Mead Corporation; *U.S. Public*, pg. 1074

REVERE 7—Vinyl Plastic Electrical Tape—Plymouth Rubber Company, Inc.; *U.S. Public*, pg. 1311

REVERE WARE—Cookware—Corning Incorporated; *U.S. Public*, pg. 448

REVERSE-A-CLEAN—Reversible Tips for Paint Spray Guns—Graco Inc.; *U.S. Public*, pg. 756

REVERSE GATEKEEPING—Specializes Medical Management Strategies—Comprehensive Care Corporation; *U.S. Public*, pg. 419

REVERSO—Watches—Jaeger-Le Coultre; *Int'l*, pg. 697

REVERSO—Wristwatch with Reversible Case—Swiss Prestige; *Int'l*, pg. 697

REVERSOL—Pharmaceutical—Organon Inc.; *Int'l*, pg. 48

REVIEW OF OPHTHALMOLOGY—National Magazine for Professionals in the Field of Ophthalmology—Reed Elsevier Business Information; *Int'l*, pg. 1095

REVIEW OF OPTOMETRY—Journal for Professionals Providing Eye Care Services & Products—Reed Elsevier Business Information; *Int'l*, pg. 1095

REVISE—NONE—FileNet Corporation; *U.S. Public*, pg. 622

REVITALIZING—Cosmetics—Maybelline, Inc.; *Int'l*, pg. 819

REVITALIZING COLOR—Lipstick, Eye Shadow & Nail Color—Maybelline, Inc.; *Int'l*, pg. 819

REVIVAL—Entry Accents—ODL Incorporated; *U.S. Private*, pg. 809

REVIVE—Deodorant—SmithKline Beecham plc; *Int'l*, pg. 1264

REVIVE-IT—Cleaning Process—Aesculap, Inc.; *Int'l*, pg. 29

REVLON—NONE—Helen of Troy Corporation; *U.S. Public*, pg. 807

REVLON—Mass Merchant Brassieres—Lilyette Brassiere Co.; *U.S. Private*, pg. 697

REVLON—Cosmetics—Revlon, Inc.; *U.S. Private*, pg. 689

REVLON TOUCH-UP—Hair Coloring Preparation—Revlon-Realistic Professional Products, Inc.; *U.S. Private*, pg. 690

REVOLUTE—Dry Ammonia Diazo Supplies—OCE-U.S.A.; *Int'l*, pg. 994

REVOLUTION—Revolving Head Miniature Flashlights—Streamlight Inc.; *U.S. Private*, pg. 1047

REVOLVA-DRAWER—Lazy Susan Lab Furniture Shelves—Fisher Scientific Company; *U.S. Private*, pg. 658

REVOLVER—Beverage Carriers & Packaging Machine—Riverwood International Corporation; *U.S. Public*, pg. 1391

REVOLVERS—Cranes—AmClyde Engineered Products Co., Inc.; *U.S. Public*, pg. 778

REVUE—Luxembourg Broadcasting—CLT-UFA; *Int'l*, pg. 561

REVUE CHIENS 2000—French Magazine about Pets—EMAP France; *Int'l*, pg. 451

REWARD—Dog Food—H.J. Heinz Company; *U.S. Public*, pg. 805

REWARD—Dog Snacks—H.J. Heinz Co. of Canada Ltd.; *U.S. Public*, pg. 806

REWARD—House Paint—PPG Industries, Inc.; *U.S. Public*, pg. 1245

REWARD—Dog Food—Star-Kist Foods Inc.; *U.S. Public*, pg. 805

REWARD—Canned Dog Food—Star-Kist Foods, Inc.; *U.S. Public*, pg. 806

REWARDS PLUS—NONE—American Express Company; *U.S. Public*, pg. 73

REWONYL—Alkyl & Sulphonic Acids—Witco Corporation; *U.S. Public*, pg. 1773

REX—Consruction Equipment—Rexworks Inc.; *U.S. Private*, pg. 926

REX—NONE—Zanussi Italia S.p.A.; *Int'l*, pg. 442

REX LIGHTS 25's—NONE—Karelia Tobacco Company Inc.; *Int'l*, pg. 724

REX NETAFIM—PVC & Polyethylene Pipes & Fittings, Drip Irrigation Sys.—CYDSA S.A.; *Int'l*, pg. 246

REX ROTARY—Copiers—Gestetner Corporation; *Int'l*, pg. 1115

REX ROTARY—Copiers—Gestetner Holdings PLC; *Int'l*, pg. 1114

REXAIR MOTOR HOME—NONE—Rexhall Industries, Inc.; *U.S. Public*, pg. 1384

REXAM—Service Mark—Rexam Inc.; *Int'l*, pg. 1106

REXCILLIUM—Dental Alloys—Customedix Corporation; *U.S. Public*, pg. 298

REXEL—Staplers—ACCO World Corporation; *U.S. Public*, pg. 674

REXEL—Soft Plastic Filing Products, Staplers & Computer Accessories—Fortune Brands, Inc.; *U.S. Public*, pg. 674

REXENE—NONE—Rexene Corporation; *U.S. Private*, pg. 549

REXOLIT—PVC & Polyethylene Pipes & Fittings—CYDSA S.A.; *Int'l*, pg. 246

REXON—NONE—Tecmar Technologies, Inc.; *Int'l*, pg. 1361

REXTAC—NONE—Rexene Corporation; *U.S. Private*, pg. 549

REXTEN—NONE—Posso S.A.; *Int'l*, pg. 1064

REXWORKS—Consruction Equipment—Rexworks Inc.; *U.S. Private*, pg. 926

REXYN—Ion-Exchange Materials—Fisher Scientific Company; *U.S. Private*, pg. 658

REYCON—Container Closing & Handling Equipment—Reynolds Metals Company; *U.S. Public*, pg. 1385

REYCURE—Underground Cable—Reynolds Metals Company; *U.S. Public*, pg. 1385

REYDOX—Aluminum & Aluminum Alloy Castings—Reynolds Metals Company; *U.S. Public*, pg. 1385

REYEM SUPER—Supercalendered—Champion International Corp.; *U.S. Public*, pg. 333

REYFLECT—Paperboard Cartons—Reynolds Metals Company; *U.S. Public*, pg. 1385

REYLINER—Laminated Foil-Paper Material for Use in Industrial Arts—Reynolds Metals Company; *U.S. Public*, pg. 1385

REYLOCK—Metallic Cans & Ends—Reynolds Metals Company; *U.S. Public*, pg. 1385

REYNO—Cigarettes-Germany—R.J. Reynolds Tobacco Intl., Inc.; *U.S. Public*, pg. 1355

REYNOBOND—Aluminum Plastic Laminates—Reynolds Metals Company; *U.S. Public*, pg. 1385

REYNODE—Sacrificial Metal Anodes—Reynolds Metals Company; *U.S. Public*, pg. 1385

REYNOGUARD—Cable—Reynolds Metals Company; *U.S. Public*, pg. 1385

REYNOLD—Shrink Film—Reynolds Metals Co.-Flexible Packaging Products Division; *U.S. Public*, pg. 1386

REYNOLDS—NONE—Ganin Tire Co., Inc.; *U.S. Private*, pg. 439

REYNOLDS—Extrusions, Aluminum, Wood & Fiberglass Ladders)—Reynolds Extrusion Company; *U.S. Public*, pg. 1387

REYNOLDS—Aluminum Alloy, Paste & Products—Reynolds Metals Company; *U.S. Public*, pg. 1385

REYNOLDS—Stencil Inks—Sherwin-Williams Diversified Brands, Inc.; *U.S. Public*, pg. 1466

REYNOLDS ALUMINUM—Aluminum Products—Reynolds Metals Company; *U.S. Public*, pg. 1385

REYNOLDS ALUMINUM LANDMARK—Building Panels—Reynolds Metals Company; *U.S. Public*, pg. 1385

REYNOLDS AND REYNOLDS—Business Forms—The Reynolds and Reynolds Company; *U.S. Public*, pg. 1384

REYNOLDS AND REYNOLDS BODY SHOP SYSTEM—Bar-Coded, Automated Estimating System—The Reynolds and Reynolds Company; *U.S. Public*, pg. 1384

REYNOLDS-DO-IT-YOURSELF ALUMINUM—Aluminum Rods, Tubes, Sheets, Track & Frame Members—Reynolds Metals Company; *U.S. Public*, pg. 1385

REYNOLDS METALS—Wrought Metal—Reynolds Metals Company; *U.S. Public*, pg. 1385

REYNOLDS REVIEW—Trade Publication—Reynolds Metals Company; *U.S. Public*, pg. 1385

REYNOLDS WRAP—Aluminum Foil—Reynolds Metals Co., Consumer Products Div.; *U.S. Public*, pg. 1386

REYNOLDS WRAP—Aluminum Foil—Reynolds Metals Company; *U.S. Public*, pg. 1385

REYNOLON—Plastic Film—Reynolds Metals Company; *U.S. Public*, pg. 1385

REYNORAIL—Metal Railing Components—Reynolds Metals Company; *U.S. Public*, pg. 1385

REYNOTREE—Underground Cable—Reynolds Metals Company; *U.S. Public*, pg. 1385

REYSEAL—Paper Laminate—Reynolds Metals Company; *U.S. Public*, pg. 1385

REZAMID—Pharmaceuticals—Rhone-Poulenc Rorer - U.S.; *Int'l*, pg. 1110

REZITRON—Closet Carriers—Josam Company; *U.S. Private*, pg. 600

REZNOR—Heaters—Thomas & Betts Corporation; *U.S. Public*, pg. 1597

REZNOR—Heaters & Furnaces—Thomas & Betts Reznor Division; *U.S. Public*, pg. 1598

REZOR UNIT HEATERS—Heaters—The Habegger Corporation; *U.S. Private*, pg. 492

REZTEMP—Synthetic Woods Such as Hardboards—Georgia-Pacific Corporation; *U.S. Public*, pg. 735

RHAPSODY—Yarn—National Spinning Co., Inc.; *U.S. Private*, pg. 786

RHEABAN—NONE—Pfizer Inc.; *U.S. Public*, pg. 1281

RHEEM—Air Conditioning & Commercial Heating—Paloma Industries Limited; *Int'l*, pg. 1022

RHEEM—Water Heaters, Air Conditioners & Furnaces—Rheem Manufacturing Co.; *Int'l*, pg. 1022

RHEEM—Appliances—Southcorp Holdings Ltd.; *Int'l*, pg. 1287

RHEMO-D—Hemorroid Treatment—Inamed Corporation; *U.S. Public*, pg. 873

RHENANIA—Forwarding, Transportation—Rhenania Schiffahrts und Speditions-Gesellschaft mbH; *Int'l*, pg. 1033

RHENOFOL—Flat-Roof Waterproofing Prod.—The Braas Group; *Int'l*, pg. 1091

RHEOBUILD—Chemical Admixture for High Strength Concrete—Master Builders Inc.; *Int'l*, pg. 1465

RHEOBUILD—Concrete Admixture—Novartis AG; *Int'l*, pg. 971

RHEOMACRODEX—Blood Flow Improver & Plasma Volume Expander—Pharmacia & Upjohn Adria Laboratories; *Int'l*, pg. 1049

RHEONETIC SYSTEMS—Fluids—Lord Corporation, Mechanical Products Division; *U.S. Private*, pg. 676

RHEUMATEX—Rheumatoid Factor Latex Slide Test—Wampole Laboratories; *U.S. Public*, pg. 310

RHEUMATON—Slide Test for Rheumatoid Factor—Wampole Laboratories; *U.S. Public*, pg. 310

RHINELANDER—Beer—Joseph Huber Brewing Co., Inc.; *U.S. Private*, pg. 545

RHINELANDER BOCK—Beer—Joseph Huber Brewing Co., Inc.; *U.S. Private*, pg. 545

RHINITIS-BAC—Swine Biologic—Salsbury Laboratories, Inc.; *Int'l*, pg. 1277

RHINITIS-BAC—Swine Biologic—Solvay Animal Health, Inc.; *Int'l*, pg. 1277

RHINITIS-BAC—Swine Biologic—Solvay S.A.; *Int'l*, pg. 1277

RHINO—Technical Intensive Use Seating—Cramer Inc.; *U.S. Private*, pg. 285

RHINO—Valves—Schrader Bellows Division; *U.S. Public*, pg. 1261

RHINO—Coated Polymer Film—Tekra Corporation; *U.S. Private*, pg. 1073

RHINO MAT—Heavy Duty Truck Bed Mats—Superior Industries International, Inc.; *U.S. Public*, pg. 1539

RHINOCORT—Anti-Inflamatory Agent—Astra AB; *Int'l*, pg. 93

RHINOCORT—Pharmaceutical Products—Astra USA, Inc.; *Int'l*, pg. 93

RHO-METER—Paper Roll Density Meter—Harnischfeger Industries, Inc.; *U.S. Public*, pg. 788

RHO SIGMA—Energy Monitering Systems, Solar Controls, Electronic Controls—Watsco, Inc.; *U.S. Public*, pg. 1745

RHODE GEAR—Bicycle Accessories—Bell Sports Corp.; *U.S. Public*, pg. 207

RHODE ISLAND MANUFACTURERS REGISTER—Register—Manufacturers' News, Inc.; *U.S. Private*, pg. 700

RHODES—Frozen Bread Dough—Rhodes International, Inc.; *U.S. Private*, pg. 927

RHODES FURNITURE—Furniture—Rhodes, Inc.; *U.S. Public*, pg. 805

RHODIGEL—Biopolymer for Food Processing—Rhone-Poulenc S.A.; *Int'l*, pg. 1108

RHODOPOL—Biopolymer for Food Processing—Rhone-Poulenc S.A.; *Int'l*, pg. 1108

RHOGAM RH (D)—Immune Globulin—Ortho Clinical Diagnostic Systems Inc.; *U.S. Public*, pg. 929

RHOPLEX—Acrylic Emulsion—Rohm and Haas Company; *U.S. Public*, pg. 1403

RHOVYL—Chlorofibers—Rhone-Poulenc S.A.; *Int'l*, pg. 1108

RHULI PRODUCTS—Dermatological—S.C. Johnson & Son, Inc.; *U.S. Private*, pg. 592

RHUM BARBANCOURT—NONE—Carillon Importers, Ltd.; *Int'l*, pg. 409

RHYMAS—Robotic Hybrid Microelectronic Assembly System—Universal Instruments Corporation; *U.S. Public*, pg. 522

RHYNECLIFF—NONE—Tandy Brands Accessories, Inc.; *U.S. Public*, pg. 1560

RHYTHMS—NONE—Pfizer Inc.; *U.S. Public*, pg. 1281

RIALTA—Motor Home—Winnebago Industries, Inc.; *U.S. Public*, pg. 1772

RIALTO—Contemporary Lighting Fixtures—IL International Inc.; *U.S. Public*, pg. 855

RIATA—Premium Cigars—Consolidated Cigar Corporation; *U.S. Public*, pg. 690

RIATRAC—Lab Control Product for Diagnostic Testing—Becton Dickinson & Company; *U.S. Public*, pg. 199

RIB—Disposable Printing Cartons—The Mead Corporation; *U.S. Public*, pg. 1074

RIB-A-TAC—Cement—Bridgestone/Firestone, Inc.; *Int'l*, pg. 213

RIB-A-TUF—Synthetic Rubber Used in Tread Rubber—Bridgestone/Firestone, Inc.; *Int'l*, pg. 213

RIB-CAGE—NONE—Berg Electronics; *U.S. Public*, pg. 212

RIB DUPLEX—Tires—Bridgestone/Firestone, Inc.; *Int'l*, pg. 213

RIB EXCAVATOR—Tires—Bridgestone/Firestone, Inc.; *Int'l*, pg. 213

RIB IMPLEMENT—Tires—Bridgestone/Firestone, Inc.; *Int'l*, pg. 213

RIB ROOM—Restaurant—Sonesta International Hotels Corporation; *U.S. Public*, pg. 1485

RIB TRAC—Tire Treads—Bandag, Incorporated; *U.S. Public*, pg. 177

RIB TRACTOR—Tires—Bridgestone/Firestone, Inc.; *Int'l*, pg. 213

RIBA HCV—Test System—Ortho Clinical Diagnostic Systems Inc.; *U.S. Public*, pg. 929

RIBA HIV-1—Test System—Ortho Clinical Diagnostic Systems Inc.; *U.S. Public*, pg. 929

RIBBON—Blender—Littleford Day Inc.; *U.S. Private*, pg. 671

RIBENA—Nutritional Fruit Drinks—SmithKline Beecham Corporation; *Int'l*, pg. 1264

RIBENA—Nutritional Healthcare—SmithKline Beecham plc; *Int'l*, pg. 1264

RIBOFOLIN—NONE—Medeva PLC; *Int'l*, pg. 852

RIBOMUSTIN—NONE—Medeva PLC; *Int'l*, pg. 852

RIBSTERS—Restaurants—Houlihan's Restaurant Group; *U.S. Public*, pg. 841

RIBZ—Dog Treats—Ralston Purina Company; *U.S. Public*, pg. 1359

RICARD—Anis—Groupe Pernod Ricard; *Int'l*, pg. 566

RICASOLI TUSCAN—Wines—Canandaigua Wine Co.; *U.S. Public*, pg. 300

RICCI-CLUB—Men's Fragrance—Accecones Ricci U.S.A., Inc.; *Int'l*, pg. 445

RICCIARELLI—NONE—SASIB Packaging North America; *Int'l*, pg. 1194

RICE-A-RONI—Flavored Rice Mixes—Golden Grain Company; *U.S. Public*, pg. 1348

RICE-A-RONI—Pasta Products—The Quaker Oats Company; *U.S. Public*, pg. 1347

RICE-A-RONI LUNCH FOR ONE—Microwavable Single-Serve Pasta Entrees—The Quaker Oats Company; *U.S. Public*, pg. 1347

RICE KRISPIES—Oven-Toasted Rice Cereal—Kellogg Company; *U.S. Public*, pg. 947

RICE KRISPIES BARS—Cereal Snacks—Kellogg Company; *U.S. Public*, pg. 947

RICE KRISPIES TREATS—Breakfast Cereal—Kellogg Company; *U.S. Public*, pg. 947

RICELAND—Rice, Oil—Riceland Foods, Inc.; *U.S. Private*, pg. 928

RICELYTE—Electrolyte Maintenance Solution—Bristol-Myers Squibb Company; *U.S. Public*, pg. 253

RICE'S BEST (PRESSED)—Twist Tobaccos—Conwood Company L.P.; *U.S. Private*, pg. 272

RICH & RARE CANDIAN WHISKEY—Spirit—Allied Domecq PLC; *Int'l*, pg. 62

RICH & CREAMY—Ice Cream & Egg Nog—Mid-America Dairymen, Inc.; *U.S. Private*, pg. 743

RICH GRAIN—Bread—Flowers Industries, Inc.; *U.S. Public*, pg. 656

RICH LASH—Cosmetics—Almay, Inc.; *U.S. Private*, pg. 689

RICH-LUX—Paint—M.A.B. Paints; *U.S. Private*, pg. 175

RICH'NING—NONE—Nestle USA; *Int'l*, pg. 916

RICH-R—Blowing Wool—Johns Manville Corporation; *U.S. Public*, pg. 927

RICH TRADITIONS—Bakery Products—The Earthgrains Company; *U.S. Public*, pg. 547

RICHARDS-WILCOX—Materials-handling Equipment—Electrolux, AB; *Int'l*, pg. 438

RICHARDSON & ROBBINS—Plum Pudding—The Pillsbury Company; *Int'l*, pg. 411

RICHARDSON FOOD CORPORATION—Ice Cream Toppings—Richardson Foods Corporation; *U.S. Public*, pg. 1347

RICHARSON FOODS—NONE—The Quaker Oats Company; *U.S. Public*, pg. 1347

RICHCO—Plastics—Richco Inc.; *U.S. Private*, pg. 929

RICHDEL—Irrigation—James Hardie Industries Ltd.; *Int'l*, pg. 596

RICHELIEU—Brandy—Distillers Corporation S.A.; *Int'l*, pg. 1129

RICHFOOD—NONE—Richfood Holdings, Inc.; *U.S. Public*, pg. 1388

RICHGLOSS—Coated Offset Paper—The Mead Corporation; *U.S. Public*, pg. 1074

RICHLAND—Cigarettes—B.A.T Industries P.L.C.; *Int'l*, pg. 110

RICHLAND—Cigarettes—Brown & Williamson Tobacco Corp.; *Int'l*, pg. 111

RICHMAN—Men's Clothing & Furnishings; Women's Career Apparel—Woolworth Corporation; *U.S. Public*, pg. 1777

RICHMAN BROTHERS—Clothing—Cliftex; *U.S. Public*, pg. 1777

RICHMAN BROTHERS—Retail Men's Clothing Stores—The Richman Brothers Co.; *U.S. Public*, pg. 1777

RICHMATTE—Coated Printing Paper—The Mead Corporation; *U.S. Public*, pg. 1074

RICHMOND—Vinyl Siding—Reynolds Metals Company; *U.S. Public*, pg. 1385

RICHMOND—Water Heaters—Rheem Manufacturing Co.; *Int'l*, pg. 1022

RICHMOND COLLEGE—International College—American Institute for Foreign Study; *U.S. Private*, pg. 56

RICHMOND GEAR—Performance Automotive Ring & Pinions & Transmissions—Regal-Beloit Corporation; *U.S. Public*, pg. 1370

RICH'S—Department Store—Federated Department Stores, Inc.; *U.S. Public*, pg. 617

RICH'S/LAZARUS—Department Stores—Rich's/Lazarus/Goldsmith's; *U.S. Public*, pg. 618

RICHTER—House Mark—The Dow Chemical Company; *U.S. Public*, pg. 522

RICHWOOD—Kitchen Cabinets—Kitchen Kompact, Inc.; *U.S. Private*, pg. 624

RICOH—Office Equip. & Cameras—Ricoh Company, Ltd.; *Int'l*, pg. 1114

RICOH—Office Equipment—Ricoh Electronics, Inc.; *Int'l*, pg. 1114

RID—NONE—Pfizer Inc.; *U.S. Public*, pg. 1281

RID-X—Septic Tank Additive—Eastman Kodak Company; *U.S. Public*, pg. 550

RID-X—Septic Tank Treatment—Reckitt & Colman Inc.; *U.S. Public*, pg. 1090

RIDALL-ZINC—Rodenticide—LiphaTech, Inc.; *Int'l*, pg. 812

RIDAURA—NONE—SmithKline Beecham Corporation; *Int'l*, pg. 1264

RIDAURA—Inflammation & Tissue Repair—SmithKline Beecham plc; *Int'l*, pg. 1264

RIDDELL—Football Equipment—Riddell Sports, Inc.; *U.S. Public*, pg. 1389

RIDDELL ATHLETIC—NONE—Signal Apparel Company, Inc.; *U.S. Public*, pg. 1472

RIDDER—Beer—Heineken N.V.; *Int'l*, pg. 608

RIDE MASTER—Shock Absorbers—Bridgestone/Firestone, Inc.; *Int'l*, pg. 213

RIDE-RITE—Air Springs—Bridgestone/Firestone, Inc.; *Int'l*, pg. 213

RIDER—Apparel—Mass Market Division; *U.S. Public*, pg. 1702

RIDERS—Jeanswear—VF Corporation; *U.S. Public*, pg. 1702

RIDGE—NONE—Beckett Papers; *U.S. Public*, pg. 903

RIDGE—Hand & Power Tools—Emerson Electric Co.; *U.S. Public*, pg. 572

RIDGE RUNNER—Attachment Equipment—Fleischer Manufacturing, Inc.; *U.S. Private*, pg. 410

RIDGELINE—Disposable Paper Products—Wisconsin Tissue Mills, Inc.; *U.S. Public*, pg. 347

RIDGETTS—Ridged Chips—C.J. Vitner Co.; *U.S. Private*, pg. 1142

RIDGEWAY—NONE—Kellwood Company; *U.S. Public*, pg. 948

RIDGEWAY—Clocks—Ridgeway Clock Company; *U.S. Public*, pg. 1343

Brand Name Index

RIDGEWOOD PARQUET—Pre-Finished Strip—Bruce Hardwood Floors; *U.S. Public,* pg. 1634

RIDGID—Professional Hand & Power Tools—Emerson Electric Co.; *U.S. Public,* pg. 572

RIDGID/KOLLMAN—Tools—Ridge Tool Co.; *U.S. Public,* pg. 574

RIDGIES—Rippled Potato Chips—Borden, Inc.; *U.S. Private,* pg. 157

RIDOLINE—Metalworking Chemical—Henkel Surface Technologies; *Int'l,* pg. 610

RIDOX—Reagent for Removing Oxygen from Gases—Fisher Scientific Company; *U.S. Private,* pg. 658

RIDSECT—Insecticide—Sara Lee Corporation; *U.S. Public,* pg. 1432

RIEGEL—Printing Papers—Fort James Corporation; *U.S. Public,* pg. 670

RIEGEL JERSEY COVER—Cover Stock—FiberMark Inc.; *U.S. Public,* pg. 620

RIESEN—Dark Chocolate Covered Caramel Candy—Storck U.S.A., L.P.; *Int'l,* pg. 1304

RIETVALLEI ESTATE—Wine—Distillers Corporation S.A.; *Int'l,* pg. 1129

RIFADIN—Prescription Antibiotic for Pulmonary Tuberculosis—Hoechst Marion Roussel North America; *Int'l,* pg. 625

RIFATER—Tuberculosis—Hoechst Marion Roussel North America; *Int'l,* pg. 625

RIFLE CABINET—NONE—American Locker Group, Inc.; *U.S. Public,* pg. 85

RIG RAYNGER—Non-asbestos oil well block—Universal Composites-U.S.C.; *U.S. Private,* pg. 1126

RIG SAVER—Air Shut-Off Valve for all Diesel Engines—Barber Industries Inc.; *Int'l,* pg. 164

RIGA-FLO—Medium & High Efficiency Air Filter—Farr Company; *U.S. Public,* pg. 613

RIGA-SORB—Commercial & Industrial Building Carbon Absorbers—Farr Company; *U.S. Public,* pg. 613

RIGAUD—Upscale Home Fragrance Candles—Tsumura International; *Int'l,* pg. 1426

RIGGS—National Bank—Riggs Bank N.A.; *U.S. Public,* pg. 1390

THE RIGHT CALL—NONE—Regions Financial Corporation; *U.S. Public,* pg. 1371

THE RIGHT CARD—NONE—Regions Financial Corporation; *U.S. Public,* pg. 1371

RIGHT COURSE—Frozen Dinners—Nestle S.A.; *Int'l,* pg. 915

RIGHT DRESS—Garden Products—Mafco Worldwide Corp.; *U.S. Private,* pg. 690

RIGHT FIELDER—Microcomputer Product—Group 1 Software, Inc.; *U.S. Public,* pg. 417

RIGHT-FIRST-TIME—Prototype, Design—LSI Logic Corp.; *U.S. Public,* pg. 971

RIGHT FIT—Booster Car Seat—Evenflo Company, Inc.; *U.S. Private,* pg. 629

RIGHT. FROM THE START—Tag Line—Alpha Microsystems; *U.S. Public,* pg. 57

RIGHT GUARD—Deodorants & Anti-Perspirants—The Gillette Company; *U.S. Public,* pg. 743

RIGHT HEIGHT—High Chair—Evenflo Company, Inc.; *U.S. Private,* pg. 629

RIGHT KIND—Oral Hygiene Aids—John O. Butler Co.; *Int'l,* pg. 1320

RIGHT-ON—Hair Preparations—The Gillette Company; *U.S. Public,* pg. 743

RIGHT-ON CURL—Hair Moisterizer & Conditioner—The Gillette Company; *U.S. Public,* pg. 743

RIGHT-ON RIGHT BACK—Curl Restorer—The Gillette Company; *U.S. Public,* pg. 743

THE RIGHT PLACE—NONE—Regions Financial Corporation; *U.S. Public,* pg. 1371

THE RIGHT PRICE—Women's Retail Specialty Store—Gateway Apparel, Inc.; *U.S. Private,* pg. 441

RIGHT START—Contact Lens Care Kits—Alcon Laboratories, Inc.; *Int'l,* pg. 916

RIGHT STUFF—Flexible Gaskets—Loctite Corp. North American Group; *Int'l,* pg. 611

THE RIGHT SUPPORT FOR YOU—Brassieres—Lilyette Brassiere Co.; *U.S. Private,* pg. 697

THE RIGHT TOUCH—NONE—OMRON Systems, Inc.; *Int'l,* pg. 1005

RIGI—Volleyball Shoe—K-Swiss Inc.; *U.S. Public,* pg. 937

RIGI-FLEX—Ureteroscope—Circon Corporation; *U.S. Public,* pg. 373

RIGID GRIP—Poultry Shackles—E.H. Titchener & Company; *U.S. Private,* pg. 1089

RIGIDENT—Denture Adhesive—Carter-Wallace, Inc.; *U.S. Public,* pg. 309

RIGIMESH—Filters—Pall Corporation; *U.S. Public,* pg. 1253

RIGIPLEAT—Hydraulics—Pall Corporation; *U.S. Public,* pg. 1253

RIGIPOR—NONE—Pall Corporation; *U.S. Public,* pg. 1253

RIGO—Pesticides & Insecticides—Rigo/Black Leaf; *U.S. Public,* pg. 1390

RIGOLLETTO—Sportswear—CGS Industries, Inc.; *U.S. Private,* pg. 194

RIGS—Rate-Integrating Gyroscopic Survey System—Baker Hughes INTEQ; *U.S. Public,* pg. 166

RIGUR—NONE—Poly Pak America, Inc.; *U.S. Private,* pg. 875

RIGUR DURALITE MAILERS—Plastic Mailers—Poly Pak America, Inc.; *U.S. Private,* pg. 875

RIKSKUPOWGER—Meal Voucher—Accor S.A.; *Int'l,* pg. 20

RILEYS—Potato Chips—Borden, Inc.; *U.S. Private,* pg. 157

RILSAN—Nylon 11 & 12—Elf Atochem North America, Inc.; *Int'l,* pg. 445

RIMACTANE—Antibiotic—Ciba Specialty Chemicals; *Int'l,* pg. 291

RIMACTANE—Antibiotc—Novartis; *Int'l,* pg. 972

RIMADYL—Carprofen—Pfizer Inc.; *U.S. Public,* pg. 1281

RIMCOR—Combustion Controls—Preferred Instruments; *U.S. Public,* pg. 881

RIMEVAX—NONE—SmithKline Beecham Corporation; *Int'l,* pg. 1264

RIMEVAX—Vaccine—SmithKline Beecham plc; *Int'l,* pg. 1264

RIMEVAX—Vaccine—SmithKline Beecham Research Limited; *Int'l,* pg. 1266

RIMFIRE—Controller Products & Disk Arrays—Ciprico, Inc.; *U.S. Public,* pg. 370

RIMFLY—Fly Reel—Cortland Line Co., Inc.; *U.S. Private,* pg. 277

RIMLEASE—Water-Based Soap Systems—The Dexter Corporation; *U.S. Public,* pg. 504

RIMSO 50—Medicine for the Treatment of Intersitial Cystitis—Baxter Research Medical, Inc.; *U.S. Public,* pg. 196

RIMTHANE—Elastomer Systems—The Dow Chemical Company; *U.S. Public,* pg. 522

RINBROS—Knit Products—Sara Lee Corporation; *U.S. Public,* pg. 1432

RINDEX—Detergents—Procter & Gamble Venezuela, C.A.; *U.S. Public,* pg. 1332

RING—Machine Tool—The Producto Machine Co.; *U.S. Private,* pg. 889

RING DINGS—Snack Cakes—Drake Bakeries, Inc.; *Int'l,* pg. 349

RING DROP—Plastic Container Closures of Caps Used on Containers—The West Company, Incorporated; *U.S. Public,* pg. 1755

RING-FLEX—Furniture Edgings—Leggett & Platt, Incorporated; *U.S. Public,* pg. 985

RING-GUN—Assembly Tool—Waldes Truarc/Industrial Retaining Ring; *U.S. Public,* pg. 1632

RING-JECTOR—Assembly Tool—Waldes Truarc/Industrial Retaining Ring; *U.S. Public,* pg. 1632

RING KING—Office Products—HON Industries Inc.; *U.S. Public,* pg. 772

RING LEADER—O-Ring Sealed Joint Chains—Diamond Chain Company; *U.S. Private,* pg. 68

RING-MOUNT—Assembly Tool—Waldes Truarc/Industrial Retaining Ring; *U.S. Public,* pg. 1632

RING-O-MAT—Assembly Tool—Waldes Truarc/Industrial Retaining Ring; *U.S. Public,* pg. 1632

RING POP LOLLIPOPS—Candy—The Topps Company, Inc.; *U.S. Public,* pg. 1621

RING RETRACT—NONE—U.S. Surgical Corp.; *U.S. Public,* pg. 1687

RING SEAL—Motor Oil Conditioner—The Shaler Company; *U.S. Private,* pg. 786

RING-TITE!—Fasteners—R&B, Inc.; *U.S. Public,* pg. 1354

RING-LOK—Easy Access System for Pool/Spa Products—Jacuzzi Bros., Jacuzzi, Inc.; *U.S. Public,* pg. 1684

RINGER—Timpani—Ludwig Industries; *U.S. Public,* pg. 1514

RINGLING BROS. BARNUM & BAILEY CIRCUS—Circuses & Retail Toys—Feld Productions; *U.S. Private,* pg. 399

RINGOOS—Pet Foods—Nestle S.A.; *Int'l,* pg. 915

RINGS & THINGS—Jewelry—World Pacific Ullenberg Corp.; *U.S. Public,* pg. 861

RINI-REGO MARKETPLACE—Retail Grocery Stores—Riser Foods, Inc.; *U.S. Private,* pg. 450

RINI-REGO STOP-N-SHOP—Retail Grocery Stores—Riser Foods, Inc.; *U.S. Private,* pg. 450

RINKER—Concrete & Cement—CSR Limited; *Int'l,* pg. 245

RINN—X-Ray Film Holders & Film Mounts—Dentsply International Inc.; *U.S. Public,* pg. 498

RINOGUTT—Antirinitic—Boehringer Ingelheim Italia S.p.A.; *Int'l,* pg. 199

RINSATE PADS—Containment Sump for Washing/Cleaning Equipment & Containing Solids—The Will-Burt Company; *U.S. Private,* pg. 1177

RINSE—Fabric Softener—Patterson Laboratories, Inc.; *U.S. Private,* pg. 843

RINSE AWAY—Rinse—Alberto-Culver Company; *U.S. Public,* pg. 37

RINSE-DRY—Fast Drying Additive—Ecolab Inc.; *U.S. Public,* pg. 562

RIO—Beach Bags, Chairs & Umbrellas—All-Luminum Products, Inc.; *U.S. Private,* pg. 34

RIO—Broadloom—Couristan Inc.; *U.S. Private,* pg. 279

RIO—Shower Head & Hand Held Shower—Interbath, Inc.; *U.S. Private,* pg. 566

RIO DE ORO—Imitation Vanilla—Clements Foods Co.; *U.S. Private,* pg. 245

RIO SUITE HOTEL & CASINO—Gaming Resort—Rio Hotel & Casino Inc.; *U.S. Public,* pg. 1390

RIO VIEJO—Sherry—Domecq Importers Inc.; *Int'l,* pg. 63

RIOPAN—NONE—Whitehall-Robins Healthcare; *U.S. Public,* pg. 80

RIOTHERM—Volute Casing Pumps—KSB Aktiengesellschaft; *Int'l,* pg. 721

RIOVAR/RIOVAR Z—Variable Speed Circulating Pump—KSB Aktiengesellschaft; *Int'l,* pg. 721

RIP-IT—NONE—Stuart Entertainment Inc.; *U.S. Public,* pg. 1526

RIP-N-PLANT—Cultivator—United Farm Tools, Inc.; *U.S. Private,* pg. 1122

RIP 'N STICK—Liner-Free Technology—Datasouth Computer Corporation; *U.S. Public,* pg. 267

RIP-OPE—Envelopes—Tension Envelope Corp.; *U.S. Private,* pg. 1077

RIP PROOF—NONE—H.C. Miller Company; *U.S. Private,* pg. 747

RIPL-FLO—Screen—Svedala Industries Inc.; *Int'l,* pg. 1325

RIPPIN' GOOD—Packaged Cookies—Ripon Foods, Inc.; *U.S. Private,* pg. 931

RIPPLE EFFECTS—Greeting Cards—Gibson Greetings, Inc.; *U.S. Public,* pg. 742

RIPPLECOAT—Coils for Electrical Rotating Machines—General Electric Canada Inc.; *U.S. Public,* pg. 713

RIPPLEFOLD—Drapery Hardware—Kirsch; *U.S. Public,* pg. 1176

RIPPLEMODE—Electronic Instrument—Intel Corporation; *U.S. Public,* pg. 886

RIPPLIN'S—Potato Chips—Keebler Company; *U.S. Public,* pg. 657

RIPWRAP—Daylight Load Package—Eastman Kodak Company; *U.S. Public,* pg. 550

RIS—Paper Products—Ris Paper Company; *U.S. Private,* pg. 932

RISC SYSTEM/6000—Computer Product—International Business Machines Corporation; *U.S. Public,* pg. 895

RISE—Shaving Cream—Carter-Wallace, Inc.; *U.S. Public,* pg. 309

RISE N' SHINE—Dry Fondant Sugars—Crompton & Knowles Ingredient Technology Corp.; *U.S. Public,* pg. 459

RISER-GARD—Riser Rated PVC Corrugated Pipe—The Lamson & Sessions Co.; *U.S. Public,* pg. 976

RISING MAN—Logo—Medtronic, Inc.; *U.S. Public,* pg. 1082

RISING STAR GRILL—NONE—Bonanza Restaurants; *U.S. Private,* pg. 736

RISK—Game—Parker Brothers; *U.S. Public,* pg. 797

RISK MAPPING—Risk Management Program—Medical Assurance, Inc.; *U.S. Public*, pg. 1079

RISLONE—Engine & Upper Cylinder Treatment—The Shaler Company; *U.S. Private*, pg. 786

RISLONE CONCENTRATE—Automotive Products—The Shaler Company; *U.S. Private*, pg. 786

RISPERDAL—Antipsychotic—Akzo Nobel N.V.; *Int'l*, pg. 42

RISPERDAL—NONE—Johnson & Johnson; *U.S. Public*, pg. 927

RISPOVAL—NONE—Pfizer Inc.; *U.S. Public*, pg. 1281

RISPOVAL—Animal Vaccine—SmithKline Beecham plc; *Int'l*, pg. 1264

RISQUE—Women's Undergarments—National Corset Supply House; *U.S. Private*, pg. 781

RISTS—NONE—LucasVarity plc; *Int'l*, pg. 819

RIT—Fabric Dyes—Best Foods; *U.S. Public*, pg. 224

RITA FEDERICI—Bed Linen—Caleffi S.p.A.; *Int'l*, pg. 252

RITALIN—Pharmaceutical—Ciba Specialty Chemicals; *Int'l*, pg. 291

RITALIN—Pharmaceutical—Novartis; *Int'l*, pg. 972

RITALINE—NONE—Novartis Pharmaceuticals; *Int'l*, pg. 973

RITASA FREIGHT SERVICES SRL—NONE—A.I. Ocean; *Int'l*, pg. 14

RITCHIE—Livestock Fountains & Hydrants—Ritchie Industries, Inc.; *U.S. Private*, pg. 933

RITE-HITE—Leveler—Rite-Hite Corporation; *U.S. Private*, pg. 933

RITE-PAK—Packings—John Crane Mechanical Seals; *Int'l*, pg. 1339

RITE SIZE—Corrugated Box Machinery—The Entwistle Company; *U.S. Private*, pg. 378

RITE SOURCE—NONE—Cleaning Solutions Group/Cello; *U.S. Public*, pg. 1466

RITE-TRAK—Track Mounted Beryllium Copper Shielding Gasket—Instrument Specialties Company; *U.S. Private*, pg. 565

RITEPOINT—Writing Instruments for Specialty Advertising—Golden Books Family Entertainment Inc.; *U.S. Public*, pg. 749

RITTAL—Electrical Enclosures—Bryant Electric Supply Company, Inc.; *U.S. Private*, pg. 177

RITZ—Soft Drink—Beverage Canners International Corp.; *U.S. Private*, pg. 106

RITZ—Crackers—Nabisco Inc.; *U.S. Public*, pg. 1355

RITZ—Cracker—RJR Nabisco Holdings Corp.; *U.S. Public*, pg. 1355

RITZ BITS—Crackers—Nabisco Inc.; *U.S. Public*, pg. 1355

RIUVERT—NONE—ETEX; *Int'l*, pg. 430

RIVA—Beauty Salon Furniture—Belvedere Company; *U.S. Private*, pg. 1008

RIVA—Power Boats—Vickers PLC; *Int'l*, pg. 1466

RIVAL—Appliances—The Rival Company; *U.S. Public*, pg. 1391

RIVAL SELECT—Appliances—The Rival Company; *U.S. Public*, pg. 1391

RIVANO—Outdoor Shoe—K-Swiss Inc.; *U.S. Public*, pg. 937

RIVCO—NONE—Riverside Millwork Company, Inc.; *U.S. Private*, pg. 934

RIVCO INSUL-TILT—Windows—Riverside Millwork Company, Inc.; *U.S. Private*, pg. 934

RIVER—Rice—Riviana Foods Inc.; *U.S. Public*, pg. 1392

RIVER HERITAGE—Riverboat Cruise Trips—American Classic Voyagers Company; *U.S. Private*, pg. 380

RIVER RANCH—Vegetables & Fruit—The Albert Fisher Group PLC; *Int'l*, pg. 491

RIVER RANCH—NONE—River Ranch Northeast, Inc.; *U.S. Private*, pg. 934

RIVERA—Wine—Paterno Imports Limited; *U.S. Private*, pg. 843

RIVERBIRCH—Manufactured Homes—Champion Enterprises, Inc.; *U.S. Public*, pg. 332

RIVERHALL—Plywood, Wood & Wood Fiber Products—Georgia-Pacific Corporation; *U.S. Public*, pg. 735

RIVERHEAD TRADE PAPERBACKS—Books—Berkley Publishing Corp.; *Int'l*, pg. 1027

RIVERSIDE MARKETS—Retail Food Outlets—The Penn Traffic Company; *U.S. Public*, pg. 1270

RIVERSIDE PLANK—Pre-Finished Laminate—Bruce Hardwood Floors; *U.S. Public*, pg. 1634

RIVES—Fine Papers—Arjo Wiggins Appleton plc; *Int'l*, pg. 567

RIVET-ALL—Consumer Rivet Tool—Marson/Creative Fastener, Inc.; *U.S. Private*, pg. 708

RIVET-TITE!—Rivets—R&B, Inc.; *U.S. Public*, pg. 1354

RIVETRITE—Shelf Framing Systems—Penco Products; *U.S. Private*, pg. 848

RIVIERA—Watches—Baume Mercier, Inc.; *U.S. Private*, pg. 124

RIVIERA—Automobile—Buick Motor Div. General Motors Corp.; *U.S. Public*, pg. 720

RIVIERA—Salad Dressing—Cains Foods, L.P.; *U.S. Private*, pg. 199

RIVIERA—Soups—Nalleys Fine Foods; *U.S. Private*, pg. 887

RIVIERA—Milk—Q.U.F. Industries Ltd.; *Int'l*, pg. 1074

RIVNITE—NONE—Banfi Vintners; *U.S. Private*, pg. 113

RIVOTRIL—Antiepilectic, Anticonvulsant—Roche Holding Ltd.; *Int'l*, pg. 1119

RIXE—Cycle—Derby International Corporation S.A.; *Int'l*, pg. 394

RIXSON—Architectural Hardware—Conrac Display Products; *U.S. Private*, pg. 264

RIZZI ARC—Folding Tables—Vecta; *U.S. Private*, pg. 1038

RO-TEL—Process Cheese Spread—Borden, Inc.; *U.S. Private*, pg. 157

ROACCUTANE—Dermatology Pharmaceutical—Roche Holding Ltd.; *Int'l*, pg. 1119

ROAD & TRACK—Automotive Magazine—Hachette Filipacchi Magazines Inc.; *Int'l*, pg. 794

ROAD KING—Tires—Bridgestone/Firestone, Inc.; *Int'l*, pg. 213

ROAD KING—Tires—Dayton Tire Company; *Int'l*, pg. 213

ROAD KING—Motorcycles—Harley-Davidson, Inc.; *U.S. Public*, pg. 786

ROAD-KING—Screening—Telsmith, Inc.; *U.S. Public*, pg. 141

ROAD MASTER—Expedited LTL Truck Service—Danzas Corporation; *Int'l*, pg. 382

ROAD MASTER—Service Products—R&B, Inc.; *U.S. Public*, pg. 1354

ROAD PAL—Emergency Car Air Compressor—Campbell Hausfeld Division of Scott Fetzer; *U.S. Public*, pg. 217

ROAD PRO—NONE—Seats Incorporated; *U.S. Private*, pg. 410

ROAD RANGER—Recreational Vehicles—Kit Manufacturing Company; *U.S. Public*, pg. 962

ROAD SAFE—Telephone Enclosures—The Lamson & Sessions Co.; *U.S. Public*, pg. 976

ROAD STAR—Shock Absorbers—Arvin Industries, Inc.; *U.S. Public*, pg. 136

ROAD TO THE NATIONAL CHAMPIONSHIP—Sports Radio Program—Westwood One Entertainment; *U.S. Private*, pg. 1763

ROAD-RUNNER—Rail Lubricators—Portec Inc., Railway Maintenance Products Div.; *U.S. Public*, pg. 1318

ROADGUARD—Automotive Paints & Lacquers—PPG Industries, Inc.; *U.S. Public*, pg. 1245

ROADKILL—War Game—Monarch Avalon, Inc.; *U.S. Public*, pg. 1123

ROADMASTER—Bicycles, Tricycles & Wagons—Brunswick Corporation; *U.S. Public*, pg. 265

ROADMASTER—Automobile—Buick Motor Div. General Motors Corp.; *U.S. Public*, pg. 720

ROADMASTER—Tires—The Cooper Tire Company; *U.S. Public*, pg. 445

ROADMASTER—Luxury Car—General Motors Corporation; *U.S. Public*, pg. 718

ROADMASTER—Motorhome Chassis—Monaco Coach Corporation; *U.S. Public*, pg. 1123

ROADMASTER—Bicycles—RDM Sports Group; *U.S. Public*, pg. 1354

ROADMASTER—Bicycle, Wagon—Roadmaster/Brunswick; *U.S. Public*, pg. 265

ROADMATE—Beverage Cooler—Igloo Products Corporation; *U.S. Public*, pg. 265

ROADMATES—Shocks, Struts, Coil Springs, Rack & Pinion Steering Units, Brakes, Suspen.—AP North American Aftermarket Division; *U.S. Private*, pg. 230

ROADRANGER—Service—Eaton Corporation, Truck Components Operations-North America; *U.S. Public*, pg. 557

ROADSTAR—Truck Service—Air Express International Corporation; *U.S. Public*, pg. 30

ROADSTER—Children's Bed—Rubbermaid Incorporated; *U.S. Public*, pg. 1411

ROAMER—Small Vacuum—Advance Machine Company; *Int'l*, pg. 932

ROAST RITE—Turkeys—Norbest, Inc.; *U.S. Private*, pg. 801

ROASTAROMA—Herb Tea—Celestial Seasonings; *U.S. Public*, pg. 319

ROASTERS—Coffee Shops—Cara Operations Limited; *Int'l*, pg. 266

ROB ROY—Children's Clothing—Garan, Incorporated; *U.S. Public*, pg. 703

ROBALO—Fishing Boats—Brunswick Corporation; *U.S. Public*, pg. 265

ROBBIE—Youth's Shirts—Arnotts plc; *Int'l*, pg. 81

ROBBY LEN—Bathing Suits & Beach Wear—Robby Len Fashions; *U.S. Public*, pg. 121

ROBERK—NONE—Plews/Edelmann; *Int'l*, pg. 1396

ROBERT ALLEN—NONE—Tandy Brands Accessories, Inc.; *U.S. Public*, pg. 1560

ROBERT BRUCE—NONE—Tandy Brands Accessories, Inc.; *U.S. Public*, pg. 1560

ROBERT CORR—Soft Drink—R.J. Corr Naturals, Inc.; *U.S. Private*, pg. 276

ROBERT E. BAYLEY—Construction—Robert E. Bayley Construction; *U.S. Private*, pg. 125

ROBERT HAVILAND C. PARLON—Limoges Porcelain—Lalique North America; *Int'l*, pg. 797

ROBERT MONDAVI—Wine—Pacific Wine Co.; *U.S. Private*, pg. 843

ROBERT MONDAVI—NONE—Robert Mondavi Winery, Inc.; *U.S. Public*, pg. 1393

ROBERT MONDAVI COASTAL—NONE—Robert Mondavi Winery, Inc.; *U.S. Public*, pg. 1393

ROBERT MONDAVI NAPA VALLEY—NONE—Robert Mondavi Winery, Inc.; *U.S. Public*, pg. 1393

ROBERT SCOTT—NONE—Kellwood Company; *U.S. Public*, pg. 948

ROBERT STEMMLER—Premium Wine—Racke USA; *Int'l*, pg. 1083

ROBERT STEMMLER WINERY—NONE—Buena Vista Winery; *Int'l*, pg. 1083

ROBERT STOCK—Men's Suits & Dress Shirts—Oxford Industries, Inc.; *U.S. Public*, pg. 1239

ROBERT TERRY—NONE—Kellwood Company; *U.S. Public*, pg. 948

ROBERT WILLIAM JAMES & ASSOC.—Executive Recruiter—Staffing Solutions; *U.S. Private*, pg. 1028

ROBERTET—Essential Oils—Robertet, Inc.; *Int'l*, pg. 1119

ROBERTS—Furniture—Masco Corporation; *U.S. Public*, pg. 1052

ROBERTS—Baby Products & Cosmetics—SmithKline Beecham plc; *Int'l*, pg. 1264

ROBERTS—Centrifuge—Western States Machine Company; *U.S. Private*, pg. 1168

ROBERTS—NONE—Whitin Roberts Co.; *U.S. Private*, pg. 309

ROBERTSON—Ready-Made Draperies & Made-to-Measure Draperies & Bedspreads—Robertson Factories, Inc.; *U.S. Private*, pg. 936

ROBERTSON—Computer Hardware—Robertson Marketing Inc.; *U.S. Private*, pg. 936

ROBERTSONS—Preserves—Ranks Hovis McDougall Limited; *Int'l*, pg. 1395

ROBESON—Manufactures & Distributes Electrical Household Appliances, Fans & Heaters—Robeson Appliance, Inc.; *U.S. Public*, pg. 1394

ROBICO—Dresses—Donnkenny, Inc.; *U.S. Public*, pg. 519

ROBIN—Industrial Engines—Fuji Heavy Industries, Ltd.; *Int'l*, pg. 522

ROBIN—Laundry Care—Reckitt & Colman plc; *Int'l*, pg. 1089

ROBIN HOOD—Flour & Mixes—General Mills, Inc.; *U.S. Public*, pg. 717

ROBIN HOOD—Consumer Mixes, Flour & Oatmeal—International Multifoods Corporation; *U.S. Public*, pg. 900

ROBIN HOOD—War Game—Monarch Avalon, Inc.; *U.S. Public*, pg. 1123

ROBIN HOOD—NONE—North America Foods; *U.S. Public*, pg. 901

ROBIN HOOD—Flour & Mixes—Robin Hood Multifoods Inc.; *U.S. Public*, pg. 901

ROBINAIR—Air Conditioning Service Equipment—SPX Corporation; *U.S. Public*, pg. 1420

ROBINSON—Ice Cream Cones & Plastic Drinking Straws—Dover Industries Limited; *Int'l*, pg. 417

ROBINSON-NUGENT—Electronic Components—Robinson Nugent, Inc.; *U.S. Public*, pg. 1394

ROBINSON R44—4-Seat Helicopter—Robinson Helicopter Company; *U.S. Private*, pg. 936

ROBINSON R22—2-Seat Helicopter—Robinson Helicopter Company; *U.S. Private*, pg. 936

ROBINSON'S—General Merchandise—Woolworth Corporation; *U.S. Public*, pg. 1777

ROBINSON'S—Apparel & other Merchandise—F.W. Woolworth Co.; *U.S. Public*, pg. 1777

ROBINSONS-MAY—Department Stores—The May Department Stores Company; *U.S. Public*, pg. 1063

ROBINTRONIC—Automatic Level Indication & Control Equipment—Litton Industries, Inc.; *U.S. Public*, pg. 1002

ROBITUSSIN—Liquids Relieve Cold And Cough Symptoms—American Home Products Corporation; *U.S. Public*, pg. 79

ROBITUSSIN—Cold & Cough Relief Liquid—Whitehall-Robins Healthcare; *U.S. Public*, pg. 80

ROBITUSSIN COUGH DROPS—Cough Drops—Whitehall-Robins Healthcare; *U.S. Public*, pg. 80

ROBITUSSIN LIQUID-GELS—NONE—Whitehall-Robins Healthcare; *U.S. Public*, pg. 80

ROBO CON—Machine Controller—Kurt Manufacturing Co. Inc.; *U.S. Private*, pg. 637

ROBOFIL—Wire Cutting EDM-Centers—Georg Fischer Ltd.; *Int'l*, pg. 488

ROBOFORM—Die Sinking EDM-Centers—Georg Fischer Ltd.; *Int'l*, pg. 488

ROBOKENT—Robotic Floor Care Equipment—The Kent Company; *Int'l*, pg. 440

ROBOLITE CARTRAC—Lightweight Car Trac System—SI Handling Systems, Inc.; *U.S. Public*, pg. 1418

ROBOT-FRI—Bakery & Restaurant Equipment—Belshaw Brothers, Inc.; *Int'l*, pg. 188

ROBOTRAC—Passive Retraction System—Aesculap, Inc.; *Int'l*, pg. 29

ROBOTRAC—Material Handling Equipment—Spartan Tool; *U.S. Private*, pg. 860

ROBT. BURNS—Cigars—General Cigar Company, Inc.; *U.S. Public*, pg. 708

ROC—NONE—Johnson & Johnson; *U.S. Public*, pg. 927

ROCA—Buttercrunch—Brown & Haley; *U.S. Private*, pg. 173

ROCA BITS—Buttercrunch—Brown & Haley; *U.S. Private*, pg. 173

ROCALTROL—Antiinflammatory, Metabolic Drug—Roche Holding Ltd.; *Int'l*, pg. 1119

ROCAN—Industrial Plastic Containers—Ropak Corporation; *Int'l*, pg. 811

ROCCHE CASTAGMAGNA BARBERA D'ALBA—Italian Wine—Laird & Company; *U.S. Private*, pg. 642

ROCCHE CASTAGMAGNA BAROLO—Italian Wine—Laird & Company; *U.S. Private*, pg. 642

ROCCHE CASTAGMAGNA DOLCETTO D'ALBA—Italian Wine—Laird & Company; *U.S. Private*, pg. 642

ROCEPHIN—Injectible Antibiotic—Hoffmann-La Roche Inc.; *Int'l*, pg. 1120

ROCEPHIN—Injectable Antibiotic, Antibacterial—Roche Holding Ltd.; *Int'l*, pg. 1119

ROCHARD—Porcelain Boxes—Syratech Corporation; *U.S. Private*, pg. 1060

ROCHAS—Perfume—Wella Group; *Int'l*, pg. 1489

ROCHE-POSAY—Dermo-Pharmacological Product—L'Oreal S.A.; *Int'l*, pg. 818

ROCHESTER—Automotive Products—General Motors Corporation; *U.S. Public*, pg. 718

ROCHFLEX—NONE—Synergistics Industries Limited; *U.S. Public*, pg. 734

ROCHIOLI—Wine—Paterno Imports Limited; *U.S. Private*, pg. 843

ROCK-A-LOUNGER—Recliners—The Berkline Corporation; *U.S. Private*, pg. 432

ROCK BOTTOM RESTAURANT & BREWERY—Brew Pub—Rock Bottom Restaurants; *U.S. Public*, pg. 1396

ROCK'EM SOCK'EM CRASH DUMMIES—Game—Tyco Toys, Inc.; *U.S. Public*, pg. 1058

ROCK'EM SOCK'EM ROBOTS—Game—Tyco Toys, Inc.; *U.S. Public*, pg. 1058

ROCK GRIP EXCAVATOR—Tires—Bridgestone/Firestone, Inc.; *Int'l*, pg. 213

ROCK GRIP ROAD BUILDER—Tires—Bridgestone/Firestone, Inc.; *Int'l*, pg. 213

ROCK MASTER—Tires—Bridgestone/Firestone, Inc.; *Int'l*, pg. 213

ROCK MASTER DEEP TREAD—Tires—Bridgestone/Firestone, Inc.; *Int'l*, pg. 213

ROCK n' ROLL—Music Series—Time-Life, Inc.; *U.S. Public*, pg. 1613

ROCK'N ROLL CHRISTMAS—Musical Item—Mr. Christmas Inc.; *U.S. Private*, pg. 765

ROCK OF AGES—Memorials & Surface Plates—Rock of Ages Corporation; *U.S. Public*, pg. 1396

ROCK PAK—Aseptic Packaged Drinks—White Rock Products Corp.; *U.S. Private*, pg. 1173

ROCK PRODUCTS—Non-Metallic Mining Industry Publication—Intertec Publishing; *U.S. Public*, pg. 1327

ROCK SPRING—Still Natural Mineral Water—Spadel SA; *Int'l*, pg. 1287

ROCKBOTTOM—Solvent Borne Nonstick Coating—The Dexter Corporation; *U.S. Public*, pg. 504

ROCKER & ROCKER II—Drum Sets & Stands—Ludwig Industries; *U.S. Public*, pg. 1514

ROCKERS—Footwear—Cherokee Inc.; *U.S. Public*, pg. 345

ROCKERS—Plastic Heads—Ludwig Industries; *U.S. Public*, pg. 1514

THE ROCKET—Music Publication—Bam Media; *U.S. Private*, pg. 113

ROCKET—Concrete Mixer—3ummit Performance Dist. Inc.; *U.S. Public*, pg. 1233

ROCKET PERMA POST—Lighting Standard—Stonco Genlyte; *U.S. Public*, pg. 730

ROCKET RED—Fluorescent Color—Day-Glo Color Corp.; *U.S. Public*, pg. 1357

ROCKET RYDER—Gym Sets—Hedstrom Corporation; *U.S. Private*, pg. 526

ROCKET TAP—Cold Forming Tap—National Twist Drill Div.; *U.S. Public*, pg. 1370

ROCKET TAP—Cold Forming Tap—Regal-Beloit Corporation; *U.S. Public*, pg. 1370

ROCKFORD ACROMATIC—Screw Machinery Products, Aircraft Parts & Machinery—Rockford Acromatic Product Co.; *U.S. Private*, pg. 938

ROCKFORD CONSTANT VELOCITY—Fwd & Driveline Parts & Accessories—Rockford Acromatic Product Co.; *U.S. Private*, pg. 938

ROCKHILL—NONE—Plews/Edelmann; *Int'l*, pg. 1396

ROCKMATE—Portable Hardness Tester—NewAge Industries Inc.; *U.S. Private*, pg. 796

ROCKMATE—Portable Hardness Tester—Newage Industries Inc., Testing Instruments Group; *U.S. Private*, pg. 796

ROCKPORT—Athletic Shoes—Reebok International Ltd.; *U.S. Public*, pg. 1369

ROCKPORT—Footwear—The Rockport Company; *U.S. Public*, pg. 1370

ROCKWELL—Aerospace, Electronic, Automotive & Graphics Products—Rockwell International Corporation; *U.S. Public*, pg. 1397

ROCKWELL—Hardness Testers—Wilson/Shore Instruments; *U.S. Public*, pg. 883

ROCKWELL AUTOMATION—NONE—Rockwell Automation; *U.S. Public*, pg. 1397

ROCKWELL INTERNATIONAL—For a Wide Variety of the Company's Products—Rockwell International Corporation; *U.S. Public*, pg. 1397

ROCKWELL SOFTWARE—Suite of Industrial Software Products—Rockwell Automation; *U.S. Public*, pg. 1397

ROCKWOOD—Guitars—Hohner/HSS Inc.; *U.S. Private*, pg. 533

ROCKWOOD GARDENS—Garden Stock by Mail—Michigan Bulb Company; *U.S. Private*, pg. 421

ROCKWOOL—Fire Retardant Rock Wool Insulation—Partek Corporation; *Int'l*, pg. 1024

ROCKY—Automobile—Daihatsu America, Inc.; *Int'l*, pg. 365

ROCKY—2000 cc (Petrol), 2800 cc (Diesel) 4WD Jeep-Type—Daihatsu Motor Corporation, Ltd.; *Int'l*, pg. 364

ROCKY—NONE—Rocky Shoes & Boots, Inc.; *U.S. Public*, pg. 1402

ROCKY—Videogame—Sega of America Inc.; *Int'l*, pg. 1218

ROCKY BOOTS—NONE—Rocky Shoes & Boots, Inc.; *U.S. Public*, pg. 1402

ROCKY CREEK—Sidings BSN—Union Camp Corporation; *U.S. Public*, pg. 1665

ROCKY MOUNTAIN BANKCARD SYSTEM—Credit Card Issuers—Colorado National Bank; *U.S. Public*, pg. 1680

ROCKY MOUNTAIN NEWS—Newspaper—The E.W. Scripps Company; *U.S. Public*, pg. 1447

ROCKY MOUNTAIN PRESTRESS—NONE—Phelps Tointon Inc.; *U.S. Private*, pg. 860

ROCKY 911 SERIES—NONE—Rocky Shoes & Boots, Inc.; *U.S. Public*, pg. 1402

ROCKY ROAD—Candy—Annabelle Candy Company, Inc.; *U.S. Private*, pg. 75

ROCKY ROAD DARK CHOCOLATE—Candy—Annabelle Candy Company, Inc.; *U.S. Private*, pg. 75

ROCKY ROAD MINT—Candy—Annabelle Candy Company, Inc.; *U.S. Private*, pg. 75

ROCKY ROCOCO—Pan Style Pizza—Rocky Rococo Corporation; *U.S. Private*, pg. 938

ROD & RINGS—Dealer Publication—Kirsch; *U.S. Public*, pg. 1176

RODA—Margarine—Vandemoortele N.V.; *Int'l*, pg. 1451

RODALE'S SCUBA DIVING—Magazine—Rodale Press, Inc.; *U.S. Public*, pg. 939

RODALE'S FITNESS SWIMMER—Magazine—Rodale Press, Inc.; *U.S. Private*, pg. 939

RODALE'S HEART & SOUL—Magazine—Rodale Press, Inc.; *U.S. Private*, pg. 939

RODAR—NONE—Carpenter Technology Corporation; *U.S. Public*, pg. 307

RODASOL—Pest Control—Reckitt & Colman plc; *Int'l*, pg. 1089

RODD—Cutlery & Silverware—McPherson's Limited; *Int'l*, pg. 852

RODDENBERY—Pickles, Table Syrup—Dean Pickle & Specialty Products Co.; *U.S. Public*, pg. 490

RODDENBERY'S—Pickles, Peanut Butter, Syrup—Dean Pickles & Specialty Products; *U.S. Public*, pg. 490

RODDIS—Flush Doors—Weyerhaeuser Forest Products Company; *U.S. Public*, pg. 1764

RODEO—Aquatic Herbicide—The Agricultural Group, Monsanto Company; *U.S. Public*, pg. 1125

RODEO—Herbicide—Monsanto Company; *U.S. Public*, pg. 1124

RODEO—Meat Products—John Morrell & Co.; *U.S. Public*, pg. 1479

RODEO DRIVE—Women's Western Boots—Georgia/Durango Boot Company; *U.S. Public*, pg. 1684

RODEWAY INNS—Main Stay Suites (Extended Stay Hotels)—Choice Hotels International, Inc.; *U.S. Public*, pg. 351

RODGERS BUILDERS—Gen. Contractors—Rodgers Builders, Inc.; *U.S. Private*, pg. 939

RODINE—Metalworking Chemical—Henkel Surface Technologies; *Int'l*, pg. 610

RODON—Fly Rod Components—Cortland Line Co., Inc.; *U.S. Private*, pg. 277

ROD'S—Salad Dressing & Dips—The Earthgrains Company; *U.S. Public*, pg. 547

ROEDERSTEIN—Film Capacitors—Vishay Intertechnology, Inc.; *U.S. Public*, pg. 1721

ROEGELEIN—Foods—Ohse Foods Inc.; *U.S. Private*, pg. 396

ROEHLEN—Embossing Rolls & Plates—Standex International Corporation; *U.S. Public*, pg. 1505

ROFERON-A—Antiviral, Antineoplastic—Roche Holding Ltd.; *Int'l*, pg. 1119

ROFFE—Ski-Wear—Gerry Sportswear Company; *U.S. Private*, pg. 449

ROFFLER—Hair Care Products For Men & Women—Framesi USA, Inc./Roffler Industries, Inc./Casa di Colore, Inc.; *U.S. Private*, pg. 419

ROGAINE—Alopecia—Pharmacia & Upjohn; *Int'l*, pg. 1048

ROGATOR—Self-Propelled Row Crop Applicator—Ag-Chem Equipment Co., Inc.; *U.S. Public*, pg. 6

ROGER & GALLET—Perfume—International Cosmetics Co., Ltd.; *Int'l*, pg. 684

ROGERS—Tobacco Pouches—Consolidated Cigar Corp.; *U.S. Private*, pg. 690

ROGERS—Silverware—Oneida Ltd.; *U.S. Public*, pg. 1225

ROGERS—Flatware—Stanley Roberts, Inc.; *U.S. Private*, pg. 936

ROGERS—Paints & Coatings—The Sherwin-Williams Company; *U.S. Public*, pg. 1465

ROGERS—Dehydrated Products—Universal Foods Corporation; *U.S. Public*, pg. 1695

ROGERS & COWAN—NONE—Shandwick International Plc; *Int'l*, pg. 1226

ROGERS BROTHERS—Seeds—Novartis AG; *Int'l*, pg. 971

ROGERS BROTHERS—Seed Wholesalers—Rogers N.K. Seed Co.; *Int'l*, pg. 974

ROY ROGERS—Restaurants—Roy Rogers Restaurants; *U.S. Public*, pg. 1069

ROY ROGERS CHICKEN—Bone-in Chicken—Hardee's Food Systems, Inc.; *U.S. Public*, pg. 278

ROGET'S II ELECTRONIC THESAURUS—Reference Work—INSO Corporation; *U.S. Public*, pg. 882

ROGUE—Sporting Goods—Brunswick Bowling & Billiards Corp.; *U.S. Public*, pg. 265

ROGUE—Weightlifting Glove—Ektelon; *U.S. Private*, pg. 884

ROH'LIX—Linear Actuators—Zero-Max, Inc.; *Int'l*, pg. 866

ROHACELL—Rigid Foam/Plastic Prods.—Rohm GmbH; *Int'l*, pg. 1454

ROHAGIT—Plastic Prods.—Rohm GmbH; *Int'l*, pg. 1454

ROHAGLAS—Plastic Products—Rohm GmbH; *Int'l*, pg. 1454

ROHAPECT—Enzymes—Rohm GmbH; *Int'l*, pg. 1454

ROHAPON—Enzymes—Rohm GmbH; *Int'l*, pg. 1454

ROHN—Towers—ROHN Industries, Inc.; *U.S. Public*, pg. 1404

ROHO SANGRIA—Wines—Adams Wine Co.; *U.S. Private*, pg. 17

ROHR—Aircraft Components—Rohr, Inc.; *U.S. Public*, pg. 751

ROHR SWIRL—Anti-Icing for Jet Engines—Rohr, Inc.; *U.S. Public*, pg. 751

ROHYPNOL—Sleep Inducing Agent—Roche Holding Ltd.; *Int'l*, pg. 1119

ROI-TANS—Domestic Cigars—Consolidated Cigar Corporation; *U.S. Private*, pg. 690

ROICA—Elastic Polyurethane Filament—Asahi Chemical Industry Co., Ltd.; *Int'l*, pg. 83

ROK-PRUF—Post Hardware—Hall Sign, Inc.; *U.S. Private*, pg. 495

ROKEACH—Kosher Foods—Rokeach Food Distributing Co.; *U.S. Private*, pg. 940

ROKITAMYCIN—Macrolide Antibiotic—Asahi Chemical Industry Co., Ltd.; *Int'l*, pg. 83

ROKOP—NONE—Rokop Corporation; *U.S. Private*, pg. 941

ROL-A-DRAW—Foundry Mold Rollover Machine—Pettibone Corporation; *U.S. Private*, pg. 859

ROL-DEK—Entrance Mats—Pawling Corporation; *U.S. Private*, pg. 844

ROL-DRI—Tennis Equipment—Aurora Electronics, Inc.; *U.S. Public*, pg. 147

ROL-DRI—Water Remover—Sport Supply Group, Inc.; *U.S. Public*, pg. 1499

ROL-IT-ON—Stencil Roller—Diagraph Corporation; *U.S. Private*, pg. 330

ROL-PAK—Retaining Rings—Waldes Truarc/Industrial Retaining Ring; *U.S. Public*, pg. 1632

ROLAIDS—Antacid—Adams U.S.A.; *U.S. Public*, pg. 1739

ROLAIDS—Antacid Tablets—Warner-Lambert Company; *U.S. Public*, pg. 1738

ROLCUT—NONE—Fiskars Oy AB; *Int'l*, pg. 492

ROLD GOLD—Pretzels—Frito-Lay Company; *U.S. Public*, pg. 1277

ROLEMODEL—Computer Programming—The Black & Decker Corporation; *U.S. Public*, pg. 233

ROLEX—Fine Watches—Rolex Watch Co. SA; *Int'l*, pg. 1126

ROLEX—Watches—Rolex Watch U.S.A., Inc.; *Int'l*, pg. 1126

ROLFS—Leather Goods—AR Accessories Group, Inc.; *U.S. Private*, pg. 7

ROLKLEEN—Rolling Oils—D.A. Stuart Company; *U.S. Private*, pg. 1048

ROLL-A-FINISH—Roller Burnishing Tool—Cogsdill Tool Products, Inc.; *U.S. Private*, pg. 250

ROLL-A-VUE—Plastic File Cards with Five Tab Styles—Continental Plastic Card Co.; *U.S. Private*, pg. 269

ROLL-A-WET—Mop—Rubbermaid Incorporated; *U.S. Public*, pg. 1411

ROLL A' SKETCH—Drawing Paper & Dispenser—The Mead Corporation; *U.S. Public*, pg. 1074

ROLL CALL—NONE—The Economist Group Limited.; *Int'l*, pg. 1026

ROLL FILTER LUBRICATION—Paper Machine—Beloit Corporation; *U.S. Public*, pg. 789

ROLL-IN 72—Refrigerator & Freezer—Foster Refrigerator Corporation; *U.S. Private*, pg. 421

ROLL LABEL—Flexographic Printing—Fred B. Johnston Company, Inc.; *U.S. Private*, pg. 595

ROLL N' GLUE—Art Materials—Pentel of America, Ltd.; *Int'l*, pg. 1035

ROLL-O-MAT—Roll Filter Media—AAF-International; *U.S. Private*, pg. 3

ROLL-O-MATIC—Air Filter—AAF-International; *U.S. Private*, pg. 3

ROLL-ON—Marking Pens—Dixon Ticonderoga Company; *U.S. Public*, pg. 514

ROLL OUT—Sport Bag—Ektelon; *U.S. Private*, pg. 884

ROLL RICH—Cigarette Tobacco—Lane Limited; *Int'l*, pg. 1129

ROLL-TOP—Cover—Coleman Spas, Inc.; *U.S. Private*, pg. 691

ROLL-TOWELS—Paper Towels—Bay West Paper Corp. Towel & Tissue Div.; *U.S. Public*, pg. 1747

ROLL-UP II—Large Format Flexible Digitizer—GTCO Corporation; *U.S. Private*, pg. 436

ROLL USA—In-Line Skates—First Team Sports Inc.; *U.S. Public*, pg. 638

ROLL VENT—Attic Ventilation System—Benjamin Obdyke, Inc.; *U.S. Private*, pg. 810

ROLLCALL—NONE—Inacom Corp.; *U.S. Public*, pg. 873

ROLLER DERBY—Roller Skates—Roller Derby Skate Corp.; *U.S. Private*, pg. 941

ROLLER KING—Sliding Windows—International Aluminum Corporation; *U.S. Public*, pg. 894

ROLLER LACER—Belt Lacing Machine—Clipper Belt Lacer Company; *U.S. Public*, pg. 413

ROLLER PERM—Home Permanent—The Gillette Company; *U.S. Public*, pg. 743

ROLLER QUEEN—Sliding Windows—International Aluminum Corporation; *U.S. Public*, pg. 894

ROLLER RACER—Sit Skate—Mattel, Inc.; *U.S. Public*, pg. 1057

ROLLER RACER—Sit Skate—Mattel Power Wheels; *U.S. Public*, pg. 1058

ROLLER-STRETCH—Film Delivery System—Lantech Inc.; *U.S. Private*, pg. 650

ROLLERBACK—Stationary Products—The Mead Corporation; *U.S. Public*, pg. 1074

ROLLERBLADE—Roller Skates—Rollerblade, Inc.; *U.S. Private*, pg. 941

ROLLERGARD—Tubular Motor Operator—Cornell Iron Works, Inc.; *U.S. Private*, pg. 276

ROLLING HILLS—Hair & Skin Care Products—Dep Corporation; *U.S. Public*, pg. 500

ROLLING ROCK—Beer—Labatt Brewing Company Limited; *Int'l*, pg. 679

ROLLING ROCK—Beer—Latrobe Brewing Co.; *Int'l*, pg. 680

ROLLING ROCK LIGHT—Beer—Labatt U.S.A.; *Int'l*, pg. 679

ROLLING ROCK PREMIUM—Beer—Labatt U.S.A.; *Int'l*, pg. 679

ROLLING STONE—Magazine—Rolling Stone Magazine; *U.S. Private*, pg. 1162

ROLLING WRITER—Pens—Pentel of America, Ltd.; *Int'l*, pg. 1035

ROLLINS—Truck Rental & Leasing—Rollins Leasing Corp.; *U.S. Public*, pg. 1405

ROLLINS PROTECTIVE SERVICES—Burglar & Fire Alarm Protection Systems & Services—Rollins, Inc.; *U.S. Public*, pg. 1404

ROLLIT—Markers—Dixon Ticonderoga Company; *U.S. Public*, pg. 514

ROLLITOS—Pet Foods—Nestle S.A.; *Int'l*, pg. 915

ROLLMIX—Roller Mills—Automatic Equipment Mfg. Co.; *U.S. Private*, pg. 101

ROLLOTRON—Air Cleaner—AAF-International; *U.S. Private*, pg. 3

ROLLS AIR MOTOR HOME—NONE—Rexhall Industries, Inc.; *U.S. Public*, pg. 1384

ROLLS-ROYCE—Ancillary Equipment for Aircraft—Rolls-Royce plc; *Int'l*, pg. 1126

ROLLS ROYCE—Motor Cars—Vickers PLC; *Int'l*, pg. 1466

ROLO—Caramels in Milk Chocolate—Hershey Chocolate U.S.A.; *U.S. Public*, pg. 812

ROLO—Candies—Hershey Foods Corporation; *U.S. Public*, pg. 811

ROLO—Chocolate Candies—Nestle-Rowntree Ltd.; *Int'l*, pg. 921

ROLOC—Twist Locking—3M; *U.S. Public*, pg. 1604

ROLODEX—Rotary Files—Newell Co.; *U.S. Public*, pg. 1176

ROLOX—Two-Part Epoxy Compounds—Hardman Division of Harcros Chemicals, Inc.; *Int'l*, pg. 598

ROLPAC—Wipers—Marcal Paper Mills, Inc.; *U.S. Private*, pg. 701

ROLTAK—Label Application Equipment—Superior Label Systems, Inc.; *U.S. Private*, pg. 1055

ROLTRA-MORSE—Auto Components—IMO Industries Inc.; *U.S. Public*, pg. 856

ROLYAT—Hot Water Storage—IMI Plc; *Int'l*, pg. 646

ROMAN LIGHT—Bread—Roman Meal Company; *U.S. Private*, pg. 942

ROMAN MEAL—Breads—Franklin Baking Co., Inc.; *U.S. Private*, pg. 424

ROMAN MEAL—Bread & Diet Bread—Metz Baking Company; *U.S. Private*, pg. 1022

ROMAN MEAL—Bread & Diet Bread—Metz Baking Company (WI); *U.S. Private*, pg. 1022

ROMAN MEAL—Bread, Waffles, Cereal, Refrigerated Products & Crackers—Roman Meal Company; *U.S. Private*, pg. 942

ROMANA SAMBUCA—Liqueur—Grand Metropolitan Plc; *Int'l*, pg. 408

ROMANA SAMBUCA—Liqueur—IDV North America; *Int'l*, pg. 411

ROMANA SAMBUCA—NONE—International Distillers Caribbean; *Int'l*, pg. 410

ROMANBURGER—Menu Item—Restaurant Developers Corp.; *U.S. Private*, pg. 925

ROMANCE—Stainless Steel & Silverplate Flatware—Dansk International Designs Ltd.; *U.S. Public*, pg. 261

ROMANCE—Intimate Apparel—Lily of France, Inc.; *U.S. Private*, pg. 140

ROMANO—Table Wines—Gibson Wine Company; *U.S. Public*, pg. 452

ROMANOFF—Cavier—T. Marzetti Company; *U.S. Public*, pg. 977

ROMANOFF—Vodka—Peerless Importers, Inc.; *U.S. Private*, pg. 847

ROMANO'S MACARONI GRILL—Upscale, Casual Italian Restaurant—Brinker International, Inc.; *U.S. Public*, pg. 253

ROMANZA—Pure, Imported Olive Oil—Pompeiian, Inc.; *U.S. Private*, pg. 875

ROMATE—Point-of-Use Water Treatment Pressure Vessel—Essef Corporation; *U.S. Public*, pg. 592

ROMBOUTS—Coffee—Ranks Hovis McDougall Limited; *Int'l*, pg. 1395

ROME—Cable & Wire—Rome Cable Corporation; *U.S. Public*, pg. 942

ROMEO JULIETA—Cigars—Rothmans UK Holdings Limited; *Int'l*, pg. 1129

ROMEX—Insulated Electrical Wire & Cable—General Cable Corporation; *Int'l*, pg. 1486

ROMI—Pasta—Borden, Inc.; *U.S. Private*, pg. 157

RON BERMUDEZ—Rum—Laird & Company; *U.S. Private*, pg. 642

RON LLAVE—Puerto Rican Rum—The Seagram Company Ltd.; *Int'l*, pg. 1214

RON ROBERTO—Rum—M.S. Walker, Inc.; *U.S. Private*, pg. 1147

RONABRITE—Powdered Iridescent-Bronze Chromate—LeaRonal, Inc.; *U.S. Public*, pg. 982

RONACAT—Preplate Process—LeaRonal, Inc.; *U.S. Public*, pg. 982

RONACAT MICROETCH—Hydrogen Peroxide Sulfuric Acid Etch—LeaRonal, Inc.; *U.S. Public*, pg. 982

RONACLEAN E900—General Purpose Electrocleaner—LeaRonal, Inc.; *U.S. Public*, pg. 982

RONACLEAN E296—Heavy Duty Electrocleaner—LeaRonal, Inc.; *U.S. Public*, pg. 982

Brand Name Index

RONACLEAN 83—Zinc Casting Electrocleaner—LeaRonal, Inc.; *U.S. Public*, pg. 982
RONACLEAN S600—General Purpose Soak for Metals—LeaRonal, Inc.; *U.S. Public*, pg. 982
RONACLEAN 333—Electrocleaner for Brass—LeaRonal, Inc.; *U.S. Public*, pg. 982
RONADEP—Versatile Electroless Copper Process—LeaRonal, Inc.; *U.S. Public*, pg. 982
RONALAC—Clear Organic Coat for Metal—LeaRonal, Inc.; *U.S. Public*, pg. 982
RONALD MCDONALD—Clown—McDonald's Corporation; *U.S. Public*, pg. 1068
RONALD MCDONALD CHILDREN'S CHARITIES—Charitable Organizations—McDonald's Corporation; *U.S. Public*, pg. 1068
RONALD MCDONALD HOUSE—Lodging for Families—McDonald's Corporation; *U.S. Public*, pg. 1068
RONABRITE L7C—Liquid Iridescent Chromate—LeaRonal, Inc.; *U.S. Public*, pg. 982
RONASALT 408—Dry Acid Salt for Pickle—LeaRonal, Inc.; *U.S. Public*, pg. 982
RONASCREEN 1550—UV Curable Plating Resists—LeaRonal, Inc.; *U.S. Public*, pg. 982
RONASCREEN 1501—UV Curable Plating Resists—LeaRonal, Inc.; *U.S. Public*, pg. 982
RONASCREEN 550—Thermal Cure Plating Resists—LeaRonal, Inc.; *U.S. Public*, pg. 982
RONASCREEN 540—Thermal Cure Plating Resists—LeaRonal, Inc.; *U.S. Public*, pg. 982
RONASCREEN 530—Thermal Cure Plating Resists—LeaRonal, Inc.; *U.S. Public*, pg. 982
RONASCREEN 750—Thermal Cure Legend Inks—LeaRonal, Inc.; *U.S. Public*, pg. 982
RONASCREEN 752—Thermal Cure Legend Inks—LeaRonal, Inc.; *U.S. Public*, pg. 982
RONASCREEN 1700—UV Curable Legend Inks—LeaRonal, Inc.; *U.S. Public*, pg. 982
RONASCREEN 660—Thermal Cure Soldermasks—LeaRonal, Inc.; *U.S. Public*, pg. 982
RONASCREEN 662—Thermal Cure Soldermasks—LeaRonal, Inc.; *U.S. Public*, pg. 982
RONASCREEN 1655—UV Curable Soldermasks—LeaRonal, Inc.; *U.S. Public*, pg. 982
RONASCREEN 1600—UV Curable Soldermasks—LeaRonal, Inc.; *U.S. Public*, pg. 982
RONASHINE 50—Chemical Polish—LeaRonal, Inc.; *U.S. Public*, pg. 982
RONASTAN—Matte or Satin Deposits—LeaRonal, Inc.; *U.S. Public*, pg. 982
RONASTRIP—Electrolytic & Powdered Stripper—LeaRonal, Inc.; *U.S. Public*, pg. 982
RONASTRIP CUF—Immersion Stripper—LeaRonal, Inc.; *U.S. Public*, pg. 982
RONCO—Pasta—Borden, Inc.; *U.S. Private*, pg. 157
RONCO—Pasta Products—Borden Italian Foods; *U.S. Private*, pg. 158
RONCO—Electric Food Dehydrator—Ronco, Inventions. LLC; *U.S. Private*, pg. 943
RONCO C&E INC.—NONE—Ronco Communications & Electronics Inc.; *U.S. Private*, pg. 943
RONCO FINANCE PRODUCTS—Popeil Pocket Fisherman—Ronco, Inventions. LLC; *U.S. Private*, pg. 943
RONDEC—Cough/Cold Preparation—Abbott Laboratories; *U.S. Public*, pg. 12
RONDELE—Cheese—Churny Company Inc.; *U.S. Public*, pg. 1288
RONDIS—Emulsifiers—Akzo Nobel N.V.; *Int'l*, pg. 42
RONDO—Office Products—Esselte AB; *Int'l*, pg. 459
RONDO—Tables—Howe Furniture Corporation; *U.S. Private*, pg. 543
RONDOS—Bite Size Ice Cream Snacks—M&M/Mars; *U.S. Private*, pg. 707
RONDOS—Chocolate Bar—Mars, Incorporated; *U.S. Private*, pg. 707
RONDURA—Office Seating—United Chair, Inc.; *U.S. Private*, pg. 512
RONETCH E372—Etch Cleaner—LeaRonal, Inc.; *U.S. Public*, pg. 982
RONFALIN—Plastics—DSM N.V.; *Int'l*, pg. 352
RONFALOY—ABS Blend—DSM N.V.; *Int'l*, pg. 352
RONILAN—Crop Protection Agent—BASF AG; *Int'l*, pg. 103

RONOVEL—Gold Electroplating Process—LeaRonal, Inc.; *U.S. Public*, pg. 982
RONPOLISH—Chemical Polish—LeaRonal, Inc.; *U.S. Public*, pg. 982
RONRICO—Rum—Fortune Brands, Inc.; *U.S. Public*, pg. 674
RONRON—Petfood—Mars Petfoods (UNISABI); *U.S. Private*, pg. 707
RONSONOL—Lighter Fuel—Ronson Corporation; *U.S. Public*, pg. 1405
RONZONI—Pasta—Hershey Foods Corporation; *U.S. Public*, pg. 811
RONZONI—Pasta—Hershey Pasta and Grocery Group; *U.S. Public*, pg. 812
RONZONI—Pasta—Kraft Foods, Inc.; *U.S. Public*, pg. 1287
ROOF FIX—Protective Coating Roof Fix—Monsey-Bakor; *U.S. Private*, pg. 757
ROOF PRO—Roof Repair Products—Macklanburg-Duncan Co.; *U.S. Private*, pg. 692
ROOF PROOF/GLASCOTE—Premium Roofing Products—The Gibson-Homans Company; *U.S. Private*, pg. 451
ROOF TITE—Roof Coating & Cements—The Gibson-Homans Company; *U.S. Private*, pg. 451
ROOFCOR—Polyurethane Spray Insulating Materials—The Dow Chemical Company; *U.S. Public*, pg. 522
ROOFING/SIDING/INSULATION—Trade Periodical—Advanstar Communications; *U.S. Private*, pg. 22
ROOFMATE—Roof Insulation—The Dow Chemical Company; *U.S. Public*, pg. 522
ROOFWALKS—Walkway Systems—Unistrut Corporation; *U.S. Public*, pg. 1651
ROOFWARE—NONE—D.C. Taylor Co.; *U.S. Private*, pg. 1070
ROOM MATES—Wallcovering—York Wallcoverings Inc.; *U.S. Private*, pg. 1196
ROOM SENSE—Carpet Deodorizer—Stanhome Inc.; *U.S. Public*, pg. 1508
ROOM SENTRY—Monitor—Westvaco Corporation; *U.S. Public*, pg. 1762
ROOM SERVICE—Wireless Video Products—Recoton Corporation; *U.S. Public*, pg. 1369
ROOM SERVICE—Hot Beverage Makers—Sunbeam Household Products; *U.S. Public*, pg. 1533
ROOMLAC—Plastic Foam—The Dow Chemical Company; *U.S. Public*, pg. 522
ROOMMATE—Powered Speaker System—Bose Corporation; *U.S. Private*, pg. 160
ROOMWORKS—Indoor Casual Furniture—Rubbermaid Incorporated; *U.S. Public*, pg. 1411
ROOS—Portfolios—The Mead Corporation; *U.S. Public*, pg. 1074
ROOSTER TAIL—Stationery Products—The Mead Corporation; *U.S. Public*, pg. 1074
ROOSVICEE—Rosehip & Fruit Syrups—CSM N.V.; *Int'l*, pg. 243
ROOT—NONE—A.I. Root Company; *U.S. Private*, pg. 944
ROOTS—NONE—Dresser Canada, Inc.; *U.S. Public*, pg. 529
ROOTS—Blowers, Gas Meters & Vacuum Pumps—Dresser Industries, Inc.; *U.S. Public*, pg. 528
ROOTS METERS—Positive Displacement Rotary Gas Meters—DMD Dresser Measurement Operation; *U.S. Public*, pg. 528
ROOTS VTC—Electronic Temperature Corrector—DMD Dresser Measurement Operation; *U.S. Public*, pg. 528
ROOTY TOOTY FRESH 'N FRUITY BREAKFAST—Restaurant—IHOP Corp.; *U.S. Public*, pg. 862
ROP NETWORKS—NONE—Metropolitan Sunday Newspapers, Inc.; *U.S. Private*, pg. 739
ROPAK—Industrial Plastic Containers—Ropak Corporation; *Int'l*, pg. 811
ROPAQUE—Hollow Sphere Pigment—Rohm and Haas Company; *U.S. Public*, pg. 1403
ROPER—Pumps & Gear—Harley Industries, Inc.; *U.S. Public*, pg. 880
ROPER—Major Appliances—Whirlpool Corporation; *U.S. Public*, pg. 1764
ROSA GRANDE—Lasagna & Pepperoni—Hormel Foods Corp.; *U.S. Public*, pg. 840
ROSALITE—Spectacle Lens Blanks—Deutsche Spezialglas AG; *Int'l*, pg. 1523

ROSARITA—Mexican Food—ConAgra, Inc.; *U.S. Public*, pg. 425
ROSARITA—Mexican Foods—Hunt-Wesson, Inc.; *U.S. Public*, pg. 428
ROSAUER'S—Supermarkets—URM Stores, Inc.; *U.S. Private*, pg. 1114
ROSAUER'S—Supermarkets—Rosauers Supermarkets, Inc.; *U.S. Private*, pg. 944
ROSCO ASPHALITE—Pothole Patcher—Rosco Manufacturing Co.; *U.S. Private*, pg. 944
ROSCOE—Dog Food—Star-Kist Foods Inc.; *U.S. Public*, pg. 805
ROSE—Pickles—International Multifoods Corporation; *U.S. Public*, pg. 900
ROSE—Pickles & Condiments—Robin Hood Multifoods Inc.; *U.S. Public*, pg. 901
ROSE—Wholesalers of Smoked Meat Prods.—Rose Packing Company; *U.S. Private*, pg. 945
ROSE ACRE FARMS—Eggs—Rose Acre Farms; *U.S. Private*, pg. 944
ROSE BUD—Plug Chewing Tobacco—Conwood Company L.P.; *U.S. Private*, pg. 272
ROSE MILK—Skin Care Moisturizer—Menley & James Laboratories, Inc.; *U.S. Public*, pg. 1086
ROSE'S LEMON—Mix Concentrates—Apollinaris & Schweppes Gmbh & Co.; *Int'l*, pg. 78
ROSE'S LIME JUICE—Mix Concentrates—Apollinaris & Schweppes Gmbh & Co.; *Int'l*, pg. 78
ROSE'S—Soft Drink—Cadbury Schweppes p.l.c.; *Int'l*, pg. 247
ROSEBUD—Matches—Diamond Brands, Inc.; *U.S. Private*, pg. 330
ROSEHIPS—Herb Tea—Celestial Seasonings; *U.S. Public*, pg. 319
ROSELI—NONE—JP Foodservice, Inc.; *U.S. Public*, pg. 918
ROSELL TRAITEUR—Catering—Accor S.A.; *Int'l*, pg. 20
ROSEMAR—Liquid Color Additives—Ferro Corporation; *U.S. Public*, pg. 618
ROSEMOUNT—Process Control Equipment—Emerson Electric Co.; *U.S. Public*, pg. 572
ROSEMOUNT ANALYTICAL—Process Instruments—Emerson Electric Co.; *U.S. Public*, pg. 572
ROSEMOUNT SMART FAMILY—Process Control Equipment—Emerson Electric Co.; *U.S. Public*, pg. 572
ROSENTHAL CLASSIC—China & Crystal—Rosenthal U.S.A. Limited; *Int'l*, pg. 1127
ROSENTHAL STUDIO -LINIE—China & Crystal—Rosenthal U.S.A. Limited; *Int'l*, pg. 1127
ROSE'S—Fruit Juices—Cadbury Beverages; *Int'l*, pg. 248
ROSE'S—Cocktail Mixes—Cadbury Beverages North America; *Int'l*, pg. 248
ROSE'S—Discount Stores—Rose's Stores, Inc.; *U.S. Public*, pg. 1405
ROSETTO—Frozen Pasta—Ore-Ida Foods, Inc.; *U.S. Public*, pg. 805
ROSIERES—Household Appliances—Candy S.p.A.; *Int'l*, pg. 259
ROSITA—Tequila, Triple Sec Liquer—Marie Brizard Wines & Spirits USA; *U.S. Private*, pg. 702
ROSITA-SI—Frozen Mexican Food—Ruiz Food Products, Inc.; *U.S. Private*, pg. 951
ROSPATCH—Bar-Coded Labels, Ribbons & Trims—PAXAR Corporation; *U.S. Public*, pg. 1266
ROSPHALT 50—Asphalt Additive (paving)—Royston Laboratories; *U.S. Public*, pg. 337
ROSPHALT50—Waterproofing Alphalt Mix—Chase Corporation; *U.S. Public*, pg. 337
ROSS—Ovens & Fume Incinerators—Kathabar Incorporated; *U.S. Public*, pg. 609
ROSS—Headphones & Accessories—Recoton Corporation; *U.S. Public*, pg. 1369
ROSS—Frozen Foods—United Biscuits (Holdings) Plc; *Int'l*, pg. 1442
ROSS—Lawn & Garden Products—Weatherly Consumer Products; *U.S. Public*, pg. 1682
ROSS & CROMARTY—Apparel—Bayer Clothing Group; *U.S. Private*, pg. 124
ROSS CATHERALL—Super Alloys—Vickers PLC; *Int'l*, pg. 1466
ROSS REPORTS—NONE—BPI Communications Inc.; *Int'l*, pg. 1446

ROSS RESULTS—Integrated Implementation Methodology—Ross Systems, Inc.; *U.S. Public*, pg. 1406

ROSS STORES—Clothing, Shoes, Luggage & Cosmetics Retailing—Ross Stores, Inc.; *U.S. Public*, pg. 1405

ROSSI—NONE—Bacardi-Martini Belgium; *U.S. Private*, pg. 109

ROSSIGNOL—Alpine & Cross Country Skis, Ski Poles, Ski Boots & Tennis Rackets—Rossignol S.A.; *Int'l*, pg. 1127

ROSSIGNOL—Skis, Boots, Snowboards—Rossignol Ski Co.; *Int'l*, pg. 1127

ROSSO ANTICO—NONE—Gio. Buton S.p.a.; *Int'l*, pg. 409

ROSSO ANTICO—Aperitif—Paterno Imports Limited; *U.S. Private*, pg. 843

ROSY—Personal Produccts—Sara Lee Corporation; *U.S. Public*, pg. 1432

ROTA-CHILL—Blast Chiller—United Service Equipment Company; *U.S. Public*, pg. 1507

ROTA-LOCK—Pipe Fitting Device—Up-Right, Inc.; *U.S. Private*, pg. 1128

ROTA-PASS—Surface Grinding Machines—Litton Industries, Inc.; *U.S. Public*, pg. 1002

ROTABROACH—Annular Hole Cutter—Hougen Manufacturing Co.; *U.S. Private*, pg. 541

ROTAC—Fluid Power Rotary Actuators—Textron Inc.; *U.S. Public*, pg. 1588

ROTAJECTOR—Vacuum Pumps—Croll-Reynolds Company, Inc.; *U.S. Private*, pg. 290

ROTALION—Rotary Seal—James Walker & Co. Limited; *Int'l*, pg. 1485

ROTARY—UPS Systems—Baylor Company; *Int'l*, pg. 1134

ROTARY-AIRE—Marine Air Conditioners—Westerbeke Corporation; *U.S. Public*, pg. 1757

ROTARY CENTRILECTOR—Air Cleaning Device—Aeroglide Corporation; *U.S. Private*, pg. 24

ROTARY MOTOR—Subfractional Horse Power Stepper Motor—Haydon Switch & Instrument, Inc.; *U.S. Private*, pg. 513

ROTARY SEPARATOR—Rader—Beloit Corporation; *U.S. Public*, pg. 789

THE ROTARY UNION—Rotating Joint—Duff-Norton; *U.S. Public*, pg. 406

ROTAX—Engines for Snowmobiles & Watercraft—Bombardier Inc.; *Int'l*, pg. 199

ROTAZYME—Diagnostic Products—Abbott Laboratories; *U.S. Public*, pg. 12

ROTECTOR—Overtemperature Protective Apparatus for Electric Motors—General Electric Canada Inc.; *U.S. Public*, pg. 713

ROTEL—Household appliances—Basel Trading Company Ltd.; *Int'l*, pg. 169

ROTEL—Food Product—International Home Foods Inc.; *U.S. Private*, pg. 526

ROTEL CANNED TOMATOES—NONE—International Home Foods Inc.; *U.S. Private*, pg. 526

ROTEX—Office Products—Esselte AB; *Int'l*, pg. 459

ROTEX—Shaft Driven Sump Pump—KSB Aktiengesellschaft; *Int'l*, pg. 721

ROTHMANS—Cigarettes—Rothmans UK Holdings Limited; *Int'l*, pg. 1129

ROTHSCHILD WINES—Wine—Heublein Inc.; *Int'l*, pg. 410

ROTICULATOR—Surgical Staplers & Laparoscopic Instruments—U.S. Surgical Corp.; *U.S. Public*, pg. 1687

ROTICULATOR 55 POLY—Surgical Staplers—U.S. Surgical Corp.; *U.S. Public*, pg. 1687

ROTIS—Photo Typesetters—AGFA EPS Division; *Int'l*, pg. 172

ROTISSERIE RECIPE—Seasoning Mixes—McCormick/Schilling; *U.S. Public*, pg. 1066

ROTO-CUT—Asphalt Cutter—Allied Construction Products, Inc.; *U.S. Public*, pg. 1339

ROTO-FLO—Cold Forming Machinery—Micromatic Textron; *U.S. Public*, pg. 1589

ROTO-FLO—Spline & Gear Cold Forming—Textron Inc.; *U.S. Public*, pg. 1588

ROTO-KONE—Liquid-Solids Separation Equipment—Komline-Sanderson Engineering Corp.; *U.S. Private*, pg. 631

ROTO LOCK—Fasteners—Southtec, Inc.; *U.S. Private*, pg. 1015

ROTO-MOP—Dry Mop—Stanhome Inc.; *U.S. Private*, pg. 1508

ROTO-RACK—Rotating Mixer—Fisher Scientific Company; *U.S. Private*, pg. 658

ROTO-ROOTER—Sewer Cleaning Machine—Roto-Rooter; *U.S. Public*, pg. 344

ROTO STOKER VCG—Stoker—Detroit Stoker Co.; *U.S. Private*, pg. 1679

ROTO-STOP—Power Products—American Honda Motor Co., Inc.; *Int'l*, pg. 634

ROTO-TELLITE—Electronic Equipment—Eaton Corp., Aerospace & Commercial Controls Div.; *U.S. Public*, pg. 557

ROTO-TRAK—Liquid-Solids Separation Equipment—Komline-Sanderson Engineering Corp.; *U.S. Private*, pg. 631

ROTOCAST—Rotational Molding Machine—McNeil & NRM., Inc.; *U.S. Private*, pg. 725

ROTOCLONE—Dust Collector—AAF-International; *U.S. Private*, pg. 3

ROTOCOTE—Rotogravure—Champion International Corp.; *U.S. Public*, pg. 333

ROTOCUT—Trimmer Head—Stihl Inc.; *Int'l*, pg. 1301

ROTOFLOW—Turboexpanders—Atlas Copco Comptec Inc.; *Int'l*, pg. 96

ROTOGRATE—Stoker—Detroit Stoker Co.; *U.S. Public*, pg. 1679

ROTOJET—Sprayer—Binks Sames Corporation; *U.S. Public*, pg. 229

ROTOLINE—Microfilming Equipment—Eastman Kodak Company; *U.S. Public*, pg. 550

ROTOLOK—Filter Housing—Pall Corporation; *U.S. Public*, pg. 1253

ROTOMATIC—Microfilming Machines—Eastman Kodak Company; *U.S. Public*, pg. 550

ROTOMAX—Sealant Dispensing System—Loctite Corporation; *Int'l*, pg. 611

ROTOREX—Tea Bag Machine—Pneumatic Scale Corporation; *U.S. Private*, pg. 118

ROTORFLOW—NONE—Gems Sensors; *U.S. Public*, pg. 481

ROTOSCAN—X-Ray Tubes—Litton Industries, Inc.; *U.S. Public*, pg. 1002

ROTOSEAL VALVE—Patented Butterfly Valve for Freeze Dryers & Sterile Machinery—Hull Corporation; *U.S. Private*, pg. 547

ROTOSTOKER—Stoker—Detroit Stoker Co.; *U.S. Public*, pg. 1679

ROTOTRACT—Lift & Cut Shaving System—Philips Electronics N.V.; *Int'l*, pg. 1051

ROTRING—Fine Art Paints & Materials Writing Instruments—Koh-I-Noor, Inc.; *U.S. Private*, pg. 629

ROTRING—Technical Pens, Drawing Inks, Drawing Instruments, Artist Materials—Koh-I-Noor, Inc.; *U.S. Private*, pg. 629

ROTRING ARTPEN—Calligraphy, Lettering, Sketching Pens—Koh-I-Noor, Inc.; *U.S. Private*, pg. 629

ROTTLUND COMPANY, INC.—Residential Home Builder—The Rottlund Company, Inc.; *U.S. Public*, pg. 1406

ROUGEMONT CASTLE—Wine—Matthew Clark Brands; *Int'l*, pg. 848

ROUGH COUNTRY—Loose Leaf Chewing & Twist Tobaccos—Conwood Company L.P.; *U.S. Private*, pg. 272

ROUGH CUT—Meat Snack—GoodMark Foods, Inc.; *U.S. Public*, pg. 751

ROUGH HEWN—Aluminum Siding—Reynolds Metals Company; *U.S. Public*, pg. 1385

ROUGH-HOUSE—Tool Boxes—The Disston Co.; *U.S. Public*, pg. 950

ROUGH RIDER—Lawn Cart—Rubbermaid Incorporated; *U.S. Public*, pg. 1411

ROUGHLYTE—Vaportight Fixtures—Stonco Genlyte; *U.S. Public*, pg. 730

ROUGHNECK—Premium Quality Flashlights—RAYOVAC Corporation; *U.S. Private*, pg. 912

ROUGHNECK—Household/Refuse Containers—Rubbermaid Incorporated; *U.S. Public*, pg. 1411

ROUGHNECK TOOLBOX STORAGE SYSTEMS—Toolboxes—The Knapheide Mfg. Co.; *U.S. Private*, pg. 626

THE ROUGHNECKS—Children's Insulated Bottles—The Thermos Company; *Int'l*, pg. 938

ROULEAU—Studded Rubber Floor Tile & Stairtreads—Burke Industries, Inc.; *U.S. Private*, pg. 183

ROULEMENT—NONE—Brammer plc; *Int'l*, pg. 212

ROUND HILL—Wine—Pacific Wine Co.; *U.S. Private*, pg. 843

ROUND METAL—Sunglasses—Bausch & Lomb Incorporated; *U.S. Public*, pg. 194

ROUND THE CLOCK—Hosiery—Pennaco Hosiery; *U.S. Public*, pg. 483

ROUND-THE-CLOCK—Room Freshener—Surco Products, Inc.; *U.S. Private*, pg. 1056

ROUND-TRIP—Envelopes—Tension Envelope Corp.; *U.S. Private*, pg. 1077

ROUND-UP—Horse Feeds—Manna Pro Corporation; *U.S. Private*, pg. 700

ROUNDTABLE—Greeting Cards—American Greetings Corporation; *U.S. Public*, pg. 77

ROUNDUP—Herbicide—The Agricultural Group, Monsanto Company; *U.S. Public*, pg. 1125

ROUNDUP—Herbicide—Monsanto Company; *U.S. Public*, pg. 1124

ROUNDY'S—Food Wholesale Distribution—Roundy's, Inc.; *U.S. Private*, pg. 948

ROUST-A-BOUT—Pipe Couplings—Victaulic Company of America; *U.S. Private*, pg. 1138

ROUST-A-BOUT—Socks & Knitted Headwear—Wigwam Mills, Inc.; *U.S. Private*, pg. 1175

ROUTE CHIEF—Refuse Collection Truck—Dempster Equipment; *U.S. Private*, pg. 1089

ROUTE COMMANDER—Computing System—Norand Mobile Systems Div.; *U.S. Public*, pg. 1699

ROUTE KING—Refuse Collection Truck—Dempster Equipment; *U.S. Private*, pg. 1089

ROUTE ONE—Greeting Cards—Fine Art Developments plc; *Int'l*, pg. 485

ROUTE 66—Men's Fragrance—Coty Inc.; *Int'l*, pg. 185

ROUTEMASTER—Paper Booklets Printed with Directional Info—American Automobile Association; *U.S. Private*, pg. 50

ROUTEMASTER SERIES—Truck Suspension Seat—Bostrom Seating, Inc.; *U.S. Public*, pg. 933

ROUTER MANAGEMENT—NONE—Check Point Software Technologies Ltd.; *U.S. Public*, pg. 342

ROUX—Hair Coloring Products & Permanent Waving Products—Revlon-Realistic Professional Products, Inc.; *U.S. Private*, pg. 690

ROVAL—NONE—Rockbottom Stores, Inc.; *U.S. Private*, pg. 938

ROVAR—Roof Over Vent-A-Ridge—Alcoa Building Products, Inc.; *U.S. Public*, pg. 61

ROVEL—Weatherable Polymer—The Dow Chemical Company; *U.S. Public*, pg. 522

ROVEMATIC—Machinery—Hollingsworth Saco Lowell Corporation, Inc.; *U.S. Private*, pg. 535

ROVER—Rust Remover—Hach Company; *U.S. Public*, pg. 773

ROVER 800 FASTBACK—Car—British Aerospace p.l.c.; *Int'l*, pg. 217

ROVER 800 SALOON—Car—British Aerospace p.l.c.; *Int'l*, pg. 217

ROVER 200—Car—British Aerospace p.l.c.; *Int'l*, pg. 217

ROVER 400—Automobile—British Aerospace p.l.c.; *Int'l*, pg. 217

ROVERALLS—Playsuits—Lands' End, Inc.; *U.S. Public*, pg. 977

ROVEX 8—Multi-Purpose Pump—KSB Aktiengesellschaft; *Int'l*, pg. 721

ROVEX U—Multi-Purpose Pump—KSB Aktiengesellschaft; *Int'l*, pg. 721

ROVIEX—Spectacle Lens Blanks—Deutsche Spezialglas AG; *Int'l*, pg. 1523

ROW RAMBLER—Farm Machinery & Equipment—Reinke Manufacturing Co., Inc.; *U.S. Private*, pg. 920

ROWASA—Pharmaceutical Product—Solvay Pharmaceuticals, Inc.; *Int'l*, pg. 1278

ROWENTA—Small Appliances—Groupe SEB; *Int'l*, pg. 568

ROWENTA—Small Household Appliances—Rowenta (USA), Inc.; *Int'l*, pg. 569

ROWMAN & LITTLEFIELD—Scholarly Books—Littlefield, Adams & Company; *U.S. Public*, pg. 1001

ROWNTREE'S—Cocoa, Jelly, Cheese Spreads—Nestle-Rowntree Ltd.; *Int'l*, pg. 921

ROWS—Computer Program—Osmonics, Inc.; *U.S. Public*, pg. 1233

ROXANE LABORATORIES—Ethical Pharmaceuticals—Roxane Laboratories, Inc.; *Int'l*, pg. 199

ROXANNE—Swim Suits—Apparel America, Inc.; *U.S. Public*, pg. 120

ROYAL—Shampoos, Bath Oils, Lotions & Conditioners—Benjamin Ansehl Company; *U.S. Private*, pg. 75

ROYAL—Margarine, Pastas—Bestfoods; *U.S. Public*, pg. 223

ROYAL—Fresh & Processed Fruits & Vegetables—Cherry Central Cooperative; *U.S. Private*, pg. 233

ROYAL—Motion Picture Cameras, Projectors, Film—Eastman Kodak Company; *U.S. Public*, pg. 550

ROYAL—Electical Wire & Cable—Essex International, Inc.; *U.S. Public*, pg. 593

ROYAL—NONE—Karelia Tobacco Company Inc.; *Int'l*, pg. 724

ROYAL—Gelatins, Sugarfree Gelatins, Pudding & Pie Fillings, & No-Bake Desserts—Nabisco Inc.; *U.S. Public*, pg. 1355

ROYAL—Ministry Services Divisions—Thomas Nelson Inc.; *U.S. Public*, pg. 1167

ROYAL—Gelatins, Instant Puddings, No Bake Desserts, SugarFree Instant Pudding—RJR Nabisco Holdings Corp.; *U.S. Public*, pg. 1354

ROYAL—Vacuum Cleaners—Royal Appliance Mfg. Co.; *U.S. Public*, pg. 1410

ROYAL—Consumer Business Products—Royal Consumer Business Products; *Int'l*, pg. 1002

ROYAL—Flush Valves—Sloan Valve Company; *U.S. Private*, pg. 1006

ROYAL—Surgical Staplers—U.S. Surgical Corp.; *U.S. Public*, pg. 1687

ROYAL ALBERT—Bone China Dinnerware & Giftware—Royal Doulton USA Inc.; *Int'l*, pg. 1135

ROYAL BRACKLA—NONE—Guinness Plc; *Int'l*, pg. 412

ROYAL CANADIAN—Whiskey—Groupe Pernod Ricard; *Int'l*, pg. 566

ROYAL CLUB—Shandy & Soft Drink—Heineken N.V.; *Int'l*, pg. 608

ROYAL COPENHAGEN—Porcelain & Crystal—Royal Copenhagen A/S; *Int'l*, pg. 1134

ROYAL COPENHAGEN—Fragrance—Tsumura International; *Int'l*, pg. 1426

ROYAL COPENHAGEN SPORT—Men's Fragrance—Tsumura International; *Int'l*, pg. 1426

ROYAL COPYSTAR—NONE—Mita Copystar America Inc.; *Int'l*, pg. 870

ROYAL CREST CHAFER—Food Chafer—The Vollrath Company, L.L.C.; *U.S. Private*, pg. 1143

ROYAL CROWN—Cola—Triarc Companies, Inc.; *U.S. Public*, pg. 1634

ROYAL CROWN COLA—Soft Drink—Grant-Lydick Beverage Co.; *U.S. Private*, pg. 470

ROYAL CROWNDERBY—Bone China Dinnerware & Giftware—Royal Doulton USA Inc.; *Int'l*, pg. 1135

ROYAL CROWN DRAFT COLA—Cola—Triarc Companies, Inc.; *U.S. Public*, pg. 1634

ROYAL DIAMOND—Cookware—Regal Ware, Inc.; *U.S. Private*, pg. 917

ROYAL DOULTON—China, Giftware & Crystal—Royal Doulton USA Inc.; *Int'l*, pg. 1135

ROYAL DOULTON GROUP—Fine China Dinnerware & Collectibles—Ebeling & Reuss Company; *U.S. Private*, pg. 358

ROYAL DUTCH—Cocoa & Chocolate Products—Barry Callebaut; *Int'l*, pg. 252

ROYAL DUTCH ADVOCAAT—Mint Cream—Groupe Pernod Ricard; *Int'l*, pg. 566

ROYAL ESTATES—Tea—Thomas J. Lipton Company; *Int'l*, pg. 1435

ROYAL FAMILY—Cabinet Hardware—Amerock Corporation; *U.S. Public*, pg. 1177

ROYAL FAMILY—Bed & Bath Products—Fieldcrest Cannon, Inc.; *U.S. Public*, pg. 1296

ROYAL FASTENERS—Fastener Products—Friedman Industries, Inc.; *U.S. Public*, pg. 682

ROYAL FLUSH—Solid Automatic Bowl Cleaner—Blue Cross Laboratories; *U.S. Private*, pg. 152

ROYAL FRIEZE—Broadloom—Couristan Inc.; *U.S. Private*, pg. 279

ROYAL GALLERY OF FRAMES—NONE—American Greetings Corporation; *U.S. Public*, pg. 77

ROYAL GARD—Paint—Graham Paint and Varnish Company; *U.S. Private*, pg. 468

ROYAL-GARD—Waterproofing Membrane—Royston Laboratories; *U.S. Public*, pg. 337

ROYAL GUARD—Cartridges—3M; *U.S. Public*, pg. 1604

ROYAL GUEST—Controlled Label Brand for Grocery Items—IGA, Inc. (Independent Grocers Alliance); *U.S. Private*, pg. 555

ROYAL HAEGER—Pottery—Haeger Industries, Inc.; *U.S. Private*, pg. 493

ROYAL JAMAICA—Cigars—Lane Limited; *Int'l*, pg. 1129

ROYAL JELLY—Health Food Product—Shiseido Company Ltd.; *Int'l*, pg. 1235

ROYAL JELLY CREAM—Skin Cream—Health Products Corporation; *U.S. Private*, pg. 514

ROYAL KERRY—Wafers & Biscuits—Atalanta Corporation; *U.S. Private*, pg. 93

ROYAL KINSDOWN—Mattress & Box Spring Sets—Kingsdown, Inc.; *U.S. Private*, pg. 622

ROYAL KONA—Coffee—C. Brewer & Company, Limited; *U.S. Private*, pg. 190

ROYAL KONA—Coffee—Superior Coffee and Foods; *U.S. Public*, pg. 1434

ROYAL LOCHNAGAR—Single Malt Scotch—Schieffelin & Somerset Co.; *Int'l*, pg. 412

ROYAL LOCHNAGAR SELECTED RESERVE—NONE—Guinness Plc; *Int'l*, pg. 412

ROYAL LUNCH—Milk Crackers—Nabisco Inc.; *U.S. Public*, pg. 1355

ROYAL MARINE—Wood & Lumber Products—Georgia-Pacific Corporation; *U.S. Public*, pg. 735

ROYAL MELROSE—Monumental Products for the Memorial Industry—Cold Spring Granite Company; *U.S. Private*, pg. 250

ROYAL MH—Plant Growth Regulants—Uniroyal Chemical Company, Inc.; *U.S. Public*, pg. 460

ROYAL OAK—Dairy Products—Labatt Brewing Company Limited; *Int'l*, pg. 679

ROYAL OAK—Charcoal—Royal Oak Enterprises, Inc.; *U.S. Private*, pg. 948

ROYAL OAK (R-O)—Form Relief Tool Grinders & CNC Cylinderical Grinders 8"x14"—Seneca Falls Technology Group; *U.S. Private*, pg. 984

ROYAL ODYSSEY—Cruise Ship—Cunard Line Ltd.; *Int'l*, pg. 773

THE ROYAL ORLEANS—Hotel—Omni Hotels; *U.S. Private*, pg. 1065

ROYAL PAD—Paper Board—Sonoco Products Company; *U.S. Public*, pg. 1485

ROYAL PAISLEY—Scotch—The Seagram Company Ltd.; *Int'l*, pg. 1214

ROYAL PALM—Men's Slacks & Shorts—Tropical Sportswear International; *U.S. Private*, pg. 1105

ROYAL PRINCE—NONE—Allen Canning Company; *U.S. Private*, pg. 36

ROYAL REEF—Seafood Products—Bumble Bee Seafoods Inc.; *U.S. Private*, pg. 526

ROYAL RESERVE CANDIAN WHISKEY—Spirt—Allied Domecq PLC; *Int'l*, pg. 62

ROYAL ROTISSERIE PLUS—NONE—Regal Ware, Inc.; *U.S. Private*, pg. 917

ROYAL SALUTE—Scotch—The House of Seagram; *Int'l*, pg. 1217

ROYAL SALUTE—Scotch—The Seagram Company Ltd.; *Int'l*, pg. 1214

ROYAL SATEEN—NONE—Crown Crafts, Inc.; *U.S. Public*, pg. 465

ROYAL SCOT—Golf Gloves—Tommy Armour Golf; *U.S. Public*, pg. 1683

ROYAL SELECTIONS—Cosmetics & Fragrances—Tristar Corp.; *U.S. Public*, pg. 1640

ROYAL SHIELD—Safety Shoes—E.J. Footwear Corp.; *U.S. Public*, pg. 1684

ROYAL SLOGRO—Agricultural Specialty Product—Uniroyal Chemical Company, Inc.; *U.S. Public*, pg. 460

ROYAL STEWART 12 YEAR OLD DE LUXE SCOTCH—Spirit—Allied Domecq PLC; *Int'l*, pg. 62

ROYAL STORE FIXTURES—Store Fixtures—Parisi Inc./Royal Store Fixture; *U.S. Private*, pg. 839

ROYAL SUEDE II—Broadloom—Couristan Inc.; *U.S. Private*, pg. 279

ROYAL TELMAST—Steel Masting—Lance Industries; *U.S. Private*, pg. 645

ROYAL VELVET—Bath & Bedding—Fieldcrest Cannon, Inc.; *U.S. Public*, pg. 1296

ROYAL VIKING LINE—Cruise Line—Cunard Line Ltd.; *Int'l*, pg. 773

ROYAL VIKING QUEEN—Cruise Ship—Cunard Line Ltd.; *Int'l*, pg. 773

ROYAL VIKING SUN—Cruise Ship—Cunard Line Ltd.; *Int'l*, pg. 773

ROYAL WORCESTER—Fine Bone China Dinnerware, Giftware; Porcelain Oven-to-Table & Dinnerware—The Royal China & Porcelain Companies Inc.; *U.S. Private*, pg. 948

ROYAL-X—Photo Film—Eastman Kodak Company; *U.S. Public*, pg. 550

ROYALAX—Broadloom—Couristan Inc.; *U.S. Private*, pg. 279

ROYALCAST—Castable Plastics—Uniroyal Chemical Company, Inc.; *U.S. Public*, pg. 460

ROYALE—Paint—ICI Paints; *Int'l*, pg. 664

ROYALE—Bath Accessories—Melard Manufacturing Corporation; *U.S. Private*, pg. 729

ROYALE—Blank Tape & Accessories—National Video, Inc.; *U.S. Public*, pg. 1755

ROYALE—NONE—SEITA, Societe Nationale D'Exploitation Industrielle des Tabacs et des Allumettes; *Int'l*, pg. 1219

ROYALE COACH BY MONACO—Bus Conversions—Monaco Coach Corporation; *U.S. Public*, pg. 1123

ROYALENE—High Performance Polymer—Uniroyal Chemical Company, Inc.; *U.S. Public*, pg. 460

ROYALFLO—NONE—Uniroyal Chemical Company, Inc.; *U.S. Public*, pg. 460

ROYALFOLD—Disposable Paper Products—Wisconsin Tissue Mills, Inc.; *U.S. Public*, pg. 347

ROYALITE—Thermoplastic Sheet & Profile Extrusions—Uniroyal Technology Corporation; *U.S. Public*, pg. 1670

ROYALPRINT—Photo Processing Apparatus, Chemicals—Eastman Kodak Company; *U.S. Public*, pg. 550

ROYALS—Mint Chocolate—Mars, Incorporated; *U.S. Private*, pg. 707

ROYALTHERM—Silicone-Modified Elastomer—Uniroyal Chemical Company, Inc.; *U.S. Public*, pg. 460

ROYALTUF—High Performance Polymer—Uniroyal Chemical Company, Inc.; *U.S. Public*, pg. 460

ROYALTY—Pineapple—Camerican International; *U.S. Public*, pg. 426

ROYALTY VODKA—Dutch Super-Premium Vodka—Carillon Importers, Ltd.; *Int'l*, pg. 409

ROYCE—Hotels, Inns, Resorts—Servico, Inc.; *U.S. Public*, pg. 1462

ROYER—Shredder/Mixer, Aerator—Royer Industries, Inc.; *Int'l*, pg. 1066

ROYLYN—Aircraft Parts—Kaiser Aerospace & Electronics Corp.; *U.S. Private*, pg. 605

ROYSTON GREENLINE—Pipeline Tape—Chase Corporation; *U.S. Public*, pg. 337

ROYTYPE—NONE—TA Triumph-Adler Vertriebs GmbH; *Int'l*, pg. 1004

ROZES—NONE—LVMH Moet Hennessy Louis Vuitton; *Int'l*, pg. 779

ROZOL—Rodenticide—LiphaTech, Inc.; *Int'l*, pg. 812

RU-TUSS GROUP—Pharmaceuticals—Knoll Pharmaceutical Company; *Int'l*, pg. 105

RUB-A-DUB DOGGIE—Dolls—Tyco Toys, Inc.; *U.S. Public*, pg. 1058

RUB-A-DUB DOLLY—Dolls—Tyco Toys, Inc.; *U.S. Public*, pg. 1058

RUB 'N PLAY—Magic Transfers—Colorforms; *U.S. Public*, pg. 1625

RUB-A-DUB—Laundry Marker—Sanford Corporation; *U.S. Public*, pg. 1178

RUBA-TECT—Diagnostic Products—Abbott Laboratories; *U.S. Public*, pg. 12

RUBACELL—Diagnostic Products—Abbott Laboratories; *U.S. Public*, pg. 12

RUBALIT—Alumina Materials—Ceramtec North America Applications, Inc.; *Int'l*, pg. 860

RUBATEX—Rubber Products—Rubatex Corporation; *U.S. Private*, pg. 56

RUBAZYME—Diagnostic Products—Abbott Laboratories; *U.S. Public*, pg. 12

RUBAZYME-M—Diagnostic Products—Abbott Laboratories; *U.S. Public*, pg. 12

RUBBER & PLASTICS NEWS—Newspaper—Crain Communications, Inc.; *U.S. Private*, pg. 284

RUBBER BASE PLUS—Printing Ink—Van Son Holland Ink Corp. of America; *U.S. Private*, pg. 1133

RUBBER CALK—Sealants—Courtaulds Aerospace; *Int'l*, pg. 339

RUBBER MATE—Rubber Injection Molding Machine—McNeil & NRM., Inc.; *U.S. Private*, pg. 725

RUBBER QUEEN—Automotive Products—Lancaster Colony Automotive Group; *U.S. Public*, pg. 977

RUBBER QUEEN—Automotive Aftermarket Products—Lancaster Colony Corporation; *U.S. Public*, pg. 976

RUBBER RED BOOK—Annual Publication—Intertec Publishing; *U.S. Public*, pg. 1328

RUBBER SATIN—NONE—Mautz Paint Co.; *U.S. Private*, pg. 715

RUBBER SLEEVE—Rubber Core Inner Barrel—Baker Hughes INTEQ; *U.S. Public*, pg. 166

RUBBERGARD—Rubber Roofing—Bridgestone/Firestone, Inc.; *Int'l*, pg. 213

RUBBERMAID—Kitchen & Bathroom Accessories—Rubbermaid Incorporated; *U.S. Public*, pg. 1411

RUBBERMAID TOYS THAT LAST—NONE—Rubbermaid Incorporated; *U.S. Public*, pg. 1411

RUBBEROLL—Rubber Surface for Printing Press Rollers—Jomac, Inc.; *U.S. Private*, pg. 595

RUBBERSET—Brushes & Rollers—Sherwin-Williams Coatings Division; *U.S. Public*, pg. 1466

RUBBERSET—Paint Applicator—Sherwin-Williams Diversified Brands, Inc.; *U.S. Public*, pg. 1466

RUBELLA-PLUS—Rubella Anitbody Detector—Wampole Laboratories; *U.S. Public*, pg. 310

RUBEX—Cancer Therapy Product—Bristol-Myers Squibb Company; *U.S. Public*, pg. 253

RUBEX—Antibiotic Used to Treat Several Types of Cancer—Bristol-Myers Squibb U.S. Pharmaceutical Group; *U.S. Public*, pg. 255

RUBICON—Writing, Text & Cover Paper—Fox River Paper Company; *U.S. Private*, pg. 422

RUBIGAN—Fungicides—The Dow Chemical Company; *U.S. Public*, pg. 522

RUBIN—Costume Jewelry, Handbags & Accessories—F.W. Woolworth Co.; *U.S. Public*, pg. 1777

RUBLE—Vodka & Gin—M.S. Walker, Inc.; *U.S. Private*, pg. 1147

RUBROC—Roll Cover—Beloit Corporation; *U.S. Public*, pg. 789

RUBY—Area Rugs—Couristan Inc.; *U.S. Private*, pg. 279

RUBY—Feminine Hygiene—Polive/Tricosteril; *U.S. Public*, pg. 673

RUBY RED SQUIRT—NONE—Cadbury Schweppes p.l.c.; *Int'l*, pg. 247

RUBY SUPERSYSTEM—Intergrated System for Service Stations & Convenience Stores—VeriFone, Inc.; *U.S. Public*, pg. 815

RUBY TUESDAY—Restaurants—Ruby Tuesday, Inc.; *U.S. Public*, pg. 1411

RUBY'S—Egg Coloring & Easter Goods—Strombecker Corporation; *U.S. Private*, pg. 1047

RUDDLES—Bitter Beer—Foster's Brewing Group Limited; *Int'l*, pg. 500

RUDE DOG—NONE—Brazos Sportswear Inc.; *U.S. Public*, pg. 251

RUDOLPH—Pork Rinds & Cracklings—Rudolph Foods Company; *U.S. Private*, pg. 950

RUDY'S FARM—Meat Product—Sara Lee Corporation; *U.S. Public*, pg. 1432

RUFCO—Plastic Sheeting—Raven Industries, Inc.; *U.S. Public*, pg. 1361

RUFEN—Pharmaceuticals—Knoll Pharmaceutical Company; *Int'l*, pg. 105

RUFF 'N TUFF—NONE—Royal Rubber & Manufacturing Co.; *U.S. Private*, pg. 949

RUFF RIDER—Beverage Carriers & Carton Opener Machine—Riverwood International Corporation; *U.S. Public*, pg. 1391

RUFFHIDES—Men's Shoes—E.J. Footwear Corp.; *U.S. Public*, pg. 1684

RUFFINI—NONE—Supreme International Corp.; *U.S. Public*, pg. 1542

RUFFINO—Chianti & Orvieto Classico Wines—Schieffelin & Somerset Co.; *Int'l*, pg. 412

RUFFLES—Potato Chips—Frito-Lay Company; *U.S. Public*, pg. 1277

RUFI—Children's Shoe—K-Swiss Inc.; *U.S. Public*, pg. 937

RUG AROMA—Carpet Freshener—Surco Products, Inc.; *U.S. Private*, pg. 1056

RUGBY WORLD—Sports Magazine—IPC Magazines Limited; *Int'l*, pg. 651

RUGER—Pistols, Revolvers, Carbines, & Shotguns—Sturm, Ruger & Co., Inc.; *U.S. Public*, pg. 1526

RUGGED—NONE—Stryker Corporation; *U.S. Public*, pg. 1525

RUGGED WEAR—Jeanswear—VF Corporation; *U.S. Public*, pg. 1702

RUGGER—Knits—Gant; *U.S. Public*, pg. 1291

RUGGIE BEAR—Stuffed Toy—Century Products Co.; *U.S. Private*, pg. 226

RUGGLES COLES—Mining & Chemical Machinery—Svedala Industries Inc.; *Int'l*, pg. 1325

RUINART—NONE—LVMH Moet Hennessy Louis Vuitton; *Int'l*, pg. 779

RUIZ—Frozen Mexican Food—Ruiz Food Products, Inc.; *U.S. Private*, pg. 951

RULE—Marine Products—Rule Industries, Inc.; *U.S. Public*, pg. 950

RULID—Infections—Hoechst Marion Roussel, Inc.; *Int'l*, pg. 624

RULID—Antibiotic—SmithKline Beecham Research Limited; *Int'l*, pg. 1266

RULON—Plastics—Furon Co.; *U.S. Public*, pg. 689

RULON—Propietary Materials—Furon Company; *U.S. Public*, pg. 688

RUM & MAPLE—Pipe Tobacco—Lane Limited; *Int'l*, pg. 1129

RUMACO—Pump—Gusher Pumps, Inc.; *U.S. Private*, pg. 488

RUMATEL—Morantel Tartrate—Pfizer Inc.; *U.S. Public*, pg. 1281

RUMBA—Software—Wall Data Incorporated; *U.S. Public*, pg. 1734

RUMENATOR—Beef Feeds—Manna Pro Corporation; *U.S. Private*, pg. 700

RUMENSIN PREMIX—Monensin Sodium, Elanco—Eli Lilly and Company; *U.S. Public*, pg. 992

RUMESIN—Animal Health—Elanco Animal Health; *U.S. Public*, pg. 993

THE RUMI SYSTEM—Gynecological Device—The Cooper Companies, Inc.; *U.S. Public*, pg. 442

RUMMIKUB—Game—Pressman Toy Corp.; *U.S. Private*, pg. 882

RUMMY RUMBLE—Board Game—Mattel Games/Puzzles; *U.S. Public*, pg. 1058

RUMMY-UP—Tile Game—Mattel Games/Puzzles; *U.S. Public*, pg. 1058

RUMPLE MINZE—Liqueur—Grand Metropolitan Plc; *Int'l*, pg. 408

RUMPLE MINZE—Peppermint Schnapps—IDV North America; *Int'l*, pg. 411

RUMPLEMINZE—Spirits—Gilbeys of Ireland; *Int'l*, pg. 409

RUNA/TAB—Carbonless Paper—The Mead Corporation; *U.S. Public*, pg. 1074

RUNAWAY—Jacket—Lands' End, Inc.; *U.S. Public*, pg. 977

RUNBIRD—Athletic Footwear—Mizuno Corporation; *Int'l*, pg. 884

RUNEQUEST-GAMEMASTERS BOX—Role Playing Game—Monarch Avalon, Inc.; *U.S. Public*, pg. 1123

RUNEQUEST-PLAYERS BOX—Role Playing Game—Monarch Avalon, Inc.; *U.S. Public*, pg. 1123

RUNNER'S WORLD—Magazine—Rodale Press, Inc.; *U.S. Private*, pg. 939

RUNNING MATE—NONE—Life Technologies, Inc.; *U.S. Public*, pg. 504

RUNNING MATE—Running Boards—Lund International Holdings, Inc.; *U.S. Public*, pg. 1020

RUNTS—Hard Candy—Nestle S.A.; *Int'l*, pg. 915

RURALITE—Incandescent Lamps—General Electric Canada Inc.; *U.S. Public*, pg. 713

RUS-ETTES—Shoestrings, Thin Cuts, Regular Cuts, Steak Cuts, Crinkle Cuts—Lamb-Weston, Inc.; *U.S. Public*, pg. 427

RUSCARD—Magnetically Encoded Access & Identification Card—CASI-RUSCO Inc.; *U.S. Private*, pg. 218

RUSCH—Invasive Disposable & Reusable Medical Devices—Teleflex Incorporated; *U.S. Public*, pg. 1569

RUSH'N'PUNCH—Tool for Russian Loop Embroidery—Wm. E. Wright Limited Partnership; *U.S. Private*, pg. 1192

RUSHES—Photo Newsletter—Eastman Kodak Company; *U.S. Public*, pg. 550

RUSKIN—White Coated C1S Cover Paper—Appleton Papers Inc.; *Int'l*, pg. 567

RUSPASS—Access Control Badge—CASI-RUSCO Inc.; *U.S. Private*, pg. 218

RUSS—Corporate Logo—Russ Berrie and Company, Inc.; *U.S. Public*, pg. 222

RUSSELL—Butcher Knives—Hyde Manufacturing Co.; *U.S. Private*, pg. 551

RUSSELL—Cutlery—Russell Harrington Cutlery Inc.; *U.S. Private*, pg. 551

RUSSELL ATHLETIC—Knit Athletic Wear—Russell Corporation; *U.S. Public*, pg. 1413

RUSSELL GREEN RIVER—Cutlery—Russell Harrington Cutlery Inc.; *U.S. Private*, pg. 551

RUSSELL INTERNATIONAL—Cutlery—Russell Harrington Cutlery Inc.; *U.S. Private*, pg. 551

RUSSELL STOVER CANDIES—Candy—Russell Stover Candies, Inc.; *U.S. Private*, pg. 953

RUSSELLSTOLL—Electrical Connector—Thomas & Betts/Amerace; *U.S. Public*, pg. 1598

RUSSELLSTOLL—Industrial Connectors—Thomas & Betts Corporation; *U.S. Public*, pg. 1597

RUSSET CHIPS—Potato Chips—Tri Valley Growers; *U.S. Private*, pg. 1101

RUSSIAN COMPREHENSIVE FORMULA 514

RUSSWIN—Hardware—The Black & Decker Corporation; *U.S. Public*, pg. 233

RUST AVENGER—Automotive Rust Converter—3M; *U.S. Public*, pg. 1604

RUST BREAKER—Penetrant—Sherwin-Williams Diversified Brands, Inc.; *U.S. Public*, pg. 1466

RUST-BUSTER—Cleaner for Ion-Exchange Resins Used in Water Softener—Ionics, Incorporated; *U.S. Public*, pg. 912

RUST FIX—Rust Convertor—Sherwin-Williams Diversified Brands, Inc.; *U.S. Public*, pg. 1466

RUST MISER—Automobile Protection System—Monsey-Bakor; *U.S. Private*, pg. 757

RUST-NOT—Primer—Jones Blair Company; *U.S. Private*, pg. 596

RUST NOT—Paint—Plasti-Kote Company Inc.; *U.S. Private*, pg. 870

RUST-O-CRYLIC—Acrylic Coating—Rust-Oleum Corporation; *U.S. Public*, pg. 1358

RUST-O-THANE—Polyurethane Coating—Rust-Oleum Corporation; *U.S. Public*, pg. 1358

RUST-OLEUM—Rust-Preventive Coatings—Rust-Oleum Corporation; *U.S. Public*, pg. 1358

RUST-OLEUM WOOD SAVER—Coatings—Rust-Oleum Corporation; *U.S. Public*, pg. 1358

RUST RID—Rust Remover—Jones Blair Company; *U.S. Private*, pg. 596

RUST SHIELD—Rust & Corrosion Protection—Lilly Industries, Inc.; *U.S. Public*, pg. 994

RUST TOUGH—Rust Preventive Enamel—Sherwin-Williams Diversified Brands, Inc.; *U.S. Public*, pg. 1466

RUST TREAT—Metal Protection—Monsey-Bakor; *U.S. Private*, pg. 757

RUST VETO—Rust-Preventive—Houghton International Inc.; *U.S. Private*, pg. 541

RUST-OLEUM—Coating—RPM, Inc.; *U.S. Public*, pg. 1356

RUSTCLEAN—Rust Removers—Octagon Process Inc.; *U.S. Private*, pg. 811

RUSTIC RIB—Siding—Reynolds Metals Company; *U.S. Public*, pg. 1385

RUSTIQUE—Stains—Colony Paints; *U.S. Public*, pg. 1.07

RUSTLER—Apparel—Mass Market Division; *U.S. Public*, pg. 1702

RUSTLER—Jeanswear—VF Corporation; *U.S. Public*, pg. 1702

RUSTLERS—Domestic Cigars—Consolidated Cigar Corporation; *U.S. Private*, pg. 690

RUSTLICK—Metal Fluid Product—ITW Fluid Products Group; *U.S. Public*, pg. 866

RUSTMASTER—Paint—ICI Paints; *Int'l*, pg. 664

RUSTMASTER METALLITE—Paint—ICI Paints; *Int'l*, pg. 664

RUSTO—Bakery & Food Oils Mixes—Park Foods L.P.; *U.S. Public*, pg. 839

RUSTON—Diesels—The General Electric Company, p.l.c.; *Int'l*, pg. 543

RUSTOP—Paint—Graham Paint and Varnish Company; *U.S. Private*, pg. 468

Brand Name Index

Brand Name Index

RUSTPHREE—Cooling Water Programs for Soft Water Applications—Calgon Corporation; *Int'l*, pg. 455

RUSTPROOF—Shower Stall—Plaskolite Inc.; *U.S. Private*, pg. 870

RUSTRIPPER—Rust Stripper—Oakite Products, Inc.; *Int'l*, pg. 861

RUSTY SCUPPER—Drinking/Dining/Dancing Restaurants—Select Restaurants, Inc.; *U.S. Private*, pg. 982

RUTHMAN PUMPS—Pumps—Gusher Pumps, Inc.; *U.S. Private*, pg. 488

RUTT CUSTOM CABINETRY—Custom-Built Wood Kitchen Cabinetry—Rutt Custom Cabinetry; *U.S. Private*, pg. 507

RUUD—Water Heaters, Air Conditioners & Furnaces—Rheem Manufacturing Co.; *Int'l*, pg. 1022

RX FIRST CLASS—Mail Order Pharmacy—Coventry Corporation; *U.S. Public*, pg. 454

RX PLACE—Deep Discount Drugstores—PharmHouse, Inc.; *U.S. Public*, pg. 1286

THE RX PLACE—Deep Discount Drug Stores—F.W. Woolworth Co.; *U.S. Public*, pg. 1777

RXLOY—EVA Containing Polymer for Medical—Ferro Corporation; *U.S. Public*, pg. 618

RY-O-LINE—Plastics—Joseph T. Ryerson & Son, Inc.; *U.S. Public*, pg. 879

RY-STAR 512 Extra—Tubing—Joseph T. Ryerson & Son, Inc.; *U.S. Public*, pg. 879

RY-WEDG—Work Order—Joseph T. Ryerson & Son, Inc.; *U.S. Public*, pg. 879

RY-WELD—Work Order—Joseph T. Ryerson & Son, Inc.; *U.S. Public*, pg. 879

RYAN—Turf Equipment—Ransomes-Cushman-Ryan; *Int'l*, pg. 1088

RYAN—Commercial Turf Machinery—Ransomes Plc; *Int'l*, pg. 1087

RYAN HOMES—NONE—NVR, Inc.; *U.S. Public*, pg. 1148

RYBO—Savory Flavor—Gilette Food Flavorings, Inc.; *U.S. Private*, pg. 453

RYCARDEN—Nicardipine Hydrochloride—Syntex; *Int'l*, pg. 1120

RYCASE—Bars—Joseph T. Ryerson & Son, Inc.; *U.S. Public*, pg. 879

RYCO—Calorifiers—IMI Plc; *Int'l*, pg. 646

RYCOLINA—Calorifiers—IMI Plc; *Int'l*, pg. 646

RYCROFT—Calorifiers—IMI Plc; *Int'l*, pg. 646

RYCROME—Bars—Joseph T. Ryerson & Son, Inc.; *U.S. Public*, pg. 879

RYCUT—Bars—Joseph T. Ryerson & Son, Inc.; *U.S. Public*, pg. 879

RYDENE—Nicardipine Hydrochloride—Syntex; *Int'l*, pg. 1120

RYDER ROAD READY—Used Vehicles—Ryder System, Inc.; *U.S. Public*, pg. 1413

RYERLUBE—Plastics—Joseph T. Ryerson & Son, Inc.; *U.S. Public*, pg. 879

RYERTEX—Plastics—Joseph T. Ryerson & Son, Inc.; *U.S. Public*, pg. 879

RYEX—Sheet—Joseph T. Ryerson & Son, Inc.; *U.S. Public*, pg. 879

RYKA—Athletic Shoes—Ryka Incorporated; *U.S. Public*, pg. 1414

RYKOFF INTERNATIONAL—Food Products—Rykoff-Sexton, Inc.; *U.S. Public*, pg. 918

RYKOFF SEXTON—Food Products—Rykoff-Sexton, Inc.; *U.S. Public*, pg. 918

RYKON—Lubricants—Amoco Corporation; *U.S. Public*, pg. 101

RYLEX—Vulcanizing Agent—Ferro Corporation; *U.S. Public*, pg. 618

RYMER—Food Products—Rymer Foods Inc.; *U.S. Public*, pg. 1414

RYMER—Foods—Rymer Meat Inc.; *U.S. Public*, pg. 1414

RYNA C—Cough/Colds—Wallace Laboratories; *U.S. Public*, pg. 310

RYNA CX—Cough/Colds—Wallace Laboratories; *U.S. Public*, pg. 310

RYNATAN PEDIATRIC SUSPENSION—Cold Without Analgesic—Wallace Laboratories; *U.S. Public*, pg. 310

RYNATAN TABLETS—Cold Without Analgesic—Wallace Laboratories; *U.S. Public*, pg. 310

RYNATUSS PEDIATRIC SUSPENSION—Cough/Cold Without Expectorant—Wallace Laboratories; *U.S. Public*, pg. 310

RYNATUSS TABLETS—Cough/Cold Without Expectorant—Wallace Laboratories; *U.S. Public*, pg. 310

RYNITE—Thermoplastic Polyester—Du Pont (E.I. Du Pont De Nemours & Co.); *U.S. Public*, pg. 530

RYNO ROLLERS—Rollers—Jomac, Inc.; *U.S. Private*, pg. 595

RYNO SPAR—Paint—Pratt & Lambert United, Inc.; *U.S. Public*, pg. 1466

RYNO-THANE—Paint—Pratt & Lambert United, Inc.; *U.S. Public*, pg. 1466

RYNSTONE—Solid Surface Countertop & Bath Fixture Material—Rynone Manufacturing Corporation; *U.S. Private*, pg. 953

RYOBI—Power Tools—Ryobi Motor Products; *Int'l*, pg. 1151

RYOLEX PERLITE—Perlite Aggregates—Silbrico Corporation; *U.S. Private*, pg. 1000

RYON'S—Boots and Saddles—Luskeys Western Stores, Inc.; *U.S. Private*, pg. 681

RYTENSE—Bars—Joseph T. Ryerson & Son, Inc.; *U.S. Public*, pg. 879

RYTEX—Disposable Fabric—Lakeland Industries, Inc.; *U.S. Public*, pg. 975

RYTHMOL—Pharmaceutical—Knoll Pharmaceutical Company; *Int'l*, pg. 105

RYTOL—White Mineral Oil—Witco Corporation; *U.S. Public*, pg. 1773

RYTON—Sulfur Containing Thermoplastic & Thermosetting Resins—Phillips Petroleum Company; *U.S. Public*, pg. 1290

S

SA—Industrial Space Heater—Rapid Engineering Inc.; *U.S. Private*, pg. 910

SAA—Computer System—International Business Machines Corporation; *U.S. Public*, pg. 895

SAA—Airway—Transnet Ltd.; *Int'l*, pg. 1417

SAAB—Automobile—Saab Cars USA, Inc.; *Int'l*, pg. 687

SAAB 900—Automobile—Saab Cars USA, Inc.; *Int'l*, pg. 687

SACI—Rust Preventative—Witco Corporation; *U.S. Public*, pg. 1773

SADIS—Semi Automatic Decoy Integrated Systems—Comptek Research, Inc.; *U.S. Public*, pg. 419

SAF—Scientific Glassware for Laboratory Use—Wheaton Inc.; *Int'l*, pg. 67

SAM—Monitor Used to Diagnose Obstructive Sleep Apnea—Criticare Systems, Inc.; *U.S. Public*, pg. 459

SAM—Columns & Chemistry Reagents—Millipore Corporation; *U.S. Public*, pg. 1112

SAP—Sine Analysis Program—GenRad, Inc.; *U.S. Public*, pg. 731

SAS—NONE—ETEX; *Int'l*, pg. 430

SAS/TUTOR SOFTWARE—Family of Online Training Causes—SAS Institute Inc.; *U.S. Private*, pg. 966

SAS/ACCESS—Individual Interfaces for Linking the SAS System with Various Data Bases—SAS Institute Inc.; *U.S. Private*, pg. 966

SAS/AF—An Interactive Facility with Menus & Screens for Applications Development—SAS Institute Inc.; *U.S. Private*, pg. 966

SAS/ASSIST—A Menu-Driven Interface to the SAS System—SAS Institute Inc.; *U.S. Private*, pg. 966

SAS/CALC—For Electronic Spreadsheets—SAS Institute Inc.; *U.S. Private*, pg. 966

SAS/CONNECT—For Cooperative and Distributed Processing—SAS Institute Inc.; *U.S. Private*, pg. 966

SAS/EIS—For Building & Maintaining Executive Information Systems—SAS Institute Inc.; *U.S. Private*, pg. 966

SAS/ENGLISH—A Natural Language Interface—SAS Institute Inc.; *U.S. Private*, pg. 966

SAS ENTERPRISE REPORTER—For Fast Design of Presentation Style & Ad Hoc Reporting—SAS Institute Inc.; *U.S. Private*, pg. 966

SAS/ETS—For Forecasting, Business Planning, Econometric and Time Series Analysis—SAS Institute Inc.; *U.S. Private*, pg. 966

SAS/FSP—For Full-Screen Data Entry, Editing, Querying, & LetterWriting Facility—SAS Institute Inc.; *U.S. Private*, pg. 966

SAS/GEO—Data Integration Solution for the Petroleum Industry—SAS Institute Inc.; *U.S. Private*, pg. 966

SAS/GIS—Visualization Of Geographic Data—SAS Institute Inc.; *U.S. Private*, pg. 966

SAS/GRAPH—For Information and Presentation Color Graphics with Image Extensions—SAS Institute Inc.; *U.S. Private*, pg. 966

SAS/IML—Interactive Matrix Programming Language—SAS Institute Inc.; *U.S. Private*, pg. 966

SAS/INSIGHT—For Graphical Data Analysis—SAS Institute Inc.; *U.S. Private*, pg. 966

SAS/INTRNET SOFTWARE—Web Enablement Software—SAS Institute Inc.; *U.S. Private*, pg. 966

SAS/LA—For Guided Data Analysis—SAS Institute Inc.; *U.S. Private*, pg. 966

SAS/OR—For Project Mngmt., Opers. Res., Scheduling & Linear Programming—SAS Institute Inc.; *U.S. Private*, pg. 966

SAS/PH-CLINICAL—Clinical Data Review System—SAS Institute Inc.; *U.S. Private*, pg. 966

SAS/QC—For Quality Improvement—SAS Institute Inc.; *U.S. Private*, pg. 966

SAS/SHARE—A Multi-User Access Tool for Concurrent Updating of Data—SAS Institute Inc.; *U.S. Private*, pg. 966

SAS/SHARE & NET—Remote ODBC Access—SAS Institute Inc.; *U.S. Private*, pg. 966

SAS/SPECTRAVIEW—3-D Scientific Data Analysis & Visualization—SAS Institute Inc.; *U.S. Private*, pg. 966

SAS/STAT—For Staticstics Analysis—SAS Institute Inc.; *U.S. Private*, pg. 966

THE SAS SYSTEM—Information Delivery Software System for Enterprise-Wide Computing—SAS Institute Inc.; *U.S. Private*, pg. 966

SAS/TOOLKIT—Tools for User-Written Extensions—SAS Institute Inc.; *U.S. Private*, pg. 966

SAS/WAREHOUSE ADMINISTRATOR—For Effectively Creating & Managing Data Warehouse Process—SAS Institute Inc.; *U.S. Private*, pg. 966

SA8—Laundry Detergent—Amway Corporation; *U.S. Private*, pg. 69

S&G—Flower Seeds & Young Plants—Novartis Seeds, Inc.; *Int'l*, pg. 974

S & H—Green Stamps—The Sperry & Hutchinson Company, Inc.; *U.S. Public*, pg. 990

S&K—Jets, Reductors, Scrubbers—Schutte & Koerting Division; *U.S. Private*, pg. 604

S & P—Holding Company—S P Company; *U.S. Private*, pg. 954

S & P COILS—Heat Exchange Coils, Air Heating & Cooling—Halma p.l.c.; *Int'l*, pg. 589

S & W—Patient Monitoring Systems—Vickers PLC; *Int'l*, pg. 1466

S & W NATURAL STYLE—Canned Fruits—Tri Valley Growers; *U.S. Private*, pg. 1101

S & W OLE'—Canned Mexican Foods—Tri Valley Growers; *U.S. Private*, pg. 1101

S & W SPRING—Canned Juices—Tri Valley Growers; *U.S. Private*, pg. 1101

SB—School Bus Chassis—Spartan Motors, Inc.; *U.S. Public*, pg. 1495

SBP-1382—Synthetic Pyrethroid—Roussel UCLAF S.A.; *Int'l*, pg. 626

SBP-1382—Synthetic Pyrethroid—Roussel Corporation; *Int'l*, pg. 625

S. B. R.—Siding & Window Caulk—Ohio Sealants Inc.; *Int'l*, pg. 802

SBS—Industrial/Institutional Hand Cleaner—SBS Products, Inc.; *U.S. Private*, pg. 955

SBS—Modified Bitumen Membrane—U.S. Intec, Inc.; *U.S. Private*, pg. 433

SBS CARE MEDICATED SKIN CREAM—Medicated Skin Cream—SBS Products, Inc.; *U.S. Private*, pg. 955

SBS DEFLECT OCCUPATIONAL SUNSCREEN—Sunscreen—SBS Products, Inc.; *U.S. Private*, pg. 955

SBS 40—Medicated Skin Cream—SBS Products, Inc.; *U.S. Private*, pg. 955

SBS 44—Protective Cream-Water Resistant—SBS Products, Inc.; *U.S. Private*, pg. 955

SBS 46—Protective Cream-Solvent Resistant—SBS Products, Inc.; *U.S. Private*, pg. 955

Brand Name Index

SBS GREEN ANTIBACTERIAL LOTION SOAP—Antibacterial Lotion Soap—SBS Products, Inc.; *U.S. Private*, pg. 955

SBS LIME HAND CLEANSER WITH NATURAL SCRUBBER—Hand Cleanser with Natural Scrubber—SBS Products, Inc.; *U.S. Private*, pg. 955

SBS NATURAL NATURAL LOTION SOAP—Natural Lotion Soap—SBS Products, Inc.; *U.S. Private*, pg. 955

SBS 100 SANITIZING GEL—Sanitizing Gel—SBS Products, Inc.; *U.S. Private*, pg. 955

SBS ORANGE HEAVY DUTY HAND CLEANSER—Heavy Duty Hand Cleanser With Natural Scrubber—SBS Products, Inc.; *U.S. Private*, pg. 955

SBS PEACH NATURAL LOTION SOAP—Natural Lotion Soap—SBS Products, Inc.; *U.S. Private*, pg. 955

SBS ROSE NATURAL LOTION SOAP—Natural Lotion Soap—SBS Products, Inc.; *U.S. Private*, pg. 955

SBS-71—Lotion Skin Cleanser—SBS Products, Inc.; *U.S. Private*, pg. 955

SBS-30—Waterless Skin Cleanser—SBS Products, Inc.; *U.S. Private*, pg. 955

S. BENT DESIGNS—NONE—S. Bent & Brothers, Inc.; *U.S. Private*, pg. 134

SC—Sales Consultants—Management Recruiters International, Inc.; *U.S. Public*, pg. 277

SCA—NONE—Enzon, Inc.; *U.S. Public*, pg. 587

SCAASI—Perfume—Revlon, Inc.; *U.S. Private*, pg. 689

SCAASI—Intimate Apparel—Warnaco Inc.; *U.S. Public*, pg. 1738

SCAN—Semiconductor Component Analysis Network—GenRad, Inc.; *U.S. Public*, pg. 731

SCAN PATHFINDER—Boundary Scan TEst Generation & Diagnostic Software for Board Test Systems—GenRad, Inc.; *U.S. Public*, pg. 731

SCD SEQUENTIAL COMPRESSION SYSTEM—Thrombosis & Pulmonary Embolism Reduction System—The Kendall Company; *U.S. Public*, pg. 1647

SCE—Electric Utility—Edison International; *U.S. Public*, pg. 564

SCF—I.V. Filter—Pall Corporation; *U.S. Public*, pg. 1253

SCF 19—NONE—Carpenter Technology Corporation; *U.S. Public*, pg. 307

SCIRAS—Sundstrand Coriolis Inertial Rate & Acceleration Sensor—AlliedSignal Commercial Avionics Systems; *U.S. Public*, pg. 50

SC JOHNSON PASTE WAX—Floor Polish—S.C. Johnson & Son, Inc.; *U.S. Private*, pg. 592

SCM—Chemicals & Metals Products—Hanson PLC; *Int'l*, pg. 592

SCP—Storage CD-Processor—Zitel Corporation; *U.S. Public*, pg. 1793

S/C ROTARY VANE—NONE—Squire-Cogswell Company; *U.S. Private*, pg. 1027

SCSI AUDIO MACHINE—NONE—Adaptec, Inc.; *U.S. Public*, pg. 19

SCSI BACK UP—NONE—Adaptec, Inc.; *U.S. Public*, pg. 19

SCSI CHANNEL—NONE—Adaptec, Inc.; *U.S. Public*, pg. 19

SCSI DIRECTION—NONE—Adaptec, Inc.; *U.S. Public*, pg. 19

SCSI MASTER—NONE—Adaptec, Inc.; *U.S. Public*, pg. 19

SCSISELECT—NONE—Adaptec, Inc.; *U.S. Public*, pg. 19

SCSI TERMINAL SERVERS—NONE—Central Data Corporation; *U.S. Private*, pg. 223

SCT (SPECTRUM CONTROL TECHNOLOGY)—Special Lens Technology—Uvex Safety, Inc.; *Int'l*, pg. 132

SCX—Digital Network Switches—Rockwell International Corporation; *U.S. Public*, pg. 1397

S-CLASS—Fish Tape—Ideal Industries, Inc.; *U.S. Private*, pg. 557

SD-100—Automotive Tires—Sime Darby Berhad; *Int'l*, pg. 1249

SD-1000—Severe Duty Control Valves—Copes-Vulcan Inc.; *U.S. Private*, pg. 274

SDRC—Engineering Data Management Software—Onyx Technologies Ltd.; *Int'l*, pg. 1007

SDRC MODAL-PLUS—NONE—Structural Dynamics Research Corp.; *U.S. Public*, pg. 1525

SDS—Safe Delivery Source Gas Delivery System—ATMI, Inc.; *U.S. Public*, pg. 12

SDS—Second Day Delivery Service—Danzas Corporation; *Int'l*, pg. 382

SD TAPS—NONE—Greenfield Industries; *U.S. Public*, pg. 950

SD/2—Computer Product—International Business Machines Corporation; *U.S. Public*, pg. 895

SEA—Radiotelephone Systems—Datamarine International, Inc.; *U.S. Public*, pg. 486

SEA—NONE—ETEX; *Int'l*, pg. 430

SEAC—Specialist Fasteners—Halma p.l.c.; *Int'l*, pg. 589

SEB—Kitchen Appliances—Groupe SEB; *Int'l*, pg. 568

SEF—Modacrylic Fibers—Monsanto Company; *U.S. Public*, pg. 1124

SE5—NONE—Stryker Corporation; *U.S. Public*, pg. 1525

SE-4—Stimulator—Medtronic, Inc.; *U.S. Public*, pg. 1082

SEMCONN—NONE—Molex Incorporated; *U.S. Public*, pg. 1121

SE Q—Television Receivers—Zenith Electronics Corp.; *U.S. Public*, pg. 1790

S.E.R.—Food Products—Rykoff-Sexton, Inc.; *U.S. Public*, pg. 918

S.E.R.V.—Safety Interlocks—Halma p.l.c.; *Int'l*, pg. 589

SETS—Severe Environment Tape System—AlliedSignal Commercial Avionics Systems; *U.S. Public*, pg. 50

S811 MICROCASSETTE—Microcassette Recorders—Olympus America Inc.; *Int'l*, pg. 1005

SF/DUROID—Electrical Insulation Materials—Rogers Corporation; *U.S. Public*, pg. 1402

SF 96—Silicone Fluids for use as Additives to Cosmetics, Toiletries & Polishes—General Electric Canada Inc.; *U.S. Public*, pg. 713

SFS—Surgical Staplers—U.S. Surgical Corp.; *U.S. Public*, pg. 1687

S.F. 6—Stress Vitamin—Health Products Corporation; *U.S. Private*, pg. 514

SFZ—Transportation Company—The Scott Fetzer Company; *U.S. Public*, pg. 217

S-FLEX—Power Transmission—Lovejoy Inc.; *U.S. Private*, pg. 677

SGD COOKIE EXPRESS—Mail Order Cookies—SGD International Corp.; *U.S. Private*, pg. 957

SGF—Catalogue—Harcourt General, Inc.; *U.S. Public*, pg. 782

SGF—Transparent Polyvinyl Chloride Film—Reynolds Metals Company; *U.S. Public*, pg. 1385

SGIA—NONE—U.S. Surgical Corp.; *U.S. Public*, pg. 1687

SGI CANADA—Property & Casualty Insurance—Saskatchewan Government Insurance, SGI; *Int'l*, pg. 1195

SGS—Rolls for use in Printing—Reynolds Metals Company; *U.S. Public*, pg. 1385

SGS-THOMPSON—NONE—Milgray Electronics, Inc.; *U.S. Public*, pg. 205

SGS-THOMSON—Microelectronics—SGS-Thomson Microelectronics, Inc.; *Int'l*, pg. 1153

SG SERIES SPIN-GLAS—Equipment Insulation—Johns Manville Corporation; *U.S. Public*, pg. 927

SH PLUS—NONE—Kellwood Company; *U.S. Public*, pg. 948

SHX—Super High Performance Antennas—Andrew Corporation; *U.S. Public*, pg. 112

SHZYK—Submersible Grinder Pump—Zoeller Co.; *U.S. Private*, pg. 1207

SI—Threaded Inserts—Penn Engineering & Manufacturing Corp.; *U.S. Public*, pg. 1269

SI-18—Tennis Shoe—K-Swiss Inc.; *U.S. Public*, pg. 937

SIL-X—Packing Material for Chromatography Columns—The Perkin-Elmer Corporation; *U.S. Public*, pg. 1279

SIM-R-WARE—Cooking Pots & Electric Heater—Robeson Appliance, Inc.; *U.S. Public*, pg. 1394

S.I.P.—Syndicated Beverage Consumption Monitor—NFO Research, Inc.; *U.S. Public*, pg. 1146

THE SIP SMARTSYSTEM—Data Management System—NFO Research, Inc.; *U.S. Public*, pg. 1146

S.I.R. GASKET—Stainless Insert Reinforced Gaskets—Norton Performance Plastics; *Int'l*, pg. 1174

SI SERIES—Solid Ink—Dataproducts Corporation; *Int'l*, pg. 620

SJ—Women's Apparel—St. John Knits; *U.S. Private*, pg. 960

SJC—Single Joint Compensator Tool—Weatherford Enterra Incorporated; *U.S. Public*, pg. 1749

S-K—Hand Tools—SK Hand Tool Corp.; *Int'l*, pg. 570

SK—Solid State Devices—Thomson Consumer Electronics Inc.; *Int'l*, pg. 1383

SKF—Bearings—MRC Bearings; *Int'l*, pg. 1157

SKF—NONE—AB SKF; *Int'l*, pg. 1156

S K SUPERSETS—Socket Set Packages—SK Hand Tool Corp.; *Int'l*, pg. 570

S. KIRK & SON—Sterling Flatware—Lenox Brands; *U.S. Public*, pg. 261

SLC—Carrier, Carrier System, Series 5 Carrier System, Fiber—Lucent Technologies Inc.; *U.S. Public*, pg. 1017

SLC-I—Stand Alone Calendar Clock & Communications Monitor—Axent Technologies; *U.S. Public*, pg. 157

SLC-II—Communications Controller/Monitor—Axent Technologies; *U.S. Public*, pg. 157

SLD—Electronic Instrument—Intel Corporation; *U.S. Public*, pg. 886

SLM POOLS—Above Ground Pools; Poly Pools—Empire of Carolina, Inc.; *U.S. Public*, pg. 579

SLM SNOW GOODS—Sleds—Empire of Carolina, Inc.; *U.S. Public*, pg. 579

SLN—Nickel—Imetal; *Int'l*, pg. 661

SL 1, 10, 100—Computer Controled Digital Switching Systems & Components—Northern Telecom Limited; *Int'l*, pg. 968

SLP—Heat-Shrinkable, Transparent Polyvinyl Chloride Film—Reynolds Metals Company; *U.S. Public*, pg. 1385

SLR—Acetate Yarn—Eastman Chemical Company; *U.S. Public*, pg. 550

SLR—Man-Made Yarn, Cellulose Acetate Yarn—Eastman Kodak Company; *U.S. Public*, pg. 550

SLR 680—Autofocus Camera—Polaroid Corporation; *U.S. Public*, pg. 1313

SL'S BLACK MAX—NONE—Molex Incorporated; *U.S. Public*, pg. 1121

SLT—NONE—Berg Electronics; *U.S. Public*, pg. 212

SLT—NONE—Surgical Laser Technologies, Inc.; *U.S. Public*, pg. 1542

SLZ—Bright Ammonium Chloride Zinc—LeaRonal, Inc.; *U.S. Public*, pg. 982

SLZ PLUS—Bright Potassium Chloride Zinc—LeaRonal, Inc.; *U.S. Public*, pg. 982

SL-20—Personnel Lift—Up-Right, Inc.; *U.S. Private*, pg. 1128

SM—Polyvinyl Chloride Film—Reynolds Metals Company; *U.S. Public*, pg. 1385

SM—Disposable Loading Units—U.S. Surgical Corp.; *U.S. Public*, pg. 1687

SMA—Video & Music Products—TSC Shannock Corporation; *Int'l*, pg. 1343

SMA—NONE—Wyeth Australia Pty. Ltd.; *U.S. Public*, pg. 82

SMA—Cow Milk-Based Infant Formula—Wyeth-Ayerst Laboratories, Inc.; *U.S. Public*, pg. 80

SMA, NURSOY—Infant Formulas—American Home Products Corporation; *U.S. Public*, pg. 79

S-MAZ—Surfactants—PPG Industries, Inc.; *U.S. Public*, pg. 1245

SMC—Sealless Strapping Tool—Illinois Tool Works Inc.; *U.S. Public*, pg. 865

SMC—Compression-Molding Process Using Fiber-Reinforced Plastic—Saint-Gobain; *Int'l*, pg. 1170

SMC—Semiconductors—Standard Microsystems Corp.; *U.S. Public*, pg. 1502

SMC-70—Computer—Sony Electronics; *Int'l*, pg. 1281

SMD—Surface Mount Devices—Philips Electronics N.V.; *Int'l*, pg. 1051

SMD—Power Fuse—S & C Electric Company; *U.S. Private*, pg. 954

SMF TRINICON—Color Video Camera—Sony Electronics; *Int'l*, pg. 1281

SM-5—Power Fuse—S & C Electric Company; *U.S. Private*, pg. 954

SM-4—Power Fuse—S & C Electric Company; *U.S. Private*, pg. 954

SMG—Dough Conditioner—Eastman Kodak Company; *U.S. Public*, pg. 550

SMP—Filter Element—Donaldson Company, Inc.; *U.S. Public*, pg. 517

SMP—Stainless Plate—Lukens Inc.; *U.S. Public*, pg. 1019

SMS—Used Needle Disposal System—Isolyser Company, Inc.; *U.S. Public*, pg. 914

SMS 1000—Proprietary Security System—Diebold, Incorporated; *U.S. Public*, pg. 506

SMS-STAR—NONE—GenRad, Inc.; *U.S. Public*, pg. 731

SMU-40—Fuse Units—S & C Electric Company; *U.S. Private*, pg. 954

SMU-20—Fuse Units—S & C Electric Company; *U.S. Private*, pg. 954

S-MATIC—Coater—Harnischfeger Industries, Inc.; *U.S. Public*, pg. 788

SNAX—Interface to SNA Networks—Tandem Computers Inc.; *U.S. Public*, pg. 417

SNC—Graphite Machining Center—Makino Inc.; *Int'l*, pg. 831

SNC—Project Mngmt., Engrng., Procurement & Construction—SNC-Lavalin Group Inc.; *Int'l*, pg. 1161

SNCM—Maritime Services—Compagnie Generale Maritime et Financiere; *Int'l*, pg. 322

SOF ROD—NONE—Applied Extrusion Technologies, Inc.; *U.S. Public*, pg. 122

S.O.F. SYSTEM—Mattress Unit—Kingsdown, Inc.; *U.S. Private*, pg. 622

SOF T-VISION—Mattress & Box Spring—Kingsdown, Inc.; *U.S. Private*, pg. 622

SOR—Pressure Switches—SOR Inc.; *U.S. Private*, pg. 957

SOR LEVEL CONTROLS—NONE—SOR Inc.; *U.S. Private*, pg. 957

S.O.S.—Glass Cleaner—Bayer AG; *Int'l*, pg. 171

S.O.S.—Steel Wool & Oven Cleaning Pads—Bayer Corporation/Consumer Care Division; *Int'l*, pg. 173

SOS—NONE—The Clorox Company; *U.S. Public*, pg. 386

S.O.S GLASS WORKS—Glass Cleaner—Bayer Corporation/Consumer Care Division; *Int'l*, pg. 173

SOSS—Invisible Hinges—Universal Industrial Products Co.; *U.S. Public*, pg. 1677

S101—Robot—BTR plc; *Int'l*, pg. 124

SP—NONE—Plantronics Inc.; *U.S. Public*, pg. 1308

SPAG—Small Particle Aerosol Generator for Virazole—ICN Pharmaceuticals, Inc.; *U.S. Public*, pg. 853

SPA1000—Ultrasound—Diasonics Ultra Sound, Inc.; *Int'l*, pg. 644

SPC—Singapore Petroleum Company—Singapore Petroleum Company Ltd.; *U.S. Public*, pg. 102

SPCC/PC+ STATISTICS—Option to SPSS/PC+—SPSS Inc.; *U.S. Public*, pg. 1420

SP DESIGN—Magnetic & Video Products & Services—Eastman Kodak Company; *U.S. Public*, pg. 550

SPEC 55—Twisted Pair Cable—Raychem Corporation; *U.S. Public*, pg. 1362

SPEER—Center Tire Pistol Ammunition Bullets—Blount, Inc. Sporting Equipment Group; *U.S. Public*, pg. 238

SPF—Small Pupil Feature, Binocular Indirect Ophthalmoscope Capability—The Cooper Companies, Inc.; *U.S. Public*, pg. 442

SPM—Single-Ply Roofing Systems—Johns Manville Corporation; *U.S. Public*, pg. 927

SP1—Computer Product—International Business Machines Corporation; *U.S. Public*, pg. 895

SPQ—Digital Loop Carrier Systems—Lucent Technologies Inc.; *U.S. Public*, pg. 1017

SPRA-MAX—Texture Coatings—Devoe Paint; *Int'l*, pg. 663

SPRA-MAX—Texture Coatings—ICI Paints; *Int'l*, pg. 664

SPRA-MAX 40—High Build Coating—Devoe Paint; *Int'l*, pg. 663

SPRA-MAX 40—High Build Coating—ICI Paints; *Int'l*, pg. 664

SPRA-MAX 12—Interior Coating—Devoe Paint; *Int'l*, pg. 663

SPRA-MENT—Aerosol Adhesives—3M; *U.S. Public*, pg. 1604

SPRA-MAX 12—Interior Coatings—ICI Paints; *Int'l*, pg. 664

S.P.S.—Stereo Equipment—Audiovox Corporation; *U.S. Public*, pg. 147

S.P.S.—Primer Sealer—Benjamin Moore & Co.; *U.S. Private*, pg. 133

SPS—Electric Utility—Southwestern Public Service Company; *U.S. Public*, pg. 1170

SPS JOINT CONTROL SYSTEMS—Computer-Controlled Tightening Equip.—SPS Technologies, Inc.; *U.S. Public*, pg. 1419

SPS MONITOR BOLT—Modified Fasteners with Sensors & Readout Devices—SPS Technologies, Inc.; *U.S. Public*, pg. 1419

SPS PAYMENT SYSTEMS—Electronic Payment Processing—Dean Witter, Discover & Co.; *U.S. Public*, pg. 1132

SPSS—Data Analysis Software For the OS/2, the Macintosh & UNIX—SPSS Inc.; *U.S. Public*, pg. 1420

SPSS CATEGORIES—Option To SPSS—SPSS Inc.; *U.S. Public*, pg. 1420

SPSS DATA ENTRY—Survey Design & Data Collection Product—SPSS Inc.; *U.S. Public*, pg. 1420

SPSS DIAMOND—Data Visualization Software—SPSS Inc.; *U.S. Public*, pg. 1420

SPSS GRAPHICS—Presentation Graphics or Option to SPSS—SPSS Inc.; *U.S. Public*, pg. 1420

SPSS/PC+—Data Analysis Software for the IBM PC/XT/AT—SPSS Inc.; *U.S. Public*, pg. 1420

SPSS/PC+ ADVANCED STATISTICS—Option to SPSS/PC+—SPSS Inc.; *U.S. Public*, pg. 1420

SPSS/PC+ CATEGORIES—Option to SPSS/PC+—SPSS Inc.; *U.S. Public*, pg. 1420

SPSS/PC+ GRAPHICS—Featuring Harvard Graphics—SPSS Inc.; *U.S. Public*, pg. 1420

SPSS/PC+ MAP—Featuring MapInfo—SPSS Inc.; *U.S. Public*, pg. 1420

SPSS/PC+ TABLES—Option to SPSS/PC+—SPSS Inc.; *U.S. Public*, pg. 1420

SPSS/PC+ TRENDS—Option to SPSS/PC+—SPSS Inc.; *U.S. Public*, pg. 1420

SPSS TABLES—Option to SPSS—SPSS Inc.; *U.S. Public*, pg. 1420

SPSS TRENDS—Option to SPSS—SPSS Inc.; *U.S. Public*, pg. 1420

SP SERIES—Ductless Split System Air Conditioner—Slant/Fin Corporation; *U.S. Private*, pg. 1005

SP TROCHES—Pharmaceuticals—Meiji Seika Kaisha, Ltd.; *Int'l*, pg. 855

SP2—Computer Product—International Business Machines Corporation; *U.S. Public*, pg. 895

SP2000—Video Recording Equipment & Supplies—Eastman Kodak Company; *U.S. Public*, pg. 550

SP2030—Video Recording Equipment & Supplies—Eastman Kodak Company; *U.S. Public*, pg. 550

SP2020—Video Recording Equipment & Supplies—Eastman Kodak Company; *U.S. Public*, pg. 550

SPX—Wide Area Data Networking System—Network Equipment Technologies, Inc.; *U.S. Public*, pg. 1168

S-PAC—DC-DC Power Source—Reliability Incorporated; *U.S. Public*, pg. 1373

S-PAK—Membrane Filter—Millipore Corporation; *U.S. Public*, pg. 1112

SQL/DS—Computer Product—International Business Machines Corporation; *U.S. Public*, pg. 895

SQL/400—Computer Product—International Business Machines Corporation; *U.S. Public*, pg. 895

SQS—Surgical Staplers—U.S. Surgical Corp.; *U.S. Public*, pg. 1687

SR—NONE—Lawter International, Inc.; *U.S. Public*, pg. 980

SRAM—Computer Peripherals—Micron Technology Inc.; *U.S. Public*, pg. 1105

SRC—Abrasion Resistant Coatings—Red Spot Paint & Varnish Co.; *U.S. Private*, pg. 915

SRDS—Media Publications—SRDS; *U.S. Private*, pg. 958

SRF—Interfacings—Specialty Textile Products; *U.S. Private*, pg. 1023

SR-500—Passive Silver Recovery Units—LogEtronics Corporation; *U.S. Public*, pg. 6

SRL—Pumps—Svedala Pumps & Process; *Int'l*, pg. 1325

SRM—Rotary Recorder—Bell & Howell Holdings; *U.S. Public*, pg. 201

SR1—Automated Immunoassay Analyzer—BioChem ImmunoSystems, Inc.; *Int'l*, pg. 196

SR1—NONE—BioChem Pharma Inc.; *Int'l*, pg. 196

SR-1000—Passive Silver Recovery Unites—LogEtronics Corporation; *U.S. Public*, pg. 6

SR SERIES—Ink Jet Imager—Videojet Systems International, Inc.; *Int'l*, pg. 545

SR-2000—Passive Silver Recovery Units—LogEtronics Corporation; *U.S. Public*, pg. 6

SRX-501—Automatic Medical Film Processor—Konica Corporation; *Int'l*, pg. 748

S-ROUNDS—Electrolytic Nickel—Inco Limited; *Int'l*, pg. 672

SS AMERIKANIS—Ship—Celebrity Cruises, Inc.; *U.S. Public*, pg. 1410

SSB—Servo Stepper Front End Brake—Electroid Co.; *U.S. Private*, pg. 369

SS BRITANIS—Ship—Celebrity Cruises, Inc.; *U.S. Public*, pg. 1410

SSD—Pharmaceuticals—Knoll Pharmaceutical Company; *Int'l*, pg. 105

S.S.H.—Stop the Smoking Habit—Health Products Corporation; *U.S. Private*, pg. 514

SSI-ADEPT—NONE—Survey Sampling, Inc.; *U.S. Private*, pg. 1056

SSI CLENSICAIR—Incontinence Management System—Hillenbrand Industries, Inc.; *U.S. Public*, pg. 828

SSI-LITE—NONE—Survey Sampling, Inc.; *U.S. Private*, pg. 1056

SSI-SNAP—On-Line Sampling Software—Survey Sampling, Inc.; *U.S. Private*, pg. 1056

SSK—Mineral Insulated Heating Cables—Thermon Manufacturing Company; *U.S. Private*, pg. 1080

SSN GUM—Anti Smoking Gum—Health Products Corporation; *U.S. Private*, pg. 514

S.S. PIERCE SPIRITS—Vodka, Gin, Scotch, Rum—M.S. Walker, Inc.; *U.S. Private*, pg. 1147

SSQ—Single Stage Quadrupole Mass Spectrometer—Finnigan Corporation; *U.S. Public*, pg. 1591

SSR—Building Materials—Varco-Pruden Buildings; *U.S. Public*, pg. 1677

SSR-100—Blended Rope—The American Group; *U.S. Private*, pg. 56

SSR-101—Blended Rope—The American Group; *U.S. Private*, pg. 56

SSR-301-R—Blended Rope—The American Group; *U.S. Private*, pg. 56

SSR-1200—NONE—The American Group; *U.S. Private*, pg. 56

S/S RADIAL—Tires—Bridgestone/Firestone, Inc.; *Int'l*, pg. 213

SSS—Cage Layer System or Cages—CTB International Corp.; *U.S. Public*, pg. 284

SST—(Single Service Cloth Towel Dispenser)—Steiner Co., Inc.; *U.S. Private*, pg. 1039

SSTE—Horizontal Process Cameras—Nuarc Company, Inc.; *U.S. Private*, pg. 808

SSVG SILICON CARBIDE SUPER VELOCITY GAS—Burner—Hauck Mfg. Co.; *U.S. Private*, pg. 510

S SCREEN—Stock Preparation—Beloit Corporation; *U.S. Public*, pg. 789

S-SERIES—Truck—Chevrolet Motor Div. General Motors Corp.; *U.S. Public*, pg. 720

S-660—Tires—Bridgestone/Firestone, Inc.; *Int'l*, pg. 213

S-SPAN—Building Systems—Behlen Mfg. Co.; *U.S. Private*, pg. 130

ST—Rotor Used in Banbury Mixer—Farrel Corporation; *U.S. Public*, pg. 614

ST—Lightguide Cable Connector—Lucent Technologies Inc.; *U.S. Public*, pg. 1017

ST—Underground Monitoring Equipment—Marley Pump; *U.S. Public*, pg. 1676

ST—Polysulfide Rubber—Morton International Inc.; *U.S. Public*, pg. 1135

ST—Automotive Tires—Sime Darby Berhad; *Int'l*, pg. 1249

STD—Video Game & PC Joysticks—Recoton Corporation; *U.S. Public*, pg. 1369

STG & DEVICE—Books—John Wiley & Sons, Inc.; *U.S. Public*, pg. 1768

STL—NONE—Western Atlas Logging Services; *U.S. Public*, pg. 1757

STM118—Sonet Transmission Manager—Network Equipment Technologies, Inc.; *U.S. Public*, pg. 1168

ST-1000—Communications Controller—Tandem Computers Inc.; *U.S. Public*, pg. 417

STP—Automotive Products—First Brands Corporation; *U.S. Public*, pg. 626

STP—Oil Treatment—STP Corporation; *U.S. Public*, pg. 627

STS 900—Squash Racquet—Ektelon; *U.S. Private*, pg. 884

STS 600—Squash Racquet—Ektelon; *U.S. Private*, pg. 884

ST SERIES—Submersible Trash Pump—The Gorman-Rupp Company; *U.S. Public*, pg. 754

S.T. 37—Liquid Antiseptic Solution—Menley & James Laboratories, Inc.; *U.S. Public*, pg. 1086

S/390—Computer System—International Business Machines Corporation; *U.S. Public*, pg. 895

S/370—Computer System—International Business Machines Corporation; *U.S. Public*, pg. 895

S25—Fertilizer—PCS Nitrogen; *Int'l*, pg. 1064

S-26—Nutritional Formula—Wyeth Australia Pty. Ltd.; *U.S. Public*, pg. 82

S-26 INFASOY—NONE—Wyeth Australia Pty. Ltd.; *U.S. Public*, pg. 82

S-26 INFASOY PROGRESS—NONE—Wyeth Australia Pty. Ltd.; *U.S. Public*, pg. 82

S-26 PROGRESS—NONE—Wyeth Australia Pty. Ltd.; *U.S. Public*, pg. 82

S-23—Coating Pigment—Engelhard Corporation; *U.S. Public*, pg. 582

S-22—Predispersed Coating Pigment—Engelhard Corporation; *U.S. Public*, pg. 582

SII—Photographic Paper & Chemicals—Eastman Kodak Company; *U.S. Public*, pg. 550

S-211—Tires—Bridgestone/Firestone, Inc.; *Int'l*, pg. 213

S-2 GLASS—Glass Yarns, Filaments, Strands and Rovings—Owens Corning; *U.S. Public*, pg. 1236

S2H2—NONE—Callaway Golf Company; *U.S. Public*, pg. 294

SU—Engine System—Echlin Inc.; *U.S. Public*, pg. 560

SUS—Clay-Coated Paperboard—Riverwood International Corporation; *U.S. Public*, pg. 1391

SVG SUPERVELOCITY GAS BURNER—Gas Burner—Hauck Mfg. Co.; *U.S. Private*, pg. 510

SVL—HID Vertical Lamp—Stonco Genlyte; *U.S. Public*, pg. 730

S.V.R. KITS—Clinical Chemistry Reagents—Dade Behring Inc.; *U.S. Private*, pg. 110

SVS APEX PLUS—Ophthalmic Laser—Summit Technology, Inc.; *U.S. Public*, pg. 1528

SX—Calendered Promotional Vinyl—Fasson Films; *U.S. Public*, pg. 153

SX—Self-Limiting Heating Cables—Thermon Manufacturing Company; *U.S. Private*, pg. 1080

SX COBRA—Sterndrive—Volvo Penta of the Americas, Inc.; *Int'l*, pg. 1477

SX DIESEL—Diesel Sterndrive—Volvo Penta of the Americas, Inc.; *Int'l*, pg. 1477

SX-50—Digital PABX—Mitel Corporation; *Int'l*, pg. 870

SXM—Computer System—International Business Machines Corporation; *U.S. Public*, pg. 895

SX-100—Telephone Switching System—Mitel Corporation; *Int'l*, pg. 870

SX-20—Telephone Switching System—Mitel Corporation; *Int'l*, pg. 870

SX-200—Analog PABX—Mitel Corporation; *Int'l*, pg. 870

SX-200 DIGITAL—Digital PABX—Mitel Corporation; *Int'l*, pg. 870

SX-200 LIGHT—Fiber Distributed PBX—Mitel Corporation; *Int'l*, pg. 870

SX-2000—Digital Switching System—Mitel Corporation; *Int'l*, pg. 870

SX-2000 LIGHT—Fiber Distributed PBX—Mitel Corporation; *Int'l*, pg. 870

SX-2000 MICRO LIGHT—Fiber Distributed PBX—Mitel Corporation; *Int'l*, pg. 870

SPX—Drilling Tool With Diamonds—Smith International, Inc.; *U.S. Public*, pg. 1478

SAAB—Military Aircraft—Saab AB; *Int'l*, pg. 686

SAASEN—Hiking/Walking Footwear—K-Swiss Inc.; *U.S. Public*, pg. 937

SABATIER—Cutlery—McPherson's Limited; *Int'l*, pg. 852

SABEL—Shoes—P.W. Minor & Son, Inc.; *U.S. Private*, pg. 751

SABENA—NONE—Sabena; *Int'l*, pg. 1168

SABENA—International World Airlines—Sabena Belgian World Airlines; *Int'l*, pg. 1168

SABER—NONE—Oshkosh Truck Corporation; *U.S. Public*, pg. 1233

SABER—Apparel & Fabric—I. Spiewak & Sons, Inc.; *U.S. Private*, pg. 1025

SABER POINT SCREWS—Self Drilling Sheetmetal Screws—Duro Dyne Corporation; *U.S. Private*, pg. 349

SABER-TOOTH—Self Drilling Anchors—Powers Fastening, Inc.; *U.S. Private*, pg. 878

SABIAN CYMBALS—Cymbals—Hohner/HSS Inc.; *U.S. Private*, pg. 533

SABIEM—NONE—Kone Corporation; *Int'l*, pg. 746

SABLE—Beauty Salon Furniture—Belvedere Company; *U.S. Private*, pg. 1008

SABLE—Car—Ford Motor Company; *U.S. Public*, pg. 661

SABLE—Ethnic Hair Care Applicances—Helen of Troy Corporation; *U.S. Public*, pg. 807

SABLE CREEK—Aluminum Siding and Accessories—Alcoa Building Products, Inc.; *U.S. Public*, pg. 61

SABLIME—Computer Programs, Software—Lucent Technologies Inc.; *U.S. Public*, pg. 1017

SABO—Walk-Behind Mowers—Deere & Company; *U.S. Public*, pg. 491

SABOR—NONE—American Greetings Corporation; *U.S. Public*, pg. 77

SABRA—Apple Juice—Brooklyn Bottling Co. of Milton, NY; *U.S. Private*, pg. 171

SABRA—Liqueur—The Seagram Company Ltd.; *Int'l*, pg. 1214

SABRE—Motorcycle—American Honda Motor Co., Inc. Motorcycle Division; *Int'l*, pg. 634

SABRE—Machining Centre—Cincinnati Milacron U.K. Limited; *U.S. Public*, pg. 368

SABRE—Electrosurgery Generator—Conmed Corporation; *U.S. Public*, pg. 431

SABRE—Lawn Tractors—Deere & Company; *U.S. Public*, pg. 491

SABRE—Engineering Resin—The Dow Chemical Company; *U.S. Public*, pg. 522

SABRE—NONE—Everest & Jennings, Inc.; *U.S. Public*, pg. 758

SABRELOC—Spatula Needles—Ethicon, Inc.; *U.S. Public*, pg. 928

SABRIL—Antiepileptic Agent—Hoechst Marion Roussel North America; *Int'l*, pg. 625

SABRINA—Toys—Hasbro; *U.S. Public*, pg. 797

SABRO—Bacteriological Analysis Equip.—Ionics, Incorporated; *U.S. Public*, pg. 912

SABRO—Decaffeinated Coffee—Reily Foods & Co.; *U.S. Public*, pg. 919

SABROSA COFFEE LIQUEUR—NONE—Barton Brands, Ltd.; *U.S. Public*, pg. 300

SABROSO—Coffee Liqueur—Barton Incorporated; *U.S. Public*, pg. 300

SACHS—Automotive Components; Clutches & Shocks—Sachs Boge of America; *Int'l*, pg. 835

SACK & SAVE—SUPERMARKET—Jitney-Jungle Stores of America, Inc.; *U.S. Private*, pg. 588

SACKNER—Automotive, Mobile Home & Boat Padding & Trim—Sackner Products; *U.S. Public*, pg. 924

SACMOBILE—Luggage—Lark Luggage Company, Inc.; *U.S. Public*, pg. 1430

SACONS.EDI—NONE—CACI International Inc; *U.S. Public*, pg. 272

SACONS-FEDERAL—Automated Contracting System, Conforms with Federal Procurement Standards—CACI International Inc; *U.S. Public*, pg. 272

SACOX—Animal Health Products—Hoechst Aktiengesellschaft; *Int'l*, pg. 624

SACRAMENTO JAGUAR, INC.—New Car Dealer—Sacramento Jaguar, Inc.; *U.S. Private*, pg. 1143

SACRAMENTO KINGS—Professional Basketball Team—Sacramento Kings; *U.S. Private*, pg. 959

SADANO'S—Dry Soup Mixes & Side Dishes—Genesee Corporation; *U.S. Public*, pg. 728

SADDLE KING—Western Jeans—Key Industries, Inc.; *U.S. Private*, pg. 618

SADDLE MATE—Cross Box—Reading Body Works, Inc.; *U.S. Private*, pg. 913

SADDLE MOUNTAIN—Wine—Stimson Lane Ltd.; *U.S. Public*, pg. 1661

SADDLE-UP—Horse Feeds—Manna Pro Corporation; *U.S. Private*, pg. 700

SADDLEBROOKE RESORT COMMUNITY—Active Adult Community In Tucson—Robson Communities; *U.S. Private*, pg. 937

SADDLEPACK—Beverage Cooler—Igloo Products Corporation; *U.S. Public*, pg. 265

SADDLER—Leather Goods—Hugo Bosca Co., Inc.; *U.S. Private*, pg. 160

SADIA—NONE—Sadia Group; *Int'l*, pg. 1168

SADIE BUFFETS—NONE—Morrison Restaurants, Inc.; *U.S. Public*, pg. 1134

SADLIER—Religious Programs & Books—William H. Sadlier, Inc.; *U.S. Public*, pg. 1422

SADLIER-OXFORD—Publications of Academic Programs—William H. Sadlier, Inc.; *U.S. Public*, pg. 1422

SAETA—Insecticides—Nuevo Federal S.A.; *Int'l*, pg. 990

SAF-EAR-SHIELD—Ear Protection—U.S. Safety; *U.S. Private*, pg. 1125

SAF-I-CHEM—Eye Protection—U.S. Safety; *U.S. Private*, pg. 1125

SAF-I-CHIPPER—Goggles—U.S. Safety; *U.S. Private*, pg. 1125

SAF-I-FLEX—Eye Protection—U.S. Safety; *U.S. Private*, pg. 1125

SAF-I-GARD—Lenses—U.S. Safety; *U.S. Private*, pg. 1125

SAF-I-WELD—Welders Helmet & Goggles—U.S. Safety; *U.S. Private*, pg. 1125

SAF-T-BLEND—Surgical Gown—Medline Industries, Inc.; *U.S. Private*, pg. 728

SAF-T-CATH—I.V. Catheter Placement Unit—Becton Dickinson & Company; *U.S. Public*, pg. 199

SAF-T-GAP—Height Contacts—Pass & Seymour/Legrand; *Int'l*, pg. 806

SAF-T-GARD—Closing Speed Governor—Cornell Iron Works, Inc.; *U.S. Private*, pg. 276

SAF-T-HOOK—Hooks—Republic Fastener Products Corp.; *U.S. Public*, pg. 923

SAF-T-LOK—Inner Safety Tires—Bridgestone/Firestone, Inc.; *Int'l*, pg. 213

SAF-T-POPS—Suckers—Spangler Candy Company; *U.S. Private*, pg. 1020

SAF-T-SWEEP—Metal Backed Push Brooms with Orange Colored Fill Material—Felton Brush Inc.; *U.S. Private*, pg. 400

SAF-TWIST—Respirator—U.S. Safety; *U.S. Private*, pg. 1125

SAF-RITE—Accounting System—Master Craft Corp.; *Int'l*, pg. 267

SAF-T-LINK—Gas Hose Connector—T & S Brass & Bronze Works, Inc.; *U.S. Private*, pg. 1061

SAF-T-PUMP—Pump—Fisher Scientific Company; *U.S. Private*, pg. 658

SAFACID—Fatty Acids—Pronova Oleochemicals a.s.; *Int'l*, pg. 961

SAFARI—Toiletries—Cosmair, Inc., Ralph Lauren Fragrance Division; *Int'l*, pg. 818

SAFARI—NONE—Guinness Plc; *Int'l*, pg. 412

SAFARI—Stationary Products—The Mead Corporation; *U.S. Public*, pg. 1074

SAFARI—Interior Walls and Countertops—Monarch Tile, Inc.; *U.S. Public*, pg. 287

SAFARI—Car—Nissan Motor Co., Ltd.; *Int'l*, pg. 943

SAFARI AWR—Tire—The Kelly-Springfield Tire Company; *U.S. Public*, pg. 753

SAFARI CSR—Tire—The Kelly-Springfield Tire Company; *U.S. Public*, pg. 753

SAFARI MSR—Tire—The Kelly-Springfield Tire Company; *U.S. Public*, pg. 753

SAFARI XT—Truck—General Motors Corporation; *U.S. Public*, pg. 718

SAFE & SOFT—Feminine Hygiene Product—The Tranzonic Companies; *U.S. Public*, pg. 1632

SAFE-GARD—Crutches—Medline Industries, Inc.; *U.S. Private*, pg. 728

SAFE-GARD—Closure Innerseal—3M; *U.S. Public*, pg. 1604

SAFE-GRIND—Scientific Glassware for Laboratory Use—Wheaton Inc.; *U.S. Private*, pg. 67

SAFE-GUARD—Slings—Macwhyte Co.; *U.S. Private*, pg. 68

SAFE MOVE—Insurance Products—U-Haul International, Inc.; *U.S. Private*, pg. 49

SAFE-PAK—NONE—Gems Sensors; *U.S. Public*, pg. 481

SAFE POWER—UPS/SPS Powerline Conditioners & Surge Suppressors; UPS Monitoring Software—Acme Electric Corporation; *U.S. Public*, pg. 16

SAFE-RELEASE—Masking Tape—3M; *U.S. Public*, pg. 1604

SAFE STOR—Insurance Products—U-Haul International, Inc.; *U.S. Private*, pg. 49

SAFE-T—Control Heads Utilized In Marine Steering Assemblies—Teleflex Incorporated; *U.S. Public*, pg. 1569

SAFE-T-GRIP—Fuse Puller—Ideal Industries, Inc.; *U.S. Private*, pg. 557

SAFE-T-LIP—Dock Levelers—Rite-Hite Corporation (WI); *U.S. Private*, pg. 933

SAFE-T-NET—Data Security Products—Tandem Computers Inc.; *U.S. Public*, pg. 417

SAFE-T-SALT—Salt—Morton Salt; *U.S. Public*, pg. 1135

SAFE-T-TOUCH—Gym Sets—Hedstrom Corporation; *U.S. Private*, pg. 526

SAFE-T-TREADS—Safety Footwear—Alba-Waldensian, Inc.; *U.S. Public*, pg. 35

SAFE-T-VAPOR—Fail-Safe Mercury Vapor Lamps—Duro-Test Corporation; *U.S. Private*, pg. 349

SAFE-T-VUE—Acrylic Sheet—ICI Acrylics Inc.; *Int'l*, pg. 663

SAFE-T-ZONE—Safety Showers—Speakman Company; *U.S. Private*, pg. 1021

SAFE-TIGUE—Vinyl Floor Matting—3M; *U.S. Public*, pg. 1604

SAFE-TOP—Closure for Composite Cans—Sonoco Products Company; *U.S. Public*, pg. 1485

SAFE-WRAP—Latex-Free Elastic Bandage—Medline Industries, Inc.; *U.S. Private*, pg. 728

SAFE-COTE—Bottle—Fisher Scientific Company; *U.S. Private*, pg. 658

SAFEBAC—Table Tracking Systems—Mikohn Gaming Corporation; *U.S. Public*, pg. 1111

SAFECO—Insurance Company—SAFECO Insurance Co. of America; *U.S. Public*, pg. 1423

SAFEGAMES—Table Tracking Systems—Mikohn Gaming Corporation; *U.S. Public*, pg. 1111

SAFEGARD—Computer Database Configuration—Beckman Instruments, Inc.; *U.S. Public*, pg. 199

SAFEGUARD—Centrifuge—Becton Dickinson Primary Care Diagnostics; *U.S. Public*, pg. 199

SAFEGUARD—Soap—The Procter & Gamble Company; *U.S. Public*, pg. 1330

SAFEGUARD—NONE—Procter & Gamble Venezuela, C.A.; *U.S. Public*, pg. 1332

SAFEGUARD—Data Security Software—Tandem Computers Inc.; *U.S. Public*, pg. 417

SAFEGUARD—Safety Device for Garage Door—Wayne Dalton of Sterling; *U.S. Private*, pg. 1155

SAFEJACK—Table Tracking Systems—Mikohn Gaming Corporation; *U.S. Public*, pg. 1111

SAFENET/ENTERPRISE—Virtual Private Networking Solutions—CyberGuard Corporation; *U.S. Public*, pg. 470

SAFER—Pest Control Products—Ringer Corporation; *U.S. Public*, pg. 1390

SAFERIM—Can Ends—Georgia-Pacific Corporation; *U.S. Public*, pg. 735

SAFESITE—Polycarbonate Ophthalmic Lenses—Sterling Vision, Inc.; *U.S. Public*, pg. 1516

SAFEST STRIPPER—Wood Refinishing Products—3M; *U.S. Public*, pg. 1604

SAFESTART—I.V. Start Kit with Gloves—Becton Dickinson & Company; *U.S. Public*, pg. 199

SAFESTEP—Vinyl Floorcoverings—Forbo Holding SA; *Int'l*, pg. 496

SAFETAP—Spinal Needle—The Kendall Company; *U.S. Public*, pg. 1647

SAFETEMP—Sterile Disposable Covers for Glass & Electronic Thermometers—Mallinckrodt Inc.; *U.S. Public*, pg. 1039

SAFETIP—Catheter—Medtronic, Inc.; *U.S. Public*, pg. 1082

SAFETRAC—NONE—SunGard Data Systems Inc.; *U.S. Public*, pg. 1534

SAFETY ALERT—Radar Detectors—Cobra Electronics Corporation; *U.S. Public*, pg. 391

SAFETY ASSURANCE LOGIC—System—General Railway Signal Corp.; *Int'l*, pg. 1194

SAFETY COUNTS—Service Products—R&B, Inc.; *U.S. Public*, pg. 1354

SAFETY CUTTERS—Safety Carton Cutter—Pacific Handy Cutter, Inc.; *U.S. Private*, pg. 831

SAFETY DRAIN—Closed Drain Used to Empty the Ventilator Circuit of Condensate—Ballard Medical Products; *U.S. Public*, pg. 171

SAFETY 1ST—Child Care & Home Security Products—Safety 1st, Inc.; *U.S. Public*, pg. 1425

SAFETY FLOAT—Flat Glass—Guardian Industries Corp.; *U.S. Private*, pg. 485

SAFETY FLOW—Lab Fume Hoods—Fisher Scientific Company; *U.S. Private*, pg. 658

SAFETY GLAZE—Flat Glass—Guardian Industries Corp.; *U.S. Private*, pg. 485

SAFETY GRIP—Utility Knife With Safety Grip and Ridges for Firm Hold—Pacific Handy Cutter, Inc.; *U.S. Private*, pg. 831

SAFETY-GRIP GRATING—NONE—CGC Inc.; *U.S. Public*, pg. 1660

SAFETY-HEAD—Centrifuge—Becton Dickinson Primary Care Diagnostics; *U.S. Public*, pg. 199

SAFETY-KLEEN—Parts Cleaner Services, Dry Cleaner Services—Safety-Kleen Corp.; *U.S. Public*, pg. 1425

SAFETY-LUBE-SUPER—Die Lubricant—Chem-Trend Incorporated; *Int'l*, pg. 235

SAFETY-MATE—Goggles—U.S. Safety; *U.S. Private*, pg. 1125

SAFETY ORANGE—Electrical Wiring Equipment: Cord Sets, Trouble Lights & Cable—General Cable Corporation; *Int'l*, pg. 1486

SAFETY POINT—Blades—Pacific Handy Cutter, Inc.; *U.S. Private*, pg. 831

SAFETY SHIELD—Health Care Workers Protection—Ballard Medical Products; *U.S. Public*, pg. 171

SAFETY SHOWER ALARM—Safety Alarms—Falcon Safety Products Inc.; *U.S. Private*, pg. 392

SAFETY SKIDS—Slippers—Medline Industries, Inc.; *U.S. Private*, pg. 728

SAFETY STRIPES—NONE—Rubbermaid Incorporated; *U.S. Public*, pg. 1411

SAFETY-TREAD GRATING—NONE—CGC Inc.; *U.S. Public*, pg. 1660

SAFETY-WALK—Antislip Surfacing Material, Pulley Lagging—3M; *U.S. Public*, pg. 1604

SAFETY YELLOW—Electrical Prods.—Woodhead Industries, Inc.; *U.S. Public*, pg. 1776

THE SAFETY ZONE—Direct Marketing of Safety & Anti-Hazard Products—Hanover Direct, Inc.; *U.S. Public*, pg. 782

SAFETYSIGNAL—Service Indicator—Donaldson Company, Inc.; *U.S. Public*, pg. 517

SAFEWATCH—Residential Security System—ADT Security Services, Inc.; *U.S. Public*, pg. 1649

SAFEWAY—Food & Non-Food Products—Safeway Inc.; *U.S. Public*, pg. 1426

SAFEWAY—Retail Stores—Safeway PLC; *Int'l*, pg. 1169

SAFEWAY—Envelopes—Westvaco Corporation; *U.S. Public*, pg. 1762

SAFEWAY SELECT—Premium Private Label Brand—Safeway Inc.; *U.S. Public*, pg. 1426

SAFFOLA—Margarine, Salad Oil & Mayonnaise—Ventura Foods LLC; *Int'l*, pg. 879

SAFLEX—Polyvinyl Butyral Sheet—Monsanto Company; *U.S. Public*, pg. 1124

SAFPOWRBAR—Electrification—Shepard Niles, Inc.; *U.S. Private*, pg. 992

SAFROTIN—Insecticide—Novartis AG; *Int'l*, pg. 971

SAFTY—NONE—Stuart Entertainment Inc.; *U.S. Public*, pg. 1526

SAG HARBOR—NONE—Kellwood Company; *U.S. Public*, pg. 948

SAGA—Ball Point Pen—Sanford Corporation; *U.S. Public*, pg. 1178

SAGAMICIN—Antibiotics—Kyowa Hakko Kogyo Company, Ltd.; *Int'l*, pg. 778

SAGE SYSTEMS—High Pressure Spray Cleaners—T & S Brass & Bronze Works, Inc.; *U.S. Private*, pg. 1061

SAGINAW—Steering Gears—General Motors Corporation; *U.S. Public*, pg. 718

THE SAGINAW NEWS—Newspaper—Booth Newspapers, Inc.; *U.S. Private*, pg. 157

SAGRES—Beer—Central de Cervejas, S.A.; *Int'l*, pg. 279

SAGROTAN—Surface Care—Reckitt & Colman plc; *Int'l*, pg. 1089

SAHARA—Pita Bread—Bestfoods; *U.S. Public*, pg. 223

SAHARA—Bread—CPC Baking Business; *U.S. Public*, pg. 224

SAHARA—Masonry Coating—Davis Paint Company; *U.S. Private*, pg. 315

SAHARA—Glazed Ceramic Tile—Porcelanite, Inc.; *Int'l*, pg. 573

SAHARA & DESIGN—Cookware—Regal Ware, Inc.; *U.S. Private*, pg. 917

SAIGON SIZZLE—Stir-Fry Sauce—Hormel Foods Corp.; *U.S. Public*, pg. 840

SAIL TOBACCO—Pipe Tobaccos—Consolidated Cigar Corporation; *U.S. Private*, pg. 690

SAILMASTER—Outboard Motors—Johnson Outboards Marine Corp.; *U.S. Private*, pg. 478

SAIMAZA—Coffee—Philip Morris Companies Inc.; *U.S. Public*, pg. 1287

SAINSBURY'S—Grocery Products—J. Sainsbury plc; *Int'l*, pg. 1169

ST. ALBRAY—Cheese—Bongrain S.A.; *Int'l*, pg. 201

ST. ANDREWS—Toiletries—International Cosmetics Co., Ltd.; *Int'l*, pg. 684

SAINT ANDREWS HOMES—Nursing Homes—Vaux Group Plc; *Int'l*, pg. 1453

ST. AUGUSTINE RECORD—Newspaper—Shivers Trading & Operating Co.; *U.S. Private*, pg. 994

ST. BRUNO—Pipe Tobacco—Hanson PLC; *Int'l*, pg. 592

ST. BRUNO—Ready Rubbed Flake Pipe Tobacco—Imperial Tobacco Group, Ltd.; *Int'l*, pg. 666

ST. CLEMENT—Winery—Sapporo Breweries Ltd.; *Int'l*, pg. 1193

ST. CROIX—Paper Pulp, Printing Papers—Georgia-Pacific Corporation; *U.S. Public*, pg. 735

ST. CYR—Sparkling Bath Oil—Benjamin Ansehl Company; *U.S. Private*, pg. 75

ST. CYR—French Brandy—Peerless Importers, Inc.; *U.S. Private*, pg. 847

ST. GENEVIEVE—Hinged Patio Door Series—Biltbest Windows; *U.S. Public*, pg. 1683

ST. HUBERT 41—Low Fat Spread—Unigate PLC; *Int'l*, pg. 1433

ST. IDES—Malt Liquor—The Stroh Brewery Company; *U.S. Private*, pg. 1047

ST. IVEL & SHAPE—Dairy Products—Unigate PLC; *Int'l*, pg. 1433

ST. IVES SWISS FORMULA—NONE—Alberto-Culver Company; *U.S. Public*, pg. 37

ST. JOHN'S BAY—Clothing—JC Penney Company, Inc.; *U.S. Public*, pg. 916

ST. JOHN'S WORT—NONE—Celestial Seasonings; *U.S. Public*, pg. 319

ST. JOSEPH—Adult Chewable Aspirin—Schering-Plough Corporation; *U.S. Public*, pg. 1438

ST. JOSEPH—Children's Aspirin Products—Schering-Plough Healthcare Products Inc.; *U.S. Public*, pg. 1438

ST. JUDE MEDICAL—Heart Valve Hemodynamic Plus Series—St. Jude Medical, Inc.; *U.S. Public*, pg. 1427

ST. JUDE MEDICAL—Mechanical Heart Valve—St. Jude Medical, Inc.; *U.S. Public*, pg. 1427

ST. JULIEN VIRGINIA—Pipe Tobacco—Imperial Tobacco Group, Ltd.; *Int'l*, pg. 666

ST. LAURENCE—Coated One-Side/Gloss & Cream Gloss—Appleton Papers Inc.; *Int'l*, pg. 567

ST. LAURENCE CIS—Coated One-Side—Appleton Papers Inc.; *Int'l*, pg. 567

ST. LAWRENCE—Corn Oil—Bestfoods; *U.S. Public*, pg. 223

ST. LEONARD—Wines & Spirits—Leonard Kreusch, Inc.; *U.S. Private*, pg. 635

SAINT-LOUIS—Crystalware—Hermes International; *Int'l*, pg. 617

SAINT LOUIS BREAD—Croissants & Bread—Au Bon Pain Co., Inc.; *U.S. Public*, pg. 146

ST. LOUIS BUSINESS JOURNAL—Business Journal—Business First of New York, Inc.; *U.S. Private*, pg. 19

ST. LOUIS CARDINALS—Baseball team—St. Louis National Baseball Club L.P.; *U.S. Private*, pg. 961

ST. LOUIS MAGAZINE—Business Magazine—Business First of New York, Inc.; *U.S. Private*, pg. 19

ST. LOUIS POST-DISPATCH—Newspapers—St. Louis Post-Dispatch; *U.S. Public*, pg. 1343

ST. MARC/MARC—Hardsurface Cleaner—Benckiser Consumer Products Inc.; *Int'l*, pg. 185

ST. MARCUS—Home Textile—CYDSA S.A.; *Int'l*, pg. 246

ST. MARYS—Blankets, Automatic Blankets, Bedspreads, Sheets, Towels, Comforters & Bath—Fieldcrest Cannon, Inc.; *U.S. Public*, pg. 1296

ST. MICHAEL—Clothing & Footwear—Marks & Spencer PLC; *Int'l*, pg. 842

ST. MICHEL—Cigarettes-Belgium/Luxembourg—R.J. Reynolds Tobacco Intl., Inc.; *U.S. Public*, pg. 1355

ST. MORITZ—Cigarettes—Rothmans UK Holdings Limited; *Int'l*, pg. 1129

ST. PAULI GIRL—Lager, Dark & Non-Alcoholic—Barton Beers, Ltd.; *U.S. Public*, pg. 300

ST. PETERSBURG TIMES—Newspaper—St. Petersburg Times; *U.S. Private*, pg. 1088

ST. PETERSBURG TIMES—Daily Newspaper—The Times Publishing Co.; *U.S. Private*, pg. 1087

ST. RAPHAEL—NONE—Bacardi-Martini Belgium; *U.S. Private*, pg. 109

ST. REGIS PAPER BAGS—Paper Bags—Puerto Rican Cement Co., Inc.; *U.S. Public*, pg. 1341

ST. SIMONS ISLAND CLUB—Residential Devel.—Sea Island Company; *U.S. Private*, pg. 977

SAIRMIX-7—Wet Temperature Air Setting Bonding Mortar—A.P. Green Industries, Inc.; *U.S. Public*, pg. 761

'SAIRSET—Mortar—A.P. Green Industries, Inc.; *U.S. Public*, pg. 761

SAIWA—Biscuits—Danone Group; *Int'l*, pg. 379

SAIZEN—Recombinant Human Growth Hormone—Ares-Serono S.A.; *Int'l*, pg. 89

SAKATA—NONE—Sakata Seed Corporation; *Int'l*, pg. 1178

SAKRETE—Cement Mixes; Driveway Sealers—American Stone-Mix, Inc.; *U.S. Private*, pg. 62

SAKRETE—Concrete Mixes—Sakrete, Inc.; *U.S. Private*, pg. 961

SAKS FIFTH AVENUE—Fashion Specialty Stores—Saks Fifth Avenue; *U.S. Public*, pg. 1429

SAKURA RST—Darkroom & Lightroom Processing Equipment—Konica Corporation; *Int'l*, pg. 748

SALAD BAR—NONE—Koo Koo Roo, Inc.; *U.S. Public*, pg. 966

SALAD CELEBRATIONS—NONE—Weight Watchers Gourmet Food Company; *U.S. Public*, pg. 806

SALAD CHEF—Croutons—Snack America; *U.S. Private*, pg. 1010

SALAD CRUNCHIES—Salad Toppings—McCormick/Schilling; *U.S. Public*, pg. 1066

SALAD FRESH—Sulfite-Free Anti-Oxidant—Crompton & Knowles Ingredient Technology Corp.; *U.S. Public*, pg. 459

SALAD LITE AND DESIGN—Salad Dressing—Cains Foods, L.P.; *U.S. Private*, pg. 199

SALAD-MATE—Shredded Cheese Substitute Products—Borden, Inc.; *U.S. Private*, pg. 157

SALAD SHOPPE—Salad Toppings—Alliant Foodservice, Inc.; *U.S. Private*, pg. 244

SALAD SUPREME—Seasoning—McCormick/Schilling; *U.S. Public*, pg. 1066

SALADENA—Goat & Feta Crumbles—Bongrain Cheese USA; *Int'l*, pg. 201

SALADMASTER—Cutler, Coffee Maker, Cookware—Regal Ware, Inc.; *U.S. Private*, pg. 917

SALADMASTER (AND DESIGN)—Cookware—Regal Ware, Inc.; *U.S. Private*, pg. 917

SALADSHOOTER—Electric Slicer/Shredder—National Presto Industries, Inc.; *U.S. Public*, pg. 1159

SALAGEN TABLETS—Drug for Treatment of Radiation-induced Xerostomia—MGI PHARMA INC.; *U.S. Public*, pg. 1026

SALAZOPYRIN—NONE—Pharmacia & Upjohn, Inc.; *Int'l*, pg. 1047

SALEM—Cash Settlement System—Brandt, Inc.; *Int'l*, pg. 387

SALEM—Cigarettes—RJR Nabisco Holdings Corp.; *U.S. Public*, pg. 1354

SALEM—Menthol Reg. & 100's, Lights 100's Menthol & Menthol Box, Ultra Menthol—R.J. Reynolds Tobacco Company; *U.S. Public*, pg. 1355

SALEM—Cigarettes—R.J. Reynolds Tobacco Intl., Inc.; *U.S. Public*, pg. 1355

SALEM—Carpets—Salem Carpet Mills, Inc.; *U.S. Public*, pg. 1464

SALEM PRODUCTS—Hydraulic Valves—The Oilgear Company; *U.S. Public*, pg. 1215

SALES & MARKETING MANAGEMENT—Business Publication—Bill Communications, Inc.; *Int'l*, pg. 1446

THE SALES MANAGER—Vendor—The Vendo Company; *Int'l*, pg. 1184

SALES TRACK—Computerized Sales Routing System—Oil-Dri Corporation of America; *U.S. Public*, pg. 1214

SALESPARTNER—Software—Information Resources, Inc.; *U.S. Public*, pg. 875

SALFLEX—Antiarthritic—Carnrick Laboratories, Inc.; *U.S. Private*, pg. 436

SALICUM—Dextrin Glues—PKL Verpackungssysteme GmbH; *Int'l*, pg. 1020

SALIGNAC—Cognac—Domecq Importers Inc.; *Int'l*, pg. 63

SALIGNAC COGNAC—Spirit—Allied Domecq PLC; *Int'l*, pg. 62

THE SALISBURY COLLECTION—Giftware—Lenox Brands; *U.S. Public*, pg. 261

SALLIE MAE—Corporation Name—SLM Holding Corp.; *U.S. Public*, pg. 1419

SALLIE MAE FIRST CLASS AWARDS—Teaching Awards—SLM Holding Corp.; *U.S. Public*, pg. 1419

SALLY FOSTER GIFTWRAP—NONE—CUC International, Inc.; *U.S. Public*, pg. 320

SALLY HANSEN—Cosmetics—Del Laboratories, Inc.; *U.S. Public*, pg. 494

SALMON CHEF—Value Added Salmon Products—Icicle Seafoods, Inc.; *U.S. Private*, pg. 556

SALON—Toiletry Products—Alberto-Culver Canada, Inc.; *U.S. Public*, pg. 38

SALON & FITNESS SYSTEMS—Mfr. Beauty Salon Furniture & Fitness Equipment—Salon & Fitness Systems; *U.S. Private*, pg. 962

SALON DESIGNS—Professional Beauty Products—Windmere-Durable Holdings; *U.S. Public*, pg. 1771

SALON EDITION—Professional Hair Care Appliances—Helen of Troy Corporation; *U.S. Public*, pg. 807

SALON FORMULA DEP—Shampoos & Conditioners—Dep Corporation; *U.S. Public*, pg. 500

SALON NEWS—Business Publication—Fairchild Publications; *U.S. Public*, pg. 513

SALON NO-LYE—Hair Relaxer—Revlon-Realistic Professional Products, Inc.; *U.S. Private*, pg. 690

SALON POWER—1250 Pro Dryer—Clairol, Inc.; *U.S. Public*, pg. 254

SALON POWER 1500—Professional Dryer—Bristol-Myers Squibb Company; *U.S. Public*, pg. 253

SALON SELECTIVES—Hair Care Line—Helene Curtis Industries, Inc.; *Int'l*, pg. 1434

SALON T-TRIM—Cordless Rechargeable Trimmer—Andis Company; *U.S. Private*, pg. 73

SALSA—Software—Wall Data Incorporated; *U.S. Public*, pg. 1734

SALSA NATURALA—Dips—McCormick/Schilling; *U.S. Public*, pg. 1066

SALT SENSE—Salt Substitute—Akzo Nobel N.V.; *Int'l*, pg. 42

SALT SENSE—Table Salt—Cargill Salt Inc.; *Int'l*, pg. 48

SALT WATER SPORTSMAN—Magazine—Times Mirror Magazines, Inc.; *U.S. Public*, pg. 1616

SALTERINI—Metal Household Furniture—Meadowcraft, Inc.; *U.S. Private*, pg. 725

SALTESEA—Seafoods—Clearwater Fine Foods Inc.; *Int'l*, pg. 297

SALTON HOTRAY—Food Warmer—Salton/Maxim Housewares, Inc.; *U.S. Public*, pg. 1430

SALTY DOG—Sportswear-Sportshirts, Sweaters, Knits, Pants & Dress Shirts—Gant; *U.S. Public*, pg. 1291

SALTY SURFERS—Snack Products—The Quaker Oats Company; *U.S. Public*, pg. 1347

SALURON—Thiazide Diuretic for Diuresis & Lowering Blood Pressure—Bristol-Myers Squibb U.S. Pharmaceutical Group; *U.S. Public*, pg. 255

SALURON—Anti-Hypertensive—Roberts Pharmaceutical Corporation; *U.S. Public*, pg. 1393

SALUTE—NONE—Wacoal Corporation; *Int'l*, pg. 1484

SALUTENSIN—Hypertension Reliever—Bristol-Myers Squibb Company; *U.S. Public*, pg. 253

SALUTENSIN—Pharmaceutical to Lower Blood Pressure—Bristol-Myers Squibb U.S. Pharmaceutical Group; *U.S. Public*, pg. 255

SALUTENSIN—Anti-Hypertensive—Roberts Pharmaceutical Corporation; *U.S. Public*, pg. 1393

SALUTENSIN-DEMI—Thiazide/Reserpine Combination with Half Concentrate—Bristol-Myers Squibb U.S. Pharmaceutical Group; *U.S. Public*, pg. 255

SALVADOR'S MARGARITA—Prepared Cocktail—Hiram Walker; *Int'l*, pg. 63

SAM—Cable Test Equipment—Wavetek Communications Div.; *U.S. Private*, pg. 1155

SAM—Cable Test Equipment—Wavetek Corporation; *U.S. Private*, pg. 1154

SAM GOODY—Pre-Recorded Audio & Video Tapes, Blank Tapes & Accessories—Musicland Group Inc.; *U.S. Public*, pg. 1142

SAMARA—Plywood—Georgia-Pacific Corporation; *U.S. Public*, pg. 735

SAMARITAN—Lift Blocks—Sanderson Plumbing Products Inc.; *U.S. Private*, pg. 964

SAMBUCA DI AMORE—NONE—Barton Brands, Ltd.; *U.S. Private*, pg. 300

SAMBUCA DI TREVI—Liquor—Peerless Importers, Inc.; *U.S. Private*, pg. 847

SAMBVCA ROMANA—Liqueur—Grand Metropolitan Plc; *Int'l*, pg. 408

SAME DAY SERVICE—Expedited Flight-Out Service—DHL Worldwide Express; *U.S. Private*, pg. 301

SAMES—Electrostatics—Binks Sames Corporation; *U.S. Public*, pg. 229

SAMMI II—Man-Machine Interface & Toolkit Software—Scientific Software-Intercomp, Inc.; *U.S. Public*, pg. 1443

SAMMONS ENTERPRISES—Indus. Equip. & Machinery; Ins. Carriers; Bottled Water—Sammons Enterprises, Inc.; *U.S. Private*, pg. 963

SAMOA—Sandals—Sao Paulo Alpargatas S.A.; *Int'l*, pg. 1193

SAMPL-KLIP—Sample Holding Clip—Buehler, Limited; *U.S. Public*, pg. 574

SAMPL-KUP—Cold Mounting Container—Buehler, Limited; *U.S. Public*, pg. 574

SAMPL-KWICK—Curing Epoxy Mounting Compound—Buehler, Limited; *U.S. Public*, pg. 574

SAMPLE MASTER—Biopsy Needles—Medtronic, Inc.; *U.S. Public*, pg. 1082

SAMPLEPOWER—Software to Determine Defensible Sample Size—SPSS Inc.; *U.S. Public*, pg. 1420

SAMPLER—Chocolates—Whitman's Candies, Inc.; *U.S. Private*, pg. 953

SAMPULE—Scientific Glassware for Laboratory Use—Wheaton Inc.; *Int'l*, pg. 67

SAMS—Computer Software—Sterling Software, Inc.; *U.S. Public*, pg. 1516

SAM'S CLUB—NONE—Wal-Mart Stores, Inc.; *U.S. Public*, pg. 1732

SAMSARA—Perfumes—Guerlain, Inc.; *Int'l*, pg. 780

SAMSARA—Fragrance—Guerlain S.A.; *Int'l*, pg. 780

SAMSON—Railroad Brake Shoes—ABC Rail Products Corp.; *U.S. Public*, pg. 2

SAMSON—NONE—The American Group; *U.S. Private*, pg. 56

SAMSON—Cigarette Rolling Tobacco—Consolidated Cigar Corporation; *U.S. Private*, pg. 690

SAMSON—NONE—Fortune Brands, Inc.; *U.S. Public*, pg. 674

SAMSON—NONE—Gallaher Tobacco Ltd.; *Int'l*, pg. 539

SAMSON—Ale—Vaux Group Plc; *Int'l*, pg. 1453

SAMSONITE—Luggage—Samsonite Corporation; *U.S. Public*, pg. 1430

SAMSON'S BIG 4—Twist Tobacco—Conwood Company L.P.; *U.S. Private*, pg. 272

SAMSUNG—Excavators, & Dozers—EEI Corporation; *Int'l*, pg. 425

SAMSUNG—Electronics—Samsung Electronics America; *Int'l*, pg. 1183

SAMUEL ADAMS—Beer—Boston Beer Company; *U.S. Public*, pg. 246

SAMUEL/LAWRENCE—Wood Bedroom Furniture—Sealy Corporation; *U.S. Private*, pg. 978

SAMUEL MEISEL & CO—Sales to Diplomatic Communities & Cruise Ships—Duty Free International, Inc.; *Int'l*, pg. 103

SAMURAI—Cameras—Kyocera Corporation; *Int'l*, pg. 775

SAN ANGELO PINOT GRIGIO—Wine—Banfi Vintners; *U.S. Private*, pg. 113

SAN ANGELO PINOT GRIGIO—NONE—Castello Banfi Srl.; *U.S. Private*, pg. 113

THE SAN ANTONIO BUSINESS JOURNAL—Business Journal—Business First of New York, Inc.; *U.S. Public*, pg. 19

SAN ANTONIO EXPRESS NEWS—Newspaper—The Hearst Corporation; *U.S. Private*, pg. 515

SAN ANTONIO EXPRESS-NEWS—Newspaper—News America Publishing Inc.; *Int'l*, pg. 925

SAN BERNARDO—Mineral Water—Nestle S.A.; *Int'l*, pg. 915

SAN-CURA OINTMENT—Pharmaceutical Product—Thompson Medical Company, Inc.; *U.S. Private*, pg. 1083

SAN DIEGO CHARGERS—Professional Football Team—San Diego Chargers; *U.S. Private*, pg. 964

THE SAN DIEGO UNION-TRIBUNE—Newspaper—San Diego Union Tribune; *U.S. Private*, pg. 275

SAN DONATO CHIANTI—Italian Wine—Laird & Company; *U.S. Private*, pg. 642

SAN FRANCISCO BUSINESS TIMES—Business Journal—Business First of New York, Inc.; *U.S. Private*, pg. 19

SAN FRANCISCO CHRONICLE—Newspaper—San Francisco Newspaper Agency; *U.S. Private*, pg. 239

SAN FRANCISCO COOKIES 'N CREAM—Liqueur—White Rock Distilleries Inc.; *U.S. Private*, pg. 1173

SAN FRANCISCO EXAMINER—Newspaper—The Hearst Corporation; *U.S. Private*, pg. 515

SAN FRANCISCO GIANTS BASEBALL CLUB—Major League Baseball—San Francisco Giants Baseball Club; *U.S. Private*, pg. 964

SAN FRANCISCO KNITWORKS—Sweaters—Hampshire Group, Ltd.; *U.S. Public*, pg. 778

SAN FRANCISCO REALTIES—Real Estate—The Hearst Corporation; *U.S. Private*, pg. 515

SAN GIORGIO—Pasta—Hershey Foods Corporation; *U.S. Public*, pg. 811

SAN GIORGIO—Pasta—Hershey Pasta and Grocery Group; *U.S. Public*, pg. 812

SAN-J—NONE—San-J Intl. Inc.; *Int'l*, pg. 1183

SAN-J GRILLING SAUCE—NONE—San-J Intl. Inc.; *Int'l*, pg. 1183

SAN-J SWEET & SOUR—NONE—San-J Intl. Inc.; *Int'l*, pg. 1183

SAN-J SZECHUAN SAUCE—NONE—San-J Intl. Inc.; *Int'l*, pg. 1183

SAN-J TAMARI REDUCED SODIUM—NONE—San-J Intl. Inc.; *Int'l*, pg. 1183

SAN-J TAMARI SOY SAUCE—NONE—San-J Intl. Inc.; *Int'l*, pg. 1183

SAN-J TERIYAKI—NONE—San-J Intl. Inc.; *Int'l*, pg. 1183

SAN-J THAI PEANUT SAUCE—NONE—San-J Intl. Inc.; *Int'l*, pg. 1183

SAN JOSE MERCURY NEWS—Newspaper—San Jose Mercury News; *U.S. Public*, pg. 964

SAN LUIS OBISPO TELEGRAM-TRIBUNE—J.P. Scripps Newspaper Group Dailies—The E.W. Scripps Company; *U.S. Public*, pg. 1447

SAN MARTIN—California Wines—Shieffelin Somerset Co.; *Int'l*, pg. 412

SAN MIGUEL—Beer—Danone Group; *Int'l*, pg. 379

SAN PEDRO WINES—Wine—Austin Nichols & Co. Inc.; *Int'l*, pg. 566

SAN REGIM—Diet Cheeses—Sancor Cooperativas Unidas Limitadas; *Int'l*, pg. 1183

SAN REMO—Genoa Sausage—Hormel Foods Corp.; *U.S. Public*, pg. 840

SAN ROCCO MERLOT—Italian Wine—Laird & Company; *U.S. Private*, pg. 642

SAN ROCCO MERLOT DOC PIAVE—Italian Wine—Laird & Company; *U.S. Private*, pg. 642

SAN ROCCO PINOT GRIGIO—Italian Wine—Laird & Company; *U.S. Private*, pg. 642

SANROCCO PINOT GRIGIO DOC PIAVE—Italian Wine—Laird & Company; *U.S. Private*, pg. 642

SAN-SIL—Synthetic Precipitated Silica for Papermaking Applications—PPG Industries, Inc.; *U.S. Public*, pg. 1245

SAN VINCENTI CHIANTI CLASSICO—Italian Wine—Laird & Company; *U.S. Private*, pg. 642

SAN VINCENTI CLASSICO RISERVA—Italian Wine—Laird & Company; *U.S. Private*, pg. 642

SANAFLOR—Cushioned Vinyl Floor Coverings—Forbo Holding SA; *Int'l*, pg. 496

SANARA—Hair & Body Care Products—Wella Group; *Int'l*, pg. 1489

SANARIUM—Soft-steambath in Sauna—Klafs Saunabau GmbH & Co. KG Medizinische Technik; *Int'l*, pg. 736

SANBORN—Air Compressors, Air Tools & Air Accessories—Coleman Powermate Compressors; *U.S. Private*, pg. 691

SANCO—Copper Plumbing Tubes Protected Against Corrosion—KM-Europa Metal Aktiengesellschaft; *Int'l*, pg. 719

SANCOR—Dairy Products—Sancor Cooperativas Unidas Limitadas; *Int'l*, pg. 1183

SAND & HIGHWAY—Tires—Bridgestone/Firestone, Inc.; *Int'l*, pg. 213

SAND & SABLE—Cologne—Coty Inc.; *Int'l*, pg. 185

SAND CHAMPION—Tires—Bridgestone/Firestone, Inc.; *Int'l*, pg. 213

SAND DOLLAR—Swimming Pool Pumps—Essef Corporation; *U.S. Public*, pg. 592

SAND PRO—Rakes for Sand Traps—The Toro Company; *U.S. Public*, pg. 1623

SAND TECHNOLOGY—NONE—Sand Technology Systems; *Int'l*, pg. 1183

SANDBERG—Toys—Strombecker Corporation; *U.S. Private*, pg. 1047

SANDCASTLE—Swimwear—Cole of California; *U.S. Public*, pg. 148

SANDELLA—Ladies & Childrens Clothes—Arnotts plc; *Int'l*, pg. 81

SANDEMAN—Ports & Sherries—Seagram Chateau & Estate Wines Co.; *Int'l*, pg. 1215

SANDEN SD—NONE—Sanden International (U.S.A.), Inc.; *Int'l*, pg. 1184

SANDERS—Defense Electronics—Sanders, A Lockheed Martin Company; *U.S. Public*, pg. 1008

SANDERSON FARMS—Fresh & Frozen Foods—Sanderson Farms, Inc.; *U.S. Public*, pg. 1430

SANDHANDLER—4" Submersible Well Pump—Jacuzzi Bros., Jacuzzi, Inc.; *U.S. Public*, pg. 1684

SANDHURST FARMS—Milk, Dairy Products, & Beverages—Q.U.F. Industries Ltd.; *Int'l*, pg. 1074

SANDI—11 1/2" Dolls, Clothes & Accessories—Totsy Manufacturing Company, Inc.; *U.S. Private*, pg. 1093

SANDIMMUN—Immunodepressant—Novartis AG; *Int'l*, pg. 971

SANDIMMUNE—Oral Solution/Gelatin Capsules for Organ Injection in Transplants—Sandoz Pharmaceuticals Corp.; *Int'l*, pg. 974

SANDOCLEAN—Pre-Treatment Chemicals—Clariant International Ltd.; *Int'l*, pg. 624

SANDOCOLOR—Metal Chemicals—Novartis AG; *Int'l*, pg. 971

SANDODERM—Dyes—Clariant International Ltd.; *Int'l*, pg. 624

SANDODERM—Leather Dye—Novartis AG; *Int'l*, pg. 971

SANDOFAN—Fungicide—Novartis AG; *Int'l*, pg. 971

SANDOFIX—Specialty Chemicals—Clariant International Ltd.; *Int'l*, pg. 624

SANDOFLAM—Additives—Clariant International Ltd.; *Int'l*, pg. 624

SANDOFLAM—Flame-Retardant Fiber Finishing Chemical—Novartis AG; *Int'l*, pg. 971

SANDOFLUOR—NONE—Clariant International Ltd.; *Int'l*, pg. 624

SANDOGEN—Dyring Chemicals—Clariant International Ltd.; *Int'l*, pg. 624

SANDOGLOBULIN—Intravenous Gammaglobulin—Novartis AG; *Int'l*, pg. 971

SANDOGLOBULIN—Primary Immunodeficiencies—Sandoz Pharmaceuticals Corp.; *Int'l*, pg. 974

SANDOLAN—Wool—Clariant International Ltd.; *Int'l*, pg. 624

SANDOLIX—Dyes—Clariant International Ltd.; *Int'l*, pg. 624

SANDOLUBE—NONE—Clariant International Ltd.; *Int'l*, pg. 624

SANDOPERM—NONE—Clariant International Ltd.; *Int'l*, pg. 624

SANDOPERSE—NONE—Clariant International Ltd.; *Int'l*, pg. 624

SANDOPUR—Dyeing Chemicals—Clariant International Ltd.; *Int'l*, pg. 624

SANDORIN—Pigments—Clariant International Ltd.; *Int'l*, pg. 624

SANDORIN—Leather Dye—Novartis AG; *Int'l*, pg. 971

SANDOSTAB—Additives—Clariant International Ltd.; *Int'l*, pg. 624

SANDOSTAB P-EPQ—Plastic Additive—Novartis AG; *Int'l*, pg. 971

SANDOSTATIN—Growth Hormone Secretion—Novartis AG; *Int'l*, pg. 971

SANDOSTATIN—Injection for Control of Symptoms of Diarrhea—Sandoz Pharmaceuticals Corp.; *Int'l*, pg. 974

SANDOZEB—Organic Fungicide—Novartis AG; *Int'l*, pg. 971

SANDOZIN—Pre-Treatment Chemicals—Clariant International Ltd.; *Int'l*, pg. 624

SANDPIPER—Plywood, Lumber, Wood & Wood Fiber Products—Georgia-Pacific Corporation; *U.S. Public*, pg. 735

SANDPIPER—Pumps—IDEX Corporation; *U.S. Public*, pg. 862

SANDRIFT—NONE—USG Corporation; *U.S. Public*, pg. 1660

SANDS OCEANFRONT RESORTS—NONE—Sands Investments, Inc.; *U.S. Private*, pg. 964

SANDSLINGER—Foundry Mold Ramming Machine—Pettibone Corporation; *U.S. Private*, pg. 859

SANDTRAP—Filter Featuring Ring-Lok Access—Jacuzzi Bros., Jacuzzi, Inc.; *U.S. Public*, pg. 1684

SANDUSKY SURETY—An On-Site Paper Machine White Water Test Program—Sandusky International Inc.; *U.S. Private*, pg. 964

SANDUVOR—NONE—Clariant International Ltd.; *Int'l*, pg. 624

SANDVIK—Specialty Steel Prods.—Sandvik AB; *Int'l*, pg. 1185

SANDVIK—Carbide Cutting Tools—Sandvik, Inc.; *Int'l*, pg. 1185

SANDVIK COROMANT—Carbide Cutting and Rockdrilling Tools—Sandvik AB; *Int'l*, pg. 1185

SANDWICH CHEF—Deli-Style Restaurant—Wall Street Deli, Inc.; *U.S. Public*, pg. 1734

SANDWICH MAKER—Deli Meats—Hormel Foods Corp.; *U.S. Public*, pg. 840

SANDWICH-MASTER—Microwave Ovens—Litton Industries, Inc.; *U.S. Public*, pg. 1002

SANDWICH-MATE—Sliced Cheese Substitute—Borden, Inc.; *U.S. Private*, pg. 157

THE SANDWICH WORKS—Fresh Sandwiches & Fast Food—White Hen Pantry, Inc.; *U.S. Private*, pg. 1172

SANECTA—Aspartame—DSM N.V.; *Int'l*, pg. 352

SANEK—Towels, Neck Strips—Kimberly-Clark Corporation; *U.S. Public*, pg. 958

SANEX—Hair Care Products—Sara Lee Corporation; *U.S. Public*, pg. 1432

SANFORD—Marks & Writing Instruments—Newell Co.; *U.S. Public*, pg. 1176

SANFORD OIL PASTELS—Art Colors—Sanford Corporation; *U.S. Public*, pg. 1178

SANFORD PLANK—Pre-Finished Laminate—Bruce Hardwood Floors; *U.S. Public*, pg. 1634

SANFORD RUBBER CEMENT—Adhesive—Sanford Corporation; *U.S. Public*, pg. 1178

SANFORD STAMP PADS—Pre-Inked Pads—Sanford Corporation; *U.S. Public*, pg. 1178

SANGEMINI—Still Mineral Water—Sangemini S.p.A.; *Int'l*, pg. 1188

SANI—Venetion Blind Components & Fabrication Equipment—Cooper Industries, Inc.; *U.S. Public*, pg. 442

SANI-AIRE—Air Fresheners—Surco Products, Inc.; *U.S. Private*, pg. 1056

SANI-DAIRY—Dairy Business—The Penn Traffic Company; *U.S. Public*, pg. 1270

SANI-FLAKES—Pet Litter Deodorant Granules—Surco Products, Inc.; *U.S. Private*, pg. 1056

SANI-FLAT—Interior Flat Paint—Benjamin Moore & Co.; *U.S. Public*, pg. 133

SANI-FLUSH—Toilet Bowl Cleaner—Reckitt & Colman Inc.; *Int'l*, pg. 1090

SANI HANKS—Facial Tissue—Marcal Paper Mills, Inc.; *U.S. Private*, pg. 701

SANI-MATIC—Trash Room Odor Control System—Surco Products, Inc.; *U.S. Private*, pg. 1056

SANI-MIST—Athlete's Foot Prevention—Sani-Mist, Inc.; *U.S. Private*, pg. 965

SANI-MISTER—Athlete's Foot Prevention—Sani-Mist, Inc.; *U.S. Private*, pg. 965

SANI-SAFE—Floor Coverings—Domco Inc.; *Int'l*, pg. 415

SANI SAFE—Glasswasher Brushes—Flo-Pac Corporation; *U.S. Private*, pg. 414

SANI SAFE—Cutlery—Russell Harrington Cutlery Inc.; *U.S. Private*, pg. 551

SANI-SCENT—Air Freshener—Surco Products, Inc.; *U.S. Private*, pg. 1056

SANI-TECH—High Purity Piping Systems—Sani-Tech Inc.; *U.S. Public*, pg. 1545

SANIFLEX—Surgical Tissues—Freudenberg & Company; *Int'l*, pg. 505

SANIGIZER—Instant Hand Sanitizer—Ecolab Inc.; *U.S. Public*, pg. 562

SANIJECTOR—Proportioning Sprayer—Ecolab Inc.; *U.S. Public*, pg. 562

SANISERV—NONE—SaniServ Manufacturing Corp.; *U.S. Private*, pg. 965

SANIT—NONE—ETEX; *Int'l*, pg. 430

SANITAIR—Air Cleaner—U.S. Bottlers Machinery Co.; *U.S. Private*, pg. 1124

SANITARY—Bakery Equipment—Belshaw Brothers, Inc.; *Int'l*, pg. 188

SANITILE—Tile-Like Coatings—Carboline Co.; *U.S. Public*, pg. 1357

SANITILE—Flooring—RPM, Inc.; *U.S. Public*, pg. 1356

SANITIVA—Anti-Bacterial Soap—Sterling Vision, Inc.; *U.S. Public*, pg. 1516

SANKA—Coffee—Philip Morris Companies Inc.; *U.S. Public*, pg. 1287

SANO2—Oxygen in Sauna—Klafs Saunabau GmbH & Co. KG Medizinische Technik; *Int'l*, pg. 736

SANOREX—Obesity Pharmaceutical—Sandoz Pharmaceuticals Corp.; *Int'l*, pg. 974

SANS-SOUCI—Life Vests—Stearns Manufacturing Company; *U.S. Public*, pg. 940

SANSABELT—Dress slacks—Hartmarx Corporation; *U.S. Public*, pg. 795

SANSABELT—Slacks, Suits & Blazers—Trans-Apparel Group; *U.S. Public*, pg. 796

SANSABELT LTD.—Slacks—Trans-Apparel Group; *U.S. Public*, pg. 796

SANSABELT SPORT—Men's Sportswear—Trans-Apparel Group; *U.S. Public*, pg. 796

SANSERT—Prevention or Reduction of Vascular Headaches—Sandoz Pharmaceuticals Corp.; *Int'l*, pg. 974

SANSUI—NONE—Semi-Tech Corporation; *Int'l*, pg. 1220

SANTA ANITA—Wine—Leonard Kreusch, Inc.; *U.S. Private*, pg. 635

SANTA BOWZ—Bows—E-Z Bowz, Inc.; *U.S. Private*, pg. 352

SANTA CAROLINA—Wine—Joseph Victori Wines, Inc.; *U.S. Private*, pg. 1139

SANTA CLARA—Prune Juice—Nestle Chocolate & Confection; *Int'l*, pg. 917

SANTA CRUZ NATURAL—Organic Fruit Juices, Fruit Spreads & Fruit Sauces—J.M. Smucker Company; *U.S. Public*, pg. 1480

SANTA FE—Area Rugs—Couristan Inc.; *U.S. Private*, pg. 279

SANTA FE—Fragrances—The Procter & Gamble Company; *U.S. Public*, pg. 1330

SANTA FE—Cigars—Swisher International Group, Inc.; *U.S. Public*, pg. 1543

SANTA FE—Fragrance—Tsumura International; *Int'l*, pg. 1426

SANTA FE SQUARE—Pre-Finished Laminate—Bruce Hardwood Floors; *U.S. Public*, pg. 1634

SANTA LUCIA—Cheese—Danone Group; *Int'l*, pg. 379

SANTA MARGHERITA—Wine—Paterno Imports Limited; *U.S. Private*, pg. 843

SANTA NINFA—Oil, Pasta, Vegetables—Colivita USA, Inc.; *U.S. Private*, pg. 252

SANTA ROSA—Jellies, Jams & Other Spreads, Tomato Sauces & Catsup—Bestfoods; *U.S. Public*, pg. 223

SANTA ROSA DOORS—Architectural Doors—Weyerhaeuser Forest Products Company; *U.S. Public*, pg. 1764

SANTAR—Organic Fungicide—Novartis AG; *Int'l*, pg. 971

SANTA'S COLLECTION—Greeting Cards; Gift Wrap & Trim; Gift Boxes—American Greetings Corporation; *U.S. Public*, pg. 77

SANTE GRAN SPUMANTE—Liquor—Peerless Importers, Inc.; *U.S. Private*, pg. 847

SANTI—Wine—Frederick Wildman & Sons Ltd.; *U.S. Private*, pg. 1176

SANTIBA—Mixers—The Coca-Cola Company; *U.S. Public*, pg. 392

SANTICIZER—Plasticizers—Solutia Inc.; *U.S. Public*, pg. 1483

SANTITAS—Tortilla Chips—Frito-Lay Company; *U.S. Public*, pg. 1277

SANTOCAT—Acid Catalysts—Monsanto Company; *U.S. Public*, pg. 1124

SANTOCURE—Rubber Processing Chemicals—Monsanto Company; *U.S. Public*, pg. 1124

SANTOCURE—Vulcanization Accelerator—Solutia Inc.; *U.S. Public*, pg. 1483

SANTOFLEX—Rubber Processing Chemicals—Monsanto Company; *U.S. Public*, pg. 1124

SANTOFLEX—Rubber Antioxidant—Solutia Inc.; *U.S. Public*, pg. 1483

SANTOGARD—Rubber Processing Chemicals—Monsanto Company; *U.S. Public*, pg. 1124

SANTOGARD—Prevulcanization Inhibitor—Solutia Inc.; *U.S. Public*, pg. 1483

SANTON—Electrical Water Heaters & Switches—IMI Plc; *Int'l*, pg. 646

SANTONOX—Antioxidant—Solutia Inc.; *U.S. Public*, pg. 1483

SANTOPRENE—Thermoplastic Rubber—Monsanto Company; *U.S. Public*, pg. 1124

SANTOPRENE—Thermoplastic Rubber—Solutia Inc.; *U.S. Public*, pg. 1483

SANTOQUIN—Ethoxyquin/Feed Antioxidant—The Agricultural Group, Monsanto Company; *U.S. Public*, pg. 1125

SANTOQUIN—Antioxidant—Monsanto Company; *U.S. Public*, pg. 1124

SANTOSOL—Dye Solvent—Solutia Inc.; *U.S. Public*, pg. 1483

SANTOTRAC—Synthetic Hydrocarbon Lubricant—Solutia Inc.; *U.S. Public*, pg. 1483

SANTOVAC—Vacuum Diffusion Pump Fluid—Solutia Inc.; *U.S. Public*, pg. 1483

SANTOVAR—Rubber Antioxidant—Solutia Inc.; *U.S. Public*, pg. 1483

SANTOWAX—Mixed Isomeric Terphenyls—Solutia Inc.; *U.S. Public*, pg. 1483

SANTOWEB—Rubber Processing Material—Solutia Inc.; *U.S. Public*, pg. 1483

SANTOWHITE—Crystals Antioxidant—Monsanto Company; *U.S. Public*, pg. 1124

SANTOWHITE—Rubber Antioxidant—Solutia Inc.; *U.S. Public*, pg. 1483

SANTYL—Pharmaceuticals—Knoll Pharmaceutical Company; *Int'l*, pg. 105

SANY—Partitions—CR LLC; *U.S. Private*, pg. 196

SANYO—All Products—Sanyo Electric Co., Ltd.; *Int'l*, pg. 1190

SANYO—NONE—Sanyo Espana S.A.; *Int'l*, pg. 1192

SANYO—Consumer & Commercial Electronics—Sanyo Fisher Company; *Int'l*, pg. 1191

SANYO—Office Automation—Sanyo Office Automation; *Int'l*, pg. 1191

SANYPLASTIC—Partitions—CR LLC; *U.S. Private*, pg. 196

SAO LOURENCO—Mineral Water—Nestle S.A.; *Int'l*, pg. 915

SAPA—Aluminium Products—Electrolux, AB; *Int'l*, pg. 438

SAPIENS—NONE—Sapiens International Corporation N.V.; *Int'l*, pg. 1193

SAPIENS IDEO—NONE—Sapiens International Corporation N.V.; *Int'l*, pg. 1193

SAPIENS OBJECTPOOL—NONE—Sapiens International Corporation N.V.; *Int'l*, pg. 1193

SAPIENS WORKSTATION—NONE—Sapiens International Corporation N.V.; *Int'l*, pg. 1193

SAPORITO—Prosciutti—Hormel Foods Corp.; *U.S. Public*, pg. 840

SAPPHIRE—Greeting Cards—American Greetings Corporation; *U.S. Public*, pg. 77

SAPPHIRE—Greeting Cards and Gift Wrap—American Greetings U.S. Greeting Card Division; *U.S. Public*, pg. 78

SAPPHIRE—X-Ray Tubes—Litton Industries, Inc.; *U.S. Public*, pg. 1002

SAPPHIRE—Electromyograph—Vickers PLC; *Int'l*, pg. 1466

SAPPHIRE VIEW—NONE—Stryker Corporation; *U.S. Public*, pg. 1525

SAPPHIRITE—Abrasion-Resistant Material Used in Sandblasting Nozzles—Diamonite Plant; *U.S. Public*, pg. 618

SAPPHIRITE—Sharpening Wheels—National Presto Industries, Inc.; *U.S. Public*, pg. 1159

SAPPORO—Beer—Sapporo Breweries Ltd.; *Int'l*, pg. 1193

SAPPORO DRAFT—NONE—Sapporo U.S.A., Inc., New York; *Int'l*, pg. 1193

SAQQARA—Wall Coverings—Amoco Corporation; *U.S. Public*, pg. 101

SAR SYSTEM—Terrain Imagery—Litton Industries, Inc.; *U.S. Public*, pg. 1002

SARA LEE—Frozen Baked Goods—Sara Lee Corporation; *U.S. Public*, pg. 1432

SARA LEE BAGELS—Frozen Bagels—Sara Lee Bakery; *U.S. Public*, pg. 1433

SARA LEE CHEESECAKE—NONE—Sara Lee Bakery; *U.S. Public*, pg. 1433

SARA LEE CINNAMON ROLLS—NONE—Sara Lee Bakery; *U.S. Public*, pg. 1433

SARA LEE COFFEE CAKES—NONE—Sara Lee Bakery; *U.S. Public*, pg. 1433

SARA LEE CROISSANTS—NONE—Sara Lee Bakery; *U.S. Public*, pg. 1433

SARA LEE DELI MEATS—Premium Processed Meats—Bil Mar Foods, Inc.; *U.S. Public*, pg. 1433

SARA LEE INDIVIDUAL PASTRIES—NONE—Sara Lee Bakery; *U.S. Public*, pg. 1433

SARA LEE LAYER CAKES—NONE—Sara Lee Bakery; *U.S. Public*, pg. 1433

SARA LEE MUFFINS—Frozen Muffins—Sara Lee Bakery; *U.S. Public*, pg. 1433

SARA LEE PIES—NONE—Sara Lee Bakery; *U.S. Public*, pg. 1433

SARAH COVENTRY—Manicure Sets—The Cook Bates Division; *Int'l*, pg. 815

SARAH COVENTRY—Jewelry & Gifts—Playboy Enterprises, Inc.; *U.S. Public*, pg. 1309

SARAN—Resin, Film, Etc.—The Dow Chemical Company; *U.S. Public*, pg. 522

SARAN 300-CELLOPHANE FILM—NONE—CYDSA S.A.; *Int'l*, pg. 246

SARAN WRAP—Plastic Film—The Dow Chemical Company; *U.S. Public*, pg. 522

SARAN WRAP—Food Storage Wrap—DowBrands, L.P.; *U.S. Public*, pg. 523

SARANAC—Beer/Lager/Stout etc.—The F.X. Matt Brewing Co.; *U.S. Private*, pg. 714

SARANEX—Plastic Film—The Dow Chemical Company; *U.S. Public*, pg. 522

SARATOGA—Electronic Components—Espey Mfg. & Electronics Corp.; *U.S. Public*, pg. 592

SARATOGA—Plywood, Lumber, Wood & Wood Fiber Products—Georgia-Pacific Corporation; *U.S. Public*, pg. 735

SARATOGA—Aircraft—The New Piper Aircraft, Inc.; *U.S. Private*, pg. 794

SARATOGA—Race Track—New York Racing Association; *U.S. Private*, pg. 795

SARATOGA—Harness Racing—Saratoga Equine Sports Center; *U.S. Private*, pg. 965

SARATOGA 120'S—Cigarettes—Philip Morris Companies Inc.; *U.S. Public*, pg. 1287

SARATOGA 120'S MENTHOL—Cigarettes—Philip Morris Companies Inc.; *U.S. Public*, pg. 1287

SARDO—Bath Oil—Schering-Plough Healthcare Products Inc.; *U.S. Public*, pg. 1438

SARGENT—Door Locks—Essex Industries, Inc.; *Int'l*, pg. 18

SARGENT—Door Locks, Door Closers & Architectural Hardware—Sargent Manufacturing Company; *Int'l*, pg. 18

SARGENTO OF WISCONSIN—Shredded, Sliced, Grated & Specialty Cheeses—Sargento Foods Inc.; *U.S. Private*, pg. 966

SARKES TARZIAN—Radio & TV Broadcasting—Sarkes Tarzian; *U.S. Private*, pg. 966

SARK'S SUPREME—Gourmet Coffee—Nestle S.A.; *Int'l*, pg. 915

SARLON QUARTZ—Cushion Vinyl Floorcoverings—Forbo Holding SA; *Int'l*, pg. 496

SARLONMOUSSE—Cushion Vinyl Floorcoverings—Forbo Holding SA; *Int'l*, pg. 496

SARNS—Blood Pumps, Cardioplegia Systems—3M; *U.S. Public*, pg. 1604

SAROMA—Pudding Mix—CSM N.V.; *Int'l*, pg. 243

SARONG—Foundation Garments—True Form Intimate Apparel; *U.S. Private*, pg. 697

SARONNO—Luggage—American Tourister, Inc.; *U.S. Public*, pg. 1430

SAROTTI—Chocolate & Confectionery—Nestle S.A.; *Int'l*, pg. 915

SARSAT—SAR/Land Composite Image—Litton Industries, Inc.; *U.S. Public*, pg. 1002

SARTORI—NONE—Banfi Vintners; *U.S. Private*, pg. 113

SASAPIRIN—CNS Agnets—Nippon Kayaku Co. Ltd.; *Int'l*, pg. 934

SASCO—NONE—ACCO World Corporation; *U.S. Public*, pg. 674

SASCO—Office Products—Fortune Brands, Inc.; *U.S. Public*, pg. 674

SASHEEN—Decorative Ribbons—3M; *U.S. Public*, pg. 1604

SASHEEN MAGIC—Pre-Cut Ribbon Forms—3M; *U.S. Public*, pg. 1604

SASONED—Bouillons, Seasonings, Spices—Bestfoods; *U.S. Public*, pg. 223

SASSI—Cotton Undergarments—National Corset Supply House; *U.S. Private*, pg. 781

SASSON—Clothing—Andover Togs, Inc.; *U.S. Public*, pg. 112

SASSON—Luggage—Monarch Luggage Co. Inc.; *U.S. Private*, pg. 757

SASSY—Magazine—MacDonald Communications; *U.S. Private*, pg. 691

SASSY—Shoes—Tober Industries, Inc.; *U.S. Private*, pg. 1089

SAT-TIN—Matte or Satin Deposits—LeaRonal, Inc.; *U.S. Public*, pg. 982

SATEL-LINK—Mobile Communications System—Union Switch & Signal Inc.; *Int'l*, pg. 77

SATELLITE—Watering System or Waterer—CTB International Corp.; *U.S. Public*, pg. 284

SATELLITE—Binoculars—Swift Instruments, Inc.; *U.S. Private*, pg. 1058

SATELLITE COMMUNICATIONS—Publication for Satellite Professionals—Intertec Publishing; *U.S. Public*, pg. 1327

SATELLITE COMMUNICATIONS—Monthly Publ.—Intertec Publishing; *U.S. Public*, pg. 1328

SATELLITE CONTROL—Electronic Assembly—Universal Instruments Corporation; *U.S. Public*, pg. 522

SATELLITE CONTROLLER—Electronic Assembly—Universal Instruments Corporation; *U.S. Public*, pg. 522

SATELLITE SERIES—Micro-Based Products Software—Dun & Bradstreet Software Services; *Int'l*, pg. 532

SATELLITE VIDEO CENTER—Instant Pay Per View Center for Home Satellite TV Users—Satellite Data Networks; *U.S. Public*, pg. 716

SATELLITE VISIONS—Photography from space into maps/globes—Replogle Globes, Inc.; *U.S. Private*, pg. 923

SATFIND-406—Emergency Position Indicating Radio Beacons—Alden Electronics, Inc.; *U.S. Private*, pg. 872

SATICON—Tube—Sony Electronics; *Int'l*, pg. 1281

SATIN—Cigarettes—Loews Corporation; *U.S. Public*, pg. 1010

SATIN—Cigarette—Lorillard Tobacco Company; *U.S. Public*, pg. 1011

SATIN CARE—Shave Gel—The Gillette Company; *U.S. Public*, pg. 743

SATIN-CATH—Medico-Surgical Tubes & Medico-Surgical Tube Appliances—Mallinckrodt Inc.; *U.S. Public*, pg. 1039

SATIN DOUGHNUT FRY—Frying Shortening—Mallet & Co.; *U.S. Private*, pg. 698

SATIN FANCIES—Bras, Panties—Olga Div.; *U.S. Public*, pg. 1738

SATIN FRY—Shortening—Mallet & Co.; *U.S. Private*, pg. 698

SATIN GLO—Ribbon for Gift Wrapping—American Greetings Corporation; *U.S. Public*, pg. 77

SATIN GLO—Pearlescent Coated Paper & Paperboard—Hazen Paper Company; *U.S. Private*, pg. 514

SATIN GLO—Shortening—Mallet & Co.; *U.S. Private*, pg. 698

SATIN GOLD—Casting Golds—Handy & Harman; *U.S. Public*, pg. 780

SATIN PLUS—Emulsified Shortening—Mallet & Co.; *U.S. Private*, pg. 698

SATIN PRIME—Paint Primers & Sealers—PPG Industries, Inc.; *U.S. Public*, pg. 1245

SATIN SHEEN—Dishwashing Detergent—Shaklee Corporation; *Int'l*, pg. 1518

SATIN-SLIP—Medico-Surgical Tubes & Medico-Surgical Tube Appliances—Mallinckrodt Inc.; *U.S. Public*, pg. 1039

SATIN-SLIP SURFACE—Surface Component of Medico Surgical Tubes—Mallinckrodt Inc.; *U.S. Public*, pg. 1039

SATIN SPAR—Plaster—Georgia-Pacific Corporation; *U.S. Public*, pg. 735

SATIN WRAP—Plastic Food Wrap—Fort James Corporation; *U.S. Public*, pg. 670

SATIN-X—Paint—Jones Blair Company; *U.S. Private*, pg. 596

SATINA—Skin & Body Care Products—Bayer AG; *Int'l*, pg. 171

SATINAL—Polishing Agent for C-39 Hard Resin Lens—Ferro Corporation; *U.S. Public*, pg. 618

SATINCOTE—Printing Paper—Georgia-Pacific Corporation; *U.S. Public*, pg. 735

SATINESQUE—Wallcoverings—Borden, Inc.; *U.S. Private*, pg. 157

SATINGLASS—Compression Rollings—CertainTeed Corporation; *Int'l*, pg. 1170

SATINGLIDE—Wire—National-Standard Co.; *U.S. Public*, pg. 1160

SATINGLO 30—Kaolin Coating Pigment—Engelhard Corporation; *U.S. Public*, pg. 582

SATINHIDE—Paint, Primers, Lacquers, Enamels & Varnishes—PPG Industries, Inc.; *U.S. Public*, pg. 1245

SATINIQUE—Personal Care Products—Amway Corporation; *U.S. Private*, pg. 69

SATINLAM—Overlay Paper—The Mead Corporation; *U.S. Public*, pg. 1074

SATINLUXE—Finish on Instant Print Film—Eastman Kodak Company; *U.S. Public*, pg. 550

SATINOX—Polishing Compounds for Plastic Lenses—Ferro Corporation; *U.S. Public*, pg. 618

SATINTONE—Gift Ties—CPS Corporation; *U.S. Private*, pg. 422

SATINTONE—Paint—Colony Paints; *U.S. Public*, pg. 1707

SATINTONE—Calcined Kaolin—Engelhard Corporation; *U.S. Public*, pg. 582

SATISFAR—Insecticide—Novartis AG; *Int'l*, pg. 971

SATORI—Ultrafast Dye Laser—Coherent, Inc.; *U.S. Public*, pg. 395

SATSTREAM—Satellite Services for Business—British Telecommunications plc; *Int'l*, pg. 222

THE SATURDAY EVENING POST—General Interest Magazine—Benjamin Franklin Literary & Medical Society, Inc.; *U.S. Private*, pg. 133

SATURDAY MATINEE—Retail Video Store—Trans World Entertainment Corporation; *U.S. Public*, pg. 1629

SATURDAY SUN COMPANY—Apparel—Fred Meyer Stores; *U.S. Public*, pg. 1103

SATURDAY'S HELPER—Electrical Apparatus & Supplies—General Cable Corporation; *Int'l*, pg. 1486

SATURN—Passenger Car—General Motors Corporation; *U.S. Public*, pg. 718

SATURN—Polyester Outdoor Sign Material—Industrial Coatings Group, Inc.; *U.S. Private*, pg. 434

SATURN—Videogame Hardware System—Sega of America Inc.; *Int'l*, pg. 1218

SATURN—Turbine Products—Solar Turbines Incorporated; *U.S. Public*, pg. 316

SATURN—Illuminated Magnifier—Stocker & Yale, Inc.; *U.S. Public*, pg. 1518

SATURN—Mass Spectrometer Systems—Varian Associates, Inc.; *U.S. Public*, pg. 1710

SATURN—Book Paper—Weyerhaeuser Company; *U.S. Public*, pg. 1764

SATURN OF DELRAY—Dealership—Ed Morse Automotive Group; *U.S. Private*, pg. 763

SATURN OF TAMPA—Dealership—Ed Morse Automotive Group; *U.S. Private*, pg. 763

SATURN OF WEST PALM BEACH—Dealership—Ed Morse Automotive Group; *U.S. Private*, pg. 763

SATURN SC—Car—General Motors Corporation; *U.S. Public*, pg. 718

SATURN SL—Car—General Motors Corporation; *U.S. Public*, pg. 718

SATURN YELLOW—Fluorescent Color—Day-Glo Color Corp.; *U.S. Public*, pg. 1357

SATZENBRAU—NONE—Guinness Plc; *Int'l*, pg. 412

SAU-SEA—Seafood Products—Sau-Sea Foods, Inc.; *U.S. Private*, pg. 967

SAUCER—Air Moving Devices—EG & G Rotron; *U.S. Public*, pg. 543

SAUCEWORKS—Cocktail, Horseradish, Sweet 'N Sour & Tartar Sauces—Philip Morris Companies Inc.; *U.S. Public*, pg. 1287

SAUCONY—Footwear—Hyde Athletic Industries, Inc.; *U.S. Public*, pg. 851

SAULAR—Cat Litter—Oil-Dri Corporation of America; *U.S. Public*, pg. 1214

SAULAR KAT KIT—Disposable Litter Tray—Oil-Dri Corporation of America; *U.S. Public*, pg. 1214

SAULAR PLUS—Cat Litter—Oil-Dri Corporation of America; *U.S. Public*, pg. 1214

SAUSAGE 'N BISCUITS—Sandwich—Owens Country Sausage, Inc.; *U.S. Public*, pg. 596

SAUSAGE MCMUFFIN—Menu Item—McDonald's Corporation; *U.S. Public*, pg. 1068

SAUSAGE SENSATIONS—Quick Breakfast Meals—Armour Swift Eckrich; *U.S. Public*, pg. 426

SAUSAGESTER—Dog Treats—The Quaker Oats Company; *U.S. Public*, pg. 1347

SAUZA—Tequila—Domecq Importers Inc.; *Int'l*, pg. 63

SAUZA TEQUILA—Spirit—Allied Domecq PLC; *Int'l*, pg. 62

SAV-A-CENTER—Food Store—The Great Atlantic & Pacific Tea Company, Inc.; *Int'l*, pg. 1375

SAV-LIN—Paper Products—Erving Industries, Inc.; *U.S. Private*, pg. 382

SAV-ON INC.—Discount Office Supplies—Tandycrafts, Inc.; *U.S. Public*, pg. 1561

SAV-U—Service Marks—Piggly Wiggly Co.; *U.S. Public*, pg. 653

SAV-U FOODS—Retail Supermarket—Schultz Sav-O Stores, Inc.; *U.S. Public*, pg. 1442

SAVADAY—Formed Fiber Plates—The Chinet Co.; *Int'l*, pg. 1146

SAVAGE—Motorcycle—American Suzuki Motor Corporation; *Int'l*, pg. 1323

SAVAGE—Magazine—Paisano Publications, Inc.; *U.S. Private*, pg. 834

SAVAGE—Guns—Savage Arms Inc.; *U.S. Private*, pg. 968

SAVANE—Men's Wear—Farah Incorporated; *U.S. Public*, pg. 612

SAVANE—Body Care Products—Sara Lee Corporation; *U.S. Public*, pg. 1432

SAVANE—Men's Toiletries—SmithKline Beecham plc; *U.S. Public*, pg. 1264

SAVANNA—Travel Trailer—Fleetwood Enterprises, Inc.; *U.S. Public*, pg. 650

SAVANNAH GAS COMPANY—Natural Gas Distribution—AGL Resources; *U.S. Public*, pg. 6

SAVANNAH LAKES VILLAGE—Recreational and Retirement Communitites—Cooper Communities, Inc.; *U.S. Private*, pg. 273

SAVANNAH MAGAZINE—Magazine—Shivers Trading & Operating Co.; *U.S. Private*, pg. 994

SAVANNAH MORNING NEWS—Newspaper—Shivers Trading & Operating Co.; *U.S. Private*, pg. 994

SAVARIN—Coffee—Tetley USA Inc.; *Int'l*, pg. 1377

SAVAS—Health Food Products—Meiji Seika Kaisha, Ltd.; *Int'l*, pg. 855

SAVAS PROTEIN XX—High-Protein Products—Meiji Seika Kaisha, Ltd.; *Int'l*, pg. 855

SAVE THE CHILDREN—Clothing—Salant Corporation; *U.S. Public*, pg. 1429

SAVETIME—Time & Attendance Systems—Control Module, Inc.; *U.S. Private*, pg. 271

SAVER'S CHOICE—Grocery & Perishable Products—Shurfine International, Inc.; *U.S. Private*, pg. 997

SAVERS CHOICE—Savings Account—NBD Bank (Indiana); *U.S. Public*, pg. 628

SAVEUR INTERNATIONAL—Cookware, Educational Services—Regal Ware, Inc.; *U.S. Private*, pg. 917

SAVILLE—Career Sportswear—Jones Apparel Group, Inc.; *U.S. Public*, pg. 933

SAVIN—Copiers—Savin Corporation; *Int'l*, pg. 1114

SAVINFAX—Facsimile Transmission Equipment—Savin Corporation; *Int'l*, pg. 1114

SAVINYL—Soluble Dyes—Clariant International Ltd.; *Int'l*, pg. 917

SAVLON—NONE—Johnson & Johnson; *U.S. Public*, pg. 927

SAVON DRUGS—Drug Stores—American Drug Stores Inc.; *U.S. Public*, pg. 93

SAVORA—Seasonings, Spices—Bestfoods; *U.S. Public*, pg. 223

SAVORA—Mustard—Refinerias de Maiz S.A.I.C.F.; *U.S. Public*, pg. 448

SAVORY—Preserves & Jellies—Clements Foods Co.; *U.S. Private*, pg. 245

SAVORY—Peanut Butter—Clements Nut Co.; *U.S. Private*, pg. 245

SAVORY—Toasters—Merco/Savory Inc.; *Int'l*, pg. 189

SAVORY—Liquid Butter Alternative—Ventura Foods LLC; *Int'l*, pg. 879

SAVORY—Rotisseries & Toasters—Welbilt Corporation; *Int'l*, pg. 188

SAVORY AND JAMES—Sherries & Ports—Charles Jacquin et Cie, Inc.; *U.S. Private*, pg. 580

SAVORY CLASSICS—Side Dish Mixes—Golden Grain Company; *U.S. Public*, pg. 1348

SAVORY CLASSICS—Rice Dinners—The Quaker Oats Company; *U.S. Public*, pg. 1347

SAVORYSOY—Food Product—Honeymead Products Co.; *U.S. Private*, pg. 537

SAVOURIN—Butter—Agropur; *Int'l*, pg. 31

SAVOY—Bathroom Tissue—Georgia-Pacific Corporation; *U.S. Public*, pg. 735

SAVOY PICTURES—NONE—USA Broadcasting; *U.S. Public*, pg. 1686

SAVOY TAYLORS GUILD—NONE—Moss Bros Group PLC; *Int'l*, pg. 895

SAW PALMETTO—NONE—Celestial Seasonings; *U.S. Public*, pg. 319

SAWASDEE—In-Flight Publication—Thai Airways Intl. Ltd.-U.S. Office; *Int'l*, pg. 1381

SAWBUCK—Field Saw—Buck Knives, Inc.; *U.S. Private*, pg. 177

SAWCAT—Power Saws—The Black & Decker Corporation; *U.S. Public*, pg. 233

SAWFORCE—Circular Saws—The Black & Decker Corporation; *U.S. Public*, pg. 233

SAWYERS—Slide Projectors—View-Master, Inc.; *U.S. Public*, pg. 1058

SAWZALL—Power Tools—Milwaukee Electric Tool Corp.; *Int'l*, pg. 96

SAX ARTS & CRAFTS—NONE—ACCO World Corporation; *U.S. Public*, pg. 674

SAXA—Table Salt Pepper—Ranks Hovis McDougall Limited; *Int'l*, pg. 1395

SAXON—NONE—Lee Pharmaceuticals; *U.S. Public*, pg. 984

SAXON—Aftershave Skin Conditioner—The Procter & Gamble Company; *U.S. Public*, pg. 1330

SAXTON WIRE & CABLE—NONE—Communication Cable, Inc.; *U.S. Public*, pg. 968

SAYETT—Electronic Projection Equipment, Software—Eastman Kodak Company; *U.S. Public*, pg. 550

SAYLOR-BEALL—Air Compressors—EEI Corporation; *Int'l*, pg. 425

SBARRO—Cafeteria Style Restaurants—Sbarro, Inc.; *U.S. Public*, pg. 1435

SBRINZ—NONE—Schweizerische Kaseunion AG; *Int'l*, pg. 1211

SCADA-MATE—Distribution Automation Switching Systems—S & C Electric Company; *U.S. Private*, pg. 954

SCALABLE POWERPARALLEL SYSTEMS—Computer System—International Business Machines Corporation; *U.S. Public*, pg. 895

SCALAMANDRE—Wallpapers, Trimmings & Custom Carpets—Scalamandre, Inc.; *U.S. Private*, pg. 969

SCALDGARD—Water Temperature Control System—Peerless Faucet Corporation; *U.S. Public*, pg. 1053

SCALE AUTO ENTHUSIAST—Magazine—Kalmbach Publishing Co.; *U.S. Private*, pg. 606

SCALE-OFF—Mineral Deposit Remover—Litton Industries, Inc.; *U.S. Public*, pg. 1002

SCALECTOR III—Tacking Iron—Seal Products Incorporated; *U.S. Private*, pg. 849

SCALEFREE—Water Heaters—Patterson-Kelley Company; *U.S. Public*, pg. 793

SCALPCAP—Laceration Cap—The Fibre-Metal Products Company; *U.S. Private*, pg. 402

SCALPICIN—Scalp Relief Medicine—Combe Incorporated; *U.S. Private*, pg. 257

SCAMP—Sporting Goods—Brunswick Bowling & Billiards Corp.; *U.S. Public*, pg. 265

SCAMP—Cat Box Filler, Cat Box Liners, Trays, Pet Accessories & Pet Food—Golden Cat Corporation; *U.S. Public*, pg. 1360

SCAMP—Car Position—Svedala Bulk Materials Handling Engineered Products; *Int'l*, pg. 1326

SCAN—Facility Management System for Parking Lots—Federal APD, Inc.; *U.S. Public*, pg. 616

SCAN GLOBE—NONE—Replogle Globes, Inc.; *U.S. Private*, pg. 923

SCAN-LINE—Electronic Instruments—Bailey, Fischer & Porter Company; *Int'l*, pg. 444

SCAN-FOLD—Folding Strip Charts—The Foxboro Company; *Int'l*, pg. 1243

SCAN-VUE—Indicator—The Foxboro Company; *Int'l*, pg. 1243

SCANCOM—Data Processing & Retrieval Network—DSC Communications Corporation; *U.S. Public*, pg. 475

SCANDINAVIAN GARMENT SERVICE—Transport & Storage of Hanging Garments—BTL AB; *Int'l*, pg. 123

SCANDINAVIAN RAIL CARGO—European Rail Transport—BTL AB; *Int'l*, pg. 123

SCANDISPA—Whirlpools—Sanitec Ltd. Oy; *Int'l*, pg. 863

SCANDO-MINI—Elevator—Alimak Elevator Company; *U.S. Public*, pg. 34

SCANMAN—Hand-Held Scaner—Logitech International SA; *Int'l*, pg. 815

SCANMARK—Machines—Markem Corporation; *U.S. Private*, pg. 704

SCANMARK—Optical Mark Readers—ScanTron Corporation; *U.S. Public*, pg. 786

SCANMASTER—Film Scanner—Houston Fearless 76 Inc.; *U.S. Private*, pg. 542

SCANNER—Annunciator—Amot Controls Corporation; *U.S. Public*, pg. 1405

SCANNER—Electronic Flow Measurement/Remote Telemetry Units—ITT Barton Instruments; *U.S. Public*, pg. 860

SCANNER-PACK—Microfilm Cartridge—Eastman Kodak Company; *U.S. Public*, pg. 550

SCANNERS—Safety Eyewear—Aearo Company; *U.S. Private*, pg. 23

SCANOE—Boat—The Canadian Coleman Co., Ltd.; *U.S. Private*, pg. 691

SCANPAL—Data collector—Metrologic Instruments, Inc.; *U.S. Public*, pg. 1102

SCANPLUS III—Scanner—CalComp Technology, Inc.; *U.S. Public*, pg. 1007

SCANRAY—X-Ray Equipment—EG & G Astrophysics; *U.S. Public*, pg. 543

SCANSPED—European Road Transport & Logistics—BTL AB; *Int'l*, pg. 123

SCANSTAR 580/590—User Programmable Portable Data Collection Terminals—CiMatrix L.L.C.; *U.S. Public*, pg. 1395

SCANTECH NEWS—Publication for Professionals in Automatic Data Collection Field—Reed Elsevier Business Information; *Int'l*, pg. 1095

SCANTEMP—Adhesive Backed Labels—Markem Corporation; *U.S. Private*, pg. 704

SCANTRON—Designs, Develops, Products & Markets—ScanTron Corporation; *U.S. Public*, pg. 786

SCANWISE—NONE—The Black & Decker Corporation; *U.S. Public*, pg. 233

SCANWORX—OCR Software—Xerox Imaging Systems, Inc.; *U.S. Public*, pg. 1785

SCARAB—Manned & Unmanned Submersibles Used in Subsea Cable Repair—Teleglobe, Inc.; *Int'l*, pg. 1373

SCARECROWZ—Bows—E-Z Bowz, Inc.; *U.S. Private*, pg. 352

SCAT—Hardware—Chips and Technologies, Inc.; *U.S. Public*, pg. 349

SCAT TRAK—Skid Steer Loader—OmniQuip International, Inc.; *U.S. Private*, pg. 500

SCATTER—Granular Deodorizers—Surco Products, Inc.; *U.S. Private*, pg. 1056

SCATTER-SAFE—NONE—Donnelly Corporation; *U.S. Public*, pg. 519

SCATTERGORIES—Game—Milton Bradley Company; *U.S. Public*, pg. 797

SCAV-EX—Fibrous Processing Aid—Hercules Incorporated; *U.S. Public*, pg. 809

SCAVENGER—Print Vapor Eliminator System, Vacuum Frame Printers—Blu-Ray; *U.S. Private*, pg. 142

SCAVENGER—Manure Spreader—Gehl Company; *U.S. Public*, pg. 704

SCENARIO—NONE—Cognos Corp.; *Int'l*, pg. 306

SCENIC AMERICA—Towels—Marcal Paper Mills, Inc.; *U.S. Private*, pg. 701

SCENT FLO—Fan Air Freshener—Surco Products, Inc.; *U.S. Private*, pg. 1056

SCENTSATION—Solid Air Freshener—Blue Cross Laboratories; *U.S. Private*, pg. 152

SCENTSCAPES—Air Fresheners—Amway Corporation; *U.S. Private*, pg. 69

SCENTSTRIP—Control Release Dispensers—Hercon Environmental Corporation; *U.S. Public*, pg. 802

SCEPTER—Herbicide—American Home Products Corporation; *U.S. Public*, pg. 79

SCHAEFER—Beer—The Stroh Brewery Company; *U.S. Private*, pg. 1047

SCHAEFER—NONE—Victoria Packing Corporation; *U.S. Private*, pg. 1139

SCHAEFER LIGHT—Beer—The Stroh Brewery Company; *U.S. Private*, pg. 1047

SCHAEVITZ—Sensors—Lucas Industries Inc.; *Int'l*, pg. 820

SCHAEVITZ—NONE—LucasVarity plc; *Int'l*, pg. 819

SCHAPIRO'S—Wine—Adams Wine Co.; *U.S. Private*, pg. 17

SCHEMA—Simulator Software—MTS Systems Corporation; *U.S. Public*, pg. 1028

SCHENLEY—NONE—Barton Brands, Ltd.; *U.S. Public*, pg. 300

SCHICK—Injector, Super II, Ultra, FX, Shaveguard Shaving Cream—Warner-Lambert K.K.; *U.S. Public*, pg. 1739

SCHICK—Shaving Razors, Blades, Disposable Razors—Warner-Lambert Shaving Products Group; *U.S. Public*, pg. 1739

SCHICK SLIM TWIN—Blade & Razor System—Warner-Lambert Company; *U.S. Public*, pg. 1738

SCHICK SUPER II—Razor Blades—Warner-Lambert Company; *U.S. Public*, pg. 1738

SCHICK TRACER RAZOR—Razor—Warner-Lambert Shaving Products Group; *U.S. Public*, pg. 1739

SCHILLING—Spices, Food Products—McCormick & Company, Incorporated; *U.S. Public*, pg. 1066

SCHIMMELPENNINCK—Cigars—Lane Limited; *Int'l*, pg. 1129

SCHIRMER—Tear Test Strips—Alcon Laboratories, Inc.; *Int'l*, pg. 916

SCHIZANDRA PLUS—Herbal Vitamin/Mineral Supplement—Herbalife International of America, Inc.; *U.S. Public*, pg. 809

SCHLAGE—Locks, Security Systems—Ingersoll-Rand Company; *U.S. Public*, pg. 876

SCHLEGEL—Sealing Systems—BTR plc; *Int'l*, pg. 124

SCHLITZ—Beer—Bass PLC; *Int'l*, pg. 169

SCHLITZ—Beer—The Stroh Brewery Company; *U.S. Private*, pg. 1047

SCHLITZ-LIGHT—Beer—The Stroh Brewery Company; *U.S. Private*, pg. 1047

SCHLITZ MALT LIQUOR—Malt Liquor—The Stroh Brewery Company; *U.S. Private*, pg. 1047

SCHLUMBERGER—Jewelry & Watches—Tiffany & Co.; *U.S. Public*, pg. 1608

SCHMIDT COUPLING—Coupling Line—Zero-Max, Inc.; *Int'l*, pg. 866

SCHOEP'S—Ice Cream—Schoep's Ice Cream, Inc.; *U.S. Private*, pg. 972

SCHOLASTIC COACH—Publication for Athletic Coaches & Trainers; 10 Issues/Yr.—Scholastic Inc.; *U.S. Public*, pg. 1440

SCHOLASTIC NEWS—Publication for Students, Grades K-8—Scholastic Inc.; *U.S. Public*, pg. 1440

SCHOLL—NONE—Scholl AG; *Int'l*, pg. 1209

SCHOLL—NONE—Scholl Plc; *Int'l*, pg. 1209

SCHOLL—Foot Care Prods.—Scholl U.S.A.; *U.S. Public*, pg. 1438

SCHONENBERGER—W. Germany—Key Handling Systems, Inc.; *U.S. Private*, pg. 618

SCHONLAND'S—Processed Meats—Kayem Foods, Inc.; *U.S. Private*, pg. 610

SCHONLANDS—Processed Meats—Labatt Brewing Company Limited; *Int'l*, pg. 679

SCHOOL ANNUAL PUBLISHING CO.—Programs, Wearables, Yearbooks—Jll/Sales Promotion Associates, Inc.; *U.S. Private*, pg. 598

SCHOOL BUS FLEET—NONE—Bobit Publishing Company; *U.S. Private*, pg. 154

SCHOOL HOUSE—Cookies—Mrs. Alison's Cookie Company; *U.S. Private*, pg. 765

SCHOOL LIBRARY JOURNAL—Magazine for Librarians Working With Children & Young Adults—Reed Elsevier Business Information; *Int'l*, pg. 1095

SCHOOL PAK—Stationary Products—The Mead Corporation; *U.S. Public*, pg. 1074

SCHOOLHOUSE PRESS—Educational Publishers—Simon & Schuster; *U.S. Private*, pg. 777

SCHOOLVIEW—Computer Product—International Business Machines Corporation; *U.S. Public*, pg. 895

SCHOONBECK—Furniture—Masco Corporation; *U.S. Public*, pg. 1052

SCHOONER—Beer—Labatt Brewing Company Limited; *Int'l*, pg. 679

SCHORR'S—Pickles—National Foods Inc.; *U.S. Public*, pg. 429

SCHOTTENSTEIN'S—NONE—Schottenstein Stores Corporation; *U.S. Private*, pg. 972

SCHRADE—Cutlery—Imperial Schrade Corp.; *U.S. Private*, pg. 559

SCHRADE—Light Weight Lockback Knives with Zytel Handles—Imperial Schrade Corp.; *U.S. Private*, pg. 559

SCHRADE EXTREME—NONE—Imperial Schrade Corp.; *U.S. Private*, pg. 559

SCHRADE STC—NONE—Imperial Schrade Corp.; *U.S. Private*, pg. 559

SCHRADE SCRIMSHAW—Limited Editions Delrin Handles—Imperial Schrade Corp.; *U.S. Private*, pg. 559

SCHRAFFT'S CANDY—Candy—Boyer Candy Company Inc.; *U.S. Private*, pg. 162

SCHRANCK'S—Cordials—NWS Inc.; *U.S. Private*, pg. 772

SCHRECK—Narrow Aisle Lift Trucks—Plymouth Industries, Inc.; *U.S. Private*, pg. 873

SCHROCK—Kitchen & Bathroom Cabinets—Electrolux, AB; *Int'l*, pg. 438

SCHROCK HANDCRAFTED CABINETRY—Cabinets—White Consolidated Industries, Inc.; *Int'l*, pg. 439

SCHUCO—NONE—Allied Healthcare Products, Inc.; *U.S. Public*, pg. 48

SCHULAMID—Plastic Compounds—A. Schulman, Inc.; *U.S. Public*, pg. 1441

SCHULT—Manufactured Housing—Schult Homes Corporation; *U.S. Public*, pg. 1442

SCHUMACHER—Fabrics, Wallcovering, Carpets—F. Schumacher & Co.; *U.S. Private*, pg. 973

SCHWAB—Fire Protective Equipment—Schwab Corp.; *U.S. Private*, pg. 974

SCHWAB ADVISOR SERVICE—NONE—Charles Schwab & Co. Inc.; *U.S. Public*, pg. 1443

SCHWAB 500 BROKERAGE—NONE—Charles Schwab & Co. Inc.; *U.S. Public*, pg. 1443

SCHWABE—Men's Work & Leisure Shirts—Movie Star, Inc.; *U.S. Public*, pg. 1140

SCHWAN'S—Ice Cream, Meats, Fish, etc.—Schwan's Sales Enterprises; *U.S. Private*, pg. 974

SCHWARZ—Paper—Schwarz Paper Company; *U.S. Private*, pg. 974

SCHWARZKOPF—Hair Care Product—Permark International (Pty.) Ltd.; *Int'l*, pg. 1036

SCHWEIGERT—Foods—Ohse Foods Inc.; *U.S. Private*, pg. 396

SCHWEITZER—Specialties for Bibles, Forms, Carbons, Cigarette Papers, Plug Wrap—Kimberly-Clark Corporation; *U.S. Public*, pg. 958

SCHWEPPES—NONE—Cadbury Beverages; *Int'l*, pg. 248

SCHWEPPES—Soft Drinks—Cadbury Beverages North America; *Int'l*, pg. 248

SCHWEPPES—Carbonated Water—Cadbury Schweppes p.l.c.; *Int'l*, pg. 247

SCHWEPPES—Soft Drink—Grant-Lydick Beverage Co.; *U.S. Private*, pg. 470

SCHWEPPES CLASSICS—Soft Drinks—Apollinaris & Schweppes Gmbh & Co.; *Int'l*, pg. 78

SCHWEPPES COOL—Lemonade—Apollinaris & Schweppes Gmbh & Co.; *Int'l*, pg. 78

SCHWEPPES DRY GRAPE—Flavored Ginger Ale—Cadbury Beverages; *Int'l*, pg. 248

SCHWEPPES LIGHTS—Low-Calorie Soft Drinks—Apollinaris & Schweppes Gmbh & Co.; *Int'l*, pg. 78

SCHWEPPES U.S.A.—Soft Drinks—Cadbury Beverages; *Int'l*, pg. 248

SCHWERINERVOLKSZEITUNG—Newspaper—Burda Holding GmbH & Co., KG; *Int'l*, pg. 233

SCHWINN—Bicycles—Schwinn Cycling & Fitness Inc.; *U.S. Private*, pg. 975

THE SCI-FI CHANNEL—Cable TV Network—USA Networks; *U.S. Public*, pg. 1686

SCICONEX—Ceramic Fibers—3M; *U.S. Public*, pg. 1604

SCIENCE AND TECHNOLOGY FOR CHILDREN—Integrated Hands On Science Program—Carolina Biological Supply Co.; *U.S. Private*, pg. 213

SCIENCE DIET—Animal Food—Hill's Pet Nutrition; *U.S. Public*, pg. 397

SCIENCE DIET LIGHT FORMULA—Food for Cats & Dogs—Hill's Pet Nutrition; *U.S. Public*, pg. 397

SCIENCE EDITIONS—Books—John Wiley & Sons, Inc.; *U.S. Public*, pg. 1768

SCIENCE FAIR—Hobby Kits—RadioShack; *U.S. Public*, pg. 1560

SCIENCE FICTION BOOK CLUB—NONE—Doubleday Direct; *Int'l*, pg. 191

THE SCIENCE OF BEAUTIFUL EYES—Electrical & Scientific Apparatus—The Cooper Companies, Inc.; *U.S. Public*, pg. 442

SCIENCEWARE—Scientific Supplies—Bel-Art Products; *U.S. Private*, pg. 130

SCIENCO—Pumping Systems—Ingersoll-Dresser Pump Company; *U.S. Public*, pg. 529

SCIENTIFIC AMERICAN—Publishing—Scientific American, Inc.; *Int'l*, pg. 1479

SCIENTIFIC ANGLERS—Fly Fishing Products—3M; *U.S. Public*, pg. 1604

SCIENTIFIC-ATLANTA—NONE—Scientific-Atlanta, Inc.; *U.S. Public*, pg. 1443

SCIENTIFIC COMPUTING & AUTOMATION—Publication for Scientists/Engineers—Reed Elsevier Business Information; *Int'l*, pg. 1095

SCIENTIFIC PROTEIN LABORATORIES, INC.—Pharmaceuticals—Scientific Protein Laboratories, Inc.; *U.S. Public*, pg. 80

SCIENTIST—Weather Instrument—Swift Instruments, Inc.; *U.S. Private*, pg. 1058

SCIMON—Software—Exabyte Corporation; *U.S. Public*, pg. 597

SCINT-A XF—Pseudocumene-Based Cocktail—Packard Instrument Co., Inc.; *U.S. Private*, pg. 833

SCINTANALYZED—Reagents—Fisher Scientific Company; *U.S. Private*, pg. 658

SCINTI PREP—Concentrated Scintillator/Solvent Mixtures—Fisher Scientific Company; *U.S. Private*, pg. 658

SCINTI VERSE—Universal Scintillation Reagent—Fisher Scientific Company; *U.S. Private*, pg. 658

SCINTILENE—Reagent—Fisher Scientific Company; *U.S. Private*, pg. 658

SCINTILLOMETER—NONE—Western Atlas Logging Services; *U.S. Public*, pg. 1757

SCIROCCO—Luggage—Andiamo, Inc.; *U.S. Private*, pg. 73

SCIROCCO—NONE—Brown & Sharpe Manufacturing Company; *U.S. Public*, pg. 260

SCIROCCO SP—NONE—Brown & Sharpe Manufacturing Company; *U.S. Public*, pg. 260

SCOOP AWAY—Clumping Cat Litter—First Brands Corporation; *U.S. Public*, pg. 626

SCOOPULA—Dispensing Implement—Fisher Scientific Company; *U.S. Private*, pg. 658

SCOOTER—Sporting Goods—Brunswick Bowling & Billiards Corp.; *U.S. Public*, pg. 265

SCOOTER STAND—Computer Furniture—Herman Miller, Inc.; *U.S. Public*, pg. 1111

SCOPE—Key System—Gai-Tronics Corporation; *U.S. Public*, pg. 1430

SCOPE—Mouthwash, Original & Peppermint Flavors—The Procter & Gamble Company; *U.S. Public*, pg. 1330

SCOPE-MOBILE—Cart—Tektronix, Inc.; *U.S. Public*, pg. 1567

SCOPEMETER SERIES II—NONE—Fluke Corporation; *U.S. Public*, pg. 659

SCOPIX—Medical Film for Electronic Imaging—AGFA Division of Bayer Corporation; *Int'l*, pg. 172

SCOPIX—Film—Bayer AG; *Int'l*, pg. 171

SCORCHER—Radio Control—Tyco Toys, Inc.; *U.S. Public*, pg. 1058

SCORE—Men's Hair Preparation—Bristol-Myers Squibb Company; *U.S. Public*, pg. 253

SCORE—NONE—Brown & Sharpe Manufacturing Company; *U.S. Public*, pg. 260

SCORE—Machine Warewashing Detergent—Ecolab Inc.; *U.S. Public*, pg. 562

SCORE—Industrial Chemical—Hercules Chemical Co., Inc.; *U.S. Private*, pg. 523

SCORE—Analysis Software—Nellcor Puritan Bennett Incorporated; *U.S. Public*, pg. 1039

SCORE—NONE—Pinnacle Brands, Inc.; *U.S. Private*, pg. 866

SCORE KING—Sporting Goods—Brunswick Bowling & Billiards Corp.; *U.S. Public*, pg. 265

SCORECARD—NONE—Marriott International, Inc.; *U.S. Public*, pg. 1047

SCORENET SERVICE—NONE—Fair, Isaac and Company, Inc.; *U.S. Public*, pg. 609

SCORESBY SCOTCH—Scotch—United Distillers USA, Inc.; *Int'l*, pg. 412

SCORPION—Screw Driver Bits—The Black & Decker Corporation; *U.S. Public*, pg. 233

SCORPION—Lager—Vaux Group Plc; *Int'l*, pg. 1453

SCORPION ANTI-SLIP—Accessories—The Black & Decker Corporation; *U.S. Public*, pg. 233

SCOT LABORATORIES—Cleaning Agents & Maintenance Chemicals—The Scott Fetzer Company; *U.S. Public*, pg. 217

SCOT-PAK—Plumbing Valves—A.Y. McDonald Industries, Inc.; *U.S. Private*, pg. 721

SCOT POT—Potentiometers—Litton Industries, Inc.; *U.S. Public*, pg. 1002

SCOTCH—NONE—Electronic Products Division; *U.S. Public*, pg. 1605

SCOTCH—Pearled Barley & Oatmeal—The Quaker Oats Company; *U.S. Public*, pg. 1347

SCOTCH—PSA Tape, Adhesive, Multiple Products—3M; *U.S. Public*, pg. 1604

SCOTCH-BRITE—Cleaning & Finishing Materials & Systems—3M; *U.S. Public*, pg. 1604

SCOTCH-CLAD—Protective Coatings for Industrial & Construction Applications—3M; *U.S. Public*, pg. 1604

SCOTCH-CORE—Syntactic Core Material—3M; *U.S. Public*, pg. 1604

SCOTCH FLEX—NONE—Electronic Products Division; *U.S. Public*, pg. 1605

SCOTCH-GRIP—Industrial Adhesives & Solvents—3M; *U.S. Public*, pg. 1604

SCOTCH-MELT—Adhesives, Hot Melt—3M; *U.S. Public*, pg. 1604

SCOTCH-MESH—Wood Floor Refinishing Discs—3M; *U.S. Public,* pg. 1604

SCOTCH-MOUNT—Double Coated Foam Tapes—3M; *U.S. Public,* pg. 1604

SCOTCH-SEAL—Sealants—3M; *U.S. Public,* pg. 1604

SCOTCH-WELD—Structural Adhesives—3M; *U.S. Public,* pg. 1604

SCOTCHBAN—Fluorochemical Treatment to Protect Paper—3M; *U.S. Public,* pg. 1604

SCOTCHBLOK—Masking Paper—3M; *U.S. Public,* pg. 1604

SCOTCHBOND—Dental Adhesive—3M; *U.S. Public,* pg. 1604

SCOTCHCAL—Film, Colored Film Vinyl, Drag Reduction Tape—3M; *U.S. Public,* pg. 1604

SCOTCHCAP—Laminating Films, Pressure Sensitive, Transparent—3M; *U.S. Public,* pg. 1604

SCOTCHCART—Broadcast Cartridge—3M; *U.S. Public,* pg. 1604

SCOTCHCAST—Cable Splicing Material, Electrical Resins, Orthopedic Casting Tape—3M; *U.S. Public,* pg. 1604

SCOTCHCODE—Wire Markers, Cable I.D.—3M; *U.S. Public,* pg. 1604

SCOTCHDAMP—Sound & Vibration Damping Products—3M; *U.S. Public,* pg. 1604

SCOTCHFIL—Electrical Insulation Putty—3M; *U.S. Public,* pg. 1604

SCOTCHFLEX—Communications & Signal Wiring Flat Cable Connector Systems, Electronic—3M; *U.S. Public,* pg. 1604

SCOTCHFOAM—Single-Coated Foam Tapes—3M; *U.S. Public,* pg. 1604

SCOTCHGARD—Fabric Protector Treatments, Carpet, Upholstery & Fabric Protector—3M; *U.S. Public,* pg. 1604

SCOTCHGEL—Dental Enamel Etchant—3M; *U.S. Public,* pg. 1604

SCOTCHKOTE—Electrical Coating, Epoxy Protective Coatings—3M; *U.S. Public,* pg. 1604

SCOTCHKUT—Stencil-Cutting Dies for Letters—3M; *U.S. Public,* pg. 1604

SCOTCHLANE—Reflective Adhesive-Backed Plastic Markings—3M; *U.S. Public,* pg. 1604

SCOTCHLENS—Reflector—3M; *U.S. Public,* pg. 1604

SCOTCHLITE—Retroreflective Adhesive Coated Sheeting, Glass Bubbles—3M; *U.S. Public,* pg. 1604

SCOTCHLOK—Compression Connectors, Electrical Splice Connectors—3M; *U.S. Public,* pg. 1604

SCOTCHMAN—Hydraulic Ironworkers, Punches & Shears—Scotchman Industries, Inc.; *U.S. Private,* pg. 636

SCOTCHMAN/BEWO—Circular Cold Saws—Scotchman Industries, Inc.; *U.S. Private,* pg. 636

SCOTCHMARK—Label Stock, Marking Films, Printable Tapes, Marker System—3M; *U.S. Public,* pg. 1604

SCOTCHMATE—Hook & Loop Fasteners—3M; *U.S. Public,* pg. 1604

SCOTCHPAD—Label Protection Tapes in Pad Form—3M; *U.S. Public,* pg. 1604

SCOTCHPAK—Heat Sealable Polyester Film—3M; *U.S. Public,* pg. 1604

SCOTCHPAR—Polyester Films, Film Backing for Pressure-Sensitive Tapes—3M; *U.S. Public,* pg. 1604

SCOTCHPLATE—Conductive Adhesive Dispersive Electrodes, Surgical, Electroplating Process—3M; *U.S. Public,* pg. 1604

SCOTCHPLY—Reinforced Composites—3M; *U.S. Public,* pg. 1604

SCOTCHPRIME—Dental Restorative Primer—3M; *U.S. Public,* pg. 1604

SCOTCHPRO—Film Backing for PSA Tapes—3M; *U.S. Public,* pg. 1604

SCOTCHRAP—Corrosion Protection Tape; Veterinary Bandage—3M; *U.S. Public,* pg. 1604

SCOTCHSHIELD—Safety & Security Film—3M; *U.S. Public,* pg. 1604

SCOTCHTAB—Peel-Open Closures—3M; *U.S. Public,* pg. 1604

SCOTCHTINT—Films—3M; *U.S. Public,* pg. 1604

SCOTCHTRAK—Circuit Reader—3M; *U.S. Public,* pg. 1604

SCOTS LION—Scotch—Laird & Company; *U.S. Private,* pg. 642

SCOTS PRIDE—NONE—American Woodmark Corporation; *U.S. Public,* pg. 96

SCOTSMAN—Ice Machines, Drink Dispensers, Bins & Crushers—Scotsman Industries, Inc.; *U.S. Public,* pg. 1444

SCOTT—NONE—Figgie International Inc.; *U.S. Public,* pg. 622

SCOTT—NONE—Kimberly-Clark Corporation; *U.S. Public,* pg. 958

SCOTT—NONE—Kruger Inc.; *Int'l,* pg. 761

SCOTT-ALERT—Portable Gas Detector—Scott Aviation; *U.S. Public,* pg. 622

SCOTT-O-VISTA—Masks—Scott Aviation; *U.S. Public,* pg. 622

SCOTT PETERSEN—Meat Products—John Morrell & Co.; *U.S. Public,* pg. 1479

SCOTT'S EMULSION—Vitamin & Tonic—SmithKline Beecham plc; *Int'l,* pg. 1264

SCOTT U.S.A.—Ski & Motorcycle Prods.—Scott U.S.A.; *U.S. Private,* pg. 977

SCOTT'S—Rolled Oats—The Quaker Oats Company; *U.S. Public,* pg. 1347

SCOTTEX—NONE—Kimberly-Clark Corporation; *U.S. Public,* pg. 958

SCOTTI BROTHERS PICTURES—Motion Picture Production—All American Communications, Inc.; *U.S. Public,* pg. 41

SCOTTI BROTHERS RECORDS—Record Production—All American Communications, Inc.; *U.S. Public,* pg. 41

SCOTTIES—NONE—Kimberly-Clark Corporation; *U.S. Public,* pg. 958

SCOTTISH AMICABLE—NONE—Prudential Corporation PLC; *Int'l,* pg. 1073

SCOTTISH DEVELOPMENT FINANCE—NONE—Scottish Enterprise; *Int'l,* pg. 1212

SCOTTISH TRADE INTERNATIONAL—NONE—Scottish Enterprise; *Int'l,* pg. 1212

SCOTTISH WIDOWS—Logo—Scottish Widows' Fund & Life Assurance Society; *Int'l,* pg. 1212

SCOTTORAMIC—Masks—Scott Aviation; *U.S. Public,* pg. 622

SCOTT'S—Emulsion, Cod Liver Oil Product—SmithKline Beecham Corporation; *Int'l,* pg. 1264

SCOTT'S EMULSION—Vitamin Food Supplement—SmithKline Beecham Consumer Healthcare, U.S.; *Int'l,* pg. 1264

SCOTT'S EMULSION—NONE—SmithKline Beecham Corporation; *Int'l,* pg. 1264

SCOTT'S LIQUID GOLD—Glass Cleaner, Wood Preservative & Cleaner—Scott's Liquid Gold-Inc.; *U.S. Public,* pg. 1447

SCOTTSDALE MOUNTAIN—Residential Community—Suncor Development Company; *U.S. Public,* pg. 1298

SCOTTY CAMERON—Titleist Putters—Fortune Brands, Inc.; *U.S. Public,* pg. 674

SCOTTY CAMERON BY TITLEIST—Putters—Acushnet Company; *U.S. Public,* pg. 675

SCOTTY CAMERON BY TITLEIST—NONE—Titleist & Foot-Joy Worldwide; *U.S. Public,* pg. 675

SCOTTY TRANSPORTABLES—NONE—Scott Specialty Gases; *U.S. Private,* pg. 977

SCOTTY'S—Hardware, House & Garden & Homebuilding Supplies—GIB Group; *Int'l,* pg. 532

SCOTTY'S—Building Supplies—Scotty's, Inc.; *Int'l,* pg. 533

SCOUPE—Automobile—Hyundai Motor America; *Int'l,* pg. 641

SCOUR POWER—Scrubbers—Magla Products; *U.S. Private,* pg. 695

SCOURGE—Pesticide-Mosquito Adulticide—Roussel Corporation; *Int'l,* pg. 625

SCOURGE—Pesticide-Mosquito Adulticide—Roussel UCLAF S.A.; *Int'l,* pg. 626

SCOURGUARD—NONE—Pfizer Inc.; *U.S. Public,* pg. 1281

SCOURGUARD—Animal Vaccine—SmithKline Beecham plc; *Int'l,* pg. 1264

SCOURMUNE-CRT—Swine Vaccine—Schering-Plough Corporation; *U.S. Public,* pg. 1438

SCOURSHIELD—NONE—Pfizer Inc.; *U.S. Public,* pg. 1281

SCOUT—Otoacoustic Emissions System—Bio-Logic Systems Corp.; *U.S. Public,* pg. 230

SCOUT—Power Electronic Charging System—C&D Charter Power Systems; *U.S. Public,* pg. 271

SCOUT—Computer Software Program—Datapoint Corporation; *Int'l,* pg. 384

SCOUT—Car Seat—Evenflo Company, Inc.; *U.S. Private,* pg. 629

SCOUT—Industrial Chemical—Hercules Chemical Co., Inc.; *U.S. Private,* pg. 523

SCOUT—Unmanned Reconnaissance Aircraft—Israel Aircraft Industries Ltd.; *Int'l,* pg. 689

SCOUT—Label & Printing Machine—Monarch Marking Systems; *U.S. Public,* pg. 1266

SCOUT—Spotting Scope—Swift Instruments, Inc.; *U.S. Private,* pg. 1058

SCOUT II—Cultivator Guidance System—Fleischer Manufacturing, Inc.; *U.S. Private,* pg. 410

SCOUTLITE—Cutlery—Buck Knives, Inc.; *U.S. Private,* pg. 177

SCRABBLE—Crossword Game—Milton Bradley Company; *U.S. Public,* pg. 797

SCRAM—Emergency Release Scrubber—ATMI, Inc.; *U.S. Public,* pg. 12

SCRAM—15 Minute Escape Respirator—Scott Aviation; *U.S. Public,* pg. 622

SCRAPE-AWAY—Concrete Floor Preparation Tool—Flo-Pac Corporation; *U.S. Private,* pg. 414

SCRAPERS—NONE—Pacific Handy Cutter, Inc.; *U.S. Private,* pg. 831

SCRAPPER—Recycle/Reclaim Extruder—Davis Standard Corporation; *U.S. Public,* pg. 459

SCRATCH-FIX—Liquid Auto Touch-Up Paint—Sherwin-Williams Diversified Brands, Inc.; *U.S. Public,* pg. 1466

SCRATCHEX—Flea & Tick Guard Products—Combe Incorporated; *U.S. Private,* pg. 257

SCRATCHGUARD—Kitchen & Bathroom Cleaner—Turtle Wax, Inc.; *U.S. Private,* pg. 1110

SCRATCHINGS—Greeting Cards, Stationery & Party Goods—American Greetings Corporation; *U.S. Public,* pg. 77

SCRATCHPROBE—NONE—GenRad, Inc.; *U.S. Public,* pg. 731

SCRATCHPROBING—Technique—GenRad, Inc.; *U.S. Public,* pg. 731

SCREAMERS—Children's Playwear—Kleinert's, Inc.; *U.S. Private,* pg. 625

SCREAMERS—Fluorescent Spray Paint—Mar-Hyde Corporation; *U.S. Public,* pg. 1357

SCREAMING YELLOW ZONKERS—Snack—Novartis Nutrition Corporation; *Int'l,* pg. 974

SCREED PRO—Construction Laser Equip.—Spectra-Physics Laserplane Inc.; *U.S. Public,* pg. 1594

SCREEN—Seed Protectant—The Agricultural Group, Monsanto Company; *U.S. Public,* pg. 1125

SCREEN—Grain Sorghum, Seed Protectants—Monsanto Company; *U.S. Public,* pg. 1124

SCREEN—NONE—Taylor Impression, Inc.; *U.S. Private,* pg. 1070

SCREEN-BAK—Abrasive Cloth Mesh—Norton Company; *Int'l,* pg. 1173

SCREEN FRONT—Grill Insert—Lund International Holdings, Inc.; *U.S. Public,* pg. 1020

SCREEN READER—Computer Product—International Business Machines Corporation; *U.S. Public,* pg. 895

SCREEN STARS—Apparel For Imprinting—Fruit of the Loom, Inc.; *U.S. Public,* pg. 685

SCREEN-TEST—Video-Based Testing Program—NFO Research, Inc.; *U.S. Public,* pg. 1146

SCREENGUARD—Perforated Rolling Door—Cornell Iron Works, Inc.; *U.S. Private,* pg. 276

SCREENMASTER—Stock Preparation—Beloit Corporation; *U.S. Public,* pg. 789

SCREENMASTER—Screen—Svedala Industries-Universal Engineering; *Int'l,* pg. 1326

SCREENPOWER—Software Allowing Blind People to Access Computers—Telesensory Corporation; *U.S. Private,* pg. 1074

SCREENSAFE—CRT Screen Cleaner for Uncoated & Multi-Coated Screens—Falcon Safety Products Inc.; *U.S. Private,* pg. 392

SCREENSERT—Filters—Pall Corporation; *U.S. Public,* pg. 1253

SCREENVIEW—Computer Product—International Business Machines Corporation; *U.S. Public,* pg. 895

SCREENWIPE—CRT Cleaning System—Aldine Technologies Industries Inc.; *U.S. Private*, pg. 33

SCREENWIPE—CRT Cleaning System—Lensclean, Inc.; *U.S. Private*, pg. 162

SCREW-DOWN—Specialty Nails—Maze Nails; *U.S. Private*, pg. 718

SCREW-LIFTS—Vertical Screw Elevators—Screw Conveyor Corp.; *U.S. Private*, pg. 977

SCREW-SHOOTERS—Power Tools—Milwaukee Electric Tool Corp.; *Int'l*, pg. 96

SCREWBALLS—Ice Cream Product—NDS; *Int'l*, pg. 918

SCREWLOOSE—Auto Products—CRC Industries, Inc.; *U.S. Private*, pg. 138

SCREWY—Hooks & Fittings for Wire Rope—Esco Corporation; *U.S. Private*, pg. 382

SCRIBBLES & GIGGLES—Retail Card & Gift Shops; Stationery; T-Shirts—American Greetings Corporation; *U.S. Public*, pg. 77

SCRIBE—Writing Paper—Kimberly-Clark Corporation; *U.S. Public*, pg. 958

SCRIPSET—Paper Coating Resin—Monsanto Company; *U.S. Public*, pg. 1124

SCRIPTMASTER—Postscript Software—Linotype-Hell Company; *Int'l*, pg. 604

SCRIPTO—Disposable Lighter—Scripto-Tokai Corp.; *U.S. Private*, pg. 977

SCRIPTO—Writing Instruments—Scripto-Tokai Corp.; *U.S. Private*, pg. 977

SCRIPTRAC—Physician Profiles—Pharmaceutical Marketing Services Inc.; *U.S. Public*, pg. 1284

SCRIPTRAC PLUS—Physician Prescribing Behavior—Pharmaceutical Marketing Services Inc.; *U.S. Public*, pg. 1284

SCRIPTURE MEMORY SONGS—NONE—Integrity Incorporated; *U.S. Public*, pg. 886

SCROLL—Beauty Salon Furniture—Belvedere Company; *U.S. Private*, pg. 1008

SCROLL EMBROIDERIES—Bras, Panties, Bodysuit, Shapewear—Olga Div.; *U.S. Public*, pg. 1738

SCRUB-ALL—Cleansing Pad—Magla Products; *U.S. Private*, pg. 695

SCRUB AND VAC—Small Vacuum—Advance Machine Company; *Int'l*, pg. 932

SCRUB-GRIT—Abrasive Rotary Brush for Scrubbing—Flo-Pac Corporation; *U.S. Private*, pg. 414

SCRUB 'N' VAC—Rug & Floor Conditioner—Hoover Company; *U.S. Public*, pg. 1065

SCRUB-VACTOR—Vacuum Pumps—Croll-Reynolds Company, Inc.; *U.S. Private*, pg. 290

SCRUB-WARE—Stainless Steel Scrub Sinks—Acorn Engineering Company; *U.S. Private*, pg. 14

SCRUBBABLE TUFFWALL—Interior/Exterior Paint—Buten, Division of Duron; *U.S. Private*, pg. 349

SCRUBBEE—Scouring Pad—Bristol-Myers Squibb Company; *U.S. Public*, pg. 253

SCRUBBING BUBBLE—Bathroom Cleaner—The Dow Chemical Company; *U.S. Public*, pg. 522

SCRUGUN—Power Tools—The Black & Decker Corporation; *U.S. Public*, pg. 233

SCUBAPRO—Snorkeling & Underwater Diving Equipment—Johnson Worldwide Associates, Inc.; *U.S. Public*, pg. 932

SCUDO—Car—Fiat Auto Ireland Ltd.; *Int'l*, pg. 481

SCUFF-BUFF—Rotary Brush for Light Scrubbing—Flo-Pac Corporation; *U.S. Private*, pg. 414

SCUFF GUARD—Deck Stain—PPG Industries, Inc.; *U.S. Public*, pg. 1245

SCUFFIE FOOTLIGHTS—Slippers—Reliable Knitting Works; *U.S. Private*, pg. 920

SCUFFIES—Slippers—Reliable Knitting Works; *U.S. Private*, pg. 920

SCUFFSHIELD—Floor Coverings—Domco Inc.; *Int'l*, pg. 415

SCULPTOR—Annuloplasty Ring—Medtronic, Inc.; *U.S. Public*, pg. 1082

SCULPTURA—Watches—Baume Mercier, Inc.; *U.S. Private*, pg. 124

SCULPTURA—Telephones—Lucent Technologies Inc.; *U.S. Public*, pg. 1017

SCULPTURE SEAT—Contour Seat Module—Interkal, Inc.; *Int'l*, pg. 759

SCULPTURED—Flexible Circuits—Advanced Circuit Technology; *U.S. Private*, pg. 21

SCYTHE—Herbicide—Mycogen Corporation; *U.S. Public*, pg. 1142

SE-QUENCER—Effects Memory System Enhancement—Tektronix-Video & Networking Div., Grass Valley Products; *U.S. Public*, pg. 1567

SEA ALASKA—Seafood—ConAgra, Inc.; *U.S. Public*, pg. 425

SEA ANGLER—Fishing Magazine—EMAP Pursuit Publishing; *Int'l*, pg. 451

SEA-BEST—Seafood—Beaver Street Fisheries, Inc.; *U.S. Private*, pg. 128

SEA BOND—Denture Adhesive—Combe Incorporated; *U.S. Private*, pg. 257

SEA BREEZE—Skin Care Product—Bristol-Myers Squibb Company; *U.S. Public*, pg. 253

SEA BREEZE—Antiseptic for the Skin, Towelettes & Moisture Lotion—Clairol, Inc.; *U.S. Public*, pg. 254

SEA BREEZE—NONE—Nordyne Inc.; *U.S. Public*, pg. 1193

SEA CLUB—Activewear—Sao Paulo Alpargatas S.A.; *Int'l*, pg. 1193

SEA DART—Medium-Range, All-Weather Missile—British Aerospace p.l.c.; *Int'l*, pg. 217

SEA-DOO—Watercraft—Bombardier Inc.; *Int'l*, pg. 199

SEA EAGLE—Long-Range Missile—British Aerospace p.l.c.; *Int'l*, pg. 217

SEA ELECTRONICS—NONE—Lowrance Electronics, Inc.; *U.S. Public*, pg. 1015

SEA-EST—Seafood—Beaver Street Fisheries, Inc.; *U.S. Private*, pg. 128

SEA FRESH—Seafood—National Sea Products Limited; *Int'l*, pg. 909

SEA HAWK—Fishing Boats—Chris-Craft Boats; *U.S. Private*, pg. 478

SEA ISLAND—Residential Resort & Devel.—Sea Island Company; *U.S. Private*, pg. 977

SEA KING—Binoculars—Swift Instruments, Inc.; *U.S. Private*, pg. 1058

SEA LORD—New Zealand Fish Fillets & Lobstertails—Mitsui Foods, Inc.; *Int'l*, pg. 879

SEA MAID—Seafood Products—Sau-Sea Foods, Inc.; *U.S. Private*, pg. 967

SEA-MERSIBLE—Motor—Franklin Electric Co., Inc.; *U.S. Public*, pg. 679

SEA MIST—Hair & Skin Care Products—Freeman Cosmetic Corp.; *U.S. Private*, pg. 426

SEA MIST PINE—Lumber & Wood Products—Georgia-Pacific Corporation; *U.S. Public*, pg. 735

SEA-NINE—Biocide—Rohm and Haas Company; *U.S. Public*, pg. 1403

SEA NYMPH—Boats—Outboard Marine Corporation; *U.S. Private*, pg. 478

SEA NYMPH—Marine Products; Boats & Pontoons—Sea Nymph Inc.; *U.S. Private*, pg. 478

SEA-OF-TILES—Technology—Gatefield Corporation; *U.S. Public*, pg. 703

SEA PASTA—Seafood Product—Hosho America Inc.; *Int'l*, pg. 733

SEA-POWER—Liquified Seaweed—Security Lawn & Garden Co.; *U.S. Private*, pg. 397

SEA RANGER—Loran Navigational & Fishing Radar—E & B Marine Incorporated; *U.S. Public*, pg. 1756

SEA RAY—Fiberglass Boats—Brunswick Corporation; *U.S. Public*, pg. 265

SEA SCAMP—Swimwear—Camp Healthcare; *Int'l*, pg. 1425

SEA SKUA—Light-Weight Sea-Skimming Missile—British Aerospace p.l.c.; *Int'l*, pg. 217

SEA STAR—Frozen Seafood—Coldwater Seafood Corporation; *U.S. Private*, pg. 251

SEA STIX SALAD STYLE—Seafood Product—Hosho America Inc.; *Int'l*, pg. 733

SEA STIX WHOLE LEG—Seafood Product—Hosho America Inc.; *Int'l*, pg. 733

SEA STRIKE—Sporting Goods—Brunswick Bowling & Billiards Corp.; *U.S. Public*, pg. 265

SEA TAILS—Seafood Product—Hosho America Inc.; *Int'l*, pg. 733

SEA-TEE—Menu Item—Tastee Freez International Inc.; *U.S. Private*, pg. 1069

SEA VIEW—Class A Motorhome—National R.V., Inc.; *U.S. Public*, pg. 1159

SEA WOLF—Binoculars—Swift Instruments, Inc.; *U.S. Private*, pg. 1058

SEA WORLD OF CALIFORNIA—Family Entertainment Park—Busch Entertainment Corp.; *U.S. Public*, pg. 114

SEA WORLD OF FLORIDA—Family Entertainment Park—Busch Entertainment Corp.; *U.S. Public*, pg. 114

SEA WORLD OF FLORIDA—Amusement Park—Sea World of Florida; *U.S. Public*, pg. 114

SEA WORLD OF OHIO—Family Entertainment Park—Busch Entertainment Corp.; *U.S. Public*, pg. 114

SEA WORLD OF TEXAS—Family Entertainment Park—Busch Entertainment Corp.; *U.S. Public*, pg. 114

SEABLENDS—Surimi Analogs—Peter Pan Seafoods, Inc.; *Int'l*, pg. 928

SEABOURN CRUISE LINE—Cruise Line—Carnival Corporation; *U.S. Public*, pg. 306

SEABREEZE—NONE—National R.V., Inc.; *U.S. Public*, pg. 1159

SEABROOK—Wicker—Avon Workshop Ficks Reed; *U.S. Private*, pg. 102

SEABULK TANKERS—NONE—Hvide Marine Incorporated; *U.S. Public*, pg. 851

SEABURY & SMITH—Insurance Program Management—Marsh & McLennan Companies, Inc.; *U.S. Public*, pg. 1048

SEACEL—Magnesium Silver Chloride Batteries—Yardney Technical Products, Inc.; *U.S. Private*, pg. 376

SEACO—Container Lessor—Sea Containers Ltd.; *Int'l*, pg. 1213

SEAFARER—Interior Floors—Monarch Tile, Inc.; *U.S. Private*, pg. 287

SEAFIRST—Bank Holding Company—Seafirst Corporation; *U.S. Public*, pg. 181

SEAFIT—Various Accessories—E & B Marine Incorporated; *U.S. Public*, pg. 1756

SEAFIT—Boating Hardware—Goldbergs Marine Distributors; *U.S. Public*, pg. 1756

SEAFIT—NONE—Iceland Seafood Corporation; *U.S. Private*, pg. 556

SEAFLEX—Marine Paint—Jotun A/S; *Int'l*, pg. 714

SEAFOOD ONE STEP—Seafood Seasoning—McCormick/Schilling; *U.S. Public*, pg. 1066

SEAFRESH—Frozen Seafoods—National Sea Products Incorporated; *Int'l*, pg. 909

SEAFRESH—NONE—Wards Cove Packing Company; *U.S. Private*, pg. 1149

SEAGRAM MIXERS—Beverages—The Coca-Cola Bottling Co. of New York, Inc.; *U.S. Public*, pg. 393

SEAGRAM'S—Gin & Wine Cooler—The House of Seagram; *Int'l*, pg. 1217

SEAGRAM'S COOLERS—Wine Coolers—The Seagram Company Ltd.; *Int'l*, pg. 1214

SEAGRAM'S COOLERS—Wine Coolers in a Variety of Flavors—Seagram Beverage Co.; *Int'l*, pg. 1215

SEAGRAM'S EXTRA DRY—Gin—The Seagram Company Ltd.; *Int'l*, pg. 1214

SEAGRAM'S MIXES—Soft Drink Mixes—Seagram Beverage Co.; *Int'l*, pg. 1215

SEAGRAM'S V.O.—Liquor—The House of Seagram; *Int'l*, pg. 1217

SEAGUARD—Close-in Weapon-Gun-System—Oerlikon-Contraves AG; *Int'l*, pg. 998

SEAGULL SUBMARINE—NONE—General Dynamics Corporation; *U.S. Public*, pg. 708

SEAHORSE—Outdoor Gas Water Heating System—Gas-Fired Products, Inc.; *U.S. Private*, pg. 440

SEAL—Heavy Knit Socks—Wigwam Mills, Inc.; *U.S. Private*, pg. 1175

SEAL-A-RIDGE—NONE—Elcor Corporation; *U.S. Public*, pg. 567

SEAL BULK—Container Liner System—TBG Management S.A.M.; *Int'l*, pg. 1335

SEAL CLEAR TECH—Counter Top Laminator—Seal Products Incorporated; *U.S. Public*, pg. 849

SEAL COAT—Heat Activated Coated Paper Used With Heat Seal Mailing Equipment—Shade/Allied, Inc.; *U.S. Public*, pg. 89

SEAL COAT—NONE—Sierra Coating Technologies; *U.S. Private*, pg. 998

SEAL EASY-PEEL—Release Paper—Seal Products Incorporated; *U.S. Public*, pg. 849

SEAL FORCE MONITOR—Sealing & Seal Testing Apparatus—The West Company, Incorporated; *U.S. Public*, pg. 1755

SEAL-GARD—Plastic Wrap—Reynolds Metals Company; *U.S. Public*, pg. 1385

SEAL-GUARD—Plastic Wrap—Reynolds Metals Company; *U.S. Public*, pg. 1385

SEAL KEENCUT—Mat Cutters—Seal Products Incorporated; *U.S. Public*, pg. 849

SEAL-LAMIN—Roller Laminator Films—Seal Products Incorporated; *U.S. Public*, pg. 849

SEAL LAMINTOR RH SERIES—Motorizcol Heated Roller Laminator—Seal Products Incorporated; *U.S. Public*, pg. 849

SEAL-LESS—Pumps—March Manufacturing Inc.; *U.S. Private*, pg. 702

SEAL-LOCK—Fascia & Flashing System—Johns Manville Corporation; *U.S. Public*, pg. 927

SEAL-LUME—Sealed Outdoor HID Units—Guth Lighting Company; *Int'l*, pg. 821

SEAL MT5—Mounting Tissue—Seal Products Incorporated; *U.S. Public*, pg. 849

SEAL N PLACE—Repair Kit—Kidde-Fenwal, Inc.; *Int'l*, pg. 1500

SEAL'N RESEAL—Envelopes—Tension Envelope Corp.; *U.S. Private*, pg. 1077

SEAL-O-MATIC—Steel Cookware—Regal Ware, Inc.; *U.S. Private*, pg. 917

SEAL OF ARIZONA—UDA Butter Label—United Dairymen of Arizona; *U.S. Private*, pg. 1121

SEAL-PAK—PTFE String Packing & Gasket Materials—Furon Fluorglas Products; *U.S. Public*, pg. 689

SEAL PROCUT—Board Cutters—Seal Products Incorporated; *U.S. Public*, pg. 849

SEAL RITE—Cookware & Design—Regal Ware, Inc.; *U.S. Private*, pg. 917

SEAL-RITE AUTOMOTIVE WEATHER STRIP—Consumer Products—Thermwell Products Co., Inc.; *U.S. Private*, pg. 1081

SEAL TECHNOLOGY SYSTEMS—Sealing Systems—Federal-Mogul Corporation; *U.S. Public*, pg. 615

SEAL-X—Conduit Fitting—Killark Electric Manufacturing Co.; *U.S. Public*, pg. 844

SEAL-UP—Laparoscopic Instruments—U.S. Surgical Corp.; *U.S. Public*, pg. 1687

SEALAIR—Windows—Kawneer Company; *U.S. Public*, pg. 60

SEALAMIN—Laminating Film—Seal Products Incorporated; *U.S. Public*, pg. 849

SEALBRITE—NONE—EcoScience Corporation; *U.S. Public*, pg. 563

SEALCLAMP—Muffler Clamp—Donaldson Company, Inc.; *U.S. Public*, pg. 517

SEALD-SWEET—Citrus Fruits—Sealed-Sweet Growers, Inc.; *U.S. Private*, pg. 978

SEALDON—NONE—CertainTeed Corporation; *Int'l*, pg. 1170

SEALED-AIRE—Tires—Bridgestone/Firestone, Inc.; *Int'l*, pg. 213

SEALED POWER—Steering & Suspension Parts—Federal-Mogul Corporation; *U.S. Public*, pg. 615

SEALER PANE—Plastic Sheets & Moldings—Bunzl Extrusion; *Int'l*, pg. 232

SEALERMATE—Impact & Nonimpact Printed Mailing System Forms—Moore Document Solutions; *Int'l*, pg. 890

SEALEZE—Roller Laminator Systems—Seal Products Incorporated; *U.S. Public*, pg. 849

SEALEZE OPTIMOUNT UV—Clear Mounting Adhesive—Seal Products Incorporated; *U.S. Public*, pg. 849

SEALEZE POWERCUT—Board Cutters—Seal Products Incorporated; *U.S. Public*, pg. 849

SEALEZE PRINTSHIELD—Pressure-Sensitive Films—Seal Products Incorporated; *U.S. Public*, pg. 849

SEALIGHT—Surmi Crab Analogues—Mitsui Foods, Inc.; *Int'l*, pg. 879

SEALIKES—Surimi Shrimp Analogues—Mitsui Foods, Inc.; *Int'l*, pg. 879

SEALIT—Cement—Fisher Scientific Company; *U.S. Private*, pg. 658

SEALKLEEN—Membrane Filters—Pall Corporation; *U.S. Public*, pg. 1253

SEALLOY—PTFE Specialty Compounded Materials—Macrotech Plyseal, Inc.; *U.S. Private*, pg. 693

SEALMARK—Memorials—Rock of Ages Corporation; *U.S. Public*, pg. 1396

SEALMASTER—Bearings—Emerson Power Transmission Corporation; *U.S. Public*, pg. 573

SEALMASTER—Plumbing Product—Radiator Specialty Company; *U.S. Private*, pg. 906

SEALSKIN—Roofing Insulation—BMCA Insulation Products, Inc.; *U.S. Private*, pg. 433

SEALSKIN—Plastic Coated Paper Stock—Georgia-Pacific Corporation; *U.S. Public*, pg. 735

SEALSTRIP—Rubber Tape—The Standard Products Company; *U.S. Public*, pg. 1504

SEALTEST—Ice Cream—Philip Morris Companies Inc.; *U.S. Public*, pg. 1287

SEALTITE—Industrial Wood Sealer/Paint—ISK BioSciences; *Int'l*, pg. 689

SEALTONIC—Wetting Agent—Seal Products Incorporated; *U.S. Public*, pg. 849

SEALTROFF—Sealed Fluorescent Troffers—Guth Lighting Company; *Int'l*, pg. 821

SEALVAR—Iron/Nickel/Cobalt—AMETEK, Inc.; *U.S. Public*, pg. 99

SEALWRAP—Institution Products Film—AEP Industries, Inc.; *U.S. Public*, pg. 4

SEALWRAP—Packaging Film—Borden, Inc.; *U.S. Private*, pg. 157

SEALY—Mattresses, Box Springs & Convertible Sofas—Sealy Corporation; *U.S. Private*, pg. 978

SEALY—Mattress—Sealy Mattress Company of Memphis; *U.S. Private*, pg. 979

SEALY POSTUREPEDIC—Mattresses—Sealy, Inc.; *U.S. Private*, pg. 979

SEALY POSTUREPEDIC—NONE—Sealy of Maryland & Virginia, Inc.; *U.S. Private*, pg. 979

SEAMATE HB—Marine Paint—Jotun A/S; *Int'l*, pg. 714

SEAMLESS—Electronic Instrument—Intel Corporation; *U.S. Public*, pg. 886

SEAMOL—Dampener Cover—Jomac, Inc.; *U.S. Private*, pg. 595

SEANAV—Sea-Based Navigation System—Kearfott Guidance & Navigation Corp.; *U.S. Private*, pg. 93

SEAPAK—Seafood—Rich Products Corp.; *U.S. Private*, pg. 928

SEAPAK—Frozen Fish—Rich SeaPak Corp.; *U.S. Private*, pg. 928

SEAPORT CAFE & BAR—Restaurant—Houlihan's Restaurant Group; *U.S. Public*, pg. 841

SEAQUEST—Diving Equipment—U.S. Divers Co., Inc.; *U.S. Private*, pg. 1125

SEARANGER—Boating Electronics—Goldbergs Marine Distributors; *U.S. Public*, pg. 1756

SEARCH—Software—Fair, Isaac and Company, Inc.; *U.S. Public*, pg. 609

SEARCH AND CREATE—Software—LSI Logic Corp.; *U.S. Public*, pg. 971

SEARCHMANAGER/2—Computer Product—International Business Machines Corporation; *U.S. Public*, pg. 895

SEAROVER—Remotely Operated Vehicle—Benthos, Inc.; *U.S. Public*, pg. 212

SEARS—NONE—Sears, Roebuck and Co.; *U.S. Public*, pg. 1452

SEARS CRAFTSMAN—Tool Storage Products—Fortune Brands, Inc.; *U.S. Public*, pg. 674

SEARS CRAFTSMAN—NONE—MasterBrand Industries, Inc.; *U.S. Public*, pg. 675

SEARS CRAFTSMAN—NONE—Waterloo Industries, Inc.; *U.S. Public*, pg. 675

SEARS CRAFTSMAN GARAGE DOOR OPENER—Garage Door Opener—The Chamberlain Group, Inc.; *U.S. Private*, pg. 344

SEARS CRAFTSMAN WAXER/POLISHERS—Waxers/Polishers—The Chamberlain Group, Inc.; *U.S. Private*, pg. 344

SEARS OPTICAL—Eyewear—Cole National Corporation; *U.S. Public*, pg. 396

SEARS POINT RACEWAY—NONE—Speedway Motorsports, Inc.; *U.S. Public*, pg. 1498

SEARS PORTRAIT STUDIOS—Portrait Photography—CPI Corp.; *U.S. Public*, pg. 283

SEARS RENT A CAR—Car Rental—Budget Rent A Car Corporation; *U.S. Private*, pg. 178

SEARS RENT A TRUCK—Truck Rental—Budget Rent A Car Corporation; *U.S. Private*, pg. 178

SEAS'N EASY—Seafood Line—McCormick/Schilling; *U.S. Private*, pg. 1066

SEAS-OLEUM—Seasoning—McCormick & Company, Incorporated; *U.S. Public*, pg. 1066

SEASCAPE—Plywood, Lumber, Wood & Wood Fiber Products—Georgia-Pacific Corporation; *U.S. Public*, pg. 735

SEASIDE—Canned Dry Packed Beans—Faribault Foods Inc.; *U.S. Private*, pg. 393

SEASON—Tissues & Sanitary Towels—Sime Darby Berhad; *Int'l*, pg. 1249

SEASON-ALL—Spices & Seasonings—McCormick & Company, Incorporated; *U.S. Public*, pg. 1066

SEASON ALL—Seasoning—McCormick/Schilling; *U.S. Public*, pg. 1066

SEASON'N FRY—Chicken Seasoning—McCormick & Company, Incorporated; *U.S. Public*, pg. 1066

SEASONITE—Stabilizing Treatment for Pressure-Treated Wood & All New Exterior Woods—The Flood Company; *U.S. Private*, pg. 414

SEASON'S BEST—Beer—The F.X. Matt Brewing Co.; *U.S. Private*, pg. 714

SEASTAR—Hydr. Fluid; Gauges & Instr. for Boats, Tachometers & Oil Pressure Gauge—Teleflex Incorporated; *U.S. Public*, pg. 1569

SEASWEPT—Glazed Ceramic Tile—Porcelanite, Inc.; *Int'l*, pg. 573

SEASWIRL—Boats—Outboard Marine Corporation; *U.S. Public*, pg. 478

SEAT—Automobile—Volkswagen AG; *Int'l*, pg. 1473

SEAT CORDOBA—Automobile—Volkswagen AG; *Int'l*, pg. 1473

SEAT IBIZA—Automobile—Volkswagen AG; *Int'l*, pg. 1473

SEAT INCA—Light Commercial Vehicle—Volkswagen AG; *Int'l*, pg. 1473

SEAT MARBELLA—Automobile—Volkswagen AG; *Int'l*, pg. 1473

SEAT TERRA—Van—Volkswagen AG; *Int'l*, pg. 1473

SEAT TOLEDO—Automobile—Volkswagen AG; *Int'l*, pg. 1473

SEATEAK—Recreational Teak Accessories—Valley Forge Corporation; *U.S. Public*, pg. 1705

SEATEX—Rubber Products—Rubatex Corporation; *U.S. Private*, pg. 56

SEATING FOR H.D. TRUCKS—NONE—Seats Incorporated; *U.S. Private*, pg. 410

SEATONE—Natural Remedy, Mussel Extract—Novo Nordisk A/S; *Int'l*, pg. 987

SEATTLE CITY LIGHT—Municipal Electric Utility—Seattle City Light; *U.S. Private*, pg. 979

SEATTLE POST-INTELLIGENCER—Newspaper—The Hearst Corporation; *U.S. Private*, pg. 515

THE SEATTLE POST-INTELLIGENCER—Newspaper—Seattle Times Company; *U.S. Private*, pg. 980

THE SEATTLE TIMES—Newspaper—Seattle Times Company; *U.S. Private*, pg. 980

SEAVIEW—Glazed Ceramic Tile—Porcelanite, Inc.; *Int'l*, pg. 573

SEAVIEW—PC Software, Document Image Management Tool—Science & Engineering Associates; *U.S. Private*, pg. 975

SEAVIEW—Wines—Southcorp Holdings Ltd.; *Int'l*, pg. 1287

SEAWARD—Cruise Ship—Norwegian Cruise Line; *U.S. Private*, pg. 808

SEAWAY—Private Label for Food Products—Riser Foods, Inc.; *U.S. Private*, pg. 450

SEAWAY SHOPPING CENTER—Shopping Center—Charan Industries, Inc.; *U.S. Private*, pg. 229

SEAWOLF—Anti-Missile Missile—British Aerospace p.l.c.; *Int'l*, pg. 217

SEAZY—NONE—Royal Waterbeds; *U.S. Private*, pg. 949

SEBA-NIL—Pharmaceutical Products—Galderma Laboratories, Inc.; *U.S. Private*, pg. 819

SEBLINE—Credit Card Purchases Processing System—Skandinaviska Enskilda Banken; *Int'l*, pg. 1258

SEBRA—Bank Terminal System for Customer Inquiries—Skandinaviska Enskilda Banken; *Int'l*, pg. 1258

SEBRING—Automobile—Chrysler Corporation; *U.S. Public*, pg. 352

SEBUCARE—Anti-Seborrheic Scalp Lotion—Westwood-Squibb Pharmaceuticals Inc.; *U.S. Public*, pg. 255

SEBULEX—Anti-Dandruff Shampoo—Bristol-Myers Squibb Company; *U.S. Public*, pg. 253

SEBULEX—Anti-Seborrheic & Dandruff Shampoo—Westwood-Squibb Pharmaceuticals Inc.; *U.S. Public*, pg. 255

SEBULON—Anti-Seborrheic & Dandruff Shampoo—Westwood-Squibb Pharmaceuticals Inc.; *U.S. Public*, pg. 255

SEBUTONE—Anti-Seborrheic Tar Shampoo—Westwood-Squibb Pharmaceuticals Inc.; *U.S. Public*, pg. 255

SEBVISION—Inquiry System for Small & Medium Sized Businesses—Skandinaviska Enskilda Banken; *Int'l*, pg. 1258

SEC*SAT—Secure Satellite Telephone—Rockwell International Corporation; *U.S. Public*, pg. 1397

SEC*SAT PLUS—Secure Satellite Terminal—Rockwell International Corporation; *U.S. Public*, pg. 1397

SECATEUR—Foot Rot Shear—Nasco Modesto; *U.S. Private*, pg. 446

SECAVER—Garden Shredders—Ransomes Plc; *Int'l*, pg. 1087

SECHRIST—Industrial Measuring Instruments—Sechrist Industries, Inc.; *U.S. Public*, pg. 980

SECONAL—Secobarbital, Lilly—Eli Lilly and Company; *U.S. Public*, pg. 992

SECONAL SODIUM—Secobarbital Sodium, Lilly—Eli Lilly and Company; *U.S. Public*, pg. 992

SECOND CUP—Coffee Shop—Cara Operations Limited; *Int'l*, pg. 266

2ND DEBUT—Cosmetics—SmithKline Beecham plc; *Int'l*, pg. 1264

SECOND FLEET—Game—Monarch Avalon, Inc.; *U.S. Public*, pg. 1123

2ND FOODS—Baby Foods & Juices—Gerber Products Company; *Int'l*, pg. 973

SECOND NATURE—Hair Grooming Gel—Bristol-Myers Squibb Company; *U.S. Public*, pg. 253

SECOND NATURE—Hair Coloring—Clairol, Inc.; *U.S. Public*, pg. 254

SECOND NATURE—No Cholesterol Egg Product—The Morning Star Group; *U.S. Public*, pg. 1527

SECOND NATURE—NONE—Wisconsin Tissue Mills, Inc.; *U.S. Public*, pg. 347

SECOND NATURE PLUS—Disposable Paper Products—Wisconsin Tissue Mills, Inc.; *U.S. Public*, pg. 347

2ND SKIN—Dressings, Compresses—Kimberly-Clark Corporation; *U.S. Public*, pg. 958

SECOND SKIN SATIN—NONE—Victoria's Secret Stores; *U.S. Public*, pg. 995

SECOND WAVE—Beach Wear—Athletic Attic Retail Company; *U.S. Public*, pg. 936

SECONDARY INDEX MAINTENANCE/DB—NONE—BMC Software, Inc.; *U.S. Public*, pg. 162

SECONDARY INDEX UTILITY—IMS Database Utility—BMC Software, Inc.; *U.S. Public*, pg. 162

SECONDARY INDEX UTILITY/EP—NONE—BMC Software, Inc.; *U.S. Public*, pg. 162

SECOROC—Drill Steel Products & Drill Bits—Atlas Copco AB; *Int'l*, pg. 95

SECRET—Antiperspirant—The Procter & Gamble Company; *U.S. Public*, pg. 1330

SECRET HUG—Bras, Daywear, Shapewear, Panties—Olga Div.; *U.S. Public*, pg. 1738

SECS—Self Clean System—Manitowoc Ice, Inc.; *U.S. Public*, pg. 1041

SECTOR—Banking Software—Jack Henry & Associates, Inc.; *U.S. Public*, pg. 808

SECTRAL—Cardiovascular Drug—American Home Products Corporation; *U.S. Public*, pg. 79

SECTRAL—Antihypertensive Agent—Wyeth-Ayerst Laboratories, Inc.; *U.S. Public*, pg. 80

SECTROL—Animal Health Pharmaceuticals—Merial Ltd.; *U.S. Public*, pg. 1092

SECTROL—Animal Health Pharmaceuticals—Merial Ltd.; *Int'l*, pg. 1109

SECUR-A-SEAL—Tape Seal for Bottle & Container Closures—3M; *U.S. Public*, pg. 1604

SECUR-FIT—NONE—Stryker Corporation; *U.S. Public*, pg. 1525

SECUR-LITE—Burglar Resistant Laminated Glass Prods.—Globe-Amerada Glass Company; *U.S. Private*, pg. 458

SECUR-LITE X—Juvenile Detention & Psychiatric Facilities—Globe-Amerada Glass Company; *U.S. Private*, pg. 458

SECUR-LOK—NONE—Ballard Medical Products; *U.S. Public*, pg. 171

SECUR-TEM + POLY—Prison Windows—Globe-Amerada Glass Company; *U.S. Private*, pg. 458

SECURE CARE—Service Mark of Insurance Product—Coventry Corporation; *U.S. Public*, pg. 454

SECURE CODE II—Non Forgable Bar Code—Control Module, Inc.; *U.S. Private*, pg. 271

SECURE FAST SPECTRUM—NONE—Cabletron Systems, Inc.; *U.S. Public*, pg. 288

SECURE HORIZONS—Medicare Risk Program—PacifiCare Health Systems, Inc.; *U.S. Public*, pg. 1250

SECURE PAK—Lyophilization Bags & Containers—The West Company, Incorporated; *U.S. Public*, pg. 1755

SECUREFAX—Facsimile Equipment—Ricoh Corporation; *Int'l*, pg. 1114

SECURELINE—Distribution Program for Life Product—Lincoln National Corporation; *U.S. Public*, pg. 997

SECUREPLEX—Security Control Systems—Rauland-Borg Corporation; *U.S. Private*, pg. 911

SECURESTAT—Security Systems—Diebold, Incorporated; *U.S. Public*, pg. 506

SECURID—NONE—Security Dynamics Technologies; *U.S. Public*, pg. 1453

SECURIFLEX—Flat Glass—Saint-Gobain; *Int'l*, pg. 1170

SECURIGUARD—NONE—Rentokil Initial plc; *Int'l*, pg. 1285

SECURITAINER—Tamper Evident Containers—Carter Holt Harvey Limited; *Int'l*, pg. 904

SECURITIES LENDING & BORROWING—NONE—American Management Systems, Inc.; *U.S. Public*, pg. 86

SECURITY—Gas, Electric & Oil Powered Heaters—Bradford-White Corporation; *U.S. Private*, pg. 164

SECURITY—Tampons—Kimberly-Clark Corporation; *U.S. Public*, pg. 958

SECURITY—Magazine for Buyers of Security Systems & Services—Reed Elsevier Business Information; *Int'l*, pg. 1095

SECURITY—Chimneys & Firepalces—Security Chimneys International Ltd.; *Int'l*, pg. 1217

SECURITY AUSTRALIA—Magazine & Directory—Reed Business Information Pty. Limited; *Int'l*, pg. 1094

SECURITY DBS—Drill Bits—Dresser Industries, Inc.; *U.S. Public*, pg. 528

SECURITY DISTRIBUTING & MARKETING—Magazine for Sellers/Service Companies of Electronic Security Systems—Reed Elsevier Business Information; *Int'l*, pg. 1095

SECURITY PARTNERSHIP SM—Hospital Income Plan—Colonial Companies, Inc.; *U.S. Public*, pg. 1699

SECURITY PLUS—Life Insurance—Old American Insurance Co.; *U.S. Public*, pg. 943

SECURITY PRO—Key Dealer Marketing Program—Interactive Technologies, Inc.; *U.S. Public*, pg. 888

SECURITY SALES—NONE—Bobit Publishing Company; *U.S. Private*, pg. 154

SECURITY-SIX—Double Action Revolvers—Sturm, Ruger & Co., Inc.; *U.S. Public*, pg. 1526

SECUROPEN—Penicillin—Bayer AG; *Int'l*, pg. 171

SECURTEM PLUS—Polycarbonate Laminates—Globe-Amerada Glass Company; *U.S. Private*, pg. 458

SEDA-PRESOMEN—Hormone Preparations—Kali-Chemie Aktiengesellschaft; *Int'l*, pg. 1278

SEDAN EXPRESSES—Cruisers—Chris-Craft Boats; *U.S. Private*, pg. 478

SEDI-STAIN—Uinalysis Stain—Becton Dickinson Primary Care Diagnostics; *U.S. Public*, pg. 199

SEDMAG—Earth Magnetic Display—Litton Industries, Inc.; *U.S. Public*, pg. 1002

SEDONA GOLF RESORT—Resort—Suncor Development Company; *U.S. Public*, pg. 1298

SEE 'N SAY—Pre-School Education Toys—Mattel, Inc.; *U.S. Public*, pg. 1057

SEE-ALL—Moisture & Liquid Indicator—Sporlan Valve Company; *U.S. Private*, pg. 1026

SEE ME, SHARE MY WORLD—Development Education Secondary Curriculum—Plan International USA, Inc.; *U.S. Public*, pg. 869

SEE & SEW—Patterns—Butterick Company, Inc.; *U.S. Private*, pg. 190

SEE-TECTOR—Plastic Bags for Preventing Pollination of Plants—Georgia-Pacific Corporation; *U.S. Public*, pg. 735

SEE-THRU—NONE—Hudson, RCI; *U.S. Private*, pg. 546

SEE WHAT DEVELOPS—NONE—Polaroid Corporation; *U.S. Public*, pg. 1313

SEECO-MUL—Drilling Mud Emulsifier—Georgia-Pacific Corporation; *U.S. Public*, pg. 735

SEECOTOL—Tall Oil & Tall Oil Emulsifier—Georgia-Pacific Corporation; *U.S. Public*, pg. 735

SEED 'N START—Seed Starting Trays—W. Atlee Burpee Co.; *U.S. Private*, pg. 187

SEEDCO—Seeds—Seed Corporation of America; *U.S. Private*, pg. 981

SEEDLING DESIGN—Printing Paper—The Mead Corporation; *U.S. Public*, pg. 1074

SEEKER—Rate-Gyro Surveying System—Baker Hughes INTEQ; *U.S. Public*, pg. 166

SEELUX—Recessed HID—Guth Lighting Company; *Int'l*, pg. 821

SEEPRO—Safety Eyewear—Aearo Company; *U.S. Private*, pg. 23

SEEQ TECHNOLOGY—Electronic Components—Interface Electronics Corporation; *U.S. Private*, pg. 567

SEEQUENCE—Disposable Contact Lens—Bausch & Lomb Incorporated; *U.S. Public*, pg. 194

SEE'S—Chocolate Candies—Berkshire Hathaway Inc.; *U.S. Public*, pg. 217

SEE'S CANDY SHOPS—Candy Stores—See's Candy Shops, Inc.; *U.S. Public*, pg. 221

SEEVIEW—Terminal Interface—Tandem Computers Inc.; *U.S. Public*, pg. 417

SEGA—Video Game—Sega of America Inc.; *Int'l*, pg. 1218

SEGA CD—Compact Disk Video Game Player—Sega of America Inc.; *Int'l*, pg. 1218

THE SEGA CARDS—Software—Sega of America Inc.; *Int'l*, pg. 1218

SEGA GENESIS—Home Video Entertainment—Konami Corporation of America Inc.; *Int'l*, pg. 746

SEGA MAGAZINE—Games Magazine—EMAP Images; *Int'l*, pg. 451

SEGMAX—Stainless Steel Powder Metal Disc Filters—Pall Corporation; *U.S. Public*, pg. 1253

SEGMET—Filters—Pall Corporation; *U.S. Public*, pg. 1253

SEGO—Diet Foods—The Pillsbury Company; *Int'l*, pg. 411

SEGWAY—Electronic Data Interchange Software—Tandem Computers Inc.; *U.S. Public*, pg. 417

SEIBERLING—Tires—Bridgestone/Firestone, Inc.; *Int'l*, pg. 213

SEIKABOND—Agent for Polyurethane Adhesives—Dainichiseika Colour & Chemicals Mfg. Co., Ltd.; *Int'l*, pg. 369

SEIKAFAST—Coloring Agent for Azoic Pigments—Dainichiseika Colour & Chemicals Mfg. Co., Ltd.; *Int'l*, pg. 369

SEIKAFIX—Coloring Agent for Dispersed Pigments—Dainichiseika Colour & Chemicals Mfg. Co., Ltd.; *Int'l*, pg. 369

SEIKO—NONE—Seiko Corporation; *Int'l*, pg. 1218

SEIKO—Watches & Clocks—SEIKO Corporation of America; *Int'l*, pg. 1218

SEISCUBE—NONE—Landmark Graphics Corporation; *U.S. Public*, pg. 776

SEISMAP—NONE—Landmark Graphics Corporation; *U.S. Public*, pg. 776

SEISWORKS—NONE—Landmark Graphics Corporation; *U.S. Public*, pg. 776

SEITZ—Packaged Meats—Sara Lee Corporation; *U.S. Public*, pg. 1432

SEITZ—Meats—Seitz Foods Inc.; *U.S. Public*, pg. 1434

SEKAI—Electronic Components—Shokai Far East Ltd.; *U.S. Private*, pg. 996

SEL-LOK—Spring Pins—SPS Technologies, Inc.; *U.S. Public*, pg. 1419

SEL-VENT—HVAC—Eljer Plumbingware; *U.S. Public*, pg. 1794

SELAIRE—HVAC—Eljer Plumbingware; *U.S. Public*, pg. 1794

SELBY—Women's Shoes—Nine West Group, Inc.; *U.S. Public*, pg. 1185

SELCO—Baler—Harris Waste Mgmt. Group, Inc.; *Int'l*, pg. 473

SELDANE—Seasonal Allergic Rhinitis—Hoechst Marion Roussel, Inc.; *Int'l*, pg. 624

SELDANE—Nonsedating Antihistamine—Hoechst Marion Roussel North America; *Int'l*, pg. 625

SELDANE-D—Antihistamine with Decongestant—Hoechst Marion Roussel North America; *Int'l*, pg. 625

SELEC-STREP—Culturing Media for Diagnostic Test—Beckman Instruments, Inc.; *U.S. Public*, pg. 199.

SELEC-T—Marine Control Assemblies Comprising a Control Head & Control Cable—Teleflex Incorporated; *U.S. Public*, pg. 1569

SELECAO—Hair & Body Shampoo—Wella Group; *Int'l*, pg. 1489

SELECT—U.K. Entertainment Magazine—EMAP Metro; *Int'l*, pg. 451

SELECT—Computerized Tomograph—Elscint Ltd.; *Int'l*, pg. 450

SELECT—Computer Furniture—Hunt Corporation; *U.S. Public*, pg. 848

SELECT—Selective Absorbent—Oil-Dri Corporation of America; *U.S. Public*, pg. 1214

SELECT—NONE—Pinnacle Brands, Inc.; *U.S. Private*, pg. 866

SELECT—Reduced-Salt Tuna Products—Star-Kist Foods Inc.; *U.S. Public*, pg. 805

SELECT-A-PAGE—Voice Paging for Telephone System—Dukane Corporation; *U.S. Private*, pg. 345

SELECT A SIZE—Children's Shoes—E.J. Footwear Corp.; *U.S. Public*, pg. 1684

SELECT AIRSTYLER—Air Blowing Adjustable Barrel Hot Curling Brush—Andis Company; *U.S. Private*, pg. 73

SELECT-AMINE—NONE—Life Technologies, Inc.; *U.S. Public*, pg. 504

SELECT B (A2)—Cold Work Die Steel—Latrobe Steel Company; *U.S. Public*, pg. 1617

SELECT COMMUNICATION SERVER—Computer Software—Attachmate; *U.S. Private*, pg. 98

SELECT CUT—Hair Clipper—Andis Company; *U.S. Private*, pg. 73

SELECT FONE—Telephone Paging & Station—Federal Signal Corporation, Signal Div.; *U.S. Public*, pg. 616

SELECT-HTLV—Diagnostic Kit—BioChem Pharma Inc.; *Int'l*, pg. 196

SELECT-O-MATIC II—Lead Holder—Koh-I-Noor, Inc.; *U.S. Private*, pg. 629

SELECT SCRUB—Automatic Battery Scrubber—The Kent Company; *Int'l*, pg. 440

SELECT SOFTWARE—NONE—Comdisco, Inc.; *U.S. Public*, pg. 407

SELECT STEAM—Steam Iron—Sunbeam Household Products; *U.S. Public*, pg. 1533

SELECT STEP—Servicing—SLM Holding Corp.; *U.S. Public*, pg. 1419

SELECT 20—Valves—Halliburton Energy Services; *U.S. Public*, pg. 776

SELECT YOUR TERMS—Servicing—SLM Holding Corp.; *U.S. Public*, pg. 1419

SELECTA-FLO—Carton Flow Rack—Interlake Material Handling Div.; *U.S. Public*, pg. 893

SELECTA SOL—Chromatography Chamber—Schleicher & Schuell, Inc.; *Int'l*, pg. 1206

SELECTABUS—Computer Product—International Business Machines Corporation; *U.S. Public*, pg. 895

SELECTAIRE—Hair Dryer—Andis Company; *U.S. Private*, pg. 73

SELECTALOY—NONE—Carpenter Technology Corporation; *U.S. Public*, pg. 307

SELECTALOY DESIGN—NONE—Carpenter Technology Corporation; *U.S. Public*, pg. 307

SELECTAVISION—Video Cassette Recorders & Players—Thomson Consumer Electronics Inc.; *Int'l*, pg. 1383

SELECTED VERTICAL CONVEYOR SYSTEM—Matl. Transport System—TransLogic Corp.; *Int'l*, pg. 1387

SELECTEMP—Curling Iron—Andis Company; *U.S. Private*, pg. 73

SELECTFIRE—NONE—Western Atlas Logging Services; *U.S. Public*, pg. 1757

SELECTGLOSS—Battery Floor Burnisher—The Kent Company; *Int'l*, pg. 440

SELECTION SUNDAY/PRELUDE TO A CHAMPIONSHIP—Sports Programming—Westwood One, Inc.; *U.S. Public*, pg. 1763

SELECTION ZEL—NONE—Provigo Inc.; *Int'l*, pg. 1072

SELECTIONS—Catalogues—Tiffany & Co.; *U.S. Public*, pg. 1608

SELECTIP ROLLING BALL—Pens—A.T. Cross Co.; *U.S. Public*, pg. 460

SELECTIVE—Greeting Cards—Fine Art Developments plc; *Int'l*, pg. 485

SELECTIVES—Nutritional Supplements—Stanhome Inc.; *U.S. Public*, pg. 1508

SELECTLINE—NONE—The Kent Company; *Int'l*, pg. 440

SELECTO—Fresh Yeast—Royal Gist-Brocades N.V.; *Int'l*, pg. 1142

SELECTO—Meats—Thorn Apple Valley, Inc.; *U.S. Public*, pg. 1602

SELECTOGEN—Reagent Red Blood Cells—Ortho Clinical Diagnostic Systems Inc.; *U.S. Public*, pg. 929

SELECTOL—Photographic Developer—Eastman Kodak Company; *U.S. Public*, pg. 550

SELECTOL-SOFT—Photo Developer—Eastman Kodak Company; *U.S. Public*, pg. 550

SELECTOMAT—Photo Developer—Eastman Kodak Company; *U.S. Public*, pg. 550

SELECTONE—System of Minimally Invasive Surgical Instruments—Conmed Corporation; *U.S. Public*, pg. 431

SELECTONE—Electric Emergency Warning Horn—Federal Signal Corporation; *U.S. Public*, pg. 616

SELECTONE—Solid Color Envelopes—Westvaco Corporation; *U.S. Public*, pg. 1762

SELECTRA—Credit/Debit Cards—Amoco Corporation; *U.S. Public*, pg. 101

SELECTRA—Hoist—Harnischfeger Industries, Inc.; *U.S. Public*, pg. 788

SELECTRA—Gas Modulation Valves—Maxitrol Co.; *U.S. Private*, pg. 716

SELECTRABAND—Circular Variable Filters—Optical Coating Laboratory, Inc.; *U.S. Public*, pg. 1227

SELECTRAC—Carpet Extractor—The Kent Company; *Int'l*, pg. 440

SELECTRIC—Typewriter—International Business Machines Corporation; *U.S. Public*, pg. 895

SELECTRIC TOUCH—Typewriter—International Business Machines Corporation; *U.S. Public*, pg. 895

SELECTRON—Filter Devices—Schleicher & Schuell, Inc.; *Int'l*, pg. 1206

SELECTRONIC—Selective Imaging & Addressing System—R.R. Donnelley & Sons Company; *U.S. Public*, pg. 517

SELECTRONIC—Mixers & Mixer Controls—Sunbeam Household Products; *U.S. Public*, pg. 1533

SELECTSET—Photo Typesetter—AGFA EPS Division; *Int'l*, pg. 172

SELECTSOURCING—NONE—Comdisco, Inc.; *U.S. Public*, pg. 407

SELENE E W/LECITHIN CAPSULES—Selenium/Lecithin Natural Anti-Oxidant Capsules—Weider Nutrition Intl.; *U.S. Private*, pg. 1159

SELEX—Melt-Blown Cartridge Filter—Osmonics, Inc.; *U.S. Public*, pg. 1233

SELEXOL—Acid Gas Treatment—Norton Company; *Int'l*, pg. 1173

SELF—Magazine—The Conde Nast Publications Inc.; *U.S. Private*, pg. 20

SELF CLEAN II—Household Products—The Black & Decker Corporation; *U.S. Public*, pg. 233

SELF-EMBEDDING—Microprocessor—LSI Logic Corp.; *U.S. Public*, pg. 971

SELF-EXPRESSIONS—Greeting Cards—American Greetings Corporation; *U.S. Public*, pg. 77

SELF EXPRESSIONS—Women's Undergarments—Maidenform Worldwide; *U.S. Private*, pg. 697

SELF PACK—Poros Column Packing System—PerSeptive Biosystems, Inc.; *U.S. Public*, pg. 1279

SELF SEAL—Tires—Bridgestone/Firestone, Inc.; *Int'l*, pg. 213

SELF-SEAL—Envelopes—Westvaco Corporation; *U.S. Public*, pg. 1762

SELF THINNED HEAVY DUTY TAPER SHANK—Taper Shank—National Twist Drill Div.; *U.S. Public*, pg. 1370

SELF-TUNE—Temperature Controls—Dwyer Instruments Inc.; *U.S. Private*, pg. 350

SELFIE—Mini System—Pioneer Electronic Corporation; *Int'l*, pg. 1057

SELFIT—Cosmetics—Shiseido Company Ltd.; *Int'l*, pg. 1235

SELFIT LIPSTICK NA—Lipstick—Shiseido Company Ltd.; *Int'l*, pg. 1235

SELFIX—Houseware Products—Home Products International, Inc.; *U.S. Public*, pg. 832

SELIG CHEMICAL IND.—Sanitation Goods—National Service Industries, Inc.; *U.S. Public*, pg. 1160

SELIX FORMAL WEAR—Formal Wear, Rental & Sales—Dick Bruhn Incorporated; *U.S. Private*, pg. 175

SELKIRK—Prefabricated Chimneys, Venting Systems, Registers—Eljer Plumbingware; *U.S. Public*, pg. 1794

THE SELL OUT—Plastic Containers—Tenneco Specialty Products; *U.S. Public*, pg. 1579

SELLERS—High Pressure Cleaning Systems—Sellers Cleaning Systems; *U.S. Public*, pg. 457

SELLERS SECURITY PLAN—Equity Advance/Assured Sale—ERA Real Estate; *U.S. Public*, pg. 321

SELLOTAPE—Packaging—Southcorp Holdings Ltd.; *Int'l*, pg. 1287

SELLS—Liver Pate—The Pillsbury Company; *Int'l*, pg. 411

SELMER—Musical Instruments—The Selmer Co., Inc.; *U.S. Public*, pg. 1514

SELO-ZOK—Cardiovascular Agent, Antianginal—Astra AB; *Int'l*, pg. 93

SELOKEN—Beta Blocker—Astra AB; *Int'l*, pg. 93

SELSCAN—Automatic Communications Processor—Rockwell International Corporation; *U.S. Public*, pg. 1397

SELSUN BLUE—Dandruff Shampoo—Abbott Laboratories; *U.S. Public*, pg. 12

SELSUN BLUE—Shampoo Prods.—Ross Products; *U.S. Public*, pg. 13

SEM-KIT—Repair Adhesives—The Dexter Corporation; *U.S. Public*, pg. 504

SEMETS—Pharmaceutical Prods.—SmithKline Beecham Laboratories; *Int'l*, pg. 1264

SEMI CONDUCTOR CIRCUITS INC—DC-DC Convertors—Astec America Inc.; *Int'l*, pg. 93

SEMI+—Circuit Boards—Litton Systems, Inc. Advanced Circuitry Div.; *U.S. Public*, pg. 1003

SEMICON—Semiconducting Treated Tape or Compound—The Okonite Company; *U.S. Private*, pg. 813

SEMICONDUCTOR INTERNATIONAL—Magazine for Engineers/Managers in Semiconductor & Integrated Circuit Field—Reed Elsevier Business Information; *Int'l*, pg. 1095

SEMIFLEX—Cable—Times Fiber Communications, Inc.; *U.S. Private*, pg. 629

SEMILENTE ILETIN—Prompt Insulin Zinc Suspension, Lilly—Eli Lilly and Company; *U.S. Public*, pg. 992

SEMINOLE—Men's Clothing—American Trouser, Inc.; *U.S. Private*, pg. 64

SEMINOLE—Aircraft—The New Piper Aircraft, Inc.; *U.S. Private*, pg. 794

SEMIPACK—Diode Modules—Semikron International, GmbH & Co. KG; *Int'l*, pg. 1220

SEMITRANS—MOSFET & IGBT Modules—Semikron International, GmbH & Co. KG; *Int'l*, pg. 1220

SEMKIT—Plastic Packaging—Courtaulds Aerospace; *Int'l*, pg. 339

SEMPAK—Mixing & Dispensing Equipment—Courtaulds Aerospace; *Int'l*, pg. 339

SEMPERIT—Tires—Continental AG; *Int'l*, pg. 327

SEMPLICE—Skin Care & Cosmetics—Stanhome Inc.; *U.S. Public*, pg. 1508

SEMPRAY-JOVENAY—Cleansing Cream—Benjamin Ansehl Company; *U.S. Private*, pg. 75

SEMRAD THORAGUIDE—Chest Tube Placement Technique—Gish Biomedical, Inc.; *U.S. Public*, pg. 745

SEMITRON—Static Dissipative Materials—DSM Engineering Plastic Products; *Int'l*, pg. 354

SEMTOL—White Mineral Oil—Witco Corporation; *U.S. Public*, pg. 1773

SEN SEN—Breath Freshener—F&F Foods; *U.S. Private*, pg. 388

SENAGE—NONE—Sta-Rite Industries, Inc.; *U.S. Public*, pg. 1767

SENATOR—Golf Clubs, Balls, Gloves & Shoes—The Austad Company; *U.S. Public*, pg. 782

SENATOR—Tires & Tubes—Bridgestone/Firestone, Inc.; *Int'l*, pg. 213

SENATOR—Pumps—Graco Inc.; *U.S. Public*, pg. 756

SENATORS CLUB—Whiskey, Gin, Vodka—Laird & Company; *U.S. Private*, pg. 642

SEND A SILK—NONE—Celebrity Incorporated; *U.S. Public*, pg. 319

SEND 'N RETURN—Envelopes—Tension Envelope Corp.; *U.S. Private*, pg. 1077

SEND SEND—Shipper—3M; *U.S. Public*, pg. 1604

SENECA—Aircraft—The New Piper Aircraft, Inc.; *U.S. Private*, pg. 794

SENECA—Endworking Equipment & Center Driven Lathes & CNC Production Lathes—Seneca Falls Technology Group; *U.S. Private*, pg. 984

SENECA—Foods—Seneca Foods Corporation; *U.S. Public*, pg. 1456

SENIOR DIMENSIONS—Medicare HMO—Sierra Health Services, Inc.; *U.S. Public*, pg. 1469

SENIOR ELECTROL—Electric Projection Screen—Da-Lite Screen Company, Inc.; *U.S. Private*, pg. 306

SENIOR GOLFER—Magazine—Weider Publications, Inc.; *U.S. Private*, pg. 1159

SENIOR KING COBRA—NONE—Cobra Golf Incorporated; *U.S. Public*, pg. 675

SENIOR KING COBRA—NONE—Fortune Brands, Inc.; *U.S. Public*, pg. 674

SENIOR ORIFICE FITTING—Fitting—Daniel Industries, Inc.; *U.S. Public*, pg. 482

SENIOR SONIC ULTRASONIC FLOW MOTOR—Gas Motor—Daniel Industries, Inc.; *U.S. Public*, pg. 482

SENKING—Industrial Laundry Equipment—Electrolux, AB; *Int'l*, pg. 438

SENNHEISER—Electronics—Sennheiser Electronic Corp.; *U.S. Private*, pg. 984

SENOKOT—Laxative—Reckitt & Colman plc; *Int'l*, pg. 1089

SENSA—Fecal Occult Blood Test Slides & Test Kit—Beckman Instruments, Inc.; *U.S. Public*, pg. 199

SENSA-RAY-200—Digital Dental CCD Sensor—AFP Imaging Corporation; *U.S. Public*, pg. 6

SENSA-SERVE—NONE—Scotsman Industries, Inc.; *U.S. Public*, pg. 1444

SENSA-TRAC—Shock Absorber—Monroe Auto Equipment Co.; *U.S. Public*, pg. 1577

SENSACION—Splash Cologne—SmithKline Beecham plc; *Int'l*, pg. 1264

SENSAI—Fragrance—Tri Tech Laboratories, Inc.; *U.S. Private*, pg. 1101

SENSAIRE—Fans—Broan Mfg. Co., Inc.; *U.S. Public*, pg. 1193

SENSALITE—Electronic Flash—Eastman Kodak Company; *U.S. Public*, pg. 550

SENSALL—Level Controls—Sensall, Div. of Rosemount, Inc.; *U.S. Public*, pg. 574

SENSAPHONE MONITORING SYSTEMS—Computerized Sensory Units—Phonetics, Inc.; *U.S. Private*, pg. 863

SENSATION—Multi-Surface Cleaner—Blue Cross Laboratories; *U.S. Private*, pg. 152

SENSATION—Sheet Vinyl Flooring—Congoleum Corporation; *U.S. Public*, pg. 69

SENSATION—Flour—Dover Industries Limited; *Int'l*, pg. 417

SENSATION—Fragrance—Jean Philippe Fragrances, Inc.; *U.S. Public*, pg. 924

SENSATIONS—Disposable Paper Products—Wisconsin Tissue Mills, Inc.; *U.S. Public*, pg. 347

SENSEMATIC—Automatic Feed Mechanical Pencil—Dixon Ticonderoga Company; *U.S. Public*, pg. 514

SENSI SANDALS—Sport Sandals—Deckers Outdoor Corporation; *U.S. Public*, pg. 491

SENSI-TEMP—Ranges & Surface Heating Units for Domestic Use—General Electric Canada Inc.; *U.S. Public*, pg. 713

THE SENSIBLE CHEF—Frozen Entrees—ConAgra Frozen Food Company; *U.S. Public*, pg. 427

SENSIBLE SEATING—Office Seating—The HON Co.; *U.S. Public*, pg. 772

SENSITIVE EYES—Daily Cleaner for Contact Lenses—Bausch & Lomb Incorporated; *U.S. Public*, pg. 194

SENSO CONTROL—Digital Pressure/Temperature Measuring System—Parker Hannifin Corp., Quick Coupling Div.; *U.S. Public*, pg. 1260

SENSO-MATIC—Detergent Dispenser—Ecolab Inc.; *U.S. Public*, pg. 562

SENSODYNE—Toothpaste for Sensitive Teeth—Block Drug Company, Inc.; *U.S. Public*, pg. 236

SENSODYNE—Tooth Brush & Tooth Paste—Stafford-Miller Limited; *U.S. Public*, pg. 237

SENSODYNE-F—Toothpaste—Block Drug Company, Inc.; *U.S. Public*, pg. 236

SENSODYNE GENTLE—Toothbrush—Block Drug Company, Inc.; *U.S. Public*, pg. 236

SENSODYNE SEARCH—Toothbrush—Block Drug Company, Inc.; *U.S. Public*, pg. 236

SENSOHM—Resistor Paste—Ferro Corporation; *U.S. Public*, pg. 618

SENSOR—Shaving System & Cartridges—The Gillette Company; *U.S. Public*, pg. 743

SENSOR—Seating—Steelcase Inc.; *U.S. Private*, pg. 1038

SENSOR EXCEL—Shaving System—The Gillette Company; *U.S. Public*, pg. 743

SENSOR FOR WOMEN—Shaving System & Cartridges for Women—The Gillette Company; *U.S. Public*, pg. 743

SENSOR GUARD—Disposable Bandages For Pulse Oximetry Sensor—Datascope Corp.; *U.S. Public*, pg. 487

SENSOR GUARD—Rip Detection Device for Conveyor Belting—The Goodyear Tire & Rubber Company; *U.S. Public*, pg. 752

SENSOR*INK—Anti-Shoplifting Tag which, If Tempered with, Releases a Non-Washable Ink—Sensormatic Electronics Corporation; *U.S. Public*, pg. 1457

SENSOR I—Portable Computerized Handtool—SPS Technologies, Inc.; *U.S. Public*, pg. 1419

SENSOR PERM—Electronic Permanent Wave Unit, Solution—Revlon-Realistic Professional Products, Inc.; *U.S. Private*, pg. 690

SENSOR*ID—Hands Free Access Control System—Sensormatic Electronics Corporation; *U.S. Public*, pg. 1457

SENSORCAINE—Pharmaceutical Products—Astra USA, Inc.; *Int'l*, pg. 93

SENSORLINK PC—Computer-Based System which Transmits Video Via Standard Phone Lines—Sensormatic Electronics Corporation; *U.S. Public*, pg. 1457

SENSORMATIC—Electronic Surveillance & Alarm System—Sensormatic Electronics Corporation; *U.S. Public*, pg. 1457

SENSORPAC—NONE—The Timken Company; *U.S. Public*, pg. 1617

SENSORTRACS—NONE—QUALCOMM; *U.S. Public*, pg. 1348

SENSORVISION—Computer Controlled Closed Circuit TV System—Sensormatic Electronics Corporation; *U.S. Public*, pg. 1457

SENTI-SWABS—Cotton Swabs—Sentinel Consumer Products, Inc.; *U.S. Private*, pg. 984

SENTINEL—Data Acquisition Units—AMETEK, Inc.; *U.S. Public*, pg. 99

SENTINEL—Measuring Instrument—Bacharach Inc.; *U.S. Private*, pg. 109

SENTINEL—Barbed Wire—CF & I Steel, L.P.; *U.S. Public*, pg. 1230

SENTINEL—Racquetball Eyewear—Ektelon; *U.S. Private*, pg. 884

SENTINEL—Security Shirts & Trousers—Horace Small Apparel Company; *Int'l*, pg. 635

SENTINEL—O.E.M. Products—Philips Consumer Electronics; *Int'l*, pg. 1054

SENTINEL—Fungicide—Sandoz Agro, Inc.; *Int'l*, pg. 974

SENTINEL—Health & Beauty Aids—Sentinel Consumer Products, Inc.; *U.S. Private*, pg. 984

SENTINEL—NONE—Seradyn, Inc.; *Int'l*, pg. 871

SENTINEL—Fire Hydrants—United States Pipe & Foundry Company, Inc.; *U.S. Public*, pg. 1736

SENTINEL—Jointing—James Walker & Co. Limited; *Int'l*, pg. 1485

SENTINEL EVE—Protects Computer Software Running on Macintosh Computers—Rainbow Technologies, Inc.; *U.S. Public*, pg. 1359

SENTINEL FAMILY OF FUNDS—Mutual Funds Owned, Managed & Distributed By Sentinel Companies—National Life Insurance Company; *U.S. Private*, pg. 785

SENTINEL GROUP FUNDS, INC.—Mutual Funds—Equity Services, Inc.; *U.S. Private*, pg. 785

SENTINEL LM—Network License Management SW—Rainbow Technologies, Inc.; *U.S. Public*, pg. 1359

SENTINEL MARK II—Shower Valve—Speakman Company; *U.S. Private*, pg. 1021

SENTINEL NEW YORK TAX FREE FUND—Mutual Fund—Equity Services, Inc.; *U.S. Private*, pg. 785

SENTINEL PA TAX FREE TRUST—Mutual Fund—Equity Services, Inc.; *U.S. Private*, pg. 785

SENTINEL II—Network Management Contractor—Ascom Timeplex; *Int'l*, pg. 86

SENTINEL U.S. TREASURY—Money Market—Equity Services, Inc.; *U.S. Private*, pg. 785

SENTINEL WIZARD—A G4I-Based Software Tool—Rainbow Technologies, Inc.; *U.S. Public*, pg. 1359

SENTINELPRO—Secures Programs Developed for IBMPC's Software Security Device—Rainbow Technologies, Inc.; *U.S. Public*, pg. 1359

SENTINEL'S BEST—Cosmetic Squares and Rounds—Sentinel Consumer Products, Inc.; *U.S. Private*, pg. 984

SENTINELSUPERPRO—Secures Programs Developed for IMB PC's, Multiple Algorithms & Memory Keys—Rainbow Technologies, Inc.; *U.S. Public*, pg. 1359

SENTRA—Automobile—Nissan Motor Corporation in U.S.A.; *Int'l*, pg. 945

SENTRIE AT—Walk-Through Metal Detector—EG & G Astrophysics; *U.S. Public*, pg. 543

SENTRIE LHS—Hand-Held Metal Detector—EG & G Astrophysics; *U.S. Public*, pg. 543

SENTRON—Racquetball Racquet—Ektelon; *U.S. Private*, pg. 884

SENTRY—Hand Portable Fire Extinguisher—Ansul Incorporated; *U.S. Public*, pg. 1648

SENTRY—Valve Position Indicators—Automatic Switch Co.; *U.S. Public*, pg. 573

SENTRY—Wash Fountain—Bradley Corporation; *U.S. Private*, pg. 164

SENTRY—Telescopes—Bushnell Corporation; *U.S. Private*, pg. 1191

SENTRY—Lumber & Hardware Stores Program—Distribution America; *U.S. Private*, pg. 335

SENTRY—Racquetball Eyewear—Ektelon; *U.S. Private*, pg. 884

SENTRY—Food Stores—Fleming Company; *U.S. Public*, pg. 653

SENTRY—Shirts & Trousers-Standards in Uniform Industry—Horace Small Apparel Company; *Int'l*, pg. 635

SENTRY—NONE—Howmedica, Inc.; *U.S. Public*, pg. 1282

SENTRY—Public Telephone Enclosure, Pedestal, Station, Post & Mounting—Lucent Technologies Inc.; *U.S. Public*, pg. 1017

SENTRY—Emergency Shutoff Valves—Maxitrol Co.; *U.S. Private*, pg. 716

SENTRY—Pillows—Medline Industries, Inc.; *U.S. Private*, pg. 728

SENTRY—NONE—Pfizer Inc.; *U.S. Public*, pg. 1281

SENTRY—Insurance Company—Sentry Insurance, A Mutual Company; *U.S. Private*, pg. 984

SENTRY—Filtration System—Serfilco, Ltd.; *U.S. Private*, pg. 985

SENTRY—Cast Iron Gas Boiler—Slant/Fin Corporation; *U.S. Private*, pg. 1005

SENTRY—Absorptive Carbon Sidcs, Orthodontic—3M; *U.S. Public*, pg. 1604

SENTRY—Tires—Western Auto Supply Company; *U.S. Public*, pg. 1452

SENTRY FIRE SAFE SECURITY CHEST—Fire Resistant Security Chest—Sentry Group; *U.S. Private*, pg. 984

SENTRY SAFES—Safe—Sentry Group; *U.S. Private*, pg. 984

SENTRY STOWAWAY—Wall Safe—Sentry Group; *U.S. Private*, pg. 984

SENTRY SUPREME SAFES—Safe—Sentry Group; *U.S. Private*, pg. 984

SENTRY SURVIVOR—Safe—Sentry Group; *U.S. Private*, pg. 984

SENTRY 2—Television Receivers—Zenith Electronics Corp.; *U.S. Public*, pg. 1790

SENTRYVISION—Traveling CCTV System—Sentry Technology Corp.; *U.S. Public*, pg. 1458

SEP-PAK—Multi-Sample Preparation System, Cartridges & Rack—Millipore Corporation; *U.S. Public*, pg. 1112

SEP TECH—Liquid Chromatographs—PPG Industries, Inc.; *U.S. Public*, pg. 1245

SEPA—Membrane Cell—Osmonics, Inc.; *U.S. Public*, pg. 1233

SEPARAN—Flocculant—The Dow Chemical Company; *U.S. Public*, pg. 522

SEPARASE G—Immobilised Penicillin G Acylase—Royal Gist-Brocades N.V.; *Int'l*, pg. 1142

SEPARATOR—Tooling Assemblies—Federal Signal Corporation; *U.S. Public*, pg. 616

SEPARIDE—NONE—Life Technologies, Inc.; *U.S. Public*, pg. 504

SEPHACEL—Biotechnology—Pharmacia & Upjohn Adria Laboratories; *Int'l*, pg. 1049

SEPHACRYL—Biotechnology—Pharmacia & Upjohn Adria Laboratories; *Int'l*, pg. 1049

SEPHADEX—Biotechnology—Pharmacia & Upjohn Adria Laboratories; *Int'l*, pg. 1049

SEPHAROSE—Biotechnology—Pharmacia & Upjohn Adria Laboratories; *Int'l*, pg. 1049

SEPHASORB—Biotechnology—Pharmacia & Upjohn Adria Laboratories; *Int'l*, pg. 1049

SEPHIA—Automobile—Kia Motors America, Inc.; *Int'l*, pg. 733

SEPPELT—Wines—Southcorp Holdings Ltd.; *Int'l*, pg. 1287

SEPRALATOR—Spiral-Wound Membrane Element—Osmonics, Inc.; *U.S. Public*, pg. 1233

SEPRO—Barrier Container for Aerosol Products—U.S. Can Company; *U.S. Public*, pg. 1681

SEPTA—Transportation System—Southeastern Pennsylvania Transportation Authority; *U.S. Private*, pg. 1015

SEPTI-SOFT—Skin Cleaner Soap—Calgon Vestal Laboratories; *U.S. Public*, pg. 1515

SEPTISOL FOAM—Antiseptic Surgical Soap—Calgon Vestal Laboratories; *U.S. Public*, pg. 1515

SEPTISOL NON-MEDICATED—Concentrated Liquid Soap—Calgon Vestal Laboratories; *U.S. Public*, pg. 1515

SEPTISOL SOLUTION—Antiseptic Soap—Calgon Vestal Laboratories; *U.S. Public*, pg. 1515

SEPTRA—Prescription Anti-Infective—Glaxo Wellcome PLC; *Int'l*, pg. 553

SEQUAZYME—Kits Use Optimized Enzyme Digestion Procedures; A Complement to Voyager—PerSeptive Biosystems, Inc.; *U.S. Public*, pg. 1279

SEQUEL—Carbonless Paper—The Mead Corporation; *U.S. Public*, pg. 1074

SEQUENCES—S&S Publication—Schleicher & Schuell, Inc.; *Int'l*, pg. 1206

SEQUENT—Computer System—Sequent Computer Systems, Inc.; *U.S. Public*, pg. 1459

SEQUOIA—Manufactured Homes—Champion Enterprises, Inc.; *U.S. Public*, pg. 332

SEQUOYA—NONE—New England Stone Industries, Inc.; *U.S. Private*, pg. 793

SEQUUS—NONE—Sequus Pharmaceuticals, Inc.; *U.S. Public*, pg. 1460

SER FOUR—NONE—Avon Products Co., Ltd.; *U.S. Public*, pg. 156

SERA—Sport Compact Car—Toyota Motor Corporation; *Int'l*, pg. 1411

SERACHEM—Blood Chemistry Controls—Fisher Scientific Company; *U.S. Private*, pg. 658

SERAFINO ENRICO—Wines—Barbero 1891 SpA; *Int'l*, pg. 164

SERALYZER—Blood Parameter—Bayer AG; *Int'l*, pg. 171

SERALYZER—Blood Chemistry Analyzer—Bayer Corporation/Consumer Care Division; *Int'l*, pg. 173

SERANO—Pickled Peppers—Trappey's Fine Foods, Inc.; *U.S. Private*, pg. 105

SERAPHIM CLASSICS COLLECTION—Scupted Angel Figures & Accessories—Roman, Inc.; *U.S. Private*, pg. 942

SERAPHOS—Insecticide—Novartis AG; *Int'l*, pg. 971

SERATEST—NONE—Seradyn, Inc.; *Int'l*, pg. 871

SERAX—Short-Term Anxiety Drug—American Home Products Corporation; *U.S. Public*, pg. 79

SERAX—Antianxiety Agent—Wyeth-Ayerst Laboratories, Inc.; *U.S. Public*, pg. 80

SERCK MARSTON—Radiators—BTR plc; *Int'l*, pg. 124

SERCO—Food Products—Rykoff-Sexton, Inc.; *U.S. Public*, pg. 918

SERDEX—Temperature & RH Recording Instruments—Bacharach Inc.; *U.S. Private*, pg. 109

SERDUCTOR—Agitation Emplying Pumps With Eductors—Serfilco, Ltd.; *U.S. Private*, pg. 985

SERENA—Car—Nissan Motor Co., Ltd.; *Int'l*, pg. 943

SERENA SAUVIGNON BLANC—NONE—Castello Banfi Srl.; *U.S. Private*, pg. 113

SERENADE—Area Rugs—Couristan Inc.; *U.S. Private*, pg. 279

SERENITY—Encoultrice—Johnson & Johnson; *U.S. Public*, pg. 927

SERENITY—Absorbent Shields—Johnson & Johnson Consumer Products; *U.S. Public*, pg. 928

SERENITY—Ceramic Floor Tile—Monarch Tile, Inc.; *U.S. Private*, pg. 287

SERENITY—Ceramic Wall Tile—Monarch Tile, Inc.; *U.S. Private*, pg. 287

SERENITY GUARDS—Urinary Maintenance Pads—Personal Products Co.; *U.S. Public*, pg. 929

SEREVENT—Asthma Treatment—Glaxo Wellcome Inc.; *Int'l*, pg. 552

SEREX GRAPHITE RTS—Racquetball Racquet—Ektelon; *U.S. Private*, pg. 884

SERFENE—PVDC Barrier Coating—Morton International Inc.; *U.S. Public*, pg. 1135

SERFILCO—Pump & Filters for Chemical Applications—Serfilco, Ltd.; *U.S. Private*, pg. 985

SERGAZ—Service Stations—Ultramar Diamond Shamrock Corporation; *U.S. Public*, pg. 1663

SERGEANT'S—Flea Collars—ConAgra, Inc.; *U.S. Public*, pg. 425

SERGIO TACCHINI—Perfume—International Cosmetics Co., Ltd.; *Int'l*, pg. 684

SERGIO TACCHINI—NONE—Luxottica Group S.p.A.; *Int'l*, pg. 822

SERICOL—Screen Printing Inks—Burmah Castrol plc; *Int'l*, pg. 234

SERIE CLUB—France Broadcasting—CLT-UFA; *Int'l*, pg. 561

SERIES 8000 AVP—Advanced Vertical Processor—Silicon Valley Group, Inc.; *U.S. Public*, pg. 1474

SERIES '80—Control Valves—Leslie Controls, Inc.; *U.S. Public*, pg. 1746

SERIES 1100—Miniature Strip Chart Recorder—Westronics, Inc.; *U.S. Public*, pg. 1593

SERIES 50—NONE—Detroit Diesel Corp.; *U.S. Private*, pg. 850

SERIES 55—NONE—Detroit Diesel Corp.; *U.S. Private*, pg. 850

SERIES 5000—Image Controller: Supports PS + Variety of Traditional Languages—Prepress Solutions, Inc.; *U.S. Private*, pg. 882

SERIES 40—NONE—Detroit Diesel Corp.; *U.S. Private*, pg. 850

SERIES 4990—Entry-Level PostScript Imagesetting System—Prepress Solutions, Inc.; *U.S. Private*, pg. 882

SERIES 4000—NONE—Detroit Diesel Corp.; *U.S. Private*, pg. 850

SERIES 4000—Image Controller: Supports PostScript Page Description Language—Prepress Solutions, Inc.; *U.S. Private*, pg. 882

SERIES 4000—Large Case Writing Recorder—Westronics, Inc.; *U.S. Public*, pg. 1593

SERIES 900—Mobile C-Arm—Diasonics Ultra Sound, Inc.; *Int'l*, pg. 644

SERIES 900—Digitizing Camera Systems—Xerox Imaging Systems, Inc.; *U.S. Public*, pg. 1785

SERIES 9000—Components—Steelcase Inc.; *U.S. Public*, pg. 1038

SERIES 9500—High Voltage Wiring—Xebec Corporation; *U.S. Private*, pg. 1194

SERIES 9600—Distributed Bus Switching—Xebec Corporation; *U.S. Private*, pg. 1194

SERIES 92—NONE—Detroit Diesel Corp.; *U.S. Private*, pg. 850

SERIES ONE—NONE—Amerimark Inc.; *U.S. Public*, pg. 1237

SERIES/1—Computer Product—International Business Machines Corporation; *U.S. Public*, pg. 895

SERIES 1000—Publishing Systems—Linotype-Hell Company; *Int'l*, pg. 604

SERIES 6000—High-Performance Integrated PostScript Imagesetting System—Prepress Solutions, Inc.; *U.S. Private*, pg. 882

SERIES 1600—100mm Programmable Recorder—Westronics, Inc.; *U.S. Public*, pg. 1593

SERIES 60—Heavy Duty, 4-Cycle, Electronically Controlled Diesel Engine—Detroit Diesel Corp.; *U.S. Public*, pg. 850

SERIES/SYSTEM 7—Open Plan Systems—Domore Corporation; *U.S. Private*, pg. 339

SERIES 10—Safety Valves—Halliburton Energy Services; *U.S. Public*, pg. 776

SERIES TEN THOUSAND—Surgical Equipment—Alcon Laboratories, Inc.; *Int'l*, pg. 916

SERIES 30G—NONE—Detroit Diesel Corp.; *U.S. Private*, pg. 850

SERIES 36—Video & Audio Routing Switcher—Meret Communications; *U.S. Public*, pg. 1233

SERIES 3200—Multipoint Programmable Recorder—Westronics, Inc.; *U.S. Public*, pg. 1593

SERIES III—Remote Mounted Aircraft Electronics—AlliedSignal Commercial Avionic Systems; *U.S. Public*, pg. 50

SERIES 3000—Software PostScript Compatible RIP on St D. Microcomputer Platform—Prepress Solutions, Inc.; *U.S. Private*, pg. 882

SERIES 3000—Panel Fasteners—SPS Technologies, Inc.; *U.S. Public*, pg. 1419

SERIES 3000—Multipoint Programmable Recorder—Westronics, Inc.; *U.S. Public*, pg. 1593

SERIES 2100—Miniature Programmable Recorder—Westronics, Inc.; *U.S. Public*, pg. 1593

SERIES 20,000—Surgical Equipment—Alcon Laboratories, Inc.; *Int'l*, pg. 916

SERIES 2000—NONE—Detroit Diesel Corp.; *U.S. Private*, pg. 850

SERIES 2000—Panel Fasteners—SPS Technologies, Inc.; *U.S. Public*, pg. 1419

SERIES 2000—Miniature Programmable Recorder—Westronics, Inc.; *U.S. Public*, pg. 1593

SERIES 2000—Benchtop Test System—Xebec Corporation; *U.S. Private*, pg. 1194

SERIES 2500—High Voltage Wiring Analyzer—Xebec Corporation; *U.S. Private*, pg. 1194

SERIES 2000i—Ion Chromatograph—Dionex Corporation; *U.S. Public*, pg. 510

SERIES 2000 VACUUM PUMPS—NONE—Kinney Vacuum Company; *U.S. Private*, pg. 1110

SERIF—NONE—Porcelanite, Inc.; *Int'l*, pg. 573

SERIGRAPH—Specialty Printed Plastics—Serigraph, Inc.; *U.S. Private*, pg. 985

SERILINK—Serializer, Deserializer or Library Element—LSI Logic Corp.; *U.S. Public*, pg. 971

SERIOUS SWEATS—Activewear—Lands' End, Inc.; *U.S. Public*, pg. 977

SERLA—Tissue Paper—Metsa-Serla Corporation; *Int'l*, pg. 863

SERMABOND—Inorganic Cermet-Type Cement for Bonding Components—Teleflex Incorporated; *U.S. Public*, pg. 1569

SERMAGARD—Corrosion & Heat Resistant Coatings—Teleflex Incorporated; *U.S. Public*, pg. 1569

SERMALOY—Inorganic Thermal Barrier Coatings—Teleflex Incorporated; *U.S. Public*, pg. 1569

SERMALUBE—All-Purpose Aqueous Inorganic Bonded Dry Film Lubricant—Teleflex Incorporated; *U.S. Public*, pg. 1569

SERMASEAL—Organic & Inorganic Bonding Coatings—Teleflex Incorporated; *U.S. Public*, pg. 1569

SERMATECH—High-Energy Plasma Coatings for Gas Turbine Engine Components—Teleflex Incorporated; *U.S. Public*, pg. 1569

SERMET—Coatings for Applying Powered Metal Parts—Teleflex Incorporated; *U.S. Public*, pg. 1569

SERMETEL—Ceramic Metallic Coatings—Teleflex Incorporated; *U.S. Public*, pg. 1569

SERMION—NONE—Pharmacia & Upjohn, Inc.; *Int'l*, pg. 1047

SERO-HIV—Single Donor HIV-1 Seroconverter Panel—Nabi; *U.S. Public*, pg. 1148

SEROFUGE II—Centrifuge—Becton Dickinson Primary Care Diagnostics; *U.S. Public*, pg. 199

SEROQUEL—Pharmaceutical—Zeneca Group Plc; *Int'l*, pg. 1524

SEROXAT—NONE—SmithKline Beecham Corporation; *Int'l*, pg. 1264

SEROXAT—Neurological Drug—SmithKline Beecham plc; *Int'l*, pg. 1264

SEROXAT—Psychotrophic—SmithKline Beecham Research Limited; *Int'l*, pg. 1266

SERP-AP-ES—NONE—Novartis Pharmaceuticals; *Int'l*, pg. 973

SERPENT—NONE—Berg Electronics; *U.S. Public*, pg. 212

SERPENTINE—Ceramic Wall Tile—Monarch Tile, Inc.; *U.S. Private*, pg. 287

SERPENTINE GRASPER—Gynecological Device—The Cooper Companies, Inc.; *U.S. Public*, pg. 442

SERROL—Bakery Ingredients—Goodman Fielder Limited; *Int'l*, pg. 555

SERTA—NONE—Royal Waterbeds; *U.S. Private*, pg. 949

SERTA—Mattress & Foundation—Serta, Inc.; *U.S. Private*, pg. 985

SERTA PERFECT NIGHT—Mattress & Foundation—Serta, Inc.; *U.S. Private*, pg. 985

SERTA PERFECT SLEEPER—Mattress & Foundation—Serta, Inc.; *U.S. Private*, pg. 985

SERUTAN—Natural Fiber Laxative—Menley & James Laboratories, Inc.; *U.S. Public*, pg. 1086

SERUTAN—Natural Fiber Laxative—SmithKline Beecham plc; *Int'l*, pg. 1264

SERV-EASE—Paper Plates—Smith-Lee Co., Inc.; *U.S. Public*, pg. 1009

SERV-ENS—Compression Sleeves & Adapters—Kearney Company; *U.S. Public*, pg. 444

SERVAAS—Cleaning & Polishing Preparations—Servaas, Inc.; *U.S. Private*, pg. 986

SERVAIDES—Dinner Napkins—Erving Industries, Inc.; *U.S. Private*, pg. 382

SERVALOT—Popcorn Warmers—Gold Medal Products Co.; *U.S. Private*, pg. 459

SERVCO—Remedial Services—Smith International, Inc.; *U.S. Public*, pg. 1478

SERVE AND VOLLEY—Tennis Shoe—K-Swiss Inc.; *U.S. Public*, pg. 937

SERVEND—Delivery Body Style—Hackney and Sons, Inc.; *U.S. Private*, pg. 1097

SERVERNET—Interconnect Technology—Tandem Computers Inc.; *U.S. Public*, pg. 417

SERVI EXPRESS—Stores—Socanav Inc.; *Int'l*, pg. 1272

SERVI PLUS—Stores—Socanav Inc.; *Int'l*, pg. 1272

SERVICE AMERICA—Food & Refreshment Services—Service America Corporation; *U.S. Private*, pg. 986

SERVICE CORPORATION INTERNATIONAL—Funeral Services & Products—Service Corporation International; *U.S. Public*, pg. 1460

SERVICE DIRECTOR—Computer Product—International Business Machines Corporation; *U.S. Public*, pg. 895

SERVICE DIRECTOR/2—Computer Product—International Business Machines Corporation; *U.S. Public*, pg. 895

SERVICE EXPRESS—NONE—Westin Hotels & Resorts; *U.S. Public*, pg. 1512

SERVICE FASTENER CENTER—Assumed Business Name in Various States—Service Supply Co. Inc. of Indiana; *U.S. Private*, pg. 987

SERVICE FIRST—Dispensing of Natural Gas Via a Pipeline & Transit Dist. of Electricity—Orange and Rockland Utilities, Inc.; *U.S. Public*, pg. 1229

SERVICE GUARD—NONE—UtiliCorp United Inc.; *U.S. Public*, pg. 1700

SERVICE LEVEL MANAGER—NONE—Network Associates, Inc.; *U.S. Public*, pg. 1168

SERVICE LINK—NONE—Detroit Diesel Corp.; *U.S. Private*, pg. 850

SERVICE MERCHANDISE—Retail Catalog Showrooms Stores—Service Merchandise Company, Inc.; *U.S. Public*, pg. 1461

SERVICE ORDER MANAGEMENT SYSTEM (SOMS)—NONE—American Management Systems, Inc.; *U.S. Public*, pg. 86

SERVICE PRO—NONE—Nordyne Inc.; *U.S. Public*, pg. 1193

SERVICE-SIX—Double-Action Revolvers—Sturm, Ruger & Co., Inc.; *U.S. Public*, pg. 1526

SERVICE SO GOOD...—NONE—Alliant Foodservice, Inc.; *U.S. Private*, pg. 244

SERVICE SPOTLIGHT W/DESIGN—Aervice Spotlight with Design—Oxford Health Plans Inc.; *U.S. Public*, pg. 1238

SERVICE-SUPPLY!—Fasteners—R&B, Inc.; *U.S. Public*, pg. 1354

SERVICE SUPPLY CO., INC. OF INDIANA—Hardware—Service Supply Co. Inc. of Indiana; *U.S. Private*, pg. 987

SERVICEBUILDER—NONE—Northern Telecom Limited; *Int'l*, pg. 968

SERVICELINE—Non Standard Socket Products Line—Service Supply Co. Inc. of Indiana; *U.S. Private*, pg. 987

SERVICEMASTER—Cleaning Service—Duskin Co., Ltd.; *Int'l*, pg. 422

SERVICEMASTER—Cleaning Service—The ServiceMaster Company; *U.S. Public*, pg. 1461

SERVICEONE—NONE—UtiliCorp United Inc.; *U.S. Public*, pg. 1700

SERVICEPAC—Computer Product—International Business Machines Corporation; *U.S. Public*, pg. 895

SERVICEPLAN—Computer Product—International Business Machines Corporation; *U.S. Public*, pg. 895

SERVICEVIEW—Network Management System—British Telecommunications plc; *Int'l*, pg. 222

SERVIN' SAVER—Food Containers—Rubbermaid Incorporated; *U.S. Public*, pg. 1411

SERVING YOU WITH ALL OUR ENERGY—Dispensing Natural Gas Via Pipeline—Orange and Rockland Utilities, Inc.; *U.S. Public*, pg. 1229

SERVISIGNAL—Service Indicator—Donaldson Company, Inc.; *U.S. Public*, pg. 517

SERVO—NONE—GenRad, Inc.; *U.S. Public*, pg. 731

SERVO—Transportation & Control Products—Servo Corporation of America; *U.S. Private*, pg. 987

SERVOCONTROL PRODUCTS—Electrohydraulic Equipment—The Oilgear Company; *U.S. Public*, pg. 1215

SERVOFLEX—Motors—MTS Systems Corporation; *U.S. Public*, pg. 1028

SERVOGLIDE—Planar Systems—Anorad Corporation; *U.S. Private*, pg. 75

SERVUS—Convenience Stores—KF/Konsum Coop Group; *Int'l*, pg. 718

SESAME PLACE—Children's Play Park—Busch Entertainment Corp.; *U.S. Public*, pg. 114

SESAME STREET—Children's Bath Products—Colgate-Palmolive Company; *U.S. Public*, pg. 397

SESAME STREET—Children's Products—Softsoap Enterprises, Inc.; *U.S. Public*, pg. 397

SESAME STREET VITAMINS—Children's Vitamins—McNeil Consumer Products Company; *U.S. Public*, pg. 928

SESAMEE—Keyless Padlocks—The Eastern Company; *U.S. Public*, pg. 548

SET-45—Chemical Action Concrete for Highways & Bridge Decks—Master Builders Inc.; *Int'l*, pg. 1465

SET IT AND FORGET IT—Slogan—Executive Software; *U.S. Private*, pg. 388

SET SAVER—IV Filter—Pall Corporation; *U.S. Public*, pg. 1253

SET-TO-GO—Hairsetters—Bristol-Myers Squibb Company; *U.S. Public*, pg. 253

SETACURE—Specialty Chemicals—Akzo Nobel Inc.; *Int'l*, pg. 47

SETAL—Modified Types of Alkyd Resins—Akzo Nobel N.V.; *Int'l*, pg. 42

SETALIET—Oil Reactive Pure Phenolic Resins Solids—Akzo Nobel N.V.; *Int'l*, pg. 42

SETALIN—Water Soluable & Dispersion Types Acrylic UV Monomers—Akzo Nobel N.V.; *Int'l*, pg. 42

SETALUX—Acrylic Resins—Akzo Nobel N.V.; *Int'l*, pg. 42

SETCO & DESIGN—Stock & Custom Bottles—McCormick & Company, Incorporated; *U.S. Public*, pg. 1066

SETH THOMAS—Clocks—General Time Corp.; *U.S. Private*, pg. 445

SETICATOR—Position Indicator—Svedala Industries Inc.; *Int'l*, pg. 1325

SETLERS—Indigestion Tablets & Liquid—SmithKline Beecham Corporation; *Int'l*, pg. 1264

SETLERS—Analgesic—SmithKline Beecham plc; *Int'l*, pg. 1264

SETLERS TUMS—Antacid Tablets—SmithKline Beecham plc; *Int'l*, pg. 1264

SETOFF—Weed Control—Novartis; *Int'l*, pg. 972

SETYRENE—Modified Types of Alkyd Resins—Akzo Nobel N.V.; *Int'l*, pg. 42

SEVCON—Electronic Controls—Tech/Ops Sevcon, Inc.; *U.S. Public*, pg. 1563

SEVCONTROL—Electronic Controls—Tech/Ops Sevcon, Inc.; *U.S. Public*, pg. 1563

SEVEN CANYONS OF SEDONA—Time Share & Golf Course Project—New Mexico & Arizona Land Co.; *U.S. Public*, pg. 1172

7 CARESSES—Body Care Products—Wella Group; *Int'l*, pg. 1489

7 CROWN—Liquor—The House of Seagram; *Int'l*, pg. 1217

7 CROWN—Blended Whisky—The Seagram Company Ltd.; *Int'l*, pg. 1214

7-ELEVEN—Convenience Food Stores—7-Eleven Stores; *Int'l*, pg. 693

7-ELEVEN—Convenience Food Stores—The Southland Corporation; *Int'l*, pg. 693

7-ELEVEN PHONE CARDS—Prepaid Phone Card Products—The Southland Corporation; *Int'l*, pg. 693

7-ELEVEN SERVICE CENTER—In-Store Work Stations for Faxing & Mailing—The Southland Corporation; *Int'l*, pg. 693

757—Airplane—The Boeing Company; *U.S. Public*, pg. 239

7-FOOTER—Socks—Wigwam Mills, Inc.; *U.S. Private*, pg. 1175

747—Socks—Wigwam Mills, Inc.; *U.S. Private*, pg. 1175

747-2—Roto Stop Hammer—ITW Ramset/Red Head; *U.S. Public*, pg. 867

747—Airplane—The Boeing Company; *U.S. Public*, pg. 239

THE 7 HABITS OF HIGHLY EFFECTIVE PEOPLE—Book & Workshop—Franklin Covey; *U.S. Public*, pg. 1264

700—Ventilator—Nellcor Puritan Bennett Incorporated; *U.S. Public*, pg. 1039

718-ER—NONE—Allvac; *U.S. Public*, pg. 43

718-OP—NONE—Allvac; *U.S. Public*, pg. 43

780—Flux—The Lincoln Electric Company; *U.S. Public*, pg. 996

711—Lubricant—Sherwin-Williams Diversified Brands, Inc.; *U.S. Public*, pg. 1466

700 SERIES—Mechanical Encoder—Oak Grigsby; *U.S. Public*, pg. 1209

760—Flux—The Lincoln Electric Company; *U.S. Public*, pg. 996

727 QTL—Lubricant—Sherwin-Williams Diversified Brands, Inc.; *U.S. Public*, pg. 1466

7-MO—NONE—Carpenter Technology Corporation; *U.S. Public*, pg. 307

7-MO PLUS—NONE—Carpenter Technology Corporation; *U.S. Public*, pg. 307

790 SERIES—Plasma Processing Systems—Plasma-Therm, Inc.; *U.S. Public*, pg. 1308

701 COLLECTION—Men's, Women's & Jr.'s Jeans—C.R. Anthony Company; *U.S. Private*, pg. 1029

707—Airplane—The Boeing Company; *U.S. Public*, pg. 239

SEVEN SEAS—Vitamins & Food Supplements—Hanson PLC; *Int'l*, pg. 592

SEVEN SEAS—Pourable Salad Dressings—Kraft Foods Inc.; *U.S. Public*, pg. 1288

SEVEN SEAS—Salad Dressings—Philip Morris Companies Inc.; *U.S. Public*, pg. 1287

SEVEN SEAS CANE—Spirits—Distillers Corporation S.A.; *Int'l*, pg. 1129

777—Airplane—The Boeing Company; *U.S. Public*, pg. 239

7-70-7 GLUE—Glue for Metal, Glass, Wood, Waterproof—Stanhome Inc.; *U.S. Public*, pg. 1508

767—Airplane—The Boeing Company; *U.S. Public*, pg. 239

SEVEN STAR—NONE—Carpenter Technology Corporation; *U.S. Public*, pg. 307

SEVEN STAR—Blended Whiskey—Laird & Company; *U.S. Private*, pg. 642

SEVEN STAR SATISFACTION GUARANTEED—NONE—Ace Hardware Corporation; *U.S. Private*, pg. 12

737—Airplane—The Boeing Company; *U.S. Public*, pg. 239

7000 SERIES—Manually Loaded Plasma Systems—Plasma-Therm, Inc.; *U.S. Public*, pg. 1308

7700—Intelligent Switching Hub—Bytex Corporation; *U.S. Public*, pg. 1522

7760—LAN Switching Hub—Bytex Corporation; *U.S. Public*, pg. 1522

7730—LAN Switching Hub—Bytex Corporation; *U.S. Public*, pg. 1522

7720—LAN Switching Hub—Bytex Corporation; *U.S. Public*, pg. 1522

7-12R—Loads Fallen Material from Railroad Tracks into a Waiting Gondola—Athey Products Corporation; *U.S. Public*, pg. 142

7-12S—Snow Remover Vehicle—Athey Products Corporation; *U.S. Public*, pg. 142

721—Tires—Bridgestone/Firestone, Inc.; *Int'l*, pg. 213

727—Airplane—The Boeing Company; *U.S. Public*, pg. 239

SEVEN-UP—NONE—Cadbury Beverages; *Int'l*, pg. 248

7 UP—Soft Drink—Cadbury Schweppes p.l.c.; *Int'l*, pg. 247

SEVEN-UP—Soft Drink—Dr. Pepper Co.; *Int'l*, pg. 248

SEVEN-UP—Soft Drink—Grant-Lydick Beverage Co.; *U.S. Private*, pg. 470

7 UP FRANCHISES—NONE—Buffalo Rock Company; *U.S. Private*, pg. 179

7XPRESS—ATG for GR2276 & Standard-Speed GR2272—GenRad, Inc.; *U.S. Public*, pg. 731

7 YEAR CAR SEAT—Car Seat—Spalding & Evenflo Companies, Inc.; *U.S. Private*, pg. 629

SEVENTEEN—Magazine—Seventeen Magazine; *U.S. Public*, pg. 1328

1780 SPECIAL RESERVE—Whiskey—The House of Seagram; *Int'l*, pg. 1217

1741 VC—Video Codec—Alcatel Telecom; *Int'l*, pg. 55

1743 VC—Video Codec—Alcatel Telecom; *Int'l*, pg. 55

1740 VC—Video Codec—Alcatel Telecom; *Int'l*, pg. 55

SEVENTEEN MAGAZINE—Consumer Magazine for Teenage Girls—Primedia Inc.; *U.S. Public*, pg. 1327

1776—Game—Monarch Avalon, Inc.; *U.S. Public*, pg. 1123

SEVENTH FLEET—Game—Monarch Avalon, Inc.; *U.S. Public*, pg. 1123

7TH STAGE—Hair Color Remover—Clairol, Inc.; *U.S. Public*, pg. 254

70—Shaft-Position Encoders—Litton Industries, Inc.; *U.S. Public*, pg. 1002

78TH STREET & DESIGN—Greeting Cards—American Greetings Corporation; *U.S. Public*, pg. 77

78TH ST...THE TALK OF THE TOWN—Greeting Cards—American Greetings Corporation; *U.S. Public*, pg. 77

7140—Processor for Photographic Materials—Prepress Solutions, Inc.; *U.S. Private*, pg. 882

77/22—Rimfire Rifles—Sturm, Ruger & Co., Inc.; *U.S. Public*, pg. 1526

7287—NONE—Eastman Kodak Company; *U.S. Public*, pg. 550

7250—Metabolic Monitor—Nellcor Puritan Bennett Incorporated; *U.S. Public*, pg. 1039

7200—Ventilator—Nellcor Puritan Bennett Incorporated; *U.S. Public*, pg. 1039

72″ LOBBY PARCEL LOCKER—Locker—American Locker Group, Inc.; *U.S. Public*, pg. 85

7260L—On-Line Processor for 5500 Image Recorder—Prepress Solutions, Inc.; *U.S. Private*, pg. 882

7210—Processor for Photographic Materials—Prepress Solutions, Inc.; *U.S. Private*, pg. 882

SEVILLE—Beauty Salon Furniture—Belvedere Company; *U.S. Private*, pg. 1008

SEVILLE—Car—Cadillac Motor Car Division; *U.S. Public*, pg. 720

SEVILLE—Area Rugs—Couristan Inc.; *U.S. Private*, pg. 279

SEVILLE—Envelopes—Dillard, A ResourceNet International Company; *U.S. Public*, pg. 901

SEVILLE—Chinaware—The Homer Laughlin China Company; *U.S. Public*, pg. 653

SEVILLE STS—Car—Cadillac Motor Car Division; *U.S. Public*, pg. 720

SEWER SENTRY CHECK VALVE—Stop Sewer Backups—A.Y. McDonald Industries, Inc.; *U.S. Private*, pg. 721

SEWING CARDS—Pre-School Sewing Activity—Colorforms; *U.S. Public*, pg. 1625

SEWOP—Lift Vessels—Halliburton Energy Services; *U.S. Public*, pg. 776

SEXTON—Food Products—Rykoff-Sexton, Inc.; *U.S. Public*, pg. 918

SEXY LIPS—Lip Balm—Health Products Corporation; *U.S. Private*, pg. 514

SEYMOUR—Coatings—Seymour of Sycamore, Inc.; *U.S. Private*, pg. 988

SFERIT—Fly Ash From Power Stations—Electrabel S.A.; *Int'l*, pg. 436

SFERNICE—Resistors/Potentiometers—Vishay Intertechnology, Inc.; *U.S. Public*, pg. 1721

SFEROFLEX—NONE—Luxottica Group S.p.A.; *Int'l*, pg. 822

SHACK'L SHIELD—Hasp—Hartwell Corporation; *U.S. Private*, pg. 1168

SHACKLE—Post Emergence Herbicide—Monsanto Company; *U.S. Public*, pg. 1124

SHADE—Suntanning Preparations—Schering-Plough Healthcare Products Inc.; *U.S. Public*, pg. 1438

SHADE UVAGUARD—Broad-Spectrum Sunscreen—Schering-Plough Corporation; *U.S. Public*, pg. 1438

SHADE UVA/UVB—Waterproof Sunblock Lotions & Gels—Schering-Plough Corporation; *U.S. Public*, pg. 1438

SHADEMESH—Packaging—Southcorp Holdings Ltd.; *Int'l*, pg. 1287

SHADES OF THE OLD WEST—Footwear—Georgia/Durango Boot Company; *U.S. Public*, pg. 1684

SHADES OF YOU—Cosmetics—Maybelline, Inc.; *Int'l*, pg. 819

SHADOW—Motorcycle—American Honda Motor Co., Inc. Motorcycle Division; *Int'l*, pg. 634

SHADOW—Wiper Cowl—Lund International Holdings, Inc.; *U.S. Public*, pg. 1020

SHADOW—Automatic Equipment Identification System—Union Switch & Signal Inc.; *Int'l*, pg. 77

SHADOW BAN—Incandescent Lamps—General Electric Canada Inc.; *U.S. Public*, pg. 713

SHADOW BROADCAST SERVICES—Traffic, Weather, Sports & News Brdcst.—Shadow Broadcast Services; *U.S. Public*, pg. 1763

SHADOW BROADCAST SERVICES, A WESTWOOD ONE COMPANY—Traffic, News, Weather, Sports & Entertainment Programming—Westwood One, Inc.; *U.S. Public*, pg. 1763

SHADOW NEWS—Broadcast Services Including News Reports—Shadow Broadcast Services; *U.S. Public*, pg. 1763

SHADOW ONLINE—Internet-Based Traffic Reports & Analysis—Shadow Broadcast Services; *U.S. Public*, pg. 1763

SHADOW PLAY—Glazed Ceramic Tile—Porcelanite, Inc.; *Int'l*, pg. 573

SHADOW RIDGE—Vinyl Siding—Georgia-Pacific Corporation; *U.S. Public*, pg. 735

SHADOW SPORTS—Broadcast Services Including Sports Updates—Shadow Broadcast Services; *U.S. Public*, pg. 1763

SHADOW TRAFFIC—Broadcast Services Including Traffic Reports—Shadow Broadcast Services; *U.S. Public*, pg. 1763

SHADOW WEATHER—Broadcast Services Including Weather Reports—Shadow Broadcast Services; *U.S. Public*, pg. 1763

SHADOW WEAVE—Wood & Lumber Products—Georgia-Pacific Corporation; *U.S. Public*, pg. 735

SHADOWCLAD—Plywood for Exterior House Cladding—Carter Holt Harvey Limited; *U.S. Public*, pg. 904

SHADY BROOK FARMS—Fresh Turkey Products—Rocco Inc.; *U.S. Private*, pg. 937

SHADY BROOK FARMS—Fresh Turkey Products—Shady Brook Farms; *U.S. Private*, pg. 937

SHADY LANE—Plywood, Lumber, Wood & Wood Fiber Products—Georgia-Pacific Corporation; *U.S. Public*, pg. 735

SHAFER—Aerospace Roller & Filament Wound Bearings—Rexnord Corporation; *Int'l*, pg. 127

SHAG—NONE—Urban Outfitters, Inc.; *U.S. Public*, pg. 1700

SHAHISTAN—Rugs—Couristan Inc.; *U.S. Private*, pg. 279

SHAKE 'N BAKE—Coatings—Philip Morris Companies Inc.; *U.S. Public*, pg. 1287

SHAKE 'N BAKE—Seasoned Coating Mix—Kraft Foods, Inc.; *U.S. Public*, pg. 1287

SHAKE 'N BAKE OVEN FRY—Coatings—Kraft Foods, Inc.; *U.S. Public*, pg. 1287

SHAKE 'N POUR—Ready to Use Pancake & Waffle Mix—General Mills, Inc.; *U.S. Public*, pg. 717

SHAKE RATTLE & ROLL—Milk Shake—Lancashire Dairies Ltd.; *Int'l*, pg. 798

SHAKEN PLANK—Solid 2 1/4-3 1/4″ Plank-Beveled—Robbins, Inc.; *U.S. Private*, pg. 934

SHAKER—Mechanical Pencil—The Pilot Pen Corp. of America; *Int'l*, pg. 1057

SHAKERTOWN SIDING—Siding & Roofing—Shakertown 1992, Inc.; *Int'l*, pg. 296

SHAKERTOWN SIDING—Siding & Roofing—Spectrum Glass Co.; *Int'l*, pg. 296

SHAKESPEARE—Cigars—General Cigar Company, Inc.; *U.S. Public*, pg. 708

SHAKESPEARE—Extruded Monofilament—K2 Inc.; *U.S. Public*, pg. 940

SHAKESPEARE—Fiberglass Utility Light & Power Poles—K2 Inc.; *U.S. Public*, pg. 940

SHAKESPEARE—Marine Radio Antennas—K2 Inc.; *U.S. Public*, pg. 940

SHAKESPEARE—Fishing Rods & Reels—K2 Inc.; *U.S. Public*, pg. 940

SHAKESPEARE—Game—Monarch Avalon, Inc.; *U.S. Public*, pg. 1123

SHAKESPEARE—Fishing Tackle—Shakespeare Fishing Tackle; *U.S. Public*, pg. 940

SHAKEY'S—Pizza Restaurants—Shakey's Incorporated; *U.S. Private*, pg. 989

SHAKLEE—Vitamins, Food Supplements, Skin, Hair & Beauty Care Products—Shaklee Corporation; *Int'l*, pg. 1518

SHAKLEE PERFORMANCE—Nutritional Products—Shaklee Corporation; *Int'l*, pg. 1518

SHALER-RISLONE—Auto. Products—The Shaler Company; *U.S. Private*, pg. 786

SHALIMAR—Hosiery for Women—Grupo Synkro, S.A. de C.V.; *Int'l*, pg. 576

SHALIMAR—Perfumes—Guerlain, Inc.; *Int'l*, pg. 780

SHALIMAR—Perfume—Guerlain S.A.; *Int'l*, pg. 780

SHALLO-TOW—Low Profile, Chain-In-Floor Conveyors—Jervis B. Webb Company; *U.S. Private*, pg. 1156

SHAM-ROCK—Top or Center Press Roll Cover—Harnischfeger Industries, Inc.; *U.S. Public*, pg. 788

SHAMPAINE—Operating/Surgical Tables & Dental Chairs—Getinge/Castle Inc.; *Int'l*, pg. 551

SHAMU—Show—Anheuser-Busch Companies, Inc.; *U.S. Public*, pg. 113

SHAND KYDD—Wallcoverings—Borden, Inc.; *U.S. Private*, pg. 157

SHANDWICK—NONE—Shandwick International Plc; *Int'l*, pg. 1226

SHANDY BASS—Soft Drink—Whitbread PLC; *Int'l*, pg. 1498

SHANGLE—NONE—CertainTeed Corporation; *Int'l*, pg. 1170

SHANI—Afro-American Fashion Dolls—Mattel, Inc.; *U.S. Public*, pg. 1057

SHANNON WITH DESIGN—Paper Goods—American Greetings Corporation; *U.S. Public*, pg. 77

SHANTU—Two-in-One Shampoo—The Procter & Gamble Company; *U.S. Public*, pg. 1330

SHAPE—Magazine—Weider Publications, Inc.; *U.S. Private*, pg. 1159

SHAPE COOKS—Magazine—Weider Publications, Inc.; *U.S. Private*, pg. 1159

SHAPE MAKERS—Stretch Knit Furniture Covers—Reeves International; *U.S. Private*, pg. 507

SHAPE 'N BLUSH—Face Make-Up—Cover Girl Cosmetics; *U.S. Public*, pg. 1330

SHAPE-UPS—Frozen Treats & Desserts—J & J Snack Foods Corporation; *U.S. Public*, pg. 916

SHAPELL—Real Estate Developer & Builder—Shapell Industries, Inc.; *U.S. Private*, pg. 990

SHAPEWEAR—Stretch Shapesuits, Briefs, Panty Girdles—Olga Div.; *U.S. Public*, pg. 1738

SHAPEWEAR SCOOPS—Control Briefs—Olga Div.; *U.S. Public*, pg. 1738

SHAPING THE FUTURE OF WOUND CLOSURE—NONE—U.S. Surgical Corp.; *U.S. Public*, pg. 1687

SHAPINGS—Hair Styling Products—Revlon-Realistic Professional Products, Inc.; *U.S. Private*, pg. 690

SHAR PAK—Ceramic Sharpeners—Fiskars-Gerber; *Int'l*, pg. 492

SHARE—Telecommunications System Software—Datapoint Corporation; *Int'l*, pg. 384

SHARK—Pulping Rotor—Harnischfeger Industries, Inc.; *U.S. Public*, pg. 788

SHARK—Vehicle Measurement System—Hein-Werner Corporation; *U.S. Public*, pg. 805

SHARK SKIN—Filter Paper—Schleicher & Schuell, Inc.; *Int'l*, pg. 1206

SHARNET—NONE—Applied Extrusion Technologies, Inc.; *U.S. Public*, pg. 122

SHARON CORR—Soft Drink—R.J. Corr Naturals, Inc.; *U.S. Private*, pg. 276

SHARP—NONE—Milgray Electronics, Inc.; *U.S. Public*, pg. 205

SHARP—Pencils—Pentel of America, Ltd.; *Int'l*, pg. 1035

SHARP—NONE—Sharp Corporation; *Int'l*, pg. 1228

SHARP—Electronics—Sharp Electronics Corporation; *Int'l*, pg. 1228

SHARP DYNAMIC—Hearing Aids—Dahlberg, Inc.; *U.S. Public*, pg. 194

SHARP'S—Nonalcohol Beer—Miller Brewing Company; *U.S. Public*, pg. 1289

SHARP'S—Beer—Philip Morris Companies Inc.; *U.S. Public*, pg. 1287

SHARPCUT—NONE—Fastenal Company; *U.S. Public*, pg. 614

SHARPE CONTROL SYSTEM (SCS)—NONE—Brown & Sharpe Manufacturing Company; *U.S. Public*, pg. 260

THE SHARPER IMAGE—High-Tech Electronics & Fitness Equipment—The Sharper Image; *U.S. Public*, pg. 1464

SHARPER IMAGE—Men's Personnel Leather—Swank, Inc.; *U.S. Public*, pg. 1543

SHARPER IMAGE SPA—NONE—The Sharper Image; *U.S. Public*, pg. 1464

SHARPIE—Permanent Marker & Litho Pen—Sanford Corporation; *U.S. Public*, pg. 1178

SHARPLAN—NONE—Laser Industries Ltd.; *Int'l*, pg. 429

SHARPLES-SUPER-D-CANTER—Solid Bowl Scroll Centrifuge—Alfa Laval Separation Inc.; *Int'l*, pg. 1378

SHARPLET-2—Pencil—Pentel of America, Ltd.; *Int'l*, pg. 1035

SHARPOINT—Surgical Instruments—Surgical Specialties; *U.S. Private*, pg. 1056

SHARPS—Toffee—Cadbury Schweppes p.l.c.; *Int'l*, pg. 247

SHARPVISION—100" LCD Projector—Sharp Electronics Corporation; *Int'l*, pg. 1228

SHARWOOD—NONE—Inkel USA Corporation; *U.S. Private*, pg. 563

SHARWOOD'S—Indian & Chinese Food—Ranks Hovis McDougall Limited; *Int'l*, pg. 1395

SHASTA—Recreational Vehicle—Coachmen Industries, Inc.; *U.S. Public*, pg. 387

SHASTA—Text & Cover Paper—The Mead Corporation; *U.S. Public*, pg. 1074

SHASTA—Soft Drinks—Shasta Beverages, Inc.; *U.S. Public*, pg. 1153

SHAVATON—Sno-Kone Machine—Gold Medal Products Co.; *U.S. Private*, pg. 459

SHAVE EASE—Aerosol Lubricant, Cleaner—Parks Products, Inc.; *U.S. Private*, pg. 840

SHAVE'R CORD—Shave Accessory—Parks Products, Inc.; *U.S. Private*, pg. 840

SHAVE STICK—Powder Stick—Parks Products, Inc.; *U.S. Private*, pg. 840

SHAVIT—M.I.C. for Checks—American Israeli Paper Mills Ltd.; *Int'l*, pg. 74

SHAVIT SECURITY—NONE—American Israeli Paper Mills Ltd.; *Int'l*, pg. 74

SHAW-BARTON—Programs & Wearables—JII/Sales Promotion Associates, Inc.; *U.S. Private*, pg. 598

SHAW BOX—Electric Wire Rope Hoist—Columbus McKinnon Corp.; *U.S. Public*, pg. 405

SHAW COMMERCIAL SYSTEMS—Carpets—Shaw Industries, Inc.; *U.S. Public*, pg. 1464

SHAW'S—Supermarkets—Shaw's Supermarkets, Inc.; *Int'l*, pg. 1170

SHAYKS—Milk—Q.U.F. Industries Ltd.; *Int'l*, pg. 1074

SHE—Magazine—The National Magazine Company Ltd.; *U.S. Private*, pg. 518

SHE—Body Care Products—Sara Lee Corporation; *U.S. Public*, pg. 1432

SHEAFFER—Writing Instruments—Sheaffer Inc.; *Int'l*, pg. 542

SHEAR-CARB—Carbide Tipped End Mills—Rogers Tool Works, Inc.; *U.S. Public*, pg. 950

SHEAR-SEAL BRAND—Directional Control Valves—Barksdale, Inc.; *U.S. Public*, pg. 457

SHEAR SPEED—Gear Shaping Machinery—Micromatic Textron; *U.S. Public*, pg. 1589

SHEAR-SPEED—Internal Gear Shaping—Textron Inc.; *U.S. Public*, pg. 1588

SHEARPROOF—Self Locking Pin—Driv-Lok, Inc.; *U.S. Public*, pg. 343

SHEATHALL—Plywood Panels—Weyerhaeuser Company; *U.S. Public*, pg. 1764

SHEBA—Catfood—Kal Kan Foods, Inc.; *U.S. Private*, pg. 707

SHEBA—Cat Food—Mars, Incorporated; *U.S. Private*, pg. 707

SHEBA—Petfood—Mars Petfoods (UNISABI); *U.S. Private*, pg. 707

SHEDD'S COUNTRY CROCK—Margarine/Spread—Chesebrough-Pond's; *Int'l*, pg. 1436

SHEDD'S SPREAD COUNTRY CROCK—NONE—Van den Bergh Foods Company; *Int'l*, pg. 1436

SHEENE—Cosmetics—International Cosmetics Co., Ltd.; *Int'l*, pg. 684

SHEER CARESS—Microfiber Hoisery—JC Penney Company, Inc.; *U.S. Public*, pg. 916

SHEER DESCENT WATERFALLS—NONE—Teledyne Laars/Jandy Products; *U.S. Public*, pg. 43

SHEER ELEGANCE—Hosiery—L'eggs Products, Inc.; *U.S. Public*, pg. 1434

SHEER ENERGY—Hosiery, Gloves & Slippers—L'eggs Products, Inc.; *U.S. Public*, pg. 1434

SHEER ENERGY—Hosiery—Sara Lee Corporation; *U.S. Public*, pg. 1432

SHEER ESSENTIALS—Make-Up—Maybelline, Inc.; *Int'l*, pg. 819

SHEER-GARD—Adhesive Bandages; face masks—Medline Industries, Inc.; *U.S. Private*, pg. 728

SHEER MIST—Hair Spray—Clairol, Inc.; *U.S. Public*, pg. 254

SHEER MOISTURE—Cosmetics—Irma Shorell, Inc.; *U.S. Private*, pg. 1101

SHEER PRIDE—Filing Cabinets—Lonrho plc; *Int'l*, pg. 817

SHEER RADIANCE FIBER OPTIC LIGHTING—NONE—Teledyne Laars/Jandy Products; *U.S. Public*, pg. 43

SHEERFILL—Permanent Architectural Fabrics—Chemfab Corporation; *U.S. Public*, pg. 344

SHEERLITE—Writing Paper—The Mead Corporation; *U.S. Public*, pg. 1074

SHEET THAT FITS—NONE—Lands' End, Inc.; *U.S. Public*, pg. 977

SHEETMETAL—NONE—Brown & Sharpe Manufacturing Company; *U.S. Public*, pg. 260

SHEETROCK—Gypsum Panels—CGC Inc.; *U.S. Public*, pg. 1660

SHEETROCK—Gypsum Wall Panels—USG Corporation; *U.S. Public*, pg. 1660

SHEETROL—Sheet Flutter Control System in Dryer Sections—Harnischfeger Industries, Inc.; *U.S. Public*, pg. 788

SHEFCUT—Precision Reamer—Cogsdill Tool Products, Inc.; *U.S. Public*, pg. 250

SHEFFIELD—NONE—Giddings & Lewis Sheffield Measurement Systems; *Int'l*, pg. 1389

SHEFFIELD—Silver—Reed & Barton Corporation; *U.S. Private*, pg. 916

SHEFFIELD—Hot Rolled Steel Bars—Sheffield Steel Corporation-Joliet; *U.S. Private*, pg. 991

SHEFFIELD MEASUREMENT—NONE—Giddings & Lewis Sheffield Measurement Systems; *Int'l*, pg. 1389

SHEIK—Latex Condoms—London International Group Inc.; *Int'l*, pg. 815

SHEILDTOX—Pest Control—Reckitt & Colman plc; *Int'l*, pg. 1089

SHELBY WILLIAMS—Chairs—Shelby Williams Industries, Inc.; *U.S. Public*, pg. 1464

SHELETS—Sox—Reliable Knitting Works; *U.S. Private*, pg. 920

SHELF ANCHOR—Hardware—Knape & Vogt Mfg. Co.; *U.S. Public*, pg. 963

SHELF NET—Extruded Plastic Net—Nalle Plastics Inc.; *U.S. Private*, pg. 773

SHELF SPACE—Medium Duty Back Room Storage System—MEG; *U.S. Private*, pg. 686

SHELF SPAN—NONE—MEG; *U.S. Private*, pg. 686

SHELFTALK/SHELFTAKE-ONE—Supermarket Shelf Advertisement—News America Marketing; *Int'l*, pg. 925

SHELL—Chairs—Herman Miller, Inc.; *U.S. Public*, pg. 1111

SHELL GASOLINE—Gasoline—Shell Oil Company; *U.S. Public*, pg. 1136

SHELL LUBRICANTS—Lubricants—Fleischli Oil Company, Inc.; *U.S. Private*, pg. 410

SHELL SIGNATURE CARD—Charge Card—Shell Oil Company; *Int'l*, pg. 1136

SHELLBAKER—NONE—The Black & Decker Corporation; *U.S. Public*, pg. 233

SHELLBURST—Photo Film—Eastman Kodak Company; *U.S. Public*, pg. 550

SHELLYGLAS—NONE—Scotsman Industries, Inc.; *U.S. Public*, pg. 1444

SHELTERING ARMS—Seat With Arms—Sanderson Plumbing Products Inc.; *U.S. Private*, pg. 964

SHENANDOAH—Plywood, Lumber, Wood & Wood Fiber Products—Georgia-Pacific Corporation; *U.S. Public*, pg. 735

SHENANDOAH—Food Products—National Fruit Product Company; *U.S. Private*, pg. 783

SHENANDOAH STACK RAIL—Pressure-Treated Fencing—Coastal Lumber Company; *U.S. Private*, pg. 248

SHEPARDS CREAM—Pharmaceuticals—Rhone-Poulenc Rorer - U.S.; *Int'l*, pg. 1110

SHEPARDS MOISTURIZING SOAP—Soap—Rhone-Poulenc Rorer - U.S.; *Int'l*, pg. 1110

SHEPARDS SKIN CREAM—Skin Cream—Rhone-Poulenc Rorer - U.S.; *Int'l*, pg. 1110

SHEPLER'S—Dept. Store & Mail Order Sales—Sheplers, Inc.; *U.S. Private*, pg. 993

SHERATON—Hotels & Motels—ITT Sheraton Corporation; *U.S. Public*, pg. 1512

SHERATON—Polishes—Kiwi Brands Pty. Ltd.; *U.S. Public*, pg. 1434

SHERBELIZER—Propylene Glycol Alginates—The NutraSweet Kelco Company; *U.S. Public*, pg. 1125

SHERBETS—Paper Napkins—Georgia-Pacific Corporation; *U.S. Public*, pg. 735

SHERIDAN'S—Black & White Liquer-White Cream & Coffee Liquer—IDV North America; *Int'l*, pg. 411

SHERIDAN'S—Spirits—Gilbeys of Ireland; *Int'l*, pg. 409

SHERLOCK—Connectors—Merit Medical Systems, Inc.; *U.S. Public*, pg. 1096

SHERLOK—Element Filter with Ring-Lok Access—Jacuzzi Bros., Jacuzzi, Inc.; *U.S. Public*, pg. 1684

SHERMAN ON THE MOUNT—Cards & Posters; Gift Items; Dolls; T-Shirts—American Greetings Corporation; *U.S. Public*, pg. 77

SHERPA—Guiding Catheters—Medtronic, Inc.; *U.S. Public*, pg. 1082

SHERTECH—Gear Pumps—Hypro Corporation; *U.S. Public*, pg. 1767

SHERTECH—NONE—WICOR, Inc.; *U.S. Public*, pg. 1767

SHERWIN WILLIAMS—Paint & Paint Prods.—The Sherwin-Williams Company; *U.S. Public*, pg. 1465

SHERWOOD—Drapery Hardware—Kirsch; *U.S. Public*, pg. 1176

SHIDLER—Real Estate Investment—The Shidler Group; *U.S. Private*, pg. 994

SHIEK—Condoms—Durex Consumer Products; *Int'l*, pg. 815

SHIELD—Flea Control Product—Carter-Wallace, Inc.; *U.S. Public*, pg. 309

SHIELD—Bar Soap—Lever Brothers Co.; *Int'l*, pg. 1435

SHIELD—Soap—Unilever Plc; *Int'l*, pg. 1433

Brand Name Index

SHIELD-ARC—Welder—The Lincoln Electric Company; *U.S. Public*, pg. 996

SHIELD-BRIGHT—NONE—ESAB Welding & Cutting Products; *Int'l*, pg. 281

SHIELDSEAL—EMI/RF Shielding Products—James Walker & Co. Limited; *Int'l*, pg. 1485

SHIELDZ—Pre-Wallcovering Primer—Wm. Zinsser & Co., Inc.; *U.S. Public*, pg. 1358

SHIFT-N-CRUISE—Transmission Cruise Control—Rockwell International Corporation; *U.S. Public*, pg. 1397

SHIFTLEX—Baseball Shoes—Mizuno Corporation; *Int'l*, pg. 884

SHIFTY'S—Men's & Women's Apparel & Footwear—Edison Brothers Stores, Inc.; *U.S. Public*, pg. 563

SHIGOTO—Electronic Components—Shokai Far East Ltd.; *U.S. Private*, pg. 996

SHILEY—Trachestony Tubes—Mallinckrodt Inc.; *U.S. Public*, pg. 1039

SHILLCRAFT—Company Name—Shillcraft, Inc.; *U.S. Private*, pg. 994

SHILOH—Orchard Grass—Green Seed Co.; *U.S. Private*, pg. 477

SHIMANO—Bicycles—Shimano Inc.; *Int'l*, pg. 1232

SHIMASHIMA—Confectionery—Meiji Seika Kaisha, Ltd.; *Int'l*, pg. 855

SHIMMER LIGHTS—Shampoo & Conditioner—Clairol, Inc.; *U.S. Public*, pg. 254

SHIMMEREEN—Nylon—BASF Corporation Fiber Products Division; *Int'l*, pg. 105

SHIMMERLIGHTS—Highlighting Shampoo—Bristol-Myers Squibb Company; *U.S. Public*, pg. 253

SHIMMERLILIES—Bras, Panties, Daywear, Shapewear—Olga Div.; *U.S. Public*, pg. 1738

SHIMMERS—Hosiery & Related Apparel—Mayer/Berkshire Corporation; *U.S. Private*, pg. 717

SHINE FREE—Cosmetics—Maybelline, Inc.; *Int'l*, pg. 819

SHINE-ON—Electric Shoe Polisher—National Presto Industries, Inc.; *U.S. Public*, pg. 1159

SHINE-ON—Co-ordinate Lingerie—Warner's; *U.S. Public*, pg. 1738

SHINGLE SHAKES—Roofing & Siding—Reynolds Metals Company; *U.S. Public*, pg. 1385

SHINGLEVENT—NONE—Air Vent Inc.; *Int'l*, pg. 1170

SHINGLEVENT—Ridge Vent—CertainTeed Corporation; *Int'l*, pg. 1170

SHINOLOGY—Systems Cleaning Equip.—Pioneer/Eclipse Corp.; *Int'l*, pg. 71

SHIP—NONE—Keyport Life Insurance Company; *U.S. Private*, pg. 666

SHIP AHOY—Frozen Seafood & Canned Seafood—Icicle Seafoods, Inc.; *U.S. Private*, pg. 556

SHIP DOCKING MODULE—Tractor Tug—Hvide Marine Incorporated; *U.S. Public*, pg. 851

SHIP SHAKE—Powdered Cereal—The Quaker Oats Company; *U.S. Public*, pg. 1347

SHIPHAM & CO.—Valves—Tomkins PLC; *Int'l*, pg. 1395

SHIPMATE—Boat Insurance—Harleysville Group; *U.S. Public*, pg. 786

SHIPPING-MATE—Packaging Aerosol Adhesives & Coatings—3M; *U.S. Public*, pg. 1604

SHIPSAFE—Dispensing Device—Calmar Inc.; *U.S. Private*, pg. 201

SHIR-BACK—Ruffled Curtain—Cameo Window Furnishings; *U.S. Private*, pg. 1094

SHIRLEY K MATERNITY—Maternity Apparel—Shirmax Leasing Ltd.; *Int'l*, pg. 1235

SHIRLEY OF HOLLYWOOD—Women's Underwear—National Corset Supply House; *U.S. Private*, pg. 781

SHIRLEY VALENTINE—Musical—Really Useful Holdings Limited; *Int'l*, pg. 1089

SHISEIDO BENEFIANCE—Skin Care—Shiseido Cosmetics (America) Ltd.; *Int'l*, pg. 1235

SHISEIDO MAKEUP—NONE—Shiseido Cosmetics (America) Ltd.; *Int'l*, pg. 1235

SHIZUKI—Film Capacitors—Shizuki Electric Corporation; *Int'l*, pg. 1236

SHLOER—Apple & Grape Juice Drinks—SmithKline Beecham plc; *Int'l*, pg. 1264

SHO-RATE—Control Measurement—Brooks Instrument; *U.S. Public*, pg. 574

SHO-PAK—Food Trays—The Chinet Co.; *Int'l*, pg. 1146

SHOBORD—Hardboard—Georgia-Pacific Corporation; *U.S. Public*, pg. 735

SHOCK-EZE—Shock Absorber—Baker Hughes INTEQ; *U.S. Public*, pg. 166

SHOCK SAFE—Extension Cords—General Cable Corporation; *Int'l*, pg. 1486

SHOCK SENTRY—Ground Fault Inte—Eagle Electric Mfg. Co., Inc.; *U.S. Private*, pg. 354

SHOCK TARTS—Candy—Nestle USA; *Int'l*, pg. 916

SHOCK TRAP—Extension Cord—Southwire Company; *U.S. Private*, pg. 1019

SHOCK WAVE—Hair Care Products—Wella Group; *Int'l*, pg. 1489

SHOCKEN—Book Imprint—Random House, Inc.; *U.S. Private*, pg. 20

SHOCKSTOPPER—Industrial Products—Email Limited; *Int'l*, pg. 450

SHOCKWATCH—Precise Impact Detector—Media Recovery, Inc.; *U.S. Private*, pg. 726

SHOE BARGAINS—Self-Service Promotional Family Shoe Stores—Woolworth Corporation; *U.S. Public*, pg. 1777

SHOE WORLD—Shoe Stores—Pic'n Pay Stores, Inc.; *U.S. Private*, pg. 864

SHOEBOX GREETINGS—Greeting Cards—Hallmark Cards, Inc.; *U.S. Private*, pg. 495

SHOFAR KOSHER—NONE—Shofar Kosher Foods; *U.S. Public*, pg. 1433

SHOGUN—Seafood—Rich SeaPak Corp.; *U.S. Private*, pg. 928

SHOGUN—Spirits—Suntory Ltd.; *Int'l*, pg. 1321

SHOJO FRIEND—Monthly Japanese Comic Magazine—Kodansha Ltd.; *Int'l*, pg. 742

SHONEN MAGAZINE—Weekly Japanese Comic Magazine—Kodansha Ltd.; *Int'l*, pg. 742

SHONEY'S—Family Restaurants—Shoney's, Inc.; *U.S. Public*, pg. 1467

SHONEY'S INNS—Hotels—Sholodge, Inc.; *U.S. Public*, pg. 1467

SHONEY'S INNS—Inns—Shoney's, Inc.; *U.S. Public*, pg. 1467

SHOOT—Magazine—BPI Communications Inc.; *Int'l*, pg. 1446

SHOOT—Sports Magazine—IPC Magazines Limited; *Int'l*, pg. 651

SHOOT-N-SCORE—Electronic Basketball Scoreboard—Lifetime Products Inc.; *U.S. Private*, pg. 667

SHOOT THE BREEZE—Compact Pro Dryer—Clairol, Inc.; *U.S. Public*, pg. 254

SHOOTING TIMES—Country Pursuits & Property Magazine—IPC Magazines Limited; *Int'l*, pg. 651

SHOOTSAVER—NONE—Eastman Kodak Company; *U.S. Public*, pg. 550

SHOP 'N SAVE—Retail Food & Drug Stores—Hannaford Bros. Co.; *U.S. Public*, pg. 781

SHOP 'N'BANK—NONE—Deposit Guaranty Corp.; *U.S. Public*, pg. 500

SHOP-RITE—Food Store—American Consumers, Inc.; *U.S. Public*, pg. 70

SHOP-RITE—Grocery Store—Foodarama Supermarkets, Inc.; *U.S. Public*, pg. 661

SHOP RITE—Independently Owned & Operated Food Stores—Roundy's, Inc.; *U.S. Private*, pg. 948

SHOPBOX—Power Tools—The Black & Decker Corporation; *U.S. Public*, pg. 233

SHOPMASTER—Computer Software for use with Numerical Control Machine Systems—General Electric Canada Inc.; *U.S. Public*, pg. 713

SHOPMAX—Industrial Operator Interfaces—Rockwell International Corporation; *U.S. Public*, pg. 1397

SHOPPERS ADVANTAGE—NONE—CUC International, Inc.; *U.S. Public*, pg. 320

SHOPPERS CASH—Controlled Markdown Program—Carlson Retail Marketing; *U.S. Private*, pg. 212

SHOPPERS DRUG MART—Pharmaceuticals—Imasco Limited; *Int'l*, pg. 112

SHOPPING CART—NONE—Drug Emporium, Inc.; *U.S. Public*, pg. 530

SHOPPING CENTER WORLD—Publication for Shopping Center Owners—Intertec Publishing; *U.S. Public*, pg. 1327

SHOPPING CENTER WORLD—Monthly Publication—Intertec Publishing; *U.S. Public*, pg. 1328

SHOPPING CENTRE PLANNER—Software—CACI International Inc; *U.S. Public*, pg. 272

SHOPRITE—Supermarket—Big V Supermarkets, Inc.; *U.S. Private*, pg. 143

SHOPSMITH—Tools—Shopsmith, Inc.; *U.S. Public*, pg. 1467

SHOPSY'S—Food Products—Maple Leaf Foods Inc.; *Int'l*, pg. 841

SHOPTRAC—NONE—Kronos Incorporated; *U.S. Public*, pg. 967

SHORAR—Family of Short-Range Acquisition Radars—Oerlikon-Contraves AG; *Int'l*, pg. 998

SHORE DUROMETERS—NONE—Wilson/Shore Instruments; *U.S. Public*, pg. 883

SHORE INSTRUMENTS—NONE—Wilson/Shore Instruments; *U.S. Public*, pg. 883

SHORE-LAND'R—Boat Trailers—Midwest Industries, Inc.; *U.S. Private*, pg. 744

SHORE-STATION—Boat Hoists & Docks—Midwest Industries, Inc.; *U.S. Private*, pg. 744

THE SHOREHAM—Hotel—Omni Hotels; *U.S. Private*, pg. 1065

SHORELINE—Phonograph Records & Tapes—A&M Records; *Int'l*, pg. 1052

SHORELINE OAK—Lumber & Wood Products—Georgia-Pacific Corporation; *U.S. Public*, pg. 735

SHORT & SASSY—Hair Conditioner—Clairol, Inc.; *U.S. Public*, pg. 254

SHORT ORDERS—Food Products—Hormel Foods Corp.; *U.S. Public*, pg. 840

SHORT PORT COLOR CARD—Computer Equipment—Emulex Corporation; *U.S. Public*, pg. 579

SHORTCUT—Surgical Knives & Blades—Alcon Laboratories, Inc.; *Int'l*, pg. 916

SHORTGOOSE—NONE—Pfizer Inc.; *U.S. Public*, pg. 1281

SHORTSTOPP II—Device for Plugging Interior of Pipe—T.D. Williamson, Inc.; *U.S. Private*, pg. 1179

SHORTSTUB—Electrode Holder—Dovatech, Ltd.; *U.S. Public*, pg. 520

SHORTY—Power Tools—The Black & Decker Corporation; *U.S. Public*, pg. 233

SHORTY VIAL—Scientific Glassware for Laboratory Use—Wheaton Inc.; *Int'l*, pg. 67

SHOSETSU GENDAI—Monthly Japanese Literary Magazine—Kodansha Ltd.; *Int'l*, pg. 742

SHOT OF STEAM—Steam Irons—Sunbeam Household Products; *U.S. Public*, pg. 1533

SHOTMASTER—35 Millimeter Autofocus Leaf Shutter Camera—Ricoh Corporation; *Int'l*, pg. 1114

SHOULDER ROLL TOP RAIL—NONE—Overholtzer Church Furniture, Inc.; *U.S. Private*, pg. 823

SHOULDER SHAPERS—Shoulder Pads—Olga Div.; *U.S. Public*, pg. 1738

SHOULDER-VAC—Commercial Vacuum Cleaner—Hoover Company; *U.S. Public*, pg. 1065

SHOUT—Laundry Soil & Stain Remover—S.C. Johnson & Son, Inc.; *U.S. Private*, pg. 592

SHOUT—Laundry Pre-Treatment—S.C. Johnson & Son, Limited; *U.S. Private*, pg. 593

SHOUT—NONE—N.V. Johnson Wax Belgium S.A.; *U.S. Private*, pg. 593

SHOUT CARPET SCIENCE—Floor Care—S.C. Johnson & Son, Inc.; *U.S. Private*, pg. 592

SHOW BEAM—Projector & Cartridges—View-Master, Inc.; *U.S. Public*, pg. 1058

SHOW BIZ PIZZA PLACE—Family Entertainment Centers—ShowBiz Pizza Time, Inc.; *U.S. Public*, pg. 1468

SHOW CARD—Video Rental Program—National Video, Inc.; *U.S. Public*, pg. 1755

SHOW OFF—Women's Retail Specialty Store—Gateway Apparel, Inc.; *U.S. Private*, pg. 441

THE SHOW OFF—Plastic Containers—Tenneco Specialty Products; *U.S. Public*, pg. 1579

SHOW OFFS—Hair Access.—Goody Products, Inc.; *U.S. Public*, pg. 1177

SHOW STAR—LCE Projector—Electrohome Ltd.; *Int'l*, pg. 438

SHOW YOUR TRUE COLORS—Photographic Film—Eastman Kodak Company; *U.S. Public*, pg. 550

SHOWBIZ—Leisure Game—Monarch Avalon, Inc.; *U.S. Public*, pg. 1123

SHOWBOAT—Canned Vegetables—Bush Brothers & Company; *U.S. Private*, pg. 189

Brand Name Index

SHOWBOAT—NONE—Showboat, Incorporated; *U.S. Public*, pg. 1469
SHOWBOATS INTERNATIONAL—Boating Magazine—Hachette Filipacchi Magazines Inc.; *Int'l*, pg. 794
SHOWCAKE—Plastic Containers—Tenneco Specialty Products; *U.S. Public*, pg. 1579
SHOWCASE—HVAC—Eljer Plumbingware; *U.S. Public*, pg. 1794
SHOWCASE—NONE—Packerland Packing Co.; *U.S. Private*, pg. 833
SHOWCASE—Plastic Packaging—Tenneco Specialty Products; *U.S. Public*, pg. 1579
SHOWCASE SUPREME—NONE—Packerland Packing Co.; *U.S. Private*, pg. 833
SHOWER MASSAGE—Personal Massager—Teledyne Water Pik; *U.S. Public*, pg. 44
SHOWER SHAVER—Razor—American Safety Razor Company; *U.S. Private*, pg. 597
SHOWER TO SHOWER—Body Powder—Johnson & Johnson; *U.S. Public*, pg. 927
SHOWER-WARE—Stainless Steel Showers—Acorn Engineering Company; *U.S. Private*, pg. 14
SHOWERALL—Bathroom Supplies—Jaclo Inc.; *U.S. Private*, pg. 349
SHOWERS OF DIAMONDS—Fountains—Irritol System; *U.S. Public*, pg. 44
SHOWFELT—Felt—Central/Shippee, Inc.; *U.S. Private*, pg. 224
SHOWPIE—Plastic Containers—Tenneco Specialty Products; *U.S. Public*, pg. 1579
SHOWTIME—Adult Cosmetic Make-Up Kits—Schering-Plough Healthcare Products Inc.; *U.S. Public*, pg. 1438
SHOWTIME—Pay Television—Showtime Networks Inc.; *U.S. Private*, pg. 779
SHOWTIME—Pay Cable Network—Viacom Inc.; *U.S. Private*, pg. 775
SHOWTIME EN ESPANOL—Showtime In Spanish—Showtime Networks Inc.; *U.S. Private*, pg. 779
SHOWTIME EVENT—Television CPPV—Showtime Networks Inc.; *U.S. Private*, pg. 779
SHOWTOONS—Knit Products—Sara Lee Corporation; *U.S. Public*, pg. 1432
SHOWTOONS—Boys Underwear—Sara Lee Knit Products; *U.S. Public*, pg. 1434
SHRED-TECH/BSD—Industrial Shredding—Global Industrial Technologies; *U.S. Public*, pg. 747
SHRED-O-MAT—Salad Maker—The Rival Company; *U.S. Public*, pg. 1391
SHREDDED WHEAT—Cereal—The Quaker Oats Company; *U.S. Public*, pg. 1347
SHREDDED WHEAT SQUARES—Breakfast Cereal—Kellogg Company; *U.S. Public*, pg. 947
SHREDMAN—Shredders—Savin Corporation; *Int'l*, pg. 1114
SHREDMASTER—Shredder—General Binding Corporation; *U.S. Public*, pg. 707
SHREVEPORT ROSE—NONE—Harrah's Entertainment, Inc.; *U.S. Public*, pg. 790
SHREVESTAR—NONE—Harrah's Entertainment, Inc.; *U.S. Public*, pg. 790
SHRINK & SEAL—Window Insulator Kit—Macklanburg-Duncan Co.; *U.S. Private*, pg. 692
SHRINK-IT—Window Sealer Kit—Warp Brothers; *U.S. Private*, pg. 412
SHRINK-N-SHIELD—Heat Shrinkable Shielding—The Zippertubing Co.; *U.S. Private*, pg. 1207
SHRUB GUARD—Wire Guard—CCX, Inc.; *U.S. Private*, pg. 193
SHUFORD MILLS—Mfr. Cotton & Synthetic Yarns—Shuford Mills, Inc.; *U.S. Private*, pg. 996
SHUGART—Floppy Disk Drives—Shugart Corporation; *U.S. Private*, pg. 997
SHUKAN GENDAI—Weekly General Interest Men's Magazine—Kodansha Ltd.; *Int'l*, pg. 742
SHULITE—Sugar-Free Carbonated Drink—Meiji Seika Kaisha, Ltd.; *Int'l*, pg. 855
SHUNTFLO—Meters—BIF; *U.S. Public*, pg. 726
SHUPERSTAR—Children's Footwear—International Seaway Trading Corporation; *U.S. Private*, pg. 572
SHUR-FLO—Anticaking Agents—Witco Corporation; *U.S. Public*, pg. 1773
SHUR-FORM—NONE—Ballard Medical Products; *U.S. Public*, pg. 171
SHUR-GAIN—Pet Foods & Livestock; Poultry Feeds—Maple Leaf Foods Inc.; *Int'l*, pg. 841

SHUR-GRIP—Extruded Plastic Net—Nalle Plastics Inc.; *U.S. Private*, pg. 773
SHUR-LOCK—Lid Opener—CTB International Corp.; *U.S. Public*, pg. 284
SHUR-STIK—Caulks, Sealants, Floor & Wallcovering Adhesives—The Gibson-Homans Company; *U.S. Private*, pg. 451
SHUR-TAB—Insert Installation Part—Shur-Lok Corporation; *U.S. Private*, pg. 997
SHUR VALU—Grocery & Perishable—Shurfine International, Inc.; *U.S. Private*, pg. 997
SHURE HIDE—Paint—Graham Paint and Varnish Company; *U.S. Private*, pg. 468
SHURFINE SELECT—Grocery Products—Shurfine International, Inc.; *U.S. Private*, pg. 997
SHURFLO—Automatic Interlock Flow Switch—Hays Fluid Controls-Division of Romac Industries; *U.S. Private*, pg. 942
SHURFLO—NONE—WICOR, Inc.; *U.S. Public*, pg. 1767
SHURFRESH—Perishable Food Products—Shurfine International, Inc.; *U.S. Private*, pg. 997
SHUTTERPLY—Solid-Faced Construction Plywood—Carter Holt Harvey Limited; *U.S. Public*, pg. 904
SHUTTLE—Home Health Care Scooter—Pride Health Care, Inc.; *U.S. Private*, pg. 883
SHUTTLE BUGGY—Mobile Self-Propelled Material Transfer Vehicle—Astec Industries, Inc.; *U.S. Public*, pg. 141
SHUTTLELIFT—Industrial Mobile Gantry, 8.5 Ton Industrial Crane—Marine Travelift, Inc.; *U.S. Private*, pg. 703
SHUTTLELOCK SERIES—Loadlocked Single or Dual Chamber Plasma Processing System—Plasma-Therm, Inc.; *U.S. Public*, pg. 1308
SIARA—Jewelry—Basel Trading Company Ltd.; *Int'l*, pg. 169
SIBARITA—Sherry—Domecq Importers Inc.; *Int'l*, pg. 63
SIBETEX—Sidmam Electron Beam Texturing—Sidmar N.V.; *Int'l*, pg. 79
SIBIO—Romanian Pork Prods.—Atalanta Corporation; *U.S. Private*, pg. 93
SICCAMAT—Actuated Valves—KSB Aktiengesellschaft; *Int'l*, pg. 721
SICCATOL—Driers, Organometallic-Based—Akzo Nobel N.V.; *Int'l*, pg. 42
SICHEL—French & German Wines—Schieffelin & Somerset Co.; *Int'l*, pg. 412
SICKLE—Herbicide—The Dow Chemical Company; *U.S. Public*, pg. 522
SICLOR—Fungicide—Caffaro S.p.A.; *Int'l*, pg. 248
SICO—NONE—Sico Inc.; *Int'l*, pg. 1239
SICO—Wallbeds & Other Space-Saving Products—Sico Incorporated; *U.S. Private*, pg. 997
SICOAC—NONE—ETEX; *Int'l*, pg. 430
SICOFLEX ABS—Polymers—The Dow Chemical Company; *U.S. Public*, pg. 522
SICOMET—Cyanoacrylate Adhesives—Henkel Corporation; *U.S. Private*, pg. 610
SICON—Silicone Coating—The Dexter Corporation; *U.S. Public*, pg. 504
SICONEX—Electronic Cable Assemblies—3M; *U.S. Public*, pg. 1604
SICOSTAB—Auxiliaries & Additives—BASF AG; *Int'l*, pg. 103
SICOSTIROLO—Polystyrene—The Dow Chemical Company; *U.S. Public*, pg. 522
SIDASE—Alpha-Amylase, Cellulase & Protease—Royal Gist-Brocades N.V.; *Int'l*, pg. 1142
SIDCA—Continuously Annealed Steel—Sidmar N.V.; *Int'l*, pg. 79
SIDE—Software—CACI International Inc; *U.S. Public*, pg. 272
SIDE BLOCKER—Awning Accessory—Carefree of Colorado; *U.S. Public*, pg. 217
SIDE I—Athletic Shoes—Nike, Inc.; *U.S. Public*, pg. 1184
SIDE-TRAC—Mobile Shelf-Type Filing Cabinets—Tab Products Co.; *U.S. Public*, pg. 1559
SIDEKICK—Sport Utility Vehicle—American Suzuki Motor Corporation; *Int'l*, pg. 1323
SIDEKICK—Recyclable 35mm Camera—Polaroid Corporation; *U.S. Public*, pg. 1313
SIDEKICK—Scooter—Pride Health Care, Inc.; *U.S. Private*, pg. 883
SIDEKICK SPORT—Sports Utility Vehicle—American Suzuki Motor Corporation; *Int'l*, pg. 1323

SIDELOADER—Automated Guide Vehicle—SI Handling Systems, Inc.; *U.S. Public*, pg. 1418
SIDEOUT—Awning—Carefree of Colorado; *U.S. Public*, pg. 217
SIDEOUT KOVER—Awning Accessory—Carefree of Colorado; *U.S. Public*, pg. 217
SIDEVISOR—accessory—Carefree of Colorado; *U.S. Public*, pg. 217
SIDEWINDER—Van Awning—Carefree of Colorado; *U.S. Public*, pg. 217
SIDEWINDER—High Chair—Evenflo Company, Inc.; *U.S. Private*, pg. 629
SIDING SAVER—Coatings—Rust-Oleum Corporation; *U.S. Public*, pg. 1358
SIDLEC—Electric Steel—Sidmar N.V.; *Int'l*, pg. 79
SIDTEC—Condenser Tube Cleaners—BetzDearborn Inc.; *U.S. Public*, pg. 226
SIEGE OF JERUSALEM—War Game—Monarch Avalon, Inc.; *U.S. Public*, pg. 1123
SIEGLING—Transmission & Convyor Belts—Forbo Holding SA; *Int'l*, pg. 496
SIEKO MAGLEV—Turbomolecular Pump—Edwards High Vacuum, International; *Int'l*, pg. 121
SIEMENS ENERGY & AUTOMATION—Energy Efficient Motors—Bryant Electric Supply Company, Inc.; *U.S. Private*, pg. 177
SIEMENS WIXDORF—NONE—Siemens AG; *Int'l*, pg. 1244
SIERO-DH—Hiking Shoe—K-Swiss Inc.; *U.S. Public*, pg. 937
SIERRA—Stainless Steelware—The Canadian Coleman Co., Ltd.; *U.S. Private*, pg. 691
SIERRA—Roofing Tiles—Carter Holt Harvey Limited; *U.S. Public*, pg. 904
SIERRA—Small Engine Parts—Echlin Inc.; *U.S. Public*, pg. 560
SIERRA—Hotels—Grupo Sidek, S.A. de C.V.; *Int'l*, pg. 576
SIERRA—Typewriters—Juki Corporation; *Int'l*, pg. 716
SIERRA—Mobile Homes—Kit Manufacturing Company; *U.S. Public*, pg. 962
SIERRA—3-Wheel Scooter—Ortho-Kinetics, Inc.; *U.S. Private*, pg. 820
SIERRA—Wall Plates—Pass & Seymour/Legrand; *Int'l*, pg. 806
SIERRA BOTTLED WATER—Bottled Water—Hinckley & Schmitt, Inc.; *Int'l*, pg. 1322
SIERRA CHOICE—Triple Option HMO—Sierra Health Services, Inc.; *U.S. Public*, pg. 1469
SIERRA DESIGNS—NONE—Kellwood Company; *U.S. Public*, pg. 948
SIERRA MODEL—Holistic Approach to the Resolution of Addictive & Mental Health Diseases—NextHealth Inc.; *U.S. Public*, pg. 1181
SIERRA PACIFIC—Lumber Mfg.—Sierra Pacific Industries; *U.S. Private*, pg. 998
SIERRA PACIFIC POWER—Multi-State Electric Utility—Sierra Pacific Power Co.; *U.S. Public*, pg. 1470
SIERRA PLANK—Pre-Finished Laminate—Bruce Hardwood Floors; *U.S. Public*, pg. 1634
SIERRA SEMICONDUCTOR—NONE—Milgray Electronics, Inc.; *U.S. Public*, pg. 205
SIERRAPINE—Medium Density Fiberboard—Willamette Industries, Inc.; *U.S. Public*, pg. 1769
SIERRAPLEX—Wiring Devices—Pass & Seymour/Legrand; *Int'l*, pg. 806
SIESTA—Beauty Salon Furniture—Belvedere Company; *U.S. Private*, pg. 1008
SIFTO—Salt—Domtar Inc.; *Int'l*, pg. 416
SIG-NATURE—Printing Coated Papers—The Mead Corporation; *U.S. Public*, pg. 1074
SIGHT & SOUND—NONE—Golden Books Family Entertainment Inc.; *U.S. Public*, pg. 749
SIGHT SAVERS—Eyeglass Cleaning & Accessory Products—Bausch & Lomb Incorporated; *U.S. Public*, pg. 194
SIGHT SEER—Booster Car Seat—Evenflo Company, Inc.; *U.S. Private*, pg. 629
SIGHT YEARS AHEAD—Technical Assistance in the Establishment & Operation of eye Care—AVC/Nu-Vision, Inc.; *U.S. Private*, pg. 9
SIGMA—Hoist—Harnischfeger Industries, Inc.; *U.S. Public*, pg. 788
SIGMA—Cable Products—Oak Industries Inc.; *U.S. Public*, pg. 1209

SIGMA—Coatings & Paints—Petrofina S.A.; *Int'l*, pg. 1043

SIGMA-F—Valves—Masoneilan North American Operations; *U.S. Public*, pg. 528

SIGMAGEL—Gel Analysis—SPSS Inc.; *U.S. Public*, pg. 1420

SIGMAPLOT—Scientific graphing software—SPSS Inc.; *U.S. Public*, pg. 1420

SIGMARK—Case Coder—Videojet Systems International, Inc.; *Int'l*, pg. 545

SIGMART—Antianginal Agent—Chugai Pharmaceutical Co., Ltd.; *Int'l*, pg. 290

SIGMASCAN PRO—Image Analysis—SPSS Inc.; *U.S. Public*, pg. 1420

SIGMASTAT—Advisory Statistical Software—SPSS Inc.; *U.S. Public*, pg. 1420

SIGN & TRAVEL—Special Form of Credit Available—American Express Company; *U.S. Public*, pg. 73

SIGN-MASTER—Software—Borland International, Inc.; *U.S. Public*, pg. 246

SIGN PENS—Porous Point Pens—Pentel of America, Ltd.; *Int'l*, pg. 1035

SIGN STUDIO APPRENTICE—Macintosh Software to Create & Maintain Professional In-House Signs—Kroy Inc.; *U.S. Public*, pg. 1339

SIGN STUDIO SPECIALIST—IBM Software to Create & Maintain Professional In-House Signs—Kroy Inc.; *U.S. Public*, pg. 1339

SIGNAL—Mouthwash—Chesebrough-Pond's USA Co.; *Int'l*, pg. 1435

SIGNAL—Sportswear—Signal Apparel Company, Inc.; *U.S. Public*, pg. 1472

SIGNAL—Toothpaste—Unilever Plc; *Int'l*, pg. 1433

SIGNAL GREEN—Fluorescent Color—Day-Glo Color Corp.; *U.S. Public*, pg. 1357

SIGNAL KICKER—Antenna—Telex Communications, Inc.; *U.S. Private*, pg. 1074

SIGNAL PROCESSING WORKBENCH—Top-Down Design Automation Software—Cadence Design Systems, Inc.; *U.S. Public*, pg. 290

SIGNAL-STAT—Lighting Products—Federal-Mogul Corporation; *U.S. Public*, pg. 615

SIGNALMAN—Control Unit, Visual Signalling Device—Lucent Technologies Inc.; *U.S. Public*, pg. 1017

SIGNALTONE—Automobile Horns—Fiamm S.p.A.; *Int'l*, pg. 480

SIGNATURE—Italian Wines—Barton Incorporated; *U.S. Public*, pg. 300

SIGNATURE—Leather Goods—Hugo Bosca Co., Inc.; *U.S. Private*, pg. 160

SIGNATURE—Chocolates—Brown & Haley; *U.S. Private*, pg. 173

SIGNATURE—Electronic Retail Theft Prevention System—Checkpoint Systems Inc.; *U.S. Public*, pg. 343

SIGNATURE—Golf Shoes—E.J. Footwear Corp.; *U.S. Public*, pg. 1684

SIGNATURE—Color Proofing Materials, Equipment & Chemicals—Eastman Kodak Company; *U.S. Public*, pg. 550

SIGNATURE—Inlaid Entrance Matting—Golden Star Inc.; *U.S. Private*, pg. 460

SIGNATURE—Bronze Casket—Hillenbrand Industries, Inc.; *U.S. Public*, pg. 828

SIGNATURE—Furniture—Kewaunee Scientific Corporation; *U.S. Public*, pg. 953

SIGNATURE—In-House IBM-Based Physicians Information System—Shared Medical Systems Corporation; *U.S. Public*, pg. 1463

SIGNATURE—Custom Cab/Chassis—Simon Engineering plc; *Int'l*, pg. 1251

SIGNATURE—Natural Graphites—Superior Graphite Co.; *U.S. Private*, pg. 1054

THE SIGNATURE COLLECTION—Handwrapped Flowers from Thailand—Celebrity Incorporated; *U.S. Public*, pg. 319

SIGNATURE GRILLS—NONE—Iceland Seafood Corporation; *U.S. Private*, pg. 556

SIGNATURE JEANS—Clothes—RetailNet B.V.; *Int'l*, pg. 750

SIGNATURE RESERVE—Line of Credit—NBD Bank (Indiana); *U.S. Public*, pg. 628

SIGNATURE SERIES—Chrome Assessories—Edelbrock Corp.; *U.S. Public*, pg. 563

SIGNATURE SERIES—Motor—The Lincoln Electric Company; *U.S. Public*, pg. 996

SIGNATURE SPECIALTIES—Specialty Frozen Food—Louis Kemp Seafood Co.; *U.S. Public*, pg. 1652

SIGNATURE II—Sofas & Sleep Sofas—La-Z-Boy Incorporated; *U.S. Public*, pg. 972

SIGNATURE II BY STAN HERMAN—NONE—Kellwood Company; *U.S. Public*, pg. 948

SIGNATURES—Mail Order House—Starcrest Products of California; *U.S. Private*, pg. 1035

SIGNATUUR—Jewelry—Vendex International N.V.; *Int'l*, pg. 1462

SIGNET—Sunglasses—Bausch & Lomb Incorporated; *U.S. Public*, pg. 194

SIGNET—Mirror—Carolina Mirror Company; *U.S. Private*, pg. 214

SIGNET—Cameras, Slide Projectors—Eastman Kodak Company; *U.S. Public*, pg. 550

SIGNET—NONE—The Hercules Tire & Rubber Company; *U.S. Private*, pg. 523

SIGNET—Adult Mass Market Paperback Books—Penguin Putnam Inc.; *Int'l*, pg. 1027

SIGNET—Flow Monitoring Equipment—Ryan Herco Products Corp.; *U.S. Private*, pg. 953

SIGNET—Surgical Staplers—U.S. Surgical Corp.; *U.S. Public*, pg. 1687

SIGNET—Skin Stapler—U.S. Surgical Corp.; *U.S. Public*, pg. 1687

SIGNET SERIES—Doors—Morgan Products Ltd.; *U.S. Public*, pg. 1132

SIGNETICS—Integrated Circuits—Philips Electronics N.V.; *Int'l*, pg. 1051

SIGNFIX—Sign Mounting Systems—IDEX Corporation; *U.S. Public*, pg. 862

SIGNORICCI—Men's Fragrance—Accecones Ricci U.S.A., Inc.; *Int'l*, pg. 445

SIGNORICCI "1"—Men's Fragrance—Accecones Ricci U.S.A., Inc.; *Int'l*, pg. 445

SIGNRIGHT—NONE—Insignia Systems, Inc.; *U.S. Public*, pg. 881

SIGNS, SYMPTOMS & CARE—NONE—Pfizer Inc.; *U.S. Public*, pg. 1281

SIGNTECH—Name of Partnership—Signtech USA, Ltd.; *U.S. Private*, pg. 999

SIGN(WARE)—Document Frame—Rubbermaid Incorporated; *U.S. Public*, pg. 1411

SIGRAFLEX—Graphite Foils—Hoechst Aktiengesellschaft; *Int'l*, pg. 624

SIGTAB—NONE—Lee Pharmaceuticals; *U.S. Public*, pg. 984

SIKADUR—Epoxy Adhesive—Sika Corporation; *Int'l*, pg. 1249

SIKAFLEX—Sealant & Adhesive—Sika Corporation; *Int'l*, pg. 1249

SIKAGARD—Epoxy Coating—Sika Corporation; *Int'l*, pg. 1249

SIKAGROUT—Gout-Multi Fluid Filler—Sika Corporation; *Int'l*, pg. 1249

SIKAMENT—Admixture Super Fluidifier—Sika Corporation; *Int'l*, pg. 1249

SIKAMIX—Admixture to Control Set of Concrete—Sika Corporation; *Int'l*, pg. 1249

SIKAPRONTO—Modified Methacrylate Repairs—Sika Corporation; *Int'l*, pg. 1249

SIKASET—Quicksets—Sika Corporation; *Int'l*, pg. 1249

SIKATOP—Cement Based Repair—Sika Corporation; *Int'l*, pg. 1249

SIKKENS—Building Paints for Exterior, Interior, Prof. & Retail Uses—Akzo Nobel N.V.; *Int'l*, pg. 42

SIKORSKY—Helicopters—United Technologies Corporation; *U.S. Public*, pg. 1689

SIL—NONE—Kiwi Brands Pty. Ltd.; *U.S. Public*, pg. 1434

SIL-CELL—Plastics Filler—Silbrico Corporation; *U.S. Private*, pg. 1000

SIL-FOS—Silver Brazing Alloy—Handy & Harman; *U.S. Public*, pg. 780

SIL-KLEER—Filter Aid—Silbrico Corporation; *U.S. Private*, pg. 1000

SIL/PAC—A Packages Adjustable Voltage Power Supply for D.C. Motors—General Electric Canada Inc.; *U.S. Public*, pg. 713

SIL-PAD—Electronic Device—The Bergquist Company; *U.S. Private*, pg. 135

SIL-STRONG—Silver Bearing Solder—Litton Industries, Inc.; *U.S. Public*, pg. 1002

SILACONE PLUS—Sealant—Dow Corning Corporation; *U.S. Public*, pg. 523

SILACURE—Lead Coating—Medtronic, Inc.; *U.S. Public*, pg. 1082

SILAPRENE—NONE—Uniroyal Technology Corporation; *U.S. Public*, pg. 1670

SILAR—Restorative Material, Dental—3M; *U.S. Public*, pg. 1604

SILASTIC—Silicone Rubber—Dow Corning Corporation; *U.S. Public*, pg. 523

SILATHANE—Gloss & Semi-Gloss Enamel—Bruning Paint Company; *U.S. Private*, pg. 176

SILBRADE—Braid Reinforced Silicone Tubing—NewAge Industries Inc.; *U.S. Private*, pg. 796

SILBRADE—Braid Reinforced Silicone Tubing—Newage Industries Inc., Plastics Technology Group; *U.S. Private*, pg. 796

SILCAD—Silver Cadmium Batteries—Yardney Technical Products, Inc.; *U.S. Private*, pg. 376

SILCARD—PVC/PET Cards—Sillcocks Plastics, Inc.; *U.S. Private*, pg. 63

SILCON—Unreinforced Silicone Tubing—NewAge Industries Inc.; *U.S. Private*, pg. 796

SILCON—Silicone Tubing—Newage Industries Inc., Plastics Technology Group; *U.S. Private*, pg. 796

SILCOR—Refractory Cement—Ferro Corporation; *U.S. Public*, pg. 618

SILCRON—Fine-Particle Silica Prolongs Shelf Life in Foods, Drugs & Cosmetics—Millennium Inorganic Chemicals; *U.S. Public*, pg. 593

SILDURA—Silicone Rubber Compound used in the Fabrication of Rubber Products—General Electric Canada Inc.; *U.S. Public*, pg. 713

SILENCER—Mufflers—Schrader Bellows Division; *U.S. Public*, pg. 1261

SILENE—Alkaline Earth Metal & Synthetic Precipitated Silica for Indust. Arts Uses—PPG Industries, Inc.; *U.S. Public*, pg. 1245

SILENT DRIVE—Dryer—Beloit Corporation; *U.S. Public*, pg. 789

SILENT FLAME—Woodburning Stove—Long MFG. NC, Inc.; *U.S. Private*, pg. 674

SILENT FLOOR—NONE—TJ International, Inc.; *U.S. Public*, pg. 1556

SILENT MAID—Concentrated Cleaner for Bathroom Care—Stanhome Inc.; *U.S. Public*, pg. 1508

SILENT MAID ECONOMIZER DISPENSER—Dispenser for Silent Maid Cleaner—Stanhome Inc.; *U.S. Public*, pg. 1508

SILENT MONITOR—96-Well Membrane Test Plates—Pall Corporation; *U.S. Public*, pg. 1253

SILENT PARTNER—Muffler—Donaldson Company, Inc.; *U.S. Public*, pg. 517

SILENT SALESMAN—Remote Control Demonstration—Zenith Electronics Corp.; *U.S. Public*, pg. 1790

SILENT SIGNAL—Hold Up-Emergency Reporting System—Linear Corporation; *U.S. Public*, pg. 1193

SILENT WATCHMAN—Security Systems—SecurityLink from Ameritech; *U.S. Public*, pg. 98

SILENTA—Salon Dryers—Belvedere Company; *U.S. Private*, pg. 1008

SILENTNIGHT—Mattresses, Bedroom Furniture—Silentnight Holdings Plc; *Int'l*, pg. 1249

SILENTVANE—Fans—The Howden Fan Co.; *U.S. Private*, pg. 543

SILFA—Silica Yarns—AMETEK, Inc.; *U.S. Public*, pg. 99

SILFAB—NONE—Flexfab Horizons International, Inc.; *U.S. Private*, pg. 412

SILFLAKE—Silver Flake—Handy & Harman; *U.S. Public*, pg. 780

SILFLEX—Ducting—HBD Industries, Inc.; *U.S. Private*, pg. 489

SILGAN—Organo-Modified Silicone Elastomer—Wacker Silicones Corporation; *Int'l*, pg. 625

SILGLAZE—Silicone Rubber Weatherproofing Sealants—General Electric Canada Inc.; *U.S. Public*, pg. 713

SILGRAIN—Silicon Metal—Elkem ASA; *Int'l*, pg. 446

SILGRIP—Silicone Adhesive—General Electric Canada Inc.; *U.S. Public*, pg. 713

SILHOUET—Pacing Lead—Medtronic, Inc.; *U.S. Public*, pg. 1082

SILHOUETTE—Regional Aircraft Seats—B/E Aerospace Seating Products Group; *U.S. Public*, pg. 159

SILHOUETTE—Range Hood—Broan Mfg. Co., Inc.; *U.S. Public*, pg. 1193

SILHOUETTE—Copyholders—Fellowes Manufacturing Co.; *U.S. Private*, pg. 400

SILHOUETTE—NONE—Harlequin Enterprises Ltd.; *Int'l*, pg. 1402

SILHOUETTE—Window Covering Product—Hunter Douglas N.V.; *Int'l*, pg. 639

SILHOUETTE—Window Coverings—Hunter Douglas N.V.; *Int'l*, pg. 639

SILHOUETTE—Sanitary Products—Johnson & Johnson Limited; *U.S. Public*, pg. 930

SILHOUETTE—Minivan—Oldsmobile Div. General Motors Corp.; *U.S. Public*, pg. 720

SILHOUETTE—Hearing Aids—Telex Communications, Inc.; *U.S. Private*, pg. 1074

SILHOUETTE BON SOIR—Room Darkening Shadings—Hunter Douglas, Inc.; *Int'l*, pg. 639

SILHOUETTE DESIRE—Romance Paperbacks—Silhouette Books; *Int'l*, pg. 1402

SILHOUETTE EXTERIORS—Vinyl Siding & Accessories—Alcoa Building Products, Inc.; *U.S. Public*, pg. 61

SILHOUETTE INTIMATE MOMENTS—Romance Paperbacks—Silhouette Books; *Int'l*, pg. 1402

SILHOUETTE ROMANCE—Romance Paperbacks—Silhouette Books; *Int'l*, pg. 1402

SILHOUETTE SPECIAL EDITIONS—Romance Paperbacks—Silhouette Books; *Int'l*, pg. 1402

SILHOUETTE III—Three-Inch Fabric Vanes Between Sheer Facings—Hunter Douglas, Inc.; *Int'l*, pg. 639

SILHOUETTE WINDOW SHADINGS—New Style Window Shading—Hunter Douglas, Inc.; *Int'l*, pg. 639

SILHOUETTES—Women's Larger Size Fashion Catalog-Career & Special Occasion—Hanover Direct, Inc.; *U.S. Public*, pg. 782

SILHOUTTE—NONE—Kewaunee Scientific Corporation; *U.S. Public*, pg. 953

SILICA PAK—Packed Liquid Chromatographic Columns/Cartridges—Millipore Corporation; *U.S. Public*, pg. 1112

SILICA-SEAL—Dielectric Paste—Ferro Corporation; *U.S. Public*, pg. 618

SILICON ENSEMBLE—Routing Up Designs with a Mix of Cell & Gate-Based Approaches—Cadence Design Systems, Inc.; *U.S. Public*, pg. 290

SILICON INTEGRATOR—Software—LSI Logic Corp.; *U.S. Public*, pg. 971

SILICON SYNTHESIS—Optimizes Logic Based on Actual Physical Implementation—Cadence Design Systems, Inc.; *U.S. Public*, pg. 290

SILICON SYSTEMS—Design/Mfg. of Silicon (ICs) for Computer Industry—Silicon Systems, Inc.; *U.S. Public*, pg. 1585

SILICONQUEST—Advanced High-Level Chip Planning Environment—Cadence Design Systems, Inc.; *U.S. Public*, pg. 290

SILINER—Air Conditioning Insulation—Carter Holt Harvey Limited; *U.S. Public*, pg. 904

SILK ACCENTS—NONE—Celebrity Incorporated; *U.S. Public*, pg. 319

SILK & SILVER—Hair Coloring—Clairol, Inc.; *U.S. Public*, pg. 254

SILK CUT—Tobacco—Fortune Brands, Inc.; *U.S. Public*, pg. 674

SILK CUT—Cigarettes—Gallaher Tobacco Ltd.; *Int'l*, pg. 539

SILK EFFECTS—Woman's Permanent Razor—Warner-Lambert Shaving Products Group; *U.S. Public*, pg. 1739

THE SILK GARDENER—NONE—Celebrity Incorporated; *U.S. Public*, pg. 319

SILK IMPRESSIONS—Women's Hosiery—Hampshire Hosiery, Inc.; *U.S. Public*, pg. 778

SILK REFLECTIONS—Hosiery—Hanes Hosiery, Inc.; *U.S. Public*, pg. 1434

SILK REFLECTIONS—Hosiery—Sara Lee Corporation; *U.S. Public*, pg. 1432

SILK SOLUTIONS—Skin Lotion—Thompson Medical Company, Inc.; *U.S. Private*, pg. 1083

SILKEE—Suede Pigskin Leather—Wolverine World Wide, Inc.; *U.S. Public*, pg. 1775

SILKEN MIST—Sheer Elegance Panty Hose—L'eggs Products, Inc.; *U.S. Public*, pg. 1434

SILKIENCE—Shampoos, Conditioners & Hair Sprays—The Gillette Company; *U.S. Public*, pg. 743

SILKTRIM—Primed MDF Mouldings—Meyer International PLC; *Int'l*, pg. 864

SILKY TOUCH—Microfiber Nylon—BASF Corporation Fiber Products Division; *Int'l*, pg. 105

SILLCOCKS—Plastic—Sillcocks Plastics, Inc.; *U.S. Private*, pg. 63

SILLY PUTTY—Toy—Binney & Smith Inc.; *U.S. Private*, pg. 496

SILLY PUTTY—Toy—Binney & Smith Ltd.; *U.S. Private*, pg. 496

SILMATE—Silicone Rubber Adhesive & Gasket Material—General Electric Canada Inc.; *U.S. Public*, pg. 713

SILOMAT—Cough Remedy—Boehringer Ingelheim Italia S.p.A.; *Int'l*, pg. 199

SILOO—Fleet Maint Products—CRC Industries, Inc.; *U.S. Private*, pg. 138

SILOX—CVD Reactors & Components—Applied Materials, Inc.; *U.S. Public*, pg. 123

SILPAC—A Packaged Adjustable Voltage Power Supply for D.C. Motors—General Electric Canada Inc.; *U.S. Public*, pg. 713

SILPLUS—RTV Room Temperature Vulcanizable) & Heat Curable Silicone Sealant—General Electric Canada Inc.; *U.S. Public*, pg. 713

SILPOWDER—Silver Powder—Handy & Harman; *U.S. Public*, pg. 780

SILPRUF—Silicone Rubber Weather Sealants & Adhesives—General Electric Canada Inc.; *U.S. Public*, pg. 713

SILPROOF—Clarifies Beverages—Millennium Inorganic Chemicals; *Int'l*, pg. 593

SILQAR—Silica Fabrics—AMETEK, Inc.; *U.S. Public*, pg. 99

SILTEC SILICON—Mfg. of Polished Silicon Wafers & Single Crystal Ingot—Mitsubishi Silicon America; *Int'l*, pg. 875

SILTEMP—High Temperature Textiles—AMETEK, Inc.; *U.S. Public*, pg. 99

SILTEX—Intimate Apparel—VF Corporation; *U.S. Public*, pg. 1702

SILUX—Restorative Material, Dental—3M; *U.S. Public*, pg. 1604

SILV-EX—Foam Agent for Forest Fires—Ansul Incorporated; *U.S. Public*, pg. 1648

SILVA—Field Compasses—Johnson Worldwide Associates, Inc.; *U.S. Public*, pg. 932

SILVA-BRITE—Silver Plating Solution—Engelhard Corporation; *U.S. Public*, pg. 582

SILVA-FIBER—Wood Fiber Used as a Soil Erosion Preventive—Weyerhaeuser Company; *U.S. Public*, pg. 1764

SILVA TALL—Cigarettes—Brown & Williamson Tobacco Corp.; *Int'l*, pg. 111

SILVA THINS—Cigarettes—Brown & Williamson Tobacco Corp.; *Int'l*, pg. 111

SILVAC—Polyester & Wire Reinforced Silicone Tubing—NewAge Industries Inc.; *U.S. Private*, pg. 796

SILVAC—Polyester & Wire Reinforced Silicone Tubing—Newage Industries Inc., Plastics Technology Group; *U.S. Private*, pg. 796

SILVACEL—Wood Fiber for Industrial and Commercial Uses—Weyerhaeuser Company; *U.S. Public*, pg. 1764

SILVADENE—Burn Cream—Hoechst Marion Roussel North America; *Int'l*, pg. 625

SILVALOY—Brazing Alloys—Engelhard Corporation; *U.S. Public*, pg. 582

SILVER—Tequila—Domecq Importers Inc.; *Int'l*, pg. 63

SILVER—Construction Metal Connectors—Rule Industries, Inc.; *U.S. Public*, pg. 950

SILVER AWARD—Pasta—Borden, Inc.; *U.S. Private*, pg. 157

SILVER, BURDETT & GINN—Educational Publishers—Simon & Schuster; *U.S. Private*, pg. 777

SILVER COAT—Metallic Marker—Sanford Corporation; *U.S. Public*, pg. 1178

SILVER COLLECTION—Economy Priced Bathroom Safety Products—Lumex Medical Products; *U.S. Public*, pg. 758

SILVER CREEK—Men's Apparel—Sheplers, Inc.; *U.S. Private*, pg. 993

SILVER CROWN—Panel Mounted Aircraft Electronics—AlliedSignal Commercial Avionic Systems; *U.S. Public*, pg. 50

SILVER CURL—Home Permanent—The Gillette Company; *U.S. Public*, pg. 743

SILVER DOLLAR CITY—America's Crafts Park—Silver Dollar City, Inc.; *U.S. Private*, pg. 1000

SILVER DOT—Plastic Heads—Ludwig Industries; *U.S. Public*, pg. 1514

SILVER FALCON—Tires—Bridgestone/Firestone, Inc.; *Int'l*, pg. 213

SILVER FLOSS—Sauerkraut—Comstock Michigan Fruit; *U.S. Private*, pg. 887

SILVER FOX—Steel Prods.—British Steel Plc; *Int'l*, pg. 220

SILVER FOX—Hair Care Product—Carme' Cosmeceutical Sciences, Inc.; *U.S. Private*, pg. 213

SILVER GLACIER—Bottled Water—Beverage Canners International Corp.; *U.S. Private*, pg. 106

SILVER GLO—Gift Ribbons—American Greetings Corporation; *U.S. Public*, pg. 77

SILVER-GRIP—Set Screw—PIC Design; *U.S. Private*, pg. 864

SILVER JET—NONE—Western Atlas Logging Services; *U.S. Public*, pg. 1757

SILVER KING—Food Service Equipment—Stevens-Lee Company; *U.S. Private*, pg. 1042

SILVER KING—Weatherstripping—W.J. & Dennis Co.; *U.S. Private*, pg. 1144

SILVER KNIGHT—Mufflers—IPC-International Parts Corp.; *U.S. Public*, pg. 1766

SILVER KNIGHTS—Pocket Knives—Fiskars-Gerber; *Int'l*, pg. 492

SILVER LINE—DC Power Supply—Best Power; *U.S. Private*, pg. 140

SILVER LINK—Investment Plans—Derbyshire Building Society; *Int'l*, pg. 394

SILVER MARK—Tires—Universal Cooperatives, Inc.; *U.S. Private*, pg. 1127

SILVER MEDAL—Food Products—McCormick & Company, Incorporated; *U.S. Public*, pg. 1066

SILVER PEAK—Lumber & Wood Products—Georgia-Pacific Corporation; *U.S. Public*, pg. 735

SILVER REY—Food Products—Rykoff-Sexton, Inc.; *U.S. Public*, pg. 918

SILVER RIM—Abrasive Discs—Gardner Abrasives; *U.S. Public*, pg. 1699

SILVER-RIM—Abrasive Wheels & Discs—Litton Industries, Inc.; *U.S. Public*, pg. 1002

SILVER ROCK—Bottled Water—Beverage Canners International Corp.; *U.S. Private*, pg. 106

SILVER ROD—Antenna—Telex Communications, Inc.; *U.S. Private*, pg. 1074

SILVER SCOT—Golf Clubs & Golf Gloves—Tommy Armour Golf; *U.S. Public*, pg. 1683

SILVER-SEAL—Ironing Board Covers—Magla Products; *U.S. Private*, pg. 695

SILVER SERVICE—Company Motto—Arnold Machinery Company; *U.S. Private*, pg. 84

SILVER SPOONS—NONE—Ruby Tuesday, Inc.; *U.S. Public*, pg. 1411

SILVER SPRINGS—Bottled Water—Hinckley & Schmitt, Inc.; *Int'l*, pg. 1322

SILVER STREAK—Mower Parts—Blount International, Inc.; *U.S. Public*, pg. 237

SILVER SWORD—Pocket Knives—Camillus Cutlery Co.; *U.S. Private*, pg. 203

SILVER THOUGHTS—Greeting Books—American Greetings U.S. Greeting Card Division; *U.S. Public*, pg. 78

SILVER THREAD FISHING LINE—Riverside Lures—EBSCO Industries, Inc.; *U.S. Private*, pg. 358

SILVER THUNDER—Malt Liquor—The Stroh Brewery Company; *U.S. Private*, pg. 1047

SILVER-WEIBULL—Food Processing—Silver-Weibull; *U.S. Public*, pg. 705

SILVERADO—Hats—Bailey Hats; *U.S. Private*, pg. 155

SILVERADO—Full Glue Installed Sheet Vinyl Flooring—Mannington Resilient Floors; *U.S. Private*, pg. 700

SILVERAMA—TV Tubes—Thomson Consumer Electronics Inc.; *Int'l*, pg. 1383

SILVERCEL—Silver Zinc Batteries—Yardney Technical Products, Inc.; *U.S. Private*, pg. 376

SILVERCOTE—Fabricator Distribution—Johns Manville Corporation; *U.S. Public*, pg. 927

SILVERCREEK—Moist Snuff Smokeless Tobacco—Swisher International Group, Inc.; *U.S. Public*, pg. 1543

SILVERCREST—Desk Accessories—Smith McDonald Corp.; *U.S. Private*, pg. 1009

SILVERGLO—High Speed Deposits from Crystal Clear Solutions—LeaRonal, Inc.; *U.S. Public*, pg. 982

SILVERJET—High Speed Bath—LeaRonal, Inc.; *U.S. Public*, pg. 982

SILVERLAKE SYSTEM—Banking Software—Jack Henry & Associates, Inc.; *U.S. Public*, pg. 808

SILVERLINE—Office Supplies—JM Company; *U.S. Private*, pg. 577

SILVERLUX—Light Reflecting Film—3M; *U.S. Public*, pg. 1604

SILVERNOSE—Spring Plunger—Vlier Engineering; *U.S. Public*, pg. 124

SILVERSTONE—No-Stick Systems—Du Pont (E.I. Du Pont De Nemours & Co.); *U.S. Public*, pg. 530

SILVERSTONE CELLARS—Wines—Gibson Wine Company; *U.S. Private*, pg. 452

SILVERWOOD—Milk Products—Labatt Brewing · Company Limited; *Int'l*, pg. 679

SILVIA—Car—Nissan Motor Co., Ltd.; *Int'l*, pg. 943

SILVIKRIN—Shampoo—SmithKline Beecham plc; *Int'l*, pg. 1264

SILVO—Metal Cleaners—Reckitt & Colman Inc.; *Int'l*, pg. 1090

SILVO—Silver Polishes—Reckitt & Colman plc; *Int'l*, pg. 1089

SILVPAC—Silver Recovery System—CPAC, Inc.; *U.S. Public*, pg. 282

SIM-PULL—Envelopes—Tension Envelope Corp.; *U.S. Private*, pg. 1077

SIMAG—NONE—Scotsman Industries, Inc.; *U.S. Public*, pg. 1444

SIMANIMATION—Animated Form Simulation Modeling Language—CACI International Inc; *U.S. Public*, pg. 272

SIMATIC—Programmable Controllers—Siemens Corporation; *Int'l*, pg. 1245

SIMBA 2—Electron Beam Power Supply—BOC Coating Technology; *Int'l*, pg. 121

SIMCO—Static Bars, Film Cleaners, Ionizing Nozzles—Simco; *U.S. Public*, pg. 865

SIME BANK—Logo for Bank—Sime Darby Berhad; *Int'l*, pg. 1249

SIME DARBY—Automotive Tires—Sime Darby Berhad; *Int'l*, pg. 1249

SIME DXP—Agricultural Products—Sime Darby Berhad; *Int'l*, pg. 1249

SIME HEALTH—Surgical, Medical, Dental & Vetinary Instruments & Apparatus—Sime Darby Berhad; *Int'l*, pg. 1249

SIME HYPOALLERGENIC—Surgical, Medical, Dental & Vetinary Instruments & Apparatus— Sime Darby Berhad; *Int'l*, pg. 1249

SIME INAX—Instruments & Material for Cleaning Purposes—Sime Darby Berhad; *Int'l*, pg. 1249

SIME LATEX—Surgical, Medical, Dental & Vetinary Instruments & Apparatus—Sime Darby Berhad; *Int'l*, pg. 1249

SIME MONZA—Automotive Tires—Sime Darby Berhad; *Int'l*, pg. 1249

SIME PAINTS—Paints—Sime Darby Berhad; *Int'l*, pg. 1249

SIME POWDERFREE—Surgical, Medical, Dental & Vetinary Instruments & Apparatus—Sime Darby Berhad; *Int'l*, pg. 1249

SIME RENGO—Paper Articles, Printed Matter & Cardboard—Sime Darby Berhad; *Int'l*, pg. 1249

SIME TREAD—Automotive Tires—Sime Darby Berhad; *Int'l*, pg. 1249

SIME TRUFEEL—Surgical, Medical, Dental & Vetinary Instruments & Apparatus—Sime Darby Berhad; *Int'l*, pg. 1249

SIME TYRES—Automobile Tires—Sime Darby Berhad; *Int'l*, pg. 1249

SIMEAC—Machines & Agricultural Implements— Sime Darby Berhad; *Int'l*, pg. 1249

SIMEBOND—Pharmaceutical, Vetinary & Sanitary Products, Chemical Products—Sime Darby Berhad; *Int'l*, pg. 1249

SIMEC—Machinery Equipment & Tools—Sime Darby Berhad; *Int'l*, pg. 1249

SIMENET—Data Communications—Sime Darby Berhad; *Int'l*, pg. 1249

SIMEPHARMA—Chemical Products—Sime Darby Berhad; *Int'l*, pg. 1249

SIMEPILLO—Bed Pillows—Sime Darby Berhad; *Int'l*, pg. 1249

SIMER—NONE—The Rival Company; *U.S. Public*, pg. 1391

SIMER PUMP—Water Pumps—The Rival Company; *U.S. Public*, pg. 1391

SIMES—Custom Marine & Other Prods.—Sterner Lighting Systems Incorporated; *U.S. Private*, pg. 1042

SIMESPRING—Mattresses—Sime Darby Berhad; *Int'l*, pg. 1249

SIMEX—Automotive Tires & Batteries—Sime Darby Berhad; *Int'l*, pg. 1249

SIMFACTORY—Simulation Modeling Language— CACI International Inc; *U.S. Public*, pg. 272

SIMFACTORY II.5—Simulation Modeling Language—CACI International Inc; *U.S. Public*, pg. 272

SIMGRAPHICS—Graphic Display Simulation Modeling Language—CACI International Inc; *U.S. Public*, pg. 272

SIMI—NONE—LVMH Moet Hennessy Louis Vuitton; *Int'l*, pg. 779

SIMI—California Premium Varietal Wine— Schieffelin & Somerset Co.; *Int'l*, pg. 412

SIMI—Winery—Simi Winery; *Int'l*, pg. 781

SIMILAC—Infant Formula—Abbott Laboratories; *U.S. Public*, pg. 12

SIMILAC—Infant Formula—Ross Products; *U.S. Public*, pg. 13

SIMILAC TODDLER'S BEST—Milk-Based Toddler's Drink—Ross Products; *U.S. Public*, pg. 13

SIMILATOR—Medical Calculator—Abbott Laboratories; *U.S. Public*, pg. 12

SIMKA KOSHER GIN—Gin—Montebello Brands Inc.; *U.S. Private*, pg. 758

SIMKA KOSHER VODKA—Vodka—Montebello Brands Inc.; *U.S. Private*, pg. 758

SIMLAB—Software—CACI International Inc; *U.S. Public*, pg. 272

SIMMENTHAL—Meats—Philip Morris Companies Inc.; *U.S. Public*, pg. 1287

SIMMER POT—Clay Cooking Vessels—Litton Industries, Inc.; *U.S. Public*, pg. 1002

SIMMER-SAFE—Electric Cooking Pots—Sunbeam Household Products; *U.S. Public*, pg. 1533

SIMMERRING—Rotating Shaft Seal—Freudenberg & Company; *Int'l*, pg. 505

SIMMONS—Scopes, Binoculars, Calls—Blount, Inc. Sporting Equipment Group; *U.S. Public*, pg. 238

SIMMONS—Gun Scopes, Binoculars—Blount International, Inc.; *U.S. Public*, pg. 237

SIMMONS FASTENER—Access Hardware for OEM Manufacturers—SouthCo. Inc.; *U.S. Private*, pg. 1014

SIMMS—Agricultural & Industrial Diesel & Fuel Injection Equipment—Lucas Industries Inc.; *Int'l*, pg. 820

SIMMS—NONE—LucasVarity plc; *Int'l*, pg. 819

SIMOBJECT—Software—CACI International Inc; *U.S. Public*, pg. 272

SIMON—Interactive Analysis & Debugging for Batch Applications with Support—Compuware Corporation; *U.S. Public*, pg. 423

SIMON—Computer Software—Medline Industries, Inc.; *U.S. Private*, pg. 728

SIMON—Electronic Game—Milton Bradley Company; *U.S. Public*, pg. 797

SIMON AND SCHUSTER—Publishers—Simon & Schuster; *U.S. Private*, pg. 777

SIMON FISCHER—Prune Butter & Apricot Butter— Sokol & Company; *U.S. Private*, pg. 1012

SIMONDS BITTER—Bitter Ale—Foster's Brewing Group Limited; *Int'l*, pg. 500

SIMONIZ—Car Care—Burmah Castrol plc; *Int'l*, pg. 234

SIMPLE—Skin Care Products—Smith & Nephew PLC; *Int'l*, pg. 1263

SIMPLE & LOGIQUE—Services Relating to Factory Automation—General Electric Canada Inc.; *U.S. Public*, pg. 713

SIMPLE PLEASURES—Greeting Cards—American Greetings Corporation; *U.S. Public*, pg. 77

SIMPLE PLEASURES—Diet Ice Cream—Monsanto Company; *U.S. Public*, pg. 1124

SIMPLE SHOES—Sport Sandals—Deckers Outdoor Corporation; *U.S. Public*, pg. 491

SIMPLE SOLUTIONS—NONE—Lechters, Inc.; *U.S. Public*, pg. 983

SIMPLESSE—All-Natural Fat Substitute— Monsanto Company; *U.S. Public*, pg. 1124

SIMPLESSE—All Natural Fat Substitute—The NutraSweet Company; *U.S. Public*, pg. 1125

SIMPLEX—Tape Dispensing Machine—Ascom Hasler Mailing Systems, Inc.; *Int'l*, pg. 86

SIMPLEX—NONE—Howmedica, Inc.; *U.S. Public*, pg. 1282

SIMPLEX—Flatwork Finishers—Raytheon Appliances; *U.S. Public*, pg. 1366 ·

SIMPLEX—Bucket Elevator—TCC Industries; *U.S. Public*, pg. 1554

SIMPLEX—Mechanical Jacks—Templeton, Kenly & Co., Inc.; *U.S. Private*, pg. 1075

SIMPLEX—Pushbutton Combination Locks— Unican Security Systems Ltd.; *Int'l*, pg. 1432

SIMPLEX—Organs—The Wurlitzer Company; *U.S. Public*, pg. 169

SIMPLEX P—NONE—Pfizer Inc.; *U.S. Public*, pg. 1281

SIMPLICITY—awning—Carefree of Colorado; *U.S. Public*, pg. 217

SIMPLICITY—Area Rugs—Couristan Inc.; *U.S. Private*, pg. 279

SIMPLICITY—Panel Systems—The HON Co.; *U.S. Public*, pg. 772

SIMPLICITY—Office Furniture—HON Industries Inc.; *U.S. Public*, pg. 772

SIMPLICITY—Feminine Pads—Kimberly-Clark Corporation; *U.S. Public*, pg. 958

SIMPLICITY—Outdoor Power Equip.—Simplicity Manufacturing, Inc.; *U.S. Private*, pg. 1002

SIMPLICITY II—NONE—The HON Co.; *U.S. Public*, pg. 772

SIMPLIFILE—NONE—Rubbermaid Incorporated; *U.S. Public*, pg. 1411

SIMPLIMET—Mounting Press—Buehler, Limited; *U.S. Public*, pg. 574

SIMPLOT—Fertilizer—J.R. Simplot Company; *U.S. Private*, pg. 1002

SIMPLOT CLASSICS—Frozen Fruits & Vegetables—J.R. Simplot Company Food Group; *U.S. Private*, pg. 1002

SIMPLOU—Potatoes & Vegetables—J.R. Simplot Company; *U.S. Private*, pg. 1002

SIMPLY FOR SPORTS—In-Store Athletic Footwear & Apparel Shops—JC Penney Company, Inc.; *U.S. Public*, pg. 916

SIMPLY FRUIT—Fruit Juice-Sweetened Fruit Spreads—J.M. Smucker Company; *U.S. Public*, pg. 1480

SIMPLY KUDOS—Granola Bars—Mars, Incorporated; *U.S. Private*, pg. 707

SIMPLY MAGIC PRODUCTIONS—Customized Business Related Messages for Telephone Answering Machines—Lucent Technologies Inc.; *U.S. Public*, pg. 1017

SIMPLY NUTRITIOUS—Fortified Fruit Juices—J.M. Smucker Company; *U.S. Public*, pg. 1480

SIMPLY PERFECT—Mousse Make-Up—Elizabeth Arden Company; *Int'l*, pg. 1435

SIMPLY PETITES—NONE—Kellwood Company; *U.S. Public*, pg. 948

SIMPLY POTATOES—Refrigerated Potato Products—Michael Foods, Inc.; *U.S. Public*, pg. 1103

SIMPLY SUPERIOR—Salad Dressings—Superior Coffee and Foods; *U.S. Public*, pg. 1434

SIMPLY YOU—Dusting Powders & Talcs—Tristar Corp.; *U.S. Public*, pg. 1640

SIMPROCESS—Software—CACI International Inc; *U.S. Public*, pg. 272

SIMPSON—Major Appliances—Email Limited; *Int'l*, pg. 450

SIMPSON—Doors—Simpson Door Company; *U.S. Private*, pg. 1003

SIMPULSE—Suction Irrigatar—Davol Inc.; *U.S. Public*, pg. 189

SIMRAX—Face Seals—Freudenberg & Company; *Int'l*, pg. 505

SIMRIT—Seals & Precision Moldings— Freudenberg & Company; *Int'l*, pg. 505

SIMRIT—Oil Seal—Freudenberg-NOK; *U.S. Private*, pg. 427

SIMSCENARIO—Software—CACI International Inc; *U.S. Public*, pg. 272

SIMSCRIPT II.5—Programming Computer Simulation Language System—CACI International Inc; *U.S. Public*, pg. 272

SIMSNIPS—Software—CACI International Inc; *U.S. Public*, pg. 272

SIMSTRUCTOR—Software—CACI International Inc; *U.S. Public*, pg. 272

SIMTRAINER—Software—CACI International Inc; *U.S. Public*, pg. 272

SIMULCAST—NONE—Compuware Corporation; *U.S. Public*, pg. 423

Brand Name Index

SIMUSOLV—Computer Program—The Dow Chemical Company; *U.S. Public*, pg. 522

SIMVIDEO—Software—CACI International Inc; *U.S. Public*, pg. 272

SIMWASH—Serum/Cell Separation System—Ortho Clinical Diagnostic Systems Inc.; *U.S. Public*, pg. 929

SINAI 48—Sausage, Cured & Smoked Meats—Bessin Corporation; *U.S. Public*, pg. 1433

SINAI 48—Kosher Meats—Sara Lee Corporation; *U.S. Public*, pg. 1432

SINAI 48 KOSHER—NONE—Shofar Kosher Foods; *U.S. Public*, pg. 1433

SINBAR—Herbicide—Du Pont (E.I. Du Pont De Nemours & Co.); *U.S. Public*, pg. 530

SINCLAIR—NONE—Betacom Plc; *Int'l*, pg. 193

SINCLAIR—NONE—ICI Paints; *Int'l*, pg. 664

SINCLAIR—Paint—Insilco Corporation; *U.S. Public*, pg. 881

SINCLAIR-COLLINS—Valves—Schrader Bellows Division; *U.S. Public*, pg. 1261

SINCLAIR FUELS—Fuels—Fleischli Oil Company, Inc.; *U.S. Private*, pg. 410

SINDY—NONE—MB Espana, S.A.; *U.S. Public*, pg. 798

SINE-AID—Sinus Medication—Johnson & Johnson; *U.S. Public*, pg. 927

SINE-AID—Proprietary Drugs—McNeil Consumer Products Company; *U.S. Public*, pg. 928

SINE-OFF—Sinus Remedy—SmithKline Beecham Consumer Healthcare, U.S.; *Int'l*, pg. 1264

SINE OFF—Cough, Cold & Influenza Treatment—SmithKline Beecham plc; *Int'l*, pg. 1264

SINEMET—Carbidopa-Levodopa—Merck & Co., Inc.; *U.S. Public*, pg. 1090

SINEMET—Pharmaceutical—Merck Human Health Division (U.S. Human Health); *U.S. Public*, pg. 1091

SINEQUAN—Doxepin—Pfizer Inc.; *U.S. Public*, pg. 1281

SINEX—Nasal Spray—Richardson-Vicks, Inc., Health Care Products; *U.S. Public*, pg. 1331

SING-A-LONG PRAISE—NONE—Integrity Incorporated; *U.S. Public*, pg. 886

SINGAPORE AIRLINES—International Airlines—Singapore Airlines; *Int'l*, pg. 1374

SINGER—Sewing Machines—Semi-Tech Corporation; *Int'l*, pg. 1220

SINGLE KIT—Eye Shadows—Cover Girl Cosmetics; *U.S. Public*, pg. 1330

SINGLE PATIENT—Surgical Accessories—Kimberly-Clark Corporation; *U.S. Public*, pg. 958

SINGLE SERV—Salt & Pepper—Diamond Crystal Specialty Foods, Inc.; *U.S. Private*, pg. 330

SINGLE-SIX—Single-Action Revolver—Sturm, Ruger & Co., Inc.; *U.S. Public*, pg. 1526

SINGLE SOURCE—Wire—National-Standard Co.; *U.S. Public*, pg. 1160

SINGLE STAGE—Self-Etching Primer—Mar-Hyde Corporation; *U.S. Public*, pg. 1357

SINGLE TAPERED BUSHING—NONE—Regal-Beloit Corporation; *U.S. Public*, pg. 1370

SINGLES—Facial Sponge—3M; *U.S. Public*, pg. 1604

SINGLESKEEPER—Reclosable/Recyclable Packaging for Borden & Bordon Lite-Line Cheese—Borden, Inc.; *U.S. Private*, pg. 157

SINGLETON—Seafood—ConAgra, Inc.; *U.S. Public*, pg. 425

THE SINGLETON OF AUCHROISK—Malt Scotch—IDV North America; *Int'l*, pg. 411

SINGLETON'S SELECTION—Super Menthol Snuff—Imperial Tobacco Group, Ltd.; *Int'l*, pg. 666

SINKMASTER—Waste Disposer—Anaheim Manufacturing Company; *U.S. Private*, pg. 70

SINOGRAFIN—Diagnostics—Bristol-Myers Squibb Company; *U.S. Public*, pg. 253

SINTECH—Electromechanical Materials Test Systems—MTS Systems Corporation; *U.S. Public*, pg. 1028

SINULIN—Sinus Headache Product—Carnrick Laboratories, Inc.; *U.S. Private*, pg. 436

SINUTAB—Analgesic/Decongestant—Warner-Lambert Company; *U.S. Public*, pg. 1738

SINUTAB—Sinus Medications—Warner-Lambert Consumer Healthcare; *U.S. Public*, pg. 1739

SINVINO JAVA TEA STRAIGHT—Beverage—Otsuka Pharmaceutical Co., Ltd.; *Int'l*, pg. 1013

SIONON—Diabetic Foods—Bayer AG; *Int'l*, pg. 171

SIOPLAS—Crosslinking Technology for Polyolefins—Dow Corning Corporation; *U.S. Public*, pg. 523

SIOUX—Portable Air & Electric Tools—Sioux Tools, Inc.; *U.S. Public*, pg. 1480

SIOUX CITY—Sarsaparilla Soft Drink—White Rock Products Corp.; *U.S. Private*, pg. 1173

SIOUX-MOX—Slippers—Wolverine World Wide, Inc.; *U.S. Public*, pg. 1775

SIPEX—Electronics—Sipex Corporation; *Int'l*, pg. 1415

SIPPIN' PAK—Aseptic Juices—Borden, Inc.; *U.S. Private*, pg. 157

SIR—Ground Fault Receptacles—Pass & Seymour/Legrand; *Int'l*, pg. 806

SIR JOHN'S—Pet Foods—Ag Processing Inc., A Cooperative; *U.S. Private*, pg. 26

SIR-PEL—PVC Coated Nonwoven—Georgia-Bonded Fibers, Inc.; *U.S. Public*, pg. 734

SIR SPEEDY—Printing Centers—Sir Speedy, Inc.; *U.S. Private*, pg. 423

SIR WALTER RALEIGH—Pipe Tobacco—B.A.T Industries P.L.C.; *Int'l*, pg. 110

SIR WALTER RALEIGH—Smoking Tobacco—Brown & Williamson Tobacco Corp.; *Int'l*, pg. 111

SIRACOM—Electronic Sirens—Federal Signal Corporation, Signal Div.; *U.S. Public*, pg. 616

SIRATONE—Electronic Warning Siren—Federal Signal Corporation, Signal Div.; *U.S. Public*, pg. 616

SIRATROL—Radio Receiver/Tone Decoder—Federal Signal Corporation, Signal Div.; *U.S. Public*, pg. 616

SIRICCA—Hiking/Walking Footwear—K-Swiss Inc.; *U.S. Public*, pg. 937

SIRLENE—Propylene Glycol U.S.P.—The Dow Chemical Company; *U.S. Public*, pg. 522

SIRLOIN STOCKADE—Restaurants—Golden Corral Corporation; *U.S. Private*, pg. 575

SIROCCO—Fans—The Howden Fan Co.; *U.S. Private*, pg. 543

SIROCCO—Ski Socks—Wigwam Mills, Inc.; *U.S. Private*, pg. 1175

SIROP DES VOSGES CAZE—Cough Remedies—SmithKline Beecham plc; *Int'l*, pg. 1264

SIRPEL—Polyvisylic Nonwoven—Bontex; *U.S. Public*, pg. 734

SISALKRAFT—Laminated Packaging—Carter Holt Harvey Limited; *U.S. Public*, pg. 904

SISI—Soft Drink—Heineken N.V.; *Int'l*, pg. 608

SISLEY—NONE—Benetton Group S.p.A.; *Int'l*, pg. 186

SISONIC SENSOR—Silicon Microphone & Integrated Circuit—Synchro-Start Products, Inc.; *U.S. Private*, pg. 627

SISSI—Perfume—International Cosmetics Co., Ltd.; *Int'l*, pg. 684

SISTO—Diaphragm Valves—KSB Aktiengesellschaft; *Int'l*, pg. 721

SISTOMAT—Actuated Valves—KSB Aktiengesellschaft; *Int'l*, pg. 721

SISU—Container Handling Systems—Partek Corporation; *Int'l*, pg. 1024

SITE—Software—CACI International Inc; *U.S. Public*, pg. 272

SITE-LOCK—TV Co-Channel Transmitter Arrangement—Emcee Broadcast Products, Inc.; *U.S. Public*, pg. 570

SITE-MAP—Software—CACI International Inc; *U.S. Public*, pg. 272

SITE OIL TOOLS—Well Completion Equipment—Camco International Inc.; *U.S. Public*, pg. 298

SITE-POTENTIAL—Software—CACI International Inc; *U.S. Public*, pg. 272

SITE RELEASE—Controlled Release Liquids, Creams & Ointments—KV Pharmaceutical Company; *U.S. Public*, pg. 941

SITE RITE—Bender—Greenlee Textron; *U.S. Public*, pg. 1589

SITE SPAN—Remote Distribution/Telecommuting Options—InteCom; *Int'l*, pg. 794

SITEGUARD—Intruder, Access Control & Closed Circuit Television Systems—Thorn Security Group, Ltd.; *Int'l*, pg. 1386

SITEWATCH—Access Control Systems—Grinnell Fire Protection Systems; *Int'l*, pg. 1386

SITEWATCH—Access Control Systems—Grinnell Fire Protection Systems; *U.S. Public*, pg. 1647

SITTING PRETTY—Interior Plant Prods.—Security Lawn & Garden Co.; *U.S. Private*, pg. 397

688 CLASS SUBMARINES—NONE—General Dynamics Corporation; *U.S. Public*, pg. 708

SIX FLAGS ASTROWORLD—Theme Park—Six Flags Theme Parks Inc.; *U.S. Public*, pg. 1611

SIX FLAGS CALIFORNIA—Theme Park/Water Park Complex—Six Flags Theme Parks Inc.; *U.S. Public*, pg. 1611

SIX FLAGS FIESTA TEXAS—NONE—Six Flags Theme Parks Inc.; *U.S. Public*, pg. 1611

SIX FLAGS GREAT ADVENTURE—Amusement Parks—Six Flags Great Adventure Theme Park & Wild Safari Animal Park; *U.S. Public*, pg. 1611

SIX FLAGS GREAT ADVENTURE—Theme Park—Six Flags Theme Parks Inc.; *U.S. Public*, pg. 1611

SIX FLAGS GREAT AMERICA—Theme Park—Six Flags Great America, Inc.; *U.S. Public*, pg. 1611

SIX FLAGS GREAT AMERICA—Theme Park—Six Flags Theme Parks Inc.; *U.S. Public*, pg. 1611

SIX FLAGS HOUSTON—Theme Park/Water Park Complex—Six Flags Theme Parks Inc.; *U.S. Public*, pg. 1611

SIX FLAGS HURRICANE HARBOR—Water Park—Six Flags Theme Parks Inc.; *U.S. Public*, pg. 1611

SIX FLAGS MAGIC MOUNTAIN—Theme Park—Six Flags Theme Parks Inc.; *U.S. Public*, pg. 1611

SIX FLAGS OVER GEORGIA—Theme Park—Six Flags Theme Parks Inc.; *U.S. Public*, pg. 1611

SIX FLAGS OVER TEXAS—Amusement Parks—Six Flags Over Texas; *U.S. Public*, pg. 1612

SIX FLAGS OVER TEXAS—Theme Park—Six Flags Theme Parks Inc.; *U.S. Public*, pg. 1611

SIX FLAGS ST. LOUIS—Theme Park—Six Flags Theme Parks Inc.; *U.S. Public*, pg. 1611

SIX FLAGS THEME PARKS—Amusement Attractions—Six Flags Theme Parks Inc.; *U.S. Public*, pg. 1611

SIX FLAGS WATER WORLD—Water Park—Six Flags Theme Parks Inc.; *U.S. Public*, pg. 1611

SIX FLAGS WILD SAFARI ANIMAL PARK—Animal Park—Six Flags Theme Parks Inc.; *U.S. Public*, pg. 1611

640—Tires—Bridgestone/Firestone, Inc.; *Int'l*, pg. 213

600 RACING, INC.—NONE—Speedway Motorsports, Inc.; *U.S. Public*, pg. 1498

600 SE—Instant Camera—Polaroid Corporation; *U.S. Public*, pg. 1313

666—Cold Tablets & Liquid—Monticello Drug Co.; *U.S. Private*, pg. 759

631-X HYDROGEN SULFIDE ANALYZER—NONE—Arizona Instrument Corporation; *U.S. Public*, pg. 129

612—VSR Hammer Drill—ITW Ramset/Red Head; *U.S. Public*, pg. 867

SIX PACK PLANT—Portable, Self-Erecting Asphalt Plants—Astec Industries, Inc.; *U.S. Public*, pg. 141

SIX-PLUS—AC & Line Protection—Porta Systems Corp.; *U.S. Public*, pg. 1317

630—Tires—Bridgestone/Firestone, Inc.; *Int'l*, pg. 213

636—Jet Transports—The Boeing Company; *U.S. Public*, pg. 239

636S—Plain Paper Copier—Dietzgen Corporation; *U.S. Private*, pg. 332

6000 SERIES—Furniture—Myrtle/Mueller, A Haworth Co.; *U.S. Private*, pg. 512

626—Car—Mazda Motor of America, Inc.; *Int'l*, pg. 849

SIXTANT—Station Automation Software—Chyron Corp.; *Int'l*, pg. 1372

SIXTEEN-D—Lint Cleaning Machine After Cotton Has Been Ginned—Continental Eagle Corporation; *U.S. Private*, pg. 267

1648 SM—Sonet Multiplexrs—Alcatel Telecom; *Int'l*, pg. 55

1600 GLASSVENT—Concealed Vent for Curtain Walls—Kawneer Company; *U.S. Public*, pg. 60

1600 TR—Liquid Scintillation Analyzer—Packard Instrument Co., Inc.; *U.S. Private*, pg. 833

1600 Wall System—Wall System—Kawneer Company; *U.S. Public*, pg. 60

1603/12 SM—Sonet Multiplexrs—Alcatel Telecom; *Int'l*, pg. 55

1664—Beer—Danone Group; *Int'l*, pg. 379

1631 SX—Digital Cross Connects—Alcatel Telecom; *Int'l*, pg. 55

1630 SX—Digital Cross Connects—Alcatel Telecom; *Int'l*, pg. 55

1633 SX—Digital Cross Connects—Alcatel Telecom; *Int'l*, pg. 55

SIXTH FLEET—Game—Monarch Avalon, Inc.; *U.S. Public*, pg. 1123

THE 60's—Greeting Cards—American Greetings Corporation; *U.S. Public*, pg. 77

60—Tires—Bridgestone/Firestone, Inc.; *Int'l*, pg. 213

60" LOBBY PARCEL LOCKER—Locker—American Locker Group, Inc.; *U.S. Public*, pg. 85

61—Paints, Varnishes, Enamels—Pratt & Lambert United, Inc.; *U.S. Public*, pg. 1466

61 SERIES—Office Chair—Vecta; *U.S. Private*, pg. 1038

60-PLUS—Crane Wheel—Harnischfeger Industries, Inc.; *U.S. Public*, pg. 788

60 SEMI GLOSS—Paint—Pratt & Lambert United, Inc.; *U.S. Public*, pg. 1466

SIZEFINDER—Grinding Machines—Landis; *U.S. Public*, pg. 1699

SIZEFINDER—Grinding Machine Apparatus—Litton Industries, Inc.; *U.S. Public*, pg. 1002

SIZING—Contouring Liquid—The Dow Chemical Company; *U.S. Public*, pg. 522

SIZZLE—Plumbing Chemical—Hercules Chemical Co., Inc.; *U.S. Private*, pg. 523

SIZZLE—Beauty Care Products—Windmere-Durable Holdings; *U.S. Public*, pg. 1771

SIZZLEAN—Breakfast Strips—Armour Swift Eckrich; *U.S. Public*, pg. 426

SIZZLEAN—Meat Products—ConAgra, Inc.; *U.S. Public*, pg. 425

SIZZLER—Casual Dining Restaurants—Sizzler International, Inc.; *U.S. Public*, pg. 1475

SIZZLER—Restaurants—Sizzler USA, Inc.; *U.S. Public*, pg. 1475

SIZZLES—Bras—Warner's; *U.S. Public*, pg. 1738

SIZZLIN' SKILLET—Microwave Browner—Nordic Ware; *U.S. Private*, pg. 806

SIZZOR LIFTS—Scissor-Type Mobile Lifting Platform—JLG Industries, Inc.; *U.S. Public*, pg. 918

SKAN-A-PAGE—Office Supplies—JM Company; *U.S. Private*, pg. 577

SKAT-PAK—5 Min. Escape Respirator—Scott Aviation; *U.S. Public*, pg. 622

SKATE ATTACK—In-Line Skates—First Team Sports Inc.; *U.S. Public*, pg. 638

SKATE CHAIR—Lounge Seating—Vecta; *U.S. Private*, pg. 1038

SKATE CHAISE—Lounge Seating—Vecta; *U.S. Private*, pg. 1038

SKATE LOUNGE—Lounge Seating—Vecta; *U.S. Private*, pg. 1038

SKATE N'SKI—Socks & Knitted Headwear—Wigwam Mills, Inc.; *U.S. Private*, pg. 1175

SKATE TABLE—NONE—Vecta; *U.S. Private*, pg. 1038

SKATEBOARDS—Children's Shoes—E.J. Footwear Corp.; *U.S. Public*, pg. 1684

SKATETILE—Rubber Flooring—Pawling Corporation; *U.S. Public*, pg. 844

SKEET—A Tactical Systems Application Submunition—Textron Systems; *U.S. Public*, pg. 1589

SKEETAL—Biological Product for Control of Mosquito & Black-Fly Larvae—Novo Nordisk A/S; *Int'l*, pg. 987

SKEETER—Bass Fishing Boats—The Coleman Company, Inc.; *U.S. Public*, pg. 690

SKELAXIN—Muscle Relaxant—Carnrick Laboratories, Inc.; *U.S. Private*, pg. 436

SKETCHER—Graphical Design Software—Harnischfeger Industries, Inc.; *U.S. Public*, pg. 788

SKEW-SHEAR—Variable Rate Designed Tap—National Twist Drill Div.; *U.S. Public*, pg. 1370

SKEW-SHEAR—Variable Rake Designed Tap—Regal-Beloit Corporation; *U.S. Public*, pg. 1370

SKI—Soft Drink—Double-Cola Co.-USA; *U.S. Private*, pg. 341

SKI—Magazine—Times Mirror Magazines, Inc.; *U.S. Public*, pg. 1616

SKI-DOO—Snowmobiles—Bombardier Inc.; *Int'l*, pg. 199

SKI-MOC—Shoes—Johnston & Murphy Co.; *U.S. Public*, pg. 728

SKI N' SKATE—Socks—Wigwam Mills, Inc.; *U.S. Private*, pg. 1175

SKI N'SKATE JR.—Socks—Wigwam Mills, Inc.; *U.S. Private*, pg. 1175

SKI NAUTIQUE—Power Boat—Correct Craft, Inc.; *U.S. Private*, pg. 276

SKI NAUTIQUE OPEN BOW—Power Boat—Correct Craft, Inc.; *U.S. Private*, pg. 276

SKI PRO—Skin Care Prod.—Tanning Research Labs., Inc.; *U.S. Private*, pg. 1068

SKI WATCH—Radio Networks—CRN International, Inc.; *U.S. Private*, pg. 197

SKID MASTER—Paper & Paperboard for Packaging & Containers—Georgia-Pacific Corporation; *U.S. Public*, pg. 735

SKID-MASTER—Paper & Paper Board Containers—Georgia-Pacific Corporation; *U.S. Public*, pg. 735

SKIERS CHOICE—Ski Handle—Outdoor Technologies Group; *U.S. Private*, pg. 822

SKIING—Magazine—Times Mirror Magazines, Inc.; *U.S. Public*, pg. 1616

SKIING TRADE NEWS—Magazine—Times Mirror Magazines, Inc.; *U.S. Public*, pg. 1616

SKIIPPACK—Integrated, Intelligent Power Semiconductors—Semikron International, GmbH & Co. KG; *Int'l*, pg. 1220

SKIL—Hand Tools—Emerson Electric Co.; *U.S. Public*, pg. 572

SKILL DYNAMICS—Computer Product—International Business Machines Corporation; *U.S. Public*, pg. 895

SKILLET CHICKEN HELPER—Main Dish Mixes—General Mills, Inc.; *U.S. Public*, pg. 717

SKILLWARE—Training Software—Manpower Inc.; *U.S. Public*, pg. 1042

SKILSAW—Precision Saw—Emerson Electric Co.; *U.S. Public*, pg. 572

SKIMPLUS—Vitamin Fortified Skim Milk—Farmland Dairies; *U.S. Private*, pg. 395

SKIN BRACER—After Shave & Pre-Electric Shave Lotion—The Mennen Company; *U.S. Public*, pg. 397

SKIN DIVER—Magazine—Petersen Publishing Company, L.L.C.; *U.S. Private*, pg. 856

SKIN-EEZ—Poly Gloves—Magla Products; *U.S. Private*, pg. 695

SKIN GLO—Almond Body Buff—Stanhome Inc.; *U.S. Public*, pg. 1508

SKIN MACHINE—NONE—Clairol, Inc.; *U.S. Public*, pg. 254

SKIN SAVER—Cosmetics—Palm Beach Beauty Products Co.; *U.S. Private*, pg. 834

SKIN SAVERS—NONE—PolyMedica Industries, Inc.; *U.S. Public*, pg. 1315

SKIN SCRUBBER—Natural Pumice Stone—Stanhome Inc.; *U.S. Public*, pg. 1508

SKIN SILK—NONE—Avon Products Co., Ltd.; *U.S. Public*, pg. 156

SKIN SO SOFT—Bath & Body Oil—Avon Products, Inc.; *U.S. Public*, pg. 155

SKINCREDIBLES—Potatoes Products—J.R. Simplot Company; *U.S. Private*, pg. 1002

SKINNER—Pasta—Hershey Foods Corporation; *U.S. Public*, pg. 811

SKINNER—Pasta—Hershey Pasta and Grocery Group; *U.S. Public*, pg. 812

SKINNER-SEAL—Pipeline Products—Schlumberger Industries; *U.S. Public*, pg. 1439

SKINNY SPIKES—Specialty Nails—Maze Nails; *U.S. Private*, pg. 718

SKINNY WAIST—Foundations—The Strouse, Adler Company; *U.S. Private*, pg. 1047

SKINPLATE—Plastic Filmed Coated Steel—Cockerill Sambre; *Int'l*, pg. 301

SKINTEGRITY—Wound Care Products—Medline Industries, Inc.; *U.S. Private*, pg. 728

SKINTIMATE—Shaving Cream—S.C. Johnson & Son, Inc.; *U.S. Private*, pg. 592

SKINTIMATE—(Shave Preparation)—S.C. Johnson & Son, Limited; *U.S. Private*, pg. 593

SKINTIMATE SHAVE GEL FOR WOMEN—Women' Shave—S.C. Johnson & Son, Inc.; *U.S. Private*, pg. 592

SKIP—Detergents—Lever S.A.; *Int'l*, pg. 1438

SKIP—Detergent—Unilever Plc; *Int'l*, pg. 1433

SKIP-BO—Card Game—Mattel Games/Puzzles; *U.S. Public*, pg. 1058

SKIP SHIFT—Transmission—Case Corporation; *U.S. Public*, pg. 311

SKIPPY—Peanut Butter—Bestfoods; *U.S. Public*, pg. 223

SKIPPY—Dog Food—H.J. Heinz Company; *U.S. Public*, pg. 805

SKIPPY—NONE—Star-Kist Foods Inc.; *U.S. Public*, pg. 805

SKIPPY—Canned Dog Food—Star-Kist Foods, Inc.; *U.S. Public*, pg. 806

SKITTLES—Fruit Chews—Mars, Incorporated; *U.S. Private*, pg. 707

SKITTLES BRAND—NONE—M&M/Mars; *U.S. Private*, pg. 707

SKOAL—NONE—United States Tobacco Company; *U.S. Public*, pg. 1661

SKOAL BANDITS—NONE—United States Tobacco Company; *U.S. Public*, pg. 1661

SKOAL LONG CUT—NONE—United States Tobacco Company; *U.S. Public*, pg. 1661

SKODA—Automobile—Volkswagen AG; *Int'l*, pg. 1473

SKODA CADDY—Automobile—Volkswagen AG; *Int'l*, pg. 1473

SKODA FAVORIT—Automobile—Volkswagen AG; *Int'l*, pg. 1473

SKODA FELICIA—Automobile—Volkswagen AG; *Int'l*, pg. 1473

SKODA FORMAN—Automobile—Volkswagen AG; *Int'l*, pg. 1473

SKODA PICKUP—Automobile—Volkswagen AG; *Int'l*, pg. 1473

SKOGCELL—Pulp—Sodra Cell AB; *Int'l*, pg. 1275

SKOGCELL Z—TCF Pulp—Sodra Cell AB; *Int'l*, pg. 1275

SKOL—NONE—Barton Brands, Ltd.; *U.S. Public*, pg. 300

SKOOL MATES—Beauty & Bath Accessories—Paris Presents; *U.S. Private*, pg. 839

SKOR—Toffee Candy Bar—Hershey Foods Corporation; *U.S. Public*, pg. 811

SKROODLES—Pasta Products—Ravarino & Freschi, Inc.; *U.S. Private*, pg. 158

SKULIGHT STUDIO—Art Supplies—American Greetings U.S. Greeting Card Division; *U.S. Public*, pg. 78

SKUM-X—Drafting Powder—Dietzgen Corporation; *U.S. Private*, pg. 332

SKWEZLOC—Lock Collars—Emerson Power Transmission Corporation; *U.S. Public*, pg. 573

SKY—U.K. Entertainment Magazine—EMAP Metro; *Int'l*, pg. 451

SKY BAR—Candy—New England Confectionery Co.; *U.S. Private*, pg. 1113

SKY BEAM—Light Fixtures—Matsushita Electric Works, Ltd.; *Int'l*, pg. 847

SKY CHEF—Restaurants—Onex Corporation; *Int'l*, pg. 1006

SKY-CLUB—Business Class Services—Malev Hungarian Airlines, Plc.; *Int'l*, pg. 833

SKY DANCER—Flying Dolls—Galoob Toys, Inc.; *U.S. Public*, pg. 698

SKY FLASH—Air-to-Air Weapon—British Aerospace p.l.c.; *Int'l*, pg. 217

SKY LITE 990—Tourist-Class Seats—B/E Aerospace Seating Products Group; *U.S. Public*, pg. 159

SKY LITE 995—First-Class Seats—B/E Aerospace Seating Products Group; *U.S. Public*, pg. 159

SKY MASK—Oxygen Mask—Scott Aviation; *U.S. Public*, pg. 622

SKY-SLOPE—Laminated Glass for Skylights & Sloped Glazing—Globe-Amerada Glass Company; *U.S. Private*, pg. 458

SKY SURFER—Gym Set Feature—Hedstrom Corporation; *U.S. Private*, pg. 526

SKY TINT—Pencils—Dixon Ticonderoga Company; *U.S. Public*, pg. 514

SKY TRAK—Rough Terrain Forklift-Variable Reach—OmniQuip International, Inc.; *U.S. Private*, pg. 500

SKYBOND—High Temperature Polyimide Resin—Monsanto Company; *U.S. Public*, pg. 1124

SKYCAP—Ceramic Capacitors—AVX Corporation; *Int'l*, pg. 775

SKYDOME—Skylight—Wasco Products, Inc.; *U.S. Private*, pg. 1152

SKYDRAGON—Basketball Shoes—Mizuno Corporation; *U.S. Public*, pg. 884

SKYDROL—Fire Resistant Hydraulic Fluid—Monsanto Company; *U.S. Public*, pg. 1124

SKYE'S HOLLOW—Wines—Canandaigua Wine Company, Inc.; *U.S. Public,* pg. 300

SKYFAX—One-Number Fax Accessibility on Your Pager—Mobile Telecommunications Technologies Corp.; *U.S. Public,* pg. 1120

SKYHAWK—NONE—The Cessna Aircraft Co.; *U.S. Public,* pg. 1589

SKYHAWK—Scissor Lift Access Platform—Simon Engineering plc; *Int'l,* pg. 1251

SKYLAND—Food Products—National Fruit Product Company; *U.S. Private,* pg. 783

SKYLANE—NONE—The Cessna Aircraft Co.; *U.S. Public,* pg. 1589

SKYLARK—Automobile—Buick Motor Div. General Motors Corp.; *U.S. Public,* pg. 720

SKYLARK BOOKS—Books for Young Readers—Bertelsmann AG; *Int'l,* pg. 189

SKYLARK GARDENS—Italian Restaurant—Skylark Co., Ltd.; *Int'l,* pg. 1262

SKYLINE—Fountain & Rollerball Pens—Eversharp Pen Co.; *U.S. Private,* pg. 386

SKYLINE—Car—Nissan Motor Co., Ltd.; *Int'l,* pg. 943

SKYLINE CHILI—Cincinnati Style Chili—Skyline Chili, Inc.; *U.S. Public,* pg. 1475

SKYLITE PYROJECTOR—Projectors—Swartwout Industries; *Int'l,* pg. 1398

SKYMILES—NONE—American Express Company; *U.S. Public,* pg. 73

SKYPAGER—Nationwide Wireless Paging—Mobile Telecommunications Technologies Corp.; *U.S. Public,* pg. 1120

SKYPHONE—Voice & Data Satellite Communications For Aircrafts—British Telecommunications plc; *Int'l,* pg. 222

SKYSHIELD 35—Advanced Technology Air Defense system—Oerlikon-Contraves AG; *Int'l,* pg. 998

SKYTALK—Toll-Free Voice Mail Accessibility & Auto Notification of Incoming Messages—Mobile Telecommunications Technologies Corp.; *U.S. Public,* pg. 1120

SKYTEL 2-WAY—Two-Way Nationwide Wireless Messaging Service—Mobile Telecommunications Technologies Corp.; *U.S. Public,* pg. 1120

SKYTEL 2-WAY—Two-Way Paging System—SkyTel Corp.; *U.S. Public,* pg. 1120

SKYTONE—Printing Paper—Georgia-Pacific Corporation; *U.S. Public,* pg. 735

SKYWALK—Roofing Material—Dodge Regupol, Inc.; *U.S. Private,* pg. 337

SKYWAY—Luggage—Skyway Luggage Co.; *U.S. Private,* pg. 1005

SKYWAY AIRLINES—NONE—Midwest Express Airlines, Inc.; *U.S. Public,* pg. 1111

SKYWAY AIRLINES—Commuter Airline Feeding—Midwest Express Holdings, Inc.; *U.S. Public,* pg. 1111

SKYWINDOW—Roof Window—Wasco Products, Inc.; *U.S. Private,* pg. 1152

SKYWORD—Nationwide Text Messaging System—Mobile Telecommunications Technologies Corp.; *U.S. Public,* pg. 1120

SLACK TUBE—U-Tube Manometer—Dwyer Instruments Inc.; *U.S. Private,* pg. 350

SLAM-A-RAMA—Card Game—Mattel Games/Puzzles; *U.S. Public,* pg. 1058

SLANT—Intraocular Lenses—Alcon Laboratories, Inc.; *Int'l,* pg. 916

SLANT—NONE—Urban Outfitters, Inc.; *U.S. Public,* pg. 1700

SLANT/FIN—Heaters, Boilers, Air-Conditioners—Slant/Fin Corporation; *U.S. Private,* pg. 1005

SLAP STIX—Suckers—Stark Candy Company; *U.S. Private,* pg. 1113

SLAPSHOT—Sports Game—Monarch Avalon, Inc.; *U.S. Public,* pg. 1123

SLATELINE SHINGLES—Architectural, Laminated Shingles—Building Materials Corporation of America; *U.S. Private,* pg. 433

SLATER PLASTIC BOXES—Switch, Outlet, Ceiling Plastic Boxes—Pass & Seymour/Legrand; *Int'l,* pg. 806

SLATES—Casual/Dressy Business Wear—Levi Strauss & Co.; *U.S. Private,* pg. 662

SLAVE SUBWOOFER—NONE—Cambridge Soundworks, Inc.; *U.S. Private,* pg. 202

SLAZENGER—NONE—Pacific Dunlop Limited; *Int'l,* pg. 1021

SLAZENGER SPORT—Toiletries—SmithKline Beecham plc; *Int'l,* pg. 1264

SLECTROL—Control Systems—Thermo Electric Co., Inc.; *U.S. Private,* pg. 1080

SLEEP CUSHION—Mattress—The Spring Air Company; *U.S. Private,* pg. 1027

SLEEP-GARD—Patient Gowns—Angelica Corporation; *U.S. Public,* pg. 113

SLEEP HAVEN—Sofa Sleeper—Flexsteel Industries, Inc.; *U.S. Public,* pg. 653

SLEEP-IN SOFA—Convertible Sleep Sofas—Kingsdown, Inc.; *U.S. Private,* pg. 622

SLEEP INNS—Main Stay Suites (Extended Stay Hotels)—Choice Hotels International, Inc.; *U.S. Public,* pg. 351

SLEEP-N-LOUNGE—Electric Bed—Kingsdown, Inc.; *U.S. Private,* pg. 622

SLEEP SHIELD—Mattress Insulator—The Spring Air Company; *U.S. Private,* pg. 1027

SLEEP WIZARD—Portable Polysomnography System—Nellcor Puritan Bennett Incorporated; *U.S. Public,* pg. 1039

SLEEPEEZEE—Beds—Sleepeezee Limited; *Int'l,* pg. 1263

SLEEPER CABS & ACCESSORIES—Cabs & Accessories—Georgia Tent & Awning Inc.; *U.S. Private,* pg. 448

SLEEPINAL CAPSULES—Sleep-Aid—Thompson Medical Company, Inc.; *U.S. Private,* pg. 1083

SLEEPINAL MEDICATED NIGHT TEA—Sleep-Aid—Thompson Medical Company, Inc.; *U.S. Private,* pg. 1083

SLEEPING BEAUTY—Mattresses—Kingsdown, Inc.; *U.S. Private,* pg. 622

SLEEPING BEAUTY ELOQUENCE—Mattress & Box Spring Sets—Kingsdown, Inc.; *U.S. Private,* pg. 622

SLEEPING BEAUTY SOFTIE—Mattress & Box Spring—Kingsdown, Inc.; *U.S. Private,* pg. 622

SLEEPING BEAUTY SYSTEM—Mattress Construction—Kingsdown, Inc.; *U.S. Private,* pg. 622

SLEEPING BEAUTY TRADITION—Mattresses & Box Springs—Kingsdown, Inc.; *U.S. Private,* pg. 622

SLEEPING BEAUTY 2000—Mattresses & Box Springs—Kingsdown, Inc.; *U.S. Private,* pg. 622

SLEEPING CALL COLLECTIONS—Telecommunications Equipment—Lucent Technologies Inc.; *U.S. Public,* pg. 1017

SLEEPQUIZ—Application Software—Nellcor Puritan Bennett Incorporated; *U.S. Public,* pg. 1039

SLEEPSCAN—Neuro-Diagnostic Instrumentation—Bio-Logic Systems Corp.; *U.S. Public,* pg. 230

SLEEPY HOLLOW NATURALS—Hair & Skin Care Products—Carme' Cosmeceutical Sciences, Inc.; *U.S. Private,* pg. 213

SLEEPY'S—Mattresses—Sleepy's The Mattress Professionals; *U.S. Private,* pg. 1005

SLEEPYTIME—Herb Tea—Celestial Seasonings; *U.S. Public,* pg. 319

SLEEPYTIME EXTRA—Blend with Valerian Root—Celestial Seasonings; *U.S. Public,* pg. 319

SLEEVELINE—Valves—Flowserve Corporation; *U.S. Public,* pg. 658

SLENDERELLA—Reduced-calorie Fruit Spreads—J.M. Smucker Company; *U.S. Public,* pg. 1480

SLENDID—Fat Replacer—Hercules Incorporated; *U.S. Public,* pg. 809

SLENDYNE—Dynamic Microphone—Shure Brothers Incorporated; *U.S. Private,* pg. 997

SLIC—Telecommunications Products—3M; *U.S. Public,* pg. 1604

SLIC E2 PROM—NONE—Xicor, Inc.; *U.S. Public,* pg. 1785

SLIC-TITE—Paste—La-Co Industries Markal Company; *U.S. Private,* pg. 640

SLIC-TITE STIK—Thread Compound—La-Co Industries Markal Company; *U.S. Private,* pg. 640

SLICE—Soft Drink—PepsiCo, Inc.; *U.S. Public,* pg. 1276

SLICE—Activewear—Sao Paulo Alpargatas S.A.; *Int'l,* pg. 1193

SLICEMATE—Slice Positioning System—Harnischfeger Industries, Inc.; *U.S. Public,* pg. 788

SLICK AIRCRAFT PRODUCTS—Aviation Ignition Equipment—Unison Industries; *U.S. Private,* pg. 1120

SLICK 50—Motor Oil Additive—Kelso Oil Company; *U.S. Public,* pg. 613

SLICKERS—Portfolios—The Mead Corporation; *U.S. Public,* pg. 1074

SLIDE-DOWN—NONE—The Crown Divisions; *U.S. Public,* pg. 1631

SLIDE-LOK—Safety Glasses—The Fibre-Metal Products Company; *U.S. Private,* pg. 402

SLIDE MASTER—Slide Controls—The Lamson & Sessions Co.; *U.S. Public,* pg. 976

SLIDE N'STACK—NONE—Rubbermaid Incorporated; *U.S. Public,* pg. 1411

SLIDE-O-MATIC—Luggage—Hartmann Luggage & Leather Goods Group; *U.S. Public,* pg. 261

SLIDE RING—Loose-Leaf Notebook—The Mead Corporation; *U.S. Public,* pg. 1074

SLIDE-SCAN—Slide Projector Screens—Eastman Kodak Company; *U.S. Public,* pg. 550

SLIDE-SHO—Office Supplies—JM Company; *U.S. Private,* pg. 577

SLIDELOCK—NONE—The Crown Divisions; *U.S. Public,* pg. 1631

SLIDEOUT—NONE—The Crown Divisions; *U.S. Public,* pg. 1631

SLIDERS—Bowling Shoes—E.J. Footwear Corp.; *U.S. Public,* pg. 1684

SLIDING SIDE DOOR—Circulating Device—Halliburton Energy Services; *U.S. Public,* pg. 776

SLIKWICK SORBENTS—Sorbent Products—The Andersons Incorporated; *U.S. Public,* pg. 111

SLIM—Seismic Lithologic Models—Litton Industries, Inc.; *U.S. Public,* pg. 1002

SLIM—Rolling Writer Pens—Pentel of America, Ltd.; *Int'l,* pg. 1035

SLIM DESIGN—Projection Television—Thomson Consumer Electronics Inc.; *Int'l,* pg. 1383

SLIM-FAST—Weight Loss Product—Slim-Fast Foods Company; *U.S. Private,* pg. 1006

SLIM GRIP—Electric Knife—The Black & Decker Corporation; *U.S. Public,* pg. 233

SLIM JIM—Meat Snacks—GoodMark Foods, Inc.; *U.S. Public,* pg. 751

SLIM LINE—Food Service Poultry Items—Tyson Foods, Inc.; *U.S. Public,* pg. 1652

SLIM N' TRIM—Low Cal Dairy Products—Hilland Dairy Company; *U.S. Private,* pg. 879

SLIM SCSI—NONE—Adaptec, Inc.; *U.S. Public,* pg. 19

SLIM SET—Food Ingredient—Firmenich; *Int'l,* pg. 486

SLIM STAMP—Pre-Inked Address Stamp—John H. Harland Company; *U.S. Public,* pg. 785

SLIM VEE PAC—Railroad Filters—Donaldson Company, Inc.; *U.S. Public,* pg. 517

SLIME-TROL—Biocides—BetzDearborn Inc.; *U.S. Public,* pg. 226

SLIMESSENCE—Labels—Avery Dennison Corporation Label Group; *U.S. Public,* pg. 153

SLIMLINE—Electric Lamps—General Electric Canada Inc.; *U.S. Public,* pg. 713

SLIMLINE—Compressor—Norwalk Co., Inc.; *U.S. Private,* pg. 807

SLIMLINE—Bed Pan Washers—Sloan Valve Company; *U.S. Private,* pg. 1006

SLIMLINE—Broom—Stanhome Inc.; *U.S. Public,* pg. 1508

SLIMLINE—Rug Shampoo Brush—Stanhome Inc.; *U.S. Public,* pg. 1508

SLIMLINE LOW FAT MILKS—NONE—Lancashire Dairies Ltd.; *Int'l,* pg. 798

SLIMLINE SLIVER DUSTER COVER—Duster—Stanhome Inc.; *U.S. Public,* pg. 1508

SLIMLINE SPONGE MOP—Sponge Mop—Stanhome Inc.; *U.S. Public,* pg. 1508

SLIMLINE WALL BRUSH—Wall Brush—Stanhome Inc.; *U.S. Public,* pg. 1508

SLIMLOOK—Foundations—The Strouse, Adler Company; *U.S. Private,* pg. 1047

SLIMLUX—Fluorescent Surface Units—Guth Lighting Company; *Int'l,* pg. 821

SLIMMING—U.K. Health Magazine—EMAP Elan; *Int'l,* pg. 451

SLIMPAC—Semi-Conductor Devices—Semtech Corporation; *U.S. Public,* pg. 1456

SLIMPLANT—Intraocular Lenses—Alcon Laboratories, Inc.; *Int'l,* pg. 916

SLING-PAK—Breathing Apparatus—Scott Aviation; *U.S. Public,* pg. 622

SLINGER—Writing Instruments—Gillette Co.-Parker Pen USA; *U.S. Public,* pg. 745

SLINKY—Original Walking Spring Toy—James Industries Inc.; *U.S. Private*, pg. 580
SLIP AND SLIDE—Water Toy—Mattel, Inc.; *U.S. Public*, pg. 1057
SLIP AND SLIDE—Water Toy—Mattel Power Wheels; *U.S. Public*, pg. 1058
SLIP-FREE—Specimen Bags—Uniflex, Inc.; *U.S. Public*, pg. 1665
SLIP 'N SPLASH—Water Slide—Mattel, Inc.; *U.S. Public*, pg. 1057
SLIP OFF—Oven Protector—Stanhome Inc.; *U.S. Public*, pg. 1508
SLIP-PLATE—Lubricant—Superior Graphite Co.; *U.S. Private*, pg. 1054
SLIPICONE—Home Maintenance Silicone Lubricant—Dow Corning Corporation; *U.S. Public*, pg. 523
SLIPLOCK—Exercise Equipment—Bollinger Industries Inc.; *U.S. Public*, pg. 243
SLIPSHEET—NONE—Chemfab Corporation; *U.S. Public*, pg. 344
SLIQUID—Level Controls—Dwyer Instruments Inc.; *U.S. Private*, pg. 350
SLITTERMATE—Auto Position Slitter Control System—Harnischfeger Industries, Inc.; *U.S. Public*, pg. 788
SLO-BID—Drug Used for the Treatment of Bronchial Disorders—Rhone-Poulenc Rorer - U.S.; *Int'l*, pg. 1110
SLO-BLO—Fuses—Littelfuse, Inc.; *U.S. Public*, pg. 1001
SLO-LAG—Fuses—Eagle Electric Mfg. Co., Inc.; *U.S. Private*, pg. 354
SLO-SPEED—Speed Drives—Sterling Electric, Inc.; *U.S. Private*, pg. 1041
SLOANE—NONE—ETEX; *Int'l*, pg. 430
SLOAN'S—External Analgesic—C. B. Fleet Co., Inc.; *U.S. Private*, pg. 410
SLOANS—Grocery Stores—Red Apple Companies; *U.S. Private*, pg. 914
SLIMTHOTICS—Orthoses for Very High-Heeled or Close-Fitting Shoes—The Langer Biomechanics Group, Inc.; *U.S. Public*, pg. 978
SLOPED CEILING DOWN-LITES—Lighting Fixture—Juno Lighting, Inc.; *U.S. Public*, pg. 935
SLOPHYLLIN—Pharmaceuticals—Rhone-Poulenc Rorer - U.S.; *Int'l*, pg. 1110
SLOTZ—Stationery Products—The Mead Corporation; *U.S. Public*, pg. 1074
SLOW FE—Once-A-Day Iron Supplement—Ciba Specialty Chemicals; *Int'l*, pg. 291
SLOW-K—NONE—Novartis Pharmaceuticals; *Int'l*, pg. 973
SLOW-MAG—Magnesium Supplement—Monsanto Company; *U.S. Public*, pg. 1124
SLOW SCAN VIDEO SYSTEM—Video Security Systems—Diebold, Incorporated; *U.S. Public*, pg. 506
SLUG-BUSTER—Punch—Greenlee Textron; *U.S. Public*, pg. 1589
SLUG SPLITTER—Punch—Greenlee Textron; *U.S. Public*, pg. 1589
SLUGSTER—Shotgun Barrels—O.F. Mossberg & Sons, Inc.; *U.S. Private*, pg. 764
SLUMBER—Mattresses—Sealy Mattress Company of Memphis; *U.S. Private*, pg. 979
SLUMBER COMFORT—Mattress—The Spring Air Company; *U.S. Private*, pg. 1027
SLUMBER KING—Mattress—Simmons Company; *Int'l*, pg. 686
SLUMBER MATES—Slumber Bags—ERO Industries, Inc.; *U.S. Private*, pg. 526
SLUMBER REST COMFORTERS—Comforters—Sunbeam Household Products; *U.S. Public*, pg. 1533
SLUMBER SOX—Bed Socks—Reliable Knitting Works; *U.S. Public*, pg. 920
SLUMBER TENTS—Bed Tents—ERO Industries, Inc.; *U.S. Private*, pg. 526
SLUMBERJACK—Sleeping Bag—American Recreation Products, Inc.; *U.S. Public*, pg. 948
SLUMBERJACK—NONE—Kellwood Company; *U.S. Public*, pg. 948
SLUMBRON—Sleep Pills—Alva/Amco Pharmacal Companies, Inc.; *U.S. Private*, pg. 47
SLURPEE—NONE—7-Eleven Stores; *Int'l*, pg. 693
SLURPEE—Frozen Carbonated Beverage—The Southland Corporation; *Int'l*, pg. 693
SLURRYSTORE—Liquid Manure Storage—A.O. Smith Corporation; *U.S. Public*, pg. 1476

SMACKERS—Snack Crackers—Austin Quality Foods; *U.S. Private*, pg. 100
SMACKS—Ready-Sweetened Puffed Wheat Cereal—Kellogg Company; *U.S. Public*, pg. 947
SMALL ANIMAL—NONE—Schering-Plough Animal Health; *U.S. Public*, pg. 1438
SMALL BUSINESS MINUTE—News Program—Westwood One, Inc.; *Int'l*, pg. 1763
SMALL CARS—NONE—Ford Motor Co. of Canada Ltd; *U.S. Public*, pg. 666
SMALL COMFORTS—Small Comforts—La-Z-Boy Incorporated; *U.S. Public*, pg. 972
SMALL FRY & DESIGN—NONE—Regal Ware, Inc.; *U.S. Private*, pg. 917
THE SMALL HOUSE LINE—Greeting Cards—American Greetings Corporation; *U.S. Public*, pg. 77
SMALL TWIN—Pumps—Hypro Corporation; *U.S. Public*, pg. 1767
SMALL WONDER—Camcorders—Thomson Consumer Electronics Inc.; *Int'l*, pg. 1383
SMALTUM—Building Paints for Exterior & Interior (Retail Uses)—Akzo Nobel N.V.; *Int'l*, pg. 42
SMARAGD—Resilient Flooring—Forbo Holding SA; *Int'l*, pg. 496
SMART—NONE—Daimler-Benz Aktiengesellschaft; *Int'l*, pg. 366
SMART—NONE—FileNet Corporation; *U.S. Public*, pg. 622
SMART—Steckel Mill Advanced Rolling Technoly—Lukens Inc.; *U.S. Public*, pg. 1019
SMART AMP—Communications Products—Shure Brothers Incorporated; *U.S. Private*, pg. 997
SMART & SIMPLE—Services Relating to Factory Automation—General Electric Canada Inc.; *U.S. Public*, pg. 713
SMART BEAT—Fat-Free & Low-Fat Foods—GFA Brands, Inc.; *U.S. Public*, pg. 435
SMART BENDER—Bender—Greenlee Textron; *U.S. Public*, pg. 1589
SMART BOLT—Not Bearing Detection System—General Railway Signal Corp.; *Int'l*, pg. 1194
SMART BRIDGE—Trust Tax Processing—Computer Language Research, Inc.; *U.S. Public*, pg. 421
SMART BUY—Non-Food Products—Smart & Final; *Int'l*, pg. 563
SMART CAT—Dry Cat Food—Ralston Purina Company; *U.S. Public*, pg. 1359
SMART CHOICE—NONE—American Greetings Corporation; *U.S. Public*, pg. 77
SMART CHOICE—NONE—The Oshawa Group Limited; *Int'l*, pg. 1012
SMART CONVEYOR—NONE—Gilman; *Int'l*, pg. 1389
SMART CORD—Extension Cords—General Cable Corporation; *Int'l*, pg. 1486
SMART CROW FLIGHT INTERNATIONAL—Combat Readiness Training Services—The Flight International Group, Inc.; *U.S. Public*, pg. 654
SMART CUISINE—Frozen Prepared Foods—Freezer Queen Foods Inc.; *Int'l*, pg. 340
SMART DOCUMENTS—Anti-counterfeit Documents—John H. Harland Company; *U.S. Public*, pg. 785
SMART FEED—Chemical Feed Systems—Diversey Water Technologies, Inc.; *U.S. Public*, pg. 1150
SMART FIT—Car seat—Century Products Co.; *U.S. Private*, pg. 226
SMART FLANGE PLUS—Mechanical Connection Between Pipes—Oceaneering International, Inc.; *U.S. Public*, pg. 1211
SMART LOAN—Consolidation Plan—SLM Holding Corp.; *U.S. Public*, pg. 1419
SMART MARKETING SUITE—Microcomputer Product—Group 1 Software, Inc.; *U.S. Public*, pg. 417
SMART MONEY—Counterfeit Detector Pen—Dri Mark Products, Inc.; *U.S. Private*, pg. 342
SMART MONEY—Magazine—The Hearst Corporation; *U.S. Private*, pg. 515
SMART MOVE—Car Seat—Century Products Co.; *U.S. Private*, pg. 226
SMART MULTIPLEXER—NONE—Westronics, Inc.; *U.S. Public*, pg. 1593
SMART NET—A Family of X.25 Multi Protocol Packet Switches and Pads—Telematics Inc.; *Int'l*, pg. 643

SMART-1—Dataset—Mitel Corporation; *Int'l*, pg. 870
SMART ONE—Controller/Integrator—Nuarc Company, Inc.; *U.S. Private*, pg. 808
SMART ONES—Frozen Meals—H.J. Heinz Co. of Canada Ltd.; *U.S. Public*, pg. 806
SMART ONES—NONE—Weight Watchers Gourmet Food Company; *U.S. Public*, pg. 806
SMART ONES—Low-Fat Frozen Food Entrees—Weight Watchers International, Inc.; *U.S. Public*, pg. 806
SMART OPTIONS—Loan Consolidation Plan—SLM Holding Corp.; *U.S. Public*, pg. 1419
SMART PACK—6 & 8 Packs of Alkaline & Heavy Duty Batteries—RAYOVAC Corporation; *U.S. Private*, pg. 912
SMART REWARDS—Servicing—SLM Holding Corp.; *U.S. Public*, pg. 1419
SMART SCHEDULER—NONE—Kronos Incorporated; *U.S. Public*, pg. 967
SMART SERIES SCALES—Electronic Postal Weighing Scales Available in 5, 10, 30 and 100 lbs. model—Ascom Hasler Mailing Systems, Inc.; *Int'l*, pg. 86
SMART SHIRTS—NONE—Kellwood Company; *U.S. Public*, pg. 948
SMART SHOPPER—Memo Books—The Mead Corporation; *U.S. Public*, pg. 1074
SMART SIZE—Baking Mixes—General Mills, Inc.; *U.S. Public*, pg. 717
SMART START—Cereal Bar—Kellogg Company; *U.S. Public*, pg. 947
SMART STRAPS—Bras—Olga Div.; *U.S. Public*, pg. 1738
SMART SYSTEM—Media Learning Center—Dukane Corporation; *U.S. Private*, pg. 345
SMART T CAR—High Speed Automatic Transfer Vehicle—Jervis B. Webb Company; *U.S. Private*, pg. 1156
SMART TEMPTATIONS—Fat Free Tortilla Chips, Salsas, Salad Dressings & BeanDips—RCB Baking Company; *U.S. Public*, pg. 1354
SMART TIME—Apparel—I. Appel Corporation; *U.S. Private*, pg. 78
SMART-TRAK—Data Acquisition & Mgmt. System—Diversey Water Technologies, Inc.; *U.S. Public*, pg. 1150
SMART-UPS—Uninterruptible Power Supplies—American Power Conversion Corporation; *U.S. Public*, pg. 89
SMART-UPS V/S—Uninterruptible Power Supplies—American Power Conversion Corporation; *U.S. Public*, pg. 89
SMART VENT—Anchored Venting Device—Oceaneering International, Inc.; *U.S. Public*, pg. 1211
SMART VIEW—Paperless Recorder—Westronics, Inc.; *U.S. Public*, pg. 1593
SMARTADDRESSER—Microcomputer Software for Canadian Mailers—Group 1 Software, Inc.; *U.S. Public*, pg. 417
SMARTBUS—Cable Network—Atlas/Soundolier; *U.S. Private*, pg. 64
SMARTCARE—Service Product—GE Capital/IT Solutions; *U.S. Public*, pg. 711
SMARTCOM EXEC—Communications Software—Hayes Microcomputer Products, Inc.; *U.S. Public*, pg. 801
SMARTCOM FOR WINDOWS—Communications Software—Hayes Microcomputer Products, Inc.; *U.S. Public*, pg. 801
SMARTCOM III—Communications Software—Hayes Microcomputer Products, Inc.; *U.S. Public*, pg. 801
SMARTCOM II FOR APPLE MACINTOSH—Communications Software—Hayes Microcomputer Products, Inc.; *U.S. Public*, pg. 801
SMARTEE—Sporting Equipment—Brunswick Bowling & Billiards Corp.; *U.S. Public*, pg. 265
SMARTFISH—NONE—Gems Sensors; *U.S. Public*, pg. 481
SMARTFOOD—Popcorn—Frito-Lay Company; *U.S. Public*, pg. 1277
SMARTFOODS—Snack Foods—Smartfoods, Inc.; *U.S. Public*, pg. 1277
SMARTIES—Sweet & Sour Candy Rolls—Ce De Candy, Inc.; *U.S. Private*, pg. 220
SMARTIES—Candies—Nestle-Rowntree Ltd.; *Int'l*, pg. 921
SMARTIES—Candy—Nestle S.A.; *Int'l*, pg. 915

SMARTIES CANDY MONEY—Sweet & Sour Coins—Ce De Candy, Inc.; *U.S. Private,* pg. 220

SMARTIES NECKLACES—Sweet & Sour Beaded Pieces—Ce De Candy, Inc.; *U.S. Private,* pg. 220

SMARTIES POPS—Sweet & Sour Lollipops-Wrapped—Ce De Candy, Inc.; *U.S. Private,* pg. 220

SMARTLEVEL—Electronic Levels—Macklanburg-Duncan Co.; *U.S. Private,* pg. 692

SMARTLINK—Host-PC Link for Masterpiece GL Data—Computer Associates International, Inc.; *U.S. Public,* pg. 420

SMARTLINK—Miniature Measurement Module—Keithley Instruments, Inc.; *U.S. Public,* pg. 946

SMARTLOOK—Traffic Characterization Sensor—The Titan Corporation; *U.S. Public,* pg. 1618

SMARTLOOKUP—Microcomputer Software for Canadian Mailers—Group 1 Software, Inc.; *U.S. Public,* pg. 417

SMARTMAILER—NONE—Pitney Bowes Inc.; *U.S. Public,* pg. 1303

SMARTMODEM OPTIMA 96 & FAX 96—Modem & Fax—Hayes Microcomputer Products, Inc.; *U.S. Public,* pg. 801

SMARTMODEM OPTIMA 144 & FAX 144—Modem & Fax—Hayes Microcomputer Products, Inc.; *U.S. Public,* pg. 801

SMARTMONEY (WITH DOW JONES)—Magazine—Hearst Magazines Division; *U.S. Private,* pg. 516

SMARTNET—NONE—ECI Telecom Ltd.; *Int'l,* pg. 643

SMARTORQUE—Hoist Control—Harnischfeger Industries, Inc.; *U.S. Public,* pg. 788

SMARTPRO DATA CENTER—Network Server UPS System—Trippe Mfg. Co.; *U.S. Private,* pg. 1104

SMARTPROBE—NONE—GenRad, Inc.; *U.S. Public,* pg. 731

SMARTRAK—System—Harnischfeger Industries, Inc.; *U.S. Public,* pg. 788

SMARTRIEVE—Text Search & Retrieval Software—Encyclopaedia Britannica, Inc.; *U.S. Private,* pg. 375

SMARTS—Area Radiation (RF) Monitor—L3 Communications Narda-Microwave Div.; *U.S. Private,* pg. 638

SMARTSONIC—Acoustic Sensors, Microprocessors—Lucent Technologies Inc.; *U.S. Public,* pg. 1017

SMARTSORT—Microcomputer Software for Canadian Mailers—Group 1 Software, Inc.; *U.S. Public,* pg. 417

SMARTSTAR—NONE—Sapiens International Corporation N.V.; *Int'l,* pg. 1193

SMARTSTART—For Underwriting Life Insurance & Loan Service—American Automobile Association; *U.S. Private,* pg. 50

SMARTSUITE—Business Applications Software—Lotus Development Corporation; *U.S. Public,* pg. 896

SMARTSUITE APPROACH—Business Applications Software—Lotus Development Corporation; *U.S. Public,* pg. 896

SMARTSUITE FREELANCE GRAPHICS—NONE—Lotus Development Corporation; *U.S. Public,* pg. 896

SMARTSUITE 1-2-3—NONE—Lotus Development Corporation; *U.S. Public,* pg. 896

SMARTSUITE ORGANIZER—NONE—Lotus Development Corporation; *U.S. Public,* pg. 896

SMARTSUITE WORDPRO—NONE—Lotus Development Corporation; *U.S. Public,* pg. 896

SMARTTOUCH—NONE—Pitney Bowes Inc.; *U.S. Public,* pg. 1303

SMARTTOUCH—Nylon Hook & Loop—YKK (U.S.A.); *Int'l,* pg. 1515

SMARTTRACK—NONE—Pitney Bowes Inc.; *U.S. Public,* pg. 1303

SMARTVANE—Pressure Compensated Pump With Electro-Hydraulic Controls—Robert Bosch Fluid Power Corporation; *Int'l,* pg. 204

SMARTVISOR—accessory—Carefree of Colorado; *U.S. Public,* pg. 217

SMARTWASHER—Parts Washer—Intelligent Systems Corp.; *U.S. Public,* pg. 888

SMARTWINDOW—NONE—LORAD Corporation; *U.S. Public,* pg. 1595

SMASH—Hair Products—Dena Corporation; *U.S. Private,* pg. 324

SMASH HITS—U.K. Entertainment Magazine—EMAP Metro; *Int'l,* pg. 451

'SMATH—Game—Pressman Toy Corp.; *U.S. Private,* pg. 882

SMEADLINK—Records Management Software—Smead Manufacturing Company; *U.S. Private,* pg. 1006

SMILE SAVER—Camera Kit—Eastman Kodak Company; *U.S. Public,* pg. 550

SMILE SAVER—Disposable Toothbrushes—Venturi Inc.; *U.S. Private,* pg. 1136

SMILEY—Cookies & Cookie Face—Eat N Park Restaurants; *U.S. Private,* pg. 358

SMIRNOFF—Spirits—Gilbeys of Ireland; *Int'l,* pg. 409

SMIRNOFF—Vodka—Grand Metropolitan Plc; *Int'l,* pg. 408

SMIRNOFF—Vodka—Heublein, Inc.; *Int'l,* pg. 410

SMIRNOFF—NONE—International Distillers Caribbean; *Int'l,* pg. 410

SMIRNOFF—NONE—Societe Pour la Vente des Produits Cinzano SA; *Int'l,* pg. 410

SMIRNOFF—NONE—Tegner & Son AB; *Int'l,* pg. 412

SMIRNOFF BLACK—NONE—Heublein, Inc.; *Int'l,* pg. 410

SMIRNOFF BLACK—NONE—The Pierre Smirnoff Company; *Int'l,* pg. 411

SMIRNOFF BLUE—NONE—The Pierre Smirnoff Company; *Int'l,* pg. 411

SMIRNOFF CITRUS—NONE—The Pierre Smirnoff Company; *Int'l,* pg. 411

SMIRNOFF CITRUS TWIST—NONE—Heublein, Inc.; *Int'l,* pg. 410

SMIRNOFF RED—NONE—The Pierre Smirnoff Company; *Int'l,* pg. 411

SMITH—Cam Follower & Cam Yoke Roller Needle Bearings—Accurate Bushing Co., Inc.; *U.S. Private,* pg. 11

SMITH—Canned Puddings, Cheese Sauces, Beverages—Major Smith Inc.; *Int'l,* pg. 201

SMITH & HARRIS—Machining Metals—Joy Mining Machinery; *U.S. Public,* pg. 789

SMITH & WESSON—Gunsmith—Tomkins PLC; *Int'l,* pg. 1395

SMITH & DAVIS—NONE—Everest & Jennings, Inc.; *U.S. Public,* pg. 758

SMITH & HAWKEN—Gardening Tools & Accessories—CML Group, Inc.; *U.S. Public,* pg. 279

SMITH & HAWKEN—Gardener's Catalog—Smith & Hawken; *U.S. Public,* pg. 279

SMITH & WESSON—Law Enforcement Equip. & Sporting Goods—Smith & Wesson Corp.; *Int'l,* pg. 1397

SMITH BARNEY INC—Financial Institution—Salomon Smith Barney Holdings, Inc.; *U.S. Public,* pg. 1633

SMITH BROTHERS—Cough Drops—F&F Foods; *U.S. Private,* pg. 388

SMITH CORONA—Typewriters—Smith Corona Corp.; *U.S. Private,* pg. 1007

SMITH FIBERGLASS—Pipe—Ryan Herco Products Corp.; *U.S. Private,* pg. 953

SMITH FLOW CONTROL—Safety Interlocks—Halma p.l.c.; *Int'l,* pg. 589

SMITH-MILLS—Boilers—H.B. Smith Co., Inc.; *U.S. Private,* pg. 1008

SMITH'S—Food & Drug Centers—Smith's Food & Drug Centers, Inc.; *U.S. Public,* pg. 1103

SMITH'S—Confections—Van Melle N.V.; *Int'l,* pg. 1450

SMITH'S FLOUR MILLS—Flour & Baking Ingredients—Northern Foods plc; *Int'l,* pg. 967

SMITHFIELD—Meats—Smithfield Foods, Inc.; *U.S. Public,* pg. 1479

SMITHFIELD BRAND—Meat Products—The Smithfield Packing Co., Inc.; *U.S. Public,* pg. 1479

SMITHFIELD SMITTY PIG—NONE—The Smithfield Companies, Inc.; *U.S. Public,* pg. 1479

SMITHFIELD TAVERN—NONE—The Smithfield Companies, Inc.; *U.S. Public,* pg. 1479

SMITHS—Snacks in Australia—United Biscuits (Holdings) Plc; *Int'l,* pg. 1442

SMITHTEMP—Personnel Recruiters—Smith's Personnel Service, Inc.; *U.S. Private,* pg. 1010

SMITHWICK—Fishing Lures—EBSCO Industries, Inc.; *U.S. Private,* pg. 358

SMITHWICK'S ALE—NONE—Guinness Plc; *Int'l,* pg. 412

SMITTEN KITTEN—Greeting Cards, Inv. & Anncnmt. Forms, Calndrs., Thank U Notes, Party Goods—American Greetings Corporation; *U.S. Public,* pg. 77

SMOG-HOG—Electrostatic Precipitator—United Air Specialists, Inc.; *U.S. Public,* pg. 382

SMOKE TEST—Smoke Detector Tester—CRC Industries, Inc.; *U.S. Private,* pg. 138

SMOKE-X—Medicated Lozenges—Alva/Amco Pharmacal Companies, Inc.; *U.S. Private,* pg. 47

SMOKEATER—NONE—Blaw-Knox Construction Equipment Corporation; *U.S. Public,* pg. 877

SMOKEETER—Electrostatic Precipitator—United Air Specialists, Inc.; *U.S. Public,* pg. 382

SMOKEHOUSE—Almonds—Blue Diamond Growers; *U.S. Private,* pg. 152

SMOKER—NONE—Health Products Corporation; *U.S. Private,* pg. 514

THE SMOKER'S CAR—Car For Smokers—Thrifty Rent-a-Car System, Inc.; *U.S. Public,* pg. 354

SMOKER'S PRIDE—Pipe Tobacco—Lane Limited; *Int'l,* pg. 1129

SMOKER'S POLIDENT—Denture Cleanser Powder & Tablets—Block Drug Company, Inc.; *U.S. Public,* pg. 236

SMOKEY JOE—Barbecue Grill—Weber-Stephen Products Co.; *U.S. Private,* pg. 1157

SMOKEY MOUNTAIN—Meat Snacks—GoodMark Foods, Inc.; *U.S. Public,* pg. 751

SMOKEY MOUNTAIN COOKER—Grill—Weber-Stephen Products Co.; *U.S. Private,* pg. 1157

SMOKING TIGER—Cigarette Papers—Kimberly-Clark Corporation; *U.S. Public,* pg. 958

SMOKY MOUNTAIN—Lumber & Wood Products—Georgia-Pacific Corporation; *U.S. Public,* pg. 735

SMOOTH.E—Arterial Blood Sampler—Radiometer America Inc.; *Int'l,* pg. 1083

SMOOTH ILLUSIONS—Hosiery—Hanes Hosiery, Inc.; *U.S. Public,* pg. 1434

SMOOTH ILLUSIONS—Hosiery—Sara Lee Corporation; *U.S. Public,* pg. 1432

SMOOTH LINE—Wall Plates—Eagle Electric Mfg. Co., Inc.; *U.S. Private,* pg. 354

SMOOTH-RITE—Lumpbreaker Roll Cover—Harnischfeger Industries, Inc.; *U.S. Public,* pg. 788

SMOOTH SILHOUETTES—Body Contouring Hosiery—L'eggs Products, Inc.; *U.S. Public,* pg. 1434

SMOOTH TOUCH—Foot Grooming Products—Schering-Plough Corporation; *U.S. Public,* pg. 1438

SMOOTH TREAD MINE SPECIAL—Tires—Bridgestone/Firestone, Inc.; *Int'l,* pg. 213

THE SMOOTHER—Foundations—The Strouse, Adler Company; *U.S. Private,* pg. 1047

SMOOTHIE—Auto Paint Additive—Marson/Creative Fastener, Inc.; *U.S. Private,* pg. 708

SMOOTHIE PEANUT BUTTER CUP—Confectionery—Boyer Candy Company Inc.; *U.S. Private,* pg. 162

SMOOTHIES—Brushes—Wilhold Inc.; *U.S. Public,* pg. 78

SMOOTHPLY—Wood & Lumber Products—Georgia-Pacific Corporation; *U.S. Public,* pg. 735

SMOOTHTOUCH—Footcare Prods.—Scholl U.S.A.; *U.S. Public,* pg. 1438

SMORCON A.R.C.—Reinforcement & Mesh—Smorgon A.R.C.; *Int'l,* pg. 1269

S'MORES GRAHAMS—Cereal—General Mills, Inc.; *U.S. Public,* pg. 717

SMORGASBIRD—Bird Feed—Manna Pro Corporation; *U.S. Private,* pg. 700

SMORGASBURGER—Dog Food—The Quaker Oats Company; *U.S. Public,* pg. 1347

SMTELECOM FUSE—Telecommuncations Fuse—Littelfuse, Inc.; *U.S. Public,* pg. 1001

SMUCKER'S—Preserves & Jellies—J.M. Smucker Company; *U.S. Public,* pg. 1480

SMUD—Toys—Mattel, Inc.; *U.S. Public,* pg. 1057

SMURF-BERRY—Crunch Cereal—Kraft Foods, Inc.; *U.S. Public,* pg. 1287

SMYTHSON OF BOND STREET—Diary Publisher & Retailer of Stationery, Gifts & Luxury Leather Goods—John Menzies plc; *Int'l*, pg. 707

SNACK & PLAY II—Portable High Chair—Evenflo Company, Inc.; *U.S. Private*, pg. 629

SNACK CHEF—Seasoned Pretzels—Snack America; *U.S. Private*, pg. 1010

SNACK ISLAND—Snacks—Snack America; *U.S. Private*, pg. 1010

SNACK OF THE MONTH—Continuity Plan—The Popcorn Factory; *U.S. Private*, pg. 421

SNACK PACK—Puddings—ConAgra, Inc.; *U.S. Public*, pg. 425

SNACK PACK—Canned Snacks—Hunt-Wesson, Inc.; *U.S. Public*, pg. 428

SNACK RITE—Chip & Vegetable Dips—FTI Foodtech International Inc.; *Int'l*, pg. 476

SNACK TO SCHOOL—Continuity Plan—The Popcorn Factory; *U.S. Private*, pg. 421

SNACK WORLD—Snacks—Snack America; *U.S. Private*, pg. 1010

SNACKER—Plastic Tableware—Amoco Corporation; *U.S. Public*, pg. 101

SNACKSTER—Electric Sandwich Maker— Toastmaster, Inc.; *U.S. Public*, pg. 1619

SNACKTIME—Snacks—Borden, Inc.; *U.S. Private*, pg. 157

SNACKWELL'S—Crackers & Cookies—Nabisco Inc.; *U.S. Public*, pg. 1355

SNACKWELL'S—Reduced Fat & Fat Free Cookies—RJR Nabisco Holdings Corp.; *U.S. Public*, pg. 1354

SNAK JAR—Insulated Food Container—The Thermos Company; *Int'l*, pg. 938

SNAK PACK—Insulated Food Container—The Thermos Company; *Int'l*, pg. 938

SNAKE EYES—NONE—Hudepohl-Schoenling Brewing Company; *U.S. Private*, pg. 545

SNAKELIGHT—Household Products—The Black & Decker Corporation; *U.S. Public*, pg. 233

SNAP—NONE—SunGard Data Systems Inc.; *U.S. Public*, pg. 1534

SNAP-CAP—Film Magazines—Eastman Kodak Company; *U.S. Public*, pg. 550

SNAP-CUT—Pruners—Vermont American Tool Corp.; *U.S. Public*, pg. 575

SNAP-FIT—Roof Flashings—Genova Products, Inc.; *U.S. Private*, pg. 447

SNAP-JOINT—Pipe Couplings—Victaulic Company of America; *U.S. Private*, pg. 1138

SNAP-LET—Sprinkler Head Fitting—Victaulic Company of America; *U.S. Private*, pg. 1138

SNAP LOC—Tamper Evident Closures—Clayton Corporation; *U.S. Private*, pg. 244

SNAP-LOC SPACERS—Conduit Spacers—The Lamson & Sessions Co.; *U.S. Public*, pg. 976

SNAP-LOCK—Plastic Bags (Europe Only)—The Dow Chemical Company; *U.S. Public*, pg. 522

SNAP-LOCK—Limit Switches—Namco Controls Corporation; *U.S. Public*, pg. 482

SNAP-LOCK—Connectors—Viking Electronics, Inc.; *U.S. Private*, pg. 1184

SNAP-ON—Mechanics Tools & Related Equip.— Snap-On Tools Corporation; *U.S. Public*, pg. 1480

SNAP-OUT—Portable Scaffold—Up-Right, Inc.; *U.S. Private*, pg. 1128

SNAP-RESEAL—Closures—White Cap, Inc.; *Int'l*, pg. 1207

SNAP-RING—Filters Bags—American Felt & Filter; *U.S. Private*, pg. 54

SNAP SHOP—Bakery Packaging—Tenneco Specialty Products; *U.S. Public*, pg. 1579

SNAP/SHOT—Computer Product—International Business Machines Corporation; *U.S. Public*, pg. 895

SNAP-TITE—Clip on Beryllium Copper Shielding Gasket—Instrument Specialties Company; *U.S. Private*, pg. 565

SNAP TITE—Fasteners—R&B, Inc.; *U.S. Public*, pg. 1354

SNAP TITE—Snap Together Hobby Kits—Revell-Monogram Inc.; *U.S. Private*, pg. 926

SNAP-TOP—Standoffs for Metal Sheets & PCB— Penn Engineering & Manufacturing Corp.; *U.S. Public*, pg. 1269

SNAP TRAC—Crib Assembly System—Cosco, Inc.; *U.S. Private*, pg. 277

SNAP-TY—Form Tieing Device—Richmond Screw Anchor Company; *U.S. Private*, pg. 932

SNAPEASE—NONE—Rubbermaid Incorporated; *U.S. Public*, pg. 1411

SNAPET—NONE—Universal Fasteners Inc.; *Int'l*, pg. 1515

SNAPFLEX—Plastic Quick Disconnect Fittings— NewAge Industries Inc.; *U.S. Private*, pg. 796

SNAPFLEX—Plastic Quick Disconnect Fittings— Newage Industries Inc., Plastics Technology Group; *U.S. Private*, pg. 796

SNAPFORM—Insulation for Pipe Fittings— CertainTeed Corporation; *Int'l*, pg. 1170

SNAPFORM—Packaging Machine System— Printpac-UEB Case Group; *U.S. Public*, pg. 905

SNAPIT—Electrical Specialties—Leviton Mfg. Co., Inc.; *U.S. Private*, pg. 663

SNAPLID—Closure for Re-using Home Canning Jar—Alltrista Corporation; *U.S. Public*, pg. 56

SNAPLOK—Packging Machine System—Printpac-UEB Case Group; *U.S. Public*, pg. 905

SNAPPERS—Refillable Highlighter—Pentel of America, Ltd.; *Int'l*, pg. 1035

SNAPPLE—Soft Drink—Grant-Lydick Beverage Co.; *U.S. Private*, pg. 470

SNAPPLE—Fruit Juice, Soda, Iced Teas & Juice Drinks—Snapple Beverage Company; *U.S. Public*, pg. 1634

SNAPPLE—Premium Beverage—Triarc Companies, Inc.; *U.S. Public*, pg. 1634

SNAPPY—Metal Ducting & Elboforming Machinery—Standex International Corporation; *U.S. Public*, pg. 1505

SNAPPY—Lemon/Lime Drink—UNICER-Uniao Cervejeira, S.A.; *Int'l*, pg. 1432

SNAPPY SET—Hair Styling Lotion—Revlon-Realistic Professional Products, Inc.; *U.S. Private*, pg. 690

SNAPS—Interior Walls and Countertops—Monarch Tile, Inc.; *U.S. Private*, pg. 287

SNAPSALE—Loan Sales—SLM Holding Corp.; *U.S. Public*, pg. 1419

SNAPSHOT—Computer With Attitude Verification—AlliedSignal Commercial Avionics Systems; *U.S. Public*, pg. 50

SNAPSHOT COPY FOR VSAM—NONE—BMC Software, Inc.; *U.S. Public*, pg. 162

SNAPSWAB—Cleaning Materials for Magnetic Tapes—Eastman Kodak Company; *U.S. Public*, pg. 550

SNAPTRACE—Extruded Flexible Heat Transfer Cement—Thermon Manufacturing Company; *U.S. Private*, pg. 1080

SNAPTROL—Variable Resistors—CTS Corporation; *U.S. Public*, pg. 285

SNAUSAGES—Dog Snacks—H.J. Heinz Company; *U.S. Public*, pg. 805

SNAUSAGES—Dog Treats—The Quaker Oats Company; *U.S. Public*, pg. 1347

SNAUSAGES—NONE—Star-Kist Foods, Inc.; *U.S. Public*, pg. 806

SNEAKS—Stationery Products—The Mead Corporation; *U.S. Public*, pg. 1074

SNEAUX—Casual & Athletic Shoes—Jack Schwartz Shoes, Inc.; *U.S. Private*, pg. 974

SNELLING & SNELLING—Franchisors—Snelling Personnel Services; *U.S. Private*, pg. 1010

SNIAMID—Nylon 6 Engineered Resins & Compounds—Nyltech North America Inc.; *Int'l*, pg. 482

SNICKERS—Candy & Ice Cream—Mars, Incorporated; *U.S. Private*, pg. 707

SNICKERS BRAND—NONE—M&M/Mars; *U.S. Private*, pg. 707

SNIDER'S—Seasonings—Bairnco Corporation; *U.S. Public*, pg. 165

SNIFFER—Measuring Instrument—Bacharach Inc.; *U.S. Private*, pg. 109

SNIFFER—RF Leakage Detection System— ComSonics, Inc.; *U.S. Private*, pg. 260

SNIFFER—Network Analyzer Software—Network Associates, Inc.; *U.S. Public*, pg. 1168

SNIFFER SLEUTH—RF Frequency Agile Leakage Detection System—ComSonics, Inc.; *U.S. Private*, pg. 260

SNIFFMASTER—Network Analyzer Software— Network Associates, Inc.; *U.S. Public*, pg. 1168

SNIP-IT—Pen Refills—Eversharp Pen Co.; *U.S. Private*, pg. 386

SNO BALLS—Snack Cake—Ralston Purina Company; *U.S. Public*, pg. 1359

SNO-CAPS—Candy—Nestle USA; *Int'l*, pg. 916

SNO-CAT—Socks & Knitted Headwear—Wigwam Mills, Inc.; *U.S. Private*, pg. 1175

SNO-EE—Cleaners—James Austin Co.; *U.S. Private*, pg. 99

SNO-FIRE—Socks & Knitted Headwear—Wigwam Mills, Inc.; *U.S. Private*, pg. 1175

SNO-HO—Socks & Knitted Headwear—Wigwam Mills, Inc.; *U.S. Private*, pg. 1175

SNO-KONER—Ice Ball Machine—Gold Medal Products Co.; *U.S. Private*, pg. 459

SNO-STRIPE—Socks & Knitted Headwear— Wigwam Mills, Inc.; *U.S. Private*, pg. 1175

SNO-WITE—NONE—Kiwi Brands Pty. Ltd.; *U.S. Public*, pg. 1434

SNOBOY—Fresh Fruit & Vegetables—Food Services of America; *U.S. Private*, pg. 987

SNOKONETTE—Sno-Kone Machine—Gold Medal Products Co.; *U.S. Private*, pg. 459

SNOLITE—Ready-Mixed White Liquid Paints & Enamel—PPG Industries, Inc.; *U.S. Public*, pg. 1245

SNOPAN—Heat Exchangers—Tranter, Inc.; *U.S. Public*, pg. 521

SNOQUALMIE—Wine—Stimson Lane Ltd.; *U.S. Public*, pg. 1661

SNORKEL—Firefighting Platform—Simon Engineering plc; *Int'l*, pg. 1251

SNORKEL—Aerial Platform, Firefighting—Snorkel; *U.S. Private*, pg. 500

SNORKEL—Gas Forced Air Convection Oven— Vulcan-Hart Corp.; *U.S. Public*, pg. 1322

SNORKELIFT—Aerial Work Platforms—Snorkel; *U.S. Private*, pg. 500

SNORKELPRO—Masks, Snorkles, Fins & Vests— Johnson Worldwide Associates, Inc.; *U.S. Public*, pg. 932

SNORKELS—Crackers—Nabisco Inc.; *U.S. Public*, pg. 1355

SNOTRACE—Snow Melting & De-Icing Systems— Thermon Manufacturing Company; *U.S. Private*, pg. 1080

SNOW BITER—Tires—Bridgestone/Firestone, Inc.; *Int'l*, pg. 213

SNOW CAPS—Candy—Nestle Chocolate & Confection; *Int'l*, pg. 917

SNOW CHIEF—Snow Blowers—TruServ Corporation; *U.S. Private*, pg. 1108

SNOW-FLOSS—Canned Foods—The Fremont Co.; *U.S. Private*, pg. 426

SNOW FRESH—Produce Stabilizer—Monsanto Company; *U.S. Public*, pg. 1124

SNOW KING—Tires—Bridgestone/Firestone, Inc.; *Int'l*, pg. 213

SNOW LILY—Bathroom Tissue—Marcal Paper Mills, Inc.; *U.S. Private*, pg. 701

SNOW-NABSTEDT—Transmission—Snow-Nabstedt Power Transmissions; *U.S. Private*, pg. 36

SNOW POWER—Tires—Bridgestone/Firestone, Inc.; *Int'l*, pg. 213

SNOW SILK—Fragrance—Jean Philippe Fragrances, Inc.; *U.S. Public*, pg. 924

SNOW-SOFT—Paper Napkins—Georgia-Pacific Corporation; *U.S. Public*, pg. 735

SNOW-SOFT EPICURE—Paper Napkins—Georgia-Pacific Corporation; *U.S. Public*, pg. 735

SNOW STALKER—NONE—Rocky Shoes & Boots, Inc.; *U.S. Public*, pg. 1402

SNOWBALL—Christmas Tree Lamp Bulbs— General Electric Canada Inc.; *U.S. Public*, pg. 713

SNOWBOARD LIFE—Magazine—Times Mirror Magazines, Inc.; *U.S. Public*, pg. 1616

SNOWBOARD/SKI RACK—Storage Rack— American Locker Group, Inc.; *U.S. Public*, pg. 85

SNOWBOARDER—Publications & Productions— For Better Living, Inc.; *U.S. Private*, pg. 417

SNOWCAP—NONE—Nestle USA; *Int'l*, pg. 916

SNOWFLAKE DESIGN—Lumber—The Mead Corporation; *U.S. Public*, pg. 1074

SNOWFLITE—Snow Removal Equip.—MTD Products, Inc.; *U.S. Private*, pg. 688

SNOWJET—Spray Nozzle—Spraying Systems Co.; *U.S. Private*, pg. 1026

SNOWLAND OPAQUE—NONE—Fraser Papers, Inc.; *Int'l*, pg. 434

SNOWMASTER—Footwear—Genfoot Inc.; *Int'l*, pg. 549

SNOW'S—NONE—Borden Foods Canada; *U.S. Private*, pg. 159

Brand Name Index

SNOW'S CLAM PRODUCTS—NONE—Castleberry/Snow's Brands Inc.; *U.S. Private*, pg. 219

SNOWY—All Fabric Bleach—Reckitt & Colman Inc.; *Int'l*, pg. 1090

SNUG—Denture Cushions—Mentholatum Company; *Int'l*, pg. 1126

SNUG FIT—Headgear for Sleep Apnea Products—Nellcor Puritan Bennett Incorporated; *U.S. Public*, pg. 1039

SNUG PLUG—Extension Cord—General Cable Corporation; *Int'l*, pg. 1486

SNUG TREDS—Slippers—R.G. Barry Corporation; *U.S. Public*, pg. 192

SNUG-UMS—Children's Sleeping Bags—ERO Industries, Inc.; *U.S. Private*, pg. 526

SNUGGABLES—Reusable Baby Diapers—Medline Industries, Inc.; *U.S. Private*, pg. 728

SNUGGEMS—Disposable Diapers—Kimberly-Clark Corporation; *U.S. Public*, pg. 958

SNUGGLE—Anti-Static Dryer Sheets—Lever Brothers Co.; *Int'l*, pg. 1435

SNUGGLE—Fabric Softener—Unilever Plc; *Int'l*, pg. 1433

SNUGGLE SINGLES—Dryer Sheets—Lever Brothers Co.; *Int'l*, pg. 1435

SNUGGLESOX—Slipper Sox—Totes Incorporated; *U.S. Private*, pg. 111

SNUGLI—Infant Products—Gerry Baby Products Company; *U.S. Private*, pg. 629

SNYDER—Breads—United States Bakery; *U.S. Private*, pg. 1124

SNYDER HEMOVAC—Infection Control System—Bristol-Myers Squibb Company; *U.S. Public*, pg. 253

SNYDER OF BERLIN—Chips & Snacks—Snyder Berlin; *U.S. Private*, pg. 887

SNYDERS—Snack Foods—Curtice Burns Foods; *U.S. Private*, pg. 887

SNYDER'S OF HANOVER—Snacks—Snyder's of Hanover, Inc.; *U.S. Private*, pg. 1011

SO-CLEAN—Filter Vessels & Pressure Filter Systems—American Felt & Filter; *U.S. Private*, pg. 54

SO FINE—Hair Conditioning Products—Wella Group; *Int'l*, pg. 1489

SO FRESH—Mattress Freshener—Surco Products, Inc.; *U.S. Private*, pg. 1056

SO FRO FABRICS, INC.—Retail Chain of Sewing Supplies Stores—House of Fabrics, Inc.; *U.S. Public*, pg. 842

SO FRUITY—Beverage—Q.U.F. Industries Ltd.; *Int'l*, pg. 1074

SO JUICY—Beverage—Q.U.F. Industries Ltd.; *Int'l*, pg. 1074

SO-LARA—Acrylic Fiber—Monsanto Company; *U.S. Public*, pg. 1124

SO-O-O SOFT & DESIGN—Paper Towels, Paper Napkins, Facial Tissue & Toilet Tissue—Georgia-Pacific Corporation; *U.S. Public*, pg. 735

SO/SAN—Biocidal Fabric Softeners—Stepan Company; *U.S. Public*, pg. 1514

SO SHEER—Interfacing—Specialty Textile Products; *U.S. Private*, pg. 1023

SO SLIM—NONE—Kiwi Brands Pty. Ltd.; *U.S. Public*, pg. 1434

SO SOFT—Facial & Bath Tissue—Georgia-Pacific Corporation; *U.S. Public*, pg. 735

SO SOFT—Fabric Labels, Label Tape—PAXAR Corporation; *U.S. Public*, pg. 1266

SOABAR—Label Machinery Tags—Avery Dennison Corporation; *U.S. Public*, pg. 152

SOACLENS—Hard Contact Lense Wetting & Soaking Solution—Alcon Laboratories, Inc.; *Int'l*, pg. 916

SOAG—Precision Machinery—Hunter Douglas N.V.; *Int'l*, pg. 639

SOAK CITY—Waterpark—Cedar Fair, L.P.; *U.S. Public*, pg. 319

SOAK CITY—NONE—Cedar Point; *U.S. Public*, pg. 319

SOAP OPERA CHALLENGE—Game—The United States Playing Card Company; *U.S. Private*, pg. 1125

SOAP OPERA DIGEST—Magazine—Soap Opera Digest; *U.S. Public*, pg. 1328

SOAP OPERA MAGAZINE—Newspaper—American Media, Inc.; *U.S. Public*, pg. 87

SOAP OPERA NEWS—Digest Size Newspaper—American Media, Inc.; *U.S. Public*, pg. 87

SOAPMASTER—Soap Dispensers—Steiner Co., Inc.; *U.S. Public*, pg. 1039

SOARER—Automobile—Toyota Motor Corporation; *Int'l*, pg. 1411

SOCCER DIGEST—Magazine—Century Publishing Company; *U.S. Private*, pg. 226

SOCCERSTARS—Sports Magazine—IPC Magazines Limited; *Int'l*, pg. 651

SOCEVEX—Peat Moss—Premier CDN Enterprises Ltd.; *Int'l*, pg. 1067

SOCIABLES—Crackers—Nabisco Inc.; *U.S. Public*, pg. 1355

SOCIAL GRACES—Greeting Cards—American Greetings Corporation; *U.S. Public*, pg. 77

SOCIAL SECURITY—Shirts Pants & Jackets Mens—M. Rubin & Sons Inc.; *U.S. Private*, pg. 949

SOCIAL TEA—Biscuits—Nabisco Inc.; *U.S. Public*, pg. 1355

SOCIAL TEA—Biscuits—RJR Nabisco Holdings Corp.; *U.S. Public*, pg. 1354

SOCIETE—Dairy Products—Compagnie Laitiere BESNIER; *Int'l*, pg. 322

SOCIETY & DESIGN—Coffee Maker, Cookware—Regal Ware, Inc.; *U.S. Private*, pg. 917

SOCIETY BRAND, LTD—Men's Apparel—Hartmarx Corporation; *U.S. Public*, pg. 795

SOCIETY FINISHES—Plumbing Products—The Black & Decker Corporation; *U.S. Public*, pg. 233

SOCKOLET—Fittings—Bonney Forge Corporation; *U.S. Private*, pg. 156

SODASORB—Gas Absorbents—W.R. Grace & Co.; *U.S. Public*, pg. 754

SODEREZE—Modified Polyurethane—Phelps Dodge Magnet Wire Co.; *U.S. Public*, pg. 1286

SODEXHO—Catering; Housekeeping; Maintenance—Sodexho S.A.; *Int'l*, pg. 1274

SODEYESUL—RDT Dye—Novartis AG; *Int'l*, pg. 971

SODIUM IODIDE I123—Capsules & Solution Thyroid Imaging—Amersham Healthcare; *Int'l*, pg. 992

SODIUM PENICILLIN G—Sodium Penicillin—Royal Gist-Brocades N.V.; *Int'l*, pg. 1142

SODNET—Turf Reinforcement Netting—Leucadia Inc. Manufacturing Division; *U.S. Public*, pg. 990

SODYESUL—Cellulose Fibers—Clariant International Ltd.; *Int'l*, pg. 624

SOF COMFORT—High Performance Insoles—Schering-Plough Corporation; *U.S. Public*, pg. 1438

SOF-LEX—Discs, Polishing, Dental—3M; *U.S. Public*, pg. 1604

SOF N' FREE—Ethnic Hair Care Products—Johnson Products Co., Inc.; *U.S. Public*, pg. 915

SOF 'N SOIL—Lawn & Garden Gypsum for Soil Conditioning—USG Corporation; *U.S. Public*, pg. 1660

SOF SPUN—Crepe Soles for Shoes—The Goodyear Tire & Rubber Company; *U.S. Public*, pg. 752

SOF STRENGTH—Bathroom Tissues, Cleansing Tissues—Georgia-Pacific Corporation; *U.S. Public*, pg. 735

SOF' STROKE—Lather Shave, Brushless Shave Creams—The Mennen Company; *U.S. Public*, pg. 397

SOF-T—Heavy Knit Athletic Socks—Wigwam Mills, Inc.; *U.S. Private*, pg. 1175

SOFA PLUS—Sleeper Mechanisms—Leggett & Platt, Incorporated; *U.S. Public*, pg. 985

SOFGRIP—Cutlery—Russell Harrington Cutlery Inc.; *U.S. Private*, pg. 551

SOFGUARD—Eye Shield—Alcon Laboratories, Inc.; *Int'l*, pg. 916

SOFI—Ice Cream Freezer—Mitsubishi Heavy Industries Ltd.; *Int'l*, pg. 873

SOFIA—Sanitary Preparations & Instructions—Sime Darby Berhad; *Int'l*, pg. 1249

SOFINA—Cosmetics—Kao Corporation; *Int'l*, pg. 717

SOFISTICARTS—Carts Designed to be used in the Kitchen or Dining Room—Ecolab Inc.; *U.S. Public*, pg. 562

SOFKEY—Elastomer Key Panel—Transico Incorporated; *U.S. Public*, pg. 1630

SOFLAN—Fabric Softeners—Colgate-Palmolive Company; *U.S. Public*, pg. 397

SOFLENS—Contact Lens—Bausch & Lomb Incorporated; *U.S. Public*, pg. 194

SOFNIT—NONE—Medline Industries, Inc.; *U.S. Private*, pg. 728

SOFPAC—Bathroom Tissue—Marcal Paper Mills, Inc.; *U.S. Private*, pg. 701

SOFRADEX—Eye Antiseptic—SmithKline Beecham Research Limited; *Int'l*, pg. 1266

SOFRAMYCIN EYE—Eye Antiseptic—SmithKline Beecham Research Limited; *Int'l*, pg. 1266

SOFRAMYCIN SKIN—Dermatological/Anti-Infective—SmithKline Beecham Research Limited; *Int'l*, pg. 1266

SOFRATULLE—Dermatological/Anti-Infective—SmithKline Beecham Research Limited; *Int'l*, pg. 1266

SOFSILK—Sutures—U.S. Surgical Corp.; *U.S. Public*, pg. 1687

SOFSPIN—Contact Lens—Bausch & Lomb Incorporated; *U.S. Public*, pg. 194

SOFT AC FORMAT—24-Hour Satellite Delivered Music Format—Westwood One, Inc.; *U.S. Public*, pg. 1763

SOFT-AIRE—Clutches & Brakes—P/A Industries, Inc.; *U.S. Private*, pg. 825

SOFT & BEAUTIFUL—Hair Products—Pro-Line Corporation; *U.S. Private*, pg. 887

SOFT & DRI—Anti-Perspirants—The Gillette Company; *U.S. Public*, pg. 743

SOFT & GENTLE—NONE—Colgate-Palmolive; *U.S. Public*, pg. 398

SOFT & THIN—Feminine Napkins—The Tranzonic Companies; *U.S. Public*, pg. 1632

SOFT BATCH—Cookies—Keebler Company; *U.S. Public*, pg. 657

SOFT BLOOM—Towels & Tissues—Dillard, A ResourceNet International Company; *U.S. Public*, pg. 901

SOFT BUBBLE—Bubble Gum—Farley Candy Company; *U.S. Public*, pg. 397

SOFT-CELL—Foam Tray—Amoco Corporation; *U.S. Public*, pg. 101

SOFT FEEL—Leather Like Coating—Red Spot Paint & Varnish Co.; *U.S. Private*, pg. 915

SOFT-FIT—Bed Linens—Medline Industries, Inc.; *U.S. Private*, pg. 728

SOFT-FLO—Aerator—The Chicago Faucet Co.; *U.S. Private*, pg. 234

SOFT-FLO—Anti-Surge Eye Wash Heads—Haws Drinking Faucet Co.; *U.S. Private*, pg. 512

SOFT IRON—Vinly Covered Iron Dumbells—Hofmann Industries, Inc.; *U.S. Private*, pg. 533

SOFT JOYS—NONE—Acushnet Company; *U.S. Public*, pg. 675

SOFT-JOYS—Golf Shoes—Fortune Brands, Inc.; *U.S. Public*, pg. 674

SOFT-JOYS—NONE—Titleist & Foot-Joy Worldwide; *U.S. Public*, pg. 675

SOFT LOOK—Protective & Decorative Industrial & Automotive Coatings—PPG Industries, Inc.; *U.S. Public*, pg. 1245

SOFT'N BACKEEZY—Rubber Products—Rubatex Corporation; *U.S. Private*, pg. 56

SOFT 'N GENTLE—Health & Beauty Aids—Penn Champ; *U.S. Private*, pg. 145

SOFT'N HANDEEZY—Rubber Products—Rubatex Corporation; *U.S. Private*, pg. 56

SOFT'N KNEEZY—Rubber Products—Rubatex Corporation; *U.S. Private*, pg. 56

SOFT NOTES—Casual Footwear—R.G. Barry Corporation; *U.S. Public*, pg. 192

SOFT-PAC—Software Module—Beckman Instruments, Inc.; *U.S. Public*, pg. 199

SOFT-PAK—Foam Tray—Amoco Corporation; *U.S. Public*, pg. 101

SOFT-PLY—Facial & Bath Tissue, Napkins & Towels—Georgia-Pacific Corporation; *U.S. Public*, pg. 735

SOFT-PULL—Starters, Recoil—Tecumseh Products Co. Engine & Transmission Group; *U.S. Public*, pg. 1566

SOFT RIDERS—Luggage—American Tourister, Inc.; *U.S. Public*, pg. 1430

SOFT SCENT—Liquid Air Freshener—Blue Cross Laboratories; *U.S. Private*, pg. 152

SOFT SCOT—Golf Gloves—Tommy Armour Golf; *U.S. Public*, pg. 1683

SOFT SCOUR—Household Scrubbing Sponge & Pad—3M; *U.S. Public*, pg. 1604

SOFT SCRUB—Mild Abrasive Liquid Cleanser Regular & with Bleach—The Clorox Company; *U.S. Public*, pg. 386

SOFT SET—Hair Setter—Andis Company; *U.S. Private*, pg. 73

SOFT SHEEN—Fabric—Narrow Fabric Industries, Inc.; *U.S. Private*, pg. 774

SOFT SILHOUETTES—Embroidered/Silkscreened Bathroom Sets—Sanderson Plumbing Products Inc.; *U.S. Private*, pg. 964

SOFT STAND—Floor Matting—3M; *U.S. Public*, pg. 1604

SOFT START—NONE—Staodyn Inc.; *U.S. Public*, pg. 1509

SOFT SWIRL—Soft Dessert—Kraft Foods, Inc.; *U.S. Public*, pg. 1287

SOFT-TECH—Soft-Sided Luggage—American Tourister, Inc.; *U.S. Public*, pg. 1430

SOFT TOUCH—Cards; Gift Items; Stationery; Stuffed Toy Figures; Wrap—American Greetings Corporation; *U.S. Public*, pg. 77

SOFT TOUCH—Photographic Cards—American Greetings U.S. Greeting Card Division; *U.S. Public*, pg. 78

SOFT-TOUCH—Egg Collection System or Finger Collector—CTB International Corp.; *U.S. Public*, pg. 284

SOFT TOUCH—Toiletries—The Gillette Company; *U.S. Public*, pg. 743

SOFT WINDOW WEAR—Fabric Treatments—Kirsch; *U.S. Public*, pg. 1176

SOFTAB—NONE—Chip Supply Inc.; *U.S. Private*, pg. 237

SOFTAIR—Detailed Replica Pistols—Daisy Manufacturing Company, Inc.; *U.S. Private*, pg. 308

SOFTASILK—Flour—General Mills, Inc.; *U.S. Public*, pg. 717

SOFTCATCH—Traps—Woodstream Corporation; *U.S. Public*, pg. 566

SOFTCO—NONE—Southern Ohio Fabricators, Inc.; *U.S. Private*, pg. 1017

SOFTEE—Occupational Protective Belt—Klein Tools Inc.; *U.S. Private*, pg. 625

SOFTENEX—Stool Softener Drops—Alva/Amco Pharmacal Companies, Inc.; *U.S. Private*, pg. 47

SOFTER THAN SOFT—Concentrated Fabric Conditioner—Shaklee Corporation; *Int'l*, pg. 1518

SOFTEX—Facial & Bath Tissue & Paper Napkins—Georgia-Pacific Corporation; *U.S. Public*, pg. 735

SOFTFIT—Nasal CPAP Mask—Nellcor Puritan Bennett Incorporated; *U.S. Public*, pg. 1039

SOFTHEAT—Electric Hot Water Baseboard Heater—Nordyne Inc.; *U.S. Public*, pg. 1193

SOFTHEAT RADIANT—Antenna De-Icing—Raychem Corporation; *U.S. Public*, pg. 1362

SOFTIES—Greeting Cards—American Greetings Corporation; *U.S. Public*, pg. 77

SOFTINA—Dolls—Goldberger Doll Mfg. Company, Inc.; *U.S. Private*, pg. 459

SOFTIQUE—Facial Tissue—Kimberly-Clark Corporation; *U.S. Public*, pg. 958

SOFTITE—Hot Dipped Galvanized Steel—WHX Corporation; *U.S. Public*, pg. 1726

SOFTITE 21—DQSK Hot Dipped Galvanized Steel—WHX Corporation; *U.S. Public*, pg. 1726

SOFTLINE—Eyeliner & Eyebrow Pencils—Cover Girl Cosmetics; *U.S. Public*, pg. 1330

SOFTLINER—Extruded Plastic Net—Nalle Plastics Inc.; *U.S. Private*, pg. 773

SOFTLIPS—Lip Protection—Mentholatum Company; *Int'l*, pg. 1126

SOFTONE—Wrist & Ankle Weights—Bollinger Industries Inc.; *U.S. Public*, pg. 243

SOFTOUCH—Wrist & Ankle Weights—Bollinger Industries Inc.; *U.S. Public*, pg. 243

SOFTOUCH—Catheters—Mallinckrodt Inc.; *U.S. Public*, pg. 1039

SOFTOUCH—Soft, Leather-like Coating—Morton Automotive Coatings; *U.S. Public*, pg. 1135

SOFTPOD—NONE—GenRad, Inc.; *U.S. Public*, pg. 731

SOFTPROBE—NONE—GenRad, Inc.; *U.S. Public*, pg. 731

SOFTSEAL-D—Disposable Respirator—U.S. Safety; *U.S. Private*, pg. 1125

SOFTSOAP—Liquid Soap—Colgate-Palmolive Co., Institutional Products Div.; *U.S. Public*, pg. 397

SOFTSOAP—Liquid Soap—Colgate-Palmolive Company; *U.S. Public*, pg. 397

SOFTSPOTS—Footwear—Morse Shoe, Inc.; *U.S. Public*, pg. 168

SOFTSPUN YARNS—For Ring Spun Cotton Yarns—Harriet & Henderson Yarns, Inc.; *U.S. Private*, pg. 504

SOFTSTIX—Cheese Filled Soft Pretzels—J & J Snack Foods Corporation; *U.S. Public*, pg. 916

SOFTSTONE—Rubber Flooring—Dodge Regupol, Inc.; *U.S. Private*, pg. 337

SOFTSTRAND—Coated Glass Fiber Technology—Owens Corning; *U.S. Public*, pg. 1236

SOFTTOUCH—Bottled Water Cooler—Sunroc Corporation; *U.S. Public*, pg. 1053

SOFTWARE DEVELOPMENT—Magazine—Miller Freeman Inc.; *Int'l*, pg. 1443

SOFTWARE ETC.—Computer Software Retailer—Babbage's Etc. LLC; *U.S. Private*, pg. 108

SOFTWARE MALL—Computer Product—International Business Machines Corporation; *U.S. Public*, pg. 895

SOFTWARE UTILITIES—NONE—MapInfo Corp.; *U.S. Public*, pg. 1042

SOFTWARE; VIDEO PROD.—Software, Video—PCI; *U.S. Private*, pg. 826

SOFTWEAR—Home & Office Products—The Mead Corporation; *U.S. Public*, pg. 1074

SOFTWELD—ELectrode—The Lincoln Electric Company; *U.S. Public*, pg. 996

SOGA—Newsprint—Haindl Papier GmbH; *Int'l*, pg. 586

SOGETI—NONE—CAP Gemini S.A.; *Int'l*, pg. 263

SOHIO—Petroleum Products—BP Oil Co.; *Int'l*, pg. 220

SOIL-BUILDER—Coulter Chisel—Brillion Iron Works, Inc.; *U.S. Public*, pg. 933

SOIL COMMANDER—Coulter Chisel—Brillion Iron Works, Inc.; *U.S. Public*, pg. 933

SOIL IMPLANT—Nitrogen Fixing Inoculant—LiphaTech, Inc.; *Int'l*, pg. 812

SOIL SENTRY—Leak Detection & Monitoring System—Arizona Instrument Corporation; *U.S. Public*, pg. 129

SOILA'WAY—Dishwashing Detergent—Ecolab Inc.; *U.S. Public*, pg. 562

SOILAX—Laundri Soil-Out, Destainer, Neutralizer, Prep—Ecolab Inc.; *U.S. Public*, pg. 562

SOILAX ALL PURPOSE CLEANER—Floor Care Product—Ecolab Inc.; *U.S. Public*, pg. 562

SOILAX PROFESSIONAL—Insecticide—Ecolab Inc.; *U.S. Public*, pg. 562

SOILECTION—Variable Blend System—Ag-Chem Equipment Co., Inc.; *U.S. Public*, pg. 6

SOILIFE—Fertilizer—Pursell Industries; *U.S. Private*, pg. 896

SOILITE—Machine Warewashing Detergent—Ecolab Inc.; *U.S. Public*, pg. 562

SOILMASTER—Heavy Duty Presoak for all Tableware in High Volume Operations—Ecolab Inc.; *U.S. Public*, pg. 562

SOILMOVER—Earth Movers—Automatic Equipment Mfg. Co.; *U.S. Private*, pg. 101

SOKALAN—Detergent Additives & Dispersants—BASF AG; *Int'l*, pg. 103

SOKREEM—Non-Dairy Sour Cream—Broughton Foods Company; *U.S. Public*, pg. 259

SOL—Mexican Beer—Guinness Import Company; *Int'l*, pg. 412

SOL—Beer—Labatt U.S.A.; *Int'l*, pg. 679

SOL—NONE—Sol Melia; *Int'l*, pg. 1277

SOL CLUB—NONE—Sol Melia; *Int'l*, pg. 1277

SOL ELITE—NONE—Sol Melia; *Int'l*, pg. 1277

SOL INN—NONE—Sol Melia; *Int'l*, pg. 1277

SOL PLUS—NONE—N.V. Johnson Wax Belgium S.A.; *U.S. Private*, pg. 593

SOL-VENT—Filtration Products—Gelman Sciences, Inc.; *U.S. Public*, pg. 1253

SOLA 700 UPS—NONE—Best Power; *U.S. Private*, pg. 140

SOLA 310 UPS—NONE—Best Power; *U.S. Private*, pg. 140

SOLAQUIN—Prescription Drug—ICN Pharmaceuticals, Inc.; *U.S. Public*, pg. 853

SOLAR—Glass—AFG Industries, Inc.; *Int'l*, pg. 84

SOLAR—Table—American Seating Company; *U.S. Private*, pg. 61

SOLAR—Reducing Apparel—Bollinger Industries Inc.; *U.S. Public*, pg. 243

SOLAR—NONE—Carpenter Technology Corporation; *U.S. Public*, pg. 307

SOLAR—Cellulose Fibers—Clariant International Ltd.; *Int'l*, pg. 624

SOLAR—Safety Floorcare Products—Namico, Inc.; *U.S. Private*, pg. 773

SOLAR—Dyes—Novartis AG; *Int'l*, pg. 971

SOLAR—Turbine Products—Solar Turbines Incorporated; *U.S. Public*, pg. 316

SOLAR MAGIC—Shoes—Trimfoot Company; *U.S. Public*, pg. 1684

SOLAR SUIT—Sauna Suit—Bollinger Industries Inc.; *U.S. Public*, pg. 243

SOLAR VISOR/LUNAR VISOR—Sun Visor for Light Truck—Lund International Holdings, Inc.; *U.S. Public*, pg. 1020

SOLARBAN—Multiple Glazed Window Units & Glass Vehicle Transparencies—PPG Industries, Inc.; *U.S. Public*, pg. 1245

SOLARBRONZE—Bronze Tinted Glass—PPG Industries, Inc.; *U.S. Public*, pg. 1245

SOLARCAINE—Sun Care Brand—Schering-Plough Corporation; *U.S. Public*, pg. 1438

SOLARCAINE—First Aid Products—Schering-Plough Healthcare Products Inc.; *U.S. Public*, pg. 1438

SOLARCOOL—Reflective Glass—PPG Industries, Inc.; *U.S. Public*, pg. 1245

SOLAREX—Photovoltaic Cells—Amoco Corporation; *U.S. Public*, pg. 101

SOLARFLEECE—Fleece Products for the Home—Dakotah, Inc.; *U.S. Public*, pg. 477

SOLARFLEX—Interlayer with Solar Rejection—Monsanto Company; *U.S. Public*, pg. 1124

SOLARGRAY—Gray Tinted Glass—PPG Industries, Inc.; *U.S. Public*, pg. 1245

SOLARIS—Socks & Knitted Headwear—Wigwam Mills, Inc.; *U.S. Private*, pg. 1175

SOLARSHIELD—Laminated Reflective Glass—Pilkington Australasia Limited; *Int'l*, pg. 1057

SOLATEX—Solar Glass—AFG Industries, Inc.; *Int'l*, pg. 84

SOLDACTONE—Pharmaceutical Products—Searle Laboratories; *U.S. Public*, pg. 1125

SOLDER BRITE—Flux & Solder—La-Co Industries Markal Company; *U.S. Private*, pg. 640

SOLDER-NU—Solder Removal—Litton Industries, Inc.; *U.S. Public*, pg. 1002

SOLDER OFF—Solder Removal—Litton Industries, Inc.; *U.S. Public*, pg. 1002

SOLDER-SAVER—Dross Recovery Chemical—Litton Industries, Inc.; *U.S. Public*, pg. 1002

SOLDER SEAL—Auto Product—Radiator Specialty Company; *U.S. Private*, pg. 906

SOLDER STRIP 8T—Tin-Lead Strip for Printed Circuit Boards—LeaRonal, Inc.; *U.S. Public*, pg. 982

SOLDERFORMS—Solder Preforms—Litton Industries, Inc.; *U.S. Public*, pg. 1002

SOLDERLOK—NONE—Berg Electronics; *U.S. Public*, pg. 212

SOLDERON—Tin-Lead Alloy Plating—LeaRonal, Inc.; *U.S. Public*, pg. 982

SOLDERPAK—Wire Termination System—Raychem Corporation; *U.S. Public*, pg. 1362

SOLDERQUIK—Tape—Raychem Corporation; *U.S. Public*, pg. 1362

SOLDERSHIELD—Splices & Feedthrus—Raychem Corporation; *U.S. Public*, pg. 1362

SOLDERSLEEVE—Closures—Raychem Corporation; *U.S. Public*, pg. 1362

SOLDERTACTS—Contacts—Raychem Corporation; *U.S. Public*, pg. 1362

SOLE—Laundry & Hand Dishwashing Detergent—Benckiser Consumer Products Inc.; *Int'l*, pg. 185

SOLE SOURCE—NONE—GTE Supply; *U.S. Public*, pg. 697

SOLECONTROL—Universal Remote Controls—Recoton Corporation; *U.S. Public*, pg. 1369

SOLEIL—Felt—American Felt & Filter; *U.S. Private*, pg. 54

SOLEIL—Women's Jewelry—Swank, Inc.; *U.S. Public*, pg. 1543

SOLENOID ACTUATED MECHANICAL CLUTCH COMBINATION—NONE—Regal-Beloit Corporation; *U.S. Public*, pg. 1370

SOLEX—Electric Machines, Equip., Supplies, Incandescent Lamps, X-Ray Apparatus—General Electric Canada Inc.; *U.S. Public*, pg. 713

SOLEX—Achitectural & Automotive Glass—PPG Industries, Inc.; *U.S. Public*, pg. 1245

SOLEXTRA—Tinted Automotive Glass—PPG Industries, Inc.; *U.S. Public*, pg. 1245

SOLEY—Coffee System—Sara Lee Corporation; *U.S. Public*, pg. 1432

SOLFRUNT—Gauges—U.S. Gauge; *U.S. Public*, pg. 100

SOLFRUNT CENTURY—Pressure Gauge—AMETEK, Inc.; *U.S. Public*, pg. 99

SOLICAM—Herbicide—Sandoz Agro, Inc.; *Int'l*, pg. 974

SOLICOR—Steel Solid Core/Non-Asbestos—Victor Products; *U.S. Public*, pg. 480

SOLID BRASS—Bath Accessories—Melard Manufacturing Corporation; *U.S. Private*, pg. 729

SOLID GOLD—Personal Care Products—Windmere-Durable Holdings; *U.S. Public*, pg. 1771

SOLID HIDE—Rustic Stain—Pratt & Lambert United, Inc.; *U.S. Public*, pg. 1466

SOLID POWER—Warewashing Detergent & Dispenser—Ecolab Inc.; *U.S. Public*, pg. 562

SOLID REGAIN—Floor Cleaner—Ecolab Inc.; *U.S. Public*, pg. 562

SOLID STATE STARTERS—Refrigeration Equipment—York International Corporation; *U.S. Public*, pg. 1789

SOLID VINYL TILE—1/8″ Commercial/Residential Vinyl Tile—Kentile Operting Co.; *U.S. Private*, pg. 615

SOLIDEX—Wireless Accessories for Cellular, Video & Computers—Unitech Industries, Inc.; *U.S. Public*, pg. 1672

SOLIDOX—Welding Torch—Sycamore Plant; *U.S. Public*, pg. 444

SOLIDS-FLOW—Valves—Patterson-Kelley Company; *U.S. Public*, pg. 793

SOLIGOR—Lens & Photographic Access.—AIC International, Inc.; *U.S. Private*, pg. 6

SOLIS—Basketball Shoe—K-Swiss Inc.; *U.S. Public*, pg. 937

SOLITAIRE—Surgical Sutures & Needles—Alcon Laboratories, Inc.; *Int'l*, pg. 916

SOLITAIRE ULTRA—Bath Fan & Fanlight—Broan Mfg. Co., Inc.; *U.S. Public*, pg. 1193

SOLITARIE—Pot & Pan Detergent—Ecolab Inc.; *U.S. Public*, pg. 562

SOLITE—Solar Glass—AFG Industries, Inc.; *Int'l*, pg. 84

SOLITEC—NONE—Solitec Wafer Processing, Inc.; *U.S. Private*, pg. 1013

SOLITEL—NONE—Magnetrol International; *U.S. Private*, pg. 696

SOLITHANE—Polyurethane; Room Tempertaure Curing System—Uniroyal Chemical Company, Inc.; *U.S. Public*, pg. 460

SOLKA FLOC—Treated Pulp—Fort James Corporation; *U.S. Public*, pg. 670

SOLKA FLOC—Pharmaceutical Excipient—Penford Corp.; *U.S. Public*, pg. 1269

SOLKWIK—Polymers—Akzo Nobel N.V.; *Int'l*, pg. 42

SOLO—Soft Drink—Cadbury Schweppes p.l.c.; *Int'l*, pg. 247

SOLO—NONE—A.T. Cross Co.; *U.S. Public*, pg. 460

SOLO—Cake & Pastry Fillings—Sokol & Company; *U.S. Private*, pg. 1012

SOLO—Disposable Cups & Dishes—Solo Cup Company; *U.S. Private*, pg. 1013

SOLO-CARE—Contact Lense One-Step Cleaning & Disinfection Product—Novartis; *Int'l*, pg. 972

SOLO CLASSIC—NONE—A.T. Cross Co.; *U.S. Public*, pg. 460

SOLO PARA TI—Cosmetics—AM Cosmetics Inc.; *U.S. Private*, pg. 6

SOLO-TRAK—Lead Introducer—Medtronic, Inc.; *U.S. Public*, pg. 1082

SOLO II—Business Telephone Providing Access to Three Outside Lines—Comdial Corporation; *U.S. Public*, pg. 407

SOLOFLEX—Solution SBR—The Goodyear Tire & Rubber Company; *U.S. Public*, pg. 752

SOLOFLEX—Flexo Printing Press—Windmoeller & Hoelscher; *Int'l*, pg. 1510

SOLOGOGGLE—Goggle—The Fibre-Metal Products Company; *U.S. Private*, pg. 402

SOLOK—NONE—Berg Electronics; *U.S. Public*, pg. 212

SOLONOX—Turbine Products—Solar Turbines Incorporated; *U.S. Public*, pg. 316

SOLOSELE—Hydraulic Seal—James Walker & Co. Limited; *Int'l*, pg. 1485

SOLOWRAP—Laminates—Reynolds Metals Company; *U.S. Public*, pg. 1385

SOLPADEINE—NONE—SmithKline Beecham Corporation; *Int'l*, pg. 1264

SOLTICE—Cold Products—Chattem, Inc.; *U.S. Public*, pg. 341

SOLTICE—Analgesic Rub—Chattem, Inc., Consumer Products Division; *U.S. Public*, pg. 341

SOLU-MEDROL—Hormone—Pharmacia & Upjohn; *Int'l*, pg. 1048

SOLUDEX—Tableting Agent for Pharmaceuticals—Penford Corp.; *U.S. Public*, pg. 1269

SOLUENE 350—Proteinaceous Tissue Solubilizer—Packard Instrument Co., Inc.; *U.S. Private*, pg. 833

SOLUS—Pacemaker—St. Jude Medical, Inc.; *U.S. Public*, pg. 1427

SOLUS 4—LED Plotter—CalComp Technology, Inc.; *U.S. Public*, pg. 1007

SOLUTION—NONE—Avon Products Co., Ltd.; *U.S. Public*, pg. 156

SOLUTION—Dry Water Soluble Selective Herbicide—Riverdale Chemical Co.; *U.S. Private*, pg. 934

SOLUTION 555—Rotor Cleaning Concentrate—Beckman Instruments, Inc.; *U.S. Public*, pg. 199

SOLUTION (SM) BUSINESS SERVICES—Dedicated & Switched-Access Commercial Services—Frontier Communications Services; *U.S. Public*, pg. 684

SOLUTIONPAC—Computer Product—International Business Machines Corporation; *U.S. Public*, pg. 895

SOLUTIONS—Seating—HON Industries Inc.; *U.S. Public*, pg. 772

SOLUTIONS SEATING—Office Seating—The HON Co.; *U.S. Public*, pg. 772

SOLVE—Computer Software—Sterling Software, Inc.; *U.S. Public*, pg. 1516

SOLVENOL—Terpene Liquid—Hercules Incorporated; *U.S. Public*, pg. 809

SOLVENT RECOVERY SYSTEM—Dry Cleaning Compound—Detrex Corporation; *U.S. Public*, pg. 501

SOLVENT III—Chemical—Vulcan Chemicals; *U.S. Public*, pg. 1725

SOLVETS—Soluble Tablets, Lilly—Eli Lilly and Company; *U.S. Public*, pg. 992

SOLVIREX—Insecticide—Novartis AG; *Int'l*, pg. 971

SOLVITOL—Industrial Consumable Aerosol Products—Meristem plc; *Int'l*, pg. 858

SOLVOCAFFARO—Solvent for Colour-Formers—Caffaro S.p.A.; *Int'l*, pg. 248

SOLVOL—Emulsion Soluble Oils—D.A. Stuart Company; *U.S. Public*, pg. 1048

SOLVSEAL—Closure Liner Sealings Materials—Tekni-Plex, Inc.; *U.S. Private*, pg. 1073

SOM-A-PRESS—Dewatering Units for Industrial Sludges—Somat Corporation; *U.S. Public*, pg. 1322

SOM-A-SYSTEM—Sludge Dewatering & Thickening Systems—Somat Corporation; *U.S. Public*, pg. 1322

SOMA—Oral Muscle Relaxant—Wallace Laboratories; *U.S. Public*, pg. 310

SOMA COMPOUND—Oral Muscle Relaxant/Analgesic—Wallace Laboratories; *U.S. Public*, pg. 310

SOMA COMPOUND WITH CODEINE—Oral Muscle Relaxant/Analgesic—Wallace Laboratories; *U.S. Public*, pg. 310

SOMAGARD—Treatment of Prostate Cancer & Children with Precocious Puberty—Roberts Pharmaceutical Corporation; *U.S. Public*, pg. 1393

SOMAT—Wastepulping Systems—Somat Corporation; *U.S. Public*, pg. 1322

SOMAT EVERGREEN—Compact Pulper—Somat Corporation; *U.S. Public*, pg. 1322

SOMATOLINE—Topical/Skincare—SmithKline Beecham plc; *Int'l*, pg. 1264

SOME-BODY—Ladies Panties & Stretch Bras—Alba-Waldensian, Inc.; *U.S. Public*, pg. 35

SOMERS—Gin—The House of Seagram; *Int'l*, pg. 1217

SOMERSET—NONE—S.D. Warren Co.; *Int'l*, pg. 1193

SOMERSET OIL—OIL—Somerset Refinery Inc.; *U.S. Private*, pg. 1013

SOMERTON—NONE—CertainTeed Corporation; *Int'l*, pg. 1170

SOMETHING ELSE—Greeting Cards—American Greetings Corporation; *U.S. Public*, pg. 77

SOMETHING SPECIAL—Women's Retail Specialty Store—Gateway Apparel, Inc.; *U.S. Private*, pg. 441

SOMETHING SPECIAL—Scotch—The Seagram Company Ltd.; *Int'l*, pg. 1214

SOMINEX—Sleep Aid—SmithKline Beecham Consumer Healthcare, U.S.; *Int'l*, pg. 1264

SOMINEX—Sleep Aid—SmithKline Beecham plc; *Int'l*, pg. 1264

SOMINEX PAIN RELIEF FORMULA—Sleep Aid/Pain Relief Medication—SmithKline Beecham Consumer Healthcare, U.S.; *Int'l*, pg. 1264

SOMOBJECTS—Computer Product—International Business Machines Corporation; *U.S. Public*, pg. 895

SOMOS—NONE—Filterwerk Mann & Hummel GmbH; *Int'l*, pg. 484

SON MAGAZINE—French Sound Magazine—EMAP France; *Int'l*, pg. 451

SON OF A GUN—Hairdryer—Bristol-Myers Squibb Company; *U.S. Public*, pg. 253

SON OF BIG CHIEF—Paper Tablets—The Mead Corporation; *U.S. Public*, pg. 1074

SON PRO—French Sound Magazine—EMAP France; *Int'l*, pg. 451

SON VIDEO MAG—French Video Magazine—EMAP France; *Int'l*, pg. 451

SONA—Beans, Vegatables, Fruit & Pickles—Campbell Soup Company; *U.S. Public*, pg. 298

SONA—Household Appliances—The Glen Dimplex Group; *Int'l*, pg. 553

SONADRY—Printing Ink—Van Son Holland Ink Corp. of America; *U.S. Private*, pg. 1133

SONAGLOSS—Printing Ink—Van Son Holland Ink Corp. of America; *U.S. Private*, pg. 1133

SONALAN—Herbicide—The Dow Chemical Company; *U.S. Public*, pg. 522

SONALERT—Audible Signal—North American Capacitor Co.; *U.S. Private*, pg. 803

SONALERT II—Audible Signal—North American Capacitor Co.; *U.S. Private*, pg. 803

SONAR—Aquatic Herbicide—The Dow Chemical Company; *U.S. Public*, pg. 522

SONAR & GPS NAVIGATIONAL EQUIPMENT—Sonar Instruments—Lowrance Electronics, Inc.; *U.S. Public*, pg. 1015

SONATA—Pre-Finished Laminate—Bruce Hardwood Floors; *U.S. Public*, pg. 1634

SONATA—Printing Paper—Georgia-Pacific Corporation; *U.S. Public*, pg. 735

SONATA—Automobile—Hyundai Motor America; *Int'l*, pg. 641

SONATA—Cool Touch Toaster—Salton/Maxim Housewares, Inc.; *U.S. Public*, pg. 1430

SONATORQ—Tension Control—P/A Industries, Inc.; *U.S. Private*, pg. 825

SONATURAL HAIR SPRAY—Electrical Apparatus System to Dispense Hair Spray—Revlon-Realistic Professional Products, Inc.; *U.S. Private*, pg. 690

SONBANOX IM—Esters—Witco Corporation; *U.S. Public*, pg. 1773

SONG AND DANCE—Musical—Really Useful Holdings Limited; *Int'l*, pg. 1089

SONG OF AMERICA—Ships—Royal Caribbean Cruises Ltd.; *U.S. Public*, pg. 1410

SONG OF NORWAY—Ships—Royal Caribbean Cruises Ltd.; *U.S. Public*, pg. 1410

SONGWRITER'S MARKET—Market Book—F & W Publications, Inc.; *U.S. Private*, pg. 388

SONIC—Company Name & Name on Restaurants—Sonic Corporation; *U.S. Public*, pg. 1485

SONIC—Restaurants—Sonic Industries, Inc.; *U.S. Public*, pg. 1485

SONIC DRIVE-IN—Restaurant Types—Sonic Corporation; *U.S. Public*, pg. 1485

SONIC HOLOGRAPHY—Stereophonic System—Carver Corporation; *U.S. Public*, pg. 310

SONIC HOLOGRAPHY-A/VP—Multi-Dimensional Stereophonic System—Carver Corporation; *U.S. Public*, pg. 310

SONIFIER—Cell Disruptor—Branson Ultrasonics Corp.-Plastics Joining Div.; *U.S. Public*, pg. 574

SONIFIER—Cell Disruptor—Branson Ultrasonics Corp. - Precision Cleaning Div.; *U.S. Public*, pg. 574

SONITRON—NONE—Sanyo Espana S.A.; *Int'l*, pg. 1192

SONNAR T—Zoom Lenses—Carl Zeiss; *Int'l*, pg. 1522

SONNEN BASSERMANN—Prepared Dishes, Pasta, Jam—Danone Group; *Int'l*, pg. 379

SONNTAG—Newspaper—Axel Springer Verlag AG; *Int'l*, pg. 102

SONO-LOC—Plastic Forms for Concrete Construction—Sonoco Products Company; *U.S. Public*, pg. 1485

SONO VU-US—Ultrasound-Visible Needle—E-Z-Em, Inc.; *U.S. Public*, pg. 540

SONO-PAL—Paper Shipping Pallets—Sonoco Products Company; *U.S. Public*, pg. 1485

SONOAIRDUCT—Fibre Duct—Sonoco Products Company; *U.S. Public*, pg. 1485

SONOBATTS—Glass Fiber Commercial Insulation—Owens Corning; *U.S. Public*, pg. 1236

SONOCARTRIDGE—Fibre & Plastic Moistureproof Cartridges—Sonoco Products Company; *U.S. Public*, pg. 1485

SONOCO SPECIAL—Premium Motor Oil—Sun Refining & Marketing Co. Lubes Div.; *U.S. Public*, pg. 1530

SONOCO ULTRA SUPER C—Heavy Duty Diesel Motor Oil—Sun Refining & Marketing Co. Lubes Div.; *U.S. Public*, pg. 1530

SONOGLO—Cones Formed of Paper—Sonoco Products Company; *U.S. Public*, pg. 1485

SONOMA GENUINE—Clothing—Kohl's Corporation; *U.S. Public*, pg. 965

SONOMOLD—Fibre Molds for Concrete Testing—Sonoco Products Company; *U.S. Public*, pg. 1485

SONOR—Drums—Hohner/HSS Inc.; *U.S. Private*, pg. 533

SONORORFF—Educational Instruments—Hohner/HSS Inc.; *U.S. Private*, pg. 533

SONOSCOPE—Inspection—Tuboscope Incorporated; *U.S. Public*, pg. 1643

SONOSCOPE-ISOLOG—Inspection—Tuboscope Incorporated; *U.S. Public*, pg. 1643

SONOTRACK—Magnetic Sound-Track Striping—Eastman Kodak Company; *U.S. Public*, pg. 550

SONOTUBE—Fibre Forms for Concrete Columns—Sonoco Products Company; *U.S. Public*, pg. 1485

SONOTUBE PLUS—Fibre Tubes for Concrete Column & Pier Construction—Sonoco Products Company; *U.S. Public*, pg. 1485

SONOVOID—Fibre Tubes for Voiding Concrete—Sonoco Products Company; *U.S. Public*, pg. 1485

SONRISAL—NONE—SmithKline Beecham Corporation; *Int'l*, pg. 1264

SONTARA—Spunlaced Fabric—Du Pont (E.I. Du Pont De Nemours & Co.); *U.S. Public*, pg. 530

SONTEX—Mineral Oils—Penreco; *U.S. Public*, pg. 1273

SONY—NONE—Milgray Electronics, Inc.; *U.S. Public*, pg. 205

SONY—Consumer Electronics—Sony Corporation; *Int'l*, pg. 1280

SONY—Radios, Stereos, Recording Equipment, Video Cameras, VCR's—Sony Electronics; *Int'l*, pg. 1281

SONY CLASSICAL—Recording Label—Sony Music Entertainment, Inc.; *Int'l*, pg. 1281

SONY COMPACT DISC PLAYERS—Disc Players—Sony Electronics; *Int'l*, pg. 1281

SONY DIGITAL S DESIGN—Digital Audio Recording Equipment—Sony Electronics; *Int'l*, pg. 1281

SONY EXPRESS—Car Stereos—Sony Electronics; *Int'l*, pg. 1281

SONY THEATRES—NONE—Loews Theatre Management Corp.; *Int'l*, pg. 1282

SONY WONDER—NONE—Sony Music Entertainment, Inc.; *Int'l*, pg. 1281

SOONER—Snacks—Borden, Inc.; *U.S. Private*, pg. 157

SOOSAN—Truck Mounted Cranes—EEI Corporation; *Int'l*, pg. 425

SOOT-A-MATIC—Boiler Tube Cleaner—Goodway Technologies Corporation; *U.S. Private*, pg. 464

SOOTH & COOL—Skin Care Products—Medline Industries, Inc.; *U.S. Private*, pg. 728

SOPALIN—Paper Napkins & Towels—Kimberly-Clark Corporation; *U.S. Public*, pg. 958

SOPARCO—NONE—ETEX; *Int'l*, pg. 430

SOPHIE—X-Ray Equipment—Fischer Imaging Corporation; *U.S. Public*, pg. 647

SOPHIST-O-TWIST—Hair Styling Accessories—Quality Special Products; *Int'l*, pg. 1075

SOPHISTACAT—Cat Products—Golden Cat Corporation; *U.S. Public*, pg. 1360

SOPIANAE—Cigarettes—B.A.T Industries P.L.C.; *Int'l*, pg. 110

SOPROSOIE—Butadiene Rubber Dispersing Agent—Rhone-Poulenc S.A.; *Int'l*, pg. 1108

SOPUR—Wheelchairs—Sunrise Medical, Inc.; *U.S. Public*, pg. 1535

SORBITS—NONE—Huhtamaki Oy; *Int'l*, pg. 638

SORBONORIT—Solvent Recovery Carbon—NORIT N.V.; *Int'l*, pg. 958

SORBSAN—Topical Wound Dressing of Calcium Alginate for Chronic Ulcers—Dow Hickam Pharmaceuticals Inc.; *U.S. Public*, pg. 1143

SOREL—Boots—Kaufman Footwear; *Int'l*, pg. 725

SORIATANE—Retinoid—Roche Holding Ltd.; *Int'l*, pg. 1119

SORRELL RIDGE—All Fruit Jam—Allied Old English, Inc.; *U.S. Private*, pg. 39

SORRENTO—Broadloom—Couristan Inc.; *U.S. Private*, pg. 279

SORRENTO—Italian Cheese—Sorrento Cheese Company, Inc.; *Int'l*, pg. 323

SORRENTO—Jewelry—Uncas Manufacturing Company; *U.S. Private*, pg. 1116

SORRENTO PARQUET—Pre-Finished Strip—Bruce Hardwood Floors; *U.S. Public*, pg. 1634

SORRY—Board Game—Parker Brothers; *U.S. Public*, pg. 797

SORT MASTER—Sortation System—ElectroCom Automation L.P.; *Int'l*, pg. 1244

SORTATION SYSTEMS—Gullwing & Flat Tray—SI Handling Systems, Inc.; *U.S. Public*, pg. 1418

SOTACOR—Antiarrhythmic—Bristol-Myers Squibb Company; *U.S. Public*, pg. 253

SOTEX—Surfactants—Morton International Inc.; *U.S. Public*, pg. 1135

SOTHEBY'S—Art & Auction House—Sotheby's Inc.; *U.S. Public*, pg. 1487

SOTRADECOL—Sodium Tetradecyl Sulfate Injection—Wyeth-Ayerst Laboratories, Inc.; *U.S. Public*, pg. 80

SOUND ADVICE—Store Tradename—Sound Advice, Inc.; *U.S. Public*, pg. 1488

SOUND & VIDEO CONTRACTOR—Technical Business Magazine—Intertec Publishing; *U.S. Public*, pg. 1327

SOUND CHOICE—Hearing Aid—Bausch & Lomb Incorporated; *U.S. Public*, pg. 194

SOUND CHOICE—Evacuation Speakers—System Sensor Division; *U.S. Public*, pg. 1306

SOUND/GARD—Sound Activated Switches—The Lamson & Sessions Co.; *U.S. Public*, pg. 976

SOUND 911—Safety Horns—Falcon Safety Products Inc.; *U.S. Private*, pg. 392

SOUND OFF—Home Entertainment Stores—Blockbuster Music; *U.S. Private*, pg. 776

SOUND SHIELD—Acoustical Covers—Hunt Corporation; *U.S. Public*, pg. 848

SOUND SOLUTION—Muffler—Walker Manufacturing Co.; *U.S. Public*, pg. 1578

SOUND VALUE—Promoting Products of Others To Auto Clubs—American Automobile Association; *U.S. Private*, pg. 50

SOUND WAREHOUSE—Home Entertainment Stores—Blockbuster Music; *U.S. Private*, pg. 776

SOUND-WRITE—Office Products—HON Industries Inc.; *U.S. Public*, pg. 772

SOUNDABOUT—Stereo Audio Tape Recorders Used with Headphones—Sony Electronics; *Int'l*, pg. 1281

SOUNDCRAFT—Professional Mixing Consoles—Harman International Industries, Inc.; *U.S. Public*, pg. 787

SOUNDESIGN—Stereos, Radios, TV's & VCR's—SDI Technologies Inc.; *U.S. Private*, pg. 956

SOUNDMASTER—Partitions—Modernfold, Inc.; *U.S. Private*, pg. 755

SOUNDOLIER—Integrated Home Electronics—Atlas/Soundolier; *U.S. Private*, pg. 64

SOUNDQUEST—Audio Installation & Interconnect Accessories—Recoton Corporation; *U.S. Public*, pg. 1369

SOUNDS GREAT—Audio Card Game—Mattel Games/Puzzles; *U.S. Public*, pg. 1058

SOUNDS OF THE SEVENTIES—Music Series—Time-Life, Inc.; *U.S. Public*, pg. 1613

SOUNDSCREEN—Acoustical Panel—United McGill Corp.; *U.S. Private*, pg. 1122

SOUNDWORKS—NONE—Cambridge Soundworks, Inc.; *U.S. Private*, pg. 202

SOUNDWORKS BY HENRY KLOSS—NONE—Cambridge Soundworks, Inc.; *U.S. Private*, pg. 202

SOUNDWORKS LISTENING ROOM—NONE—Cambridge Soundworks, Inc.; *U.S. Private*, pg. 202

SOUNPAK—Industrial & HVAC Silencers—United McGill Corp.; *U.S. Private*, pg. 1122

SOUP STARTER—Dry Mixes—Borden, Inc.; *U.S. Private*, pg. 157

SOUP SUPREME—Frozen Soup Varieties—Norpac Foods, Inc.; *U.S. Private*, pg. 802

SOUPER SOUP—Menu Item-Soup—Dunkin' Donuts Incorporated; *U.S. Private*, pg. 63

SOUPLINE—Fabric Softeners—Colgate-Palmolive Company; *U.S. Public*, pg. 397

SOUR TREAT—Imitation Sour Cream—Friendship Dairies, Inc.; *U.S. Private*, pg. 429

THE SOURCE—News Program for Youth-Oriented Music Stations—Westwood One, Inc.; *U.S. Public*, pg. 1763

SOURCE RECORD PUNCH—Data Collection Devices—The Standard Register Company; *U.S. Public*, pg. 1505

THE SOURCE REPORT—News Program—Westwood One, Inc.; *U.S. Public*, pg. 1763

SOURCE 3000—Computer System—SEI Investments; *U.S. Public*, pg. 1417

SOURCELINE—Video Information Service—SBC Communications Inc.; *U.S. Public*, pg. 1415

SOURCES—NONE—Capintec Inc.; *U.S. Private*, pg. 205

SOURCY—Soft Drink—Heineken N.V.; *Int'l*, pg. 608

SOURDOUGH—Pizza—Straw Hat Cooperative Corp.; *U.S. Private*, pg. 1046

SOUTH CAROLINA—Insurance—South Carolina Insurance Company; *U.S. Public*, pg. 1453

SOUTH CAROLINA MANUFACTURERS REGISTER—Register—Manufacturers' News, Inc.; *U.S. Private*, pg. 700

SOUTH CHESTER TUBE—NONE—SouthCo. Inc.; *U.S. Private*, pg. 1014

SOUTH DAKOTA MANUFACTURERS REGISTER—Register—Manufacturers' News, Inc.; *U.S. Private*, pg. 700

SOUTH FLORIDA BUSINESS JOURNAL—Business Journal—Business First of New York, Inc.; *U.S. Public*, pg. 19

SOUTH SEAS—hair Access.—Goody Products, Inc.; *U.S. Public*, pg. 1177

SOUTH STREET—NONE—Alliant Foodservice, Inc.; *U.S. Private*, pg. 244

SOUTH WIND—Heat Transfer Equipment—BTR plc; *Int'l*, pg. 124

SOUTH WIND—Heat Exchangers & Heaters—Stewart-Warner South Wind Corp.; *Int'l*, pg. 127

SOUTHBEND—Cooking & Steam Equipment—The Middleby Corporation; *U.S. Public*, pg. 1109

SOUTHCO—Access Hardware for OEM Manufacturers—SouthCo. Inc.; *U.S. Private*, pg. 1014

SOUTHCO INTERNATIONAL—Access Hardware for OEM Manufacturers—SouthCo. Inc.; *U.S. Private*, pg. 1014

SOUTHEAST FARM PRESS—Publication for Local Farming Issues—Intertec Publishing; *U.S. Public*, pg. 1327

SOUTHEAST FARM PRESS—NONE—Intertec Publishing; *U.S. Public*, pg. 1328

SOUTHEASTERN ACCESS CONTROL—Access Control Equipment—Reeves Southeastern Corporation; *U.S. Private*, pg. 916

SOUTHEASTERN GALVANIZING—Commercial Galvanizing—Reeves Southeastern Corporation; *U.S. Private*, pg. 916

SOUTHEASTERN SPECIALTY PRODUCTS—Ornamental Fencing—Reeves Southeastern Corporation; *U.S. Private*, pg. 916

SOUTHEASTERN WIRE—Welded Wire Mesh—Reeves Southeastern Corporation; *U.S. Private*, pg. 916

SOUTHERN—Railroad Wheels—ABC Rail Products Corp.; *U.S. Public*, pg. 2

SOUTHERN ACCENTS—Bi-Monthly Magazine—Southern Progress Corporation; *U.S. Public*, pg. 1612

SOUTHERN ACCENTS—Magazine—Time Warner Inc.; *U.S. Public*, pg. 1610

SOUTHERN BEAUTY—Fresh & Frozen Chicken—Sanderson Farms, Inc.; *U.S. Public*, pg. 1430

SOUTHERN BELLE—NONE—Harrah's Entertainment, Inc.; *U.S. Public*, pg. 790

SOUTHERN CALIFORNIA GAS—Public Utility Distributing Natural Gas—Southern California Gas Co.; *U.S. Public*, pg. 1249

SOUTHERN COMFORT—Liqueur—Brown-Forman Beverages Worldwide; *U.S. Public*, pg. 261

SOUTHERN COMFORT—Liqueur—Brown-Forman Corporation; *U.S. Public*, pg. 261

SOUTHERN COMFORT—Mens' Wear—Tootal Group plc; *Int'l*, pg. 300

SOUTHERN COMFORT & COLA—NONE—Brown-Forman Beverages Worldwide; *U.S. Public*, pg. 261

THE SOUTHERN COMPANY—Regional Electric Utility—Southern Company; *U.S. Public*, pg. 1489

SOUTHERN FARMS—Kettle-Cooked Potato Chips—Golden Flake Snack Foods, Inc.; *U.S. Public*, pg. 750

SOUTHERN GEM—Canned Vegetables—Bush Brothers & Company; *U.S. Private*, pg. 189

SOUTHERN GOLD—Plywood—Georgia-Pacific Corporation; *U.S. Public*, pg. 735

SOUTHERN GRAVURE SERVICE—Printing—Reynolds Metals Company; *U.S. Public*, pg. 1385

SOUTHERN LIVING—Monthly Magazine—Southern Progress Corporation; *U.S. Public*, pg. 1612

SOUTHERN LIVING—Magazine—Time Warner Inc.; *U.S. Public*, pg. 1610

SOUTHERN LIVING VACATIONS—Quarterly Travel Guides—Southern Progress Corporation; *U.S. Public*, pg. 1612

SOUTHERN MOST—Food Service Prods.—Savannah Foods & Industries, Inc.; *U.S. Public*, pg. 872

SOUTHERN OUTDOORS—Magazine—B.A.S.S., Inc.; *U.S. Public*, pg. 105

SOUTHERN PACIFIC LINES—Railroad & Trucking Operations—Southern Pacific Rail Corporation; *U.S. Public*, pg. 1668

SOUTHERN PAVING—NONE—LeGrand Johnson Construction Co.; *U.S. Private*, pg. 591

SOUTHERN STAR—NONE—Harrah's Entertainment, Inc.; *U.S. Public*, pg. 790

SOUTHERN STEEL COMPANY—NONE—Phelps Tointon Inc.; *U.S. Private*, pg. 860

SOUTHERN TURF & LANDSCAPE PRESS—NONE—Intertec Publishing; *U.S. Public*, pg. 1328

SOUTHERN TURF MANAGEMENT—NONE—Farm Press; *U.S. Public*, pg. 1328

SOUTHERN WINDS—Name for Edible Food—H.J. Baker & Bro., Inc.; *U.S. Private*, pg. 112

SOUTHPAW—Beer—Miller Brewing Company; *U.S. Public*, pg. 1289

SOUTHTEC INC.—Access Hardware for OEM Manufacturing—SouthCo. Inc.; *U.S. Private*, pg. 1014

SOUTHWEST ART—NONE—Cowles Enthusiast Media, Inc.; *U.S. Private*, pg. 281

SOUTHWEST CANYON—NONE—Niches, Inc.; *U.S. Public*, pg. 1181

SOUTHWEST CHEMICAL SERVICES—Polymer Compounding Inc.—M.A. Hanna Company; *U.S. Public*, pg. 780

SOUTHWEST CLIMATE SOLUTIONS—Heat Pumps—APS; *U.S. Public*, pg. 1297

SOUTHWEST FARM PRESS—Publication for Local Farming Issues—Intertec Publishing; *U.S. Public*, pg. 1327

SOUTHWEST FARM PRESS—NONE—Intertec Publishing; *U.S. Public*, pg. 1328

SOUTHWEST KITCHENS—Electric Cooking—APS; *U.S. Public*, pg. 1297

SOUTHWESTERN—Life Insurance—Southwestern Life Insurance Company; *U.S. Private*, pg. 1018

SOUTHWIND—Motor Home—Fleetwood Enterprises, Inc.; *U.S. Public*, pg. 650

SOUTHWIRE—Electrical Wire—Bryant Electric Supply Company; *U.S. Public*, pg. 177

SOUVENYEAR TASSEL—Graduation Tassel—E.R. Moore Co.; *U.S. Private*, pg. 759

SOVA—Source of Volume Analysis—BASES Worldwide; *U.S. Private*, pg. 120

SOVAKLOR—Coatings—The Valspar Corp. Protective Coatings Div.; *U.S. Public*, pg. 1707

SOVAPON—Epoxy Coating—The Valspar Corp. Protective Coatings Div.; *U.S. Public*, pg. 1707

SOVEREIGN—Fabrics—Dan River Inc.; *U.S. Public*, pg. 478

SOVEREIGN—NONE—Fortune Brands, Inc.; *U.S. Public*, pg. 674

SOVEREIGN OF THE SEAS—Ships—Royal Caribbean Cruises Ltd.; *U.S. Public*, pg. 1410

SOVEREIGN SERIES—3-Tab Fiberglass Shingles—Building Materials Corporation of America; *U.S. Public*, pg. 433

SOVRAN BANK—Banking & Related Services—NationsBank Virginia; *U.S. Public*, pg. 1163

SOXCAT—Cracking Catalyst—Engelhard Corporation; *U.S. Public*, pg. 582

SOYAFLUFF—Flour—Central Soya Company, Inc.; *Int'l*, pg. 324

SOYARICH—Flour & Soy Products—Central Soya Company, Inc.; *Int'l*, pg. 324

SOYBEAN DIGEST—Publication of the American Soybean Association—Intertec Publishing; *U.S. Public*, pg. 1327

SOYCO—Casein & Soy Based Cheese Product—Galaxy Food Company; *U.S. Public*, pg. 697

SOYMAGE—Tofu & Soybean Based Cheese Product—Galaxy Food Company; *U.S. Public*, pg. 697

SOYOLA—Margarine—Sabanci Holding A.S.; *Int'l*, pg. 1167

SPA & FRUIT—Juice-Based Carbonates—Spadel SA; *Int'l*, pg. 1287

SPA BARISART—Sparkling Natural Mineral Water—Spadel SA; *Int'l*, pg. 1287

SPA CITRON—Extract-Based Carbonate—Spadel SA; *Int'l*, pg. 1287

SPA MARI-HENRIETTE—Low Sparkling Natural Mineral Water—Spadel SA; *Int'l*, pg. 1287

SPA REINE—Still Natural Mineral Water—Spadel SA; *Int'l*, pg. 1287

SPAC—Insert Nuts—RB&W Corporation; *U.S. Public*, pg. 1259

SPACE CAP—Pick-Up Cap—Reading Body Works, Inc.; *U.S. Private*, pg. 913

SPACE-CASE—Office Supplies—JM Company; *U.S. Private*, pg. 577

SPACE COMMAND—TV Receivers—Zenith Electronics Corp.; *U.S. Public*, pg. 1790

SPACE FLEET—Sweet & Sour Novelty—Ce De Candy, Inc.; *U.S. Private*, pg. 220

SPACE-GARD—Whole-House Air Cleaners—Research Products Corporation; *U.S. Private*, pg. 924

SPACE HARRIER—Videogame—Sega of America Inc.; *Int'l*, pg. 1218

SPACE JR.—Test Equipment—Tenney Environmental; *U.S. Private*, pg. 1076

SPACE MAKERS—Luggage—American Tourister, Inc.; *U.S. Public*, pg. 1430

SPACE MANAGEMENT SYSTEMS—Office Systems Furniture—Trendway Corporation; *U.S. Private*, pg. 1099

SPACE MASTER—Document Management Products—Bell & Howell Holdings; *U.S. Public*, pg. 201

SPACE PHONE—TV Receivers—Zenith Electronics Corp.; *U.S. Public*, pg. 1790

SPACE PLACE—Portfolios—The Mead Corporation; *U.S. Public*, pg. 1074

SPACE POLICE—Children's Building Sets—LEGO Systems, Inc.; *U.S. Public*, pg. 805

SPACE-RAY—Radiant Gas Heating Systems—Gas-Fired Products, Inc.; *U.S. Private*, pg. 440

SPACE-SAVER—Boxes—Kimberly-Clark Corporation; *U.S. Public*, pg. 958

SPACE-SAVER—Indexing—Knoll, Inc.; *U.S. Private*, pg. 627

SPACE-SAVER—Filtration System—Serfilco, Ltd.; *U.S. Private*, pg. 985

SPACEBANK—Timeshare Exchange Iventory—Resort Condominiums International; *U.S. Public*, pg. 322

SPACEFINDER—Filing Cabinets—Tab Products Co.; *U.S. Public*, pg. 1559

SPACELABS MEDICAL—Medical Patient Monitoring Equip. & Clinical Information Systems Mfr.—SpaceLabs Medical, Inc.; *U.S. Public*, pg. 1494

SPACEMAKER—Household Products—The Black & Decker Corporation; *U.S. Public*, pg. 233

SPACEMAKER—Microwave Ovens—General Electric Canada Inc.; *U.S. Public*, pg. 713

SPACEMAKER—NONE—TJ International, Inc.; *U.S. Public*, pg. 1556

SPACEMAKER OPTIMA—Household Products—The Black & Decker Corporation; *U.S. Public*, pg. 233

SPACEMASTER—Spotting Scope—Bausch & Lomb Incorporated; *U.S. Public*, pg. 194

SPACEMASTER—Telescopes—Bushnell Corporation; *U.S. Private*, pg. 1191

SPACEMASTER—Store Fixtures—RHC/Spacemaster Corporation; *U.S. Private*, pg. 904

SPACESAVER—Glass Fiber Building Insulation and Packaging—Owens Corning; *U.S. Public*, pg. 1236

SPACESAVER DONUT SYSTEM—Bakery Equipment—Belshaw Brothers, Inc.; *Int'l*, pg. 188

SPACESAVER FRYERS—Bakery Equipment—Belshaw Brothers, Inc.; *Int'l*, pg. 188

SPACESETTER—Partitions/Operable Walls; Portable Office Panels—Modernfold, Inc.; *U.S. Private*, pg. 755

SPACETRAK—Electrical Power Distribution System—RHC/Spacemaster Corporation; *U.S. Private*, pg. 904

SPACEWAY—Ka-band Broadband Satellite System/Service—Hughes Communications, Inc.; *U.S. Public*, pg. 721

SPADE GRIP—Tires—Bridgestone/Firestone, Inc.; *Int'l*, pg. 213

SPAGEDDIES—Full Service, Modest Priced Italian Restaurant—Brinker International, Inc.; *U.S. Public*, pg. 253

SPAFAS—NONE—Spafas, Inc.; *U.S. Public*, pg. 195

SPAGEDDIES ITALIAN KITCHEN—Restaurant—Quality Dining Inc.; *U.S. Public*, pg. 1349

SPAGHETTIO'S—Canned food—Campbell Soup Company; *U.S. Public*, pg. 298

SPAGMOS—Floral Moss—Premier Brands, Inc.; *Int'l*, pg. 1068

SPAGULAX—Laxative—SmithKline Beecham plc; *Int'l*, pg. 1264

SPAKO—Cooking String—The Dow Chemical Company; *U.S. Public*, pg. 522

SPALDING—Headwear—AJD; *U.S. Private*, pg. 510

SPAM—Luncheon Meat—Hormel Foods Corp.; *U.S. Public*, pg. 840

SPAN—NONE—Akzo Nobel N.V.; *Int'l*, pg. 42

SPAN-AIDS—Patient Positioners—Span-America Medical Systems Inc.; *U.S. Public*, pg. 1495

SPAN-CARE—Liquid Fill Products—Span-America Medical Systems Inc.; *U.S. Public*, pg. 1495

SPAN-TRACK—Shelf-less Carton Flow Track—Unex Conveying Systems, Inc.; *U.S. Private*, pg. 1117

SPANDRELITE—Coated Glass for Structural Applications—PPG Industries, Inc.; *U.S. Public*, pg. 1245

SPANEL—Hosiery—Sara Lee Corporation; *U.S. Public*, pg. 1432

SPANGLE—Neutral Floor Cleaner—3M; *U.S. Public*, pg. 1604

SPANISH LEDER—Natural Soap—Wella Group; *Int'l*, pg. 1489

SPANISH MASTER—Language Dictionary—Franklin Electronic Publishers, Inc.; *U.S. Public*, pg. 679

SPARC LT—Laptop Computer—Toshiba Corporation; *Int'l*, pg. 1402

SPARCAL—Custom, Self-Adhesive Decorative Products & Moldings for Marine & Leisure—Spartan International Inc.; *U.S. Private*, pg. 1020

SPARCO—Office Products—Genuine Parts Company; *U.S. Public*, pg. 732

SPARCOM—Thin Route Earth Station—Spar Aerospace Limited; *Int'l*, pg. 1287

SPARKIT—Chipset—LSI Logic Corp.; *U.S. Public*, pg. 971

SPARKLE—Paper Towels & Napkins—Georgia-Pacific Corporation; *U.S. Public*, pg. 735

SPARKLE—Dog Food—Triple F, Inc.; *U.S. Private*, pg. 1104

SPARKLE JR.—Dog Food—Triple F, Inc.; *U.S. Private*, pg. 1104

SPARKLE TIP—Light Bulb—Duro-Test Corporation; *U.S. Private*, pg. 349

SPARKLEEN—Detergent—Fisher Scientific Company; *U.S. Private*, pg. 658

SPARKLERS—Interior Wall—Monarch Tile, Inc.; *U.S. Private*, pg. 287

SPARKLETTS—Processed, Purified Bottled Water—McKesson Corporation; *U.S. Public*, pg. 1072

SPARKLON—Packaging Adhesive—Morton International Inc.; *U.S. Public*, pg. 1135

SPARKY THE FIREDOG—Fire Safety Education—National Fire Protection Association; *U.S. Private*, pg. 782

SPARLUX—Polycarbonate Plates—Solvay S.A.; *Int'l*, pg. 1334

SPARTA—Machinery—AE Goetze-North America; *Int'l*, pg. 1334

SPARTA PINK—NONE—New England Stone Industries, Inc.; *U.S. Private*, pg. 793

SPARTAN—Plastic Pipe—Cresline Plastic Pipe Co. Inc.; *U.S. Private*, pg. 289

SPARTAN—Air Moving Devices—EG & G Rotron; *U.S. Public*, pg. 543

SPARTAN—Soldering Materials—Litton Industries, Inc.; *U.S. Public*, pg. 1002

SPARTAN—Product of The Fineline Process, Needs Little or No Heating Before Welding—Lukens Steel Company; *U.S. Public*, pg. 1020

SPARTAN—Disposable-HPLC Filters—Schleicher & Schuell, Inc.; *Int'l*, pg. 1206

SPARTAN—Sewer Cleaners—Spartan Tool; *U.S. Private*, pg. 860

SPARTON—Electro-Mechanical Equip., Horns—Sparton Corporation; *U.S. Public*, pg. 1496

SPARVAR—Spray Paints—Sherwin-Williams Diversified Brands, Inc.; *U.S. Public*, pg. 1466

SPATIALWARE—Stores & Manages Spatial Data in Corporate National Databases—MapInfo Corp.; *U.S. Public*, pg. 1042

SPATINI SAUCE MIX—Gravy Mixes—Thomas J. Lipton Company; *Int'l*, pg. 1435

SPATULA SMART—Household Products—The Black & Decker Corporation; *U.S. Public*, pg. 233

SPAZZY—Trash Bags—The Dow Chemical Company; *U.S. Public*, pg. 522

SPEAK EASY—Breath Freshener—American Safety Razor Company; *U.S. Private*, pg. 597

SPEAK-EZEE—Communication Equip.—Scott Aviation; *U.S. Public*, pg. 622

SPEAKEASY—Microcassette—Sony Electronics; *Int'l*, pg. 1281

SPEAKER'S—Scotch—Laird & Company; *U.S. Private*, pg. 642

SPEAKING ACE—Speller—Franklin Electronic Publishers, Inc.; *U.S. Public*, pg. 679

SPEAKING DICTIONARY—Electronic Dictionary—Franklin Electronic Publishers, Inc.; *U.S. Public*, pg. 679

SPEAKING WORDMASTER—Thesaurus—Franklin Electronic Publishers, Inc.; *U.S. Public*, pg. 679

SPEARHEAD—High Alkaline Powdered Detergent for Machine Washing—Ecolab Inc.; *U.S. Public*, pg. 562

SPEARMINT—Herb Tea—Celestial Seasonings; *U.S. Public*, pg. 319

SPEARMINTLETS—Candy—Brach & Brock Confections Inc.; *U.S. Private*, pg. 163

SPEARS—Pipe & Fittings—Ryan Herco Products Corp.; *U.S. Private*, pg. 953

SPEAS FARM—Apple Products—Knouse Foods Inc.; *U.S. Private*, pg. 627

SPEAS FARM—Fruit Juices, Fruit Juice Blends-Shelf Stable—Sundor Brands Inc.; *U.S. Private*, pg. 1331

SPEC AID—Finished Fuel Additives—BetzDearborn Inc.; *U.S. Public*, pg. 226

SPEC MANAGER—NONE—Detroit Diesel Corp.; *U.S. Private*, pg. 850

SPEC-MASTER—Wiring Devices—Leviton Mfg. Co., Inc.; *U.S. Public*, pg. 663

SPEC-SELECT—Sand Classifying Tanks With Programmable Controls—Portec, Inc.-Construction Equipment Div.; *U.S. Public*, pg. 1318

SPEC-T—Cough Suppressant & Decongestant—Bristol-Myers Squibb Company; *U.S. Public*, pg. 253

SPEC 200—Control System—The Foxboro Company; *Int'l*, pg. 1243

SPEC WIZARD—NONE—Detroit Diesel Corp.; *U.S. Private*, pg. 850

SPECCHIP—Surface Mount Capacitors—Spectrum Control, Inc.; *U.S. Public*, pg. 1497

SPECFIL—Urethane Components—The Dow Chemical Company; *U.S. Public*, pg. 522

SPECFLEX—Polyurethane Components—The Dow Chemical Company; *U.S. Public*, pg. 522

SPECI-GARD—Liquid-Tight, Disposable Specimen Transport Bags—Uniflex, Inc.; *U.S. Public*, pg. 1665

SPECIAL AIR TUFF—NONE—Uniflex, Inc.; *U.S. Public*, pg. 1665

SPECIAL ALTERNATIVES—Insurance Claims Management Service—Lincoln National Corporation; *U.S. Public*, pg. 997

SPECIAL CRISP—Candy Bar—Hershey Foods Corporation; *U.S. Public*, pg. 811

SPECIAL CUTS—Dog Food—H.J. Heinz Company; *U.S. Public*, pg. 805

SPECIAL DARK—Sweet Chocolate Bar—Hershey Foods Corporation; *U.S. Public*, pg. 811

SPECIAL DINNERS—Cat Food—Ralston Purina Company; *U.S. Public*, pg. 1359

SPECIAL EDITION—Cajun Snack Sticks—Lawry's Foods, Inc.; *Int'l*, pg. 1435

SPECIAL EFFECTS—Greeting Cards—American Greetings Corporation; *U.S. Public*, pg. 77

SPECIAL EYES—Sunglasses—Goody Products, Inc.; *U.S. Public*, pg. 1177

SPECIAL K—High-Protein Low-Sugar Rice & Wheat Cereal—Kellogg Company; *U.S. Public*, pg. 947

SPECIAL MALT—NONE—Grolsch N.V.; *Int'l*, pg. 559

SPECIAL MOMENTS—NONE—Oxford Health Plans Inc.; *U.S. Public*, pg. 1238

SPECIAL OCCASIONS—Wedding Flowers—Celebrity Incorporated; *U.S. Public*, pg. 319

SPECIAL ORDER—Pizza—Tombstone Pizza Corporation; *U.S. Public*, pg. 1288

SPECIAL PURCHASE ACCOUNT—NONE—American Express Company; *U.S. Public*, pg. 73

SPECIAL RECIPE—Ice Cream Toppings—J.M. Smucker Company; *U.S. Public*, pg. 1480

SPECIAL-T—Metallic Reloading Press—Lyman Products Corporation; *U.S. Public*, pg. 683

SPECIAL 10'S—Cigarettes—Brown & Williamson Tobacco Corp.; *Int'l*, pg. 111

SPECIAL TOFFEE—Sugar Confectionery—Thorntons PLC; *Int'l*, pg. 1386

SPECIAL VALUE—Food Products—Certified Grocers of California; *U.S. Private*, pg. 226

SPECIALIST—Fly Line, Leaders, Reels, Rods—Outdoor Technologies Group; *U.S. Private*, pg. 822

SPECIALIST DIRECT—Open Access HMO—Sierra Health Services, Inc.; *U.S. Public*, pg. 1469

SPECIALTY LIGHTING—Lighting—JJI Lighting Group Inc.; *Int'l*, pg. 821

SPECIALTY SLEEP—NONE—Simmons Company; *Int'l*, pg. 686

SPECIALTY SUPREME—Sandwiches—Hardee's Food Systems, Inc.; *U.S. Public*, pg. 278

SPECIFICATION LINE—NONE—Scotsman Industries, Inc.; *U.S. Public*, pg. 1444

SPECK CHEK ORANGE—Duct Connector Fabric—Duro Dyne Corporation; *U.S. Private*, pg. 349

SPECKLED SMUD—Toys—Mattel, Inc.; *U.S. Public*, pg. 1057

SPECMAKER—Screening—Telsmith, Inc.; *U.S. Public*, pg. 141

SPECTA CLEAR—Anti Reflective Ophthalmic Lens Treatment—Sterling Vision, Inc.; *U.S. Public*, pg. 1516

SPECTAR—Polyester; Copolymer—Eastman Chemical Company; *U.S. Public*, pg. 550

SPECTATOR—Sunglasses—Bausch & Lomb Incorporated; *U.S. Public*, pg. 194

SPECTATOR—Binoculars—Bushnell Corporation; *U.S. Private*, pg. 1191

SPECTATOR SERIES—Binoculars—Bausch & Lomb Incorporated; *U.S. Public*, pg. 194

SPECTAZOLE—Cream—Ortho-McNeil Pharmaceutical Corporation; *U.S. Public*, pg. 929

SPECTER—Racquetball Eyewear—Ektelon; *U.S. Private*, pg. 884

SPECTIACAIR—NONE—MEDIQ Incorporated; *U.S. Public*, pg. 1081

SPECTRA—Color Slide Duplicator—AFP Imaging Corporation; *U.S. Public*, pg. 6

SPECTRA—Educational & Consulting Services—Alcon Laboratories, Inc.; *Int'l*, pg. 916

SPECTRA—High Performance Fibers—AlliedSignal Inc., Engineered Materials; *U.S. Public*, pg. 51

SPECTRA—Book Imprint—Bertelsmann AG; *Int'l*, pg. 189

SPECTRA—Car Care—Burmah Castrol plc; *Int'l*, pg. 234

SPECTRA—Software—CACI International Inc; *U.S. Public*, pg. 272

SPECTRA—Ultrasound System—Diasonics Ultra Sound, Inc.; *Int'l*, pg. 644

SPECTRA—Office Chairs—HON Industries Inc.; *U.S. Public*, pg. 772

SPECTRA—Nickel Process—LeaRonal, Inc.; *U.S. Public*, pg. 982

SPECTRA—Open Cross-Development Backplane—Microtec Division; *U.S. Public*, pg. 1086

SPECTRA—Floodlights—Wide-Lite; *U.S. Public*, pg. 730

SPECTRA-CHIP—Floor Coverings—Domco Inc.; *Int'l*, pg. 415

SPECTRA FOCUS—System for Spectral UV/VIS Analysis—Thermo Separation Products; *U.S. Public*, pg. 1594

SPECTRA NET—Data System Communication Network—Thermo Separation Products; *U.S. Public*, pg. 1594

SPECTRA NEWS—Magazine—Alcon Laboratories, Inc.; *Int'l*, pg. 916

SPECTRA 900—Yarn—AlliedSignal Inc.; *U.S. Public*, pg. 49

SPECTRA 1000—Yarn—AlliedSignal Inc.; *U.S. Public*, pg. 49

SPECTRA PHORESIS—System for Capillary Electrophoresis—Thermo Separation Products; *U.S. Public*, pg. 1594

SPECTRA POINT—Broadloom—Couristan Inc.; *U.S. Private*, pg. 279

SPECTRA 6000—Disk Arrays—Ciprico, Inc.; *U.S. Public*, pg. 370

SPECTRA SYSTEM—Instant Camera & Film—Polaroid Corporation; *U.S. Public*, pg. 1313

SPECTRA SYSTEM—Liquid Chromatography System—Thermo Separation Products; *U.S. Public*, pg. 1594

SPECTRA II SERIES—Table System—Howe Furniture Corporation; *U.S. Private*, pg. 543

SPECTRACHECK—Software for Color Evalutation—Ferro Corporation; *U.S. Public*, pg. 618

SPECTRACLAD—Architectural Glass Panels—PPG Industries, Inc.; *U.S. Public*, pg. 1245

SPECTRACOAT—Color Products—Universal Foods Corporation; *U.S. Public*, pg. 1695

SPECTRACOLOR—Art Materials—Sanford Corporation; *U.S. Public*, pg. 1178

SPECTRAFLO—Liquid Colorants—Ferro Corporation; *U.S. Public*, pg. 618

SPECTRAGLAZE—Brick—Justin Industries, Inc.; *U.S. Public*, pg. 936

SPECTRAGUIDE—Optical Fiber—SpecTran Corporation; *U.S. Public*, pg. 1497

SPECTRALERT—Fire Alarm Notification Equipment—Pittway Corporation; *U.S. Public*, pg. 1305

SPECTRALIFE—Combines Lower Costs of Term Life Ins. withTaxDeferred Cash Value Whole-New York Life Insurance Company; *U.S. Private*, pg. 794

SPECTRALOG—NONE—Western Atlas Logging Services; *U.S. Public*, pg. 1757

SPECTRANALYZED—Solvents—Fisher Scientific Company; *U.S. Private*, pg. 658

SPECTRATECH—Color Concentrates, Additives & Compound Resins—Millennium Petrochemicals, Inc.; *Int'l*, pg. 594

SPECTRATECH—Printing Papers—S.D. Warren Co.; *Int'l*, pg. 1193

SPECTRAX—Pacemaker—Medtronic, Inc.; *U.S. Public*, pg. 1082

SPECTRAX S—Pacemaker—Medtronic, Inc.; *U.S. Public*, pg. 1082

SPECTRAX SX-HT—Pacemaker—Medtronic, Inc.; *U.S. Public*, pg. 1082

SPECTRAX SX—Pacemaker—Medtronic, Inc.; *U.S. Public*, pg. 1082

SPECTRAX SXT—Pacemaker—Medtronic, Inc.; *U.S. Public*, pg. 1082

SPECTRAX VL—Pacemaker—Medtronic, Inc.; *U.S. Public*, pg. 1082

SPECTRAX VM—Pacemaker—Medtronic, Inc.; *U.S. Public*, pg. 1082

SPECTRE HDL—Analog Behavioral Simulation System for Analog & Mixed-Signal Applications—Cadence Design Systems, Inc.; *U.S. Public*, pg. 290

SPECTRE RF—Simulation Software for Design of Radio Frequency Applications—Cadence Design Systems, Inc.; *U.S. Public*, pg. 290

SPECTRIM—Reaction Maldable Products—The Dow Chemical Company; *U.S. Public*, pg. 522

SPECTRIS—Direct Access Storage Devices—Amdahl Corporation; *Int'l*, pg. 527

SPECTRIS MR—Injection System—Medrad, Inc.; *Int'l*, pg. 1204

SPECTRO MONITOR—UV/VIS Detection System—Thermo Separation Products; *U.S. Public*, pg. 1594

SPECTROL—Electronic Controls—Spectrol Electronics Corporation; *U.S. Private*, pg. 351

SPECTROLINE—Ultraviolet Equipment—Spectronics Corporation; *U.S. Private*, pg. 1024

SPECTRON—HMWPE Fiber Rope—The American Group; *U.S. Private*, pg. 56

SPECTRON—Braided Fishing Line—Cortland Line Co., Inc.; *U.S. Private*, pg. 277

SPECTRON—NONE—The Titan Corporation; *U.S. Public*, pg. 1618

SPECTRON 3000—Helium Mass Spectrometer Leak Detector—Edwards High Vacuum, International; *Int'l*, pg. 121

SPECTROPREP—NONE—CEM Corporation; *U.S. Public*, pg. 277

SPECTROPURE—Dental Mercury—Engelhard Corporation; *U.S. Public*, pg. 582

SPECTROSCOPY—Trade Periodical—Advanstar Communications; *U.S. Private*, pg. 22

SPECTRUM—NONE—Bachmann Industries, Inc.; *U.S. Private*, pg. 109

SPECTRUM—Spa—Coleman Spas, Inc.; *U.S. Private*, pg. 109

SPECTRUM—Kitchen Tools—Ekco Housewares, Inc.; *U.S. Public*, pg. 566

SPECTRUM—Integrated Control System—The Foxboro Company; *Int'l*, pg. 1243

SPECTRUM—Prefinished Interior Wall Paneling—Georgia-Pacific Corporation; *U.S. Public*, pg. 735

SPECTRUM—Printing Paper—Georgia-Pacific Corporation; *U.S. Public*, pg. 735

SPECTRUM—Jib & Gantry Crane—Harnischfeger Industries, Inc.; *U.S. Public*, pg. 788

SPECTRUM—Canister Vacuum Cleaner With Power Nozzle—Hoover Company; *U.S. Public*, pg. 1065

SPECTRUM—Employer-Sponsored Life Product—Lincoln National Corporation; *U.S. Public*, pg. 997

SPECTRUM—Welding & Cutting Equip.—Miller Electric Manufacturing Co.; *U.S. Public*, pg. 867

SPECTRUM—Home & Small Business Communications Systems—Mitel Corporation; *Int'l*, pg. 870

SPECTRUM—Automatic Call Distributor—Rockwell International Corporation; *U.S. Public*, pg. 1397

SPECTRUM—Automatic Call Distributor—Rockwell Switching Systems Div.; *U.S. Public*, pg. 1398

SPECTRUM—Flat Colored Glass—Spectrum Glass Co.; *Int'l*, pg. 296

SPECTRUM—Generators—Valley Detroit Diesel Allison; *U.S. Private*, pg. 1132

SPECTRUM AUTOSYNC—High Resolution, Multi-Frequency Color Monitors—Aydin Corporation; *U.S. Public*, pg. 158

SPECTRUM CHROMAX—Printing Paper—Georgia-Pacific Corporation; *U.S. Public*, pg. 735

SPECTRUM CONTROL—NONE—Milgray Electronics, Inc.; *U.S. Public*, pg. 205

SPECTRUM DP—Xerographic Paper—Georgia-Pacific Corporation; *U.S. Public*, pg. 735

SPECTRUM DUPL/LTT—Printing Paper—Georgia-Pacific Corporation; *U.S. Public*, pg. 735

SPECTRUM LASER DP—Printing Paper—Georgia-Pacific Corporation; *U.S. Public*, pg. 735

SPECTRUM MASTER—Gamma Spectroscopy System—EG & G Ortec; *U.S. Public*, pg. 543

SPECTRUM MIMEO—Printing Paper—Georgia-Pacific Corporation; *U.S. Public*, pg. 735

SPECTRUM OFFSET—Printing Paper—Georgia-Pacific Corporation; *U.S. Public*, pg. 735

SPECTRUM I—Thread—Coats North America; *Int'l*, pg. 300

SPECTRUM RAZOR TOOLS—A Division of P H C—Pacific Handy Cutter, Inc.; *U.S. Private*, pg. 831

SPECTRUM TOOLS—A Division of P H C—Pacific Handy Cutter, Inc.; *U.S. Private*, pg. 831

SPECTRUM 2000—Multimode Commuinication System—Rockwell International Corporation; *U.S. Public*, pg. 1397

SPECULAR+—Silver-sputtered, coated DTI specialty film—Material Sciences Corporation; *U.S. Public*, pg. 1056

SPECWAVE—Microwave Products—Spectrum Control, Inc.; *U.S. Public*, pg. 1497

SPEECHMAKER—Electronic Equipment—Cognitronics Corporation; *U.S. Public*, pg. 394

SPEECHVIEWER—Computer Product—International Business Machines Corporation; *U.S. Public*, pg. 895

SPEED—Portland Cement—Essroc Cement, Corp.; *U.S. Private*, pg. 384

SPEED—High Density Plasma CRD—Novellus Systems, Inc.; *U.S. Public*, pg. 1204

SPEED-A-MATIC—Solid State D.C. Controller—U.S. Electrical Motor Division; *U.S. Public*, pg. 573

SPEED BENDER—Bender—Greenlee Textron; *U.S. Public*, pg. 1589

SPEED CHOICE—High Speed Data Communications Systems—People's Choice TV Corp.; *U.S. Public*, pg. 1274

SPEED CIRCUIT—Game—Monarch Avalon, Inc.; *U.S. Public*, pg. 1123

SPEED-COMPOUNDER—Battery Paste Mixer—Pettibone Corporation; *U.S. Private*, pg. 859

SPEED-CRO-SHEEN—Needlework Yarn—Coats & Clark Inc.; *Int'l*, pg. 300

SPEED CUSHION—Bicycle Tires—Bridgestone/Firestone, Inc.; *Int'l*, pg. 213

SPEED-D—Switchboards & Motor Control Centers—Square D Company; *Int'l*, pg. 1208

SPEED-DRY—Int./Ext. Primer & Enamels—Devoe Paint; *Int'l*, pg. 663

SPEED DRY—Int./Ext. Primer & Enamels—ICI Paints; *Int'l*, pg. 664

SPEED-FEED—Electrode—The Lincoln Electric Company; *U.S. Public*, pg. 996

SPEED GRILL—Multisurface Cooking Device—Toastmaster, Inc.; *U.S. Public*, pg. 1619

SPEED KING—Tires—Bridgestone/Firestone, Inc.; *Int'l*, pg. 213

SPEED KING—Bass Drum Pedal—Ludwig Industries; *U.S. Public*, pg. 1514

SPEED KING—Valves—Schrader Bellows Division; *U.S. Public*, pg. 1261

SPEED LINE—CAD Software—The Falk Corporation; *U.S. Public*, pg. 1534

SPEED-LOCK—Toggle Bolt—Powers Fastening, Inc.; *U.S. Private*, pg. 878

SPEED-MILL—Diamond Sidetracking/Window-Cutting Bit—Baker Hughes INTEQ; *U.S. Public*, pg. 166

SPEED-PAK—Unfilled Plastic & Glass Ampules and Vials for Pharmaceuticals—The West Company, Incorporated; *U.S. Public*, pg. 1755

SPEED-PRO—Performance Products—Federal-Mogul Corporation; *U.S. Public*, pg. 615

SPEED QUEEN—Laundry Appliances & Equipment—Raytheon Appliances; *U.S. Public*, pg. 1366

SPEED QUOTE—Software Selection Program—The Falk Corporation; *U.S. Public*, pg. 1534

SPEED-REX—Epoxy Ester Enamel—Devoe Paint; *Int'l*, pg. 663

SPEED-REX—Epoxy Ester Enamel—ICI Paints; *Int'l*, pg. 664

SPEED SCRUB—NONE—Castex Incorporated; *U.S. Public*, pg. 1577

SPEED SEAL—Primer—Jones Blair Company; *U.S. Private*, pg. 596

SPEED SENSORS—NONE—Philips Automotive Electronics; *Int'l*, pg. 1054

SPEED SET—Joint Compound—Georgia-Pacific Corporation; *U.S. Public*, pg. 735

SPEED SHINE—NONE—Castex Incorporated; *U.S. Public*, pg. 1577

SPEED-SIX—Double-Action Revolvers—Sturm, Ruger & Co., Inc.; *U.S. Public*, pg. 1526

SPEED SPRAY—Antiperspirant Deodorant—The Mennen Company; *U.S. Public*, pg. 397

SPEED STAR—NONE—Carpenter Technology Corporation; *U.S. Public*, pg. 307

SPEED STICK—Deodorant & Anti-Perspirant—The Mennen Company; *U.S. Public*, pg. 397

SPEED TRAP—Diesel Engine Overspeed Protection Systems—Amot Controls Corporation; *U.S. Public*, pg. 1405

SPEED-TROL—Speed Drives—Sterling Electric, Inc.; *U.S. Private*, pg. 1041

SPEED II—4th Generation Application Devel. Tool & Data Base Mngmt. System—APPX Software Inc.; *U.S. Public*, pg. 1634

SPEED-WALL—Paint—ICI Paints; *Int'l*, pg. 664

SPEED WELD—Ceramic Fiber Module—A.P. Green Industries, Inc.; *U.S. Public*, pg. 761

SPEED ZONE—Licensed NASCAR Apparel—K2 Inc.; *U.S. Public*, pg. 940

SPEEDAIRE—Air Compressor—W.W. Grainger, Inc.; *U.S. Public*, pg. 758

SPEEDBALL—Lettering Matls, Art & Drawing—Hunt Corporation; *U.S. Public*, pg. 848

SPEEDBOR 2000—Woodboring Bits—American Tool Companies, Inc.; *U.S. Private*, pg. 63

SPEEDCART—Rack—Speedrack Products Group, Ltd.; *U.S. Private*, pg. 1024

SPEEDCAST—Fishing Competition—Outdoor Technologies Group; *U.S. Private*, pg. 822

SPEEDCOTE—Paint—ICI Paints; *Int'l*, pg. 664

SPEEDCRAFT—Interior & Exterior Latex & Oil-Based Enamels—PPG Industries, Inc.; *U.S. Public*, pg. 1245

SPEEDET—Laundry Products & Related Dispensing Equipment for OPL Laundries—Puritan/Churchill Chemical Company; *U.S. Private*, pg. 895

SPEEDFLOW—Process Continuous Mixer—Pettibone Corporation; *U.S. Private*, pg. 859

SPEEDFLOW—NONE—Pfizer Inc.; *U.S. Public*, pg. 1281

SPEEDFLOW, JR.—NONE—Pfizer Inc.; *U.S. Public*, pg. 1281

SPEEDHIDE—Paints, Enamels, Rollers & Roller Covers—PPG Industries, Inc.; *U.S. Public*, pg. 1245

SPEEDI-BOOT!—Split Boots & Clamps—R&B, Inc.; *U.S. Public*, pg. 1354

SPEEDI-DRI-OIL—Grease Absorbent—Engelhard Corporation; *U.S. Public*, pg. 582

SPEEDIMAILER—Self-Mailer—Moore Corporation Limited; *Int'l*, pg. 888

SPEEDIPLY—Carbonless Form Set—Moore Corporation Limited; *Int'l*, pg. 888

SPEEDISEALER—Self-Mailing System—Moore Document Solutions; *Int'l*, pg. 890

SPEEDISET—Snap-Apart Sets—Moore Corporation Limited; *Int'l*, pg. 888

SPEEDLINE—Paint Brushes, Cleaning, Polishing, Smoothing & Dusting Brushes—PPG Industries, Inc.; *U.S. Public*, pg. 1245

SPEEDMASTER—Hair Clipper—Andis Company; *U.S. Private*, pg. 73

SPEEDMASTER—Automatic Labeling Equipment—Exact Equipment Corporation; *U.S. Private*, pg. 387

SPEEDMULLOR—Foundry Sand Mullor—Pettibone Corporation; *U.S. Private*, pg. 859

SPEEDNOTCH—Roll Forming Material—Lockformer Company; *U.S. Public*, pg. 1100

SPEEDOLET—Conduit Fitting—Killark Electric Manufacturing Co.; *U.S. Public*, pg. 844

SPEEDOMAX—Recorders—Honeywell, Inc.; *U.S. Public*, pg. 834

SPEEDPLUS—Option—GenRad, Inc.; *U.S. Public*, pg. 731

SPEEDPOST—Post Support Devices—Rule Industries, Inc.; *U.S. Public*, pg. 950

SPEEDSTER—Deep Fryer—American Wyott Corporation; *U.S. Private*, pg. 1193

SPEEDSTICK—NONE—Colgate-Palmolive S.A.I.C.; *U.S. Public*, pg. 399

SPEEDSTORE—Vertical Plate Storage Rack—Jarke Corporation; *U.S. Private*, pg. 583

SPEEDTRON—Electronic Var. Speed—Sterling Electric, Inc.; *U.S. Public*, pg. 1041

SPEEDWAY MOTOR SPORTS—NONE—Speedway Motorsports, Inc.; *U.S. Public*, pg. 1498

SPEEDY—Brake & Muffler—Speedy Car-X, Inc.; *U.S. Public*, pg. 1578

SPEEDY AUTO GLASS—Automotive Replacement Glass—TCG International Inc.; *Int'l*, pg. 1336

SPEEDYVAP—Covers—Fisher Scientific Company; *U.S. Private*, pg. 658

SPEER—Center Fire Pistol Ammunition Bullets—Blount International, Inc.; *U.S. Public*, pg. 237

SPEKOL 1100—Diode Array Spectral Photometer—Carl Zeiss; *Int'l*, pg. 1522

SPEL-BINDER—Office Supplies—JM Company; *U.S. Private*, pg. 577

SPELL-WRITE—Notebooks—The Mead Corporation; *U.S. Public*, pg. 1074

SPELLING ACE—Electronic Speller—Franklin Electronic Publishers, Inc.; *U.S. Public*, pg. 679

SPELLJAMMER—Games & Books—TSR, Inc.; *U.S. Public*, pg. 1185

SPELLMASTER—Electronic Dictionary—Franklin Electronic Publishers, Inc.; *U.S. Public*, pg. 679

SPENCE—Valves—Watts Industries, Inc.; *U.S. Public*, pg. 1746

SPENCER—Food Stores—Spencer Companies Inc.; *U.S. Private*, pg. 1024

SPENCER—Slacks—The Spencer Group Inc.; *U.S. Private*, pg. 1025

SPENCER—Air Blowers, Exhausters & Gas Boosters—The Spencer Turbine Co.; *U.S. Private*, pg. 1025

SPENCER GIFTS—Retail Gift Stores—Spencer Gifts, Inc.; *Int'l*, pg. 1216

SPENCER'S—Children's Wear—Spencer's Inc.; *U.S. Private*, pg. 1025

SPENCO—Insoles Dressings, Padding & Exercise Aids—Kimberly-Clark Corporation; *U.S. Public*, pg. 958

SPHERICEL—Hollow Glass Beads for Plastics—Potters Industries, Inc.; *U.S. Private*, pg. 827

SPERRY-SUN—Drilling Services—Dresser Industries, Inc.; *U.S. Public*, pg. 528

SPERRY TOPSIDERS—Footwear—The Stride Rite Corporation; *U.S. Public*, pg. 1524

SPEXX—NONE—The Timken Company; *U.S. Public*, pg. 1617

SPEY—Military Engine—Rolls-Royce Military Aero Engines Ltd.; *Int'l*, pg. 1127

SPEYBURN SINGLE MALT—NONE—Barton Brands, Ltd.; *U.S. Public*, pg. 300

SPEZYME—Enzymes for the Starch Industry—Cultor Ltd.; *Int'l*, pg. 349

SPHERE-ROL—Spherical Roller Bearings—McGill Manufacturing Company, Inc.; *U.S. Public*, pg. 573

SPHEREX—Medical—Pharmacia & Upjohn Adria Laboratories; *Int'l*, pg. 1049

SPHERIGLASS—Solid Glass Spheres for Plastics—Potters Industries, Inc.; *U.S. Private*, pg. 827

SPHERILOK—Lip Systems for Earthmoving Buckets—Esco Corporation; *U.S. Private*, pg. 382

SPHEROGEL—Liquid Chromatography Columns—Beckman Instruments, Inc.; *U.S. Public*, pg. 199

SPHINX PRODUCTS—Paper—Unisource; *U.S. Public*, pg. 1671

SPI-ARGENT—Infection Resistant Coating—Spire Corporation; *U.S. Public*, pg. 1499

SPI-ARRAY TESTER 750—Outdoor Module & Array Tester—Spire Corporation; *U.S. Public*, pg. 1499

SPI-ASSEMBLER 500—Automated Solar Cell Assembly—Spire Corporation; *U.S. Public*, pg. 1499

SPI-ASSEMBLER 5000—Automated Solae Cell Assembly—Spire Corporation; *U.S. Public*, pg. 1499

SPI-CELL QC6—Cell Tester—Spire Corporation; *U.S. Public*, pg. 1499

SPI-CELL TEST 150—Solar Cell Tester—Spire Corporation; *U.S. Public*, pg. 1499

SPI-CERAMIC—Ceramic Coatings for Medical Devices—Spire Corporation; *U.S. Public*, pg. 1499

SPI-CONNECT 1000—Cell Connector—Spire Corporation; *U.S. Public*, pg. 1499

SPI-FRET—Mechanical Fretting Simulation System—Spire Corporation; *U.S. Public*, pg. 1499

SPI-ION 3Q00ME—Metal Ion Implantation Equipment—Spire Corporation; *U.S. Public*, pg. 1499

SPI-LAMINATOR 460—Photovoltaic Module Laminator—Spire Corporation; *U.S. Public*, pg. 1499

SPI-LAMINATOR 660—Photovoltaic Module Laminator—Spire Corporation; *U.S. Public*, pg. 1499

SPI-LAMINATOR 350—Photovoltaic Module Laminator—Spire Corporation; *U.S. Public*, pg. 1499

SPI-LAMINATOR 240—Module Laminator—Spire Corporation; *U.S. Public*, pg. 1499

SPI-LASE50-50—Watt Diode Laser 780-810nm—Spire Corporation; *U.S. Public*, pg. 1499

SPI-LINE 100MSU—Semiautomated Photovoltaic Module Manufacturing—Spire Corporation; *U.S. Public*, pg. 1499

SPI-LINE 1000C—Solar Cell Manufacturing Line—Spire Corporation; *U.S. Public*, pg. 1499

SPI-LINE 1000M—Photovoltaic Module Manufacturing Line—Spire Corporation; *U.S. Public*, pg. 1499

SPI-LINE 1000W—Silicon Wafer Manufacturing Line—Spire Corporation; *U.S. Public*, pg. 1499

SPI-MET—Low Temperature Coating Process—Spire Corporation; *U.S. Public*, pg. 1499

SPI-POLYMER—Slippery, Thromboresistant Surface Treatment—Spire Corporation; *U.S. Public*, pg. 1499

SPI-PULSE—NONE—Spire Corporation; *U.S. Public*, pg. 1499

SPI-SIGHT—Radiopaque Coatings for Medical Devices—Spire Corporation; *U.S. Public*, pg. 1499

SPI-SPECTRUM—Color Coatings on Metallic Components—Spire Corporation; *U.S. Public*, pg. 1499

SPI-SUN SIMULATOR 660—Photovoltaic Module Tester—Spire Corporation; *U.S. Public*, pg. 1499

SPI-SUN SIMULATOR 460—Photovoltaic Module Tester—Spire Corporation; *U.S. Public*, pg. 1499

SPI-SUN SIMULATOR 240APV—Module Tester—Spire Corporation; *U.S. Public*, pg. 1499

SPI-TAB 500—Semi Automated Solar Cell Tabber—Spire Corporation; *U.S. Public*, pg. 1499

SPI-TAB 1000—Cell Tabber—Spire Corporation; *U.S. Public*, pg. 1499

SPI-TEXT—Material Treatment System—Spire Corporation; *U.S. Public*, pg. 1499

SPI-TRIBOTESTER—Mechanical Wear Simulator & Friction Measurement Systems—Spire Corporation; *U.S. Public*, pg. 1499

SPI-VAC PIK 240—Vacuum Transfer Machine—Spire Corporation; *U.S. Public*, pg. 1499

SPIAGGIA—Private Dining & Conference Center—The Levy Organization; *U.S. Private*, pg. 664

SPIC & SPAN—Cleaner—The Procter & Gamble Company; *U.S. Public*, pg. 1330

SPICE-CAP—Spice Alternatives—McCormick Flavor Division-U.S.A.; *U.S. Public*, pg. 1066

SPICE ISLAND—Spices—Specialty Brands; *Int'l*, pg. 237

SPICE ISLANDS—Herbs & Spices—Burns, Philp & Company Limited; *Int'l*, pg. 236

SPICER—Axles, Clutches, Transmissions, Universal Joints, Driveshafts—Dana Corporation; *U.S. Public*, pg. 479

SPICER CLARK-HURTH—Off-Highway Components—Dana Corporation; *U.S. Public*, pg. 479

SPICES OF THE WORLD—Leisure Game—Monarch Avalon, Inc.; *U.S. Public*, pg. 1123

SPIDER & GTV—Car—Fiat Auto Ireland Ltd.; *Int'l*, pg. 481

SPIDER VELOCE—Sports Car—Fiat Auto S.p.A.; *Int'l*, pg. 481

SPIDER-WEB—Filter Medium—Donaldson Company, Inc.; *U.S. Public*, pg. 517

SPIDERWIRE—Fishing Line—Johnson Worldwide Associates, Inc.; *U.S. Public*, pg. 932

SPIDERWIRE ICE LINE—Fishing Line—Johnson Worldwide Associates, Inc.; *U.S. Public*, pg. 932

SPIEGELAU—Glassware—WMF/USA; *U.S. Private*, pg. 1144

SPIEWAK—Apparel—I. Spiewak & Sons, Inc.; *U.S. Private*, pg. 1025

SPIFFITS—Moist Cleaning Towels—The Dow Chemical Company; *U.S. Public*, pg. 522

SPIFFY SPOOL—Automotive Products—Standard Motor Products, Inc.; *U.S. Public*, pg. 1503

SPIKE—Herbicide—The Dow Chemical Company; *U.S. Public*, pg. 522

SPIKE—Steel Anchor—Powers Fastening, Inc.; *U.S. Private*, pg. 878

SPIKE ENERGY—Vibration Measurement—IRD Mechanalysis, Inc. (U.S.A.); *U.S. Public*, pg. 789

SPIKEMASTER—Saige Protection Modules—Recoton Corporation; *U.S. Public*, pg. 1369

SPILL MATE—Towels—Fort James Corporation; *U.S. Public*, pg. 670

SPILL-X—Spil Control Products for Hazardous Spills—Ansul Incorporated; *U.S. Public*, pg. 1648

SPILLBUSTER—Household Products—The Black & Decker Corporation; *U.S. Public*, pg. 233

SPI-MOCVD 400S—Single Wafer MOCVD Reactor—Spire Corporation; *U.S. Public*, pg. 1499

SPIN—Curlers—The Gillette Company; *U.S. Public*, pg. 743

SPIN BLEND—Salad Dressing—GFA Brands, Inc.; *U.S. Private*, pg. 435

SPIN CHEM—Chemical Reagents—Beckman Instruments, Inc.; *U.S. Public*, pg. 199

SPIN-EASE—NONE—Life Technologies, Inc.; *U.S. Public*, pg. 504

SPIN-GLAS—HTB Fiberglass Blanket Insulation—Johns Manville Corporation; *U.S. Public*, pg. 927

SPIN PHYSICS—Magnetic & Video Products & Services—Eastman Kodak Company; *U.S. Public*, pg. 550

SPIN RADIO NETWORK—Music & Talk Radio Program—Westwood One Entertainment; *U.S. Public*, pg. 1763

SPIN RADIO NETWORK—Alternative Rock Program—Westwood One, Inc.; *U.S. Public*, pg. 1763

SPIN SOFT—Fabric Softener Sheet—Blue Cross Laboratories; *U.S. Private*, pg. 152

SPIN-VAP—Scientific Glassware for Laboratory Use—Wheaton Inc.; *Int'l*, pg. 67

SPIN-AID—Agricultural Chemical—AgrEvo USA Company; *Int'l*, pg. 1203

SPINAFLEX—Back Support Brace—Camp Healthcare; *Int'l*, pg. 1425

SPINAL AID—Mattresses—Kingsdown, Inc.; *U.S. Private*, pg. 622

SPINAL GUARD—Sleep Products—King Koil Licensing Company Inc.; *U.S. Private*, pg. 621

SPINAL-STIM—Noninvasive Spinal Fusion Stimulator System—Orthofix Int'l; *Int'l*, pg. 1011

SPINAL-STIM—Bone Growth Stimulator—Orthofix International N.V.; *Int'l*, pg. 1011

SPINALLOY—Magnetic & Video Heads—Eastman Kodak Company; *U.S. Public*, pg. 550

SPINBAR—Magneting Stirring Bars—Bel-Art Products; *U.S. Private*, pg. 130

SPINCHRON—Centrifuge—Beckman Instruments, Inc.; *U.S. Public*, pg. 199

SPINCRAFT—Power Metal Spinning—Standex International Corporation; *U.S. Public*, pg. 1505

SPINDLE-TITE!—Axle Spindle Nuts—R&B, Inc.; *U.S. Public*, pg. 1354

SPINE SUPPORT SLEEP CENTER—Retail Gallery—King Koil Licensing Company Inc.; *U.S. Private*, pg. 621

SPINESCOPE—NONE—Laserscope Surgical Systems; *U.S. Public*, pg. 979

SPINESTAT—NONE—Laserscope Surgical Systems; *U.S. Public*, pg. 979

SPINGUARD—Ceramic Capacitors—AVX Corporation; *Int'l*, pg. 775

SPINHALER—Turbo-Inhaler (For Use with Intal Capsules)—Medeva Pharmaceuticals; *Int'l*, pg. 852

SPINKOTE—Lubricant—Beckman Instruments, Inc.; *U.S. Public*, pg. 199

SPINLOCK—Spinning Nut Type Linear Activator—P.L. Porter Co.; *U.S. Private*, pg. 876

SPINNER BASKER—Mini-Bioreactor—New Brunswick Scientific Co., Inc.; *U.S. Public*, pg. 1169

SPINNING ARROWS AND DETROIT—NONE—Detroit Diesel Corp.; *U.S. Private*, pg. 850

SPINNING ARROWS AND DIESEL—NONE—Detroit Diesel Corp.; *U.S. Private*, pg. 850

SPINNING ARROWS DESIGN—NONE—Detroit Diesel Corp.; *U.S. Private*, pg. 850

SPINNING WHEEL—Fabrics—Thomaston Mills, Inc.; *U.S. Public*, pg. 1599

SPINNSTER—Machinery—Hollingsworth Saco Lowell Corporation, Inc.; *U.S. Private*, pg. 535

SPINOMATIC—Machinery—Hollingsworth Saco Lowell Corporation, Inc.; *U.S. Private*, pg. 535

SPINPRO—Ultracentrifuge Expert System—Beckman Instruments, Inc.; *U.S. Public*, pg. 199

SPINTEX—Blowing Wool—Johns Manville Corporation; *U.S. Public*, pg. 927

SPIR'ATOR—Constant Torque Spring—AMETEK, Inc.; *U.S. Public*, pg. 99

SPIRA-PAK—Cathodic Protection—Corrpro Companies, Inc.; *U.S. Public*, pg. 451

SPIRACOUSTIC—Pre-Formed Round Fiber Glass Duct Liner—Johns Manville Corporation; *U.S. Public*, pg. 927

SPIRAFLEX—Hose—The Goodyear Tire & Rubber Company; *U.S. Public*, pg. 752

SPIRAL—Air Moving Devices—EG & G Rotron; *U.S. Public*, pg. 543

SPIRAL—Paper Tablets, Account, Data & Order Books—The Mead Corporation; *U.S. Public*, pg. 1074

SPIRAL—School Supplies—Mead School & Office Products; *U.S. Public*, pg. 1074

SPIRAL-CURVE—Continuous Vertical Spiral Belt Conveyor Turn—Flomaster Div.; *U.S. Public*, pg. 1318

SPIRAL-LIFT—Continuous Vertical Spiral Belt Conveyor—Flomaster Div.; *U.S. Public*, pg. 1318

SPIRAL LOCK—Notebooks—The Mead Corporation; *U.S. Public*, pg. 1074

THE SPIRAL ORGANIZER—Stationery Products—The Mead Corporation; *U.S. Public*, pg. 1074

SPIRALS—Snack—Borden, Inc.; *U.S. Private*, pg. 157

SPIRALTEK—Liquid Separation Filters—Eastman Kodak Company; *U.S. Public*, pg. 550

SPIRALTEK—Rolled Filters—Osmonics, Inc.; *U.S. Public*, pg. 1233

SPIRALUX—Compact Fluorescent Lamp—Duro-Test Corporation; *U.S. Private*, pg. 349

SPIRATREX—Point of Use UF/MF Systems—Osmonics, Inc.; *U.S. Public*, pg. 1233

SPIRATUBE—Hose—Flexible Technologies Inc.; *Int'l*, pg. 1267

SPIREX—Reamer—Greenfield Industries; *U.S. Public*, pg. 950

SPIRIT—Awning—Carefree of Colorado; *U.S. Public*, pg. 217

SPIRIT—Mixing Consoles—Harman International Industries, Inc.; *U.S. Public*, pg. 787

SPIRIT—Catheter—Medtronic, Inc.; *U.S. Public*, pg. 1082

SPIRIT—NONE—Molex Incorporated; *U.S. Public*, pg. 1121

SPIRIT—Evoked Potential Testing System—Nicolet Analytical; *U.S. Public*, pg. 1593

SPIRIT—Motor Homes—Winnebago Industries, Inc.; *U.S. Public*, pg. 1772

SPIRIT OF BOSTON—Cruise & Dining Ship—Spirit Cruises, Inc.; *Int'l*, pg. 1274

SPIRIT OF CHICAGO—Cruise & Dining Ship—Spirit Cruises, Inc.; *Int'l*, pg. 1274

THE SPIRIT OF FAMILY—Casual Clothing—Gitano Fashions Ltd.; *U.S. Public*, pg. 686

SPIRIT OF NEW JERSEY—Cruise & Dining—Spirit Cruises, Inc.; *Int'l*, pg. 1274

SPIRIT OF NEW YORK—Cruise & Dining Ship—Spirit Cruises, Inc.; *Int'l*, pg. 1274

SPIRIT OF NORFOLK—Cruise & Dining Ship—Spirit Cruises, Inc.; *Int'l*, pg. 1274

SPIRIT OF PAGET SOUND—Cruise & Dining Ship—Spirit Cruises, Inc.; *Int'l*, pg. 1274

SPIRIT OF PHILADELPHIA—Cruise & Dining Ship—Spirit Cruises, Inc.; *Int'l*, pg. 1274

SPIRIT OF WASHINGTON—Cruise & Dining Ship—Spirit Cruises, Inc.; *Int'l*, pg. 1274

SPIRO-PAC—Composite Containers & Corner Posts, Paper Shipping Drums—Sonoco Products Company; *U.S. Public*, pg. 1485

SPIRO-TEX—Extruded Plastic Net—Nalle Plastics Inc.; *U.S. Public*, pg. 773

SPIRO-LUBE—Spindle Lubricant for Paper Tube & Can Winding—Sonoco Products Company; *U.S. Public*, pg. 1485

SPIROCORT—Respiratory Pharmaceutical—Astra AB; *Int'l*, pg. 93

SPIROFLEX—Diaphragm For Regulators—Leslie Controls, Inc.; *U.S. Public*, pg. 1746

SPIROL—Fasteners—Spirol International Corp.; *U.S. Private*, pg. 1026

SPIROLITE—High-Density Polyethylene Pipe—Chevron Chemical Co.; *U.S. Public*, pg. 348

SPIROPENT—Bronchodilator—Boehringer Ingelheim GmbH; *Int'l*, pg. 199

SPIROSENSE—Spirometry System—Burdick, Inc.; *U.S. Private*, pg. 181

SPIRULINA—Vitamins—Health Products Corporation; *U.S. Private*, pg. 514

SPITFIRE—Power Tools—The Black & Decker Corporation; *U.S. Public*, pg. 233

SPLASH—Cologne—Nuevo Federal S.A.; *Int'l*, pg. 990

SPLASH—Carbonated Juices—Ocean Spray Cranberries, Inc.; *U.S. Private*, pg. 811

SPLASHDANCE—Shower Radio—Pollenex; *U.S. Public*, pg. 1391

SPLASHGON—Splash Eliminator—Fisher Scientific Company; *U.S. Private*, pg. 658

SPLASHPAK—Pool System—Jacuzzi Bros., Jacuzzi, Inc.; *U.S. Public*, pg. 1684

SPLENDA—NONE—Johnson & Johnson; *U.S. Public*, pg. 927

SPLENDAIDES—Bathroom Tissue, Paper Napkins & Towels—Georgia-Pacific Corporation; *U.S. Public*, pg. 735

SPLENDOR—Pasta—Borden, Inc.; *U.S. Private*, pg. 157

SPLICE-SAVER—Splice Connections—Delphi Packard Electric Systems; *U.S. Public*, pg. 719

SPLICE WRAP—Low Voltage Splice Kits—Plymouth Rubber Company, Inc.; *U.S. Public*, pg. 1311

SPLINE DRIVE INVERTED SPOTFACER—Inverted Cutter—National Twist Drill Div.; *U.S. Public*, pg. 1370

SPLINE-TAPER DRIVE COUNTERBORE & HOLDER—Counterbore & Holder—National Twist Drill Div.; *U.S. Public*, pg. 1370

SPLIT-COUPLING—Speed Union for Joining Two Threaded Rigid Metal Conduits—O-Z/Gedney Co.; *U.S. Public*, pg. 727

SPLIT-LESS—Specialty Nails—Maze Nails; *U.S. Private*, pg. 718

SPLIT SECOND—Convenience Stores—Amoco Corporation; *U.S. Public*, pg. 101

SPLITFIRE—Sparkplugs—Old World Industries, Inc.; *U.S. Private*, pg. 814

SPLITFORM—Split Bobbin Power Transformers—Tamura Corp. of America, Microtran Div.; *U.S. Private*, pg. 1067

SPLUGEN—Basketball Shoe—K-Swiss Inc.; *U.S. Public*, pg. 937

SPODE—Fine Bone & Stone China;Imperialware; Oven-to-Tableware, Giftware—The Royal China & Porcelain Companies Inc.; *U.S. Private*, pg. 948

SPOILED GIRLS—Apparel—Clothestime Stores, Inc.; *U.S. Public*, pg. 387

SPOILER BARS—Dryer—Beloit Corporation; *U.S. Public*, pg. 789

SPOKESMAN—Telephone Loudspeaker—Lucent Technologies Inc.; *U.S. Public*, pg. 1017

SPONGOSTAN—Gelatine Sponge—Novo Nordisk A/S; *Int'l*, pg. 987

SPONTEX—Cellulose Sponges—Spontex, Inc.; *Int'l*, pg. 1409

SPONTIN—Syrup—Spadel SA; *Int'l*, pg. 1287

SPONTO—Agricultural Emulsifiers—Witco Corporation; *U.S. Public*, pg. 1773

SPOODLE—Portion Control Server—The Vollrath Company, L.L.C.; *U.S. Private*, pg. 1143

SPOOL-PAC—Products in the Electronics & Communications Industry—General Cable Corporation; *U.S. Public*, pg. 1486

SPOOLARC—NONE—ESAB Welding & Cutting Products; *Int'l*, pg. 281

SPOONULA—Combination Spoon & Spatula—Fisher Scientific Company; *U.S. Private*, pg. 658

SPOONULET—Spoon/spatula—Fisher Scientific Company; *U.S. Private*, pg. 658

SPOORNET—Railway Network—Transnet Ltd.; *Int'l*, pg. 1417

SPORANOX—NONE—Johnson & Johnson; *U.S. Public*, pg. 927

SPORSTER II—Stove—The Canadian Coleman Co., Ltd.; *U.S. Private*, pg. 691

SPORT—Magazine—Petersen Publishing Company, L.L.C.; *U.S. Private*, pg. 856

SPORT AUTO—French Motoring Magazine—EMAP France; *Int'l*, pg. 451

SPORT BILD—Magazine—Axel Springer Verlag AG; *Int'l*, pg. 102

SPORT CRUISER—38' & 47' Sport Boats—Fountain Powerboat Industries, Inc.; *U.S. Public*, pg. 678

SPORT ELITE—Sport Bag—Ektelon; *U.S. Private*, pg. 884

SPORT EVENT MANAGEMENT—NONE—Intertec Publishing; *U.S. Public*, pg. 1486

SPORT FISHING—23', 27' & 31' Sport Fishing Boats—Fountain Powerboat Industries, Inc.; *U.S. Public*, pg. 678

SPORT GRIP—Steering Wheel Covers—Superior Industries International, Inc.; *U.S. Public*, pg. 1539

SPORT LAVIT—Toiletries—SmithKline Beecham plc; *Int'l*, pg. 1264

SPORT MASTER—Shoes—E.J. Footwear Corp.; *U.S. Public*, pg. 1684

SPORT MATE 1200—Blower/Dryer—Sunbeam Household Products; *U.S. Public*, pg. 1533

SPORT NAUTIQUE—Power Boat—Correct Craft, Inc.; *U.S. Private*, pg. 276

SPORT OF STYLE—Lifestyle—L.A. Gear, Inc.; *U.S. Public*, pg. 969

SPORT PLUS MASSAGE—Shower head & Hand Held Shower—Interbath, Inc.; *U.S. Private*, pg. 566

SPORT PREMIUM—Tires—Bridgestone/Firestone, Inc.; *Int'l*, pg. 213

SPORT SET—Athletic Shoes—E.J. Footwear Corp.; *U.S. Public*, pg. 1684

SPORT SHAKE—NONE—Mid-America Dairymen, Inc.; *U.S. Private*, pg. 743

SPORT SOX—Socks—Ridgeview, Inc.; *U.S. Private*, pg. 930

SPORT TRUCK—Magazine—Petersen Publishing Company, L.L.C.; *U.S. Private*, pg. 856

SPORTAGE—Sport-Utility Vehicle—Kia Motors America, Inc.; *Int'l*, pg. 733

SPORTCARRIER—Soft Baby Carrier—Evenflo Company, Inc.; *U.S. Private*, pg. 629

SPORTCORT—Hydrocortisone Creme—Mueller Sports Medicine, Inc.; *U.S. Private*, pg. 766

SPORTCRAFT—Athletic Team Equip. & Backyard Games—Sportcraft Ltd.; *U.S. Private*, pg. 1026

SPORTELAST—Flooring Compositions—The Dow Chemical Company; *U.S. Public*, pg. 522

SPORTELLE—Women's Casual Apparel Stores—F.W. Woolworth Co.; *U.S. Public*, pg. 1777

SPORTELLE/KARUBA—Women's Casual Apparel Stores—Woolworth Corporation; *U.S. Public*, pg. 1777

SPORTER—NONE—Weatherby, Inc.; *U.S. Private*, pg. 1155

SPORTHOMSON—Sportswear—Thomson Company, Inc.; *U.S. Public*, pg. 1429

SPORTHOTICS—Biodynamic Sport Orthotic Devices—The Langer Biomechanics Group, Inc.; *U.S. Public*, pg. 978

SPORTING GOODS BUSINESS—Magazine—Miller Freeman Inc.; *Int'l*, pg. 1443

SPORTING GUN—Shooting Magazine—EMAP Pursuit Publishing; *Int'l*, pg. 451

SPORTING GUN—Country Pursuits & Property Magazine—IPC Magazines Limited; *Int'l*, pg. 651

THE SPORTING LIFE—NONE—Mirror Group plc; *Int'l*, pg. 869

THE SPORTING NEWS—Magazine—Times Mirror Magazines, Inc.; *U.S. Public*, pg. 1616

THE SPORTING NEWS—Magazine—The Sporting News Publishing Company; *U.S. Public*, pg. 1616

SPORTIQUES—Shoes—Tober Industries, Inc.; *U.S. Private*, pg. 1089

SPORTIS—Breakfast Cereal—Nestle S.A.; *Int'l*, pg. 915

SPORTIVA—Tents & Sports Bags—Jinwoong Inc.; *Int'l*, pg. 706

SPORTLIFE—Chewing Gum—Huhtamaki Oy; *Int'l*, pg. 638

SPORTLINER—Cargo Tray—Lund International Holdings, Inc.; *U.S. Public*, pg. 1020

SPORTMAT—Molded Floor Tray—Lund International Holdings, Inc.; *U.S. Public*, pg. 1020

SPORTOCASINS—Shoes—G.H. Bass & Co.; *U.S. Public*, pg. 1291

SPORTPLUS—Soft Drink—Cadbury Schweppes p.l.c.; *Int'l*, pg. 247

SPORTS AFIELD—Magazine—The Hearst Corporation; *U.S. Private*, pg. 515

SPORTS AFIELD—Magazine—Hearst Magazines Division; *U.S. Private*, pg. 516

SPORTS CARD TRADER—Magazine—Century Publishing Company; *U.S. Private*, pg. 226

SPORTS CENTRAL USA—Sports News Programming—Westwood One, Inc.; *U.S. Public*, pg. 1763

SPORTS CUSHION—Shock-Absorbing Shoe Inserts—Schering-Plough Corporation; *U.S. Public*, pg. 1438

SPORTS FAN GOING TO THE GAME—Licensed Athletic Team Apparel—Woolworth Corporation; *U.S. Public*, pg. 1777

SPORTS GIFT DIGEST—Catalogue-Magazine—Century Publishing Company; *U.S. Private*, pg. 226

SPORTS ILLUSTRATED—Magazine—Time Warner Inc.; *U.S. Public*, pg. 1610

SPORTS ILLUSTRATED FOR KIDS—Magazine—Time Warner Inc.; *U.S. Public*, pg. 1610

SPORTS PAD FOOTBALL—Videogame—Sega of America Inc.; *Int'l*, pg. 1218

SPORTS PAD SOCCER—Videogame—Sega of America Inc.; *Int'l*, pg. 1218

SPORTS REPORT—Daily Sportscast—Westwood One, Inc.; *U.S. Public*, pg. 1763

SPORTS SCENES—Stationery Items - Paper Pads—The Mead Corporation; *U.S. Public*, pg. 1074

SPORTS SCOREBOARD—Weekend News Recap Programming—Westwood One, Inc.; *U.S. Public*, pg. 1763

SPORTS TERRAIN—Tires—Bridgestone/Firestone, Inc.; *Int'l*, pg. 213

SPORTS TIME—Watches & Clocks—Bulova Corporation; *U.S. Public*, pg. 1010

SPORTS WORLD ROUNDUP—Sports Programming—Westwood One, Inc.; *U.S. Public*, pg. 1763

SPORTSBAND—AM/FM Radio with Headband—Sony Electronics; *Int'l*, pg. 1281

SPORTSBRA—Bra—Olga Div.; *U.S. Public*, pg. 1738

SPORTSCHANNEL AMERICA—Regional Cable Sports Channel—National Broadcasting Co., Inc.; *U.S. Public*, pg. 712

SPORTSCREME—Pharmaceutical Products—Thompson Medical Company, Inc.; *U.S. Private*, pg. 1083

SPORTSCREME ICE—Pharmaceutical Product—Thompson Medical Company, Inc.; *U.S. Private*, pg. 1083

SPORTSFLIES 2000—NONE—Pinnacle Brands, Inc.; *U.S. Private*, pg. 866

SPORTSMAN—Sporting Goods—Brunswick Bowling & Billiards Corp.; *U.S. Public*, pg. 265

SPORTSMAN—Flashlights, Search Lights & Area Lights—RAYOVAC Corporation; *U.S. Private*, pg. 912

SPORTSMASTER—Recreational Vehicles—Kit Manufacturing Company; *U.S. Public*, pg. 962

SPORTSMASTER CLASSIC—Recreational Vehicle—Kit Manufacturing Company; *U.S. Public*, pg. 962

SPORTSTER—Sport Bag—Ektelon; *U.S. Private*, pg. 884

SPORTSTER—Gyms—Hedstrom Corporation; *U.S. Private*, pg. 526

SPORTSTER—Fax & Computer Modems—3Com Personal Communications Div.; *U.S. Public*, pg. 1604

SPORTSTIME—Sports News Commentary—Westwood One, Inc.; *U.S. Public*, pg. 1763

SPORTSTRAINER—Multi-Station Weight Training For up to 11 People—Paramount Fitness Corp.; *U.S. Public*, pg. 838

SPORTSTRAX—Pager & Paging Service—Motorola, Inc.; *U.S. Public*, pg. 1136

SPORTSTRIPE—Marine, R.V. & Leisure Decorative Utilitarian Products—Spartan International Inc.; *U.S. Public*, pg. 1020

SPORTSTYLE—Business Publication—Fairchild Publications; *U.S. Public*, pg. 513

SPORTVAN—Truck—Chevrolet Motor Div. General Motors Corp.; *U.S. Public*, pg. 720

SPORTVIEW—Binoculars, Riflescopes—Bushnell Corporation; *U.S. Private*, pg. 1191

SPORTWOOD—Glue-Down Flooring—Robbins, Inc.; *U.S. Private*, pg. 934

SPORTWOOD PLUS—Glue-Down Flooring—Robbins, Inc.; *U.S. Private*, pg. 934

SPORTWOOD PLUS ULTRA—Suspended/Anchored Sports Flooring—Robbins, Inc.; *U.S. Private*, pg. 934

SPORTX—Nerve Stimulating Units in the Field of Sports Medicine—Staodyn Inc.; *U.S. Public*, pg. 1509

SPOT—NONE—BBC Magazines; *Int'l*, pg. 114

SPOT-BILT—Footwear—Hyde Athletic Industries, Inc.; *U.S. Public*, pg. 851

SPOT DTEK—Pipe & Cable Locator—McLaughlin Manufacturing Company; *U.S. Private*, pg. 724

SPOT GLUE—Gaskets—Tranter, Inc.; *U.S. Public*, pg. 521

SPOT O'GOLD—NONE—Berg Electronics; *U.S. Public*, pg. 212

SPOT RAIN—Stationery Sprinklers—L.R. Nelson Corporation; *U.S. Private*, pg. 790

SPOTBRADS—Fasteners—Spotnails, *U.S. Private*, pg. 845

SPOTCHECK—Dye Penetrant—ITW Magnaflux; *U.S. Public*, pg. 866

SPOTLIGHT ON VIDEO—Video Rental Program—National Video, Inc.; *U.S. Public*, pg. 1755

SPOTLIGHTER—Merchandiser Display—The Mead Corporation; *U.S. Public*, pg. 1074

SPOTLITER—Rechargable Utility Lights—The Black & Decker Corporation; *U.S. Public*, pg. 233

SPOTLITER—Highlighting Marker—The Pilot Pen Corp. of America; *Int'l*, pg. 1057

SPOTNAILERS—Tool—Spotnails; *U.S. Private*, pg. 845

SPOTPINNER/BRADDER—Tool—Spotnails; *U.S. Private*, pg. 845

SPOTPINS—Fasteners—Spotnails; *U.S. Private*, pg. 845

SPOTS—Channel Unit—Lucent Technologies Inc.; *U.S. Public*, pg. 1017

SPOTSCRUBBER—Major Appliances-Mostly Washing Machines—General Electric Canada Inc.; *U.S. Public*, pg. 713

SPOTSTAPLERS—Tool—Spotnails; *U.S. Private*, pg. 845

SPOTSTAPLES—Fasteners—Spotnails; *U.S. Private*, pg. 845

SPOTWHEEL—Roller Applicators for Hot Melt Adhesives—Graco Inc.; *U.S. Public*, pg. 756

SPOUT PAK—Juice & Milk Containers—International Paper Company; *U.S. Public*, pg. 901

SPOW—Transparent Thermoplastic Stretch Film—Reynolds Metals Company; *U.S. Public*, pg. 1385

SPOX—NONE—Molex Incorporated; *U.S. Public*, pg. 1121

SPRABABBITT—Metallizing Wire—Sulzer Metco (Westbury) Inc.; *Int'l*, pg. 1307

SPRABOND WIRE—Metallizing Wire for Bonding—Sulzer Metco (Westbury) Inc.; *Int'l*, pg. 1307

SPRABRASS—Metallizing Wire—Sulzer Metco (Westbury) Inc.; *Int'l*, pg. 1307

SPRABRONZE—Metallizing Wire—Sulzer Metco (Westbury) Inc.; *Int'l*, pg. 1307

SPRAGUE—Heavy Duty Windshield Wiper Systems—Echlin Inc.; *U.S. Public*, pg. 560

SPRAGUE—Tantalum Capacitors—Vishay Intertechnology, Inc.; *U.S. Public*, pg. 1721

SPRASTEEL—Metallizing Wire—Sulzer Metco (Westbury) Inc.; *Int'l*, pg. 1307

SPRAY-CYTE—Cytological Fixative—Becton Dickinson Primary Care Diagnostics; *U.S. Public*, pg. 199

SPRAY-DAY-LITE—Paint—ICI Paints; *Int'l*, pg. 664

SPRAY-DOC—Metal & Plastic Tank Sprayers—Vermont American Tool Corp.; *U.S. Public*, pg. 575

SPRAY GRIP—Handle for Aerosol Cans—Rust-Oleum Corporation; *U.S. Public*, pg. 1358

SPRAY MIST—Irons—Sunbeam Household Products; *U.S. Public*, pg. 1533

SPRAY-MOUNT—Adhesive Aerosol—3M; *U.S. Public*, pg. 1604

SPRAY-N-GLUE—Adhesive—DAP Inc.; *Int'l*, pg. 1486

SPRAY 'N STARCH—Fabric Finish—The Dow Chemical Company; *U.S. Public*, pg. 522

SPRAY 'N WASH—Soil & Stain Remover—The Dow Chemical Company; *U.S. Public*, pg. 522

SPRAY 'N WASH STAIN STICK—Stain Removal Laundry Stick—DowBrands, L.P.; *U.S. Public*, pg. 523

SPRAY 'N WIPE—Cleaner—Colgate-Palmolive Company; *U.S. Public*, pg. 397

SPRAY SATIN—Predispersed Coating Pigment—Engelhard Corporation; *U.S. Public*, pg. 582

SPRAY SENSATIONS—Shower Access.—Waxman Industries, Inc.; *U.S. Public*, pg. 1748

SPRAY-TAINER—Oil Spray Booth—Binks Sames Corporation; *U.S. Public*, pg. 229

SPRAYBABBITT—Coating Materials for Thermal Spray Application—The Perkin-Elmer Corporation; *U.S. Public*, pg. 1279

SPRAYBOND—Coating Materials for Thermal Spray Application—The Perkin-Elmer Corporation; *U.S. Public*, pg. 1279

SPRAYBRASS—Coating Materials for Thermal Spray Application—The Perkin-Elmer Corporation; *U.S. Public*, pg. 1279

SPRAYBRONZ—Coating Materials for Thermal Spray Application—The Perkin-Elmer Corporation; *U.S. Public*, pg. 1279

SPRAYIT—Paint Sprayers & Air Compressors—Thomas Industries Inc.; *U.S. Public*, pg. 1598

SPRAYON—Aerosols—Pegasus International Corporation; *U.S. Private*, pg. 1046

SPRAYON—Industrial Aerosol—Sherwin-Williams Diversified Brands, Inc.; *U.S. Public*, pg. 1466

SPRAYPRO—Roller Pumps—Hypro Corporation; *U.S. Public*, pg. 1767

SPRAYSOL—Trigger Pumps—Carter Holt Harvey Limited; *U.S. Public*, pg. 904

SPRAYSTEEL—Coating Materials for Thermal Spray Application—The Perkin-Elmer Corporation; *U.S. Public*, pg. 1279

SPRAYWALL—Spray Applied Corrosive Resistant Manhole & Pipe Reconstruction—Enviroq; *U.S. Public*, pg. 881

SPREADARC—Welder—The Lincoln Electric Company; *U.S. Public*, pg. 996

SPREADERY—Spreadable Cheese—Kraft Foods Inc.; *U.S. Public*, pg. 1288

SPREADMASTER—Gas Lift Valves—Halliburton Energy Services; *U.S. Public*, pg. 776

SPREAN—Washing Compound—Enthone-OMI, Inc.; *U.S. Public*, pg. 138

SPRECHER + SCHUH—Contractors, Relays & Starters—Rockwell International Corporation; *U.S. Public*, pg. 1397

SPRED—Paint—ICI Paints; *Int'l*, pg. 664

SPRED-DURA—Paint—ICI Paints; *Int'l*, pg. 664

SPRED ENAMEL—Paint—ICI Paints; *Int'l*, pg. 664

SPRED FLAT—Paint—ICI Paints; *Int'l*, pg. 664

SPRED GLOSS—Paint—ICI Paints; *Int'l*, pg. 664

SPRED HOUSE—Paint—ICI Paints; *Int'l*, pg. 664

SPRED KITCHEN AND BATH—Paint—ICI Paints; *Int'l*, pg. 664

SPRED LO-LUSTRE—Paint—ICI Paints; *Int'l*, pg. 664

SPRED LUSTRE—Paint—ICI Paints; *Int'l*, pg. 664

SPRED SATIN—Paint—ICI Paints; *Int'l*, pg. 664

SPRED SILK—Paint—ICI Paints; *Int'l*, pg. 664

SPRED SOLO—Paint—ICI Paints; *Int'l*, pg. 664

SPRED SUPREME—Paint—ICI Paints; *Int'l*, pg. 664

SPRED 2000—No-Voc Paint—ICI Paints; *Int'l*, pg. 664

SPREDA-COTE—Roll Coater Distributor Roll Cover—Harnischfeger Industries, Inc.; *U.S. Public*, pg. 788

SPREE—Motorscooter—American Honda Motor Co., Inc. Motorcycle Division; *Int'l*, pg. 634

SPREE—Luggage—American Tourister, Inc.; *U.S. Public*, pg. 1430

SPREE—Candy—Nestle S.A.; *Int'l*, pg. 915

SPREE—NONE—Nestle USA; *Int'l*, pg. 916

SPREE—All Natural Sodas—Shasta Beverages, Inc.; *U.S. Public*, pg. 1153

SPIRAGAN—Gas Seperation Elements—AlliedSignal Inc.; *U.S. Public*, pg. 49

SPRING—Cigarette—Lorillard Tobacco Company; *U.S. Public*, pg. 1011

SPRING ACTION—Eyeglass Frames—AVC/Nu-Vision, Inc.; *U.S. Private*, pg. 9

SPRING AIR—Mattresses—The Spring Air Company; *U.S. Private*, pg. 1027

SPRING GARDEN—Cookware—Regal Ware, Inc.; *U.S. Public*, pg. 917

SPRING-GREEN—Lawn & Tree Care Service—Spring-Green Lawn Care Corporation; *U.S. Private*, pg. 1027

SPRING-GRIP—Anchoring Device—U.S. Surgical Corp.; *U.S. Public*, pg. 1687

SPRING HEARTH—Spring Wheat Flour—Cargill Flour Div.; *U.S. Private*, pg. 210

SPRING HILL—Nurseries—Spring Hill Nurseries Co.; *U.S. Private*, pg. 420

SPRING IRIS—Kitchen Tools—Ekco Housewares, Inc.; *U.S. Public*, pg. 566

SPRING LEMON LIGHTS—Cigarettes—Lorillard Tobacco Company; *U.S. Public*, pg. 1011

SPRING-O-PEDIC—Mattress—The Spring Air Company; *U.S. Private*, pg. 1027

SPRING SCENT—Cleaner—The Dow Chemical Company; *U.S. Public*, pg. 522

SPRING SOFT DRINKS—Soft Drinks—Vaux Group Plc; *Int'l*, pg. 1453

SPRING TECTOR—NONE—Western Atlas Logging Services; *U.S. Public*, pg. 1757

SPRING-TITE!—Multi-purpose Springs—R&B, Inc.; *U.S. Public*, pg. 1354

SPRINGBOK—Puzzles—Hallmark Cards, Inc.; *U.S. Private*, pg. 495

SPRINGBROOK—Hair & Body—Levlad, Inc.; *U.S. Private*, pg. 663

SPRINGBROOK—Mobile Homes—Wick Bldg. Systems Inc. Manufactured Homes Div.; *U.S. Private*, pg. 1174

SPRINGENERATOR—Spring Machines—The U.S. Baird Corporation; *U.S. Private*, pg. 1124

SPRINGER—NONE—Clarks International; *Int'l*, pg. 296

SPRINGER—Motorcycle—Harley-Davidson, Inc.; *U.S. Public*, pg. 786

SPRINGER-VERLAG NEW YORK—Publisher: Scientific, Medical, Technical Books & Journals—Springer-Verlag New York Inc.; *Int'l*, pg. 1291

SPRINGFIELD—Food Products & General Merchandise—Certified Grocers of California; *U.S. Private*, pg. 226

SPRINGFIELD—Vertical Universal Grinders—Motch Corporation; *Int'l*, pg. 1128

SPRINGFIELD—Weather Products—Springfield Precision Instruments, Inc.; *U.S. Private*, pg. 1027

SPRINGFIELD BITTER—Bitter—Bass PLC; *Int'l*, pg. 169

SPRINGFIELD ROYALE—Food Products & General Merchandise—Certified Grocers of California; *U.S. Private*, pg. 226

SPRINGFIELD VGC—Vertical Grinding Center—Motch Corporation; *Int'l*, pg. 1128

SPRINGFLEX—Ducts—Callahan Mining Corporation; *U.S. Public*, pg. 394

SPRINGFLEX—Innersole Material—Texon Materials Inc.; *U.S. Private*, pg. 1079

SPRINGFORM—Fiberglass Reinforced Plastic Column Forms—Symons Corporation; *U.S. Private*, pg. 932

SPRINGFRESH—NONE—Cleaning Solutions Group/Cello; *U.S. Private*, pg. 1466

SPRINGHILL—Printing & Reprographic Papers—International Paper Company; *U.S. Public*, pg. 901

SPRINGHILL MIRA-GLOSS—Wood-Free Coated Printing Paper—International Paper Company; *U.S. Public*, pg. 901

SPRINGHILL MIRA-WEB—Wood-Free Coated Printing Papers—International Paper Company; *U.S. Public*, pg. 901

SPRINGLOCK—NONE—CertainTeed Corporation; *Int'l*, pg. 1170

SPRINGMAID—Bed & Bath Linens & Accessories—Springs Industries, Inc.; *U.S. Public*, pg. 1499

SPRINGWALL—Mattress & Box Spring—The Springwall Mattress Co.; *U.S. Private*, pg. 973

SPRINKLE—Granular Deodorizer—Surco Products, Inc.; *U.S. Private*, pg. 1056

SPRINKL'INS—Yogurt with Rainbow Sprinkles—The Dannon Co.; *Int'l*, pg. 379

SPRINT—Saw Blades—American Tool Companies, Inc.; *U.S. Private*, pg. 63

SPRINT—Soft Top—Bestop, Inc.; *Int'l*, pg. 830

SPRINT—Delivery Body Style—Hackney and Sons, Inc.; *U.S. Private*, pg. 1097

SPRINT—Sheet-Fed Press—Komori America Corporation; *Int'l*, pg. 745

SPRINT—Paper Handling Equipment—Michael Business Machines Corporation; *U.S. Private*, pg. 740

SPRINT—Lower Cost Version of Bio-CAD—PerSeptive Biosystems, Inc.; *U.S. Public*, pg. 1279

SPRINT WIRE—8mm Spark Plug Wire—Mallory, Inc.; *U.S. Private*, pg. 698

SPRINTA—Lubricant—Petroliam Nasional Berhad (Petronas); *Int'l*, pg. 1046

SPRINTER CARIB—Automobile—Toyota Motor Corporation; *Int'l*, pg. 1411

SPRINTER VITEX—Bakery Ingredient—Royal Gist-Brocades N.V.; *Int'l*, pg. 1142

SPRINTSCAN—Digital Slide Scanner—Polaroid Corporation; *U.S. Public*, pg. 1313

SPRITE—Small Vacuum—Advance Machine Company; *Int'l*, pg. 932

SPRITE—Soft Drink—The Coca-Cola Bottling Co. of New York, Inc.; *U.S. Public*, pg. 393

SPRITE—Soft Drink—The Coca-Cola Company; *U.S. Public*, pg. 392

SPRITZER—Carbonated Fruit Juices—J.M. Smucker Company; *U.S. Public*, pg. 1480

SPROING—Action Game—Mattel Games/Puzzles; *U.S. Public*, pg. 1058

SPRUCE SPRAY—Coatings—Seymour of Sycamore, Inc.; *U.S. Private*, pg. 988

SPRUNCH—Setting Agent—Redmond Products, Inc.; *U.S. Public*, pg. 254

SPRY—Shortening—Lever Brothers Co.; *Int'l*, pg. 1435

SPRY—Shortening—Unilever Plc; *Int'l*, pg. 1433

SPUD-NU—Anti-oxidants—Diamond Crystal Specialty Foods, Inc.; *U.S. Private*, pg. 330

SPUD-SKIN—Thin Fries, Thin Cuts, Regular Cuts, Steak Cuts, Rounds, Wedges—Lamb-Weston, Inc.; *U.S. Public*, pg. 427

SPUN DEE SSP—Thread—Coats North America; *Int'l*, pg. 300

SPUN DOLA—Yarn—National Spinning Co., Inc.; *U.S. Private*, pg. 786

SPUN-GEE—Yarn—National Spinning Co., Inc.; *U.S. Private*, pg. 786

SPUN PAK—Yarn—National Spinning Co., Inc.; *U.S. Private*, pg. 786

SPUNGUARD—Disposable Medical Accessories—Kimberly-Clark Corporation; *U.S. Public*, pg. 958

SPUNLINE—Pipe Lining Service—Ameron Concrete & Steel Pipe Group; *U.S. Public*, pg. 99

SPUNRAY—Fabrics—Dan River Inc.; *U.S. Public*, pg. 478

SPUR—Petroleum Products in the United States & Canada—Murphy Oil Corporation; *U.S. Public*, pg. 1141

SPUR—Magazine—Shivers Trading & Operating Co.; *U.S. Private*, pg. 994

SPUTOLYSIN KITS—Clinical Chemistry Reagents—Dade Behring Inc.; *U.S. Private*, pg. 110

SPUTTER-RING—Vacuum Equip.—BOC Coating Technology; *Int'l*, pg. 121

SPY-PROOF—Combination Lock Dial—Sargent & Greenleaf, Inc.; *U.S. Private*, pg. 965

SPY TECH TOYS—Toys—Tyco Toys, Inc.; *U.S. Public*, pg. 1058

SPYGLASS—Catheter—St. Jude Medical, Inc.; *U.S. Public*, pg. 1427

SPYRO—NONE—PolyMedica Industries, Inc.; *U.S. Public*, pg. 1315

SPYROFLEX—Wound Dressing Products—PolyMedica Industries, Inc.; *U.S. Public*, pg. 1315

SQUAD LEADER—Game—Monarch Avalon, Inc.; *U.S. Public*, pg. 1123

SQUADRON—Herbicide—American Home Products Corporation; *U.S. Public*, pg. 79

SQUALL—Jacket—Lands' End, Inc.; *U.S. Public*, pg. 977

SQUARE-CAP—Specialty Nails—Maze Nails; *U.S. Private*, pg. 718

SQUARE D—Motor Control & Distribution Equipment—Bryant Electric Supply Company, Inc.; *U.S. Private*, pg. 177

SQUARE D—Electrical Apparatus—W.A. Roosevelt Co.; *U.S. Private*, pg. 943

SQUARE D—Electrical & Industrial Control—Schneider S.A.; *Int'l*, pg. 1207

SQUARE RIGGER—Luggage & Jeans—Lands' End, Inc.; *U.S. Public*, pg. 977

SQUARESHOOTER—Hard Candy & Suckers—Gilliam Candy Brands; *U.S. Public*, pg. 454

SQUEEZ-KLIP—Fasteners, Tools, Cutters, Kits—Republic Fastener Products Corp.; *U.S. Private*, pg. 923

SQUEEZE POP—Candy—Amurol Confections Co.; *U.S. Public*, pg. 1781

SQUEEZE POP SPORTS BOTTLE—NONE—Amurol Confections Co.; *U.S. Public*, pg. 1781

SQUEEZE SIX—Juice—McCain Citrus Inc.; *Int'l*, pg. 850

SQUEEZIT—Fruit Juice Drinks—General Mills, Inc.; *U.S. Public*, pg. 717

SQUEEZIT—NONE—Snacks Unlimited Division; *U.S. Public*, pg. 718

SQUEEZIT 100—Fruit Juice Drinks—General Mills, Inc.; *U.S. Public*, pg. 717

SQUEEZONS—Compression Connectors—Kearney Company; *U.S. Public*, pg. 444

SQUEGEES—Squeegees—W.J. & Dennis Co.; *U.S. Private*, pg. 1144

SQUIBB—Mineral Oil & Suppositories—Bristol-Myers Squibb Company; *U.S. Public*, pg. 253

SQUIER—Guitars, Amplfiers—Fender Musical Instruments; *U.S. Private*, pg. 400

SQUIRMS—Candy—Brach & Brock Confections Inc.; *U.S. Private*, pg. 163

SQUIRREL—Peanut Butters—Bestfoods; *U.S. Public*, pg. 223

SQUIRREL—NONE—Sulcus Computer Corp.; *U.S. Public*, pg. 1527

SQUIRT—NONE—Cadbury Beverages; *Int'l*, pg. 248

SQUIRT—Soft Drink—Cadbury Schweppes p.l.c.; *Int'l*, pg. 247

SQUIRT—Soft Drink—Grant-Lydick Beverage Co.; *U.S. Private*, pg. 470

SQUIRT—Welder—The Lincoln Electric Company; *U.S. Public*, pg. 996

SQURT—Boom Articulated Watertower (Firefighting)—Snorkel; *U.S. Private*, pg. 500

SQUIRTGUN—Welder—The Lincoln Electric Company; *U.S. Public*, pg. 996

SQUIRTMOBILE—Welder—The Lincoln Electric Company; *U.S. Public*, pg. 996

SQUISH GRIP—Children's Toothbrush—Oral-B Laboratories; *U.S. Public*, pg. 743

SSDI & DESIGN—Semiconductor Devices—Solid State Devices, Inc.; *U.S. Private*, pg. 1012

SSIPS—Aseptic Fruit Juices—Johanna Foods Inc.; *U.S. Public*, pg. 589

SSIPS—Juices—Labatt Brewing Company Limited; *Int'l*, pg. 679

STA-BIL PLUS—NONE—Gold Eagle Company; *U.S. Private*, pg. 459

STA-FLEX—NONE—Medline Industries, Inc.; *U.S. Private*, pg. 728

STA FLO LIQUID STARCH—NONE—The Dial Corporation; *U.S. Public*, pg. 505

STA-FORM 60—Urea Formaldehyde Reaction Product—Georgia-Pacific Corporation; *U.S. Public*, pg. 735

STA-FRESH—Sodium Bisulfate Treated Silage—AlliedSignal Inc.; *U.S. Public*, pg. 49

STA-KLEEN—Wall Plates—Pass & Seymour/Legrand; *Int'l*, pg. 806

STA-KON—Installing Tools—Thomas & Betts Corporation; *U.S. Public*, pg. 1597

STA-LOK—Positive Locking Bearing Locknuts—Shur-Lok Corporation; *U.S. Private*, pg. 997

STA-LUBE—Greases & Gear Oils—CRC Industries, Inc.; *U.S. Private*, pg. 138

STA-PRO—Soy Concentrate—Central Soya Company, Inc.; *Int'l*, pg. 324

STA-PUT—Plumbing Chemical—Hercules Chemical Co., Inc.; *U.S. Private*, pg. 523

STA-RITE—Under Shields—Kleinert's, Inc.; *U.S. Private*, pg. 625

STA-RITE—Pumps—Ryan Herco Products Corp.; *U.S. Private*, pg. 953

STA-RITE—Swimming Pool Pumps & Filters—Sta-Rite Industries, Inc.; *U.S. Public*, pg. 1767

STA-RITE—NONE—Sta-Rite Water Systems; *U.S. Public*, pg. 1767

STA-RITE—NONE—WICOR, Inc.; *U.S. Public*, pg. 1767

STA-SLIM—Dietary Product—Dean Foods Company; *U.S. Public*, pg. 489

STA-SOF—NONE—Acushnet Company; *U.S. Public*, pg. 675

STA-SOF—Golf Gloves—Fortune Brands, Inc.; *U.S. Public*, pg. 674

STA-SOF—NONE—Titleist & Foot-Joy Worldwide; *U.S. Public*, pg. 675

STA-SOF-FRO—Ethnic Hair Care Products—Johnson Products Co., Inc.; *U.S. Public*, pg. 915

STA-SOFT—Fabric Softeners—Colgate-Palmolive Company; *U.S. Public*, pg. 397

STA-TAC—Synthetic Resins—Arizona Chemical Div.; *U.S. Public*, pg. 901

STABIL-9—Food Leavening Agent—Monsanto Company; *U.S. Public*, pg. 1124

STABILAN—Plant Protectives—DSM Chemie Linz GmbH; *Int'l*, pg. 356

STABILAS—Fly Ash From Power Stations—Electrabel S.A.; *Int'l*, pg. 436

STABILENKA—Heavy-Duty Reinforcing Fabric of Polyester & Polymide Fiber—Akzo Nobel N.V.; *Int'l*, pg. 42

STABILITE—Antioxidants—Arizona Chemical Div.; *U.S. Public*, pg. 901

STABILITE—Laminated, Resin-Impregnated Plywood—Georgia-Pacific Corporation; *U.S. Public*, pg. 735

STABILIZER—Golf Shoe—Aritmos AB; *Int'l*, pg. 1072

STABILIZER—Plastic Case—International Container Systems; *Int'l*, pg. 685

STABL-NIP—Calender Roll Offset Adjuster—Harnischfeger Industries, Inc.; *U.S. Public*, pg. 788

STABL-TIP—Fourdrinier Ceramic Foil Insert—Harnischfeger Industries, Inc.; *U.S. Public*, pg. 788

STABLE-ARC—Electrode—The Lincoln Electric Company; *U.S. Public*, pg. 996

STABLE-RITE—Labeling Products—Avery Dennison Corporation; *U.S. Public*, pg. 152

STABLE STIX—Solid Supplement For Horses—Feed Service Corp.; *U.S. Private*, pg. 399

STABLE TABLE—Ironing Board—Magla Products; *U.S. Private*, pg. 695

STABRITE—Caps For Cosmetic Containers—Risdon Corporation; *U.S. Public*, pg. 463

STAC PAC—Semi-Conductor Devices—Semtech Corporation; *U.S. Public*, pg. 1456

STACER—Boats—Outboard Marine Corporation; *U.S. Public*, pg. 478

STACK ALL—Food Storage Container—Carlisle Food Service Products; *U.S. Public*, pg. 305

STACK PACK—Pallets of Electrical Extension Cords Sold as Complete Retail Displays—General Cable Corporation; *Int'l*, pg. 1486

STACK PAK—Ovenable Paperboard Containers—Westvaco Corporation; *U.S. Public*, pg. 1762

STACKALL—Storage Racks for Audio/Video—Recoton Corporation; *U.S. Public*, pg. 1369

STACKHOUSE—Surgical & Oxygen Equipment & Supplies—Bird Products Corporation; *U.S. Public*, pg. 1591

STACKING WINDOWSILL GREENHOUSE—Garden Products—Jiffy Products of America, Inc.; *Int'l*, pg. 706

STACKOR—High Performance Linenboard—Stone Container Corporation; *U.S. Public*, pg. 1520

STACKPACK—Bench-Scale Multi-Chamber ED Laboratory Equip.—Ionics, Incorporated; *U.S. Public*, pg. 912

STACY-ADAMS—Shoes—Weyco Group, Inc.; *U.S. Public*, pg. 1763

STADELMAN'S—NONE—Stadelman Fruit L.L.C.; *U.S. Private*, pg. 1028

STADIA TURF—Artificial Turf—Southwest Recreational Industries Inc.; *U.S. Private*, pg. 1018

STADIUM CLUB SPORTS CARDS—Baseball, Football, Basketball & Hockey Cards—The Topps Company, Inc.; *U.S. Public*, pg. 1621

STADOL—Nasal Spray—Bristol-Myers Squibb Company; *U.S. Public*, pg. 253

STADOL IM/IV—Agonist-Antagonist Analgesic—Bristol-Myers Squibb U.S. Pharmaceutical Group; *U.S. Public*, pg. 255

STADOL NS—Central Nervous System Therapy—Bristol-Myers Squibb Company; *U.S. Public*, pg. 253

STAEFA CONTROL SYSTEM—Building Automation & Temperature Control—Peoples Electric Contractor, Inc.; *U.S. Private*, pg. 851

STAFAC—Virginiamycin—Pfizer Inc.; *U.S. Public*, pg. 1281

STAFAC—Animal Productivity Enhancer—SmithKline Beecham plc; *Int'l*, pg. 1264

STAFF BUILDERS—NONE—Staff Builders Inc.; *U.S. Public*, pg. 1501

STAFFORD—Men's Suits & Trousers—JC Penney Company, Inc.; *U.S. Public*, pg. 916

STAFFORD STRIP—Pre-Finished Laminate—Bruce Hardwood Floors; *U.S. Public*, pg. 1634

STAFILEX—Tablets,Powder & Liquid Disinfectants—Akzo Nobel N.V.; *Int'l*, pg. 42

STAFLO—Polymers—Akzo Nobel N.V.; *Int'l*, pg. 42

STAFOR—Tall Oil Rosin Sizing—Westvaco Corporation; *U.S. Public*, pg. 1762

STAG'S LEAP—Wine—Pacific Wine Co.; *U.S. Private*, pg. 843

STAGE—NONE—Stage Stores, Inc.; *U.S. Private*, pg. 1028

STAGES—Baby Food—Beech-Nut Nutrition Corporation; *U.S. Public*, pg. 1359

STAGES—NONE—Ralcorp Holdings Inc.; *U.S. Public*, pg. 1359

STAGG—Chili & Corned Beef Hash—Hormel Foods Corp.; *U.S. Public*, pg. 840

STAHL—Metal Products—The Scott Fetzer Company; *U.S. Public*, pg. 217

STAHL USA—Stitchers—Baum USA; *Int'l*, pg. 1293

STAHL USA—Stitchers—Stahl GmbH & Co.; *Int'l*, pg. 1293

STAIN ENDER—Gynecological Device—The Cooper Companies, Inc.; *U.S. Public*, pg. 442

STAIN-RESISTANT BOUNCE—Fabric Softener—The Procter & Gamble Company; *U.S. Public*, pg. 1330

STAIN STICK—Laundry Soil & Stain Remover—The Dow Chemical Company; *U.S. Public*, pg. 522

STAINGUARD—NONE—Elcor Corporation; *U.S. Public*, pg. 567

STAINLESS—NONE—Weatherby, Inc.; *U.S. Private*, pg. 1155

STAINLESS-TITE!—Stainless Steel Fasteners—R&B, Inc.; *U.S. Public*, pg. 1354

STAINMASTER—Carpeting—Du Pont (E.I. Du Pont De Nemours & Co.); *U.S. Public*, pg. 530

STAINSHIELD—Stain—Pratt & Lambert United, Inc.; *U.S. Public*, pg. 1466

STAINWELD—Electrode—The Lincoln Electric Company; *U.S. Public*, pg. 996

STAK PACK—NONE—Life Technologies, Inc.; *U.S. Public*, pg. 504

STAK-PAK—Open Sided Bulk Shipping Container—Buckeye Corrugated Inc.; *U.S. Private*, pg. 177

STAKEHOLDER INFORMATION SYSTEMS—Consulting Tools Used to Assess Client Needs—Franklin Covey; *U.S. Public*, pg. 679

STAKMASTER—Stacking Cranes—Abell-Howe Company; *U.S. Private*, pg. 10

STAKMORE—Folding Furniture—Stakmore Inc.; *U.S. Private*, pg. 1029

STALEY—Margarine, Salad Dressing—Borden, Inc.; *U.S. Private*, pg. 157

STALGARD—Corrosion-Resistant Screws—Elco Textron; *U.S. Public*, pg. 1590

STALLIONS—Truck Blowers—MD Pneumatics; *U.S. Private*, pg. 1111

STAM—Herbicide—Rohm and Haas Company; *U.S. Public*, pg. 1403

STAMARK—Pavement Marking Film—3M; *U.S. Public*, pg. 1604

STAMINADE—NONE—Kiwi Brands Pty. Ltd.; *U.S. Public*, pg. 1434

STAMISOL—Roof Insulation Sheeting—Forbo Holding SA; *Int'l*, pg. 496

STAMOID—Coated Fabrics—Forbo Holding SA; *Int'l*, pg. 496

STAMOLUX—Coated Fabrics—Forbo Holding SA; *Int'l*, pg. 496

STAMP 'N LEARN—Children's Rubber Stampers—Mattel Games/Puzzles; *U.S. Public*, pg. 1058

STAMPOS—Children's Rubber Stampers—Mattel Games/Puzzles; *U.S. Public*, pg. 1058

STAMSKIN—Artificial Leather—Forbo Holding SA; *Int'l*, pg. 496

STAMTEX—Light-Duty Conveyor Belts—Forbo Holding SA; *Int'l*, pg. 496

STAMYLAN—Polypropylene—DSM N.V.; *Int'l*, pg. 352

STAMYLAN HD—Linear Low Density Polyethylene—DSM N.V.; *Int'l*, pg. 352

STAMYLAN LD—Linear Low Density Polyethylene—DSM N.V.; *Int'l*, pg. 352

STAMYLAN P—Polypropylene Homo & Co-Polymers—DSM N.V.; *Int'l*, pg. 352

STAMYLEX—Low Density Polyethylene—DSM N.V.; *Int'l*, pg. 352

STAMYROID—Polypropylene Compounds—DSM N.V.; *Int'l*, pg. 352

STAN HERMAN—NONE—Kellwood Company; *U.S. Public*, pg. 948

STAN MAG—Magnesium Oxides—Harwick Standard Distribution Corporation; *U.S. Private*, pg. 509

STAN-PAC—Industrial Cleaning Preparations—Stanhome Inc.; *U.S. Public*, pg. 1508

STAN TONE—Colors—Harwick Standard Distribution Corporation; *U.S. Private*, pg. 509

STANART—Tradename—Esselte Meto Kimball Systems; *Int'l*, pg. 460

STANART—Esselte Meto—Meto, USA; *Int'l*, pg. 460

STANAX—Durable Antistat—Henkel Corporation; *Int'l*, pg. 610

STANBACK—Stimulant Powders—Stanback Company; *U.S. Private*, pg. 1030

STANBACK HEADACHE POWDERS—Analgesic Powders—Stanback Company; *U.S. Private*, pg. 1030

STANBEE—Shoe Components—Stanbee Company, Inc.; *U.S. Private*, pg. 1030

STANBOOK—Sales Books—The Standard Register Company; *U.S. Public*, pg. 1505

STANCE—Floor Finish—3M; *U.S. Public*, pg. 1604

STANCE INDUSTRIES—Combs & Brushes—Winstar Global Products, Inc.; *U.S. Public*, pg. 1772

STANCLERE—Plastic Stabilizers—Akzo Nobel N.V.; *Int'l*, pg. 42

STANCUT—Continuous Tab Cards—The Standard Register Company; *U.S. Public*, pg. 1505

STAND-COTE—Bolts—Standco Industries, Inc.; *U.S. Private*, pg. 1032

STANDAFIN—Fabric Hand Modifiers—Henkel Corporation; *Int'l*, pg. 610

STANDAPHOS—Phosphated Alcohols—Henkel Corporation; *Int'l*, pg. 610

STANDAPOL—Fiber Lubricants—Henkel Corporation; *Int'l*, pg. 610

STANDAPON—Detergents, Wetting Agents—Henkel Corporation; *Int'l*, pg. 610

STANDARD—Plumbing Products—American Standard Inc.; *U.S. Public*, pg. 91

STANDARD—Petroleum Products—Amoco Corporation; *U.S. Public*, pg. 101

STANDARD—Barbed Wire—CF & I Steel, L.P.; *U.S. Public*, pg. 1230

STANDARD—Anti-Glare CRT Filter—Optical Coating Laboratory, Inc.; *U.S. Public*, pg. 1227

STANDARD—Coffee Service—William B. Reily & Co., Inc.; *U.S. Private*, pg. 919

STANDARD—Religious Publishing—Standex International Corporation; *U.S. Public*, pg. 1505

Brand Name Index

STANDARD—NONE—Taylor Impression, Inc.; *U.S. Private*, pg. 1070

STANDARD ARCHITECTRUAL SERIES—1/8″ & 3/32″ Commercial Vinyl Composition Tile—Kentile Operting Co.; *U.S. Private*, pg. 615

STANDARD CRESSALL—High Power Electrical Resistors & Shoe Machinery—Halma p.l.c.; *Int'l*, pg. 589

STANDARD DIARY—Hardbound Diaries—The At-A-Glance Group; *U.S. Private*, pg. 295

STANDARD DIRECTORY OF ADVERTISERS—Business Directory—National Register Publishing; *Int'l*, pg. 1096

STANDARD DIRECTORY OF ADVERTISING AGENCIES—Business Directory—National Register Publishing; *Int'l*, pg. 1096

STANDARD DIRECTORY OF INTL. ADVERTISERS & AGENCIES—Business Directory—National Register Publishing; *Int'l*, pg. 1096

STANDARD ELECTRIC TIME—Clock Systems & Timers—Faraday, Inc.; *Int'l*, pg. 1246

STANDARD 500—Anti Glare Filter—Optical Coating Laboratory, Inc.; *U.S. Public*, pg. 1227

STANDARD INSERT—NONE—Penn Engineering & Manufacturing Corp.; *U.S. Public*, pg. 1269

STANDARD MAGNETIC SYSTEM—Magnetic Ribbon-Based EAS System Designed to Protect Light Hard Goods—Sensormatic Electronics Corporation; *U.S. Public*, pg. 1457

STANDARD MICROSYSTEMS—NONE—Milgray Electronics, Inc.; *U.S. Public*, pg. 205

STANDARD POWER—Switchmode Power Supplies—Acme Electric Corporation; *U.S. Public*, pg. 16

STANDARD REGISTER—Printing—The Standard Register Company; *U.S. Public*, pg. 1505

STANDEX—Reed Switches & Relays—Standex International Corporation; *U.S. Public*, pg. 1505

STANDING OVATIONS—Mugs—Stanhome Inc.; *U.S. Public*, pg. 1508

STANDOX—Vehicle Refinishing Lacquers—Herberts GmbH; *Int'l*, pg. 625

STANFAST—Cut Sheet Printing—The Standard Register Company; *U.S. Public*, pg. 1505

STANFIX—Waterbased Adhesive—Henkel Corporation; *Int'l*, pg. 610

STANFLAKE—Flake Textile Softeners—Henkel Corporation; *Int'l*, pg. 610

STANFLEX—Construction Business Forms—The Standard Register Company; *U.S. Public*, pg. 1505

STANFORD—Champagne—Weibel Winery; *U.S. Private*, pg. 1159

STANFORD TELECOM—NONE—Stanford Telecommunications; *U.S. Public*, pg. 1508

STANGUARD—Check Paper—The Standard Register Company; *U.S. Public*, pg. 1505

STANLEY—Thermos—Aladdin Industries, Incorporated; *U.S. Private*, pg. 30

STANLEY—Furniture Cream & Floor Wax—Stanhome Inc.; *U.S. Public*, pg. 1508

STANLEY—Tools & Hardware—The Stanley Works; *U.S. Public*, pg. 1508

STANLEY BLACKER—Apparel—Bayer Clothing Group; *U.S. Private*, pg. 124

STANLEY ELECTRIC—NONE—Milgray Electronics, Inc.; *U.S. Public*, pg. 205

STANLEY FOR HER—Cologne Spray—Stanhome Inc.; *U.S. Public*, pg. 1508

STANLEY FOR HIM—Cologne—Stanhome Inc.; *U.S. Public*, pg. 1508

STANLEY ROBERTS—Cutlery—Stanley Roberts, Inc.; *U.S. Private*, pg. 936

STANNAVER—Chemical Reagant—Hach Company; *U.S. Public*, pg. 773

STANSET—Construction Forms—The Standard Register Company; *U.S. Public*, pg. 1505

STANSOFT—Liquid Textile Softeners—Henkel Corporation; *Int'l*, pg. 610

STANSTRIP—Rubber Garage Door Bottom—The Standard Products Company; *U.S. Public*, pg. 1504

STANTEST—Enamel—Jones Blair Company; *U.S. Private*, pg. 596

STANTEX—Textile Chemicals—Henkel Corporation; *Int'l*, pg. 610

STANTON-COOPER—Sofas—Woodmark Originals Inc.; *U.S. Private*, pg. 747

STANWELL—Pipes—Lane Limited; *Int'l*, pg. 1129

STANWOOD—Home Furniture—Spectrum Industries, Inc.; *U.S. Private*, pg. 1024

STANYL—Engineering Plastics—DSM N.V.; *Int'l*, pg. 352

STANZALL—Outdoor Signs—Chicago Show Printing Co.; *U.S. Private*, pg. 235

STAODERM—NONE—Staodyn Inc.; *U.S. Public*, pg. 1509

STAODYN—Biomedical Engineering—Staodyn Inc.; *U.S. Public*, pg. 1509

STAONAL—Marking Crayons—Binney & Smith Inc.; *U.S. Private*, pg. 496

STAPH VAX—Vaccine for Staph epi Infections—Nabi; *U.S. Public*, pg. 1148

STAPAC—Road Machinery-Compactor—Rosco Manufacturing Co.; *U.S. Private*, pg. 944

STAPAK—Fiber Pails, Drums & Cheese Boxes—Sonoco Products Company; *U.S. Public*, pg. 1485

STAPH-CHEK—Hospital Product—Herculite Products, Inc.; *U.S. Public*, pg. 802

STAPH-CHEK COMFORT—Fabrics—Herculite Products, Inc.; *U.S. Public*, pg. 802

STAPH-CHEK FLEX—Fabrics—Herculite Products, Inc.; *U.S. Public*, pg. 802

STAPH-CHEK MICROVENT COMFORT—Fabrics—Herculite Products, Inc.; *U.S. Public*, pg. 802

STAPH-CHEK SOFT—Fabrics—Herculite Products, Inc.; *U.S. Public*, pg. 802

STAPH-CHEK XL—Fabrics—Herculite Products, Inc.; *U.S. Public*, pg. 802

STAPHCILLIN—Antibiotic—Bristol-Myers Squibb Company; *U.S. Public*, pg. 253

STAPHERE—Germicidal Detergent—Calgon Vestal Laboratories; *U.S. Public*, pg. 1515

STAPHGAM—Staph A & Staph epi Infections—Nabi; *U.S. Public*, pg. 1148

STAPLCOTN—Cotton Cooperative—Staple Cotton Cooperative Association; *U.S. Private*, pg. 1033

STAPLDISCOUNT—Lending Cooperative—Staple Cotton Cooperative Association; *U.S. Private*, pg. 1033

STAPLEOSCOPY—Laparoscopic Instruments—U.S. Surgical Corp.; *U.S. Public*, pg. 1687

STAPLES THE OFFICE SUPERSTORE—Discount Office Supply Stores—Staples, Inc.; *U.S. Public*, pg. 1509

STAPLIZER—Surgical Instruments—3M; *U.S. Public*, pg. 1604

STAPRON—Engineering Plastics—DSM N.V.; *Int'l*, pg. 352

STAR—NONE—Aqua Care Systems Inc.; *U.S. Public*, pg. 126

STAR—Meat Prods.—Armour Food Company; *U.S. Public*, pg. 427

STAR—NONE—CEM Corporation; *U.S. Public*, pg. 277

STAR—Soft Drink—Central de Cervejas, S.A.; *Int'l*, pg. 279

STAR—Medium-Duty Bus—Champion Enterprises, Inc.; *U.S. Public*, pg. 332

STAR—Grocery Products—Danone Group; *Int'l*, pg. 379

STAR—Cameras—Eastman Kodak Company; *U.S. Public*, pg. 550

STAR—Ventilator—Nellcor Puritan Bennett Incorporated; *U.S. Public*, pg. 1039

STAR—Television Receivers—Philips Consumer Electronics; *Int'l*, pg. 1054

STAR—Lumber & Supply—Star Lumber & Supply Company, Inc.; *U.S. Private*, pg. 1034

STAR—NONE—Thiokol Corporation; *U.S. Public*, pg. 1596

STAR—Sewing Thread—Tootal Group plc; *Int'l*, pg. 300

STAR BRAND—Screening—CCX, Inc.; *U.S. Private*, pg. 193

STAR BRAND PRODUCTS—Olive Oil, Olives, Wine Vinegar, Capers, Pepperocini & Maraschino Cherries)—Star Fine Foods, Inc.; *U.S. Private*, pg. 1034

STAR BRANDS—Thread—Coats North America; *Int'l*, pg. 300

STARCFW—Concealed Fastener Wall System—Star Building Systems; *U.S. Public*, pg. 1394

STAR CELL—Vacuum Pumps & Power Supplies—Varian Associates, Inc.; *U.S. Public*, pg. 1710

STAR CODY—Apparel—Clothestime Stores, Inc.; *U.S. Public*, pg. 387

STAR CONNECT—Door-to Door International Air Service—Danzas Corporation; *Int'l*, pg. 382

STAR CRANES—Dockside Container Handling Cranes—Ederer Inc.; *U.S. Private*, pg. 363

STAR DUST LINGERIE—Ladies Apparel—Movie Star, Inc.; *U.S. Public*, pg. 1140

STAR FRONTIERS—Game—TSR, Inc.; *U.S. Private*, pg. 1185

A STAR IS BORN—Musical—Really Useful Holdings Limited; *Int'l*, pg. 1089

STAR-KAP—Chimney Caps—Field Controls Co.; *U.S. Private*, pg. 860

STAR KIST—Tuna Products—H.J. Heinz Company; *U.S. Public*, pg. 805

STAR-KIST—Tuna—Star-Kist Foods Inc.; *U.S. Public*, pg. 805

STAR-KIST EATWELL—Sardines & Mackerel—Star-Kist Foods Inc.; *U.S. Public*, pg. 805

STAR KLEEN—Gasolines—Coastal Refining & Marketing; *U.S. Public*, pg. 390

STAR LINK—Electronic Control Unit for Ultra High Vacuum Pumping Systems—Varian Associates, Inc.; *U.S. Public*, pg. 1710

STAR LUMEN—NONE—Hudson, RCI; *U.S. Private*, pg. 546

STAR MAGAZINE—Newspaper—American Media, Inc.; *U.S. Public*, pg. 87

STAR MARKET—Supermarkets—Star Markets Company, Inc.; *U.S. Private*, pg. 1035

STAR-MAX—NONE—Carpenter Technology Corporation; *U.S. Public*, pg. 307

STAR MIST—NONE—Nellcor Puritan Bennett Incorporated; *U.S. Public*, pg. 1039

STAR NYLON—Thread—Coats North America; *Int'l*, pg. 300

STAR PERFORMERS—NONE—Carpenter Technology Corporation; *U.S. Public*, pg. 307

STAR PRINT BANDS—Character Print Bands—Aspen Imaging International, Inc.; *U.S. Public*, pg. 1339

STAR READY-WOUND BOBBINS—Bobbins—Coats North America; *Int'l*, pg. 300

STAR SAPPHIRE—X-Ray Tubes—Litton Industries, Inc.; *U.S. Public*, pg. 1002

STAR SHIELD—Sporting Equipment—Brunswick Bowling & Billiards Corp.; *U.S. Public*, pg. 265

STAR SHUTTER—NONE—Nellcor Puritan Bennett Incorporated; *U.S. Public*, pg. 1039

STAR VI—Computer Processor—Datapoint Corporation; *Int'l*, pg. 384

STAR SYNC—Patient Triggered Interface—Nellcor Puritan Bennett Incorporated; *U.S. Public*, pg. 1039

STAR TELEGRAM—Newspaper—Star-Telegram Newspaper, Inc.; *U.S. Public*, pg. 964

STAR TRACK—NONE—Nellcor Puritan Bennett Incorporated; *U.S. Public*, pg. 1039

STAR TRIBUNE—Newspaper—Cowles Media Company; *U.S. Private*, pg. 280

STAR TRIBUNE—Newspaper—Star Tribune, Minneapolis-St. Paul; *U.S. Private*, pg. 281

STAR ULTRA DEE—Thread—Coats North America; *Int'l*, pg. 300

STAR VALLEY CHEESE—Italian Cheeses—Western Dairymen Cooperative, Inc.; *U.S. Private*, pg. 1165

STARALUM—Aluminum Wire Cloth—CCX, Inc.; *U.S. Private*, pg. 193

STARALUM—Screening Prods.—Hanover Wire Cloth; *U.S. Private*, pg. 193

STARANE—Agricultural Product—The Dow Chemical Company; *U.S. Public*, pg. 522

STARBASE—Electronic Components—General Instrument Corporation; *U.S. Public*, pg. 716

STARBASE 2000—NONE—Plantronics Inc.; *U.S. Public*, pg. 1308

STARBEAM—Laser Printer Computer System Peripheral—Datapoint Corporation; *Int'l*, pg. 384

STARBRITE—Wire Cloth—CCX, Inc.; *U.S. Private*, pg. 193

STARBRITE—Screening Prods.—Hanover Wire Cloth; *U.S. Private*, pg. 193

STARBRITE—NONE—Ocean Bio-Chem Inc.; *U.S. Public*, pg. 1211

STARBRITE OPAQUE—1671

STARBUCKS COFFEE—Coffee—Starbucks Coffee Company; *U.S. Public*, pg. 1510

STARBUILDER—Family of Computer Interconnectivity Prods.—Datapoint Corporation; *Int'l*, pg. 384

STARBURST—Multi-Color Displays—Daktronics, Inc.; *U.S. Public*, pg. 478

STARBURST—Fruit Chews—Mars, Incorporated; *U.S. Private*, pg. 707

STARBURST BRAND—NONE—M&M/Mars; *U.S. Private*, pg. 707

STARBUS—Data and Control Transfer Path for Computer System—Datapoint Corporation; *Int'l*, pg. 384

STARCHE—Tailoring Spritz—The Dow Chemical Company; *U.S. Public*, pg. 522

STARCLUSTER—Computer Processor, Networking & Videoconferencing System—Datapoint Corporation; *Int'l*, pg. 384

STARCOM—Cable TV Addressable Systems & Set-Top Terminals—Broadband Networks Group; *U.S. Public*, pg. 716

STARCOM—Electronic Components—General Instrument Corporation; *U.S. Public*, pg. 716

STARCON—Container Handling Rubber Tired Cranes—Ederer Inc.; *U.S. Private*, pg. 363

STARCON 2000—Container Handling Rubber-Tired Cranes—Ederer Inc.; *U.S. Private*, pg. 363

STARCRAFT—Vehicle Conversions—Starcraft Corporation; *U.S. Public*, pg. 1510

STARCREST—Mail Order House—Starcrest Products of California; *U.S. Private*, pg. 1035

STARDANCE—Full Glue Installed Sheet Vinyl Flooring—Mannington Resilient Floors; *U.S. Private*, pg. 700

STARDUST—Broadloom—Couristan Inc.; *U.S. Private*, pg. 279

STARDYNE—NONE—The Titan Corporation; *U.S. Public*, pg. 1618

STARFAST—Thread—Coats North America; *Int'l*, pg. 300

STARFELT—Felt—Central/Shippee, Inc.; *U.S. Private*, pg. 224

STARFICHE—Microfiche Reader-Printers—Eastman Kodak Company; *U.S. Public*, pg. 550

STARFIGHTER—Jogging Shoes—Mizuno Corporation; *Int'l*, pg. 884

STARFILE—Microfilm Machine—Eastman Kodak Company; *U.S. Public*, pg. 550

STARFIRE—Sporting Equipment—Brunswick Bowling & Billiards Corp.; *U.S. Public*, pg. 265

STARFIRE—Tires—The Cooper Tire Company; *U.S. Public*, pg. 445

STARFIRE—Overhead Projector—Dukane Corporation; *U.S. Private*, pg. 345

STARFLASH—Camera—Eastman Kodak Company; *U.S. Public*, pg. 550

STARFLEET—Family of Computer System Prods. & Logo—Datapoint Corporation; *Int'l*, pg. 384

STARFLEX—Camera—Eastman Kodak Company; *U.S. Public*, pg. 550

STARFLO—Valves—The Wm. Powell Company; *U.S. Public*, pg. 877

STARFONE—Electronic Components—General Instrument Corporation; *U.S. Public*, pg. 716

STARGLASS—Screening Prods.—Hanover Wire Cloth; *U.S. Private*, pg. 193

STARGUARD—Lighting Fixture—Guth Lighting Company; *Int'l*, pg. 821

STARIL—Cardiovascular Therapy Product—Bristol-Myers Squibb Company; *U.S. Public*, pg. 253

STARK—Sugar Specialties; Gummies—New England Confectionery Co.; *U.S. Private*, pg. 1113

STARK DINOSAURS—Gummi Candy—Stark Candy Company; *U.S. Private*, pg. 1113

STARK GUMMI FRUITS—Gummi Candy—Stark Candy Company; *U.S. Private*, pg. 1113

STARKEEPER—Computer Programs—Lucent Technologies Inc.; *U.S. Public*, pg. 1017

STARKIST TUNA—NONE—Star-Kist Foods, Inc.; *U.S. Public*, pg. 806

STARLET—Camera—Eastman Kodak Company; *U.S. Public*, pg. 550

STARLET—Automobile—Toyota Motor Corporation; *Int'l*, pg. 1411

STARLIFE—Wire Cloth—CCX, Inc.; *U.S. Private*, pg. 193

STARLIFE—Screening Prods.—Hanover Wire Cloth; *U.S. Private*, pg. 193

STARLIFE—Computer Software for Engineering & Structural Analysis—The Titan Corporation; *U.S. Public*, pg. 1618

STARLIFT—Multi-User Computer System—Datapoint Corporation; *Int'l*, pg. 384

STARLIFTER—Aerospace Manufacturing—Lockheed Aeronautical Systems Company; *U.S. Public*, pg. 1007

STARLIGHT—Dance Floor—Sico Incorporated; *U.S. Private*, pg. 997

STARLIGHT EXPRESS—Musical—Really Useful Holdings Limited; *Int'l*, pg. 1089

STARLIGHT GLOBE—NONE—Replogle Globes, Inc.; *U.S. Private*, pg. 923

STARLIGHT ROMANCE BOOKS—Book Imprint—Bertelsmann AG; *Int'l*, pg. 189

STARLIN—Bathroom Tissue, Paper Napkins—Georgia-Pacific Corporation; *U.S. Public*, pg. 735

STARLINE—Cable TV Distribution Line Equipment—Broadband Networks Group; *U.S. Public*, pg. 716

STARLINE—Electronic Components—General Instrument Corporation; *U.S. Public*, pg. 716

STARLINE—Cable TV Distribution Equipment—General Instrument of Canada Ltd.; *U.S. Public*, pg. 716

STARLINE—Paint—Pratt & Lambert United, Inc.; *U.S. Public*, pg. 1466

STARLINK—Computer Software—Eastman Kodak Company; *U.S. Public*, pg. 550

STARLINK—Electronics—National Semiconductor Corporation; *U.S. Public*, pg. 1159

STARLITE—Deluxe Aluminum Storm Doors—Binning's Building Products, Inc.; *U.S. Public*, pg. 67

STARLITE—Microscope Illuminator—Leica, Inc.; *Int'l*, pg. 806

STARLOCK—Exercise Equipment—Bollinger Industries Inc.; *U.S. Public*, pg. 243

STARLUX—Grocery Products—Danone Group; *Int'l*, pg. 379

STARLYTT—White Mineral Oil—Witco Corporation; *U.S. Public*, pg. 1773

STARMAP—Computer Software—The Titan Corporation; *U.S. Public*, pg. 1618

STARMARK—Wall Panel—Star Building Systems; *U.S. Public*, pg. 1394

STARMASTER—Networking System—Gandalf Technologies Inc.; *Int'l*, pg. 540

STARMATE—Cameras, Microfilm Readers—Eastman Kodak Company; *U.S. Public*, pg. 550

STARMATIC—Cameras—Eastman Kodak Company; *U.S. Public*, pg. 550

STARMETER—Camera—Eastman Kodak Company; *U.S. Public*, pg. 550

STARMITE—Camera—Eastman Kodak Company; *U.S. Public*, pg. 550

STARMODAL—NONE—GenRad, Inc.; *U.S. Public*, pg. 731

STARNIKE—Computer Software—The Titan Corporation; *U.S. Public*, pg. 1618

STARNODE—Personal Computer Bar Code Data Collection Network—CiMatrix L.L.C.; *U.S. Public*, pg. 1395

STARPAC—Valves—Flowserve Corporation; *U.S. Public*, pg. 658

STARPAC—Packaging Machin System—Printpac-UEB Case Group; *U.S. Public*, pg. 905

STARPACK—Electronic Components—General Instrument Corporation; *U.S. Public*, pg. 716

STARPHIRE—Glass for the Manufacture of Furniture, Shelving & Cabinets—PPG Industries, Inc.; *U.S. Public*, pg. 1245

STARPLEX—Electronics—National Semiconductor Corporation; *U.S. Public*, pg. 1159

STARPORT—Computer System—Datapoint Corporation; *Int'l*, pg. 384

STARPROBE—Network Mgmnt. System—Datapoint Corporation; *Int'l*, pg. 384

STARPULSE—NONE—Laserscope Surgical Systems; *U.S. Public*, pg. 979

STARQUEST—Vehicle Conversions—Starcraft Corporation; *U.S. Public*, pg. 1510

STARR WIRE—NONE—Carpenter Technology Corporation; *U.S. Public*, pg. 307

STARRETT—Steel Tapes—Evans Rule Co., Inc.; *U.S. Public*, pg. 1511

STARRETT—Steel Tapes Logo—Evans Rule Co., Inc.; *U.S. Public*, pg. 1511

STARS & STRIPES—Sporting Equipment—Brunswick Bowling & Billiards Corp.; *U.S. Public*, pg. 265

STARSERVER—Computer File Server System—Datapoint Corporation; *Int'l*, pg. 384

STARSHIELD—Standing Seam Roof System—Star Building Systems; *U.S. Public*, pg. 1394

STARSHIP—Family of High Performance Computer Prods.—Datapoint Corporation; *Int'l*, pg. 384

STARSHIP I—Computer Processor—Datapoint Corporation; *Int'l*, pg. 384

STARSHIP II—Computer Processor—Datapoint Corporation; *Int'l*, pg. 384

STARSIGHT—Patented Technology for Integration & Licensing—StarSight Telecast, Inc.; *U.S. Public*, pg. 705

STARSOUND—Electronic Components—General Instrument Corporation; *U.S. Public*, pg. 716

STARSPAN—Digital Telephone Equipment & Telecommunications Equipment—DSC Communications Corporation; *U.S. Public*, pg. 475

STARSPUN—Fabrics—Dan River Inc.; *U.S. Public*, pg. 478

STARSTACKER—Long Span Rail Mounted Container Gantry Crane—Ederer Inc.; *U.S. Private*, pg. 363

STARSTRUCK—NONE—GenRad, Inc.; *U.S. Public*, pg. 731

START!—Alternator & Starter Repair Parts—R&B, Inc.; *U.S. Public*, pg. 1354

START 5—Exterior Alkyd Primer—Paragon Paint & Varnish Corp.; *U.S. Private*, pg. 838

START 4—Exterior Latex Primer—Paragon Paint & Varnish Corp.; *U.S. Private*, pg. 838

START 1—Interior Latex Primer—Paragon Paint & Varnish Corp.; *U.S. Private*, pg. 838

START SMART—NONE—Molex Incorporated; *U.S. Public*, pg. 1121

START 3—Rust Preventive Primer—Paragon Paint & Varnish Corp.; *U.S. Private*, pg. 838

START 2—Interior Alkyd Primer—Paragon Paint & Varnish Corp.; *U.S. Private*, pg. 838

STARTECH—Processor, Photographic Film—Eastman Kodak Company; *U.S. Public*, pg. 550

STARTER—Sportswear—Starter Corp.; *U.S. Public*, pg. 1511

STARTER LOGGS—Fire Logs—First Brands Corporation; *U.S. Public*, pg. 626

STARTHANE—Automotive Coatings—PPG Industries, Inc.; *U.S. Public*, pg. 1245

STARTHERM II—Insulated Roof & Wall System—Star Building Systems; *U.S. Public*, pg. 1394

STARTING POINT—Service Mark for Chemical Dependency Programs—Comprehensive Care Corporation; *U.S. Public*, pg. 419

STARTLER & DESIGN—NONE—Regal Ware, Inc.; *U.S. Private*, pg. 917

STARTOPAZ—Computer Software—The Titan Corporation; *U.S. Public*, pg. 1618

STARVUE—Microfilm Readers & Reader-Printers—Eastman Kodak Company; *U.S. Public*, pg. 550

STARVUE—Electronic Components—General Instrument Corporation; *U.S. Public*, pg. 716

STARWARS—NONE—Hasbro; *U.S. Public*, pg. 797

STARWEB—Internet Web Site—The Free Lance-Star Publishing Co.; *U.S. Private*, pg. 424

STARWHITE VICKSBURG—Writing, Text & Cover Paper—Fox River Paper Company; *U.S. Private*, pg. 422

STARWIND—NONE—The Titan Corporation; *U.S. Public*, pg. 1618

STARWOOD LODGING—NONE—Starwood Hotels & Resorts; *U.S. Public*, pg. 1512

STARWOOD LODGING TRUST—NONE—Starwood Hotels & Resorts; *U.S. Public*, pg. 1512

STARZONE—NONE—The Titan Corporation; *U.S. Public*, pg. 1618

STASH TOP—Stopper—The Thermos Company; *Int'l*, pg. 938

STASIS—Isolation Gowns—The Dexter Corporation; *U.S. Public*, pg. 504

STAT BLUE—Resuscitators—Vital Signs, Inc.; *U.S. Public*, pg. 1723

STAT CAP—Airway Carbon Dioxide Indicator—Nellcor Puritan Bennett Incorporated; *U.S. Public*, pg. 1039

STAT-CRIT—Hematacrit & Hemoglobin Device—Wampole Laboratories; *U.S. Public*, pg. 310

STAT-EX—Computer Software Feature—Beckman Instruments, Inc.; *U.S. Public*, pg. 199

Brand Name Index

Brand Name Index

STAT-O-SEAL—Fatener Seal—Seal Group; *U.S. Public*, pg. 1262

STAT PACK—Diagnostic Products—Abbott Laboratories; *U.S. Public*, pg. 12

STAT-PACK KITS—Clinical Chemistry Reagents—Dade Behring Inc.; *U.S. Private*, pg. 110

STAT PADZ MULTI-FUNCTION ELECTRODES—Non-Invasive Cardiac Device—Zoll Medical Corporation; *U.S. Private*, pg. 1207

STAT-PREP—NONE—Medline Industries, Inc.; *U.S. Private*, pg. 728

STAT PRIME—Filters—Pall Corporation; *U.S. Public*, pg. 1253

STAT SAT—Oxymeter—Gish Biomedical, Inc.; *U.S. Public*, pg. 745

STAT STRIPS—Adhesive Bandages—American White Cross; *U.S. Public*, pg. 694

STAT-X—Static Dissipating Reel Spool or Paper Carrying Roll Cover—Harnischfeger Industries, Inc.; *Int'l*, pg. 788

STAT-X-ATOR—A.C. Motors & Generators—General Electric Canada Inc.; *U.S. Public*, pg. 713

STATAK SOFT—Tissue Attachment Device—Bristol-Myers Squibb Company; *U.S. Public*, pg. 253

STATE BRAND—Dairy Products, Puddings & Cheese Sauce—North Central AMPI, Inc.; *U.S. Private*, pg. 804

STATE EXPRESS 555—NONE—Ardath Tobacco Co. Ltd.; *Int'l*, pg. 111

STATE FAIR FOODS—Food Products—Sara Lee Corporation; *U.S. Public*, pg. 1432

STATE OF SMALL BUSINESS—NONE—The Goldhirsh Group; *U.S. Private*, pg. 461

STATE-SENSITIVE—NONE—GenRad, Inc.; *U.S. Public*, pg. 731

STATEMENT—Dinnerware—Dansk International Designs Ltd.; *U.S. Private*, pg. 261

STATEMENT—Building Products—ODL Incorporated; *U.S. Private*, pg. 809

THE STATES—Test Switches & Blocks—AVO International; *Int'l*, pg. 1335

STATESMAN—Lockers—American Locker Group, Inc.; *U.S. Public*, pg. 85

STATESMAN—Power Equipment—Southern States Cooperative, Inc.; *U.S. Private*, pg. 1017

STATESMAN JUNIOR—Locker—American Locker Group, Inc.; *U.S. Public*, pg. 85

STAYFLATS—Heavy Duty Mailers—Calumet Carton Company; *U.S. Private*, pg. 201

STATGRAPHICS—NONE—Manugistics Group, Inc.; *U.S. Public*, pg. 1042

STATIC—After Shave—The Gillette Company; *U.S. Public*, pg. 743

STATIC GUARD—Static Remover—Alberto-Culver Canada, Inc.; *U.S. Public*, pg. 38

STATIC GUARD—Anti-Static Spray—Alberto-Culver Company; *U.S. Public*, pg. 37

STATIC O RING—Pressure Switches—SOR Inc.; *U.S. Private*, pg. 957

STATICIN—Erythromycin-Antibiotic—Westwood-Squibb Pharmaceuticals Inc.; *U.S. Public*, pg. 255

STATION POST—High Voltage Porcelain Insulators—Lapp Insulator Company; *U.S. Private*, pg. 473

STATIONAIR 6—NONE—The Cessna Aircraft Co.; *U.S. Public*, pg. 1589

STATIONARY STIFE STOOL—Stationary Stife Stool—Cramer Inc.; *U.S. Private*, pg. 285

STATIONMASTER—Bus Heat/Cool Units—Remcor Products Co.; *Int'l*, pg. 646

STATLAN OACIS—Clinical Information System—Oacis Healthcare Systems, Inc.; *U.S. Public*, pg. 1208

STATMASTER—Software for SPC—Air Gage Company; *U.S. Public*, pg. 1676

STATPAL—Blood Gas Monitoring/Testing Unit—PPG Industries, Inc.; *U.S. Public*, pg. 1245

STATROL—Polymyxin B Sulfate/Neomycin Sulfate Suspension & Ointment—Alcon Laboratories, Inc.; *Int'l*, pg. 916

STATS SUNGARD—NONE—SunGard Data Systems Inc.; *U.S. Public*, pg. 1534

STATURE—Static Control Additives—The Dow Chemical Company; *U.S. Public*, pg. 522

STAUFFER—Seeds—Novartis AG; *Int'l*, pg. 971

STAUFFER—Communications—Stauffer Communications, Inc.; *U.S. Private*, pg. 995

STAX—Layered Elastomeric Connection Elements—Elastomeric Technologies, Inc.; *U.S. Public*, pg. 1598

STAX-ON-STEEL—Filing System—Fellowes Manufacturing Co.; *U.S. Private*, pg. 400

STAY BRIGHT—Interior & Exterior Flat Latex Paint—Perry & Derrick Co.; *U.S. Private*, pg. 854

STAY DRY—Ice Pack—Kimberly-Clark Tecnol; *U.S. Public*, pg. 959

STAY DRY—Ballasts—MagneTek Lighting Products Group; *U.S. Public*, pg. 1037

STAY-FORM—Leave-in-Place Concrete Form—Alabama Metal Industries Corporation; *U.S. Private*, pg. 30

STAY FRESH TUBE—Athletic Packaging—Bike Athletic Co.; *U.S. Private*, pg. 143

STAY MOIST—Moisturizing Lip Conditioner—Stanback Company; *U.S. Private*, pg. 1030

STAY PUT—Eyeglass Frames—AVC/Nu-Vision, Inc.; *U.S. Private*, pg. 9

STAY SLIM—Foundations—The Strouse, Adler Company; *U.S. Private*, pg. 1047

STAY-STRATE—Doors—Georgia-Pacific Corporation; *U.S. Public*, pg. 735

STAYBELITE—Rosin—Hercules Incorporated; *U.S. Public*, pg. 809

STAYBRIGHT—Electric Discharge Lamp—General Electric Canada Inc.; *U.S. Public*, pg. 713

STAYFLATS PLUS—Heavy Duty Mailers—Calumet Carton Company; *U.S. Private*, pg. 201

STAYFREE—Maxi & Mini Sanitary Napkins—Johnson & Johnson; *U.S. Public*, pg. 927

STAYFREE SILHOUETTES—Body Shape Maxipads—Personal Products Co.; *U.S. Public*, pg. 929

STAYING @ WORK—Proven process For Integrating Disability Management ToImprove Productivity—Watson Wyatt Worldwide; *U.S. Private*, pg. 1154

STAYMADE—Fitted Sheets—Springs Industries, Inc.; *U.S. Public*, pg. 1499

STAYNEW—Spin Filter—Pneumatic Products Corp.; *U.S. Public*, pg. 1676

STAYSHARP—Cutlery—McPherson's Limited; *Int'l*, pg. 852

STAYSTRATE—Hardboard Siding—Georgia-Pacific Corporation; *U.S. Public*, pg. 735

STAZON—Buckles—Eagle Button Co., Inc.; *U.S. Private*, pg. 354

STBL2—NONE—Life Technologies, Inc.; *U.S. Public*, pg. 504

STEADY EDDY—Recyclables seperator—COUNTEC Recycling Systems Division; *U.S. Public*, pg. 1318

STEADY LIFT—Replacement Parts—R&B, Inc.; *U.S. Public*, pg. 1354

STEAK & BURGER—Fine Dining Restaurants—Cara Operations Limited; *Int'l*, pg. 266

STEAK AND ALE—Nation's Largest Chain of Upscale Steakhouses(156 units)—Bennigan's; *U.S. Private*, pg. 736

STEAK 'N SHAKE—Restaurants—Consolidated Products, Inc.; *U.S. Public*, pg. 436

STEAK 'N SHAKE—Restaurants—Steak 'n Shake, Inc.; *U.S. Public*, pg. 437

STEAK-UMMS—Sandwiches & Sandwich Steaks—Ore-Ida Foods, Inc.; *U.S. Public*, pg. 805

STEAKWICH—Sliced Wafer Steak—DeVault Foods; *U.S. Private*, pg. 329

STEALTH—Electric Lawn & Garden Tools—The Black & Decker Corporation; *U.S. Public*, pg. 233

STEALTH—Radar Detectors—Cobra Electronics Corporation; *U.S. Public*, pg. 391

STEALTH—Long-Circulating Liposomes—Sequus Pharmaceuticals, Inc.; *U.S. Public*, pg. 1460

STEALTH—Cable Tester—Wavetek Corporation; *U.S. Private*, pg. 1154

STEAM CUISINE—Electric Food Steamer—The Metal Ware Corp.; *U.S. Private*, pg. 734

STEAM 'N DRI—Curling Brush—Sunbeam Household Products; *U.S. Public*, pg. 1533

STEAM RAILWAY—U.K. Train Magazine—EMAP Apex; *Int'l*, pg. 451

STEAM-SAFE 20—Cleaning Products—Clayton Industries Co.; *U.S. Private*, pg. 245

STEAM VALET—Clothes Wrinkle Remover—Sunbeam Household Products; *U.S. Public*, pg. 1533

STEAM WORLD—U.K. Train Magazine—EMAP Apex; *Int'l*, pg. 451

STEAMATE—Corrosion Inhibitors—BetzDearborn Inc.; *U.S. Public*, pg. 226

STEAMER/DEHYDRATOR DESIGN—Food Processors, Etc.—Regal Ware, Inc.; *U.S. Private*, pg. 917

STEAMERS—NONE—The Smithfield Companies, Inc.; *U.S. Public*, pg. 1479

STEAMFOIL—Thermal Shower—Thermo Fibertek, Inc.; *U.S. Public*, pg. 1593

STEAMIN DEMON—Cleaning Products—Clayton Industries Co.; *U.S. Private*, pg. 245

STEAMIN' HOT—Hot Water Dispenser—In-Sink-Erator; *U.S. Public*, pg. 573

STEAMMASTER—Steam Cooking Equipment—The Middleby Corporation; *U.S. Public*, pg. 1109

STEAMVAC—Deep Cleaner—Hoover Company; *U.S. Public*, pg. 1065

STEAMVAC DELUXE—Deep Cleaner—Hoover Company; *U.S. Public*, pg. 1065

STEAMVAC JR.—Compact Spot Cleaner—Hoover Company; *U.S. Public*, pg. 1065

STEAMVAC ULTRA—Deep Cleaner with Power Hand Nozzle—Hoover Company; *U.S. Public*, pg. 1065

STEAMWORKS—Wallpaper Stripper—The Black & Decker Corporation; *U.S. Public*, pg. 233

STEARNS—Personal Flotation Devices—K2 Inc.; *U.S. Public*, pg. 940

STEARNS—Brakes & Clutches—Rexnord Corporation; *Int'l*, pg. 127

STEARNS—Personal Flotation Gear—Stearns Manufacturing Company; *U.S. Public*, pg. 940

STEARNS & FOSTER—Mattresses & Box Springs—Sealy Corporation; *U.S. Private*, pg. 978

STEARNS & FOSTER—Bedding—The Stearns & Foster Bedding Company; *U.S. Private*, pg. 979

STEDI-DRIVE—Motors—Emerson Electric Co.; *U.S. Public*, pg. 572

STEDI-DRIVE—Motor Speed Control—Emerson Motor Company; *U.S. Public*, pg. 573

STEDI-FLO—In-Line Water Conserving Apparatus—The Chicago Faucet Co.; *U.S. Private*, pg. 234

STEDI-R—Insulating Foamboard—Georgia-Pacific Corporation; *U.S. Public*, pg. 735

STEDY-FLO—Automatic Indus. Filters—Detrex Corporation; *U.S. Public*, pg. 501

STEEGO—Diversified Services—Steego Corporation; *Int'l*, pg. 216

STEEL & WIRE—NONE—MNP Corp.; *U.S. Private*, pg. 687

STEEL BOWERS—Boxes, Covers & Conduit Fittings—Thomas & Betts Corporation; *U.S. Public*, pg. 1597

STEEL BRIDGE—Pitless Trucking Scale—Weigh-Tronix, Inc.; *Int'l*, pg. 1299

STEEL CITY—Boxes & Covers & Fittings—Thomas & Betts Corporation; *U.S. Public*, pg. 1597

STEEL COMMANDER—Boxes, Covers & Conduit Fittings—Thomas & Betts Corporation; *U.S. Public*, pg. 1597

STEEL HAWG—Power Tools—Milwaukee Electric Tool Corp.; *Int'l*, pg. 96

STEEL-LITE—Shovels—Ames Company; *U.S. Public*, pg. 1683

STEEL MONSTERS—Male Action Toys—Tonka Corporation; *U.S. Public*, pg. 797

STEEL-PLY—Concrete Forming System—Symons Corporation; *U.S. Private*, pg. 932

STEELCASE—Commercial Office Furniture—A. Pomerantz & Company; *U.S. Private*, pg. 875

STEELCASE—Office Furniture—Steelcase Inc.; *U.S. Private*, pg. 1038

STEELCRAFT—Commerical Steel Doors & Frames—Steelcraft Manufacturing Company; *U.S. Public*, pg. 877

STEELEX—Boat Storage—Star Building Systems; *U.S. Public*, pg. 1394

STEELFLEX—Machine Tool Covers—A&A Manufacturing Co.; *U.S. Private*, pg. 1

STEELFLEX—Couplings—The Falk Corporation; *U.S. Public*, pg. 1534

STEELHEAD—Sprinkler—Rain Bird Sprinklers Manufacturing Corp.; *U.S. Private*, pg. 907

STEELMASTER—Office Product—American Trading and Production Corporation; *U.S. Private*, pg. 63

STEELMASTER—Metal Organizers & Cabinets—ATAPCO Office Products Group; *U.S. Private*, pg. 64

STEELMASTER—Tools—The Stanley Works; *U.S. Public*, pg. 1508

STEELMOBILE—Positioning Table—Jarke Corporation; *U.S. Private*, pg. 583

STEELNET—Iron & Steel Service—Conrail, Inc.; *U.S. Public*, pg. 431

STEELOK—Grooved Piping Systems—NIBCO, Inc.; *U.S. Public*, pg. 798

STEELON—Wire & Leaders—Outdoor Technologies Group; *U.S. Private*, pg. 822

STEELOX BUILDING SYSTEMS—NONE—Steelox Systems Inc.; *U.S. Private*, pg. 1038

STEELOX ROOFING SYSTEMS—NONE—Steelox Systems Inc.; *U.S. Private*, pg. 1038

STEELPAW—Wire Rope Isolator—Enidine Incorporated; *U.S. Private*, pg. 377

STEELTEX—Tires—Bridgestone/Firestone, Inc.; *Int'l*, pg. 213

STEELTEX RADIAL ASR—Tires—Bridgestone/Firestone, Inc.; *Int'l*, pg. 213

STEELTEX RADIAL FSR—Tires—Bridgestone/Firestone, Inc.; *Int'l*, pg. 213

STEELTEX RADIAL RTH—Tires—Bridgestone/Firestone, Inc.; *Int'l*, pg. 213

STEELTEX RADIAL 23 DEGREES—Tires—Bridgestone/Firestone, Inc.; *Int'l*, pg. 213

STEELTITE—Enclosed/Gasketed Fixtures—Guth Lighting Company; *Int'l*, pg. 821

STEELTRAIN—Dedicated Train Service for Coil Steel Shippers in Chicago-Detroit Corridor—Conrail, Inc.; *U.S. Public*, pg. 431

STEELTREE—Cantilever Rack—Jarke Corporation; *U.S. Private*, pg. 583

STEELWAY—Fensecure—Glynwed International PLC; *Int'l*, pg. 554

STEELWELD—Welding Equipment—Ambac B.V.; *Int'l*, pg. 71

STEELWOOD—Pole Buildings—Chief Industries, Inc.; *U.S. Private*, pg. 236

STEEMER—Rug Extractor—Oreck Manufacturing Company; *U.S. Private*, pg. 819

STEEMPAN—Heat Exchangers—Tranter, Inc.; *U.S. Public*, pg. 521

STEER-KLEER—Windshield Washer Solvent—Patterson Laboratories, Inc.; *U.S. Private*, pg. 843

STEERO—Bouillon & Broth Products—Borden, Inc.; *U.S. Private*, pg. 157

STEFANO MAN—Menswear—Charming Shoppes, Inc.; *U.S. Public*, pg. 335

STEFANSBACK—Sweet Baked Snack & Specialty Breads—Borden, Inc.; *U.S. Private*, pg. 157

STEFFEN'S—Dairy Products—Hilland Dairy Company; *U.S. Private*, pg. 879

STEG LIGHT—Low Calorie Beer—The Lion Brewery, Inc.; *U.S. Public*, pg. 1000

STEGEMAN—Packaged Meats—Sara Lee Corporation; *U.S. Public*, pg. 1432

STEGGLES—Poultry—Goodman Fielder Limited; *Int'l*, pg. 555

STEGMAIER—Beer—The Lion Brewery, Inc.; *U.S. Public*, pg. 1000

STEGMAIER 1857—Premium Line—The Lion Brewery, Inc.; *U.S. Public*, pg. 1000

STEIGER—4 Wheel Drive Tractors—Case Corporation; *U.S. Public*, pg. 311

STEINBACH—Department Stores—Steinbach Stores, Inc.; *U.S. Public*, pg. 461

STEINBACH STORES—Department Stores—Crowley, Milner & Company; *U.S. Public*, pg. 461

STEINBERG—Supermarkets—Socanav Inc.; *Int'l*, pg. 1272

STEINER—Commercial Turf Machinery—Ransomes Plc; *Int'l*, pg. 1087

STEINFELS—Cleaning Agents—Coop Switzerland; *Int'l*, pg. 329

STEINLAGER—Beer, Japan Only—Asahi Breweries Ltd.; *Int'l*, pg. 83

STEINLAGER—Lager—Bass PLC; *Int'l*, pg. 169

STEINWAY—pianos—Steinway & Sons; *U.S. Public*, pg. 1514

STEL—NONE—Stanford Telecommunications; *U.S. Public*, pg. 1508

STELANNEAL—Galvanneal—Stelco Inc.; *Int'l*, pg. 1299

STELAZINE—NONE—SmithKline Beecham Corporation; *Int'l*, pg. 1264

STELAZINE—Neurosciences—SmithKline Beecham plc; *Int'l*, pg. 1264

STELAZINE—Psychotropic—SmithKline Beecham Research Limited; *Int'l*, pg. 1266

STELCOAT—Hot-Dipped Galvanized Steel—Stelco Inc.; *Int'l*, pg. 1299

STELCOLOUR—Prefinished Steel—Stelco Inc.; *Int'l*, pg. 1299

STELL*R DIMMERS—Thin Profile Slide Dimmers—The Lamson & Sessions Co.; *U.S. Public*, pg. 976

STELLA ARTOIS—Lager—Interbrew S.A.; *Int'l*, pg. 679

STELLA ARTOIS—Ale—Whitbread PLC; *Int'l*, pg. 1498

STELLA D'ORO—Baked Goods—Nabisco Inc.; *U.S. Public*, pg. 1355

STELLAR—Theatre Seating—American Seating Company; *U.S. Private*, pg. 61

STELLAR—Computer Programming—The Black & Decker Corporation; *U.S. Public*, pg. 233

STELLAR—1/16" Residential Vinyl Composition Tile—Kentile Operting Co.; *U.S. Private*, pg. 615

STELLAR—Floor Finish—3M; *U.S. Public*, pg. 1604

STELLAR 2000—Air Conditioning Equipment—York International Corporation; *U.S. Public*, pg. 1789

STELLENRYCK—Wine—Distillers Corporation S.A.; *Int'l*, pg. 1129

STELVETITE—Sheet Steel—British Steel Plc; *Int'l*, pg. 220

STEMCO—Truck Prods.—Coltec Industries Inc.; *U.S. Public*, pg. 401

STEMI 1000—Stereomicroscope—Carl Zeiss; *Int'l*, pg. 1522

STEMI 2000—Stereo Microscope—Carl Zeiss; *Int'l*, pg. 1522

STEMPRO—NONE—Life Technologies, Inc.; *U.S. Public*, pg. 504

STEMPRO-34—NONE—Life Technologies, Inc.; *U.S. Public*, pg. 504

STEMU—Fittings for Water Supply Systems—Georg Fischer Ltd.; *Int'l*, pg. 488

STEN—NONE—Posso S.A.; *Int'l*, pg. 1064

STENCIL FACTORY—Stencils—Highlights for Children, Inc.; *U.S. Private*, pg. 528

STENDHAL—Cosmetics—International Cosmetics Co. Ltd.; *Int'l*, pg. 684

STENDHAL—Skin Treatment & Cosmetics—Sanofi Beaute, Inc.; *Int'l*, pg. 445

STENGER—Canned Beaf Stew, Chili, Mock Turtle Soup—Stegner Food Products Co.; *U.S. Private*, pg. 1039

STENMARK—Stencil Cutting Machine—Weber Marking Systems, Inc.; *U.S. Private*, pg. 1157

STENOCRAFT—Copy Paper—Georgia-Pacific Corporation; *U.S. Public*, pg. 735

STENORAM—Computer-Aided Transcription Systems—Photomatrix Corporation; *U.S. Public*, pg. 1292

STENTOR—NONE—Carpenter Technology Corporation; *U.S. Public*, pg. 307

STEOL—Surfactant-Ether Sulfates—Stepan Company; *U.S. Public*, pg. 1514

STEP—Computers—Everex Systems Inc.; *Int'l*, pg. 498

STEP—Vinyl Floorcoverings—Forbo Holding SA; *Int'l*, pg. 496

STEP AHEAD—Educational Workbooks—Golden Books Publishing; *U.S. Public*, pg. 749

STEP DECK—Step Stool Work Platform for Home Projects—Cosco, Inc.; *U.S. Private*, pg. 277

STEP-LITE—Decorative Vehicle Lighting—Superior Industries International, Inc.; *U.S. Public*, pg. 1539

STEP-PETTE—Scientific Glassware for Laboratory Use—Wheaton Inc.; *Int'l*, pg. 67

STEP REEBOK—Athletic Shoes—Reebok International Ltd.; *U.S. Public*, pg. 1369

STEP SAVER—Floor Cleaner—S.C. Johnson & Son, Inc.; *U.S. Private*, pg. 592

STEPAN-MILD—Surfactant—Stepan Company; *U.S. Public*, pg. 1514

STEPANATE—Surfactant-Sulfonate—Stepan Company; *U.S. Public*, pg. 1514

STEPANFLO—Organic Chemicals—Stepan Company; *U.S. Public*, pg. 1514

STEPANFOAM—Urethane Systems—Stepan Company; *U.S. Public*, pg. 1514

STEPANFORM—Surfactant—Stepan Company; *U.S. Public*, pg. 1514

STEPANLUBE—Organic Chemicals—Stepan Company; *U.S. Public*, pg. 1514

STEPANOL—Surfactant—Stepan Company; *U.S. Public*, pg. 1514

STEPANPOL—Polymer Resins—Stepan Company; *U.S. Public*, pg. 1514

STEPANQUAT—Organic Chemicals—Stepan Company; *U.S. Public*, pg. 1514

STEPANTAN—Surfactant—Stepan Company; *U.S. Public*, pg. 1514

STEPANTEX—Organic Chemicals—Stepan Company; *U.S. Public*, pg. 1514

STEPFAC—Organic Chemicals—Stepan Company; *U.S. Public*, pg. 1514

STEPHANIE THOMAS—Large Size Dresses & Sportswear—Jerell, Inc.; *U.S. Private*, pg. 586

STEPMASTER—Step on Receptacle—United Receptical, Inc.; *U.S. Private*, pg. 1123

STEPMATE—Pick Up Step—Lund International Holdings, Inc.; *U.S. Public*, pg. 1020

STEPOSOL—Surfactant—Stepan Company; *U.S. Public*, pg. 1514

STEPPER MOTORS—NONE—Philips Automotive Electronics; *Int'l*, pg. 1054

STEPSPERSE—Surfactant-Agricultural Emulsion—Stepan Company; *U.S. Public*, pg. 1514

STEPWET—Surfactant-Aricultural Emulsion—Stepan Company; *U.S. Public*, pg. 1514

STER-L 10—Gynecological Device—The Cooper Companies, Inc.; *U.S. Public*, pg. 442

STERADENT—Denture Care—Reckitt & Colman plc; *Int'l*, pg. 1089

STERALCON—Flexible Food Packaging—Alusuisse-Lonza Holding Ltd.; *Int'l*, pg. 66

STEREO REVIEW—Home Entertainment Magazine—Hachette Filipacchi Magazines Inc.; *Int'l*, pg. 794

STEREO SURROUND—Home Theater Sound—Shure Brothers Incorporated; *U.S. Private*, pg. 997

STEREO ZOOM—Microscope—Leica, Inc.; *Int'l*, pg. 806

STEREOGUIDE—NONE—LORAD Corporation; *U.S. Public*, pg. 1595

STEREOLOC II—NONE—LORAD Corporation; *U.S. Public*, pg. 1595

STEREON—Copolymers of Butadiene & Styrene—Bridgestone/Firestone, Inc.; *Int'l*, pg. 213

STEREOSTAR ZOOM—Stereoscopic Zoom Microscope—Leica, Inc.; *Int'l*, pg. 806

STERGIST—Fresh Yeast—Royal Gist-Brocades N.V.; *Int'l*, pg. 1142

STERI-DET—Liquid Detergent—Oakite Products, Inc.; *Int'l*, pg. 861

STERI-DRAPE—Surgical Drapes—3M; *U.S. Public*, pg. 1604

STERI-GAS—Ethylene Oxide Cartridges—3M; *U.S. Public*, pg. 1604

STERI-LOK—Sterilization Packaging—3M; *U.S. Public*, pg. 1604

STERI-PAD—Wound Dressings—Johnson & Johnson; *U.S. Public*, pg. 927

STERI-SHIELD—NONE—Stryker Corporation; *U.S. Public*, pg. 1525

STERI-STRIP—Skin Closures—3M; *U.S. Public*, pg. 1604

STERI-UNITS—Ophthalmic Solutions—Alcon Laboratories, Inc.; *Int'l*, pg. 916

STERI-VAC—Gas Sterilizers Aeration Cabinet, Drying Cabinet—3M; *U.S. Public*, pg. 1604

STERI-WRAP—Sterilization Products—Propper Manufacturing Co., Inc.; *U.S. Private*, pg. 891

STERICLOTH—Surgical Gowns—Medline Industries, Inc.; *U.S. Private*, pg. 728

STERIFIL—Filter System—Millipore Corporation; *U.S. Public*, pg. 1112

STERILCONTAINER—Sterile Processing Containers—Aesculap, Inc.; *Int'l*, pg. 29

STERILCONTAINER SYSTEM 2000—NONE—Aesculap, Inc.; *Int'l*, pg. 29

STERILE-GUARD—Technical Papers—MACtac Scranton Facility; *U.S. Public*, pg. 210

STERION—NONE—Johnson & Johnson; *U.S. Public*, pg. 927

STERISAFE—Sterilizer Treatment—BetzDearborn Inc.; *U.S. Public*, pg. 226

STERISEAL—NONE—Medline Industries, Inc.; *U.S. Private*, pg. 728

STERITEST—Sterility Test System—Millipore Corporation; *U.S. Public*, pg. 1112

STERITRON—Ultraviolet Sterilization Equip.—Hanovia Colight; *Int'l*, pg. 17

STERIVEX—Filter Unit—Millipore Corporation; *U.S. Public*, pg. 1112

STERLING—Salt & Salt Products—Akzo Nobel Inc.; *Int'l*, pg. 47

STERLING—Table Salt—Cargill Salt Inc.; *Int'l*, pg. 48

STERLING—Blackboard Chalk—Dixon Ticonderoga Company; *U.S. Public*, pg. 514

STERLING—Pistons—Federal-Mogul Corporation; *U.S. Public*, pg. 615

STERLING—Nails—Northwestern Steel & Wire Co.; *U.S. Public*, pg. 1201

STERLING—Cigarettes—RJR Nabisco Holdings Corp.; *U.S. Public*, pg. 1354

STERLING—Cigarettes—R.J. Reynolds Tobacco Company; *U.S. Public*, pg. 1355

STERLING—Gasket—Standco Industries, Inc.; *U.S. Private*, pg. 1032

STERLING—Electronics—Sterling Electronics Corporation; *U.S. Public*, pg. 1051

STERLING—Hardware—John Sterling Corporation; *U.S. Private*, pg. 1041

STERLING—Scooters—Sunrise Medical, Inc.; *U.S. Public*, pg. 1535

STERLING—Drills—Wahl Clipper Corp.; *U.S. Private*, pg. 1146

STERLING—NONE—Wayne Dalton of Sterling; *U.S. Private*, pg. 1155

STERLING—Printing Paper—Westvaco Corporation; *U.S. Public*, pg. 1762

STERLING & HUNT—Women's & Men's Apparel—Hartmarx Corporation; *U.S. Public*, pg. 795

STERLING AIR SERVICES—Ground Handling Arrangement Services—Air Malta Co. Ltd.; *Int'l*, pg. 37

STERLING BUILDING SYSTEMS—NONE—Wausau Homes, Inc.; *U.S. Private*, pg. 1154

STERLING CHOICE—Bed & Bath Products—Fieldcrest Cannon, Inc.; *U.S. Public*, pg. 1296

THE STERLING EDITION—Mattress & Box Spring Sets—Kingsdown, Inc.; *U.S. Private*, pg. 622

STERLING FILL—Automotive Body Filler—PPG Industries, Inc.; *U.S. Public*, pg. 1245

STERLING LINE—Sleep Sofas—Kingsdown, Inc.; *U.S. Private*, pg. 622

STERLING OPTICAL—Retail Optical Goods & Services—Sterling Vision, Inc.; *U.S. Public*, pg. 1516

STERLING PRESTIGE PLANK—Pre-Finished Strip—Bruce Hardwood Floors; *U.S. Public*, pg. 1634

STERLING PRESTIGE PLANK—3/4" Solid Plank—Bruce Hardwood Floors; *U.S. Public*, pg. 1634

STERLING RADIATOR—Heating & Ventilation Equipment—Mestek, Inc.; *U.S. Public*, pg. 1099

STERLING-STIEFF—Sterling Flatware—Lenox Brands; *U.S. Public*, pg. 261

STERLING STRIP—Pre-Finished Strip—Bruce Hardwood Floors; *U.S. Public*, pg. 1634

STERLING VINEYARDS—Wine—The Seagram Company Ltd.; *Int'l*, pg. 1214

STERN'S—Department Store—Federated Department Stores, Inc.; *U.S. Public*, pg. 617

STERNO—Canned Heat—Colgate-Palmolive Co., Institutional Products Div.; *U.S. Public*, pg. 397

STERNO—Portable Fuel & Related Equip. for Food Warming—Colgate-Palmolive Company; *U.S. Public*, pg. 397

STERNO—Cooking Fuel—Sterno, Inc.; *U.S. Public*, pg. 397

STERO—Food Equipment—Premark International, Inc.; *U.S. Public*, pg. 1321

STEROX—Surface Active Agent—Monsanto Company; *U.S. Public*, pg. 1124

STERRAD—NONE—Johnson & Johnson; *U.S. Public*, pg. 927

STERRAD—Sterilization System—Johnson & Johnson Medical, Inc.; *U.S. Public*, pg. 928

STERZI—Wines—Barbero 1891 SpA; *Int'l*, pg. 164

STETSON—Men's fragrance—Coty Inc.; *Int'l*, pg. 185

STETSON—Leather Goods—Enger-Kress Company; *U.S. Private*, pg. 376

STETSON—Hats—HATCO, Inc.; *U.S. Private*, pg. 510

STETSON—Men's Hats—Stetson Hat Co.; *U.S. Private*, pg. 510

STEUBEN—Glassware—Corning Incorporated; *U.S. Public*, pg. 448

STEVEN—Toys—Steven Manufacturing Co.; *U.S. Private*, pg. 1042

STEVENS—Hydrologic Instruments—Leupold & Stevens, Inc.; *U.S. Private*, pg. 662

STEVENS—Guns—Savage Arms Inc.; *U.S. Private*, pg. 968

STEVENS—Centrifuge Components—Western States Machine Company; *U.S. Private*, pg. 1168

STEVENS—Bed & Bath Products—WestPoint Stevens Inc.; *U.S. Public*, pg. 1762

STEVENS INTERNATIONAL—Mfr. Printing Presses—Stevens International, Inc.; *U.S. Public*, pg. 1517

STEVE'S—Ice Cream—Integrated Brands Inc.; *U.S. Public*, pg. 883

STEVES GEOMEMBRANES—NONE—JPS Elastomerics Corp.; *U.S. Private*, pg. 578

STEVE'S GOURMET LIGHT—Ice Cream—Integrated Brands Inc.; *U.S. Public*, pg. 883

STEVE'S OUTRAGEOUS ICE CREAM THINGS—Ice Cream—Integrated Brands Inc.; *U.S. Public*, pg. 883

STEVES ROOFING SYSTEMS—NONE—JPS Elastomerics Corp.; *U.S. Private*, pg. 578

STEW STARTER—Dry Mixes—Borden, Inc.; *U.S. Private*, pg. 157

STEWART-WARNER—Automotive Gauges, Hoses, Belts & Other Industrial Equipment—Stewart Warner Instruments Corporation; *U.S. Private*, pg. 1042

STEWART'S—Premium Beverage—Triarc Companies, Inc.; *U.S. Public*, pg. 1634

STEWART'S CREAM OF THE BARLEY SCOTCH WHISKY—Spirit—Allied Domecq PLC; *Int'l*, pg. 62

STICHMAT—Classic Reinforcements—CertainTeed Corporation; *Int'l*, pg. 1170

STICK 'EM—Disposable Yellow Jacket Trap—Security Lawn & Garden Co.; *U.S. Private*, pg. 397

STICK IT—Snowboard Gloves—The Grandoe Corp.; *U.S. Private*, pg. 469

STICK MATES—Magnetic & Self-Adhesive Plastic Novelties & Buttons—American Greetings Corporation; *U.S. Public*, pg. 77

STICK-TITE—Counter Security Ballpoint Pens—Eversharp Pen Co.; *U.S. Private*, pg. 386

STICKER FUN—Children's Stickers—Golden Books Family Entertainment Inc.; *U.S. Public*, pg. 749

STICKNEY—Film Cleaning Equipment—Eastman Kodak Company; *U.S. Public*, pg. 550

STICKY FINGERS—Adhesive Backed EMI Shielding Gaskets—Instrument Specialties Company; *U.S. Private*, pg. 565

STIEFF LADY CLAIRE—Flatware—Lenox Brands; *U.S. Public*, pg. 261

STIFFEL—Lamps—The Stiffel Company; *U.S. Private*, pg. 1043

STIGA—Tractors & Lawn Mowers—Aritmos AB; *Int'l*, pg. 1072

STIGGLES—Stickers—Highlights for Children, Inc.; *U.S. Private*, pg. 528

STIHL—NONE—Stihl Inc.; *Int'l*, pg. 1301

STIHL DUROMATIC—Guide Bars—Stihl Inc.; *Int'l*, pg. 1301

STIHL FARM BOSS—Chain Saw—Stihl Inc.; *Int'l*, pg. 1301

STIHL MAGNUM—Chain Saw—Stihl Inc.; *Int'l*, pg. 1301

STIHL MAGNUM II—Chain Saw—Stihl Inc.; *Int'l*, pg. 1301

STIHL PICCO—Saw Chain—Stihl Inc.; *Int'l*, pg. 1301

STIHL RAPID—Saw Chain—Stihl Inc.; *Int'l*, pg. 1301

STIHL ROLLOMATIC—Guide Bars—Stihl Inc.; *Int'l*, pg. 1301

STIHL TOPIC—Saw Chain—Stihl Inc.; *Int'l*, pg. 1301

STIHL WOOD BOSS—Chain Saw—Stihl Inc.; *Int'l*, pg. 1301

STIK-EESE—Office Supplies—JM Company; *U.S. Private*, pg. 577

STIKFAST—Label Gummers—Diagraph Corporation; *U.S. Private*, pg. 330

STIKIT—Unlined Pressure-Sensitive Coated Abrasives—3M; *U.S. Public*, pg. 1604

STILAN—Polymer—Raychem Corporation; *U.S. Public*, pg. 1362

STILETTO—NONE—Morse Controls; *U.S. Public*, pg. 857

STILL—Food Equipment—Premark International, Inc.; *U.S. Public*, pg. 1321

STILL-SEAL—Gaskets & Flange Seals—Hutchenson Seal Corporation; *U.S. Private*, pg. 550

STILLVER—Chemical Reagant—Hach Company; *U.S. Public*, pg. 773

STILLWATER TROUT ANGLER—Special Interest Magazine—IPC Magazines Limited; *Int'l*, pg. 651

STILNOX—Pharmaceutical—L'Oreal S.A.; *Int'l*, pg. 818

STILPHOSTROL—Pharmaceutical—Bayer Corporation/Pharmaceutical Division; *Int'l*, pg. 173

STILWELL—Frozen Vegetables & Pies—Flowers Industries, Inc.; *U.S. Public*, pg. 656

STIM-U-DENT—Dental Prods.—Johnson & Johnson Consumer Products; *U.S. Public*, pg. 928

STIM-U-PLANT—Plant Stands & Containers—Kay Home Products, Inc.; *U.S. Public*, pg. 622

STIMATE—(Desmopressin Acetate) Nasal Spray, 1.5 mg/ml—Centeon, L.L.C.; *Int'l*, pg. 626

STIMORAL—Gum—Kraft Jacobs Suchard; *U.S. Public*, pg. 1290

STIMSONITE—Reflective Prods.—Thomas & Betts/Amerace; *U.S. Public*, pg. 1598

STIMSONITE 88—Reflective Roadway & Hwy. Markers—Thomas & Betts/Amerace; *U.S. Public*, pg. 1598

STIMULAIRE—Aroma Therapy System—Surco Products, Inc.; *U.S. Private*, pg. 1056

STIMULON—Adjuvant—Aquila Biopharmaceuticals, Inc.; *U.S. Public*, pg. 126

STIMULUS PROGRESSION—Programming Format—Muzak Limited Partnership; *U.S. Private*, pg. 222

STING—Card Game—Mattel Games/Puzzles; *U.S. Public*, pg. 1058

STING-A-WAY—Relief From Insect Bites—Bethurum Research & Development, Inc.; *U.S. Private*, pg. 141

STING ANTI DRAWSINESS GUM—Anti-Drausiness Gum—Warner-Lambert K.K.; *U.S. Public*, pg. 1739

STING-EZE—Lotion for Insect Bites—Wisconsin Pharmacal Co., Inc.; *U.S. Private*, pg. 1185

STING KILL—Topical Analgesic—Kiwi Brands; *U.S. Public*, pg. 1433

STINGER—Fiberglass Handled Tools—Ames Company; *U.S. Public*, pg. 1683

STINGER—Computer Alignment Unit—Bee Line Company; *U.S. Private*, pg. 129

STINGER—Herbicide—The Dow Chemical Company; *U.S. Public*, pg. 522

STINGER—Production Test Systems—GenRad, Inc.; *U.S. Public*, pg. 731

STINGER—Auto Sound Accessories—Recoton Corporation; *U.S. Public*, pg. 1369

STINGER—Telescopic Crane—Simon Engineering plc; *Int'l*, pg. 1251

STINGRAY—Tracked Armored Vehicle—Textron Inc.; *U.S. Public*, pg. 1588

STIPEND—Insecticide—The Dow Chemical Company; *U.S. Public*, pg. 522

STIR CRAZY—Popcorn Maker—The West Bend Co.; *U.S. Public*, pg. 1322

STIR-N-SERV—Dinner Mix—Golden Grain Company; *U.S. Public*, pg. 1348

STIR-N-SERVE—Easy Serve Meals—The Quaker Oats Company; *U.S. Public*, pg. 1347

STIRATOR—Grain Stirrer (In Bin)—David Manufacturing Company (DMC); *U.S. Private*, pg. 436

STIRLING—Steam Boilers—Babcock & Wilcox Co.; *U.S. Public*, pg. 1068

STITCH N' SEW QUILTS—Crafts Publications—House of White Birches, Inc.; *U.S. Private*, pg. 542

STITCHES MAGAZINE—Magazine for Ebroidery & Monogramming Industry—Intertec Publishing; *U.S. Public*, pg. 1327

STITCHLESS—Billfolds—DHP Limited Partnership; *U.S. Private*, pg. 302

STITCHTEX—Innersole Material—Texon Materials Inc.; *U.S. Private*, pg. 1079

STIVAL CHARDONNAY LE RIVE—Italian Wine—Laird & Company; *U.S. Private*, pg. 642

STIVAL LE RIVE MERLOT—Italian Wine—Laird & Company; *U.S. Private*, pg. 642

STIVAL PINOT GRIGIOM MERLOT—Italian Wine—Laird & Company; *U.S. Private*, pg. 642

STIX-ALL—Adhesive—Borden, Inc.; *U.S. Private*, pg. 157

STOCK-AID—Base—McCormick & Company, Incorporated; *U.S. Public*, pg. 1066

STOCK-AID—Liquid & Dry Meat Flavors—McCormick Flavor Division-U.S.A.; *U.S. Public*, pg. 1066

STOCK CAR RACING—Magazine—General Media International Inc.; *U.S. Private*, pg. 444

STOCK LOCKS—Packaged Locks For Retail Market—National Cabinet Lock, Inc.; *U.S. Private*, pg. 270

THE STOCK MARKET—Game—Monarch Avalon, Inc.; *U.S. Public*, pg. 1123

STOCK YARDS CHICAGO—Gourmet Food Gifts—Stock Yards Packing Co., Inc.; *U.S. Private*, pg. 1043

STOCKADE—Livestock Feeds & Feed Supplements—Altair Corporation; *U.S. Private*, pg. 46

STOCKI—Potato Dumpling & Pancake Mix—Bestfoods; *U.S. Public*, pg. 223

STOCKMASTER—Conical Refiner—Harnischfeger Industries, Inc.; *U.S. Public*, pg. 788

STOCKO—Snap Fasteners—Stocko Corp.; *Int'l*, pg. 1301

STOCKS & BONDS—Game—Monarch Avalon, Inc.; *U.S. Public*, pg. 1123

STOKELY'S FINEST—Canned & Frozen Vegetables—Stokely USA, Inc.; *U.S. Public*, pg. 1518

STOLICHNAYA—Imported Vodka—PepsiCo, Inc.; *U.S. Public*, pg. 1276

STOLICHNAYA CRISTALL—Ultra-Premium Vodka—Carillon Importers, Ltd.; *Int'l*, pg. 409

STOLICHNAYA LIMONNAYA—Citrus Flavored Vodka—Carillon Importers, Ltd.; *Int'l*, pg. 409

STOLICHNAYA OHRANJ—Orange Flavored Vodka—Carillon Importers, Ltd.; *Int'l*, pg. 409

STOLICHNAYA OKHOTNICHYA—NONE—Carillon Importers, Ltd.; *Int'l*, pg. 409

STOLICHNAYA PERTSOVKA—Pepper Flavored Vodka—Carillon Importers, Ltd.; *Int'l*, pg. 409

STOLICHNAYA VODKA—NONE—Carillon Importers, Ltd.; *Int'l*, pg. 409

STOMAHESIVE—Skin Barriers—Bristol-Myers Squibb Company; *U.S. Public*, pg. 253

STOMASEAL—Adhesive Discs, Colostomy Dressings—3M; *U.S. Public*, pg. 1604

STONBLEND—Multi-Colored Textured Industrial/Commercial Flooring Systems—Stonhard, Inc.; *U.S. Public*, pg. 1358

STONCHEM—Heavy duty reinforced coatings—Stonhard, Inc.; *U.S. Public*, pg. 1358

STONCLAD—Flooring—RPM, Inc.; *U.S. Public*, pg. 1356

STONCLAD—Heavy Duty Industrial Flooring—Stonhard, Inc.; *U.S. Public*, pg. 1358

STONCO—Lighting Fixtures—The Genlyte Group Incorporated; *U.S. Public*, pg. 729

STONCO—Outdoor Lighting & Access.—Stonco Genlyte; *U.S. Public*, pg. 730

STONE & WEBSTER—Engineering Services—Stone & Webster Engineering & Constructors Corp.; *U.S. Public*, pg. 1519

STONE HOUSE—Natural Zeolite—The Goldfield Corporation; *U.S. Public*, pg. 750

STONE LITE COR—Corrugated Board—Stone Container Corporation; *U.S. Public*, pg. 1520

STONE TONES—NONE—Porcelanite, Inc.; *Int'l*, pg. 573

STONEBRIDGE—Paneling—Weyerhaeuser Forest Products Company; *U.S. Public*, pg. 1764

STONEBRIDGE VILLAGE—Recreational & Retirement Communities—Cooper Communities, Inc.; *U.S. Private*, pg. 273

STONECRAFT—Pocket Knives—Camillus Cutlery Co.; *U.S. Private*, pg. 203

STONEHAVEN—Mens Apparel—The Richman Brothers Co.; *U.S. Public*, pg. 1777

STONEHOUSE FARM—NONE—Weston Bakeries Limited; *Int'l*, pg. 1495

STONELINK—Computer Software—Stone & Webster, Incorporated; *U.S. Public*, pg. 1519

STONES—Ginger Wine—Banfi Vintners; *U.S. Private*, pg. 113

STONES—Tires—Bridgestone/Firestone, Inc.; *Int'l*, pg. 213

STONES BB—Bitter/Ale—Bass PLC; *Int'l*, pg. 169

STONEWALL—Corrugated Boxes—Stone Container Corporation; *U.S. Public*, pg. 1520

STONEWALL JACKSON'S WAY—War Game—Monarch Avalon, Inc.; *U.S. Public*, pg. 1123

STONEWEAVE—NONE—Royal Rubber & Manufacturing Co.; *U.S. Private*, pg. 949

STONEWOOL—NONE—EcoScience Corporation; *U.S. Public*, pg. 563

STONEWORKS—Computer Software Tools—Stone & Webster, Incorporated; *U.S. Public*, pg. 1519

STONEX—Mineral Compound—Raschig GmbH; *U.S. Private*, pg. 827

STONGLAZE—High Build Wall Systems for Industrial & Commercial Use—Stonhard, Inc.; *U.S. Public*, pg. 1358

STONHARD—Flooring—RPM, Inc.; *U.S. Public*, pg. 1356

STONLINER—Heavy-Duty Industrial Lining System—Stonhard, Inc.; *U.S. Public*, pg. 1358

STONLUX—Flooring—RPM, Inc.; *U.S. Public*, pg. 1356

STONLUX—Free Flowing Flooring for Static Protection—Stonhard, Inc.; *U.S. Public*, pg. 1358

STONSHIELD—Comm. & Light Duty Flooring Systems For Max. Skid-Resistance—Stonhard, Inc.; *U.S. Public*, pg. 1358

STOOPID STICK-ONS—Printed Adhering Appliques—American Greetings Corporation; *U.S. Public*, pg. 77

STOP—Toxic Gas Detection & Respiratory Protection—Camco International Inc.; *U.S. Public*, pg. 297

STOP & SHOP—Supermarket—Koninklijke Ahold NV; *Int'l*, pg. 749

STOP & SHOP—Supermarkets—The Stop & Shop Companies, Inc.; *Int'l*, pg. 750

STOP LEAK—Foundation Coatings—Monsey-Bakor; *U.S. Private*, pg. 757

STOP-N-FLOW—Light/Medium Duty Power-and-Free Conveyors—Jervis B. Webb Company; *U.S. Private*, pg. 1156

STOP N GO—Convenience Store with Gasoline Outlets—Ultramar Diamond Shamrock Corporation; *U.S. Public*, pg. 1663

STOP SCALD—Fruit Spray—Monsanto Company; *U.S. Public*, pg. 1124

STOP-STEP LADDERS—Aluminium Rolling Step Ladders—Cramer Inc.; *U.S. Private*, pg. 285

STOP TOU—Medicated Cough Drops—Cadbury Schweppes p.l.c.; *Int'l*, pg. 247

STOP-X37—Automatically Detects Potential Space Abends, Takes Preventive Action—Boole & Babbage, Inc.; *U.S. Public*, pg. 244

STOPAMATIC—Sprinklers—Rain Bird Sprinklers Manufacturing Corp.; *U.S. Private*, pg. 907

STOPHOEST—Candy—CSM N.V.; *Int'l*, pg. 243

STOPMASTER—Brakes—Rockwell International Corporation; *U.S. Public*, pg. 1397

STOPS RUST—Coatings—Rust-Oleum Corporation; *U.S. Public*, pg. 1358

STOR/DRAWER—Filing System—Fellowes Manufacturing Co.; *U.S. Private*, pg. 400

STOR-E-Z—Nesting Racks—Cres-Cor; *U.S. Private*, pg. 288

STORA—Matte Paper—Appleton Papers Inc.; *Int'l*, pg. 567

STORA PAPYRUS—Multi Art Paper/G-Print Paper—Appleton Papers Inc.; *Int'l*, pg. 567

STORAGE STACKERS—Stackable Storage Organizers—Hirsh Company; *U.S. Public*, pg. 963

STORAGEMASTER—Floppy Discs—Anacomp, Inc.; *U.S. Public*, pg. 106

STORAGESMART—Computer Product—International Business Machines Corporation; *U.S. Public*, pg. 895

STORAGETEK—Data Storage Systems—Storage Technology Corporation; *U.S. Public*, pg. 1522

STORBORD—Lumber—Georgia-Pacific Corporation; *U.S. Public*, pg. 735

STORE N POUR—Bar Storage/Serving Containers—Carlisle Food Service Products; *U.S. Public*, pg. 305

STORE-RITE—NONE—EcoScience Corporation; *U.S. Public*, pg. 563

STORE-SMART MARKETING—NONE—American Greetings Corporation; *U.S. Public*, pg. 77

STORE 2000—Food Stores—Koninklijke Ahold NV; *Int'l*, pg. 749

STORE 2000 THE STORE OF THE FUTURE—NONE—Ace Hardware Corporation; *U.S. Private*, pg. 12

STOREWORKS—Modular Frame System—Marketing Displays International; *U.S. Private*, pg. 705

STOREYS—Wallcoverings—Borden, Inc.; *U.S. Private*, pg. 157

STORK ENGINEERED PUMPS—Pumps—BW/IP International, Inc.; *U.S. Public*, pg. 658

STORK ENGINEERED PUMPS—Pumps—Flowserve Corporation; *U.S. Public*, pg. 658

STORM—Monitor—Akron Brass Company; *Int'l*, pg. 1068

STORM—Motor Home—Fleetwood Enterprises, Inc.; *U.S. Public*, pg. 650

STORM CHOKE—Valves—Halliburton Energy Services; *U.S. Public*, pg. 776

STORM KING—NONE—Huhtamaki Oy; *Int'l*, pg. 638

STORM OVER ARNHEM—War Game—Monarch Avalon, Inc.; *U.S. Public*, pg. 1123

STORM TRACK—Insulated Clothing—Refrigiwear, Inc.; *U.S. Private*, pg. 917

STORMGUARD—Specialty Nails—Maze Nails; *U.S. Private*, pg. 718

STORMSCOPE—Weather Mapping Systems—BF Goodrich Avionic Systems, Inc.; *U.S. Public*, pg. 751

STORMSHED—Treated Fabric for Outerwear—Reeves International; *U.S. Private*, pg. 507

STORMSTAIN—Exterior Wood Stain—California Products Corp.; *U.S. Private*, pg. 201

STORTZ—NONE—American Home Products Corporation; *U.S. Public*, pg. 79

STORY—Magazine—F & W Publications, Inc.; *U.S. Private*, pg. 388

STORY MAGIC—Activity—Tyco Toys, Inc.; *U.S. Public*, pg. 1058

STORY PRESS—Book Publishers—F & W Publications, Inc.; *U.S. Private*, pg. 388

STORYBOARD—Software—International Business Machines Corporation; *U.S. Public*, pg. 895

STORYQUESTS SERIES—NONE—Broderbund Software, Inc.; *U.S. Public*, pg. 258

STOUFFER'S—Frozen Foods & Ice Cream—Nestle S.A.; *Int'l*, pg. 915

STOUFFER'S—Frozen Entrees—Nestle USA; *Int'l*, pg. 916

STOUFFER'S CREATIVE RECIPES—NONE—Nestle USA; *Int'l*, pg. 916

STOUFFER'S HEARTY PORTIONS—NONE—Nestle USA; *Int'l*, pg. 916

STOUFFER'S HOMESTYLE—NONE—Nestle USA; *Int'l*, pg. 916

STOUFFER'S LEAN CUISINE—NONE—Nestle USA; *Int'l*, pg. 916

STOUFFER'S LEAN CUISINE CAFE CLASSICS—NONE—Nestle USA; *Int'l*, pg. 916

STOUFFER'S LEAN CUISINE HEARTY PORTIONS—NONE—Nestle USA; *Int'l*, pg. 916

STOUFFER'S LEAN CUISINE LUNCH EXPRESS—NONE—Nestle USA; *Int'l*, pg. 916

STOUFFER'S LUNCH EXPRESS—NONE—Nestle USA; *Int'l*, pg. 916

STOUT—Beer—The F.X. Matt Brewing Co.; *U.S. Private*, pg. 714

STOUT—Trucks & Buses—Toyota Motor Corporation; *Int'l*, pg. 1411

STOVE TOP—Stuffing Mix—Kraft Foods, Inc.; *U.S. Public*, pg. 1287

STOVE TOP—Stuffing Mixes—Philip Morris Companies Inc.; *U.S. Public*, pg. 1287

STOVER—Lock Nuts—RB&W Corporation; *U.S. Public*, pg. 1259

STOW-ALL—Storage Prods.—Grayline Housewares; *U.S. Private*, pg. 472

STOWAWAY—Horizontal Furnace—Lennox International Inc.; *U.S. Private*, pg. 659

Brand Name Index

STOWAWAY—Telephones—Lucent Technologies Inc.; *U.S. Public*, pg. 1017
STOWE WOODWARD—Roll Covering—BTR plc; *Int'l*, pg. 124
STRACHAN—Silverware—McPherson's Limited; *Int'l*, pg. 852
STRADA—Shoes—Bostonian Shoe Co.; *Int'l*, pg. 297
STRADA—Executive Side Chair—Domore Corporation; *U.S. Private*, pg. 339
STRADAL—Concrete Products—Poliet; *Int'l*, pg. 1177
STRAIGHT APPLE B-I-B—Brandy—Laird & Company; *U.S. Private*, pg. 642
STRAIGHT ARROW—NONE—Stadelman Fruit L.L.C.; *U.S. Private*, pg. 1028
STRAIGHT ARROW—Publishers—Wenner Media; *U.S. Private*, pg. 1162
STRAIGHT SHOT—Cardioplegia Delivery System—Gish Biomedical, Inc.; *U.S. Public*, pg. 745
STRAIGHT TALK—Automatic Voice Delivery System—Dictaphone Corp.; *U.S. Private*, pg. 1045
STRAIGHT TALK PLUS—Digital Voice Delivery System—Dictaphone Corp.; *U.S. Private*, pg. 1045
STRAIGHT-THROUGH PRESS—Press—Beloit Corporation; *U.S. Public*, pg. 789
STRAIT-LINE—Marking Tools—American Tool Companies, Inc.; *U.S. Private*, pg. 63
STRANDFOAM—Plastic Foam—The Dow Chemical Company; *U.S. Public*, pg. 522
STRANDLINK—Automatic Connecting Device—Maclean-Fogg Co.; *U.S. Private*, pg. 692
STRANDVISE—Automatic Connecting Device—Maclean-Fogg Co.; *U.S. Private*, pg. 692
STRATA—NONE—American Management Systems, Inc.; *U.S. Public*, pg. 86
STRATA—Air Cleaning System—Donaldson Company, Inc.; *U.S. Public*, pg. 517
STRATA—High Selectivity Etch System—GaSonics International; *U.S. Public*, pg. 703
STRATA—NONE—Howmedica, Inc.; *U.S. Public*, pg. 1282
STRATA DIP—NONE—Western Atlas Logging Services; *U.S. Public*, pg. 1757
STRATA-FLO—Multi-Ply Headbox—Harnischfeger Industries, Inc.; *U.S. Public*, pg. 788
STRATA-GRIT—Abrasive Rotary Brush for Scrubbing & Stripping—Flo-Pac Corporation; *U.S. Private*, pg. 414
STRATA II—Decorative Laminates—Pioneer Plastics Corporation; *U.S. Private*, pg. 867
STRATA SCAN—NONE—Del Mar Avionics; *U.S. Private*, pg. 321
STRATABASE—Rings—Regal Ware, Inc.; *U.S. Private*, pg. 917
STRATACRAWLER SERIES—Crawler Mounted Machines—Telsmith, Inc.; *U.S. Public*, pg. 141
STRATAGLAZE—NONE—Regal Ware, Inc.; *U.S. Private*, pg. 917
STRATAGON—NONE—Western Atlas Logging Services; *U.S. Public*, pg. 1757
STRATALAB—Microscope—Leica, Inc.; *Int'l*, pg. 806
STRATALOGIK—NONE—Western Atlas Logging Services; *U.S. Public*, pg. 1757
STRATAMESH—Athletic Apparel—Bike Athletic Co.; *U.S. Private*, pg. 143
STRATASHEEN—Athletic Apparel—Bike Athletic Co.; *U.S. Private*, pg. 143
STRATASTRETCH—Athletic Apparel—Bike Athletic Co.; *U.S. Private*, pg. 143
STRATATROL—Filter System—Pall Corporation; *U.S. Public*, pg. 1253
STRATEGIC APPLICATION MODELER—Enterprise Modeling Tool—Ross Systems, Inc.; *U.S. Public*, pg. 1406
STRATEGIC CUSTOMER SERVICES—Warehousing & Forms Management—Moore Document Solutions; *Int'l*, pg. 890
STRATEGIC POINTER 2000 CUSTOMER MODULE—Business Product—International Business Machines Corporation; *U.S. Public*, pg. 895
STRATEGIC POINTER 2000/2—Business Product—International Business Machines Corporation; *U.S. Public*, pg. 895

STRATEGIC REWARDS—Incentive Plans To Align Employee Performance/Behavior With Company Goals—Watson Wyatt Worldwide; *U.S. Private*, pg. 1154
STRATEGO—Game—Milton Bradley Company; *U.S. Public*, pg. 797
STRATEGY SERIES—Loudspeaker Mounting System—Atlas/Soundolier; *U.S. Private*, pg. 64
STRATEGYWARE—Decision Support System for Account Origination—Fair, Isaac and Company, Inc.; *U.S. Public*, pg. 609
STRATELINE—Plywood Siding—Georgia-Pacific Corporation; *U.S. Public*, pg. 735
STRATFORD—Upholstered Furniture—Consolidated Furniture Corporation; *U.S. Private*, pg. 265
STRATFORD COURT—NONE—Marriott International, Inc.; *U.S. Public*, pg. 1047
STRATHMORE—Clothing—Cliftex; *U.S. Public*, pg. 1777
STRATHMORE—Fine Paper—International Paper Company; *U.S. Public*, pg. 901
STRATHMORE—Paper—Strathmore Paper; *U.S. Public*, pg. 903
STRATMASTER—Rotary Drilling Rigs—The George E. Failing Company; *U.S. Private*, pg. 153
STRATO-STREAK—Tires—Bridgestone/Firestone, Inc.; *Int'l*, pg. 213
STRATOFLEX—Aerospace Hose—Parker Hannifin Corporation; *U.S. Public*, pg. 1259
STRATOLOUNGER—Lounge Chair—Consolidated Furniture Corporation; *U.S. Private*, pg. 265
STRATOPEDIC—Sofa Beds, Sleepers—Consolidated Furniture Corporation; *U.S. Private*, pg. 265
STRATOROUTE 2000—Satellite Network—BCE Inc.; *Int'l*, pg. 114
STRATOS—Boats—Outboard Marine Corporation; *U.S. Private*, pg. 478
STRATUS—Automobile-Dodge Car/Truck Division—Chrysler Corporation; *U.S. Public*, pg. 352
STRATUS—Air Handlers—Daw Technologies, Inc.; *U.S. Public*, pg. 489
STRATUS—NONE—Porcelanite, Inc.; *Int'l*, pg. 573
STRATWORKS—Geological Tools—Landmark Graphics Corporation; *U.S. Public*, pg. 776
STRAUS-FRANK COMPANY—Wholesale Distribution of Auto Parts—STRAFCO, Inc.; *U.S. Private*, pg. 1046
STRAWBERRY—Women's Apparel—A&E Stores, Inc.; *U.S. Private*, pg. 1
STRAWBERRY FIELDS—Herb Tea—Celestial Seasonings; *U.S. Public*, pg. 319
STRAWBERRY SHORTCAKE—NONE—American Greetings Corporation; *U.S. Public*, pg. 77
STRAWBERRY SQUARES—Strawberry-Filled Whole Wheat Biscuit—Kellogg Company; *U.S. Public*, pg. 947
STRAWBRIDGE'S—Department Stores—The May Department Stores Company; *U.S. Public*, pg. 1063
STRAX—NONE—Jotun A/S; *Int'l*, pg. 714
STREAM MASTER—Monitor—Akron Brass Company; *Int'l*, pg. 1068
STREAM MATE—Cutlery—Buck Knives, Inc.; *U.S. Private*, pg. 177
STREAMER—Business Product—International Business Machines Corporation; *U.S. Public*, pg. 895
STREAMER TAG—Outdoor Game—Mattel Games/Puzzles; *U.S. Public*, pg. 1058
STREAMERICA—Men's Accessories Collection—Tiffany & Co.; *U.S. Public*, pg. 1608
STREAMJET—Spray Nozzle—Spraying Systems Co.; *U.S. Private*, pg. 1026
STREAMLIGHT JR.—Miniature Aluminum Flashlight—Streamlight Inc.; *U.S. Private*, pg. 1047
STREAMLINE—Intravenous Catheters—Johnson & Johnson Medical, Inc.; *U.S. Public*, pg. 928
STREAMLINE—Copper Tube & Fittings—Mueller Industries, Inc.; *U.S. Public*, pg. 1141
STREAMLINE—NONE—Tri-Clover Inc.; *Int'l*, pg. 1379
STREET & SMITH—Magazine—The Conde Nast Publications Inc.; *U.S. Private*, pg. 20
STREET HEAT—Heads, Automotive—The Will-Burt Company; *U.S. Private*, pg. 1177

STREET MACHINE—Car Magazine—EMAP Nationals; *Int'l*, pg. 451
STREET SKEES—Boots—International Seaway Trading Corporation; *U.S. Private*, pg. 572
STREET/SOCKET—Plumbing Fittings—Genova Products, Inc.; *U.S. Private*, pg. 447
STREET TUNNEL RAMS—Manifolds—Edelbrock Corp.; *U.S. Public*, pg. 563
STREETFINDER—Street Map Book—Rand McNally & Company; *U.S. Private*, pg. 908
STREETHAWK—Vehicle Warning Light Bar—Federal Signal Corporation; *U.S. Public*, pg. 616
STREETJAM—NONE—Mattel, Inc.; *U.S. Public*, pg. 1057
STREETS OF FIRE—Game—Monarch Avalon, Inc.; *U.S. Public*, pg. 1123
STREETTGUARD—AntiFreeze—J.D. Streett & Co., Inc.; *U.S. Private*, pg. 1047
STREETTS SUPERIOR—Motor Oil & Lubricants—J.D. Streett & Co., Inc.; *U.S. Private*, pg. 1047
STREPCILLIN F-25—Feed Additives—Salsbury Laboratories, Inc.; *Int'l*, pg. 1277
STREPSILS—NONE—Boots Healthcare International; *Int'l*, pg. 202
STREPTASE—Cardiovascular Agent—Astra AB; *Int'l*, pg. 93
STREPTASE—NONE—Astra USA, Inc.; *Int'l*, pg. 93
STREPTASE—Therapeutics in Field of Fibrinolysis—Behringwerke AG; *Int'l*, pg. 624
STREPTOKINASE—Pharmaceutical—Hoechst Aktiengesellschaft; *Int'l*, pg. 624
STREPTOMYCIN—Streptomycin Sulfate—Royal Gist-Brocades N.V.; *Int'l*, pg. 1142
STREPTOSIL—Disinfectant—Boehringer Ingelheim Italia S.p.A.; *Int'l*, pg. 199
STREPTOZYME—Slide Test for Streptococcal Antigens—Wampole Laboratories; *U.S. Public*, pg. 310
STRESKYD—NONE—Lawter International, Inc.; *U.S. Public*, pg. 980
STRESS WRAP—Splice & Termination Kits—Plymouth Rubber Company, Inc.; *U.S. Public*, pg. 1311
STRESSGARD—Vitamins—Bayer AG; *Int'l*, pg. 171
STRESSGARD—Vitamins—Bayer Corporation/Consumer Care Division; *Int'l*, pg. 173
STRESSPROOF—Steel Bar Products—LaSalle Steel Company; *U.S. Public*, pg. 1181
STRESSPROOF—Type of Cold Finished Steel Bar—Quanex Corporation; *U.S. Public*, pg. 1349
STRESSTABS—NONE—Whitehall-Robins Healthcare; *U.S. Public*, pg. 80
STRETCH—Disposable Underwater Camera—Eastman Kodak Company; *U.S. Public*, pg. 550
STRETCH—Delivery Trailer Style—Hackney and Sons, Inc.; *U.S. Private*, pg. 1097
STRETCH-BOARD—Aluminum Extrusions—Reynolds Metals Company; *U.S. Public*, pg. 1385
STRETCH 'N DUST—Sweeping Tools & Cleaning Cloths—Chicopee Inc.; *Int'l*, pg. 113
STRETCH 'N SEAL—Plastic Film—The Dow Chemical Company; *U.S. Public*, pg. 522
STRETCH-TITE—Plastic Food Wrap—Polyvinyl Films, Inc.; *U.S. Public*, pg. 875
STRETCHRITE—Stretch Film—Brawny Plastics West; *U.S. Private*, pg. 166
STRIBORD—Striated Hardboard—Georgia-Pacific Corporation; *U.S. Public*, pg. 735
STRIDE—Fiber-Cement Siding—GAF Premium Products, Inc.; *U.S. Private*, pg. 433
STRIDE RITE—Childrens Shoes—The Stride Rite Corporation; *U.S. Public*, pg. 1524
STRIDERS—Plastic Heads—Ludwig Industries; *U.S. Public*, pg. 1514
STRIK-T—Marine Steering Assemblies—Teleflex Incorporated; *U.S. Public*, pg. 1569
STRIKER—Sporting Equipment—Brunswick Bowling & Billiards Corp.; *U.S. Public*, pg. 265
STRIMMER—Outdoor Products—The Black & Decker Corporation; *U.S. Public*, pg. 233
STRING KING—Industrial Adhesives—H.B. Fuller Company; *U.S. Public*, pg. 686
STRINGS & MACHINES—Necessities—Prince Sports Group Inc.; *U.S. Private*, pg. 884
STRIP AWAY—Stain Remover—Ecolab Inc.; *U.S. Public*, pg. 562

STRIP/AWAY—Tape Cassette Labels—Ludlow Corporation; *U.S. Public*, pg. 1651

STRIP-N-SEAL—Envelopes—Tension Envelope Corp.; *U.S. Private*, pg. 1077

STRIP-N-STICK—Security Envelope—KCL Corporation; *U.S. Public*, pg. 603

STRIP-SEAL—Weather Cord—Tremco, Inc.; *U.S. Public*, pg. 1358

STRIP-TAC—Pressure Sensitive Sheet & Roll Products—Brown-Bridge; *U.S. Public*, pg. 1022

STRIP-TAC—Adhesive Coated Paper & Cloth—Kimberly-Clark Corporation; *U.S. Public*, pg. 958

STRIP-TAC PLUS—Pressure Sensitive Sheets—Brown-Bridge; *U.S. Public*, pg. 1022

STRIPE—NONE—Zebra Technologies Corporation; *U.S. Public*, pg. 1790

STRIPED—Tube Bubble Gum—Amurol Confections Co.; *U.S. Public*, pg. 1781

STRIPED GRIPPERS—PVC Striped Gripping Gloves—Jomac, Inc.; *U.S. Private*, pg. 595

STRIPES OF QUALITY—Logo—Allen Telecom Inc.; *U.S. Public*, pg. 45

STRIPMASTER—Outdoor Products—The Black & Decker Corporation; *U.S. Public*, pg. 233

STRIPMASTER—Wire Strippers—Ideal Industries, Inc.; *U.S. Private*, pg. 557

STRIPPER-LIP—Lip Systems for Earthmoving Buckets—Esco Corporation; *U.S. Private*, pg. 382

STRIPPGARD—Strippable Coating for Substrate Protection—PPG Industries, Inc.; *U.S. Public*, pg. 1245

STRIPPIT—Machine Tools & Accessories for Punching Sheet Materials—IDEX Corporation; *U.S. Public*, pg. 862

STRIPSWITCH—Miniature Printed Circuit Board Switch—Transico Incorporated; *U.S. Public*, pg. 1630

STRIPTROL—Variable Resistors—CTS Corporation; *U.S. Public*, pg. 285

STRIPTRON—Photoresist Stripper—The Dow Chemical Company; *U.S. Public*, pg. 522

STROB-SAW—Circular Blade Saws—Weyerhaeuser Company; *U.S. Public*, pg. 1764

STROBATAC—NONE—GenRad, Inc.; *U.S. Public*, pg. 731

STROBE—MVS Software For Measuring Application Performance—Programart Corporation; *U.S. Private*, pg. 890

STROBE—NONE—S.D. Warren Co.; *Int'l*, pg. 1193

STROBEHAWK—Vehicle Warning Light Bar—Federal Signal Corporation, Signal Div.; *U.S. Public*, pg. 616

STROBOLUME—NONE—GenRad, Inc.; *U.S. Public*, pg. 731

STROBOSLAVE—NONE—GenRad, Inc.; *U.S. Public*, pg. 731

STRODEX—Multifunctional-Balanced Detergent—Dexter Chemical Corp.; *U.S. Private*, pg. 329

STROEHMANN—Baked Goods—George Weston Limited; *Int'l*, pg. 1494

STROH'S—Beer—The Stroh Brewery Company; *U.S. Private*, pg. 1047

STROH'S LIGHT—Beer—The Stroh Brewery Company; *U.S. Private*, pg. 1047

STROMBERG—Time Equip.—New Haven Mfg. Corp.; *U.S. Private*, pg. 793

STRONG ARM—Gas-Charged Lift Supports—Arvin Industries, Inc.; *U.S. Public*, pg. 136

STRONG HOLD—Olefin—Bemis Company, Inc.; *U.S. Public*, pg. 210

STRONG HOLDER—Carry Trays—The Chinet Co.; *Int'l*, pg. 1146

STRONGARM—Electric Winches—Dutton-Lainson Co.; *U.S. Private*, pg. 350

STRONGBARN—Steel Roofing & Siding—National Steel Corp., Granite City Division; *Int'l*, pg. 902

STRONGDRAIN—Steel Raingoods—National Steel Corp., Granite City Division; *Int'l*, pg. 902

STRONGHEART—Pet Food—Allied Foods, Inc.; *U.S. Private*, pg. 39

STRONGID—NONE—Pfizer Inc.; *U.S. Public*, pg. 1281

STRONGPANEL—Steel Roofing & Siding—National Steel Corp., Granite City Division; *Int'l*, pg. 902

STRONGTRIM—Steel Accessories—National Steel Corp., Granite City Division; *Int'l*, pg. 902

STROUDS—Specialty Retail Stores—Strouds, Inc.; *U.S. Public*, pg. 1525

STROUDS LINEN OUTLET—NONE—Strouds, Inc.; *U.S. Public*, pg. 1525

STROUDS, THE LINEN EXPERTS—NONE—Strouds, Inc.; *U.S. Public*, pg. 1525

STRUC-ONE—Wood Composite—Weyerhaeuser Company; *U.S. Public*, pg. 1764

STRUC-ONE—Boards & Sheets of Composite Material—Weyerhaeuser Forest Products Company; *U.S. Public*, pg. 1764

STRUCTAFLOR—Flooring—CSR Limited; *Int'l*, pg. 245

STRUCTO-LITE—Floor Trucks—Faultless Nutting; *Int'l*, pg. 473

STRUCTO-LITE—Gypsum Plaster—USG Corporation; *U.S. Public*, pg. 1660

STRUCTOGLAS—USDA Accepted Fiberglas Reinforced Wall/Ceiling Panels—Sequentia Inc.; *U.S. Private*, pg. 985

STRUCTUREPAK—Paperboard—Weyerhaeuser Company; *U.S. Public*, pg. 1764

STRUCTURFRAME—Frame Stock For Upholstered Furniture—Weyerhaeuser Forest Products Company; *U.S. Public*, pg. 1764

STRUCTURIX—Nondestructive Testing Films, Chemistry & Processors—AGFA Division of Bayer Corporation; *Int'l*, pg. 172

STRUCTURSEAL—Edge Sealer form Concrete Formant—Weyerhaeuser Forest Products Company; *U.S. Public*, pg. 1764

STRUCTURWOOD—Wood Composite—Weyerhaeuser Company; *U.S. Public*, pg. 1764

STRUCTURWOOD—Wood Fiber Panels—Weyerhaeuser Forest Products Company; *U.S. Public*, pg. 1764

STRUT CUSHION—Compression Bumpers & Dust Boots—Arvin Industries, Inc.; *U.S. Public*, pg. 136

STRUT-LOK—Folding Struts—Hartwell Corporation; *U.S. Private*, pg. 1168

STRUT MASTER—Shock Absorbers—Bridgestone/Firestone, Inc.; *Int'l*, pg. 213

STRUT-TITE!—Strut Mounts & Related Parts—R&B, Inc.; *U.S. Public*, pg. 1354

STRUTHERS—Various Company Products—Struthers Industries Inc.; *U.S. Private*, pg. 1048

STRUTHERS INDUSTRIES—NONE—Struthers Industries Inc.; *U.S. Private*, pg. 1048

STRUTHERS WELLS CORPORATION—NONE—Struthers Industries Inc.; *U.S. Private*, pg. 1048

STRYGLOSS—Paper—Champion International Corp.; *U.S. Public*, pg. 333

STRYKER—NONE—Stryker Corporation; *U.S. Public*, pg. 1525

STRYPEEZE—Paint Remover Semi Paste—The Savogran Company; *U.S. Private*, pg. 968

STUART—Imported Food Products—World Finer Foods, Inc.; *U.S. Private*, pg. 1190

STUART ANDERSON'S—Restaurants—Stuart Anderson's Black Angus/Cattle Company Restaurants; *U.S. Private*, pg. 61

STUART AUSTIN—Clocks—Tropar Mfg. Co., Inc.; *U.S. Public*, pg. 1176

STUART HALL—Office Products—Newell Co.; *U.S. Public*, pg. 1176

STUART HALL—School Supplies—Stuart Hall Co., Inc.; *U.S. Public*, pg. 1178

THE STUART NEWS—Newspaper—The E.W. Scripps Company; *U.S. Public*, pg. 1447

STUARTNATAL PLUS—NONE—American Home Products Corporation; *U.S. Public*, pg. 79

STUARTS—NONE—Petrie Retail, Inc.; *U.S. Private*, pg. 858

STUBBLE DEVICE—Shaver—Wahl Clipper Corp.; *U.S. Private*, pg. 1146

STUBBY—Spring Plunger—Vlier Engineering; *U.S. Public*, pg. 124

STUCCO—Fome-Cor—Monsanto Company; *U.S. Public*, pg. 1124

STUCCO-SHIELD II—Residential Polyiso Foam Insulation—Atlas Roofing Corp.; *U.S. Private*, pg. 96

STUD-TITE!—Double-ended Studs—R&B, Inc.; *U.S. Public*, pg. 1354

STUDENT CARD—NONE—American Express Company; *U.S. Public*, pg. 73

STUDENT INFORMATION SYSTEM (SIS)—NONE—American Management Systems, Inc.; *U.S. Public*, pg. 86

STUDENT PRIVILEGES—NONE—American Express Company; *U.S. Public*, pg. 73

STUDER—Analog & Digital Tape Machines, Broadcast Mixing Consoles—Harman International Industries, Inc.; *U.S. Public*, pg. 787

STUDIO—French Television/Cinema Magazine—EMAP France; *Int'l*, pg. 451

STUDIO—Paint—Graham Paint and Varnish Company; *U.S. Public*, pg. 468

STUDIO—Knitting Machines—VWS, Inc.; *Int'l*, pg. 440

STUDIO CARDS—Greeting Cards—Fine Art Developments plc; *Int'l*, pg. 485

STUDIO COORDINATES—Drapery Hardware—Kirsch; *U.S. Public*, pg. 1176

STUDIO EASE—NONE—Kellwood Company; *U.S. Public*, pg. 948

STUDIO EXPRESS—NONE—Polaroid Corporation; *U.S. Public*, pg. 1313

STUDIO III—Glazed Ceramic Decorative Wall Tile—Precision Die & Engineering, Inc.; *U.S. Public*, pg. 1322

STUDIO LINE DAILY EXPRESS—Shampoo—Cosmair, Inc.; *Int'l*, pg. 818

STUDIO LINE HAIR—Styling Products—Cosmair, Inc.; *Int'l*, pg. 818

STUDIO POLAROID—NONE—Polaroid Corporation; *U.S. Public*, pg. 1313

STUDIO 36—Apparel—I. Appel Corporation; *U.S. Private*, pg. 78

STUDIOSET—Photo Typesetter—AGFA EPS Division; *Int'l*, pg. 172

STUDY MATE—Filmstrip Projector—Telex Communications, Inc.; *U.S. Private*, pg. 1074

STUFF-IT—Body Filler—Marson/Creative Fastener, Inc.; *U.S. Private*, pg. 708

STUFFED CRUST PIZZA—NONE—Pizza Hut, Inc.; *U.S. Public*, pg. 1636

STUFFINS—Stuffed Toy Figures—American Greetings Corporation; *U.S. Public*, pg. 77

STULSKI—Vodka—Laird & Company; *U.S. Private*, pg. 642

STUN—Card Game—Mattel Games/Puzzles; *U.S. Public*, pg. 1058

STUPP—Carbon Pipe & Steel Products—Thomas Pipe & Steel, Inc.; *U.S. Private*, pg. 508

STUR-D-LACE—Electronic Lacing Tape—Gudebrod, Inc.; *U.S. Private*, pg. 486

STURACO—Gear Lubricants—D.A. Stuart Company; *U.S. Private*, pg. 1048

STURBRIDGE—Lumber & Wood Products—Georgia-Pacific Corporation; *U.S. Public*, pg. 735

STURD-I-FLOOR—Underlayment—Boise Cascade Corporation; *U.S. Public*, pg. 242

STURDI-SIDE—Klamath Falls Hardboard Siding—Weyerhaeuser Forest Products Company; *U.S. Public*, pg. 1764

STURDI-TOP—Fiberboard—Georgia-Pacific Corporation; *U.S. Public*, pg. 735

STURDI-WOOD—Pelican Oriented Strand Board—Weyerhaeuser Forest Products Company; *U.S. Public*, pg. 1764

STURDILITE—Engineering Work Station—Kewaunee Scientific Corporation; *U.S. Public*, pg. 953

STURDY JUG—Ice Chest—Igloo Products Corporation; *U.S. Public*, pg. 265

STURDYWARE—Disposable Dinnerware—Amoco Chemicals; *U.S. Public*, pg. 102

STURM, RUGER—Pistols & Revolvers—Sturm, Ruger & Co., Inc.; *U.S. Public*, pg. 1526

STURTEVANT—Fans—The Howden Fan Co.; *U.S. Private*, pg. 543

STYCAST—One & Two Component Epoxy Impregnant & Casting Resins—Emerson & Cuming Specialty Polymers; *Int'l*, pg. 1435

STYL-SAFE—Spectacle—U.S. Safety; *U.S. Private*, pg. 1125

STYLE—Cigarettes—Lorillard Tobacco Company; *U.S. Public*, pg. 1011

STYLE-AIRE—Styler/Dryer—Sunbeam Household Products; *U.S. Public*, pg. 1533

STYLE AUTO—Clothing—Gilrichco, Inc.; *U.S. Private*, pg. 454

STYLE AUTO RACING BEARS—Toys—Gilrichco, Inc.; *U.S. Private*, pg. 454

STYLE CHIEF—Leisure Wear—Duck Head Apparel; *U.S. Public*, pg. 498

STYLE HIDE—Paints—Pratt & Lambert United, Inc.; *U.S. Public*, pg. 1466

STYLE-LITE—Lightweight Carrying Case—Zero Corporation; *U.S. Public,* pg. 1791

STYLE SETTER—Heated Rollers—Bristol-Myers Squibb Company; *U.S. Public,* pg. 253

STYLE 360—Pipe Repair Clamp—DMD; *U.S. Public,* pg. 528

STYLE WRITER II—Ink Jet Printer—Apple Computer, Inc.; *U.S. Public,* pg. 121

STYLEBORD—Hardboard & Hardboard Paneling—Georgia-Pacific Corporation; *U.S. Public,* pg. 735

STYLELITE—Camera—Eastman Kodak Company; *U.S. Public,* pg. 550

STYLERITE—Seating—HON Industries Inc.; *U.S. Public,* pg. 772

STYLESETTER—Handmade & Machine-Made Glass & Lead Crystal—Crystal Clear Industries; *U.S. Private,* pg. 293

STYLEWRITER PLUS—Lettering System—General Binding Corporation; *U.S. Public,* pg. 707

STYLINER—Trimmer—Andis Company; *U.S. Private,* pg. 73

STYLO SPORT LIPSTICK—Cosmetics—Cosmair, Inc.; *Int'l,* pg. 818

STYLUS—NONE—Insignia Systems, Inc.; *U.S. Public,* pg. 881

STYLUS—Nonwoven Interfacings—Specialty Textile Products; *U.S. Private,* pg. 1219

STYLUS COLOR—Inkjet Printer—Epson America Inc.; *Int'l,* pg. 1219

STYLUS EIGHT HUNDRED—Inkjet Printer—Epson America Inc.; *Int'l,* pg. 1219

STYMER—Textile Sizing Resin—Monsanto Company; *U.S. Public,* pg. 1124

STYMER—Textile Sizing Resin—Solutia Inc.; *U.S. Public,* pg. 1483

STYRAGEL—GPC Columns, Bulk Packing—Millipore Corporation; *U.S. Public,* pg. 1112

STYREX—Petrochemical Processing Aids—BetzDearborn Inc.; *U.S. Public,* pg. 226

STYROBOARD—Insulation Board—The Dow Chemical Company; *U.S. Public,* pg. 522

STYROBOHSUI—Insulation Board—The Dow Chemical Company; *U.S. Public,* pg. 522

STYROCONPANE—Insulation Board—The Dow Chemical Company; *U.S. Public,* pg. 522

STYRODANNETSU—Insulation Board—The Dow Chemical Company; *U.S. Public,* pg. 522

STYROFLEX—Flexibilized Insulation Materials—The Dow Chemical Company; *U.S. Public,* pg. 522

STYROFOAM—Plastic Foam—The Dow Chemical Company; *U.S. Public,* pg. 522

STYROFUSUMA—Sliding Door—The Dow Chemical Company; *U.S. Public,* pg. 522

STYROGUARD—Insulation Board—The Dow Chemical Company; *U.S. Public,* pg. 522

STYROLATH—Lath—The Dow Chemical Company; *U.S. Public,* pg. 522

STYRON—Polystyrene Resins—The Dow Chemical Company; *U.S. Public,* pg. 522

STYROPANEL—Insulation Panel—The Dow Chemical Company; *U.S. Public,* pg. 522

STYROSLIT—Foam Panels—The Dow Chemical Company; *U.S. Public,* pg. 522

STYROSPAN—Insulation—The Dow Chemical Company; *U.S. Public,* pg. 522

STYROTATAMI—Tatami Mat—The Dow Chemical Company; *U.S. Public,* pg. 522

STYROTATAMIDOKO—Tatami Mat Bases—The Dow Chemical Company; *U.S. Public,* pg. 522

STYROVAN—Insulation Board—The Dow Chemical Company; *U.S. Public,* pg. 522

STYROWALL—Metal-Surfaced Insulation Materials—The Dow Chemical Company; *U.S. Public,* pg. 522

STYVEX—Styrenic Compounds—Ferro Corporation; *U.S. Public,* pg. 618

SU-PRO—Pressure Sensitive Films—Sun Process Converting Company; *U.S. Private,* pg. 1051

SUAVE—Hair Products, Antiperspirant, Deodorant, Skin Lotion & Hair Care—Helene Curtis Industries, Inc.; *Int'l,* pg. 1434

SUB-G—Oral Hygiene Aids—John O. Butler Co.; *Int'l,* pg. 1320

SUB-Q—Subcutaneous Needles & Syringes—Becton Dickinson & Company; *U.S. Public,* pg. 199

SUB-SOILER—Deep V-Chisel—Brillion Iron Works, Inc.; *U.S. Public,* pg. 933

SUB-ZERO—EPDM Weatherstrip—Macklanburg-Duncan Co.; *U.S. Private,* pg. 692

SUB-ZERO FREEZER—Freezers & Built in Refrigerator Equip.—Sub-Zero Freezer Co., Inc.; *U.S. Private,* pg. 1048

SUB-SIEVE SIZER—Particle-Size Apparatus—Fisher Scientific Company; *U.S. Private,* pg. 658

SUBARU—Compact Cars—Fuji Heavy Industries, Ltd.; *Int'l,* pg. 522

SUBARU—Automobile—Subaru of America, Inc.; *Int'l,* pg. 523

SUBCENTER—Subwoofer & Center Channel System—Atlas/Soundolier; *U.S. Private,* pg. 64

SUBCLONING EFFICIENCY—NONE—Life Technologies, Inc.; *U.S. Public,* pg. 504

SUBDEW—Heat Exchanger—Crown Andersen Inc.; *U.S. Public,* pg. 462

SUBLIMAZE—Pharmaceutical—Janssen Pharmaceutica, Inc.; *U.S. Public,* pg. 928

SUBMARINE—Game—Monarch Avalon, Inc.; *U.S. Public,* pg. 1123

SUBMATIC—Sump Pump Motor—Franklin Electric Co., Inc.; *U.S. Public,* pg. 679

SUBS 2 GOGO—Sandwich Shops—Cara Operations Limited; *Int'l,* pg. 266

SUBSIDIARY BANKING—NONE—HongKong Bank of Canada; *Int'l,* pg. 583

SUBSITE—NONE—Charles Machine Works, Inc.; *U.S. Private,* pg. 230

SUBTRACT—Pharmaceutical Prods.—Alva/Amco Pharmacal Companies, Inc.; *U.S. Private,* pg. 47

SUBTRACT—Foundation Garments—True Form Intimate Apparel; *U.S. Private,* pg. 697

SUBTRACT ELITE—Foundation Garment—True Form Intimate Apparel; *U.S. Private,* pg. 697

SUBTRACT FLIRTATIONS—Control Garments—True Form Intimate Apparel; *U.S. Private,* pg. 697

SUBURBAN—Truck—Chevrolet Motor Div. General Motors Corp.; *U.S. Public,* pg. 720

SUBURBAN COOK COUNTY BUSINESS DIRECTORY—Directory—Manufacturers' News, Inc.; *U.S. Private,* pg. 700

SUBURBAN PETITES—Women's Apparel—Hartmarx Corporation; *U.S. Public,* pg. 795

SUBWAY—Sporting Equipment—Brunswick Bowling & Billiards Corp.; *U.S. Public,* pg. 265

SUBWAY—Sandwiches & Salads—Subway Franchise Advertising Fund Trust; *U.S. Private,* pg. 1048

SUCCESS—Rice—Riviana Foods Inc.; *U.S. Public,* pg. 1392

SUCCESS DEVELOPMENT INTERNATIONAL—Financial Information Program—Success Development International; *U.S. Private,* pg. 1048

SUCCESSFUL FARMING—Magazine—Meredith Corporation; *U.S. Public,* pg. 1094

SUCCESSFUL MEETINGS—Business Publication—Bill Communications, Inc.; *Int'l,* pg. 1446

SUCCESSORIES—NONE—The At-A-Glance Group; *U.S. Private,* pg. 295

SUCCINYLCHOLIN CHLORIDE—Pharmaceutical—Organon Inc.; *Int'l,* pg. 48

SUCHARD—Chocolates—Andes Candies Inc.; *U.S. Private,* pg. 163

SUCHARD—Chocolate—Kraft Jacobs Suchard; *U.S. Public,* pg. 1290

SUCHARD—Chocolate—Kraft Jacobs Suchard AG; *U.S. Public,* pg. 1288

SUCKLE—Dairy Feeds—Manna Pro Corporation; *U.S. Private,* pg. 700

SUCRETS—Sore Throat Lozenges & Spray—SmithKline Beecham Consumer Healthcare, U.S.; *Int'l,* pg. 1264

SUCRETS—NONE—SmithKline Beecham Corporation; *Int'l,* pg. 1264

SUCRETS—Coughs, Colds & Influenza Product—SmithKline Beecham plc; *Int'l,* pg. 1264

SUCTION COMMAND—Cotton Trailer Unloading System—Continental Eagle Corporation; *U.S. Private,* pg. 267

SUDAFED—Decongestant—Glaxo Wellcome PLC; *Int'l,* pg. 553

SUDAFED—Allergy/Cold/Flu/Sinus Medication—Warner-Lambert Consumer Healthcare; *U.S. Public,* pg. 1739

SUDAFED PLUS—Decongestant—Glaxo Wellcome PLC; *Int'l,* pg. 553

SUDAFED SEVERE COLD FORMULA—Decongestant—Glaxo Wellcome PLC; *Int'l,* pg. 553

SUDAFED SINUS—Decongestant—Glaxo Wellcome PLC; *Int'l,* pg. 553

SUDBURY—Marine Chemicals—Rule Industries, Inc.; *U.S. Public,* pg. 950

SUDBURY—Soil Test Kits—Security Lawn & Garden Co.; *U.S. Private,* pg. 397

SUDDEN CHANGE—NONE—CCA Industries, Inc.; *U.S. Public,* pg. 276

SUDDEN IMPACT—Women's Clothing—Niches, Inc.; *U.S. Public,* pg. 1181

SUDDEN SERVICE—Computerized Parts & Service—Taylor Machine Works, Inc.; *U.S. Private,* pg. 1070

SUDDENLY SALAD—Dry Boxed Salad Mixes—General Mills, Inc.; *U.S. Public,* pg. 717

SUDDENLY SLIM—Shapewear—Olga Div.; *U.S. Public,* pg. 1738

SUDDENLY SLIM SUPREME—Control Brief Bodysuit—Olga Div.; *U.S. Public,* pg. 1738

SUDDENLY SMOOTH—Bra, Braslip & Shapesuit—Olga Div.; *U.S. Public,* pg. 1738

SUDENGA INDUSTRIES—Farm Equipment Sales & Service—Adair Feed & Grain Company; *U.S. Private,* pg. 16

SUE BEE—Honey—Sioux Honey Association; *U.S. Private,* pg. 1003

SUEDETOUCH—Soft, Suede-like Appearance Coating—Morton Automotive Coatings; *U.S. Public,* pg. 1135

SUESSEN—Equipment for Ring & O.E. Spinning; Parafil, Plyfil, Flomax, Ring Can Syste—Spindelfabrik Suessen; *Int'l,* pg. 1290

SUFENTA—Pharmaceutical—Janssen Pharmaceutica, Inc.; *U.S. Public,* pg. 928

SUGAR—Women's Apparel—International Cosmetics Co., Ltd.; *Int'l,* pg. 684

SUGAR BABIES—Chocolate/Caramel Candies—Tootsie Roll Industries, Inc.; *U.S. Public,* pg. 1621

SUGAR BABY—Vegetable—A. Duda & Sons Inc.; *U.S. Private,* pg. 344

SUGAR CUBE—Electronic Instrument—Intel Corporation; *U.S. Public,* pg. 886

SUGAR DADDIES—Chocolate/Caramel Candies—Tootsie Roll Industries, Inc.; *U.S. Public,* pg. 1621

SUGAR DELIGHT—Sugar Sweetener Blend—The NutraSweet Company; *U.S. Public,* pg. 1125

SUGAR FREE CREAMSICLE—Ice Pops—Good Humor/Breyers Ice Cream; *Int'l,* pg. 1435

SUGAR FREE FUDGSICLE—Ice Pops—Good Humor/Breyers Ice Cream; *Int'l,* pg. 1435

SUGAR FREE POPSICLE—Ice Pops—Good Humor/Breyers Ice Cream; *Int'l,* pg. 1435

SUGAR FROSTED FLAKES—Cereal—Malt-O-Meal Company; *U.S. Public,* pg. 699

SUGAR LOAF—Pickles—Cains Foods, L.P.; *U.S. Private,* pg. 199

SUGAR-PAK—I Column—Millipore Corporation; *U.S. Public,* pg. 1112

SUGAR PUFFS—Presweetened Puffed Wheat—Malt-O-Meal Company; *U.S. Private,* pg. 699

SUGAR PUFFS—Cereal—The Quaker Oats Company; *U.S. Public,* pg. 1347

SUGAR TWIN—Artificial Sweetener—Alberto-Culver Canada, Inc.; *U.S. Public,* pg. 38

SUGAR TWIN—Sugar Substitute—Alberto-Culver Company; *U.S. Public,* pg. 37

SUGARCANE—Yarn—Lion Brand Yarn Co.; *U.S. Private,* pg. 669

SUGARDALE—Meats—Fresh Mark, Inc.; *U.S. Private,* pg. 427

SUGARPLUM—Ham—Armour Swift Eckrich; *U.S. Public,* pg. 426

SUGARY SAM—NONE—Allen Canning Company; *U.S. Private,* pg. 36

SUGUS—Candy—Kraft Jacobs Suchard AG; *U.S. Public,* pg. 1288

THE SUIT COMPANY—NONE—Moss Bros Group PLC; *Int'l,* pg. 895

SUL-PERM—Lubricant Additives—Ferro Corporation; *U.S. Public,* pg. 618

SULCUS—NONE—Sulcus Computer Corp.; *U.S. Public,* pg. 1527

SULFA-PAK—Pharmaceuticals—Rhone-Poulenc Rorer - U.S.; *Int'l,* pg. 1110

Brand Name Index

SULFACET-R—Pharmaceutical—Dermik Laboratories, Inc.; *Int'l*, pg. 1110

SULFAMYLON—Mafenide Acetate Topical Burn Cream—Dow Hickam Pharmaceuticals Inc.; *U.S. Public*, pg. 1143

SULFASAN—Rubber Vulcanizing Agent— Monsanto Company; *U.S. Public*, pg. 1124

SULFAVER—Chemical Reagant—Hach Company; *U.S. Public*, pg. 773

SULFOAM—Medicated Anti-Dandruff Shampoo; Control of Dandruff—Bradley Pharmaceuticals; *U.S. Public*, pg. 249

SULFOAM—Medicated Anti-Dandruff Shampoo; Control of Dandruff—Doak Dermatologics; *U.S. Public*, pg. 250

SULFOBETAINE—Amphoteric Sulfobetaine— Henkel Corporation; *Int'l*, pg. 610

SULFODENE—Dog/Cat Skin Medication—Combe Incorporated; *U.S. Private*, pg. 257

SULFOMAT—ED Equipment for Treating Sulfate Solution—Ionics, Incorporated; *U.S. Public*, pg. 912

SULFORCIN—Pharmaceutical Products— Galderma Laboratories, Inc.; *Int'l*, pg. 819

SULFOTEX—Sulphaten—Henkel Corporation; *Int'l*, pg. 610

SULFRAMINE—Alkyl Sulfate—Witco Corporation; *U.S. Public*, pg. 1773

SULLISCREW—Compressors—Sullair Corporation; *U.S. Public*, pg. 1534

SULLIVAN—Gynecological Device—The Cooper Companies, Inc.; *U.S. Public*, pg. 442

SULPERAZON—Sulbactam/Cefoperazone—Pfizer Inc.; *U.S. Public*, pg. 1281

SULPHO-LAC—Acne Medication; Medicated Soap; Treatment of Acne—Bradley Pharmaceuticals; *U.S. Public*, pg. 249

SULPHO-LAC—Medicated Soap; Treatment of Acne—Doak Dermatologics; *U.S. Public*, pg. 250

SULTRIN—Triple Sulfa Cream—Ortho-McNeil Pharmaceutical Corporation; *U.S. Public*, pg. 929

SULTRIN—Triple Sulfa Vaginal Tablets—Ortho-McNeil Pharmaceutical Corporation; *U.S. Public*, pg. 929

SUMCASE—Bit Set—American Tool Companies, Inc.; *U.S. Private*, pg. 63

SUMITOMO—State Bank—Sumitomo Bank of California; *Int'l*, pg. 1309

SUMITOMO—Carbon Pipe & Steel Products— Thomas Pipe & Steel, Inc.; *U.S. Private*, pg. 508

SUMITOMO SITIX—NONE—Sumitomo Sitix Corporation; *Int'l*, pg. 1317

SUMMA-SINO—Rugs—Couristan Inc.; *U.S. Private*, pg. 279

SUMMAGRAPHICS—Digitizing Tablets, Plotters, Cutters—CalComp Technology, Inc.; *U.S. Public*, pg. 1007

SUMMER BLONDE—Hair Lightener—Clairol, Inc.; *U.S. Public*, pg. 254

SUMMER CLOUDS—Lumber & Wood Products— Georgia-Pacific Corporation; *U.S. Public*, pg. 735

SUMMER COUNTRY CONCERT SERIES— Country Music Radio Program—Westwood One Entertainment; *U.S. Public*, pg. 1763

SUMMER COUNTRY CONCERT SERIES— Country Music Programming—Westwood One, Inc.; *U.S. Public*, pg. 1763

SUMMER GARDEN—NONE—The Smithfield Companies, Inc.; *U.S. Public*, pg. 1479

SUMMER LEGG'S—Hosiery—L'eggs Products, Inc.; *U.S. Public*, pg. 1434

SUMMER NATURALS—NONE—Frozfruit Corporation; *U.S. Private*, pg. 430

SUMMER SENSATIONS—Cosmetics—Cosmair, Inc.; *Int'l*, pg. 818

SUMMER SHEER—Pantyhose—Hanes Hosiery, Inc.; *U.S. Public*, pg. 1434

SUMMERAIRE—Cleaning Products—Clayton Industries Co.; *U.S. Private*, pg. 245

SUMMERIZER—Lawn Fertilizer—The Scotts Company; *U.S. Public*, pg. 1446

SUMMERLOC—Produce Packaging—The Dow Chemical Company; *U.S. Public*, pg. 522

SUMMER'S EVE—Douche & External Cleansers— C. B. Fleet Co., Inc.; *U.S. Private*, pg. 410

SUMMER'S EVE FEMININE BATH—Shower & Bath Moisturizing Cleanser—C. B. Fleet Co., Inc.; *U.S. Private*, pg. 410

SUMMERWOOD—Wood & Lumber Products— Georgia-Pacific Corporation; *U.S. Public*, pg. 735

SUMMIT—Forms & Converting Paper—Boise Cascade Corporation; *U.S. Public*, pg. 242

SUMMIT—Cigarettes—Brown & Williamson Tobacco Corp.; *Int'l*, pg. 111

SUMMIT—Oxygen Concentrator—CAIRE, Inc.; *U.S. Private*, pg. 751

SUMMIT—Investment Plans—Derbyshire Building Society; *Int'l*, pg. 394

SUMMIT—Communication Systems—Executone Information Systems, Inc.; *U.S. Public*, pg. 599

SUMMIT—Roofing Shingles—Georgia-Pacific Corporation; *U.S. Public*, pg. 735

SUMMIT—Single Wheel Caster—ITW Plastiglide; *U.S. Public*, pg. 867

SUMMIT—Windows—Jeld-Wen, Inc.; *U.S. Private*, pg. 585

SUMMIT—(Mobile Radio)—E.F. Johnson Radio Systems; *U.S. Public*, pg. 1630

SUMMIT—Drapery Hardware—Kirsch; *U.S. Public*, pg. 1176

SUMMIT—Luggage—Lands' End, Inc.; *U.S. Public*, pg. 977

SUMMIT—Candy—Mars, Incorporated; *U.S. Private*, pg. 707

SUMMIT—NONE—Seats Incorporated; *U.S. Private*, pg. 1767

SUMMIT—Paperback Books—Simon & Schuster; *U.S. Private*, pg. 777

SUMMITT—Magnetic Computer Tape—Anacomp Magnetics, Inc.; *U.S. Public*, pg. 107

SUMNER SUITES—Hotels—Sholodge, Inc.; *U.S. Public*, pg. 1467

SUMP—NONE—Sta-Rite Industries, Inc.; *U.S. Public*, pg. 1767

SUMP-VAC—Mobile Sludge Vacuum—The Spencer Turbine Co.; *U.S. Private*, pg. 1025

SUMYCIN—Infectious Disease Therapy—Bristol-Myers Squibb Company; *U.S. Public*, pg. 253

SUN—Pool Product—Olin Corporation; *U.S. Public*, pg. 1218

SUN—Automotive Diagnostic Equipment Utilizing Advanced Electronics—Sun Electric; *U.S. Public*, pg. 1480

SUN—Computer Software & Hardware—Sun Microsystems, Inc.; *U.S. Public*, pg. 1531

SUN ADHESIVES—Wood Adhesives—Patrick Industries Inc.; *U.S. Public*, pg. 1264

SUN-AIRE—Venetian Blinds—Kirsch; *U.S. Public*, pg. 1176

SUN & SAND CHAIRS—Aluminum Beach Chairs— Telescope Casual Furniture, Inc.; *U.S. Private*, pg. 1074

SUN BAN—Sun Protection Lip Conditioner— Stanback Company; *U.S. Private*, pg. 1030

SUN BLOCKER—Awning/Accessory—Carefree of Colorado; *U.S. Public*, pg. 217

SUN CHASER—Recreational Vehicles—Kit Manufacturing Company; *U.S. Public*, pg. 962

SUN CHIPS—Multi-Grain Snack Food—PepsiCo, Inc.; *U.S. Public*, pg. 1276

SUN COUNTRY—Coolers—Canandaigua Wine Company, Inc.; *U.S. Public*, pg. 300

SUN COUNTRY—Role Playing—Monarch Avalon, Inc.; *U.S. Public*, pg. 1123

SUN COUNTRY—Granola—The Quaker Oats Company; *U.S. Public*, pg. 1347

SUN CREST—Soft Drink—The Monarch Company, Inc.; *U.S. Private*, pg. 756

SUN CRUNCHERS—Cereal—General Mills, Inc.; *U.S. Public*, pg. 717

SUN DANCER ROOF WINDOW—NONE— Benjamin Obdyke, Inc.; *U.S. Private*, pg. 810

SUN DAY BEST—Optical—D.O.C. Optics Corporation; *U.S. Public*, pg. 305

SUN-DROP—Soft Drink—Cadbury Beverages North America; *Int'l*, pg. 248

SUN-DROP—Soft Drinks—The Procter & Gamble Company; *U.S. Public*, pg. 1330

SUN E SERIES—NONE—Detroit Diesel Corp.; *U.S. Private*, pg. 850

SUN ESSENCE—Developer Lotion—Clairol, Inc.; *U.S. Public*, pg. 254

SUN-FLO—Fruit Juices—Dean Foods Company; *U.S. Public*, pg. 489

SUN GEMS—Salt & Salt Products—Akzo Nobel Inc.; *Int'l*, pg. 47

SUN GEMS—Water Softener Salt—Cargill Salt Inc.; *Int'l*, pg. 48

SUN-GLEAM—Automotive Finishes—PPG Industries, Inc.; *U.S. Public*, pg. 1245

SUN GRAIN—Bread—Roman Meal Company; *U.S. Private*, pg. 942

THE SUN-HERALD—NONE—John Fairfax Holdings Limited; *Int'l*, pg. 477

SUN HILL—Devel., Mfg. & Mktg. of Consumer Products—Sun Hill Industries, Inc.; *U.S. Private*, pg. 1051

SUN-IN—Hair Lightener—Chattem, Inc.; *U.S. Public*, pg. 341

SUN LAKES RESORT COMMUNITY—Activ Adult Community In Phoenix—Robson Communities; *U.S. Private*, pg. 937

SUN LINE—Luxury Cruises—Royal Olympic Cruises; *U.S. Public*, pg. 1411

SUN LUBRICANTS—Lubricants—Fleischli Oil Company, Inc.; *U.S. Private*, pg. 410

SUN-MAID—Raisin Loaf—Meneba N.V.; *Int'l*, pg. 555

SUN-MAID—Raisins & Cut Dried Fruit—Sun Diamond Growers of California; *U.S. Private*, pg. 1051

SUN-MAID GROWERS OF CALIFORNIA—Raisin Growers—Sun-Maid Growers of California; *U.S. Private*, pg. 1051

SUN MART—Retail Grocery Stores—Nash Finch Company; *U.S. Public*, pg. 1151

SUN MITE—Electric Infrared Comfort Heating Equipment—Fostoria Industries, Inc.; *U.S. Private*, pg. 421

SUN-OF-A-GUN—Antenna—Telex Communications, Inc.; *U.S. Private*, pg. 1074

SUN OIL—Industrial & Engine Oils, Gear Lube & Greaser—Kelso Oil Company; *U.S. Private*, pg. 613

SUN-PAC—Photodegradable Plastic Loose-Fill— The Dow Chemical Company; *U.S. Public*, pg. 522

SUN PACER—Sun Care Products—Amway Corporation; *U.S. Private*, pg. 69

SUN-PATS—Confections, Nuts—Nestle-Rowntree Ltd.; *Int'l*, pg. 921

SUN PORT—Soft Top—Bestop, Inc.; *Int'l*, pg. 830

SUN PRIDE—NONE—Sun City Industries, Inc.; *U.S. Public*, pg. 1529

SUN PRO—Automotive Test Equipment—Actron Manufacturing Company; *U.S. Private*, pg. 16

SUN PRO—Horse & Dog Foods—Intermountain Farmers Association; *U.S. Private*, pg. 568

SUN-PROOF—Paint—PPG Industries, Inc.; *U.S. Public*, pg. 1245

SUN RIDGE CANYON—Residential Community— Suncor Development Company; *U.S. Public*, pg. 1298

SUN RIPE—Glace (Candied Fruit)—Paradise, Inc.; *U.S. Public*, pg. 1256

SUN-SENTINEL—Daily Newspaper—Tribune Company; *U.S. Public*, pg. 1635

SUN SENTURY—Car Alarm Systems—Actron Manufacturing Company; *U.S. Private*, pg. 16

SUN SERIES—NONE—Detroit Diesel Corp.; *U.S. Private*, pg. 850

SUN 600—Camera—Polaroid Corporation; *U.S. Public*, pg. 1313

SUN 660—Autofocus Camera—Polaroid Corporation; *U.S. Public*, pg. 1313

SUN SPLASH—NONE—Friendly Holidays Inc.; *U.S. Private*, pg. 428

SUN-TEX—Wallcoverings—Borden, Inc.; *U.S. Private*, pg. 157

THE SUN—Newspaper—The Baltimore Sun Newspapers; *U.S. Public*, pg. 1616

SUN-TIMES—Daily Newspaper—Chicago Sun Times; *Int'l*, pg. 632

SUN TUNE—Automotive Test Equipment—Actron Manufacturing Company; *U.S. Private*, pg. 16

SUN VAC—Vacumn/broom Street Sweeper— Vactor Mfg. Inc.; *U.S. Public*, pg. 617

SUN VALLEY—Cosmetics—Cosmetic Group, U.S.A.; *U.S. Private*, pg. 277

SUN VIKING—Ships—Royal Caribbean Cruises Ltd.; *U.S. Public*, pg. 1410

SUN VISTA—Canned Beans—Tri Valley Growers; *U.S. Private*, pg. 1101

Brand Name Index

SUNAMERICA—Life Insurance & Financial Services—SunAmerica Inc.; *U.S. Public*, pg. 1532

SUNBEAM—Bread & Rolls—Franklin Baking Co., Inc.; *U.S. Private*, pg. 424

SUNBEAM—Bread, Buns & Sweet Goods—Metz Baking Company; *U.S. Private*, pg. 1022

SUNBEAM—Bread, Buns, Sweet Goods—Metz Baking Company (WI); *U.S. Private*, pg. 1022

SUNBEAM—White Bread, Buns & Rolls & Varieties—Quality Bakers of America Cooperative, Inc.; *U.S. Private*, pg. 898

SUNBEAM—Snack Cakes—Quality Bakers of America Cooperative, Inc.; *U.S. Private*, pg. 898

SUNBEAM—Appliances—Sunbeam Corporation; *U.S. Public*, pg. 1533

SUNBEAM AIR CLEANERS—Ionizer, Heap, Furnace Mounts—Sunbeam Household Products; *U.S. Public*, pg. 1533

SUNBEAM BATH SCALES—Mechanical & Electronic Bath Scales—Sunbeam Household Products; *U.S. Public*, pg. 1533

SUNBEAM BOOKS—Greeting Card Books—American Greetings U.S. Greeting Card Division; *U.S. Public*, pg. 78

SUNBEAM CHILL-IT—Gel-Packs, Ice Bags, Cold Therapy Products—Sunbeam Household Products; *U.S. Public*, pg. 1533

SUNBEAM HAIR DRYERS—Wall-Mount, Hand Held Grounded Hair Dryers—Sunbeam Household Products; *U.S. Public*, pg. 1533

SUNBEAM HEAT TO GO—Portable Heating Pads—Sunbeam Household Products; *U.S. Public*, pg. 1533

SUNBEAM KITCHEN SCALES—Mechanical & Digital Scales—Sunbeam Household Products; *U.S. Public*, pg. 1533

SUNBEAM LITE—Diet Bread—Quality Bakers of America Cooperative, Inc.; *U.S. Private*, pg. 898

SUNBEAM MESSAGERS—Hand Held, Home/Auto, Portable Messagers—Sunbeam Household Products; *U.S. Public*, pg. 1533

SUNBEAM SHOWER MESSAGERS—Wall Mount, Hand Held Shower Messagers—Sunbeam Household Products; *U.S. Public*, pg. 1533

SUNBEAM—Timers, Clocks & Kitchen Gadgets—Springfield Precision Instruments, Inc.; *U.S. Private*, pg. 1027

SUNBELT—Snacks—McKee Foods Corporation; *U.S. Private*, pg. 723

SUNBIRD—Boats—Outboard Marine Corporation; *U.S. Private*, pg. 478

SUNBIRD RESORT COMMUNITY—Active Adult Community In Phoenix—Robson Communities; *U.S. Private*, pg. 937

SUNBONDED—Fluorescent Paints—Day-Glo Color Corp.; *U.S. Public*, pg. 1357

SUNBONNET KIDS—Greeting Cards—American Greetings Corporation; *U.S. Public*, pg. 77

SUNBOW—Prefinished Wall Paneling—Georgia-Pacific Corporation; *U.S. Public*, pg. 735

SUNBRAND—NONE—Willcox & Gibbs, Inc.; *U.S. Private*, pg. 1177

SUNBRED—Sunflower Seeds—Northrup King Co.; *Int'l*, pg. 974

SUNBRELLA—Solution-dyed Acrylic Fabric for Awnings, Boat Covers &Outdoor Furniture—Glen Raven Mills, Inc.; *U.S. Private*, pg. 456

SUNBURST—Recycled Envelopes—Champion International Corp.; *U.S. Public*, pg. 333

SUNBURST C—Herb Tea—Celestial Seasonings; *U.S. Public*, pg. 319

SUNCARE—Sun Protection Products—Schering-Plough Healthcare Products Inc.; *U.S. Public*, pg. 1438

SUNCHEE—Drink Concentrates & Juices—Armour Swift Eckrich; *U.S. Public*, pg. 426

SUNCHIPS MULTIGRAIN SNACKS—Multigrain Snacks—Frito-Lay Company; *U.S. Public*, pg. 1277

SUNCLOUD—Sunglasses—Outlook Eyewear Company; *U.S. Public*, pg. 195

SUNCOAST—Dairy Products & Milk—Q.U.F. Industries Ltd.; *Int'l*, pg. 1074

SUNCOAST MOTION PICTURE CO.—Video for Sale Store—Musicland Group Inc.; *U.S. Public*, pg. 1142

SUNCOOL—Reflective High Performance Glass—Pilkington Australasia Limited; *Int'l*, pg. 1057

SUNCOR—NONE—Suncor Development Company; *U.S. Public*, pg. 1298

SUNCRUISER—Boats—Outboard Marine Corporation; *U.S. Private*, pg. 478

SUNCRUISER—Motor Homes—Winnebago Industries, Inc.; *U.S. Private*, pg. 1772

SUNDAE SYRUP—Fat-Free Ice Cream Toppings—J.M. Smucker Company; *U.S. Public*, pg. 1480

SUNDAES—Children's Shoes—Jumping Jacks; *U.S. Private*, pg. 767

SUNDANCE—Digital Color Printer—Astro-Med, Inc.; *U.S. Public*, pg. 141

SUNDANCE—Text & Cover Paper—Fox River Paper Company; *U.S. Private*, pg. 422

SUNDANCE—Siding—Georgia-Pacific Corporation; *U.S. Public*, pg. 735

SUNDANCE—Skin Cream—Lee Pharmaceuticals; *U.S. Public*, pg. 984

SUNDANCE CHANNEL—NONE—Showtime Networks Inc.; *U.S. Private*, pg. 779

SUNDANCER—Home Health Care Scooter—Pride Health Care, Inc.; *U.S. Private*, pg. 883

SUNDANCER—Boat—Sea Ray; *U.S. Public*, pg. 266

SUNDANCER—Motor Homes—Winnebago Industries, Inc.; *U.S. Public*, pg. 1772

THE SUNDAY AGE—NONE—John Fairfax Holdings Limited; *Int'l*, pg. 477

SUNDAY EXAMINER & CHRONICLE—Newspaper—San Francisco Newspaper Agency; *U.S. Private*, pg. 239

SUNDAY EXPRESS—NONE—Express Newspapers plc; *Int'l*, pg. 1443

SUNDAY EXPRESS MAGAZINE—NONE—Express Newspapers plc; *Int'l*, pg. 1443

SUNDAY MAGAZINE NETWORK—NONE—Metropolitan Sunday Newspapers, Inc.; *U.S. Private*, pg. 739

SUNDAY MAIL—NONE—Mirror Group plc; *Int'l*, pg. 869

SUNDAY MIRROR—NONE—Mirror Group plc; *Int'l*, pg. 869

THE SUNDAY SUN—Newspaper—The Baltimore Sun Newspapers; *U.S. Public*, pg. 1616

SUNDEX—Premium Process Oil—Sun Refining & Marketing Co. Lubes Div.; *U.S. Public*, pg. 1530

SUNDIAL—Paint—Jones Blair Company; *U.S. Private*, pg. 596

SUNDOME 7X7—Tent—The Canadian Coleman Co., Ltd.; *U.S. Private*, pg. 691

SUNDOME 10X10—Tent—The Canadian Coleman Co., Ltd.; *U.S. Private*, pg. 691

SUNDOWN—Sunscreen—Johnson & Johnson; *U.S. Public*, pg. 927

SUNDOWN—Vitamins—Rexall Sundown Inc.; *U.S. Public*, pg. 1384

SUNDOWN CANDLES—Disposable Oil Lanterns—Wisconsin Pharmacal Co., Inc.; *U.S. Private*, pg. 1185

SUNDOWNER—Outdoor Bracket—Guth Lighting Company; *Int'l*, pg. 821

SUNDROP—NONE—Cadbury Beverages; *Int'l*, pg. 248

SUNDURA—Coatings for Woods—PPG Industries, Inc.; *U.S. Public*, pg. 1245

SUNDY—Chocolate Bar—Nestle S.A.; *Int'l*, pg. 915

SUNDYNE—Pumps—Sundstrand Corporation; *U.S. Public*, pg. 1533

SUNFILM—Silage Wrap—AEP Industries, Inc.; *U.S. Public*, pg. 4

SUNFIRE—Car—Pontiac-GMC Division; *U.S. Public*, pg. 720

SUNFLAIR—Ladies & Childrens Clothes—Arnotts plc; *Int'l*, pg. 81

SUNFLEX—Window Covering Product—Hunter Douglas N.V.; *Int'l*, pg. 639

SUNFLEX—Window Coverings—Hunter Douglas N.V.; *Int'l*, pg. 639

SUNFLO—Compressors & Blowers—Sundstrand Corporation; *U.S. Public*, pg. 1533

SUNFLOUR—Flour—Hopkinsville Milling Co.; *U.S. Private*, pg. 538

SUNFLOWER—Plaster—Georgia-Pacific Corporation; *U.S. Public*, pg. 735

SUNFLOWER—Cornmeal—Hopkinsville Milling Co.; *U.S. Private*, pg. 538

SUNFLOWERS—Fragrance—Elizabeth Arden Company; *Int'l*, pg. 1435

SUNFLYER—Motor Homes—Winnebago Industries, Inc.; *U.S. Public*, pg. 1772

SUNFURAL—Anti-Cancer Agent—Asahi Chemical Industry Co., Ltd.; *Int'l*, pg. 83

SUNGARD—NONE—SunGard Data Systems Inc.; *U.S. Public*, pg. 1534

SUNGATE—Low-Emissivity Coated Glass & Windshields—PPG Industries, Inc.; *U.S. Public*, pg. 1245

SUNGLASSES FOR WINDOWS—Optix Transparent Blinds—Wausau Metals, Nanik Division; *U.S. Public*, pg. 1500

SUNICAL—Land & Livestock Division—The Hearst Corporation; *U.S. Private*, pg. 515

SUNIL—Detergent—Unilever Plc; *Int'l*, pg. 1433

SUNJUNS—Shoes—G.H. Bass & Co.; *U.S. Public*, pg. 1291

SUNKIST—Soft Drink—Buffalo Rock Company; *U.S. Private*, pg. 179

SUNKIST—NONE—Cadbury Beverages; *Int'l*, pg. 248

SUNKIST—Soft Drinks—Cadbury Beverages North America; *Int'l*, pg. 248

SUNKIST—Soft Drinks—Cadbury Schweppes p.l.c.; *Int'l*, pg. 247

SUNKIST—Vitamin C—Ciba Specialty Chemicals; *Int'l*, pg. 291

SUNKIST—Soft Drink—Grant-Lydick Beverage Co.; *U.S. Private*, pg. 470

SUNKIST—(Juice)—Morinaga Milk Industry Co., Ltd.; *Int'l*, pg. 895

SUNKIST—Citrus Fruits—Sunkist Growers, Inc.; *U.S. Private*, pg. 1052

SUNKIST—Fruit Juices, Food Additives, Flavorings & Products—Sunkist Growers, Processed Products; *U.S. Private*, pg. 1052

SUNKIST JUICES—Line Of Sunkist not From Concentrate Juices—Lykes Brothers Inc.; *U.S. Private*, pg. 682

SUNKIST ORANGE SODA—Orange Soda—The Coca-Cola Bottling Co. of New York, Inc.; *U.S. Public*, pg. 393

SUNLAND BEEF—Boned Beef Product—Packerland Packing Co.; *U.S. Private*, pg. 833

SUNLIGHT—Dishwashing Liquid—Lever Brothers Co.; *Int'l*, pg. 1435

SUNLIGHT—Soap Prod.—Unilever Plc; *Int'l*, pg. 1433

SUNLINE—NONE—Sunline Coach Co., Inc.; *U.S. Private*, pg. 1053

SUNLINE SLIPPER—Felt—American Felt & Filter; *U.S. Private*, pg. 54

SUNLINE 2000—Air Conditioning Equipment—York International Corporation; *U.S. Public*, pg. 1789

SUNMARK—Hard Candies—Nestle S.A.; *Int'l*, pg. 915

SUNN—Amplifiers, Professional Lighting & Sound Reinforcement—Fender Musical Instruments; *U.S. Private*, pg. 400

SUNNE—Temperature Controls—Peco Mfg. Co., Inc.; *U.S. Private*, pg. 846

SUNNEN—Industrial Honing Machines & Auto Engine—Sunnen Products Company; *U.S. Private*, pg. 1053

SUNNET—NONE—SunGard Data Systems Inc.; *U.S. Public*, pg. 1534

SUNNY—Car—Nissan Motor Co., Ltd.; *Int'l*, pg. 943

SUNNY DELIGHT—Soft Drink—Grant-Lydick Beverage Co.; *U.S. Private*, pg. 470

SUNNY DELIGHT—Fruit Drinks, Nectors—Sundor Brands Inc.; *U.S. Public*, pg. 1331

SUNNY DOODLES—NONE—Drake Bakeries, Inc.; *Int'l*, pg. 349

SUNNY FRESH—Egg Products—Cargill; *U.S. Private*, pg. 210

SUNNY GOLD—Vegetable Corn Oil—Mallet & Co.; *U.S. Private*, pg. 698

SUNNY MAID—Chewable Vitamins For Children—Pharmavite Corp.; *U.S. Private*, pg. 860

SUNNY SQUARE—Food Products—P & C Food Markets, Inc.; *U.S. Private*, pg. 1270

SUNNY TEXAS—Institutional Flour—Cargill Flour Div.; *U.S. Private*, pg. 210

SUNNYLAND—Syrup—Dean Pickles & Specialty Products; *U.S. Public*, pg. 490

SUNNYLAND AMERICA—Pork Products—Sunnyland Inc.; *U.S. Public*, pg. 1479

SUNOCO—Petroleum Prods.—Sun Company, Inc.; *U.S. Public*, pg. 1530

SUNOCO—Petroleum, Motor Oil Products—Sun Company, Inc. (R&M); *U.S. Public*, pg. 1530

SUNOLA CORN OIL—Cooking Oil—Quality Food Oils, Inc.; *Int'l*, pg. 92

SUNOLA ITALIAN STYLE VEGETABLE OIL—Cooking Oil—Quality Food Oils, Inc.; *Int'l*, pg. 92

SUNOLA NON-AEROSOL COOKING SPRAYS—Cooking Oil—Quality Food Oils, Inc.; *Int'l*, pg. 92

SUNOLA VEGETABLE OIL—Cooking Oil—Quality Food Oils, Inc.; *Int'l*, pg. 92

SUNOLITE—PVC Plast Lubricant—Witco Corporation; *U.S. Public*, pg. 1773

SUNPAR—Premium Process Oil—Sun Refining & Marketing Co. Lubes Div.; *U.S. Public*, pg. 1530

SUNPROOF—Wax—Uniroyal Chemical Company, Inc.; *U.S. Public*, pg. 460

SUNRABIN—Anti-Cancer Agent—Asahi Chemical Industry Co., Ltd.; *Int'l*, pg. 83

SUNRAY—Printing Papers—Georgia-Pacific Corporation; *U.S. Public*, pg. 735

SUNRINSE FRESH DOWNY—Liquid Fabric Softener—The Procter & Gamble Company; *U.S. Public*, pg. 1330

SUNRISE—Bath Tissue, Towels—Marcal Paper Mills, Inc.; *U.S. Private*, pg. 701

SUNRISE—Instant Coffee—Nestle S.A.; *Int'l*, pg. 915

SUNRISE—Bottled Water COoler—Sunroc Corporation; *U.S. Private*, pg. 1053

SUNRISE—Motor Homes—Winnebago Industries, Inc.; *U.S. Public*, pg. 1772

SUNRISE DESIGNS—Patterns—EZ International; *U.S. Private*, pg. 1192

SUNRISE PLUS—Software Program For Microlab Instruments—Hamilton Co., Inc.; *U.S. Private*, pg. 497

SUNRON—Non-Stick Coatings—Sunbeam Household Products; *U.S. Public*, pg. 1533

SUNSASH—Architectural Lineal Components; Jambs, Heads, Sills, Sashes, ect.—PPG Industries, Inc.; *U.S. Public*, pg. 1245

SUNSET—Paints, Enamels, Varnishes & Lacquers—PPG Industries, Inc.; *U.S. Public*, pg. 1245

SUNSET—Magazine & Books—Sunset Publishing Corporation; *U.S. Public*, pg. 1613

SUNSET—NONE—Tabacalera, S.A.; *Int'l*, pg. 1345

SUNSET BLUE'S—Women's Apparel—Henry I. Siegel Company, Inc.; *U.S. Private*, pg. 998

SUNSET BLVD—Musical—Really Useful Holdings Limited; *Int'l*, pg. 1089

SUNSET HARVEST—Retail Variety Breads—Four-S Baking Company; *U.S. Private*, pg. 422

SUNSHADE—Awning Accessory—Carefree of Colorado; *U.S. Public*, pg. 217

SUNSHADE—Tinted Automotive Glass—PPG Industries, Inc.; *U.S. Public*, pg. 1245

SUNSHINE—Canned Vegetables—Allen Canning Company; *U.S. Private*, pg. 36

SUNSHINE—Fabric Softener—Knomark, Inc.; *U.S. Private*, pg. 627

SUNSHINE ALLEY—NONE—Kellwood Company; *U.S. Public*, pg. 948

SUNSHINE COUNTRY—NONE—John B. Sanfilippo & Son, Inc.; *U.S. Public*, pg. 1431

SUNSHOWER—Prepasted Vinyl Coated Strippable Wallcovering—York Wallcoverings Inc.; *U.S. Private*, pg. 1196

SUNSPLASH—Overhead Projector—Dukane Corporation; *U.S. Public*, pg. 345

SUNSPOT—Incandescent Displays—Daktronics, Inc.; *U.S. Public*, pg. 478

SUNSTAR—Gas Room Heaters—Gas-Fired Products, Inc.; *U.S. Private*, pg. 440

SUNSTAR—Management Software—SunGard Data Systems Inc.; *U.S. Public*, pg. 1534

SUNSWEET—Prunes, Prune Juice, Cut Dried Fruit—Sun Diamond Growers of California; *U.S. Private*, pg. 1051

SUNTAN—Converting Paper—Champion International Corp.; *U.S. Public*, pg. 333

SUNTEC—Manual Wheelchairs—Sunrise Medical, Inc.; *U.S. Public*, pg. 1535

SUNTEC—Fuel Oil Pumps—Suntec Industries Inc.; *U.S. Private*, pg. 1054

SUNTEC-HD—High-Density Polyethylene—Asahi Chemical Industry Co., Ltd.; *Int'l*, pg. 83

SUNTEC-LD—Low-Density Polyethylene—Asahi Chemical Industry Co., Ltd.; *Int'l*, pg. 83

SUNTEC-LL—Linear-Low-Density Polyethylene—Asahi Chemical Industry Co., Ltd.; *Int'l*, pg. 83

SUNTECFOAM—Polyethylene Foam—Asahi Chemical Industry Co., Ltd.; *Int'l*, pg. 83

SUNTHENE—Premium Process Oil—Sun Refining & Marketing Co. Lubes Div.; *U.S. Public*, pg. 1530

SUNTORY—Vodka—Suntory International Corp.; *Int'l*, pg. 1321

SUNTORY—Bottled Water—Suntory Water Group, Inc.; *Int'l*, pg. 1321

SUNTORY DRAFT—Beer—Suntory International Corp.; *Int'l*, pg. 1321

SUNTORY MIDORI—Melon Liqueur—Hiram Walker; *Int'l*, pg. 63

SUNTORY OLD WHISKY—Whisky—Suntory International Corp.; *Int'l*, pg. 1321

SUNTORY RESERVE—Whisky—Suntory International Corp.; *Int'l*, pg. 1321

SUNTORY ROYAL—Whisky—Suntory International Corp.; *Int'l*, pg. 1321

SUNTORY SIGNATURE—Whisky—Suntory International Corp.; *Int'l*, pg. 1321

SUNTRACKER—Electronic Lighting Control—Paragon Electric Co., Inc.; *Int'l*, pg. 1243

SUNTRON—Automotive Refinish Coatings—PPG Industries, Inc.; *U.S. Public*, pg. 1245

SUNVAULT—Off-Premises Transaction Duplication Technology—SunGard Data Systems Inc.; *U.S. Public*, pg. 1534

SUNVIEW II—Manufactured Homes—Champion Enterprises, Inc.; *U.S. Public*, pg. 332

SUNWALL 54—Wallcovering—Borden, Inc.; *U.S. Private*, pg. 157

SUNWALL 27—Wallcoverings—Borden, Inc.; *U.S. Private*, pg. 157

SUNWEB—Paper—Champion International Corp.; *U.S. Public*, pg. 333

SUNWOOD—Wood Preservative—Osmose Wood Preserving, Inc.; *U.S. Private*, pg. 821

SUNWOOD—Wood preservative—Osmose Wood Preserving, Inc.; *U.S. Private*, pg. 821

SUNWORTHY—Wallcoverings—Borden, Inc.; *U.S. Private*, pg. 157

SUNYLITE—High Expanded Polyethylene Panel for Residential Insulation—Asahi Chemical Industry Co., Ltd.; *Int'l*, pg. 83

SUP-R-BELT—Tires—Bridgestone/Firestone, Inc.; *Int'l*, pg. 213

SUP-R-CAULK—Expansion Screw Anchors—Gunnebo Fastening Corp.; *U.S. Private*, pg. 488

SUP-R-DRILL—Self Drilling Masonry Anchor—Gunnebo Fastening Corp.; *U.S. Private*, pg. 488

SUP-R-DROP—Masonry Anchor—Gunnebo Fastening Corp.; *U.S. Private*, pg. 488

SUP-R-HOLLY—Metal Hollow Wall Fastener—Gunnebo Fastening Corp.; *U.S. Private*, pg. 488

SUP-R-LAG—Lag Shields—Gunnebo Fastening Corp.; *U.S. Private*, pg. 488

SUP-R-LEAD—Lead Anchors—Gunnebo Fastening Corp.; *U.S. Private*, pg. 488

SUP-R-POSTURE—NONE—Restonic Mattress Corporation; *U.S. Private*, pg. 925

SUP-R-RESIN—Polyester & Epoxy Resin Adhesive—Gunnebo Fastening Corp.; *U.S. Private*, pg. 488

SUP-R-SET—Capsule Anchors—Gunnebo Fastening Corp.; *U.S. Private*, pg. 488

SUP-R-SLEEVE—Masonry Anchor—Gunnebo Fastening Corp.; *U.S. Private*, pg. 488

SUP-R-STUD—Masonry Anchor—Gunnebo Fastening Corp.; *U.S. Private*, pg. 488

SUP-R-TOGGLES—Toggle Bolts—Gunnebo Fastening Corp.; *U.S. Private*, pg. 488

SUP-R-TUF—Synthetic Rubber Used in Tread Rubber—Bridgestone/Firestone, Inc.; *Int'l*, pg. 213

SUPA—Abrasive Blast Hose—Aerolyte Systems; *U.S. Private*, pg. 24

SUPAGRAF—Packing/Jointing—James Walker & Co. Limited; *Int'l*, pg. 1485

SUPANOVA—NONE—SaniServ Manufacturing Corp.; *U.S. Private*, pg. 965

SUPER "G"—Fishing Line—Gudebrod, Inc.; *U.S. Private*, pg. 486

SUPER AGITENE—Cleaning Fluid—Graymills Corp.; *U.S. Private*, pg. 473

SUPER ALL TRACTION—Tires—Bridgestone/Firestone, Inc.; *Int'l*, pg. 213

SUPER ALL TRACTION DUPLEX—Tires—Bridgestone/Firestone, Inc.; *Int'l*, pg. 213

SUPER-ALUMINUM ALBAL—Aluminum Foil—The Dow Chemical Company; *U.S. Public*, pg. 522

SUPER ARCOFLEX—Ungummed Paper Tape for Binding Pads, Binders & Books—FiberMark Inc.; *U.S. Public*, pg. 620

SUPER ARROW-FLEX—Kink-Resistant Catheter Sheath—Arrow International, Inc.; *U.S. Public*, pg. 135

SUPER AVALANCHE—Coal Car—Thrall Car Mfg. Co.; *U.S. Private*, pg. 344

SUPER BECKACITE—Terpene Phenolic Resin—Arizona Chemical Div.; *U.S. Public*, pg. 901

SUPER BETAMOVIE—Video Camera—Sony Electronics; *Int'l*, pg. 1281

SUPER BIG GULP—44 oz. Fountain Soft Drink—The Southland Corporation; *Int'l*, pg. 693

SUPER BLOCKS—Pre-School Blocks—Tyco Toys, Inc.; *U.S. Public*, pg. 1058

SUPER BOCK—Beer—UNICER-Uniao Cervejeira, S.A.; *Int'l*, pg. 1432

SUPER-BOND 300—Floor Decking—Wheeling Corrugating Co.; *U.S. Public*, pg. 1727

SUPER-BOND 200—Floor Decking—Wheeling Corrugating Co.; *U.S. Public*, pg. 1727

SUPER BOOSTER—Aluminum Hose Reel—Hannay Reels; *U.S. Private*, pg. 499

SUPER BREEZER—Shorts—Lands' End, Inc.; *U.S. Public*, pg. 977

SUPER-BRITE—Sporting Equipment—Brunswick Bowling & Billiards Corp.; *U.S. Public*, pg. 265

SUPER BRUTES—Medium Size Toy Vehicles—Empire of Carolina, Inc.; *U.S. Public*, pg. 579

SUPER BUBBLE—Bubble Gum—Huhtamaki Oy; *Int'l*, pg. 638

SUPER C—Muffler—Arvin Industries, Inc.; *U.S. Public*, pg. 136

SUPER C D—Pharmaceutical Prods.—Durex Consumer Products; *Int'l*, pg. 815

SUPER CAMU PLUS—Chewable Vitamin C—Nature's Bounty Inc.; *U.S. Public*, pg. 1166

SUPER-CARBON PATCH—Refractory—CFB Industries, Inc.; *U.S. Private*, pg. 194

SUPER-CARBON PATCH—Refractory—Chicago Fire Brick Co.; *U.S. Private*, pg. 194

SUPER CARD—NONE—CSP Inc.; *U.S. Public*, pg. 283

SUPER CE-RITE—High Speed Polish For Glass—Ferro Corporation; *U.S. Public*, pg. 618

SUPER CENTRIFUGE—Solid Bowl Centrifuge—Alfa Laval Separation Inc.; *Int'l*, pg. 1378

SUPER CEROXYLON—Thread Waxing Compound—Markem Corporation; *U.S. Private*, pg. 704

SUPER-CHEMINERT—Filter Cartridges—Pall Corporation; *U.S. Public*, pg. 1253

SUPER CLEAN—Automotive Engine Cleaner—Burmah Castrol plc; *Int'l*, pg. 234

SUPER CLEAN—Automotive Engine Cleaner—Castrol North America; *Int'l*, pg. 235

SUPER-COLD—Ultra Low Freezers—The Jewett Refrigerator Co., Inc.; *U.S. Private*, pg. 952

SUPER COMPOSTER—Compost Starter—Security Lawn & Garden Co.; *U.S. Private*, pg. 397

SUPER-CONICAL—Tooth Equipment for Earthmoving Buckets—Esco Corporation; *U.S. Private*, pg. 382

SUPER CROSS—Bras—Warner's; *U.S. Public*, pg. 1738

SUPER-CUSHION—Automotive & Industrial Air Springs—The Goodyear Tire & Rubber Company; *U.S. Public*, pg. 752

SUPER D—NONE—Lee Pharmaceuticals; *U.S. Public*, pg. 984

SUPER DEEP TREAD—Tires—Bridgestone/Firestone, Inc.; *Int'l*, pg. 213

SUPER DEEP TREAD LOADER DOZER—Tires—Bridgestone/Firestone, Inc.; *Int'l*, pg. 213

SUPER DOGEROO—Hot Dog Machine—Gold Medal Products Co.; *U.S. Private*, pg. 459

SUPER DOME—Ceramic Waste Treatment Systems—Ferro Corporation; *U.S. Public*, pg. 618

SUPER DOUGH—Modeling Compounds—Tyco Toys, Inc.; *U.S. Public*, pg. 1058

SUPER DRY—Beer—Asahi Breweries Ltd.; *Int'l*, pg. 83

SUPER DRY—Disposable Diapers—Kimberly-Clark Corporation; *U.S. Public*, pg. 958

SUPER-DUAL—Portable Crushing & Screening Plant—Svedala Industries Inc.; *Int'l*, pg. 1325

SUPER DUPER DOUBLE LOOPER—Race Set—Tyco Toys, Inc.; *U.S. Public*, pg. 1058

SUPER DURABRAKE II—Switchgear Enclosure Finish—S & C Electric Company; *U.S. Private*, pg. 954

SUPER DUTY—Tune-Up Prods.—Mallory, Inc.; *U.S. Private*, pg. 698

SUPER DVORA—Fast Patrol Boat—Israel Aircraft Industries Ltd.; *Int'l*, pg. 689

SUPER EMT—Tires—Bridgestone/Firestone, Inc.; *Int'l*, pg. 213

SUPER E Z KLEEN—Aluminum Air Filters—Research Products Corporation; *U.S. Private*, pg. 924

SUPER 8 MOTELS, INC.—Hotel Chain—HFS, Incorporated; *U.S. Public*, pg. 321

SUPER EMT II—Tires—Bridgestone/Firestone, Inc.; *Int'l*, pg. 213

SUPER EPOXYCOP—Anti-Fouling Paints & Coatings—Rule Industries, Inc.; *U.S. Public*, pg. 950

SUPER-ETCH—Filters—Pall Corporation; *U.S. Public*, pg. 1253

SUPER FINE PENTEL—Pens—Pentel of America, Ltd.; *Int'l*, pg. 1035

SUPER 500AR—Plate—Joseph T. Ryerson & Son, Inc.; *U.S. Public*, pg. 879

SUPER-FLEX—Elevator Electrical Control Cable—Siecor Corporation; *U.S. Public*, pg. 449

SUPER-FLEX—Elevator Electrical Control Cable—Siecor Corporation; *Int'l*, pg. 1245

SUPER-FLO—Drains & Sinks—Josam Company; *U.S. Private*, pg. 600

SUPER-FLO—Chain & Flight Type Conveyors—Screw Conveyor Corp.; *U.S. Private*, pg. 977

SUPER-FLO-SEPTOR—Sanitary Floor Sink With A.R. Interiors—Josam Company; *U.S. Private*, pg. 600

SUPER FLOSS—Dental Floss—Oral-B Laboratories; *U.S. Public*, pg. 743

SUPER FOAL—Horse Feed—Manna Pro Corporation; *U.S. Private*, pg. 700

SUPER 40—Waveguide Having 40 dB Return Loss—Airtron; *U.S. Public*, pg. 1003

SUPER-40—Photographic Shutters—Eastman Kodak Company; *U.S. Public*, pg. 550

SUPER-49—Green & Clear Fertilizer—PCS Phosphate - Raleigh; *Int'l*, pg. 1064

SUPER FRESH—Food Store—The Great Atlantic & Pacific Tea Company, Inc.; *Int'l*, pg. 1375

SUPER G—Manufacturing & Distributing—Giant Food Inc.; *U.S. Public*, pg. 741

SUPER G—Plastic—A.P. Green Industries, Inc.; *U.S. Public*, pg. 761

SUPER G—Valves—Leslie Controls, Inc.; *U.S. Public*, pg. 1746

SUPER GARD LAMINATE—For Pressure Sensitive Labels—Superior Label Systems, Inc.; *U.S. Private*, pg. 1055

SUPER-GEL—NONE—Lawter International, Inc.; *U.S. Public*, pg. 980

SUPER GENTHERM—Insulated Electrical Wires—General Cable Corporation; *Int'l*, pg. 1486

SUPER GROUND GRIP—Tires—Bridgestone/Firestone, Inc.; *Int'l*, pg. 213

SUPER GROUND GRIP LOADER DOZER—Tires—Bridgestone/Firestone, Inc.; *Int'l*, pg. 213

SUPER GROUND GRIP ROAD BUILDER—Tires—Bridgestone/Firestone, Inc.; *Int'l*, pg. 213

SUPER H—Plastic—A.P. Green Industries, Inc.; *U.S. Public*, pg. 761

SUPER HARD SHELL—Car Wax—Turtle Wax, Inc.; *U.S. Private*, pg. 1110

SUPER HAWK—Motorcycle—American Honda Motor Co., Inc. Motorcycle Division; *Int'l*, pg. 634

SUPER HG—Video Cassette—Konica Corporation; *Int'l*, pg. 748

SUPER HI-POLYMER—Leads—Pentel of America, Ltd.; *Int'l*, pg. 1035

SUPER HIFI—Video Casette—Konica Corporation; *Int'l*, pg. 748

SUPER HIGHWAY—Tires—Bridgestone/Firestone, Inc.; *Int'l*, pg. 213

SUPER HIGHWAY LOW PLATFORM—Tires—Bridgestone/Firestone, Inc.; *Int'l*, pg. 213

SUPER HIGHWAY II—Tires—Bridgestone/Firestone, Inc.; *Int'l*, pg. 213

SUPER HORSE—Horse Feed—Manna Pro Corporation; *U.S. Private*, pg. 700

SUPER HYSLIK—Polyester Base Coated Magnet Wire—Rea Magnet Wire Company, Inc.; *U.S. Private*, pg. 913

SUPER ILLU—Magazine—Burda Holding GmbH & Co., KG; *Int'l*, pg. 233

SUPER JUICE—Frozen Treats & Desserts—J & J Snack Foods Corporation; *U.S. Public*, pg. 916

SUPER-K—Photographic Paper—Eastman Kodak Company; *U.S. Public*, pg. 550

SUPER KLEAN—Thinner—Grow Group, Inc.; *Int'l*, pg. 663

SUPER KLEAN—Thinner—ICI Paints; *Int'l*, pg. 664

SUPER KLEANED WHEAT—Edible Wheat—King Milling Company; *Int'l*, pg. 621

SUPER KLEEN—Sewer & Draincleaning Businesses—The Dwyer Group, Inc.; *U.S. Public*, pg. 537

SUPER-KOTE—Paint—Jones Blair Company; *U.S. Private*, pg. 596

SUPER L—Complete Line of Winders—Beloit Lenox, Div.; *U.S. Public*, pg. 789

SUPER L—Bags—Grace Packaging; *U.S. Public*, pg. 755

SUPER LII PLUS—Large Format, Opaque Digitizer—GTCO Corporation; *U.S. Private*, pg. 436

SUPER LINK—NONE—CSP Inc.; *U.S. Public*, pg. 283

SUPER-LITE—Combination Running; Courtesy Lights—Superior Industries International, Inc.; *U.S. Public*, pg. 1539

SUPER-M—Flash Lighting Apparatus—Eastman Kodak Company; *U.S. Public*, pg. 550

SUPER MAG—Magneto—Mallory, Inc.; *U.S. Private*, pg. 698

SUPER MARIO BROS.—Videogame—Nintendo of America; *Int'l*, pg. 932

SUPER MARK-X—Marking Pens—Diagraph Corporation; *U.S. Private*, pg. 330

SUPER MATH DX/SX—NONE—Chips and Technologies, Inc.; *U.S. Public*, pg. 349

SUPER MIX—Animal Feed / Feed Supplies—Ag Processing Inc., A Cooperative; *U.S. Private*, pg. 26

SUPER MP—8mm Tape—Konica Corporation; *Int'l*, pg. 748

SUPER MSS—Magnetic Cores—The Arnold Engineering Company; *U.S. Public*, pg. 1420

SUPER NEOTEX—Mens Rain Wear—Rainfair, Inc.; *U.S. Private*, pg. 907

SUPER NES—Home Video Entertainment System—Konami Corporation of America Inc.; *Int'l*, pg. 746

SUPER NIBS—Candy—Hershey Foods Corporation; *U.S. Public*, pg. 811

SUPER 99—Urethane Roller Cover—Samuel Bingham Co; *U.S. Private*, pg. 144

SUPER NINTENDO ENTERTAINMENT SYSTEM—Videogame Hardware System—Nintendo of America; *Int'l*, pg. 932

SUPER NYLOGARD—Mens Rain Wear—Rainfair, Inc.; *U.S. Private*, pg. 907

SUPER ONE—Service Marks—Piggly Wiggly Co.; *U.S. Public*, pg. 653

SUPER 1—Foods—URM Stores, Inc.; *U.S. Private*, pg. 1114

SUPER 125—Tires—Bridgestone/Firestone, Inc.; *Int'l*, pg. 213

SUPER-PAC—Actuator—Duff-Norton; *U.S. Public*, pg. 406

SUPER PAL—Portable Air Power Source—The Scott Fetzer Company; *U.S. Public*, pg. 217

SUPER PAN—Food Service Hotel Pan—The Vollrath Company, L.L.C.; *U.S. Private*, pg. 1143

SUPER PELLENS—Rust Remover Pellets—Morton International Inc.; *U.S. Public*, pg. 1134

SUPER PELLENS—Salt—Morton Salt; *U.S. Public*, pg. 1135

SUPER PERM—Contact Lenses—40 Fort Eye Associates; *U.S. Private*, pg. 420

SUPER PILOT—Valves—The Wm. Powell Company; *U.S. Private*, pg. 877

SUPER POLAR PETE—Slush Machine—Gold Medal Products Co.; *U.S. Private*, pg. 459

SUPER POLI-GRIP—Denture Adhesive—Block Drug Company, Inc.; *U.S. Public*, pg. 236

SUPER POLY-SOFT—X-Ray Film Packet—Eastman Kodak Company; *U.S. Public*, pg. 550

SUPER POP—Popcorn—Comstock Michigan Fruit; *U.S. Private*, pg. 887

SUPER POP—Popcorn—Curtice Burns Foods; *U.S. Private*, pg. 887

SUPER-POR-SEAL—Water Repellent Sealer—Devoe Paint; *Int'l*, pg. 663

SUPER-POR-SEAL—Water Repellent Sealer—ICI Paints; *Int'l*, pg. 664

SUPER-PRECISION—Machines & Machine Tools—Hardings, Inc.; *U.S. Private*, pg. 502

SUPER PREMIUM—Beer—Asahi Breweries Ltd.; *Int'l*, pg. 83

SUPER PRO—Institutional Mower—The Toro Company; *U.S. Public*, pg. 1623

SUPER PUMA—Helicopter—American Eurocopter Corp.; *Int'l*, pg. 29

SUPER-Q—Water System—Millipore Corporation; *U.S. Public*, pg. 1112

SUPER QUINK—Ink—Gillette Co.-Parker Pen USA; *U.S. Public*, pg. 745

SUPER RTL—German Broadcasting—CLT-UFA; *Int'l*, pg. 561

SUPER REVIEW—Magazine—Reed Business Information Pty. Limited; *Int'l*, pg. 1094

SUPER RICH—Lawn Food—The Chas. H. Lilly Co.; *U.S. Private*, pg. 667

SUPER RITE FOODS, INC.—Wholesale & Retail Grocery—Richfood Pennsylvania; *U.S. Public*, pg. 1389

SUPER ROCK GRIP—Tires—Bridgestone/Firestone, Inc.; *Int'l*, pg. 213

SUPER ROCK GRIP DEEP TREAD—Tires—Bridgestone/Firestone, Inc.; *Int'l*, pg. 213

SUPER ROCK GRIP DEEP TREAD LOADER DOZER—Tires—Bridgestone/Firestone, Inc.; *Int'l*, pg. 213

SUPER ROCK GRIP DEEP TREAD ROAD BUILDER—Tires—Bridgestone/Firestone, Inc.; *Int'l*, pg. 213

SUPER ROCK GRIP INDUSTRIAL MINING SERVICE—Tires—Bridgestone/Firestone, Inc.; *Int'l*, pg. 213

SUPER ROCK GRIP LOADER DOZER—Tires—Bridgestone/Firestone, Inc.; *Int'l*, pg. 213

SUPER-S—Animal Feeds—International Multifoods Corporation; *U.S. Public*, pg. 900

SUPER S—Water Soluble Air Freshener—Surco Products, Inc.; *U.S. Public*, pg. 1056

SUPER SABRE—Copying Equipment—Dietzgen Corporation; *U.S. Private*, pg. 332

SUPER SAFE—Money Transfer Envelopes—Uniflex, Inc.; *U.S. Public*, pg. 1665

SUPER SAGLESS—Recliner & Bed Mechanisms—Consolidated Furniture Corporation; *U.S. Private*, pg. 265

SUPER SAMPSON—NONE—Carpenter Technology Corporation; *U.S. Public*, pg. 307

SUPER SATIN—Paint—Mautz Paint Co.; *U.S. Private*, pg. 715

SUPER SAVER—Shower—Teledyne Water Pik; *U.S. Public*, pg. 44

SUPER SCANNER—CB Antenna—Allen Telecom Inc.; *U.S. Public*, pg. 45

SUPER-SCRUBBER—Rotary Washer—Telsmith, Inc.; *U.S. Public*, pg. 141

SUPER-7—Convenience Store Chain—The Southland Corporation; *Int'l*, pg. 693

SUPER 77—High Strength Aerosol Adhesive—3M; *U.S. Public*, pg. 1604

SUPER SEWER—Sewer & Drain Pipes—The Lamson & Sessions Co.; *U.S. Public*, pg. 976

SUPER SEWER VANTAGE—Drain Pipe & Fittings—The Lamson & Sessions Co.; *U.S. Public*, pg. 976

SUPER SHADES—Stationery Products—The Mead Corporation; *U.S. Public*, pg. 1074

SUPER SHOTS—Stationery Products—The Mead Corporation; *U.S. Public*, pg. 1074

SUPER SHOW PROJECTOR—Activity—Tyco Toys, Inc.; *U.S. Public*, pg. 1058

SUPER SHUTTLE—Airport Shuttle Service—Supershuttle Inc.; *U.S. Public*, pg. 1056

SUPER SIGN—Sale Sign—ERA Real Estate; *U.S. Public*, pg. 321

SUPER SIPPER—Automatic Sampling System For Analytical Instruments—The Perkin-Elmer Corporation; *U.S. Public*, pg. 1056

SUPER 6—Environmental Control System—CTB International Corp.; *U.S. Public*, pg. 284

SUPER SIX—Pressure Cooker & Canner—National Presto Industries, Inc.; *U.S. Public*, pg. 1159

SUPER 600—Residential & Commercial Sprinklers—The Toro Company; *U.S. Public*, pg. 1623

SUPER 60—Socks—Wigwam Mills, Inc.; *U.S. Private*, pg. 1175

SUPER 60 JR.—Socks—Wigwam Mills, Inc.; *U.S. Private*, pg. 1175

SUPER SKY—Skylights—BTR plc; *Int'l*, pg. 124

SUPER SLAW—Seasoning Mix—McCormick/Schilling; *U.S. Public*, pg. 1066

SUPER SOAP—Liquid Soap—SmithKline Beecham plc; *Int'l*, pg. 1264

SUPER SOFT—Mono—Outdoor Technologies Group; *U.S. Private*, pg. 822

SUPER-SONIC HORN—Safety Horns—Falcon Safety Products Inc.; *U.S. Private*, pg. 392

SUPER SOUND—Air Horn—Falcon Safety Products Inc.; *U.S. Private*, pg. 392

SUPER SOUND RACING—Race Set—Tyco Toys, Inc.; *U.S. Public*, pg. 1058

SUPER SOURCE—Electron Beam Source—BOC Coating Technology; *Int'l*, pg. 121

SUPER SPAR—Varnish—Jones Blair Company; *U.S. Private*, pg. 596

SUPER-SPEC—Specification Grade Wiring Devices—Eagle Electric Mfg. Co., Inc.; *U.S. Private*, pg. 354

SUPER SPEED—Aluminum Paint—Jones Blair Company; *U.S. Private*, pg. 596

SUPER SPORT GRIP—Steering Wheels Covers—Superior Industries International, Inc.; *U.S. Public*, pg. 1539

SUPER SPORTS—Notebooks—American Greetings Corporation; *U.S. Public*, pg. 77

SUPER SPORTS—Tires—Bridgestone/Firestone, Inc.; *Int'l*, pg. 213

SUPER SPORTS WITH DESIGN—Bed & Bath Linens—American Greetings Corporation; *U.S. Public*, pg. 77

SUPER SR—Videocassette—Konica Corporation; *Int'l*, pg. 748

SUPER STA-TAC—Synthetic Resin—Arizona Chemical Div.; *U.S. Public*, pg. 901

SUPER STAR—NONE—Carpenter Technology Corporation; *U.S. Public*, pg. 307

SUPER STAR—Beer—Sapporo Breweries Ltd.; *Int'l*, pg. 1193

SUPER STATE—NONE—Chips and Technologies, Inc.; *U.S. Public*, pg. 349

SUPER STEP—Aerobic Bench—Empire of Carolina, Inc.; *U.S. Public*, pg. 579

SUPER STICK—Bubble Gum—Clark Gum Company; *U.S. Private*, pg. 243

SUPER STIX—Antenna—Telex Communications, Inc.; *U.S. Private*, pg. 1074

SUPER STOCK & DRAG ILLUSTRATED—Magazine—General Media International Inc.; *U.S. Private*, pg. 444

SUPER STONE COR—Corrugated Board—Stone Container Corporation; *U.S. Public*, pg. 1520

SUPER STRETCH—Labels—Avery Dennison Corporation Label Group; *U.S. Public*, pg. 153

SUPER STRIKER—NONE—Ace Hardware Corporation; *U.S. Private*, pg. 12

SUPER STRIP—Nonflammable Paint Remover—The Savogran Company; *U.S. Private*, pg. 968

SUPER STRIP—Anti-theft Target—Sentry Technology Corp.; *U.S. Public*, pg. 1458

SUPER STRIP 100—Strip for Gold & Silver—LeaRonal, Inc.; *U.S. Public*, pg. 982

SUPER STRIP 101—Strip For Gold & Silver—LeaRonal, Inc.; *U.S. Public*, pg. 982

SUPER STRUT—Suspension Unit—Monroe Auto Equipment Co.; *U.S. Public*, pg. 1577

SUPER SUDS—Soap Powder—Colgate-Palmolive Company; *U.S. Public*, pg. 397

SUPER SUN IN—Hair Lightener—Chattem, Inc., Consumer Products Division; *U.S. Public*, pg. 341

SUPER SUPREME—Vanilla—David Michael & Co. Inc.; *U.S. Private*, pg. 740

SUPER SYNERGIZER—Sporting Equipment—Brunswick Bowling & Billiards Corp.; *U.S. Public*, pg. 265

SUPER-T—Shirts—Lands' End, Inc.; *U.S. Public*, pg. 977

SUPER TV—Magazine—Burda Holding GmbH & Co., KG; *Int'l*, pg. 233

SUPER-10—Telephone Switching System—Mitel Corporation; *Int'l*, pg. 870

SUPER TENNIS—Videogame—Sega of America Inc.; *Int'l*, pg. 1218

SUPER 386 DX/SX—NONE—Chips and Technologies, Inc.; *U.S. Public*, pg. 349

SUPER TOP—Soft Top for Jeep—Bestop, Inc.; *Int'l*, pg. 830

SUPER TOUCHCOAT—Paint—Sherwin-Williams Consumer Brands Division; *U.S. Public*, pg. 1466

SUPER-TOUGH—NONE—Milwaukee Electric Tool Corp.; *Int'l*, pg. 96

SUPER TOWN & COUNTRY—Tires—Bridgestone/Firestone, Inc.; *Int'l*, pg. 213

SUPER TRACK—Phonograph Cartridge—Shure Brothers Incorporated; *U.S. Private*, pg. 997

SUPER TRACTION DUPLEX—Tires—Bridgestone/Firestone, Inc.; *Int'l*, pg. 213

SUPER TRACTION LOADER—Tires—Bridgestone/Firestone, Inc.; *Int'l*, pg. 213

SUPER-TRANSTRAY—Overlay Films for Graphic Arts (Anti-Static, Anti-HaloPoly. Layout Base—Transilwrap Company, Inc.; *U.S. Private*, pg. 1097

SUPER-TREAD—Scraper Matting - Rubber—Golden Star Inc.; *U.S. Private*, pg. 460

SUPER TRUMP—Manual Warewashing Detergent for Dispensers—Ecolab Inc.; *U.S. Public*, pg. 562

SUPER TRUSS—Uprights for Selective & Drive-In Rack—Speedrack Products Group, Ltd.; *U.S. Private*, pg. 1024

SUPER TUBE—Socks—Wigwam Mills, Inc.; *U.S. Private*, pg. 1175

SUPER TUF CUT END MILLS—Rex 76 End Mills—Regal-Beloit Corporation; *U.S. Public*, pg. 1370

SUPER TUFF—Mens Rain Wear—Rainfair, Inc.; *U.S. Private*, pg. 907

SUPER TUFF-LINE—Can Liners—Amcel Corp.; *U.S. Private*, pg. 48

SUPER TUGGER—Puller—Greenlee Textron; *U.S. Public*, pg. 1589

SUPER 12M—Lubricating Oil—Universal Cooperatives, Inc.; *U.S. Private*, pg. 1127

SUPER TWIZZLERS—Candy—Hershey Chocolate U.S.A.; *U.S. Public*, pg. 812

SUPER TWIZZLERS—Candy—Hershey Foods Corporation; *U.S. Public*, pg. 811

SUPER 2 WATE-ON—Tablets—Lee Pharmaceuticals; *U.S. Public*, pg. 984

SUPER-V—Vinyl Siding, Accessories & Soffit—Alcoa Building Products, Inc.; *U.S. Public*, pg. 61

SUPER VAC-U-FLEX—Hose—Flexible Technologies Inc.; *Int'l*, pg. 1267

SUPER VALUE—Pipe Tobacco—Consolidated Cigar Corp.; *U.S. Private*, pg. 690

SUPER VALUE—Pipe Tobaccos, Cigarette Rolling Tobacco—Consolidated Cigar Corporation; *U.S. Private*, pg. 690

SUPER VALUE HAND MADES—Premium Cigars—Consolidated Cigar Corporation; *U.S. Private*, pg. 690

SUPER VALUE LITTLE CIGARS—Domestic Cigars—Consolidated Cigar Corporation; *U.S. Private*, pg. 690

SUPER VALUE PIPE TOBACCO CIGARS—Domestic Cigars—Consolidated Cigar Corporation; *U.S. Private*, pg. 690

SUPER VISIBILITY—Accessory—The Lincoln Electric Company; *U.S. Public*, pg. 996

SUPER WATE-ON—Tablets—Lee Pharmaceuticals; *U.S. Public*, pg. 984

SUPER WERNET'S—Denture Adhesive Powder—Block Drug Company, Inc.; *U.S. Public*, pg. 236

SUPER WESTCHAR—Activated Carbon for Water & Waste Water Treatment—Osmonics, Inc.; *U.S. Public*, pg. 1233

SUPER WIRE—7mm Spark Plug Wire—Mallory, Inc.; *U.S. Public*, pg. 698

SUPER-XX—Photographic Film—Eastman Kodak Company; *U.S. Public*, pg. 550

SUPERASE—Bond Paper, Copy & Writing Paper—The Mead Corporation; *U.S. Public*, pg. 1074

SUPERATHLETE—Athletic Shoes—Mizuno Corporation; *Int'l*, pg. 884

SUPERB—Soft Drink Extract—Universal Flavors-U.S.A.; *U.S. Public*, pg. 1696

SUPERB DRAWING—Pencils—Dixon Ticonderoga Company; *U.S. Public*, pg. 514

SUPERBA—Salon Dryers—Belvedere Company; *U.S. Private*, pg. 1008

SUPERBAND—Lenses—Optical Coating Laboratory, Inc.; *U.S. Public*, pg. 1227

SUPERBEARCAT—Single Action Revolver—Sturm, Ruger & Co., Inc.; *U.S. Public*, pg. 1526

SUPERBEE—Painting Outfit—Binks Sames Corporation; *U.S. Public*, pg. 229

SUPERBETA—VCR—Sony Electronics; *Int'l*, pg. 1281

SUPERBETA HI-FI—VCR—Sony Electronics; *Int'l*, pg. 1281

SUPERBETAMAX—VCR—Sony Electronics; *Int'l*, pg. 1281

SUPERBLADE—Medical—Pharmacia & Upjohn Adria Laboratories; *Int'l*, pg. 1049

SUPERBLEND—NONE—Alliant Foodservice, Inc.; *U.S. Private*, pg. 244

SUPERBRANDS—NONE—Gitano Fashions Ltd.; *U.S. Public*, pg. 686

SUPERBUFF—Buffing Pad—3M; *U.S. Public*, pg. 1604

SUPERCAL—NONE—Avenor, Inc.; *Int'l*, pg. 101

SUPERCAL—Hot Water Storage—IMI Plc; *Int'l*, pg. 646

SUPERCALC—Integrated Spreadsheet with Graphics & Data Management—Computer Associates International, Inc.; *U.S. Public*, pg. 420

SUPERCALE—Sheets & Pillow Cases—Springs Industries, Inc.; *U.S. Public*, pg. 1499

SUPERCARGO—Truck—Iveco-Ford Truck Ltd.; *Int'l*, pg. 484

SUPER CARGOMASTER—NONE—The Cessna Aircraft Co.; *U.S. Public*, pg. 1589

SUPERCAVITY—Optical Spectrum Analyzer—Newport Corporation; *U.S. Public*, pg. 1179

SUPERCELLS—Computer Chip—Standard Microsystems Corp.; *U.S. Public*, pg. 1502

SUPERCHANGER—Plate and Frame Heat Exchangers—Tranter, Inc.; *U.S. Public*, pg. 521

SUPERCHARGER—Power Tools—The Black & Decker Corporation; *U.S. Public*, pg. 233

SUPERCHARGER—UV Lamp—Spectronics Corporation; *U.S. Private*, pg. 1024

SUPERCHARGER III—12-48 Volt Battery Chargers—Hydrolectric Lift Trucks Inc.; *U.S. Public*, pg. 61

SUPERCHLOR—Alloy—Flowserve Corporation; *U.S. Public*, pg. 658

SUPERCLEAN—Gasoline—Phillips Petroleum Company; *U.S. Public*, pg. 1290

SUPERCLEAR—Label—Avery Dennison Corporation; *U.S. Public*, pg. 152

SUPERCOLD—Ultra Low Temp Freezers-85 degrees celcius—Ruslander & Sons, Inc.; *U.S. Public*, pg. 952

SUPERCOLOR—Videocassettes—Polaroid Corporation; *U.S. Public*, pg. 1313

SUPERCRISPS—French Fries—McCain Foods Limited; *Int'l*, pg. 850

SUPERCURED—NONE—Alliant Foodservice, Inc.; *U.S. Private*, pg. 244

SUPERCUT—Scribing Knife System—Karl M. Reich Maschinenfabrik GmbH; *Int'l*, pg. 1101

SUPERCUT—Trimmer Head—Stihl Inc.; *Int'l*, pg. 1301

SUPERCUTS—Owned & Franchised Hair Salons—Supercuts, Inc.; *U.S. Public*, pg. 1373

SUPERDIE—Zinc Alloy—Belmont Metals, Inc.; *U.S. Private*, pg. 132

SUPERDOE—Home Furnishings—Vendex International N.V.; *Int'l*, pg. 1462

SUPERDRUG—Drugstores—Kingfisher plc; *Int'l*, pg. 733

SUPERDYNE—Pharmaceutic—Salsbury Laboratories, Inc.; *Int'l*, pg. 1277

SUPERDYNE—Pharmaceutic—Solvay Animal Health, Inc.; *Int'l*, pg. 1277

SUPERDYNE—Pharmaceutic—Solvay S.A.; *Int'l*, pg. 1277

SUPERECTIFIER—Electronic Components—General Instrument Corporation; *U.S. Public*, pg. 716

SUPERF4—NONE—SunGard Data Systems Inc.; *U.S. Public*, pg. 1534

SUPERFAST—Semi-Conductor Devices—Semtech Corporation; *U.S. Public*, pg. 1456

SUPERFECTA—Electronic Components—General Instrument Corporation; *U.S. Public*, pg. 716

SUPERFILER—Filing & Storage Products—GF Office Furniture; *U.S. Private*, pg. 435

SUPERFINE—Processed Foods—Hanover Foods Corporation; *U.S. Private*, pg. 499

SUPERFINE—Drapery Hardware—Kirsch; *U.S. Public*, pg. 1176

SUPERFLEX—Translating Mass Accelerometer—AlliedSignal Commercial Avionics Systems; *U.S. Public*, pg. 50

SUPERFLEX—Electrical Cable—General Cable Corporation; *Int'l*, pg. 1486

SUPERFLO—Centrifugal Pumps—Graymills Corp.; *U.S. Private*, pg. 473

SUPERFLOR—Floor Coverings—Domco Inc.; *Int'l*, pg. 415

SUPERFOAM—Proprietary of Carbon Graphite Material—The Langer Biomechanics Group, Inc.; *U.S. Public*, pg. 978

SUPERFORTE—Catalyzed Varnish—Lilly Industries, Inc.; *U.S. Public*, pg. 994

SUPERFRIES—NONE—McCain Foods Inc.; *Int'l*, pg. 850

SUPERFROST—Microscope Slide with Advanced Marking Surface—Erie Scientific Co.; *U.S. Public*, pg. 1545

SUPERFROST—Microscope Slide—Sybron International Corporation; *U.S. Public*, pg. 1544

SUPERGELO—Freezer Bags—The Dow Chemical Company; *U.S. Public*, pg. 522

SUPERGLAS—Safety Hats—The Fibre-Metal Products Company; *U.S. Private*, pg. 402

SUPERGLUE 4—NONE—Bostik Ltd.; *Int'l*, pg. 1409

SUPERGOLD—Adult Contempory Radio Program—Westwood One Entertainment; *U.S. Public*, pg. 1763

SUPERGOLD—Oldies Programming—Westwood One, Inc.; *U.S. Public*, pg. 1763

SUPERGOLD NEW YEAR'S EVE—Adult Contemporary Radio Program—Westwood One Entertainment; *U.S. Public*, pg. 1763

SUPERGOLD NEW YEAR'S EVE—Oldies Programming—Westwood One, Inc.; *U.S. Public*, pg. 1763

SUPERHOSE—Flexible Capillary for Refrigeration Systems—Johnson Controls, Inc., Controls Group; *U.S. Public*, pg. 932

SUPERIOR—Carbonless Paper—Arjo Wiggins Appleton plc; *Int'l*, pg. 567

SUPERIOR—NONE—Consolidated Papers, Inc.; *U.S. Public*, pg. 436

SUPERIOR—Meats—Fresh Mark, Inc.; *U.S. Private*, pg. 427

SUPERIOR—Mexican Beer—Guinness Import Company; *Int'l*, pg. 412

SUPERIOR—Tires—The Hercules Tire & Rubber Company; *U.S. Private*, pg. 523

SUPERIOR—Food Service Coffee & Tea—Sara Lee Corporation; *U.S. Public*, pg. 1432

SUPERIOR—Crushers—Svedala Industries Inc.; *Int'l*, pg. 1325

SUPERIOR—Dry Snuff—Swisher International Group, Inc.; *U.S. Public*, pg. 1543

SUPERIOR—Linkage—Tuthill Corporation; *U.S. Private*, pg. 1110

SUPERIOR BENCHMARK—Coffee—Superior Coffee and Foods; *U.S. Public*, pg. 1434

SUPERIOR BRITE—NONE—Avenor, Inc.; *Int'l*, pg. 101

SUPERIOR CAFE ROYAL—Coffee—Superior Coffee and Foods; *U.S. Public*, pg. 1434

SUPERIOR SUCAF—Naturally DecaffeinatedCoffee—Superior Coffee and Foods; *U.S. Public*, pg. 1434

SUPERIOR WORLD'S FINEST—Coffee—Superior Coffee and Foods; *U.S. Public*, pg. 1434

SUPERKINGS—Cigarettes—Hanson PLC; *Int'l*, pg. 592

SUPERKINGS—Superking Light Menthol Filter Cigarettes—Imperial Tobacco Group, Ltd.; *Int'l*, pg. 666

SUPERKOOL—Cutting Fluids & Lubricants—D.A. Stuart Company; *U.S. Private*, pg. 1048

SUPERKROME—Wrenches—SK Hand Tool Corp.; *Int'l*, pg. 570

SUPERL—Winder—Beloit Corporation; *U.S. Public*, pg. 789

SUPERLAN—NONE—UB Networks; *Int'l*, pg. 924

SUPERLECTRIC—Safety Hats—The Fibre-Metal Products Company; *U.S. Private*, pg. 402

SUPERLIFE—NONE—Lancashire Dairies Ltd.; *Int'l*, pg. 798

SUPERLIGHTS—Cigarettes—Philip Morris Companies Inc.; *U.S. Public*, pg. 1287

SUPERLINK—Data Analysis, Proving & Reporting Services—John H. Harland Company; *U.S. Public*, pg. 785

SUPERLINK—Centralized Merchandising, Programming & Monitoring Systems—Mikohn Gaming Corporation; *U.S. Public*, pg. 1111

SUPERLIRA—NONE—GS Societa Generale Supermercati; *Int'l*, pg. 186

SUPERLITE—Vapor Recovery Hose—HBD Industries, Inc.; *U.S. Private*, pg. 489

SUPERLITE—Concrete Masonry Block, Aluminum Windows & Doors—Hanson PLC; *Int'l*, pg. 592

SUPERLITE 1—Fire Protective Glass—O'Keeffe's, Inc.; *U.S. Private*, pg. 813

SUPERLITE 11—Fire Protective Glass—O'Keeffe's, Inc.; *U.S. Private*, pg. 813

SUPERLOCK—Gaskets—Tranter, Inc.; *U.S. Public*, pg. 521

SUPERLOID—Ammonium Alginate—The NutraSweet Kelco Company; *U.S. Public*, pg. 1111

SUPERLUX—NONE—Sico Inc.; *Int'l*, pg. 1239

SUPERMAN—Action Figures—Hasbro; *U.S. Public*, pg. 797

SUPERMARKET NEWS—Business Publication—Fairchild Publications; *U.S. Public*, pg. 513

SUPERMATCH—Barbecue Starter—Diamond Brands, Inc.; *U.S. Private*, pg. 330

SUPERMATIC—Shutters, Slide Projectors, Processing Apparatus, Chemicals, Microfilming M—Eastman Kodak Company; *U.S. Public*, pg. 550

SUPERMATIC-STAR—Processing Apparatus—Eastman Kodak Company; *U.S. Public*, pg. 550

SUPERMERCADOS—Supermarkets—Controladora Comercial Mexicana, S.A. de C.V.; *Int'l*, pg. 328

SUPERMET—Capacitors—Aerovox Inc.; *U.S. Public*, pg. 25

SUPERMET—High-Speed Abrasive Disc Grinder—Buehler, Limited; *U.S. Public*, pg. 574

SUPERMILL—Horizontal Media Mill—Premier Mill Corp.; *U.S. Private*, pg. 881

SUPERMITE—Flash Lighting Apparatus—Eastman Kodak Company; *U.S. Public*, pg. 550

SUPERMOIST—Cake Mixes—General Mills, Inc.; *U.S. Public*, pg. 717

SUPERNEG—Photographic Film—Eastman Kodak Company; *U.S. Public*, pg. 550

SUPERNODE—Telecommunications—Northern Telecom Limited; *Int'l*, pg. 968

SUPERNUMBER—For Hotel & Motel Reservations Service—American Automobile Association; *U.S. Private*, pg. 50

SUPERNUTS—Lug Nuts—Superior Industries International, Inc.; *U.S. Public*, pg. 1539

SUPEROHM—Plastic Compounds—A. Schulman, Inc.; *U.S. Public*, pg. 1441

SUPEROLLER—Non-suspension Files—The HON Co.; *U.S. Public*, pg. 772

SUPERONI—Protein Fortified Pasta—Borden, Inc.; *U.S. Private*, pg. 157

SUPERPAINT—Coatings—The Sherwin-Williams Company; *U.S. Public*, pg. 1465

SUPERPAN—Bakers' Sundries—Royal Gist-Brocades N.V.; *Int'l*, pg. 1142

SUPERPATTIES—Speciality—McCain Foods Limited; *Int'l*, pg. 850

SUPERPILA—NONE—Duracell International Inc.; *U.S. Public*, pg. 743

SUPERPRETZEL—Soft Pretzels—J & J Snack Foods Corporation; *U.S. Public*, pg. 916

SUPERPUMP—Vacuum Pumping Systems for Corrosive Semiconductor Applications—Edwards High Vacuum, International; *Int'l*, pg. 121

SUPERSAVER—Food Stores—Fleming Company; *U.S. Public*, pg. 653

SUPERSCONTO—NONE—GS Societa Generale Supermercati; *Int'l*, pg. 186

SUPERSCOPE—Flexible Borescope—Circon Corporation; *U.S. Public*, pg. 373

SUPERSCRIPT—NONE—Life Technologies, Inc.; *U.S. Public*, pg. 504

SUPERSEAL—Driveway Sealer Product—Monsey-Bakor; *U.S. Private*, pg. 757

SUPERSEED—NONE—Elkem ASA; *Int'l*, pg. 446

SUPERSET 4—Advanced Business Telephones—Mitel Corporation; *Int'l*, pg. 870

SUPERSET 1—Single Line Telephone—Mitel Corporation; *Int'l*, pg. 870

SUPERSET 7—Attendant Console for SX-2000—Mitel Corporation; *Int'l*, pg. 870

SUPERSET 3—Advanced Business Telephones—Mitel Corporation; *Int'l*, pg. 870

SUPERSET 2—Single Line Telephone—Mitel Corporation; *Int'l*, pg. 870

SUPERSHEATH—Insulated Wires & Cables—General Cable Corporation; *Int'l*, pg. 1486

SUPERCHIPS—ATC 100 Series RF/Microwave Multilayer Porcelain Capacitors—American Technical Ceramics Corp.; *U.S. Public*, pg. 93

SUPERSITE—Software—CACI International Inc; *U.S. Public*, pg. 272

SUPERSKIN—Leather Steering Wheel Covers—Superior Industries International, Inc.; *U.S. Public*, pg. 1539

SUPERSLIMS FROM VIRGINIA SLIMS—Cigarettes—Philip Morris U.S.A.; *U.S. Public*, pg. 1289

SUPERSLIX—NONE—Chemfab Corporation; *U.S. Public*, pg. 344

SUPERSOFT—Ear Plugs—Aearo Company; *U.S. Private*, pg. 23

SUPERSPORT—Motorcycle—American Honda Motor Co., Inc. Motorcycle Division; *Int'l*, pg. 634

SUPERSTAR—French Fries—McCain Foods Limited; *Int'l*, pg. 850

SUPERSTAR—Athletic Clothing—Mizuno Corporation; *Int'l*, pg. 884

SUPERSTAR BASEBALL—Game—Monarch Avalon, Inc.; *U.S. Public*, pg. 1123

SUPERSTAR CONCERT SERIES—Rock Music Radio Program—Westwood One Entertainment; *U.S. Public*, pg. 1763

SUPERSTAR CONCERT SERIES—Rock Programming—Westwood One, Inc.; *U.S. Public*, pg. 1763

SUPERSTAR ESTEGRAL—Athletic Clothing—Mizuno Corporation; *Int'l*, pg. 884

SUPERSTEP—Universal Truck Steps—Lund International Holdings, Inc.; *U.S. Public*, pg. 1020

SUPERSTIK—Pressure Sensitive Tapes—Gould Packaging, Inc.; *U.S. Private*, pg. 466

SUPERSTRUT—Hanger & Support Systems—Thomas & Betts Corporation; *U.S. Public*, pg. 1597

SUPERSWEET—Pet Foods—Ag Processing Inc., A Cooperative; *U.S. Private*, pg. 26

SUPERSWEET FEEDS—Formula Feeds For Animals-US—Ag Processing Inc., A Cooperative; *U.S. Private*, pg. 26

SUPERTAUT PLUS—Screens—Sweco; *U.S. Public*, pg. 574

SUPERTENAX—High Strength Steel—Cockerill Sambre; *Int'l*, pg. 301

SUPERTEX—Nonwoven—Bontex; *U.S. Public*, pg. 734

SUPERTEX—Computer Management System—Gaston County Dyeing Machine Co.; *U.S. Private*, pg. 441

SUPERTEX—NONE—Milgray Electronics, Inc.; *U.S. Public*, pg. 205

SUPERTEX, HC, III—Supercalendar—Beloit Corporation; *U.S. Public*, pg. 789

SUPERTHANE—Unreinforced Polyurethane Tubing—NewAge Industries Inc.; *U.S. Private*, pg. 796

SUPERTHANE SOLIDS—Urethane Rod, Sheet, Tube & Bar—Newage Industries Inc., Plastics Technology Group; *U.S. Private*, pg. 796

SUPERTHERM—Gauges—U.S. Gauge; *U.S. Public*, pg. 100

SUPERTRACKER—Hand Held Tracker—FDX Corporation; *U.S. Public*, pg. 603

SUPERTUFF—Graphic Arts Paper—Appleton Papers Inc.; *U.S. Public*, pg. 567

SUPERTURF—Lawn Seed & Lawn Food—Mock Seed Company; *U.S. Private*, pg. 981

SUPERTYFON—Signalling Apparatus—Leslie Controls, Inc.; *U.S. Public*, pg. 1746

SUPERVAN—Vanillin Replacement—David Michael & Co. Inc.; *U.S. Private*, pg. 740

SUPERVAR—Catalyzed Varnish—Lilly Industries, Inc.; *U.S. Public*, pg. 994

SUPERVISION—Sunglasses—Goody Products, Inc.; *U.S. Public*, pg. 1177
SUPERVISION—Computerized Security/Facilities Management System—Litton Industries, Inc.; *U.S. Public*, pg. 1002
SUPERVISOR—Control Products—Bailey, Fischer & Porter Company; *Int'l*, pg. 449
SUPERVISOR PC—Control Products—Bailey, Fischer & Porter Company; *Int'l*, pg. 449
SUPERWEB—NONE—Taylor Impression, Inc.; *U.S. Private*, pg. 1070
SUPERWIPE—Disposable Cellulose Wiping Sheets—Georgia-Pacific Corporation; *U.S. Public*, pg. 735
SUPERWOOD—Fiber Composition Board—Georgia-Pacific Corporation; *U.S. Public*, pg. 735
SUPOR—NONE—Elcor Corporation; *U.S. Public*, pg. 567
SUPOR—High Flow Rate Membrane—Gelman Sciences, Inc.; *U.S. Public*, pg. 1253
SUPOR CAP—Filtration Products—Gelman Sciences, Inc.; *U.S. Public*, pg. 1253
SUPOR FLOW—Process Filtration—Gelman Sciences, Inc.; *U.S. Public*, pg. 1253
SUPP-HOSE—Support Dress Socks for Men—Kayser-Roth Corporation, Inc.; *Int'l*, pg. 576
SUPPLEX—Water-Resistant Fabric—Du Pont (E.I. Du Pont De Nemours & Co.); *U.S. Public*, pg. 530
SUPPLY CHAIN MANAGEMENT REVIEW—Professional Journal for the Field of Moving Materials & Products—Reed Elsevier Business Information; *Int'l*, pg. 1095
SUPPLY HOUSE TIMES—Magazine for Air-Conditioning/Heating/Plumbing Supply House & Wholesalers—Reed Elsevier Business Information; *Int'l*, pg. 1095
SUPPLY POINT—Supply Chain & Consulting Services—EA Industries; *U.S. Public*, pg. 541
SUPPLY STATION—NONE—Cardinal Health Inc.; *U.S. Public*, pg. 304
SUPPORTED 100—Graft Product—Meadox Medicals, Inc.; *U.S. Public*, pg. 247
SUPPORTLINK—NONE—Eastman Kodak Company; *U.S. Public*, pg. 550
SUPPORTNET—Network Services—Olsy North America Inc.; *Int'l*, pg. 1002
SUPPRELIN—LHRH Superagonist—Roberts Pharmaceutical Corporation; *U.S. Public*, pg. 1393
SUPPRESSINOL—Pharmaceutical Prods.—Alva/Amco Pharmacal Companies, Inc.; *U.S. Private*, pg. 47
SUPR-LOK—Post Hardware—Hall Sign, Inc.; *U.S. Private*, pg. 495
SUPRA—Photographic Paper—Eastman Kodak Company; *U.S. Public*, pg. 550
SUPRA—NONE—Eljer Plumbingware; *U.S. Public*, pg. 1794
SUPRA—Car—Toyota Motor Sales, U.S.A., Inc.; *Int'l*, pg. 1412
SUPRA-DOM—Welded Drawn Over Mandrel Steel Tubing—J.H. Roberts Industries Inc.; *U.S. Private*, pg. 935
SUPRA SLATE—Replacement for Slate—GAF Premium Products, Inc.; *U.S. Private*, pg. 433
SUPRA-SOCKET—Reinforcement Connection—Flo-Pac Corporation; *U.S. Private*, pg. 414
SUPRA-TONES—Fiber-Cement Siding—GAF Premium Products, Inc.; *U.S. Private*, pg. 433
SUPRA-WELD—Drawn Electric Weld or Butt Weld Steel Tubing—J.H. Roberts Industries Inc.; *U.S. Private*, pg. 935
SUPRACAP—Ceramic Capacitors—AVX Corporation; *Int'l*, pg. 775
SUPRAFERM—Extrusion Coated Laminates—PKL Verpackungssysteme GmbH; *Int'l*, pg. 1020
SUPRAHOLD—Oil Tools—Weatherford Enterra Incorporated; *U.S. Public*, pg. 1749
SUPRAL—Super Plastic Aluminum Pressings—Alcan Aluminium Limited; *Int'l*, pg. 50
SUPRALATE—Alkyl Sulfate—Witco Corporation; *U.S. Public*, pg. 1773
SUPRALIFE—Alkaline Batteries—Eastman Kodak Company; *U.S. Public*, pg. 550
SUPRAMESH—Filters—Pall Corporation; *U.S. Public*, pg. 1253
SUPRAMILKER—Milking Machine—Carter Holt Harvey Limited; *U.S. Public*, pg. 904
SUPRANE—Desflurane—Ohmeda; *Int'l*, pg. 121

SUPRAPEN—Broad-Spectrum Antibiotics—SmithKline Beecham plc; *Int'l*, pg. 1264
SUPRASLATE II—Replacement for Slate—GAF Premium Products, Inc.; *U.S. Private*, pg. 433
SUPRAVALVE—Check Valve—Vernay Laboratories, Inc.; *U.S. Private*, pg. 1137
SUPRAX—Anti-Infective—American Home Products Corporation; *U.S. Public*, pg. 79
SUPRAZELL—Dispersion Coated Laminates—PKL Verpackungssysteme GmbH; *Int'l*, pg. 1020
SUPRE SWEETS—Domestic Cigars—Consolidated Cigar Corporation; *U.S. Private*, pg. 690
SUPREME—Tires, Tubes, Tire Repair Material, Batteries—Bridgestone/Firestone, Inc.; *Int'l*, pg. 213
SUPREME—Cake & Bar Mixes—General Mills, Inc.; *U.S. Public*, pg. 717
SUPREME—Stationery—Georgia-Pacific Corporation; *U.S. Public*, pg. 735
SUPREME—Aluminum Paint—Jones Blair Company; *U.S. Private*, pg. 596
SUPREME—Paints—Masury Paint; *U.S. Public*, pg. 1707
SUPREME—Vanilla—David Michael & Co. Inc.; *U.S. Private*, pg. 740
SUPREME—Mens Rain Wear—Rainfair, Inc.; *U.S. Private*, pg. 907
SUPREME—Truck Bodies & Related Equip.—Supreme Corporation; *U.S. Public*, pg. 1542
SUPREME ASR—Tires—Bridgestone/Firestone, Inc.; *Int'l*, pg. 213
SUPREME ASR-12—Tires—Bridgestone/Firestone, Inc.; *Int'l*, pg. 213
SUPREME ASR II—Tires—Bridgestone/Firestone, Inc.; *Int'l*, pg. 213
SUPREME AU CREME—Margarine Spread—Lever Brothers Co.; *Int'l*, pg. 1435
SUPREME DISPLAY—Graphic Displays—Mikohn Gaming Corporation; *U.S. Public*, pg. 1111
SUPREME GARDEN FERTILIZERS—Fertilizing Systems—Ringer Corporation; *U.S. Public*, pg. 1390
SUPREME LAWN FERTILIZERS—Fertilizing System—Ringer Corporation; *U.S. Public*, pg. 1390
SUPREME MPB—Business Papers—Georgia-Pacific Corporation; *U.S. Public*, pg. 735
SUPREME MICROWAVE MEAT PIES—Meat Pies—ConAgra Frozen Food Company; *U.S. Public*, pg. 427
SUPREMEKOTE—Cover Cast Coated Printing Paper—Georgia-Pacific Corporation; *U.S. Public*, pg. 735
SUPRETTE DELHAIZE—Supermarkets—Etablissements Delhaize Freres Et Cie "Le Lion" S.A.; *Int'l*, pg. 462
SUPRI—Fortified Sugar-Free Drink Mix in Fruit Flavors—Kraft Foods, Inc.; *U.S. Public*, pg. 1287
SUPRIMA DI AVELLINO—NONE—Suprema Specialties, Inc.; *U.S. Public*, pg. 1541
SUPRIME—Paint—Pratt & Lambert United, Inc.; *U.S. Public*, pg. 1466
SUPRMIX—Dry Liquid Concentrate—The C.P. Hall Company; *U.S. Private*, pg. 495
SUPRO—Soy Proteins—Ralston Purina Company; *U.S. Public*, pg. 1359
SUPRO PLUS—Soy Proteins—Ralston Purina Company; *U.S. Public*, pg. 1359
SUR-FIT—Irrigation Product—Bristol-Myers Squibb Company; *U.S. Public*, pg. 253
SUR-FIT FLEXIBLE—Two-Piece Ostomy Product—Bristol-Myers Squibb Company; *U.S. Public*, pg. 253
SUR-FIT SYSTEM—Two-Piece Ostomy Product—Bristol-Myers Squibb Company; *U.S. Public*, pg. 253
SUR RUN—White Bond, Mimeo & Duplicator Paper—Georgia-Pacific Corporation; *U.S. Public*, pg. 735
SUR-TEN—Surfactants—DuCoa L.P.; *U.S. Private*, pg. 301
SUR-V-LON—PVC Coated Bontex—Bontex; *U.S. Public*, pg. 734
SUR-V-LON—PVC Coated Bontex—Georgia-Bonded Fibers, Inc.; *U.S. Public*, pg. 734
SURAN—Fertilizer—PCS Nitrogen; *Int'l*, pg. 1064
SURCO FRAGRANCES—Perfume Bases—Surco Products, Inc.; *U.S. Private*, pg. 1056
SURCOTECH—Odor Control Systems—Surco Products, Inc.; *U.S. Private*, pg. 1056

SURCOTTA—Solid Air Freshener—Surco Products, Inc.; *U.S. Private*, pg. 1056
SURE—Deodorant—The Procter & Gamble Company; *U.S. Public*, pg. 1330
SURE & NATURAL—Maxishields Breathable Panty Liners—Personal Products Co.; *U.S. Public*, pg. 929
SURE & NATURAL—NONE—Fort James Corporation; *U.S. Public*, pg. 670
SURE & NATURAL—Sanitary Product—Johnson & Johnson; *U.S. Public*, pg. 927
SURE-FOOT—Safety Plate—Lukens Steel Company; *U.S. Public*, pg. 1020
SURE-GAIT—Crutches, Walkers & Rollators—Lumex Medical Products; *U.S. Public*, pg. 758
SURE-GARD—Ground Fault Interrupter—Leviton Mfg. Co., Inc.; *U.S. Private*, pg. 663
SURE-GRIP—Slip Resistant Footwear—Georgia/Durango Boot Company; *U.S. Public*, pg. 1684
SURE-GRIP—Slippers—Medline Industries, Inc.; *U.S. Private*, pg. 728
SURE-GREY GRIP—Handle—Regal Ware, Inc.; *U.S. Private*, pg. 917
SURE-GUARD—Scientific Glassware for Laboratory Use—Wheaton Inc.; *Int'l*, pg. 67
SURE HEAT—Cold Weather Products—The Budd Company; *Int'l*, pg. 1388
SURE-JEL—Fruit Pectin—Kraft Foods, Inc.; *U.S. Public*, pg. 1287
SURE-JELL—NONE—Philip Morris Companies Inc.; *U.S. Public*, pg. 1287
SURE-LITES—Emergency Lighting—Cooper Industries, Inc.; *U.S. Public*, pg. 442
SURE-LOCK—Device That Locks Stake Racks To Platform—The Knapheide Mfg. Co.; *U.S. Private*, pg. 626
SURE MAKE—Electrical Cable Connectors—General Electric Canada Inc.; *U.S. Public*, pg. 713
SURE PULL—Trailer Hitches—Echlin Inc.; *U.S. Public*, pg. 560
SURE SALADS—Surimi Analog Items—Louis Kemp Seafood Co.; *U.S. Public*, pg. 1652
SURE SCALE—Polyester Drafting Film—OCE-U.S.A.; *Int'l*, pg. 994
SURE SEAL—Sealer—Jones Blair Company; *U.S. Private*, pg. 596
SURE-SEAL—Reclosable Plastic Bags—Reynolds Metals Company; *U.S. Public*, pg. 1385
SURE SEAL FLOAT EQUIPMENT—Float Equipment—Weatherford Enterra Incorporated; *U.S. Public*, pg. 1749
SURE SEAT—Valve Springs—Edelbrock Corp.; *U.S. Public*, pg. 563
SURE SHOT—Camera—Canon U.S.A., Inc.; *Int'l*, pg. 262
SURE-SNAP—Scientific Glassware for Laboratory Use—Wheaton Inc.; *Int'l*, pg. 67
SURE-SORBER—Filter—Donaldson Company, Inc.; *U.S. Public*, pg. 517
SURE-STAND—Agricultural Seeder—Brillion Iron Works, Inc.; *U.S. Public*, pg. 933
SURE STEAM—Household Products—The Black & Decker Corporation; *U.S. Public*, pg. 233
SURE STEP—Walker/Jumper with Floor Sensor Base—Cosco, Inc.; *U.S. Private*, pg. 277
SURE-TRAC—Quarry Tile Cleaning System—Bristol-Myers Squibb Company; *U.S. Public*, pg. 253
SUREBEAM SM—Material Irradiation Services—The Titan Corporation; *U.S. Public*, pg. 1618
SUREBIND—Strip Binding System—General Binding Corporation; *U.S. Public*, pg. 707
SURECELL—Diagnostic Test Kits—Eastman Kodak Company; *U.S. Public*, pg. 550
SUREFIRE—Industrial Torches—BernzOmatic; *U.S. Public*, pg. 1177
SUREFIRE—NONE—Blaw-Knox Construction Equipment Corporation; *U.S. Public*, pg. 877
SUREFLOW—Face Velocity/Room Pressure Controller—TSI Incorporated; *U.S. Public*, pg. 1559
SUREFOOT—Fingermats—Pawling Corporation; *U.S. Private*, pg. 844
SUREGLIDE—Locks—American Tourister, Inc.; *U.S. Public*, pg. 1430
SUREGRIP—Screwdrivers—SK Hand Tool Corp.; *Int'l*, pg. 570
SUREKOTE—Paint—Progress Paint Mfg. Co.; *U.S. Private*, pg. 890

SURELINE—Hose—The Goodyear Tire & Rubber Company; *U.S. Public*, pg. 752

SURELL—Solid Surfacing Material—Formica Corporation; *Int'l*, pg. 129

SURELOCK 95—Beverage Cooler—Igloo Products Corporation; *U.S. Public*, pg. 265

SUREMAKE—High Voltage Electrical Connectors—The Chardon Rubber Co.; *U.S. Private*, pg. 229

SURENA—Beer—Central de Cervejas, S.A.; *Int'l*, pg. 279

SUREPAGE—Display & Message Retrieval Paging System—Paging Network, Inc.; *U.S. Public*, pg. 1252

SUREPATH—Business Product—International Business Machines Corporation; *U.S. Public*, pg. 895

SUREPOP—Sprinkler—Rain Bird Sprinklers Manufacturing Corp.; *U.S. Private*, pg. 907

SURESITE—NONE—Gems Sensors; *U.S. Public*, pg. 481

SURESPOT—Halogen Light—Philips Electronics N.V.; *Int'l*, pg. 1051

SURESTEP—Vinyl Floorcoverings—Forbo Holding SA; *Int'l*, pg. 496

SURESTOP—Needle Depth Stop—Medtronic, Inc.; *U.S. Public*, pg. 1082

SURETEST—Rolling Steel Fire Door—Raynor Garage Doors; *U.S. Private*, pg. 912

SURETY LIFE—Annuities & Savings—The Allstate Corporation; *U.S. Public*, pg. 55

SUREVIEW—Mammography—Picker International, Inc.; *Int'l*, pg. 545

SUREVUE—Daily-Wear Contact Lenses—Vistakon Johnson & Johnson Vision Products, Inc.; *U.S. Public*, pg. 929

SUREWELD—NONE—ESAB Welding & Cutting Products; *Int'l*, pg. 281

SURF—Detergent—Lever Brothers Co.; *Int'l*, pg. 1435

SURF—Detergent—Unilever Plc; *Int'l*, pg. 1433

SURF AND SAIL—Nautical Shoe—K-Swiss Inc.; *U.S. Public*, pg. 937

SURF-COTE—Roll Coater Applicator Roll Cover—Harnischfeger Industries, Inc.; *U.S. Public*, pg. 788

SURF-FORM—Natural & Synthetic Wood Fiber—Georgia-Pacific Corporation; *U.S. Public*, pg. 735

SURFA-ETCH—Etching Solution—Rust-Oleum Corporation; *U.S. Public*, pg. 1358

SURFA-SELE—Coating—Rust-Oleum Corporation; *U.S. Public*, pg. 1358

SURFACE SAVER—Lens Surfacing Systems—3M; *U.S. Public*, pg. 1604

SURFACE-SAVER—Tempered Glass Cutting Boards—Vance Industries, Inc.; *U.S. Private*, pg. 1133

SURFACE SCATTER—Turbidimeter, On-Line—Hach Company; *U.S. Public*, pg. 773

SURFACE SYSTEMS—Architectural Wall Finish System—Marlite; *U.S. Private*, pg. 705

SURFADONE—Non-Ionic Surfactant—International Specialty Products, Inc.; *U.S. Public*, pg. 858

SURFAMAX—Porous Stainless Steel Filters—Pall Corporation; *U.S. Public*, pg. 1253

SURFBOARDS—Multi-Purpose Tennis Shoes—International Seaway Trading Corporation; *U.S. Private*, pg. 572

SURFCUBE—NONE—Landmark Graphics Corporation; *U.S. Public*, pg. 776

SURFER—NONE—Brown & Sharpe Manufacturing Company; *U.S. Public*, pg. 260

SURFER—Publications & Productions—For Better Living, Inc.; *U.S. Private*, pg. 417

SURFEX—Lampholders—Pass & Seymour/Legrand; *Int'l*, pg. 806

SURFLAN—Herbicide—The Dow Chemical Company; *U.S. Public*, pg. 522

SURFLO—I.V. Products—Terumo Medical Corporation; *Int'l*, pg. 1376

SURFMET—Belt Surfacing Machine—Buehler, Limited; *U.S. Private*, pg. 574

SURFOAM—Cushion Foam—Bontex; *U.S. Public*, pg. 734

SURFORM—Tools—The Stanley Works; *U.S. Public*, pg. 1508

SURFPLANK—Plywood—Georgia-Pacific Corporation; *U.S. Public*, pg. 735

SURFTRAN—Industrial Deburring—Robert Bosch Corporation; *Int'l*, pg. 204

SURFWOOD—Plywood—Georgia-Pacific Corporation; *U.S. Public*, pg. 735

SURFYNOL—Surfactants—Air Products and Chemicals, Inc.; *U.S. Public*, pg. 30

SURGALLOY—Needles—U.S. Surgical Corp.; *U.S. Public*, pg. 1687

SURGAM—Anti-Inflammatory—SmithKline Beecham Research Limited; *Int'l*, pg. 1266

SURGE—Soft Drink—The Coca-Cola Company; *U.S. Public*, pg. 392

SURGE-GARD—Thermistors—Ketema, Inc.; *U.S. Private*, pg. 604

SURGE GUARD—NONE—Harris Calorific Co.; *U.S. Public*, pg. 996

SURGEARREST—Network-Grade, Multistage Surge Protection—American Power Conversion Corporation; *U.S. Public*, pg. 89

SURGEBLOC—Surge Protection Receptacle—Eagle Electric Mfg. Co., Inc.; *U.S. Private*, pg. 354

SURGEXPRESS—NONE—The Black & Decker Corporation; *U.S. Public*, pg. 233

SURGI-BAC—Cleansing Soap for Washing Hands—Ecolab Inc.; *U.S. Public*, pg. 562

SURGI-CREAM—Depilatory—American International Industries; *U.S. Private*, pg. 57

SURGIBRITE—Liquid Light Cable—U.S. Surgical Corp.; *U.S. Public*, pg. 1687

SURGICAL PRODUCTS—Industry Publication for Decision-Makers Involved with the Operating Room—Reed Elsevier Business Information; *Int'l*, pg. 1095

SURGICEL—Absorbable Hemostat—Johnson & Johnson Medical, Inc.; *U.S. Public*, pg. 928

SURGICLIP—Clip Appliers—U.S. Surgical Corp.; *U.S. Public*, pg. 1687

SURGIDAC—Sutures—U.S. Surgical Corp.; *U.S. Public*, pg. 1687

SURGIDAY SYSTEM—Ambulatory Care Products—Kimberly-Clark Corporation; *U.S. Public*, pg. 958

SURGIGRIP—Laparoscopic Instruments—U.S. Surgical Corp.; *U.S. Public*, pg. 1687

SURGIGUT—Sutures—U.S. Surgical Corp.; *U.S. Public*, pg. 1687

SURGILAV—NONE—Stryker Corporation; *U.S. Public*, pg. 1525

SURGINE—Face Masks—Johnson & Johnson Medical, Inc.; *U.S. Public*, pg. 928

SURGINEEDLE—Laparoscopic Instruments—U.S. Surgical Corp.; *U.S. Public*, pg. 1687

SURGINET—Surgery Information System—Cerner Corporation; *U.S. Public*, pg. 331

SURGIPATCH—Device—U.S. Surgical Corp.; *U.S. Public*, pg. 1687

SURGIPORT—Laparoscopic Instruments—U.S. Surgical Corp.; *U.S. Public*, pg. 1687

SURGIPRO—Sutures—U.S. Surgical Corp.; *U.S. Public*, pg. 1687

SURGISCREEN—Reagent Red Blood Cells—Ortho Clinical Diagnostic Systems Inc.; *U.S. Public*, pg. 929

SURGISPIKE—Trocar—U.S. Surgical Corp.; *U.S. Public*, pg. 1687

SURGITIE—Ligating Loops—U.S. Surgical Corp.; *U.S. Public*, pg. 1687

SURGIVA—Water—Paterno Imports Limited; *U.S. Private*, pg. 843

SURGIWAND—Laparoscopic Instruments—U.S. Surgical Corp.; *U.S. Public*, pg. 1687

SURGIWIP—Ligating Loops—U.S. Surgical Corp.; *U.S. Public*, pg. 1687

SURGIYEK—Percutaneous Nephrostomy Kit—Bristol-Myers Squibb Company; *U.S. Public*, pg. 253

SURICEF—Oral Cephalosporin—Bristol-Myers Squibb Company; *U.S. Public*, pg. 253

SURLYN—Ionomer Resin—Du Pont (E.I. Du Pont De Nemours & Co.); *U.S. Public*, pg. 530

SURMAX—Avilamycin, Elanco—Eli Lilly and Company; *U.S. Public*, pg. 992

SURMONTIL—Antidepressant Agent—Wyeth-Ayerst Laboratories, Inc.; *U.S. Public*, pg. 80

SURPASS—Intraocular Lenses—Alcon Laboratories, Inc.; *Int'l*, pg. 916

SURPRISE—Infant & Toddler Sportswear—Seibel & Stern Inc.; *U.S. Private*, pg. 981

SURPRISE HOLDER—Gift Wrap Paper—American Greetings Corporation; *U.S. Public*, pg. 77

SURROUND—Technology for Stickies Control in Paper Making—Calgon Corporation; *Int'l*, pg. 455

THE SURROUND—NONE—Cambridge Soundworks, Inc.; *U.S. Private*, pg. 202

SURROUND AIR—Paint Spray Booth—Binks Sames Corporation; *U.S. Public*, pg. 229

THE SURROUND AND DESIGN—NONE—Cambridge Soundworks, Inc.; *U.S. Private*, pg. 202

THE SURROUND BY HENRY KLOSS—NONE—Cambridge Soundworks, Inc.; *U.S. Private*, pg. 202

SURTEX—Fiber—Bontex; *U.S. Public*, pg. 734

SURTONE—Printing Paper—Georgia-Pacific Corporation; *U.S. Public*, pg. 735

SURTONE II—Printing Paper—Georgia-Pacific Corporation; *U.S. Public*, pg. 735

SURUGYOR—Mini-Dome, Closed-Circuit Television Equipment—Vicon Industries, Inc.; *U.S. Public*, pg. 1719

SURVALENT—NONE—Graham-Field Health Products, Inc.; *U.S. Public*, pg. 757

SURVANTA—Lung Surfactant—Abbott Laboratories; *U.S. Public*, pg. 12

SURVIVAIR—Self Contained Breathing Apparatus—U.S. Divers Co., Inc.; *U.S. Private*, pg. 1125

SURVIVAL GEAR FOR CARS—Application of Protection Products, Accessories & Automotive Detailing—Ziebart International Corporation; *U.S. Private*, pg. 1205

SURVIVE AIR—Respirators—Kimmins Corp.; *U.S. Public*, pg. 960

SURVIVOR—Envelopes Made of Tyvek—American Business Products, Inc.; *U.S. Public*, pg. 70

SURVIVOR—Tyvek Envelopes—International Envelope Company; *U.S. Public*, pg. 70

SURVIVOR—Safety-Approved Rechargeable Flashlight—Streamlight Inc.; *U.S. Private*, pg. 1047

SURVIVOR—Bearings—The Torrington Co.; *U.S. Public*, pg. 877

SURVIVOR LIFE—Second to Die Product—The Life Insurance Co. of Virginia; *U.S. Public*, pg. 712

SUSAN SCHEEWE—Art Materials—Martin/F. Weber Company; *U.S. Private*, pg. 710

SUSANNA WITH DESIGN—Greeting Cards—American Greetings Corporation; *U.S. Public*, pg. 77

SUSICO—Subsurface Signs—Castcraft Industries, Inc.; *U.S. Private*, pg. 219

SUSIE'S—Women's Apparel—Woolworth Corporation; *U.S. Public*, pg. 1777

SUSIE'S—Women's Clothing Stores—F.W. Woolworth Corporation; *U.S. Public*, pg. 1777

SUSIE'S CASUALS—Junior Apparel Stores—Kinney Shoe Corporation; *U.S. Public*, pg. 1777

SUSPAMAT—Suspension System for Automotive Washing Machines—Suspa Compart AG; *Int'l*, pg. 1322

SUSPANDER—Gas Springs for the Automotive Industry and Others—Suspa Compart AG; *Int'l*, pg. 1322

SUSPEND-R—Insulated Ceilings—Johns Manville Corporation; *U.S. Public*, pg. 927

SUSPENDEX—Plastic Loose-Fill—The Dow Chemical Company; *U.S. Public*, pg. 522

SUSQUANNA TRAIL—NONE—Tandy Brands Accessories, Inc.; *U.S. Public*, pg. 1560

SUSSANDE—Premium-Price Chocolates—Mars, Incorporated; *U.S. Private*, pg. 707

SUSSEX—Weather instrument—Swift Instruments, Inc.; *U.S. Private*, pg. 1058

SUSTACAL—Adult Vitamins—Bristol-Myers Squibb Company; *U.S. Public*, pg. 253

SUSTACAL—Supplemental Food with High Protein & Low Fat—Mead Johnson Nutritional Group; *U.S. Public*, pg. 254

SUSTAGEN—Nutritional Supplements—Bristol-Myers Squibb Company; *U.S. Public*, pg. 253

SUSTAIN—Fabric—Narrow Fabric Industries, Inc.; *U.S. Private*, pg. 774

SUTLIFF—Private Stock—Consolidated Cigar Corp.; *U.S. Private*, pg. 690

SUTORBILT—Displacement Blowers—Gardner Denver Machinery Inc.; *U.S. Public*, pg. 703

SUTTER GRANT—NONE—Tandy Brands Accessories, Inc.; *U.S. Public*, pg. 1560

SUTTER HOME—Wines—Sutter Home Winery, Inc.; *U.S. Private*, pg. 1057

SUTTOCIDE—Cosmetic Preservatives—International Specialty Products, Inc.; *U.S. Public*, pg. 858

SUTTON—Carpets—Salem Carpet Mills, Inc.; *U.S. Public*, pg. 1464

SUTTON PLANK—Pre-Finished Strip—Bruce Hardwood Floors; *U.S. Public*, pg. 1634

SUTTONS—Seeds—Groupe Limagrain; *Int'l*, pg. 566

SUTUPAK—Pre-cut Sterile Sutures—Ethicon, Inc.; *U.S. Public*, pg. 928

SUTURE RIB—Medico-Surgical Tubes & Medico-Surgical Tube Appliances—Mallinckrodt Inc.; *U.S. Public*, pg. 1039

SUZE—Aperitif—Groupe Pernod Ricard; *Int'l*, pg. 566

SUZORITE MICA—Phlogopite Mica—Zemex Corporation; *Int'l*, pg. 1523

SUZUKI—Automobiles, Motorcycles, Outboard Motors, Snowmobiles—American Suzuki Motor Corporation; *Int'l*, pg. 1323

SUZUKI—Cars—Champion Motors (1975) Pte. Ltd.; *Int'l*, pg. 672

SUZUKI—Motorcycles & Automobiles—Suzuki Motor Corporation; *Int'l*, pg. 1322

SUZUKI TDCC—Motorcycle—American Suzuki Motor Corporation; *Int'l*, pg. 1323

SUZUKI TSCC—Motorcycle—American Suzuki Motor Corporation; *Int'l*, pg. 1323

SUZY—Cakes, Biscuits, Waffles—GrandMet Foods Southern Europe; *Int'l*, pg. 409

SUZY Q—Snack Cakes—Ralston Purina Company; *U.S. Public*, pg. 1359

SVENSKA—Paints—Masury Paint; *U.S. Public*, pg. 1707

SVENSKA FODOR—NONE—Suomen Rehu Oy; *Int'l*, pg. 349

SVS APEX—Ophthalmic Laser—Summit Technology, Inc.; *U.S. Public*, pg. 1528

SWAG 'N TAILS—drapery hardware—Kirsch; *U.S. Public*, pg. 1176

SWAGEFORM—Thread Roilling Screws For Plastic—Parker Kalon; *U.S. Public*, pg. 233

SWALLOW HOTELS—Hotels—Vaux Group Plc; *Int'l*, pg. 1453

SWAMP BUGGY—Tires—Bridgestone/Firestone, Inc.; *Int'l*, pg. 213

SWAN—Hose—Dayco Swan Corporation; *U.S. Public*, pg. 1045

SWAN—NONE—Moulinex S.A.; *Int'l*, pg. 896

SWANK—Gifts, Leather Accessories, Belts, Jewelry—Swank, Inc.; *U.S. Public*, pg. 1543

SWANS DOWN—Flour—Dover Industries Limited; *Int'l*, pg. 417

SWANS DOWN—Cake Flour—Kraft Foods, Inc.; *U.S. Public*, pg. 1287

SWANSDOWN—Cake Flour—Reily Foods Company; *U.S. Private*, pg. 919

SWANSON—Food Products—Campbell Soup Company Ltd.; *U.S. Public*, pg. 299

SWANSON—NONE—Swanson; *U.S. Public*, pg. 299

SWANSON CANNED—Ready to Serve Brothes, Main Dishes—Campbell Soup Company; *U.S. Public*, pg. 298

SWANSON FROZEN—Prepared Frozen Entrees—Campbell Soup Company; *U.S. Public*, pg. 298

SWARFEGA—Heavy Duty Gel Hand Cleanser—SBS Products, Inc.; *U.S. Private*, pg. 955

SWASHBUCKLER—Sporting Equipment—Brunswick Bowling & Billiards Corp.; *U.S. Public*, pg. 265

SWATCH—Watches—SMH Swiss Corporation for Micro Electronics & Watchmaking Indus. Ltd.; *Int'l*, pg. 1160

SWATCH—Watches—Swatch Watch U.S.A.; *Int'l*, pg. 1161

SWEAT/DROP DESIGN—Socks & Knitted Headwear—Wigwam Mills, Inc.; *U.S. Private*, pg. 1175

SWEATBUSTERS—Socks—Wigwam Mills, Inc.; *U.S. Private*, pg. 1175

SWEDCO—NONE—Southwestern Petroleum Corporation; *U.S. Private*, pg. 1019

SWEDISH GOLD—Danish Pastry Margarine—Ventura Foods LLC; *Int'l*, pg. 879

SWEEP EASY—Carpet Sweeper—Bissell Inc.; *U.S. Private*, pg. 145

SWEEP-ON—Oxygen Masks—Nellcor Puritan Bennett Incorporated; *U.S. Public*, pg. 1039

SWEEPA—Rubber Cleaning Products—Quality Special Products; *Int'l*, pg. 1075

SWEEPAID—Gas Production—Amoco Chemicals; *U.S. Public*, pg. 102

SWEEPOLET—Fittings—Bonney Forge Corporation; *U.S. Private*, pg. 156

SWEEPS—NONE—Tattersalls; *Int'l*, pg. 1357

SWEEPSTAKES BINGO—NONE—Stuart Entertainment Inc.; *U.S. Public*, pg. 1526

SWEEPZONE TECHNOLOGY—Ultrasonic Cleaning System—L&R Manufacturing Co.; *U.S. Private*, pg. 638

SWEET CELEBRATION—Beverage—H.J. Heinz Co. of Canada Ltd.; *U.S. Public*, pg. 806

SWEET CHOICE—Candy—Farley Candy Company; *U.S. Private*, pg. 397

SWEET CRYSTALS—Condiment—Diamond Crystal Specialty Foods, Inc.; *U.S. Private*, pg. 330

SWEET DREAMS—Book Imprint—Bertelsmann AG; *Int'l*, pg. 189

SWEET'EES—Almonds—Blue Diamond Growers; *U.S. Private*, pg. 152

SWEET MARIE—Chocolate Bar—George Weston Limited; *Int'l*, pg. 1494

SWEET 'N LOW—Sugar Substitute—Cumberland Packing Corp.; *U.S. Private*, pg. 295

SWEET ONE—Artificial Sweetener—Cumberland Packing Corp.; *U.S. Private*, pg. 295

SWEET PRETENDERS—Dietetic Cookies & Candies—Novartis Nutrition Corporation; *Int'l*, pg. 974

SWEET RELY—Horse Feed—Manna Pro Corporation; *U.S. Private*, pg. 700

SWEET REWARDS—Cake Mixes & Snack Bars—General Mills, Inc.; *U.S. Public*, pg. 717

SWEET SHIRLEY—Indoor & Outdoor Pet Shampoo & Flea & Tick Powder—Bethurum Research & Development, Inc.; *U.S. Private*, pg. 141

SWEET SLUMBER—Bedding—Jamison Bedding, Inc.; *U.S. Private*, pg. 581

SWEET SPOT—Sporting Equipment—Brunswick Bowling & Billiards Corp.; *U.S. Public*, pg. 265

SWEET SUCCESS—Diet Drink Mix—Nestle USA; *Int'l*, pg. 916

SWEET SUE—Meat Products—Sara Lee Corporation; *U.S. Public*, pg. 1432

SWEET TIP—Pacemaker Leads—Guidant Corporation-Cardiac Rhythm Management Group; *U.S. Public*, pg. 768

SWEET TOPS—Ladies Apparel—Movie Star, Inc.; *U.S. Public*, pg. 1140

SWEETARTS—Candy—Nestle S.A.; *Int'l*, pg. 915

SWEETARTS—Candy—Nestle USA; *Int'l*, pg. 916

SWEETEX—NONE—Boots Healthcare International; *Int'l*, pg. 202

SWEETHEART—Stout—Bass PLC; *Int'l*, pg. 169

SWEETHEART—Bread—Interstate Brands Corporation; *U.S. Public*, pg. 909

SWEETHEART—Turkeys & Turkey Products—Norbest, Inc.; *U.S. Private*, pg. 801

SWEETHEARTS—Household Products—The Black & Decker Corporation; *U.S. Public*, pg. 233

SWEETHEARTS—Candy—Stark Candy Company; *U.S. Private*, pg. 1113

SWEETHEARTS—Conversation Hearts—New England Confectionery Co.; *U.S. Private*, pg. 1113

SWEETLIX—Animal Nutrition—Tate & Lyle PLC; *Int'l*, pg. 1356

SWEETMATE—Low Calorie Tabletop Sweetener—The NutraSweet Company; *U.S. Public*, pg. 1125

SWEETWORLD LOLLIES—Sweet & Sour Lollipops-unwrapped—Ce De Candy, Inc.; *U.S. Private*, pg. 220

SWENSEN'S—Ice Cream & Food Parlour Restaurants—Swensen's Ice Cream Co.; *U.S. Public*, pg. 883

SWEP—Brazed Heat Exchangers—Tranter, Inc.; *U.S. Public*, pg. 521

SWEPCO—Pipe & Tubing—Swepco Tube Corporation; *U.S. Private*, pg. 1058

SWIF—Industrial Chemical—Hercules Chemical Co., Inc.; *U.S. Private*, pg. 523

SWIF 95—Industrial Chemical—Hercules Chemical Co., Inc.; *U.S. Private*, pg. 523

SWIFT—Automobile—American Suzuki Motor Corporation; *Int'l*, pg. 1323

SWIFT—NONE—Brown & Sharpe Manufacturing Company; *U.S. Public*, pg. 260

SWIFT—Meat Products—ConAgra, Inc.; *U.S. Public*, pg. 425

SWIFT—Textiles—Dominion Textile Inc.; *Int'l*, pg. 415

SWIFT—Binoculars, Spotting Scopes, Telescopes—Swift Instruments, Inc.; *U.S. Private*, pg. 1058

SWIFT LIFT SYSTEM—Hardware—Dayton Superior Corporation; *U.S. Private*, pg. 931

SWIFT PREMIUM—Processed Meats—Armour Swift Eckrich; *U.S. Public*, pg. 426

SWIFT WATER—Seafood Products—Bumble Bee Seafoods Inc.; *U.S. Private*, pg. 526

SWIFT-STRIP—Blue Print Base Paper—MACtac Scranton Facility; *U.S. Public*, pg. 210

SWIFT'NING—Shortening—Armour Swift Eckrich; *U.S. Public*, pg. 426

SWIGGLE SEAL—Insulating Glass Sealant—Tremco, Inc.; *U.S. Public*, pg. 1358

SWIM WAYS—NONE—Mattel, Inc.; *U.S. Public*, pg. 1057

SWIMMING POOL/SPA AGE—Publication for Swimming Pool & Spa Industry—Intertec Publishing; *U.S. Public*, pg. 1327

SWIMMING POOL/SPA AGE—Monthly Publication—Intertec Publishing; *U.S. Public*, pg. 1328

SWIMQUIP—Swimming Pool Equip.—Sta-Rite Industries, Inc.; *U.S. Public*, pg. 1767

SWIMQUIP—Pool Equip. & Parts—Sta-Rite Water Systems; *U.S. Public*, pg. 1767

SWIMWAYS—Pool Products—Mattel Power Wheels; *U.S. Public*, pg. 1058

SWINE LEPTO-BAC—Swine Biologic—Salsbury Laboratories, Inc.; *Int'l*, pg. 1277

SWINE LEPTO-BAC—Swine Biologic—Solvay Animal Health, Inc.; *Int'l*, pg. 1277

SWINE LEPTO-BAC—Swine Biologic—Solvay S.A.; *Int'l*, pg. 1277

SWING A-WAY OVER-THE-DOOR IRONING BOARD—Ironing Board—Magla Products; *U.S. Private*, pg. 695

SWING ARM—Corner System—Reinke Manufacturing Co., Inc.; *U.S. Private*, pg. 920

SWING EASY—Wind-Up Infant Swing—Cosco, Inc.; *U.S. Private*, pg. 277

SWING-OUT—Valves—Akron Brass Company; *Int'l*, pg. 1068

SWING OUT—Valves—Premier Farnell; *Int'l*, pg. 1068

SWING-REACH—Turrett—The Raymond Corporation; *Int'l*, pg. 123

SWING SEARCH—VTR Component Bi-Directional Playback Apparatus—Sony Electronics; *Int'l*, pg. 1281

SWING WEST—Skiwear—Raven Industries, Inc.; *U.S. Public*, pg. 1361

SWING WEST—Skiwear—Raven Industries Sportswear Div.; *U.S. Public*, pg. 1361

SWINGER—Class A Motor Home—Georgie Boy Manufacturing, Inc.; *U.S. Public*, pg. 388

SWINGER—Grooved & Swing Check Valve—Victaulic Company of America; *U.S. Private*, pg. 1138

SWINGER CHAFER—Food Chafer—The Vollrath Company, L.L.C.; *U.S. Private*, pg. 1143

SWINGER CUSTOM—Class A Motor Home—Georgie Boy Manufacturing, Inc.; *U.S. Public*, pg. 388

SWINGLINE—Stapler—ACCO Brands, Inc.; *U.S. Public*, pg. 674

SWINGLINE—Staplers—ACCO World Corporation; *U.S. Public*, pg. 674

SWINGLINE—Staplers—Fortune Brands, Inc.; *U.S. Public*, pg. 674

SWINGSET—Patio Doors—Morgan Products Ltd.; *U.S. Public*, pg. 1132

SWINGSTER—Loged Apparel & Promotional Products—American Marketing Industries, Inc.; *U.S. Private*, pg. 58

SWINGSTER—Apparel & Ad Specialty Merchandise—Swingster Company; *U.S. Private*, pg. 58

SWINNEX—Disc Filter Holder—Millipore Corporation; *U.S. Public*, pg. 1112

SWIPER—Herbicide Applicator—Security Lawn & Garden Co.; *U.S. Private*, pg. 397

Brand Name Index

S'WIPE'S—Moist Towels—The Dow Chemical Company; *U.S. Public*, pg. 522

SWIRE—NONE—Swire Pacific Limited; *Int'l*, pg. 1328

SWIRL—Household Cleaning Products—Melitta Unternehmensgruppe Bentz KG; *Int'l*, pg. 856

SWIRL DIRECTIONS—Loungewear—Swirl, II LTD; *U.S. Private*, pg. 1059

SWIRL-OUT—Exhaust—Swartwout Industries; *Int'l*, pg. 1398

SWIRLMETER—Gas Flowmeter—Bailey, Fischer & Porter Company; *Int'l*, pg. 449

SWISH—Cup Watering System or Waterer—CTB International Corp.; *U.S. Public*, pg. 284

SWISH—Window Treatments—Newmond PLC; *Int'l*, pg. 924

SWISH—NONE—Swish Products Ltd.; *Int'l*, pg. 925

SWISHER SWEETS—Cigar—Swisher International Group, Inc.; *U.S. Public*, pg. 1543

SWISS AIR—Deodorizing Dispensers—Steiner Co., Inc.; *U.S. Private*, pg. 1039

SWISS CHALET—Chicken & Ribs Restaurants—Cara Operations Limited; *Int'l*, pg. 266

SWISS CHEESE—Snack Crackers—Nabisco Inc.; *U.S. Public*, pg. 1355

SWISS COLONY—Gourmet Food Stores—The Swiss Colony, Inc; *U.S. Private*, pg. 1059

SWISS CREME—Soft Drink—Select Canfield; *U.S. Private*, pg. 982

SWISS METROSENE METTLER—Thread—Wm. E. Wright Limited Partnership; *U.S. Private*, pg. 1192

SWISS MISS—Cocoa—ConAgra, Inc.; *U.S. Public*, pg. 425

SWISS MISS—Cocoa & Puddings—Hunt-Wesson, Inc.; *U.S. Public*, pg. 428

SWISS 'N BACON—Chick N Quick—Tyson Foods, Inc.; *U.S. Public*, pg. 1652

SWISSAIR—Airline—The Swissair Group; *Int'l*, pg. 1333

SWISSMETAL—NONE—UMS Swiss Metalworks Holding Ltd; *Int'l*, pg. 1427

SWITCH-CART—Tow Chain Conveying Equipment—SI Handling Systems, Inc.; *U.S. Public*, pg. 1418

SWITCHES—Heavy Duty for Space, or Very Rough Environments—Haydon Switch & Instrument, Inc.; *U.S. Private*, pg. 513

SWITCHMASTER—NONE—Master International Corp.; *U.S. Private*, pg. 713

SWITCHMUX—Switching Multiplexer—Gandalf Technologies Inc.; *Int'l*, pg. 540

SWITCHPLAN—Occupancy Sensing Controls—Pass & Seymour/Legrand; *Int'l*, pg. 806

SWITCHSERVER/2—Computer Sytem—International Business Machines Corporation; *U.S. Public*, pg. 895

SWITCHSERVER—Computer System—International Business Machines Corporation; *U.S. Public*, pg. 895

SWIV-L-CUT—Windshield Removing Tools & Replacement Parts—PPG Industries, Inc.; *U.S. Public*, pg. 1245

SWIVEL—Disposable Pivoting Head Razor—The Gillette Company; *U.S. Public*, pg. 743

SWIVEL-BLADE—Cable Stripper—Ideal Industries, Inc.; *U.S. Private*, pg. 557

SWIVEL-LOCK—Utility Knife—The Stanley Works; *U.S. Public*, pg. 1508

SWIVEL SCRUB—Swivel Hand Abrasive Brush—Flo-Pac Corporation; *U.S. Private*, pg. 414

SWIX—Sporting Goods—Tiedemanns - Joh.H.Andresen ANS; *Int'l*, pg. 1389

SWIZEN—Tap Fittings & Sanitaryware—Sime Darby Berhad; *Int'l*, pg. 1249

SWOOPEE POPS—Frozen Dessert—Land-O-Sun Dairies, Inc.; *U.S. Private*, pg. 646

SY BONDEZE—Modified Polyurethane with Polyamide Overcoat and Polyvinyl Butyral Cement—Phelps Dodge Magnet Wire Co.; *U.S. Public*, pg. 1286

SY/GATE—LAN Interface—Square D Automation Products; *Int'l*, pg. 1208

SY/GATE—LAN Interface—Square D Company; *Int'l*, pg. 1208

SY/LINK—Software Interface—Square D Automation Products; *Int'l*, pg. 1208

SY/LINK—Software Interface—Square D Company; *Int'l*, pg. 1208

SY/MATE—Programming Software—Square D Automation Products; *Int'l*, pg. 1208

SY/MATE—Programming Software—Square D Company; *Int'l*, pg. 1208

SY/MATIC—Field Control Family—Square D Automation Products; *Int'l*, pg. 1208

SY/MATIC—Field Control Family—Square D Company; *Int'l*, pg. 1208

SY/MAX—Programmable Controller Family—Square D Automation Products; *Int'l*, pg. 1208

SY/MAX—Programmable Controllers—Square D Company; *Int'l*, pg. 1208

SY/MOTION—Motion Control Family—Square D Automation Products; *Int'l*, pg. 1208

SY/MOTION—Motion Control Family—Square D Company; *Int'l*, pg. 1208

SY/NET—Local Area Network—Square D Automation Products; *Int'l*, pg. 1208

SY/NET—Local Communications Network—Square D Company; *Int'l*, pg. 1208

SY/VIEW—Operator Interface—Square D Automation Products; *Int'l*, pg. 1208

SY/VIEW—Operator Interface—Square D Company; *Int'l*, pg. 1208

SYBASE—Database, Middleware & Tool Software—Sybase, Inc.; *U.S. Public*, pg. 1544

SYCAMORE HILLS—Clothing—The Austad Company; *U.S. Public*, pg. 782

THE SYDNEY MORNING HERALD—NONE—John Fairfax Holdings Limited; *Int'l*, pg. 477

SYLFAN—Fatty Nitriles—Arizona Chemical Div.; *U.S. Public*, pg. 901

SYLFAT—Tall Oil Products—Arizona Chemical Div.; *U.S. Public*, pg. 901

SYLGARO—Elastomers—Dow Corning Corporation; *U.S. Public*, pg. 523

SYLKO—Sewing Thread—Tootal Group plc; *Int'l*, pg. 300

SYLKO EMBROIDER THREAD—Thread—Coats North America; *Int'l*, pg. 300

SYLLACT—Bulk Laxative—Wallace Laboratories; *U.S. Public*, pg. 310

SYLLAMALT—Bulk Laxative—Wallace Laboratories; *U.S. Public*, pg. 310

SYLOFF—Release Coating—Dow Corning Corporation; *U.S. Public*, pg. 523

SYLOID—Desiccants—W.R. Grace & Co.; *U.S. Public*, pg. 754

SYLPHON—Bellows—Robertshaw Tennessee; *Int'l*, pg. 1243

SYLVA-CELL—Micro Batteries—Gold Peak Industries (Holdings) Limited; *Int'l*, pg. 537

SYLVAC—Measuring Tools—Fred V. Fowler Company, Inc.; *U.S. Private*, pg. 422

SYLVACOTE—Dispersants—Arizona Chemical Div.; *U.S. Public*, pg. 901

SYLVADYM—Dimer—Arizona Chemical Div.; *U.S. Public*, pg. 901

SYLVAMID—Polyamide Resins—Arizona Chemical Div.; *U.S. Public*, pg. 901

SYLVAN—Swimming Pools & Pool Equip.—Anthony and Sylvan Pools Corporation; *U.S. Public*, pg. 593

SYLVAN—Learning Centers—Sylvan Learning Systems Inc.; *U.S. Public*, pg. 1545

SYLVAN OAK—Paneling—Georgia-Pacific Corporation; *U.S. Public*, pg. 735

SYLVANIA—Audio-Video Products—Philips Consumer Electronics; *Int'l*, pg. 1054

SYLVANIA—Consumer Electronics—Philips Electronics N.V.; *Int'l*, pg. 1051

SYLVAROS—Tall Oil Resins—Arizona Chemical Div.; *U.S. Public*, pg. 901

SYLVATAC—Resin Esters—Arizona Chemical Div.; *U.S. Public*, pg. 901

SYLVATAL—Tall Oil Products—Arizona Chemical Div.; *U.S. Public*, pg. 901

SYLVIA ANN—Mother Of The Bride Dresses—S.A.S.I. Corporation; *U.S. Private*, pg. 955

SYMBIOS—Pacemaker—Medtronic, Inc.; *U.S. Public*, pg. 1082

SYMBOL JET—Ink Jet Systems—Marsh Company; *U.S. Private*, pg. 707

SYMBOLLINK 320/350—Interface—Symbol Technologies, Inc.; *U.S. Public*, pg. 1546

SYMBOLLINK 200/210/300—Interface—Symbol Technologies, Inc.; *U.S. Public*, pg. 1546

SYMIX—Software—Symix Systems, Inc.; *U.S. Public*, pg. 1546

SYMMETREL—Anti-Viral Drug—Du Pont (E.I. Du Pont De Nemours & Co.); *U.S. Public*, pg. 530

SYMMETRY—Computer Systems—Sequent Computer Systems, Inc.; *U.S. Public*, pg. 1459

SYMMIX—Neurological Lead—Medtronic, Inc.; *U.S. Public*, pg. 1082

SYMPATEX—Membrane Materials—Akzo Nobel Inc.; *Int'l*, pg. 47

SYMPATEX—Breathable Membrane for Wind & Waterproof Garments—Akzo Nobel N.V.; *Int'l*, pg. 42

SYMPHONY—Chocolate Bar—Hershey Chocolate U.S.A.; *U.S. Public*, pg. 812

SYMPHONY—Milk Chocolate Bar—Hershey Foods Corporation; *U.S. Public*, pg. 811

SYMPHONY—Interior Floor Tile—Monarch Tile, Inc.; *U.S. Private*, pg. 287

SYMPHONY COLLECTION—Shoes—Tober Industries, Inc.; *U.S. Private*, pg. 1089

SYMS—Apparel Stores—Syms Corporation; *U.S. Public*, pg. 1547

SYN-A-CRYL—Varnish—Lilly Industries, Inc.; *U.S. Public*, pg. 994

SYN-CHEK—Chlorinated Fatty Ester—Ferro Corporation; *U.S. Public*, pg. 618

SYNACLYN—Anti-Rhinitis—Otsuka Pharmaceutical Co., Ltd.; *Int'l*, pg. 1013

SYNALAR—Fluocinolone Acetonide—Syntex; *Int'l*, pg. 1120

SYNALOX—Polyglycol Compositions—The Dow Chemical Company; *U.S. Public*, pg. 522

SYNANTHIC—Veterinary Pharmaceuticals—American Home Products Corporation; *U.S. Public*, pg. 79

SYNANTHIC—Oxfendazole—Syntex; *Int'l*, pg. 1120

SYNAREL—Nafarelin Acetate—Syntex; *Int'l*, pg. 1120

SYNC—Electronics—Hanover Direct Pennsylvania, Inc.; *U.S. Public*, pg. 782

SYNC—Missy Sportswear—Seattle Pacific Industries, Inc.; *U.S. Private*, pg. 980

SYNCHOSHIFT—Transmission—Case Corporation; *U.S. Public*, pg. 311

SYNCHRO-START—Speed Switches—Synchro-Start Products, Inc.; *U.S. Private*, pg. 627

SYNCHROMED—Drug Pump—Medtronic, Inc.; *U.S. Public*, pg. 1082

SYNCHRON—Clinical Analytical Instruments & Reagents—Beckman Instruments, Inc.; *U.S. Public*, pg. 199

SYNCHRON AS—Stat Routine Analyzers & Reagents—Beckman Instruments, Inc.; *U.S. Public*, pg. 199

SYNCHRON CX—Clinical Analytical Instruments & Reagents—Beckman Instruments, Inc.; *U.S. Public*, pg. 199

SYNCHRON EL-ISE—Electrolyte System—Beckman Instruments, Inc.; *U.S. Public*, pg. 199

SYNCHRONY—Pacemaker—St. Jude Medical, Inc.; *U.S. Public*, pg. 1427

SYNCHROPOWER CONTROL SYSTEM—Control System—Automatic Switch Co.; *U.S. Public*, pg. 573

SYNCOM—Stereo Test Equipment—Bose Corporation; *U.S. Private*, pg. 160

SYNCOM—NONE—ECI Telecom Ltd.; *Int'l*, pg. 643

SYNCORDIA—Telecommunications Managed Network Services—British Telecommunications plc; *Int'l*, pg. 222

SYNCORE—Low Density Structural Film—The Dexter Corporation; *U.S. Public*, pg. 504

SYNCRO—Industrial Instrumentation—Moore Products Co.; *U.S. Public*, pg. 1128

SYNCROGEAR—Gearmotors & Gears—U.S. Electrical Motor Division; *U.S. Public*, pg. 573

SYNCROMATIC—NONE—Martin Universal Design, Inc.; *U.S. Private*, pg. 709

SYNCROUSEL—NONE—Gilman; *Int'l*, pg. 1389

SYNCROWAVE—Welding & Cutting Equip.—Miller Electric Manufacturing Co.; *U.S. Public*, pg. 867

SYNCURE—Moisture Initiated Cross-Linkable Polyethylene Compound—Synergistics Industries Limited; *U.S. Public*, pg. 734

SYNEDOL—Thermosetting Acrylic Resins—DSM N.V.; *Int'l*, pg. 352

SYNERA—Yarn—Amoco Chemicals; *U.S. Public*, pg. 102

SYNERA PLUS—Yarn—Amoco Chemicals; *U.S. Public*, pg. 102

SYNERGIE 100—Test System—MTS Systems Corporation; *U.S. Public*, pg. 1028

SYNERGITE—Fiberboard—Georgia-Pacific Corporation; *U.S. Public*, pg. 735

SYNERGIZER—Sporting Equipment—Brunswick Bowling & Billiards Corp.; *U.S. Public*, pg. 265

SYNERGY—Circuit Synthesis & Optimization— Cadence Design Systems, Inc.; *U.S. Public*, pg. 290

SYNERGY—Flame Retardant Fabrics—Springs Industries, Inc.; *U.S. Public*, pg. 1499

SYNERGYST II—Pacemaker—Medtronic, Inc.; *U.S. Public*, pg. 1082

SYNEROL—Insecticide—Roussel Corporation; *Int'l*, pg. 625

SYNEROL—Insecticide—Roussel UCLAF S.A.; *Int'l*, pg. 626

SYNERGYST—Pacemaker—Medtronic, Inc.; *U.S. Public*, pg. 1082

SYNFLEX—Hose & Tubing—Eaton International Corp.; *U.S. Public*, pg. 558

SYNFLEX—Hose & Tubing—Furon Company; *U.S. Public*, pg. 688

SYNFLEX—Naproxen Sodium, Pain/ Inflammation—Recordati Industria Chimica e Farmaceutica S.p.A.; *Int'l*, pg. 1090

SYNFLEX—NONE—Synergistics Industries Limited; *U.S. Public*, pg. 734

SYNFONET—SDN Transmission Equipment—Oy Nokia Ab/Nokia Group; *Int'l*, pg. 951

SYNGARD—Enprostil—Syntex; *Int'l*, pg. 1120

SYNITE—Mixed Metal Hydroxy Composition—The Dow Chemical Company; *U.S. Public*, pg. 522

SYNKAD—Lubricants—Ferro Corporation; *U.S. Public*, pg. 618

SYNOLATE—Plasticizer—DSM N.V.; *Int'l*, pg. 352

SYNOLITE—Unsaturated Polyester Resins For Plastics—DSM N.V.; *Int'l*, pg. 352

SYNOPHYLATE—Pharmaceutical Products— Schwarz Pharma Manufacturing, Inc.; *Int'l*, pg. 1211

SYNOTEX—Cyclized Rubber—DSM N.V.; *Int'l*, pg. 352

SYNOVEX—Veterinary Pharmaceuticals—American Home Products Corporation; *U.S. Public*, pg. 79

SYNOVEX—Growth Promoting Agents—Syntex; *Int'l*, pg. 1120

SYNPHASE—Norethindrone/ethinyl Estradiol— Syntex; *Int'l*, pg. 1120

SYNPRENE—NONE—Synergistics Industries Limited; *U.S. Public*, pg. 734

SYNRESATE—Alkyd Resins—DSM N.V.; *Int'l*, pg. 352

SYNRESENINE—Phenol Resins—DSM N.V.; *Int'l*, pg. 352

SYNRESINE—Amino Resins—DSM N.V.; *Int'l*, pg. 352

SYNRESOL—Hard Resins—DSM N.V.; *Int'l*, pg. 352

SYNRESON—Unsaturated Polyester Powder— DSM N.V.; *Int'l*, pg. 352

SYNROSYL—Emulsions—DSM N.V.; *Int'l*, pg. 352

SYNRX—NONE—Medeva PLC; *Int'l*, pg. 852

SYNSILATE—Water Soluble Resins—DSM N.V.; *Int'l*, pg. 352

SYNSKIN—Composite Surfacing Film—The Dexter Corporation; *U.S. Public*, pg. 504

SYNTALLIC—Motorcycle—American Honda Motor Co., Inc. Motorcycle Division; *Int'l*, pg. 634

SYNTEQ—Filter Medium—Donaldson Company, Inc.; *U.S. Public*, pg. 517

SYNTEQ AIR—Air Filter—Donaldson Company, Inc.; *U.S. Public*, pg. 517

SYNTH-O-SAVER—Solvent—Detrex Corporation; *U.S. Public*, pg. 501

SYNTHAPULVIN—NONE—DSM N.V.; *Int'l*, pg. 352

SYNTHETIC MARK V—Rifle Bolt Action— Weatherby, Inc.; *U.S. Private*, pg. 1155

SYNTHOL—NONE—SmithKline Beecham Corporation; *Int'l*, pg. 1264

SYNTHOL—Topical/Skincare—SmithKline Beecham plc; *Int'l*, pg. 1264

SYNTHROID—Pharmaceuticals—Knoll Pharmaceutical Company; *Int'l*, pg. 105

SYNTOCINON—Initiation or Improvement of Uterine Contractions—Sandoz Pharmaceuticals Corp.; *Int'l*, pg. 974

SYNTOCINON—Nasal Spray—Sandoz Pharmaceuticals Corp.; *Int'l*, pg. 974

SYNTODUR—Polyurethane Resins—DSM N.V.; *Int'l*, pg. 352

SYNTON—Synthetic Lubricant—Uniroyal Chemical Company, Inc.; *U.S. Public*, pg. 460

SYNTOOL—NONE—Landmark Graphics Corporation; *U.S. Public*, pg. 776

SYNTOP—Seating—GF Office Furniture; *U.S. Private*, pg. 435

SYNTOPHTONE—Antibiotics—The Dow Chemical Company; *U.S. Public*, pg. 522

SYNULOX—Animal Antibacterial—SmithKline Beecham plc; *Int'l*, pg. 1264

SYNVISC—Byopolimer—Recordati Industria Chimica e Farmaceutica S.p.A.; *Int'l*, pg. 1090

SYNVISE—Osteo Arthritis—American Home Products Corporation; *U.S. Public*, pg. 79

SYQUEST—NONE—Milgray Electronics, Inc.; *U.S. Public*, pg. 205

SYRINGE SHIELDS—NONE—Capintec, Inc.; *U.S. Private*, pg. 205

SYROCO—Casual Resin Furniture—Marley PLC; *Int'l*, pg. 843

SYROCO—Decorative Accessories—Syroco Inc.; *Int'l*, pg. 844

SYROCO FURNITURE—Resin Furn.; Chairs, Tables, Chaises, Access.—Syroco Inc.; *Int'l*, pg. 844

SYSCAD—Computer Software for Computer Aided Electronic Design—Lucent Technologies Inc.; *U.S. Public*, pg. 1017

SYSCO—NONE—Sysco Corporation; *U.S. Public*, pg. 1550

SYSCOM—Pre-Matched Component Systems— Pioneer Electronics (USA) Inc.; *Int'l*, pg. 1058

SYSCON—Syscon Software Development Services—Harnischfeger Industries, Inc.; *U.S. Public*, pg. 788

SYSTAT—Desktop Statistics & Graphics Package—SPSS Inc.; *U.S. Public*, pg. 1420

SYSTECH—Wall Merchandising System— Columbus Show Case Company; *U.S. Private*, pg. 257

THE SYSTEM—Combination Notebook—The Mead Corporation; *U.S. Public*, pg. 1074

SYSTEM—Fly Fishing Products—3M; *U.S. Public*, pg. 1604

SYSTEM ADVANTAGE—Warranty Services on Roofing Materials—Owens Corning; *U.S. Public*, pg. 1236

SYSTEM APPLICATION ARCHITECTURE— Computer Product—International Business Machines Corporation; *U.S. Public*, pg. 895

SYSTEM COMMANDER—Electronic Components—General Instrument Corporation; *U.S. Public*, pg. 716

SYSTEM E BIOLAGE—Hair Care—Matrix Essentials, Inc.; *U.S. Public*, pg. 254

SYSTEM E4A—Clinical Analyzer & Reagents— Beckman Instruments, Inc.; *U.S. Public*, pg. 199

SYSTEM E3A—Clinical Analyzer & Reagents— Beckman Instruments, Inc.; *U.S. Public*, pg. 199

SYSTEM E2A—Clinical Analyzer & Reagents— Beckman Instruments, Inc.; *U.S. Public*, pg. 199

SYSTEM 8000—Hematology Cell Counter— BioChem ImmunoSystems, Inc.; *Int'l*, pg. 196

SYSTEM/88—Computer System—International Business Machines Corporation; *U.S. Public*, pg. 895

SYSTEM 11—Tape Care & Maintenance Products—Recoton Corporation; *U.S. Public*, pg. 1369

SYSTEM 59—Composite Processing—The Budd Company; *Int'l*, pg. 1388

SYSTEM FINEX—FDDI Equipment—N Base Communications; *U.S. Public*, pg. 1027

SYSTEM 5—DOS Based Corporation Tax Processing—Computer Language Research, Inc.; *U.S. Public*, pg. 421

SYSTEM 500—Emergency Audio Evacuation System—Dukane Corporation; *U.S. Private*, pg. 345

SYSTEM-4—Chute Feeding for Card Room-Textile Mills—Continental Eagle Corporation; *U.S. Private*, pg. 267

SYSTEM 4—Transaction Processing System Software—Equitrac Corporation; *U.S. Public*, pg. 590

SYSTEM 4—Greenhouse/Solarium Aluminum Product—Four Seasons Solar Products Corp.; *U.S. Private*, pg. 422

SYSTEM 4000—Ink Jet Imager—Videojet Systems International, Inc.; *Int'l*, pg. 545

SYSTEM 14—Closed-Circuit Television Equipment—Vicon Industries, Inc.; *U.S. Public*, pg. 1719

SYSTEM GOLD—Liquid Chromatograph Equipment—Beckman Instruments, Inc.; *U.S. Public*, pg. 199

SYSTEM INTEGRATOR—Software—LSI Logic Corp.; *U.S. Public*, pg. 971

SYSTEM KING—Skeleton (Open Frame) Motors— Groschopp, Inc.; *Int'l*, pg. 559

SYSTEM MF—Fasteners—Maclean-Fogg Co.; *U.S. Private*, pg. 692

SYSTEM MANAGEMENT ADVISORY—System Evolution Program—Executive Software; *U.S. Private*, pg. 388

SYSTEM MATE—Engineering Plain Paper Copier & Supplies—OCE-U.S.A.; *Int'l*, pg. 994

SYSTEM 9000—Automated Hematology Cell Counter—BioChem ImmunoSystems, Inc.; *Int'l*, pg. 196

SYSTEM 9000—NONE—BioChem Pharma Inc.; *Int'l*, pg. 196

SYSTEM 19—Single Moniter with Plug-In Module Capability—Vicon Industries, Inc.; *U.S. Public*, pg. 1719

SYSTEM 9900 YAG OPTHALMIC LASER— Medical Instrument—Coherent, Inc.; *U.S. Public*, pg. 395

SYSTEM 9100—NONE—BioChem Pharma Inc.; *Int'l*, pg. 196

SYSTEM 93 PLUS—Mass Memory Subsystem— Zitel Corporation; *U.S. Public*, pg. 1793

SYSTEM 93 PLUS SPLIT—Mass Memory Subsystem—Zitel Corporation; *U.S. Public*, pg. 1793

SYSTEM I—Space-Frame—Unistrut Corporation; *U.S. Public*, pg. 1651

SYSTEM 100—Clinical Analytical Instruments & Accessories—Beckman Instruments, Inc.; *U.S. Public*, pg. 199

SYSTEM 1-2-3—Men's Electric Shaver—Braun, North America; *U.S. Public*, pg. 743

SYSTEM SAVER—Water Conditioning Salt— Morton International Inc.; *U.S. Public*, pg. 1134

SYSTEM SAVER—Air Dryer—Rockwell International Corporation; *U.S. Public*, pg. 1397

SYSTEM SENSOR—Commercial Fire Detection Sensors—Pittway Corporation; *U.S. Public*, pg. 1305

SYSTEM SENTRY—Controller/Monitor for Automatic Lubrication Systems—Lincoln Industrial; *U.S. Public*, pg. 1273

SYSTEM 7—Cookware—Regal Ware, Inc.; *U.S. Private*, pg. 917

SYSTEM 700—Clinical Analytical Instruments & Accessories—Beckman Instruments, Inc.; *U.S. Public*, pg. 199

SYSTEM 700/800—Electronic Access Control System—Unican Security Systems Ltd.; *Int'l*, pg. 1432

SYSTEM 70—Fiber Optic Platforms & Products— Scientific-Atlanta, Inc.; *U.S. Public*, pg. 1443

SYSTEM-SIX—6" Aluminum Gutter & Downspouts—Alcoa Building Products, Inc.; *U.S. Public*, pg. 61

SYSTEM 631—Exposure System—Nuarc Company, Inc.; *U.S. Private*, pg. 808

SYSTEM 64-LOCK—NONE—Chicago Lock Company; *U.S. Private*, pg. 235

SYSTEM 10—Closed-Circuit Television Equipment—Vicon Industries, Inc.; *U.S. Public*, pg. 1719

SYSTEM THINKING—Brand Promise—Owens Corning; *U.S. Public*, pg. 1236

SYSTEM/38—Computer System—International Business Machines Corporation; *U.S. Public*, pg. 895

SYSTEM 37—NONE—Matria Healthcare, Inc.; *U.S. Public*, pg. 1057

SYSTEM/36—Computer System—International Business Machines Corporation; *U.S. Public*, pg. 895

SYSTEM 3—Router Control Software—Chyron Corp.; *Int'l*, pg. 1372

Brand Name Index

SYSTEM 3—Voice/Data Response System—Electronic Tele-Communications, Inc.; *U.S. Public*, pg. 570

SYSTEM 3—Dos-Based Transaction Processing System Software—Equitrac Corporation; *U.S. Public*, pg. 590

SYSTEM 3—Gasoline Product—Texaco Inc.; *U.S. Public*, pg. 1582

SYSTEM III—Space-Frame—Unistrut Corporation; *U.S. Public*, pg. 1651

SYSTEM 3—TV Receivers—Zenith Electronics Corp.; *U.S. Public*, pg. 1790

SYSTEM 350—Electronic Modular Controls—Johnson Controls, Inc., Controls Group; *U.S. Public*, pg. 932

SYSTEM/390—Computer System—International Business Machines Corporation; *U.S. Public*, pg. 895

SYSTEM/370—Computer System—International Business Machines Corporation; *U.S. Public*, pg. 895

SYSTEM/360—Computer System—International Business Machines Corporation; *U.S. Public*, pg. 895

SYSTEM 12—NONE—Stuart Entertainment Inc.; *U.S. Public*, pg. 1526

SYSTEM 29—Double Moniter with Plug-In Module Capability—Vicon Industries, Inc.; *U.S. Public*, pg. 1719

SYSTEM II—Space-Frame—Unistrut Corporation; *U.S. Public*, pg. 1651

SYSTEM 2000—Routing Switcher System—Meret Communications; *U.S. Public*, pg. 1233

SYSTEM 2000—Data Management Software—SAS Institute Inc.; *U.S. Private*, pg. 966

SYSTEM W—Fin. Modeling & Forecasting System for IBM Mainframe & Micro or DEC VAX—Comshare, Incorporated; *U.S. Public*, pg. 425

SYSTEMATCH—Medical Accounting System—Master Craft Corp.; *Int'l*, pg. 267

SYSTEMATIC—Filing System—Fellowes Manufacturing Co.; *U.S. Private*, pg. 400

SYSTEMATIC PREMIUM LIFE—Life Product—Lincoln National Corporation; *U.S. Public*, pg. 997

SYSTEMETRICS—NONE—Medline Industries, Inc.; *U.S. Private*, pg. 728

SYSTEMEXTRA—Computer Product—International Business Machines Corporation; *U.S. Public*, pg. 895

SYSTEMPAC—Computer Product—International Business Machines Corporation; *U.S. Public*, pg. 895

SYSTEMPLAN—Computer Product—International Business Machines Corporation; *U.S. Public*, pg. 895

SYSTEMPRO—Computer—COMPAQ Computer Corporation; *U.S. Public*, pg. 417

SYSTEMS AND SOLUTIONS—Smart Card; Namely, Plastic Encapsulated Integrated Circuits—Lucent Technologies Inc.; *U.S. Public*, pg. 1017

SYSTEMS COAT 3000—Coatings Systems for Metal Office Furniture—Akzo Nobel Coatings Inc. (KY); *Int'l*, pg. 47

SYSTEMS IN SILICON—Circuit, Design or Integrated Circuit Products—LSI Logic Corp.; *U.S. Public*, pg. 971

SYSTEMS SCAFFOLDS—Modular Scaffolds—Safway Steel Products Inc.; *Int'l*, pg. 1389

SYSTEMS VALIDATION SERVICES—Computer Product—International Business Machines Corporation; *U.S. Public*, pg. 895

SYSTEMVIEW—Computer Product—International Business Machines Corporation; *U.S. Public*, pg. 895

SYSTHANE—Fungicide—Rohm and Haas Company; *U.S. Public*, pg. 1403

SYSTIMAX—Premises Distribution System Products—Lucent Technologies Inc.; *U.S. Public*, pg. 1017

SYSTRON DONNER INERTIALS—Rate Sensors & Accelerometers—BEI Sensors and Systems Company; *U.S. Public*, pg. 160

SYSWAY—System Gateway Software—Tandem Computers Inc.; *U.S. Public*, pg. 417

SYTELINE—Software—Symix Systems, Inc.; *U.S. Public*, pg. 1546

SYTEN—Hydraulic Steering Systems—Teleflex Incorporated; *U.S. Public*, pg. 1569

T

T—Wire Striper—Ideal Industries, Inc.; *U.S. Private*, pg. 557

TA—Surgical Staplers—U.S. Surgical Corp.; *U.S. Public*, pg. 1687

TAC—Air Valves—Humphrey Products Company; *U.S. Public*, pg. 547

T.A.C.—Microcomputer Game—Monarch Avalon, Inc.; *U.S. Public*, pg. 1123

TACC—Timed Access Cash Controllers-Electronic Cash Handling System—Tidel Engineering, Inc.; *U.S. Public*, pg. 1608

TACL—Prompt—Tandem Computers Inc.; *U.S. Public*, pg. 417

T.A.G.—Lager—Bass PLC; *Int'l*, pg. 169

TAJ—International Hotels—Taj International Hotels; *U.S. Private*, pg. 1067

T.A.L.-5—Extra-Strength Synthetic Spray Lubricant for Heavy Duty Applicants—WD-40 Company; *U.S. Public*, pg. 1726

TALL—Terminal Application Level Language—CiMatrix L.L.C.; *U.S. Public*, pg. 1395

TA 90 B—Surgical Staplers—U.S. Surgical Corp.; *U.S. Public*, pg. 1687

TA 90 BN—Surgical Staplers—U.S. Surgical Corp.; *U.S. Public*, pg. 1687

TAP—Transient Analysis Program—GenRad, Inc.; *U.S. Public*, pg. 731

TA II—Surgical Staplers—U.S. Surgical Corp.; *U.S. Public*, pg. 1687

T/AUTONOM—Software/Service Integrating Third Party Back Office Systems—Eastern Utilities Associates; *U.S. Public*, pg. 549

TBA—Helicopter Transportable Drilling rigs—Parker Drilling Company; *U.S. Public*, pg. 1259

TBG—Bags—Grace Packaging; *U.S. Public*, pg. 755

TBQ—Germicidal Detergent—Calgon Vestal Laboratories; *U.S. Public*, pg. 1515

TBRT—NONE—Western Atlas Logging Services; *U.S. Public*, pg. 1757

TBS—Entertainment Network—Turner Broadcasting System Inc.; *U.S. Public*, pg. 1614

TBZ—Thiabendazole—Merck & Co., Inc.; *U.S. Public*, pg. 1090

T. BERD—NONE—Dynatech Corporation; *U.S. Public*, pg. 539

T. BIRD—Manual Wheelchair—Theradyne Corporation; *U.S. Private*, pg. 637

T-BOND II—Semi-Regid Foam Spacer System—Norton Performance Plastics; *Int'l*, pg. 1174

TCB—Hair Care Products—Alberto-Culver Company; *U.S. Public*, pg. 37

TCBY—Frozen Yogurt, Ice Cream Specialties & Refrigerated Yogurt—TCBY Enterprises Inc.; *U.S. Public*, pg. 1553

TCBY TREATS—Frozen Yogurt & Ice Cream—TCBY Enterprises Inc.; *U.S. Public*, pg. 1553

TCC—Bacteriostatic Agent—Solutia Inc.; *U.S. Public*, pg. 1483

TCE—Photographic Film & Paper—Eastman Kodak Company; *U.S. Public*, pg. 550

TCF—Photographic Film & Paper—Eastman Kodak Company; *U.S. Public*, pg. 550

TCF7—Photographic Film & Paper—Eastman Kodak Company; *U.S. Public*, pg. 550

TCK—NONE—Chemfab Corporation; *U.S. Public*, pg. 344

TCK-UVR—NONE—Chemfab Corporation; *U.S. Public*, pg. 344

TCM—Transcutaneous Monitoring of Bloodgases—Radiometer A/S; *Int'l*, pg. 1083

TCN—NONE—Chemfab Corporation; *U.S. Public*, pg. 344

TCN-UVR—NONE—Chemfab Corporation; *U.S. Public*, pg. 344

TCP—Thermocouples & RTD's—Desco Corporation; *U.S. Private*, pg. 326

TCP—Photographic Film & Paper—Eastman Kodak Company; *U.S. Public*, pg. 550

TCP—NONE—Pfizer Inc.; *U.S. Public*, pg. 1281

TCP—NONE—Western Atlas Logging Services; *U.S. Public*, pg. 1757

TCPM II—Pneumatic Touniquet System—Medtronics Inc.; *U.S. Public*, pg. 1083

TC ROUNDS—Biscuits—George Weston Limited; *Int'l*, pg. 1494

TCS—Process Control Systems—Computer Products, Inc.; *U.S. Public*, pg. 422

TCT—Twin Coating Tower—Harnischfeger Industries, Inc.; *U.S. Public*, pg. 788

TCT GOLD LINE—Super Precision Spindles—Setco; *U.S. Private*, pg. 987

TC TRACTION—Tires—Bridgestone/Firestone, Inc.; *Int'l*, pg. 213

T C 2000—Precured Tread Rubber—Oliver Rubber Co.; *U.S. Public*, pg. 1504

T-CARB—Carbonate—Harcros Chemicals Inc.; *Int'l*, pg. 598

T-D—Dust Collector—Donaldson Company, Inc.; *U.S. Public*, pg. 517

TDA CD-R RECORDABLE COMPACT DISCS—Recordable Compact Discs—TDK Electronics Corporation; *Int'l*, pg. 1336

TDC—Filtration Products—Gelman Sciences, Inc.; *U.S. Public*, pg. 1253

TDF—Photographic Film & Paper—Eastman Kodak Company; *U.S. Public*, pg. 550

TDF7—Photographic Film & Paper—Eastman Kodak Company; *U.S. Public*, pg. 550

T-D-I—Terminal Digital Indexing—Smead Manufacturing Company; *U.S. Private*, pg. 1006

TDK—Recording Tapes, Magnetic Components, Floppy Discs—TDK Corporation; *Int'l*, pg. 1336

TDK—Recording Tapes—TDK Electronics Corporation; *Int'l*, pg. 1336

TDK DATA CARTRIDGES—Data Cartridges—TDK Electronics Corporation; *Int'l*, pg. 1336

TDK FLOPPY DISKS—Floppy Disks—TDK Electronics Corporation; *Int'l*, pg. 1336

TDK MAGNETO-OPTICAL DISKS—Magneto Optical Disks—TDK Electronics Corporation; *Int'l*, pg. 1336

TDK QK CARTRIDGES—QK Cartridges—TDK Electronics Corporation; *Int'l*, pg. 1336

TDK SUPER AVILYN—Video Cassettes VHS & Beta—TDK Electronics Corporation; *Int'l*, pg. 1336

TD MECHANICAL—NONE—TD Industries Inc.; *U.S. Private*, pg. 1063

TDQ—NONE—Landmark Graphics Corporation; *U.S. Private*, pg. 776

TD SERVICE—NONE—TD Industries Inc.; *U.S. Private*, pg. 1063

TD-3000—Optical Time Domain Reflectometer—GN Nettest Fiber Optic Division; *Int'l*, pg. 536

TDW—Tires, Tread Rubber—The Hercules Tire & Rubber Company; *U.S. Private*, pg. 523

TDX—Diagnostic Products—Abbott Laboratories; *U.S. Public*, pg. 12

T/DEALMAKR—Gas Pipeline Capacity Trading System—Eastern Utilities Associates; *U.S. Public*, pg. 549

T/DERM—Tar Emollient—Neutrogena Corporation; *U.S. Public*, pg. 928

T-DET—Surfactants—Harcros Chemicals Inc.; *Int'l*, pg. 598

T/DISPATCHR—Communications System for Gas Pipeline & Distribution Companies—Eastern Utilities Associates; *U.S. Public*, pg. 549

T.E.C.—Carpet Yarn—AlliedSignal Inc.; *U.S. Public*, pg. 49

TEC 100—Squash Racquet—Ektelon; *U.S. Private*, pg. 884

TEC 700—Squash Racquet—Ektelon; *U.S. Private*, pg. 884

T.E.D.—Antiembolism Surgical Stockings—The Kendall Company; *U.S. Public*, pg. 1647

TEK—Series Resistance Heating Cables—Thermon Manufacturing Company; *U.S. Private*, pg. 1080

TEL—Fiberglass Manufacturing system—Saint-Gobain; *Int'l*, pg. 1170

TEREC—Tactical Electronic reconnaisance Systems—Comptek Research, Inc.; *U.S. Public*, pg. 419

TERPES—Tactical Electronic Reconnaissance Processing Evaluation Systems—Comptek Research, Inc.; *U.S. Public*, pg. 419

TEV—Today's English Version—American Bible Society; *U.S. Private*, pg. 51

T-EDJER—Trimmer Razor—Andis Company; *U.S. Private*, pg. 73

T800—Trucks—Kenworth Truck Company; *U.S. Public*, pg. 1246

TFC MAGNUM 60—Osmosus Spiral Wound Elements—AlliedSignal Inc.; *U.S. Public*, pg. 49

TFG—Thru Feed Grinder—SpeedFan International, Inc.; *U.S. Public*, pg. 1497

TFS—Thick Film Pastes for Electronic Circuits—Ferro Corporation; *U.S. Public*, pg. 618

TFS—Surge Protectors—TII Industries, Inc.; *U.S. Public*, pg. 1556

TFX MEDICAL—Invasive Disposable & Reusable Medical Devices—Teleflex Incorporated; *U.S. Public*, pg. 1569

T50—Staple Gun—Arrow Fastener Co., Inc.; *U.S. Private*, pg. 85

T-589—Tires—Bridgestone/Firestone, Inc.; *Int'l*, pg. 213

T-545 RADIAL—Tires—Bridgestone/Firestone, Inc.; *Int'l*, pg. 213

T-506—Tires—Bridgestone/Firestone, Inc.; *Int'l*, pg. 213

T-520—Tires—Bridgestone/Firestone, Inc.; *Int'l*, - pg. 213

T-FLECTOR—Pesticide Applicator—The Dow Chemical Company; *U.S. Public*, pg. 522

T-FOAM—Rehabilitation Product—Alimed, Inc.; *U.S. Private*, pg. 34

T-40—Thinner—Devoe Paint; *Int'l*, pg. 663

T-40—Thinner—ICI Paints; *Int'l*, pg. 664

T450—Trucks—Kenworth Truck Company; *U.S. Public*, pg. 1246

T4 RIA—Diagnostic Products—Abbott Laboratories; *U.S. Public*, pg. 12

TGAL—Format—Tandem Computers Inc.; *U.S. Public*, pg. 417

T.G. BEARWICH—Graham Sandwiches—Nabisco Inc.; *U.S. Public*, pg. 1355

TGC-THE GIFT COMPANY—Magnets, Musical Box, Pencil Holders, Doorknobs, Toy Playsets & Dolls—American Greetings Corporation; *U.S. Public*, pg. 77

TGF—Total Geriatric Formula Vitamin—Health Products Corporation; *U.S. Private*, pg. 514

TGI FRIDAY'S—Restaurants—Carlson Companies, Inc.; *U.S. Private*, pg. 211

TGI FRIDAYS—Restaurants—Whitbread PLC; *Int'l*, pg. 1498

T.G.I. FRIDAY'S FROZEN COCKTAILS—Frozen Cocktails—Heublein, Inc.; *Int'l*, pg. 410

T.G. LEE—Milk—Dean Foods Company; *U.S. Public*, pg. 489

TGUI9440—NONE—Trident Microsystems, Inc.; *U.S. Public*, pg. 1637

TGUI9680—NONE—Trident Microsystems, Inc.; *U.S. Public*, pg. 1637

T/GEL—Therapeutic Shampoo & Conditioner—Neutrogena Corporation; *U.S. Public*, pg. 928

T-GRAIN—Photographic Emulsions—Eastman Kodak Company; *U.S. Public*, pg. 550

TH—Sprinkler—Rain Bird Sprinklers Manufacturing Corp.; *U.S. Private*, pg. 907

TH JR.—Test Equipment—Tenney Environmental; *U.S. Private*, pg. 1076

TI-KOTE—Coating Product—Texas Instruments Incorporated; *U.S. Public*, pg. 1585

T.I.M.—Integrated Manufacturing Environment—Tandem Computers Inc.; *U.S. Public*, pg. 417

T-J—Fluid Power Cylinders—Aeroquip-Vickers, Inc.; *U.S. Public*, pg. 24

T-J—Cylinders—Vickers Actuator Products; *U.S. Public*, pg. 24

T.J. CINNAMON'S—Food Concept—Triarc Companies, Inc.; *U.S. Public*, pg. 1634

TJI JOISTS—NONE—Trus Joist MacMillan; *Int'l*, pg. 829

TJI JOISTS—NONE—Trus Joist MacMillan; *U.S. Public*, pg. 1556

TJ INTERNATIONAL—Company Name—TJ International, Inc.; *U.S. Public*, pg. 1556

TJM—Company Logo—TJ International, Inc.; *U.S. Public*, pg. 1556

T.J. MAXX—Retail Stores—T.J. Maxx; *U.S. Public*, pg. 1557

T.J. MAXX—Off-Price Family Apparel—The TJX Companies, Inc.; *U.S. Public*, pg. 1556

T-K—NONE—Carpenter Technology Corporation; *U.S. Public*, pg. 307

TK—Coating—Tuboscope Incorporated; *U.S. Public*, pg. 1643

TKC—Connection—Tuboscope Incorporated; *U.S. Public*, pg. 1643

T.K. MAXX—Off-Price Family Retailer in the United Kingdom—The TJX Companies, Inc.; *U.S. Public*, pg. 1556

TL—Automobile—American Honda Motor Co., Inc.; *Int'l*, pg. 634

TLA—Transmission Line Assembly—3M; *U.S. Public*, pg. 1604

TLC—NONE—Berg Electronics; *U.S. Public*, pg. 212

TLC—PRW and Transportation—Christiana Companies, Inc.; *U.S. Public*, pg. 352

TLC—Infant Car Seat/Carrier—Cosco, Inc.; *U.S. Private*, pg. 277

TLC—Filing Claims Service—The Mead Corporation; *U.S. Public*, pg. 1074

TLC—Crossflow Filter—Osmonics, Inc.; *U.S. Public*, pg. 1233

TLC CHAIR—Bath Chair—Ortho-Kinetics, Inc.; *U.S. Private*, pg. 820

TLC-D99—Doxorubicin—Pfizer Inc.; *U.S. Public*, pg. 1281

TLN—Treated Lumber Nails to Reduce Corrosion—Paslode; *U.S. Public*, pg. 867

T.L. SMITH MACHINE—Concrete Mixers—T.L. Smith Machine; *U.S. Private*, pg. 1009

T-LINE—Golf Clubs—Tommy Armour Golf; *U.S. Public*, pg. 1683

T-LOCK—Concrete Sewer Pipe Lining—Ameron Concrete & Steel Pipe Group; *U.S. Public*, pg. 99

T-LOCK—Concrete Sewer Pipe Lining—Ameron International Corporation; *U.S. Public*, pg. 98

"T" LOGO—Computer Hardware—Thinking Machines Corporation; *U.S. Private*, pg. 1081

T-LOK—Vinyl Siding and Accessories—Alcoa Building Products, Inc.; *U.S. Public*, pg. 61

TMA—Truck-Mounted Attenuator—Quixote Corporation; *U.S. Public*, pg. 1353

TMF—Planting Seeds-Corn—Mycogen Corporation; *U.S. Public*, pg. 1142

TMF—Planting Seeds—Mycogen Seeds; *U.S. Public*, pg. 1142

TMF—Transaction Recovery Software—Tandem Computers Inc.; *U.S. Public*, pg. 417

TM-40—NONE—Molex Incorporated; *U.S. Public*, pg. 1121

TMK—Woodworking Machinery—Makita Corporation; *Int'l*, pg. 831

TMO—Optical Disk Equipment—Eastman Kodak Company; *U.S. Public*, pg. 550

TM-147T—Temperature Monitor—Medtronics Inc.; *U.S. Public*, pg. 1083

TMPD—Glycol—Eastman Chemical Company; *U.S. Public*, pg. 550

TMPD—Glycol Chemicals—Eastman Kodak Company; *U.S. Public*, pg. 550

TMS—Digitizing Machine—Makino Inc.; *Int'l*, pg. 831

TMS—Markers, Identification Sleeves—Raychem Corporation; *U.S. Public*, pg. 1362

TMS 40—Tightening Tools—SPS Technologies, Inc.; *U.S. Public*, pg. 1419

TMS STOCKS—Customized Stock Market Listings for Newspapers—Tribune Media Services, Inc.; *U.S. Public*, pg. 1636

TMS 3000—Frame Delay Switch/Multiplexer—General Datacomm Industries, Inc.; *U.S. Public*, pg. 708

TMS TV LISTINGS—Customized TV Program Listings for Newspapers—Tribune Media Services, Inc.; *U.S. Public*, pg. 1636

TMS WEATHER SERVICE—Weather Information for Newspapers—Tribune Media Services, Inc.; *U.S. Public*, pg. 1636

TMS WEBPOINT—Customized Iternet Services for Newspapers—Tribune Media Services, Inc.; *U.S. Public*, pg. 1636

TM SERIES—Analog Router—Chyron Corp.; *Int'l*, pg. 1372

TM-33—Mist Eliminator—Farr Company; *U.S. Public*, pg. 613

TMX—Tricycle—Roadmaster/Brunswick; *U.S. Public*, pg. 265

T-MAG—Metallic Reloading Press—Lyman Products Corporation; *U.S. Private*, pg. 683

T-MAT—X-Ray Film—Eastman Kodak Company; *U.S. Public*, pg. 550

T-MAX—Photographic Film, Plates, Chemicals—Eastman Kodak Company; *U.S. Public*, pg. 550

T-MAZ—Surfactants—PPG Industries, Inc.; *U.S. Public*, pg. 1245

T-MULZ—Emulsifiers—Harcros Chemicals Inc.; *U.S. Public*, pg. 598

TNF RECEPTOR/ENBREL—Immunological Therapeutic—Immunex Corporation; *U.S. Public*, pg. 871

TNS—Temporary Nursing Services—Continental Health Affiliates, Inc.; *U.S. Public*, pg. 440

TNT—X-Ray System Training Simulator—EG & G Astrophysics; *U.S. Public*, pg. 543

TNT—Spray Pump Dispensers—Risdon Corporation; *U.S. Public*, pg. 463

TNT—Entertainment Network—Turner Broadcasting System Inc.; *U.S. Public*, pg. 1614

T/NOMINATR—Software Enabling Gas Users to Make Pipeline Capacity Nominations—Eastern Utilities Associates; *U.S. Public*, pg. 549

TOA-THRONE—NONE—AGA Gas, Inc.; *Int'l*, pg. 13

TOFC SPECIAL—Tires—Bridgestone/Firestone, Inc.; *Int'l*, pg. 213

TORQR—Catheter—Medtronic, Inc.; *U.S. Public*, pg. 1082

T-O-T—Sealing Pipe Compound—La-Co Industries Markal Company; *U.S. Private*, pg. 640

T1 & T2—Thermocouple Alloys (Typek)—Driver-Harris Company; *U.S. Public*, pg. 530

T100—Pickup—Toyota Motor Sales, U.S.A., Inc.; *Int'l*, pg. 1412

T-OUTLINER—Hair Trimmer—Andis Company; *U.S. Private*, pg. 73

TP—Plastic Squeeze Tubes Sold Empty for Food, Cosmetic & Drug Industry—McCormick & Company, Incorporated; *U.S. Public*, pg. 1066

TP—Plasticizers—Morton International Inc.; *U.S. Public*, pg. 1135

T.P.A.—Third Party Administration—Universal Standard Healthcare, Inc.; *U.S. Public*, pg. 1697

TP INK—NONE—Stuart Entertainment Inc.; *U.S. Public*, pg. 1526

TPL—Third Party Liability Processing—Health Management Systems, Inc.; *U.S. Public*, pg. 802

TPM—Slide Test for Toxo Antibodies—Wampole Laboratories; *U.S. Public*, pg. 310

TPP—Dry Adhesive Systems—H.B. Fuller Company; *U.S. Public*, pg. 686

TPR—Thermoplastic Elastomer—Monsanto Company; *U.S. Public*, pg. 1124

'T+ SERIES—Self Priming Centrifugal Trash Pump Solids Handling—The Gorman-Rupp Company; *U.S. Public*, pg. 754

"T" PORT—Adapter—Becton Dickinson & Company; *U.S. Public*, pg. 199

T/POSTER—FERC & GISB Complient Information Posting Service—Eastern Utilities Associates; *U.S. Public*, pg. 549

TRAC—Tooless Reenterable Aerial Closure—Raychem Corporation; *U.S. Public*, pg. 1362

TRC—Horse Health Care Product—Farnam Companies, Inc.; *U.S. Private*, pg. 396

TRC AIR EXPERT—Software to Manage Air Emissions Inventories—TRC Companies, Inc.; *U.S. Public*, pg. 1557

TR FLEX—Pipe & Fittings—United States Pipe & Foundry Company, Inc.; *U.S. Public*, pg. 1736

TR-LL—Time-Resolved Liquid Scintillation Counting—Packard Instrument Co., Inc.; *U.S. Private*, pg. 833

TR-LSC—Time-Resolved Liquid Scintillation Counting—Packard Instrument Co., Inc.; *U.S. Private*, pg. 833

TR RACING—NONE—LDI, Ltd.; *U.S. Private*, pg. 639

TR TELE FLEX—Extendable, Flexible, Restrained Joint Assembly—United States Pipe & Foundry Company, Inc.; *U.S. Public*, pg. 1736

TR-10—Herbicide—The Dow Chemical Company; *U.S. Public*, pg. 522

TRW—Engine & Chassis Parts—Federal-Mogul Corporation; *U.S. Public*, pg. 626

TRW—Automotive Replacement Parts; Computer & Engineering Services—TRW Inc.; *U.S. Public*, pg. 1558

T/RELEASR—System for Pipelines & Local Gas Distribution—Eastern Utilities Associates; *U.S. Public*, pg. 549

T-REX—Serving Trays—Menasha Corporation; *U.S. Private*, pg. 731

TSA—A Suspension Assembly Having Integrated Electrical Leads—Hutchinson Technology Inc.; *U.S. Public*, pg. 850

TSA—Test Equipment—Tenney Environmental; *U.S. Private*, pg. 1076

Brand Name Index

TSCE—Service Creation Environment—Tandem Computers Inc.; *U.S. Public*, pg. 417

TSCE-1000—Service Creation Environment—Tandem Computers Inc.; *U.S. Public*, pg. 417

TSCP—Service Control Point—Tandem Computers Inc.; *U.S. Public*, pg. 417

TSCP-1000—Service Control Point—Tandem Computers Inc.; *U.S. Public*, pg. 417

TSDS—Instructional Manuals re: Driver Training—Lucent Technologies Inc.; *U.S. Public*, pg. 1017

TSI—Company Name—TSI Incorporated; *U.S. Public*, pg. 1559

TSK-GEL—NONE—TosoHaas Company; *U.S. Public*, pg. 1403

TSK-GEL—NONE—TosoHaas Company; *Int'l*, pg. 1408

TSMS—Service Management System—Tandem Computers Inc.; *U.S. Public*, pg. 417

TSMS-1000—Service Management System—Tandem Computers Inc.; *U.S. Public*, pg. 417

TSMT—Transportation—Tri-State Motor Transit Co.; *U.S. Private*, pg. 1101

TSP—Steel Components—Xtek, Inc.; *U.S. Private*, pg. 1194

TSP-90—Cleaner—Red Devil Inc.; *U.S. Private*, pg. 915

TSQ—High Resolution Organic Mass Spectrometer, Isotope Ratio Mass Spectrometer—Finnigan Corporation; *U.S. Public*, pg. 1591

TSR—Books—TSR, Inc.; *U.S. Private*, pg. 1185

TSRH—Spinal Implant Devices—Sofamor Danek Group, Inc.; *U.S. Public*, pg. 1482

TSS-TASK SEATING SYSTEM—Ergonomic Seating—Domore Corporation; *U.S. Private*, pg. 339

TS SERIES—Analog Router—Chyron Corp.; *Int'l*, pg. 1372

T/SAL—Shampoo—Neutrogena Corporation; *U.S. Public*, pg. 928

T-SCANWHEEL—Scanning Earth Sensor & Momentum Wheel—Ithaco Inc.; *U.S. Private*, pg. 576

T-SENTRY—Performance Monitoring System—ADC Telecommunications, Inc.; *U.S. Public*, pg. 4

T600A—Trucks—Kenworth Truck Company; *U.S. Public*, pg. 1246

T600B—Trucks—Kenworth Truck Company; *U.S. Public*, pg. 1246

T 663—Tires—Bridgestone/Firestone, Inc.; *Int'l*, pg. 213

T-65—Toluene Di Isociante—CYDSA S.A.; *Int'l*, pg. 246

T-STAT—Topical Erythromycin—Bristol-Myers Squibb Company; *U.S. Public*, pg. 253

T-STAT—Antibiotic Pads—Westwood-Squibb Pharmaceuticals Inc.; *U.S. Public*, pg. 255

T-STUD—Fasteners—R&B, Inc.; *U.S. Public*, pg. 1354

TTD—Dust Collector—Donaldson Company, Inc.; *U.S. Public*, pg. 517

TT-44—Band Saw Blades—Sandvik/Milford Corporation; *Int'l*, pg. 1185

TT LITE—Outdoor Products—The Black & Decker Corporation; *U.S. Public*, pg. 233

TTR—Transformer Turn Ratio Test Sets—Avo International; *U.S. Private*, pg. 9

TTRM—NONE—Western Atlas Logging Services; *U.S. Public*, pg. 1757

TTSI-NET—Intelligent Netwoking Products—Tandem Computers Inc.; *U.S. Public*, pg. 417

T/10—Network Products—GTE Internetworking; *U.S. Public*, pg. 696

T/300—Network Products—GTE Internetworking; *U.S. Public*, pg. 696

T300—Trucks—Kenworth Truck Company; *U.S. Public*, pg. 1246

T3 RIA—Diagnostic Products—Abbott Laboratories; *U.S. Public*, pg. 12

T/20—Network Products—GTE Internetworking; *U.S. Public*, pg. 696

TII—Logo—TII Industries, Inc.; *U.S. Public*, pg. 1556

T/200—Network Products—GTE Internetworking; *U.S. Public*, pg. 696

TUPH—PH/ORP Sensors—Rosemount Analytical, Uniloc Div.; *U.S. Public*, pg. 574

TV—Private Label Grocery, Perishables & Frozen Items—Fleming Companies, Inc.; *U.S. Public*, pg. 652

TV & SATELLITE WEEK—Weekly TV Magazine—IPC Magazines Limited; *Int'l*, pg. 651

TVGA8900DR—NONE—Trident Microsystems, Inc.; *U.S. Public*, pg. 1637

TVGA9000I—NONE—Trident Microsystems, Inc.; *U.S. Public*, pg. 1637

TVG9470—NONE—Trident Microsystems, Inc.; *U.S. Public*, pg. 1637

TV HOST MONTHLY—Cable Publication with Pay & Satellite Network Listings—TV Host Inc.; *U.S. Private*, pg. 1066

TV HOST WEEKLY—Comprehensive Program Guide with Broadcast & Cable Program Services Listed—TV Host Inc.; *U.S. Private*, pg. 1066

TVI EDITIONS—Belgium Broadcasting—CLT-UFA; *Int'l*, pg. 561

TV NEU—Magazine—Axel Springer Verlag AG; *Int'l*, pg. 102

TVS—Window Glazing Units—PPG Industries, Inc.; *U.S. Public*, pg. 1245

TVTIMES—Weekly TV Magazine—IPC Magazines Limited; *Int'l*, pg. 651

TV WARS—Leisure—Monarch Avalon, Inc.; *U.S. Public*, pg. 1123

TWA—Commercial Airlines—Trans World Airlines, Inc.; *U.S. Public*, pg. 1629

TXO—Operatin System Software & Development Tools—VeriFone, Inc.; *U.S. Public*, pg. 815

TXP—Computers—Tandem Computers Inc.; *U.S. Public*, pg. 417

TX 220—Master Control Switcher—Chyron Corp.; *Int'l*, pg. 1372

T-ZOID—Golf Equipment—Mizuno USA, Inc.; *Int'l*, pg. 885

T&B—Cable Tray Systems—Thomas & Betts Corporation; *U.S. Public*, pg. 1597

T-LINE—Pumps, Valves—Flowserve Corporation; *U.S. Public*, pg. 658

3D OCR—Page Recognition Technology—Caere Corporation; *U.S. Public*, pg. 291

3-36—General Purpose Lubricant—CRC Industries, Inc.; *U.S. Private*, pg. 138

TRIPLEDECKER PIZZA—Layered Pizza—Pizza Hut, Inc.; *U.S. Public*, pg. 1636

TRUE PAGE—Page Recognition Technology—Caere Corporation; *U.S. Public*, pg. 291

2800 TRUSSWALL—NONE—Kawneer Company; *U.S. Public*, pg. 60

2-26—General Purpose Lubricant—CRC Industries, Inc.; *U.S. Private*, pg. 138

TA'POT—Slidewire Potentiometer—Howell Instruments Inc.; *U.S. Private*, pg. 543

TA TAPER—Tapered Bushing—The Falk Corporation; *U.S. Public*, pg. 1534

TA-KETTE—Tachometer—AMETEK, Inc.; *U.S. Public*, pg. 99

TA-NON-KA—Premium No. 1—Badger Paper Mills, Inc.; *U.S. Public*, pg. 165

TAB—Diet & Diet Caffeine-Free Cola—The Coca-Cola Company; *U.S. Public*, pg. 392

TAB LOCK—Dispensing Cartons for Rolls of Sheet Material—Reynolds Metals Company; *U.S. Public*, pg. 1385

TAB MARKER INDEXING SYSTEM—VCR Feature—Sony Electronics; *Int'l*, pg. 1281

TAB-ON—Marking Stencils—Weber Marking Systems, Inc.; *U.S. Private*, pg. 1157

TAB-TRAC—Mobile Filing Equip.—Tab Products Co.; *U.S. Public*, pg. 1559

TAB-BLU—Drop In Toilet Tablet—Blue Cross Laboratories; *U.S. Private*, pg. 152

TABASCO—Pepper Sauce, Bloody Mary Mix, & Picante Sauce—McIlhenny Company; *U.S. Private*, pg. 722

TABBIES—NONE—Stuart Entertainment Inc.; *U.S. Public*, pg. 1526

TABBY—Premium Cat Food—Alpo Pet Foods, Inc.; *Int'l*, pg. 917

TABCIN—Effervescent Cold Medicine—Bayer AG; *Int'l*, pg. 171

TABFOLIO—Stationary Products—The Mead Corporation; *U.S. Public*, pg. 1074

TABLE PAC—Packaging & Containers for Food—Sonoco Products Company; *U.S. Public*, pg. 1485

TABLE QUEEN—Food Products—Smart & Final; *Int'l*, pg. 563

TABLE TAILORS—Tables for Industry—John Boos & Company; *U.S. Private*, pg. 156

TABLE TALK—Poultry—Goodman Fielder Limited; *Int'l*, pg. 555

TABLECURVE 3D—Surface-Fitting Software—SPSS Inc.; *U.S. Public*, pg. 1420

TABLECURVE 2D—Curve-Fitting Software—SPSS Inc.; *U.S. Public*, pg. 1420

TABLERITE—Controlled Label for Fresh Meat & Processed Meat Prods.—IGA, Inc. (Independent Grocers Alliance); *U.S. Private*, pg. 555

TABLETIME—Baby Food—Beech-Nut Nutrition Corporation; *U.S. Public*, pg. 1359

TABLETOP—Conveying Chain—Rexnord Corporation; *Int'l*, pg. 127

TABLETOX—Tabletop Computerized Instrumentation—Beckman Instruments, Inc.; *U.S. Public*, pg. 199

TABQUIK—Creates Color-Coded Labels—Tab Products Co.; *U.S. Public*, pg. 1559

TABSCRIPT—Photo Typesetter—AGFA EPS Division; *Int'l*, pg. 172

TABU—Perfume—Dana Perfumes Corp.; *U.S. Private*, pg. 922

TABU LIPSTICK—Lipcolor—Dana Perfumes Corp.; *U.S. Private*, pg. 922

TABULABEL—Labels—Avery Dennison Corporation; *U.S. Public*, pg. 152

TAC AIR—War Game—Monarch Avalon, Inc.; *U.S. Public*, pg. 1123

TAC-FAST CARPET SYSTEMS—Carpet Installation System—3M; *U.S. Public*, pg. 1604

TAC-OLE—Mexican Food—Bruce Foods Corp.; *U.S. Private*, pg. 175

TAC TABS—NONE—Barton Nelson Inc.; *U.S. Private*, pg. 120

TAC 3—Electric Air Valves—Humphrey Products Company; *U.S. Private*, pg. 547

TAC 2—Air Valves—Humphrey Products Company; *U.S. Private*, pg. 547

TACA INTERNATIONAL—Airlines—Taca International Airlines, S. A.; *Int'l*, pg. 1346

TACARYL—Tablets & Syrup-Antipruritic Antihistamine—Westwood-Squibb Pharmaceuticals Inc.; *U.S. Public*, pg. 255

TACHOMETERS—NONE—Philips Automotive Electronics; *Int'l*, pg. 1054

TACK-MATE—Horse Clipper—Andis Company; *U.S. Private*, pg. 73

TACK N TOGS—Trade Magazine—Farm Progress Publications; *U.S. Public*, pg. 513

TACKLE—Household Cleaner Disinfectant—The Clorox Company; *U.S. Public*, pg. 386

TACKLE—Household Paper Goods—Orchids Paper Products Co.; *U.S. Private*, pg. 819

TACKLE—Acifluorfen Herbicide—Rhone-Poulenc S.A.; *Int'l*, pg. 1108

TACO BELL—Grocery Products—Kraft Foods, Inc.; *U.S. Public*, pg. 1287

TACO BELL—Mexican Style Fast Food Chain—PepsiCo, Inc.; *U.S. Public*, pg. 1276

TACO BRAVO—2 Shell Taco—Taco John's International, Inc.; *U.S. Private*, pg. 1066

TACO JOHN'S—Restaurants—Taco John's International, Inc.; *U.S. Private*, pg. 1066

TACO JOHN'S MEXPRESS—Alternative Distribution Unit—Taco John's International, Inc.; *U.S. Private*, pg. 1066

TACO-MATE—Shredded Cheese Subsititute Products—Borden, Inc.; *U.S. Private*, pg. 157

TACO TUESDAY—Promotion—Taco John's International, Inc.; *U.S. Private*, pg. 1066

TACOMA—Titling Equipment—Eastman Kodak Company; *U.S. Public*, pg. 550

TACOMA—sacrum conjunction with TSRH—Sofamor Danek Group, Inc.; *U.S. Public*, pg. 1482

TACOMA—Compact Pickup Truck—Toyota Motor Sales, U.S.A., Inc.; *Int'l*, pg. 1412

TACOMA NEWS TRIBUNE—Newspaper—The News Tribune; *U.S. Public*, pg. 1066

TACONIC—Tea Bag Paper—Kimberly-Clark Corporation; *U.S. Public*, pg. 958

TACTICS—War Game—Monarch Avalon, Inc.; *U.S. Public*, pg. 1123

TACTICS II—Game—Monarch Avalon, Inc.; *U.S. Public*, pg. 1123

TACTIFLEX—Catheter—Medtronic, Inc.; *U.S. Public*, pg. 1082

TACTIX—High Performance Resins—The Dow Chemical Company; *U.S. Public*, pg. 522

TADS—Fashion Slacks for Toddlers & Boys—H. R. Kaminsky & Sons, Inc.; *U.S. Private*, pg. 606

TAEKEUK—Representing National Carrier—Korean Airlines Co., Ltd.; *Int'l*, pg. 758

TAFFY TAPE—NONE—Nestle USA; *Int'l*, pg. 916

TAFFY TARTS—NONE—Nestle USA; *Int'l*, pg. 916

TAG-ALONG—Beverage Cooler—Igloo Products Corporation; *U.S. Public*, pg. 265

TAG-O-GRAPH—Duplicating Ink—Weber Marking Systems, Inc.; *U.S. Private*, pg. 1157

TAGAMET—Stomach Remedies—SmithKline Beecham Consumer Healthcare, U.S.; *Int'l*, pg. 1264

TAGAMET—Gastrointestinal Treatment—SmithKline Beecham Corporation; *Int'l*, pg. 1264

TAGAMET—NONE—SmithKline Beecham Laboratorios Ltda.; *Int'l*, pg. 1266

TAGAMET—Gastrointestinal Drug—SmithKline Beecham plc; *Int'l*, pg. 1264

TAGAMET—Anti-Ulcerant—SmithKline Beecham Research Limited; *Int'l*, pg. 1266

TAHITI—NONE—Colgate-Palmolive; *U.S. Public*, pg. 398

TAHOE—Sport Utility—Chevrolet Motor Div. General Motors Corp.; *U.S. Public*, pg. 720

TAHSIS—NONE—Avenor, Inc.; *Int'l*, pg. 101

TAIKOO—NONE—Swire Pacific Limited; *Int'l*, pg. 1328

TAIKOO SHING—Paint—Swire Pacific Limited; *Int'l*, pg. 1328

TAIKOO SUGAR—Sugar Products—Swire Pacific Limited; *Int'l*, pg. 1328

TAILGATOR—Fiberglass Tailgater—Lund International Holdings, Inc.; *U.S. Public*, pg. 1020

TAILLEFINE—Cheese—Danone Group; *Int'l*, pg. 379

TAILLEUR INDUSTRIE—NONE—GEODIS; *Int'l*, pg. 549

TAILMATE—Rear Valance—Lund International Holdings, Inc.; *U.S. Public*, pg. 1020

TAILOR-MADE—Fertilizer—Security Lawn & Garden Co.; *U.S. Private*, pg. 397

TAILORED PROTECTION—Insurance—American Republic Insurance Co.; *U.S. Private*, pg. 61

TAILORED SHEERS—Bras, Panties, Bodysuit—Olga Div.; *U.S. Public*, pg. 1738

TAILORS ROW—Labels—S & K Famous Brands, Inc.; *U.S. Public*, pg. 1414

TAJ MAHAL—Broadloom—Couristan Inc.; *U.S. Private*, pg. 279

TAKE-A-NUMBER—Queuing System—Esselte Meto Kimball Systems; *Int'l*, pg. 460

TAKE-A-NUMBER—Take A Number Queing System—Meto, USA; *Int'l*, pg. 460

TAKE A STEP ABOVE THE CROWD—Recruiting & Advertising Package—RE/MAX International, Inc.; *U.S. Private*, pg. 912

TAKE CHARGE—Dog and Cat Collars—Carter-Wallace, Inc.; *U.S. Public*, pg. 309

TAKE-OFF—Make-up & Facial Cleansers—Advanced Polymer Systems; *U.S. Public*, pg. 22

TAKE OFF—Make-Up Remover Cloths—Johnson & Johnson; *U.S. Public*, pg. 927

TAKE-OFF—NONE—Premier, Inc.; *U.S. Private*, pg. 647

TAKECONTROL—Software—Brock International Inc.; *U.S. Public*, pg. 258

TAKECONTROL CONSUMER AFFAIRS—NONE—Brock International Inc.; *U.S. Public*, pg. 258

TAKECONTROL CUSTOMER SUPPORT—NONE—Brock International Inc.; *U.S. Public*, pg. 258

TAKECONTROL MARKETING—NONE—Brock International Inc.; *U.S. Public*, pg. 258

TAKECONTROL SALES—NONE—Brock International Inc.; *U.S. Public*, pg. 258

TAKHOMASAK—Restaurants—Consolidated Products, Inc.; *U.S. Public*, pg. 436

TAKHOMASAK—Restaurants—Steak 'n Shake, Inc.; *U.S. Public*, pg. 437

TAL-STRIP—Paint Remover—Mar-Hyde Corporation; *U.S. Public*, pg. 1357

TAL TEK ELECTRONICS—Point of Sale Verification Terminals—NBS Technologies, Inc.; *Int'l*, pg. 898

TALBOT—Automobile—Peugeot S.A.; *Int'l*, pg. 1020

TALBOTS—Retail Stores—Talbots, Inc.; *Int'l*, pg. 28

TALCID—Stomach Remedy—Bayer AG; *Int'l*, pg. 171

TALENS—Jointing Materials & Sealants, Painters Equipment & Tools—Akzo Nobel N.V.; *Int'l*, pg. 42

TALENTI BRUNELLO—Wine—Paterno Imports Limited; *U.S. Private*, pg. 843

TALES FROM THE FLOATING VAGABOND—Role Playing Game—Monarch Avalon, Inc.; *U.S. Public*, pg. 1123

TALFINO TALEGGIO CHEESE—NONE—Cucina Classica Italiana, Inc.; *U.S. Public*, pg. 1435

TALIN—Sweetener—Tate & Lyle PLC; *Int'l*, pg. 1356

TALIS—Sedatives—Kali-Chemie Aktiengesellschaft; *Int'l*, pg. 1278

TALIS—Benzodiazepine—Solvay S.A.; *Int'l*, pg. 1277

TALISKER—NONE—Guinness Plc; *Int'l*, pg. 412

TALISMAN—Refrigerators, Dishwashers, Electric Washers, Electric Dryers—General Electric Canada Inc.; *U.S. Public*, pg. 713

TALISMAN—Jeans—Sheplers, Inc.; *U.S. Private*, pg. 993

TALISMAN AMERICANA—Ranges, Refrigerators, Dishwashers for Domestic Use—General Electric Canada Inc.; *U.S. Public*, pg. 713

TALISMAN ROYALE—Ranges, Refrigerators, Dishwashers, Garbage Compactors for Domestic Use—General Electric Canada Inc.; *U.S. Public*, pg. 713

TALISMAN VERSATRON—Clothes Washers, Clothes Dryers for Domestic Use—General Electric Canada Inc.; *U.S. Public*, pg. 713

TALK TO—Home & Small Business Communication Systems—Mitel Corporation; *Int'l*, pg. 870

TALK TO THE SOURCE—Provide Educational Information Materials & Services Related to Energy—Orange and Rockland Utilities, Inc.; *U.S. Public*, pg. 1229

TALK-A-PHONE—Intercom Systems—Talk-A-Phone Co.; *U.S. Private*, pg. 1067

TALKALONG—Telephone Service—AirTouch Cellular - Western Region; *U.S. Public*, pg. 34

TALKING FAMILY DOLLHOUSE—Dollhouse—Tyco Toys, Inc.; *U.S. Public*, pg. 1058

TALKING PAGES—Telephone Information Service—British Telecommunications plc; *Int'l*, pg. 222

TALKING TINA—Toy—Toymax International Inc.; *U.S. Public*, pg. 1626

TALKING VIEW MASTER—Viewers & Reels—View-Master, Inc.; *U.S. Public*, pg. 1058

TALLADEGA SERIES—Suspension Seat—Bostrom Seating, Inc.; *U.S. Public*, pg. 933

TALLEX—Tall Oil Pitch—Westvaco Corporation; *U.S. Public*, pg. 1762

TALLEY—Defense Products—Talley Defense Systems, Inc.; *U.S. Public*, pg. 308

TALLIS—Consultancy Service—British Telecommunications plc; *Int'l*, pg. 222

TALLSO—Crude Tall Oil—Westvaco Corporation; *U.S. Public*, pg. 1762

TALLY-HO—Deodorants—SmithKline Beecham plc; *Int'l*, pg. 1264

TALLY-HO—Playing Cards—The United States Playing Card Company; *U.S. Private*, pg. 1125

TALON—Zippers—Coats & Clark Inc.; *Int'l*, pg. 300

TALPEN—Broad-Spectrum Antibiotic—SmithKline Beecham plc; *Int'l*, pg. 1264

TALSOL—Auto Finishing Products—RPM, Inc.; *U.S. Public*, pg. 1356

TAM—Natural Laxative—Nature's Bounty Inc.; *U.S. Public*, pg. 1166

TAM TAM—Crackers—The B. Manischewitz Company; *U.S. Private*, pg. 699

TASMANIAN—Cheese—Bongrain S.A.; *Int'l*, pg. 201

TAMARACK—Manufactured Homes—Champion Enterprises, Inc.; *U.S. Public*, pg. 332

TAMARI—Sauce—San-J Intl. Inc.; *Int'l*, pg. 1183

TAMBOCOR—Flecainide Acetate Antiarrythmic Prescription Drug—3M; *U.S. Public*, pg. 1604

TAMBOURINE—Books—The Hearst Corporation; *U.S. Private*, pg. 515

TAMBOURINE BOOKS—Juvenile Books—William Morrow & Co., Inc.; *U.S. Private*, pg. 515

TAMDHU—Single Malt Scotch—The Highland Distilleries Company plc; *Int'l*, pg. 619

TAME—Hair Preparations—The Gillette Company; *U.S. Public*, pg. 743

TAMERLANE—Area Rugs—Couristan Inc.; *U.S. Private*, pg. 279

TAMISEE—Flour—Grands Moulins de Paris S.A.; *Int'l*, pg. 556

TAMOL—Detergent Additives & Dispersants—BASF AG; *Int'l*, pg. 103

TAMOR—Houseware Products—Home Products International, Inc.; *U.S. Public*, pg. 832

TAMPA BAY BUSINESS JOURNAL—Business Journal—Business First of New York, Inc.; *U.S. Private*, pg. 19

TAMPALERT—Tamper-Evident Innerseals—Zimmer Custom-Made Packaging Co.; *U.S. Private*, pg. 802

TAMPAMARK—Adhesive Backed Labels—Markem Corporation; *U.S. Private*, pg. 704

TAMPAX—Petal Soft and Tampons—Tambrands Inc.; *U.S. Public*, pg. 1331

TAMPAX SATIN TOUCH—Tampons—Tambrands Inc.; *U.S. Public*, pg. 1331

TAMPERPROOF—Front-Loading Frames—Marketing Displays International; *U.S. Private*, pg. 705

TAMPONA—Tampons—VP-Schickedanz AG; *U.S. Public*, pg. 1333

TANA—Shoe Polishes—Kiwi Brands; *U.S. Public*, pg. 1433

TANA—Specialty Shoe Care—Kiwi Brands Pty. Ltd.; *U.S. Public*, pg. 1434

TANA—Shoe Care Products—Sara Lee Corporation; *U.S. Public*, pg. 1432

TANAC—For Canker Sores & Blisters—Del Pharmaceuticals, Inc.; *U.S. Public*, pg. 494

TANATEX—Dyehouse & Finishing Textile Chemicals—Sybron Chemicals Inc.; *U.S. Public*, pg. 1544

TANDEM—Valve Trim—Copes-Vulcan Inc.; *U.S. Private*, pg. 274

TANDEM—Selective Herbicide—The Dow Chemical Company; *U.S. Public*, pg. 522

TANDEM—Filing System—Fellowes Manufacturing Co.; *U.S. Private*, pg. 400

TANDEM—Premium Quality Flashlights—RAYOVAC Corporation; *U.S. Private*, pg. 912

TANDEM LOGO—Company Name & Trademark—Tandem Computers Inc.; *U.S. Public*, pg. 417

TANDEM UNIPASS ACME TAP—Taps with a Roughing & Finishing Section—Regal-Beloit Corporation; *U.S. Public*, pg. 1370

TANDERIL—Antirheumatic—Novartis; *Int'l*, pg. 972

TANDETRON—Ion Implant Accelerator—Genus Inc.; *U.S. Public*, pg. 732

TANDY—Microcomputers—RadioShack; *U.S. Public*, pg. 1560

TANDY—Leather Goods—Tandycrafts, Inc.; *U.S. Public*, pg. 1561

TANG—Regular & Sugar-Free Instant Breakfast Beverage—Kraft Foods, Inc.; *U.S. Public*, pg. 1287

TANG—Powdered Soft Drink—Kraft Jacobs Suchard; *U.S. Public*, pg. 1290

TANG—Salad Dressing—Nalleys Fine Foods; *U.S. Private*, pg. 887

TANG—Powdered Beverage—Philip Morris Companies Inc.; *U.S. Public*, pg. 1287

TANG FRUIT BOXES—Single Serve Aseptic Packages With 30% Fruit Juices—Kraft Foods, Inc.; *U.S. Public*, pg. 1287

TANG KUEI—Herbal Tablets—Herbalife International of America, Inc.; *U.S. Public*, pg. 809

TANGENT—Stainless Steel Flatware—Dansk International Designs Ltd.; *U.S. Public*, pg. 261

TANGLE-PROOF—Battery Booster Cable—General Cable Corporation; *Int'l*, pg. 1486

TANGLE RIDGE—NONE—Fortune Brands, inc.; *U.S. Public*, pg. 674

TANGLE TWIST—Toys—Mattel, Inc.; *U.S. Public*, pg. 1057

TANGO—Software—Veritas DGC Inc; *U.S. Private*, pg. 1136

TANGO BY MAX RAAB—NONE—J.G. Hook, Inc.; *U.S. Private*, pg. 538

TANGRAM—Cooperative Processing Software—Safeguard Scientifics, Inc.; *U.S. Public*, pg. 1424

TANGY—Catsup & Tomato Juice—Brooks Foods; *U.S. Private*, pg. 887

TANGY-C—Chewable Vitamin C—Nature's Bounty Inc.; *U.S. Public*, pg. 1166

TANGY TAFFY—Candy—Nestle USA; *Int'l*, pg. 916

TANK TOP INSUL—Rigid Board Insulation—Johns Manville Corporation; *U.S. Public*, pg. 927

TANKATITE—Marine Tank-Lid Packing—James Walker & Co. Limited; *Int'l*, pg. 1485

TANKHIDE—Liquid & Paste Paints, Primers, Enamels, Lacquers & Varnishes—PPG Industries, Inc.; *U.S. Public*, pg. 1245

TANKMASTER—Hose—HBD Industries, Inc.; *U.S. Private*, pg. 489

TANKTRAIN—Interconnected Tank Cars—GATX Corporation; *U.S. Public*, pg. 690

TANNER—Misses Dresses—Tanner Co.; *U.S. Private*, pg. 1068

TANNER SPORT—Misses Sportswear—Tanner Co.; *U.S. Private*, pg. 1068

TANNIVER—Chemical Reagant—Hach Company; *U.S. Public*, pg. 773

TANN'S—Eyewear—Logo of the Americas; *Int'l*, pg. 462

TANON EXPRESS—Quick Turn/Proto Type Services—EA Industries; *U.S. Public*, pg. 541

TANOSHII YOCHIEN—Monthly Japanese Children's Magazine—Kodansha Ltd.; *Int'l*, pg. 742

TANQUERAY—Gin—Guinness Import Company; *Int'l*, pg. 412

TANQUERAY—NONE—Guinness Plc; *Int'l*, pg. 412

TANQUERAY—Gin & Vodka—Schieffelin & Somerset Co.; *Int'l*, pg. 412

TANQUERAY—Gin—Shieffelin Somerset Co.; *Int'l*, pg. 412

TANQUERAY STERLING VODKA—NONE—Guinness Plc; *Int'l*, pg. 412

TANTUM—Antirheumatics—Kali-Chemie Aktiengesellschaft; *Int'l*, pg. 1278

TANTUNG—Alloys Carbide Tools & Dies—Fansteel, Inc.; *U.S. Public*, pg. 612

TANTUNG—Proprietery Alloy—Fansteel VR/Wesson-Plantsville; *U.S. Public*, pg. 612

TAORMINA—Broadloom—Couristan Inc.; *U.S. Private*, pg. 279

TAOS—Low Alcohol Beverage—Seagram Beverage Co.; *Int'l*, pg. 1215

TAP AIR—Commercial Airline—TAP Air Portugal; *Int'l*, pg. 1418

TAP-IT—Nylon Drive Anchor—Gunnebo Fastening Corp.; *U.S. Private*, pg. 488

TAP TUNES—AM/FM Water Resistant Radio with LCD Clock—Sony Electronics; *Int'l*, pg. 1281

TAPAZOLE—Thyroid Hormone—Jones Medical Industries Inc.; *U.S. Public*, pg. 933

TAPAZOLE—Methimazole, Lilly—Eli Lilly and Company; *U.S. Public*, pg. 992

TAPDEK—Roof Fastening System—Elco Textron; *U.S. Public*, pg. 1590

TAPE CABLE—Multiple Wire Electrical Conductor—BICC Brand-Rex; *Int'l*, pg. 120

TAPE DOPE—Plumbing Chemical—Hercules Chemical Co., Inc.; *U.S. Private*, pg. 523

TAPE-ID—Labels for Tape Reels—Tab Products Co.; *U.S. Public*, pg. 1559

TAPE-ON—Storm Window Kit—Warp Brothers; *U.S. Private*, pg. 412

TAPE-PAK—Fish Tape—Ideal Industries, Inc.; *U.S. Private*, pg. 557

TAPE TWISTERS—Chewing Gum—Amurol Confections Co.; *U.S. Public*, pg. 1781

TAPE 250 TAPE DRIVE—NONE—Iomega Corporation; *U.S. Public*, pg. 912

TAPE-UP!—Service Products—R&B, Inc.; *U.S. Public*, pg. 1354

TAPE WORLD—Retail Music Store—Trans World Entertainment Corporation; *U.S. Public*, pg. 1629

TAPECOAT—Corrosion Protection Tape Products—T C Manufacturing Company, Inc.; *U.S. Private*, pg. 1062

TAPER BOLT—Masonry Anchor—Gunnebo Fastening Corp.; *U.S. Private*, pg. 488

TAPER CELL—Flow Cell Design—Millipore Corporation; *U.S. Public*, pg. 1112

TAPERASER—Typwriter Correction Tape—Dixon Ticonderoga Company; *U.S. Public*, pg. 514

TAPERCUT—Surgical Needles—Ethicon, Inc.; *U.S. Public*, pg. 928

TAPERFIT—Ear Plugs—Aearo Company; *U.S. Private*, pg. 23

TAPERLINE—Brush Head—John O. Butler Co.; *Int'l*, pg. 1320

TAPERLOCK—Sprockets & Related Hardware—Rockwell International Corporation; *U.S. Public*, pg. 1397

TAPESHOOTER—Tape Dispensing Machine—Ascom Hasler Mailing Systems, Inc.; *Int'l*, pg. 86

TAPESTRIES—Dinnerware—Dansk International Designs Ltd.; *U.S. Public*, pg. 1136

TAPESTRY—Printing Paper—Georgia-Pacific Corporation; *U.S. Public*, pg. 735

TAPESTRY—Value-Oriented Home Entertainment Catalog—Hanover Direct, Inc.; *U.S. Public*, pg. 782

TAPESTRY—Home Decorating—Hanover Direct Pennsylvania, Inc.; *U.S. Public*, pg. 782

TAPESTRY—Paperback Books—Simon & Schuster; *U.S. Private*, pg. 777

TAPPAN—NONE—Electrolux, AB; *Int'l*, pg. 438

TAPPAN—Appliances—Frigidaire Home Products; *Int'l*, pg. 439

TAPPAN—Major Appliances—White Consolidated Industries, Inc.; *U.S. Public*, pg. 439

TAPTITE—Bolts & Screws—Continental/Midland, Inc.; *U.S. Private*, pg. 268

TAPTONE—Container Inspection Systems—Benthos, Inc.; *U.S. Public*, pg. 212

TAR-GARD—Cigarette Filters—Venturi Inc.; *U.S. Private*, pg. 1068

TARA—Shirts & Pajamas—Arnotts plc; *Int'l*, pg. 81

TARAMET STERLING—Lead-Free Solders—Taracorp, Inc.; *U.S. Private*, pg. 1068

TARCA—Track—Shepard Niles, Inc.; *U.S. Private*, pg. 992

TARCIL—Antibiotic—SmithKline Beecham plc; *Int'l*, pg. 1264

TAREYTON—Cigarettes—Brown & Williamson Tobacco Corp.; *Int'l*, pg. 111

TARGA—Mobile Audio—Inkel USA Corporation; *U.S. Private*, pg. 563

TARGA—Car—Porsche Cars North America, Inc.; *Int'l*, pg. 1063

TARGA—Digital Video Editing—Truevision, Inc.; *U.S. Public*, pg. 1642

TARGA BY SHEAFFER—Writing Instruments—Sheaffer Inc.; *Int'l*, pg. 542

TARGET—NONE—Coles Myer Ltd.; *Int'l*, pg. 306

TARGET—Software—GenRad, Inc.; *U.S. Public*, pg. 731

TARGET—Brushes—Mill-Rose Company; *U.S. Private*, pg. 746

TARGET—Pest Control—Reckitt & Colman plc; *Int'l*, pg. 1089

TARGET—Discount Stores—Target Stores; *U.S. Public*, pg. 489

TARGET EUROPA—NONE—Market Facts, Inc.; *U.S. Public*, pg. 1046

TARGET LIFE—Universal Life Insurance—New York Life Insurance Company; *U.S. Private*, pg. 794

TARGET MARKETING—Magazine—North American Publishing Company; *U.S. Private*, pg. 803

TARGET RX—In-Store Pharmacy Advertising—News America Marketing; *Int'l*, pg. 925

TARGET TIP—Leads—Medtronic, Inc.; *U.S. Public*, pg. 1082

TARGET TUNING—Radio & Television Sets—Zenith Electronics Corp.; *U.S. Public*, pg. 1790

TARGETEER—Beverage Carriers & Packaging Machine—Riverwood International Corporation; *U.S. Public*, pg. 1391

TARGETER—Software—Information Resources, Inc.; *U.S. Public*, pg. 875

TARIVID—Infections—Hoechst Marion Roussel, Inc.; *Int'l*, pg. 624

TARNI-SHIELD—Tarnish Preventing Metal Cleaner—3M; *U.S. Public*, pg. 1604

TARNIBAN—Antitarnish for Silver—Technic Incorporated; *U.S. Private*, pg. 1071

TARN-X—Tarnish Remover, Metal Glazes, Tarn-X Jewelry Cleaner—Jelmar Company; *U.S. Private*, pg. 585

TARO—Light Commercial Vehicle—Volkswagen AG; *Int'l*, pg. 1473

TARVO—Baked Goods—Meneba N.V.; *Int'l*, pg. 555

TASC—Cathodic Protection—Corrpro Companies, Inc.; *U.S. Public*, pg. 451

TASCAM—Professional Sound Equip.—Teac America, Inc.; *Int'l*, pg. 1360

TASCO—Consumer Optical Products—Irwin Toy Ltd.; *Int'l*, pg. 688

TASCO—Company Name—Tasco Sales Inc.; *U.S. Private*, pg. 928

TASCOM—Automated Message System—Conrac Display Products; *U.S. Private*, pg. 264

TASCOR—Outsourcing Division—Norrell Corporation; *U.S. Public*, pg. 1192

TASHAN—Cream—Block Drug Company, Inc.; *U.S. Public*, pg. 236

TASKCARD—Electrical Technology—Dranetz-BMI; *U.S. Private*, pg. 1144

TASKITS—NONE—Medline Industries, Inc.; *U.S. Private*, pg. 728

TASKVIEW—Handheld Status Display—Nellcor Puritan Bennett Incorporated; *U.S. Public*, pg. 1039

TASMAR—Parkinson's Disease Drug Therapy—Hoffmann-La Roche Inc.; *Int'l*, pg. 1120

TASMAR—Parkinson's Disease Tablets—Roche Holding Ltd.; *Int'l*, pg. 1119

TASSELLI—Food Equipment—Premark International, Inc.; *U.S. Public*, pg. 1321

TASTE O'SEA—Frozen Seafood—ConAgra, Inc.; *U.S. Public*, pg. 425

TASTE O'SEA—Frozen Dinners & Foodservice—O'Donnell-Usen Fisheries Corp.; *U.S. Public*, pg. 427

TASTE OF AMERICA—Cigarettes—Liggett Group Inc.; *U.S. Public*, pg. 259

TASTE OF HOME—NONE—Richfood Holdings, Inc.; *U.S. Public*, pg. 1388

TASTE OF PARADISE—Papaya—Calavo Growers of California; *U.S. Private*, pg. 199

TASTE OF THE ALPS—Hot Cocoa Mix—Genesee Corporation; *U.S. Public*, pg. 728

TASTE OF THE MISSISSIPPI—Riverboat Cruise Trips—American Classic Voyagers Company; *U.S. Private*, pg. 380

TASTEE—Corn, Cane, Pancake & Waffle Syrup—Whitfield Foods, Inc.; *U.S. Private*, pg. 1173

TASTEE CRISP—Menu Item—Tastee Freez International Inc.; *U.S. Private*, pg. 1069

TASTEE FREEZ—Restaurants & Menu Items—Tastee Freez International Inc.; *U.S. Private*, pg. 1069

TASTEMATE—Water Filter—Parker Hannifin Corporation; *U.S. Public*, pg. 1259

TASTER'S CHOICE—Instant Coffee—Nestle S.A.; *Int'l*, pg. 915

TASTER'S CHOICE—Coffee—Nestle USA; *Int'l*, pg. 916

THE TASTES OF SUNSET—Multi-Market Highlighting Presentation—Sunset Publishing Corporation; *U.S. Public*, pg. 1613

TASTI-LEAN—Turkeys & Turkey Products—Norbest, Inc.; *U.S. Private*, pg. 801

TASTIT—Imitation Vanilla—Adams Extract Co., Inc.; *U.S. Private*, pg. 16

TASTONE—Yeast—Universal Foods Corporation; *U.S. Public*, pg. 1695

TASTY BASTED—Poultry Items—Tyson Foods, Inc.; *U.S. Public*, pg. 1652

TASTY BIRD—Food Service Poultry Items—Tyson Foods, Inc.; *U.S. Public*, pg. 1652

TASTY WINGS—Poultry Items—Tyson Foods, Inc.; *U.S. Public*, pg. 1652

TASTYBIRD—Foodservice Poultry Items—Louis Kemp Seafood Co.; *U.S. Public*, pg. 1652

TASTYBIRD IQF—Foodservice Frozen Items—Louis Kemp Seafood Co.; *U.S. Public*, pg. 1652

TASTYKAKE—Bakery Goods—Tasty Baking Company; *U.S. Public*, pg. 1561

TATA SAFARI—NONE—Tata Engineering & Locomotive Co. Ltd. (TELCO); *Int'l*, pg. 369

TATA SHERPARI—NONE—Tata Engineering & Locomotive Co. Ltd. (TELCO); *Int'l*, pg. 369

TATA SPORT—NONE—Tata Engineering & Locomotive Co. Ltd. (TELCO); *Int'l*, pg. 369

TATA SUMO—NONE—Tata Engineering & Locomotive Co. Ltd. (TELCO); *Int'l*, pg. 369

TATCH-A-CLEAT—Conveyor Belt Cleats—Flexible Steel Lacing Company; *U.S. Private*, pg. 413

TATE—Flooring Systems—Carter Holt Harvey Limited; *U.S. Public*, pg. 904

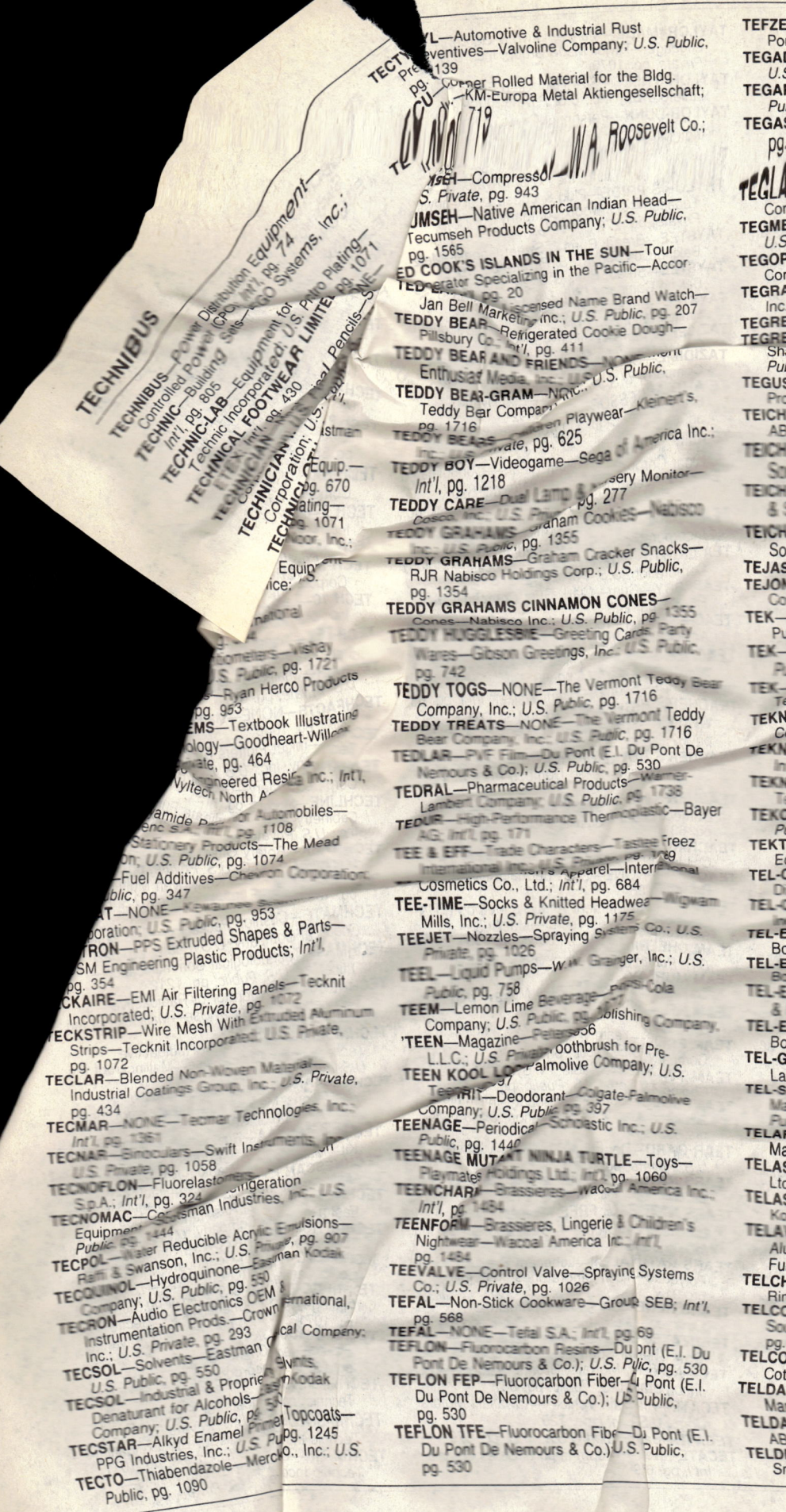

TECHNIBUS

TECHNIBUS—Power Distribution Equipment—Controlled Power Co.; *Int'l*, pg. 74

TECHNIC—Building Sets—LEGO Systems, Inc.; pg. 805

TECHNIC-LAB—Equipment for Plating—Technic Incorporated; *U.S. Priv* pg. 1071

TECHNICAL FOOTWEAR LIMITED—

TECHNICIAN—Eastman ... ETEX; pg. 430 ... Corporation; *U.S. P...*

TECHNICIAN—... Equip.— ... pg. 670

TECHNI... ... Plating— ... 1071 ...cor, Inc.;

...

...Automotive & Industrial Rust ...eventives—Valvoline Company; *U.S. Public*, pg. ...139 pg. ... ...Corner Rolled Material for the Bldg. ...KM-Europa Metal Aktiengesellschaft; ... 719

...W.A. Roosevelt Co.;

...SEH—Compressor... *S. Pivate*, pg. 943

...UMSEH—Native American Indian Head— Tecumseh Products Company; *U.S. Public*, pg. 1565

...ED COOK'S ISLANDS IN THE SUN—Tour ...erator Specializing in the Pacific—Accor ... pg. 20

...Jan Bell ...icensed Name Brand Watch— Marketing, Inc.; *U.S. Public*, pg. 207

TEDDY BEAR—Refrigerated Cookie Dough— Pillsbury Co.; *Int'l*, pg. 411

TEDDY BEAR AND FRIENDS—NONE... Enthusias Media, Inc.; *U.S. Public*,

TEDDY BEAR-GRAM—NR... Teddy Bear Compan... pg. 1716

TEDDY BEARS...ren Playwear—Kleinert's, Inc.; ...rivate, pg. 625

TEDDY BOY—Videogame—Sega of America Inc.; *Int'l*, pg. 1218

TEDDY CARE—Dual Lamp & ...sery Monitor— Cosco, Inc.; *U.S. P...* pg. 277

TEDDY GRAHAMS—...Graham Cookies—Nabisco Inc.; *U.S. Public*, pg. 1355

TEDDY GRAHAMS—Graham Cracker Snacks— RJR Nabisco Holdings Corp.; *U.S. Public*, pg. 1354

TEDDY GRAHAMS CINNAMON CONES— Cones—Nabisco Inc.; *U.S. Public*, pg. 1355

TEDDY HUGGLESBIE—Greeting Cards, Party Wares—Gibson Greetings, Inc.; *U.S. Public*, pg. 742

TEDDY TOGS—NONE—The Vermont Teddy Bear Company, Inc.; *U.S. Public*, pg. 1716

TEDDY TREATS—NONE—The Vermont Teddy Bear Company, Inc.; *U.S. Public*, pg. 1716

TEDLAR—PVF Film—Du Pont (E.I. Du Pont De Nemours & Co.); *U.S. Public*, pg. 530

TEDRAL—Pharmaceutical Products—Warner-Lambert Company; *U.S. Public*, pg. 1738

TEDUR—High-Performance Thermoplastic—Bayer AG; *Int'l*, pg. 171

TEE & EFF—Trade Characters—Tastee Freez International Inc.; ...

...Apparel—International Cosmetics Co., Ltd.; *Int'l*, pg. 684

TEE-TIME—Socks & Knitted Headwear—Wigwam Mills, Inc.; *U.S. Private*, pg. 1175

TEEJET—Nozzles—Spraying Systems Co.; *U.S. Private*, pg. 1026

TEEL—Liquid Pumps—W.W. Grainger, Inc.; *U.S. Public*, pg. 758

TEEM—Lemon Lime Beverage—PepsiCola Company; *U.S. Public*, pg. ...

'TEEN—Magazine—Peters... L.L.C.; *U.S. P...* ...oothbrush for Pre-Palmolive Company; *U.S.*

TEEN KOOL L... ... ...RIT—Deodorant—Colgate-Palmolive Company; *U.S. Public*, pg. 397

TEENAGE—Periodical—Scholastic Inc.; *U.S. Public*, pg. 1440

TEENAGE MUTANT NINJA TURTLE—Toys— Playmates Holdings Ltd.; *Int'l*, pg. 1060

TEENCHARM—Brassieres—Wacoal America Inc.; *Int'l*, pg. 1484

TEENFORM—Brassieres, Lingerie & Children's Nightwear—Wacoal America Inc.; *Int'l*, pg. 1484

TEEVALVE—Control Valve—Spraying Systems Co.; *U.S. Private*, pg. 1026

TEFAL—Non-Stick Cookware—Group SEB; *Int'l*, pg. 568

TEFAL—NONE—Tefal S.A.; *Int'l*, pg. 69

TEFLON—Fluorocarbon Resins—Du Pont (E.I. Du Pont De Nemours & Co.); *U.S. Public*, pg. 530

TEFLON FEP—Fluorocarbon Fiber—Du Pont (E.I. Du Pont De Nemours & Co.); *U.S. Public*, pg. 530

TEFLON TFE—Fluorocarbon Fiber—Du Pont (E.I. Du Pont De Nemours & Co.); *U.S. Public*, pg. 530

TEFZEL—Fluoropolymer Resins—Du Pont (E.I. Du Pont De Nemours & Co.); *U.S. Public*, pg. 530

TEGADERM—Transparent Dressing, Medical—3M; *U.S. Public*, pg. 1604

TEGAPORE—Wound Contact Material—3M; *U.S. Public*, pg. 1604

TEGASORB—Ulcer Dressing—3M; *U.S. Public*, pg. 1604

TEGLAR—Flexible Planar Radomes—Andrew Corporation; *U.S. Public*, pg. 112

TEGMER—Plasticizers—The C.P. Hall Company; *U.S. Private*, pg. 495

TEGOPEN—Antibiotic—Bristol-Myers Squibb Company; *U.S. Public*, pg. 253

TEGRA—Polycarbonate Lens—BMC Industries, Inc.; *U.S. Public*, pg. 162

TEGRETOL—Antiepileptic—Novartis; *Int'l*, pg. 972

TEGRETOL—NONE—Novartis Pharmaceuticals; Shampoos—Block Drug Company, Inc.; *U.S. Public*, pg. 236

TEGUSOL—Clay Roof Tile—GAF Premium Products, Inc.; *U.S. Private*, pg. 433

TEICHERT—Picture-Framing Products—Esselte AB; *Int'l*, pg. 459

TEICHERT AGGREGATES—NONE—A. Teichert & Son, Inc.; *U.S. Private*, pg. 1072

TEICHERT CONSTRUCTION—NONE—A. Teichert & Son, Inc.; *U.S. Private*, pg. 1072

TEICHERT PRECAST—NONE—A. Teichert & Son, Inc.; *U.S. Private*, pg. 1072

TEJAS DE CHENA—NONE—ETEX; *Int'l*, pg. 430

TEJON RANCH—General Farming—Tejon Ranch Company; *U.S. Public*, pg. 1566

TEK—Toothbrushes—Playtex Products Corp.; *U.S. Public*, pg. 1311

TEK—Toothbrushes—Playtex Products Inc.; *U.S. Public*, pg. 1310

TEK—Electronic Test & Measurement Equip.— Tektronix, Inc.; *U.S. Public*, pg. 1567

TEKNA—Flashlights & Sunglasses—RAYOVAC Corporation; *U.S. Private*, pg. 912

TEKNAR—Biological Insecticide—Novartis AG; *Int'l*, pg. 971

TEKNISEAL—Closure Liner Sealings Materials— Tekni-Plex, Inc.; *U.S. Private*, pg. 1073

TEKONSHA—Brake Parts—Echlin Inc.; *U.S. Public*, pg. 560

TEKTRONIX—Electronic Test & Measurement Equip.—Tektronix, Inc.; *U.S. Public*, pg. 1567

TEL-CHARGE—Telephone Billing System—Conrac Display Products; *U.S. Private*, pg. 264

TEL-CRAFT—Telephone Access.—Waxman Industries, Inc.; *U.S. Public*, pg. 1748

TEL-E-BALL—Sporting Equipment—Brunswick Bowling & Billiards Corp.; *U.S. Public*, pg. 265

TEL-E-BRITE—Sporting Equipment—Brunswick Bowling & Billiards Corp.; *U.S. Public*, pg. 265

TEL-E-FOUL—Sporting Equip.—Brunswick Bowling & Billiards Corp.; *U.S. Public*, pg. 265

TEL-E-SCORE—Sporting Equip.—Brunswick Bowling & Billiards Corp.; *U.S. Public*, pg. 265

TEL-GARD—Prelubricated PVC Conduit—The Lamson & Sessions Co.; *U.S. Public*, pg. 976

TEL-STIK—Equipment for Lifting & Lowering Materials—Blount International, Inc.; *U.S. Public*, pg. 237

TELAFLEX—Machine Tool Covers—A&A Manufacturing Co.; *U.S. Private*, pg. 1

TELASOL—Soluble Dyes—Clariant International Ltd.; *Int'l*, pg. 624

TELASSISTANCE—Computer Network—Eastman Kodak Company; *U.S. Public*, pg. 550

TELAWEAVE VINYL MESH—Indoor/Outdoor Aluminum Furniture—Telescope Casual Furniture, Inc.; *U.S. Private*, pg. 1074

TELCHIME—Replacement Signal for Telephone Ringers—Wheelock Inc.; *U.S. Private*, pg. 1171

TELCOM-PAC—Telecommunications Power Source—Reliability Incorporated; *U.S. Public*, pg. 1373

TELCOT—Electronic Marketing System—Plains Cotton Co-op Association; *U.S. Private*, pg. 868

TELDANE—Seasonal Allergic Rhinitis—Hoechst Marion Roussel, Inc.; *Int'l*, pg. 624

TELDANEX—Repiratory Pharmaceutical—Astra AB; *Int'l*, pg. 93

TELDRIN—Cough, Cold & Influenza Treatment— SmithKline Beecham plc; *Int'l*, pg. 1264

TELE-CUSTOMER—Product Information Service—Eastman Kodak Company; *U.S. Public*, pg. 550

TELE-EKTRA—Cameras—Eastman Kodak Company; *U.S. Public*, pg. 550

TELE-EKTRALITE—Cameras—Eastman Kodak Company; *U.S. Public*, pg. 550

TELE-FI—Headphone—Telex Communications, Inc.; *U.S. Private*, pg. 1074

TELE-INSTAMATIC—Camera—Eastman Kodak Company; *U.S. Public*, pg. 550

TELE-POCHE—French Television Magazine—EMAP France; *Int'l*, pg. 451

TELE-STYLELITE—Cameras—Eastman Kodak Company; *U.S. Public*, pg. 550

TELE TRACK—Theater of Racing—General Instrument Corporation; *U.S. Public*, pg. 716

TELE-TWIN—Paperboard Carton—Georgia-Pacific Corporation; *U.S. Public*, pg. 735

TELE-THERMOMETER—Scientific Instruments—YSI Incorporated; *U.S. Private*, pg. 1195

TELECARE—Health Information Solution for Hospitals—Brite Voice Systems, Inc.; *U.S. Public*, pg. 257

TELECENTER—Telephone Communication Systems—Rauland-Borg Corporation; *U.S. Private*, pg. 911

TELECHECK—Check Verification Services—TeleCheck Services, Inc.; *U.S. Public*, pg. 631

TELECOM ASIA—Trade Periodical—Advanstar Communications; *U.S. Private*, pg. 22

TELECOMM-DUCT—PE Duct—Tamaqua Cable Products Corp.; *Int'l*, pg. 417

TELECONNECT—Diversified Long Distance Service—MCI Systemhouse; *U.S. Public*, pg. 1024

TELEDYNE RELAYS—NONE—Milgray Electronics, Inc.; *U.S. Public*, pg. 205

TELEFLEX—Automobile, Marine & Industrial Equipment—Teleflex Incorporated; *U.S. Public*, pg. 1569

TELEFLORA—Flowers By Wire—Teleflora, LLC; *U.S. Private*, pg. 941

TELEGAN GAS MONITORING—Gas Detection Instruments—Halma p.l.c.; *Int'l*, pg. 589

TELEGLOBE—Data Communication Service—Teleglobe, Inc.; *Int'l*, pg. 1373

TELEGLOBE INTERNATIONAL—Data Communiacation Service—Teleglobe, Inc.; *Int'l*, pg. 1373

TELEGLOBE MARINE—Subsea Cable Engineering Service—Teleglobe, Inc.; *Int'l*, pg. 1373

TELEGYR 8500—EMS-Energy Management Systems—Landis & Staefa, Inc.; *Int'l*, pg. 800

TELEK—Accessory Lenses & Industrial Publication—Eastman Kodak Company; *U.S. Public*, pg. 550

TELELECT—Hydraulic Platform—Simon Engineering plc; *Int'l*, pg. 1251

TELEMARK—Ink Jet Printer—Diagraph Corporation; *U.S. Private*, pg. 330

TELEMASTER—Spotting Scope/Telephoto Lens—Swift Instruments, Inc.; *U.S. Private*, pg. 1058

TELEMATCH—Computerized Phone Directory & Data Base Service—Gannett Offset-Springfield Plant; *U.S. Public*, pg. 700

TELEMECANIQUE—Electrical & Industrial Control—Schneider S.A.; *Int'l*, pg. 1207

TELEMESSAGE—Messaging Service—British Telecommunications plc; *Int'l*, pg. 222

TELEMETRAC—Copier Count Tracking System—Equitrac Corporation; *U.S. Public*, pg. 590

TELEMIX—Telephone interface—Harris Broadcast Division; *U.S. Public*, pg. 791

TELENATION—NONE—Market Facts, Inc.; *U.S. Public*, pg. 1046

TELENGARD—Microcomputer Game—Monarch Avalon, Inc.; *U.S. Public*, pg. 1123

TELENURSE—Nurse Call Communications System—Rauland-Borg Corporation; *U.S. Private*, pg. 911

TELEPAGE NORTHWEST—Paging Service Provider—AT&T Wireless Services; *U.S. Public*, pg. 11

TELEPART—Electronic Ordering Terminal—CCI/Triad Automotive; *U.S. Private*, pg. 193

TELEPARTNER—Modems—Lucent Technologies Inc.; *U.S. Public*, pg. 1017

TELEPHONY—Publication for Telecommunication Systems—Intertec Publishing; *U.S. Public*, pg. 1327

TELERACK—Telecommunications Power Supply Rack—Lambda Electronics Inc.; *Int'l*, pg. 1241

TELERAY—CRT Terminals—Research, Incorporated; *U.S. Public*, pg. 1382

TELESCIENCES—Telecommunication Equipment—Axiom Inc.; *U.S. Public*, pg. 157

TELESCOPING DRAIN—Holding Tank Evacuation System—Thetford Corporation; *U.S. Private*, pg. 352

TELESCRIPT GRAPHICAL EDITOR—Icon-based Software for Managing Call Routing Parameters—Rockwell Switching Systems Div.; *U.S. Public*, pg. 1398

TELESET—Headphone—Telex Communications, Inc.; *U.S. Private*, pg. 1074

TELESPAR—Tubing—Unistrut Corporation; *U.S. Public*, pg. 1651

TELESQURT—Telescopic Boom Watertower (Firefighting)—Snorkel; *U.S. Private*, pg. 500

TELESSENTIALS—Educational Services—Lucent Technologies Inc.; *U.S. Public*, pg. 1017

TELESURVEILLANCE—NONE—Nellcor Puritan Bennett Incorporated; *U.S. Public*, pg. 1039

TELETAPE—Flat Undercarpet Telephone Cable—BICC Brand-Rex; *Int'l*, pg. 120

TELETHIN—Earphone—Telex Communications, Inc.; *U.S. Private*, pg. 1074

TELETRACE—Phone Monitor—Medtronic, Inc.; *U.S. Public*, pg. 1082

TELETRAM—Mining Equipment—Atlas Copco Wagner Inc.; *Int'l*, pg. 96

TELEVATOR—Trim Tabs, Power Boats—Teleflex Incorporated; *U.S. Public*, pg. 1569

TELEVIDEO SYSTEMS, INC.—Computer Systems—Televideo, Inc.; *U.S. Public*, pg. 1572

TELEVISION ASIA—Publication Covering Asian Television Broadcasting & Programming—Reed Elsevier Business Information; *Int'l*, pg. 1095

TELEVISION EUROPE—London-Based Publication Covering International Television Industry—Reed Elsevier Business Information; *Int'l*, pg. 1095

TELEVISION PROGRAMMING SOURCEBOOK—Programming Guide—North American Publishing Company; *U.S. Private*, pg. 803

TELHORN—Accessory Signal on Telephone (High Noise Areas)—Wheelock Inc.; *U.S. Private*, pg. 1171

TELKEE—Key Control Systems—Telkee; *U.S. Private*, pg. 1053

TELKEM—Solder Fluxes & Solvents—Litton Industries, Inc.; *U.S. Public*, pg. 1002

TELL-A-PHONE—Bill Pay by Phone—Downey Savings & Loan Association, F.A.; *U.S. Public*, pg. 526

TELL/BEACON—Weed Control—Novartis; *Int'l*, pg. 972

TELL-I-VISION—Guides and Folders—Smead Manufacturing Company; *U.S. Private*, pg. 1006

TELL ME ON SUNDAY—Musical—Really Useful Holdings Limited; *Int'l*, pg. 1089

TELLABS—Telecommunications Products—Tellabs Operations, Inc.; *U.S. Public*, pg. 1572

TELLICO VILLAGE—Recreational and Retirement Communities—Cooper Communities, Inc.; *U.S. Private*, pg. 273

TELLITE—Electronic Equipment—Eaton Corp., Aerospace & Commercial Controls Div.; *U.S. Public*, pg. 557

TELLOY—Special Steels—Inland Steel Industries, Inc.; *U.S. Public*, pg. 879

TELMA—Soups, Sauces, Bouillons, Mayonnaise, Cereals—Bestfoods; *U.S. Public*, pg. 223

TELME—Electric Retarders for Businesses—Labinal SA; *Int'l*, pg. 785

TELONE—Soil Fumigant—The Dow Chemical Company; *U.S. Public*, pg. 522

TELSMITH—Quarry Plants—Telsmith, Inc.; *U.S. Public*, pg. 141

TELSTA—Telecommunications Products—American Financial Group; *U.S. Public*, pg. 75

TELSTAR—Coated Printing Paper—The Mead Corporation; *U.S. Public*, pg. 1074

TELSTROBE—Auxiliary Flashing Signal for Telephone—Wheelock Inc.; *U.S. Private*, pg. 1171

TELXON—Computer Equipment—Telxon Corporation; *U.S. Public*, pg. 1573

TELZON—Cross-Connection Devices—Thomas & Betts Corporation; *U.S. Public*, pg. 1597

TEM-U-LAC—Screw Conveyor Coupling Bolts—Screw Conveyor Corp.; *U.S. Private*, pg. 977

TEMA—Mechanical Design Standards—American Precision Industries Inc.; *U.S. Public*, pg. 90

TEMAC—Books—Encyclopaedia Britannica, Inc.; *U.S. Private*, pg. 375

TEMCO—NONE—Graham-Field Health Products, Inc.; *U.S. Public*, pg. 757

TEMCO—NONE—The Kent Company; *Int'l*, pg. 440

TEMCO—Fireplace Systems—Temco Fireplace Products, Inc.; *U.S. Public*, pg. 1576

TEMCO—Zero Clearance Metal Fireplaces, Gas Fireplaces & Gas Logs—Temtex Industries Inc.; *U.S. Public*, pg. 1575

TEMCO AMERICAN DREAM—NONE—Temtex Industries Inc.; *U.S. Public*, pg. 1575

TEMESCAL—Vacuum Equipment—BOC Coating Technology; *Int'l*, pg. 121

TEMFLEX—Electrical Tape—3M; *U.S. Public*, pg. 1604

TEMGESIC—Analgesic—Boehringer Mannheim GmbH; *Int'l*, pg. 331

TEMGESIC—Strong Analgesic—Reckitt & Colman plc; *Int'l*, pg. 1089

TEMIC—NONE—Daimler-Benz Aktiengesellschaft; *Int'l*, pg. 366

TEMOPEN—Treatment of Urinary & Respiratory Tract Infections—SmithKline Beecham plc; *Int'l*, pg. 1264

TEMOVATE—Dermatology Cream & Ointment—Glaxo Wellcome Inc.; *Int'l*, pg. 552

TEMP-ALARM—Temperature Signaling Paint—Tempil Inc.; *U.S. Private*, pg. 90

TEMP-LACE—Electronic Lacing Tape—Gudebrod, Inc.; *U.S. Private*, pg. 486

TEMP-PLATE—Heat Transfer System—Paul Mueller Company; *U.S. Public*, pg. 1141

TEMP-RITE—Insulated Tray Systems—Aladdin Synergetics, Inc.; *U.S. Private*, pg. 31

TEMP-RITE II—Cook/Chill Meal Service Systems—Aladdin Synergetics, Inc.; *U.S. Private*, pg. 31

TEMP RITE II EXCEL—Cook/Chill Meal Service Systems—Aladdin Synergetics, Inc.; *U.S. Private*, pg. 31

TEMP-TONE—Cookware—Regal Ware, Inc.; *U.S. Private*, pg. 917

TEMPA SPARE—Mini Spare Tire—Bridgestone/Firestone, Inc.; *U.S. Public*, pg. 213

TEMPCAL—Tester—Howell Instruments Inc.; *U.S. Private*, pg. 543

TEMPCO—Controllers—Barnstead/Thermolyne Corporation; *U.S. Public*, pg. 1545

TEMPCOR—Magnetic Steel Laminations—Tempel Steel Company; *U.S. Public*, pg. 1075

TEMPER-TUF—Glass Tempuring—Gemtron Corporation; *Int'l*, pg. 1523

TEMPERATURE PROBES—Rectal/Esophageal Temperature Probe—Datascope Corp.; *U.S. Public*, pg. 487

TEMPERFOAM—Rehabilitation Product—Alimed, Inc.; *U.S. Private*, pg. 34

TEMPERNO—Greek Pepperoncini—Trappey's Fine Foods, Inc.; *U.S. Private*, pg. 105

TEMPEST/2—Tables—Howe Furniture Corporation; *U.S. Private*, pg. 543

TEMPGARD—Test Equipment—Tenney Environmental; *U.S. Public*, pg. 1076

TEMPIL MARKER—Paint in a Tube—Tempil Inc.; *U.S. Private*, pg. 90

TEMPILABEL—Temperature Monitors—Tempil Inc.; *U.S. Private*, pg. 90

TEMPILAQ—Temperature Indicating Liquid—Tempil Inc.; *U.S. Private*, pg. 90

TEMPILINK—Sterilization Indicator Ink—Tempil Inc.; *U.S. Private*, pg. 90

TEMPILSTIK—Temperature Indicating Chalk—Tempil Inc.; *U.S. Private*, pg. 90

TEMPLE HALL—Cigars—General Cigar Company, Inc.; *U.S. Public*, pg. 708

TEMPO—Insecticide—Bayer AG; *Int'l*, pg. 171

TEMPO—Power Sources—Bowthorpe plc; *Int'l*, pg. 207

TEMPO—Personal Computers—Everex Systems Inc.; *Int'l*, pg. 498

TEMPO—Women's Retail Specialty Store—Gateway Apparel, Inc.; *U.S. Private*, pg. 441

TEMPO—Stick Vacuum Cleaner & Attached Tools—Hoover Company; *U.S. Public*, pg. 1065

TEMPO—Bathtub Wall Kit—Plaskolite Inc.; *U.S. Private*, pg. 870

TEMPO—Marine Aftermarket Prods.—Plasti-Kote Company Inc.; *U.S. Private*, pg. 870

TEMPO—Antacid—Thompson Medical Company, Inc.; *U.S. Private*, pg. 1083

TEMPO—Sanitary Paper Products—VP-Schickedanz AG; *U.S. Public*, pg. 1333

TEMPO 400—Watch Cleaning Machine—L&R Manufacturing Co.; *U.S. Private*, pg. 638

TEMPO MECHANICAL—NONE—TD Industries Inc.; *U.S. Private*, pg. 1063

TEMPO-TEK—Thermometers—Medline Industries, Inc.; *U.S. Private*, pg. 728

TEMPO 3—Open Office System—Knoll, Inc.; *U.S. Private*, pg. 627

TEMPOINT—Measuring Instrument—Bacharach Inc.; *U.S. Private*, pg. 109

TEMPORA—Felt—Central/Shippee, Inc.; *U.S. Private*, pg. 224

TEMPOSONICS—Transducers—MTS Systems Corporation; *U.S. Public*, pg. 1028

TEMPRA—Analgesics—Bristol-Myers Squibb Company; *U.S. Public*, pg. 253

TEMPRA—Mid-Sized Family Sedan—Fiat Auto SpA; *Int'l*, pg. 480

TEMPRESIST—NONE—Carpenter Technology Corporation; *U.S. Public*, pg. 307

TEMPRINT—Sublistatic Ink—Raffi & Swanson, Inc.; *U.S. Private*, pg. 907

TEMPROBE—Temperature Indicating Kit—Tempil Inc.; *U.S. Private*, pg. 90

TEMPROOF—Vibration Mounts—Lord Corporation; *U.S. Private*, pg. 675

TEMPSCRIBE—Measuring Instrument—Bacharach Inc.; *U.S. Private*, pg. 109

TEMPSTAR—HVAC Equipment—International Comfort Products; *U.S. Public*, pg. 898

TEMPSTAR—Heating & Cooling Products—International Comfort Products Corp.; *U.S. Public*, pg. 898

TEMPSTAR—Temperature Controller—Thermo Electric Co., Inc.; *U.S. Private*, pg. 1080

TEMPSTIK TEST KIT—Temperature Indicating Kit—Tempil Inc.; *U.S. Private*, pg. 90

TEMPTRON—Lead—Medtronic, Inc.; *U.S. Public*, pg. 1082

TEMRO—Cold Weather Products for Automobiles—The Budd Company; *Int'l*, pg. 1388

TEMTROL—Air Conditioners—Nortek, Inc.; *U.S. Public*, pg. 1192

TEN & ALWAYS—San-Napkins—Procter & Gamble Venezuela, C.A.; *U.S. Public*, pg. 1332

10-BENZAGEL—Pharmaceuticals—Rhone-Poulenc Rorer - U.S.; *Int'l*, pg. 1110

TEN HIGH—NONE—Barton Brands, Ltd.; *U.S. Public*, pg. 300

TEN HIGH—Bourbon—Barton Incorporated; *U.S. Public*, pg. 300

TEN HIGH BOURBON—Spirit—Allied Domecq PLC; *Int'l*, pg. 62

TEN-K—NONE—Novartis Pharmaceuticals; *Int'l*, pg. 973

10-K—Isotonic Sports Drink—Suntory Water Group, Inc.; *Int'l*, pg. 1321

TEN PEAKS—Tents, Backpacks & Sleeping Bags—Jinwoong Inc.; *Int'l*, pg. 706

'10+ SERIES—Self Priming Centrifugal Pumps—The Gorman-Rupp Company; *U.S. Public*, pg. 754

TEN POUNDER—Antenna—Telex Communications, Inc.; *U.S. Private*, pg. 1074

TEN STAR—NONE—Carpenter Technology Corporation; *U.S. Public*, pg. 307

TEN TERRIFIC NAILS—Applied Nails—Cover Girl Cosmetics; *U.S. Public*, pg. 1330

TEN-TUF ENVELOPES—Envelopes—Tension Envelope Corp.; *U.S. Private*, pg. 1077

10/22—Autoloading Carbine—Sturm, Ruger & Co., Inc.; *U.S. Public*, pg. 1526

TEN-X—Routing Switchers—Tektronix-Video & Networking Div., Grass Valley Products; *U.S. Public*, pg. 1567

TEN YEAR HOUSE PAINT—Paint—Pratt & Lambert United, Inc.; *U.S. Public*, pg. 1466

TENAMENE—Chemicals for use in Synthetic Resins—Eastman Kodak Company; *U.S. Public*, pg. 550

TENARO—Pizza—Little Lady Foods, Inc.; *U.S. Private*, pg. 671

TENAX—Plastic Products—Tenax Corporation; *Int'l*, pg. 193

TEND-R-FRESH—Poultry—Maple Leaf Foods Inc.; *Int'l*, pg. 841

TENDENSER—Trade Magazine—ICA Forlaget AB; *Int'l*, pg. 643

TENDER—Decubis Prevention—Graham-Field Health Products, Inc.; *U.S. Public*, pg. 757

TENDER AIR—Air Mattresses & Cushions—Graham-Field Health Products, Inc.; *U.S. Public*, pg. 757

TENDER CHOPS—Dry Dog Food—H.J. Heinz Company; *U.S. Public*, pg. 805

TENDER CHUNKS DINNERS—Dog Food—The Quaker Oats Company; *U.S. Public*, pg. 1347

TENDER CLOUD—Static Air Mattress—Graham-Field Health Products, Inc.; *U.S. Public*, pg. 757

TENDER DELITE—Snack Foods—Wyandot Inc.; *U.S. Private*, pg. 1193

TENDER FLO—Water Mattresses & Cushion—Graham-Field Health Products, Inc.; *U.S. Public*, pg. 757

TENDER GEL—Gel Mattresses & Cushions—Graham-Field Health Products, Inc.; *U.S. Public*, pg. 757

TENDER LEAF—House Plant Care—Dexol; *U.S. Public*, pg. 1390

TENDER LEAF—Tea—The Folger Coffee Company; *U.S. Public*, pg. 1331

TENDER MEATY CHUNX—Dog Food—The Jim Dandy Co., Inc.; *Int'l*, pg. 918

TENDER MOIST CHUNX—Dog Food—The Jim Dandy Co., Inc.; *Int'l*, pg. 918

TENDER REST—Sheets & Pillow Cases—Thomaston Mills, Inc.; *U.S. Public*, pg. 1599

TENDER TOUCH—Cotton Wool—Smith & Nephew PLC; *Int'l*, pg. 1263

TENDER TOUCH—Bread & Rolls—Stroehmann Bakeries; *Int'l*, pg. 1495

TENDER VITTLES—Cat Food—Ralston Purina Company; *U.S. Public*, pg. 1359

TENDEROAST—Precooked Entrees—Vienna Sausage Mfg. Co.; *U.S. Private*, pg. 1139

TENDERS AUSTRALIA—Manufacturing Magazine—Reed Business Information Pty. Limited; *Int'l*, pg. 1094

TENDERSWEET—Canned Vegetables—Owatonna Canning Company; *U.S. Private*, pg. 349

TENDRIL—Pacemaker Lead—St. Jude Medical, Inc.; *U.S. Public*, pg. 1427

TENET—NONE—Tenet Healthcare Corporation; *U.S. Public*, pg. 1576

TENET HEALTH SYSTEM—NONE—Tenet Healthcare Corporation; *U.S. Public*, pg. 1576

TENET HEALTHCARE—NONE—Tenet Healthcare Corporation; *U.S. Public*, pg. 1576

TENET SELECT—NONE—Tenet Healthcare Corporation; *U.S. Public*, pg. 1576

TENEX—Cardiovascular Drug—American Home Products Corporation; *U.S. Public*, pg. 79

TENEX—Sporting Ammunitionn—IMI Plc; *Int'l*, pg. 646

TENEX—Antihypertensive Agent—Wyeth-Ayerst Laboratories, Inc.; *U.S. Public*, pg. 80

TENFORM—Sheet Steel & Strip—British Steel Plc; *Int'l*, pg. 220

TENITE—Plastics—Eastman Chemical Company; *U.S. Public*, pg. 550

TENITE—Molding & Sheetforming Plastic Materials—Eastman Kodak Company; *U.S. Public*, pg. 550

TENITE HIFOR—Plastics Polymer—Eastman Chemical Company; *U.S. Public*, pg. 550

TENKAY—Self-Cleaning Dust Collector—Farr Company; *U.S. Private*, pg. 613

TENN-TOM—Printing Papers—Weyerhaeuser Company; *U.S. Public*, pg. 1764

TENNANT—Industrial Floor Sweepers, Floor Scrubbers, Floor Coatings—Tennant Company; *U.S. Public*, pg. 1577

TENNECO—Gas & Oil Services; Land Management Services—Tenneco Inc.; *U.S. Public*, pg. 1577

TENNENT'S 80 TRADITIONAL ALE—Ale—Bass PLC; *Int'l*, pg. 169

TENNENT'S EXPORT ALE—Premium Ale—Bass PLC; *Int'l*, pg. 169

TENNENT'S EXPORT LAGER—Lager—Bass PLC; *Int'l*, pg. 169

TENNENT'S EXTRA—Lager—Bass PLC; *Int'l*, pg. 169

TENNENT'S GOLD BIER—Lager—Bass PLC; *Int'l*, pg. 169

TENNENT'S LA—Lager—Bass PLC; *Int'l*, pg. 169

TENNENT'S LAGER—Lager—Bass PLC; *Int'l*, pg. 169

TENNENT'S LIGHT ALE—Ale—Bass PLC; *Int'l*, pg. 169

TENNENT'S MILK/XXX STOUT—Stout—Bass PLC; *Int'l*, pg. 169

TENNENT'S PILSNER—Lager—Bass PLC; *Int'l*, pg. 169

TENNENT'S 60 PALE ALE—Ale—Bass PLC; *Int'l*, pg. 169

TENNENT'S SPECIAL 70—Ale—Bass PLC; *Int'l*, pg. 169

TENNENT'S STOUT—Stout—Bass PLC; *Int'l*, pg. 169

TENNENT'S STRONG ALE—Strong Ale—Bass PLC; *Int'l*, pg. 169

TENNENT'S SUPER—Lager—Bass PLC; *Int'l*, pg. 169

TENNESSEE MANUFACTURERS REGISTER—Register—Manufacturers' News, Inc.; *U.S. Private*, pg. 700

TENNEY JR.—Test Equipment—Tenney Environmental; *U.S. Private*, pg. 1076

TENNEYMITE—Test Equipment—Tenney Environmental; *U.S. Private*, pg. 1076

TENNIS RACQUETS—NONE—Prince Sports Group Inc.; *U.S. Private*, pg. 884

THE TENNIS SPOT—Tennis Program—Westwood One, Inc.; *U.S. Public*, pg. 1763

TENNTROL—Institute Control System—Tenney Environmental; *U.S. Private*, pg. 1076

TENORETIC—Pharmaceutical—Zeneca Group Plc; *Int'l*, pg. 1524

TENORMIN—Pharmaceutical—Zeneca Group Plc; *Int'l*, pg. 1524

TENOX—Food-Grade Antioxidants—Eastman Chemical Company; *U.S. Public*, pg. 550

TENOX—Food-Grade Antioxidants—Eastman Kodak Company; *U.S. Public*, pg. 550

TENSABARRIER—Adjustable Spring Loaded Webbing Belt to Direct Crowds—Lawrence Metal Products, Inc.; *U.S. Private*, pg. 654

TENSETTE—Automatic Pipet—Hach Company; *U.S. Public*, pg. 773

TENSILBOND 125—Floor Decking—Wheeling Corrugating Co.; *U.S. Public*, pg. 1727

TENSILLITE—Steel Plate—WHX Corporation; *U.S. Public*, pg. 1726

TENSILOCK—Nuts—RB&W Corporation; *U.S. Public*, pg. 1259

TENSIOMAT—Tensiometer—Fisher Scientific Company; *U.S. Private*, pg. 658

TENSION GROOVED ENVELOPES—Envelopes—Tension Envelope Corp.; *U.S. Private*, pg. 1077

TENSION TAMER—Blend with St. John's Wort—Celestial Seasonings; *U.S. Public*, pg. 319

TENSIONERS—Tensioners—Electroid Co.; *U.S. Private*, pg. 369

TENSIONET—Packaging Net—Leucadia Inc. Manufacturing Division; *U.S. Public*, pg. 990

TENSOR—Elastic Bandages—The Kendall Company; *U.S. Public*, pg. 1647

TENSOR I—Portable Computerized Handtool—SPS Technologies, Inc.; *U.S. Public*, pg. 1419

TENTHSET—Adjustable Boring Bars—Kennametal Inc.; *U.S. Public*, pg. 950

TENTRON—Herbicide—The Dow Chemical Company; *U.S. Public*, pg. 522

TENUATE—Diet Pill—Hoechst Marion Roussel North America; *Int'l*, pg. 625

TENZCARE—Transcutaneous Electrical Nerve Stimulation Products—3M; *U.S. Public*, pg. 1604

TEPEE—Socks & Knitted Headwear—Wigwam Mills, Inc.; *U.S. Private*, pg. 1175

TEQUILA YUCATAN—Tequila—Groupe Pernod Ricard; *Int'l*, pg. 566

TER HUURNE—Chainstores—Koninklijke Ahold NV; *Int'l*, pg. 749

TERA SEARCH—COTS Imaging System for Organizing & Retrieving Large Databases—BTG, Inc.; *U.S. Public*, pg. 164

TERAHUB—High Capacity Broadband Telecommunications Switching Apparatus—DSC Communications Corporation; *U.S. Public*, pg. 475

TERATE—Resin—Hercules Incorporated; *U.S. Public*, pg. 809

TERAZOL—NONE—Johnson & Johnson; *U.S. Public*, pg. 927

TERAZOL 7—Vaginal Cream 0.4%—Ortho-McNeil Pharmaceutical Corporation; *U.S. Public*, pg. 929

TERAZOL 3—Vaginal Suppositories & Cream—Ortho-McNeil Pharmaceutical Corporation; *U.S. Public*, pg. 929

TERCEL—Automobile—Toyota Motor Corporation; *Int'l*, pg. 1411

TERCEL—Car—Toyota Motor Sales, U.S.A., Inc.; *Int'l*, pg. 1412

TERCOD—Refractory Crucibles—Ferro Corporation; *U.S. Public*, pg. 618

TEREX—Articulated Rigid Off-Highway Haulers—Terex Corporation; *U.S. Public*, pg. 1581

TEREX—Off-Highway Articulated & Rigid Dump Trucks—Terex Trucks; *U.S. Public*, pg. 1581

TEREX AERIALS—Aerial Work Platforms—Terex Corporation; *U.S. Public*, pg. 1581

TEREX-RO—Boom Trucks—Terex Corporation; *U.S. Public*, pg. 1581

TEREX TELELECT—Utility Aerial Devices—Terex Corporation; *U.S. Public*, pg. 1581

TERGITOL—Surfactants—Union Carbide Corporation; *U.S. Public*, pg. 1666

TERGOLIX—Dyes—Clariant International Ltd.; *Int'l*, pg. 624

TERI—Paper Towels, Washcloths—Kimberly-Clark Corporation; *U.S. Public*, pg. 958

TERIOS—1300 cc (Petrol) 4WD—Daihatsu Motor Corporation, Ltd.; *Int'l*, pg. 364

TERLON—NONE—Lawter International, Inc.; *U.S. Public*, pg. 980

TERMALENE—Oil Lubricant—Bel-Ray Company, Inc.; *U.S. Private*, pg. 130

TERMAPOST—Wiring Termination System—Raychem Corporation; *U.S. Public*, pg. 1362

TERMINIX—Pest Control Service—Duskin Co., Ltd.; *Int'l*, pg. 422

TERMINIX—Termite & Pest Control—The ServiceMaster Company; *U.S. Public*, pg. 1461

TERMINUS—Burglar Alarm Systems—Litton Industries, Inc.; *U.S. Public*, pg. 1002

TERMSEAL—Terminal Lug Caps—Raychem Corporation; *U.S. Public*, pg. 1362

TERMSHARE—Unstaffed MRI Service—Mobile Technology Inc.; *U.S. Private*, pg. 754

TERNELIN—Pharamceutical—Novartis AG; *Int'l*, pg. 971

TERPAL—Crop Protection Agent—BASF AG; *Int'l*, pg. 103

TERPINEOL 318—Terpene Alcohol—Hercules Incorporated; *U.S. Public*, pg. 809

TERRA—NONE—Comare Products; *U.S. Public*, pg. 1771

TERRA—Women's Walking Shoe—K-Swiss Inc.; *U.S. Public*, pg. 937

TERRA-CORTRIL—NONE—Pfizer Inc.; *U.S. Public*, pg. 1281

TERRA-GATOR—Full Flotation Applicator of Fertilizers & Nutrients to Crops—Ag-Chem Equipment Co., Inc.; *U.S. Public*, pg. 6

TERRA-GREEN—Soil Conditioner—Oil-Dri Corporation of America; *U.S. Public*, pg. 1214

TERRA-TIRE—High Flotation Tires—The Goodyear Tire & Rubber Company; *U.S. Public*, pg. 752

TERRACE—Prefinished Wall Paneling—Georgia-Pacific Corporation; *U.S. Public*, pg. 735

TERRACE—Panel System—The HON Co.; *U.S. Public*, pg. 772

TERRACLOR—Fungicide—Uniroyal Chemical Company, Inc.; *U.S. Public*, pg. 460

TERRACOTTA—Cosmetic Bronzing Collection—Guerlain, Inc.; *Int'l*, pg. 780

TERRAGUARD—Fungicide—Uniroyal Chemical Company, Inc.; *U.S. Public*, pg. 460

TERRAIN—Drainage Systems—Caradon Plc; *Int'l*, pg. 266

TERRALOK—Brake Fluid—The Dow Chemical Company; *U.S. Public*, pg. 522

TERRAMYCIN—Oxytetracycline—Pfizer Inc.; *U.S. Public*, pg. 1281

TERRAMYCIN LA (LA-200)—Oxytetracycline—Pfizer Inc.; *U.S. Public*, pg. 1281

TERRANO—Car—Nissan Motor Co., Ltd.; *Int'l*, pg. 943

TERRASPHERE—NONE—Replogle Globes, Inc.; *U.S. Private*, pg. 923

TERRATI—Outdoor Shoe—K-Swiss Inc.; *U.S. Public*, pg. 937

TERRAZOLE—Fungicide—Uniroyal Chemical Company, Inc.; *U.S. Public*, pg. 460

TERREON—Solid Surface Material—Bradley Corporation; *U.S. Private*, pg. 164

TERRI—Tracked Vehicles—Bombardier Inc.; *Int'l*, pg. 199

TERRI BROGAN—Ophthalmic—Optimaxx International; *U.S. Private*, pg. 818

TERRY—Travel Trailers—Fleetwood Enterprises, Inc.; *U.S. Public*, pg. 650

TERRY TOGS—Infant Wear—Spencer's Inc.; *U.S. Private*, pg. 1025

TERRY-TREADS—Safety Footwear—Alba-Waldensian, Inc.; *U.S. Public*, pg. 35

TERRY'S OLD FASHION DONUTS—Bakery—The Levy Organization; *U.S. Private*, pg. 664

TERSAN—Turf Fungicides—Du Pont (E.I. Du Pont De Nemours & Co.); *U.S. Public*, pg. 530

TERSASEPTIC—Skin Cleanser—Bradley Pharmaceuticals; *U.S. Public*, pg. 249

TERSASEPTIC—Skin Cleanser—Doak Dermatologics; *U.S. Public*, pg. 250

TERUFLEX—Transfusion Products—Terumo Medical Corporation; *Int'l*, pg. 1376

TERUFUSION—I.V. Products—Terumo Medical Corporation; *Int'l*, pg. 1376

TERUMO—Hypodermic Syringes—Terumo Medical Corporation; *Int'l*, pg. 1376

TESA—Film—Beiersdorf Group; *Int'l*, pg. 182

TESA—Tools—Brown & Sharpe Manufacturing Company; *U.S. Public*, pg. 260

TESABAND—Electrical Tapes—Tesa Tuck Inc.; *Int'l*, pg. 182

TESAFILM—Office Supply Tapes, Packaging Tapes—Tesa Tuck Inc.; *Int'l*, pg. 182

TESAFIX—Double-Coated Tapes—Tesa Tuck Inc.; *Int'l*, pg. 182

TESAFLEX—Electrical Tapes—Tesa Tuck Inc.; *Int'l*, pg. 182

TESAKREPP—Bandoliering, Masking Tapes—Tesa Tuck Inc.; *Int'l*, pg. 182

TESAMOLL—Foam Tapes—Tesa Tuck Inc.; *Int'l*, pg. 182

TESAPACK—Polypropylene Strapping Tapes—Tesa Tuck Inc.; *Int'l*, pg. 182

TESCO—Retail Stores—Tesco PLC; *Int'l*, pg. 1376

TESLAC—Cancer Therapy Product—Bristol-Myers Squibb Company; *U.S. Public*, pg. 253

TESLAC—Synthetic Agent Similar to Testosterone Used in Treatment of Brest Cancer—Bristol-Myers Squibb U.S. Pharmaceutical Group; *U.S. Public*, pg. 255

TESLIN—Microporous Sheets, Films & Membranes for Industrial Uses—PPG Industries, Inc.; *U.S. Public*, pg. 1245

TESMA—Automotive Parts—Magna International Inc.; *Int'l*, pg. 829

TESORO—Petroleum Prods.—Tesoro Petroleum Corporation; *U.S. Public*, pg. 1581

TESORO—Jewelry, Watches—Tiffany & Co.; *U.S. Public*, pg. 1608

TESSA—Tissues & Sanitary Towels—Sime Darby Berhad; *Int'l*, pg. 1249

TESSALON—Cough Suppressant—Forest Laboratories, Inc.; *U.S. Public*, pg. 670

TESSERA—Shampoo & Rinse—Shiseido Company Ltd.; *Int'l*, pg. 1235

TEST & MEASUREMENT EUROPE—Magazine Reporting on Quality Control in the Electronics Industry in Europe—Reed Elsevier Business Information; *Int'l*, pg. 1095

TEST & MEASUREMENT WORLD—Magazine Reporting on Quality Control in the Electronics Industry Worldwide—Reed Elsevier Business Information; *Int'l*, pg. 1095

TEST LINK—Disk-driven Diagnostic Engine Analyzer—Sun Electric; *U.S. Public*, pg. 1480

TEST PALETTE—PC-Based Color Interface to GR227X & GR228X Board Testers—GenRad, Inc.; *U.S. Public*, pg. 731

TEST PILOT—Computer Programs for Computer Aided Design—Lucent Technologies Inc.; *U.S. Public*, pg. 1017

TEST:RIGHT—Pelleted Dairy Feed—Agway, Inc.; *U.S. Private*, pg. 27

TEST XPRESS—PC/UNIX-Based Software Designed to Speed Test Programming for Complex PCB's—GenRad, Inc.; *U.S. Public*, pg. 731

TESTFLO—Layered Application Under Test Palette for J11-Based GR2275 & GR2276 Users—GenRad, Inc.; *U.S. Public*, pg. 731

TESTMASTER—Inspector's Test Module—Victaulic Company of America; *U.S. Private*, pg. 1138

TESTMATE—Continuity Tester Flashlight—Bright Star Industries, Inc.; *U.S. Public*, pg. 1341

TESTNET—Circuit Tester—Teradyne, Inc.; *U.S. Public*, pg. 1580

TESTODERM—Testosterone Transdermal System—Alza Corporation; *U.S. Public*, pg. 62

TESTOR—Models & Hobby Supplies—RPM, Inc.; *U.S. Public*, pg. 1356

TESTOR—Brush-On Spray Enamel Paints, Model Kits—The Testor Corporation; *U.S. Public*, pg. 1358

TESTPACK—Diagnostic Test—Abbott Laboratories; *U.S. Public*, pg. 12

TESTRED—Prescription Drug—ICN Pharmaceuticals, Inc.; *U.S. Public*, pg. 853

TESTSTAR—Materials Test Systems—MTS Systems Corporation; *U.S. Public*, pg. 1028

TESTWARE—Material Testing Software—MTS Systems Corporation; *U.S. Public*, pg. 1028

TESTWORKS—Material Testing Software—MTS Systems Corporation; *U.S. Public*, pg. 1028

TETKOMAT—Tensiometer—Tetko, Inc.; *U.S. Private*, pg. 1078

TETLEY—Tea Bags, Instant & Liquid Tea—Tetley USA Inc.; *Int'l*, pg. 1377

TETLEY ROUND TEA BAGS—Tea—Tetley USA Inc.; *Int'l*, pg. 1377

TETLEY TEA—Soft Drink—Grant-Lydick Beverage Co.; *U.S. Private*, pg. 470

TETON—Text & Cover Paper—Fox River Paper Company; *U.S. Private*, pg. 422

TETON—Hardboard Siding—Georgia-Pacific Corporation; *U.S. Public*, pg. 735

TETORON—Polyester Fiber, Polyester Film—Teijin Limited; *Int'l*, pg. 1362

TETRA—Home Aquarium Products—Warner-Lambert Company; *U.S. Public*, pg. 1738

TETRA BOND—Amorphous Diamond Coatings—Andal Corp.; *U.S. Public*, pg. 111

TETRABEAD—Diagnostic Products—Abbott Laboratories; *U.S. Public*, pg. 12

TETRACAINE—Tetracaine Hcl—Alcon Laboratories, Inc.; *Int'l*, pg. 916

TETRAGREEN—Annual Ryegrass—Green Seed Co.; *U.S. Private*, pg. 477

TETRAMET—Mold Closure Assembly—Buehler, Limited; *U.S. Public*, pg. 574

TETRAMUNE—Vaccine—American Home Products Corporation; *U.S. Public*, pg. 79

TETRATHAL—Flame Retardant—Monsanto Company; *U.S. Public*, pg. 1124

TETRATHAL—Flame Retardant for Polyester Resins—Solutia Inc.; *U.S. Public*, pg. 1483

TETRAZYME—Diagnostic Products—Abbott Laboratories; *U.S. Public*, pg. 12

TETRINOX—Resistance Film—Caddock Electronics, Inc.; *U.S. Private*, pg. 198

TETRON—NONE—Lawter International, Inc.; *U.S. Public*, pg. 980

TETROX—Manual Warewashing Product—Ecolab Inc.; *U.S. Public*, pg. 562

TEVA—Sport Sandals—Deckers Outdoor Corporation; *U.S. Public*, pg. 491

TEX/CAP—Financial Program—Medline Industries, Inc.; *U.S. Private*, pg. 728

TEX-KNIT—Ironing Board Cover—Magla Products; *U.S. Private*, pg. 695

TEX TAN—Menswear—Tandy Brands Accessories, Inc.; *U.S. Public*, pg. 1560

TEXACO—Anti-Freeze Coolant—Texaco Inc.; *U.S. Public*, pg. 1582

TEXACO SUPER UNLEADED—Gasoline—Texaco Inc.; *U.S. Public*, pg. 1582

TEXACOTE—Logo—Textile Rubber & Chemical Company; *U.S. Private*, pg. 1079

TEXACRO—Hook & Loop Fasteners—Velcro Industries N.V.; *Int'l*, pg. 1462

TEXACRO—NONE—Velcro USA Inc.; *Int'l*, pg. 1462

TEXALON—NONE—Lawter International, Inc.; *U.S. Public*, pg. 980

TEXAN—Confections—Nestle-Rowntree Ltd.; *Int'l*, pg. 921

TEXANOL—Ester Alcohol—Eastman Chemical Company; *U.S. Public*, pg. 550

TEXANOL—Ester Alcohol, Chemical Intermediate & Coalescing Agent—Eastman Kodak Company; *U.S. Public*, pg. 550

TEXARKANA WIRE & CABLE—NONE—Communication Cable, Inc.; *U.S. Public*, pg. 968

TEXAS AA—Instant Rice—American Rice Inc.; *U.S. Public*, pg. 591

TEXAS BIRCH—Wood & Lumber Products—Georgia-Pacific Corporation; *U.S. Public*, pg. 735

TEXAS CLAY INDUSTRIES—Residential & Commercial Face Brick (Clay)—Temtex Industries Inc.; *U.S. Public*, pg. 1575

TEXAS FARMER-STOCKMAN—Monthly Agricultural Publication—Farm Progress Publications; *U.S. Public*, pg. 513

TEXAS MANUFACTURERS REGISTER—Register—Manufacturers' News, Inc.; *U.S. Private*, pg. 700

TEXAS MICRO—Industrial PCs for Rackmount, Benchtop, Mobile & Telecommunications—Texas Micro, Inc.; *U.S. Public*, pg. 1586

TEXAS MONTHLY—Magazine—Mediatex Communications Corporation; *U.S. Private*, pg. 727

TEXAS MOTOR SPEEDWAY—NONE—Speedway Motorsports, Inc.; *U.S. Public*, pg. 1498

TEXAS PRIDE—Beer—Pearl Brewing Company; *U.S. Private*, pg. 954

TEXAS TUBULAR PRODUCTS—Tubular Goods—Friedman Industries, Inc.; *U.S. Public*, pg. 682

TEXIZE—House Mark—The Dow Chemical Company; *U.S. Public*, pg. 522

TEXLINER—Extruded Plastic Net—Nalle Plastics Inc.; *U.S. Private*, pg. 773

TEXTLITER—Flat Style Highlighters—Sanford Corporation; *U.S. Public*, pg. 1178

TEXMADE—Bed Linens—Springs Industries, Inc.; *U.S. Public*, pg. 1499

TEXMAT—Industrial—Texon Materials Inc.; *U.S. Private*, pg. 1079

TEXMET—Polishing Cloth—Buehler, Limited; *U.S. Public*, pg. 574

TEXO—Multi-strand Textured Fiber Glass Strand & Yarn—PPG Industries, Inc.; *U.S. Public*, pg. 1245

TEXOPRINT—Durable Paper—Kimberly-Clark Corporation; *U.S. Public*, pg. 958

TEXORIST—Innersole Material—Texon Materials Inc.; *U.S. Private*, pg. 1079

TEXPERTO—Wool Finishing Consulting Service—Novartis AG; *Int'l*, pg. 971

TEXSKIN—Rubber Products—Rubatex Corporation; *U.S. Private*, pg. 56

TEXSUN—Fruit Juices—Citrus World Inc.; *U.S. Private*, pg. 241

TEXTAMER—Polymeric Acrylates—Henkel Corporation; *Int'l*, pg. 610

TEXTAMINE—Cationic Amines—Henkel Corporation; *Int'l*, pg. 610

TEXTAMINE OXIDE—Amine Oxides—Henkel Corporation; *Int'l*, pg. 610

TEXTBOOK PUBLISHES—Grades 6-12 & Post Secondary—Glencoe/Mc-Graw Hill; *U.S. Public*, pg. 1070

TEXTBRIDGE—OCR Software—Xerox Imaging Systems, Inc.; *U.S. Public*, pg. 1785

TEXTERGE—Detergents—Henkel Corporation; *Int'l*, pg. 610

TEXTILE WORLD—Reports on New Market Trends—Intertec Publishing; *U.S. Public*, pg. 1327

TEXTILENE—Vinyl Coated Poly Thread—Ludlow Corporation; *U.S. Public*, pg. 1651

TEXTILENE—Woven Fabrics—Tyco International Ltd.; *U.S. Public*, pg. 1647

TEXTILENE SUNSURE—Vinyl Coated Poly Thread—Ludlow Corporation; *U.S. Public*, pg. 1651

TEXTOFOAM—Detergents—Henkel Corporation; *Int'l*, pg. 610

TEXTONE—NONE—Vulcan Chemicals; *U.S. Public*, pg. 1725

TEXTOOL—NONE—Electronic Products Division; *U.S. Public*, pg. 1605

TEXTOOL—Flat Pack Socket—3M; *U.S. Public*, pg. 1604

TEXTSMART—Complete Analysis of Open-Ended Survey Questions—SPSS Inc.; *U.S. Public*, pg. 1420

TEXTURE-FLEX—Plastic Product—Uniflex, Inc.; *U.S. Public*, pg. 1665

TEXTURE LITE—Food Emulsifier—Eastman Kodak Company; *U.S. Public*, pg. 550

TEXTURE SILK—Conditioner—Revlon-Realistic Professional Products, Inc.; *U.S. Private*, pg. 690

TEXTURE 2000—Plywood Exterior Cladding—Carter Holt Harvey Limited; *U.S. Public*, pg. 904

TEXTURES—Appointment Jounals—American Greetings Corporation; *U.S. Public*, pg. 77

TEXWRITE—Cleanroom Stationery—The Texwipe Co., Inc.; *U.S. Private*, pg. 1079

TEZIER—NONE—Groupe Limagrain; *Int'l*, pg. 566

TGREEN—Fertilizer—PCS Phosphate - Raleigh; *Int'l*, pg. 1064

THAI ACCENTS—Thai Sauces & Marinades—Pacific Foods, Inc.; *U.S. Private*, pg. 831

THALASSA INTERNATIONAL—Seawater Spas—Accor S.A.; *Int'l*, pg. 20

THALLOUS CHLORIDE TI 201—Cardiac Studies—Amersham Healthcare; *Int'l*, pg. 992

THAM—Chemical Reagent—Fisher Scientific Company; *U.S. Private*, pg. 658

THAMES SIDE-MAYWOOD—Load Cells & Strain Gauges—Halma p.l.c.; *Int'l*, pg. 589

THANK YOU—Pie Fillings & Puddings Vegetables & Specialty Fruits—Curtice Burns Foods; *U.S. Private*, pg. 887

THANK YOU BRAND—Desserts—Comstock Michigan Fruit; *U.S. Private*, pg. 887

THAT'S LOVE—NONE—American Greetings Corporation; *U.S. Public*, pg. 77

THAT'S MY BABY—Baby Doll Clothes & Accessories—Totsy Manufacturing Company, Inc.; *U.S. Private*, pg. 1093

THAT'S MY GIRL—Cologne Spray—Stanhome Inc.; *U.S. Public*, pg. 1508

THAYER—Weighing Devices—Hyer Industries Inc./Thayer Scale; *U.S. Private*, pg. 552

THE FUN TO READ CATALOG—NONE—The Sportsman's Guide, Inc.; *U.S. Public*, pg. 1499

THE HERALD NEWS—NONE—The Lorain Journal Company-The Morning Journal; *U.S. Public*, pg. 935

THE MORNING JOURNAL—NONE—The Lorain Journal Company-The Morning Journal; *U.S. Public*, pg. 935

THE RECORD—NONE—The Lorain Journal Company-The Morning Journal; *U.S. Public*, pg. 935

THE SPORTSMAN'S GUIDE—NONE—The Sportsman's Guide, Inc.; *U.S. Public*, pg. 1499

THE TIMES—NONE—The Lorain Journal Company-The Morning Journal; *U.S. Public*, pg. 935

THE WALNUT BREWERY—Brew Pub—Rock Bottom Restaurants; *U.S. Public*, pg. 1396

THEAKSTON—Ales—Scottish & Newcastle plc; *Int'l*, pg. 1211

THEAKSTON'S OLD PECULIER—Ale—Scottish & Newcastle Importers Co.; *Int'l*, pg. 1212

THEATER—Color Cosmetics—Coty Inc.; *Int'l*, pg. 185

THEATRE CRAFTS INTERNATIONAL—Publication for Performing Arts—Intertec Publishing; *U.S. Public*, pg. 1327

THEBE—Stainless Steel Flatware—Dansk International Designs Ltd.; *U.S. Public*, pg. 261

THEMEL—Software to Manipulate Stored Landscape—Evans & Sutherland Computer Corporation; *U.S. Public*, pg. 595

THEO-DUR—Antiasthma Agent—Astra AB; *Int'l*, pg. 93

THEO-DUR—Theophylline, Respiratory—Recordati Industria Chimica e Farmaceutica S.p.A.; *Int'l*, pg. 1090

THEO-DUR—Sustained-Release Theophylline Bronchodilator—Schering-Plough Corporation; *U.S. Public*, pg. 1438

THEO-24—Pharmaceutical—Monsanto Company; *U.S. Public*, pg. 1124

THEO-24—Bronchodilator—Searle & Co.; *U.S. Public*, pg. 1125

THEO-24—Bronchodilator—Searle Laboratories; *U.S. Public*, pg. 1125

THEO-X—Asthma Control—Carnrick Laboratories, Inc.; *U.S. Private*, pg. 436

THEOCHRON—Pharmaceutical—Forest Laboratories, Inc.; *U.S. Public*, pg. 670

THEOCLEAR—Pharmaceutical Products—Schwarz Pharma Manufacturing, Inc.; *Int'l*, pg. 1211

THEOLAIR—Theophylline, Prescription Drug—3M; *U.S. Public*, pg. 1604

THEONOMICS—Warewashing & Laundry Products—Theochem Labs., Inc.; *U.S. Private*, pg. 1079

THEORIE—Premium Hair Care & Styling Products—Dep Corporation; *U.S. Public*, pg. 500

THERA—Pacemaker—Medtronic, Inc.; *U.S. Public*, pg. 1082

THERA D—Pacemaker—Medtronic, Inc.; *U.S. Public*, pg. 1082

THERA DR—Pacemaker—Medtronic, Inc.; *U.S. Public*, pg. 1082

THERA I—Pacemaker—Medtronic, Inc.; *U.S. Public*, pg. 1082

THERA S—Pacemaker—Medtronic, Inc.; *U.S. Public*, pg. 1082

THERA SR—Pacemaker—Medtronic, Inc.; *U.S. Public*, pg. 1082

THERA SCRIBE—NONE—John Wiley & Sons, Inc.; *U.S. Public*, pg. 1768

THERA VDD—Pacemaker—Medtronic, Inc.; *U.S. Public*, pg. 1082

THERACHEM—Therapeutic Drug Control—Fisher Scientific Company; *U.S. Private*, pg. 658

THERACYS—BCG-Live Intravesicle—Connaught Laboratories, Inc.; *Int'l*, pg. 1109

THERAFLU—Flu Cough & Cold Medicine—Sandoz Pharmaceuticals Corp.; *Int'l*, pg. 974

THERAGRAN—Stress Formula—Bristol-Myers Squibb Company; *U.S. Public*, pg. 253

THERAGRAN—Multivitamin Supplement—Mead Johnson Nutritional Group; *U.S. Public*, pg. 254

THERAGRAN-M—Stress Formula—Bristol-Myers Squibb Company; *U.S. Public*, pg. 253

THERAHEALTH-M—Vitamins—Health Products Corporation; *U.S. Private*, pg. 514

THERALAX—Pharmaceutical Products—SmithKline Beecham Laboratories; *Int'l*, pg. 1264

THERALIN VMP—Pet Food Supplement—Carter-Wallace, Inc.; *U.S. Public*, pg. 309

THERAMIC—Hot Plate Top—Fisher Scientific Company; *U.S. Private*, pg. 658

THERAPEUTIC MINERAL ICE—Lozenges—Bristol-Myers Squibb Company; *U.S. Public*, pg. 253

THERAPY MANAGEMENT INNOVATIONS (TMI)—NONE—American Rehability Services, Inc.; *U.S. Public*, pg. 1257

THERARAD—Medical Instrument—Capintec Inc.; *U.S. Private*, pg. 205

THERASONIC—Lithotripsy Treatment System—Diasonics Ultra Sound, Inc.; *Int'l*, pg. 644

THERM-A-BIND—Adhesive Binding System—General Binding Corporation; *U.S. Public*, pg. 707

THERM-A-LECTRIC—High Performance Tapes—Norton Performance Plastics; *Int'l*, pg. 1174

THERM-CHEK—Heat Stabilizers—Ferro Corporation; *U.S. Public*, pg. 618

THERM-L-VEYOR—Heat Exchangers—Svedala Pumps & Process; *Int'l*, pg. 1325

THERM-LOCK—Pressure Sensitive Closure Tape—Johns Manville Corporation; *U.S. Public*, pg. 927

THERM-O-DISC—Temperature Controls, Sensors & Overload Protection Devices—Emerson Electric Co.; *U.S. Public*, pg. 572

THERM-TITRATOR—Natural Gas Instrumentation—Badger Meter, Inc.; *U.S. Public*, pg. 164

THERM-O-SCOPE—Industrial Instrument—Capintec Inc.; *U.S. Private*, pg. 205

THERMA—Household Appliances—Electrolux, AB; *Int'l*, pg. 438

THERMA-CEL—Rubber Products—Rubatex Corporation; *U.S. Private*, pg. 56

THERMA-JOINT—Bridge-Joint Repair—Linear Dynamics Inc.; *U.S. Private*, pg. 668

THERMA-PLOT—Thermal Plotter Media—Dietzgen Corporation; *U.S. Private*, pg. 332

THERMA-STOR—Heat Recovery Systems—Bou-Matic; *U.S. Private*, pg. 301

THERMA-TRIEVE—Packers—Halliburton Energy Services; *U.S. Public*, pg. 776

THERMA-TRU CRYSTALLINE SERIES—Beveled Leaded Glass Door Lites—Therma-Tru Corp.; *U.S. Private*, pg. 1079

THERMA-TUF—Heat Strengthened Glass—Gemtron Corporation; *Int'l*, pg. 1523

THERMABOND—Adhesive—3M; *U.S. Public*, pg. 1604

THERMACLAD—Moisture-Proof Coating for Pipes—Raychem Corporation; *U.S. Public*, pg. 1362

THERMACOLOR—Video Print Paper, Cartridge, Kit—Eastman Kodak Company; *U.S. Public*, pg. 550

THERMADOOR—Cold Storage & Fire Door Combination—Clark Door Co., Inc.; *U.S. Private*, pg. 242

THERMADOR—Ovens, Household Equipment—Masco Corporation; *U.S. Public*, pg. 1052

THERMADOR—Appliances—Thermador; *U.S. Public*, pg. 1053

THERMADORE-WASTE KING—Appliance Division—NI Industries, Inc.; *U.S. Public*, pg. 1054

THERMADRAPE—Heat Retentive & Insulating Surgical Drape—Vital Signs, Inc.; *U.S. Public*, pg. 1723

THERMADRY—Insulating Drainage Panel—The Dow Chemical Company; *U.S. Public*, pg. 522

THERMAFIBER—Insulation—USG Corporation; *U.S. Public*, pg. 1660

THERMAFIBER—Ceiling & Wall Products—USG Interiors, Inc.; *U.S. Public*, pg. 1660

THERMAFIN—Barrel Heater—Davis Standard Corporation; *U.S. Public*, pg. 459

THERMAFLEX—Air Conditioning Duct—Flexible Technologies, Inc.; *Int'l*, pg. 1267

THERMAFLEX—Household Ducting—Smiths Industries plc; *Int'l*, pg. 1266

THERMAGLAS—Glass Fiber Residential Insulation—Owens Corning; *U.S. Public*, pg. 1236

THERMAL-CARE—Boilers & Chillers—MFRI Inc.; *U.S. Public*, pg. 1026

THERMAL CLAD—Circuit Board Product—The Bergquist Company; *U.S. Private*, pg. 135

THERMAL DISC—Indirect Dryer & Processor—The Bethlehem Corporation; *U.S. Public*, pg. 225

THERMAL FLUID MIZER—Ball Valves-Thermal Fluid—Worcester Controls Corp.; *Int'l*, pg. 128

THERMAL OPTION—Disposable Biopsy/Coagulating Forceps—Ballard Medical Products; *U.S. Public*, pg. 171

THERMAL SENSORS—NONE—Philips Automotive Electronics; *Int'l*, pg. 1054

THERMAL TEX—Hot Oil Treatment—Revlon-Realistic Professional Products, Inc.; *U.S. Private*, pg. 690

THERMALBOND—Thermal Barrier System—Norton Performance Plastics; *Int'l*, pg. 1174

THERMALEX—Insulated Electrical Wire—General Electric Canada Inc.; *U.S. Public*, pg. 713

THERMALEZE N—THEIC Modified Polyester with Polyamide Overcoat—Phelps Dodge Magnet Wire Co.; *U.S. Public*, pg. 1286

THERMALEZE T—Solderable Polyesterimide—Phelps Dodge Magnet Wire Co.; *U.S. Public*, pg. 1286

THERMALEZE/BONDEZE—THEIC Modified Polyester with Modified Polyester Cement—Phelps Dodge Magnet Wire Co.; *U.S. Public*, pg. 1286

THERMALINE—Thermal Printers—Printronix, Inc.; *U.S. Public*, pg. 1329

THERMALITE—Aerated Concrete Blocks—Marley PLC; *Int'l*, pg. 843

THERMALLOY—Heatsinks—Bowthorpe plc; *Int'l*, pg. 207

THERMALLOY—Semiconductor Access.—Thermalloy, Inc.; *Int'l*, pg. 208

THERMAPRINT—Paper—Nashua Corporation; *U.S. Public*, pg. 1152

THERMARK—Wood Grain Foils—Avery Dennison Corporation; *U.S. Public*, pg. 152

THERMASEAL—Seals & Gaskets—Metex Corporation; *U.S. Public*, pg. 1674

THERMASHIELD—Thermal Shock Resistant Paper Carry Roll Cover—Harnischfeger Industries, Inc.; *U.S. Public*, pg. 788

THERMASOTE—Nail Base Roof Insulation—Homasote Company; *U.S. Public*, pg. 831

THERMATEL—Thermal Dispersion Flow or Level Switch—Magnetrol International; *U.S. Private*, pg. 696

THERMATIC—Extruder—Davis Standard Corporation; *U.S. Public*, pg. 459

THERMATTACH—Thermally Conductive Adhesive Tapes—Chomerics Inc.; *U.S. Public*, pg. 1262

THERMAVIEW—Communication Products—Arkwright, Inc; *Int'l*, pg. 994

THERMAX—Chart Paper—Ludlow Corporation; *U.S. Public*, pg. 1651

THERMAX—X-Ray Tubes & Housings—Varian Associates, Inc.; *U.S. Public*, pg. 1710

THERMAZIP—Pipe Insulation—The Zippertubing Co.; *U.S. Private*, pg. 1207

THERMEVAP—Multiple & Single-Effect Stills—Osmonics, Inc.; *U.S. Public*, pg. 1233

THERMEX—NONE—Lawter International, Inc.; *U.S. Public*, pg. 980

THERMEX—Hot Die & Forging Compounds—D.A. Stuart Company; *U.S. Private*, pg. 1048

THERMIC RAY—Cookware—Regal Ware, Inc.; *U.S. Private*, pg. 917

THERMICE—Chemical—Publicker Industries Inc.; *U.S. Public*, pg. 1341

THERMIFIC—Commercial Gas Boiler—Patterson-Kelley Company; *U.S. Public*, pg. 793

THERMINOL—Heat Transfer Fluid—Monsanto Company; *U.S. Public*, pg. 1124

THERMINOL—Heat Transfer Fluid—Solutia Inc.; *U.S. Public*, pg. 1483

THERMISER—Insulated Rolling Door—Cornell Iron Works, Inc.; *U.S. Private*, pg. 276

THERMISOL—Oil—Fuchs Petrolub AG Oel + Chemie; *Int'l*, pg. 517

THERMISTEMP—Industrial Instruments—YSI Incorporated; *U.S. Private*, pg. 1195

THERMIVOLT—Industrial Instruments—YSI Incorporated; *U.S. Private*, pg. 1195

THERMIX—Stirrer/Hot Plate—Fisher Scientific Company; *U.S. Public*, pg. 658

THERMIZER—Holding Furnace—Seco Warwick Corporation; *U.S. Private*, pg. 980

THERMO-BUFF—Mop-on Gloss Restorer—Rochester-Midland ICL; *U.S. Private*, pg. 937

THERMO-CABLE—Cable—Thermo Electric Co., Inc.; *U.S. Private*, pg. 1080

THERMO-CLEAN—Neutal Cleanser—Rochester-Midland ICL; *U.S. Private*, pg. 937

THERMO COMFORTER—NONE—Futuro Inc.; *Int'l*, pg. 182

THERMO CORE—Cookware—Regal Ware, Inc.; *U.S. Private*, pg. 917

THERMO-DUCER—Infrared Sensor—Watlow Electric Manufacturing Company; *U.S. Private*, pg. 1153

THERMO-FIX—Heatseal Coated Laminates—PKL Verpackungssysteme GmbH; *Int'l*, pg. 1020

THERMO-GLOSS—Ultra High Speed Floor Finish—Rochester-Midland ICL; *U.S. Private*, pg. 937

THERMO KING—NONE—Illinois Auto Electric Co.; *U.S. Private*, pg. 557

THERMO KING—Refrigeration Systems—Thermo King Corporation; *U.S. Public*, pg. 877

THERMO-LOCK—Insulation System—Coleman Spas, Inc.; *U.S. Private*, pg. 691

THERMO-MILL—Color Products—Universal Foods Corporation; *U.S. Public*, pg. 1695

THERMO-PAK BURNER—Forced Draft Industrial 881

THERMO-PLY—Insulative Sheating—K2 Inc.; *U.S. Public*, pg. 940

THERMO-PURE—Purified Graphites—Superior Graphite Co.; *U.S. Private*, pg. 1054

THERMO-SPAN—NONE—Carpenter Technology Corporation; *U.S. Public*, pg. 307

THERMO-STA—Color Products—Universal Foods Corporation; *U.S. Public*, pg. 1695

THERMO-TEK—Industrial Filter—Donaldson Company, Inc.; *U.S. Public*, pg. 517

THERMO 12 BLUE—Pipe & Block Insulation—Johns Manville Corporation; *U.S. Public*, pg. 927

THERMO VINYL FRAME—Windows—Thermal Industries, Inc.; *U.S. Private*, pg. 490

THERMOBARB—Injection Molded Barbed Fittings—NewAge Industries Inc.; *U.S. Private*, pg. 796

THERMOBARB—Plastic Barbed Fittings—Newage Industries Inc., Plastics Technology Group; *U.S. Private*, pg. 796

THERMOBOND—Document Heat Sealing Device—The Standard Register Company; *U.S. Public*, pg. 1505

THERMOCHROME—NONE—Lawter International, Inc.; *U.S. Public*, pg. 980

THERMOCON—Temperature Measuring Device—Alnor Instrument Company; *U.S. Public*, pg. 1559

THERMOCRIMP—Connector—Raychem Corporation; *U.S. Public*, pg. 1362

THERMODENT—Sensitive Teeth Toothpaste—Lee Pharmaceuticals; *U.S. Public*, pg. 984

THERMODENT—Toothpaste—Mentholatum Company; *Int'l*, pg. 1126

THERMOFIT—Heat-Shrinkable Molded Parts & Tubing—Raychem Corporation; *U.S. Public*, pg. 1362

THERMOFLEECE—Polar Fleece Products for the Home—Dakotah, Inc.; *U.S. Public*, pg. 477

THERMOFLEX—Extruded Silicon Tubing & Cord—Minor Rubber Co., Inc.; *U.S. Private*, pg. 751

THERMOFLON—Bendable Rod Heaters for Corrosive Liquids—Norton Performance Plastics; *Int'l*, pg. 1174

THERMOFOIL—Air Floatation Dryer—Thermo Fibertek, Inc.; *U.S. Public*, pg. 1593

THERMOFORM—Paste & Liquid Adhesives—The Dexter Corporation; *U.S. Public*, pg. 504

THERMOGAS—Propane—Mapco Inc.; *U.S. Public*, pg. 1042

THERMOGAS—LP Gas—Mapco Natural Gas Liquids Inc.; *U.S. Public*, pg. 1042

THERMOGEL—NONE—Lawter International, Inc.; *U.S. Public*, pg. 980

THERMOGENETIC—Thermal Storage—Precision Parts Corp.; *U.S. Private*, pg. 879

THERMOGRIP—Accessories—The Black & Decker Corporation; *U.S. Public*, pg. 233

THERMOGUARD—Flame Retardant—Elf Atochem North America, Inc.; *Int'l*, pg. 445

THERMOGUN—Hot Air Convection Heater—Raychem Corporation; *U.S. Public*, pg. 1362

THERMOID—Belts & Hoses—Bryant Electric Supply Company, Inc.; *U.S. Private*, pg. 177

THERMOID—NONE—HBD Industries, Inc.; *U.S. Private*, pg. 489

THERMOJETICS—Herbal Tablets—Herbalife International of America, Inc.; *U.S. Public*, pg. 809

THERMOJETICS—Herbal Tea—Herbalife International of America, Inc.; *U.S. Public*, pg. 809

THERMOLACTYL—Warmth-Keeping Synthetic Fabric—Damart; *Int'l*, pg. 376

THERMOLACTYL—Warmth-Keeping Synthetic Fabric—Damart S.A.; *Int'l*, pg. 376

THERMOLDS—Shoes—P.W. Minor & Son, Inc.; *U.S. Private*, pg. 751

THERMOLENE—NONE—AGA Gas, Inc.; *Int'l*, pg. 13

THERMOLIER—Pipe Fittings—Grinnell Corporation; *U.S. Public*, pg. 1651

THERMOLIMIT—Heater—Raychem Corporation; *U.S. Public*, pg. 1362

THERMOLINC—NONE—Thermo Jarrell Ash Corporation; *U.S. Public*, pg. 1594

THERMOLINE—Fuel Line Heater—Raychem Corporation; *U.S. Public*, pg. 1362

THERMOLINER—System Roof & Wall Insulation—Johns Manville Corporation; *U.S. Public*, pg. 927

THERMOLOFT—Insulated Materials—Du Pont (E.I. Du Pont De Nemours & Co.); *U.S. Public*, pg. 530

THERMOMAT—Heat-Formable Materials—FiberMark Inc.; *U.S. Public*, pg. 620

THERMOMETRICS—Thermistors—Bowthorpe plc; *Int'l*, pg. 207

THERMOMIX—Kitchen Appliances—Vorwerk & Co.; *Int'l*, pg. 1480

THERMOPANEL—Radiators—Blue Circle Industries PLC; *Int'l*, pg. 197

THERMOPOINT—NONE—Agema Infrared Systems AB; *Int'l*, pg. 1289

THERMOPROFILE—NONE—Agema Infrared Systems AB; *Int'l*, pg. 1289

THERMORAIL—Contact Rail Heaters—Raychem Corporation; *U.S. Public*, pg. 1362

THERMORON—Heat Exchangers for Corrosive Liquids—Norton Performance Plastics; *Int'l*, pg. 1174

THERMOS—Insulated Containers—The Thermos Company; *Int'l*, pg. 938

THERMOS SPEC—NONE—Thermo Jarrell Ash Corporation; *U.S. Public*, pg. 1594

THERMOSEAL—Glass Sealants—H.B. Fuller Company; *U.S. Public*, pg. 686

THERMOSHIELD—Coaxial Cable Repair System—Raychem Corporation; *U.S. Public*, pg. 1362

THERMOSPEED—Film Splicer & Splicing Tape—Eastman Kodak Company; *U.S. Public*, pg. 550

THERMOSPRAY—Flame Spray Guns—The Perkin-Elmer Corporation; *U.S. Public*, pg. 1279

THERMOSPRAY—Ceramic & Hard Face Coating—Sulzer Metco (Westbury) Inc.; *Int'l*, pg. 1307

THERMOSTONE—Ceramic Ovens—A & S Tribal Industries; *U.S. Private*, pg. 1

THERMOSWITCH—Temperature Detector—Kidde-Fenwal, Inc.; *Int'l*, pg. 1500

THERMOTABS—Buffered Salt Tablets—Menley & James Laboratories, Inc.; *U.S. Public*, pg. 1086

THERMOTAINER—Food Holding Equipment—Duke Manufacturing Co., Inc.; *U.S. Private*, pg. 346

THERMOTUBE—Pre-Insulated Tubing—Thermon Manufacturing Company; *U.S. Private*, pg. 1080

THERMOVISION—NONE—Agema Infrared Systems AB; *Int'l*, pg. 1289

THERMOWEAR—NONE—Carpenter Technology Corporation; *U.S. Public*, pg. 307

THERMTRAC—Skin Effect Heating Systems—Thermon Manufacturing Company; *U.S. Private*, pg. 1080

THERMX—Synthetic Resins, Copolyester Plastics—Eastman Chemical Company; *U.S. Public*, pg. 550

THERMX—Synthetic Resins, Copolyester Plastics—Eastman Kodak Company; *U.S. Public*, pg. 550

THETFORD 775MSD—Marine Head—Thetford Corporation; *U.S. Private*, pg. 352

THETFORD 735MSD—Marine Head—Thetford Corporation; *U.S. Private*, pg. 352

THEUNISKRAAL ESTATE—Wine—Distillers Corporation S.A.; *Int'l*, pg. 1129

THEX-FORTE—Pharmaceuticals—Medtech Inc.; *U.S. Public*, pg. 728

THIBENZOLE—Thiabendazole—Merck & Co., Inc.; *U.S. Public*, pg. 1090

THICK & EASY—Pureed Line—Hormel Foods Corp.; *U.S. Public*, pg. 840

THE THICK & JUICY BURGER—Hamburger Patties—Harker's Distribution, Inc.; *U.S. Private*, pg. 502

THICK LASH 2—Mascara—Cover Girl Cosmetics; *U.S. Public*, pg. 1330

THICK 'N CRISPY—Frozen Poultry—Tyson Foods, Inc.; *U.S. Public*, pg. 1652

THICK 'N THIN—Eye Color Pencils—Cover Girl Cosmetics; *U.S. Public*, pg. 1330

THIEL CHEESE—Cheese Spreads—Thiel Cheese Co.; *U.S. Private*, pg. 1081

THIERRY MUGLER—Perfume—Clarins; *Int'l*, pg. 295

THILMANY—Industrial Paper—Thilmany Division; *U.S. Public*, pg. 903

THIMET—Insecticide—American Home Products Corporation; *U.S. Public*, pg. 79

THIN CHANNEL—Headbox—Beloit Corporation; *U.S. Public*, pg. 789

THIN-FLEX—Single-Stage Venous Return Catheters—Baxter Research Medical, Inc.; *U.S. Public*, pg. 196

THIN ICE—Game—Pressman Toy Corp.; *U.S. Private*, pg. 882

THIN-LINE—Brush Head—John O. Butler Co.; *Int'l*, pg. 1320

THIN LITE—Accessory—Carefree of Colorado; *U.S. Public*, pg. 217

THIN 'N LIGHT—Pretzels—Bachman Company; *U.S. Private*, pg. 109

THIN 'N RIGHT—Pretzels—Bachman Company; *U.S. Private*, pg. 109

THINCAST—Cast-In Heater—Watlow Electric Manufacturing Company; *U.S. Private*, pg. 1153

THINCRUST—Pizza—Tombstone Pizza Corporation; *U.S. Public*, pg. 1288

THINEX—Blossom Thinner—Mycogen Corporation; *U.S. Public*, pg. 1142

A THING FOR YOU—Greeting Cards—American Greetings Corporation; *U.S. Public*, pg. 77

THINGS ARE POPPING—Video Equipment—National Video, Inc.; *U.S. Public*, pg. 1755

THINGS REMEMBERED—Gifts—Cole National Corporation; *U.S. Public*, pg. 396

THINK—Computer System—International Business Machines Corporation; *U.S. Public*, pg. 895

THINK GAMES—Solitaire Games—Pressman Toy Corp.; *U.S. Private*, pg. 882

THINKABLE—Computer Product—International Business Machines Corporation; *U.S. Public*, pg. 895

THINKING MACHINES—Computer Hardware—Thinking Machines Corporation; *U.S. Private*, pg. 1081

THINKING OF YOU—Greeting Cards—American Greetings Corporation; *U.S. Public*, pg. 77

THINKPAD—Computer Product—International Business Machines Corporation; *U.S. Public*, pg. 895

THINKPAD PROVEN—Computer Product—International Business Machines Corporation; *U.S. Public*, pg. 895

THINSULATE—Insulation Material, Thermal—3M; *U.S. Public*, pg. 1

THINTECH—Waterproof Breathable Garment Insert—3M; *U.S. Public*, pg. 1604

THINZ—Appetite Suppressant—Alva/Amco Pharmacal Companies, Inc.; *U.S. Private*, pg. 47

THINZ—Drilling Mud Additive—Georgia-Pacific Corporation; *U.S. Public*, pg. 735

THINZ BACK TO NATURE—Appetite Suppressant—Alva/Amco Pharmacal Companies, Inc.; *U.S. Private*, pg. 47

THINZ FIBRE NATURALE—Reducing Plan Tablets—Alva/Amco Pharmacal Companies, Inc.; *U.S. Private*, pg. 47

THINZ GRAPEFRUIT & FIBER—Reducing Plan Tablets—Alva/Amco Pharmacal Companies, Inc.; *U.S. Private*, pg. 47

THINZ-SPAN—Timed Release Reducing Capsules & Water Caplets—Alva/Amco Pharmacal Companies, Inc.; *U.S. Private*, pg. 47

THIOCLEAR—Flue Gas Desulfurization Technology—Dravo Corporation; *U.S. Public*, pg. 527

THIOCLEAR—Fine Gas Treatment Technology—Dravo Lime Company; *U.S. Public*, pg. 527

THIODAN—Insecticides—Hoechst Aktiengesellschaft; *Int'l*, pg. 624

THIOFIDE—Rubber Vulcanization Accelerator—Monsanto Company; *U.S. Public*, pg. 1124

THIOFIX E—Leveling Agent/Fixative—Morton International Inc.; *U.S. Public*, pg. 1135

THIOGUANINE—Pharmaceutical Product—Glaxo Wellcome PLC; *Int'l*, pg. 553

THIOKOL—Insulating Glass Sealant—Morton International Inc.; *U.S. Public*, pg. 1135

THIOKOL—Rocket Motors, Rocket Motor Parts & Accessories—Thiokol Corporation; *U.S. Public*, pg. 1596

THIOLENT—Plant Protectives—DSM Chemie Linz GmbH; *Int'l*, pg. 356

THIOLUX—Sulphur-Based Fungicides—Novartis AG; *Int'l*, pg. 971

THIOLUX—Fungicide—Sandoz Agro, Inc.; *Int'l*, pg. 974

THIOPLEX—Oncology Therapy—American Home Products Corporation; *U.S. Public*, pg. 79

THIOSORBIC—Scrubber Lime—Dravo Corporation; *U.S. Public*, pg. 527

THIOSORBIC—Lime—Dravo Lime Company; *U.S. Public*, pg. 527

THIOTAX—Rubber Vulcanization Accelerator—Monsanto Company; *U.S. Public*, pg. 1124

THIOVIT—Sulphur-Based Fungicides—Novartis AG; *Int'l*, pg. 971

3RD FOODS—Baby Foods & Juices—Gerber Products Company; *Int'l*, pg. 973

THE THIRD REICH—Book Series—Time-Life, Inc.; *U.S. Public*, pg. 1613

THIRST QUENCH'R—Powder Drink Mixer—Genesee Corporation; *U.S. Public*, pg. 728

THIRST THRASHER—NONE—Triarc Companies, Inc.; *U.S. Public*, pg. 1634

THIRSTBUSTER—Fountain Soft Drinks—The Circle K Company; *U.S. Public*, pg. 1624

THIRSTEE SMASH—Fruit Drinks—Borden, Inc.; *U.S. Private*, pg. 157

1320 NM—Network Manage Unit Platform—Alcatel Telecom; *Int'l*, pg. 55

38—Varnish—Pratt & Lambert United, Inc.; *U.S. Public*, pg. 1466

35MM/SKYGUARD—Air Defense System for Permanent Surveillance—Oerlikon-Contraves AG; *Int'l*, pg. 998

30 MILLIONS D'AMIS—French Pet Magazine—EMAP France; *Int'l*, pg. 451

3090—Computer System—International Business Machines Corporation; *U.S. Public*, pg. 895

3100—Industrial Space Heater—Rapid Engineering Inc.; *U.S. Private*, pg. 910

37E—Small Character Ink Jet Printer—Videojet Systems International, Inc.; *Int'l*, pg. 545

37EZ—Small Character Ink jet Printer—Videojet Systems International, Inc.; *Int'l*, pg. 545

37PLUS—Small Character Ink Jet Printer—Videojet Systems International, Inc.; *Int'l*, pg. 545

30/30—Air Filter Medium Efficiency—Farr Company; *U.S. Public*, pg. 613

33—Beer—Heineken N.V.; *Int'l*, pg. 608

3300—Blood Gas Monitors—Nellcor Puritan Bennett Incorporated; *U.S. Public*, pg. 1039

33 METAL PRODUCING—Periodical—Penton Publishing, Inc.; *U.S. Public*, pg. 1306

33 NON-FERROUS—Periodical—Penton Publishing, Inc.; *U.S. Public*, pg. 1306

3270 SUPEROPTIMIZER/CICS—Network Optimization—BMC Software, Inc.; *U.S. Public*, pg. 162

3270 SUPEROPTIMIZER/CICS FOR VSE—Network Optimization—BMC Software, Inc.; *U.S. Public*, pg. 162

3270 SUPEROPTIMIZER/VM—Network Optimization—BMC Software, Inc.; *U.S. Public*, pg. 162

THIS BUD'S FOR YOU—Trademark—The Florists Assn. of Greater Cleveland, Inc.; *U.S. Private*, pg. 415

THISTLE—Stainless Steel Flatware—Dansk International Designs Ltd.; *U.S. Public*, pg. 261

THIURAD—Rubber Vulcanization Accelerator—Solutia Inc.; *U.S. Public*, pg. 1483

THIXAMID—NONE—Lawter International, Inc.; *U.S. Public*, pg. 980

THIXMOLDING—Injection Molding Process for Semi-Solid Metal—Lindberg Corporation; *U.S. Public*, pg. 999

THIXON—Rubber-to-Metal Bonding Agents—Morton International Inc.; *U.S. Public*, pg. 1134

THIXX—NONE—Lawter International, Inc.; *U.S. Public*, pg. 980

THO-ROBRED—Braids—Eagle Button Co., Inc.; *U.S. Private*, pg. 354

THOMAS—Specialty Baked Goods, Breads—Bestfoods; *U.S. Public*, pg. 223

THOMAS'—English Muffins & Bagels—CPC Baking Business; *U.S. Public*, pg. 224

THOMAS—Flexible Disc Couplings—Rexnord Corporation; *Int'l*, pg. 127

THOMAS—Lighting Fixtures—Thomas Industries, Consumer Lighting Division; *U.S. Public*, pg. 1599

THOMAS—Decorative Lighting Fixtures—Thomas Industries Inc.; *U.S. Public*, pg. 1598

THOMAS & BETTS—Electrical Fittings—Bryant Electric Supply Company, Inc.; *U.S. Private*, pg. 177

THOMAS & BETTS—Customer-Specific Interconnects & Components, Fittings & Heating—Thomas & Betts Corporation; *U.S. Public*, pg. 1597

THOMAS BY ROSENTHAL—China & Crystal—Rosenthal U.S.A. Limited; *Int'l*, pg. 1127

THOMAS ENGINEERING—Pharmaceutical Tablet Pressess & Coaters, Marking & Printing Devices—Thomas Engineering Inc.; *U.S. Private*, pg. 1082

THOMAS-SCHREDER—Tunnel Lighting—Thomas Industries Inc.; *U.S. Public*, pg. 1598

THOMASTON—Fabrics—Thomaston Mills, Inc.; *U.S. Public*, pg. 1599

THOMASVILLE—Furniture—Furniture Brands International Inc.; *U.S. Public*, pg. 688

THOMASVILLE—Furniture—Thomasville Furniture Industries, Inc.; *U.S. Public*, pg. 688

THOMPSON—Vitamins & Mineral Products—Thompson Nutritional Products; *U.S. Public*, pg. 1384

THOMPSON & FORMBY—NONE—Eastman Kodak Company; *U.S. Public*, pg. 550

THOMPSON GRINDER—Machine Tools—Waterbury Farrel Technologies; *U.S. Private*, pg. 461

THOMPSON'S WATER SEAL—Waterproofer—The Thompson's Company; *U.S. Public*, pg. 1466

THOMPSON'S WATER SEAL STAIN—Exterior Stain—The Thompson's Company; *U.S. Public*, pg. 1466

THOMSON—Clothing—Salant Corporation; *U.S. Public*, pg. 1429

THOMSON—Women's Wear—Thomson Company, Inc.; *U.S. Public*, pg. 1429

THOMSON—Business Information—Thomson Holdings Inc.; *U.S. Public*, pg. 1601

THOMSON SLACKS—Slacks—Thomson Company, Inc.; *U.S. Public*, pg. 1429

THOMY—Culinary Products—Nestle S.A.; *Int'l*, pg. 915

THOR—Industrial Products—BTR plc; *Int'l*, pg. 124

THORA-KLEX—Chest Drainage Unit—Davol Inc.; *U.S. Public*, pg. 189

THORACOPORT—Laparoscopic Instruments—U.S. Surgical Corp.; *U.S. Public*, pg. 1687

THORAZINE—Neurosciences—SmithKline Beecham plc; *Int'l*, pg. 1264

THORAZINE—Psychotropic—SmithKline Beecham Research Limited; *Int'l*, pg. 1266

THOREAU—Paper—Kimberly-Clark Corporation; *U.S. Public*, pg. 958

THORITE—Patching Material For Concrete & Masonry—Thoro; *U.S. Private*, pg. 505

THORKOM—Connectors—Viking Electronics, Inc.; *U.S. Private*, pg. 1184

THORN APPLE VALLEY—Meats—Thorn Apple Valley, Inc.; *U.S. Public*, pg. 1602

THORN AUTOMATED SYSTEMS—Fire Alarm Systems—EEI Corporation; *Int'l*, pg. 425

THORNEL—Carbon Fibers & Composites—Amoco Chemicals; *U.S. Public*, pg. 102

THORNEL—Carbon Graphite Fiber—Amoco Corporation; *U.S. Public*, pg. 101

THORNET—Fire Systems Network—Thorn Security Group, Ltd.; *Int'l*, pg. 1386

THORNGATE—Uniforms—Hartmarx Corporation; *U.S. Public*, pg. 795

THORNMASTER—Integrated Systems—Thorn Security Group, Ltd.; *Int'l*, pg. 1386

THORNTONS—Confectionery—Thorntons PLC; *Int'l*, pg. 1386

THORO FARE—NONE—Richfood Pennsylvania; *U.S. Public*, pg. 1389

THORO-TRED—Tire Repair Materials—Bridgestone/Firestone, Inc.; *Int'l*, pg. 213

THOROBRED—Tires, Tubes, Batteries & Shock Absorbers—Bridgestone/Firestone, Inc.; *Int'l*, pg. 213

THOROBRED—Hose Fly Spray—Universal Cooperatives, Inc.; *U.S. Private*, pg. 1127

THOROBRED POLY—Tires—Bridgestone/Firestone, Inc.; *Int'l*, pg. 213

THOROCRETE—Cement Base Patching Material For Concrete & Masonry—Thoro; *U.S. Private*, pg. 505

THOROFARE—Tires & Tubes—Bridgestone/Firestone, Inc.; *Int'l*, pg. 213

THOROGARD—Safety Shoes—Weinbrenner Shoe Company, Inc.; *U.S. Private*, pg. 1160

THOROGOOD—Uniform Work & Safety Shoes—Weinbrenner Shoe Company, Inc.; *U.S. Private*, pg. 1160

THOROGRIP—Waterproof Anchoring Cement For Concrete & Masonry—Thoro; *U.S. Private*, pg. 505

THOROLASTIC—Acrylic Emulsion Finish For Concrete & Masonry—Thoro; *U.S. Private*, pg. 505

THOROSEAL—Bag Filter Housing—Pall Corporation; *U.S. Public*, pg. 1253

THOROSEAL—Waterproof Coating For Concrete & Masonry—Thoro; *U.S. Private*, pg. 505

THOROSEAL PLASTER MIX—Waterproof Texture Coating For Concrete & Masonry—Thoro; *U.S. Private*, pg. 505

THOROSHEEN—Acrylic Emulsion Paint For Concrete & Masonry—Thoro; *U.S. Private*, pg. 505

THOROUGH BRED FENCE—Pressure Creosoted Round Post Wood Fence & 1" x 6" Rails—Seaman Timber Company, Inc.; *U.S. Private*, pg. 979

THOROUGHBRED—Wheelbarrows—Ames Company; *U.S. Public*, pg. 1683

THORTEX—Industrial Maintenance Products—Meristem plc; *Int'l*, pg. 858

THE THOS. D. MURPHY CO.—Programs & WearablesAlbums—JII/Sales Promotion Associates, Inc.; *U.S. Private*, pg. 598

THOUGHTFULNESS IS A GIFT OF LOVE—Greeting Cards—American Greetings Corporation; *U.S. Public*, pg. 77

THOUSAND OAKS NEWS-CHRONICLE—J.P. Scripps Newspaper Group Dailies—The E.W. Scripps Company; *U.S. Public*, pg. 1447

THREAD-EASY—Film Reels, Magazines—Eastman Kodak Company; *U.S. Public*, pg. 550

THREAD TITE!—Fasteners—R&B, Inc.; *U.S. Public*, pg. 1354

THREADEZY—Oil—Curtis-Toledo, Inc.; *U.S. Private*, pg. 298

THRED-O-MATIC—Pipe Thread Cutting Machines—Rothenberger Group GmbH; *Int'l*, pg. 1127

THRED SEAL—Fastener Seal—Seal Group; *U.S. Public*, pg. 1262

THREDKUT—Cutting Fluids & Lubricants—D.A. Stuart Company; *U.S. Private*, pg. 1048

THREDOLET—Fittings—Bonney Forge Corporation; *U.S. Private*, pg. 156

THREE A—For Auto Association Prints & Publications—American Automobile Association; *U.S. Private*, pg. 50

THREE BEES—Honey—Sioux Honey Association; *U.S. Private*, pg. 1003

3-CHIP—NONE—Stryker Corporation; *U.S. Public*, pg. 1525

THREE COWS—Cheese—MD Foods; *Int'l*, pg. 826

THREE D BED & BATH STORES—Retail Bed & Bath Stores—Three D Departments, Inc.; *U.S. Public*, pg. 1604

3-D CREATURE KIT MOLD PACKS—Toy—Toymax International Inc.; *U.S. Public*, pg. 1626

3D DESIGN MAGAZINE—Magazine—Miller Freeman Inc.; *Int'l*, pg. 1443

3D HOME ARCHITECT, EDITION 2—NONE—Broderbund Software, Inc.; *U.S. Public*, pg. 258

3D STUDIO MAX—3D Modeling, Graphics & Animation Software—Autodesk, Inc.; *U.S. Public*, pg. 148

3DVI—3D Volume Interpretation—Landmark Graphics Corporation; *U.S. Public*, pg. 776

386 SERIES—Computer Systems—Acer/Altos Computer Systems; *Int'l*, pg. 22

351 ACCESS POINT MANAGER—Access Control System—Interactive Technologies, Inc.; *U.S. Public*, pg. 888

THREE FOR ALL—Espresso/Cappuccino Maker—Salton/Maxim Housewares, Inc.; *U.S. Public*, pg. 1430

300 FS POWERSTEEL—Flattened Strand—Broderick & Bascom Rope Co.; *U.S. Private*, pg. 68

309 A.B.Q.—NONE—Carpenter Technology Corporation; *U.S. Public*, pg. 307

372—Rubber Products—Rubatex Corporation; *U.S. Private*, pg. 56

360—Levels & Plumb Vials—The Stanley Works; *U.S. Public*, pg. 1508

360 CHAIRS—Chairs—Knoll, Inc.; *U.S. Public*, pg. 627

366—Shotshell Press—Hornady Manufacturing Company; *U.S. Private*, pg. 539

303 A1 MODIFIED—NONE—Carpenter Technology Corporation; *U.S. Public*, pg. 307

303DQ—NONE—Carpenter Technology Corporation; *U.S. Public*, pg. 307

302HQ-FM—NONE—Carpenter Technology Corporation; *U.S. Public*, pg. 307

3-IN-ONE—All Purpose Oil—Reckitt & Colman Inc.; *Int'l*, pg. 1090

3-IN-ONE—Drip Oil Lubricant—WD-40 Company; *U.S. Public*, pg. 1726

THREE KIT—Eye Shadows—Cover Girl Cosmetics; *U.S. Public*, pg. 1330

3M—Tapes, Abrasive and Adhesive—Camalloy, Incorporated; *U.S. Private*, pg. 202

3M—NONE—Electronic Products Division; *U.S. Public*, pg. 1605

3M—Abrasives, Adhesives, Chemical Additives, Etc.—3M; *U.S. Public*, pg. 1604

THREE-M-ITE—Aluminum Oxide Coated Abrasives—3M; *U.S. Public*, pg. 1604

3M-MATIC—Automatic & Semi-Automatic Business Equipment, Seals Boxes—3M; *U.S. Public*, pg. 1604

3M SCOTCHPLY—Rail Joint—Portec Inc., Railway Maintenance Products Div.; *U.S. Public*, pg. 1318

3M THERMABOND-INSULATED—Rail Joint—Portec Inc., Railway Maintenance Products Div.; *U.S. Public*, pg. 1318

3 MUSKETEERS—Candy & Ice Cream Bars—Mars, Incorporated; *U.S. Private*, pg. 707

3 MUSKETEERS BRAND—NONE—M&M/Mars; *U.S. Private*, pg. 707

3-NITRO—Feed Chemicals—Salsbury Laboratories, Inc.; *Int'l*, pg. 1277

THREE NUNS—Pipe Tobaccos—Imperial Tobacco Group, Ltd.; *Int'l*, pg. 666

316L-SCQ—NONE—Carpenter Technology Corporation; *U.S. Public*, pg. 307

THREE OVAL DESIGN LOGO—Color Television—Sony Electronics; *Int'l*, pg. 1281

3PL—Warehousing Services—Van Waters & Rogers; *Int'l*, pg. 1147

THREE-PLY COMFORT—Fabrics—Herculite Products, Inc.; *U.S. Public*, pg. 802

THREE SISTERS—NONE—Petrie Retail, Inc.; *U.S. Private*, pg. 858

365—For Placing Insurance With Underwriters—American Automobile Association; *U.S. Private*, pg. 50

THREE STAR—Pipe Tobacco—Consolidated Cigar Corp.; *U.S. Private*, pg. 690

THREE STAR—Pipe Tobaccos—Consolidated Cigar Corporation; *U.S. Private*, pg. 690

333HT—Fly Lines—Cortland Line Co., Inc.; *U.S. Private*, pg. 277

3000A—Vital Signs Monitor—Datascope Corp.; *U.S. Public*, pg. 487

3000GT—Automobile—Mitsubishi Motor Sales of America, Inc.; *Int'l*, pg. 875

3000GT Spyder—Automobile—Mitsubishi Motor Sales of America, Inc.; *Int'l*, pg. 875

3100 SERIES—Conveyers—Dorner Manufacturing Corp.; *U.S. Public*, pg. 340

3001X—Wafer Probers—Electroglas, Inc.; *U.S. Public*, pg. 727

3000 SERIES—Eductors—Akron Brass Company; *Int'l*, pg. 1068

THREE TIGERS—Cement—The Siam Cement Public Company Limited; *Int'l*, pg. 1237

THREE TUNING FORKS IN A CIRCLE—Logo—Yamaha Corporation of America; *Int'l*, pg. 1516

3UV—Multiple Wavelengths in One Unit—UVP, Inc.; *U.S. Private*, pg. 1115

THRESHER—Off-License Liquor Store—Whitbread PLC; *Int'l*, pg. 1498

THRESHOLD—Electronic Access Control System—Checkpoint Systems Inc.; *U.S. Public*, pg. 343

THRIFT—Grocery Stores—URM Stores, Inc.; *U.S. Private*, pg. 1114

THRIFT FLO—Depanning Compound—Mallet & Co.; *U.S. Private*, pg. 698

THRIFT KING—Grocery Products—Shurfine International, Inc.; *U.S. Private*, pg. 997

THRIFTEE—Depanning Compound—Mallet & Co.; *U.S. Private*, pg. 698

THRIFTWAY—Supermarkets—Associated Grocers, Inc.; *U.S. Private*, pg. 90

THRIFTWAY—Supermarkets & Drug Stores—Thriftway, Inc.; *U.S. Public*, pg. 1771

THRIFTY—Car Rental—Thrifty Rent-a-Car System, Inc.; *U.S. Public*, pg. 354

THRIFTY RENT-A-CAR—Car Rental—Thrifty Rent-a-Car System, Inc.; *U.S. Public*, pg. 354

THRIFTY-RIB—Roofing & Siding—Reynolds Metals Company; *U.S. Public*, pg. 1385

THRIVE—Dry Cat Food—Ralston Purina Company; *U.S. Public*, pg. 1359

THOROCOAT—Acrylic Textured Coating—Thoro; *U.S. Private*, pg. 505

THROMBINAR—Topical Hemostatic Product—Jones Medical Industries Inc.; *U.S. Public*, pg. 933

THROMBOSCINT—NONE—Cytogen Corporation; *U.S. Public*, pg. 471

Brand Name Index

THROMBOSIL APTT REAGENT—Coagulation Assay—Ortho Clinical Diagnostic Systems Inc.; *U.S. Public*, pg. 929

THROMBOTECT—Diagnostic Products—Abbott Laboratories; *U.S. Public*, pg. 12

THRU-EMBOSSED—Paper Towels—Georgia-Pacific Corporation; *U.S. Public*, pg. 735

THRU-WAY—Tires—Bridgestone/Firestone, Inc.; *Int'l*, pg. 213

THRUFLEX—Catheter—Medtronic, Inc.; *U.S. Public*, pg. 1082

THRUFLEX II—Catheter—Medtronic, Inc.; *U.S. Public*, pg. 1082

THRUGLASS—Touch Products for Retail Store Windows—Microtouch Systems, Inc.; *U.S. Public*, pg. 1108

THRULUMEN—NONE—Cordis, a Johnson & Johnson Company; *U.S. Public*, pg. 928

THULE—Bicycle Carrier—Eldon AB; *Int'l*, pg. 436

THUMB FUN LOLLIPOPS—Candy—The Topps Company, Inc.; *U.S. Public*, pg. 1621

THUMB SUCKERS—Suckers—Amurol Confections Co.; *U.S. Public*, pg. 1781

THUMBER—NONE—Medline Industries, Inc.; *U.S. Private*, pg. 728

THUMBPOT—Voltage Divider—Transico Incorporated; *U.S. Public*, pg. 1630

THUMBS UP—Disposable Isolation Gown—Medline Industries, Inc.; *U.S. Private*, pg. 728

THUNDER BEAM—Outdoor Warning Siren—Federal Signal Corporation, Signal Div.; *U.S. Public*, pg. 616

THUNDER CRUNCH—Kettle Chips—Snyder Berlin; *U.S. Private*, pg. 887

THUNDERBIRD—Wine—E. & J. Gallo Winery; *U.S. Private*, pg. 438

THUNDERBIRD—Antenna—Telex Communications, Inc.; *U.S. Private*, pg. 1074

THUNDERBOLT—Electrically Operated Sirens—Federal Signal Corporation, Signal Div.; *U.S. Public*, pg. 616

THUNDERBOLT—Welding & Cutting Equip.—Miller Electric Manufacturing Co.; *U.S. Public*, pg. 867

THUNDERLAN—NONE—Texas Instruments Incorporated; *U.S. Public*, pg. 1585

THUNDERSWITCH—NONE—Texas Instruments Incorporated; *U.S. Public*, pg. 1585

THUNDERVOLT—24 Volt Industrial Products—The Black & Decker Corporation; *U.S. Public*, pg. 233

THURICIDE—Biological Insecticide—Novartis AG; *Int'l*, pg. 971

THURICIDE—Insecticide—Sandoz Agro, Inc.; *Int'l*, pg. 974

THURMADUKE—Food Warmer—Duke Manufacturing Co., Inc.; *U.S. Private*, pg. 346

THYBONY—Wall Coverings—Thybony Wall Coverings Co.; *U.S. Private*, pg. 1084

THYE HONG—Biscuits—Danone Group; *Int'l*, pg. 379

THYME MATERNITY—Maternity Apparel—Shirmax Leasing Ltd.; *Int'l*, pg. 1235

THYMITAQ—Thymidylate Synthase Inhibitor for Treatment of Malignant Solid Tumors—Agouron Pharmaceuticals, Inc.; *U.S. Public*, pg. 28

THYMONE—Protirelin—Abbott Laboratories; *U.S. Public*, pg. 12

THYPINONE—Diagnostic Products—Abbott Laboratories; *U.S. Public*, pg. 12

THYRIG—SCR Motor Controls—Baylor Company; *Int'l*, pg. 1134

THYRIGGER—Small Rig SCR—Baylor Company; *Int'l*, pg. 1134

THYROGEN—Treatment for Thyroid Cancer—Genzyme Corporation; *U.S. Public*, pg. 733

THYROID UPTAKE SYSTEMS—NONE—Capintec Inc.; *U.S. Private*, pg. 205

THYROLAR—Thyroid Medicine, U.S. Rights Only—Forest Laboratories, Inc.; *U.S. Public*, pg. 670

THYROLAR—Pharmaceuticals—Rhone-Poulenc Rorer - U.S.; *Int'l*, pg. 1110

TI-CO—Galvanized Sheet Steel—Inland Steel Industries, Inc.; *U.S. Public*, pg. 879

TI-CO GALVANIZED BLAC-KLAD CULVERT—Sheet Steel—Inland Steel Industries, Inc.; *U.S. Public*, pg. 879

TI-CO GALVANIZED CULVERT—Sheet Steel—Inland Steel Industries, Inc.; *U.S. Public*, pg. 879

TI-CO PAINT-TITE—Galvanized Steel Sheets—Inland Steel Industries, Inc.; *U.S. Public*, pg. 879

TI-GRIP—NONE—Lawter International, Inc.; *U.S. Public*, pg. 980

TI-NAMEL—High Strength Enamelling Sheet Steel—Inland Steel Industries, Inc.; *U.S. Public*, pg. 879

TIA MARIA—Liqueur—Allied Domecq PLC; *Int'l*, pg. 62

TIA MARIA—NONE—Allied Domecq Spirits & Wine (UK) Ltd.; *Int'l*, pg. 63

TIA MARIA—Liqueur—Hiram Walker; *Int'l*, pg. 63

TIA ROSA—Flour, Corn Tortillas—Grupo Industrial Bimbo S.A. de C.V.; *Int'l*, pg. 575

TIAMUTIN—Veterinary Antibiotic—Novartis AG; *Int'l*, pg. 971

TIARA—Luggage—American Tourister, Inc.; *U.S. Public*, pg. 1430

TIARA—Party-Plan Giftware—Lancaster Colony Corporation; *U.S. Public*, pg. 976

TIARA DESSERTS—Lower-Calorie Dessert Mixes—The Procter & Gamble Company; *U.S. Public*, pg. 1330

TIA'S TEX-MEX—Tex-Mex Restaurant—Ruby Tuesday, Inc.; *U.S. Public*, pg. 1411

TIBERAL—Antimicrobial—Roche Holding Ltd.; *Int'l*, pg. 1119

TIBET—Broadloom—Couristan Inc.; *U.S. Private*, pg. 279

TIBOND—Anodes—IMI Plc; *Int'l*, pg. 646

TIBOR—Titanium Boron Aluminum Alloys—KB Alloys, Inc.; *U.S. Private*, pg. 249

TIBROPARK—Wallcovering & Borders—Forbo Holding SA; *Int'l*, pg. 496

TIC TAC—Breath Mints—Ferrero U.S.A., Inc.; *Int'l*, pg. 480

TIC TACS—Candy Breath Mints—Ferrero; *Int'l*, pg. 480

TICAR—Titanium Carbon Aluminum Alloys—KB Alloys, Inc.; *U.S. Private*, pg. 249

TICAR—Pharmaceutical Prods.—SmithKline Beecham Laboratories; *U.S. Public*, pg. 1264

TICAR—Anti-Infective—SmithKline Beecham plc; *Int'l*, pg. 1264

TICARPARIN—Treatment of Gram-Negative Bacterial Infections—SmithKline Beecham plc; *Int'l*, pg. 1264

TICARPENNIN—Treatment of Gram-Negative Bacterial Infection—SmithKline Beecham plc; *Int'l*, pg. 1264

TICE BCG—Pharmaceutical—Organon Inc.; *Int'l*, pg. 48

TICK STOP—Repellent—Health Products Corporation; *U.S. Private*, pg. 514

TICK STOP D-20—Repellent—Health Products Corporation; *U.S. Private*, pg. 514

TICKET RESTAURANT—Meal Vouchers—Accor S.A.; *Int'l*, pg. 20

TICKETCHEK—Computerized Transportation System—Rand McNally & Company; *U.S. Private*, pg. 908

TICKETMASTER—Computerized Ticketing Services—Ticketmaster Corporation; *U.S. Private*, pg. 1084

TICKETS—Casual Dresses—Chorus Line Corporation; *U.S. Private*, pg. 238

TICKLE—Deodorant—Bristol-Myers Squibb Company; *U.S. Public*, pg. 253

TICKLER—Memory Board—Sanford Corporation; *U.S. Public*, pg. 1178

TICLID—Anti Stroke Drug—Roche Holding Ltd.; *Int'l*, pg. 1119

TICO—Avocados—Calavo Growers of California; *U.S. Private*, pg. 199

TICO ADJUSTAMOUNTS—Machine Mounts—James Walker & Co. Limited; *Int'l*, pg. 1485

TICODE-12—Metals—Titanium Metals Corporation; *U.S. Private*, pg. 270

TICONDEROGA—Pencils—Dixon Ticonderoga Company; *U.S. Public*, pg. 514

TICONDEROGA—Plywood, Wood & Wood Fiber Products—Georgia-Pacific Corporation; *U.S. Public*, pg. 735

TIDALWAVE—NONE—Packaging Resources, Incorporated; *U.S. Private*, pg. 833

TIDE—Laundry Product—The Procter & Gamble Company; *U.S. Public*, pg. 1330

TIDEGUARD—Protective Cladding—Ameron International Corporation; *U.S. Public*, pg. 98

TIDI-BENCH—Sports Maintenance Equipment—Sport Supply Group, Inc.; *U.S. Public*, pg. 1499

TIDI-COURT—Sports Maintenance Equipment—Sport Supply Group, Inc.; *U.S. Public*, pg. 1499

TIDY CAT—Cat Box Fillers, Cat Box Liners & Deodorizers—Golden Cat Corporation; *U.S. Public*, pg. 1360

TIDY CAT MC—Cat Litter—Golden Cat Corporation; *U.S. Public*, pg. 1360

TIDY SACK—Disposable Sacks & Bags—Georgia-Pacific Corporation; *U.S. Public*, pg. 735

TIDY SCOOP—Scooping Cat Box Filler—Golden Cat Corporation; *U.S. Public*, pg. 1360

TIDY SCOOP MULTIPLE CAT—Scooping Cat Box Filler—Golden Cat Corporation; *U.S. Public*, pg. 1360

TIE-DIE—Neckwear Interlining Die-Cut Process—Specialty Textile Products; *U.S. Private*, pg. 1023

TIE-SERIES—T1 Network Access Multiplexers—Osicom Technologies Inc.; *U.S. Public*, pg. 1233

TIELINE—NONE—American Management Systems, Inc.; *U.S. Public*, pg. 86

TIEMPO—Radial Tires—The Goodyear Tire & Rubber Company; *U.S. Public*, pg. 752

TIER 1—Sleeping Bags—The Canadian Coleman Co., Ltd.; *U.S. Private*, pg. 691

TIER 3—Sleeping Bags—The Canadian Coleman Co., Ltd.; *U.S. Private*, pg. 691

TIER 2—Sleeping Bags—The Canadian Coleman Co., Ltd.; *U.S. Private*, pg. 691

TIFFANY—Jewelry, Fragrance—Tiffany & Co.; *U.S. Public*, pg. 1608

TIFFANY & CO.—Jewelry, Fragrance, China, Crystal, Silver—Tiffany & Co.; *U.S. Public*, pg. 1608

TIFFANY'S—Pies—Ranks Hovis McDougall Limited; *Int'l*, pg. 1395

TIGACLAD II—Prefinished Doors & Panels Composed of Wood Products—Weyerhaeuser Company; *U.S. Public*, pg. 1764

TIGACLAD II—Prefinished Doors & Panels—Weyerhaeuser Forest Products Company; *U.S. Public*, pg. 1764

TIGAN—Anti-Emebic—Roberts Pharmaceutical Corporation; *U.S. Public*, pg. 1393

TIGAN—Pharmaceutical Prods.—SmithKline Beecham Laboratories; *Int'l*, pg. 1264

TIGAN—Control of Nausea—SmithKline Beecham plc; *Int'l*, pg. 1264

TIGEAR—Mechanical Speed Reducing Units—Rockwell International Corporation; *U.S. Public*, pg. 1397

TIGER—Sporting Goods—ASICS Tiger Corporation; *U.S. Private*, pg. 89

TIGER—Gruyere Cheese—Atalanta Corporation; *U.S. Private*, pg. 93

TIGER—Thread—Coats North America; *Int'l*, pg. 300

TIGER—Beer—Heineken N.V.; *Int'l*, pg. 608

TIGER—Saw—Pentair, Inc.; *U.S. Public*, pg. 1273

TIGER—Admixed & White Admixed Cement—The Siam Cement Public Company Limited; *Int'l*, pg. 1237

TIGER—Electronic Hand-Held Games/Toys—Tiger Electronics, Inc.; *U.S. Private*, pg. 1086

TIGER—NONE—Tiger Medicals Ltd.; *Int'l*, pg. 603

TIGER—Vacuum Cleaner—Vorwerk & Co.; *Int'l*, pg. 1480

TIGER BALM—NONE—Tiger Medicals Ltd.; *Int'l*, pg. 603

TIGER-CUB—Compact Saw—Pentair, Inc.; *U.S. Public*, pg. 1273

TIGER EXPRESS—NONE—Imperial Oil Limited; *U.S. Public*, pg. 602

TIGER FORCE—Carbide Circular Saw Blades & Handsaws—The Disston Co.; *U.S. Public*, pg. 950

TIGER GRIP—Caulks, Adhesives, Sealants—Sherwin-Williams Coatings Division; *U.S. Public*, pg. 1466

TIGER-GRIT—Made in a Wide Range of Grit Sizes—Felton Brush Inc.; *U.S. Private*, pg. 400

TIGER MEDICATED PLASTER—NONE—Tiger Medicals Ltd.; *Int'l*, pg. 603

TIGER MUSCLE RUB—NONE—Tiger Medicals Ltd.; *Int'l*, pg. 603

TIGER PLUS—Fiberglass Handled Shovels—Ames Company; *U.S. Public*, pg. 1683

TIGER RIVER SPAS—Spas—Watkins Manufacturing Corp./Hot Spring Portable Spas; *U.S. Public*, pg. 1054

TIGER TEETH—Mining Teeth—GH Hensley Industries, Inc.; *U.S. Private*, pg. 439

TIGER TOP—Soft Top—Bestop, Inc.; *Int'l*, pg. 830

TIGER-TUF—Power Brush Products in Nylon, Horsehair and Tampico—Felton Brush Inc.; *U.S. Private*, pg. 400

TIGERHOOD—Welding Helmets—The Fibre-Metal Products Company; *U.S. Private*, pg. 402

TIGERVISION—Video Software—Tiger Electronics, Inc.; *U.S. Private*, pg. 1086

TIGHTENING-TASKMASTER—Microprocessor-Based Controllers for Fastener Tightening Tools—SPS Technologies, Inc.; *U.S. Public*, pg. 1419

TIGON—Voice Messaging—Lucent Netcare Messaging Services; *U.S. Public*, pg. 1018

TIGRA—NONE—Vauxhall; *U.S. Public*, pg. 724

TIJUANA SMALLS—Cigars—General Cigar Company, Inc.; *U.S. Public*, pg. 708

TIKES PEAK—Road & Rail Set—Rubbermaid Incorporated; *U.S. Public*, pg. 1411

TIKI—NONE—Cruspi S.A.; *Int'l*, pg. 348

TIKKELS—Licorice Candy—CSM N.V.; *Int'l*, pg. 243

TILADE—Inhaler (Nedocromil Sodium Inhalation Aerosol)—Medeva Pharmaceuticals; *Int'l*, pg. 852

TILCOTIL—Anti-Inflammatory Agent—Roche Holding Ltd.; *Int'l*, pg. 1119

TILDIEM—Pharmaceutical—L'Oreal S.A.; *Int'l*, pg. 818

TILDIEM—Pharmaceutical Products—Searle Laboratories; *U.S. Public*, pg. 1125

TILE PASTE—Adhesive—Red Devil Inc.; *U.S. Private*, pg. 915

TILEX—Instant Mildew Remover—The Clorox Company; *U.S. Public*, pg. 386

TILLAMOOK—Cheese—Tillamook County Creamery Assn.; *U.S. Private*, pg. 1086

TILLER—Ag Chemical—AgrEvo USA Company; *Int'l*, pg. 1203

TILLERS—Garden Tractors—MTD Products, Inc.; *U.S. Private*, pg. 688

TILLON—Aggregates—BTR plc; *Int'l*, pg. 124

TILLYER—Magnifying Ophthalmic Lenses—American Optical Corporation; *U.S. Private*, pg. 60

TILT—Fungicide—Ciba Specialty Chemicals; *Int'l*, pg. 291

TILT—Fungicide—Novartis; *Int'l*, pg. 972

TILT N' TUMBLE—Game—Pressman Toy Corp.; *U.S. Private*, pg. 882

TILT-TOP—Anvil—U.S. Surgical Corp.; *U.S. Public*, pg. 1687

TILT-WHEEL STEERING—Power Boats—Teleflex Incorporated; *U.S. Public*, pg. 1569

TILT-WHEEL—Adjustable Steering Columns—Delphi Saginaw Steering Systems; *U.S. Public*, pg. 719

TIM MEE—Toys—Processed Plastic Company; *U.S. Private*, pg. 888

TIMATION—Computer Product—International Business Machines Corporation; *U.S. Public*, pg. 895

TIMBER CREEK—Casual Pants—VF Corporation; *U.S. Public*, pg. 1702

TIMBER RIDGE—Prefinished Wall Paneling—Georgia-Pacific Corporation; *U.S. Public*, pg. 735

TIMBER STRAND—Laminated Strand Lumber—Trus Joist MacMillan; *Int'l*, pg. 829

TIMBER STRAND—Laminated Strand Lumber—Trus Joist MacMillan; *U.S. Public*, pg. 1556

TIMBER TOPPER—Apparel—Fred Meyer Stores; *U.S. Public*, pg. 1103

TIMBERLAKE—NONE—American Woodmark Corporation; *U.S. Public*, pg. 96

TIMBERLAND—Outdoor Wear—Sao Paulo Alpargatas S.A.; *Int'l*, pg. 1193

TIMBERLAND—Footwear, Apparel Accessories & Licensed Products—The Timberland Company; *U.S. Public*, pg. 1609

TIMBERLAND WATCHES—Licensee—Timex Corporation; *U.S. Private*, pg. 1088

TIMBERLINE—Vehicle Conversion—Starcraft Corporation; *U.S. Public*, pg. 1510

TIMBERLINE—Wood Window Coverings—Wausau Metals, Nanik Division; *U.S. Public*, pg. 1500

TIMBERLINE SERIES—Heavyweight Laminated Shingles—Building Materials Corporation of America; *U.S. Public*, pg. 433

TIMBERMAX—Laminated Veneer Lumber—TJ International, Inc.; *U.S. Public*, pg. 1556

TIMBERSTRAND—Laminated Strand Lumber—TJ International, Inc.; *U.S. Public*, pg. 1556

TIMBERTONE—NONE—Amerimark Inc.; *U.S. Public*, pg. 1237

TIMBERWOLF—Power Tools—The Black & Decker Corporation; *U.S. Public*, pg. 233

TIMBLEND—Composition Wood Panels—Weyerhaeuser Company; *U.S. Public*, pg. 1764

TIMBLEND—Industrial Grade Particleboard—Weyerhaeuser Forest Products Company; *U.S. Public*, pg. 1764

TIME—Insurance—Time Insurance; *Int'l*, pg. 499

TIME—Magazine—Time Warner Inc.; *U.S. Public*, pg. 1610

TIME-A-MATIC—Sprinklers—Melnor Inc.; *U.S. Public*, pg. 1234

TIME AND PLACE—Computer Product—International Business Machines Corporation; *U.S. Public*, pg. 895

TIME CRITICAL MANUFACTURING—NONE—Effective Management Systems; *U.S. Public*, pg. 565

TIME-LIFE BOOKS—Book Publ.—Time Warner Inc.; *U.S. Public*, pg. 1610

TIME-LIFE MUSIC—Music Publ.—Time Warner Inc.; *U.S. Public*, pg. 1610

TIME-LIFE VIDEO RECORDINGS—Videos—Time-Life, Inc.; *U.S. Public*, pg. 1613

TIME MANAGER—Software Program—Barrister Information Systems Corporation; *U.S. Public*, pg. 192

TIME RETAIL FINANCE—Credit Services—Kingfisher plc; *Int'l*, pg. 733

TIME SAVER—Convenience Stores—E-Z Serve Convenience Stores, Inc.; *U.S. Public*, pg. 540

TIME SAVER—Convenience Stores—E-Z Serve Corp.; *U.S. Public*, pg. 540

TIME SAVERS—24 Hour Telephone Banking—The Troy Savings Bank; *U.S. Private*, pg. 1106

TIME SAVOR LINE—Soup Cubes, Salad Dices, Small Whole Peeled Potatoes, SuperSlices—Lamb-Weston, Inc.; *U.S. Public*, pg. 427

TIME SPECTRUM—Computer Equipment—Emulex Corporation; *U.S. Public*, pg. 579

TIME/SYSTEM—Personal Planning Systems—Amer Group Ltd.; *Int'l*, pg. 72

TIME TAPE—Tape Labels—TimeMed Labeling Systems, Inc.; *U.S. Public*, pg. 1087

TIME/VIEW—Network Mgt. System—Ascom Timeplex; *Int'l*, pg. 86

TIME WARNER AUDIO & VIDEO RECORDINGS—Audio & Videos—Time Warner Inc.; *U.S. Public*, pg. 1610

TIMEBINATION—Time-Delay Combination Lock—Sargent & Greenleaf, Inc.; *U.S. Private*, pg. 965

TIMEBLEND PLUS—Super Smooth Surfaced Industrial Grade Particleboard—Weyerhaeuser Forest Products Company; *U.S. Public*, pg. 1764

TIMEKEEPER—NONE—Kronos Incorporated; *U.S. Public*, pg. 967

TIMEKEEPER CENTRAL—NONE—Kronos Incorporated; *U.S. Public*, pg. 967

TIMELINE—NONE—The At-A-Glance Group; *U.S. Private*, pg. 295

TIMEMASTER—Investment Plans—Derbyshire Building Society; *Int'l*, pg. 394

TIMENTIN—Antibiotic—SmithKline Beecham Corporation; *Int'l*, pg. 1264

TIMENTIN—Pharmaceutical Prods.—SmithKline Beecham Laboratories; *Int'l*, pg. 1264

TIMEOUT—Activewear—King Louie International; *U.S. Private*, pg. 621

TIMEPAC—Packet Switching—Ascom Timeplex; *Int'l*, pg. 86

TIMEPEACE—Calenders—The At-A-Glance Group; *U.S. Private*, pg. 295

TIMEPLEXER—Time Div. Multiplexer—Ascom Timeplex; *Int'l*, pg. 86

TIMES—Book Imprint—Random House, Inc.; *U.S. Private*, pg. 20

TIMESLINE—Audiotext Service—St. Petersburg Times; *U.S. Private*, pg. 1088

TIMESPAN—Digital Telephone Equipment—DSC Communications Corporation; *U.S. Public*, pg. 475

TIMETAL—Metals—Titanium Metals Corporation; *U.S. Private*, pg. 270

TIMETER—Home RespiratoryCare Products—Allied Healthcare Products, Inc.; *U.S. Public*, pg. 48

TIMETIN—Anti-Infective—SmithKline Beecham plc; *Int'l*, pg. 1264

TIMEX—Watches & Clocks—Timex Corporation; *U.S. Private*, pg. 1088

TIMKEN—Bearings, Steels—The Timken Company; *U.S. Public*, pg. 1617

TIMOLIDE—Timolol Maleate with Hydrochlorothiazide—Merck & Co., Inc.; *U.S. Public*, pg. 1090

TIMOPTIC—Timolol Maleate—Merck & Co., Inc.; *U.S. Public*, pg. 1090

TIMOPTIC—Pharmaceutical—Merck Human Health Division (U.S. Human Health); *U.S. Public*, pg. 1091

TIMOTEI—Shampoo—Unilever Plc; *Int'l*, pg. 1433

TIN STRIP 9T—Tin Strip for Printed Circuit Boards—LeaRonal, Inc.; *U.S. Public*, pg. 982

TINA—Transcutaneous Monitor—Radiometer America Inc.; *Int'l*, pg. 1083

TINACTIN—Antifungal Products—Schering-Plough Corporation; *U.S. Public*, pg. 1438

TINACTIN—Anti-Fungal Agent—Schering-Plough Healthcare Products, Inc.; *U.S. Public*, pg. 1438

TINDLE MILLS FEEDS—Formula Feeds For Animals-US—Ag Processing Inc., A Cooperative; *U.S. Private*, pg. 26

TINE—NONE—Tine-Vestlandsmeieriet; *Int'l*, pg. 1390

TINEL—Shape Memory Alloys—Raychem Corporation; *U.S. Public*, pg. 1362

TINEL-LOCK—Rings—Raychem Corporation; *U.S. Public*, pg. 1362

TINGLE FEET—Insoles & Foot Pads—Sentinel Consumer Products, Inc.; *U.S. Private*, pg. 984

TINGLEY RUBBER—Rubber Footwear—Tingley Rubber Corporation; *U.S. Private*, pg. 1088

TINGLO CULMO—Bright Acid Tin—LeaRonal, Inc.; *U.S. Public*, pg. 982

TINGLO CULMO HS—High Speed Plating Bath—LeaRonal, Inc.; *U.S. Public*, pg. 982

TINGLO CULMO SPECIAL F—Semi-to-Bright Acid Tin—LeaRonal, Inc.; *U.S. Public*, pg. 982

TINKERTOYS—Construction Toys—Hasbro, Inc.; *U.S. Public*, pg. 797

TINNERMAN—Spring Steel & Plastic—Eaton Corporation, Engineered Fasteners Division; *U.S. Public*, pg. 556

TINNERMAN—Fasteners—Engineered Fasteners Div.; *U.S. Public*, pg. 557

TINNOL—Cooling Lubricants for Reduction of Metal for Metal Containers—Quaker Chemical Corporation; *U.S. Public*, pg. 1346

TINOSTAT—Feed Chemicals—Salsbury Laboratories, Inc.; *U.S. Public*, pg. 1277

TINSEL TOWN—Dining Experience—Ogden Corporation; *U.S. Public*, pg. 1213

TINSLEY ADVERTISING—NONE—Tinsley Advertising; *U.S. Private*, pg. 1088

TINSLEY PUBLIC RELATIONS—NONE—Tinsley Advertising; *U.S. Private*, pg. 1088

TINSLEY SPORTS NETWORK—NONE—Tinsley Advertising; *U.S. Private*, pg. 1088

TINSLEY YELLOW PAGE SERVICES—NONE—Tinsley Advertising; *U.S. Private*, pg. 1088

TINTEX—Fabric Dye—Kiwi Brands; *U.S. Public*, pg. 1433

TINTOLITES—Opthalmic Lenses—American Optical Corporation; *U.S. Private*, pg. 60

TINTOMATIC—Photochromic Ophthalmic Lenses—American Optical Corporation; *U.S. Private*, pg. 60

TINUVIN 123—Light Stabilizer—Ciba Specialty Chemicals; *Int'l*, pg. 291

TINY TALK—Greeting Cards—American Greetings Corporation; *U.S. Public*, pg. 77

TINY TIM COLLECTION—Greeting Cards—American Greetings Corporation; *U.S. Public*, pg. 77

TINY TOONS—Breakfast Cereal—The Quaker Oats Company; *U.S. Public*, pg. 1347

TINY-TUFT—Small Tuft Pad Drivers—Felton Brush Inc.; *U.S. Private*, pg. 400

TINY WHACKER—Insect Control—Bushwhacker Associates, Inc.; *U.S. Private*, pg. 141

TIO MATEO—Sherry—Allied Domecq PLC; *Int'l*, pg. 62

TIO PEPE—Spirits—Mercian Corporation; *Int'l,* pg. 858

TIO PEPE'S—Churros—J & J Snack Foods Corporation; *U.S. Public,* pg. 916

TIO SOTO—Fortified Wine—Leonard Kreusch, Inc.; *U.S. Private,* pg. 635

TIOGA—Motor Home—Fleetwood Enterprises, Inc.; *U.S. Public,* pg. 650

TIOGA—Men's Cologne & Skin Conditioner—Shaklee Corporation; *Int'l,* pg. 1518

TIONA—Used in Coatings, Paints, Plastics etc. for Superior Whitening—Millennium Inorganic Chemicals; *Int'l,* pg. 593

TIOXIDE—Titanium Dioxide Pigaments—Tioxide Group Limited; *Int'l,* pg. 663

TIP—Tailored Insurance Protection—Harleysville Group; *U.S. Public,* pg. 786

TIP AND POUR—Small Vacuum—Advance Machine Company; *Int'l,* pg. 932

TIP-OFF—Closure Caps Used For Sealing Containers of Serum—The West Company, Incorporated; *U.S. Public,* pg. 1755

TIP-ON—Plastic Sheet for Bond Paper—Plastic Suppliers Inc.; *U.S. Private,* pg. 871

TIP-TO-TIP—Catheters with a Radiopaque Line—Mallinckrodt Inc.; *U.S. Public,* pg. 1039

TIP TONI—Home Permanent—The Gillette Company; *U.S. Public,* pg. 743

TIP TOP—Foods—Seneca Foods Corporation; *U.S. Public,* pg. 1456

TIP2—Turbine Ice Peaking Power—Burns & McDonnell Engineers-Architects-Consultants; *U.S. Private,* pg. 187

TIPAQUE—Titanium Dioxide—Ishihara Sangyo Kaisha, Ltd.; *Int'l,* pg. 689

TIPARILLO—Cigars—General Cigar Company, Inc.; *U.S. Public,* pg. 708

TIPS—Outsourced Solution for Reengineering Trade Fund & Deduction Management—Gelco Information Network, Inc.; *U.S. Private,* pg. 442

TIRE AMERICA—NONE—Sears, Roebuck and Co.; *U.S. Public,* pg. 1452

TIRE BUSINESS—Newspaper—Crain Communications, Inc.; *U.S. Private,* pg. 284

TIRESEAL—Tire Sealant for Off Road—Texas Refinery Corp.; *U.S. Private,* pg. 1078

TIRIS—NONE—Texas Instruments Incorporated; *U.S. Public,* pg. 1585

TIRS—Computer Product—International Business Machines Corporation; *U.S. Public,* pg. 895

TISCHLER-KEVORKIAN—Gynecological Device—The Cooper Companies, Inc.; *U.S. Public,* pg. 442

TISCHLER-MORGAN—Gynecological Device—The Cooper Companies, Inc.; *U.S. Public,* pg. 442

TISS—Facial Tissue, Bathroom Tissue, Cocktail & Table Napkins—Kimberly-Clark Corporation; *U.S. Public,* pg. 958

TISSOT—Watches—SMH Swiss Corporation for Micro Electronics & Watchmaking Indus. Ltd.; *Int'l,* pg. 1160

TISSUE DIGESTER—Holding Tank Tissue Digester—Thetford Corporation; *U.S. Private,* pg. 352

TISSUE-PREP—Tissue Embedding Material—Fisher Scientific Company; *U.S. Private,* pg. 658

TITAL—Titanium Aluminum Alloys—KB Alloys, Inc.; *U.S. Private,* pg. 249

TITAN—Door Locksets—The Black & Decker Corporation; *U.S. Public,* pg. 233

TITAN—Manufactured Homes & Motor Homes—Champion Enterprises, Inc.; *U.S. Public,* pg. 332

TITAN—BALL VALVES—Crane Limited U.K.; *U.S. Public,* pg. 458

TITAN—Electric Revolving Warning/Signal Light—Federal Signal Corporation, Signal Div.; *U.S. Public,* pg. 616

TITAN—Plastic Block Utility Brush—Flo-Pac Corporation; *U.S. Private,* pg. 414

TITAN—Automotive Lubricants—Fuchs Petrolub AG Oel + Chemie; *Int'l,* pg. 517

TITAN—Trucks—Le Tourneau, Inc.; *U.S. Public,* pg. 1410

TITAN—Electric Shavers—Matsushita Electric Works, Ltd.; *Int'l,* pg. 847

TITAN—NONE—The Middleby Corporation; *U.S. Public,* pg. 1109

TITAN—Fantasy Game—Monarch Avalon, Inc.; *U.S. Public,* pg. 1123

TITAN—Commercial Grade Steel Shelving—Penco Products; *U.S. Private,* pg. 848

TITAN—Conditioning Systems & Burn-in Boards & Sockets—Reliability Incorporated; *U.S. Public,* pg. 1373

TITAN—Portable Electric Heater—The Rival Company; *U.S. Public,* pg. 1391

TITAN—Turbine Products—Solar Turbines Incorporated; *U.S. Public,* pg. 316

TITAN—Apparel & Fabric—I. Spiewak & Sons, Inc.; *U.S. Private,* pg. 1025

TITAN—Off-Highway Wheels & Tires—Titan International, Inc.; *U.S. Public,* pg. 1618

TITAN—Fertilizer Applicator—Tyler Industries; *U.S. Private,* pg. 1112

TITAN—Above Nema Frame Motors—U.S. Electrical Motor Division; *U.S. Public,* pg. 573

TITAN—Centrifuge—Western States Machine Company; *U.S. Private,* pg. 1168

TITAN/CENTAUR LAUNCH VEHICLE—NONE—General Dynamics Corporation; *U.S. Public,* pg. 708

TITAN & DESIGN—Communications Consulting & Computer Hardware Design—The Titan Corporation; *U.S. Public,* pg. 1618

TITAN LINKABIT—Communication Apparatus—The Titan Corporation; *U.S. Public,* pg. 1618

TITAN SCAN SM—Material Irradiation Services—The Titan Corporation; *U.S. Public,* pg. 1618

TITAN TEQCOM—Computer Software & Network—The Titan Corporation; *U.S. Public,* pg. 1618

TITAN 90—Filter-Permanent Media, Automatic Backwash—Serfilco, Ltd.; *U.S. Private,* pg. 985

TITANIUM HEAD BUBBLE DRIVER—Titanium Golf Driver—Taylor Made Golf Co. Inc.; *Int'l,* pg. 1181

TITANIUM PLUS—Alkaline Batteries—VARTA Batteries Inc.; *Int'l,* pg. 1452

THE TITANIUM—Cutlery—Buck Knives, Inc.; *U.S. Private,* pg. 177

TITE-LOC—Coping System—Petersen Aluminum Corporation; *U.S. Private,* pg. 856

TITE-R-BOND—Adhesion Promotors—Norton Performance Plastics; *Int'l,* pg. 1174

TITESEAL—Oil Treatment—Radiator Specialty Company; *U.S. Private,* pg. 906

TITESEAL—Closure Liner Sealings Materials—Tekni-Plex, Inc.; *U.S. Private,* pg. 1073

TITLE BOUT—Game—Monarch Avalon, Inc.; *U.S. Public,* pg. 1123

TITLEIST—Golf Equipment—Acushnet Company; *U.S. Public,* pg. 675

TITLEIST—Golf Balls—Fortune Brands, Inc.; *U.S. Public,* pg. 674

TITLEIST—Golf Prods.—Titleist & Foot-Joy Worldwide; *U.S. Public,* pg. 675

TITLEIST DT—NONE—Fortune Brands, Inc.; *U.S. Public,* pg. 674

TITLEIST DCI IRONS—Golf Equipment—Fortune Brands, Inc.; *U.S. Public,* pg. 674

TITLEIST DT—NONE—Acushnet Company; *U.S. Public,* pg. 675

TITLEIST DT—NONE—Titleist & Foot-Joy Worldwide; *U.S. Public,* pg. 675

TITLEIST HP2—NONE—Fortune Brands, Inc.; *U.S. Public,* pg. 674

TITLEIST PROFESSIONAL—NONE—Acushnet Company; *U.S. Public,* pg. 675

TITLEIST PROFESSIONAL—NONE—Fortune Brands, Inc.; *U.S. Public,* pg. 674

TITLEIST PROFESSIONAL—NONE—Titleist & Foot-Joy Worldwide; *U.S. Public,* pg. 675

TITLEIST TOUR BALATA—NONE—Fortune Brands, Inc.; *U.S. Public,* pg. 674

TITOX—Synthetic Rutile—Hitox Corporation of America; *U.S. Public,* pg. 829

TITRALAB—High Performance Titration System—Radiometer America Inc.; *Int'l,* pg. 1083

TITRALAC—Antacid—3M; *U.S. Public,* pg. 1604

TITRALYZER—Titrating Apparatus—Fisher Scientific Company; *U.S. Private,* pg. 658

TITRASTIR—Magnetic Stirrer—Hach Company; *U.S. Public,* pg. 773

TITRIMETER—Apparatus—Fisher Scientific Company; *U.S. Private,* pg. 658

TITRIVER—Chemical Reagant—Hach Company; *U.S. Public,* pg. 773

TIV PLUS—Resin Removing Skin Cleaner—SBS Products, Inc.; *U.S. Private,* pg. 955

TIVOLI—Dinnerware—Dansk International Designs Ltd.; *U.S. Public,* pg. 261

TIVOLI—Bathroom Supplies—Jaclo Inc.; *U.S. Private,* pg. 349

TIZON—Zirconium Chemicals for Glass Polishing—Ferro Corporation; *U.S. Public,* pg. 618

TIZOX—Silicon Polish—Ferro Corporation; *U.S. Public,* pg. 618

TO LIFE!—Magazine—Kimberly-Clark Corporation; *U.S. Public,* pg. 958

TO THE NINTH DEGREE—NONE—Norwest Corporation; *U.S. Public,* pg. 1201

TO YOUR TASTE—NONE—JP Foodservice, Inc.; *U.S. Public,* pg. 918

TO-RICOS—Poultry—ConAgra, Inc.; *U.S. Public,* pg. 425

TOAST!CAFE—Upscale Cafe—Cara Operations Limited; *Int'l,* pg. 266

TOAST'EM—Toaster Pastries Products—Schulze & Burch Biscuit Company; *U.S. Private,* pg. 973

TOAST 4—Toast—Metz Baking Company (WI); *U.S. Private,* pg. 1022

TOAST-R-CAKES—Cakes—CPC Baking Business; *U.S. Public,* pg. 224

TOAST-R-OVEN—Toaster Ovens—The Black & Decker Corporation; *U.S. Public,* pg. 233

TOASTED OAT CEREAL—NONE—Malt-O-Meal Company; *U.S. Private,* pg. 699

TOASTETTES—Toaster Pastries—Nabisco Inc.; *U.S. Public,* pg. 1355

TOASTIES—Breakfast Cereal—Kraft Foods, Inc.; *U.S. Public,* pg. 1287

TOASTMASTER—Cooking & Warming Equipment—The Middleby Corporation; *U.S. Public,* pg. 1109

TOASTMASTER—Mfr. of Small Kitchen Appliances, Heaters, Humidifiers & Fans—Toastmaster, Inc.; *U.S. Public,* pg. 1619

TOASTY O'S—Toasted Oat Cereal—Malt-O-Meal Company; *U.S. Private,* pg. 699

TOASTY-O'S—Toasted Oat Cereal—Malt-O-Meal Company; *U.S. Private,* pg. 699

TOASTY SPICE—Herbal Tea Bags—Thomas J. Lipton Company; *Int'l,* pg. 1435

TOBACCO—Making and Packaging Machinery—G.D. Packaging Machinery Inc.; *Int'l,* pg. 531

TOBIN FIRST PRIZE—Meat Products—John Morrell & Co.; *U.S. Public,* pg. 1479

TOBLER—Chocolate—Kraft Jacobs Suchard AG; *U.S. Public,* pg. 1288

TOBLERONE—Chocolate—Kraft Foods Inc.; *U.S. Public,* pg. 1288

TOBLERONE—Chocolate—Kraft Jacobs Suchard; *U.S. Public,* pg. 1290

TOBLERONE—Chocolate—Kraft Jacobs Suchard AG; *U.S. Public,* pg. 1288

TOBLERONE—Chocolate Bar—Philip Morris Companies Inc.; *U.S. Public,* pg. 1287

TOBRADEX—Antibiotic/Anti-Inflammatory Drops & Ointment—Alcon Laboratories, Inc.; *Int'l,* pg. 916

TOBRAMYCIN—Infectious Disease Therapy—Bristol-Myers Squibb Company; *U.S. Public,* pg. 253

TOBREX—Tobramycine Solution & Ointment—Alcon Laboratories, Inc.; *Int'l,* pg. 916

TOBREX—Antibiotic—Nestle S.A.; *Int'l,* pg. 915

TOBY ALE—Ale—Bass PLC; *Int'l,* pg. 169

TOBY BITTER—Bitters—Bass PLC; *Int'l,* pg. 169

TOBY BROWN—Ale—Bass PLC; *Int'l,* pg. 169

TOBY LIGHT—Ale—Bass PLC; *Int'l,* pg. 169

TOCCO—Induction Hte Systems—Park-Ohio Industries, Inc.; *U.S. Public,* pg. 1258

TOCCOTRON—Oscillator—Tocco, Inc.; *U.S. Public,* pg. 1259

TODAY—Veterinary Pharmaceuticals—American Home Products Corporation; *U.S. Public,* pg. 79

TODAY—Homes—Centex Corporation; *U.S. Public,* pg. 322

TODAY—Electric Irons—Sunbeam Household Products; *U.S. Public,* pg. 1533

TODAY'S CHRISTIAN WOMAN—Magazine—Christianity Today, Inc.; *U.S. Private,* pg. 238

TODAY'S GOLFER—Golf Magazine—EMAP Pursuit Publishing; *Int'l,* pg. 451

TODAY'S HEALTH MINUTE—Health Magazine Program—Westwood One, Inc.; *U.S. Public,* pg. 1763

TODAY'S HOMEOWNER—Magazine—Times Mirror Magazines, Inc.; *U.S. Public,* pg. 1616

TODAY'S KIDS—Toys—Spang & Company; *U.S. Private*, pg. 1020

TODAY'S MAN—Clothing Retailer—Today's Man, Inc.; *U.S. Public*, pg. 1619

TODAY'S RUNNER—Running Magazine—EMAP Pursuit Publishing; *Int'l*, pg. 451

TODAY'S TRAVELER—Travel Tips News Programming—Westwood One, Inc.; *U.S. Public*, pg. 1763

TODCO—Vehicular Door Products—Overhead Door Corporation; *U.S. Private*, pg. 822

TODD—Auctioneers—J.L. Todd Auction Co.; *U.S. Private*, pg. 1090

TODD-AO—Sound Recording for Motion Pictures—The Todd-AO Corporation; *U.S. Public*, pg. 1619

TODD SHIPYARDS—Ship Repair, Conversion, Building—Todd Pacific Shipyards Corp.; *U.S. Public*, pg. 1619

TODDLE TOTS—Building Block Toys—Rubbermaid Incorporated; *U.S. Public*, pg. 1411

TODDLER SOFT SHAPES—Toddler Playground Accessories—Stainless Incorporated; *U.S. Private*, pg. 1029

TODDYNHO—Chocolate Beverage—The Quaker Oats Company; *U.S. Public*, pg. 1347

TOFFEE CRISP—Candies—Nestle-Rowntree Ltd.; *Int'l*, pg. 921

TOFFIFAY—Candy—Storck U.S.A., L.P.; *Int'l*, pg. 1304

TOFFO—Confections—Nestle-Rowntree Ltd.; *Int'l*, pg. 921

TOFRANIL—NONE—Novartis Pharmaceuticals; *Int'l*, pg. 973

TOG—Women's Apparel—The Tog Shop; *U.S. Private*, pg. 1090

TOG-L-LOK—One Hand Clamping Tool—Channellock, Inc.; *U.S. Private*, pg. 229

TOGA-TOPPER—Window Treatment—Robertson Factories, Inc.; *U.S. Private*, pg. 936

TOGAR—Herbicide—The Dow Chemical Company; *U.S. Public*, pg. 522

TOGETHER—Fashion Clothes for the Older—Spiegel, Inc.; *U.S. Public*, pg. 1498

TOGGENBURGER SWISS BUTTER COOKIES—Imported Swiss Butter Cookies—The Promotion in Motion Companies; *U.S. Private*, pg. 890

TOGGENBURGER SWISS WAFERS—Imported Swiss Wafers—The Promotion in Motion Companies; *U.S. Private*, pg. 890

TOGGI SWISS CHOCOLATE COVERED WAFERS—Imported Swiss Wafers—The Promotion in Motion Companies; *U.S. Private*, pg. 890

TOHI-BANK-BY-PHONE—Banking By Phone—Standard Bank Investment Corporation Limited; *Int'l*, pg. 1293

TOILET/BATHROOM DUCK—Cleanser—S.C. Johnson & Son, Inc.; *U.S. Private*, pg. 592

TOILET DUCK—Household Cleaner—S.C. Johnson & Son, Limited; *U.S. Private*, pg. 593

TOILETTE—Child's Toilet—Cosco, Inc.; *U.S. Private*, pg. 277

TOILETTE PLUS—Toilet Trainer & Step Stool—Cosco, Inc.; *U.S. Private*, pg. 277

TOKO—NONE—Toko Inc.; *Int'l*, pg. 1393

TOKRON—Millenium XB—LeaRonal, Inc.; *U.S. Public*, pg. 982

TOKUTOKU KUN—Automatic Development System—Konica Corporation; *Int'l*, pg. 748

TOKYO EXPRESS—Game—Monarch Avalon, Inc.; *U.S. Public*, pg. 1123

TOKYO SHAPIRO—TV-Audio, Electronics—Luskin's, Inc.; *U.S. Private*, pg. 681

TOLECTIN DS CAPSULES—NONE—Ortho-McNeil Pharmaceutical Corporation; *U.S. Public*, pg. 929

TOLECTIN TABLETS—NONE—Ortho-McNeil Pharmaceutical Corporation; *U.S. Public*, pg. 929

TOLEDO—Rugs—Couristan Inc.; *U.S. Private*, pg. 279

TOLEDO TOOL—Pipe Tools—Curtis-Toledo, Inc.; *U.S. Private*, pg. 298

TOLHURST—NONE—Bird Machine Company; *U.S. Public*, pg. 166

TOLHURST—Centrifuges—Ketema, Inc.; *U.S. Private*, pg. 604

TOLL BROTHERS—Homes—Toll Brothers, Inc.; *U.S. Public*, pg. 1620

TOLL HOUSE—Baking Chocolate—Nestle USA; *Int'l*, pg. 916

TOLL HOUSE CAFE—NONE—Nestle USA; *Int'l*, pg. 916

TOLL HOUSE CHOCOBAKE—NONE—Nestle USA; *Int'l*, pg. 916

TOLLET—Air Fresheners—Sara Lee Corporation; *U.S. Public*, pg. 1432

TOLLMAN/HUNDLEY—Hotels—Tollman/Hundley Hotels; *U.S. Public*, pg. 1090

TOLLTAG—Electronic Identification Device—Amtech Corporation; *U.S. Public*, pg. 105

TOLLYCRAFT—All Power Boats—Tollycraft Yacht Corporation; *U.S. Public*, pg. 1620

TOLMICEN—Agent for Epidermis—Kyowa Hakko Kogyo Company, Ltd.; *Int'l*, pg. 778

TOLRA—Frabrics—Tradicion Textil, S.A.; *Int'l*, pg. 1474

TOM & CO—Specialty Pet Care Stores—Etablissements Delhaize Freres Et Cie "Le Lion" S.A.; *Int'l*, pg. 462

THE TOM BROKAW REPORT—90 Second Feature Programming—Westwood One, Inc.; *U.S. Public*, pg. 1763

TOM CAT—Chore Gloves—Boss Manufacturing Company; *U.S. Private*, pg. 1142

THE TOM LEYKIS SHOW—Talk Radio Program—Westwood One Entertainment; *U.S. Public*, pg. 1763

THE TOM LEYKIS SHOW—Talk Show Programming—Westwood One, Inc.; *U.S. Public*, pg. 1763

TOM MOORE—NONE—Barton Brands, Ltd.; *U.S. Public*, pg. 300

TOM MOORE—Bourbon & Whiskey—Barton Incorporated; *U.S. Public*, pg. 300

TOM SAWYER—Boyswear—Elder Manufacturing Company; *U.S. Private*, pg. 367

TOM SAWYER—Meat Products—John Morrell & Co.; *U.S. Public*, pg. 1479

TOM SCOTT—Nuts—The Procter & Gamble Company; *U.S. Public*, pg. 1330

TOM THUMB—Cigars—Hanson PLC; *Int'l*, pg. 592

TOM TOM—Medicated Cough Drops—Cadbury Schweppes p.l.c.; *Int'l*, pg. 247

TOM WATSON—Golf Equipment—RAM Golf Corporation; *U.S. Private*, pg. 908

TOM'S—Nuts, Crackers, Snack Foods—Nestle-Rowntree Ltd.; *Int'l*, pg. 921

TOMAPEP—Seasoning—Cadbury Nigeria PLC; *Int'l*, pg. 248

TOMATIN—Scotch Whiskey—John Gross & Co.; *U.S. Private*, pg. 483

TOMATO GARD—Welded Wire Fabric—Gilbert & Bennett Manufacturing Company; *U.S. Private*, pg. 453

TOMATO TOWER—Plant Support—Gilbert & Bennett Manufacturing Company; *U.S. Private*, pg. 453

TOMATOR—Tomato Sauce—Danone Group; *Int'l*, pg. 379

TOMBEL—Insecticide—Novartis AG; *Int'l*, pg. 971

TOMBOLINI VERDICCHIO—Liquor—Peerless Importers, Inc.; *U.S. Private*, pg. 847

TOMBSTONE—Frozen Pizza—Kraft Foods Inc.; *U.S. Public*, pg. 1288

TOMBSTONE—Frozen Pizza—Philip Morris Companies Inc.; *U.S. Public*, pg. 1287

TOMBSTONE ORIGINAL—Pizza & Beef Sticks—Tombstone Pizza Corporation; *U.S. Public*, pg. 1288

TOMCAT—PTCA Guidewires—Merit Medical Systems, Inc.; *U.S. Public*, pg. 1096

TOMCO CARBURETORS—NONE—Tomco Auto Products, Inc.; *U.S. Private*, pg. 1090

TOMEX—Drilling Technology—Litton Industries, Inc.; *U.S. Public*, pg. 1002

TOMIC—Fittings—Pass & Seymour/Legrand; *Int'l*, pg. 806

TOMLYN—O.T.C. Animal Health & Grooming Aids—IGI, Inc.; *U.S. Public*, pg. 855

TOMMY—NONE—Tommy Hilfiger Corporation; *Int'l*, pg. 1398

TOMMY HILFIGER—Men's Dress Shirts & Golf Shirts—Oxford Industries, Inc.; *U.S. Public*, pg. 1239

TOMORROW—Veterinary Pharmaceuticals—American Home Products Corporation; *U.S. Public*, pg. 79

TOMORROW—Refrigerator—Foster Refrigerator Corporation; *U.S. Private*, pg. 421

TOMOSCAN—Imaging Systems—Philips Electronics N.V.; *Int'l*, pg. 1051

TOM'S—Toasted, Roasted, Salted Peanuts—Tom's Foods, Inc.; *U.S. Private*, pg. 1090

TOM'S GREAT AMERICAN—Potato Chips & Snacks—Tom's Foods, Inc.; *U.S. Private*, pg. 1090

TOMTOM—Sugar Confectionary—Cadbury Nigeria PLC; *Int'l*, pg. 248

TOMUDEX—Pharmaceutical—Zeneca Group Plc; *Int'l*, pg. 1524

TONDENA MANILA—Rum—La Tondena Distillers, Inc.; *Int'l*, pg. 785

TONE BAR SOAP—NONE—The Dial Corporation; *U.S. Public*, pg. 505

TONE BODY WASH—NONE—The Dial Corporation; *U.S. Public*, pg. 505

TONE UP—Temporary Hair Color—Revlon-Realistic Professional Products, Inc.; *U.S. Private*, pg. 690

TONE'S—Herbs & Spices—Burns, Philp & Company Limited; *Int'l*, pg. 236

TONES—On Location Taped Music—Muzak Limited Partnership; *U.S. Private*, pg. 222

TONE'S—Spices, Extracts, Kitchen Ingredients—Tone Brothers Inc.; *U.S. Private*, pg. 237

TONETIC—Wood Stains—Pratt & Lambert United, Inc.; *U.S. Public*, pg. 1466

TONETTE—Bow Machines—CPS Corporation; *U.S. Private*, pg. 422

TONETTE—Children's Home Permanent—The Gillette Company; *U.S. Public*, pg. 743

TONGEL—Cellulose Prods. used in Bldg. Matls., Earthenware—Akzo Nobel N.V.; *Int'l*, pg. 42

TONGUE DIPPERS—Bubble Gum—Amurol Confections Co.; *U.S. Public*, pg. 1781

TONI LIGHTWAVES—Home Permanent—The Gillette Company; *U.S. Public*, pg. 743

TONI SILKWAVE—Home Permanent—The Gillette Company; *U.S. Public*, pg. 743

TONIGUM—Gum—Kraft Jacobs Suchard; *U.S. Public*, pg. 1290

TONKA—Toys—Andover Togs, Inc.; *U.S. Public*, pg. 112

TONKA—NONE—Hasbro; *U.S. Public*, pg. 797

TONKA—Walk-in Coolers & Freezers—The Manitowoc Company, Inc.; *U.S. Public*, pg. 1040

TONKA TRUCKS—Playskool Preschool & Infant Toys—Hasbro, Inc.; *U.S. Public*, pg. 797

TONKAFLO—High Pressure Centrifugal Pumps—Osmonics, Inc.; *U.S. Public*, pg. 1233

TONOCARD—Antiarrhythmic Agent—Astra AB; *Int'l*, pg. 93

TONOCARD—Tocainide—Merck & Co., Inc.; *U.S. Public*, pg. 1090

TONOCARD—Pharmaceutical—Merck Human Health Division (U.S. Human Health); *U.S. Public*, pg. 1091

TONOX—Specialty Chemical—Uniroyal Chemical Company, Inc.; *U.S. Public*, pg. 460

TONY LAMA—Footwear—Justin Industries, Inc.; *U.S. Public*, pg. 936

TONY LAMA—Western Wear—Tony Lama Co., Inc.; *U.S. Public*, pg. 937

TONY ROMA'S FAMOUS FOR RIBS—Restaurant—NPC International, Inc.; *U.S. Public*, pg. 1146

TONY ROMA'S FAMOUS FOR RIBS—Restaurants—Romacorp, Inc.; *U.S. Public*, pg. 1147

TONY'S—Frozen Pizza—Schwan's Sales Enterprises; *U.S. Private*, pg. 974

TOOKIT—Ada Application Components—Harnischfeger Industries, Inc.; *U.S. Public*, pg. 788

TOOL MATES—Tool Boxes—Reading Body Works, Inc.; *U.S. Private*, pg. 913

TOOL PRODUCTS—Aluminum Die Casting—Quadion Corporation; *U.S. Private*, pg. 898

TOOL STOOL—Carryall for Tools & Supplies—Hirsh Company; *U.S. Private*, pg. 963

TOOLMASTER—Small Tool Storage Cases—Delta Consolidated Industries, Inc. (Co. Headquarters); *U.S. Public*, pg. 481

TOOLO—Children's Building Sets—LEGO Systems, Inc.; *U.S. Public*, pg. 805

TOOLSHOP—Tools Provided With Software—Brock International Inc.; *U.S. Public*, pg. 258

TOOLVAC—NONE—AGA Gas, Inc.; *Int'l*, pg. 13

Brand Name Index

TOOTAL—Mens' Wear—Tootal Group plc; *Int'l*, pg. 300

TOOTER—Voice Response Units—Home Shopping Network, Inc.; *U.S. Public*, pg. 1685

TOOTIE—Voice Response Units—Home Shopping Network, Inc.; *U.S. Public*, pg. 1685

TOOTIE FRUITIE'S—Sweetened Fruit Flavored Cereal—Malt-O-Meal Company; *U.S. Private*, pg. 699

TOOTIE FRUITIES—Fruit-Flavored Cereal—Malt-O-Meal Company; *U.S. Private*, pg. 699

TOOTSIE POP—Candy—Tootsie Roll Industries, Inc.; *U.S. Public*, pg. 1621

TOOTSIE POP—Candy—World Trade & Marketing, LTD.; *U.S. Public*, pg. 1621

TOOTSIE ROLL—Candy—Tootsie Roll Industries, Inc.; *U.S. Public*, pg. 1621

TOOTSIE ROLL—Candy—World Trade & Marketing, LTD.; *U.S. Public*, pg. 1621

TOOTSIETOY—Toys—Strombecker Corporation; *U.S. Private*, pg. 1047

TOP BILLING—Personnel Management—Top Billing Inc.; *U.S. Private*, pg. 1091

TOP CARE—HBA—Topco Associates, Inc.; *U.S. Private*, pg. 1091

TOP CREST—General Merchandise—Topco Associates, Inc.; *U.S. Private*, pg. 1091

TOP DOG—Pet Foods—Ag Processing Inc., A Cooperative; *U.S. Private*, pg. 26

TOP DRIVE CENTRIFUGE—NONE—Bird Machine Company; *U.S. Public*, pg. 166

TOP DRUM—Separator—The Spencer Turbine Co.; *U.S. Private*, pg. 1025

TOP FLITE—Golf Ball—Spalding & Evenflo Companies, Inc.; *U.S. Private*, pg. 629

TOP FLITE 2ND GENERATION—Golf Balls—Spalding Sports Worldwide; *U.S. Private*, pg. 630

TOP FLITE TOUR SERIES—Golf Balls—Spalding Sports Worldwide; *U.S. Private*, pg. 630

TOP FROST—Frozen Foods—Topco Associates, Inc.; *U.S. Private*, pg. 1091

TOP GEAR—NONE—BBC Magazines; *Int'l*, pg. 114

TOP GUN—Static Neutralizing Gun—Illinois Tool Works Inc.; *U.S. Public*, pg. 865

TOP HANDZ—Barcode Label Printer—Astro-Med, Inc.; *U.S. Public*, pg. 141

TOP HAT—Frozen Foods—Danone Group; *Int'l*, pg. 379

TOP HAT—Tube Retainers—Litton Industries, Inc.; *U.S. Public*, pg. 1002

TOP HAT SERVICE—Quality & Level of Service Definition—Interstate Van Lines, Inc.; *U.S. Private*, pg. 573

TOP JOB—Cleaner—The Procter & Gamble Company; *U.S. Public*, pg. 1330

TOP NOTCH—Inserts For Metalcutting Tools—Kennametal Inc.; *U.S. Public*, pg. 950

TOP OF THE POPS—NONE—BBC Magazines; *Int'l*, pg. 114

TOP QUALITY—Fresh Potatoes—Idaho Supreme Company; *U.S. Private*, pg. 557

TOP QUARTILE—Quarry Tile Floor Cleaner—Ecolab Inc.; *U.S. Public*, pg. 562

TOP RAMEN—Instant Noodles—Nissin Foods (U.S.A.) Co. Ltd.; *Int'l*, pg. 949

TOP-RIDER—Two-Tiered Organizers—Vance Industries, Inc.; *U.S. Private*, pg. 1133

TOP SECRET—Granular Cat Box Deodorized Additive—Ralston Purina Company; *U.S. Public*, pg. 1359

TOP-SPEC—After Market Truck Components—Eaton Corporation; *U.S. Public*, pg. 555

TOP STOP—Length-Adjustable Gas Cylinder for Office Chairs—Suspa Compart AG; *Int'l*, pg. 1322

TOP THAT—Card Game—Mattel Games/Puzzles; *U.S. Public*, pg. 1058

TOP-TOWLS—Paper Towels—Bay West Paper Corp. Towel & Tissue Div.; *U.S. Public*, pg. 1747

TOP UP—Clinical Nutrition—Novo Nordisk A/S; *Int'l*, pg. 987

TOPAS—Fungicide—Novartis; *Int'l*, pg. 972

TOPAZ—Rugs—Couristan Inc.; *U.S. Private*, pg. 279

TOPAZ—X-Ray Tubes—Litton Industries, Inc.; *U.S. Public*, pg. 1002

TOPAZ—Adult Mass Market Paperback Books—Penguin Putnam Inc.; *Int'l*, pg. 1027

TOPAZIO—Beer—Central de Cervejas, S.A.; *Int'l*, pg. 279

TOPAZIO—Women's Shoes—Nine West Group, Inc.; *U.S. Public*, pg. 1185

TOPCHIC—Permanent Haircolor—Goldwell Cosmetics (USA) Inc.; *Int'l*, pg. 718

TOPCOAT—Body Filler—Marson/Creative Fastener, Inc.; *U.S. Private*, pg. 708

TOPCOUNT—Microplate Scintillation Counter—Packard Instrument Co., Inc.; *U.S. Private*, pg. 833

TOPDROP—Candy—CSM N.V.; *Int'l*, pg. 243

TOPEKA CAPITAL JOURNAL—Newspapers—Shivers Trading & Operating Co.; *U.S. Private*, pg. 994

TOPEX—Acne Remedy—Richardson-Vicks, Inc. Personal Care Products Div.; *U.S. Public*, pg. 1331

TOPFLITE—Lawn Equip.—MTD Products, Inc.; *U.S. Private*, pg. 688

TOPGARD—A, B, C, F Roof Coatings—Johns Manville Corporation; *U.S. Public*, pg. 927

TOPGUARD—All Products—DMI Furniture Inc.; *U.S. Public*, pg. 473

TOPGUN—Premium Laser, Inkjet Paper—Union Camp Corporation; *U.S. Public*, pg. 1665

TOPHEL—NONE—Carpenter Technology Corporation; *U.S. Public*, pg. 307

TOPHET—NONE—Carpenter Technology Corporation; *U.S. Public*, pg. 307

TOPI—Ball Valves—KSB Aktiengesellschaft; *Int'l*, pg. 721

TOPI MAT—Actuated Valves—KSB Aktiengesellschaft; *Int'l*, pg. 721

TOPIC—NONE—Nestle USA; *Int'l*, pg. 916

TOPICYCLINE—Dermatological Product—Roberts Pharmaceutical Corporation; *U.S. Public*, pg. 1393

TOPIFRAM—Lotions, Creams—E.T. Browne Drug Co., Inc.; *U.S. Private*, pg. 175

TOPIK—Wheat Herbicide—Novartis; *Int'l*, pg. 972

TOPKAPI—Women's Fashion Accessories Stores—Claire's Stores Inc.; *U.S. Public*, pg. 381

TOPKICK—Trucks—General Motors Corporation; *U.S. Public*, pg. 718

TOPLINER—Vacuum-Formed Liners—Hedwin Corporation; *Int'l*, pg. 1278

TOPOL—Whitenning Toothpaste Products—Dep Corporation; *U.S. Public*, pg. 500

TOPPER—Athletic Footwear—Sao Paulo Alpargatas S.A.; *Int'l*, pg. 1193

TOPPER—Trailer-Mounted Access Platform—Simon Engineering plc; *Int'l*, pg. 1251

TOPPITS—Food Wraps & Foils—Melitta Unternehmensgruppe Bentz KG; *Int'l*, pg. 856

TOPPLE—Game—Pressman Toy Corp.; *U.S. Private*, pg. 882

TOPPS—Comics—The Topps Company, Inc.; *U.S. Public*, pg. 1621

TOPPS ARCHIVES—Sports Cards—The Topps Company, Inc.; *U.S. Public*, pg. 1621

TOPPS FINEST—Sports Cards—The Topps Company, Inc.; *U.S. Public*, pg. 1621

TOPPS GALLERY—Sports Cards—The Topps Company, Inc.; *U.S. Public*, pg. 1621

TOPPS SPORTS CARDS—Baseball, Football, Basketball & Hockey Cards—The Topps Company, Inc.; *U.S. Public*, pg. 1621

TOPROL-XL—Cardiovascular Pharmaceutical—Astra AB; *Int'l*, pg. 93

TOPROL XL—Pharmaceutical Products—Astra USA, Inc.; *U.S. Public*, pg. 93

TOPS—Semi-Automatic Telephone Switchboard—Northern Telecom Limited; *Int'l*, pg. 968

TOPS APPLIANCE CITY—Retail Outlet—Tops Appliance City; *U.S. Public*, pg. 1622

TOPS MARKETS—Food Stores—Koninklijke Ahold NV; *Int'l*, pg. 749

TOPS MILD—Dry Snuff—Swisher International Group, Inc.; *U.S. Public*, pg. 1543

TOPS 'N BOTTOMS—Junior & Young Men's Fashions—Deb Shops, Inc.; *U.S. Public*, pg. 491

TOPS SWEET—Dry Snuff—Swisher International Group, Inc.; *U.S. Public*, pg. 1543

TOPSIDER—Industrial Safety Eyewear—Uvex Safety, Inc.; *Int'l*, pg. 132

TOPSIN—Fungicide—Elf Atochem North America, Inc.; *Int'l*, pg. 445

TOPSPIN—Occasional Tables, ai Collection—Vecta; *U.S. Private*, pg. 1038

TOPSPOT—Transformable Handsfree Flashlight—Streamlight Inc.; *U.S. Private*, pg. 1047

TOPSY'S—Food Service & Franchise Co.—Topsy's International Inc.; *U.S. Private*, pg. 1092

TOPTICAL—Color Filters for LCDs—Toray Industries, Inc.; *Int'l*, pg. 1399

TOPTIP—Furniture—Coop Switzerland; *Int'l*, pg. 329

TOPVIEW—Computer Product—International Business Machines Corporation; *U.S. Public*, pg. 895

TOR BOOKS—Books—St. Martins Press, Inc.; *Int'l*, pg. 1479

TOR-TICOS—Tortilla Chips—Borden, Inc.; *U.S. Private*, pg. 157

TORADOL—Ketorolac, Pain—Recordati Industria Chimica e Farmaceutica S.p.A.; *Int'l*, pg. 1090

TORADOL—Nonsteroidal Antirheumatic Drug—Roche Holding Ltd.; *Int'l*, pg. 1119

TORADOL—Ketorolac Tromethamine—Syntex; *Int'l*, pg. 1120

TORAY TETORON—Polyester Fibre—Toray Industries, Inc.; *Int'l*, pg. 1399

TORAYCA—Carbon Fibre—Toray Industries, Inc.; *Int'l*, pg. 1399

TORAYLON—Acrylic Fibre—Toray Industries, Inc.; *Int'l*, pg. 1399

TORBEAM—Girder—Harnischfeger Industries, Inc.; *U.S. Public*, pg. 788

TORBOFLOR—Peat Products—DSM Chemie Linz GmbH; *Int'l*, pg. 356

TORBUTROL—Oral Cough Suppressant—Bristol-Myers Squibb Company; *U.S. Public*, pg. 253

TORCH CANDLE—Candle Torchlight—Will & Baumer Incorporated; *U.S. Private*, pg. 1176

TORCO MPZ—Racing Oil—D.A. Stuart Company; *U.S. Private*, pg. 1048

TORDON—Herbicide—The Dow Chemical Company; *U.S. Public*, pg. 522

TORDUCTOR—Torque-Meter—ABB AB; *Int'l*, pg. 7

TORINO—Sporting Equipment—Brunswick Bowling & Billiards Corp.; *U.S. Public*, pg. 265

TORINO—Bread & Bakery Products—Gonnella Baking Co.; *U.S. Private*, pg. 463

TORIT—Environmental Control Apparatus—Donaldson Company, Inc.; *U.S. Public*, pg. 517

TORIT-BUILT—Air Filtration & Contaminant Collection System—Donaldson Company, Inc.; *U.S. Public*, pg. 517

TORIT DOWNFLO—In-Plant Air Filtration System—Donaldson Company, Inc.; *U.S. Public*, pg. 517

TORK—Time Control & Photoelectric Controls—Tork, Inc.; *U.S. Private*, pg. 1092

TORK ALERT—Audible & Visual Signals—Tork, Inc.; *U.S. Private*, pg. 1092

TORKER II—Manifolds—Edelbrock Corp.; *U.S. Public*, pg. 563

TORLON—Engineering Resins—Amoco Corporation; *U.S. Public*, pg. 101

TORLON POLYAMIDE-IMIDE—High Temperature Engineering Resins—Amoco Chemicals; *U.S. Public*, pg. 102

TORMORE MALT SCOTCH WHISKEY—Whiskey—Allied Domecq PLC; *Int'l*, pg. 62

TORNADO—Carpet Care Machines & Industrial Vacuum Cleaners—Breuer/Tornado; *U.S. Private*, pg. 167

TORNADO—Military Aircraft—British Aerospace p.l.c.; *Int'l*, pg. 217

TORNADO—Herbicide—The Dow Chemical Company; *U.S. Public*, pg. 522

TORNADO—Garden Equipment, Floor Care Products—Electrolux, AB; *Int'l*, pg. 438

TORNADO—Cotton Candy Machine—Gold Medal Products Co.; *U.S. Private*, pg. 459

TORNADO—NONE—Wind River Systems, Inc.; *U.S. Public*, pg. 1770

TORO—Outdoor Maintenance & Irrigation Equipment—The Toro Company; *U.S. Public*, pg. 1623

TORO BRAVO—NONE—M. Rubin & Sons Inc.; *U.S. Private*, pg. 949

TORO-TENDER—NONE—Zero-Max, Inc.; *Int'l*, pg. 866

TOROFORM—Transformers—Kuhlman Corporation; *U.S. Public*, pg. 968

TORON GRAPHITE RTS—Racquetball Racquet—Ektelon; *U.S. Private*, pg. 884

TORONTO BLUE JAYS—NONE—Toronto Blue Jays Baseball Club, Inc.; *Int'l*, pg. 680

TORONTO SPV—Tissue Heart Valve—St. Jude Medical, Inc.; *U.S. Public*, pg. 1427

TOROWARE—Cooking Utensils—Vollrath-Kewaunee Plant; *U.S. Private*, pg. 1143

TORQ-FLEX—Packless Swivel Joints, Rotary Joints; Shaft & Mechanical Couplings—Marquette Coppersmithing Co., Inc.; *U.S. Private*, pg. 706

TORQ-SET—Fastening System—Rule Industries, Inc.; *U.S. Public*, pg. 950

TORQ-TENDER—Overload Coupling—Zero-Max, Inc.; *Int'l*, pg. 866

TORQK MASTER—Gear Motors—Groschopp, Inc.; *Int'l*, pg. 559

TORQOMETER—Torque Wrenches—Snap-On Tools Corporation; *U.S. Public*, pg. 1480

TORQROD—Electromagnet—Ithaco Inc.; *U.S. Private*, pg. 576

TORQSYN—Electronic Components—Axsys Technologies, Inc.; *U.S. Public*, pg. 157

TORQUE-CHEK—Torque/Force Gauges—AMETEK, Inc.; *U.S. Public*, pg. 99

TORQUE COMMANDER—Compact Tool Kits—Klein Tools Inc.; *U.S. Private*, pg. 625

TORQUE-ON-DEMAND—NONE—Borg Warner Automotive, Inc.; *U.S. Public*, pg. 245

TORQUE TEAM—Power Transmission Belting—The Goodyear Tire & Rubber Company; *U.S. Public*, pg. 752

TORQUER MTRS.—NONE—Philips Automotive Electronics; *Int'l*, pg. 1054

TORR SEAL—Sealing Kit—Varian Associates, Inc.; *U.S. Public*, pg. 1710

TORRAMET—Specimen Dryer—Buehler, Limited; *U.S. Private*, pg. 574

TORREX II—Cabinet X-Ray Inspection System—EG & G Astrophysics; *U.S. Public*, pg. 543

TORREX II—Specialty X-Ray Equipment—EG & G, Inc.; *U.S. Public*, pg. 542

TORRIDO—Santa Fe Grande—Trappey's Fine Foods, Inc.; *U.S. Private*, pg. 105

TORRIDS—NONE—Bristol-Myers Squibb Company; *U.S. Public*, pg. 253

TORRIDS—Hair Coloring—Clairol, Inc.; *U.S. Public*, pg. 254

TORRINGTON—Bearings—Bryant Electric Supply Company, Inc.; *U.S. Private*, pg. 177

TORRINGTON—Bearings—Ingersoll-Rand Company; *U.S. Public*, pg. 876

TORRINGTON—Bearings & Precision Components—The Torrington Co.; *U.S. Public*, pg. 877

TORSION-FLOW—Axle Shafts—Rockwell International Corporation; *U.S. Public*, pg. 1397

TORTUGA—Sunglasses—Bausch & Lomb Incorporated; *U.S. Public*, pg. 194

TORTULIT—Adhesive Tapes—The Braas Group; *Int'l*, pg. 1091

TORUN—Stainless Steel & Silverplate Flatware—Dansk International Designs Ltd.; *U.S. Public*, pg. 261

TORUS—Couplings—The Falk Corporation; *U.S. Public*, pg. 1534

TORX HI/LOW—Bolts & Screws—Continental/Midland, Inc.; *U.S. Private*, pg. 268

TOSCANA—Baking Company—San Francisco French Bread Company; *U.S. Public*, pg. 909

TOSCO—Petroleum Prods.—Tosco Corporation; *U.S. Public*, pg. 1624

TOSHIBA—Consumer Electronic Equipment—Hamburg Brothers; *U.S. Private*, pg. 497

TOSHIBA—Televisions, Tape Recorders, Microwave Ovens, Cassette Players—Toshiba Corporation; *Int'l*, pg. 1402

TOSHIBA PORTABLE COMPUTER—Portable Computer—Toshiba America Inc.; *Int'l*, pg. 1405

TOSS ACROSS—Game—Tyco Toys, Inc.; *U.S. Public*, pg. 1058

TOSS-N-GO—Soluble Bags—Du Pont (E.I. Du Pont De Nemours & Co.); *U.S. Public*, pg. 530

TOSTITOS—Tortilla Chips—Frito-Lay Company; *U.S. Public*, pg. 1277

TOSUXACIN—Quinolone Anti-Infective—Abbott Laboratories; *U.S. Public*, pg. 12

TOT-LOK—Magnetic Cabinet Locking System—Rev-A-Shelf; *U.S. Private*, pg. 925

TOTACILLIN—Pharmaceutical Prods.—SmithKline Beecham Laboratories; *Int'l*, pg. 1264

TOTACILLIN—Antibiotic—SmithKline Beecham plc; *Int'l*, pg. 1264

TOTAL—Cereal—General Mills, Inc.; *U.S. Public*, pg. 717

TOTAL—Wireless, Programmable Remote Controls—Recoton Corporation; *U.S. Public*, pg. 1369

TOTAL—NONE—Ultramar Diamond Shamrock Corporation; *U.S. Public*, pg. 1663

TOTAL ADVANTAGE—NONE—Adaptec, Inc.; *U.S. Public*, pg. 19

TOTAL ANTIOXIDANT—Blend with Grapeseed—Celestial Seasonings; *U.S. Public*, pg. 319

TOTAL CAMERA III—CAMERA—GraphLine Inc.; *U.S. Private*, pg. 471

TOTAL CD—NONE—Adaptec, Inc.; *U.S. Public*, pg. 19

TOTAL CHARGE—Charge System for Golf Carts & Small Vehicles—E-Z-GO Textron; *U.S. Public*, pg. 1589

TOTAL CLEAN—Can Openers—Sunbeam Household Products; *U.S. Public*, pg. 1533

TOTAL CONNECT—NONE—Adaptec, Inc.; *U.S. Public*, pg. 19

TOTAL CORN FLAKES—Cereal—General Mills, Inc.; *U.S. Public*, pg. 717

TOTAL DATA—NONE—Adaptec, Inc.; *U.S. Public*, pg. 19

TOTAL ECLIPSE—Floor Coating—Pioneer/Eclipse Corp.; *Int'l*, pg. 71

TOTAL FORMULA—Vitamins—Health Products Corporation; *U.S. Private*, pg. 514

TOTAL HOME—Automated Home Climate—Honeywell Inc.; *U.S. Public*, pg. 833

TOTAL HOME—NONE—Honeywell Limited; *U.S. Public*, pg. 835

TOTAL IMAGE—Uniforms—Angelica Corporation; *U.S. Public*, pg. 113

TOTAL IMMERSION—Intensive Language Training—Berlitz International, Inc.; *U.S. Public*, pg. 221

TOTAL NETWORK VISIBILITY—NONE—Network Associates, Inc.; *U.S. Public*, pg. 1168

TOTAL NUTRITION—Vitamins—Health Products Corporation; *U.S. Private*, pg. 514

TOTAL PACKAGING—Graphic Design—Weyerhaeuser Company; *U.S. Public*, pg. 1764

TOTAL PLANT—Process Automation—Honeywell Inc.; *U.S. Public*, pg. 833

TOTAL PLANT—NONE—Honeywell Limited; *U.S. Public*, pg. 835

TOTAL PRACTICE PROTECTION—Package Liability/Insurance—Medical Assurance, Inc.; *U.S. Public*, pg. 1079

TOTAL PREP—Cleaner—Mar-Hyde Corporation; *U.S. Public*, pg. 1357

TOTAL RAISIN BRAN—Cereal—General Mills, Inc.; *U.S. Public*, pg. 717

TOTAL RECALL REPORTS—Software for Information Access—Rockwell Switching Systems Div.; *U.S. Public*, pg. 1398

TOTAL SITE MANAGEMENT—Environmental Management—GZA GeoEnvironmental Technologies, Inc.; *U.S. Public*, pg. 697

TOTAL TABLETOP—NONE—World Tableware, Inc.; *Int'l*, pg. 1056

TOTALINE—Air Conditioner Parts & Supplies—The Climatic Corp.; *U.S. Private*, pg. 246

TOTALSPEC—Sand Processing Equipment—Telsmith, Inc.; *U.S. Public*, pg. 141

TOTALSTAT—Electrostatic Spraying System—United Air Specialists, Inc.; *U.S. Public*, pg. 382

TOTALTRAK—NONE—Stuart Entertainment Inc.; *U.S. Public*, pg. 1526

TOTE—Electronic Components—General Instrument Corporation; *U.S. Public*, pg. 716

TOTE TORCH—Cutting/Welding Torch—BernzOmatic; *U.S. Public*, pg. 1177

TOTEL FAILSAFE—Surge Protectors—TII Industries, Inc.; *U.S. Public*, pg. 1556

TOTELINE—Food Service & Bakery Display Trays, Boxes & Pans—Molded Fiber Glass Companies; *U.S. Public*, pg. 755

TOTES—NONE—Tandy Brands Accessories, Inc.; *U.S. Public*, pg. 1560

TOTES—Waterproof Accessories, Footwear, Umbrellas—Totes Incorporated; *U.S. Private*, pg. 111

TOTEWHEELS—Totelocker (Meets Airline Requirements for Checked Baggage)—Rubbermaid Incorporated; *U.S. Public*, pg. 1411

TOTINO'S—Frozen Pizza—Grand Metropolitan Plc; *Int'l*, pg. 408

TOTINO'S—Frozen Pizza & Pizza Snacks—The Pillsbury Company; *Int'l*, pg. 411

TOTT'S—Champagne—E. & J. Gallo Winery; *U.S. Private*, pg. 438

TOUCH-A-MATIC—Switches—Eagle Electric Mfg. Co., Inc.; *U.S. Private*, pg. 354

TOUCH ACTIVITY CENTER—Business Product—International Business Machines Corporation; *U.S. Public*, pg. 895

TOUCH DRY—Ink—Markem Corporation; *U.S. Private*, pg. 704

TOUCH DRY PLUS—Inks & Ink Rolls—Markem Corporation; *U.S. Private*, pg. 704

TOUCH-FREE—NONE—Scotsman Industries, Inc.; *U.S. Public*, pg. 1444

TOUCH MIXER—Lab Mixer For Test Tubes—Fisher Scientific Company; *U.S. Private*, pg. 658

TOUCH MOTION—Recliners—The Berkline Corporation; *U.S. Private*, pg. 432

TOUCH 'N FOAM—One Component Expanding Polyurethane Foam—Clayton Corporation; *U.S. Private*, pg. 244

TOUCH-N-GLUE—Adhesive—DAP Inc.; *Int'l*, pg. 1486

TOUCH 'N SEAL—One or Two Component Expanding or Reduced Expanding Polyurethane Foam—Clayton Corporation; *U.S. Private*, pg. 244

TOUCH 'N SEAL—Envelopes—Tension Envelope Corp.; *U.S. Private*, pg. 1077

TOUCH 'N STICK—Spray Adhesive for Household & Industrial Use—Clayton Corporation; *U.S. Private*, pg. 244

TOUCH O' GOLD PEANUT OIL—Vegetable Oil—Mallet & Co.; *U.S. Private*, pg. 698

TOUCH-O-MATIC—Luggage—Hartmann Luggage & Leather Goods Group; *U.S. Public*, pg. 261

TOUCH OF BUTTER—NONE—Nabisco Inc.; *U.S. Public*, pg. 1355

A TOUCH OF COTTON—Bond Paper—The Mead Corporation; *U.S. Public*, pg. 1074

A TOUCH OF GLASS—Ranges & Refrigerators—General Electric Canada Inc.; *U.S. Public*, pg. 713

TOUCH OF GLOSS—Bras—Warner's; *U.S. Public*, pg. 1738

TOUCH-OF-SCENT—Room Air Freshener—Scott's Liquid Gold-Inc.; *U.S. Public*, pg. 1447

TOUCH-OF-SCENT-TOO—Air Freshener—Scott's Liquid Gold-Inc.; *U.S. Public*, pg. 1447

TOUCH TAPER—Tape Machine—Marsh Company; *U.S. Private*, pg. 707

TOUCH WELD—Resistance Computer Control—Sciaky, Inc.; *U.S. Private*, pg. 862

TOUCH-WELD PLUS—Resistance Computer Control—Sciaky, Inc.; *U.S. Private*, pg. 862

THE TOUCHABLES—Mattress—Therapedic Associates, Inc.; *U.S. Private*, pg. 1079

TOUCHBLEND—NONE—Dynamics Corporation of America; *U.S. Public*, pg. 286

TOUCHCOAT—Paints—Sherwin-Williams Consumer Brands Division; *U.S. Public*, pg. 1466

TOUCHLESS ACRYLIC—NONE—Blue Coral/Slick 50; *U.S. Public*, pg. 1348

TOUCHMATE—Platform-Based Touch Terminals—Microtouch Systems, Inc.; *U.S. Public*, pg. 1108

TOUCHMATIC—Keyboard Mailing Machine—Pitney Bowes Inc.; *U.S. Public*, pg. 1303

TOUCHMOBILE—Business Product—International Business Machines Corporation; *U.S. Public*, pg. 895

TOUCHPEN—Input Devices for Pen Compuuting—Microtouch Systems, Inc.; *U.S. Public*, pg. 1108

TOUCHSELECT—Computer Product—International Business Machines Corporation; *U.S. Public*, pg. 895

TOUCHSTONE—Motion Picture & Television Production Company—The Walt Disney Company; *U.S. Public*, pg. 511

TOUCHSTONE—Paperback Books—Simon & Schuster; *U.S. Private*, pg. 777

TOUCHTIME—Computer Software—Harnischfeger Industries, Inc.; *U.S. Public*, pg. 788

Brand Name Index

Brand Name Index

TOUGH—Herbicides—Agrolinz Melamin GmbH; *Int'l*, pg. 356

TOUGH—Plant Protectives—DSM Chemie Linz GmbH; *Int'l*, pg. 356

TOUGH—Herbicide—Sandoz Agro, Inc.; *Int'l*, pg. 974

TOUGH ACT—Heavy Duty Bathroom Cleaner—The Dow Chemical Company; *U.S. Public*, pg. 522

TOUGH ACT—Heavy Duty Bathroom Cleaner—DowBrands, L.P.; *U.S. Public*, pg. 523

TOUGH BIRD—Sprinkler—Rain Bird Sprinklers Manufacturing Corp.; *U.S. Private*, pg. 907

TOUGH CAT—Cloths—Kimberly-Clark Corporation; *U.S. Public*, pg. 958

TOUGH-GLASS—Fiberglass-Based Asphalt Roofing—Georgia-Pacific Corporation; *U.S. Public*, pg. 735

TOUGH-GUARD—Eaves Flashing—Georgia-Pacific Corporation; *U.S. Public*, pg. 735

TOUGH ONE—Batteries—Western Auto Supply Company; *U.S. Public*, pg. 1452

TOUGH TEX—Printing Ink—Van Son Holland Ink Corp. of America; *U.S. Private*, pg. 1133

TOUGH-TIP—Steel Tapes—Evans Rule Co., Inc.; *U.S. Public*, pg. 1511

TOUGHLINE—Heavy Industrial Vinyl Gloves—Phoenix Medical Technology, Inc.; *U.S. Public*, pg. 1292

TOUR—NONE—Hansberger Precision Golf Inc.; *U.S. Private*, pg. 499

TOUR—Golf Balls—MacGregor Golf Company; *Int'l*, pg. 72

TOUR & TRAVEL NEWS—Newspaper—Miller Freeman Inc.; *Int'l*, pg. 1443

TOUR EDITION—Golf Clubs & Balls—Spalding Sports Worldwide; *U.S. Private*, pg. 630

TOUR 400—Golf Equipment—RAM Golf Corporation; *U.S. Private*, pg. 908

TOUR GLIDE—Motorcycles—Harley-Davidson, Inc.; *U.S. Public*, pg. 786

TOUR HOCKEY SKATES—Hockey Skates—Roller Derby Skate Corp.; *U.S. Private*, pg. 941

TOUR SPORT—Motorcycle Accessories—American Honda Motor Co., Inc. Motorcycle Division; *Int'l*, pg. 634

TOURING PRO—Sport Bag—Ektelon; *U.S. Private*, pg. 884

TOURISM MALAYSIA—NONE—Malaysia Tourism Promotion Board (MTPB); *Int'l*, pg. 832

TOURISTER—Luggage—American Tourister, Inc.; *U.S. Public*, pg. 1430

TOURLOCK—Revolving Doors—Boon Edam Inc.; *Int'l*, pg. 202

TOURNAMENT—Sporting Equipment—Brunswick Bowling & Billiards Corp.; *U.S. Public*, pg. 265

TOURNAMENT—Racquetball Racquet—Head USA, Inc.; *U.S. Private*, pg. 514

TOURNAMENT ACE—Sport Bag—Ektelon; *U.S. Private*, pg. 884

TOURNAMENT GOLF—Microcomputer Game—Monarch Avalon, Inc.; *U.S. Public*, pg. 1123

TOURNAMENT PLUS—Softball—Spalding & Evenflo Companies, Inc.; *U.S. Private*, pg. 629

TOURNAMENT 20—Tennis Racquet Strings—Head USA, Inc.; *U.S. Private*, pg. 514

TOURNEAU—Watches, Clocks & Jewelry—Tourneau Inc.; *U.S. Private*, pg. 1093

TOURNEX—Revolving Doors—Boon Edam Inc.; *Int'l*, pg. 202

TOURNIKET—Revolving Doors—Boon Edam Inc.; *Int'l*, pg. 202

TOURTEL—Alcohol-Free Beer—Danone Group; *Int'l*, pg. 379

TOURTRAIN—Cheese—Bongrain S.A.; *Int'l*, pg. 201

TOVENE—Treatment of Varicose Veins—Kali-Chemie Aktiengesellschaft; *Int'l*, pg. 1278

TOWARD MAN'S FULL LIFE—Service—Medtronic, Inc.; *U.S. Public*, pg. 1082

TOWEL SILVERSMITH—NONE—Carvel Hall; *U.S. Private*, pg. 1061

TOWER—Carpets—Carriage Industries, Inc.; *U.S. Public*, pg. 514

TOWER—NONE—Hibernia Corporation; *U.S. Public*, pg. 825

TOWER—Record Stores—Tower Records; *U.S. Private*, pg. 688

TOWER BY HENRY KLOSS—NONE—Cambridge Soundworks, Inc.; *U.S. Private*, pg. 202

TOWER OF DOOM—Action Game—Mattel Games/Puzzles; *U.S. Public*, pg. 1058

TOWER OF TREATS—Five Gift Boxes of Fruit, Candy & Nuts—Harry and David; *Int'l*, pg. 1518

TOWER TRAILER—Tower for Antenna—Telex Communications, Inc.; *U.S. Private*, pg. 1074

TOWERBROM—Cooling Water Microbiological Control Systems—Calgon Corporation; *Int'l*, pg. 455

TOWING OPERATORS PROTECTOR PLAN—Insurance Packege Program—Poe & Brown, Inc.; *U.S. Public*, pg. 1312

TOWLE SILVERSMITHS—Flatware, Holloware—Syratech Corporation; *U.S. Private*, pg. 1060

TOWLER PRODUCTS—Hydraulic Systems & Components—The Oilgear Company; *U.S. Public*, pg. 1215

TOWMASTER—Towing Unit—Todco; *U.S. Private*, pg. 823

TOWN & COUNTRY—Mens Apparel—Gordon & Ferguson of Delaware, Inc.; *U.S. Private*, pg. 465

TOWN & COUNTRY—Magazine—The Hearst Corporation; *U.S. Private*, pg. 515

TOWN ACE—Trucks & Buses—Toyota Motor Corporation; *Int'l*, pg. 1411

TOWN & COUNTRY—Van—Chrysler Corporation; *U.S. Public*, pg. 352

TOWN & COUNTRY—Magazine—Hearst Magazines Division; *U.S. Private*, pg. 516

TOWN & COUNTRY—Magazine Publication—Town & Country; *U.S. Private*, pg. 517

TOWN & COUNTRY—Shoes—Wolverine World Wide, Inc.; *U.S. Public*, pg. 1775

TOWN CLASSICAL—Kitchen Cabinets—Georgia-Pacific Corporation; *U.S. Public*, pg. 735

TOWN & COUNTRY—Tires—Bridgestone/Firestone, Inc.; *Int'l*, pg. 213

TOWN & COUNTRY PET FOODS—Pet Food—Doane Products Co., Branded Sales Div.; *U.S. Private*, pg. 337

TOWN & COUNTRY STEEL BELTED RADIAL RS—Tires—Bridgestone/Firestone, Inc.; *Int'l*, pg. 213

TOWN HOUSE—Crackers—Keebler Company; *U.S. Public*, pg. 657

TOWN HOUSE—Disposable Paper Products—Wisconsin Tissue Mills, Inc.; *U.S. Public*, pg. 347

TOWN HOUSE & CHEDDAR—Cracker Snacks—Keebler Company; *U.S. Public*, pg. 657

TOWN HOUSE CLASSIC JRS.—Bite-Size Snack Crackers—Keebler Company; *U.S. Public*, pg. 657

TOWNE—NONE—London Fog Industries, Inc.; *U.S. Private*, pg. 673

TOWNLEY—Liquid-Solids Separation Equipment—Komline-Sanderson Engineering Corp.; *U.S. Private*, pg. 631

TOWNSEND—Gynecological Device—The Cooper Companies, Inc.; *U.S. Public*, pg. 442

TOWNSEND—NONE—A.T. Cross Co.; *U.S. Public*, pg. 460

TOWNSEND—NONE—Glynwed International PLC; *Int'l*, pg. 554

TOWNTALK—Ladies & Childrens Clothes—Arnotts plc; *Int'l*, pg. 81

TOWVEYOR—Conveyor Floor—Jervis B. Webb Company; *U.S. Private*, pg. 1156

TOX ELUT—Conalytical Extraction Columns—Varian Associates, Inc.; *U.S. Public*, pg. 1710

TOXCART—Mobile Computerized Instrumentation—Beckman Instruments, Inc.; *U.S. Public*, pg. 199

TOXIC CRUSADERS—Toys—Playmates Holdings Ltd.; *Int'l*, pg. 1060

TOXICHEM—Toxicology Controls—Fisher Scientific Company; *U.S. Private*, pg. 658

TOXIMUL—Surfactant-Agricultural Emulsion—Stepan Company; *U.S. Public*, pg. 1514

TOXO-G EIA—Diagnostic Products—Abbott Laboratories; *U.S. Public*, pg. 12

TOXO-M EIA—Diagnostic Products—Abbott Laboratories; *U.S. Public*, pg. 12

TOXSTRIP—Control Release Dispensers—Hercon Environmental Corporation; *U.S. Public*, pg. 802

TOXSYS—Information System—Beckman Instruments, Inc.; *U.S. Public*, pg. 199

TOYBARS—Toys—Century Products Co.; *U.S. Private*, pg. 226

TOYBOX—NONE—BBC Magazines; *Int'l*, pg. 114

TOYE—Motor Homes—Winnebago Industries, Inc.; *U.S. Public*, pg. 1772

TOYO ACE—Trucks & Buses—Toyota Motor Corporation; *Int'l*, pg. 1411

TOYOCERIN—Probiotic Feed Additive—Asahi Chemical Industry Co., Ltd.; *Int'l*, pg. 83

TOYOPEARL—NONE—TosoHaas Company; *U.S. Public*, pg. 1403

TOYOPEARL—NONE—TosoHaas Company; *Int'l*, pg. 1408

TOYOTA—Automobiles—Northway Motorcar Corporation; *U.S. Private*, pg. 806

TOYOTA—Automobiles, Trucks & Vans—Toyota Motor Sales, U.S.A., Inc.; *Int'l*, pg. 1412

TOYOTA—NONE—Toyota Norge A/S; *Int'l*, pg. 1414

TOYOTA CENTURY—Automobile—Toyota Motor Corporation; *Int'l*, pg. 1411

TOYOTA CROWN—Automobile—Toyota Motor Corporation; *Int'l*, pg. 1411

TOYS "R" US—Retail Toy Supermarkets—Toys "R" Us, Inc.; *U.S. Public*, pg. 1626

TRABON—Lubrication Equipment—IDEX Corporation; *U.S. Public*, pg. 1411

TRAC—Torque Reactive Anti-Dive Control—American Honda Motor Co., Inc. Motorcycle Division; *Int'l*, pg. 634

TRAC—Financial Management Information Service—Eastman Kodak Company; *U.S. Public*, pg. 550

TRAC—System for Computerized Maintenance Management—Raytheon Engineers & Constructors International, Inc.; *U.S. Public*, pg. 1366

TRAC-BALL—Toy—Wham-O, Inc.; *U.S. Private*, pg. 1170

TRAC CONVERTAMATIC—Small Vacuum—Advance Machine Company; *U.S. Public*, pg. 932

TRAC-MASTER—NONE—Juno Lighting, Inc.; *U.S. Public*, pg. 935

TRAC12—Financial Management Information Service—Eastman Kodak Company; *U.S. Public*, pg. 550

TRAC II—Razors & Blades—The Gillette Company; *U.S. Public*, pg. 743

TRAC-BALL—Toy—Mattel, Inc.; *U.S. Public*, pg. 1057

TRACE—Automated Meter Reading System—American Meter Company; *Int'l*, pg. 1149

TRACE—Upholstery Yarn—Amoco Chemicals; *U.S. Public*, pg. 102

TRACE—A Process Used in Manufacturing TSA Suspensions—Hutchinson Technology Inc.; *U.S. Public*, pg. 850

TRACE-BACK—NONE—Brown & Sharpe Manufacturing Company; *U.S. Public*, pg. 260

TRACE-KLEAN—Cleaning Solution—Beckman Instruments, Inc.; *U.S. Public*, pg. 199

TRACECALC—Software—Raychem Corporation; *U.S. Public*, pg. 1362

TRACECLAD—Pipe Coverings—Raychem Corporation; *U.S. Public*, pg. 1362

TRACECUT—Software—Renishaw plc; *Int'l*, pg. 1103

TRACELECTRIC—Communications for Buyers & Suppliers of Large Used Electrical Equipment—Data Transmission Network Corporation; *U.S. Public*, pg. 486

TRACETEK—Process Systems for Leak Detection—Raychem Corporation; *U.S. Public*, pg. 1362

TRACH CARE—Suctioning Device—Ballard Medical Products; *U.S. Public*, pg. 171

TRACH CARE DOUBLE SWIVEL ELBOW—Calibrated Closed Suction Catheter—Ballard Medical Products; *U.S. Public*, pg. 171

TRACH CARE MAC—Medical Tool—Ballard Medical Products; *U.S. Public*, pg. 171

TRACH CARE WET PAK—NONE—Ballard Medical Products; *U.S. Public*, pg. 171

TRACIN—Material for Supplying Trace Minerals to Plants—Georgia-Pacific Corporation; *U.S. Public*, pg. 735

TRACKER—Remote Analyzer—General Railway Signal Corp.; *Int'l*, pg. 1194

TRACKER—Therapy Beam Evaluation System—Keithley Instruments Inc.-Radiation Measurements Div.; *U.S. Public*, pg. 946

TRACKMAN—Stationary Input Device—Logitech International SA; *Int'l*, pg. 815

TRACKPOINT—Computer Product—International Business Machines Corporation; *U.S. Public*, pg. 895

TRACKPOINT II—Computer Product—International Business Machines Corporation; *U.S. Public*, pg. 895

TRACPLUS—Computerized Tracking System—Weyerhaeuser Company; *U.S. Public*, pg. 1764

TRACRIUM—Muscle Relaxant—Glaxo Wellcome PLC; *Int'l*, pg. 553

TRACS—Test & Repair Analysis Control System—GenRad, Inc.; *U.S. Public*, pg. 731

TRACTION DRIVE—Tires—Bridgestone/Firestone, Inc.; *Int'l*, pg. 213

TRACTION EQUALIZER—Differential Mechanisms—Rockwell International Corporation; *U.S. Public*, pg. 1397

TRACTION FIELD & ROAD—Tires—Bridgestone/Firestone, Inc.; *Int'l*, pg. 213

TRACTION LUG—Tires—Bridgestone/Firestone, Inc.; *Int'l*, pg. 213

TRACTION RELEASE—Orthodontic Headgear—3M; *U.S. Public*, pg. 1604

TRACTIONEER—Trucks—FWD/Seagrave Fire Apparatus, Inc.; *U.S. Private*, pg. 390

TRACTIONITE—Tires—Bridgestone/Firestone, Inc.; *Int'l*, pg. 213

TRADE—Muzzle Loading Rifle—Lyman Products Corporation; *U.S. Private*, pg. 683

TRADE-MARK—Vinyl Siding and Accessories—Alcoa Building Products, Inc.; *U.S. Public*, pg. 61

TRADE MATE—Sealants—Dow Corning Corporation; *U.S. Public*, pg. 523

TRADE WINDS—Wood & Lumber Products—Georgia-Pacific Corporation; *U.S. Public*, pg. 735

TRADE WINDS—Seafood—Rich SeaPak Corp.; *U.S. Private*, pg. 928

TRADEARBED—Rolled Steel Prods.—Arbed S.A.; *Int'l*, pg. 78

TRADEPRO—NONE—Stuart Entertainment Inc.; *U.S. Public*, pg. 1526

TRADER BAY—NONE—Sears, Roebuck and Co.; *U.S. Public*, pg. 1452

TRADER JOE'S—Gourmet Market—TACT Holding; *U.S. Private*, pg. 1067

TRADESHOW WEEK—Weekly Publication for Show Organizers & Corporate Exhibitors—Reed Elsevier Business Information; *Int'l*, pg. 1095

TRADESMAN—Reel Stands—Greenlee Textron; *U.S. Public*, pg. 1589

TRADESMAN—Quality Cutting Tools—Imperial Schrade Corp.; *U.S. Private*, pg. 559

TRADESTAR—Insurance Product—Eagle Star; *Int'l*, pg. 110

TRADEWINDS—Beer—Hudepohl-Schoenling Brewing Company; *U.S. Private*, pg. 545

TRADEWINDS—Evaporative Coolers—Justin Industries, Inc.; *U.S. Public*, pg. 936

TRADEWINDS—Class A Diesel Pusher Motorhome—National R.V., Inc.; *U.S. Public*, pg. 1159

TRADEX—Pine Timber—CSR Limited; *Int'l*, pg. 245

TRADINCO—Equipment for Calibration of Pressure Instruments—Halma p.l.c.; *Int'l*, pg. 589

TRADITION—Mattresses—Kingsdown, Inc.; *U.S. Private*, pg. 622

TRADITIONAL CLASSICS—Broadloom—Couristan Inc.; *U.S. Private*, pg. 279

TRADITIONAL HOME—Magazine—Meredith Corporation; *U.S. Public*, pg. 1094

TRADITIONAL STRIP—Laminated 2 1/4" Strip Flooring-Square Edge—Robbins, Inc.; *U.S. Private*, pg. 934

TRADITIONALS—Ray-Ban Sunglasses—Bausch & Lomb Incorporated; *U.S. Public*, pg. 194

TRADITIONS—Candy—Pangburn Candy Company; *U.S. Private*, pg. 836

TRADITIONS—Mail Order House—Starcrest Products of California; *U.S. Private*, pg. 1035

TRADITIONS BY MAGNALITE—Cookware—General Housewares Corp.; *U.S. Public*, pg. 715

TRADWINDS—Label for Edible Food—H.J. Baker & Bro., Inc.; *U.S. Private*, pg. 112

TRAFALGAR—Belts & Brakes—Trafalgar Gurkha Ltd.; *U.S. Private*, pg. 1095

TRAFFIC BLASTER—Electric Activated Vehicular Horn—Federal Signal Corporation, Signal Div.; *U.S. Public*, pg. 616

TRAFFIC JAMMER—Providing Advertising Aids—Georgia-Pacific Corporation; *U.S. Public*, pg. 735

TRAFFIC-LINE—Traffic Paint—Devoe Paint; *Int'l*, pg. 663

TRAFFIC LINE—Traffic Paint—ICI Paints; *Int'l*, pg. 664

TRAFFIC-LINE-WB—Waterborne Traffic Marking Paint—Devoe Paint; *Int'l*, pg. 663

TRAFFIC LINE WB—Waterborne Traffic Marking Paint—ICI Paints; *Int'l*, pg. 664

TRAFFIC MASTER—Office Systems—General Railway Signal Corp.; *Int'l*, pg. 1194

TRAFFIC TILES—Carpet-to-Rubber Tiles—The Akro Corporation; *U.S. Public*, pg. 399

TRAFFICCAM—Remote Pan & Zoom Cameras that Monitor Traffic—Shadow Broadcast Services; *U.S. Public*, pg. 1763

TRAFLOMATIC III—Microprocessor Control for Gearless Traction Elevators—Dover Elevator Systems, Inc.; *U.S. Public*, pg. 521

TRAFLOMATIC III—Microprocessor Control for Geared Traction Elevators—Dover Elevator Systems, Inc.; *U.S. Public*, pg. 521

TRAFLOMATIC II—Microprocessor Control for Gearless Traction Elevators—Dover Elevator Systems, Inc.; *U.S. Public*, pg. 521

TRAFO—Ankle Foot Orthoses—The Langer Biomechanics Group, Inc.; *U.S. Public*, pg. 978

TRAIL BITS—Pet Foods—Ag Processing Inc., A Cooperative; *U.S. Private*, pg. 26

TRAIL BLAZER—Lumber & Wood Products—Georgia-Pacific Corporation; *U.S. Public*, pg. 735

TRAIL BOSS—NONE—Seats Incorporated; *U.S. Private*, pg. 410

TRAIL KINGS—Men's Shoes—E.J. Footwear Corp.; *U.S. Public*, pg. 1684

TRAIL MIX—Beer—The F.X. Matt Brewing Co.; *U.S. Private*, pg. 714

TRAIL QUEENS—Women's Shoes—E.J. Footwear Corp.; *U.S. Public*, pg. 1684

TRAIL VAN—Intermodal Service; Highway Trailer & Marine Shipping Container on Flatcars—Conrail, Inc.; *U.S. Public*, pg. 431

TRAIL WALKER—Walking Magazine—EMAP Pursuit Publishing; *Int'l*, pg. 451

TRAILBLAZER—Welding & Cutting Equip.—Miller Electric Manufacturing Co.; *U.S. Public*, pg. 867

TRAILBREAKERS—Men's Shoes—E.J. Footwear Corp.; *U.S. Public*, pg. 1684

TRAILBUXE—Men's Footwear—J. Baker, Inc.; *U.S. Public*, pg. 167

TRAILER/BODY BUILDERS—Truck & Truck Equipment Publication—Intertec Publishing; *U.S. Public*, pg. 1327

TRAILMASTER—Tents & Backpacks—Jinwoong Inc.; *Int'l*, pg. 706

TRAILPAK—Comml. Line of Meals Ready-to-Eat—Star Food Processing, Inc.; *U.S. Private*, pg. 1034

TRAINING—Business Publication—Bill Communications, Inc.; *Int'l*, pg. 1446

TRAINING DEVICE, ATROPINE INJECTION—Training Device for US Military—Meridian Medical Technology, Inc.; *U.S. Public*, pg. 1095

TRAINING DEVICE, PRALIDOXIME CHLORIDE INJECTION—Training Device for US Military—Meridian Medical Technology, Inc.; *U.S. Public*, pg. 1095

TRAINING KIT, NERVE AGENT ANTIDOTE, MARK I—Training Kit for US Military—Meridian Medical Technology, Inc.; *U.S. Public*, pg. 1095

TRAINING SIMULATORS—Complete Air Defense Training Systems—Oerlikon-Contraves AG; *Int'l*, pg. 998

TRAINS—Magazine—Kalmbach Publishing Co.; *U.S. Private*, pg. 606

TRAK—Digital Readout Systems—Southwestern Industries, Inc.; *U.S. Private*, pg. 1019

TRAK 1—Single Circuit Track—Progress Lighting; *U.S. Public*, pg. 1684

TRAK 3—Three Circuit Track—Progress Lighting; *U.S. Public*, pg. 1684

TRAK TRED—Men's Shoes—E.J. Footwear Corp.; *U.S. Public*, pg. 1684

TRAKKER—Portable Bar Code Readers—Intermec Technologies Corporation; *U.S. Public*, pg. 1699

TRAKODE—Track Circuit—General Railway Signal Corp.; *Int'l*, pg. 1194

TRAKPRO—Data Analysis Software—TSI Incorporated; *U.S. Public*, pg. 1559

TRAKSTAR—NONE—Cordis, a Johnson & Johnson Company; *U.S. Public*, pg. 928

TRAKSTAR—Portable Rail Drill—Hougen Manufacturing Inc.; *U.S. Private*, pg. 541

TRAMPOLINE CUSHION SYSTEM—Shoes—Johnston & Murphy Co.; *U.S. Public*, pg. 728

TRAN SCRIBER—Accessories—Recoton Corporation; *U.S. Public*, pg. 1369

TRAN-STAY—Clear Polyester Layout Base Sheet—Transilwrap Company, Inc.; *U.S. Private*, pg. 1097

TRANDATE—Cardiovascular Treatment—Glaxo Wellcome Inc.; *Int'l*, pg. 552

TRANE—Air Conditioning Equip.—American Standard Inc.; *U.S. Public*, pg. 91

TRANQUIL DAY—Anti Aniety-Stress Relief Tablets—Alva/Amco Pharmacal Companies, Inc.; *U.S. Private*, pg. 47

TRANQUIL PLUS—Relaxant Capsules—Alva/Amco Pharmacal Companies, Inc.; *U.S. Private*, pg. 47

TRANQUIL-SPAN—Relaxant Capsules—Alva/Amco Pharmacal Companies, Inc.; *U.S. Private*, pg. 47

TRANS—Photographic Paper—Konica Corporation; *Int'l*, pg. 748

TRANS-ADAPTOR—Filter Assembly—Pall Corporation; *U.S. Public*, pg. 1253

TRANS-AID—Chemical—Westvaco Corporation; *U.S. Public*, pg. 1762

TRANS AM—Sports Car—General Motors Corporation; *U.S. Public*, pg. 718

TRANS AMERICA GLASS—Automotive Replacement Glass—TCG International Inc.; *Int'l*, pg. 1336

TRANS BRITANNIA GLASS—Automotive Replacement Glass—TCG International Inc.; *Int'l*, pg. 1336

TRANS CANADA GLASS—Automotive Replacement Glass—TCG International Inc.; *Int'l*, pg. 1336

TRANS/COPY—Carbonless Copy Paper—The Mead Corporation; *U.S. Public*, pg. 1074

TRANS-EZE—Heat Transfer Printing Paper—Kimberly-Clark Corporation; *U.S. Public*, pg. 958

TRANS/IMAGE—Carbonless Copy Paper—The Mead Corporation; *U.S. Public*, pg. 1074

TRANS-KOTE—Thermal Laminating Film—Transilwrap Company, Inc.; *U.S. Private*, pg. 1097

TRANS-LUX COLORWALL—Advertising Displays—Trans-Lux Corporation; *U.S. Public*, pg. 1628

TRANS-LUX DATAWAH—Programmable LED Display for Posting Frequently Updated Information—Trans-Lux Corporation; *U.S. Public*, pg. 1628

TRANS-LUX GRAPHICSWALL—Versatile 3 Color Display for Animation & Graphics via Personal Computer—Trans-Lux Corporation; *U.S. Public*, pg. 1628

TRANS-LUX INFO WALL—Programmable LED Display for Custom Messages—Trans-Lux Corporation; *U.S. Public*, pg. 1628

TRANS-LUX LED JET—Large Scale LED Display for Stocks & Commodities—Trans-Lux Corporation; *U.S. Public*, pg. 1628

TRANS-LUX LED NEWS JET—Large Scale LED Display for Business News—Trans-Lux Corporation; *U.S. Public*, pg. 1628

TRANS-LUX MENUWALL—Programmable LED Display for Custom Messages—Trans-Lux Corporation; *U.S. Public*, pg. 1628

TRANS-LUX PICTUREWALL—Trading Display Systems—Trans-Lux Corporation; *U.S. Public*, pg. 1628

TRANS-MEDIC—Stops Transmission Trouble—Radiator Specialty Company; *U.S. Private*, pg. 906

TRANS-MYND-R—Transmission Filter Moniter—Pall Corporation; *U.S. Public*, pg. 1253

TRANS NATIONAL GROUP SERVICES—Travel Agency; Special Membership Services—TNT Vacations; *U.S. Private*, pg. 1065

TRANS-PAK—Solid Waste Compactor—Harris Waste Mgmt. Group, Inc.; *Int'l*, pg. 473

TRANS-PAK—Spring Assemblies—Kuhlman Corporation; *U.S. Public*, pg. 968

TRANS-PORT—NONE—Life Technologies, Inc.; *U.S. Public*, pg. 504

TRANS-PRESS—Press—Harnischfeger Industries, Inc.; *U.S. Public*, pg. 788

TRANS-RIB—Tires—Bridgestone/Firestone, Inc.; *Int'l*, pg. 213

TRANS RIB LT—Tires—Bridgestone/Firestone, Inc.; *Int'l*, pg. 213

TRANS/RITE—Carbonless Copy Paper—The Mead Corporation; *U.S. Public*, pg. 1074

TRANS-RUPTER—Circuit Interrupter for Transformer Protection—S & C Electric Company; *U.S. Private*, pg. 954

TRANS-SEAL—Skin Packaging Equipment—Stone Container Corporation; *U.S. Public*, pg. 1065

TRANS SPORT—Mini-Van—Pontiac-GMC Division; *U.S. Public*, pg. 720

TRANS/TAB—Carbonless Copy Paper—The Mead Corporation; *U.S. Public*, pg. 1074

TRANS/TRAC—Tires—Bridgestone/Firestone, Inc.; *Int'l*, pg. 213

TRANS TRAC LT—Tires—Bridgestone/Firestone, Inc.; *Int'l*, pg. 213

TRANS-VAN COMMUTER—Medium-Duty Buses—Champion Enterprises, Inc.; *U.S. Public*, pg. 332

TRANS-VER-SAL—Wart Remover Kit; Dermal Patch Delivery System for Wart Removal—Bradley Pharmaceuticals; *U.S. Public*, pg. 249

TRANS-VER-SAL—Wart Remover Kit; Dermal Patch Delivery System for Wart Removal—Doak Dermatologics; *U.S. Public*, pg. 250

TRANS VISION—Infrastructure Management—General Railway Signal Corp.; *Int'l*, pg. 1194

TRANS VISTA—TV Receivers—Thomson Consumer Electronics Inc.; *Int'l*, pg. 1383

TRANS-SEAL—Sealant & Adhesive—Ohio Sealants Inc.; *Int'l*, pg. 802

TRANSA-BIND—Paper—Schleicher & Schuell, Inc.; *Int'l*, pg. 1206

TRANSALP—Motorcycle—American Honda Motor Co., Inc. Motorcycle Division; *Int'l*, pg. 634

TRANSAMERICA—Insurance—TIG Holdings, Inc.; *U.S. Public*, pg. 1555

TRANSBAY—Building Materials—Varco-Pruden Buildings; *U.S. Public*, pg. 1677

TRANSBOND—Orthodontic Adhesive—3M; *U.S. Public*, pg. 1604

TRANSBOT—Videogame—Sega of America Inc.; *Int'l*, pg. 1218

TRANSCAR—Self-Propelled, Battery-Powered Towing Vehicle—TransLogic Corp.; *Int'l*, pg. 1387

TRANSCEND—Ceramic Bracket System—3M; *U.S. Public*, pg. 1604

TRANSCODE—NONE—Avery Dennison Corporation; *U.S. Public*, pg. 152

TRANSCOP—Scopolamine Patch, Motion Sickness—Recordati Industria Chimica e Farmaceutica S.p.A.; *Int'l*, pg. 1090

TRANSDERM-NITRO—Nitroglycerin—Ciba Specialty Chemicals; *Int'l*, pg. 291

TRANSDERM-NITRO—NONE—Novartis Pharmaceuticals; *Int'l*, pg. 973

TRANSDERM SCOP—Motion Sickness Product—Ciba Specialty Chemicals; *Int'l*, pg. 291

TRANSDERM-NITRO—Pharmaceutical—Novartis; *Int'l*, pg. 972

TRANSDERM-SCOP—Conquers Seasickness—Novartis; *Int'l*, pg. 972

TRANSEAL—Transmission Sealer—Radiator Specialty Company; *U.S. Public*, pg. 906

TRANSFER—Time-Staged Delivery Software—Tandem Computers Inc.; *U.S. Public*, pg. 417

TRANSFERITE—Tape—American Biltrite Inc.; *U.S. Public*, pg. 68

TRANSFERLINE—NONE—Gilman; *Int'l*, pg. 1389

TRANSFERTECH—Dry Transfer Lettering Sheets—Castcraft Industries, Inc.; *U.S. Private*, pg. 219

TRANSFLOW—Flexible, Clear Plastic Tubing—Norton Performance Plastics; *Int'l*, pg. 1174

TRANSFORM—Cardiomyoplasty Pulse Generator—Medtronic, Inc.; *U.S. Public*, pg. 1082

TRANSFORMER—Junior Knit Sportswear—Niches, Inc.; *U.S. Public*, pg. 1181

TRANSFORMERS—NONE—Hasbro; *U.S. Public*, pg. 797

TRANSGRAPHICS—Adhesive-backed and OHP Films—Dietzgen Corporation; *U.S. Private*, pg. 332

TRANSGUARD—Transient Voltage Suppressor—AVX Corporation; *Int'l*, pg. 775

TRANSIL—Electrical Steel Sheet—British Steel Plc; *Int'l*, pg. 220

TRANSIL G.A.—Precoated Acetate to Accept Inks & Water Colors—Transilwrap Company, Inc.; *U.S. Private*, pg. 1097

TRANSILMASK—Vinyl Masking Film—Transilwrap Company, Inc.; *U.S. Private*, pg. 1097

TRANSILMATTE—Drafting Film—Transilwrap Company, Inc.; *U.S. Private*, pg. 1097

TRANSILON—Conveyor Belts—Forbo Holding SA; *Int'l*, pg. 496

TRANSILPRINT—Paper Backed Plastic Sheets to Facilitate Printing—Transilwrap Company, Inc.; *U.S. Private*, pg. 1097

TRANSIT—NONE—Cordis, a Johnson & Johnson Company; *U.S. Public*, pg. 928

TRANSIT MASTER—Information Management Systems—Rockwell International Corporation; *U.S. Public*, pg. 1397

TRANSIT VINYL—Calendered Film for Transit Advertising—Fasson Films; *U.S. Public*, pg. 153

TRANSITIONS—Vinyl Windows—Owens Corning; *U.S. Public*, pg. 1236

TRANSITIONS—Eyewear Lenses & Blanks—PPG Industries, Inc.; *U.S. Public*, pg. 1245

TRANSITIONS CMS—Wood Case Goods for Computers & Cables—Helikon Furniture Co., Inc.; *U.S. Private*, pg. 520

TRANSITIONS LENSES—NONE—Transitions Optical, Inc.; *U.S. Public*, pg. 1245

TRANSITIONS XTRACTIVE LENSES—NONE—Transitions Optical, Inc.; *U.S. Public*, pg. 1245

TRANSLATOR—Bi-Fuel Electronic CNG Conversion System—Synchro-Start Products, Inc.; *U.S. Private*, pg. 627

TRANSLINE—Herbicide—The Dow Chemical Company; *U.S. Public*, pg. 522

TRANSLINK—Extender & Refinforcing Materials—Engelhard Corporation; *U.S. Public*, pg. 582

TRANSLITE—Photo Film—Eastman Kodak Company; *U.S. Public*, pg. 550

TRANSMARK—Year 2000 Conversion Methodology—Computer Task Group, Inc. (CTG); *U.S. Public*, pg. 423

TRANSMAT—Metal Forming Presses—Verson Division; *U.S. Public*, pg. 48

TRANSMEDIA—Network—Transmedia Network Inc.; *U.S. Public*, pg. 1631

TRANSMISSION—Photo Film—Eastman Kodak Company; *U.S. Public*, pg. 550

TRANSMISSION & DISTRIBUTION WORLD—Electrical Power Industry—Intertec Publishing; *U.S. Public*, pg. 1327

TRANSMISSION TROUBLESHOOTER—Diagnostic Scan Tool Line—Snap-On Tools Corporation; *U.S. Public*, pg. 1480

TRANSOCEANIC—Radio Receiving Sets—Zenith Electronics Corp.; *U.S. Public*, pg. 1790

TRANSOL—NONE—Lawter International, Inc.; *U.S. Public*, pg. 980

TRANSOUND STEREO—Portable Stereos—Sony Electronics; *Int'l*, pg. 1281

TRANSPAC II—Transducer—Abbott Laboratories; *U.S. Public*, pg. 12

TRANSPAK—Field-Mounted Process 2-Wire Transmitters—Action Instruments, Inc.; *U.S. Private*, pg. 15

TRANSPALOCK—NONE—Boon Edam Inc.; *Int'l*, pg. 202

TRANSPORE—Surgical Tape—3M; *U.S. Public*, pg. 1604

TRANSPORT—Tires—Bridgestone/Firestone, Inc.; *Int'l*, pg. 213

TRANSPORT ALL TRACTION—Tires—Bridgestone/Firestone, Inc.; *Int'l*, pg. 213

TRANSPORT APS—Tires—Bridgestone/Firestone, Inc.; *Int'l*, pg. 213

TRANSPORT DUPLEX—Tires—Bridgestone/Firestone, Inc.; *Int'l*, pg. 213

TRANSPORT 500 WIDE OVAL—Tires—Bridgestone/Firestone, Inc.; *Int'l*, pg. 213

TRANSPORT MATERIAL—Tires—Bridgestone/Firestone, Inc.; *Int'l*, pg. 213

TRANSPORT 1—Tires—Bridgestone/Firestone, Inc.; *Int'l*, pg. 213

TRANSPORT 110—Tires—Bridgestone/Firestone, Inc.; *Int'l*, pg. 213

TRANSPORT 1 WIDE OVAL—Tires—Bridgestone/Firestone, Inc.; *Int'l*, pg. 213

TRANSPORT RIB—Tires—Bridgestone/Firestone, Inc.; *Int'l*, pg. 213

TRANSPORT RIB TR—Tires—Bridgestone/Firestone, Inc.; *Int'l*, pg. 213

TRANSPORT SUPREME—Tires—Bridgestone/Firestone, Inc.; *Int'l*, pg. 213

TRANSPORT 2000—Tires—Bridgestone/Firestone, Inc.; *Int'l*, pg. 213

TRANSPORT WIDE OVAL—Tires—Bridgestone/Firestone, Inc.; *Int'l*, pg. 213

TRANSPORTATION & DISTRIBUTION—Periodical—Penton Publishing, Inc.; *U.S. Public*, pg. 1306

TRANSPORTER—Hose—HBD Industries, Inc.; *U.S. Private*, pg. 489

TRANSPORTER—Van—Volkswagen AG; *Int'l*, pg. 1473

TRANSPORTNODE—Telecommunications—Northern Telecom Limited; *Int'l*, pg. 968

TRANSPORTSS—Loan Servicing—SLM Holding Corp.; *U.S. Public*, pg. 1419

TRANSTAR—Photo Paper, Sensitized Materials—Eastman Kodak Company; *U.S. Public*, pg. 550

TRANSTAR—Pressure Transducer—Medex Inc.; *U.S. Public*, pg. 689

TRANSTEC—Aftermarket Rebuild Kit Distribution Division—Freudenberg-NOK; *U.S. Private*, pg. 427

TRANSTEEL—Tires—Bridgestone/Firestone, Inc.; *Int'l*, pg. 213

TRANSTEEL TRACTION DRIVE T506—Tires—Bridgestone/Firestone, Inc.; *Int'l*, pg. 213

TRANSUS—Freight—Transus Intermodal L.L.C.; *U.S. Private*, pg. 1097

TRANSVENE—Leads—Medtronic, Inc.; *U.S. Public*, pg. 1082

TRANSVENE PCD—Device—Medtronic, Inc.; *U.S. Public*, pg. 1082

TRANSVUE—Slide Trays—Eastman Kodak Company; *U.S. Public*, pg. 550

TRANSWAY—Transfer Gateway Software—Tandem Computers Inc.; *U.S. Public*, pg. 417

TRANSWORLD SKATEBOARDING—MAGAZINE—Times Mirror Magazines, Inc.; *U.S. Public*, pg. 1616

TRANSWORLD SNOWBOARDING—Magazine—Times Mirror Magazines, Inc.; *U.S. Public*, pg. 1616

TRANSWRAP—Vertical Form/Fill/Seal Machines—Package Machinery Co.; *U.S. Private*, pg. 832

TRANSYT IV—Computer Program—Litton Industries, Inc.; *U.S. Public*, pg. 1002

TRANXENE—Tranquilizer—Abbott Laboratories; *U.S. Public*, pg. 12

TRANZ—Transaction Systems—VeriFone, Inc.; *U.S. Public*, pg. 815

TRAP-STIK—Glue Device Rodenticide—LiphaTech, Inc.; *Int'l*, pg. 812

TRAPEZOIDAL BOOM—Material Handling Equip.—Grove WorldWide; *Int'l*, pg. 593

TRAPICHE—Cabernet Sauvignon/Chardonnay—Penaflor S.A.; *Int'l*, pg. 1032

TRAPICHE MALBEC ROBLE—Wine—Penaflor S.A.; *Int'l*, pg. 1032

TRAPICHE MEDALLA—Wine—Penaflor S.A.; *Int'l*, pg. 1032

TRAPPER—Stationery products—The Mead Corporation; *U.S. Public*, pg. 1074

TRAPPER KEEPER—Stationery Products—The Mead Corporation; *U.S. Public*, pg. 1074

TRAPPER XL—Notebook—The Mead Corporation; *U.S. Public*, pg. 1074

TRAPPEY—NONE—Allen Canning Company; *U.S. Private*, pg. 36

TRAPPEY'S—Peppers in Vinegar—Trappey's Fine Foods, Inc.; *U.S. Private*, pg. 105

TRAPPEY'S—Sliced Banana Hot Pepper Slices—Trappey's Fine Foods, Inc.; *U.S. Private*, pg. 105

TRAPPEY'S—Banana Mild Peppers—Trappey's Fine Foods, Inc.; *U.S. Private*, pg. 105

TRAPPEY'S—Hot Cherry Peppers—Trappey's Fine Foods, Inc.; *U.S. Private*, pg. 105

TRAPPEY'S—Mild Cherry Peppers—Trappey's Fine Foods, Inc.; *U.S. Private*, pg. 105

TRAPPEY'S—Whole Jalapeno Peppers—Trappey's Fine Foods, Inc.; *U.S. Private*, pg. 105

TRAPPEY'S—Sliced Jalapeno Peppers—Trappey's Fine Foods, Inc.; *U.S. Private*, pg. 105

TRAPPEY'S—Mild Cocktail Okra—Trappey's Fine Foods, Inc.; *U.S. Private*, pg. 105

TRAPPEY'S—Hot Cocktail Okra—Trappey's Fine Foods, Inc.; *U.S. Private*, pg. 105

TRAPPEYS—Pepper Sauce—Trappey's Fine Foods, Inc.; *U.S. Private*, pg. 105

TRAPPINGS—Apparel—I. Spiewak & Sons, Inc.; *U.S. Private*, pg. 1025

TRAPSHOOTER—Radar Detectors—Cobra Electronics Corporation; *U.S. Public*, pg. 391

TRASAR—TV Transmitting Antennas—Andrew Corporation; *U.S. Public*, pg. 112

TRASE MILLER SOLUTIONS—Technology Consulting Services—MTI Vacations, Inc.; *U.S. Private*, pg. 688

TRASE MILLER TECHNOLOGIES—Call Center Outsourcing Services For The Travel Industry—MTI Vacations, Inc.; *U.S. Private*, pg. 688

TRASE MILLER TELESERVICES—Event Reservations & Ticketing Services—MTI Vacations, Inc.; *U.S. Private*, pg. 688

TRASH CAT—NONE—Ellicott Machine Corporation International; *U.S. Private*, pg. 372

TRASH-HOG—Pumps—ITT A-C Pump/ITT Marlow; *U.S. Public*, pg. 860

TRASH MAGNET—NONE—Koo Koo Roo, Inc.; *U.S. Public*, pg. 966

TRASYLOL—Pharmaceutical—Bayer Corporation/Pharmaceutical Division; *Int'l*, pg. 173

TRAUB—Mill Turning Centers—Traub AG; *Int'l*, pg. 1419

TRAUMACAL—Adult Vitamin—Bristol-Myers Squibb Company; *U.S. Public*, pg. 253

TRAUMACAL—High Nitrogen Liquid Formula for Burn Patients—Mead Johnson Nutritional Group; *U.S. Public*, pg. 254

TRAUMEX—X-Ray Equipment—Fischer Imaging Corporation; *U.S. Public*, pg. 647

TRAV-LER—Interdental Brush—John O. Butler Co.; *Int'l*, pg. 1320

TRAV-START—Control—Harnischfeger Industries, Inc.; *U.S. Public*, pg. 788

TRAV-A-DIAL—Analog Readout Systems—Southwestern Industries, Inc.; *U.S. Private*, pg. 1019

TRAVAGLINI—Wine—Wine World Estates Company; *Int'l*, pg. 917

TRAVASAK—Sleeping System—American Recreation Products, Inc.; *U.S. Public*, pg. 948

TRAVCLEAN—Traveling Cleaners—Luwa Bahnson, Inc.; *U.S. Private*, pg. 682

TRAVEL ALL—Sport Bag—Ektelon; *U.S. Private*, pg. 884

TRAVEL AMERICA—Magazine—Century Publishing Company; *U.S. Private*, pg. 226

TRAVEL AMERICA AT HALF PRICE—Coupon Books—Entertainment Publications, Inc.; *U.S. Public*, pg. 320

TRAVEL & LEISURE—Magazine—American Express Company; *U.S. Public*, pg. 73

TRAVEL & LEISURE—Magazine—American Express Publishing Corporation; *U.S. Public*, pg. 74

TRAVEL CANADA AT HALF PRICE—Coupon Books—Entertainment Publications, Inc.; *U.S. Public*, pg. 320

THE TRAVEL CHANNEL—NONE—The Travel Channel; *U.S. Private*, pg. 647

TRAVEL CHEQUES—NONE—American Express Service Europe Ltd.; *U.S. Public*, pg. 74

TRAVEL HOLIDAY—Magazine—The Reader's Digest Association, Inc.; *U.S. Public*, pg. 1367

TRAVEL INNS—Hotels—Whitbread PLC; *Int'l*, pg. 1498

TRAVEL MAGIC COPIER—Activity—Tyco Toys, Inc.; *U.S. Public*, pg. 1058

TRAVEL MANAGEMENT SERVICES—NONE—American Express Service Europe Ltd.; *U.S. Public*, pg. 74

TRAVEL MATES—Beauty & Bath Accessories—Paris Presents; *U.S. Private*, pg. 839

TRAVEL-MATIC—NONE—Melnor Inc.; *U.S. Public*, pg. 1234

TRAVEL PLAZAS BY MARRIOTT—Restaurants—Marriott International, Inc.; *U.S. Public*, pg. 1047

TRAVEL PORTS—Fuel Operations—Travel Ports of America Inc.; *U.S. Public*, pg. 1632

TRAVEL TANDEM—Infant Car Seat—Evenflo Company, Inc.; *U.S. Private*, pg. 629

TRAVEL TUB—Full-Sized Baby Bath That Folds for Travel—Cosco, Inc.; *U.S. Private*, pg. 277

TRAVELER—NONE—Clarify Inc.; *U.S. Public*, pg. 382

TRAVELER—NONE—Everest & Jennings, Inc.; *U.S. Public*, pg. 758

TRAVELER EXPRESS—Neuro Diagnostic Instrumentation—Bio-Logic Systems Corp.; *U.S. Public*, pg. 230

TRAVELER 2000—Anti Glare Filter—Optical Coating Laboratory, Inc.; *U.S. Public*, pg. 1227

TRAVELERS ADVANTAGE—Membership Based Full Service Travel Agency—CUC International, Inc.; *U.S. Public*, pg. 320

TRAVELERS CHEQUES—NONE—American Express Company; *U.S. Public*, pg. 73

TRAVELERS EXPRESS—Money Order—Viad Corp; *U.S. Public*, pg. 1718

TRAVELETTER DIRECT—Travel Expense Management Featuring Touch-Tone Reporting—Gelco Information Network, Inc.; *U.S. Private*, pg. 442

TRAVELID—Lids for Paper & Plastic Cups—Sweetheart Cup Company Inc.; *U.S. Private*, pg. 1058

TRAVELIFT—Intermodal Handling Equipment—MI-Jack Products, Inc.; *U.S. Private*, pg. 740

TRAVELING BRIDGE FILTER—Automated Gravity Filtration of Municipal/Industrial Water & Wastewater—U.S. Filter/Davis Water & Waste Industries, Inc.; *U.S. Public*, pg. 1682

TRAVELITE—Stroller—Century Products Co.; *U.S. Private*, pg. 226

TRAVELLER—Tires—Tractor Supply Co.; *U.S. Public*, pg. 1627

TRAVELMASTER—Recreational Vehicles—Coachmen Industries, Inc.; *U.S. Public*, pg. 387

TRAVELMASTER—Electronics Storage/Specialty Luggage—Delta Consolidated Industries, Inc. (Co. Headquarters); *U.S. Public*, pg. 481

TRAVELMATCH—For Travel Agency—American Automobile Association; *U.S. Private*, pg. 50

TRAVELMATE—Computer Terminal—Texas Instruments Incorporated; *U.S. Public*, pg. 1585

TRAVELODGE—NONE—HFS, Incorporated; *U.S. Public*, pg. 321

TRAVELODGE—Hotel Chain—Travelodge; *U.S. Public*, pg. 322

TRAVELREACH—Paging Service—Frontier Communications Services; *U.S. Public*, pg. 684

TRAVELTRADE—Travel Magazine—Reed Business Information Pty. Limited; *Int'l*, pg. 1094

TRAVELTRADE VISA GUIDE—Directory—Reed Business Information Pty. Limited; *Int'l*, pg. 1094

TRAVELTRADE YEARBOOK—Directory—Reed Business Information Pty. Limited; *Int'l*, pg. 1094

TRAVELWORLD—Deluxe Escorted Tours; Orient, China, Africa, S. America, India, S. Pacific—Noel Olson Group; *U.S. Private*, pg. 800

TRAVERSANIP—Film Haul Off—Battenfeld Gloucester Engineering Co. Inc.; *U.S. Private*, pg. 123

TRAVERSANO—NONE—Porcelanite, Inc.; *Int'l*, pg. 573

TRAVERSE BAY FRUIT CO.—Dried Fruit—Cherry Central Cooperative; *U.S. Private*, pg. 233

TRAVERTINE—Vinyl Composition Tile—Kentile Operting Co.; *U.S. Private*, pg. 615

TRAVL-MATES—Food Preparation Appliances—The Metal Ware Corp.; *U.S. Private*, pg. 734

TRAX—Cooler Cart—Igloo Products Corporation; *U.S. Private*, pg. 265

TRAX—Game—The United States Playing Card Company; *U.S. Private*, pg. 1125

TRAX-DRIVE—Tires—Bridgestone/Firestone, Inc.; *Int'l*, pg. 213

TRAX MUSIC—Retail Stores—TSC Shannock Corporation; *Int'l*, pg. 1343

TRAX PLUS—Tires—Bridgestone/Firestone, Inc.; *Int'l*, pg. 213

TRAX 12—Tires—Bridgestone/Firestone, Inc.; *Int'l*, pg. 213

TRAXX—Tires—Bridgestone/Firestone, Inc.; *Int'l*, pg. 213

TRAXX ASR—Tires—Bridgestone/Firestone, Inc.; *Int'l*, pg. 213

TRAYCO—Bath Prods.—Delta Faucet Corporation; *U.S. Public*, pg. 1053

TRAYFRESH—Ovenable Paperboard Containers—Westvaco Corporation; *U.S. Public*, pg. 1762

TRAYLOR—Crushers, Kilns, Mills—Fuller Company; *Int'l*, pg. 475

TRAYMATE—Canned Beverage Tray—International Container Systems; *Int'l*, pg. 685

TRE CI LUCE—Contemporary Lighting Fixtures—IL International Inc.; *U.S. Public*, pg. 855

TREADEASY—Shoes—P.W. Minor & Son, Inc.; *U.S. Private*, pg. 751

TREASURE CAVE—Blue Cheese & Feta—Beatrice Cheese Co.; *U.S. Public*, pg. 426

TREASURE CAVE—Cheese—ConAgra, Inc.; *U.S. Public*, pg. 425

TREASURE CHEST—Casino—Boyd Gaming Corporation; *U.S. Public*, pg. 249

TREASURED MEMORIES—Figurines & Musicals—Stanhome Inc.; *U.S. Public*, pg. 1508

TREASURES IN NEEDLEWORK—Magazine—Meredith Corporation; *U.S. Public*, pg. 1094

TREASURY & RISK MANAGEMENT—NONE—The Economist Group Limited.; *Int'l*, pg. 1026

TREAT—Snack Foods—Bachman Company; *U.S. Private*, pg. 109

TREATMEAL—Combination Meal for Children—International Dairy Queen, Inc.; *U.S. Public*, pg. 220

TREBOR—Mints—Cadbury Schweppes p.l.c.; *Int'l*, pg. 247

TREBOR GINGER—Sugar Confectionary—Cadbury Nigeria PLC; *Int'l*, pg. 248

TREBOR KOFFSTICKS—Sugar Confectionary—Cadbury Nigeria PLC; *Int'l*, pg. 248

TREBOR LUCKIES—Sugar Confectionary—Cadbury Nigeria PLC; *Int'l*, pg. 248

TREBOR PEPPERMINTS—Sugar Confectionary—Cadbury Nigeria PLC; *Int'l*, pg. 248

TRECON—NONE—Trebla Chemical Company; *U.S. Private*, pg. 282

TREDAIRE—Carpet Underlay—The Gates Rubber Company Ltd.; *Int'l*, pg. 1397

TREDLOC—Woven Tire Belt Design—Pirelli Armstrong Tire Corporation; *Int'l*, pg. 1058

TREE—Pickles—Dean Foods Company; *U.S. Public*, pg. 489

THE TREE GROWING COMPANY—Wood Fiber—Weyerhaeuser Company; *U.S. Public*, pg. 1764

TREE OF LIFE—Health Food Products—Koninklijke BolsWessanen nv; *Int'l*, pg. 750

TREE RIPE—Refrigerated Juice—Johanna Foods Inc.; *U.S. Private*, pg. 589

TREE SWEET—Frozen Juices—Seneca Foods Corporation; *U.S. Public*, pg. 1456

TREE TOP—Juice, Sauce & Blend—Tree Top, Inc.; *U.S. Private*, pg. 1098

TREE TOP—Fruit Drink—Unilever Plc; *Int'l*, pg. 1433

TREE WISHES—Educational & Entertainment Services—Georgia-Pacific Corporation; *U.S. Public*, pg. 735

TREEFRESH—Juice—Home Juice Co.; *U.S. Private*, pg. 537

THE TREEHOUSE—NONE—Broderbund Software, Inc.; *U.S. Public*, pg. 258

TREESOURCE—Lumber & Lumber By-Products—WTD Industries, Inc.; *U.S. Public*, pg. 1729

TREESWEET—Juices—Erly Industries, Inc.; *U.S. Public*, pg. 591

TREET—Razor Blades—American Safety Razor Company; *U.S. Private*, pg. 597

TREEVIEW—Software—Fair, Isaac and Company, Inc.; *U.S. Public*, pg. 609

TREFLAN—Herbicide—The Dow Chemical Company; *U.S. Public*, pg. 522

TREFLE—NONE—Wacoal Corporation; *Int'l*, pg. 1484

TREGALON—Staple Fiber—Bayer AG; *Int'l*, pg. 171

TREKK—NONE—Kellwood Company; *U.S. Public*, pg. 948

Brand Name Index

TREKKER—Wearable Personal Computer—Rockwell International Corporation; *U.S. Public*, pg. 1397

TRELEX NATURAL—Graft Product—Meadox Medicals, Inc.; *U.S. Public*, pg. 247

TRELLIS—Dinnerware—Dansk International Designs Ltd.; *U.S. Public*, pg. 261

TRELOC—Cardiovascular Pharmaceutical—Astra AB; *Int'l*, pg. 93

TRELUX—NONE—Trebla Chemical Company; *U.S. Public*, pg. 282

TREN-SHORE—Aluminum Hydraulic Shoring—Allied Construction Products, Inc.; *U.S. Public*, pg. 1339

TRENCHCOAT—Poleolefin Film—The Dow Chemical Company; *U.S. Public*, pg. 522

TREND—Security, Fire, Control Systems—Caradon Plc; *Int'l*, pg. 266

TREND CLUB—Apparel—Clothestime Stores, Inc.; *U.S. Public*, pg. 387

TRENDFINDER—Software—Fair, Isaac and Company, Inc.; *U.S. Public*, pg. 609

TRENDLINE—Newsletter—The Mead Corporation; *U.S. Public*, pg. 1074

TRENDSETTER—Professional Hair Styling Tools—Andis Company; *U.S. Private*, pg. 73

TRENDWALL—Floor to Ceiling Moveable Partitions—Trendway Corporation; *U.S. Private*, pg. 1099

TRENDWAY—Company Name—Trendway Corporation; *U.S. Private*, pg. 1099

TRENDWAY XPRESS—Quick Shipment Delivery—Trendway Corporation; *U.S. Private*, pg. 1099

TRENT 800—Civil Engine—Rolls-Royce-Commercial Aero Engines Ltd.; *Int'l*, pg. 1127

TRENT 500—Civil Engine—Rolls-Royce-Commercial Aero Engines Ltd.; *Int'l*, pg. 1127

TRENT 900—Civil Engine—Rolls-Royce-Commercial Aero Engines Ltd.; *Int'l*, pg. 1127

TRENT 700—Civil Engine—Rolls-Royce-Commercial Aero Engines Ltd.; *Int'l*, pg. 1127

TRENTAL—Vascular Disorders—Hoechst Marion Roussel, Inc.; *Int'l*, pg. 624

TRENTAL—Treatment for Intermittent Claudication—Hoechst Marion Roussel North America; *Int'l*, pg. 625

TRENTON STONE—Apparel—Fred Meyer Stores; *U.S. Public*, pg. 1103

TREO—Women's Shoes—Nine West Group, Inc.; *U.S. Public*, pg. 1185

TREO—NONE—Pharmacia & Upjohn, Inc.; *Int'l*, pg. 1047

TREPAN—NONE—Trebla Chemical Company; *U.S. Public*, pg. 282

TRES NINAS—Dairy Products—Sancor Cooperativas Unidas Limitadas; *Int'l*, pg. 1183

TRESADERM—Animal Health Pharmaceuticals—Merial Ltd.; *U.S. Public*, pg. 1092

TRESADERM—Animal Health Pharmaceuticals—Merial Ltd.; *Int'l*, pg. 1109

TRESADO—Cigars—Lane Limited; *Int'l*, pg. 1129

TRESEMME—Hair Products—Alberto-Culver Company; *U.S. Public*, pg. 37

TRESOR—Fragrance—Cosmair, Inc.; *Int'l*, pg. 818

TRESOR—Perfume—L'Oreal S.A.; *Int'l*, pg. 818

TRETORN—Tennis Shoes & Balls—Aritmos AB; *Int'l*, pg. 1072

TRETORN—Casual Footwear—Tretorn; *Int'l*, pg. 1072

TRETORN—Tennis Shoes & Balls—Tretorn AB; *Int'l*, pg. 1072

TRETORN XL PLUS—Tennis Ball—Aritmos AB; *Int'l*, pg. 1072

TRETORN XL PLUS—Tennis Ball—Tretorn AB; *Int'l*, pg. 1072

TREVIRA—Polyester Fibre—Hoechst Aktiengesellschaft; *Int'l*, pg. 624

TREVIS—Lactic Acid Bacteria—Novo Nordisk A/S; *Int'l*, pg. 987

TREWAX—Wood & Floorcare Retail Products—Namico, Inc.; *U.S. Private*, pg. 773

TRI—Company Name—TSI Incorporated; *U.S. Public*, pg. 1559

TRI-AXIS FEED—Electronic & Mechanical Feeds for Transmat Presses—Verson Division; *U.S. Public*, pg. 48

TRI-BLENDER—NONE—Tri-Clover Inc.; *Int'l*, pg. 1379

TRI-CARB TR/LL—Liquid Scintillation Counting—Packard Instrument Co., Inc.; *U.S. Private*, pg. 833

TRI-CARB 2500—Liquid Scintillation Analyzer—Packard Instrument Co., Inc.; *U.S. Private*, pg. 833

TRI-CHECK—Electrophoresis Serum-Based Controls—Beckman Instruments, Inc.; *U.S. Public*, pg. 199

TRI-CHEM—All Purpose Cleaners—Ecolab Inc.; *U.S. Public*, pg. 562

TRI-CHEM—Paint—Tri-Chem, Inc.; *U.S. Private*, pg. 1100

TRI-CLAMP—NONE—Tri-Clover Inc.; *Int'l*, pg. 1379

TRI-CLEAN—Liquid Soap—Calgon Vestal Laboratories; *U.S. Public*, pg. 1515

TRI-C.L.O.P.S.—Element Filter with Ring-Lok Access—Jacuzzi Bros., Jacuzzi, Inc.; *U.S. Public*, pg. 1684

TRI-CLOVER—Sanitary Stainless Steel Fittings, Pipe & Pumps—Crouch Supply Company, Inc.; *U.S. Private*, pg. 291

TRI-CODE—Electronics—National Semiconductor Corporation; *U.S. Public*, pg. 1159

TRI-CORE—3″ thick thermal break & expanded polystyrene insulatedcommercial door—Raynor Garage Doors; *U.S. Private*, pg. 912

TRI-D—Super Mini Computer Products—Modcomp; *U.S. Public*, pg. 283

TRI-DERM S.E.—Cosmetic Ingredient—Tri-K Industries, Inc.; *U.S. Private*, pg. 1100

TRI-DERM T—Comsmetic Ingredient—Tri-K Industries, Inc.; *U.S. Private*, pg. 1100

TRI-DET—NONE—Western Atlas Logging Services; *U.S. Public*, pg. 1757

TRI DRUM—3 Drum Rack—Jarke Corporation; *U.S. Public*, pg. 583

TRI-ETHANE—Methyl Chloroform Industrial Solvents—PPG Industries, Inc.; *U.S. Public*, pg. 1245

TRI-FET—Trimmed Resistor/Implanted Field Effect Transistor—Analog Devices, Inc.; *U.S. Public*, pg. 107

TRI-FLASH—Snap-On Mirror Assembly—Federal Signal Corporation, Signal Div.; *U.S. Public*, pg. 616

TRI-FLAT—Flowmeter—Bailey, Fischer & Porter Company; *Int'l*, pg. 449

TRI-FLEX—Security Envelopes—Uniflex, Inc.; *U.S. Public*, pg. 1665

TRI-FLEX 2—Panel System for Triaxial Permeability Testing—ELE International, Inc./Soiltest; *Int'l*, pg. 1287

TRI-FLO—NONE—Tri-Clover Inc.; *Int'l*, pg. 1379

TRI-FLOW—Lubricant—The Thompson's Company; *U.S. Public*, pg. 1466

TRI-FORCE—Line of Men's Woods & Irons—Square Two Golf Incorporated; *U.S. Public*, pg. 1501

TRI-GARD—Sealing System for Right Angle Reducers—Rockwell International Corporation; *U.S. Public*, pg. 1397

TRI-GLAS—Fiberglass Products—TRI-GLAS; *U.S. Private*, pg. 848

TRI-GRIP—Screwdrivers—Greenlee Textron; *U.S. Public*, pg. 1589

TRI-GUARD—Moisture-Handling System for Capnographs—Nellcor Puritan Bennett Incorporated; *U.S. Public*, pg. 1039

TRI-IMMUNOL—Vaccine—American Home Products Corporation; *U.S. Public*, pg. 79

TRI-K HMP—Cosmetic Ingredients—Tri-K Industries, Inc.; *U.S. Private*, pg. 1100

TRI-LIMINATOR—Water Filter—Manitowoc Ice, Inc.; *U.S. Public*, pg. 1041

TRI-LOK—Press-Fit Connector Technology—SAE Engineering, Inc.; *U.S. Private*, pg. 955

TRI-M-ITE—Silicon Carbide Coated Abrasives—3M; *U.S. Public*, pg. 1604

TRI MAG—NONE—Western Atlas Logging Services; *U.S. Public*, pg. 1757

TRI-MATE—Pig Milk Replacer—Manna Pro Corporation; *U.S. Private*, pg. 700

TRI-METAL—Flexible Circuits—Advanced Circuit Technology; *U.S. Private*, pg. 21

TRI-MILTOX—Fungicide—Novartis AG; *Int'l*, pg. 971

TRI-MINULET—Oral Contraceptives—American Home Products Corporation; *U.S. Public*, pg. 79

TRI MINULET—Triphasic Oral Contraceptive—Wyeth-Ayerst Laboratories, Inc.; *U.S. Public*, pg. 80

TRI-NORINYL—Norethindrone/Ethinyl Estradiol—Syntex; *Int'l*, pg. 1120

TRI OMINOS—Game—Pressman Toy Corp.; *U.S. Private*, pg. 882

TRI-PALM ESTATES—Mobile Home Community—GWP, Inc.; *U.S. Private*, pg. 437

TRI-PIN—NONE—Berg Electronics; *U.S. Public*, pg. 212

TRI-POINT—Temperature & Pressure Switches—Ascolectric Limited; *U.S. Public*, pg. 575

TRI-POINT—Pressure & Temperature Switches—Automatic Switch Co.; *U.S. Public*, pg. 573

TRI-POLY—Electronics—National Semiconductor Corporation; *U.S. Public*, pg. 1159

TRI-SOCKET—NONE—Berg Electronics; *U.S. Public*, pg. 212

TRI-SPEED—Control—Harnischfeger Industries, Inc.; *U.S. Public*, pg. 788

TRI-STAR—In-Plant Laundry System—Ecolab Inc.; *U.S. Public*, pg. 562

TRI-STAR—Movies—Sony Corporation; *Int'l*, pg. 1280

TRI-STAR L—2000-Detergent Emulsion for Tough Fabric Soils—Ecolab Inc.; *U.S. Public*, pg. 562

TRI-STAR PICTURES—Motion Pictures—Sony Pictures Studios; *Int'l*, pg. 1283

TRI-STAR PICTURES—Motion Pictures—Tri-Star Pictures, Inc.; *Int'l*, pg. 1282

TRI-STATE—Electronics—National Semiconductor Corporation; *U.S. Public*, pg. 1159

TRI-STEEL—Special Steels—Inland Steel Industries, Inc.; *U.S. Public*, pg. 879

TRI-TAB—Tricalcium Phosphate Anhydrous—Rhone-Poulenc Basic Chemicals Co.; *Int'l*, pg. 1110

TRI-TEC—Three Spring Edge Support System-Patented Mattress Design—Therapedic Associates, Inc.; *U.S. Private*, pg. 1079

TRI-TORRAT—Beta-Blocker—Boehringer Mannheim GmbH; *Int'l*, pg. 331

TRI-VI-FLOR—Three Vitamins With Floride—Mead Johnson Nutritional Group; *U.S. Public*, pg. 254

TRI-VI-SOL—Vitamins for Children—Mead Johnson Nutritional Group; *U.S. Public*, pg. 254

TRI-VI-SOL WITH IRON—Vitamins with Iron for Children—Mead Johnson Nutritional Group; *U.S. Public*, pg. 254

TRI-WELD—NONE—Tri-Clover Inc.; *Int'l*, pg. 1379

TRI-WING—Fastening System—Rule Industries, Inc.; *U.S. Public*, pg. 950

TRI-X—Photo Film, Plates—Eastman Kodak Company; *U.S. Public*, pg. 550

TRI-CLOVER—Industrial & Sanitary Fittings—Tri-Clover Inc.; *Int'l*, pg. 1379

TRI-ONIC—Low Voltage Fuse—Gould Electronics Inc., Shawmut Circuit Protection Division; *U.S. Public*, pg. 1592

TRI-POWER—Selective Herbicide—Riverdale Chemical Co.; *U.S. Private*, pg. 934

TRI-WALL PAK—Corrugated Fiberboard Containers—TBG Management S.A.M.; *Int'l*, pg. 1335

TRIA—Graphic Art Supplies—Esselte AB; *Int'l*, pg. 459

TRIABON—Slow-Release Fertilizer—BASF AG; *Int'l*, pg. 103

TRIAC—Centrifuge—Becton Dickinson Primary Care Diagnostics; *U.S. Public*, pg. 199

TRIAD—Control Sera—Beckman Instruments, Inc.; *U.S. Public*, pg. 199

TRIAD—Solvents—Detrex Corporation; *U.S. Public*, pg. 501

TRIAD—Communications System—Executone Information Systems, Inc.; *U.S. Public*, pg. 599

TRIAD—Adaptive Control System—Fair, Isaac and Company, Inc.; *U.S. Public*, pg. 609

TRIAD—Bond Paper—Fort James Corporation; *U.S. Public*, pg. 670

TRIAD—X-Ray Field Service & Quality Assurance Kit—Keithley Instruments Inc.-Radiation Measurements Div.; *U.S. Public*, pg. 946

TRIAD—Ballasts, Transformers—MagneTek, Inc.; *U.S. Public*, pg. 1037

TRIAD—Cut-Off, Grooving & Tracing Tool—Rogers Tool Works, Inc.; *U.S. Public*, pg. 950

TRIAD-IL—Adaptive Control System—Fair, Isaac and Company, Inc.; *U.S. Public*, pg. 609

TRIAD PERSONNEL SERVICES—Employment Agency—General Empioyment Enterprises, Inc.; *U.S. Public*, pg. 714

TRIADE FILM SYSTEM—Photographic Film—AGFA Division of Bayer Corporation; *Int'l*, pg. 172

TRIAL RUN—Design of Experiment Software—SPSS Inc.; *U.S. Public*, pg. 1420

TRIAMBIENT—Lighting—Haworth, Inc.; *U.S. Private*, pg. 511

TRIAMINE—Herbicide—Riverdale Chemical Co.; *U.S. Private*, pg. 934

TRIAMINIC—Cough & Cold Medicine—Sandoz Pharmaceuticals Corp.; *Int'l*, pg. 974

TRIAMINIC-DM—Cold Syrup—Sandoz Pharmaceuticals Corp.; *Int'l*, pg. 974

TRIAMINIC-12—Tablets—Sandoz Pharmaceuticals Corp.; *Int'l*, pg. 974

TRIAMINICIN—Cough & Cold Medicine—Sandoz Pharmaceuticals Corp.; *Int'l*, pg. 974

TRIAMINICOL—Multi-Symptom Cold Syrup, Multi-Symptom Cold Tablets—Sandoz Pharmaceuticals Corp.; *Int'l*, pg. 974

TRIANGLE—Veterinary Pharmaceuticals—American Home Products Corporation; *U.S. Public*, pg. 79

TRIANGLE—Fitness Equipment—Empire of Carolina, Inc.; *U.S. Public*, pg. 579

TRIAX—Engineering Thermoplastic Alloys—Monsanto Company; *U.S. Public*, pg. 1124

TRIAX—AS/R Systems—Jervis B. Webb Company; *U.S. Private*, pg. 1156

TRIBIOTIC—Pharmaceutical—Thompson Medical Company, Inc.; *U.S. Private*, pg. 1083

TRIBONETICS—Bearings—L & S Bearing Co.; *U.S. Public*, pg. 970

TRIBUNE—Information & Entertainment—Tribune Company; *U.S. Public*, pg. 1635

TRIBUNO—Vermouth—The Wine Group; *U.S. Private*, pg. 1182

TRIBUTE—Termicide—Roussel Corporation; *Int'l*, pg. 625

TRIBUTE—Termiticide—Roussel UCLAF S.A.; *Int'l*, pg. 626

TRICENTRIC VALVES—Sealing Metal Seated Valves—Atwood & Morrill Co., Inc.; *Int'l*, pg. 1489

TRICHANNEL ARCHITECTURE—Multiple Network Potocols Within The Same Hub—3Com Corporation; *U.S. Public*, pg. 1604

TRICHOTINE—NONE—Schwarz Pharma Inc.; *Int'l*, pg. 1211

TRICITY-BENDIX—NONE—Electrolux, AB; *Int'l*, pg. 438

TRICO—Oilfield Equipment—Paccar Inc.; *U.S. Public*, pg. 1246

TRICO—Pumps, Tanks & Oil Machinery—Trico Industries, Inc.; *U.S. Public*, pg. 1247

TRICO—Windshield Wipers, Arms & Refills—Trico Products Corporation; *Int'l*, pg. 1397

TRICOL—Refiners Syrup—Crompton & Knowles Ingredient Technology Corp.; *U.S. Public*, pg. 459

TRICON CONVEYOR—Modular Roller Conveyor Systems—ElectroCom Automation L.P.; *Int'l*, pg. 1244

TRICONE—Mining & Chemical Machinery—Svedala Industries Inc.; *Int'l*, pg. 1325

TRICORD—NONE—Tricord Systems, Inc.; *U.S. Public*, pg. 1637

TRICOSTERIL—Adhesive Bandages—Polive/Tricosteril; *U.S. Public*, pg. 673

TRIDANE—Linear Alkyl Benzene—Monsanto Company; *U.S. Public*, pg. 1124

TRIDENT—Chewing Gum—Adams U.S.A.; *U.S. Public*, pg. 1739

TRIDENT—Clocks—Litton Industries, Inc.; *U.S. Public*, pg. 1002

TRIDENT—Forms Press—Rockwell International Corporation; *U.S. Public*, pg. 1397

TRIDENT—Chewing Gum—Warner-Lambert Company; *U.S. Public*, pg. 1738

TRIDENT GUM—Chewing Gum—Warner-Lambert K.K.; *U.S. Public*, pg. 1739

TRIDENT STEEL STRIP—NONE—Glynwed International PLC; *Int'l*, pg. 554

TRIDENT SUBMARINE—NONE—General Dynamics Corporation; *U.S. Public*, pg. 708

TRIDESILON 0.05 PERCENT CREME—Pharmaceutical—Bayer Corporation/Pharmaceutical Division; *Int'l*, pg. 173

TRIDYNE—Stock Preparation—Beloit Corporation; *U.S. Public*, pg. 789

TRIFAB—Storefront Framings for Low-Rise Applications—Kawneer Company; *U.S. Public*, pg. 60

TRIFECTA—Electronic Components—General Instrument Corporation; *U.S. Public*, pg. 716

TRIFLES—Catalogue—Harcourt General, Inc.; *U.S. Public*, pg. 782

TRIFLEX—Gloves for Use in Medical Procedures—Allegiance Healthcare Corp.; *U.S. Public*, pg. 44

TRIFLUID—PPN Basic Solution—Otsuka Pharmaceutical Co., Ltd.; *Int'l*, pg. 1013

TRIFURCON—NONE—Molex Incorporated; *U.S. Public*, pg. 1121

TRIGAC—Convertor—Kearfott Guidance & Navigation Corp.; *U.S. Private*, pg. 93

TRYGG-HANSA—Life and Non-Life Insurance—Trygg-Hansa; *Int'l*, pg. 1425

TRIGGER-LOCK—Latch & Trigger Action—Hartwell Corporation; *U.S. Private*, pg. 1168

TRIGGER START—Torches—BernzOmatic; *U.S. Public*, pg. 1177

TRIGGER-TRAC—NONE—National-Standard Co.; *U.S. Public*, pg. 1160

TRIGON—Triple Crucible Electron Beam Source—BOC Coating Technology; *Int'l*, pg. 121

TRIGONAL—UV Sensitisers, Radiation, Curing—Akzo Nobel N.V.; *Int'l*, pg. 42

TRIGUARD—Boiler Deposit Inhibitor—Diversey Water Technologies, Inc.; *U.S. Public*, pg. 1150

TRILAFON—Antipsychotic Concentrate, Injection & Tablets—Schering-Plough Corporation; *U.S. Public*, pg. 1438

TRILAG—Gyroscope—Kearfott Guidance & Navigation Corp.; *U.S. Private*, pg. 93

TRILAN—Local Area Network—Dukane Corporation; *U.S. Public*, pg. 345

TRILENE—Mono—Outdoor Technologies Group; *U.S. Private*, pg. 822

TRILENE—Liquid Polymer—Uniroyal Chemical Company, Inc.; *U.S. Public*, pg. 460

TRILENE BIG GAME—Mono—Outdoor Technologies Group; *U.S. Private*, pg. 822

TRILENE XL—Mono—Outdoor Technologies Group; *U.S. Private*, pg. 822

TRILENE XT—Mono—Outdoor Technologies Group; *U.S. Private*, pg. 822

TRILEX—Wheels—Georg Fischer Ltd.; *Int'l*, pg. 488

TRILLIONAIRES—Candy—Pangburn Candy Company; *U.S. Private*, pg. 836

TRILOGY—NONE—James Hardie Industries Ltd.; *Int'l*, pg. 596

TRILOGY—Multi-Channel Infusion Pump—Medex Inc.; *U.S. Public*, pg. 689

TRILOGY—Pacemaker—St. Jude Medical, Inc.; *U.S. Public*, pg. 1427

TRILON—Sequestering Agents—BASF AG; *Int'l*, pg. 103

TRILON—PTFE Sheet, Rod & Tube, Tape—Furon Fluorglas Products; *U.S. Public*, pg. 689

TRILOX—Herbicides—Agrolinz Melamin GmbH; *Int'l*, pg. 356

TRILOX—Plant Protectives—DSM Chemie Linz GmbH; *Int'l*, pg. 356

TRILUDAN—Seasonal Allergic Rhinitis—Hoechst Marion Roussel, Inc.; *Int'l*, pg. 624

TRILUDAN—Terfenadine—Hoechst Marion Roussel North America; *Int'l*, pg. 625

TRILYTE—Roof Prism Binoculars—Swift Instruments, Inc.; *U.S. Private*, pg. 1058

TRIM—Manicure Implements—The W.E. Bassett Company; *U.S. Private*, pg. 122

TRIM—Milk, Yogurt, Dairy Products, UHT Milk—Q.U.F. Industries Ltd.; *Int'l*, pg. 1074

TRIM & TERRIFIC—Milk—Q.U.F. Industries Ltd.; *Int'l*, pg. 1074

TRIM-CRAFT—Vehicle Trim Adhesives—PPG Industries, Inc.; *U.S. Public*, pg. 1245

TRIM-FIT—Drawer Dividers—Vance Industries, Inc.; *U.S. Private*, pg. 1133

TRIM/LIGHT—NONE—Reynolds Metals Co.-Can Division Headquarters; *U.S. Public*, pg. 1386

TRIM/LIGHT—Metallic Cans—Reynolds Metals Company; *U.S. Public*, pg. 1385

TRIM-LINE—Surgical Instruments—Alcon Laboratories, Inc.; *U.S. Public*, pg. 916

TRIM LINE—Poultry—Tyson Foods, Inc.; *U.S. Public*, pg. 1652

TRIM'N'EDGE—Outdoor Products—The Black & Decker Corporation; *U.S. Public*, pg. 233

TRIM-TO-SIZE—Air Conditioner Filter—Research Products Corporation; *U.S. Public*, pg. 924

TRIM-TOWLS—Paper Towels—Bay West Paper Corp. Towel & Tissue Div.; *U.S. Public*, pg. 1747

TRIM TYTE—Fittings—United States Pipe & Foundry Company, Inc.; *U.S. Public*, pg. 1736

TRIM TYTON—Fittings—United States Pipe & Foundry Company, Inc.; *U.S. Public*, pg. 1736

TRIMAR FAST RECOVERY UTILITY—IMS Database Utility—BMC Software, Inc.; *U.S. Public*, pg. 162

TRIMAR ONLINE DEDB IMAGE COPY—IMS Database Utility—BMC Software, Inc.; *U.S. Public*, pg. 162

TRIMAR RESTART CONTROL FACILITY—IMS Database Utility—BMC Software, Inc.; *U.S. Public*, pg. 162

TRIMAX—Furniture Max, Copy Max & Office Max—OfficeMax; *U.S. Public*, pg. 1212

TRIMAX—Monofilament Fishing Line—Outdoor Technologies Group; *U.S. Private*, pg. 822

TRIMAX—Medical X-Ray Film, Screening System, Intensifying Screen Combination—3M; *U.S. Public*, pg. 1604

TRIMBACH-ALSACE—Wines—Seagram Chateau & Estate Wines Co.; *U.S. Public*, pg. 1215

TRIMBRITE—Auto Decor Self-Adhesive Side Wheel & Door Molding Products Do-It-Yourself—Spartan International Inc.; *U.S. Private*, pg. 1020

TRIMCAT—Power Tools—The Black & Decker Corporation; *U.S. Public*, pg. 233

TRIMCO—Tradename—Triangle Brass Manufacturing; *U.S. Private*, pg. 1101

TRIMFLEX—Instrumentation Systems—Teleflex Incorporated; *U.S. Public*, pg. 1569

TRIMFOLD—Paper Towels—Georgia-Pacific Corporation; *U.S. Public*, pg. 735

TRIMFOOT—Infant's Footwear—E.J. Footwear Corp.; *U.S. Public*, pg. 1684

TRIMIDAL—Fungicide—The Dow Chemical Company; *U.S. Public*, pg. 522

TRIMKIDS—Shoes—Trimfoot Company; *U.S. Public*, pg. 1684

TRIMLINE—Pencils—Dixon Ticonderoga Company; *U.S. Public*, pg. 514

TRIMLINE—Dial-in-Handset Phone—Lucent Technologies Inc.; *U.S. Public*, pg. 1017

TRIMLITE—Cameras, Microfilm Readers—Eastman Kodak Company; *U.S. Public*, pg. 550

TRIMLOOK—Foundations—The Strouse, Adler Company; *U.S. Private*, pg. 1047

TRIMMATE—Lenses, Photographic Paper, Microfilm Equipment Accessories—Eastman Kodak Company; *U.S. Public*, pg. 550

TRIMOS—Measuring Tools—Fred V. Fowler Company, Inc.; *U.S. Private*, pg. 422

TRIMPRINT—Instant Color Film & Cameras—Eastman Kodak Company; *U.S. Public*, pg. 550

TRIMRITE—NONE—Carpenter Technology Corporation; *U.S. Public*, pg. 307

TRIMSTEPS—Shoes—Trimfoot Company; *U.S. Public*, pg. 1684

TRIMTEC—Thermoplastic Rubber Seals—The West Company, Incorporated; *U.S. Public*, pg. 1755

TRIMTEX—Braided, Knitted & Woven Trimmings & Tapes—Trimtex Co. Inc.; *U.S. Private*, pg. 1103

TRIMTITE 150—150 Class High-Performance Valves—Fisher Controls International, Inc.; *U.S. Public*, pg. 573

TRINALIN—Antihistamine—Schering-Plough Corporation; *U.S. Public*, pg. 1438

TRINARANJUS—Non-Carbonated Fruit Drink—Cadbury Schweppes p.l.c.; *Int'l*, pg. 247

TRINICON—Color Video Cameras—Sony Electronics; *Int'l*, pg. 1281

TRINITONE—Color Temp Switch—Sony Electronics; *Int'l*, pg. 1281

TRINITRON—Color Television Receivers—Sony Electronics; *Int'l*, pg. 1281

TRINITY—Anti-Perspirant—The Gillette Company; *U.S. Public*, pg. 743

TRINITY—Metal Stampings, Railroad Car & Ship Building—Trinity Industries Inc.; *U.S. Public*, pg. 1638

TRINITY SQUARE—Luggage—American Tourister, Inc.; *U.S. Public*, pg. 1430

TRIO—Herbicides—Agrolinz Melamin GmbH; *Int'l*, pg. 356

TRIO—Low Profile In The Ear Hearing Aid—Beltone Electronics Corporation; *U.S. Private*, pg. 132

TRIO—Plant Protectives—DSM Chemie Linz GmbH; *Int'l*, pg. 356

TRIO—Food Products—Nestle USA; *Int'l*, pg. 916

TRIO ITALIANO—Pasta—Hershey Foods Corporation; *U.S. Public*, pg. 811

TRIO SUPREME—NONE—Nestle USA; *Int'l*, pg. 916

TRIOBEAD—Diagnostic Products—Abbott Laboratories; *U.S. Public*, pg. 12

TRIOGRAN—Herbicides—Agrolinz Melamin GmbH; *Int'l*, pg. 356

TRIOGRAN—Plant Protectives—DSM Chemie Linz GmbH; *Int'l*, pg. 356

TRION—Electronic Air Cleaners—Trion, Inc.; *U.S. Public*, pg. 1639

TRION RX—Console HEPA Class II Medical Device Air Cleaner—Trion, Inc.; *U.S. Public*, pg. 1639

TRIONOL—NONE—Lawter International, Inc.; *U.S. Public*, pg. 980

TRIOSTAT—Thyroid Hormone—Jones Medical Industries Inc.; *U.S. Public*, pg. 933

TRIPAC—Kitchen & Vanity Cabinets—Triangle Pacific Corporation; *U.S. Public*, pg. 1634

TRIPAREN—Basic Solution for TPN—Otsuka Pharmaceutical Co., Ltd.; *Int'l*, pg. 1013

TRIPASSIST—For life & Health Insurance Administration Services—American Automobile Association; *U.S. Private*, pg. 50

TRIPCLIK—Disposable Photographic Camera—American Automobile Association; *U.S. Private*, pg. 50

TRIPEDIA—Diptheria & Tetanus Toxoids—Connaught Laboratories, Inc.; *Int'l*, pg. 1109

TRIPFAX—Computer Software—Rockwell International Corporation; *U.S. Public*, pg. 1397

TRIPHASIL—Levonorgestrel - Low-dose Triphasic Oral Contraceptive—American Home Products Corporation; *U.S. Public*, pg. 79

TRIPHASIL—Oral Contraceptive—Wyeth-Ayerst Laboratories, Inc.; *U.S. Public*, pg. 80

TRIPLE A—For Auto Association Prints & Publications—American Automobile Association; *U.S. Private*, pg. 50

TRIPLE BLASTS—Candy-Coated Bubble Gum Pop—The Topps Company, Inc.; *U.S. Public*, pg. 1621

TRIPLE-COVER—House Paint—Devoe Paint; *Int'l*, pg. 663

TRIPLE COVER—House Paint—ICI Paints; *Int'l*, pg. 664

TRIPLE CROWN—Sporting Equipment—Brunswick Bowling & Billiards Corp.; *U.S. Public*, pg. 265

TRIPLE CROWN—Fence—CTB International Corp.; *U.S. Public*, pg. 284

TRIPLE CROWN—Intermodal Rail Service—Norfolk Southern Corporation; *U.S. Public*, pg. 1190

TRIPLE CROWN SL—Tires—Bridgestone/Firestone, Inc.; *Int'l*, pg. 213

TRIPLE DUTY—Joint Finishing Compound—Georgia-Pacific Corporation; *U.S. Public*, pg. 735

TRIPLE EDGE—Mattress—Therapedic Associates, Inc.; *U.S. Private*, pg. 1079

TRIPLE FLEX—Electronic Component—Shure Brothers Incorporated; *U.S. Private*, pg. 997

TRIPLE FRUITS—Jam Type Spread—E.D. Smith; *Int'l*, pg. 1263

TRIPLE GOLD—Investment Plans—Derbyshire Building Society; *Int'l*, pg. 394

TRIPLE M—Processed Meats—Kayem Foods, Inc.; *U.S. Private*, pg. 610

TRIPLE MMM—Meats—Thorn Apple Valley, Inc.; *U.S. Public*, pg. 1602

TRIPLE I—Customer Computer System—Landauer, Inc.; *U.S. Public*, pg. 977

TRIPLE PACK—Poultry Netting—Gilbert & Bennett Manufacturing Company; *U.S. Private*, pg. 453

TRIPLE PLUS PAK—Caedboard Shipping & Packaging Materials—PPG Industries, Inc.; *U.S. Public*, pg. 1245

TRIPLE SEAL—Plumbing Products—Radiator Specialty Company; *U.S. Private*, pg. 906

TRIPLE THICK BUBBLE STICK—NONE—Amurol Confections Co.; *U.S. Public*, pg. 1781

TRIPLE-X—Pediculicide—Carter-Wallace, Inc.; *U.S. Public*, pg. 309

TRIPLE ZOOM—Binoculars—Bushnell Corporation; *U.S. Private*, pg. 1191

TRIPLES—Cereal—General Mills, Inc.; *U.S. Public*, pg. 717

TRIPLET—Selective Herbicide—Riverdale Chemical Co.; *U.S. Private*, pg. 934

TRIPLEX—Microfilmers—Eastman Kodak Company; *U.S. Public*, pg. 550

TRIPLEX—Laminated Safety Glass—Pilkington Australasia Limited; *Int'l*, pg. 1057

TRIPLEX—Liquid Packaging Board—Stora Billerud AB; *Int'l*, pg. 1302

TRIPLEX CLEATFORMER—Roll Forming Material—Lockformer Company; *U.S. Public*, pg. 1100

TRIPMASTER—Performance Monitoring & Data Acquisition Systems for Vehicles—Rockwell International Corporation; *U.S. Public*, pg. 1397

TRIPOD BANGERS—Insulation Fasteners—Duro Dyne Corporation; *U.S. Private*, pg. 349

TRIPOLINK—Fuse Links—Kearney Company; *U.S. Public*, pg. 444

TRIPOLYMER—Mono—Outdoor Technologies Group; *U.S. Private*, pg. 822

TRIPS—Tuscarora's Returnable Integrated Pallet System—Tuscarora Incorporated; *U.S. Public*, pg. 1646

TRISCUIT—Wafer—Nabisco Inc.; *U.S. Public*, pg. 1355

TRISCUIT—Crackers—RJR Nabisco Holdings Corp.; *U.S. Public*, pg. 1354

TRISEQUENS—Product for Gynaecological Use—Novo Nordisk A/S; *Int'l*, pg. 987

TRISORALEN—Prescription Drug—ICN Pharmaceuticals, Inc.; *U.S. Public*, pg. 853

TRISTACK—Lab Exhaust Fans—Met-Pro Corporation; *U.S. Public*, pg. 1100

TRISTAR—Herbicides—Agrolinz Melamin GmbH; *Int'l*, pg. 356

TRISTAR—Thread—Coats North America; *Int'l*, pg. 300

TRISTAR—Plant Protectives—DSM Chemie Linz GmbH; *Int'l*, pg. 356

TRISTAR—Cutlery—Lifetime Hoan Corp.; *U.S. Public*, pg. 992

TRISTAR EXTRA—Herbicides—Agrolinz Melamin GmbH; *Int'l*, pg. 356

TRISTAR MUSIC GROUP—NONE—Sony Music Entertainment; *Int'l*, pg. 1281

TRISTAT BNP—Cosmetic Ingredient—Tri-K Industries, Inc.; *U.S. Private*, pg. 1100

TRISTAT IU—Cosmetic Ingredient—Tri-K Industries, Inc.; *U.S. Private*, pg. 1100

TRI-STRIPE—Toilet Suites, Basins & Taps—James Hardie Industries Ltd.; *Int'l*, pg. 596

TRITACE—Hypertension—Hoechst Marion Roussel, Inc.; *Int'l*, pg. 624

TRITAN—Topical Antifungal Products—Schering-Plough Corporation; *U.S. Public*, pg. 1438

TRITHAC—Fungicide—The Dow Chemical Company; *U.S. Public*, pg. 522

TRITIEL PRETZELS—NONE—Anderson Bakery Co., Inc.; *U.S. Private*, pg. 65

TRITLE'S—Cream/Lotion—Blistex, Inc.; *U.S. Private*, pg. 149

TRITON—Intensive Task Seating—Cramer Inc.; *U.S. Private*, pg. 285

TRITON—Swimming Pool Accessories—Essef Corporation; *U.S. Public*, pg. 592

TRITON BARRIER—Highway Barrier—Quixote Corporation; *U.S. Public*, pg. 1353

TRITON MAX—Intensive Task—Cramer Inc.; *U.S. Private*, pg. 285

TRITON TOWER—Computer Enclosure Line—Triton Industries, Inc.; *U.S. Private*, pg. 1104

TRITOUR—Revolving Doors—Boon Edam Inc.; *Int'l*, pg. 202

TRIUMPH—Luggage—American Tourister, Inc.; *U.S. Public*, pg. 1430

TRIUMPH—Tires—Bridgestone/Firestone, Inc.; *Int'l*, pg. 213

TRIUMPH—Inlaid Sheet Vinyl Flooring—Congoleum Corporation; *U.S. Public*, pg. 69

TRIUMPH—Cycle—Derby International Corporation S.A.; *Int'l*, pg. 394

TRIUMPH—Cigarettes—Loews Corporation; *U.S. Public*, pg. 1010

TRIUMPH—Cigarette—Lorillard Tobacco Company; *U.S. Public*, pg. 1011

TRIUMPH—Paper Cutter—Michael Business Machines Corporation; *U.S. Private*, pg. 740

TRIUMPH—3 Wheeled Scooter—Ortho-Kinetics, Inc.; *U.S. Private*, pg. 820

TRIUMPH—Dry & Canned Dog & Cat Foods-Treats—Triumph Pet Industries, Inc.; *U.S. Private*, pg. 1104

TRIUMPH—Bag Machines—Windmoeller & Hoelscher; *Int'l*, pg. 1510

TRIUMPH-ADLER—Office Machines—TA Triumph-Adler Vertriebs GmbH; *Int'l*, pg. 1004

TRIUMPH IMPERIAL—Writing Instruments—Sheaffer Inc.; *Int'l*, pg. 542

TRIUMPH PICTURES—Motion Picture Production Company—Sony Pictures Entertainment; *Int'l*, pg. 1281

TRIUNFO—Biscuits—Danone Group; *Int'l*, pg. 379

TRIVALVE—Delivery Systems—ATMI, Inc.; *U.S. Public*, pg. 12

TRIVAX—NONE—Medeva PLC; *Int'l*, pg. 852

TRIVENT—Press—Beloit Corporation; *U.S. Public*, pg. 789

TRIVIAL PURSUIT—Board Game—Parker Brothers; *U.S. Public*, pg. 797

TRIX—Cereal—General Mills, Inc.; *U.S. Public*, pg. 717

TRIX YOGURT—Yogurt—General Mills, Inc.; *U.S. Public*, pg. 717

TRIXY—Pudding Mix—CSM N.V.; *Int'l*, pg. 243

TRO LUBE—Lubricants—Mallet & Co.; *U.S. Private*, pg. 698

TROFAK—Human Protein Used in Treatment of Chronic Skin Ulcers—Amgen Boulder, Inc.; *U.S. Public*, pg. 101

TROFECO—Two-Door Sedan—General Motors Corporation; *U.S. Public*, pg. 718

TROGARD—Trocar for Mini Access Surgery—Conmed Corporation; *U.S. Public*, pg. 431

TROJAN—Condoms—Carter Products, Canada; *U.S. Public*, pg. 310

TROJAN—Condoms & Personal Lubricant—Carter-Wallace, Inc.; *U.S. Public*, pg. 309

TROJAN—Yachts—Carver Boat Corp.; *U.S. Private*, pg. 447

TROJAN—ACTUATORS—Crane Limited U.K.; *U.S. Public*, pg. 458

TROJAN—Livestock Watering Equip.—Ritchie Industries, Inc.; *U.S. Private*, pg. 933

TROJAN-ENZ—Condom—Carter-Wallace, Inc.; *U.S. Public*, pg. 309

TROJAN VERY THIN—Condom—Carter-Wallace, Inc.; *U.S. Public*, pg. 309

TROLEX—Switches—CTS Corporation; *U.S. Public*, pg. 285

TRONA—Chemicals—Kerr-McGee Chemical Corp.; *U.S. Public*, pg. 952

TRONA MANG—Manganese Metalo—Kerr-McGee Chemical Corp.; *U.S. Public*, pg. 952

TRONOLANE—Antihemorrhoidal—Abbott Laboratories; *U.S. Public*, pg. 12

TRONOLANE—Hemorrhoid Remedy—Ross Products; *U.S. Public*, pg. 13

TRONOX—Pigments—Kerr-McGee Chemical Corp.; *U.S. Public*, pg. 952

TROOPER—Car Seat—Evenflo Company, Inc.; *U.S. Private*, pg. 629

TROOPER—Glyphosate & Dicamba Production—Monsanto Company; *U.S. Public*, pg. 1124

TROOPER—Hand-Held Vehicular GPS Receiver—Rockwell International Corporation; *U.S. Public*, pg. 1397

TROOST—Pipe Tobacco—Lane Limited; *Int'l*, pg. 1129

TROP-ARTIC—Motor Oil—Phillips Petroleum Company; *U.S. Public*, pg. 1290

TROPHY—Riflescopes—Bausch & Lomb Incorporated; *U.S. Public*, pg. 194

TROPHY—Tires—Bridgestone/Firestone, Inc.; *Int'l*, pg. 213

TROPHY—Telescopes & Riflescopes—Bushnell Corporation; *U.S. Private*, pg. 1191

TROPHY—Horse Feeds—Manna Pro Corporation; *U.S. Private*, pg. 700

TROPHY—Plastic Drinking Cups—Sweetheart Cup Company Inc.; *U.S. Private*, pg. 1058

TROPHY PREMIUM—Tires—Bridgestone/Firestone, Inc.; *Int'l*, pg. 213

TROPHY SERIES—Western Boots—Genesco Inc.; *U.S. Public*, pg. 728

TROPIC ISLE—Frozen Coconut—Curtice Burns Foods; *U.S. Private*, pg. 887

TROPIC ISLE—Frozen Food—Southern Frozen Foods; *U.S. Private*, pg. 887

TROPICAL—NONE—National R.V., Inc.; *U.S. Public*, pg. 1159

TROPICAL BLEND—Sun Care Brand—Schering-Plough Corporation; *U.S. Public*, pg. 1438

TROPICAL BLEND—Suntanning Preparations—Schering-Plough Healthcare Products Inc.; *U.S. Public*, pg. 1438

TROPICAL ESCAPE—Herb Tea—Celestial Seasonings; *U.S. Public*, pg. 319

TROPICAL FREEZES—Wine-Based & Daiquiris, Margaritas & Punches—Brown-Forman Beverages Worldwide; *U.S. Public*, pg. 261

TROPICAL FREEZES—Specialty Items—Brown-Forman Corporation; *U.S. Public*, pg. 261

TROPICAL PALM—NONE—Celebrity Incorporated; *U.S. Public*, pg. 319

TROPICAL SQUEEZE—Fruit Juice Blend—Chiquita Banana North America; *U.S. Public*, pg. 349

TROPICAL TWISTS—Bubble Gum—Amurol Confections Co.; *U.S. Public*, pg. 1781

TROPICANA—Hotels—Aztar Corporation; *U.S. Public*, pg. 158

TROPICANA—Casino & Resort—Tropicana Casino & Resort; *U.S. Public*, pg. 159

TROPICANA—Pure Premium Juices—Tropicana Dole Beverages North America; *Int'l*, pg. 1217

TROPICANA—Juice—Tropicana Dole Beverages North America; *Int'l*, pg. 1217

TROPICANA DOLE—Juice & Juice Beverage—Joseph E. Seagram & Sons, Inc.; *Int'l*, pg. 1215

TROPICANA SEASON'S BEST JUICES—Juices—Tropicana Dole Beverages North America; *Int'l*, pg. 1217

TROPITONE—Suntan Preparations—Permark International (Pty.) Ltd.; *Int'l*, pg. 1036

TROPITONE—Pool & Patio Casual Furniture—Tropitone Furniture Co. Inc.; *U.S. Private*, pg. 1105

TROPWORLD—Hotels—Aztar Corporation; *U.S. Public*, pg. 158

TROSYD—Tioconazole—Pfizer Inc.; *U.S. Public*, pg. 1281

TROSYD AF—NONE—Pfizer Inc.; *U.S. Public*, pg. 1281

TROTTERS—Shoes—Penobscot Shoe Company; *U.S. Public*, pg. 1273

TROUBLE TICKET—Computer Product—International Business Machines Corporation; *U.S. Public*, pg. 895

TROUT & SALMON—Fishing Magazine—EMAP Pursuit Publishing; *Int'l*, pg. 451

TROUT FISHERMAN—Fishing Magazine—EMAP Pursuit Publishing; *Int'l*, pg. 451

TROVAN—Trovafloxacin—Pfizer Inc.; *U.S. Public*, pg. 1281

TROVAN IV—Alatrofloxacin—Pfizer Inc.; *U.S. Public*, pg. 1281

TROY—Chemicals—Troy Corporation; *U.S. Private*, pg. 1105

TROY-BILT—Rototillers, Shredders, Sicklebar & High Wheel Mowers—Garden Way, Inc.; *U.S. Private*, pg. 440

TROY POWDERMATE—Powder Coating Additives—Troy Corporation; *U.S. Private*, pg. 1105

TROY UNIFILM—Rheology Modifiers—Troy Corporation; *U.S. Private*, pg. 1105

TROYKYD—Defoamers & Anti Skinning Agents on Napthenate Driers—Troy Corporation; *U.S. Private*, pg. 1105

TROYMAX—Sythic Driers—Troy Corporation; *U.S. Private*, pg. 1105

TROYSAN—Broad Spectrum Non-Metallic Organic Biocides—Troy Corporation; *U.S. Private*, pg. 1105

TROYSAN POLYPHASE—Broad Spectrum Non-Metallic Fungicide—Troy Corporation; *U.S. Private*, pg. 1105

TROYSOL—Dispersants & Specialty Surfactancts—Troy Corporation; *U.S. Private*, pg. 1105

TROYTHIX—Rheology Modifiers—Troy Corporation; *U.S. Private*, pg. 1105

TRU-BILT—Plywood, Wallboard & Doors—Georgia-Pacific Corporation; *U.S. Public*, pg. 735

TRU BLU—Cookies—Sunshine Biscuits, Inc.; *U.S. Private*, pg. 434

TRU BLU—Cookies—Sunshine Biscuits, Inc.; *U.S. Public*, pg. 657

TRU-BOND—Roofing Shingles with Sealant—Owens Corning; *U.S. Public*, pg. 1236

TRU-BORE—NONE—Callaway Golf Company; *U.S. Public*, pg. 294

TRU-FEED 50—Automatic Powdered Detergent Cleansing System—Ecolab Inc.; *U.S. Public*, pg. 562

TRU-FIL—Candles in Glass—Will & Baumer Incorporated; *U.S. Private*, pg. 1176

TRU-FIT—Muffler—Walker Manufacturing Co.; *U.S. Public*, pg. 1578

TRU-FLATE—NONE—Plews/Edelmann; *Int'l*, pg. 1396

TRU-FLEX FASTENERS—Screws, Bolts—SPS Technologies, Inc.; *U.S. Public*, pg. 1419

TRU-FORM PLASTICS—Vacuum Formed Plastics—Elixir Industries; *U.S. Private*, pg. 371

TRU-GLAZE—Epoxy Coatings—Devoe Paint; *Int'l*, pg. 663

TRU-GLAZE—Epoxy Coatings—ICI Paints; *Int'l*, pg. 664

TRU-GLAZE 4—Epoxy Coating—Devoe Paint; *Int'l*, pg. 663

TRU-GLAZE 4—Epoxy Coatings—ICI Paints; *Int'l*, pg. 664

TRU-GLAZE 2—Warterborne Epoxy Coatings—ICI Paints; *Int'l*, pg. 664

TRU-GLAZE-WB—Waterborne Epoxy Coating—Devoe Paint; *Int'l*, pg. 663

TRU-GUIDE—Gas Lift Mandrels—Halliburton Energy Services; *U.S. Public*, pg. 776

TRU KLEEN—Soft Goods Cleaner—Camp Healthcare; *Int'l*, pg. 1425

TRU-LEVEL—Filter—American Felt & Filter; *U.S. Private*, pg. 54

TRU-LOK—Steel Tapes—Evans Rule Co., Inc.; *U.S. Public*, pg. 1511

TRU-LOK—Mounting Abrasive Discs—Gardner Abrasives; *U.S. Public*, pg. 1699

TRU-LOK—Grinding Wheel Mounting Plates—Litton Industries, Inc.; *U.S. Public*, pg. 1002

TRU-MASS—Coriolis Mass Meter—Bailey, Fischer & Porter Company; *U.S. Public*, pg. 449

TRU PAC—Road Machinery-Compactor—Rosco Manufacturing Co.; *U.S. Private*, pg. 944

TRU POISE—Leisure Wear—Camp Healthcare; *Int'l*, pg. 1425

TRU SCOPE—Boresighter—Bushnell Corporation; *U.S. Private*, pg. 1191

TRU-SEAL—Hydraulic Component—Miller Fluid Power Corp.; *U.S. Private*, pg. 747

TRU-SPOKE—Wheels—Cragar Industries, Inc.; *U.S. Public*, pg. 456

TRU-STITCH—Slippers—Wolverine World Wide, Inc.; *U.S. Public*, pg. 1775

TRU-TEMP—Tempered Glass—AFG Industries, Inc.; *Int'l*, pg. 84

TRU-TEST—Paint—TruServ Corporation; *U.S. Private*, pg. 1108

TRU-THERM—Natural Gass Instrumentation—Badger Meter, Inc.; *U.S. Public*, pg. 164

TRU-TINT—Carnations—Denver Wholesale Florists Company; *U.S. Private*, pg. 326

TRU TOGUE—Auto Parts—JPE, Inc.; *U.S. Public*, pg. 919

TRU-TORQ—High Grade Fastening Systems—Lawson Products, Inc.; *U.S. Public*, pg. 980

TRU TRAC—Sporting Equipment—Brunswick Bowling & Billiards Corp.; *U.S. Public*, pg. 265

TRU-TRAC—Wire—National-Standard Co.; *U.S. Public*, pg. 1160

TRU-TRAC—Passenger & Light Truck Tires—Pirelli Armstrong Tire Corporation; *Int'l*, pg. 1058

TRU-VIEW MAST—Lift Truck Mast—Baker Material Handling Corp.; *Int'l*, pg. 810

TRU VUE—Custom Picture Framing Glass & Matboard—Apogee Enterprises, Inc.; *U.S. Public*, pg. 120

TRU-WEFT—Interlinings—Specialty Textile Products; *U.S. Private*, pg. 1023

TRU-GLU—Glucose Tolerance Test Beverages—Fisher Scientific Company; *U.S. Private*, pg. 658

TRU-TEST—Gummed Tape—Intertape Polymer Group; *Int'l*, pg. 685

TRU/BLU—Protocol Converter—Ascom Timeplex; *Int'l*, pg. 86

TRUARC—Retaining Rings—Waldes Truarc/Industrial Retaining Ring; *U.S. Public*, pg. 1632

TRUBYTE—Artificial Teeth—Dentsply International Inc.; *U.S. Public*, pg. 498

TRUCAST—Turbocharger Wheels—Vickers PLC; *Int'l*, pg. 1466

TRUCE—Non-Selective Herbicide—Riverdale Chemical Co.; *U.S. Private*, pg. 934

TRUCK AUSTRALIA—Transport Magazine—Reed Business Information Pty. Limited; *Int'l*, pg. 1094

TRUCK.COMM—Quarterly Supplement to Fleet Owner—Intertec Publishing; *U.S. Public*, pg. 1327

TRUCK GUARD—Motor Oil—Shell Oil Company; *Int'l*, pg. 1136

TRUCK LOAD SYSTEM—Mailing Efficiency System—Group 1 Software, Inc.; *U.S. Public*, pg. 417

TRUCK PLUG—NONE—Champion Ignition Products; *U.S. Public*, pg. 442

TRUCKERS BANK PLAN—Truck Leasing / Financing For Individual & Fleet—1st Source Corporation; *U.S. Public*, pg. 638

TRUCKLINE SPORT GRIP—Steering Wheel Covers—Superior Industries International, Inc.; *U.S. Public*, pg. 1539

TRUDRIL—Electronic Control Equipment—Advanced Controls, Inc.; *U.S. Private*, pg. 21

TRUDRIL—Downhole Motors—National-Oilwell/Dreco; *U.S. Public*, pg. 1158

TRUE—Cigarettes—Loews Corporation; *U.S. Public*, pg. 1010

TRUE—Cigarette—Lorillard Tobacco Company; *U.S. Public*, pg. 1011

TRUE ALARM—Safety System—Simplex Time Recorder Co.; *U.S. Private*, pg. 1002

TRUE BLUE PRINTS—Newsletter—The Dow Chemical Company; *U.S. Public*, pg. 522

TRUE COLOR—Ophthalmic Lenses & Sunglasses—American Optical Corporation; *U.S. Private*, pg. 60

TRUE G—Surface Plates—Rock of Ages Corporation; *U.S. Public*, pg. 1396

TRUE IMAGE RENDERING SYSTEM—Laser Printer Controller Software—Imaging Technologies Corp.; *U.S. Public*, pg. 870

TRUE-LITE—Sunlight Simulating Fluorescent Tube—Duro-Test Corporation; *U.S. Private*, pg. 349

TRUE LOVE—Women's Fragrance—Elizabeth Arden Company; *Int'l*, pg. 1435

TRUE PINE—Pine Cleaner—Blue Cross Laboratories; *U.S. Private*, pg. 152

TRUE SPOT—Measuring Instrument—Bacharach Inc.; *U.S. Private*, pg. 109

TRUE TEMPER—Outdoor Products—The Black & Decker Corporation; *U.S. Public*, pg. 233

TRUE TEMPER—Lawn & Garden Tools—Huffy Corporation; *U.S. Public*, pg. 846

TRUE TEMPER—Hardware—True Temper Hardware Company; *U.S. Public*, pg. 846

TRUE-TO-LIGHT—Makeup Mirrors—Bristol-Myers Squibb Company; *U.S. Public*, pg. 253

TRUE TO LIGHT—Mirror—Clairol, Inc.; *U.S. Public*, pg. 254

TRUE TRIM—Boxed Beef—BeefAmerica Operating Co., Inc.; *U.S. Private*, pg. 130

TRUE VALU—Hardware—Allens Of Hastings, Inc.; *U.S. Private*, pg. 37

TRUE VALUE—Retail Grocery—Covington Foods, Inc.; *U.S. Private*, pg. 280

TRUE VALUE HARDWARE STORES—Retail Stores—TruServ Corporation; *U.S. Private*, pg. 1108

TRUE VIEW—Satellite Systems—Lance Industries; *U.S. Private*, pg. 645

TRUE WHITE GEL—NONE—Health Products Corporation; *U.S. Private*, pg. 514

TRUEDGE—Aluminum Seals for Pharmaceutical Closures—The West Company, Incorporated; *U.S. Public*, pg. 1755

TRUEMAN CLUB HOTEL—Midscale Lodging—Red Roof Inns, Inc.; *U.S. Public*, pg. 1369

TRUESTE—Fragrance—Tiffany & Co.; *U.S. Public*, pg. 1608

TRUETORQUE—Polyurethane-Coated Wire Guide—Arrow International, Inc.; *U.S. Public*, pg. 135

TRUEWAVE—Optical Fiber—Lucent Technologies Inc.; *U.S. Public*, pg. 1017

TRUFFON—Chocolate & Confectionery—Nestle S.A.; *Int'l*, pg. 915

TRUFLOW—Asphalt Coatings—Owens Corning; *U.S. Public*, pg. 1236

TRUGREEN—Lawn Care Products & Services—TruGreen-ChemLawn; *U.S. Public*, pg. 1461

TRUGREEN-CHEMLAWN—Lawn Care—The ServiceMaster Company; *U.S. Public*, pg. 1461

TRUGUARD—Asphalt-Based Sealant for Pavements—Owens Corning; *U.S. Public*, pg. 1236

TRULY FITTING—Bras—Warner's; *U.S. Public*, pg. 1738

TRULY LACE—Women's fragrance—Coty Inc.; *Int'l*, pg. 185

TRUMBULL—Asphalt Coatings—Owens Corning; *U.S. Public*, pg. 1236

TRUMELT—Asphalt Sold in a Disposable Package—Owens Corning; *U.S. Public*, pg. 1236

TRUMP—Warewashing Detergent—Ecolab Inc.; *U.S. Public*, pg. 562

TRUNK 2000—Fume Exhauster—Donaldson Company, Inc.; *U.S. Public*, pg. 517

TRUNKLINE—Fume Exhauster—Donaldson Company, Inc.; *U.S. Public*, pg. 517

TRUNZ—Meat Prods.—Worldwide Food Products Inc.; *U.S. Private*, pg. 1191

TRUON—NONE—Berg Electronics; *U.S. Public*, pg. 212

TRUPRINT—Photo Processing—Nashua Corporation; *U.S. Public*, pg. 1152

TRUS JOIST MACMILLIAN—Limited Partnership—TJ International, Inc.; *U.S. Public*, pg. 1556

TRUSPEC—NONE—Pico Products, Inc.; *U.S. Public*, pg. 1294

TRUST—Convenience Stores—E-Z Serve Corp.; *U.S. Public*, pg. 540

TRUST ALLOCATION & TAX SYSTEM—NONE—SunGard Data Systems Inc.; *U.S. Public*, pg. 1534

TRUST EASE—Trust Tax Processing—Computer Language Research, Inc.; *U.S. Public*, pg. 421

TRUST 3000—Computer System—SEI Investments; *U.S. Public*, pg. 1417

TRUSTS & ESTATES—Monthly Publication—Intertec Publishing; *U.S. Public*, pg. 1328

TRUSTS & ESTATES DIRECTORY—Annual Publication—Intertec Publishing; *U.S. Public*, pg. 1328

TRUSTS & ESTATES—Estate Planning Publication—Intertec Publishing; *U.S. Public*, pg. 1327

TRUSTWORTHY—Hardware Stores Program—Distribution America; *U.S. Private*, pg. 335

TRUSTWORTHY—Retail Hardware Stores—United Hardware Distributing Co.; *U.S. Private*, pg. 335

TRUSTWORTHY HOWE—Hardware Store—Frederick Trading Company; *U.S. Private*, pg. 335

TRUTASTE—Compound Liquid Flavors—Crompton & Knowles Ingredient Technology Corp.; *U.S. Public*, pg. 459

TRUVISION—Ophthalmic Lenses—American Optical Corporation; *U.S. Private*, pg. 60

TRY-IT—Concentrated All-Purpose Cleaner—Stanhome Inc.; *U.S. Public*, pg. 1508

TRYCITE—Plastic Film—The Dow Chemical Company; *U.S. Public*, pg. 522

TRYMER—Rigid Foam Insulation—The Dow Chemical Company; *U.S. Public*, pg. 522

TRYPTAN—Prescription Drug—ICN Pharmaceuticals, Inc.; *U.S. Public*, pg. 853

TRYPTOPHAN—Amino Acids—Nippon Kayaku Co. Ltd.; *Int'l*, pg. 934

TSAR—NONE—James Hardie Industries Ltd.; *Int'l*, pg. 596

TSARS/SYNGENES—In Vitro & In Vivo Applications—Cytogen Corporation; *U.S. Public*, pg. 471

TSINGTAO—Beer Imported From China—Barton Beers, Ltd.; *U.S. Public*, pg. 300

TUACA—Liqueur—Hiram Walker; *Int'l*, pg. 63

TUB-GUARD—Bathroom Safety Rails—Lumex Medical Products; *U.S. Public*, pg. 758

TUB TIME—Accessory Items—Boscarale/Tom Togs; *U.S. Private*, pg. 160

TUBAR—Lock—Chicago Lock Company; *U.S. Private*, pg. 235

TUBBLE GUM—Tube Bubble Gum—Amurol Confections Co.; *U.S. Public*, pg. 1781

TUBE-KOTE—Coating—Tuboscope Incorporated; *U.S. Public*, pg. 1643

TUBE-LOK THREAD COMPOUND—Pipe Thread Lubricant—Weatherford Enterra Incorporated; *U.S. Public*, pg. 1749

TUBE MASTER—NONE—Richardson Electronics, Ltd.; *U.S. Public*, pg. 1387

TUBE ROSE—Snuff—Brown & Williamson Tobacco Corp.; *Int'l*, pg. 111

TUBE TOASTER—Radiant Heater for Slender, Cylindrical Products—Research, Incorporated; *U.S. Public*, pg. 1382

TUBE TOPPER—Hand Held Centrifuge Tube Sealing Accessory—Beckman Instruments, Inc.; *U.S. Public*, pg. 199

TUBEMARKER 600—Industrial Thermal Transfer Printer—Kroy Inc.; *U.S. Public*, pg. 1339

TUBEMASTERS—Hot Finished Steel Hollow Sections—British Steel Tubes & Pipes; *Int'l*, pg. 221

TUBERSOL—Tuberculin Purfied Protein Derivative—Connaught Laboratories, Inc.; *Int'l*, pg. 1109

TUBETEX—Circular Woven Mesh—Tetko, Inc.; *U.S. Private*, pg. 1078

TUBETRACE—Preinsulated Heat Traced Tubing—Thermon Manufacturing Company; *U.S. Private*, pg. 1080

TUBEX—Generic Drug—American Home Products Corporation; *U.S. Public*, pg. 79

TUBEX—Closed Injection System—Wyeth-Ayerst Laboratories, Inc.; *U.S. Public*, pg. 80

TUBLEX—Wheel Rims—Georg Fischer Ltd.; *Int'l*, pg. 488

TUBOGAGE—Ultrasonic Inspection—Tuboscope Incorporated; *U.S. Public*, pg. 1643

TUBORG—Beer—UNICER-Uniao Cervejeira, S.A.; *Int'l*, pg. 1432

TUBOSCAN—Inspection—Tuboscope Incorporated; *U.S. Public*, pg. 1643

TUBULAR EXHAUST SYSTEMS—Exhaust Systems—Edelbrock Corp.; *U.S. Public*, pg. 563

TUC—Biscuits—Danone Group; *Int'l*, pg. 379

TUCANO—Military Trainer Aircraft—Bombardier Inc.; *Int'l*, pg. 199

TUCK HILL—Verietal Wines—The Beverage Source, Inc.; *U.S. Public*, pg. 591

TUCKAWAY—Adhesive Labels—Litton Industries, Inc.; *U.S. Public*, pg. 1002

TUCKER—Fasteners—The Black & Decker Corporation; *U.S. Public*, pg. 233

TUCKS—Premoistened Pads—Warner-Lambert Company; *U.S. Public*, pg. 1738

TUCKS—Hemmorrhoidal Personal Wipes—Warner-Lambert Consumer Healthcare; *U.S. Public*, pg. 1739

TUDOR—Fine Watches—Rolex Watch Co. SA; *Int'l*, pg. 1126

TUDOR—Watches—Rolex Watch U.S.A., Inc.; *Int'l*, pg. 1126

TUESDAY MORNING—Variety Stores—Tuesday Morning Corporation; *U.S. Public*, pg. 1644

TUF—Math Game—Monarch Avalon, Inc.; *U.S. Public*, pg. 1123

TUF-FORM—MDO Plywood—Riverwood International Corporation; *U.S. Public*, pg. 1391

TUFF KIKS—Footwear—Genfoot Inc.; *Int'l*, pg. 549

TUF-LINK—Chain Link Fence—MMI Products, Inc.; *U.S. Private*, pg. 687

TUF-LITE—Axial Fan—McDermott International, Inc.; *U.S. Public*, pg. 1067

TUF-LOK—Vandal-Proof Exit System—Triangle Brass Manufacturing; *U.S. Private*, pg. 1101

TUF-LYTE—Neckwear Interlinings—Specialty Textile Products; *U.S. Private*, pg. 1023

TUF'N EGA—Hand Cleanser with Polygrit—SBS Products, Inc.; *U.S. Private*, pg. 955

TUF-NUT—Men's Clothing—Key Industries, Inc.; *U.S. Public*, pg. 618

TUF-SHIELD—Corregated Vinyl Building Sheet—Georgia-Pacific Corporation; *U.S. Public*, pg. 735

TUF-SKIN—Equipment Insulation—Johns Manville Corporation; *U.S. Public*, pg. 927

TUF-TEMP—Process For Toughening Glass—Fisher Scientific Company; *U.S. Private*, pg. 658

TUF-TEST—Electronic Lacing Tape—Gudebrod, Inc.; *U.S. Private*, pg. 486

TUF-TIP—Dragline Bucket Hardware—Harnischfeger Industries, Inc.; *U.S. Public*, pg. 788

TUF-TOTE—Trash Bags—Tenneco Packaging, Consumer Products Group; *U.S. Public*, pg. 1579

TUF WOOD—Wood Fencing-General—MMI Products, Inc.; *U.S. Private*, pg. 687

TUF WOOD "PLUS"—Water Resistant Wood Fencing—MMI Products, Inc.; *U.S. Private*, pg. 687

TUFABET—Literary Game—Monarch Avalon, Inc.; *U.S. Public*, pg. 1123

TUFBAK—Waterproof Sandpaper—Norton Company; *Int'l*, pg. 1173

TUFF BELLS—Hand-Held Weights—Empire of Carolina, Inc.; *U.S. Public*, pg. 579

TUFF-BOND—Bonding Gum & Repair Material—Oliver Rubber Co.; *U.S. Public*, pg. 1504

TUFF CORD—Telephone Handset Cords—Lucent Technologies Inc.; *U.S. Public*, pg. 1017

TUFF CURE—Rubber Products Retread System—Oliver Rubber Co.; *U.S. Public*, pg. 1504

TUFF CUT—High Grade Saw Blades—Lawson Products, Inc.; *U.S. Public*, pg. 980

TUFF GEAR COLLECTION—Tactical Shirt, Trousers, Vest, Cap, Gloves & Primary Underlayer Clothing—Horace Small Apparel Company; *Int'l*, pg. 635

TUFF GRIP—Work Gloves—Boss Manufacturing Company; *U.S. Private*, pg. 1142

TUFF GUARD—Non-Stick Coatings—Sunbeam Household Products; *U.S. Public*, pg. 1533

TUFF-KOTE—Barn Paint—Jones Blair Company; *U.S. Private*, pg. 596

TUFF-KOTE—NONE—Regal Ware, Inc.; *U.S. Private*, pg. 917

TUFF-LITE—Sterile Processing Container Lid—Aesculap, Inc.; *Int'l*, pg. 29

TUFF LITE—Epoxy Adhesives—TEC Incorporated; *U.S. Public*, pg. 687

TUFF 'N RUFF—Rubber Prods.—Miller Products Company, Inc.; *U.S. Private*, pg. 747

TUFF-N-TIDY—Disposable Plastic Bags—Georgia-Pacific Corporation; *U.S. Public*, pg. 735

TUFF 1—Ratchets—SK Hand Tool Corp.; *Int'l*, pg. 570

TUFF-SAK—Garbage Bags—Distribution America; *U.S. Private*, pg. 335

TUFF SEAL—Plumbing Chemical—Hercules Chemical Co., Inc.; *U.S. Private*, pg. 523

TUFF-SKIN—Coated Lamp Bulbs—General Electric Canada Inc.; *U.S. Public*, pg. 713

TUFF-SPUN—Shred-Resistant Lightly Waxed & Unwaxed Dental Floss—John O. Butler Co.; *Int'l*, pg. 1320

TUFF STUFF—Disposable Tableware—The Chinet Co.; *Int'l*, pg. 1146

TUFF STUFF—Pre-School Role-Play Toys—Mattel, Inc.; *U.S. Public*, pg. 1057

TUFF TAC—Cement—Oliver Rubber Co.; *U.S. Public*, pg. 1504

TUFF TANK—Container—Hoover Group, Inc.; *U.S. Private*, pg. 538

TUFF-TORQ—High Grade Fastening Systems—Lawson Products, Inc.; *U.S. Public*, pg. 980

TUFF TOWELS—Foodservice Towel—Chicopee Inc.; *Int'l*, pg. 113

TUFF TRAC—Industrial Retread Rubber & System—Oliver Rubber Co.; *U.S. Public*, pg. 1504

TUFF TRED—Men's Shoes—E.J. Footwear Corp.; *U.S. Public*, pg. 1684

TUFFAK—Plastic—Rohm and Haas Company; *U.S. Public*, pg. 1403

TUFFBOND—Thermocouple Wire—Thermo Electric Co., Inc.; *U.S. Private*, pg. 1080

TUFFCOAT—Roofing Tiles—Carter Holt Harvey Limited; *U.S. Public*, pg. 904

TUFFCOTE—Wire—Tensolite Company; *U.S. Public*, pg. 305

TUFFDOM—Drawn Over Mandrel Steel Mechanical Tubing—Copperweld Fayetteville Division; *Int'l*, pg. 662

TUFFGARDS—Disposable Plastic Bags—Handgards Inc.; *U.S. Private*, pg. 499

TUFFLEX—Tape—Dillard, A ResourceNet International Company; *U.S. Public*, pg. 901

TUFFLEX—Cushioning & Padding—Leucadia Inc. Manufacturing Division; *U.S. Public*, pg. 990

TUFFLINK—Adapter—Becton Dickinson & Company; *U.S. Public*, pg. 199

TUFFLITE—Insulated Wire—Tensolite Company; *U.S. Public*, pg. 305

TUFFRYN—Filtration Products—Gelman Sciences, Inc.; *U.S. Public*, pg. 1253

TUFFTOP—Work Bench Top—Penco Products; *U.S. Private*, pg. 848

TUFFY—Plastic Mesh Scouring Pads—Bayer AG; *Int'l*, pg. 171

TUFFY—Plastic Mesh Scouring Pads—Bayer Corporation/Consumer Care Division; *Int'l*, pg. 173

TUFFY—Mesh Scrubber—The Clorox Company;. *U.S. Public*, pg. 386

TUFFY—Liquid Level Switch—Magnetrol International; *U.S. Private*, pg. 696

TUFFY—Fishing Rods and Reels—Martin Reels, A Division of Zebco; *U.S. Public*, pg. 265

TUFFY—XM-20 Type Products—Sanderson Plumbing Products Inc.; *U.S. Private*, pg. 964

TUFFY—Mufflers—Tuffy Associates Corp.; *U.S. Private*, pg. 1109

TUFFY—Audio, Video & Computer Furniture—H. Wilson Company; *U.S. Private*, pg. 359

TUFFY'S—Snacks—Lever Brothers Co.; *Int'l*, pg. 1435

TUFFY'S—Dry Dog Food—Star-Kist Foods Inc.; *U.S. Public*, pg. 805

TUFFY'S—Snacks—Unilever Plc; *Int'l*, pg. 1433

TUFLEXX—Lens—Bright Star Industries, Inc.; *U.S. Public*, pg. 1341

TUFRAM—Synergistic Coating Process—General Magnaplate Corporation; *U.S. Public*, pg. 717

TUFTANE—Film Products—Lord Corporation; *U.S. Private*, pg. 675

TUFTEC—Hydrogenated Thermoplastic Elastomer—Asahi Chemical Industry Co., Ltd.; *Int'l*, pg. 83

TUFTEX—Particleboard of Wood—Georgia-Pacific Corporation; *U.S. Public*, pg. 735

TUFTEX—Ducting—HBD Industries, Inc.; *U.S. Private*, pg. 489

TUFWITE—Tag Stock—FiberMark Inc.; *U.S. Public*, pg. 620

TUGGER—Puller—Greenlee Textron; *U.S. Public*, pg. 1589

TUINAL—Secobarbital Sodium & Amobarbital Sodium, Lilly—Eli Lilly and Company; *U.S. Public*, pg. 992

TUKON—Micro Hardness Testers—Wilson/Shore Instruments; *U.S. Public*, pg. 883

TULIP COLLECTION—Teakwood—Dansk International Designs Ltd.; *U.S. Public*, pg. 261

TULLAMORE DEW—Whiskey—Cantrell & Cochrane Group; *Int'l*, pg. 63

TULLAMORE DEW—Irish Whiskey—Hiram Walker; *Int'l*, pg. 63

TULSA—Endodontic Materials & Instruments—Dentsply International Inc.; *U.S. Public*, pg. 498

TULTEX—Men's & Ladies' Fleece Activewear—Tultex Corporation; *U.S. Public*, pg. 1644

TULTEX MAXIMUM SWEATS—Midweight Men's & Women's Fleecewear—Tultex Corporation; *U.S. Public*, pg. 1644

TULTEX SUPERWEIGHT—Heavyweight Men's & Women's Fleecewear—Tultex Corporation; *U.S. Public*, pg. 1644

TUMBLING WATERS—Beverage—Q.U.F. Industries Ltd.; *Int'l*, pg. 1074

TUMM-EE-BREEF—Stretch Brief—Olga Div.; *U.S. Public*, pg. 1738

TUMS—Antacid Tablets—SmithKline Beecham Consumer Healthcare, U.S.; *Int'l*, pg. 1264

TUMS—NONE—SmithKline Beecham Corporation; *Int'l*, pg. 1264

TUMS—Stomach/Indigestion Remedy—SmithKline Beecham plc; *Int'l*, pg. 1264

TUMS E-X—Extra Strength Antacid—SmithKline Beecham Consumer Healthcare, U.S.; *Int'l*, pg. 1264

TUNA HELPER—Main Dish Mixes—General Mills, Inc.; *U.S. Public*, pg. 717

TUNEX—Joint Venture Name—Tandem Computers Inc.; *U.S. Public*, pg. 417

TUNG-I—Instant Noodles—President Enterprises Corp.; *Int'l*, pg. 1068

TUNING STICKS—Apparatus for Placing Capacitor in Electronic Circuit—American Technical Ceramics Corp.; *U.S. Public*, pg. 93

TUPERSAN—Herbicide—Du Pont (E.I. Du Pont De Nemours & Co.); *U.S. Public*, pg. 530

TUPIC—Perfume—Rhone-Poulenc S.A.; *Int'l*, pg. 1108

TUPLA—Chocolate Bar—Huhtamaki Oy; *Int'l*, pg. 638

TUPPERCARE—Kids Feeding Line—Tupperware Corporation; *U.S. Public*, pg. 1644

TUPPERFUN—Food Storage & Serving Containers—Tupperware Corporation; *U.S. Public*, pg. 1644

TUPPERKIDS—Kids Feeding Line—Tupperware Corporation; *U.S. Public*, pg. 1644

TUPPERWARE—Plastic Food Containers—Premark International, Inc.; *U.S. Public*, pg. 1321

TUPPERWARE—Food Storage & Serving Containers—Tupperware Corporation; *U.S. Public*, pg. 1644

TUPPERWAVE—Microwave—Tupperware Corporation; *U.S. Public*, pg. 1644

TUPS—Stress Skin Roof Panels—Homasote Company; *U.S. Public*, pg. 831

TURA—Tennis Shoe—K-Swiss Inc.; *U.S. Public*, pg. 937

TURBI TIMESYSTEM—Analyzer—Dade Behring Inc.; *U.S. Private*, pg. 110

TURBIQUANT KITS—Turbidimetric Reagents—Dade Behring Inc.; *U.S. Private*, pg. 110

TURBO-BIT—Hardware Products—Rule Industries, Inc.; *U.S. Public*, pg. 950

TURBO CHARGER—Reactivator for Polishing Media—Lyman Products Corporation; *U.S. Private*, pg. 683

TURBO HOPPER—Radio-Control Toys—Tyco Toys, Inc.; *U.S. Public*, pg. 1058

TURBO-LIFT—Scientific Glassware for Laboratory Use—Wheaton Inc.; *Int'l*, pg. 67

TURBO 1000—Walkie Talkies—Thomson Consumer Electronics Inc.; *Int'l*, pg. 1383

TURBO SERIES—High Performance Car Speakers—Kraco Enterprises, Inc.; *U.S. Private*, pg. 634

TURBO TUMBLERS—Brass Polishing Systems—Lyman Products Corporation; *U.S. Private*, pg. 683

TURBO 2000—Dry Vacuum System—Air Techniques, Inc.; *U.S. Private*, pg. 28

TURBO-2000 AIR DRYERS—Air Dryers—CR Services; *U.S. Private*, pg. 1157

TURBOCALCIN—NONE—SmithKline Beecham Corporation; *Int'l*, pg. 1264

TURBOCALCIN—Inflammation & Tissue Repair—SmithKline Beecham plc; *Int'l*, pg. 1264

TURBODYNE—Self-Cleaning Air Filter System—Pall Corporation; *U.S. Public*, pg. 1253

TURBOFIRE—Burners, Low Nox—Donlee Technologies Inc.; *U.S. Private*, pg. 339

TURBOHALER—Respiratory Agent—Astra AB; *Int'l*, pg. 93

TURBOJET—Nozzles—Akron Brass Company; *Int'l*, pg. 1068

TURBOMAX—Drill Bits—American Tool Companies, Inc.; *U.S. Private*, pg. 63

TURBOMECA—Gas Turbines for Aircraft & Helicopters—Labinal SA; *Int'l*, pg. 785

TURBOPAK—Reciprocating Chillers—York International Corporation; *U.S. Public*, pg. 1789

TURBOPREP—Liquid Chromatography Software—PPG Industries, Inc.; *U.S. Public*, pg. 1245

TURBOSONICS—Surgical Instruments—Alcon Laboratories, Inc.; *Int'l*, pg. 916

TURBOSTALTIC—Surgical Instruments—Alcon Laboratories, Inc.; *Int'l*, pg. 916

TURBOTECH—NONE—Ganin Tire Co., Inc.; *U.S. Private*, pg. 439

TURBOVANE—Fans—The Howden Fan Co.; *U.S. Private*, pg. 543

TURBOWAYS—Computer Product—International Business Machines Corporation; *U.S. Public*, pg. 895

TURBUHALER—Respiratory Agent—Astra AB; *Int'l*, pg. 93

TURBULATOR—Chemical Process Systems—Ferguson International, Inc.; *U.S. Private*, pg. 401

TURBULATOR—Axially-Placed Steel Bars Placed Inside Rotating Paper-Drying Cylinders—The Johnson Corporation; *U.S. Private*, pg. 591

TURCAM—Specialty Chemical—AgrEvo USA Company; *Int'l*, pg. 1203

TURCAM 2 1/2 G—Specialty Chemical—AgrEvo USA Company; *Int'l*, pg. 1203

TURF & FIELD—Tires—Bridgestone/Firestone, Inc.; *Int'l*, pg. 213

TURF & LANDSCAPE DIGEST—NONE—Farm Press; *U.S. Public*, pg. 1328

TURF & LANDSCAPE DIGEST—NONE—Intertec Publishing; *U.S. Public*, pg. 1328

TURF & LANDSCAPE PRESS—NONE—Farm Press; *U.S. Public*, pg. 1328

TURF BIRD—Sprinkler—Rain Bird Sprinklers Manufacturing Corp.; *U.S. Private*, pg. 907

TURF BUILDER—Fertilizer—The Scotts Company; *U.S. Public*, pg. 1446

TURF BUILDER PLUS HALTS—Fertilizer—The Scotts Company; *U.S. Public*, pg. 1446

TURF BUILDER PLUS 2—Fertilizer—The Scotts Company; *U.S. Public*, pg. 1446

TURF & FIELD NHS—Tires—Bridgestone/Firestone, Inc.; *Int'l*, pg. 213

TURF KING—Garden Supplies—Fred Meyer Stores; *U.S. Public*, pg. 1103

TURF-MAKER—Precision Seeder—Brillion Iron Works, Inc.; *U.S. Public*, pg. 933

TURF MANAGEMENT DIGEST—NONE—Farm Press; *U.S. Public*, pg. 1328

TURF ROTORS—NONE—Weather Tec Corporation; *U.S. Private*, pg. 1155

TURF TAMER—Lawn Care Equip.—Lawn Doctor Inc.; *U.S. Private*, pg. 653

TURF-TIL—Garden Tillers—Universal Cooperatives, Inc.; *U.S. Private*, pg. 1127

TURF-TRAC—Lawn & Garden Tractors—Universal Cooperatives, Inc.; *U.S. Private*, pg. 1127

TURF-TRIM—Lawn Mowers—Universal Cooperatives, Inc.; *U.S. Private*, pg. 1127

TURFLON—Herbicide—The Dow Chemical Company; *U.S. Public*, pg. 522

TURFMASTER—Fertilizer—Lebanon Seaboard Corporation; *U.S. Private*, pg. 656

TURFTREET—Liquid Fertilizer—Mapco Natural Gas Liquids Inc.; *U.S. Public*, pg. 1042

TURISIMO—Tires—Bridgestone/Firestone, Inc.; *Int'l*, pg. 213

TURKEY BAR—NONE—Koo Koo Roo, Inc.; *U.S. Public*, pg. 966

TURKEY BAR CARVING STATION—NONE—Koo Koo Roo, Inc.; *U.S. Public*, pg. 966

TURKEY BY GEORGE—Prepared Meat Product—Hormel Foods Corp.; *U.S. Public*, pg. 840

TURKEY CLUB—Turkey Sandwich—Hardee's Food Systems, Inc.; *U.S. Public*, pg. 278

TURKEY HILL—Dairy Products—Turkey Hill Dairy, Inc.; *U.S. Public*, pg. 1109

TURKEY QUICK—Poultry Items—Tyson Foods, Inc.; *U.S. Public*, pg. 1652

TURKEY SELECTS—Turkey Products—Armour Food Company; *U.S. Public*, pg. 427

TURKEY STORE—Fresh Turkey—Jerome Foods Inc.; *U.S. Private*, pg. 586

TURKPETROL—Fuels—Burmah Castrol plc; *Int'l*, pg. 234

TURMOIL—Fragrance—Parfums De Coeur Ltd.; *U.S. Private*, pg. 839

TURMOLUBE/LUBCON—Specialty Lubricants—LubeCon Systems, Inc.; *U.S. Private*, pg. 679

TURN-O-MATIC—Take-a-Number Machine—Esselte AB; *Int'l*, pg. 459

TURN-TOWLS—Paper Towels—Bay West Paper Corp. Towel & Tissue Div.; *U.S. Public*, pg. 1747

TURNER BROADCASTING SYSTEM—Television Broadcasting & Cable Production—Turner Broadcasting System Inc.; *U.S. Public*, pg. 1614

TURNER TEMPEST—Torches & Cylinders—Sycamore Plant; *U.S. Public*, pg. 444

TURNER TORNADO—Torches & Cylinders—Sycamore Plant; *U.S. Public*, pg. 444

TURNING LEAF—NONE—E. & J. Gallo Winery; *U.S. Private*, pg. 438

TURNING POINT: STALINGRAD—Wargame—Monarch Avalon, Inc.; *U.S. Public*, pg. 1123

TURNLOK—Wiring Devices—Pass & Seymour/Legrand; *Int'l*, pg. 806

Brand Name Index

TURNOVER CHOO CHOO—Preschool—Tyco Toys, Inc.; *U.S. Public*, pg. 1058

TURPENOID—Turpentine Substitute—Martin/F. Weber Company; *U.S. Private*, pg. 710

TURPENOID NATURAL—Non-Toxic Cleaner—Martin/F. Weber Company; *U.S. Private*, pg. 710

TURQUOISE—Drafting Instruments—Empire Berol U.S.A.; *U.S. Public*, pg. 1178

TURQUOISE—Drawing & Sketching—Sanford Corporation; *U.S. Public*, pg. 1178

TURTLE—PVC Liquid Proof Gloves—Jomac, Inc.; *U.S. Private*, pg. 595

TURTLE—Chocolate Candy—Nestle Chocolate & Confection; *Int'l*, pg. 917

TURTLE MAGAZINE—Magazine for Pre-School Children—Benjamin Franklin Literary & Medical Society, Inc.; *U.S. Private*, pg. 133

TURTLE WAX—Automotive—Bloch/New England, Inc.; *U.S. Public*, pg. 149

TURTLE WAX—Car Wax & Shoe Polish—Turtle Wax, Inc.; *U.S. Private*, pg. 1110

TURTLE WAX PLUS WITH TEFLON—Car Wax—Turtle Wax, Inc.; *U.S. Private*, pg. 1110

TURTLE WAXER—Car Polisher—WEN Products, Inc.; *U.S. Private*, pg. 1144

TURTLE'S—Confections—Nestle-Rowntree Ltd.; *Int'l*, pg. 921

TURTLES—Frozen Novelties—Borden, Inc.; *U.S. Private*, pg. 157

TURTLES—Candy—Nestle S.A.; *Int'l*, pg. 915

TURTLES—Candy—Nestle USA; *Int'l*, pg. 916

TUS—Insecticides—SmithKline Beecham plc; *Int'l*, pg. 1264

TUSS-ORNADE—NONE—SmithKline Beecham Corporation; *Int'l*, pg. 1264

TUSS-ORNADE—Allergy/Cough/Cold Product—SmithKline Beecham plc; *Int'l*, pg. 1264

TUSSAR—Pharmaceuticals—Rhone-Poulenc Rorer - U.S.; *Int'l*, pg. 1110

TUSSI-ORGANIDIN—Newly Reformulated Cough Medicine—Wallace Laboratories; *U.S. Public*, pg. 310

TUSSI-ORGANIDIN DM—Newly Reformulated Cough Medicine—Wallace Laboratories; *U.S. Public*, pg. 310

TUSSIONEX PENNKINETIC—Ext.-Rel. Suspension (Hydrocodone Polistirex & Chlorpheniramine Polistirex—Medeva Pharmaceuticals; *Int'l*, pg. 852

TUTHILL—Industrial Pumps, Linkage Components & Push-Pull Cables—Tuthill Corporation; *U.S. Private*, pg. 1110

TUTOR—Training Table System—Howe Furniture Corporation; *U.S. Private*, pg. 543

TUTOR—Safety Products—Rentokil Initial plc; *Int'l*, pg. 1285

TUTOURIAL—Computer Product—International Business Machines Corporation; *U.S. Public*, pg. 895

THE TUTTLE—NONE—Callaway Golf Company; *U.S. Public*, pg. 294

TUTTLE STERLING—Flatware, Holloware—Syratech Corporation; *U.S. Public*, pg. 1060

TUTTNAUER—Autoclaves—Brinkmann Instruments, Inc.; *U.S. Private*, pg. 169

TUWAVE—NONE—Staodyn Inc.; *U.S. Public*, pg. 1509

TUXAN—Shoe Care Products—Sara Lee Corporation; *U.S. Public*, pg. 1432

TUXEDO—Luggage—Andiamo, Inc.; *U.S. Private*, pg. 73

TUXEDO—Food Products—Bumble Bee Seafoods Inc.; *U.S. Private*, pg. 526

TV GUIDE MAGAZINE—Magazine—TV Guide Magazine; *Int'l*, pg. 925

TV INDEX—NONE—BPI Communications Inc.; *Int'l*, pg. 1446

TV WEEK INTERACTIVE—TV Listings Service for Newspapers Online & the InterNet—Tribune Media Services, Inc.; *U.S. Public*, pg. 1636

TWARON—Aromatic Polyamide—Akzo Nobel N.V.; *Int'l*, pg. 42

TWEED—Multicolor Paint—Raffi & Swanson, Inc.; *U.S. Private*, pg. 907

TWEED—Lentheric-Men's Fragrance—Yardley of London, Inc.; *Int'l*, pg. 819

TWEEDS—European Inspired Women's Fashion Catalog—Hanover Direct, Inc.; *U.S. Public*, pg. 782

12 BEERS OF CHRISTMAS—Beer—The F.X. Matt Brewing Co.; *U.S. Private*, pg. 714

12 HOUR C TABLETS—500 Mg. Controlled-Release Vitamin C Tablets—Weider Nutrition Intl.; *U.S. Private*, pg. 1159

20CB-3—NONE—Carpenter Technology Corporation; *U.S. Public*, pg. 307

21st SENTRY—Security System—Linear Corporation; *U.S. Public*, pg. 1193

24 HOUR CITY HALL—Computer Product—International Business Machines Corporation; *U.S. Public*, pg. 895

24 HOUR ODOR ABSORBER—Odor Neutralizer—Surco Products, Inc.; *U.S. Public*, pg. 1056

2400/2500—Air Cleaner—Donaldson Company, Inc.; *U.S. Public*, pg. 517

20MO-4—NONE—Carpenter Technology Corporation; *U.S. Public*, pg. 307

20MO-6—NONE—Carpenter Technology Corporation; *U.S. Public*, pg. 307

TWENTY MULE TEAM BORAX—NONE—The Dial Corporation; *U.S. Public*, pg. 505

2100—Industrial Space Heater—Rapid Engineering Inc.; *U.S. Private*, pg. 910

21000—Programmable Operator—Clark Door Co., Inc.; *U.S. Private*, pg. 242

2033—Self-Propelled Aerial Work Platform—Mayville Engineering Co., Inc.; *U.S. Private*, pg. 718

20/20—Easy to Read Pen—Sanford Corporation; *U.S. Public*, pg. 1178

TWI-LIGHT—Energy Control Laminated Bronze Glass—Globe-Amerada Glass Company; *U.S. Private*, pg. 458

TWICE—Business Trade Newspaper—Reed Elsevier Business Information; *Int'l*, pg. 1095

TWIGLETS—Snacks—Danone Group; *Int'l*, pg. 379

TWIGS—Sesame & Cheese Snack Sticks—Nabisco Inc.; *U.S. Public*, pg. 1355

TWILIGHTER—Family of Low Wattage HIP—Stonco Genlyte; *U.S. Public*, pg. 730

TWIN—Soya Based Specialties—Nestle S.A.; *Int'l*, pg. 915

TWIN BEAR—Lumber Products—Georgia-Pacific Corporation; *U.S. Public*, pg. 735

TWIN CAP CAPACITORS—Two Capacitors on One Substrate—American Technical Ceramics Corp.; *U.S. Public*, pg. 93

TWIN CENTS—Bath Products—Smith Enterprises; *U.S. Private*, pg. 1007

TWIN CHANNEL—NONE—Adaptec, Inc.; *U.S. Public*, pg. 19

TWIN FALLS CHEESE—Natural Cheeses—Western Dairymen Cooperative, Inc.; *U.S. Private*, pg. 1165

TWIN GRIP—Centreless Grinding Machine—Cincinnati Milacron U.K. Limited; *U.S. Public*, pg. 368

TWIN-LAP—Fiber-Cement Siding—GAF Premium Products, Inc.; *U.S. Private*, pg. 433

TWIN-PAK—Aircraft Engine—Pratt & Whitney Canada Inc.; *U.S. Public*, pg. 1690

TWIN PASTEL—Women's Shaving Razor—BIC Corporation; *Int'l*, pg. 1273

TWIN PET—Pet Food—Allied Foods, Inc.; *U.S. Private*, pg. 39

TWIN PIN—Dragline Bucket Accessory—Harnischfeger Industries, Inc.; *U.S. Public*, pg. 788

TWIN POWER—Generators & Electric Plants—Winpower Inc.; *U.S. Private*, pg. 350

TWIN-SHELL—Blenders—Patterson-Kelley Company; *U.S. Public*, pg. 793

TWIN STAR—Motorcycle—American Honda Motor Co., Inc. Motorcycle Division; *Int'l*, pg. 634

TWIN STRIKE—Sporting Goods—Brunswick Bowling & Billiards Corp.; *U.S. Public*, pg. 265

TWIN-TAC—Envelopes—Westvaco Corporation; *U.S. Public*, pg. 1762

TWIN TANK—Steel Tank Within Another Steel Tank—Kennedy Tank & Manufacturing Co., Inc.; *U.S. Private*, pg. 614

TWIN-TAPER—Tape Machine—Marsh Company; *U.S. Private*, pg. 707

TWIN TONE—Decorative Light Bulb—Duro-Test Corporation; *U.S. Private*, pg. 349

TWIN-TONE—Hair Brushes—Goody Products, Inc.; *U.S. Public*, pg. 1177

TWIN-TRAC—Tires—Bridgestone/Firestone, Inc.; *Int'l*, pg. 213

TWIN-VENT PRESS—Press—Harnischfeger Industries, Inc.; *U.S. Public*, pg. 788

TWIN WIRE—Looseleaf Notebooks—The Mead Corporation; *U.S. Public*, pg. 1074

TWIN-FLOW—Gas Leak Detectors—Balzers; *Int'l*, pg. 997

TWINAC—Joint Venture Name—Tandem Computers Inc.; *U.S. Public*, pg. 417

TWINARC—Welder—The Lincoln Electric Company; *U.S. Public*, pg. 996

TWINCO—Grooming Tools for Pets—Carter-Wallace, Inc.; *U.S. Public*, pg. 309

TWINCOS—Joint Venture Name—Tandem Computers Inc.; *U.S. Public*, pg. 417

TWINDOW—Insulating Glass Units—PPG Industries, Inc.; *U.S. Public*, pg. 1245

TWINFILE—Rotating File Cabinet—Tab Products Co.; *U.S. Public*, pg. 1559

TWININGS—Tea—Grosvenor Marketing Ltd.; *Int'l*, pg. 92

TWINKIES—Snack Cake—Ralston Purina Company; *U.S. Public*, pg. 1359

TWINKLE—Copper & Silver Cleaner—Bristol-Myers Squibb Company; *U.S. Public*, pg. 253

TWINKLE—Chocolate Novelty—Meiji Seika Kaisha, Ltd.; *Int'l*, pg. 855

TWINKLE SHEEN—Gift Wrapping Ribbon—American Greetings Corporation; *U.S. Public*, pg. 77

TWINKLE T-LITES—Candle Containers—Will & Baumer Incorporated; *U.S. Private*, pg. 1176

TWINKLEBOARD—Hardboard—Georgia-Pacific Corporation; *U.S. Public*, pg. 735

TWINKLES—Toy—Toymax International Inc.; *U.S. Public*, pg. 1626

TWINLINE—Liquid Type Enteral Formula—Otsuka Pharmaceutical Co., Ltd.; *Int'l*, pg. 1013

TWINLOCK—Hanging Files—ACCO World Corporation; *U.S. Public*, pg. 674

TWINLOCK—Hanging Files, Ring Binders & Accounting Supplies—Fortune Brands, Inc.; *U.S. Public*, pg. 674

TWINMATE—Plastic Bags—Sonoco Products Company; *U.S. Public*, pg. 1485

TWINPRO—Joint Venture Name—Tandem Computers Inc.; *U.S. Public*, pg. 417

TWINSONIC—Vehicle Warning Light Bar—Federal Signal Corporation; *U.S. Public*, pg. 616

TWINSTAR—Helicopter—American Eurocopter Corp.; *Int'l*, pg. 29

TWINTONE—Armoured Stator Bars—General Electric Canada Inc.; *U.S. Public*, pg. 713

TWINTOUR—NONE—Boon Edam Inc.; *Int'l*, pg. 202

TWINTRON—Automotive Battery Booster Cable—General Cable Corporation; *Int'l*, pg. 1486

TWINVANE—Double Vane Pump Pressure Compensaters—Robert Bosch Fluid Power Corporation; *Int'l*, pg. 204

TWINVER PRESS—Press—Beloit Corporation; *U.S. Public*, pg. 789

TWIRLY TYE—Gift Wrapping Ribbon—American Greetings Corporation; *U.S. Public*, pg. 77

TWIST & VAC—Hand-held Vacuum—Hoover Company; *U.S. Public*, pg. 1065

TWIST-LIFT SYSTEM—Hardware—Dayton Superior Corporation; *U.S. Private*, pg. 931

TWIST-LITE—Electronic Equipment—Eaton Corp., Aerospace & Commercial Controls Div.; *U.S. Public*, pg. 557

TWIST LOK—Cleanout Plug—Genova Products, Inc.; *U.S. Private*, pg. 447

TWIST-LOK—Cleaning Pad Holder—3M; *U.S. Public*, pg. 1604

TWIST-MATE—Terminals—The Lincoln Electric Company; *U.S. Public*, pg. 996

TWIST-OFF—Closures—White Cap, Inc.; *Int'l*, pg. 1207

TWIST'S SHANDY—Beer Cooler—Labatt Brewing Company Limited; *Int'l*, pg. 679

TWISTAGUIDE—Twistable, Flexible Waveguide—Airtron; *U.S. Public*, pg. 1003

TWISTAGUIDE—Microwave Flexible Wave Guides—Litton Industries, Inc.; *U.S. Public*, pg. 1002

TWISTAIR—Oil-Free Rotary Screw Compressor—Gardner Denver Machinery Inc.; *U.S. Public*, pg. 703

TWISTED SHEILA'S LIME TEQUILA—NONE—Barton Brands, Ltd.; *U.S. Public*, pg. 300

TWISTER—Game—Hasbro, Inc.; *U.S. Public*, pg. 797

TWISTER—Wire Connector—Ideal Industries, Inc.; *U.S. Private*, pg. 557

TWISTER—Game—Milton Bradley Company; *U.S. Public*, pg. 797

TWISTER FRIES—Natural (Fryable), Natural (Ovenable), Private Reserve—Lamb-Weston, Inc.; *U.S. Public*, pg. 427

TWISTER JUICE BLENDS—Juices—Tropicana Dole Beverages North America; *Int'l*, pg. 1217

TWISTOMATIC—Machinery—Hollingsworth Saco Lowell Corporation, Inc.; *U.S. Private*, pg. 535

TWIX—Cookie Bars—Mars, Incorporated; *U.S. Private*, pg. 707

TWIX COOKIE BAR—NONE—M&M/Mars; *U.S. Private*, pg. 707

TWIXT—Game—Monarch Avalon, Inc.; *U.S. Public*, pg. 1123

TWIZZLERS—Candy—Hershey Chocolate U.S.A.; *U.S. Public*, pg. 812

TWIZZLERS—Licorice—Hershey Foods Corporation; *U.S. Public*, pg. 811

IIC—Personal Computer—Apple Computer, Inc.; *U.S. Public*, pg. 121

2-CALORIE QUEST—Beverage—Seagram Beverage Co.; *Int'l*, pg. 1215

IIE—Personal Computer—Apple Computer, Inc.; *U.S. Public*, pg. 121

250G GRAPHITE RTS—Racquetball Racquet—Ektelon; *U.S. Private*, pg. 884

240SX (NISSAN)—Sports Coupe—Nissan Motor Corporation in U.S.A.; *Int'l*, pg. 945

TWO GETHERNESS—Greeting Cards—American Greetings Corporation; *U.S. Public*, pg. 77

200 APS—Photoresist Processing System—Silicon Valley Group, Inc.; *U.S. Public*, pg. 1474

214 ST SUPER TRANSPORT—20 Place Twin Engine Helicopter—Bell Helicopter Textron; *U.S. Public*, pg. 1588

200SE (NISSAN)—Sports Coupe—Nissan Motor Corporation in U.S.A.; *Int'l*, pg. 945

200 SERIES—Banquet Tables—Howe Furniture Corporation; *U.S. Private*, pg. 543

206LT—7 Place Light Twin Engine Helicopter—Bell Helicopter Textron; *U.S. Public*, pg. 1588

230—Ten Place Twin Engine Helicopter—Bell Helicopter Textron; *U.S. Public*, pg. 1588

230—Sealant—DAP Inc.; *Int'l*, pg. 1486

212—15 Place Twin Engine Helicopter—Bell Helicopter Textron; *U.S. Public*, pg. 1588

TWO-IN-ONE—Mailing Bags—Bemis Company, Inc.; *U.S. Public*, pg. 210

2-IN-1—Indoor Fluorescent Bracket—Guth Lighting Company; *Int'l*, pg. 821

2 N 1—Reversible Driver—Hold-E-Zee, Ltd.; *U.S. Private*, pg. 229

2-IN-1—Wick-Equipped Drip Bottle Deodorant—Surco Products, Inc.; *U.S. Private*, pg. 1056

2-IN-1 WAGON—NONE—Rubbermaid Incorporated; *U.S. Public*, pg. 1411

2KB/2KC—Two-Component High-Performance Coatings—Morton Automotive Coatings; *U.S. Public*, pg. 1135

2K-PERM—NONE—Goldwell Cosmetics (USA) Inc.; *Int'l*, pg. 718

THE TWO-MEGA CARTRIDGE—Videogames—Sega of America Inc.; *Int'l*, pg. 1218

TWO OCEANS—Wine—Distillers Corporation S.A.; *Int'l*, pg. 1129

TWO PEPPER—Jeans—Tropical Sportswear International; *U.S. Private*, pg. 1105

2 PLEX—Laminated Exterior Engravable Plastic—New Hermes Incorporated; *U.S. Private*, pg. 793

2 PLUS 4—Warranty & Protection—Volvo Penta of the Americas, Inc.; *Int'l*, pg. 1477

TWO + TWO—Packaging Machines—Reynolds Metals Company; *U.S. Public*, pg. 1385

2.4-D—Weedkilling Compound—Riverdale Chemical Co.; *U.S. Private*, pg. 934

2-PYROL—2-Pyrrolidone—International Specialty Products, Inc.; *U.S. Public*, pg. 858

TWO SHOT SOLES—Shoes—Knapp Shoes Inc.; *U.S. Private*, pg. 401

260 VOLT-OHM—Volt-Ohm-Milliammeter—Simpson Electric Co.; *U.S. Private*, pg. 1002

TWO STEP—Folding Two-Step Stool with Handle—Cosco, Inc.; *U.S. Private*, pg. 277

TWO-STEP—Office Furniture—HON Industries Inc.; *U.S. Public*, pg. 772

2 TAB—Filing Cabinets & Related Hardware, Keypunch Apparatus—Tab Products Co.; *U.S. Public*, pg. 1559

2 TEMP—Power Tool Accessories—The Black & Decker Corporation; *U.S. Public*, pg. 233

234 LINK—Factory Automation Spreadsheet Software—Square D Automation Products; *Int'l*, pg. 1208

234 LINK—Factory Automation Spreadsheet Software—Square D Company; *Int'l*, pg. 1208

2000 A—Flatbed Trailer—Utility Trailer Manufacturing Co.; *U.S. Private*, pg. 1130

2001—Tile Mastic—DAP Inc.; *Int'l*, pg. 1486

2011-V-TEL VIDEO—NONE—TIE/Communications, Inc.; *U.S. Private*, pg. 1085

2000 FLUSHES—Toilet Bowl Cleaners—Block Drug Company, Inc.; *U.S. Public*, pg. 236

2100 SERIES—Conveyers—Dorner Manufacturing Corp.; *U.S. Private*, pg. 340

2001X—Wafer Probers—Electroglas, Inc.; *U.S. Public*, pg. 727

2000 R—Refrigerated Van Trailer—Utility Trailer Manufacturing Co.; *U.S. Private*, pg. 1130

2000 RX—Refrigerated Van Trailer—Utility Trailer Manufacturing Co.; *U.S. Private*, pg. 1130

2000 SERIES—Hinges—Amerock Corporation; *U.S. Public*, pg. 1177

2000 SERIES—Highly Durable Pliers—Klein Tools Inc.; *U.S. Private*, pg. 625

2000/SUPER BULK—Carpet Yarn—Amoco Corporation; *U.S. Public*, pg. 101

2010X—Wafer Probers—Electroglas, Inc.; *U.S. Public*, pg. 727

2251—Oil—Penreco; *U.S. Public*, pg. 1273

TWO TONE—NONE—Amerimark Inc.; *U.S. Public*, pg. 1237

TWO-TWENTY—Womens Apparel—Blair Corporation; *U.S. Public*, pg. 236

TWO-TWENTY—Mail Order for Apparel—Blair Corporation; *U.S. Public*, pg. 236

2UV—Multiple Wavelengths in One Unit—UVP, Inc.; *U.S. Private*, pg. 1115

TWO-WAY—Fasteners—Maclean-Fogg Co.; *U.S. Private*, pg. 692

TXIB—Plasticizer—Eastman Chemical Company; *U.S. Public*, pg. 550

TY-D-BOL—Toilet Bowl Cleaner—Kiwi Brands; *U.S. Public*, pg. 1433

TY-D-BOL—Toilet Cleaners—Knomark, Inc.; *U.S. Private*, pg. 627

TY-D-BOL—Toilet Cleaner—Sara Lee Corporation; *U.S. Public*, pg. 1432

TY-FAST—Cable Ties—Thomas & Betts Corporation; *U.S. Public*, pg. 1597

TY-LON—Line of Boiler & Loading Tower Products—Calgon Vestal Laboratories; *U.S. Public*, pg. 1515

TY-RAP—Cable Ties—Thomas & Betts Corporation; *U.S. Public*, pg. 1597

TYANNO EX—Strategy Game—Monarch Avalon, Inc.; *U.S. Public*, pg. 1123

TYBON—Synthetic Resins—Georgia-Pacific Corporation; *U.S. Public*, pg. 735

TYBRITE—Packaging Films—The Dow Chemical Company; *U.S. Public*, pg. 522

TYCO—Toys—Tyco Toys, Inc.; *U.S. Public*, pg. 1058

TYCO PREESCHOOL—Toys—Tyco Toys, Inc.; *U.S. Public*, pg. 1058

TYCO SUPER DOUGH—Activity—Tyco Toys, Inc.; *U.S. Public*, pg. 1058

TYCOON—Game—Monarch Avalon, Inc.; *U.S. Public*, pg. 1123

TYCOON—Japanese Food—Mutual Trading Co., Inc.; *U.S. Private*, pg. 770

TYCOTE—Coated Spun Bound Polyolefin—Tekra Corporation; *U.S. Private*, pg. 1073

TYDEX—Flocculant—The Dow Chemical Company; *U.S. Public*, pg. 522

TYE—Tillage Equipment, Planters—AGCO Corporation; *U.S. Public*, pg. 28

TYGAFLOR—NONE—Chemfab Corporation; *U.S. Public*, pg. 344

TYGALAM—NONE—Chemfab Corporation; *U.S. Public*, pg. 344

TYGATAPE—NONE—Chemfab Corporation; *U.S. Public*, pg. 344

TYGON—Non-Metallic Tubing—Norton Company; *Int'l*, pg. 1173

TYGON—Flexible, Clear Plastic Tubing—Norton Performance Plastics; *Int'l*, pg. 1174

TYGOTHANE—Polyurethane Tubing—Norton Performance Plastics; *Int'l*, pg. 1174

TYLAN—Animal Health—Elanco Animal Health; *U.S. Public*, pg. 993

TYLAN CONCENTRATE—Granulated Tylosin Phosphate Concentrate, Elanco—Eli Lilly and Company; *U.S. Public*, pg. 992

TYLAN 50 INJECTION—Tylosin, Elanco—Eli Lilly and Company; *U.S. Public*, pg. 992

TYLAN 40 PREMIX—Tylosin, Elanco—Eli Lilly and Company; *U.S. Public*, pg. 992

TYLAN 40 SULFA PREMIX—Tylosin Phosphate & Sulfamethazine, Elanco—Eli Lilly and Company; *U.S. Public*, pg. 992

TYLAN INJECTION—Animal Health—Elanco Animal Health; *U.S. Public*, pg. 993

TYLAN INJECTION—Tylosin, Elanco—Eli Lilly and Company; *U.S. Public*, pg. 992

TYLAN SOLUBLE—Tylosin, Elanco—Eli Lilly and Company; *U.S. Public*, pg. 992

TYLAN SULFA-G—Tylosin Phosphate & Sulfamethazine, Elanco—Eli Lilly and Company; *U.S. Public*, pg. 992

TYLAN 10 PREMIX—Tylosin, Elanco—Eli Lilly and Company; *U.S. Public*, pg. 992

TYLAN 10 SULFA PREMIX—Tylosin Phosphate & Sulfamethazine, Elanco—Eli Lilly and Company; *U.S. Public*, pg. 992

TYLAN 200 INJECTION—Tylosin, Elanco—Eli Lilly and Company; *U.S. Public*, pg. 992

TYLENOL—Analgesic—Johnson & Johnson; *U.S. Public*, pg. 927

TYLENOL—Proprietary Drugs—McNeil Consumer Products Company; *U.S. Public*, pg. 928

TYLENOL COLD FORMULA—Cold Medicine—Johnson & Johnson; *U.S. Public*, pg. 927

TYLENOL COUGH/COLD/FLU—Proprietary Drugs—McNeil Consumer Products Company; *U.S. Public*, pg. 928

TYLENOL HEADACHE PLUS—Pain Reliever—McNeil Consumer Products Company; *U.S. Public*, pg. 928

TYLENOL PM—Nighttime Pain Reliever—McNeil Consumer Products Company; *U.S. Public*, pg. 928

TYLENOL SINUS/ALLERGY SINUS—Sinus Medication—McNeil Consumer Products Company; *U.S. Public*, pg. 928

TYLENOL WITH CODEINE—Tablets—Ortho-McNeil Pharmaceutical Corporation; *U.S. Public*, pg. 929

TYLOSE—Cellulose Ethers—Hoechst Aktiengesellschaft; *Int'l*, pg. 624

TYLOX CAPSULES—NONE—Ortho-McNeil Pharmaceutical Corporation; *U.S. Public*, pg. 929

TYNA-MYTE—Electric Air Valve—Humphrey Products Company; *U.S. Private*, pg. 547

TYNE BRAND—Meat Product—Master Foods; *U.S. Private*, pg. 707

TYNEX—Nylon—Du Pont (E.I. Du Pont De Nemours & Co.); *U.S. Public*, pg. 530

TYPE DIRECTOR—Photo Typesetter—AGFA EPS Division; *Int'l*, pg. 172

TYPE JC—Home Series—Toyota Motor Corporation; *Int'l*, pg. 1411

TYPE K—Bakery Equipment—Belshaw Brothers, Inc.; *Int'l*, pg. 188

TYPE R—Thermo Plastic Insulation—Thermo Electric Co., Inc.; *U.S. Public*, pg. 1080

TYPE-SET—Photographic Papers & Chemicals—Eastman Kodak Company; *U.S. Public*, pg. 550

TYPE 30—Glass Fiber Roving—Owens Corning; *U.S. Public*, pg. 1236

TYPECODER—Word Processing Machine—Sony Electronics; *Int'l*, pg. 1281

TYPESTYLER—Overhead Maker—Varitronic Systems, Inc.; *U.S. Public*, pg. 250

TYPHOON—NONE—Brown & Sharpe Manufacturing Company; *U.S. Public*, pg. 260

TYPOSITOR 4000—Headline Typesetter—GraphLine Inc.; *U.S. Private*, pg. 471

TYRIL—Resins—The Dow Chemical Company; *U.S. Public*, pg. 522

TYRIN—Chlorinated Polyethylene—The Dow Chemical Company; *U.S. Public*, pg. 522

TYRITE—Adhesive—Lord Corporation; *U.S. Private*, pg. 675

TYRONE—Greeting Cards—American Greetings Corporation; *U.S. Public*, pg. 77

Brand Name Index

TYSCRU—Form Tieing Device—Richmond Screw Anchor Company; *U.S. Private*, pg. 932

TYSON—Frozen Poultry—Louis Kemp Seafood Co.; *U.S. Public*, pg. 1652

TYSON—Frozen Poultry—Tyson Foods, Inc.; *U.S. Public*, pg. 1652

TYSON—Fresh Poultry—Louis Kemp Seafood Co.; *U.S. Public*, pg. 1652

TYSON COUNTRY FRESH CHICKEN—Fresh Poultry—Louis Kemp Seafood Co.; *U.S. Public*, pg. 1652

TYSON COUNTRY FRESH CHICKEN—Fresh Poultry—Tyson Foods, Inc.; *U.S. Public*, pg. 1652

TYSON HOLLY FARMS—Fresh Poultry—Tyson Foods, Inc.; *U.S. Public*, pg. 1652

TYSON TASTYBIRD IQF—Foodservice Frozen Items—Louis Kemp Seafood Co.; *U.S. Public*, pg. 1652

TYSON'S PRIDE—Poultry Items—Louis Kemp Seafood Co.; *U.S. Public*, pg. 1652

TYSON'S 28—Poultry Items—Tyson Foods, Inc.; *U.S. Public*, pg. 1652

TYTON—Fixing & Securing Components—Bowthorpe plc; *Int'l*, pg. 207

TYTON—NONE—Clouth Gummiwerke AG; *Int'l*, pg. 297

TYTON JOINT—Pipe—United States Pipe & Foundry Company, Inc.; *U.S. Public*, pg. 1736

TYTRON—Test System—MTS Systems Corporation; *U.S. Public*, pg. 1028

TYVEK—Envelopes—American Business Products, Inc.; *U.S. Public*, pg. 70

TYVEK—Spunbonded Olefin—Du Pont (E.I. Du Pont De Nemours & Co.); *U.S. Public*, pg. 530

TYZINE—Nasal Decongestant—Bradley Pharmaceuticals; *U.S. Public*, pg. 249

TYZINE—Nasal Decongestant—Doak Dermatologics; *U.S. Public*, pg. 250

TYZOR—Organic Titanates—Du Pont (E.I. Du Pont De Nemours & Co.); *U.S. Public*, pg. 530

U

UADBU—Unattended Automatic Dial Back Up—Microtel International Inc.; *U.S. Public*, pg. 1108

UB—NONE—UB Networks; *Int'l*, pg. 924

U.B. ANYWEAR—Childrenswear—Woolworth Corporation; *U.S. Public*, pg. 1777

U.B.I.—Cable TV/Interactive TV—The Hearst Corporation; *U.S. Private*, pg. 515

UBIQ—Personal Computer Terminals—The Mead Corporation; *U.S. Public*, pg. 1074

UB NETWORKS—NONE—UB Networks; *Int'l*, pg. 924

UBS—Brake Parts—Echlin Inc.; *U.S. Public*, pg. 560

U-BAG-IT—Produce Bags On Roll—Tenneco Packaging, Consumer Products Group; *U.S. Public*, pg. 1579

U-BIX—PlainPaper Photocopiers—Konica Corporation; *Int'l*, pg. 748

U-BOLTS—Bolts—Ripon Foods, Inc.; *U.S. Private*, pg. 931

U BONDAGEL—E-125, E-500, E-1000, E-High A, E-Linear Aqueous GPC Column—Millipore Corporation; *U.S. Public*, pg. 1112

U BONDAPAK—C18, Phenyl, NH2 Cartridge, Column, Packing & Packing Family—Millipore Corporation; *U.S. Public*, pg. 1112

U-BRAND—Copper Tube & Fittings—Mueller Industries, Inc.; *U.S. Public*, pg. 1141

UC—NONE—Thiokol Corporation; *U.S. Public*, pg. 1596

UCF—Photographic Film—Eastman Kodak Company; *U.S. Public*, pg. 550

UCFS—Finance Company—The Scott Fetzer Company; *U.S. Public*, pg. 217

UCF7—Photographic Film—Eastman Kodak Company; *U.S. Public*, pg. 550

UCG BETA SLIDE—Pregnancy Test—Wampole Laboratories; *U.S. Public*, pg. 310

UCG SLIDE TEST—Pregnancy Test—Wampole Laboratories; *U.S. Public*, pg. 310

UCG TEST—Pregnancy Test—Wampole Laboratories; *U.S. Public*, pg. 310

UCP—Graphic Arts Paper—Eastman Kodak Company; *U.S. Public*, pg. 550

UDF—Photographic Film—Eastman Kodak Company; *U.S. Public*, pg. 550

UDF7—Photographic Film—Eastman Kodak Company; *U.S. Public*, pg. 550

UDM UPHOLSTERY DESIGN & MANUFACTURING—Magazine for Manufacturers of Upholstered Furniture & Bedding—Reed Elsevier Business Information; *Int'l*, pg. 1095

U.D.R.—NONE—Carpenter Technology Corporation; *U.S. Public*, pg. 307

U.E.S.—Vitamin Shampoo—Health Products Corporation; *U.S. Public*, pg. 514

UF—NONE—Uniflex, Inc.; *U.S. Public*, pg. 1665

UF—Food Product—Universal Foods Corporation; *U.S. Public*, pg. 1695

UFO—Instant Chow Mein Noodles in a Bowl—Nissin Food Products Co., Ltd.; *Int'l*, pg. 949

UFO-USER FRIENDLY OFFICE—Ergonomically Designed Computer Accessories—Rubbermaid Incorporated; *U.S. Public*, pg. 1411

UFT—Farm Equip.—United Farm Tools, Inc.; *U.S. Private*, pg. 1122

U-FLEX—Connector System—Parlex Corporation; *U.S. Public*, pg. 1264

U 46 PRODUCTS—Crop Protection Agent—BASF AG; *Int'l*, pg. 103

UGF—Photographic Film—Eastman Kodak Company; *U.S. Public*, pg. 550

UGF7—Photographic Film—Eastman Kodak Company; *U.S. Public*, pg. 550

UGM—Photographic Film—Eastman Kodak Company; *U.S. Public*, pg. 550

UGX—Ultra Gain Antennas—Andrew Corporation; *U.S. Public*, pg. 112

UHD—Engine Air Filter for Off-Highway—Farr Company; *U.S. Public*, pg. 613

UHF—Photographic Film—Eastman Kodak Company; *U.S. Public*, pg. 550

UHF2—Photographic Film—Eastman Kodak Company; *U.S. Public*, pg. 550

UHN—Photographic Film—Eastman Kodak Company; *U.S. Public*, pg. 550

UHQ—Fax Ultra High Quality—Canon U.S.A., Inc.; *Int'l*, pg. 262

UHS—Material Handling Systems—Litton Industries, Inc.; *U.S. Public*, pg. 1002

UHS-NET—Security Network—Vindicator Technologies; *U.S. Private*, pg. 1141

UHT—Milk—Parmalat USA Corporation; *Int'l*, pg. 1023

UHT—Milk Products—Q.U.F. Industries Ltd.; *Int'l*, pg. 1074

UHX—Ultra High Performance Antennas—Andrew Corporation; *U.S. Public*, pg. 112

UHX II—Ultra High Performance Antennas—Andrew Corporation; *U.S. Public*, pg. 112

U-HAUL—NONE—Amerco; *U.S. Private*, pg. 48

U-HAUL—Rental Trucks & Trailers—U-Haul International, Inc.; *U.S. Private*, pg. 49

UICS—Universal Instruments Control Software—Universal Instruments Corporation; *U.S. Public*, pg. 522

UID/RCL—Rotary Switches—ITW Switches; *U.S. Public*, pg. 867

UITKYK ESTATE—Wine—Distillers Corporation S.A.; *Int'l*, pg. 1129

U-INSTALL—Garage Door Openers & Residential Steel Replacement Doors—The Stanley Works; *U.S. Public*, pg. 1508

UK KOMPASS REGISTER—Business Directory—Reed Business Information-East Grinstead; *Int'l*, pg. 1094

U-LINE—Aluminum & Malleable Iron Receptacles—Appleton Electric Co.; *U.S. Public*, pg. 572

UMS—NONE—Brown & Sharpe Manufacturing Company; *U.S. Public*, pg. 260

UMX—Multiband Antennas—Andrew Corporation; *U.S. Public*, pg. 112

U-MOBILE—Stock Transport Cart—Jarke Corporation; *U.S. Private*, pg. 583

UNI-FLEX—Textured Coating—Jones Blair Company; *U.S. Private*, pg. 596

UNUM—Insurance—UNUM Corporation; *U.S. Public*, pg. 1699

U-NINE—Digestive Organs Agents—Nippon Kayaku Co. Ltd.; *Int'l*, pg. 934

U-NO BAR—Candy—Annabelle Candy Company, Inc.; *U.S. Private*, pg. 75

U-NO MINT BAR—Candy—Annabelle Candy Company, Inc.; *U.S. Private*, pg. 75

UPC PRE-PAC—Scalesline for Supermarket Back Rooms—Exact Equipment Corporation; *U.S. Private*, pg. 387

UPF—Photographic Film—Eastman Kodak Company; *U.S. Public*, pg. 550

UPI—Electronic Instrument—Intel Corporation; *U.S. Public*, pg. 886

UPL 500—Paint—Pratt & Lambert United, Inc.; *U.S. Public*, pg. 1466

UPS—Parcel Deliveries—United Parcel Service of America, Inc.; *U.S. Private*, pg. 1123

'U+ SERIES—Self Priming Centrifugal High Efficiency Pump—The Gorman-Rupp Company; *U.S. Public*, pg. 754

U PORASIL—GPC 60A Column & LC Bulk Packing—Millipore Corporation; *U.S. Public*, pg. 1112

U-PRINT—Label—Avery Dennison Corporation; *U.S. Public*, pg. 152

URBA—Water Pumps—Echlin Inc.; *U.S. Public*, pg. 560

UREX—Methenamine Hippurate, Prescription Drug—3M; *U.S. Public*, pg. 1604

URS—Engineering & Other Business Services—URS Corporation; *U.S. Public*, pg. 1655

USA—Urology Systems America—Circon Corporation; *U.S. Public*, pg. 373

USA OVERNIGHT—Domestic Express Delivery—DHL Worldwide Express; *U.S. Private*, pg. 301

USA TIME—Time, Temperature & Weather Announcement System—Electronic Tele-Communications, Inc.; *U.S. Public*, pg. 570

USC—Ultra Sonic Cleaning—SpeedFam International, Inc.; *U.S. Public*, pg. 1497

USC—Ultra Selective Conversion—Stone & Webster, Incorporated; *U.S. Public*, pg. 1519

USCI—Medical Instruments—C.R. Bard, Inc.; *U.S. Public*, pg. 189

USD—Fuse Holders & Terminal Blocks—Bussmann Division; *U.S. Public*, pg. 443

USD—Fuseholders, Electrical Interconnect Devices & Miniature Circuit Breakers—Cooper Industries, Inc.; *U.S. Public*, pg. 442

USF&G—Insurance & Asset Management—United States Fidelity & Guaranty Company; *U.S. Public*, pg. 1659

USG—NONE—USG Corporation; *U.S. Public*, pg. 1660

USIP20—Multichannel Ultrasonic Flaw Detector—Krautkramer-Branson, Inc.; *U.S. Public*, pg. 574

USK7D—Ultrasonic Flaw Detector—Krautkramer-Branson, Inc.; *U.S. Public*, pg. 574

U.S. LOCK—Security Hardware—Waxman Industries, Inc.; *U.S. Public*, pg. 1748

USN52—Ultrasonic Flaw Detector—Krautkramer-Branson, Inc.; *U.S. Public*, pg. 574

USP—Lumber & Wood Products—Georgia-Pacific Corporation; *U.S. Public*, pg. 735

US PACKS—Suture Packaging—U.S. Surgical Corp.; *U.S. Public*, pg. 1687

U.S. PLYWOOD—Wood & Lumber Products—Georgia-Pacific Corporation; *U.S. Public*, pg. 735

U.S. ROBOTICS—NONE—Texas Instruments Incorporated; *U.S. Public*, pg. 1585

USSC—NONE—U.S. Surgical Corp.; *U.S. Public*, pg. 1687

U STYRAGEL—100A, 500A, 10 3-6A GPC Column—Millipore Corporation; *U.S. Public*, pg. 1112

UTAX—Office Communications Equipment—Basel Trading Company Ltd.; *Int'l*, pg. 169

UT AUTOMOTIVE—NONE—United Technologies Corporation; *U.S. Public*, pg. 1689

UTC—NONE—OPT Industries, Inc.; *U.S. Public*, pg. 1624

UTC 5253 POS TERMINALS—NONE—Ultimate Technology Corporation; *U.S. Public*, pg. 1637

UTC PD SERIES OF CUSTOMER DISPLAYS—NONE—Ultimate Technology Corporation; *U.S. Public*, pg. 1637

UTC SERIES 500 COMPACT POS KEYBOARD—NONE—Ultimate Technology Corporation; *U.S. Public*, pg. 1637

UTILX—Corporate Name—UTILX Corporation; *U.S. Public*, pg. 1701

UTK—Dental Stone—3M; *U.S. Public*, pg. 1604

UTK-FM—Generators, Milker Kits, Dispensers & Evacuated Vials—Mallinckrodt Inc.; *U.S. Public*, pg. 1039

UTR—Grounds Equipment—Excel Industries, Inc.; *U.S. Private*, pg. 387

UTS—Unix Software Product—Amdahl Corporation; *Int'l*, pg. 527

UT 2000—Tires—Bridgestone/Firestone, Inc.; *Int'l*, pg. 213

U-TEACH—Hand-held Programmer—Universal Instruments Corporation; *U.S. Public*, pg. 522

U-THANE—Rigid Foam Insulation—The Dow Chemical Company; *U.S. Public*, pg. 1643

U-TRON—Ultrasonic Inspection—Tuboscope Incorporated; *U.S. Public*, pg. 1643

U-2—Acrylic Urethane Catalyst—Mar-Hyde Corporation; *U.S. Public*, pg. 1357

UV/BAKE—Registered Trademark—Eaton Corporation, Semi-Conductor; *U.S. Public*, pg. 557

UV-CHEK—Light Stabilizers—Ferro Corporation; *U.S. Public*, pg. 618

UVT—Flo Meters—BIF; *U.S. Public*, pg. 726

UV/ULTRA—Translucent Paper—Kimberly-Clark Corporation; *U.S. Public*, pg. 958

UVX2000—Computer System—Van Waters & Rogers; *Int'l*, pg. 1147

UBENA—Sauces, Mealmakers, Seasonings, Spices—Bestfoods; *U.S. Public*, pg. 223

UCAR—Chemicals—Union Carbide Corporation; *U.S. Public*, pg. 1666

UCON—Thermofluids—Union Carbide Corporation; *U.S. Public*, pg. 1666

UDDER-WIZE—Skin Care—Palm Beach Beauty Products Co.; *U.S. Private*, pg. 834

UDEL—Polysulfone High Temperature Engineering Resins—Amoco Chemicals; *U.S. Public*, pg. 102

UDEL—High-Tech Polymer—Amoco Corporation; *U.S. Public*, pg. 101

UETA, INC—U.S./Mexican Border Shops—Duty Free International, Inc.; *Int'l*, pg. 103

UFT-MOHAWK—Rotary Cutters, Levee Plows—United Farm Tools, Mohawk; *U.S. Private*, pg. 1122

UGAUGE—Electronic Gauge with Set Points—Amot Controls Corporation; *U.S. Public*, pg. 1405

UGLY DUCKLING RENT-A-CAR—Car Rental—Ugly Duckling Corp.; *U.S. Public*, pg. 1662

UGLY STIK—Fishing Rod—K2 Inc.; *U.S. Public*, pg. 940

ULBRASEAL—Stainless Steel & Special Metal Strips—Ulbrich Stainless Steels & Special Metals, Inc.; *U.S. Private*, pg. 1115

ULBRAVAR—Stainless Steel & Special Metal Strips—Ulbrich Stainless Steels & Special Metals, Inc.; *U.S. Private*, pg. 1115

ULBRICH—Stainless Steel & Special Metal Strips & Round & Flat Shaped Wire—Ulbrich Stainless Steels & Special Metals, Inc.; *U.S. Private*, pg. 1115

ULMA—Smart Web Inspection System—ABB Industrial Systems, Inc.; *Int'l*, pg. 4

ULRICH'S INTERNATIONAL PERIODICALS DIRECTORY—Reference Book for Serials—R.R. Bowker; *Int'l*, pg. 1096

ULTARA I—Car Seat—Evenflo Company, Inc.; *U.S. Private*, pg. 629

ULTARA V—Car Seat—Evenflo Company, Inc.; *U.S. Private*, pg. 629

ULTEC—Dressings—American Home Products Corporation; *U.S. Public*, pg. 79

ULTEM—Polyetherimide Resin—General Electric Canada Inc.; *U.S. Public*, pg. 713

ULTEM—Engineered Plastics—General Electric Company; *U.S. Public*, pg. 709

ULTERIOR MOTIVES—Juniors' Dresses—Niches, Inc.; *U.S. Public*, pg. 1181

ULTI-MATE—NONE—Molex Incorporated; *U.S. Public*, pg. 1121

ULTICAM—CAD/CAM System—Hurco Companies, Inc.; *U.S. Public*, pg. 850

ULTIMA—Paper Towels, Soap & Bath Tissue—Georgia-Pacific Corporation; *U.S. Public*, pg. 735

ULTIMA—Stationery Products—The Mead Corporation; *U.S. Public*, pg. 1074

ULTIMA—Cosmetics—Revlon, Inc.; *U.S. Private*, pg. 689

ULTIMA & ULTRA—Dinnerware—World Tableware, Inc.; *Int'l*, pg. 1056

ULTIMA GOLD—Biodegradable Cocktail—Packard Instrument Co., Inc.; *U.S. Private*, pg. 833

ULTIMA GOLD XR—Biodegradable Cocktail—Packard Instrument Co., Inc.; *U.S. Private*, pg. 833

ULTIMA 2000—Photocoagulator—Coherent, Inc.; *U.S. Public*, pg. 395

ULTIMA 2000—Versatile Label Merchandising System for the Grocers Meat Counter—Premark International, Inc.; *U.S. Public*, pg. 1321

ULTIMA 80—Hi Power Behind the Hearing Aid—Beltone Electronics Corporation; *U.S. Private*, pg. 132

ULTIMAG—Magnetic Computer Tape—Anacomp Magnetics, Inc.; *U.S. Public*, pg. 107

ULTIMATE—Gasoline—Amoco Corporation; *U.S. Public*, pg. 101

ULTIMATE—Premium Gasoline—Amoco Oil Company; *U.S. Public*, pg. 102

ULTIMATE—Shoes—Aritmos AB; *Int'l*, pg. 1072

ULTIMATE—Reagent—Beckman Instruments, Inc.; *U.S. Public*, pg. 199

ULTIMATE—NONE—McCain Foods Inc.; *Int'l*, pg. 850

ULTIMATE—Interior Plant Prods.—Security Lawn & Garden Co.; *U.S. Private*, pg. 397

ULTIMATE—De-Icer—Simon Engineering plc; *Int'l*, pg. 1251

ULTIMATE—Shoes—Tretorn AB; *Int'l*, pg. 1072

ULTIMATE BLONDE—NONE—Bristol-Myers Squibb Company; *U.S. Public*, pg. 253

ULTIMATE CHOICE—Grocery & Perishable Products—Shurfine International, Inc.; *U.S. Private*, pg. 997

ULTIMATE COMBO—Menu Item—Chi-Chi's Inc.; *U.S. Private*, pg. 393

ULTIMATE DEEP DISH—Deep Dish Pizza—Domino's Pizza Inc.; *U.S. Private*, pg. 339

THE ULTIMATE GOURMET BURGER—Hamburger Patties—Harker's Distribution, Inc.; *U.S. Private*, pg. 502

ULTIMATE OUTLET—Outlet Merchandise through Catalogs—Spiegel, Inc.; *U.S. Public*, pg. 1498

ULTIMATIC—Dispensers for Paper Towels, Bath Tissue, Soap & Room Deodorant—Georgia-Pacific Corporation; *U.S. Public*, pg. 735

ULTIMAX—Thread—Coats North America; *Int'l*, pg. 300

ULTIMAX—Computer Numerical Controls System—Hurco Companies, Inc.; *U.S. Public*, pg. 850

ULTIMAX—Socks—Wigwam Mills, Inc.; *U.S. Private*, pg. 1175

ULTIMEDIA—Computer Product—International Business Machines Corporation; *U.S. Public*, pg. 895

ULTIMET—Metals Class 6—Haynes International, Inc.; *U.S. Public*, pg. 801

ULTIMO!—Pizza Sauces & Cheese—International Multifoods Corporation; *U.S. Public*, pg. 900

ULTIMOTION—Computer Product—International Business Machines Corporation; *U.S. Public*, pg. 895

ULTIPOR—Filters—Pall Corporation; *U.S. Public*, pg. 1253

ULTIPOR GF—Filters—Pall Corporation; *U.S. Public*, pg. 1253

ULTIPOR II—Filter Media—Pall Corporation; *U.S. Public*, pg. 1253

ULTISPERSE—Suspension for Aqueous Film Coating—Crompton & Knowles Ingredient Technology Corp.; *U.S. Public*, pg. 459

ULTR-CASE—Contour Gear Hardening—Ajax Magnethermic Corp.; *Int'l*, pg. 113

ULTRA—Plastic Cutlery—Amcel Corp.; *U.S. Private*, pg. 48

ULTRA—Salon Re-Sale Line Of Hair Care Electric Appliances—Andis Company; *U.S. Private*, pg. 73

ULTRA—Heavy Duty Liquid Laundry Detergent—Blue Cross Laboratories; *U.S. Private*, pg. 152

ULTRA—Liquid Laundry Detergent—Blue Cross Laboratories; *U.S. Private*, pg. 152

ULTRA—Air Filter—Donaldson Company, Inc.; *U.S. Public*, pg. 517

ULTRA—Photographic Paper—Eastman Kodak Company; *U.S. Public*, pg. 550

ULTRA—Gel Coats—Ferro Corporation; *U.S. Public*, pg. 618

ULTRA—Electronic Sprayers—Graco Inc.; *U.S. Public*, pg. 756

ULTRA—Paint—ICI Paints; *Int'l*, pg. 664

ULTRA—Refrigerated Trailers & Truck Bodies—Kidron Inc.; *U.S. Private*, pg. 619

ULTRA—NONE—Medex Inc.; *U.S. Public*, pg. 689

ULTRA—Paint—Plasti-Kote Company Inc.; *U.S. Private*, pg. 870

ULTRA—MP&G Accelerator—Sigma Designs, Inc.; *U.S. Public*, pg. 1472

ULTRA—Petroleum Products—Sun Company, Inc.; *U.S. Public*, pg. 1530

ULTRA AIRE—Air Filter—Donaldson Company, Inc.; *U.S. Public*, pg. 517

ULTRA AJAX—Detergent—Colgate-Palmolive Company; *U.S. Public*, pg. 397

ULTRA BABY SOFT LAUNDRY DETERGENT—NONE—The Dial Corporation; *U.S. Public*, pg. 505

ULTRA BAN—Anti-Perspirant-Solid & Lotion—Bristol-Myers Squibb Company; *U.S. Public*, pg. 253

ULTRA BAN II—Anti-Perspirant Spray—Bristol-Myers Squibb Company; *U.S. Public*, pg. 253

ULTRA BINDERS—Seal & Cut Binders—Rundel Products, Inc.; *U.S. Private*, pg. 951

ULTRA BLOCK—NONE—CertainTeed Corporation; *Int'l*, pg. 1170

ULTRA BLUE—Hair Lightener—Clairol, Inc.; *U.S. Public*, pg. 254

ULTRA-BLUE—Silicone—Loctite Corporation; *Int'l*, pg. 611

ULTRA BRITE—Toothpaste—Colgate-Palmolive Company; *U.S. Public*, pg. 397

ULTRA-BUFF—Rotary Brush for Burnishing—Flo-Pac Corporation; *U.S. Private*, pg. 414

ULTRA CHO—Serum-Free Media—BioWhittaker, Inc.; *U.S. Public*, pg. 297

ULTRA CAP—Capnograph & Pulse Oximeter—Nellcor Puritan Bennett Incorporated; *U.S. Public*, pg. 1039

ULTRA CHEER—Detergent—The Procter & Gamble Company; *U.S. Public*, pg. 1330

ULTRA CLEAN—Water Filtration System—Regal Ware, Inc.; *U.S. Private*, pg. 917

ULTRA-CLEAR—Centrifuge Tubes—Beckman Instruments, Inc.; *U.S. Public*, pg. 199

ULTRA-CLEAR—Clarification Aid—Oil-Dri Corporation of America; *U.S. Public*, pg. 1214

ULTRA CLIFF HANGERS—Race Set—Tyco Toys, Inc.; *U.S. Public*, pg. 1058

ULTRA COLLECTION—NONE—Regal Ware, Inc.; *U.S. Private*, pg. 917

ULTRA-COM—Microcontroller for Plastics Assembly—Dukane Corporation; *U.S. Private*, pg. 345

ULTRA COTE—Clays For Coating & Filling Paper & Board—Engelhard Corporation; *U.S. Public*, pg. 582

ULTRA-CUT—Knife-cut Indirect Embroidery—Voyager Emblems, Inc.; *U.S. Private*, pg. 1143

ULTRA DEO BASE—Odor Counteractant Concentrate—Surco Products, Inc.; *U.S. Private*, pg. 1056

ULTRA-DRY—Continuous Flow Drying System—CTB International Corp.; *U.S. Public*, pg. 284

ULTRA-DUCT—Modular Wiring Management System—Pass & Seymour/Legrand; *Int'l*, pg. 806

ULTRA EDGE—Bedding—The Stearns & Foster Bedding Company; *U.S. Private*, pg. 979

ULTRA ELITE & HYDRO ELITE—Printing Roller Covers—Samuel Bingham Co; *U.S. Private*, pg. 144

ULTRA-FIBER—High Fiber Dietary Supplement Tablets—Alva/Amco Pharmacal Companies, Inc.; *U.S. Private*, pg. 47

ULTRA-FINE—Needles—Becton Dickinson & Company; *U.S. Public*, pg. 199

ULTRA FINE FLAIR—Porous Point Pen—The Gillette Company; *U.S. Public*, pg. 743

ULTRA FLEX—Beryllium Copper Kinitted Wire Mesh—Instrument Specialties Company; *U.S. Private*, pg. 565

ULTRA-FLEX—Envelope Printing Service—Westvaco Corporation; *U.S. Public*, pg. 1762

ULTRA FLOSS—Dental Floss—Oral-B Laboratories; *U.S. Public*, pg. 743

Brand Name Index

ULTRA-FLOW—High Quality Tapes—Recoton Corporation; *U.S. Public*, pg. 1369

ULTRA GAIN—Detergent—The Procter & Gamble Company; *U.S. Public*, pg. 1330

ULTRA-GARD—Industrial Fasteners—Mid-Continent Screw Products Company; *U.S. Private*, pg. 743

ULTRA GEAR—NONE—Sport Obermeyer Ltd., USA; *U.S. Private*, pg. 1026

ULTRA-GLAS 6500—High-Temperature Glass Lining—Pfaudler, Inc.; *U.S. Public*, pg. 1393

ULTRA-GLIDE—Push-Pull Controls—Latshaw Enterprises, Inc.; *U.S. Public*, pg. 979

ULTRA GLOSS 90—Clays For Coating & Filling Paper & Board—Engelhard Corporation; *U.S. Public*, pg. 582

ULTRA GRAPHICS—Paperboard Containers—Union Camp Corporation; *U.S. Public*, pg. 1665

ULTRA-GREEN—Ultralow Cement Castables—A.P. Green Industries, Inc.; *U.S. Public*, pg. 761

ULTRA GREEN—Lawn Turf Seed—The Chas. H. Lilly Co.; *U.S. Private*, pg. 667

ULTRA GREEN LAWN FOOD—Lawn Fertilizer—The Chas. H. Lilly Co.; *U.S. Private*, pg. 667

ULTRA GUARD—Exhibit Quality Film—Seal Products Incorporated; *U.S. Public*, pg. 849

ULTRA-HIDE—Coating—ICI Paints; *Int'l*, pg. 664

ULTRA HYDROGEL COLUMNS—Porous GPC Family—Millipore Corporation; *U.S. Public*, pg. 1112

ULTRA-KAP—Capacitors—Philips Components; *Int'l*, pg. 1054

ULTRA-LAST—Roller Ball Pens—Eversharp Pen Co.; *U.S. Private*, pg. 386

ULTRA-LIFE—Ultrafine Filters—Pall Corporation; *U.S. Public*, pg. 1253

ULTRA-LINER—Fiber Glass Insulation for Ducts—CertainTeed Corporation; *Int'l*, pg. 1170

ULTRA LITE—Binoculars & Microscopes—Swift Instruments, Inc.; *U.S. Private*, pg. 1058

ULTRA-LITE—Fiberwood—Weyerhaeuser Company; *U.S. Public*, pg. 1764

ULTRA-LITE—Panels—Weyerhaeuser Forest Products Company; *U.S. Public*, pg. 1764

ULTRA-LITHO—Envelope Printing Service—Westvaco Corporation; *U.S. Public*, pg. 1762

ULTRA-LOC—Precision Servo—BEI Sensors and Systems Company; *U.S. Public*, pg. 160

ULTRA-LOK—Panel Filter—Donaldson Company, Inc.; *U.S. Public*, pg. 517

ULTRA LOW POROSITY WOVEN—Woven Polyester Vascular Prosthesis—Datascope Corp.; *U.S. Public*, pg. 487

ULTRA/M & M-II—Commercial Roof Insulation—Homasote Company; *U.S. Public*, pg. 831

ULTRA-MAG—Level Controls—Dwyer Instruments Inc.; *U.S. Private*, pg. 350

ULTRA-MAGNETICS—Styli Line—Recoton Corporation; *U.S. Public*, pg. 1369

ULTRA-MAT—Class 19 Fiberglass Backing—Elcor Corporation; *U.S. Public*, pg. 567

ULTRA-MAT—Class 24 Filter Media—Elcor Corporation; *U.S. Public*, pg. 567

ULTRA-MATE—Hook Fastener—Velcro Industries N.V.; *Int'l*, pg. 1462

ULTRA-MATE—High-Tech Fastener Hook—Velcro USA Inc.; *Int'l*, pg. 1462

ULTRA*MAX—Powerful EAS System Which Protects Hard Goods In Businesses With Wide Doors—Sensormatic Electronics Corporation; *U.S. Public*, pg. 1457

ULTRA-MAX ANNUITY—NONE—Keyport Life Insurance Company; *U.S. Private*, pg. 666

ULTRA-MICRON—Can Liners—Amcel Corp.; *U.S. Private*, pg. 48

ULTRA MILK—NONE—Agropur; *Int'l*, pg. 31

ULTRA OXYDOL—Detergent—The Procter & Gamble Company; *U.S. Public*, pg. 1330

ULTRA PAMPERS PLUS—Disposable Diaper—The Procter & Gamble Company; *U.S. Public*, pg. 1330

ULTRA PEP-BACK—Stimulant Caplets—Alva/Amco Pharmacal Companies, Inc.; *U.S. Private*, pg. 47

ULTRA-PERFORMER—Plastic Protective Wrap for Breakable Containers—Kerr Group, Inc.; *U.S. Public*, pg. 952

ULTRA PLUS—NONE—Ganin Tire Co., Inc.; *U.S. Private*, pg. 439

ULTRA PRECISE—Eye Pencils—Cover Girl Cosmetics; *U.S. Public*, pg. 1330

ULTRA PURE—Anodes, Solder—Litton Industries, Inc.; *U.S. Public*, pg. 1002

ULTRA PURE LOGO—NONE—Life Technologies, Inc.; *U.S. Public*, pg. 504

ULTRA PUREX LAUNDRY DETERGENT—NONE—The Dial Corporation; *U.S. Public*, pg. 505

ULTRA PUREX LAUNDRY DETERGENT BLEACH ALTERNATIVE—NONE—The Dial Corporation; *U.S. Public*, pg. 505

ULTRA PUREX LIQUID LAUNDRY FREE AND CLEAR—NONE—The Dial Corporation; *U.S. Public*, pg. 505

ULTRA/R—Insulating Sidewall Sheathing—Homasote Company; *U.S. Public*, pg. 831

ULTRA REPAIR DEP—Deep Conditioners—Dep Corporation; *U.S. Public*, pg. 500

ULTRA RES—Reticle Manufacturing Process—Photronics, Inc.; *U.S. Public*, pg. 1293

ULTRA RETRIEVE—On-Line Document Storage & Retrieval System—CACI International Inc; *U.S. Public*, pg. 272

ULTRA-REZ—NONE—Lawter International, Inc.; *U.S. Public*, pg. 980

ULTRA-RIDE—Seat—Peterbilt Motors Co.; *U.S. Public*, pg. 1247

ULTRA SAFE—Bath & Shower Valves—T & S Brass & Bronze Works, Inc.; *U.S. Private*, pg. 1061

ULTRA SATIN—Paint—Mautz Paint Co.; *U.S. Private*, pg. 715

ULTRA-SEAL—Membrane Closure for Cans—Sonoco Products Company; *U.S. Public*, pg. 1485

ULTRA SERIES—NONE—Therapedic Associates, Inc.; *U.S. Private*, pg. 1079

ULTRA SEVEN—Sleeper Mattresses—Kingsdown, Inc.; *U.S. Private*, pg. 622

ULTRA SHARP—Knives—Douglas/Quikut; *U.S. Public*, pg. 217

ULTRA SHEEN—Cosmetic & Hair Products—Johnson Products Co., Inc.; *U.S. Public*, pg. 915

ULTRA-SHIELD—Lead Shield for Radiosotope Generator for Clinical Laboratory—Mallinckrodt Inc.; *U.S. Public*, pg. 1039

ULTRA-SHIELD—Radiosotope Generators for Clinical Laboratory Use—Mallinckrodt Inc.; *U.S. Public*, pg. 1039

ULTRA-SIL—Siliconized Polyester—Lilly Industries, Inc.; *U.S. Public*, pg. 994

ULTRA SILK—Hosiery—Hanes Hosiery, Inc.; *U.S. Public*, pg. 1434

ULTRA SLIM-FAST—Weight Loss Product—Slim-Fast Foods Company; *U.S. Private*, pg. 1006

ULTRA SLIM-FAST CRUNCH BARS—Low-Calorie Snacks—Slim-Fast Foods Company; *U.S. Private*, pg. 1006

ULTRA SLIM FAST FROZEN ENTREES—Frozen Entrees—ConAgra Frozen Food Company; *U.S. Public*, pg. 427

ULTRA SLIM-FAST LITE N' TASTY SNACKS—Low-Calorie Snacks—Slim-Fast Foods Company; *U.S. Private*, pg. 1006

ULTRA SLIM-FAST NUTRITION BARS—Low-Calorie Snack—Slim-Fast Foods Company; *U.S. Private*, pg. 1006

ULTRA SLIM-FAST PLUS—Weight Loss Product—Slim-Fast Foods Company; *U.S. Private*, pg. 1006

ULTRA SLIM-FAST PUDDING—Low-Calorie Snack—Slim-Fast Foods Company; *U.S. Private*, pg. 1006

ULTRA SLIM-FAST READY-TO-DRINK—Weight Loss Product—Slim-Fast Foods Company; *U.S. Private*, pg. 1006

ULTRA SLIMPAK—Signal Conditioners & Unit Alarms—Action Instruments, Inc.; *U.S. Private*, pg. 15

ULTRA SOFT—Low Force Beryllium Copper EMI Shielding Gaskets—Instrument Specialties Company; *U.S. Private*, pg. 565

ULTRA-SPAN—Steel Truss System—MiTek, Inc.; *Int'l*, pg. 1106

ULTRA SPARK—Automotive Spark Plug Wires—AutoZone, Inc.; *U.S. Public*, pg. 150

ULTRA-SPEED—Dental Film—Eastman Kodak Company; *U.S. Public*, pg. 550

ULTRA SPIC AND SPAN—Cleaning Powder—The Procter & Gamble Company; *U.S. Public*, pg. 1330

ULTRA STAR—Texturizer & Maintenance Prod.—Johnson Products Co., Inc.; *U.S. Public*, pg. 915

ULTRA STEEL—Bedding—The Stearns & Foster Bedding Company; *U.S. Private*, pg. 979

ULTRA STEP—Truck & Van Accessories—Kenco; *U.S. Public*, pg. 1769

ULTRA SUEDE—Suede Like Coating—Red Spot Paint & Varnish Co.; *U.S. Private*, pg. 915

ULTRA SUN FORMULA—Skin Care Prods.—Tanning Research Labs., Inc.; *U.S. Private*, pg. 1068

ULTRA TAPER—Tape Machine—Marsh Company; *U.S. Private*, pg. 707

ULTRA TEARS—Hydroxpropyl Methylcellulose—Alcon Laboratories, Inc.; *Int'l*, pg. 916

ULTRA TEC—Pesticides—Roussel UCLAF S.A.; *Int'l*, pg. 626

ULTRA TECH—NONE—Ganin Tire Co., Inc.; *U.S. Private*, pg. 439

ULTRA-TECHNEKOW—Generators, Milker Kits, Dispensers & Evacuated Vials—Mallinckrodt Inc.; *U.S. Public*, pg. 1039

ULTRA-TEK—Industrial Filter—Donaldson Company, Inc.; *U.S. Public*, pg. 517

ULTRA-THERM—NONE—CertainTeed Corporation; *Int'l*, pg. 1170

ULTRA 3s—NONE—Blaw-Knox Construction Equipment Corporation; *U.S. Public*, pg. 877

ULTRA TIDE—Detergent—The Procter & Gamble Company; *U.S. Public*, pg. 1330

ULTRA TORQUE—Angiographic Catheters & Component Parts—Mallinckrodt Inc.; *U.S. Public*, pg. 1039

ULTRA TOUCH—Nylon—BASF Corporation Fiber Products Division; *Int'l*, pg. 105

ULTRA TREND LAUNDRY DETERGENT—NONE—The Dial Corporation; *U.S. Public*, pg. 505

ULTRA TREND POWDER DETERGENT BLEACH ALTERNATIVE—NONE—The Dial Corporation; *U.S. Public*, pg. 505

ULTRA TUGGER—Puller—Greenlee Textron; *U.S. Public*, pg. 1589

ULTRA 24 WITH EXPRESS 96—Modem—Hayes Microcomputer Products, Inc.; *U.S. Public*, pg. 801

ULTRA TWIN—Paper Towel Dispensers—Georgia-Pacific Corporation; *U.S. Public*, pg. 735

ULTRA TWIST—NONE—Thiokol Corporation; *U.S. Public*, pg. 1596

ULTRA 2000—Wavesoldering System—Electrovert; *Int'l*, pg. 328

ULTRA ULTIMATE—High-Strength & High Wet-Abrasion Resistant—The American Group; *U.S. Private*, pg. 56

ULTRA-VAULT—NONE—Uniflex, Inc.; *U.S. Public*, pg. 1665

ULTRA VELVET—Paint—Mautz Paint Co.; *U.S. Private*, pg. 715

ULTRA VUE—Optical Device—Galileo Corp.; *U.S. Public*, pg. 698

ULTRA-WEAR—UHMWPE Parts—DSM Engineering Plastic Products; *Int'l*, pg. 354

ULTRA-WEB—Filter Medium—Donaldson Company, Inc.; *U.S. Public*, pg. 517

ULTRA-WEB (STYLIZED BLUE)—Air Filter—Donaldson Company, Inc.; *U.S. Public*, pg. 517

ULTRA WHITE 90—Pre Dispersed Coating Pigment—Engelhard Corporation; *U.S. Public*, pg. 582

ULTRA-WISP—Chromotography Systems—Millipore Corporation; *U.S. Public*, pg. 1112

ULTRA-WRAP—Upscale Coordinated Gift Wrap—CPS Corporation; *U.S. Private*, pg. 422

ULTRABAC—Animal Vaccine—SmithKline Beecham plc; *Int'l*, pg. 1264

ULTRABANK—Typesetting Computer, Memory Apparatus—Eastman Kodak Company; *U.S. Public*, pg. 550

ULTRABASE 7—Acrylic Urethane Basecoat—The Sherwin-Williams Company; *U.S. Public*, pg. 1465

ULTRABIN—Corrugated Board Shipping Boxes—Georgia-Pacific Corporation; *U.S. Public*, pg. 735

ULTRABIX—Chemical—Warner-Jenkinson Co.; *U.S. Public*, pg. 1696

ULTRABOND—Perm—Zotos International; *Int'l*, pg. 1236

Brand Name Index

ULTRACAL—Enteral Nutritionals—Bristol-Myers Squibb Company; *U.S. Public*, pg. 253

ULTRACAL—Tube Feeding Formula High in Fiber—Mead Johnson Nutritional Group; *U.S. Public*, pg. 254

ULTRACARE—Contact Lens Care Product—Allergan, Inc.; *U.S. Public*, pg. 46

ULTRACEF—Antibiotic for Infections, Tonsillitis & Pharyngitis—Bristol-Myers Squibb U.S. Pharmaceutical Group; *U.S. Public*, pg. 255

ULTRACLEAN—NONE—Domco Inc.; *Int'l*, pg. 415

ULTRACLEAN—Air Cleaning Machine—Pneumatic Scale Corporation; *U.S. Private*, pg. 118

ULTRACOM—Key Systems—TIE/Communications, Inc.; *U.S. Private*, pg. 1085

ULTRACOMP—Typesetting Keyboards—Eastman Kodak Company; *U.S. Public*, pg. 550

ULTRACOTE—NONE—Kerry Group PLC; *Int'l*, pg. 731

ULTRACOUNT—Typesetting Terminals & Computers—Eastman Kodak Company; *U.S. Public*, pg. 550

ULTRACOUSTIC—NONE—CertainTeed Corporation; *Int'l*, pg. 1170

ULTRACULTURE—Serum-Free Media—BioWhittaker, Inc.; *U.S. Public*, pg. 297

ULTRADEX—Skills Assessment Software—Manpower Inc.; *U.S. Public*, pg. 1042

ULTRADOMA—Serum-Free Media—BioWhittaker, Inc.; *U.S. Public*, pg. 297

ULTRADOMA PF—Serum-Free Media—BioWhittaker, Inc.; *U.S. Public*, pg. 297

ULTRADOSE—Unit Dose Ultrasonic Cleaning Powders—L&R Manufacturing Co.; *U.S. Private*, pg. 638

ULTRADRAW—Drawing Ink—Koh-I-Noor, Inc.; *U.S. Private*, pg. 629

ULTRADUCT—Insulation—CertainTeed Corporation; *Int'l*, pg. 1170

ULTRADUR—Switchgear Enclosure Finishing System—S & C Electric Company; *U.S. Private*, pg. 954

ULTRADURA—Industrial Safety Eyewear—Uvex Safety, Inc.; *Int'l*, pg. 132

ULTRAFFINITY—Affinity Chromatography Columns—Beckman Instruments, Inc.; *U.S. Public*, pg. 199

ULTRAFINER—Water Softening & Purification Equipment—RainSoft Water Treatment Systems; *U.S. Private*, pg. 78

ULTRAFIT—Ear Plugs—Aearo Company; *U.S. Private*, pg. 23

ULTRAFLEX—Chemical AGV Guidepath—Litton Industries, Inc.; *U.S. Public*, pg. 1002

ULTRAFLEX—Furnace—Nordyne Inc.; *U.S. Public*, pg. 1193

ULTRAFLEX SERIES—Multiple Output Modular Power Supplies—Lambda Electronics Inc.; *Int'l*, pg. 1241

ULTRAFLO—Feeding System or Feeder—CTB International Corp.; *U.S. Public*, pg. 284

ULTRAFLOW—Surgical Instruments—Alcon Laboratories, Inc.; *Int'l*, pg. 916

ULTRAFOAM—Television Transmission Cable—General Cable Corporation; *Int'l*, pg. 1486

ULTRAFREE—Cartridge Filter—Millipore Corporation; *U.S. Public*, pg. 1112

ULTRAFUSE—Couplers—Raychem Corporation; *U.S. Public*, pg. 1362

ULTRAGARD—Hybrid Security & Home Automation System—Interactive Technologies, Inc.; *U.S. Public*, pg. 888

ULTRAGARD—Ultrafiltration System—Millipore Corporation; *U.S. Public*, pg. 1112

ULTRAGARD GOLD—Roof Insulation—Johns Manville Corporation; *U.S. Public*, pg. 927

ULTRAGOLD—ULtra High Strength Polyolefin Rope—The American Group; *U.S. Private*, pg. 56

ULTRAGRAF—Computer Graphics Display Workstations—Landmark Systems Inc.; *U.S. Private*, pg. 649

ULTRAGUARD—Industrial Goggles (Safety)—Uvex Safety, Inc.; *Int'l*, pg. 132

ULTRAJECT—Prefilled Syringe—Mallinckrodt Inc.; *U.S. Public*, pg. 1039

ULTRAJECT—Prefilled Plastic Syringes Containing Injectable Pharmaceuticals—Mallinckrodt Inc.; *U.S. Public*, pg. 1039

ULTRAKAN—Containers—Sealright Company, Inc.; *U.S. Public*, pg. 1451

ULTRAKAR—NONE—CTB International Corp.; *U.S. Public*, pg. 284

ULTRALEATHER—Fabric—Springs Industries, Inc.; *U.S. Public*, pg. 1499

ULTRALIGHT—Light Cream Cheese Based Products—BC-USA; *Int'l*, pg. 201

ULTRALINE—High Strength Polyolefin Rope—The American Group; *U.S. Private*, pg. 56

ULTRALINE—Grinder—Bryant Grinder Corp.; *U.S. Private*, pg. 461

ULTRALINE—Graphic Arts Films & Chemicals—Eastman Kodak Company; *U.S. Public*, pg. 550

ULTRALINER—Polymer Liner—Fasson Films; *U.S. Public*, pg. 153

ULTRALITE—Cooling Towers—Baltimore Aircoil Company; *U.S. Private*, pg. 68

ULTRALITE—NONE—CertainTeed Corporation; *Int'l*, pg. 1170

ULTRALITE—Cooling Towers—Justin Industries, Inc.; *U.S. Public*, pg. 936

ULTRALITE—Auto Finishing—RPM, Inc.; *U.S. Public*, pg. 1356

ULTRALOC—Seat Recline System—Enidine Incorporated; *U.S. Private*, pg. 377

ULTRALUX—NONE—Chemfab Corporation; *U.S. Public*, pg. 344

ULTRA-LYTE—Menswear Interlining—Specialty Textile Products; *U.S. Private*, pg. 1023

ULTRAM TABLETS—NONE—Ortho-McNeil Pharmaceutical Corporation; *U.S. Public*, pg. 929

ULTRAMAR—Service Stations—Ultramar Diamond Shamrock Corporation; *U.S. Public*, pg. 1663

ULTRAMET—Ultrasonic Cleaner—Buehler, Limited; *U.S. Public*, pg. 574

ULTRAMET-L GASKLEEN—Filter Assembly—Pall Corporation; *U.S. Public*, pg. 1253

ULTRAMIN—Filters—Wavetek Communications Div.; *U.S. Private*, pg. 1155

ULTRAMITE—Multifunction Ind. Cal.—Thermo Electric Co., Inc.; *U.S. Private*, pg. 1080

ULTRAMOVABLE—Steel Wall Panel—Clestra Hauserman, Inc.; *U.S. Public*, pg. 569

ULTRAOAK—Premium Prefinished Moulding—ABT Building Products Corporation; *Int'l*, pg. 20

ULTRAPAK—Column Packing Materials & Columns—Beckman Instruments, Inc.; *U.S. Public*, pg. 199

ULTRAPAK—Wavesoldering System—Electrovert; *Int'l*, pg. 328

ULTRAPAK—Maximum Furniture Protection—Interstate Van Lines, Inc.; *U.S. Private*, pg. 573

ULTRAPHAN—Laminated Products—Alusuisse-Lonza Holding Ltd.; *Int'l*, pg. 66

ULTRAPHONE—Wireless Telecommunications System—InterDigital Communications Corp.; *U.S. Public*, pg. 889

ULTRAPLACE—SMC Placement System—Universal Instruments Corporation; *U.S. Public*, pg. 522

ULTRAPLAS—Additive for Masonry Cement—Westvaco Corporation; *U.S. Public*, pg. 1762

ULTRAPLY 78—Tires—Bridgestone/Firestone, Inc.; *Int'l*, pg. 213

ULTRAPORE—Column Packing Materials & Columns—Beckman Instruments, Inc.; *U.S. Public*, pg. 199

ULTRAPREP—Preparative Liquid Chromatography Columns—Beckman Instruments, Inc.; *U.S. Public*, pg. 199

ULTRAPULSE—Surgical Laser—Coherent, Inc.; *U.S. Public*, pg. 395

ULTRAPURE—Anodes—Kester Solder; *U.S. Public*, pg. 1003

ULTRASCAN—Ultrasonic Imaging Apparatus—Alcon Laboratories, Inc.; *Int'l*, pg. 916

ULTRASEAL—Engine System Parts—Echlin Inc.; *U.S. Public*, pg. 560

ULTRASEED—High Quality Seed—Asgrow Seed Company; *Int'l*, pg. 1048

ULTRASIL—Column Packing Material & Columns—Beckman Instruments, Inc.; *U.S. Public*, pg. 199

ULTRASIL-HM—High Modulus Silicone Construction Sealant—Ohio Sealants Inc.; *Int'l*, pg. 802

ULTRASIL-LM—Low Modulus Silicone Construction Sealant—Ohio Sealants Inc.; *Int'l*, pg. 802

ULTRASIL II—Silicone Bath Panel Sealant—Ohio Sealants Inc.; *Int'l*, pg. 802

ULTRASKILL—Skill Assessment Program—Manpower Inc.; *U.S. Public*, pg. 1042

ULTRASPONGE—Superabsorbent—IGI, Inc.; *U.S. Public*, pg. 855

ULTRASONIC—Phaco Handpieces—Alcon Laboratories, Inc.; *Int'l*, pg. 916

ULTRASONIC DIPLOG—NONE—Western Atlas Logging Services; *U.S. Public*, pg. 1757

ULTRASPEC—Industrial Safety Eyewear—Uvex Safety, Inc.; *Int'l*, pg. 132

ULTRASPERSE—Boiler Treatment Products—BetzDearborn Inc.; *U.S. Public*, pg. 226

ULTRASPHERE—Column Packing Material & Columns—Beckman Instruments, Inc.; *U.S. Public*, pg. 199

ULTRASPHEROGEL—Column Packing Materials & Columns—Beckman Instruments, Inc.; *U.S. Public*, pg. 199

ULTRASTAK—Packaging Materials & Container Board—Georgia-Pacific Corporation; *U.S. Public*, pg. 735

ULTRASTAK—Stack Plate—Millipore Corporation; *U.S. Public*, pg. 1112

ULTRASTEEL—Chrome Truck Wheels—Redco Corporation; *U.S. Private*, pg. 915

ULTRASTRENGTH—Burst Strength PET Label—Kal Grafx; *U.S. Public*, pg. 387

ULTRASTRONG—High-Strength & High-Abrasion Resistant Rope—The American Group; *U.S. Private*, pg. 56

ULTRASTYRAGEL—Linear Column—Millipore Corporation; *U.S. Public*, pg. 1112

ULTRASUEDE—Fabric—Springs Industries, Inc.; *U.S. Public*, pg. 1499

ULTRASWIM—Specialty Shampoo, Conditioner, Soap—Chattem, Inc.; *U.S. Public*, pg. 341

ULTRASWIM—Shampoo, Conditioner & Skin Bar—Chattem, Inc., Consumer Products Division; *U.S. Public*, pg. 341

ULTRASWITCH—Actuators—Flowserve Corporation; *U.S. Public*, pg. 658

ULTRASYSTEM—Typesetting Terminals & Computers—Eastman Kodak Company; *U.S. Public*, pg. 550

ULTRATAG—Diagnostic Agents for use in Humans—Mallinckrodt Inc.; *U.S. Public*, pg. 1039

ULTRATAG RBC—Diagnostic Kit—Mallinckrodt Inc.; *U.S. Public*, pg. 1039

ULTRATARD—Product for Diabetes Care—Novo Nordisk A/S; *Int'l*, pg. 987

ULTRATEC—Graphic Arts Films, Papers, Chemicals & Contract Screen—Eastman Kodak Company; *U.S. Public*, pg. 550

ULTRATECH—Uncoated Paper—The Mead Corporation; *U.S. Public*, pg. 1074

ULTRATHENE—Ethylene-VinylAcetate Copolymer Resins—Millennium Petrochemicals, Inc.; *Int'l*, pg. 594

ULTRATHERM—Beverage Cooler—Igloo Products Corporation; *U.S. Public*, pg. 265

ULTRATONES—NONE—Kerry Group PLC; *Int'l*, pg. 731

ULTRATORCH—Soldering Iron, Torch, Flameless Heat Tool-Butane FiredPowered—Master Appliance Corp.; *U.S. Private*, pg. 713

ULTRAVATE—Dermatological Therapy Product—Bristol-Myers Squibb Company; *U.S. Public*, pg. 253

ULTRAVENT—Aerosol Delivery System—Mallinckrodt Inc.; *U.S. Public*, pg. 1039

ULTRAVENT—Medical Instruments-Aerosol Delivery Apparatus—Mallinckrodt Inc.; *U.S. Public*, pg. 1039

ULTRAVISION—Illuminated Assembly Magnifier—Stocker & Yale, Inc.; *U.S. Public*, pg. 1518

ULTRAVUE—Ophthalmic Lenses—American Optical Corporation; *U.S. Private*, pg. 60

ULTRAWALL—Wall Product—USG Interiors, Inc.; *U.S. Public*, pg. 1660

ULTRAWHEELS—In-Line Skates—First Team Sports Inc.; *U.S. Public*, pg. 638

ULTRAZINC—Cyanide Zinc Brighteners—LeaRonal, Inc.; *U.S. Public*, pg. 982

ULTRAZYME—Contact Lens Care Product—Allergan, Inc.; *U.S. Public*, pg. 46

ULTREFINER—Water Softening & Purification Equipment—RainSoft Water Treatment Systems; *U.S. Private*, pg. 78

ULTRESS—Haircolor—Bristol-Myers Squibb Company; *U.S. Public*, pg. 253

ULTREX—NONE—Burlington Industries, Inc.; *U.S. Public*, pg. 268

ULTREX—Razor Blades—Warner-Lambert Company; *U.S. Public*, pg. 1738

ULTRO—Electrical Wire & Cable—BICC Brand-Rex; *Int'l*, pg. 120

ULTRON—3D Nylon—Monsanto Company; *U.S. Public*, pg. 1124

ULTRON—Staple Nylon Yarns—Solutia Inc.; *U.S. Public*, pg. 1483

ULTRONIX—Resistors/Potentiometers—Vishay Intertechnology, Inc.; *U.S. Public*, pg. 1721

ULTRX—Stylized Composite Enclosures—Hoffman Engineering Company; *U.S. Public*, pg. 1273

ULYSSE—Car—Fiat Auto Ireland Ltd.; *Int'l*, pg. 481

UMBRELLA COVERAGE—NONE—Elcor Corporation; *U.S. Public*, pg. 567

UNARCO MATERIAL HANDLING—Storage Racks—Hy-Tek Material Handling, Inc.; *U.S. Private*, pg. 550

UNASYN IM/IV—Sulbactam/Ampicillin—Pfizer Inc.; *U.S. Public*, pg. 1281

UNASYN ORAL—Sultamicillin—Pfizer Inc.; *U.S. Public*, pg. 1281

UNBRAKO—Range of Socket Screws—Precision Fasteners Ltd.; *U.S. Public*, pg. 1420

UNBRAKO—Socket Screw Prods.—SPS Technologies, Inc.; *U.S. Public*, pg. 1419

UNCANNY—Can & Bag Opener—The Rival Company; *U.S. Public*, pg. 1391

UNCLE BEN'S—Rice—Master Foods; *U.S. Private*, pg. 707

UNCLE BEN'S BEANS & RICE—NONE—Uncle Ben's, Inc.; *U.S. Private*, pg. 707

UNCLE BEN'S CINNAMON & RAISINS RICE PUDDING—NONE—Uncle Ben's, Inc.; *U.S. Private*, pg. 707

UNCLE BEN'S CONVERTED BRAND—Rice—Uncle Ben's, Inc.; *U.S. Private*, pg. 707

UNCLE BEN'S COOKIN' SAUCES—Packaged Sauce Mixes—Uncle Ben's, Inc.; *U.S. Private*, pg. 707

UNCLE BEN'S COUNTRY INN RICE DISHES—NONE—Uncle Ben's, Inc.; *U.S. Private*, pg. 707

UNCLE BEN'S HEARTY SOUP—NONE—Uncle Ben's, Inc.; *U.S. Private*, pg. 707

UNCLE BEN'S LONG GRAIN & WILD RICE—NONE—Uncle Ben's, Inc.; *U.S. Private*, pg. 707

UNCLE BEN'S SPECIALTY RICES—NONE—Uncle Ben's, Inc.; *U.S. Private*, pg. 707

UNCLE BEN'S STUFFING MIX TRADITIONAL SAGE—NONE—Uncle Ben's, Inc.; *U.S. Private*, pg. 707

UNCLE HENRY KNIVES—Pocket, Hunting & Fillet Knives w/ Staglon Handles—Imperial Schrade Corp.; *U.S. Private*, pg. 559

UNCLE TOBYS—Snack Foods, Breakfast Cereals—Goodman Fielder Limited; *Int'l*, pg. 555

UNCOLOR—Hair Color Remover—Clairol, Inc.; *U.S. Public*, pg. 254

UNCOPPER—PB Tubing & Fittings—Genova Products, Inc.; *U.S. Private*, pg. 447

UNCUT—Music & Lifestyle Magazine—IPC Magazines Limited; *Int'l*, pg. 651

UNDER CONTROL BY FLEXEES—Control Garments—True Form Intimate Apparel; *U.S. Private*, pg. 697

UNDER PRIME LINE—Facilities Line of Credit—SLM Holding Corp.; *U.S. Public*, pg. 1419

UNDER WONDER BY FLEXEES—Control Garments—True Form Intimate Apparel; *U.S. Private*, pg. 697

UNDERCOUNTER—Refrigerator & Freezer—Foster Refrigerator Corporation; *U.S. Private*, pg. 421

UNDERCOVER—Labels—Avery Dennison Corporation Label Group; *U.S. Public*, pg. 153

UNDERDAWG—Cable Puller for Underground Cable—Sherman & Reilly, Inc.; *U.S. Private*, pg. 993

UNDERGEAR—Men's Activewear & Fashion Underwear Catalog—Hanover Direct, Inc.; *U.S. Public*, pg. 782

UNDERGEAR—Undergarments for Men—Hanover Direct Pennsylvania, Inc.; *U.S. Public*, pg. 782

UNDERGRADER—Under-Ground Grader—Arnold Machinery Company; *U.S. Private*, pg. 84

UNDEROOS—Children's Underwear—Fruit of the Loom, Inc.; *U.S. Public*, pg. 685

UNDERSEAL—Auto Underbody Protective Coatings—3M; *U.S. Public*, pg. 1604

UNDERSTANDING TECHNOLOGY—Basic Text Explaining Industrial Technology—Goodheart-Willcox Publisher; *U.S. Private*, pg. 464

UNDERWOOD—Deviled Meat Spreads—The Pillsbury Company; *Int'l*, pg. 411

UNDO—Pet Odor Decontaminant—Surco Products, Inc.; *U.S. Private*, pg. 1056

UNEEDA—Biscuit—Nabisco Inc.; *U.S. Public*, pg. 1355

UNFORGETTABLE—Fragrance—Revlon, Inc.; *U.S. Private*, pg. 689

UNGAR—Soldering Equipment—Cooper Industries, Inc.; *U.S. Public*, pg. 442

UNGARO—Intimate Apparel—Warnaco Inc.; *U.S. Public*, pg. 1738

THE UNGARO COLLECTION—NONE—Crown Crafts, Inc.; *U.S. Public*, pg. 465

UNGERMANN-BASS—NONE—UB Networks; *Int'l*, pg. 924

UNGLASS—Polycarbonate Water Cooler Bottles—Liqui-Box Corporation; *U.S. Public*, pg. 1000

UNGUENTINE—Burn Relief—Mentholatum Company; *Int'l*, pg. 1126

UNI—Side Chair—Vecta; *U.S. Private*, pg. 1038

UNI BALL—Liquid Prover—Perry Equipment Corporation; *U.S. Private*, pg. 855

UNI-BALL—Rolller Ball Pens—Sanford Corporation; *U.S. Public*, pg. 1178

UNI-BAST—Basting Blend for Poultry—Crompton & Knowles Ingredient Technology Corp.; *U.S. Public*, pg. 459

UNI-BOX—Plastic Product—Uniflex, Inc.; *U.S. Public*, pg. 1665

UNI-BRAID—Combines Single Plaits of Small Diameter, Tiesed, Tension Controlled—Titeflex Corporation; *Int'l*, pg. 1340

UNI-CAL—Industrial Colorant—Veba AG; *Int'l*, pg. 1454

UNI-CAM—Muffler—Arvin Industries, Inc.; *U.S. Public*, pg. 136

UNI-COAT—Titanium Carbide Coated Inserts—Rogers Tool Works, Inc.; *U.S. Public*, pg. 950

UNI-COAT—PVC Coated Duct & Fittings—United McGill Corp.; *U.S. Private*, pg. 1122

UNI-CORD—Plastic Product—Uniflex, Inc.; *U.S. Public*, pg. 1665

UNI-DAMP—Dampener Cover—Jomac, Inc.; *U.S. Private*, pg. 595

UNI-DOSE—Scientific Glassware for Laboratory Use—Wheaton Inc.; *Int'l*, pg. 67

UNI-DRILL—Single Flute Solid Carbide Drill—National Twist Drill Div.; *U.S. Public*, pg. 1370

UNI-DRILL—Single Flute Solid Carbide Drill—Regal-Beloit Corporation; *U.S. Public*, pg. 1370

UNI-DRUM—Bulk Transfer, Pump & Store—Graco Inc.; *U.S. Public*, pg. 756

UNI-DYME—NONE—Union Camp Chemicals; *U.S. Public*, pg. 1666

UNI FIT—Couplers—Rain Bird Sprinklers Manufacturing Corp.; *U.S. Private*, pg. 907

UNI-FRAME—Cage System Floor Stand—CTB International Corp.; *U.S. Public*, pg. 284

UNI-FRAME—Upholstered Furniture Frame Stock—Union Camp Corporation; *U.S. Public*, pg. 1665

UNI-GRIP—Multi Surface Dry Fog—Devoe Paint; *Int'l*, pg. 663

UNI-GRIP—Multi Surface Dry Fog—ICI Paints; *Int'l*, pg. 664

UNI-GRIP—Acrylic Duct Sealer—United McGill Corp.; *U.S. Private*, pg. 1122

UNI-GRIP-WB—Acrylic Dry Fog—Devoe Paint; *Int'l*, pg. 663

UNI-HOUSING—Pressurized Enclosure Panel Systems—United McGill Corp.; *U.S. Private*, pg. 1122

UNI-LIFT—Mechanical Actuators—Templeton, Kenly & Co., Inc.; *U.S. Private*, pg. 1075

UNI-MATE—NONE—Union Camp Chemicals; *U.S. Public*, pg. 1666

UNI-MOD—Standard Pre-Engineered Water Treatment Products—Cochrane, Inc.; *U.S. Public*, pg. 456

UNI-MODULE-DIP—Inserter—Universal Instruments Corporation; *U.S. Public*, pg. 522

UNI-PAC—Standard Pre-Engineered Water Treatment Products—Cochrane, Inc.; *U.S. Public*, pg. 456

UNI-PAK—NONE—Allied Diagnostic Imaging Resources, Inc.; *U.S. Public*, pg. 282

UNI-PAK—Zinc-Rich Coating—The Valspar Corp. Protective Coatings Div.; *U.S. Public*, pg. 1707

UNI-PLUG—Plastic Screen Anchor—Gunnebo Fastening Corp.; *U.S. Private*, pg. 488

UNI-PLUS—Multi-Purpose Drill Bits—American Tool Companies, Inc.; *U.S. Private*, pg. 63

UNI-PRIME—Electrodeposition Coatings—PPG Industries, Inc.; *U.S. Public*, pg. 1245

UNI-RACK—Merchandise Displays—The Stanley Works; *U.S. Public*, pg. 1508

UNI-REZ—NONE—Union Camp Chemicals; *U.S. Public*, pg. 1666

UNI-REZ—Synthetic Resins—Union Camp Corporation; *U.S. Public*, pg. 1665

UNI-RIB—Standing Ribbed Duct—United McGill Corp.; *U.S. Private*, pg. 1122

UNI-RUPTER—Single-Pole Load Switching Device—S & C Electric Company; *U.S. Private*, pg. 954

UNI-SEAL—Spiral Duct—United McGill Corp.; *U.S. Private*, pg. 1122

UNI-SYN—Carburetor Synchronizer—Edelbrock Corp.; *U.S. Public*, pg. 563

UNI-TAC—NONE—Union Camp Chemicals; *U.S. Public*, pg. 1666

UNI-TAP—Nylon Drive Anchor—Gunnebo Fastening Corp.; *U.S. Private*, pg. 488

UNI-TOTE—Plastic Product—Uniflex, Inc.; *U.S. Public*, pg. 1665

UNI-TRAC—Mobile Filing Cabinets—Tab Products Co.; *U.S. Public*, pg. 1524

UNI-TREAT—Process Used On Bars—Joseph T. Ryerson & Son, Inc.; *U.S. Public*, pg. 879

UNI-TURF—Synthetic Sports Surfaces—American Biltrite Inc.; *U.S. Public*, pg. 68

UNI-VAULT—NONE—Uniflex, Inc.; *U.S. Public*, pg. 1665

UNI-WELD—Cement & Duct Fittings—United McGill Corp.; *U.S. Public*, pg. 1122

UNIBAR—Common Bar Belt Fasteners—Clipper Belt Lacer Company; *U.S. Private*, pg. 413

UNIBEACON—Lights—Unity Manufacturing Co.; *U.S. Private*, pg. 1126

UNIBEAM—Conveyor Components—Jervis B. Webb Company; *U.S. Private*, pg. 1156

UNIBILT—Cab Sleeper System—Peterbilt Motors Co.; *U.S. Public*, pg. 1247

UNIBILT—Conveyors, Enclosed Track—Jervis B. Webb Company; *U.S. Private*, pg. 1156

UNIBIT—Step Drills—American Tool Companies, Inc.; *U.S. Private*, pg. 63

UNIBRASS—Tubing Access.—Outokumpu American Brass Co.; *Int'l*, pg. 1016

UNIC—NONE—Bentley Leathers Inc.; *Int'l*, pg. 187

UNIC—Franchised Supermarkets—GIB Group; *Int'l*, pg. 532

UNICABLE—Insulated Wires & Cables—General Cable Corporation; *Int'l*, pg. 1486

UNICAN—Key Blanks—Ilco Unican Corp.; *Int'l*, pg. 1432

UNICAN—Key Blanks—Unican Security Systems Ltd.; *Int'l*, pg. 1432

UNICAP—Vitamins—Pharmacia & Upjohn; *Int'l*, pg. 1048

UNICAP—NONE—Pharmacia & Upjohn, Inc.; *Int'l*, pg. 1047

UNICEL—Vibration Monitor—IRD Mechanalysis, Inc. (U.S.A.); *U.S. Public*, pg. 789

UNICHEM—Pharmaceuticals—Alliance UniChem PLC; *Int'l*, pg. 57

UNICHEM—NONE—BJ Services Company; *U.S. Public*, pg. 161

UNICHEM—Pump—Union Pump Company; *U.S. Private*, pg. 1119

UNICHIPS—Highlander Potato Chips—Armando Testa S.p.A; *Int'l*, pg. 1377

UNICIRCLE—Retread System—The Goodyear Tire & Rubber Company; *U.S. Public*, pg. 752

UNICLEAN—Clean Room Services—UniFirst Corporation; *U.S. Public*, pg. 1665

UNICOAT—Universal Automotive Coating Systems—Morton Automotive Coatings; *U.S. Public*, pg. 1135

UNICOAT—Coating—Morton International Inc.; *U.S. Public*, pg. 1135

UNICODE—IEC Listed Products—Appleton Electric Co.; *U.S. Public*, pg. 572

UNICOIL—Transformer/reactor—Tech-Tran Corporation; *U.S. Private*, pg. 560

UNICOM—Conveyors—The Buschman Co.; *U.S. Private*, pg. 188

UNICOMB—Drill & Tap Combination—National Twist Drill Div.; *U.S. Public*, pg. 1370

UNICOMB—Type of Drill & Tap Combination—Regal-Beloit Corporation; *U.S. Public*, pg. 1370

UNICOMMANDER—Remote Control—Sony Electronics; *Int'l*, pg. 1281

UNICONTRAST—Photo Paper—Eastman Kodak Company; *U.S. Public*, pg. 550

UNICORN—Darts Equip.—Sportcraft Ltd.; *U.S. Private*, pg. 1026

UNICRAFT—Mausoleums—Rock of Ages Corporation; *U.S. Public*, pg. 1396

UNICREPE—Resins Used in the Manufacture of Paper—Georgia-Pacific Corporation; *U.S. Public*, pg. 735

UNICURE—Retread Equipment—Admiral Heintz, Inc.; *U.S. Public*, pg. 1143

UNIDAD HERMETICA—Compressors—Electrolux, AB; *Int'l*, pg. 438

UNIDEX—Rotary Switches—Oak Grigsby; *U.S. Public*, pg. 1209

UNIDOZEN—Packaging Machines, Folding Cartons—The Mead Corporation; *U.S. Public*, pg. 1074

UNIDRESS—One-Piece Ostomy Product—Bristol-Myers Squibb Company; *U.S. Public*, pg. 253

UNIDYNE—Directional Dynamic Microphone—Shure Brothers Incorporated; *U.S. Private*, pg. 997

UNIFACE—NONE—Compuware Corporation; *U.S. Public*, pg. 423

UNIFILO—Continuous Strand Mat—CertainTeed Corporation; *Int'l*, pg. 1170

UNIFIX—Photgraphic Fixer—Eastman Kodak Company; *U.S. Public*, pg. 550

UNIFLAKE—Particle Board—Union Camp Corporation; *U.S. Public*, pg. 1665

UNIFLEX—Flexible Machining Equip.—Liberty Precision Industries; *U.S. Private*, pg. 666

UNIFLEX—Power Transmission—Lovejoy Inc.; *U.S. Private*, pg. 677

UNIFLEX—NONE—Uniflex, Inc.; *U.S. Public*, pg. 1665

UNIFLEX GRIDS—Metallic Grids Inside Mattresses—Kingsdown, Inc.; *U.S. Private*, pg. 622

UNIFLO—Sterile Disposable Syringe Filter—Schleicher & Schuell, Inc.; *Int'l*, pg. 1206

UNIFLOOD—Sealed Beam Incandescent Lamps—General Electric Canada Inc.; *U.S. Public*, pg. 713

UNIFORCE—Staffing Service—Comforce/Uniforce Staffing Services; *U.S. Public*, pg. 409

THE UNIFORM PEOPLE—Uniform Programs—Cintas Corporation; *U.S. Public*, pg. 370

UNIFY—Computer Software—Unify Corporation; *U.S. Public*, pg. 1665

UNIFY VISION—Computer Software—Unify Corporation; *U.S. Public*, pg. 1665

UNIGAP—Arrester—Kearney Company; *U.S. Public*, pg. 444

UNIGARD—Insurance Service—Unigard Indemnity Co.; *Int'l*, pg. 345

UNIGARD—Insurance Services—Unigard Insurance Co.; *Int'l*, pg. 345

UNIGATE—Milk—Unigate PLC; *Int'l*, pg. 1433

UNIGRAPHICS—Cad/Cam System—McDonnell Aircraft & Missile Systems Div.; *U.S. Public*, pg. 241

UNIGRO—Soil Products—L & L Nursery Supply, Inc.; *U.S. Private*, pg. 638

UNIGROUP—Office Interior Systems—Haworth, Inc.; *U.S. Public*, pg. 511

UNIHIB—Water Treatment Chemicals—Lonza Inc.; *Int'l*, pg. 67

UNIJET—Spray Nozzle—Spraying Systems Co.; *U.S. Private*, pg. 1026

UNILAM—Casing—Devro-Teepak, Inc.; *Int'l*, pg. 408

UNILETS—Conduit Bodies—Appleton Electric Co.; *U.S. Public*, pg. 572

UNILIGN—Pump—Union Pump Company; *U.S. Private*, pg. 1119

UNILINE—Wormgear Reducer Series—Regal-Beloit Corporation; *U.S. Public*, pg. 1370

UNILINE—Special Synthetic Rope—Sherman & Reilly, Inc.; *U.S. Private*, pg. 993

UNILINTEL—Lintels—British Steel Plc; *Int'l*, pg. 220

UNILITE—Cooling Towers—Baltimore Aircoil Company; *U.S. Private*, pg. 68

UNILITE—Veneered Doors & Plywood Panels—Georgia-Pacific Corporation; *U.S. Public*, pg. 735

UNILITE—Electronic Ignition Kit/System—Mallory, Inc.; *U.S. Private*, pg. 698

UNILITE—Lights—Unity Manufacturing Co.; *U.S. Private*, pg. 1126

UNILITE-LSERIES—Cooling Towers—Baltimore Aircoil Company; *U.S. Private*, pg. 68

UNILOC—Filter Cartridge—Pall Corporation; *U.S. Public*, pg. 1253

UNILOC—Industrial Instrumentation—Rosemount Analytical, Uniloc Div.; *U.S. Public*, pg. 574

UNILON—Plastic Casing—Devro-Teepak, Inc.; *Int'l*, pg. 408

UNILOY—Blowmolding Machinery—Johnson Controls, Inc.; *U.S. Public*, pg. 932

UNILUX—Paint—Pratt & Lambert United, Inc.; *U.S. Public*, pg. 1466

UNIMAC—On-Premise Laundry Equipment—Raytheon Appliances; *U.S. Public*, pg. 1366

UNIMATCH—NONE—Jason Industrial, Inc.; *U.S. Private*, pg. 583

UNIMATCH—Microphones & Plugs—Sony Electronics; *Int'l*, pg. 1281

UNIMATIC—High Voltage Electrical Splices—The Chardon Rubber Co.; *U.S. Private*, pg. 229

UNIMAX—Material for Model Aircraft Kits—Baltek Corporation; *U.S. Public*, pg. 171

UNIMODE—Fire Alarm System—ADT Security Services, Inc.; *U.S. Public*, pg. 1649

UNIMODULE—One Piece Electric Clutch/Brake—Warner Electric Industrial Products Division; *U.S. Public*, pg. 480

UNIMOG—NONE—Daimler-Benz Aktiengesellschaft; *Int'l*, pg. 366

UNIMOUNT—Stock Preparation—Beloit Corporation; *U.S. Public*, pg. 789

UNIMOUNT—Modular Electric Motors—U.S. Electrical Motor Division; *U.S. Public*, pg. 573

UNINIP—Calendar—Beloit Corporation; *U.S. Public*, pg. 789

UNION—Valves—The Wm. Powell Company; *U.S. Private*, pg. 877

UNION—Non-Metallic Outlet Boxes—Thomas & Betts Corporation; *U.S. Public*, pg. 1597

UNION—Underwear—Union Underwear Co., Inc.; *U.S. Public*, pg. 686

UNION—Farm & Garden Tools—UnionTools, Inc.; *U.S. Public*, pg. 17

UNION—Wire Rope—Wire Rope Corporation of America, Inc.; *U.S. Private*, pg. 1184

UNION CITY—Chairs—Union City Chair Co.; *U.S. Private*, pg. 170

UNION ELECTRIC COMPANY—Electric Generation & Distribution—AmerenUE; *U.S. Public*, pg. 66

UNION GOLD—Farm & Garden Tools—UnionTools, Inc.; *U.S. Public*, pg. 17

UNION LOCK—Locks & Keys—Sime Darby Berhad; *Int'l*, pg. 1249

UNION PLANTERS—Bank—Union Planters Bank; *U.S. Public*, pg. 1669

UNION SPECIAL—Industrial Sewing Machines—Union Special Corp.; *Int'l*, pg. 716

UNION SPECIAL INTERNATIONAL TRADE CORP.—Used Machinery—Union Special Corp.; *Int'l*, pg. 716

UNION STEEL—Metal Products—Email Limited; *Int'l*, pg. 450

UNION WORKMAN—Loose Leaf Chewing Tobacco—Conwood Company L.P.; *U.S. Private*, pg. 272

UNIONBAY—Young Men's, Young Contemporary & Boys Sportswear—Seattle Pacific Industries, Inc.; *U.S. Private*, pg. 980

UNIPAC—Induction Melting Systems—Inductotherm Corp.; *U.S. Private*, pg. 560

UNIPAC—NONE—The Timken Company; *U.S. Public*, pg. 1617

UNIPAK—Surgical Kits—Alcon Laboratories, Inc.; *Int'l*, pg. 916

UNIPAK—Software—Data I/O Corporation; *U.S. Public*, pg. 486

UNIPASS DRILL 'N' TAP—Drill & Tap on the Same Blank—Regal-Beloit Corporation; *U.S. Public*, pg. 1370

UNIPASS TAPER PIPE DRILL 'N' TAP—Drill & Tap on the Same Blank Tapered—Regal-Beloit Corporation; *U.S. Public*, pg. 1370

UNIPECO—Writing Instruments—Union Pen Company; *U.S. Private*, pg. 1119

UNIPEDIC—Mattress—The Spring Air Company; *U.S. Private*, pg. 1027

UNIPHASE—Coalescer Filter—Pneumatic Products Corp.; *U.S. Public*, pg. 1676

UNIPHYL—Sustained Release Theophyline Preparation—Otsuka Pharmaceutical Co., Ltd.; *Int'l*, pg. 1013

UNIPIX—Picks—Ilco Unican Corp.; *Int'l*, pg. 1432

UNIPIX—Picks—Unican Security Systems Ltd.; *Int'l*, pg. 1432

UNIPLEX—Casing—Devro-Teepak, Inc.; *Int'l*, pg. 408

UNIPOL—Polyethylene Production Process—Union Carbide Corporation; *U.S. Public*, pg. 1666

UNIPORT—Telephony Middleware—Precision Systems, Inc.; *U.S. Public*, pg. 1321

UNIPOWER—Coml. & Indus. Heating Equip.—Midco International Inc.; *U.S. Private*, pg. 744

UNIPREP—General Sample Filtration—Whatman Inc.; *Int'l*, pg. 1498

UNIPRODUX—NONE—Mineralac Co.; *U.S. Private*, pg. 750

UNIQUAT—Water Treatment Chemicals—Lonza Inc.; *Int'l*, pg. 67

UNIQUE—Smokeless Powder—Hercules Incorporated; *U.S. Public*, pg. 809

UNIQUE—Catfood—Ralston Purina Company; *U.S. Public*, pg. 1359

UNIQUE DESIGNER SERIES—Bakery Show Cases—Columbus Show Case Company; *U.S. Private*, pg. 257

UNIQUOTE—Mortgage Score Service—Fair, Isaac and Company, Inc.; *U.S. Public*, pg. 609

UNIRACK—Tobacco Holding Racks—Gas-Fired Products, Inc.; *U.S. Private*, pg. 440

UNIRACK—Lights—Unity Manufacturing Co.; *U.S. Private*, pg. 1126

UNIRETIC—NONE—Schwarz Pharma Inc.; *Int'l*, pg. 1211

UNIROYAL—Tires—Continental AG; *Int'l*, pg. 327

UNIROYAL—Passenger & Light Truck Tires—Michelin Americas Small Tires (MAST); *Int'l*, pg. 322

UNIROYAL—Tires—Michelin North America; *Int'l*, pg. 322

UNIROYAL PASSENGER & LIGHT TRUCK TIRES—NONE—Michelin North America (Canada) Inc.; *Int'l*, pg. 322

UNISAN—Private Label Sanitation Products—United Stationers Inc.; *U.S. Public*, pg. 1689

UNISEA—Seafood Products—UniSea Foods, Inc.; *Int'l*, pg. 940

UNISET—Powder Actuated Products—Gunnebo Fastening Corp.; *U.S. Private*, pg. 488

UNISETTER—Photo Typesetters—AGFA EPS Division; *Int'l*, pg. 172

UNISIL—Electrical Steel Sheet—British Steel Plc; *Int'l*, pg. 220

UNISITE—Hardware—Data I/O Corporation; *U.S. Public*, pg. 486

UNISOL—Pres. Free Unit Dose Saline Solution—Alcon Laboratories, Inc.; *Int'l*, pg. 916

UNISOL—Preservative-free, pH-Balanced Saline Solution—Wesley-Jessen; *U.S. Private*, pg. 111

UNISOL 4—Preservative-free Saline Solution—Alcon Laboratories, Inc.; *Int'l*, pg. 916

UNISOL PLUS—NONE—Alcon Laboratories, Inc.; *Int'l*, pg. 916

UNISOL PLUS—Preservative-free, pH Balanced Aerosol Saline Solution—Wesley-Jessen; *U.S. Private*, pg. 111

UNISOM/ULTRABAC—NONE—Pfizer Inc.; *U.S. Public*, pg. 1281

UNISON—On-Line UPS Systems—Trippe Mfg. Co.; *U.S. Private*, pg. 1104

UNISON—Aircraft Engine Electrical Components—Unison Industries; *U.S. Private*, pg. 1120

UNISON MUSIC—Books—Thomas Nelson Inc.; *U.S. Public*, pg. 1167

UNISPENSE—Scientific Glassware for Laboratory Use—Wheaton Inc.; *Int'l*, pg. 67

UNISPHERE—Microphones—Shure Brothers Incorporated; *U.S. Private*, pg. 997

UNISPORT—Multi-Purpose Car Racks—Barrecrafters; *U.S. Private*, pg. 991

UNISTAR—Quarter-Mask Respirator—Aearo Company; *U.S. Private*, pg. 23

UNISTAT—Analytical Instrument—Leica, Inc.; *Int'l*, pg. 806

UNISTAT—Feed Chemicals—Salsbury Laboratories, Inc.; *Int'l*, pg. 1277

UNISTATABLE—NONE—Vecta; *U.S. Private*, pg. 1038

UNISTEEL—Truck, Off-the-Road & Earth Moving Tires—The Goodyear Tire & Rubber Company; *U.S. Public*, pg. 752

UNISTOKER—Stoker—Detroit Stoker Co.; *U.S. Public*, pg. 1679

UNISTRUT—Metal Framing—Unistrut Corporation; *U.S. Public*, pg. 1651

UNISYN—Telephone System—Comdial Corporation; *U.S. Public*, pg. 407

UNISYS—Computers & Data Processing Systems—Unisys Corporation; *U.S. Public*, pg. 1671

UNIT BLOCK—Pre-Finished Strip—Bruce Hardwood Floors; *U.S. Public*, pg. 1634

UNIT-LOCK—Corrugated Boxes—Westvaco Corporation; *U.S. Public*, pg. 1762

UNIT MARINER—Cranes—AmClyde Engineered Products Co., Inc.; *U.S. Public*, pg. 778

UNIT RIG—Off-Highway Articulated & Rigid Dump Trucks—Terex Corporation; *U.S. Public*, pg. 1581

UNIT RIG—Electric Drive Haulers for Surface Mining—Terex Trucks; *U.S. Public*, pg. 1581

UNIT RIG-LECTRA HAUL—Electric Drive Haulers for Surface Mining—Terex Corporation; *U.S. Public*, pg. 1581

UNITE—Functionalized Polypropylene—Aristech Chemical Corporation; *Int'l*, pg. 872

UNITED AIRLINES—Commercial Airline—UAL Corporation; *U.S. Public*, pg. 1652

UNITED ARTISTS—NONE—Metro-Goldwyn-Mayer Inc.; *U.S. Public*, pg. 1101

UNITED AUTO GROUP—Car Dealerships—United Auto Group, Inc.; *U.S. Private*, pg. 1095

UNITED BRAKE SYSTEMS—Brake Parts—Echlin Inc.; *U.S. Public*, pg. 560

UNITED CENTRIFUGAL PUMPS—Centrifugal Pumps—BW/IP International, Inc.; *U.S. Public*, pg. 658

UNITED CENTRIFUGAL PUMPS—Centrifugal Pumps—Flowserve Corporation; *U.S. Public*, pg. 658

UNITED CHAIR—Office Furniture—United Chair, Inc.; *U.S. Private*, pg. 512

UNITED CHEMI-CON—NONE—Milgray Electronics, Inc.; *U.S. Public*, pg. 205

UNITED COLORS OF BENETON—Women's, Men's & Children's Clothing—Benetton U.S.A. Corporation; *Int'l*, pg. 186

UNITED COLORS OF BENETTON—NONE—Benetton Group S.p.A.; *Int'l*, pg. 186

UNITED DOMINION REALTY TRUST—Real Estate Investment Trust—United Dominion Realty Trust, Inc.; *U.S. Public*, pg. 1677

UNITED EXPRESS—Air Transportation—Air Wis Services, Inc.; *U.S. Public*, pg. 1653

UNITED FUNDS, INC.—NONE—Waddell & Reed, Inc.; *U.S. Public*, pg. 1623

UNITED HEALTH PLAN—Health Maintenance Organization—UHP Healthcare; *U.S. Private*, pg. 1113

UNITED INTERLOCK—Plank Grating—Unistrut Corporation; *U.S. Public*, pg. 1651

UNITED INVESTORS LIFE INSURANCE COMPANY—NONE—Waddell & Reed, Inc.; *U.S. Public*, pg. 1623

UNITED PARCEL SERVICE—Parcel Deliveries—United Parcel Service of America, Inc.; *U.S. Private*, pg. 1123

UNITED SHADE—Pleated Blinds & Shades—Patrick Industries Inc.; *U.S. Public*, pg. 1264

US AIRWAYS—Airline—US Airways Group, Inc.; *U.S. Public*, pg. 1680

U.S. AXLE—Regular & Customer Specification Axle Shafts & Custom Machined Shafts—U.S. Axle, Inc.; *U.S. Private*, pg. 1124

UNITED STATES COLD STORAGE—Refrigerated Warehousing—United States Cold Storage, Inc.; *U.S. Private*, pg. 1124

U.S. DIVERS—Underwater Diving Equipment—U.S. Divers Co., Inc.; *U.S. Private*, pg. 1125

U.S. ELECTRICAL MOTORS—Electric Motors—Emerson Electric Co.; *U.S. Public*, pg. 572

US HEALTHCARE—Health Maintenance Organization—U.S. Healthcare, Inc.; *U.S. Public*, pg. 26

U.S. KIDS—Magazine for Children—Benjamin Franklin Literary & Medical Society, Inc.; *U.S. Private*, pg. 133

U.S. NEWS & WORLD REPORT—Magazines & Books—U.S. News & World Report; *U.S. Public*, pg. 1125

U.S. NEWS WASHINGTON BUSINESS REPORT—Report—U.S. News & World Report; *U.S. Private*, pg. 1125

U.S. OAK—Wood Flooring Product Line—Premark International, Inc.; *U.S. Public*, pg. 1321

USA TODAY—National Newspaper—Gannett Company, Inc.; *U.S. Public*, pg. 698

USA TRAINING—Video Tape Training Products—ITC Learning Corp.; *U.S. Public*, pg. 859

USA WEEKEND—Newspaper Magazine—USA Weekend; *U.S. Public*, pg. 701

U.S. RANGE—Ranges & Ovens—Welbilt Corporation; *Int'l*, pg. 188

U.S. REGULATORY REPORTER—Newsletter—PAREXEL International Corporation; *U.S. Public*, pg. 1257

UNITED STATES STEEL SUPPLY CO.—NONE—Interstate Steel Supply Company; *U.S. Public*, pg. 1100

US STITCHLINE—Blindstitch Machines—Union Special Corp.; *Int'l*, pg. 716

UNITED STATES SURGICAL CORPORATION—NONE—U.S. Surgical Corp.; *U.S. Public*, pg. 1687

UNITED STATES TESTING—NONE—SGS U.S. Testing Company, Inc.; *U.S. Public*, pg. 1153

US WATER HEATER COMPANY—Water Heaters—Southcorp Holdings Ltd.; *Int'l*, pg. 1287

UNITED STATIONERS—Office Supplies—United Stationers Inc.; *U.S. Public*, pg. 1689

UNITED TECHNOLOGIES—All Products—United Technologies Automotive; *U.S. Public*, pg. 1691

UNITED VAN LINES—Trucking—Johnson Storage Moving Co; *U.S. Private*, pg. 594

UNITED VAN LINES—Moving Company—United Van Lines, Inc.; *U.S. Private*, pg. 1117

UNITEK—Orthodontic Products—3M; *U.S. Public*, pg. 1604

UNITEK—Dental Materials—3M Unitek Corporation; *U.S. Public*, pg. 1606

UNITEX—Flocked Surface Paper Carriers—Sonoco Products Company; *U.S. Public*, pg. 1485

UNITOG—Men's & Women's Clothing—Unitog Company; *U.S. Public*, pg. 1693

UNITOME—Disposable Knife—Becton Dickinson & Co., Massachusetts Div.; *U.S. Public*, pg. 199

UNITOR—Suspension—Shepard Niles, Inc.; *U.S. Private*, pg. 992

UNITORQUE—Fasteners—Maclean-Fogg Co.; *U.S. Private*, pg. 692

UNITRACK—Garment Tracking System—UniFirst Corporation; *U.S. Public*, pg. 1665

UNITRAX—Computer Program, Software—Lucent Technologies Inc.; *U.S. Public*, pg. 1017

UNITRAY—Food Service Equipment—United Service Equipment Company; *U.S. Public*, pg. 1507

UNITROL—Induction Melting Power Control—Inductotherm Corp.; *U.S. Private*, pg. 560

UNITROL—Chair Apparatus—Steelcase Inc.; *U.S. Private*, pg. 1038

UNITRON—Closet Carriers—Josam Company; *U.S. Private*, pg. 600

UNITRON—Children's Building Sets—LEGO Systems, Inc.; *Int'l*, pg. 805

UNITRON—Food Service Equipment—United Service Equipment Company; *U.S. Public*, pg. 1507

UNITUBE—Tubing Access.—Outokumpu American Brass Co.; *Int'l*, pg. 1016

UNITURN LATHES—Lathes—WCI Machine Tools & Systems; *Int'l*, pg. 440

UNITY—Network Control & Management Products—Bytex Corporation; *U.S. Public*, pg. 1522

UNITY—Telephone Sets—Northern Telecom Limited; *Int'l*, pg. 968

UNITY—Full Functioned DEC & IBM-Based Healthcare Informaion System Series—Shared Medical Systems Corporation; *U.S. Public*, pg. 1463

UNITY—NMR Spectrometer & Accessories—Varian Associates, Inc.; *U.S. Public*, pg. 1710

UNIVAR EUROPE—Industrial Chemicals—Van Waters & Rogers; *Int'l*, pg. 1147

UNIVASC—NONE—Schwarz Pharma Inc.; *Int'l*, pg. 1211

UNIVENDOR—Vendor—The Vendo Company; *Int'l*, pg. 1184

UNIVENDOR-2—Vendor—The Vendo Company; *Int'l*, pg. 1184

UNIVER—Chemical Reagant—Hach Company; *U.S. Public*, pg. 773

UNIVERSAL—Labeler—Avery Dennison Corporation; *U.S. Public*, pg. 152

UNIVERSAL—Livestock Equipment—Behlen Mfg. Co.; *U.S. Public*, pg. 130

UNIVERSAL—X-Ray Systems—Del Global Technologies; *U.S. Public*, pg. 493

UNIVERSAL—Microform Reader—Dukane Corporation; *U.S. Private*, pg. 345

UNIVERSAL—NONE—ETEX; *Int'l*, pg. 430

UNIVERSAL—Greeting Cards—Fine Art Developments plc; *Int'l*, pg. 485

UNIVERSAL—Suction Pumps—Hollister Medical Systems Division; *U.S. Private*, pg. 535

UNIVERSAL—Ballasts—MagneTek, Inc.; *U.S. Public*, pg. 1037

UNIVERSAL—Private Label Office Supplies—United Stationers Inc.; *U.S. Public*, pg. 1689

UNIVERSAL—Pesticides, Various Products—Universal Cooperatives, Inc.; *U.S. Private*, pg. 1127

UNIVERSAL—Relays—Universal Relay; *U.S. Private*, pg. 839

UNIVERSAL—Security Instruments—Universal Security Instruments Inc.; *U.S. Public*, pg. 1697

UNIVERSAL—Marine Engines—Westerbeke Corporation; *U.S. Public*, pg. 1757

UNIVERSAL—Level Transit—David White, L.L.C.; *U.S. Public*, pg. 1765

UNIVERSAL—Level Transit—David White, L.L.C.; *U.S. Private*, pg. 1765

UNIVERSAL CITY STUDIO TOURS—Studio Tours—Universal Studios Hollywood; *Int'l*, pg. 1216

UNIVERSAL DATA STATION—Computer Desk—Virco Mfg. Corporation; *U.S. Public*, pg. 1721

UNIVERSAL DRILL PRESS TRIMMER—Precision Cartridge Case for Use With Drill Press—Lyman Products Corporation; *U.S. Private*, pg. 683

UNIVERSAL ELECTRIC—Motors—MagneTek, Inc.; *U.S. Public*, pg. 1037

UNIVERSAL ENGINEERING—NONE—DeVlieg-Bullard Inc.; *U.S. Public*, pg. 502

UNIVERSAL FILTER—Bakery & Restaurant Equipment—Belshaw Brothers, Inc.; *Int'l*, pg. 188

UNIVERSAL GENEVE—Watches—Wittnauer International, Inc.; *U.S. Public*, pg. 273

UNIVERSAL NOLIN—Commercial Refrigeration Equipment—Electrolux, AB; *Int'l*, pg. 438

UNIVERSAL NOLIN—Commercial Refrigeration—White Consolidated Industries, Inc.; *Int'l*, pg. 439

UNIVERSAL-PLUS—Ballasts—MagneTek, Inc.; *U.S. Public*, pg. 1037

UNIVERSAL PLUS—Hybrid Ballasts—MagneTek Lighting Products Group; *U.S. Public*, pg. 1037

UNIVERSAL PRESSURE—Boilers—Babcock & Wilcox Co.; *U.S. Public*, pg. 1068

UNIVERSAL-RUNDLE—Bath Fixtures & Faucets—Universal-Rundle Corp.; *U.S. Public*, pg. 1193

UNIVERSAL SOURCE PROTECTION (USP)—NONE—Sentry Technology Corp.; *U.S. Public*, pg. 1458

UNIVERSAL SPLICE—Disconnectable Cable Splicing Systems—G & W Electric Co.; *U.S. Private*, pg. 683

UNIVERSAL TRIMMER—Precision Cartridge Case Trimer—Lyman Products Corporation; *U.S. Private*, pg. 683

UNIVERSAL UNDERWRITERS—Insurance Company—Universal Underwriters Insurance Co.; *Int'l*, pg. 1530

UNIVERSE—32-Bit Super Microcomputer—Charles River Data Systems, Inc.; *U.S. Private*, pg. 230

VRS 2000—Graphical Interface Integrating CCTV, Access Control & Alarm Monitoring—Sensormatic Electronics Corporation; *U.S. Public*, pg. 1457

VRT—Valves—Masoneilan North American Operations; *U.S. Public*, pg. 528

VRTX/OS—3.0 Convigurable Real-Time Operating System—Microtec Division; *U.S. Public*, pg. 1086

VRTX-VELOCITY—C Cross-Development Environment for VRTX-Based Applications—Microtec Division; *U.S. Public*, pg. 1086

VRTX32—Software Components—Microtec Division; *U.S. Public*, pg. 1086

V-ROHTO—Eye Lotions—Rohto Pharmaceutical Co.; *Int'l*, pg. 1126

V*S—Electric Adjustable Speed Motors Drives—Rockwell International Corporation; *U.S. Public*, pg. 1397

VS—Mini Computer—Wang Laboratories, Inc.; *U.S. Public*, pg. 1737

VSBX—Connectors—Viking Electronics, Inc.; *U.S. Private*, pg. 1184

VSE/ESA—Computer System—International Business Machines Corporation; *U.S. Public*, pg. 895

VSM—Vehicle System Manager—Jervis B. Webb Company; *U.S. Private*, pg. 1156

VSM STEEL—NONE—Carpenter Technology Corporation; *U.S. Public*, pg. 307

V-SERIES SMARTMODEM 9600—Modem—Hayes Microcomputer Products, Inc.; *U.S. Public*, pg. 801

V-SERIES ULTRA SMARTMODEM 9600—Modem—Hayes Microcomputer Products, Inc.; *U.S. Public*, pg. 801

V-SERIES ULTRA SMARTMODEM 14400—Modem—Hayes Microcomputer Products, Inc.; *U.S. Public*, pg. 801

VTAM—Computer System—International Business Machines Corporation; *U.S. Public*, pg. 895

VT400—Plain-Paper PostScript Imagesetter—Prepress Solutions, Inc.; *U.S. Private*, pg. 882

VTR—Motorcycle—American Honda Motor Co., Inc. Motorcycle Division; *Int'l*, pg. 634

VT600W—Plain-Paper PostScript Imagesetter—Prepress Solutions, Inc.; *U.S. Private*, pg. 882

VT3—Lawn Equipment—The Toro Company; *U.S. Public*, pg. 1623

V32Cell—Modem Chipset—Lucent Technologies Inc.; *U.S. Public*, pg. 1017

V386S, A—AT Compatible—Victor Technology; *U.S. Private*, pg. 1139

V-25—Dentifrice Polishing Agent—Rhone-Poulenc Basic Chemicals Co.; *Int'l*, pg. 1110

V2500—Civil Engine—Rolls-Royce-Commercial Aero Engines Ltd.; *Int'l*, pg. 1127

V-22—TiltRotor Aircraft Twin Engine—Bell Helicopter Textron; *U.S. Public*, pg. 1588

V286—AT Compatible Microcomputer—Victor Technology; *U.S. Private*, pg. 1139

V286S, C, A—AT Compatible—Victor Technology; *U.S. Private*, pg. 1139

VVE—Vertical Process Camera—Nuarc Company, Inc.; *U.S. Private*, pg. 808

V800—NONE—NEC Electronics Inc.; *Int'l*, pg. 900

V805—NONE—NEC Electronics Inc.; *Int'l*, pg. 900

V810—NONE—NEC Electronics Inc.; *Int'l*, pg. 900

V820—NONE—NEC Electronics Inc.; *Int'l*, pg. 900

V50—NONE—NEC Electronics Inc.; *Int'l*, pg. 900

V40—NONE—NEC Electronics Inc.; *Int'l*, pg. 900

VV PUBLISHING—Publisher of Village Voice Weekly Newspaper—VV Publishing Corp.; *U.S. Private*, pg. 1131

V SERIES—NONE—NEC Electronics Inc.; *Int'l*, pg. 900

V30—NONE—NEC Electronics Inc.; *Int'l*, pg. 900

V30H—NONE—NEC Electronics Inc.; *Int'l*, pg. 900

V20—NONE—NEC Electronics Inc.; *Int'l*, pg. 900

V25—NONE—NEC Electronics Inc.; *Int'l*, pg. 900

V20H—NONE—NEC Electronics Inc.; *Int'l*, pg. 900

V VIAL—Scientific Glassware for Laboratory Use—Wheaton Inc.; *Int'l*, pg. 67

VR4000—NONE—NEC Electronics Inc.; *Int'l*, pg. 900

VR4000PC—NONE—NEC Electronics Inc.; *Int'l*, pg. 900

VR4000SC—NONE—NEC Electronics Inc.; *Int'l*, pg. 900

VR4400—NONE—NEC Electronics Inc.; *Int'l*, pg. 900

VR4400MC—NONE—NEC Electronics Inc.; *Int'l*, pg. 900

VR4400PC—NONE—NEC Electronics Inc.; *Int'l*, pg. 900

VR4400SC—NONE—NEC Electronics Inc.; *Int'l*, pg. 900

VR4200—NONE—NEC Electronics Inc.; *Int'l*, pg. 900

VR4200LP—NONE—NEC Electronics Inc.; *Int'l*, pg. 900

VR4200PC—NONE—NEC Electronics Inc.; *Int'l*, pg. 900

VR SERIES—NONE—NEC Electronics Inc.; *Int'l*, pg. 900

V/W—Auto—Loeber Motors, Inc.; *U.S. Private*, pg. 672

V-WALL—Floor-to-Ceiling Partitions—Herman Miller, Inc.; *U.S. Public*, pg. 1111

V-X—Scaffolds—Up-Right, Inc.; *U.S. Private*, pg. 1128

VXR—Nuclear Magnetic Resonance Spectrometers & Accessories—Varian Associates, Inc.; *U.S. Public*, pg. 1710

VX WORKS—NONE—Wind River Systems, Inc.; *U.S. Public*, pg. 1770

VICS—Service Verifying Billable Calls & Reducing Fraud—Intellicall, Inc.; *U.S. Public*, pg. 887

VXISCAN—NONE—GenRad, Inc.; *U.S. Public*, pg. 731

VA-TRO-NOL—Nose Drops—Richardson-Vicks, Inc., Health Care Products; *U.S. Public*, pg. 1331

VAALIA—Milk Based Beverages—Q.U.F. Industries Ltd.; *Int'l*, pg. 1074

VAASAN—Bread—Cultor Ltd.; *Int'l*, pg. 349

VAASAN RAPEAT—Crisp Crackerbread—Cultor Ltd.; *Int'l*, pg. 349

VAASAN VOIMA—Crisp Bread—Cultor Ltd.; *Int'l*, pg. 349

VABE—Aperitif—Groupe Pernod Ricard; *Int'l*, pg. 566

VAC-ARC—Vacuum Arc Remelted—Latrobe Steel Company; *U.S. Public*, pg. 1617

VAC ELUT—LaboratoryEquipment; Vacuum Processing Units—Varian Associates, Inc.; *U.S. Public*, pg. 1710

VAC-HACK—Power Hack Saw Blades—Sandvik/Milford Corporation; *Int'l*, pg. 1185

VAC ION—Vacuum Ion Implanter—Varian Associates, Inc.; *U.S. Public*, pg. 1710

VAC KOTE—Lubricant—Ball Corporation; *U.S. Public*, pg. 170

VAC'N'MULCH—Outdoor Products—The Black & Decker Corporation; *U.S. Public*, pg. 233

VAC-U-FLEX—Hose—Flexible Technologies Inc.; *Int'l*, pg. 1267

VAC-U-FLEX—Flexible Hosing for Vaccum Cleaners—Smiths Industries plc; *Int'l*, pg. 1266

VAC-U-LIFT—Vacuum Lifters & Transfer Systems—Acco Chain & Lifting Products; *Int'l*, pg. 473

VAC-U-LOK—Hose—Flexible Technologies Inc.; *Int'l*, pg. 1267

VAC-U-RIG—Power Tools—Milwaukee Electric Tool Corp.; *Int'l*, pg. 96

VACATION DESTINATION—Prerecorded Audio Tapes Containing Travel Information—American Automobile Association; *U.S. Private*, pg. 50

VACATION ESCAPES—Vacation Product—Resort Condominiums International; *U.S. Public*, pg. 322

VACATION PASSPORT—Travel Club Offering Hotel, Car Rental, Airline & Vacation Discounts—Damark International, Inc.; *U.S. Public*, pg. 478

VACATIONER—Family Tent—The Canadian Coleman Co., Ltd.; *U.S. Private*, pg. 691

VACATIONER—NONE—Holiday Rambler; *U.S. Public*, pg. 1123

VACHON—Snack Cakes—Culinar Inc.; *Int'l*, pg. 348

VACLOCK—Syringe—Merit Medical Systems, Inc.; *U.S. Public*, pg. 1096

VACO—Tools and Terminals—Klein Tools Inc.; *U.S. Private*, pg. 625

VACOMBO—Tool Kits—Klein Tools Inc.; *U.S. Private*, pg. 625

VACPAC—Medium-Voltage Vacuum Switch—Kearney Company; *U.S. Public*, pg. 444

VACSORB—Vacuum Forepump—Varian Associates, Inc.; *U.S. Public*, pg. 1710

VACSTAR—Suction—Air Techniques, Inc.; *U.S. Private*, pg. 28

VACSYS—Manufacturing Process Analysis System—Science Management Corporation; *U.S. Public*, pg. 1717

VACTOR—Vacuum Trucks—Federal Signal Corporation; *U.S. Public*, pg. 616

VACTOR—Indus. Street & Basin Cleaner—Vactor Mfg. Inc.; *U.S. Public*, pg. 617

VACTOR KEENER KLEENER—In Plant Vacumn—Vactor Mfg. Inc.; *U.S. Public*, pg. 617

VACTROL—Medico-Surgical Tubing Connector—Mallinckrodt Inc.; *U.S. Public*, pg. 1039

VACU-DRY—Low-Moisture Fruit, Apple Snacks—Vacu-Dry Company; *U.S. Public*, pg. 1704

VACU-MAID—Central Vacuum Systems—Lindsay Manufacturing Inc.; *U.S. Private*, pg. 668

VACU QUEEN—Vacuum Cleaners—HMI Industries; *U.S. Public*, pg. 771

VACU-SPONGE—Continuous Suctioning Surgical Sponge—Baxter Research Medical, Inc.; *U.S. Public*, pg. 196

VACU-TITE!—Vacuum Tees, Connectors & Tubing—R&B, Inc.; *U.S. Public*, pg. 1354

VACUATOR—Valve—Donaldson Company, Inc.; *U.S. Public*, pg. 517

VACUCAP—Filtration Products—Gelman Sciences, Inc.; *U.S. Public*, pg. 1253

VACUDYNE—Process Control Equipment—Altair Corporation; *U.S. Private*, pg. 46

VACUDYNE—Vacuum Conditioning Equip.—Vacudyne Inc.; *U.S. Private*, pg. 46

VACUFLOW—Powder Fillers—Pneumatic Scale Corporation; *U.S. Private*, pg. 118

VACULE—Scientific Glassware for Laboratory Use—Wheaton Inc.; *Int'l*, pg. 67

VACUMATE—Scientific Glassware for Laboratory Use—Wheaton Inc.; *Int'l*, pg. 67

VACUMELTROL—NONE—Carpenter Technology Corporation; *U.S. Public*, pg. 307

VACUMET—NONE—Carpenter Technology Corporation; *U.S. Public*, pg. 307

VACUSEAL SERIES—Combination Vaccum Press—Seal Products Incorporated; *U.S. Public*, pg. 849

VACUSHIE—Filtration Products—Gelman Sciences, Inc.; *U.S. Public*, pg. 1253

VACUTAINER—Blood Collection Tubes & Needles—Becton Dickinson & Company; *U.S. Public*, pg. 199

VACUUM DYNAMICS—Chip Vacuum Systems—Mayfran International, Inc.; *Int'l*, pg. 1397

VAGABOND—Electronic Component—Shure Brothers Incorporated; *U.S. Private*, pg. 997

THE VAGABOND INNS—Motor Inns—The Vagabond Inns; *U.S. Private*, pg. 558

VAGISIL—Feminine Itching Medication—Combe Incorporated; *U.S. Private*, pg. 257

VAGISTAT-1—NONE—Bristol-Myers Squibb Company; *U.S. Public*, pg. 253

VAJRA BAROLO—Wine—Wine World Estates Company; *Int'l*, pg. 917

VAL-AN—Instrument Carrying Case—Zero Corporation; *U.S. Public*, pg. 1791

VAL-REX—NONE—Fortune Brands, Inc.; *U.S. Public*, pg. 674

VAL-U-PLUS—Household Paper Goods—Orchids Paper Products Co.; *U.S. Private*, pg. 819

VAL-CHEM—Coatings—The Valspar Corp. Protective Coatings Div.; *U.S. Public*, pg. 1707

VAL-U-LINE—Hardware & Housewares—Distribution America; *U.S. Private*, pg. 335

VALANTI—Pleasure Boat Name—Regal Marine Industries Inc.; *U.S. Private*, pg. 917

VALASSIS IMPACT PROMOTIONS—Specialty & Solo Printing; Media Planning & Placement—Valassis Communications, Inc.; *U.S. Public*, pg. 1704

VALASSIS INSERTS—4/Color Free-Standing Inserts—Valassis Communications, Inc.; *U.S. Public*, pg. 1704

VALASSIS ROP SOLUTIONS—Advertising Placed Directly on Pages of Newspapers—Valassis Communications, Inc.; *U.S. Public*, pg. 1704

VALASSIS SAMPLING—Newspaper Delivered Product Samples—Valassis Communications, Inc.; *U.S. Public*, pg. 1704

VALBAZAN—Animal Health Product—SmithKline Beecham plc; *Int'l*, pg. 1264

Brand Name Index

Brand Name Index

VALBAZEN—Albendazole—Pfizer Inc.; *U.S. Public*, pg. 1281
VALBOND—Chemical—Air Products; *U.S. Public*, pg. 30
VALCAT—Chemical—Air Products; *U.S. Public*, pg. 30
VALCO ENGINEERING—Valves—Davies Shephard Pty. Ltd.; *Int'l*, pg. 2
VALCOR—NONE—Thermal Ceramics Inc.; *Int'l*, pg. 894
VALDA PASTILLES—NONE—SmithKline Beecham Research Limited; *Int'l*, pg. 1266
VALDI DISCOUNT FOOD STORES—Grocery Stores—Socanav Inc.; *Int'l*, pg. 1272
VALDISPERT—Sedatives—Kali-Chemie Aktiengesellschaft; *Int'l*, pg. 1278
VALE—Computer System—International Business Machines Corporation; *U.S. Public*, pg. 895
VALE DISPENSAS—Meal Vouchers—Accor S.A.; *Int'l*, pg. 20
VALENTINA—Perfume ine—Stanhome Inc.; *U.S. Public*, pg. 1508
VALENTINO—NONE—Luxottica Group S.p.A.; *Int'l*, pg. 822
VALENTINO VENDETTA—Fragrance—Elizabeth Arden Company; *Int'l*, pg. 1435
VALEREX—High Performance Plastic Drums—Van Leer Containers, Inc.; *Int'l*, pg. 1146
VALET AUTO-STROP—Blades—The Gillette Company; *U.S. Public*, pg. 743
VALETHENE—High Performance Composite Drums—Van Leer Containers, Inc.; *Int'l*, pg. 1146
VALFOR—Zeolites—PQ Corporation; *U.S. Private*, pg. 827
VALI—Volleyball Shoe—K-Swiss Inc.; *U.S. Public*, pg. 937
VALI-DINE—Data Terminal—Griffin Technology Incorporated; *U.S. Public*, pg. 506
VALIANT—NONE—Acclaim Comics; *U.S. Public*, pg. 15
VALIANT—Roofing Shingles—Georgia-Pacific Corporation; *U.S. Public*, pg. 735
VALIANT—Writing Paper & Bond Paper—The Mead Corporation; *U.S. Public*, pg. 1074
VALISE—Plugs—Hubbell Incorporated; *U.S. Public*, pg. 844
VALISONE—Medium Potency Topical Steroid Cream, Lotion & Ointment—Schering-Plough Corporation; *U.S. Public*, pg. 1438
VALIUM ROCHE—Central Nervous System Pharmaceutical—Roche Holding Ltd.; *Int'l*, pg. 1119
VALK—Truck Mounted Snowplows, Plowparts & Accessories—Valk Manufacturing Company; *U.S. Private*, pg. 1131
VALKOTE—Enamel—The Valspar Corp. Protective Coatings Div.; *U.S. Public*, pg. 1707
VALLE—Fruit Juice—Jugos del Valle, S.A. de C.V.; *Int'l*, pg. 716
VALLEY—Faucets—Eljer Plumbingware; *U.S. Public*, pg. 1794
VALLEY—Irrigation Equipment—Valmont Industries, Inc.; *U.S. Public*, pg. 1706
VALLEY CHEF—Chicken Products—Rocco Inc.; *U.S. Private*, pg. 937
VALLEY FAIR—NONE—Schottenstein Stores Corporation; *U.S. Private*, pg. 972
VALLEY FARMS—French Fries—McCain Foods Limited; *Int'l*, pg. 850
VALLEY FORGE—Prefinished Wall Paneling—Georgia-Pacific Corporation; *U.S. Public*, pg. 735
VALLEY FORGE PARCHMENT—Writing, Text & Cover Paper—Fox River Paper Company; *U.S. Private*, pg. 422
VALLEY MAID—Potato Chips—Bachman Company; *U.S. Private*, pg. 109
VALLEY PAK—Ice Cream—Kemps Foods, Inc.; *Int'l*, pg. 752
VALLEYDALE—Processed Meats—Smithfield Foods, Inc.; *U.S. Public*, pg. 1479
VALLEYFAIR—Amusement Park—Cedar Fair, L.P.; *U.S. Public*, pg. 319
VALMA—Car Care Products—Sara Lee Corporation; *U.S. Public*, pg. 1432
VALMANE—Sedatives—Kali-Chemie Aktiengesellschaft; *Int'l*, pg. 1278
VALMEL—Chemical—Air Products; *U.S. Public*, pg. 30

VALMET—Straddle Carriers—Partek Corporation; *Int'l*, pg. 1024
VALMET—Machinery—Valmet Corporation; *Int'l*, pg. 1447
VALMET SYM-CONCEPT—Paper Making Machinery—Valmet Corporation; *Int'l*, pg. 1447
VALON—Electrical Maintenance Products—Thomas & Betts Corporation; *U.S. Public*, pg. 1597
VALONTAN—Motion Sickness Product—Recordati Industria Chimica e Farmaceutica S.p.A.; *Int'l*, pg. 1090
VALOR—Electrical Components—GTI Corporation; *U.S. Public*, pg. 767
VALOR—Space Heating—Newmond PLC; *Int'l*, pg. 924
VALOROS—Luggage—Andiamo, Inc.; *U.S. Private*, pg. 73
VALOX—Polyester Resins for Injection Moulding Purpose—General Electric Canada Inc.; *U.S. Public*, pg. 713
VALOX—Engineered Plastics—General Electric Company; *U.S. Public*, pg. 709
VALREZ—Chemical—Air Products; *U.S. Public*, pg. 30
VALSA—Coated Mechanical Papers—Haindl Papier GmbH; *Int'l*, pg. 586
VALSOF—Chemical—Air Products; *U.S. Public*, pg. 30
VALSPAR—Paint—The Valspar Corporation; *U.S. Public*, pg. 1707
VALSPEX—Chemical—Air Products; *U.S. Public*, pg. 30
VALSPIN—Chemical—Air Products; *U.S. Public*, pg. 30
VALTAC—Chemical—Air Products; *U.S. Public*, pg. 30
VALTEC—Storage Products—Lyon Metal Products, Inc.; *U.S. Private*, pg. 638
VALTEC—Polypropylene Resin—Montedison S.p.A.; *Int'l*, pg. 324
VALTEK—Valves—Flowserve Corporation; *U.S. Public*, pg. 658
VALTRA-VALMET—Tractors—Partek Corporation; *Int'l*, pg. 1024
VALU-KING—NONE—Telsmith, Inc.; *U.S. Public*, pg. 141
VALU RITE—Pharmaceuticals—Allens Of Hastings, Inc.; *U.S. Private*, pg. 37
VALU-RITE/CARE MAX—Independent Pharmacy Network—McKesson U.S. Health Care; *U.S. Public*, pg. 1073
VALU-TIME—Foods & Non-Foods—Topco Associates, Inc.; *U.S. Private*, pg. 1091
VALUE—NONE—Lennox International Inc.; *U.S. Private*, pg. 659
VALUE ADDED CLASSIFIEDS—Services for Classified Advertisers—Brite Voice Systems, Inc.; *U.S. Public*, pg. 257
VALUE CALL SERVICES—Enhanced Public Switched Telephone Network Service—British Telecommunications plc; *Int'l*, pg. 222
VALUE CITY—NONE—Schottenstein Stores Corporation; *U.S. Public*, pg. 972
VALUE CITY—Department Store—Value City Department Stores, Inc.; *U.S. Private*, pg. 972
VALUE CLASSICS—NONE—Weight Watchers Gourmet Food Company; *U.S. Public*, pg. 806
VALUE CREATION PROCESS—4-Step process To Getting The Best Value For Your Company's Health Care—Watson Wyatt Worldwide; *U.S. Private*, pg. 1154
VALUE EXPRESS—Window Fashions—Hunter Douglas, Inc.; *Int'l*, pg. 639
VALUE FOR MONEY—Derby—Souza Cruz, S.A.; *Int'l*, pg. 112
VALUE GROUP—Computer Furniture—Hunt Corporation; *U.S. Public*, pg. 848
VALUE LINE—Investment Advisory Publisher & Money Manager—Value Line, Inc.; *U.S. Private*, pg. 137
VALUE-LINE—NONE—Zebra Technologies Corporation; *U.S. Public*, pg. 1790
VALUE LINE ASSET MANAGEMENT—Management Services for Mutual Funds & Institutional Accounts—Value Line, Inc.; *U.S. Private*, pg. 137
VALUE LINE INVESTMENT SURVEY—Stock Analysis Software—Value Line, Inc.; *U.S. Private*, pg. 137

VALUE-MASTER—Platform Model—The Knapheide Mfg. Co.; *U.S. Private*, pg. 626
VALUE-MASTER-X—Platform Model—The Knapheide Mfg. Co.; *U.S. Private*, pg. 626
VALUE MATE—Packaging System—Sanderson Plumbing Products Inc.; *U.S. Private*, pg. 964
VALUE PAK—Garden Products—Jiffy Products of America, Inc.; *Int'l*, pg. 706
THE VALUE STACKER—Plastic Stack Chair—Virco Mfg. Corporation; *U.S. Public*, pg. 1721
VALUE-LINE—Valves & Actuators—Neles-Jamesbury Corp.; *Int'l*, pg. 1428
VALUCRAFT—Automotive Hard Parts Including Starters, Alternators & Brakes—AutoZone, Inc.; *U.S. Public*, pg. 150
VALUED—Cutting, Power & Hand Tool Accessories—Vermont American Tool Corp.; *U.S. Public*, pg. 575
VALUELINK—Hospital Inventory & Equipment Management Services—Allegiance Healthcare Corp.; *U.S. Public*, pg. 44
VALUEMASTER—Horizontal Blinds—Hunter Douglas, Inc.; *Int'l*, pg. 639
VALUENET—NONE—FileNet Corporation; *U.S. Public*, pg. 622
VALUEPOINT—Computer Product—International Business Machines Corporation; *U.S. Public*, pg. 895
VALUETIME—Generic Label—Smith's Food & Drug Centers, Inc.; *U.S. Public*, pg. 1103
VALUFLOR—Sheet Vinyl Flooring—Congoleum Corporation; *U.S. Public*, pg. 69
VALUGARDS—Disposable Plastic Gloves & Aprons—Handgards Inc.; *U.S. Private*, pg. 499
VALULINE—Aluminum Carrying Case—Zero Corporation; *U.S. Public*, pg. 1791
VALUMARKET—Supermarket Chain—Valu Discount, Incorporated; *U.S. Private*, pg. 1132
VALUMED—Generic Drugs—Moore Medical Corp.; *U.S. Public*, pg. 1128
VALUTASK—Office Seating—The HON Co.; *U.S. Public*, pg. 772
VALV-POWR—Actuators—Neles-Jamesbury Corp.; *Int'l*, pg. 1428
VALVACTOR—Valve Positioner—The Foxboro Company; *Int'l*, pg. 1243
VALVAIR—Valves—Schrader Bellows Division; *U.S. Public*, pg. 1261
VALVE MEDIC—Valve Lubricant—Radiator Specialty Company; *U.S. Private*, pg. 906
VALVERT—Mineral Water—Nestle S.A.; *Int'l*, pg. 915
VALVOLET—Fittings—Bonney Forge Corporation; *U.S. Private*, pg. 156
VALVOLINE—Motor Oils, Filters & Lubricants—Valvoline Company; *U.S. Public*, pg. 139
VALVOLINE INSTANT OIL CHANGE—Quick Lube Outlets—Ashland, Inc.; *U.S. Public*, pg. 138
VALVTRON—Flow Control Products—Keystone International, Inc.; *U.S. Public*, pg. 1650
VAMAC—Ethylene/acrylic Elastomer—Du Pont (E.I. Du Pont De Nemours & Co.); *U.S. Public*, pg. 530
VAMPIRE—Next-Generation Verification—Cadence Design Systems, Inc.; *U.S. Public*, pg. 290
VAN—Utility Vehicle—Toyota Motor Sales, U.S.A., Inc.; *Int'l*, pg. 1412
VAN CAMP—Beans—Hunt-Wesson, Inc.; *U.S. Public*, pg. 428
VAN CAMP BEANS—Pork & Beans—Hunt-Wesson, Inc.; *U.S. Public*, pg. 428
VAN CAMP'S PORK & BEANS—Pork and Beans—The Quaker Oats Company; *U.S. Public*, pg. 1347
VAN CLEEF & ARPELS—Jewelry—Van Cleef & Arpels, Inc.; *U.S. Private*, pg. 1132
VAN CORTLANDT—NONE—Wechsler Coffee Corp.; *U.S. Private*, pg. 1158
VAN GOGH—Paints & Colours—Akzo Nobel N.V.; *Int'l*, pg. 42
VAN HEUSEN COLLECTION—Apparel—Phillips-Van Heusen Corporation; *U.S. Public*, pg. 1291
VANMARK—Highway Striper—M-B Companies Inc. of Wisconsin; *U.S. Private*, pg. 684
VAN MELLE—Confections—Van Melle N.V.; *Int'l*, pg. 1450
VAN NELLE—Coffee System—Sara Lee Corporation; *U.S. Public*, pg. 1432
VAN RAALTE—Gloves—Honey Fashions Ltd.; *U.S. Private*, pg. 537

VAN SON—NONE—Taylor Impression, Inc.; *U.S. Private*, pg. 1070

VAN STRAATEN—Lubricants—Burmah Castrol plc; *Int'l*, pg. 234

VAN WAGENEN & SCHICKHAUS—Franks & Processed Meat Products—Armour Swift Eckrich; *U.S. Public*, pg. 426

VAN WATERS & ROGERS—Industrial Chemicals—Van Waters & Rogers; *Int'l*, pg. 1147

VANART—NONE—Pfizer Inc.; *U.S. Public*, pg. 1281

VANCE-MIRROR—Finish Brass, Copper & Stainless Bar Sinks With Mirror Polish—Vance Industries, Inc.; *U.S. Private*, pg. 1133

VANCENASE—Asthma Products—Schering-Plough Corporation; *U.S. Public*, pg. 1438

VANCERIL—Oral Inhaled Steroid for Asthma-Related Inflammation—Schering-Plough Corporation; *U.S. Public*, pg. 1438

VANCOCIN HCl—Vancomycin Hydrochloride, Lilly—Eli Lilly and Company; *U.S. Public*, pg. 992

VANCOCINA—Vancomycin—Eli Lilly Italia, S.p.A.; *U.S. Public*, pg. 994

VANCOMYCIN HCl—Generic Drug—American Home Products Corporation; *U.S. Public*, pg. 79

VANCOUR—Cross Court Shoe—K-Swiss Inc.; *U.S. Public*, pg. 937

VANCRYL—Chemical—Air Products; *U.S. Public*, pg. 30

VANCRYL—Acrylic Polymers—Air Products and Chemicals, Inc.; *U.S. Public*, pg. 30

VANDA HI—Orchids/Leis, Hawaiian Tropicals—Flowers of Hawaii; *U.S. Private*, pg. 415

VANDAMME—Pastries—Danone Group; *Int'l*, pg. 379

VANDAR—Polybutylene Terephtalate—Hoechst Aktiengesellschaft; *Int'l*, pg. 624

VANDEMOORTELE—Mayonnaise & Oil—Vandemoortele N.V.; *Int'l*, pg. 1451

VANDERBILT—NONE—Ganin Tire Co., Inc.; *U.S. Private*, pg. 439

VANDERVELL—Bearings—T & N Plc; *Int'l*, pg. 1334

VANEOMETER—Anemometer—Dwyer Instruments Inc.; *U.S. Private*, pg. 350

VANESSA—Flow Control Products—Keystone International, Inc.; *U.S. Public*, pg. 1650

VANGARD—Recreational Van Conversion Fabrics—Guilford Mills, Inc.; *U.S. Public*, pg. 768

VANGARD—Rear Window Vehicle Lens—3M; *U.S. Public*, pg. 1604

VANGRACK—Line of Athletic Shoes & Apparel—Adidas International; *Int'l*, pg. 24

VANGUARD—Engine Line—Briggs & Stratton Corporation; *U.S. Public*, pg. 252

VANGUARD—Manufactured Homes—Champion Enterprises, Inc.; *U.S. Public*, pg. 332

VANGUARD—NONE—Ecolab Inc.; *U.S. Public*, pg. 562

VANGUARD—Endovascular Graft—Meadox Medicals, Inc.; *U.S. Public*, pg. 247

VANGUARD—Vanilla—David Michael & Co. Inc.; *U.S. Private*, pg. 740

VANGUARD—Golf Clubs—Mizuno Corporation; *Int'l*, pg. 884

VANGUARD—Steel Lockers—Penco Products; *U.S. Private*, pg. 848

VANGUARD—NONE—Pfizer Inc.; *U.S. Public*, pg. 1281

VANGUARD—Vaccine For Canine Distemper & Other Diseases—SmithKline Beecham Corporation; *Int'l*, pg. 1264

VANGUARD—Animal Vaccine—SmithKline Beecham plc; *Int'l*, pg. 1264

VANGUARD—Binoculars—Swift Instruments, Inc.; *U.S. Private*, pg. 1058

VANGUARD 500—CNC Controls—WCI Machine Tools & Systems; *Int'l*, pg. 440

VANGUARD 5000—Computerized Engraving—New Hermes Incorporated; *U.S. Private*, pg. 793

VANGUARD 1000—Computerized Engraving—New Hermes Incorporated; *U.S. Private*, pg. 793

VANGUARD PUPPY—NONE—Pfizer Inc.; *U.S. Private*, pg. 1281

VANGUARD TECHNOLOGIES—Automatic Data Processing Services—Information & Engineering Technology; *U.S. Private*, pg. 351

VANGUARD 3000—Computerized Engraving—New Hermes Incorporated; *U.S. Private*, pg. 793

VANILLA FIELDS—Women's Fragrance—Coty Inc.; *Int'l*, pg. 185

VANILLA MUSK—Women's fragrance—Coty Inc.; *Int'l*, pg. 185

VANISH—Laundry Additive—Benckiser Consumer Products Inc.; *Int'l*, pg. 185

VANISH—Toilet Bowl Cleaner—Bristol-Myers Squibb Company; *U.S. Public*, pg. 253

VANISH—Bathroom Care—S.C. Johnson & Son, Inc.; *U.S. Public*, pg. 592

VANISH—Toilet Cleaner—S.C. Johnson & Son, Limited; *U.S. Private*, pg. 593

VANISHING POINT—Retractable Point—The Pilot Pen Corp. of America; *Int'l*, pg. 1057

VANITY—Vegetable—A. Duda & Sons Inc.; *U.S. Private*, pg. 344

VANITY FAIR—Magazine—The Conde Nast Publications Inc.; *U.S. Private*, pg. 20

VANITY FAIR—Napkins—Fort James Corporation; *U.S. Public*, pg. 670

VANITY FAIR—Women's Apparel—International Cosmetics Co., Ltd.; *Int'l*, pg. 684

VANITY FAIR—Intimate Apparel—VF Corporation; *U.S. Public*, pg. 1702

VANITY-FLAIR—Bathroom Sink Tops—Leucadia National Corporation; *U.S. Public*, pg. 989

VANO—Blowers—Coppus Murray Group, Tuthill Corporation; *U.S. Private*, pg. 1110

VANO LIQUID STARCH—NONE—The Dial Corporation; *U.S. Public*, pg. 505

VANOXIDE—Pharmaceuticals—Rhone-Poulenc Rorer - U.S.; *Int'l*, pg. 1110

VANTAGE—NONE—AAH Pharmaceuticals Limited; *Int'l*, pg. 1

VANTAGE—Sporting Equipment—Brunswick Bowling & Billiards Corp.; *U.S. Public*, pg. 265

VANTAGE—Software—CSC Financial Services Group; *U.S. Public*, pg. 422

VANTAGE—Daily-Wear Soft Contact Lens—The Cooper Companies, Inc.; *U.S. Public*, pg. 442

VANTAGE—Card Game—Mattel Games/Puzzles; *U.S. Public*, pg. 1058

VANTAGE—Vascular Graft—Meadox Medicals, Inc.; *U.S. Public*, pg. 247

VANTAGE—Key Telephone Systems—Northern Telecom Limited; *Int'l*, pg. 968

VANTAGE—Cigarettes—RJR Nabisco Holdings Corp.; *U.S. Public*, pg. 1354

VANTAGE—Filter, Menthol, 100's Reg. & Menthol, Ultra Lights Reg. & 100's Cigarettes—R.J. Reynolds Tobacco Company; *U.S. Public*, pg. 1355

VANTAGE—Cigarettes—R.J. Reynolds Tobacco Intl., Inc.; *U.S. Public*, pg. 1355

VANTAGE ACCENTS—Daily-Wear Soft Contact Lens—The Cooper Companies, Inc.; *U.S. Public*, pg. 442

VANTAGE-ONE—Software—CSC Financial Services Group; *U.S. Public*, pg. 422

VANTAGE THIN—Flexible-Wear Soft Contact Lens—The Cooper Companies, Inc.; *U.S. Public*, pg. 442

VANTAGE THIN ACCENTS—Flexible Wear Soft Contact Lens—The Cooper Companies, Inc.; *U.S. Public*, pg. 442

VAPE-SORBER—Liquid/Gas Coalescer—Osmonics, Inc.; *U.S. Public*, pg. 1233

VAPEX—Paint & Varnish—Pratt & Lambert United, Inc.; *U.S. Public*, pg. 1466

VAPONA—Insecticide—Sara Lee Corporation; *U.S. Public*, pg. 1432

VAPONICS—Distillation Equipment—Osmonics, Inc.; *U.S. Public*, pg. 1233

VAPOR-VACUUM—Cappers—White Cap, Inc.; *U.S. Public*, pg. 1207

VAPORFLO—Test Equipment—Tenney Environmental; *U.S. Private*, pg. 1076

VAPORGARD—Anti-Transpirant—Miller Chemical & Fertilizer Corp.; *U.S. Private*, pg. 33

VAPORIZER IN A BOTTLE—Portable Decongestant—Columbia Laboratories, Inc.; *U.S. Public*, pg. 405

VAPORTAPE—Control Release Dispensers—Hercon Environmental Corporation; *U.S. Public*, pg. 802

VAPORUB—Vapor Ointment—Richardson-Vicks, Inc., Health Care Products; *U.S. Public*, pg. 1331

VAPOSEAL—Closure Liner Sealings Materials—Tekni-Plex, Inc.; *U.S. Private*, pg. 1073

VAPOSTEAM—Liquid Medication for Steam—Richardson-Vicks, Inc., Health Care Products; *U.S. Public*, pg. 1331

VAPSTOP—Cold Store & Swimming Pool Vapor Barrier—Carter Holt Harvey Limited; *U.S. Public*, pg. 904

VAPURE—Vapor Compression Still—Paul Mueller Company; *U.S. Public*, pg. 1141

VAQUEIRO—Margarine—FIMA-Productos Alimentares, Lda; *Int'l*, pg. 471

VARAMIDES—Alkanolamide—Witco Corporation; *U.S. Public*, pg. 1773

VARASHIELD—Air Deflector—Peterbilt Motors Co.; *U.S. Public*, pg. 1247

VARATHANE—Liquid Plastics—The Flecto Co., Inc.; *U.S. Private*, pg. 410

VARATHANE ELITE DIAMOND FINISH—Transparent IPN Coating—The Flecto Co., Inc.; *U.S. Private*, pg. 410

VARATORQ—Tension Control—P/A Industries, Inc.; *U.S. Private*, pg. 825

VARBUSINESS—Magazine—CMP Media, Inc.; *U.S. Public*, pg. 279

VARCO—Top Drive Drilling Systems & Other Oil Tools—Varco International, Inc.; *U.S. Public*, pg. 1709

VARDEX—Steel Wire Reinforced PVC Tubing—NewAge Industries Inc.; *U.S. Private*, pg. 796

VARDEX—Wire Reinforced PVC Hose—Newage Industries Inc., Plastics Technology Group; *U.S. Private*, pg. 796

VAREC—Tank Liquid Level Measurement—Emerson Electric Co.; *U.S. Public*, pg. 572

VAREL—Drilling Bits—Varel Manufacturing Co.; *U.S. Private*, pg. 1134

VAREX—Blown Film Line—Windmoeller & Hoelscher; *Int'l*, pg. 1510

VARI-BLADE—Blades—Becton Dickinson & Co., Massachusetts Div.; *U.S. Public*, pg. 199

VARI CAM—Gamma Camera—Elscint Ltd.; *Int'l*, pg. 450

VARI-CELL—Robotic Unit—Universal Instruments Corporation; *U.S. Public*, pg. 522

VARI-INTENSE—Horns with SPL Correction for Long-Throw—Altec Lansing Corp.; *U.S. Private*, pg. 479

VARI-SPEED—Mechanical, Adjustable Speed Pulleys—Rockwell International Corporation; *U.S. Public*, pg. 1397

VARI-TAP—Transformers—Atlas/Soundolier; *U.S. Private*, pg. 64

VARI-TEMP—Hold Over Plate Refrigeration System For Truck Bodies—Kidron Inc.; *U.S. Private*, pg. 619

VARI-TEMP—Cold Plate Refrigeration Systems—Transportation Technologies, Inc.; *U.S. Private*, pg. 1097

VARIABLE INCLINING POSITIONS BED—Electric Bed—Kingsdown, Inc.; *U.S. Private*, pg. 622

VARIAC—NONE—GenRad, Inc.; *U.S. Public*, pg. 731

VARIAN TEM—Surgical Medical & Radio-Therapeutic Apparatus & Instruments—Varian Associates, Inc.; *U.S. Public*, pg. 1710

VARIANCE—Women's Apparel—International Cosmetics Co., Ltd.; *Int'l*, pg. 684

VARIANCE—Intimate Apparel—VF Corporation; *U.S. Public*, pg. 1702

VARIANT—Adjustable Height Table—Howe Furniture Corporation; *U.S. Private*, pg. 543

VARIATION V—Stainless Steel Flatware—Dansk International Designs Ltd.; *U.S. Public*, pg. 261

VARIATIONS—Contact Lens—Essilor International Compagnie Generale d'Optique; *Int'l*, pg. 462

VARIATIONS—Magazine—General Media International Inc.; *U.S. Private*, pg. 444

VARIAX—NONE—Giddings & Lewis Automation Technology; *Int'l*, pg. 1389

VARICEL—Air Filter—AAF-International; *U.S. Private*, pg. 3

VARIDRIVE—Mechanical Speed Drive—U.S. Electrical Motor Division; *U.S. Public*, pg. 573

VARIDYNE—Inverter Duty Motors—U.S. Electrical Motor Division; *U.S. Public*, pg. 573

VARIETY—Cereal Assortment in 10 Single-Serving Packages—Kellogg Company; *U.S. Public*, pg. 947

VARIETY—Global Newspaper for the Entertainment Industry—Reed Elsevier Business Information; *Int'l*, pg. 1095

VARIETY'S ON PRODUCTION—Magazine Reporting on Production & Post-Production Technology in Film/TV—Reed Elsevier Business Information; *Int'l*, pg. 1095

VARIFUEL—Gaseous Fuel Systems for Large Industrial Engines—IMPCO AirSensors Technologies; *U.S. Public*, pg. 34

VARIG—Brazilian Airlines—Varig Brazilian Airlines; *Int'l*, pg. 1451

VARIHUE—Digital Memo Board Pricing System—American Sign & Marketing Services, Inc.; *U.S. Public*, pg. 1309

VARILUX—Lens—Essilor International Compagnie Generale d'Optique; *Int'l*, pg. 462

VARILUX-MULTI-DESIGN (VMD)—Lens—Essilor International Compagnie Generale d'Optique; *Int'l*, pg. 462

VARIMIXER—Welbilt Mixer—Welbilt Corporation; *Int'l*, pg. 188

VARIO-RETINAR—Lenses—Eastman Kodak Company; *U.S. Public*, pg. 550

VARIOLAC 83, 95, 99—Bio-Product—Kali-Chemie Aktiengesellschaft; *Int'l*, pg. 1278

VARIOTIN—Antibiotic Preparations—Nippon Kayaku Co. Ltd.; *Int'l*, pg. 934

VARIPAK—Valves—Masoneilan North American Operations; *U.S. Public*, pg. 528

VARISOFT—Main Conditioning Ingredients—Witco Corporation; *U.S. Public*, pg. 1773

VARITEMP HEAT GUN—Flameless Heat Gun—Master Appliance Corp.; *U.S. Private*, pg. 713

VARITRAC—Mechanical Traction Drive—U.S. Electrical Motor Division; *U.S. Public*, pg. 573

VARITY ZECAL—Copper to Ceramic Bonding for Electroinics—LucasVarity Inc.; *Int'l*, pg. 820

VARITYPER COLOR MANAGEMENT SYSTEM—System Calibration Software—Prepress Solutions, Inc.; *U.S. Private*, pg. 882

VARITYPER COLOR PROOFING SYSTEMS—Commercial & Desktop Models Available—Prepress Solutions, Inc.; *U.S. Private*, pg. 882

VARITYPER IMAGE MANAGEMENT—Sophisticated Network Image Management Software—Prepress Solutions, Inc.; *U.S. Private*, pg. 882

VARITYPER PRINTMASTER—Imagesetter Control Software—Prepress Solutions, Inc.; *U.S. Private*, pg. 882

VARITYPER TOOLBOX—Imagesetter Calibration Software—Prepress Solutions, Inc.; *U.S. Private*, pg. 882

VARIVENT—Valve—Tuchenhagen GmbH; *Int'l*, pg. 1426

VARIZONE—Air Conditioning/Heating VAV—Lennox International Inc.; *U.S. Private*, pg. 659

VARMOR—Paint—Pratt & Lambert United, Inc.; *U.S. Public*, pg. 1466

VARNITE—Electrical Steel Sheet—British Steel Plc; *Int'l*, pg. 220

VARNVILLE DOORS—Architectural Doors—Weyerhaeuser Forest Products Company; *U.S. Public*, pg. 1764

VAROX—Amine Oxides—Witco Corporation; *U.S. Public*, pg. 1773

VARSITY—Stationery Products—The Mead Corporation; *U.S. Public*, pg. 1074

VARTA—Batteries & Plastics—VARTA AG; *Int'l*, pg. 1451

VARTA—Batteries—VARTA Batteries Inc.; *Int'l*, pg. 1452

VAS—Skis—Rossignol Ski Co.; *Int'l*, pg. 1127

VASCO DIE—Tool & Die Steel—Allvac; *U.S. Public*, pg. 43

VASCO HYPERCUT—High Speed Steel—Allvac; *U.S. Public*, pg. 43

VASCO SUPREME—High Speed Steel—Allvac; *U.S. Public*, pg. 43

VASCO TUF—Tool & Die Steel—Allvac; *U.S. Public*, pg. 43

VASCO WEAR—Tool & Die Steel—Allvac; *U.S. Public*, pg. 43

VASCOMAX—18% Nickel Maraging Steel—Allvac; *U.S. Public*, pg. 43

VASCOR TABLETS—NONE—Ortho-McNeil Pharmaceutical Corporation; *U.S. Public*, pg. 929

VASCORAY—X-Ray Contrast Media—Mallinckrodt Inc.; *U.S. Public*, pg. 1039

VASCUCLUDER—Internal Balloon Blood Vessel Occluder—Baxter Research Medical, Inc.; *U.S. Public*, pg. 196

VASCUSHUNT—Balloon-Tipped Vascular Shunt—Baxter Research Medical, Inc.; *U.S. Public*, pg. 196

VASELINE—Petroleum Jelly—Chesebrough-Pond's USA Co.; *Int'l*, pg. 1435

VASELINE DERMASIL—Dry Skin Treatment Lotion—Chesebrough-Pond's USA Co.; *Int'l*, pg. 1435

VASELINE INTENSIVE CARE—Hand & Body Lotions, UV Lotio, Overnight Moisture Treatment Cream—Chesebrough-Pond's USA Co.; *Int'l*, pg. 1435

VASELINE INTENSIVE CARE HAND 'N' NAIL—Lotion—Unilever Plc; *Int'l*, pg. 1433

VASELINE INTENSIVE CARE NO BURN NO BITE—Moisturizing Sunblock Lotion—Chesebrough-Pond's USA Co.; *Int'l*, pg. 1435

VASELINE LIP THERAPY—Lip Care Prods.—Chesebrough-Pond's USA Co.; *Int'l*, pg. 1435

VASERETIC—Enalapril Maleate & Hydrochlorothiazide—Merck & Co., Inc.; *U.S. Public*, pg. 1090

VASERETIC—Pharmaceutical—Merck Human Health Division (U.S. Human Health); *U.S. Public*, pg. 1091

VASODILAN—Pharmaceutical Product to Increase Blood Flow in Some Vascular Disorders—Bristol-Myers Squibb U.S. Pharmaceutical Group; *U.S. Public*, pg. 255

VASONASE—Nicardipine Hydrochloride—Syntex; *Int'l*, pg. 1120

VASOSEAL—Vascular Hemostasis Device for Sealing of Wounds—Datascope Corp.; *U.S. Public*, pg. 487

VASOTEC—Enalapril Maleate—Merck & Co., Inc.; *U.S. Public*, pg. 1090

VASOTEC—Pharmaceutical—Merck Human Health Division (U.S. Human Health); *U.S. Public*, pg. 1091

VASOXYL—Pharmaceutical Product—Glaxo Wellcome PLC; *Int'l*, pg. 553

VASPORT—Implantable Port for Chemotherapy, Intravenous Feeding & Delivery of Drugs—Gish Biomedical, Inc.; *U.S. Public*, pg. 745

VASQUE—Hiking & Mountaineering Shoes—Red Wing Shoe Co., Inc.; *U.S. Private*, pg. 915

VAASA—NONE—Suomen Rehu Oy; *Int'l*, pg. 349

VASSAR PIONEER TIMES—Newspaper—The Hearst Corporation; *U.S. Private*, pg. 515

VASSARETTE—Intimate Apparel—VF Corporation; *U.S. Public*, pg. 1702

VAST—Variable Accuracy & Speed Probing Technology for Meteorology—Carl Zeiss; *Int'l*, pg. 1522

VAUBAN—Food Products—Rykoff-Sexton, Inc.; *U.S. Public*, pg. 918

VAUGHN-BASSETT—NONE—Royal Waterbeds; *U.S. Private*, pg. 949

THE VAULT—Alternative Rock Programming—Westwood One, Inc.; *U.S. Public*, pg. 1763

VAUXHALL—Passenger Cars—General Motors Corporation; *U.S. Public*, pg. 718

VAVOOM—Hair Care Prods.—Matrix Essentials, Inc.; *U.S. Public*, pg. 254

VBALL—Rolling Ball Pen—The Pilot Pen Corp. of America; *Int'l*, pg. 1057

VEAL-GLO—Veal Feeds—Manna Pro Corporation; *U.S. Private*, pg. 700

VECOS—Vehicle Electrical Checkout System—GenRad, Inc.; *U.S. Public*, pg. 731

VECTIS—Cameras—Minolta Corporation; *Int'l*, pg. 869

VECTOBAC—Insecticide—Abbott Laboratories; *U.S. Public*, pg. 12

VECTOR—Writing Instruments & Desk Sets—Gillette Co.-Parker Pen USA; *U.S. Public*, pg. 745

VECTOR—Engines Rotary Mowers—Tecumseh Products Co. Engine & Transmission Group; *U.S. Public*, pg. 1566

VECTOR—Office Seating—United Chair, Inc.; *U.S. Private*, pg. 512

VECTOR BY JUNO—Trac Lighting Fixtures—Juno Lighting, Inc.; *U.S. Public*, pg. 935

VECTOR MODE—Writing Instruments—Gillette Co.-Parker Pen USA; *U.S. Public*, pg. 745

VECTOR TECHNOLOGY—Wet Scrubber—ATMI, Inc.; *U.S. Public*, pg. 12

VECTORCAM—Line of Professional Products—Vicon Industries, Inc.; *U.S. Public*, pg. 1719

VECTRA—NONE—Vauxhall; *U.S. Public*, pg. 724

VECTRA—Motor Homes—Winnebago Industries, Inc.; *U.S. Public*, pg. 1772

VECTRA GRAND TOUR—Motor Home—Winnebago Industries, Inc.; *U.S. Public*, pg. 1772

VECTRIN—Insecticide—Roussel Corporation; *Int'l*, pg. 625

VECTRIN—Insecticide—Roussel UCLAF S.A.; *Int'l*, pg. 626

VECTRIN FOUR PLUS ONE—Insecticide—Roussel Corporation; *Int'l*, pg. 625

VECTRIN FOUR PLUS ONE—Insecticide—Roussel UCLAF S.A.; *Int'l*, pg. 626

VEDOC—Organic Powder Coatings—Ferro Corporation; *U.S. Public*, pg. 618

VEDOC HI-Q—Finsishing Materials—Ferro Corporation; *U.S. Public*, pg. 618

VEE-BALL—U-NotchRotary Valves—Fisher Controls International, Inc.; *U.S. Public*, pg. 573

VEE PAC—Engine Air Filter—Donaldson Company, Inc.; *U.S. Public*, pg. 517

VEEDOL—Lubricants—Burmah Castrol plc; *Int'l*, pg. 234

VEEJET—Spray Nozzle—Spraying Systems Co.; *U.S. Private*, pg. 1026

VEELOK GOLD—Non-asbestos woven clutch facing liner—Universal Composites-U.S.C.; *U.S. Private*, pg. 1126

VEELOS-V—Belts—Fenner Drives; *U.S. Private*, pg. 400

VEET—Depilatories—Reckitt & Colman plc; *Int'l*, pg. 1089

VEG-ALL—Canned Vegetables—Dean Foods Company; *U.S. Public*, pg. 489

VEG-ALL—Canned & Frozen Vegetables—Dean Foods Vegetable Company; *U.S. Public*, pg. 490

VEGA—NONE—Carpenter Technology Corporation; *U.S. Public*, pg. 307

VEGA LUBE—Bread Pan Oils—Mallet & Co.; *U.S. Private*, pg. 698

VEGA II—Full Glue Installed Sheet Vinyl Flooring—Mannington Resilient Floors; *U.S. Private*, pg. 700

VEGALUBE—Pan Oil—Mallet & Co.; *U.S. Private*, pg. 698

VEGAMINE—Hydrolyzed Vegetable Protein—Griffith Laboratories Worldwide, Inc.; *U.S. Private*, pg. 481

VEGAS INSTANT PAGE—Paging Service Provider—AT&T Wireless Services; *U.S. Public*, pg. 11

VEGAS NITE—Casino Game—Mattel Games/Puzzles; *U.S. Public*, pg. 1058

VEGETABLE CRISPS—Breaded Vegetables—Ore-Ida Foods, Inc.; *U.S. Public*, pg. 805

THE VEGETABLE STAND SALADS—NONE—Koo Koo Roo, Inc.; *U.S. Public*, pg. 966

VEGETABLE SUPREME—Seasoning—McCormick & Company, Incorporated; *U.S. Public*, pg. 1066

VEGETABLE THINS—Snack Crackers—Nabisco Inc.; *U.S. Public*, pg. 1355

VEGETABLES N' PASTRY—Vegetables in Puffed Pastry—Pepperidge Farm, Incorporated; *U.S. Public*, pg. 299

VEGETARIAN TIMES—Periodical—Cowles Enthusiast Media, Inc.; *U.S. Private*, pg. 281

VEGISNAX—Vegetable Snacks—DNAP Holding Corp.; *Int'l*, pg. 454

VEHICLE/N—Topical Vehicle Systems for Compounding—Neutrogena Corporation; *U.S. Public*, pg. 928

VEHICLE/N MILD—Topical Vehicle Systems for Compounding—Neutrogena Corporation; *U.S. Public*, pg. 928

LE VEILLEES DES CHAUMIERES—French Outdoor Pursuits Magazine—EMAP France; *Int'l*, pg. 451

VEL—Soap—Colgate-Palmolive Company; *U.S. Public*, pg. 397

VELAMINTS—Sugarfree Mints—Ragold, Inc.; *Int'l*, pg. 1084

VELAN—Seismic Exploration & Data Analysis— Litton Industries, Inc.; *U.S. Public*, pg. 1002

VELATE—Coalescing Agent—Velsicol Chemical Corporation; *U.S. Private*, pg. 1135

VELBAN—Vinblastine Sulfate, Lilly—Eli Lilly and Company; *U.S. Public*, pg. 992

VELCRO—Hook & Loop Fasteners—Velcro Industries N.V.; *Int'l*, pg. 1462

VELCRO—Fasteners—Velcro USA Inc.; *Int'l*, pg. 1462

VELDEX—Industrial Coating—The Dexter Corporation; *U.S. Public*, pg. 504

VELDOWN—Facial Tissue, Bathroom Tissue— Kimberly-Clark Corporation; *U.S. Public*, pg. 958

VELDURA—NONE—Royal Rubber & Manufacturing Co.; *U.S. Private*, pg. 949

VELLUX—Bed & Bath Products—WestPoint Stevens Inc.; *U.S. Public*, pg. 1762

VELOCE 500—Women's Apparel—A&E Stores, Inc.; *U.S. Private*, pg. 1

VELOCICALC—Portable Velocity Meter—TSI Incorporated; *U.S. Public*, pg. 1559

VELOCICHECK—Air Velocity Meter—TSI Incorporated; *U.S. Public*, pg. 1559

VELOCITRON—Automatic Packager—Pneumatic Scale Corporation; *U.S. Public*, pg. 118

VELOCITY—NONE—Evans & Sutherland Computer Corporation; *U.S. Public*, pg. 595

VELOCITY MODULATION—Scanning Apparatus— Sony Electronics; *Int'l*, pg. 1281

VELOMETER—Air Velocity Measuring Device— Alnor Instrument Company; *U.S. Public*, pg. 1559

VELOSEF—Infectious Disease Therapy—Bristol-Myers Squibb Company; *U.S. Public*, pg. 253

VELOSTAT—Electrically Conductive Plastics—3M; *U.S. Public*, pg. 1604

VELOSULIN—Product for Diabetes Care—Novo Nordisk A/S; *Int'l*, pg. 987

VELOUR—Alkyd Enamel—Devoe Paint; *Int'l*, pg. 663

VELOUR—Alkyd enamel—ICI Paints; *Int'l*, pg. 664

VELOURS NOIR—Coffee—Kraft Jacobs Suchard; *U.S. Public*, pg. 1290

VELOUTINE—Sauce Binders—Bestfoods; *U.S. Public*, pg. 223

VELOX—Photo Paper & Printers—Eastman Kodak Company; *U.S. Public*, pg. 550

VELPAR—Herbicide—Du Pont (E.I. Du Pont De Nemours & Co.); *U.S. Public*, pg. 530

VELSICURE—Benzophenone—Velsicol Chemical Corporation; *U.S. Private*, pg. 1135

VELTEX—Surface Treated Cones for Textiles— Sonoco Products Company; *U.S. Public*, pg. 1485

VELV-IT—Wood Stain—Jones Blair Company; *U.S. Private*, pg. 596

VELVA-GLO—Enamel—Jones Blair Company; *U.S. Private*, pg. 596

VELVA-GRAIN—Wood Stain—Jones Blair Company; *U.S. Private*, pg. 596

VELVACHOL—Pharmaceutical Products— Galderma Laboratories, Inc.; *Int'l*, pg. 819

VELVEETA—Pasteurized Process Cheese Loaf— Kraft Foods Inc.; *U.S. Public*, pg. 1288

VELVEETA—Pasteurized Process Cheese, Packaged Dinners—Philip Morris Companies Inc.; *U.S. Public*, pg. 1287

VELVET—Household Paper Goods—Orchids Paper Products Co.; *U.S. Private*, pg. 819

VELVET—Woodcase Pencil—Sanford Corporation; *U.S. Public*, pg. 1178

VELVET—Cones & Tubes—Sonoco Products Company; *U.S. Public*, pg. 1485

VELVET DRIVE TRANSMISSIONS—NONE— Regal-Beloit Corporation; *U.S. Public*, pg. 1370

VELVET-FAB—Flocked Gift Ribbon—American Greetings Corporation; *U.S. Public*, pg. 77

VELVET-RIB—Flocked Gift Ribbon—American Greetings Corporation; *U.S. Public*, pg. 77

VELVET SERIES—Carpet Tile—Interface Inc.; *U.S. Public*, pg. 889

VELVET-TIP—Oral Hygiene Aids—John O. Butler Co.; *Int'l*, pg. 1320

VELVETEX—Amphoteric Betaine—Henkel Corporation; *Int'l*, pg. 610

VELVETOUCH—Friction Metal Plate—The S.K. Wellman Friction Products Co.; *U.S. Private*, pg. 511

VELVETTA—Processed Cheese Product—Alliant Foodservice, Inc.; *U.S. Private*, pg. 244

VELVEX—Pattern Glass—AFG Industries, Inc.; *Int'l*, pg. 84

VELVO—Printing Papers—Westvaco Corporation; *U.S. Public*, pg. 1762

VENCAT—Telecommunications Channel Access Test Sets—3M; *Int'l*, pg. 1604

VENCO—Liquorice—CSM N.V.; *Int'l*, pg. 243

VENDCART—Mobile Food Service Vending Carts—Kidron Inc.; *U.S. Private*, pg. 619

VENDING MACHINE VINYL—Special Film for Vending Machine Graphics—Fasson Films; *U.S. Public*, pg. 153

VENDOME—Jewelry—Richton International Corporation; *U.S. Public*, pg. 1389

VENDOR'S SELECT—Coffee—International Multifoods Corporation; *U.S. Public*, pg. 900

VENDORNET—Inventory Control—Graybar Electric Company, Inc.; *U.S. Private*, pg. 472

VENEMAN—Cast Aluminum Contract Seating— Tropitone Furniture Co. Inc.; *U.S. Private*, pg. 1105

VENERABLE—Sherry—Domecq Importers Inc.; *Int'l*, pg. 63

VENES—NONE—Futuro Inc.; *Int'l*, pg. 182

VENETEX—Plywood—Georgia-Pacific Corporation; *U.S. Public*, pg. 735

VENGEANCE—Rodenticide—Roussel Corporation; *Int'l*, pg. 625

VENGEANCE—Rodenticide—Roussel UCLAF S.A.; *Int'l*, pg. 626

VENI-GARD—Disposable, Sterile I.V. Products— Conmed Corporation; *U.S. Public*, pg. 431

VENO'S—Coughs, Colds & Influenza Product— SmithKline Beecham plc; *Int'l*, pg. 1264

VENOGLOBULIN-I—NONE—Alpha Therapeutic Corp.; *Int'l*, pg. 558

VENOGLOBULIN-S—NONE—Alpha Therapeutic Corp.; *Int'l*, pg. 558

VENOJECT—Blood Collection Products—Terumo Medical Corporation; *Int'l*, pg. 1376

VENOJECT II—Blood Collection Products— Terumo Medical Corporation; *Int'l*, pg. 1376

VENT-A-RIDGE—Attic Ventilation System—Alcoa Building Products, Inc.; *U.S. Public*, pg. 61

VENT-A-SYSTEM—Attic Ventilation System— Alcoa Building Products, Inc.; *U.S. Public*, pg. 61

VENTAIR—Blowers—Coppus Murray Group, Tuthill Corporation; *U.S. Private*, pg. 1110

VENTAK AICD—Implantable Defibrillator Systems—Guidant Corporation-Cardiac Rhythm Management Group; *U.S. Public*, pg. 768

VENTAMATIC—Residential Ventilation Products— Butler Ventamatic Corp.; *U.S. Private*, pg. 190

VENTANIP—Press—Beloit Corporation; *U.S. Public*, pg. 789

VENTECH—Dyed & Reconstructed Natural Wood Veneer—Carter Holt Harvey Limited; *U.S. Public*, pg. 904

VENTED PICO HOLDER—High-Density Polyethylene Holder for Miniature Vials— Packard Instrument Co., Inc.; *U.S. Private*, pg. 833

VENTEX—Polymeric Roll Cover used for Grooved Press Rolls—Harnischfeger Industries, Inc.; *U.S. Public*, pg. 788

VENTFAB—NONE—Flexfab Horizons International, Inc.; *U.S. Private*, pg. 412

VENTI-COMP—NONE—Hudson, RCI; *U.S. Private*, pg. 546

VENTILITE—Shoe Upper Material—Reebok International Ltd.; *U.S. Public*, pg. 1369

VENTMASTER—Ventilation Equipment—Garland Commercial Ranges, Ltd.; *Int'l*, pg. 189

VENTO—Automobile—Volkswagen AG; *Int'l*, pg. 1473

VENTOLIN—Asthma Treatment—Glaxo Wellcome Inc.; *Int'l*, pg. 552

VENTOLIN—Pharmaceutical—Glaxo Wellcome plc; *Int'l*, pg. 552

VENTREX—Pleated Cartridge Filters—Osmonics, Inc.; *U.S. Public*, pg. 1233

VENTROL—Medico-Surgical Tube Appliances— Mallinckrodt Inc.; *U.S. Public*, pg. 1039

VENTSULATION—Roof Felt—Johns Manville Corporation; *U.S. Public*, pg. 927

VENTSURE—Ridge Vents—Owens Corning; *U.S. Public*, pg. 1236

VENTURA—Pleasure Boat Name—Regal Marine Industries Inc.; *U.S. Private*, pg. 917

VENTURA COUNTY STAR-FREE PRESS—J.P. Scripps Newspaper Group Dallies—The E.W. Scripps Company; *U.S. Public*, pg. 1447

VENTURA PUBLISHER—Computer Software— Xerox Corporation; *U.S. Public*, pg. 1783

VENTURE—Small Business Risk Scoring Service—Fair, Isaac and Company, Inc.; *U.S. Public*, pg. 609

VENTURE—Liquid Men's Hair Dressing—Menley & James Laboratories; *U.S. Public*, pg. 1086

VENTURE—Financial Card Game—Monarch Avalon, Inc.; *U.S. Public*, pg. 1123

VENTURE—Manual Wheelchair—Theradyne Corporation; *U.S. Private*, pg. 637

VENTURE—NONE—Venture Stores, Inc.; *U.S. Public*, pg. 1716

VENTURE DOLLAR—NONE—Venture Stores, Inc.; *U.S. Public*, pg. 1716

VENTURI—Flow Meters—BIF; *U.S. Public*, pg. 726

VENTURI—4 Week Stop Smoking System— Venturi Inc.; *U.S. Private*, pg. 1136

VENTURI-RECYCLE TRAY—High-Velocity Liquid Recycle Gas/Liquid Contact Plate—Beco Engineering Company; *U.S. Private*, pg. 129

VENTURION—High Efficiency Industrial Unit Heaters—Thomas & Betts Reznor Division; *U.S. Public*, pg. 1598

VENTURIVENT—NONE—Air Vent Inc.; *Int'l*, pg. 1170

VENTUS—Liposomal Prostaglandin E1—The Liposome Company, Inc.; *U.S. Public*, pg. 1000

VENTWOOD—Wood Arch Panels—Howard Manufacturing; *U.S. Private*, pg. 477

VENUS—Message/Animation Display Control System—Daktronics, Inc.; *U.S. Public*, pg. 478

VENZ—Sweet Sandwich Fillings—CSM N.V.; *Int'l*, pg. 243

VEPESID—Anti-Cancer Agent—Bristol-Myers Squibb Company; *U.S. Public*, pg. 253

VEPESID—Pharmaceutical Used in Treatment of Lung Cancer—Bristol-Myers Squibb U.S. Pharmaceutical Group; *U.S. Public*, pg. 255

VERA—Mineral Water—Nestle S.A.; *Int'l*, pg. 915

VERA—Clothing—Salant Corporation; *U.S. Public*, pg. 1479

VERA CRUZ—Mexican Food Products—Don Miguel Mexican Foods, Inc.; *U.S. Private*, pg. 339

VERABILL—Telephone Company Billing System— Moscom Corporation; *U.S. Public*, pg. 1136

VERAFLEX—Electronic Component—Shure Brothers Incorporated; *U.S. Private*, pg. 997

VERAL DE BELVAL—Textile—Hermes International; *Int'l*, pg. 617

VERANDA—Rattan—Avon Workshop Ficks Reed; *U.S. Private*, pg. 102

VERASEAL—Trocar Seal—U.S. Surgical Corp.; *U.S. Public*, pg. 1687

VERATRAN—Sedatives—Kali-Chemie Aktiengesellschaft; *Int'l*, pg. 1278

VERATREX—Filter—Osmonics, Inc.; *U.S. Public*, pg. 1233

VERATRONICS—NONE—Taylor Impression, Inc.; *U.S. Private*, pg. 1070

VERCOOPE—Verde, Wine from Cooperatives— Vercoope-Uniao Das Adegas Cooperativas da Regiao Dos Vinhoa Verdes, U.C.R.L.; *Int'l*, pg. 1463

VERDEGAR—NONE—Vercoope-Uniao Das Adegas Cooperativas da Regiao Dos Vinhoa Verdes, U.C.R.L.; *Int'l*, pg. 1463

VERDICHTER OE—Compressor—Electrolux, AB; *Int'l*, pg. 438

VERDICT—Grass Killer—The Dow Chemical Company; *U.S. Public*, pg. 522

VEREDUS—Surface Flaw Detection & Analysis System—Eastman Kodak Company; *U.S. Public*, pg. 550

VERELAN—Cardiovascular Drug—American Home Products Corporation; *U.S. Public*, pg. 79

VERELAN—NONE—Elan Corporation Plc; *Int'l*, pg. 435

VERGE—Magazine—Times Mirror Magazines, Inc.; *U.S. Public*, pg. 1616

VERI-LITE—Distribution Insulators—The Ohio Brass Co.; *U.S. Public*, pg. 845

Brand Name Index

VERI-SHARP—Cutlery—Imperial Schrade Corp.; *U.S. Private*, pg. 559

VERI-SOFT—Vascular Graft—Meadox Medicals, Inc.; *U.S. Public*, pg. 247

VERI TEST—Destructive Machine Software—Weigh-Tronix, Inc.; *Int'l*, pg. 1299

VERIBEST—Canned Meats—Armour Food Company; *U.S. Public*, pg. 427

VERIBROM—Photographic Developer—Eastman Kodak Company; *U.S. Public*, pg. 550

VERICAP—Pharmaceutical Weighing & Sorting System—Modern Controls, Inc.; *U.S. Public*, pg. 1120

VERICHROME—Photo Film—Eastman Kodak Company; *U.S. Public*, pg. 550

VERICOLOR—Photo Color Film, Chemicals—Eastman Kodak Company; *U.S. Public*, pg. 550

VERIDATE—Tablet Dispenser—Ortho-McNeil Pharmaceutical Corporation; *U.S. Public*, pg. 929

VERIFAX—Photocopying Equipment, Paper & Chemicals, Copy Paper—Eastman Kodak Company; *U.S. Public*, pg. 550

VERIFIER—Pipe & Cable Locator—McLaughlin Manufacturing Company; *U.S. Private*, pg. 724

THE VERIFIER—Central Station Alarm Verification System—Vicon Industries, Inc.; *U.S. Public*, pg. 1719

VERIFILE—Microfilm—Eastman Kodak Company; *U.S. Public*, pg. 550

VERIFINE—Milk—Dean Foods Company; *U.S. Public*, pg. 489

VERIFORE FOLIO—Transaction Storage Device for Restaurant Table Service—VeriFone, Inc.; *U.S. Public*, pg. 815

VERIFY—Temporary Screening Lead—Medtronic, Inc.; *U.S. Public*, pg. 1082

VERIGOOD—Blotter Paper—FiberMark Inc.; *U.S. Public*, pg. 620

VERIGOOD—Toilet Tissue—Georgia-Pacific Corporation; *U.S. Public*, pg. 735

VERILITH—Sensitized Photo Materials, Chemicals, Photo Copying & Processing Apparatus—Eastman Kodak Company; *U.S. Public*, pg. 550

VERILOG XL—Verilog HDL Logic Simulator—Cadence Design Systems, Inc.; *U.S. Public*, pg. 290

VERINO—Women's Fragrance—Coty Inc.; *Int'l*, pg. 185

VERITAB—Pharmaceutical Weighing & Sorting System—Modern Controls, Inc.; *U.S. Public*, pg. 1120

VERITRAC—Communications Logger—Dictaphone Corp.; *U.S. Private*, pg. 1045

VERKADE—Chocolate Blocks—United Biscuits (Holdings) Plc; *Int'l*, pg. 1442

VERMEER—Farm Equipment; Rubber Tire Trencher, Brush Chipper & Track Trencher—Vermeer Manufacturing Company; *U.S. Private*, pg. 1137

VERMONT AMERICAN—Cutting Tools, Screwdrivers & Power Tool Access.—Vermont American Tool Corp.; *U.S. Public*, pg. 575

VERMONT BEAR-GRAM—NONE—The Vermont Teddy Bear Company, Inc.; *U.S. Public*, pg. 1716

VERMONT MAID—Syrup—Nabisco Inc.; *U.S. Public*, pg. 1355

VERMONT MAID—Syrup—RJR Nabisco Holdings Corp.; *U.S. Public*, pg. 1354

VERMONT MAPLE ORCHARDS—Pure Maple Syrup—Borden, Inc.; *U.S. Private*, pg. 157

VERMONT MARBLE—Marble—Pluess-Staufer AG; *Int'l*, pg. 1061

VERMONT TAP & DIE—Indus. Taps, Dies & Drills—Vermont American Tool Corp.; *U.S. Public*, pg. 575

THE VERMONT TEDDY BEAR COMPANY—Stuffed Toys—The Vermont Teddy Bear Company, Inc.; *U.S. Public*, pg. 1716

VERMOUTH—NONE—Gio. Buton S.p.a.; *Int'l*, pg. 409

VERMOX—Pharmaceutical—Janssen Pharmaceutica, Inc.; *U.S. Public*, pg. 928

VERNACHLOR—Chloreen Compound—Vernay Laboratories, Inc.; *U.S. Private*, pg. 1137

VERNALITE—Needle Valves—Vernay Laboratories, Inc.; *U.S. Private*, pg. 1137

VERNALON—Compound—Vernay Laboratories, Inc.; *U.S. Private*, pg. 1137

VERNEL—Detergent—Henkel KGaA; *Int'l*, pg. 609

VERNITECH—Electronic Components—Axsys Technologies, Inc.; *U.S. Public*, pg. 157

VERNORS—NONE—Cadbury Beverages; *Int'l*, pg. 248

VERNORS—NONE—Cadbury Schweppes p.l.c.; *Int'l*, pg. 247

VERON—Enzymes—Rohm GmbH; *Int'l*, pg. 1454

VERONA—Luggage—American Tourister, Inc.; *U.S. Public*, pg. 1430

VERONES CENTRIFUGE—NONE—Dorr-Oliver Incorporated; *Int'l*, pg. 839

VERONICA—Netherlands Broadcasting—CLT-UFA; *Int'l*, pg. 561

VEROSOL—Interior Window Coverings—Blydenstein-Willink N.V.; *Int'l*, pg. 198

VERS-O-TOOL—Die Heads, Blocks, Chasers—Greenfield Industries; *U.S. Public*, pg. 950

VERSA-BENCH—Mobile Work Bench—Kennedy Manufacturing Company; *U.S. Private*, pg. 614

VERSA-CAL—Thermocouple Calibrators—Avo International; *U.S. Private*, pg. 9

VERSA-CART—Tool Carts—Kennedy Manufacturing Company; *U.S. Private*, pg. 614

VERSA-CLUTCH—Power Tools—The Black & Decker Corporation; *U.S. Public*, pg. 233

VERSA-CRIMP—Compression Connectors & Tools—Square D Company; *Int'l*, pg. 1208

VERSA-FX—Compression Hip Fixation System—Bristol-Myers Squibb Company; *U.S. Public*, pg. 253

VERSA-FILE—Liquid Scintillation Feature—Beckman Instruments, Inc.; *U.S. Public*, pg. 199

VERSA-KOTE—Paint—Pratt & Lambert United, Inc.; *U.S. Public*, pg. 1466

VERSA-LAM—Laminated Veneer Lumber Beams—Boise Cascade Corporation; *U.S. Public*, pg. 242

VERSA-LAM PLUS—Laminated Veneer Lumber Beams—Boise Cascade Corporation; *U.S. Public*, pg. 242

VERSA LATCH—Fasteners—Southtec, Inc.; *U.S. Private*, pg. 1015

VERSA-LOADER—Load Frame—ELE International, Inc./Soiltest; *Int'l*, pg. 1287

VERSA-RACK—Sampling Handling Apparatus—Beckman Instruments, Inc.; *U.S. Public*, pg. 199

VERSA-STAND—Candle Stand—Will & Baumer Incorporated; *U.S. Private*, pg. 1176

VERSA-STIM—Disposable Electrodes—Conmed Corporation; *U.S. Public*, pg. 431

VERSA-TESTER—Construction Test Equipment—ELE International, Inc./Soiltest; *Int'l*, pg. 1287

VERSA-TINT—Tinting Colors—Jones Blair Company; *U.S. Private*, pg. 596

VERSA-TOGGLE—Plastic Screw Anchor—Gunnebo Fastening Corp.; *U.S. Private*, pg. 488

VERSA-TOOLS—Kitchen tools—Ekco Housewares, Inc.; *U.S. Public*, pg. 566

VERSA 22—Lounge Seating And Tables—United Chair, Inc.; *U.S. Private*, pg. 512

VERSA-BATH—Bath Heater & Controller—Fisher Scientific Company; *U.S. Private*, pg. 658

VERSA-TABLE—Modular Lab Table—Fisher Scientific Company; *U.S. Private*, pg. 658

VERSABACS—Carpet Backing System—The Dow Chemical Company; *U.S. Public*, pg. 522

VERSABOARD—Particleboard—Weyerhaeuser Company; *U.S. Public*, pg. 1764

VERSACAD—CAD Systems Software—Parametric Technology Corporation; *U.S. Public*, pg. 1257

VERSACONTROLLER—Computer Based Control System for Semiconductor Equip.—Applied Materials, Inc.; *U.S. Public*, pg. 123

VERSADET—Detergent—Oakite Products, Inc.; *Int'l*, pg. 861

VERSADYME—Dimerized Fatty Acids—Henkel Corporation; *Int'l*, pg. 610

VERSAFIT—Heat-Shrinkable Tubing—Raychem Corporation; *U.S. Public*, pg. 1362

VERSAFLO—Photo Chemicals—Eastman Kodak Company; *U.S. Public*, pg. 550

VERSAFORM—Microfilming Apparatus—Eastman Kodak Company; *U.S. Public*, pg. 550

VERSAGUARD—Commodes, Raised Toilet Seats & Grab Bars—Lumex Medical Products; *U.S. Public*, pg. 758

VERSALAB—Laboratory Furniture—Kewaunee Scientific Corporation; *U.S. Public*, pg. 953

VERSALITE—Photographic Film & Papers—Eastman Kodak Company; *U.S. Public*, pg. 550

VERSALITE—Shotshell Wads—Hornady Manufacturing Company; *U.S. Private*, pg. 539

VERSALOCK—Plasma Systems—Plasma-Therm, Inc.; *U.S. Public*, pg. 1308

VERSALON—Polyamide Hot Melt Adhesive Resins—Henkel Corporation; *Int'l*, pg. 610

VERSALTM—Alumina Product—LaRoche Industries Inc.; *U.S. Private*, pg. 651

VERSAMAT—Retread Equipment—Admiral Heintz, Inc.; *U.S. Public*, pg. 1143

VERSAMAT—Photo Processing Equipment & Chemicals—Eastman Kodak Company; *U.S. Public*, pg. 550

VERSAMATIC—Machinery—Hollingsworth Saco Lowell Corporation, Inc.; *U.S. Private*, pg. 535

VERSAMID—Polyamide Resins—Henkel Corporation; *Int'l*, pg. 610

VERSAMIX—Stirrer—Fisher Scientific Company; *U.S. Private*, pg. 658

VERSAMOUNT—Dry Mounting Tissue—Eastman Kodak Company; *U.S. Public*, pg. 550

VERSAPAK—Power tools—The Black & Decker Corporation; *U.S. Public*, pg. 233

VERSAPOINT—Braille Printer—Telesensory Corporation; *U.S. Private*, pg. 1074

VERASAPORT—Trocar—U.S. Surgical Corp.; *U.S. Public*, pg. 1687

VERSAPOT—Calibrators/Potentiometers—Avo International; *U.S. Private*, pg. 9

VERSAPULSE—Surgical Laser—Coherent, Inc.; *U.S. Public*, pg. 395

VERSAPULSE SELECT—Surgical Laser—Coherent, Inc.; *U.S. Public*, pg. 395

VERSAPUR—Filtration Products—Gelman Sciences, Inc.; *U.S. Public*, pg. 1253

VERSATACK—Surgical Staplers—U.S. Surgical Corp.; *U.S. Public*, pg. 1687

VERSATAN—Shoes—E.J. Footwear Corp.; *U.S. Public*, pg. 1684

VERSATENN—Digital Programmer—Tenney Environmental; *U.S. Private*, pg. 1076

VERSATILE—Tractors—New Holland Ltd.; *Int'l*, pg. 484

VERSATILE 11—Rod Wrapper—Gudebrod; Inc.; *U.S. Private*, pg. 486

VERSATOL—Photo Developer—Eastman Kodak Company; *U.S. Public*, pg. 550

VERSATOL—Electrical Wires, Cables & Conductors—General Electric Canada Inc.; *U.S. Public*, pg. 713

VERSATONE—Photo Processing Chemicals—Eastman Kodak Company; *U.S. Public*, pg. 550

VERSATRONIC—Ranges, Refrigerators, Dishwashers, Washers & Dryers—General Electric Canada Inc.; *U.S. Public*, pg. 713

VERSATRYME—Trimer Acid—Henkel Corporation; *Int'l*, pg. 610

VERSENE—Chelating Agent—The Dow Chemical Company; *U.S. Public*, pg. 522

VERSENEX—Chelating Agent—The Dow Chemical Company; *U.S. Public*, pg. 522

VERSENOL—Chelating Agent—The Dow Chemical Company; *U.S. Public*, pg. 522

VERSETERM—Date Collector—Harnischfeger Industries, Inc.; *U.S. Public*, pg. 788

VERSICAN—Hose—HBD Industries, Inc.; *U.S. Private*, pg. 489

VERSICOPY—Cut Size Copy Paper—Network Services Company; *U.S. Private*, pg. 791

VERSIFEEDER—Vibrating Screw Feeder—Vibra Screw Inc.; *U.S. Private*, pg. 1138

VERSIFORM—Concrete Forming System—Symons Corporation; *U.S. Private*, pg. 932

VERSILOK—Acrylic Adhesive—Lord Corporation; *U.S. Private*, pg. 675

VERSITRON—Hardness Tester—NewAge Industries Inc.; *U.S. Public*, pg. 796

VERSITRON—Hardness Tester—Newage Industries Inc., Testing Instruments Group; *U.S. Private*, pg. 796

VERSON—Metal Forming Presses—Allied Products Corporation; *U.S. Public*, pg. 48

VERSON-WHEELON—Fluid Forming Rubber Bag Hydraulic Presses—Verson Division; *U.S. Public*, pg. 48

VERSTAT—Glass Wool for Thermal & Accoustic Insulation—The Dow Chemical Company; *U.S. Public*, pg. 522

VERT-LOCK—Vises—Wilton Corporation; *U.S. Private*, pg. 1181

VERTAGREEN—Fertilizer—Pursell Industries; *U.S. Private*, pg. 896

VERTEX—Satellite Antennas—Vertex Communications Corporation; *U.S. Public*, pg. 1717

VERTI-LINE—Pumps—Aurora Pump; *U.S. Public*, pg. 726

VERTI-SHIELD—Electrode—The Lincoln Electric Company; *U.S. Public*, pg. 996

VERTICAL FORM, FILL, SEAL—Bagmaking Equipment—G.D. Packaging Machinery Inc.; *Int'l*, pg. 531

VERTICAL PROFILE—Vertical Scanning Weather Radar—AlliedSignal Commercial Avionic Systems; *U.S. Public*, pg. 50

VERTICON—Thin Film Evaporator—Groen, A Dover Industries Co.; *U.S. Public*, pg. 521

VERTICOOL—Counterflow Cooler—Aeroglide Corporation; *U.S. Private*, pg. 24

VERTIFINER—Vertical Two-Disk Refiner—Harnischfeger Industries, Inc.; *U.S. Public*, pg. 788

VERTIFLEX—Stock Preparation—Beloit Corporation; *U.S. Public*, pg. 789

VERTIGAGE—Industrial Instrumentation—Moore Products Co.; *U.S. Public*, pg. 1128

VERTIGO—Book & Magazine Publishing Imprint—DC Comics, Inc.; *U.S. Public*, pg. 1614

VERTIGO—Records—Philips Electronics N.V.; *Int'l*, pg. 1051

VERTILOC—NONE—Western Atlas Logging Services; *U.S. Public*, pg. 1757

VERTOMAX—Vertical Carton Machinery—G.D. Packaging Machinery Inc.; *Int'l*, pg. 531

VERVE—Faucets, Valves & Fittings—The Black & Decker Corporation; *U.S. Public*, pg. 233

VERVE—Records—Philips Electronics N.V.; *Int'l*, pg. 1051

VERY OLD BARTON—Bourbon—Barton Incorporated; *U.S. Public*, pg. 300

VERY OLD BARTON BOURBON—NONE—Barton Brands, Ltd.; *U.S. Public*, pg. 300

THE VERY THING—Mail Order Women's Apparel—DM Management Company; *U.S. Public*, pg. 473

VERYFINE—Fruit Juices & Drinks—Veryfine Products, Inc.; *U.S. Private*, pg. 1137

VES-PHENE—Germ Detergent—Calgon Vestal Laboratories; *U.S. Public*, pg. 1515

VESCAN—Liposomal Formula—Nexstar Pharmaceuticals, Inc.; *U.S. Public*, pg. 1180

VESDIL—Cardiovascular Pharmaceutical—Astra AB; *Int'l*, pg. 93

VESPEL—Polyimide Parts & Shapes—Du Pont (E.I. Du Pont De Nemours & Co.); *U.S. Public*, pg. 530

VESTA DUB—NONE—Pfizer Inc.; *U.S. Public*, pg. 1281

VESTA GLASS—Floor Wax—Calgon Vestal Laboratories; *U.S. Public*, pg. 1515

VESTA INSURANCE—Germicidal Cleaner Concentrate—Calgon Vestal Laboratories; *U.S. Public*, pg. 1515

VESTA IODINE PREP—Iodine Skin Prep—Calgon Vestal Laboratories; *U.S. Public*, pg. 1515

VESTA LOTION SOAP—Cosmetic Quality Liquid Soap—Calgon Vestal Laboratories; *U.S. Public*, pg. 1515

VESTAL MEIDCATED LOTION SOAP—Antimcrobial Lotion Soap—Calgon Vestal Laboratories; *U.S. Public*, pg. 1515

VESTAL 1776—Floor Finish—Calgon Vestal Laboratories; *U.S. Public*, pg. 1515

VESTBAK—Clothing—OshKosh B'Gosh, Inc.; *U.S. Public*, pg. 1232

VESTRA—Dental Material—3M; *U.S. Public*, pg. 1604

VESTURE—Thermal Heating Pads—R.G. Barry Corporation; *U.S. Public*, pg. 192

VESTURIT—Monomer & Coating Resin—Veba AG; *Int'l*, pg. 1454

VET-KEM—Pet-Care Insecticide—Novartis AG; *Int'l*, pg. 971

VETBOND—Veterinary Tissue Adhesive—3M; *U.S. Public*, pg. 1604

VETCAST—Casting Tape, Veterinary—3M; *U.S. Public*, pg. 1604

VETERAN—Industrial Vegetation Control—Riverdale Chemical Co.; *U.S. Private*, pg. 934

THE VETERINARIAN—Magazine—Reed Business Information Pty. Limited; *Int'l*, pg. 1094

VETIMAST—Pharmaceutical—Novartis; *Int'l*, pg. 972

VETO—Farm Machinery—Thrige Agro A/S; *Int'l*, pg. 1386

VETRAP—Veterinarian Bandaging Tape—3M; *U.S. Public*, pg. 1604

VETROLIN—Body Wash—Farnam Companies, Inc.; *U.S. Private*, pg. 396

VETROTEX—Glass Fiber—Saint-Gobain; *Int'l*, pg. 1170

VETS—Dog Food—H.J. Heinz Company; *U.S. Public*, pg. 805

VETS—Dog Food—Star-Kist Foods Inc.; *U.S. Public*, pg. 805

VETSAT—Vetinary Sensor Clip—Nellcor Puritan Bennett Incorporated; *U.S. Public*, pg. 1039

VETTA PASTA—Pasta—Goodman Fielder Limited; *Int'l*, pg. 555

VETTER—Vynlalum Windows—SNE Enterprises, Inc.; *U.S. Public*, pg. 1193

VEUVE AMIOT—NONE—Bacardi-Martini Belgium; *U.S. Private*, pg. 109

VEUVE CLICQUOT—Champagne—Veuve Clicquot Ponsardin; *Int'l*, pg. 781

VEUVE CLICQUOT PONSARDIN—NONE—LVMH Moet Hennessy Louis Vuitton; *Int'l*, pg. 779

VEVOZYME—Viscosity Reducing Enzyme used to Reduce the Volume of Manure—Royal Gist-Brocades N.V.; *Int'l*, pg. 1142

VEXTRA—Salmon Feed—Cultor Ltd.; *Int'l*, pg. 349

VGI/VIKAY—NONE—Milgray Electronics, Inc.; *U.S. Public*, pg. 205

VI-CORR—Composite Material Pump—Viking Pump, Inc.; *U.S. Public*, pg. 862

VI-DAYLIN—Multiple Vitamins—Abbott Laboratories; *U.S. Public*, pg. 12

VI-DAYLIN—Vitamins—Ross Products; *U.S. Public*, pg. 13

VI-FLOR—Vitamins—Bristol-Myers Squibb Company; *U.S. Public*, pg. 253

VI-SOL—Vitamins—Bristol-Myers Squibb Company; *U.S. Public*, pg. 253

VIA—NONE—Ekco Group, Inc.; *U.S. Public*, pg. 566

VIA LATINA—NONE—Vercoope-Uniao Das Adegas Cooperativas da Regiao Dos Vinhoa Verdes, U.C.R.L.; *Int'l*, pg. 1463

VIA MAX—Apparel—Clothestime Stores, Inc.; *U.S. Public*, pg. 387

VIACOM—Broadcast Stations—Viacom Broadcasting Inc.; *U.S. Private*, pg. 778

VIACOM—Communication Services—Viacom Inc.; *U.S. Private*, pg. 775

VIADENT—Anti-Plaque Toothpaste, Gel & Oral Rinse—Colgate Oral Pharmaceutical; *U.S. Public*, pg. 397

VIAGRA—Sildenafil—Pfizer Inc.; *U.S. Public*, pg. 1281

VIAGRID—Multi-Layer Laminate System—Sheldahl, Inc.; *U.S. Public*, pg. 1465

VIAL FILE—Scientific Glassware for Laboratory Use—Wheaton Inc.; *Int'l*, pg. 67

VIALE—Premium Wine—Racke USA; *Int'l*, pg. 1083

VIALETTO—NONE—Cruspi S.A.; *Int'l*, pg. 348

VIALON—Biomaterial—Becton Dickinson & Company; *U.S. Public*, pg. 199

VIANAIN—Treatment of Severe Burns—Genzyme Corporation; *U.S. Public*, pg. 733

VIASORB—Dressings—American Home Products Corporation; *U.S. Public*, pg. 79

VIATHIN—Semiconductor Substrates—Sheldahl, Inc.; *U.S. Public*, pg. 1465

VIAU—Cookies—Culinar Inc.; *Int'l*, pg. 348

VIBCO—Industrial Vibrators—Vibco Inc.; *U.S. Private*, pg. 1138

VIBRA-BLENDER—Continuous Blender—Vibra Screw Inc.; *U.S. Private*, pg. 1138

VIBRA-COTE—Roll Coater Oscillator Roll Cover—Harnischfeger Industries, Inc.; *U.S. Public*, pg. 788

VIBRA-FLEX—Vibratory Conveyors—TCC Industries; *U.S. Public*, pg. 1554

VIBRA-GRATE—Stoker—Detroit Stoker Co.; *U.S. Public*, pg. 1679

VIBRA-METRIC—Weigh-Belt Feeder—Vibra Screw Inc.; *U.S. Private*, pg. 1138

VIBRA-SHAKE—Industrial Dust Collector—Donaldson Company, Inc.; *U.S. Public*, pg. 517

VIBRA SHANK—Cultivators—Case Corporation; *U.S. Public*, pg. 311

VIBRA TINE—Cultivators—Case Corporation; *U.S. Public*, pg. 311

VIBRALERT—End of Service Indicator—Scott Aviation; *U.S. Public*, pg. 622

VIBRALOK—Locking Nuts—RB&W Corporation; *U.S. Public*, pg. 1259

VIBRAMYCIN—Doxycycline—Pfizer Inc.; *U.S. Public*, pg. 1281

VIBRANCE—Hair Care—Helene Curtis Industries, Inc.; *Int'l*, pg. 1434

VIBRANETICS—Vibrating Feeders, Bin & Pile Dischargers—Carrier Vibrating Equipment, Inc.; *U.S. Private*, pg. 215

VIBRANT—Dry Bleach—The Procter & Gamble Company; *U.S. Public*, pg. 1330

VIBRAPAC—Vibrating Concrete-Block Machine—Besser Company; *U.S. Private*, pg. 139

VIBRASENSE—Vibration Transmitters—Amot Controls Corporation; *U.S. Public*, pg. 1405

VIBRASTAT—Road Machinery-Compactor—Rosco Manufacturing Co.; *U.S. Private*, pg. 944

VIBRATECH—Vibration Control Mechanisms—IDEX Corporation; *U.S. Public*, pg. 862

VIBRATHANE—Liquid Castable, Sprayable & Millable Urethane—Uniroyal Chemical Company, Inc.; *U.S. Public*, pg. 460

VIBRATION MOUNTINGS & CONTROLS—Shock & Vibration—Aeroflex Incorporated; *U.S. Public*, pg. 23

VIBRATONE—Electrical Audible Signal/Alarm—Federal Signal Corporation, Signal Div.; *U.S. Public*, pg. 616

VIBRAVET—Doxycycline Hyclate—Pfizer Inc.; *U.S. Public*, pg. 1281

VIBRO-ENERGY—Finishing Equip., Separators, Grinding Mills—Sweco; *U.S. Public*, pg. 574

VIBRO-GUARD—Vibration Sensing Valves & Switches—Amot Controls Corporation; *U.S. Public*, pg. 1405

VIBRO-KING—Screening—Telsmith, Inc.; *U.S. Public*, pg. 141

VIBROMET—Polishing Machine—Buehler, Limited; *U.S. Public*, pg. 574

VIBROXIDE—Polishing Grade Powders—Ferro Corporation; *U.S. Public*, pg. 618

VIC-ADJUSTABLE—Tool For Cut Grooving Pipes—Victaulic Company of America; *U.S. Private*, pg. 1138

VIC-BALL—Grooved End Ball Valve—Victaulic Company of America; *U.S. Private*, pg. 1138

VIC-BOLTLESS—Pin Assembled Grooved Pipe Coupling—Victaulic Company of America; *U.S. Private*, pg. 1138

VIC-CHECK—Grooved End Check Valve—Victaulic Company of America; *U.S. Private*, pg. 1138

VIC-EASY—Tool For Roll Grooving Pipe—Victaulic Company of America; *U.S. Private*, pg. 1138

VIC-FLANGE—Flange-to-groove Adapter—Victaulic Company of America; *U.S. Private*, pg. 1138

VIC-GROOVER—Tool For Cut Grooving Individual Pipes—Victaulic Company of America; *U.S. Private*, pg. 1138

VIC JENSENS—Family Shoe Stores—Woolworth Corporation; *U.S. Public*, pg. 1777

VIC-LET—One Nut Outlet—Victaulic Company of America; *U.S. Private*, pg. 1138

VIC-O-WELL—Thermometer Outlet—Victaulic Company of America; *U.S. Private*, pg. 1138

VIC-PLUG—Grooved End Eccentric Plug Valve—Victaulic Company of America; *U.S. Private*, pg. 1138

VIC-RING—Applied Collar Adapter—Victaulic Company of America; *U.S. Private*, pg. 1138

VIC-STRAINER—Grooved End Tee-type Strainer—Victaulic Company of America; *U.S. Private*, pg. 1138

VIC-TAP—Victaulic Hot Tapping Device—Victaulic Company of America; *U.S. Private*, pg. 1138

VIC-TAP II—Victaulic Hot Tapping Device—Victaulic Company of America; *U.S. Private*, pg. 1138

VIC-300—Grooved End Butterfly Valve—Victaulic Company of America; *U.S. Private*, pg. 1138

VICCILLIN-S—Antibiotics—Meiji Seika Kaisha, Ltd.; *Int'l*, pg. 855

VICCILLIN(AMPICILLIN)—Anitbiotics—Meiji Seika Kaisha, Ltd.; *Int'l*, pg. 855

Brand Name Index

VICENTE COLLECTION—Men's Shoes—E.J. Footwear Corp.; *U.S. Public*, pg. 1684
VICEROY—Cigarettes—B.A.T Industries P.L.C.; *Int'l*, pg. 110
VICEROY—Cigarettes—Brown & Williamson Tobacco Corp.; *Int'l*, pg. 111
VICEROY—Brandy—Distillers Corporation S.A.; *Int'l*, pg. 1129
VICHEM—Extruded Flouroelastomer Tubing & Cord—Minor Rubber Co., Inc.; *U.S. Private*, pg. 751
VICHON WINERY—NONE—Robert Mondavi Winery, Inc.; *U.S. Public*, pg. 1393
VICHY—Cosmetics—L'Oreal S.A.; *Int'l*, pg. 818
VICKERS DEFENSE SYSTEM—NONE—Vickers PLC; *Int'l*, pg. 1466
VICKERS MEDICAL—Electro-Physiology Equip.—Vickers PLC; *Int'l*, pg. 1466
VICKS—Pharmaceutical Preparation—Permark International (Pty.) Ltd.; *Int'l*, pg. 1036
VICKS—NONE—Procter & Gamble Espana S.A.; *U.S. Public*, pg. 1332
VICKS BLUE—Cough Drops—Richardson-Vicks, Inc., Health Care Products; *U.S. Public*, pg. 1331
VICKS DAYCARE—Daytime Cough & Cold Medicine—Richardson-Vicks, Inc.; *U.S. Public*, pg. 1331
VICKS FORMULA 44—Cough & Cold Medicine—The Procter & Gamble Company; *U.S. Public*, pg. 1330
VICKS FORMULA 44D—Cough Mixture—Richardson-Vicks, Inc.; *U.S. Public*, pg. 1331
VICKS NYQUIL—Cough & Cold Medicine—The Procter & Gamble Company; *U.S. Public*, pg. 1330
VICKS SINEX—Cough & Cold Medicine—The Procter & Gamble Company; *U.S. Public*, pg. 1330
VICKS THROAT DROPS—Cold Medicine—The Procter & Gamble Company; *U.S. Public*, pg. 1330
VICKS VAPORUB—Cough & Cold Medicine—The Procter & Gamble Company; *U.S. Public*, pg. 1330
VICKS VAPORUB—NONE—Procter & Gamble Venezuela, C.A.; *U.S. Public*, pg. 1332
VICKS VICTORS—Cough Drops—Richardson-Vicks, Inc.; *U.S. Public*, pg. 1331
VICKY—Greeting Cards—American Greetings Corporation; *U.S. Public*, pg. 77
VICOAX—Closed-Circuit Television Equipment—Vicon Industries, Inc.; *U.S. Public*, pg. 1719
VICODIN—Pharmaceuticals—Knoll Pharmaceutical Company; *Int'l*, pg. 105
VICODIN-TUSS—Pharmaceuticals—Knoll Pharmaceutical Company; *Int'l*, pg. 105
VICODINES—Pharmaceutical—Knoll Pharmaceutical Company; *Int'l*, pg. 105
VICRTEX—Wallcoverings—Forbo Holding SA; *Int'l*, pg. 496
VICRYL—Suture/mesh—Ethicon, Inc.; *U.S. Public*, pg. 928
VICTABRITE—Polishing Agent for Aluminum—Rhone-Poulenc Basic Chemicals Co.; *Int'l*, pg. 1110
VICTOCOR—Steel/Non-Asbestos—Victor Products; *U.S. Public*, pg. 480
VICTOCOTE—Rubber Coating—Victor Products; *U.S. Public*, pg. 480
VICTOR—NONE—AST Research Inc.; *Int'l*, pg. 1181
VICTOR—Bioanalytic Assay Instrument—EG & G, Inc.; *U.S. Public*, pg. 542
VICTOR—Photographic Processors—Eastman Kodak Company; *U.S. Public*, pg. 550
VICTOR—Plastic Storage Containers: Tool Boxes, Tackle Boxes & Gun Cases—Ekco Group, Inc.; *U.S. Public*, pg. 566
VICTOR—Farm Equip—Miller-St. Nazianz, Inc.; *U.S. Private*, pg. 748
VICTOR—Industrial Chemicals—Rhone-Poulenc Basic Chemicals Co.; *Int'l*, pg. 1110
VICTOR—Electronic Products—Thomson Consumer Electronics Inc.; *Int'l*, pg. 1383
VICTOR—Non Poisonous Control Products—Woodstream Corporation; *U.S. Public*, pg. 566
VICTOR 9000—Desk Top Micro Computer—Victor Technology; *U.S. Private*, pg. 1139
VICTOR REINZ—Gaskets, Sealing Products—Dana Corporation; *U.S. Public*, pg. 479

VICTOR REINZ—NONE—Victor Products; *U.S. Public*, pg. 480
VICTOR SERIES—Manifolds—Edelbrock Corp.; *U.S. Public*, pg. 563
VICTORIA—Bath Accessories—Baldwin Hardware Corporation; *U.S. Public*, pg. 1053
VICTORIA—Magazine—The Hearst Corporation; *U.S. Private*, pg. 515
VICTORIA—Magazine—Hearst Magazines Division; *U.S. Private*, pg. 516
VICTORIA—NONE—Victoria Packing Corporation; *U.S. Private*, pg. 1139
VICTORIA BITTER—Bitter Ale—Carlton & United Breweries Ltd.; *Int'l*, pg. 500
VICTORIA BITTER—Bitter Ale—Foster's Brewing Group Limited; *Int'l*, pg. 500
VICTORIA STATION—Restaurants—A.S. Management Corporation; *U.S. Private*, pg. 7
VICTORIA WOOD—Homebuilding/Canada—Kaufman and Broad Home Corporation; *U.S. Public*, pg. 944
VICTORIA'S SECRET—Lingerie Shops—Victoria's Secret Stores; *U.S. Public*, pg. 995
VICTORIA'S SECRET UNDERWARE—Lingerie—Victoria's Secret Stores; *U.S. Public*, pg. 995
VICTORIAN SAMPLER—Consumer Magazine Featuring Victorian Decorating—Sampler Publications Inc.; *U.S. Private*, pg. 963
VICTORS—Vapor Cough Drops—Richardson-Vicks, Inc., Health Care Products; *U.S. Public*, pg. 1331
VICTORY—Insecticide Products for Pets—Carter-Wallace, Inc.; *U.S. Public*, pg. 309
VICTORY—Cast Iron Gas Boiler—Slant/Fin Corporation; *U.S. Private*, pg. 1005
VICTORY—Comml. Refrigerators & Freezers—Victory Refrigeration Co. LC; *U.S. Private*, pg. 1139
VICTORY AT SEA VIDEO—Video Series—Time-Life, Inc.; *U.S. Public*, pg. 1613
VICTORY IN THE PACIFIC—Game—Monarch Avalon, Inc.; *U.S. Public*, pg. 1123
VICTORY SERIES—Orthodontic Tubes—3M; *U.S. Public*, pg. 1604
VICTROLA—Electronic Products—Thomson Consumer Electronics Inc.; *Int'l*, pg. 1383
VIDAL SASSOON—Retail Hair Care Appliances—Helen of Troy Corporation; *U.S. Public*, pg. 807
VIDAL SASSOON—Hair Care Products—The Procter & Gamble Company; *U.S. Public*, pg. 1330
VIDAL SASSOON—NONE—Procter & Gamble Espana S.A.; *U.S. Public*, pg. 1332
VIDAL SASSOON—Haircare Products—Procter & Gamble (Health & Beauty Care) Limited; *U.S. Public*, pg. 1332
VIDAL SASSOON—Chain of Beauty Salons—Vidal Sassoon; *U.S. Public*, pg. 1330
VIDAL SASSOON CONDITIONERS—Hair Conditioners—Helen of Troy Corporation; *U.S. Public*, pg. 807
VIDAR INC—Registered—Vidar, Inc.; *U.S. Private*, pg. 1139
VIDCOMP—Video Compression Data Links—Litton Applied Technology; *U.S. Public*, pg. 1003
VIDEK—Image Sensing Vision Equipment—Eastman Kodak Company; *U.S. Public*, pg. 550
VIDEO BROADCAST—French Video Magazine—EMAP France; *Int'l*, pg. 451
VIDEO BUSINESS—Magazine for Retailers Who Sell/Rent Pre-Recorded Video Products—Reed Elsevier Business Information; *Int'l*, pg. 1095
VIDEO COMPUTE ENGINE—Semiconductor Device—LSI Logic Corp.; *U.S. Public*, pg. 971
VIDEO DIRECTOR—Video Tape Recorders/Players—Zenith Electronics Corp.; *U.S. Public*, pg. 1790
VIDEO DISPLAY—Cathode Ray Tubes—Video Display Corporation; *U.S. Public*, pg. 1720
VIDEO EP—Prerecorded Video Tapes—Sony Electronics; *Int'l*, pg. 1281
VIDEO KING—NONE—Stuart Entertainment Inc.; *U.S. Public*, pg. 1526
VIDEO LP—Prerecorded Video Tapes—Sony Electronics; *Int'l*, pg. 1281
VIDEO MASTER—Video Control Centers—Lance Industries; *U.S. Private*, pg. 645
VIDEO-PAK—Video Storage Boxes—Plastic Reel Corp. of America; *U.S. Private*, pg. 871

VIDEO PASSPORT—Televison Encoders & Decoders—The Titan Corporation; *U.S. Public*, pg. 1618
VIDEO ROOMMATE—Powered Speaker System—Bose Corporation; *U.S. Private*, pg. 160
VIDEO SPAN—Interactive Video Technology—Paradyne; *U.S. Private*, pg. 838
VIDEO STORE—Trade Periodical—Advanstar Communications; *U.S. Private*, pg. 22
VIDEO SYSTEMS—Publication for Video Production Activities—Intertec Publishing; *U.S. Public*, pg. 1327
VIDEO SYSTEMS—Professional Video Equipment—Toshiba America Inc.; *Int'l*, pg. 1405
VIDEO-VAULT—Video Shipping Cases—Plastic Reel Corp. of America; *U.S. Private*, pg. 871
VIDEO WINDOW—Video Multimeter—ComSonics, Inc.; *U.S. Private*, pg. 260
THE VIDEO WIZARD—Video Equipment—National Video, Inc.; *U.S. Public*, pg. 1755
VIDEO 45—Video Cassettes—Sony Electronics; *Int'l*, pg. 1281
VIDEO 8—Video Camera/Recorder & Other 8mm Video Products—Sony Electronics; *Int'l*, pg. 1281
VIDEOCIPHER—Scrambling Descrambling Technology Used by Major US and Candian Programmers—Satellite Data Networks; *U.S. Public*, pg. 716
VIDEOCIPHER—NONE—The Titan Corporation; *U.S. Public*, pg. 1618
VIDEOCONCEPTS—Stores—Tandy Corporation; *U.S. Public*, pg. 1560
VIDEOFAX—Wide-Band Facsimile System—Litton Industries, Inc.; *U.S. Public*, pg. 1002
VIDEOFILM NOTES—Technical Publication—Eastman Kodak Company; *U.S. Public*, pg. 550
VIDEOGUARD—Protection Program—National Video, Inc.; *U.S. Public*, pg. 1755
VIDEOJET—Marking Machines—The General Electric Company, p.l.c.; *Int'l*, pg. 543
VIDEOJET—Packaging—Southcorp Holdings Ltd.; *Int'l*, pg. 1287
VIDEOKEY—NONE—Intelligent Controls Inc.; *U.S. Private*, pg. 566
VIDEOLINK—Transmission System—Vicon Industries, Inc.; *U.S. Public*, pg. 1719
VIDEOMASK—Interdiction System—Blonder-Tongue Laboratories, Inc.; *U.S. Public*, pg. 237
VIDEOMATIC—Television Receivers—Philips Consumer Electronics; *Int'l*, pg. 1054
VIDEOPAL LOGO—Artwork to Describe Instant Pay Per View Ordering Device for Home Satellite—Satellite Data Networks; *U.S. Public*, pg. 716
VIDEOPRINTER—Instant Color Film Recorder—Polaroid Corporation; *U.S. Public*, pg. 1313
VIDEOSCOPE—Projection Television Sets—Sony Electronics; *Int'l*, pg. 1281
VIDEOSCOPE—Indus. Video Inspection System—Telesensory Corporation; *U.S. Private*, pg. 1074
VIDEOSETTER—Photo Typesetters—AGFA EPS Division; *U.S. Public*, pg. 172
VIDEOTENN—Touch Screen Programmer—Tenney Environmental; *U.S. Private*, pg. 1076
VIDEOTRAX—Tape Controller Board—Alpha Microsystems; *U.S. Public*, pg. 57
VIDEOTRAX AND DESIGN—NONE—Alpha Microsystems; *U.S. Public*, pg. 57
VIDEX—Infectious Disease Therapy—Bristol-Myers Squibb Company; *U.S. Public*, pg. 253
VIDMAR—Storage Equipment—The Stanley Works; *U.S. Public*, pg. 1508
VIDOR—Dry Cell Batteries & Flashlights—RAYOVAC Corporation; *U.S. Private*, pg. 912
VIE DE FRANCE—Wholesale Bakeries & Retail cafe Bakeries—Cuisine Solutions, Inc.; *U.S. Public*, pg. 466
VIEJA ABADIA—Wine—Penaflor S.A.; *Int'l*, pg. 1032
VIENETTA—Frozen Dessert—Good Humor/Breyers Ice Cream; *Int'l*, pg. 1435
VIENNA—All Beef Prods—Vienna Sausage Mfg. Co.; *U.S. Private*, pg. 1139
VIENNA FINGERS—Cookies—Keebler Company; *U.S. Public*, pg. 657
VIENNA FINGERS—Cookies—Sunshine Biscuits, Inc.; *U.S. Private*, pg. 434
VIENNA FINGERS—Cookies—Sunshine Biscuits, Inc.; *U.S. Public*, pg. 657

VIENNA TEA BISCUITS—Petit Tea Biscuits From Austria—The Promotion in Motion Companies; *U.S. Private*, pg. 890

VIENNALINE—Ophthalmic & Sunglasses—Optimaxx International; *U.S. Private*, pg. 818

VIENNETTA—Ice Cream Dessert—Unilever Plc; *Int'l*, pg. 1433

VIENNO—Bakery Ingredients—Royal Gist-Brocades N.V.; *Int'l*, pg. 1142

VIETNAM—Periodical—Cowles Enthusiast Media, Inc.; *U.S. Private*, pg. 281

VIETNAM VIDEO—Video Series—Time-Life, Inc.; *U.S. Public*, pg. 1613

VIEW—Commercial Fire Detection System—Pittway Corporation; *U.S. Public*, pg. 1305

VIEW-MASTER—Audio-Visual Viewers & Reels—Tyco Toys, Inc.; *U.S. Public*, pg. 1058

VIEW PACK—Packaging System—Sanderson Plumbing Products Inc.; *U.S. Private*, pg. 964

VIEW SAVER—Windshield Washer Solvent—Patterson Laboratories, Inc.; *U.S. Private*, pg. 843

VIEW VAC—Vacuum Viewing Parts—BOC Coating Technology; *Int'l*, pg. 121

VIEWCAM—LCD Viewscreen Camcorder—Sharp Electronics Corporation; *Int'l*, pg. 1228

VIEWMASTER—Viewers & Reels—View-Master, Inc.; *U.S. Public*, pg. 1058

VIEWPAC—Recorder—Moore Products Co.; *U.S. Public*, pg. 1128

VIEWPOINT—POS Monitoring System—Checkpoint Systems Inc.; *U.S. Public*, pg. 343

VIEWPOINT—Operations Console Facility—Tandem Computers Inc.; *U.S. Public*, pg. 417

VIEWPOINT—Portable Overhead Projector—Varitronic Systems, Inc.; *U.S. Private*, pg. 250

VIEWSYS—System Resource Monitoring Facility—Tandem Computers Inc.; *U.S. Public*, pg. 417

VIGIL—Clincial Chemistry Reagents—Beckman Instruments, Inc.; *U.S. Public*, pg. 199

VIGIL LIGHT—Devotional Candles—Will & Baumer Incorporated; *U.S. Private*, pg. 1176

VIGIL PRX—Clinical Chemistry Reagents—Beckman Instruments, Inc.; *U.S. Public*, pg. 199

VIGILANT—Rail Crossing Monitoring Systems—Rockwell International Corporation; *U.S. Public*, pg. 1397

VIGILON—Primary Wound Dressing—C.R. Bard, Inc.; *U.S. Public*, pg. 189

VIGNETTE WINDOW SHADINGS—Soft Fabric Shades on Easy Operating Clutch System—Hunter Douglas, Inc.; *Int'l*, pg. 639

VIGNETTI PITTARO—Table Wine—Paterno Imports Limited; *U.S. Private*, pg. 843

VIGOPAS—Cured Polyester Resin—Raschig GmbH; *U.S. Private*, pg. 827

VIGOR—Pacemaker Systems—Guidant Corporation-Cardiac Rhythm Management Group; *U.S. Public*, pg. 768

VIGOR-LIGHT—Fluorescent Lamps—General Electric Canada Inc.; *U.S. Public*, pg. 713

VIGORO—Lawn & Garden Fertilizer—IMC Agribusiness; *U.S. Public*, pg. 856

VIGORO—Fertilizer Products—The Vigoro Corporation; *U.S. Public*, pg. 856

VIGORPAK—High Quality Seed—Asgrow Seed Company; *Int'l*, pg. 1048

VIGORTONE AG—Blended Vitamins for Livestock Industry—Vigortone AG Products, Inc.; *Int'l*, pg. 1357

VIKANE—Space Fumigant, Hybrid & Barietal Seeds—The Dow Chemical Company; *U.S. Public*, pg. 522

VIKING—Camping Trailers—Coachmen Industries, Inc.; *U.S. Public*, pg. 387

VIKING—Sewing Machines—Electrolux, AB; *Int'l*, pg. 438

VIKING—Pumps—IDEX Corporation; *U.S. Public*, pg. 862

VIKING—(Handheld & Mobile Radios)—E.F. Johnson Radio Systems; *U.S. Public*, pg. 1630

VIKING—Adult Hardcover Books—Penguin Putnam Inc.; *Int'l*, pg. 1027

VIKING—Ariene 4 Engine—SNECMA - Societe Nationale d'Etude et de Construction de Moteurs d'Aviation; *Int'l*, pg. 1165

VIKING—Sewing Machines—VWS, Inc.; *Int'l*, pg. 440

VIKING—Rotary Pump—Viking Pump, Inc.; *U.S. Public*, pg. 862

VIKING—Gas Cooking Stoves—Viking Range Corp.; *U.S. Private*, pg. 1140

VIKING—Yachts—Viking Yacht Co.; *U.S. Private*, pg. 1140

VIKING AIR—Power Tools—The Black & Decker Corporation; *U.S. Public*, pg. 233

VIKING ANCHOR—Anchor—Attwood Corporation; *U.S. Private*, pg. 1038

VIKING & NORDSMAN—Cutlery—Douglas Stephen Plastics, Inc.; *U.S. Private*, pg. 341

VIKING BUILT-IN OVENS—Built in Single & Double Gas & Electric Ovens—Viking Range Corp.; *U.S. Private*, pg. 1140

VIKING COOKTOP—Sealed Burner Cooktops—Viking Range Corp.; *U.S. Private*, pg. 1140

VIKING DISHWASHER—"Quiet Clean" Dishwashers—Viking Range Corp.; *U.S. Private*, pg. 1140

VIKING DUAL FUEL RANGES—Gas Surface Cooking With Electric Oven—Viking Range Corp.; *U.S. Private*, pg. 1140

VIKING HANGING SCALES—Utility & Sportsman's Scales—Sunbeam Household Products; *U.S. Public*, pg. 1533

VIKING ICE MACHINE—NONE—Viking Range Corp.; *U.S. Private*, pg. 1140

VIKING KESTREL—Children's Hardcover Books—Penguin Putnam Inc.; *Int'l*, pg. 1027

VIKING LID-EASE—In-Line Liquid Strainers—Viking Pump, Inc.; *U.S. Public*, pg. 862

VIKING MAG DRIVE—Magnetically Coupled Pump—Viking Pump, Inc.; *U.S. Public*, pg. 862

VIKING "100"—High Strength Steel—Nelsen Steel & Wire Co.; *U.S. Private*, pg. 790

VIKING OUTDOOR GAS GRILLS—Premium Outdoor Grills—Viking Range Corp.; *U.S. Private*, pg. 1140

VIKING RANGEHOOD—Wall & Island Ventilators—Viking Range Corp.; *U.S. Private*, pg. 1140

VIKING RANGETOP—Comml. Type Gas Cooktops—Viking Range Corp.; *U.S. Private*, pg. 1140

VIKING REFRIGERATOR—Side By Side Refrigerators Freezers—Viking Range Corp.; *U.S. Private*, pg. 1140

VIKING SERENADE—Ships—Royal Caribbean Cruises Ltd.; *U.S. Public*, pg. 1410

VIKING SHIP BRAND—NONE—Hydro Agri North America; *Int'l*, pg. 961

VIKING SNOWPLOWS—NONE—Cives Corporation; *U.S. Private*, pg. 241

VIKING T-BAR—Off-Hwy. Suspension Seat—Bostrom Seating, Inc.; *U.S. Public*, pg. 933

VIKING II—Electromyographic Testing System—Nicolet Analytical; *U.S. Public*, pg. 1593

VIKING WINE COOLER—Fifty Bottle Wine Cooler—Viking Range Corp.; *U.S. Private*, pg. 1140

VIKOR—Insecticide—Roussel Corporation; *Int'l*, pg. 625

VILDONA—Synthetic Leather, Leather, Non-Wovens—Freudenberg & Company; *Int'l*, pg. 505

VILEDA—Household Cloths—Freudenberg & Company; *Int'l*, pg. 505

VILEDON—Non-Woven Company—Freudenberg & Company; *Int'l*, pg. 505

VILEDON—Industrial Products—Freudenberg Nonwovens; *Int'l*, pg. 505

VILEDON COMPACT—Non-Woven Table Cover—Freudenberg & Company; *Int'l*, pg. 505

VILEDON FILTER—Non-Woven Air Filter—Freudenberg & Company; *Int'l*, pg. 505

VILENE—Freudenberg Non-Wovens—Freudenberg & Company; *Int'l*, pg. 505

VILENE—Interlining—Freudenberg Nonwovens; *Int'l*, pg. 505

VILLA ABA—Italian Wines—Marie Brizard Wines & Spirits USA; *U.S. Private*, pg. 702

VILLA MASSA LIQUORE DI LIMONI—Liqueur—Laird & Company; *U.S. Private*, pg. 642

VILLA MT. EDEN—Wine—Stimson Lane Ltd.; *U.S. Public*, pg. 1661

VILLA NICOLA OF LEE IACOCCA—Wine—Paterno Imports Limited; *U.S. Private*, pg. 843

VILLA NOVA PLANK—Pre-Finished Laminate—Bruce Hardwood Floors; *U.S. Public*, pg. 1634

VILLA SPINELLI—Italian Wines—Barton Incorporated; *U.S. Public*, pg. 300

VILLABOARD—External Cladding—James Hardie Industries Ltd.; *Int'l*, pg. 596

VILLAGE—Wallcovering, Fabrics—F. Schumacher & Co.; *U.S. Private*, pg. 973

VILLAGE—Bath Foam—Softsoap Enterprises, Inc.; *U.S. Public*, pg. 397

VILLAGE—Grocery Stores—Village Super Market Inc.; *U.S. Public*, pg. 1721

VILLAGE BATH—Bath Products—Colgate-Palmolive Company; *U.S. Public*, pg. 397

VILLAGE INN—Restaurants—Vicorp Restaurants, Inc.; *U.S. Public*, pg. 1719

VILLAGE INN—Restaurants—Village Inn Restaurants; *U.S. Public*, pg. 1719

VILLAGE PANTRIES—Convenience Stores—Marsh Supermarkets, Inc.; *U.S. Public*, pg. 1049

VILLAGE PLANK—Pre-Finished Laminate—Bruce Hardwood Floors; *U.S. Public*, pg. 1634

VILLAGE PRODUCTS—NONE—Aliments Flamingo; *Int'l*, pg. 57

VILLAGER—Drapery Hardware—Kirsch; *U.S. Public*, pg. 1176

VILLAGER LODGE—NONE—HFS, Incorporated; *U.S. Public*, pg. 1176

VILLARD—Book Imprint—Random House, Inc.; *U.S. Private*, pg. 20

VILLAS OF THE WORLD—Promoting Resorts of Others—Encore Marketing International, Inc.; *U.S. Public*, pg. 580

VILLEPARK—NONE—Forbo Holding SA; *Int'l*, pg. 496

VILLEROY & BOCH—NONE—Villeroy & Boch AG; *Int'l*, pg. 1468

VILLOS/SALLOS—Candy—Huhtamaki Oy; *Int'l*, pg. 638

VILMORIN—NONE—Groupe Limagrain; *Int'l*, pg. 566

VILON—Luggage—American Tourister, Inc.; *U.S. Public*, pg. 1430

VILTEC—Shirt Interlining—Freudenberg Nonwovens; *Int'l*, pg. 505

VILTER—Refrigeration Products—Vilter Manufacturing Corporation; *U.S. Private*, pg. 1140

VIM—Soap Product—Lever Brothers Co.; *Int'l*, pg. 1435

VIM—Soap Prod.—Unilever Plc; *Int'l*, pg. 1433

VIM/NET—Computer Systems Marketed to Automobile Dealers—The Reynolds and Reynolds Company; *U.S. Public*, pg. 1384

VIMCO—Pasta—Borden, Inc.; *U.S. Private*, pg. 157

VIMRXYN—Synthetic Hypericin—VIMRx Pharmaceuticals, Inc.; *U.S. Public*, pg. 1702

VIMS—Logistics Services for Industrial Chemicals—Van Waters & Rogers; *Int'l*, pg. 1147

VINAC—Polyvinyl Acetate Emulsions—Air Products and Chemicals, Inc.; *U.S. Public*, pg. 30

VINAL SIDE—NONE—CertainTeed Corporation; *Int'l*, pg. 1170

VINCE—Mouthwash Rinse—Lee Pharmaceuticals; *U.S. Public*, pg. 984

VINCENZO—Jewelry—Uncas Manufacturing Company; *U.S. Private*, pg. 1116

VINCOTE—Spray Booth Coating—Detrex Corporation; *U.S. Public*, pg. 501

VINDICATOR LOCK—Electronic Lock System for Safes & Vaults—Vindicator Technologies; *U.S. Private*, pg. 1141

VINELAND LABORATORIES—Poultry Vaccines—IGI, Inc.; *U.S. Public*, pg. 855

VINEYARD—Plywood, Paneling, Siding & Roofing—Georgia-Pacific Corporation; *U.S. Public*, pg. 735

VINEYARD GARDEN COLLECTION—Wrought Aluminum Outdoor Furniture—Telescope Casual Furniture, Inc.; *U.S. Private*, pg. 1074

VINIDUR—Polyvinyl Chloride—BASF AG; *Int'l*, pg. 103

VINO KULAFU—Chinese Wine—La Tondena Distillers, Inc.; *Int'l*, pg. 785

VINOFLEX—Polyvinyl Chloride PVC—BASF AG; *Int'l*, pg. 103

VINOFLEX COMPOUNDS—Polyvinyl Chloride Compounds—BASF AG; *Int'l*, pg. 103

VINSALYN—Resin—Hercules Incorporated; *U.S. Public*, pg. 809

VINSOL—Resin—Hercules Incorporated; *U.S. Public*, pg. 809

VINTAGE—High Density Copolymer Shutters—Alcoa Building Products, Inc.; *U.S. Public*, pg. 61

VINTAGE—Dispenser Line of Fruit Juices—Citrus World Inc.; *U.S. Private*, pg. 241

VINTAGE—Drapery Hardware—Kirsch; *U.S. Public*, pg. 1176

VINTAGE—Lifestyle—L.A. Gear, Inc.; *U.S. Public*, pg. 969

VINTAGE—Book Imprint—Random House, Inc.; *U.S. Private*, pg. 20

VINTAGE BLUE—NONE—Kellwood Company; *U.S. Public*, pg. 948

VINTAGE GOURMET—Super Premium Ice Cream—Barber Ice Cream Company; *U.S. Private*, pg. 115

VINTAGE STUDIO—NONE—Kellwood Company; *U.S. Public*, pg. 948

VINTNER—Table & Dessert Wines, Champagnes & Sparkling Wines—Warner Vineyards; *U.S. Private*, pg. 1151

VINTNER'S CHOICE—Wines—Canandaigua Wine Company, Inc.; *U.S. Public*, pg. 300

VINTNER'S LABEL—Paper to be Used to Make Labels for Bottles—Georgia-Pacific Corporation; *U.S. Public*, pg. 735

VINURAN—Polyvinyl Chloride—BASF AG; *Int'l*, pg. 103

VINYL EASE—Full Glue Installed Sheet Vinyl Flooring—Mannington Resilient Floors; *U.S. Private*, pg. 700

VINYL GARD—Fence Prod.—Gilbert & Bennett Manufacturing Company; *U.S. Public*, pg. 453

VINYL KING—Weatherstripping—W.J. & Dennis Co.; *U.S. Private*, pg. 1144

VINYL-PANE—Window Material—Warp Brothers; *U.S. Public*, pg. 412

VINYL PRIME—Vinyl Windows—Binning's Building Products, Inc.; *U.S. Public*, pg. 67

VINYL SHIELD—Prefinished Wall Paneling—Georgia-Pacific Corporation; *U.S. Public*, pg. 735

VINYL SIDING WASH—Vinyl Siding Cleaner—Armor All Products Group; *U.S. Public*, pg. 387

VINYL-TUF—Aluminum Siding—Reynolds Metals Company; *U.S. Public*, pg. 1385

VINYLCREST—Sheet Vinyl Flooring—Congoleum Corporation; *U.S. Public*, pg. 69

VINYLGARD—Vinyl Siding & Gutters—Georgia-Pacific Corporation; *U.S. Public*, pg. 735

VINYLIRON—PVC Pressure Pipe—CertainTeed Corporation; *Int'l*, pg. 1170

VINYLPLUS—Floor Coverings—Domco Inc.; *Int'l*, pg. 415

VINYLSEAL—Closure Liner Sealings Materials—Tekni-Plex, Inc.; *U.S. Private*, pg. 1073

VINYLUBE—Plastic Additives—Lonza Inc.; *Int'l*, pg. 67

VIP—Grills—The Thermos Company; *Int'l*, pg. 938

VIP SERIES—Ink Jet System—Videojet Systems International, Inc.; *Int'l*, pg. 545

VIPER—Military Engine—Rolls-Royce Military Aero Engines Ltd.; *Int'l*, pg. 1127

VIPER—Heat Treated Through Hardened Cutting Edges—Valk Manufacturing Company; *U.S. Private*, pg. 1131

VIQUIN FORTE—Prescription Drug—ICN Pharmaceuticals, Inc.; *U.S. Public*, pg. 853

VIRACEPT—HIV Protease Inhibitor for Treatment of HIV Infection & AIDS—Agouron Pharmaceuticals, Inc.; *U.S. Public*, pg. 28

VIRAZOLE (RIBAVIRIN)—Antiviral—ICN Pharmaceuticals, Inc.; *U.S. Public*, pg. 853

VIREX—Disinfectant—S.C. Johnson & Son, Inc.; *U.S. Private*, pg. 592

VIRGINIA—Paneling, Siding & Plywood—Georgia-Pacific Corporation; *U.S. Public*, pg. 735

VIRGINIA BLUE CRYSTAL—Kyanite—Kyanite Mining Corporation; *U.S. Private*, pg. 638

VIRGINIA CHOICE—NONE—The Smithfield Companies, Inc.; *U.S. Public*, pg. 1479

VIRGINIA DARE—Wines—Canandaigua Wine Company, Inc.; *U.S. Public*, pg. 300

VIRGINIA IS FOR LOVERS—Travel Slogan—Virginia Tourism Corp.; *U.S. Private*, pg. 1141

VIRGINIA MANUFACTURERS DIRECTORY—Directory—Manufacturers' News, Inc.; *U.S. Private*, pg. 700

VIRGINIA METAL IND., INC.—Movable Metal Partitions—Virginia Metal Industries, Inc.; *U.S. Private*, pg. 1141

VIRGINIA POWER—Electric Utility—Virginia Electric and Power Company; *U.S. Public*, pg. 516

VIRGINIA REEL—Meat Products—Bar-S Foods Co.; *U.S. Private*, pg. 114

VIRGINIA SLIM LIGHTS 100'S—Cigarettes—Philip Morris Companies Inc.; *U.S. Public*, pg. 1287

VIRGINIA SLIMS—Cigarettes—Philip Morris U.S.A.; *U.S. Public*, pg. 1289

VIRGINIA SLIMS LIGHTS 100'S MENTHOL—Cigarettes—Philip Morris Companies Inc.; *U.S. Public*, pg. 1287

VIRGINIA SLIMS LIGHTS 120'S—Cigarettes—Philip Morris Companies Inc.; *U.S. Public*, pg. 1287

VIRGINIA SLIMS LIGHTS 120'S MENTHOL—Cigarettes—Philip Morris Companies Inc.; *U.S. Public*, pg. 1287

VIRGINIA SLIMS 100'S—Cigarettes—Philip Morris Companies Inc.; *U.S. Public*, pg. 1287

VIRGINIA SLIMS 100'S MENTHOL—Cigarettes—Philip Morris Companies Inc.; *U.S. Public*, pg. 1287

VIRGINIA SLIMS SUPER SLIMS—Cigarettes—Philip Morris Companies Inc.; *U.S. Public*, pg. 1287

VIRGO RO—Reverse Osmosis Home Unit—Ionics, Incorporated; *U.S. Public*, pg. 912

VIRHORIN D—Antibiotic Preparations—Nippon Kayaku Co. Ltd.; *Int'l*, pg. 934

VIROFRAL—Antiparkinsonism—Novo Nordisk A/S; *Int'l*, pg. 987

VIROGEN ROTATEST—Test—Wampole Laboratories; *U.S. Public*, pg. 310

VIROPTIC—Ophthalmic Antiviral Product—Glaxo Wellcome PLC; *Int'l*, pg. 553

VIROSURE—NONE—Nabi; *U.S. Public*, pg. 1148

VIRTUAL CRANE—Crane Operator Training—Advanced Marine Enterprises, Inc.; *U.S. Public*, pg. 1182

VIRTUAL MACHINE/ENTERPRISE SYSTEMS ARCHITECTURE—Computer System—International Business Machines Corporation; *U.S. Public*, pg. 895

VIRTUAL MACHINE/EXTENDED ARCHITECTURE—Computer System—International Business Machines Corporation; *U.S. Public*, pg. 895

VIRTUAL SHIP—Shiphandling Software—Advanced Marine Enterprises, Inc.; *U.S. Public*, pg. 1182

VIRTUOSO—Custom IC Layout & Library Development—Cadence Design Systems, Inc.; *U.S. Public*, pg. 290

VIS-A-VIS—Projector Pen—Sanford Corporation; *U.S. Public*, pg. 1178

VIS-CON—Fluid Heaters—Graco Inc.; *U.S. Public*, pg. 756

VISA—Central Station Monitor—Datascope Corp.; *U.S. Public*, pg. 487

VISA—Progressive Lens—Essilor International Compagnie Generale d'Optique; *Int'l*, pg. 462

VISA BUSINESS CARD—Bank-Issued Card For Business Use—Visa U.S.A. Inc.; *U.S. Private*, pg. 1141

VISA CLASSIC CARD—Standard Bank Issued Credit Card—Visa U.S.A. Inc.; *U.S. Private*, pg. 1141

VISA DEBIT CARD—Bank-Issued Card That Pays From Customers Deposit Account—Visa U.S.A. Inc.; *U.S. Private*, pg. 1141

VISA GOLD CARD—Upscale Bank-Issued Card—Visa U.S.A. Inc.; *U.S. Private*, pg. 1141

VISA TRAVEL VOUCHERS—Travelers Vouchers—Visa U.S.A. Inc.; *U.S. Private*, pg. 1141

VISA TRAVELERS CHEQUES—Travelers Checks—Visa U.S.A. Inc.; *U.S. Private*, pg. 1141

VISA-PAC—Passport & Visa Application Service—DHL Worldwide Express; *U.S. Private*, pg. 301

VISADRON—Eye Drops—Boehringer Ingelheim Italia S.p.A.; *Int'l*, pg. 199

VISAGE—Electronic Image Processing Apparatus—Eastman Kodak Company; *U.S. Public*, pg. 550

VISAGE—Cosmetics—Revlon, Inc.; *U.S. Private*, pg. 689

VISALERT—Stationary Warning Light—Federal Signal Corporation, Signal Div.; *U.S. Public*, pg. 616

VISC—Semiconductor Device—LSI Logic Corp.; *U.S. Public*, pg. 971

VISCOAT—Sterile Viscoelastic Solution—Alcon Laboratories, Inc.; *Int'l*, pg. 916

VISCOLENS—Medical—Pharmacia & Upjohn Adria Laboratories; *Int'l*, pg. 1049

VISCOMAT—Motion Picture Photo Processing Apparatus & Chemicals—Eastman Kodak Company; *U.S. Public*, pg. 550

VISCOPLEX—Oil-Additive—Rohm GmbH; *Int'l*, pg. 1454

VISCOSURGERY PACK—Medical—Pharmacia & Upjohn Adria Laboratories; *Int'l*, pg. 1049

VISCOUNT—Sporting Equipment—Brunswick Bowling & Billiards Corp.; *U.S. Public*, pg. 265

VISCOUNT—Photographic Processing Apparatus—Eastman Kodak Company; *U.S. Public*, pg. 550

VISCOUNT—Fish Sticks & Portions—Frionor U.S.A. Inc.; *Int'l*, pg. 516

VISCOUNT—Pump—Graco Inc.; *U.S. Public*, pg. 756

VISCOUNT 44 (H13)—Hot Work Die Steel (Prehardened)—Latrobe Steel Company; *U.S. Public*, pg. 1617

VISE-GRIP—Locking Pliers, Clamps & Wrenches—American Tool Companies, Inc.; *U.S. Private*, pg. 63

VISENZA—Eyeglass Lenses & Blanks—PPG Industries, Inc.; *U.S. Public*, pg. 1245

VISGARD—Viscosity Control—Graymills Corp.; *U.S. Private*, pg. 473

VISHAY—Liteon Power Semiconductor—Diodes Incorporated; *U.S. Public*, pg. 510

VISHAY—Precision Resistive Components—Vishay Intertechnology, Inc.; *U.S. Public*, pg. 1721

VISHAY BULK METALS—Foil Resistors—Vishay Intertechnology, Inc.; *U.S. Public*, pg. 1721

VISI-BELLE—Office Supplies—JM Company; *U.S. Private*, pg. 577

VISI-BLACK—Surgical Needle—Ethicon, Inc.; *U.S. Public*, pg. 928

VISI-FLOAT—Flowmeter—Dwyer Instruments Inc.; *U.S. Private*, pg. 350

VISI FLOW—Irrigation Product—Bristol-Myers Squibb Company; *U.S. Public*, pg. 253

VISI PLAS—Plastic Embedments—Fisher Scientific Company; *U.S. Public*, pg. 658

VISI-TRIP—Circuit Breaker Trip Indicator—Square D Company; *Int'l*, pg. 1208

VISIBAR—Electrical Safety Signal Apparatus—Federal Signal Corporation, Signal Div.; *U.S. Public*, pg. 616

VISIBEAD—Solid Glass Beads for Wet-Night Reflecting—Potters Industries, Inc.; *U.S. Private*, pg. 827

VISIBEAM—Search Light For Vehicles—Federal Signal Corporation, Signal Div.; *U.S. Public*, pg. 616

VISIBLE CATCHING OPERATING SYSTEM—Computer Software for Real Time Operation of Digital Signal Processors—Lucent Technologies Inc.; *U.S. Public*, pg. 1017

VISIBLE DIFFERENCE—Skin Care—Elizabeth Arden Company; *Int'l*, pg. 1435

VISIKOM—Telephone Intercom—Atlas/Soundolier; *U.S. Private*, pg. 64

VISILUX—Dental Curing Unit—3M; *U.S. Public*, pg. 1604

VISINE—NONE—Pfizer Inc.; *U.S. Public*, pg. 1281

VISION—Diagnostic Products—Abbott Laboratories; *U.S. Public*, pg. 12

VISION—Active Mobility Wheelchairs—Everest & Jennings, Inc.; *U.S. Public*, pg. 758

VISION—Light Bar—Federal Signal Corporation; *U.S. Public*, pg. 616

VISION—Motor Home—Fleetwood Enterprises, Inc.; *U.S. Public*, pg. 650

VISION—Oxygenator—Gish Biomedical, Inc.; *U.S. Public*, pg. 745

VISION—Sail Boats—Hunter Marine Corporation; *U.S. Private*, pg. 549

VISION—NONE—Rexhall Industries, Inc.; *U.S. Public*, pg. 1384

VISION—Roller Ball Pens—Sanford Corporation; *U.S. Public*, pg. 1178

VISION—Computer Software—Sterling Software, Inc.; *U.S. Public*, pg. 1516

VISION—NONE—Vision Financial Corporation; *U.S. Private*, pg. 1141

VISION—NONE—Western Atlas Logging Services; *U.S. Public*, pg. 1757

VISION AIRE—Rolling Grille—Cornell Iron Works, Inc.; *U.S. Private*, pg. 276

VISION CARE—Enzymatic Cleaner—Alcon Laboratories, Inc.; *Int'l*, pg. 916

VISION-EASE—Opthalmic Lenses—BMC Industries, Inc.; *U.S. Public*, pg. 162

VISION GLIDE—Side-Folding Grille—Cornell Iron Works, Inc.; *U.S. Private*, pg. 276

VISION NET—Centralized Systems Management—Apertus Technologies Incorporated; *U.S. Public*, pg. 119

VISION POINT—Stationery Products—The Mead Corporation; *U.S. Public*, pg. 1074

VISION SYSTEM—Crop Management System—Rockwell International Corporation; *U.S. Public*, pg. 1397

VISION VUE—All Glass Wall System—Kawneer Company; *U.S. Public*, pg. 60

VISIONAID—Lens Cleaning Products—Lensclean, Inc.; *U.S. Private*, pg. 162

VISIONAIRE—NONE—Kewaunee Scientific Corporation; *U.S. Public*, pg. 953

VISIONAIRE—Computer Programs—Lucent Technologies Inc.; *U.S. Public*, pg. 1017

VISIONS—Cookware—Corning Incorporated; *U.S. Public*, pg. 448

VISIONS—Medical Laser Technology Seminars—Summit Technology, Inc.; *U.S. Public*, pg. 1528

VISIONS—Craft Products—The Testor Corporation; *U.S. Public*, pg. 1358

VISIPAK—Digital Process Indicators—Action Instruments, Inc.; *U.S. Private*, pg. 15

VISIPORT—Optical Trocar—U.S. Surgical Corp.; *U.S. Public*, pg. 1687

VISIPOUR—Automatic Pouring Control System—Inductotherm Corp.; *U.S. Private*, pg. 560

VISKALDIX—Pharmaceutical—Novartis AG; *Int'l*, pg. 971

VISKASE—Cellulosic Casings & Shrinkable Plastic Bags—Viskase Corporation; *U.S. Public*, pg. 586

VISKEN—Pharmaceutical—Novartis AG; *Int'l*, pg. 971

VISKEN—Cardiovascular Pharmaceutical—Sandoz Pharmaceuticals Corp.; *Int'l*, pg. 974

VISLON—Zipper—YKK (U.S.A.); *Int'l*, pg. 1515

VISONARY—Advanced Medical Laser Technology Seminars—Summit Technology, Inc.; *U.S. Public*, pg. 1528

VISOR—Herbicide—Rohm and Haas Company; *U.S. Public*, pg. 1403

VISTA—Battery Operated Swing Without Overhead Crossbar—Cosco, Inc.; *U.S. Private*, pg. 277

VISTA—Floor Coverings—Domco Inc.; *Int'l*, pg. 415

VISTA—NONE—Everest & Jennings, Inc.; *U.S. Public*, pg. 758

VISTA—Communications System—Executone Information Systems, Inc.; *U.S. Public*, pg. 599

VISTA—Prefinished Wall Paneling—Georgia-Pacific Corporation; *U.S. Public*, pg. 735

VISTA—Vacuum Cleaner—HMI Industries; *U.S. Public*, pg. 771

VISTA—Lighting—JJI Lighting Group Inc.; *Int'l*, pg. 821

VISTA—Nurse Station—Mennen Medical Inc.; *Int'l*, pg. 858

VISTA—Ring & Presentation Binders & Tabs—H.C. Miller Company; *U.S. Private*, pg. 747

VISTA—Skylights—ODL Incorporated; *U.S. Private*, pg. 809

VISTA—Security System—Pittway Corporation; *U.S. Public*, pg. 1305

VISTA—Appliances—Sunbeam Household Products; *U.S. Public*, pg. 1533

VISTA—Computer Enlarging System—Telesensory Corporation; *U.S. Private*, pg. 1074

VISTA—Automobile—Toyota Motor Corporation; *Int'l*, pg. 1411

VISTA—Recycled School & Office Products—Union Camp Corporation; *U.S. Public*, pg. 1665

VISTA-AGENDA—Calendar & Activity Mgmnt. Software—Datapoint Corporation; *Int'l*, pg. 384

VISTA BRITE TIP—NONE—Cordis, a Johnson & Johnson Company; *U.S. Public*, pg. 928

VISTA-CHROME—NONE—Printing House, Inc.; *U.S. Private*, pg. 886

VISTA-CONNECT—Personal Network Software—Datapoint Corporation; *Int'l*, pg. 384

VISTA-FILE—File Mngmt. Computer Software—Datapoint Corporation; *Int'l*, pg. 384

VISTA-FINDER—Information Retrieval & File Mngmt. Computer Software—Datapoint Corporation; *Int'l*, pg. 384

VISTA-GATE—Network Communications Server System—Datapoint Corporation; *Int'l*, pg. 384

VISTA GLIDE—Side-Folding Closure—Cornell Iron Works, Inc.; *U.S. Private*, pg. 276

VISTA-GUIDE—Advanced Computer System User Interface Software—Datapoint Corporation; *Int'l*, pg. 384

VISTA-IMAGE—Image Management Tools—Datapoint Corporation; *Int'l*, pg. 384

VISTA-LAB—Laboratory Automation Computer Software Systems—Datapoint Corporation; *Int'l*, pg. 384

VISTA-LAW—Law Office Automation Computer Software System—Datapoint Corporation; *Int'l*, pg. 384

VISTA-MAIL—Advanced Electronic Message System Software—Datapoint Corporation; *Int'l*, pg. 384

VISTA-OFFICE—Office Automation Computing System—Datapoint Corporation; *Int'l*, pg. 384

VISTA-PC—Computer System—Datapoint Corporation; *Int'l*, pg. 384

VISTA-PHONE—Telemarketing System—Datapoint Corporation; *Int'l*, pg. 384

VISTA-PLAN—Fin. Modeling & Spreadsheet Computer Software—Datapoint Corporation; *Int'l*, pg. 384

VISTA-PRINT—Printer Mngmt. Facility Software—Datapoint Corporation; *Int'l*, pg. 384

VISTA-SCRIPT—Computer System User Interface Software—Datapoint Corporation; *Int'l*, pg. 384

VISTA-SPELL—Spelling Checking, Verificaiton & Hyphenation Computer Software—Datapoint Corporation; *Int'l*, pg. 384

VISTA-SPELL I—Spelling, Verification & Hyphenation Computer Software—Datapoint Corporation; *Int'l*, pg. 384

VISTA-SPELL II—Spelling, Verification & Hyphenation Computer Software—Datapoint Corporation; *Int'l*, pg. 384

VISTA-STATION XX—Computer System Workstation—Datapoint Corporation; *Int'l*, pg. 384

VISTA-STATION-82—Computer System Workstation—Datapoint Corporation; *Int'l*, pg. 384

VISTA-STATION-84—Computer System Workstation—Datapoint Corporation; *Int'l*, pg. 384

VISTA SUNROOMS—Aluminum Frame Sunrooms—Lindal Cedar Homes, Inc.; *U.S. Public*, pg. 998

VISTA-TELEX—Telex Mngmt. Computer System—Datapoint Corporation; *Int'l*, pg. 384

VISTA-VIEW—Multitasking Window/Context Mngmt. Computer Software—Datapoint Corporation; *Int'l*, pg. 384

VISTA/WIZARD—Porcelain Furnace—Air Techniques, Inc.; *U.S. Private*, pg. 28

VISTA-WORD—Enhance Word Processing Computer Software—Datapoint Corporation; *Int'l*, pg. 384

VISTA-36—Computer System—Datapoint Corporation; *Int'l*, pg. 384

VISTACAM & OMNI—Intra Oral Video Camera System—Air Techniques, Inc.; *U.S. Private*, pg. 28

VISTAFLEX—Plastic Strip Doors—Pawling Corporation; *U.S. Private*, pg. 844

VISTAGUARD—Rolling Grille—Cornell Iron Works, Inc.; *U.S. Private*, pg. 276

VISTAKON—NONE—Johnson & Johnson; *U.S. Public*, pg. 927

VISTAL—Translucent Ceramic—Coors Ceramics Company; *U.S. Public*, pg. 3

VISTALITE—Bicycle Accessories—Bell Sports Corp.; *U.S. Private*, pg. 207

VISTAMARC—Soft Contact Lenses—Vistakon Johnson & Johnson Vision Products, Inc.; *U.S. Public*, pg. 929

VISTAMARC TORIC—Soft Contact Lens—Johnson & Johnson; *U.S. Public*, pg. 927

VISTAMYCIN—Antibiotics—Meiji Seika Kaisha, Ltd.; *Int'l*, pg. 855

VISTAR—Magnetic Resonance—Picker International, Inc.; *Int'l*, pg. 545

VISTASCAN—Information Systems for Scanning Electron Microscopes—The Perkin-Elmer Corporation; *U.S. Public*, pg. 1279

VISTATRIM—Decorative Vinyl Trim—The Standard Products Company; *U.S. Public*, pg. 1504

VISU-GLOW—Fluorescent Gas Leak Detector—La-Co Industries Markal Company; *U.S. Private*, pg. 640

VISUAL AUTO TELLER—Remote Banking—Diebold, Incorporated; *U.S. Public*, pg. 506

VISUAL CONNECT—Internet Connectivity Device—InterVoice, Inc.; *U.S. Public*, pg. 910

VISUAL EXPLORER—Graphical User Interface—Cerner Corporation; *U.S. Public*, pg. 331

VISUAL IMPACT—Traditional & Image-Enabled Item Processing—Broadway & Seymour, Inc.; *U.S. Public*, pg. 258

VISUAL SOLUTIONS—Telecommunications Services—Lucent Technologies Inc.; *U.S. Public*, pg. 1017

VISUAL VOICE—Computer Telephony—Artisoft, Inc.; *U.S. Public*, pg. 136

VISUAL WORKFLO—NONE—FileNet Corporation; *U.S. Public*, pg. 622

VISUALAGE—Computer Product—International Business Machines Corporation; *U.S. Public*, pg. 895

VISUALINFO—Computer Product—International Business Machines Corporation; *U.S. Public*, pg. 895

VISUFLO—Surgical Site Visualization Wand—Baxter Research Medical, Inc.; *U.S. Public*, pg. 196

VITA—NONE—Groupe Limagrain; *Int'l*, pg. 566

VITA—Soya Based Specialties—Nestle S.A.; *Int'l*, pg. 915

VITA—Fish Prods.—Vita Food Products, Inc.; *U.S. Private*, pg. 1142

VITA—Juices & Tea—Vitasoy (U.S.A.) Inc.; *Int'l*, pg. 1469

VITA-C—Nutritional Products—Shaklee Corporation; *Int'l*, pg. 1518

VITA-CAL—Nutritional Products—Shaklee Corporation; *Int'l*, pg. 1518

VITA-E—Nutritional Products—Shaklee Corporation; *Int'l*, pg. 1518

VITA FUSION—Hair Care—Palm Beach Beauty Products Co.; *U.S. Private*, pg. 834

VITA GOLD—Juice—McCain Citrus Inc.; *Int'l*, pg. 850

VITA-LEA—Nutritional Products—Shaklee Corporation; *Int'l*, pg. 1518

VITA-LITE—Sunlight-Simulating Fluorescent Bulb—Duro-Test Corporation; *U.S. Private*, pg. 349

VITA-LITE—Dairy Products—Vitamilk Dairy, Inc.; *U.S. Private*, pg. 1142

VITA PEDIC—Bedding—Jamison Bedding, Inc.; *U.S. Private*, pg. 581

VITA PLUS—Milk—Q.U.F. Industries Ltd.; *Int'l*, pg. 1074

VITABATH—Upscale Gelees, Personal Care—Tsumura International; *Int'l*, pg. 1426

VITABATH NATURALS—NONE—Tsumura International; *Int'l*, pg. 1426

VITACHROME—Biological Supplies—Carolina Biological Supply Co.; *U.S. Private*, pg. 213

VITAFLO—NONE—Uniroyal Chemical Company, Inc.; *U.S. Public*, pg. 460

VITAFREZE—Frozen Confections—Crystal Cream & Butter Company; *U.S. Private*, pg. 294

VITAGARD RUST-NO-MORE—Paint—Masury Paint; *U.S. Public*, pg. 1707

VITAL DEFENSE—Dental Disinfecting & Sterilizing Solution Line—Block Drug Company, Inc.; *U.S. Public*, pg. 236

VITAL E—Vitamin E Supplement (Equine & Bovine)—Schering-Plough Corporation; *U.S. Public*, pg. 1438

VITAL FIBER—Fiber Product—Novo Nordisk A/S; *Int'l*, pg. 987

VITAL IV—Simulation Systems—McDonnell Aircraft & Missile Systems Div.; *U.S. Public*, pg. 241

VITAL PAK—Anesthesia Kits—Vital Signs, Inc.; *U.S. Public*, pg. 1723

VITAL-PERFECTION—Skin Care—Shiseido Cosmetics (America) Ltd.; *Int'l*, pg. 1235

VITALAIT—Low Fat Cheese—Cabot Creamery Co-Operative Inc.; *U.S. Private*, pg. 26

VITALASTIC—Flashing Cement—Gulf States Asphalt Company, Inc.; *U.S. Private*, pg. 487

VITALIS—Men's Hair Care Preparation—Bristol-Myers Squibb Company; *U.S. Public*, pg. 253

VITALIS—Water—UNICER-Uniao Cervejeira, S.A.; *Int'l*, pg. 1432

VITALITE—Electric Signal Light—Federal Signal Corporation, Signal Div.; *U.S. Public*, pg. 616

VITALITY—Line of Foodservice Juices & Coffee—Lykes Brothers Inc.; *U.S. Private*, pg. 682

VITALITY—Hair Care—Palm Beach Beauty Products Co.; *U.S. Private*, pg. 834

VITALVIEW—Telemetry System that Links Bedside Pulse Oximeters to a Central Station—Criticare Systems, Inc.; *U.S. Public*, pg. 459

VITAMASTER—Fitness Equipment—RDM Sports Group; *U.S. Public*, pg. 1354

VITAMASTER—Exercise Equipment—Roadmaster/Brunswick; *U.S. Public*, pg. 265

VITAMILHO—Corn Flour—Bestfoods; *U.S. Public*, pg. 223

VITAMILK—Dairy Products—Vitamilk Dairy, Inc.; *U.S. Private*, pg. 1142

VITAMIN E & LANOLIN—Soap—The Andrew Jergens Company; *Int'l*, pg. 717

VITAMIN WORLD—Vitamin Products—Nature's Bounty Inc.; *U.S. Public*, pg. 1166

VITAMITE—Non-Dairy Low Fat Beverage—Diehl Inc.; *U.S. Private*, pg. 332

VITAMITE—Non-Dairy Beverage—Diehl Specialties International; *U.S. Private*, pg. 332

VITAPOINTE—Hair Conditioner—Clairol, Inc.; *U.S. Public*, pg. 254

VITAPOINTE—NONE—Kiwi Brands Pty. Ltd.; *U.S. Public*, pg. 1434

VITARICH ICE CREAM—NONE—Vitamilk Dairy, Inc.; *U.S. Private*, pg. 1142

VITASHEEN—Beauty Products—DeMert & Dougherty, Inc.; *U.S. Private*, pg. 323

VITASNELLA—Low-Fat Yogurt—Danone Group; *Int'l*, pg. 379

VITASOY—Soft Drink—Vitasoy (U.S.A.) Inc.; *Int'l*, pg. 1469

VITASPA—Spa/Bath Personal Care—Tsumura International; *Int'l*, pg. 1426

VITATRON—NONE—Medtronic, Inc.; *U.S. Public*, pg. 1082

VITAVEL—Vitamin Supplements—SmithKline Beecham plc; *Int'l*, pg. 1264

VITEK—Specialty Chemicals—Akzo Nobel Inc.; *Int'l*, pg. 47

VITELMA—Margarine—Vandemoortele N.V.; *Int'l*, pg. 1451

VITNERS PRIZE WINNING SNACKS—Snack Foods—C.J. Vitner Co.; *U.S. Private*, pg. 1142

VITO—Musical Instruments—G. Leblanc Corporation; *U.S. Private*, pg. 656

VITON—Fluoroelastomer—Du Pont (E.I. Du Pont De Nemours & Co.); *U.S. Public*, pg. 530

VITR-AU-LESS—Conductor Paste—Ferro Corporation; *U.S. Public*, pg. 618

VITRA-SHIELD—Stipple Finish—Pratt & Lambert United, Inc.; *U.S. Public*, pg. 1466

VITRAFOS—Glassy Phosphate—Rhone-Poulenc Basic Chemicals Co.; *Int'l*, pg. 1110

VITRALITE—Paint—Pratt & Lambert United, Inc.; *U.S. Public*, pg. 1466

VITRALON—Paint, Powder Coating—Pratt & Lambert United, Inc.; *U.S. Public*, pg. 1466

VITRASIL—Paint—Pratt & Lambert United, Inc.; *U.S. Public*, pg. 1466

VITRICOLOR—Multicolor Wall Coating—Polymer Plastics Corporation; *U.S. Private*, pg. 875

VITRICON—Wall & Floor Finishes—Polymer Plastics Corporation; *U.S. Private*, pg. 875

VITRITURF—Safety Floor System—Polymer Plastics Corporation; *U.S. Private*, pg. 875

VITROFILM—Automotive Ornamentation—3M; *U.S. Public*, pg. 1604

VITROKE—Paint—Swire Pacific Limited; *Int'l*, pg. 1328

VITROMEX—Vitreous China Sanitaryware, Ceramic Floor & Wall Tile—Vitromex, S.A.; *Int'l*, pg. 1469

VITRONIC—Promotional Vinyl Business Products—Golden Books Family Entertainment Inc.; *U.S. Public*, pg. 749

VITROTRIM—Automotive Body Trim—3M; *U.S. Public*, pg. 1604

VITTEL—Mineral Water—Nestle S.A.; *Int'l*, pg. 915

VITUBE—Viton Flexible Tubing—NewAge Industries Inc.; *U.S. Private*, pg. 796

VITUBE—Tubing of DuPont's Viton—Newage Industries Inc., Plastics Technology Group; *U.S. Private*, pg. 796

VIVA—Lowfat & Extra-Calcium Milks, Cottage Cheese & Yogurt—Borden, Inc.; *U.S. Private*, pg. 157

VIVA—NONE—Medical Meadow Gold Dairies, Inc.; *U.S. Private*, pg. 1016

VIVA—Bath Accessories—Melard Manufacturing Corporation; *U.S. Private*, pg. 729

VIVAK—Extruded PETG—DSM Sheffield Plastics; *Int'l*, pg. 354

VIVALP—NONE—Tefal S.A.; *Int'l*, pg. 569

VIVANA—Nylon—BASF Corporation Fiber Products Division; *Int'l*, pg. 105

VIVARIN—Stimulant—SmithKline Beecham Consumer Healthcare, U.S.; *Int'l*, pg. 1264

VIVARIN—Stimulant—SmithKline Beecham Corporation; *Int'l*, pg. 1264

VIVARIN—Stimulant—SmithKline Beecham plc; *Int'l*, pg. 1264

VIVELLE—NONE—Novartis Pharmaceuticals; *Int'l*, pg. 973

VIVI—Monthly General Interest Women's Magazine—Kodansha Ltd.; *Int'l*, pg. 742

VIVID—Bleach—The Dow Chemical Company; *U.S. Public*, pg. 522

VIVID—Color Safe All Fabric Bleach—DowBrands, L.P.; *U.S. Public*, pg. 523

VIVID PROTEIN—Health Food Products—Meiji Seika Kaisha, Ltd.; *Int'l*, pg. 855

VIVIMED—Analgesic—Bausch & Lomb Incorporated; *U.S. Public*, pg. 194

VIVITAR—Photographic Equipment—Gestetner Holdings PLC; *Int'l*, pg. 1114

VIVITAR—Photographic & Electronic Equipment—Vivitar Corporation; *Int'l*, pg. 1060

VIVRA PHYSICIAN SERVICES—Primary Car Physician Practice Management—Vivra Incorporated; *U.S. Public*, pg. 1723

VIVRA SPECIALTY PARTNERS—Specialty Network Management—Vivra Incorporated; *U.S. Public*, pg. 1723

VIYELLA—NONE—Coats Viyella plc; *Int'l*, pg. 299

VIZIR—Detergent—Procter & Gamble GmbH; *U.S. Public*, pg. 1332

VLADIMIR—Vodka—Montebello Brands Inc.; *U.S. Private*, pg. 758

VLADIVAR—Vodka—Fortune Brands, Inc.; *U.S. Public*, pg. 674

VLADIVAR—Vodka—The Whyte & Mackay Group Plc.; *U.S. Public*, pg. 675

VLASIC—Pickles & Relishes—Campbell Soup Company; *U.S. Public*, pg. 298

VLEMASQUE—Pharmaceuticals—Rhone-Poulenc Rorer - U.S.; *Int'l*, pg. 1110

VLIESELINE—Non-Wovens for the Apparel Industry—Freudenberg & Company; *Int'l*, pg. 505

VO—Canadian Whisky—The Seagram Company Ltd.; *Int'l*, pg. 1214

VOC ABATOR—Air Pollution Controle Equipment—Donaldson Company, Inc.; *U.S. Public*, pg. 517

VOCAL IMAGES—NONE—Image Entertainment, Inc.; *U.S. Public*, pg. 870

VOCAL'NET—Internet Protocol Telephony Gateway System—Inter-Tel, Incorporated; *U.S. Public*, pg. 888

VOCOL—Rubber Accelerator—Monsanto Company; *U.S. Public*, pg. 1124

VOCOL—Rubber Accelerator—Solutia Inc.; *U.S. Public*, pg. 1483

VODKA GORDON'S—NONE—Guinness Plc; *Int'l*, pg. 412

VODKA HUZZAR—Vodka—Groupe Pernod Ricard; *Int'l*, pg. 566

VODKA KARINSKAYA—Vodka—Groupe Pernod Ricard; *Int'l*, pg. 566

VODKA PETROFF—Vodka—Groupe Pernod Ricard; *Int'l*, pg. 566

VODSTOK—Vodka—Marie Brizard Wines & Spirits USA; *U.S. Private*, pg. 702

VOGEL—NONE—Quality Bakers New Zealand Ltd.; *Int'l*, pg. 556

VOGEL & OCHSNER—European Industrial Pumps—Goulds Pumps, Incorporated; *U.S. Public*, pg. 860

VOGEL'S—Bakery Products—Goodman Fielder Limited; *Int'l*, pg. 555

VOGEL'S—NONE—Quality Bakers Australia Ltd.; *Int'l*, pg. 555

VOGT—Valves & Pipe Fittings—Henry Vogt Machine Co.; *U.S. Public*, pg. 1143

VOGUE—Stationery—American Greetings U.S. Greeting Card Division; *U.S. Public*, pg. 78

VOGUE—Patterns—Butterick Company, Inc.; *U.S. Private*, pg. 190

VOGUE—Magazine—The Conde Nast Publications Inc.; *U.S. Private*, pg. 20

VOGUE—Facial Tissue—Kimberly-Clark Corporation; *U.S. Public*, pg. 958

VOGUE—Cookware—Regal Ware, Inc.; *U.S. Private*, pg. 917

VOGUE—Ready-Made Curtains & Draperies—Robertson Factories, Inc.; *U.S. Private*, pg. 936

VOGUE—Periodical—Vogue Magazine; *U.S. Private*, pg. 20

VOGUE AND DESIGN—Cookware—Regal Ware, Inc.; *U.S. Private*, pg. 917

VOICE+—Trade Periodical—Advanstar Communications; *U.S. Private*, pg. 22

VOICE + ASIA PACIFIC—Trade Periodical—Advanstar Communications; *U.S. Private*, pg. 22

VOICE CONTROL—Loudspeakers—Atlas/Soundolier; *U.S. Private*, pg. 64

VOICE DIRECTORIES—Talking Yellow Pages for Phone Directory Publishers—Brite Voice Systems, Inc.; *U.S. Public*, pg. 257

VOICE ENHANCER—In-The-Canal Instrument—Beltone Electronics Corporation; *U.S. Private*, pg. 132

VOICE EXPRESS—Business Telephone—Comdial Corporation; *U.S. Public*, pg. 407

VOICE GUN—Portable Loud Speaker—Federal Signal Corporation, Signal Div.; *U.S. Public*, pg. 616

VOICE LOGGER—Telephone & Radio Communication Recorder—Lanier Worldwide Inc.; *U.S. Public*, pg. 791

VOICE MANAGEMENT FACILITY/2—Business System—International Business Machines Corporation; *U.S. Public*, pg. 895

VOICE∗MASSAGING—Storage & Forwarding of Voice Messages—Intellicall, Inc.; *U.S. Public*, pg. 887

VOICE MEMO—Voice Messaging & Call Processing Capabilities—Centigram Communications Corporation; *U.S. Public*, pg. 323

VOICE NEWS NETWORK—Audio News & Information Accessed by Telephone—Tribune Media Services, Inc.; *U.S. Public*, pg. 1636

VOICE/PHONE ASSISTANT—Business System—International Business Machines Corporation; *U.S. Public*, pg. 895

VOICE SELECT—Voice Activated System for Cellular Users—Brite Voice Systems, Inc.; *U.S. Public*, pg. 257

VOICE SERVER—Platform/Hardware that Runs Infomail Express 2.1—Digital Sound Corporation; *U.S. Public*, pg. 508

VOICE SPAN—Simultaneous Voice & Data Technology—Paradyne; *U.S. Private*, pg. 838

VOICE SYSTEM 4000—Digital Dictation System—Philips Speech Processing; *Int'l*, pg. 1055

VOICE/TONE—Signal Devices—Atlas/Soundolier; *U.S. Private*, pg. 64

VOICEWRITER 160—Dictation Equipment—Lanier Worldwide Inc.; *U.S. Public*, pg. 791

VOICEBANK—Voice Message Retrieval Service—British Telecommunications plc; *Int'l*, pg. 222

VOICEMAX PLUS—Voice Response Health Information—National Health Enhancement Systems, Inc.; *U.S. Public*, pg. 1157

VOICEPRINT—Photographic Film—Qualex Inc.; *U.S. Public*, pg. 551

VOICETYPE—Business System—International Business Machines Corporation; *U.S. Public*, pg. 895

VOICEWRITER 800 & 1600—Digital Dictation—Lanier Worldwide Inc.; *U.S. Public*, pg. 791

VOICEWRITER EXECUTIVE—Digital Dictation Equipment—Lanier Worldwide Inc.; *U.S. Public*, pg. 791

VOICEWRITER OS—Open System Digital System—Lanier Worldwide Inc.; *U.S. Public*, pg. 791

VOICEWRITER 110—Dictation Equipment—Lanier Worldwide Inc.; *U.S. Public*, pg. 791

VOICEWRITER 650—Dictation Equipment—Lanier Worldwide Inc.; *U.S. Public*, pg. 791

VOIT—Physical Equipment—Aurora Electronics, Inc.; *U.S. Public*, pg. 147

VOIT—Baseball Equipment—Sport Supply Group, Inc.; *U.S. Public*, pg. 1499

VOIT—Sports Equipment—Voit Sports, Inc.; *U.S. Private*, pg. 1143

VOL-CON—Voltage/Continuity Tester—Ideal Industries, Inc.; *U.S. Private*, pg. 557

VOL DE NUIT—Fragrance—Guerlain S.A.; *Int'l*, pg. 780

VOL-U-METER—Control Measurement—Brooks Instrument; *U.S. Public*, pg. 574

VOLANTE—Chairs—Knoll, Inc.; *U.S. Private*, pg. 627

VOLCLAY PANELS—Moisture Impedance Material—AMCOL International Corp.; *U.S. Public*, pg. 63

VOLDROP—Candy—CSM N.V.; *Int'l*, pg. 243

VOLDYNE—Incentive Breathers—American Home Products Corporation; *U.S. Public*, pg. 79

VOLENTI—Wheels—Cragar Industries, Inc.; *U.S. Public*, pg. 456

VOLK OPTICAL—Ophthalmic Aspheric Lenses—Halma p.l.c.; *Int'l*, pg. 589

VOLKSWAGEN—Automobile—Autogerma S.p.A.; *Int'l*, pg. 1474

VOLKSWAGEN—Automobile—Volkswagen AG; *Int'l*, pg. 1473

VOLKSWAGEN CARAVELLE—Commercial Vehicle—Volkswagen AG; *Int'l*, pg. 1473

VOLKSWAGEN EUROVAN—Van—Volkswagen of America, Inc.; *Int'l*, pg. 1474

VOLKSWAGEN GTI—Car—Volkswagen of America, Inc.; *Int'l*, pg. 1474

VOLKSWAGEN GOLF—Automobile—Volkswagen of America, Inc.; *Int'l*, pg. 1474

VOLKSWAGENINDUSTRIAL—Industrial Diesel & Gas Engines-Sales; Parts & Service—McDonald Equipment Co.; *U.S. Private*, pg. 721

VOLKSWAGEN JETTA—Car—Volkswagen of America, Inc.; *Int'l*, pg. 1474

VOLKSWAGEN PASSAT—Car—Volkswagen of America, Inc.; *Int'l*, pg. 1474

VOLKSWAGEN SHARAN—Multi Purpose Vehicle—Volkswagen AG; *Int'l*, pg. 1473

VOLLMAR—NONE—Filterwerk Mann & Hummel GmbH; *Int'l*, pg. 484

VOLLEYS—NONE—Venture Stores, Inc.; *U.S. Public*, pg. 1716

VOLLHUMON—Peat Products—DSM Chemie Linz GmbH; *Int'l*, pg. 356

VOLLKORN—Fertilizers—DSM Chemie Linz GmbH; *Int'l*, pg. 356

VOLMAC—NONE—CAP Gemini S.A.; *Int'l*, pg. 263

VOLMAX—Oral Solid Bronchodilator—Muro Pharmaceutical, Inc.; *U.S. Private*, pg. 767

VOLTA—Floor Care Equipment—Electrolux, AB; *Int'l*, pg. 438

VOLTA—NONE—Zanussi Italia S.p.A.; *Int'l*, pg. 442

VOLTALEF—Resin used in Oils & Greases—Elf Atochem North America, Inc.; *Int'l*, pg. 445

VOLTAREN—Antirheomatic—Ciba Specialty Chemicals; *Int'l*, pg. 291

VOLTAREN—Antirheumatic—Novartis; *Int'l*, pg. 972

VOLTAREN—NONE—Novartis Pharmaceuticals; *Int'l*, pg. 973

VOLTMASTER—Coil—Mallory, Inc.; *U.S. Private*, pg. 698

VOLUETTE—Chemical Standard Solution—Hach Company; *U.S. Public*, pg. 773

VOLUFLEX—Hose—HBD Industries, Inc.; *U.S. Private*, pg. 489

VOLUMATIC—Retail Security Products—Halma p.l.c.; *Int'l*, pg. 589

VOLUMATOR—NONE—Manufacturers Technologies, Inc.; *U.S. Public*, pg. 701

VOLUME MAXIMIZER—Turbo Dryer—Remington Products Company, L.L.C.; *U.S. Private*, pg. 921

VOLUME SERVER—Computer Software System—Datapoint Corporation; *Int'l*, pg. 384

VOLUMEASURE—Soil Density Tester—ELE International, Inc./Soiltest; *Int'l*, pg. 1287

VOLUMETRIC CONCEPT SCREENING BY MAIL—Evaluate Early-State Product Ideas & Concepts—BASES Worldwide; *U.S. Private*, pg. 120

VOLUPTE—Fragrances—Sanofi Beaute, Inc.; *Int'l*, pg. 445

VOLVIC—Mineral Water—Danone Group; *Int'l*, pg. 379

VOLVIC—Non-Carbonated Water—The Perrier Group of America; *U.S. Public*, pg. 919

VOLVO—Truck—Buffalo Truck Center; *U.S. Private*, pg. 179

VOLVO—Cars, Trucks, Buses, Construction Equipment & Engines—AB Volvo; *Int'l*, pg. 1476

VOLVO—Passenger Cars/Parts & Accessories—Volvo Car UK Ltd.; *Int'l*, pg. 1477

VOLVO—Automobile & Logo—Volvo Cars of North America, Inc.; *Int'l*, pg. 1477

VOLVO—NONE—Volvo Construction Equipment; *Int'l*, pg. 1477

VOLVO—Class 7 Truck & Tractors—Volvo Truck North America, Inc.; *Int'l*, pg. 1477

VOLVO BM—Articulated Haulers—Euclid Hitachi; *Int'l*, pg. 622

VOLVO ON CALL—Road Service Program—Volvo Cars of North America, Inc.; *Int'l*, pg. 1477

VOLVO PENTA—Marine & Industrial Engines—Volvo Penta of the Americas, Inc.; *Int'l*, pg. 1477

VON DUPRIN—Door Exit Hardware—Exit Device Division; *U.S. Public*, pg. 876

VON DUPRIN—Door Closers—Ingersoll-Rand Company; *U.S. Public*, pg. 876

VON GAL—Palletizers, Depalletizers—Litton Industries, Inc.; *U.S. Public*, pg. 1002

VON HOUSEN—Auto Parts—Von Housen Motors; *U.S. Private*, pg. 1143

VONS—Supermarkets—The Vons Companies, Inc.; *U.S. Public*, pg. 1426

VONS FOOD & DRUG STORES—Supermarkets—The Vons Companies, Inc.; *U.S. Public*, pg. 1426

VOPLEXER—Voice/Data Multiplexer—Ascom Timeplex; *Int'l*, pg. 86

VORACEL—Urethane Carpet Backing—The Dow Chemical Company; *U.S. Public*, pg. 522

VORACOR—Polyurethane Components—The Dow Chemical Company; *U.S. Public*, pg. 522

VORAL—Hose—Alsons Corporation; *U.S. Public*, pg. 1053

VORALAST—Polyurethane Components—The Dow Chemical Company; *U.S. Public*, pg. 522

VORANATE—Isocyante Adducts—The Dow Chemical Company; *U.S. Public*, pg. 522

VORANOL—Polyol—The Dow Chemical Company; *U.S. Public*, pg. 522

VORATEC—Polyurethane Components—The Dow Chemical Company; *U.S. Public*, pg. 522

VOROBA—Hearing Aids—Bausch & Lomb Incorporated; *U.S. Public*, pg. 194

VORTEMP—Air Heating Device—3M; *U.S. Public*, pg. 1604

VORTEX—Regenerative Blower—The Spencer Turbine Co.; *U.S. Private*, pg. 1025

VORTEX—Respirator Cooling Device—3M; *U.S. Public*, pg. 1604

VORTEX BBQ GRILL—NONE—Kay Home Products, Inc.; *U.S. Public*, pg. 1258

VORTEX SMOKE-RING SCRUBBER—Submicron Particulate Spray Scrubber—Beco Engineering Company; *U.S. Private*, pg. 129

VOSENE—Shampoo—SmithKline Beecham plc; *Int'l*, pg. 1264

VOSOL—Ear Infections—Wallace Laboratories; *U.S. Public*, pg. 310

VOSOL HC—Ear Infections—Wallace Laboratories; *U.S. Public*, pg. 310

VOTICANDLES—Votive Candles—Will & Baumer Incorporated; *U.S. Private*, pg. 1176

VOX—Music & Lifestyle Magazine—IPC Magazines Limited; *Int'l*, pg. 651

VOYAGE THROUGH THE UNIVERSE—Book Series—Time-Life, Inc.; *U.S. Public*, pg. 1613

VOYAGER—Van—Chrysler Corporation; *U.S. Public*, pg. 352

VOYAGER—Cameras—Eastman Kodak Company; *U.S. Public*, pg. 550

VOYAGER—Biospectrometry Workstations—PerSeptive Biosystems, Inc.; *U.S. Public*, pg. 1279

VOYAGER—Swiss Embroidered Emblems—Voyager Emblems, Inc.; *U.S. Private*, pg. 1143

VOYAGER ORIGINIALS—Swiss Embroidered Emblems—Voyager Emblems, Inc.; *U.S. Private*, pg. 1143

VOYAGEUR—NONE—Consolidated Papers, Inc.; *U.S. Public*, pg. 436

VOYAGR—Catheter—Medtronic, Inc.; *U.S. Public*, pg. 1082

VOYANT—Washable Velvet—Guilford Mills, Inc.; *U.S. Public*, pg. 768

VOYCO—Swiss Embroidered Emblems & Caps—Voyager Emblems, Inc.; *U.S. Private*, pg. 1143

VOYEZ—Beauty & Bath Accessories—Paris Presents; *U.S. Private*, pg. 839

VRIECO-NAUTA—Mixing & Drying Equipment—Hosokawa Micron International Inc.; *Int'l*, pg. 635

VRIECO-NAUTA—NONE—Hosokawa Micron Powder Systems; *Int'l*, pg. 636

VROOM & DREESMANN—Clothing—Vendex International N.V.; *Int'l*, pg. 1462

VROOM BOOKS—NONE—Broderbund Software, Inc.; *U.S. Public*, pg. 258

VU-MAX—Gynecological Device—The Cooper Companies, Inc.; *U.S. Public*, pg. 442

VU-MORE—Gynecological Device—The Cooper Companies, Inc.; *U.S. Public*, pg. 442

VU-TRON—Insulated Wire & Cable—General Cable Corporation; *Int'l*, pg. 1486

VU-TRON 7—Insulated Wire & Cable—General Cable Corporation; *Int'l*, pg. 1486

VUEMIX—Stirrer—Fisher Scientific Company; *U.S. Private*, pg. 658

VUL-CUP—Peroxide Catalyst—Hercules Incorporated; *U.S. Public*, pg. 809

VULCA SEAL—Machine Tool Covers—A&A Manufacturing Co.; *U.S. Private*, pg. 1

VULCAIN—Ariene 5 Engine—SNECMA - Societe Nationale d'Etude et de Construction de Moteurs d'Aviation; *Int'l*, pg. 1165

VULCAN—Plasma Cutting Tables—Lockformer Company; *U.S. Public*, pg. 1100

VULCAN—Cookware—Premark International, Inc.; *U.S. Public*, pg. 1321

VULCAN—Compressible Offset Blankets—Reeves International; *U.S. Private*, pg. 507

VULCAN—Appliances—Southcorp Holdings Ltd.; *Int'l*, pg. 1287

VULCAN—Lawnmowers—Southland Mower Corp.; *U.S. Private*, pg. 1144

VULCAN—Traffic Control Signs—Vulcan Inc.; *U.S. Private*, pg. 1144

VULCAN OIL & CHEMICAL—Industrial Bulb Oils—Kelso Oil Company; *U.S. Private*, pg. 613

VULCAN RADIATOR—Radiator—Mestek, Inc.; *U.S. Public*, pg. 1099

VULCANEER—Laminated Material—Georgia-Pacific Corporation; *U.S. Public*, pg. 735

VULCANITE—NONE—CertainTeed Corporation; *Int'l*, pg. 1170

VULCATHENE—NONE—Glynwed International PLC; *Int'l*, pg. 554

VULCRAFT—Steel Joist & Joist Girders, Steel Roof & Floor Decking—Nucor Corporation; *U.S. Public*, pg. 1205

VULKASHIELD—High Voltage Electrical Distr. Protection Equip.-Ground Shields—General Electric Canada Inc.; *U.S. Public*, pg. 713

VULKEM—Polyurethatne Sealant—RPM, Inc.; *U.S. Public*, pg. 1356

VULKENE—Electrical Wire & Cable—General Electric Canada Inc.; *U.S. Public*, pg. 713

VULKOLLAN—Polyurethane—Merkel Kunststoff GmbH; *Int'l*, pg. 859

VULNOPOL—Synthetic Rubber Production Chemicals—Alco Chemical; *Int'l*, pg. 1435

VULT-ACET—Polyvinyl Acetate Latices—General Latex & Chemical Corporation; *U.S. Private*, pg. 444

VULT-ACRYL—Acrylic Latices—General Latex & Chemical Corporation; *U.S. Private*, pg. 444

VULTAFOAM—Urethane Prepolymers & Foam Systems—General Latex & Chemical Corporation; *U.S. Private*, pg. 444

VULTEX—Latex Compounds—General Latex & Chemical Corporation; *U.S. Private*, pg. 444

VULTEX—Mens Rain Wear—Rainfair, Inc.; *U.S. Private*, pg. 907

VULTEX II—Bowling Pins—Vulcan International Corporation; *U.S. Public*, pg. 1725

VUMON—Cancer Therapy Product—Bristol-Myers Squibb Company; *U.S. Public*, pg. 253

VYBEX—Polyester Compounds—Ferro Corporation; *U.S. Public*, pg. 618

VYBRAN—Yarn—National Spinning Co., Inc.; *U.S. Private*, pg. 786

VYCOR—Indus. & Laboratoryware—Corning Incorporated; *U.S. Public*, pg. 448

VYDATE—Insecticide/Nematicide—Du Pont (E.I. Du Pont De Nemours & Co.); *U.S. Public*, pg. 530

VYDAX—Fluorocarbon Telomer—Du Pont (E.I. Du Pont De Nemours & Co.); *U.S. Public*, pg. 530

VYDYNE—Nylon Molding/Extrusion Resins—Monsanto Company; *U.S. Public*, pg. 1124

VYDYNE R—Nylon Molding/Extrusion Resins—Monsanto Company; *U.S. Public*, pg. 1124

VYKMIN—Vitamin & Tonic—SmithKline Beecham plc; *Int'l*, pg. 1264

VYLON PIPE—High Capacity, Large Diameter Sewer Main—The Lamson & Sessions Co.; *U.S. Public*, pg. 976

VYNATHENE—Vinyl Acetate-Ethylene Copolymer Resins & Elastomers—Millennium Petrochemicals, Inc.; *Int'l*, pg. 594

VYRAM—Thermoplastic Elastomer—Monsanto Company; *U.S. Public*, pg. 1124

VYTONE CREAM—Pharmaceuticals—Rhone-Poulenc Rorer - U.S.; *Int'l*, pg. 1110

W

W—Consumer Publication—Fairchild Publications; *U.S. Public*, pg. 513

WAN ONE—Networking Software—V-Band Corporation; *U.S. Public*, pg. 1701

WAVS—Waters Automated Valve Station—Millipore Corporation; *U.S. Public*, pg. 1112

W & B—Grinding Lubricants & Cutting Oils—Dryden Oil of New England; *Int'l*, pg. 235

W&G—NONE—Willcox & Gibbs, Inc.; *U.S. Private*, pg. 1177

WBAL-AM—Broadcasting—The Hearst Corporation; *U.S. Private*, pg. 515

WBAL-TV—Broadcasting—The Hearst Corporation; *U.S. Private*, pg. 515

WBFI—Finance Company—The Scott Fetzer Company; *U.S. Public*, pg. 217

WBS—Wood Based Building Components—Weyerhaeuser Company; *U.S. Public*, pg. 1764

WBSS—FM Broadcasting Station—Press Communications, LLC; *U.S. Private*, pg. 882

WBUD—AM Broadcasting Station—Press Communications, LLC; *U.S. Private*, pg. 882

WC EEND—NONE—N.V. Johnson Wax Belgium S.A.; *U.S. Private*, pg. 593

WCIX-TV—Television Broadcasting—WFOR-TV Channel 4; *U.S. Public*, pg. 275

WCVB-TV—Broadcasting—The Hearst Corporation; *U.S. Private*, pg. 515

WD-40—Lubricant, Penetrant, Rust Preventative, Moisture Displacer & Cleaner—WD-40 Company; *U.S. Public*, pg. 1726

WDS—NONE—Western Atlas Logging Services; *U.S. Public*, pg. 1757

WDTN-TV—Broadcasting—The Hearst Corporation; *U.S. Private*, pg. 515

W/DESIGN—NONE—Berg Electronics; *U.S. Public*, pg. 212

W DESIGN—Metal Caps, Lids, Closures & Liners for Containers—The West Company, Incorporated; *U.S. Public*, pg. 1755

WE—Electrical Connectors—Litton Industries, Inc.; *U.S. Public*, pg. 1002

WEA—Globe & Butterfly Control Valves—Dwyer Instruments Inc.; *U.S. Private*, pg. 350

W.E. ANDERSON—Flow and Level Controls—Dwyer Instruments Inc.; *U.S. Private*, pg. 350

W.E. GARRETT—Scotch & Sweet Snuffs—Conwood Company L.P.; *U.S. Private*, pg. 272

WF—Ferrous & Nonferrous Forgings—Jervis B. Webb Company; *U.S. Private*, pg. 1156

W1500—NONE—J.M. Process Systems Inc.; *U.S. Private*, pg. 577

WIBI—Pharmaceutical Products—Galderma Laboratories, Inc.; *Int'l*, pg. 819

WIBW AM/FM—Radio—Shivers Trading & Operating Co.; *U.S. Private*, pg. 994

WINS—Processing System for P&C Insurance Companies—Avemco Corporation; *U.S. Public*, pg. 151

WINS-FIS—Financial Information System, Including GL, AP, AR—Avemco Corporation; *U.S. Public*, pg. 151

WINS-RE—Facultative & Treaty Reinsurance Administration System—Avemco Corporation; *U.S. Public*, pg. 151

WIPS—Word Image Processing System Software—Xerox Imaging Systems, Inc.; *U.S. Public*, pg. 1785

WIPS EDITOR—Word Image Processing System Software Editor—Xerox Imaging Systems, Inc.; *U.S. Public*, pg. 1785

W.I.S.E.—WorkPlace Insurance For Employees—Utica Mutual Insurance Company; *U.S. Private*, pg. 1129

WISN-AM—Broadcasting—The Hearst Corporation; *U.S. Private*, pg. 515

WISN-TV—Broadcasting—The Hearst Corporation; *U.S. Private*, pg. 515

WISP—Waters Intelligent Sample Processor—Millipore Corporation; *U.S. Public*, pg. 1112

WIYY-FM—Broadcasting—The Hearst Corporation; *U.S. Private*, pg. 515

WJR-AM—Radio Station—WJR-AM; *U.S. Public*, pg. 512

WKCF—TV Broadcasting Station—Press Communications, LLC; *U.S. Private*, pg. 882

WLTQ-FM—Broadcasting—The Hearst Corporation; *U.S. Private*, pg. 515

W.L. WELLER—Bourbon—Shieffelin Somerset Co.; *Int'l*, pg. 412

W.L. WELLER—Bourbon—United Distillers USA, Inc.; *Int'l*, pg. 412

WMF/USA—Stainless Steel Hollow & Flatware—WMF/USA; *U.S. Private*, pg. 1144

WM. H. MCGEE—Marine Insurance—Orion Capital Companies, Inc.; *U.S. Public*, pg. 1231

WMI—Socks & Knitted Headwear—Wigwam Mills, Inc.; *U.S. Private*, pg. 1175

WMO—Precision Machinery—Hunter Douglas N.V.; *Int'l*, pg. 639

WMS GAMING—Slot Machines & Video Lottery Terminals—WMS Industries Inc.; *U.S. Public*, pg. 1727

WMTP—Radio Paging Equipment & Related Software—Glenayre Technologies, Inc.; *U.S. Public*, pg. 746

WMAPI—Computer Gateways & Related Software—Glenayre Technologies, Inc.; *U.S. Public*, pg. 746

W900B—Trucks—Kenworth Truck Company; *U.S. Public*, pg. 1246

W900B AERODYNE—Trucks—Kenworth Truck Company; *U.S. Public*, pg. 1246

WOB-L—Piston-Type Air Compressor—Thomas Industries Inc.; *U.S. Public*, pg. 1598

W.O.G.R.—NONE—Fox River Paper Company; *U.S. Private*, pg. 422

WP—Water-Resistant Chain—U.S. Tsubaki, Inc.; *Int'l*, pg. 1425

WPD—Women's Power Design Oversize Irons & Metal Woods—Square Two Golf Incorporated; *U.S. Public*, pg. 1501

W-P FEEDS—Livestock Feeds & Feed Supplements—Altair Corporation; *U.S. Private*, pg. 46

WPIX—Television Station—WPIX, Inc.; *U.S. Public*, pg. 1636

WPLINK—Document Exchange Product—Tandem Computers Inc.; *U.S. Public*, pg. 1547

WPHINK—Transcription Interface—Cerner Corporation; *U.S. Public*, pg. 331

WRM SYSTEMS—Sprayable, Trowelable Urethanes—Uniroyal Chemical Company, Inc.; *U.S. Public*, pg. 460

WR-12—Tires—Bridgestone/Firestone, Inc.; *Int'l*, pg. 213

W. RAY CRABB—NONE—Phelps Tointon Inc.; *U.S. Private*, pg. 860

W. S.—Valves—The Wm. Powell Company; *U.S. Private*, pg. 877

W 6 DRIVER—Screwdriver—Wilton Corporation; *U.S. Private*, pg. 1181

WTAE-AM—Broadcasting—The Hearst Corporation; *U.S. Private*, pg. 515

WTAE-TV—Broadcasting—The Hearst Corporation; *U.S. Private*, pg. 515

WTTW—Television Station—WTTW (Channel 11); *U.S. Private*, pg. 1145

W2000—Computer Control for AcuWeld & E.B. Systems—Sciaky, Inc.; *U.S. Private*, pg. 862

WVTY-FM—Broadcasting—The Hearst Corporation; *U.S. Private*, pg. 515

WWF WRESTLEMANIA—Interactive Entertainment Software—Acclaim Entertainment, Inc.; *U.S. Public*, pg. 15

W-W GRINDER—Chipper/Shredders, Sprayers—Garden Way, Inc.; *U.S. Private*, pg. 440

W.W. NORTON—Books—W.W. Norton & Company, Inc.; *U.S. Private*, pg. 807

WWUS-FM—Radio Station—Crain Communications, Inc.; *U.S. Private*, pg. 284

W WING—Heat Recovery Equipment—Mestek, Inc.; *U.S. Public*, pg. 1099

W.W. FLYERS—Foodservice Poultry Items—Louis Kemp Seafood Co.; *U.S. Public*, pg. 1652

W.W. FLYERS—Foodservice Poultry Items—Tyson Foods, Inc.; *U.S. Public*, pg. 1652

WA SE CO—Lubricant Products—Waterloo Service Company; *U.S. Private*, pg. 1152

WABASH—Electronic Devices & Components—Wabash Magnetics; *U.S. Private*, pg. 351

WABASSO—Bed Linens—Springs Industries, Inc.; *U.S. Public*, pg. 1499

WABCO—Commercial & Utility Vehicle Braking Equipment & Control Systems—American Standard Inc.; *U.S. Public*, pg. 91

WACKENHUT—Security & Investigation Services—The Wackenhut Corporation; *U.S. Public*, pg. 1731

WACKY FROOTZ—Candy—Nabisco Inc.; *U.S. Public*, pg. 1355

WACKY MAC—Macaroni—Foulds Inc.; *U.S. Private*, pg. 421

WACOAL—Women's Apparel—International Cosmetics Co., Ltd.; *Int'l*, pg. 684

WACOAL—Brassieres & Lingerie—Wacoal America Inc.; *Int'l*, pg. 1484

WACOAL BLOUSE—Women's Apparel—International Cosmetics Co., Ltd.; *Int'l*, pg. 684

WADDELL & REED—Brokerage & Insurance Services—Waddell & Reed, Inc.; *U.S. Public*, pg. 1623

WADDELL & REED FUNDS, INC.—NONE—Waddell & Reed, Inc.; *U.S. Public*, pg. 1623

WADKINS—Woodworking Machinery—Thomas Robinson Group Plc; *Int'l*, pg. 231

WADSWORTH—Textbooks & Software—Wadsworth Publishing co.; *U.S. Public*, pg. 1600

WAFER—Tables—Howe Furniture Corporation; *U.S. Private*, pg. 543

WAFER SPHERE—Butterfly Valves—Neles-Jamesbury Corp.; *Int'l*, pg. 1428

WAFERCON—NONE—Molex Incorporated; *U.S. Public*, pg. 1121

WAFERGARD—In-Line Filter Unit, Cartridge—Millipore Corporation; *U.S. Public*, pg. 1112

WAFERLITE—Anti-theft Target—Sentry Technology Corp.; *U.S. Public*, pg. 1458

WAFERMARK—Marking Systems—Lumonics Inc.; *Int'l*, pg. 1314

WAFERPURE—Gas Purifier—Millipore Corporation; *U.S. Public*, pg. 1112

WAFFLE HOUSE—Restaurant—Waffle House, Incorporated; *U.S. Private*, pg. 1146

WAFFLEMASTER—Waffle Baker with Audio Signal—Toastmaster, Inc.; *U.S. Public*, pg. 1619

WAGNER—Automotive Brakes & Lights—Cooper Industries, Inc.; *U.S. Public*, pg. 442

WAGNER—Halogen Sealed Beam & Miniature Lamps—Wagner Lighting Products; *U.S. Public*, pg. 442

WAGNER—Paint Spraying Equip.—Wagner Spray Tech Corp.; *U.S. Private*, pg. 1146

WAGNER LIGHTING—NONE—Cooper Automotive Division; *U.S. Public*, pg. 443

WAGNER'S 1891 ORIGINAL CAST IRON—Cookware—General Housewares Corp.; *U.S. Public*, pg. 715

WAGO—Terminal Blocks, Connectors & Electronic Modules—Bowthorpe plc; *Int'l*, pg. 207

WAGON-LITS FERROVIAIRE—Railway Services—Accor S.A.; *Int'l*, pg. 20

WAGON-LITS TOURISME—Hotels—Accor S.A.; *Int'l*, pg. 20

WAGON-LITS TRAVEL—Travel Agencies—Accor S.A.; *Int'l*, pg. 20

WAGON MASTER PORK & BEANS—Food Products—Allen Canning Company; *U.S. Private*, pg. 36

Brand Name Index

WAGON TRAIL—Imitation Peanut Butter—Ventura Foods; *U.S. Private*, pg. 508

WAGTIME BEEF BASTED BISCUITS—Dog Treats—Superior Brands, Inc.; *Int'l*, pg. 917

WAIST-WATCHER—Shapewear—Olga Div.; *U.S. Public*, pg. 1738

WAISTLETS—Reducing Gum Plan—Alva/Amco Pharmacal Companies, Inc.; *U.S. Private*, pg. 47

WAIT-LESS PRINTING—Computer Equipment—Emulex Corporation; *U.S. Public*, pg. 579

WAL-MART—Discount Department Stores—Wal-Mart Stores, Inc.; *U.S. Public*, pg. 1732

WALBAR—Jet Engine Turbine Blades, Vanes, Discs—Coltec Industries Inc.; *U.S. Public*, pg. 401

WALBRO—Motor Vehicle Parts & Access.—Walbro Corporation; *U.S. Public*, pg. 1733

WALDBAUM—Food Stores—The Great Atlantic & Pacific Tea Company, Inc.; *Int'l*, pg. 1375

WALDENBOOKS—Retail Book Outlets—Walden Book Company; *U.S. Public*, pg. 245

WALDRON—Coaters—Kathabar Incorporated; *U.S. Private*, pg. 609

WALGREENS—Drugs, Toiletries, Sundries—Walgreen Co.; *U.S. Public*, pg. 1733

WALITA—Local Products—Philips do Brasil-Walita Div.; *Int'l*, pg. 1055

WALK IV—Socks—Wigwam Mills, Inc.; *U.S. Private*, pg. 1175

WALK'N'ROLL—Dispenser—Kimberly-Clark Corporation; *U.S. Public*, pg. 958

WALK I—Socks—Wigwam Mills, Inc.; *U.S. Private*, pg. 1175

WALK III—Socks—Wigwam Mills, Inc.; *U.S. Private*, pg. 1175

WALK II—Socks—Wigwam Mills, Inc.; *U.S. Private*, pg. 1175

WALKABOUT—Laptop Computer—Data General Corporation; *U.S. Public*, pg. 485

WALKCHWIL—Hiking/Walking Footwear—K-Swiss Inc.; *U.S. Public*, pg. 937

WALKER—Exhaust Products—Midwest Tire & Muffler, Inc.; *U.S. Private*, pg. 745

WALKER—Mufflers & Other Aftermarket Equipment for Automobiles—Tenneco Inc.; *U.S. Public*, pg. 1577

WALKER CLARITY—Amplified Telephone for Hearing Impaired—Plantronics Inc.; *U.S. Public*, pg. 1308

WALKER HILL—All Types Footwear—International Seaway Trading Corporation; *U.S. Private*, pg. 572

WALKER'S DELUXE—Bourbon—Hiram Walker; *Int'l*, pg. 63

WALKERBOX—Floorboxes—Walker Systems, Inc.; *U.S. Private*, pg. 1184

WALKERCELL—Cellular Raceway—Walker Systems, Inc.; *U.S. Private*, pg. 1184

WALKERDECK—Electrifiedl Steel Deck—Walker Systems, Inc.; *U.S. Private*, pg. 1184

WALKERDUCT—Underfloor Electrical Distr. Systems—Walker Systems, Inc.; *U.S. Private*, pg. 1184

WALKERFLEX—Flexible Wiring System—Walker Systems, Inc.; *U.S. Private*, pg. 1184

WALKERSELE—Rotary Seal—James Walker & Co. Limited; *Int'l*, pg. 1485

WALKING MAGAZINE—NONE—Cowles Enthusiast Media, Inc.; *U.S. Private*, pg. 281

WALKING WARDROBE—Luggage—American Tourister, Inc.; *U.S. Public*, pg. 1430

WALKMAN—Personal Portable Stereos—Sony Electronics; *Int'l*, pg. 1281

WALL COVER—Latex Flat Wall Paint—Bruning Paint Company; *U.S. Private*, pg. 176

WALL HUGGER—Recliner Mechanisms—Leggett & Platt, Incorporated; *U.S. Public*, pg. 985

WALL KING—Air Conditioners/Heat Pump For Modular Buildings—Nordyne Inc.; *U.S. Public*, pg. 1193

WALL-LITER—Lighting Fixtures—Guth Lighting Company; *Int'l*, pg. 821

WALL PLATE—Latex Flat & Eggshell Enamel—Bruning Paint Company; *U.S. Private*, pg. 176

WALL RECLINA-ROCKER—NONE—La-Z-Boy Incorporated; *U.S. Public*, pg. 972

WALL RECLINER—NONE—La-Z-Boy Incorporated; *U.S. Public*, pg. 972

WALL SELL—Wall Merchandising System—Columbus Show Case Company; *U.S. Private*, pg. 257

WALL SELL BASIC—Wall Merchandising System—Columbus Show Case Company; *U.S. Private*, pg. 257

WALL STARS—Basketball Posters—The Upper Deck Company, LLC; *U.S. Private*, pg. 1129

WALL STREET JOURNAL—Daily Business & Financial Newspaper—Dow Jones & Company, Inc.; *U.S. Public*, pg. 524

WALL STREET JOURNAL EUROPE—Daily Business & Financial Newspaper Circulated in Europe—Dow Jones & Company, Inc.; *U.S. Public*, pg. 524

WALL STREET JOURNAL—Newspaper—The Wall Street Journal; *U.S. Public*, pg. 524

WALL STREET TECHNOLOGY—Magazine—Miller Freeman Inc.; *Int'l*, pg. 1443

WALL-TEX—Wall Coverings—Borden, Inc.; *U.S. Private*, pg. 157

WALL TITE—Wall Coverings—Evans Adhesive Corp.; *U.S. Private*, pg. 384

WALL TO WALL—Rug Shampoo—Bissell Inc.; *U.S. Private*, pg. 145

WALL TO WALL—Protective Plan & Home Warranty—National Real Estate Services, Inc.; *Int'l*, pg. 909

WALLABEE—Shoes—Clark Shoe Co.; *Int'l*, pg. 297

WALLABY—Designer Chair Line—Harter; *U.S. Private*, pg. 581

WALLABY—Sorter—Interlake Material Handling Div.; *U.S. Public*, pg. 893

WALLACE—Tools—Fiskars Oy AB; *Int'l*, pg. 492

WALLACE—Manufacturers of Silver & Silver Plate—Wallace International Silversmiths, Inc.; *U.S. Private*, pg. 1061

WALLACE SILVERSMITHS—Flatware, Holloware—Syratech Corporation; *U.S. Private*, pg. 1060

WALLACES FARMER—Farm Publication—Farm Progress Publications; *U.S. Public*, pg. 513

WALLAROOS—Stationery Products—The Mead Corporation; *U.S. Public*, pg. 1074

WALLAWAY—Recliners—The Berkline Corporation; *U.S. Private*, pg. 432

WALLCHOICE—Wallcovering—Appleton Papers Inc.; *Int'l*, pg. 567

WALLHIDE—Paints, Primers, Enamels, Lacquers, Shellacs, Stains, Varnishes & Thinners—PPG Industries, Inc.; *U.S. Public*, pg. 1245

WALLMATE—Plastic Foam Insulation—The Dow Chemical Company; *U.S. Public*, pg. 522

WALLPAPERS TO GO—Stores Featuring In-Stock & Special Order Wallcoverings & Home Decor Prods.—Wicks 'n Sticks, Ltd; *U.S. Private*, pg. 1175

WALLSTENT—NONE—Pfizer Inc.; *U.S. Public*, pg. 1281

WALNUT CREST—Varietal Wines—Banfi Vintners; *U.S. Private*, pg. 113

WALNUT CREST—Wine—Banfi Vintners; *U.S. Private*, pg. 113

WALNUT FLAKE—Pipe Tobacco—Imperial Tobacco Group, Ltd.; *Int'l*, pg. 666

THE WALNUT TRADITION—Cutlery—General Housewares Corp.; *U.S. Public*, pg. 715

WALNUT WHIP—Confections—Nestle-Rowntree Ltd.; *Int'l*, pg. 921

WALSALL—Electrical Distribution Equipment—The General Electric Company, p.l.c.; *Int'l*, pg. 543

WALT DISNEY—Motion Picture & Television Production Company—The Walt Disney Company; *U.S. Public*, pg. 511

WALT DISNEY WORLD—Amusement Park—The Walt Disney Company; *U.S. Public*, pg. 511

WALTER DRAKE & SONS—Mail Order Goods—Walter Drake, Inc.; *U.S. Private*, pg. 421

WALTER-MORTON—Clothing—Hickey-Freeman/Bobby Jones; *U.S. Public*, pg. 795

WALTER READE THEATRES—Motion Picture Theaters—Cineplex Odeon Corporation; *Int'l*, pg. 292

WALWORTH—Indus. Valves—The Walworth Company USA; *U.S. Private*, pg. 1149

WAMPLER FOODS—Further Processed Poultry Products—WLR Foods, Inc.; *U.S. Public*, pg. 1727

WAMSUTTA—Bed & Bath Linens & Accessories—Springs Industries, Inc.; *U.S. Public*, pg. 1499

WAN FU—French Wine—Schieffelin & Somerset Co.; *Int'l*, pg. 412

WANCER—Machining Centre—Cincinnati Milacron U.K. Limited; *U.S. Public*, pg. 368

WANDA—Building Paints for Exterior, Interior, Prof. & Retail Uses—Akzo Nobel N.V.; *Int'l*, pg. 42

WANDERER—Paperback Books—Simon & Schuster; *U.S. Public*, pg. 777

WANDERLODGE—Motor Homes—Blue Bird Corporation; *U.S. Private*, pg. 151

WANGDAT—DAT Tape Drives—Tecmar Technologies, Inc.; *Int'l*, pg. 1361

WANGTEK—QIC Tape Drives—Tecmar Technologies, Inc.; *Int'l*, pg. 1361

WAR & PEACE—War Game—Monarch Avalon, Inc.; *U.S. Public*, pg. 1123

WAR AT SEA—Game—Monarch Avalon, Inc.; *U.S. Public*, pg. 1123

WAR BIRD—NONE—Callaway Golf Company; *U.S. Public*, pg. 294

WARD'S AUTO WORLD—OEM Publication—Intertec Publishing; *U.S. Public*, pg. 1327

WARD'S AUTO WORLD—Automotive Equipment Publication—Intertec Publishing; *U.S. Public*, pg. 1327

WARD'S AUTOMOTIVE INTERNATIONAL—Twice-Monthly Newsletter—Intertec Publishing; *U.S. Public*, pg. 1327

WARD'S AUTOMOTIVE REPORTS—Weekly Newsletter—Intertec Publishing; *U.S. Public*, pg. 1327

WARD'S AUTOMOTIVE YEARBOOK—Statistical Source Book—Intertec Publishing; *U.S. Public*, pg. 1327

WARD'S ENGINE & VEHICLE TECHNOLOGY UPDATE—Twice Monthly Newsletter—Intertec Publishing; *U.S. Public*, pg. 1327

WARDS' SHEFFIELD BESTBITTER—Ale—Vaux Group Plc; *Int'l*, pg. 1453

WAREHOUSE MARKET—Retail Grocery Stores—Nash Finch Company; *U.S. Public*, pg. 1151

WAREHOUSE PRO—Software System—American Software, Inc.; *U.S. Public*, pg. 91

WAREHOUSING MANAGEMENT—Publication Providing Analysis, News, Trends, Equipment & Events—Reed Elsevier Business Information; *Int'l*, pg. 1095

WARING—Food Mixers—Dynamics Corporation of America; *U.S. Public*, pg. 286

WARING CAN-VERTIBLE—Can Opener—Waring Products; *U.S. Public*, pg. 286

WARING VORTEX—Blenders—Waring Products; *U.S. Public*, pg. 286

WARM & DRY—Mens Rain Wear—Rainfair, Inc.; *U.S. Private*, pg. 907

WARM AIR—Hyper-Thermia Unit—Cincinnati Sub-Zero Products, Inc.; *U.S. Private*, pg. 240

WARM & GENTLE—Perm—Zotos International; *Int'l*, pg. 1236

WARM-EZE—Wool Fleece Insulating Insoles—Schering-Plough Corporation; *U.S. Public*, pg. 1438

WARM MORNING—Gas Space Heaters/Furnaces—Martin Industries, Inc. (AL); *U.S. Private*, pg. 709

WARMING TUBE—Provides Heat for Warm Air Unit—Cincinnati Sub-Zero Products, Inc.; *U.S. Private*, pg. 240

WARMTOUCH—Medical Apparatus (Patient Warming Blanket)—Mallinckrodt Inc.; *U.S. Public*, pg. 1039

WARMTRACE—Domestic Hot Water Systems—Thermon Manufacturing Company; *U.S. Private*, pg. 1080

WARN—Light Truck Accessories—Warn Industries, Inc.; *U.S. Private*, pg. 1150

WARN INDUSTRIAL—Industrial Winches, Hoists & Accessories—Warn Industries, Inc.; *U.S. Private*, pg. 1150

WARNE—Beatrix Potter Books—Penguin Putnam Inc.; *Int'l*, pg. 1027

WARNER—Woven Labels—PAXAR Corporation; *U.S. Public*, pg. 1266

WARNER—Table & Dessert Wines, Champagnes—Warner Vineyards; *U.S. Private*, pg. 1151

WARNER ASPECT—Books—Warner Books, Inc.; *U.S. Public*, pg. 1614

WARNER BALLSCREWS—Precision Ball Screws—Warner Electric Industrial Products Division; *U.S. Public*, pg. 480

WARNER BOOKS—Books—Warner Books, Inc.; *U.S. Public*, pg. 1614

WARNER BROS. LICENSING—Licensing Company—Warner Bros. Consumer Products; *U.S. Public*, pg. 1610

WARNER-CHILCOTT—Pharmaceuticals—Warner-Chilcott Laboratories, Inc.; *Int'l*, pg. 436

WARNER ELECTRIC—Linear Actuators, Photoelectric Switches & Air Conditioner Clutches—Dana Corporation; *U.S. Public*, pg. 479

WARNER ELECTRIC—Elec. & Mech. Brakes & Clutches, Precision Ball Bearing Screws, Step Motors—Warner Electric Industrial Products Division; *U.S. Public*, pg. 480

WARNER-JENKINSON—Color Products—Universal Foods Corporation; *U.S. Public*, pg. 1695

WARNER SWASEY—NONE—Giddings & Lewis Automation Technology; *Int'l*, pg. 1389

WARNER'S—Intimate Apparel—Warnaco Inc.; *U.S. Public*, pg. 1738

WARP—Magazine—Times Mirror Magazines, Inc.; *U.S. Public*, pg. 1616

WARPS—Window Material—Flex-O-Glass, Inc.; *U.S. Private*, pg. 412

WARREN—Fasteners—The Black & Decker Corporation; *U.S. Public*, pg. 233

WARREN—NONE—IMO Pump; *U.S. Public*, pg. 857

WARREN—Commercial Printing Papers—S.D. Warren Co.; *Int'l*, pg. 1193

WARREN COUNTY—Twist Tobacco & Tobacco Rolls—Conwood Company L.P.; *U.S. Private*, pg. 272

WARREN GLOSS/WARREN DULL/AERO—NONE—S.D. Warren Co.; *Int'l*, pg. 1193

WARREN PUMPS—Pumps—IMO Industries Inc.; *U.S. Public*, pg. 856

WARREN RUPP—Pumps—IDEX Corporation; *U.S. Public*, pg. 862

WARRENGAS—Liquefied Petroleum Gas—Warren Petroleum Company; *U.S. Public*, pg. 1146

WARRIOR—Bicycles—Bridgestone/Firestone, Inc.; *Int'l*, pg. 213

WARRIOR—Training Wear—Mizuno Corporation; *Int'l*, pg. 884

WARRIOR—Aircraft—The New Piper Aircraft, Inc.; *U.S. Private*, pg. 794

WARRIOR—Hotel & Restaurant Flour—The Uhlmann Co.; *U.S. Private*, pg. 1115

WARRIOR—Motor Homes—Winnebago Industries, Inc.; *U.S. Public*, pg. 1772

WARSTEINER FRESH—Non-Alcoholic—Warsteiner Importers Agency; *Int'l*, pg. 1486

WARSTEINER PREMIUM—Pilsner—Warsteiner Importers Agency; *Int'l*, pg. 1486

WART-OFF—NONE—Pfizer Inc.; *U.S. Public*, pg. 1281

WARTICON—Genitial Wart Medication—Perstorp Pharma Ltd. Wound Care Division; *Int'l*, pg. 1037

WARTSILA DIESEL—Diesel Engines—Metra Corporation; *Int'l*, pg. 862

WARWICK—Paper Napkins, Paper Towels, Toilet Tissue & Wrapping Paper—Georgia-Pacific Corporation; *U.S. Public*, pg. 735

WASA—Crispbread—Novartis AG; *Int'l*, pg. 971

WASA—Crispbread—Novartis Nutrition Corporation; *Int'l*, pg. 974

WASCOMAT—Industrial Laundry Equipment—Electrolux, AB; *Int'l*, pg. 438

WASH & CLEAN—Prewash—Blue Cross Laboratories; *U.S. Private*, pg. 152

WASH 'N CURL—Hair Care Prods.—CCA Industries, Inc.; *U.S. Public*, pg. 276

WASH 'N DRI—Anti-Bacterial Towelettes—Softsoap Enterprises, Inc.; *U.S. Public*, pg. 397

WASH 'N WEAR—Enamel—Jones Blair Company; *U.S. Private*, pg. 596

WASH-UP—Cleansing & Refreshing Towelette—The Clinipad Corporation; *U.S. Private*, pg. 246

WASH WARE—Multi-Lavatories and Wash Fountains—Acorn Engineering Company; *U.S. Private*, pg. 14

WASHEX—Industrial Laundry Equipment—Electrolux, AB; *Int'l*, pg. 438

WASHEX—Commercial & Industrial Laundry Equipment—White Consolidated Industries, Inc.; *Int'l*, pg. 439

WASHINGTON—Cranes—Ederer Inc.; *U.S. Private*, pg. 363

WASHINGTON—Flour—Wilkins-Rogers Incorporated; *U.S. Private*, pg. 1176

WASHINGTON ALERT—Complete Database of Up-to-Date Congressional Activity & Biographical Data—The Times Publishing Co.; *U.S. Private*, pg. 1087

WASHINGTON ALL PURPOSE—Flour—Wilkins-Rogers Incorporated; *U.S. Private*, pg. 1176

WASHINGTON BUSINESS JOURNAL—Business Journal—Business First of New York, Inc.; *U.S. Private*, pg. 19

WASHINGTON CAKE MIXES—Cake Mix—Wilkins-Rogers Incorporated; *U.S. Private*, pg. 1176

WASHINGTON CIRCLE THEATRES—Motion Picture Theaters—Cineplex Odeon Corporation; *Int'l*, pg. 292

WASHINGTON FEDERAL SAVINGS—Savings Institution—Washington Federal Savings; *U.S. Public*, pg. 1740

WASHINGTON FROSTING MIX—Frosting Mixes—Wilkins-Rogers Incorporated; *U.S. Private*, pg. 1176

WASHINGTON HOMES—NONE—Washington Homes, Inc.; *U.S. Public*, pg. 1741

WASHINGTON MUFFIN MIXES—Muffin Mix—Wilkins-Rogers Incorporated; *U.S. Private*, pg. 1176

THE WASHINGTON POST—Newspaper—The Washington Post Company; *U.S. Public*, pg. 1742

THE WASHINGTON POST—Daily Newspaper—The Washington Post; *U.S. Public*, pg. 1743

WASHINGTON SELF RISING CORN MEAL—Corn Meal—Wilkins-Rogers Incorporated; *U.S. Private*, pg. 1176

WASHINGTON SELF RISING FLOUR—Flour—Wilkins-Rogers Incorporated; *U.S. Private*, pg. 1176

WASHINGTON SPECIALTY METALS—Stainless Steel—Lukens Inc.; *U.S. Public*, pg. 1019

WASHINGTON SQUARE PRESS—Adult Trade Paperback Books—Pocket Books; *U.S. Private*, pg. 777

WASHINGTON SQUARE PRESS—Books—Simon & Schuster; *U.S. Private*, pg. 777

WASHINGTON STEEL—Stainless Steel—Lukens Inc.; *U.S. Public*, pg. 1019

WASHJET—Spray Nozzle—Spraying Systems Co.; *U.S. Private*, pg. 1026

WASHMASTER—Laundry Washer/Extractors—Ecolab Inc.; *U.S. Public*, pg. 562

WASP—Atmospheric Diving Suit—Oceaneering International, Inc.; *U.S. Public*, pg. 1211

WASTE KING—Hot Water Dispensers & Disposers—Anaheim Manufacturing Company; *U.S. Private*, pg. 70

WASTE KING—Garbage Disposals & Trash Compactors—Masco Corporation; *U.S. Public*, pg. 1052

WASTEMASTER—Swing Top Receptacle—United Receptical, Inc.; *U.S. Private*, pg. 1123

WASTEMATE—Sewage Pump—Zoeller Co.; *U.S. Private*, pg. 1207

WAT 2000—Tires—Bridgestone/Firestone, Inc.; *Int'l*, pg. 213

WATCH 'EM GROW—Pre-Planted Floral Bulbs in Containers—Bachman's, Inc.; *U.S. Private*, pg. 109

WATCH US—Zenith Products—Zenith Electronics Corp.; *U.S. Public*, pg. 1790

WATCH/GUARD—Holder—Fisher Scientific Company; *U.S. Private*, pg. 658

WATCHCAM—Security System—Sony Electronics; *Int'l*, pg. 1281

WATCHDOG—Programmable Timer Transformers—Square D Company; *Int'l*, pg. 1208

WATCHER—NONE—KLA Tencor Corporation; *U.S. Public*, pg. 939

WATCHGUARD—Laminated Safety Glass—PPG Industries, Inc.; *U.S. Public*, pg. 1245

WATCHMAN—Micro Television—Sony Electronics; *Int'l*, pg. 1281

WATCHMASTER—Marine/Clock—Swift Instruments, Inc.; *U.S. Private*, pg. 1058

WATCHMATE—Marine/Weather Instrument—Swift Instruments, Inc.; *U.S. Private*, pg. 1058

WATCO—Finishes, Sealers & Waxes—The Thompson-Minwax Company; *U.S. Public*, pg. 1466

WATCO DANISH OIL FINISH—NONE—The Flecto Co., Inc.; *U.S. Private*, pg. 410

WATE-ON—Tablets & Emulsion—Lee Pharmaceuticals; *U.S. Public*, pg. 984

WATER ACE—Pumps for Retail—F.E. Myers; *U.S. Public*, pg. 1273

WATER BABIES—Leading Sun Care Brand—Schering-Plough Corporation; *U.S. Public*, pg. 1438

WATER BABIES—Sun Care Products—Schering-Plough Healthcare Products Inc.; *U.S. Public*, pg. 1438

WATER BUSTER—Portable, Submersible Pump—Attwood Corporation; *U.S. Private*, pg. 1038

WATER COUNTRY U.S.A.—Water Theme Park—Busch Entertainment Corp.; *U.S. Public*, pg. 114

WATER EATER—Accessory—Little Giant Pump Company; *U.S. Public*, pg. 1566

WATER-GLO—Fluorescent Additive—Spectronics Corporation; *U.S. Private*, pg. 1024

WATER HEATER SPIN-GLAS—Insulation—Johns Manville Corporation; *U.S. Public*, pg. 927

WATER MAID—Rice—Riviana Foods Inc.; *U.S. Public*, pg. 1392

WATER MAIN RESTRAINTS—NONE—Ford Meter Box Company; *U.S. Private*, pg. 418

WATER PIK—Dental Hygiene Prod.—Teledyne Water Pik; *U.S. Public*, pg. 44

WATER RIDD'R II—Submersible Sump Pump—Zoeller Co.; *U.S. Private*, pg. 1207

WATER-TOUGH—NONE—Carpenter Technology Corporation; *U.S. Public*, pg. 307

WATER-WEAR—NONE—Carpenter Technology Corporation; *U.S. Public*, pg. 307

WATER WIZARD—Steam/Water Heater Line—Aerco International Inc.; *U.S. Public*, pg. 23

WATER WORKS BRASS—NONE—Ford Meter Box Company; *U.S. Private*, pg. 418

WATER-HARD—NONE—Carpenter Technology Corporation; *U.S. Public*, pg. 307

WATERBURY FARREL—Machine Tools—Waterbury Farrel Technologies; *U.S. Private*, pg. 461

WATERBURY HEADERS—Cold Heading or Threading Machines—Seneca Falls Technology Group; *U.S. Private*, pg. 984

WATERCOLOR—Magazine—BPI Communications Inc.; *Int'l*, pg. 1446

WATERCOM—Telcommunication Network—CSX Corporation; *U.S. Public*, pg. 284

WATERFORD—Vinyl Siding—ABT Building Products Corporation; *Int'l*, pg. 20

WATERFORD—Crystal—Waterford Wedgwood Plc; *Int'l*, pg. 1487

WATERFORD—Hand-cut Crystal—Waterford Wedgwood UK Plc; *Int'l*, pg. 1487

WATERFORD SYSTEMS—Swimming Pool Equipment—Sta-Rite Industries, Inc.; *U.S. Public*, pg. 1767

WATERFOWL—NONE—Tandy Brands Accessories, Inc.; *U.S. Public*, pg. 1560

WATERGUN—Pressure Pump—Goulds Pumps, Incorporated; *U.S. Public*, pg. 860

WATERLOO—Tool Storage Products—Fortune Brands, Inc.; *U.S. Public*, pg. 674

WATERLOO—Tool Storage Products, Metal & Plastic Storage Products—MasterBrand Industries, Inc.; *U.S. Public*, pg. 675

WATERLOO—War Game—Monarch Avalon, Inc.; *U.S. Public*, pg. 1123

WATERLOO—Tool Storage Products—Waterloo Industries, Inc.; *U.S. Public*, pg. 675

WATERMAN—Premium Fountain & Ball Point Pens—The Gillette Company; *U.S. Public*, pg. 743

WATERMAN—Pens—Stationery Products Division; *U.S. Public*, pg. 744

WATERMASTER—Fire Hydrant—East Jordan Iron Works; *U.S. Private*, pg. 356

WATERMATE—Processor Wash Water Recirculator—LogEtronics Corporation; *U.S. Public*, pg. 6

WATERMILL—Water Treatment System—Herbalife International of America, Inc.; *U.S. Public*, pg. 809

WATERNIFE—Intensifier Pump—Flow International Corporation; *U.S. Public*, pg. 656

WATEROUTER—Hand Tool—Flow International Corporation; *U.S. Public*, pg. 656

WATERPLUG—Hydraulic Cement For Concrete & Masonry—Thoro; *U.S. Private*, pg. 505

WATERQUEST KDF—Filters—Energy Brokers Guild; *U.S. Private*, pg. 376

WATERS QA-1—Analyzer—Millipore Corporation; *U.S. Public*, pg. 1112

WATERS SYSTEMS PRO CHANNEL—NONE—Sta-Rite Industries, Inc.; *U.S. Public*, pg. 1767

WATERSHED—Water Repellant—Jones Blair Company; *U.S. Private*, pg. 596

WATERSHED—Liquid Rinse-Aid—LeaRonal, Inc.; *U.S. Public*, pg. 982

WATERTIGHT—Railroad Devices—Maclean-Fogg Co.; *U.S. Private*, pg. 692

WATERTITE—Plugs & Connectors—Woodhead Industries, Inc.; *U.S. Public*, pg. 1776

WATERVALLEY—Fresh Turkey Products—ConAgra, Inc.; *U.S. Public*, pg. 425

WATERWAY GUIDE—Directories—Intertec Publishing; *U.S. Public*, pg. 1327

WATERWAY GUIDE, GREAT LAKES—Annual Publication—Intertec Publishing; *U.S. Public*, pg. 1328

WATERWAY GUIDE, MID-ATLANTIC—Annual Publication—Intertec Publishing; *U.S. Public*, pg. 1328

WATERWAY GUIDE, NORTHERN—Annual Publication—Intertec Publishing; *U.S. Public*, pg. 1328

WATERWAY GUIDE, SOUTHERN—Annual Publication—Intertec Publishing; *U.S. Public*, pg. 1328

WATKINS—Hot Tubs—Masco Corporation; *U.S. Public*, pg. 1052

WATKINS CONTRACTING—Environmental Remediation Services—Rexx Environmental Corp.; *U.S. Public*, pg. 1384

WATNEYS BEERS—Red Barrel, Cream Stout—Wisdom Imports Sales Co. Inc.; *Int'l*, pg. 679

WATNEYS CREME STOUT—Stout—Scottish & Newcastle Importers Co.; *Int'l*, pg. 1212

WATNEYS RED BARREL—Ale—Scottish & Newcastle Importers Co.; *Int'l*, pg. 1212

WATROD—Electric Tubular Element—Watlow Electric Manufacturing Company; *U.S. Private*, pg. 1153

WATSCO COMPONENTS—Air Conditioning & Refrigeration Components—Watsco, Inc.; *U.S. Public*, pg. 1745

WATSON-GUPTILL—Art Instructions Books—BPI Communications Inc.; *Int'l*, pg. 1446

WATT—Magazine Publishing—Watt Publishing Co.; *U.S. Private*, pg. 1154

WATT-MISER—Fluorescent Lamps; Fluorescent Lamp Ballasts—General Electric Canada Inc.; *U.S. Public*, pg. 713

WATT REDUCER—Energy Saving Ballasts—MagneTek Lighting Products Group; *U.S. Public*, pg. 1037

WATT SAVER—Energy-Saving Incandescent & Fluorescent Light Bulb—Duro-Test Corporation; *U.S. Public*, pg. 349

WATTBOX—Quad Output Powersupply—Lambda Electronics Inc.; *U.S. Public*, pg. 1241

WATTIES—NONE—H.J. Heinz Company Australia Ltd.; *U.S. Public*, pg. 807

WATTMIZER—Solenoid—Snap-Tite, Inc.; *U.S. Private*, pg. 1010

WATTS REGULATOR—Valves—Watts Industries, Inc.; *U.S. Public*, pg. 1746

WAUKESHA—Engines & Prime Power Systems—Dresser Industries, Inc.; *U.S. Public*, pg. 528

WAUKESHA—Transformers—MagneTek, Inc.; *U.S. Public*, pg. 1037

WAUKESHA 88—Nongalling Corrosion Resistant Alloy Used in Food & Chemical Industries—Waukesha Foundry Inc.; *U.S. Private*, pg. 1154

WAUKESHA 88 METAL—Anti-Gallery Alloy used where Gallery & Sizing are a Problem—Waukesha Foundry Inc.; *U.S. Private*, pg. 1154

WAUSAU—Machinery—AE Goetze-North America; *Int'l*, pg. 1334

WAUSAU—Insurance Companies—Employers Insurance of Wausau; *U.S. Private*, pg. 788

WAUSAU—Homes—Wausau Homes, Inc.; *U.S. Private*, pg. 1154

WAUSAU INSURANCE—Commercial Insurance Services—Nationwide Insurance Enterprise; *U.S. Private*, pg. 788

WAVE—Vinyl Emulsions—Air Products and Chemicals, Inc.; *U.S. Public*, pg. 30

WAVE—Radio—Bose Corporation; *U.S. Private*, pg. 160

WAVE—Toothbrush—Colgate-Palmolive Company; *U.S. Public*, pg. 397

WAVE—Running Footwear—Mizuno USA, Inc.; *Int'l*, pg. 885

WAVE MASTER—Marine Coatings—Seymour of Sycamore, Inc.; *U.S. Private*, pg. 988

WAVE RUNNER—Personal Water Craft—Yamaha Motor Corp., U.S.A.; *Int'l*, pg. 1516

THE WAVE—Objects D'Art—Lava World International/Haggerty Enterprises, Inc.; *U.S. Private*, pg. 653

WAVECORE—Polyethylene Foam—The Dow Chemical Company; *U.S. Public*, pg. 522

WAVELENGTH CONVERSION EFFECT SURFACE TREATMENTS—NONE—Surgical Laser Technologies, Inc.; *U.S. Public*, pg. 1542

WAVELINK—Fiber Optic Communications Systems—Tektronix-Video & Networking Div., Grass Valley Products; *U.S. Public*, pg. 1567

WAVEMAGNET—Antennas—Zenith Electronics Corp.; *U.S. Public*, pg. 1790

WAVERLY—Crackers—Nabisco Inc.; *U.S. Public*, pg. 1355

WAVERLY—Fabrics, Wallcovering—F. Schumacher & Co.; *U.S. Private*, pg. 973

WAVETEK RF—Signal Generators—Wavetek Communications Div.; *U.S. Private*, pg. 1155

WAXMASTER WAXER—Waxer/Polisher—The Chamberlain Group, Inc.; *U.S. Private*, pg. 344

WAY TO GO—Stroller—Century Products Co.; *U.S. Private*, pg. 226

WAYCOOL—Wafer Platen—Varian Associates, Inc.; *U.S. Public*, pg. 1710

WAYFARER—Sunglasses—Bausch & Lomb Incorporated; *U.S. Public*, pg. 194

WAYFARER MAX—Sunglasses—Bausch & Lomb Incorporated; *U.S. Public*, pg. 194

WAYFLOW—Automatic Vacuum Lock—Varian Associates, Inc.; *U.S. Public*, pg. 1710

WAYLITE—Emergency Luminaires—JSB Electrical PLC; *Int'l*, pg. 453

WAYMOR—Pharmaceutical Prods.—Alva/Amco Pharmacal Companies, Inc.; *U.S. Private*, pg. 47

WAYNE—Vehicle Fueling Systems—Dresser Industries, Inc.; *U.S. Public*, pg. 528

WAYNE—Gasoline Dispensing Systems—Dresser Industries Wayne Division; *U.S. Public*, pg. 528

WAYNE—Home Equipment—The Scott Fetzer Company; *U.S. Public*, pg. 217

WAYNE—School Bus—TBG Management S.A.M.; *Int'l*, pg. 1335

WAYNE FARMS—Broiler Chickens—Continental Grain Company; *U.S. Private*, pg. 268

WAYNE FEEDS—Animal Feed—Continental Grain Company; *U.S. Private*, pg. 268

WAYSIDE INN—Plywood—Georgia-Pacific Corporation; *U.S. Public*, pg. 735

WE ARE RADIO—Logo—CRN International, Inc.; *U.S. Private*, pg. 197

WE BRING GOOD THINGS TO LIFE—Major Appliances-Ranges, Washers, Dryers, Refrigerators, Dishwashers—General Electric Canada Inc.; *U.S. Public*, pg. 713

WE CAN—Composite Can Capabilities—Sonoco Products Company; *U.S. Public*, pg. 1485

WE CAPTURE THE STRENGTH—NONE—Continental Medical Systems, Inc.; *U.S. Public*, pg. 839

WE HELP MAKE MIRACLES HAPPEN—NONE—U.S. Surgical Corp.; *U.S. Public*, pg. 1687

WE MAKE IT EASY TO DO IT RIGHT—NONE—Browning-Ferris Industries, Inc.; *U.S. Public*, pg. 262

WE MAKE LIFE A LITTLE EASIER—NONE—Ballard Medical Products; *U.S. Public*, pg. 171

WE POWER THE WORLD—NONE—Detroit Diesel Corp.; *U.S. Private*, pg. 850

WE'VE GOT YOU COVERED—NONE—Elcor Corporation; *U.S. Public*, pg. 567

WE WORK MAGIC WITH FRESH FLOWERS—Trademark—The Florists Assn. of Greater Cleveland, Inc.; *U.S. Private*, pg. 415

WEAPONS & WARRIORS—Game—Pressman Toy Corp.; *U.S. Private*, pg. 882

WEAR—Pipe Restraint—Enidine Incorporated; *U.S. Private*, pg. 377

WEAR-ARC—NONE—ESAB Welding & Cutting Products; *Int'l*, pg. 281

WEAR-DATED—Textile Products Made from Monsanto Fibers—Monsanto Company; *U.S. Public*, pg. 1124

WEAR-DATED—Textile Products Made From Monsanto Fibers—Solutia Inc.; *U.S. Public*, pg. 1483

WEAR IT OUT—Tagline—Chico's Fas Inc; *U.S. Public*, pg. 349

WEAR-O-MATIC—NONE—ESAB Welding & Cutting Products; *Int'l*, pg. 281

WEARABLE CRAFTS—Wearable Art Magazine—House of White Birches, Inc.; *U.S. Public*, pg. 542

WEARDIE—Die Blocks—McInnes Steel Company; *U.S. Private*, pg. 722

WEAREVER—Pens & Other Writing Instruments—Dixon Ticonderoga Company; *U.S. Public*, pg. 514

WEAREVER—Commercial Cookware—Lincoln Foodservice Products, Inc.; *Int'l*, pg. 188

WEAREVER—Cookware—Mirro Company; *U.S. Public*, pg. 1177

WEAREVER—Cookware—Newell Co.; *U.S. Public*, pg. 1176

WEARHOUSE OF FASHIONS—Women's Retail Specialty Store—Gateway Apparel, Inc.; *U.S. Private*, pg. 441

WEARMASTER—Pre-Finished Plank—Bruce Hardwood Floors; *U.S. Public*, pg. 1634

WEARMASTER COMMERCIAL CONCENTRATE—Cleaner for Acrylic Impregnated—Bruce Hardwood Floors; *U.S. Public*, pg. 1634

WEARSHIELD—Electrode—The Lincoln Electric Company; *U.S. Public*, pg. 996

WEASLER—Mfr. PTO Drive Lines—Weasler Engineering Inc.; *U.S. Private*, pg. 249

WEATHER BEATER—NONE—Sears, Roebuck and Co.; *U.S. Public*, pg. 1452

WEATHER BEST II—Thermoformed Exterior Solutions—ABT Building Products Corporation; *Int'l*, pg. 20

WEATHER CHEK—Aluminum Roof Coating—Monsey-Bakor; *U.S. Private*, pg. 757

WEATHER FIGHTER—Tires—Bridgestone/Firestone, Inc.; *Int'l*, pg. 213

WEATHER-FLEX—Waterproof Coating—Pratt & Lambert United, Inc.; *U.S. Public*, pg. 1466

WEATHER 4 OUTERWEAR—Waterproof, Breathable Jacket, Parka & Overpant—Horace Small Apparel Company; *Int'l*, pg. 635

WEATHER-GUARD—Covers, Curtains—Refrigiwear, Inc.; *U.S. Public*, pg. 917

WEATHER LEATHER—Leather—Wolverine World Wide, Inc.; *U.S. Public*, pg. 1775

WEATHER MARK—Tires & Batteries—Universal Cooperatives, Inc.; *U.S. Private*, pg. 1127

WEATHER MASTER—Water Resistant Electronics—Alaron Inc.; *U.S. Public*, pg. 31

WEATHER MASTER—Plastic Heads—Ludwig Industries; *U.S. Public*, pg. 1514

WEATHER-MATIC—Underground Sprinkler System—Telsco Industries; *U.S. Private*, pg. 1074

WEATHER-OMETER—Accelerated Laboratory Test Chamber For Weathering—Atlas Electric Devices Co.; *U.S. Private*, pg. 96

WEATHER PACK—Sealed Connections—Delphi Packard Electric Systems; *U.S. Public*, pg. 719

WEATHER SHEDDER—NONE—Ace Hardware Corporation; *U.S. Private*, pg. 12

WEATHER-SOF—Gloves—Acushnet Company; *U.S. Public*, pg. 675

WEATHER-SOF—Golf Gloves—Fortune Brands, Inc.; *U.S. Public*, pg. 674

WEATHER-SOF—NONE—Titleist & Foot-Joy Worldwide; *U.S. Public*, pg. 675

WEATHER STRIP—Fluorescent Outdoor Strips—Guth Lighting Company; *Int'l*, pg. 821

WEATHER TEC AGRI SPRINKLERS—Sprinklers—Weather Tec Corporation; *U.S. Private*, pg. 1155

WEATHER TEC ELECTRIC & HYDRAULIC VALVES—Valves—Weather Tec Corporation; *U.S. Private*, pg. 1155

WEATHER-TECH—Apparel—I. Spiewak & Sons, Inc.; *U.S. Private*, pg. 1025

Brand Name Index

WEATHERADAR—Remote Facsimile Radar Display—Alden Electronics, Inc.; *U.S. Private*, pg. 872

WEATHERBAN—Air Drying & Moisture Curing Liquid Sealants—3M; *U.S. Public*, pg. 1604

WEATHERBY HEALTH CARE—Recruits M.D.'s & Medical Personnel—Weatherby Health Care; *U.S. Private*, pg. 1155

WEATHERBY LOCUMS INC—Temporary Physican Staffing—Weatherby Health Care; *U.S. Private*, pg. 1155

WEATHERCAPS—Vertical Exhaust Stack Covers for Trucks, Off-Road Vehicles & Indus. Equip.—Gleason Corporation; *U.S. Public*, pg. 746

WEATHERFAX—Facsimile Transmitters & Receivers—Litton Industries, Inc.; *U.S. Public*, pg. 1002

WEATHERFORD—Oil Field Products, Equipment & Service—Weatherford Enterra Incorporated; *U.S. Public*, pg. 1749

WEATHERGARD—Wood Columns—Weyerhaeuser Forest Products Company; *U.S. Public*, pg. 1764

WEATHERGLAZE—Residential Exterior/Interior Fiberglass Reinforced Panles—Sequentia Inc.; *U.S. Private*, pg. 985

WEATHERGUARD—Weathered Rolling Door—Cornell Iron Works, Inc.; *U.S. Private*, pg. 276

WEATHERGUARD—All Weather Electrical Extension Cords—General Cable Corporation; *Int'l*, pg. 1486

WEATHERHEAD—Brass & Steel Fittings, Hose Products—Dana Corporation; *U.S. Public*, pg. 479

WEATHERITE—Heat Pump—Nordyne Inc.; *U.S. Public*, pg. 1193

WEATHERLOCK—Self-Adhesive Waterproofing Underlayment—Owens Corning; *U.S. Public*, pg. 1236

WEATHERMASTER—Asphalt Shingles—Atlas Roofing Corp.; *U.S. Public*, pg. 96

WEATHERMASTER—Corrosion-Resistant Screws—Elco Textron; *U.S. Public*, pg. 1590

WEATHERMASTER—Weather Instrument—Swift Instruments, Inc.; *U.S. Private*, pg. 1058

WEATHERMATIC A—Watertight 110 Camera—Minolta Corporation; *Int'l*, pg. 869

WEATHERPAD—Felt—American Felt & Filter; *U.S. Private*, pg. 54

WEATHERPANE—Multiple Glazed Window Units—PPG Industries, Inc.; *U.S. Public*, pg. 1245

WEATHERSEAL—Shingles—Johns Manville Corporation; *U.S. Public*, pg. 927

WEATHERSHIELD—Wood preservative—Osmose Wood Preserving, Inc.; *U.S. Private*, pg. 821

WEATHERSTONE—NONE—CertainTeed Corporation; *Int'l*, pg. 1170

WEATHERTEL—Weather Forecasting Package—Electronic Tele-Communications, Inc.; *U.S. Public*, pg. 570

WEATHERTITE—Premier Insulating Sheathing—Johns Manville Corporation; *U.S. Public*, pg. 927

WEATHERVANE—Women's Apparel—Hartmarx Corporation; *U.S. Public*, pg. 795

WEATHERVANE—Sportswear—International Women's Apparel Group; *U.S. Public*, pg. 796

WEATHERVANE PETITES—Coordinated Sportswear—International Women's Apparel Group; *U.S. Public*, pg. 796

WEAVER—Optics, Rings, Bases, Scopes & Binoculars—Blount, Inc. Sporting Equipment Group; *U.S. Public*, pg. 238

WEAVER—Gun Scopes, Mounts & Rings—Blount International, Inc.; *U.S. Public*, pg. 237

WEAVER—Frozen & Refrigerated Items—Louis Kemp Seafood Co.; *U.S. Public*, pg. 1652

WEAVER—Frozen & Refrigerated Items—Tyson Foods, Inc.; *U.S. Public*, pg. 1652

WEAVER—Producer & Processor of Popcorn—Weaver Popcorn Company, Inc.; *U.S. Private*, pg. 1156

WEAVER ORIGINAL MOVIE POPCORN—Microwave; Portion Pak; 501156

WEAVETEX—Plywood—Georgia-Pacific Corporation; *U.S. Public*, pg. 735

WEAVINGS—Journal of Christian Spiritual Life—The Upper Room; *U.S. Private*, pg. 1129

WEB—Electric Insect Killers—Weber-Stephen Products Co.; *U.S. Private*, pg. 1157

WEB FOCUS—Internet Report Generator—Information Builders; *U.S. Private*, pg. 561

WEBASTO—Sunroofs—Magna International Inc.; *Int'l*, pg. 829

WEBB—Fasteners—Tomkins PLC; *Int'l*, pg. 1395

WEBB—Conveyors & Corporate Name—Jervis B. Webb Company; *U.S. Private*, pg. 1156

WEBB ALLOY II—Special Steel Track—Jervis B. Webb Company; *U.S. Private*, pg. 1156

WEBB IVORY—Gifts & Greeting Cards—Fine Art Developments plc; *Int'l*, pg. 485

WEBB-KEY—Disconnect Conveyor Screws—Jervis B. Webb Company; *U.S. Private*, pg. 1156

WEBB-X—Conveyor Chain—Jervis B. Webb Company; *U.S. Private*, pg. 1156

WEBBALLOY—Special Steel, Double-Channel Track—Jervis B. Webb Company; *U.S. Private*, pg. 1156

WEBBER FARMS—Processed Meats—Armour Food Company; *U.S. Public*, pg. 427

WEBCON—NONE—PolyMedica Industries, Inc.; *U.S. Public*, pg. 1315

WEBCRAFT—Technologies—Webcraft Technologies, Inc.; *U.S. Public*, pg. 228

WEBDRI—Clothing—Tingley Rubber Corporation; *U.S. Private*, pg. 1088

WEBER—Baked Sweet Snacks—Borden, Inc.; *U.S. Private*, pg. 157

WEBER—Processed Meats—Kayem Foods, Inc.; *U.S. Private*, pg. 610

WEBER—Aircraft Interior Equipment—Weber Aircraft, Inc.; *Int'l*, pg. 572

WEBER—Barbeques—Weber-Stephen Products Co.; *U.S. Private*, pg. 1157

WEBER BREAD—Retail White Bread—Four-S Baking Company; *U.S. Private*, pg. 422

WEBER ET BROUTIN—Construction Mortar—Poliet; *Int'l*, pg. 1177

WEBER'S—Bread—Interstate Brands Corporation; *U.S. Public*, pg. 909

WEBFLEX—Book Papers—Weyerhaeuser Company; *U.S. Public*, pg. 1764

WEBGLAZE—NONE—Lawter International, Inc.; *U.S. Public*, pg. 980

WEBLINE—Furniture Seating Systems—Leggett & Platt, Incorporated; *U.S. Public*, pg. 985

WEBLOY—Iron with Additives—Webster Industries Inc.; *U.S. Private*, pg. 1157

WEBQ—Universal Access to Customer Information Utilizing A Web Browser—Quintus Corporation; *U.S. Private*, pg. 901

WEBRAD—Medical Image Delivery System—Analogic Corporation; *U.S. Public*, pg. 109

WEBREX—Agent for Web-Offset Printing Ink—Dainichiseika Colour & Chemicals Mfg. Co., Ltd.; *Int'l*, pg. 369

WEBSERT—Personalized Multi-Offer Mailing Package—Webcraft Technologies, Inc.; *U.S. Public*, pg. 228

WEBSOURCE—Marketing Program—Ikon Office Solutions, Inc.; *U.S. Public*, pg. 862

WEBSTER—Fluid Controls, Dukes, Danfoss—Danfoss Fluid Power; *Int'l*, pg. 377

WEBSTER—Film Cleaning Equipment—Eastman Kodak Company; *U.S. Public*, pg. 550

WEBSTERS—Yorkshire Bitter—Foster's Brewing Group Limited; *Int'l*, pg. 500

WEBSTER'S NEW WORLD DICTIONARIES—Reference Books—Simon & Schuster; *U.S. Private*, pg. 777

WEBVAR—NONE—Lawter International, Inc.; *U.S. Public*, pg. 980

WECHSLER—(Coffee & Food Products)—Wechsler Coffee Corp.; *U.S. Private*, pg. 1158

WECKSTAT—Skin Staplers—Bristol-Myers Squibb Company; *U.S. Public*, pg. 253

WECOBEE—Organic Chemicals—Stepan Company; *U.S. Public*, pg. 1514

WEDAC—Rust Remover—Wechco, Inc.; *U.S. Private*, pg. 1158

WEDAC—Rust Remover—West Chemical Products, Inc.; *U.S. Private*, pg. 1158

WEDDING AND HOME—Women's Special Interest Magazine—IPC Magazines Limited; *Int'l*, pg. 651

WEDDING CAKES—NONE—Reed Business Information Pty. Limited; *Int'l*, pg. 1094

WEDDING CHECKLIST—NONE—Reed Business Information Pty. Limited; *Int'l*, pg. 1094

WEDDING FLOWERS—NONE—Reed Business Information Pty. Limited; *Int'l*, pg. 1094

WEDDING PLANNER—NONE—Reed Business Information Pty. Limited; *Int'l*, pg. 1094

WEDGE—Erasers—Dixon Ticonderoga Company; *U.S. Public*, pg. 514

WEDGE-LOCK—NONE—Blaw-Knox Construction Equipment Corporation; *U.S. Public*, pg. 877

WEDGE-LOCK—Vault Door—Diebold, Incorporated; *U.S. Public*, pg. 506

WEDGE X—Display Stands—The Mead Corporation; *U.S. Public*, pg. 1074

WEDGROL—Electrical Connection—Litton Industries, Inc.; *U.S. Public*, pg. 1002

WEDGWOOD—China—Waterford Crystal, Inc.; *Int'l*, pg. 1487

WEDGWOOD—Ceramics—Waterford Wedgwood Plc; *Int'l*, pg. 1487

WEDGWOOD—Fine Bone China, Tableware, Giftware, Jewelry—Waterford Wedgwood UK Plc; *Int'l*, pg. 1487

WEE—Juvenile Wheel Goods—Roadmaster/Brunswick; *U.S. Public*, pg. 265

WEE FOOT FASHIONS—Children's Shoes—E.J. Footwear Corp.; *U.S. Public*, pg. 1684

WEE KIDS—Infant's Footwear—E.J. Footwear Corp.; *U.S. Public*, pg. 1684

WEE KIDS—Shoes—Trimfoot Company; *U.S. Public*, pg. 1684

WEE SING—Children's Books & Cassettes—Price Stern Sloan Inc.; *Int'l*, pg. 1215

WEE SPORTS—Children's Shoes—E.J. Footwear Corp.; *U.S. Public*, pg. 1684

WEE WAFFLE—Building Block Toys—Rubbermaid Incorporated; *U.S. Public*, pg. 1411

WEE WALKER—Infant's Footwear—E.J. Footwear Corp.; *U.S. Public*, pg. 1684

WEE WALKER—Shoes—Trimfoot Company; *U.S. Public*, pg. 1684

WEE-Z—Independance Bond—General Railway Signal Corp.; *Int'l*, pg. 1194

WEEBOK—Infant & Children's Footwear & Apparel—Reebok International Ltd.; *U.S. Public*, pg. 1369

WEED—Tire Chains—Acco Chain & Lifting Products; *Int'l*, pg. 473

WEED EATER—Trimmers, Blowers—Frigidaire Home Products-Specialty Power Equipment; *Int'l*, pg. 440

WEED EATER—Lawn & Garden Products—White Consolidated Industries, Inc.; *Int'l*, pg. 439

WEED-OUT—Insecticide—Dexol; *U.S. Public*, pg. 1390

WEEDCAT—NONE—Ellicott Machine Corporation International; *U.S. Private*, pg. 372

WEEDMASTER—Herbicide—Sandoz Agro, Inc.; *Int'l*, pg. 974

WEEFRY—Skillet—National Presto Industries, Inc.; *U.S. Public*, pg. 1159

WEEJUNS—Shoes—G.H. Bass & Co.; *U.S. Public*, pg. 1291

WEEK-END—Confections—Nestle-Rowntree Ltd.; *Int'l*, pg. 921

THE WEEK IN REVIEW—News Program—Westwood One, Inc.; *U.S. Public*, pg. 1763

WEEKEND—Disposable Camera with Wider Lens—Eastman Kodak Company; *U.S. Public*, pg. 550

WEEKEND—Spray Paints—Sherwin-Williams Diversified Brands, Inc.; *U.S. Public*, pg. 1466

WEEKEND HEADLINER—News Program—Westwood One, Inc.; *U.S. Public*, pg. 1763

WEEKEND HEADLINER—News Program—Westwood One Radio Networks; *U.S. Public*, pg. 1763

WEEKENDER—Boat—Sea Ray; *U.S. Public*, pg. 266

THE WEEKENDER—NONE—Mirror Group plc; *Int'l*, pg. 869

WEEKENDERS—Men's Apparel—International Cosmetics Co., Ltd.; *Int'l*, pg. 684

WEEKLY COUNTRY MUSIC COUNTDOWN—Country Music Radio Program—Westwood One Entertainment; *U.S. Public*, pg. 1763

THE WEEKLY COUNTRY MUSIC COUNTDOWN—Country Music Programming—Westwod One, Inc.; *U.S. Public*, pg. 1763

WEEKLY READER—School Periodical—Primedia Inc.; *U.S. Public*, pg. 1327

WEEKLY WORLD NEWS—Newspaper—American Media, Inc.; *U.S. Public*, pg. 87

WEEKS—Ice Cream—Koninklijke BolsWessanen nv; *Int'l*, pg. 750

WEEKS—Ice Cream—Weeks Dairy Foods, Inc.; *Int'l*, pg. 752

WEEMS & PLATH—Nautical Instruments—Litton Industries, Inc.; *U.S. Public*, pg. 1002

WEETABIX—Cereals—The Weetabix Company, Inc.; *Int'l*, pg. 1488

WEGENER—Welders—Ryan Herco Products Corp.; *U.S. Private*, pg. 953

WEGMANS—Retail Supermarkets—Wegmans Food Markets, Inc.; *U.S. Private*, pg. 1158

WEIBEL—Sparkling & Table Wines—Weibel Winery; *U.S. Private*, pg. 1159

WEICHERT—NONE—Weichert Company; *U.S. Private*, pg. 1159

WEIGH BAR—Sensing Device—Weigh-Tronix, Inc.; *Int'l*, pg. 1299

WEIGH-MATIC—Weigh System, Bin, or Scale— CTB International Corp.; *U.S. Public*, pg. 284

WEIGH PACKER—Fruit & Vegetable Machine— Aeroglide Corporation; *U.S. Private*, pg. 24

WEIGH SCALE FILLER—Liquid Filling—U.S. Bottlers Machinery Co.; *U.S. Private*, pg. 1124

WEIGHT LOSS TODAY—Television Program Series—Nutri/System Inc.; *U.S. Private*, pg. 859

WEIGHT WATCHERS—Frozen Foods—H.J. Heinz Company; *U.S. Public*, pg. 805

WEIGHTWATCHERS—NONE—H.J. Heinz Company Australia Ltd.; *U.S. Public*, pg. 807

WEIGHT WATCHERS—Diet—H.J. Heinz Company, Limited; *U.S. Public*, pg. 806

WEIGHT WATCHERS—Frozen Meals, Snacks & Desserts—H.J. Heinz Co. of Canada Ltd.; *U.S. Public*, pg. 806

WEIGHT WATCHERS—Bi-Monthly Magazine— Southern Progress Corporation; *U.S. Public*, pg. 1612

WEIGHT WATCHERS—NONE—Weight Watchers Gourmet Food Company; *U.S. Public*, pg. 806

WEIGHT WATCHERS—Low-Calorie Food—Weight Watchers International, Inc.; *U.S. Public*, pg. 806

WEIGHT WATCHERS—Consumer Magazine— Weight Watchers Magazine; *U.S. Public*, pg. 1612

WEIGHT WATCHERS—NONE—Weston Bakeries Limited; *Int'l*, pg. 1495

WEIGHT WATCHERS INTERNATIONAL—Weight Loss Program—H.J. Heinz Company; *U.S. Public*, pg. 805

WEIGHTLESS—Eyeglass Frames—AVC/Nu-Vision, Inc.; *U.S. Private*, pg. 9

WEISER—Locks—Masco Corporation; *U.S. Public*, pg. 1052

WEISER—Door Locks—Weiser Inc.; *U.S. Public*, pg. 1055

WEISER—Door Locks & Hardware—Weiser Lock; *U.S. Public*, pg. 1053

WEISER BRILLIANCE—Door Lock Hardware with Anti-Tarnish Finish—Weiser Lock; *U.S. Public*, pg. 1053

WEISERBOLT—Door Lock Hardware—Weiser Lock; *U.S. Public*, pg. 1053

WEISERLOCK—Door Lock Hardware—Weiser Lock; *U.S. Public*, pg. 1053

WEISFLOG APERITIF—NONE—Societe Pour la Vente des Produits Cinzano SA; *Int'l*, pg. 410

WEISS—Investment Advisors—Weiss Group.; *U.S. Private*, pg. 1160

WEISZ GRAPHICS—Screenprinting—Fred B. Johnston Company, Inc.; *U.S. Private*, pg. 595

WEJLOC—Clamp Device—Josam Company; *U.S. Private*, pg. 600

WEL-PRESS—Blind-drilled Felted Press Roll Covers—Harnischfeger Industries, Inc.; *U.S. Public*, pg. 788

WELBY—Clocks—Elgin National Industries, Inc.; *U.S. Private*, pg. 370

WELCH'S—Carbonated Soft Drink—Dr. Pepper Co.; *Int'l*, pg. 248

WELCH'S—Juices, Drinks & Cocktails—Welch Foods Inc., A Cooperative; *U.S. Private*, pg. 784

WELCH'S FRUIT JUICE BARS—Frozen Juice Bars—Welch Foods Inc., A Cooperative; *U.S. Private*, pg. 784

WELCH'S SQUEEZABLES—Squeezable Jellies, Jams & Preserves—Welch Foods Inc., A Cooperative; *U.S. Private*, pg. 784

WELCH'S TOTALLY FRUIT—Spreadable Fruit Spreads—Welch Foods Inc., A Cooperative; *U.S. Private*, pg. 784

WELCHADE—Drink—Welch Foods Inc., A Cooperative; *U.S. Private*, pg. 784

WELCHEM—Oil & Gas Production Chemical— Amoco Corporation; *U.S. Public*, pg. 101

WELCHOS PRODUCTS—Soft Drink—Grant-Lydick Beverage Co.; *U.S. Private*, pg. 470

WELCH'S—NONE—Cadbury Beverages; *Int'l*, pg. 248

WELCH'S FRUIT JUICE BARS—Licensed Ice Pops—Eskimo Pie Corporation; *U.S. Public*, pg. 592

WELCH'S JUICEMAKERS—NONE—Welch Foods Inc., A Cooperative; *U.S. Private*, pg. 784

WELCOME HOME—Door Hardware—Weiser Lock; *U.S. Public*, pg. 1053

WELCOME ICE CREAM—NONE—Vitamilk Dairy, Inc.; *U.S. Private*, pg. 1142

WELCOME WAGON—NONE—CUC International, Inc.; *U.S. Public*, pg. 320

WELCOME WAGON—Community Introduction Program—Welcome Wagon-Intl., Inc.; *U.S. Public*, pg. 321

WELDANPOWER—Welder—The Lincoln Electric Company; *U.S. Public*, pg. 996

WELDCOOL—Welding Lens—Aearo Company; *U.S. Private*, pg. 23

WELDCRAFT—TIG Welding Torches and Accessories—Dovatech, Ltd.; *U.S. Public*, pg. 520

WELDING DESIGN & FABRICATION— Periodical—Penton Publishing, Inc.; *U.S. Public*, pg. 1306

WELDOLET—Fittings—Bonney Forge Corporation; *U.S. Public*, pg. 156

WELDRAWN—Metal Tubing—Superior Tube Company; *U.S. Private*, pg. 1056

WELDROD WITH 3 DOTS—Electrode—The Lincoln Electric Company; *U.S. Public*, pg. 996

WELDRON—Wood & Lumber Products—Georgia-Pacific Corporation; *U.S. Public*, pg. 735

WELDVIEW—Goggles—Aearo Company; *U.S. Private*, pg. 23

WELDWOOD—Adhesives—DAP Inc.; *Int'l*, pg. 1486

WELDWRITE—NONE—Material Sciences Corporation; *U.S. Public*, pg. 1056

WELL—Stockings & Tights—Courtaulds Textiles Plc; *Int'l*, pg. 339

WELL DATA SYSTEM—Software—Litton Industries, Inc.; *U.S. Public*, pg. 1002

WELL DATA SYSTEM—NONE—Western Atlas Logging Services; *U.S. Public*, pg. 1757

WELL-GARD—Discharge Guard—CTB International Corp.; *U.S. Public*, pg. 284

WELL MATE—Well Water Reservoir Vessel— Essef Corporation; *U.S. Public*, pg. 592

WELL OF YOUTH—Cosmetics—Palm Beach Beauty Products Co.; *U.S. Private*, pg. 834

WELLA BALSAM—Hair Care Products—The Wella Corporation; *Int'l*, pg. 1489

WELLA BALSAM—Hair Care Prods.—Wella Group; *Int'l*, pg. 1489

WELLA PRIVAT—Hair Care Products—Wella Group; *Int'l*, pg. 1489

WELLAFLEX—Hair Lacquer Products—Wella Group; *Int'l*, pg. 1489

WELLAID—Oil & Gas Production Chemical— Amoco Corporation; *U.S. Public*, pg. 101

WELLBASE—NONE—Landmark Graphics Corporation; *U.S. Public*, pg. 776

WELLBECK GOLIN/HARRIS—NONE—Shandwick International Plc; *Int'l*, pg. 1226

WELLBUTRIN—Anti-Depressant—Glaxo Wellcome PLC; *Int'l*, pg. 553

WELLCO—Footwear—Wellco Enterprises, Inc.; *U.S. Public*, pg. 1752

WELLCOVORIN—Prescription Drug—Glaxo Wellcome PLC; *Int'l*, pg. 553

WELLCRAFT—Fiberglass Boats—Genmar Holdings, Inc.; *U.S. Private*, pg. 447

WELLER—Soldering, Desoldering, Rework/Repair Tools and Torches—Cooper Hand Tools; *U.S. Public*, pg. 444

WELLER—Soldering Guns & Irons—Cooper Industries, Inc.; *U.S. Public*, pg. 442

WELLER 107—Bourbon—Shieffelin Somerset Co.; *Int'l*, pg. 412

WELLESLEY INNS—Hotels—Prime Hospitality Corp.; *U.S. Public*, pg. 1326

WELLFERON—Anti-Viral—Glaxo Wellcome PLC; *Int'l*, pg. 553

WELLINGTON—Webbing Kits—Wellington Home Products; *U.S. Private*, pg. 1161

WELLS—Automotive Prods.—Wells Mfg. Corp.; *U.S. Private*, pg. 1113

WELLS/BLOOMFIELD—Commercial Coffee & Tea Brewers—Wells/Bloomfield; *U.S. Public*, pg. 1497

WELLS FARGO—Security Services—Borg-Warner Security Corporation; *U.S. Public*, pg. 245

WELLS FARGO—Alarms—Wells Fargo Alarm Services, Inc.; *U.S. Public*, pg. 246

WELLS FARGO GUARD SERVICES—Security Services—Borg-Warner Protective Services Corporation; *U.S. Public*, pg. 245

WELLSEIS—Seismic Surveying System for Gas & Oil Drilling—Bolt Technology Corporation; *U.S. Public*, pg. 244

WELLSTREAM—Flexible Pipe & Riser Systems— Dresser Industries, Inc.; *U.S. Public*, pg. 528

WELOCATOR—Stairway Lift—Access Industries; *U.S. Private*, pg. 11

WELONDA—Hairdressing Salon Equipment—Wella Group; *Int'l*, pg. 1489

WELSCO—Industrial Gases—Welsco Inc.; *U.S. Private*, pg. 1161

WELT AM SONTAG—Newspaper—Axel Springer Verlag AG; *Int'l*, pg. 102

WEMAC—Illuminated Mirrors—Nellcor Puritan Bennett Incorporated; *U.S. Public*, pg. 1039

WEN—Electric Hand Power Tools, Sodering Guns, Elec. Chain Saws, Bench Prods.—WEN Products, Inc.; *U.S. Private*, pg. 1144

WENDY—Fruit Juice—Nestle S.A.; *Int'l*, pg. 915

WENDY'S—Hamburger Restaurant—Southern Hospitality Corporation; *U.S. Public*, pg. 488

WENDY'S—Old Fashioned Hamburgers Restaurants—Wendy's International Inc.; *U.S. Public*, pg. 1754

WENDY'S—Fast Food Hamburgers—BR Associates, Inc.; *U.S. Private*, pg. 107

WENTE—Wine—Pacific Wine Co.; *U.S. Private*, pg. 843

WENZEL—Sleeping Bags & Tents—American Recreation Products, Inc.; *U.S. Public*, pg. 948

WENZEL—NONE—Kellwood Company; *U.S. Public*, pg. 948

WE'RE BULLISH ON BUSINESS—Slogan— Service Supply Co. Inc. of Indiana; *U.S. Private*, pg. 987

WE'RE WARNING YOU—Indicators—Projects Unlimited, Inc.; *U.S. Private*, pg. 890

WE'RE WITH YOU EVERY STEP OF THE WAY— Life Insurance—Gerber Products Company; *Int'l*, pg. 973

WERNET'S—Adhesive Cream, Powder & Denture Brush—Block Drug Company, Inc.; *U.S. Public*, pg. 236

WERTHEIM—Department Store—Hertie Waren-und Kaufhaus GmbH; *Int'l*, pg. 724

WERTHER'S ORIGINAL—Butter Toffee Candies—Storck U.S.A., L.P.; *Int'l*, pg. 1304

WESCODYNE—Disinfectant/Germicide—Wechco, Inc.; *U.S. Private*, pg. 1158

WESCODYNE—Disinfectant/Germicide—West Chemical Products, Inc.; *U.S. Private*, pg. 1158

WESLOCK—Door Locks—Weslock National, Inc.; *U.S. Private*, pg. 1163

WESP—Security/Fire Detection—Allied Research Corporation; *U.S. Public*, pg. 48

WESPER—International CII Airside Products—AAF McQuay, Inc.; *U.S. Private*, pg. 2

WESSANEN—Food Prods.—Koninklijke BolsWessanen nv; *Int'l*, pg. 750

WESSON—Vegetable Oil—ConAgra, Inc.; *U.S. Public*, pg. 425

WESSON—NONE—Glynwed International PLC; *Int'l*, pg. 554

WESSON—Oils—Hunt-Wesson, Inc.; *U.S. Public*, pg. 428

WESSON OILS—NONE—Hunt-Wesson, Inc.; *U.S. Public*, pg. 428

WEST—Cigarettes—Reemtsma Cigarettenfabriken GmbH, Hamburg; *Int'l*, pg. 1100

WEST—Metal Caps, Lids, Closures & Liners For Containers—The West Company, Incorporated; *U.S. Public*, pg. 1755

WEST AIR-CRIMP—Power-Operated Tools for Applying Closures or Seals to Containers—The West Company, Incorporated; *U.S. Public*, pg. 1755

WEST BEND—Cookware—Premark International, Inc.; *U.S. Public*, pg. 1321

WEST BIODIRECT—Catalogue for Supplies & Services For the Biotechnology Industry—The West Company, Incorporated; *U.S. Public*, pg. 1755

WEST BRAE NATURAL—Cookies, Pasta, Japanese Products, Condiments, Potato Chips, Canned Foods—Westbrae Natural, Inc.; *U.S. Public*, pg. 774

WEST CD-ROM LIBRARIES—CD-ROM—West Information Publishing Group; *U.S. Public*, pg. 1602

WEST COAST—Video—West Coast Entertainment Inc.; *U.S. Public*, pg. 1755

WEST COAST LIFE—Insurance Co.—West Coast Life Insurance Co.; *U.S. Public*, pg. 1336

THE WEST COMPANY AND DIAMOND DESIGN—Metal Caps, Lids, Closures & Liners for Containers—The West Company, Incorporated; *U.S. Public*, pg. 1755

WEST OF ALAMEIN—War Game—Monarch Avalon, Inc.; *U.S. Public*, pg. 1123

WEST SOY—Non Dairy Beverages—Westbrae Natural, Inc.; *U.S. Public*, pg. 774

WEST VIRGINIA—Ham, Bacon & Smoked Meat Prods.—Hygrade Food Products Corporation; *U.S. Public*, pg. 1433

WEST VIRGINIA MANUFACTURERS REGISTER—Register—Manufacturers' News, Inc.; *U.S. Private*, pg. 700

WEST'S DESKTOP PRACTICE SYSTEMS—Disk—West Information Publishing Group; *U.S. Public*, pg. 1602

WESTA—Premium Quality Masonry Tools—Vermont American Tool Corp.; *U.S. Public*, pg. 575

WESTAFF—Staffing Office/Light Industrial—Western Staff Services; *U.S. Public*, pg. 1760

WESTAINER—Container & Closures Made of Plastic—The West Company, Incorporated; *U.S. Public*, pg. 1755

WESTAMERICA BANK—NONE—Westamerica Bancorporation; *U.S. Public*, pg. 1756

WESTAR—Ready to Use Stoppers or Metal Seals Lined With Rubber—The West Company, Incorporated; *U.S. Public*, pg. 1755

WESTAR—Mining, Timber & Petroleum—Westar Group Ltd.; *Int'l*, pg. 1491

WESTAR—NONE—Western Resources, Inc.; *U.S. Public*, pg. 1759

WESTAT—Statistical Survey Research—Westat Inc.; *U.S. Private*, pg. 1163

WESTCAN—Electric Heaters - Canada—The Glen Dimplex Group; *Int'l*, pg. 553

WESTCAPPER—Bottle & Vial Capping Machines—The West Company, Incorporated; *U.S. Public*, pg. 1755

WESTCHESTER—Luggage—American Tourister, Inc.; *U.S. Public*, pg. 1430

WESTCHESTER CLASSIC—Leisure Wear—Duck Head Apparel; *U.S. Public*, pg. 498

WESTCLOX—Clocks—General Time Corp.; *U.S. Private*, pg. 445

WESTCLOX—Clocks—Westclox; *U.S. Private*, pg. 445

WESTCO—Bakery Ingredients—CSM N.V.; *Int'l*, pg. 243

WESTCON—Digital Panel Meters—Desco Corporation; *U.S. Private*, pg. 326

WESTCORT—Topical Steroid—Bristol-Myers Squibb Company; *U.S. Public*, pg. 253

WESTCORT CREAM—Topical Steroid—Westwood-Squibb Pharmaceuticals Inc.; *U.S. Public*, pg. 255

WESTCORT OINTMENT—Topical Steroid—Westwood-Squibb Pharmaceuticals Inc.; *U.S. Public*, pg. 255

WESTCOTT—Rulers—Acme United Corporation; *U.S. Public*, pg. 17

WESTCOTT COMMUNICATIONS—Satellite Television Provider—Primedia Workplace Learning; *U.S. Public*, pg. 1328

WESTERBEKE—Marine Engines & Generator Sets—Westerbeke Corporation; *U.S. Public*, pg. 1757

WESTERN—Dressings—Bestfoods; *U.S. Public*, pg. 223

WESTERN ACCOUNTING SERVICES—Accounting Staffing—Western Staff Services; *U.S. Public*, pg. 1760

WESTERN AUTO—NONE—Sears, Roebuck and Co.; *U.S. Public*, pg. 1452

WESTERN COMBINE—Combines—AGCO Corporation; *U.S. Public*, pg. 28

WESTERN CUTLERY—NONE—Camillus Cutlery Co.; *U.S. Private*, pg. 203

WESTERN DIGITAL—NONE—Milgray Electronics, Inc.; *U.S. Public*, pg. 205

WESTERN DIGITAL—Specialized Semiconductors—Western Digital Corporation; *U.S. Public*, pg. 1758

WESTERN ENTERPRISES—Welding Products, Home Health Care & Hospital Products, Plastics—The Scott Fetzer Company; *U.S. Public*, pg. 217

WESTERN FAMILY—NONE—Associated Food Stores Inc.; *U.S. Private*, pg. 90

WESTERN FAMILY—Mexican Food Products—Wilson Products Co.; *U.S. Private*, pg. 1181

WESTERN FLYER—Bicycles—Western Auto Supply Company; *U.S. Public*, pg. 1452

WESTERN FORGE—Private Labeled Hand Tools—Emerson Electric Co.; *U.S. Public*, pg. 572

WESTERN GEOPHYSICAL—Resource Exploration—Litton Industries, Inc.; *U.S. Public*, pg. 1002

WESTERN LOGANBERRY—Sparkling Mineral Water—Clearly Canadian Beverage Corp.; *Int'l*, pg. 297

WESTERN MEDICAL SERVICES—Medical Staffing—Western Staff Services; *U.S. Public*, pg. 1760

WESTERN MEDICAL SERVICES HOME HEALTH AGENCY—Home Healthcare—Western Staff Services; *U.S. Public*, pg. 1760

WESTERN METERS—Dialysis Meters—Mesa Laboratories, Inc.; *U.S. Public*, pg. 1099

WESTERN OAK—Aluminum Siding—Alcoa Building Products, Inc.; *U.S. Public*, pg. 61

WESTERN OUTSOURCING SERVICES—Outsourcing—Western Staff Services; *U.S. Public*, pg. 1760

WESTERN PRECIPITATION—Air Pollution Control—Joy Mining Machinery; *U.S. Public*, pg. 789

WESTERN RESERVE—Private Brand Paper—The Cincinnati Cordage & Paper Company; *U.S. Private*, pg. 264

WESTERN SHAKE—Weathered Wood Shakes—GAF Premium Products, Inc.; *U.S. Private*, pg. 433

WESTERN STAFF SERVICES—Staffing—Western Staff Services; *U.S. Public*, pg. 1760

WESTERN STATES—Envelopes—Western States Envelope Co.; *U.S. Private*, pg. 1168

WESTERN STEER FAMILY STEAKHOUSE—Restaurant—WSMP, Inc.; *U.S. Public*, pg. 1729

WESTERN STEER STEAKS BUFFET & BAKERY—Restaurant—WSMP, Inc.; *U.S. Public*, pg. 1729

WESTERN SUN—Farm Supplies & Feeds—Intermountain Farmers Association; *U.S. Private*, pg. 568

WESTERN TECHNICAL SERVICES—Technical Staffing—Western Staff Services; *U.S. Public*, pg. 1760

WESTERN TEMPORARY SERVICES—Office & Light Industrial Staffing—Western Staff Services; *U.S. Public*, pg. 1760

WESTERN TURF & LANDSCAPE PRESS—NONE—Intertec Publishing; *U.S. Public*, pg. 1328

WESTERN TURF MANAGEMENT—NONE—Farm Press; *U.S. Public*, pg. 1328

WESTERN UNION MONEY TRANSFER—Money Services—New Valley Corporation; *U.S. Public*, pg. 1173

WESTERN UNION MONEY TRANSFER—Money Services—Western Union Financial Services, Inc.; *U.S. Public*, pg. 631

WESTERSTROOP—Sugar Syrup—CSM N.V.; *Int'l*, pg. 243

WESTFILLER—Machine for Filling Containers—The West Company, Incorporated; *U.S. Public*, pg. 1755

WESTIES—Women's Shoes—Nine West Group, Inc.; *U.S. Public*, pg. 1185

WESTIN—Hotels & resorts—Westin Hotels & Resorts; *U.S. Public*, pg. 1512

WESTIN—Food Products—Westin, Inc.; *U.S. Private*, pg. 1169

WESTIN CONNECTIONS—NONE—Westin Hotels & Resorts; *U.S. Public*, pg. 1512

WESTIN KID'S CLUB—NONE—Westin Hotels & Resorts; *U.S. Public*, pg. 1512

WESTIN PREMIER—NONE—Westin Hotels & Resorts; *U.S. Public*, pg. 1512

WESTIN'S GUEST OFFICE—Room Featuring Business Machines—Westin Hotels & Resorts; *U.S. Public*, pg. 1512

WESTINGHOUSE—Open Office Systems—Carter Holt Harvey Limited; *U.S. Public*, pg. 904

WESTINGHOUSE—Major Appliances—Email Limited; *Int'l*, pg. 450

WESTLAW—Electronic Publishing—West Information Publishing Group; *U.S. Public*, pg. 1602

WESTLEY'S—Cleaners—Blue Coral/Slick 50; *U.S. Public*, pg. 1348

WESTMINSTER—Glazed Ceramic Tile—Porcelanite, Inc.; *Int'l*, pg. 573

WESTMINSTER HOMES—NONE—Washington Homes, Inc.; *U.S. Public*, pg. 1741

WESTMORELAND—Coal Mining, Processing & Marketing—Westmoreland Coal Co.; *U.S. Public*, pg. 1761

WESTOMER—Seals for Use on Pharmaceutical Containers—The West Company, Incorporated; *U.S. Public*, pg. 1755

WESTON—Eye Protection—U.S. Safety; *U.S. Private*, pg. 1125

THE WESTON GALLERY—Picture Frames—Wilton Industries, Inc.; *U.S. Private*, pg. 1181

WESTON'S—NONE—Weston Bakeries Limited; *Int'l*, pg. 1495

WESTPINE—Disinfectant—Knomark, Inc.; *U.S. Private*, pg. 627

WESTPORT—Travel Trailer—Fleetwood Enterprises, Inc.; *U.S. Public*, pg. 650

WESTPORT—Travel Trailers—Fleetwood Travel Trailers of Nebraska, Inc.; *U.S. Public*, pg. 652

WESTPORT, LTD.—NONE—The Dress Barn, Inc.; *U.S. Public*, pg. 528

WESTRAK—Data Transfer System—Westvaco Corporation; *U.S. Public*, pg. 1762

WESTRAK EXPRESS—Computer Software Program—Westvaco Corporation; *U.S. Public*, pg. 1762

WESTRAN—PVDF Membrane—Schleicher & Schuell, Inc.; *Int'l*, pg. 1206

WESTREE—Lumber—Georgia-Pacific Corporation; *U.S. Public*, pg. 735

WESTREZ—Adhesive Tacifiers—Westvaco Corporation; *U.S. Public*, pg. 1762

WEST'S LEGAL DIRECTORY—Online Directory—West Information Publishing Group; *U.S. Public*, pg. 1602

WEST'S PREMISE RESEARCH SOFTWARE—Search Software—West Information Publishing Group; *U.S. Public*, pg. 1602

WESTVACO—Paper, Paperboard, Corrugated Boxes, Milk Cartons, Envelops; Chemicals—Westvaco Corporation; *U.S. Public*, pg. 1762

WESTVACO DIACID—Specialty Chemicals—Westvaco Corporation; *U.S. Public*, pg. 1762

WESTVACO-OVENWARE—Paperboard Trays & Lids—Westvaco Corporation; *U.S. Public*, pg. 1762

WESTVIEW—Dairy Products—Vitamilk Dairy, Inc.; *U.S. Private*, pg. 1142

WESTWIND—Business Jet—Israel Aircraft Industries Ltd.; *Int'l*, pg. 689

WESTWOOD—Consumer Turf Machinery—Ransomes Plc; *Int'l*, pg. 1087

WESTWOOD—Mobile Home—Wick Bldg. Systems Inc. Manufactured Homes Div.; *U.S. Private*, pg. 1174

WESTWOOD ONE COLLEGE FOOTBALL BOWLS—Sports Radio Program—Westwood One Entertainment; *U.S. Public*, pg. 1763

WESTWOOD ONE COLLEGE FOOTBALL BOWLS—Seasonal Sports Program—Westwood One, Inc.; *U.S. Public*, pg. 1763

THE WESTWOOD ONE/HBO BOXING SERIES—Sports Radio Program—Westwood One Entertainment; *U.S. Public*, pg. 1763

THE WESTWOOD ONE/HBO BOXING SERIES—Boxing Program—Westwood One, Inc.; *U.S. Public*, pg. 1763

WESTWOOD ONE NEWS—News Updates & Newsfeeds—Westwood One, Inc.; *U.S. Public*, pg. 1763

WESTWOOD ONE 70'S FORMAT—24-Hour Satellite Delivered Music Format—Westwood One, Inc.; *U.S. Public*, pg. 1763

WESVAR—Statistical Software—Westat Inc.; *U.S. Private*, pg. 1163

WESVAR PC—Statistical Software For The PC—Westat Inc.; *U.S. Private*, pg. 1163

WET & DRY—2 Part Screen Cleaner—The Texwipe Co., Inc.; *U.S. Private*, pg. 1079

WET 'N' WILD—Cosmetics—AM Cosmetics Inc.; *U.S. Private*, pg. 6

WET BREWERS GRAIN—Dairy Feed—Labatt Brewing Company Limited; *Int'l*, pg. 679

WET BREWERS GRAIN—Dairy Feed—Miracle Feeds Inc.; *U.S. Private*, pg. 432

WET CASSETTE—Shower Cassette Player/Radio—Salton/Maxim Housewares, Inc.; *U.S. Public*, pg. 1430

WET CEL—Fishing Lines—3M; *U.S. Public*, pg. 1604

WET GUARD AND DESIGN—Gypsum Wallboard—Weyerhaeuser Forest Products Company; *U.S. Public*, pg. 1764

WET-NAP—Moist Towelettes—Nice-Pak Products, Inc.; *U.S. Private*, pg. 798

WET PAK—Ice Cream Carry Out Bags—Tenneco Packaging, Consumer Products Group; *U.S. Public*, pg. 1579

WET REFLECTIONS—Shower Mirror & AM/FM Radio—Salton/Maxim Housewares, Inc.; *U.S. Public*, pg. 1430

WET SET PVC PLASTIC PIPE CEMENT—Industrial Chemical—Hercules Chemical Co., Inc.; *U.S. Private*, pg. 523

WET STICK—Labels—Avery Dennison Corporation Label Group; *U.S. Public*, pg. 153

WET SURFACE—Air Coolers—Niagara Blower Company; *U.S. Private*, pg. 798

WETHERGARD—Lumber—Weyerhaeuser Forest Products Company; *U.S. Public*, pg. 1764

WETORDRY—Waterproof Resin Bonded Coated Abrasives—3M; *U.S. Public*, pg. 1604

WEYCO—Paper, Lumber—Weyerhaeuser Company; *U.S. Public*, pg. 1764

WEYCO—Green Lumber—Weyerhaeuser Forest Products Company; *U.S. Public*, pg. 1764

WEYENBERG—Shoes—Weyco Group, Inc.; *U.S. Public*, pg. 1763

WEYER-PAK—Kraft Containerboard—Weyerhaeuser Company; *U.S. Public*, pg. 1764

WEYERHAEUSER—Wood Pulp, Boxes, Cartons & Wood Fiber—Weyerhaeuser Company; *U.S. Public*, pg. 1764

WEYERHAEUSER CORPORATE SYMBOL—Plywood & Wood Fiber—Weyerhaeuser Company; *U.S. Public*, pg. 1764

WEYERHAEUSER FIRST CHOICE PAPER—Premium Laser Paper-Reprographic Papers—Weyerhaeuser Company; *U.S. Public*, pg. 1764

WEYERHAEUSER LASER COPY—Premium Xerocopy-Reprographic Papers—Weyerhaeuser Company; *U.S. Public*, pg. 1764

WEYERHAEUSER LASER WEB—Reprographic Roll Feed Papers—Weyerhaeuser Company; *U.S. Public*, pg. 1764

WEYERHAEUSER OFFICE PAPER—Xerocopy-Reprographic Papers—Weyerhaeuser Company; *U.S. Public*, pg. 1764

WEYERHAEUSER RECYCLED LASER COPY—Premium Xerocopy-Reprographic Papers—Weyerhaeuser Company; *U.S. Public*, pg. 1764

WEYERHAEUSER WOODSHED—Paneling—Weyerhaeuser Forest Products Company; *U.S. Public*, pg. 1764

WHALE—Writing Instruments—Dixon Ticonderoga Company; *U.S. Public*, pg. 514

WHAM—Plumbing Chemical—Hercules Chemical Co., Inc.; *U.S. Private*, pg. 523

WHAM-O-RANG—Toy—Mattel, Inc.; *U.S. Public*, pg. 1057

WHAT BIKE?—Motorcycle Magazine—EMAP Nationals; *Int'l*, pg. 451

WHAT CAMERA—Special Interest Magazine—IPC Magazines Limited; *Int'l*, pg. 651

WHAT PERSONAL COMPUTER—NONE—EMAP Business Communications Division; *Int'l*, pg. 451

WHATABURGER—Hamburgers—Whataburger, Inc.; *U.S. Private*, pg. 1170

WHATCHAMACALLIT—Candy Bar—Hershey Chocolate U.S.A.; *U.S. Public*, pg. 812

WHATCHAMACALLIT—Candy Bar—Hershey Foods Corporation; *U.S. Public*, pg. 811

WHATMAN—NONE—Whatman plc; *Int'l*, pg. 1498

WHAT'S NEWS—Column Heading—Dow Jones & Company, Inc.; *U.S. Public*, pg. 524

WHAT'S ON TV—Weekly TV Magazine—IPC Magazines Limited; *Int'l*, pg. 651

WHEAT—Rechargeable Lanterns—Koehler Manufacturing Company; *U.S. Private*, pg. 706

WHEAT CRUNCHIES—Snacks—Borden, Inc.; *U.S. Private*, pg. 157

WHEAT HEARTS—Cereal—General Mills, Inc.; *U.S. Public*, pg. 717

WHEAT 'N BRAN—Baked Goods—George Weston Limited; *Int'l*, pg. 1494

WHEAT THINS—Snack Crackers—Nabisco Inc.; *U.S. Public*, pg. 1355

WHEATABLES—Crackers—Keebler Company; *U.S. Public*, pg. 657

WHEATENA—Hot Cereal—International Home Foods Inc.; *U.S. Private*, pg. 526

WHEATIES—Cereal—General Mills, Inc.; *U.S. Public*, pg. 717

WHEATLAND TUBE—Pipe Valve—The Gage Company; *U.S. Private*, pg. 437

WHEATLEY—Valves, Pumps, Meters & Measuring Equipment—Dresser Industries, Inc.; *U.S. Public*, pg. 528

WHEATLEY—Pumps & Plunger—Harley Industries, Inc.; *U.S. Public*, pg. 880

WHEATON AUTOSTILL—Scientific Glassware for Laboratory Use—Wheaton Inc.; *Int'l*, pg. 67

WHEATON 33—Scientific Glassware for Laboratory Use—Wheaton Inc.; *Int'l*, pg. 67

WHEATON WORLDWIDE MOVING—Moving of Household Goods—Wheaton Van Lines, Inc.; *U.S. Private*, pg. 1171

WHEATSWORTH—Wheat Crackers—Nabisco Inc.; *U.S. Public*, pg. 1355

WHEEL CHROME TITE!—Fasteners—R&B, Inc.; *U.S. Public*, pg. 1354

WHEEL-DRAGON—Bucketwheel Dredge—Ellicott Machine Corporation International; *U.S. Private*, pg. 372

WHEEL HORSE—Lawn & Garden Tractors—Toro-Wheel Horse; *U.S. Public*, pg. 1624

WHEEL-TITE!—Wheel Studs & Nuts—R&B, Inc.; *U.S. Public*, pg. 1354

WHEELFORCE—Wheel Service Equipment—SPX Corporation; *U.S. Public*, pg. 1420

WHEELWRITER—Typewriter—International Business Machines Corporation; *U.S. Public*, pg. 895

WHELAND—Gray Iron & Ductile Iron—North American Royalties, Inc.; *U.S. Private*, pg. 803

WHEN IT'S IMPORTANT ENOUGH TO SIGN YOUR NAME—Bond & Business Papers—The Mead Corporation; *U.S. Public*, pg. 1074

WHERE IN THE USA IS CARMEN SANDIEGO?—NONE—Broderbund Software, Inc.; *U.S. Public*, pg. 258

WHERE IN THE WORLD IS CARMEN SANDIEGO?—NONE—Broderbund Software, Inc.; *U.S. Public*, pg. 258

WHEREHOUSE—Home Entertainment Products—Wherehouse Entertainment, Inc.; *U.S. Private*, pg. 1171

WHEREMI—NONE—Excelled Sheepskin & Leather Coat Corporation; *U.S. Private*, pg. 387

WHILE YOU WAIT—Maternity Panties & Hosiery—Alba-Waldensian, Inc.; *U.S. Public*, pg. 35

WHIP—Specialty Chemical—AgrEvo USA Company; *Int'l*, pg. 1203

WHIP—Pesticide—Hoechst Aktiengesellschaft; *Int'l*, pg. 624

WHIP TOPPING—Non-Dairy Topping—Rich Products Corp.; *U.S. Private*, pg. 928

WHIPPED DELUXE—Frostings—General Mills, Inc.; *U.S. Public*, pg. 717

WHIPPER MIX—NONE—Nestle USA; *Int'l*, pg. 916

WHIPPS—Granola Snacks—The Quaker Oats Company; *U.S. Public*, pg. 1347

WHIRL-PAK—Sterile Sampling Bags—Nasco; *U.S. Private*, pg. 446

WHIRL-PAK—Sampling Bags—Nasco Modesto; *U.S. Private*, pg. 446

WHIRLAMATIC—Small Vacuum—Advance Machine Company; *Int'l*, pg. 932

WHIRLAWAY—Waste Disposer & Instant Hot Water Dispenser—Anaheim Manufacturing Company; *U.S. Private*, pg. 70

WHIRLBUSTER—Anti-Whirl PDC—Baker Hughes INTEQ; *U.S. Public*, pg. 166

WHIRLETTES—Derricks—AmClyde Engineered Products Co., Inc.; *U.S. Public*, pg. 778

WHIRLEYS—Cranes—AmClyde Engineered Products Co., Inc.; *U.S. Public*, pg. 778

WHIRLIMET—Automatic Polishing Device—Buehler, Limited; *U.S. Public*, pg. 574

WHIRLJET—Spray Nozzle—Spraying Systems Co.; *U.S. Private*, pg. 1026

WHIRLOUT—Exhaust—Swartwout Industries; *Int'l*, pg. 1398

WHIRLPOOL—Power Spa—Pollenex; *U.S. Public*, pg. 1391

WHIRLPOOL—Major Appliances—Whirlpool Corporation; *U.S. Public*, pg. 1764

WHIRLWIND—Sweeper—Elgin Sweeper Company; *U.S. Public*, pg. 617

WHIRLWIND—Cotton Candy Machine—Gold Medal Products Co.; *U.S. Private*, pg. 459

WHIRLWIND—Gas Torch—Sycamore Plant; *U.S. Public*, pg. 444

WHISKAS—Premium Cat Food-Meat & Dry—Kal Kan Foods, Inc.; *U.S. Private*, pg. 707

WHISKAS—Premium Cat Food—Mars, Incorporated; *U.S. Private*, pg. 707

WHISKAS—Petfood—Mars Petfoods (UNISABI); *U.S. Private*, pg. 707

WHISKAS CAT MILK—Premium Cat Food—Mars, Incorporated; *U.S. Private*, pg. 707

WHISKAS CRUNCH—Premium Cat Food—Mars, Incorporated; *U.S. Private*, pg. 707

WHISKEY—Ready Rubbed Pipe Tobacco—Imperial Tobacco Group, Ltd.; *Int'l*, pg. 666

WHISPER—Ladies Shaver—American Safety Razor Company; *U.S. Private*, pg. 597

WHISPER—Hosiery—Sara Lee Corporation; *U.S. Public*, pg. 1432

WHISPER-FLEX—Elevator Compensating Cable—Siecor Corporation; *U.S. Public*, pg. 449

WHISPER-FLEX—Elevator Compensating Cable—Siecor Corporation; *Int'l*, pg. 1245

WHISPER PRINTS—Wallcovering—York Wallcoverings Inc.; *U.S. Private*, pg. 1196

WHISPER-TIP—Brushes & Combs—Wilhold Inc.; *U.S. Public*, pg. 78

WHISPER TRIM—Noise Abatement Valve—Monsanto Company; *U.S. Public*, pg. 1124

WHISPER WEFT—Interfacings—Specialty Textile Products; *U.S. Private*, pg. 1023

WHISPERCOOL—Ventilater—CertainTeed Corporation; *Int'l*, pg. 1170

WHISPERDYNE—Centrifuge Components—Western States Machine Company; *U.S. Private*, pg. 1168

WHISPERFLO—Swimming Pool Pumps—Essef Corporation; *U.S. Public*, pg. 592

WHISPERTAPE—Electromagnetic Detection System—3M; *U.S. Public*, pg. 1604

WHISPERTOUCH—Impedance-Matching Stereo Volume Control—Atlas/Soundolier; *U.S. Private*, pg. 64

WHISTLE DOWN THE WIND—Musical—Really Useful Holdings Limited; *Int'l*, pg. 1089

WHITAK—Disinfectants—SmithKline Beecham plc; *Int'l*, pg. 1264

WHITCO—Building Products—Email Limited; *Int'l*, pg. 450

WHITE—Tractors—AGCO Corporation; *U.S. Public*, pg. 28

WHITE—NONE—Key Handling Systems, Inc.; *U.S. Private*, pg. 618

WHITE—Disinfectants—SmithKline Beecham plc; *Int'l*, pg. 1264

WHITE—Sewing & Knitting Machines—VWS, Inc.; *Int'l*, pg. 440

WHITE BIRCH—Peppermint Schnapps—Marie Brizard Wines & Spirits USA; *U.S. Private*, pg. 702

Brand Name Index

WHITE BOND—Premium Grade Single Part Stock Computer Paper—Shade/Allied, Inc.; *U.S. Public*, pg. 89

WHITE CAP—Aerosol Pan Coating, Bakery Shortening Chocolate—Ventura Foods LLC; *Int'l*, pg. 879

WHITE CAP—Closures—White Cap, Inc.; *Int'l*, pg. 1207

WHITE CASTLE—Fast Food Restaurants—White Castle System, Inc.; *U.S. Private*, pg. 1171

WHITE CHRISTMAS—NONE—Bachmann Industries, Inc.; *U.S. Private*, pg. 109

WHITE CLOUD—Bathroom Tissue—The Procter & Gamble Company; *U.S. Public*, pg. 1330

WHITE DIAMOND—Fragrance—Parfums International Ltd.; *Int'l*, pg. 1435

WHITE ELECTRICAL—Electrical Construction—White Electrical Construction Co.; *U.S. Private*, pg. 1172

WHITE ELEPHANT—White Portland Cement—The Siam Cement Public Company Limited; *Int'l*, pg. 1237

WHITE FILL—Body Filler—Marson/Creative Fastener, Inc.; *U.S. Private*, pg. 708

WHITEGMC WG—Class 8 Truck & Tractors—Volvo Truck North America, Inc.; *Int'l*, pg. 1477

WHITEGMC AERO SERIES—Class 8 Truck & Tractors—Volvo Truck North America, Inc.; *Int'l*, pg. 1477

WHITEGMC CONVENTIONALS—Class 8 Truck & Tractors—Volvo Truck North America, Inc.; *Int'l*, pg. 1477

WHITEGMC HIGH CABOVERS—Class 8 Truck & Tractors—Volvo Truck North America, Inc.; *Int'l*, pg. 1477

WHITEGMC INTEGRAL SLEEPER—Class 8 Truck & Tractors—Volvo Truck North America, Inc.; *Int'l*, pg. 1477

WHITE GILL—Bow & Stern Thrusters—Elliott Company; *U.S. Private*, pg. 373

WHITE GOLD—Body Filler—Marson/Creative Fastener, Inc.; *U.S. Private*, pg. 708

WHITE HEATHER—Blended Scotch Whiskey—Groupe Pernod Ricard; *Int'l*, pg. 566

WHITE HORSE FINE OLD—NONE—Guinness Plc; *Int'l*, pg. 412

WHITE HOUSE—Bath Accessories—Melard Manufacturing Corporation; *U.S. Private*, pg. 729

WHITE HOUSE—Food Products—National Fruit Product Company; *U.S. Private*, pg. 783

WHITE KING—NONE—Kiwi Brands Pty. Ltd.; *U.S. Public*, pg. 1434

WHITE KING—Specialty Detergent—Sara Lee Corporation; *U.S. Public*, pg. 1432

WHITE LABEL—Low-Alcohol Bitter—Whitbread PLC; *Int'l*, pg. 1498

WHITE LIGHTNIN'—Body Filler—Marson/Creative Fastener, Inc.; *U.S. Private*, pg. 708

WHITE LILY—Flour, Mixes & Corn Meal—The White Lily Foods Co.; *U.S. Private*, pg. 866

WHITE MAGIC—Faucets, Valves & Fittings—The Black & Decker Corporation; *U.S. Public*, pg. 233

WHITE MOUNTAIN—Ice Cream Freezers—The Rival Company; *U.S. Public*, pg. 1391

WHITE MOUNTAIN BOND—Bond Paper—Fort James Corporation; *U.S. Public*, pg. 670

WHITE-NEW IDEA—Implements, Planters, Manure Spreaders, Hay Tools—AGCO Corporation; *U.S. Public*, pg. 28

WHITE OWL—Cigars—General Cigar Company, Inc.; *U.S. Public*, pg. 708

WHITE PLUME—Flour—ADM Milling Co.; *U.S. Public*, pg. 128

WHITE RAIN—Hair Preparations—The Gillette Company; *U.S. Public*, pg. 743

WHITE RIVER FARMS—Catalog & Food Products—Alltrista Corporation; *U.S. Public*, pg. 56

WHITE ROSE—Flour—ADM Milling Co.; *U.S. Public*, pg. 128

WHITE ROSE—Food Products—Di Giorgio Corporation; *U.S. Private*, pg. 330

WHITE SATIN—Sugar—The Amalgamated Sugar Company LLC; *U.S. Private*, pg. 48

WHITE SHIELD—Ale—Bass PLC; *Int'l*, pg. 169

WHITE SHOULDERS—Toiletries—Parfums International Ltd.; *Int'l*, pg. 1435

WHITE STAG—Sportswear—Warnaco Inc.; *U.S. Public*, pg. 1738

WHITE STAR—Valves—The Wm. Powell Company; *U.S. Private*, pg. 877

WHITE STAR—Sugar—Savannah Foods & Industries, Inc.; *U.S. Public*, pg. 872

WHITE-SUNDSTRAND—NONE—DeVlieg-Bullard Inc.; *U.S. Public*, pg. 502

WHITE SWAN—Glace (Candied Fruit)—Paradise, Inc.; *U.S. Public*, pg. 1256

WHITE SWAN—NONE—Portland Food Products Company; *U.S. Private*, pg. 876

WHITE SWAN—Healthcare Uniforms—Whiteswan/Meta; *U.S. Private*, pg. 342

WHITE SWAN-META UNIFORMS—NONE—Whiteswan/Meta; *U.S. Private*, pg. 342

WHITE SYSTEM—White Board Markers—Dixon Ticonderoga Company; *U.S. Public*, pg. 514

WHITE WATER—World's Best Water Adventures—Silver Dollar City, Inc.; *U.S. Private*, pg. 1000

WHITE-WESTINGHOUSE—Major Appliances—Electrolux, AB; *Int'l*, pg. 438

WHITE-WESTINGHOUSE—Appliances—Frigidaire Home Products; *Int'l*, pg. 439

WHITE-WESTINGHOUSE—Major Appliances—White Consolidated Industries, Inc.; *Int'l*, pg. 439

WHITE WINGS—Groceries—Goodman Fielder Limited; *Int'l*, pg. 555

WHITEMAN—Concrete Equipment—MultiQuip, Inc.; *Int'l*, pg. 695

WHITEWHEAT—Bread—Flowers Industries, Inc.; *U.S. Public*, pg. 656

WHITFIELD—Pickles—Dean Foods Company; *U.S. Public*, pg. 489

WHITIN—NONE—Whitin Roberts Co.; *U.S. Private*, pg. 309

WHITING—Service Station—Kaibab Industries; *U.S. Private*, pg. 605

WHITING—Cranes, Railroad Maintenance & Metallurgical Equipment—Whiting Corporation; *U.S. Private*, pg. 1173

WHITLENGE—NONE—Scotsman Industries, Inc.; *U.S. Public*, pg. 1444

WHITLOCK—Heat Exchangers—Ketema, Inc.; *U.S. Private*, pg. 604

WHITMAN—Books & Games—Golden Books Family Entertainment Inc.; *U.S. Public*, pg. 749

WHITMAN—Umbrella Brand for Coin Collecting Books & Albums—Golden Books Publishing; *U.S. Public*, pg. 749

WHITMAN—Chocolates—Whitman's Candies, Inc.; *U.S. Private*, pg. 953

WHITMAN'S—Candies—The Pillsbury Company; *Int'l*, pg. 411

WHITMAN'S SAMPLER—Candies—The Pillsbury Company; *Int'l*, pg. 411

WHITMOR—Brandname for all Products—Earle Industries, Inc.; *U.S. Private*, pg. 356

WHITNEY—NONE—Petrie Retail, Inc.; *U.S. Private*, pg. 858

WHITNEY LIBRARY OF DESIGN—Books for Designers—BPI Communications Inc.; *Int'l*, pg. 1446

WHITTAKER—Electronic & Fluid Controls—Whittaker Corporation; *U.S. Public*, pg. 1766

WHIZ—Shampoo Bowl Spray—Belvedere Company; *U.S. Private*, pg. 1008

WHIZ—Automotive Chemicals—Malco Products, Inc.; *U.S. Private*, pg. 698

WHIZ BANG—Popcorn Machine—Gold Medal Products Co.; *U.S. Private*, pg. 459

WHIZLOCK—Fasteners—Maclean-Fogg Co.; *U.S. Private*, pg. 692

WHIZZ WITCH—BrushCutter/Power Scythe—Hoffco/Comet Industries, Inc.; *U.S. Private*, pg. 532

WHIZZER—Bag Closer—Corn States Hybrid Service, Inc.; *U.S. Public*, pg. 1124

WHIZZER—Mat & Equip. Disinfectant—Mueller Sports Medicine, Inc.; *U.S. Private*, pg. 766

WHO—Wisconsin Health Organization—Humana Wisconsin Health Organization Insurance Corporation; *U.S. Public*, pg. 848

WHOLE GRAIN TOTAL—Cereal—General Mills, Inc.; *U.S. Public*, pg. 717

WHOLE GRAIN WHEATIES—Cereal—General Mills, Inc.; *U.S. Public*, pg. 717

WHOLE LIFE—Life Insurance—Pan-American Life Insurance Company; *U.S. Private*, pg. 836

WHOLE RICE TIME RELEASE SINGLE DAY—Chelated Multi-Vitamin & Mineral—Weider Nutrition Intl.; *U.S. Private*, pg. 1159

WHOLE WHEAT HOT NATURAL CEREAL—Hot Cereal—The Quaker Oats Company; *U.S. Public*, pg. 1347

WHOLESALE BAKING REPORT—Report Delivering Industry Information for Wholesale Baking Executives—Reed Elsevier Business Information; *Int'l*, pg. 1095

WHOLESALERS-DISTRIBUTORS INSURANCE PROGRAM—Insurance Package Program—Poe & Brown, Inc.; *U.S. Public*, pg. 1312

WHOLESOME ACCENTS—NONE—Cookie Tree Inc.; *U.S. Private*, pg. 273

WHOPPER—Burger—Burger King Corporation; *Int'l*, pg. 411

WHOPPERS—Malted Milk Balls; Candy—Huhtamaki Oy; *Int'l*, pg. 638

WHO'S NEWS—Column Heading—Dow Jones & Company, Inc.; *U.S. Public*, pg. 524

WHYTE & MACKAY—Scotch Whisky—Lonrho plc; *Int'l*, pg. 817

WHYTE & MACKAY SPECIAL RESERVE—Blended Scotch Whisky—The Whyte & Mackay Group Plc; *U.S. Public*, pg. 675

WHYTE & MACKAY SPECIAL RESERVE—Blended Scotch Whiskey—Fortune Brands, Inc.; *U.S. Public*, pg. 674

WICHITA—Air Clutches & Brakes—Warner Electric Industrial Products Division; *U.S. Public*, pg. 480

WICHITA BUSINESS JOURNAL—Business Journal—Business First of New York, Inc.; *U.S. Private*, pg. 19

THE WICHITA EAGLE—Newspaper—The Wichita Eagle and Beacon Publishing Co., Inc.; *U.S. Public*, pg. 964

WICK FOWLER'S—2-Alarm Chili—Reily Foods Company; *U.S. Private*, pg. 919

WICKERBORD—Hardboard—Georgia-Pacific Corporation; *U.S. Public*, pg. 735

WICKES LUMBER—NONE—Wickes Inc.; *U.S. Public*, pg. 1391

WICKFORD—Weather Instrument—Swift Instruments, Inc.; *U.S. Private*, pg. 1058

WICKMAN—Diamond/Borazon Wheels, Hones—The Wickman Corp.; *U.S. Private*, pg. 1175

WICKS 'N' STICKS—Retail Candle Stores—Wicks 'n Sticks, Ltd; *U.S. Private*, pg. 1175

WICO—Amusement & Vending Supplies—WICO; *U.S. Private*, pg. 1144

WICU—Insulated Tubes—KM-Europa Metal Aktiengesellschaft; *Int'l*, pg. 719

WIDDER—Cutting Tools—Rule Industries, Inc.; *U.S. Public*, pg. 950

THE WIDE BODY BURGER—Hamburger Patties—Harker's Distribution, Inc.; *U.S. Private*, pg. 502

WIDE GLIDE—Motorcycles—Harley-Davidson, Inc.; *U.S. Public*, pg. 786

WIDE-LITE—NONE—The Genlyte Group Incorporated; *U.S. Public*, pg. 729

WIDE/PLY—Spiral Tubes—Sonoco Products Company; *U.S. Public*, pg. 1485

WIDE TRAK—Ironing Board—Magla Products; *U.S. Private*, pg. 695

WIDESIDE—Fabrics—Herculite Products, Inc.; *U.S. Public*, pg. 802

WIDESIDES—Fender Extenders—Lund International Holdings; *U.S. Public*, pg. 1020

WIDETRACK BIG BAJA—Tires—Bridgestone/Firestone, Inc.; *Int'l*, pg. 213

WIDETRACK DRIVE—Tires—Bridgestone/Firestone, Inc.; *Int'l*, pg. 213

WIDETRACK RADIAL—Tires—Bridgestone/Firestone, Inc.; *Int'l*, pg. 213

WIDETRACK RADIAL BAJA—Tires—Bridgestone/Firestone, Inc.; *Int'l*, pg. 213

WIDETRACK RADIAL GT—Tires—Bridgestone/Firestone, Inc.; *Int'l*, pg. 213

WIDETRACK RADIAL S/R—Tires—Bridgestone/Firestone, Inc.; *Int'l*, pg. 213

WIDETRACK RIB—Tires—Bridgestone/Firestone, Inc.; *Int'l*, pg. 213

WIDETRACK RIB L/P—Tires—Bridgestone/Firestone, Inc.; *Int'l*, pg. 213

WIDETRACK STEEL BELTED 70—Tires—Bridgestone/Firestone, Inc.; *Int'l*, pg. 213

WIDETRACK SUPER—Tires—Bridgestone/Firestone, Inc.; *Int'l*, pg. 213

WIDETRACK SUPER THING—Tires—Bridgestone/Firestone, Inc.; *Int'l*, pg. 213

WIDEWALL—Fiber Glass Plastic Continuous Flat Sheet—Molded Fiber Glass Companies; *U.S. Private*, pg. 755

WIDGET—Scraper & Cutter—The Gillette Company; *U.S. Public*, pg. 743

WIDMANN—NONE—Schottenstein Stores Corporation; *U.S. Private*, pg. 972

WIDMER'S—Wine—Widmer's Wine Cellars, Inc.; *U.S. Public*, pg. 300

WIDMER'S—Wines—Canandaigua Wine Company, Inc.; *U.S. Public*, pg. 300

WIECKSE WITTE—White Beer—Heineken N.V.; *Int'l*, pg. 608

WIEJSKE WYROBY—Polish Pickles—Campbell Sales; *U.S. Public*, pg. 299

WIENIE PAK—Casing—Devro-Teepak, Inc.; *Int'l*, pg. 408

WIGGLE N' GIGGLE—Action Game—Mattel Games/Puzzles; *U.S. Public*, pg. 1058

WIGRAINE—Pharmaceutical—Organon Inc.; *Int'l*, pg. 48

WIGWAM—Foodservice Items—Performance Food Group Company; *U.S. Public*, pg. 1278

WIGWAM—Socks & Knit Headwear—Wigwam Mills, Inc.; *U.S. Private*, pg. 1175

WIKTOR—Stent—Medtronic, Inc.; *U.S. Public*, pg. 1082

WIL-CREAM—Porcelain & Ceramic Alloys—Williams Advanced Materials, Inc.; *U.S. Public*, pg. 266

WILBUR & WILLIAMS—Industrial Maintenance Coatings—California Products Corp.; *U.S. Private*, pg. 201

WILBUR COON—Shoes—P.W. Minor & Son, Inc.; *U.S. Private*, pg. 751

WILBUR-ELLIS—Agricultural Chemicals—Wilbur-Ellis Company & Connell Brothers Company; *U.S. Private*, pg. 1175

WILCH—NONE—Grindmaster Corporation; *U.S. Private*, pg. 482

WILD ASIA—Area Rugs & Broadloom—Couristan Inc.; *U.S. Private*, pg. 279

WILD BERRY WHEAT—Beer—The F.X. Matt Brewing Co.; *U.S. Private*, pg. 714

WILD BERRY ZINGER—Herb Tea—Celestial Seasonings; *U.S. Public*, pg. 319

WILD BUNCH—Fruit Flavored Soft Drinks—PepsiCo, Inc.; *U.S. Public*, pg. 1276

WILD BUNCH—Boys' Wear—Tootal Group plc; *Int'l*, pg. 300

WILD CAT—Twist Tobacco—Conwood Company L.P.; *U.S. Private*, pg. 272

WILD CHERRY—Sparkling Mineral Water—Clearly Canadian Beverage Corp.; *Int'l*, pg. 297

WILD DUCK—Handbags—C.R. Daniels, Inc.; *U.S. Private*, pg. 310

WILD FOREST BLACKBERRY—Herb Tea—Celestial Seasonings; *U.S. Public*, pg. 319

WILD IRISH ROSE—Wines—Canandaigua Wine Company, Inc.; *U.S. Public*, pg. 300

WILD NUMBER—NONE—Stuart Entertainment Inc.; *U.S. Public*, pg. 1526

THE WILD PAIR—Shoes—Edison Brothers Stores, Inc.; *U.S. Public*, pg. 563

WILD RAIN—Men's Cologne—The Gillette Company; *U.S. Public*, pg. 743

WILD RICE—Shoes for Women—Topline Imports, Inc.; *U.S. Private*, pg. 1091

WILD THINGS—Stationery Products—The Mead Corporation; *U.S. Public*, pg. 1074

WILD TURKEY—Bourbon Whiskey—Groupe Pernod Ricard; *Int'l*, pg. 566

WILD TURKEY—Bourbon Whiskey—Austin Nichols & Co. Inc.; *Int'l*, pg. 566

WILD TURKEY BOURBON—Bourbon—Heublein, Inc.; *Int'l*, pg. 410

WILD WEST—Periodical—Cowles Enthusiast Media, Inc.; *U.S. Private*, pg. 281

WILD'N RARE—Preserves—Harry and David; *Int'l*, pg. 1518

WILDCAT—Power Tools—The Black & Decker Corporation; *U.S. Public*, pg. 233

WILDCAT—Scissor Lifts—Snorkel; *U.S. Private*, pg. 500

WILDCATS—Shoes—Brown Group, Inc.; *U.S. Public*, pg. 262

WILDE—Sauces—Refinerias de Maiz S.A.I.C.F.; *U.S. Public*, pg. 448

WILDERNESS—Fillings & Toppings—Comstock Michigan Fruit; *U.S. Private*, pg. 887

WILDERNESS—Travel Trailers—Fleetwood Enterprises, Inc.; *U.S. Public*, pg. 650

WILDERNESS—Footgear—Wolverine World Wide, Inc.; *U.S. Public*, pg. 1775

WILDERNESS GRILL—Restaurant & Dining Experience—Ogden Corporation; *U.S. Public*, pg. 1213

WILDLIFE—Paneling—Weyerhaeuser Forest Products Company; *U.S. Public*, pg. 1764

WILEY—Cranes—AmClyde Engineered Products Co., Inc.; *U.S. Public*, pg. 778

WILEY—Audio Cassettes, Computer Programs, Books—John Wiley & Sons, Inc.; *U.S. Public*, pg. 1768

WILEY CPA EXAMINATION REVIEW—Audio Cassettes, Computer Programs, Books—John Wiley & Sons, Inc.; *U.S. Public*, pg. 1768

WILEY PROFESSORS' RESOURCE PROGRAM—Books—John Wiley & Sons, Inc.; *U.S. Public*, pg. 1768

WILFLEX—Silk-Screen Ink for Textiles—Flexible Products Company; *U.S. Private*, pg. 412

WILHOLD—Hair Accessories—Wilhold Inc.; *U.S. Public*, pg. 78

WILKERSON—Instrumentation—Associated Process Controls; *U.S. Private*, pg. 92

WILKINSON—Razor Blades—Warner-Lambert Shaving Products Group; *U.S. Public*, pg. 1739

WILKINSON SWORD—NONE—Fiskars Oy AB; *Int'l*, pg. 492

WILL & BAMUER—Candles & Related Access.—Will & Baumer Incorporated; *U.S. Private*, pg. 1176

WILL-BURT—Masts, Telescoping, Stokers—The Will-Burt Company; *U.S. Private*, pg. 1177

WILL COUNTY (IL) BUSINESS DIRECTORY—Directory—Manufacturers' News, Inc.; *U.S. Private*, pg. 700

WILL-DO—Concentrated Mildew Cleaner—Stanhome Inc.; *U.S. Public*, pg. 1508

WILLCOX & GIBBS—Industrial Sewing Machines, Equipment & Accessories—Rexel, Inc.; *Int'l*, pg. 1107

WILLIAM ADAMS—Tableware—Waterford Wedgwood UK Plc; *Int'l*, pg. 1487

WILLIAM FISHER—NONE—Fischer Packing Co.; *Int'l*, pg. 201

WILLIAM HARVEY—Membrane Oxygenator—C.R. Bard, Inc.; *U.S. Public*, pg. 189

WILLIAM HILL CALIFORNIA—Wine—The Wine Alliance; *Int'l*, pg. 63

WILLIAM HOUSE—Greeting Cards, Business Envelopes & School Supplies—Williamhouse-Regency, Inc.; *U.S. Public*, pg. 89

WILLIAM LAWSON'S—NONE—Bacardi-Martini Belgium; *U.S. Private*, pg. 109

WILLIAM M. MERCER—Employee Benefits Services—Marsh & McLennan Companies, Inc.; *U.S. Public*, pg. 1048

WILLIAM MORROW & COMPANY, INC.—Books—The Hearst Corporation; *U.S. Private*, pg. 515

WILLIAM PENN—Blended Whiskey—Laird & Company; *U.S. Private*, pg. 642

WM. ROGERS & SON—Flatware—Syratech Corporation; *U.S. Public*, pg. 1060

WILLIAM SAURIN—Ready-to-Serve Dishes—Danone Group; *Int'l*, pg. 379

WILLIAMS—Body Care Products—Sara Lee Corporation; *U.S. Public*, pg. 1432

WILLIAMS—Men's Toiletries—SmithKline Beecham Corporation; *Int'l*, pg. 1264

WILLIAMS—Shaving Products, Cosmetics—SmithKline Beecham plc; *Int'l*, pg. 1264

WILLIAMS—Breads—United States Bakery; *U.S. Private*, pg. 1124

WILLIAMS—Arcade Games—WMS Industries Inc.; *U.S. Public*, pg. 1727

WILLIAMS—Pinball Games—Williams Electronics Games, Inc.; *U.S. Public*, pg. 1727

WILLIAM'S—Seasonings—Williams Foods Inc.; *U.S. Private*, pg. 1178

WILLIAMS-SONOMA—Grande Cuisine—Williams-Sonoma, Inc.; *U.S. Public*, pg. 1770

WILLIAMS-SONOMA GUIDE TO GOOD COOKING—NONE—Broderbund Software, Inc.; *U.S. Public*, pg. 258

WILLIAMS THE SHOEMEN—Family Shoe Stores—Woolworth Corporation; *U.S. Public*, pg. 1777

WILLIAMS THE SHOEMEN—Family Shoe Stores—F.W. Woolworth Co.; *U.S. Public*, pg. 1777

WILLIAMSBURG—Meat Products—Gwaltney of Smithfield, Ltd.; *U.S. Public*, pg. 1479

WILLIAMSBURG—Paints—Sherwin-Williams Consumer Brands Division; *U.S. Public*, pg. 1466

WILLIAMSBURG—Offset Printing Papers—Union Camp Corporation; *U.S. Public*, pg. 1665

WILLIE G'S—Restaurant Chain—Landry's Seafood Restaurants Inc.; *U.S. Public*, pg. 977

WILLOUGHBY'S—Cameras, Binoculars—Willoughby's; *U.S. Private*, pg. 1180

WILLOWBROOK FARMS—Poultry Items—Louis Kemp Seafood Co.; *U.S. Public*, pg. 1652

WILLOWBROOK FARMS—Poultry Items—Tyson Foods, Inc.; *U.S. Public*, pg. 1652

WILLSON—Safety Products—WGM Safety Corporation; *Int'l*, pg. 462

WILLY WATER BUG—Toy—Mattel, Inc.; *U.S. Public*, pg. 1057

WILLY WONKA—Candy—Nestle S.A.; *Int'l*, pg. 915

WILLY WONKA'S—Chocolate—Nestle USA; *Int'l*, pg. 916

WILLY WONKA'S DINASOUR EGGS—NONE—Nestle USA; *Int'l*, pg. 916

WILLY WONKA'S DWEEBS—NONE—Nestle USA; *Int'l*, pg. 916

WILLY WONKA'S FIZZY BOTTLE CAPS—NONE—Nestle USA; *Int'l*, pg. 916

WILLY WONKA'S GOBSTOPPERS—NONE—Nestle USA; *Int'l*, pg. 916

WILLY WONKA'S HEART BREAKERS—NONE—Nestle USA; *Int'l*, pg. 916

WILLY WONKA'S MIX UPS—NONE—Nestle USA; *Int'l*, pg. 916

WILLY WONKA'S NERDS—NONE—Nestle USA; *Int'l*, pg. 916

WILLY WONKA'S RUNTS—NONE—Nestle USA; *Int'l*, pg. 916

WILLY WONKA'S SWEET & SOUR HEARTS—NONE—Nestle USA; *Int'l*, pg. 916

WILLY WONKA'S TANGY BUNNYS—NONE—Nestle USA; *Int'l*, pg. 916

WILLY WONKA'S TART'N TINYS—NONE—Nestle USA; *Int'l*, pg. 916

WILLY WONKA'S WACKY WAFERS—NONE—Nestle USA; *Int'l*, pg. 916

WILMER ONE-WRITE PEGBOARD—Accounting Systems—The Reynolds and Reynolds Company; *U.S. Public*, pg. 1384

WILSEARCH—Software for Direct Patron Access—The H.W. Wilson Co.; *U.S. Private*, pg. 1180

WILSON—Color Concentrates, Dispersion Agents—Akzo Nobel Inc.; *Int'l*, pg. 47

WILSON—Tennis, Golf & Team Sports Equipment—Amer Group Ltd.; *Int'l*, pg. 72

WILSON—Worldwide Air & Sea Freight—BTL AB; *Int'l*, pg. 123

WILSON—Clinical Stainless Steel Accessories—Getinge/Castle Inc.; *Int'l*, pg. 551

WILSON—Test Blocks and Brales—Wilson/Shore Instruments; *U.S. Public*, pg. 883

WILSON COLOR—Color Additive Concentrates—M.A. Hanna Company; *U.S. Public*, pg. 780

WILSON INNS—Limited Service Hotels—Kemmons Wilson, Inc.; *U.S. Private*, pg. 613

WILSON JONES—Stapler—ACCO Brands, Inc.; *U.S. Public*, pg. 674

WILSON JONES—Loose-Leaf Binders & Columnar Pads—ACCO World Corporation; *U.S. Public*, pg. 674

WILSON JONES—Binders, Indexes, Business Forms & Shredders—Fortune Brands, Inc.; *U.S. Public*, pg. 674

WILSON/MOURAN—NONE—Sadia Group; *Int'l*, pg. 1168

WILSON PUBLICATIONS—Publishing—PCI; *U.S. Private*, pg. 826

WILSON-SNYDER—Pumps—Flowserve Corporation; *U.S. Public*, pg. 658

WILSON-SNYDER PUMPS—Pumps—BW/IP International, Inc.; *U.S. Public*, pg. 658

WILSON WORLDS—Full Service Hotels—Kemmons Wilson, Inc.; *U.S. Private*, pg. 613

WILSON'S—Supermarkets—Hannaford Bros. Co.; *U.S. Public*, pg. 781

WILSONART—Decorative Plastic Laminate—Premark International, Inc.; *U.S. Public*, pg. 1321

WILSONDISC—CD-ROM Retrieval System—The H.W. Wilson Co.; *U.S. Private*, pg. 1180

WILSONDOC—Document Delivery Service—The H.W. Wilson Co.; *U.S. Private*, pg. 1180

WILSONLINE—Online Retrieval System—The H.W. Wilson Co.; *U.S. Private*, pg. 1180

WILSONTAPE—Database Licencing Service—The H.W. Wilson Co.; *U.S. Private*, pg. 1180

WILSONWEB—Web Site Delivery Service—The H.W. Wilson Co.; *U.S. Private*, pg. 1180

WILTON ENTERPRISES—Baking & Decorating Products—Wilton Industries, Inc.; *U.S. Private*, pg. 1181

WILTRON—Electronic Test Instruments, Systems & Components—Wiltron Company; *Int'l*, pg. 77

WILTSHIRE—Knives—McPherson's Limited; *Int'l*, pg. 852

WIMBLEDON—Radio Networks—CRN International, Inc.; *U.S. Private*, pg. 197

WIMS—NONE—Landmark Graphics Corporation; *U.S. Public*, pg. 776

WIMZEES—Casual Footwear—Wolverine World Wide, Inc.; *U.S. Public*, pg. 1775

WIN—Nozzle—The Dow Chemical Company; *U.S. Public*, pg. 522

WIN-CODE—NONE—Stuart Entertainment Inc.; *U.S. Public*, pg. 1526

WIN COM—Electrical Connectors—Litton Industries, Inc.; *U.S. Public*, pg. 1002

WIN-PIN—Electrical Connectors—Litton Industries, Inc.; *U.S. Public*, pg. 1002

WIN, PLACE & SHOW—Game—Monarch Avalon, Inc.; *U.S. Public*, pg. 1123

WIN YOU—Pie Fillings—Clements Foods Co.; *U.S. Private*, pg. 245

WIN-OS/2—Computer Product—International Business Machines Corporation; *U.S. Public*, pg. 895

WINADOL—NONE—SmithKline Beecham Research Limited; *Int'l*, pg. 1266

WINALOT PRIME—Pet Food—Dalgety Plc; *Int'l*, pg. 376

WINCAIRS—Computer Aided Inspection Reporting System for Windows—Oceaneering International, Inc.; *U.S. Public*, pg. 1211

WINCANTON—Transportation & Distribution—Unigate PLC; *Int'l*, pg. 1433

WINCENTER PRO—Software—Network Computing Devices, Inc.; *U.S. Public*, pg. 1168

WINCHESTER—NONE—Fire King International, Inc.; *U.S. Private*, pg. 406

WINCHESTER—Civil Shotgun & Ammunition—Herstal S.A.; *Int'l*, pg. 617

WINCHESTER—Ammunition—Olin Corporation; *U.S. Public*, pg. 1218

WINCHESTER—Electronics—Winchester Electronics; *U.S. Public*, pg. 1003

WINCHESTER ELECTRONICS—Electrical Connectors—Litton Industries, Inc.; *U.S. Public*, pg. 1002

WINCO—Generators & Accessories—WINCO; *U.S. Private*, pg. 350

WIND—French Sailing Magazine—EMAP France; *Int'l*, pg. 451

WIND DANCER—Spring Horses—Hedstrom Corporation; *U.S. Private*, pg. 526

WIND JAMMER—Air Deflector—Lund International Holdings, Inc.; *U.S. Public*, pg. 1020

WIND RIDGE—Hardboard Siding—Georgia-Pacific Corporation; *U.S. Public*, pg. 735

WIND RIVER—Hats—Bailey Hats; *U.S. Private*, pg. 155

WIND RIVER SYSTEMS—NONE—Wind River Systems, Inc.; *U.S. Public*, pg. 1770

WIND SONG—Fragrance—Parfums De Coeur Ltd.; *U.S. Private*, pg. 839

THE WINDCURRENT COLLECTION—Giftware—Custom Decor, Inc.; *U.S. Private*, pg. 298

WINDERMATE—Roll Structure Control System—Harnischfeger Industries, Inc.; *U.S. Public*, pg. 788

WINDEX—Glass Cleaner—Bristol-Myers Squibb Company; *U.S. Public*, pg. 253

WINDEX—Cleaners—S.C. Johnson & Son, Inc.; *U.S. Private*, pg. 592

WINDEX—Window Cleaner—S.C. Johnson & Son, Limited; *U.S. Private*, pg. 593

WINDFALL BOOKS—Book Imprint—Bertelsmann AG; *Int'l*, pg. 189

WINDGUARD—NONE—Elcor Corporation; *U.S. Public*, pg. 567

WINDHAM CUSHION COLLECTION—Aluminum Outdoor Cushion Furniture—Telescope Casual Furniture, Inc.; *U.S. Private*, pg. 1074

WINDHAM STRAP COLLECTION—Aluminum Outdoor Strap Furniture—Telescope Casual Furniture, Inc.; *U.S. Private*, pg. 1074

WINDJAMMER—Blowers—AMETEK, Inc.; *U.S. Public*, pg. 99

WINDJAMMER—Marine Flotation Line—Stearns Manufacturing Company; *U.S. Public*, pg. 940

WINDMASTER—Curb Displays—Marketing Displays International; *U.S. Private*, pg. 705

WINDMERE—Personal Care Products—Windmere-Durable Holdings; *U.S. Public*, pg. 1771

WINDMILL—Bread—Ranks Hovis McDougall Limited; *Int'l*, pg. 1395

WINDO-WELD—Auto Window Sealers & Primer, Sealant—3M; *U.S. Public*, pg. 1604

WINDOGRAF—Portable Recorder; Includes Real Time Monitor and Disk Storage—Gould Instrument Systems, Inc.; *U.S. Public*, pg. 1592

WINDOLENE—Window Cleaners—Reckitt & Colman plc; *Int'l*, pg. 1089

WINDOW—NONE—Alliance Semiconductor Corp.; *U.S. Public*, pg. 47

WINDOW—Automated Signal Level Meter System—ComSonics, Inc.; *U.S. Private*, pg. 260

WINDOW CLEAR—Window Cleaner—Blue Cross Laboratories; *U.S. Private*, pg. 152

WINDOW IDEAS—Drapery/Window Stores—Montgomery Ward & Co., Inc.; *U.S. Private*, pg. 758

WINDOW SELLER—Marketing Software—Complast, Inc.; *U.S. Private*, pg. 259

WINDOW SYSTEM II—Screen & Storm Window Kits—Macklanburg-Duncan Co.; *U.S. Private*, pg. 692

WINDOW VISIONS—Wood Windows—Lindal Cedar Homes, Inc.; *U.S. Public*, pg. 998

WINDOW WORKS—NONE—Swish Products Ltd.; *Int'l*, pg. 925

WINDOWLITE INSTALLER—Signal Level Meter—ComSonics, Inc.; *U.S. Private*, pg. 260

WINDOWLITE PLUS—Automated Signal Level Meter System with Modularity—ComSonics, Inc.; *U.S. Private*, pg. 260

WINDOWS—Greeting Card—Hallmark Cards, Inc.; *U.S. Private*, pg. 495

WINDOWS—Computer Operating System—Microsoft Corporation; *U.S. Public*, pg. 1107

WINDOWS BEAUTIFUL—Publication—Kirsch; *U.S. Public*, pg. 1176

WINDOWS MAGAZINE—Magazine—CMP Media, Inc.; *U.S. Public*, pg. 279

WINDOWS '95—Computer Operating System—Microsoft Corporation; *U.S. Public*, pg. 1107

WINDOWTOOL—Computer Product—International Business Machines Corporation; *U.S. Public*, pg. 895

WINDRIFT—Nominal 4″ Sculptured Glazed Surface with a Matte Finish—United States Ceramic Tile Co.; *U.S. Private*, pg. 1124

WINDRIFT REFLECTIONS—Nominal 4″ Sculptured Glazed Surface with a Bright Glaze Finish—United States Ceramic Tile Co.; *U.S. Private*, pg. 1124

WINDSOR—Faucets, Valves & Fittings—The Black & Decker Corporation; *U.S. Public*, pg. 233

WINDSOR—Blended Canadian Whiskey—Fortune Brands, Inc.; *U.S. Public*, pg. 674

WINDSOR—Injection Molding Machines—Klockner-Werke AG; *Int'l*, pg. 736

WINDSOR CASTLE—Table Salt—Morton International Inc.; *U.S. Public*, pg. 1134

WINDSOR WALKERS—Men's Shoes—E.J. Footwear Corp.; *U.S. Public*, pg. 1684

WINDSPOILER—Premium Design Wiper Blades—Trico Products Corporation; *Int'l*, pg. 1397

WINDSTAR—Mini-Van—Ford Motor Company; *U.S. Public*, pg. 661

WINDSTAR CRUISES—Cruise Line—Carnival Corporation; *U.S. Public*, pg. 306

WINDSTONE—Book Imprint—Bertelsmann AG; *Int'l*, pg. 189

WINDSURFER—Computer Product—International Business Machines Corporation; *U.S. Public*, pg. 895

WINDSWEPT—Women's Fragrance—Avon Products, Inc.; *U.S. Public*, pg. 155

WINDTUNNEL—Upright Vacuum Cleaner—Hoover Company; *U.S. Public*, pg. 1065

WINDWARD STRIP—Pre-Finished Strip—Bruce Hardwood Floors; *U.S. Public*, pg. 1634

WINE RACK—Off-License Liquor Stores—Whitbread PLC; *Int'l*, pg. 1498

WINELINE—Hose—The Goodyear Tire & Rubber Company; *U.S. Public*, pg. 752

WINFALL—NONE—Stuart Entertainment Inc.; *U.S. Public*, pg. 1526

WINFIELD—Locks—Masco Corporation; *U.S. Public*, pg. 1052

WINFIELD—Mens Apparel—The Richman Brothers Co.; *U.S. Public*, pg. 1777

WINFINIT—Graphics Interface Software—Chyron Corp.; *Int'l*, pg. 1372

WING—Mark—American Honda Motor Co., Inc. Motorcycle Division; *Int'l*, pg. 634

WING—Records—Philips Electronics N.V.; *Int'l*, pg. 1051

WING AND CIRCLE—Restaurant Logo—Consolidated Products, Inc.; *U.S. Public*, pg. 436

WING AND CIRCLE—Restaurant Logo—Steak 'n Shake, Inc.; *U.S. Public*, pg. 437

WING ELITE—Motorcycle—American Honda Motor Co., Inc. Motorcycle Division; *Int'l*, pg. 634

WING-FIL—Tire Filling Compound—The Goodyear Tire & Rubber Company; *U.S. Public*, pg. 752

WING NUT—Wire Connectors—Ideal Industries, Inc.; *U.S. Private*, pg. 557

WINGATE INN—NONE—HFS, Incorporated; *U.S. Public*, pg. 321

WINGCURE—Rubber Curing Agents—The Goodyear Tire & Rubber Company; *U.S. Public*, pg. 752

WINGCURE—Cure Blend For SBR—The Goodyear Tire & Rubber Company; *U.S. Public*, pg. 752

WINGERS—Hot Sauce—Van den Bergh Foods Company; *Int'l*, pg. 1436

WINGLOCK—NONE—Boon Edam Inc.; *Int'l*, pg. 202

WINGROAD—Car—Nissan Motor Co., Ltd.; *Int'l*, pg. 943

WINGS—Sunglasses—Bausch & Lomb Incorporated; *U.S. Public*, pg. 194

WINGS—Perfume—Giorgio Beverly Hills; *U.S. Public*, pg. 1331

WINGS—Leather Luggage & Accessories—Hartmann Luggage & Leather Goods Group; *U.S. Public*, pg. 261

WINGS—Incontinent Briefs—The Kendall Company; *U.S. Public*, pg. 1647

WINGS LUGGAGE—Luggage—Brown-Forman Corporation; *U.S. Public*, pg. 261

WINGS OF FIRE—Further-processed Poultry Items—Louis Kemp Seafood Co.; *U.S. Public*, pg. 1652

WINGS OF FIRE—Further-processed Poultry Items—Tyson Foods, Inc.; *U.S. Public*, pg. 1652

WINGSTAY—Rubber Antidegradants—The Goodyear Tire & Rubber Company; *U.S. Public*, pg. 752

WINGSTOP—Polymar Short Stop—The Goodyear Tire & Rubber Company; *U.S. Public*, pg. 752

WINGTACK—C-5 Hyrocarbon Resin—The Goodyear Tire & Rubber Company; *U.S. Public*, pg. 752

WINKLEMAN—NONE—Petrie Retail, Inc.; *U.S. Private*, pg. 858

WINKS—NONE—Alimentation Couche Tard Inc.; *Int'l*, pg. 57

WINLINER—Printers—Datasouth Computer Corporation; *U.S. Public*, pg. 267

WINLINER—Vacuum-Formed Liners—Hedwin Corporation; *Int'l*, pg. 1278

WINN-DIXIE—Grocery Stores—Winn-Dixie Stores, Inc.; *U.S. Public*, pg. 1771

WINNEBAGO—Motor Homes & Outdoor Prods.—Winnebago Industries, Inc.; *U.S. Public*, pg. 1772

WINNER—Cameras—Eastman Kodak Company; *U.S. Public*, pg. 550

Brand Name Index

WINNERS APPAREL LTD.—Off-Price Family Apparel Retailer in Canada—The TJX Companies, Inc.; *U.S. Public*, pg. 1556

WINNERS CIRCLE—Sales Awards—ERA Real Estate; *U.S. Public*, pg. 321

WINNIE THE POOH FOR DISNEY—Gloves, Mittens & Headwear—Heyman Corporation; *U.S. Private*, pg. 524

WINNING STREAK—NONE—Harrah's Entertainment, Inc.; *U.S. Public*, pg. 790

THE WINNIPEG SUN—Newspaper—Quebecor Inc.; *Int'l*, pg. 1075

WINNWELL—Hockey Products—Irwin Toy Ltd.; *Int'l*, pg. 688

WINONA—NONE—Winona Knits; *U.S. Private*, pg. 1183

WINPAK—Blow Molded Containers—Hedwin Corporation; *Int'l*, pg. 1278

WINPOWER—Tractor Driven Generators—Winpower Inc.; *U.S. Private*, pg. 350

WINRHO SD—Treatment for ITP & Suppresses Rh Isoimmunization—Nabi; *U.S. Public*, pg. 1148

WINS—Marine Navigation Services—Litton Industries, Inc.; *U.S. Public*, pg. 1002

WINSERVER—Computer System—Sequent Computer Systems, Inc.; *U.S. Public*, pg. 1459

WINSLOW—NONE—Giddings & Lewis Automation Technology; *Int'l*, pg. 1389

WINSLOW'S GOURMET—Coffee—New England Coffee Company; *U.S. Private*, pg. 792

WINSOM—Pasta Sauce—Borden, Inc.; *U.S. Private*, pg. 157

WINSOR WHITE—Side Chair—Vecta; *U.S. Private*, pg. 1038

WINSTAR—Safety System—Simplex Time Recorder Co.; *U.S. Private*, pg. 1002

WINSTON—Cigarettes—RJR Nabisco Holdings Corp.; *U.S. Public*, pg. 1354

WINSTON—Reg., Box, 100's & 100's Lts., Lts. 80's & 100's Box, Ultra Lts. Reg & 100—R.J. Reynolds Tobacco Company; *U.S. Public*, pg. 1355

WINSTON—Cigarettes—R.J. Reynolds Tobacco Intl., Inc.; *U.S. Public*, pg. 1355

WINSTON—Tires—Winston Tire Company; *U.S. Private*, pg. 514

WINSTON SELECT—Cigarettes—R.J. Reynolds Tobacco Company; *U.S. Public*, pg. 1355

WINSTON SELECT LIGHTS—Cigarettes—R.J. Reynolds Tobacco Company; *U.S. Public*, pg. 1355

WINTER HAVEN NEWS CHIEF—Newspapers—Shivers Trading & Operating Co.; *U.S. Private*, pg. 994

WINTER HILL—Natural Juices—Sundor Brands Inc.; *U.S. Public*, pg. 1331

WINTER LEGG'S—Hosiery—L'eggs Products, Inc.; *U.S. Public*, pg. 1434

WINTER MORN—Wood & Lumber Products—Georgia-Pacific Corporation; *U.S. Public*, pg. 735

WINTER START—Cold Weather Oil Conditioner—The Shaler Company; *U.S. Private*, pg. 786

WINTER WASSAIL—Beer—The F.X. Matt Brewing Co.; *U.S. Private*, pg. 714

WINTER WEAVE—Wood & Lumber Products—Georgia-Pacific Corporation; *U.S. Public*, pg. 735

WINTER WONDERLAND—Greeting Cards; Gift Wrap & Trim; Gift Boxes—American Greetings Corporation; *U.S. Public*, pg. 77

WINTERFEST—Holiday Beer, Stout Lager—Adolph Coors Company; *U.S. Public*, pg. 445

WINTERGARD—Comml. Freeze Protection Heater—Raychem Corporation; *U.S. Public*, pg. 1362

WINTERGARTEN—Peppermint & Apple Schnapps—Marie Brizard Wines & Spirits USA; *U.S. Private*, pg. 702

WINTERGREEN—Annual Ryegrass—Green Seed Co.; *U.S. Private*, pg. 477

WINTERKING—Rye—Green Seed Co.; *U.S. Private*, pg. 477

WINTERS CHOCOLATES—Chocolate—Boyer Candy Company Inc.; *U.S. Private*, pg. 162

WINTERSEAL—Cold Weather Clothing—Refrigiwear, Inc.; *U.S. Private*, pg. 917

WINTERVORST—NONE—Grolsch N.V.; *Int'l*, pg. 559

WINTERWEIGHTS—Apparel—Phillips-Van Heusen Corporation; *U.S. Public*, pg. 1291

WINTRISS—Safety Equip. for Punch Press Machines—Data Instruments, Inc.; *U.S. Private*, pg. 312

WIPE AWAY—Cleaner—James Austin Co.; *U.S. Private*, pg. 99

WIRE GLASS—Pattern Glass—AFG Industries, Inc.; *Int'l*, pg. 84

WIRE LOKT—Abrasive Discs & Locks—Gardner Abrasives; *U.S. Public*, pg. 1699

WIRE-LOKT—Abrasive Wheels & Discs—Litton Industries, Inc.; *U.S. Public*, pg. 1002

WIRE LUBE—Wire Pulling Lubricant—Ideal Industries, Inc.; *U.S. Public*, pg. 557

WIRE NUT—Wire Connectors—Ideal Industries, Inc.; *U.S. Public*, pg. 557

WIRE-O—Table Top Booklet Binding Machines—James Burn Intl.; *U.S. Public*, pg. 1506

WIRE-O—Machinery & Complete Binding Systems—Standex International Corporation; *U.S. Public*, pg. 1505

WIRE-WRAP—Wire-Wrapping Tools—Cooper Hand Tools; *U.S. Public*, pg. 444

WIRE-WRAP—Solderless Connection Equipment—Cooper Industries, Inc.; *U.S. Public*, pg. 442

WIRECO—Wire Rope—Wire Rope Corporation of America, Inc.; *U.S. Private*, pg. 1184

WIREFORMS BY JUNO—Lighting Fixtures—Juno Lighting, Inc.; *U.S. Public*, pg. 935

WIRELESS DESIGN & DEVELOPMENT—New-Product Tabloid—Reed Elsevier Business Information; *Int'l*, pg. 1095

WIRELESS NEATBOOK—Notebooks—The Mead Corporation; *U.S. Public*, pg. 1074

WIRELESS SYSTEMS DESIGN—Periodical—Penton Publishing, Inc.; *U.S. Public*, pg. 1306

WIRELESS WEEK—Weekly Newspaper for Cellular, PCS, Paging & Mobile Radio Industry—Reed Elsevier Business Information; *Int'l*, pg. 1095

WIRELESS WORLD—Publication for Communications Personnel—Intertec Publishing; *U.S. Public*, pg. 1327

WIRELINK—Automatic Connecting Devices—Maclean-Fogg Co.; *U.S. Private*, pg. 692

WIRELITE—Dairy Industry Case—Cannon Equipment; *Int'l*, pg. 646

WIREPLAY—Interactive Videogames Network—British Telecommunications plc; *Int'l*, pg. 222

WIREVISE—Automatic Connecting Device—Maclean-Fogg Co.; *U.S. Private*, pg. 692

WIREWORKS—NONE—USG Corporation; *U.S. Public*, pg. 1660

WIRUS—Wood Particle Board, Interior Doors & Windows—Pfleiderer Industrie GmbH Wirus-Werke Guetersloh; *Int'l*, pg. 1047

WIRUTEX—Malemine Faced Particle Board & Furniture Components—Pfleiderer Industrie GmbH Wirus-Werke Guetersloh; *Int'l*, pg. 1047

WIRY JOE—Automotive Harness, Battery Cable Leads & High Tension Ignition Cable—General Cable Corporation; *Int'l*, pg. 1486

WIS-TONE—Disposable Paper Products—Wisconsin Tissue Mills, Inc.; *U.S. Public*, pg. 347

WISARD—NONE—KLA Tencor Corporation; *U.S. Public*, pg. 939

WISCOFOLD—Disposable Paper Products—Wisconsin Tissue Mills, Inc.; *U.S. Public*, pg. 347

WISCOLD—PRW—Christiana Companies, Inc.; *U.S. Public*, pg. 352

WISCONSIN—Gasoline Engines—Harley Industries, Inc.; *U.S. Public*, pg. 880

WISCONSIN AGRICULTURIST—Farm Publication—Farm Progress Publications; *U.S. Public*, pg. 513

WISCONSIN CLUB—Beer—Joseph Huber Brewing Co., Inc.; *U.S. Private*, pg. 545

WISCONSIN LAND O'LAKES—Bond Paper—The Mead Corporation; *U.S. Public*, pg. 1074

WISCONSIN MANUFACTURERS REGISTER—Register—Manufacturers' News, Inc.; *U.S. Private*, pg. 700

WISCONSIN STATE JOURNAL—Newspaper—Madison Newspapers, Inc.; *U.S. Public*, pg. 984

WISDOM—Computer Programs—Eastman Kodak Company; *U.S. Public*, pg. 550

WISDOM—Marine Navigation Systems—Litton Industries, Inc.; *U.S. Public*, pg. 1002

WISDOM & WARTER—Sherry—Banfi Vintners; *U.S. Private*, pg. 113

WISE—Potato Chips & Related Products—Borden, Inc.; *U.S. Private*, pg. 157

WISE—Potato Chips—Wise Foods, Inc.; *U.S. Private*, pg. 157

WISE CHOICE—Premium Popcorn—Borden, Inc.; *U.S. Private*, pg. 157

WISER'S CANADIAN WHISKY—Spirit—Allied Domecq PLC; *Int'l*, pg. 62

WISH-BONE—Salad Dressings—Thomas J. Lipton Company; *Int'l*, pg. 1435

WISH-BONE LITE—Low-Calorie Salad Dressings—Thomas J. Lipton Company; *Int'l*, pg. 1435

WISH-BONE RANCH—Salad Dressing—Thomas J. Lipton Company; *Int'l*, pg. 1435

WISHING WELL—Stationery; Cards & Posters; Calendars; Photo Albums—American Greetings Corporation; *U.S. Public*, pg. 77

WISK—Detergent—Lever Brothers Co.; *Int'l*, pg. 1435

WISK—Detergent—Unilever Plc; *Int'l*, pg. 1433

WISMATIC—Metal Cutting Equipment & Machinery—Wisconsin Machine and Tool Corporation; *U.S. Private*, pg. 1185

WISMER SERIES 2—Investment Accounting & Portfolio Management System—SunGard Data Systems Inc.; *U.S. Public*, pg. 1534

WISP—Ladies & Childrens Clothes—Arnotts plc; *Int'l*, pg. 81

WISPA THINS—Polycarbonate Ophthalmic Lenses—Sterling Vision, Inc.; *U.S. Public*, pg. 1516

WISS—Snips and Scissors—Cooper Hand Tools; *U.S. Public*, pg. 444

WISS—Scissors, Shears & Snips—Cooper Industries, Inc.; *U.S. Public*, pg. 442

WISS—NONE—Cooper Tools; *U.S. Public*, pg. 444

WISSOLL—Grocery Store—Tengelmann Warenhandelsgesellschaft; *Int'l*, pg. 1375

WITCAMIDE—Alkanolamide—Witco Corporation; *U.S. Public*, pg. 1773

WITCH DOCTOR—Liquid, Pads, Stick, Gel—C. B. Fleet Co., Inc.; *U.S. Private*, pg. 410

WITCHOL—Alcohols—Witco Corporation; *U.S. Public*, pg. 1773

WITCO—Corrosion Inhibitors—Witco Corporation; *U.S. Public*, pg. 1773

WITCODET—Detergent Concentrates, Intermediates, Stearates, Organosulfonio Acids—Witco Corporation; *U.S. Public*, pg. 1773

WITE-OUT CORRECTION FLUIDS—NONE—BIC Corporation; *Int'l*, pg. 1273

WITH—Monthly General Interest Women's Magazine—Kodansha Ltd.; *Int'l*, pg. 742

WITHIN—Multivitamins With Calcium—Bayer Corporation/Consumer Care Division; *Int'l*, pg. 173

WITHSTAND—Paint—Pratt & Lambert United, Inc.; *U.S. Public*, pg. 1466

WIT'S END & DESIGN—Greeting Cards, Invits. & Anncmnts., Thank U Notes, Calenders, Party Goods—American Greetings Corporation; *U.S. Public*, pg. 77

WITTNAUER—Watches—Wittnauer International, Inc.; *U.S. Public*, pg. 273

WITWOT—Winder—Beloit Corporation; *U.S. Public*, pg. 789

WIX—Oil, Air, Fuel Filters—Dana Corporation; *U.S. Public*, pg. 479

WIX—Filters—Wix Div.; *U.S. Public*, pg. 479

WIZ BUCKS—Discount Coupons—Nobody Beats the Wiz; *U.S. Private*, pg. 800

WIZARD—Ink Compounds—Markem Corporation; *U.S. Private*, pg. 704

WIZARD—Pneumatic Pressure Controller—Monsanto Company; *U.S. Public*, pg. 1124

WIZARD—Room Deodorizer, Charcoal Lighter—Reckitt & Colman Inc.; *Int'l*, pg. 1090

WIZARD—Punch Laminator—Seal Products Incorporated; *U.S. Public*, pg. 849

WIZARD—Electronic Organizer—Sharp Electronics Corporation; *Int'l*, pg. 1228

WIZARD—Lawn & Garden Power Equipment—Western Auto Supply Company; *U.S. Public*, pg. 1452

WIZARD'S QUEST—Fantasy Game—Monarch Avalon, Inc.; *U.S. Public*, pg. 1123

WM. PENN—Cigars—General Cigar Company, Inc.; *U.S. Public*, pg. 708

WOBBLE—NONE—Astro Dairy Products Ltd.; *Int'l*, pg. 95
WOBBLE BLOCK—Visible Files—Knoll, Inc.; *U.S. Private*, pg. 627
WOLCO—NONE—Allen Canning Company; *U.S. Private*, pg. 36
WOLF—Food Equipment—Premark International, Inc.; *U.S. Public*, pg. 1321
WOLF BRAND—Chili, Hot Dog Sauce, Chili-Mac, Beef Stew, Tamales, Homestyle Chili Fixins—Wolf Brand Products; *U.S. Public*, pg. 428
WOLF BRAND CHILI—NONE—Hunt-Wesson, Inc.; *U.S. Public*, pg. 428
WOLF BRAND CHILI & TAMALES—Chili—The Quaker Oats Company; *U.S. Public*, pg. 1347
WOLF CREEK—Backpacks—JanSport; *U.S. Public*, pg. 1702
WOLF CREEK—Daypacks—VF Corporation; *U.S. Public*, pg. 1702
WOLF'S HEAD—Oil—Wolf's Head Oil Company; *U.S. Public*, pg. 1273
WOLFE—Biological Products—Carolina Biological Supply Co.; *U.S. Private*, pg. 213
WOLFERMAN—Bakery Products—Sara Lee Corporation; *U.S. Public*, pg. 1432
WOLFSCHMIDT—Vodka—Fortune Brands, Inc.; *U.S. Public*, pg. 674
WOLMANIT—Wood Preservative—BASF AG; *Int'l*, pg. 103
WOLMANIZED—Pressure-Treated Wood—Hickson Corporation; *Int'l*, pg. 619
WOLMANOL—Wood Preservative—BASF AG; *Int'l*, pg. 103
WOLOHAN—Lumber—Wolohan Lumber Co.; *U.S. Public*, pg. 1774
WOLVERINE—Oil & Gas Drilling & Exploration Services—Amerac Energy Corp.; *U.S. Public*, pg. 1490
WOLVERINE—NONE—CertainTeed Corporation; *Int'l*, pg. 1170
WOLVERINE—Hunting Wear—Duck Head Apparel; *U.S. Public*, pg. 498
WOLVERINE—Boots & Shoes—Wolverine World Wide, Inc.; *U.S. Public*, pg. 1775
WOMAN—Women's Weekly Magazine—IPC Magazines Limited; *Int'l*, pg. 651
WOMAN & HOME—Women's General Interest Magazine—IPC Magazines Limited; *Int'l*, pg. 651
WOMAN TO WOMAN—Greeting Cards—American Greetings Corporation; *U.S. Public*, pg. 77
WOMAN'S DAY—Women's Service Field Magazine—Hachette Filipacchi Magazines Inc.; *Int'l*, pg. 794
WOMAN'S DAY—Magazine—Woman's Day; *Int'l*, pg. 795
WOMAN'S DAY SPECIALS—Women's Magazine—Hachette Filipacchi Magazines Inc.; *Int'l*, pg. 794
WOMAN'S JOURNAL—Fashion & Beauty Magazine—IPC Magazines Limited; *Int'l*, pg. 651
WOMAN'S OWN—Women's Weekly Magazine—IPC Magazines Limited; *Int'l*, pg. 651
WOMAN'S REALM—Women's Weekly Magazine—IPC Magazines Limited; *Int'l*, pg. 651
A WOMAN'S TOUCH—Greeting Cards—American Greetings Corporation; *U.S. Public*, pg. 77
WOMAN'S WEEKLY—Women's Weekly Magazine—IPC Magazines Limited; *Int'l*, pg. 651
WOMEN & GOLF—Sports Magazine—IPC Magazines Limited; *Int'l*, pg. 651
WOMEN'S HEALTH BOUTIQUE—Health Care Needs—International Center for Entrepreneurial Development, Inc.; *U.S. Private*, pg. 568
WOMEN'S CIRCLE—General Interest Publication—House of White Birches, Inc.; *U.S. Private*, pg. 542
WOMEN'S HISTORY—NONE—Cowles Enthusiast Media, Inc.; *U.S. Private*, pg. 281
WOMEN'S HOUSEHOLD CROCHET—Crafts Publications—House of White Birches, Inc.; *U.S. Private*, pg. 542
WOMEN'S WEAR DAILY—Business Publication—Fairchild Publications; *U.S. Public*, pg. 513
WON TON—Won Ton Soup—Maruchan Inc.; *U.S. Private*, pg. 710
WONDER—Rice—American Rice Inc.; *U.S. Public*, pg. 591

WONDER—Bread—Interstate Brands Corporation; *U.S. Public*, pg. 909
WONDER—Batteries (French)—Ralston Purina Company; *U.S. Public*, pg. 1359
WONDER—Toys—Strombecker Corporation; *U.S. Private*, pg. 1047
WONDER—Baked Goods—George Weston Limited; *Int'l*, pg. 1494
WONDER BASE—Acrylic Wallcovering Primer—Wm. Zinsser & Co., Inc.; *U.S. Public*, pg. 1358
WONDER BOND—Adhesive—Borden, Inc.; *U.S. Private*, pg. 157
WONDER BOND—Bonding Coat—Devoe Paint; *Int'l*, pg. 663
WONDER BOND—Bonding Coat—ICI Paints; *Int'l*, pg. 664
WONDER BOY—Videogame—Sega of America Inc.; *Int'l*, pg. 1218
WONDER BREADS—NONE—Weston Bakeries Limited; *Int'l*, pg. 1495
WONDER CUSHION—Gel Wheelchair Cushion—Graham-Field Health Products, Inc.; *U.S. Public*, pg. 757
WONDER FOAM—Polyurethane Expanding Foam—Ohio Sealants Inc.; *Int'l*, pg. 802
WONDER-GUARD—House & Masonry Paint—Devoe Paint; *Int'l*, pg. 663
WONDER GUARD—House & Masonry Paint—ICI Paints; *Int'l*, pg. 664
WONDER-HIDE—Interior Latex Semi-Gloss Enamel—Devoe Paint; *Int'l*, pg. 663
WONDER HIDE—Interior Latex Semi-Gloss Enamel—ICI Paints; *Int'l*, pg. 664
WONDER-PRIME—Interior Latex Primer-Sealer—Devoe Paint; *Int'l*, pg. 663
WONDER-PRUF—Waterproofing Coating—Devoe Paint; *Int'l*, pg. 663
WONDER-PRUF—Waterproofing Coating—ICI Paints; *Int'l*, pg. 664
WONDER-SHIELD—House Paint—Devoe Paint; *Int'l*, pg. 663
WONDER SHIELD—House Paint—Grow Group, Inc.; *Int'l*, pg. 663
WONDER SHIELD—House Paint—ICI Paints; *Int'l*, pg. 664
WONDER-SPEED—Interior Latex Paint—Devoe Paint; *Int'l*, pg. 663
WONDER-SPEED—Interior Latex Paint—ICI Paints; *Int'l*, pg. 664
WONDER-STICK—Wallcovering Adhesive & Primer—Devoe Paint; *Int'l*, pg. 663
WONDER-STICK—Wallcovering Adhesive & Primer—ICI Paints; *Int'l*, pg. 664
WONDER TINT—Colorants—Devoe Paint; *Int'l*, pg. 663
WONDER TINT—Colorants—ICI Paints; *Int'l*, pg. 664
WONDER-TONES—Interior Primer & Paint—Devoe Paint; *Int'l*, pg. 663
WONDER TONES—Interior Primer & Paint—ICI Paints; *Int'l*, pg. 664
WONDER TOOLS—NONE—Mattel, Inc.; *U.S. Public*, pg. 1057
WONDER WARE—Cookware—Regal Ware, Inc.; *U.S. Private*, pg. 917
WONDER-WICK—Socks & Knitted Headwear—Wigwam Mills, Inc.; *U.S. Private*, pg. 1175
WONDER WOODTONES—Wall Paint—Grow Group, Inc.; *Int'l*, pg. 663
WONDER WOODTONES—Wall Paint—ICI Paints; *Int'l*, pg. 664
WONDER-PRIME—Interior Latex Primer-Sealer—ICI Paints; *Int'l*, pg. 664
WONDERART—Craft Kits—Caron International; *U.S. Private*, pg. 786
WONDERBRA—Lingerie—Sara Lee Corporation; *U.S. Public*, pg. 1432
A WONDERFUL YEAR—NONE—American Greetings Corporation; *U.S. Public*, pg. 77
WONDERKLEEN—All Purpose Household Cleaners—Permark International (Pty.) Ltd.; *Int'l*, pg. 1036
WONDERLAWN—Grass Seed—Barenbrug Northeast; *Int'l*, pg. 167
WONDERLAWN GRASS & SEED FERTILIZER—NONE—Barenbrug Northeast; *Int'l*, pg. 167
WONDERLOOM—Fabric—E.R. Moore Co.; *U.S. Private*, pg. 759
WONDERS OF THE WILD—24% of Full Lead Crystal Animals—Princess House, Inc.; *U.S. Public*, pg. 399

WONDERSOFT—Facial Tissue, Disposable Household Towels, Bathroom Tissue—Kimberly-Clark Corporation; *U.S. Public*, pg. 958
WONDERWARE FACTORY SUITE—Suite of Industrial Automation Tools—Wonderware Corporation; *U.S. Public*, pg. 1775
WONDERWASH—Cleaning Products—Clayton Industries Co.; *U.S. Private*, pg. 245
WONDERWEAR—Control Briefs, Shapesuit—Olga Div.; *U.S. Public*, pg. 1738
WONDRA—Flour—General Mills, Inc.; *U.S. Public*, pg. 717
WONDRA—Skin Lotion—The Procter & Gamble Company; *U.S. Public*, pg. 1330
WOOD—Magazine—Meredith Corporation; *U.S. Public*, pg. 1094
WOOD ACE—Shrubbery & Potted Plant Fertilizer Mixes—IMC Agribusiness; *U.S. Public*, pg. 856
WOOD DRI—Semi Transparent Water Repellant Wood Stain—Perry & Derrick Co.; *U.S. Private*, pg. 854
WOOD ESSENCE—NONE—Amerimark Inc.; *U.S. Public*, pg. 1237
WOOD N' STREAM—Outdoor/Casual Shoes—Weinbrenner Shoe Company, Inc.; *U.S. Private*, pg. 1160
WOOD NU'N'LITE—Consumer Wood Cleaner & Brightner—ISK BioSciences; *Int'l*, pg. 689
WOOD PANELS—Medium Density Fiberboard, Particle Board- Raw, Vinyl & Melamine Overlays—California Panel & Veneer Company; *U.S. Private*, pg. 201
WOOD PLUS—Cleaner—The Dow Chemical Company; *U.S. Public*, pg. 522
WOOD PREEN—Floor Wax—Kiwi Brands; *U.S. Public*, pg. 1433
THE WOOD PRESERVER—Clear Wood Preservative—Star Bronze Company; *U.S. Private*, pg. 1034
WOOD PRO—Semi Transparent Wood Stain—Perry & Derrick Co.; *U.S. Private*, pg. 854
WOOD PRO TECH—Wood Preservation—Monsey-Bakor; *U.S. Private*, pg. 757
WOOD SLAT COLLECTION—Indoor/Outdoor Wood Furniture—Telescope Casual Furniture, Inc.; *U.S. Private*, pg. 1074
WOOD TECHNOLOGY—Magazine—Miller Freeman Inc.; *Int'l*, pg. 1443
WOOD TONE II STAIN—Stain—Mautz Paint Co.; *U.S. Private*, pg. 715
WOOD WINDOW FURNITURE—Wood Blinds—Wausau Metals, Nanik Division; *U.S. Public*, pg. 1500
WOODACE—Lawn Products—The Vigoro Corporation; *U.S. Public*, pg. 856
WOODARD—Wrought Iron, Contemporary Steel & Contemporary Aluminum—Woodard Inc.; *U.S. Private*, pg. 192
WOODBINE—Graphic Arts Papers—Appleton Papers Inc.; *Int'l*, pg. 567
WOODBINE—Cigarettes—Imperial Tobacco Group, Ltd.; *Int'l*, pg. 666
WOODBRIDGE BY ROBERT MONDAVI—NONE—Robert Mondavi Winery, Inc.; *U.S. Public*, pg. 1393
WOODBROOK VINEYARDS—Wines—Gibson Wine Company; *U.S. Private*, pg. 452
WOODBURY—Soap—The Andrew Jergens Company; *Int'l*, pg. 717
WOODBUXE—Men's Footwear—J. Baker, Inc.; *U.S. Public*, pg. 167
WOODCLASSICS—Office Furniture—DMI Furniture Inc.; *U.S. Public*, pg. 473
WOODCLIFF—Wood & Lumber Products—Georgia-Pacific Corporation; *U.S. Public*, pg. 735
WOODCRAFT—Pocket Knives—Camillus Cutlery Co.; *U.S. Private*, pg. 203
WOODCRAFT—Futon Frames & Accompanying Tables—Spectrum Industries, Inc.; *U.S. Private*, pg. 1024
WOODCRAFT—Wood products—Woodcraft Industries, Inc.; *U.S. Private*, pg. 1187
WOODEN SHIPS & IRON MEN—War Game—Monarch Avalon, Inc.; *U.S. Public*, pg. 1123
WOODFIELD SUITES—NONE—The Marcus Corporation; *U.S. Public*, pg. 1044
WOODFORD RESERVE—Bourbon Whiskey—Brown-Forman Beverages Worldwide; *U.S. Public*, pg. 261

Brand Name Index

WOODGLEN—Wood & Lumber Products—Georgia-Pacific Corporation; *U.S. Public*, pg. 735

WOODGLO—Hardwood Paneling—Weyerhaeuser Forest Products Company; *U.S. Public*, pg. 1764

WOODGREEN—Consumer Wood Preservative—ISK BioSciences; *Int'l*, pg. 689

WOODGUARD—Wood Preservative—ISK BioSciences; *Int'l*, pg. 689

WOODHUE—Luan Paneling—Weyerhaeuser Forest Products Company; *U.S. Public*, pg. 1764

WOODLAC—Insulation Board/Plastic Foam—The Dow Chemical Company; *U.S. Public*, pg. 522

WOODLAC-PANEL—Display Panel—The Dow Chemical Company; *U.S. Public*, pg. 522

WOODLAKE—Manufactured Homes—Champion Enterprises, Inc.; *U.S. Public*, pg. 332

WOODLAND FRIENDS—Calendars, Party Goods & Gift Wrap—American Greetings Corporation; *U.S. Public*, pg. 77

WOODLAND PANTRY—NONE—The Smithfield Companies, Inc.; *U.S. Public*, pg. 1479

WOODLANDS—Roof Shingles—Johns Manville Corporation; *U.S. Public*, pg. 927

WOODLIFE—Wood Preservative—DAP Inc.; *Int'l*, pg. 1486

WOODLINES—Horizontal Blinds—Springs Industries, Inc.; *U.S. Public*, pg. 1499

WOODLINK—Chain Link with Wood Slats Fencing—MMI Products, Inc.; *U.S. Private*, pg. 687

WOODLOK—Adhesive—Unilever Plc; *Int'l*, pg. 1433

WOODMAN'S—Sauces—International Multifoods Corporation; *U.S. Public*, pg. 900

WOODMAN'S—Condiments—Robin Hood Multifoods Inc.; *U.S. Public*, pg. 901

WOODMARK—Indoor Illuminated Sign Series—American Sign & Marketing Services, Inc.; *U.S. Public*, pg. 1309

WOODMARK ORIGINALS—Upholstered Furniture—Woodmark Originals Inc.; *U.S. Private*, pg. 747

WOODMASTER—Corrosion-Resistant Screws—Elco Textron; *U.S. Public*, pg. 1590

WOODMASTER—Interior Stains—ICI Paints; *Int'l*, pg. 664

WOODMASTER—Partitions—Modernfold, Inc.; *U.S. Private*, pg. 755

WOODMATE—Treated Wood & Deck Adhesive—Ohio Sealants Inc.; *Int'l*, pg. 802

WOODRIFT—Sporting Equipment—Brunswick Bowling & Billiards Corp.; *U.S. Public*, pg. 265

WOODSCAPE—Standards for Electric Lighting Fixtures—Weyerhaeuser Forest Products Company; *U.S. Public*, pg. 1764

WOODSCAPES—Do-It-Yourself Landscape Building Product—Weyerhaeuser Forest Products Company; *U.S. Public*, pg. 1764

WOODSEAL—Consumer Wood Preservative—ISK BioSciences; *Int'l*, pg. 689

WOODSENSE—Windows Having Wood Frames—Georgia-Pacific Corporation; *U.S. Public*, pg. 735

WOODSHADES—Pre-Stained Pressure Treated Wood—Osmose Wood Preserving, Inc.; *U.S. Private*, pg. 821

WOODSMAN—Land Clearing Machinery—Royer Industries, Inc.; *Int'l*, pg. 1066

WOODSTOCK'S—Wild Bird Feed—ConAgra, Inc.; *U.S. Public*, pg. 425

WOODSTREAM—Plastic Storage Containers: Tool Boxes, Tackle Boxes & Gun Cases—Ekco Group, Inc.; *U.S. Public*, pg. 566

WOODTECH—Coating Products—Columbia Paint & Coatings; *U.S. Private*, pg. 256

WOODTEX—NONE—CertainTeed Corporation; *Int'l*, pg. 1170

WOODTONE—Garage Doors—Wayne Dalton of Sterling; *U.S. Private*, pg. 1155

WOODTRIM—Wood Veneer Strips—DAP Inc.; *Int'l*, pg. 1486

WOODTUFF—Consumer Wood Protectant—ISK BioSciences; *Int'l*, pg. 689

WOODWELD—Pressed Wood Resins—Georgia-Pacific Corporation; *U.S. Public*, pg. 735

WOODWIND COMPANY—Mouthpieces—G. Leblanc Corporation; *U.S. Private*, pg. 656

WOODWORKER'S BOOK CLUB—NONE—F & W Publications, Inc.; *U.S. Private*, pg. 388

WOODWORKERS WAREHOUSE—Woodworking Catalog—Trend-Lines Inc.; *U.S. Private*, pg. 1099

WOODWORKS—Interior Wood Stain & Clear Finishes—Devoe Paint; *Int'l*, pg. 663

WOODY POP—Videogame—Sega of America Inc.; *Int'l*, pg. 1218

WOODY'S BBQ SAUCE—Barbeque Sauce—Reily Foods Company; *U.S. Public*, pg. 919

WOODY'S—Cheese—Churny Company Inc.; *U.S. Public*, pg. 1288

WOODZIG—Power Pruners—Blount International, Inc.; *U.S. Public*, pg. 237

WOOL-EASE—Yarn—Lion Brand Yarn Co.; *U.S. Private*, pg. 669

WOOL MIX—NONE—Kiwi Brands Pty. Ltd.; *U.S. Public*, pg. 1434

WOOLCO—Full-Line Promotional Department Stores—Woolworth Corporation; *U.S. Public*, pg. 1777

WOOLCO—Full Line Discount Stores—F.W. Woolworth Co.; *U.S. Public*, pg. 1777

WOOLITE—Carpet/Upholstery Cleaner—Playtex Products Inc.; *U.S. Private*, pg. 1310

WOOLITE—Fine Fabric Wash, Rug & Upholstery Cleaner—Reckitt & Colman Inc.; *Int'l*, pg. 1090

WOOLITE—Fine Fabric Wash—Reckitt & Colman plc; *Int'l*, pg. 1089

WOOL'N CARE—Cold Water Wash—Blue Cross Laboratories; *U.S. Private*, pg. 152

WOOLRICH—Mfr. Men's & Ladies' Sportswear—Woolrich, Inc.; *U.S. Private*, pg. 1188

WOOLSEY—Marine Coatings—RPM, Inc.; *U.S. Public*, pg. 1356

WOOLTONS—Mfr. of Curtains, Blinds—Lonrho plc; *Int'l*, pg. 817

WOOLWORTH—General Merchandise Stores—Woolworth Corporation; *U.S. Public*, pg. 1777

WOOLWORTH—Retail Gen. Mdse. Store—F.W. Woolworth Co.; *U.S. Public*, pg. 1777

WOOLWORTH EXPRESS—General Mdse. Convenience Stores—F.W. Woolworth Co.; *U.S. Public*, pg. 1777

WOOLWORTH EXPRESS/MINI SHOPS—General Mdse. Convenience Stores—Woolworth Corporation; *U.S. Public*, pg. 1777

WOOLWORTHS—Variety Stores—Kingfisher plc; *Int'l*, pg. 733

WOOSTER—NONE—The Wooster Brush Company; *U.S. Private*, pg. 1188

WOOSTER MAGIKOTER—NONE—The Wooster Brush Company; *U.S. Private*, pg. 1188

WORCESTER—Ball Valves & Actuators—Associated Process Controls; *U.S. Private*, pg. 92

WORD—Label—A&M Records; *Int'l*, pg. 1052

WORD—Computer Word Processing Software—Microsoft Corporation; *U.S. Public*, pg. 1107

WORD—Records & Books—Word, Incorporated; *U.S. Public*, pg. 704

WORD PALETTE—Greeting Cards—American Greetings Corporation; *U.S. Public*, pg. 77

WORD PORTRAITS—Greeting Cards—American Greetings Corporation; *U.S. Public*, pg. 77

WORD POWER—Game—Monarch Avalon, Inc.; *U.S. Public*, pg. 1123

WORD TANK—Endless Loop Recorder—Dictaphone Corp.; *U.S. Private*, pg. 1045

WORD YAHTZEE—Game—Milton Bradley Company; *U.S. Public*, pg. 797

WORDMANAGER—Advanced Word Processing Systems—Barrister Information Systems Corporation; *U.S. Public*, pg. 192

WORDMASTER—Thesaurus & Phonetic Speller—Franklin Electronic Publishers, Inc.; *U.S. Public*, pg. 679

WORDPERFECT—Computer Software—Corel Corporation; *Int'l*, pg. 331

WORDS OF FAITH—Greeting Cards—American Greetings Corporation; *U.S. Public*, pg. 77

WORDS ON CASSETTE—Guide to Audiocassette Collections—R.R. Bowker; *Int'l*, pg. 1096

WORK—Records—Sony Music Entertainment, Inc.; *Int'l*, pg. 1281

WORK HORSE—Packaging Machine—Exact Equipment Corporation; *U.S. Public*, pg. 387

WORK DAY—Super Comfort Insoles—Schering-Plough Corporation; *U.S. Public*, pg. 1438

WORK-FACTOR—Manufacturing Process Analysis System—Science Management Corporation; *U.S. Public*, pg. 1717

WORK FORCE EXPEDITION—Professional Apparel—Barco of California; *U.S. Private*, pg. 115

WORK HORSE—Canvas Truck—C.R. Daniels, Inc.; *U.S. Private*, pg. 310

WORK MANAGER—Office Furniture & Accessories—Rubbermaid Incorporated; *U.S. Public*, pg. 1411

WORK MASTER—Steel Commercial Pickup Caps—Gem Top Mfg., Inc.; *U.S. Private*, pg. 443

WORKBENCH—Reservoir Engineering Software—Scientific Software-Intercomp, Inc.; *U.S. Public*, pg. 1443

WORKBRUTES—PVC Over-The-Shoe Boots—Tingley Rubber Corporation; *U.S. Private*, pg. 1088

WORKDAY—Heavy Duty Insoles—Scholl U.S.A.; *U.S. Public*, pg. 1438

WORKFLO—NONE—FileNet Corporation; *U.S. Public*, pg. 622

WORKFLO/FAX—NONE—FileNet Corporation; *U.S. Public*, pg. 622

WORKFLO/PRINT—NONE—FileNet Corporation; *U.S. Public*, pg. 622

WORKFLO/SCAN—NONE—FileNet Corporation; *U.S. Public*, pg. 622

WORKFLOW/WORDFLOW—NONE—The Titan Corporation; *U.S. Public*, pg. 1618

WORKFORCE—Faucets—Delta Faucet Corporation; *U.S. Public*, pg. 1053

WORKFORCE DESKTOP—NONE—FileNet Corporation; *U.S. Public*, pg. 622

WORKHORSE—Premium Quality Flashlights, Lanterns, Minilights & Area Lights—RAYOVAC Corporation; *U.S. Private*, pg. 912

THE WORKING BALL—Sporting Equipment—Brunswick Bowling & Billiards Corp.; *U.S. Public*, pg. 265

WORKING IMAGES—Uniforms—Sketchley Plc; *Int'l*, pg. 1261

WORKING MOTHER MAGAZINE—Magazine—MacDonald Communications; *U.S. Private*, pg. 691

WORKING PAPER...NOT PAPER WORK—Business Product—International Business Machines Corporation; *U.S. Public*, pg. 895

WORKING TO MAKE LIFE BETTER—NONE—Continental Medical Systems, Inc.; *U.S. Public*, pg. 839

WORKING WARDROBE—Uniforms—Angelica Corporation; *U.S. Public*, pg. 113

WORKING WITH YOUNG CHILDREN—Textbook Designed to Develop Skills for a Career in Child Care—Goodheart-Willcox Publisher; *U.S. Private*, pg. 464

WORKING WOMAN MAGAZINE—Magazine—MacDonald Communications; *U.S. Private*, pg. 691

WORKING WOMAN'S DREAM HOME—Real Estate—Weyerhaeuser Company; *U.S. Public*, pg. 1764

WORKING WORLD—Greeting Cards—American Greetings Corporation; *U.S. Public*, pg. 77

WORKLOAD DELAY MONITER—System Moniter for both Physical & Logical System Resources—Boole & Babbage, Inc.; *U.S. Public*, pg. 244

WORKMASTER—Screwdrivers & Tools—The Stanley Works; *U.S. Public*, pg. 1508

WORKMATE—Work Bench—The Black & Decker Corporation; *U.S. Public*, pg. 233

WORKNET—Computer Systems—Acer/Altos Computer Systems; *Int'l*, pg. 22

WORKOUT—High-Tech Energy Drink—White Rock Products Corp.; *U.S. Private*, pg. 1173

WORKOUT LIGHT—High-Tech Energy Drink—White Rock Products Corp.; *U.S. Private*, pg. 1173

WORKPAD—Computer Product—International Business Machines Corporation; *U.S. Public*, pg. 895

WORKPLACE SHELL—Computer System—International Business Machines Corporation; *U.S. Public*, pg. 895

WORKSAFE—Biodegradable Degreasers—The Brulin Corporation; *U.S. Private*, pg. 176

Brand Name Index

WORKSAFE—NONE—Eastco Industrial Safety Corp.; *U.S. Public*, pg. 548
WORKSHOP—NONE—FileNet Corporation; *U.S. Public*, pg. 622
WORKSPACE—Design Software—Alias Wavefront; *U.S. Public*, pg. 1474
WORKSTATION—Information Processing Products—Fellowes Manufacturing Co.; *U.S. Private*, pg. 400
WORKSTATION ONE—Computer System—International Business Machines Corporation; *U.S. Public*, pg. 895
WORLD—Hand & Hair Dryers, Faucets, Hand Wash Station—World Dryer Corp.; *U.S. Public*, pg. 1497
WORLD AIRWAYS—Charter Airline—WorldCorp, Inc.; *U.S. Public*, pg. 1779
THE WORLD ALMANAC—Annual Reference Work—Primedia Inc.; *U.S. Public*, pg. 1327
WORLD BAND RADIO—Short Wave Radios—Sony Electronics; *Int'l*, pg. 1281
WORLD BOND—Printing & Writing Paper—Georgia-Pacific Corporation; *U.S. Public*, pg. 735
WORLD BOOK—Encyclopedias—Berkshire Hathaway Inc.; *U.S. Public*, pg. 217
WORLD BOOK—Encyclopedia, Dictionary—World Book, Inc.; *U.S. Public*, pg. 218
WORLD BOOK MULTIMEDIA ENCYCLOPEDIA—NONE—World Book, Inc.; *U.S. Public*, pg. 218
WORLD BROADCAST NEWS—Broadcast Industry Publication—Intertec Publishing; *U.S. Public*, pg. 1327
WORLD BUSINESS CLASS—Formerly Executive Class—Northwest Airlines, Inc.; *U.S. Public*, pg. 1200
WORLD CARPETS, INC.—Carpet—World Carpets, Inc.; *U.S. Private*, pg. 1190
WORLD CHAMPIONSHIP WRESTLING—Wrestling Production—Turner Broadcasting System Inc.; *U.S. Public*, pg. 1614
WORLD CLASS—Ski Rope—Outdoor Technologies Group; *U.S. Private*, pg. 822
WORLD CLASSICS—Foods—Topco Associates, Inc.; *U.S. Private*, pg. 1091
WORLD CRISA—NONE—World Tableware, Inc.; *Int'l*, pg. 1056
WORLD-FAMOUS—Wooden Dir. Chairs—Telescope Casual Furniture, Inc.; *U.S. Private*, pg. 1074
WORLD 4 KIDS—NONE—Coles Myer Ltd.; *Int'l*, pg. 306
WORLD LAMB—Electric Motor-Blowers—AMETEK, Inc.; *U.S. Public*, pg. 99
WORLD LAMINATION—Electric Motors—AMETEK, Inc.; *U.S. Public*, pg. 99
WORLD*LINE—Automated International Calling—Intellicall, Inc.; *U.S. Public*, pg. 887
WORLD MUSIC THEATRE—Concert Theatre—The Levy Organization; *U.S. Private*, pg. 664
WORLD OF COLOR—Print Applicators—Linzer Products Corp.; *U.S. Private*, pg. 669
WORLD OVENS—NONE—7-Eleven Stores; *Int'l*, pg. 693
WORLD OVENS—Bakery Products—The Southland Corporation; *Int'l*, pg. 693
WORLD PACIFIC—NONE—IWI Holding Limited; *U.S. Public*, pg. 861
WORLD RECORD LINE—Mono—Outdoor Technologies Group; *U.S. Private*, pg. 822
WORLD SOCCER—Sports Magazine—IPC Magazines Limited; *Int'l*, pg. 651
WORLD SOFTWARE—Computer Software—J.D. Edwards & Company; *U.S. Private*, pg. 365
THE WORLD TONIGHT—News Program—Westwood One, Inc.; *U.S. Public*, pg. 1763
WORLD TRADE—Magazine Publication—Freedom Communication Inc.; *U.S. Private*, pg. 425
WORLD VIEW—Camera System For Aircraft—Nellcor Puritan Bennett Incorporated; *U.S. Public*, pg. 1039
WORLD WAR 3-D—3-D Videogame—Sega of America Inc.; *Int'l*, pg. 1218
WORLD WAR II—Periodical—Cowles Enthusiast Media, Inc.; *U.S. Private*, pg. 281
WORLD WAR II VIDEO—Video Series—Time-Life, Inc.; *U.S. Public*, pg. 1613
WORLD WASTES—Publication for Waste-Management Professionals—Intertec Publishing; *U.S. Public*, pg. 1327

WORLD WASTES INTERNATIONAL—Monthly Publication—Intertec Publishing; *U.S. Public*, pg. 1328
WORLD WILDLIFE FUND—Clothing—Salant Corporation; *U.S. Public*, pg. 1429
WORLDCLUBS—Airport Lounges—Northwest Airlines, Inc.; *U.S. Public*, pg. 1200
WORLDGUIDE—Programming Guide—North American Publishing Company; *U.S. Private*, pg. 803
WORLDMAIL—Re-Mail Service—DHL Worldwide Express; *U.S. Private*, pg. 301
WORLDPERKS—Free Travel Programs—Northwest Airlines, Inc.; *U.S. Public*, pg. 1200
WORLDPLANE—747-400 Aircraft Commemorating 50th Anniversary of Service to Asia—Northwest Airlines, Inc.; *U.S. Public*, pg. 1200
THE WORLD'S BIGGEST, BEST BREAKFAST BUFFET—All-You-Can-Eat Buffet—Ponderosa Steakhouse; *U.S. Public*, pg. 736
THE WORLD'S BIGGEST, BEST SALAD BUFFET—All-You-Can-Eat Buffet—Ponderosa Steakhouse; *U.S. Public*, pg. 736
WORLD'S FINEST—Chocolate Candy—World's Finest Chocolate, Inc.; *U.S. Private*, pg. 1191
WORLD'S FRIENDLIEST DRIVER—NONE—Callaway Golf Company; *U.S. Public*, pg. 294
WORLD'S FRIENDLIEST FAIRWAY WOODS—NONE—Callaway Golf Company; *U.S. Public*, pg. 294
WORLD'S FRIENDLIEST IRONS—NONE—Callaway Golf Company; *U.S. Public*, pg. 294
WORLD'S LARGEST CRUISE AGENCY—NONE—Cruises Only Inc.; *U.S. Private*, pg. 293
WORLDS OF FUN—Amusement Park—Cedar Fair, L.P.; *U.S. Public*, pg. 319
WORLDTRAK—Sales Force & Mktg. Automation System—Group 1 Software, Inc.; *U.S. Public*, pg. 417
WORLDVACATIONS—Packaged Vacations—Northwest Airlines, Inc.; *U.S. Public*, pg. 1200
WORLDVANE—Vane Pump with International Mounting Capability—Robert Bosch Fluid Power Corporation; *Int'l*, pg. 204
WORLDWEB—Internet Website—Northwest Airlines, Inc.; *U.S. Public*, pg. 1200
WORLDWIDE—NONE—Harlequin Enterprises Ltd.; *Int'l*, pg. 1402
WORLDWIDE PRIORITY EXPRESS—Express Package & Freight—DHL Worldwide Express; *U.S. Private*, pg. 301
WORMALD—Fire Protection Equipment—Tyco International Ltd.; *U.S. Public*, pg. 1647
WORTHINGTON BEST BITTER—Bitters—Bass PLC; *Int'l*, pg. 169
WORTHINGTON—NONE—ComPair LeRoi; *Int'l*, pg. 1242
WORTHINGTON—Pumps—Ingersoll-Dresser Pump Company; *U.S. Public*, pg. 529
WORTHINGTON—NONE—Ingersoll-Rand Company; *U.S. Public*, pg. 876
WORTHINGTON—Women's Careerwear—JC Penney Company, Inc.; *U.S. Public*, pg. 916
WORTHINGTON—NONE—Worthington Foods Inc.; *U.S. Public*, pg. 1780
WORTHINGTON ALE—Ale—Bass PLC; *Int'l*, pg. 169
WORTHINGTON DARK MILD/"-"—Dark Mild Beer—Bass PLC; *Int'l*, pg. 169
WORTHINGTON E—Premium Ale—Bass PLC; *Int'l*, pg. 169
WOVCO—Valve-Utility—Worcester Controls Corp.; *Int'l*, pg. 128
WOW—Collecting & Recycling Office Wastepaper—Weyerhaeuser Company; *U.S. Public*, pg. 1764
WOW!, MULTIMEDIA SUPERSTORE—Jointly Operated with The Good Guys, Tower Records & Includes a Coffee Bar—The Good Guys, Inc.; *U.S. Public*, pg. 750
WOW! WHAT A DIFFERENCE—Slogan for Advertising—Blockbuster Entertainment Group; *U.S. Private*, pg. 775
WRANGLER—Western Headwear—AJD; *U.S. Private*, pg. 510
WRANGLER—Light Truck Tires—The Goodyear Tire & Rubber Company; *U.S. Public*, pg. 752
WRANGLER—Men's Apparel—Mass Market Division; *U.S. Public*, pg. 1702
WRANGLER—Jeanswear—VF Corporation; *U.S. Public*, pg. 1702

WRANGLER LIMITED—Apparel—Mass Market Division; *U.S. Public*, pg. 1702
WRANGLERS—Smoked Bacon & Ham—Hormel Foods Corp.; *U.S. Public*, pg. 840
WRAP-A-DAX—Computer Software And An Electronic Switch—DSC Communications Corporation; *U.S. Public*, pg. 475
WRAP-KING—Wrapping Machinery—G.D. Packaging Machinery Inc.; *Int'l*, pg. 531
WRAP TAMER—Wrap Dispenser—The Rival Company; *U.S. Public*, pg. 1391
THE WRAP—Bras—Warner's; *U.S. Public*, pg. 1738
WRAP'N CRAFT—Box to Store Wrapping, Cards, Bows etc.—Rubbermaid Incorporated; *U.S. Public*, pg. 1411
WRAPCAP—Packaging Machines for Packaging Atricles into Corrugated Paperboard—The Mead Corporation; *U.S. Public*, pg. 1074
WRAPPER—Notebook Cover—The Mead Corporation; *U.S. Public*, pg. 1074
WRASSLIN'—Sports—Monarch Avalon, Inc.; *U.S. Public*, pg. 1123
WRATTEN—Light Filter—Eastman Kodak Company; *U.S. Public*, pg. 550
WREN—Air Brush—Binks Sames Corporation; *U.S. Public*, pg. 229
WRIGHT—Hoists & Trolleys—Acco Chain & Lifting Products; *Int'l*, pg. 473
WRIGHT—Smoked Meat Products—Wright Brand Foods, Inc.; *U.S. Private*, pg. 1192
WRIGHT LINE—Office Systems—Applied Power Inc.; *U.S. Public*, pg. 124
WRIGHT'S—Liquid Smoke—Nabisco Inc.; *U.S. Public*, pg. 1355
WRIGHT'S—Liquid Smoke—RJR Nabisco Holdings Corp.; *U.S. Public*, pg. 1354
WRIGHTS—Tapes & Braids, Decorator Trims, Laces, Trims—Wm. E. Wright Limited Partnership; *U.S. Private*, pg. 1192
WRIGLEYGUIBTT—NONE—Cruspi S.A.; *Int'l*, pg. 348
WRIGLEY'S SPEARMINT—Gum—Wm. Wrigley Jr. Company; *U.S. Public*, pg. 1781
WRIGLEY'S SPEARMINT—Chewing Gum—Wrigley Canada Inc.; *U.S. Public*, pg. 1781
WRINKL-SHED—Fabrics—Dan River Inc.; *U.S. Public*, pg. 478
WRINKLE CONTROL CREME—Cosmetics—Palm Beach Beauty Products Co.; *U.S. Private*, pg. 834
WRINKLE FREE COTTONS—Slacks—Haggar Corporation; *U.S. Public*, pg. 774
WRITE-A-NOTES—Note Paper—American Greetings Corporation; *U.S. Public*, pg. 77
WRITE-A-NOTES—Stationery—American Greetings U.S. Greeting Card Division; *U.S. Public*, pg. 78
WRITE BROS.—Retractable & Stick Pens—The Gillette Company; *U.S. Public*, pg. 743
WRITE, CAMERA, ACTION!—NONE—Broderbund Software, Inc.; *U.S. Public*, pg. 258
WRITE RIGHT—School, Art & Stationery Products—Union Camp Corporation; *U.S. Public*, pg. 1665
WRITER'S DIGEST—Magazine—F & W Publications, Inc.; *U.S. Private*, pg. 388
WRITER'S DIGEST BOOKS—Book Publishers—F & W Publications, Inc.; *U.S. Private*, pg. 388
WRITER'S DIGEST SCHOOL—Home Study—F & W Publications, Inc.; *U.S. Private*, pg. 388
WRITER'S MARKET—Market Book—F & W Publications, Inc.; *U.S. Private*, pg. 388
WRITERS' ASSISTANT—Software—International Business Machines Corporation; *U.S. Public*, pg. 895
WRITER'S DIGEST BOOK CLUB—Book Club—F & W Publications, Inc.; *U.S. Private*, pg. 388
WRITING ASSISTANT—Software—International Business Machines Corporation; *U.S. Public*, pg. 895
WRITING TO READ—Software—International Business Machines Corporation; *U.S. Public*, pg. 895
WRITING TO WRITE—Software—International Business Machines Corporation; *U.S. Public*, pg. 895
WUHRER—Beer—Danone Group; *Int'l*, pg. 379
WUL-LYTE—Neckwear Interfacings—Specialty Textile Products; *U.S. Private*, pg. 1023

WUNDA WEVE—Carpet—World Carpets, Inc.; *U.S. Private*, pg. 1190

WUNDALINER—Drapery Liners—Cameo Window Furnishings; *U.S. Private*, pg. 1094

WUNDERLICH—Clay Roof Tiles—CSR Limited; *Int'l*, pg. 245

WURLITZER—Pianos & Organs—Baldwin Piano & Organ Company; *U.S. Public*, pg. 169

WYANDOT—Snack Foods—Wyandot Inc.; *U.S. Private*, pg. 1193

WYANDOTTE—Automotive Coatings—Akzo Nobel N.V.; *Int'l*, pg. 42

WYBOROWA—Vodka—The House of Seagram; *Int'l*, pg. 1217

WYCLIP—Scraper Ring—James Walker & Co. Limited; *Int'l*, pg. 1485

WYCO—Mark-Line—The Wyco Tool Co.; *U.S. Private*, pg. 906

WYDASE—Generic Drug—American Home Products Corporation; *U.S. Public*, pg. 79

WYKO—Metrology Systems—Veeco Instruments, Inc.; *U.S. Public*, pg. 1711

WYLER—Measuring Tools—Fred V. Fowler Company, Inc.; *U.S. Private*, pg. 422

WYLER'S—Bouillons—Borden, Inc.; *U.S. Private*, pg. 157

WYMAN-GORDON—Forgings & Other Engineered Metal Prods.—Wyman-Gordon; *U.S. Public*, pg. 1782

WYNN'S—Auto Chemical Additives—Wynn Oil Company; *U.S. Public*, pg. 1782

WYNNS COONAWARRA ESTATE—Wines—Southcorp Holdings Ltd.; *Int'l*, pg. 1287

WYNWOOD—NONE—DMI Furniture Inc.; *U.S. Public*, pg. 473

WYO LP GAS—Liquid Propane Gas Distribution Operations—Energy West Inc.; *U.S. Public*, pg. 581

WYROBY—Pickles—Campbell Sales; *U.S. Public*, pg. 299

WYSE—Computer—Wyse Technology Inc.; *U.S. Private*, pg. 1194

WYTEBORD—Dry-Erase Maker—The Pilot Pen Corp. of America; *Int'l*, pg. 1057

WYTENSIN—Antihypertensive Agent—Wyeth-Ayerst Laboratories, Inc.; *U.S. Public*, pg. 80

X

X—Equipment—Halliburton Energy Services; *U.S. Public*, pg. 776

XAGA—Heat-Shrinkable Splice Closures—Raychem Corporation; *U.S. Public*, pg. 1362

X-ACTO—Knives, Blades & Tools—Hunt Corporation; *U.S. Public*, pg. 848

X-BLOX—Module Synthesis System—Xilinx, Inc.; *U.S. Public*, pg. 1786

X-CELL—Tissue Heart Valve—St. Jude Medical, Inc.; *U.S. Public*, pg. 1427

XDC—Blade Coated Backup or Applicator Roll Cover—Harnischfeger Industries, Inc.; *U.S. Public*, pg. 788

XDC 3200—Control Products—Bailey, Fischer & Porter Company; *Int'l*, pg. 449

XD SERIES—Digital Router—Chyron Corp.; *Int'l*, pg. 1372

XFP 2000—Com System—Anacomp, Inc.; *U.S. Public*, pg. 106

XFT—Chelation & Stabilization of Silver Ions—Isolyser Company, Inc.; *U.S. Public*, pg. 914

X-15R—Cotton Candy Machine—Gold Medal Products Co.; *U.S. Private*, pg. 459

X-14—Mildew Stain Remover, Soap Scum Remover, Rust & Mineral Stain Remover—Block Drug Company, Inc.; *U.S. Public*, pg. 236

XGA—Computer System—International Business Machines Corporation; *U.S. Public*, pg. 895

XGR-II—Oversize Irons—Square Two Golf Incorporated; *U.S. Public*, pg. 1501

X-HYDRA—Anti-Perspirant—The Gillette Company; *U.S. Public*, pg. 743

XI ARCHERY—NONE—Escalade Sports; *U.S. Public*, pg. 591

XIDEX—Film—Anacomp, Inc.; *U.S. Public*, pg. 106

XILINX—Software—Xilinx, Inc.; *U.S. Public*, pg. 1786

X IPER—NONE—GS Societa Generale Supermercati; *Int'l*, pg. 186

XJ-12—NONE—Lawter International, Inc.; *U.S. Public*, pg. 980

XJ-2000—Stationery Products—The Mead Corporation; *U.S. Public*, pg. 1074

X-JUMBO—Biological Supplies—Carolina Biological Supply Co.; *U.S. Private*, pg. 213

XL—NONE—GenRad, Inc.; *U.S. Public*, pg. 731

XL—Rail Anchor—Portec Ltd.; *U.S. Public*, pg. 1318

X.L.—Roller Ball Pens—Sanford Corporation; *U.S. Public*, pg. 1178

XL DATACOMP—Computer Equip. & Services—Distributed Systems Division; *U.S. Public*, pg. 1522

XL8—Storage Product—Tandem Computers Inc.; *U.S. Public*, pg. 417

XL80—Storage Products—Tandem Computers Inc.; *U.S. Public*, pg. 417

XLH SPORTSTER—Motorcycle—Harley-Davidson, Inc.; *U.S. Public*, pg. 786

XL MAGNETIC LAMINATING TAPE—Extended Life Magnetic Tape For Plastic Transaction Cards—Schlumberger Malco Inc.; *Int'l*, pg. 1206

XL-19—Scissor Lift—Up-Right, Inc.; *U.S. Private*, pg. 1128

XL-1 FAIR—Rail Anchor—Portec Ltd.; *U.S. Public*, pg. 1318

XL-100—TV Receivers—Thomson Consumer Electronics Inc.; *Int'l*, pg. 1383

XLP—Filter Element—Donaldson Company, Inc.; *U.S. Public*, pg. 517

XLP MAGNETIC TAPE—Ultra Low Stripe Profile Magnetic Tape For Plastic Transaction Cards—Schlumberger Malco Inc.; *Int'l*, pg. 1206

XL SERIES—Printers—Datasouth Computer Corporation; *U.S. Public*, pg. 267

XL SERIES—Scooters—Pride Health Care, Inc.; *U.S. Private*, pg. 883

XLT—Circuit Tester—Teradyne, Inc.; *U.S. Public*, pg. 1580

XL-TRACE—Heating Cable—Raychem Corporation; *U.S. Public*, pg. 1362

XL-TC—Electrical Wire & Cable—BICC Brand-Rex; *Int'l*, pg. 120

X-LINE—Equip.—Halliburton Energy Services; *U.S. Public*, pg. 776

X LINK TC—Tray Cable—Rockbestos-Supranant Cable Corp.; *U.S. Private*, pg. 938

XMC—Fiber Glass Reinforced Compositions & Fibers—PPG Industries, Inc.; *U.S. Public*, pg. 1245

XML-125—Wire—Rockbestos-Supranant Cable Corp.; *U.S. Private*, pg. 938

XMOS—Electronics—National Semiconductor Corporation; *U.S. Public*, pg. 1159

XM SERIES END MILL—M42 Cobalt End Mill—National Twist Drill Div.; *U.S. Public*, pg. 1370

XM SERIES END MILL—M42 Cobalt End Mill—Regal-Beloit Corporation; *U.S. Public*, pg. 1370

X-MEN: CHILDREN OF THE ATOM—Interactive Entertainment Software—Acclaim Entertainment, Inc.; *U.S. Public*, pg. 15

X-90—Sports Utility Vehicle—American Suzuki Motor Corporation; *Int'l*, pg. 1323

X-90—Sport Utility Vehicle—Suzuki Motor Corporation; *Int'l*, pg. 1322

XO-2—Printing & Writing Paper—The Mead Corporation; *U.S. Public*, pg. 1074

X-OMAT—X-ray Processing Apparatus, Films & Chemicals—Eastman Kodak Company; *U.S. Public*, pg. 550

X-OMATIC—Intensifying Screens, X-ray Film, Cassettes—Eastman Kodak Company; *U.S. Public*, pg. 550

XP—Extended Performance—GenRad, Inc.; *U.S. Public*, pg. 731

XP—Cracking Catalysts—W.R. Grace & Co.; *U.S. Public*, pg. 754

XP/PM—Particle Metal End Mill—National Twist Drill Div.; *U.S. Public*, pg. 1370

XP/PM—Particle Metal End Mill—Regal-Beloit Corporation; *U.S. Public*, pg. 1370

XP/PMC—Particle Metal End Mill With Cobalt—National Twist Drill Div.; *U.S. Public*, pg. 1370

XP/PMC—Particle Metal End Mill with Cobalt—Regal-Beloit Corporation; *U.S. Public*, pg. 1370

XPRE GRAPHITE RTS—Racquetball Racquet—Ektelon; *U.S. Private*, pg. 884

XP-20—Animal Repellents—Weatherly Consumer Products; *U.S. Public*, pg. 1682

X-PAC—Explosion Detection & Suppression Systems—Kidde-Fenwal, Inc.; *Int'l*, pg. 1500

X-PRESS MILL—NONE—Hosokawa Micron Powder Systems; *Int'l*, pg. 636

XR—Motorcycle—American Honda Motor Co., Inc. Motorcycle Division; *Int'l*, pg. 634

XR4 RADIAL—Tires—Bridgestone/Firestone, Inc.; *Int'l*, pg. 213

XR4 TRACTION DRIVE—Tires—Bridgestone/Firestone, Inc.; *Int'l*, pg. 213

XRM—Gear Oil Prod.—The Lubrizol Corporation; *U.S. Public*, pg. 1016

XR PACK—Power Tools—The Black & Decker Corporation; *U.S. Public*, pg. 233

XR-7—Poromeric Insole Material—Bontex; *U.S. Public*, pg. 734

X-RITE 820—Transmission/Reflection Densitometer—X-Rite, Incorporated; *U.S. Public*, pg. 1783

X-RITE 410—Transmission Densitometer—X-Rite, Incorporated; *U.S. Public*, pg. 1783

X-RITE 428—Reflection Densitometer—X-Rite, Incorporated; *U.S. Public*, pg. 1783

XS—NONE—Lee Pharmaceuticals; *U.S. Public*, pg. 984

XSD—Halogen Specific Detector—O.I. Corporation; *U.S. Public*, pg. 1208

X-SERIES SLR'S—Cameras—Minolta Corporation; *Int'l*, pg. 869

X-SITE—Portable X-Ray Analyzer—Kevex Instruments; *U.S. Public*, pg. 1594

XT—Computer—International Business Machines Corporation; *U.S. Public*, pg. 895

XT—Automobile—Subaru of America, Inc.; *Int'l*, pg. 523

XTC—Printing Paper, Copier Paper & Personal Computer Paper—Georgia-Pacific Corporation; *U.S. Public*, pg. 735

XTC—Energy Drink—Global Beverage Co.; *U.S. Private*, pg. 457

XTC TRANSMITTER—Controller—Moore Products Co.; *U.S. Public*, pg. 1128

XT-8000 FAMILY—Disk Drives—Maxtor Corporation; *Int'l*, pg. 641

XT-4000 FAMILY—Disk Drives—Maxtor Corporation; *Int'l*, pg. 641

XTP—Pistol Bullet—Hornady Manufacturing Company; *U.S. Private*, pg. 539

XT POLYMER—Acrylic Based Multipolymer Compound—Cyro Industries; *Int'l*, pg. 1454

X-TAL LOCK—Quartz Crystal Receiver for Car Stereo—Sony Electronics; *Int'l*, pg. 1281

X-TEND—Petrochemical—Wynn Oil Company; *U.S. Public*, pg. 1782

X-TENDED LIFE SPRING SEATING—NONE—Overholtzer Church Furniture, Inc.; *U.S. Private*, pg. 823

X-TREL—Implantable Electrode—Medtronic, Inc.; *U.S. Public*, pg. 1082

X25NET—Computer System—International Business Machines Corporation; *U.S. Public*, pg. 895

X2—NONE—Texas Instruments Incorporated; *U.S. Public*, pg. 1585

X UVEX—Goggles/Spectacles—Uvex Safety, Inc.; *Int'l*, pg. 132

XWAY—Electronic Data Interchange Software—Tandem Computers Inc.; *U.S. Public*, pg. 417

XX-SPAN—Dressing Retainer—Alba-Waldensian Health Products Div.; *U.S. Public*, pg. 36

XX-SPAN—Dressing Retainers—Alba-Waldensian, Inc.; *U.S. Public*, pg. 35

XZ—Sack Kraft—Stora Billerud AB; *Int'l*, pg. 1302

X-SAM—Hoist Safety System—Ederer Inc.; *U.S. Private*, pg. 363

XACT—Steering—Volvo Penta of the Americas, Inc.; *Int'l*, pg. 1477

XACT-STEP ALLIANCE SOLUTION—NONE—Xilinx, Inc.; *U.S. Public*, pg. 1786

XACT-STEP FOUNDATION SOLUTION—NONE—Xilinx, Inc.; *U.S. Public*, pg. 1786

XACT-PERFORMANCE—Allows Set Performance Requirements at the Schematic Level for FPGA Designs—Xilinx, Inc.; *U.S. Public*, pg. 1786

XALATAN—NONE—Pharmacia & Upjohn, Inc.; *Int'l*, pg. 1047

XAMAMINA—Stimulant—SmithKline Beecham plc; *Int'l*, pg. 1264

XANADU—Timers—Valcor Engineering Corp.; *U.S. Private*, pg. 1131

XANAX—Prescription Anti-Anxiety Agent—Pharmacia & Upjohn; *Int'l*, pg. 1048

XANTAR—Polycarbonate—DSM N.V.; *Int'l*, pg. 352

XATRAL—Pharmaceutical—L'Oreal S.A.; *Int'l*, pg. 818

XBIOX—Software—Xilinx, Inc.; *U.S. Public*, pg. 1786

XCELITE—Screwdrivers, Nutdrivers, Tool Kits and Stes, Pliers, and Cutters—Cooper Hand Tools; *U.S. Public*, pg. 444

XCELITE—Screwdrivers, Nutdrivers & Pliers—Cooper Industries, Inc.; *U.S. Public*, pg. 442

XCHECKER—Universal Download Cable that Supplies XL2000, 3000 and 4000 FPGA Families—Xilinx, Inc.; *U.S. Public*, pg. 1786

XENACRYL—Acrylic Resins—Witco Corporation; *U.S. Public*, pg. 1773

XENICAL—Fat Absorption Blocker—Hoffmann-La Roche Inc.; *Int'l*, pg. 1120

XENON 133 GAS—Ventilation Studies—Amersham Healthcare; *Int'l*, pg. 992

XENON-PULSE—Technology—Millipore Corporation; *Int'l*, pg. 1112

XENOTRON—Medical Apparatus for Transferring Xenon Gas—Mallinckrodt Inc.; *U.S. Public*, pg. 1039

XENOY—Engineered Plastics—General Electric Company; *U.S. Public*, pg. 709

XENTARI—Biologically Derived Insecticide—Abbott Laboratories; *U.S. Public*, pg. 12

XERIGATION—Sprinklers—Rain Bird Sprinklers Manufacturing Corp.; *U.S. Private*, pg. 907

XEROX—Business Products—Xerox Corporation; *U.S. Public*, pg. 1783

XEROX COPIERS—NONE—Xerox South Africa; *U.S. Public*, pg. 1785

XEROX LASER PRINTERS—NONE—Xerox South Africa; *U.S. Public*, pg. 1785

XEROX OFFICE SUPPLIES—NONE—Xerox South Africa; *U.S. Public*, pg. 1785

XEROX PRINTING SYSTEMS—NONE—Xerox South Africa; *U.S. Public*, pg. 1785

XETRON—Access Control Systems—Pittway Corporation; *U.S. Public*, pg. 1305

XHD—Extra Heavy Duty Truck Wheels—Redco Corporation; *U.S. Private*, pg. 915

XHLLAPI—Computer System—International Business Machines Corporation; *U.S. Public*, pg. 895

XICOR—NONE—Xicor, Inc.; *U.S. Public*, pg. 1785

XIMATRON—Radiotherapy Treatment Centers—Varian Associates, Inc.; *U.S. Public*, pg. 1710

XLINK—Resin—Unilever Plc; *Int'l*, pg. 1433

XO—Turbine Meters—Schutte & Koerting Division; *U.S. Private*, pg. 604

XODUST—Dust Control Products—3M; *U.S. Public*, pg. 1604

XOMED—Medical Devices—Xomed Surgical Products; *U.S. Public*, pg. 253

XOMOX—Specialized Flow Control Products—Emerson Electric Co.; *U.S. Public*, pg. 572

XOOR—NONE—Polaroid Corporation; *U.S. Public*, pg. 1313

XPEDITER—Program Editing, Analysis & Debugging Product for OS/2—Compuware Corporation; *U.S. Public*, pg. 423

XPEDITOR—Refuse Vehicle—Volvo Truck North America, Inc.; *Int'l*, pg. 1477

XPELAIR—Extractor fans—The General Electric Company, p.l.c.; *Int'l*, pg. 543

XPERT—Nuclear Medicine Workstation—Elscint Ltd.; *Int'l*, pg. 450

XPERT—Paint—ICI Paints; *Int'l*, pg. 664

XPLOIT—NONE—The Titan Corporation; *U.S. Public*, pg. 1618

XPLORER—Motor Homes, Cargo Vans & Commercial Vehicles—Frank Industries, Inc.; *U.S. Private*, pg. 423

XPOGRAPH—Foam Display Board—The Dow Chemical Company; *U.S. Public*, pg. 522

XPRESS CONNECT—Remote Access/Internet Working—Gandalf Technologies Inc.; *Int'l*, pg. 540

XPRESS MODEL—NONE—GenRad, Inc.; *U.S. Public*, pg. 731

XPRESS NAIL—NONE—GenRad, Inc.; *U.S. Public*, pg. 731

XPRESS STACK—Remote Access Concentration—Gandalf Technologies Inc.; *Int'l*, pg. 540

XPRESSWAY—Milking Parlor Systems—Bou-Matic; *U.S. Private*, pg. 301

XPRESSWAY—Remote Office Network System—Gandalf Technologies Inc.; *Int'l*, pg. 540

XSTATION MANAGER—Software—International Business Machines Corporation; *U.S. Public*, pg. 895

XTALSCINT—Solid Scintillator—Beckman Instruments, Inc.; *U.S. Public*, pg. 199

XTENDED-LIFE—Color TV Receiver—Thomson Consumer Electronics Inc.; *Int'l*, pg. 1383

XTOL—Tall Oil Fatty Acids & Tall Oil Byproducts—Georgia-Pacific Corporation; *U.S. Public*, pg. 735

XTRA-CATOR—Fertilizer Applicators—Agrotec, Williams Inc.; *U.S. Public*, pg. 1769

XTRA FOOD—Supermarkets—Socanav Inc.; *Int'l*, pg. 1272

XTRA-GUARD—Cable—Alpha Wire Company; *U.S. Public*, pg. 201

XTRA-SERV—Paper Toilet Tissue—Georgia-Pacific Corporation; *U.S. Public*, pg. 735

XTRA SUPER FOOD CENTERS—Super stores—Pueblo Xtra International, Inc.; *U.S. Private*, pg. 894

XTRALIFE—Batteries—Eastman Kodak Company; *U.S. Public*, pg. 550

XXXTRA—Household Paper Goods—Orchids Paper Products Co.; *U.S. Private*, pg. 819

XXXX FOUREX—Condoms—Durex Consumer Products; *Int'l*, pg. 815

XYCON—Hybrid Resins—Amoco Corporation; *U.S. Public*, pg. 101

XYDAR—Liquid Crystal Polymers High Temperature Engineering Resins—Amoco Chemicals; *U.S. Public*, pg. 102

XYDAR—Polymers—Amoco Corporation; *U.S. Public*, pg. 101

XYLIFRESH—Xylitol Chewing Gum—Huhtamaki Oy; *Int'l*, pg. 638

XYLITOLJENKKI—Chewing gum—Huhtamaki Oy; *Int'l*, pg. 638

XYLO-TOL—NONE—Ballard Medical Products; *U.S. Public*, pg. 171

XYLOCAINE—Anesthetic—Astra AB; *Int'l*, pg. 93

XYLOCAINE—Pharmaceutical Products—Astra USA, Inc.; *Int'l*, pg. 93

XYLOCARD—Antiarrhythmic Agent—Astra AB; *Int'l*, pg. 93

XYMARK—Marking System—Lumonics Inc.; *Int'l*, pg. 1314

XYREL—Pacemaker—Medtronic, Inc.; *U.S. Public*, pg. 1082

Y

YAG—Laser Product—AlliedSignal Inc.; *U.S. Public*, pg. 49

Y&S—Candy—Hershey Chocolate U.S.A.; *U.S. Public*, pg. 812

YF-VAX—Yellow Fever Vaccine—Connaught Laboratories, Inc.; *Int'l*, pg. 1109

YM—Magazine—Gruner + Jahr USA Publishing, Inc.; *Int'l*, pg. 190

YSL—Cigarettes—R.J. Reynolds Tobacco Intl., Inc.; *U.S. Public*, pg. 1355

YS SPORT—Apparel—Young Stuff Apparel Group, Inc.; *U.S. Private*, pg. 1202

YS STUDIO—Apparel—Young Stuff Apparel Group, Inc.; *U.S. Private*, pg. 1202

YA YA—Cosmetics—Health Products Corporation; *U.S. Private*, pg. 514

YABON—Desserts, Baking Aids—Bestfoods; *U.S. Public*, pg. 223

YACHTING—Magazine—Times Mirror Magazines, Inc.; *U.S. Public*, pg. 1616

YACHTING MONTHLY—Yachting Magazine—IPC Magazines Limited; *Int'l*, pg. 651

YACHTING WORLD—Yachting Magazine—IPC Magazines Limited; *Int'l*, pg. 651

YAHTZEE—Game—Milton Bradley Company; *U.S. Public*, pg. 797

YAKIMA DOOR—Doors—Jeld-Wen, Inc.; *U.S. Private*, pg. 585

YALE—Hoists—Columbus McKinnon Corp.; *U.S. Public*, pg. 405

YALE—Fork-Lift Trucks & Related Service Parts—NACCO Industries, Inc.; *U.S. Public*, pg. 1149

YALE MATERIALS HANDLING—Fork Lifts—Hy-Tek Material Handling, Inc.; *U.S. Private*, pg. 550

YALE UNIVERSITY PRESS—Book Publishers—Yale University Press; *U.S. Private*, pg. 1195

YAMAHA—Sporting Goods & Athletic Goods—Yamaha Corp. of America, Sporting Goods Div.; *Int'l*, pg. 1516

YAMAHA—Musical Instruments, Sports Equip.—Yamaha Corporation; *Int'l*, pg. 1515

YAMAHA—Musical Instruments & Sporting Goods—Yamaha Corporation of America; *Int'l*, pg. 1516

YAMAHA—Stereo Components—Yamaha Electronics Corp. USA; *Int'l*, pg. 1516

YAMAHA—Motorcycles, Snowmobiles, A.T.V's, Outboard Motors—Yamaha Motor Canada Ltd.; *Int'l*, pg. 1516

YAMAHA—NONE—Yamaha Motor Co., Ltd.; *Int'l*, pg. 1516

YAMAHA—Motorized Products—Yamaha Motor Corp., U.S.A.; *Int'l*, pg. 1516

YAMAHA CONTROLLERS—NONE—Milgray Electronics, Inc.; *U.S. Public*, pg. 205

YAMAZAKI PURE MALT WHISKY—Whisky—Suntory International Corp.; *Int'l*, pg. 1321

YAN YAN—Chocolate Snacks—Meiji Seika Kaisha, Ltd.; *Int'l*, pg. 855

YANAGISAWA—Musical Instruments & Accessories—G. Leblanc Corporation; *U.S. Private*, pg. 656

YANKEE—Mens Rain Wear—Rainfair, Inc.; *U.S. Private*, pg. 907

YANKEE—Monthly Magazine, New England Region—Yankee Publishing Incorporated; *U.S. Private*, pg. 1195

YANKEE DOODLES—Snack Cakes—Drake Bakeries, Inc.; *Int'l*, pg. 349

YANKEE GIRL—Loose Leaf Chewing Tobacco—Conwood Company L.P.; *U.S. Private*, pg. 272

YANKEE HANDYMAN—Tools—The Stanley Works; *U.S. Public*, pg. 1508

YANKEE MAGAZINES TRAVEL GUIDE TO NEW ENGLAND—Annual New England Regional Travel Guide—Yankee Publishing Incorporated; *U.S. Private*, pg. 1195

YANKEE TRAVELER—Newsletter, 9 Editions Annually—Yankee Publishing Incorporated; *U.S. Private*, pg. 1195

YANKEECLIPPER—Sharpening Stones—Norton Company; *Int'l*, pg. 1173

YAPRE—Men's Apparel—H. Freeman & Son, Inc.; *U.S. Private*, pg. 426

YARD CARE—Organic Ground Covers—MWCA; *U.S. Public*, pg. 804

YARD GUARD—Fence Prod.—Gilbert & Bennett Manufacturing Company; *U.S. Private*, pg. 453

YARD-MAN—Power Mowers/Snow Equipment—MTD Products, Inc.; *U.S. Private*, pg. 688

YARDCLEANER—Blower/Vacuum—The Black & Decker Corporation; *U.S. Public*, pg. 233

YARDKING—Yard Ramps—B & P Manufacturing; *U.S. Private*, pg. 105

YARDLEY—Soaps, Cosmetics, Toiletries, Perfumes—Yardley of London, Inc.; *Int'l*, pg. 819

YARDLEY LEATHER—Colognes & Toiletries—Yardley of London, Inc.; *Int'l*, pg. 819

YARDLEY MUSK—Colognes & Toiletries—Yardley of London, Inc.; *Int'l*, pg. 819

YARDLEY SPICE—Men's Fragrance Products—Yardley of London, Inc.; *Int'l*, pg. 819

YARDPRO—Garden Equipment—Electrolux, AB; *Int'l*, pg. 438

YARDS 2000—Retarder Yard Control Systems—General Railway Signal Corp.; *Int'l*, pg. 1194

YARMOR—Pine Oil—Hercules Incorporated; *U.S. Public*, pg. 809

YARNSAVER—Paper Cones—Sonoco Products Company; *U.S. Public*, pg. 1485

YARWAY—Flow Control Products—Keystone International, Inc.; *U.S. Public*, pg. 1650

YASHICA—Cameras & Photographic Accessories—Kyocera Corporation; *Int'l*, pg. 775

YASHICA—35 mm Cameras—Kyocera International, Inc.; *Int'l*, pg. 775

YASHICA—Cameras—Yashica, Inc.; *Int'l*, pg. 776

YATES—Coatings—Burmah Castrol plc; *Int'l*, pg. 234

Yazoo Vari Mulch—Mulching Lawnmower—Yazoo Power Equipment, LLC; *U.S. Private*, pg. 1195

YEACO—Yeast—Universal Foods Corporation; *U.S. Public*, pg. 1695

YEAR END TAX TIPS—News Program—Westwood One, Inc.; *U.S. Public*, pg. 1763

YEARBOOK OF INTERNATIONAL ORGANIZATIONS—Index of Worldwide Organizations—R.R. Bowker; *Int'l*, pg. 1096

YEARS YOUNGER—Cosmetics—Irma Shorell, Inc.; *U.S. Private*, pg. 1101

YEAST VITE—Vitamin & Mineral Supplements—SmithKline Beecham plc; *Int'l*, pg. 1264

YEBISU—Beer—Sapporo Breweries Ltd.; *Int'l*, pg. 1193

YELLO-BOLE—Smoking Pipes & Related Products—S.M. Frank & Co., Inc.; *U.S. Private*, pg. 423

YELLO-JAKET—Pocket & Hunting Knives—Camillus Cutlery Co.; *U.S. Private*, pg. 203

YELLOW BIRCH—Paper Towels—Georgia-Pacific Corporation; *U.S. Public*, pg. 735

YELLOW JACKET—Plastic Screw Anchor—Gunnebo Fastening Corp.; *U.S. Private*, pg. 488

YELLOW JACKET—Glass Fiber Insulation—Owens Corning; *U.S. Public*, pg. 1236

YELLOW LABEL—Honey Flavored Syrup—Whitfield Foods; *U.S. Private*, pg. 1173

YELLOW PAGES—Telephone Directories—BCE Inc.; *Int'l*, pg. 114

YELLOW PAGES—Classified Telephone Directory, U.K. Only—British Telecommunications plc; *Int'l*, pg. 222

YELLOW RIM—Abrasive Discs—Gardner Abrasives; *U.S. Public*, pg. 1699

YELLOW-RIM—Abrasive Tools, Wheels & Discs—Litton Industries, Inc.; *U.S. Public*, pg. 1002

YELLOW 77—Wire Pulling Lubricant—Ideal Industries, Inc.; *U.S. Private*, pg. 557

YELLOW STRAND—Wire Rope—Broderick & Bascom Rope Co.; *U.S. Private*, pg. 68

YELLOW TAG—Twist Tobacco—Conwood Company L.P.; *U.S. Private*, pg. 272

YELLOWLINE—Reinforcing Mesh—Smorgon A.R.C.; *Int'l*, pg. 1269

YELLOWSTONE—Strategy—Monarch Avalon, Inc.; *U.S. Public*, pg. 1123

YELOMINE—Mine Piping—CertainTeed Corporation; *Int'l*, pg. 1170

YENKIN-MAJESTIC—Paints, Resins, Varnishes & Enamels—Yenkin-Majestic Paint Corporation; *U.S. Private*, pg. 1195

YEOMAN—Instant Potatoes—Master Foods; *U.S. Private*, pg. 707

YES—Detergent—The Dow Chemical Company; *U.S. Public*, pg. 522

YES—Laundry Detergent Plus Fabric Softener—DowBrands, L.P.; *U.S. Public*, pg. 523

YES—Cakes—Nestle S.A.; *Int'l*, pg. 915

YESTERDAY—Casual Dining—Skylark Co., Ltd.; *Int'l*, pg. 1262

YE$YSTEM—Banking Services Package—Bank of the Hudson; *U.S. Public*, pg. 1319

YIJIANXI—Oral Care Products—Sara Lee Corporation; *U.S. Public*, pg. 1432

YIKES!—Pencils & School Supplies—Empire Berol U.S.A.; *U.S. Public*, pg. 1178

YIMPACT—Explosive Welding Services—IMI Plc; *Int'l*, pg. 646

YO CREAM—Frozen Yogurt—Norpac Foods, Inc.; *U.S. Private*, pg. 802

YO-FLEX—NONE—Chr. Hansen, Inc.; *Int'l*, pg. 288

YO YO—Lip Balm & Nail Polish Remover—Health Products Corporation; *U.S. Private*, pg. 514

YODELS—Snack Cakes—Drake Bakeries, Inc.; *Int'l*, pg. 349

YODORA—Cream Deodorant—Menley & James Laboratories, Inc.; *U.S. Public*, pg. 1086

YOGEN FRUZ—Frozen Yogurt—Yogen Fruz Worldwide Inc.; *Int'l*, pg. 1520

YOGURET—A Yogurt Flavored Candy—Meiji Seika Kaisha, Ltd.; *Int'l*, pg. 855

YOGURT DRINKABLES—NONE—Alta-Dena Certified Dairy; *Int'l*, pg. 201

YOGURT TO GO—Fresh Fruit Flavored Yogurt Drink—Dean Foods Company; *U.S. Public*, pg. 489

YOKOHAMA BRAND—Tires—Yokohama Tire Corporation; *Int'l*, pg. 1521

YONDERHILL—Lumber & Wood Products—Georgia-Pacific Corporation; *U.S. Public*, pg. 735

YOO-HOO—Chocolate Drink—Groupe Pernod Ricard; *Int'l*, pg. 566

YOO-HOO—Soft Drink—Grant-Lydick Beverage Co.; *U.S. Private*, pg. 470

YOO-HOO—Chocolate, Coconut & Strawberry Drinks—Yoo Hoo Chocolate Beverage Corp.; *Int'l*, pg. 567

YOPA—Frozen Desserts—Nestle S.A.; *Int'l*, pg. 915

YOPLAIT—Yogurt—Agropur; *Int'l*, pg. 31

YOPLAIT—NONE—Avenmore Waterford Foods plc; *Int'l*, pg. 102

YOPLAIT—Yogurt—General Mills, Inc.; *U.S. Public*, pg. 717

YOPLAIT CRUNCH'N YOGURT—Yogurt—General Mills, Inc.; *U.S. Public*, pg. 717

YOPLAIT CUSTARD STYLE—Yogurt—General Mills, Inc.; *U.S. Public*, pg. 717

YOPLAIT LIGHT—Yogurt—Yoplait USA; *U.S. Public*, pg. 718

YORCALBRO—Tubes—IMI Plc; *Int'l*, pg. 646

YORK—Peppermint Patties—Hershey Chocolate U.S.A.; *U.S. Public*, pg. 812

YORK—Peppermint Patty—Hershey Foods Corporation; *U.S. Public*, pg. 811

YORK—Food Prods.—Maple Leaf Foods Inc.; *Int'l*, pg. 841

YORK—Air Conditioners & Furnaces—Unitary Products Group; *U.S. Public*, pg. 1788

YORK—Fitness Products—York Barbell Co., Inc.; *U.S. Private*, pg. 1196

YORK—Air Conditioning Equip.—York International Corporation; *U.S. Public*, pg. 1789

YORK NEWS TIMES—Newspapers—Shivers Trading & Operating Co.; *U.S. Private*, pg. 994

YORK PHOTO LABS—Photo Processing—Nashua Corporation; *U.S. Public*, pg. 1152

YORK USA—Fitness Products—York Barbell Co., Inc.; *U.S. Private*, pg. 1196

YORKE—Shirtmakers—Hartmarx Corporation; *U.S. Public*, pg. 795

YORKER—Plastic Closures—Alltrista Corporation; *U.S. Public*, pg. 56

YORKIE—Chocolates—Nestle-Rowntree Ltd.; *Int'l*, pg. 921

YORKMESH—Mist Eliminators—Koch Otto H. York Co., Inc.; *U.S. Private*, pg. 628

YORKSHIRE—Pipes & Pipe Fittings—IMI Plc; *Int'l*, pg. 646

YORKTOWN—Plywood & Building Products—Georgia-Pacific Corporation; *U.S. Public*, pg. 735

YORKTOWN—Paper for Office & Personal Copiers—Union Camp Corporation; *U.S. Public*, pg. 1665

YORKTOWNE—Cabinets—Yorktowne, Inc.; *U.S. Private*, pg. 1196

YOU & I—NONE—Names for Dames, Inc.; *U.S. Private*, pg. 773

YOU AND YOUR MONEY—Financial Advice Program—Westwood One, Inc.; *U.S. Public*, pg. 1763

YOU BABES—Girls & Juniors Sportswear & Dresses—Fritzi of California Manufacturing Corp.; *U.S. Private*, pg. 429

YOU CAN'T ARGUE WITH PHYSICS—NONE—Callaway Golf Company; *U.S. Public*, pg. 294

YOU DESERVE OUR BEST—Product Mark—D & W Food Centers, Inc.; *U.S. Private*, pg. 300

YOU JUST CAN'T GET IT ANYWHERE ELSE—NONE—Cambridge Soundworks, Inc.; *U.S. Private*, pg. 202

YOU: LIVING LEARNING & CARING—Textbook Designed to Help Students Learn About Themselves & Environment—Goodheart-Willcox Publisher; *U.S. Private*, pg. 464

YOUNG AMERICA BY STANLEY—Youth Furniture—Stanley Furniture Co.; *U.S. Public*, pg. 1508

YOUNG AMERICAN—Studio Beds—Kingsdown, Inc.; *U.S. Private*, pg. 622

YOUNG CLASSICS—NONE—Tandy Brands Accessories, Inc.; *U.S. Public*, pg. 1560

YOUNG CURL—Hair Waving Solution—Revlon-Realistic Professional Products, Inc.; *U.S. Private*, pg. 690

YOUNG DEBS—Brassieres, Lingerie & Children's Nightwear—Wacoal America Inc.; *Int'l*, pg. 1484

YOUNG HAIR—Hair Coloring Preparation—Revlon-Realistic Professional Products, Inc.; *U.S. Private*, pg. 690

YOUNG KENT—Men's Apparel—International Cosmetics Co., Ltd.; *Int'l*, pg. 684

YOUNG MODEL BUILDERS CLUB—Children's Club—Gruner + Jahr USA Publishing, Inc.; *Int'l*, pg. 190

YOUNG ROMANTICS—Home Fashions—Croscill, Inc.; *U.S. Private*, pg. 290

YOUNG SMOOTHIE—Foundations—The Strouse, Adler Company; *U.S. Private*, pg. 1047

YOUNG STUFF—Large-Size Womens' Apparel—Young Stuff Apparel Group, Inc.; *U.S. Private*, pg. 1202

YOUNG 'UNS—Shoes—Tober Industries, Inc.; *U.S. Private*, pg. 1089

YOUNGER'S—Ales & Beers—Scottish & Newcastle plc; *Int'l*, pg. 1211

YOUNGER'S TARTAN SPECIAL—Ale—Scottish & Newcastle Importers Co.; *Int'l*, pg. 1212

YOUNGER'S TARTAN ALE—NONE—Scottish & Newcastle Importers Co.; *Int'l*, pg. 1212

YOUNG'S—Frozen & Chilled Foods—United Biscuits (Holdings) Plc; *Int'l*, pg. 1442

YOUR CAT—Pet Magazine—EMAP Pursuit Publishing; *Int'l*, pg. 451

YOUR CHURCH—Magazine—Christianity Today, Inc.; *U.S. Private*, pg. 238

YOUR DOG—Pet Magazine—EMAP Pursuit Publishing; *Int'l*, pg. 451

YOUR DOLLARS—News Program—Westwood One, Inc.; *U.S. Public*, pg. 1763

YOUR GARDEN—Special Interest Magazine—IPC Magazines Limited; *Int'l*, pg. 651

YOUR GLOBAL CONNECTION—NONE—Berg Electronics; *U.S. Public*, pg. 212

YOUR GLOBAL CONNECTION AND YOUR GLOBAL DESIGN—NONE—Berg Electronics; *U.S. Public*, pg. 212

YOUR GREATEST GUIDE TO CALORIES—U.K. Health Magazine—EMAP Elan; *Int'l*, pg. 451

YOUR HOME YOUR WAY—Calton's Home Customization Program—Calton, Inc.; *U.S. Public*, pg. 296

YOUR MONEY MINUTE—News Program—Westwood One, Inc.; *U.S. Public*, pg. 1763

YOUR PARTNER IN PRINTING—Printing Franchise—American Speedy Printing Centers, Inc.; *U.S. Private*, pg. 62

YOUR PARTNER IN PRODUCTIVITY—Company Slogan—Beloit Corporation; *U.S. Public*, pg. 789

YOUR PARTNERS IN PAPERMAKING—Company Slogan—Beloit Corporation; *U.S. Public*, pg. 789

YOUR PASSPORT TO THE STARS—Video Rental Program—National Video, Inc.; *U.S. Public*, pg. 1755

YOURS—U.K. Retirement Magazine—Choice Publications Ltd; *Int'l*, pg. 451

YOUTH RESTRICTED VIEWING—Video Tape—Blockbuster Entertainment Group; *U.S. Private*, pg. 775

YOUTHENING HAND & BODY LOTION—Cosmetics—Irma Shorell, Inc.; *U.S. Private*, pg. 1101

YUASA—NONE—Yuasa-Exide, Inc.; *Int'l*, pg. 1522

YUASA-GBC—NONE—Yuasa-Exide, Inc.; *Int'l*, pg. 1522

YUBAN—Coffee—Kraft Foods, Inc.; *U.S. Public*, pg. 1287

YUBAN—Coffee—Philip Morris Companies Inc.; *U.S. Public*, pg. 1287

YUCAIPA VALEY—Shell Eggs—McAnally Enterprises, Inc.; *U.S. Private*, pg. 718

YUCCA—Food Products—Rykoff-Sexton, Inc.; *U.S. Public*, pg. 918

YUKON—Hose—The Goodyear Tire & Rubber Company; *U.S. Public*, pg. 752

YUKON JACK CANADIAN LIQUEUR—NONE—Heublein, Inc.; *Int'l*, pg. 410

YUNSA—Textiles—Sabanci Holding A.S.; *Int'l*, pg. 1167

YUTOPAR—NONE—Astra AB; *Int'l*, pg. 93

YUTOPAR—Pharmaceutical Products—Astra USA, Inc.; *Int'l*, pg. 93

YVES ROCHE—Wine & Spirits—Leonard Kreusch; *U.S. Private*, pg. 635

YVES SAINT LAURENT—Menswear—Arrow Shirt Company; *Int'l*, pg. 194

YVES SAINT LAURENT—NONE—Luxottica Group S.p.A.; *Int'l*, pg. 822

Brand Name Index

YVES ST. LAURENT—Shoes—Schwartz & Benjamin, Inc.; *U.S. Private*, pg. 974

Z

Z—Photo Typesetters—AGFA EPS Division; *Int'l*, pg. 172

Z—Beer—Asahi Breweries Ltd.; *Int'l*, pg. 83

Z—Mining Chemicals—The Dow Chemical Company; *U.S. Public*, pg. 522

Z—NONE—Elcor Corporation; *U.S. Public*, pg. 567

Z—Distributorship Services—The Mead Corporation; *U.S. Public*, pg. 1074

ZB50—Motorcycle—American Honda Motor Co., Inc. Motorcycle Division; *Int'l*, pg. 634

ZCX—Full Line of Woods & Irons—Square Two Golf Incorporated; *U.S. Public*, pg. 1501

Z-CHLOR—Disinfection Product—Bailey, Fischer & Porter Company; *Int'l*, pg. 449

Z-COAT—Steel Tubing—Bundy North America; *Int'l*, pg. 1340

Z-DENSILOG—NONE—Western Atlas Logging Services; *U.S. Public*, pg. 1757

Z-54—Heavy Duty Wallcovering Primer—Wm. Zinsser & Co., Inc.; *U.S. Public*, pg. 1358

Z50R—Motorcycle—American Honda Motor Co., Inc. Motorcycle Division; *Int'l*, pg. 634

Z-14—Fragrances—Halston Enterprises, Inc.; *U.S. Private*, pg. 690

ZGA—NONE—Berg Electronics; *U.S. Public*, pg. 212

ZGS—Photo Typesetters—AGFA EPS Division; *Int'l*, pg. 172

ZHN—Photo Typesetters—AGFA EPS Division; *Int'l*, pg. 172

ZHP—Photo Typesetters—AGFA EPS Division; *Int'l*, pg. 172

ZHS—Photo Typesetter—AGFA EPS Division; *Int'l*, pg. 172

ZIF—Zero Insertion Force Printed Circuit Board Retainer—Dynamics Corporation of America; *U.S. Public*, pg. 286

ZIF—Zero Insertion Force P/C Board Retainers—International Electronic Research Corp.; *U.S. Public*, pg. 286

Z-KOHO—Metal fittings—The Dow Chemical Company; *U.S. Public*, pg. 522

ZLP—Photo Typesetters—AGFA EPS Division; *Int'l*, pg. 172

Z-LIGHT—Microspheres—3M; *U.S. Public*, pg. 1604

ZMC—Injection-Molding Process Utilizing Fiber-Reinforced Plastic—Saint-Gobain; *Int'l*, pg. 1170

ZMI-1000—NONE—Zygo Corporation; *U.S. Public*, pg. 1795

ZMR—Photo Typesetters—AGFA EPS Division; *Int'l*, pg. 172

ZMS—Intramedullary Fixation System—Bristol-Myers Squibb Company; *U.S. Public*, pg. 253

Z-MODULE—Radial Compression Separation System—Millipore Corporation; *U.S. Public*, pg. 1112

ZPL—Zebra Programming Language—Zebra Technologies Corporation; *U.S. Public*, pg. 1790

Z-PAC—Powered Roller Conveyors—Litton Industries, Inc.; *U.S. Public*, pg. 1002

Z-PAC—DC-DC Power Source—Reliability Incorporated; *U.S. Public*, pg. 1373

Z-PAK—NONE—Pfizer Inc.; *U.S. Public*, pg. 1281

Z-PAL—Conveyors—Litton Industries, Inc.; *U.S. Public*, pg. 1002

ZPLATE-ATL—Anterior Fixation of the Thoracic and/or Lumbar Spine—Sofamor Danek Group, Inc.; *U.S. Public*, pg. 1482

ZSTAR—Electronics—National Semiconductor Corporation; *U.S. Public*, pg. 1159

Z-SCAN—3-D X-Ray Imaging Technology—EG & G Astrophysics; *U.S. Public*, pg. 543

Z-SCAN—Specialty X-Ray—EG & G, Inc.; *U.S. Public*, pg. 542

Z SEAL—Bi-Material Rod Seal—Macrotech Plyseal, Inc.; *U.S. Public*, pg. 693

Z SERIES—Marine Transmissions—Regal-Beloit Corporation; *U.S. Public*, pg. 1370

Z-SPAR—Marine Coatings—RPM, Inc.; *U.S. Public*, pg. 1356

ZT—Jacketing For Cables—The Zippertubing Co.; *U.S. Private*, pg. 1207

ZTOF—Zink Thermal Oxidizer Flare—John Zink Co.; *U.S. Private*, pg. 628

Z-TAC—Subscription TV Equipment—Zenith Electronics Corp.; *U.S. Public*, pg. 1790

Z-UP80RC—Automatic 35mm Camera—Konica Corporation; *Int'l*, pg. 748

Z-UP28W—Camera—Konica Corporation; *Int'l*, pg. 748

Z-VIEW—For Two-Way Cable TV System—Zenith Electronics Corp.; *U.S. Public*, pg. 1790

Z. ZILDJIAN—Cymbals—Avedis Zildjian Company; *U.S. Private*, pg. 1206

Z-MAP PLUS—NONE—Landmark Graphics Corporation; *U.S. Public*, pg. 776

ZAAP—Golf Clubs—Tommy Armour Golf; *U.S. Public*, pg. 1683

ZACKY FARMS—Chicken Turkey Further Processed—Zacky Farms, Inc.; *U.S. Private*, pg. 1203

ZACUBA—Clay Bricks—CSR Limited; *Int'l*, pg. 245

ZADITEN—Asthma Prophylactic—Novartis AG; *Int'l*, pg. 971

ZAGNUT—Chocolate—Huhtamaki Oy; *Int'l*, pg. 638

ZAGREB—Canned Hams—M.H. Greenebaum, Inc.; *U.S. Private*, pg. 477

ZALES—Jewelry & Stores—Zale Corporation; *U.S. Public*, pg. 1789

ZALUTITE—COATED Steel Strip—British Steel Plc; *Int'l*, pg. 220

ZANAFLEX—NONE—Elan Corporation Plc; *Int'l*, pg. 435

ZANDVLIET ESTATE—Wine—Distillers Corporation S.A.; *Int'l*, pg. 1129

ZANIES—Hair Accessories—Goody Products, Inc.; *U.S. Public*, pg. 1177

ZANITRIN—Cefatrizine—Bristol-Myers Squibb Company; *U.S. Public*, pg. 253

ZANKER—NONE—Zanussi Italia S.p.A.; *Int'l*, pg. 442

ZANTAC—Anti-ulcer Treatment—Glaxo Wellcome Inc.; *Int'l*, pg. 552

ZANTAC—Pharmaceutical—Glaxo Wellcome plc; *Int'l*, pg. 552

ZANTAC—Antacid—Warner-Lambert Company; *U.S. Public*, pg. 1738

ZANUSSI—Appliances—Electrolux, AB; *Int'l*, pg. 438

ZANUSSI—NONE—Zanussi Italia S.p.A.; *Int'l*, pg. 442

ZANUSSI ELETTROMECCANICA—Compressors—Electrolux, AB; *Int'l*, pg. 438

ZANXX—Lighting Products—Cooper Industries, Inc.; *U.S. Public*, pg. 442

ZAP!—NONE—Landmark Graphics Corporation; *U.S. Public*, pg. 776

ZAP CAP—Bottle Top Filter—Schleicher & Schuell, Inc.; *Int'l*, pg. 1206

ZAP-IT—Masonry Drive Anchor—Gunnebo Fastening Corp.; *U.S. Private*, pg. 488

ZAPATA—Offshore Drilling—Zapata Corporation; *U.S. Public*, pg. 1789

ZAPATA WHITE & GOLD—Tequila—Laird & Company; *U.S. Private*, pg. 642

ZAPPETITES—Microwaveable Snacks—Philip Morris Companies Inc.; *U.S. Public*, pg. 1287

ZAPSET—Setting Agent—Redmond Products, Inc.; *U.S. Public*, pg. 254

ZAROXOLYN—Tablets (Metolazone Tablets, USP)—Medeva Pharmaceuticals; *Int'l*, pg. 852

ZARSIL—Zirconium Silicate Grinding Beads—Ferro Corporation; *U.S. Public*, pg. 618

ZAURUS—Personal Digital Assistants—Sharp Electronics Corporation; *Int'l*, pg. 1228

ZAX ELECTRIC SAFETY CHILDREN'S PROGRAM—NONE—Duke Energy Corporation; *U.S. Public*, pg. 534

ZAXXON 3-D—3-D Videogame—Sega of America Inc.; *Int'l*, pg. 1218

ZAZCH—Men's Apparel—International Cosmetics Co., Ltd.; *Int'l*, pg. 684

ZEBBIES—Batters, Breadings—McCormick/Schilling; *U.S. Public*, pg. 1066

ZEBCO—Fishing Equipment—Brunswick Corporation; *U.S. Public*, pg. 265

ZEBCO—Fishing Tackle—Zebco; *U.S. Public*, pg. 265

ZEBO—Grate Polish—Reckitt & Colman plc; *Int'l*, pg. 1089

ZEBRA—Photo Typesetters—AGFA EPS Division; *Int'l*, pg. 172

ZEBRA—Golf Clubs—RAM Golf Corporation; *U.S. Private*, pg. 908

ZEC—Color Monitors—Zenith Electronics Corp.; *U.S. Public*, pg. 1790

ZEDA—Pickled Food Products—Purity Products Inc.; *U.S. Private*, pg. 896

ZEE—Paper Towels and Napkins—Consumer Products Business; *U.S. Public*, pg. 671

ZEE—Towels, Napkins—Fort James Corporation; *U.S. Public*, pg. 670

ZEE ADVANTAGE—Training Series—Zee Medical, Inc.; *U.S. Public*, pg. 1073

ZEE CAP—Zinc Wine Bottle Closures—Alltrista Corporation; *U.S. Public*, pg. 56

ZEEOSPHERES—Hollow Spheres—3M; *U.S. Public*, pg. 1604

ZEFLUOR—Filtration Products—Gelman Sciences, Inc.; *U.S. Public*, pg. 1253

ZEFSPORT—Nylon—BASF Corporation Fiber Products Division; *Int'l*, pg. 105

ZEFTRON—Nylon—BASF Corporation Fiber Products Division; *Int'l*, pg. 105

ZEFTRON 500—Solution-Dyed Nylon—BASF Corporation Fiber Products Division; *Int'l*, pg. 105

ZEFTRON 200—Nylon—BASF Corporation Fiber Products Division; *Int'l*, pg. 105

ZEFTRON 2000—Solution-Dyed Nylon—BASF Corporation Fiber Products Division; *Int'l*, pg. 105

ZEL—NONE—Provigo Inc.; *Int'l*, pg. 1072

ZEL-O-PAQUE—Printing Paper—The Mead Corporation; *U.S. Public*, pg. 1074

ZELCON—Fabric Conditioner—Du Pont (E.I. Du Pont De Nemours & Co.); *U.S. Public*, pg. 530

ZELEX—NONE—Alltrista Corporation; *U.S. Public*, pg. 56

ZELEX—Coextruded Plastic Sheet—Ball Corporation; *U.S. Public*, pg. 170

ZELIG—Open Office Systems—Carter Holt Harvey Limited; *U.S. Public*, pg. 904

ZELITE—Polyethylene Tubing—NewAge Industries Inc.; *U.S. Private*, pg. 796

ZELITE—Polyethylene Tubing—Newage Industries Inc., Plastics Technology Group; *U.S. Private*, pg. 796

ZELL—Plastic Drinking Cups—The Mead Corporation; *U.S. Public*, pg. 1074

ZELLER—Specialty Closures—Carter Holt Harvey Limited; *U.S. Public*, pg. 904

ZELLER—Machine Parts—Zeller Corp.; *U.S. Private*, pg. 1204

ZELLERBACH—Distributorship Services—The Mead Corporation; *U.S. Public*, pg. 1074

ZEMOPLAST—Cement Sand Binder—Raschig GmbH; *U.S. Private*, pg. 827

ZEMURON—Muscle Relaxant—Akzo Nobel N.V.; *Int'l*, pg. 42

ZEMURON—Pharmaceutical—Organon Inc.; *Int'l*, pg. 48

ZEN—Fragrance—Shiseido Cosmetics (America) Ltd.; *Int'l*, pg. 1235

ZENA—Jeans—MUDD Jeans, Inc.; *U.S. Private*, pg. 766

ZENATE—Pharmaceutical Products—Solvay Pharmaceuticals, Inc.; *Int'l*, pg. 1278

ZENDEL—High-Tech Polymer—Amoco Corporation; *U.S. Public*, pg. 101

ZENDIUM—Oral Care Products—Sara Lee Corporation; *U.S. Public*, pg. 1432

ZENGER-MILLER—Educational/Instructional Materials—Zenger-Miller; *U.S. Public*, pg. 1617

ZENITH—Pumps—Parker Hannifin Corporation; *U.S. Public*, pg. 1259

ZENITH—Chiropractic Tables—Standex International Corporation; *U.S. Public*, pg. 1505

ZENITH—TM for Zenith Prods.—Zenith Electronics Corp.; *U.S. Public*, pg. 1790

ZENITH—Sheet Metal Fabrication—Zenith Products Corp.; *U.S. Private*, pg. 1054

ZENITH BOOKS—Book Imprint—Bertelsmann AG; *Int'l*, pg. 189

ZENITH CARPETS—Carpet—World Carpets, Inc.; *U.S. Private*, pg. 1190

ZENITH DATA SYSTEMS—P C Compatible Computers—Zenith Data Systems; *Int'l*, pg. 317

ZENOX—Flea & Tick Shampoo—Carter-Wallace, Inc.; *U.S. Public*, pg. 309

ZENTEL—NONE—SmithKline Beecham Corporation; *Int'l*, pg. 1264

ZENTEL—Anti-Infective—SmithKline Beecham plc; *Int'l*, pg. 1264

ZENTEL—Anthelmintic—SmithKline Beecham Research Limited; *Int'l*, pg. 1266

ZENTRON—High Strength Glass Fiber—Owens Corning; *U.S. Public*, pg. 1236

ZEOLEX—White Fillers—Rhone-Poulenc S.A.; *Int'l*, pg. 1108

ZEOSIL—White Fillers—Rhone-Poulenc S.A.; *Int'l*, pg. 1108

ZEP MFG. CO.—Sanitation Goods—National Service Industries, Inc.; *U.S. Public*, pg. 1160

ZEPEL—Fabric Fluoridizer—Du Pont (E.I. Du Pont De Nemours & Co.); *U.S. Public*, pg. 530

ZEPHAIRE—Full-Size Convertion Oven—The Blodgett Oven Co., Inc.; *U.S. Public*, pg. 1064

ZEPHYR—Self-Contained Industrial Dust Collector—Farr Company; *U.S. Public*, pg. 613

ZEPHYR—Gasoline—J.D. Streett & Co., Inc.; *U.S. Private*, pg. 1047

ZEPHYR BOOKS—Book Imprint—Bertelsmann AG; *Int'l*, pg. 189

ZEPHYRHILLS—Mineral Water—Nestle S.A.; *Int'l*, pg. 915

ZEPHYRHILLS—Mineral Water—The Perrier Group of America; *Int'l*, pg. 919

ZER-LON—Plastic Coated Picture Hanging Wire—Elco Textron; *U.S. Public*, pg. 1590

ZEREX—Automotive Antifreeze—Ashland, Inc.; *U.S. Public*, pg. 138

ZERO CENTURION—Aluminum Carrying Case—Zero Corporation; *U.S. Public*, pg. 1791

ZERO-FLEX—Rigid Grooved Pipe Coupling—Victaulic Company of America; *U.S. Private*, pg. 1138

ZERO GUARDIAN—Cabinet Line—Zero Corporation; *U.S. Public*, pg. 1791

ZERO H2O—Laminate Flooring Edge Treatment, Providing Seal to Resist Moisture—Pickering Inc.; *U.S. Private*, pg. 864

ZERO HALLIBURTON—Luggage, Cases & Photo & Video Cases—Zero Corporation; *U.S. Public*, pg. 1791

ZERO-MAX—Speed Transmission—Zero-Max, Inc.; *Int'l*, pg. 866

ZERO PAK—Alumimum & Steel Chassis—Zero Corporation; *U.S. Public*, pg. 1791

ZERO PRODUCTS DIVISON—Blast Cabinets, Automatic Blast Cabinets & Industrial Blast Rooms—Clemco Industries Corp.; *U.S. Private*, pg. 24

012 Benetton—NONE—Benetton Group S.p.A.; *Int'l*, pg. 186

02 LOTTO—NONE—Tattersalls; *Int'l*, pg. 1357

00—I.D. for Hardware Items—Loos & Co., Inc.; *U.S. Public*, pg. 675

00-7—Reloading Press—Hornady Manufacturing Company; *U.S. Private*, pg. 539

ZEROHAL—Cable Jacketing—Raychem Corporation; *U.S. Public*, pg. 1362

ZEROMATIC—pH Meter—Beckman Instruments, Inc.; *U.S. Public*, pg. 199

ZEROPACK—Hot Melt Adhesive—H.B. Fuller Company; *U.S. Public*, pg. 686

ZEROSTAT—Static Elimination Guns—Recoton Corporation; *U.S. Public*, pg. 1369

ZEROTONDO—Infant's Clothing—Benetton U.S.A. Corporation; *Int'l*, pg. 186

ZEROWATT—Household Appliances—Candy S.p.A.; *Int'l*, pg. 259

ZERTELL—Insecticide—The Dow Chemical Company; *U.S. Public*, pg. 522

ZEST—Magazine—The National Magazine Company Ltd.; *U.S. Private*, pg. 518

ZEST—Soap—The Procter & Gamble Company; *U.S. Public*, pg. 1330

ZEST FREE—Fragrance Free Bar Soap—The Procter & Gamble Company; *U.S. Public*, pg. 1330

ZESTA—Crackers—Keebler Company; *U.S. Public*, pg. 657

ZESTEE—Foods—Ventura Foods; *U.S. Private*, pg. 508

ZESTI SMOKE NATURAL SMOKE FLAVOR—Hickory & Mesquite Liquid Smoke Flavors On Liquid, Oil & Powder Bases—Hickory Specialties, Inc.; *U.S. Public*, pg. 596

ZESTON—2000 PVC Insulated Fitting Covers—Johns Manville Corporation; *U.S. Public*, pg. 927

ZESTORETIC—Pharmaceutical—Zeneca Group Plc; *Int'l*, pg. 1524

ZESTRIL—Pharmaceutical—Zeneca Group Plc; *Int'l*, pg. 1524

ZETABON—Tape—The Dow Chemical Company; *U.S. Public*, pg. 522

ZETALITE—Emergency Luminaires—JSB Electrical PLC; *Int'l*, pg. 453

ZETAMETER—Liquid-Solids Separation Equipment—Komline-Sanderson Engineering Corp.; *U.S. Private*, pg. 631

ZETAR—Pharmaceuticals—Rhone-Poulenc Rorer - U.S.; *Int'l*, pg. 1110

ZETEX—NONE—PAXAR Corporation; *U.S. Public*, pg. 1266

ZETRA—Roller Skates—Rollerblade, Inc.; *U.S. Private*, pg. 941

ZEUS—Fly Fishing Reels—Martin Reels, A Division of Zebco; *U.S. Public*, pg. 265

ZEVCO—Valves—Circle Seal Controls, Inc.; *U.S. Public*, pg. 1746

ZEZE—Mechanical Pencil & Ball Point Pen—Sanford Corporation; *U.S. Public*, pg. 1178

ZHENKA—Vodka—Jenkins Spirits Corp. Ltd.; *U.S. Private*, pg. 585

ZIAC—Cardiovascular Drug—American Home Products Corporation; *U.S. Public*, pg. 79

ZIEBART—Rust Protection, Paint Protection & Interior Protection—Ziebart International Corporation; *U.S. Private*, pg. 1205

ZIEBART TOYCAR—Application of Protection Products & Accessories—Ziebart International Corporation; *U.S. Private*, pg. 1205

ZIFCON—NONE—Molex Incorporated; *U.S. Public*, pg. 1121

ZIFGRIP—NONE—Berg Electronics; *U.S. Public*, pg. 212

ZIFTAC—NONE—Hypertronics Corporation; *Int'l*, pg. 1268

ZIG-ZAG—Blenders—Patterson-Kelley Company; *U.S. Public*, pg. 793

ZILBEL—Bells—Avedis Zildjian Company; *U.S. Private*, pg. 1206

ZILDJIAN—Drumsticks—Avedis Zildjian Company; *U.S. Private*, pg. 1206

ZILDJIAN—Cymbals—Avedis Zildjian Company; *U.S. Private*, pg. 1206

ZIM-AMERICAN ISRAELI SHIPPING—Cargo Shipping Line—Zim-American Israeli Shipping Co.; *U.S. Private*, pg. 1206

ZIMA CLEARMALT—Premium Clear Malt Beverage—Adolph Coors Company; *U.S. Public*, pg. 445

ZIMMATIC—NONE—Lindsay Manufacturing Company; *U.S. Public*, pg. 999

ZIMMER—Pelvic Plates—Bristol-Myers Squibb Company; *U.S. Public*, pg. 253

ZIMMERMAN—Ergonomic Handling Systems—Tool & Hoist Division; *U.S. Public*, pg. 877

ZIN-TECH—Agricultural Chemicals—IMC Agribusiness; *U.S. Public*, pg. 856

ZINACEF—Antibiotic—Glaxo Wellcome Inc.; *Int'l*, pg. 552

ZINC CALCINE—NONE—Horsehead Resource Development Company, Inc.; *U.S. Private*, pg. 540

ZINC RENU—Aerosol Zinc—CRC Industries, Inc.; *U.S. Private*, pg. 138

ZINC-SELE—Zinc Coating—Rust-Oleum Corporation; *U.S. Public*, pg. 1358

ZINCAHMEX—Galvanized Products—Altos Hornos de Mexico, S.A.; *Int'l*, pg. 66

ZINCAL—Zinc Process—LeaRonal, Inc.; *U.S. Public*, pg. 982

ZINCFRIN—Zinc Sulfate/Phenylephrine—Alcon Laboratories, Inc.; *Int'l*, pg. 916

ZINCLAD—Specialty Nails—Maze Nails; *U.S. Private*, pg. 718

ZINCOR-NOVOZINC—NONE—Cockerill Sambre; *Int'l*, pg. 301

ZINCOVER—Chemical Reagant—Hach Company; *U.S. Public*, pg. 773

ZINCPRIME 100—Zinc Rich Primers—Grow Group, Inc.; *Int'l*, pg. 663

ZINCPRIME 100—Zinc Rich Primers—ICI Paints; *Int'l*, pg. 664

ZINCROMETAL—Zinc Painted Sheet Steel—Inland Steel Industries, Inc.; *U.S. Public*, pg. 879

ZINN—Special Wine—Eckes AG; *Int'l*, pg. 432

ZINNANTI SURGICAL—Surgical Products—BEI Medical Systems Company; *U.S. Private*, pg. 106

ZINNAT/CEFTIN—Pharmaceutical—Glaxo Wellcome plc; *Int'l*, pg. 552

ZINSSER—Shellac—RPM, Inc.; *U.S. Public*, pg. 1356

ZINSSER—NONE—Wm. Zinsser & Co., Inc.; *U.S. Public*, pg. 1358

ZINTAN—Herbicides—Agrolinz Melamin GmbH; *Int'l*, pg. 356

ZINTEC—Coated Steel Ship—British Steel Plc; *Int'l*, pg. 220

ZIP—Wax Hair Removal System & Creme Bleach—Lee Pharmaceuticals; *U.S. Public*, pg. 984

ZIP—Fire Lighter—Reckitt & Colman plc; *Int'l*, pg. 1089

ZIP—NONE—Texas Instruments Incorporated; *U.S. Public*, pg. 1585

ZIP-A-DEE-DOO-DA—Suckers—Charms Company, *U.S. Private*, pg. 1621

ZIP BOX BLUE—Outlets & Switch Boxes—The Lamson & Sessions Co.; *U.S. Public*, pg. 976

ZIP CLAMP—Integral Clamp—The Lamson & Sessions Co.; *U.S. Public*, pg. 976

ZIP CLIP—Outlet & Switch Boxes—The Lamson & Sessions Co.; *U.S. Public*, pg. 976

ZIP DEMOGRAPHICS—Marketing Information Software—CACI International Inc; *U.S. Public*, pg. 272

ZIP GELO—Plastic Bags—The Dow Chemical Company; *U.S. Public*, pg. 522

ZIP-GUARD—Urethane Clear Wood Finish—Star Bronze Company; *U.S. Private*, pg. 1034

ZIP-GUARD WOOD STAIN—Interior Wood Stain—Star Bronze Company; *U.S. Private*, pg. 1034

ZIP-IT—Hollow Wall Anchor—Powers Fastening, Inc.; *U.S. Private*, pg. 878

ZIP-KLEEN—Brush Cleaner—Star Bronze Company; *U.S. Private*, pg. 1034

ZIP-LIFT—Hoist—Harnischfeger Industries, Inc.; *U.S. Public*, pg. 788

ZIP-LOK—Runners—Pawling Corporation; *U.S. Private*, pg. 844

ZIP MOUNT—Swing Clamp—The Lamson & Sessions Co.; *U.S. Public*, pg. 976

ZIP-ON—Jacketing for Cables—The Zippertubing Co.; *U.S. Private*, pg. 1207

ZIP-PAC—Resealable Packaging—The Dow Chemical Company; *U.S. Public*, pg. 522

ZIP-SANDER—Liquid Paint Sander—Star Bronze Company; *U.S. Private*, pg. 1034

ZIP SORTER—Package Conveying Machinery—Alvey Systems, Inc; *U.S. Public*, pg. 47

ZIP-STRIP—Paint & Varnish Remover—Star Bronze Company; *U.S. Private*, pg. 1034

ZIP-STRIP LIQUID—Refinisher & Remover—Star Bronze Company; *U.S. Private*, pg. 1034

ZIP STRIP WATER RINSABLE—Paint & Varnish Remover—Star Bronze Company; *U.S. Private*, pg. 1034

ZIP SWITCH—Package Conveying Machinery—Alvey Systems, Inc; *U.S. Public*, pg. 47

ZIP III—Hoist—Harnischfeger Industries, Inc.; *U.S. Public*, pg. 788

ZIP-TITE—Hand-Operated Tools—Reynolds Metals Company; *U.S. Public*, pg. 1385

ZIP-TOWLS—Paper Towels—Bay West Paper Corp. Towel & Tissue Div.; *U.S. Public*, pg. 1747

ZIP II—Hoist—Harnischfeger Industries, Inc.; *U.S. Public*, pg. 788

ZIP WAX—Car Wash—Turtle Wax, Inc.; *U.S. Private*, pg. 1110

ZIPCARD—Forms—The Standard Register Company; *U.S. Public*, pg. 1505

ZIPCON—NONE—Molex Incorporated; *U.S. Public*, pg. 1121

ZIPF'S CANDIES—Confectionery—Boyer Candy Company Inc.; *U.S. Private*, pg. 162

ZIPGARDS—Disposable Plastic Resealable Bags—Handgards Inc.; *U.S. Public*, pg. 499

ZIPLIP—Reclosable Poly Bag—KCL Corporation; *U.S. Private*, pg. 603

ZIPLOC—Plastic Bags—The Dow Chemical Company; *U.S. Public*, pg. 522

ZIPLOC—Plastic Food Bags—DowBrands, L.P.; *U.S. Public*, pg. 523

ZIPLON—Zipper—YKK (U.S.A.); *Int'l*, pg. 1515

ZIPLOX—NONE—Life Technologies, Inc.; *U.S. Public*, pg. 504

ZIPMAILER—Business Forms—The Standard Register Company; *U.S. Public*, pg. 1505

ZIPPAK—Forms Holder—The Standard Register Company; *U.S. Public*, pg. 1505

ZIPPER-LIP—Lip Systems for Earthmoving Buckets—Esco Corporation; *U.S. Private*, pg. 382

ZIPPERTUBING—Zip on Jacketing—The Zippertubing Co.; *U.S. Public*, pg. 1207

ZIPPIE—Mexican Food Products—Don Miguel Mexican Foods, Inc.; *U.S. Private*, pg. 339

ZIPSET—Business Forms—The Standard Register Company; *U.S. Public*, pg. 1505

ZIPTAPE—Marking Tapes—The Zippertubing Co.; *U.S. Private*, pg. 1207

ZIPY—Plastic Bags—The Dow Chemical Company; *U.S. Public*, pg. 522

ZIRCINOC—NONE—Elkem ASA; *Int'l*, pg. 446

ZIRCO—Driers, Organometallic Based—Akzo Nobel N.V.; *Int'l*, pg. 42

ZIRLANE—High Temperature Blanket—Kerlane; *Int'l*, pg. 1176

ZIRMAG—Refractories—Resco Products, Inc.; *U.S. Private*, pg. 924

ZIRMET—Zirconia-Alumina Abrasive Belts & Papers—Buehler, Limited; *U.S. Public*, pg. 574

ZIRMONITE—Zirconia Advanced Material System—Diamonite Plant; *U.S. Public*, pg. 618

ZITEL—Trademark—Zitel Corporation; *U.S. Public*, pg. 1793

ZITEL PRIMARY STORAGE—Solid State Mass Memory System—Zitel Corporation; *U.S. Public*, pg. 1793

ZITEX—Fibrous-Porous TFE Rolls, Tapes & Filter Discs—Norton Performance Plastics; *Int'l*, pg. 1174

ZITHROMAX—Azithromycin—Pfizer Inc.; *U.S. Public*, pg. 1281

ZOCO—Aperitif—Groupe Pernod Ricard; *Int'l*, pg. 566

ZOCOR—Simvastatin—Merck & Co., Inc.; *U.S. Public*, pg. 1090

ZOCOR—Pharmaceutical—Merck Human Health Division (U.S. Human Health); *U.S. Public*, pg. 1091

ZODIAC—GPS Receiver Chipsets—Rockwell International Corporation; *U.S. Public*, pg. 1397

ZODIAC—Watches—Wittnauer International, Inc.; *U.S. Public*, pg. 273

ZODIAC USA—Shoes & Boots—Encore Shoe Corporation; *U.S. Private*, pg. 375

ZOEGAS KAFFE—Gourmet Coffee—Nestle S.A.; *Int'l*, pg. 915

ZOFRAN—Anti-Nausea Drug—Glaxo Wellcome Inc.; *Int'l*, pg. 552

ZOFRAN—Pharmaceuticals—Glaxo Wellcome plc; *Int'l*, pg. 552

ZOHAR—White Printing Papers for Color Printing of Books, Maps, Stationery, etc.—American Israeli Paper Mills Ltd.; *Int'l*, pg. 74

ZOHAR COLORED—NONE—American Israeli Paper Mills Ltd.; *Int'l*, pg. 74

ZOHAR COPIER—Woodfree White Papers for Copiers—American Israeli Paper Mills Ltd.; *Int'l*, pg. 74

ZOHAR COPIER COLORED—NONE—American Israeli Paper Mills Ltd.; *Int'l*, pg. 74

ZOHAR IMPROVED COPIER AND LASER—NONE—American Israeli Paper Mills Ltd.; *Int'l*, pg. 74

ZOHAR OPTICAL—NONE—American Israeli Paper Mills Ltd.; *Int'l*, pg. 74

ZOHAR PAZ—Recycled for Printing—American Israeli Paper Mills Ltd.; *Int'l*, pg. 74

ZOLADEX—Pharmaceutical—Zeneca Group Plc; *Int'l*, pg. 1524

ZOLICEF—Infectious Disease Therapy—Bristol-Myers Squibb Company; *U.S. Public*, pg. 253

ZOLOFT/LUSTRAL—Sertraline—Pfizer Inc.; *U.S. Public*, pg. 1281

ZOMERGOUD—NONE—Grolsch N.V.; *Int'l*, pg. 559

ZON—Transaction Computer/Terminal—VeriFone, Inc.; *U.S. Public*, pg. 815

ZON-O-DOR—Non Mechanical Deodorant Diffuser—Surco Products, Inc.; *U.S. Private*, pg. 1056

ZONAREZ—Polyterpene Resins—Arizona Chemical Div.; *U.S. Public*, pg. 901

ZONATAC—Tackifying Resins—Arizona Chemical Div.; *U.S. Public*, pg. 901

ZONE-A-MATIC—Motorized Control Valves—Edwards Engineering Corporation; *U.S. Private*, pg. 365

ZONE PHONE—Wireless Remote Telephone—Sony Electronics; *Int'l*, pg. 1281

ZONEMASTER—Air Conditioning—Lennox International Inc.; *U.S. Private*, pg. 659

ZONESTER—Resin Esters—Arizona Chemical Div.; *U.S. Public*, pg. 901

ZONEX—Security System—Radionics, Inc.; *U.S. Public*, pg. 501

ZONITE—Vaginal Douche—Menley & James Laboratories, Inc.; *U.S. Public*, pg. 1086

ZONK—Greeting Cards & Gift Wrap—American Greetings Corporation; *U.S. Public*, pg. 77

ZONOLITE—NONE—Grace Construction Products; *U.S. Public*, pg. 755

ZOO—Animal Crackers—Austin Quality Foods; *U.S. Private*, pg. 100

THE ZOO FOOD FESTIVAL—Restaurant—The Levy Organization; *U.S. Private*, pg. 664

ZOO-KINI'S BUFFET—Buffet—Furr's/Bishops, Inc.; *U.S. Public*, pg. 689

ZOOM BROOM—Carpet Sweeper—Bissell Inc.; *U.S. Private*, pg. 145

ZOOM/FAX MODEM—NONE—Zoom Telephonics, Inc.; *U.S. Public*, pg. 1794

ZOOM/MODEM—Computer Modems—Zoom Telephonics, Inc.; *U.S. Public*, pg. 1794

ZOOM 2000—Microscope—Leica, Inc.; *Int'l*, pg. 806

ZOPPAS—NONE—Zanussi Italia S.p.A.; *Int'l*, pg. 442

ZORB-IT-ALL—Hygienic Fluid Absorber—Surco Products, Inc.; *U.S. Private*, pg. 1056

ZORBIT—Baby Products—Courtaulds Textiles Plc; *Int'l*, pg. 339

ZORIAL—Cotton Herbicide—Novartis AG; *Int'l*, pg. 971

ZORIAL—Herbicide—Sandoz Agro, Inc.; *Int'l*, pg. 974

ZORPRIN—Pharmaceuticals—Knoll Pharmaceutical Company; *Int'l*, pg. 105

ZORRO—Liquid & Powder Detergent—Nuevo Federal S.A.; *Int'l*, pg. 990

ZOSYN—Nosocomial Pneumonia Drug—American Home Products Corporation; *U.S. Public*, pg. 79

ZOTON—NONE—Wyeth Australia Pty. Ltd.; *U.S. Public*, pg. 82

ZOTOS RX—Salon Hair-Care Products—Shiseido Company Ltd.; *Int'l*, pg. 1235

ZOVIRAX—Antiviral Product—Glaxo Wellcome PLC; *Int'l*, pg. 553

ZOVIRAX—Gential Herpes Treatment—Warner-Lambert Consumer Healthcare; *U.S. Public*, pg. 1739

ZOX—Glass & Plastic Polish—Ferro Corporation; *U.S. Public*, pg. 618

ZU-PREEM—Zoo Foods—Hill's Pet Nutrition; *U.S. Public*, pg. 397

ZUMA BEACH—Girls' Swimwear—Jantzen; *U.S. Public*, pg. 1702

ZIPPER—Cutlery—Buck Knives, Inc.; *U.S. Private*, pg. 177

ZURICH INSURANCE—NONE—Zurich Insurance Company; *Int'l*, pg. 1529

ZURICH INSURANCE GROUP—NONE—Zurich Insurance Company; *Int'l*, pg. 1529

ZURICH INTERNATIONAL—NONE—Zurich Insurance Company; *Int'l*, pg. 1529

ZURICH INVESTMENT MANAGEMENT—NONE—Zurich Insurance Company; *Int'l*, pg. 1529

ZURICH LIFE—NONE—Zurich Insurance Company; *Int'l*, pg. 1529

ZURICH REINSURANCE—NONE—Zurich Insurance Company; *Int'l*, pg. 1529

ZURION—NONE—Health Products Corporation; *U.S. Private*, pg. 514

ZWAARDEMAKER—Jams & Marmalades—CSM N.V.; *Int'l*, pg. 243

ZWIEBACK—Crackers—Nabisco Inc.; *U.S. Public*, pg. 1355

ZWITSAL—Baby-Care Products—Sara Lee Corporation; *U.S. Public*, pg. 1432

ZYGLO—Fluorescent Penetrant—ITW Magnaflux; *U.S. Public*, pg. 866

ZYGO—NONE—Zygo Corporation; *U.S. Public*, pg. 1795

ZYLAR SERIES—Clear Acrylic Terpolymers for Injection Molding—Nova Chemicals, Inc.; *Int'l*, pg. 971

ZYLOPRIM—Prescription Gout Treatment—Glaxo Wellcome PLC; *Int'l*, pg. 553

ZYMACAP—NONE—Lee Pharmaceuticals; *U.S. Public*, pg. 984

ZYMASE—Pharmaceutical—Organon Inc.; *Int'l*, pg. 48

ZYPREX—NONE—Eli Lilly and Company; *U.S. Public*, pg. 992

ZYRTEC—Cetirizine—Pfizer Inc.; *U.S. Public*, pg. 1281

ZYTEL—Nylon Resins—Du Pont (E.I. Du Pont De Nemours & Co.); *U.S. Public*, pg. 530

ZYTRON—Herbicide—The Dow Chemical Company; *U.S. Public*, pg. 522

MASTER GEOGRAPHIC INDEX TO U.S. LOCATED COMPANIES

ALABAMA

Addison

Cavalier Industries, Inc., P.O. Box 300, 35540, pg. 318 **PB**
Cavalier Manufacturing, Inc., P.O. Box 300, 35540, pg. 318 **PB**

Alabaster

Specification Rubber Products Inc., P.O. Box 568, 35007, pg. 52 **PV**

Albertville

Reeves Rubber, Marshall & McDonald, 35950, pg. 127 **IT**
Regions Bank/Albertville/Guntersville/Arab, P.O. Box 10, 35950-0010, pg. 1371 **PB**

Alexander City

RUSSELL CORPORATION, 755 Lee St., 35010, pg. 1413 **PB**

Aliceville

Aliceville Casting Co., One Baptist Line Rd., 35442, pg. 456 **PB**

Andalusia

ALABAMA ELECTRIC COOPERATIVE, INC., Hwy. 29 N., 36420, pg. 30 **PV**
Andalusia & Conecuh Railroad, Inc., P.O. Box 550, Hwy. 29 N., 36420, pg. 30 **PV**
First Alabama Bank/Covington/Conecuh/Monroe Counties, P.O. Box 608, 36401-0608, pg. 1371 **PV**
Lakeside Coal Company, P.O. Box 550, Hwy. 29 N., 36420, pg. 30 **PV**
Neste Resins Corporation, Hwy. 84 West, P.O. Box 1377, 36420, pg. 913 **IT**
Power South, P.O. Box 550, Hwy. 29 N., 36420, pg. 30 **PV**
Shorewood Packaging Corporation Of Alabama, One Shorewood Dr., 36420-6420, pg. 1468 **PB**
United Energy Corporation, P.O. Box 550, Hwy. 29 N., 36420, pg. 30 **PV**
Waters Coal Company, P.O. Box 550, Hwy. 29 N., 36420, pg. 30 **PV**

Anniston

Barbour Threads, Inc., 20 Blue Mountain Ave., 36201, pg. 618 **IT**
Central Castings Corporation, 2660 Old Gadsden Hwy., 36206, pg. 327 **PB**
CONSOLIDATED PUBLISHING COMPANY, 216 W. Tenth St., 36201, pg. 266 **PV**
R & G Plumbing, 230 G St., 36201, pg. 847 **PB**
Regions Bank/Anniston, P.O. Box 2128, 36202-2128, pg. 1371 **PB**
Sentinel Consumer Products, Inc., Greenbriar Ind. Park, 100 Sentinel Dr., 36201, pg. 984 **PV**
Steel Products Div., 2101 W. 10th St., 36201, pg. 213 **PV**
SuperValu, Inc.-Southeast Div., Roberts Dr., Industrial Park, 36201, pg. 1541 **PB**

Arab

ATRION CORPORATION, P.O. Box 587, 1426 Curtis Francis Rd., 35016, pg. 146 **PB**
IEC Arab Alabama Operations, 350 11th St. S.W., 35016, pg. 855 **PB**
Ryder International, P.O. Box 564, 1426 Curt Francis Rd., 35016, pg. 146 **PB**

Ardmore

IWG-Ardmore, 29290 Mangum Dr., 35739, pg. 526 **PV**

Athens

ConAgra Broiler Co., P.O. Box 349, 35612, pg. 427 **PB**
Eaton Corp. Div., 200 E. Elm St., 35611, pg. 556 **PB**
Regions Bank/Athens/Lauderdale County/Florence, P.O. Box 1189, 35611-9986, pg. 1371 **PB**
Stone & Webster Engineering, P.O. Box 949, Browns Ferry Nuclear, 35611-0949, pg. 1519 **IT**
Sweet Sue Kitchens, 222 N.E. MacArthur Dr., 35611, pg. 1434 **PB**

Atmore

Frontier Communications of the South, Inc., 210 Brookwood Road, 36502, pg. 684 **PB**

Attalla

AAA Plumbing Pottery Corp., Pleasant Valley Rd., 35954, pg. 449 **PV**

Auburn

Regions Bank/Lee County, P.O. Box 1712, 36831-1712, pg. 1372 **PB**
SMC South, 1955 McMillan St., 36832, pg. 1014 **PV**

Axis

Courtaulds Fibers Inc., P.O. Box 141, 36505, pg. 339 **IT**
Du Pont/Shell, P.O. Box 525, 36505-0525, pg. 531 **PB**

Bay Minette

Regions Bank/Baldwin County, P.O. Box 850, 36507-0850, pg. 1371 **PB**
Uniroyal Chemical Co., Inc., P.O. Box 147, Highway 225, 36507, pg. 460 **PB**

Bayou La Batre

QF, Inc., Shell Belt Rd., 36509, pg. 940 **IT**

Bessemer

Coil-Tec Corporation, 2101 18th Ave., N., 35020, pg. 79 **IT**
Earle M. Jorgensen Company/Birmingham, 200 Kilsby Circle, 35023, pg. 600 **PV**
USX Fairfield Works, 1500 Concord Mines Rd., 35023-1011, pg. 1662 **PB**

Birmingham

ABB Environmental Systems (Utilities), 31 Inverness Center Parkway, 35243, pg. 4 **IT**
Ahlstrom Process Equipment Inc., Two Perimeter Park S., Ste. 250E, 35243, pg. 34 **IT**
Air Systems Div., 211 Summit Pkwy., Ste. 108, 35201, pg. 1794 **PB**
Akzo Nobel Coatings Inc., 1629 Vanderbilt Rd., 35234, pg. 48 **IT**
Alabama Gas Corporation, 2101 Sixth Ave. N., 35203, pg. 581 **PB**
ALABAMA METAL INDUSTRIES CORPORATION, 3245 Fayette Ave., 35208, pg. 30 **PB**
Alabama Power Co., 600 N. 18th St., 35291, pg. 1489 **PB**
Allright Birmingham, Inc., 1919 Morris Ave., Ste. 555, 35203, pg. 42 **PV**
ALTEC INDUSTRIES, INC., 210 Inverness Ctr. Dr., 35242, pg. 47 **PV**

American Carbon Industries, 2714 Second Ave. North, 35203, pg. 891 **IT**
AMERICAN CAST IRON PIPE CO., 2930 N. 16th St., 35207, pg. 51 **PV**
American Centrifugal, 2930 16th St. N., 35207, pg. 52 **PV**
American Ductile Iron Pipe Div., 2930 16th St. N., 35207, pg. 52 **PV**
American Flow Control, 2930 16th St. N., 35207, pg. 52 **PV**
American Foundation Life Insurance Company, 2801 Hwy. 280 S., 35223, pg. 1336 **PB**
American Steel Pipe Div., 2930 16th St. N., 35207, pg. 52 **PV**
AMSOUTH BANCORPORATION, 1901 6th Ave. N., Ste. 500, 35203, pg. 105 **PB**
AmSouth Bank, P.O. Box 11007, 35288, pg. 105 **PB**
AmSouth Bank N.A., P.O. Box 11007, 1900 5th Ave. N., Suite 1400, 35288, pg. 105 **PB**
Amsouth Investment Services, Inc., P.O. Box 830329, 1900 5th Ave. N., 35283, pg. 105 **PB**
ASSOCIATED GROCERS OF THE SOUTH, INC., 3600 Vanderbilt Rd., 35217, pg. 91 **PV**
BE & K, INC., 2000 International Park Dr., 35243, pg. 106 **PV**
Barbary Coast Steel Co., 9 Corp. Office, 35201, pg. 232 **PB**
BARBER DAIRIES, INC., 36 Barber Court, 35209, pg. 115 **PV**
Barber Ice Cream Company, 126 Barber Ct., 35209, pg. 115 **PV**
Barber Pure Milk Co., 36 Barber Ct., 35209, pg. 115 **PV**
Basin Pipeline Corp., 2101 6th Ave. N., 35203, pg. 581 **PB**
Bergen Brunswig Medical Corporation, 107 Walter Davis Dr., 35209, pg. 214 **PB**
Birmingham AL Steel Division, 2301 F.L. Shuttlesworth Dr., 35234-1335, pg. 232 **PB**
Birmingham Baseball Club, Inc., 100 Ben Chapman Dr. Bassemer, 35244, pg. 1321 **IT**
Birmingham Cable Communications, Inc., 6429 First Ave. S., 35212, pg. 1610 **PB**
Birmingham Post-Herald Company, 2200 4th Ave. N., P.O. Box 2553, 35202, pg. 1447 **PB**
Birmingham South, 2013 Canyon Rd., pg. 1297 **PB**
BIRMINGHAM STEEL CORPORATION, 1000 Urban Center Drive, Ste. 300, 35242-2516, pg. 232 **PB**
Birmingham Steels Overseas, Ltd., 3000 Riverchase Galleria, Ste. 1000, 35244, pg. 232 **PB**
Birmingham Ventures Inc., 3000 Riverchase Galleria, Ste. 1000, 35201, pg. 232 **PB**
BOOKS-A-MILLION, INC., 402 Industrial Ln., 35211, pg. 244 **PB**
BRICE BUILDING CO., INC., 2721 Second Ave. N., 35203, pg. 167 **PV**
Brown-Service Funeral Homes Co., Inc., 1340 26th Ave., N., 35234, pg. 1622 **PB**
Browning-Ferris Industries of Alabama, Inc., P.O. Box 10104, 35202, pg. 263 **PB**
Bruno's Birmingham, 300 Research Pkwy., 35211, pg. 265 **PB**
BRUNO'S INC., 800 Lakeshore Pkwy., 35211, pg. 265 **PB**
BUFFALO ROCK COMPANY, 111 Oxmoor Rd., 35209, pg. 179 **PV**
CITATION CORPORATION, Two Office Park Cir., Ste. 204, 35223, pg. 376 **PB**
COCA-COLA BOTTLING CO. UNITED, INC., 4600 East Lake Blvd., 35217, pg. 248 **PV**
Comdata Saunders Incorporated, 300 Riverchase Pkwy. E., 35244, pg. 331 **PB**
COMPASS BANCSHARES, INC., 15 S. 20th St., 35233, pg. 418 **PB**
Compass Bank, 15 S. 20th St., 35233, pg. 418 **PB**
CONSOLIDATED PIPE & SUPPLY COMPANY, 1205 Hilltop Pkwy., 35204, pg. 266 **PV**
Constar Inc., 1400 Urban Center Dr., Ste. 200, 35242, pg. 605 **IT**
Copperweld Birmingham Division, 1500 N. 50th St., 35212, pg. 662 **IT**
Courier Dispatch Division, 2729 Third Ave. S., 35233, pg. 450 **PB**

PB - *U.S. Public Companies Volume*
PV - *U.S. Private Companies Volume*
IT - *International Public & Private Companies Volume*

Geographic Index-U.S.

COWIN & COMPANY, INC., 301 Industrial Dr., 35211, pg. 280   **PV**

Dayton Superior Corp., 1400-Fifth Ave. S., 35201, pg. 931   **PV**

Denver Thomas, Inc., P.O. Box 96, 35201, pg. 1325   **IT**

Dillard, A ResourceNet International Company, 541 Republic Circle, P. O. Box 11367, 35202, pg. 902   **PB**

Dixie Insurance Company, 2204 Lakeshore Dr., 35209, pg. 75   **PB**

Dixie Type & Supply Co., Inc., 124 Citation Ct., 35209, pg. 1329   **PB**

DUNN INVESTMENT CO., 3900 Airport Hwy., 35222, pg. 347   **PV**

EBSCO INDUSTRIES, INC., P.O. Box 1943, 35201, pg. 358   **PB**

Ebsco Investment Services, Inc., P.O. Box 1943, 35201, pg. 359   **PB**

Empire General Life Assurance Corporation, 2801 Highway 280 S., 35223, pg. 1336   **PB**

ENERGEN CORPORATION, 2101 Sixth Ave. N., 35203, pg. 581   **PB**

Enviroq, 3918 Montclair Rd., 35213, pg. 881   **PB**

Ericsson Network Systems, Inc., 1901 Sixth Ave. North, Ste 1530, 35203, pg. 1365   **IT**

FMP-Rauma Company, 104 Inverness Center Pl., 35242, pg. 1428   **IT**

Fairview Nursing Home, 1028 Bessemer Superhighway, 35228, pg. 1256   **PB**

Feralloy Southern Div., 100 Finley Ave., 35204, pg. 1070   **PV**

First Protective Insurance Group, 2801 Hwy. 280 S., 35223, pg. 1336   **PB**

L.B. Foster Company-Birmingham Plant, 3135-B Daniel Payne Dr., 35214, pg. 676   **PB**

J. Gordon Gaines, Inc., 3760 River Run Dr., 35243, pg. 1622   **PB**

Gayle Supply Inc., 321 11th Ave. N., 35234, pg. 847   **PB**

GOLDEN ENTERPRISES, INC., 2101 Magnolia Ave., S., Ste. 212, 35205, pg. 749   **PB**

GRIMMER REALTY CO. INC., 200 Green Springs Hwy., 35209, pg. 482   **PV**

Guzzler Manufacturing, Inc., 575 N. 37th St., 35222, pg. 616   **PB**

HARBERT CORPORATION, One River Chase Pkwy., 35244, pg. 500   **PV**

HEALTHSOUTH CORPORATION, One Healthsouth Pkwy., 35243, pg. 803   **PV**

Hewlett-Packard Company, Bldg. 100, Ste. 118, 2100 Riverchase Ctr., 35244, pg. 813   **PB**

Hilb, Rogal and Hamilton Company of Alabama, Inc., 600 Luckie Dr., Suite 300, 35253, pg. 827   **PB**

Hillhaven Convalescent Center Birmingham, 2728 Tenth Ave. S., 35205, pg. 1713   **PB**

Ikon Office Solutions-Alabama, 217 Oxmoor Circle, 35209, pg. 863   **PB**

Incor of Alabama, 511 Volcan Dr., Ste. 109, 35210, pg. 309   **PV**

Intergraph Corporation, 300 W. Vestavia Pkwy., Ste: 2300, 35216, pg. 891   **PB**

Intergraph Corporation, 5532 1st Ave. S., 35216, pg. 891   **PB**

JASPER CORP., 530 Beacon Pkwy., Ste. 503, 35209, pg. 583   **PV**

A.C. LEGG PACKING COMPANY, INC., 2319 First Ave., N., 35203, pg. 658   **PV**

Liberty Management Services, Inc., 2008 Third Ave. S., 35233, pg. 1622   **PB**

Liberty National Auto Club, Inc., 2001 Third Ave. S., 35233, pg. 1623   **PB**

Liberty National Fire Insurance Co., 2008 Third Ave. S., 35233, pg. 1623   **PB**

Liberty National GroupCare, Inc., 2001 Third Ave. S., 35233, pg. 1623   **PB**

Liberty National Insurance Corp., 2008 Third Ave. So., 35233, pg. 1623   **PB**

Liberty National Life Insurance Co., 2001 Third Ave. S., 35233, pg. 1622   **PB**

LONG'S ELECTRONICS, INC., 2630 Fifth Ave. S., 35210, pg. 675   **PV**

Manulife Financial - Birmingham, 3800 Colonnade Pkwy., Ste. 260, 35243, pg. 840   **IT**

McWane Cast Iron Pipe Co., 1201 Vanderbilt Rd., 35234, pg. 725   **PV**

McWane Cast Iron Pipe Co., P.O. Box 607, 35201, pg. 725   **PV**

MCWANE, INC., 2900 Hwy. 280, Ste. 300, 35233, pg. 725   **PV**

MEADOWCRAFT, INC., 1401 Meadowcraft Rd., 35215, pg. 725   **PV**

Media Services, Inc., 820 Shades Creek Hwy., 35202, pg. 1613   **PB**

MEDICAL ASSURANCE, INC., 100 Brookwood Pl., Ste. 500, 35209, pg. 1079   **PB**

MEDPARTNERS INC., 3000 Galleria Towers, Ste. 1000, 35244, pg. 1082   **PB**

Mutual Assurance, Inc., P.O. Box 590009, 35209, pg. 1080   **PB**

NATIONAL COMPUTER PRINT, INC., 5200 E. Lake Blvd., 35217, pg. 780   **PV**

National Mine Service Company, Alabama Div., 128 Citation Ct., Suite C, 35209, pg. 281   **IT**

Nichols Select, Midtown Center, 1801 First Ave. S., Ste. 400, 35233, pg. 1182   **PB**

O'NEAL STEEL INC., 744 N. 41 St., 35222, pg. 817   **PV**

Oxmoor House, Inc., 820 Shades Creek Hwy., 35202, pg. 1613   **PB**

Parisian, Inc., 750 Lakeshore Pkwy., 35211, pg. 1333   **PB**

PENCO-Alabama, 529 Beacon Pkwy. W., Ste. 207, 35219, pg. 1508   **IT**

President Baking Co., 4500 1st Ave. N., 35222, pg. 1069   **IT**

ProEquities, Inc., 2801 Hwy. 280 S., 35223, pg. 1336   **PB**

Progressive Farmer, Inc., 820 Shades Creek Hwy., 35202, pg. 1613   **PB**

Progressive Farmer Insurance Service, Inc., 820 Shades Creek Hwy., 35202, pg. 1613   **PB**

Progressive Farmer Network, Inc., 820 Shades Creek Hwy., 35202, pg. 1613   **PB**

Protective Benefits Communications, 2801 Hwy. 280 S., 35223, pg. 1336   **PB**

PROTECTIVE LIFE CORPORATION, 2801 Hwy. 280, S., 35223-2448, pg. 1336   **PB**

Protective Life Insurance Co., 2801 Hwy. 280 S., 35223, pg. :336   **PB**

Regions Bank/Birmingham, P.O. Box 10247, 35202-0247, pg. 1371   **PB**

REGIONS FINANCIAL CORPORATION, 417 N. 20th St., 35203, pg. 1371   **PB**

Regions Investments, Inc., P.O. Box 10247, 35202-0247, pg. 1371   **PB**

River Oaks Bancorporation, 701 S. 20th St., 35233, pg. 419   **PB**

Rust Engineering & Construction Co., 100 Corporate Pkwy., 35242, pg. 1366   **PB**

Rust International Inc., 100 Corporate Pkwy., 35242, pg. 1366   **PB**

SMI Steel, Inc., 101 S. 50th St., 35212, pg. 412   **PB**

St. Clair Manufacturing Co., 4000 10th Ave. North, 35202, pg. 1044   **PB**

Sheffield Insurance Corporation, 2008 Third Ave. S., 35233, pg. 1623   **PB**

The Sloan-Major Agency, Inc., 110 S. 6th St., 35202, pg. 750   **PB**

Sonat Energy Services Company, 1900 Fifth Ave. N., 35203, pg. 1485   **PB**

SONAT INC., P.O. Box 2563, 35202-2563, pg. 1484   **PB**

Southern Accents, Inc., 820 Shades Creek, 35202, pg. 1613   **PB**

Southern Beauty Enterprises, 411 37th St. N., 35222, pg. 128   **PV**

Southern Electric Generating Co., 600 N. 18th St., 35291, pg. 1490   **PB**

Southern Electric Supply Co., Inc., 3000 Fifth Ave. S., 35233, pg. 1107   **IT**

Southern Life and Health Insurance Company, 2101 Highland Ave., 35205, pg. 447   **PB**

Southern Living, Inc., 820 Shades Creek Hwy., 35202, pg. 1613   **PB**

Southern Living Real Estate, Inc., 820 Shades Creek Hwy., 35202, pg. 1613   **PB**

Southern Natural Gas Company, 1900 Fifth Ave. N., 35203, pg. 1485   **PB**

Southern Nuclear, 40 Inverness Ctr. Pkwy., 35242, pg. 1490   **PB**

Southern Progress Corporation, 2100 Lakeshore Dr., 35209, pg. 1612   **PB**

SOUTHTRUST CORPORATION, 420 N. 20th St., 35203, pg. 1491   **PB**

SouthTrust Data Services, Inc., 6434 First Ave. N., 35212, pg. 1492   **PB**

SouthTrust Insurance Agency, Inc., 420 N. 20th St., 35203, pg. 1492   **PB**

SouthTrust Leasing, Inc., 420 N. 20th St., 35203, pg. 1492   **PB**

SouthTrust Life Insurance Co., 420 N. 20th St., 35203, pg. 1492   **PB**

SouthTrust Mobile Services, 112 N. 20th St., 35203, pg. 1492   **PB**

SouthTrust Mortgage Corp., 100 Office Park Dr., 35223, pg. 1492   **PB**

SouthTrust Securities Inc., 112 N. 20th St., 35203, pg. 1492   **PB**

Sprayroq, Inc., P.O. Box 11169, 35202, pg. 882   **PB**

Statewide Mortgage Company, 500 Riverhills Business Park, Ste. 590, 35241, pg. 1202   **PB**

STOCKHAM VALVES & FITTINGS, INC., 4000 10th Ave. N., 35212, pg. 1043   **PV**

Stonewall Insurance Co., P.O. Box 1688, 2204 Lakeshore Dr., 35201-1688, pg. 75   **PB**

SULLIVAN LONG & HAGERTY, INC., 801 5th Ave., N., 35203, pg. 1050   **PV**

Sunds Defibrator Woodhandling, Inc., 104 Inverness Center Pl., Ste. 300, 35242, pg. 1428   **IT**

SunGard Asset Management Systems, 210 Automation Way, 35283-0600, pg. 1535   **PB**

SunGard Employee Benefits Systems, 210 Automation Way, 35210, pg. 1534   **PB**

SunGard Mailing Services, 210 Automation Way, 35201, pg. 1534   **PB**

Sunnyland Refining Co., Inc., 3330 Tenth Ave. N., 35234, pg. 607   **PV**

TMK/United Oil Management Company, 2001 Third Ave. S., 35233, pg. 1623   **PB**

TXEN, Ten Inverness Ctr. Pkwy., Ste. 500, 35242, pg. 1182   **PB**

Taurus Exploration, Inc., 2101 6th Ave. S., 35203, pg. 581   **PB**

THOMPSON TRACTOR COMPANY, 2401 Pinson Hwy., 35202, pg. 1083   **PV**

TORCHMARK CORPORATION, 2001 Third Ave. S., 35233, pg. 1622   **PB**

Torchmark Investment Advisory Company, Inc., 2001 Third Ave. South, 35233, pg. 1623   **PB**

TV Alabama, Inc., 800 Concourse Pkwy., Ste 300, 35244, pg. 854   **PB**

United Investors Equity Services, Inc., 2001 Third Ave. S., 35233, pg. 1623   **PB**

United Investors Life Insurance Co., 2001 Third Ave. So., 35233, pg. 1623   **PB**

United Land Corp., 3300 First Avenue N., 35222, pg. 1736   **PB**

United States Pipe & Foundry Company, Inc., 3300 First Ave. N., 35222, pg. 1736   **PB**

Unitog Rental Facility, 501 S. 24th, 35233, pg. 1693   **PB**

VESTA INSURANCE GROUP, INC., 3760 River Run Dr., 35243, pg. 1718   **PB**

Vulcan Chemicals, One Metroplex Dr., 35209, pg. 1725   **PB**

Vulcan Gulf Coast Materials, Inc., One Metroplex Dr., 35209, pg. 1726   **PB**

Vulcan Lands, Inc., One Metroplex Dr., 35215, pg. 1726   **PB**

Vulcan Life Insurance Co., 105 Vulcan Road, 35209, pg. 433   **PB**

VULCAN MATERIALS COMPANY, One Metroplex Dr., 35209, pg. 1725   **PB**

Vulcan Materials Company-Southern Div., One Metroplex Dr., 35209, pg. 1726   **PB**

WBMG-TV, 2075 Golden Crest Dr., 35209, pg. 1078   **PB**

WVTM-TV, Inc., 1732 Valley View Dr., 35209, pg. 712   **PB**

WALL STREET DELI, INC., One Independence Plaza, Ste. 100, 35209, pg. 1734   **PB**

Wall Street Deli, Inc., One Independence Plaza, Ste. 100, 35209, pg. 1734   **PB**

Weight Watchers Magazine, P.O. Box 12847, 35202-2847, pg. 1612   **PB**

Willis Corroon Administrative Services Corporation, 1927 First Ave. N., 35203, pg. 1504   **IT**

Willis Corroon Corp. of Birmingham, 1927 First Ave. N., 35203, pg. 1505   **IT**

Wright & Lopez of Alabama, Inc., 3965 Lorna Crest Rd., 35244, pg. 844   **PV**

Zellerbach Division, 220 Distribution Dr., 35209, pg. 1075   **PB**

Blue Mountain

Barbour Thread, Inc., 20 Blue Mountain Ave., 36204, pg. 618   **IT**

Boaz

Boaz Plant, 300 Wagner Dr., 35957, pg. 443   **PB**

Chandeleur Homes, Inc., P.O. Box 557, 35957, pg. 333   **PB**

Tocco, Inc., 1506 Industrial Park, 35957, pg. 1259   **PB**

Brookwood

Black Warrior Methane Corp., Rte. 1, Hwy. 216, 35444, pg. 1737   **PB**

Black Warrior Transmission Corp., Rte. 1, Hwy. 216, 35444, pg. 1485   **PB**

Butler

Butler Telephone Company, Inc., 203 Academy St., 36904, pg. 1571   **PB**

Fort James Corporation, P.O. Box 428, 36908, pg. 672   **PB**

Regions Bank/Choctaw County, P.O. Box 537, 36904-0537, pg. 1372   **PB**

Centre

Regions Bank/Cherokee County, P.O. Box 615, 35960-0615, pg. 1372   **PB**

Citronelle

Gulf Coast Galvanizing Inc., P.O. Box 325, 36522, pg. 159   **PB**

Claiborne

Alabama Pine Pulp Company, Inc., Country Rd. 39, off Hwy. 84, 36460, pg. 841   **PV**

Alabama River Chip Mills, Inc., Country Rd. 39, off Hwy. 84, 36460, pg. 841   **PV**

Alabama River Crude Tall Oil, Inc., Country Rd. 39, off Hwy. 84, 36460, pg. 841   **PV**

Alabama River Pulp Company, Inc., Country Rd. 39, off Hwy. 84, 36460, pg. 841   **PV**

Coden

Shell Offshore, 13700 A Dauphin Island Pkwy., 36523-2920, pg. 1142   **IT**

Coosa Pines

U.S. Pulp and Newsprint, Hwy. 235 N., 35044, pg. 959   **PB**

Cordova

Vulcan Asphalt Refining Company, P.O. Box 388, 35550, pg. 915   **PV**

Courtland

Courtland Mill, Champion International Corporation, P.O. Box 189, 35618, pg. 334   **PB**

Cullman

Americold Compressor Co., 2340 Second Ave. N.W., 35055, pg. 439   **IT**

CULLMAN PRODUCTS CORPORATION, 1909 Beach Ave. S.E., 35056, pg. 294   **PV**

Cullman Supply Company, P.O. Box 908, 601 2nd Ave. N.E., 35056-0908, pg. 763   **PB**

Geographic Index-U.S.

IMI Cash Valve, Inc., 2400 7th Ave. S.W., 35055-0278, pg. 646 **IT**
Nicholson File, P.O. Box 946, 2125 Second Ave. S.W., 35055, pg. 444 **PB**
Regions Bank/Cullman/Walker County, P.O. Box 100, 35056-0100, pg. 1372 **PB**
Speedring, Inc., 6717 Alabama Hwy. 157, 35057, pg. 158 **PB**
Wal Mart Distribution Center, 2200 7th Ave. S.W., 35055-6333, pg. 1733 **PB**

Dadeville

Shape South, Inc., 170 Rice Ave., P.O. Box 186, 36853, pg. 990 **PV**

Daleville

Daleville Learning Center, 24 Industrial Ave., 36322, pg. 218 **PB**
TRI-GLAS, Industrial Park, 110 Robert C. Barnes St., 36322, pg. 848 **PV**

Decatur

ALABAMA FARMERS CO-OP, 121 Somerville Rd. N.E., 35609, pg. 30 **PV**
Atlas Cylinders, 1021 Brooks St. S.E., 35601, pg. 1261 **PB**
Automatic Screw Machines Products Company, 709 2nd Ave., S.E., 35601, pg. 980 **PB**
Chemland Industries, Inc., P.O. Box 1584, 35602, pg. 975 **PB**
Fireland Industries, Inc., P.O. Box 1584, 35602, pg. 975 **PB**
Highland International, Inc., 202 Pride Lane, S.W., 35603, pg. 975 **PB**
HISPAN Corp., P.O. Box 2247, 35609, pg. 810 **PB**
Interstate Billing Service, Inc., P.O. Box 2250, 35602, pg. 1373 **PB**
Regions Bank/Decatur/Hartselle, P.O. Box 2229, 35602-2229, pg. 1372 **PB**
Southern Electric Supply Co., Inc., 1420 Church St., NE, 35601, pg. 1107 **IT**
SouthTrust Bank, Hartselle, 254 E. Moulton St., 35601, pg. 1491 **PB**
Union Planters Bank of Alabama, 255 Grant St. S.E., 35601, pg. 1669 **PB**
United Foam Plastics Corporation, P.O. Box 1207, 1528 Church St., 35602-1207, pg. 1112 **PV**

Dothan

AmSouth Bank N.A., P.O. Box 1150, 36302, pg. 105 **PB**
Charter Woods Behavioral Health System, Inc., 700 Cottonwood Rd., 36301, pg. 1035 **PB**
Custom Lumber Mfg. Co., 819 Cowarts Rd., 36303, pg. 680 **PV**
Dothan Auto Auction, 3664 S. Oates St., 36301, pg. 1649 **PB**
Dothan Learning Center, 600 FlightSafety Dr., 36322, pg. 218 **PB**
Dunbarton Corporation, 868 Murray Rd., 36303, pg. 194 **PV**
FLAVOR HOUSE PRODUCTS, INC., 2700 Horace Shepherd Dr., 36303, pg. 410 **PV**
Lilly Industries, Inc., 1771 Industrial Rd., 36303, pg. 994 **PB**
LUMBER GROUP INC., 819 Cowarts Rd., 36303, pg. 680 **PV**
Regions Bank/Dothan, P.O. Box 6507, 36302-6507, pg. 1372 **PB**
Rock-Tenn, 3775 Napier Field Rd., 36303, pg. 1397 **PB**
Wholesale Wood Products, 819 Cowarts Rd., pg. 680 **PV**

Elba

Dorsey Trailers, Inc., 1409 Hickman St., 36323, pg. 520 **PB**
Kleinert's, Inc., of Alabama, 2251 Old Curtis Rd., 36323, pg. 625 **PV**
SouthTrust Bank of Elba, 402 Collier St., 36323, pg. 1492 **PB**

Elkmont

Alabama Fine Wire, P.O. Box 350, 18771 Carter Circle, 35620, pg. 526 **PB**
Ross Breeders, Inc., P.O. Box 155, Hwy. 127, 35620, pg. 619 **IT**

Enterprise

ConAgra Broiler Co., County Rd. 636, 36330, pg. 427 **PB**
Enterprise Electronics Corp., 128 S. Industrial Blvd., 36331, pg. 1563 **PB**
Regions Bank/Enterprise, P.O. Box 1260, 36331-1260, pg. 1372 **PB**

Eufaula

ABC Transportation Co., State Docks Rd., 36027, pg. 69 **PB**
AMERICAN BUILDINGS CO., 1150 State Docks Rd., 36027, pg. 69 **PB**
Eufaula Plant, Four Hummingbird Ln., 36027, pg. 444 **PB**
Techsonic Industries, Inc., Five Humminbird Ln., 36027, pg. 1570 **PB**

Evergreen

Landstar Poole, Inc., PO Drawer 500, Bates Rd., 36401, pg. 978 **PB**

Fairhope

Rohr Aero Services, Inc., P.O. Drawer 1107, 36533-1107, pg. 751 **PB**

Florence

ABCO, 4121 Rushton St., 35630, pg. 581 **PV**
Broilmaster Division, 301 E. Tennessee St., 35631, pg. 709 **PV**
Domco Inc. Floor Products (Alabama), 3420 Church Rd., Florence Industrial Pk., 35630, pg. 415 **IT**
Martin Gas, 301 E. Tennessee Rd., 35631, pg. 709 **PV**
MARTIN INDUSTRIES, INC. (AL), 301 E. Tennessee St., 35631, pg. 709 **PV**
Monarch Tile, Inc., 834 Rickwood Rd., 35630, pg. 287 **PV**
NAFCO National Floor Company, Florence Industrial Pk., 3420 Church Rd., 35630, pg. 415 **IT**
SunTrust Bank, Alabama, N.A., 201 South Court St., 35631, pg. 1538 **PB**
TSP Newspapers, Inc., 219 W. Tennessee St., 35630, pg. 1175 **PB**
Times Daily, Inc., 219 W. Tennessee St., 35630, pg. 1175 **PB**

Foley

Rohr Industries, Foley Plant, 1300 W. Fern, 36535, pg. 751 **PB**
Solutia Inc., P. O. Drawer 730, 36535, pg. 1484 **PB**
VULCAN INC., 410 E. Berry, 36535, pg. 1144 **PV**

Fort Payne

DeSoto Mills, Inc., P.O. Box 720, 35967, pg. 1413 **PB**
Game Time, Inc., 150 Gametime Dr., 35967, pg. 1543 **PB**
Heil Environmental Industries (H.E.I.L.), P.O. Box 109, 35967, pg. 520 **PB**
Plastex Extruders Inc., USA, P.O. Box 717, 120-55th St., N.E., 35967, pg. 378 **PV**

Fort Rucker

Community Bank & Trust of S.E. Alabama, P.O. Box 309, 36362, pg. 1549 **PB**

Frisco City

FARMERS CO-OP MARKET INC., 20 Houston St., 36445, pg. 395 **PV**

Gadsden

DAWSON CONSTRUCTION CO., INC., 350 Locust St., 35901, pg. 316 **PV**
Flowers Baking Co. of Gadsden, Inc., 1605 W. Grand Ave., 35901, pg. 657 **PB**
The Gadsden Times, 401 Locust St., 35901, pg. 1175 **PB**
GULF STATES STEEL, INC., 174 S. 26th St., 35904, pg. 488 **PV**
Regions Bank/Gadsden, P.O. Box 308, 35999-2301, pg. 1372 **PB**
Southern Electric Supply Co., Inc., 433 Locust, 35902, pg. 1107 **IT**

Geneva

CMI Industries, Inc., P.O. Box 699, 36340, pg. 195 **PV**
DIXIELAND FOOD STORES INC., 1015 W. Magnolia Ave., 36340, pg. 337 **PV**
Fleming Foods of Alabama, Inc., 1015 W. Magnolia Ave., 36340, pg. 653 **PB**

Goshen

Goshen Telephone Company, Inc., P.O. Box 159, 104 N. Star St., 36035, pg. 1571 **PB**

Greensboro

DAIRY FRESH CORP., 903 Tuscaloosa St., 36744, pg. 307 **PV**
Dairy Fresh Ice Cream, P.O. Box 39, 36744, pg. 307 **PV**

Grove Hill

Grove Hill Telephone Co., 121 Church St., 36451, pg. 1571 **PB**

Guntersville

C.I.S. Co. of Alabama, 2600 Railroad Ave., 35976, pg. 223 **PV**
KAPPLER SAFETY GROUP, INC., P.O. Box 490, 35976-0491, pg. 607 **PV**
Kappler USA, 70 Grimes St., 35976, pg. 607 **PV**

Haleyville

American Door Company of Michigan, Inc.-Flush Door Plant, P.O. Drawer F, 300 Industrial Park, 33565, pg. 1067 **IT**
Haleyville Drapery Manufacturing Division, P.O. Box 695, 35565, pg. 491 **PB**
Haleyville Office, 1012 20th St., pg. 1297 **PB**
Riverchase Homes, P.O. Box 676, 35569, pg. 319 **PB**

Hamilton

Buccaneer Homes, Inc., P.O. Box 1418, 35570, pg. 318 **PB**
Cavalier Acceptance Corporation, P.O. Box 300, Industrial Dr., 35540, pg. 318 **PB**
Cavalier Insurance Agency, Inc., P.O. Box 300, Industrial Dr., 35540, pg. 318 **PB**
Fleetwood Homes of Alabama, Inc., 406 Airport Rd., 35570-8697, pg. 651 **PB**

Harpersville

HyCon, Inc., 2200 U.S. 280 West, 35078, pg. 1304 **PB**

Homewood

BIFP, Inc., Two Metroplex Dr., Ste. 214, 35209, pg. 669 **PB**

Hoover

Community Bio-Resources, 2197 Parkway Lake Dr., 35244, pg. 196 **PB**

Hope Hull

MILTOPE GROUP, INC., 500 Richardson Rd. S., 36043, pg. 1114 **PB**

Huntsville

ADS Environmental Services Inc., 5025 Bradford Blvd., 35805-9949, pg. 709 **IT**
ADTRAN, INC., 901 Explorer Blvd., N.W., 35814, pg. 20 **PB**
Alabama Oil Company, 120 Woodson St. N.W., 35801, pg. 1025 **PV**
All American Semiconductor of Huntsville, Inc., 4900 University Sq., Ste. 34, 35816, pg. 41 **PB**
American Bread Co., 7200 Governors West, 35807, pg. 547 **PB**
AmSouth Bank N.A., P.O. Box 507, 35804, pg. 105 **PB**
Arrow/Schweber Electronics, 1015 Henderson Rd., 35816, pg. 134 **PB**
AVEX Electronics, Inc., 4807 Bradford Dr., 35805, pg. 545 **PV**
Birmingham News, 2317 Memorial Pkwy., 35801-5623, pg. 20 **PV**
Browning-Ferris Industries of Alabama, Inc., P.O. Box 11280, 35814, pg. 263 **PB**
Central CPVC Corporation, 3415-B Stanwood Blvd. N.E., 35811, pg. 327 **PB**
Cinram Inc., 4905 Moores Mill Rd., 35811, pg. 293 **IT**
Control Dynamics Division, 600 Blvd. S., Ste. 304, 35802, pg. 106 **PV**
Disc Manufacturing Cinram, 4905 Moors Mill Rd., 35810, pg. 293 **IT**
Dun & Bradstreet Software (Huntsville), Research Park, 670 Discovery Dr., 35806, pg. 532 **IT**
Dunlop Tire Corporation (Huntsville), P.O. Box 1141, 35807, pg. 1317 **IT**
EDD-Huntsville, 555 Sparman Dr., Ste. 600D, 35816, pg. 205 **PB**
Encore Computer-Huntsville, 555 Sparkman Dr., Ste. 1028, 35816, pg. 580 **PB**
First Commercial Bank, 2123 Whitesburg Dr., 35804-1002, pg. 1549 **PB**
General Shale Products Corp., P.O. Box 4558, Haysland Station, 35815, pg. 844 **IT**
Goldstar of America, Inc., 201 James Record Rd., 35824, pg. 779 **IT**
Stephen Gould of Alabama, Inc., 4960 Corporate Dr., Ste. 130-6, 35806, pg. 467 **PV**
Hickory Capital Corporation, 200 W. Court Sq., Ste. 100, 35801, pg. 639 **PB**
Hickory Venture Capital Corporation, 200 W. Court Sq., Ste. 100, 35801, pg. 639 **PB**
Hokuriku U.S.A. Co., Ltd., 2995-B Wall Treiana Hwy., 35824, pg. 628 **IT**
Huntsville Electronics Div., 100 Electronics Blvd., 35824, pg. 353 **PV**
Huntsville Space Operations, P.O. Box 9033, 35812, pg. 1170 **PB**
Huntsville Times, 2317 S. Memorial Pkwy., 35801, pg. 20 **PV**
Instrumentation Connectors Div., 9400 S. Memorial Pkwy., 35802-1504, pg. 1261 **PB**
INTERGRAPH CORPORATION, 35894-0001, pg. 890 **PB**
MTI Systems Div., Ste. 120, 4950 Corporate Dr., 37211, pg. 135 **PV**
MidSouth Ice Co., 120 Woodson St. N.W., 35801, pg. 1025 **PV**
Missiles & Space Division, 499 Boeing Blvd., 35806, pg. 241 **PB**
NICHOLS RESEARCH CORPORATION, 4040 S. Memorial Pkwy., 35802, pg. 1182 **PB**

PB - *U.S. Public Companies Volume*
PV - *U.S. Private Companies Volume*
IT - *International Public & Private Companies Volume*

Onan Corporation, 10001 James Record Rd., 35807, pg. 468 **PB**

Poli-Twine Southern Inc., 4950 Gilmer Dr., 35805, pg. 1362 **IT**

Regions Bank/Huntsville, P.O. Box 680, 35804-0680, pg. 1372 **PB**

SCI Manufacturing, Inc., 2101 W. Clinton, 35807, pg. 1417 **PB**

SCI SYSTEMS, INC., 2101 W. Clinton Ave., 35805, pg. 1416 **PB**

SCI Technology, Inc., 2101 Clinton Ave. W., 35805, pg. 1417 **PB**

Science and Engineering Huntsville Office, P.O. Box 9033, 35812, pg. 1597 **PB**

SPENCER COMPANIES INC., 120 Woodson St. N.W., 35801, pg. 1024 **PV**

TDK Electronics, Huntsville, 250 Finney Rd., 35824, pg. 1336 **IT**

TecSyn P.M.P. Inc., 4950 Gilmer Dr., 35805, pg. 1362 **IT**

Teledyne Advanced Materials, 7300 Hwy. 20 W., 35806-2052, pg. 43 **PB**

Teledyne Brown Engineering, 300 Sparkman Dr., N.W., 35805-1912, pg. 43 **PB**

United Space Boosters, Inc., P.O. Box 1900, 188 Sparkman Dr., 35807, pg. 1690 **PB**

Universal Construction Co., 356 James Record Rd., 35806, pg. 1646 **PB**

VeriBest Inc., One Madison Industrial Park, 35824-1112, pg. 891 **PB**

WHNT-TV, 200 Holmes Ave., 35801, pg. 1174 **PB**

WOLVERINE TUBE INC., 1525 Perimeter Park, Ste. 210, 35806, pg. 1774 **PB**

Wyle Laboratories-Eastern Operations, 7800 Governors Dr. W., 35807, pg. 1193 **PV**

Irondale

Motion Industries, Inc., 1605 Alton Rd., 35210, pg. 732 **PB**

Jacksonville

Instrumentation Valve Division, 2651 Al Hwy. 21 N., P.O. Box 69, 36265-9681, pg. 1261 **PB**

Jasper

AmSouth Bank of Walker County, 310 Hwy. 78 E., 35502, pg. 105 **PB**

DRUMMOND COMPANY, INC., P.O. Box 1549, 35501, pg. 343 **PV**

First National Bank, 200 West 18th St., 35501, pg. 1549 **PB**

Mall Office, 204 Hwy. 78 E., pg. 1297 **PB**

PINNACLE BANK, 1811 Second Ave., 35501, pg. 1297 **PV**

SouthTrust Bank, Jasper, 205 W. 19th St., 35501, pg. 1491 **PB**

Lafayette

TALLAPOOSA RIVER ELECTRIC CO-OP, 15163 U.S. Hwy. 431 S., 36862, pg. 1067 **PV**

Lanett

SKINNER CORP., 1009 N. Lanier Ave., 36863, pg. 1005 **PV**

Leeds

ALLTEL Alabama, 624 First Ave. S.E., P.O. Box 67, 35094, pg. 55 **PB**

United Chair, Inc., 114 Churchill Ave. N.W., 35094, pg. 512 **PV**

Leesburg

Mid-Western of Alabama Division, County Rd. Seven, 35983, pg. 60 **PV**

Livingston

Regions Bank/Sumter County, P.O. Box S, 35470-0349, pg. 1373 **PB**

Madison

Athens Paper Co., Inc., 9312 Highway 20 W., 35758, pg. 94 **PV**

Milgray/Huntsville, Inc., 8215 Hwy. 20 West, 35758, pg. 206 **PB**

Transport, Inc., 127 Jetplex Cir., 35758, pg. 482 **PB**

Marion

Southland Nursing Home, 500 Shivers Terrace, 36756, pg. 1257 **PB**

Meridianville

Halliburton Energy Services, P.O. Box 380, 35759-0380, pg. 776 **PB**

Millport

Frontier Communication of Lamar County, Inc., P.O. Box 469, 121 New Columbus, 35576, pg. 683 **PB**

Mobile

Allright Birmingham Inc., 101 N. Royal St., 36602, pg. 42 **PV**

AmSouth Bank N.A., 31 N. Royal St., 36601, pg. 105 **PB**

ASSOCIATED EQUIPMENT COMPANY OF DELAWARE, 1230 N. Beltline Hwy., 36607, pg. 90 **PV**

BENDER SHIPBUILDING & REPAIR COMPANY, INC., 265 S. Water St., 36603, pg. 132 **PV**

Bergen Brunswig Medical Corporation, 85 Sidney Phillips Dr., 36607, pg. 214 **PB**

Bergen Brunswig Medical Corporation, 210 Cox St., 36607, pg. 214 **PB**

Browning-Ferris Industries of Alabama, Inc., 920 Navco Rd., 36606, pg. 263 **PB**

W.C. Caye & Co., 560 St. Emanuel St., 36603, pg. 220 **PV**

Charter Hospital of Mobile, Inc., 5800 Southland Dr., 36609, pg. 1034 **PB**

Coca-Cola Bottling Co. of Mobile, Inc., 5300 Coca-Cola Rd., 36619, pg. 391 **PB**

Cooper Smith, Inc., 1201 N. Belt Line Hwy., 36618, pg. 547 **PV**

Crown Door Corp., 3218 Crichton St., 36607, pg. 1067 **IT**

Delchamps, Inc., 305 Delchamps Dr., 36602, pg. 588 **PV**

Financial Collection Agencies (1990) Inc., 3446 Demetropolis Rd., 36693, pg. 471 **IT**

FOLMAR & ASSOCIATES, 3472 Springhill Ave., 36608, pg. 417 **PV**

Gayfers, Springdale Plaza, 36623, pg. 1090 **PB**

GULF LUMBER COMPANY, INC., 1850 Conception St., 36610, pg. 487 **PV**

Hillhaven Convalescent Center Mobile, 1758 Springhill Ave., 36607, pg. 1713 **PB**

INTEGRITY INCORPORATED, 1000 Cody Rd., 36695, pg. 886 **PB**

International Paper Co., Papermill Rd., 36652, pg. 902 **PB**

Jeffrey Steel Products, 210 Saint Joseph St., 36602, pg. 1100 **PB**

Kimberly-Clark, Mobile, P.O. Box 24117, Bay Bridge Rd., 36652, pg. 958 **PB**

MGS Energy Services, Inc., 2828 Dauphin St., 36606, pg. 1120 **PB**

MGS Storage Services, Inc., 2828 Dauphin St., 36606, pg. 1120 **PB**

MCCONNELL AUTOMOTIVE, 3150 Dauphin St., 36606, pg. 720 **PV**

MOBILE GAS SERVICE CORP., 2828 Dauphin St., 36606, pg. 1120 **PB**

Mozzarella's Restaurants, 4721 Morrison Dr., 36609, pg. 1412 **PB**

QMS, INC., One Magnum Pass, 36618, pg. 1346 **PB**

RHG Mobile, P.O. Box 2492, 701a South Conception, 36603, pg. 1151 **IT**

Regions Bank/Mobile, P.O. Box 2527, 36622, pg. 1372 **PB**

Riedel-Smith Environmental Services, 1660 S. Beltline Hwy., 36609, pg. 1478 **PB**

RUBY TUESDAY, INC., 4721 Morrison Dr., 36609, pg. 1411 **PB**

Ruby Tuesday Restaurants, 4721 Morrison Dr., 36609, pg. 1412 **PB**

KELLER SMITH SUPPLY, INC., 855 E. Lakeside Dr., 36693, pg. 1008 **PV**

Sodexho USA South, P.O. Box 160266, 4721 Morrison Dr., 36625, pg. 1274 **IT**

Southern Electric Supply Co., Inc., 3307 Moffat Rd., 36607, pg. 1107 **IT**

Supermarket Cigarette Sales, Inc., 305 Delchamps Dr., 36602, pg. 588 **PV**

Teledyne Continental Motors, 2000 Ninth St., 36615-1293, pg. 43 **PB**

Tia's Tex-Mex Restaurants, 4721 Morrison Dr., 36609, pg. 1412 **PB**

TURNER SUPPLY COMPANY, 250 N. Royal St., 36602, pg. 1110 **PV**

United Companies Lending Corp. (Alabama), 857 Downtowner Blvd., 36609, pg. 1675 **PB**

WALA-TV, 210 Government St., 36602, pg. 1685 **PB**

WPMI-TV, 661 Azalea Rd., 36609, pg. 385 **PB**

White Electrical Construction Co., 554 Saint Louis St., 36601, pg. 1172 **PV**

Willis Corroon Administrative Services Corporation, 51 Saint Joseph St., 36602, pg. 1504 **IT**

Willis Corroon Corp. of Mobile, 51 St. Joseph St., 36602, pg. 1506 **IT**

Woodward-Clyde, 1015 Montlimar Dr., Ste. A-100, 36609, pg. 1656 **PB**

Monroeville

Design Systems Inc., P.O. Box 1572, 36461-1572, pg. 13 **IT**

Frontier Communications of Alabama, Inc., 210 S. Alabama Ave., 36460, pg. 683 **PB**

Montevallo

King Fisher, Inc., P.O.Box 372, 35115, pg. 979 **PV**

SEAMAN TIMBER COMPANY, INC., P.O. Box 372, 35115, pg. 979 **PV**

Montgomery

The Advertiser Co., 200 Washington Ave., 36102, pg. 699 **PB**

ALFA CORPORATION, 2108 E. South Blvd., 36116-2015, pg. 40 **PB**

Alfa Financial Corporation, P.O. Box 11000, 36191-0001, pg. 40 **PB**

Alfa General Insurance Corp., P.O. Box 11000, 36191-0001, pg. 40 **PB**

Alfa Insurance Corp., P.O. Box 11000, 36191-0001, pg. 40 **PB**

Alfa Investment Corp. & Builders Inc., P.O. Box 11000, 36191-0001, pg. 40 **PB**

Alfa Life Insurance Corp., P.O. Box 11000, 36191-0001, pg. 40 **PB**

Alfa Realty, Inc., P.O. Box 11000, 36191-0001, pg. 40 **PB**

ALGERNON BLAIR INTERNATIONAL, 2821 Eastern Blvd., 36116, pg. 33 **PV**

Augat, Inc., Wiring Systems, 2745 Gunter Park Dr., 36109, pg. 1598 **PB**

Augat, Inc., Wiring Systems & Components Group, 2745 Gunter Park Dr., 36109, pg. 1598 **PB**

B.A.S.S., INC., 5845 Carmichael Rd., 36117, pg. 105 **PV**

B.A.S.S. Times, 5845 Carmichael Rd., 36117, pg. 105 **PV**

BI Holdings Corp., 4520 Executive Park Dr., 36116, pg. 238 **PB**

Bass Angler Sportsman Society, 5845 Carmichael Rd., 36117-2329, pg. 105 **PV**

Bassmaster Magazine, P.O. Box 17116, 36141, pg. 105 **PV**

The Bassmaster Television Series, 5845 Carmichael Rd., 36117, pg. 105 **PV**

Bassmaster Tournament Trail, 5845 Carmichael Rd., 36117, pg. 105 **PV**

Bergen Brunswig Medical Corporation, 2061 W. Fairview Ave., 36108, pg. 214 **PB**

Bergen Brunswig Medical Corporation (Durr Drug), 2061 W. Fairview Ave., 36108, pg. 214 **PB**

Bes-Pak & Co., Inc., 2705 Gunter Park Dr. W., 36109, pg. 231 **PV**

Blount Development Corp., 4520 Executive Park Dr., 36116-1602, pg. 239 **PB**

Blount, Inc., 4520 Executive Park Dr., 36116-1602, pg. 238 **PB**

BLOUNT INTERNATIONAL, INC., 4520 Executive Park Dr., 36116-1602, pg. 237 **PB**

Capital Alliance Insurance Company, Inc., 2911 Zelda Rd., 36111, pg. 1258 **IT**

Carolina Steel-Montgomery Plant, 1085 Parker St., 36108, pg. 214 **PV**

Cedar Crest, 4490 Virginia Loop Rd., 36116, pg. 1256 **PB**

The Cedars, 3300 Lynchburg Dr., 36116, pg. 1256 **PB**

The Colonial BancGroup Building Corporation, One Commerce St., 36104, pg. 400 **PB**

THE COLONIAL BANCGROUP, INC., Colonial Financial Ctr., One Commerce St., 36104, pg. 400 **PB**

Colonial Bank, One Commerce St., 36104, pg. 400 **PB**

Colonial Capital I, One Commerce St., 36104, pg. 400 **PB**

Colonial Mortgage Company, 32 Commerce St., 36104, pg. 400 **PB**

Dillard, A ResourceNet International Company, 2720 Gunter Park Dr. W., Stes. E & F, 36109, pg. 902 **PV**

Ellis Communications, 201 Monroe St., Ste. 710, 36104, pg. 912 **PV**

Fishing Tackle Retailer, P.O. Box 17151, 36141, pg. 105 **PV**

Flowers Specialty Foods of Montgomery, Inc., 140 Folmar Pkwy., 36105, pg. 657 **PB**

4520 Corp., Inc., 4520 Executive Park Dr., 36116-1602, pg. 239 **PB**

Gayfers, 3063 E. South Blvd., 36111, pg. 1090 **PB**

Green Tree Acceptance of Alabama, Inc., 324 Interstate Park Dr., 36109, pg. 762 **PB**

Herff Jones Yearbooks, P.O. Box 17, 2800 Selma Hwy., 36101, pg. 524 **PV**

Humana Health Plan of Alabama, Inc., 2350 Fairlane Dr., Ste. 120, 36116, pg. 848 **PB**

Kimball Furniture Reproductions, 1919 Bell St., 36104, pg. 957 **PB**

Kinpak, Inc., 2780 Gunter Park Dr. E., 36109, pg. 1211 **PB**

John R. Kitchens Insurance, Inc., 2911 Zelda Rd., 36111, pg. 1258 **IT**

Miltope Corporation, 500 Richardson Rd. S., 36043-0000, pg. 1174 **PB**

Mocenplaza Development Corporation, 4520 Executive Park Dr., 36116-1602, pg. 239 **PB**

National Industries, Inc., 2745 Gunter Park W., 36109, pg. 1598 **PB**

Peachtree Wynfrey Associates, c/o Peachtree Corner Assoc., 300 Water St., 36104, pg. 362 **PB**

PIKNIK PRODUCTS COMPANY, INC., 3806 Day St., 36108, pg. 865 **PV**

RAYCOM MEDIA, INC., 201 Monroe St., Ste. 710, 36104, pg. 911 **PV**

Regions Bank/Montgomery/Alexander City, P.O. Box 511, 36101-0511, pg. 1372 **PB**

Regions Mortgage, Inc., P.O. Box 669, 36101-0669, pg. 1373 **PB**

Rheem Water Heater, P.O. Box 244020, 36124, pg. 1022 **IT**

Rheem Water Heater-Division Headquarters, 101 Bell Rd., 36117, pg. 1022 **IT**

RUSSELL PETROLEUM CORPORATION, 3378 Tankview Ct., 36108, pg. 953 **PV**

Benjamin F. Shaw Co., 4520 Executive Park Dr., 36116-1602, pg. 239 **PB**

SMITH INDUSTRIES, INC., 2781 Gunter Park Dr. E., 36109, pg. 1008 **PV**

J.R. Smith Manufacturing Company, 2781 Gunter Park Dr. E., 36109, pg. 1008 **PV**

South Haven Manor Nursing Home, 1300 E. South Blvd., 36116, pg. 1257 **PB**

Southern Electric Supply Co., Inc., 1141 Holloway Park, 36117, pg. 1107 **IT**

Southern Guaranty Insurance Companies, 2545 Taylor Rd., 36123-5004, pg. 346 **IT**

Southern Outdoors Magazine, P.O. Box 17915, 36141, pg. 106 **PV**

PB - *U.S. Public Companies Volume*
PV - *U.S. Private Companies Volume*
IT - *International Public & Private Companies Volume*

Geographic Index-U.S.

Sterling Bank, 4121 Carmichael Rd., 36123-0849, pg. 1549 **PB**
Thermal Components, Inc., 2760 Gunter Park, West, P.O. Box 3253, 36193, pg. 881 **PB**
Trinity-Structural Steel, P.O. Box 1984, 36102-1984, pg. 1639 **PB**
WSFA-TV, P.O. Box 2566, 10 E. Delano St., 36105, pg. 992 **PB**
WEIL BROTHERS COTTON INC., 4444 Park Blvd., 36116, pg. 1159 **PV**
WHITFIELD FOODS, INC., 1101 N. Court St., 36104, pg. 1173 **PV**
Willis Corroon Corp. of Birmingham, 423 S. Hull St., 36104, pg. 1505 **IT**
JIM WILSON & ASSOCIATES, INC., 4121 Carmichael Rd., Ste. 501, 36106, pg. 1181 **PV**
Winn-Dixie Montgomery, Inc., 1550 Jackson Ferry Rd., 36104, pg. 1771 **PB**
Woodley Manor Nursing Home, 3312 Woodley Rd., 36116, pg. 1257 **PB**

Montrose

Montrose Bay Health Care Center, P.O. Box 2177, 36559, pg. 1257 **PB**

Muscle Shoals

Alabama Tennessee Natural Gas Company, 3230 Second St., 35661, pg. 1109 **PB**
General Precision Tool & Die Division, P.O. Box 2523, 2721 Avalon Ave., 35662, pg. 986 **PB**
Manufacturing Technology Laboratory, 3326 E. Second St., 35561-1258, pg. 1386 **PB**
Midcoast Marketing Company, 3230 Second St., 35661, pg. 1109 **PB**
Tennessee River Intrastate Gas Company, 3230 Second St., 35661, pg. 1109 **PB**

Oakman

Oakman Telephone Company, Box 305, Market St., 35579, pg. 1571 **PB**

Odenville

International Forest Seed Company, P.O. Box 490, Simpson Rd., 35120, pg. 973 **IT**

Oneonta

Regions Bank/Blount County, P.O. Box 669, 35121-0669, pg. 1372 **PB**

Opelika

Flowers Baking Co. of Opelika, Inc., 101 Simmons St., 36803, pg. 657 **PB**

Opp

Opp Micolas Mills Inc., 1800 Cummings Ave., 36467, pg. 933 **PB**
SouthTrust Bank, Covington County, P.O. Drawer A, 110 S. Main St., 36467, pg. 1491 **PB**

Oxford

Central Bank, N.A., 700 Quintard & Dodson, 36203, pg. 418 **PB**

Ozark

SouthTrust Bank, Ozark, 242 W. Reynolds St., 36360, pg. 1492 **PB**

Pelham

AmeriSource-Birmingham Div., 172 Cahaba Valley Pkwy., 35124, pg. 96 **PB**
Cole Hall Lumber Co., 2500 Oak St., 35124, pg. 680 **PV**
JUST FOR FEET, INC., 153 Cahaba Valley Pkwy. N., 35124, pg. 935 **PB**
Keystone Morin, Inc., 110 Commerce Dr., 35124-1838, pg. 1650 **PB**
MOORE-HANDLEY, INC., 3140 Pelham Pkwy., 35124, pg. 1128 **PB**
Regions Bank/Shelby County, P.O. Box 216, 35124-0216, pg. 1373 **PB**
Reliable/Bethea Power Products Inc., 3098 Hwy. 31 S., 35124, pg. 692 **PV**
SEALING EQUIPMENT PRODUCTS CO., INC., 2790 Montgomery Hwy., 35124, pg. 978 **PV**

Pell City

Ahlstrom Kamyr Services Inc., P.O. Box 767, Cogswell Avenue Industrial Pk., 35125, pg. 34 **IT**
Benjamin Moore & Co., 109 Bamberg Dr., 35125-9142, pg. 133 **PV**
Energy Absorption Systems, Inc.-Pell City, 250 Bamberg Dr., 35125, pg. 1353 **PB**
Tri-Lite Plastics South, Inc., 3901 Research Way, 35125, pg. 233 **IT**

Pennington

Naheola Board, HC. 66, Box 305, 36916, pg. 671 **PB**

Phenix City

CB & T Bank of Russell County, P.O. Box 2400, 36868, pg. 1549 **PB**
Continental Carbon Company, 1500 E. State Bocks Rd., 36869, pg. 286 **IT**
Johnston Industries Composite Reinforcements, 3503 Lakewood Dr., 36867, pg. 933 **PB**
Lotus Carpet Division, 3018 Lakewood Dr., 36869, pg. 257 **PB**
Phenix City Nursing Home, 3900 Lakewood Dr., 36867-2499, pg. 1257 **PB**
Regions Bank/Phenix City, P.O. Box 550, 36868-0550, pg. 1372 **PB**
Southern Phenix Textiles, Inc., 300 Gen. Colin Powell Pkwy., 36867, pg. 933 **PB**

Piedmont

Bostrom Seating, Inc., Vigo Rd., P.O. Box 566, 36272, pg. 933 **PB**

Prattville

CONTINENTAL EAGLE CORPORATION, Gin Shop Hill Rd., 36067, pg. 267 **PV**
Prattville Mfg., Inc., 1085 Selma Hwy., 36067, pg. 561 **PB**
Prattville Progress, 36067, pg. 699 **PB**
Ring Around Products, Inc., Rynolds Mill Rd., 36067, pg. 1210 **PB**
Wabash Fibre Box Co.-Montgomery, 947 Washington Ferry Rd., Route 5, Box 852A, 36067, pg. 1170 **PV**

Prichard

AUTRY GREER & SONS, INC., 2850 W. Main St., 36612, pg. 479 **PV**

Red Bay

TIFFIN MOTOR HOMES, INC., 502 Fourth St., N.W., 35582, pg. 1086 **PV**

Reform

Durbin-Durco, 113 21st Ave., S.W., 35481, pg. 406 **PB**

Roanoke

Snyder Southeast Div., 182 Industrial Ave., 36274, pg. 1011 **PV**

Saraland

Masland Carpets, Inc., 716 Bill Myles Dr., 36571, pg. 514 **PB**

Scottsboro

McQuay Int'l, P.O. Box 466, RR 2, 35768-9676, pg. 3 **PV**

Selma

American Fine Wire Corp., P.O. Box 966, 907 Ravenwood Dr., 36701, pg. 969 **PV**
Assurance Glass Co. of Alabama, Selfield Industrial Park, 36701, pg. 458 **PV**
Borg Warner Automotive-Alabama Div., 455 Water Ave., 36702, pg. 245 **PB**
Bush Hog Division, 2501 Griffin Ave., 36701, pg. 48 **PB**
Dunn Nursing Home, 515 Mabry St., 36701, pg. 1256 **PB**
MILLER & CO., 500 Hooper Dr., 36702, pg. 746 **PV**
Regions Bank/Selma, P.O. Box 479, 36702, pg. 1372 **PB**
Warren Manor Nursing Home, 11 Bell Rd., 36701, pg. 1257 **PB**

Sheffield

Hardin County Gas Company, 100 E. Second St., 35660, pg. 146 **PB**
North Mississippi Natural Gas Corporation, 100 E. Second St., 35660, pg. 146 **PB**
Southern Reclamation Company, Rte. 1, Box 1B, River Road, 35660, pg. 1386 **PB**
Vulcan Oil & Gas Company, 100 E. Second St., 35660, pg. 146 **PB**
Warrior Basin Gas Company, 100 E. Second St., 35660, pg. 146 **PB**

Sumiton

Sumiton Office, Bryan Rd. & U.S., pg. 1297 **PB**

Sylacauga

Avondale Foreign Sales Corporation, 900 Avondale Ave., 35150, pg. 103 **PV**
Avondale Mills, Inc., 900 Avondale Ave., 35150, pg. 102 **PV**
PURSELL INDUSTRIES, 201 W. Fourth St., 35150, pg. 896 **PV**

SouthTrust Bank, Sylacauga, 911 W. Ft. Williams St., 35150, pg. 1492 **PB**

Talladega

Regions Bank/Talladega County, P.O. Box 856, 35160-0856, pg. 1373 **PB**
SPECIALTY TEXTILE PRODUCTS, 1211 Ft. Lashley Ave., 35160, pg. 1023 **PV**

Tallassee

Dow United Technologies, Hwy. 229 S., 36078, pg. 523 **PB**
Mount Vernon Mills, Inc., Tallassee, AL, 36078, pg. 835 **PV**

Theodore

BARNETT MILLWORKS, INC., 4915 Hamilton Blvd., 36582, pg. 116 **PV**
Huls America Inc., Theodore Industrial Park, Degussa Road, 36582, pg. 1455 **IT**
Ultraform Company, Theodore Industrial Pk., 36582, pg. 105 **IT**

Thorsby

Regions Bank/Chilton County, P.O. Box 339, 35171-0339, pg. 1372 **PB**

Troy

Miltope Corporation Alabama Facility, 1101 S. Brundidge St., 36081, pg. 1114 **PB**
Regions Bank/Troy, P.O. Box 569, 36081-0569, pg. 1373 **PB**

Trussville

Continental Electric, P.O. Box 385, 6655 Hwy. 11 N., 35173, pg. 692 **PV**

Tuscaloosa

AmSouth of Tuscaloosa, P.O. Box 2028, 35403, pg. 105 **PB**
Bank of Tuscaloosa, 2209 Ninth St., 35403, pg. 1549 **PB**
Elk Corp. of Alabama, Old Sanders Ferry Rd., 35403, pg. 568 **PB**
GULF STATES PAPER CORPORATION, 1400 River Rd., N.E., 35404, pg. 487 **PV**
Hardin's Bakery, Inc., 546 15th St., 35403, pg. 657 **PB**
Hunt Refining Company, 1855 Fairlawn Rd., 35401, pg. 549 **PV**
JVC Disc America, Co., #2 JVC Rd., 35405-3598, pg. 847 **IT**
JVC Magnets America, Co., #1 JVC Rd., 35405-3597, pg. 847 **IT**
Regions Bank/Tuscaloosa, P.O. Box 2509, 35403-2509, pg. 1373 **PB**
Southern Electric Supply Co., Inc., 2006 Tenth Ave., 35401, pg. 1107 **IT**
The Tuscaloosa News, 2001 Sixth St., 35401, pg. 1175 **PB**
Tuscaloosa Steel Corp., 1700 Holt Rd., 35404, pg. 221 **IT**
WEST JEWEL INC., 1608 Queen City Ave., 35401, pg. 1163 **PV**
Westervelt Land Co., 1400 River Rd., 35404, pg. 488 **PV**
R.L. ZEIGLER CO. INC., 3201 Kauloosa Ave., 35401, pg. 1204 **PV**

Tuscumbia

Elixir Industries, Hwy. 20, Alt. 72 East, 35674, pg. 371 **PV**
Marley Floors (USA) Inc., P.O. Box 553, 35674, pg. 843 **IT**

Union Springs

DIXIE ELECTRIC COOPERATIVE, 402 E. Blackman St., 36089, pg. 337 **PV**

Valley

Wellington Sears Co., 3101 Twenty-Third Dr., 36854, pg. 933 **PB**

Vernon

Marathon Equipment Company, P.O. Box 1798, 35592-1798, pg. 521 **PB**

Wetumpka

Artee-Wrap Spun, P.O. Box 70, 36092, pg. 467 **PB**

Winfield

Continental Conveyor & Equipment Company, 438 Industrial Dr., 35594, pg. 791 **PV**

Geographic Index-U.S.

ALASKA

Anchorage

AFSC Signature Flight Support, c/o Butler Aviation Intl., P.O. Box 190246, 99519-0246, pg. 700 **IT**
ASCG, Inc., 301 Arctic Slope Ave., 99518, pg. 80 **PV**
ASCG Inspection Services, 301 Arctic Slope Ave., Ste. 100, 99518, pg. 80 **PV**
ASRC Parsons Engineering, LLC., 6700 Arctic Spur Rd., 99518, pg. 80 **PV**
AT&T Alascom, 210 E. Bluff Rd., 99501-1100, pg. 10 **PB**
AGRA Earth & Environmental, Inc., 711 H St., Ste. 450, 99501-3442, pg. 31 **PV**
ALASKA INDUSTRIAL HARDWARE INC., 2192 Viking Dr., 99501, pg. 31 **PV**
Alaska Lube and Fuel, 301 Arctic Slope Ave., 99518, pg. 80 **PV**
Alaska Pacific Assurance Company, 2525 C St., Ste. 400, 99503, pg. 366 **PB**
Alaska Petroleum Contractors, 6700 Arctic Spur Rd., 99518, pg. 80 **PV**
Alaska Pipeline Co., 3000 Spenard Rd., 99503, pg. 1450 **PB**
Alaska Tool & Equipment Service, 3207 Arctic Blvd., 99503, pg. 31 **PV**
Alaska-West Express, Inc., 660 Ocean Dock Rd., 99501, pg. 683 **PV**
ALYESKA PIPELINE SERVICE COMPANY, 1835 S. Bragaw St., 99512, pg. 47 **PV**
America North Inc., 201 E. 56th, Ste. 300, 99518, pg. 571 **PB**
Anchorage Cold Storage Co., 240 W. First Ave., 99501, pg. 812 **PV**
ARCO Alaska, Inc., 700 G. St., 99501, pg. 144 **PB**
ARCO Transportation Alaska, Inc., 550 W. 7th Ave., Ste. 1850, 99501, pg. 144 **PB**
BP Exploration (Alaska) Inc., 900 E. Benson Blvd., 99503, pg. 220 **IT**
Bank of America Alaska, N.A., 550 W. Seventh Ave., Ste. 1700, 99510, pg. 180 **PB**
CARR GOTTSTEIN FOODS, 6411 A Street, 99518, pg. 308 **PB**
Charter North Behavioral Health System, Inc., 2530 DeBarr Rd., 99508-2996, pg. 1035 **PB**
Charter North Counseling Center, Inc., 2530 DeBarr Rd., 99508-2996, pg. 1035 **PB**
China Airlines Ltd., P.O. Box 191013, Anchorage Intl. Airport, 99519, pg. 285 **IT**
Cominco Alaska Incorporated, 5660 '8' Street, 99518, pg. 307 **IT**
EA Engineering, Science & Technology, Inc., 4401 Business Park Blvd., Ste. 26, 99503, pg. 541 **PB**
ERA Aviation, Inc., 6160 S. Airpark Dr., 99502, pg. 1410 **PB**
Enstar Natural Gas Co., 3000 Spenard Rd., 99503, pg. 1450 **PB**
First American Co. of Alaska, 510 W. Tudor Rd., Ste. 101, 99503, pg. 625 **PB**
GTE Alaska Incorporated, 4300 B. St., Ste. 303, 99503, pg. 697 **PB**
Galen Hospital-Alaska, 2801 DeBarr Rd., 99508, pg. 404 **PB**
GCI Cable, Inc., 5151 Fairbanks St., 99503, pg. 708 **PB**
GENERAL COMMUNICATION, INC., 2550 Denali St., Ste. 1000, 99503, pg. 708 **PB**
General Hardware Distributors, 2192 Viking Dr., 99501, pg. 31 **PV**
Hewlett-Packard Company, 1 Aleut Plaza, 4000 Old Seward Hwy., Ste. 101, 99503, pg. 813 **PV**
Hoffman Construction Company of Alaska, 3201 C St., Ste. 610, 99503, pg. 532 **PV**
Houston Contracting Company-Alaska, Ltd., 6700 Arctic Spur Rd., 99518, pg. 80 **PV**
Key Bank of Alaska, P.O. Box 100420, 101 W. Benson Blvd., 99510, pg. 954 **PB**
Key Trust Company of Alaska, 101 West Benson Blvd, Ste. 302, 99510-0900, pg. 954 **PB**
Lynden Incorporated, 6441 S. Airpark Pl., 99501-1981, pg. 683 **PV**
Manulife Financial - Anchorage, 1225 E. Intl. Airport Rd., Ste. 205, 99518, pg. 840 **IT**
Nabors Alaska Drilling, Inc., 4300 B St., 99503, pg. 1148 **PB**
Nabors Alaska Petroleum Svcs., 4300 B St., Ste. 600, 99503, pg. 1148 **PB**
NANA REGIONAL CORPORATION, INC., 1001 E. Benson Blvd., 99508, pg. 774 **PV**
Natchiq, Inc., 6700 Arctic Spur Rd., 99518, pg. 80 **PV**
NATIONAL BANCORP OF ALASKA, INC., 301 W. Northern Lights, 99503, pg. 1153 **PB**
National Bank of Alaska, 301 W. Northern Lights Blvd., 99503, pg. 1153 **PB**
Peak Oilfield Services Company, 4300 B Street, 99503, pg. 1149 **PV**
Petro Star Inc., 301 Arctic Slopve Ave., 99518, pg. 80 **PV**
Piquniq Management Corp., 6613 Brayton Dr., 99507-2127, pg. 80 **PV**
Pool Arctic Alaska, 5801 Silverado Way, 99518, pg. 1316 **PB**
Republic Automotive Parts Sales, Inc., 5491 Minnesota Dr., 99518, pg. 1378 **PB**
Rowan Drilling Co., Inc.-Alaska Div., 2555 Merrill Field Dr., 99501-4126, pg. 1410 **PB**
SKW/Eskimos Inc., 620 E. Whitney Rd., 99501, pg. 80 **PV**
Security Pacific Bank Alaska, N.A., 550 W. Seventh St., 99501, pg. 180 **PB**
Sodexho Alaska Inc., Bldg. A, Unit 1, 5610 Silverado Way, 99518, pg. 1274 **IT**

Tesoro Alaska Petroleum Co., P.O. Box 190272, 3230 C St., 99519-0272, pg. 1582 **PB**
Tesoro Alaska Pipeline Company, P.O. Box 190272, 3230 C Street, 99519-0272, pg. 1582 **PB**
Tesoro Northstore Company, 4450 Cordova, Ste. 200, 99503, pg. 1582 **PB**
3M Alaska, 11151 Calaska Cir., 99516, pg. 1605 **PB**
Unocal Agricultural Products Group, 909 W. 9th Ave., 99501, pg. 1698 **PB**
Western Arctic Coal, 301 Arctic Slope Ave., Ste. 100, 99518-3035, pg. 80 **PV**
Willis Corroon Corp. of Anchorage, 4220 B St., 99503-5995, pg. 1505 **IT**
Woodward-Clyde, 3501 Denali St., Ste. 101, 99503, pg. 1656 **PB**
Yukon Pacific Corporation, 1049 W. Fifth Ave., 99501, pg. 284 **PB**

Barrow

ARCTIC SLOPE REGIONAL CORPORATION, P.O. Box 129, 99801, pg. 80 **PV**
Barrow Cable TV, P.O. Box 489, 99723, pg. 80 **PV**
Eskimos, Inc., P.O. Box 536, 99723, pg. 80 **PV**
Top of the World Hotel, P.O. Box 189, 99723, pg. 80 **PV**
Tundra Tours, Inc., P.O. Box 189, 99723, pg. 80 **PV**

Fairbanks

Alyeska Pipeline Service Company, Fairbanks Business Unit, 701 Bidwell, 99701, pg. 48 **PV**
Arctic Alaska Testing Laboratories, 2055 Hill Rd., P.O. Box 70843, 99707, pg. 989 **PV**
EA Engineering, Science & Technology, Inc., 3540 International Way, 99701, pg. 541 **PB**
Interior Fuels Company, P.O. Box 70199, 3569 S. Cushman, 99701, pg. 1582 **PB**
Sourdough Fuel, Inc., P.O. Box 70288, 99707, pg. 80 **PV**
Willis Corroon Corp. of Fairbanks, Tanana Chiefs Building, 122 First Ave., Ste. 301, 99701, pg. 1505 **IT**

Healy

USIBELLI COAL MINE, INC., 100 River Rd., 99743, pg. 1129 **PV**

Juneau

Echo Bay Alaska Inc., c/o R.M.E., 801 W. 10th St., Ste. 300, 99801, pg. 562 **PB**
Greens Creek Unit, P.O. Box 32199, 99803-2199, pg. 804 **PB**
SEALASKA CORPORATION, One Sealaska Plaza, Ste. 400, 99801-1276, pg. 978 **PV**

Kenai

Kenai LNG Corporation, Mile 21.5, N. Rd. Spur, 99611, pg. 1291 **PB**
Tesoro Alaska Petroleum Company, P.O. Box 3369, 99611, pg. 1582 **PB**

Ketchikan

Ketchikan Pulp Co., P.O. Box 6600, 99901, pg. 1015 **PB**
Sealaska Timber Corporation, 2030 Sea Level Dr., 99901, pg. 978 **PV**

Kotzebue

Nana Development Corporation, P.O. Box 49, 99752, pg. 774 **PV**
Red Dog, P.O. Box 1230, 99752, pg. 308 **IT**

Nikiski

Weatherford, Mi 26.5 Kenai Spur Hwy., 99635, pg. 1749 **PB**

North Pole

Alaska Refinery, 1150 H & H Lane, 99705, pg. 1042 **PB**

Searcy

First National Bank of Searcy, 200 W. Race St., 72143, pg. 630 **PB**

Skagway

White Pass & Yukon Route, P.O. Box 435, 99840-2214, pg. 1151 **IT**

Unalaska

Alyeska Seafoods, Inc., P.O. Box 275, 99685, pg. 845 **IT**

Valdez

Alyeska Pipeline Service Company, Valdez Marine Terminal, P.O. Box 300, 99686, pg. 48 **PV**

ARIZONA

Apache Junction

W.J. Flyte Corporation, 3690 S. Cactus, 85219, pg. 49 **PB**

Bagdad

Cyprus Bagdad Copper Corporation, P.O. Box 245, 86321, pg. 471 **PB**

Buckeye

Golden Eagle Distributors, Inc., P.O. Box 697, 85326, pg. 460 **PV**
Schult Homes Corporation, 201 Apache Rd., 85326, pg. 1442 **PB**

Bullhead City

Citizens Utilities Company, 927 E. Hancock Road, Ste. 1, 86442, pg. 380 **PB**
SunRidge Hotel & Conference Center, 839 Landon Dr., 86430, pg. 673 **PV**

Casa Grande

ARIZONA GRAINS INC., 601 E. Main Ave., 85222, pg. 81 **PV**
Casa Grande Mfg. Division, 1145 Gila Bend Hwy., 85222, pg. 518 **PB**
Cyprus Tohono Corporation, P.O. Box 15009, 85230-5009, pg. 471 **PB**
First American Title Insurance Agency of Pinal, 1415 N. Trekell Rd., 85222, pg. 626 **PB**
Golden Eagle Distributors, Inc., 1000 N. Jefferson, 85222, pg. 460 **PV**
Nestle Beverage Company, 602 S. Swanson, 85222, pg. 917 **IT**
Strick Corp., 1112 N. VIP Blvd., 85222-3015, pg. 1787 **PB**
Valley Seed Co., 601 E. Main Ave., 85222, pg. 82 **PV**

Chandler

ADFLEX SOLUTIONS, INC., 2001 W. Chandler Rd., 85244, pg. 20 **PB**
Aircraft Gear Corporation-Arizona Division, 1800 So. Price Rd., 85248, pg. 938 **PV**
Alpha Omega Publications, 300 N. McKemy Ave., 85226, pg. 168 **PV**
Arizona Auction Services, Inc., 400 N. Beck Ave., 85226, pg. 282 **PV**
BASHAS, 22402 S. Basha Rd., 85248, pg. 120 **PV**
BRIDGESTONE MULTI-MEDIA GROUP, 300 North McKemy Ave., 85226, pg. 168 **PV**
Charter Medical of East Valley, Inc., 2190 N. Grace Blvd., 85224, pg. 1035 **PB**
Chickasha Cotton Oil Co., 1347 N. Alma School Rd., Ste. 200, 85224, pg. 1395 **IT**
Circuit Materials Division, 100 N. Dobson Rd., 85244, pg. 1402 **PB**
Coleman Spas, Inc., 25605 S. Arizona Ave., 85248, pg. 691 **PV**
Crafco, Inc., 6975 W. Crafco Way, 85226, pg. 381 **PV**
Durel Corporation, 2225 W. Chandler Blvd., 85224, pg. 1403 **PB**
Energy Dynamics Division, 7073 W. Willis Dr., 85226, pg. 1250 **PB**
Inter-Tel Integrated Systems, Inc., 7300 W. Boston St., 85226, pg. 888 **PB**
MICROCHIP TECHNOLOGY, INC., 2355 W. Chandler Blvd., 85224, pg. 1105 **PB**
Microwave Materials Group-Microwave Materials Div., 100 S. Roosevelt, 85224, pg. 1402 **PB**
Nimtec Inc., 125 N. Price Rd., 85224, pg. 702 **IT**
Oberg Arizona, 208 S. McKemy, 85226, pg. 810 **PV**
Pimalco Inc., Box 5050, 6833 W. Willis Rd., 85226, pg. 61 **PB**
SMP II, L.P., One San Marcos Place, 85224, pg. 1537 **PB**
Snavely Forest Products, Inc., 302 S. 56th St., 85226, pg. 1010 **PV**
SpeedFam Corporation, 305 N. 54th St., 85226-2416, pg. 1498 **PB**
SPEEDFAM INTERNATIONAL, INC., 305 North 54th Street, 85226-2416, pg. 1497 **PB**

Claypool

Cyprus Miami Mining Corporation, P.O. Box 4444, 85532, pg. 471 **PB**

Douglas

Shure Electronics Of AZ, P.O. Box 4140W, 7th & K Av., 85607, pg. 997 **PV**

Eloy

Eloy Detention Center, 1705 E. Hanna Rd., 85231, pg. 450 **PB**

Flagstaff

The Arizona Daily Sun, P.O. Box 1849, 86002, pg. 1343 **PB**

PB - U.S. Public Companies Volume
PV - U.S. Private Companies Volume
IT - International Public & Private Companies Volume

EMPIRE Machinery - California, 4900 E. Empire Ave., 86004-2814, pg. 375 **PV**
Fairfield Flagstaff, 1900 N. Country Club Dr., 86004, pg. 611 **PB**
First American Title Insurance Agency of Coconino, Inc., 403 N. Agassiz, 86002, pg. 626 **PB**
Golden Eagle Distributors, Inc., 1850 E. Butler, 86002, pg. 460 **PV**
New England Business Service, 1801 W. Hwy. 66, 86001, pg. 1171 **PB**
Northland Publishing Co., Hwy. 80 N, P.O. Box N, 86001, pg. 937 **PB**
Peabody Western Coal Company, 1300 South Yale, 86001-6385, pg. 594 **PB**
Super Services Waste Management Inc., 18600 W. Klabab, 86002, pg. 49 **PB**
Wisconsin Tissue, 1601 E. Butler Ave., 86001, pg. 347 **PB**

Florence

Central Arizona Detention Center, P.O. Box 1048, 85232, pg. 450 **PB**

Fountain Hills

MCO Properties Inc., 16838 E. Palisades Blvd., 85269, pg. 1062 **PB**

Gilbert

CERPROBE CORPORATION, 1150 N. Fiesta Blvd., 85233, pg. 332 **PB**
Coast RV, Inc., 1400 N. Fiesta Blvd., 85234, pg. 388 **PB**
Earnhardt Dodge, 1301 N. Arizona Ave., 85233, pg. 356 **PV**
EARNHARDT'S MOTOR COMPANIES, 1301 N. Arizona Ave., 85233, pg. 356 **PV**
HUNTER CONTRACTING COMPANY, 701 N. Cooper Rd., 85233, pg. 549 **PV**
INTESYS TECHNOLOGIES, 1300 N. Fiesta Blvd., 85233-1604, pg. 574 **PV**
Materials Research Corporation, 2120 W. Guadalupe Rd., 85233, pg. 1283 **IT**

Glendale

BIDDULPH AUTOMOTIVE GROUP, 4611 W. Glendale, 85301, pg. 142 **PV**
Charter Medical of North Phoenix, Inc., 6015 W. Peoria Ave., 85302, pg. 1035 **PB**
Fleetwood Homes of Arizona, Inc., 6112 North 56th Ave., 85301, pg. 651 **PB**
Miller Brands of Phoenix, 5061 N. 51st Ave., 85301, pg. 1289 **PB**
National Bedding Co., 10950 W. Northview Ave., 80317, pg. 780 **PB**
Newport Landing, 5205 W. Thunderbird, 85306, pg. 163 **PV**
SANDS MOTOR COMPANY, INC., 5418 N.W. Grand Ave., 85301, pg. 964 **PV**
SCHUCK & SONS CONSTRUCTION CO., 8205 N. 67th Ave., 85302, pg. 973 **PV**
Zellerbach Division, 4710 W. Camelback Rd., 85301, pg. 1076 **PB**

Globe

Golden Eagle Distributors, Inc., 550 S. Broad St., 85501, pg. 460 **PV**

Goodyear

Arizona Galvanizing Inc., 15775 Elwood St., 85338, pg. 159 **PB**
Lockheed Martin Tactical Defense Systems (Arizona), 1300 S. Litchfield Rd., 85338, pg. 1009 **PB**

Green Valley

Cyprus Sierrita, P.O. Box 527, 85622-0527, pg. 471 **PB**
Piper Jaffray Inc., 180 W. Continental Rd., Ste. 120, 85614-1997, pg. 1301 **PB**

Holbrook

Golden Eagle Distributors, Inc., P.O. Box 209, 86025, pg. 460 **PV**

Keams Canyon

Universal Telephone Southwest-Arizona, P.O. Box 125, Hwy. 264, 86034, pg. 330 **PB**

Kingman

Citizens Utilities Company, 2730 E. Andy Devine Ave., 86401, pg. 380 **PB**
Citizens Utilities Company, 2202 Stockton Hill Rd., 86401, pg. 380 **PB**
EMPIRE Machinery - Kingman, 3140 Airway Ave., 86401-3655, pg. 375 **PV**
First American Title Insurance Agency of Mohave, Inc., 2213 Stockton Hill Rd., 86401, pg. 626 **PB**
Tucker Housewares, 4625 Interstate Way, W., 86401, pg. 1118 **PB**

Lake Havasu City

Havasu Water Company, McCullough Blvd., 86403, pg. 380 **PB**

Laveen

Arnold Machinery Company of Arizona, 6024 W. Southern Ave., 85339, pg. 84 **PV**

Litchfield Park

IMSAMET, Inc., 505 East Plaza Circle, Ste. D, 85340, pg. 587 **PB**
Wigwam Resort, 300 E. Wigwam Blvd., 85340, pg. 721 **IT**

Lukeville

La Choya Unit, P.O. Box 510, 85341, pg. 804 **PB**

Mesa

American Land Cruisers, 11 W. Hampton Ave., 85210, pg. 178 **PV**
Boeing Helicopter Division, 5000 E. McDowell Rd., 85215, pg. 241 **PB**
BROWN & BROWN VENTURE GROUP, LLC, P.O. Box 1059, 85211, pg. 172 **PV**
BROWN EVANS DISTRIBUTING CO., 306 S. Country Club Dr., 85210, pg. 174 **PV**
Cruise America, Inc., 11 W. Hampton Ave., 85210, pg. 388 **PV**
Earnhardt RV, 2222 E. Main St., 85213, pg. 356 **PV**
Elixir Industries, 219 S. Mulberry, 85202, pg. 371 **PV**
EMPIRE Hydraulic Service, 37 W. Iron Ave., 85210-6102, pg. 374 **PV**
EMPIRE Machinery, 1725 S. Country Club Dr., 85210-6099, pg. 374 **PV**
EMPIRE SOUTHWEST CO., 1725 S. Country Club Dr., 85210-6003, pg. 374 **PV**
EMPIRE Transport, 40 W. Iron Ave., 85210-6103, pg. 375 **PV**
Epitronics, Inc., 550 W. Juanita Ave., pg. 12 **PB**
FARNSWORTH COMPANIES, 460 S. Greenfield Rd., 85206, pg. 397 **PV**
Farnsworth Development Co., 460 S. Greenfield, 85206, pg. 397 **PV**
Farnsworth Homes, 8355 E. Baseline Rd., 85208, pg. 397 **PV**
Golden West Homes, 2222 S. Dobson Rd., Ste. 302, 85202, pg. 1209 **PB**
Green Tree Acceptance, Inc., 1930 S. Alma School Rd., Ste. A-207, 85210, pg. 762 **PB**
IKOS Systems, Inc., 1201 S. Alma School Rd., #7550, 85210, pg. 864 **PB**
Las Flores Nursing Center, 6458 E. Broadway, 85206, pg. 1257 **PB**
MESA CITRUS GROWERS, 254 W. Broadway, 85210, pg. 733 **PV**
NCS Education Software & Services, 827 W. Grove Ave., 85210-4931, pg. 1155 **PB**
Northern Trust Bank of Arizona, N.A., 1525 S. Greenfield Rd., 85206, pg. 1196 **PB**
Price Woods, Inc., 2610 E. University Dr., Ste. 102, 85213, pg. 1187 **PV**
System Management Group, 11 W. Hampton Ave., 85210, pg. 178 **PV**
Talley Defense Systems, Inc., 3500 N. Greenfield Rd., 85205, pg. 198 **PB**
Tractor Machining Co., 41 W. Iron Ave., 85210-6196, pg. 375 **PV**
The Tribune, 120 W. First Ave., 85202, pg. 1601 **PB**
WJW Constructors, LLC, 63 E. Main St., Ste. 401, 85201-7417, pg. 1187 **PV**
JOE E. WOODS, INC., 63 E. Main St., Ste. 401, 85201-7417, pg. 1187 **PV**
Z-SEVEN FUND, INC., 2651 W. Guadalupe Rd., Ste. B-233, 85202, pg. 1789 **PB**

Miami

Magma-Pinto Valley Mining Division, P.O. Box 100, 85539, pg. 224 **IT**

Morenci

Phelps Dodge Morenci Inc., 4521 U.S. Hwy. 191, 85540, pg. 1287 **PB**
Sumitomo Metal Mining Arizona Inc., P.O. Box S, 85540, pg. 1316 **IT**

Nogales

Alcatel Network System, Inc., P.O. Box 2078, 85628-2078, pg. 55 **IT**
Citizens Utilities Company, 260 Mariposa Rd., 85621, pg. 380 **PB**
Jeffers Electronics, 1331 W. Fairway Dr., 85621, pg. 1722 **PB**

Parker

Dayton Superior Corp., Mohave Rd., 85344, pg. 932 **PV**

Payson

Broken Bow Gas Co., 200 W. Longhorn, 85541, pg. 581 **PB**
First American Title Insurance Agency of Gila, Inc., 610 E. Hwy. 260, 85541, pg. 626 **PB**

Phoenix

A & B Plastics-Southwest, Inc., 4101 W. Gibson Ln., 85009, pg. 232 **IT**
A S H, INC., 2630 W. Buckeye Rd., 85009, pg. 2 **PV**
AMP Inc. Lytel Division, 21220 N. 19th Ave., 85027-2702, pg. 8 **PB**
APS, M/S 8585, 400 N. Fifth St., 85004, pg. 1297 **PB**
ABCO MARKETS, INC., 3001 W. Indian School Rd., 85017, pg. 10 **PV**
Acoustic Imaging Technologies, Inc., 10027 S. 51st St., 85044, pg. 368 **IT**
ACTION PERFORMANCE COMPANIES, INC., 4707 E. Baseline Rd., 85040, pg. 17 **PB**
AGRA Earth & Environmental, Inc., 3232 W. Virginia Ave., 85009, pg. 31 **PB**
Allied Security Inc., The Green Gables, 2345 E. Thomas Rd., Ste. 205, 85016, pg. 41 **PB**
AlliedSignal Airline Services, 4601 E. Hilton Ave., 85034, pg. 50 **PB**
AlliedSignal Engines, 111 S. 34th St., 85010, pg. 50 **PB**
Allright Corporation of Delaware, 3101 N. Central Ave., Ste. 970, 85012, pg. 42 **PV**
Amerco Real Estate Company, 2727 N. Central Ave., 85004, pg. 49 **PV**
America West Airlines, Inc., 4000 E. Sky Harbor Blvd., 85034, pg. 67 **PB**
AMERICA WEST HOLDINGS CORPORATION, 4000 E. Sky Harbor Blvd., 85034, pg. 66 **PB**
American Color, 3202 E. Harbour Dr., 85034, pg. 1133 **PV**
AMERICAN FENCE & SECURITY COMPANY, 2920 N. 7th St., 85014, pg. 54 **PV**
AmeriSource-Phoenix Div., 107 S. 41st Ave., 85009, pg. 97 **PV**
Anasazi Inc., 7500 Dreamy Draw Dr., 85020, pg. 1098 **IT**
Anasazi Travel Resources Inc., 7500 N. Dreamy Draw Dr., Ste. 120, 85020, pg. 1098 **IT**
APOLLO GROUP, INC., 4615 E. Elmwood St., 85040, pg. 120 **PB**
Aquapure Moisture Systems, Inc., 610 S. 80th Ave., 85043, pg. 1066 **IT**
Arizona Auto Auction Services, 3420 S. 48th St., 85040, pg. 282 **PV**
ARIZONA CARDINALS, P.O. Box 888, 85001-0888, pg. 81 **PV**
Arizona Dairy, 2228 N. Black Canyon Hwy., 85009, pg. 989 **PV**
Arizona Elevator, Inc., 1634 N. 19th Ave., 85009, pg. 521 **PB**
Arizona Health Plan, Inc., 11001 N. Black Canyon Hwy., 85029, pg. 359 **PB**
Arizona Institutional Foods, 2540 N. 29th Ave., 85009, pg. 989 **PV**
ARIZONA INSTRUMENT CORPORATION, 4114 E. Wood St., 85040-1941, pg. 129 **PB**
Arizona Life Insurance Co., 377 N. Third Ave., 85003, pg. 739 **PV**
Arizona Refrigeration Supplies, Inc., 5020 S. 36th St., 85040, pg. 624 **PV**
Arizona Sports Programming Network, 17602 N. Black Canyon, Ste. 111, 85203, pg. 455 **PB**
ARIZONA WHOLESALE SUPPLY COMPANY, 2020 E. University Dr., 85034, pg. 82 **PV**
Arrow/Schweber Electronics, 4134 E. Wood St., 85040, pg. 134 **PB**
Atlas Weathering DSET Laboratories, 45601 N. 47th Ave., 85027, pg. 96 **PV**
AZTAR CORPORATION, 2390 E. Camelback Rd., Ste. 400, 85016-3452, pg. 158 **PB**
Banc Life Insurance Corporation, 4700 E. Thomas Rd., Ste. 204, 85018, pg. 140 **PB**
Bank of America, 101 N. First Ave., 85003, pg. 180 **PB**
Bank One, Arizona, NA, 241 N. Central Ave., 85004, pg. 173 **PB**
BankAmerica Sutter Mortgage Corporation, 3101 N. Central, Ste. 1200, 85012, pg. 181 **PB**
BAR-S FOODS CO., 4041 N. Central, Ste. 1300, 85012, pg. 114 **PV**
BEDROOM SUPERSTORES, 5015 N. 19th Ave., 85015, pg. 129 **PV**
Bell Atlantic Financial Overseas Corporation, 11811 N. Tatum Blvd., Ste. 2000, 85028-1601, pg. 202 **PB**
Bell Atlantic Systems Leasing International, Inc., 11811 N. Tatum Blvd., Ste. 2000, 85028-1601, pg. 203 **PB**
Bergen Brunswig Drug Company, 2101 W. Roosevelt St., 85009, pg. 213 **PB**
BEST WESTERN INTERNATIONAL, INC., 6201 N. 24th Pkwy., 85016-2023, pg. 140 **PV**
BOWMAR INSTRUMENT CORPORATION, 3601 E. University Dr., 85034, pg. 248 **PB**
Browning-Ferris Industries of Arizona, Inc., P.O. Box 21596, 85036, pg. 263 **PB**
Bud West, Inc., P.O. Box 41190, 85080, pg. 178 **PV**
Bulldog VSI, 2225 S. 43rd Ave., 85009, pg. 1176 **PB**
Burgess & Niple, Inc., 5025 E. Washington St., Ste. 212, 85034, pg. 182 **PB**
Burns & Wilcox - Phoenix Office, 3344 East Camelback Rd., Ste. 101, 85018, pg. 610 **PV**
Business Journal Publications, Inc., 2910 N. Central Ave., 85012, pg. 19 **PV**
C S K Auto Inc., 645 E. Missouri, 85012, pg. 1108 **PV**

Geographic Index-U.S.

Geographic Index-U.S.

CFE Company, 111 S. 34th St., Dept. 93-21, MS 503-3J, 85010-5274, pg. 51 PB

Cameron Ashley, 4820 W. Colter St., 85301, pg. 298 PB

A.M. Castle & Co., 2302 E. Magnolia #A, 85034, pg. 313 PB

Cavco Industries, Inc., 1001 N. Central Ave., Ste. 800, 85004, pg. 323 PB

Central Commissary, Inc., 610 S. 56th Ave., 85043, pg. 276 PV

Central Pennsylvania Life Insurance Co., 1421 E. Thomas Rd., 85014, pg. 1222 PB

Chase Bank of Arizona, P.O. Box 29791, 85038-9791, pg. 338 PB

Chemonics Fire-Trol, Inc., 734 E. Southern Pacific Dr., P.O. Drawer 21568, 85034, pg. 591 PB

Cigna Community Choice, Inc., 1101 N. Black Canyon Blvd., pg. 359 PB

Cigna Healthcare of Arizona, Inc., 11001 N. Black Canyon Hwy., 85029, pg. 359 PB

Circle Freight International USA, 4620 E. Elwood, Ste. 6, 85040, pg. 371 PB

The Circle K Company, Phoenix Corporate Ctr., 3003 N. Central Ave., Ste. 1600, 85012, pg. 1624 PB

City Meats & Provisions Co., 1418 N. 27th Ave., 85009, pg. 244 PV

CONTINENTAL CIRCUITS CORP., 3502 E. Roeser, 85040, pg. 440 PB

Continental/Murray, 1805 E. Jefferson, 85036, pg. 268 PV

CONVAIR COOLER CORP., 100 W. Clarendon Ave., Ste. 1260, 85013, pg. 271 PV

Conventry Homes of Phoenix, 6001 N. 24th St., 85016, pg. 495 PB

Cox Communications-Phoenix, 17602 N. Black Canyon Hwy., Ste. 111, 85023, pg. 455 PV

CRAGAR INDUSTRIES, INC., 4636 N. 43rd Ave., 85031, pg. 456 PB

Cramer-Krasselt, 829 N. First Ave., 85003, pg. 285 PV

Cross-Country Life Insurance Company, 1421 E. Thomas Rd., 85014, pg. 27 IT

CUMMINS SOUTHWEST INC., 2239 N. Black Canyon Hwy., 85009, pg. 296 PV

Cupertino Electric, Inc., 3050 S. Country Club Dr., Ste. 8, 85210, pg. 1060 PV

Cutter Deer Valley, 530 W. Deer Valley Rd., 85027-2136, pg. 299 PV

D.C. TAYLOR CO., 2224 W. Shangnea Rd., 85029, pg. 300 PV

D.S., Inc., 11811 N. Tatum Blvd., Ste. 2000, 85028-1601, pg. 203 PB

Daher Golden Eagle - Phoenix, 3904 E. Air Lane, 85034, pg. 749 PB

Daily Racing Form, Inc., 2231 E. Camelback Rd., Ste. 100, 85016, pg. 1327 PB

DavisElen Advertising, Inc., 1702 E. Highland #130, 85016, pg. 316 PV

Dealers Auto Auction of Phoenix Inc., 200 North 83rd Ave., 85043, pg. 1648 PV

Dean's Grand Canyon Photos, 702 W. Camelback Rd., 85013, pg. 319 PB

DEL WEBB CORPORATION, 6001 N. 24th St., 85016, pg. 494 PB

Del Webb's Coventry Homes, 6001 N. 24th St., 85016, pg. 495 PB

Derlan Inc./Phoenix Facility, 401 South 36th Street, 85034, pg. 395 IT

Desert Haven Nursing Center, 2645 E. Thomas Rd., 85017, pg. 1256 PB

Desert Production Center, 2235 W. Alice Ave., 85021, pg. 685 PV

Desert Terrace Nursing Center, 2509 N. 24 St., 85008, pg. 1256 PB

Design Center, 3040 N. 44th St., Ste. 201, 85018, pg. 495 PB

DeVRY Institute of Technology, 2149 Dunlap Ave., 85021, pg. 504 PB

THE DIAL CORPORATION, 15501 N. Dial Blvd., 85260-1619, pg. 505 PB

Dolphin, Inc., 740 S. 59th Ave, 85043, pg. 608 PV

El Dorado Investment Company, 400 E. Van Buren, Ste. 750, 85004, pg. 1298 PB

Eller Media Company, 2850 E. Camelback Rd., Ste. 300, 85016, pg. 383 PB

EMCON Southwest, Inc., 4636 E. Elwood, Ste., #8, 85040, pg. 571 PB

EMPIRE METRO, 2222 W. Grant St., 85009-5857, pg. 375 PB

EMPIRE Power Systems, 2211 W. McDowell Rd., 85009-3074, pg. 375 PV

EMPLOYEE SOLUTIONS, INC., 2929 E. Camelback Rd., Ste. 220, 85016, pg. 579 PB

Encore Computer-Phoenix, 120 N. 44 Street, Ste. 360, 85034, pg. 580 PB

F&B MANUFACTURING CO., 4316 N. 39th Ave., 85019, pg. 388 PV

Fairmont Mortgage, Inc., 6001 N. 24th Ave., 85016, pg. 495 PB

Fan Fueler Sports Marketing, 4707 E. Baseline Rd., 85040, pg. 17 PV

FARNAM COMPANIES, INC., 301 W. Osborn Rd., 85013, pg. 396 PV

Financial Collection Agencies, Inc., 100 West Clarendon, Ste. 1010, 85013, pg. 471 PB

FINOVA Capital Corporation, 1850 N. Central Ave., 85002, pg. 624 PB

THE FINOVA GROUP INC., 1850 N. Central Ave., 85004, pg. 624 PB

First Interstate Bank of Arizona, N.A., 100 W. Washington, 85003, pg. 1753 PB

FLETCHER COBRE TIRE CO. INC., 2601 N. 32nd Ave., 85009, pg. 411 PV

FLORI CORP., 3622 S. 30th St., 85040, pg. 414 PV

Fujitsu Business Communication Systems, Inc. - Sales & Marketing, 7776 S. Pointe Pkwy. W., Ste. 200, 85044, pg. 526 IT

G-2 Office Furniture Market, 841 E. Jefferson St, 85002, pg. 464 PV

GCC Far East, Inc., 11811 N. Tatum Blvd., Ste. 2000, 85028-1601, pg. 203 PB

Galen of Arizona, Inc., 2231 E. Camelback, Ste. #208, 85019, pg. 404 PB

Garrett Airline Services Division, 2612 S. 46th St., 85034, pg. 50 PV

General Employment Enterprises, Inc., 100 W. Clarendon, Ste. 1700, 85013, pg. 714 PB

GIFFELS ASSOCIATES, INC., 3003 North Central Ave., Ste. 2001, 85012-2902, pg. 452 PV

GOODMANS, INC., 1400 E. Indian School Rd., 85014, pg. 464 PV

Gosnell Builders, 2728 N. 24th St., 85008, pg. 873 PV

W.M. GRACE DEVELOPMENT, 7575 N. 16th St., Ste. 1, 85020, pg. 468 PV

Graphic Arts Supply Division, 3321 E. Atlanta Ave., 85040, pg. 205 PB

Harris/Arizona Rebar Inc., 2101 W. Jackson St., 85009, pg. 598 IT

H.E.I.L., 108 E. Pioneer Rd., 85040, pg. 521 PB

Heil-Brice Retail Advertising, Inc., 2139 E. Tecoma Rd., 85044, pg. 519 PV

HENSLEY & CO., 4201 N. 45th Ave., 85031, pg. 523 PV

Hewlett-Packard Company, 8080 Pointe Pkwy., W., 85044, pg. 813 PB

Highland Manor Nursing Home, 4635 N. 14th St., 85014, pg. 1257 PB

Hilb, Rogal and Hamilton Company of Arizona, 3003 N. Central Ave., Ste. 300, 85012, pg. 827 PB

Hillhaven Healthcare, Phoenix, 531 W. Thomas Rd., 85013, pg. 1713 PB

HOLSUM BAKERY, INC., 408 S. 23rd Ave., 85009-5852, pg. 536 PV

HOMES & SON CONTRACTORS, INC., 4105 N. 20th St., Ste. 130, 85016, pg. 537 PV

Huber, Hunt & Nichols, Inc., 426 N. 44th St., Ste. 410, 85008, pg. 548 PV

Hydro Conduit Corp., P.O. Box 6220, 4242 W. Buckeye Rd., 85005, pg. 245 IT

ILA Financial Services, Inc., 337 N. 3rd Ave., 85002, pg. 680 PB

Idea Courier, Inc., 2121 E. Magnolia, 85034, pg. 557 PB

IMPERIAL LITHO & DRYOGRAPHY, INC., 210 S. Fourth Ave., 85003, pg. 558 PV

Industrial Automation & Control Division, 16404 N. Black Canyon Hwy., 85023, pg. 833 PB

Info Enterprises, Inc., 426 N. 44th St., Ste. 250, 85008, pg. 1137 PB

Institute for Professional Development, 4615 E. Elwood St., 85040, pg. 120 PB

Inter-Tel DataComm, Inc., 120 N. 44th St., Ste. 200, 85034, pg. 888 PB

INTER-TEL, INCORPORATED, 120 N. 44th St., Ste. 200, 85034-1822, pg. 888 PB

Inter-Tel, Incorporated-New Jersey, 120 N. 44th St., Ste. 200, 85034, pg. 888 PB

Inter-Tel Leasing, Inc., 120 n. 44th St., Ste. 200, 85034, pg. 888 PB

Inter-Tel Midwest, Inc., 120 N. 44th St., Ste. 200, 85034, pg. 888 PB

Inter-Tel Net Solutions, 120 N. 44th St., Ste. 200, 85039, pg. 888 PB

Inter-Tel Technologies, Inc., 120 N. 44th St., Ste. 200, 85034, pg. 888 PB

INTERNATIONAL FIBERCOM, 3615 S. 28th St., 85040, pg. 898 PV

International Turbine Engine Corporation (ITEC), 111 S. 34th St., 85072-2181, pg. 51 PB

International Window-Arizona, Inc., 2500 E. Chambers, 85040, pg. 895 PB

Interstate Bakeries Corporation-Western Division, 4100 E. Broadway, Ste. 150, 85040-8810, pg. 909 PB

Iowa Fidelity Life Insurance Co., 2929 N. 44th St., Ste. 120, 85018, pg. 27 IT

Jaco Electronics, Inc., 2432 W. Peoria Ave., Ste. 1344, 85029, pg. 920 PB

Jay Incorporated-Phoenix Division, 4544 E. Chisum Trail, 85016, pg. 583 PV

Earle M. Jorgensen Company/Phoenix, 5445 W. Madison, 85043, pg. 600 PV

KKLT-FM, 5300 N. Central Ave., 85012, pg. 1344 PB

KMVP-AM, 5300 N. Central Ave., 85012, pg. 1344 PB

KNXV-TV, 4625 S. 33rd Place, 85040, pg. 1448 PB

KPHO-TV, 4016 N. Black Canyon, 85017, pg. 1094 PB

KPNX-TV, 1101 N. Central Ave., 85004, pg. 702 PB

KTAR-AM, 5300 N. Central Ave., 85012, pg. 1344 PB

KUTP Television, Inc., 4630 S. 33rd St., 85040, pg. 352 PB

KAIBAB INDUSTRIES, 4602 E. Thomas Rd., 85018, pg. 605 PV

Kaibab Metals, Inc., 4602 E. Thomas Rd., 85018, pg. 605 PV

Karsten Engineering Corp., 2201 W. Desert Cove, 85029, pg. 608 PV

KARSTEN MANUFACTURING CORPORATION, 2201 W. Desert Cove, 85029, pg. 608 PV

Kaufman and Broad of Arizona, Inc., 432 N. 44th St., Ste. 115, 85008, pg. 945 PB

Kintetsu World Express, Inc., 4425 E. Elwood St., Ste. 107, 85040, pg. 735 IT

KITCHELL CORPORATION, 1707 E. Highland, Ste. 100, 85016, pg. 624 PV

LNG Energy, Inc., One Deer Valley Rd., Ste. 107, 85027, pg. 1493 PB

Lake Investment Co., P.O. Box 50, 85924, pg. 1563 PB

Lane Graphics Products Div., 21039 N. 27th Ave., 85027, pg. 707 PB

Lennar Homes of Arizona, Inc., 1610 W. Camelback Rd., 85015, pg. 988 PB

Lodgistix, Inc., 2150 E. Highland Ave., Ste. 102, 85016, pg. 1527 PB

Jennifer Loomis & Associates, 7878 N. 16th St., Ste. 235, 85068-6930, pg. 1267 PB

M & I Marshall & Ilsley Trust Company of Arizona, One E. Camelback Rd., Ste. 340, 85012, pg. 1051 PB

M & I Thunderbird Bank, One E. Camelback Rd., 85012, pg. 1050 PB

MAC AMERICA COMMUNICATIONS, INC., 5555 N. 7th Ave., 85013, pg. 685 PB

M M Systems Corporation, 2985 W. Whitton Ave., 85009, pg. 685 PV

Madison Industries Inc. of Arizona, 2100 S. 11th Ave., 85007, pg. 428 PV

Magma-Superior Mining Division, P.O. Box 37, 85273, pg. 224 IT

Mail Media Companies, 7815 S. 46th Ave., 85044, pg. 1509 PB

MANHATTAN PARTNERS L.P., 215 S. 28th St., 85034, pg. 699 PV

Manulife Financial - Phoenix, 2398 E. Camelback Rd., Ste. 610, 85016, pg. 841 IT

Masterview Window Company, Inc., 3065 S. 43rd Ave., 85009, pg. 1341 PV

Materials Research Corporation, 3821 E. Broadway Rd., 85040, pg. 1283 IT

Maximet, 5925 W. Monroe, 85043, pg. 608 PV

MEDICIS PHARMACEUTICAL CORP., 4313 E. Camelback Rd., 85018, pg. 1080 PB

Microsi, 10028 S. 51st St., 85044, pg. 1234 IT

Moon Valley Country Club, 151 Westmoon Valley Dr., 85023, pg. 608 PV

Motor Coach Industries, Inc., 1850 N. Central Ave., 85004, pg. 326 PB

Motor Coach Industries International, Inc., 1850 N. Central Ave., 85004, pg. 326 IT

Motorola CPSTG, Sensors Products Division, 5005 E. McDowell Rd., 85008, pg. 1137 PB

Motorola CVD, Inc., 3821 E. Broadway, 85040, pg. 1138 PB

Mutoh America Inc., 3007 E. Chambers St., 85040-3796, pg. 897 IT

NRG Management, 3875 N. 44th St., Ste. 220, 85018, pg. 1527 PB

NZ Development Corporation, 3033 N. 44th St., Ste. 270, 85018, pg. 1172 PB

NZ Properties, Inc., 3033 N. 44th St., Ste. 270, 85018, pg. 1172 PB

NATIONAL BRANDS, INC., 4633 W. Polk, 85043, pg. 780 PV

NATIONAL HEALTH ENHANCEMENT SYSTEMS, INC., 3200 N. Central Ave., 85012, pg. 1157 PB

National Security Containers, 1001 N. Central Ave., Ste. 401, 85004, pg. 323 PB

Nationwide Commercial Co., 2721 No. Central Ave., 85004, pg. 49 PV

New CII Computer, Inc., 11811 N. Tatum Blvd., Ste. 2000, 85028-1601, pg. 203 PB

NEW MEXICO & ARIZONA LAND CO., 3033 N. 44th St., Ste. 270, 85018-7228, pg. 1172 PB

Northern Pipeline Construction Co., One W. Deer Vallley Rd., Ste. 101, 85027-2130, pg. 1493 PB

Northern Trust Bank of Arizona, N.A., 2398 E. Camelback Rd., 85016, pg. 1196 PB

J.R. NORTON COMPANY, 3200 E. Camelback Rd., Ste. 389, 85018, pg. 807 PV

Norwest Bank Arizona, N.A., 3300 N. Central Ave., 85012, pg. 1202 PB

W.E. O'Neil Construction Company of Arizona, 4602 E. University Dr., Ste. 120, 85034, pg. 817 PV

OUTDOOR SYSTEMS, INC., 2502 N. Black Canyon Hwy., 85009, pg. 1235 PB

Oxford Life Insurance Co., 2721 N. Central Ave., 85004, pg. 49 PV

Ozone Research & Equipment Corp., 4953 W. Missouri Ave., 85301, pg. 1234 PV

PA Sun Life Insurance Company, 100 W. Clarenon, Ste. 800, 85013, pg. 1529 PB

PS Insurance Co., 2929 N. 44th St., Suite 120, 85018, pg. 1341 PB

Pacific Century Bank, 1001 N. Central Ave., 85004, pg. 1248 PB

Pacificare of Arizona, 410 44th St., 85006, pg. 1251 PB

The Pavilion Venture, 2525 E. Arizona Biltmore Cir., 85029, pg. 365 PB

Penco, 7600 N. 15th St., Ste. 220, 85020, pg. 1504 IT

PENCO-Arizona, 7600 N. 15th St., 85020, pg. 1508 IT

Penn-Ohio Life Insurance Company, 3101 N. Central Ave., Ste. 770, 85012-2640, pg. 607 PB

Penn Racquet Sports, 306 S. 45th Ave., 85043, pg. 706 PB

People's Choice-TV Corp. of Phoenix, Inc., 2921 N. 30th Ave., 85017, pg. 1274 PB

Perini Building Co., Inc. Western U.S. Division, 360 E. Coronado, 85004, pg. 1278 PB

Peter Piper, Inc., 2036 E. Camelback Rd., 85016, pg. 157 IT

PETSMART, INC., 19601 N. 27th Ave., 85027, pg. 1281 PB

PHARMACEUTICAL MARKETING SERVICES INC., 2394 E. Camelback Rd., 85016, pg. 1284 PB

Phelps Dodge Copper Products Company, 2600 N. Central Ave., 85004, pg. 1287 PB

PHELPS DODGE CORPORATION, 2600 N. Central Ave., 85004-3014, pg. 1286 PB

Phelps Dodge Exploration Corporation, 2660 N. Central Ave., 85004, pg. 1287 PB

PB - *U.S. Public Companies Volume*
PV - *U.S. Private Companies Volume*
IT - *International Public & Private Companies Volume*

Phelps Dodge Industries, 2600 N. Central Ave., 85004-3089, pg. 1286 PB
Phelps Dodge Mining Company, 2600 N. Central Ave., 85004-3089, pg. 1286 PB
Phoenix Concrete Cutting, 3301 E. Wood St., 85040, pg. 849 PV
PHOENIX FUEL COMPANY, INC., 2343 N. 27th Ave., 85005, pg. 863 PV
Phoenix Magazine, 5555 N. Seventh Ave., Ste. B-200, 85013, pg. 685 PV
Phoenix Manufacturing, Inc., 3655 E. Roeser Rd., 85036, pg. 441 PB
Phoenix Metallics, Inc., 2308 S. 11th St., 85007, pg. 428 PV
Phoenix Newspapers, Inc., 120 E. VanBuren St., 85004, pg. 326 PB
Physician Sales & Services Inc., 3740 E. LaSalle, 85040, pg. 1294 PB
PINNACLE WEST CAPITAL CORPORATION, 400 E. Van Buren St., Ste. 800, 85004, pg. 1297 PB
Piper Jaffray Inc., 2525 E. Camelback Rd., Ste. 900, 85016-4244, pg. 1301 PB
Poe & Brown of Arizona, Citibank Plaza, 4041 N. Central Ave., Ste. 1400, 85012, pg. 1312 PB
POINTE GROUP LTD., 2728 N. 24th St., 85008, pg. 873 PV
Ponderosa Holdings Inc., 2721 N. Central Ave., 85004, pg. 49 PV
Post-Newsweek Cable Division, 4742 N. 24 St., Ste. 270, 85016, pg. 1743 PB
Pure Solutions, 4101 E. Wood St., 85040, pg. 912 PB
QDI, 2020 E. University Dr., 85034, pg. 82 PV
R&R Advertising, 4745 N. 7th St., Ste. 429, 85014, pg. 902 PV
Racing Collectables Club of America, 4707 E. Baseline Rd., 85040, pg. 17 PB
Rapid Rail Systems, 2441 S. 40th St., 85034, pg. 521 PB
REDBURN TIRE COMPANY, 3801 W. Clarendon, 85019, pg. 915 PV
Republic Vanguard (of Arizona) Insurance Co., 1600 W. Camelback Rd., 85015, pg. 346 IT
Republic Western Insurance Co., 2721 No. Central Ave., 85004, pg. 49 PV
RETIREMENT COMMUNITY SPECIALISTS, INC., 3101 North Central, Ste. 1120, 85012, pg. 925 PV
RezSolutions, Inc., 7500 N. Dreamy Draw Dr., Ste. 120, 85020, pg. 1098 IT
Ringier America, Phoenix Division, 2802 W. Palm Lane, 85009, pg. 1778 PB
ROAD MACHINERY COMPANY, 716 S. Seventh St., 85034, pg. 934 PV
CHAS ROBERTS AIR CONDITIONING, INC., 9828 N. 19th Ave., 85021, pg. 935 PV
J.B. RODGERS MECHANICAL CONTRACTORS, 2825 W. Thomas Rd., 85017, pg. 939 PV
ROOFING WHOLESALE CO., INC., 1918 W. Grant, 85009, pg. 943 PV
STS, Inc., 6523 N. Black Canyon Hwy., 85015, pg. 538 PB
SabreTech, Inc., Sky Harbor Intl. Airport, 3737 E. Bonanza Way, 85034, pg. 959 PV
SCHUFF STEEL CO., 420 S. 19th Ave., 85009, pg. 973 PV
Sealy Mattress Company - Phoenix, 4802 West Van Buren St., 85043, pg. 979 PV
Sequent Computer Systems, Inc., 2390 E. Camelback, 85016, pg. 1459 PB
SHAMROCK FOODS COMPANY, 2228 N. Black Canyon Hwy., 85009, pg. 989 PV
Shorrock Inc., 11811 N. Tatum Blvd., Ste. 2000, 85028-1601, pg. 203 PB
RUSSELL SIGLER INC., 3451 N. 34th Ave., 85017, pg. 999 PV
SIMULA, INC., 2700 N. Cential Ave. S-1000, 85004, pg. 1475 PB
Singapore Airlines Ltd., 4350 E. Camelback Rd., Ste. 100F-27, 85018, pg. 1374 IT
SMITH PIPE & STEEL CO., 735 N. 19th Ave., 85009, pg. 1009 PV
Smith Specialty Metals, 1716 W. McKinley Ave., 85009, pg. 1009 PV
Sonee Heat Treating, 3900 N. 31st Ave., 85017, pg. 608 PV
Southwest Equity Life Insurance Co., 2929 N. 44th St., Ste. 120, 85018, pg. 27 IT
Southwest Powder Coating, Inc., 5923 Westman Row, 85043, pg. 608 PV
Southwest Risk Services Inc., 1801 N. Tatum Blvd., Ste. 223, 85028, pg. 215 PB
Southwest Telephone Systems, Inc., 120 N. 44th St., Ste. 200, 85034, pg. 888 PB
Southwest Villages, 777 N. 59th Ave., 85043, pg. 1250 PB
Standard Restaurant Equipment Co., 2922 E. McDowell Rd., 85008, pg. 1031 PV
Star Container, Co., 2525 E. Magnolia, 85034, pg. 1071 PV
STARWOOD HOTELS & RESORTS, 2231 E. Camelback Rd., Ste. 410, 400, 85016, pg. 1512 PB
Steris Laboratories, Inc., 620 N. 51st Ave., 85043, pg. 969 PV
Sterling Electronics, 3312 E. Broadway Rd., 85040, pg. 1051 PB
Stewart Smith West, Inc., Point Corridor Ctr. H, 7600 N. 15th St., Ste. 280, 85020, pg. 1508 IT
SunAmerica Securities, Inc., 2800 N. Central, Ste. 1900, 85004, pg. 1533 PB
SunBuilt Homes, Inc., 1001 N. Central Ave., Ste. 800, 85004, pg. 323 PB
Suncor Development Company, 3838 N. Central Ave., Ste. 1500, 85012, pg. 1298 PB
Sundstrand Aerospace Operations, 18008B No. Black Canyon Hwy., 85023, pg. 1533 PB
SUPERSHUTTLE INC., 4610 S. 35th St., 85040, pg. 1056 PV
Swift Leasing Co., 2200 S. 75th St., 85043, pg. 1543 PB
SYNTELLECT, INC., 20401 N. 29th Ave., 85027, pg. 1550 PB
Sysco Food Services of Arizona, Inc., 611 S. 80th Ave., 85043, pg. 1551 PB
TMO Holdings of Canada, Ltd., 1850 N. Central Ave., 85004, pg. 326 IT
Talley Industries, Inc., 2702 N. 44th St., Ste. 100A, 85008, pg. 307 PB
Talley Realty Group, 2702 N. 44th St., Ste. 100A, 85008, pg. 308 PB
Talley Realty Investment Group, Inc., 2702 N. 44th St., 85008, pg. 308 PB
Terra Tech Labs, Inc., 3902 E. University Dr., Ste. 4, 85034, pg. 1594 PB
Time Index, Inc., 825 East University, 85034, pg. 1087 PV
TIME SYSTEMS, INC., 5353 N. 16th St., Ste. 400, 85016, pg. 1086 PV
Tip Top Nursery, 2941 No. 43rd Ave., 85031, pg. 715 PB
Tire Mileage, Incorporated, 3035 East Weldon, 85016, pg. 177 PB
Top-Seal Corp., 2236 E. University Dr., 85034, pg. 1071 PV
Town & Country Tours, 808 E. Osborn St., 85014-5216, pg. 23 PV
Tradewind Technologies, Inc., 616 S. 55th Ave., Ste. 1, 85043, pg. 937 PB
Transico Inc., Membrane Switch Operations, 5436 W. Latham St., 85043, pg. 1631 PB
Transico Inc., Switch Division, 5436 W. Latham St., 85043, pg. 1631 PB
Transport Technology Corp., 1850 N. Central Ave., 85004, pg. 326 IT
Transportation Manufacturing Operations, Inc., 1850 N. Central Ave., 85004, pg. 326 IT
Triumph Air Repair, 4010 S. 43rd Pl., 85040, pg. 1640 PB
Tucchetti, 2135 E. Camelback Rd., 85016, pg. 661 PV
Turf Paradise, Inc., 1501 W. Bell Rd., 85023, pg. 831 PB
Tussenderlo Kerley Inc., 2801 W. Osborn Rd., 85017, pg. 619 IT
20th Century Insurance Co. of Arizona, 5353 N. 16th St., Ste. 150, 85016, pg. 85 PB
U-Haul International, Inc., 2727 No. Central Ave., 85004, pg. 49 PV
U-Haul Leasing & Sales Company, 2727 No. Central Ave., 85004, pg. 49 PV
URS Greiner, Inc., 7310 N. 16th St., 85020-2402, pg. 1658 PB
UGLY DUCKLING CORP., 2525 E. Camelback Rd., Ste. 1150, 85016, pg. 1662 PB
UNITED PRODUCERS & CONSUMERS CO-OP, 1821 E. Jackson St., 85034, pg. 1123 PV
Universal Homes, Inc., 3875 N. 44th St., 85018, pg. 495 PB
Universal Propulsion Co., Inc., 25401 N. Central Ave., 85027, pg. 308 PB
University of Phoenix, P.O. Box 52076, 4605 E. Elmwood St., 85072-2076, pg. 120 PB
VAW of America, Inc., P.O. Box 6726, 85005, pg. 1466 IT
VIAD CORP, 1850 N. Central Ave., 85077, pg. 1718 PB
The Weitz Company, Inc., 2255 N. 44th St., Ste. 125, 85008, pg. 1161 PV
Westco Products/Phoenix, 5720 W. Jefferson St., 85043, pg. 244 IT
Western Ash Company, 5020 N. Eighth Pl., 85014, pg. 203 IT
Western Direct, 4041 N. Central C-200, 85012, pg. 1166 PV
Western International Media Corporation, 4041 N. Central C 200, 85012, pg. 1167 PV
Western International University, 9215 N. Black Canyon Hwy., 85021, pg. 120 PB
WESTERN STATES PETROLEUM INC., 450 S. 15th Ave., 85007, pg. 1169 PV
WestEx, Inc., 2929 N. 44th St., Ste. 410, 85018-7242, pg. 1788 PB
White Microelectronics, 3601 E. University Dr., 85034, pg. 248 PB
Williams Detroit Diesel-Allison S.W., Inc., 2602 S. 19th Ave., 85009, pg. 1179 PV
Willis Corroon Corp. of Arizona, 7310 N. 16th St., Ste. 300, 85020-5299, pg. 1505 IT
WINCUP, 7980 W. Buckeye Rd., 85043, pg. 1182 PV
Winona Research, 8800 N. 22nd Ave., 85021-4258, pg. 1483 IT
WOODSTUFF MANUFACTURING, INC., 1635 S. 43rd Ave., 85005, pg. 1187 PV
Woodward-Clyde, Gateway 111, 410 N. 44th St., Ste. 350, 85008, pg. 1656 PB
Wyle Electronics-Phoenix, 4602 E. University Dr., Ste. 100, 85034, pg. 1457 IT
Yesawich, Pepperdine & Moss, 3800 N. Central Ave., 85012, pg. 1196 PV
Zeneca Specialties, 3259 E. Harbour Dr., Ste. 100, 85034, pg. 1525 IT

Pinetop

First American Title Insurance Agency, Inc., P.O. Box 1030, 1684 E. White Mountain Blvd., Ste. 4, 85935, pg. 626 PB

Prescott

AlliedSignal Avionics Communications Systems, Global Wulfsberg, 6400 Wilkinson Dr., 86301-6164, pg. 51 PB
EMPIRE Machinery - Prescott, 5919 Wilkinson Dr., 86301-6161, pg. 375 PV
First American Title Insurance Agency of Yavapai, Inc., 600 W. Gurley St., 86301, pg. 626 PB
Ruger Investment Castings, 200 Ruger Rd., 86301, pg. 1526 PB
Sturm, Ruger & Co., Inc., Ruger Road, 86301, pg. 1526 PB

San Manuel

Magma-San Manuel Mining Division, P.O. Box M, 85631, pg. 224 IT

Scottsdale

ALLIED WASTE INDUSTRIES, 15880 N. Greenway-Hayden Loop, Ste. 100, 85260, pg. 49 PB
American Reliable Insurance Company, 14805 North 73rd St., 85260, pg. 67 PB
BV&K Direct, 4311 N. Miller Rd., 85251, pg. 108 PV
Bankers Financial Life Insurance Company, 6710 E. Camelback Rd., 85251, pg. 27 IT
Bellasera, 14901 N. Scottsdale Rd., Ste. 200, 85254, pg. 495 PB
Blackeyed Pea Restaurants Inc., 7373 N. Scottsdale Rd., Ste. D-120, 85253, pg. 498 PB
CDI Telecommunications, Inc., 8700 E. Via de Ventura, Ste. 250, 85258-4308, pg. 277 PB
CH Mortgage Company, 7001 N. Scottsdale Rd., Ste. 2050, 85253, pg. 441 PB
CHI Finance Corp., 7001 N. Scottsdale Rd., Ste. 2050, 85253, pg. 441 PB
Candela Skin Care Center, 6939 E. Main St., 85251, pg. 300 PB
Casa Lupita, 4725 N. Scottsdale Rd., Ste. 350, 85251, pg. 393 PV
CHAPMAN AUTOMOTIVE GROUP INC., P.O. Box 11550, 85271, pg. 229 PV
Clear Channel Radio Works, 11508 E. Quartz Rock Rd., 85255, pg. 383 PB
Club Med, 7975 N. Hayden, #C300, 85258, pg. 298 IT
COMAV, 14555 N. Scottsdale Rd., Ste. 240, 85254, pg. 1423 PB
CONTINENTAL HOMES HOLDING CORP., 7001 N. Scottsdale Rd., Ste. 2050, 85253, pg. 440 PB
Continental Homes, Inc., 7001 N. Scottsdale Rd., Ste. 2050, 85254, pg. 440 PB
CyData, Inc., 7001 N. Scottsdale Rd., Ste. 1000, 85253, pg. 770 PB
Data Com, 350 N. Hayden Rd., 85257, pg. 1421 PB
DENAMERICA CORP., 7373 N. Scottsdale Rd., Ste. D-120, 85253, pg. 498 PB
DISCOUNT TIRE, 14631 N. Scottsdale Rd., 85254, pg. 334 PV
Don and Charlie's, 7501 E. Camelback Rd., 85251, pg. 661 PV
DOUBLE AA BUILDERS, LTD., 6040 E. Thomas Rd., 85251, pg. 341 PV
DRUG EMPORIUM OF ARIZONA, 13802 N. Scottsdale Rd., 85254, pg. 343 PV
EDD-Phoenix, 10611 N. HAyden Rd., Ste. D-103, 85260, pg. 205 PB
Educational Management Group, 6710 E. Camelback, 85251, pg. 778 PV
FAMOUS RESTAURANTS INC., 6210 E. Thomas Rd., Ste.203, 85251, pg. 393 PV
FENDER MUSICAL INSTRUMENTS, 7975 N. Hayden Rd., C-100, 85258-3241, pg. 400 PV
FOREVER LIVING PRODUCTS INTERNATIONAL, INC., 7501 E. McCormick Pkwy., 85258, pg. 418 PV
FRANCHISE FINANCE CORP. OF AMERICA, 17207 N. Perimeter Dr., 85255, pg. 679 PB
Garcia's Mexican Restaurants, 4725 No. Scottsdale Rd., Ste. 350, 85251, pg. 393 PV
General Employment Enterprises, Inc., 8283 N. Hayden Rd., Ste. 279, 85258, pg. 715 PB
Giant Industries Arizona, Inc., 23733 N. Scottsdale Rd., 85255, pg. 742 PB
GIANT INDUSTRIES INC., 23733 N. Scottsdale Rd., 85255, pg. 741 PB
GO-VIDEO, INC., 7835 E. McClain Dr., 85260-1732, pg. 748 PB
Great Divide Insurance Company, 7273 E. Butherus Dr., 85260, pg. 216 PB
HBO & Company/Cycare Business Group, 7001 N. Scottsdale Rd., #100, 85253-3644, pg. 770 PB
Harris Life Insurance Company, 6263 N. Scottsdale Rd., Ste. 100, 85250, pg. 154 IT
Harris Trust Bank of Arizona, 6263 N. Scottsdale Rd., Ste. 100, 85250-5401, pg. 155 IT
In-Stat Incorporated, Helm Drive Corp. Offices, 7418 E. Helm Dr., 85260-2418, pg. 1096 IT
Juice Works Development, Inc., 8283 Hayden Rd., Ste. 250, 85258, pg. 1554 PB
Kroy Inc., 14555 N. Hayden Rd., 85260, pg. 1339 PB
LAIDLAW CORPORATION, 6625 N. Scottsdale Rd., 85250, pg. 642 PV
Market Facts, Inc., 15020 N. Hayden Rd., Ste. 202-14, 85260, pg. 1047 PB
MARTA COOPERATIVE OF AMERICA INC., 15150 N. Hayden Rd., Ste. 106, 85260, pg. 708 PV
Microsemi Corp.-Scottsdale, 8700 E. Thomas Rd., P.O. Box 1390, 85252, pg. 1107 PB
Monterey Nursing Center, 7303 E. Monterey, 85251, pg. 1257 PB
Motorola Government Electronics Group, 8201 E. McDowell Rd., 85252, pg. 1137 PB
Motorola Military & Aerospace Electronics, Inc., 8201 E. McDowell Rd., 85252, pg. 1138 PB
Motorola RFID, Inc., 8201 E. McDowell Rd., 85252, pg. 1138 PB

Geographic Index-U.S.

PB - *U.S. Public Companies Volume*
PV - *U.S. Private Companies Volume*
IT - *International Public & Private Companies Volume*

Nautilus Insurance Company, 7273 E. Butherus Dr., 85260, pg. 216 **PB**
NYLIFE Insurance Company of Arizona, 6263 N. Scottsdale Rd., Ste. 300, 85250, pg. 795 **PV**
Northern Trust Bank of Arizona, N.A., 7001 N. Scottsdale Rd., 85253, pg. 1196 **PB**
PCS Health Systems, Inc., 9501 E. Shea Blvd., 85260, pg. 993 **PB**
PADDOCK POOL CONSTRUCTION CO., INC., 6525 E. Thomas Rd., 85251-8849, pg. 833 **PB**
Paradise Valley Water Co., P.O. Box 158, 7500 E. McDonald Dr., Ste. 200-A, 85250, pg. 95 **PB**
Piper Jaffray Inc., 7333 E. Doubletree Ranch Rd., Ste. 105, 85258-2023, pg. 1301 **PB**
RURAL METRO CORPORATION, 8401 E. Indian School Rd., 85251, pg. 1412 **PB**
Sandoz Pharmaceuticals Corp., 7373 N. Scottsdale Rd., Ste. 244, 85253-3550, pg. 974 **IT**
Scottsdale Insurance Company, 8370 E. Via de Ventura, 85258, pg. 789 **PB**
Shea Homes Arizona, 8800 N. Gainey Center Dr., Ste. 350, 85258, pg. 991 **PV**
Solidex, 15035 N. 75th. St., 85260, pg. 1672 **PB**
Sonic Couriers of Arizona, Inc., 15150 N. Hayden Rd., Ste. 200, 85260, pg. 1123 **PV**
Sunburst Resort, 4925 N. Scottsdale Rd., 85251, pg. 800 **PV**
TMP Worldwide, Inc., 8787 East Pinnacle Peak Rd., Ste. # 200, 85255, pg. 1064 **PV**
THE TECH GROUP, 7975 N. Hayden Rd., Ste. D100, 85258, pg. 1071 **PV**
Tech Group Scottsdale, Inc., 14677 N. 74th St., 85260, pg. 1071 **PV**
Terravita Corp., 14901 N. Scottsdale Rd., Ste. 200, 85254, pg. 495 **PB**
Tundra Mesa Constructors, P.O. Box 4550, 85267, pg. 80 **PV**
United Planners' Financial Services of America, 7333 E. Doubletree Rd., Ste. 120, 85258-2023, pg. 831 **PV**

Sedona

Great Vacations International, 52 W. Cortez Dr., 86351, pg. 1172 **PB**

Show Low

EMPIRE Machinery - Show Low, 1501 E. Thornton, 85901, pg. 375 **PV**

Snowflake

The Apache Railway Company, P.O. Drawer E, 85937, pg. 1521 **PV**

Springdale

First National Bank of Springdale, P.O. Box 249, 72765, pg. 639 **PB**

Sun City

Northern Trust Bank of Arizona, N.A., Fountainbell Sq., 10220 W. Bell Rd., Ste 120, 85351, pg. 1196 **PB**
Northern Trust Bank of Arizona, N.A., 10015 Royal Oak Rd., 85351, pg. 1196 **PB**
Piper Jaffray Inc., 10220 W. Bell Rd., Ste. 108, 85351-1179, pg. 1301 **PB**
Sun City Water Company, 15626 N. Del Webb Blvd., 85372, pg. 380 **PB**

Sun City West

Northern Trust Bank of Arizona, N.A., 19432 R.H. Johnson Blvd., 85375, pg. 1196 **PB**
Sun City Grand, 13950 Meeker Blvd., 85375, pg. 495 **PB**
Sun City West, 13950 Meeker Blvd., 85375, pg. 495 **PB**

Sun Lakes

ROBSON COMMUNITIES, 9532 E. Riggs Rd., 85248, pg. 937 **PV**

Tempe

AlliedSignal Fluid Systems, 1300 W. Warner Rd., 85285, pg. 50 **PB**
Arizona Service Center, 1600 West Broadway, Ste. 121, 85282, pg. 829 **PV**
Avnet Computer, 1626 S. Edwards Dr., 85281, pg. 155 **PB**
BTR Med/Vet, 4025 S. McClintock Dr., Ste. 210, 85282, pg. 127 **IT**
California Micro Devices Corporation - Tempe, 2000 W. 14th St., 85281, pg. 293 **PB**
Cascade Controls, Inc., 1403 W. Tenth Pl., Ste. B101, 85281, pg. 1060 **PV**
CITADEL COMMUNICATIONS CORPORATION, 140 S. Ash Ave., 85281, pg. 241 **PV**
Comtech Communications Corp., 4666 S. Ash Ave., 85282, pg. 425 **PB**
CONTINENTAL PROMOTION GROUP, 422 S. Madison Dr., 85281, pg. 269 **PV**
Crompton Metermaster Inc., 2507 W. Erie Dr., 85282, pg. 125 **IT**
Cyprus Climax Metals Company, 1501 W. Fountainhead Pkwy., Ste. 290, 85282, pg. 891 **PB**
Cytec Fiberite Inc., 2055 E. Technology Cir., 85284, pg. 471 **PB**

Dale Electronics, Tempe Div., 1155 23rd St., 85282-1883, pg. 1722 **PB**
EF Data Corp., 2105 W. Fifth Pl., 85281, pg. 293 **PB**
Earnhardt Chrysler/Plymouth-Jeep/Eagle, 577 E. Baseline Rd., 85282, pg. 356 **PV**
Earnhardt Ford, 777 E. Baseline Rd., 85282, pg. 356 **PV**
Elliot Grove Associates, 4041 S. McClintock, Ste. 303, 85282, pg. 361 **PB**
Emtek Health Care Systems, Inc., 1501 W. Fountainhead Pkwy., Ste. 190, 85282, pg. 1137 **PB**
General Employment Enterprises, Inc., 4500 S. Lakeshore Dr., Ste. 490, 85282, pg. 715 **PB**
Stephen Gould of Arizona, Inc., 4041 S. McClintock, Ste. 312, 85282, pg. 467 **PV**
Hoffman-Miller Engineers, Inc., 2323 W. 14th St., Ste. 601, 85281, pg. 842 **PV**
HOMES BY DAVE BROWN, 2164 E. Broadway, Ste. 300, 85282, pg. 537 **PV**
IMC Magnetics Corp., 1900 E. Fifth St., 85281, pg. 868 **IT**
Ikon Office Solutions-Arizona, 1702 W. 3rd St., 85281, pg. 863 **PB**
Infincom, 1702 West Third St., 85281, pg. 864 **PB**
Intergraph Corporation, 1400 E. Southern Ave., Ste. 700, 85282, pg. 891 **PB**
JMI-Phoenix Laboratories, Inc., 405 S. Siesta Lane, 85260, pg. 934 **PB**
Marmid Life Insurance Company, 1414 W. Broadway, Ste. 200, 85282, pg. 581 **PB**
Medtronic Micro-Rel, 2343 W. Tenth Pl., 85281, pg. 1083 **PB**
MicroAge Enterprises, Inc., 2308 S. 55th St., 85282, pg. 1104 **PV**
MICROAGE, INC., 2400 S. Microage Way, 85282, pg. 1104 **PB**
MicroAge International Inc., 2308 S. 55th St., 85282, pg. 1104 **PV**
Microsource Corp., 1555 W. Tenth Pl., Ste. 106, 85281, pg. 1105 **PV**
Motorola Computer Group, 2900 S. Diablo Way, 85282, pg. 1137 **PB**
Nelco Technology, Inc., 1130 W. Geneva Dr., 85282, pg. 1258 **PB**
ORTHOLOGIC CORPORATION, 1475 W. Washington St., 85281, pg. 1232 **PB**
Pulte Phoenix Division, 1430 W. Broadway, Ste. A 200, 85282-1107, pg. 1345 **PB**
JACK ROSS MOTORS INC., 2700 N. Scottsdale Rd., 85271, pg. 946 **PV**
SALT RIVER PROJECT AGRICULTURAL IMPROVEMENT AND POWER DISTRICT, 1521 Project Dr., 85281, pg. 962 **PV**
Sonic Messenger Service, 2223 S. 48th St., Ste. E, 85282, pg. 1123 **PV**
TIE Systems Arizona, 1800 W. Broadway Rd., Ste. A, 85282, pg. 1085 **PB**
Tech Group Phoenix, Inc., 470 W. Vaughn St., 85283, pg. 1071 **PV**
Tech Group Tempe Inc., 640 S. Rockford Dr., 85281, pg. 1071 **PV**
Tech Mold, 1735 W. 10th St., 85281, pg. 1071 **PV**
Tecomet-Tempe, 1425 South Clark, 85281, pg. 1592 **PB**
Tempe Electronics Center, 615 S. River Dr. # R, 85281-3024, pg. 1710 **PB**
THREE-FIVE SYSTEMS, 1600 N. Desert Dr., 85281-1230, pg. 1604 **PB**
Turner/On-Site, 1016 E. Guadalaupe Rd., 85283, pg. 1646 **PB**
UNITECH INDUSTRIES, INC., 444 W. Geneva Dr., 85282, pg. 1672 **PB**
UNITED DAIRYMEN OF ARIZONA, 2008 S. Hardy Dr., 85282, pg. 1121 **PV**
Unitog Rental Facility, 214 S. Rockford Drive, 85281, pg. 1693 **PV**
Walbar of Arizona, Inc., 811 W. Broadway, 85281, pg. 402 **PB**
Wynn's-Precision, Inc., Arizona Div., 708-A W. 22nd St., Ste. 101, 85282, pg. 1783 **PV**
XTEK/Arizona Division, 1710 W. Broadway, P.O. Box 27288, 85282, pg. 1194 **PV**

Tolleson

Sun Land Beef Company, P.O. Box 99, 651 S. 91St Ave., 85353, pg. 833 **PV**

Tucson

ADP Fluor Daniel, 2480 N. Arcadia Ave., 85712, pg. 660 **PB**
ATC Healthcare, 1661 N. Swan, Ste. 214, 85712, pg. 8 **PV**
Advanced Energy Technologies, 220 W. Sixth St., 85701, pg. 1670 **PB**
AlliedSignal Controls & Accessories, 11100 N. Oracle Rd., 85737-9588, pg. 50 **PB**
American Church, P.O. Box 26100, 85726, pg. 60 **PV**
The Arizona Daily Star, 4850 S. Park Ave., 85714, pg. 1343 **PB**
ARTISOFT, INC., 2202 N. Forbes Blvd., 85745, pg. 136 **PB**
Avent, Inc., 3701 E. Colombia St., 85714-2896, pg. 959 **PB**
BHP Copper North America, 7400 N. Oracle Rd., Ste. 200, 85704, pg. 224 **IT**
Barone Foods, 345 S. Kino Pkwy., 85719, pg. 244 **PV**
Battle Mountain Exploration Company, 2700 E. Executive Dr., Ste. 150, 85706-7151, pg. 193 **PB**
Blue Coral Systems, 4775 S. Butterfield Dr., Ste. 175, 85714, pg. 1348 **PV**
BURR-BROWN CORPORATION, 6730 S. Tucson Blvd., 85706, pg. 270 **PB**

Citizen Publishing Co., 4850 S. Park Ave., 85726, pg. 700 **PB**
City Meat Alliant, 1045 S. Highland, 85719, pg. 244 **PV**
Coherent Tucson Research Center, 4605 S. Palo Verde, Ste. 607, 85714, pg. 395 **PB**
Coventry Homes of Tucson, Inc., 1565 E. Rancho Vistoso Blvd., 85737, pg. 495 **PV**
Data Forth, 3331 E. Hemisphere Loop, 85706, pg. 270 **PB**
Delta V Technologies, Inc., 7775 N. Casa Grande Hwy., 85743, pg. 1324 **PB**
Documentation Services-CIM LAB, 3714 E. Columbia St., Ste. 120, pg. 518 **PB**
Donnelly Optics Corporation, 4400 S. Santa Rita Ave., 85714-1642, pg. 519 **PB**
EMPIRE Machinery - Tucson, 7600 S. Nogales Hwy., 85706-9676, pg. 375 **PV**
EMPIRE Power Systems - Tucson, 7600 S. Nogales Hwy., 86004-2814, pg. 375 **PV**
Familian Southwest, Inc., 1101 E. 18th St., 85719, pg. 1512 **IT**
Global Atmospherics, Inc., 2705 E. Medina Rd., Ste. 111, 85706, pg. 1189 **IT**
Global Solar Energy, 220 W. Sixth St., 85701, pg. 1670 **PB**
GOLDEN EAGLE DISTRIBUTORS, INC., P.O. Box 27506, 85713, pg. 460 **PV**
Granite Construction Inc.-Arizona Div., 4115 E. Illinois St., 95714, pg. 759 **PB**
Graphic Arts Supply Division, 1520 E. Broadway, 85719, pg. 205 **PB**
Helian Occupational-Central, 2545 E. Adams, 85716, pg. 1715 **PB**
Helian Occupational-North, 2001 W. Orange Grove, Ste. 504, 85704, pg. 1715 **PB**
Helian Occupational-South, 4600 S. Park Ave., Ste. 5, 85714, pg. 1715 **PB**
Henkel Corporation Minerals Industry Div., 1844 W. Grant Rd., Ste. 104, 85745, pg. 610 **IT**
Hewlett-Packard Company, Bldg. C, Ste. 124, 3400 E. Britannia Dr., 85706, pg. 813 **PB**
HOLDERNESS SUPPLIES, 450 E. Irvington Rd., 85734, pg. 534 **PV**
HOLMES TUTTLE FORD, INC., 660 W. Auto Mall Dr., 85705, pg. 535 **PV**
Huck International, Inc., 3724 E. Columbia St., 85714, pg. 1597 **PB**
Intelligent Instrumentation Inc., 6550 S. Bay Colony Dr., 85706, pg. 270 **PB**
Intergroup Health Corporation, 1010 N. Finance Center Dr., 85710, pg. 678 **PV**
KGUN-TV, 7280 E. Rosewood St., 85710, pg. 983 **PB**
KOLD-TV, 7831 N. Business Park, 85743, pg. 912 **PV**
KTTU-TV, 1855 N. Sixth Ave., 85705, pg. 384 **PB**
Lambda Electronics, 1150 W. Drexel Rd., 85706, pg. 1241 **IT**
Magma Metals Company, 7400 N. Oracle Rd., 85704, pg. 224 **IT**
Miraval, 16600 N. Lago del Oro Pkwy., 85732, pg. 1181 **PB**
National Bank of Arizona, 335 N. Wilmot, 85711, pg. 1793 **PB**
Nations Energy Corporation, 220 W. Sixth St., 85701, pg. 1670 **PB**
NEXTHEALTH INC., 16600 N. Lago del Oro Pkwy., 85739, pg. 1181 **PB**
North Tucson Business Center, 3895 N. Business Center Dr., Ste. 105, 85705, pg. 1250 **PB**
Northern Trust Bank of Arizona, N.A., 6373 E. Tanque Verde Rd., Ste. 100, 85715, pg. 1196 **PB**
Partek Operation, 7075 E. Southpoint Rd., 85706-9407, pg. 1262 **PB**
People's Choice-TV Corp., 5301 E. Broadway Blvd., 85711, pg. 1274 **PB**
People's Choice TV of Tucson, Inc., 3740 E. 43rd Pl., 85713, pg. 1274 **PB**
Piper Jaffray Inc., 5255 E. Williams Cir., Ste. 6600, 85711-7402, pg. 1301 **PB**
Preferred Properties, 1890 E. River Rd., 85718, pg. 1109 **PV**
QUEBEDEAUX PONTIAC, INC., 3566 E. Speedway, 85716, pg. 900 **PV**
R&R Advertising, 1200 N. El Dorado, Ste. F-690, 85715, pg. 902 **PV**
Radisson Suite Hotel, 6555 E. Speedway Blvd., 85710, pg. 1250 **PB**
Richmond American Homes, Inc., 7493 N. Oracle Rd., Ste. 207, 85704, pg. 1025 **PB**
Sargent Controls, 5675 W. Burlingame Rd., 85743, pg. 521 **PB**
Schuller Intl. Inc., 6455 N. Thornydale Rd., 85741-2805, pg. 927 **PB**
Sierra Tucson, Inc., 16600 N. Lago del Oro Pkwy., 85739, pg. 1181 **PB**
Smith Pipe & Steel, 1501 S. Euclid Ave., 85713, pg. 1009 **PV**
Southwest Energy Solutions, 220 W. Sixth St., 85701, pg. 1670 **PB**
Southwest Power Products, 220 W. Sixth St., 85701, pg. 1670 **PB**
Sun City Tucson, 1565 E. Rancho Vistoso Blvd., 85737, pg. 495 **PB**
SUNDT CORP., 4101 E. Irvington Rd., 85714, pg. 1051 **PV**
Sunflower, 1565 E. Rancho Vistoso Blvd., 85737, pg. 495 **PB**
Texas Aluminum Industries Inc., 1603 W. Grant Rd., 85745, pg. 1101 **PB**
TRICO ELECTRIC CO-OP, 5100 W. Ina Rd., 85743, pg. 1102 **PV**
Triple S Plastics, Southwest, 6885 E. Southpoint Rd., 85706, pg. 1640 **PB**

PB - U.S. Public Companies Volume
PV - U.S. Private Companies Volume
IT - International Public & Private Companies Volume

Tucson Electric Power Company, 220 W. Sixth St., 85701, pg. 1670 **PB**

Tucson Learning Center, 6870 S. Plumer Ave., 85706, pg. 219 **PB**

Tucson Newspapers, Inc., P.O. Box 26887, 85726, pg. 701 **PB**

TUCSON REALTY & TRUST CO., 1890 E. River Rd., 85718, pg. 1109 **PV**

Turner/CAS Laboratories, Inc., 1895 W. Prince Rd., 85705, pg. 571 **PB**

Turner Laboratories, 1844 W. Grant Rd., Ste. 104, 85745, pg. 571 **PB**

URS Greiner, Inc. Southwest, 4742 N. Oracle Rd., Ste. #310, 85704, pg. 1659 **PB**

UNISOURCE ENERGY CORPORATION, 220 W. Sixth St., 85701, pg. 1670 **PB**

Valley House Healthcare, 5545 E. Lee St., 85712, pg. 1715 **PB**

Valley Manor Apartments, 5545 E. Lee St., 85712, pg. 1715 **PB**

Vulcan Peroxidation Systems, Inc., 5151 E. Broadway, 85711, pg. 1726 **PB**

Weiser Lock, 6700 Weiser Lock Dr., 85746, pg. 1053 **PB**

Yuma

EC III, Bldg. 2023-D, Yuma Proving Ground, 85365, pg. 543 **PB**

EMPIRE Machinery - Yuma, 3050 E. US Hwy. 95, 85365-2312, pg. 375 **PB**

First American Title Insurance Agency of Yuma, Inc., 2501 Arizona Ave., 85364, pg. 626 **PB**

The Yuma Daily Sun, 2055 Arizona Ave., 85364, pg. 1601 **PB**

ARKANSAS

Alexander

Russell Development Corp., Lee St., 35010, pg. 1413 **PB**

Alma

Commercial Bank at Alma, P.O. Box 2199, Highways 64 & 71, 72921, pg. 641 **PB**

Arkadelphia

Alumacraft Boat Co., Hwy. 67 N., P.O. Box 180, 71923, pg. 1088 **PV**

Citizens First Bank, Fifth & Main, 71923, pg. 630 **PB**

Reynolds Metals Company-Gum Springs, P.O. Box 520, 71923, pg. 1385 **PB**

Atkins

Dean Pickle & Specialty Products, 602 S.E. First St., P.O. Box 158, 72823, pg. 490 **PB**

Batesville

Arkansas Eastman Co., P.O. Box 2357, 72503, pg. 550 **PB**

Arkansas Lime Co., P.O. Box 2356, 72503, pg. 1685 **PB**

Concord Specialty Corp., 101 Industrial Dr., 72503, pg. 177 **PV**

NationsBank of Batesville, 250 S. Broad St., P.O. Box 2557, 72503, pg. 1164 **PB**

Bauxite

Manitowoc Re-Manufacturing, Inc., P.O. Box 8, Route 1 Sardis Rd., 72011, pg. 1041 **PB**

Bearden

BEARDEN LUMBER COMPANY, INC., 111 N. Plum St., 71720, pg. 127 **PV**

Bella Vista

Apartment Ventures, Inc., 1801 Forest Hills Blvd., 72714, pg. 274 **PV**

Blair Tower Limited Partnership, 1801 Forest Hills Blvd., 72714, pg. 274 **PV**

COOPER COMMUNITIES, INC., 1801 Forest Hills Blvd., 72714, pg. 273 **PV**

Cooper Ventures, Inc., 1801 Forest Hills Blvd., 72714, pg. 274 **PV**

Essex House Limited Partnership, 1801 Forest Hills Blvd., 72714, pg. 274 **PV**

Gardenwood Limited Partnership, 1801 Forest Hills Blvd., 72714, pg. 274 **PV**

Highlands at Briarcliff Limited Partnership, 1801 Forest Hills Blvd., 72714, pg. 274 **PV**

Benton

Benton State Bank, 46 W. South St., 72015, pg. 630 **PB**

Bentonville

Colgate-Palmolive (Arkansas), 1309 S. Walton Blvd., Ste. 9, 72712, pg. 397 **PB**

Electrocomponents, 1300 S.E. Eighth St., 72712, pg. 285 **PB**

Hypermart USA, 702 S. W. Eighth St., 72716, pg. 1733 **PB**

North Arkansas Wholesale Co., Inc., 702 S.W. Eighth St., 72716, pg. 1733 **PB**

Sam's Clubs Div., 608 S.W. Eighth St., 72716, pg. 1733 **PB**

Super Center Warehouse Club, Inc., 702 S.W. Eight St., 72716, pg. 1733 **PB**

Wal-Mart Home/Seasonal Div., 702 S.W. Eighth St., 72716, pg. 1733 **PB**

Wal-Mart Jewelry Div., 702 S.W. Eighth St., 72716, pg. 1733 **PB**

Wal-Mart Merchandising Div., 702 S.W. Eighth St., 72716, pg. 1733 **PB**

Wal-Mart Properties, Inc., 702 S.W. Eighth St., 72716, pg. 1733 **PB**

Wal-Mart Realty Company, 702 S.W. Eighth St., 72716, pg. 1733 **PB**

Wal-Mart Shoe Div., 702 S.W. Eight St., 72716, pg. 1733 **PB**

Wal-Mart Softlines Div., 702 S.W. Eighth St., 72716, pg. 1733 **PB**

WAL-MART STORES, INC., 702 S.W. Eighth St., 72716-8611, pg. 1732 **PB**

Blytheville

ACCO Controls Inc., 1 ACCO Dr., 72315-6832, pg. 472 **IT**

Bush Brothers & Company Plant, 400 W. Locust St., 72315, pg. 189 **PV**

Nucor Steel-Arkansas, 7301 E. County Rd. 142, 72315, pg. 1205 **PB**

Nucor-Yamato Steel Company, Hwy. 18 & 137 Armorel, 72316, pg. 1206 **PB**

Booneville

Ace Comb Company Inc., P.O. Box 118, 72927, pg. 1177 **PV**

Spang & Company-Booneville Plant, Hwy. 10 E., 72927, pg. 1020 **PV**

Today's Kids, Hwy. 10 E., 72927, pg. 1020 **PV**

Bryant

Broad, Vogt & Conant S.W., Inc., 1200 Reynolds Rd., 72022, pg. 170 **PV**

Camden

ARC Propulsion Division, Highland Industrial Park, Bldg. M 85 Complex, 71701, pg. 1458 **PB**

Chicopee, P.O. Box 3107, 71701-1207, pg. 113 **IT**

Merchant & Planters Bank N.A. of Camden, P.O. Box 1017, 123 Washington, 71701, pg. 641 **PB**

NationsBank of Camden, 125 Washington St., P.O. Drawer 977, 71701, pg. 1164 **PB**

Chandler

Image Technology Corporation, 2873 N. Nevada St., 85225, pg. 1219 **PB**

Clarksville

Arkansas State Bank, P.O. Box 100, 72830, pg. 630 **PB**

Baldor Electric Company, One R.S. Boreham Dr., 72830, pg. 169 **PB**

Clinton

Clinton Plant, P.O. Box H, Factory Rd., 72031, pg. 201 **PB**

Clinton State Bank, 202 S. Court, 72031, pg. 630 **PB**

UPB of Central Arkansas NA, Hwy. 65 S., 72031, pg. 1669 **PB**

Conway

AMW Industries Inc., P.O. Box 1364, 584 Commerce Rd., 72032, pg. 457 **PB**

ACXIOM CORPORATION, P.O. Box 2000, 301 Industrial Blvd., 72033-2000, pg. 18 **PB**

Acxiom Transportation Services, Inc., 301 Industrial Blvd., 72032, pg. 18 **PB**

Aeromotor Pump, Inc., 584 Commerce Rd., 72032, pg. 538 **IT**

AmTran Corporation, 751 South Harkrider, 72032, pg. 1167 **PB**

CONWAY CORPORATION, 1307 Prairie, 72032, pg. 272 **PV**

First National Bank of Conway, Main & Chestnut, 72032, pg. 630 **PB**

Frigidaire Commercial Refrigeration, 707 Robins St., 72032, pg. 439 **IT**

Frigidaire Home Products, Robins St. & Hwy. 65 S., 72032, pg. 439 **IT**

Infobase Services, 301 Industrial Blvd., 72033-2000, pg. 18 **PB**

Kimberly-Clark Consumer Products, 480 Exchange Ave., 72032-7808, pg. 959 **PB**

NABHOLZ CONSTRUCTION CORP., 612 Garland, 72032, pg. 772 **PV**

NationsBank of Conway, P.O. Box 729, Harkrider Pl., 72032, pg. 1164 **PB**

Wonder State Box Co., P.O. Box 418, 72033, pg. 1017 **PV**

Crossett

Ashley, Drew & Northern Railway Co., Hwy. 82, P.O. Box 757, 71635, pg. 736 **PB**

Formaldehyde, P.O. Box 520, 71635, pg. 737 **PB**

Georgia-Pacific Mid-Continent Wood Prods. Mfg. Div., 105 W. 2nd Ave., 71635, pg. 735 **PB**

Poly Coating Plant, P. O. Box 520, Hwy. 82, 71635, pg. 737 **PB**

Primary Pulp & Paper Plant, P.O. Box 520, Hwy. 82, Paper Mill Rd., 71635, pg. 736 **PB**

De Witt

CORMIER RICE MILLING COMPANY, INC., 501 W. Third St., 72042, pg. 276 **PV**

Decatur

Decatur Telephone Company, P.O. Box 98, 72722-0098, pg. 1571 **PB**

PETERSON FARMS, 250 S. Main St., 72722, pg. 857 **PV**

Dumas

Barton's of Dumas, 1020 Hwy. 165 E., 71639, pg. 119 **PV**

Earle

EARLE INDUSTRIES, INC., Hwy. 64 & 149, 72331, pg. 356 **PV**

El Dorado

ANTHONY FOREST PRODUCTS CO., INC., P.O. Box 1877, 71730, pg. 76 **PV**

Arkansas Chemicals, Inc., Rt. 6, Box 98, 71730, pg. 760 **PB**

Citizens First Bank, 201 E. Peach, 71731, pg. 630 **PB**

ConAgra Broiler Co., P.O. Box 1758, 71730, pg. 427 **PB**

ConAgra Poultry Company, P.O. Box 1758, 71730, pg. 427 **PB**

ConAgra Turkey Company, P.O. Box 1758, 71730, pg. 427 **PB**

Cooper Tire & Rubber Company, El Dorado Plant, P.O. Box 1608, 166 Cooper Dr., 71730, pg. 445 **PB**

DELTIC TIMBER CORPORATION, 210 E. Elm, 71730, pg. 498 **PB**

Engineered Wood Div., P.O. Box 1877, 71730, pg. 76 **PV**

First National Bank of El Dorado, P.O. Box 751, Main at Washington, 71730, pg. 641 **PB**

FIRST UNITED BANCSHARES, INC., 101 W. Main St., 71730, pg. 641 **PB**

KTVE, Inc., Channel 10, 400 W. Main St., 71730, pg. 759 **PB**

MURPHY OIL CORPORATION, 200 Peach St., 71730-5836, pg. 1142 **PB**

Murphy Oil Trading Co. (Eastern), 200 Peach Street, 71730, pg. 1142 **PB**

Murphy Oil USA, Inc., 200 Peach St., 71730, pg. 1142 **PB**

Professional Food Systems, Washington & Oak, 71730, pg. 427 **PB**

Professional Food Systems, P.O. Box 1758, 71730, pg. 427 **PB**

Zeneca Specialties, Hwy. 82 W., 1709 W. Hillsboro St., 71730, pg. 1525 **IT**

Eudora

Barton's of Eudora, 218 S. Main, 71640, pg. 119 **PV**

Fairfield Bay

Fairfield Bay, P.O. Box 1008, 72088, pg. 610 **PB**

Fayetteville

A.W. Realty Co., 1083 Sain St., 72701, pg. 1494 **PB**

Arkansas Western Gas Co., 1001 Sain St., 72703, pg. 1494 **PB**

Arkansas Western Pipeline Company, P.O. Box 1408, 1083 Sain St., 72702-1408, pg. 1494 **PB**

Campbell Soups (Fayetteville Plant), 1100 W. 15th St., 72701, pg. 299 **PB**

Charter Behavioral Health System of Northwest Arkansas, Inc., 4253 Crossover Rd., 72703, pg. 1034 **PB**

Citizens Bank of Northwest Arkansas, 3500 N. College, pg. 163 **PB**

Kearney Company, 3660 S. School St., 72701, pg. 444 **PB**

NationsBank of Northwest Arkansas, One Center St., P.O. Box 1287, 72701, pg. 1164 **PB**

NORTHWEST TOBACCO & CANDY CO., 612 W. Center, 72701, pg. 806 **PV**

Pace Industries, Inc., One McIlroy Pl., 72701, pg. 986 **PB**

SEECO, Inc., P.O. Box 1408, 1083 Sain St., 72703, pg. 1494 **PB**

SOUTHWESTERN ENERGY COMPANY, 1083 Sain St., 72703, pg. 1494 **PB**

Southwestern Energy Pipeline Company, P.O. Box 1408, 1083 Sain St., 72702, pg. 1494 **PB**

Superior Industries-Fayetteville, 1901 Commerce Dr., 72701, pg. 1539 **PB**

Transmontaigne, 280 N. College, Ste. 500, 72701, pg. 1631 **PB**

Fordyce

Citizens First Bank, 611 W. 4th St., 71742, pg. 630 **PB**

Fordyce & Princeton R.R. Co., 301 E. 3rd St., P.O. Box 392, 71742, pg. 736 **PB**

Geographic Index-U.S.

Forman

Ash Grove Cement Plant, P.O. Box 130, 71836, pg. 88 **PV**

Forrest City

GES Inc., 2300 N. Washington, 72360, pg. 434 **PV**
WOODRUFF ELECTRIC CO-OP, 3190 N. Washington, 72335, pg. 1187 **PV**
Yale Industrial Products, 3105 N. Washington, 72335, pg. 406 **PB**

Fort Smith

ABF Freight System, Inc., 3801 Old Greenwood Rd., 72903, pg. 130 **PB**
Acme Brick Co., P.O. Box 3886, 2723 Old Greenwood Rd., 72913, pg. 936 **PB**
Alcoa Proppants, Inc., 5300 Gerber Rd., 72904, pg. 61 **PB**
ARKANSAS BEST CORPORATION, 3801 Old Greenwood Rd., 72903-10048, pg. 130 **PB**
BALDOR ELECTRIC COMPANY, 5711 R.S. Boreham Jr. St., 72908, pg. 168 **PB**
Baldor Electric Company, 4900 Wheeler, 72902, pg. 169 **PB**
Baldor Electric Company, 5711 R.S. Boreham Jr. St., 72908, pg. 169 **PB**
BEVERLY ENTERPRISES, INC., 5111 Rogers Ave., Ste. 40-A, 72919, pg. 227 **PB**
CARCO INTERNATIONAL, INC., 2721 Midland Blvd., 72904, pg. 208 **PV**
City National Bank of Fort Smith, 1222 Rogers Ave., 72902, pg. 641 **PB**
Data-Tronics Corp., 900 Rogers Ave., 72901, pg. 130 **PB**
Federal Savings Bank, 524 Garrison Ave., 72901, pg. 614 **PV**
FLANDERS INDUSTRIES, INC., 1901 Wheeler Ave., 72901, pg. 410 **PV**
Hydro Conduit Corp., P.O. Box 403, 3723 Spradling Ave., 72901, pg. 245 **IT**
Industrial Plastics Company, 8307 Ball Rd., 72903-8435, pg. 56 **PB**
KFSM-TV, 318 N. 13th St., 72901, pg. 1174 **PB**
Label Art, Inc., 5721 S. Zero St., 72903, pg. 782 **PV**
MacSteel Div., 5225 Planters Rd., P.O. Box 1592, 72916, pg. 1349 **PB**
Merchant's Investment Center, Inc., P.O. Box 1007, 72917, pg. 501 **PB**
Merchants National Bank, P.O. Box 1007, 72917, pg. 501 **PB**
Neste Polyester Inc., 5106 Wheeler Ave., 72901, pg. 913 **IT**
Norton-Alcoa Proppants, 5300 Gerber Rd., 72904, pg. 1174 **IT**
Okla Homer Smith Furniture Co., P.O. Box 1148, 72902, pg. 226 **PV**
Plastics Research & Development Co., 3601 Jenny Land, 72901, pg. 359 **PB**
Quikrete Materials, Inc., 4907 Claton Pkwy., 72914, pg. 88 **PV**
Rheem Air Conditioning Div., 5600 Old Greenwood Rd., 72903, pg. 1022 **IT**
Southwestern Die Casting, Inc., 4900 Wheeler, 72902, pg. 169 **PB**
SUPERIOR FEDERAL BANK, 5000 Rogers Ave., 72903, pg. 1054 **PB**
The Times Southwest Broadcasting, Inc., 318 N. 13th St., 72901, pg. 1173 **PB**
Treadco, Inc., 1101 So. 21st St., 72901, pg. 131 **PB**
Unitog Company, 5721 N. 6th St., 72901, pg. 1693 **PB**
WELDON, WILLIAMS & LICK, INC., 711 N. A St., 72902, pg. 1161 **PV**

Green Forest

Automatic Castings Division, P.O. Box 1400, Highway 62 W., 72638, pg. 986 **PB**

Hardy

Century Telephone Company, P.O. Box 636, 100 Woodland Hills Dr., 72542, pg. 329 **PB**
Century Telephone of Arkansas, Inc., P.O. Box 306, 100 Woodland Hills Dr., 72542, pg. 329 **PB**
Century Telephone, Region II, 100 Woodland Hills, 72542, pg. 329 **PB**
TOWN & COUNTRY SUPERMARKET, 102 Jackson, 72542, pg. 1093 **PV**

Harrisburg

Barton's of Harrisburg, 208 Station St., 72432, pg. 119 **PV**

Harrison

AMERICAN FREIGHTWAYS CORPORATION, 2200 Forward Dr., 72601, pg. 75 **PB**
Anchor Die Cast, P.O. Box 1197, 72601, pg. 687 **PV**
CUO, 103 Industrial Park Rd., Ste C, 72601, pg. 1659 **PB**
NationsBank of North Central Arkansas, Rush & Walnut Sts., P.O. Box 730, 72601, pg. 1164 **PB**
The Security Bank, Harrison, 300 N. Main, 72601, pg. 630 **PB**
Wood Products Division, P.O. Box 2552, 72601, pg. 654 **PB**

Heber Springs

Rohr Industries, Heber Springs Plant, 424 Industrial Park Rd., 72543, pg. 752 **PB**

Helena

MID SOUTH SALES, 520 Walnut St., 72342, pg. 744 **PV**

Hope

Bruner-Ivory Handle Company, P.O. Box 647, 71802, pg. 669 **PV**
KLIPSCH, INC., 137 County Rd. 278, 71802, pg. 626 **PV**
SMI Joist Company, Box 2000, 71802-2000, pg. 413 **PB**

Hot Springs National Park

Arkansas Aluminum Alloys, P.O. Box 1410, 71902, pg. 1076 **PV**
Engineered Specialty Plastics, 5111 JFK, 72116, pg. 583 **PB**
Lake Catherine, 190 Elmwood Rd., 71902, pg. 767 **PV**
Mountain Valley Spring Company, 150 Central Ave., 71901, pg. 963 **PV**
MUNRO & COMPANY, INC., 190 Elmwood Rd., 71901, pg. 767 **PV**
NationsBank of Hot Springs, P.O. Box 1000, 71901, pg. 1164 **PB**
Reynolds Metals Company-Hot Springs, P.O. Box 1155, 71901, pg. 1385 **PB**
KEITH SMITH COMPANY, 915 Gaines Ave., 71901, pg. 1008 **PV**

Hot Springs Village

Arkansas Bank & Trust, 935 Central Ave., 71902, pg. 630 **PB**

Huntsville

Butterball Turkey Company, P.O. Box 665, 1200 N. College, 72740, pg. 426 **PB**

Jacksonville

Crosby-National Swage Co., P.O. Box 906, 2511 W. Main St., 72078, pg. 473 **IT**
FIRST ELECTRIC COOPERATIVE, CORP., 901 N. First St., 72076, pg. 407 **PV**
Kitchen Fair, 1090 Redmond Rd., 72076, pg. 917 **PV**
Regal Ware, Inc., 1100 Redmond Rd., 72076, pg. 917 **PV**

Jefferson

Acurex Environmental Corp., Incineration Research Facility, Natl. Ctr. for Toxicol. Res., Bldg. #45, 72079, pg. 607 **IT**

Jonesboro

Agricultural Machinery Div., 5601 E. Highland Dr., 72401, pg. 605 **PB**
E.C. BARTON & COMPANY, 2929 Brown's Ln., 72401, pg. 119 **PV**
Barton's of Jonesboro, 3023 Brown's Lane, 72403, pg. 119 **PV**
Builders Material Company, 102 N. Gee St., 72403, pg. 119 **PV**
Delta Consolidated Industries, Inc. (Co. Headquarters), 4800 Kruger Dr., 72401, pg. 481 **PB**
E.C.B. Brokerage, 2929 Brown's Ln., 72403, pg. 119 **PV**
First Bank of Arkansas, 2400 E. Highland Dr., 72401, pg. 630 **PB**
Frolic Footwear Div., 1020 Aggie Rd., 72401, pg. 1775 **PB**
J and O Diesel, 1333 E. Parker Rd., 72401, pg. 1101 **PV**
KAIT-TV, Hwy.141 N., 72401, pg. 992 **PB**
Ringier America, Jonesboro Division, 4708 Krueger Dr., 72401, pg. 1778 **PB**
Surplus Warehouse-Jonesboro, 215 Union St., 72403, pg. 120 **PV**
UPB of Northeast Arkansas, 300 S. Church, 72401, pg. 1669 **PB**
Wabash Fibre Box Company, 4401 Sarah, 72401, pg. 1170 **PV**

Lake Village

Barton's of Lake Village, Hwys. 65 & 86 S., 71653, pg. 119 **PV**

Leachville

Barton's of Leachville, 109 S. Main St., 72438, pg. 119 **PV**

Lepanto

Barton's of Lepanto, 111 Burney St., 72354, pg. 119 **PV**

Lewisville

Falcon-Lewisville, Hwy. 82 E., P.O. Box 70, 71845, pg. 611 **PB**

Little Rock

AFFILIATED FOODS SOUTHWEST, 12103 Interstate 30, 72209, pg. 26 **PV**
Allright L.R., Inc., 209 W. 6th, 72201, pg. 42 **PV**
ALLTEL Arkansas, Inc., One Allied Dr., P.O. Box 2177, 72203, pg. 55 **PB**
ALLTEL CORPORATION, One Allied Dr., 72202, pg. 55 **PB**
ALLTEL Finance Corporation, One Allied Dr., 72203, pg. 55 **PB**
Alltel Information Services, Inc., 4001 Rodney Parham Rd., 72212, pg. 56 **PB**
ALLTEL Mobile Communications, Inc., One Allied Dr., 72202, pg. 56 **PB**
ALLTEL Services, Inc., One Allied Dr., P.O. Box 2177, 72203, pg. 56 **PB**
ALLTEL Telephone Services Corporation, One Allied Dr., 72202, pg. 56 **PB**
Ameron Protective Coatings Group, 11605 Vimy Ridge Rd., 72209, pg. 99 **PB**
ANDY'S RESTAURANTS INC., 11521 W. Markham St., 72211, pg. 74 **PV**
Arkansas Casualty Investment, 10720 Kanis Rd., 72211, pg. 82 **PV**
ARKANSAS ELECTRIC COOPERATIVES INC., 8000 Scott Hamilton Dr., 72209, pg. 82 **PV**
ARKANSAS FARM BUREAU FEDERATION, 10720 Kanis Rd., 72211, pg. 82 **PV**
Arkansas Farm Bureau Investment, 10720 Kanis Rd., 72211, pg. 82 **PV**
Arkla, P.O. Box 751, 400 E. Capitol Ave., 72203, pg. 843 **PB**
Ash Grove Cement Company Sales Office, 10025 W. Markham, 72205, pg. 87 **PV**
BV&K Direct, #4 Shackleford Plaza, West Edge Bldg., Ste. 210, 72211, pg. 108 **PV**
Babcock & Wilcox ST Company, 8900 Fourche Dam Pike, 72206-3806, pg. 1068 **PB**
Boatmen's Mortgage Company, 200 W. Capitol Ave., P.O. Box 1681, 72203, pg. 1164 **PB**
Boatmen's Trust Company, Inc., P.O. Box 1681, 72203, pg. 1164 **PB**
Browning-Ferris Industries of Arkansas, Inc., P.O. Box 9156, 72219, pg. 263 **PB**
Cleveland Electric Company of Arkansas, 3401 W. 65th St., 72209, pg. 246 **PV**
The Climatic Corporation, 3700 W. 65th St., 72209, pg. 246 **PV**
M.M. Cohn Co., Inc., 300 S. University Ave., 72201, pg. 346 **PV**
COLEMAN DAIRY LLC, 5801 Asher Ave., 72204, pg. 251 **PV**
Community Psychiatric Centers Of Arkansas, Inc., CPC Pinnacle Point Hospital, 11501 Fin. Center Pkwy., 72211, pg. 1712 **PB**
Construction Developers Inc., 1600 Cantrell Rd., 72201, pg. 509 **PB**
CRANFORD JOHNSON ROBINSON WOODS, 303 W. Capitol Ave., 72201-3593, pg. 286 **PV**
DEMOCRAT PRINTING & LITHOGRAPH COMPANY, 114 E. 2nd St., 72201, pg. 323 **PV**
Dillard Investment Co. Inc., 1600 Cantrell Rd., 72201, pg. 509 **PB**
Dillard National Bank, 1600 Cantrell Rd., 72203, pg. 509 **PB**
DILLARD'S, INC., 1600 Cantrell Rd., 72201, pg. 509 **PB**
DYKE INDUSTRY, INC., 309 Center St., 72201, pg. 350 **PV**
Entergy Arkansas, Inc., 425 W. Capitol Ave., 40th Fl., 72201, pg. 586 **PB**
Fairfield Acceptance Corporation, 11001 Executive Ctr. Dr., 72211, pg. 611 **PB**
FAIRFIELD COMMUNITIES, INC., 11001 Executive Ctr. Dr., 72211, pg. 610 **PB**
Farm Bureau Building Inc., 10720 Kanis Rd., 72211, pg. 82 **PV**
Farm Bureau Casualty Insurance Co., 10720 Kanis Rd., 72203, pg. 82 **PV**
Farm Bureau Mutual Insurance Co. of Arkansas, 10720 Kanis Road, 72203, pg. 82 **PV**
First Commercial Bank, N.A., 400 W. Capitol Ave., 72203, pg. 630 **PB**
FIRST COMMERCIAL CORPORATION, 400 W. Capitol Ave., 72203-3464, pg. 630 **PB**
First Commercial Mortgage Co., Capitol & Broadway, 72203, pg. 630 **PB**
Georg Fischer Sloane Inc., 7777 Sloane Dr., 72206, pg. 490 **IT**
Globe Insurance Agency, Inc., 417 Spring St., 72201, pg. 1622 **PB**
Green Tree Acceptance, Inc., P.O. Box 8511, 72215, pg. 762 **PB**
Healthsource Arkansas, Inc., 333 Executive Ct., 72215, pg. 360 **PB**
Hewlett-Packard Company, Conway Bldg., Ste. 116, 10816 Executive Center Dr., 72211, pg. 813 **PB**
Hillhaven, Little Rock, 5720 W. Markham, 72205, pg. 1713 **PB**
Integrated Distributions, Inc., 6001 Lindsey Rd., 72206, pg. 131 **PB**
Interstate Highway Sign, 6005 Scott Hamilton Dr., 72209, pg. 1045 **PB**
Jacuzzi Bros., Jacuzzi, Inc., 12401 Interstate 30, 72219, pg. 1684 **PB**
Jannock Steel Fabricating, Inc., 7420 Enmar Dr., 72219, pg. 699 **IT**
Earle M. Jorgensen Company/Little Rock, 5207 Scott Hamilton Dr., 72209, pg. 600 **PV**
KLRT-TV, 1711 W. Markham, 72211, pg. 384 **PB**

PB - *U.S. Public Companies Volume*
PV - *U.S. Private Companies Volume*
IT - *International Public & Private Companies Volume*

1118

Geographic Index-U.S.

KATV, LLC, P.O. Box 77, 72203, pg. 854 **PV**
Leisure Arts, Inc., 5701 Ranch Dr., 72212, pg. 1613 **PB**
Lilly Industries, Inc., 1900 E. 145th St., 73206, pg. 994 **PB**
Manulife Financial - Little Rock, 425 W. Capital Ave., Ste. 3822, 72201, pg. 840 **IT**
National Old Line Insurance Co., 501 Wood Lane, 72201, pg. 27 **IT**
NationsBank of Arkansas, 200 W. Capitol Ave., P.O. Box 1681, 72201, pg. 1164 **PB**
NationsBank Services Corporation, 200 W. Capitol Ave., P.O. Box 1681, 72203, pg. 1164 **PB**
ORBIT VALVE INTERNATIONAL, INC., 7200 Interstate 30, 72209, pg. 819 **PV**
Pirelli Armstrong Extruded Products Division, 5701 Murray St., 72209, pg. 1058 **PV**
Quality Bearing Service of Missouri, Inc., 4301 Pratt Remmel Rd., 72114, pg. 1711 **PB**
QUALITY FOODS INC., 4901 Asher Ave., 72204, pg. 898 **PV**
J.A. RIGGS TRACTOR CO., 9125 Interstate 30, 72209, pg. 930 **PV**
George Fischer Sloane, Inc., 7777 Sloane Dr., 72206, pg. 430 **IT**
Smith Fiberglass Products Inc., 2700 W. 65th St., 72209, pg. 1477 **PB**
Supplemental Insurance Division, Inc., 1020 W. Fourth St., 72201, pg. 27 **IT**
Sysco Food Services of Arkansas, Inc., 5800 Frozen Rd., 72209, pg. 1551 **PB**
TCBY ENTERPRISES INC., 1200 TCBY Tower, 425 W. Capitol Ave., 72201, pg. 1553 **PB**
TCBY Systems, Inc., 425 W. Capitol, 72201, pg. 1554 **PB**
TIE Systems Arkansas/Gulfcoast, 1601 Westpark Dr., Ste. 6, 72204, pg. 1085 **PV**
Tencarva Machinery Co., 3520 W. 69th St., Ste. 102, 72209, pg. 1076 **PV**
Tri-State Mack Inc., 4616 Thibault Rd, 72206, pg. 1101 **PV**
WEHCO MEDIA, INC., 115 E. Capitol St., 72201, pg. 1159 **PV**
Wehco Video Inc., 115 E. Capitol St., 72203, pg. 1159 **PB**
Windsor Door, 5800 Scott Hamilton Dr., 72209, pg. 69 **PB**
WINROCK ENTERPRISES, INC., 2222 Cottondale Ln. #300, 72202-2055, pg. 1183 **PV**
Woodward-Clyde, Three Financial Ctr., 900 S. Shakleford, Ste. 412, 72211, pg. 1656 **PB**

Lonoke

GUNNEBO FASTENING CORP., One Gunnebo Dr., 72086, pg. 488 **PV**
Gunnebo Fastening Corporation, 1 Gunnebo Dr., 72086, pg. 578 **IT**

Lowell

J.B. Hunt Transport, Inc., P.O. Box 130, 72745, pg. 849 **PB**
J.B. HUNT TRANSPORT SERVICES, INC., 615 J.B. Hunt Corporate Dr., 72745, pg. 849 **PB**

Magnolia

AMERICAN FUEL CELL & COATED FABRICS CO. (AMFUEL), 601 Firestone Dr., 71753, pg. 55 **PV**
First National Bank of Magnolia, P.O. Box 400, 101 S. Court Sq., 71753, pg. 641 **PB**
Quail Piping Products, Inc., 2410 S. Washington St., 71753, pg. 137 **PB**
SMI Steel-Arkansas, Box 1147, 71753, pg. 413 **PB**
Southern Post Company, Box 1147, 71753, pg. 412 **PB**

Malvern

Acme Brick Co., P.O. Box 250, Grigshy Ford Road, 72104, pg. 936 **PB**
Acme Brick Co., P.O. Box 100, Old Hwy. 67 North, 72104, pg. 936 **PB**
Precision Industries Division, P.O. Box 220, 1002 E. Section Line, 72104, pg. 986 **PB**

Manila

Barton's of Manila, 116 W. Concord, 72442, pg. 119 **PV**

Marianna

Douglas & Lomason Company, P.O. Box 628, Olive St., 72360, pg. 830 **IT**
GES INC., Hwy. One Lee Shopping Center, 72360, pg. 434 **PV**

Marked Tree

Mid-South Manufacturing Co., 301 Industrial Park, 72365, pg. 1113 **PV**
Snyder-Crown, Inc., 602 Industrial St., 72365, pg. 1011 **PV**

Maumelle

Charter Little Rock Behavioral Health System, Inc., 1601 Murphy Dr., 72113, pg. 1035 **PB**

McGehee

Barton's of McGehee, 601 N. First St., 71654, pg. 119 **PV**

Melbourne

The Bank of North Arkansas, P.O. Box 70, Main & Spring, 72556, pg. 641 **PB**

Mena

Sterling Machinery Co., Inc., 104 Port Arthur, 71953, pg. 746 **IT**

Monette

Barton's of Monette, 145-49 Drew Ave., 72447, pg. 119 **PV**

Monticello

Barton's of Monticello, Hwy. 425 N., 71655, pg. 119 **PV**

Morrilton

Morrilton Security Bank, N.A., 300 N. Moose, 72110, pg. 630 **PB**

Mountain Home

The Baxter Bulletin, 16 W. 6th St., 72653, pg. 699 **PB**
Baxter County Newspapers, Inc., P.O. Box A, 72653, pg. 699 **PB**
Century Telephone of Mountain Home, P.O. Drawer E, 503 Baker St., 72653, pg. 330 **PB**

Nashville

Boral Gypsum Inc., Hwy. 369 N., 71852, pg. 203 **IT**
First National Bank, Nashville, 101 N. Main, 71852, pg. 630 **PB**
Graysonia, Nashville & Ashdown Railroad Co., P.O. Box 588, 71852, pg. 628 **PV**

Newark

NationsBank of Newark, Front St., P.O. Box 320, 72562, pg. 1164 **PB**

Newport

Norandal U.S.A., Hwy. 67 North, 72112, pg. 434 **IT**

North Little Rock

Bridgeway Hospital, 21 Bridgeway Rd., 72113, pg. 1696 **PB**
Chicopee, P.O. Box 39, 72115-0039, pg. 113 **IT**
Hydro Conduit Corp., 401 N. Palm St., 72114, pg. 245 **IT**
KDDK-FM, 314 Main St., 72114, pg. 384 **PB**
Midland Color Company, 1309 North Hills, 72114, pg. 1311 **IT**
BRUCE OAKLEY, INC., 3700 Lincoln Ave., 72114, pg. 809 **PV**
President Baking-Little Rock, 113 S. Olive St., 72115, pg. 1069 **IT**
Quikrete Materials, Inc., P.O. Box 17209, 72117, pg. 88 **PV**
SF SERVICES, 824 N. Palm St., 72119, pg. 956 **PV**
TARCO, 9515 Hwy. 165 S., 72117, pg. 1068 **PV**
A. TENENBAUM CO. INC., 4500 W. Bethany Rd., 72117, pg. 1076 **PV**
WELSCO INC., 9006 Crystal Hill Rd., 72113, pg. 1161 **PV**
Zeneca Ag Products, 824 E. 12th St., 72115, pg. 1525 **IT**

Osceola

Barton's of Osceola, 314 S. Pecan St., 72370, pg. 119 **PV**
Cyro Industries, PO Box 388, Highway 61, 72370, pg. 1454 **IT**
Southwire Specialty Products, P.O. Box 643, 72370-0643, pg. 1019 **PV**

Ozark

Baldor Electric Company, 1910 Baldor Dr., 72949, pg. 169 **PB**

Paragould

Barton's of Paragould, 1203 Hwy. 49B N., 72451, pg. 119 **PV**

Pine Bluff

Barton's of Pine Bluff, 2900 W. 6th Ave., 71611, pg. 119 **PV**
Camden Wire Co., Inc., 3411 N. Hutchinson, 71611, pg. 526 **PV**
Coca-Cola/Dr. Pepper Bottling Co. Of South Arkansas, 205 E. Second Ave., 71601, pg. 393 **PB**
STEPHEN LAFRANCE HOLDINGS, INC., 3017 N. Midland Dr., 71603, pg. 642 **PV**
THE MAD BUTCHER, INC., 2001 W. Fifth, 71601, pg. 693 **PV**
NationsBank of Pine Bluff, P.O. Box 6208, Fifth & Pine Sts., 71611, pg. 1164 **PB**
Shunt Technology, Jefferson Industrial Park, 3411 N. Hutchinson, 71611, pg. 526 **PV**

Super D Drugs Acquisition Co., 3017 N. Midland Dr., 71603, pg. 642 **PV**
TrefilARBED Arkansas Inc., 5100 Industrial Drive S., 71602, pg. 80 **IT**

Pocahontas

MacLean Esna, 611 Country Club Rd., 72455, pg. 692 **PV**
Magee Co., U.S. Highway 67, 72455, pg. 1561 **PB**

Prairie Grove

Arkansas Galvanizing Inc., 998 Escue Dr., 72753, pg. 159 **PB**

Prescott

Firestone Building Products Company-Prescott, 1406 Hwy. 24 W., 71857, pg. 214 **IT**

Redfield

Primedica, 100 E. Boone St., 72132, pg. 733 **PB**

Rison

Cleveland County Telephone Company, Inc., P.O. Box 366, 206 Pine St., 71665, pg. 1571 **PB**

Rogers

Bekaert Corporation, One Bekaert Dr., 72757, pg. 184 **IT**
BRASS EAGLE INC., 1203 A N. Sixth St., 72756, pg. 250 **PB**
DAISY MANUFACTURING COMPANY, INC., 2111 S. 8th St., 72757, pg. 308 **PV**
Farmers & Merchants Bank, Fourth & Chestnut Sts., 72756, pg. 630 **PB**
Foam Molding Corp., P.O. Box 1720, 72757-1720, pg. 605 **PB**
Rogers Tool Works, Inc., 205 N. 13th St., 72756, pg. 950 **PB**
Superior Industries-Rogers, 1301 N. Dixieland Rd., 72756, pg. 1539 **PB**

Russellville

BIBLER BROTHERS, INC., P.O. Box 490, 72811, pg. 142 **PV**
Firestone Tube Company, 2700 E. Main, 72801, pg. 214 **IT**
Firestone Tube Company-Russellville Plant, Veterans Pkwy. & Fort Jesse Rd., 72801, pg. 214 **IT**
First National Bank of Russellville, Second & Denver, 72801, pg. 630 **PB**
NationsBank of Russellville, Main & Commerce Sts., P.O. Box 220, 72801, pg. 1164 **PB**
Sugar Creek Foods, P.O. Box 747, 72811, pg. 592 **PB**
Taber Metals, Inc., P.O. Box 1418, 72801, pg. 1068 **PV**

Searcy

Identification Systems, 501 Lincoln St., 72143, pg. 1059 **PB**
Road Systems, Inc, 2001 Benton Ave., 72143, pg. 281 **PB**

Sheridan

Centria, P.O. Box 99, 72150, pg. 225 **PV**
Rohr Industries, Sheridan Plant, Hwy. 270 E., Rte. 5, Box 505, 72150, pg. 752 **PB**
Sterling Faucet Co., P.O. Box 427, S. Oklahoma St., 72150, pg. 630 **PB**

Sherwood

RUSSELL CHEVROLET COMPANY, 6100 Landers Rd., 72117, pg. 952 **PV**

Siloam Springs

ALLEN CANNING COMPANY, 305 E. Main St., 72761, pg. 36 **PV**
BYRON Valve Facility, P.O. Box 458, 2547 Waukesha, 72761-8696, pg. 1260 **PB**
Cobb-Vantress, Inc., P.O. Box 249, 72761, pg. 1652 **PB**
La-Z-Boy Arkansas, 2601 N. Country Club Rd., 72761, pg. 973 **PB**

Springdale

BRUNNER & LAY, INC., P.O. Box 1190, 72765, pg. 176 **PV**
Cannon Express Corp., P.O. Box 364, 72765, pg. 301 **PB**
CANNON EXPRESS INC., 1457 E. Robinson, 72764, pg. 301 **PB**
HARP'S FOOD STORES, INC., 1004 S. Gutensohn Rd., 72764, pg. 504 **PV**
Jannock Steel Fabricating, Inc., P.O. Box 6280, 72766, pg. 699 **IT**
Keystone Fasteners, 1407 S. Powell, 72764, pg. 956 **PB**
SCHMIEDING ENTERPRISES INC., 2330 N. Thompson, 72765, pg. 971 **PV**
Tyson Export Sales, Inc., P.O. Box 2020, 72765, pg. 1652 **PB**
TYSON FOODS, INC., 2210 W. Oaklawn Dr., 72762-6999, pg. 1652 **PB**

Geographic Index-U.S.

Tyson Foods of Texas, Inc., P.O. Box 2020, 72765, pg. 1652 **PB**

Stuttgart

Barton's of Stuttgart, W. Second & Porter Sts., 72160, pg. 119 **PV**

Comet Rice, Inc.-Stuttgart, 501 E. 19th St., 72160, pg. 591 **PV**

First Stuttgart Bank & Trust, P.O. Drawer 908, 412 S. Main, 72160, pg. 641 **PB**

Jacob Hartz Seed Company, Inc., P. O. Box 946, North Park Ave., 72160, pg. 1125 **PB**

PRODUCERS RICE MILL INC., 518 E. Harrison St., 72160, pg. 888 **PB**

RICELAND FOODS, INC., 21205 Park Ave., 72160, pg. 928 **PV**

Texarkana

BUHRMAN-PHARR HARDWARE COMPANY, 212-222 Laurel St., 75502, pg. 179 **PV**

Cooper Tire & Rubber Company, Texarkana Plant, 3500 E. Washington Rd., 71854-5894, pg. 445 **PV**

State First National Bank, Arkansas, 300 Olive St., 75502, pg. 630 **PB**

Texarkana Wire & Cable, 3717 Old Post Rd., 75502, pg. 968 **PB**

Tontitown

P.A.M. TRANSPORT, INC., Hwy. 412 W., 72770, pg. 825 **PV**

Trumann

Barton's of Trumann, 739 Hwy. 63 S., 72472, pg. 119 **PV**

Urbana

Anthony Forest Div., 1236 Urbana Rd., 71768, pg. 76 **PV**

Van Buren

Bekaert Corporation, 1881 Bekaert Dr., 72956-6801, pg. 184 **IT**

Therma-Tru Western Mfg. Opers., Industrial Park Rd., 72956, pg. 1080 **PV**

Waldron

Graseby STI, 45 Fir St., 72958, pg. 1268 **IT**

Walnut Ridge

Barton's of Walnut Ridge, 607 Hwy. 67 N., 72476, pg. 119 **PV**

Douglas/Quikut, P.O. Box 29, 118 E. Douglas Rd., 72476, pg. 217 **PB**

Douglas/Quikut, Hwy. 67 North, 72476, pg. 217 **PB**

Warren

The Prescott & Northwestern Railroad Co., P.O. Box 390, 71671, pg. 1318 **PB**

Warren & Saline River Railroad Co., P.O. Box 390, 71671, pg. 1318 **PB**

Weiner

Barton's of Weiner, 415-25 Fourth St., 72479, pg. 119 **PV**

West Helena

Helena Sportswear Co., 107 S. Sebastian St., 72390, pg. 795 **PB**

West Memphis

American Cablevision of West Memphis, Inc., 308 N. 5th St., 72301, pg. 1610 **PB**

Barton's of West Memphis, 215 W. Broadway, 72301, pg. 119 **PV**

Coastal Unilube, Inc., 310 Mid Continent Plaza, 72301, pg. 390 **PB**

Eclipse Combustion, Inc., 803 W. Barton Ave., 72301, pg. 360 **PV**

ELITE LAMP, INC., P.O. Box 936, 72303, pg. 371 **PV**

General Shale Products Corp.-Arkalite Products Div., P.O. Box 1567, 72303, pg. 844 **IT**

Superior Industries-Memphis, 1515 S. Avalon St., 72301, pg. 1539 **PB**

Surplus Warehouse-West Memphis, 3000 E. Broadway, 72301, pg. 120 **PV**

Wilton

Braswell Sand & Gravel Company, Inc., P.O. Box 66, 71865, pg. 628 **IT**

Wynne

Halstead Industrial Prods. Div., Hwy. 1, 72396, pg. 497 **PV**

CALIFORNIA

Adelanto

Aerochem, Inc./El Mirage, 4011 El Mirage Road, 92301, pg. 534 **PB**

General Atomics, Aeronautics, 73 El Mirage Airport Rd Ste B, 92301-9540, pg. 709 **PB**

Molded Fiber Glass/West, 9400 Holly Rd., 92301-0370, pg. 756 **PV**

National-Arnold Magnetics Company, 17030 Muskrat Ave., 92301, pg. 1420 **PB**

Agoura

PAISANO PUBLICATIONS, INC., 28210 Dorothy Dr., 91301, pg. 834 **PV**

Agoura Hills

Command, Control & Communications Systems, 29851 Agoura Rd., 91301-0500, pg. 1002 **PB**

Data Command Systems, 29851 W. Agoura Rd., 91301-0500, pg. 1002 **PB**

PACIFIC CREST CAPITAL, INC., 30343 Canwood St., Ste. 100, 91301, pg. 1248 **PB**

Pip Printing, 27001 Agoura Rd., Ste. 200, 91301, pg. 423 **PV**

J.D. POWER AND ASSOCIATES, 30401 Agoura Rd., 91301, pg. 878 **PV**

Teradyne Semiconductor Test Division, 30801 Agoura Rd., 91301, pg. 1581 **PB**

USA PETROLEUM CORPORATION, 30101 Agoura Ct., Ste. 200, 91301-4311, pg. 1125 **PV**

Alameda

ASCEND COMMUNICATIONS, INC., One Ascend Plaza, 1701 Harbor Bay Pkwy., 94502, pg. 138 **PB**

Autodesk Alameda, 1301 Marina Village Pkwy., 94501, pg. 149 **PB**

IDX Systems Corporation-San Francisco, 1420 Harbor Bay Pkwy., Ste. 290, 94502, pg. 854 **PB**

Norman Levy Associates, Inc., 885 Island Dr., Ste. 207, 94502, pg. 664 **PV**

NETOPIA, INC., 2470 Mariner Square Loop, 94501, pg. 1168 **PB**

OAKLAND RAIDERS, 1220 Harbor Bay Pkwy., 94502-6501, pg. 809 **PV**

Riedel-Smith Environmental Services, 2900 Main St., Bldg. 140, 94501, pg. 1478 **PB**

Sodexho USA West, 1001 Marina Village Pkwy., Ste. 400, 94501-1068, pg. 1247 **IT**

SYBEX, INC., 1151 Marina Village, 94501, pg. 1059 **PV**

WIND RIVER SYSTEMS, INC., 1010 Atlantic Ave., 94501, pg. 1770 **PB**

Alhambra

Brown & Root Inc., P.O. Box 3900, 1000 S. Fremont Ave., 91802, pg. 775 **PB**

California State Bank-Alhambra, 123 S. Chapel Ave., pg. 294 **PB**

Carrier North America, P.O. Box 1234, 91802-1234, pg. 1689 **PB**

Design USA, 949 S. Meridian Ave., 91803, pg. 580 **PV**

International Extrusion Corp., 1000 Meridian Ave., 91801, pg. 895 **PB**

Jacmar Builders Inc., 949 S. Meridian Ave., 91803, pg. 580 **PV**

JACMAR COMPANIES, INC., 2200 W. Valley Blvd., 91803, pg. 580 **PV**

Moran Company, 2121 Orange St., 91803, pg. 84 **PV**

ORTEL CORPORATION, 2015 W. Chestnut St., 91803, pg. 1232 **PB**

SFIC Properties, Inc., 1000 S. Fremont Ave., 91802, pg. 765 **IT**

Santa Fe Drilling Co., 1000 S. Fremont Ave., P.O. Box 4000, 91802, pg. 765 **IT**

Santa Fe for Engineering & Petroleum Projects Company K.S.C., 1000 S. Fremont, 91802, pg. 765 **IT**

Santa Fe Shaft Drilling Co., 1000 So. Fremont Ave., 91802, pg. 765 **IT**

Aliso Viejo

American Zettler Inc., 75 Columbia, 92656, pg. 1528 **IT**

GHN, 31 Columbia, 92656, pg. 386 **PV**

MarketSource Corporation, 85 Argonaut, Ste. 120, 92656, pg. 705 **PV**

MEDSTONE INTERNATIONAL, INC., 100 Columbia, Ste. 100, 92656, pg. 1082 **PB**

Vivra Renal Care, 115 Columbia, 92656, pg. 1724 **PB**

Altadena

CHARLES PANKOW BUILDERS, LTD., 2476 N. Lake Ave., 91001, pg. 836 **PV**

American Canyon

Pechiney Cork & Seal of California, 5415 Napa Vallejo Hwy., 94589, pg. 1029 **IT**

Zeneca Resins, 501 Green Island Rd., 94589, pg. 1525 **IT**

Anaheim

AHF Salons, Inc., 1400 N. Kellogg Dr., 92807, pg. 818 **PV**

ATL Products, Inc., 1515 S. Manchester, 92802, pg. 1212 **PB**

Acurex Environmental Corp., 4883 E. LaPalma Ave., Ste. 505, 92807, pg. 607 **IT**

Advanced Polymers Division, 3340 E. La Palma Ave., 92806, pg. 689 **PB**

AGRA Earth & Environmental, Inc., P.O. Box 19079, 92817, pg. 31 **IT**

Amano Cincinnati - Los Angeles Branch Office, 1485 N. Manassero St., 92807-1943, pg. 70 **IT**

AMERICAN SECURITY DISTRIBUTION, 4411 E. La Palma Ave., 92807, pg. 61 **PV**

Anaheim Extrusion Co., 1330 N. Kraemer Blvd., 92816, pg. 1127 **PV**

ANAHEIM MANUFACTURING COMPANY, 4240 E. La Palma Ave., 92807, pg. 70 **PV**

Bancomm, 1363 S. State College Blvd., 92806, pg. 488 **PB**

BASSANI MANUFACTURING, 2900 La Jolla, 92806, pg. 122 **PV**

Boeing North America, Autonetics Electronic Systems Division, 3370 E. Miraloma Ave., 92803, pg. 241 **PB**

Boeing North America, North American Aircraft Modification Division, 3370 Miraloma Ave., 92803, pg. 241 **PB**

Boston Pacific, Inc., 1200 N. Harbor Blvd., 92803, pg. 278 **PB**

Bridgford Distributing Co., 1308 N. Patt St., 92801, pg. 252 **PB**

BRIDGFORD FOODS CORPORATION, 1308 N. Patt St., 92801, pg. 252 **PB**

Bunnell Plastics Division, 3336 E. La Palma Ave., 92806, pg. 689 **PB**

Burns & Wilcox - Anaheim Office, Ste. 160, 4175 E. La Palma Ave., 92807, pg. 609 **PV**

CKE RESTAURANTS INC., P.O. Box 4349, 1200 N. Harbor Blvd., 92803-4349, pg. 278 **PB**

CalComp Technology, Inc., 2411 W. La Palma Ave., 92801, pg. 1007 **PB**

California Auto Dealers Exchange, Inc., 1320 N. Tustin Ave., 92817, pg. 282 **PV**

California School Book Fairs, Inc., 1221 N. Lakeview Ave., 92806, pg. 1440 **PB**

California State Bank-Anaheim, 2099 S. State College Blvd., 92806, pg. 294 **PB**

Carl's Jr., 1200 N. Harbor Blvd., 92803, pg. 278 **PB**

Cinram Inc., 3400 E. La Palma Ave., 92806, pg. 293 **IT**

CLOTHESTIME STORES, INC., 5325 E. Hunter Ave., 92807, pg. 387 **PB**

Colonial Insurance Company of California, 2390 Orangewood Ave., 92803, pg. 788 **PV**

CYBER SYSTEMS, INC., 2031 E. Cerritos Ave., 92806, pg. 299 **PV**

DSC, 1230 N. Simon Cir. No. A, 92806-1814, pg. 475 **PB**

Data I/O (Manufacturing Automation Div.), 2570 E. Cerritos Ave., 92806, pg. 486 **PB**

Disc Manufacturing Cinram, 1120 Cosby Way, 92806, pg. 293 **IT**

Walt Disney Attractions Division, 1313 Harbor Blvd., 92803, pg. 511 **PB**

Walt Disney Travel Co., Inc., 1150 W. Cerritos Ave., 92802, pg. 513 **PB**

Disneyland, 1313 Harbor Blvd., 92803, pg. 511 **PB**

Disneyland Hotel, 1150 W. Cerritos Ave., 92802, pg. 513 **PB**

DON MIGUEL MEXICAN FOODS, INC., 2125 E. Orangewood, 92803, pg. 339 **PV**

ECONOLITE CONTROL PRODUCTS, INC., 3360 E. La Palma Ave., 92806, pg. 361 **PV**

Electra-Gear Div., 1110 N. Lemon St., 92801, pg. 1370 **PV**

Ericsson Business Communications, Inc., 1900 W. Crescent Ave., 92801, pg. 1364 **IT**

Everest Enclosures, 2100 E. Orange Wood Ave., 92806, pg. 124 **PV**

FS Concepts, Inc., 1400 N. Kellogg Dr., Ste. E, 92807, pg. 818 **PV**

Falcon-Anaheim, 411 E. Julianna St., 92801, pg. 611 **PB**

Firmenich, 424 S. Atchison, 92805, pg. 486 **IT**

Fremont Investment & Loan, 175 N. Riverview Dr., 92808, pg. 681 **PB**

Fujitsu Business Communication Systems, 3190 Mira Loma Ave., 92806, pg. 526 **IT**

GANAHL LUMBER COMPANY, 1220 E. Ball Rd., 92805-5993, pg. 439 **PV**

Golden West Baseball Club, State College Blvd., 92805, pg. 461 **PV**

Great States, 2099 S. State College Blvd., Ste. 500, 92806, pg. 1251 **PB**

Gyyr, Inc., 1515 S. Manchester Ave., 92802, pg. 1212 **PB**

Haircuts Plus, Inc., 1400 N. Kellogg Dr., 92807, pg. 818 **PV**

Hexcel Composites, 5115 E. La Palma Ave., 92807-2018, pg. 824 **PB**

Hitachi Consumer Products of America, Inc., 901 E., South St., 92805, pg. 622 **IT**

Intelligent Technologies & Services, Inc., 2211 E. Winston Rd.,Ste. F, 92806, pg. 404 **PV**

Interstate Electronics Corp., 1001 E. Ball Rd., 92803, pg. 622 **PB**

INTERSTATE ENGINEERING, 522 E. Vermont Ave., 92805, pg. 573 **PB**

Carl Karcher Enterprises, Inc., 1200 N. Harbor Blvd., 92803-4349, pg. 278 **PB**

Kaufman and Broad Inland Empire, 180 N. Riverview Dr., Ste. 300, 92808, pg. 945 **PB**

Kester Solder Co., P. O. Box 188, 92805, pg. 1003 **PB**

Las Palma Nursing Center, 1130 W. La Palma, 92801, pg. 1714 **PB**

PB - *U.S. Public Companies Volume*
PV - *U.S. Private Companies Volume*
IT - *International Public & Private Companies Volume*

1120

Geographic Index-U.S.

Lasco Bathware, 3255 E. Miraloma Ave., 92806, pg. 1397 **IT**

LASCO Bathware, 3255 E. Miraloma Ave., 92806, pg. 1398 **IT**

Ling Electronics Inc., 4890 E. LaPalma Ave., 92806, pg. 1077 **PB**

MTI TECHNOLOGY CORPORATION, 4905 E. LaPalma Ave., 92807, pg. 1028 **PB**

Martin Luther Hospital Anaheim, 1830 W. Romneya Dr., 92801, pg. 1118 **PV**

McLean, 3409 E. Miraloma Ave., 92806-2102, pg. 1791 **PV**

Medtronic Cardiopulmonary, 4633 E. La Palma Ave., pg. 1083 **PB**

Midwest Beauty L.P., 1400 N. Kellogg Dr., 92807, pg. 818 **PV**

The Mighty Ducks of Anaheim, 2695 Katella Ave., 92806, pg. 513 **PV**

MODEL GLASS COMPANY, 4887 E. La Palma Ave., Ste. 704, 92807, pg. 754 **PB**

Moore & Taber Grouting Services, P.O. Box 19079, 92817, pg. 31 **PV**

N.O.A. Airscrew Howden Inc., 1380 No. McCan St., 92806, pg. 636 **IT**

Nelco International, 2401 E. Katella, Ste. 370, 92806, pg. 1258 **PB**

ODETICS INC., 1515 S. Manchester Ave., 92802-2907, pg. 1212 **PB**

OPAL CONCEPTS, INC., 1400 N. Kellogg Dr., 92807, pg. 817 **PV**

PENHALL INTERNATIONAL, 1801 Penhall Way, 92803, pg. 849 **PV**

Pro-cuts, Inc., 1400 N. Kellogg Dr., 92807, pg. 818 **PV**

Programmed Composites, Inc., 5605 E. La Palma Ave., 62807, pg. 882 **PV**

Quad/West Pre-Press, 1174 N. Grove, Ste. A., 92806-2198, pg. 898 **PV**

RTI Electronics Inc., 2900 Blue Star St., 92806, pg. 1455 **PB**

SAFEGUARD HEALTH ENTERPRISES, INC., 505 N. Euclid St., Ste. 200, 92803, pg. 1424 **PB**

Safeguard Health Plans, Inc., 505 N. Euclid St., Ste. 200, 92803, pg. 1424 **PV**

SECHRIST INDUSTRIES, INC., 4225 E. La Palma Ave., 92807, pg. 980 **PV**

Setco, Inc., 4875 E. Hunter, P.O. Box 68008, 92817, pg. 1066 **PB**

SPECIALTY RESTAURANTS CORPORATION, 4155 E. LaPalma Ave., Ste. 250, 92807, pg. 1022 **PV**

Sumitomo Machinery Corporation of America, 1645 S. Sinclair St., 92806, pg. 1314 **IT**

Sundor Brands Inc., 1230 N. Tustin Ave., 92806, pg. 1331 **PB**

Superior Pool Products, Inc., 4900 E. Landon Dr., 92807, pg. 1219 **PB**

Trans Asian Insurance Services, Inc., 2400 E. Katella Ave., 92806, pg. 366 **PB**

UNOCO, 1441 S. West St., 92803, pg. 514 **PB**

Volt Alphanumeric Publication Systems, 3430 E. Miraloma, 92806, pg. 1724 **PB**

Watlow Aov, Inc., 4545 E. La Palma Ave., 92807, pg. 1153 **PV**

Anderson

Anderson Solid Waste, Inc., 18703 Cambridge Rd., 96007, pg. 1379 **PB**

SIERRA PACIFIC INDUSTRIES, 19794 Riverside Ave., 96007, pg. 998 **PV**

Angels Camp

Stockton Savings Bank-Angels Camp, 479 S. Main St., 95222, pg. 1575 **PB**

Antioch

Ledger Dispatch, 1650 Cavallo Rd., 94509, pg. 964 **PB**

Aptos

Newmans Own Organics, 7010 Soquel Dr., Ste. 200, 95003, pg. 797 **PV**

Arcadia

Autronics Corporation, 312-314 E. Live Oak Ave., 91006, pg. 208 **IT**

California State Bank-Arcadia, 444 E. Huntington Dr., pg. 294 **PB**

Commercial Metals Company, 1929 S. Sixth Ave., 91006, pg. 412 **PB**

Downey Savings & Loan Association, F.A., 101 E. Foothill Blvd., 91006, pg. 526 **PB**

Los Angeles Turf Club, Inc., 285 W. Huntington Dr., 91007, pg. 1081 **PB**

Pavilions, 618 Michillinda Ave., 91007, pg. 1426 **PB**

Penny & Giles Drives Technology Inc., 314 E. Live Oak Ave., 91006, pg. 208 **IT**

The Santa Anita Companies, 285 W. Huntington Dr., 91007, pg. 1081 **PB**

Santa Anita Enterprises, Inc., 301 W. Huntington Dr., Ste. 405, 91066-6025, pg. 1081 **PB**

The Vons Companies, Inc., 618 Michillinda Ave., 91007, pg. 1426 **PB**

Arcata

Sierra Pacific Industries-Arcata Division, Samoa Road, 95521, pg. 998 **PV**

Arleta

Vintage Blue, 12822 Rangoon St., 91331, pg. 948 **PB**

Arlington

Alta Vista Healthcare, 9020 Garfield, 92503, pg. 1711 **PB**

Arroyo Grande

Corbett Canyon Vineyards, 1295 Corbett Canyon, 93420, pg. 1183 **PV**

Maison Deutz Winery, 453 Deutz Dr., 93420, pg. 917 **IT**

Artesia

CALIFORNIA MILK PRODUCERS, 11709 E. Artesia Blvd., 90701, pg. 201 **PV**

Twin Palms Care Center, 11900 E. Artesia Blvd., 90701, pg. 733 **PV**

Arvin

Tejon Farming Company, 500 Laval Rd., 93203, pg. 1566 **PB**

Atascadero

WEATHERBY, INC., 3100 El Camino Real, 93422, pg. 1155 **PV**

Atwater

Stockton Savings Bank-Atwater, 1329 Broadway Ave., 95301, pg. 1575 **PB**

J.R. WOOD INC., P.O. Box 545, 95301, pg. 1186 **PV**

Auburn

Coherent, Inc.-Auburn Group, 2303 Lindbergh St., 95602-9562, pg. 395 **PB**

FOR BETTER LIVING, INC., 13620 Lincoln Way, Ste. 380, 95603, pg. 417 **PV**

NELLA OIL COMPANY, 2349 Rickenbacker Way, 95602, pg. 790 **PV**

Sutter Auburn Faith Community Hospital, 11815 Education St., 95604, pg. 1057 **PV**

Avenal

The Avenal Progress, 524 E. Mercer St., 93204, pg. 1343 **PB**

Azusa

Aerojet Azusa Operations, 1100 W. Hollyvale St., 91702, pg. 706 **PB**

Avery International Converting Group, 777 E. Foothill Blvd., 91702, pg. 152 **PB**

MONROVIA NURSERY CO., 18331 E. Foothill Blvd., 91702, pg. 757 **PV**

Optical Radiation Corporation, 1300 Optical Dr., 91702, pg. 160 **PB**

Pierre Fabre, 1055 W. 8th St., 91702, pg. 1056 **IT**

Wynn Oil Company, 1050 W. Fifth St., 91702, pg. 1782 **PB**

Bakersfield

All American Pipeline Company, P.O. Box 40160, 10000 Ming Ave., 93384-0160, pg. 753 **PB**

THE BAKERSFIELD CALIFORNIAN, 1707 Eye St., 93302-0440, pg. 112 **PB**

Blackwell Land Co., P.O. Box 2393, 93303, pg. 1027 **IT**

WM. BOLTHOUSE FARMS, INC., 7200 E. Brundage Ln., 93307, pg. 155 **PV**

Bowman Distribution, 4401 Stine Rd., 93301, pg. 190 **PB**

CALCOT, LTD., 1601 E. Brundage, 93307, pg. 200 **PB**

Casey Co., 7845 E. Panama Ln., 93307, pg. 218 **PV**

Celeron Corporation, P.O. Box 41060, 10000 Ming Ave., 93309, pg. 753 **PB**

Cox Communications-Bakersfield, 820 22nd St., 93301, pg. 454 **PB**

Dole Citrus & Dole Deciduous, 10000 Ming Ave., 93311, pg. 515 **PB**

Downey Savings & Loan Association, F.A., 1530 Truxton Ave., 93301, pg. 527 **PB**

Granite Construction Inc.-Bakersfield Div., 3000 James Rd., 93308, pg. 759 **PB**

Holiday RV Superstores West, Inc., 5810 S. Union Ave., 93307, pg. 830 **PB**

Hood Industries, 2459 Fruitdale Ave., Unit 3, 93313, pg. 215 **PV**

KBAK-TV, 1901 Westwind Dr., 93301, pg. 1170 **PV**

KERO-TV, Television Ctr., 321 21st St., 93301, pg. 1070 **PV**

KGET-TV, 2831 Eye St., 93301, pg. 16 **PB**

Kern County Land Co., P.O. Box 9380, 201 New Stine Rd., 93389, pg. 1578 **PB**

Kern Livestock Supplement Co., Inc., P.O. Box 70056, 93387-0056, pg. 46 **PV**

M&N Valve, 1834 Norris Road, 93308, pg. 1449 **IT**

Mercury Air Center, 1550 Skyway Dr., 93308, pg. 1093 **PB**

MILLS & CLEMENT INC., 208 Kentucky St., 93305-4228, pg. 749 **PV**

Mojave Pipeline Company, P.O. Box 10269, 93389-0269, pg. 567 **PB**

Occidental Oil & Gas Corporation, 1200 Discovery Dr., 93389-2021, pg. 1210 **PB**

Paramount Farming Company, P.O. Box 1107, 93308, pg. 941 **PV**

Pool California Energy Services, Inc., 1001 Tower Way, # 110, 93309, pg. 1316 **PB**

Square D Co., 7600 District Blvd., 93313, pg. 1208 **IT**

Texaco USA, P.O. Box 5197X, 93388-5197, pg. 1583 **PB**

VIDEO CITY INC., 6840 District Blvd., 93313, pg. 1719 **PB**

Welenco, Inc., 4817 District Blvd., 93313, pg. 1019 **IT**

WESTWIND COMMUNICATIONS, 1901 Westwind Dr., 93301, pg. 1170 **PV**

Zellerbach Division, 110 S. Montclair St., Ste. 202, 93309, pg. 1076 **PB**

Baldwin Park

RELIEF PRINTING, 5160 Rivergrade Rd., 91706, pg. 921 **PV**

STEINY & COMPANY, INC., P.O. Box 8100, 12907 E. Garvey, 91706, pg. 1039 **PV**

SUES, YOUNG & BROWN INC., 5151 Commerce Dr., 91706, pg. 1049 **PV**

Beaumont

California State Bank-Beaumont, 385 E. Sixth St., pg. 294 **PB**

Bell Gardens

BICYCLE CLUB CASINO, 7301 Eastern Ave., 90201, pg. 142 **PV**

Chrome Crankshaft Company, P.O. Box 2126, 6845 E. Florence Pl., 90201, pg. 1710 **PB**

Wei-Chuan Foods U.S.A., 6655 S. Garfield Ave., 90201, pg. 1488 **IT**

Bellflower

Fabric King, 17434 Bellflower Blvd., 90706, pg. 842 **PB**

Belmont

Belmedco Pharmacy, 1301 Ralston Ave., 94032, pg. 1712 **PB**

KG Land California Corporation, 301 Island Parkway, Ste. 100, 94002, pg. 764 **IT**

Nikon Precision Inc., 1399 Shoreway Rd., 94002-4107, pg. 931 **IT**

Oral-B Laboratories, 600 Clipper Dr., 94002, pg. 743 **PB**

Oral-B Laboratories, Inc., 600 Clipper Dr., 94002, pg. 743 **PB**

Wadsworth International, 10 Davis Dr., 94002, pg. 1600 **PB**

Wadsworth Publishing co., 10 Davis Dr., 94002, pg. 1600 **PB**

Wadsworth Publishing Co., 10 Davis Dr., 94002, pg. 1600 **PB**

Wesgo, 477 Harbor Blvd., 94002, pg. 893 **IT**

Benicia

COPART, INC., 5500 E. Second St., 94510, pg. 446 **PB**

Institutional Financing Services, 5100 Park Rd., 94510, pg. 1652 **PV**

Keystone Northern California Warehouse-Benicia, 3919 Oregon St., 94510, pg. 955 **PB**

M&N Valve, 524 Stone Road, Unit E, 94510, pg. 1449 **IT**

NHT, 535 Getty Ct., Bldg. B, 94510, pg. 1369 **PB**

Now Hear This (NHT), 537 Stone Rd., Ste. E, 94510, pg. 1369 **PB**

Pro Shop (Northern California), 94510, pg. 861 **PB**

UNDERGROUND CONSTRUCTION CO., INC., 5145 Industrial Way, 94510, pg. 1116 **PV**

YLA, Inc., 2970 C Bay Vista Ct., 94510, pg. 1037 **IT**

Berkeley

ANDROS INCORPORATED, 2332 Fourth St., 94710-2402, pg. 74 **PV**

Andros Incorporated International, 2332 Fourth St., 94710, pg. 74 **PV**

BARRA, INC., 2100 Milvia St., 94704-1113, pg. 191 **PB**

Bayer Corp. Pharmaceuticals, Fourth & Parker, 94710, pg. 173 **IT**

Bendix Environmental Research, 1950 Addison St., 94704-1182, pg. 51 **PV**

Berkeley Marina Restaurant Corp., 199 Seawall Dr., 94710, pg. 1022 **PV**

ELECTRO-COATINGS, INC., 893 Carleton St., 94710, pg. 368 **PV**

EXPERIENCE IN SOFTWARE, INC., 2000 Hearst Ave. Ste 202, 94709, pg. 388 **PV**

HAWS DRINKING FAUCET CO., 1435 Fourth St., 94710-1499, pg. 512 **PV**

Kodak Berkeley Research, 2120 Haste St., 94704, pg. 555 **PB**

The Nature Company, 750 Hearst Ave., 94710, pg. 334 **PV**

Osborne/McGraw-Hill, 2600 Tenth St., 94710, pg. 1071 **PB**

Outdoor Systems, Inc. of Northern California, 1695 Eastshore Hwy., 94710, pg. 1235 **PB**

Geographic Index-U.S.

PACIFIC STEEL CASTING CO., 1333 Second St., 94710, pg. 832 — PV
PEERLESS LIGHTING CORP., 2246 Fifth St., 94710, pg. 847 — PV
Risk Management Technologies, 2150 Shattuck Ave., 94704, pg. 610 — PB
Tailored Solutions, 2001 Center St., 94704, pg. 1602 — PB
XOMA CORPORATION, 2910 Seventh St., 94710, pg. 1786 — PB
Zeneca Specialty Inks, 635 Cedar St., 94710, pg. 1525 — IT

Beverly Hills

Advanced Electronic Systems, 360 N. Crescent Dr., 90210-4867, pg. 1002 — PB
After Dark Video, Inc., 9242 Beverly Blvd., 90210, pg. 1310 — PB
Alta Loma Productions, Inc., 9242 Beverly Blvd., 90210, pg. 1310 — PB
Bank Leumi le-Israel B.M., 8383 Wilshire Blvd., Ste. 400, 90211, pg. 150 — IT
THE BEVERLY HILLS HOTEL, 9641 Sunset Blvd., 90210, pg. 164 — PV
CAPUCCI CREATIONS INTERNATIONAL, INC., 9565 Santa Monica Blvd., 90210, pg. 207 — PV
City National Bank, 400 N. Roxbury Dr., 90210, pg. 381 — PB
CITY NATIONAL CORPORATION, 400 N. Roxbury Dr., 90210, pg. 380 — PB
Components and Industrial Products, 360 N. Crescent Dr., 90210-4867, pg. 1002 — PB
Entertainment Industries Group, 9777 Wilshire Blvd., Ste. 610, 90212, pg. 871 — PV
FIRST GRAY LINE CORPORATION, 335 N. Maple, Ste. 273, 90210, pg. 407 — PV
Fox Broadcasting Company (FBC), P.O. Box 900, 90213, pg. 926 — IT
GRAMERCY PICTURES, 9333 Wilshire Blvd., 90210, pg. 468 — PV
Merv Griffin Enterprises, 9860 Wilshire Blvd., 90210, pg. 1282 — IT
Hilton Equipment Corp., 9336 Civic Center Dr., 90210, pg. 829 — PB
HILTON HOTELS CORPORATION, 9336 Civic Center Dr., 90210, pg. 828 — PB
Hilton Inns, Inc., 9336 Civic Center Dr., 90210, pg. 829 — PB
Impulse Productions, Inc., 9242 Beverly Blvd., 90210, pg. 1310 — PB
Interlease Management Corporation, 8484 Wilshire Blvd., 90211, pg. 85 — PB
Interlease Trading Corp., 8484 Wilshire Blvd., 90211, pg. 85 — PB
JB OXFORD HOLDINGS INC., 9665 Wilshire Blvd., 3rd Fl., 90212, pg. 916 — PB
Lambert Smith Hampton, 2nd Fl., American Savings Bank, 9090 Wilshire Blvd., Ste. 200, 90211, pg. 797 — IT
Pacific Crest Investment & Loan (Beverly Hills Branch), 9320 Wilshire Blvd., Ste. 105, 90212, pg. 1249 — PB
Playboy Entertainment Group, Inc., 9242 Beverly Blvd., 90210, pg. 1310 — PB
Playboy Models, Inc., 9242 Beverly Blvd., 90210, pg. 1310 — PB
Playboy Shows, Inc., 9242 Beverly Blvd., 90210, pg. 1310 — PB
Playboy Video Enterprises, Inc., 9242 Beverly Blvd., 90210, pg. 1310 — PB
RNF MEDIA CORPORATION INC., 9440 Santa Monica Blvd., 90210, pg. 905 — PV
RETROSPETTIVA, INC., 8825 W. Olympic Blvd., 90211, pg. 1383 — PB
EARL SCHEIB, INC., 8737 Wilshire Blvd., 90211-2795, pg. 1437 — PB
Earl Scheib Realty Corp., 8737 Wilshire Blvd., 90211, pg. 1437 — PB
SHAPELL INDUSTRIES, INC., 8383 Wilshire Blvd., Ste. 700, 90211, pg. 990 — PV
Singapore Tourist Promotion Board - Los Angeles, 8484 Wilshire Blvd., Ste. 510, 90211, pg. 1254 — IT
M.L. STERN & COMPANY, INC., 8350 Wilshire Blvd., 90211, pg. 1041 — PV
UNOVA, INC., 360 N. Crescent Dr., 90210-4867, pg. 1698 — PB
Virgin Records America Inc., Foothill Boulevard, 90210, pg. 427 — IT
WESTMINSTER CAPITAL INC., 9665 Wilshire Blvd. Ste. M 10, 90212, pg. 1761 — PB

Brea

Advance Engineering, 895 Beacon St., 92621, pg. 553 — PV
American Suzuki Motor Corporation, 3251 E. Imperial Hwy., 92621, pg. 1323 — PV
Ameron Protective Coatings Div., 201 N. Berry St., 92622, pg. 99 — PB
Ameron Protective Linings Division, 201 N. Berry St., 92622, pg. 99 — PB
Asset Based Financing, 2650 E. Imperial Hwy., 92621, pg. 287 — PV
Binks Manufacturing Company, 1405 Pioneer St., 92621-3721, pg. 229 — PB
BRISTOL INDUSTRIES, 630 E. Lambert Rd., 92621, pg. 168 — PV
CB Partners, 265 S. Randolph, 92621, pg. 357 — PV
California State Bank-Brea, 390 N. Brea Blvd., 92718, pg. 294 — PB
Central Sprink Inc., 3170 Nasa St., 92621, pg. 327 — PB
Central Sprinkler Company, 3170 Nasa St., 92621, pg. 327 — PB
Computer Furniture & Accessories, 895 Beacon St., 92621, pg. 553 — PV

Danaher Controls, 3350 E. Birch St. Ste. 243, 92621-6264, pg. 480 — PB
Equifax Check Service, 2601 Saturn St., Ste. 301, 92821, pg. 588 — PB
HiChem Diagnostics, Inc., 231 N. Puente St., 92621, pg. 436 — IT
IAC INDUSTRIES, 895 Beacon St., 92621, pg. 553 — PV
EARLE M. JORGENSEN COMPANY, 3050 E. Birch, 92821, pg. 600 — PB
KRAUSE'S FURNITURE INC., 200 N. Berry St., 92821, pg. 967 — PB
Krause's Sofa Factory, 200 N. Berry St., 92621, pg. 967 — PB
Lucas Aircraft Cargo Systems, 610 Neptune Ave., 92622-2207, pg. 820 — IT
Molycorp, Inc., 376 S. Valencia, 92823, pg. 1698 — PB
Multiplex Technology, Inc., 3200 E. Birch St., 92621-6258, pg. 1705 — PB
North Specialty Products, 2664-B Saturn St., 92621, pg. 1243 — PV
PEC Los Angeles, 1125 Beacon St., 92821, pg. 871 — PV
PennySaver, P.O. Box 8900, 92622, pg. 794 — PB
Racet Computes Limited, 3150 E. Birch St., 92621, pg. 740 — IT
Shea Homes Southern California, 603 S. Valencia, Ste. 200, 92823, pg. 991 — PV
Thetford Corp., Warehouse Div., 2700-B Saturn, 92621, pg. 352 — PV
Unocal Carbon & Minerals, 376 S. Valencia, 92823, pg. 1698 — PB

Brisbane

Circle International, 240 Valley Dr., 94005, pg. 372 — PB
GEORGE LITHOGRAPH, 460 Valley Dr., 94005, pg. 448 — PB
THE GOOD GUYS, INC., 7000 Marina Blvd., 94005-1840, pg. 750 — PB
International Paint Western Div., 3785 Bayshore Blvd., 94005, pg. 339 — IT
Western Fire Equip., 440 Valley Dr., Crocker Indus. Park, 94005, pg. 1068 — IT
Y.K.K. (U.S.A.) Inc., 150 North Hill Dr., 94005, pg. 1515 — IT

Buena Park

Anchor Wire Rope Div., 6900 8th St., 90620, pg. 1001 — IT
Con-Way Western Express, Inc., 6301 Beach Blvd., Ste. 300, 90621, pg. 281 — PB
Esselte Pendaflex, Artegio Blvd., 90620, pg. 460 — IT
Global Van & Storage Co., 6800 Orangethorp, Suite C, 90620, pg. 458 — PV
KNOTT'S BERRY FARM, 8039 Beach Blvd., 90620, pg. 627 — PV
Knottsberry Fair, 8039 Beach Blvd., 90620, pg. 319 — PV
LEACH INTERNATIONAL, 6900 Orangethorpe Ave., 90622-5032, pg. 655 — PV
Lucky Stores Southern California Division, 6565 Knott Ave., 90620, pg. 93 — PB
MEDIEVAL TIMES DINNER & TOURNAMENT, INC., 7662 Beach Blvd., 90622, pg. 728 — PV
NutriLite Products, Inc., P.O. Box 5940, 90622-5940, pg. 69 — PV
PCI Tandem Div., 6905 Aragon Cl., 90620, pg. 1504 — PB
Stanfast, Inc., 5743 Rostrata Ave. Ste. 101, 90621, pg. 1505 — PV
Sunclipse, Inc., 6600 Valley View St., 90260, pg. 72 — IT
Tera Pharmaceuticals, 6920 Stanton Ave., 90621, pg. 196 — PB
U.N. Alloy Steel Div., 6900 8th St., 90620, pg. 1001 — IT
U.S. Amada, 7025 Firestone Blvd., 90621, pg. 70 — IT
Yamaha Corporation of America, 6600 Orangethorpe, 90620, pg. 1516 — IT

Burbank

ASCO Music, 3400 Riverside Dr., 91505, pg. 282 — PV
Allianz Underwriters Insurance Co., 3400 Riverside Dr., Ste. 300, 91505-4669, pg. 58 — IT
Aramark Uniform Services, 115 N. First St., 91502, pg. 79 — PV
AVIBANK MFG., INC., 210 S. Victory Blvd., 91502, pg. 101 — PV
BET West Coast Operations, 2801 W. Olive Ave., 91505, pg. 235 — PB
Barry Controls Aerospace, 2323 Valley St., 91505, pg. 124 — PV
BeePee Music, 3400 Riverside Dr., 91505, pg. 282 — PV
Buena Vista Home Video, 350 S. Buena Vista St., 91521, pg. 513 — PB
Buena Vista International, Inc., 350 S. Buena Vista St., 91521, pg. 513 — PB
Buena Vista Pictures Distribution Inc., 3900 W. Alameda Ave., Ste. 2400, 91505, pg. 513 — PB
CADAM Inc., 1935 N. Buena Vista, 91504, pg. 896 — PB
Dick Clark Corporate Productions, Inc., 3003 W. Olive Ave., 91510-7811, pg. 382 — PB
Dick Clark Media Archives, 3003 W. Olive Ave., 91510-7811, pg. 382 — PB
DICK CLARK PRODUCTIONS, INC., 3003 W. Olive Ave., 91510-7811, pg. 382 — PB
Dick Clark Restaurants, Inc., 3003 W. Olive Ave., 91510-7811, pg. 382 — PB
Columbia Tri-Star Home Video, 3400 Riverside Dr., 91505, pg. 1282 — IT
Columbia Tri-Star Television Distribution, 3400 Riverside Dr., 91505, pg. 1282 — IT
Bing Crosby Productions, Inc., 3400 Riverside Dr., 91505, pg. 282 — PV

DIC Entertainment, 303 N. Glenoaks Blvd., 91502, pg. 513 — PB
The Disney Channel, 3800 W. Alameda Ave., 91505, pg. 513 — PB
Disney Educational Productions, 500 S. Buena Vista St., 91521, pg. 513 — PB
Disney Publishing Group, 3900 W. Alameda, 29th Fl., 91201, pg. 511 — PB
THE WALT DISNEY COMPANY, 500 S. Buena Vista St., 91521, pg. 511 — PB
Walt Disney Consumer Products, 3900 W. Alameda Blvd., 91521, pg. 511 — PB
Walt Disney Music Co., 500 S. Buena Vista St., 91521, pg. 511 — PB
Walt Disney Network Television, 500 S. Buena Vista St., 91521, pg. 511 — PB
Walt Disney Pictures and Television, 500 S. Buena Vista St., 91521, pg. 513 — PB
Downey Savings & Loan Association, F.A., 1750 W. Olive Ave., 91506, pg. 527 — PB
Elmo Semiconductor Corp., 7590 N. Glen Oaks Blvd., 91504-1052, pg. 957 — PB
EMCON Southwest, Inc., 3300 N. San Fernando Blvd., 91504, pg. 571 — PB
Entertainment Partners, 3601 W. Olive St., 91505, pg. 554 — PV
Financial Indemnity, Burbank Airport Center, 2550 Hollywood Way, 91505, pg. 1694 — PV
FLO CONTROL, INC., 3210 Winona Ave., 91504, pg. 414 — PV
FOUR MEDIA COMPANIES, 2813 W. Alameda Ave., 91505, pg. 422 — PV
FRIEDLAND JACOBS COMMUNICATIONS, 3601 W. Olive Ave., 1st Fl., 91505, pg. 428 — PV
GC & Co.-Mobile Field Shop & Garage, pg. 1692 — IT
The Guber Peters Entertainment Company (Burbank), Studio Plaza, 3400 Riverside Dr., 7th Fl., 91505, pg. 1283 — IT
Haskel Control, 100 E. Graham Pl., 91502, pg. 798 — PB
HASKEL INTERNATIONAL, INC., 100 E. Graham Pl., 91502, pg. 798 — PB
Hydro-Aire, 3000 Winona Ave., 91510, pg. 457 — PB
International Electronic Research Corp., 135 W. Magnolia Blvd., 91502-7704, pg. 286 — PB
IWERKS ENTERTAINMENT, 4540 W. Valerio St., 91505, pg. 915 — PB
Kodak Cineßite, 303 N. Glenoaks Blvd., Ste. 200, 91502-1143, pg. 555 — PV
Lockheed Finance Corporation, 303 N. Glenoaks Blvd., Ste. 800, 91502, pg. 1008 — PB
Lorimar Television, 4000 Warner Blvd., 91522, pg. 1611 — IT
MARTINO'S BAKERY, INC., 901 W. Alameda Ave., 91506, pg. 710 — PV
MATTHEWS STUDIO EQUIPMENT, 2405 Empire Ave., 91504, pg. 1060 — PV
J.H. McCORMICK, INC., 2507 Empire Ave., 91504, pg. 720 — PV
Menasco California Operation, 100 Cedar St., 91502, pg. 402 — PB
Mercury Air Center, 4301 Empire Ave., 91505, pg. 1093 — PV
Norman Enterprises, Inc., 2601 Empire Ave., 91504, pg. 1292 — PB
OROAMERICA, INC., 443 N. Varney St., 91502, pg. 1232 — PB
PacAero, 2810-20 N. Lima St., 91504, pg. 187 — PB
PolyGram Records, Inc., 3800 Alameda Ave., Ste. 1500, 91505, pg. 1052 — IT
Products Research & Chemical Corp. Research Laboratories, 2820 Empire Avenue, 91504, pg. 339 — IT
RYAN HERCO PRODUCTS CORP., 3010 North San Fernando Blvd., 91504, pg. 953 — PV
SHAMROCK HOLDINGS, INC., Shamrock Center, 4444 Lakeside Dr., 91505, pg. 989 — PV
Shamrock Holdings Of California, Inc., 4444 Lakeside Dr., 91505, pg. 989 — PV
SWANER HARDWOOD COMPANY, INC., Five W. Magnolia Blvd., 91502, pg. 1057 — PV
TriStar Pictures Western Division, 3400 Riverside Dr., 91505, pg. 1283 — IT
UNIHEALTH, 3400 Riverside Dr., 91505, pg. 1117 — PV
Unimed Management Services, 3400 Riverside Dr., 91505, pg. 1118 — PV
Verdugo Restaurant Corp., 1250 Harvard Rd., 91503, pg. 1022 — PV
WEA Corp., 111 N. Hollywood Way, 91505, pg. 1612 — IT
Warner Bros. Consumer Products, 4000 Warner Blvd., 91522, pg. 1610 — PB
Warner Bros. Records, Inc., 3300 Warner Blvd., 91505, pg. 1611 — PB
Warner Bros. Studios, Inc., 4000 Warner Blvd., 91522, pg. 1611 — PB
Warner Bros. Television, Inc., 4000 Warner Blvd., 91505, pg. 1611 — PB
Warner Home Video, 400 Warner Blvd., 91505, pg. 1611 — PB
Warner Special Products, 4000 Warner Blvd., 91505, pg. 1612 — PB
Western International Media Corporation, 500 S. Buena Vista St., 91521, pg. 1166 — PV
Winston Tire Company, 900 W. Alameda, 91506, pg. 514 — PV
Wonderland Music Co., Inc., 500 S. Buena Vista St., 91521, pg. 514 — PB

Burlingame

ACSIA, 1840 Ogden Dr., 94010, pg. 499 — IT
Binks Manufacturing Company, One Edwards Ct., Ste 202, 94010, pg. 229 — PB

PB - U.S. Public Companies Volume
PV - U.S. Private Companies Volume
IT - International Public & Private Companies Volume

1122

Geographic Index-U.S.

Cott Corporation International Operations, 1350 Old Bayshore Highway, Suite 210, 94010, pg. 338 **IT**
Cott Corporation - Pacific Central Region, 1350 Old Bayshore Highway, Ste. 210, 94010, pg. 338 **IT**
GYMBOREE CORPORATION, 700 Airport Blvd., Ste. 200, 94010, pg. 770 **PB**
Hillhaven Convalescent Hospital Burlingame, 1609 Trousdale Dr., 94010, pg. 1713 **PB**
The Imagination Network, 577 Airport Blvd., Ste. 300, 94010, pg. 66 **PB**
Kintetsu World Express Inc., 1811 Adrian Rd., 94010, pg. 735 **IT**
Kirin U.S.A. c/o Nomusa & Co., 1350 Old Bayshore Hwy., Ste. 650, 94010, pg. 736 **IT**
Metropolitan Furniture Corporation, 1635 Rollins Rd., 94010, pg. 1038 **PV**
Mitsui Foods Export, 1350 Bayshore Hwy., 94010, pg. 879 **IT**
Mitsui Foods, Inc., Western Div., 1350 Bayshore Hwy., 94010, pg. 879 **IT**
Nakano Foods, 851 Bull Way, Ste. 515, 94010, pg. 883 **IT**
NIECO CORPORATION, 15 Guittard Rd., 94010, pg. 799 **PV**
PMT of the Southwest, Inc., 1766 El Camino Real, 94010, pg. 1668 **PB**
Pacific Motor Transport Co., 1766 El Camino Real, 94010, pg. 1668 **PB**
Pacific Motor Trucking Co., 1766 El Camino Real, 94010, pg. 1668 **PB**
Pay-Fone Systems, Inc., 1601 Old Bayshore Hwy. 101, 94010, pg. 1267 **PB**
Union-Transport Corporation-San Francisco Office, 1535 Rollins Rd., 94010, pg. 1120 **PV**
THE WORNICK COMPANY, 345 Lorton Ave., 94010, pg. 1191 **PV**
YAR West, 1799 Bayshore Hwy., Ste. 210, 94010, pg. 1195 **PV**

Burney

Dicalite Corporation, 36994 Summit Lake Rd., 96013, pg. 903 **PV**

Byron

Underground Technologies, P.O. Box 160, 3800 Byron Hwy., Bldg. B, 94514, pg. 1598 **PB**

Calabasas

AMWEST INSURANCE GROUP, INC., 5320 Las Virgenes Rd., 91302, pg. 106 **PB**
Amwest Surety Insurance Company, 5320 Las Virgenes Rd., 91302, pg. 106 **PB**
DATAMETRICS CORPORATION, 26604 Agoura Rd., 91302, pg. 487 **PB**
ENVIRONMENTAL INDUSTRIES, INC., 24121 Ventura Blvd., 91302, pg. 378 **PV**
Far West Insurance Company, 5230 Las Virgenes Rd., 91302, pg. 106 **PB**
Hewlett-Packard Company, 26701 W. Argoura Rd., 91302, pg. 813 **PB**
International Flavors & Fragrances, Inc., 23621 Park Sorrento, Ste. 202, 91302, pg. 899 **PB**
NATIONAL TECHNICAL SYSTEMS, INC., 24007 Ventura Blvd., 91302, pg. 1161 **PB**
PRIME MATRIX WIRELESS COMMUNICATIONS, 26635 W. Agoura Rd., 91302, pg. 884 **PV**
Rantec Microwave and Electronics, Inc., 24003 Ventura Blvd., 91302, pg. 546 **PB**
TEKELEC, 26580 W. Agoura Rd., 91302, pg. 1566 **PB**
WESTERN DATA SYSTEMS, 26707 W. Agoura Rd., 91302, pg. 1165 **PV**
Wyle Electronics-Los Angeles, 26010 Mureau Rd., Ste. 150, 91302, pg. 1457 **IT**

Calabasas Hills

CHEESECAKE FACTORY INCORPORATED, 26950 Agoura Rd., 91301, pg. 343 **PB**

Calexico

Goldstar Mexico S.A. de C.V., 355 W. 2nd St., #265, 92231, pg. 779 **IT**

Calistoga

Calistoga Water Co., 865 Silverado Trail, 94515, pg. 919 **IT**
CRYSTAL GEYSER, 501 Washington, 94515, pg. 294 **PV**
Crystal Geyser Water Company, 501 Washington St., 94515, pg. 1013 **IT**

Camarillo

ACT NETWORKS, INC., 188 Camino Ruiz, 93012, pg. 3 **PB**
Harris Network Support Systems, 809 Calle Plano, 93010, pg. 792 **PB**
Lumonics Corp., 3629 Vista Mercado, 93010, pg. 1315 **IT**
MEDICAL ANALYSIS SYSTEMS INC., 542 Flynn Rd., 93012, pg. 727 **PV**
POWER-ONE, INC., 740 Calle Plano, 93012, pg. 878 **PV**
3 dbm, Inc., 975 Flynn Rd., 93012, pg. 534 **PB**
VITESSE SEMICONDUCTOR CORPORATION, 741 Calle Plano, 93012, pg. 1723 **PB**

Campbell

Day-Lee Foods (San Francisco), Inc., 496 Salmar Ave., 95008, pg. 936 **IT**
Downey Savings & Loan Association, F.A., 1480 W. Campbell Ave., 95008, pg. 527 **PB**
HaL Computer Systems, Inc., 1315 Dell Ave., 95008, pg. 526 **PB**
Ionics Ultrapure Water Corporation, 1160 Dell Ave., 95008, pg. 912 **PB**
Mountaingate Engineering, Inc., 540 Division St., 95008, pg. 1188 **PB**
OddzOn Products, Inc., 1696 Dell Ave., 95008-6901, pg. 797 **PB**
Recognition Systems Inc., 1520 Dell Ave, 95008, pg. 507 **PV**
South Bay Tech Center Associates, 511 Division St., 95008, pg. 365 **PB**
WESTERN MICRO TECHNOLOGY, INC., 254 E. Hacienda Ave., 95008-6617, pg. 1759 **PB**

Canoga Park

ANGELES HOUSING CONCEPTS, 6700 Fallbrook Ave., Ste. 191, 91307-3569, pg. 74 **PV**
Boeing North America, Rocketdyne Division, 6633 Canoga Ave., 91303, pg. 241 **PB**
Encore Computer Corp., 21515 Vanowen St., Ste. 100, 91303, pg. 580 **PB**
FABER ENTERPRISES, INC., 6606 Variel Ave., 91303, pg. 390 **PV**
Golden State/CAS, Inc., 6925 Canoga Ave., 91303, pg. 571 **PB**
Leadtec Systems, Inc., 6800 Owensmouth Ave., Ste. 320, 91303-2091, pg. 1177 **PV**
SunGard Financial Systems, Inc., 22134 Sherman Way, 91303, pg. 1534 **PB**
Tedea Inc., 7800 Deering Avenue, 91304, pg. 644 **IT**

Canyon Country

Ampex Corporation, 27342 Dewdrop Ave., 91351, pg. 104 **PB**

Capitola

NETWORK REAL ESTATE INC., 2121 41 Ave., Ste. 102, 95010, pg. 791 **PV**

Carlsbad

Artecon, Inc., 6305 El Camino Real, 92018, pg. 409 **PV**
Astec America Inc., 6339 Paseo del Lago, 92009, pg. 93 **IT**
Asymtek, 2762 Loker Ave., W., 92008, pg. 1188 **PB**
Barratt American Inc., 2035 Corte Del Nogal, Ste. 160, 92009, pg. 168 **IT**
Calcitek, Inc., 2320 Faraday Ave., 92008, pg. 1307 **IT**
CALLAWAY GOLF COMPANY, 2285 Rutherford Rd., 92008, pg. 294 **PB**
Cobra Golf Incorporated, 1818 Aston Ave., 92008, pg. 675 **PB**
Dentsply New Image, 2283 Cosmos Ct., 92009, pg. 499 **PB**
GEC Plessey Naval Systems Inc., 5927 Landau Ct., 92008-3854, pg. 545 **IT**
GW Services, Inc., 2261 Cosmos Ct., 92009, pg. 745 **PB**
GLACIER WATER SERVICES INC., 2261 Cosmos Ct., 92009, pg. 745 **PB**
Glacier Water Services, Inc., 2261 Cosmos Ct., 92009, pg. 745 **PB**
Hughes-JVC Technology Corp., 2310 Camino Vida Roble, 92009, pg. 846 **IT**
INTERNATIONAL LOTTERY & TOTALIZATOR SYSTEMS, INC., 2131 Faraday Ave., 92008, pg. 900 **PB**
JM Television Productions, 2808 Roosevelt St., 92008, pg. 584 **PV**
JAZZERCISE, INC., 2808 Roosevelt St., 92008, pg. 584 **PV**
Kaiser Electro Optics, 2752 Loker Ave. W., 92008-6603, pg. 605 **PV**
Linear Corporation, 2055 Corte del Nogal, 92009, pg. 1193 **PB**
Planet Earth Products, 2221 Las Palmas Dr., Ste. B, 92009, pg. 940 **PV**
Rohm Electronics South-West Sales Division, 701 Palomar Airport Rd., 92009, pg. 1125 **IT**
Smith & Nephew DonJoy Inc., 2777 Loker Ave. W., Ste. 100, 92008, pg. 1263 **PB**
Stillman Seal, 6020 Avenida Encinas, 92009, pg. 550 **PV**
SUNRISE MEDICAL, INC., 2382 Faraday Ave. Ste. 200, 92008, pg. 1535 **PB**
Taylor Made Golf Co. Inc., 2271 Cosmos Court, 92009, pg. 1181 **IT**
THE UPPER DECK COMPANY, LLC, 5909 Sea Otter Pl., 92008, pg. 1129 **PV**
VOIT SPORTS, INC., 5927 Priestly Dr., Ste. 200, 92008, pg. 1143 **PV**

Carmel

First National Bank of Central California, 26380 Carmel Rancho Ln., 93922-2017, pg. 1248 **PB**
Templeton Investment Services, Inc., 26335 Carmel Rancho Blvd., 93923, pg. 680 **PB**

Carpinteria

Astro Aerospace Corp., 6384 Via Real, 93013-2993, pg. 1288 **IT**
BENTON OIL & GAS COMPANY, 1145 Eugenia Pl., Ste. 200, 93013, pg. 212 **PB**
Bio Enterics Corporation, 1035 Cindy Ln., 93013, pg. 873 **PB**
DIGITAL SOUND CORPORATION, 6307 Carpinteria Ave., 93013, pg. 508 **PB**
Hall Surgical Division, 1170 Mark Ave., 93013, pg. 254 **PB**
Kilovac Corporation, 550 Linden Ave., 93013, pg. 259 **PV**
QAD INC, 6450 Via Real, 93013, pg. 1345 **PB**

Carson

Anemostat-West, 1220 Watson Center Rd., 90745, pg. 286 **PB**
Barton Brands of California, Inc., P.O. Box 6267, 90769, pg. 300 **PB**
BEACH PATROL INC., 1165 E. 230th St., 90745, pg. 125 **PV**
Carson Terminal, 2000 E. Sepulveda Blvd., 90810, pg. 692 **PB**
CORMIER CHEVROLET COMPANY, INC., 2201 E. 223 St., 90810, pg. 276 **PV**
Crest Steel Corp., 1250 E. 223rd St., Ste. 108, 90745, pg. 845 **IT**
DUCOMMUN INCORPORATED, 23301 S. Wilmington Ave., 90745, pg. 533 **PB**
EDUCATIONAL INSIGHTS, INC., 16941 Keegan Ave., 90746, pg. 565 **PV**
GOOD COMPANIES, 1118 E. 223rd St., 90745, pg. 463 **PV**
Hewlett-Packard Company, 1210 E. 223rd St., Ste. 306, 90745, pg. 813 **PB**
Huck International Aerospace Fastener Division, P.O. Box 5268, 900 Watsoncenter Rd., 90749, pg. 1597 **PB**
Jay-El Products, Inc., 23301 Wilmington Ave., 90745, pg. 534 **PB**
Kintetsu Intermodal Inc., 1231 E. 230th St., 90745, pg. 735 **IT**
Kintetsu Intermodal (U.S.A.), Inc., 1035 Watson Ctr. Rd., 90745, pg. 735 **IT**
LEINER HEALTH PRODUCTS, INC., 901 E. 233rd St., 90745-6204, pg. 659 **PV**
Little Bear Organic Foods, Inc., 1065 E. Walnut St., 90746, pg. 774 **PB**
Maxitile Inc., 17141 Kingsview Ave., 90746, pg. 1171 **IT**
MultiQuip, Inc., 18910 Wilmington Ave., 90746, pg. 695 **IT**
PENBERTHY LUMBER COMPANY, 2011 E. Carson, 90810, pg. 848 **PV**
PURITAN BAKERY, INC., 1624 E. Carson St., 90745, pg. 895 **PV**
Sanyo Logistics Corporation, 22010 S. Wilmington Ave., Ste. 401, 90745, pg. 1191 **IT**
Sharp Electronics Corporation, Sharp Plaza, 20600 S. Alameda St., 90810, pg. 1229 **IT**
Sunkyong America, Inc.-Los Angeles Branch, 17106 Avalon Blvd., 90746, pg. 1320 **IT**
Van Leeuwen Pipe & Tube Corp., 1250 E. 223rd St., Ste. 110, 90745, pg. 1450 **IT**
Westbrae Natural Foods, Inc., 1065 E. Walnut St., 90746, pg. 774 **PB**
Westbrae Natural, Inc., 1065 E. Walnut St., 90746, pg. 774 **PV**
Zynolite Products Company, 2320 E. Dominguez St., 90749, pg. 663 **IT**

Castroville

ARTICHOKE INDUSTRIES, INC., 10838 Cara Mia Pkwy., 95012, pg. 86 **PV**
OCEAN MIST FARMS CORP., 11500 Del Monte Ave., 95012, pg. 811 **PV**

Cathedral City

ADAMS BUSINESS MEDIA, 68-860 Perez Rd., 92234, pg. 16 **PV**
Charter Canyon Springs Behavioral Health Systems, Inc., 69696 Ramon Rd., 92234, pg. 1034 **PB**

Century City

ABC Productions, 2020 Ave. of the Stars, 90067, pg. 5 **PB**
HERBALIFE INTERNATIONAL OF AMERICA, INC., 1800 Century Park E., 90067-1501, pg. 809 **PB**
KABC-TV, 2040 Ave. of the Stars, 90067, pg. 512 **PB**
Rogers & Cowan, Inc., 1888 Century Park East, Ste. 500, 90067, pg. 1227 **IT**

Cerritos

BEREL INDUSTRIES INC., 13845 Artesia Blvd., 90703, pg. 135 **PV**
Calhac, Inc., 16220 Bloomfield Ave., 90701, pg. 634 **PV**
CALIFORNIA PANEL & VENEER COMPANY, 14055 Artesia Blvd., 90701, pg. 226 **PV**
CERRITOS FORD, INC., 18900 Studebaker Rd., 90703, pg. 226 **PV**
Downey Savings & Loan Association, F.A., 11350 E. South St., 90701, pg. 526 **PB**
Foam Craft, Inc., 16016 Arthur St., 90703, pg. 433 **PV**
Hyosung America, Inc., 18000 Studebaker Rd., Ste. 550, 90703, pg. 641 **IT**

Geographic Index-U.S.

IMPCO AirSensors Technologies, 16804 Gridley Pl., 90703, pg. 34 **PB**
Klockner-Moeller, 13939 Equitable Rd., 90703, pg. 736 **IT**
NPR of America Inc., 16704 Marquardt Ave., 90701, pg. 938 **IT**
Pay-Fone Systems, Inc., 17326 Edwards Rd., Ste. A-115, 90701, pg. 1267 **PB**
Prestige Stations Inc., 17215 Studebaker Rd., 90701, pg. 144 **PB**
Revere Transducers Inc., 14030 Bolsa Lane, 90701, pg. 790 **PB**
Sasco Electric, 12900 Alondra Blvd., 90701, pg. 967 **PV**
SASCO GROUP, 12900 Alondra Blvd., 90701, pg. 967 **PV**
Strategic Technology Services, 12750 Center Court Dr., Ste. 700, 90701-4566, pg. 1154 **IT**
WEBB AUTOMOTIVE GROUP, 18700 Studebaker Rd., 90703, pg. 1156 **PV**
Y.K.K. (U.S.A.) Inc., 16410 Bloomfield Ave., 90701, pg. 1515 **IT**

Chatsworth

Advanced Products Division, 9320 Mason Ave., 91311, pg. 1101 **PB**
ALATEC PRODUCTS, INC., 21123 Nordhoff St., 91311, pg. 31 **PV**
Amperif Corporation, 9232 Eton Ave., 91311, pg. 1523 **PB**
Ampersand, 9180 Kelvin Ave., 91311, pg. 1369 **PB**
Arrow/Schweber Electronics, 19748 Dearborn St., 91311, pg. 134 **PB**
Bryant Financial Corp., 9200 Oakdale, 91311, pg. 1741 **PB**
Burton Medical Products Corporation, 21100 Lassen St., 91311, pg. 821 **IT**
CCB/NILS, Inc., 21625 Prairie St., 91311, pg. 512 **PB**
California Reconveyance Co., 9200 Oakdale, 91311-6519, pg. 1741 **PB**
CHAD THERAPEUTICS, 21622 Plummer St., 91311, pg. 332 **PB**
CHATSWORTH DATA CORPORATION, 20701 Lassen St., 91311, pg. 231 **PV**
Christie Design, 9424 Eton Ave., 91311, pg. 1369 **PB**
Clinishare, 20600 Nordhoff, 91311, pg. 1118 **PV**
Coast Fed Services, 19900 Plummer St., 91311, pg. 389 **PB**
Computer Optical Products Inc., 9305 Eton Ave., 91311, pg. 799 **PB**
CUSTOM CONTROL SENSORS, INC., 21111 Plummer St., 91311, pg. 298 **PV**
David Dart, 20500 Plummer St., 91311, pg. 948 **PB**
Dataproducts Supplies Div., 9657 Mason Ave., 91311, pg. 621 **IT**
Fadal Engineering Company, Inc., 20701 Plummer St., 91311, pg. 1389 **PB**
Fiber-Resin Corporation, 20701 Nordhoff Ave., 91311, pg. 686 **PB**
Geonex, 9200 Eton Ave., 91311, pg. 448 **PV**
Graphic Research, Inc., 9334 Mason Ave., 91311, pg. 1101 **PB**
Great Western Bank, 9200 Oakdale Ave., 91311-6519, pg. 1741 **PB**
Great Western Financial Corporation, 9200 Oakdale Ave., NII-31, 91311, pg. 1741 **PB**
Great Western Mortgage Corporation, 9200 Oakdale Ave., 91311-6519, pg. 1742 **PB**
Hitachi Power Tools U.S.A. Ltd., 09409 Owens Mouth Ave., 91311, pg. 620 **IT**
HYDRAULICS INTERNATIONAL, INC., 9000 Mason Ave., 91311, pg. 551 **PV**
Hydro-Mill Co., 9301 Mason Ave., 91311, pg. 1640 **PB**
IMAGE ENTERTAINMENT, INC., 9333 Oso Ave., 91311, pg. 870 **PB**
Infinity Systems, Inc., 9409 Owensmouth Ave., 91311, pg. 787 **PB**
K-SWISS INC., 20664 Bahama St., 91311-6101, pg. 937 **PB**
LEVLAD, INC., 9200 Mason Ave., 91311, pg. 663 **PV**
MCRB SERVICE BUREAU, INC., 9171 Oso Ave., 91311, pg. 686 **PB**
MRV COMMUNICATIONS, INC., 20415 Nordhoff St., 91311, pg. 1027 **PB**
Manchester Plastics Co., Inc., 20401 Prairie St., 91311, pg. 1527 **PB**
Melrose, 9419 Mason Ave., 91311, pg. 948 **PB**
MERCURY DISTRIBUTING CO., INC., 9600 Lurline Ave., 91311, pg. 732 **PV**
MICROPOLIS CORPORATION, 21211 Nordhoff St., 91311, pg. 742 **PB**
N Base Comunications, 8943 Fullbright Ave., 91311, pg. 1027 **PB**
NMB Corporation, 9730 Independence Ave., 91311, pg. 868 **IT**
NMB (USA) Inc., 9730 Independence Ave., 91311, pg. 868 **IT**
New Hampshire Ball Bearings, Precision Products Group, 9730 Independence Ave., 91311, pg. 868 **IT**
NILS Publishing Company, 21625 Prairie St., 91311, pg. 1513 **IT**
Retix, 9600 Topanga Canyon Blvd., 91311, pg. 1717 **PB**
RONCO, INVENTIONS, LLC, 9457 DeSoto Ave., 91311, pg. 943 **PV**
Sanyo Fisher Company, 21605 Plummer St., 91311, pg. 1191 **PB**
Sanyo Office Automation, 21350 Lassen St., 91311, pg. 1191 **PB**
Tecom Industries, Inc., 9324 Topanga Canyon Blvd., 91311-5728, pg. 1563 **PB**
TimeMed Labeling Systems, Inc., 9566 Vassar St., 91311, pg. 1087 **PV**
TRIKON TECHNOLOGIES INC., 9255 Deering Ave., 91311, pg. 1638 **PB**

Viking Electronics, Inc., 9250 Independence Ave., 91311, pg. 1184 **PV**

Chico

DuckBack Products, 2644 Hegan Lane, 95927, pg. 944 **PB**
Fleetwood Motor Homes of California, Inc./Chico, 300 E. Ryan Ave., 95926, pg. 651 **PB**
Knudsen & Sons, Inc., P.O. Box 369, 95928, pg. 1480 **PB**
Mid Valley Title & Escrow Co., 601 Main St., 95928, pg. 626 **PB**

Chino

ACI Kimtruss Corp., 13950 Yorba Ave., 91710, pg. 129 **PB**
AEP Industries, Inc., 14000 Monte Vista Ave., 91710, pg. 5 **PB**
Acorn Custom Molding/Cal Tube, 13818 Oaks Ave., 91710, pg. 14 **PV**
Agribusiness Department, 12808 Central Ave., 2nd Fl., 91710, pg. 287 **PV**
COWDEN METAL SPECIALTIES, INC., 4626 Eucalyptus Ave., 91710, pg. 280 **PV**
El Doraco National, 13900 Sycamore Way, 91710, pg. 1502 **PV**
Great American Oak, Inc., 13477 Benson, 91710, pg. 280 **PV**
Harrington Industrial Plastics Inc., P.O. Box 5128, 14480 Yorba Ave., 91708-5128, pg. 554 **IT**
Hitek Product Finishing, Inc., 14450 Yorba Ave., 91710, pg. 280 **PV**
L & L NURSERY SUPPLY, INC., 5350 G St., 91710, pg. 638 **PV**
Los Angeles Cellular Telephone Co., 2256 Point Vista Ave., 91710, pg. 11 **PB**
ROBESON APPLIANCE, INC., 14375 Telephone Ave., 91710, pg. 1394 **PB**
USA Casualty Company, P.O. Box 5131, 91708, pg. 1116 **PV**

Chowchilla

Friction Inc., 711 S. Third St., 93610, pg. 560 **PB**

Chula Vista

Bourns De Mexico, 1055 Bay Blvd., Ste. D, 91911-1628, pg. 161 **PV**
California-American Water Co., 800 Kuhn Dr., 91914, pg. 95 **PV**
Crown Chemical Corporation, 1888 Nirvana Ave., 91911, pg. 1458 **PV**
HYSPAN PRECISION PRODUCTS, INC., 1685 Brandywine Ave., 91911, pg. 552 **PV**
KSWB-TV, 1696 Frontage Rd., 91911, pg. 1636 **PB**
Rohr Credit Corporation, 850 Lagoon Dr., 91910-2098, pg. 751 **PB**
Rohr, Inc., 850 Lagoon Dr., 91910-2098, pg. 751 **PB**

Citrus Heights

Benihana Sunrise Corp., 5489F Sunrise Blvd., 95610, pg. 212 **PB**

City of Commerce

A K H COMPANY, INC., 5800 Southeastern Ave., 90040, pg. 2 **PV**
All Clubman, 2220 Gaspar Ave., 90040, pg. 57 **PV**
Aaron Brothers, Inc., 1270 S. Goodrich Blvd., 90022, pg. 1104 **PV**
AMERICAN INTERNATIONAL INDUSTRIES, 2220 Gaspar Ave., 90040, pg. 57 **PV**
Andrea International, 2220 Gaspar Ave., 90040, pg. 57 **PV**
Anthony Macaroni Co., Inc., 5733 Rickenbacker Ave., 90040, pg. 153 **PV**
Banco Popular, N.A. (California), 6001 E. Washington Blvd., 90040, pg. 176 **PB**
Delore, 2220 Gaspar Ave., 90040, pg. 57 **PV**
Double H West Shoe Wholesale, 2300 S. Garfield Ave., 90040, pg. 217 **PV**
Dunbar Sales Inc., 2746 Vail Ave., 90040, pg. 1720 **PB**
E.N.C., 6330 Chalet Dr., 90040, pg. 948 **PB**
FORTUNE FASHION INC., 6501 Flotilla St., 90040, pg. 419 **PV**
GATX Freight Systems-California, L.A. Dupont, 5500 Union Pacific Ave., 90022, pg. 691 **PB**
GATX Logistics, Inc.-California (Dupont), 5500 Union Pacific Ave., 90022, pg. 691 **PB**
GiGi, 2220 Gaspar Ave., 90040, pg. 57 **PV**
Graphic Arts Supply Division, 4425 Sheila St., 90023, pg. 205 **PB**
PRESSURE SYSTEMS, INC., 6033 E. Bandini Blvd., 90040, pg. 882 **PV**
Rembrandt Photo Services, 6049 Slauson Ave., 90040, pg. 222 **PV**
Sackner-West Div., 3400 Malt Ave., 90040, pg. 924 **PB**
Senior Engineering Company-USA, 5701 S. Eastern Ave., 90040, pg. 1222 **IT**
Standard Flour Co., 2425 Saybrook Ave., 90040, pg. 24 **IT**
Stewart & Stevenson Power, Inc., 5840 Dahlia St., 80022, pg. 1518 **PB**
SuperNail, 2220 Gaspar Ave., 90040, pg. 57 **PV**
2110 Davie Corporation, 2110 Davie Ave., 90040, pg. 94 **PV**
Unisource, 2600 S. Commerce Way, 90040, pg. 1671 **PB**
Wellman Nonwovens Div., 2748 Tanager Ave., 90040, pg. 1753 **PB**

Western Globe Products, Inc., 5733 Rickenbacker Rd., 90040, pg. 158 **PV**
WOLFER PRINTING COMPANY, 6670 E. Flotilla St., 90040, pg. 1186 **PV**

City of Industry

ACORN ENGINEERING COMPANY, 15125 Proctor Ave., 91746, pg. 14 **PV**
ADAMS RITE MANUFACTURING CO., 4040 S. Capital Ave., 91749, pg. 17 **PV**
Allfast Facility, 15200 E. Don Julian Rd., 91745, pg. 37 **PV**
ALLFAST FASTENING SYSTEMS, INC., 15200 E. Don Julian Rd., 91745, pg. 37 **PV**
Alta-Dena Certified Dairy, P.O. Box 388, 91747-0388, pg. 201 **IT**
Alta Dena Inc., 17637 E. Valley Blvd., 91744, pg. 201 **IT**
American Modular Technologies, LLC, 18233 E. Railroad, 91744, pg. 69 **PB**
Anvil Cases, Inc., 15650 Salt Lake Ave., 91745, pg. 1791 **PB**
Ardell International, Inc., 2220 Gaspar Ave., 90040, pg. 57 **PV**
Belwith International Div., 18071 Arenth Ave., 91748, pg. 473 **IT**
Benihana Puente Hills Corp., 17877 Gale Ave., 91748, pg. 212 **PB**
Bentley Mills, Inc., 14641 E. Don Julian Rd., 91746, pg. 889 **PB**
CME, 19481 San Jose Ave., 91748, pg. 201 **PV**
Cacique, P.O. Box 91330, 14940 Procter, 91715-1330, pg. 995 **PB**
CACIQUE, INC., 14940 Proctor Ave., 91744, pg. 198 **PV**
California State Bank-City of Industry, 17700 Castleton St., 91715, pg. 294 **PB**
CALMAR INC., 333 S. Turnbull Canyon Rd., 91745, pg. 201 **PV**
Coastal Wood Products, Inc., 13285 Temple Ave., 91746, pg. 720 **PV**
Consolidated Device Inc., 19220 San Jose Ave., 91748, pg. 1481 **PB**
CROWN PRINCE, INC. (CA), 17031 Green Dr., 91745, pg. 293 **PV**
DTK COMPUTER INC., 770 Epperson Dr., 91748-1336, pg. 306 **PV**
Dexter Electronic Materials Division, 15051 E. Don Julian Rd., 91746-3398, pg. 504 **PB**
Dreyer's Southern California Region, 351 Cheryl Ln., 91789, pg. 529 **PB**
Dreyer's Southwest Division, 351 Cheryl Ln., 91789, pg. 529 **PB**
EXCELSIOR INC., 2211 Saybrook Ave., 90040, pg. 387 **PV**
Falcon-City of Industry, 16040 Stephens St., 91745, pg. 611 **PV**
GS Battery (U.S.A.), Inc., 17253 Chestnut St., 91748, pg. 702 **PV**
Great Dane Los Angeles, Inc., 1500 E. Nelson Ave., 91744, pg. 1030 **PV**
HITCHCOCK AUTOMOTIVE RESOURCES, P.O. Box 8367, 91748, pg. 1777 **PV**
Holtzman's Little Folk Shop, Inc., 801 Sentous Ave., 91748, pg. 1777 **PB**
ITT Barton Instruments, P.O. Box 1882, 900 S. Trumbull Canyon Rd., 91749, pg. 860 **PB**
Ingram Paper Company, 17411 Valley Blvd., 91744, pg. 904 **PB**
INTERBATH, INC., 665 N. Baldwin Park Blvd., 91746, pg. 566 **PV**
KERN INDUSTRIES, 13000 E. Temple Ave., 91749-1207, pg. 616 **PV**
LA VICTORIA FOODS, INC., P.O. Box 3884, 91744, pg. 641 **PV**
Lincoln Products, 17711 E. Railroad St., 91748, pg. 1512 **IT**
Liuski International California, Inc., 18567 East Gale Avenue, 91748, pg. 1005 **PV**
LYNX GOLF, INC., 16017 E. Valley Blvd., 91744, pg. 684 **PV**
M M M SALES, INC., 14314 Lomitas Ave., 91744, pg. 685 **PV**
Ondine Div., 665 N. Baldwin Park Blvd., 91746, pg. 566 **PV**
Plastron, 19555 E. Arenth Ave., 91748, pg. 15 **PV**
Plaxicon Company, 14351 Bonelli St., 91744, pg. 1481 **IT**
Presto Food Products, Inc., 18275 Arenth Ave., 91748, pg. 1527 **PB**
Pro Shop (Los Angeles, CA), 3951 Capitol Ave., 91749, pg. 861 **PB**
Quadrastat Corp., 4040 S. Capitol Ave., 91749, pg. 17 **PV**
QUALITY NATURALLY FOODS, 18830 E. San Jose Ave., 91748, pg. 899 **PV**
REULAND ELECTRIC COMPANY, 17969 E. Railroad St., 91749, pg. 925 **PV**
Richmond Screw Anchor Division, 17051 E. Green Drive, 91716, pg. 932 **PV**
Sanwa Foods, Inc., 331 N. Vineland Ave., 91746, pg. 299 **PB**
Sierra Craft, Inc., 18825 E. San Jose Ave., 91748-1326, pg. 1512 **IT**
STROUDS, INC., 780 S. Nogales St., 91748-1364, pg. 1525 **PB**
SUSIE'S DEALS, 1115 John Reed Ct., 91745, pg. 1056 **PV**
TECSTAR INC., 15251 E. Don Julian Rd., 91745-1002, pg. 1072 **PV**
TULIP CORPORATION, 14955 E. Salt Lake Ave., 91746-3133, pg. 1109 **PV**
UTILITY TRAILER MANUFACTURING CO., 17295 E. Railroad Ave., 91748-1022, pg. 1130 **PV**
VALLEY DETROIT DIESEL ALLISON, 425 S. Hecienta Blvd., 91745, pg. 1132 **PB**

Ventura Foods LLC, 14840 E. Don Julian Rd., 91746, pg. 879 **IT**
WWF Paper Corporation - West (California), 2727 Workman Mill Rd., 91746, pg. 1145 **PV**
Western Specialty Container, 17955 E. Ajax Circle, 91748, pg. 559 **PV**
Whitehall Manufacturing Inc., 15058 Proctor Ave., 91744, pg. 14 **PV**
Williamhouse of California, Inc., 705 N. Baldwin Park Blvd., 91746, pg. 89 **PB**
YALE/CHASE MATERIALS HANDLING, INC., 2615 Pellissier Pl., 91742, pg. 1195 **PV**
YUM YUM DONUT SHOP, INC., 18830 E. San Jose Ave., 91748, pg. 1203 **PV**

Claremont

Claremont Service Center, 725 Wharton Dr., 91711, pg. 287 **PB**
Downey Savings & Loan Association, F.A., 935 West Foothill Blvd., 91711, pg. 526 **PB**
GREEN SPOT PACKAGING INC., 100 S. Cambridge, 91711-4842, pg. 477 **PV**
Hillhaven Convalescent Hospital Claremont, 590 S. Indian Hill Blvd., 91711, pg. 1713 **PB**
ServiceLine, Customer Service Info. Ctr., 91711, pg. 287 **PB**

Cloverdale

Clover Springs, 200 Hot Springs Rd., 95425, pg. 495 **PB**

Clovis

Clovis Independent, P.O. Box 189, 1321 Railroad Ave., 93612, pg. 1065 **PB**
Manulife Financial - Fresno, 8501 N. Chamise Lane, 93611, pg. 840 **IT**
McClatchy Printing Service, P.O. Box 189, 93612, pg. 1066 **PB**
Nichimen America, Inc., Fresno Office, 3097 Willow Ave., Ste. 16, 93612, pg. 928 **IT**

Coachella

AMCOR CAPITAL CORPORATION, 52300 Enterprise Way, 92236, pg. 64 **PB**
Armtec Defense Products Co., 85-901 Ave. 53, 92236, pg. 594 **PB**

Coalinga

The Coalinga Record, 152 E. Elm St., 93210, pg. 1343 **PB**
HARRIS FARMS, INC., Rte. 1, Box 420, 93210, pg. 505 **PV**
Harris Feeding Co., Rte. 1, Box 400, 93210, pg. 505 **PV**
Harris Ranch Restaurant, Rte. 1 Box 777, Interstate 5 & Hwy. 198, 93210, pg. 506 **PV**
Inn at Harris Ranch, Rte. 1 Box 777, Interstate 5 & Hwy. 198, 93210, pg. 506 **PV**

Colfax

TOMS SIERRA COMPANY, 333 N. Canyon, 95713, pg. 1090 **PV**

Colton

Hydro Conduit Corp., P.O. Box 1237, 1205 S. Rancho Ave., 92324, pg. 245 **IT**
Stater Bros. Inc., 21700 Barton Rd., 92324, pg. 456 **PB**
Stater Brothers Holdings, 21700 Barton Rd., 92324, pg. 456 **PB**
Williams Furnace Co., 225 Acacia, 92324, pg. 441 **PB**

Colusa

Pirelli Cable, Power Div. Service Center, 346 Fifth St., Ste 200, 95932, pg. 1059 **IT**

Compton

Arden-Mayfair, Inc., 2020 S. Central Ave., 90220, pg. 129 **PB**
BEAUCHAMP DISTRIBUTING COMPANY, 1911 S. Santa Fe Ave., 90221, pg. 127 **PV**
Box USA Inc., 301 W. Walnut St., 90220, pg. 421 **PV**
BROOKHURST, INC., 107 W. Carob, 90220, pg. 171 **PV**
CONTINENTAL FORGE COMPANY, 512 E. Carlin St., 90222, pg. 268 **PV**
Crystal Park Casino, 111 E. Srtesia Blvd., 90220, pg. 831 **PV**
Daewoo International America Corp. - Los Angeles, 1055 W. Victoria St., 90220, pg. 357 **IT**
Food 4 Less, Inc., 100 W. Artesia Blvd., 90220, pg. 1202 **PV**
GKN Westland Aerospace North America Inc., 15800 S. Avalon, 90220, pg. 535 **IT**
Harvard Sports, Inc., 2640 E. Del Amo Blvd., 90221, pg. 591 **PB**
Hitachi Home Electronics, Western Region, 401 W. Artesia Blvd., 90220, pg. 622 **IT**
HOUSTON FEARLESS 76 INC., 203 W. Artesia Blvd., 90220-5550, pg. 542 **PV**
Kawai America Corporation, 2055 E. University Dr., 90220, pg. 725 **IT**
KLEER-VU PLASTICS, INC., 921 West Artesia Blvd., 90220, pg. 962 **PB**

Kleer-Vu Plastics Corp., 921 West Artesia Blvd., 90220, pg. 962 **PB**
KRACO ENTERPRISES, INC., 505 E. Euclid Ave., 90224, pg. 634 **PV**
M&N Valve, 2044 Gladwick Street, 90220, pg. 1449 **IT**
Ralphs Grocery Company, 1100 W. Artesia Blvd., 90220, pg. 1202 **PV**
Sanyo Fisher Service Corp., 1200 West Artesia Blvd., 90220, pg. 1191 **IT**
Sermatech West, Airfoil Management Co., 18502 Laurel Park Rd., 90220-6053, pg. 1570 **PB**
Robert Skeels & Co., 19216 S. Laurel Pk. Rd., 90220, pg. 1782 **PV**
Tylan General, Inc.-Flow Division, 19617 Broadwick Dr., 90220, pg. 1112 **PB**
Wolf Range Co., 19600 S. Alameda St., 90224, pg. 1322 **PB**
Y.K.K. (U.S.A.) Inc., 510 W. Carob St., 90220, pg. 1515 **IT**

Concord

Air Conditioning Co, Inc, 2150 John Glenn Dr., 94520, pg. 28 **PV**
BOC Coating Technology, 4020 Pike Ln., 94520, pg. 121 **IT**
Business Information Technology, 1800 Sutter St., Ste. 770, 94520, pg. 356 **IT**
CPI Prints Plus, Inc., 2500 Bisso Ln., Bldg. 200, 94520, pg. 283 **PB**
EMCON Associates, pg. 571 **PB**
J.E. HIGGINS LUMBER CO., 1485 Enea Ct., Ste. 1100, 94520, pg. 527 **PV**
Klockner-Moeller, 4041 Pike Ln., Ste. A, 94520, pg. 736 **IT**
Systron Donner-Inertial Division, 2700 Systron Dr., 94518-1399, pg. 160 **PB**
Transdyn Controls, Inc., 4040 Pike Ln., 94520, pg. 1111 **PB**
Tuthill Pump Company of California, 5143 Port Chicago Hwy., 94520, pg. 1111 **PV**
Valley Manor Care Center, 3806 Clayton Rd., 94521, pg. 733 **PV**

Corning

Premdor Wood Products, P.O. Box 285, 96021, pg. 1067 **IT**

Corona

BWD Automotive Corp., 235 N. Sherman Ave., 91720, pg. 560 **PB**
Bergen Brunswig Drug Company, 1851 Califorina Ave., 91719-3379, pg. 213 **PB**
CALIFORNIA MANUFACTURING ENTERPRISES, 248 Glider Cir., 91720, pg. 201 **PV**
CASE-SWAYNE CO. INC., 1930 California Ave., 91719, pg. 218 **PV**
Charter Behavioral Health System of the Inland Empire, Inc., 2055 Kellogg Dr., 91719, pg. 1034 **PB**
Circle Seal Controls, Inc., 2301 Wardlow Circle, 91720, pg. 1746 **PB**
Coast RV, Inc., 231 N. Sherman Ave., 91720, pg. 388 **PB**
Corona Clipper, 1540 E. Sixth St., 91719, pg. 506 **PV**
FLEETWOOD ALUMINUM PRODUCTS, 2485 Railroad St., 91720, pg. 410 **PV**
M.A. Hanna Engineered Materials, 13435 Estelle St., 91720, pg. 781 **PB**
Hayden, 1241 Old Temsecal Rd., 91720, pg. 1503 **PB**
Higgins Riverside Operations, 1521 Pomona Rd., 91720, pg. 527 **PV**
Noah Howden, Inc., 2616 Research, 91720, pg. 636 **IT**
Hydro Conduit Corp., P.O. Box 939, 23200 Temescal Canyon Rd., 91718, pg. 245 **IT**
Kolmar Laboratories, 450 N. Sheridan St., 91720, pg. 239 **IT**
NATURE'S RECIPE PET FOODS, 341 Bonnie Circle, 91720, pg. 789 **PV**
Ny-Glass Plastics, Inc., 1255 Railroad St., 91720, pg. 1527 **PB**
Oclassen Pharmaceuticals, 311 Bonnie Cir., 91720, pg. 1746 **PB**
Pacific Clay Products, P.O. Box 1149, 91720, pg. 831 **PB**
Power Systems Group, 1521 Pomona Rd., 91720, pg. 927 **PV**
Roof Tile Manufacturing Co., 1230 Railroad St., 91720, pg. 905 **PB**
Schnadig Corp., 1350 Railroad Ave., 91720, pg. 971 **PV**
Spirol West, 645 E. Harrison St., Ste. 100, 91719, pg. 1026 **PV**
Uni-Line Div., 402 S. Temescal St., 91720, pg. 1243 **PB**
Waterworks Equipment Co. (WECO) Div., c/o-Western Operations OFC., 1660 E. Sixth St., 91719, pg. 1682 **PB**
Watson Laboratories, Inc., 311 Bonnie Cir., 91720, pg. 1746 **PB**
WATSON PHARMACEUTICALS, INC., 311 Bonnie Cir., 91720, pg. 1746 **PB**

Corona Del Mar

The Accor Group, Inc., 1101 Bayside Dr., Ste. 201, 92625, pg. 21 **PB**
COMPREHENSIVE CARE CORPORATION, 1111 Bayside Dr., Ste. 100, 92625, pg. 419 **PB**
Comprehensive Care Integration, 1111 Bayside Dr., Ste. 100, 92625, pg. 419 **PB**
Five Crowns, 3801 E. Coast Hwy., 92625, pg. 654 **PV**
MEDIASPOT, INC., 1550 Bayside Dr., 92625, pg. 727 **PV**

Corte Madera

Comdisco Financial Services, 770 Tamalpais Dr., Suite 300, 94925, pg. 408 **PB**
IL FORNAIO AMERICA CORPORATION, 770 Tamalpais Dr., 94925, pg. 864 **PB**
Midwest Agri-Commodities, 100 Tamal Plaza, Ste. 180, 94925, pg. 53 **PV**
Portal Publications, Ltd., 770 Tamalpais Dr., 94925, pg. 503 **PB**

Costa Mesa

APRIA HEALTHCARE GROUP INC., 3560 Hyland Ave., 92626, pg. 125 **PB**
Avco Financial Services, Plaza Tower, 600 Anton Blvd., 92628-5011, pg. 1589 **PB**
Bank of America Capital, 650 Town Center Dr., 17th Fl., 92626, pg. 180 **PB**
Canon Business Machines Inc., 3191 Red Hill Ave., 92626, pg. 261 **IT**
Canon Computer Systems, Inc., 2995 Red Hill Ave., 92626, pg. 262 **IT**
Canon Information Systems, Inc., 3188 Pullman St., 92626, pg. 261 **IT**
J.C. Carter Company, Inc., 671 W. 17th St., 92627, pg. 81 **PV**
CENTRIS GROUP INC., 650 Town Center Dr., Ste. 1600, 92626, pg. 328 **PB**
CERADYNE, INC, 3169 Redhill Ave., 92626, pg. 330 **PB**
Computerized Security Systems, Inc., 1020 W. 17th St., 92627, pg. 1053 **PB**
Ted Cook Tours Islands in the Sun, 760W. 16th St., 92627, pg. 21 **PV**
Coventry Homes of Southern California, Suite 3187-H, 3187 Airway Ave., 92626, pg. 495 **PV**
Del Webb Homes, Inc., 3187 Airway Ave., Ste. 3187-H, 92626, pg. 495 **PB**
Digital House, Ltd., 3545 Harbor Blvd., 92626, pg. 579 **PB**
Downey Savings & Loan Association, F.A., 3200 Bristol St., 92626, pg. 526 **PB**
Downey Savings & Loan Association, F.A., 360 E. 17th St., 92627, pg. 526 **PB**
Eaton Corp., Aerospace & Commercial Controls Div., 1640 Monrovia Ave., 92627, pg. 557 **PB**
EMULEX CORPORATION, 3535 Harbor Blvd., 92626, pg. 579 **PB**
FILENET CORPORATION, 3565 Harbor Blvd., 92626, pg. 622 **PB**
Friendly Holidays Inc.-West, 575 Anton Blvd., 92629, pg. 429 **PV**
Glendale Associates, 3200 Bristol St., Ste. 660, 92626, pg. 361 **PV**
Glendale Limited Partnership Associates - II, 3200 Bristol St., Ste. 660, 92626, pg. 361 **PV**
GRISWOLD INDUSTRIES, INC., 1701 Placentia Ave., 92627, pg. 482 **PV**
ICN PHARMACEUTICALS, INC., 3300 Hyland Ave., 92626, pg. 853 **PB**
ITT Jabsco, 1485 Dale Way, 92626, pg. 860 **PB**
Imperial Real Estate Ventures, 695 Town Center Dr., 92626, pg. 831 **PV**
InteSys of California, 265 Briggs Ave., 92626, pg. 574 **PV**
IRVINE SENSORS CORPORATION, Bldg. 3, 3001 Redhill Ave., 92626, pg. 913 **PB**
Katin, 1751 Placentia Ave., 92627, pg. 940 **PV**
Knight Equipment International Inc., 2945 Airway Ave., 92627, pg. 862 **PV**
MacNeal-Schwendler Corp., 2975 Red Hill Ave., 92626, pg. 1031 **PB**
Mercury Air Center, 3000 Airway Ave. B-3A, 92626, pg. 1093 **PB**
Nadel Architects, Inc., 3080 Bristol St., Ste. 500, 92626, pg. 773 **PV**
Oki, 151 Kalmus Dr., Ste. M-1, 92626-5988, pg. 1000 **IT**
One Stop Mortgage, Inc., 200 Baker St., pg. 12 **PV**
PACIFIC HANDY CUTTER, INC., 2968 Randolph Ave., 92626-4312, pg. 831 **PV**
Pacific One Dealer Center, Inc., 950 S. Coast Dr., Ste. 270, 92626, pg. 635 **PV**
PacifiCare Life & Health Insurance Co., 3515 Harbor Blvd., 92626, pg. 1251 **PB**
Playmates Toys Inc., 611 Anton Blvd., Ste. 60, 92626, pg. 1060 **IT**
Prescription Solutions, 3515 Harbor Blvd., 92626, pg. 1251 **PB**
Principal Portfolio Services, Inc., 3150 Bristol St., Ste. 250, 92626, pg. 886 **PB**
Prudential Real Estate Affiliates Inc., 3200 Park Center Dr., Ste. 1400, 92628, pg. 892 **PV**
QUIKSILVER, INC., 1740 Monrovia Avenue, 92627, pg. 1353 **PB**
ROCKWELL INTERNATIONAL CORPORATION, 600 Anton Blvd., Ste. 700, 92628-5090, pg. 1397 **PB**
Satellite Technical Management, 3530 Hyland Ave., 92626-1469, pg. 1154 **IT**
Secon Properties, 3315 Fairview Rd., 92626, pg. 362 **PB**
Sequent Computer Systems, Inc., 949 S. Coast Dr., Ste. 155, 92626, pg. 1459 **PB**
Sony Trans Com Systems Inc., 2729 S. Bristol, 92626, pg. 1281 **IT**
Spectron Development Labs, 3535 Hyland Ave., Ste. 102, 92626, pg. 1618 **PB**
Spectrum Razor Tools, 2968 Randolph Ave., 92626-4312, pg. 831 **PV**
Stacoswitch, Inc., 1139 Baker St., 92626, pg. 260 **PV**
STANDARD PACIFIC CORP., 1565 W. MacArthur Blvd., 92626, pg. 1503 **PB**

Geographic Index-U.S.

StanPac Corp, 1565 W. Mac Arthur Blvd., 92626, pg. 1504 — PB
StanPac Partners, 1565 W. Mac Arthur Blvd., 92626, pg. 1504 — PB
Symbol Technologies, Portable Systems Division, 300 Fischer Ave., 92626, pg. 1546 — PB
THREE D DEPARTMENTS, INC., 3535 Highland Ave., Ste. 200, 92626-1808, pg. 1604 — PB
Turner Construction Company, 575 Anton Blvd., Ste. 250, 92626, pg. 1645 — PB
USF Re Insurance Company, 650 Town Ctr. Dr., Ste. 1600, 92626, pg. 328 — PB
US Benefits Insurance Services, Inc., 650 Town Ctr. Dr., Ste. 1600, 92626, pg. 328 — PB
WARMINGTON HOMES, 3090 Pullman Ave., Ste. A, 92626, pg. 1150 — PV
Westmark Mortgage Corporation, 535 Anton Blvd., Ste. 500, 92626, pg. 1761 — PB
WHITE CAP INDUSTRIES, INC., 3120 Airway Ave., 92626, pg. 1765 — PB

Cotati

Precision Lamp, Inc., 720 Portal St., 94931, pg. 856 — PB

Cottonwood

Wood Moulding Plant, P. O. Box 2090, 96022, pg. 738 — PB

Covina

Avery Converted Products Group, 818 Oak Park Rd., 91724, pg. 152 — PB
California State Bank-Covina Downtown, 301 N. Second Ave., pg. 294 — PB
California State Bank-Covina Main, 925 W. Badillo St., pg. 294 — PB
Charter Oak Behavioral Health System, Inc., 1161 E. Covina Blvd., 91724, pg. 1035 — PB
EG & G Optoelectronics-Covina, 1330 E. Cypress St., 91724, pg. 543 — PB
Grocers and Merchants Insurance, Inc., 874 S. Village Oak Dr., 91724, pg. 227 — PV
Grocers & Merchants Management Co., 874 S. Village Oaks Drr., 91724-3614, pg. 227 — PV
Springfield Insurance Company, 874S Village Oaks Dr., 91724, pg. 227 — PV

Crockett

California & Hawaiian Sugar Company Inc., 830 Loring Ave., 94525-1199, pg. 39 — PB

Crows Landing

Grisez Warehouse Co., Inc., 22124 Hwy. 33, 95313, pg. 428 — PB

Cucamonga

General Latex & Chemical Corporation, P.O. Box 748, 91729, pg. 444 — PV
Rolock of California, 9155 Archibald Ave., #503, 91730, pg. 942 — PV
Shelter Products Group-Western Div., 9141 Arrow Hwy., 91730, pg. 1398 — IT

Cudahy

CONSOLIDATED FOUNDRIES, 8333 Wilcox St., 90201, pg. 265 — PV
Downey Savings & Loan Association, F.A., 7220 Atlantic Blvd., 90201, pg. 527 — PB

Culver City

Body Drama, Inc., 5840 Uplander Way, Ste. 202, 90230, pg. 1182 — PB
Capy U.S.A. Inc., 5730 Uplander Way-Suite 110, 90230, pg. 253 — IT
Columbia Pictures, 10202 W. Washington Blvd., 90232, pg. 1281 — IT
Columbia Pictures Western Division, 10202 W. Washington Blvd., 90232, pg. 1281 — IT
Columbia Tri-Star Film Distributors International, 10202 W. Washington Blvd., 90232, pg. 1281 — IT
Columbia Tri-Star International Releasing Corp., 10202 W. Washington Blvd., 90232, pg. 1281 — IT
Columbia Tri-Star International Television, 10202 W. Washington Blvd., 90232, pg. 1281 — IT
Columbia TriStar Television, 9336 W. Washington Blvd., CSOB-1100, 90232, pg. 1282 — IT
Culver Studios, 9336 W. Washington Blvd., 90232, pg. 1283 — IT
DATA DIMENSIONS, INC., 5839 Green Valley Cir., Ste. 104, 90230, pg. 485 — PB
Hamilton Hallmark, 10950 Washington Blvd., 90230, pg. 155 — PB
IDB WorldCom, Inc., 10525 W. Washington Blvd., 90232-1922, pg. 1779 — PB
KENT & SPIEGEL DIRECT, 6133 Bristol Pkwy., Ste. 150, 90230, pg. 615 — PV
MGM Entertainment Company, 10202 W. Washington Blvd., 90232, pg. 1614 — PB
NEC Business Communication Systems (West), Inc., 6025 Slauson Ave., 90230, pg. 900 — IT
JACK NADEL, INC., 9950 W. Jefferson Blvd., 90232, pg. 773 — PV

Overhill Farms, Inc., 5730 Uplander Way, Suite 201, 90230, pg. 1315 — PB
L. POWELL CO., INC., 8631 Hayden Pl., 90232, pg. 877 — PV
Resin Formulators, 8500 Steller Dr., 90232, pg. 935 — PV
E.V. ROBERTS & ASSOCIATES, INC., 8500 Steller Dr., 90232, pg. 935 — PV
Sony Pictures Entertainment, 10202 W. Washington Blvd., 90232, pg. 1281 — IT
Sony Pictures Entertainment Television Group, 10202 W. Washington Blvd., 90232, pg. 1282 — IT
Sony Pictures Studios, 10202 W. Washington Blvd., 90232, pg. 1283 — IT
Tri-Star Pictures, Inc., 10202 W. Washington Blvd., 90232, pg. 1282 — IT
TriStar Pictures, 10202 W. Washington Blvd., 90232, pg. 1283 — IT
Value Priced Clothing Inc., 8660 Hayden Pl., 90232, pg. 1086 — PB

Cupertino

APPLE COMPUTER, INC., One Infinite Loop, 95014, pg. 121 — PB
CKS GROUP, 10443 Bandley Dr., 95014, pg. 195 — PV
DSP COMMUNICATIONS INC., 20300 Stevens Creek Blvd., 95014, pg. 475 — PB
Downey Savings & Loan Association, F.A., 10381 S. DeAnza Blvd., 95014, pg. 526 — PB
Honeywell-Measurex Corporation, One Results Way, 95014-5991, pg. 833 — PB
Honeywell-Measurex Credit Corporation, One Results Way, 95014, pg. 833 — PB
Honeywell-Measurex Foreign Sales Corporation, One Results Way, 95014-5991, pg. 833 — PB
Honeywell-Measurex (Ireland) Finance Unlimited, One Results Way, 95014-5991, pg. 833 — PB
Honeywell-Measurex (Ireland) Service Ltd., c/o Measurex Corp., One Results Way, 95014-5991, pg. 833 — PB
Honeywell-Measurex Systems Inc., One Results Way, 95015, pg. 833 — PB
IKOS SYSTEMS, INC., 19050 Pruneridge Ave., 95014, pg. 864 — PB
Medtronic Aneu Rx, 10231 Bubb Rd., 95014, pg. 1083 — PB
MISSION WEST PROPERTIES, 10050 Bandley Dr., 95014, pg. 1117 — PB
Motorola Radius, Computer Group, 10700 N. De Anza Blvd., 95014-2082, pg. 1138 — PB
Olivetti Advanced Technology Center, Inc., 20300 Stevens Creek Blvd., 95014, pg. 1002 — IT
Orchard Glen Venture, 20300 Stevens Creek, Ste. 100, 95014, pg. 361 — IT
PowerTV, Inc., 20833 Stevens Creek Blvd., Ste. 100, 95014-2154, pg. 1443 — PB
RATIONAL SOFTWARE CORPORATION, 18880 Homestead Rd., 95014, pg. 1361 — PB
Ridge Vineyards Inc., 17100 Monte Bello Rd., 95015, pg. 1013 — IT
Siemens Components, Inc., 10950 N. Tantan Ave., 95014, pg. 1245 — IT
SYMANTEC CORPORATION, 10201 Torre Ave., 95014-2132, pg. 1545 — PB
Tandem Computers Americas Div., 19191 Vallco Pkwy., 95014-2494, pg. 417 — PB
Tandem Computers Inc., 19333 Vallco Pkwy., 95014-2599, pg. 417 — PB

Cypress

Bandai America, Inc., 5551 Katalla Ave., 90630, pg. 145 — IT
Ferrari North America, Inc., 6780 Katella Ave., 90630, pg. 483 — IT
KYB Corp. of America, 6601 Darin Way, 90630, pg. 727 — IT
Mary Kay Cosmetics, Inc., 6300 Katella Ave., 90630, pg. 872 — PV
Mitsubishi Electric America, Inc., 5665 Plaza Dr., 90630, pg. 872 — IT
Mitsubishi Electric Sales America, P.O. Box 6007, 5757 Plaza Dr., 90630, pg. 872 — IT
Mitsubishi Electronics America, 5665 Plaza Dr., 90630, pg. 872 — IT
Mitsubishi Motor Sales of America, Inc., 6400 Katella Ave., 90630, pg. 875 — IT
Mitsubishi Motors Credit of America, Inc., 6363 Katella Ave., 90630, pg. 875 — IT
PACIFICARE HEALTH SYSTEMS, INC., 5995 Plaza Dr., 90630-5028, pg. 1250 — PB
Pacificare of California, 3165 Plaza Dr., 92134, pg. 1118 — PB
PacifiCare of California, 5701 Katella Ave., 90630, pg. 1265 — PB
Toyo Tire (U.S.A.) Corporation, 6415 Katella Ave., 2nd Fl., 90630, pg. 1411 — IT
The Voucher Corporation, 5836 Corporate Ave., Ste. 150, 90630, pg. 21 — IT
Whessoe Varec, 10800 Valley View St., 90630, pg. 1498 — IT

Daggett

Calnev Pipeline Company, P.O. Box 188, 92327, pg. 692 — PB

Daly City

Monterey Construction Company, P.O. Box 1758, 94014-1758, pg. 143 — PB

Dana Point

Downey Savings & Loan Association, F.A., Dana Point Branch, 33621 Del Obispo, Ste. A, 92629, pg. 526 — PB
Surfer Publications, Inc., P.O. Box 1028, 92629, pg. 417 — PV

Danville

James E. Roberts-Obayashi Corporation, 20 Oak Ct., 94526, pg. 995 — IT

Davis

Calgene LLC, 1920 Fifth St., 95616, pg. 1124 — PB
Novo Nordisk Biotech, Inc., 1445 Drew Ave., 95616, pg. 987 — IT
Novo Nordisk Entotech, Inc., 1497 Drew Ave., 95616-4880, pg. 987 — IT
CHUCK SWIFT SALES & LEASING, 1500 Chiles Rd., 95616, pg. 1058 — PV

Del Mar

BV&K Direct, 445 Marine View Ave., Ste. 300, 92014, pg. 108 — PV
Brookfield Homes, 12865 Pointe Del Mar Way, 92014, pg. 228 — IT
Hexcel-Fyfe Company, Inc., 1341 Ocean Ave., 92014, pg. 824 — PB
LAMBESIS, 100 Via de la Valle, 92014, pg. 644 — PV

Di Giorgio

Heck Cellars Winery, 15401 Bear Mountain Winery Rd., 93217, pg. 632 — PV

Diamond Bar

Ahmanson Commercial Development Co., 1370 S. Valley Vista Dr., Ste. 200, 21765, pg. 29 — PB
Riverside Cement Co., P.O. Box 4904, 91765, pg. 1293 — IT
Ssangyong Pacific, P.O. Box 4904, 91765, pg. 1292 — IT

Dinuba

BLUE ANCHOR, INC., 200 N. N St., 93618, pg. 150 — PV
RUIZ FOOD PRODUCTS, INC., 501 S. Alta Ave., 93618, pg. 951 — PV

Dixon

Heil West, Inc., 1450 N. First St., 95620, pg. 521 — PB

Downey

ALL AMERICAN HOME CENTER, 7201 E. Firestone Blvd., 90241, pg. 34 — PV
Boeing North America, Space Systems Division, 12214 Lakewood Blvd., 90241, pg. 241 — PB
Downey Savings & Loan Association, F.A., 8444 Florence Ave., 90241, pg. 526 — PB
DURAY/J.F. DUNCAN INDUSTRIES, INC., 9301 Steward & Gray Rds., 90241, pg. 348 — PV
HUTCHENSON SEAL CORPORATION, 11634 Patton Rd., 90241-5295, pg. 550 — PV
Massey Cadillac, Inc., 10700 Studebaker Rd., 90241, pg. 713 — PV
Massey Chevrolet Geo, Inc., 10700 Studebaker Rd., 90241, pg. 713 — PV

Duarte

Dowty Aerospace, Los Angeles, 1700 Business Center Dr., 91010, pg. 1337 — IT
HTL/Kin-Tech Division, 1800 Highland Ave., 91010, pg. 1250 — PB
VARI TRONICS COMPANY, INC., 2745 E. Huntington Dr., 91010, pg. 1134 — PV
Zack Electronics/Tele-Com Products, Inc., 1070 Hamilton Rd., 91010, pg. 1203 — PV

Dublin

Heat Transfer Systems, P.O. Box 2819, 6747-D Sierra Ct., 94568, pg. 360 — PV
SmithKline Beecham Clinical Laboratories of Northern California, 6511 Golden Gate Dr., 94568, pg. 1265 — IT
STRAW HAT COOPERATIVE CORP., 6400 Village Pkwy., 94568, pg. 1046 — PV

Edison

GIUMARRA VINEYARDS, 11220 Edison Hwy., 93220, pg. 455 — PV

El Cajon

BUCK KNIVES, INC., 1900 Weld Blvd., 92020, pg. 177 — PV
Chartwell Leisure, 1973 Friendship Dr., 92020, pg. 462 — PV
Chem-tronics, Inc., 1150 W. Bradley, 92022, pg. 893 — PB
EG & G Frank Hill Associates, 474 Raleigh Ave., 92020, pg. 543 — PV

EG & G KT Aerofab, 203 N. Johnson Ave., 92020, pg. 542 · PB
Ketema Division, 790 Greenfield Dr., 92021, pg. 1222 · IT
SoniForm, Inc., 1908 Friendship Dr., 92020-1129, pg. 689 · PV
Travelodge, 1973 Friendship Dr., 92020, pg. 322 · PB

El Centro

Republic Automotive Parts Sales, Inc., 641 State St., 92243, pg. 1378 · PB

El Dorado Hills

International Billing Services, 5220 Robert J. Mathews Pkwy., 95762, pg. 1659 · PB
TRACK 'N TRAIL, 4961-A Windplay Dr., 95762, pg. 1626 · PB
WETSEL-OVIATT LUMBER COMPANY, P.O. Box 5530, 95762, pg. 1170 · PV

El Monte

Birtcher, 3445 Fletcher Ave., 91731, pg. 1791 · PB
BROWN JORDAN COMPANY, 9860 Gidley St., 91731, pg. 174 · PV
Cetec Corporation, 9900 Baldwin Place, 91731, pg. 1045 · PB
CHADWICK-HELMUTH COMPANY, INC., 4601 N. Arden Dr., 91731, pg. 227 · PV
CLAYTON INDUSTRIES CO., 4213 N. Temple City Blvd., 91731, pg. 245 · PB
Clayton Manufacturing Div., Dynamic Equipment, 4213 N. Temple City Blvd., 91713, pg. 245 · PV
DBM HATCH, INC., 2304 Troy Ave., 91733, pg. 300 · PV
M.C. GILL CORPORATION, 4056 Easy St., 91731, pg. 453 · PV
GREGG INDUSTRIES, INC., 10460 Hickson St., 91734, pg. 480 · PV
James Jones Company, 4127 Temple City Blvd., 91731, pg. 1650 · PB
KELLER CONSTRUCTION COMPANY LTD., 9950 E. Baldwin Pl., 91734, pg. 612 · PV
MARSHALL INDUSTRIES, 9320 Telstar Ave., 91731-2895, pg. 1051 · PB
MCCONNELL CABINETS, INC., 3017 N. Rumford Ave., 91732-3698, pg. 720 · PV
NAVCOM DEFENSE ELECTRONICS, INC., 4323 N. Arden Dr., 91731-1997, pg. 789 · PV
Pay-Fone Systems, Inc., 9386 Telstar Ave., 91731, pg. 1267 · PB
Sargent-Fletcher Inc., 9400 Flair Dr., 91731, pg. 301 · IT
Signet Scientific Co., P.O. Box 5770, 3401 Aerojet Avenue, 91734-1770, pg. 489 · IT
Texaco Research Center, 329 Durfee Ave., 91733-4398, pg. 1583 · PB

El Segundo

AEROSPACE CORPORATION, 2350 E. El Segundo Blvd., 90245-4691, pg. 24 · PV
Air New Zealand Ltd. (U.S.A.), 1960 E. Grand Ave., 90245, pg. 38 · IT
Aromat Southwest Sales Office, 300 N. Sepulveda Blvd., Ste. 1010, 90245, pg. 848 · IT
AURA SYSTEMS, INC., 2335 Alaska Ave., 90245, pg. 147 · PB
Aviva Sport, Inc., 333 Continental Blvd., 90245, pg. 1058 · PB
BELL INDUSTRIES, INC., 2201 E. El Segundo Blvd., 90245, pg. 204 · PB
Burton Electrical Engineering, 111 Maryland St., 90245, pg. 1193 · PV
COMPUTER SCIENCES CORPORATION, 2100 E. Grand Ave., 90245, pg. 422 · PB
Daher Golden Eagle - Los Angeles, 200 Center St., 90245, pg. 749 · PB
DirecTV Inc., 2230 E. Imperial Hwy., 90245, pg. 720 · PB
Eaton Corporation, Defense Valve and Actuator Division, 2338 Alaska Ave., 90245, pg. 556 · PB
FARR COMPANY, 2201 Park Pl., 90245-4900, pg. 613 · PB
Harco, 557 S. Douglas St., 90245, pg. 187 · PB
Health Care Microsystems, Inc., 200 N. Sepulveda Blvd., Ste. 600, 90245, pg. 802 · PB
IR International Holdings, Inc., 247 Kansas St., 90245, pg. 907 · PB
ITOCHU Aviation, Inc., 222 N. Sepulveda Blvd., Ste. 1400, 90245, pg. 694 · IT
IMPERIAL HOTELS, 2361 Rosecrans Ave., Ste. 375, 90245, pg. 558 · PV
INTERNATIONAL RECTIFIER CORPORATION, 233 Kansas St., 90245, pg. 906 · PB
Kokusai Electric Co., Ltd. America, 363 Coral Circle, 90245, pg. 743 · IT
Mattel Funding Corporation, 333 Continental Blvd., 90245, pg. 1058 · PB
Mattel G, Inc., 333 Continental Blvd., 90245, pg. 1058 · PB
Mattel Games/Puzzles, 333 Continental Blvd., M1-1113, 90245, pg. 1058 · PB
Mattel Holding, Inc., 333 Continental Blvd., 90245, pg. 1058 · PB
Mattel I., Inc., 333 Continental Blvd., 90245, pg. 1058 · PB
MATTEL, INC., 333 Continental Blvd., 90245-5012, pg. 1057 · PB
Mattel International Limited, 333 Continental Blvd., 90245, pg. 1058 · PB
Mattel Overseas, Inc., 333 Continental Blvd., 90245, pg. 1058 · PB
Mattel Realty Corporation, 333 Continental Blvd., 90245, pg. 1058 · PB

MERISEL, INC., 200 Continental Blvd., 90245-0984, pg. 1095 · PB
Military Aircraft Systems Division, One Hornet Way, 90245-2804, pg. 1198 · PB
Polaroid Copy Services, 625 S. Douglas St., 90245-4812, pg. 1313 · PB
Qantas Airways Ltd., 841 Apollo St., Ste. 400, 90245, pg. 1075 · IT
Sensors & Electronic Systems, 2000 E. El Segundo Blvd., 90245-0902, pg. 1365 · PB
Team One Advertising, 1960 E. Grand Ave., Ste. 700, 90245, pg. 1422 · PB
Thai Airways Intl. Ltd.-El Segundo, 1960 E. Grand Ave., Ste. 222, 90245, pg. 1381 · IT
Thai Airways Intl. Ltd.-U.S. Office, 222 N. Sepulveda Blvd., Ste. 1950, 90245, pg. 1381 · IT
UNOCAL CORPORATION, 2141 Rosecrans Ave., Ste. 4000, 90245, pg. 1698 · PB
WYLE LABORATORIES, INC., 128 Maryland St., 90245, pg. 1193 · PV
Wyle Laboratories-Western Operations, 128 Maryland St., 90245, pg. 1193 · PV
Xerox Special Markets Group, 101 Continental Blvd., 90245, pg. 1785 · PB

El Toro

Morgan Matroc Inc.-West Coast Sales Division, 22865 Lake Forest Dr., Ste. 18, 92630, pg. 893 · IT
Motorola Radius, 23861 El Toro Rd., Ste. 209, 92630-4733, pg. 1138 · PB

Elk Grove

Downey Savings & Loan Association, F.A., Elk Grove Branch, 5000 Laguna Blvd., 95758, pg. 526 · PB
MSC Western Regional Office, Bldg. 1, 8788 Elk Grove Blvd., Ste. 1, 95624, pg. 1031 · PB
Stockton Savings Bank-Elk Grove, 9611 Stockton Blvd., 95624, pg. 1575 · PB

Emeryville

Biocine Company, c/o Chiron Corporation, 4560 Horton St., 94608, pg. 973 · PB
The Biocine Company, 4560 Horton St., 94680-2916, pg. 350 · PB
Cetus Oncology, 4560 Horton St., 94608-2916, pg. 350 · PB
CHIRON CORPORATION, 4560 Horton St., 94608-2916, pg. 349 · PB
Chiron Diagnostics, 4560 Horton St., 94608-2916, pg. 350 · PB
Chiron Technologies, 4560 Horton St., 94680-2916, pg. 350 · PB
Chiron Therapeutics, 4560 Horton St., 94608-2916, pg. 350 · PB
ENVIRON International Corporation-Emeryville, 5820 Shellmound St., Ste. 700, 94608, pg. 1285 · PB
IA CORPORATION, 1900 Powell St., Ste. 600, 94608, pg. 553 · PV
NADY SYSTEMS, INC., 6701 Bay St., 94608, pg. 773 · PV
SCOPUS TECHNOLOGY, INC., 1900 Powell St., Ste. 900, 94608, pg. 1444 · PB
Sodexho USA-Westcoast Headquarters, 2000 Powell St., Ste. 950, 94608-1804, pg. 1274 · IT
SYBASE, INC., 6475 Christie Ave., 94608, pg. 1544 · PB
ZD Press, 5903 Christie Ave., 94608, pg. 1276 · IT

Empire

Vilmorin Inc., P.O. Box 707, 95319, pg. 566 · IT

Encinitas

Autodesk, Inc., Rancho Professional Plaza, 2235 Encinitas Blvd., Ste. 111, 92024, pg. 149 · PB
Downey Savings & Loan Association, F.A., 485 Santa Fe Dr., 92024, pg. 526 · PB
PAUL ECKE RANCH, 441 Saxony Rd., 92024, pg. 359 · PV
Equifax National Decision Systems, 539 Encinitas Blvd., 92024, pg. 588 · PB
Media That Works, 11045 Neptune Ave., 92024, pg. 727 · PV

Encino

Bank Leumi le-Israel B.M., 16530 Ventura Blvd., 91436, pg. 150 · IT
Becker CPA Review, 15760 Ventura Blvd., Ste. 1101, 91436, pg. 504 · PB
Benihana Encino Corp., 16226 Ventura Blvd., 91316, pg. 212 · PV
Cinamerica Service Corp., 16530 Ventura Blvd., Ste. 500, 91436, pg. 239 · PV
CINAMERICA THEATRES, L.P., 16530 Ventura Blvd., Ste. 500, 91436, pg. 239 · PV
Dentsply/Implant Division, 15821 Ventura Blvd., Ste. 420, 91436, pg. 499 · PB
Downey Savings & Loan Association, F.A., 17250 Ventura Blvd., 91316, pg. 526 · PB
FIRST FINANCIAL GROUP, INC., 16830 Ventura Blvd., Ste. 401, 91436, pg. 407 · PV
Gelson's Markets, 16400 Ventura Blvd., 91436, pg. 129 · PB
Intergraph Corporation, 15821 Ventura Blvd., Ste. 160, 91436, pg. 891 · PB
LARWIN COMPANY, 16633 Ventura Blvd., Ste. 1300, 91436, pg. 652 · PV
Mann Theatres, P.O. Box 20077, 91416-0077, pg. 239 · PV

Market Facts, Inc., 16133 Ventura Blvd., 91436, pg. 1047 · PB
Pacific Crest Investment & Loan (Encino Branch), 17656 Ventura Blvd., 91316, pg. 1249 · PB
PINKERTON'S INC., 15910 Ventura Blvd., Ste. 900, 91436, pg. 1296 · PV
Rathbone, King & Seeley Insurance Services, 15760 Ventura Blvd., Ste. 1023, 91436, pg. 610 · PV
Rutter Group, 15760 Ventura Blvd., Suite 630, 91436-3011, pg. 1602 · PB
Showcase Technologies, 16255 Ventura Blvd., Ste. 450, 91436, pg. 872 · PV

Escalon

Stockton Savings Bank-Escalon, 1701 Main St., 95320, pg. 1575 · PB

Escondido

A.T.I. Tools, Inc., 2425 W. Vineyard Ave., 92025, pg. 1480 · PB
Advanced Software Concepts, Inc., 2430 Vineyard Ave., Ste. 101, 92029, pg. 1309 · PB
Advanced Structures, Inc., 2181 Meyers Ave., 92029, pg. 592 · PB
Downey Savings & Loan Association, F.A., 2369 E. Valley Parkway, 92027, pg. 526 · PB
Robert F. Driver & Co., Inc., 420 S. Broadway, 92025, pg. 343 · PV
Ferro Msi, 2310 Aldergrove Ave., 92029-1935, pg. 619 · PB
Hawthorne Lift Systems, 1330A Mission Rd., 92029, pg. 513 · PV
Pacific Pride Bakeries, 2069 Aldergrove Ave., 92029, pg. 575 · IT
Palomar Systems, Inc., 2310 Aldergrove Ave., 92029-1935, pg. 1285 · PB
POLESTAR LABS, INC., 955 S. Andreasen Dr., 92902, pg. 874 · PV
San Diego Wild Animal Park, 15500 San Pasqual Valley Rd., 92027, pg. 1207 · PV
Structural North America, 2181 Meyers Ave., 92029, pg. 593 · PB
WARREN PROPERTIES, P.O. Box 469114, 92025, pg. 1151 · PV

Eureka

Arcata Redwood Company, 5151 Highway 101 N., 95501, pg. 1003 · PV
Cox Communications-Humboldt Bay, 911 W. Wabash, 95501, pg. 454 · PB
General Hospital, 2200 Harrison Ave., 95501, pg. 169 · PV
Simpson Redwood Company, 5151 Hwy. 101, 95501, pg. 1003 · PV
Utility Tree Service, 104 W. Street, 95501, pg. 119 · PV
Zellerbach Division, 1030 W. Del Norte St., 95501, pg. 1075 · PB

Exeter

JACK GRIGGS INC., 1149 S. Kaweah, 93221, pg. 482 · PV
Sequoia-Pacific Systems Corp., 1030 N. Anderson Rd., 93221, pg. 1270 · IT

Fairfield

BOC Coating Technologies, 2700 Maxwell Way, 94533, pg. 121 · IT
BOC Coating Technology, 2700 Maxwell Way, 94533, pg. 121 · IT
Household Products, 2600 Huntington Dr., 94533, pg. 387 · PB
OEA Aerospace, Inc., ET Rd. & Hwy. 12, 94533, pg. 1207 · PB
URS Greiner, Inc., 1455 Oliver Rd., Ste. 200, 94533, pg. 1658 · PB
WESTAMERICA BANCORPORATION, 4550 Mangels Blvd., 94585-1200, pg. 1756 · PB

Fallbrook

Overly Manufacturing, 1501 S. Mission Rd., 92028, pg. 823 · PV

Fillmore

Ameron Pole Products & Systems, 1020 B St., 93015, pg. 99 · PB

Folsom

L3 Communications Narda-Microwave West Div., 107 Woodmere Rd., 95630, pg. 638 · PV
OBJECTIVE SYSTEMS INTEGRATORS, INC., 100 Blue Ravine Rd., 95630, pg. 1209 · PB
West Coast Correct Craft, Inc., Three Auto-Plaza Dr., Bldg. B, 95630, pg. 277 · PV

Fontana

AMI Metals, Inc., 10606 Commerce Way, 92337, pg. 1375 · PB
AMICO-West Distr. Center, 11093 Beech St., 92335, pg. 30 · PV
Curtis 1000, Inc., 10887 Commerce Way, Ste. A, 92337-3730, pg. 70 · PB

PB - *U.S. Public Companies Volume*
PV - *U.S. Private Companies Volume*
IT - *International Public & Private Companies Volume*

Dart Trucking Company, Inc., 10505 Almond Ave., 92335, pg. 94 **PB**
Flo-Pac Pacific, 11690 Pacific Ave., 92337, pg. 414 **PV**
Fontana, 131 Marlay Ave., 92335, pg. 730 **PB**
James Hardie Building Products Inc., 10901 Elm Ave., 92335, pg. 597 **IT**
NIBCO, 10516 Commerce Way, 92337, pg. 798 **PV**
Pacific Forge, Inc., 10641 Etiwanda Ave., 92337, pg. 102 **PV**
Plasti-Line West, 13489 Slover Ave., Bldg. B, 92337, pg. 1309 **PB**
Premier Metal Products, 16641 Orange Way, 92335, pg. 881 **PV**
SCRIPTO-TOKAI CORP., 11591 Etiwanda Ave., 92337, pg. 977 **PV**
Southern California Auto Auction, 10700 Beech Ave., 92335, pg. 282 **PV**

Fort Bragg

West Coast Redwood Sawmill, 90 W. Redwood Ave., 95437, pg. 739 **PB**

Foster City

Applied Biosystems, 850 Lincoln Ctr. Dr., 94404, pg. 1279 **PB**
Bull Data AB, 323 Vintage Park Dr., 94404, pg. 317 **IT**
Diab Data Inc., 323 Vintage Park Dr., 94404, pg. 317 **IT**
Ebara America Corporation, 1065 E. Hillsdale Blvd., Ste. 215, 94404, pg. 431 **IT**
Foster's Landing, 700 Bounty Dr., 94404, pg. 163 **PV**
Hewlett-Packard Company, 353 Lakeside Dr., Ste. B, 94404, pg. 813 **PB**
IDG Books Worldwide, 919 E. Hillsdale, 4th. Fl., 94404, pg. 569 **PV**
Information Access Co., 362 Lakeside Dr., 94404, pg. 1600 **PV**
KAISER AEROSPACE & ELECTRONICS CORP., 950 Tower Ln., Ste. 800, 94404, pg. 605 **PV**
LINC Quantum Analytics, 363 Vintage Park Dr., 94404, pg. 996 **PV**
Lincoln Property Co., Northern California, 101 Lincoln Center Dr., 94404, pg. 668 **PV**
LYON'S RESTAURANTS, INC., 1165 Triton Dr., 94404, pg. 684 **PV**
MacUser, 110 Marsh Dr., Ste. 250, 94404, pg. 1276 **IT**
Otari Corporation, 378 Vintage Park Drive, 94404, pg. 1013 **IT**
Oxford Instruments, 331c Lakeside Dr., 94404, pg. 1018 **IT**
PC Computing, 950 Tower Lane, 94404, pg. 1276 **IT**
RUDOLPH AND SLETTEN, INC., 989 E. Hillsdale Blvd., 94404, pg. 950 **PV**
Tosoh Medics, Inc., 373 Vintage Park Dr. Ste. D, 94404, pg. 1407 **IT**
Varilux Corporation, 363 Vintage Pk. Dr., 94404, pg. 462 **IT**

Fountain Valley

AST Research Inc., 17665 Newhope, 92728, pg. 1182 **IT**
ANDIAMO, INC., 11520 Warner Ave., 92708, pg. 73 **PV**
ASICS TIGER CORPORATION, 10540 Talbert Ave., 92708, pg. 89 **PV**
Downey Savings & Loan Association, F.A., 17150 Magnolia Ave., 92708, pg. 526 **PB**
4DAY TIRE STORES, 16650 Harbor Blvd., 92708, pg. 421 **PV**
Gerard L. Greer Co., 11175 Condor Ave., 92708, pg. 891 **PV**
Hyundai Motor America, 10550 Talbert Ave., 92728, pg. 641 **IT**
Hyundai Motor America Western Regional Office, 10550 Talbert, 92708, pg. 641 **IT**
KINGSTON TECHNOLOGY CORPORATION, 17600 Newhope St., 92708, pg. 622 **PV**
PM Group Life Insurance Company, 17360 Brookhurst St., 92708-3755, pg. 831 **PV**
Southern California Service Center, 17150 Newhope St., Ste. 502, 92708, pg. 829 **PV**
Sycamore Valley, 10349 Slater Ave., 92708, pg. 163 **PB**
Systems Tax Service, Inc., 17390 Brookhurst Street, 90021, pg. 331 **PB**

Fremont

ASI CORP., 48289 Fremont Blvd., 94538, pg. 8 **PV**
Access Business Unit, 45550 Northport Loop E., 94538, pg. 1568 **PB**
Altron Systems Corporation, 48621 Warm Springs Blvd., 94539, pg. 59 **PB**
Apex Data, 4305 Cushing Pkwy., 94538, pg. 1476 **PB**
ASCOR, Inc., 47790 Westinghouse Dr., 94539, pg. 743 **PB**
AVANTI, 46871 Bayside Pkwy., 94538, pg. 151 **PB**
Bentley & Bentley, 113 Auburn, 94539-0417, pg. 1186 **PV**
Big Valley Marketing Corp., 1133 Auburn, 94539-0417, pg. 1186 **PV**
CXR Telcom Corporation, 47233 Freemont Blvd., 94536, pg. 1108 **PV**
Cablelink-California, 41946 Christy St., 94538, pg. 1394 **PB**
California Microwave-TeleCom Transmission Systems, Inc., pg. 293 **PB**
CIRRUS LOGIC, INC., 3100 W. Warren Ave. Dr., 94538, pg. 375 **PB**
Computer Products, National Accounts Division, 3797 Spinnaker Ct., 94538, pg. 422 **PB**
Cyantek Corporation, 3055 Osgood Court, 94538, pg. 802 **IT**

DSP TECHNOLOGY INC., 48500 Kato Rd., 94538-7385, pg. 475 **PB**
Dexter Magnetic Materials, 48460 Kato Rd., 94538-7337, pg. 504 **PB**
Downey Savings & Loan Association, F.A. 41298 Paseo Padre Pkwy., 94539, pg. 527 **PB**
DYWIDAG Systems International, USA, Inc., 39059 Guardino Dr., Ste. 107, 94538, pg. 424 **IT**
EFI Corporation, 5357 Randall Pl., 94538, pg. 1082 **IT**
ELMA Electronic Inc., 4435 Grimmer Blvd., 94538-6385, pg. 1305 **IT**
Elo TouchSystems, Inc., 41752 Christy St., 94538, pg. 1362 **IT**
Everex Systems Inc., 5020 Brandin Ct., 94538, pg. 498 **IT**
EXAR CORPORATION, 48720 Kato Rd., 94538, pg. 597 **PB**
Fremont Division, 44250 Osgood Rd., 94539, pg. 518 **PB**
Fuji Hi-Tech, 47520 Westinghouse Dr., 94538, pg. 522 **IT**
GATEFIELD CORPORATION, 47100 Bayside Pkwy., 94538-9942, pg. 703 **PB**
General Signal Thinfilm Company, 48603 Warm Spring Blvd., 94539, pg. 727 **PB**
Golden Gate Auto Auction Inc., 6700 Stevenson Blvd., 94538, pg. 1649 **PB**
Stephen Gould of California, 45541 Northport Loop W., 94538, pg. 467 **PV**
HMT TECHNOLOGY CORPORATION, 1055 Page Ave., 94538-7342, pg. 771 **PB**
IPC Peripherals, Inc., 48041 Fremont Blvd., 94538, pg. 651 **PV**
Kao Infosystems Company, 800 Corporate Way, 94538, pg. 717 **IT**
Kaufman and Broad-South Bay Inc., 2201 Walnut St., Ste. 150, 94538, pg. 945 **PV**
Lafayette Precast, 4177 Boyce Rd., 94538, pg. 1149 **PV**
LAM RESEARCH CORPORATION, 4650 Cushing Pkwy., 94538, pg. 975 **PB**
LOGISTIX, 48021 Warm Springs Blvd., 94539, pg. 673 **PV**
Logitech Inc., 6505 Kaiser Dr., 94555, pg. 815 **IT**
Lucas NovaSensor Inc., 1055 Mission Ct., 94539, pg. 820 **IT**
Makita U.S.A. Inc.-San Francisco, 41850 Christy St., 94538-5107, pg. 831 **IT**
MATTSON TECHNOLOGY, INC., 3550 W. Warren Ave., 94538, pg. 1060 **PB**
Maxoptix Corp., 3342 Gateway Blvd., 94538, pg. 762 **IT**
McKenzie Technology, 910 Page Ave., 94538, pg. 776 **IT**
MedaSonics, Inc., 47233 Fremont Blvd., 94539-4903, pg. 1225 **IT**
MEN'S WEARHOUSE, 40650 Encyclopedia Cir., 94538, pg. 1086 **PB**
MICRONICS COMPUTERS, INC., 45365 Northport Loop W., 94538, pg. 1106 **PB**
MYLEX CORPORATION, 34551 Ardenwood Blvd., 94555, pg. 1143 **PB**
Network Power & Light, 34551 Ardenwood Blvd., 94555, pg. 1144 **PB**
New United Motor Manufacturing Inc., 45500 Fremont Blvd., 94538, pg. 1413 **PV**
Nitto Denko America, Inc., 48500 Fremount Blvd., 94538, pg. 950 **IT**
Penright!, 47358 Fremont Blvd., 94538-6501, pg. 1573 **PB**
Performance Elastomers Division, 326 E. Warren Ave., 94538, pg. 689 **PB**
The Pilot Corporation of America, 4200 Business Dr., 94538, pg. 1057 **IT**
Power Conversion-North America West, 173 Benicia St., 94538, pg. 422 **PB**
PREMISYS COMMUNICATIONS, INC., 48664 Milmont Dr., 94538, pg. 1323 **PB**
QUINTUS CORPORATION, 47212 Mission Falls Ct., 94538, pg. 901 **PV**
Read-Rite Corporation, 44100 Osgood Rd., 94538, pg. 1367 **PB**
Red Hawk Ranch, 1401 Red Hawk Cir., 94538, pg. 163 **PB**
Rehabilitation & Nursing Care Center, 2400 Parkside Dr., 94536, pg. 733 **PV**
Robinson Nugent, Inc., 41946 Christy St., 94538, pg. 1394 **PB**
SEEQ TECHNOLOGY INC., 47200 Bayside Pkwy., 94538, pg. 1417 **PB**
Seagate Recording Media, 47010 Kato Rd., 94538, pg. 1421 **PB**
SEE Technologies Inc., 47823 Westinghouse Dr., 94539, pg. 1421 **PB**
SIGMA DESIGNS, INC., 46501 Landing Pkwy., 94538, pg. 1472 **PB**
SMART MODULAR TECHNOLOGIES, 4305 Cushing Pkwy., 94538, pg. 1476 **PB**
StarSight Telecast, Inc., 39650 Liberty St., 3rd Fl., 94538, pg. 705 **PB**
Sumitomo Sitix Silicon, Inc., 49090 Milmont Drive, 94538, pg. 1317 **IT**
Supply Point, Inc., 46360 Fremont Blvd., 94538-6406, pg. 1186 **PV**
SYQUEST TECHNOLOGY, INC., 47071 Bayside Pkwy., 94538, pg. 1550 **PB**
Sysco Food Services of San Francisco, Inc., 5900 Stewart Ave., 94538, pg. 1552 **PB**
TASHA, 43285 Auto Mall Cir., 94538-3186, pg. 1069 **PV**
Terminal Division, 4181 Business Center Dr., 94538-6355, pg. 563 **PV**
TRIGON ADCOTECH, 41332 Christy St., 94538-3115, pg. 1103 **PV**
Valmark Industries, Inc., 3393 West Warren Ave., 94538, pg. 598 **PV**
Viking Semiconductor Equipment, Inc., 44249 Old Warm Springs Blvd., 94538, pg. 743 **PB**

VISIONEER, INC., 34800 Campus Dr., 94555, pg. 1722 **PB**
WALTERS & WOLF, 41450 Boscell Rd., 94538, pg. 1149 **PV**
ZITEL CORPORATION, 47211 Bayside Pkwy., 94538, pg. 1793 **PB**

French Camp

Granite Construction Inc.-Stockton Div., 10500 S. Harlan Rd., 95231, pg. 759 **PB**

Fresno

ATAPCO Globe-Weis/Fresno, 2851 E. Florence St., 93721, pg. 64 **PV**
Atcot Corp., Inc., 211 W. Shields, 93705, pg. 300 **IT**
Bergen Brunswig Drug Company, 4586 E. Commerce Ave., 93725, pg. 213 **PB**
CAL EMBLEM LABELS, INC., 4790 W. Jacquelyn Ave., 93722, pg. 199 **PV**
Calwest Compress & Warehouse Co., Inc., 4254 N. Weber Ave., 93722, pg. 694 **IT**
DC Company, 5180 N. Channing, 93711, pg. 736 **PB**
DANISH CREAMERY ASSOCIATION, 755 F St., 93706, pg. 310 **PV**
David & Sons, 5626 E. Shields, 93727, pg. 917 **IT**
Dow CHEM Co.- Fresno Plant, 4787 E. Date Ave., 93725-2102, pg. 523 **PB**
Dunavant Enterprises, 8225 N. Fresno St., 93720, pg. 346 **PV**
EMCON Associates, 4233 W. Sierra Madre Ave., #109, 93711, pg. 571 **PB**
Farmers Insurance Group, 4944 E. Clinton Way Ste. 112, 93727-1527, pg. 111 **IT**
Fiserv Fresno, Inc., 1385 E. Shaw, 93710, pg. 647 **PB**
Fleming Foods West - Fresno Div., 2797 S. Orange, 93772, pg. 653 **PB**
Fresno Auto Dealers Auction, 278 N. Marks, 93706, pg. 282 **PV**
The Fresno Bee, 1626 E St., 93786, pg. 1065 **PV**
GOTTSCHALKS INC., Seven River Park Pl. E., 93720, pg. 754 **PB**
Hewlett-Packard Company, 1907 N. Gateway Blvd., 93727, pg. 813 **PB**
Higgins Fresno Operations, 4734 E. Jensen Ave., 93725, pg. 527 **PV**
Hilb, Rogal and Hamilton Insurance Services of Central California, Inc., 265 W. Bullard, Ste. 101, 93704, pg. 827 **PB**
Hydro Conduit Corp., 4150 North Brawley, 93722, pg. 245 **IT**
KFSN-TV, 1777 G St., 93706, pg. 512 **PB**
Mercury Air Center, 5045 E. Anderson Ave., 932707, pg. 1093 **PB**
Occupational Health Associates-North, 6042 N. Fresno St., Ste. 101, 93710, pg. 1715 **PB**
Occupational Health Associates-South, 1235 E St., 93706, pg. 1715 **PB**
PDM Steel Service Center-Fresno, 4005 E. Church St., 93725, pg. 1305 **PB**
Piper Jaffray Inc., 7108 N. Fresno St., Ste. 410, 93720-9955, pg. 1303 **PB**
RANCHERS COTTON OIL, 2691 S. Cedar Ave., 93725, pg. 908 **PV**
Rathbone, King & Seeley Insurance Services, 2547 W. Shaw Ave., Ste. 113, 93711, pg. 610 **PB**
STAR FINE FOODS, INC., 4652 E. Date Ave., 93725, pg. 1034 **PV**
Stockton Savings Bank-Fresno, 1015 W. Shaw Ave., 93711, pg. 1575 **PB**
Sunrise Medical Mobility Products, 2842 Business Park Ave., 93727, pg. 1536 **PB**
TODCO Door Div., 4771 E. Date Ave., 93725, pg. 823 **PV**
The Twin Cities Times/Riverdale Free Press, 2357 W. Tahoe, 93609, pg. 1343 **PV**
Ulbrich of California, Inc., 5455 E. Home Ave., 93727, pg. 1115 **PV**
Uniroyal Chemical Co., Inc,, 1530 E. Shaw, Ste. 105, 93710, pg. 460 **IT**
United States Cold Storage of Calif., 2003 S. Cherry St., 93718, pg. 1125 **PV**
Valley Fig Growers, 2028 S. Third St., 93718, pg. 1051 **PV**
The Vendo Company, 7209 N. Ingram Ave., 93650, pg. 1184 **IT**
Vendo International Div., 7209 No. Ingram, 93650, pg. 1184 **IT**
WEATHER TEC CORPORATION, 5645 E. Clinton Ave., 93727, pg. 1155 **PV**
Weir Floway Inc., 2494 S. Railroad Ave., P.O. Box 164, 93707, pg. 1489 **IT**
Westair Commuter Airlines, Inc., 5588 Air Corp Way, 93727, pg. 1099 **PB**
Zellerbach Division, 4603 E. Vine St., 93725, pg. 1075 **PB**

Fullerton

AEI HOLDING CO., INC., 1600 E. Valencia Dr., 92631, pg. 4 **PV**
American Electronics, Inc., 1600 E. Valencia Dr., 92631, pg. 5 **PV**
Beckman Industrial Corporation, 4200 Bonita Pl., 92635, pg. 574 **PB**
BECKMAN INSTRUMENTS, INC., 2500 Harbor Blvd., 92834-3100, pg. 199 **PB**
Carriage House Manor, 245 E. Wilshire, 92632, pg. 733 **PV**
D/B Cameras Microcheck Division, 1600 E. Valencia Dr., 92631, pg. 5 **PV**

PB - *U.S. Public Companies Volume*
PV - *U.S. Private Companies Volume*
IT - *International Public & Private Companies Volume*

1128

Geographic Index-U.S.

Electro-Mechanical Instruments Div., 1600 E. Valencia Dr., 92631, pg. 5 PV
Engineered Construction-Fullerton, 2600 E. Nutwood Ave., Ste. 750, 92631, pg. 1304 PB
Favorite Foods, Inc., 1901 E. Via Burton, 92634, pg. 1527 PB
Grinnell Supply Sales Division, 801 S. Placentia Ave., 92631-5154, pg. 1648 PB
Ground Systems Group, P.O. Box 3310, 92634-3310, pg. 1364 PB
Harte-Hanks Direct Mail/California, 2337 W. Commonwealth Ave., 92633, pg. 794 PB
Hewlett-Packard Company, 1421 S. Manhattan Ave., 92631, pg. 813 PB
Hunt-Wesson Consumer Advertising Div., 1645 W. Valencia Dr., 92634, pg. 428 PB
Hunt-Wesson Foodservice Division, 1645 W. Valencia Dr., 92634, pg. 428 PB
Hunt-Wesson Grocery Sales Division, 1645 W. Valencia Dr., 92634, pg. 428 PB
Hunt-Wesson, Inc., 1645 W. Valencia Dr., 92833, pg. 428 PB
Hunt-Wesson Marketing Services Division, 1645 W. Valencia Dr., 92634, pg. 428 PB
Hunt-Wesson Refrigerated Foods Div., 1645 W. Valencia Dr., 92634, pg. 426 PB
Hunt-Wesson Tomato Products Division, 1645 W. Valencia Dr., 92634, pg. 428 PB
J. Hungerford Smith Company, 1645 W. Valencia Dr., 92833, pg. 428 PB
JONATHAN MANUFACTURING CORP., 1101 S. Acacia Ave., 92631, pg. 595 PV
Kaynar/K-Fast/APS, 800 S. State College Blvd., 92834, pg. 940 PB
LABEL-AIRE INC., 550 Burning Tree Rd., 92633, pg. 641 PV
Nelco Products, Inc., 1411 E. Orangethorpe Ave., 92633, pg. 1258 PB
North American Enclosures, Inc., 1401 E. Orange Thorpe Ave., 92631, pg. 803 PV
Penhall Diamond Products Company, 1345 S. Acacia Ave., 92631, pg. 1176 IT
Plastic Suppliers Inc., 2340 E. Walnut Ave., 92831, pg. 871 PV
Precision Power Div., 1600 E. Valencia Dr., 92634, pg. 5 PV
Ropak Corporation, 660 S. State College Blvd., 92631, pg. 811 IT
Weber Aircraft, Inc., 1300 E. Valencia Dr., 92831, pg. 572 IT
Wesson/Peter Pan Foods Co., 1645 W. Valencia Dr., 92634, pg. 428 PB
Wolf Brand Products, Mail Station 848, 1645 W. Valencia Dr., 92833, pg. 428 PB
Yokohama Corporation of America, 601 S. Acacia Ave., 92631, pg. 1521 IT
Yokohama Tire Corporation, 601 S. Acacia Ave., 92834-4550, pg. 1521 IT

Garden Grove

Accord Contract Services, 12442 Knott Ave., 92841, pg. 1458 IT
AIR INDUSTRIES CORPORATION, 12570 Knott St., 92641, pg. 28 PV
Cosmar Corp., 11700 Monarch St., 92841, pg. 922 PV
Costco, Inc.-Los Angeles Region, 11000 Garden Grove, #201, 92643, pg. 452 PB
Data Aire, Inc., 7442 Orangewood, 92675, pg. 266 PV
Gregg Foods of Garden Grove, Inc., 12572 Monarch St., 92641, pg. 158 PV
Linfinity Microelectronics Inc., 11861 Western Ave., 92641-2119, pg. 1547 PB
New Hermes Inc.-West Coast, 11711 Monarch St., 92641, pg. 794 PV
RICHEY ELECTRONICS, INC., 7441 Lincoln Way, Ste. 100, 92641, pg. 1388 PB
Ssangyong Engineering & Construction (America), Inc., 12101 Western Ave., 92641, pg. 1292 IT
Ssangyong International Inc., 12101 Western Ave., 92641, pg. 1292 IT
Ssangyong Sacramento Ltd., 12101 Western Ave., 92641, pg. 1292 IT
Subaru Research & Design, Inc., 12601 Western Ave., 92641, pg. 523 IT
Todd Pipe & Supply Garden Grove, 13591 Harbor Blvd., 92643, pg. 1090 PV

Gardena

AHF-Ducommun Incorporated, 131 E. Gardena Blvd., 90247, pg. 534 PB
AMELCO CORPORATION, 19208 S. Vermont Ave., 90248, pg. 65 PB
American Marketing Work, Inc., 14501 S. Figueroa St., 90248, pg. 1472 PB
APPAREL VENTURES, INC., 204 W. Rosecrans, 90248, pg. 78 PV
Asatsu America Inc., 1411 W. 190th St., Ste. 570, 90248, pg. 86 IT
Astro Business Solutions, Inc., 110 W. Walnut St., 90248, pg. 262 IT
BARCO OF CALIFORNIA, 350 W. Roscrans Ave., 90248, pg. 115 PV
Beemak Plastics, 16639 South Gramercy Pl., 90247, pg. 598 PV
BENJAMIN METALS COMPANY, 14400 S. Figueroa St., 90248, pg. 133 PV
Camino Real Foods, Inc., 2001 W. Rosecrans Ave., 90249, pg. 949 IT
Clarion Corporation of America, 661 W. Redondo Beach Blvd., 90247, pg. 296 IT
Clarion Sales Corporation, 661 W. Redondo Beach Blvd., 90247, pg. 296 IT
COASTCAST CORPORATION, 14831 Maple Ave., 90247, pg. 391 PB
Cosco Fire Protection Inc., 321 E. Gardena Blvd., 90247, pg. 1795 PB
Dean Industries, Inc., 14501 S. Broadway, 90248, pg. 188 IT
Deutsch Metal Components, 14800 S. Figueroa St., 90248, pg. 328 PV
ERNST W. DORN CO., INC., 15905 S. Broadway, 90248, pg. 340 PV
E-Z Lok, 240 E. Rosencrans Ave., 90247-0069, pg. 1063 PV
ELIXIR INDUSTRIES, 17925 S. Broadway, 90248, pg. 371 PV
The Emmac, Inc., 1025 W. 190th St., Ste. 215, 90248, pg. 364 IT
Freeman Products West, 14700 S. San Pedro St., 90248, pg. 1105 PV
FROZFRUIT CORPORATION, 14805 S. San Pedro St., 90248, pg. 430 PV
Garden Insurance Companies, 17809 S. Broadway, 90248, pg. 371 PV
Charles Leonard Western, Inc., 13130 S. Normandie Ave., 90249, pg. 660 PV
Lilly Industries, Inc., 210 E. Alondra Blvd., 90248, pg. 995 PB
LORBER INDUSTRIES OF CALIFORNIA, 17908 S. Figueroa St., 90248, pg. 675 PV
J.W. Miller Div., 306 E. Alondra Blvd., 90221, pg. 205 PB
Nissan Motor Corporation in U.S.A., 18501 S. Figueroa St., 90248, pg. 945 IT
Nissin Foods (U.S.A.) California Plant, 2001 W. Rosecrans Ave., 90249, pg. 949 IT
Nissin Foods (U.S.A.) Co. Ltd., 2001 W. Rosecrans Ave., 90249, pg. 949 IT
NITEC (U.S.A.), Inc., 2001 W. Rosecrans Ave., 90249, pg. 950 IT
OVERTON MOORE & ASSOCIATES, 1125 W. 190th St., Ste. 200, 90248, pg. 823 PV
Pace Die Cast Products, Inc., 621 W. Rosecrans Ave., 90248, pg. 986 PB
Pacific Electricord Co., 747 W. Redondo Beach Blvd., 90247, pg. 663 PV
Removal, Inc., P.O. Box 2348, 90247, pg. 264 PB
Rotational Molding, Inc., 17038 S. Figueroa St., 90248, pg. 1406 PB
Rotoflow Corporation, 540 E. Rosecrans Ave., 90248, pg. 96 IT
ROTONICS MANUFACTURING INC., 17022 S. Figeroa St., 90248, pg. 1406 PB
Southern California Air Gas, 1122 W. Rosecrans Ave., 90247, pg. 33 PB
SWIFT-COR TOOL ENGINEERING, 344 W. 157th St., 90248, pg. 1058 PV
TCI ALUMINUM, 240 E. Rosecrans Ave., 90248, pg. 1063 PV
Tulon Co., 15209 S. Broadway, 90248, pg. 594 PB
WEISS SHEET METAL COMPANY, 1715 W. 135th St., 90249, pg. 1160 PV

Gilroy

Gilroy Dispatch, P.O. Box 22365, 6400 Monterey Street, 95021, pg. 225 PV
Gilroy Energy Company, 1400 Pacheco Pass Hwy., 95020, pg. 296 PB
Gilroy Foods, Inc., 1350 Pacheco Pass Hwy., 95020, pg. 428 PB
NOB HILL GENERAL STORE, INC., 200 E. Tenth St., 95020, pg. 799 PV
South Valley National Bank, 8000 Santa Teresa Blvd., 95020, pg. 1248 PB

Glendale

Adams Rite Sabre International, 540 W. Chevy Chase Dr., 91204, pg. 1203 PV
Advanced Risk Management Services, 801 N. Brand Blvd., Ste. 400, 91203, pg. 1505 IT
AIR CONDITIONING CO., INC., 6265 San Fernando Rd., 91201, pg. 28 PV
Airport Group International, Inc., 330 N. Brand Blvd., Ste. 300, 91203, pg. 1009 PB
Baskin-Robbins Incorporated, 31 Baskin-Robbins Pl., 91201, pg. 63 IT
Baskin-Robbins International Co., 31 Baskin-Robbins Pl., 91201, pg. 63 IT
Baskin-Robbins USA Co., 31 Baskin-Robbins Pl., 91201, pg. 63 IT
Baxter-Hyland, 550 N. Brand Blvd., 14th Fl., 91203, pg. 196 PB
A. Biederman, Inc., 1425 Grant Central Ave., 91201, pg. 1640 PB
COP COMMUNICATIONS, 620 W. Elk Ave., 91204-1404, pg. 196 PV
California Offset Printers, Inc., 620 W. Elk Ave., 91204-1404, pg. 196 PV
Carnation Grocery Products Div., 800 N. Brand Blvd., 91203, pg. 916 IT
Carnation Products Div., 800 N. Brand Blvd., 91203, pg. 916 IT
Cigna Healthcare of California, Inc., 505 N. Brand Blvd., Ste. 400, 91203, pg. 359 PB
Citadel Realty, Inc., P.O. Box 1631, 91209-1631, pg. 456 PB
Contadina Dalla Casa Buitoni, 800 Brand Blvd., 91203, pg. 916 IT
Contadina Fresh, 800 N. Brand St., 91203, pg. 918 IT
Courtaulds Aerospace, P.O. Box 1800, 91209, pg. 339 IT
Culinary Foods Group, 800 N. Brand Blvd., 91203, pg. 917 IT
DMR Group, Inc., 550 N. Brand Blvd., Ste. 1060, 91203, pg. 528 IT
Walt Disney Imagineering, 1401 Flower St., 91221-5020, pg. 513 PB
Earthrise Farms, 418 Magnolia AVe., 91204, pg. 369 IT
EXECUTIVE SOFTWARE, 701 N. Brand Blvd., 91203-1242, pg. 388 PV
First American Title Co. of Los Angeles, 520 N. Central Ave., 91203, pg. 625 PB
Food Services Division, 800 N. Brand Blvd., 91203, pg. 917 IT
Foreign Trade Division, 800 N. Brand Blvd., 91203, pg. 917 IT
Friskies PetCare Div., 800 N. Brand St., 91203, pg. 917 IT
GLENDALE FEDERAL BANK, F.S.B., P.O. Box 1709, 91209, pg. 747 PB
Glendale Memorial Hospital and Medical Center, 1420 Central & Los Feliz, 91204-2594, pg. 1118 PV
GLENFED Brokerage Services, 700 N. Brand Blvd., Ste. 220, 91203, pg. 747 PB
GLENFED Insurance Services, Inc., 413 North Brand Blvd., 91203, pg. 747 PB
Herff Jones Photography, 2219 Broadview Dr., 91208-1395, pg. 524 PV
IHOP CORP., 525 N. Brand Blvd., 3rd Fl., 91203, pg. 862 PB
IHOP Realty Corp., 525 N. Brand Blvd., 3rd Fl., 91203, pg. 862 PB
International House of Pancakes, Inc., 525 N. Brand Blvd., 3rd Fl., 91203-1903, pg. 862 PB
Lockheed Martin Librascope, 811 Sonora Ave., 91201-2433, pg. 1008 PB
MCC Behavioral Care of California, Inc., 801 N. Brand Blvd., Ste. 1150, 91203, pg. 362 PB
Mason Electric Company, 440 W. Los Feliz Rd., 91204, pg. 127 IT
MINARIK CORP, 905 E. Thompson St., 91201, pg. 749 PV
Nestle Beverage Company, 800 N. Brand Ave., 18th Fl., 91203, pg. 917 IT
Nestle Chocolate & Confection, 800 North Brand Blvd., 91203, pg. 917 IT
Nestle USA, 800 N. Brand Blvd., 91203, pg. 916 IT
Pasta & Cheese, Inc., 800 N. Brand Blvd., 91203, pg. 918 IT
Products Research & Chemical Corp., Semco Division, 5454 San Fernando Rd., 91203, pg. 339 IT
Public Storage Commercial Properties Group, Inc., 600 N. Brant Blvd., Ste. 300, 91203, pg. 1341 PB
PUBLIC STORAGE, INC., 701 Western Ave., Ste. 200, 91201-2397, pg. 1340 PB
Ross-Loos Health Plan of California, 505 N. Brand Blvd., Ste. 300, 91203, pg. 359 PB
TA Mfg. Co., 375 W. Arden Ave., 91203, pg. 594 PB
Transo Envelope Co./Glendale, 6501 San Fernando Rd., 91201, pg. 1077 PV
Van Deventer & Hoch, 800 N. Brand Blvd., 91203, pg. 339 PB
West Coast Creative, 1100A Airway, 91201, pg. 503 PB
Willis Corroon Aerospace-Western Region, 801 N. Brand Blvd., Ste. 400, 91203, pg. 1505 IT
Willis Corroon Corp. of Los Angeles, 801 N. Brand Blvd., Ste. 400, 91203, pg. 1506 IT
Willis Corroon Financial Services Corp., 801 N. Brand Blvd., Ste. 400, 91203, pg. 1507 IT
Willis Corroon International/Americas, 801 N. Brand Blvd., Ste. 400, 91203, pg. 1507 IT
Willis Corroon Japan Limited, 801 N. Brand Blvd., Ste. 400, 91203, pg. 1509 IT
Willis Corroon Marine & Energy, 801 N. Brand Blvd., Ste. 400, 91203, pg. 1508 IT
Wirth Gas Equipment, Inc., 1233 W. Glenoaks Blvd., 91201, pg. 360 PV
ZMP, INC., 540 W. Chevy Chase Dr., 91204-1814, pg. 1203 PV

Glendora

California State Bank-Glendora, 655 S. Grand Ave., pg. 294 PB
CALTROL, INC., 2011 E. Financial Way, 91741, pg. 201 PV
MILLHOUSE GROUP, 1160 Nicole Ct., 91740, pg. 748 PV
Onoda U.S.A., Inc., 2025 E. Financial Way, 91741, pg. 284 IT
RAIN BIRD SPRINKLERS MANUFACTURING CORP., 145 N. Grand, 91741, pg. 907 PV
Sybron Dental Specialties, Inc., 1332 S. Lone Hill Ave., 91740, pg. 1545 PB
Treasure Chest Advertising Co., Inc., 511 W. Citrus Edge, 91740, pg. 228 PB

Gold River

Sacramento Branch Office, 2366 Gold Meadow Way, Ste. 110, 95670, pg. 1683 PB

Goleta

APPLIED MAGNETICS CORPORATION, 75 Robin Hill Rd., 93117, pg. 123 PB
Cox Communications-Santa Barbara, 22 S. Fairview, 93117, pg. 455 PB

Geographic Index-U.S.

PB - *U.S. Public Companies Volume*
PV - *U.S. Private Companies Volume*
IT - *International Public & Private Companies Volume*

DECKERS OUTDOOR CORPORATION, 495A S. Fairview, 93117, pg. 491 — PB
Delco Systems Operation, 6767 Hollister Ave., 93117, pg. 720 — PB
Electromagnetic Systems Div., 6380 Hollister Ave., 93117, pg. 1364 — PB
Hewlett-Packard Company, 130 Cremona, 93117, pg. 813 — PB
Joslyn Electronic Systems Corporation, 6868 Cortona Dr., P.O. Box 817, 93116, pg. 481 — PB
MAGNETICS DATA INC., 445 Pine Ave., 93117, pg. 695 — PV
Mercury Air Center, 404 Moffet Rd., 89502, pg. 1093 — PB
Platinum Technology - Santa Barbara Laboratory, 340 S. Kellogg Ave., 93117, pg. 1309 — PB
Santa Barbara Research Center, 75 Coromar Dr., 93117, pg. 1365 — PB
Softool Development Laboratory, 340 S. Kellogg Ave., 93117, pg. 1309 — PB

Granada Hills

Mission Hills Restaurant Corp., 15600 Odyssey Dr., 91344, pg. 1022 — PV
Penguin's Industries, 16902 Devonshire St., 91344, pg. 201 — IT

Grand Terrace

Hood Communications, Inc., 21496 Main St., 92324, pg. 673 — PV

Greenbrae

OACIS HEALTHCARE SYSTEMS, INC., 100 Drake's Landing Rd., Ste. 100, 94904, pg. 1208 — PB

Gridley

Mathews Readymix, Inc., Oroville & Gridley Hwy., 95948, pg. 323 — PB

Guerneville

F. KORBEL BROS. INC., 13250 River Rd., 95446, pg. 632 — PV
Russian River Brewing Company, 13250 River Rd., 95446, pg. 632 — PV

Hacienda Heights

Duskin USA, Inc., 2440 Hacienda Blvd., #215, 91745, pg. 422 — IT

Hanford

Granite Construction Inc.-Central Valley Div., 11280 Ave. 101/2, 94230, pg. 759 — PB
The Hanford Sentinel, 300 W. 6th, 93232, pg. 1343 — PB
Pirelli Armstrong Pacific Coast Division, 10700 Idaho Ave., 93232, pg. 1058 — IT

Hawaiian Gardens

Charter Community Hospital, Inc., 21530 S. Pioneer Blvd., 90716, pg. 1034 — PB

Hawthorne

Aircraft Division, One Northrop Ave., 90250-3277, pg. 1198 — PB
Aircraft Systems Division, Los Angeles, 4880 W. Rosencrans Ave., 90250, pg. 71 — PV
ANCRA INTERNATIONAL LLC, 4880 W. Rosencrans Ave., 90250, pg. 71 — PV
BGW SYSTEMS, INC., 13130 Yukon Ave., 90250, pg. 107 — PV
Dav-El West, 3216 W. El Secundo Blvd., 90250, pg. 314 — PV
Electronics Systems Division, 2301 W. 120th St., 90250, pg. 1198 — PB
Kyotaru USA, 2180 Hawthorne Blvd., 90503, pg. 778 — IT
MARCO COLOR LABS, INC., 12410 Wilkie Ave., 90250, pg. 702 — PV
OSI SYSTEMS, INC., 12525 Chadron Ave., 92050, pg. 1208 — PB
TODD PIPE & SUPPLY HAWTHORNE, 4828 W. 145th St., 90251, pg. 1090 — PV
UDT SENSORS, INC., 12525 Chadron Ave., 90250, pg. 1112 — PV

Hayward

ANNABELLE CANDY COMPANY, INC., 27211 Industrial Blvd., 94545, pg. 75 — PV
Arrow Commercial Systems Div., 1502 Crobker Ave., 94544, pg. 133 — PB
Autocam Acquisition, Inc., 31069 Genstar Rd., 94544, pg. 148 — PB
Autocam Laser Technologies, Inc., 31065 Genstar Rd., 94544, pg. 148 — PB
Bay Cities Auto Auction, 29900 Auction Way, 94544, pg. 282 — PV
Branson International Plasma Corp., 31172 Huntwood Ave., Box 4136, 94544, pg. 574 — PB
Samuel Cabot, Inc., 23284 Eichler St., 94545, pg. 198 — PV
Central Sprinkler Company, 1266 San Luis Obispo Ave., 94544, pg. 327 — PB

CHEMCENTRAL/San Francisco, 31702 Hayman St., 94544, pg. 232 — PB
EKC Technology, Inc., 2520 Barrington Ct., 94545-3703, pg. 344 — PB
Elkey Plastics Co., Inc., Stock Service Center, 23841 Foley St., 94545, pg. 372 — PV
ETEC SYSTEMS, INC., 26460 Corporate Ave., 94545, pg. 594 — PB
Friden Alcatel, 30955 Huntwood Ave., 94544, pg. 55 — IT
HEAT & CONTROL, INC., 21121 Cabot Blvd., 94545, pg. 518 — PB
Henkel Adhesives Corporation, 25817 Clawiter Rd., 94545, pg. 610 — IT
International Window-Northern California, 30526 San Antonio St., 94544, pg. 895 — PB
Ito Cariani Sausage Co., Inc., 3190 Corporate Pl., 94545, pg. 695 — IT
Earle M. Jorgensen Company/Hayward, 31100 Weigman Rd., 94544, pg. 600 — PV
Majestic Pines Care Center, 1628 B St., 94541, pg. 733 — PV
Mervyn's California, 25001 Industrial Blvd., 94545, pg. 489 — PB
MULTIPLE ALLIED SERVICES, INC., 3157 Corporate Pl., 94545, pg. 767 — PB
Safe-Hit Corporation, 1930 W. Winton Ave., Bldg. 11, 94545, pg. 1353 — PB
SASI3-West, 31800 Hayman St., 94544, pg. 1194 — IT
SELECTONE, INC., 3501 Breakwater Ave., 94545, pg. 982 — PV
Shasta Beverages, Inc., 26901 Industrial Blvd., 94545, pg. 1153 — PB
SMARTRUNK SYSTEMS, INC., 23278 Bernhardt St., 94545, pg. 1006 — PV
TIE Systems Northern California, 21020 Alexander Ct., 94545, pg. 1085 — PV
Telna Retarder, Inc., 3488-3490 Diablo Ave., 94545, pg. 786 — IT
Trimac Transportation Services (Western) Inc., 3453 Enterprise Ave., 94545, pg. 1424 — IT
U.C. Moving Services, Inc., 26999 Industrial Blvd., 94545, pg. 458 — PV
Western Region, 31145 San Antonio St., 94544, pg. 744 — IT

Healdsburg

Simi Winery, 16275 Healdsburg Ave., 95448, pg. 781 — IT
The Wine Alliance, P.O. Box 948, 95448, pg. 63 — IT

Hemet

Cloverleaf Healthcare, 275 N. San Jacinto, 92543, pg. 1712 — PB
Deutsch Engineered Connecting Devices Co., 36033 Whittier Ave., 92545, pg. 328 — PV
Deutsch Industrial Product Division, 3850 Industrial Ave., 92545-9050, pg. 328 — PV
McCrometer Inc., 3255 W. Stetson Ave., 92545, pg. 482 — PB

Hercules

Bio-Rad Clinical Div., 4000 Alfred Nobel Dr., 94547, pg. 230 — PB
BIO-RAD LABORATORIES, INC., 1000 Alfred Nobel Dr., 94547, pg. 230 — PB

Highland

Hillhaven Highland House, 7534 Palm Ave., 92346, pg. 1713 — PB

Hollister

Hollister Free Lance, P.O. Box 1417, 360 Sixth St., 95023, pg. 225 — PV
Ozeki Sake (U.S.A.) Inc., 249 Hillcrest Rd., 95023, pg. 1019 — IT
Quantic Industries Inc., 2751 San Juan Rd., 95023, pg. 839 — PV

Hollywood

A&M Records, 1416 N. La Brea Ave., 90028, pg. 1052 — IT
Burda Publications, Inc., 6430 Sunset Blvd., Ste. 1225, 90028-7975, pg. 233 — IT
C & L Marketing Inc., 1750 No. Vine St., 90028, pg. 428 — IT
Capitol Data Systems, 1750 N. Vine St., 90028, pg. 428 — IT
Capitol Industries-EMI Inc., 1750 N. Vine St., 90028, pg. 427 — IT
Capitol Records, Inc., 1750 N. Vine St., 90028, pg. 428 — IT
Deluxe Laboratories, Inc., 1377 N. Serrano Ave., 90027, pg. 1087 — IT
FPC, Inc., 6677 Santa Monica Blvd., 90038-0939, pg. 551 — IT
FREDERICK'S OF HOLLYWOOD, INC., 6608 Hollywood Blvd., 30028, pg. 424 — PB
Hanna-Barbera Productions, Inc., 3400 Cahuenga Blvd. W., 90068-1376, pg. 1614 — PB
The Hollywood Reporter, 6715 Sunset Blvd., 90028, pg. 1446 — PB
Hollywood Supply Company, 1021 N. Seward St., 90038, pg. 1619 — PB
J & R FILM / MOVIOLA DIGITAL CO., 1135 N. Mansfield Ave., 90038, pg. 576 — PV

Magnasync Moviola Corporation, 1135 Mansfield Ave., 90038, pg. 576 — PV
Pacific Title/Mirage, 6350 Santa Monica Blvd., 90038, pg. 1425 — PV
PARKS PRODUCTS, INC., 3611 Cahuenga Blvd., 90068, pg. 840 — PV
Shorewood Packaging of California, Inc., 7080 Hollywood Blvd., Ste. 914, 90028, pg. 1468 — PB
THE TODD-AO CORPORATION, 900 N. Seward St., 90038, pg. 1619 — PB
Todd-AO Hollywood Digital, 669 Sunset Blvd., 90028, pg. 1619 — PB
Todd-AO Preservation Services, 900 N. Seward St., 90038, pg. 1619 — PB
Todd-AO Studios, 900 N. Seward St., 90038, pg. 1619 — PB
Todd-AO Video Services, 1135 Mansfield Ave., 90038, pg. 1619 — PB

Hopland

Fetzer Vineyards California Wines, 13501 US Hwy. 101, S., 95449, pg. 261 — PV

Huntington Beach

Aqua Chem Division, 16390 Pacific Coast Hwy., 92649, pg. 663 — IT
CAMBRO MANUFACTURING COMPANY, 7601 Clay Ave., 92648, pg. 203 — PV
Circle International, 15602 Producer Ln., 92649, pg. 372 — PB
Cost Care, Inc., 7711 Center Ave., Ste. 100, 92647, pg. 589 — PV
Customer Development Corporation, 17011 Beach Blvd., Ste. 800, 92647, pg. 298 — PV
Du Pont NDT Systems Inc., 15751 Graham St., 92649-1630, pg. 531 — PB
Hochiki America Corporation, 15412 Electronic Ln., Ste. 201, 92649-1334, pg. 623 — IT
INTERTRADE INDUSTRIES, 15301 Transistor Ln., 92649, pg. 573 — PV
Jani King of California, Inc., 7755 Center Ave., Ste. 720, 92647, pg. 581 — PV
Jeta Power Systems, Inc., 5252 Bolsa Ave., 92649, pg. 422 — PB
Precision Resource California Div., 5803 Engineer Dr., 92649, pg. 880 — PV
Weiser Lock Division, 5555 McFadden Ave., 92649, pg. 1053 — PB
Winfield Locks, Inc., 5555 McFadden Ave., 92649, pg. 1053 — PB

Huntington Park

Maxon Advanced Vehicle Systems, 1960 Slauson Ave., 90255, pg. 717 — PV
Maxon Compactor Corp., 1960 Slauson Ave., 90255, pg. 717 — PV
MAXON INDUSTRIES, INC., 1960 E. Slauson Ave., 90255, pg. 717 — PV
Maxon International, Inc., 1960 Slauson Ave., 90255, pg. 717 — PV
Maxon Refuse Chassis Corp., 1960 Slauson Ave., 90255, pg. 717 — PV
Solid Waste Control Corp., 1960 Slauson Ave., 90255, pg. 717 — PV
Xon Leasing, 1960 Slauson Ave., 90255, pg. 717 — PV

Imperial

EMPIRE Machinery - Imperial, 3393 Hwy. 86, 92251, pg. 375 — PV

Imperial Beach

Republic Imperial and El Centro Sanitation Service Co., 104 E. Robinson, 92251, pg. 1379 — PB

Indio

Downey Savings & Loan Association, F.A., 81-020 Highway 111, 92201, pg. 527 — PB
Granite Construction Inc.-Southern California Reg. Div., 38000 Monroe St., 92203, pg. 759 — PB
Sun City Palm Springs, 39755 Berkeley Rd., 92203, pg. 495 — PB

Inglewood

ALAN LITHOGRAPH, INC., 550 N. Oak St., 90302, pg. 31 — PV
Cal Litho Color, 550 N. Oak St., 90302, pg. 31 — PV
Circle Freight International USA, 300 N. Oak St., 90301, pg. 371 — PB
Circle Freight International USA, 8411 S. La Cienega Blvd., 90301, pg. 371 — PB
Circle International, 300 N. Oak St., 90301, pg. 371 — PB
H.F. Coors China Co., 8729 Aviation Blvd., 90301, pg. 1506 — PB
Herbalife Dominicana, S.A., 9800 LaCienega Blvd., 90301, pg. 809 — PB
Herbalife International of America, Inc., 9800 La Cienega Blvd., 90301, pg. 809 — PB
Hollywood Park Casino, 3883 W. Century Blvd., 90303, pg. 831 — PB
HOLLYWOOD PARK, INC., 1050 S. Prairie Ave., 90301, pg. 830 — PB
Hollywood Park Operating Company, P.O. Box 369, 1050 South Prairie Ave., 90301, pg. 831 — PB

PB - *U.S. Public Companies Volume*
PV - *U.S. Private Companies Volume*
IT - *International Public & Private Companies Volume*

IMPERIAL BANCORP, 9920 S. La Cienega Blvd., 90301, pg. 871 PB
Imperial Bank, 9920 South La Cienga Blvd., 90301, pg. 871 PB
International Aero-Sea Forwarders, Inc., 630 S. Glasgow Ave., 90301, pg. 683 IT
Kintetsu World Express Inc., 711 Glasglow Ave., 90301, pg. 734 IT
Locus Development Laboratory, 9800 LaCienega, 90301, pg. 1309 PB
L.A. COMPUTER CENTER, 450 N. Oak St., 90302, pg. 676 PV
MARVIN ENGINEERING COMPANY, INC., 260 W. Beach Ave., 90302, pg. 710 PV
Platinum Solutions, 9800 La Cienega Blvd., 90301-4440, pg. 1309 PB
SIGNATURE EYEWEAR, INC., 498 N. Oak St., 90302, pg. 1473 PB
STANDUN, INC., 201 Hindry Ave., 90307, pg. 1032 PV
UHP HEALTHCARE, 3405 W. Imperial Hwy., 90303, pg. 1113 PV
YOUR MAN TOURS, INC., 8331 Aviation Blvd., 90301, pg. 1202 PV
Zephyr Mfg. Co., 201 Hindry Ave., 90307, pg. 1032 PV

Ione

Toms Sierra Company, 117 W. Jackson St., 95640, pg. 1090 PV

Irvine

AST Bearings, 3A Faraday St., 92718, pg. 157 PB
AST Research Inc., 16215 Alton Pkwy., 92618-3618, pg. 1181 IT
AST Research Inc., P.O. Box 57005, 16215 Alton Pkwy., 92619-7005, pg. 1181 IT
AST Research, Inc., 19000 MacArthur Blvd., Ste. 100, 92715, pg. 1182 IT
Adaptec - Southwestern Region, 9701 Geronimo Rd., 92618, pg. 19 PB
ADVANCED CONTROLS, INC., 16901 Jamboree Blvd., 92714, pg. 21 PV
Advanced Logic Research, Inc., 9401 Jeronimo Rd., 92618, pg. 703 PB
Air & Fuel Div., 18321 Jamboree Rd., 92612-1073, pg. 1262 PB
Alcone Marketing Group, 15 Whatney, 92718, pg. 1223 PB
ALLERGAN, INC., 2525 DuPont Dr., 92715, pg. 46 PB
American Adjustment Company, Inc., 18581 Teller Ave., 92715, pg. 365 PB
American Lenders Facilities, Inc., 18581 Teller Ave., 92715, pg. 366 PB
AMERICAN SPORTING GOODS CORPORATION, 2323 Main St., 92614, pg. 62 PV
Anes Security, Inc., 2825 Warner Ave., 92714, pg. 394 PB
AURORA ELECTRONICS, INC., 2030 Main St., Ste. 1120, 92714-7241, pg. 147 PB
Avco Insurance Services/Balboa Life & Casualty, 18581 Teller Ave., 92715-1627, pg. 1589 PB
Avia, 2323 Main St., 92614, pg. 62 PV
B/E Aerospace, Inc./In Flight Entertainment Group, Redhill Ave., pg. 159 PB
BAX Global, 16808 Armstrong Ave., 92606, pg. 1305 PB
Battenfeld of America, Inc., 33 Hammond, Ste. 204, 92718, pg. 825 IT
Belmont Plastics Co., 1821 Langley Ave., 92714, pg. 415 PV
The Boeing Travel Company, 2171 Campus Dr., Ste. 380, 92715, pg. 241 PB
Buehler Ltd., 9272 Jeronimo Rd., Ste. 107B, 92718, pg. 574 PB
CIE America, Inc., 2515 McCabe Way, 92714, pg. 694 IT
CIE America, Inc., P.O. Box 16579, 2502 McCabe Way, 92713, pg. 694 IT
CIE Systems, P.O. Box 19628, 2515 McCabe Way, 92714, pg. 694 IT
CMI-California, 18662 MacArthur Blvd., Ste. 440, 92715, pg. 287 PV
California State Bank-Irvine, 15771 Rockfield Blvd., 92718, pg. 294 PB
California State Bank-Lake Forest Irvine, 15771 Rockfield Blvd., 92718, pg. 294 PB
Calsonic Climate Control, Inc., Nine Holland, 92718, pg. 944 IT
Calsonic International, Inc., Nine Holland, 92718, pg. 944 IT
Castrol Inc., Specialty Products Div., 16715 Von Karman Ave.,Ste. 230, 92714, pg. 235 IT
Catellus Residential Group, 5 Park Plaza, 92714, pg. 315 PB
Cerner Corporation -Southwest Region, 2603 Main St., Ste. 700, 92714, pg. 331 PB
Chiron Vision, 9342 Jeronimo Rd., 92718, pg. 350 PB
Ciba Corning Diagnostics Corporation, 17392 Daimler St., 92714, pg. 973 IT
Coco's & Carrows Restaurants, 3333 Michelson Dr., Ste. 550, 92612, pg. 23 PB
COLORBUS INC., 18261 McDurmott W., 92614, pg. 255 PV
Comarco Wireless Technologies, Inc., Five Jenner, Ste. 100, 92718, pg. 406 PB
Control Systems Div.-Military, 14300 Alton Pkwy., 92618-1898, pg. 1262 PB
THE COOPER COMPANIES, INC., Ten Faraday Dr., 92618, pg. 442 PB
CooperVision, Inc., 10 Faraday, 92718, pg. 442 PB
CORNUCOPIA, INC., 2450 White Rd., 92614, pg. 276 PV
CORVEL CORPORATION, 2010 Main St., Ste. 1020, 92614, pg. 451 PB
Coscan Stewart Limited Partnership, 1920 Main St., 92714, pg. 228 IT
Crow-O.C. Fund T, 333 Michelson Dr., Ste. 500, 92715, pg. 365 PB
Daiwa House Corporation, 2082 Business Centre Dr., Ste. 170, 92715, pg. 374 IT
DATUM INC., 9975 Toledo Way, 92718-1819, pg. 488 PB
DEL MAR AVIONICS, 1621 Alton Pkwy., 92606, pg. 321 PV
Desktop Networks Business Unit, 6 Hughes, 92718, pg. 1503 PB
Discovision Associates, 2355 Main St., Ste. 200, 92714, pg. 1057 IT
DOT PRINTER, INC., 2424 McGaw Ave., 92714, pg. 341 PV
EDD-Orange County, 220 Technology Dr., Ste. 100, 92618, pg. 205 PB
Edison Capital, 18101 Von Karmon Ave., Ste. 1700, 92715-1046, pg. 564 PB
Edison Mission Energy, 18101 Von Karman Ave., Ste. 1700, 92715-1046, pg. 564 PB
El Pollo Loco, 3333 Michelson Dr., Ste. 350, 92612, pg. 23 PB
El Torito Restaurants Inc., 18831 Von Karman Ave., 92612, pg. 393 PV
ENERGY & ENVIRONMENTAL RESEARCH CORP., 18 Mason St., 92718, pg. 376 PV
ENVIRON Corporation, One Park Plaza, Ste. 700, 92714, pg. 1285 PB
Environmental Landscape Products, 3007 Main St., 92714, pg. 378 PV
Epoxylite Corporation-Equipment Div., 9400 Toledo Way, 92718, pg. 379 PV
EPOXYLITE CORPORATION-RESIN DIV., 9400 Toledo Way, 92618, pg. 379 PV
EXAR Corp.-West, 23 Riverrun, 92714, pg. 598 PB
FAMILY RESTAURANTS, INC., 18831 Von Karman Ave., 92715, pg. 393 PV
FIDELITY NATIONAL FINANCIAL, INC., 17911 Von Karman Ave., Ste. 300, 92614-6253, pg. 620 PB
Fidelity National Title Insurance Company, 17911 Von Karman Ave., Ste. 300, 92614, pg. 620 PB
FLOJET CORPORATION, 12 Morgan, 92718, pg. 414 PV
Fluor Constructors International, Inc., 3353 Michelson Dr., 92730, pg. 660 PB
FLUOR CORPORATION, 3353 Michelson Dr., 92698, pg. 659 PB
Fluor Daniel Inc., 3353 Michelson Dr., 534Q, 92730, pg. 660 PB
FOAM PRO MANUFACTURING, 1821 Langley Ave., 92714, pg. 415 PV
FREEDOM COMMUNICATION INC., 17666 Fitch, 92714, pg. 425 PV
Friction Inc., 17152 Dainler St., Irvine Industrial Park, 92713, pg. 560 PB
Futaba Corporation of America, Four Studebaker, 92718, pg. 531 IT
G.E. Capital Mortgage Services, 2301 Dupont Dr., Ste. 200, 92715, pg. 712 PB
GENERAL AUTOMATION, INC., 17731 Mitchell N., 92714, pg. 706 PB
General Employment Enterprises, Inc., 4 Venture, Ste. 290, 92618, pg. 714 PB
General Power Systems, Inc., 17881 Cartwright Rd., 92714, pg. 260 PV
Geosystems Division, 2030 Main St., Ste. 300, pg. 518 PB
GISH BIOMEDICAL, INC., 2681 Kelvin Ave., 92614, pg. 745 PB
Gish International, Inc., 2681 Kelvin Ave., 92714, pg. 745 PB
GOLDEN STATE FOODS, 18301 Von Karman Ave., Ste. 1100, 92612, pg. 460 PV
Stephen Gould, Inc./LA, Two Corporate Pk., Ste. 210, 92714, pg. 467 PV
Gradco (USA), Inc., 39 Parker, 92618, pg. 757 PB
HIH America, P.O. Box 19544, 92623, pg. 153 PV
HNTB Design & Build, 36 Executive Park, 92714, pg. 492 PV
Heraeus/Kulzer, Inc. - Kulzer Div., 10005 Muilands Boulevard, Unit G, 92618-2595, pg. 616 IT
Hewlett-Packard Company, 9800 Murlands Ave., 92718, pg. 813 PB
HOMEBASE, INC., 3345 Michelson Dr., 92715, pg. 832 PB
Hot'n Now, 17901 Ron Karman, 92714, pg. 1637 PB
HYCOR BIOMEDICAL, INC., 18800 Von Karman, 92612, pg. 851 PB
ICL, Inc., 9801 Muirlands Blvd., 92718, pg. 529 IT
ICS Intangibles Holding Company, 18400 Von Karman Ave., 92715, pg. 783 PB
IKOS Systems, Inc., Six Venture, Ste. 100, 92718, pg. 864 PB
Icon International, Inc., 18301 Von Karman Ave., Ste. 750 Ave., 92715, pg. 1191 IT
Ikon Office Solutions-Southern California, 16715 Van Karman, Ste. 100, 92606, pg. 864 PB
Intergraph Corporation, 26 Technology Dr., 92618-2301, pg. 891 PB
Interplay OEM, Inc., 16815 Von Karman Ave., Ste. 100, 92606, pg. 573 PV
INTERPLAY PRODUCTIONS, INC., 16902 Millikan Ave., 92606, pg. 572 PV
Irvine World News Newspaper Company, 2712 McGraw Ave., 92714, pg. 575 PV
JAE Electronics, Inc., 142 Technology Dr., Bldg. 100, 92618, pg. 701 IT
Jacuzzi Whirlpool Bath Inc., 1922 Barranca Pkwy., 92714-4826, pg. 1684 PB
The Johnny Rockets Group, Inc, 15635 Alton Pkwy., 92618, pg. 222 PV
KVB, 17819 Gillette Ave., 92714, pg. 29 PB
Kawasaki Motors Corp., U.S.A., 9950 Jeronimo Rd., 92718, pg. 725 IT
Kia Motors America, Inc., 22 Cromwell, 92718, pg. 733 IT
Kwikset Corporation, One Park Plaza, Ste. 1000, 92614, pg. 233 PB
LG & E Power Systems Inc., 2030 Main St., 92714-7240, pg. 970 PB
Arthur D. Little, Inc, 2500 Michelson Dr., Ste 110, 92612, pg. 670 PV
LoanWorks, 16265 Laguna Canyon Dr., 92718, pg. 858 PB
LUSK, 16592 Hale Ave., 92606-5005, pg. 681 PV
MTI Systems Div., 17152 Armstrong, 92714, pg. 135 PB
Manulife Financial - Orange County, 18301 Von Karman Ave., 300, 92612, pg. 841 IT
MARUCHAN INC., 15800 Laguna Canyon Rd., 92618, pg. 710 PV
Mazda Motor of America, Inc., 7755 Irvine Center Dr., 92618, pg. 849 IT
Mazda Motor of America, Inc. Western Region, 9451 Toledo Way, 92618-1896, pg. 849 IT
Mazda (North America), Inc., 1444 McGaw Ave., 92614, pg. 849 IT
Mazda Research & Development of North America, Inc., 1421 Reynolds Ave., 92614, pg. 849 IT
Medtronic Heart Valve Division, 18011 S. Mitchell, 92714, pg. 1083 PB
Mercedes-Benz Advanced Design of North America, Inc., 17742 Cowan, 92614, pg. 368 IT
Micropolis Corporation, 19782 MacArthur Blvd., Ste. 320, 92715, pg. 742 PV
Milgray/Orange County, Inc., 25 Mauchly, 92718, pg. 206 PB
The Mission Group, 18101 Von Karmon Ave., Ste. 1700, 92715-1007, pg. 564 PB
Mission Land Company, 18101 Von Karmon Ave., Ste. 1700, 92715-1007, pg. 564 PB
Mock Resources, Inc., Five Park Plaza, Ste. 1400, 92714, pg. 1175 PV
Monier Inc., Jamboree Ctr., 1 Park Plaza, Ste. 900, 92714, pg. 1091 IT
NETG Holding, Inc., 18400 Von Karman Ave., 92715, pg. 784 PB
National Education Credit Corporation, 18400 Von Karman Ave., 92715, pg. 784 PB
National Education Payroll Corp., 18400 Von Karman Ave., 92715, pg. 784 PB
National Educational International Corp., 18400 Von Karman Ave., 92715, pg. 784 PB
NEWPORT CORPORATION, 1791 Deere Ave., 92606, pg. 1179 PB
NewsEdge Corp., 18300 Van Karman Ave., Ste. 405, 92715, pg. 1180 PB
OAC Inc., 17536 Von Karman Ave., 92714, pg. 947 IT
Office Automation Corp., 17922 Sky Park Circle, Ste. L, 92714, pg. 706 IT
Packard Hughes Interconnect, 17150 Von Karman Ave., 92614, pg. 719 PB
Pepper Construction Company, 17941 Fitch, 92714, pg. 851 PV
Pepsi-Cola West, 2600 Michelson Dr., Ste. 1700, 92715, pg. 1277 PB
Petro-Diamond, Inc., 18401 Von Karman Ave., 92713, pg. 872 IT
Phoenix Technologies Ltd., 135 Technology Dr., 92618, pg. 1292 PB
POST Buckley Schuh & Jernigan, 18022 Cowan St., Ste. 100A, 92614, pg. 826 PV
PRINTRONIX, INC., 17500 Cartwright Rd., 92623, pg. 1329 PB
Quantum Corporation, 2301 Dupont Dr., Ste. 500, 92612, pg. 1350 PB
The Quikset Organization, 2301 Dupont Dr., Ste. 100, 92612, pg. 417 PV
Racal Instruments, Inc., Four Goodyear St., 92718, pg. 1083 IT
Racal Recorders Inc., 15375 Barranca Pkwy., Ste. H-101, 92718, pg. 1083 IT
RAINBOW TECHNOLOGIES, INC., 50 Technology Dr., 92618, pg. 1359 PB
RAM Optical Instrumentation, Inc., 1791 Deere Ave., 92714, pg. 1179 PB
Red Robin International Inc., 28 Executive Park, Ste. 200, 92714, pg. 1262 IT
Respiratory Support Products Inc., 2552 McGaw Ave., 92714, pg. 1268 IT
Review Co., 15326 Alton Pkwy., 92713, pg. 678 PB
Richmond American Homes of California, Inc., 17310 Redhill Ave., Ste. 320, 92714, pg. 1025 PB
Roanoke Valley Plant, 2030 Main St., 92714-7240, pg. 970 PB
Rogerson Aircraft Controls, 2201 Alton Pkwy., 92606, pg. 940 PV
ROGERSON AIRCRAFT CORPORATION, 2201 Alton Pkwy., 92606, pg. 940 PV
Rogerson Aircraft Systems, 2201 Alton Pkwy., 92606, pg. 940 PV
Rogerson ATS, 2201 Alton Pkwy., 92606, pg. 940 PV
Rosemount Analytical, Inc., 2400 Barranca Pkwy., 92714, pg. 574 PB
Rosemount Analytical, Uniloc Div., 2400 Barranca Pkwy., 92606, pg. 574 PB
STM WIRELESS, INC., One Mauchly Ave., 92618, pg. 1421 PB
ST. JOHN KNITS, 17422 Derian Ave., 92614, pg. 960 PV
Sanyo, 18301 Von Karman Ave., 92715-1009, pg. 1191 IT
Security Pacific State Bank, 14222 Culver Dr., 92714, pg. 182 PB
Separation & Recovery Systems, 1762 McGaw Ave., 92714-4962, pg. 74 IT

PB - *U.S. Public Companies Volume*
PV - *U.S. Private Companies Volume*
IT - *International Public & Private Companies Volume*

SHAFER, 18200 Von Karman Ave., 8th Fl., 92612, pg. 988 **PV**
SHAKEY'S INCORPORATED, 2201 Dupont Dr., Ste. 100, 92612-1515, pg. 989 **PV**
Sharp Digital Information Products, Inc., 16841 Armstrong Ave., 92714-4979, pg. 1229 **IT**
Shiley Incorporated, 16700 Red Hill Ave., 92606, pg. 1284 **PB**
Shiley International, Shiley Heart Valve Rsrch. Ctr., 7672-B Cowan Ave., 92714, pg. 1284 **PB**
Shimano American Corporation, One Shimano Dr., 92718, pg. 1232 **IT**
SHUR-LOK CORPORATION, 2541 White Rd., 92614, pg. 997 **PV**
Sorin Biomedica, 17600 Gillette Ave., 92714, pg. 483 **IT**
Southwest Diversified Coscan Partnerships, 19200 Von Karman Ave., Ste. 400, 92715, pg. 228 **IT**
STERLING ELECTRIC, INC., 16752 Armstrong Ave., 92606, pg. 1041 **PV**
Sterling Electronics, 15215 Alton Pkwy., Ste. 100, 92618, pg. 1051 **PB**
Subaru Western Region, 12A Whatney Dr., 92718-2895, pg. 523 **IT**
TIE Systems Southern California, 18902 Bardeen Ave., 92612, pg. 1085 **PV**
TRC Environmental Solutions, Inc., 21 Technology Dr., 92718, pg. 1558 **PB**
Taco Bell Corp., 17901 Von Karman Rd., 92614, pg. 1637 **PB**
Toppan Interamerica Inc.-Irvine Office, 20 Executive Park, Ste. 130, 92614, pg. 1399 **IT**
Toshiba America Electronic Components, Inc., 9775 Toledo Way, 92718, pg. 1405 **IT**
Toshiba America, Inc., 9740 Irvine Blvd., 92718, pg. 1405 **IT**
Toshiba America Information Systems, Inc., 9740 Irvine Blvd., 92718, pg. 1405 **IT**
Trans Leasing International, Inc.-Western Region, 2030 Main St., Ste. 210, 92714, pg. 1628 **IT**
TROPITONE FURNITURE CO. INC., Five Marconi, 92618, pg. 1105 **PV**
Turner Construction Company, 36 Executive Park, Ste. 150, 92714, pg. 1645 **PB**
Turntec, 2323 Main St., 92614, pg. 62 **PV**
TUTTLE-CLICK AUTOMOBILE GROUP, 14 Auto Center Dr., 92718-2802, pg. 1111 **PV**
Ultrasystems Defense, 16775 Von Karman Ave., 82714, pg. 1199 **IT**
UniCARE Financial Corp., 2201 Dupont Dr., Ste. 600, 92715, pg. 152 **PV**
UniCARE Insurance Company, 2201 Dupont Dr., Ste. 600, 92715, pg. 152 **PV**
Virgin Interactive Entertainment Inc., 18061 Fitch Ave., 92614, pg. 776 **PV**
WFS Financial, Inc., P.O. Box 19733, 23 Pasteur, 92178-3804, pg. 1757 **PB**
WESTCORP, 23 Pasteur, 92618-3816, pg. 1756 **PB**
Westec Security Inc., 5 Mason, 92718, pg. 1217 **IT**
Western Consumer Services, Inc., P.O. Box 19733, 23 Pasteur, 92178-3804, pg. 1757 **PB**
Western Design Corporation, 16952 Milliken Ave., 92714, pg. 636 **PV**
WESTERN DIGITAL CORPORATION, 8105 Irvine Center Dr., 92618, pg. 1758 **PB**
Western Financial Auto Loans, Inc., P.O. Box 19733, 23 Pasteur, 92178-3804, pg. 1757 **PB**
Western Financial Auto Loans 2, Inc., P.O. Box 19733, 23 Pasteur, 92178-3804, pg. 1757 **PB**
Western Financial Bank, P.O. Box 19733, 23 Pasteur, 92718, pg. 1757 **PB**
Western Reconveyance Company, Inc., P.O. Box 19733, 23 Pasteur, 92178-3804, pg. 1757 **PB**
Westhrift Life Insurance Company, P.O. Box 19733, 23 Pasteur, 92178-3804, pg. 1757 **PB**
Westplan Insurance Agency, Inc., P.O. Box 19733, 23 Pasteur, 92178-3804, pg. 1757 **PB**
THE WET SEAL, INC., 64 Fairbanks, 92718, pg. 1763 **PB**
Wisdom Imports Sales Co. Inc., 17401 Eastman, 92714, pg. 679 **IT**
WONDERWARE CORPORATION, 100 Technology Dr., 92618, pg. 1775 **PB**
Wyle Data Services, 15370 Barranco Pkwy., 92618, pg. 1457 **IT**
Wyle Electronics, 1356 Barranca Pkwy., 92618, pg. 1457 **IT**
Zee Medical, Inc., 2575 McCabe Way, 92606, pg. 1073 **PB**

Irwindale

H.F. AHMANSON & CO., 4900 Rivergrade Rd., 91706, pg. 29 **PV**
Ahmanson Mortgage Company, 4900 Rivergrade, 91706, pg. 29 **PB**
Allied Diagnostic Imaging Resources, Inc., 16018 Adelante St., Ste. D, 91706, pg. 282 **PB**
Automotive Worldwide Sector, 5462 N. Irwindale Ave., 91706-2058, pg. 1558 **PB**
Davis Wire Corp., 5555 N. Irwindale Ave., 91706, pg. 859 **PV**
Fey Mfg. Co., Inc., 15854 Ornelas, 91706, pg. 1751 **PB**
Home Savings of America, FSB, 4900 Rivergrade Rd., 91706, pg. 29 **PB**
Hughes Family Markets, Inc., 14005 Live Oak Ave., 91706, pg. 1349 **PV**
Kifuki U.S.A. Co., Inc., 15547 First St., 91706, pg. 1074 **IT**
Leisure Time Industries, 5800 Awala Ave., 91706, pg. 802 **IT**
Miller Brewing Company, 15801 E. First St., 91706, pg. 1289 **PB**
Q & B Foods, Inc., 15547 E. 1st St., 91706, pg. 1074 **IT**

Savings of America Inc., 4900 Rivergrade Rd., 91706, pg. 29 **PB**
Wedgestone Automotive Corp., 15854 Ornelas St., 91706, pg. 1751 **PB**
WEDGESTONE FINANCIAL INC., 5200 N. Irwindale Ave., Ste. 168, 91706, pg. 1751 **PB**

Jackson

Amador Central Railroad Company, P.O. Box 66, Hwy. 49, 95642, pg. 736 **PB**
Amador Ledger-Dispatch, P.O. Box 907, 95642, pg. 225 **PV**
PROSPECT MOTORS, INC., 645 Hwy. 49-88, 95642, pg. 891 **PV**
Stockton Savings Bank-Jackson, 11992 State Hwy. 88, Ste. 2048, 95652, pg. 1575 **PB**

Kenwood

Chateau St. Jean Winery, P.O. Box 293, 8555 Sonoma Hwy., 95452, pg. 1321 **IT**

Kerman

Helm Bean & Seed Warehouse, Inc., 1100 S. Madera Ave., 93630, pg. 428 **PB**

Kingsburg

Nutrius Dairy Feed Supplements Div., 39494 Clarkson Dr., 93631, pg. 145 **PV**

La Habra

Business Banking Group, 441 W. Whittier Blvd., 90631, pg. 294 **PV**
California State Bank-La Habra, 401 W. Whittier Blvd., 90631-3713, pg. 294 **PV**
HOWARDS TV & APPLIANCES, INC., 901 E. Imperial Hwy., 91776, pg. 543 **PV**
Master-Halco, Inc., 110 East La Habra Blvd., 90631, pg. 695 **IT**
Stockc Corp., 1140 G & H S. Cypress St., 90631, pg. 1301 **IT**

La Jolla

AGOURON PHARMACEUTICALS, INC., 10350 N. Torrey Pines Rd., 92037-1020, pg. 28 **PV**
Blood Cells, Inc., 2050 Via Ladeta, 92037, pg. 855 **PB**
Computer Intelligence, 3344 N. Torrey Pines Ct., 92037, pg. 1276 **IT**
THE COPLEY PRESS, INC., 7776 Ivanhoe Ave., 92037, pg. 275 **PV**
DavisElen Advertising, Inc., 7825 Fay Ave., Ste. 200, 92037, pg. 316 **PV**
Fourth Generation Technology Inc., 10280 N. Torrey Pines Rd., 92037, pg. 1199 **PV**
Frontier Pacific Insurance Company, 4250 Executive Sq., Ste. 200, 92037, pg. 685 **PV**
Fujitsu Systems of America, Inc., 11085 N. Torry Pines Rd., #200, 92037-1007, pg. 685 **PV**
Gemini Science, Inc., 11077 N. Torrey Pines Rd., 92037, pg. 736 **PV**
I.C.H. CORPORATION, 9404 Genesee Ave., Suite 330, 92037, pg. 853 **PV**
JENNY CRAIG, INC., 11355 N. Torrey Pines Rd., 92037, pg. 926 **PB**
SMC, 1437 Caminito Halago, 92037-7172, pg. 1503 **PB**
Spencer Douglass Insurance Associates, 4250 Executive Sq., Ste. 200, 92037, pg. 685 **PV**
WESTERN PACIFIC DATA SYSTEMS, 7590 Fay Ave., 92037, pg. 1168 **PV**

La Mesa

Charter Alvarado Behavioral Health Systems, Inc., 7050 Parkway Dr., 91942-2352, pg. 1033 **PB**
Pacific Bell, 5601 Grossmont Ctr. Dr., 91942-3025, pg. 1416 **PB**

La Mirada

Alchem Plastics Inc.-California, 14263 Gannet St., 90638, pg. 1495 **IT**
Amada Cutting Technologies, Inc., 14921 E. Northam St., 90638, pg. 70 **IT**
Amada Engineering & Service Co., Inc., 14921 E. Northam St., 90638, pg. 70 **IT**
Associated Wholesale Electric Co., Artesia Blvd., 90638, pg. 92 **PV**
Flexible Technologies Inc., 14657 Industry Cir., 90638, pg. 1257 **IT**
G.I. Trucking Co., 14727 Alondra Blvd., 90638, pg. 131 **PB**
Graphic Arts Supply Division, 16870 Valley View Ave., 90638, pg. 205 **PV**
Industrial Coatings Div., P.O. Box 608, 16421 Phoebe Ave., 90638, pg. 687 **PB**
INKEL USA CORPORATION, 14830 Alondra Blvd., 90638, pg. 563 **PV**
Makita U.S.A., Inc., 14930 Northam St., 90638-5753, pg. 831 **IT**
Makita U.S.A. Inc.-Los Angeles, 14930 Northam St., 90638-5753, pg. 831 **IT**
Manitowoc Western Company, Inc., 14683 E. Industry Circle, 90637, pg. 1041 **PB**

Rohm & Haas Co. Research Labs, 14445 Alondra Blvd., 90638-5504, pg. 1403 **PB**
Ropak West, 14720 Alondra Blvd., 90638, pg. 812 **IT**
Samsung Pacific International, Inc., 14251 East Firestone Blvd. Rm. 201, 90638, pg. 1183 **IT**
Shasta Beverage Inc., 14405 Artesia Blvd., 90638-5804, pg. 1153 **PB**
SOLID STATE DEVICES, INC., 14830 Valley View Ave., 90638, pg. 1012 **PV**

La Palma

California State Bank-La Palma, 4875 La Palma Ave., 90623, pg. 294 **PV**
La Palma Intercommunity Hospital, 7901 Walker St., 90623-1764, pg. 1118 **PV**

La Puente

Suburban Water Systems, 16340 E. Maplegrove St., 91744-1399, pg. 1494 **PB**

La Verne

CCL Label Product Development, 1925 D. Wright Ave., 91750, pg. 238 **IT**

Lafayette

BELL-CARTER FOODS, INC., 3742 Mt. Diablo Blvd., 94549, pg. 131 **PV**
EA Engineering, Science & Technology, Inc., 3468 Mt. Diablo Blvd., Ste. B-100, 94549, pg. 541 **PB**

Laguna Beach

Shiny Entertainment Inc., The Laguna Design Center, 1088 North Coast Hwy., 92651-1338, pg. 573 **PB**
TELONIC BERKELEY, INC., 2825 Laguna Canyon Rd., 92651, pg. 1074 **PV**

Laguna Hills

CPC Pharmacy, Inc., 2450 Pacific Park Dr., 92656, pg. 1712 **PB**
Community Psychiatric Centers of California, 24502 Pacific Park Dr., 92656, pg. 1712 **PB**
Community Psychiatric Centers Properties, Inc., 24502 Pacific Park Dr., 92656, pg. 1712 **PB**
DEL TACO, INC., 23041 Ave. de la Carlota, 92653, pg. 321 **PV**
PacifiCare Behavioral Health, 23046 Avenida De La Carlota, Ste. 700, 92653-7961, pg. 1251 **PB**
Taylor Woodrow Homes California Limited, 24461 Ridge Route Dr., 92653-1686, pg. 1359 **IT**

Laguna Niguel

Downey Savings & Loan Association, F.A., Laguna Niguel Branch, 27120-A Alicia Pkwy., 92677, pg. 526 **PB**
FURON COMPANY, 29982 Ivy Glenn Dr., 92677, pg. 688 **PB**

Lake Forest

ARB INC., 26000 Commercentre Dr., 92630, pg. 7 **PV**
ARB, Inc.-Building Division, 2600 Commercentre Dr., 92630, pg. 7 **PV**
Downey Savings & Loan Association, F.A., 21781 Lake Forest Dr., 92630, pg. 526 **PB**
I-FLOW CORPORATION, 20202 Wind Dr., 92630, pg. 851 **PB**

Lake View Terrace

Pico Macom Inc., 12500 Foothill Blvd., 91342, pg. 1294 **PB**
PICO PRODUCTS, INC., 12500 Foothill Blvd., 91342, pg. 1294 **PB**

Lakeport

Bank of Lake County, N.A., 150 S. Main St., 95453, pg. 1756 **PB**

Lakewood

Southern California Air Gas, 4007 Paramount Blvd., Ste.100, 90712, pg. 33 **PB**

Lancaster

Downey Savings & Loan Association, F.A., 1000 E. Ave. J, 93535, pg. 527 **PB**
Downey Savings & Loan Association, F.A., 44401 Valley Central Way, 93536, pg. 527 **PB**
LANCE CAMPER MANUFACTURING CORPORATION, 43120 Oventure St., 93535-4510, pg. 645 **PV**
REXHALL INDUSTRIES, INC., 46147 Seventh St. W., 93534, pg. 1384 **PB**
Science and Engineering Lancaster Office, Essex Ctr., 858 W. Jackman, Ste. 202, 93534, pg. 1597 **PB**
United Technologies Chemical System Division, 44300 Lowtree Ste. 118, 93534-4168, pg. 1690 **PB**

Larkspur

SYNON CORPORATION, 1100 Larkspur Landing Cir., 94939, pg. 1060   **PV**

Lathrop

J.R. Simplot Company Lathrop Plant, P.O. Box 198, 95330, pg. 1002   **PV**
Yosemite Express Co., 18500 Louise Ave., 95330, pg. 968   **PV**

Lawndale

Union-Transport Corporation-Los Angeles, 5422 Rosecrans Ave., 90260, pg. 1119   **PV**

Lebec

Tejon Agricultural Corp., P.O. Box 1000, 93243, pg. 1566   **PB**
TEJON RANCH COMPANY, P.O. Box 1000, 4436 Lebec Rd., 93243, pg. 1566   **PB**

Lemoore

The Lemoore Advance, 339 W. D St., Ste. A, 93245, pg. 1343   **PB**

Lincoln

Lincoln News Messenger, P.O. Box 368, 627 Fifth St., 95648, pg. 167   **PV**

Lindsay

Champion Home Builders Co., P.O. Box 429, 840 Palm Ave., 93247, pg. 332   **PB**

Livermore

CCI/Triad Automotive, 3055 Triad Dr., 94550, pg. 193   **PV**
Costco, Inc.-Northern California Region, 2820 Independence Dr., 94550, pg. 452   **PB**
Davey Tree Surgery Co., 2617 S. Vasco Rd., 94550, pg. 314   **PV**
De La Rue Faraday - West, P.O. Box 5029, 266 Lindberg Ave., 94550-5300, pg. 387   **IT**
MCGRATH RENTCORP, 5700 Las Positas Rd., 94550, pg. 1069   **PB**
Orleans Leasing Corporation, 3055 Triad Dr., 84550, pg. 193   **PV**
Pella Window & Door Company, 4771 Arroyo Vista, Ste. E, 94550, pg. 528   **PV**
Triad Systems Financial Corp., 3055 Triad Dr., 94550, pg. 193   **PV**

Livingston

FOSTER FARMS, 1000 Davis St., 95334, pg. 421   **PV**

Lodi

APACHE PLASTICS, L.P., 300 S. Beckman, 95240, pg. 77   **PV**
California Custom Foods, 631 N. Cluff Ave., 95240, pg. 831   **PV**
FARMERS & MERCHANTS BANK OF CENTRAL CALIFORNIA, 121 W. Pine St., 95240, pg. 394   **PB**
Holz Rubber Inc., Call Box 241002, 1129 S. Sacramento St., 95241, pg. 113   **IT**
PACIFIC COAST PRODUCERS, 631 N. Cluff Ave., 95240, pg. 830   **PB**
PROFESSIONAL APARTMENT MANAGEMENT, INC., 2020 W. Kettleman Ln., 95241, pg. 889   **PV**
Stockton Savings Bank-Lodi, 1150 W. Kettleman Ln., 95240, pg. 1575   **PB**
Stockton Savings Bank-Lodi, 200 N. Church St., 95240, pg. 1575   **PB**
WEIBEL WINERY, One Winemasters Way, 95240, pg. 1159   **PV**

Lompoc

GREFCO, Inc., P.O. Box 637, 93438, pg. 903   **PV**
Harborlite Corporation, 137 W. Central Ave., 93436, pg. 42   **PB**

Long Beach

AFSA Data Corp., 2277 E. 220th St., 90810, pg. 649   **PB**
Acapulco Restaurants, 4001 Via Oro Ave., Ste. 200, 90810, pg. 925   **PV**
Alflex, 2630 El Presidio St., 90810, pg. 415   **PB**
Allright Long Beach Parking, 107 B W. Broadway, 90802, pg. 42   **PV**
American Bank Note Company, 711 E. Wardlow Rd., Ste. 301, 90807, pg. 68   **PB**
ARCO Marine, Incorporated, 300 Oceangate, 90802, pg. 144   **PV**
ARGOSystems, Inc., 3901 Via Oro Ave., 90810, pg. 240   **PV**
BHP Trading Inc., 111 W. Ocean Blvd., Ste. 1200, 90802, pg. 226   **IT**
BW/IP International, Inc., 200 Oceangate Blvd.- #900, 90802, pg. 658   **PB**

Bandag Licensing Corporation, 2500 Thompson, 90805, pg. 177   **PB**
BEACH CITY CHEVROLET CO., 3001 E. Pacific Coast Hwy., 90804, pg. 125   **PV**
Boeing Capital Corp., 4060 Lakewood Blvd., 90808, pg. 240   **PB**
Boeing Realty Corporation, 4060 Lakewood Blvd., 6th Fl., 90808, pg. 241   **PB**
CASEY CO., 180 E. Ocean Blvd., Ste. 910, 90802, pg. 218   **PV**
Certified Alloy Products, Inc., 3245 Cherry Ave., 90801, pg. 1467   **IT**
Conroy's Flowers, 6621 East Pacific Coast Hwy., Ste. 280, 90803, pg. 366   **PV**
CROSBY & OVERTON, INC., 1610 W. 17th St., 90813, pg. 290   **PV**
CROWN FENCE CO., 4130 Cherry Ave., 90807, pg. 292   **PV**
Denso Sales California, 3900 Via Oro Ave., 90810, pg. 1412   **IT**
Dillingham Construction N.A., Inc., 135 Victoria St., 90805, pg. 333   **PB**
DOMINGUEZ SERVICES CORPORATION, 21718 S. Alameda St., 90810, pg. 516   **PB**
Dominguez Water Company, 21718 S. Alameda St., 90810, pg. 516   **PB**
DYWIDAG Systems International, USA, Inc., 2154 South St., 90805, pg. 424   **IT**
E & L Engineering, 4001 Via Oro Ave., 90810, pg. 1587   **PV**
EG & G Astrophysics, P.O. Box 22709, 4031 Via Oro Ave., 90801-5709, pg. 543   **PB**
Earth Technology Corp. USA, 100 W. Broadway, Ste. 5000, 90802-4443, pg. 1648   **PB**
Edgington Oil Company, 2400 E. Artesia Blvd., 90805, pg. 77   **PV**
Enthone OMI-Long Beach, 2779 El Presidio St., 90810, pg. 138   **PB**
FINNAIR, P.O. Box 7335, 90807, pg. 486   **IT**
FlowSeal, 3201 Walnut Ave., 90807, pg. 457   **PB**
Flowserve Corporation, 200 Oceangate Blvd., Ste. 900, 90802, pg. 658   **PB**
Gary Steel Co., Inc., 2400 E. Dominguez St., 90810, pg. 884   **PV**
Grayson Controls Div., 100 W. Victoria St., 90805, pg. 1243   **IT**
Hanjin Co., Ltd., 44 W. Ocean Blvd., Ste. 1200, 90802, pg. 592   **IT**
Hewlett-Packard Company, 2525 Grand Ave., 90815, pg. 813   **PB**
Hughes Communications, Inc., P.O. Box 9712, 1500 Hughes Way, 90810, pg. 721   **PB**
Hyundai Steel Industries Inc., 6505 Paramount Blvd., 90805, pg. 642   **IT**
INTEX CORP., 4130 Santa Fe Ave., 90810, pg. 574   **PV**
Jetro Cash & Carry, 20300 E. 60th St., 90805, pg. 587   **PV**
Kaufman and Broad Multi-Housing Group, 320 Golden Shore, Ste. 200, 90802-4217, pg. 945   **PB**
Kenwood Americas Corporation, 2201 E. Dominguez, 90801-5745, pg. 730   **PB**
Kenwood Service Corporation, P.O. Box 22745, 2201 E. Dominguez St., 90801-3745, pg. 730   **PB**
Kenwood USA, 2201 E. Dominguez, 90801-5745, pg. 730   **PB**
KIT MANUFACTURING COMPANY, 530 E. Wardlow Rd., 90801, pg. 962   **PB**
Lafayette Metal Service Corporation, 3025 E. Dominguez St., 90810, pg. 695   **IT**
Lomita Gasoline Company, 301 E. Ocean Blvd., 90801, pg. 1085   **PV**
Long Beach Community Hospital, 1720 Termino Ave., 90804-2180, pg. 1118   **PV**
Long Beach Learning Center, Long Beach Municipal Airport, 4330 Donald Douglas Dr., 90808, pg. 218   **PB**
Long Beach Press-Telegram, 604 Pine Ave., 90844, pg. 727   **PV**
M&N Valve, 2875 64th Avenue, 90802, pg. 1449   **IT**
MANESS INDUSTRIES, INC., 1101 E. Spring St., 90806, pg. 699   **PV**
Max Food & Drug Div., 4700 Cherry Ave., 90807, pg. 38   **PB**
Neste Oil, MTBE, 301 E. Ocean Blvd., Ste. 300, 90802, pg. 914   **IT**
Nuway Linen & Industrial Rental, 3001 E. Anaheim, 90804, pg. 1693   **PB**
Pacific Fuel Trading Corporation, 111 W. Ocean Blvd., #1950, 90802, pg. 700   **IT**
Pacific Valves, 3201 Walnut Ave., 90807, pg. 457   **PB**
Payson Bronco, Inc., 6900 Cherry Ave., 90805, pg. 844   **PV**
Pioneer Electronics (USA) Inc., 2265 E. 220th St., 90810, pg. 1058   **PB**
PIONEER NEW MEDIA TECHNOLOGIES, P.O. Box 93128, 90809, pg. 866   **PV**
Preferred Health Network, 301 E. Ocean Blvd., Ste. 900, 90802, pg. 678   **PB**
RHG Long Beach, 1965 E. Spring St., 90806, pg. 1151   **PV**
Raytheon Support Systems, 1510 Hughes Way, 90810-0399, pg. 1364   **PB**
SCS ENGINEERS, 3711 Long Beach Blvd., 90807-3315, pg. 955   **PV**
SCS Field Services, Inc., 4014 Long Beach Blvd., 90807-3315, pg. 956   **PV**
Sony Logistics Service Co., 2201 E. Carson St., 90810-1227, pg. 1284   **IT**
SOUTHLAND INDUSTRIES, 1661 E. 32nd St., 90807, pg. 1018   **PV**
TABC, Inc., 6375 Paramount Blvd., 90801, pg. 1412   **IT**
Taisei America Corp., 301 E. Ocean Blvd. Ste. 400, 90802, pg. 1347   **IT**

Taisei Construction Corp., 301 E. Ocean Blvd., Ste. 400, 90802, pg. 1347   **IT**
Tatung Company of America, 2850 El Presidio St., 90810, pg. 1357   **IT**
TIDELANDS OIL PRODUCTION CO., 301 East Ocean, Ste. 300, 90802, pg. 1084   **PV**
Topko, Tidelands Oil Production Company, 301 E. Ocean Blvd., P.O. Box 1330, 90801, pg. 913   **IT**
Turco Products Division, 4907 E. Arbor Rd., 90808-1037, pg. 446   **IT**
VIBRO-METER CORP., 3995 Via Oro Ave., 90810, pg. 1138   **PV**
WCO Port Properties, Inc., P.O. Box 8, 92802, pg. 514   **PV**
Westcode Semiconductors Inc. (U.S.A.), 3270 Cherry Ave., 90807, pg. 127   **IT**

Los Alamitos

Daihatsu America, Inc., 4422 Corporate Center Dr., 90720, pg. 365   **IT**
TREND OFFSET PRINTING SERVICES, 3791 Catalina St., 90720, pg. 1099   **PV**

Los Altos

Stuart Anderson's Black Angus/Cattle Company Restaurants, 4410 El Camino Real, Ste. 201, 94022, pg. 61   **PV**

Los Angeles

A A CATER TRUCK MANUFACTURING COMPANY, INC., 750 E. Slauson Ave., 90011, pg. 1   **PV**
ABC Inc., 2040 Ave. of the Stars, 90067, pg. 511   **PB**
ABC/Watermark, Inc., 3575 Cahuenga Blvd. W. 90068, pg. 511   **PB**
ABN AMRO Bank, N.V. (Los Angeles), 300 S. Grand Ave., Ste. 1115, 90071-7519, pg. 10   **IT**
AST Research, Inc., 1990 S. Bundy Dr., Ste. 500, 90025, pg. 1181   **PB**
AAMES FINANCIAL CORPORATION, 3731 Wilshire Blvd., 10th Fl., 90010, pg. 12   **PB**
ABBOTT ELECTRONICS, INC., 2727 S. La Cienega, 90034, pg. 9   **PV**
Ad Americas, 865 S. Figueroa, 90017, pg. 316   **PV**
Adidas America, 10866 Wilshire Blvd., Ste. 900, 90024, pg. 24   **IT**
Aero Peru, 5959 W. Century Blvd., Ste. 556, 90045, pg. 24   **IT**
Air France (U.S. Pacific Region), 725 S. Figueroa, Ste. 3250, 90017, pg. 561   **IT**
Aircraft Bearing Corp., 2238 Cotner Ave., 90064, pg. 187   **PB**
Alexander & Alexander Inc., 801 S. Figuroa, Ste. 700, 90017, pg. 117   **PB**
Allied Concrete, Inc., P.O. Box 2950, 90051, pg. 295   **PB**
Allied Security Inc., Wilshire Windsor Bldg., 4311 Wilshire Blvd., #311, 90010, pg. 40   **PV**
Allright Cal. Inc., 631 S. Olive, Ste. 210, 90014, pg. 42   **PV**
Alpha Therapeutic Corp., 5555 Valley Blvd., 90032, pg. 558   **IT**
American Interactive Media, Inc., 11111 Santa Monica Blvd., 90025, pg. 1052   **PV**
American Trading Real Estate Properties, Inc., Wilshire-Bixel Bldg., Ste.1504, 1055 Wilshire Blvd., 90017, pg. 64   **PV**
Ampco Auto System Parking, 808 S. Olive St., 90014, pg. 2   **PB**
Ampex Data Systems Corporation, 5230 Pacific Concourse Dr., #200, 90045, pg. 104   **PB**
AMVAC Chemical Corporation, 4100 E. Washington Blvd., 90023, pg. 94   **PB**
Analytic TSA Global Asset Management Inc., 700 S. Flower St., Ste. 2400, 90017, pg. 1672   **IT**
Anchor National Life Insurance Co., One SunAmerica Center, Century City, 90067-6022, pg. 1533   **PB**
ANDERSON LITHOGRAPH COMPANY, 3217 S. Garfield Ave., 90040, pg. 72   **PV**
Angeles Funding Corporation, 10301 W. Pico Bvld., 90064, pg. 74   **PV**
APARTMENT SERVICE CO., 3699 Wilshire Blvd., 90010, pg. 77   **PV**
APPERSON BUSINESS FORMS, INC., 6855 E. Gage Ave., 90040, pg. 78   **PV**
Applied Graphics, 340 N. Madison Ave., 90004, pg. 125   **PV**
ARCO Products Co., 333 S. Hope, 90071, pg. 144   **PB**
ARDEN GROUP, INC., P.O. Box 512256, 90051-0256, pg. 128   **PB**
Area Reyclers, 4020 Bandini Blvd., 90023, pg. 111   **PV**
ARGONAUT GROUP, INC., 1800 Ave. of the Stars, Ste. 1175, 90067, pg. 129   **PB**
Arnold Advertising, 10866 Wilshire Blvd., Ste. 565, 90024, pg. 84   **PV**
Arrosto Coffee Company, 11075 Santa Monica Blvd., Ste. 225, 90025, pg. 966   **PB**
Asahi Bank of California, 350 S. Grand Ave., 33810, pg. 82   **PB**
Asahi Breweries U.S.A., Inc., 2920 Via Pacheco, 90017, pg. 83   **IT**
ASHER/GOULD ADVERTISING, INC., 5900 Wilshire Blvd., 90036, pg. 88   **PV**
ASIANA AIRLINES, 3530 Wilshire Blvd., #1450, 90010, pg. 89   **PV**
ASSOCIATED OF LOS ANGELES, 2585 E. Olympic Blvd., 90023, pg. 92   **PV**
ATLANTIC RICHFIELD COMPANY, 515 S. Flower St., 90071, pg. 144   **PB**
ATLAPAC TRADING COMPANY, INC., 2240 S. Garfield Ave., 90040, pg. 96   **PV**

PB - U.S. Public Companies Volume
PV - U.S. Private Companies Volume
IT - International Public & Private Companies Volume

Geographic Index-U.S.

1133

AUTHENTIC FITNESS CORP., 6040 Bandini Blvd., 90040, pg. 147 **PB**

Auto Trend Products, 1911 E. 51st St., 90058, pg. 895 **PV**

Azusa Rock, Inc., P.O. Box 2950, 90051, pg. 295 **PB**

BA Investment Managers, 300 S. Grand Ave., 90071, pg. 180 **PB**

BCI Coca-Cola Bottling Company of Los Angeles, 1334 S. Central Ave., 90021, pg. 393 **PB**

BGM Health Communications, Inc., 10960 Wilshire Blvd., Ste. 600, 90024, pg. 1223 **PB**

BHF (Los Angeles), P.O. Box 32186, 111 W. Ocean Blvd., Ste. 1325, 90832-2186, pg. 119 **IT**

BMW of North America, Inc.-Western Region, 12541 Beatrice St., 90066, pg. 177 **IT**

BNY Western Trust Company, 700 S. Flower St., 2nd Fl., 90017, pg. 179 **PB**

BSA Advertising, Inc., 1875 Century Park E., Ste 1970, 90067, pg. 108 **PV**

BAKER COMMODITIES, INC., 4020 Bandini Blvd., 90023, pg. 111 **PV**

Banca Commerciale Italiana, 555 S. Flower St., Ste. 2400, 90071-2364, pg. 652 **IT**

Banca Nazionale Del Lavoro (Los Angeles), 660 S. Figueroa St., Ste. 1900, 90017, pg. 136 **IT**

Banca Nazionale Del Lavoro (Overseas), 660 S. Figueroa St., Ste. 1900, 90017, pg. 136 **IT**

Banca Serfin, S.N.C., Los Angeles Agency, One Wilshire Bldg., 624 S. Grand, Ste. 1706, 90017, pg. 138 **IT**

Banco Di Napoli-Los Angeles, 333 S. Grand Ave., 90071, pg. 140 **IT**

Banco di Sicilia, 333 S. Grant Ave., Ste. 3600, 90071, pg. 140 **IT**

Banco do Brasil S.A.-Los Angeles, 811 Wilshire Blvd., 90017-2624, pg. 141 **IT**

Banco Nacional de Mexico, 811 Wilshire Blv., 90017, pg. 574 **IT**

Bancomer Los Angeles International Banking Branch, 444 S. Flower St., Ste. 100, Plaza Level, 90071, pg. 652 **IT**

BANDINI FERTILIZER COMPANY, 4139 Bandini Blvd., 90023, pg. 113 **PV**

Bank Hapoalim (Los Angeles), 6222 Wilshire Blvd., 90048, pg. 149 **IT**

Bank of America, 333 S. Grand Ave., Ste. 1700, 90071, pg. 180 **PB**

Bank of America Public Finance, 555 S. Flower St., 48th Fl., 90071, pg. 181 **PB**

Bank of China, 444 Flower St., Ste. 3900, 90071, pg. 152 **IT**

Bank of Montreal - Los Angeles, 707 Wilshire Blvd., 90017, pg. 154 **IT**

The Bank of New York, 10990 Wilshire Blvd., Ste. 1125, 90024, pg. 179 **IT**

The Bank of Tokyo-Mitsubishi, Ltd. (Los Angeles Branch), 777 S. Figueroa St., 90017, pg. 157 **IT**

Bank of Yokohama Los Angeles, 777 S. Figueroa St., Ste. 700, 90017, pg. 159 **IT**

Bankers Trust Company of California, N.A., 400 S. Hope St., 90071, pg. 185 **IT**

Banque Paribas-Los Angeles, 2029 Century Park East - Suite 3900, 90067, pg. 319 **IT**

Barksdale, Inc., 3211 Fruitland Ave., 90058, pg. 457 **PB**

Barris Music, Inc., 1990 Bundy Dr., 90025, pg. 1283 **IT**

Barris Productions, Inc., 1990 S. Bundy, 90025, pg. 1283 **IT**

THEODORE BARRY & ASSOCIATES, 515 S. Figueroa St., Ste. 1500, 90071, pg. 118 **PV**

The Baywatch Production Company, 5433 Beethoven St., 90066, pg. 41 **PB**

Beacon Communications, 1041 N. Formosa Ave., 90046, pg. 138 **PB**

Bear, Stearns & Co. Inc., Los Angeles, 1999 Ave. of the Stars, 90067-6100, pg. 198 **IT**

Beiersdorf, Inc., pg. 182 **IT**

BERGELECTRIC CORPORATION, 5650 W. Centinela Ave., 90045, pg. 135 **PV**

The Beverage Source, Inc., 10990 Wilshire Blvd., Ste. 1800, 90024, pg. 591 **PB**

Blue Chip Stamps, 5801 S. Eastern Ave., 90040, pg. 217 **PB**

Bowne of Los Angeles, Inc., 633 W. Fifth Ave., 90015, pg. 249 **PB**

BRIDGEWATER RESOURCES CORPORATION, 1801 Century Park E., Ste. 1101, 90067, pg. 168 **PV**

Brierley & Partners, 5700 Wilshire Blvd., Ste. 300, 90036, pg. 166 **PB**

BRUSH RESEARCH MANUFACTURING COMPANY, 4642 E. Floral Dr., 90022, pg. 176 **PV**

Bundy Properties, Teleflora Plaza, 12233 W. Olympic Blvd., 90064, pg. 941 **PV**

Leo Burnett U.S.A., 10900 Wilshire Blvd., Ste. 700, 90024, pg. 184 **PV**

CB COMMERCIAL REAL ESTATE, 533 Fremont Ave., Ste. 1000, 90071, pg. 272 **PB**

CB Commercial Real Estate Group, Inc., 533 Fremont Ave., Ste. 1000, 90071, pg. 272 **PB**

CBS Entertainment, 7800 Beverly Blvd., 90036, pg. 274 **PB**

CC Plaza Co., P.O. Box 2950, 90051, pg. 295 **PB**

CFI Insurers, Ltd., 12655 W. Jefferson Blvd., 90066, pg. 1475 **PB**

CFI Pty., Ltd., 12655 W. Jefferson Blvd., 90066, pg. 1475 **PB**

CLT USA, 1933 Avenue of the Stars, Ste. 2590, 90067, pg. 561 **IT**

Cableco, 4333 Maywood Ave., 90058, pg. 215 **PV**

CalAmerica Life Insurance Co., SunAmerica Ctr., Century City, 90067-6022, pg. 1533 **PB**

California Cho Hung Bank, 3000 W. Olympic Blvd., 90006, pg. 287 **IT**

California Commerce Bank, 2029 Century Park E., 42nd Fl., 90067, pg. 574 **IT**

California Commerce Bank, 5438 E. Whittier Blvd., 90022, pg. 574 **IT**

California Drop Forge, 1033 Alhambra Ave., 90012, pg. 612 **PV**

CALIFORNIA FASHION INDUSTRIES INC., 3434 S. Grand Ave., 90007, pg. 200 **PV**

California Hospital Medical Center, 1401 S. Grand Ave., 90015-3063, pg. 1118 **PV**

California MEC, Inc., 777 Tower, 777 S. Figueroa St. Ste. 3900, 90071, pg. 873 **IT**

California Pizza Kitchen Inc., 1640 S. Sepulveda Blvd., Ste. 200, 90025, pg. 1277 **PB**

CALMAT CO., 3200 San Fernando Rd., 90065, pg. 295 **PB**

CalMat Co. of Arizona, P.O. Box 2950, 90051, pg. 295 **PB**

CalMat Co. of New Mexico, P.O. Box 2950, 90051, pg. 295 **PB**

CalMat Land Co., P.O. Box 2950, 90051, pg. 295 **PB**

CalMat Leasing Co., P.O. Box 2950, 90051, pg. 295 **PB**

CalMat of Central California, P.O. Box 2950, 90051, pg. 295 **PB**

CalMat Properties Co., P.O. Box 2950, 90051, pg. 295 **PB**

Canadian Imperial Bank of Commerce (California), 300 So. Grand Ave., 90071, pg. 257 **IT**

THE CAPITAL GROUP COMPANIES INC., 333 S. Hope St., 52nd Fl., 90071, pg. 206 **PV**

The Capital Group International, 333 S. Hope St., 49th Fl., 90071, pg. 206 **PV**

Capital Management Sciences, 11766 Wilshire Blvd., Ste. 300, 90025, pg. 484 **PV**

The Capital Research & Management Co., 333 S. Hope St., 90071, pg. 206 **PV**

CARAT ICG, 1925 Century Park E., Ste. 1850, 90067, pg. 207 **PV**

Carat ICG Retail/Co-op Div. of Carat ICG, 1925 Century Park E., Ste. 1850, 90067, pg. 207 **PV**

Castelazo & Associates, 5420 W. 104th St., 90045, pg. 1071 **PV**

CASTLE & COOKE INC., 10900 Wilshire Blvd., 90024, pg. 313 **PB**

Catellus Development Corporation, 304 S. Broadway, 4th Fl., 90012, pg. 315 **PB**

Central Japan Railway Company-Los Angeles Office, Ste. 2620, Security Pacific, Plaza, 333 S. Hope St., 90071, pg. 279 **IT**

Central Plants, Inc., 633 W. 5th St., Ste. 5400, 90071, pg. 1249 **IT**

Century Dialysis Corporation, 8201 Beverly Blvd., 90048-4520, pg. 1525 **PV**

CERTIFIED GROCERS OF CALIFORNIA, 2601 S. Eastern Ave., 90040, pg. 226 **PV**

CHARLES DUNN COMPANY, INC., 1200 Wilshire Blvd., 1st Floor, 90017, pg. 229 **PV**

Charter Oak Ventures, 2222 Corinth Ave., 90064, pg. 361 **PV**

CHARTWELL PARTNERS, 1999 Ave. of the Stars, Ste. 3050, 90067-6001, pg. 230 **PV**

Chiba Bank, Ltd.-Los Angeles Agency, 444 S. Flower St., 90071, pg. 283 **IT**

China Airlines Ltd., 6053 W. Century Blvd., Ste. 800, 90045, pg. 284 **IT**

China Airlines Ltd., Cargo Center, 11201 Aviation Blvd., 90045, pg. 285 **IT**

CIBA Specialty Chemicals-Performance Polymers Division, Formulated Materials Group, 5121 San Fernando Rd. W., 90039-1011, pg. 291 **IT**

Cigna Excess & Surplus Insurance Services, Inc. (CA), 3700 Wilshire Blvd., Ste. 900, 90010, pg. 362 **PB**

Cigna Hospital of Los Angeles, Inc., 1711 W. Temple St., 90026, pg. 360 **PB**

Cineplex Odeon Corporation -Los Angeles, 1925 Century Park E., Ste. 300, 90067, pg. 293 **IT**

Citadel Holdings Corp., 550 S. Hope St., Ste. 1825, 90071, pg. 456 **PB**

Citicorp Business Credit, Inc., 515 S. Flower, 90071, pg. 378 **IT**

City National Bank - Fairfax Regional Office, 300 N. Fairfax Ave., 90036, pg. 381 **PB**

City National Bank - Olympic Plaza Regional Office, 11500 West Olympic Blvd., 90064, pg. 381 **PB**

Clearly Canadian Beverage Corp., 90067, pg. 297 **PB**

Coast Asphalt, Inc., P.O. Box 2950, 90051, pg. 295 **PB**

Coast Business Credit, 12121 Wilshire Blvd., Ste. 1111, 90025, pg. 872 **PB**

Coast Federal Bank FSB, 1000 Wilshire Blvd., 90055, pg. 389 **PB**

COAST SAVINGS FINANCIAL, INC., 1000 Wilshire Blvd., 90017-2457, pg. 388 **PB**

Comet Ventures, Inc., 10990 Wilshire Blvd., Ste. 1800, 90024, pg. 591 **PB**

Commerzbank Aktiengesellschaft Los Angeles Office, 633 W. Fifth St., Ste. 6600, 90071, pg. 310 **IT**

Comprehensive Cancer Centers, 8201 Beverly Blvd., 90048-4520, pg. 1525 **PV**

Computer Service Company, P.O. Box 74901, 90004, pg. 1040 **PV**

Concord Fabrics, Los Angeles, 13435 S. Main St., 90061, pg. 430 **PV**

Conde Nast Publications, 6300 Wilshire Blvd., 90048, pg. 20 **PV**

Contempo Casuals, 5433 W. Jefferson Blvd., 90016, pg. 1763 **PV**

Continental Graphics Corporation, 4525 Wilshire Blvd., Ste. 203, 90010, pg. 268 **PV**

CONTINENTAL GRAPHICS HOLDINGS, INC., 4525 Wilshire Blvd., Ste. 203, 90010, pg. 268 **PV**

CRAIG CORPORATION, 550 S. Hope St., Ste. 1825, 90071, pg. 456 **PB**

Crain Communications, Los Angeles, 6500 Wilshire Blvd., Ste. 2300, 90048-4947, pg. 285 **PV**

CROWELL, WEEDON & CO., One Wilshire Blvd., 90017, pg. 291 **PV**

Crown Grocers, Inc., 2601 S. Eastern Ave., 90040, pg. 227 **PV**

Crystal Cruises, Inc., 2121 Avenue of the Stars, Ste. 200, 90067, pg. 941 **IT**

DMB&B Los Angeles, 6500 Wilshire Blvd., Ste. 1000, 90048, pg. 303 **IT**

Dai-Ichi Kangyo Bank, Ltd.-Los Angeles, 555 W. Fifth St., 90013, pg. 359 **IT**

Dai-Ichi Kangyo Bank of California-Los Angeles, 555 W. Fifth St., 90013, pg. 360 **IT**

Dai-ichi Life Insurance Agency (U.S.A.), Inc.-Los Angeles, 633 W. Fifth St., Ste. 6700, 90071, pg. 362 **IT**

Dames & Moore Inc., 911 Wilshire Blvd., 90017, pg. 624 **PV**

DAVIS COMPANIES, 2121 Ave. of the Stars, Ste. 2800, 90067, pg. 315 **PV**

DAVISELEN ADVERTISING, INC., 865 S. Figueroa, 90017, pg. 316 **PV**

DEARDEN'S, 700 S. Main St., 90014, pg. 319 **PV**

Defense Technology Group, 6053 W. Century Blvd., 90045-6430, pg. 1199 **PB**

Dentsply Ransom & Randolph, 2337 S. Yates St., 90040, pg. 499 **PB**

Dentsu Burson Marsteller, Inc. Los Angeles Office, 3333 Wilshire Blvd., 90010, pg. 393 **IT**

Deutsche Bank AG (Los Angeles Branch) 300 S. Grand Ave. Ste. 3950, 90071, pg. 403 **IT**

DIAGNOSTIC PRODUCTS CORPORATION, 5700 W. 96th St., 90045, pg. 505 **PB**

Diversified Compounders, 5701 E. Union Pacific Blvd., 90022, pg. 324 **PV**

Doodle Art Div., 11835 W. Olympic Blvd., 90064, pg. 1215 **PV**

Down River Forest Products, Inc., 2920 Tanager Ave., 90040, pg. 763 **PB**

DreamWorks Interactive, P.O. Box 251677, 90025, pg. 342 **PV**

Dresdner Bank AG (Los Angeles), 725 S. Figueroa St., Ste. 3950, 90017, pg. 418 **IT**

Dun & Bradstreet Software (Los Angeles), 12121 Wilshire Blvd., 90025, pg. 532 **IT**

DUNN-EDWARDS CORPORATION, 4885 East 52nd Place, 90040, pg. 347 **PV**

E & E Steel, Inc., 2187 S. Garfield Ave., 90040, pg. 941 **PV**

EJL Advertising/Los Angeles, 5700 Wilshire Blvd., 90036, pg. 673 **PV**

EcoTrans OEM Transportation, 555 W. Fifth St., 90013, pg. 1249 **PB**

Edelman Worldwide, Inc., 5670 Wilshire Blvd., 90024, pg. 362 **PV**

Elite Information Systems, Inc., 3415 South Sepulveda Blvd., Ste. 500, 90034, pg. 258 **PB**

ELKAY PLASTICS COMPANY, INC., 4380 Ayers Ave., 90023, pg. 372 **PV**

Elof Hansson Wood Products, Inc., 7039 E. Slauson Ave., 90040, pg. 595 **IT**

Emery Group Henkel Corp., 5568 E. 61st St., 90040-3406, pg. 611 **PV**

Empty Chair Productions, Inc., 2020 Ave. of the Stars, 90067, pg. 511 **PV**

Energy Pacific, 633 W. Fifth St., Ste. 5400, 90071-2006, pg. 584 **PB**

ROBERT ENGLEKIRK, INC., 2116 Arlington, 90018, pg. 377 **PV**

Englekirk & Sabol, Inc., 2116 Arlington Avenue, 90018, pg. 377 **PV**

ERLY INDUSTRIES, INC., 10990 Wilshire Blvd., Ste. 1800, 90024, pg. 591 **PB**

Euro Global Travel Inc., 5670 Wilshire Blvd., Ste. 120B, 90036, pg. 90 **PV**

Europ Assistance International Inc., 5670 Wilshire Blvd., Ste. 120, 90036, pg. 90 **IT**

EvansGroup, Museum Sq., Ste. 240, 5757 Wilshire Blvd., 90036, pg. 385 **PV**

EVY OF CALIFORNIA, INC., 10755 Venice Blvd., 90034, pg. 387 **PV**

Executive Car Leasing Company, 7807 Santa Monica Blvd., 90046, pg. 388 **PV**

EXECUTIVE CAR LEASING, INC., 7807 Santa Monica Blvd., 90046, pg. 388 **PV**

The Export-Import Bank of Korea, 600 Wilshire Blvd., Ste. 1650, 90017, pg. 467 **IT**

F.C. Properties Co., World Savings Bldg., Wilshire Blvd., 90025, pg. 668 **PB**

Farmers Group, Inc., 4680 Wilshire Blvd., 90010, pg. 110 **PV**

Feralloy Reliance Company Ltd. Partnership, 2550 E. 25th St., 90058, pg. 1070 **PV**

Feralloy Reliance Management Corp., 2550 E. 25th St., 90058, pg. 1070 **IT**

Fiduciary Trust International of California, 444 S. Flower St., Ste. 3010, 90071-2961, pg. 621 **PB**

Fields & Devereaux/HEPY, Inc., 116 N. Robertson Blvd., Ste. 802, 90048, pg. 503 **PV**

Filtrol Corporation, 3200 E. Washington Blvd., 90023, pg. 47 **PB**

Financial Insurance Marketing Group, 6171 W. Century Blvd., 90045, pg. 588 **PB**

Financial Management, 300 S. Grand Ave., Ste. 2500, 90071, pg. 181 **PV**

Fire Underwriters Association, 4680 Wilshire Blvd., 90010, pg. 110 **PV**

FIRST COMPUTER CORPORATION, 1740 Westwood Blvd., 90024, pg. 406 **PV**

First Interstate Bank of California, 633 W. 5th St., 90071, pg. 1753 **PB**

Geographic Index-U.S.

First Pacific Advisors, Inc., 11400 W. Olympic Blvd., Ste. 1200, 90064, pg. 1673 — PB
Fishking Processors, Inc., 1320 Newton St., 90021, pg. 940 — IT
Fleishman-Hillard, Inc., Arco Tower, 515 S. Flower St., 7th Fl., 90071-2200, pg. 411 — PB
The Foothill Group, Inc., 11111 Santa Monica Blvd., 90025, pg. 1201 — PB
Ford Life Insurance Company, One SunAmerica Ctr., Century City, 90067-6022, pg. 1533 — PB
Forest City Properties Corporation, World Savings Bldg., Wilshire Blvd., 90025, pg. 669 — PB
FOUR-S BAKING COMPANY, 1771 Blake Ave., 90031, pg. 422 — PV
Four Seasons Hotel, 300 So. Doheny Dr., 90048, pg. 502 — PV
Four Star Holdings Corp., 1440 S. Sepulveda Blvd., 90025, pg. 689 — PV
Fox, Inc., 10201 W. Pico Blvd., 90035, pg. 926 — PV
Fox Kids Worldwide, 10960 Wilshire Blvd., 90025, pg. 927 — IT
Fox Net, 5746 Sunset Blvd., 90028, pg. 926 — IT
Fox Television Stations Inc., 1999 South Bundy Dr., 90025, pg. 926 — IT
Frankfurt Balkind Partners, 6135 Wilshire Blvd., 90048, pg. 424 — PV
FREEMAN COSMETIC CORP., 10000 Santa Monica Blvd., Ste. 400, 90067, pg. 426 — PV
JOHN S. FREY ENTERPRISES, 1900 E. 64th St., 90001, pg. 428 — PV
Fuji Bank, Los Angeles, 333 S. Hope St., Ste. 3900, 90071, pg. 520 — IT
GWP, INC., 9080 Santa Monica Blvd., 90069, pg. 437 — PV
GANS INK & SUPPLY COMPANY, INC., 1441 Boyd St., 90033, pg. 440 — PV
Garment Center Region, Ste. B-270, 110 E. 9th St., 90079, pg. 872 — PV
Geffen Records, 9130 Sunset Blvd., 90069, pg. 1215 — IT
GILMORE ENVELOPE CORP., 4540 Worth St., 90063, pg. 454 — PV
GOLDEN STATE MUTUAL LIFE INSURANCE COMPANY, 1999 W. Adams Blvd., 90018, pg. 461 — PV
Golden Tiger, 6711 Alameda St., 90001, pg. 1182 — PV
GOLDEN WEST BROADCASTERS, 1645 N. Vine St., Ste. 200, 90028, pg. 461 — PV
Goldman, Sachs & Co., 333 S. Grand Ave., 19th Fl., 90071, pg. 462 — PV
THE SAMUEL GOLDWYN COMPANY, 10203 Santa Monica Blvd., 90067, pg. 463 — PV
Graco Western Regional Sales & Distribution Center, 3165 S. Garfield Ave., 90040-3287, pg. 757 — PV
Great Scott Advertising Co., Inc., 6671 Sunset Blvd., Ste. 1523, 90028, pg. 476 — PV
Green Equity Investors II, L.P., 11111 Santa Monica Blvd., Ste 2000, 90025, pg. 477 — PV
Green Equity Investors L.P., 11111 Santa Monica Blvd., Ste. 2000, 90025, pg. 477 — PV
LEONARD GREEN & PARTNERS, 11111 Santa Monica Blvd., Ste. 2000, 90025, pg. 477 — PV
Grey Advertising Inc., Western Div., 6100 Wilshire Blvd., 90048, pg. 764 — PV
Grey Directory Marketing Inc., 6100 Wilshire Blvd., 90048, pg. 764 — PB
Grizzard/Los Angeles, 1480 Colorado Blvd., 90041, pg. 482 — PV
Grocers Capital Co., 2601 So. Eastern Ave., 90040, pg. 227 — PV
Grocers Development Co., 2601 S. Eastern Ave., 90040, pg. 227 — PV
Grocers Equipment Co., 2601 S. Eastern Ave., 90040, pg. 227 — PV
Grocers General Merchandise Co., 2601 S. Eastern Ave., 90040, pg. 227 — PV
Grocers Specialty Co., 2601 S. Eastern Ave., 90040, pg. 227 — PV
Group 3 Design, 9080 Santa Monica Blvd., 90069, pg. 437 — PV
The Guber Peters Entertainment Company, 1990 S. Bundy Dr., Penthouse Ste., 90025, pg. 1283 — IT
GUESS ?, INC., 1444 S. Alameda, 90021, pg. 768 — PV
Guilford Mills (Apparel, Home & Industrial Fabrics), 124 E. Olympic Blvd., 90015, pg. 769 — PB
HB Entertainment Co., 3400 Cahuenga Blvd., 90068, pg. 1615 — PB
Hamlet Group, Inc., 11075 Santa Monica Blvd., Ste. 225, 90025, pg. 966 — PB
HARDEN INDUSTRIES, INC., 13915 S. Main St., 90061, pg. 501 — PV
Harris Trust Company of California, 707 Wilshire Ave. 4840, 90017, pg. 155 — IT
Haseko (California) Inc., 350 So. Figueroa St., #601, 90071, pg. 600 — PV
Haseko Realty (California), Inc., 350 S. Figueroa St., Ste. 601, 90071, pg. 600 — PV
Haseko (USA) Corporation, 350 South Figueroa St., Ste. 610, 90071, pg. 600 — IT
The Haworth Group, Inc., 10900 Wilshire Blvd., Ste. 410, 90024, pg. 511 — PV
Hawthorne Communications, Inc.-Western Regional Office, 6500 Wilshire Blvd., Ste. 500, 90045, pg. 512 — PV
Hearst Entertainment Productions, Inc., 1640 S. Sepulveda Blvd., 90025, pg. 516 — PV
W. Heath & Co., 3225 Lacy St., 90031, pg. 84 — PB
HEHR INTERNATIONAL INC., 3333 Casitas Ave., 90039, pg. 519 — PV
Heil Steel Fabricating, Inc., 3121 Fruitland Ave., 90058, pg. 521 — PB
J. Hellman Frozen, Inc., 1601 E. Olympic Blvd., Ste. 200, 90021, pg. 520 — PV
J. HELLMAN PRODUCE, INC., 1601 E. Olympic Blvd., Ste. 200, 90021, pg. 520 — PV

Hewlett-Packard Company, 5651 W. Manchester Ave., 90009, pg. 813 — PB
Hidden Valley Coal Company, P.O. Box 2950, 90051, pg. 296 — PB
The Hokkaido Takushoku Bank, Ltd.-Los Angeles Agency, 550 S. Hope St., Ste. 1700, 90071, pg. 627 — IT
The Holden Group, 11365 W. Olympic Blvd., 90064, pg. 435 — IT
THE LEWIS HORWITZ ORGANIZATION, 1840 Century Park E., 90067, pg. 540 — PV
Household Products, 4333 Bandini Blvd., 90023, pg. 387 — PB
Houston Helm and Company, 11755 Wilshire Blvd., Ste. 2000, 90025, pg. 542 — PV
Hudson Aviation Services Inc., California, Los Angeles Intl. Airport, 7025 West Imperial Hwy., 90045, pg. 845 — PV
Hudson General Coach Lines, Inc., Los Angeles Intl. Airport, 7025 West Imperial Hwy., 90058, pg. 845 — PV
R.S. Hughes Co., 3410 San Fernando Rd., 90065, pg. 547 — PV
Hughes Space & Communications Group, P.O. Box 92919, 90009, pg. 721 — PV
Huntmix, Inc., P.O. Box 2950, 90051, pg. 296 — PB
ICG Direct, Inc., 1925 Century Park, E., Ste. 1850, 90067, pg. 208 — PB
ICG Media Consultants, Inc., 1925 Century Park E., Ste. 1850, 90067, pg. 208 — PV
IMI Marston Inc., 6033 Century Blvd., Ste. 1200, 90045, pg. 646 — IT
ING Capital, 333 South Grand Avenue, 90071, pg. 648 — IT
Iberia Air Lines of Spain, 6300 Wilshire Blvd., 90048, pg. 575 — IT
IDEA MAN, INC., 1945 S. La Cienega Blvd., 90034, pg. 557 — PV
IMAGINE ENTERTAINMENT, 1925 Century Park E., Ste. 2300, 90067, pg. 558 — PV
Imperial Bank Realty Company, P.O. Box 92991, Century Blvd. & San Diego Fwy., 90009, pg. 872 — PB
Imperial Credit Commercial Mortgage Investment Corp., 11601 Wilshire Blvd., Ste. 2080, 90025, pg. 872 — PB
Imperial Trust Co., 201 N. Figueroa St.; Ste. 610, 90012, pg. 872 — PV
Imperial Ventures, Inc., P.O. Box 92991, Century Blvd. & San Diego Fwy., 90009, pg. 872 — PB
The Industrial Bank of Japan, Limited (Los Angeles Agency), 350 S. Grand Ave., Ste. 1500, 90071, pg. 674 — IT
Integrated Systems, 444 S. Flower St., Ste. 2100, 90071-2922, pg. 1791 — PB
InterAmerican-Star Group, 6277 E. Slauson Ave., 90040, pg. 1529 — PV
The International Commercial Bank of China, 445 S. Figueroa St., Ste. 1900, 90071, pg. 683 — IT
International Creative Management, Inc., 8942 Wilshire Blvd., 90211, pg. 554 — PV
International Lease Finance Corporation, 1999 Ave. of the Stars, 39th Fl., 90067, pg. 85 — PV
International Surplus Adjusting Services, 3700 Wilshire Blvd., Ste. 520, 90010, pg. 366 — PB
Island Music, Inc., 6525 Sunset Blvd., 90028, pg. 1052 — IT
ITALIA/GAL ADVERTISING, 5750 Wilshire Blvd., Ste. 480, 90036, pg. 576 — PV
JCB International Credit Card Co., Ltd., 626 Wilshire Blvd., Ste. 200, 90017, pg. 846 — IT
The JCM Group, 10866 Wilshire Blvd., Ste. 600, 90024, pg. 696 — PV
JANIK & ASSOCIATES, INC., 1901 Ave. of the Stars, Ste. 610, 90067, pg. 582 — PV
The Japan Development Bank-Los Angeles Representative Office, 601 S. Figueroa St., Ste. 4450, 90017-5748, pg. 701 — IT
Japan Energy USA Inc., 2049 Century Park Ste 2530, 90067, pg. 702 — IT
Jay Incorporated-Los Angeles Division, 6300 Wilshire Blvd., Ste. 1600, 90048, pg. 583 — PV
Jefferies & Company, Inc., 11100 Santa Monica Blvd., 90025, pg. 925 — PV
Jefferies & Company, Inc., 11100 Santa Monica Blvd., 10th Fl., 90025, pg. 925 — PB
JEFFERIES GROUP, INC., 11100 Santa Monica Blvd., 11th Fl., 90025, pg. 924 — PV
Jensen Industries, 1946 E 46th St., 90058, pg. 1193 — PB
Quincy Jones Entertainment, 7250 Beverly Blvd., Ste. 207, 90036, pg. 1611 — PV
KABC-AM Radio, Inc., 2040 Ave. of the Stars, 90067, pg. 512 — PV
KCBS-TV, 6121 Sunset Blvd., 90028, pg. 275 — PB
KCOP Television, Inc., 915 N. La Brea, 90038, pg. 352 — PB
KFI, Inc., 610 S. Ardmore Ave., 90005, pg. 282 — PV
KFWB Radio, 6230 Yucca St., 90028, pg. 274 — PV
KLOS-FM Radio, 2040 Ave. of the Stars, 90067, pg. 512 — PV
KTLA, Inc., 5800 Sunset Blvd., 90078, pg. 1636 — PB
KTTV, 5746 W. Sunset Blvd., 90028, pg. 926 — IT
K2 INC., 4900 S. Eastern Ave. Ste. 200, 90040-2962, pg. 940 — PV
KAUFMAN AND BROAD HOME CORPORATION, 10990 Wilshire Blvd., 7th Fl., 90024, pg. 944 — PB
Kelly Paper Company, 1441 E. 16th St., 90021, pg. 757 — IT
Ketchum Public Relations, 11755 Wilshire Blvd., Ste. 1900, 90025, pg. 617 — PV
Kimmel Motz Refrigeration Corp., 4100 Goodwin Ave., 90039, pg. 1400 — IT
King World Productions, 12400 Wilshire Blvd., Ste. 1200, 90025, pg. 961 — PB
Kirin USA, Inc., 1000 Wilshire Blvd., Ste. 220, 90017, pg. 736 — IT
Kirst Construction Co., Inc., P.O. Box 2950, 90051, pg. 296 — PB

KNAR GOLD & SILVER EXCHANGE, 640 S. Hill St., Ste. 241, 90014, pg. 626 — PV
Kobe Steel USA Inc. (Los Angeles),-300 So. Grand Ave., Suite 2620, 90017, pg. 740 — IT
KOO KOO ROO, INC., 11075 Santa Monica Blvd., Ste. 225, 90025, pg. 966 — PB
KORN/FERRY INTERNATIONAL, 1800 Century Park E., #900, 90067, pg. 632 — PV
Korn/Ferry International, 601 S. Figueroa, Ste. 1900, 90017, pg. 633 — PV
Korn/Ferry International, 1800 Century Park E., Ste. 900, 90067, pg. 633 — PV
Kredietbank Representative Office (Los Angeles), 550 S. Hope St., Ste. 1775, 90071, pg. 760 — IT
Kubota America Corp., 523 West Sixth St., Ste. 723, 90014, pg. 762 — IT
Kubota Corp.-Los Angeles Office, 523 W. Sixth St., Ste. 723, 90014, pg. 762 — IT
Kuwait Airways, West Coast Region, 510 W. 6th St., 90014, pg. 764 — IT
LA REINA, INC., 316 N. Ford Blvd., 90022, pg. 640 — PV
Light Signatures, Inc., 6171 W. Century Blvd., 90045, pg. 588 — PB
Lindberg Heat Treating Co., 2900 S. Sunol Dr., 90023, pg. 999 — PB
LITHOGRAPHIX, INC., 13500 S. Figueroa St., 90061, pg. 670 — PV
LLOYD PROPERTIES, 12400 Wilshire Blvd., Ste. 1180, 90025, pg. 672 — PV
Logicon R & D Associates, 6053 W. Century Blvd., 90045, pg. 1199 — PB
Lois/EJL, 5700 Wilshire Blvd., #600, 90036, pg. 1011 — PB
Lois/EJL Los Angeles, 5700 Wilshire Blvd., 6th Fl., 90036, pg. 1011 — PB
LOIS/EJL LOS ANGELES, 5700 Wilshire Blvd., 90036, pg. 673 — PV
Los Angeles Branch Office, 445 S. Figueroa St., Ste. 3700, 90071, pg. 935 — PB
THE LOS ANGELES DEPARTMENT OF WATER AND POWER (DWP), Box 51111 Rm. 1550, 90051-0100, pg. 676 — PV
Los Angeles Die Casting, 340 Crocker St., 90013, pg. 142 — PB
Los Angeles Division, 11766 Wilshire Blvd., 18th Fl., 90025, pg. 1613 — PB
Los Angeles Magazine, 11100 Santa Monica Blvd., 7th Fl., 90025, pg. 513 — PB
Los Angeles Smoking & Curing Company, 778 Kohler St., 90021, pg. 810 — PB
Los Angeles Times, Times Mirror Square, 90053, pg. 1616 — PB
Los Angeles Times Syndicate, Times Mirror Square, 90053, pg. 1616 — PB
Los Angeles Times-Washington Post News Service, Inc., 145 Spring St., 90053, pg. 1743 — PB
Los Angeles Union Terminal, Inc., 746 S. Central Ave., Rm. 250, 90021, pg. 1668 — PV
Lufkin Industries, Gear Div., 12555 W. Jefferson, Ste. 345, 90066-7037, pg. 1019 — PB
THE MACNEAL-SCHWENDLER CORP., 815 Colorado Blvd., 90041-1777, pg. 1030 — PV
MADISON GRAHAM COLORGRAPHICS, INC., 150 N. Myers St., 90033, pg. 694 — PV
Madison Industries, 1900 E. 64th St., 90001, pg. 428 — PV
MAGUIRE PARTNERS, 355 S. Grande Ave., Ste. 4500, 90071, pg. 696 — PV
Manufacturers Bank, 515 S. Figueroa St., 90071, pg. 1179 — IT
Manulife Financial - Los Angeles, 10877 Wilshire Blvd., Ste. 700, 90024, pg. 841 — IT
MARK FABRICKS, INC., 1555 Newton St., 90021, pg. 704 — PV
Mars-Los Angeles, Crossroads of The World, 6671 Sunset Blvd., Ste. 1591, 90028, pg. 706 — PV
AC MARTIN PARTNERS, 811 W. Seventh St., 90017, pg. 708 — PV
GILDA MARX INC., 5340 Alla Rd., 90066, pg. 710 — PV
Master Products Mfg. Co., 3841 E. 14th St., 90023, pg. 304 — PV
MAXICARE HEALTH PLANS, INC., 1149 S. Broadway, 90015, pg. 1061 — PV
MAXINE OF HOLLYWOOD, INC., 2424 E. 28th St., 90058, pg. 716 — PV
Robert E. McKee, Inc., 4701 San Fernando Rd. W., 90039, pg. 921 — PV
The Meijiseimei Insurance Services of California, Inc., 777 S. Figueroa St., Ste 1300, 90017, pg. 854 — IT
Mellon Financial Services, 300 S. Grand Ave., Ste. 1200, 90071, pg. 1085 — IT
Mellon First Business Bank, One Bunker Hill Bldg., 601 W. Fifth St., 90071, pg. 1085 — PB
MENDELSOHN/ZIEN ADVERTISING, INC., Westwood Gateway, 11111 Santa Monica Blvd., 22nd Fl., 90025-3356, pg. 731 — PV
Mercury Air Cargo, 6851 W. Imperial Hwy., 90045, pg. 1093 — PB
MERCURY AIR GROUP INC., 5456 McConnell Ave., 90066, pg. 1092 — PV
MERCURY GENERAL CORPORATION, 4484 Wilshire Blvd., 90010, pg. 1093 — PB
Mercury Refueling, Inc., 6851 W. Imperial Hwy., 90045, pg. 1093 — PB
MERLE NORMAN COSMETICS, INC., 9130 Bellanca Ave., 90045, pg. 733 — PV
Merrill Corporation, 1926 E. 14th, 90021, pg. 1097 — PB
J.W. Messner, Inc., 4929 Wilshire Blvd., Ste. 570, 90010-3819, pg. 734 — PV
Mexicana Airlines, 9841 Airport Blvd., Ste. 200, 90045, pg. 332 — IT
Miss Universe, L.P., 1801 Century Park E., Ste. 2100, 90067, pg. 1108 — PV

Geographic Index-U.S.

Mission Valley Development Co., P.O. Box 2950, 90051, pg. 295 — PB

The Mitsubishi Trust & Banking Corporation, 801 S. Figueroa St., Ste. 2400, 90017, pg. 876 — IT

Mitsui & Co. (U.S.A.), Inc., 6015 Figueroa St., 90017, pg. 879 — IT

The Mitsui Trust and Banking Company - Los Angeles, 611 W. Sixth St., Ste. 3800, 90017, pg. 883 — IT

Mitsui Trust & Banking Company, Limited, 611 West Sixth St., Ste. 3800, 90017, pg. 883 — IT

MOBILE TECHNOLOGY INC., 9841 Airport Blvd., 12th Fl., 90045, pg. 754 — PV

MONICO ALLOYS, INC., 2301 E. 15th St., 90021-4848, pg. 757 — PV

Monogram Aerospace Fasteners, Inc., 3423 S. Garfield Ave., 90022-0547, pg. 1054 — PB

Montgomery & Collins, Inc., 3700 Wilshire Blvd., 4th Fl., 90010-2905, pg. 366 — PB

Montgomery & Collins, Inc. of Florida, 3700 Wilshire Blvd., 90010-2905, pg. 366 — PB

Montgomery & Collins, Inc. of Indiana, 3700 Wilshire Blvd., Ste. 400, 90010-2905, pg. 366 — PB

Montgomery & Collins, Inc. of Massachusetts, 3700 Wilshire Blvd., Ste. 400, 90010-2905, pg. 366 — PB

Morgan Guaranty Trust Company, 444 S. Flower St., 90071, pg. 1129 — PB

J.P. Morgan & Co. Incorporated, 444 Flower St., 90071, pg. 1129 — PB

J.P. Morgan California, 444 S. Flower St., 90071, pg. 1129 — PB

J.P. Morgan Investment Management Inc., 444 S. Flower St., 90071, pg. 1129 — PB

Morgan Stanley Los Angeles, 1999 Ave. of the Stars, Ste. 2400, 90067, pg. 1132 — PB

MUTUAL TRADING CO., INC., 431 Crocker St., 90013, pg. 770 — PV

BEN MYERSON CANDY COMPANY, INC., 928 Towne Ave., 90021, pg. 771 — PV

NLI Properties West, Inc., 445 S. Figueroa St., Ste. 2850, 90071, pg. 935 — IT

NTS Engineering, 5300 West 104th St., 90045, pg. 1161 — PB

NTS-Los Angeles Division, 5320 W. 104th St., 90045, pg. 1161 — PB

NWQ Investment Managaement Company, 655 S. Hope St., 11th Fl., 90017, pg. 1673 — PB

NADEL ARCHITECTS, INC., 1990 S. Bundy Dr. Ste. 400, 90025, pg. 773 — PV

National Aerosol Products Co., 2193 E. 14th St., 90021, pg. 663 — PB

NATIONAL CORSET SUPPLY HOUSE, 3240 E. 26th St., 90023, pg. 781 — PV

Neutrogena Corporation, 5760 W. 96th St., 90045-5544, pg. 928 — PB

New Line Cinema-Los Angeles, 116 N. Robertson Blvd., 90048, pg. 1615 — IT

New World Entertainment, Inc., 1440 S. Sepulveda Blvd., 90025, pg. 926 — IT

Nichimen America, Inc., Los Angeles Branch, Citicorp Center, 725 S. Figueroa St., Ste. 1535, 90017-5415, pg. 928 — IT

Nihon Keizai Shimbun America, Inc., 725 S. Figueroa St., Ste. 1515, 90017, pg. 929 — IT

Nikko Securities Co., Los Angeles, 800 Wilshire Blvd., Ste 1050, 90017, pg. 930 — IT

Nippon Credit Bank Ltd., Los Angeles, 550 S. Hope St., #2500, 90071, pg. 932 — IT

Nippon Steel U.S.A., Inc., 601 S. Figueroa, Ste. 4470, 90017-3405, pg. 940 — IT

Nittetsu Shoji America, Inc., 725 S. Figueroa St., Ste. 1860, 90017, pg. 939 — IT

Nordisk Aviation Products, Inc., 5450 W. 102nd. St., 90045, pg. 961 — IT

Northern Trust Bank of California, N.A., 355 S. Grand Ave., Ste. 2600, 90071, pg. 1196 — PB

Northern Trust Bank of California, N.A., 10877 Wilshire Blvd., Ste. 100, 90024, pg. 1196 — PB

NORTHROP GRUMMAN CORPORATION, 1840 Century Park E., 90067, pg. 1197 — PB

OC America Construction, Inc., 420 E. Third St., Ste. 600, 90013, pg. 995 — IT

OC Real Estate Management, Inc., 420 E. Third St., Ste 600, 90013, pg. 995 — IT

ONC Company, 1990 S. Bundy Dr., 90025, pg. 1283 — IT

Obayashi Corporation-Los Angeles, 420 E. Third St., Ste. 600, 90013, pg. 995 — IT

OCCIDENTAL PETROLEUM CORPORATION, 10889 Wilshire Blvd., 90024, pg. 1210 — PB

Oldcastle, Inc., 11777 San Vicente Blvd., Ste. 747, 90049, pg. 242 — IT

One More Time Inc., 4020 BandiniBlvd., 90023, pg. 111 — PV

O'Neil Data Systems, Inc., 2005 Armacost Ave., 90025, pg. 817 — PV

WILLIAM O'NEIL & CO., INC., 12655 Beatrice St., 90066, pg. 817 — PV

ORIX USA Corporation-Los Angeles, 500 S. Hope St., Ste. 1600, 90017, pg. 1009 — IT

Outdoor Systems, Inc., 1731 Workman St., 90031, pg. 1235 — PB

Outdoor Systems, Inc.-New York, 1731 Workman St., 90031, pg. 1235 — PB

OWEN PACIFIC, 1236 S. Compton Ave., 90021, pg. 824 — PV

PHC Holdings, Inc., 10900 Wilshire Blvd., Ste. 1600, 90024, pg. 831 — PV

Pacific Combining Corp., 3055 E. Fruitland Ave., 90058, pg. 802 — PB

PACIFIC ENTERPRISES, 555 W. Fifth St., Ste. 2900, 90013, pg. 1249 — PB

Pacific Enterprises International, 555 W. 5th St., Ste. 2900, 90013-1011, pg. 1249 — PB

Pacific Enterprises Leasing Co., 633 W. 5th St., Ste. 5400, 90071, pg. 1249 — PB

PACIFIC HOLDING CORPORATION, Murdock Plaza, Ste. 1600, 10900 Wilshire Blvd., 90024, pg. 831 — PV

Pacific Indemnity Co., 6500 Wilshire Blvd., 90048, pg. 355 — PB

Pacific Insurance Co., 420 Wilshire Blvd., 90010, pg. 1011 — PB

Pacific Interstate Company, 633 W. Fifth St., Ste. 5400, 90071, pg. 1249 — PB

Pacific Interstate Mojave Company, 633 W. Fifth St., Ste. 5400, 90071-2006, pg. 1249 — PB

Pacific Interstate Offshore Company, 633 W. Fifth St., Ste. 5400, 90071-2006, pg. 1249 — PB

Pacific Interstate Transmission Company, 633 W. Fifth St., 90071-2006, pg. 1249 — PB

Pacific Interstate Transmission Company (Arctic), 633 W. Fifth St., Ste. 5400, 90071-2006, pg. 1249 — PB

Pacific Library Tower, 633 W. Fifth St., Ste. 5400, 90071-2006, pg. 1249 — PB

Pacific Lighting Gas Development Co., 633 W. Fifth St., Ste. 5400, 90071-2006, pg. 1249 — PB

Pacific Lighting Real Estate Group, 633 W. 5th St., Ste. 5400, 90071, pg. 1249 — PB

Pacific Offshore Pipeline Company, 633 W. Fifth St., Ste. 5400, 90071-2006, pg. 1249 — PB

Pacific Synthetic Fuel Company, 633 W. Fifth St., Ste. 5400, 90071-2006, pg. 1249 — PB

Pacific Western Resources Co., 633 W. Fifth St., Ste. 5400, 90071-2006, pg. 1249 — PB

Palomar Transit Mix Co., P.O. Box 2950, 90051, pg. 296 — PB

PARAMOUNT FITNESS CORP., 6450 E. Bandini Blvd., 90040-3185, pg. 838 — PV

Paramount Pictures Corporation, 5555 Melrose Ave., 90038, pg. 776 — PV

Parcwood-Sacramento Joint Venture, 2049 Century Pk. E., Ste. 755, 90067, pg. 362 — PV

Pardee Construction Company, 10880 Wilshire Blvd., Ste. 1400, 90024, pg. 1764 — PB

PECK JONES CONSTRUCTION, 10866 Wilshire Blvd., 7th Fl., 90024, pg. 846 — PV

Pedus Aviation, 3500 W. First St., 90004, pg. 846 — PV

Pedus Building Services, 3500 W. First St., 90004, pg. 846 — PV

Pedus Food Services, 3500 W. First St., 90004, pg. 846 — PV

Pedus Office Services, 3500 W. First St., 90004, pg. 846 — PV

Pedus Security Services, 3500 W. First St., 90004, pg. 846 — PV

PEDUS SERVICES, INC., 3500 W. First St., 90004, pg. 846 — PV

The Pep Boys-Manny, Moe & Jack of California, 1122 W. Washington Blvd., 90015, pg. 1276 — PV

THE PERVO PAINT COMPANY, 6624 Stanford Ave., 90001, pg. 856 — PV

PETERSEN PUBLISHING COMPANY, L.L.C., 6420 Wilshire Blvd., 90048-5515, pg. 856 — PV

PIONEER ALUMINUM, INC., 3800 E. 26th St., 90023, pg. 866 — PV

PIONEER FOODS, INC., 1625 Sunset Blvd., 90026, pg. 866 — PV

Pitney Bowes Management Services, 1400 S. Grand, Ste. 101, 90015-3011, pg. 1304 — PB

PLATINUM EQUITY HOLDINGS, LLC, 2049 Century Park E., Ste. 2710, 90067, pg. 872 — PV

Playboy Shows, Inc., 8560 Sunset Blvd., 90069, pg. 1310 — PB

POLY PAK AMERICA, INC., 2939 E. Washington Ave., 90023, pg. 875 — PV

Precision Specialty Metals, Inc., 3301 Medford St., 90063, pg. 344 — PV

Preferred Public Storage Co., 2601 S. Eastern Ave., 90040, pg. 227 — PV

Presley-Home Mac Finance Co., Inc., 633 W. 5th St., Ste. 5400, 90071, pg. 1249 — PB

Presley RAC Finance Co., Inc., 633 W. Fifth St., Ste. 5400, 90071, pg. 1249 — PB

Price Stern Sloan Inc., 11835 Olympic Blvd., 5th Fl., 90064, pg. 1215 — IT

Princess Cruise Lines, 10100 Santa Monica Blvd., 90067, pg. 1035 — IT

Procter & Gamble Productions, Inc., 9200 Sunset Blvd., Ste. 525, 90069, pg. 1331 — PV

Promotional Broadcast Services, 8544 Sunset Blvd., 90069, pg. 1166 — PV

The Prudential - Jon Douglas Company, 11900 W. Olympic Blvd., Ste. 499, 90064, pg. 892 — PV

PUNCH PRESS PRODUCTS, INC., 1911 E. 51st St., 90058, pg. 895 — PV

Quantum Media International, Inc., 10990 Wilshire Blvd., 90024, pg. 899 — PV

Questron Div., 11835 W. Olympic Blvd., 90064, pg. 1215 — IT

RLI Southern California Regional Office, 3435 Wilshire Blvd., Ste. 970, 90010, pg. 1356 — PB

RNL/Interplan, 611 W. 6th St., Ste. 350, 90017, pg. 905 — PV

Radar Systems Group, P. O. Box 92426, 90009-2426, pg. 1364 — PB

Rahn Industries, 7720 Maie Ave., 90001-2693, pg. 1632 — PV

Railroad Insurance Brokers, Inc., 3700 Wilshire Blvd., Ste. 900, 90010, pg. 366 — PB

Red Calliope & Associates, Inc., 13003 S. Figueroa, 90061, pg. 465 — PV

Reed Travel Publishing-Los Angeles, 9911 W. Pico Blvd., 11th Fl., 90035, pg. 1097 — IT

REHRIG PACIFIC COMPANY, 4010 E. 26th St., 90023, pg. 919 — PV

Reliance Land Co., P.O. Box 2950, 90051, pg. 296 — PB

RELIANCE STEEL & ALUMINUM CO., 2550 E. 25th St., 90058, pg. 1375 — PB

Reliance Transport Co., P.O. Box 2950, 90051, pg. 296 — PB

Republic Entertainment, Inc., 5700 Wilshire Blvd., Ste. 525, 90036, pg. 776 — PV

Republic Factors Corp., 1605 W. Olympic Blvd., 90015, pg. 1380 — PV

George Rice & Sons, 2001 N. Soto St., 90032, pg. 1779 — PB

Rio Norte Este Co., P.O. Box 2950, 90051, pg. 296 — PB

River Bend Corp., P.O. Box 2950, 90051, pg. 296 — PB

River Ranch - Los Angeles, 777 South Mission Road, 90023, pg. 491 — IT

River Vista Development Co., 3200 San Fernando Rd., 90065, pg. 296 — PB

ROLL INTERNATIONAL CORPORATION, 11444 W. Olympic Blvd., 90064, pg. 941 — PV

ROLLED STEEL PRODUCTS CORPORATION, 2187 S. Garfield Ave., 90040, pg. 941 — PV

Ross Loos Hospital, Inc., 1711 W. Temple St., 90026, pg. 360 — PB

Runway Two Five Corporation, 11022 Aviation Blvd., 90045, pg. 1022 — PV

SFM/Los Angeles, 11444 W. Olympic Blvd., 90064-1544, pg. 957 — PV

SOCO-Lynch Corp., 3270 E. Washington Blvd., 90023, pg. 1458 — IT

SABAN ENTERTAINMENT, 10960 Wilshire Blvd., 90024, pg. 959 — PV

Sakura Bank - Los Angeles Agency, 515 S. Figueroa St., 90071, pg. 1179 — IT

Salick Health Care, Inc., 8201 Beverly Blvd., 90048-4520, pg. 1524 — IT

Sanger Rock and Sand, P.O. Box 2950, 90051, pg. 296 — PB

Sanpaolo-Los Angeles Branch, 444 S. Flower St., 45th Fl., 90071, pg. 691 — IT

Santee Dairies, 231 E. 23rd St., 90011, pg. 1349 — PB

Sanwa Bank California, 601 S. Figueroa St., 90017, pg. 1189 — IT

CECIL SAYDAH COMPANY, 2935 E. 12th St., 90023, pg. 969 — PV

L.M. SCOFIELD COMPANY, 6533 Bandini Blvd., 90040, pg. 976 — PV

ScotiaMocatta, 606 South Olive St., Ste. 2140, 90014, pg. 156 — IT

Sealright Mfg. West, Inc., 4209 E. Noakes St., 90023, pg. 1452 — PV

Sequent Computer Systems, Inc., 11100 Santa Monica Blvd., Ste. 200, 90025, pg. 1459 — PB

Servco California Inc., 2222 Davie Ave., 90040, pg. 986 — PB

SERVICE PACKING COMPANY-UNITED FOOD GROUP, 3425 E. Vernon Ave., 90058, pg. 986 — PV

SHIELD SECURITY, INC., 200 N. Westmoreland Ave., 90004, pg. 994 — PV

Shimizu America Corporation, 1055 W. Seventh St, 1800, 90017, pg. 1233 — IT

Shimizu Land Corporation-Los Angeles Office, 1055 W. Seventh St, 1800, 90017, pg. 1233 — IT

Shuwa Investments Corp., Arco Plaza, 515 S. Flower St., Ste. 1270, 90071, pg. 1237 — IT

Sierra Capital Management Corporation, 888 S. Figueroa St., Ste. 1100, 90017, pg. 1742 — IT

SIMON MARKETING, INC., 1900 Ave. of the Stars, Ste. 400, 90067, pg. 1001 — PV

Sinclair/Ameritone Paint Corp., 6100 S. Garfield, 90040, pg. 663 — PV

Sinclair Paint Co., 6100 S. Garfield Ave., 90040, pg. 663 — IT

SINCLAIR PRINTING & LITHO, INC., 4005 Whiteside St., 90063, pg. 1003 — PV

Singapore Airlines, 5670 Wilshire Blvd., Ste. 1800, 90036, pg. 1374 — IT

SIZZLER INTERNATIONAL, INC., 12655 W. Jefferson Blvd., 90066, pg. 1475 — PB

Sizzler USA, Inc., 12655 W. Jefferson Blvd., 90066, pg. 1475 — PB

Skadden, Arps, Slate, Meagher & Flom LLP, 300 S. Grand Ave., 90071, pg. 1004 — PV

Sloan Canyon Sand Co., P.O. Box 2950, 90051, pg. 296 — PB

SMITH-EMERY COMPANY, 781 E. Washington Blvd., 90021, pg. 1007 — PV

SNACK AMERICA, 6190 E. Slauson Av., 90040, pg. 1010 — PV

Societe Generale, 2029 Century Park E. Ste. 2900, 90067, pg. 1273 — IT

THE SOLENDER GROUP, INC., 1950 Sawtelle Blvd., #304, 90025, pg. 1012 — PV

SOURCE CAPITAL, INC., 11400 W. Olympic Blvd., Ste. 1200, 90064, pg. 1488 — PV

Southern California Gas Co., 555 W. Fifth St., 90013-1011, pg. 1249 — PB

Southern California Gas Tower, 555 W. Fifth St., 90013, pg. 1249 — PB

Southern Pacific Bank, 12300 Wilshire Blvd., Ste. 200, 90025, pg. 872 — PB

Spelling Entertainment Group, Inc., 5700 Wilshire Blvd., 90036-3659, pg. 776 — PV

Spelling Television, 5700 Wilshire Blvd., 90036, pg. 776 — PV

Standard Chartered Bank (Los Angeles), First Interstate Tower, 707 Wilshire Blvd. W14-12, 90017, pg. 1294 — IT

STARVING STUDENTS, INC., 8525 W. Pico Blvd., 2nd Fl., 90035, pg. 1035 — PV

PB - U.S. Public Companies Volume
PV - U.S. Private Companies Volume
IT - International Public & Private Companies Volume

1136

Geographic Index-U.S.

Starwood Lodging Corporation, 11835 W. Olympic Blvd., Ste. 675, 90064, pg. 1512 — PB

Stewart Smith West, Inc., 3200 Wilshire Blvd., 90010, pg. 1508 — IT

Stocker Resources, Inc., 5640 S. Fairfax Ave., 90056, pg. 1308 — PB

Strategic Compensation Associates, 644 S. Figueroa St., 2nd Fl., 90017, pg. 633 — PV

SUISSA MILLER ADVERTISING, INC., 11601 Wilshire Blvd., 16th Fl., 90025, pg. 1049 — PV

Sumikin Bussan International Corp. - Los Angeles Branch, 500 S. Grand Ave., Ste. 1640, 90071, pg. 1308 — IT

The Sumitomo Bank, Ltd.-Los Angeles Branch, 777 S. Figueroa St., Ste. 2600, 90017, pg. 1308 — IT

Sumitomo Corporation of America, 444 S. Flower St., Ste. 1600, 90071, pg. 1312 — IT

The Sumitomo Trust & Banking Co., Ltd., Wells Fargo Ctr. (North Tower), 333 S. Grand Ave., Ste. 5300, 90071, pg. 1317 — IT

SunAmerica Financial, One SunAmerica Center, Century City, 90067-6022, pg. 1533 — PB

SUNAMERICA INC., One Sun America Ctr., 90067-6022, pg. 1532 — PB

SunAmerica Life Insurance Company, One SunAmerica Center, Century City, 90067-6022, pg. 1533 — PB

Suntory International Corp., 515 S. Figueroa St., Ste. 1030, 90071, pg. 1321 — IT

SUPERBA, INC., 1735 S. Santa Fe Ave., 90021, pg. 1054 — PV

Swiss Bank Corporation, 300 S. Grand Ave., Ste.3850, 90071, pg. 1329 — IT

SYSTEMS PARKING, INC., 417 S. Hill St., Ste. 200, 90013, pg. 1061 — PV

TMP Worldwide/Recruitment Division, 10635 Santa Monica Blvd., Ste. 360, 90025, pg. 1065 — PV

Takenaka (U.S.A.) Corporation, Los Angeles Office, 801 S. Figueroa St., Ste. 1070, 90017, pg. 1351 — IT

Tall Wall Media, 8544 Sunset Blvd., 90069-2310, pg. 1166 — PV

Tam O'Shanter Inn, 2980 Los Feliz Blvd., 90039, pg. 654 — PV

Telecredit Collection Service, 6171 W. Century Blvd., 90045, pg. 588 — PB

Telecredit Service Center, Inc., 6171 W. Century Blvd., 90045, pg. 588 — PB

Teledyne Electronic Technologies, 12964 Panama St., 90066-6534, pg. 43 — PB

Teleflora, LLC, 11444 Olympic Blvd., 90064, pg. 941 — PV

Thermador, 5119 District Blvd., 90040, pg. 1053 — PB

Thermo Process Systems Inc./Cal-Doran Metallurgical, Inc., 2830 E. Washington Blvd., 90023, pg. 1594 — PB

Thomas & Betts Automotive, 4371 Valley Blvd., 90032-3632, pg. 1597 — PB

Thomas Lighting-C&I Accent Division, 6430 E. Slauson Ave., 90040, pg. 1599 — PB

Time Publishing Ventures, Inc., Rosbury at Westwood, 11100 Santa Monica Blvd., 90025, pg. 1613 — PB

THE TIMES MIRROR COMPANY, Times Mirror Sq., 90053, pg. 1615 — PB

Todd Pipe & Supply-West L.A., 2331 Predue, 90003, pg. 1090 — PV

Tokai Bank of California, 300 S. Grand Ave., 90071, pg. 1391 — IT

Tokyo Gas, 633 W. 5th St., 90071, pg. 1394 — IT

TOMCO AUTO PRODUCTS, INC., 4330 E. 26th St., 90023, pg. 1090 — PV

TOPA EQUITIES LTD, INC., 1800 Ave. of the Stars, Ste. 1400, 90067, pg. 1091 — PV

TOTTEN TUBES, INC., 1555 Los Palos St., 90023, pg. 1093 — PV

Tourism Malaysia - L.A. Office, Ste. 804, 818 W. 7th St., 90017, pg. 833 — IT

Transamerica Finance Group, Inc., 1150 S. Olive St., 90015, pg. 1630 — PB

Transamerica Investment Services, Inc., 1150 S. Olive St., 90015, pg. 1630 — PB

Transamerica Life Companies, 1150 S. Olive St., 90015, pg. 1630 — PB

Transmix Corporation, 4760 Valley Blvd., 90032, pg. 1489 — PB

TRIANGLE BRASS MANUFACTURING, 3528 Emery St., 90023, pg. 1101 — PV

Triangle Rocks Products, Inc., P.O. Box 2950, 90051, pg. 296 — PB

Tribune Entertainment Company, 5800 Sunset Blvd., 90028, pg. 1636 — PB

Triumph Releasing Corporation, 3801 Barham Blvd., 3rd Fl., 90068, pg. 1282 — IT

Triumph Releasing Corporation - Pacific Territory, 3801 Barham Blvd., 3rd Fl., 90068-1046, pg. 1282 — IT

Truck Underwriters Association, 4680 Wilshire Blvd., 90010, pg. 110 — IT

Turner Construction Co., 555 W. Fifth St., 90013, pg. 1645 — PB

Turner Entertainment Company, 1888 Century Park E., 90067, pg. 1615 — PB

Twentieth Century Fox Film Corp., 10201 W. Pico Blvd., 90035, pg. 926 — IT

20th Century Fox Home Entertainment, 2121 Ave. of the Stars, 25th Fl., 90067, pg. 275 — PB

20th Century Products Div., 3628 Crenshaw Blvd., 90016, pg. 153 — PB

UPN-United Paramount Network, 11800 Wilshire Blvd., 90025, pg. 352 — PB

UPN-United Paramount Network, 11800 Wilshire Blvd., 90025, pg. 777 — PV

URS Greiner, Inc., 445 S. Figueroa St., Ste. 2700, 90071, pg. 1658 — PB

USHAWL, Inc., 8201 Beverly Blvd., 90048-4520, pg. 1525 — IT

Union Bank of Switzerland, 444 S. Flower St., 45th Fl., 90071, pg. 1440 — IT

USA Network, 2049 Century Park East, 90067, pg. 1686 — PB

U.S. Yellow Pages, 8544 Sunset Blvd., 90069, pg. 1168 — PV

Unitel Video, Inc. - Studio, Post-Production & Computer Facilities, 729 N. Highland, pg. 1692 — PB

Universal Paper Goods, 7171 Telegraph Rd., 90040, pg. 460 — IT

Utell International-Los Angeles, 9911 W. Pico Blvd., 11th Fl., 90035, pg. 1098 — IT

Vickers Sterer Engineering, 4690 Colorado Blvd., 90039-1106, pg. 25 — PB

Vitt Media International, Inc. - Los Angeles, 12400 Wilshire Blvd., Ste. 610, 90025, pg. 1142 — PV

Wako Securities (America), Inc., 515 South Flower St., Ste. 1670, 90071, pg. 1485 — IT

Warner/Chappell Music Inc., 10585 Santa Monica Blvd., 90025-4950, pg. 1612 — PV

Warrior, Inc., 11766 Wishire Blvd., Ste. 720, 90025-6538, pg. 782 — PB

Waste King, 6100 Bandini Blvd., 90058, pg. 1053 — PB

Wells Fargo & Company, 633 W. Fifth St., 90071, pg. 1753 — PB

WESLOCK NATIONAL, INC., 13344 S. Main St., 90061, pg. 1163 — PB

West Coast Conversion Co., Inc., 5456 McConnell Ave., 90066, pg. 296 — PB

West Dallas, 110 E. Ninth St., Ste. C425, 90076, pg. 1429 — PB

Western Environmental Contracting, Inc., P.O. Box 2950, 90051, pg. 296 — PB

Western Interactive Media, 8544 Sunset Blvd., 90069, pg. 1166 — PV

WESTERN INTERNATIONAL MEDIA CORPORATION, 8544 Sunset Blvd., 90069, pg. 1165 — PV

Western Motivational Incentives Group, Inc., 8544 Sunset Blvd., 90069, pg. 1167 — PV

Western Multicultural Group, 8544 Sunset Blvd., 90069, pg. 1167 — PV

Western Product Placement, 8544 Sunset Blvd., 90069, pg. 1167 — PV

WESTERN REINSURANCE BROKERS, INC., 3435 Wilshire Blvd., Ste. 123, 90010, pg. 1168 — PV

Western States Assoc., 4601 Wilshire Blvd., Ste. 110, 90010, pg. 719 — PV

Western Thermal Soils Co., P.O. Box 2950, 90051, pg. 296 — PB

WestLB Los Angeles, 633 W. 5th St., 90071, pg. 1493 — IT

Westpac Banking Corporation (Los Angeles Branch), 300 S. Grand Ave., Ste. 3800, 90017-3165, pg. 1496 — IT

Wigand Fabric Wall Systems, 612 Moulton Ave., Studio 5, 90031, pg. 1038 — PB

WINDSOR FASHIONS, 3901 S. Broadway, 90037, pg. 1182 — PV

Worldvision Enterprises, Inc., 5700 Wilshire Blvd., 5th Fl., 90036, pg. 776 — PV

Xerox Computer Services, 5310 Beethoven St., 90066, pg. 1784 — PB

Yamaichi International (America) Inc.-Los Angeles Branch, 333 South Hope St., Ste. 2430, 90071, pg. 1517 — IT

Yamazaki California Inc., 826 E. Third St., 90013, pg. 1519 — IT

Year 2K Communications, 5700 Wilshire Blvd., # 600, 90036, pg. 1011 — PV

THE YUCAIPA COMPANIES, 10000 Santa Monica Blvd., 5th Fl., 90067-7007, pg. 1202 — PV

Z. CAVARICCI INC., 2535 E. 12th St., Unit A, 90021, pg. 1203 — PV

Zenith Media Services, Inc., 6300 Wilshire Blvd., 90048, pg. 1204 — PV

ZERO CORPORATION, 444 S. Flower, Ste. 2100, 90071-2922, pg. 1791 — PB

THE ZIPPERTUBING CO., 13000 S. Broadway, 90061, pg. 1207 — PV

Los Banos

FRL, Inc., 200 W. Willmott, 93635, pg. 396 — PB

Los Gatos

CAERE CORPORATION, 100 Cooper Ct., 95032, pg. 291 — PB

Maxxim Medical, 14300 Winchester Blvd., 95030, pg. 1063 — PB

SCM MICROSYSTEMS, INC., 131 Albright Way, 95030, pg. 1417 — PV

XKD CORPORATION, 101 Cooper Court, 95030, pg. 1194 — PV

Los Olivos

The Firestone Vineyard, Zaca Station Rd., 93441, pg. 1321 — IT

Nord Resources Corp., 2963 Grand Ave., 93441, pg. 1188 — PV

Lower Lake

McLaughlin Mine, 26775 Morgan Valley Rd., 95457-1010, pg. 833 — PB

Lucerne Valley

Pluess-Staufer (California), Inc., Crystal Creek Rd., 92356, pg. 1061 — IT

Lynwood

Goldenberg Group, Inc., 11852 S. Alameda St., 90262, pg. 1193 — PB

Earle M. Jorgensen Company/Los Angeles, 10650 Alameda St., 90262, pg. 600 — PV

UNIVERSAL MOLDING COMPANY, 10807 Stanford Ave., 90262, pg. 1127 — PV

W.G.C. Corp., 2600 E. Imperial Hwy., 90262, pg. 1206 — PV

Madera

Bisceglia Brothers Wine Co., 25427 Ave. 13, 93637, pg. 300 — PB

Carris of California, Inc., 2100 W. Almond, 93637, pg. 215 — PV

Corrugated Packaging, 24600 Ave. 13, P.O. Box 1327, 93637, pg. 737 — PB

Malibu

Hughes Research Laboratories, 3011 Malibu Canyon Rd., 90265, pg. 721 — PB

JAKKS PACIFIC, INC., 24955 Pacific Coast Hwy., B202, 90265, pg. 923 — PB

Manhattan Beach

Manhattan Beach, 1800 Rosecrans Ave., 90266, pg. 795 — IT

Piper Jaffray Inc., 225 S. Sepulveda Blvd., Ste. 310, 90266-6866, pg. 1303 — PB

Manteca

DELICATO VINEYARDS, 12001 S. Hwy. 99, 95336, pg. 322 — PV

Stockton Savings Bank-Manteca, 201 N. Main St., 95336, pg. 1575 — PB

Suprema Specialties West, Inc., 14253 S. Airport Way, 95336, pg. 1541 — PB

Marina Del Rey

Aurora Electronics, 4755 Alla Rd., 90292-6378, pg. 296 — PB

CALPROP CORPORATION, 13160 Mindanao Way, Ste. 180, 90292, pg. 296 — PB

Del Rey Restaurant Corp., 13813 Fiji Way, 90291, pg. 1022 — PV

Dentsu Corporation of America, Los Angeles Office, 310 Washington Blvd., # 1, 90292, pg. 393 — PV

Fattal & Collins (F&C), 4640 Admiralty Way, # 900, 90292, pg. 765 — PB

QUARTERDECK CORP., 13160 Mindanao Way, 90292, pg. 1350 — PB

Syseca Inc., 4553 Glencoe Ave., Ste. 100, 90292, pg. 1384 — IT

Toppan Printing Co. (America) Inc.-Los Angeles, Marina Business Center, 4451 Glencoe Ave., Ste. 230, 90292, pg. 1399 — IT

Martinez

Foster Wheeler Martinez, 550 Solano Way, 94553, pg. 677 — PB

Plant Maintenance, Inc., 201 Berrellesa St., 94553, pg. 1011 — PV

Pohang Steel America Pty., Ltd (POSAM), 2530 Arnold Dr., Ste. 170, 94553, pg. 1062 — IT

Van Leeuwen Pipe & Tube Corp., 370 Ferry St., 94553, pg. 1450 — IT

Marysville

Windsor Door, 1370 Furneaux Dr., 95901, pg. 69 — PB

Mc Kittrick

Shell West Exploration & Production Inc., P.O. Box 4, 19590 Seventh Standard Rd., 93251-9709, pg. 1142 — IT

Texaco USA, 3646 Reward Rd., 93251-9734, pg. 1583 — PB

Menlo Park

Accountemps, 2884 Sand Hill Rd., 94025, pg. 775 — PB

The Affiliates, 2884 Sand Hill Rd., 94025, pg. 775 — PB

Argonaut Co., 350 Middlefield, 94025, pg. 129 — PB

The Benjamin/Cummings Publishing Company, 2725 Sand Hill Rd., 94025, pg. 1026 — IT

CBT SYSTEMS USA LTD., 1005 Hamilton Ct., 94025, pg. 275 — PB

CARCO ELECTRONICS, 195 Constitution Dr., 94025, pg. 208 — PV

CONSOLIDATED FREIGHTWAYS CORP., 175 Linfield Dr., 94025, pg. 435 — PB

Environmental Health Strategies, 149 Commonwealth Dr., 94025, pg. 609 — PB

Ericsson-Raynet, 155 Constitution Dr., 94025, pg. 1365 — IT

THE FAILURE GROUP, INC., 149 Commonwealth Dr., 94025, pg. 609 — PB

GeneTrace Systems, Inc., 333 Ravenswood Ave., 94025, pg. 958 — PV

Guidant Corporation-Cardiac & Vascular Surgery Group, 135 Constitution Dr., 94025, pg. 768 — PB

Robert Half, 2884 Sand Hill Rd., 94025, pg. 775 — PB

Geographic Index-U.S.

ROBERT HALF INTERNATIONAL INC., 2884 Sand Hill Rd., Ste. 200, 94025, pg. 774 PB

Hillhaven Convalescent Hospital Menlo Park, 16 Coleman Place, 94025, pg. 1713 PB

Indosuez Ventures, 2180 Sand Hill Rd., Ste. 450, 94025, pg. 314 IT

INFORMIX SOFTWARE, P.O. Box 60000, 4100 Bohannon Dr., 94025, pg. 876 PB

Kohlberg Kravis Roberts, 2800 Sandhill Rd., Ste.200, 94025, pg. 629 PV

L3 Communications Randtron Systems, 130 Constitution Dr., 94025, pg. 639 PV

MSC Menlo Park Office, 120 Independence Dr., 94025, pg. 1031 PB

Menlo Logistics, 1020 Marsh Rd., Ste. 210, 94025, pg. 281 PB

METCAL, INC., 1530 O'Brien Dr., 94025, pg. 735 PB

Morgan Stanley Menlo Park, 3000 Sand Hill Rd., Bldg 4, Ste. 250, 94025, pg. 1132 PV

Nuance Communications, 1380 Willow Road, 94025, pg. 958 PV

OfficeTeam, 2884 Sand Hill Rd., 94025, pg. 775 PB

PHARMCHEM LABORATORIES, INC., 1505 A O'Brien Dr., 94025, pg. 1285 PB

Pharmetrix Corporation, 1330 O'Brien Dr., 94025, pg. 1090 IT

Pilkington Visioncare, 2420 Sand Hill Rd., Ste. 200, 94025, pg. 1056 IT

Piper Jaffray Inc., 2500 Sand Hill Rd., Ste. 200, 94025-7016, pg. 1301 PB

PowerHouse Systems, Inc., 190 Independence Dr., 94025, pg. 261 IT

RHI Consulting, 2884 Sand Hill Rd., 94025, pg. 775 PB

RHI Management Resources, 2884 Sand Hill Rd., 94025, pg. 775 PB

RAYCHEM CORPORATION, 300 Constitution Dr., 94025-1164, pg. 1362 PB

Raychem International Corporation, 300 Constitution Dr., 94025, pg. 1362 PB

Raychem International Manufacturing Corp., 300 Constitution Dr., 94025, pg. 1362 PB

Recovery Inn of Menlo Park, 570 Willow Rd., 94025, pg. 1715 PB

Redwood Systems, 175 Linfield Dr., 94025, pg. 435 PB

Ricoh California Research Center, 2882 Sandhill Rd. Ste. 115, 94025-7022, pg. 1114 IT

SRI Consulting, 333 Ravenswood Ave., 94025-3493, pg. 958 PV

SRI Development Corp., 333 Ravenswood Ave., 94025, pg. 958 PV

SRI INTERNATIONAL, 333 Ravenswood Ave., 94025-3493, pg. 958 PV

SEQUUS PHARMACEUTICALS, INC., 960 Hamilton Ct., 94025, pg. 1460 PB

Sunset Publishing Corporation, 80 Willow Rd., 94025, pg. 1613 PB

Merced

Stockton Savings Bank-Merced, 3065 G St., 95350, pg. 1575 PB

Mill Valley

S & P COMPANY, Bldg. B, 100 Shoreline Hwy., Ste. 395, 94941, pg. 954 PV

Smith & Hawken, 117 E. Strawberry Dr., 94941, pg. 279 PB

Milpitas

ADAC LABORATORIES INC., 540 Alder Dr., 95035, pg. 3 PB

Adaptec - Corporate Headquarters, 691 S. Milpitas Blvd., 95035, pg. 19 PB

ADAPTEC, INC., 691 S. Milpitas Blvd., 95035, pg. 19 PB

Allied Security Inc., 1900 McCarthy Blvd., Ste. 302, 95035, pg. 41 PV

Atari Games Corporation, 675 Sycamore Dr., 95035, pg. 1727 PB

C-CUBE MICROSYSTEMS, 1778 McCarthy Blvd., 95035, pg. 272 PB

CALIFORNIA MICRO DEVICES, 215 Topaz St., 95035, pg. 293 PB

California Micro Devices Corporation - Milpitas, 215 Topaz St., 95035-5430, pg. 293 PB

EMBEDDED PERFORMANCE, INC., 1860 Barber Ln., 95034, pg. 373 PV

INTERNATIONAL MICROCIRCUITS, INC., 525 Los Coches St., 95035, pg. 571 PV

LSI LOGIC CORP., 1551 McCarthy Blvd., 95035, pg. 971 PB

LifeScan, Inc., 1000 Gilbraltar Dr., 95035-6314, pg. 928 PB

LINEAR TECHNOLOGY CORP., 1630 McCarthy Blvd., 95035-7417, pg. 1000 PB

Lockheed Martin Fairchild Imaging Sensors, 1801 McCarthy Blvd., 95053, pg. 1008 PB

B.T. MANCINI CO., INC., 876 So. Milpitas Blvd., 95036, pg. 699 PV

T. Marzetti Company - West, 876 Yosemite Dr., 95035, pg. 977 PB

Maxtor Corporation, 510 Cottonwood Dr., 95035, pg. 641 IT

NETWORK PERIPHERALS INC., 1371 McCarthy Blvd., 95035, pg. 1169 PB

North American Transformer, Inc., 1200 Piper Dr., 95035, pg. 1398 PB

Octel Messaging Division, 1001 Murphy Ranch Rd., 95035-7912, pg. 1017 PB

Quartum, 500 McCarthy Blvd., 95035, pg. 1350 PB

QUANTUM CORPORATION, 500 McCarthy Blvd., 95035, pg. 1350 PB

Quartum Corporation, 1900 McCarthy Blvd., Ste. 210, 95035, pg. 1350 PB

Quartum Intl. Disc., Inc., 500 McCarthy Blvd., 95035, pg. 1350 PB

READ-RITE CORPORATION, 345 Los Coches St., 95035, pg. 1366 PB

Solectron California Corporation, 847 Gibraltar Dr., 95035, pg. 1483 PB

SOLECTRON CORPORATION, 777 Gibraltar Dr., 95035, pg. 1483 PB

STORAGE DIMENSIONS, INC., 1656 McCarthy Blvd., 95035, pg. 1522 PB

Sun Microsystems Federal Inc., 1100 Cadillas Ct., 95035-3025, pg. 1531 PB

Tatung Science & Technology, Inc., 1840 McCarthy Blvd., 95035, pg. 1357 IT

Telecommunications Technology, 195 S. Milpitas Blvd., 95035, pg. 1658 PB

URS Greiner, Inc., 100 N. Milpitas Blvd., Ste. 160, 95035, pg. 1682 PB

U.S. Filter/Polymetrics, 960 Ames Ave., 95035, pg. 1682 PB

XICOR, INC., 1511 Buckeye Dr., 95035, pg. 1785 PB

Mira Loma

ADVANCE BUSINESS GRAPHICS, 3810 Wabash Dr., 91752, pg. 18 PV

Harte-Hanks Shoppers, 3885 Wabash St/Harte Hanks, 91752-1143, pg. 794 PB

Penn Emblem Co., 1199 Inland Ave., 91752, pg. 849 PV

Mission Hills

Facey Medical Foundation, 11165 Sepulveda, 91345, pg. 118 PV

PHARMAVITE CORP., 15451 San Fernando Mission Blvd., 91345, pg. 860 PV

Pharmavite Corporation, 15451 San Fernando Mission Blvd., 91345, pg. 1013 IT

Mission Viejo

Adaptive Information Systems, 26001 Pala, 92691, pg. 946 IT

Basic Vegetable Products, 27758 Santa Margarita Pkwy., 92691-6709, pg. 121 PV

Charter Mission Viejo Behavioral Health System, Inc., 23228 Madero, 92691, pg. 1035 PB

Comprehensive Business Services Inc., 26722 Plaza Dr., 92691 , pg. 423 PV

Downey Savings & Loan Association, F.A., Crown Valley Ctr. Branch, 27529 Puerta Real, 92691, pg. 526 PB

FRANCHISE SERVICES, INC., 26722 Plaza Dr., 92691, pg. 423 PV

James Hardie USA, 2630 La Alameda, Ste. 250, 92691, pg. 557 IT

Mission Viejo Company, 26137 La Paz Rd., 92691, pg. 1289 PB

SHUGART CORPORATION, 26431 Crown Valley Pkwy., Ste 200, 92691, pg. 997 PV

Sir Speedy, Inc., 26722 Plaza Dr., 92691, pg. 423 PV

Modesto

Ballatore Champagne Cellars, 600 Yosemite Blvd., 95354, pg. 438 PV

Basic Vegetable Products, 705 E. Whitmore, 95358-9408, pg. 121 PV

Bell Carter Distributing, 806 Kiernan Ave., 95356, pg. 1350 PV

Bergen Brunswig Medical Corporation, 2084 Yosemite Blvd., 95354, pg. 214 PB

Brake Parts, Inc., 4000 Finch Rd., 95357, pg. 560 PB

Bridgford Distributing Co., 227 Maze Blvd., 95351, pg. 252 PB

Corrugated Packaging, Lampham & Doherty Sts., P.O. Box 3182, 95353, pg. 736 PB

CuraCare, Inc., 1400 Lone Palm Ave., 95351, pg. 91 PB

E & J Distillers Brandy, 600 Yosemite Blvd., 95354, pg. 438 PV

Ferry-Morse Seed Company, 555 Codoni St., 95354, pg. 566 IT

Fisher Graphic Industries, 1137 Graphics Dr., 95351, pg. 267 PV

E & J Gallo, 600 Yosemite Blvd., 95354, pg. 438 PV

E. & J. GALLO WINERY, 600 Yosemite Blvd., 95354, pg. 438 PV

Kaufman and Broad Central Valley Div., 4701 Sisk Rd., 95356, pg. 945 PB

Major Sysco Food Services Inc., 136 S. Mariposa Rd., 95354, pg. 1551 PB

The Modesto Bee, 1325 H St., 95352, pg. 1065 PB

Nasco Modesto, 1524 Princeton Ave., 95352, pg. 446 PV

National Health Plans, 1005 W. Orangeburg Ave., Ste. B, 95350-6773, pg. 1577 PB

OVERHOLTZER CHURCH FURNITURE, INC., 626 Kearney Ave., 95350, pg. 823 PV

Racor Division, 3400 Finch Rd., 95353-3208, pg. 1260 PV

SAVE MART SUPERMARKETS, 1800 Standiford Ave., 95350, pg. 968 PV

Stockton Savings Bank-Modesto, 3013 McHenry Ave., 95350, pg. 1575 PB

Stockton Savings Bank-Modesto, 2601 T Oakdale Rd., 95354, pg. 1575 PB

Stockton Savings Bank-Modesto, 1101 J St., 95350, pg. 1575 PB

Tott's Champagne Cellars, 600 Yosemite Blvd., 95354, pg. 438 PV

Wood Colony Millworks, 1436 Lone Palm Ave., 95351, pg. 823 PV

Mojave

International Polymer Corp., 11601 United St., 93501, pg. 339 IT

Products Research & Chemical Corp. Manufacturing Facilities Div., 11601 United St., 93501, pg. 339 IT

Scaled Composites, Inc., Hanger 78, Airport, 93501, pg. 1782 PB

Tracor Flight Systems, Inc., 1434 Flight Line, Bldg. 58B, 93501-1665, pg. 1627 PB

Monrovia

AEROVIRONMENT, INC., 222 E. Huntington Dr., Ste. 200, 91016, pg. 25 PV

Alcoa Composites, Inc., 605 E. Huntington Dr., 91016, pg. 60 PB

BARRY'S JEWELERS, INC., 111 W. Lemon Ave., 91016, pg. 192 PB

CCL Label, 1616 S. California Ave., 91016, pg. 238 IT

CCL Labeling Equipment, 1616 S. California Ave., 91016, pg. 238 IT

Circle Machine Co., 1323 S. Shamrock Ave., 91016, pg. 950 PV

CONRAC DISPLAY PRODUCTS, 730 E. Cypress Ave., 91106, pg. 264 PV

THE CONVERSE PROFESSIONAL GROUP, INC., 222 E. Huntington Dr., Ste. 211, 91016-3500, pg. 271 PV

Decco Div., 1713 S. California Ave., 91016, pg. 446 IT

Lawry's Foods, Inc., 222 East Huntington Dr., 91016, pg. 1435 IT

Miura Boiler West, Inc. (U.S.A.), 1945 S. Myrtle Ave., 91016-4854, pg. 884 IT

Pachmayr LTD, 1875 S. Mountain Ave., 91016, pg. 683 PV

3M Unitek Corporation, 2724 S. Peck Rd., 91017-7118, pg. 1606 PB

Xerox Medical Systems, 1425 S. Shamrock, 91016, pg. 1784 PB

Montebello

Lilly Industries, Inc., 901 W. Union St., 90640, pg. 994 PB

Mrs. Cubbison's Foods, Inc., 1325 S. Peerless Way, 90640, pg. 909 PB

Peerless Pump, 1441 Peerless Way, 90640, pg. 1335 IT

ROYAL PAPER BOX OF CALIFORNIA, 1105 S. Maple Ave., 90640, pg. 949 PV

Sterling Fluid, 1200 Sycamore St., 90640, pg. 1335 IT

Teac America, Inc., 7733 Telegraph Rd., 90640, pg. 1360 IT

Montecito

Piper Jaffray Inc., 585 Stone Meadow Ln., 93108, pg. 1303 PB

Monterey

AT&T Language Line Services, One Lower Ragsdale Dr., 93940-5749, pg. 11 PB

CSX Lis, 2511 Garden Rd. A 120, 93940-5330, pg. 284 PB

CTB/McGraw Hill, 20 Ryan Ranch Rd., 93940, pg. 1070 PB

California Capital Insurance Company, 2300 Garden Rd., 93940, pg. 613 PV

CENTURY ALUMINUM COMPANY, 2511 Garden Rd., 93940, pg. 328 PB

Design Professional Insurance Co., P.O. Box DPIC, 93942, pg. 1231 PB

First National Bank of Central California, 495 Washington St., 93942-2718, pg. 1248 PB

Gloria Jean's and Coffee Plantation, 395 Del Monte Center, Ste. 152, 93940, pg. 266 IT

Helian ASC of Northridge, Inc., 9600 Blue Larkspur, 93940, pg. 1715 PB

Helian Health Group, Inc., 9600 Blue Larkspur Ln., Ste. 201, 93940, pg. 1715 PB

Helian Health Group of Fresno, Inc., 9600 Blue Larkspur, 93940, pg. 1715 PB

Helian Recovery Corp., 9600 Blue Larkspur, 93940, pg. 1715 PB

Hewlett-Packard Company, Trident Executive Ctr., 2600 Garden Rd., Ste. 110, 93940, pg. 813 PB

Jekel Vineyards, P.O. Box 336, 93927, pg. 261 PB

PRO-LOG CORPORATION, 12 Upper Ragsdale Dr., 93940, pg. 887 PV

Rehabilitative Back Center of Atlanta, Inc., 9600 Blue Larkspur, 93940, pg. 1715 PB

Southcorp Wines USA/Canada, 60 Garden Ct., Ste. 220, 93940, pg. 1287 IT

Monterey Park

AL & ED'S AUTO SOUND CENTER, 516 Monterey Pass Rd., 91754, pg. 30 PV

Arrowhead Mountain Spring Water Company, 601 Potrero Grande Dr., 91754, pg. 919 IT

CAMINO REAL CHEVROLET & GEO, 2401 S. Atlantic Blvd., 91754, pg. 203 PV

Casuda Canyon Restaurant Corp., 3500 Ramona Blvd., 91754, pg. 1022 PV

PB - U.S. Public Companies Volume
PV - U.S. Private Companies Volume
IT - International Public & Private Companies Volume

1138

Geographic Index-U.S.

U.S. LOCATED COMPANIES CALIFORNIA

H. SALT OF SOUTHERN CALIFORNIA, INC., 2540 Corporate Pl., Ste. B 102, 91754, pg. 489 PV
INTERNATIONAL ALUMINUM CORPORATION, 767 Monterey Pass Rd., 91754, pg. 894 PB
Kajima Development Corp., 901 Corporate Ctr. Dr. Ste 201, 91754, pg. 722 IT
REFRIGERATION SUPPLIES DISTRIBUTORS, 1201 Monterey Pass Rd., 91754, pg. 917 PV
Rothenberger USA, Inc., 955 Monterey Pass Rd., 91754, pg. 1129 IT
Specialty Restaurant Corporation, 3700 Ramona Blvd., 91754, pg. 1022 PV
Ultra Industries, Inc., 777 Monterey Pass Rd., 91754, pg. 692 PV
Union Bank, 1980 Saturn St., 91755, pg. 157 IT

Moorpark

ADK Pressure Equipment Corporation, 5297 Maureen Ln., 93021, pg. 481 PB
Aero Products Div., 6101 Condor Dr., 93021-2699, pg. 1002 PB
Aerospace Bearing Support, Inc., 11953 Challenger Ct., 93021, pg. 187 PB
Air-Dry Corporation of America, 5297 Maureen Lane, 93021, pg. 481 PB
American Products, Inc., 10951 W. Los Angeles Ave., 93021, pg. 593 PB
General Aquatics Corporation, 10951 W. Los Angeles Ave., 93201, pg. 592 PB
The Sunbank Family of Companies, Inc., 5297 Maureen Lane, 93021, pg. 482 PB
Teledyne Laars, 6000 Condor Dr., 93021-2601, pg. 43 PB

Moreno Valley

Maestro Products Inc., 14050 Day St., 92553, pg. 895 PB
Supreme Truck Bodies of California, Inc., 22211 Alessandro Blvd., 92388, pg. 1542 PB
Thor California, Inc., 14255 Elsworth St., 92553-9013, pg. 1602 PB

Morgan Hill

Abbott Critical Care Systems, 755 Jarvis Dr., 95037, pg. 13 PB
Anritsu America, Inc.-Western Region, 490 Jarvis Dr., 95037, pg. 77 IT
Anritsu Wiltron, 685 Jarvis Dr., 95037, pg. 77 IT
Custom Chrome Inc., 16100 Jacqueline Ct., 95037, pg. 748 PB
GLOBAL MOTOR SPORT GROUP, INC., 16100 Jacqueline Ct., 95037, pg. 748 PB
Microwave Measurement Division, 490 Jarvis Dr., Bldg. 12C, 95037, pg. 77 IT
Morgan Hill Times, P.O. Box 757, 30 E. Third St., 95037, pg. 1065 PB
Sakata Seed America, Inc., 18095 Serene Dr., 95038, pg. 1178 IT
Wiltron Company, 490 Jarvis Dr., 95037, pg. 77 IT

Mountain View

Abbott Laboratories, 1212 Terra Bella, 94043, pg. 13 PB
Acurex Environmental Corp., 555 Clyde Ave., 94039, pg. 607 IT
ACUSON CORPORATION, 1220 Charleston Rd., 94043, pg. 18 PB
Axent Technologies, 201 Ravendale Dr., 94043, pg. 157 PB
Biotrack, 1058 Hulf Ave., 94043, pg. 973 IT
Cognex Regional Technology Center, 1949 Landings Dr., 94043, pg. 394 PB
Compool Corporation, 599 Fairchild Drive, 94043, pg. 592 PB
CONSILIUM, INC., 485 Clyde Ave., 94043, pg. 434 PB
Core Research, Inc., 1500 Salado Dr., Ste. 101, 94043, pg. 1003 PB
CREATIVE PUBLICATIONS, 1300 Villa St., 94041, pg. 288 PV
Creative Publications, 1300 Villa St., 94041, pg. 288 PV
The DIALOG Corporation, 2440 El Camino Real, 94040-1040, pg. 412 IT
Dow Jones Markets Systems, Inc., 2091 Landings Dr., 94043, pg. 525 PB
Downey Savings & Loan Association, F.A., 1570 Grant Rd., 94040, pg. 527 PB
Eidesign Technologies, Inc., 1923 Landings Dr., 94043, pg. 940 IT
Esselte Meto, 2672 Bay Shore Parkway, Ste. 514, 94043, pg. 460 IT
FROST & SULLIVAN, 2525 Charleston Rd., 94043, pg. 430 PV
GENXON Power Systems LLC, 430 Ferguson Dr., 94043, pg. 1776 PB
Integrated Media, 555 Ellis St., 94043-2205, pg. 188 PB
INTELLICORP INC., 1975 El Camino Real W., 94040, pg. 887 PB
Intergraph Electronics, 381 E. Evelyn Ave., 94041, pg. 891 PB
Interop, Inc., 480 San Antonio Rd., Ste. 100, 94040, pg. 1600 PB
INTUIT, INC., 2535 Garcia Ave., 94043, pg. 911 PB
Japan Energy USA, Inc., 650 Castro St., Ste. 220, 94041, pg. 702 IT
Karakas, Vansickle, Ouellette Advertising & Public Relations, 1172 Castro St., 94041, pg. 607 PV
Litton Computer Services Div., 1300 Villa St., P.O. Box 7113, 94039-7113, pg. 1002 PB
MIPS Technologies, Inc., 2011 N. Shoreline Blvd., 64043, pg. 1473 PB
NETSCAPE COMMUNICATIONS CORP., 501 E. Middlefield Rd., 94043, pg. 1168 PB
NETWORK COMPUTING DEVICES, INC., 350 N. Bernardo Ave., 94043, pg. 1168 PB
PINNACLE SYSTEMS, INC., 280 N. Bernardo Ave., 94043, pg. 1297 PB
Precision Metalcraft, 2637 Marine Way, 94043, pg. 205 PB
PROXIM, INC., 295 N. Bernardo Ave., 94043, pg. 1338 PB
Sasco/Valley Electric, 2288 Charleston Rd., 94043, pg. 967 PV
SCIOS INC., 2450 Bayshore Pkwy., 94043-1173, pg. 1444 PB
SILICON GRAPHICS, INC., 2011 N. Shoreline Blvd., 94043-1389, pg. 1473 PB
Spectra-Physics Lasers, Inc., 1335 Terra Bella Ave., 94039-7013, pg. 1594 PB
Spectra-Physics Optics Corp., 1330 Middlefield Dr., 94039, pg. 1594 PB
Sun Microsystems Computer Corporation, 2550 Garcia Ave., 94043, pg. 1531 PB
Sun Microsystems Laboratories, Inc., 2550 Garcia Ave., 94043, pg. 1531 PB
Sun Technology Business, 2550 Garcia Ave., 94043, pg. 1531 PB
SunSoft, 2550 Garcia Ave., 94043, pg. 1531 PB
Surface Science Instruments, 465 National Ave., 94043, pg. 1111 IT
Surface Science Laboratories, 1206 Charleston Rd., 94043, pg. 1111 IT
SYNOPSYS, INC., 700 E. Middlefield Rd., 94043, pg. 1548 PB
Tatung Telecom Corp., 1060 Terra Bella Ave., 94043, pg. 1357 IT
TELCOM SEMICONDUCTOR, INC., 1300 Terra Bella Ave., 94043-1836, pg. 1569 PB
TRIDENT MICROSYSTEMS, INC., 189 N. Bernardo Ave., 94043-5203, pg. 1637 PB
VeriBest Inc., 381 E. Evelyn Ave., 94041, pg. 891 PB

Napa

Basalt Precast Division, 2301 Napa Vallejo Hwy., P.O. Box 2490, 94558, pg. 333 PV
CARME' COSMECEUTICAL SCIENCES, INC., 620 Airpack Rd., 94558, pg. 213 PV
Dey Laboratories Inc., 2751 Napa Valley Corp. Dr., 94558, pg. 812 IT
Domaine Carneros, P.O. Box 5420, 94581, pg. 1348 IT
Howard, (c/o Brian Roberts), 1434 3rd St., 94559, pg. 1387 IT
Hydro Conduit Corp., P.O. Box 3508, Tower Rd. & Hwy. 29, 94558, pg. 246 IT
Marinco/AFI, 265 Napa Valley Corp. Dr., 94558, pg. 1705 PB
Napa Pipe Corporation, 1025 Kaiser Rd., 94559, pg. 1230 PB
Napa Valley Bank, One Financial Plaza, 94558, pg. 1756 PB
The Napa Valley Register, 1615 2nd St., 94559, pg. 1343 PB
Real Time Solutions, 831 LaTour Ct., 94558, pg. 866 PV
Silverado Convalescent Hospital, 2300 Brown St., 94558, pg. 1714 PB
Stone Products Corporation, Hwy 29, N. Tower Rd., 94559, pg. 1237 PB
SYAR INDUSTRIES, INC., 2301 Napa Vallejo Hwy., 94558-0542, pg. 1059 PV

National City

Marine Systems, Inc.-West Coast, 2626 Southport Way, Ste. A, 91950, pg. 961 PB
Pacord, 206 W. 35th St., 92050, pg. 957 PV
Zellerbach Division, 1010 W. 19th St., 91950-5490, pg. 1076 PB

Nevada City

TDK Systems Development Group, 136 New Mohawk Rd., 95959-3262, pg. 1336 IT
Tektronix-Video & Networking Div., Grass Valley Products, 13024 Bitney Springs Rd., 95959, pg. 1567 PB

Newark

Cargill Salt, 7220 Central Ave., 94560-4206, pg. 210 PV
Fireside Thrift, 5600 Mowry School Rd., 94560, pg. 1694 PB
Gas Tech, 8407 Central Ave., 94560-3431, pg. 1593 PB
General Employment Enterprises, 39899 Balentine Dr., Ste. 200, 94560, pg. 714 PB
Newark Mfg. Division, 7447 Morton Ave., Unit A, 94560, pg. 518 PB
ROSS STORES, INC., 8333 Central Ave., 94560, pg. 1405 PB

Newbury Park

DDL ELECTRONICS, INC., 2151 Anchor Ct., 91320, pg. 473 PB
Hexcel Chemical Products Div., 3547 Old Canejo Rd., Ste. 102, 91320, pg. 824 PB
PTI Technolgies, Inc., 950 Rancho Conejo Blvd., 91320, pg. 546 PB
SEMTECH CORPORATION, 652 Mitchell Rd., 91320, pg. 1456 PB
Semtech Western Region, 652 Mitchell Rd., 91320, pg. 1456 PB
Sight Systems, Inc., 3541 Old Conejo Rd. #119, 91320, pg. 1795 PB
Vivitar Corporation, 1280 Rancho Conejo Blvd., 91320, pg. 1060 IT

Newcastle

CIMS Development Laboratory, 1150 Kentucky Greens Way, 95658-9798, pg. 1309 PB

Newhall

Newhall Refining Co., 22674 N. Clampitt Rd., 91321, pg. 818 IT
SPECIAL DEVICES, INCORPORATED, 16830 W. Placerita Canyon Rd., 91321, pg. 1496 PB

Newport Beach

Airpark Associates, 4343 Von Karman Ave., 92660, pg. 361 PB
Airwave Communications Corp., 5000 Birch St., Ste. 5500, 92660, pg. 1137 PB
AMERICAN RESTAURANT GROUP, INC., 450 Newport Ctr. Dr., Ste. 600, 92660, pg. 61 PV
AMERICAN VANGUARD CORPORATION, 4695 MacArthur Ct., Ste. 1250, 92660, pg. 94 PB
BIP SUB1, Inc., 610 Newport Ctr. Dr., Ste. 1150, 92660, pg. 1166 PB
BOYLE ENGINEERING CORP., 1501 Quail St., 92658, pg. 163 PV
BROMAR INC., 15 Corporate Plaza, Ste. 200, 92660, pg. 171 PV
California State Bank-Newport Beach, 2101 E. Coast Hwy., pg. 294 PB
Calty Design Research, Inc., 2810 Jamboree Rd., 92660, pg. 1412 IT
CAPITAL PACIFIC HOLDINGS, 4100 MacArthur Blvd., Ste. 200, 92660, pg. 302 PB
Centrum South Partners, 1400 Dove St., 92660, pg. 361 PB
CLAYTON, WILLIAMS & SHERWOOD, INC., 800 Newport Ctr. Dr., Ste. 400, 92660, pg. 245 PV
Cognos Corp.-Los Angeles Sales Office, 4675 MacArthur Ct., Ste. 300, 92660, pg. 306 IT
Costain Homes Inc., 620 Newport Centre Dr., Ste. 400, 92660, pg. 337 IT
DSL Service Co., 3501 Jamboree Rd., 92660, pg. 527 PB
DVI Business Credit, Inc., 4041 MacArthur Blvd., Ste. 401, 92660, pg. 476 PB
DVI Financial Services Inc., 4041 MacArthur Blvd., Ste. 401, 92660, pg. 476 PB
Donahue Schriber, South Tower, 3501 Jamboree Rd., Ste. 300, 92660, pg. 253 IT
DOWNEY FINANCIAL CORP., 3501 Jamboree Rd., 92660, pg. 525 PB
Downey Savings & Loan Association, F.A., 3501 Jamboree Rd., 92660, pg. 526 PB
Robert F. Driver & Co., Inc., 3636 Birch St., Ste. 230, 92660-2619, pg. 343 PV
Environmental Mediation, Inc., 4695 MacArthur Ct., Ste. 1250, 92660, pg. 94 PB
First American Capital Management, Inc., 567 San Nicolas Pl., Ste. 101, 92660, pg. 625 PB
Four Seasons Hotel, 690 Newport Center Dr., 92660, pg. 502 IT
Gage Marketing Group-West Coast, 3620 Birch St., 92660, pg. 437 PV
GALARDI GROUP, INC., 4440 Von Karman Ave., 92660, pg. 437 PV
Gemchem, Inc., 4695 MacArthur Ct., Ste. 1250, 92660, pg. 94 PB
Glendale Ohrbach's Associates, 0601 Jamboree Rd., #300 S. Tower, 92660, pg. 365 PB
HEALTH CARE PROPERTY INVESTORS, INC., 4675 MacArthur Ct., 7th Fl., 92660, pg. 801 PB
HEIL-BRICE RETAIL ADVERTISING, Four Corporate Plaza Dr., 92660, pg. 519 PV
Household Bank F.S.B., 4301 MacArthur Blvd., 92660, pg. 842 PB
INSIGHT HEALTH SERVICES CORP., 4400 MacArthur Blvd., Ste. 800, 92660, pg. 880 PB
Irvine Apartment Communities Incorporated, 500 Newport Ct. Dr., 92660, pg. 575 PV
THE IRVINE COMPANY, 550 Newport Center Dr., 92660, pg. 575 PV
Kaufman and Broad Coastal, 100 Bayview Cir., S. Tower, Ste. 100, 92660, pg. 945 PB
Koll Center Irvine No. 2 Partnership, 4343 Vonkarmen Ave., 92660, pg. 361 PB
KOLL CO., 4343 Von Karmen Ave., 92660, pg. 631 PV
Koll-Tustin Business Center, c/o Koll Company, 4343 Vonkarmen Ave., 92660, pg. 361 PB
Korn/Ferry International, 1300 Dove St., Ste. 300, 92660, pg. 633 PV
Kyowa Hakko-West Coast Office, 4695 MacArthur Ct., Ste. 1540, 92660, pg. 778 IT
LINC Medical Imaging, 3991 MacArthur Blvd., Ste. 310, 92660, pg. 996 PB
WILLIAM LYON COMPANY, 4490 Von Karman, 92660, pg. 684 PV
Mendoza, Dillon & Asociados, Inc., 4100 Newport Pl., Ste. 600, 92660, pg. 1483 IT
Meridian Neuro Care, 1001 Dove St., Ste. 180, 92660-2816, pg. 839 PB
Mission Viejo Associates, 1400 Bristol St. S., Ste. 245, 92660, pg. 361 PB
MONEX DEPOSIT CO., 4910 Birch St., 92660, pg. 757 PV

PB - *U.S. Public Companies Volume*
PV - *U.S. Private Companies Volume*
IT - *International Public & Private Companies Volume*

Geographic Index-U.S.

National Sports Grill, 450 Newport Ctr., Dr., 92660, pg. 61 — PV

Nationwide Health Properties Finance Corp., 4675 MacArthur Ct., Ste. 1170, 92660, pg. 1166 — PB

NATIONWIDE HEALTH PROPERTIES INC., 610 Newport Center Dr., Ste. 1150, 92660, pg. 1166 — PB

Nationwide Health Properties Inc., Kansas, 610 Newport Ctr. Dr., Ste. 1150, 92660, pg. 1166 — PB

Northern Trust Bank of California, N.A., Ste. 200, 620 Newport Center Dr., 92660, pg. 1196 — PB

P and G Specialty Insurance Services, 4590 MacArthur Blvd., Ste. 400, 92660, pg. 354 — PV

PM Realty Advisors Inc., 800 Newport Center Dr., Ste 300, 92660-5000, pg. 831 — PV

PACIFIC LIFE INSURANCE COMPANY, 700 Newport Ctr. Dr., 92660-6397, pg. 831 — PV

Pacific Mezzanine Investors, 610 Newport Center Dr., 92660-6460, pg. 831 — PV

Pacific Mutual Distributors, 700 Newport Center Dr., 92660-6397, pg. 831 — PV

PACIFIC SCIENTIFIC COMPANY, 620 Newport Ctr. Dr., Ste. 700, 92660-8007, pg. 1250 — PB

J.M. Peters Co., 4100 Mac Arthur Blvd., Ste. 200, 92660, pg. 302 — PV

PIMCO Advisors L.P., 840 Newport Center Dr., 92660-6397, pg. 832 — PV

Pulte Southern California Division, 270 Newport Ctr. Dr., 92660, pg. 1345 — PV

Radiosurgery Centers, Inc., 4440 Von Karman Ave., Ste. 320, 92660, pg. 881 — PB

Road and Track, 1499 Monrovia Ave., 92663, pg. 795 — IT

SRS TECHNOLOGIES, 1811 Quail St., 92660, pg. 958 — PV

Saddleback Associates, Ste. 245, 1400 Bristol St. South, pg. 362 — PB

Saddleback II Associates, 1420 Bristol St. N., Ste. 100, 92660, pg. 362 — PB

Secomerica, Inc., 620 Newport Center Dr., Ste. 1450, 92660, pg. 1217 — IT

Service Assets Corp., 15 Corporate Plaza, 92660, pg. 171 — PV

Southern California Bank, 4100 Newport Pl., # 900, 92666, pg. 1758 — PB

Spectrum, 450 Newport Ctr., Dr., 92660, pg. 61 — PV

Spoons, 450 Newport Ctr., Dr., 92660, pg. 61 — PV

Standard Pacific Savings, F. A., 4950 Mac Arthur Bvld., 92660, pg. 1504 — PB

TTA/Newport, Inc., 1201 Dove St., Ste. 650, 92660, pg. 1083 — PV

Tyler Mall Associates, c/o Donahue Schreiber, 3501 Jamboree Rd., Ste. 300, 92660, pg. 362 — PB

Warner Newhope Associates, 4343 Vonkarmen Ave., 92660, pg. 362 — PV

WEST COAST BANCORP, 4770 Campus Dr., Ste. 250, 92660-1833, pg. 1755 — PB

WESTERN BANCORP, 4100 Newport Pl., Ste. 900, 92660, pg. 1757 — PB

Western International Media Corporation, 4000 Westerly Pl., Ste. 150, 92660, pg. 1167 — PV

Wienerschnitzel, 4440 Von Karman, 92660, pg. 437 — PV

Zimmerman & Partners Advertising, Inc., 3990 Westerly Pl., Ste. 115, 92660, pg. 1206 — PV

Nipomo

Speedling Incorporated Nipomo Nursery, 1040 N. Thompson Rd., 93444, pg. 1024 — PV

Norco

Wyle Laboratories-Western Operations, 1841 Hillside Dr., 91760, pg. 1193 — PV

North Highlands

Burnup & Sims of California, Inc., 6445 32nd St., 95660, pg. 1056 — PB

Citizens Utilities Company of California, 3335 Long View Dr., 95660, pg. 380 — PB

North Hills

GALPIN MOTORS, 15505 Roscoe Blvd., 91343, pg. 438 — PV

North Hollywood

Adolph's Ltd., 5355 Cartwright Ave., 91601, pg. 1435 — IT

Arrow Thompson Metals, 6880 Troost Ave., 91605, pg. 1083 — PV

BVK/McDonald, 10921 Morrison St., #4, 91601, pg. 108 — PV

Hewlett-Packard Company, 5161 Lankershim Blvd., 91601, pg. 813 — PV

M & C Remco Tape Products Co., 5547 Vineland Ave., 91601, pg. 684 — PV

MARTIN LAWRENCE LIMITED EDITIONS, INC., 13443 Sherman Way, 91605, pg. 709 — PV

Media Recovery Inc.-California, 13407 Saticoy, 91605-3417, pg. 727 — PV

Robinsons-May, 6160 Laurel Canyon Blvd., 91606-3247, pg. 1064 — PB

TMP Worldwide, Inc., 12800 Riverside Dr., 91607, pg. 1064 — PV

Technicolor, Inc., 4050 Lankershim Blvd., 91608, pg. 272 — IT

Technicolor Professional Film Div., 4050 Lankershim Blvd., 91608, pg. 689 — PV

Technicolor Videocassette Inc., 4050 Lankershim Blvd., 91608, pg. 689 — PV

Whittaker Controls, Inc., 12838 Saticoy St., 91605, pg. 1767 — PB

Northridge

Great Western Financial Securities, 9301 Corbin Ave., Ste. 333, 91324-2498, pg. 1742 — PB

Harman Electronics, Inc., 8500 Balboa Blvd., 91329, pg. 787 — PV

Harman Speaker Manufacturing, 8500 Balboa Blvd., 91329, pg. 787 — PV

JBL Professional, 8400 Balboa Blvd., 91329, pg. 787 — PV

Mikuni American Corporation, 8910 Mikuni Ave., 91324, pg. 867 — PV

Northridge Hospital-Roscoe Blvd. Campus, 18300 Roscoe Blvd., 91328, pg. 1118 — PV

Northridge Surgery Center, 8327 Reseda Blvd., 91325, pg. 1715 — PV

Sierra Capital Management, 9301 Corbin Ave., Ste. 333, 91324-2498, pg. 1742 — PB

Norwalk

Contico Container Company, 15510 Blackburn Ave., 90650-6845, pg. 267 — PV

Downey Savings & Loan Association, F.A., Norwalk Civic Ctr. Branch, 12305 E. Imperial Hwy., 90650, pg. 526 — PB

Zellerbach Division, 12501 E. Imperial Hwy., 90651-1050, pg. 1076 — PB

Novato

Alfa-Laval, Inc., 23 Pimentel Ct., 94947, pg. 1378 — IT

Associated Indemnity Corp., 777 San Marin Dr., 94998, pg. 59 — IT

BRIGHTWARE, INC., 350 Ignacio Blvd., 94949, pg. 68 — PV

BRODERBUND SOFTWARE, INC., 500 Redwood Blvd., 94948-6101, pg. 258 — PB

California Newspapers, Inc., 150 Alameda Del Prado, 94949, pg. 700 — PV

Devon Publishing Group, 201 Alameda Del Prado, 94948, pg. 503 — PV

FAMEX, Inc., 777 San Marin Dr., 94998, pg. 59 — IT

C.R. Fedrick, Inc., P.O. Box 688, 94948, pg. 1052 — PV

Fireman's Fund Insurance Company, 777 San Marin Dr., 94998, pg. 58 — PV

Fireman's Fund Risk Management Services, Inc., 777 San Marin' Dr., 94998, pg. 59 — PV

Harding Lawson Associates, 7655 Redwood Blvd., 94945, pg. 735 — PB

HARDING LAWSON ASSOCIATES GROUP, INC., 7655 Redwood Blvd., 94948, pg. 785 — PB

Harris Corp., Digital Telephone Systems Div., 300 Bel Marin Keys Blvd., 94949, pg. 791 — PB

IPC Interactive, Inc., 105 Digital Dr., 94949, pg. 651 — IT

Mindscape, Inc., 88 Rowland Way, 94945, pg. 1026 — IT

Photocentron Inc., 35 Leveroni Ct., 94947, pg. 462 — IT

San Francisco Reinsurance Co., 777 San Marin Dr., 94998, pg. 59 — IT

Teledyne Laars/Jandy Products, 21 Pimentel Ct., 94949-6101, pg. 43 — PV

WineQuest, 330 Ignacio Blvd., Ste. 201, 94949, pg. 322 — PV

Oakdale

Hershey Chocolate U.S.A.-Western Plant, Yosemite Ave., 95361, pg. 812 — PB

Oakland

APL Land Transport Service Inc., 1111 Broadway, 94607, pg. 912 — IT

APL Limited, 1111 Broadway, 94607, pg. 912 — IT

Admiral Remco, Inc., 1200 65th St., 94662, pg. 1505 — PB

Allied Security Inc. (CA), 519 17th St., Ste. 410, 94612, pg. 40 — PV

American Consolidation Services Ltd., 1111 Broadway, 94607, pg. 912 — IT

American President Lines, Canada, Ltd., 1111 Broadway, 94607, pg. 912 — IT

American President Lines, China Co., Ltd., 1111 Broadway, 94607, pg. 912 — IT

American President Lines, Delaware, Ltd., 1111 Broadway, 94607, pg. 912 — IT

American President Real Estate Co., Ltd., 1111 Broadway, 94607, pg. 912 — IT

American President Trucking Company, Ltd., 1111 Broadway, 94607, pg. 912 — IT

Armor All Products Group, 1221 Broadway St., 94612, pg. 387 — PB

BHP Trading Inc., 475 14th St., Ste. 1150, 94612, pg. 226 — IT

Baxter Novacor Division, 7799 Pardee Ln., 94621, pg. 196 — PB

Bay Park, Inc., 1624 Franklin St., Rm. 722, 94612, pg. 43 — PV

Bovis International California, 1330 Broadway, Ste. 1017, 94612, pg. 1035 — IT

Brita (USA), Inc., 1221 Broadway, 94612, pg. 387 — PB

Candlestick Waterfront Rest. Corp., 30 Jack London Sq., 94607, pg. 1022 — PV

Citicorp Savings, A Federal Savings & Loan Assn., 100 Grand Ave., 15th Fl., 94612, pg. 378 — PB

Citicorp Savings of California, 180 Grand Ave., 94604, pg. 377 — PB

THE CLOROX COMPANY, 1221 Broadway, 94612, pg. 386 — PB

The Clorox International Co., 1221 Broadway, 94612, pg. 387 — PB

Clorox Professional Products Company, 1221 Broadway, 94612, pg. 387 — PB

CommAir Mechanical Services, 1266 14th St., 94607, pg. 2 — PB

CROWLEY MARITIME CORPORATION, 155 Grand Ave., 94612, pg. 292 — PV

CROWN VANTAGE INC., 300 Lakeside Dr., 14th Fl., 94612, pg. 465 — PB

L.N. CURTIS & SONS, 1800 Peralta St., 94607, pg. 297 — PV

DNA Plant Technology Corp., 6701 San Pablo Ave., 94608, pg. 454 — IT

DNAP Holding Corp., 6701 San Pablo Ave., 94608, pg. 454 — IT

DREYER'S GRAND ICE CREAM, INC., 5929 College Ave., 94618, pg. 529 — PB

Dreyer's Grand Ice Cream, Inc., 5929 College Ave., 94618, pg. 529 — PB

Eagle Marine Services, Ltd., 1111 Broadway, 94607, pg. 912 — IT

Eagle Packaging Corp., 2107 Livingston St., 94606-5218, pg. 1156 — IT

Eagle Packaging Group, 2107 Livingston St., 94606-5218, pg. 832 — PV

Fabco Automotive, P.O. Box 8276, 94662, pg. 933 — PB

First American Title Guaranty Co., 1939 Harrison St., 94612, pg. 625 — PB

THE FLECTO CO., INC., 1000 45th St., 94608, pg. 410 — PV

GOLDEN WEST FINANCIAL CORPORATION, 1901 Harrison St., 94612, pg. 750 — PB

GRANNY GOOSE FOODS, INC., 930 98th Ave., 94603, pg. 469 — PV

Harza Engineering Company of California, 425 Roland Way, 94621, pg. 509 — PV

Hillhaven Convalescent Hospital Oakland, 3030 Webster St., 94609, pg. 1713 — PB

Household Products Co., 1221 Broadway, 94612, pg. 387 — PB

ICF Kaiser Engineers, Inc., 1800 Harrison St., 94612, pg. 853 — PB

KTVU Inc., Two Jack London Sq., 94607, pg. 282 — PV

KAISER PERMANENTE, One Kaiser Plaza, 94612, pg. 605 — PV

Kaiser Permanente, California Division, 1950 Franklin St., 94612, pg. 605 — PV

The Kingsford Products Company, P.O. Box 24305, 94623, pg. 387 — PB

Kovel Kresser & Partners/Oakland Office, 500 12th St., Ste. 350, 94607, pg. 634 — PV

Lips Propellers West/Coast Operations, 1899 Seventh St., 94607, pg. 812 — IT

Longview Fibre Co. Western Container Div., 8511 Blaine St., 94621, pg. 1014 — PB

Manetti-Farrow Incorporated, 31 Fourth St., 94607, pg. 461 — PV

J.W. Messner, Inc., 1814 Franklin St., Ste. 1100, 94612, pg. 734 — PV

MONTEREY MECHANICAL COMPANY, 8275 San Leandro St., 94621, pg. 758 — PV

NATIONAL AIRMOTIVE CORPORATION, 7200 Earhart Rd., Bldg. 815, 94621, pg. 775 — PV

Nautical Express, Ltd., 1111 Broadway, 94607, pg. 912 — IT

Packaging Division, 6617 San Leanolro St., 94612, pg. 226 — IT

PORT OF OAKLAND, 530 Water St., 94607, pg. 876 — PV

Property Development Associates, 7677 Oakport St., Ste. 520, 94621, pg. 1426 — PV

RHG San Francisco, 1552 Beach St., Ste. F, 94608, pg. 1151 — IT

SMS-Oakland, 2201 Broadway, 94612, pg. 1463 — PB

Safeway U.S. Holdings, Inc., Fourth & Jackson Sts., 94660, pg. 1426 — PB

San Francisco French Bread Company, 7801 Edgewater Dr., 94621, pg. 909 — PB

VASCOR, 1111 Broadway, 94607, pg. 912 — IT

Woodward-Clyde, 500 12th St., Ste. 100, 94607, pg. 1656 — PB

World Savings Bank, FSB, 1901 Harrison St., 94612, pg. 750 — PB

World Savings & Loan Association, FSLA, 1901 Harrison St., 94612, pg. 750 — PB

Yankee Whaler Company, Berth 75, 90731, pg. 1023 — PV

Zellerbach Division, 2230 Willow St., 94607, pg. 1076 — PB

Oakville

ROBERT MONDAVI WINERY, INC., 7801 St. Helena Hwy., 94562, pg. 1393 — PB

Oceanside

ASTEC America Corp., 401 Jones Rd., 92054, pg. 573 — PB

HOBIE CAT COMPANY, 4925 Oceanside Blvd., 92056, pg. 531 — PV

Hydranautics, 401 Jones Rd., 92054, pg. 950 — IT

Monitor Products Company Inc., 502 Via Del Monte, 92054, pg. 208 — IT

P & M Manufacturing, 4056 Calle Palatino, 92056, pg. 1145 — PV

San Diego Auto Auction Inc., 4691 Calle Joven, 92057, pg. 1649 — PB

Titeflex Industrial Americas, 1995 Peacock Blvd., 92054, pg. 1340 — IT

Ojai

Ojai Manor, 1306 Maricopa Hwy., 93023, pg. 1714 — PB

PB - U.S. Public Companies Volume
PV - U.S. Private Companies Volume
IT - International Public & Private Companies Volume

Geographic Index-U.S.

1140

U.S. LOCATED COMPANIES CALIFORNIA

Olancha

Crystal Geyser Roxane Water L.P., 1210 State Hwy. 395, 93549, pg. 1013 IT

Ontario

Agricultural Products, Inc., 5001 East Philadelphia, 91761, pg. 1527 PB
Arthrotek, Inc., 4861 E. Airport Dr., 91761, pg. 231 PB
Auxitrol Co., Bld. 15, Ste. G, 1898 S. Carlos Ave., 91761, pg. 594 PB
Avery Dennison Corporation Label Group, 3633 East Inland Empire Blvd., Ste. 450, 91764, pg. 153 PB
BMCA Insulation Products, Inc., 300 N. Haven Ave., 91761, pg. 433 PV
Bank Card Services Department, 701 North Haven Ave., Ste. 310, 91764, pg. 287 PB
CVB FINANCIAL CORP., 701 N. Haven Ave., Ste. 350, 91764, pg. 286 PB
California Hardware Company, 3601 E. Jurupa, 91761, pg. 335 PV
California State Bank-Ontario, 3401 Centrelake Dr., pg. 294 PB
Clover Insurance Agency, Inc., 2551 S. Euclid Ave., 91762, pg. 826 PB
COAST GRAIN COMPANY, INC., 5355 E. Airport Dr., 91761, pg. 248 PV
Construction Loans, 701 N. Haven Ave., 91764, pg. 287 PB
Developmental Sciences Corp., 1930 S. Vinyard Ave., 91761, pg. 544 IT
Eagle Mountain Reclamation, Inc., 3633 E. Inland Empire Blvd., Ste. 850, 91764, pg. 941 PB
Excel/Digitran, 4290 E. Brickel St., 91761, pg. 1108 PB
Fontana Water Resources, Inc., 3633 E. Inland Empire Blvd., Ste. 850, 91764, pg. 941 PB
GATX Logistics, Inc.-(Colgate), 5351 Jurupa St., 91761, pg. 691 PB
GESTRA Inc., 430 N. Vineyard Ave., Ste. 451, 91764, pg. 549 IT
Hewlett-Packard Company, 3400 Inland Empire Blvd., Ste. 150, 91764, pg. 813 PB
HOLLYTEX CARPET MILLS, INC., 1251 S. Rockefeller, 91761, pg. 535 PV
HOOKER INDUSTRIES, 1024 W. Brooks St., 91761, pg. 538 PV
ICEE-USA Corp., 4701 Airport Dr., 91761, pg. 916 PB
International Services Department, 701 North Haven Ave., Ste. 310, 91764, pg. 287 PB
Investment Services Department, 701 North Haven Ave., Ste. 350, 91764, pg. 287 PB
Kaiser Eagle Mountain, Inc., 3633 E. Inland Empire Blvd., Ste. 850, 91764, pg. 941 PB
Kaiser Recycling Corp., 3633 E. Inland Empire Blvd., Ste. 850, 91764, pg. 941 PB
Kaiser Steel Corporation, 3633 E. Inland Empire Blvd., Ste. 850, 91764, pg. 941 PB
Kaiser Steel Land Development, Inc., 3633 E. Inland Empire Blvd., Ste 850, 91764, pg. 941 PB
KAISER VENTURES, INC., 3633 E. Inland Empire Blvd., Ste. 850, 91764, pg. 941 PB
Kaiser Waste Treatment, Inc., 3633 E. Inland Empire Blvd., Ste.850, 91764, pg. 941 PB
KIPP GROUP, 930 Wanamaker Ave., 91761, pg. 623 PV
Lake Tamarisk Development Corporation, 3633 E. Inland Empire Blvd., Ste. 850, 91764, pg. 941 PB
Mercury Air Center, 2161 E. Avion St., 91761, pg. 1093 PB
Mico West, 701 E. Francis St., 91761, pg. 742 PV
MICROTEL INTERNATIONAL INC., 4290 E. Brickell St., 91761, pg. 1108 PB
National Bedding Co., 4774 E. Airport Way, 91761, pg. 780 PV
Neste Polyester Inc., 1720 Monticello Ct., 91762, pg. 913 IT
Smith Engineering Co., 2837 E. Cedar St., 91761, pg. 586 IT
Spectrol Electronics Corporation, 4051 Greystone Dr., 91761, pg. 351 PV
Speedway Development Corp., 3633 E. Inland Empire Blvd., Ste. 850, 91764, pg. 941 PB
Tamms Industries Co., 5741 E. Santa Ana St., 91761, pg. 803 IT
Telemation Productions Inc., 3833 Ebony St., 91761, pg. 1686 PB
Thor West, 4750 Zinfandel Ct., 91761, pg. 1602 PB

Orange

Aerochem, Inc., 1885 N. Batavia St., 92665, pg. 534 PB
American Cablevision of Orange, Inc., 154 No. Glassell, 92666, pg. 1610 PB
B/E Services, 230 W. Blueridge, 92865, pg. 159 PB
BERGEN BRUNSWIG CORPORATION, 4000 Metropolitan Dr., 92668-3510, pg. 213 PB
Bergen Brunswig Drug Company, 4000 Metropolitan Dr., 92668, pg. 213 PB
Bergen Brunswig Medical Corporation, 4000 Metropolitan Dr., 92868, pg. 214 PB
BISCO INDUSTRIES, INC, 704 W. Southern Ave., 92865, pg. 145 PV
California State Bank-Orange, 170 S. Main St., 92668, pg. 294 PB
Continental Auxiliary Company Trustee, P.O. Box 6026, 92667, pg. 181 PB
Donnelley Information Publishing, Inc., 681 S. Parker St., 92668, pg. 535 PB
First Security Thrift, 803 E. Katella Ave., 92667, pg. 626 PB
Frankel & Company, 333 City Blvd. W., Ste. 720, 92668, pg. 424 PV
Fremont Life Insurance Co., 790 The City Dr. S., Ste. 210, 92613, pg. 681 PB
General Employment Enterprises, Inc., One City Blvd. W., Ste. 300, 92868, pg. 714 PB
GLOBAL VAN LINES, INC., 810 W. Taft, 92865, pg. 458 PV
Hillhaven Convalescent Hospital Orange, 920 W. La Veta, 92668, pg. 1713 PB
Inteplex, 4000 Metropolitan Dr., 92668-3510, pg. 215 PB
KTI, 500 N. State College Blvd., Ste. 1000, 92868-1638, pg. 939 PB
MSC Orange County Office, 1915 W. Orangewood Ave., 92668, pg. 1031 PB
Monier Inc., 750 The City Drive S., Ste. 200, 92668, pg. 1091 IT
Orange County Metal Works, 341 W. Collins Ave., 92667, pg. 411 PB
Orange Hill Restaurant Corp., PO Box 2307, 6410 E. Chapman, 92669, pg. 1022 PV
RTS Packaging, 749 N. Poplar, 92668, pg. 1397 PB
SVG Thermco Systems, 1465 N. Batavia St., 92667, pg. 1474 PB
Southern California Air Gas, 538 W. Katella Ave., 92667, pg. 33 PB
SPIRES RESTAURANTS INC., 303 W. Katella Ave., Ste. 205, 92867, pg. 1026 PV
Syndicated Office Systems, Inc., 770 The City Drive, Ste. 7000-90, 92613, pg. 1577 PB
TMP Worldwide/Recruitment Division, 500N. State College Blvd., Ste. 1470, 92867, pg. 1065 PV
TRW Information Systems & Services, 505 City Pkwy. W., 92868, pg. 557 IT
Tekra Corp., West Coast Div., 331 Levers Pl., 92667, pg. 1073 PV
Toto Kiki USA, Inc. - Los Angeles Branch, 415 West Taft Ave., Unit A, 92665, pg. 1410 IT
Ulti-Mate, Inc., 641 Poplar St., 92868, pg. 1122 PB
Varco BJ Drilling Systems, 743 N. Eckhoff St., 92613-6626, pg. 1709 PB
Varco BJ Oil Tools, 743 N. Eckhoff St., 92668, pg. 1709 PB
VARCO INTERNATIONAL, INC., 743 N. Eckhoff St., 92868, pg. 1709 PB
Volt Technical Services-West, 2401 N. Glassel St., 92865, pg. 1724 PB
Volt Temporary Services, 2401 N. Glassell St., 92665, pg. 1724 PB
Volt VIEWtech, Inc., 2401 N. Glassell St., 92665, pg. 1724 PB
WYNN'S INTERNATIONAL, INC., 500 N. State College Blvd., Ste. 700, 92868, pg. 1782 PB
Yoh Scientific, 500 S. Main St., Ste. 550, 92668, pg. 317 PV
YOUNG'S HOLDINGS INC., 2164 N. Batavia St., 92865, pg. 1202 PV
Young's Market Company, 2164 N. Batavia St., 92665, pg. 1202 PV

Orinda

BancTec, Inc.-Los Angeles, 27 Woodland Rd., 94563, pg. 177 PB

Orland

Hydro Conduit Corp., P.O. Box 817, 4 Miles E. of Orland-Hwy. 32, 95963, pg. 245 IT

Oroville

Setzer Forest Products-Oroville Plant, 1980 Kusel Rd., 95966, pg. 988 PV

Oxnard

Aigner Products Division, 350 Cactus Dr., 93031, pg. 152 PB
Condor D.C. Power Supplies Inc., 2311 Statham Pkwy., 93033, pg. 1419 PB
DEARDORFF-JACKSON COMPANY, 1120 Mountain View Ave., 93030, pg. 319 PV
Foga Systems, 800 Del Norte Blvd., 93030, pg. 496 IT
GILRICHCO, INC., 500 Spectrum Cir., 93030, pg. 454 PV
Higgins Ventura, 524 Pacific Ave., 93030, pg. 527 PV
Gene Jackson Farms, P.O. Box 5147, 93031, pg. 344 PV
Maywood Acres Healthcare, 2641 S. C St., 93030, pg. 1714 PB
Merchants Home Delivery Service Inc., 2400 Latigo St., 93030, pg. 901 IT
The Optical Corporation, 1800 Lockwood St., 93030, pg. 599 PB
Pacific Coast Laminating, 539 Montgomery Ave., 93030, pg. 528 PV
Ransco Industries, Inc., 1400 E. Statham Pkwy., 93033, pg. 327 PV
Raytheon, 4347 Raytheon Rd., 93033-8230, pg. 1365 PB
TFP Data Systems, 3451 Jupiter G., 93030, pg. 1070 PV
Telair International, 1950 Williams Dr., 93030, pg. 1570 PB
Telair International Cargo Systems, 1950 Williams Dr., 93030-2600, pg. 1570 PB

Pacheco

BRADY MARKETING COMPANY, 80 Berry Dr., 94553, pg. 165 PV

Pacific Grove

Brooks/Cole Publishing Co., 511 Forest Lodge Rd., 93950, pg. 1600 PB

Pacoima

Brice Manufacturing Company, Inc., 10262 Norris Ave., 91331, pg. 534 PB
Higgins San Fernando Valley Operations, 13290 Paxton St., 91331, pg. 527 PV
Price Pfister, Inc., 13500 Paxton St., 91331, pg. 234 PB
Stantron/PFT/EMI, 12224 Montague St., 91331, pg. 1791 PB
Zero Stantron Cabinets, 12224 Montague St., 91331, pg. 1791 PB

Palm Desert

Downey Savings & Loan Association, F.A., 72-260 Hwy. 111, 92260, pg. 527 PB
Greenberg Financial Insurance Services, Inc., P.O. Box 1996, 41550 Eclectric St., Ste. 200, 92261, pg. 1334 PB
GUTHY-RENKER CORP., 41-550 Eclectic St., Ste. 200, 92260, pg. 488 PV
HRH Insurance Services of the Coachella Valley, Inc., 77-564 Country Club Dr., Ste. 150, 92211, pg. 826 PB
Sun City Palm Desert, 39755 Berkey Dr., 92211, pg. 495 PB
Tarmac California, Inc., 77564 Country Club Dr., 92260, pg. 1355 IT
Tarmac-Massey, 77564 Country Club Dr., 92260, pg. 1356 IT
U.S. Filter, 40-004 Cook St., 92211, pg. 61 PB
UNITED STATES FILTER CORPORATION, 40-004 Cook St., 92211, pg. 1681 PB

Palm Springs

Bird Products Corporation, 1100 Bird Center Dr., 92262, pg. 1591 PB
California Energy International, Ltd., 950 W. Lindsey Rd., 92233, pg. 292 PB
The Desert Sun, 611 S. Palm Canyon Dr., 92263, pg. 700 PB
Downey Savings & Loan Association, F.A., 1793 E. Palm Canyon Dr., 92264, pg. 527 PB
Western International Media Corporation, 1111 Tahquitz Cyn Way, Ste. 108, 92262, pg. 1167 PV

Palmdale

Anderson-Barrows Metals Corp., 2800 Anderson Ave., 93550, pg. 1746 PB
Kaufman and Broad-Antelope Valley Regional Office, 38345-A 30th St. E., 93550, pg. 945 PB
Lockheed Advanced Development Company, 1011 Lockheed Way, 93599, pg. 1007 PB
Lockheed Martin Skunk Works, 1011 Lockheed Way, 93599, pg. 1007 PB
WESTERN PACIFIC ROOFING, 2229 E. Avenue Q, 93550, pg. 1168 PV

Palo Alto

ALZA CORPORATION, 950 Page Mill Rd., 94304, pg. 62 PB
ALZA Development Corporation, 950 Page Mill Rd., 94303-0802, pg. 62 PB
ALZA International, P.O. Box 10950, 950 Page Mill Rd., 94303, pg. 62 PB
ALZA, Ltd., P.O. Box 10950, 950 Page Mill Rd., 94303, pg. 62 PB
Andersen Consulting, 1661 Page Mill Rd., 94304, pg. 72 PV
Beckman Instruments, 1050 Page Mill Rd., 94304, pg. 199 PB
CNF TRANSPORTATION INC., 3240 Hillview Ave., 94304, pg. 281 PB
Canon Research Center America, Ltd., Stanford Research Park, 4009 Miranda Ave., 94304, pg. 261 IT
Cetia Inc., 350 Cambridge Ave., #100, 94306, pg. 1383 IT
Ciba Corning Diagnostics Corporation, 490 San Antonio Rd., 94306, pg. 973 IT
Coherent, Inc.-Medical Group, 3290 W. Bayshore Rd., 94303-0810, pg. 395 PB
COLLAGEN CORPORATION, 2500 Faber Pl., 94303, pg. 399 PB
Con-Way Transportation Services, 3340 Hillview Ave., 94304, pg. 281 PB
Edelman Worldwide, Inc., 260 Sheridan Ave., Ste. 200, 94306, pg. 362 PV
General Employment Enterprises, Inc., 430 Cowper St., Ste. 223, 94301, pg. 715 PB
Gigamax, 45 Sherman Ave., Ste. 120, 94306, pg. 1347 IT
HEWLETT-PACKARD COMPANY, 3000 Hanover St., 94304, pg. 813 PB
Hillhaven Convalescent Hospital Palo Alto, 911 Bryant St., 94301, pg. 1713 PB
JEOL (U.S.A.), Inc., 1015 E. Meadow Cir., 94303, pg. 697 IT
Korn/Ferry International, 2180 Sand Hill Rd., Ste. 440, 94025, pg. 633 PV
LVL ADVERTISING, 431 Florence St., #100, 94301, pg. 640 PV
LVL Interactive, 480 Cowper St., 94301, pg. 640 PV

Geographic Index-U.S.

PB - *U.S. Public Companies Volume*
PV - *U.S. Private Companies Volume*
IT - *International Public & Private Companies Volume*

LEGATO SYSTEMS, INC., 3210 Porter Dr., 94304, pg. 984 — PB
Logistics Worldwide, 3350 W. Bayshore Rd., 94303, pg. 281 — PB
Mitsubishi Silicon America, 2445 Faber Pl., Ste. 100, 94303-0912, pg. 875 — IT
Nuclear Magnetic Resonance Instruments, 3120 Hansen Way, 94304, pg. 1710 — PB
Oncology Systems, 911 Hansen Way, 94304, pg. 1710 — PB
Palo Alto Research Center, 3333 Coyote Hill Rd., 94304, pg. 1784 — PB
PETE'S BREWING COMPANY, 514 High St., 94301, pg. 1280 — PB
Raylan, 2525 E. Bayshore Dr., Ste. 2, 94303, pg. 8 — PB
Rollins Hudig Hall of Northern California, Inc., 2595 E. Bayshore, 94303, pg. 117 — PB
SmithKline Diagnostics, 1050 Page Mill Rd., 94304, pg. 199 — PB
Space Systems/Loral, Inc., 3825 Fabian Way, 94303-4697, pg. 1014 — PB
SUN MICROSYSTEMS, INC., 901 San Antonio Rd., 94043-4900, pg. 1531 — PB
Surgecenter of Palo Alto, 400 Forest Ave., 94301, pg. 1716 — PB
Syntex, 3401 Hillview Ave., 94304, pg. 1120 — IT
Syntex Agribusiness, Inc., 3401 Hillview Ave., 94304, pg. 1120 — IT
SyStemix, Inc., 3155 Porter Dr., 94304, pg. 974 — IT
Systems Control Technology, 2300 Geng Rd., 94303, pg. 976 — PV
TAB PRODUCTS CO., 1400 Page Mill Rd., 94304, pg. 1559 — PB
Tab Sales Corp. (International), 1400 Page Mill Rd., 94304, pg. 1559 — PB
VARIAN ASSOCIATES, INC., 3050 Hansen Way, 94304-1000, pg. 1710 — PB
WATKINS-JOHNSON COMPANY, Stanford Research Park, 3333 Hillview Ave., 94304-1223, pg. 1745 — PB
Watkins-Johnson International, 3333 Hillview Ave., 94304, pg. 1745 — PB
The Weber Group, 101 University Ave., 94301, pg. 1157 — PV
Wireless Products Group, 3333 Hillview Ave., 94304, pg. 1745 — PB
Xerox Imaging Systems, Inc., 3400 Hillview Ave., 94303, pg. 1785 — PB

Paramount

A.M. Castle & Co., 14001 Orange Ave., 90723, pg. 313 — PB
Roger Cleveland Golf Company, 14508 S. Garfield Ave., 90723, pg. 1127 — IT
Graphite & Specialty Products, Inc., 7350 Adams St., 90723, pg. 891 — IT
PARAMOUNT PETROLEUM CORP., 14700 Downey Ave., 90723, pg. 838 — PV
The Producto Machine Co., 15958 S. Downey Ave., 90723, pg. 889 — PV

Pasadena

Acxiom Corporation, 924 E. Green St., Ste. 200, 91106-2907, pg. 18 — PB
Agbabian Associates, Inc., 1111 S. Arroyo Pkwy., Ste. 405, 91105, pg. 1019 — PB
AMERON INTERNATIONAL CORPORATION, 245 S. Los Robles Ave., 91101-2894, pg. 98 — PB
AVERY DENNISON CORPORATION, 150 N. Orange Grove Ave., 91103, pg. 152 — PB
Avon Sales & Distribution Branch, 2940 E. Foothill Blvd., 91121, pg. 156 — PB
CARLSBERG FINANCIAL CORP., 2 N. Lake Ave., Ste. 800, 91101, pg. 211 — PV
Construction Lending Corporation of America-Builder Division, 35 N. Lake Ave., 91101, pg. 857 — PB
Countrywide Agency, Inc., 155 N. Lake Ave., 91101-1857, pg. 452 — PB
Countrywide Asset Management Corporation, 155 No. Lake Ave., 91101-1857, pg. 452 — PB
Countrywide Capital Markets, Inc., P.O. Box 7137, 155 N. Lake Ave., 91109-7137, pg. 453 — PB
Countrywide Funding Corporation, 155 N. Lake Ave., 91109, pg. 453 — PB
COUNTRYWIDE HOME LOANS INC., P.O. Box 7137, 155 N. Lake Ave., 91101-1857, pg. 452 — PB
Countrywide Partnership Investments, Inc., 155 N. Lake Ave., 91109, pg. 453 — PB
Countrywide Securities Corporation, 155 N. Lake Ave., 91101-1857, pg. 453 — PB
Countrywide Servicing Exchange, 155 N. Lake Ave., 91101-1857, pg. 453 — PB
Countrywide Title Corporation, P.O. Box 7137, 155 N. Lake Ave., 91109-7137, pg. 453 — PB
DUFFORD MARKETING, 2233 Brigden Rd., 91104, pg. 345 — PV
FSEC, Inc., 100 E. Corson St., 91103, pg. 80 — PV
FLOWERS OF HAWAII, P.O. Box 93933, 91109, pg. 415 — PV
GEMSTAR INTERNATIONAL GROUP LIMITED, 135 N. Los Robles Ave., Ste. 800, 91101, pg. 705 — PB
Graphics Arts Center, 2181 E. Foothill Blvd., 91107, pg. 1038 — PB
Huntington Provider Management Services, 141 S. Lake Ave., Ste. 200, 91101, pg. 1118 — PV
HUTCHINS MANUFACTURING COMPANY, 49 N. Lotus Ave., 91107, pg. 550 — PB
INMC MORTGAGE HOLDINGS, INC., 35 N. Lake Ave., 91101, pg. 857 — PB
Indimac, 35 N. Lake Ave., 91101, pg. 857 — PB

Indimac Mortgage Obligations, II, Inc., 35 N. Lake Ave., 91101, pg. 858 — PB
Indimac Mortgage Obligations, Inc., 35 N. Lake Ave., 91101, pg. 858 — PB
Indimac Third Party Construction Lending Division, 35 North Lake Ave., 91101, pg. 857 — PB
JACOBS ENGINEERING GROUP INC., 1111 S. Arroyo Pkwy., 91105, pg. 921 — PB
Kajima Engineering and Construction Inc., 200 S. Los Robles Ave., Ste. 400, 91101-2431, pg. 722 — IT
Kinemetrics, Inc., 222 Vista Ave., 91107, pg. 1019 — IT
Kleinwort Benson Capital Management Incorporated, 200 S. Los Robles Ave., Ste. 210, 91101, pg. 420 — IT
Kleinwort Benson Cross Financing Incorporated, 200 S. Los Robles Ave., Ste. 210, 91101, pg. 420 — IT
LandSafe Title Agency, Inc., P.O. Box 7137, 155 N. Lake Ave., 91109-7137, pg. 453 — PB
LAWRY'S RESTAURANTS, INC., 234 E. Colorado Blvd., Ste. 500, 91101, pg. 654 — PV
Lindenmeyr Central, 140 S. Lake Ave., Ste. 269, 91101, pg. 224 — PV
Lockheed Martin Electro-Optical Systems, 300 N. Halstead St., 91107, pg. 1008 — PB
McKesson Water Products Company, 3280 E. Foothill Blvd., Ste. 400, 91107, pg. 1073 — PB
MONTGOMERY WATSON, 300 N. Lake St., Ste. 1200, 91101, pg. 759 — PB
Mutual Savings & Loan Association, 315 E. Colorado Blvd., 91101, pg. 217 — PB
Osaka Gas Co.-Los Angeles, 300 N. Lake Ave., Ste. 920, 91101, pg. 1012 — IT
PACIFIC AMERICAN INCOME SHARES, INC., 117 E. Colorado Blvd., Sixth Fl., 91105, pg. 1247 — PB
PACIFICA SERVICES, INC., 106 S. Mentor Ave., Ste. 200, 91106-2936, pg. 832 — PV
Parsons Constructors Inc., P.O. Box 7036, 91109, pg. 842 — PV
PARSONS CORPORATION, 100 W. Walnut St., 91124, pg. 841 — PV
Parsons Development Company, 100 W. Walnut St., 91124, pg. 842 — PV
Parsons Engineering Science, Inc., 100 W. Walnut St., 91124, pg. 842 — PV
Parsons Infrastructure & Technology Group Inc., 100 W. Walnut St., 91124, pg. 842 — PV
Parsons Water Resources, Inc., 100 W. Walnut St., 91124, pg. 842 — PV
PAULA FINANCIAL, 300 N. Lake Ave., Ste. 300, 91101, pg. 1266 — PB
Provident Investment Counsel, Inc., 300 N. Lake Ave., 91101, pg. 1674 — PB
Rogerson Kratos, 403 S. Raymond Ave., 91109, pg. 940 — PV
RUSS REID COMPANY, INC., Two N. Lake Ave., Ste. 600, 91101, pg. 952 — PV
A. Schulman, Inc., 600 S. Lake Ave., Ste. 506, 91106, pg. 1441 — PB
Sparkletts Drinking Water Corp., 3280 E. Foothill Dr., Ste. 400, 91107, pg. 1073 — PB
Specialty Tapes and Adhesives Group, 150 N. Orange Grove Blvd., 91103, pg. 153 — PB
Symons Corporation, 251 S. Lake Ave., Ste. 606, 91101, pg. 932 — PV
Telos Information Systems, 320 N. Halstead, Ste. 260, 91107, pg. 1573 — PB
TETRA TECH, INC., 670 N. Rosemead Blvd., 91107-2190, pg. 1582 — PB
Tokai Credit Corporation, 1111 S. Arroyo Pkwy., Ste. 500, 91105, pg. 1391 — IT
Tokio Marine Management Inc. - Western Regional Office, 800 E. Colorado Blvd., 91101-2132, pg. 1392 — IT
Warehouse Lending Corporation of America, 35 N. Lake Ave., 91101, pg. 857 — PB
Wasteco, Inc., 1600 N. Lincoln Ave., 91103, pg. 264 — PB
Wesco Financial Corporation, 315 E. Colorado Blvd., 91109, pg. 217 — PB
Wesco-Financial Insurance Company, 315 E. Colorado Blvd., 91109, pg. 217 — PB
Western Asset Management, 117 E. Colorado Blvd., 91105, pg. 985 — PB
Woodward-Clyde, 566 El Dorado St., Ste. 100, 91101, pg. 1656 — PB
Xerox Special Information Systems, 250 N. Halstead St., 91107, pg. 1784 — PB
Zahorik Co., Inc., 251 S. Lake Ave., 91101, pg. 28 — IT

Paso Robles

Ennis Western Div., P.O. Box 7004, 93447-7004, pg. 583 — PB
Hearst Real Estate Division, 5165 Estrella Rd., 93446, pg. 518 — PV
Sunbank Joslyn, Inc., 1740 Commerce Way, 93446, pg. 482 — PB
Wilkins-Regulator Div., 1747 Commerce Way, 93446, pg. 1794 — PB

Patterson

PATTERSON FROZEN FOODS, INC., 100 W. Las Palmas, 95363, pg. 843 — PV

Perris

Handsome Rewards, 3660 Brennan Ave., 92370, pg. 1035 — PV
MODTECH, INC., 2830 Barret Ave., 92572, pg. 1121 — PB
NATIONAL R.V., INC., 3411 N. Perris Blvd., 92571, pg. 1159 — PB
Signatures, 3660 Brennan Ave., 92370, pg. 1035 — PV

Starcrest of California, 3660 Brennan Ave., 92370, pg. 1035 — PV
STARCREST PRODUCTS OF CALIFORNIA, 3660 Brennan Ave., 92571, pg. 1035 — PV

Petaluma

Argus-Courier, 830 N. Petaluma Blvd., 94952, pg. 1343 — PB
DSC, 1310 Redwood Way Ste. C, 94954-6514, pg. 475 — PB
Earthrise Trading Co., 424 Payran St., 94952, pg. 369 — IT
LEGACY MARKETING GROUP, 1179 N. McDowell Blvd. N., 94954, pg. 658 — PV
Northern California Laboratory, 1455 McDowell Blvd. N., Ste. D, 94954, pg. 829 — PV
Old TG Corp., 2201 S. McDowell Blvd., 94953-6020, pg. 1138 — PV
Parmatech Corporation, 2211 Pine View Way, 94954, pg. 307 — PV
Tele-Quote Corporation, 2199 S. McDowell Extension, 94954, pg. 28 — PV
Textron Optoelectronics, 1309 Dynamic St., 94954-1420, pg. 1589 — PV
WILLITTS DESIGN, 1129 Industrial Ave., 94952, pg. 1180 — PV

Pico Rivera

Advanced Technology and Design Center, 8900 E. Washington Blvd., 90660-3783, pg. 1198 — PB
B-2 Division, 8900 E. Washington Blvd., 90660-3737, pg. 1198 — PB
General Felt Industries, Inc., 8320 Rex Rd., 90660, pg. 1094 — PV
Harwick Standard Distribution Corp., 7225 Paramount Blvd., 90660, pg. 509 — PV
MCLAUGHLIN INDUSTRIAL DISTRIBUTORS, INC., 7141 Paramount Blvd., 90660, pg. 724 — PV
Westco Products, Inc., 7351 Crider Ave., 90660, pg. 244 — IT
Windsor Art, Inc., 9101 Perkins St., 90660, pg. 212 — PB

Pittsburg

Dexter Aerospace Materials Division, 2850 Willow Pass Rd., 94565-3299, pg. 504 — PB
GSI of California, 1503 Loveridge Rd., 94565, pg. 487 — PV
USS-POSCO Industries, 900 Loveridge Rd., 94565, pg. 1662 — PB

Placentia

AC Products, Inc., 172 E. La Jolla St., 92670, pg. 1346 — PB
ACI America Holdings Inc., 231-A Lakeview, 92670, pg. 129 — IT
Argus Publishers, 774 S. Placentia Ave., 92670-6846, pg. 1328 — PB
California State Bank-Placentia, 111 E. Yorba Linda Blvd., 92670, pg. 294 — PB
Hartwell Commercial Division, 620 S. Jefferson St., Unit A, 92670-4783, pg. 1168 — PV
Hartwell Corporation, 900 S. Richfield Rd., 92670-6788, pg. 1168 — PV
Hilb, Rogal and Hamilton Insurance Services of Orange County, Inc., 701 Kimberly Ave., Ste. 200, 92670, pg. 827 — PV
Instrument Specialties - Western Division, 505 Porter Way, 92670, pg. 565 — PV
McMullen/Argus Publishers, 774 S. Placentia Ave., 92670-6846, pg. 1328 — PB
Microdot/Recoil, 190 W. Crowther, 92670, pg. 940 — PV
Switching Systems International, 500 Porter Way, 92870, pg. 208 — IT

Pleasant Hill

BAM MEDIA, 3470 Buskirk Ave., 94523, pg. 113 — PV
BROWN AND CALDWELL, 3480 Buskirk Ave., 94523-1220, pg. 173 — PV
COLOR SPOT NURSERY, INC., 3478 Buskirk Ave., 94523, pg. 254 — PV
Morrison Homes, 2255 Contra Costa Bvld., 94523, pg. 1510 — IT

Pleasanton

AT&T Communications, 4460 Rosewood Dr. # 6222, 94588-3050, pg. 10 — PB
ASSOCIATED PROCESS CONTROLS, 7150 Koll Center Pkwy., 94566, pg. 92 — PV
Associates National Bank, 4301-09 Hacienda Dr., 94566, pg. 663 — PV
BMW of North America, Inc.-Northwestern Region, 6606 Owens Dr., 94566, pg. 177 — IT
Cognos Corp.-San Francisco Sales Office, 5994 W. Las Positas Blvd., Ste. 215, 94588-3350, pg. 306 — IT
DILLINGHAM CONSTRUCTION CORPORATION, 5960 Inglewood Dr., 94588-8535, pg. 333 — PV
Dreyer's Northern California Region, 4234 Hacienda Dr., Ste. 212, 94588, pg. 1348 — PB
Golden Grain Company, 4576 Willow Rd., 94588, pg. 529 — PB
Hewlett-Packard Company, 5725 W. Las Positas Blvd., 94588, pg. 824 — PB
HEXCEL CORPORATION, 5794 W. Las Positas Blvd., 94588, pg. 529 — PB
Huls America Inc., 5555 Sunol Blvd., 94566, pg. 1455 — IT
Intelligent Technologies & Services, Inc., 1031 Serpentine Ln., 94566, pg. 404 — PV
Intisys, Inc., 7150 Koll Ctr. Pkwy., 94566, pg. 93 — PV

Kaiser Aluminum & Chemical Corporation, 6177 Sunol Blvd., 94566-7769, pg. 1062 **PB**

Kaiser Cement Corporation, P.O. Box 309, 3000 Busch Rd., 94566, pg. 593 **IT**

Nellcor Puritan Bennett Incorporated, 4280 Hacienda Dr., 94588, pg. 1039 **PB**

Netwave Technologies, Inc., 6663 Owens Dr., 94588, pg. 1564 **PB**

PEOPLESOFT, INC., 4440 Rosewood Dr., 94588-3031, pg. 1276 **PB**

PROBUSINESS SERVICES, INC., 5934 Gibraltar Dr., 94588, pg. 1330 **PB**

Pulte Northern California Division, 5976 W. Las Positas Blvd., Ste. 100, 94566, pg. 1345 **PB**

SMS-San Francisco, 6000 Stoneridge Mall Rd., 94588, pg. 1463 **PB**

SAFEWAY INC., 5918 Stoneridge Mall Rd., 94588-3229, pg. 1426 **PB**

Smith Environmental Technologies Corp., 7901 Stoneridge Dr., Ste. 100, 94588, pg. 1477 **PB**

Standard Pacific-No. California, 3825 Hopgard Rd., Ste. 195, 94566, pg. 1503 **PB**

Stanfast, Inc., 7069 Commerce Circle, 94588, pg. 1505 **PB**

SUN DIAMOND GROWERS OF CALIFORNIA, P.O. Box 9024, 94566, pg. 1051 **PV**

URS Greiner, Inc., 5890 Stoneridge Dr., 94588, pg. 1658 **PB**

Valley Times, 127 Spring St., 94566, pg. 964 **PB**

VANSTAR CORPORATION, 5964 W. Las Positas Blvd., 94588, pg. 1708 **PB**

Wine World Estates, Inc., 6140 Stoneridge Mill Rd., Ste. 175, 94558, pg. 917 **IT**

Xerox Diablo Supplies, 5724 W Las Positas Ste. 110, 94588-4083, pg. 1784 **PB**

Pomona

AMP Inc. Lytel Division, 3333 N. Corporate Terrace Dr., 91765-4701, pg. 8 **PB**

Ahmanson Developments, Inc., 1370 Valley Vista Dr., 91765-3921, pg. 29 **PB**

Basic Vegetable Products, 1186 S. Diamond Bar Blvd., 91765-2203, pg. 121 **PV**

Boral Resources Inc., 1301 E. Lexington Ave., 91766, pg. 203 **IT**

Casablanca Fan Company, 761 Corporate Center Dr., 91768, pg. 549 **PB**

DeVRY Institute of Technology, 901 Corporate Center Dr., 91768, pg. 504 **PB**

Everett/Charles Automation Systems, Inc., 700 E. Harrison, 91767, pg. 386 **PV**

Everett/Charles Contact Products, Inc., 700 E. Harrison, 91767, pg. 386 **PV**

EVERETT CHARLES TECHNOLOGIES, P.O. Box 2632, 700 E. Harrison Ave., 91769-2632, pg. 386 **PV**

Everett/Charles Test Equipment, 2887 N. Towne Ave., 91767, pg. 386 **PV**

Fundamental Management, Inc., 3880 W. Valley Blvd., 91769, pg. 561 **PV**

GEMINI ALUMINUM CORPORATION, 3255 Pomona Blvd., 91768, pg. 443 **PV**

Hehr Glass Company Inc., 1021 Walnut Ave., 91766, pg. 519 **PV**

Huntington Tile, Inc., 1315 E. Third St., 91766, pg. 831 **PV**

ITT Pomona, 1500 E. Ninth St., 91776, pg. 859 **PB**

Industrial Alloys, Inc., 3880 W. Valley Blvd., 91769, pg. 561 **PV**

INDUSTRIAL WIRE PRODUCTS CORPORATION, 3880 W. Valley Blvd., 91769, pg. 561 **PV**

KEYSTONE AUTOMOTIVE INDUSTRIES, INC., 700 E. Bonita Ave., 91767, pg. 955 **PB**

Western Marketing Div., 2350 S. Garey Ave., 91766, pg. 296 **PV**

Western Sales Office, 2350 S. Garey Ave., 91766, pg. 296 **PV**

Zenith West Corp., 2675 Pomona Blvd., 91768, pg. 1054 **PB**

Pope Valley

Juliana Vineyards, P.O. Box 77, 94567, pg. 1383 **PB**

Treegrove Management Corp., P.O. Box 77, 94567, pg. 1383 **PB**

Porterville

Wal Mart Distribution Center, 1300 N. S. F. St., 93257-5969, pg. 1733 **PB**

Poway

Johnson Storage & Moving, San Diego, 12525 Stowe Dr., 92064, pg. 594 **PV**

Quartz Hill

Antelope Valley Water Company, 5015 W. Ave. L14, Ste. 5, 93536, pg. 516 **PB**

Norton Performance Plastics Co., 42263 50th St. W. 1006, 93536-3500, pg. 1176 **IT**

Quincy

Nugget Motors, 116 E. Main St., 93971, pg. 713 **PV**

Ramona

Ampex Data Systems Corporation, 16512 Daza Dr., 92065, pg. 104 **PB**

Davy McKee Corporation, San Francisco, 2440 Camino, 92065, pg. 774 **IT**

Rancho Cordova

ASRC Contacting Company, Inc. (ACCI), 3033 Gold Canal Rd., 95670, pg. 80 **PV**

Aerojet, Hwy. 50 & Aerojet Rd., 95670, pg. 706 **PV**

Air Conditioning Co. Inc., 3329 Fitzgerald Rd., 95742, pg. 28 **PV**

Associated Claims Management, Inc. of California, 3400 Data Dr., 95670, pg. 678 **PB**

BLAGGE ENTERPRISES, 3295 Ste. B, Mononier Circle, 95742, pg. 148 **PB**

Business Insurance Corporation, 3400 Data Dr., 95670, pg. 678 **PB**

Cabledata, Inc., 11020 Sun Center Dr., 95670, pg. 1659 **PB**

CableLease, Inc., 2969 Prospect Park Dr., 95670, pg. 1659 **PB**

DentiCare of California, Inc., 3400 Data Dr., 95670, pg. 678 **PB**

Foundation Health, A California Health Plan, 3400 Data Dr., 95670, pg. 678 **PB**

Foundation Health Benefit Life Insurance Company, 3400 Data Dr., 95670, pg. 678 **PB**

Foundation Health Federal Services, Inc., 3400 Data Dr., 95670, pg. 678 **PB**

Foundation Health Pharmaceutical Services, Inc., 3400 Data Dr., 95670, pg. 678 **PB**

Foundation Health Preferred Administrators, 3400 Data Dr., 95670, pg. 678 **PB**

Foundation Health PsychCare Services, 3400 Data Dr., 95670, pg. 678 **PB**

Foundation Insurance Company, 3400 Data Dr., 95670, pg. 678 **PB**

Geo-Con, Inc., 3039 Kilgore Rd., Ste. 190, 95670, pg. 1657 **PB**

Higgins Sacramento/Purch, 2550 Mercantile Dr., Ste. C, 95670, pg. 527 **PV**

INAC Corp. of California, 10860 Gold Center Dr., 2nd Fl., 95741, pg. 366 **PV**

KVP Systems, Inc., 11255 Pyrites Way, 95670, pg. 1527 **PB**

McLaren/Hart Environmental Engineering Company, 11101 Wright Rock Rd., 95670, pg. 1465 **IT**

C.C. MYERS, INC., 3286 Fitzgerald Rd., 95742, pg. 770 **PV**

Occupational Health Services, Inc., 3400 Data Dr., 95670, pg. 678 **PB**

Quality Medical Adjudication, Inc., 2897 Kilgore Rd., 95670, pg. 602 **PB**

Storage Management Division, 11050 White Rock Rd., Ste. 100, 95670-6095, pg. 1516 **PB**

USCS INTERNATIONAL, INC., 2969 Prospect Park Dr., 95670, pg. 1659 **PB**

Wyle Electronics-Sacramento, 2951 Sunrise Blvd., Ste. 175, 95742, pg. 1457 **IT**

Rancho Cucamonga

BHP Coated Steel Corp., 11200 Arrow Route, 91730, pg. 226 **IT**

California State Bank-Rancho Cucamonga, 6351 N. Haven Ave., pg. 294 **PB**

Carson Industries, 10220 Fourth St., 91730, pg. 748 **PV**

Concrete & Steel Pipe Group (Southern Div.), 10681 Foothill Rd., Ste. 450, 91730, pg. 99 **PB**

Electrohome U.S.A. (1989), Inc., 9216 Bally Ct., 91730-5835, pg. 438 **IT**

FORECAST GROUP, 10670 Civic Ctr. Dr., 91730, pg. 418 **PB**

Green Tree Acceptance, Inc., 9600 Center Ave., Ste. 160, 91730, pg. 762 **PB**

Industrial Wire Products, 12459 Arrow Rd., 91730, pg. 561 **PV**

Intertrace Technology, Inc., 10282 6th St., 91730, pg. 1101 **PB**

Monitor Dynamics Inc., 9518 Ninth St., 91730, pg. 1663 **PB**

Pacific Tri-View Corporation, 9000 9th St., Ste. 140, 91730, pg. 990 **PB**

SCHLOSSER FORGE COMPANY, 11711 Arrow Rte., 91730, pg. 970 **PV**

Tamco, P.O. Box 325, 91739, pg. 99 **PB**

Voltelcon, 9785 Crescent Center Dr., 91730, pg. 1724 **PB**

Zeneca Pharmaceuticals, 10681 Foothill Blvd., Ste. 297, 91730, pg. 1525 **IT**

Rancho Dominguez

Ablestik Laboratories, 20021 Susana Rd., 90221, pg. 1435 **IT**

Air Cargo Equipment Corporation, 2930 E. Maria St., 90221, pg. 1791 **PB**

Aydin Molded Devices Div., 2757 E. Del Amo Blvd., 90221, pg. 158 **PV**

Beck/Arnley Worldparts Corp., 3130 E. Maria St., 90221, pg. 561 **PV**

CCC Steel, Inc., 2576 E. Victoria, 90220, pg. 1375 **PB**

Danielson Indemnity Company, 19100 Susana Rd., 90221, pg. 483 **PB**

Danielson Insurance Company, 19100 Susana Rd., 90221, pg. 483 **PB**

Danielson National Insurance Company, 19100 Susana Rd., 90221, pg. 483 **PB**

Danielson Reinsurance Corporation, 19100 Susana Rd., 90221, pg. 483 **PB**

DEP CORPORATION, 2101 E. Via Arado, 90220, pg. 500 **PB**

Dep International, Ltd., 2101 E. Via Arado, 90220, pg. 500 **PB**

Electronic Systems Packaging Corp., 2525 Vista Industria, 90220, pg. 370 **PV**

ELECTRONICS STAMPING CORP., 19920 S. Alameda St., 90220, pg. 370 **PV**

Eskimo Flavors, 18831 Laurel Park Rd., 90220, pg. 592 **PB**

Griffin Technology Inc., Amsec Div., 17621 Susana Rd., 90221, pg. 506 **PB**

ITW Plastiglide, 19440 Dominguez Hills Dr., 90220, pg. 867 **PB**

KCP Holding Company, 19100 Susana Rd., 90221, pg. 483 **PB**

Kramer Capital Consultants, Inc., 19100 Susana Rd., 90221, pg. 483 **PB**

Mac Frugal's Bargains Close-Outs Inc., 2430 E. Del Amo Blvd., 90220-6306, pg. 437 **PB**

Medtronic Avalon Laboratories, Inc., 2610 E. Homestead Pl., 90220, pg. 1083 **PB**

Mission American Insurance Company, 19100 Susana Rd., 90221, pg. 483 **PB**

National American Insurance Company of California, 19100 Susana Rd., 90221, pg. 483 **PB**

Sequa Can Machinery-West Coast Operations, 2943 E. Las Hermanas St., 90221, pg. 1458 **PV**

SOUTHWESTERN INDUSTRIES, INC., 2605 Homestead Pl., 90220, pg. 1019 **PV**

Strand Lighting Inc., 18111 S. Santa Fe Ave., 90224, pg. 1087 **IT**

Tokyo Printing Ink Corporation U.S.A., Suite 101, 18710 S. Wilmington Ave., 90220, pg. 1394 **IT**

UNION-TRANSPORT CORPORATION, 19443 Laurel Park Rd., Ste. 107, 90220, pg. 1119 **PV**

West Coast Liquidators, Inc., 2430 E. Del Amo Blvd., 90220-6306, pg. 437 **PB**

Rancho Mirage

Farmers Insurance Group, 72057 Hwy. 11, 92270, pg. 111 **IT**

Rancho Santa Fe

Investment Research Company, 16236 San Dieguito Rd., Ste. 2-20, 92067, pg. 1673 **PB**

Motorola Radius, SPS, P.O. Box 3811, 92067-3811, pg. 1138 **PB**

Rancho Santa Margarita

Control Components, Inc., 22591 Avenida Emoressa, 92688, pg. 646 **IT**

Downey Savings & Loan Association, F.A., Rancho Santa Margarita Branch, 22012 El Paseo, 92688, pg. 526 **PB**

Noel Joanna, Inc., 22942 Arroyo Vista, 92688, pg. 465 **PB**

Raymond

Raymond Granite Co., 36772 Rd. 606, 93653, pg. 251 **PB**

Redding

Arthrotek, Inc., 779 Twin View Blvd., 96003, pg. 231 **PB**

Higgins Redding, 6819 C Eastside Rd., 96099-4286, pg. 527 **PV**

McColls Dairy, 2500 Angelo Ave., 96001, pg. 294 **PV**

Pacific Bell, 1805 Hilltop Dr. Ste. 105, 96002-0279, pg. 1416 **PB**

Pirelli Tri-State Inc., 7611 Sands Ln., 96099, pg. 1059 **IT**

Redding Record Searchlight, 1101 Twin View Blvd., 96003, pg. 1448 **PB**

Redlands

Climet Instruments Co., 1320 W. Colton Ave., 92374, pg. 1136 **PV**

Downey Savings & Loan Association, F.A., 640 Orange St., 92374, pg. 527 **PB**

Inland Surgery Center, 1620 Laurel Ave., 92373, pg. 803 **PB**

La-Z-Boy West, 301 Tennessee, 92373, pg. 973 **PB**

RICHMOND TECHNOLOGY INC., 1897 Colton Ave., 92374, pg. 929 **PV**

Redondo Beach

MCKINNEY & MCKINNEY ADVERTISING, 1719 Via El Prado, 90277, pg. 723 **PV**

TRW Space & Electronics Group, One Space Park, 90278-1001, pg. 1558 **PB**

TIERNAY METALS, 2600 Marine Ave., 90278, pg. 1085 **PV**

West Rockies Inc., 143 S. Broadway, 90277, pg. 1255 **IT**

Redwood City

Adecco Employment Services, 100 Redwood Shores Pkwy., 94065, pg. 24 **IT**

ADVANCED POLYMER SYSTEMS, 3696 Haven Ave., 94063, pg. 22 **PB**

AMPEX CORPORATION, 500 Broadway, M.S. 4205, 94063-3199, pg. 104 **PB**

Ampex Data Systems, 500 Broadway, 94063, pg. 104 **PB**

BAY AREA BANCSHARES, 900 Veterans Blvd., 94063, pg. 124 **PV**

BROADVISION, INC., 585 Broadway, 94063, pg. 258 **PB**

PB - U.S. Public Companies Volume
PV - U.S. Private Companies Volume
IT - International Public & Private Companies Volume

Geographic Index-U.S.

Check Point Software Technologies Inc., Three Lagoon Dr., Ste. 400, 94065, pg. 342 **PB**
CHECK POINT SOFTWARE TECHNOLOGIES LTD., Three Lagoon Dr., Ste. 400, 94065, pg. 342 **PB**
DHL Airways, Inc., 333 Twin Dolphin Dr., 94065, pg. 302 **PV**
DHL WORLDWIDE EXPRESS, 333 Twin Dolphin Dr., 94065, pg. 301 **PV**
DPR CONSTRUCTION, INC., 555 Twin Dolphin Dr., Ste. 200, 94065, pg. 305 **PV**
Downey Savings & Loan Association, F.A., 1475 Woodside Rd., 94061, pg. 527 **PB**
Emery Global Logistics, One Lagoon Dr., 94065, pg. 281 **PB**
Emery Worldwide, One Lagoon Dr., Ste. 400, 94065, pg. 281 **PB**
EXCITE, INC., 555 Broadway St., 94063-3132, pg. 599 **PB**
Harte Hanks Shoppers, 555 Twin Dlson Dr. Ste. 120, 94065, pg. 794 **PB**
Hydro Agri San Francisco, Inc., 303 Twin Dolphin Dr., Ste. 500, 94065, pg. 961 **IT**
KG Construction, Ten Twin Dolphin Dr., Ste. B-270, 94065, pg. 764 **IT**
Marketing Resources Plus, 555 Twin Dolphin Drive, 94065, pg. 1447 **IT**
NETWORK EQUIPMENT TECHNOLOGIES, INC., 800 Saginaw Dr., 94063, pg. 1168 **PB**
ORACLE CORPORATION, 500 Oracle Pkwy., 94065, pg. 1227 **PB**
RESOUND CORPORATION, 220 Saginaw Dr., 94063, pg. 1382 **PB**
Scientific Systems Division, 303 Twin Dolphin Dr., Ste 510, 94065, pg. 1516 **PB**
Sega of America Inc., 255 Shoreline Dr., 94065, pg. 1218 **IT**
Shorewood Packaging of California, 333 Twin Dolphin Dr., 94065-1401, pg. 1468 **PB**
Trinzic Development Laboratory, 555 Twin Dolphin Dr., Ste. 400, 94065, pg. 1309 **PB**
VeriFone, Inc., Three Lagoon Dr., 94065, pg. 815 **PB**

Reedley

SALWASSER MANUFACTURING COMPANY, INC., 1949 E. Manning, 93654, pg. 963 **PV**

Rialto

Boral Concrete Products Inc., 3511 N. Riverside Ave., 92376, pg. 203 **IT**

Richmond

Amot Controls Corporation, 401 First St., 94801, pg. 1405 **PB**
Chevron Research and Technology Company, P.O. Box 1627, 94802, pg. 348 **PB**
Navistar International, P.O. Box 4041, 94804-0041, pg. 1146 **PB**
PIXAR ANIMATION STUDIOS, 1001 W. Cutting Blvd., Ste. 200, 94804, pg. 1307 **PB**
Richmond Terminal, 1140 Canal Blvd., 94804-0007, pg. 692 **PB**
Sealy Mattress Company - Clarion, 1130 Seventh St., 94801-2103, pg. 979 **PV**
SHOE PAVILION, 3200 Regatta Blvd., Ste. F, 98404, pg. 996 **PV**
Tinsley Corp., 3900 Lakeside Dr., 94806, pg. 1474 **PB**
West County Times, 4301 Lakeside Dr., 94806, pg. 964 **PB**
Zeneca Ag Products, 1415 S. 47th St., 94804, pg. 1525 **IT**

Ridgecrest

California Energy Operating Company, 900 N. Heritage Dr., Bldg. D, 93555, pg. 292 **PB**
Carriage Inn, 901 China Lake Blvd., 93555, pg. 96 **PB**
MTTC, P.O. Box 1420, 93556, pg. 406 **PB**

Rio Linda

ECW, Inc., 6828 Seventh Ave., 95673, pg. 523 **PB**

Ripon

Franzia Brothers Winery, 17000 E. Hwy. 120, 95366, pg. 1183 **PV**
Nestle Beverage Company, 230 Industrial Ave., 95366, pg. 918 **IT**
NULAID FOODS, 200 W. Fifth St., 95366, pg. 809 **PV**

Riverside

Associated Plastics, Inc., 2626 Kansas Ave., 92507, pg. 417 **PV**
BOURNS, INC., 1200 Columbia Ave., 92507-2114, pg. 161 **PV**
Bourns Pressure Products, 1200 Columbia Ave., 92507, pg. 161 **PV**
CADDOCK ELECTRONICS, INC., 1717 Chicago Ave., 92507, pg. 198 **PV**
Caddock Network Division, 1717 Chicago Ave., 92507, pg. 198 **PV**
Continental Lumber, 3125 Myers St., 92503, pg. 651 **PB**
J.D. DIFFENBAUGH, INC., 2375 Chicago Ave., 92507, pg. 332 **PV**
Fleetwood Canada Ltd., 3125 Myers St., 92523, pg. 651 **PB**

FLEETWOOD ENTERPRISES, INC., 3125 Myers St., 92513, pg. 650 **PB**
Fleetwood Motor Homes of California, Inc.-Riverside Plant/ Via Ricardo, 2350 Fleetwood Dr., 92502, pg. 651 **PB**
General Employment Enterprises, Inc., 6700 Indiana Ave., Ste. 245, 92506, pg. 714 **PB**
Gold Shield Fiberglass, Inc., 1850 Atlanta Ave., 92509, pg. 652 **PB**
Harmon Industries-Riverside, 7337 Central Ave., 92504, pg. 788 **PB**
Hunter Engineering Co., Inc., 6147 River Crest Dr., 92507, pg. 474 **PV**
Inland Concrete Constructors, 2375 Chicago Ave., 92507, pg. 332 **PV**
Irritol System, P.O. Box 489, 92502, pg. 1624 **PB**
Luxfer USA Ltd., 1995 Third St., 92507, pg. 50 **IT**
Motor Home Service Facility-Riverside, California, 1975 Third St., 92507, pg. 652 **PB**
Press Enterprise Company, 3512 14th St., 92501-3878, pg. 209 **PB**
Resistor Division, 3127 Chicago Ave., 92507, pg. 198 **PV**
Rohr Industries, Riverside Plant, 8200 Arlington Ave., 92503-1499, pg. 752 **PB**
Stackhouse Inc., 2059 Atlanta Ave., 92507, pg. 1591 **PB**
Swiss Dairy, 12171 Madera Way, 92503, pg. 1527 **PV**
The Toro Company Irrigation Products, 5825 Jasmine St., 92504, pg. 1624 **PB**
Treasure Chest Advertising, 7190 Jurupa Ave., 92504, pg. 228 **PB**
URS Greiner, Inc., Bldg. 200, #253, 5225 Canyon Crest Dr., 92507, pg. 1658 **PV**
Western Metal Lath, 6510 General Dr., 92509, pg. 845 **IT**

Robbins

Yosuba Farms, Reclamation & Everglades Rds., 95676, pg. 1062 **PB**

Rocklin

Energy Absorption Systems, Inc.-Rocklin, 3617 Cincinnati Ave., 95667, pg. 1353 **PB**
Formica Corp., 3500 Cincinnati Ave., 95677, pg. 129 **IT**
Reynolds Metals Company-Rocklin, 3939 Cincinatti Ave., 95765, pg. 1386 **PB**

Rodeo

Asbury Graphite Inc. of California, 2855 Franklin Canyon Rd., 94572, pg. 87 **PV**

Rohnert Park

Compumotor Division, 5500 Business Park Dr., 94928-7904, pg. 1259 **PB**
Higgins Santa Rosa Operations, 5620 State Farm Dr., 94928, pg. 527 **PV**
Transworld Systems, Inc., 5880 Commerce Blvd., 94928, pg. 1667 **PV**

Rolling Hills Estates

Cox Communications-Palos Verdes, 43 Peninsula Ctr., 90274, pg. 455 **PB**

Rosemead

Durham Transportation Inc., 2713 N. River Ave., 91770-3303, pg. 348 **PV**
EDISON INTERNATIONAL, 2244 Walnut Grove Ave., 91770, pg. 564 **PB**
Energy Services, Inc., P.O. Box 800, 91770, pg. 564 **PB**
HCC INDUSTRIES, 4232 Temple City Blvd., 91770, pg. 490 **PV**
Hermetic Seal Corp., 4232 Temple City Blvd., 91770, pg. 490 **PV**
Los Angeles Dealers Auto Auctions, 8001 Garvey Ave., 92770-1053, pg. 282 **PV**
Mono Power Company, P.O. Box 800, 91770, pg. 564 **PB**
SCE Capital Company, P.O. Box 800, 91770, pg. 564 **PB**
Southern California Edison Company, 2244 Walnut Grove Ave., 91770, pg. 564 **PB**

Roseville

Charter Behavioral Health System of Northern California, Inc., 101 Cirby Hills Dr., 95678, pg. 1034 **PB**
Del Webb California Corporation, 2999 Douglas Blvd., Ste. 135, 95661-3828, pg. 495 **PB**
EDD-Sacramento, 3001 Douglas Blvd., Ste. 205, 95661, pg. 205 **PB**
Hewlett Packard, Research & Development, 8000 Foothills Blvd., 95747-6502, pg. 816 **PB**
SIERRAFINE LIMITED, 2151 Professional Dr., Ste. 200, 95661, pg. 999 **PV**
Sun City Roseville, 198 Cirby Way, Ste. 155, 95678, pg. 495 **PB**
Trans Leasing International, Inc.-Northwest Region, 2140 Professional Dr., Ste. 105, 95661, pg. 1628 **PB**
URS Greiner, Inc., 1380 Lead Hill Rd., Ste. #100, 95661, pg. 1658 **PV**
Zeneca Ag Products, 2999 Douglas Blvd., Ste. 300, 95661, pg. 1525 **IT**

Rubidoux

Fleetwood Travel Trailers of California, Inc.-Rubidoux, 6001 20th St., 92519, pg. 652 **PB**

Rutherford

Beaulieu Vineyard, 1960 St. Helena Hwy., 94573, pg. 410 **IT**

Sacramento

AT&T Communications, Marketing, 8950 California Ctr. Dr., 95826, pg. 10 **PB**
Aerojet, P.O. Box 13222, 95813-6000, pg. 706 **PB**
Airco Commercial Services, Inc., 5700 Alder Ave., 95828, pg. 29 **PV**
AIRCO MECHANICAL INC., 5720 Alder Ave., 95828, pg. 29 **PV**
Allright Sacramento, 708 10th St., Ste. 140, 95814, pg. 43 **PV**
AMERICAN RECREATION CENTERS, INC., 11171 Sun Center Dr., Ste. 120, 95670, pg. 90 **PB**
Banta Global Turnkey, 8380 Tiogawoods Dr., 95828, pg. 188 **PB**
Bell Atlantic Services, 4640 N. Gate Blvd. Ste. 100, 95834-1126, pg. 203 **PB**
Bell Distributing, 8180 Signal Ct., 95824, pg. 664 **PV**
Bergen Brunswig Drug Company, 1281 National Dr., 95834, pg. 213 **PB**
BEUTLER HEATING & AIR CONDITIONING INC., 9605 Oates Dr., 95827, pg. 141 **PV**
BIO-CYPHER LABORATORIES, 3301 C St., Ste. 100E, 95816, pg. 145 **PV**
BLUE DIAMOND GROWERS, 1802 C St., 95814, pg. 152 **PV**
Burns & Wilcox - Sacramento Office, 1610 Arden Way, #230, 95815, pg. 610 **PV**
Cable/Cisco, 771 B Northport Dr., 95691, pg. 215 **PV**
Cal-Ag Insurance Services, Inc., 1601 Exposition Blvd., 95815, pg. 1791 **PB**
CalFarm Insurance Agency, 1601 Exposition Blvd., 95815, pg. 1791 **PB**
CalFarm Insurance Company, 1601 Exposition Blvd., 95815, pg. 1791 **PB**
CLARK PACIFIC, 1980 S. River Rd. W., 95691, pg. 243 **PV**
CRYSTAL CREAM & BUTTER COMPANY, 1013 D St., 95814, pg. 294 **PV**
Custom-Made Packaging, Inc., 7640 Wilbur Way, 95828, pg. 803 **PV**
Dade Behring-Microscan Div., 1584 Enterprise Blvd., 95691, pg. 110 **PV**
MIKE DAUGHERTY'S CHEVROLET GEO, INC., 2449 Fulton Ave., 95825, pg. 313 **PV**
DE VONS JEWELERS, 1910 29th St., 95816, pg. 318 **PV**
THE DORRIS LUMBER & MOULDING CO., 2601 Redding Ave., 95820, pg. 341 **PV**
Down River International, Inc., P.O. Box 15290, 95851-1290, pg. 763 **PV**
Downey Savings & Loan Association, F.A., Sacramento Watt Ave. Brach, 2150 Watt Ave., 95825, pg. 526 **PV**
EA Engineering, Science & Technology, Inc., 3841 N. Freeway Blvd., Ste. 145, 95834, pg. 541 **PB**
Ebara Technologies Inc., 51 Main Ave., 95838, pg. 432 **IT**
Edelman Worldwide, Inc., 1121 L St., Ste. 803, 95814, pg. 362 **PV**
Elixir Industries, 3321 Airport Rd., 95834, pg. 371 **PV**
Engineered Construction-Sacramento, 9719 Lincoln Village Dr., Ste. 301, 95827, pg. 1304 **PB**
FILCO, INC., 1433 Fulton Ave., Ste. D, 95825, pg. 404 **PV**
First Bank of California, 865 Howe Ave., 3rd. Fl., 95825, pg. 626 **PB**
First Banks, Inc., 865 Howe Ave., Ste. 310, 95825, pg. 626 **PB**
Fleishman-Hillard, Inc., 555 Capitol Mall, Ste. 785, 95814-4502, pg. 411 **PV**
Geonex, 5979 Freeport Blvd., 95822, pg. 448 **PV**
Golden State Flooring, 1015 N. Market Blvd., 95834, pg. 527 **PV**
Granite Construction Inc.-Sacramento Div., 4001 Bradshaw Rd., 95827, pg. 759 **PB**
Graphic Arts Supply Division, 1700 Enterprise Blvd., Ste. D, 95691, pg. 205 **PB**
Green Tree Acceptance, Inc., P.O. Box 255524, 95865, pg. 762 **PV**
Grinnell Supply Sales Division, 431 Richards Blvd., 95814-0219, pg. 1648 **PB**
Harland Bartholomew & Associates Inc., 2233 Watt Ave. Ste. 330, 95825, pg. 842 **PV**
Hewlett-Packard Company, 4244 S. Market Ct., Ste. A, 95852, pg. 813 **PB**
Higgins Sacramento Operations, 1122 Joellis Way, 95815, pg. 527 **PV**
Hillhaven Convalescent Hospital Sherwood, 4700 Elvis Ave., 95819, pg. 1713 **PB**
Holiday RV Superstores West, Inc., 2020 Taylor Rd., 95678, pg. 830 **PB**
Hospital Staffing Services of California, Inc., 9700 Business Park Dr., Ste. 402, 95827, pg. 840 **PB**
HUBACHER, CADILLAC & LANDROVER INC., One Cadillac Dr., 95825, pg. 543 **PV**
Ikon Office Solutions-North California, 4515 Auburn Blvd., 95841-9000, pg. 863 **PB**
Intergraph Corporation, 777 Campus Commons Dr., 95825, pg. 891 **PB**
KFBK (AM) & KAER (FM) Radio, 1440 Ethan Way, Ste. 200, 95825, pg. 335 **PB**
KTXL Channel 40, 4655 Fruitridge Rd., 95820, pg. 1636 **PB**
KXTV Inc., 400 Broadway, 95818, pg. 209 **PB**
LAWSON MECHANICAL CONTRACTORS, 6090 S. Watt Ave., 95829, pg. 654 **PV**
Legi-Tech, 1029 J Street, Ste. 450, 95814, pg. 1066 **PB**

PB - *U.S. Public Companies Volume*
PV - *U.S. Private Companies Volume*
IT - *International Public & Private Companies Volume*

Geographic Index-U.S.

1144

A. LEVY & J. ZENTNER CO., P.O. Box 292307, 95829, pg. 663 **PV**
Liqui-Box Corp., 5000 Warehouse Way, 95826, pg. 1001 **PB**
MacFarms of Hawaii, Inc., 1802 C St., 95814, pg. 299 **PB**
Manulife Financial - Sacramento, 8810 Cal Center Dr., Ste. 250, 95826, pg. 841 **IT**
MCCLATCHY NEWSPAPERS INC., 2100 Q St., 95816, pg. 1065 **PB**
Merryhill Country Schools, Inc., Point West Executive III, 1451 River Park Dr., Ste. 141, 95815, pg. 1186 **PB**
THE MONEY STORE, 3301 C St., Suite 100 M, 95816, pg. 1124 **PB**
Moroch & Associates, Inc., 1812 J. St., Ste. 2, 95814, pg. 762 **PV**
Nadel Architects, Inc., 1760 Creekside Oaks Dr., Ste. 140, 95833, pg. 773 **PV**
OHD Corp.-California Div., 2701 47th St., 95822, pg. 822 **PV**
PACIFIC COAST BUILDING PRODUCTS INC., 3001 I St., 95816, pg. 830 **PV**
PACKARD BELL NEC, One Packard Bell Way, 95828, pg. 833 **PV**
PERFORMANCE CHEVROLET & GEO, 4811 Madison Ave., 95841, pg. 853 **PV**
Piper Jaffray Inc., One Capitol Mall, Ste. 800, 95814-3229, pg. 1303 **PB**
Pitt-Des Moines, Inc., 9719 Lincoln Village Dr., Ste. 301, 95827, pg. 1305 **PB**
RGA Products Inc., P.O. Box 958, 95812, pg. 927 **PV**
MEL RAPTON HONDA, 2820 Fulton Ave., 95821, pg. 911 **PV**
REYNEN, BARDIS & WINN, 9985 Folsom Blvd., 95827, pg. 926 **PV**
SAIC, 3800 Watt Ave., Ste. 210, 95821, pg. 976 **PV**
The Sacramento Bee, 2100 Q St., 95852, pg. 1066 **PB**
Sacramento Cable, 4350 Pell Dr., 95838, pg. 1448 **PB**
Sacramento Jaguar, Inc., 2052 Fulton Ave., 95825, pg. 1143 **PV**
SACRAMENTO KINGS, One Sports Pkwy., 95834, pg. 959 **PV**
SACRAMENTO MUNICIPAL UTILITY DISTRICT, 6201 S St., 95817-1899, pg. 959 **PV**
Saylor Lane Convalescent Hospital, 3500 Folsom Blvd., 95816, pg. 1714 **PB**
Scripps Howard Cable Co. of Sacramento, 4350 Pell Dr., 95838, pg. 1448 **PB**
SENATOR FORD, 3801 Florin Rd., 95823, pg. 983 **PV**
Senior Spectrum, P.O. Box 13456, 9261 Folsom Blvd., 95813, pg. 1066 **PB**
Sequent Computer Systems, Inc., 980 Ninth St., 16th Fl., 95814, pg. 1459 **PB**
SETZER FOREST PRODUCTS, 2555 Third St., 95818, pg. 987 **PV**
Sherwood Convalescent Hospital, 4700 Elvas Ave., 95819, pg. 1714 **PB**
Sierra Spring Water Company, 8631 Younger Creek Dr., 95828, pg. 322 **IT**
SUTTER HEALTH, One Capitol Mall, 95814, pg. 1057 **PV**
TIE Systems-Sacramento, 3140 Gold Camp Dr., Ste 130, 95670, pg. 1085 **PV**
A. TEICHERT & SON, INC., 3500 American River Dr., 95864, pg. 1072 **PV**
Teichert Land Co., 3500 American River Dr., 95864, pg. 1073 **PV**
U.S. Bank of California, P.O. Box 1020, 402 F St., 95502, pg. 1681 **PB**
VIDEO PRODUCTS DISTRIBUTORS, INC., 6051 S. Watt Ave., 95829, pg. 1139 **PV**
Vitafreze Frozen Confections, P.O. Box 1313, 95806, pg. 294 **PV**
VON HOUSEN MOTORS, 1810 Howe Ave., 95825, pg. 1143 **PV**
Walsh Construction Company (West), 10365 Old Placerville Rd., Ste. 210, 95827, pg. 143 **PB**
Walsh Power Group, 10365 Old Placerville Rd., Ste. 210, 95827, pg. 143 **PB**
Westco Products/Sacramento, 11350 Sunrise Park Dr., 95742, pg. 244 **IT**
Western Farm Credit Bank, 3636 American River Dr., 95864, pg. 398 **PV**
Western International Media Corporation, 601 University Ave., Ste. 275, 95825, pg. 1167 **PV**
WICKLAND CORPORATION, 3640 American River Dr., 95864, pg. 1174 **PV**
Wickland Oil Company, Inc., 3640 American River Dr., 95864, pg. 1175 **PV**
Wickland Properties, 3640 American River Dr., 95864, pg. 1175 **PV**
Willis Corroon Corp. of Sacramento, 960 Fulton Ave., 95825, pg. 1507 **IT**
WINTER VOLVO & LINCOLN MERCURY, P.O. Box 232210, 95823-0420, pg. 1183 **PV**
Woodward-Clyde, 10370 Old Placerville Rd., Ste. 104, 95827, pg. 1656 **PB**
Xerox Research, 560 J St. Ste. 300, 95814-2342, pg. 1784 **PB**
Zellerbach Division, 1100 Richards Blvd., 95814, pg. 1075 **PB**

Saint Helena

Beringer Wine Estates Holdings, Inc., P.O. Box 111, 1000 Pratt Ave., 94574, pg. 1078 **PV**
Markham Vineyards, 2812 No. St. Helena Hwy., 94574, pg. 858 **IT**
St. Clement Vineyards, 2867 St. Helena Hwy. North, 94574, pg. 1193 **IT**
SUTTER HOME WINERY, INC., P.O. Box 248, 94574, pg. 1057 **PV**
Wine World Estates Company, 2000 Main St., 94574, pg. 917 **IT**

Salinas

Administration Center, 307 Main St., 93902-1786, pg. 1248 **PB**
DICK BRUHN INCORPORATED, 300 Main St., 93901, pg. 175 **PV**
Credit Administration Center, 17547 Vierra Canyon Rd., 93907-1329, pg. 1248 **PB**
The Dickinson Family, Inc., c/o The J.M. Smucker Co., 1275 Hansen St., 93901, pg. 1480 **PB**
Dole Fresh Vegetables, 639 S. Sanborn Rd., 93901, pg. 515 **PB**
First National Bank of Central California, 1001 S. Main St., 93902-1786, pg. 1248 **PB**
First National Bank of Central California, 307 Main St., 93902-1786, pg. 1248 **PB**
First National Bank of Central California, 307 Main St., 93901, pg. 1248 **PB**
Fresh Western International, 931 A. Blanco Circle, 93901, pg. 491 **IT**
Household Bank, N.A., 1441 Schilling Place, 93901, pg. 842 **PB**
Household Credit Services, 1441 Schilling Place, 93901, pg. 842 **PB**
KCBA-TV, P.O. Box 3560, 93912, pg. 16 **PB**
KSBW, Inc., 238 John St., 93901, pg. 389 **PV**
Kaufman and Broad-Monterey Bay, Inc., 1604 N. Main St., 93906, pg. 945 **PB**
Mary Ellen, Inc., P.O. Box 458, 93902, pg. 1480 **PB**
Nestle Chocolate & Confections Company, 900 E. Blanco Rd., 93901, pg. 917 **IT**
PACIFIC CAPITAL BANCORP, 307 Main St., 93901, pg. 1247 **PB**
Radionics, Inc., 1800 Abbott St., 93901, pg. 501 **PB**
River Ranch - Salinas, 1156 Abbott Street, 93901, pg. 491 **IT**
Salinas Californian, 123 W. Alisal St., 93912, pg. 701 **PB**
Salinas Care Center, 637 E. Romie Ln., 93901, pg. 733 **PV**
Schilling Plant, 1311 Schilling Place, 93901, pg. 1066 **PB**
Smucker Salinas Plant, 1275 Hansen St., 93901, pg. 1480 **PB**
Static RAM Div., 1566 Moffett St., 93905, pg. 884 **PB**

Samoa

Louisiana Pacific Western Div., P.O. Box 158, 95564, pg. 1015 **PB**

San Bernardino

Baldwin Stobb San Bernardino, 1351 E. Riverview Dr., 92408, pg. 170 **PB**
Calnev Pipeline Company, 348 W. Hospitality Ln., Ste. 100, 92408, pg. 692 **PB**
Cott Corporation - Pacific South West Region, 336 Central Avenue, 92408, pg. 338 **IT**
Foamex, 1400 A East Victoria Ave., 92406, pg. 1094 **PV**
Franklin Press, 1001 S. Arrowhead Ave., 92408, pg. 268 **PV**
GATE CITY BEVERAGE DISTRIBUTORS, 2505 Steele St., 92408, pg. 441 **PV**
The Sun Co., 399 N. D St., 92401, pg. 701 **PB**
Temco Fireplace Products, Inc. (Perris), 23560 Oleander, 92370, pg. 1576 **PB**
URS Greiner, Inc., 225 W. Hospitality Ln., Ste. 24, 92408, pg. 1659 **PB**

San Bruno

ATKINSON, 1001 Bayhill Dr., 2nd Fl., 94066, pg. 143 **PB**
Atkinson Construction, 1100 Grundy Ln., 94066, pg. 143 **PB**
FASTRAC Systems, Inc., 1250 Bayhill Dr., Ste. 100, 94066, pg. 1158 **PB**
First DataBank, 1111 Bayhill Dr., Ste. 350, 94066, pg. 515 **PV**
Gap Stores Division, 900 Cherry Ave., 94066, pg. 702 **PB**
GapKids Division, 900 Cherry Ave., 94066, pg. 702 **PB**
Great Pacific Insurance Company, 1250 Bayhill Dr., 94066, pg. 1158 **PB**
Krames Communications, 1100 Grundy Ln., 94066, pg. 1616 **PB**
Pinnacle Data Corporation, 1250 Bayhill Dr., Ste. 100, 94066, pg. 1158 **PB**
SCHOOL APPAREL, INC., 1099 Sneath Ln., 94066, pg. 972 **PV**

San Carlos

Air Conditioning Co., Inc., 1700 Industrial Rd., 94070, pg. 28 **PV**
Benefit Consultants, Inc. (CT), 1125 Industrial Rd., 94070, pg. 320 **PB**
Electronic Devices and Materials, 960 Industrial Rd., 94070-1303, pg. 1003 **PB**
Genzyme Diagnostics, Medix Biotecth, 1531 Industrial Rd., 94070, pg. 733 **PB**
KELLY-MOORE PAINT COMPANY, INC., 987 Commercial St., 94070, pg. 613 **PV**
QUANTIC INDUSTRIES, INC., 990 Commercial St., 94070, pg. 899 **PV**

San Clemente

Daden-Anthony Associates, Inc., 1001 Calle Amanecer, 92673-6260, pg. 1563 **PB**
SUNSTONE HOTEL INVESTORS, INC., 115 Calle de Industrias, Ste. 201, 92672, pg. 1536 **PB**
Veravision, 1046 Calle Recodo, Ste. 1, 92673, pg. 1663 **PB**

San Diego

A/CD-West, 10060 Carrol Canyon Rd., 92131, pg. 859 **PB**
ABB Hafo Inc., 11501 Rancho Bernardo Rd., 92127, pg. 4 **IT**
ADC Wireless Systems, Inc., 9645 Scranton Rd., 92121, pg. 4 **PB**
Abbott Ambulatory Infusion, 1522-B Ave. of Science, Ste. B, 92118, pg. 13 **PB**
Academic Press, Inc., 1250 Sixth Ave., 92101, pg. 783 **PB**
ACTION INSTRUMENTS, INC., 8601 Aero Dr., 92123, pg. 15 **PV**
Advanced Digital Systems Inc., 3033 Science Park Rd., 92121, pg. 1618 **PB**
Air Conditioning Co., Inc., 7179 Construction Ct., Ste. A, 92121, pg. 28 **PV**
Alanex Corporation, 3550 General Atomics Ct., 92121, pg. 28 **PB**
ALARIS MEDICAL, INC., 10221 Wateridge Circle, 92121, pg. 35 **PB**
ALARIS Medical Systems, Inc., 10221 Wateridge Circle, 92121-1579, pg. 35 **PB**
Alcoa Electronic Packaging, Inc., 16750 Via Del Campo Ct., 92127, pg. 60 **PB**
Allied Security Inc., 6151 Fairmont Ave., Ste. 207, 92120, pg. 40 **PV**
AlliedSignal Fluid Systems, 10054 Old Grove Rd., 92131, pg. 51 **PB**
Allright San Diego Parking, Inc., 3740 Fifth Ave., 92103, pg. 43 **PV**
Alvarado Convalescent & Rehabilitation Hospital San Diego, 6599 Alvarado Rd., 92120, pg. 1711 **PB**
American Rigging & Supply, 2317 Newton Ave., 92113, pg. 215 **PV**
AmeriStar Financial Corporation, 5405 Morehouse Dr., Ste. 330, 92121, pg. 987 **PB**
APPLIED DIGITAL ACCESS, 9855 Scranton Rd., 92121, pg. 122 **PB**
Applied Super Conetics, Inc., 8980 Crestmar Point, 92121, pg. 1405 **IT**
Arnolds Interiors, Inc., 7069 Consolidated Way, 92121, pg. 546 **PV**
Arrow/Schweber Electronics, 9511 Ridgehaven Ct., 92121, pg. 134 **PB**
Arts & Crafts Press, 1949 W. Walnut, 92101, pg. 268 **PV**
ATLAS HOTELS, INC., 500 Hotel Circle N., 92108, pg. 96 **PV**
Aurora Electronics, 11085 Sorrento Valley Ct., 92121, pg. 147 **PB**
The Austad Company, 741 F St., 92101, pg. 782 **PB**
Auxiliary Power International Corporation (APIC), P.O. Box 939090, 8985 Balboa Ave., 92193, pg. 787 **IT**
BMS, Inc., 7322 Convoy St., 92111, pg. 396 **PB**
BSA Advertising, Inc., 3111 Camino Del Rio N., Ste. 202, 92108, pg. 108 **PV**
Ball Systems Engineering Operations, 5580 Morehouse Dr., 92121-1709, pg. 171 **PB**
Bank of America, 9918 Hibert St., 92131, pg. 180 **PB**
Bank of America Business Credit, 10174 Old Grove Rd., 92131, pg. 180 **PB**
BankAmerica Financial Services System, Inc., 10124 Old Grove Rd., 92131, pg. 181 **PB**
BankAmerica Insurance Group, 10174 Old Grove, 92131, pg. 181 **PB**
Beckman-IPD/Doric, 3883 Ruffin Rd., 92123, pg. 574 **PB**
Bilstein Corporation of America, 8845 Rehco Rd., 92121, pg. 507 **IT**
Blue Devil Industries, Inc., 9485-A Customhouse Plaza, 92173, pg. 802 **IT**
Books for Professionals, Inc., 1250 Sixth Ave., 92101, pg. 783 **PB**
Brawn of California, Inc., 741 F St., 92101, pg. 782 **PB**
BREHM COMMUNICATIONS INC., 17065 Via Del Campo, Ste. 200, 92127, pg. 166 **PV**
Brooktree Rockwell Semiconductor Systems Div., 9868 Scranton Rd., 92121-3707, pg. 1398 **PB**
Bull, Inc., 10260 Campus Point Dr., 92121, pg. 976 **PV**
Bumble Bee Seafoods Inc., 3990 Ruffin Rd., 92123, pg. 526 **PV**
JOHN BURNHAM & CO., 610 W. Ash, 92101, pg. 186 **PV**
Burns & Wilcox - San Diego Office, 2650 Camino del Rio North, Ste. 308, 92108, pg. 610 **PV**
Cable/Home Communications Corp., 6262 Lusk Blvd., 92121, pg. 716 **PB**
Cade Composites, Inc., 4075 Ruffin Rd., 92123, pg. 290 **PB**
Califia Company, 101 Ash St., 92101, pg. 584 **PB**
Calterm, 9220 Activity Rd., 92126, pg. 124 **PB**
Campbell Industries, Inc., P.O. Box 1870, Harbor Dr. & Eighth Ave., 92112, pg. 703 **PV**
Campus Point Realty Corporation, 10260 Campus Point Dr., 92121, pg. 976 **PV**
Carriage House Inns, 500 Hotel Circle, 92186, pg. 96 **PV**
Casio Manufacturing Corporation, 1840 Dornoch Ct., 92173, pg. 274 **IT**
A.M. Castle & Co., 4340 Vandever Ave., 92120, pg. 313 **PB**
Caterpillar Capital Company, Inc., 2200 Pacific Hwy., 92101, pg. 315 **PB**

Geographic Index-U.S.

PB - *U.S. Public Companies Volume*
PV - *U.S. Private Companies Volume*
IT - *International Public & Private Companies Volume*

Geographic Index-U.S.

Chapman Warwick Inc., 2445 Fifth Ave., Ste. 401, 92101-1665, pg. 1152 PV
Charter San Diego Behavioral Health System, Inc., 11878 Ave. of Industry, 92128, pg. 1035 PB
Chiron Mimotopes Peptide Systems, 3550 General Atomics Ct., 92121, pg. 350 PB
Chiron Viagene, Inc., 11055 Roselle St., 92121, pg. 350 PB
Christiana Community Builders, 10825 Carbet Pl., 92124, pg. 352 PB
Chugai Biopharmaceuticals, Inc., 6275 Nancy Ridge Dr., 92121, pg. 291 IT
Chugai Pharma U.S.A., Inc., 6275 Nancy Ridge Dr., 92121, pg. 291 IT
City Meats & Provisions - San Diego, 5235 Lovelock St., 92110, pg. 244 PV
COHU, INC., 5755 Kearny Villa Rd., 92123-1170, pg. 396 PB
Comdisco Electronics Group, Herst Towne Center, 3655 Nobel Dr., Ste. 600, 92122, pg. 408 PB
Compsolven Corporation, 2200 Pacific Hwy., 92101, pg. 316 PB
Comstream Corporation, 10180 Barnes Canyon Rd., 92121, pg. 1288 PB
Continental Homes of California, 12636 High Bluff Dr., Ste. 300, 92130, pg. 441 PB
Continental Ranch, Inc., 12636 High Bluff Dr., Ste. 300, 92130, pg. 441 PB
Convair Div., P.O. Box 85357, 92138, pg. 709 PB
Coordinated Healthcare Systems, P.O. Box 85088, 92138, pg. 361 PB
Costco, Inc.-San Diego Region, 4455 Morena Blvd., 92117, pg. 452 PB
Cox Communications-San Diego, 5159 Federal Blvd., 92105, pg. 455 PB
Cubic Communications, 9535 Waples St., 92121, pg. 466 PB
CUBIC CORPORATION, 9333 Balboa Ave., 92123, pg. 466 PB
Cubic Defense Systems, 9333 Balboa Ave., 92123, pg. 466 PB
Cubic Worldwide Technical Services, Inc., 4285 Ponderosa Ave., 92123, pg. 466 PB
DRS Technical Services, Inc., 2535 Camino Del Rio S., Ste. 300, 92110, pg. 474 PB
Davidson Coscan Partners, 12520 High Bluff Dr., Ste. 300, 92130, pg. 228 IT
DEAN'S PHOTO SERVICE, 4575 Mission Gorge Pl., 92120, pg. 319 PV
Delta Design, Inc., 5775 Kearny Villa Rd., 92123, pg. 396 PB
Deltec, 2727 Kurtz St., 92110, pg. 126 IT
Deltec Corporation, 2727 Kurtz St., 92110, pg. 492 IT
Deposition Technologies, Inc., 4540 Viewbridge Ave., 92123, pg. 1056 PB
Digitree, Inc., P.O. Box 26260, 9889 Willow Creek Rd., 92196, pg. 1600 PB
Doctor Design, 10505 Sorrento Valley Rd. #1, 92121, pg. 886 PB
Dowty O Rings North America, 2498 Roll Dr. #906, 92173, pg. 1338 IT
ROBERT F. DRIVER CO., INC., 1620 Fifth Ave., 92101-2703, pg. 343 PV
EDD-San Diego, 5520 Ruffin Rd., Ste. 205, 92123, pg. 205 PB
Edge Semiconductor, 10021 Willow Creek Rd., 92131, pg. 1456 PB
Electronic Materials Division, 10080 Willow Creek Rd., 92131, pg. 713 IT
Electronic Solutions, 6790 Flanders Dr., 92121, pg. 1791 PB
Elgar Corporation, 9250 Brown Deer Rd., 92121, pg. 789 PB
Encore Computer Corp., 5230 Carroll Canyon Rd., Ste. 224, 92121, pg. 580 PB
ENOVA CORP., P.O. Box 129400, 101 Ash St., 92112-9400, pg. 583 PB
FHI Benefit Systems, Inc., 1620 Fifth Ave., 92101, pg. 343 PV
FPA MEDICAL MANAGEMENT, INC., 3636 Nobel Dr., 2nd Fl., 92122, pg. 608 PB
Factory 2-U, 4000 Ruffin Rd., 92123, pg. 612 PB
FAMILY BARGAIN CORPORATION, 4000 Ruffin Rd., 92123, pg. 612 PB
H.G. FENTON MATERIAL COMPANY, 7220 Trade St., Ste. 300, 92121, pg. 400 PV
Financial Collection Agencies (1990), Inc., 3160 Camino Del Rio South, Ste. 200B, 92108, pg. 471 PB
First American Appraisal Services, 3570 Camino Del Rio N., 92108, pg. 625 PB
First American CREDCO, 9444 Balboa Ave., Ste. 550, 92123, pg. 625 PB
FOODMAKER, INC., 9330 Balboa Ave., 92123-1516, pg. 661 PB
Foster Wheeler Energy Services, Inc., 8925 Rehco Rd., 92121, pg. 677 PB
FOTOBALL USA, INC., 3738 Ruffin Rd., 92123, pg. 678 PB
Frazee Industries Inc., 6625 Miramar Rd., 92121, pg. 1501 IT
GDE Systems, Inc., P.O. Box 509009, 92150-9009, pg. 1627 PB
Gen-Probe Inc., 9880 Campus Point Dr., 92121, pg. 291 IT
GENERAL ATOMICS, 3550 General Atomics Ct., 92186-9784, pg. 443 PV
General Employment Enterprises, Inc., 12526 High Bluff Dr., Ste. 300, 92130, pg. 715 PV
GENERAL TEXTILES, 4000 Ruffin Rd., Ste. B, 92123-1866, pg. 445 PV

Genstar Development Company, Pacific Tower, 4365 Executive Dr., Ste. 1470, 92121, pg. 112 IT
Global Moving Systems, Inc., 8925 Carroll Way, 92121, pg. 458 PV
Graphic Arts Supply Division, 6160 Marindustry Dr., Ste. A, 92121, pg. 205 PV
Green Tree Acceptance, Inc., 9968 Hibert St., Ste. 204, 92131, pg. 762 PV
Grossmont Bank, 4320 La Jolla Dr., Ste. 355, 92122, pg. 1793 PB
GTI CORPORATION, 9715 Business Park Ave., 92131-1642, pg. 767 PB
HK Systems, 10509 Vista Sorrento Pkwy., 92121, pg. 491 PV
Ernest W. Hahn Inc., 700-4350 LaJolla Village Dr., 92122-1233, pg. 229 PB
Hartley Courseware, 9920 Pacific Heights Blvd., 92121, pg. 601 PV
HAWTHORNE MACHINERY COMPANY, P.O. Box 708-92112, 16945 Camina San Bernardo, 92127, pg. 512 PV
Hawthorne Power Systems, P.O. Box 708, 8050 Othello Ave., 92112, pg. 513 PV
Hazard Center Associates, c/o Trammell Crow Company, 701 B St., Ste. 200, 92101-8199, pg. 361 PV
Heating and Cooling Supply Inc., 3970 Home Ave., 92105, pg. 1746 PV
Hewlett-Packard Company, 9606 Aero Dr., 92123, pg. 813 PV
Higgins San Diego Operations, 3612 Kurtz St., 92110, pg. 527 PV
HomeFed Trust, 625 Broadway, Ste. 906, 92185, pg. 1742 PB
Humphrey, Inc., 9212 Balboa Ave., 92123, pg. 1376 PB
I-Bus Division, 9174 Sky Park Court, 92123, pg. 1062 PB
IDX Systems Corporation-San Diego, 4370 La Jolla Village Dr., Ste. 400, 92122, pg. 854 PB
IVHS Technologies Inc., 10802 Willow Ct., 92127, pg. 558 PB
Ikon Office Solutions-San Diego, 7520 Convoy Ct., 92111, pg. 364 PB
Imagery & Information Systems, P.O. Box 509008, 92150-9008, pg. 1627 PB
IMAGING TECHNOLOGIES CORP., 11031 Via Frontera, 92127, pg. 870 PB
Imperia Business Credit, 16935 W. Bernardo Dr. #150, 92127, pg. 872 PB
Indimac Agency, Inc., 15050 Ave. of Science, Ste. 101, 92128, pg. 857 PB
Indimac Manufactured Housing Division, 15050 Avenue of Science, Ste. 101, 92128, pg. 857 PB
Industrial Computer Source, Inc., 9950 Barnes Canyon Rd., 92121-2720, pg. 539 PB
Innovative Steam Technologies, 4180 Ruffin Rd., Ste. 250, 92123, pg. 316 PB
Insight Electronics Inc., 9980 Huennekens St., 92121, pg. 1457 PB
Intergraph Corporation, 9988 Hibert St., Ste. 201, 92131, pg. 851 PB
Iomega Tape Co., 15110 Ave. of Science, 92128-3405, pg. 912 PB
Jacor, Inc., 9775 Towne Centre Dr., 92121, pg. 584 PV
Jacor Networks Inc., 9775 Towne Centre Dr., 92121, pg. 584 PV
Jani King of California, Inc., 3465 Camino del Rio S., Ste. 330, 92108, pg. 581 PV
JAYMARK, INC., 9775 Towne Centre Dr., 92121, pg. 584 PV
Jostens Home Learning, 9920 Pacific Heights Blvd., 92121, pg. 601 PV
JOSTENS LEARNING CORPORATION, 9901 Pacific Heights Blvd., 92121, pg. 601 PV
KGTV, 47th St. & Freeway 94, 92102, pg. 1070 PB
KNSD-TV, 8330 Engineer Rd., 92111-2493, pg. 712 PB
KSON AM & FM, P.O. Box 15036, 92115, pg. 926 PV
Kaufman and Broad of San Diego, Inc., 12626 High Bluff Dr., Ste. 400, 92130, pg. 945 PB
Kintetsu World Express Inc., 9060 Activity Rd., Ste. F, 92126, pg. 735 IT
Kyocera America, Inc., 8611 Balboa Ave., 92123, pg. 775 IT
Kyocera International, Inc., 8611 Balboa Ave., 92123, pg. 775 IT
L3 Communications Conic Div., 9020 Balboa Ave., 92193-3507, pg. 638 PV
L3 Communications Telemetry & Instrumentation Div., 15378 Avenue of Science, 92128-3407, pg. 639 PV
LA MESA R V CENTER, INC., 7430 Copley Pk. Pl., Hwy. 52, 92111, pg. 640 PV
Lambert Smith Hampton, 3200 4th Ave., Ste. 101, 92103, pg. 797 IT
LASER POWER CORPORATION, 12777 High Bluff Dr., 92130, pg. 652 PV
Logicon Tactical and Training Systems Division, 4010 Sorrento Valley Blvd., 92121, pg. 1199 PB
Magnet Controls Div., 160 Precision Park Ln., 92073, pg. 157 PB
Mail Boxes Etc., 6060 Cornerstone Ct. W., 92121, pg. 1687 PB
Major Pharmaceuticals, 8330 Arjons Dr., 92126, pg. 475 PV
Manulife Financial - San Diego, 7676 Hazard Center Dr., Ste. 1450, 92108, pg. 841 IT
Martinique Holdings, P.O. Box 420220, 92124, pg. 352 PB
Mattel Toys Mexico, 1333 30th St., 92154-3404, pg. 1058 PB
Maxwell Federal Division, 8888 Balboa Ave., 92123, pg. 1062 PB
Maxwell Technologies-Federal Division, 8888 Balboa Ave., 92123, pg. 1062 PB

MAXWELL TECHNOLOGIES, INC., 9275 Sky Park Ct., 92123-1506, pg. 1061 PB
Maxwell Technologies-Information Systems Division, 8888 Balboa Ave., 92123, pg. 1062 PB
MCKELLAR COMPANIES, 12526 High Bluff Dr., Ste. 100, 92130, pg. 723 PV
Medtronic Interventional Vascular, 9410 Carroll Park Dr., 92121, pg. 1083 PB
Meret Communications, 9990 Mesa Rim Rd., 92121, pg. 1233 PB
Milgray/San Diego, Inc., 6835 Flanders Dr., 92121, pg. 207 PB
Miller Accounting Publications, Inc., 1250 Sixth Ave., 92101, pg. 784 PB
Millipore Tylan Products, 15330 Ave. of Science, Ste. 200, 92128, pg. 1112 PB
Mission Management Systems, P.O. Box 509008, 92150-9008, pg. 1627 PB
Mitchell International, 9889 Willow Creek Rd., 92126, pg. 1601 PB
MITEK SYSTEMS, INC., 10070 Carroll Canyon Rd., 92131-1108, pg. 1117 PB
Mitsubishi Foods (MC), Inc., 5355 Mira Sorrento Pl., Ste. 700, 92138, pg. 872 IT
Monterey Kelp Corp., P.O. Box 23076, 92123, pg. 1125 IT
MONTICELLO MANAGEMENT CO., 2505 Congress St., Ste. 220, 92110, pg. 759 PV
MYCOGEN CORPORATION, 5501 Oberlin Dr., 92121-1718, pg. 1142 PB
Mycogen Crop Protection, 5501 Oberlin Dr., 92121, pg. 1142 PB
NATIONAL STEEL & SHIPBUILDING COMPANY, Harbor Dr. at 28th, 92113, pg. 787 PV
NELSON PHOTO SUPPLIES, 722 33rd St., 92102, pg. 791 PV
NICHES, INC., 10280 Camino Santa Fe Rd., 92121, pg. 1181 PB
Nielsen Dillingham Builders, Inc., 3127 Jefferson St., 92110, pg. 333 PV
Ninteman Construction Company, Inc., 4375 Jutland Dr., #200, 92138, pg. 1052 PV
Nissan Design International, Inc., 9800 Campus Point Dr., 92121, pg. 944 IT
Nokia Mobile Phones, Inc., 9605 Scranton Rd., Ste. 450, 92121, pg. 952 IT
Northern Trust Bank of California, N.A., 4370 La Jolla Village Dr.-Ste. 1000, 92122, pg. 1196 PB
NuEar Electronics, 10070 Mesa Rim Rd., 92121, pg. 1035 PB
Nurseryland Garden Centers, 5985 Santa Fe St., 92109, pg. 715 PV
The NutraSweet Kelco Company, 8355 Aero Dr., 92193, pg. 1125 PB
O-Seal Div., 7664 Panasonic Way, 92173-4206, pg. 1262 PB
OTSG, Inc., 2200 Pacific Hwy., 92101, pg. 316 PB
OmniTRACS Division, 6455 Lusk Blvd., 92121, pg. 1349 PB
PMR CORPORATION, 501 Washington St., 5th Fl., 92103, pg. 1242 PB
PS GROUP HOLDINGS, 4370 La Jolla Village Dr., Ste. 1050, 92122, pg. 1245 PB
PSICOR, Inc., 16818 Via Del Campo Ct., 92127, pg. 196 PB
Pacific Communication Sciences, Inc., 10075 Barnes Canyon Rd., 92121, pg. 375 PB
Pacific Crest Investment & Loan (San Diego Branch), 1501 5th Ave., Ste. 100, 92101, pg. 1249 PB
PAREXEL International Corporation, 8910 University Center Lane, Ste. 500, 92122, pg. 1258 PB
Pay-Fone Systems, Inc., 7204 Claremont Mesa Blvd., 92111, pg. 1267 PB
Penco West, 3838 Camino Del Rio N., #222, 92108, pg. 1504 IT
PHOTOMATRIX CORPORATION, 11065 Sorrento Valley Ct., 92121, pg. 1292 PB
Phyxis Corporation, 9380 Carroll Park Ave., 92121, pg. 305 PB
Pilkington Barnes Hind (PBH), 7979 Vickers St., 92111, pg. 111 PV
Pointe Builders, 3130 Bonita Rd., 92114, pg. 873 PV
Polese Company, 10103 Carroll Canyon Rd., 06790, pg. 1456 PB
Pow Con, 8123 Miralani Dr., 92126, pg. 867 PB
Pre-Mix Concrete Co., 7220 Trade St., Ste.300, 92121, pg. 400 PB
Premium Advance Company, 1620 5th Ave., P.O. Box 670, 92101, pg. 343 PV
PRICE ENTERPRISES, INC., 4649 Morena Blvd., 92117-3650, pg. 1324 PB
PRICESMART INC., 4649 Morena Blvd., 92117, pg. 1324 PB
Products, P.O. Box 509008, 92150-9008, pg. 1627 PB
PROXIMA CORPORATION, 9440 Carroll Park Dr., 92121-2298, pg. 1339 PB
Pueblo Mall Limited Partnership, c/o Hahn Prop. Mngmt., 3666 Kearny Villa Rd., 92123, pg. 362 PB
Pulse Engineering, Inc., 12220 World Trade Dr., 92128, pg. 1564 PB
Pure Pulse Technologies, Inc., 4241 Ponderosa Ave., 92123, pg. 1062 PB
QUALCOMM, 6455 Lusk Blvd., 92121-2779, pg. 1348 PB
Qualidyne Systems Inc., 3055 Del Sol Blvd., 92154, pg. 1241 IT
QUIDEL CORPORATION, 10165 McKellar Ct., 92121, pg. 1352 PB
RF Microsystems, 9454 Chesapeake Dr., 92123, pg. 1376 PB
RLI Professional Risk, 9820 Willow Creek Rd., Ste. 30, 92131, pg. 1356 PB

PB - U.S. Public Companies Volume
PV - U.S. Private Companies Volume
IT - International Public & Private Companies Volume

1146

Raytheon Semiconductor-La Jolla, 4243 Campus Point Ct., 92121, pg. 1365 **PB**
REMEC, INC., 9404 Chesapeake Dr., 92123, pg. 1376 **PB**
Revenue Collection Group, P.O. Box 85587, 5650 Kearny Mesa Rd., 92186-5587, pg. 466 **PB**
Revenue Collection Group World Headquarters, 5650 Kearny Mesa Rd., 92111, pg. 466 **PB**
Rice, Hall, James & Associates, 600 W. Broadway, Ste. 1000, 92101-3383, pg. 1674 **PB**
Robot Research, Inc., 5636 Ruffin Rd., 92123, pg. 1457 **PB**
Rush Press, 8835 Complex Dr., 92123, pg. 268 **PV**
SAIC Commercial Enterprises, Inc., 10260 Campus Point Dr., 92121, pg. 976 **PV**
SDRC Engineering Services Inc., 11995 El Camino Real, Ste. 200, 92130-2566, pg. 1525 **PB**
SKF Condition Monitoring Inc., 4141 Ruffin Rd., 92123-1841, pg. 1157 **IT**
SAFESKIN CORPORATION, 12671 High Bluff Dr., 92138, pg. 1425 **PB**
SAN DIEGO CHARGERS, 4020 Murphy Canyon Rd., 92123, pg. 964 **PV**
San Diego Division, 10790 Roselle St., 92121, pg. 27 **PB**
San Diego Gas & Electric Company, 101 Ash St., 92101, pg. 584 **PB**
San Diego Learning Center, P.O. Box 368-002, 92136-8002, pg. 219 **PB**
San Diego Union Tribune, 350 Camino de la Reina, 92108-4106, pg. 275 **PV**
Sanyo, 1201 Sanyo Ave., 92173, pg. 1191 **IT**
Sanyo E & E Corporation, 2001 Sanyo Ave., 92173, pg. 1191 **IT**
Sanyo Energy (U.S.A.) Corporation, 2001 Sanyo Ave., 92173, pg. 1191 **IT**
Sanyo Video Components (USA) Corporation, 2001 Sanyo Ave., 92173, pg. 1191 **IT**
Satellite Data Networks, 6262 Lusk Blvd., 92121, pg. 716 **PB**
SCIENCE APPLICATIONS INTERNATIONAL CORP., 10260 Campus Point Dr., 92121-1522, pg. 975 **PV**
John P. Scripps Newspapers, 525 C St., Ste. 306, 92101, pg. 1448 **PB**
Sea World of California, 1720 S. Shores Rd., 92109, pg. 114 **PV**
Seafood Importers, Inc., 8899 University Center Ln., 92122, pg. 526 **PV**
Security Pacific Housing Services, Inc., 10680 Treena St., Ste. 500, 92131, pg. 182 **PB**
Security Pacific Information Services Corporation, 10174 Old Grove Rd., 92131, pg. 182 **PB**
Security Pacific International Finance, Inc., 10089 Willow Creek Rd., 92131, pg. 182 **PB**
Security Pacific Services Corporation, 10124 Old Grove Rd., 92131, pg. 182 **PB**
Shea Homes San Diego, 10721 Treena St., Ste. 200, 92131-1039, pg. 991 **PV**
Shimizu America Corporation, 1202 Kettner Blvd., Ste. 3100, 92101, pg. 1233 **IT**
Shimizu Land Corporation-San Diego Office, 1202 Kettner Blvd., Ste. 3100, 92101, pg. 1233 **IT**
Smith Laboratories, 9425 Chesapeake Dr., 92123, pg. 405 **PB**
Soladyne Division, 5037 Ruffner St., 92111, pg. 1097 **PB**
Solar Turbines Incorporated, 2200 Pacific Hwy., 92101, pg. 316 **PB**
Solar Turbines International Company, 2200 Pacific Hwy., 92138, pg. 316 **PB**
Sony Engineering & Manufacturing of America, 16450 W. Bernardo Dr., 92127-1804, pg. 1284 **IT**
Southwest Marine, Inc., P.O. Box 13308, 92170, pg. 213 **PV**
Specialty Restaurants Corp, 8885 Balboa Ave., 92123, pg. 1022 **PV**
Sprint's Local Telecommunication Division, 2650 Camino De La Reina, 92108, pg. 1500 **PB**
Standard Pacific of San Diego, 7290 Clairmont Mesa Bvld., 92111, pg. 1503 **PB**
Sterling Electronics, 9340 Hazard Way, Ste. 3A, 92123, pg. 1051 **PB**
Sundstrand Power Systems, P.O. Box 85757, 4400 Ruffin, 92123 **PB**
SYSTECH COMPUTER CORPORATION, 11021 Via Frontera, 92127, pg. 1061 **PV**
TMP Worldwide/Recruitment Division, 9645 Granite Ridge Dr., Ste. 330, 92123-2659, pg. 1065 **PV**
Tanabe Group Service U.S.A., Inc., 7930 Convoy Ct., 92111, pg. 1354 **IT**
Tanabe Research Laboratories U.S.A., Inc., 4540 Towne Centre Ct., 92121, pg. 1354 **IT**
Tanabe Research Laboratories U.S.A., Inc., pg. 1354 **IT**
Tanabe Seiyaku Co., Ltd.-International Information Division, 4540 Towne Centre Ct., 92121, pg. 1354 **IT**
Tanabe U.S.A., Inc.-San Diego Office, 7930 Convoy Ct., 92111, pg. 1354 **IT**
Teal Electronics, 10305 Sorrento Valley Rd., 92121, pg. 1419 **PB**
Teledyne Ryan Aeronautical, 2701 Harbor Dr., 92101-1085, pg. 43 **PB**
Test & Space Systems Division, P.O. Box 509009, 92150-9009, pg. 1627 **PB**
Thermolase, 10455 Pacific Ctr. Ct., 92121-4339, pg. 1595 **PB**
ThermoTrex, 10455 Pacific Center Ct., 92121-4339, pg. 1595 **PB**
Thomson Software Products, 10251 Vista Sorrento Pkwy., #300, 92121-2706, pg. 1384 **IT**
THE TITAN CORPORATION, 3033 Science Park Rd., 92121-1199, pg. 1618 **PB**
Titan Information Systems, 3033 Science Park Rd., 92121, pg. 1618 **PB**

Titan Linkabit, 3033 Science Park Rd., 92121, pg. 1618 **PB**
Titan Research & Technology, 3033 Science Park Rd., 92121, pg. 1618 **PB**
Titan Systems, Inc., 3033 Science Park Rd., 92121, pg. 1618 **PB**
TOLLYCRAFT YACHT CORPORATION, 17 Horton Plaza, Ste. 251, 92101, pg. 1620 **PB**
Toppan West, Inc., 7770 Miramar Road, 92126, pg. 1399 **IT**
Town & Country Hotel, 500 Hotel Circle, 92186, pg. 96 **PV**
Tracor Information Systems Company, P.O. Box 509009, 92150-9009, pg. 1627 **PB**
TrizecHahn Centers Inc., 4350 La Jolla Village Dr., Ste. 400, 92122-1233, pg. 1425 **PB**
Union Bank of California, 1201 Fifth Ave., 92101, pg. 157 **IT**
Union Bank of California, 530 B St., Ste. 303, 92101, pg. 157 **IT**
Unisys Semiconductor, 10850 Via. Frontera, 92127-1705, pg. 1671 **PB**
Unitog Rental Facility, 675 32nd St., 92102, pg. 1693 **PB**
University Mechanical & Engineering Contractors, Inc., 4464 Alvarado Canyon Rd., 92120, pg. 572 **PB**
Valor Electronics, Inc., 9715 Business Park Ave., 92131-1642, pg. 768 **PB**
Verbatim Tape Corporation, 10170 Sorrento Valley Rd., 92121, pg. 872 **IT**
Vernitron Controls Div., 1601 Precision Park Ln., 92173, pg. 158 **PB**
Vision Cable Ties Co., 9220 Activity Rd., 92126, pg. 124 **PB**
WD-40 COMPANY, 1061 Cudahy Pl., 92110-3929, pg. 1726 **PB**
Washington Inventory Service, 9265 Sky Park Ctr., Ste. 100, 92193-9080, pg. 846 **PB**
Watkins Contracting, Inc., 8690 Aero Dr., Ste. M327, 92123, pg. 1384 **PB**
Wavetek Corp., P.O. Box 85265, 9045 Balboa Ave., 92123, pg. 1155 **PV**
WAVETEK CORPORATION, 11995 El Camino Real, Ste. 301, 92130, pg. 1154 **PV**
Wavetek Export Corp., 11995 El Camino Real, 92123, pg. 1155 **PV**
Western American Manufacturing, Inc., 9255 Custom House Plaza Dr., Suites I&J, 92173, pg. 1749 **PV**
Western American Manufacturing, Inc., 9255 Customhouse Plaza, Dr. Ste. I & J, 92173, pg. 1749 **PV**
Western International Media Corporation, 550 West C St., Ste. 1400, 92101, pg. 1167 **PV**
Weststar Engineering Inc., 2001 Kettner Blvd., Ste. B, 92101, pg. 65 **PB**
Willis Corroon Administrative Services Corporation, 438 Camino Del Rio S., Ste. B223, 92108, pg. 1504 **IT**
Willis Corroon Corp. of San Diego, 1615 Murray Canyon Rd., Ste. 800, 92108-4322, pg. 1507 **IT**
THE WOODFIN SUITE HOTELS, 9255 Town Center Dr., Ste. 900, 92121, pg. 1187 **PV**
Woodward-Clyde, Sunroad Plaza 3, Ste. 1000, 1615 Murray Canyon Rd., 92108, pg. 1657 **PV**
Wyle Electronics-San Diego, 9525 Chesapeake Dr., 92123, pg. 1458 **IT**
ZOOLOGICAL SOCIETY OF SAN DIEGO, 2920 Zoo Dr., 92103, pg. 1207 **PV**

San Dimas

Bindley Western, Southern California Division, 542 Covina Blvd., 91773, pg. 229 **PB**
Louis Vuitton US Manufacturing Inc., 321 Covina Blvd., 91773, pg. 781 **IT**
SOUTHERN CALIFORNIA WATER COMPANY, 630 E. Foothill Blvd., 91773, pg. 1489 **PB**
Wenco Inc., 433 W. Allen Ave. Ste. 113, 91773-4705, pg. 1754 **PB**

San Fernando

Avica Inc., 1175 Aviation Pl., 91340, pg. 853 **IT**
BERNARDS BROTHERS, INC., 610 Ilex St., 91340, pg. 136 **PV**
Mason Electric Co., 605 Eighth St., 91340, pg. 594 **PV**
Nature Made Nutritional Products Inc., 15451 San Fernando Mission Blvd., 91345, pg. 860 **PV**
OH BOY CORPORATION, 1516 First St., 91340, pg. 812 **PV**
Paramount Citrus Association, P.O. Box 8599, 91346, pg. 941 **PV**
PRECISION DYNAMICS CORPORATION, 13880 Del Sur St., 91340-3490, pg. 879 **PB**
Precision Dynamics International Inc., 13880 Del Sur St., 91340-3490, pg. 879 **PV**
SAMCO Scientific, Inc., 1050 Arroyo, 91340, pg. 448 **PB**

San Francisco

ABI Management, Inc., 160 Spear St., Ste. 1540, 94105, pg. 74 **PV**
ABM INDUSTRIES, 50 Fremont St., Ste. 2600, 94105, pg. 2 **PB**
ABN AMRO Bank, N.V. (San Francisco), 555 California St., Ste. 2750, 94104-1603, pg. 10 **IT**
ANA Hotel, 50 Third St., 94103, pg. 57 **IT**
Adapt Electronic Publishing, 150 Spear St., Ste. 1125, 94105, pg. 191 **PV**
Air Fresh Trucking, 2351 Powell St., 94133, pg. 1180 **PV**
AIRLEASE LTD., 555 California St., 4th Fl., 94104, pg. 33 **PB**
Airlease Management Services, Inc., P.O. Box 193985, 733 Front St., 94119, pg. 33 **PB**

AIRTOUCH COMMUNICATIONS, INC., One California St., 94111, pg. 34 **PB**
Alexander & Alexander Inc., 333 Bush St., Ste. 600, 94104, pg. 117 **PB**
Allied Security Inc., 50 First Street Bldg., Ste. 511, 94105, pg. 40 **PV**
Allright San Francisco Parking, Inc., 655 Fourth St., 94107, pg. 43 **PV**
American Bank Note Company, 55 New Montgomery St., Ste. 206, 94105, pg. 68 **PB**
American Bldg. Maintenance Co., 510 Howard, 94105, pg. 2 **PB**
American Commercial Security & Investigative Services, 50 Fremont St., Ste. 2600, 94105, pg. 2 **PB**
American Industrial Partners, One Maritime Plaza, 94111, pg. 56 **PV**
American Shared-CuraCare, Four Embarcadero Ctr. #3620, 94111, pg. 91 **PB**
AMERICAN SHARED HOSPITAL SERVICES, Four Embarcadero Ctr., Ste. 3620, 94111, pg. 91 **PB**
American Shared Radiosurgery Services, Four Embarcadero Ctr. #3620, 94111, pg. 91 **PB**
AMERICAN SIGHTSEEING INTERNATIONAL, 490 Post St., Ste. 1701A, 94102-2703, pg. 61 **PV**
Analysts International, Western Region, 44 Montgomery St., Ste. 2365, 94104-4710, pg. 110 **PB**
Arkansas & Memphis Railway Bridge and Terminal Co., Southern Pacific Bldg., One Market Plaza, 94105, pg. 1568 **PB**
Asahi Bank San Francisco Representative Office, 345 California St., Ste. 2550, 94104, pg. 82 **IT**
BA Agency, Inc., 433 California St., Ste.502, 94104, pg. 180 **PB**
BA ATM, Inc., P.O. Box 37000, 94137, pg. 181 **PB**
BA Cheque Corp., One Powell St., 94102, pg. 180 **PB**
BA Insurance Company, Inc., 433 California St.,Ste.502, 94104, pg. 180 **PB**
BA Leasing & Capital Corporation, P.O. Box 37000, 94137, pg. 181 **PB**
BA Mortgage & International Realty Corp., 500 Washington St.,4th Fl., 94111, pg. 180 **PB**
BA Ventures, Inc., 555 California St., 94104, pg. 180 **PB**
BEI TECHNOLOGIES, INC., One Post St., Ste. 2500, 94104, pg. 160 **PB**
BHP Copper, 550 California St., 94104, pg. 227 **IT**
The BHP Copper Group, 550 California St., 94104, pg. 224 **IT**
BHP World Minerals, 550 California St., 94104, pg. 224 **IT**
BRE PROPERTIES, INC., One Montgomery St., Ste. 2500, 94104, pg. 163 **PB**
Babcock & Brown, Inc., Two Harrison St., 6th Fl., 94105, pg. 956 **IT**
Banana Republic, Two Harrison St., 94105, pg. 702 **PV**
Bancroft-Whitney Co., 3250 Van Ness Ave., 94109, pg. 1602 **PB**
Bank Hapoalim (San Francisco), 250 Montgomery St., Ste. 700, 94104, pg. 149 **IT**
Bank of America California, 555 California St., 94137, pg. 180 **PB**
Bank of America NT&SA, 55 California St., 94137, pg. 180 **PB**
The Bank of Nova Scotia, 580 California St., Ste. 2100, 94104, pg. 156 **IT**
Bank of San Francisco, 550 Montgomery St., 94111, pg. 1430 **PB**
Bank of San Francisco Securities Brokerage, 550 Montgomery St., 94111, pg. 1430 **PB**
The Bank of Tokyo-Mitsubishi, Ltd. (San Francisco Branch), 350 California St., 94104, pg. 157 **IT**
BankAmerica, Four Embarcadero Ctr., Ste. 1200, 94111, pg. 181 **PB**
BankAmerica Capital Corp., 555 California St., 94104, pg. 181 **PB**
BankAmerica Capital Investments, Inc., 555 California St., 94104, pg. 181 **PB**
BANKAMERICA CORPORATION, One S. Vanness Ave., 94103, pg. 179 **PB**
BankAmerica Realty Services, Inc., 555 California St., 94104, pg. 181 **PB**
Banque Paribas-San Francisco, 101 California St. - Suite 3150, 94111, pg. 319 **IT**
Baring Asset Management Inc., 353 Sacramento St., Ste. 618, 94111, pg. 647 **IT**
Bear, Stearns & Co. Inc., San Francisco, Citicorp Ctr., One Sansome St., 94104, pg. 198 **PB**
Bechtel Civil, Inc., 50 Beale St., 94105, pg. 128 **PV**
Bechtel Enterprises, Inc., 50 Beale St., 94105-1895, pg. 128 **PV**
Bechtel Financing Services, Inc., 50 Beale St., 94105, pg. 128 **PV**
BECHTEL GROUP, INC., 50 Beale St., 94105, pg. 128 **PV**
Bechtel Mining & Metals, 50 Beale St., 94105, pg. 128 **PV**
Bechtel National, Inc., 50 Beale St., 94105, pg. 128 **PV**
Bendix Environmental Research, 1390 Market St. Bldg. 418, 94102-5406, pg. 51 **PV**
Berry, Hartell, Evers & Osborne, Inc., 580 California St., Ste. 1900, 94104, pg. 1196 **PV**
BLUE SHIELD OF CALIFORNIA, 50 Beal St., 94105, pg. 153 **PV**
Burns Philp Company of San Francisco, 750 Bryant St., 94107, pg. 236 **IT**
Burns, Philp Inc., 222 Sutter St., 94120, pg. 236 **IT**
Business Journal Publications, Inc., 275 Battery, Ste. 940, 94107, pg. 19 **PV**
BYER CALIFORNIA, 66 Potrero Ave., 94103, pg. 191 **PV**
CF2GS, 222 Sutter St., Ste. 500, 94108, pg. 194 **PV**
CKS Partners/San Francisco, 345 Spear St., Ste. 500, 94105, pg. 195 **PV**
CSE INSURANCE GROUP, 989 Market St., 94120, pg. 197 **PV**

PB - *U.S. Public Companies Volume*
PV - *U.S. Private Companies Volume*
IT - *International Public & Private Companies Volume*

Geographic Index-U.S.

1147

California Closet Company, Inc., 1700 Montgomery St., 94111, pg. 1770 — PB
California Federal Bank, 135 Main St., 94105-1817, pg. 690 — PV
CALIFORNIA FRESH APRICOT COUNCIL, 847 Sansome St., Ste. 200, 94111, pg. 200 — PV
California Physicians Insurance Corp., 50 Beal St., 94105, pg. 153 — PV
Canadian Imperial Bank of Commerce (California), 580 California St., Ste. 1500, 94104, pg. 257 — IT
Carat ICG (San Francisco), 201 Filbert St., Ste. 201, 94133, pg. 208 — PV
Cariplo (Los Angeles), 44 Montgomery St., 94104, pg. 275 — IT
THE CARPENTER GROUP, 222 Napolean St., 94124, pg. 215 — PV
Carpenter Rigging, 222 Napolean St., 94124, pg. 215 — PV
CATELLUS DEVELOPMENT CORPORATION, 201 Mission St., 94105, pg. 314 — PB
Central California Traction Co., One Market Plaza, 94105, pg. 1668 — PB
Chase & Sanborn Coffee, Inc., 345 Spear St., 94105, pg. 917 — IT
The Chase Manhattan Trust Co. of California, N.A., One Embarcadero Ctr., 94111, pg. 338 — PB
CHEMOIL, Four Embarcadero Ctr., Ste. 1800, 94111, pg. 233 — PV
Chevron Capital U.S.A. Inc., 225 Bush St., 94104, pg. 348 — PB
CHEVRON CORPORATION, 575 Market St., 94105-2856, pg. 347 — PB
Chevron Land & Development Company, 575 Market St., 94104, pg. 348 — PB
Chevron Oil Finance Company, 225 Bush St., 94104, pg. 348 — PB
Chevron Shipping Co., 555 Market St., 94105, pg. 348 — PB
Chevron Stations, Inc., 225 Bush St., 94104, pg. 348 — PB
Chevron U.S.A. Inc., 575 Market St., 94105, pg. 348 — PB
Chevron USA Products Co., P.O. Box 740339, 575 Market St., 94105, pg. 348 — PB
China Airlines Ltd., 391 Sutter St. 2nd Floor, 94108, pg. 285 — IT
Cho Hung Bank - San Francisco, Ste. 1502, 601 California St., 94108, pg. 287 — IT
CHRONICLE PUBLISHING CO. INC., 901 Mission St., 94103, pg. 239 — PV
Circle Freight International (U.S.A.), 260 Townsend St., 94107, pg. 370 — PB
Circle International, 260 Townsend St., 94107-1719, pg. 371 — PB
Circle International, 260 Townsend St., 94107, pg. 372 — PB
CIRCLE INTERNATIONAL GROUP, INC., 260 Townsend St., 94107, pg. 370 — PB
CITRON HALIGMAN BEDECARRE, 1160 Battery St., 94111, pg. 241 — PV
Civil Service Employees Insurance Co., 989 Market St., 94103, pg. 197 — PV
Clearwater Commodity Corp., One Maritime Plaza, 94111, pg. 1318 — PB
Club Med Boutique, 222 Sutter St., 94108, pg. 298 — IT
Cohn & Wells, 909 Montgomery St., Ste. 300, 94133, pg. 601 — IT
Corporate National Accounts Pacific Southwest, 201 Spear St., 6th Fl., 94105, pg. 1024 — PB
CORPORATE TRAVEL SERVICES, 550 California St., 3rd Fl., 94104, pg. 276 — PV
Corrugated Packaging, 249 E. Grand Ave., P.O. Box 2407, 94080, pg. 736 — PB
Credit Agricole (CNCA) San Francisco, 101 California St., 94111, pg. 341 — IT
Creditanstaldt-Bankverein, San Francisco Representative Office, Four Embarcadero Center, Ste. 1630, 94111, pg. 347 — IT
DMR Group, Inc., 50 Fremont St., Ste. 1410, 94105, pg. 528 — PV
Dai-Ichi Kangyo Bank, Ltd.-San Francisco, 101 California Street, Suite 4000, 94111, pg. 359 — IT
Dallas Terminal Railway and Union Depot Co., One Market Plaza, Southern Pacific Bldg., 94105, pg. 1668 — PB
DARTFORD PARTNERSHIP, 456 Montgomery St., Ste. 20200, 94104, pg. 312 — PV
David Corporation, 180 Howard St., 6th Fl., 94105, pg. 872 — PV
DEL MONTE FOODS, One Market Plaza, 94105, pg. 321 — PV
DeLeuw, Cather & Company, 120 Howard St., Ste. 850, 94105, pg. 841 — PV
Dockers Brand, 1155 Battery St., 94111, pg. 663 — PV
EQE INTERNATIONAL, 44 Montgomery St., Ste. 3200, 94104, pg. 354 — PV
Easterday Janitorial Supply Co., 355 7th St., 94103, pg. 2 — PB
Edelman Worldwide, Inc., 350 California St., Ste. 1600, 94104, pg. 362 — PV
Enso International, Inc., 2550 Leavenworth St., Ste. 2, 94133, pg. 457 — IT
Epsilon/West, 601 Montgomery, Ste. 725, 94111, pg. 74 — PB
Esprit Accessories, 900 Minnesota St., 94107, pg. 383 — PV
ESPRIT DE CORP., 900 Minnesota St., 94107, pg. 383 — PV
Esprit Department, 900 Minnesota St., 94107, pg. 383 — PV
Esprit Kids, 900 Minnesota St., 94107, pg. 383 — PV
Esprit Sport, 900 Minnesota St., 94107, pg. 383 — PV
EvansGroup, 160 Pacific Ave., Ste. 200, 94111, pg. 385 — PV
FCB HealthCare, Headquarters: One Lombard St., Ste. 300, 94111, pg. 1641 — PB
THE FAIRMONT HOTELS, 950 Mason St., 94108, pg. 391 — PV

Financial Security Assurance Inc., Steuart Tower, One Market, 94105, pg. 623 — PB
FINNAIR, 291 Geary St., 94102, pg. 486 — IT
First Trust of California, National Association, 101 California St., Ste. 1150, 94111, pg. 1681 — IT
Fleischmann's Yeast Consumer Products Div., 222 Sutter St., 94108, pg. 237 — IT
Four Seasons Clift Hotel, Geary at Taylor, 94102, pg. 502 — IT
Frankel & Company, 731 Sansome St., 5th Fl., 94111, pg. 424 — PV
Frankfurt Balkind Partners, 369 Pine St., 94104, pg. 424 — PV
THE FREMONT GROUP, 50 Fremont St., Ste. 3600, 94105-2271, pg. 427 — PV
FRITZ COMPANIES, INC., 706 Mission St., 94103, pg. 683 — PB
FRITZI OF CALIFORNIA MANUFACTURING CORP., 199 First St., 94105, pg. 429 — PV
Fuji Bank International, Inc., International Bldg., 601 California St., 94108, pg. 519 — IT
Fuji Bank, San Francisco, Intl. Bldg., Ste. 500, 601 California St., 94108, pg. 520 — IT
GATX Capital Corporation, Four Embarcadero Ctr., Ste. 2200, 94111, pg. 690 — PB
GATX Financial Services, Four Embarcadero Center, Ste. 2200, 94111, pg. 690 — PB
GK Financing, LLC, Four Embarcadero Ctr. #3620, 94111, pg. 91 — PB
G.T. Global, Inc., 50 California St., 27th fl., 94111, pg. 809 — IT
THE GAP, INC., One Harrison St., 94105, pg. 702 — PB
General Electric Capital Aviation Services, 201 Mission St., 27th Fl., 94105, pg. 712 — PV
General Employment Enterprises, Inc., 455 Market St., Ste. 1170, 94105, pg. 714 — PV
Global Special Risks Insurance Services California, 44 Montgomery St., Ste. 3880, 94104, pg. 1503 — IT
GOLDBERG MOSER O'NEILL, 77 Maiden Ln., 94108, pg. 459 — PV
Goldman, Sachs & Co., 555 California St., 45th Fl., 94104, pg. 462 — PV
Golin/Harris Technologies, 101 Howard St., 2nd Fl., 94105-1616, pg. 1227 — PV
Goodby, Silverstein & Partners, 720 California St., 94108, pg. 1224 — PV
Gump's, 135 Post St., 94108, pg. 782 — PB
Gump's By Mail, Inc., 135 Post St., 94108, pg. 782 — PB
HS RESOURCES, One Maritime Plaza, 15th Fl., 94111, pg. 772 — PB
HAMBRECHT & QUIST LLC., One Bush St., 94104, pg. 778 — PB
Hampel/Stefanides, 111 Maiden Ln., Ste. 301, 94108, pg. 498 — PV
HarperCollins San Francisco, 1160 Battery St., 94111, pg. 927 — IT
HEALD COLLEGES, 1453 Mission St., 4th Fl., 94103, pg. 514 — PV
Hewlett-Packard Company, 50 Fremont St., Ste. 200, 94105, pg. 838 — PB
Highway One Communications, Integrated Marketing Services, 601 California St., 94108, pg. 303 — PV
Hillhaven-Lawton Convalescent Hospital, P.O. Box 22249, 94122, pg. 1713 — PV
HOFFMAN/LEWIS, 1725 Montgomery St., 94111, pg. 552 — PV
Hold Everything, Inc., 100 N. Point St., 94133, pg. 1770 — PB
HOMESTAKE MINING COMPANY, 650 California St., 94108-2788, pg. 832 — PB
Hotel Nikko San Francisco, 275 O' Farrel St., 94102, pg. 700 — IT
Huntington Beach Co., 225 Bush St., 94104, pg. 348 — PB
IHI Inc., 50 Fremont St., Sge. 3200, 94105, pg. 689 — PV
ING Baring (U.S.) Securities:, 456 Montgomery St., Ste. 2250, 94104, pg. 647 — IT
Iberia Air Lines of Spain, 360 Post St. Ste. 505, 94108, pg. 575 — IT
The Industrial Bank of Japan, Limited (San Francisco), 555 California St., Ste. 3110, 94104, pg. 674 — IT
Industrial Indemnity Company, 255 California St., 94111, pg. 681 — PB
Industrial Indemnity Financial Corporation, 255 California St., 94111, pg. 681 — PB
Industrial Indemnity Insurance Services, Inc., 255 California St., 94111, pg. 681 — PB
Ingalls Moranville Advertising, 530 Bush St., 94108, pg. 316 — PV
InPower Inc., 525 Market Street, 11th. Floor, 94105, pg. 242 — IT
Inso Corporation, 601 Van Ness Ave., #E3819, 94102, pg. 882 — PB
Interbrand Schechter, 170 Maiden Ln., 94108, pg. 1224 — PV
Intergraph Corporation, 100 Spear St., Ste. 1525, 94105, pg. 891 — PV
Intermedia Capital Partners IV, L.P., 235 Montgomery St., 94104, pg. 222 — PV
Ishihara Corporation (U.S.A.), Transamerica Pyramid, 38th Fl., 600 Montgomery St., 94111, pg. 934 — IT
JCB International Credit Card Co., Ltd.-USA, 240 Stockton St., 10th Fl., 94108, pg. 696 — IT
JMD Development Corporation, 388 Market St., Ste. 1450, 94111, pg. 976 — PV
JWG Associates, Inc., 655 Montgomery St., Ste. 1010, 94110, pg. 579 — PV
JARAN INC., 275 Brannan St., 94107, pg. 582 — PV
Jefferies & Company, Inc., 580 California St., Ste. 2085, pg. 925 — PB
John Hancock Capital Growth Management, Inc., 1140 Taylor St., 94108, pg. 590 — PV

Jossey-Bass, Inc., 350 Sansome Street, 5th Fl., 94104-1342, pg. 778 — PV
KBHK Television, Inc., 650 California St., 94108, pg. 352 — PB
KGO-AM Radio, Inc., 900 Front St., 94111, pg. 512 — PB
KGO Television, Inc., 900 Front St., 94111, pg. 512 — PB
KPIX-TV, 855 Battery St., 94111, pg. 275 — PB
Kabuto International Phoenix Inc., One Daniel Burnham Court, Ste. 205C, 94109, pg. 721 — IT
Kaiser Electronics, 2710 Orchard Pkwy., 94134, pg. 605 — PV
Keller & Gannon, 1453 Mission St., 94103, pg. 626 — PV
KENETECH CORP., 500 Sansome St., 94111, pg. 950 — PB
Ketchum Advertising/San Francisco, 55 Union St., 94107, pg. 624 — PV
Kirshenbaum Bond & Partners/West, 300 Bramman St., pg. 683 — PV
KORET OF CALIFORNIA, INC., 611 Mission St., 94105, pg. 632 — PV
Korn/Ferry International, The Transamerica Pyramid, 600 Montgomery St., 31st Fl., 94111, pg. 633 — PV
Kvaerner Hydro Power, Inc.-West Coast Sales Division, 49 Stevenson St., Ste. 1075, 94120, pg. 770 — IT
LGT Asset Management, Inc., 50 California St., 27th fl., 94111, pg. 809 — IT
LANZ, INC., 525 Brannan St., Ste. 300, 94107, pg. 650 — PV
LEVI STRAUSS & CO., 1155 Battery St., 94111, pg. 662 — PV
Levi's Brand, 1155 Battery St., 94111, pg. 663 — PV
Lilli Ann Corporation, 275 Brannan St., 94107, pg. 582 — PV
Arthur D. Little, Inc., Ste. 600, Four Embarcadero Center, 6th Floor, 94111-4173, pg. 670 — PV
Logica Inc., 353 Sacramento St. Ste. 2300, 94111-3650, pg. 814 — IT
MBT ARCHITECTURE, 185 Berry St., Ste. 5700, 94107, pg. 686 — PV
MMRI Inc., Four Embarcadero Ctr. #3620, 94111, pg. 91 — PB
Macworld, 501 2nd St., 94107, pg. 569 — PB
Macy's West, 50 O'Farrel St., 94102, pg. 618 — PB
Mandarin Oriental, San Francisco, 222 Sansome St., 94104-2792, pg. 704 — IT
Manulife Financial - San Francisco, 101 California St., Ste. 2850, 94111-5840, pg. 841 — IT
Market Facts, Inc., Two Embarcadero Ctr., Ste. 200, 94111, pg. 1047 — PV
Matson Intermodal System, Inc., 333 Market St., 94105, pg. 40 — PB
Matson Navigation Company, Inc., 333 Market St., 94105, pg. 39 — PB
Matson Terminals, Inc., 333 Market St., 94105, pg. 40 — PB
JESSICA McCLINTOCK INC., 1400 16th St., 94103-5110, pg. 719 — PV
The McGuire Furniture Company, 1201 Bryant St., 94103, pg. 630 — PV
MCKESSON CORPORATION, One Post St., 94104, pg. 1072 — PB
McKesson Health Systems, One Post St., pg. 1073 — PB
McKesson Home Health Care Division, One Post St., 94104, pg. 1073 — PB
McKesson Medical Supply, One Post St., 94104, pg. 1073 — PB
McKesson U.S. Health Care, One Post St., 94104, pg. 1073 — PB
The Meijiseimei Insurance Services of California, Inc., 235 Montgomery St., Ste. 850, 94104, pg. 854 — IT
Mellon Capital Management Corporation (MFSC #6), 595 Market St., 94105, pg. 1085 — PV
Merrill Corporation, 345 California St., Ste. 1600, 94104, pg. 1097 — PB
Miller Freeman Inc., Corporate Headquarters, 600 Harrison St., 94107, pg. 1443 — IT
MILLER/KADANOFF/HUBER DIRECT & INTERACTIVE, 470 Carolina St., 94107, pg. 747 — PV
Mitsui & Co. (U.S.A.), Inc., One California St., Ste. 3000, 94111, pg. 879 — IT
Modem media San Francisco, 15 Lombard St., 94111, pg. 1641 — PB
MONTGOMERY ST. INCOME SECURITIES, INC., 101 California St., Ste. 4100, 94111, pg. 1127 — PB
Morgan Guaranty Trust Company, 101 California St., 94111, pg. 1129 — PB
J.P. Morgan & Co. Incorporated, 101 California St., 94111, pg. 1129 — PB
J.P. Morgan California, 101 California St., 94111, pg. 1129 — PB
J.P. Morgan Capital Corporation, 101 California St., 94111, pg. 1129 — PB
J.P. Morgan Futures Inc., 101 California St., 94111, pg. 1129 — PB
J.P. Morgan Securities Inc., 101 California St., 94111, pg. 1129 — PB
Morgan Stanley San Francisco, 555 California St., Ste. 2200, 94104, pg. 1132 — PB
NAC Reinsurance Corporation-San Francisco, One Embarcadero Ctr., Ste. 3810, 94111-3607, pg. 1144 — PB
National Yellow Pages Monitor (NYPM), 44 Montgomery St., 94104, pg. 1146 — PB
NationsBank Montgomery Securities LLC, 600 Montgomery St., 94111, pg. 1162 — PB
New Business Development, 550 California St., 94104, pg. 224 — IT
Nichimen America, Inc., San Francisco Branch, 235 Montgomery St., 94104, pg. 928 — IT
Nippon Express Travel U.S.A. Inc., 720 Market St., 94102, pg. 934 — IT
Nippon Oil (U.S.A.) Limited - San Francisco Office, 555 Market St., Rm. 1200, 94105, pg. 937 — IT
NORCAL WASTE SYSTEMS, Five Thomas Mellon Cir., Ste. 304, 94134, pg. 1188 — PB

PB - *U.S. Public Companies Volume*
PV - *U.S. Private Companies Volume*
IT - *International Public & Private Companies Volume*

Geographic Index-U.S.

Northern Trust Bank of California, N.A., 580 California St., Ste. 1800, 94104, pg. 1196 **PB**
Northwestern Pacific Railroad Co., One Market Plaza, Southern Pacific Bldg., 94105, pg. 1668 **PB**
O'KEEFFE'S, INC., 75 Williams Ave., 94124, pg. 813 **PV**
Old Navy Stores, Two Harrison St., 94105, pg. 703 **PB**
Olicom Americas - West, 1072 Folsom St., Ste. 247, 94103, pg. 1001 **IT**
Omega Performance Group, 50 Freemont St., Ste. 1800, 94105, pg. 816 **PV**
Organic Online, 510 3rd St., Ste. 540, 94107, pg. 1224 **PV**
ORIX USA Corporation-San Francisco, One Bush St., Ste. 250, 94104, pg. 1009 **IT**
Bob Ostrow Co., 437 Kaufmann Ct., 94080, pg. 75 **PV**
Otsuka America, Inc., One Embarcadero Center, Ste. 2020, 94111, pg. 1013 **IT**
Outdoor Services, 410 Pacific Ave., 94133, pg. 1166 **PV**
Overseas Assets Holdings Inc., c/o WBG Financial #5025, 555 California St., 3rd Fl., 94104, pg. 181 **IT**
PC World, 501 2nd St., 94107, pg. 569 **PV**
PG&E CORPORATION, One Market, Spear Tower, Ste. 2400, 94105, pg. 1240 **PB**
PG&E Energy Services, 345 California St., Ste. 3200, 94104, pg. 1241 **PB**
PG&E Gas Transmission, One Market, Spear Tower, Ste. 2400, 94105, pg. 1241 **PB**
PLM Financial Services, Inc., One Market, Steuart St. Tower, Ste. 800, 94105, pg. 1241 **PB**
PLM INTERNATIONAL, INC., One Market, Steuart St. Tower, Ste. 800, 94105-1301, pg. 1241 **PB**
PLM Trailer Leasing, One Market, Steuart Tower, Ste. 800, 94105-1301, pg. 1241 **PB**
Pacific Bell, 140 New Montgomery St., 94105, pg. 1416 **PB**
Pacific Gas & Electric Company, 77 Beale St., 94177, pg. 1241 **PB**
PACIFIC GATEWAY PROPERTIES, One Rincon Ctr., 101 Spear St., Ste. 215, 94105, pg. 1250 **PB**
Pacific International Brokers, Ltd., 50 California St., 94111, pg. 1504 **IT**
Pacific Telesis Foundation, 130 Kearny St., 94108, pg. 1416 **PB**
Pacific Telesis Group, 130 Kearny St., 94105, pg. 1415 **PB**
Parisian Bakeries, 1995 Evans Ave., 94124, pg. 909 **PV**
Perstorp Xytec, Inc., Ste. 490, 50 Francisco St., 94133, pg. 1037 **IT**
Philippine Airlines, Inc., 447 Sutter St., 94108, pg. 1051 **IT**
Pine Towers Convalescent Hospital, 2707 Pine St., 94115, pg. 1714 **PV**
Piper Jaffray Inc., 345 California St., Ste. 2200, 94104-2606, pg. 1301 **PB**
Pitney Bowes Management Services, 660 Fourth St., 94107-1618, pg. 1304 **PB**
Placer Dome U.S. Inc., One California St., Ste. 2500, 94111-5472, pg. 1060 **IT**
Poe & Brown of California, 101 California St. 27th Fl., 94111-5830, pg. 1312 **PB**
Promotion House, 500 Sansome, Ste. 100, 94111, pg. 1166 **PV**
PROVIDIAN FINANCIAL CORPORATION, 201 Missouri St., 94105, pg. 1338 **PB**
RCM Capital Management, Four Embarcadero Ctr., Ste. 2800, 94111, pg. 418 **IT**
RLI Northern California Regional Office, 425 California St., Ste. 2101, 94104, pg. 1356 **PB**
Rainoldi, Kerzner & Radcliffe, 343 Sansome St., 94104, pg. 1224 **PB**
Rathbone, King & Seeley Insurance Services, Inc., 350 California St., Ste. 1950, 94104, pg. 610 **PV**
Red Sky Interactive, 921 Front St., 94111, pg. 1224 **PB**
Redgate Communications Corp., 221 Main St., Ste. 480, 94105, pg. 66 **PB**
Reed Travel Publishing-San Francisco, 49 Stevenson #460, 94015-2909, pg. 1097 **IT**
Resource Marketing, Inc., 100 Bush St., Ste. 2200, 94104, pg. 924 **PV**
HAL RINEY & PARTNERS, INC., 735 Battery St., 94111, pg. 931 **PV**
The Royal Bank of Scotland plc, The Pyramid, 600 Montgomery St., 94111, pg. 1133 **IT**
SBG Enterprise, 1725 Montgomery St., 94111, pg. 1483 **IT**
SEI Corporation, 444 Market St., Ste. 1250, 94111, pg. 1417 **PB**
SEMIA, Inc., One California St., Ste. 3000, 94111, pg. 1313 **IT**
SFM/San Francisco, 1 Sansome St., Ste. 2000, 94104, pg. 957 **PV**
SQL Software Development Laboratory, 100 Spear St., Ste. 680, 94105, pg. 1309 **IT**
Safety And Fire Technology, Inc., 75 Williams Ave, 94124, pg. 813 **PV**
St. Louis Southwestern Railway Co., One Market Plaza, Southern Pacific Bldg., 94105, pg. 1668 **PB**
Sakura Bank - San Francisco Agency, 345 California St., Ste. 1100, 94104, pg. 518 **IT**
THE SAN FRANCISCO CO., 550 Montgomery St., 94111, pg. 1430 **PV**
San Francisco Convalescent Center, 1359 Pine St., 94109, pg. 1714 **PV**
San Francisco Examiner, 110 Fifth St., 94103, pg. 518 **PV**
SAN FRANCISCO GIANTS BASEBALL CLUB, 3-COM Park, Candlestick Point, 94124, pg. 964 **PV**
San Francisco Knitworks, 345 Alabama St., 94110, pg. 779 **PV**
San Francisco Newspaper Agency, 925 Mission St., 94103, pg. 239 **PV**
San Francisco Realties, 200 Hearst Building, Five Third St., 94103, pg. 518 **PV**
San Ramon Partners, 55 Green St., pg. 362 **PB**

Sanwa Bank California, 444 Market St., 94111, pg. 1189 **IT**
Charles Schwab & Co. Inc., 101 Montgomery St., 94104, pg. 1443 **PB**
THE CHARLES SCHWAB CORPORATION, 101 Montgomery St., 94104, pg. 1442 **PB**
The Charles Schwab Trust Company, One Montgomery St., 7th Fl., 94104, pg. 1443 **PB**
Schwab Holdings, Inc., 101 Montgomery St., 94104, pg. 1443 **PB**
Scottish & Newcastle Importers Co., 444 De Haro, Ste. 209, 94107-2347, pg. 1212 **IT**
Sea Containers West Inc., 88 Kearny St., #1800, 94108, pg. 1214 **IT**
Sequent Computer Systems, Inc., One Market, Spear Tower, Ste. 700, 94105, pg. 1459 **PB**
Settsu USA, 360 Post Street, Ste. 406, 94108, pg. 1225 **IT**
Shafer, 170 Maiden Ln., 5th Fl., 94108, pg. 988 **PV**
Shaklee Corporation, 444 Market St., 94111, pg. 1518 **IT**
Shaklee U.S., Shaklee Terraces, 444 Market St., 94111, pg. 1518 **IT**
THE SHARPER IMAGE, 650 Davis St., 94111, pg. 1464 **PB**
Sherwood Insurance Services, Inc., 201 California St., 10th Fl., 94111, pg. 118 **PB**
SHORENSTEIN COMPANY, 555 California St., Ste. 4900, 94104, pg. 996 **PV**
THE SIERRA CAPITAL COMPANIES, 50 California St., Ste. 2020, 94111, pg. 998 **PV**
Singapore Airlines Ltd., 333 Bush St., Ste. 1500, 94104, pg. 1374 **IT**
Skadden, Arps, Slate, Meagher & Flom LLP, Four Embarcadero Ctr., 94111, pg. 1004 **PV**
Skandia America Reinsurance Corp., San Francisco Branch Office, 100 California St., Ste. 1360, 94111, pg. 1257 **IT**
Slates Brand, 1155 Battery St., 94111, pg. 663 **PV**
Snow Brand America Co., Ltd., 44 Montgomery St., Ste. 3580, 94104, pg. 1272 **IT**
Southern Pacific Rail Corporation, One Market Plaza, Southern Pacific Bldg., 94105, pg. 1668 **PB**
Southern Pacific Warehouse Co., One Market Plaza, Southern Pacific Bldg., 94105, pg. 1668 **PB**
Specialty Brands, 222 Sutter St., 94108, pg. 237 **PB**
Stewart Smith West, Inc., 350 California St., Ste. 1940, 94104, pg. 1508 **IT**
The Sumitomo Bank, Ltd.-San Francisco Branch, 555 California St., Ste. 3350, 94104, pg. 1309 **IT**
Sumitomo Bank of California, 320 California St., 94104, pg. 1309 **IT**
Sumitomo Chemical America, Inc.-San Francisco Office, One California St., 23rd Fl., 94111, pg. 1311 **IT**
Sumitomo Corporation of America, One California St., Ste. 2300, 94111, pg. 1312 **IT**
Sunical Land & Livestock Division, 200 Hearst Bldg., Five Third St., 94103, pg. 518 **PV**
Sunset Railway Co., One Market Plaza, Southern Pacific Bldg., 94105, pg. 1668 **PB**
Supercuts, Inc., 550 California St., 94104, pg. 1373 **PB**
SWINERTON INC., 580 California St. 94104, pg. 1059 **PV**
Swiss Bank Corporation, 101 California St., 94111, pg. 1329 **IT**
TBWA Chiat/Day San Francisco, 225 Bush St., 94104, pg. 1062 **PV**
TMP Worldwide/Recruitment Division, 221 Main St., Ste. 1400, 94104, pg. 1065 **PV**
Takenaka (U.S.A.) Corporation, San Francisco Office, 350 California St., Ste. 1450, 94104; pg. 1351 **IT**
Taylor Woodrow of California Inc., 333 Third Street, 94107, pg. 1359 **IT**
Taylor Woodrow of San Francisco Inc., 333 Third Street, 94107, pg. 1359 **IT**
TENERA Energy, LLC, One Market, Ste. 1850, Spear Tower, 94105, pg. 1576 **PB**
TENERA, INC., One Market, Spear Tower, Ste. 1850, 94105, pg. 1576 **PB**
Thai Airways Intl. Ltd., 88 Kearny St., Ste. 810, 94108, pg. 1381 **IT**
Time Inc. Health, 301 Howard St., 94105, pg. 1613 **PB**
Tokio Marine Management Inc. - San Francisco, Ste. 2725, 100 Pine St., 94111, pg. 1392 **IT**
Toshiba America MRI Inc., 280 Utah Ave., 94103, pg. 1405 **IT**
Toshiba International Corporation, Utility Division, 350 California St., Ste. 700, 94104, pg. 1405 **IT**
Tosoh USA, Inc.-San Francisco Office, 383 E. Grand Ave., Ste. E, 94080-6209, pg. 1407 **IT**
Trans-American Steamship Agency, 340 Pine St., #405, 94104-3221, pg. 1418 **IT**
TRANSAMERICA CORPORATION, 600 Montgomery St., 94111, pg. 1629 **PB**
Transamerica HomeFirst, Inc., 505 Sansome St., 11th Fl., 94111, pg. 1630 **PB**
Transamerica Realty Services, Inc., 600 Montgomery St., 94111, pg. 1630 **PB**
Transportation Equipment Corporation, One Market, Steuart Tower, Ste. 800, 94105-1301, pg. 1241 **PB**
Transportation Equipment Indemnity Co. Ltd., One Market, Steuart St. Tower, Ste. 800, 94105, pg. 1242 **IT**
Turner Construction Co., 353 Sacramento St., 94111, pg. 1645 **PV**
255 California Corporation, 255 California St., 94111, pg. 681 **PB**
UBS Representative Office, 555 California St., Ste. 4660, 94104, pg. 1440 **IT**
URS CORPORATION, 100 California St., Ste. 500, 94111, pg. 1655 **PB**
Union Bank of California, 350 California St., 94104-1476, pg. 157 **IT**

United Cogen, Inc., UA Maintenance Operations Ctr., San Francisco Intl. Airport, 94128, pg. 1653 **PB**
United States Airlease, Incorporated, 733 Front St., 94111, pg. 1653 **PB**
U.S. HOME & GARDEN INC., 655 Montgomery St., Ste. 830, 94111, pg. 1682 **PB**
U.S. Yellow Pages, 440 Pacific Ave., 94133, pg. 1168 **PV**
Utell International-San Francisco, 3145 Geary #205, 94118-3300, pg. 1098 **IT**
Vestek Systems, Inc., 388 Market St., Ste. 700, 94111, pg. 1325 **PB**
Victorian Convalescent Hospital, 2121 Pine St., 94115, pg. 1715 **PV**
VISA U.S.A. INC., P.O. Box 8999, 94128-8999, pg. 1141 **PV**
Visalia Electric Railroad Co., One Market Plaza, Southern Pacific Bldg., 94105, pg. 1668 **PB**
WELLS FARGO & COMPANY, 420 Montgomery St., 94163, pg. 1753 **PB**
Wells Fargo Bank, National Assn., 420 Montgomery St., 94163, pg. 1753 **PB**
West Coast Life Insurance Co., 343 Sansome St., 94104, pg. 1336 **PB**
Westchester Specialty Group, 275 Battery St., Ste. 1500, 94111, pg. 681 **PB**
Western Direct, 440 Pacific Ave., 94133, pg. 1166 **PV**
Western International Media Corporation, 440 Pacific Ave., 94133, pg. 1167 **PV**
Western States Assoc., 101 California St., 94111, pg. 739 **PV**
Westpac Banking Corporation (San Francisco Branch), 101 California St., 38th Fl., 94111, pg. 1496 **IT**
WHAM-O, INC., 155 Montgomery St., 94104, pg. 1170 **PV**
WILBUR-ELLIS COMPANY & CONNELL BROTHERS COMPANY, 345 California St., 27th Fl., 94104, pg. 1175 **PV**
WILLIAMS-SONOMA, INC., 3250 Van Ness Ave., 94109, pg. 1770 **PB**
Willis Corroon Corp. of California, 50 California St., Ste. 2200, 94111, pg. 1505 **IT**
Willis Faber North America, Inc.-California, 50 California St., Ste. 2100, 94111, pg. 1503 **IT**
WILSEY BENNETT CO., 2351 Powell St., Ste. 500, 94133, pg. 1180 **PV**
Wilsey Bennett Real Estate Division, 2351 Powell St., 94133, pg. 1180 **PV**
THE WINE GROUP, 240 Stockton St., Ste. 800, 94108, pg. 1182 **PV**
WINKLER ADVERTISING, 301 Howard Ct., 21st Fl., 94105, pg. 1183 **PV**
Winterland Productions, 100 Harrison St., 94105, pg. 1215 **PV**
XTRA International Ltd., 333 Market St., 3rd Fl., 94105, pg. 1786 **PB**
Young & Rubicam San Francisco, 100 First St., 94105, pg. 1198 **PV**
Zenith Media Services, Inc., 1010 Battery St., 94111, pg. 1204 **PV**
Zimmerman & Partners Advertising, Inc., 605 Market St., 94105, pg. 1206 **PV**

San Gabriel

San Gabriel Valley Medical Center, 218 S. Santa Anita St., 91776-1137, pg. 1118 **PV**

San Jose

AST Research, Inc., 2055 Gateway Pl., #750, 95110, pg. 1181 **IT**
ATMI Ecosys Corp., 617 River Oaks Pkwy., 95134, pg. 12 **PB**
Acer/Altos Computer Systems, 2641 Orchard Pkwy., 95134, pg. 22 **PB**
Acer America Corporation, 2641 Orchard Pkwy., 95134, pg. 22 **IT**
ADEPT TECHNOLOGY, INC., 150 Rose Orchard Way, 95134, pg. 19 **PB**
ADOBE SYSTEMS INCORPORATED, 345 Park Ave., 95110, pg. 20 **PB**
Advanced Information Technology Center, 1060 Rincon Circle, 95131, pg. 1405 **IT**
Akashic Memories Corporation, 305 W. Tasman Dr., 95134, pg. 762 **IT**
Alantec Corp., 2115 O'Nel Dr., 95131, pg. 667 **PB**
All American Semiconductor of Northern California, Inc., 230 Devon Dr., 95131, pg. 41 **IT**
ALLIANCE SEMICONDUCTOR CORP., 3099 N. First St., 95134, pg. 47 **PB**
ALTERA CORPORATION, 101 Innovation Dr., 95134-2020, pg. 59 **PB**
AMATI Communications Corp., 2043 Smaritan Dr., 95124-4401, pg. 1585 **PB**
Analog Division, 555 River Oaks Pkwy., 95134, pg. 290 **PB**
Answer Systems Development Laboratory, Two N. 2nd St., Ste. 1000, 95113, pg. 1309 **IT**
Anthem Electronics Inc., 1160 Ridder Park Dr., 95131, pg. 134 **PB**
Anthem Technology, 1160 Ridder Park Dr., 95131, pg. 134 **PB**
Applied Technology, 4747 Hellyer Ave., 91538, pg. 1002 **PB**
Aromat Northwestern Sales Office, 401 River Oaks Pkwy., 95134, pg. 848 **IT**
Atalla Corporation, 2304 Zanker Rd., 95131, pg. 417 **PB**
ATMEL CORPORATION, 2325 Orchard Pkwy., 95131, pg. 145 **PB**
Aydin Corporation West, 30 Great Oaks Blvd., 95119, pg. 158 **PB**

Geographic Index-U.S.

BSA Advertising, Inc., 101 Metro Drive, Ste. 660, 95110, pg. 108 **PV**
Balco, 3550 Snell Ave., 95136, pg. 1480 **PB**
Ball Screws & Actuators Co., Inc., 3616 Snell Ave., 95136-1305, pg. 482 **PB**
Bancomm, 6541 Via Del Oro, 95119-1294, pg. 488 **PB**
Becton Dickinson Immunocytometry Systems, 2350 Qume Dr., 95131-1893, pg. 199 **PB**
BELL SPORTS CORP., 6350 San Ignacio Ave., 95119, pg. 207 **PB**
Bergen Brunswig Drug Company, 450 Charcot Ave., 95131, pg. 213 **PB**
BOOLE & BABBAGE, INC., 3131 Zanker Rd., 95134, pg. 244 **PB**
British Telecom Tymnet, 2560 N. 1st St., 95131-1015, pg. 223 **IT**
Browning-Ferris Industries of California, Inc., P.O. Box 1987, 95109, pg. 263 **PB**
Burke Flooring Products Div., 2250 S. 10th St., 95112, pg. 183 **PV**
BURKE INDUSTRIES, INC., 2250 S. Tenth St., 95112, pg. 183 **PV**
Burke Rubber Co., 2250 S. 10th St., 95112, pg. 183 **PV**
CAE Division, 2655 Seely Rd., 95134, pg. 290 **PB**
CADENCE DESIGN SYSTEMS, INC., 555 River Oaks Pkwy., 95134, pg. 290 **PB**
CALIFORNIA WATER SERVICE CO., 1720 N. First St., 95112, pg. 294 **PB**
CALPINE CORPORATION, 50 W. San Fernando St., 95113, pg. 296 **PB**
Capstone Electronics Div., 1180 Murphy Ave., 95131, pg. 134 **PB**
CardioRhythm, 130 Rio Robles, 95134, pg. 1083 **PB**
Ceitronics, Inc., 775 Commercial St., 95112, pg. 1060 **PV**
CENTIGRAM COMMUNICATIONS CORPORATION, 91 E. Tasman Dr., 95134, pg. 323 **PB**
Charter Behavioral Health System of San Jose, Inc., 455 Silicon Valley Blvd., 95138, pg. 1034 **PB**
CHIPS AND TECHNOLOGIES, INC., 2950 Zanker Rd., 95134, pg. 349 **PB**
Chips and Technologies, Inc., 2950 Zanker Road, 95134, pg. 349 **PB**
CISCO SYSTEMS, INC., 170 W. Tasman Dr., 95134-1706, pg. 375 **PB**
Citation Insurance Company, One Almaden Blvd., 95113, pg. 376 **PB**
CITATION INSURANCE GROUP, One Almaden Blvd., 95113, pg. 376 **PB**
Citation National Insurance Company, One Almaden Blvd., 95113, pg. 376 **PB**
CLARIFY INC., 2125 O'Nel Dr., 95131, pg. 382 **PB**
THE COAKLEY HEAGERTY ADVERTISING & PUBLIC RELATIONS CO., 1155 N. First St., Ste. 201, 95112-4925, pg. 248 **PB**
THE COAST DISTRIBUTION SYSTEM, 1982 Zanker Rd., 95112, pg. 388 **PB**
Coast RV, Inc., 1705 Junction St., 95112, pg. 388 **PB**
Comerica Bank California, 333 W. Santa Clara St., 95113, pg. 409 **PB**
Compass Design Automation Inc., 1865 Lundy Ave., 95131, pg. 1703 **PB**
Convergent, Inc., 2700 N. First St., 95150-6685, pg. 1671 **PB**
Conway Import Co. Inc., 610 Trimble Rd., 95131, pg. 272 **PV**
Cowden Metal-San Jose, 2157 S. Tenth St., 95112, pg. 280 **PV**
Custom Process, 2250 S. Tenth St., 95112, pg. 183 **PV**
CYPRESS SEMICONDUCTOR CORPORATION, 3901 N. First St., 95134, pg. 470 **PB**
DRS Ahead Technology, Inc., 6410 Via Del Oro, 95119, pg. 475 **PB**
Dai-Ichi Kangyo Bank of California-San Jose, 190 Park Center Plz., 95113, pg. 360 **IT**
Dataquest Incorporated, 1290 Ridder Park Drive, 95131-2398, pg. 535 **PB**
DIAMOND MULTIMEDIA SYSTEMS, INC., 2880 Junction Ave., 95134, pg. 505 **PB**
DIGITAL MICROWAVE CORPORATION, 170 Rose Orchard Way, 95134, pg. 508 **PB**
Downey Savings & Loan Association, F.A., 2945 Villages Pkwy., 95135, pg. 527 **PB**
Duel Systems, 1750 Junction Ave., 95112, pg. 1101 **PB**
EMS-West, 2248 N. 1st St., 95131, pg. 565 **PB**
Eagle Technology, 2865 Zanker Rd., 95134, pg. 1105 **PB**
ESPRIT SYSTEMS, INC., 2115 Ringwood Ave., 95131, pg. 383 **PV**
Exel Microelectronics, Inc., 2150 Commerce Dr., 95131, pg. 1125 **IT**
Exsil, Inc., 6541 Via Del Oro, 95119, pg. 802 **IT**
Exsil, Inc., 6541 Via Del Oro, Ste. C, 95119, pg. 802 **IT**
FIFO Division, 2670 Seeley Rd., 95134, pg. 884 **PB**
Fine Pitch Technology, Inc., 2450 Autumnvale Dr., 65131, pg. 1483 **PB**
Finnigan Corporation, 355 River Oaks Pkwy., 95134-1991, pg. 1591 **PB**
Finnigan MAT, 335 River Oaks Pkwy., 95134, pg. 1591 **PB**
Finnigan MAT Instruments, Inc., 355 River Oaks Pkwy., 95134, pg. 1591 **PB**
Finnigan Properties, Inc., 355 River Oaks Pkwy., 95134, pg. 1591 **PB**
First American Records Management, 559 Charcot Ave., 95131, pg. 625 **PB**
Four-Phase Systems International, Inc., 2001 Logic Dr., 95124, pg. 1137 **PB**
The Foxboro Company, 199 Riveroaks Pkwy., 95134, pg. 1243 **IT**
FRY'S ELECTRONICS, INC., 600 Brokaw Rd., 95112, pg. 430 **PV**
Fujitsu America, Inc., 3055 Orchard Dr., 95134, pg. 526 **IT**

Fujitsu America - Information Systems Group, 3055 Orchard Dr., 95134, pg. 526 **IT**
Fujitsu America - Super Computer Group, 3055 Orchard Dr., 95134, pg. 526 **IT**
Fujitsu Compound Semiconductor, Inc., 50 Rio Robles, 55104-1806, pg. 526 **IT**
Fujitsu Computer Packaging Technologies, Inc., 3811 Zanker Rd., 95134, pg. 526 **IT**
Fujitsu Computer Products of America, Inc., 2904 Orchard Pkwy., 95134, pg. 526 **IT**
Fujitsu Laboratories of America, inc., 77 Rio Robles, 95134-1307, pg. 526 **IT**
Fujitsu Microelectronics, Inc., 3545 N. First Street, 95134, pg. 527 **IT**
Fujitsu Open Systems Solutions, Inc., 3055 Orchard Dr., 95134, pg. 526 **IT**
G.E. Nuclear Energy, 175 Curtner Ave., 95125, pg. 711 **PB**
GASONICS INTERNATIONAL, 2540 Junction Ave., 95134-1609, pg. 703 **PB**
General Employment Enterprises, Inc., 2540 N. First St., Ste. 110, 95131, pg. 714 **PB**
Granite Construction Inc.-San Jose Div., 120 Granite Rock Way, 95136, pg. 759 **PB**
Harman Interactive Group, 111 W. St. John St., Ste. 900, 95113, pg. 787 **PB**
Hitachi Instruments, Inc., 3100 N. First St., 95134, pg. 622 **IT**
Hyundai Electronics America, 3101 N. First St., 95134, pg. 641 **IT**
INFORMATION STORAGE DEVICES, 2045 Hamilton Ave., 95125, pg. 876 **PB**
Integrated Circuits Division, 555 River Oaks Pkwy., 95134, pg. 290 **PB**
International Components Technology Corporation (CMD), 2360 Zanker Rd., 95131-1198, pg. 530 **PB**
International Disposal Corp. of California, P.O. Box 1987, 95109, pg. 264 **PB**
JTS CORPORATION, 166 Baypoint Pkwy., 95134, pg. 919 **PB**
Jabil Circuit, Inc./West, 2220 Lundy Ave., 95131, pg. 320 **PB**
Jaco Electronics, Inc., 2880 Zanker Rd., 95134, pg. 921 **PB**
Jinwoong Inc., 569 Charcot Ave., 95131, pg. 707 **IT**
Joslyn Jennings Corporation, 970 McLaughlin Ave., 95122, pg. 481 **PB**
KLA TENCOR CORPORATION, 160 Rio Robles, 95134, pg. 939 **PB**
Kellogg Convenience Food Plant, 475 Eggo Way, 95116, pg. 547 **PB**
Kent Landsberg, 2124 Bering Dr., 95131, pg. 72 **PB**
Kokusai Electric Co., Ltd. America, 1961 Concourse Dr., Ste. C, 95131, pg. 743 **IT**
KOMAG, INCORPORATED, 1704 Automation Pk., 95131, pg. 956 **PB**
Landis & Gyr Systems, Inc., 1730 Technology Dr., 95110, pg. 800 **IT**
Laserscope Inc., 3052 Orchard Drive, 95134-2011, pg. 6 6 **PB**
LASERSCOPE SURGICAL SYSTEMS, 3052 Orchard Dr., 95134-2011, pg. 979 **PB**
LEASING SOLUTIONS, INC., Ten Almaden Blvd., Ste. 1500, 95113-2238, pg. 982 **PB**
Leasing Solutions Receivables, Inc., 10 Almaden Blvd., Ste. 1500, 95113, pg. 983 **PB**
Litton Applied Technology, 4747 Hellyer Ave., 95138, pg. 1003 **PB**
Lockheed Martin Western Development Labs, 3200 Zanker Rd., 95134, pg. 1009 **PB**
Madison Acceptance Corporation, One Almaden Blvd., 95113, pg. 376 **PB**
Matsubo Company (America), Inc., 109 Bonaventurea Drive, 95134, pg. 432 **IT**
Matsushita Electric Works Research & Development Laboratory Inc., 401 River Oaks Pkwy., 95134, pg. 84E **IT**
George S. May International Co., 991 W. Hedding St., 94126-206, pg. 717 **PV**
MEDIA ARTS GROUP, INC., 521 Charcot Ave., 95131, pg. 1077 **PB**
Microdyne Corp., 1140 Ringwood Ave., 95131, pg. 1105 **PB**
Micropolis Corporation, 100 Century Center Ct., Ste. 410, 95112-4512, pg. 742 **PV**
Microtec Division, 880 Ridder Park Dr., 95131, pg. 1086 **PB**
Milgray/Northern California, 2880 Zanker Rd., 95134, pg. 206 **PB**
Motorola Computer Sales & Services, Inc., 2001 Logic Dr., 95124, pg. 1138 **PB**
Motorola Indala Corporation, 3041 Orchard Pkwy., 95134, pg. 1138 **PB**
Motorola Information Systems, Inc., 2001 Logic Dr., 95124, pg. 1138 **PB**
MR. WRIGHT'S AMAZING COFFEE FACTORY, 3870 Charter Park Dr., 95136, pg. 765 **PV**
Multichip Technology, 3901 N. First St., 95134, pg. 470 **PB**
Multigen Inc, 550 S. Winchester Blvd., Ste. 500, 95128, pg. 1425 **PB**
NEC Systems Laboratory, Inc., 110 Rio Robles Ave., 95134-1899, pg. 900 **IT**
Namco-America, Inc., 150 Charcot Ave., 95131, pg. 905 **IT**
Namco-Holding, Corp., 150 Charcot Ave., 95131, pg. 905 **IT**
Namco Hometek, Inc., 150 Charcot Ave., Ste. A, 95131, pg. 905 **IT**
NavSymm, 85 W. Tasman Dr., 95134-1703, pg. 1547 **PB**
NewsEdge Corporation, 4880 Stevens Creek Blvd., Ste. 206, 95129, pg. 1180 **PB**

Nextron, 6830 Via Del Oro, Ste. 240, 95119, pg. 1424 **PB**
94th Aero Squadron of San Jose, Inc., 1160 Coleman Ave., 95110, pg. 1022 **PV**
NOVELLUS SYSTEMS, INC., 3970 N. First St., 95134, pg. 1204 **PB**
Nu Horizons/Merit Electronics Corp., 2070 Ringwood Ave., 95131, pg. 1205 **PB**
Oki Advanced Technology Division, 2087 Ringwood Ave., 95131-1703, pg. 1000 **IT**
OnTrak Systems, Inc., 1010 Rincon Cir., 95131, pg. 975 **PB**
Orchard Supply Hardware, 6450 Via Del Oro, 95119, pg. 1452 **PB**
PARADIGM TECHNOLOGY, INC., 71 Vista Montana, 95134, pg. 1256 **PB**
Perkins Corporation, 1980 Zanker Road, 95112, pg. 1229 **IT**
PHOENIX TECHNOLOGIES LTD., 411 E. Plumeria Dr., 95134, pg. 1292 **PB**
Plus Logic, 2100 Logic Drive, 95124, pg. 1786 **PB**
Quebecor Printing San Jose Inc., 696 E. Trimble Rd., 95131-1222, pg. 1077 **PB**
Read-Rite Corporation, 530 Race St., 95126, pg. 1367 **PB**
Red Wing Company, 665 Lenfast Rd., 95133, pg. 1398 **IT**
Richardson Electronics Ltd.-Western, 1762 Technology Dr., Ste. 226, 95110, pg. 1388 **PB**
Rohm Corporation, 2150 Commerce Dr., 95131, pg. 1125 **IT**
Rohm Electronics North-West Sales Division, 226 Airport Pkwy., Ste. 390, 95110, pg. 1125 **IT**
Rohm LSI Systems Inc., 1740 Technology Dr., Ste. 210, 95110, pg. 1125 **IT**
Rohm U.S.A., Inc., 2150 Commerce Dr., 95131, pg. 1125 **IT**
ROSENDIN ELECTRIC, INC., 880 Mabury Rd., 95133, pg. 945 **PV**
S MOS Systems, Inc., 150 River Oaks Pkwy., 95134, pg. 1219 **IT**
SJNB FINANCIAL CORP., P.O. Box 1957, 95109, pg. 1418 **PB**
SJW CORP., 374 W. Santa Clara, 95196, pg. 1418 **PB**
SJW Land Company, 374 W. Santa Clara, 95196, pg. 1418 **PB**
SVG Track Systems, 2240 Ringwood Ave., 95131, pg. 1474 **PB**
Samsung Semiconductors, Inc., 3655 N. First St., 95134-1708, pg. 1183 **IT**
San Jose Mercury News, 750 Ridder Park Dr., 95190, pg. 964 **PB**
San Jose National Bank, One N. Market St., 95113, pg. 1418 **PB**
San Jose Water Company, 374 W. Santa Clara, 95196, pg. 1418 **PB**
SANMINA CORPORATION, 355 E. Trimble Ave., 95131, pg. 1431 **PB**
Sanmina Corporation-San Jose, 4405 Fortran Ct., 95134, pg. 1431 **PB**
Semi-Gas Systems, Inc., 625 Wool Creek Dr., 95112, pg. 938 **IT**
Sharp Electronics Corporation, 1980 Zanker Rd., 95112, pg. 1229 **IT**
Shea Homes Northern California, 25 Metro Dr., Ste. 300, 95110, pg. 991 **PV**
SIERRA SEMICONDUCTOR, 2222 Qume Dr., 95131, pg. 1470 **PB**
SILICON VALLEY GROUP, INC., 101 Metro Dr., Ste. 400, 95110, pg. 1474 **PB**
SOLITEC WAFER PROCESSING, INC., 685 River Oaks Pkwy., 95134-1907, pg. 1013 **PV**
Sony Microelectronics, 3300 Zanker Rd., 95134-1940, pg. 1284 **PB**
Spectra Diode Laboratories, 80 Rose Orchard Way, 95134-1356, pg. 1785 **PB**
THE STEPHENZ GROUP, INC., 150 Almaden Blvd., 95113, pg. 1040 **PB**
Sterling Electronics, 2159 Bering Dr., 95131, pg. 1051 **PB**
Stryker Corporation Endoscopy, 210 Baypointe Pkwy., 95134-1621, pg. 1526 **PB**
SYMMETRICOM, INC., 2300 Orchard Pkwy., 95131, pg. 1547 **PB**
Systems Design Division, 555 River Oaks Pkwy., 95134, pg. 290 **PB**
Technical Service Center, 99 Tasman Ave., Ste. 200, 95134, pg. 871 **PB**
Technology Solutions Inc., 101 Park Center Plaza, #1300, 95113, pg. 1157 **PV**
Telecom Solutions, 2300 Orchard Pkwy., 95131, pg. 1547 **PB**
TELEVIDEO, INC., 2345 Harris Way, 95131, pg. 1572 **PB**
Thermo Separation Products, 355 River Oaks Pkwy., 95134, pg. 1594 **PB**
TRACE MOUNTAIN PRODUCTS, 1040 E. Brokaw Rd., 95131, pg. 1095 **PV**
Trace Optical LLC, 1040 E. Brokaw Rd., 95131, pg. 293 **IT**
Trillium Digital Division, 3930 N. First St., 95134, pg. 972 **PB**
Turner Construction Company, 101 Park Center Plaza, Ste. 1100, 95113, pg. 1645 **PB**
ULTRATECH STEPPER, INC., 3050 Zanker Rd., 95134, pg. 1663 **PB**
UNIFY CORPORATION, 181 Metro Dr., Ste. 300, 95110, pg. 1665 **PB**
UNIPHASE CORPORATION, 163 Baypointe Pkwy., 95134, pg. 1670 **PB**
United Technologies, Chemical Systems Div., 600 Metcalf Rd., 95138, pg. 1690 **PB**
Universal Fleet, 1733 Rogers Ave., 95112, pg. 939 **PV**
VLSI TECHNOLOGY, INC., 1109 McKay Dr., 95131, pg. 1703 **PB**

PB - U.S. Public Companies Volume
PV - U.S. Private Companies Volume
IT - International Public & Private Companies Volume

Viking Freight System, Inc., 410 E. Plumeria Dr., 95134, pg. 604 **PB**
Weiss Glass Technologies, Inc., 2300 Zanker Rd., Ste. A, 95131, pg. 1408 **IT**
Western Digital Drive Engineering Inc., 5863 Rueferrai Rd., 95138, pg. 1758 **PB**
Western Region Sales, 2365 Hanis Way, pg. 1572 **PB**
Willis Corroon Administrative Services Corporation, 1871 The Alameda, Ste. 350, 95126, pg. 1504 **PB**
Willis Corroon Corp. of San Jose, 1735 Technology Dr., Ste. 500, 95110, pg. 1507 **IT**
Woodward-Clyde, 55 S. Market St., Ste. 1650, 95113, pg. 1657 **PB**
WYSE TECHNOLOGY INC., 3471 N. First St., 95134, pg. 1194 **PV**
Xerox Colorgraphics, 5853 Rue Ferrari, 95138, pg. 1784 **PB**
XILINX, INC., 2100 Logic Dr., 95124, pg. 1786 **PB**
Yamamoto Mfg. (USA) Inc., 2290 N. First St., Ste. 202, 95131, pg. 295 **IT**
ZACK ELECTRONICS, 2514 Channing Ave., 95131, pg. 1203 **PB**
Zenger-Miller, 1735 Technology Drive, 6th Fl., 95110-1313, pg. 1617 **PB**

San Juan Bautista

Amycel, Inc., P.O. Box 1260, 95045, pg. 758 **PV**
Speedling Incorporated San Juan Bautista Nursery, 2640 San Juan Highway, pg. 1024 **PV**

San Juan Capistrano

ChromaVision Medical Systems, Inc., 33171 Paseo Cerveza, 92690, pg. 1424 **PB**
Cox Communications-Orange County, 26181 Avenida Aeropuerto, 92675, pg. 455 **PB**
Endevco Corporation, 30700 Rancho Viejo Rd., 92675, pg. 853 **IT**
Orange County Plant, P.O. Box 249, 92693-0249, pg. 1213 **PB**
REMEDYTEMP, INC., 32122 Camino Capistrano, 92675, pg. 1376 **PB**

San Leandro

Bridgestone Cycle (U.S.A.), Inc., 15021 Wicks Blvd., 94577, pg. 213 **IT**
California Pretzel Company, 2235 Polvorosa, Ste. 200, 94577, pg. 434 **PV**
Elcat Corporation, 14299 Wicks Blvd., 94577, pg. 369 **PV**
Harris Rebar Oakland, Inc., 1105 Aladdin Ave., 94577, pg. 598 **PB**
Kallista, Inc., 2701 Merced St., 94577, pg. 630 **PB**
Lighting Corporation of America, 1251 Doolittle Dr., 94577-2221, pg. 1684 **PB**
Lucky Stores Northern California Division, 1701 Marina Blvd., 94577, pg. 93 **PB**
MDL Information Systems, Inc., 14600 Catalina St., 94577, pg. 1100 **PB**
MDL Information Systems-Western Sales, 14600 Catalina St., 94577, pg. 1100 **IT**
PETERSON TRACTOR COMPANY, 955 Marina Blvd., 94577, pg. 858 **PV**
Physics International Co., 2700 Merced St., 94577, pg. 1219 **PB**
Prescolite Moldcast Lighting Company, 1251 Doolittle Dr., 94577, pg. 1684 **PB**
Pulse Sciences, Inc., 600 McCormick St., 94577, pg. 1618 **PB**
Sealright Mfg. West, Inc., 2450 Alvarado St., 94577, pg. 1452 **PB**
Thomas Lighting-C&I Outdoor Division, 2661 Alvarado St., 94577, pg. 1599 **PB**
Wyman-Gordon Investment Castings, 414 Hester St., 94577, pg. 1782 **PB**

San Lorenzo

Gallo/Galileo Salame, 2411 Baumann Ave., 94580, pg. 1433 **PB**

San Luis Obispo

FOSTERS FREEZE INTERNATIONAL, INC., 3701 S. Higuera St., Ste. 102, 93401-7462, pg. 677 **PB**
San Luis Obispo Telegram-Tribune, 3825 S. Higuera, 93401, pg. 964 **PB**
Seagate Software, Inc., 708 Fiero Commerce Park, Ste. 5, 93401, pg. 1449 **PB**
Seagate Technology Holdings, 708 Fiero Commerce Park, Ste. 5, 93401, pg. 1449 **PB**
Wings West Airlines, 1194 Pacific St., Ste. #200, 93403, pg. 9 **PB**

San Marcos

NAPP Systems, 360 S. Pacific, 92069, pg. 875 **PV**
NAPP Systems Inc., 360 S. Pacific St., 92069, pg. 984 **PB**
POLARIS POOL SYSTEMS, INC., 1709 LaCosta Meadows Dr., 92069-5194, pg. 873 **PV**
Structron Corporation, 1980 Diamont St., pg. 988 **PV**
Xentek, Inc., 1770 La Costa Meadows, 92069, pg. 1349 **IT**

San Marino

ZIMMERMAN HOLDINGS, INC., 2600 Mission St., Ste. 100, 91108, pg. 1206 **PV**

San Mateo

ACTUATE SOFTWARE CORPORATION, 999 Baker Way, Ste. 330, 94404, pg. 16 **PV**
BLC Corp., 2655 Campus Dr., 94403, pg. 377 **PB**
BLFC Securities Corporation, 2655 Campus Dr., 94403, pg. 377 **PB**
Bankers Leasing Corp., 2655 Campus Dr., 94403, pg. 377 **PB**
J.H. BAXTER & COMPANY, 1700 S. El Camino Real, 94402, pg. 124 **PV**
Bay Meadows Race Track, P.O. Box 5050, 2600 S. Delaware St., 94403, pg. 1265 **PB**
Bay View Bank, 2121 S. El Camino Real, 94403, pg. 197 **PB**
BAY VIEW CAPITAL CORPORATION, 2121 S. El Camino Real, 94403, pg. 197 **PB**
The Burke Co., 2655 Campus Dr., 94403, pg. 1423 **IT**
CitiCorp Del-Lease, Inc., 2655 Campus Dr., 94403, pg. 377 **PB**
Commetro Leasing Corp., 2655 Campus Dr., 94403, pg. 377 **PB**
Commonwealth Control, Inc., 2655 Campus Dr., 94403, pg. 377 **PB**
The Commonwealth Plan, Inc., 2655 Campus Dr., 94403, pg. 377 **PB**
The Commonwealth System, Inc., 2655 Campus Dr., 94403, pg. 377 **PB**
ComPlan, Inc., 2655 Campus Dr., 94403, pg. 377 **PB**
CONNECTIX CORPORATION, 2655 Campus Dr., Ste. 100, 94403, pg. 264 **PB**
Coyote Restaurant Corp., Coyote Point Dr., 94401, pg. 1022 **PV**
DBC West, 1900 S. Norfolk St., 94403, pg. 484 **PB**
ELECTRONIC ARTS, 1450 Fashion Island Blvd., 94404, pg. 569 **PB**
ELECTRONICS FOR IMAGING, INC., 2855 Campus Dr., 94403, pg. 570 **PB**
EMCON, 400 S. El Camino Real-Ste. 1200, 94402, pg. 571 **PB**
Financial Leasing Corp., 2655 Campus Dr., 94403, pg. 377 **PB**
Franklin Bank, 777 Mariners Island Blvd., 94404, pg. 680 **PB**
Franklin Properties, Inc., 777 Mariners Island Blvd., 94404, pg. 680 **PB**
FRANKLIN RESOURCES, INC., 777 Mariners Island Blvd., 94404, pg. 679 **PB**
Franklin/Templeton Distributors, Inc., 777 Mariners Island Blvd., 94404, pg. 680 **PB**
Franklin Templeton Investor Services, Inc., 777 Mariners Island Blvd., 94404, pg. 680 **PB**
Franklin Templeton Trust Company, 777 Mariners Island Blvd., 94404, pg. 680 **PB**
GF INDUSTRIES, INC., 999 Baker Way, Ste. 200, 94404, pg. 434 **PV**
GF Properties, Inc., 999 Baker Way, Ste. 200, 94404, pg. 434 **PV**
J. Gordon Gaines Insurance Services, Inc., 2988 Campus Dr., #345, 94403, pg. 1622 **PV**
GamePro, 951 Mariner's Island Blvd., Ste. 700, 94404, pg. 569 **PV**
GLENBOROUGH REALTY TRUST INCORPORATED, 400 S. El Camino Real, 11th Fl., 94402-1708, pg. 747 **PB**
HYPERMEDIA COMMUNICATIONS, INC., 901 Mariners Island Blvd., Ste. 365, 94404, pg. 851 **PV**
Infoworld Publishing, Inc., 155 Bovet Rd., Ste. 800, 94402, pg. 569 **PV**
JT America Inc., 1825 South Grant Street, Suite 220, 94402, pg. 703 **IT**
Jani King of California, Inc., 1875 S. Grant St., Ste. 240, 94402, pg. 581 **PV**
La Prensa Asociada, Inc., 207 Second Ave., 94401, pg. 92 **PV**
Lakeshore Landing, 2717 S. Norfolk St., 94403, pg. 1724 **PB**
Manulife Financial - San Mateo, 1777 Borel Place, Ste. 104, 94402, pg. 841 **PB**
Master Builders Inc., 1730 S.Amphlett Blvd., Ste. 127, 94402, pg. 1465 **IT**
The Pacific Plan, Inc., 2655 Campus Dr., 94403, pg. 377 **PB**
Patriot American Hospitality Operating Company, P.O. Box 5050, 2600 S. Delaware St., 94402, pg. 1265 **PB**
The Seagram Classics Wine Company, 2600 Campus Drive, Suite 160, 94403-2523, pg. 1215 **IT**
Showa Denko America, Inc., 951 Mariner's Island Blvd., Ste. 680, 94404, pg. 1237 **IT**
SunGard Shareholder Systems Inc., 951 Mariners Island Blvd., 94404, pg. 1535 **PB**
Tokuyama America Inc., 1875 South Grant St., Ste. 570, 94402, pg. 1394 **IT**
United States Fleet Leasing, Inc., Two Waters Park Dr., 94403, pg. 664 **PB**
Viva Specialty Partners, 1850 gateway Dr., Ste. 500, 94404, pg. 1724 **PB**
VIVRA INCORPORATED, 1850 Gateway Dr., Ste. 500, 94404, pg. 1723 **PB**
The Worcester Plan, Inc., 2655 Campus Dr., 94403, pg. 377 **PB**

San Pedro

GATX Terminals Corp.-San Pedro, Berth 70-71, Signal St., 90731, pg. 692 **PB**
Information Technology Group, 222 W. 6th St., 90731-0471, pg. 1199 **PB**
Krupp MaK Diesel Inc., 723 Basin St., Unit C, 90731, pg. 509 **IT**

Logicon Strategic and Information Systems Division, 222 W. Sixth St., 90731, pg. 1199 **PB**
Los Angeles Harbor Terminal, 1900 Wilmington-San Pedro Rd., 90733, pg. 692 **PB**
The News-Pilot, 362 W. Seventh St., 90731, pg. 275 **PB**
Ports O'Call Restaurant Corp., Berth 76, 90731, pg. 1022 **PV**
SILICON POWER CUBE CORPORATION, 1891 N. Gaffey Unit M, 90731, pg. 1000 **PV**
Trans-American Steamship Agency, 140 W. Sixth St., 90731-3314, pg. 1418 **IT**

San Rafael

Amex Life Assurance Co., 1650 Los Gamos Dr., 94903, pg. 712 **PB**
AUTODESK, INC., 111 McInnis Pkwy., 94903, pg. 148 **PB**
Autodesk, Inc., 111 McInnis Pkwy., 94903, pg. 149 **PB**
FAIR, ISAAC AND COMPANY, INC., 120 N. Redwood Dr., 94903, pg. 609 **PB**
Fifth Avenue Convalescent House, 1601 Sawtelle Blvd., 94903, pg. 1712 **PB**
HRH Insurance Services of Northern California, Inc., 160 Mitchell Blvd., 94903, pg. 827 **PB**
Hanson Investment Management Company, 4000 Civic Ctr. Dr., Ste. 200, 94903, pg. 1673 **PB**
Hillhaven Convalescent Hospital San Rafael, 233 W. End Ave., 94901, pg. 1713 **PB**
Hillside Manor Convalescent Hospital, 81 Professional Center Pkwy., 94903, pg. 1714 **PB**
Johnson-Loft Engineering, Inc., 3100 Kerner Blvd., Ste. C, 94901, pg. 1378 **PB**
Komori West Incorporated, 3000 Kerner Blvd., 94901, pg. 745 **IT**
LUCASFILM LTD., P.O. Box 2009, 94912, pg. 679 **PV**
Phoenix American Alarm Affiliates, Inc., 2401 Kerner Blvd., 94901-5527, pg. 862 **PV**
PHOENIX AMERICAN INCORPORATED, 2401 Kerner Blvd., 94901, pg. 862 **PV**
Phoenix Cable Incorporated, 2401 Kerner Blvd., 94901, pg. 862 **PV**
Phoenix Fiber Link Inc., 2401 Kerner Blvd., 94901, pg. 863 **PV**
Phoenix Growth Capital Corp., 2401 Kerner Blvd., 94901, pg. 863 **PV**
Phoenix Leasing Incorporated, 2401 Kerner Blvd., 94901, pg. 863 **PV**
Phoenix Securities, Inc., 2401 Kerner Blvd., 94901, pg. 863 **PV**
Phoenix Systems Exchange, Inc., 2401 Kerner Blvd., 94901, pg. 863 **PV**
Polycold Systems International, Inc., 67 Mark Dr., 94903, pg. 894 **PB**
RETZLAFF INCORPORATED, 50 Mitchell Blvd., 94903, pg. 925 **PV**
VALLEY FORGE CORPORATION, 100 Smith Ranch Rd., Ste. 326, 94903, pg. 1705 **PB**
Westamerica Bank, P.O. Box 600, 1108 Fifth Ave., 94901, pg. 1756 **PB**

San Ramon

Aerotest Operations, Inc., 3455 Fostoria Way, 94583, pg. 1207 **PB**
BASES Services & Durables Division, 200 Porter Dr., Ste. 210, 94583, pg. 120 **PV**
Chandeleur Pipe Line Co., P.O. Box 5059, 94583, pg. 348 **PB**
Chevron Chemical Co., 6001 Bollinger Canyon Rd., 94583, pg. 348 **PB**
Chevron Overseas Petroleum, Inc., 6001 Bollinger Canyon Rd., 94583, pg. 348 **PB**
Chevron Pipe Line Company, P.O. Box 5059, 94583, pg. 348 **PB**
Comverse Network Systems, 19799 San Ramon Valley Blvd., 94583, pg. 425 **PB**
Davy International, San Francisco, 2440 Camino Ramon, 94583, pg. 774 **IT**
GIGA-TRONICS INCORPORATED, 4650 Norris Canyon Rd., 94583, pg. 742 **PB**
Kaufman and Broad of Northern California, Inc., 3130 Crow Canyon Pl., Ste. 300, 94583, pg. 945 **PB**
Lindenmeyr Paper, 2694 Bishop Dr., Ste. 290, 94583, pg. 224 **PV**
MFS Intelenet Companies, 2678 Bishop St., Ste. 200, 94583, pg. 1779 **PB**
Nortel Communications, 2400 Camino Ramon, Ste. 100, 94583, pg. 969 **IT**
Nortel Communications, 2400 Camino Ramon, Ste. 100, 94583, pg. 1416 **PB**
Pacific Bell, 2600 Camino Ramon, 94583, pg. 1416 **PB**
Promontory Point Apartments, 1700 Promontory Ln., 94583, pg. 163 **PB**
ROBERTSON-CECO CORPORATION, 5000 Exec. Pk., Ste. 425, 94583, pg. 1394 **PB**
SBE, INC., 4550 Norris Canyon Rd., 94583-1369, pg. 1416 **PB**
Standard Pipe Line Co., P.O. Box 5059, 94583, pg. 348 **PB**
Symbol, 3130 Crow Canyon Pl., Ste. 200, 94583, pg. 1546 **PB**
Tech Data Finance, 5000 Exec. Pkwy., Ste. 490, 94583, pg. 1562 **PB**
TRI VALLEY GROWERS, 12667 Alcosta Blvd., 94583, pg. 1101 **PV**
VECTRA TECHNOLOGIES, INC., 2333 San Ramon Valley Blvd., Ste. 225, 94583, pg. 1711 **PB**

Geographic Index-U.S.

San Ysidro

California Commerce Bank, 418 W. San Ysidro Blvd., 92173, pg. 574 IT
Ertl de Mexico, P.O. Box 13-B, 92073, pg. 1684 PB
J.E. Higgins Lumber Company, 3330 Beyer Blvd., Ste. E, 92173, pg. 527 PV
Kintetsu Intermodal Inc., 9163 Siempre Viva Rd., Ste. I-1, 92173, pg. 735 IT
O&S California, Inc., 9731 Siempre Viva Rd., Ste. E, 92173-3217, pg. 1313 IT
Square D Company-Pacifico, Box 3436, 92073, pg. 1208 IT

Sand City

Slautterback Corp., 709 California Ave., 93955, pg. 1188 PB

Sanger

GIBSON WINE COMPANY, 1720 Academy Ave., 93657, pg. 452 PV
McCall Wineries & Distillers, 1042 S. McCall Ave., 93657, pg. 1321 IT

Santa Ana

AAI/ACL Technologies, 1505 E. Warner Ave., 92705, pg. 1679 PB
Adhesive Films, 2811 Harbor Blvd., 92702, pg. 165 PB
Admar, Inc., 1551 N. Tustin Ave., Ste. 300, 92705, pg. 885 PV
ALPHA MICROSYSTEMS, 2722 S. Fairview St., 92704, pg. 57 PB
Alta Pacific Constructors, 2002 E. McFadden Ave., 92705, pg. 907 PV
AMERIQUEST TECHNOLOGIES, Three Imperial Promenade, Ste. 300, 92707, pg. 96 PB
AMPLICON, INC., Five Hutton Centre Dr., Ste. 500, 92707, pg. 104 PB
Architectural Landscape Lighting, 2930 S. Fairview St., 92704-6598, pg. 821 IT
Associated Concrete Products, Inc., 4301 W. MacArthur Blvd., 92704, pg. 417 PV
BFI Constructors, 1415 N. Susan St., 92703, pg. 263 PB
BENMAR MARINE ELECTRONICS, INC., 3207 W. Warner Ave., 92704-5314, pg. 133 PV
Brawny Plastics West, 2120 S. Susan St., 92704-4494, pg. 166 PV
Brookfield Homes California Inc., Three Imperial Promenade, Ste. 860, 92707, pg. 228 IT
Brookfield Homes-Orange County, Three Imperial Promenade, Ste. 860, 92707, pg. 228 IT
CDB INFOTEC INC., 6 Hutton Center Dr., 92707, pg. 193 PV
Calavo Foods, Inc., 2530 Red Hill Ave., 92705-5542, pg. 199 PV
CALAVO GROWERS OF CALIFORNIA, 2530 Red Hill Ave., 92705-5542, pg. 199 PV
Cannon Military/Aerospace, 666 E. Dyer Rd., 92702, pg. 859 PB
Cherry Textron, 1224 E. Warner Ave., 92707-0157, pg. 1589 PB
ConAgra Consumer Direct, Inc., 1801-B Parkcourt Place, 92701, pg. 426 PB
Derlan Inc./Santa Ana Facility, 2040 E. Dyer Rd., 92705-5777, pg. 395 IT
THE FIRST AMERICAN FINANCIAL CORPORATION, 114 E. Fifth St., 92701, pg. 624 PB
First American Title Insurance Co., 114 E. Fifth St., 92701, pg. 625 PB
First American Trust Co., 421 N. Main St., 92701, pg. 626 PB
GST Industries, Inc., 3601 W. Central Ave., 92704, pg. 1527 PB
GT BICYCLES, INC., 2011 E. Dyer Rd., 92705, pg. 695 PB
Hillhaven Convalescent Hospital Santa Ana, 2210 E. First St., 92705, pg. 1713 PB
ITT Cannon, 666 E. Dyer Rd., 92705, pg. 859 PB
INGRAM MICRO INC., 1600 E. St. Andrew Pl., 92705, pg. 878 PB
Irvine Scientific Sales Co., Ltd., 2511 Daimler St., 92705-5588, pg. 702 IT
Lam Lighting Systems Inc., 2930 S. Fairview St., 92704-6598, pg. 821 IT
Liqui-Box Film Div., 3117 W. Alpine Ave., 92704, pg. 1000 PB
MAG INNOVISION CO., INC., 2801 S. Yale St., 92704, pg. 694 PV
MICROSEMI CORPORATION, 2830 S. Fairview St., 92704, pg. 1107 PB
Mitsubishi Consumer Electronics America, 2001 E. Carnegie Ave., 92705, pg. 872 IT
Newport Electronics, Inc., 2229 S. Yale St., 92704, pg. 816 PV
North Canadian Power, 1551 N. Tustin Ave., Bentall Executive Ctr., Ste. 900, 92701, pg. 434 IT
The Orange County Register, 625 N. Grand Ave., 92701, pg. 425 PV
Pacific Diversified Capital Company, 3600 W. Segerstrom Ave., 92704, pg. 584 PB
Pacificare Health Systems, 3120 Lake Center Dr., 92704, pg. 1251 PB
PacifiCare Life Assurance, 3120 Lake Center Dr., 92704, pg. 1251 PB
Panel Concepts, L.P., 3001 S. Yale, 92704, pg. 1504 PB
Pricrity Healthcare-W. Coast Division, 3201 MacArthur Blvd., 92704, pg. 229 PB
REC Equipment Corp., 2002 E. McFadden Ave., 92705, pg. 907 PV
THE RADOS COMPANIES, 2002 E. McFadden Ave., 92705, pg. 907 PV
Steve P. Rados, Inc., 2002 E. McFadden Ave., 92705, pg. 907 PV
RHOADES DEVELOPMENT, 1801 C Parkcourt Pl., 92701, pg. 927 PV
SAFECO Select Insurance Services, 2677 N. Main St., Ste. 600, 92705, pg. 1423 PB
Schuller Intl. Inc., 3750 S. Susan St., Ste. 110, 92704-6963, pg. 927 PB
Shurflo Pump Manufacturing Co., 12650 Westminster Ave., 92706-2100, pg. 1767 PB
Standard Concrete, 117 W. Fourth St., 92701, pg. 605 IT
Symix Systems Inc., 6 Hutton Ctr., Ste. 200, 92707, pg. 1547 PB
Terra Tech Labs, Inc., 1920 E. Deere Ave., 92705, pg. 1594 PB
TRANSICO INCORPORATED, 1800 E. Wilshire Ave., 92705, pg. 1630 PB
Transico Inc., Key Pad Div., 1601 E. Chestnut Ave., 92701, pg. 1630 PB
URS Greiner, Inc., 1241 E. Dyer Rd., Ste. 250, 92705, pg. 1658 PB
U.S. DIVERS CO., INC., 3323 W. Warner Ave., 92704, pg. 1125 PV
Universal Management Corp., 2002 E. McFadden Ave., 92705, pg. 907 PV
Vista Lighting, 2200 South Anne St., 92704, pg. 821 IT
Willis Corroon Corp. of Orange County, 1551 N. Tustin Ave., Ste. 1000, 92701, pg. 1506 IT
Winchell's Donut Houses, L.P., 1800 E. 16th St., 92701, pg. 1230 IT
Woodward-Clyde, 2020 E. First St., Ste. 400, 92705, pg. 1657 PB

Santa Barbara

Advanced Computer Communications (ACC), 315 Bollay Dr., 93117, pg. 924 IT
Anarad, Inc., 534 E. Ortega St., 93103-3091, pg. 1563 PB
Beaver Free Corp., 1033 Anacapa St., 93101, pg. 832 PV
BIG DOG HOLDINGS INC., 121 Gray Ave., 93101, pg. 227 PB
Casino Realty Inc., 524 Chapala St., 93101, pg. 563 IT
Casino U.S.A., Inc., 524 Chapala St., 93101, pg. 563 IT
Celite Corporation, 130 Castilian Dr., 93117, pg. 42 PB
Channel Industries, Inc., 839 Ward Dr., 93111, pg. 228 PV
CHANNEL TECHNOLOGIES, INC., 839 Ward Dr., 93111, pg. 228 PV
CIRCON CORPORATION, 6500 Holister Ave., 93117-3019, pg. 373 PB
Circon Video Div., 460 Ward Dr., 93111, pg. 373 PB
Electro Kinetics Div., 402 E. Gutierrez, 93101, pg. 1250 PB
Electro Optical Ind., 859 Ward Dr., 93111, pg. 228 PV
EVANS, HARDY & YOUNG, INC., 829 De la Vina St., 93101-3285, pg. 384 PV
Farmers Insurance Group, 123 W. Padre Ste. E., 93105-3960, pg. 111 IT
SUE FIRESTONE & ASSOC., 4141 State St. 1313, 93110, pg. 406 PV
Frontier Communications of the West, Inc., 135 E. Ortega St., 93101, pg. 684 PB
Granite Construction Inc.-Santa Barbara Div., 5335 Debbie Ln., 93111, pg. 759 PB
Howden Fluid Systems, 72 Santa Felicia, 93117, pg. 1045 PB
International Transducer Corporation, 869 Ward Dr., 93111, pg. 228 PV
Invest West Financial Corporation, 1033 Anacapa St., 93101, pg. 832 PV
Arthur D. Little, Inc., Ste. 2A, 3916 State St., 93105-3137, pg. 670 PV
McGhan Medical Corporation, 700 Ward Dr. S., 93111, pg. 873 PB
MENTOR CORPORATION, 5425 Hollister Ave., 93111, pg. 1086 PB
Mentor H/S Inc., 5425 Hollister, 93111, pg. 1086 PB
Mentor Opthalmics, Inc., 5425 Hollister, 93111, pg. 1086 PB
Mentor Urology, Inc., 5425 Hollister Ave., 93111, pg. 1086 PB
Mission Linen Supply, 2936 De La Vina St., 93105, pg. 753 PV
Northern Trust Bank of California, N.A., 206 E. Anapamu St., 93101, pg. 1196 PB
Pacifica Hotel Company, 1033 Anacapa St., 93101, pg. 832 PV
PACIFICA REAL ESTATE GROUP, 1033 Anacapa St., 93101, pg. 832 PV
SMS-Santa Barbara, 4231 State St., 93110, pg. 1463 PB
Santa Barbara News-Press, 715 Anacapa St., 93101, pg. 1175 PB
Sloan Technology, 602 E. Montecito St., 93103, pg. 1711 PB
Sonatech, Inc., 879 Ward Dr., 93111, pg. 229 PV
JACOB STERN & SONS, INC., 1464 E. Valley Rd., 93108, pg. 1041 PV
TENET HEALTHCARE CORPORATION, 3820 State St., 93105, pg. 1576 PB
THE TERRITORY AHEAD, 419 State St., 93101, pg. 1077 PV
Woodward-Clyde, 130 Robin Hill Rd., Ste. 100, 93116, pg. 1657 PB
World Minerals Inc., 130 Castilian Dr., 93117, pg. 42 PB

Santa Clara

ACCPAC International, 2525 Augustine Dr., 95054, pg. 420 PB
ACTIVE SOFTWARE, INC., 325 5-1 Scott Blvd., 95054, pg. 15 PV
Analog Devices, 1500 Space Park Dr., 95052, pg. 108 PB
Analog Devices, Santa Clara, 1550 Space Park Dr., 95052, pg. 108 PB
Applied Materials Asia Pacific, Ltd., 2350 Mission College Blvd., #850, 95054, pg. 123 PB
APPLIED MATERIALS, INC., 3050 Bowers Ave., 95054, pg. 123 PB
BAY NETWORKS, INC., 4401 Great America Pky., 95054-8185, pg. 196 PB
Cascade Design Automation, 2041 Mission College Blvd., Ste. #160, 95054-1553, pg. 1000 IT
CELERITEK, INC., 3236 Scott Blvd., 95054, pg. 319 PB
Claris Corporation, 5201 Patrick Henry Dr., 95054, pg. 121 PB
COHERENT, INC., 5100 Patrick Henry Dr., 95056, pg. 395 PB
Coherent, Inc.-Laser Group, 5100 Patrick Henry Dr., 95054, pg. 395 PB
DRS Precision Echo, Inc., 3105 Patrick Henry Dr., 95054, pg. 474 PB
Daewoo International America Corp. - Santa Clara, 4701 Patrick Henry Dr. #501, 95054, pg. 357 IT
Data I/O (Sales & Service), 2620 Augustine Dr., Ste. 245, 95054, pg. 486 PB
Data Systems Group, 3105 Patrick Henry Dr., 95054, pg. 474 PB
Diasonics Credit Corporation, 2860 De La Cruz Blvd., 95050-2619, pg. 644 IT
Diasonics Ultra Sound, Inc., 2860 De la Cruz Blvd., 95050, pg. 644 IT
Disco Hi-Tec America Inc., 3395 Woodward Ave., 95054, pg. 413 IT
DistribuPro, Inc., 2525 Augustine Dr., Ste. 201, 95054, pg. 420 PB
Downey Savings & Loan Association, F.A., Santa Clara Branch, 2730 Homestead Rd., Ste. 19, 95051, pg. 526 PB
Du Pont Photomasks, 2920 Coronado, 95054-3203, pg. 531 PB
Electroglas, 3141 Coronado Dr., 95054, pg. 727 PB
FRESH CHOICE, INC., 2901 Tasman Dr., Ste. 109, 95054, pg. 682 PB
Fujitsu Personal Systems, Inc., 5200 Patrick Henry Dr., 95054, pg. 526 IT
Fujitsu Systems Business of America, Inc., 5200 Patrick Henry Dr., 95054, pg. 526 IT
Funai Electric Silicon Valley, 3000 Scott Blvd., Ste. 111, 95054, pg. 530 IT
Furukawa Electric Technologies Inc. (FET), 900 Lafayette St., Ste. 401, 95050, pg. 530 IT
Greylands Business Park, Phase 2, c/o McCandless Companies, 3945 Freedom Cir., Ste. 1000, 95054, pg. 361 PB
Guidant Corporation-Vascular Intervention Group, 3200 Lakeside Dr., P.O. Box 58167, 95052-8167, pg. 768 PB
Hadco Corporation, 445 El Camino Real, 95050, pg. 773 PB
Hewlett-Packard Company, 3003 Scott Blvd., 95054, pg. 813 PB
Hitachi Chemical Co. America Ltd., 1333 Lawrence Expwy., Ste. 212, 95051, pg. 622 IT
Hitachi Data Systems Corporation, 750 Central Expwy., 95050, pg. 622 IT
InfoCorp, 2880 Lakeside Dr., Ste. 300, 95056, pg. 1276 IT
INTEGRATED DEVICE TECHNOLOGY, INC., 2975 Stender Way, 95054, pg. 884 PB
INTEL CORPORATION, 2200 Mission College Blvd., 95052, pg. 886 PB
JVC Information Products Company of America, 2903 Bunker Hill Lane, Ste. 102, 95054, pg. 847 IT
JVC Laboratory of America, 2903 Bunker Hill Lane, Ste.102, 95054, pg. 847 IT
Kubota Corp.-Silicon Valley Office, 2880 Lakeside Dr., Ste. 131, 95051, pg. 762 IT
Kulicke & Soffa U.S. Western Regional Office, 2210 Martin Ave., 95050, pg. 969 PB
Lambda Advanced Analog, 2270 Martin Ave., 95050, pg. 1241 IT
Larscom Inc., 4600 Patrick Henry Dr., 95054, pg. 710 IT
Larse Corporation, 4600 Patrick Henry Dr., 95054, pg. 710 IT
Litton Solid State, 3251 Olcott St., 95054-3095, pg. 1003 PB
Marubeni International Electronics Corp., 3285 Scott Blvd., 95054, pg. 845 IT
Materials Research Corp., Unit 16, Marriott Center, 4701 Patrick Henry Dr., 95054, pg. 1283 IT
Matra Design Semiconductor Corp., 2840 San Thomas Expwy., Ste. 100, 95051, pg. 795 IT
Meridian Communications Systems Div., 2305 Mission College Blvd., 95054, pg. 970 IT
Micron Quantum Devices, Inc., 2338 Walsh Ave., 95051, pg. 1105 PB
NEC Electronics Inc., P.O. Box 58062, 2880 Scott Blvd., 95052-8062, pg. 900 IT
NATIONAL SEMICONDUCTOR CORPORATION, 2900 Semiconductor Dr., 95052, pg. 1159 PB
NETWORK ASSOCIATES, INC., 2805 Bowers Ave., 95051-0963, pg. 1168 PB
Numetrix Inc., 5201 Great America Pkwy., Ste. 320, 95054, pg. 990 IT
OMRON Advanced Systems, Inc., 3945 Freedom Cir., Ste. 410, 95054, pg. 1005 IT

Geographic Index-U.S.

PB - *U.S. Public Companies Volume*
PV - *U.S. Private Companies Volume*
IT - *International Public & Private Companies Volume*

OMRON Office Automation Products, Inc., 3945 Freedom Cir., Ste. 700, 95054, pg. 1005   **IT**
On Command Video, 3301 Olcott St., 95054, pg. 138   **PB**
Oriental Motor U.S.A. Corp., 1600 Wyatt Dr., Ste. Two, 95054, pg. 1008   **IT**
PDM Steel Service Center-Santa Clara, 3500 Bassett St., 95054, pg. 1305   **PB**
Parallax Graphics, Inc., 2500 Condensa St., 95051, pg. 539   **PB**
Potpourri (Harte-Hanks Northern California CDM, Inc.), 1350 Duane Ave., 95054, pg. 794   **PB**
Prima International, 3350 Scott Blvd., Bldg. 7, 95054, pg. 870   **PB**
Quantronix Corp., 2310 J Walsh Ave., 95050, pg. 599   **PB**
S3 INCORPORATED, P.O. Box 58058, 2831 Mission College Blvd., 95052-8058, pg. 1415   **PB**
SAE ENGINEERING, INC., 282 Brokaw Rd., 95050, pg. 955   **PV**
Semitec, Inc., 3025 Stender Way, 95054, pg. 969   **PB**
Sequent Computer Systems, Inc., 2350 Mission College Blvd., Ste. 600, 95054, pg. 1459   **IT**
Siemens Business Communication Systems, Inc., 4900 Old Ironsides Dr., 95054, pg. 1245   **IT**
Signal Science, 2985 Kaifer Rd., 95051, pg. 46   **IT**
Siliconix, P.O. Box 54951, 95056-0951, pg. 367   **IT**
Sumitomo Chemical America, Inc.-Santa Clara, 2350 Mission College Blvd., Ste. 360, 95054, pg. 1311   **IT**
Synergy Computer Graphics Corporation, 2945 Oakmead Village Ct., 95051, pg. 940   **PV**
TMP Worldwide/Recruitment Division, 3032 Bunker Hill Ln., 95054, pg. 1065   **PV**
Telos Consulting Services, 3333 Bowers Ave., Ste. 151, 95054, pg. 1573   **PB**
Tempress, 3111 Coronado Dr., 95051, pg. 727   **PB**
3COM CORPORATION, 5400 Bayfront Plaza, 95052-8145, pg. 1603   **PB**
Toppan Electronics (U.S.A.), Inc., 3032 Bunker Hill Ln., Ste. 108, 95054, pg. 1399   **IT**
TRUEVISION, INC., 2500 Walsh Ave., 95051, pg. 1642   **PB**
UB Networks, 3990 Freedom Circle, 95054, pg. 924   **PB**
Viewlogic Systems, Inc., The Regency Plaza, 2350 Mission College Blvd., Ste. 1000, 95024, pg. 1548   **PB**
West Tech Expo Corp., 4701 Patrick Henry Dr., 95054, pg. 326   **PB**
Western Digital Media Inc., 2119 Tassman Dr., 95054, pg. 1758   **PB**
Westinghouse Commercial Security, 5452 Betsy Ross Dr., 95054, pg. 273   **PB**
Whittaker Communications, Inc., 2200 Lausen Rd., 93103, pg. 1767   **PB**
Wyle Electronics-Santa Clara, 3000 Bowers Ave., 95051, pg. 1458   **PB**
Wyle Electronics-Research Div., 3000 Bowers Ave., 95051, pg. 1457   **IT**
YAHOO!, INC., 3400 Central Expwy., Ste. 201, 95051, pg. 1787   **PB**

Santa Clarita

JOHN PAUL MITCHELL SYSTEMS, P.O. Box 10597, 264555 Golden Valley Rd., 91530, pg. 753   **PV**

Santa Cruz

Computer & Mobile Systems, 345 Encinal St., 95060, pg. 1308   **PB**
Giro Sports Design, Inc., 380 Encinal St., 95060, pg. 207   **PB**
HARMONY FOODS CORPORATION, 2200 Delaware Ave., 95060, pg. 503   **PV**
Hillhaven Extended Care, 1115 Capitola Rd., 95062, pg. 1713   **PB**
PLANTRONICS INC., 337 Encinal St., 95061, pg. 1308   **PB**
SALZ LEATHERS, INC., P.O. Box 1840, 95061, pg. 963   **PV**
Simian Company, Inc., 298 Harvey West Blvd., 95060, pg. 1357   **PB**
Speedling Incorporated, 56 Peckam Rd., 95076, pg. 1024   **PB**

Santa Fe Springs

A & A Associates, 12118 Bloomfield, 90670, pg. 1206   **PV**
Alimak Elevator Company, 11912 Rivera Rd., 90670, pg. 34   **PV**
Alloy Tool Steel Inc., 13525 E. Freeway Dr., 90670, pg. 947   **IT**
CHEMCENTRAL/Los Angeles, 13900 S. Carmenita Rd., 90670-4997, pg. 232   **PV**
Chemifax, 11641 Pike St., 90670, pg. 774   **PV**
Day-Lee Foods Inc., 13055 E. Molette St., 90670, pg. 936   **IT**
Dayton Superior Corp., 9415 S. Sorenson Ave., 90670, pg. 932   **PV**
Jon Donaire Desserts, Inc., 942 Sorenson Ave., 90670, pg. 1527   **PB**
FEDCO, INC., 9300 Santa Fe Springs Rd., 90670, pg. 398   **PV**
Frigid Coil West, 13711 Freeway Dr., 90670, pg. 1789   **PB**
Golden West Refining Company, 13534 E. Foster Rd., 90670, pg. 1084   **PV**
Grabner Pacific Co., 10330 Pioneer Blvd., Ste. 170, 90670-3795, pg. 165   **PV**
Griffin Financial Services, 10100 Pioneer Ave., Ste. 1000, 90670, pg. 29   **PB**
M.A. Hanna Rubber Compounding, Wakeman Blvd., 90670, pg. 781   **PB**

Juki Electronics Corp., 14518 Best Ave., 90670, pg. 716   **IT**
Juki Union Special, Inc.-California Office, 14518 Best Ave., 90670, pg. 716   **IT**
LeFebure, Area West, 9945 Pioneer Blvd., 90670, pg. 387   **IT**
Maruichi American Corp., 11529 S. Greenstone, 90670, pg. 947   **IT**
Metalcenter, Inc., 12034 Greenstone Ave., 90670, pg. 1375   **IT**
Morton Chemical Div., 11733 E. Slauson Ave., 90670, pg. 1135   **IT**
National Computer Supplies, 13827 Carmenita Rd., 90670, pg. 927   **PV**
Norgren/Los Angeles, 13151 Florence Ave., 90670, pg. 647   **IT**
NuArc Western Div., 12130 Mora Dr., Unit # 1, 90670, pg. 809   **PV**
PIPE FABRICATING & SUPPLY COMPANY, 9703 S. Norwalk Blvd., 90670, pg. 867   **PV**
PYRO Engineering Division, 14801 S. Anson Ave., 90670, pg. 924   **PV**
REINHOLD INDUSTRIES INC., 12827 E. Imperial Hwy., 90670, pg. 920   **PV**
RICCOBON & COMPANY, INC., 13827 Carmenita Rd., 90670, pg. 927   **PV**
Salem Carpet Mills, 14911 Valleyview St., 90620, pg. 1464   **PV**
Santa Fe Springs Holding Company, 13100 Arctic Cir., 90670, pg. 526   **PV**
Spicers Paper, 12310 E. Slasson Ave., 90670, pg. 72   **IT**
Tatch-A-Cleat Products, 9830 Norwalk Blvd. #140, 90670, pg. 413   **PV**
THRIFTY OIL CO., 13534 E. Foster Rd., 90670, pg. 1084   **PV**
Transilwrap Company, Inc., 11875 Burke St., 90670, pg. 1097   **PV**
TRIANGLE DISTRIBUTING COMPANY, 12065 E. Pike St., 90670, pg. 1101   **PV**
Tuftex, 15305 Valley View Dr., 90670, pg. 900   **PV**
Turbine Engine Components Textron, 8839 S. Pioneer Blvd., 90670, pg. 1588   **PB**
Uddeholm Corporation, 9331 Santa Fe Springs Rd., 90670, pg. 1472   **IT**
Votaw Precision Technologies, 13153 Lakeland Rd., 90670, pg. 605   **PV**
WGM Eastman, P.O. Box 3704, 12805 Busch Place, 94080, pg. 551   **PB**
Williams Scotsman Group, Inc., 11811 Greenstone Ave., 90670, pg. 977   **PV**
Winkler Forming, P.O. Box 2369, 90670, pg. 827   **PV**

Santa Margarita

Lockheed Martin Aeronutronic, 29947 Avenidae Las Banderas Rancho, 92688-7004, pg. 1008   **PB**

Santa Maria

DEN-MAT CORPORATION, 2727 Skyway Dr., 93455, pg. 324   **PV**
Higgins Santa Maria, 939 W. Boone, 93454, pg. 527   **PV**
QUINTRON SYSTEMS, INC., 2105 S. Blosser, 93454, pg. 901   **PV**
Santa Maria Times, P.O. Box 400, 93455, pg. 1343   **PB**
Seagate Tape Technologies, Inc., 1290 W. McCoy Ln., 93455, pg. 1449   **PB**
Zellerbach Division, 327 E. Plaza Dr., Ste. 3E, 93454, pg. 1076   **PB**

Santa Monica

A-MARK FINANCIAL, 100 Wilshire Blvd., 3rd Fl., 90401, pg. 2   **PV**
ACTIVISION, 3100 Ocean Park Blvd., 90405-3032, pg. 17   **PB**
ALL AMERICAN COMMUNICATIONS, INC., 808 Wilshire Blvd., 90401-1810, pg. 41   **PB**
AMERICAN GOLF CORPORATION, 2951 28th St., 90405, pg. 55   **PV**
BET West Coast Media/Affiliate Sales & BET Action Pay Per View, 2425 W. Olympic Blvd., Ste. 4050, 90404, pg. 235   **PB**
Bel-Air Patrol, 3220 Nebraska Ave., 90404, pg. 245   **PB**
Benchmark Contractors, Inc., 2901 28th St., 90405, pg. 761   **PV**
BOMAINE CORPORATION, 2716 Ocean Park Blvd., Ste. 1065, 90405, pg. 155   **PB**
CANDLE CORPORATION, 2425 Olympic Blvd., 90404, pg. 204   **PV**
Canon Communications, 3340 Ocean Pk. Blvd. Ste. 1000, 90405-3207, pg. 261   **PV**
The Cinram POP DVD Centre, 730 Arizona Ave., 90401, pg. 293   **IT**
Citizen America Corp., 2450 Broadway, Ste. 600, 90404-3060, pg. 294   **IT**
Climatemaster Corp., 2314 Michigan Ave., 90404, pg. 970   **PV**
Dance France Ltd., 2503 Main St., 90405, pg. 483   **PB**
Dentsu USA-Los Angeles, 120 Broadway, Ste. 260, 90401, pg. 393   **IT**
THE DEUTSCH COMPANY, 2444 Wilshire Blvd., Ste. 600, 90403, pg. 328   **PV**
Deutsch LA, 1315 Third St. Promenade, 90401, pg. 328   **PV**
Dext Company, 233 Wilshire Blvd., Ste. 790, 90401, pg. 1444   **PB**
Dext Company of AZ, 233 Wilshire Blvd., Ste. 310, 90401, pg. 1444   **PB**

First Federal Bank of California, FSB, 401 Wilshire Blvd., 90401-1490, pg. 646   **PB**
Firstcorp, 3250 Ocean Park Blvd., Ste. 325, 90405, pg. 408   **PV**
FIRSTFED FINANCIAL CORP., 401 Wilshire Blvd., 90401-1490, pg. 645   **PB**
FOCUS MEDIA, 2401 Colorado Ave., Ste. 120, 90404, pg. 415   **PV**
Fremont Financial Corporation, 2020 Santa Monica Blvd., Ste. 600, 90404, pg. 681   **PV**
FREMONT GENERAL CORPORATION, 2020 Santa Monica Blvd., Ste. 600, 90404-2208, pg. 681   **PB**
Fremont Indemnity Co./Medical Professional Liab. Div., 2020 Santa Monica Blvd., Ste. 600, 90404, pg. 681
Fremont Indemnity Corp., 2020 Santa Monica Blvd., Ste. 500, 90404, pg. 681   **PB**
Fremont Premium Finance Corp., 2020 Santa Monica Blvd., Ste. 410, 90404, pg. 681   **PV**
G & H Technology, Inc., 1649 17th St., 90404, pg. 75   **PB**
Giorgio Beverly Hills, 2400 Broadway, Ste. 400, 90404, pg. 1331   **PV**
GROUND ZERO, 1558 10th St., 90401, pg. 484   **PV**
Guthy-Renker Corp., 3340 Ocean Park Blvd., Ste. 300, 90405, pg. 488   **PV**
Harvey Titanium Ltd., 1330 Colorado Ave., 90404, pg. 1100   **PV**
Intervisual Communications Inc., 1452 2nd St., pg. 518   **PB**
KENNEDY-WILSON, INC., 530 Wilshire Blvd., Ste. 101, 90401, pg. 951   **PB**
KOVEL KRESSER & PARTNERS, 2501 Colorado Ave., 2nd Fl., 90404-3585, pg. 634   **PV**
L.A. Gear California, Inc., 2850 Ocean Park Blvd., 90405, pg. 969   **PB**
L.A. GEAR, INC., 2850 Ocean Park Blvd., 90405, pg. 969   **PB**
Lacos Land Company, 233 Wilshire Blvd., Suite 310, 90401, pg. 1444   **PV**
The Leap Partnership, 3000 W. Olympic Blvd #1412, 90404, pg. 655   **PV**
Lear Astronics Corp., 3400 Airport Ave., 90406, pg. 544   **IT**
MGM/UA Distribution Co., 2500 Broadway St., 90404, pg. 1102   **PB**
MGM/UA Home Entertainment, Inc., 2500 Broadway, 90404, pg. 1102   **PB**
MGM/UA Licensing & Merchandising, 2500 Broadway, 90404, pg. 1102   **PB**
MGM/UA Music, 2500 Broadway, 90404, pg. 1102   **PB**
MGM/UA Telecommunications Group, 2500 Broadway, 90404, pg. 1102   **PB**
MRI Los Angeles, 100 Wilshire Blvd., 90401, pg. 727   **PV**
THE MACERICH COMPANY, 401 Wilshire Blvd., Ste. 700, 90401, pg. 1030   **PB**
Marinello Schools of Beauty, 233 Wilshire Blvd., Ste. 790, 90401, pg. 1444   **PB**
Master Distributors, 1301 Olympic Blvd., 90404, pg. 714   **PV**
MASTER INTERNATIONAL CORP., 1301 Olympic Blvd., 90404, pg. 713   **PV**
Media Marketing Technologies, Inc., 100 Wilshire Blvd., Ste. 800, 90401, pg. 331   **PB**
Merat Optical Communications, 1800 Stewart St., 90404, pg. 1233   **PV**
METRO-GOLDWYN-MAYER INC., 2500 Broadway St., 90404-3061, pg. 1101   **PB**
Metro-Goldwyn-Mayer Pictures, Inc., 2500 Broadway, 90404, pg. 1102   **PB**
MGM Worldwide Television, Group., 2500 Broadway, 90404, pg. 1102   **PB**
MORLEY BUILDERS, 2901 28th St., Ste. 100, 90405, pg. 761   **PV**
Morley Construction Co., 2901 28th St., 90405, pg. 761   **PV**
The New Yorker - California, 3201 Wilshire Boulevard, 90403-2337, pg. 796   **PV**
OSICOM TECHNOLOGIES INC., 2800 28th Ave., Ste. 100, 90405, pg. 1233   **PB**
The Outlook, 1920 Colorado Ave., 90406, pg. 275   **PV**
PALISADES MEDIA GROUP, INC., 1620 26th St., Ste. 2050 N., 90404, pg. 834   **PV**
Penny & Giles Aerospace Inc., Ste. 1005, 2716 Ocean Park Blvd., 90405, pg. 208   **IT**
Penny & Giles Inc., 2716 Ocean Park Blvd., Ste. 1005, 90405, pg. 208   **IT**
Protellicos Software Development Laboratory, 429 Santa Monica Blvd., Ste. 460, 90401, pg. 1309   **PB**
PSOMAS & ASSOCIATES, 3420 Ocean Park Blvd., 90405, pg. 893   **PV**
RP alpha, 201 Santa Monica Blvd., 90401, pg. 950   **PV**
RALEIGH ENTERPRISES, INC., 100 Wilshire Blvd., 8th Fl., 90401, pg. 907   **PV**
RAND, 1700 Main St., 90401, pg. 908   **PV**
Reader's Digest, 2400 Broadway Ave., Ste. 260, 90404, pg. 1367   **PB**
Rodeo Drive Properties, Inc., 1250 Sixth St., Ste. 102, 90401, pg. 1349   **IT**
RUBIN POSTAER & ASSOCIATES, 1333 2nd St., 90401, pg. 949   **PV**
Rubin Postaer & Associates, 201 Santa Monica Blvd., 90401, pg. 950   **PV**
SF Broadcasting Companies, 2425 Olympic Blvd., 90404, pg. 1685   **PB**
Santa Monica Bank, 1251 Fourth St., 90401, pg. 1757   **PB**
SANTA MONICA FORD COMPANY, 1230 Santa Monica Blvd., 90404, pg. 965   **PV**
Santa Monica Place, 395 Santa Monica Pl., 90401, pg. 1408   **PB**
Scope Energy Resources, Inc., 233 Wilshire Blvd., 90401, pg. 1444   **PB**
SCOPE INDUSTRIES, 233 Wilshire Blvd., Ste. 310, 90401, pg. 1444   **PB**

PB - *U.S. Public Companies Volume*
PV - *U.S. Private Companies Volume*
IT - *International Public & Private Companies Volume*

Geographic Index-U.S.

Scope Products, Inc., 233 Wilshire Blvd., Suite 310, 90401, pg. 1444 **PB**
Scope Properties, Inc., 233 Wilshire Blvd., Suite 310, 90401, pg. 1444 **PB**
Scotti Brothers Entertainment Industries, 2114 Pico Blvd., 90405, pg. 41 **PB**
Scripps Howard Productions, 2425 Olympic Blvd., Ste. 5005, 90404, pg. 1448 **PB**
Seaside Financial Corporation, 401 Wilshire Blvd., 90401-1490, pg. 646 **PB**
SHAPCO, INC., 1666 20th St., Ste. 100, 90404, pg. 989 **PV**
SNYDER-DIAMOND, 1399 Olympic Blvd., 90404, pg. 1011 **PV**
Sony Music Entertainment, 2100 Colorado Ave., 90404-3504, pg. 1284 **IT**
STORM PRODUCTS COMPANY, INC., 429 Santa Monica Blvd., 95050, pg. 1045 **PV**
Takashimaya (California), Inc., 1250 Sixth St., Ste. 102, 90401, pg. 1349 **PB**
TECHNOLOGY TRANSFER INSTITUTE, 741 10th St., 90402, pg. 1072 **PV**
Todd-AO Hollywood Digital West, 1661 Lincoln Blvd., 90405, pg. 1619 **PB**
Todd-AO Studios West, Bldg. One, 3000 W. Olympic Blvd., 90404, pg. 1619 **PB**
Transaction Technology Inc., 3100 Ocean Park Blvd., 90405, pg. 377 **PB**
TRIMARK HOLDINGS, INC., 2644 30th St., 90405-3009, pg. 1638 **PB**
Trimark Interactive, 2644 30th St., 90405-3009, pg. 1638 **PB**
Trimark Pictures, 2644 30th St., 90405-3009, pg. 1638 **PB**
Trimark Television, 2644 30th St., 90405-3009, pg. 1638 **PB**
United Artists Pictures, Inc., 2500 Broadway, 90404, pg. 1102 **PB**
WILLIAMS WORLDWIDE, 3130 Wilshire Blvd., 4th Fl., 90403, pg. 1179 **PV**

Santa Paula

Santa Paula Healthcare, 220 W. Main St., 93060, pg. 1714 **PB**
Twin Pines Healthcare, 250 March St., 93060, pg. 1715 **PB**
Weatherford US Inc., 201 S. Hallock Dr., 93060, pg. 1749 **PB**

Santa Rosa

BIW Cable Systems-Connector Systems Div., 500 Tesconi Circle, 95401, pg. 417 **IT**
Custodis-Ecodyne, P.O. Box 1267, 95402, pg. 29 **PB**
EXCHANGE BANK, 545 Fourth St., 95402, pg. 599 **PB**
Flex Products, Inc., 1402 Mariner Way, 95407-7370, pg. 1227 **PB**
Hewlett-Packard Company, 818 Mendocino Ave., Ste. A, 95404, pg. 813 **PB**
Komag Material Technology Inc., 93 Stony Circle, 95401, pg. 966 **PB**
Lemo U.S.A. Inc., 335 Tesconi Cir., 95406, pg. 806 **IT**
Milk Products Holdings (North America) Inc., 3645 Westwind Blvd., 95403, pg. 923 **IT**
OPTICAL COATING LABORATORY, INC., 2789 Northpoint Pkwy., 95407-7397, pg. 1227 **PB**
Polaroid MAG Media, 3636 N. Laughlin Rd., 95403-1027, pg. 1314 **PB**
The Press Democrat, 427 Mendocino Ave., 95401, pg. 1175 **PB**
SANTA ROSA STEEL FORMING, INC., 1219 Briggs Ave., 95401, pg. 965 **PV**
Weigh-Tronix, 2320 Airport Blvd., 95403, pg. 1299 **IT**

Santee

Bird-Katema, 10769 Woodside Ave., Ste. 207, 92071, pg. 166 **PB**
County Tool & Abrasive, 9263 Abraham Way, 92071, pg. 177 **PV**
Toyota Lift, Inc., 11446 Woodside Ave., N., 92071, pg. 1412 **IT**

Saticoy

Petoseed Co., 1905 Lirio, 93007, pg. 188 **PV**

Saugus

Allou Personal Care Corp., 25655 Springbrook Ave., #6, 91350, pg. 55 **PB**
BLUE CROSS LABORATORIES, 26411 N. Golden Valley Rd., 91350, pg. 152 **PB**
KEYSOR CENTURY CORPORATION, 26000 Springbrook Ave., 91350, pg. 618 **PV**

Sausalito

Essex Polytech, Inc., 3030 Bridgeway, 94965, pg. 523 **PB**
Nokia Display Products Inc., 1505 Bridgeway Blvd., Ste. 128, 94965, pg. 954 **IT**
OMEGA PERFORMANCE GROUP, Three Harbor Dr., Ste. 200, 94965, pg. 816 **PV**

Scotia

The Pacific Lumber Company, P.O. Box 37, 125 Main St., 95565, pg. 1062 **PB**

Scotts Valley

BORLAND INTERNATIONAL, INC., 100 Borland Way, 95066, pg. 246 **PB**
Borland Latin America, 100 Borland Way, 95066, pg. 246 **PB**
Kevex X-Ray, 320 El Pueblo Rd., 95066, pg. 1594 **PB**
Oxford Instruments-X-Ray Technology Group, 275 Technology Cir., 95066, pg. 1018 **IT**
SEAGATE TECHNOLOGY INC., 920 Disc Dr., 95066, pg. 1449 **PB**
Semiconductor Equipment Group, 440 Kings Village Rd., 95066, pg. 1745 **PB**

Seal Beach

Boeing North America, North American Aircraft Division, 2600 Westminster Blvd., 90740, pg. 241 **PB**
Boeing North America, Systems Development Center, 2800 Westminster Blvd., 90740, pg. 241 **PB**
Boeing North American, 2201 Seal Beach Blvd., 90740-3250, pg. 241 **PB**
Masco Building Products Corp., 3030 Ranch Pkwy. Ste. 400, 90740-2752, pg. 1053 **PB**
NI Industries, Inc., 3030 Old Ranch Pkwy., Ste. 400, 90740-2752, pg. 1054 **PB**
SMS-Los Angeles, 3010 Old Ranch Pkwy., Ste. 450, 90740, pg. 1463 **PB**

Sebastopol

HearthSong, Inc., 400 Morris St., 95473, pg. 421 **PV**
VACU-DRY COMPANY, 7765 Healdsburg Ave., 95472, pg. 1704 **PV**
Vacu-Dry Company Plant, Hwy. 116 N., 2064 Gravenstein Hwy., 95472, pg. 1704 **PB**

Selma

Harris Ranch Beef Co., P.O. Box 220, 93662, pg. 505 **PV**
UP-FIGHT, INC., 1775 Park St., 93662, pg. 1128 **PV**

Sherman Oaks

BCIS Services, Inc., 15301 Ventura Blvd., 91403, pg. 175 **PV**
Carriage Inn, 5525 Seplvida Blvd., 91411, pg. 96 **PV**
Fabricland, Inc., 13400 Riverside Dr., 91352, pg. 842 **PB**
FRUIT GROWERS SUPPLY CO., 14130 Riverside Dr., 91423, pg. 430 **PV**
GORES TECHNOLOGY GROUP, 15260 Ventura Blvd., Ste. 1000, 91403, pg. 465 **PV**
HOUSE OF FABRICS, INC., 13400 Riverside Dr., 91423, pg. 842 **PB**
Outdoor Services, 15315 Magnolia Blvd., Ste. 301, 91403, pg. 1166 **PV**
So Fro Fabrics, Inc., 13400 Riverside Dr., 91423, pg. 842 **PB**
SUNKIST GROWERS, INC., 14130 Riverside Dr., 91423-2392, pg. 1052 **PV**

Signal Hill

Almega Corporation-CA, 2301 E. 28th St., Ste. 307, 90806, pg. 546 **PV**
Norwest Financial Coast, Inc., 2525 Cherry Ave., Ste. 110, 90806, pg. 1202 **PV**
Signal Hill Service Center, 2248 Obispo Ave., Ste. 210, 90806, pg. 1180 **PV**

Simi Valley

BUGLE BOY INDUSTRIES, INC., 2900 Madera Rd., 93065, pg. 179 **PV**
Cardkey Systems, Inc., 1757 Tapo Canyon Rd., 93065, pg. 105 **PV**
CERWIN VEGA, INC., 555 E. Easy St., 93065, pg. 227 **PV**
Dataproducts Corporation, 1757 Tapo Canyon Rd., 93063, pg. 620 **IT**
Dragon International, 2900 Madera Rd., 93065, pg. 179 **PV**
Gibraltar Savings, 2800 N. Madera Rd., 93065, pg. 181 **PB**
Guardian Products, Inc., 4175 Guardian St., 93063, pg. 1535 **PV**
Hirose Electric (U.S.A.), Inc., 2688 West Hills Ct., 93065-6235, pg. 620 **IT**
Knurr USA, Inc., 1890 N. Voyager Ave., 93063, pg. 739 **IT**
MICOM Communications Corp., 4100 Los Angeles Ave., 93063, pg. 969 **PB**
N-Lynx Andrew, 2267 Agate Ct., 93065, pg. 112 **IT**
Seagate Technology Simi Valley, 5898 Condor Dr., 93021, pg. 1450 **PB**
SunMed Finance Inc., P.O. Box 3559, 93093-3559, pg. 1536 **PV**
Sunrise Medical, Inc., Intl. Sales Dept., 4175 Guardian St., 93063, pg. 1536 **PB**
View Engineering, 1650 N. Voyager Ave., 93063, pg. 72 **PV**
WHITTAKER CORPORATION, 1955 N. Surveyor Ave., 93063-3386, pg. 1766 **PB**
Whittaker Electronic Systems, P.O. Box 8000, 1785 Voyager Ave., 93063, pg. 1767 **PB**

Solana Beach

ROBINHOOD HOMES, INC., 265 Santa Helena, #100, 92075, pg. 936 **PV**
Stacey's/J. K. Gill Retail Stores, 990 Highland Dr., Ste. 100, 92075-2472, pg. 170 **PV**

Sonoma

Buena Vista Winery, 27000 Ramal Rd., 95476, pg. 1083 **IT**
GLEN ELLEN WINERY, 21468 Eighth St. E., 95476, pg. 455 **PV**
Nicholas Turkey Breeding Farms, 19449 Riverside Dr., 95476, pg. 202 **IT**
Piper Jaffray Inc., 552 Broadway St., 95476, pg. 1303 **PB**
Racke USA, 27000 Ramal Rd., 95476, pg. 1083 **IT**
Sears Point Raceway, Hwys. 37 & 121, 95476, pg. 1498 **PB**
SONOMA MISSION INN & SPA, 18140 Sonoma Hwy., 95416, pg. 1014 **PV**
SONOMA VALLEY BANK, 202 W. Napa St., 95476, pg. 1487 **PB**
Robert Stemmler Winery, 27000 Ramal Rd., 95476, pg. 1083 **IT**

Sonora

Stockton Savings Bank-Sonora, 13755-A Mono Way, 95370, pg. 1575 **PB**

South El Monte

Amtech Lighting Services Co., 9637 Remer St., 91733, pg. 2 **PB**
BURKE ENGINEERING COMPANY, 9700 Factorial Way, 91733, pg. 183 **PV**
Integrated Grain & Milling, 2000 N. Tyler Ave., 91733, pg. 1203 **PV**
Jarvis (West), 2300 Merced Ave., 91733, pg. 1506 **PB**
Lee Consumer Products, 1444 Santa Anita Ave., 91733, pg. 984 **PB**
Lee Dental & Orthodontics Div., 1444 Santa Anita Ave., 91733, pg. 984 **PB**
LEE PHARMACEUTICALS, 1444 Santa Anita Ave., 91733, pg. 984 **PB**
Stockton Further Processing, 2000 N. Tyler Ave., 91733, pg. 1203 **PV**
Taylor-Jett Div., 2075 S. Peck Rd., 91733, pg. 1682 **PB**
ZACKY FARMS, INC., 2000 N. Tyler Ave., 91733, pg. 1203 **PV**
Zacky Foods, 2000 N. Tyler Ave., 91733, pg. 1203 **PV**

South Gate

Artistic Brass Div., 4100 Ardmore Ave., 90280, pg. 1054 **PB**
Flewelling Div., 12411 Industrial Ave., Box 2247, 90280, pg. 353 **PB**
International California Glass Corp., 4232 Santa Ana St., 90280, pg. 895 **PB**
International Window Corp., 5625 E. Firestone Blvd., 90280, pg. 895 **PB**
ROYAL RUBBER & MANUFACTURING CO., 5951 E. Firestone Blvd., 90280, pg. 949 **PV**
SCHULTZ STEEL COMPANY, 5321 Firestone Blvd., 90280, pg. 973 **PV**
Sealy Mattress Company - Southgate, 436 E. Firestone Blvd., 90280, pg. 979 **PV**
WORLD OIL CORP., 9302 Garfield, 90280, pg. 1190 **PV**

South Pasadena

ATC Cablevision of San Marino, Inc., 909 El Central St., 91030, pg. 1610 **PB**
ATC Cablevision of South Pasadena, Inc., 909 El Central St., 91030, pg. 1610 **PB**
FORD GRAPHICS, 900 Palm Ave., 91030, pg. 418 **PV**
TACT HOLDING, 538 Mission St., 91030, pg. 1067 **PV**
Trader Joe's Co., 538 Mission St., 91030, pg. 1067 **PV**

South San Francisco

Aesculap, Inc., 1000 Gateway Blvd., 94080, pg. 29 **IT**
Atkinson Dynamics Company, 405 Eccles Ave., 94080, pg. 143 **PB**
Banner Aircraft International, in. 21 Airport Blvd., 94080, pg. 187 **PB**
Brookfield Homes-San Francisco, 651 Gateway Blvd., Ste. 400, 94080, pg. 228 **IT**
CBT Systems USA, 400 Oyster Point Blvd., 94080, pg. 276 **PB**
Claricom, 850 Dubuque Ave., 94080, pg. 111 **PV**
CORE-MARK INTERNATIONAL, 395 Oyster-Point Blvd., Ste. 415, 94080, pg. 275 **PV**
Daher Golden Eagle - San Francisco, 333 Oyster Point Blvd., Unit # 6, 94080, pg. 749 **PB**
Datascan Technology, 121 Main St., 94080, pg. 45 **PV**
FASTRAC Systems, Inc.-Insurance Agent & Broker, 395 Oyster Point Blvd., Ste. 500, 94080, pg. 1158 **PB**
GALOOB TOYS, INC., 500 Forbes Blvd., 94080, pg. 698 **PB**
Genentech, Inc., One DNA Way, 94080-4990, pg. 1120 **IT**
Golden State Flooring, 449 Littlefield Ave., 94083, pg. 527 **PV**
LITHOTYPE COMPANY, INC., 333 Pt. San Bruno Blvd., 94080, pg. 670 **PV**

PB - *U.S. Public Companies Volume*
PV - *U.S. Private Companies Volume*
IT - *International Public & Private Companies Volume*

Geographic Index-U.S.

1154

NASAM International, Incorporated, 601 Gateway Blvd., Suite 1155, 94080, pg. 187
NATIONAL INSURANCE GROUP, 395 Oyster Point Blvd., Ste. 500, 94080, pg. 1157 **PB**
Obayashi Corporation-San Francisco, 345 Allenon Ave., 94080, pg. 995 **IT**
Sapporo U.S.A., Inc., San Francisco, 601 Gateway Blvd., Ste. 450, 94080, pg. 1194 **IT**
See's Candies, Inc., 210 El Camino Real, 94080, pg. 221 **PB**
See's Candy Shops, Inc., 210 El Camino Real, 94080, pg. 221 **PB**
TransCoast Envelope Co., 240 Littlefield Ave., 94083, pg. 1077 **PV**
Treadway Corporation, 601 Gateway Blvd., Ste. 650, 94080, pg. 1312 **IT**
Vitasoy (U.S.A.) Inc., 400 Oyster Point Blvd., Ste. 201, 94080, pg. 1469 **IT**
WARRENS WALLER PRESS, INC., 339 Harbor Way, 94080, pg. 1151 **PV**
Zellerbach Division, 245 S. Spruce Ave., 94083, pg. 1075 **PB**

Spring Valley

U.S. Elevator, 10728 U.S. Elevator Rd., 91978, pg. 1387 **PV**

Standard

Sierra Pacific Industries-Standard Division, P.O. Box 218, 95373, pg. 999 **PV**

Stanton

Custom Pipe & Coupling Co., 10560 Fern, P.O. Box 978, 90680, pg. 1512 **IT**
LSP Specialty Products Co., 8380 Cerritos, 90680, pg. 1145 **PB**
ORCO BLOCK COMPANY, 8042 Katella Ave., 90680, pg. 819 **PV**

Stockton

ALPINE PACKING COMPANY, 9900 Lower Sacramento Rd., 95210-3995, pg. 45 **PV**
BANK OF AGRICULTURE & COMMERCE, 221 W. March Lane, 2nd Fl., 95207, pg. 114 **PV**
CALIFORNIA CEDAR PRODUCTS, INC., 400 Fresno Ave., 95203, pg. 200 **PV**
A.M. Castle & Co., 2701 E. Hammer, 95826, pg. 313 **PB**
CHASE CHEVROLET CO., INC., 6441 Holman Rd., 95212, pg. 230 **PV**
Diamond Walnut Growers, Inc., 1050 S. Diamond St., 95205, pg. 1051 **PV**
DURAFLAME, INC., 2894 Monte Diablo Ave., 95203, pg. 348 **PV**
FMC FoodTech/Fran Rica, 2807 South Hwy. 99, 95205, pg. 605 **PB**
Ferro Union, Inc., Northern California, 2881 Navuone Rd., 95215, pg. 402 **PV**
L.B. Foster Company-Stockton Yard, 2710 Heinz St., 95206, pg. 676 **PB**
Hillhaven Rehabilitation & Convalescent Hospital, 1630 N. Edison Ave., 95204, pg. 1713 **PB**
KBC Trading & Processing, 2389 W. March Ln., 95207, pg. 428 **PV**
Klein Brothers Ltd., Snack & Packaged Nut Div., 1515 S. Fresno Ave., 95206, pg. 428 **PB**
PDM Steel Service Center-Stockton, 3535 E. Myrtle St., 95205, pg. 1305 **PB**
PDM Strocal, Inc., 2324 Navy Dr., 95206, pg. 1305 **PB**
Premier Drywall Tool Company, 119 Val Dervin Pkwy., Ste. 1, 95206, pg. 613 **PV**
THE SPANOS COMPANIES, 1341 W. Robinhood Dr., 95207, pg. 1020 **PV**
Stockton Culvert, Steel Service Headquarters, 3535 E. Myrtle St., 95205, pg. 1305 **PB**
Stockton Restaurant Corp., 321 W. Weber St., 95203, pg. 1022 **PB**
Stockton Savings Bank, 501 W. Weber Ave., 95203-3169, pg. 1575 **PB**
Stockton Savings Bank-Stockton, 131 N. San Joaquin St., 95202, pg. 1575 **PB**
Stockton Savings Bank-Stockton, 1110 W. Robinhood Dr., 95207, pg. 1575 **PB**
Stockton Savings Bank-Stockton, 1782 W. Hammer Ln., 95209, pg. 1575 **PB**
Stockton Savings Bank-Stockton, 2562 Pacific Ave., 95204, pg. 1575 **PB**
Stockton Savings Bank-Stockton, 2287 W. March Ln., 95207, pg. 1575 **PB**
Stockton Savings Bank-Stockton, 8135 N. West Ln., 95210, pg. 1575 **PB**
Stockton Savings Bank-Stockton, Loan Dept., 501 W. Weber Ave., 95203, pg. 1575 **PB**
Sumiden Wire Products Corp., 1412 El Pinal Dr., 95208, pg. 1313 **IT**
Triptych CD Corp., 1604 Tillie Lewis Dr., 95201, pg. 539 **PV**
Willis Corroon Administrative Services Corporation, 6702 Inglewood Ave., Ste. H, 95207, pg. 1504 **IT**
Zellerbach Division, 1551 N. Broadway, 95205, pg. 1076 **PB**

Studio City

CBS/MTM Company, 4024 Radford, Ste. 290, 91604, pg. 275 **PB**

CARSEY-WERNER COMPANY, LLC, 4024 Radford Ave., Bldg. 3, 91604-2101, pg. 216 **PV**
MTM Enterprises, Inc., 12700 Ventura Blvd., Ste. 200, 91604, pg. 927 **IT**
Todd-AO Scoring, CBS Studios Ctr., 4024 Radford Ave., 91604, pg. 1619 **PB**

Sun City

Mathews International, P.O. Box 460, 92586, pg. 1059 **PB**

Sun Valley

AVX Filters Div., 11144 Penrose St., 91352-3921, pg. 775 **IT**
Automated Studio Lighting, Inc., 10848 Cantara St., 91352, pg. 1283 **IT**
W. Braun Co., 9455 Chivers Ave., Shadow Mountain Industrial Pk., 91352, pg. 166 **PV**
Burbank Aircraft Supply Inc., 10679 Lanark, 91352, pg. 187 **PB**
COSMETIC GROUP, U.S.A., 11312 Penrose St., 91352, pg. 277 **PV**
Gauss Div., 9130 Glenoaks Blvd., 91352, pg. 479 **PB**
Hi-Profit Distributors, Inc., 9505 El Dorado, 91352, pg. 752 **IT**
L.A. Gauge Co., 7440 San Fernando Rd., 91352, pg. 1640 **PB**
PMC, INC., 12243 Branford St., 91352, pg. 827 **PB**
Red-E-Crete, Inc., 8401 Tujunga Blvd., 91353, pg. 818 **IT**

Sunnyvale

AMD Corporation, One AMD Pl., 94088, pg. 21 **PB**
AMD Far East, Ltd., One AMD Pl., 94086, pg. 21 **PB**
AMD Properties, 901 Thompson Pl., 94086, pg. 21 **PB**
Advanced Micro Computers Export Corporation, Inc., One AMD Pl., 94086, pg. 21 **PB**
Advanced Micro Devices Export Corporation, One AMD Pl., 94086, pg. 21 **PB**
ADVANCED MICRO DEVICES, INC., One AMD Pl., 94086, pg. 21 **PB**
Advanced Micro Devices Overseas Corporation, One AMD Pl., 94086, pg. 21 **PB**
Advanced Micro, Ltd., One AMD Pl., 94086, pg. 21 **PB**
Aerometrics, Inc., 755 N. Mary Ave., 94086, pg. 1559 **PB**
Amdahl Corporation, 1250 E. Arques Ave., 94088-3470, pg. 527 **IT**
American Peptide Company, Inc., 777 E. Evelyn Ave., 94086, pg. 695 **IT**
Application Specific Products Group, P.O. Box 3409, 94088, pg. 1053 **IT**
ARBOR SOFTWARE CORPORATION, 1344 Crossman Ave., 94089, pg. 127 **PB**
ARGOSystems, Inc., 324 N. Mary Avenue, 94088-3452, pg. 240 **PB**
ARGOSystems, Inc., 324 N. Mary Ave., 94088-3452, pg. 240 **PB**
Arrow/Schweber Electronics, 1180 Murphy Ave., 94089, pg. 134 **PB**
ASPEC TECHNOLOGY, INC., 830 E. Arques Ave., 94086, pg. 89 **PV**
BR Communications, 222 Caspian Dr., 94089-1014, pg. 1555 **PB**
CTX International, 115 Sobrante, 94086, pg. 1137 **PB**
California Microwave Foreign Sales Corporation, 990 Almanor Ave., 94089, pg. 293 **PB**
CALIFORNIA MICROWAVE, INC., 1143 Borregas Ave., 94089, pg. 293 **PB**
California Microwave, Inc.-Government Grp., 1143 Borregas Ave., 94089, pg. 293 **PB**
California Microwave, Inc.-Wireless Products Grp., 1143 Borregas Ave., 94089, pg. 293 **PB**
Cascade Controls, Inc., 712 E. Evelyn Ave., 94086, pg. 1060 **PV**
Computer Curriculum Corporation, 1287 Lawrence Station Road, 94089, pg. 778 **PV**
Cupertino Electric, Inc., 714 E. Evelyn Ave., 94086, pg. 1060 **PV**
Cylink Corp., 910 Hermosa Ct., 94086, pg. 1306 **PB**
Defense Products Division, 1143 Borregas Ave., 94089, pg. 293 **PB**
Diablo Research Corporation, 825 Stewart Dr., 94086, pg. 1424 **PB**
Digi International, 1299 Orleans Dr., 94089, pg. 507 **PB**
DIGITAL LINK CORPORATION, 217 Humboldt Ct., 94089-1300, pg. 508 **PB**
DIONEX CORPORATION, P.O. Box 3603, 1228 Titan Way, 94088-3603, pg. 510 **PB**
EDD-Sunnyvale, 1161 N. Fairoaks Ave., 94089, pg. 205 **PB**
EG & G Optoelectronics Reticon, 345 Potrero Ave., 94086, pg. 543 **PB**
ESL, Inc., P.O. Box 3510, 94089, pg. 1558 **PB**
FAROUDJA, INC., 750 Palomar Ave., 94086, pg. 613 **PB**
Formtek, 602 Baltic Way, 94089, pg. 1008 **PB**
Fujitsu AMD Semi-Conductor, Ltd., One AMD Pl., 94088-3453, pg. 21 **PB**
GENUS INC., 1139 Karlstad Dr., 94089, pg. 732 **PB**
GLOBAL VILLAGE COMMUNICATION, 1144 E. Arques Ave., 94086, pg. 748 **PB**
Greyland Business Park, Phase I, 710 Lakeway, Ste. 200, 94086, pg. 361 **PB**
Handar, Inc., 1288 Reamwood Ave., 94089, pg. 1559 **PB**
HARMONIC LIGHTWAVES, 549 Baltic Way, 94089, pg. 788 **PB**
Healthsouth Corporation, 1322 Orleans Dr., 94089, pg. 803 **PB**
R.S. HUGHES CO., INC., 1162 Sonoma Ct., 94086, pg. 547 **PV**

ILC TECHNOLOGY, INC., 399 Java Dr., 94089, pg. 856 **PB**
Icore International Inc., 180 N. Wolfe Rd., 94086, pg. 1268 **PB**
INFOSEEK CORPORATON, 1399 Moffett Park Dr., 94089-1134, pg. 876 **PB**
INTEGRATED SYSTEMS, INC., 201 Moffett Park Dr., 94089, pg. 885 **PB**
Konica Technology, Inc., 777 N. Pastoria Ave., 94086, pg. 748 **IT**
Linear Div., P.O. Box 3409, 94088, pg. 1054 **IT**
Lockheed Martin Missiles & Space, 1111 Lockheed Way, 94088-3504, pg. 1008 **IT**
Lockheed Martin Space & Range Systems, 1260 Crossman Ave., 94089-1198, pg. 1009 **IT**
Lockheed Technical Operations Company, 1309 Moffett Park Blvd., 94089-9929, pg. 1009 **IT**
MMC NETWORKS, INC., 1134 E. Arques Ave., 94086, pg. 1007 **PV**
MAXIM INTEGRATED PRODUCTS, INC., 120 San Gabriel Dr., 94086, pg. 1061 **PB**
McCandless San Tomas No. 1, 710 Lakeway, Ste. 200, 94086, pg. 361 **PB**
McCandless San Tomas No. 2, 710 Lakeway, Ste. 200, 94086, pg. 361 **PB**
McCandless Towers, Phase II, 710 Lakeway, Ste. 200, 94086, pg. 365 **PB**
MERCURY INTERACTIVE CORP., 470 Potrero Ave., 94086, pg. 1093 **PB**
Microelectronics Center, 1220 Midas Way, 94088-3509, pg. 1405 **IT**
Microprocessor & Microcontroller Div., P.O. Box 3409, 94088, pg. 1054 **IT**
Military Products Div., P.O. Box 3409, 94088, pg. 1054 **IT**
NANOMETRICS INCORPORATED, 310 Deguigne Dr., 94086, pg. 1151 **PB**
National Nuclear Corporation, 1275 Hammerwood Ave., 94089, pg. 1594 **PB**
Oki Semiconductor Group, 785 N. Mary Ave., 94086, pg. 1000 **IT**
ORBIT SEMICONDUCTOR, INC., 169 Java Dr., 94089, pg. 819 **PV**
PATSON'S PRESS, 508 Tasman Dr., 94089, pg. 843 **PB**
Pen-Stock, Inc., 520 Mercury Dr., 94085, pg. 155 **PB**
Performance Elastomers Division, 1032 Morse St., 94089, pg. 689 **PB**
Philips Semiconductors, 811 E. Arques Ave., 94088-3409, pg. 1054 **IT**
Pico Design, Inc., 1150 Kifer Rd., 94086, pg. 1138 **PB**
The Plexus Group, 1310 Chesapeake Ter., 94089, pg. 177 **PB**
QT OPTOELECTRONICS, 610 N. Mary Ave., 94086-2906, pg. 897 **PB**
QUICKLOGIC CORPORATION, 1277 Orleans Dr., 94089-1138, pg. 901 **PV**
RADIUS INC., 215 Moffett Park Dr., 94089-1374, pg. 1358 **PB**
Reactor Experiments, Inc., 1275 Hammerwood Ave., 94089-2231, pg. 1594 **PB**
Resumix, 890 Ross Dr., 94089, pg. 331 **PB**
Revo, Inc., 1315 Chesapeake Terrace, 94089, pg. 195 **PB**
San Tomas No. 1 Limited Partnership, 710 Lakeway, Ste. 200, 94086, pg. 361 **PB**
San Tomas No. 2 Limited Partnership, McCandless Group, 710 Lakeway, Ste. 200, 94086, pg. 362 **PB**
Semi-Custom Products Div., P.O. Box 3409, 94088, pg. 1054 **IT**
SenSym Inc., 1244 Roamwood Ave., 94089, pg. 127 **IT**
Services Division, 1143 Borregas Ave., 94089, pg. 293 **PB**
Spectrace Instruments, 1275 Hammerwood Ave., 94089, pg. 1593 **PB**
Standard Products Group, P.O. Box 3409, 94088, pg. 1054 **IT**
STANFORD TELECOMMUNICATIONS, 1221 Crossman Ave., 94089-1117, pg. 1508 **PB**
Sumitomo Electric Interconnect Products Inc., 155 C-1 Moffet Pk. Dr., 94089, pg. 1313 **IT**
SUPERTEX, INC., 1235 Bordeaux Dr., 94088-3607, pg. 1060 **PB**
SYNERGISM, INC., 722 E. Evelyn Ave., 94086, pg. 1539 **PV**
TCI INTERNATIONAL INC., 222 Caspian Dr., 94089-1014, pg. 1555 **PB**
TCI Wireless, 222 Caspian Dr., 94089, pg. 1555 **PB**
Technical Instrument Company, 650 N. Mary Ave., 94086, pg. 1795 **PB**
Technology for Communications International, 222 Caspian Dr., 94089, pg. 1555 **PB**
TELESENSORY CORPORATION, 520 Almancr, 94086, pg. 1074 **PV**
Trimble Navigation International Foreign Sales Corporation, c/o Trimble Navigation Limited, 585 North Mary Ave., 94086, pg. 1638 **PB**
Trimble Navigation International Limited, 910 Benicia, 94086, pg. 1638 **PB**
TRIMBLE NAVIGATION LIMITED, 645 N. Mary Ave., 94088, pg. 1638 **PB**
Western Multiplex Corporation, 1196 Borregas Ave., 94089-1302, pg. 747 **PB**
Whisper Communications, 825 Stewart Ave., 94086, pg. 1425 **PV**
Xetex, Inc., 1275 Hammerwood Ave., 94089, pg. 1594 **PB**

Sutter Creek

Amador Motors, P.O. Box 278, 95685, pg. 891 **PV**

Geographic Index-U.S.

Sylmar

AlliedSignal Ocean Systems, 15825 Roxford St., 91342-3597, pg. 50 **PB**
BEI Sensors and Systems Company, 13100 Telfair Ave., 91342, pg. 160 **PB**
LANCE INDUSTRIES, 13001 Bradley Ave., 91342, pg. 645 **PV**
Pacesetter Inc., 15900 Valley View Ct., 91392-9221, pg. 1428 **PB**
Regency-Sonnell Greetings, 13291 Ralston Ave., 91342, pg. 89 **PV**
Santee Manufacturing, 12950 San Fernando Rd., 91342, pg. 748 **PV**
SIERRACIN CORPORATION, 12780 San Fernando Rd., 91342-3796, pg. 999 **PV**
Sierracin/Sylmar Corporation, 12780 San Fernando Rd., 91342, pg. 999 **PV**
Sierracin/Trans Tech, 12780 San Fernando Rd., 91342, pg. 999 **PV**
TUTOR-SALIBA CORPORATION, 15901 Olden St., 91342, pg. 1111 **PV**
Valley-Todeco, Inc., 12975 Bradley Ave., 91342, pg. 852 **IT**

Taft

BERRY PETROLEUM COMPANY, 28700 Hovey Hills Rd., 93268, pg. 223 **PB**

Tarzana

Unilab Corporation, 18448 Oxnard St., 91356, pg. 1352 **PB**

Tecate

Rockwell Automation Tecate S.A. de C.V., P.O. Box 57, 91980-0057, pg. 1398 **PB**

Temecula

Callaway Vineyard & Winery, P.O. Box 9014, 32720 Rancho California Rd., 92589-9014, pg. 63 **IT**
HEXFET America, 41915 Business Park Drive, 92390, pg. 906 **PB**
HUDSON, RCI, P.O. Box 9020, 27711 Diaz Road, 92589-9020, pg. 546 **PV**
TAMURA CORPORATION OF AMERICA, 4352 Business Park Dr., 92590-6624, pg. 1067 **PV**

Terminal Island

Hugo Neu-Proler Co., 901 New Dock St., 90731, pg. 1440 **PB**
AL LARSON BOAT SHOP, INC., 1046 S. Seaside Ave., 90731, pg. 652 **PV**

Thousand Oaks

Amgen Development Corporation, 1840 Dehavilland Dr., 91320-1789, pg. 101 **PB**
The Amgen Foundation, Inc., 1840 Dehavilland Dr., 91320-1789, pg. 101 **PB**
Amgen Holding, Inc., 1840 Dehavilland Drive, 91320-1789, pg. 101 **PB**
AMGEN INC., One Amgen Ctr. Dr., 91320-1789, pg. 100 **PB**
Amgen International Inc., 1840 Dehavilland Dr., 91320-1789, pg. 101 **PB**
Amgen Ventures, 1840 Dehavilland Dr., 91320-1789, pg. 101 **PB**
Autologic Information International, Inc., 1050 Rancho Conejo Blvd., 91320, pg. 1724 **PB**
BV&K Direct, 3169 White Cedar Pl., 91362, pg. 108 **PV**
Centronic Inc., 1829 B. De Havilland Dr., 91320-1702, pg. 892 **IT**
Du Pont NDT Systems, 2517 Azurite, 91320-1202, pg. 531 **PB**
Kirin Amgen, Inc., 1840 DeHavilland Dr., 91320-1789, pg. 101 **IT**
Medical Management Associates, Inc., 566 St. Charles St., 91360, pg. 839 **PB**
Milgray/California, Inc., 275 E. Hillcrest Dr., 91360, pg. 206 **PB**
Practical Peripherals, P.O. Box 5024, 91360, pg. 801 **PB**
Science Center, 1049 Camino Dos Rios, 91360, pg. 1398 **PB**
Thousand Oaks News-Chronicle, 2595 Thousand Oaks Blvd., 91362, pg. 1448 **PB**

Thousand Palms

Tri-Palm Estate, 32700 Desert Moon Dr., 92276, pg. 437 **PV**

Tiburon

American Software, Inc., Western, 1801 Tiburon Blvd., Ste. 700, 94920, pg. 91 **PB**

Toluca Lake

American Bank Note Company, 3900 W. Alameda Ave., Ste. 1700, 91505, pg. 68 **PB**

Torrance

Advanced Products & Systems Corp., 2829 Maricopa St., 90503, pg. 1365 **PB**
Aerospace Systems & Equipment, 2525 W. 190th St., 90504-6099, pg. 1127 **PB**
Aisin World Corp. of America, 24330 Garnier St., 90505, pg. 39 **IT**
Ajinomoto U.S.A., Inc., Los Angeles Branch, 19675 Mariner Ave., 90503, pg. 40 **IT**
All American Semiconductor of California, Inc., 369 Van Ness Way, Ste. 701, 90501, pg. 41 **PB**
AlliedSignal Aerospace, 2525 W. 190th St., 90504-6099, pg. 50 **PB**
AlliedSignal Airline Services, 18700 Crenshaw Blvd., 90504, pg. 50 **PB**
AlliedSignal Ceramic Components, 2525 W. 190th St., 90504-6099, pg. 50 **PB**
AlliedSignal Turbocharging & Truck Brake Systems, 3201 W. Lomita Blvd., 90505-5064, pg. 51 **PB**
Alpine Electronics of America, Inc., 19145 Gramercy Pl., 90501, pg. 65 **IT**
American Honda Motor Co., Inc., 1919 Torrance Blvd., 90501-2746, pg. 634 **IT**
American Honda Motor Co., Inc. Automobile Sales Division, 1919 Torrance Blvd., 90501, pg. 634 **IT**
American Honda Motor Co., Inc. Motorcycle Division, 1919 Torrance Blvd., 90501-2746, pg. 634 **IT**
Archer Pipe & Tube Co., Inc., 2780 Sky Park Dr., Ste. 315, 90505, pg. 845 **IT**
Auto Marketing Network, Inc., Bldg. 1, 23550 Hawthorne Blvd., Ste. 110, 90505, pg. 872 **PV**
BD SYSTEMS, INC, 385 Van Ness Ave., Ste. 200, 90501, pg. 106 **PV**
BPA International - Torrance, Pacific Gateway II, 19191 S. Vermont Ave., Ste. 350, 90502, pg. 107 **PV**
BOEIT PUBLISHING COMPANY, 21061 S. Western Ave., 90501, pg. 154 **PV**
Bridgestone (U.S.A.), 2000 W. 190th St., 90504, pg. 214 **IT**
CCH Computax Inc., 21250 Hawthorne Blvd., 90503, pg. 1513 **IT**
CAPITOL METALS COMPANY, 20000 S. Western Ave., 90501, pg. 206 **PV**
Casic Phone-Mate, Inc., 20665 Manhattan Pl., 90501, pg. 274 **PV**
CBM America Corp., 365 Van Ness Way, Ste. 510, 90501, pg. 192 **PV**
Chugai Boyeki Co., Ltd., 1830 W. 208th St., 90501, pg. 290 **IT**
Cosworth Engineering Inc., 23205 Early Ave., 90505, pg. 1468 **IT**
CREATIVE COMPUTERS, INC., 2555 W. 190th St., 90504, pg. 458 **PB**
Dai-Ichi Kangyo Bank of California-Torrance, 21525 Hawthorne Blvd., 90503, pg. 360 **IT**
The Daily Breeze, 5215 Torrance Blvd., 90509, pg. 275 **PV**
Davidson & Associates, Inc., 19840 Pioneer Ave., 90503, pg. 320 **PV**
Del Amo Hospital, 23700 Camino del Sol, 90505-5060, pg. 1697 **PB**
Dexol, 1450 W. 228th St., 90501, pg. 1390 **PB**
E For M Corp., 625 Alaska Ave., 90503, pg. 1047 **PB**
Eclipse Mobile Electronics, 19600 S. Vermont Ave., 90502, pg. 526 **IT**
EDELBROCK CORP., 2700 California St., 90503, pg. 563 **PB**
Encore Computer-Los Angeles, 2601 Airport Dr., Ste. 249, 90505, pg. 580 **PB**
Epson America Inc., 20770 Madrona Ave., 90503, pg. 219 **IT**
Excellon Automation Co., 24751 Crenshaw Blvd., 90505, pg. 594 **PB**
FBC Finance Co., 20333 S. Normandic Ave., 90502, pg. 613 **PB**
FARMER BROTHERS COMPANY, 20333 S. Normandie Ave. 90502, pg. 613 **PB**
FERRO UNION, INC., 1000 W. Francisco St., 90502, pg. 402 **PV**
FINANCIAL NETWORK INVESTMENT CORP, 2780 Skypark Dr., Ste. 300, 90505, pg. 404 **PV**
Fujitsu Ten Corp. of America, 19600 S. Vermont, 90502, pg. 526 **IT**
Gamma-f Corporation, 3111-T Fujita St., 90505, pg. 1718 **PB**
General Employment Enterprises, Inc., 21535 Hawthorne Blvd., Ste. 330, 90503, pg. 714 **PB**
Goodring International Inc., 21250 Hawthorne Blvd., Ste. 760, 90503-5502, pg. 1255 **IT**
GREFCO, Inc., 23705 Crenshaw Blvd., 90509, pg. 903 **PV**
The C.P. Hall Company, 444 Alaska Ave., 90503, pg. 495 **PV**
Hi-Shear Corp., 2600 Skypark Dr., 90505, pg. 825 **PB**
Honda North America Inc., 1919 Torrance Blvd., 90501, pg. 635 **IT**
Honda R&D North America, Inc., 1900 Harpers Way, 90501, pg. 634 **IT**
IMPERIAL CREDIT INDUSTRIES, INC., Bldg. 1, 23550 Hawthorne Blvd., Ste. 110, 90505, pg. 872 **PB**
Industrial Electronics Group, 3110 W. Lomita Blvd., 90509, pg. 1364 **PB**
ITOCHU Digital Products, Inc., 19750 S. Vermont St., Ste. 220, 90502, pg. 695 **IT**
JT International U.S.A. Inc., 2441 205th St., Ste. C-102, 90501, pg. 703 **IT**
JTUSA, Inc., 3655 Torrance Blvd, Ste. 430, 90503, pg. 926 **IT**
Japan Oxygen, Inc., 22301 S. Western Ave., Ste. 106, 90501, pg. 938 **IT**

K & M Products Division, 525 Maple Ave., 90503, pg. 152 **PB**
Kubota Credit Corporation U.S.A., 3401 Del Amo Blvd., 90503, pg. 762 **IT**
Kubota Tractor Corp., 3401 Del Amo Blvd., 90503, pg. 762 **IT**
LaundryMart, Inc., 3812 Sepulveda Blvd., Ste 510, 90505, pg. 222 **PV**
Logicon Geodynamic, 21171 Western Ave., Ste. 110, 90501, pg. 1199 **PB**
Logicon Geodynamics Western Division, 21171 Western Ave., Ste. 110, 90501, pg. 1199 **PB**
Logicon, Inc., 3701 Skypark Dr., 90505, pg. 1198 **PB**
Logicon, Inc., 3701 Skypark Dr., 90505-4794, pg. 1199 **PB**
Los Angeles Mfg. Division, 19681 Pacific Gateway Dr., 90502-1168, pg. 518 **PB**
M K DIAMOND PRODUCTS, INC., 1315 Storm Pkwy., 90501-2803, pg. 684 **PV**
Matrix Science Corporation, 435 Maple Ave., 90503, pg. 8 **PB**
Moog Torrance, 20263 Western Ave., 90501, pg. 1127 **PB**
Morinaga Nutritional Foods, Inc., 2050 W. 190th St., Ste. 110, 90504, pg. 895 **IT**
MOTORCAR PARTS & ACCESSORIES, 2727 Maricopa St., 90503, pg. 1136 **PB**
Motorola Rf Devices, 325 Maple Ave., 90503-2602, pg. 1138 **PB**
Mykotronx, 357 Van Ness Way, Ste. 200, 90501, pg. 1359 **PB**
NYK Bulkship-Los Angeles, 21535 Hawthorne Blvd., Ste. 325, 90503, pg. 941 **IT**
Nikon Inc., 19601 Hamilton Ave., 90502, pg. 931 **IT**
Nippo Marketing & Advertising, Inc., 970 W. 190th St., Ste. 290, 90502, pg. 932 **IT**
Nissan Motor Acceptance Corp., 990 W. 190th St., 90502, pg. 945 **IT**
Nissan North America, Inc., 990 W. 190th St., 90502, pg. 945 **IT**
Oriental Motor U.S.A. Corp., 2580 W. 237th St., 90505, pg. 1008 **IT**
PRGR USA Corporation, 3051 Fujita St., 90505, pg. 1521 **IT**
Pacific Optical Division, 2660 Columbia St., 90503, pg. 914 **PV**
PELICAN PRODUCTS, 23215 Early Ave., 90505, pg. 848 **PV**
Pentel of America, Ltd., 2805 Columbia St., 90509, pg. 1035 **IT**
Piper Jaffray Inc., 2780 Skypark Dr., Ste. 400, 90505-5350, pg. 1301 **PB**
PLASMA TECHNOLOGY, INC., 1754 Crenshaw Blvd., 90501, pg. 870 **PV**
POSTRADE LA Office, 21515 Hawthorne Blvd., Union Bank Tower, STe. 640, 90503, pg. 1062 **PB**
Reynolds Metals Company-Torrance, 500 Crenshaw Blvd., 90509, pg. 1386 **PB**
Riedel-Smith Environmental Services, 19500 S. Normandy, 90502, pg. 1478 **IT**
ROBINSON HELICOPTER COMPANY, 2901 Airport Dr., 90505, pg. 936 **PV**
ST Piping, Inc., 3011 W. Lomita Blvd., 90505, pg. 1460 **PB**
Sakata Inx USA Corp., 4040 Spencer St., Ste. E, 90503, pg. 1311 **IT**
Samsteel, Inc., 1000 W. Francisco St., 90502, pg. 402 **PV**
Sankosha U.S.A., Inc., 406 Amapola Ave., Ste. 135, 90501, pg. 1189 **IT**
Serv-Tech, Inc., Western Area, 3011 W. Lomita Blvd., 90505, pg. 1460 **PB**
Shimadzu Precision Instruments, Inc., 20410 Earl St., 90503, pg. 1232 **IT**
Shimadzu Precision Instruments, Inc.-Medical System Div., 20101 S. Vermont Ave., 90502, pg. 1232 **IT**
Shionogi & Co., Ltd. - Los Angeles, 3848 Carson St., Ste. 206, 90503, pg. 1235 **IT**
Shionogi USA, Inc., 3848 Carson St., Ste. 206, 90503, pg. 1235 **IT**
Sikkens Aerospace Finishers, 20846 S. Normandie Ave., 90502, pg. 48 **IT**
SOUTHERN CALIFORNIA AUTO GROUP, 3233 Pacific Coast Hwy., 90505, pg. 1016 **PV**
Standard Communications Corp., 1111 Knox St., 90502, pg. 841 **IT**
Sumitomo Rubber Industries, 438 Amapola Ave., Ste. 100, 90501, pg. 1317 **IT**
SUMMA INDUSTRIES, 21250 Hawthorne Blvd., Ste. 500, 90503, pg. 1527 **PB**
Taisho Pharmaceutical California Inc., 3878 Carson St., Ste. 216, 90503, pg. 1348 **IT**
Torrance Care Center, 4315 Torrance Blvd., 90503, pg. 733 **PV**
Torrance Nissan, Inc., 20710 Hawthorne Blvd., 90503, pg. 1380 **IT**
TOTAL RENAL CARE HOLDINGS, INC., 21250 Hawthorne Blvd., 90503-5517, pg. 1625 **PB**
Toyota Motor Credit Corp., 1515 W. 190th St., 90509, pg. 1413 **IT**
Toyota Motor Sales, U.S.A., Inc., 19001 W. Western Ave., 90509, pg. 1412 **IT**
Trico Industries, Inc., P.O. Box 4358, 90502, pg. 1247 **PB**
VIKING OFFICE PRODUCTS, 950 W. 190th St., 90502, pg. 1720 **PB**
VIRCO MFG. CORPORATION, 2027 Harpers Way, 90501, pg. 1721 **PB**
West Torrance Care Center, 4333 Torrance Blvd., 90503, pg. 733 **PV**
Western Waste Industries, 21061 S. Western Ave., 90501, pg. 1686 **PB**
WHEREHOUSE ENTERTAINMENT, INC., 19701 Hamilton Ave., 90502, pg. 1171 **PV**
Yonex Corporation, 3520 Challenger St., 90503, pg. 1522 **IT**

PB - *U.S. Public Companies Volume*
PV - *U.S. Private Companies Volume*
IT - *International Public & Private Companies Volume*

Geographic Index-U.S.

Tracy

Stockton Savings Bank-Tracy, 1070 N. Tracy Blvd., 95376, pg. 1575 **PB**

Trona

CR Briggs Corporation, Briggs Mine, P.O. Box 668, 93592, pg. 302 **PB**

Truckee

SIERRA WEST BANCORP, 10181 Truckee-Tahoe Airport Rd., 96161, pg. 1470 **PB**
Sierra West Bank, P.O. Box BD, 10181 Truckee-Tahoe Airport Road, 96160, pg. 1470 **PB**

Turlock

ConAgra Turkey Co., 5th & F St., 95381, pg. 427 **PB**
Rogers Foods, 151 S. Walnut, 95380, pg. 1696 **PB**
Star Building Systems, 1301 South Ave., 95380, pg. 1394 **PB**
Stockton Savings Bank-Turlock, 2846 Geer Rd., 95380, pg. 1575 **PB**
Stockton Savings Bank-Turlock, 501 E. Olive St., 95380, pg. 1575 **PB**
Trine Manufacturing Co., 650 Trade Way, 95381-8328, pg. 558 **PV**
Universal Foods Corp.-Dehydrated Products Div., 151 S. Walnut, Drawer R, 95381, pg. 1696 **PB**
VALLEY FRESH, INC., 680 D St., 95381-5498, pg. 1132 **PV**

Tustin

Airshow, 15222 Del Amo Ave., 92680, pg. 539 **PB**
Arrow Commercial Systems Div., 14242 Timbers Rd., 92680, pg. 133 **PB**
Arrow/Schweber Electronics, 2961 Dow Ave., 92680, pg. 134 **PB**
Capstone Electronics Div., 2961 Dow Ave., 92680, pg. 134 **PB**
THE CERPLEX GROUP, INC., 1382 Bell Ave., 92780, pg. 332 **PB**
CHEROKEE INTERNATIONAL LLC, 2841 Dow Ave., 92780, pg. 233 **PV**
Georg Fischer Inc., 2882 Dow Ave., 92680-7285, pg. 489 **IT**
Heritage Hills, 14452 Franklin Ave., 92680, pg. 957 **PB**
Jaco Electronics, Inc., 1541 Parkway Loop, Ste. A, 92680, pg. 921 **PB**
LAMP POST FRANCHISE CORPORATION, 3002 Dow Ave., Ste. 320, 92780, pg. 644 **PV**
Meridian Lamps Development, Inc., 1582 Parkway Loop, Ste. F, 92680, pg. 314 **PV**
PacifiCare Dental & Vision, 14471 Chambers Rd., 92780-6902, pg. 1251 **PB**
PAIRGAIN TECHNOLOGIES INC., 14402 Franklin Ave., 92780, pg. 1253 **PB**
Ricoh Development of California, Inc., One Ricoh Sq., 1100 Valencia Ave., 92680, pg. 1114 **IT**
Ricoh Electronics, Inc., One Ricoh Sq., 1100 Valencia Ave., 92780, pg. 1114 **IT**
ScanTron Corporation, 1361 Valencia Ave., 92780, pg. 786 **PB**
Silicon Systems, Inc., 14351 Myford Rd., 92780-7068, pg. 1585 **PB**
Southwest Aerospace, 2672 Dow Ave., 92780, pg. 853 **IT**
Sunwest Bank, 535 E. First St., 92780, pg. 1755 **PB**
Sunwest Leasing Corp. (SLC), 535 E. First St., 92680, pg. 1755 **PB**
Tatung Electric Co. of America, Inc., 14381 Chambers Rd., 92780, pg. 1357 **IT**
Toshiba America Medical Systems, Inc., 2441 Michelle Dr., 92680, pg. 1405 **IT**
Vishay Resistor Products, 14032 Enderle Center Dr. Ste. 202, 92680, pg. 1722 **PB**
VITATECH INTERNATIONAL, INC., 2832 Dow Ave., 92780, pg. 1142 **PV**

Ukiah

First American Title Co. of Mendocino County, 551 S. Orchard Ave., 95482, pg. 625 **PB**

Union City

All-American Co., 2831 Faber St., 94578, pg. 1389 **PB**
Higgins Lumber Purchasing, 600 Daggett Ave., 94587, pg. 527 **PV**
Higgins Union City Operations, 600 Daggett Ave., 94587, pg. 527 **PV**
MJB Rice Company, 1550 Atlantic St., 94587, pg. 917 **IT**
Nestle Beverage Company, 1555 Atlantic St., 94587, pg. 917 **IT**
Rapid Mounting & Finishing, 33195 Lewis Ave., 94587-2201, pg. 910 **PV**
Shade Foods, Inc., 33063 Western Ave., 94587, pg. 802 **PV**
Shin-Etsu Polymer America, Inc., 34135 7th St., 94587, pg. 1234 **IT**
TapeTech Tool Co., Inc., 30009 Ahern Ave., 94587, pg. 103 **PV**
Unitog Rental Facility, 33483 Western Ave., 94587, pg. 1693 **PB**
Westco Products/Bay Area, 32621 Central Ave., 94587, pg. 244 **IT**

Universal City

DREAMWORKS SKG, 100 Universal Plaza, 91608, pg. 342 **PV**
Getty Oil Exploration Co., 10 Universal City Plaza, Ste. 602, 91601, pg. 1583 **PB**
MCA Records, Inc., 70 Universal City Plaza, 91608, pg. 1215 **IT**
MCA/Universal Merchandising, 100 Universal City Plaza, 91608, pg. 1215 **IT**
Merchandising Corp. of America, Inc., 100 Universal City Plaza, 91608, pg. 1216 **IT**
Rollins Hudig Hall of Southern California, Ten Universal City Plaza, Ste. 3400, 91608, pg. 117 **PB**
UNI Distribution Corp., 60 Universal City Plaza, 91608, pg. 1215 **IT**
Universal Amphitheatre, 100 Universal City Plaza, 91608, pg. 1216 **IT**
Universal City Studios (DISC), Inc., 100 Universal City Plaza, 91608, pg. 1216 **IT**
Universal Education & Visual Arts, 100 Universal City Plaza, 91608, pg. 1216 **IT**
Universal Pictures, 100 Universal City Plaza, 91608, pg. 1216 **IT**
Universal Studios Development Co., 100 Universal City Plaza, 91608, pg. 1216 **IT**
Universal Studios Enterprises, 100 Universal City Plaza, 91608, pg. 1215 **IT**
Universal Studios Hollywood, 100 Universal City Plaza, 91608, pg. 1216 **IT**
Universal Studios Home Entertainment Group, 70 Universal City Plaza, 91608, pg. 1215 **IT**
Universal Studios, Inc., 100 Universal City Plaza, 91608, pg. 1215 **IT**
Universal Studios Mfg., 100 Universal City Plaza, 91608, pg. 1216 **IT**
Universal Studios Music Entertainment Group, 70 Universal City Plaza, 91608, pg. 1215 **IT**
Universal Studios New Ventures, Inc., 100 Universal City Plaza, 91608, pg. 1216 **IT**
Universal Studios Publishing Group, 100 Universal City Plaza, 91608, pg. 1216 **IT**
Universal Studios Recreation Services Group, 100 Universal City Plaza, 91608, pg. 1216 **IT**
Universal Studios Television Ltd., 100 Universal City Plaza, 91608, pg. 1216 **IT**
Universal Studios TV, 100 Universal City Plaza, 91608, pg. 1215 **IT**
Universal Studios Videodisc, Inc., 100 Universal City Plaza, 91608, pg. 1216 **IT**
Universal Television Div., 100 Universal City Plaza, 91608, pg. 1216 **IT**
Viacom Entertainment, 10 Universal City Plaza, 91608, pg. 778 **PV**
Viacom Productions Inc., 10 Universal City Plaza, 91608, pg. 779 **PV**
Womp's Restaurant Bar & Grill, Universal City Plaza, 91608, pg. 1216 **IT**

Upland

Advanco Constructors, Inc., 1500 W. 9th St., 91785, pg. 1795 **PB**
Lewis Construction Co., Inc., 1156 N. Mountain Ave., 91786, pg. 665 **PV**
Lewis Development Co., 1156 N. Mountain Ave., 91786, pg. 665 **PV**
LEWIS HOMES MANAGEMENT CORP., 1156 N. Mountain Ave., 91786, pg. 665 **PV**
Lewis Homes of California, 1156 N. Mountain Ave., 91786, pg. 665 **PV**
MACE Products, 2022 W. 11th St., 91786, pg. 1234 **PV**
NEW BEDFORD PANORAMEX CORPORATION, 1037 W. 9th St., 91786, pg. 792 **PV**
Nuevo Camino Constructors Co., 1500 W. 9th, 91786, pg. 1795 **PB**
Pyramid Western Mouldings, 1111 E. 8th St., 91786, pg. 1335 **IT**
Republic Sales Co., 1156 N. Mountain Ave., 91786, pg. 665 **PV**
Shugart Corp., 1501 W. Ninth St., Ste. E, 91786, pg. 997 **PV**
UVP, INC., 2066 W. 11th St., 91786, pg. 1115 **PV**
Western Land Properties, 1156 N. Mountain Ave., 91786, pg. 665 **PV**
Western Supply Corp., 1156 N. Mountain Ave., 91786, pg. 666 **PV**
Zurn Constructors, Inc., 1500 W. Ninth St., 91786, pg. 1795 **PB**

Vacaville

Chiron, 2010 Cessna Dr., 95688, pg. 350 **PB**
Insolair Industries, 909 Aldridge Rd., 95688, pg. 120 **PB**
SERTA MATTRESS COMPANY, 3777 Vaca Valley Pkwy., 95688, pg. 985 **PV**
SIMPSON DURA-VENT CO., INC., 902 Aldridge Rd., 95688, pg. 1474 **PB**

Valencia

Airvision, 25136 West Anza Dr., 91355-1203, pg. 1053 **IT**
Answer Products, Inc., 27460 Ave. Scott, 91355, pg. 639 **PV**
Applied Research Labs, 24911 Ave. Stanford, 91355, pg. 1111 **IT**
Bergen Brunswig Drug Company, 24903 Ave. Kearney, 91355, pg. 213 **PB**

Vallejo

MARINE WORLD AFRICA USA, Marine World Pkwy., 94589, pg. 703 **PV**
SAIC Comsystems, 100 Corporate Pl., 94590-6968, pg. 976 **PV**
TIMEC COMPANY, 155 Corporate Pl., 94590, pg. 1087 **PV**

Van Nuys

ARBCO Electronics, 7820 Gloria Ave., 91406, pg. 664 **IT**
CHEROKEE INC., 6835 Valjean Ave., 91406, pg. 345 **PB**
Cigna Dental Health of California, Inc., 5990 Sepulveda Blvd., 5th fl., 91411, pg. 358 **PB**
Color Me Mine, Inc., 14721 Califa St., 91411, pg. 966 **PV**
Com Corp Factors, Inc., 14761 Calife St., 91411, pg. 615 **PV**
CONTINENTAL COIN CORPORATION, 5627 Sepulveda Blvd., 91411, pg. 267 **PV**
Dale Electronics, Techro, 7803 Lemona Ave., 91405-1139, pg. 1722 **PB**
Data Rental/Sales, Division, 6060 Sepulveda Blvd., 91411, pg. 568 **PB**
Dayton Rogers of California, 13630 Saticoy St., 91402, pg. 318 **PV**
ELECTRO RENT CORPORATION, 6060 Sepulveda Blvd., 91411-2512, pg. 568 **PB**
Equipment Sales Division, 6060 Sepulveda Blvd., 91411-2512, pg. 568 **PB**
Familian Corp., 13704 Saticoy St., 91402, pg. 1512 **IT**
Familian Pipe & Supply Co., 7651 Woodman Ave., 91402, pg. 1512 **IT**
Familian Pipe Inc., P.O. Box 9082, 91409, pg. 1512 **IT**
First American Home Buyers Protection Corp., 7833 Haskell Ave., 91406, pg. 625 **PB**
Gilcron Corporation, 7821 Orion Ave., 91409, pg. 860 **PB**
Holga Inc., 7901 Woodley Ave., 91408, pg. 772 **PB**
ITT Gilfillan, 7821 Orion Ave., 91409, pg. 859 **PB**
INDUSTRIAL ELECTRONIC ENGINEERS, INC., 7740 Lemona Ave., 91409, pg. 561 **PV**
KENNINGTON LTD., INC., 14761 Calife St., 91411, pg. 615 **PV**
KEYES MOTORS, INC., 5855 Van Nuys Blvd., 91401, pg. 618 **PV**
Laidlaw Transit, Inc, 5725 Sepulveda Blvd., 91411, pg. 259 **IT**
LIVE ENTERTAINMENT INC., 15400 Sherman Way, Ste. 500, 91406, pg. 671 **PV**
LIVE Film & Mediaworks, 15400 Sherman Way, 91406, pg. 671 **PV**
Martin Lawrence Limited Editions of California, Inc., 16250 Stagg St., 91406, pg. 709 **PV**
Northridge Hospital-Sherman Way Campus, 14500 Sherman Circle, 91405, pg. 1118 **PV**
Puroflow Corp., 16559 Saticoy St., 91406-1739, pg. 1345 **PB**
PUROFLOW INCORPORATED, 16559 Saticoy St., 91406-1739, pg. 1345 **PB**
Republic American Corporation, 15821 Ventura Blvd., 91436, pg. 75 **PB**
Stanleigh International, Inc., 14761 Calife St., 91411, pg. 615 **PV**
Sun-Litho, 7950 Haskell Ave., 91406, pg. 762 **PV**
SUPERIOR INDUSTRIES INTERNATIONAL, INC., 7800 Woodley Ave., 91406, pg. 1539 **PB**
USECO, 13536 Saticoy St., 91402-6428, pg. 1003 **PB**
Van Nuys Airport Restaurant Corp., 16320 Raymer Ave., 91406, pg. 1022 **PV**
Yoh Health Care Services, 16600 Sherman Way, Ste. 230, 91406, pg. 317 **PV**

Vandenberg AFB

CSD, Vandenberg AFB, P.O. Box 5549, 93437, pg. 1690 **PB**

Venice

TBWA Chiat/Day Los Angeles, 340 Main St., 90291, pg. 1062 **PV**

Ventura

General Magnaplate California, 2707 Palma Dr., 93003, pg. 717 **PB**
Hewlett-Packard Company, 5280 Valentine Rd., Ste. 205, 93003, pg. 813 **PB**

Geographic Index-U.S.

KINKO'S CORPORATION, 255 W. Stanley Ave., 93001, pg. 622   PV
Kinko's Service Corp., 255 W. Stanley Ave., 93001-1300, pg. 622   PV
LOST ARROW CORPORATION, 259 W. Santa Clara, 93001, pg. 676   PV
Oceaneering Technologies, 2055 N. Ventura Ave., 93001, pg. 1211   PB
Patagonia, 259 W. Santa Clara, 93001, pg. 677   PV
PEMKO MANUFACTURING COMPANY, 4226 Transport St., 93003, pg. 848   PV
Texaco USA, P.O. Box 811, 93002-0811, pg. 1583   PB
Valex Corp., 6080 Leland St., 93003, pg. 1375   PB
VENTURA COASTAL CORPORATION, 2325 Vista Del Mar, 93001, pg. 1136   PV
Ventura County Star-Free Press, 5250 Ralston St., 93003, pg. 1448   PB

Vernon

A.J. Brandon, 4480 Pacific Blvd., 90058, pg. 948   PB
CHORUS LINE CORPORATION, 4505 Bandini Blvd., 90040, pg. 238   PV
COAST PACKING COMPANY, 3275 E. Vernon Ave., 90058, pg. 248   PV
International Baking Co., 5200 S. Alameda St., 90058, pg. 1433   PB
Ivy, 4480 Pacific Blvd., 90058, pg. 948   PB
J & J Snack Foods Corp. of California, 5353 Downey Rd., 90058, pg. 916   PB
Kal Kan Foods, Inc., P.O. Box 58853, 3250 E. 44th St., 90058, pg. 707   PV
National Distributors, 2608 E. 37th. St., 90058, pg. 781   PV
Smart & Final, 4700 S. Boyle Ave., 90058, pg. 563   IT
United States Aluminum Corp., 3663 Bandini Blvd., 90023, pg. 895   PB
VIVIAN & ELLIETTE, INC., 4701 S. Santa Fe Ave, 90058, pg. 1142   PV

Victorville

California State Bank-Victorville, 12470 Hesperia Rd., 93294   PB
Comarco Staffing, Inc., 14011 Park Ave., Ste. 170, 92392, pg. 406   PB

Visalia

Brite Vue Glass Systems, P.O. Box 3148, 7200 Doe Ave., 93291, pg. 60   PB
Continental Eagle Visalia, CA, 6678 Ave. 304 Ste. B, 93291, pg. 267   PB
Early California Foods, 315 E. Tulare Ave., 93277, pg. 591   PV
HOUCK INDUSTRIES, INC., 317 W. Oak Ave., 93291, pg. 541   PV
Ivex Packaging Corporation-Visalia, 7101 Avenue 304, 93291, pg. 915   PB
The Mangano Company, Inc., 1840 S. Central Ave., 93291, pg. 323   PB
Nash DeCamp Company, P.O. Box 3127, 6825 W. Mineral King Ave., 93278, pg. 1152   PV
Sunkist Growers, Inc.-Western Division, 2929 W. Main St., Ste. K, 93291-5730, pg. 1052   PB
Visalia Times-Delta, 330 N. West St., 93277, pg. 702   PB

Vista

Armor Safe Technologies, 2580 Progress St., 92083, pg. 861   PV
Cox Communications-Vista, 2790 Business Park Dr., 92083, pg. 455   PB
Magnedyne Div., 1360 Park Ctr. Ln., 92083, pg. 999   PV
J.W. Messner, Inc., 644 Lado De Loma Dr., 92084, pg. 734   PV
Tactyl Technologies, Inc., 2595 Commerce Way, 92083, pg. 1425   PB
Taiyo Yuden (U.S.A) Inc., 2580 Pioneer Ave., 92083, pg. 1349   IT
Watkins Manufacturing Corp./Hot Spring Portable Spas, 1280 Park Ctr. Dr., 92083, pg. 1054   PB

Walnut

Circuit City Western Div., 680 S. Lemon Ave., 91789, pg. 374   PB
GATX Logistics, Inc.-California (Kellogg), 20450 E. Business Pkwy., 91789, pg. 691   PB
GATX Logistics, Inc.-California (TCE), 20002 E. Business Pkwy., 91789, pg. 691   PB
LIGHTS OF AMERICA, INC., 611 Reyes Dr., 91789, pg. 667   PV
SHEA HOMES, 655 Brea Canyon Rd., 91789, pg. 990   PV

Walnut Creek

Air Liquide Corporation Bulk Gases Division, 2121 N. California Blvd., 94596, pg. 37   IT
AirTouch Cable, 2999 Oak Road, 94596, pg. 34   PB
AirTouch Cellular, 2999 Oak Rd., 94596, pg. 34   PB
AirTouch International, 2999 Oak Rd., 94596, pg. 34   PB
AirTouch Properties, 2999 Oak Road, 94596, pg. 34   PB
Alphagaz Division, 2121 N. California Blvd., 94596, pg. 37   IT
Amistad Gathering Co., 1333 N. California, 94596, pg. 593   IT
BWC FINANCIAL CORP., 1400 Civic Dr., 94596, pg. 108   PV
Bank of the West, 1450 Treat Blvd., 94596, pg. 163   IT

BASIC AMERICAN FOODS, 2999 Oak Rd., 94596, pg. 121   PV
Best Temporaries Federal Systems, Inc., 301 Lennon Lane, 94598, pg. 1760   PB
Bouygues Offshore USA, 31 Fraser Ct., 94596, pg. 206   IT
Calaveras Cement Company, 2033 N. Main St., Ste. 500, 94596, pg. 605   IT
Cardox Division, California Plaza, 2121 N. California Blvd., 94596, pg. 37   IT
Chromatography Systems, 2700 Mitchell Dr., 94598, pg. 1710   PB
Citicorp National System, Data Ctr. 1400 Treat Bouleva, 94596, pg. 378   PB
Contra Costa Newspapers, Inc., 2640 Shadeland Dr., 94598, pg. 964   PB
Contra Costa Times, 2640 Shadeland Dr., 94598, pg. 964   PB
General Employment Enterprises, Inc., 675 Ygnacio Valley Rd., Ste. B206, 94596, pg. 715   PB
Harbor Financial/New America, 2175 N. California Blvd., Ste. 800, 94596, pg. 644   PB
Integral Systems, Inc., 2730 Shadelands Dr., 94598, pg. 242   IT
Integrated Health Concepts, 141 N. Civic Dr., 94596, pg. 1013   PB
Jacuzzi, Inc., 100 N. Wiget Ln., 94598, pg. 1684   PB
Kaiser International Services Corp., 1333 N. California, 94596, pg. 593   IT
Kaiser Pacific Properties Corp., 1333 N. California, 94596, pg. 593   IT
Liquid Air Corporation, Package Gases Div., 2121 N. California Blvd., 94596, pg. 37   IT
LONGS DRUG STORES CORPORATION, 141 N. Civic Dr., 94596, pg. 1013   PB
Maxis, 2121 N. California Blvd., Ste. 600, 94596-3572, pg. 569   PB
Northern California Region, 1333 N. California, 94596, pg. 593   IT
Pacific Region, 2175 N. California Blvd., Ste. 303, 94596, pg. 1024   IT
Safeway Supply, Inc., 2800 Ignacio Valley Rd., 94598, pg. 1426   PB
Tampella Power Corp., 3325 Arbolado Dr., 94598, pg. 1353   IT
Teradyne Assembly Test/West Division, 2625 Shadelands Dr., 94598, pg. 1581   PB
Vitalaire Corporation, California Plaza, 2121 N. California Blvd., 94596, pg. 37   IT
Walnut Creek Restaurant Corp., 3800 Valle Vista, 94598, pg. 1022   PV
Western Medical Services Inc., 301 Lennon Ln., 94598-2404, pg. 1760   PB
Western Permanent Services Agency, Inc., 301 Lennon Ln., 94598-2404, pg. 1760   PB
WESTERN STAFF SERVICES, 301 Lennon Ln., 94598-2453, pg. 1760   PB
Western Staff Services (USA), Inc., 301 Lennon Ln., 94598-2453, pg. 1760   PB
Western Temporary Services Div., 301 Lennon Ln., 94598-2404, pg. 1760   PB

Walnut Grove

CGG American Services, Inc., 14440 Walnut Grove Thornton Rd., 95690, pg. 241   IT

Watsonville

California Farm Products, 423 Salinas Rd., 95076, pg. 1480   PB
CALIFORNIA STRAWBERRY COMMISSION, 41 Hangar Way, 95076-0269, pg. 201   PV
Cornerstone Propane G.P. Inc., 432 Westridge Dr., 95076, pg. 1201   PB
Dean Foods Vegetable Company, P.O. Box 1339, 345 Harvest Dr. Dr., 95077, pg. 490   PB
First National Bank of Central California, 655 Main St., 95077-1540, pg. 1248   PB
MARTY FRANICH AUTO CENTER, 550 Arthur Rd., Auto Center Dr., 95076, pg. 423   PV
Granite Construction Inc.-Heavy Construction Div., 24 San Juan Rd. Extension, 95076, pg. 759   PB
Granite Construction Inc.-Monterey Bay Div., 735 W. Beach St., 95076, pg. 759   PB
GRANITE CONSTRUCTION INCORPORATED, 585 W. Beach St., 95076, pg. 759   PB
Higgins Monterey Bay Operations, 417 Salinas Rd., 95076, pg. 527   PV
MONTEREY MUSHROOMS, INC., 260 Westgate Dr., 95076, pg. 758   PV
SKYWAY FREIGHT SYSTEMS, INC., 225 Westridge Dr., 95076, pg. 1005   PV
Skyway Systems, Inc., 225 Westbridge Dr., 95076, pg. 1005   PV
Smucker Oxnard Plant, 423 Salinas Rd., 95076, pg. 1430   PB
Watlow Anafaze, 334 Westridge Dr., 95076, pg. 1153   PV
WEST MARINE, INC., 500 Westridge Dr., 95076-4100, pg. 1756   PB

West Covina

CALIFORNIA STATE BANK, 100 N. Barranca St., 91791, pg. 294   PB
California State Bank-West Covina, 100 N. Barranca St., pg. 294   PB
Citrus State Development Corp., 100 N. Barranca St., 91791, pg. 294   PB

Granada Realty Services, Inc., 100 N. Barranca St., 91791, pg. 294   PB
SOUTHWEST WATER COMPANY, 225 N. Barranca Ave., Ste. 200, 91791-1605, pg. 1494   PB

West Hills

Guaranty Asset Protection Services, Inc., 6700 Fallbrook Ave., 91307, pg. 857   PB

West Hollywood

Dailey & Associates, 8687 Melrose Ave., 90069, pg. 909   PB
TICKETMASTER CORPORATION, 8800 Sunset Blvd., 7th Fl., 90069, pg. 1084   PV

West Sacramento

The Affordable Medical Networks, 750 Riverpoint Dr., 95605, pg. 635   PB
AmeriSource-Sacramento Div., 3910 Seaport Blvd., 95691, pg. 97   PB
BHP Steel Building Products USA Ltd., 2110 Enterprise Blvd., 95691, pg. 226   IT
Bel Air Markets, 500 W. Capital Ave., 95605, pg. 908   PV
California Woodfiber Corp., 1880 S. River Rd., 95691, pg. 845   IT
Earl Construction Company, 3940 Industrial Blvd., Ste. 100-D, 95691, pg. 1051   PB
Fleming Foods West - Sacramento Div., 3771 Channel Dr., 95691, pg. 653   PB
MTS, INC., 2500 Del Monte St., Bldg. C, 95691, pg. 688   PV
REX MOORE ELECTRICAL CONTRACTORS & ENGINEERS, P.O. Box 980010, 95798-0010, pg. 801   PV
NOR-CAL BEVERAGE CO., INC., 2286 Stone Blvd., 95691, pg. 801   PV
Occupational-Urgent Care Health Systems (OUCH), 750 Riverpoint Dr., 95605, pg. 635   PB
Pulse Magazine, 2500 Del Monte St., 95691, pg. 688   PV
RALEY'S & BEL AIR, 500 W. Capital Ave., 95605, pg. 907   PV
RICE GROWERS ASSOCIATION OF CALIFORNIA, 1550 Harbor Blvd., Ste. 200, 95691, pg. 927   PB
Tower Records, 2500 Del Monte St., 95691, pg. 688   PV
Turner Construction Company, 1450 Harbor Blvd., Ste. 1100, 95691, pg. 1645   PB
Warehouse Concepts, Inc., 500 W. Capital Ave., 95605, pg. 908   PV

Westchester

Hughes Electronics Corporation, 7200 Hughes Terrace, 90045, pg. 720   PB

Westlake Village

American Nucleonics Corp., 696 Hampshire Rd., 91361, pg. 556   PB
Bank of America Auto Lease Center, 2660 Townsgate Rd., 91361, pg. 181   PB
CONDOR PACIFIC INDUSTRIES, INC., 31829 La Tienda Dr., 91362-4011, pg. 262   PV
CONSOLIDATED ELECTRICAL DISTRIBUTORS, 31356 Via Colinas #107, 91362, pg. 265   PV
COYOTE NETWORK SYSTEMS, INC., 4360 Park Ter. Dr., 91361, pg. 455   PB
Dimeric Development Labortory, 340 N. Westlake Blvd., Ste. 120, 91362, pg. 1309   PB
DIODES INCORPORATED, 3050 E. Hill Crest Dr., Ste. 200, 91362, pg. 510   PB
DOLE FOOD COMPANY, INC., 31365 Oak Crest Dr., 91361, pg. 515   PB
Dole Fresh Fruit Company, 5795 Lindero Cyn Dr., 91361, pg. 515   PB
Dole Packaged Food Company, 5795 Lindero Canyon Rd., 91362, pg. 515   PB
EDD-Ventura, 125 Auburn Ct., Ste. 110, 91362, pg. 205   PB
Entree Corporation, 4360 Park Ter. Dr., 91361, pg. 455   PB
Jaco Electronics, Inc., 2260 Townsgate Rd., 91361, pg. 921   PB
Newcom, Inc., 31166 Via Colinas, 91362, pg. 147   PB
Raypak, Inc., 31111 Agoura Rd., 91361, pg. 1022   IT
RIGHT START, INC., 5334 Sterling Center Dr., 91361, pg. 930   PB
Sato Kogyo U.S.A. Corporation, 2659 Townsgate Rd., Ste. 101, 91361, pg. 1197   IT
Sato Kogyo U.S.A. Corporation - Los Angeles, 2659 Townsgate Rd., Ste. 101, 91361, pg. 1197   IT
Standard Pacific Ventura, 32123 Lindero Canyon Rd., 94017, pg. 1504   PB
Sterling Electronics, 31200 Via Colinas, Ste. 110, 91362, pg. 1051   PB
Sunrise Medical Mobility Products, 5601 Lindale Canyon Rd., Ste. 205, 91362, pg. 1536   PB
TMP Worldwide, Inc., 2801 Townsgate Rd., Ste. 215, 91361, pg. 1064   PV
Volkswagen of America Administration Center West, 5388 No. Sterling Center Dr., 91361, pg. 1474   IT
Westlake Medical Center, 4415 S. Lakeview Canyon Rd., 91361, pg. 1697   PB

Westminster

Alum-A-Therm, 7474 Garden Grove Blvd., 92683, pg. 999   PB

PB - *U.S. Public Companies Volume*
PV - *U.S. Private Companies Volume*
IT - *International Public & Private Companies Volume*

1158

Geographic Index-U.S.

Levolor Home Fashions, 7150 Fenwick Ln., 92683, pg. 1177 **PB**

Turco Products Division, 7320 Bolsa Ave., 92683-5211, pg. 446 **IT**

Whittier

American Isuzu Motors Inc., 2300 Pellisier Pkwy. N., 4th Fl., 90608, pg. 692 **IT**

Amtech Elevator Services, 13215 E. Penn St., Ste. 630, 90602, pg. 2 **IT**

CAL-AIR INC., 12393 Slausom Ave., 90606, pg. 199 **PV**

CALCOR SPACE FACILITY, INC., 12031 E. Philadelphia St., 90601, pg. 200 **PV**

Consolidated Converting Co., 2601 Workman Mill Rd., 90601, pg. 466 **PB**

Delta Contractor Equipment Rental, Inc., 8205 S. Sorenson Ave., 90670, pg. 673 **PV**

Eastman Kodak Company Distribution, 12100 Rivera Rd., 90606-2602, pg. 555 **PB**

First Strategic Group, 7032 Comstock Ave., 90602, pg. 1157 **PB**

Hood Corporation, 8205 S. Sorensen Ave., 90606, pg. 673 **PV**

LOMBARDI HOLDINGS INC., 8201 S. Sorenson Ave., 90606, pg. 673 **PV**

OLTMANS CONSTRUCTION COMPANY, 10005 Mission Mill Rd., 90608-0985, pg. 815 **PV**

PECK ROAD FORD TRUCK SALES, 2450 Kella Ave., 90601, pg. 846 **PV**

Scope Beauty Ent., Inc., 6538 Greenleaf Ave., 90601, pg. 1444 **PB**

Unitog Rental Facility, 2829 Workman Mill Rd., 90601, pg. 1693 **PB**

Western Region, P.O. Box 922, 90606, pg. 687 **PV**

ZIEMAN MANUFACTURING COMPANY, 7909 S. Painter Ave., 90602, pg. 1205 **PV**

Wildomar

Inland Valley Regional Medical Center, 36485 Inland Valley Dr., 92595, pg. 1697 **PB**

Williams

Colusa County Canning Co., 6229 Myers Rd., 95987, pg. 1396 **IT**

Willits

ADVANCED MANUFACTURING & DEVELOPMENT, 300 E. Hill Rd., 95490, pg. 22 **PV**

Wilmington

ASSOCIATED POWER, INC., 1741 Colon St., 90744, pg. 92 **PV**

IT Corp., 336 W. Anaheim St., 90744, pg. 908 **PB**

Los Angeles Marine Terminal, Berth 172, 90744, pg. 692 **PB**

TRMI Holdings Inc., P.O. Box 817, 90748-0817, pg. 1583 **PB**

Winterhaven

American Girl, P.O. Box 879, 92283, pg. 804 **PB**

Wofford Heights

Arden Water Company, 721 Sierra Vista Dr., 93285, pg. 516 **PB**

Kernville Domestic Water Company, 721 Sierra Vista Dr., 93285, pg. 516 **PB**

Woodland

Ames Co., Inc., 1485 Tanforan Ave., 95776, pg. 1746 **PB**

The Lamson & Sessions Co., 1776 E. Beamer St., 95695, pg. 976 **PB**

VALLEY RECORD DISTRIBUTORS, INC., 1280 Santa Anita Ct., 95776, pg. 1132 **PV**

Western Passage Express, 281 N. County Rd., 95695, pg. 1122 **PV**

Woodland Hills

APPLAUSE INC., 6101 Variel Ave., 91365, pg. 78 **PV**

BLUE CROSS OF CALIFORNIA, 21555 Oxnard St., 91367, pg. 152 **PB**

M.J. Brock & Sons, Inc., 21800 Burbank Blvd., 3rd. Fl., 91367, pg. 1414 **PB**

Care America-Southern CA, 6300 Canoga Ave., 91367, pg. 153 **PB**

CATALINA YACHTS, INC., 21200 Victory Blvd., 91367, pg. 219 **PV**

Cigna Specialty Insurance Company, 21860 Burbank Blvd., 90010, pg. 366 **PB**

Cooke Media Group, Inc., P.O. Box 4200, 91365, pg. 273 **PV**

Courtaulds Aerospace Inc., 21800 Burbank Blvd. 3rd Fl., 91367, pg. 339 **IT**

EL CAMINO RESOURCES, LTD., 21051 Warner Ctr. Ln., 91367-6512, pg. 366 **PV**

Federal Home Loan Mortgage Corporation (Freddie Mac)-Western Region, 21700 Oxnard St., 91367, pg. 615 **PB**

General Employment Enterprises, Inc., 5850 Canoga Ave., 91367, pg. 715 **PB**

Government Electronics Div., P.O. Box 2800, 91365, pg. 293 **PB**

GuestInformant, Inc., 21220 Erwin St., 91367, pg. 11 **PB**

Guidance & Control Systems Div., 5500 Canoga Ave., 91367-6698, pg. 1002 **PB**

Information Management Division, 5900 Canoga Ave., 91367, pg. 1516 **PB**

Kaufman and Broad Mortgage Co., 21650 Oxnord St., Ste. 300, 91367, pg. 945 **PB**

Litton Computer Services-Western Regional Data Center, P.O. Box 4040, 5490 Canoga Ave., 91365-4040, pg. 1002 **PB**

LITTON INDUSTRIES, INC., 21240 Burbank, 91367-6675, pg. 1002 **PB**

Manulife Financial - San Fernando Valley, 21800 Oxnard St., Ste. 200, 91367, pg. 841 **IT**

Navigation, Guidance & Control Systems, 5500 Canoga Ave., 91367-6698, pg. 1002 **PB**

PAC RIM HOLDING CORPORATION, 6200 Canoga Ave., 91367-2402, pg. 1246 **PB**

The Pacific Rim Assurance Company, 6200 Canoga Ave., 91367-2402, pg. 1246 **PB**

P.L. PORTER CO., 6355 De Soto Ave., 91367, pg. 876 **PV**

REAL Applications, Ltd., 21011 Warner Ctr. Ln., 91367, pg. 366 **PV**

Richardson Electronics Ltd.-Western, 21243 Ventura Blvd., 91364, pg. 1388 **PB**

Silgan Container Corp., 21800 Oxnard St., Ste. 600, 91367, pg. 1473 **PB**

SYNCOR INTERNATIONAL CORPORATION, 6464 Canoga Ave., 91367-2407, pg. 1548 **PB**

TIG Insurance Co., 6300 Canoga Ave., 91367, pg. 1556 **PB**

Thomson Passive Components Corp., 6203 Variel Ave., Unit A, P.O. Box 4051, 91365-4051, pg. 1384 **IT**

20TH CENTURY INDUSTRIES, 6301 Owensmouth Ave., Ste. 700, 91367, pg. 1646 **PB**

20th Century Insurance Co., 6301 Owensmouth Ave., 91367, pg. 1646 **PB**

21st Century Casualty Co., 6301 Owensmouth Ave., 91367, pg. 1646 **PB**

Underwriters Reinsurance, 22801 Ventura Blvd., Ste. 300, 91364, pg. 42 **PB**

United Insurance Company of America, 20931 Burbank Blvd., 91367, pg. 1694 **PB**

Value Property Trust, 22120 Clarendon St., Ste 230, 91367, pg. 1707 **PB**

VERTEL, 21300 Victory Blvd., Ste. 1200, 91267, pg. 1717 **PB**

Vertel, 21300 Victory Blvd., #1200, 91367, pg. 1717 **PB**

WEIDER PUBLICATIONS, INC., 21100 Erwin St., 91367, pg. 1159 **PV**

Wellpoint Health Networks, Inc., 21555 Oxnard St., 91367-4943, pg. 152 **PV**

Weyerhaeuser Mortgage Company, 6320 Canoga Ave., 91367, pg. 1764 **PB**

ZENITH NATIONAL INSURANCE CORP., 21255 Califa St., 91367-5021, pg. 1790 **PB**

Yorba Linda

COMARCO, INC., 22800 Savi Ranch Pkwy., Ste. 214, 92687, pg. 406 **PB**

Fleetwood Credit Corp., 22840 Savi Ranch Rd., 92686, pg. 663 **PB**

Jaco Electronics, 22815 Savi Ranch Pkwy., Ste. E, 92887, pg. 920 **PB**

A.J. Oster West, Inc., 22833 LaPalma Ave., 92687, pg. 1219 **PB**

TACTech, Inc., 22700 Savi Ranch Pkwy., 92687, pg. 1792 **PV**

Wine World Estates, Inc., 22800 Savi Ranch Pkwy., 92687, pg. 917 **IT**

Yosemite National Park

Yosemite Concession Services Co., 95389, pg. 1216 **IT**

Yountville

Domaine Chandon, Inc., California Dr., 94599, pg. 781 **IT**

Yucaipa

MCANALLY ENTERPRISES, INC., 12215 Seventh St., 92399, pg. 718 **PV**

COLORADO

Arvada

ADDWEST MINERALS, INC., 5460 Ward Rd., Ste. 202, 80002, pg. 17 **PV**

COBE Cardiovascular Inc., 14401 W. 65th Way, 80004, pg. 667 **IT**

Graco Contractor Equipment Div., 5280 Vivian St., 80002-1921, pg. 757 **PB**

MK Centennial, 15000 W. 64th Ave., 80001, pg. 1134 **PB**

Sunstrand Fluid Handling, 14845 W. 64th Ave., 80004, pg. 1534 **PB**

Aspen

Colorado National Bank Aspen, 420 E. Main St., 81611, pg. 1680 **PB**

Pitkin County Bank & Trust Company, 534 E. Hyman Ave., 81611, pg. 1793 **PB**

SPORT OBERMEYER LTD., USA, 115 AABC, 81611, pg. 1026 **PV**

Aurora

ADT Security Services, Inc., 14200 E. Exposition Ave., 80012, pg. 1649 **PB**

Aurora Regional Medical Center, 1501 S. Potomac St., 80012, pg. 403 **PB**

Brown-Strauss Steel, 20400 E. 26th Ave., 80011, pg. 153 **PB**

Burns & Wilcox - Aurora Office, 2950 South Jamaica Court, Ste. 200, 80014, pg. 609 **PV**

Capstone Electronics Corp., 3254 Fraser St., 80011, pg. 134 **PB**

Colorado Air Restaurant Corp., 10081 E. 25th Ave., 80010, pg. 1023 **PV**

Daher Golden Eagle - Denver, 3390 Peoria St., #300, 80010, pg. 749 **PB**

Denver Auto Auction, 17400 E. 31st Ave., 80011, pg. 282 **PV**

Elkay Plastics Co., Inc., Stock Service Center, 14600 E. 35th Pl., Unit H, 80011, pg. 372 **PV**

Frederic Printing Company, 14701 E. 38th Ave., 80011, pg. 265 **PV**

Johnson Storage & Moving, Aurora, 5050 Havana, 80239, pg. 594 **PV**

The Louisiana Purchase, 80016, pg. 105 **PB**

M&N Valve, 14704 E. 33rd Place, 80011, pg. 1449 **IT**

Montgomery & Collins, Inc. of Wyoming, 3151 S. Vaughn Way, Ste. 505, 80014, pg. 366 **PB**

OEA Automotive Safety Products Division, 34501 E. Quincy Ave., 80015, pg. 1207 **PB**

OEA, INC., 34501 E. Quincy Ave., 80015, pg. 1206 **PB**

Pulte Colorado Division, 15150 E. Iliff Ave., 80014, pg. 1344 **PB**

RP alpha/Denver, 3151 S. Vaughn Way, Ste. 512, 80014, pg. 950 **PV**

Sable Care Center, 656 Dillon Way, 80011, pg. 836 **PB**

Silver-Weibull, 14800 E. Moncrieff Place, 80011, pg. 705 **PB**

Subaru Central Region, Inc., 15000 E. 39th Ave., 80011, pg. 523 **IT**

XEL Corporation, 17101 E. Ohio Dr., 80017-3878, pg. 1430 **PB**

Berthoud

Titan Homes Div., P.O. Box 10, 2221 Clayton, 80513, pg. 332 **PB**

Boulder

AMERICAN EDUCATIONAL PRODUCTS, 5350 Manhattan Cir., Ste. 210, 80301, pg. 71 **PB**

Amgen Boulder, Inc., 3200 Walnut St., 80301, pg. 101 **PB**

Amrion Inc., 6565 Odell Pl., 80301-3330, pg. 1767 **PB**

Applied Films Corp., 6797 Winchester Cir., 80501, pg. 519 **PB**

Artemis Management Systems, 6260 Lookout Rd., 80301, pg. 465 **PV**

AutoSystems Development Laboratory, 1050 Walnut St., Ste. 515, 80302, pg. 1309 **PV**

BEI Graphics, 3550 Frontier Ave., 80301, pg. 796 **PB**

Ball Aerospace Systems Division, 1600 Commerce St., 80301-1062, pg. 171 **PB**

Binks Research & Development Corp., 1791 Range St., 80301-2714, pg. 229 **PB**

Boulder Publishing, Inc., 1048 Pearl, 80302, pg. 1447 **PB**

CareerTrack Inc., 3080 Center Green Dr., 80301, pg. 1555 **PB**

Cattle Feeding Div., 5408 Idylwild Trail, 80301, pg. 268 **PV**

Celestial Beverages, Inc., 4600 Sleepytime Dr., 80301-3292, pg. 320 **PB**

CELESTIAL SEASONINGS, 4600 Sleepytime Dr., 80301-3292, pg. 319 **PB**

COLORADO MEDTECH, INC., 6175 Longbow Dr., 80301, pg. 401 **PB**

Denver Autometrics, 6235 Lookout Rd., 80301, pg. 1325 **IT**

EUA Cogenex West, 2970 Wilderness Pl., Ste. 110, 80301, pg. 549 **PB**

Eastman Software Storage Management Group, Inc., 4760 Walnut St., 80301, pg. 555 **PB**

EXABYTE CORPORATION, 1685 38th St., 80301, pg. 597 **PB**

Exabyte FSC Ltd., 1685 38th St., 80301, pg. 597 **PB**

Gensym Corporation, Western Regional Office, 4940 Pearl E. Cir., Ste. 200, 80301, pg. 731 **PB**

Graftele, 6260 Lookout Rd., 80301, pg. 465 **PV**

Hewlett-Packard Company, 2945 Center Green Ct., S., Ste. A, 80301, pg. 813 **PB**

Hewlett-Packard Company, 3005 Center Green Dr., Ste. 205, 80301, pg. 813 **PB**

Highline Financial Services, Inc., Canyon Ctr., 1881 Ninth St., Ste. 300, 80302, pg. 1785 **PB**

Link-VTC, Inc., 6350 Nautilus Court S., 80301, pg. 684 **PB**

MacDonald Dettwiler Technologies Inc., 1877 Broadway, Ste. 405, 80302, pg. 1229 **PB**

Micro Motion Inc., 7070 Winchester Circle, 80301, pg. 574 **PB**

Mountain Chai, 4699 Nautilus Ct. S., #404, 80301, pg. 320 **PB**

Mountain Optech Inc., 4775 Walnut St., Ste. A, 80301, pg. 862 **PV**

NEXSTAR PHARMACEUTICALS, INC., 2860 Wilderness Pl., 80301, pg. 1180 **PB**

Nexstar Pharmaceuticals, Inc., 2860 Wilderness Pl., 80301, pg. 1180 **PB**

PB - U.S. Public Companies Volume
PV - U.S. Private Companies Volume
IT - International Public & Private Companies Volume

Geographic Index-U.S.

COLORADO DIRECTORY OF CORPORATE AFFILIATIONS

Object Technology Group, 4900 Pearl East Circle, 80301, pg. 1154 IT
Piper Jaffray Inc., Garden Level N., 1877 Broadway, Ste. Three, 80302-5222, pg. 1302 PB
RELA, Inc., 6175 Longbow Dr., 80301, pg. 401 PB
Schwinn Cycling & Fitness Inc., 1690 38th St., 80301, pg. 975 PV
SCHWINN HOLDINGS, 1690 38th St., 80301, pg. 975 PV
Senetics, 1035 Pearl St., Ste. 201, 80302, pg. 1755 PB
STAFFING SOLUTIONS, 2741 Mapleton Ave., 80304, pg. 1028 PV
Syntex Chemicals, Inc., 2075 N. 55th St., 80301, pg. 1120 IT
Tea Direct, 4600 Sleepytime Dr., 80301-3292, pg. 320 PB
VeriBest Inc., 6101 Lookout Rd., Ste. A, 80301, pg. 891 PB
Vesta Medical, Inc., 5920 Longbow Dr., 80301-9015, pg. 1284 PB
Wenco Inc., 21267 Juniper Ave., 80304, pg. 1754 PB
Western Aggregates, Inc., 11728 Hwy. 93, 80303, pg. 672 IT
Westpeak Investment Advisors, Inc., 1011 Walnut St., Ste. 400, 80302, pg. 738 PV
Xlinx, Inc., Boulder, 2300 55th St., 80301, pg. 1786 PB

Brighton

Kuner-Empson Company, 221 No. Kuner Rd., 80601, pg. 393 PV
MetalWest LLC, 1229 S. Fulton Ave., 80601, pg. 817 PV
VALLEY BANK & TRUST, 30 N. 4th Ave., 80601, pg. 1132 PV

Broomfield

Ball Aerospace & Technologies Corp., Ten Longs Peak Dr., 80020-2510, pg. 171 PB
Ball Telecommunication Products Division, Ten Longs Peak Dr., 80021-2510, pg. 171 PB
Bestop, Inc., 2100 W. Midway Blvd., 80020, pg. 830 IT
Carefree of Colorado, 2145 W. 6th Ave., 80020, pg. 217 PB
CORPORATE EXPRESS, INC., One Environmental Way, 80021-3416, pg. 449 PB
Geneva Pharmaceuticals, Inc., 2555 W. Midway Blvd., 80038, pg. 973 IT
Green Tree Acceptance, Inc., 9030 Yukon, 80021, pg. 762 PB
Key Products, 2780 Industrial Ln., 80020, pg. 446 PV
Marshall Erdman & Assoc., Inc., 891 Interlocken Pkwy., 80020, pg. 380 PV
Microsemi Corp.-Colorado, 800 Hoyt St., 80020, pg. 1107 PB
Pentax Technologies Corp., 100 Technology Dr., Ste. 200, 80021, pg. 85 IT

Canon City

DFC Ceramics Inc., P.O. Box 110, 81215-0110, pg. 893 IT
Morgan Refractories Inc., P.O. Box 110, 81215-0110, pg. 893 IT

Castle Rock

Woolrich Store Co., c/o Castle Rock Factory Shops, 5050 Factory Shops Blvd., Ste. 400, 80104, pg. 1188 PV

Colorado Springs

AMI Industries, Inc., 1275 N. Newport Rd., 80916, pg. 401 PB
AVX Corp., 2435 Executive Circle, 80905, pg. 775 IT
Ackerman McQueen, Inc., 400 Plaza of the Rockies, 111 S. Tejan St., 80903, pg. 13 PV
Akzo Electronics Materials Co., 2853 Janitell Rd., 80906, pg. 48 IT
AMERICAN TELECASTING, INC., 5575 Tech Center Dr., Ste. 300, 80919, pg. 93 PB
Ampex Corporation, 600 Wooten Rd., 80915-3597, pg. 104 PB
ANALYTICAL SURVEYS, INC., 1935 Jamboree Dr., Ste. 100, 80920, pg. 110 PB
Banta Global Turnkey, 116 W. Las Vegas, 80903, pg. 188 PB
BROADMOOR HOTEL, INC., One Lake Ave., 80906, pg. 170 PV
Castle Concrete Co., P.O. Box 2379, 7250 Allegheny Dr., 80919, pg. 441 PB
Colorado Interstate Gas Co., 2 N. Nevada Ave., 80903, pg. 390 PB
Colorado Springs Auto Auction Inc., 1-25 & Exit 132 E., 80931, pg. 1648 PB
Colorado Springs Cablevision, Inc., 213 N. Union, 80909, pg. 1610 PB
COOK COMMUNICATION MINISTRIES, 4050 Leevance View, 80918, pg. 272 PV
Coventry Homes of Colorado, 6915 Ashely Dr., 80922, pg. 495 PB
Current, Inc., P.O. Box 2559, 80901, pg. 498 PB
El Paso Restaurant Corp., 230 Point of the Pines Dr., 80907, pg. 1023 PV
Ford Microelectronics, Inc., 10440 State Hwy. 83, 80908, pg. 664 PB
Gates Land Co., 202 E. Cheyenne Mountain Blvd., Ste. I, 80906, pg. 249 PV
Gazette Telegraph, P.O. Box 1779, 80901, pg. 425 PV
Hewlett-Packard Company, 8245 N. Union, 80918, pg. 813 PB
ITT Federal Services Corporation, P.O. Box 15012, 1330 Inverness Dr., 80935-5012, pg. 859 PB
G.E JOHNSON CONSTRUCTION CO., INC., 310 S. 14th St., 80904, pg. 591 PV
Johnson Storage & Moving, Colorado Springs, 4226 N. Sinton Rd., 80907, pg. 594 PV
KKTV-TV, 3100 N. Nevada, 80907, pg. 16 PB
Kaman Instrumentation Corp., 1500 Garden of the Gods Rd., 80933, pg. 942 PB
Kaman Sciences Corp., P.O. Box 7463, 1500 Garden of the Gods Rd., 80933, pg. 942 PB
Lockheed Martin Command & Control Systems, 9970 Federal Dr., 80921-3697, pg. 1008 PB
Logicon Geodynamics Central Division, 5450 Tech Center Dr., Ste 301, 80919, pg. 1199 PB
PHIL LONG FORD, 1212 Motor City Dr., 80906, pg. 675 PV
MCI Software Development & Information Technology, 2424 Garden of the Gods Rd., 80919, pg. 1024 PB
Martin Marietta Range Services, 1150 Academy Park Loop, Ste. 204, 80910-3716, pg. 1007 PB
MAXCOR MANUFACTURING, INC., 3020 N. Stone Ave., 80907, pg. 716 PV
Maytag Aircraft Corp., 6145 Lehman Dr., #300, 80932-2759, pg. 1093 PB
MOUNTAIN STATES PIPE & SUPPLY COMPANY, 111 W. Las Vegas, 80903, pg. 764 PV
NATIONAL SYSTEMS & RESEARCH CO., 5475 Mark Dabling, Ste. 200, 80918, pg. 787 PV
NXTREND TECHNOLOGY, INC., 5225 N. Academy Blvd., 80918, pg. 809 PV
The Ohio Mattress Company Licensing & Components Group, 6275 Lake Shore Ct., 80915, pg. 979 PV
Philip Laser Magnetic Storage, 4425 ArrowsWest Dr., 80907-7900, pg. 1054 IT
Piper Jaffray Inc., 25 N. Cascade Ave., Ste. 100, 80903-1642, pg. 1302 PB
ProSoft International Co., Inc., 444 E. Costilla St., 80903, pg. 441 PB
Qualifed Plans for Health-Colorado Springs, 5575 Tech Ctr Dr., Ste. 120, 80919, pg. 678 PB
Quantum Corporation, 1110 Bayfield Dr., 80906, pg. 1350 PB
Richmond Homes, Inc. II, 6455 N. Union Blvd., Ste. 200, 80918, pg. 1025 PB
Schlage Lock Company, 1915 Jamboree, Ste. 165, 80920, pg. 876 PB
Shepard's, 555 Middle Creek Pkwy., 80921, pg. 1095 IT
Shepard's, 555 Middle Creek Pkwy., 80921, pg. 1616 PB
Svedala Pumps & Process, 621 S. Sierra Madre, 80903, pg. 1325 IT
Transit Mix Concrete Co., 444 E. Costilla St., 80903, pg. 441 PB
UMB Bank Colorado, 2 North Nevada Ave, Suite 100, 80903, pg. 1654 PB
UMB Bank of the West, N.A., 5910 E. Galley Rd., 80915, pg. 1654 PB
VELCON FILTERS, INC., 4525 Centennial Blvd., 80919, pg. 1135 PV
Walter Drake, Inc., Drake Bldg., 4510 Edison Ave., 80915, pg. 421 PV
Weitz-Cohen Construction Co., 5575 Tech Center Dr., Ste. 310, 80919, pg. 1161 PV
Western Forge Div., 4607 Forge Rd., 80907, pg. 575 PB
Western International Media Corporation, 102 S. Tejon St. #1100, 80903, pg. 1167 PV
WESTMORELAND COAL CO., Holly Sugar Bldg., 14th Fl., Two N. Cascade Ave., 80903-1614, pg. 1761 PB
Wigand Corporation, 850 Elkton Dr., 80907, pg. 1038 PV

Commerce City

Browning-Ferris Industries of Colorado, Inc., 8484 Tower Rd., 80022, pg. 263 PB
Colorado Auction Services Corporation, 6955 E. 50th Ave., 80022, pg. 282 PV
Colorado Institutional Foods, 5199 Ivy St., 80022, pg. 989 PV
Dayton Superior Corp., 4975 Pontiac St., 80022, pg. 932 PV
Jeffco Land Reclamation, Inc., 8480 Tower Rd., 80022, pg. 264 PB
Kintetsu World Express Inc., 6717 E. 50th Ave., 80022, pg. 705 IT
Republic Paperboard Co.-Commerce City Mill, P.O. Box 1268, 5501 Brighton Blvd., 88022-1268, pg. 1378 PB
Secoroc Inc., 3700 E. 68th Ave., 80022, pg. 96 IT
STEEL, INC., 6245 Clermont St., 80022, pg. 1037 PV
Western Filter, 4545 E. 60th Ave., 80022-3137, pg. 1234 PB
Whale Scientific Inc., 4945 Monaco, 80022, pg. 1595 PB

Cortez

EMPIRE ELECTRIC ASSOCIATION, Drawer K, 81321, pg. 374 PV
Valley National Bank of Cortez, 350 W. Montezuma, 81321, pg. 1793 PB

Craig

Cyprus Empire Corporation, P.O. Box 68, 81626, pg. 471 PB

Crested Butte

Crested Butte Marriott Resort, 500 Gothic Rd., 81225, pg. 289 PV
CRESTED BUTTE MOUNTAIN RESORT, INC., 500 Gothic Rd., 81225, pg. 289 PV

Denver

A Bar A Ranch, 900 S. Broadway, 80209, pg. 249 PV
AiC Tech West, 7800 E. Union Ave., Ste. 630, 80237-2755, pg. 110 PB
APG SECURITY, INC., 10170 E. Mississippi, 80231, pg. 7 PV
AWS Remediation, Inc., 3190 S. Wadsworth Blvd., 80227, pg. 94 PB
Advertising Promotions, Inc., 4880 Havana St., 80239, pg. 1447 PB
Affiliated Banks Building Co., 1125 17th St., Ste. 1500, 80202, pg. 173 PB
Affiliated First Colorado Lease Company, 1125 17th St., Ste. 1500, 80202, pg. 173 PB
Agrium U.S., 4582 S. Ulster St., Ste. 1400, 80237, pg. 31 IT
AKZO Dreeland, 1600 Broadway, Ste. 2050, 80202, pg. 48 IT
Allen-Lewis Manufacturing Co., Inc., 5601 E. Logan, 80216, pg. 1554 PB
Allright Colorado, Inc., 1616 Glenarm Pl., Ste. 1910, 80202, pg. 42 PV
AMERICAN WATER WORKS ASSOCIATION, 6666 W. Quincy Ave., 80235, pg. 94 PB
AmeriServe of Denver, 1881 Bassett St., 80202, pg. 533 PV
ANSCHUTZ CORPORATION, 555 17th St., Ste. 2400, 80202, pg. 75 PV
The Anschutz Overseas Corp., 2400 Anaconda Tower, 555 17th St., 80202, pg. 75 PV
ARCO Coal Company, 555-17th St., 80202, pg. 144 PB
ASCENT ENTERTAINMENT GROUP, INC., 1200 17th St., Ste. 2800, 80202, pg. 138 PB
Aspen Pet Products, Inc., 11701 E. 53rd. Ave., 80239, pg. 566 PB
AUTO-TROL TECHNOLOGY CORPORATION, 12500 N. Washington St., 80241-2400, pg. 148 PB
Bakers Square Restaurants, 400 W. 48th Ave., 80216, pg. 1719 PB
Band-It-Idex, Inc., 4799 Dahlia St., 80216, pg. 862 PB
Bank One, Colorado, 1125 17th St., Ste. 1500, 80202, pg. 173 PB
Barrett Fuels Corporation, 1515 Arapahoe St., Twr. 3, Ste. 1000, 80202, pg. 191 PB
BARRETT RESOURCES CORPORATION, 1515 Arapahoe St., Twr. 3, Ste. 1000, 80202, pg. 191 PB
Benham & Company, P.O. Box 22139, 80222, pg. 1103 PV
Bergen Brunswig Drug Company, 501 W. 44th Ave., 80216, pg. 213 PB
Bergen Brunswig Medical Corporation, 5401 Oswego, 80239, pg. 214 PB
BROE COMPANIES, 252 Clayton St., Ste. 400, 80206, pg. 171 PV
Burro Pipeline Corp., 633 17th St., Ste. 1550, 80202, pg. 1618 PB
CGF Sign, Inc., 2930 W. Ninth Ave., 80204, pg. 194 PV
CRSS Constructors, Inc., 1670 Broadway, Ste. 3200, 80202, pg. 922 PB
Cable Car Beverage Corporation, 717 17th St., Ste. 1475, 80202-3314, pg. 1635 PB
Cal Emblem, Inc., 1455 S. Platte River Dr., 80223, pg. 199 PV
Calco International, Inc., Two Denver Highlands, 10065 E. Harvard Ave., Ste. 501, 80231, pg. 695 IT
Case Paper Co. of Colorado, 4900 Dahlia St., 80216, pg. 218 PV
Centre Court Travel, 12200 N. Pecos St., 80234, pg. 1758 PB
CHAMPION BOXED BEEF, 5900 York St., 80216, pg. 228 PV
Cigna Healthcare of Colorado, Inc., 3900 E. Mexico Ave., Ste. 1100, 80222, pg. 359 PB
Coast RV, Inc., 11575B E. 40th St., 80239, pg. 388 PB
CODY COMPANY, 3773 Cherry Creek N. Dr., 80209, pg. 249 PV
Cody Energy, Inc., 7555 E. Hampden, Ste. 600, 80231, pg. 249 PV
Cognos Corp.-Denver Sales Office, 4600 S. Ulster St., Ste. 700, 80237-7200, pg. 306 IT
College for Financial Planning, 4695 S. Monaco St., 80237, pg. 120 PB
Colorado Avalanche, 1200 17th St., Ste. 1000, 80202, pg. 138 PB
Colorado Business Bank, 821 17th St., 80202, pg. 255 PV
COLORADO BUSINESS BANKSHARES, INC., P.O. Box 8779, 80201, pg. 255 PV
Colorado Business Leasing, Inc., 999 18th St., Ste. 2400, 80202, pg. 255 PV
Colorado National Bank, 950 17th St., 80202, pg. 1680 PB
Colorado National Bankshares, Inc., 950 17th St., Ste. 2100, 80202, pg. 1680 PB
Columbine JDS Systems, Inc., 1999 Broadway, Suite 4000, 80202-3050, pg. 228 PB
CONVENIENCE PLUS PARTNERS LTD., 1055 Auraria Pkwy., Ste. 100, 80204, pg. 271 PV
CORAM HEALTHCARE CORPORATION, 1125 17th St., Ste. 2100, 80202, pg. 446 PB
DAKOTA MINING CORPORATION, 1560 Braodway, Ste. 880, 80202-1000, pg. 477 PB
Denver Baby Doe's Rest. Corp., 2530 23rd Ave., 80211, pg. 1023 PV
The Denver Business Journal, LLC, 1700 Broadway, Ste. 515, 80290, pg. 19 PV
Denver District Office, 9520 E. Jewell Ave., 80231, pg. 1106 PB
Denver Freeway Restaurant Corp., 2150 Bryant St., 80211, pg. 1023 PV

PB - *U.S. Public Companies Volume*
PV - *U.S. Private Companies Volume*
IT - *International Public & Private Companies Volume*

Geographic Index-U.S.

Denver Moving & Storage Co., 2153 S. Wabash St., 80231, pg. 594 PV
Denver Nuggets Limited Partnership, McNichols Arena, 1635 Clay St., 80204, pg. 138 PB
The Denver Publishing Company, 400 W. Colfax Ave., 80204, pg. 1447 PB
Denver Recycling Center, 4525 Ironton St., 80239, pg. 1378 PB
DENVER WHOLESALE FLORISTS COMPANY, 4800 Dahlia St., 80216, pg. 326 PV
Design-Build West, 1515 Arapahoe St., Tower 3, Ste. 700, 80202, pg. 905 PV
Dext Company of CO, 5801 Franklin St., 80216, pg. 1444 PB
Dixon Paper Co., P.O. Box 5285, T.A., 410 Raritan Way, 80217, pg. 902 PB
DRIVE TRAIN INDUSTRIES, 3301 Brighton Blvd., 80216, pg. 343 PV
Duke Energy Field Services, Inc., 370 17th St., Ste. 900, 80202, pg. 534 PB
E Prime, Inc., 1331 17th St., Ste. 601, 80202, pg. 1170 PB
Earth Sciences Consultants, Inc. (Rocky Mountain Opers.), 3190 S. Wadsworth Blvd., 80227, pg. 94 PB
EATON METAL PRODUCTS COMPANY, 4800 York St., 80216, pg. 358 PV
J.D. EDWARDS & COMPANY, 8055 E. Tufts Ave., Ste. 1331, 80237, pg. 365 PV
ENECO TECH GROUP, 1580 Lincoln St., Ste. 1000, 80203, pg. 376 PV
Equity Oil Company, Ste. 2110 S., Dominion Plaza, 600 17th St., 80202, pg. 590 PB
EvansGroup, Independence Plaza, 1050 17th St., Ste. 700, 80265, pg. 385 PV
Financial Asset Management Corporation, 3600 S. Yosemite St., Ste. 900, 80237, pg. 1025 PB
First Colorado Bankshares Insurance Co., 1125 17th St., Ste. 1500, 80202, pg. 173 PB
First Trust Corporation, 717 17th St., 80203, pg. 647 PB
FISCHER IMAGING CORPORATION, 12300 N. Grant St., 80241, pg. 647 PB
FOREST OIL CORPORATION, 1600 Broadway, Ste. 2200, 80202-4922, pg. 670 PB
1480 Welton, Inc., 1225 17th St., 80202, pg. 1170 PB
GATX Logistics, Inc.-Colorado, 5077 Kingston St., 80239, pg. 691 PB
Garden State Newspapers, Inc., 1560 Broadway, Ste. 1450, 80202, pg. 727 PV
GARY-WILLIAMS ENERGY CORPORATION, 370 17th St., Ste. 5300, 80202, pg. 440 PV
Gary-Williams Energy Corporation, 370 17th St., Ste. 5300, 80202, pg. 440 PV
The Gates Corporation, 900 S. Broadway, 80209, pg. 1396 IT
The Gates Rubber Company, 900 S. Broadway, 80209, pg. 1396 IT
General Atomics, 5000 S. Quebec St. #600, 80237-2705, pg. 709 PB
Geo-Con, Inc., 4582 S. Ulster St., Ste. 600, 80237, pg. 1657 PB
Geraghty & Miller, Inc., 1099 18th St., Ste. 2100, 80202, pg. 607 IT
Sheldon Good & Company-Colorado, 4600 S. Ulster St., Ste. 700, 80737, pg. 464 PV
Stephen Gould of Colorado, Inc., Unit 3, 4860 Ironton St., 80239, pg. 467 PV
Granges, Inc., 370 17th St., Ste. 3000, 80202, pg. 1723 PB
Graphic Arts Supply Division, 4100 Jackson St., 80216, pg. 205 PB
GREASE MONKEY INTERNATIONAL INC., 216 16th St., Ste. 1100, 80202, pg. 759 PB
Greeley Gas Co., 1301 Pennsylvania St., Ste. 800, 80203, pg. 145 PB
Green & Clear Lakes, 1225 17th St., 80202, pg. 1170 PB
Group Insurance of Colorado, 2140 S. Ivanhoe St., Ste. G12, 80222, pg. 484 PV
Hallwood Energy Partners, L.P., 4582 South Ulster St. Pkwy. Ste. 1700, 80237, pg. 778 PB
Hilb, Rogal and Hamilton Company of Denver, 455 Sherman, Ste. 390, 80203, pg. 827 PB
HomeAmerican Mortgage Corp., 3600 S. Yosemite St., Ste. 600 & 700, 80237, pg. 1025 PB
Hydro Conduit Corp., 8600 No. Welby Rd.; P.O. Box 29039, 80229, pg. 245 IT
IMA of Colorado Inc., 999 18th St., Ste. 2800, 80202, pg. 565 PV
Ikon Office Solutions-Colorado, 5285 Fox St., 80216, pg. 863 PB
Intermountain Bankshares of Colorado, Inc., 1125 17th St., Ste. 1500, 80202, pg. 173 PB
International Insurance Underwriters, Inc., 7551 W. Alameda, 80217, pg. 220 PB
Interplan, 1515 Arapahoe St., Tower 3, Ste. 700, 80202, pg. 905 PV
Invesco Funds Group, 7800 E. Union Ave., 80237, pg. 685 IT
Jacobs Engineering Group Inc., 600 17th St., Ste. 1100 N., 80202, pg. 921 PB
Jani King of Colorado, Inc., 518 17th St., 80203, pg. 582 PV
Janus Capital Corporation, 100 Fillmore St., Suite 300, 80206, pg. 944 PB
Jetstream Systems Inc., 4690 Joliet, 80239, pg. 118 PV
JOHNS MANVILLE CORPORATION, 717 17th St., 80202-5108, pg. 927 PB
JOHNSON STORAGE MOVING CO, 221 Broadway, 80203, pg. 594 PV
Earle M. Jorgensen Company/Denver, 6050 Downing St., 80216, pg. 600 PV
Joslins, 595 W. Hampden Ave., 80110, pg. 1090 PB
KDA/HEPY, P.C., 1201 18th St., Ste. 200, 80202, pg. 503 PV
KEZW-AM, Bldg. B, Ste. 131, 10200 E. Girard Ave., 80231, pg. 1636 PB
KHOW-AM/FM, 8975 E. Kenyon, 80237, pg. 922 PB
KIMN AM & KYGO FM, 1095 S. Monaco Pkwy., 80224, pg. 926 PB
KKHK, 10200 E. Girard Ave., Ste. B131, 80231, pg. 1636 PB
KMGH-TV, 123 Speer Blvd., 80203, pg. 1070 PB
KOA-AM, 1380 Lawrence St., Ste. 1300, 80204, pg. 922 PB
KOSI-FM, Bldg. B, Ste. 131, 10200 E. Girard Ave., 80231, pg. 1636 PB
KRFX-FM, 1380 Lawrence St., Ste. 1300, 80204, pg. 922 PB
KTM HOLDINGS CORP., 501 S. Cherry St., Ste. 600, 80222, pg. 604 PV
KUSA-TV, 1089 Bannock St., 80217, pg. 702 PB
KYGO AM & FM/KWMX AM & FM, 1095 S. Monaco Pkwy., 80224, pg. 926 PB
Kaiser Permanente, Rocky Mountain Division, 10350 E. Dakota Ave., 80231-1314, pg. 605 PV
Kaufman and Broad Colorado Division, 8101 E. Belleview Ave., Ste. G, 80237, pg. 945 PB
Keebler Co./Denver Bakery, 5000 Osage St., 80221, pg. 657 PB
KEPCO Resources America, 216 Sixteenth Street Mall, Ste. 810, 80202, pg. 758 IT
Ketema, Inc., 501 S. Cherry St., Ste. 600, 80222, pg. 604 PV
Kevaland Corp., 950 17th St., 80202, pg. 628 IT
Kevaland Texas Corp., 950 17th St., 80202, pg. 628 IT
KEY PRODUCTION COMPANY, INC., 707 17th St., Ste. 3300, 80202, pg. 953 PB
Kwal-Howells, Inc.(Denver), 3900 Joliet St., 80239, pg. 1501 IT
Lark Luggage Company, Inc., 11200 E. 45th Ave., 80239-3018, pg. 1430 PB
LEPRINO FOODS, 1830 W. 38th Ave., 80211, pg. 660 PV
Louisiana Nevada Transit Co., 950 17th St., 80202, pg. 628 IT
Ed J. Lyng Company, P.O. Box 22139, 80222, pg. 1103 PV
M.D.C. HOLDINGS, INC., 3600 S. Yosemite St., Ste. 900, 80237, pg. 1025 PB
MIGC, Inc., 12200 N. Pecos, 80234, pg. 1758 PB
MSC Denver Office, 11178 Huron St., 80234, pg. 1031 PB
Makita U.S.A. Inc.-Denver, 11839 E. 51st Ave., 80239-2709, pg. 831 IT
Manna Pro Partner L.P. (Limited Partnership), 4545 Madison St., 80216, pg. 700 PV
Manville Sales Corporation, P.O. Box 5018, 80217, pg. 927 PB
Martin Marietta Astronautics, P.O. Box 179, 80201, pg. 1007 PB
Martin Marietta Astronautics Space Systems, P.O. Box 179, 80201, pg. 1007 PB
MEDIANEWS GROUP INC., 1560 Broadway, #1485, 80202, pg. 727 PV
Merrill/Denver, 410 17th St., 80202, pg. 1097 PB
Micromedex, Inc., 600 Grant St., 80203-3527, pg. 1601 PB
Mile High Equipment Co., 11100 E. 45th Ave., 80239, pg. 189 IT
Morgan Technical Ceramics, 50 S. Steele, No. 222, 80209, pg. 893 IT
Mountain Gas Reources, Inc., 12200 N. Pecos St., 80234, pg. 1758 PB
Multifoods Specialty Distribution Inc., One Denver Highlands, 10375 E. Harvard Ave., 80217, pg. 901 PB
NW TRANSPORT SERVICE, INC., 717 17th St., 80202, pg. 772 PV
National Bedding Co., 6501 Stapleton N. Dr., 80216, pg. 780 PV
Natural Fuels Corporation, 1225 17th St., 80202, pg. 1170 PB
Nelson, Benson & Zellmer, Inc., 455 Sherman St., 80203, pg. 1673 PB
Neoteric Cosmetics, Inc., 4880 Havana, 80239, pg. 1447 PB
NEW CENTURY ENERGIES, INC., 1225 17th St., 80202, pg. 1170 PB
Newmont Exploration Ltd., 1700 Lincoln St., 80203, pg. 1179 PB
Newmont Gold Company, 1700 Lincoln St., 80203, pg. 1179 PB
NEWMONT MINING CORPORATION, 1700 Lincoln St., 80203, pg. 1178 PB
Nobel/Sysco Food Services Company-Denver, 1101 W. 48th Ave., 80217, pg. 1551 PB
North Mining Inc., Ste. 1200, 475 17th St., 80202, pg. 967 IT
Norwest Bank Colorado N.A., 1740 Broadway, 80274, pg. 1202 PB
OMNI Industry, 1801 Broadway, 80202, pg. 458 PV
Outdoor Systems, Inc.-Colorado, 4647 Leyden, 80238, pg. 1235 PB
Outlook Eyewear Company, 1444 Wazee St., Ste. 320, 80202, pg. 195 PB
P.S. Colorado Credit Corp., 1225 17th St., 80202, pg. 1170 PB
P.S.R. Investments, Inc., 1225 17th St., 80202, pg. 1170 PB
PAMCO, P.O. Box 39068, 10777 E. 45th, 80239, pg. 1517 PB
Park Foods, L.P., 1485 E. 61st. Ave., 82016, pg. 839 PV
PATINA OIL & GAS CORP., 1625 Broadway, Ste. 2000, 80202, pg. 1264 PB
Frank Paxton Lumber Company, 4837 Jackson St., Box 16343, 80216, pg. 585 PV
PEERLESS TYRE CO., 5000 Kingston St., 80239, pg. 847 PV
PEPSI-COLA BOTTLING CO., 3801 Brighton Blvd., 80216, pg. 1276 PB
Performance Building System, 5098 Paris St., 80239, pg. 905 PV
Pharmaceutical Basics, Inc., 301 S. Cherokee St., P.O. Box 9327, 80209, pg. 48 IT
GERALD H. PHIPPS, INC., 1530 W. 13th Ave., 80204, pg. 862 PV
Phoenix Industries, P.O. Box 22139, 80222, pg. 1103 PV
Pinnacle Gas Treating, Inc., 12200 N. Pecos St., 80234, pg. 1758 PB
Piper Jaffray Inc., 1050 17th St., Ste. 2100, 80265-2101, pg. 1301 PB
Piper Jaffray Inc., Metropoint Bldg., 4600 S. Ulster St., Ste. 880, 80237-2873, pg. 1303 PB
Pitney Bowes Management Services, 1050 17th St., Ste. 1250, 80265-1201, pg. 1304 PB
Plains Petroleum Company, 1515 Arapahoe St., Twr. 3, Ste. 1000, 80303, pg. 191 PB
PRECISION STANDARD, INC., 1225 17th St., Ste. 1800, 80202, pg. 1321 PB
PRIMA ENERGY CORPORATION, Ste. 500, 1801 Broadway, 80202, pg. 1325 PB
Prima Natural Gas Marketing, Inc., Ste. 500, 1801 Broadway, 80202, pg. 1325 PB
Prima Oil and Gas Company, Ste. 500, 1801 Broadway, 80202, pg. 1325 PB
PROPERTY ASSET MANAGEMENT, 1873 S. Bellaire St., Ste. 1700, 80222, pg. 891 PV
Public Service Company of Colorado, 1225 17th St., Ste. 900, 80202, pg. 1170 PB
QDI, Inc., 11585 E. 53rd Ave., Unit G, 80239, pg. 82 PV
Quality Education Data (QED), 1600 Broadway, Ste. 1200, 80202, pg. 858 PV
QualMed Plans for Health-Denver, 14001 E. Iliff Ave., Ste. 118, 80014, pg. 678 PB
QUARK INC., 1800 Grant St., 80203, pg. 900 PV
RCR Publications, 777 E. Spear Blvd., 80203-4214, pg. 285 PV
RK MECHANICAL, INC., 9300 E. Smith Rd., 80207, pg. 904 PV
RNL Design, 1515 Arapahoe St., Tower 3, Ste. 700, 80202, pg. 905 PV
RNL FACILITIES CORPORATION, 1515 Arapahoe St., Tower 3, Ste. 700, 80202, pg. 905 PV
Railco, Inc., 252 Clayton St., Ste. 400, 80206, pg. 171 PV
Raynor Distribution Center, 10625 E. 51st Ave., 80239, pg. 912 PV
Red Seal Quality Foods, Inc., 4300 Oneida, 80216, pg. 158 PV
Republic Automotive Parts Sales, Inc., P.O. Box 4640, 2550 W. Fifth Ave., 80204, pg. 1378 PB
Resurrection Mining Co., 1700 Lincoln St., 80203, pg. 1179 PB
Richmond Homes, Inc. I, 4600 S. Ulster., Ste. 400, 80237, pg. 1025 PB
Rio Grande Land Co., 1515 Arapahoe St., 80202, pg. 1668 PB
Rocky Mountain BankCard System, Inc., P.O. Box 5952, 80217, pg. 1680 PB
Rocky Mountain News, 400 W. Colfax Ave., 80202, pg. 1448 PB
Rocky Mountain Prestress, 5801 N. Pecos St., 80221, pg. 861 PV
Roth Corporation, 11440 E. 56th Avenue Suite 100, 80239, pg. 1099 PV
SLG Chemicals, Inc., 4880 Havana St., 80239, pg. 1447 PB
SLG Plastics, Inc., 4880 Havana St., 80239, pg. 1447 PB
SMS-Denver, 1355 S. Colorado Blvd., 80222, pg. 1463 PB
SAMSONITE CORPORATION, 11200 E. 45th Ave., 80239, pg. 1430 PB
Schuller International, Inc., P.O. Box 5108, 80217-5108, pg. 927 PB
SCIENTIFIC SOFTWARE-INTERCOMP, INC., 633 17th St., Ste. 1600, 80202, pg. 1443 PB
Scientific Software-Intercomp, Inc.-Exploration and Production Products Div., 1801 California St., Ste. 295, 80202, pg. 1443 PB
SCOTT'S LIQUID GOLD-INC., 4880 Havana St., 80239, pg. 1447 PB
Sealy Mattress Company - Denver, 12555 East 39 Ave., 80239, pg. 979 PV
Security Life of Denver Reinsurance Company, 1290 Broadway, 80203, pg. 648 IT
Sequent Computer Systems, Inc., 4100 E. Mississippi Ave., Ste. 1800, 80222, pg. 1459 PB
SHAFER COMMERCIAL SEATING INC., 4101 E. 48th Ave., 80216-3298, pg. 988 PV
Snavely Forest Products, Inc., P.O. Box 16107, 80216, pg. 1010 PV
Sociedad Industrial Minera Yamin Ltda., 370 17th St., Ste. 3000, 80202, pg. 1723 PB
Stant Corporation, 900 S. Broadway, 80209, pg. 1396 IT
SuperValu, Inc.-Denver Div., 80011, pg. 1540 PB
SWENCO-Western, Inc., 1801 Broadway, 80202, pg. 1543 PB
TIE Systems Colorado, 1080 Cherokee St., 80204, pg. 1085 PV
TMP Worldwide/Recruitment Division, Century Towers, Ste. 480, 720 S. Colorado Blvd., 80246, pg. 1065 PV
Tamrock EJC USA Inc., P.O. Box 39395, 4720 Lima St., 80239, pg. 1353 IT
Texaco Trading & Transportation Inc., 1670 Broadway, Ste. 2900, 80202, pg. 1583 PB
Thorstenberg Materials Co., Inc., 950 17th St., 80201, pg. 628 IT
TIMPTE INDUSTRIES, INC., 700 Broadway, Ste. 800, 80203, pg. 1088 PV

PB - *U.S. Public Companies Volume*
PV - *U.S. Private Companies Volume*
IT - *International Public & Private Companies Volume*

Geographic Index-U.S.

TIPPERARY CORPORATION, 633 17th St., Ste. 1550, 80202, pg. 1618 PB
Tipperary Oil & Gas Corp., 633 17th St., Ste. 1550, 80202, pg. 1618 PB
Titanium Metals Corporation, 1999 Broadway, Ste. 4300, 80202, pg. 270 PV
TOOL KING, 299 Bryant St., 80219-1636, pg. 1091 PV
Total Crude Oil Transport, Inc., 999 18th Street, 80202, pg. 1663 PB
Total Petroleum, Inc., 900 19th St., 80202, pg. 1663 PB
Total Pipeline Corporation, P.O. Box 500, 80201, pg. 1663 PB
TransLogic Corp., 10825 E. 47th Ave., 80239, pg. 1387 IT
TRANSMONTAIGNE OIL COMPANY, 2750 Republic Plaza, 370 17th St., Ste. 2750, 80202, pg. 1631 PB
Trautman & Shreve, Inc., 4406 Race St., 80216, pg. 572 PB
Tremont Corporation, 1999 Broadway, 43rd Fl., 80202, pg. 270 PV
Tribune Denver Radio, Inc., Bldg. B, Ste. 131, 10200 E. Girard Ave., 80231, pg. 1636 PB
Trinidad Bean & Elevator Co., P.O. Box 22139, 80222, pg. 1103 PV
TRINIDAD/BENHAM CORP., P.O. Box 22139, 80222, pg. 1103 PV
Turner Construction Company, 4155 E. Jewell Ave., Ste. 405, 80222, pg. 1645 PB
UMB Columbine National Bank, 6900 E. Hampden Ave., 80223, pg. 1654 PB
URS Greiner, 1099 18th St., Ste. 700, 80202-1907, pg. 1655 PB
URS Greiner Engineering, Inc., 1099 18th St., Ste. 700, 80202-1907, pg. 1658 PB
Union-Transport Corporation-Denver Office, 12445 E. 39th Ave., Unit A517, 80239, pg. 1119 PV
Unisource, 12601 E. 38th Ave., 80239, pg. 1671 PB
U S West DEX, 10375 E. Harvard St, 80231, pg. 1689 PB
Uranerz USA Inc., 216 16th St. Mall Ste. 810, 80202, pg. 1070 IT
VSA, Inc., 370 17th St., 80217, pg. 901 PB
VICOM Production and Distribution Co., 400 W. 48th Ave., 80216, pg. 1719 PB
VICORP RESTAURANTS, INC., 400 W. 48th Ave., 80216, pg. 1719 PB
Village Inn Restaurants, 400 W. 48th Ave., 80216, pg. 1719 PB
VISTA GOLD CORP., 370 17th St., Ste. 3000, 80202, pg. 1723 PB
Vista Gold Holdings Inc., 370 17th St., Ste. 3000, 80202, pg. 1723 PB
Weitz-Cohen Construction Co., 899 Logan St., Ste. 600, 80203, pg. 1161 PV
Wells Fargo Bank, 633 17th St., 80270, pg. 1753 PB
Wendy's of Denver Inc., 5250 Leetsdale Dr., 80222, pg. 1754 PB
Westana Gathering Company, 12200 N. Pecos St., 80234, pg. 535 PB
WESTERN GAS RESOURCES, INC., 12200 N. Pecos St., 80234-3439, pg. 1758 PB
Western Gas Resources Storage, Inc., 12200 N. Pecos St., 80234, pg. 1759 PB
Western Gas Resources-Louisiana, Inc., 12200 N. Pecos St., 80234, pg. 1758 PB
Western Gas Resources-Oklahoma, Inc., 12200 N. Pecos St., 80234, pg. 1758 PB
Western Gas Resources-Texas, Inc., 122000 N. Pecos St., 80234, pg. 1759 PB
Western International Media Corporation, 1200 17th St., Ste. 2620, 80202, pg. 1167 PV
Western Mobile Inc., P.O. Box 21588, 1400 W. 64th Ave., 80221, pg. 1091 IT
The Western Sugar Company, 1700 Broadway, Ste. #1600, 80290, pg. 1357 IT
WestGas Interstate, Inc., 1225 17th St., 80202-8533, pg. 1170 PB
Westlam Foods, P.O. Box 22139, 80222, pg. 1103 PV
Whittaker Power Storage Division, 3850 Olive St., 80207, pg. 1767 PB
Williamhouse of Colorado, Inc., 4825 Nome St., P.O. Box 39926, 80239, pg. 89 PB
Willis Corroon Financial Services Corp., Hudson's Bay Centre, 1600 Stout St., Ste. 1220, 80202-3126, pg. 1507 IT
Woodward-Clyde, Stanord Pl. Three, Ste. 1000, 4582 S. Ulster St., 80237, pg. 1656 PB
Woodward-Clyde Consultants, 4582 S. Ulster St., Ste. 600, 80237, pg. 1657 PB
Woodward-Clyde Federal Services, 4584 S. Ulster St., Ste. 600, 80237, pg. 1657 PB
Woodward-Clyde Group, Inc., Stanford Pl. Three, 4582 S. Ulster St., Ste. 600, 80237-2637, pg. 1655 PB
Woodward-Clyde International, 4584 S. Ulster St., Ste. 600, 80237, pg. 1657 PB
Woodward-Constructors, 4582 S. Ulster St., Ste. 600, 80237, pg. 1657 PB
Y.K.K. (U.S.A.) Inc., 4990 Nome St., 80229, pg. 1515 IT
Young Electric Signs Denver Div., 3770 Joliet St., 80239, pg. 1201 PV
Young Gas Storage Company, 1225 17th St., 80202, pg. 1170 PB
Zellerbach Division, 12770 E. 39th Ave., 80239, pg. 1075 PB

Durango

Centennial Federal Savings Bank F.S.B., 1101 E. Second Ave., 81301, pg. 1793 PB
Piper Jaffray Inc., 1199 Main Ave., Ste. 201, 81301-5170, pg. 1301 PB
Tamarron Division, P.O. Box 3131, 81302, pg. 1036 PV
United Pipeline System USA, Inc., 135 Turner Dr., 81301, pg. 882 PB

Englewood

Alcoa Packaging Machinery, Inc., 4535 S. Santa Fe Dr., 80110, pg. 60 PB
Amax Energy, Inc., 9100 E. Mineral Cir., 80112, pg. 470 PB
Amax Exploration, Inc., 9100 E. Mineral Cir., 80112, pg. 470 PB
Amex Gold Inc., 9100 E. Mineral Cir., 80112, pg. 470 PB
Amex Research & Development Inc., 9100 E. Mineral Cir., 80112, pg. 470 PB
American Cablevision Holdings, Inc., 160 Inverness Dr. W., 80112, pg. 1610 PB
American Mail-Well Envelope, 23 Inverness Way E., Ste. 150, 80112, pg. 1038 PB
Antarctic Support Associates, Ste. 300, 61 Inverness Dr. E., 80112-5121, pg. 544 PB
Antec Group, 8101 E. Prentice Ave., 80111, pg. 117 PB
Aspen Laboratories, Inc., 7211 S. Eagle St., 80122, pg. 431 PB
BPA International - Englewood, 5299 DTC Blvd., #532, 80111, pg. 107 PV
BSA Advertising, Inc., 7600 East Orchard Ave., Ste. 320, 80111, pg. 108 PV
Big O Tires Incorporated, 11755 E. Peakview Ave., Ste. A, 80111, pg. 1553 PB
Binswanger West, 5690 DTC Blvd., Ste. 315, 80111, pg. 144 PV
Bolt Geophysical Corporation, 6890 S. Tucson Way, 80112, pg. 244 PB
Bretec Inc., 12742 E. Caley Ave., Unit A, 80111, pg. 1352 IT
Tom Brown, Inc., 5613 DTC Pkwy., Ste. 750, 80111-3065, pg. 262 PB
C-COR Electronics, Inc., 5299 DTC Blvd., Ste. 552, 80111, pg. 272 PB
CSG SYSTEMS INTERNATIONAL, INC., 7887 E. Belleview Ave., Ste. 1000, 80111, pg. 283 PB
Cable Management Corp., 5619 DTC Pkwy., 80111, pg. 1555 PB
Cadmus Direct Marketing, 6400 S. Fiddler Green Circle, 80111, pg. 290 PB
Cambiar Investors, Inc., 8400 E. Prentice Ave., Ste. 460, 80111, pg. 1672 PB
Cambior USA, Inc., 8101 E. Prentice Ave., Ste. 800, 80111, pg. 253 IT
CAP Gemini America (Denver Branch), 5299 DTC Blvd., Ste. 610, 80111, pg. 264 IT
CHATEAU COMMUNITIES, INC., 6430 S. Quebec St., 80111, pg. 341 PB
Chevron Shale Oil Co., 6400 S. Fiddler's Green Circle, 80111, pg. 348 PB
CIBEF, INC., 5251 DTC Pkwy., Ste. 1400, 80111, pg. 356 PB
CoBank, 5500 S. Quebec St., 80111, pg. 398 PV
Colorado Data Systems Inc., 3301 W. Hampden Ave., Unit C, 80110, pg. 1567 PB
COMMNET CELLULAR INC., 8350 E. Crescent Pkwy., Ste. 400 80111, pg. 414 PB
Continental Divide Insurance Co., 7935 E. Prentice, 80111, pg. 221 PB
Continental Homes of Denver, 7120 E. Orchard Rd., Ste. 300, 80111, pg. 441 PB
Cosmicar Lens Div., 35 Inverness Dr., E., P.O. Box 6509, 80155-6509, pg. 85 IT
Cyprus Amax Coal Co., 9100 E. Mineral Cir., 80112, pg. 470 PB
CYPRUS AMAX MINERALS COMPANY, 9100 E. Mineral Cir., 80112, pg. 470 PB
Cyprus Exploration & Development Corporation, 9100 E. Mineral Cir., 80112, pg. 471 PB
Cyprus Mines Corp., 9100 East Mineral Circle, 80112, pg. 471 PB
Denver Technological Center, 7887 E. Bellview Ave., Ste. 1200, 80111, pg. 1035 IT
Descente America Inc., 6900 S. Peoria St., 80112, pg. 395 IT
ECHO BAY MINES LTD., 6400 S. Fiddlers Green Cir., Ste. 1000, 80111-4957, pg. 561 PB
Finora Company, Inc., 6312 S. Fiddler's Green Cir., 80111, pg. 802 PV
First Interstate Bank of Englewood, N.A., 3333 S. Bannock St., 80110, pg. 1753 PB
Fischbach Corporation, 2775 S. Vallejo St., 80110, pg. 84 PB
Frontier Holdings Inc., 5340 S. Quebec St., Ste. 200 N., 80111-1911, pg. 1732 PB
Frontier Oil & Refining Company, 5340 S. Quebec St., Ste. 200 N., 80111-1911, pg. 1732 PB
Frontier Oil Corporation, 5340 S. Quebec St., Ste. 200 N., 80111-1911, pg. 1732 PB
Frontier Pipeline Inc., 5340 S. Quebec St., Ste. 200 N., 80111-1911, pg. 1732 PB
Full Service Beverage Company of Colorado, 2840 S. Zuni, 80110, pg. 34 PV
GWL Properties Inc., 8505-8515 E. Orchard Rd., 80111, pg. 558 IT
Genesee Wester, 1600 West Yale Ave., 80110, pg. 446 PV
GETCHELL GOLD CORP., 5460 S. Quebec, Ste. 240, 80111, pg. 740 PB
Great-West Life & Annuity Insurance Co., 8505-8515 E. Orchard Rd., 80111, pg. 558 IT
The Great-West Life Assurance Company, 8505-8515 E. Orchard Rd., 80111, pg. 558 IT
Great-West Realty Investments, Inc., 8505-8515 E. Orchard Rd., 80111, pg. 558 IT
Guarantee National Insurance Company, 9800 S. Meridan Blvd., 80112, pg. 1231 PB
Hewlett-Packard Company, 24 Inverness Pl., E., 80112, pg. 813 PB
The Hotsy Corporation, 21 Inverness Way E., 80112, pg. 500 PV
Information Handling Services, 15 Inverness Way E., P.O. Box 1154, 80150, pg. 1335 IT
Integrated Payment Systems, 6200 S. Quebec St., Ste. 310BA, 80111, pg. 631 PB
Intergraph Corporation, 7400 E. Orchard Rd., Ste. 3000, 80301, pg. 891 PB
Intertec Presentations, 6300 S. Syracuse Way, Ste. 650, 80111, pg. 1328 PB
Jeppesen Sanderson, 55 Inverness Dr. E., 80112-5498, pg. 1616 PB
Johnson Storage & Moving, Englewood, 6989 S. Jordan Rd., 80112, pg. 594 PV
Jones Capital Markets, Inc., 9697 E. Mineral Ave., 80112, pg. 597 PV
Jones Galactic Radio, 9697 E. Mineral Ave., 80112, pg. 597 PV
Jones Interactive, Inc., 9697 E. Mineral Ave., 80112, pg. 597 PV
Jones Intercable, Inc., 9697 E. Mineral Ave., 80112, pg. 597 PV
JONES INTERNATIONAL, LTD., 9697 E. Mineral Ave., 80112, pg. 597 PV
Jones International Securities, Ltd., 9697 E. Mineral Ave., 80112, pg. 597 PV
Jones Programming Services, Inc., 9697 E. Mineral Ave., 80112, pg. 597 PV
Jones Properties, Inc., 9697 E. Mineral Ave., 80112, pg. 597 PV
Jones Spacelink, Ltd., 9697 E. Mineral Ave., 80112, pg. 597 PV
KWGN Inc., 6160 S. Wabash Way, 80111, pg. 1636 PB
KATY INDUSTRIES, INC., 6300 S. Syracuse Way, Ste. 300, 80111, pg. 944 PB
Kilborn SNC-Lavalin, 5775 DTC Blvd., Suite 200, 80111-3227, pg. 1162 IT
Kinetic Systems Test Management Systems Group, 7308 S. Alton Way, Bldg. 2, 80112, pg. 620 PV
Krupp Robins, Inc., 7730 E. Belleview Ave., Ste. 404, 80111, pg. 511 IT
LGC MANAGEMENT, 5200 S. Broadway, 80110, pg. 639 PV
Liberty Banking Service, 7400 E. Arapahoe Rd., Ste. 100, 80112, pg. 809 PB
Liberty Cable, Inc., 8101 Prentice Ave., Ste 500, 80111, pg. 1555 PB
Liberty Holdings, Inc., 8101 Prentice Ave., Ste. 500, 80111, pg. 1555 PB
Liberty Media Corporation, 8101 E. Prentice Ave., Ste. 500, 80111, pg. 1555 PB
Liberty Program Investments, Inc., 8101 Prentice Ave., Ste. 500, 80111, pg. 1555 PB
Liberty Programming Corporation, 8101 Prentice Ave., Ste. 500, 80111, pg. 1555 PB
Liberty Sports, Inc., 8101 Prentice Ave., Ste. 500, 80111, pg. 1555 PB
Lincoln Holdings, Inc., 6312 S. Fiddlers Green Cir., Ste. 400E, 80111, pg. 647 PB
Logicon Geodynamics Services Corporation, 304 Inverness Way South, Ste. 300, 80112, pg. 1199 PB
MAIL-WELL INC., Ste. 160, 23 Inverness Way East, 80112, pg. 1037 PB
Don Massey Buick-Pontiac, 9701 E. Arapahoe Rd., 80112, pg. 712 PV
Don Massey Cadillac, Inc., 9400 E. Arapahoe Rd., 80112, pg. 713 PV
Meadowlark, Inc., P.O. Box 3299, 80112-3299, pg. 471 PB
Measurement Science, Inc., 5300 DTC Pkwy., Ste. 150, 80111, pg. 826 PV
Media Recovery Inc.-Colorado, 6860 S. Yosemite Ct., Ste. 102 C, 80112, pg. 727 PV
Monitor Labs, Inc., 74 Inverness Dr. E., 80112-5189, pg. 208 IT
Mountain Operations Land Division, 5970 Greenwood Plaza, Ste. 310, 80111, pg. 1683 PB
Mullen Environmental Services, Inc., 5613 DTC Pkwy., Ste. 630, 80111, pg. 94 PB
Natkin Group, Inc., 2700 S. Zuni St., 80110, pg. 84 PB
The Natkin Service Co., 2700 S. Zuni, 80150, pg. 84 PB
Nordstrom Credit, Inc., 13531 E. Caley Ave., 80111, pg. 1190 PB
Operations Management International, Inc., 5299 DTC Blvd., Ste. 1200, 80111-3333, pg. 195 PV
Outokumpu Mintec U.S.A., Inc., 109 Inverness Dr. E., Ste. F, 80112, pg. 1017 IT
PPV Venture Productions, 160 Inverness Dr. W., 80112, pg. 1610 PB
Pacificare of Colorado, 7455 S. Josimite St., 80111, pg. 1251 PB
Penford Food Ingredients Company, 11011 E. Peakview Ave., 80111, pg. 1269 PB
Pentax Corporation, 35 Inverness Dr., E., 80112, pg. 85 IT
The Pittsburg & Midway Coal Mining Co., 6400 S. Fiddlers Green Cir., 80111, pg. 348 PB
POST Buckley International Inc., 5300 DTC Pkwy., Ste. 150, 80111, pg. 826 PV
Presidio Exploration, Inc., 5613 DTC Pkwy., Ste. 750, 80111, pg. 262 PB
PRO GROUP, INC., 9137 E. Mineral Cir., Third Fl., 80112, pg. 887 PV
Product Information Network, 9697 E. Mineral Ave., 80155-3309, pg. 597 PV
Production Operators, Inc. (Denver Office), P.O. Box 4553, 80155, pg. 298 PB

Geographic Index-U.S.

PB - *U.S. Public Companies Volume*
PV - *U.S. Private Companies Volume*
IT - *International Public & Private Companies Volume*

QUANTERRA ENVIRONMENTAL SERVICES, 5251 DTC Pkwy., Ste. 415, 80111, pg. 899 — PV

Raytheon Engineers & Constructors, Inc., 5555 Greenwood Plaza Blvd., 80111, pg. 1366 — PB

RE/MAX INTERNATIONAL, INC., P.O. Box 2907, 80155-3907, pg. 912 — PV

Resources Trust Company, 8051 E. Maplewood, 80111, pg. 1533 — PV

RICHFIELD HOSPITALITY SERVICES, 5775 DTC Blvd., Ste. 300, 80111, pg. 929 — PB

Sceptre Hospitality Resources, Inc., 5775 DTC Blvd., Ste. 300, 80111, pg. 929 — PV

ServiceMaster Energy Management, 5340 S. Quebec St., 80111, pg. 1462 — PV

Smith Environmental Technologies Corp., 94 Inverness Ter. E., Ste. 100, 80112, pg. 1477 — PB

Standard & Poor's Compustat Services, Inc., 7400 S. Alton Court, 80112, pg. 1071 — PB

Sterling Electronics, 101 Inverness Dr. E., Ste. 140, 80112, pg. 1052 — PB

T-NETIX, INC., 67 Inverness E., 80112, pg. 1553 — PB

TCI COMMUNICATIONS, INC., 5619 DTC Pkwy., 80111, pg. 1554 — PB

TCI Development Corp., 5619 BTC Pkwy., 80111, pg. 1555 — PB

UNITED ARTISTS THEATRE CIRCUITS INCORPORATED, 9110 E. Nichols Ave., Ste. 200, 80112, pg. 1120 — PV

U S West Business Resources, 6892 S. Yosemite St., 80112, pg. 1689 — PB

U S West Cellular, 7800 E. Orchard Rd., Ste. 300, 80111, pg. 1689 — PB

U S West Communications Federal Services Inc., 7800 E. Orchard Rd., Ste. 3000, 80111, pg. 1689 — PB

U S West Communications Group, Inc., 7800 E. Orchard Rd., 80111, pg. 1689 — PB

U S WEST INC., 7800 E. Orchard Rd., 80111-2522, pg. 1688 — PB

U S West Media Group, 7800 E. Orchard Rd., Ste. 300, 80111, pg. 1689 — PB

Vista Cablevision, Inc., 160 Inverness Dr. W., 80112, pg. 1611 — PB

Vital Signs, 11039 E. Lansing Cir., 80112, pg. 1723 — PB

Wall Street Deli, Inc., 14 Inverness Dr. E., Ste. F148, 80112, pg. 1734 — PB

Wenatchee Mountains, Inc., 160 Inverness Dr. W., 80112, pg. 1611 — PB

West Region, MCI Plaza, 6312 S. Fiddlers Green Cir., Ste. 600 E., 80111, pg. 1024 — PB

WINDSOR INDUSTRIES, INC., 1351 W. Stanford Ave., 80110, pg. 1182 — PV

Zeneca Pharmaceuticals, 8400 E. Prentice Ave., 80111, pg. 1525 — IT

Zenith Media Services, Inc., 8400 E. Prentice Ave., Ste. 804, 80111, pg. 1204 — PV

Erie

Jaco Electronics Inc., 695 Pierce St., 80516, pg. 920 — PB

Fort Collins

ADVANCED ENERGY INDUSTRY, 1625 Sharp Point Dr., 80525, pg. 20 — PV

ALLIANCE CONSTRUCTION SOLUTIONS, INC., 301 E. Lincoln Ave., 80524, pg. 38 — PV

Comlinear Corporation, 4800 Wheaton Dr., 80525, pg. 1160 — PB

Elscint MR Inc., 2555 Midpoint Dr., 80525, pg. 450 — IT

Fort Collins Newspapers, Inc., 1212 Riverside Ave., 80522, pg. 700 — PB

HESKA CORPORATION, 1825 Sharp Point Dr., 80525, pg. 812 — PB

Hewlett-Packard Company, Boardwalk Business Ctr., 748 Whalers Way, Bldg. E, Ste. 100, 80525, pg. 813 — PB

Key Bank of Colorado, 300 W. Oak St., 80521, pg. 954 — PB

LGT Real Estate Advisors, Stanford Plaza, Ste. 100, 355 Stanford Rd., 80525, pg. 809 — PB

Otsuka Electronics (U.S.A.) Inc., 2607 Midpoint Dr., 80525, pg. 1013 — IT

Phelps Tointon Millwork, 1001 Buckingham St., 80524, pg. 861 — PV

RANCH-WAY FEED INC., 416 Linden St., 80524, pg. 908 — PV

Scott Resources, 40 Hickory St., 80522, pg. 71 — PB

Teledyne Water Pik, 1730 E. Prospect Rd., 80553-0001, pg. 44 — PB

Welding Systems Division, 4600 Innovation Dr., 30525, pg. 4 — IT

Fort Morgan

Colorado Plains Medical Center, 1000 Lincoln St., 80701, pg. 169 — PV

Frisco

Copper Mountain Resort, 209 Tenmile Cir., 80443, pg. 685 — IT

Glenwood Springs

Glenwood Post, P.O. Box 550, 2014 Grand Ave., 81602-0550, pg. 995 — PV

HOLY CROSS ELECTRIC ASSOCIATION, INC., 3799 Hwy. 82, 81601, pg. 536 — PV

Rocky Mountain Natural Gas Co., P.O. Box 670, 81602, pg. 937 — PB

Golden

ACX TECHNOLOGIES INC., 16000 Table Mountain Pkwy., 80403, pg. 3 — PB

ANR Freight System, Inc., Bldg. 26, 1819 Denver W. Dr., 80401, pg. 389 — PB

Aramark Educational Resources Inc. Inc., 573 Park Point Dr., 80401, pg. 79 — PV

BOSTON CHICKEN, INC., 14103 Denver W. Pkwy., 80401, pg. 247 — PB

CR Minerals Corporation, Corporate Office, 14142 Denver W. Pkwy., Ste. 101, 80401, pg. 302 — PV

CANYON RESOURCES CORPORATION, 14142 Denver W. Pkwy., Ste. 250, 80401, pg. 301 — PB

The Coleman Company, Inc., 1526 Cole Blvd., Ste. 300, 80401, pg. 690 — PV

ADOLPH COORS COMPANY, 311 Tenth St., 80401, pg. 445 — PB

Coors Brewing Company, BC 300, 80401-1295, pg. 445 — PB

Coors Ceramics Company, 600 Ninth St., 80401, pg. 3 — PB

Coors Distributing Co., P.O. Box 4030, 80401, pg. 445 — PB

Coors Energy Co., 14062 Denver W. Pkwy., Bldg. 52, Ste. 300, 80401, pg. 446 — PB

Ecova Corporation, 800 Jefferson County Pkwy., 80401-6001, pg. 103 — PB

Einstein/Noah Bagel Corp., 14203 Denver W. Pkwy., 80401, pg. 247 — PB

EMICH OLDSMOBILE, INC., 16400 W. Colfax Ave., 80401, pg. 373 — PV

IGT-Colorado Corporation, 301 Commercial Rd., 80401, pg. 900 — PB

P-T Templet Company, 15680 W. Fifth Ave., 80401, pg. 1145 — PB

PolyMedica Healthcare, Inc., 581 Conference Pl., 80401, pg. 1315 — PB

PolyMedica Wound Care Company, 581 Conference Pl., 80401, pg. 1315 — PB

Rocky Mountain Water Co., 80401, pg. 445 — PB

Rust Federal Services Inc., Building 15, 1597 Cole Blvd., Ste. 350, 80401, pg. 1366 — PB

Sunrise Leasing Corporation, 1746 Cole Blvd., Ste. 225, 80401, pg. 1535 — PB

Grand Junction

AMETEK Dixson Division, 287-27 Rd., 81503-1900, pg. 100 — PB

DYWIDAG Systems International, USA, Inc., 483-1/2 Anjou Dr., 81504, pg. 424 — IT

Grand Junction Newspapers, Inc., 734 S. Seventh St., 81501, pg. 281 — PV

GAY JOHNSON'S INC., 1154 N. Fourth St., 81501, pg. 595 — PV

Scientific Measurement Systems, Inc., 2527 Foresight Circle, 81505, pg. 1593 — PB

Steel, Inc., 2334 Interstate Ave., 81515, pg. 1038 — PB

Sundstrand Aerospace Operations, 2800 Sundstrand Way, 81506, pg. 1533 — PB

Greeley

ConAgra Agri-Products Co., Box 1286, 80632, pg. 426 — PB

ConAgra Red Meat Companies, 1918 AA St., 80631, pg. 427 — PB

R.R. Donnelley Norwest Div.-Greeley, 259 - 30th St., 80631-7435, pg. 518 — PB

HENSEL PHELPS CONSTRUCTION CO., 420 Sixth Ave., 80632, pg. 523 — PV

Mapelli Brothers Company, 1918 AA St., 80631, pg. 427 — PB

Monfort, Inc., 1930 AA St., 80631, pg. 427 — PB

PHELPS TOINTON INC., 822 Seventh St., Ste. 700, 80631, pg. 860 — PV

ROCHE CONSTRUCTORS, INC., 361 71st. Ave., 80634, pg. 937 — PV

Swift & Company, 1903 AA St., 80631-9663, pg. 426 — PB

Swift & Co., 1904 AA St., 80631, pg. 426 — PB

United Agri Products Co., P.O. Box 1286, 80632, pg. 426 — PB

Unitog Rental Facility, 523 10th St., 80631, pg. 1693 — PB

Greenwood Village

CH2M HILL COMPANIES, LTD., 6060 S. Willow Dr., 80111-5142, pg. 195 — PV

CH2M Hill, Inc., 6060 S. Willow Dr., 80111, pg. 195 — PV

NATIONAL CATTLEMEN'S BEEF ASSOCIATION, 5020 S. Quebec St., 80111, pg. 780 — PV

Pulte Financial Companies, Inc., 6061 S. Willow Dr., Ste. 301, 80111, pg. 1345 — PB

Pulte Mortgage Corporation, 6061 S. Willow Dr., Ste. 300, 80111, pg. 1345 — PB

Telemation Productions Inc., 8745 East Orchard Rd., 80111, pg. 1685 — PB

Henderson

Pioneer Steel & Tube, 9520 E. 104th Ave., 80640, pg. 1150 — IT

Sturgeon Electric Company, 12150 E. 112th Ave., 80640, pg. 1029 — PB

Highlands Ranch

Reed Elsevier Business Information-Denver, 8773 S. Ridgeline Blvd., 80126, pg. 1095 — IT

Shea Homes-Colorado, 8822 S. Ridgeline Blvd., 80126, pg. 991 — PV

Holyoke

Jacks Bean Company, 127 E. Denver St., 80734, pg. 428 — PB

La Junta

Dean Foods Vegetable Company, Second & Grand, 81050, pg. 490 — PB

La Salle

Action Oilfield Services, Inc., 24020 WCR 46, 80645, pg. 1325 — PB

ICI Seeds, 17658 Weld County Rd. 48, 80645, pg. 1524 — IT

Lafayette

DYNAMIC MATERIALS CORPORATION, 551 Aspen Ridge Dr., 80026, pg. 539 — PB

Lakewood

AMS Operations Corporation, Inc., 6th St., Ent. W16, 80226, pg. 86 — PB

Allied Security Inc., 363 S. Harlan St., #100, 80226, pg. 40 — PV

Atkinson Underground Group, 200 Union Blvd., Ste. 400, 80228, pg. 143 — PV

CAPITAL ASSOCIATES, INC., 7175 W. Jefferson Ave., Ste. 4000, 80235, pg. 302 — PB

Carquest Corp., 12596 W. Bayaud Ave., Ste. 400, 80228, pg. 445 — PV

CARQUEST CORPORATION, 12596 W. Bayard Ave., 80228, pg. 215 — PV

The Check Store, 11100 W. 8th Ave., 80215, pg. 785 — PB

COBE Laboratories, Inc., 1185 Oak St., 80215, pg. 667 — IT

Cotter Corp., 12596 W. Bayaud Ave., Ste. 350, 80228, pg. 1664 — PB

Dreyer's Rocky Mountain Region, 5567 W. Sixth Ave., 80214, pg. 529 — PB

Ericsson Network Systems, Inc., 215 Union Blvd., Ste. 415, 80228, pg. 1364 — IT

Gambro Healthcare, 1185 Oak Street, 80215, pg. 667 — IT

Holnam Inc. (West Division), 3609 S. Wadsworth Blvd., Ste. 200, 80235, pg. 628 — IT

Houston International Minerals Corp., P.O. Box 27F, 300 Union Blvd.,Ste. 300, 80227, pg. 1578 — IT

International Communications (Denver), 7114 W. Jefferson Ave., Ste. 100, 80227, pg. 208 — PV

K N ENERGY, INC., 370 Van Gordon St., 80228, pg. 937 — PB

K N Field Services, Inc., P.O. Box 281304, 80228-8304, pg. 937 — PB

K N Gas Gathering, Inc., P.O. Box 281304, 80228-8304, pg. 937 — PB

K N Gas Marketing, Inc., P.O. Box 281304, 80228-8304, pg. 937 — PB

K N Interstate Gas Transmission Co., P.O. Box 281304, 80228-8304, pg. 937 — PB

K N Services, Inc., P.O. Box 281304, 80228-8304, pg. 937 — PB

Litchfield Financial Corporation, 13701 W. Jewell Ave., Ste. 200, 80228, pg. 1001 — PB

Plains Petroleum Operating Co., 12596 W. Bayaud, #400, 80228, pg. 191 — PB

Slaybaugh-Thompson, Inc., 8646 W. Colfax Ave., Ste. 203, 80215, pg. 360 — PV

The Sygma Network, Inc.-Denver Central, 7125 W. Jefferson Ave., Ste. 460, 80235, pg. 1551 — PB

Tenneco Minerals Co., 300 Union Blvd., Ste. 300, 80227, pg. 1579 — PB

Lamar

CARDER, INC., 700 E. Crystal St., 81052, pg. 208 — PV

RANCHERS SUPPLY COMPANY, INC., P.O. Box 721, 81052, pg. 908 — PV

Larkspur

Micropolis Corporation, 13694 W. Woodmoor Dr., 80118, pg. 742 — PV

Las Animas

Bent Co. Colorado Correctional Facility, 11560 Rd. FF.75, 81054-9598, pg. 450 — PB

Littleton

ABB Hydro Power Div., 7921 S. Park Plaza, Ste. 208, 80120, pg. 4 — IT

CARDER CONCRETE PRODUCTS CO., 8311 W. Carder Court, 80125, pg. 208 — PV

Colorado Business Bank of Littleton, N.A., 101 W. Mineral Ave., 80120, pg. 255 — PB

ELECTRON CORP., 5101 S. Rio Grande St., 80120, pg. 370 — PV

FlightSafety Services Corporation, 10184 W. Belleview Ave., Ste. 300, 80127, pg. 218 — PB

GLOBUS & COSMOS, 5301 S. Federal Circle, 80123, pg. 458 — PV

PB - *U.S. Public Companies Volume*
PV - *U.S. Private Companies Volume*
IT - *International Public & Private Companies Volume*

1163

HATHAWAY CORPORATION, 8228 Park Meadows Dr., 80124, pg. 798   PB
Hathaway Systems Corporation, 8228 Park Meadows Dr., 12422, pg. 799
Intergraph Corporation, Ana Tech Div., 10499 Bradford Rd., 80127, pg. 891   PB
LE PEEP'S GRILL INC., Four W. Dry Creek Circle, Ste. 201, 80120, pg. 655   PV
Martin Marietta Field Services, 1101 W. Mineral Ave., Ste. 115, 80120, pg. 1007   PB
Norgren Co., 5400 S. Delaware, 80120, pg. 647   IT
Reedex Corporation, 5400 S. Delaware St., 80120, pg. 647   IT
Video King Gaming Systems, Inc., 8122 Southpark Ln. #300, 80120, pg. 1526   PB

Longmont

Adaptec - Rocky Mountain Region, 1951 S. Fordham St., 80503, pg. 19   PB
Advanced Forming Technology, Inc., 2150 Miller Dr., 80502-6744, pg. 1320   PB
Binks Manufacturing Facility, 2605 Trade Ctr., 80503, pg. 229   PB
Codar Technology Inc., 2405 Trade Centre Ave., 80503, pg. 1144   PB
Fujitsu Computer Products of America - Research & Development, 2402 Clover Rd. Basin, 80503, pg. 526   IT
Hilleshog Mono-Hy Inc., 11939 Sugar Mill Road, 80501, pg. 973   IT
Johnson Moving & Storage, Boulder/Longmont, 900 S. Sunset St., 80501, pg. 594   PV
Longmont Foods, P.O. Box 1479, 80502-1479, pg. 426   PB
Micro Products, 1285 S. Fordham St., 80503, pg. 1465   PB
NexStar Automation, Inc., 2505-A Trade Centre Ave., 80501, pg. 1795   PB
Read-Rite Corporation, 1880 Industrial Cir., Ste. B-3, 80501, pg. 1367   PB
Scripps Howard Cable Company, 434 Kimbark St., 80501, pg. 1448   PB
STAODYN INC., 1225 Ken Pratt Blvd., 80501, pg. 1509   PB
StorageTek Peripherals, 1351 S. Sunset St., 80501, pg. 1523   PB
Sunrise Mobility Products Division, 7477 E. Dry Creek Pkwy., 80503, pg. 1536   PB
Tecmar Technologies, Inc., 1900 Pike Rd., Bldg. E, 80501, pg. 1361   IT
Universal Transport-Western Division, c/o Universal Transport Inc., pg. 1424   IT

Louisville

Charter Centennial Peaks Behavioral Health System, Inc., 2255 S. 88th St., 80027, pg. 1034   PB
EFI Division, 1301 Courtesy Rd., 80027, pg. 539   PB
Quantum Peripherals Colorado, 2270 S. 88th St., 80028, pg. 1350   PB
ROCK BOTTOM RESTAURANTS, 248 Centennial Pkwy., Ste. 100, 80027, pg. 1396   PB
STORAGE TECHNOLOGY CORPORATION, 2270 S. 88th St., 80028, pg. 1522   PB
TENERA Rocky Flats, LLC, 500 Cherry St., Ste. C, 80027, pg. 1576   PB

Loveland

HACH COMPANY, 5600 Lindbergh Dr., 80537, pg. 773   PB
Hach International Foreign Sales Co., Inc., 5600 Lindbergh Dr., 80539, pg. 773   PB

Lyons

Baseline Industries, North Star Route, Box 649, 80540, pg. 1114   PB

Meeker

Texaco USA, 7265 Rbc 9, 81641, pg. 1583   PB

Monte Vista

MONTE VISTA CO-OP ASSOCIATION, INC., 1901 E. Hwy. 160, 81144, pg. 758   PV

Morrison

Ampex Data Systems Corporation, 6228 S. Willow Springs Dr., 80465, pg. 104   PB

Pagosa Springs

Century Telephone Co. of Colorado, P.O. Box 359, 81147, pg. 330   PB
Fairfield Pagosa, P.O. Box 4040, 42 Pinon Causeway, 81157, pg. 611   PB
Universal Telephone Co. of Colorado, P.O. Box 359, 421 Lewis St., 81147, pg. 330   PB
Universal Telephone Co. of Colorado, P.O. Box 359, 398 Bastille Ave., 81147, pg. 330   PB

Paonia

Delta County Tele-Comm, Inc., 132 Grand Ave., 81428, pg. 1571   PB

Parker

DYWIDAG Systems International, USA, Inc., P.O. Box 422, 11479 S. Pine Dr., 80134, pg. 424   IT
Medtronics Inc., 18501 E. Plaza Dr., 80134, pg. 1083   PB

Pueblo

C & W Railway Co., 225 Canal St., 81002, pg. 1230   PB
CF & I Steel, L.P., 1612 E. Abriendo, 81004, pg. 1230   PB
FOUNDATION HEALTH SYSTEMS, INC., 225 N. Main St., 81003, pg. 678   PB
Piper Jaffray Inc., 119 W. Fifth St., 81003-3161, pg. 1301   PB
Qual-Med, Inc., 225 N. Main St., 81003, pg. 678   PB
QualMed Plans for Health-Pueblo, 225 N. Main St., 81003, pg. 678   PB
Southern Colorado Health Plan, 41 Montebello St., H, 81001, pg. 678   PB
West Plains Energy, P.O. Box 75, 200 W. First St., 81002-0075, pg. 1701   PB

Security

UMB Bank Colorado, 502 Security Blvd., 80911, pg. 1654   PB

Sedalia

Schlumberger Satellite, 7147 Reynolds Dr., 80135-8805, pg. 1439   PB

Silverton

Sunnyside Gold Corporation, One Gladstone St., 81433, pg. 562   PB

Steamboat Springs

TIC, 40185 County Rd. # 129, 80487, pg. 1064   PV

Thornton

Affiliated Banks Service Co., 445 E. 124th Ave., 80241, pg. 173   PB
Audio King Corporation, 321 A W. 84th Ave., 80221, pg. 1662   PB
EDD-Denver, 9351 Grant St., Ste. 460, 80229, pg. 205   PB
Elms Haven Care Center, 12080 Bellaire Way, 80241-3600, pg. 836   PB
Gerry Baby Products Company, 1500 E. 128th Ave., 80241, pg. 629   PV
North Denver Hill Corp., 9350 Grant St., 80229, pg. 1023   PB
ULTIMATE ELECTRONICS, 321 A W. 84th Ave., 80221, pg. 1662   PB
WESTERN DAIRYMEN COOPERATIVE, INC., 12450 N. Washington St., 80241, pg. 1165   PV

Vail

Lodge Properties, Inc. (Lodge at Vail), 174 Gore Creek Dr., 81657, pg. 1213   IT
Vail Associates, Inc., P.O. Box 78, 81658, pg. 1704   PB
VAIL RESORTS, INC., 137 Benchmark Rd., 81658, pg. 1704   PB

Walsenburg

Navajo Western Land Co., 502 W. 7th, 81089, pg. 1153   PV

Westminster

ARGOSystems, Inc., 9101 Harlan St., Ste. 210, 80030, pg. 240   PB
Ball Metal Beverage Container Corp., 9300 W. 108th Cir., 80021, pg. 171   PB
Ball Metal Food Container Corp., 9300 W. 108th Cir., 80021-3682, pg. 171   PB
Ball Packaging Holdings Corp., 9300 W. 108th Circle, 80021-3682, pg. 171   PB
ConferTech International, 12110 N. Pecos St., 80234-2076, pg. 683   PB
General Cable Apparatus Division, 5600 W. 88th Ave., 80030, pg. 1487   IT
HOMESTEAD HOUSE INC., 9410 Wadsworth Pkwy., 80021, pg. 537   PV
Mecor, Inc., 12200 N. Pecos St., Ste. 100, 80234, pg. 855   IT
Milgray/Colorado, Inc., 8787 Turnpike Dr., 80030, pg. 206   PB
Mobil Tool International, 5600 W. 88th Ave., 80030, pg. 1486   IT

Weston

Basin Resources, 14300 Hwy. 12, 81091, pg. 1127   PB

Wheat Ridge

American Copper & Nickel Company, Inc., 4860 Robb St., Ste 201, 80033, pg. 672   PB
MESA LABORATORIES, INC., 3904 Youngfield St., 80033, pg. 1099   PB

Windsor

Eastman Kodak Kcd, P.O. Box 909, 80550-0909, pg. 555   PB

CONNECTICUT

Ansonia

FARREL CORPORATION, 25 Main St., 06401, pg. 614   PB

Avon

Atcor Engineering Systems, 6411 Ivy Lane, Ste. 204, 20774, pg. 694   PB
Computer Systems Research, Inc., Avon Park S., 06001, pg. 1070   PB
EASTERN COLOR PRINTING COMPANY, 60 Security Dr., 06001, pg. 357   PV
MINTZ & HOKE INC., 40 Tower Ln., 06001, pg. 751   PV
M.H. RHODES, INC., 99 Thompson Rd., 06001, pg. 927   PV
SpecTran Specialty Optics, P.O. Box 1260, 150 Fisher Dr., 06001, pg. 1497   PB
TUPMAN THURLOW CO. INC., 40 Tower Ln., 06001, pg. 1109   PV

Baltic

M.S. Chambers Engraving Group, 132 W. Main St., 06330, pg. 351   PV

Beacon Falls

Bakers Choice Products, Inc., Railroad Ave., 06403, pg. 1386   PB
Hardware & Components Operation, 158 Pinesbridge Rd., 06403, pg. 1177   PB

Berlin

THE BERLIN STEEL CONSTRUCTION COMPANY, 76 Depot Rd., 06037, pg. 136   PV
Charter Oak Energy, Inc., Selden St., 06037, pg. 1194   PB
The Connecticut Light & Power Co., 107 Selden St., 06037, pg. 1194   PB
Connecticut Yankee Atomic Power Co., 107 Belden St., 06037, pg. 325   PB
Corbin Russwin, Inc., P.O. Box 4004, 225 Episcopal Rd., 06037, pg. 1499   IT
EIS Brake Parts Div., P.O. Box 1315, 129 Worthington Ridge, 06037, pg. 1503   IT
Lindberg Heat Treating Co., 675 Christian Lane, 06037, pg. 999   PB
Mazzucchelli Inc., Christian Ln., 400, 06037, pg. 849   IT
Northeast Nuclear Energy Co., Selden St., 06037, pg. 1195   PB
NORTHEAST UTILITIES, 107 Selden St., 06037, pg. 1194   PB
Northeast Utilities Service Co., Selden St., 06037, pg. 1195   PB

Bethel

CANNONDALE CORPORATION, 16 Trowbridge Dr., 06801, pg. 301   PB
Culligan, C.I. Div., Five Second Ln., 06801-2852, pg. 467   PB
DCG PRECISION MANUFACTURING CORPORATION, Nine Trowbridge Dr., 06801, pg. 301   PV
Duracell International Inc., Berkshire Corporate Pasrk, 8 Research Dr., 06801, pg. 743   PB
Duracell U.S.A., Berkshire Corporate Park, 06801, pg. 743   PB
Eaton Corporation, Pressure Sensors Division, 15 Durant Ave., 06801, pg. 557   PB
The Kanthal Corporation, 119 Wooster St., P.O. Box 281, 06801-0281, pg. 723   IT

Bloomfield

Amplex/SGNIC, 66 Douglas St., 06002, pg. 1173   IT
ANDERSEN GROUP, INC., Ney Industrial Pk., Two Douglas St., 06002, pg. 111   PB
BARTLETT BRAINARD EACOTT, INC., 30 Tobey Rd., 06002, pg. 118   PV
BEACON GROUP, 85 Granby St., 06002, pg. 126   PV
Beacon Group, 85 Granby St., 06002, pg. 126   PV
Beacon Winch Company, 85 Granby St., 06002, pg. 126   PV
CG Equity Ventures, Inc., 900 Cottage Grove Rd., 06002, pg. 365   PB
CG Individual Tax Benefits Payments, Inc., 900 Cottage Grove Rd., 06002, pg. 358   PB
CG Life Pension Benefits Payments, Inc., 900 Cottage Grove Rd., 06002, pg. 358   PB
CG Lina Pension Benefits Payments, Inc., 900 Cottage Grove Rd., 06002, pg. 358   PB
California Seven Associates Limited Partnership, 900 Cottage Grove Rd., S-226, 06002, pg. 359   PB
Calisar Associates, 900 Cottage Grove Rd., 06002, pg. 361   PB
Cambridge Products Corporation, 244 Woodland Ave., 06002, pg. 598   PV
Cigna Advisory Partners, Inc., 900 Cottage Grove Rd., 06002, pg. 357   PB

PB - *U.S. Public Companies Volume*
PV - *U.S. Private Companies Volume*
IT - *International Public & Private Companies Volume*

Geographic Index-U.S.

Cigna Associates, Inc., 900 Cottage Grove Rd., 06002, pg. 358 **PB**

Cigna Benefits Processing Ireland Ltd., 900 Cottage Grove Rd., 06082, pg. 358 **PB**

Cigna Capital Brokerage, Inc., 900 Cottage Grove Rd., 06002, pg. 357 **PB**

Cigna Employee Benefits Services, Inc., 900 Cottage Grove Rd., 06002, pg. 358 **PB**

Cigna Energy Partners 1985-A Ltd. Partnership, c/o Cigna Energy Resources, 900 Cottage Grove Rd., S-226, 06003, pg. 359 **PB**

Cigna Energy Partners 1986-A Ltd. Partnership, 900 Cottage Grove Rd., S-215, 06002, pg. 358 **PB**

Cigna Energy Partners 1986-B Ltd. Partnership, 900 Cottage Grove Rd., S-215, 06002, pg. 358 **PB**

Cigna Energy Resources, Inc., 900 Cottage Grove Rd., 06002, pg. 358 **PB**

Cigna Financial Advisors, Inc., 900 Cottage Grove Rd., 06002, pg. 358 **PB**

Cigna Financial Futures, Inc., 900 Cottage Grove Rd., 06002, pg. 357 **PB**

Cigna Financial Partners, Inc., 900 Cottage Grove Rd., 06002, pg. 358 **PB**

Cigna Funding Limited Partnership, 900 Cottage Grove Rd., 06002, pg. 357 **PB**

Cigna Health Corporation, 900 Cottage Grove Rd., 06002, pg. 359 **PB**

Cigna Healthcare, Inc., 900 Cottage Grove Rd., 06002, pg. 359 **PB**

Cigna Hotel Associates-I Limited Partnership, c/o CT Gen. Realty-4th, 900 Cottage Grove Rd., S-226, 06002, pg. 359 **PB**

Cigna Income Realty-I Limited Partnership, c/o Cigna Tenth, 900 Cottage Grove Rd., S-226, 06002, pg. 359 **PB**

Cigna International Finance Inc., 900 Cottage Grove Rd., 06002, pg. 357 **PB**

Cigna Investment Advisory Company, Inc., 900 Cottage Grove Rd., 06002, pg. 357 **PB**

Cigna Investment Group, Inc., 900 Cottage Grove Rd., 06002, pg. 357 **PB**

Cigna Investments & Placements Company, 900 Cottage Grove Rd., 06002, pg. 357 **PB**

Cigna Investments, Inc., 900 Cottage Grove Rd., 06002, pg. 357 **PB**

Cigna Leveraged Capital Fund, Inc., 900 Cottage Grove Rd., 06002, pg. 357 **PB**

Cigna Life Insurance Company, 900 Cottage Grove Rd., 06002, pg. 361 **PB**

Cigna Mezzanine Capital, Inc., 900 Cottage Grove Rd., 06002, pg. 357 **PB**

Cigna Mezzanine Partners III, Inc., 900 Cottage Grove Rd., 06002, pg. 357 **PB**

Cigna Mezzanine Partners II, L.P., 900 Cottage Grove Rd., 06002, pg. 357 **PB**

Cigna Mortgage Securities, Inc., 900 Cottage Grove Rd., 06002, pg. 361 **PB**

Cigna Re Corporation, 900 Cottage Grove Rd., 06002, pg. 360 **PB**

Cigna Real Estate Fund S Ltd. Partnership, 950 Cottage Grove Rd., 06002, pg. 365 **PB**

Cigna Real Estate Fund T Ltd. Partnership, c/o CII, 900 Cottage Grove Rd., 06002, pg. 365 **PB**

Cigna Realty Resources, Inc. - Eighth, 900 Cottage Grove Rd., 06002, pg. 358 **PB**

Cigna Realty Resources, Inc. - Eleventh, 900 Cottage Grove Rd., 06002, pg. 358 **PB**

Cigna Realty Resources, Inc. - Fifteenth, 900 Cottage Grove Rd., 06002, pg. 359 **PB**

Cigna Realty Resources, Inc. - Fifth, 900 Cottage Grove Rd., 06002, pg. 359 **PB**

Cigna Realty Resources, Inc. - Fourteenth, 900 Cottage Grove Rd., 06002, pg. 359 **PB**

Cigna Realty Resources, Inc. - Ninth, 900 Cottage Grove Rd., 06002, pg. 359 **PB**

Cigna Realty Resources, Inc. - Seventh, 900 Cottage Grove Rd., 06002, pg. 359 **PB**

Cigna Realty Resources, Inc. - Sixteenth, 900 Cottage Grove Rd., 06002, pg. 359 **PB**

Cigna Realty Resources, Inc. - Sixth, 900 Cottage Grove Rd., 06002, pg. 359 **PB**

Cigna Realty Resources, Inc. - Tenth, 900 Cottage Grove Rd., 06002, pg. 359 **PB**

Cigna Realty Resources, Inc. - Twelfth, 900 Cottage Grove Rd., 06002, pg. 359 **PB**

Cigna Securities, Inc., 900 Cottage Grove Rd., 06002, pg. 360 **PB**

Cigna/Willowbrook Associates Limited Partnership, c/o Cigna 11th, 900 Cottage Grove Rd., S-226, 06002, pg. 359 **PB**

Cigna/Willowbrook II Associates Limited Partnership, c/o CRR-XIV, 900 Cottage Grove Rd., 06152, pg. 359 **PB**

CONGEN Properties, Inc., 900 Cottage Grove Rd., 06002, pg. 365 **PB**

Connecticut General Benefit Payments, Inc., 900 Cottage Grove Rd., 06002, pg. 360 **PB**

Connecticut General Corporation, 900 Cottage Grove Rd., 06002, pg. 358 **PB**

Connecticut General Equity Properties-I Limited Partnership, c/o CGRR Third, 900 Cottage Grove Rd., S-226, 06002, pg. 359 **PB**

Connecticut General Life Insurance Company, 900 Cottage Grove Rd., 06002, pg. 360 **PB**

Connecticut General Pension Services, Inc., 900 Cottage Grove Rd., 06002, pg. 360 **PB**

Connecticut General Realty Investors Limited Partnership, c/o CRR Inc., 900 Cottage Grove Rd., S-226, 06002, pg. 359 **PB**

Connecticut General Realty Investors-III Limited Partnership, c/o CRR-Fifth, 900 Cottage Grove Rd., S-226, pg. 359 **PB**

Connecticut General Realty Investors-II Limited Partnership, c/o CRR-Second, 900 Cottage Grove Rd., S-226, 06002, pg. 359 **PB**

Connecticut General Realty Resources, Inc., 900 Cottage Grove Rd., 06002, pg. 359 **PB**

Connecticut General Realty Resources, Inc. - Fourth, 900 Cottage Grove Rd., 06002, pg. 359 **PB**

Connecticut General Realty Resources, Inc. - Second, 900 Cottage Grove Rd., 06002, pg. 359 **PB**

Connecticut General Realty Resources, Inc. - Third, 900 Cottage Grove Rd., 06002, pg. 359 **PB**

Disability Claim Services, Inc., 900 Cottage Grove Rd., 06002, pg. 362 **PB**

First Equicor Life Insurance Company, 900 Cottage Grove Rd., 06002, pg. 361 **PB**

General Cigar Company, Inc., 320 W. Newbury Rd., 06002-1398, pg. 708 **PB**

General Graphics, Inc., 900 Cottage Grove Rd., 06002, pg. 362 **PB**

Howden Compressors, 23 Old Windsor Rd., 06002, pg. 636 **IT**

James Howden America Inc., 23 Old Windsor Rd., 06002, pg. 636 **IT**

IFD Properties, Inc.-First, 900 Cottage Grove Rd., 06002, pg. 359 **PB**

Jacobs Brake Division, 22 E. Dudley Town Rd., 06002, pg. 481 **PB**

Jacobs Vehicle Equipment Company, 22 E. Dudley Town Rd., 06002, pg. 481 **PB**

Kaman Aerospace Corp., Old Windsor Rd., P.O. Box 2, 06002-0002, pg. 942 **PB**

KAMAN CORPORATION, 1332 Blue Hills Ave., 06002-0001, pg. 941 **PB**

Kaman Diversified Technologies Corp., 1332 Blue Hills Ave., 06002, pg. 942 **PB**

Kaman Industrial Technologies Corp., 1332 Blue Hills Ave., 06002-0001, pg. 942 **PB**

Kaman Music Corp., 20 Bllue Olde Windsor Rd., 06002, pg. 942 **PB**

Kaman Music International, 1330 Blue Hills Ave., 06002, pg. 942 **PB**

Kamatics Corp., Blue Hills Ave., P.O. Box 3, 06002-0003, pg. 942 **PB**

Knolls Associates Limited Partnership, c/o CRR-12th, 900 Cottage Grove Rd., S-226, 06002, pg. 359 **PB**

Knollwood Associates Limited Partnership, c/o CRR-11th, 900 Cottage Grove Rd., S-226, 06002, pg. 359 **PB**

LINA Benefit Payments, Inc., 900 Cottage Grove Rd., 06002, pg. 362 **PB**

Metal Stamping Equip. Div., 522 Cottage Grove Rd., 06002, pg. 825 **PV**

Ney Dental International, 1280 Blue Hills Ave., 06002, pg. 388 **IT**

The J.M. Ney Company, Ney Industrial Pk., 06002, pg. 111 **PB**

Ney Ultrasonics, Inc., 1280 Blue Hills Ave., 06002, pg. 111 **PB**

100 Gold Street Limited Partnership, c/o Cigna Realty Resources-6th, 900 Cottage Grove Rd., S-226, 06002, pg. 359 **PB**

P/A INDUSTRIES, INC., 522 Cottage Grove Rd., 06002-3111, pg. 825 **PV**

Power Systems Inc., 45 Griffin Rd. S., 06002, pg. 868 **IT**

Quebec Street Investments, Inc., 900 Cottage Grove Rd., 06002, pg. 361 **PB**

Regional Mall CII, L.P., 900 Cottage Grove Rd., 06002, pg. 357 **PB**

Regional Mall Development Partners L.P., c/o Investment Law Dept., 900 Cottage Grove Rd., 06002, pg. 359 **PB**

San Ramon Corporation, 900 Cottage Grove Rd., 06002, pg. 361 **PB**

Silver Brook Real Estate Development Company, 900 Cottage Rd., 06002, pg. 358 **PB**

Smyth Manufacturing Company, 85 Granby St., 06002, pg. 126 **PV**

Ten-Ten Jefferson Corporation, 900 Cottage Grove Rd., 06002, pg. 361 **PB**

James P. Toner Company, Inc., 900 Cottage Grove Rd., 06002, pg. 358 **PB**

The Tulsa Corporation, 900 Cottage Grove Rd., S-313, 06002, pg. 359 **PB**

Web Processing Equip. Div., 522 Cottage Grove Rd., 06002, pg. 825 **PV**

Westford Office Venture, c/o Cigna Inv., Inc., 900 Cottage Grove Rd., 06002, pg. 359 **PB**

Bolton

SIMONIZ USA, INC., 201 Boston Turnpike, 06043, pg. 1001 **PV**

Branford

The Advertiser, 230 E. Main St., P.O. Box 829, 06405, pg. 934 **PB**

Automotive Controls Corp., Echlin Rd. & U. S. Rte. No. 1, 06405, pg. 560 **PB**

Branford Review, 230 E. Main St., 06405, pg. 934 **PB**

BRANFORD SAVINGS BANK, 45 S. Main St., 06405, pg. 250 **PB**

Branford Savings Bank-Branford, 568 E. Main St., 06405, pg. 250 **PB**

Dryden & Palmer Company, 16 Business Park Dr., 06405, pg. 471 **PV**

ECHLIN INC., 100 Double Beach Rd., 06405, pg. 560 **PB**

Electrostatic Technology, Inc., Four Pin Oak Dr., 06405, pg. 1189 **PB**

GRAVYMASTER INC., 16 Business Park Dr., 06405, pg. 471 **PV**

Howmet Turbine Component Corporation, Four Commercial St., 06405, pg. 213 **PV**

Interspiro Inc., 31 Business Park Dr., 06405, pg. 1289 **IT**

Micropolis Corporation, 24 Flat Rock Extension, 06405, pg. 742 **PV**

NEUROGEN CORPORATION, 35 N.E. Industrial Rd., 06405, pg. 1169 **PB**

Sandvik/Milford Corporation, 30 Thompson Rd., 06405, pg. 1185 **IT**

Bridgeport

ALIMAK ELEVATOR COMPANY, 1100 Boston Ave., 06601-1950, pg. 34 **PV**

AQUARION COMPANY, 835 Main St., 06604-2353, pg. 126 **PB**

Aquarion Management Services, 835 Main St., 06604, pg. 126 **PB**

Aquarion Management Services, Inc., 835 Main St., 06604, pg. 126 **PB**

BHC Company, 600 Lindley St., 06610, pg. 126 **PB**

BEAD INDUSTRIES INC., 110 Mountain Grove, 06605, pg. 154 **PV**

BODINE ASSEMBLY AND TEST SYSTEMS, 317 Mountain Grove, 06605-2046, pg. 154 **PV**

BRIDGEPORT MACHINES, INC., 500 Lindley St., 06606, pg. 251 **PB**

Casco Products Corporation, 380 Horace St., 06610-0241, pg. 1458 **PB**

Chase Manhattan Bank of Connecticut, 961 Main St., 06601, pg. 338 **PB**

Cobra Components, 347 Railroad Ave., 06604, pg. 839 **PV**

Componenta International Inc., 1100 Boston Avenue, 06610, pg. 1421 **IT**

CONNECTICUT ENERGY CORPORATION, 855 Main St., 06604, pg. 431 **PB**

The Cornwall & Patterson Co., 1155 Railroad Ave., 06605, pg. 879 **PV**

COUNTRY HOME BAKERY, INC., 1700-1722 Barnum Ave., 06610, pg. 278 **PV**

EMSON, INC., 1100 Boston Ave., 06610, pg. 375 **PV**

Highfield Manufacturing Co., 380 Mountain Grove St., 06601, pg. 127 **IT**

Hydrocorp, Inc., 835 Main St., 06601, pg. 126 **PB**

Lacey Mfg. Co., 1146 Barnum Ave., 06610, pg. 468 **IT**

Main Street South Corp., 835 Main St., 06601, pg. 126 **PB**

Moore Tool Company, Inc., 800 Union Ave., 06607-0088, pg. 889 **PV**

Olga Div., 325 Lafayette St., 06601, pg. 1738 **PB**

PARK DISTRIBUTORS, INC., 347 Railroad Ave., 06604, pg. 839 **PV**

PEOPLE'S BANK, 850 Main St., 06604, pg. 1274 **PB**

People's Securities Incorporated, 815 Main St., 06601, pg. 1274 **PB**

PRATT-READ CORPORATION, 1155 Railroad Av., 06605, pg. 879 **PV**

Precision Arc Co., 60 Radel St., 06607, pg. 1008 **PV**

THE PRODUCTO MACHINE CO., 990 Housatonic Ave., 06601, pg. 889 **PV**

REMINGTON PRODUCTS COMPANY, L.L.C., 60 Main St., 06604, pg. 921 **PV**

Safari Tool, 1155 Railroad Ave., 06605, pg. 879 **PV**

The Southern Connecticut Gas Company, 855 Main St., 06604-4918, pg. 431 **PB**

Universal Relay, 347 Railroad Ave., 06604, pg. 839 **PV**

WCI Machine Tools, 286 Canfield Ave., 06605, pg. 440 **IT**

Warner's, 325 Lafayette Ave., 06601, pg. 1738 **PB**

Bristol

Accurate Forging Corp., 201 Pine St., 06010, pg. 391 **IT**

Associated Spring, 18 Main St., 06010, pg. 190 **PB**

BARNES GROUP INC., 123 Main St., 06011-0489, pg. 189 **PB**

The Bristol Press, 99 Main St., 06010, pg. 934 **PB**

ESPN, Inc., ESPN Plaza, 935 Middle St., 06010-7454, pg. 512 **PB**

Imprint Newpapers, 99 Main St., 06010, pg. 935 **PB**

Brookfield

Beta Squared, Inc., 15 Secor Rd., 06804, pg. 1293 **PB**

PHOTRONICS, INC., 15 Secor Rd., 06804, pg. 1293 **PB**

Quebecor Printing Modern Inc., P.O. Box 207, 1000 Federal Rd., 06804, pg. 1078 **IT**

Quebecor Printing Modern Inc., 1000 Federal Rd., 06804, pg. 1078 **IT**

RAPID POWER TECHNOLOGIES, INC., 18 Graysbridge Rd., 06804, pg. 910 **PV**

Cheshire

AB-Small Business Investment Company, Inc., 275 School House Rd., 06410, pg. 249 **PB**

Advanced Compounding, 617 W. Johnson Ave., 06410, pg. 68 **PV**

AlliedSignal Guidance & Control, 250 Knotter Dr., 06410, pg. 50 **PB**

Bloomingdale's By Mail, Ltd., 475 Knotter Dr., 06410, pg. 618 **PB**

Boz-White Hills Inc., 275 Schoolhouse Rd., 06410, pg. 249 **PB**

BOZZUTO'S INC., 275 Schoolhouse Rd., 06410, pg. 249 **PB**

CONSOLIDATED INDUSTRIES, INC., 677 Mixville Rd., 06410, pg. 265 **PV**

Dual-Lite, 90 Fieldstone Ct., 06410, pg. 726 **PB**

Edwards Systems Tech, 90 Fieldstone Ct., 064110, pg. 726 **PB**

Geographic Index-U.S.

Fresh-Line Distributors, Inc., 275 Schoolhouse Road, 06410, pg. 249 **PB**
Greenery Extended Care Center at Cheshire, 50 Hazel Dr., 06410, pg. 836 **PB**
McGuire Manufacturing, 60 Grandview Ct., 06410, pg. 126 **PV**
Philips Automotive Electronics, 150 Knotter Dr., 06410-0868, pg. 1054 **IT**
Superior Steel Acquisition Corporation, Peck Ln., 06410, pg. 75 **IT**
Tolland Supermarket, Inc., Schoolhouse Rd., 06410, pg. 249 **PB**
Waterbury Farrel Technologies, 60 Fieldstone St., 06410, pg. 461 **PV**

Clinton

Chesebrough Pond's, Johns Street, 06413, pg. 1435
The Connecticut Water Company, 93 W. Main St., 06413, pg. 431 **PB**
CONNECTICUT WATER SERVICE, INC., 93 W. Main St., 06413-1600, pg. 431 **PB**

Colchester

ALPHA Q, INC., 87 Upton Rd., 06415, pg. 45 **PV**
The Regional Standard, Eighth Norwich Ave., P.O. Box 510, 06415, pg. 935 **PB**

Collinsville

Foothills Trader, Inc., 85 River Rd., 06022, pg. 934 **PB**
Inertia Dynamics Inc., 146 Powder Mill Rd., 06022, pg. 1398 **PB**

Coventry

First Federal Savings, Rtes. 31 & 275, 06238, pg. 632 **PB**

Danbury

A & M Products, 83 Wooster Heights Rd., 06810, pg. 627 **PB**
ATMI, INC., 7 Commerce Dr., 06810, pg. 12 **PB**
Banta Direct Marketing Group, Prindle, Ln., 06813-2479, pg. 188 **PB**
The Barden Corporation, 200 Park Ave., 06813, pg. 468 **PB**
Barden Precision Bearings, 200 Park Ave., P.O. Box 2449, 06813, pg. 468 **PB**
Beginning Readers' Program, Sherman Turnpike, 06816, pg. 794 **IT**
Branson Ultrasonics, 33 Eagle Rd., Commerce Park, 06810, pg. 574 **PB**
Branson Ultrasonics Corp.-Plastics Joining Div., 41 Eagle Rd., 06813-1961, pg. 574 **PB**
Branson Ultrasonics Corp. - Precision Cleaning Div., 41 Eagle Rd., 06813-1961, pg. 574 **PB**
Bread & Rolls Distribution, 60 Mill Plain Rd., 06810, pg. 299 **PB**
Childrens Press Inc., 90 Sherman Turnpike, 06816-0001, pg. 794 **IT**
COGNITRONICS CORPORATION, Three Corporate Dr., 06810-4130, pg. 394 **PB**
Color Cosmetics Group, Old Newtown Rd., 06810, pg. 464 **PB**
Ethan Allen, Inc., Ethan Allen Dr., 06813, pg. 595 **PB**
ETHAN ALLEN INTERIORS INC., Ethan Allen Dr., 06813, pg. 595 **PB**
FAG Bearings Corporation, 200 Park Ave., 06813-1933, pg. 469 **IT**
Federated Credit Corp., Sherman Tpke., 06816, pg. 794 **IT**
FIRST BRANDS CORPORATION, 83 Wooster Heights Rd., 06813, pg. 626 **PB**
G.E. Capital Vendor Financial Services, Corporate Ctr. One, 55 Federal Rd., 06810, pg. 712 **PB**
Grolier Educational Corporation, Sherman Tpke., 06816, pg. 794 **IT**
Grolier Electronic Publishing, Inc., Sherman Turnpike, 06816, pg. 794 **IT**
Grolier Enterprises Corporation, Sherman Tpke., 06816, pg. 794 **IT**
Grolier Enterprises Inc., 90 Sherman Turnpike, 06816-0001, pg. 794 **IT**
Grolier Inc., 90 Sherman Turnpike, 06816-0001, pg. 794 **IT**
Grolier International, Inc., Sherman Tpke., 06816, pg. 794 **IT**
Grolier Interstate, Inc., Sherman Turnpike, 06816, pg. 794 **IT**
Grolier Overseas Inc., Sherman Tpke., 06816, pg. 794 **IT**
Grolier Publishing Inc., Sherman Tpke., 06816, pg. 794 **IT**
Grolier Reading Programs, Inc., Sherman Tpke., 06816, pg. 794 **IT**
Grolier TeleMarketing, Inc., Sherman Tpke., 06816, pg. 794 **IT**
Grolier Year Book, Inc., Sherman Tpke., 06816, pg. 794 **IT**
HFS Mobility Services, 40 Apple Ridge Rd., 06810, pg. 321 **PB**
Himolene Corp., 83 Wooster Heights Rd., 06813, pg. 627 **PB**
KIRK & MATZ LTD., 95 Golden Hill Rd., 06811, pg. 623 **PV**
Latco II Inc., Sherman Tpke., 06816, pg. 794 **IT**
Lexicon Publications, Inc., Sherman Tpke., 06816, pg. 794 **IT**

LORAD Corporation, 36 Apple Ridge Rd., 06810, pg. 1595 **PB**
Novo Nordisk Bioindustrials, Inc., 33 Turner Rd., 06813-1907, pg. 987 **IT**
Nuclear Energy Services, Inc., 46 Shelter Rock Rd., 06810, pg. 75 **PB**
POWER DESIGNS, INC., Commerce Dr., Commerce Park, 06810, pg. 878 **PV**
PRAXAIR INC., 39 Old Ridgeburg Rd., 06817, pg. 1319 **PB**
Preferred Instruments, 31-35 South St., 06810, pg. 881 **PV**
PREFERRED UTILITIES MANUFACTURING CORP., 31-35 S. St., 06810, pg. 881 **PV**
Prestone Products Corporation, 39 Old Ridgeberry Rd., 06810-5109, pg. 51 **PB**
Proner Comatel USA Inc., Commerce Park, 22 Eagle Rd., 06810, pg. 1241 **IT**
Publishers World Trade Corporation, Sherman Tpke., 06816, pg. 795 **IT**
Raytheon Optical Systems, Incorporated, 100 Wooster Heights Rd., 06810, pg. 1364 **PB**
Rodenstock USA, Inc., P.O. Box 3709, 69 Kenosia Ave., 06813-3709, pg. 1007 **IT**
STP Consumer Services, 83 Wooster Heights Rd., 06813, pg. 627 **PB**
STP Corporation, 83 Wooster Heights Rd., Bldg. 301, 06813-1911, pg. 627 **PB**
STP Products, Inc., 83 Wooster Heights Rd., 06813, pg. 627 **PB**
Schwing America, Inc., Sludge Pump Div., 98 Mill Plain Rd., Ste. #2A, 06811, pg. 1211 **IT**
Seadrift Pipeline Corp., 39 Old Ridgebury Rd., 06817, pg. 1667 **IT**
Sealed Air Engineered Products Division, 10 Old Sherman Tpke., 06810, pg. 1451 **PB**
Sperry Rail Services, 46 Shelter Rock Rd., 06810, pg. 75 **PB**
Tenax Corporation, Four Old Newtown Rd., 06810, pg. 193 **IT**
Trex Medical Corporation, 36 Apple Ridge Rd., 06810, pg. 1595 **PB**
Ucar Pipeline, Inc., 39 Old Ridgebury Rd., 06817, pg. 1667 **IT**
UCAR Global Enterprises Inc., 39 Old Ridgebury Rd., 06817, pg. 1662 **PB**
UCAR INTERNATIONAL INC., 39 Old Ridgebury Rd., Section J4, 06817, pg. 1662 **PB**
UNION CARBIDE CORPORATION, 39 Old Ridgebury Rd., 06817-0001, pg. 1666 **PB**
Union Carbide Inter-America, 39 Old Ridgebury Road, 06817, pg. 1667 **PB**
W.N. Best, 31-35 S. St., 06810, pg. 881 **PV**

Danielson

DELTA RUBBER COMPANY, P.O. Box 300, 06239, pg. 323 **PV**
SPIROL INTERNATIONAL CORP., 30 Rock Ave., 06239-1434, pg. 1026 **PV**

Darien

AEI Ocean Services, 120 Tokeneke Rd., 06820, pg. 30 **PB**
Air Express Intl. Agency, Inc., 120 Tokeneke Rd., 06820, pg. 30 **PB**
AIR EXPRESS INTERNATIONAL CORPORATION, 120 Tokeneke Rd., 06820, pg. 30 **PB**
Air Express Intl. USA, Inc., 120 Tokeneke Rd., 06820, pg. 30 **PB**
Brink's, Inc., One Thorndal Cir., 06820, pg. 1305 **PB**
HEATING OIL PARTNERS L.P., 1120 Post Rd., 06820, pg. 518 **PV**
Labatt U.S.A., 23 Old Kings Hwy. S., 06820, pg. 679 **IT**
Lee & Steel Inc., P.O. Box 2007, 06820, pg. 359 **PV**
Milupa Company, P.O. Box 4062, 06820, pg. 991 **IT**
PARFUMS DE COEUR LTD., 85 Old Kings Highway N., 06820, pg. 839 **PV**
Software Security, Inc., 6 Thorndal Cir., 06820, pg. 1359 **PB**
Surface Freight Corp., 120 Tokeneke Rd., 06820, pg. 30 **PB**
SWISHER INTERNATIONAL GROUP, INC., 20 Thorndal Cir., 06820, pg. 1543 **PB**
Trammochem Division, 19 Old Kings Hwy. S., 06820, pg. 1096 **PV**
Zotos International, 100 Tokeneke Road, 06820, pg. 1236 **IT**

Dayville

American White Cross, P.O. Box Box 419, 349 Lake Rd., 06241, pg. 694 **PB**
Wilson Machine Knife Co., Inc., Louisa Viens Dr., 06241, pg. 551 **PV**

Derby

Browning-Ferris Industries of Connecticut, Inc., P.O. Box 871, 06418, pg. 263 **PB**

East Berlin

Albi Manufacturing Division, 401 Berlin St., 06023, pg. 1030 **PV**
STANCHEM INC., 401 Berlin St., 06023, pg. 1030 **PV**

East Granby

Beckett Papers, Two Gateway Blvd., 06026, pg. 903 **PB**

DELTA INDUSTRIES, 39 Bradley Park Rd., 06026, pg. 322 **PV**
Windsor Airmotive, Seven Connecticut S. Dr., 06026, pg. 190 **PB**
YESCo Industrial Energy Services, Inc., 11 C. Kripes Rd., 06026, pg. 1788 **PB**

East Hartford

BKM ENTERPRISES, INC., 300 E. River Dr., 06108, pg. 107 **PV**
BKM Total Office, 300 E. River Dr., 06108, pg. 107 **PV**
Eastman Kodak Riverbend, 77 Hartland St., 06108-3259, pg. 555 **PB**
FIRST FEDERAL SAVINGS, 1137 Main St., 06108, pg. 632 **PB**
First Federal Savings, 1137 Main St., 06103, pg. 632 **PB**
First Federal Savings, Silver Ln., pg. 632 **PB**
The General Building Supply Company, 367 Ellington Rd., Rt. 5, 06108, pg. 403 **PB**
Konica Photo Service U.S.A., Inc., 88 Prestige Park Circle, 06108, pg. 748 **IT**
Media Recovery Inc.-Connecticut, 330 Robert St., Ste. 403, 06108, pg. 727 **PB**
Staveley Sensors Division, 91 Prestige Park Circle, 06108, pg. 1299 **IT**
Thermal Industries Inc., 91 Prestige Park Cir., 06108-1918, pg. 491 **PV**
WWF Paper Corporation - N.E., 45 Belden St., 06108, pg. 1145 **PV**

East Haven

Branford Savings Bank-East Haven, 263 Hemingway Ave., 06512, pg. 250 **PB**
Branford Savings Bank-Foxon, 430 Foxon Rd., 06512, pg. 250 **PB**

East Lyme

Ozone Industries Inc., 29 Industrial Park Rd., 06333, pg. 113 **IT**

East Windsor

Central Metal Products, Inc., Nine Thompson Rd., 06088, pg. 190 **PB**
Marshall Erdman & Assoc., Inc., Seven Thompson Rd., 06088, pg. 380 **PV**
Surface Technology Business, 12 Thompson Rd., 06088-9696, pg. 582 **PB**

East Woodstock

Poron Materials Unit, 245 Woodstock Rd., 06281, pg. 1403 **PB**

Ellington

Accu-Time System, P.O. Box 630, 06029, pg. 11 **PV**
First Federal Savings, Meadowview Plaza, Rte. 83, 06029, pg. 632 **PB**
P.S.I. Division, P.O. Box 536, 06029, pg. 832 **PV**
TRI-S Incorporated, 25 Pinney St., 06029, pg. 546 **PB**

Enfield

August Max Woman, 107 Phoenix Ave., 06082, pg. 219 **PV**
Carris of Connecticut, Inc., P.O. Box 1104, 06083, pg. 215 **PV**
CASUAL CORNER GROUP, INC., 100 Phoenix Ave., 06082, pg. 219 **PV**
Casual Corner Group Inc., 107 Phoenix Ave., 06082, pg. 219 **PV**
Casual Corner Outlet, 107 Phoenix Ave., 06082, pg. 219 **PV**
Casual Corner Woman, 107 Phoenix Ave., 06082, pg. 219 **PV**
Cigna Healthcare of Connecticut, Inc., 5700 Bigelow Commons, 06082, pg. 359 **PB**
CONTROL MODULE, INC., 227 Brainard Rd., 06082, pg. 271 **PV**
Dairy Mart Farms, Inc., One Vision Dr., 06082, pg. 476 **PB**
Dairy Mart, Inc., One Vision Dr., 06082, pg. 476 **PB**
Enfield Distribution Center, P.O. Box 2100, 25 Bacon Rd., 06082, pg. 496 **PV**
Financial Opportunities, Inc., 240 South Rd., 06082, pg. 477 **PB**
Jagenberg, Inc., 175 Freshwater Blvd., 06083-1250, pg. 1108 **IT**
LEGO Systems, Inc., 555 Taylor Rd., 06082-3298, pg. 805 **IT**
PTR-Precision Technologies, Inc., 120 Post Road, 06082, pg. 679 **IT**
Parkway Pavilion Healthcare, 1157 Enfield St., 06082, pg. 1714 **PB**
Petite Sophisticate, 107 Phoenix Ave., 06082, pg. 219 **PV**
Petite Sophisticate Outlet, 107 Phoenix Ave., 06082, pg. 219 **PV**
SPRINGBORN TESTING & RESEARCH, INC., 10 Water St., 06082, pg. 1027 **PV**

Fairfield

ACME UNITED CORPORATION, 75 Kings Highway Cut Off, 06430, pg. 17 **PB**
FKI Industries. Inc., 425 Post Rd., 06430, pg. 472 **IT**

Geographic Index-U.S.

Fairprene Ind. Products Company, 85 Mill Plain Rd., 06430, pg. 113 IT
G.E. Industrial & Power Systems Sales, 3135 Easton Tpke., 06431, pg. 711 PB
GENERAL ELECTRIC COMPANY, 3135 Easton Tpke., 06431, pg. 709 PB
Intellisource, 55 Walls Rd., 06430, pg. 1425 PB
Measurement Systems, Inc., 777 Commerce Dr., 06432, pg. 1431 IT
PUBLICKER INDUSTRIES INC., One Coast Rd., 06430, pg. 1341 PB
ROLOCK, INC., 1350 Kings Hwy. E., 06432, pg. 942 PV
SURVEY SAMPLING, INC., One Post Road, 06430, pg. 1056 PV

Farmington

The Connecticut Indemnity Co., Nine Farm Springs Dr., 06032, pg. 1231 PB
Connecticut Specialty Insurance Company, 9 Farm Springs Dr., 06032, pg. 1231 PB
CONNECTICUT SPRING & STAMPING CORPORATION, 48 Spring Lane, 06034, pg. 263 PV
EBI Consulting Services, Inc., 9 Farm Springs Dr., 06032, pg. 1231 PB
EBI Indemnity Company, Nine Farm Springs Dr., 06032, pg. 1231 PB
Employee Benefits Insurance Company, 9 Farm Springs Dr., 06032, pg. 1231 PB
The Fire & Casualty Co. of Connecticut, Nine Farm Springs Dr., 06032, pg. 1231 PB
Healthsource Connecticut, 40 Stamford Dr., 06032, pg. 360 PB
IDV North America, P.O. Box 388, 16 Munson Rd., 06034-0388, pg. 409 IT
Kaiser Permanente, Northeast Division, 76 Batterson Park Rd., 06034-4011, pg. 605 PV
KEILER & COMPANY, 304 Main St., 06032-2957, pg. 611 PV
Micro Networks of America, Inc., P.O. Box 859, 320 Main St., 06034, pg. 711 PB
Microsoft Consulting Services, 74 Batterson Park Rd., 06032-2565, pg. 1108 PB
THE ROBERT E. MORRIS COMPANY, 17 Talcott Notch Rd., 06034, pg. 762 PV
THE MOTORLEASE CORP., 1506 New Britain Ave., 06032, pg. 764 PV
Nation's Care, Inc., 9 Farm Springs Dr., 06032, pg. 1231 PB
O-Z/Gedney Co., 199 Scott Swamp Rd., 06034-4044, pg. 727 PB
Orion Capital Companies, Inc., Nine Farm Springs Dr., 06032, pg. 1231 PB
Otis Elevator Company, Ten Farm Springs, 06032, pg. 1690 PB
Peninsula Excess Insurance Brokers, Inc., 9 Farm Springs Rd., 06032, pg. 1231 PB
Security Insurance Co. of Hartford, Nine Farm Springs Dr., 06032, pg. 1231 PB
Security Insurance Co. (U.K.) Ltd., Nine Farm Springs Dr., 06032, pg. 1231 PB
Security Reinsurance Co., Nine Farm Springs Dr., 06032, pg. 1231 PB
Stanley Access Technologies, Rte. 6 Corner Hyde Rd., 06032, pg. 1509 PB
Stewart Smith East, Inc., Ten Stanford Dr., 06032, pg. 1508 IT
TRUMPF INC., 111 Hyde Rd., Farmington Industrial Park, 06032, pg. 1108 PV
Vanguard Division, 16 Munson Rd., 06034-0388, pg. 917 IT
Willis Corroon Construction Svcs. Corp. of CT, 160 Farmington Ave., 06032, pg. 1504 IT

Forestville

Locknetics Security Engineering, 575 Birch St., 06011, pg. 507 PV

Georgetown

GILBERT & BENNETT MANUFACTURING COMPANY, North Main St., 06829, pg. 453 PV

Gilman

Kaman Aerospace Corporation-Gilman Plant, Thames Rd., 06336, pg. 942 PB

Glastonbury

Arbor Acres Farm, Inc., Marlborough Rd., 06033, pg. 202 IT
Equator Holdings Ltd., Equator House, 45 Glastonbury Blvd., 06033, pg. 580 IT
Equator Limited, Equator House, 45 Glastonbury Blvd., 06033, pg. 580 IT
First Federal Savings, 2510 Main St., 06033, pg. 632 PB
Fleet Capital Corporation, 200 Glastonbury Blvd., 06033, pg. 649 PB
Harte-Hanks, 95 Oak St., 06033-2315, pg. 793 PB
Hewlett-Packard Company, 115 Glastonbury Blvd., 06033, pg. 813 PB
Ikon Office Solutions-New England, 755 Winding Brook Dr., 06033, pg. 863 PB
Montgomery & Collins, Inc. of Connecticut, 655 Winding Brook Dr., 1st Fl., 06033-4337, pg. 366 PB
MOTT'S HOLDINGS, INC., 655 Winding Brook Dr., 06033-4337, pg. 764 PV
Motts Supermarkets, 655 Winding Brook Dr, 06033, pg. 764 PV
Poe & Brown of Connecticut, 703 Helron Ave., 3rd Fl., 06033, pg. 1312 PB
RLI Special Risk, 655 Winding Brook Rd., 06032, pg. 1356 PB

Granby

Imperial Nurseries Inc., 90 Salmon Brook St., P.O. Box 120, 06035, pg. 707 PB
Strathmore Paper, 2 Gateway Blvd., 06026, pg. 903 PB

Greenwich

Abitibi-Consolidated Paper Sales Corporation, Two Soundview Dr., 06830, pg. 20 IT
Academic Year In America, Greenwich Park Bldg.#1, 51 Weaver St., 06831, pg. 56 PV
R.L. ALBERT & SON, INC., 19 W. Elm St., 06830, pg. 32 PV
AMERICAN INSTITUTE FOR FOREIGN STUDY, 102 Greenwich Ave., 06830, pg. 56 PV
American Landmark Springs, 777 W. Putnam Ave., 06830, pg. 919 IT
AMERICAN OPTICAL CORPORATION, 80 Field Point Rd., 06830, pg. 60 PV
Au Pair in America, 102 Greenwich Ave., 06830, pg. 56 PV
Bank of Ireland Asset Management Limited, Two Greenwich Plaza, 06830, pg. 152 IT
Benckiser Consumer Products Inc., Greenwich American Ctr., Five American Ln., 06831, pg. 185 IT
Berkley Dean & Company, Inc., 165 Mason St., 06836, pg. 216 PB
W.R. BERKLEY CORPORATION, 165 Mason St., 06830, pg. 215 PB
BLYTH INDUSTRIES, 100 Field Point Rd., 06830-6451, pg. 239 PB
Brandeis Division of PWT (USA) Inc., 475 Steamboat Rd., 06830, pg. 1029 IT
Brandeis Services Inc., 475 Steamboat Rd., 06830, pg. 1029 IT
BRANT ALLEN INDUSTRIES, INC., 80 Field Point Rd., 06830, pg. 165 PV
Brighton Communication Corp., Eight Sound Shore Dr., 06830, pg. 1021 PB
H.H. Brown Shoe Company, Inc., 124 W. Putnam Ave., 06830, pg. 217 PB
CA Communications, Two Greenwich Plaza, 06830, pg. 287 PV
CS BROOKS CANADA INC., One Lafayette Pl., 06830, pg. 197 PV
Camp America, 102 Greenwich Ave., 06830, pg. 57 PV
Chesebrough-Pond's USA Co., 33 Benedict Pl., 06830, pg. 1435 IT
A.T. CLAYTON & COMPANY, INC., Two Pickwick Plaza, 06830, pg. 244 PV
CLIGGOTT PUBLISHING, P.O. Box 4010, 55 Holly Hill Ln., 06831-0010, pg. 246 PV
Compendium Systems, 75 Holly Hill Ln., 06830-6098, pg. 259 PV
COMPENDIUM SYSTEMS CORPORATION, 75 Holly Hill Lane, 06830-6098, pg. 259 PV
Connecticut-American Water Co., 75 Holly Hill Lane, 06830, pg. 95 PB
Curtis Bay Towing Company Of Pennsylvania, Two Greenwich Plaza, 3rd Fl., 06830, pg. 760 PV
Curtis Bay Towing Company Of Virginia, Two Greenwich Plaza, 3rd FL., 06830, pg. 760 PV
DECORATIVE CRAFTS, INC., 50 Chestnut St., 06830, pg. 320 PV
Diamond Lease U.S.A. Inc., Two Soundview Dr., 06830, pg. 413 IT
Douglas Elliman Pickering Assoc., Inc., 30 Milbank Ave., 06830, pg. 341 PV
DRIBECK IMPORTERS, INC., 57 Old Post Road No. 2, 06830, pg. 343 PV
DUBIN-CLARK & COMPANY, 289 Greenwich Ave., 06830, pg. 344 PV
Dynamics Corporation of America, 475 Steamboat Rd., 06830-7197, pg. 286 PB
The Ericcson Corporation, Greenwich Office Park 3, P.O. Box 2630, 06836-2630, pg. 1364 IT
Ericsson Network Systems, Inc., Greenwich Office Park #3, 06831, pg. 1364 IT
Ericsson Paging Systems Inc., 3 Greenwich Office Park, Ste. 300, 06870, pg. 1365 IT
Florida Towing Company, Two Greenwich Plaza, 3rd Fl., 06830, pg. 760 PV
Franchise Mortgage Acceptance Company, 5 Greenwich Office Park, 06831, pg. 872 PB
Gestetner Corporation, P.O. Box 2656, 599 W. Putnam Ave., 06836, pg. 1115 IT
Great Bear Spring Company, 777 W. Putnam Ave., 06830, pg. 919 IT
Great Waters of France, 777 W. Putnam Ave., 06830, pg. 919 IT
Greenwich Capital Markets, Inc., 600 Steamboat Rd., 3rd Fl., 06830, pg. 911 IT
Greenwich Insurance Company, One Greenwich Plaza, 06836, pg. 1144 PB
Greenwich Times, 20 East Elm St., 06830, pg. 1616 PB
Greystone Realty Corporation, Two Pickwick Plaza, 3rd Fl., 06830, pg. 795 PV
Hachette Filipacchi Magazines Inc., 1 Fawcet Pl., 06830, pg. 794 IT
Hampton Roads Land Co., Ltd, Two Greenwich Plaza, 3rd Fl., 06830, pg. 760 PV
Harvey Electronics, 19 W. Putnam Ave., 06830, pg. 797 PB
HELM RESOURCES INC., 537 Steamboat Rd., 06830-7153, pg. 808 PB
HOLBERG INDUSTRIES, INC., 545 Steamboat Rd., 06830, pg. 533 PV
Howmet Corporation, 475 Steamboat Rd., 06830, pg. 213 PV
Howmet Corporation, 475 Steamboat Rd., 06830, pg. 1597 PB
Indian Harbor Insurance Company, One Greenwich Plaza, 06836, pg. 1144 PB
INTERLAKEN CAPITAL, INC., 165 Mason St., 06830, pg. 567 PV
International Wine & Spirits Ltd., 100 W. Putnam Ave., 06830, pg. 1661 PB
J.B.N. Finance Corporation, Eight Sound Shore Dr., 06830, pg. 1021 PB
JJI Lighting Group Inc., 67 Holly Hill Ln., 06830, pg. 821 IT
Jakobson Shipyard, Inc, Two Greenwich Plaza, 3rd Fl., 06830, pg. 760 PV
Kerry Kelly Thompson, One Sound Shore Dr., 06830, pg. 174 PV
Lynch Capital Corporation, Eight Sound Shore Dr., Ste. 290, 06830, pg. 1021 PB
LYNCH CORPORATION, Eight Sound Shore Dr., Ste. 290, 06830, pg. 1021 PB
Lynch Entertainment Corporation, Eight Sound Shore Dr., 06830, pg. 1021 PB
Lynch Entertainment Corporation II, 8 Sound Shore Dr., 06830, pg. 1021 PB
Lynch Manufacturing Corporation, Eight Sound Shore Dr., 06830, pg. 1022 PB
Lynch Multimedia Corporation, 8 Sound Shore Dr., 06830, pg. 1022 PB
Lynch Telecommunications Corporation, Eight Sound Shore Dr., 06830, pg. 1022 PB
Lynch Telephone Corporation, Eight Sound Shore Dr., 06905, pg. 1022 PB
Lynch Telephone Corporation IV, 8 Sound Shore Dr., 06830, pg. 1021 PB
Lynch Telephone Corporation VII, 8 Sound Shore Dr., 08830, pg. 1021 PB
Lynch Telephone Corporation VI, 8 Sound Shore Dr., 06830, pg. 1021 PB
Lynch Telephone Corporation III, 8 Sound Shore Dr., 06830, pg. 1022 PB
Lynch Telephone Corporation II, Eight Sound Shore Dr., 06830, pg. 1022 PB
Marsh & McLennan Risk Capital Corp., 20 Horseneck Ln., 06830, pg. 1049 PB
Moran Barge Corporation, Two Greenwich Plaza, 3rd Fl., 06830, pg. 760 PV
Moran Bulk Corporation, Two Greenwich Plaza, 3rdFl., 06830, pg. 760 PV
Moran Insurance Company Limited, Two Greenwich Plaza, 3rd Fl., 06830, pg. 760 PV
Moran Services Corporation, Two Greenwich Plaza, 3rd Fl., 06830, pg. 760 PV
Moran Shipyard Corporation, Two Greenwich Plaza, 3rd Fl., 06830, pg. 761 PV
Moran Towing & Transportation, Two Greenwich Plaza, 06830, pg. 761 PV
Moran Towing Corporation, Two Greenwich Plaza, 06830, pg. 760 PV
Moran Towing Of Delaware, Inc, Two Greenwich Plaza, 3rd Fl., 06830, pg. 760 PV
Moran Towing Of Texas Corporation, Two Greenwich PLaza, 3rd Fl., 06830, pg. 761 PV
MORAN TRANSPORTATION COMPANY, Two Greenwich Plaza, 06830, pg. 760 PV
NAC RE CORP., One Greenwich Plaza, P.O. Box 2568, 06836-2568, pg. 1144 PB
NAC Reinsurance Corporation, One Greenwich Plaza, 06836-2568, pg. 1144 PB
NFO RESEARCH, INC., Two Pickwick Plaza, Ste. 400, 06830, pg. 1146 PB
NTC GROUP, Three Pickwick Plaza, 06830, pg. 772 PV
Nebco Evans Holding Co., 545 Steamboat Rd., 06830, pg. 533 PV
NORTHERN NAVIGATION INTERNATIONAL INC., 77 Full Point Rd., 06830, pg. 805 PV
Northstar Investment Management Corporation, Two Pickwick Plaza, 06830, pg. 1375 PB
OSV Partners, 2 Greenwich Office Park, 06831, pg. 1673 PB
Organo Silicones Group, One American Ln., 06831-2559, pg. 1774 PB
PTC Partners, 475 Steamboat Rd., 06830, pg. 1029 IT
The Perrier Group of America, 777 W. Putnam Ave., 06830, pg. 919 IT
Petroleum Specialties Group, One American Ln., 06831-2559, pg. 1774 PB
Petroleum Transportation Corporation, Two Greenwich Plaza, 3rdFl., 06830, pg. 761 PV
Poland Spring Corporation, 777 W. Putnam Ave., 06830, pg. 919 IT
Polymer Chemicals Group, One American Ln., 06831-2559, pg. 1774 PB
Portsmouth Navigation Corporation, Two Greenwich Plaza, 3rd Fl., 06830, pg. 761 PV
Premier, Inc., Greenwich Office Park One, 06831, pg. 647 PV
Preussag North America, 55 Railroad Ave., 06830, pg. 1070 IT
QUALITY BAKERS OF AMERICA COOPERATIVE, INC., 70 Riverdale Ave., 06831, pg. 898 PV
Quebecor Printing (USA) Corp., 777 W. Putnam Ave., 06830, pg. 1078 IT

Geographic Index-U.S.

PB - *U.S. Public Companies Volume*
PV - *U.S. Private Companies Volume*
IT - *International Public & Private Companies Volume*

Seaboard Barge Corporation, Two Greenwich Plaza, 3rd Fl., 06830, pg. 761 **PV**
Seaways Leasing Co., 66 Field Point Rd., 06830, pg. 304 **IT**
Sempra Energy Trading, One Greenwich Plaza, 06830, pg. 1249 **PB**
Shorewood Packaging Corporation, 166 W. Putnam Ave., 06830-5241, pg. 1468 **PB**
Skanska (U.S.A.) Inc., 60 Arch St., 06830, pg. 1261 **IT**
Solvay Performance Chemicals, 41 W. Putnam Ave., 06830, pg. 1278 **IT**
Spectrum Skanska Inc., 60 Arch Street, 06830, pg. 1261 **IT**
STARWOOD CAPITAL GROUP LLC, Three Pickwick Plaza, Ste. 250, 06830, pg. 1036 **PV**
Teletrak Advanced Technology Systems, Inc., 537 Steamboat Rd., 06830, pg. 808 **PB**
TENNECO INC., 1275 King St., 06831, pg. 1577 **PB**
Triangle Geophysical Co., 66 Field Point Rd., 06830, pg. 808 **PB**
UMEX Company, Greenwich Office Park, Bldg. 1, 51 Weaver St., 06831, pg. 1435 **IT**
UST INC., 100 W. Putnam Ave., 06830, pg. 1660 **PB**
USTC Kansas, Inc., Eight Sound Shore Dr., 06830, pg. 1021 **PB**
THE UNION CORPORATION, 145 Mason St., 06830, pg. 1667 **PB**
UNION PEN COMPANY, 70 Riverdale Ave., 06831-5030, pg. 1119 **PV**
United States Tobacco Company, 100 W. Putnam Ave., 06830, pg. 1661 **PB**
URSTADT BIDDLE PROPERTIES, INC., 321 Railroad Ave., 2nd Fl., 06830-6306, pg. 1700 **PB**
Valois of America, Inc., 15 Valley Dr., 06831, pg. 125 **PV**
WWF Paper Corporation - International, 35 Mason St., 06830, pg. 1145 **PV**
WITCO CORPORATION, One American Ln., 06831-2559, pg. 1773 **PB**
WORLD COLOR PRESS, INC., 340 Pemberwick Rd., 06831, pg. 1778 **PB**
Yachting, 20 E. Elm St., 06830, pg. 1617 **PB**

Groton

The Dolphin, Naval Submarine Base-New London, 06349, pg. 934 **PB**
General Dynamics Electric Boat, 75 Eastern Point Rd., 06340, pg. 709 **PB**
MAN Roland, Inc., 115 Poheganut Dr.-Suite 101, 06340-3221, pg. 825 **IT**
Pfizer Products Corporation, Eastern Point Rd., 06340, pg. 1284 **PB**
Proto-Power Corporation, 15 Thames St., 06340, pg. 965 **PB**
Wyman-Gordon Investment Castings, Inc., Poquonnock Rd., 06340, pg. 1782 **PB**

Guilford

Clinton Recorder, 705 Boston Post Rd., 06437, pg. 934 **PB**
Kenyon Marine, Inc., P.O. Box 308, New Whitfield St., 06437-0308, pg. 1462 **PB**
Lewmar Marine Marketing, P.O. Box 308, New Whitfield St., 06437-0308, pg. 1461 **IT**
NAVTEC (A Div. of Kenyon Marine, Inc.), P.O. Box 388, New Whitfield St., 06437-0388, pg. 1462 **IT**
Niantic News, 120 N. Fair St., 06437, pg. 935 **PB**
The Pictorial Gazette, 120 N. Fair St., 06437, pg. 935 **PB**
Shore Line Newspaper, 705 Boston Post Rd., 06437, pg. 935 **PB**

Hamden

American Payment Systems, Inc., One Hamden Ctr., 2319 Whitney Ave., 06518, pg. 1678 **PB**
CRN INTERNATIONAL, INC., One Circular Ave., 06514, pg. 197 **PV**
Clear Channel Radio, Inc., 495 Benham St., 06514, pg. 383 **PB**
Entoleter, Inc., 251 Welton St., 06517, pg. 1022 **PB**
Hamden Chronicle, 2348 Whitney Ave., 06518, pg. 935 **PB**
Meyer Wire & Cable Company, 1072 Sherman Ave., 06514, pg. 251 **PV**
Precision Power, Inc., One Hamden Ctr., 2319 Whitney Ave., 06518, pg. 1678 **PB**
Research Center, Inc., One Hamden Ctr., 2319 Whitney Ave., 06518, pg. 1678 **PB**
Souwestcon Properties, Inc., One Hamden Ctr., 2319 Whitney Ave., 06518, pg. 1679 **PB**
Thermal Energies, Inc., One Hamden Ctr., 2319 Whitney Ave., 06518, pg. 1679 **PB**
United Energy International, Inc., One Hamden Ctr., 2319 Whitney Ave., 06518, pg. 1678 **PB**
United Resources, Inc., One Hamden Ctr., 2319 Whitney Ave., 06518, pg. 1678 **PB**
Vibra-Metrics, Inc., 1014 Sherman Ave., 06514, pg. 622 **PV**
Vibrametric, 1014 Sherman Ave., pg. 622 **PV**
WAVZ-AM, 495 Benham St., 06514, pg. 384 **PB**
WELI-AM, 495 Benham, 06415, pg. 384 **PB**
WKCI-FM, 495 Brenham St., 06514, pg. 385 **PB**

Hartford

AT&T Communications, One Corporate Ctr. 14th Fl., 06103-3206, pg. 10 **PB**
THE ADVEST GROUP, INC., 90 State House Sq., 06103, pg. 23 **PB**
Advest, Inc., 90 State House Sq., 06103, pg. 23 **PB**

Aeltus Investment Management, Inc., 242 Trumball St., 06156, pg. 27 **PB**
Aetna Financial Services Inc., 151 Farmington Ave., 06156, pg. 26 **PB**
AETNA INC., 151 Farmington Ave., 06156, pg. 26 **PB**
Aetna International, Inc., 151 Farmington Ave., 06156, pg. 26 **PB**
Aetna Life Insurance and Annuity Co., 151 Farmington Ave., 06156, pg. 26 **PB**
Aetna Life Insurance Company, 151 Farmington Ave., 06156, pg. 26 **PB**
Aetna Life Insurance Company of America, 151 Farmington Ave., 06156-0001, pg. 26 **PB**
Aetna Realty Investors, Inc., 242 Trumball St., 06156, pg. 26 **PB**
American Brokerage Corporation, One American Row, 06115, pg. 863 **PB**
W.E. Andrews Co., Inc., of Connecticut, 206 Murphy Rd., 06114, pg. 1735 **PB**
Bank of Boston Connecticut, 220 Pearl St., 06103, pg. 184 **PB**
Bank of Boston Connecticut, 31 Pratt St., 06103, pg. 184 **PB**
BEAUTY ENTERPRISES INC., 150 Meadow St., 06114, pg. 128 **PV**
Billings & Co., Inc., 90 State House Sq., 06103, pg. 23 **PB**
CGI Partners LP, 900 Cottage Grove Rd., 06152, pg. 357 **PB**
CNG Realty Co., P.O. Box 1500, 06144-1500, pg. 285 **PB**
CTG RESOURCES, INC., 100 Columbus Blvd., 06144-1500, pg. 285 **PB**
The Charter Oak Fire Insurance Co., One Tower Square, 06183, pg. 1633 **PB**
Connecticut Natural Gas Corporation, 100 Columbus Blvd., 06144, pg. 285 **PB**
Conning, 185 Asylum St., 06103, pg. 443 **PV**
Cornerstone Real Estate, One Financial Plaza, Ste. 1700, 06103-2604, pg. 712 **PV**
Downtown Cogeneration Associates, 100 Columbus Blvd., 06144, pg. 285 **PB**
ENI Gas Services, Inc., P.O. Box 1500, 06144-1500, pg. 285 **PB**
Energy Networks, Inc. (ENI), 60 Columbus Blvd., 06144-1500, pg. 285 **PB**
FIRST INTERNATIONAL BANCORP, INC., One Comercial Plaza, 06103, pg. 635 **PB**
First National Bank of New England, One Commercial Plaza, 06103, pg. 636 **PB**
Fleet Bank, N.A., One Constitution Plaza, 06115, pg. 649 **PB**
Fleet National Bank of Connecticut, 777 Main St., 06115, pg. 649 **PB**
HSB Reliability Technologies, 1 State St., 06102, pg. 795 **PB**
The Hartford Courant Company, 285 Broad St., 06115, pg. 1616 **PB**
Hartford District Office, Seven Waterside Crossing, Ste. 250, 06095, pg. 1106 **PB**
Hartford Europe, Inc., Hartford Plaza, 06115, pg. 795 **PB**
THE HARTFORD FINANCIAL SERVICES GROUP INC., Hartford Plaza, 690 Asylum Ave., 06115, pg. 794 **PB**
Hartford Fire Insurance Co., Hartford Plaza, 06115, pg. 794 **PB**
Hartford International Insurance Company, Hartford Plaza, 06115, pg. 795 **PB**
Hartford Life & Accident Insurance Company, Hartford Plaza, 06115, pg. 795 **PB**
THE HARTFORD STEAM BOILER INSPECTION & INSURANCE CO., P.O. Box 5024, One State St., 06102-5024, pg. 795 **PB**
Hartford Steam Co., P.O. Box 1500, 60 Columbus Blvd., 06144, pg. 285 **PB**
Heublein Inc., P.O. Box 778, 450 Columbus Blvd., 06142-0778, pg. 410 **IT**
Heublein, Inc., 450 Columbus Blvd., 06142-0778, pg. 410 **IT**
LEWTAN INDUSTRIES CORP., 30 High St., 06103, pg. 666 **PV**
Mafco, Inc., P.O. Box 2104, 69 Fishfry St., 06145-2104, pg. 711 **PB**
Massachusetts Mutual Life Insurance Company, 140 Garden St., 06154, pg. 712 **PV**
NAC Reinsurance Corporation-Hartford, Goodwin Sq., 225 Asylum St., 27th Fl., 06103-4306, pg. 1144 **PV**
NEW ENGLAND DAIRIES, INC., 255 Homestead Ave., 06112, pg. 793 **PB**
Nielsen/Sessions, 770 Wethersfield St., 06141, pg. 1791 **PB**
PM Holdings, Inc., One American Row, 06115, pg. 863 **PB**
Phoenix American Life Ins. Co., One American Row, 06115, pg. 863 **PV**
Phoenix Founders, Inc, One American Row, 06115, pg. 863 **PB**
Phoenix Home Life Mutual Insurance Co., One American Row, 06102, pg. 863 **PV**
PHOENIX HOME LIFE MUTUAL INSURANCE COMPANY, One American Row, 06102, pg. 863 **PV**
Phoenix Investment Counsel Inc., One American Row, 06115, pg. 863 **PV**
Post-Newsweek Stations, Connecticut, Inc., 3 Constitution Plaza, 06115, pg. 1743 **PB**
Post-Newsweek Stations, Inc., Three Constitution Plaza, 06115, pg. 1743 **PB**
The Quinnehtuk Company, P.O. Box 270, 06141, pg. 1195 **PV**
Reflections Partners Corp., 900 Cottage Grove Rd., 06152, pg. 361 **PB**
Rocky River Realty Company, P.O. Box 270, 06141, pg. 1195 **PV**
M. SWIFT & SONS INC., 10 Love Lane, 06141, pg. 1059 **PV**

The Travelers Asset Management Intl. Corp., One Tower Sq., 06115, pg. 1633 **PB**
The Travelers Life & Annuity Co., One Tower Square, 06183, pg. 1633 **PB**
The Travelers Life Insurance Co., One Tower Square, 06183, pg. 1633 **PB**
Travelers Property Casualty Corp., One Tower Square, 06183, pg. 1633 **PB**
United HealthCare Insurance Company, 450 Columbus Blvd., 06115-0450, pg. 1678 **PB**
UNITED TECHNOLOGIES CORPORATION, One Financial Plaza, 06101, pg. 1689 **PB**
WFSB-TV, 3 Constitution Plaza, 06115, pg. 1743 **PB**
WTIC, Chase Broadcasting of Hartford, One Corporate Ctr., 06103, pg. 1636 **PB**
WINDSOR SHADE TOBACCO COMPANY, INC., 158 Woodland St., 06105, pg. 1182 **PV**

Lakeville

ITW Deltar, 194 Main St., 06039, pg. 866 **PB**

Litchfield

B/E Aerospace Seating Products Group, 607 Bantam Rd., 06759, pg. 159 **PB**

Madison

MAGELLAN PETROLEUM CORPORATION, Oak Park, Unit 31, 149 Durham Rd., 06443, pg. 1036 **PV**

Manchester

ALLIED PRINTING SERVICES, INC., 579 Middle Tpke. W., 06040, pg. 40 **PV**
Cox Communications-Greater Hartford, 801 Parker St., 06040, pg. 454 **PB**
DYNAMIC METAL PRODUCTS COMPANY, 967 Parker St., 06040, pg. 350 **PV**
First Federal Savings, 1007 Main St., 06103, pg. 632 **PB**
First Federal Savings, 23 Main St., 06106, pg. 632 **PB**
First Federal Savings, Spencer St., pg. 632 **PB**
First Federal Savings, 344 W. Middle Tpke., 06040, pg. 632 **PB**
GUNVER MANUFACTURING CO., 255 Sheldon Rd., 06040, pg. 488 **PV**
HARTFORD DISTRIBUTORS INC., 131 Chapel Rd., 06040, pg. 507 **PV**
Lydall & Foulds Div., P.O. Box 151, 580 Parker St., 06045-0151, pg. 1021 **PB**
Lydall Express, Inc., P.O. Box 151, 580 Parker St., 06045-0151, pg. 1021 **PB**
LYDALL, INC., One Colonial Rd., 06040, pg. 1020 **PB**
Lydall, Inc., P.O. Box 151, One Colonial Rd., 06045-0151, pg. 1021 **PB**
Manhattan/CDT, 203 Progress Dr., 06040, pg. 287 **PB**
Molding Materials Div., Mill & Oakland Sts., 06040, pg. 1403 **PB**
Phalo/CDT, 90 Progress Dr., 06040, pg. 287 **PB**
Pro/Mark, 220 Chapel Rd., 06040, pg. 867 **PB**
THE PURDY CORPORATION, 586 Hilliard St., 06045-1898, pg. 895 **PV**
SCAN-OPTICS, INC., 169 Progress Dr., 06040, pg. 1436 **PB**
Sermatech Klock, 1366 Tolland Tpke., 06040-1696, pg. 1570 **PB**
Tyco Engineered Systems, 50 Harrison St., 06040, pg. 1648 **PB**
Wing Industries Northeastern, 60 Progress Dr., Bldg. 4, 06040, pg. 1183 **PV**

Meriden

ABS Pumps Inc., 140 Pond View Dr., 06450, pg. 270 **IT**
Atlantic Guest, Inc., 48 Elm St., 06450, pg. 1705 **PB**
Bob's Stores, Inc., 160 Corporate Ct., 06450, pg. 287 **PB**
Braodband Communications Division, 999 Research Pkwy., 06450, pg. 4 **PB**
CNF Constructors Inc., 355 Research Pkwy., 06450, pg. 950 **PB**
CNF Industries Inc., 355 Research Pkwy., 06460, pg. 950 **PB**
Cox Communications-Meriden, 683-685 E. Main St., 06450, pg. 455 **PB**
Housatonic Corporation, 599 Research Parkway, 06450-1030, pg. 1787 **PB**
THE LANE CONSTRUCTION CORP., 965 E. Main St., 06450, pg. 649 **PV**
THE MILLER COMPANY, 290 Pratt St., 06450, pg. 746 **PV**
THE NAPIER CO., 74 Cambridge St., 06450, pg. 774 **PV**
Norconn Properties, Inc., 599 Research Parkway, 06450-1030, pg. 1787 **PB**
Packard Bioscience, 800 Research Pkwy., 06450, pg. 833 **PV**
PACKARD BIOSCIENCE COMPANY, 800 Research Pkwy., 06450, pg. 833 **PV**
Packard Instrument Co., Inc., 800 Research Pkwy., 06450, pg. 833 **PV**
R.M. Services, Inc., 639 Research Pkwy., 06450-1030, pg. 1787 **PB**
THE RECORD-JOURNAL PUBLISHING COMPANY, 11 Crown St., 06450, pg. 914 **PV**
Virginia Paving Co., 965 E. Main St., 06450, pg. 649 **PV**
Yankee Energy Financial Services Company, 599 Research Pkwy., 06450-1030, pg. 1787 **PB**
Yankee Energy Production Services, Inc., 599 Research Pkwy., 06450-1030, pg. 1787 **PB**

Geographic Index-U.S.

Yankee Energy Services Company, 639 Research Pkwy., 06450-1030, pg. 1788 **PB**

YANKEE ENERGY SYSTEM, INC., 599 Research Pkwy., 06450-1030, pg. 1787 **PB**

Yankee Gas Services Company, 599 Research Pkwy., 06450-1030, pg. 1788 **PB**

YESCo Energy Consulting Services, Inc., 639 Research Pkwy., 06450-1030, pg. 1788 **PB**

Middlebury

DataComm Leasing Corp., 1579 Straits Tpke., 06762, pg. 708 **PB**

General DataComm, Inc., 1579 Straits Tpke., 06762, pg. 708 **PB**

GENERAL DATACOMM INDUSTRIES, INC., 1579 Straits Tpke., 06762-1299, pg. 708 **PB**

General DataComm Intl. Corp., 1579 Straits Tpke., 06762, pg. 708 **PB**

PIC DESIGN, 86 Benson Rd., 06762, pg. 864 **PV**

TIMEX CORPORATION, Park Rd. Extension, 06762, pg. 1088 **PV**

Uniroyal Chemical Company, Inc., World Headquarters, 06749, pg. 460 **PB**

Uniroyal Chemical Corporation, World Headquarters, 06749, pg. 459 **PB**

Vital Network Service, Inc., 1579 Straits Tpke., 06762, pg. 708 **PB**

Middlefield

COOPER INSTRUMENT CORP., 33 Reeds Gap Rd., 06455-0450, pg. 274 **PV**

ZYGO CORPORATION, Laurel Brook Rd., 06455, pg. 1795 **PB**

Middletown

BIDWELL INDUSTRIAL GROUP, INC., 2055 S. Main St., 06457, pg. 142 **PV**

Blu-Ray, 2055 S. Main St., 06457, pg. 142 **PB**

LYMAN PRODUCTS CORPORATION, 475 Smith St., 06457, pg. 683 **PV**

Magnagrip, 2055 S. Main St., 06457, pg. 142 **PB**

The Middletown Press, Two Main St., 06457, pg. 935 **PB**

NORTH & JUDD, 699 Middle St., 06457, pg. 804 **PV**

Power-Dyne, 2055 S. Main St., 06457-6151, pg. 142 **PV**

PRIMAC CORP., 760 Newfield St., 06457, pg. 883 **PV**

Primary Steel, Inc., 760 Newfield St., 06457, pg. 884 **PV**

Rapid Print, 2055 S. Main St., 06457, pg. 142 **PV**

Raymond Engineering, 217 Smith St., 06457, pg. 942 **PB**

Raych Industries Division, 475 Smith St., 06457, pg. 683 **PV**

Safeway Products, Inc., 440 Middlefield St., 06457-3551, pg. 752 **PB**

U.S. Healthcare (Connecticut), Middlesex Corporate Center, 213 Court St., 7th Fl., 06457, pg. 26 **PB**

Weekly Reader Corp., 245 Long Hill Rd., 06457, pg. 1328 **PB**

Milford

BIC Corporation, 500 Bic Dr., 06460, pg. 1273 **IT**

BIC Sport, 565 Bic Dr., 06460, pg. 1273 **IT**

Bryant Electrical, Inc., 185 Plains Rd., 06460-2465, pg. 844 **PB**

CONNECTICUT DRIVE SHAFT, INC., 470 Naugatuck Ave., 06460-5049, pg. 263 **PV**

Dorr-Oliver Incorporated, 612 Wheeler's Farm Rd., 06460, pg. 839 **IT**

EAO Switch Corporation, 198 Pepe's Farm Rd., 06460, pg. 444 **IT**

Elm City Newspaper, 349 New Haven Ave., 06460, pg. 934 **PB**

EXECUTONE INFORMATION SYSTEMS, INC., 478 Wheelers Farm Rd., 06460, pg. 599 **PB**

Marse Care Inc., 57 Plains Rd., 06460, pg. 1157 **PB**

MILFORD FASTENING SYSTEMS, 857 Bridgeport Ave., 06460, pg. 745 **PV**

Milford Office, 39 Orlando St., 06460, pg. 274 **IT**

Milgray/Connecticut, Inc., 326 W. Main St., 06460, pg. 206 **PB**

New England Controls Corp., 110 Arton Dr., 06460, pg. 124 **PB**

New England Health Care, 57 Plains Rd., 06460, pg. 1157 **PB**

Olympic Steel - Connecticut Division, One Eastern Steel Rd., 06460, pg. 1221 **PB**

SUBWAY FRANCHISE ADVERTISING FUND TRUST, 325 Bic Drive, 06460, pg. 1048 **PV**

T-Bar, Inc., 540 New Haven Ave., 06484, pg. 727 **PB**

Warner-Lambert Shaving Products Group, 10 Leighton Rd., 06460, pg. 1739 **PB**

Warner-Lambert Worldwide Shaving Products Group, 10 Webster Rd., 06460, pg. 1739 **PB**

Milldale

Allied Security Inc., P.O. Box 526, 1573 Meriden-Waterbury Rd., 06467, pg. 41 **PV**

Firoillo A. Co. Inc., 396 Clark St., 06467, pg. 1449 **PB**

Monroe

Mikron Corp. Monroe, P.O. Box 268, 600 Pepper St., 06468, pg. 866 **IT**

Vitramon, Incorporated, #10-Route 25, 06468, pg. 1722 **PB**

Moosup

Kaman Aerospace Corporation-Moosup Plant, 100 S. Main St., 06354, pg. 942 **PB**

Mystic

Mystic Color Lab, Inc., Mason's Island Rd., 06355, pg. 501 **IT**

Naugatuck

Baldwin Dampening Systems, 141 Sheridan Dr., 06770, pg. 170 **PB**

Banco Totta & Acores, 215 Church St., 06770, pg. 145 **IT**

THE EASTERN COMPANY, 112 Bridge St., 06770, pg. 548 **PB**

Lewis Engineering Company, 238 Water St., 06770, pg. 402 **PB**

NAUGATUCK GLASS COMPANY, Church & Bridge Sts., 06770, pg. 789 **PV**

Peter Paul, P.O. Box 310, New Haven Road, 06770, pg. 812 **PB**

Risdon Corporation, One Risdon St., 06770, pg. 463 **PB**

Seal Products Incorporated, 550 Spring St., 06770-9985, pg. 849 **PB**

Uniroyal Chemical Co., Inc., Elm St., 06770, pg. 460 **PB**

New Britain

ABB Electro Mechanics Inc., 150 John Downey Dr., 06051-2904, pg. 3 **IT**

ACMAT CORPORATION, 233 Main St., 06050, pg. 16 **PB**

ACSTAR Insurance Company, 233 Main St., 06050-2350, pg. 16 **PB**

Amins, Inc., 233 Main St., 06050-2350, pg. 16 **PB**

Andrew House Healthcare, 66 Clinic Dr., 06051, pg. 1711 **PB**

Branford Vibrator Company, 150 John Downey Dr., 06051, pg. 4 **IT**

CCL Security Products, 199 Whiting St., 06050-4360, pg. 548 **PB**

Geremia Electric Co., Inc., 233 Main St., 06050, pg. 16 **PB**

Hardware City Rock Cats, Beehive Field, Willowbrook Park Complex, 06051, pg. 751 **PV**

The Herald, One Herald Sq., 06050, pg. 935 **PB**

ITT Cannon Sealectro, 565 E. Main St., 06051, pg. 859 **PB**

MACRISTY INDUSTRIES, INC., 206 Newington Ave., 06051, pg. 693 **PV**

Maguire Group Architects, Inc., One Court St., 06051, pg. 696 **PV**

MOORE MEDICAL CORP., 389 John Downey Dr., 06050, pg. 1128 **PB**

Skinner Valve Division, 95 Edgewood Ave., 06051, pg. 1260 **PB**

Stanley Customer Support Div., 480 Myrtle St., 06053, pg. 1509 **PB**

Stanley Hardware Div., 480 Myrtle St., 06053, pg. 1509 **PB**

Stanley Home Decor Div., 480 Myrtle St., 06053, pg. 1509 **PB**

Stanley Tools Div., 600 Myrtle, 06053, pg. 1509 **PB**

THE STANLEY WORKS, 1000 Stanley Dr., 06053, pg. 1508 **PB**

TILCON, INC., Black Rock Ave., 06052, pg. 1086 **PB**

United Coastal Insurance Company, 233 Main St., 06050-2350, pg. 16 **PB**

THE WEATHERVANE RETAIL CORP., 300 John Downey Dr., 06051, pg. 1156 **PV**

New Canaan

Centennial Cellular Corp., 50 Locust Ave., 06840, pg. 329 **PB**

CENTURY COMMUNICATIONS CORP., 50 Locust Ave., 06840, pg. 329 **PB**

Laing Construction Services, 272 West Hills Rd., 06840, pg. 797 **IT**

Town Brooke Associates, 34 Elm St., 06840, pg. 365 **PV**

New Hartford

HITCHCOCK CHAIR COMPANY LTD., 31 Industrial Park Rd., Greenwood Industrial Pk., Rte. 219, 06057, pg. 531 **PV**

Ovation Instruments, Greenwoods Rd., 06057, pg. 942 **PV**

Qualheim, Inc., 283 Main St., 06057, pg. 286 **PB**

Waring Products, 283 Main St., 06057-0319, pg. 286 **PB**

New Haven

Acme Chemicals & Insulation Co., 166 Chapel St., 06505, pg. 565 **PV**

APPAREL AMERICA, INC., 1175 State St., 06511, pg. 120 **PB**

CHR Division, 407 E. St., 06509, pg. 689 **PB**

CHR Industries, Inc., 407 East St., 06509-9988, pg. 689 **PB**

Clifton House Rehabilitation Center, 181 Clifton St., 06513, pg. 836 **PB**

Essex Industries, 110 Sargent Dr., 06511, pg. 18 **PB**

Essex Industries, Inc., 110 Sargent Dr., 06511, pg. 18 **IT**

THE FUSCO CORPORATION, 555 Long Wharf Dr., 06511, pg. 432 **PV**

The G & O Manufacturing Co., 100 Gando Dr., 06508, pg. 1631 **PB**

GO/DAN Industries, 100 Gando Dr., 06513, pg. 1631 **PB**

Insurance Management Incorporated, 545 Long Wharf Dr., 6th Fl., 06511, pg. 827 **PB**

NEW HAVEN MFG. CORP., 446 Blake St., 06515, pg. 793 **PV**

New Haven Register, Inc., 40 Sargent Dr., Long Wharf, 06511, pg. 935 **PB**

NEW HAVEN SAVINGS BANK, 195 Church St., 06510, pg. 793 **PB**

Outdoor Systems, Inc.-Connecticut, 119 Water St., 06530, pg. 1235 **PB**

Perri Sausage, Inc., P.O. Box 8327, 06530, pg. 595 **PV**

Pirelli Armstrong Tire Corporation, 500 Sargent Dr., 06536, pg. 1058 **IT**

SNET Diversified Group, Inc., 227 Church St., 06506, pg. 1491 **PB**

SNET MobileCom, Inc., 555 Long Wharf Dr., 06511, pg. 1491 **PB**

SNET Paging, Inc., 555 Long Warf Dr., 06511, pg. 1491 **PB**

SNET Real Estate Inc., 555 Long Wharf Dr., 06511, pg. 1491 **PB**

SNET Systems Inc., 6 Devine St., 06473, pg. 1491 **PB**

Sargent Manufacturing Company, 100 Sargent Dr., 06511, pg. 18 **IT**

Scientific Imaging Systems, 4 Science Park West, 06511, pg. 550 **PB**

SIMKINS INDUSTRIES, INC., 260 East St., 06511, pg. 1000 **PV**

Simkins New Haven Board, 259 East St., 06511, pg. 1000 **PV**

SOUTHERN NEW ENGLAND TELECOMMUNICATIONS CORPORATION, 227 Church St., 06510, pg. 1490 **PB**

The Southern New England Telephone Company, 227 Church St., 06510, pg. 1491 **PB**

STARTER CORP., 370 James St., 06513-3051, pg. 1511 **PB**

THE STROUSE, ADLER COMPANY, 78 Olive St., 06507, pg. 1047 **PV**

TRANSPRO, INC., 100 Gando Dr., 06513, pg. 1631 **PB**

UNITED ILLUMINATING COMPANY, 157 Church St., 06506, pg. 1678 **PB**

U.S. REPEATING ARMS COMPANY, 344 Winchester Ave., 06511, pg. 1125 **PV**

WYATT ENERGY INCORPORATED, Wyatt Executive Bldg., 280 Waterfront St., 06512, pg. 1193 **PV**

YALE UNIVERSITY PRESS, 302 Temple St., 06511, pg. 1195 **PV**

New London

Citizens Bank Of Connecticut, 63 Eugene O'Neill Dr., 06320, pg. 1132 **IT**

Nutmeg Pavilion Healthcare, 78 Viets St. Extension, 06320, pg. 1714 **PB**

New Milford

FIDCO (Food Ingredient Development Company), 201 Housatonic Ave., 06776, pg. 917 **IT**

Quality Food Oils, Inc., 87 Pickett District Rd., 06776, pg. 92 **IT**

Newington

AMERICAN RADIO RELAY LEAGUE, 225 Main, 06111, pg. 60 **PV**

ARBURG, INC., 125 Rockwell Rd., 06111, pg. 79 **PV**

Fenn Manufacturing Co., 300 Fenn Rd., 06111-2299, pg. 1676 **PB**

Five Star Group, Inc., 81 Alumni Dr., 06111, pg. 694 **PB**

KEENEY MANUFACTURING CO., 1170 Main St., 06111, pg. 611 **PV**

E. Rabinowe & Company, Inc., 81 Alumni Dr., 06111, pg. 694 **PB**

Tube Bend, 610 N. Mountain Rd., 06111, pg. 693 **PV**

Newtown

Emergency Lighting Div., P.O. Box 468, 06470, pg. 726 **PB**

Hubbell Plastics, Inc., 14 Prospect Dr., 06470, pg. 844 **PB**

North Branford

Branford Savings Bank-North Branford, 1717 Foxon Rd., 06512, pg. 250 **PB**

Tilcon Tomasso Services Inc., P.O. Box 67, 06471-0067, pg. 1086 **PV**

North Grosvenordale

Kenyon Oil Company, Inc., P.O. Box 866, 221 Quinebaug Rd., 06255, pg. 1151 **PV**

Sanitary-Dash Manufacturing Co., Inc., P.O. Box 815, 929 Riverside Dr., 06255-0815, pg. 1795 **PB**

North Haven

American Refractories & Crucible Corporation, P.O. Box 338, 345 Washington Ave., 06473, pg. 893 **IT**

The Burton Company, Sturbridge Commons, 250 State St., 06473, pg. 826 **PB**

CABLEWAVE SYSTEMS, 60 Dodge Ave., 06473, pg. 197 **PV**

CIRCUIT-WISE, INC., 400 Sackett Point Rd., 06473, pg. 240 **PV**

CONNECTICUT CONTAINER CORPORATION, 455 Sackett Point Rd., 06473, pg. 263 **PV**

Custom Products Corporation, 457 State St., 06473, pg. 244 **PB**

Gamma One, Inc., 12 Corporate Dr., 06473, pg. 228   **PB**
The Humphrey Chemical Company, Inc., 45 Devine St., 06473, pg. 297   **PB**
Methode New England Co., Inc., 50 McDermott Rd., 06473, pg. 1101   **PB**
O.F. MOSSBERG & SONS, INC., Seven Grasso Ave., 06473, pg. 764   **PV**
PLASTICRETE BLOCK & SUPPLY CORP., P.O. Box 513, 99 Stoddard Ave., 06473, pg. 871   **PV**
ULBRICH STAINLESS STEELS & SPECIAL METALS, INC., 57 Dodge Ave., 06473, pg. 1115   **PV**
Ulbrich Wire, Inc., 55 Defco Park Ave., 06473, pg. 1115   **PV**
UNITED ALUMINUM CORPORATION, 100 United Dr., 06473, pg. 1120   **PV**

North Stonington

ANALYSIS & TECHNOLOGY, INC., P.O. Box 220, Rte. 2, Technology Park, 06359-0220, pg. 109   **PB**
Fisher Controls International, Inc., Rte. 49 & US 95, 06359, pg. 573   **PB**
Integrated Performance Decisions, Technology Park, Rte. 2, 06359-0220, pg. 110   **PB**
S.A. USA, Ste. 2 & 184, North Stonington Professional Center, 06359, pg. 994   **PV**
SHIP ANALYTICS, INC., 183 Providence-New London Tpke., 06378, pg. 994   **PV**

Northford

Fire Lite Alarms, Inc./Notifier Co., 12 Clintonville Rd., 06472-1653, pg. 1306   **PB**

Norwalk

ABB Inc., 501 Merritt 7, 06856, pg. 3   **IT**
American Natl. Can Co.-Tube Packaging, P.O. Box 5121, 101 Merritt 7, 06856-5121, pg. 1029   **IT**
Appleton & Lange, Four Stamford Plaza, 06912, pg. 778   **PV**
BALDWIN TECHNOLOGY COMPANY, INC., One Norwalk West, 40 Richards Ave., 06854, pg. 169   **PB**
Bedford Associates, Inc., 101 Merritt Seven, 06851, pg. 219   **IT**
Beiersdorf, Inc., 360 Martin Luther King Dr., 06856, pg. 182   **PV**
BOLT TECHNOLOGY CORPORATION, Four Duke Place, 06854, pg. 244   **PB**
W. Braun Co., 535 Connecticut Ave., 06854, pg. 166   **PB**
CALDOR, INC., 20 Glover Ave., 06856-5620, pg. 292   **PB**
Cardinal Business Media, Vision Care Grp., 50 Washington St., 06854, pg. 1116   **PV**
The Chinet Co., 101 Merritt 7, 06856, pg. 1146   **IT**
Consumer Products Business, 800 Connecticut Ave., 06856, pg. 671   **PB**
CONTINENTAL CAN CO., 301 Merritt Seven, Corporate Park, 06856, pg. 439   **PB**
Continental Plastic Containers, Inc., Riverpark, 800 Connecticut Ave., 06856, pg. 440   **PB**
Crestline Div., 345 Ely Ave., 06854, pg. 1543   **PB**
CULLMAN VENTURES, INC., 101 Merritt 7, 7th Fl., 06851, pg. 294   **PV**
Dixie Foodservice, 800 Connecticut Ave., 06856, pg. 671   **PB**
Easton Press Books, 677 Connecticut Ave., 06854, pg. 685   **PV**
Easton Press Videos, 677 Connecticut Ave., 06854, pg. 685   **PV**
EMCOR GROUP, INC., 101 Merritt Seven Corp. Pk., 7th Fl., 06851, pg. 571   **PB**
Fibreweb International, Ltd., 33 Marlborough Rd., 06851, pg. 467   **PV**
Ford Consumer Finance Company, Inc., 101 Merritt 7, 06851, pg. 664   **PB**
Franklin Advisers, Inc., 16 S. Main St., Ste. 303, 06854, pg. 680   **PB**
C.R. Gibson Co., 32 Knight St., 06856, pg. 1168   **PB**
HART HOLDING COMPANY, INC., Seven Corporate Pk., 401 Merritt, 06856-5063, pg. 507   **PV**
ILS, Shore Pointe, One Selleck St., 06855, pg. 331   **PB**
INTERNATIONAL MICROWAVE CORPORATION, 25 Van Zant St., 06855, pg. 571   **PV**
KING INDUSTRIES, INC., P.O. Box 588, Science Rd., 06852, pg. 620   **PV**
MBI INC., 47 Richards Ave., 06857, pg. 685   **PV**
Marine Midland Business Loans, Inc., 40 Richards Avenue, 06856, pg. 581   **IT**
Media Partnership Corporation, 40 Richards Ave., 3rd Fl., 06854, pg. 1168   **PV**
Mercedes-Benz Credit Corp., 201 Merritt 7, Ste. 700, 06856, pg. 368   **PB**
MICRO WAREHOUSE, INC., 535 Connecticut Ave., 06854, pg. 1104   **PB**
MICROPHASE CORPORATION, 587 Connecticut Ave., 06854, pg. 742   **PV**
Mobil Chemical Co., P.O. Box 5445, 06856-5445, pg. 1118   **PB**
News America Marketing, 301 Merritt Seven, 06856-5102, pg. 925   **IT**
NORWALK CO., INC., 20 N. Water St., 06854, pg. 807   **PV**
NORWALK POWDERED METALS, INC., Muller Park, 06852, pg. 808   **PV**
Numetrix, Inc., 101 Merritt 7, 2nd Fl., 06851, pg. 990   **IT**
OLIN CORPORATION, 501 Merritt 7, 06856-4500, pg. 1218   **PB**
Olin Microelectronic Materials, Inc., P.O. Box 4500, 06856-4500, pg. 1219   **PB**

Oxford Health Centers, 800 Connecticut Ave., 06854, pg. 1239   **PB**
Oxford Health Insurance, Inc., 800 Connecticut Ave., 06854, pg. 1239   **PB**
Oxford Health Plans (CT), Inc., 800 Connecticut Ave., 06854, pg. 1239   **PB**
OXFORD HEALTH PLANS INC., 800 Connecticut Ave., 06854, pg. 1238   **PB**
Oxford Health Plans (NJ), Inc., 800 Connecticut Ave., 06854, pg. 1239   **PB**
Oxford Health Plans (NY), Inc., 800 Connecticut Ave., 06854, pg. 1239   **PB**
PE Biosystems, 761 Main Ave., 06859-0001, pg. 1279   **PB**
Pepperidge Farm, Incorporated, 595 Westport Ave., 06856, pg. 299   **PB**
THE PERKIN-ELMER CORPORATION, 761 Main Ave., 06859-0001, pg. 1279   **PB**
Pitney Bowes Credit Corporation, 201 Merritt Seven, pg. 1303   **PB**
Pitney Bowes Financial Services, 201 Merritt Seven, 06856, pg. 1303   **PB**
Pitney Bowes Real Estate Financing Corporation, 201 Merritt Seven, 068656, pg. 1303   **PB**
Plastic Containers, Inc., P.O. Box 5410, 301 Merritt Seven Corp. Pk., 06856, pg. 440   **PB**
Postal Commemorative Society Collection, 47 Richards Ave., 06856, pg. 685   **PV**
R.F. Technology, Inc., 16 Testa Pl., 06854-4613, pg. 1289   **IT**
Reed Exhibition Companies-North America, Merrit View, 383 Main Ave., 06851, pg. 1096   **IT**
REX MARINE CENTER, INC., 144-146 Water St., 06854, pg. 926   **PV**
Saunders Realty Corporation, 110 Richards Ave., 06854, pg. 1629   **PB**
Skandia America Reinsurance Corp., Norwalk Branch, Shorepoint Bldg., 1 Selleck St., Ste. 200, 06855-1120, pg. 1257   **IT**
Spadone-Alfa Corporation, 507 Westport Ave., 06856, pg. 1020   **PV**
SPADONE INC., 507 Westport Ave., 06856, pg. 1019   **PV**
TAUBE/VIOLANTE, INC., P.O. Box 1259, 94 Taylor Ave., Ste. 2, 06856, pg. 1069   **PV**
Thimble Collectors Club Collections, 677 Connecticut Ave., 06854, pg. 685   **PV**
Thomson Software Products, U3S Corp. of America, 101 Merrit Seven, 06856, pg. 1384   **IT**
TRAFALGAR GHURKA LTD., 300 Wilson Ave., 06854, pg. 1095   **PV**
Trans-Lux Consulting Corporation, 110 Richards Ave., 06856-5090, pg. 1629   **PB**
TRANS-LUX CORPORATION, 110 Richards Ave., 06854, pg. 1628   **PB**
Trans-Lux Credit Terminal Corporation, 110 Richards Ave., 06856-5090, pg. 1629   **PB**
Trans-Lux Experience Corp., 110 Richards Ave., 06854, pg. 1629   **PB**
Trans-Lux Investment Corporation, 110 Richards Ave., 06856-5090, pg. 1629   **PB**
Trans-Lux Loma Corporation, 110 Richards Ave., 06856-5090, pg. 1629   **PB**
Trans-Lux Multimedia Corp., 110 Richards Ave., 06854, pg. 1629   **PB**
Trans-Lux Pennsylvania Corporation, 110 Richards Ave., 06854, pg. 1629   **PB**
Trans-Lux Seaport Corporation, 110 Richards Ave., 06854, pg. 1629   **PB**
Trans-Lux Service Corp., 110 Richards Ave., 06854, pg. 1629   **PB**
Trans-Lux Sign Corporation, 110 Richards Ave., 06856-5090, pg. 1629   **PB**
Trans-Lux Syndicated Programs Corp., 110 Richards Ave., 06854, pg. 1629   **PB**
Trans-Lux Theatres Corporation, 110 Richards Ave., 06856-5090, pg. 1629   **PB**
U.S. SURGICAL CORP., 150 Glover Ave., 06856, pg. 1687   **PB**
Usertech, One Selleck St., 06855, pg. 331   **PB**
VALLERIE'S TRANSPORT SERVICE, INC., 465 Connecticut Ave., 06852, pg. 1131   **PV**
R.T. VANDERBILT COMPANY, INC., 30 Winfield St., 06855, pg. 1133   **PV**
Vectron Labs, Inc., 166 Glover Ave., 06850, pg. 522   **PB**
WEATHERBY HEALTH CARE, 25 Van Zant St., 06855, pg. 1155   **PV**

Norwich

The Bulletin Company, 66 Franklin St., 06360, pg. 700   **PB**
The Clinipad Corp., 243 Vergason Ave., 06360, pg. 247   **PV**
Hamilton Pavilion Healthcare, 60 Palmer St., 06360, pg. 1713   **PB**
NORWICH FINANCIAL CORP., Four Broadway, 06360, pg. 1203   **PB**
The Norwich Savings Society, Four Broadway, 06360, pg. 1203   **PB**
Rubber Molding Division, 19 Ohio Ave., 06360, pg. 355   **PV**
Sybron Chemicals, Inc., Norwich Industrial Pk., 29 Stott Ave., 06360, pg. 1544   **PB**
VISION ONE, Three Hilltop Rd., 06360, pg. 1141   **PV**

Oakville

Hoboken Floors-Connecticut Div., 290 Sylvan Lake Rd., 06779, pg. 532   **PV**
Seymour Smith & Son, 900 Main St., 06779, pg. 575   **PB**

Old Greenwich

ABCO, Inc., 1700 E. Putnam Ave., 06870, pg. 674   **PB**
Domecq Importers Inc., 143 Sound Beach Ave., 06870, pg. 63   **IT**
FORTUNE BRANDS, INC., 1700 E. Putnam Ave., 06870-0811, pg. 674   **PB**
Fortune Brands International Corporation, 1700 East Putnam Ave., 06870, pg. 675   **PB**
MCM Products, Inc., 1700 East Putnam Ave., 06870, pg. 675   **PB**

Old Lyme

Neumann (USA), Six Vista Dr., 00371, pg. 984   **PV**
SENNHEISER ELECTRONIC CORP., Six Vista Dr., 06371, pg. 984   **PV**

Old Saybrook

Cramer Company, 139 Mill Rock Rd. E., 06475-1261, pg. 1238   **PB**
Northeastern Div.-Old Saybrook, 50 School House Rd., 06475-4007, pg. 518   **PB**

Orange

ALARMGUARD HOLDINGS, INC., 125 Frontage Rd., 06477, pg. 35   **PB**
Bindley Western, Orange Division, 181 Marsh Hill Rd., 06477, pg. 228   **PB**
Stephen Gould of Connecticut Corp., 291 Lambert Rd., 06477, pg. 467   **PV**
HUBBELL INCORPORATED, 584 Derby Milford Rd., 06477, pg. 844   **PB**
Saab-Scania Financial Services Corp, P.O. Box 697, Saab Drive, 06477, pg. 687   **IT**
Scania USA Inc., P.O. Box 538, Edison Rd., 06477, pg. 687   **IT**

Oxford

PTA CORPORATION, 178 Christian St., 06478, pg. 828   **PV**

Pawcatuck

Alupower, Inc., 82 Mechanic St., 06379-2154, pg. 376   **PV**
Davis Standard Corporation, One Extrusion Dr., 06379, pg. 459   **PB**
Douglas-Randall, Inc., 6 Pawcatack Ave., 06379, pg. 1341   **PB**
ENER-TEK INTERNATIONAL CORPORATION, 82 Mechanic St., 06379-2154, pg. 376   **PV**
Lithion, Inc., 82 Mechanic St., 06379-2154, pg. 376   **PV**
Ortronics, Inc., 595 Greenhaven Rd., 06379, pg. 806   **IT**
United Foam Plastics Corporation, 213 Mechanic St., 06379-2196, pg. 1112   **PV**
Yardney Technical Products, Inc., 82 Mechanic St., 06379-2154, pg. 376   **PV**

Plainville

Gems Sensors, One Cowles Rd., 06062, pg. 481   **PB**
PECK SPRING COMPANY, 89 Whiting St., 06062, pg. 846   **PV**
Pratt & Whitney, 74 Northwest Dr., 06062-0900, pg. 1128   **PB**

Plantsville

Fansteel VR/Wesson-Plantsville, 389 Marion Ave., 06479, pg. 612   **PB**

Pomfret

LOOS & CO., INC., 1 Cable Rd., 06258, pg. 675   **PV**

Portland

STANDARD-KNAPP, INC., 127 Main St., 06480, pg. 1031   **PV**

Preston

Spafas, Inc., 190 Rte. 165, 06365, pg. 195   **PB**

Putnam

Pallflex, Inc., Kennedy Dr., 06260, pg. 1254   **PB**

Ridgefield

Ammex Tax & Duty Free Shops, 63 Copps Hill Rd., 06877, pg. 103   **IT**
Ammex Tax & Duty Free Shops West, Inc., 63 Copps Hill Rd., 06877, pg. 103   **IT**
Ammex Warehouse Company, Inc., 63 Copps Hill Rd., 06877, pg. 103   **IT**
Boehringer Ingelheim Corporation, 900 Ridgebury Rd., 06877, pg. 199   **IT**
Boehringer Ingelheim Pharmaceuticals, Inc., 900 Ridgebury Rd., 06877, pg. 199   **IT**
DFI/Inflight, Inc., 63 Copps Hill Rd., 06877, pg. 103   **IT**
Duty Free International, Inc., 63 Copps Hill Rd., 06877, pg. 103   **IT**

PB - U.S. Public Companies Volume
PV - U.S. Private Companies Volume
IT - International Public & Private Companies Volume

Pyramid Services, Inc., Executive Pavilion, 90 Grove St., Ste. 207, 06877, pg. 118 **PB**
QSP, Inc., 38A Grove St., 06877, pg. 1367 **PB**
TMP Worldwide, Inc., 38C Grove St., 06877, pg. 1064 **PV**

Rockville

AMERBELLE CORPORATION, 104 E. Main St., 06066, pg. 48 **PB**
ANO-COIL CORPORATION, 60 E. Main St., 06066, pg. 75 **PV**

Rocky Hill

AMES DEPARTMENT STORES, INC., 2418 Main St., 06067, pg. 99 **PB**
THE CLINIPAD CORPORATION, 175 Capital Blvd., 06067, pg. 246 **PV**
Lilly Industries, Inc., 145 Dividend Rd., 06067, pg. 994 **PB**
Loctite Corp. North American Group, 1001 Trout Brook Crossing, 06067, pg. 611 **IT**
Loctite Corporation, 1001 Trout Brook Crossing, 06067-3910, pg. 611 **IT**
SNET Mobility, Inc., 500 Enterprise Dr., 06067, pg. 1491 **PB**
Sun Microsystems, 175 Capital Blvd., Ste. 202, 06067-3578, pg. 1531 **PB**
Sysco Food Services of Connecticut, 100 Inwood Rd., 06067, pg. 1551 **PB**

Rogers

Composite Materials Div., One Technology Dr., 06263, pg. 1402 **PB**
ROGERS CORPORATION, One Technology Dr., 06263-0188, pg. 1402 **PB**

Rowayton

COLDWATER SEAFOOD CORPORATION, 133 Rowayton Ave., 06853, pg. 251 **PV**

Seymour

EGA, 42 Silvermine Rd., 06483, pg. 436 **IT**
Fleet Bank, P.O. Box 456, 115 Main St., 06483, pg. 649 **PB**
The Kerite Company, 49 Day St., 06483, pg. 844 **PB**

Shelton

ADC NewNet, Inc., Two Enterprise Dr., Ste. 400, 06484, pg. 4 **PB**
American Skandia Business Services Corporation, Tower One, Corporate Dr., 06484-0883, pg. 1257 **IT**
American Skandia Information Services & Tecnology Corp., P.O. Box 883, One Corporate Drive, 06484-0883, pg. 1257 **IT**
American Skandia Investment Holding Corporation, Tower One, Corporate Dr., 06484-0883, pg. 1257 **IT**
American Skandia Investment Services, Inc., P.O. Box 883, One Corporate Drive, 06484-0883, pg. 1257 **IT**
American Skandia Life Assurance Corporation, P.O. Box 883, Corporate Drive, 06484-0883, pg. 1257 **IT**
American Skandia Marketing, Inc., P.O. Box 883, One Corporate Drive, 06484-0883, pg. 1257 **IT**
Ascom Hasler Mailing Systems, Inc., 19 Forest Pkwy., 06484, pg. 86 **PV**
AUTOSWAGE PRODUCTS, INC., 726 River Rd., 06484, pg. 101 **PV**
Barnes Engineering, 88 Long Hill Cross Rd., 06484-0867, pg. 542 **IT**
THE W.E. BASSETT COMPANY, 100 Trap Falls Rd. Ext., 06484, pg. 122 **PV**
Black & Decker Household Products Group, Six Armstrong Rd., 06484, pg. 238 **PB**
CCL Label, Inc., P.O. Box 511, 15 Controls Dr., 06484-0511, pg. 238 **PB**
CooperSurgical Inc., 15 Forest Pkwy., 06484, pg. 442 **PB**
R.H. Forschner Division, One Research Dr., 06484-0874, pg. 1544 **PB**
General Signal Networks, One Waterview Dr., 06484, pg. 727 **PB**
Hudson Life Reassurance Corporation, P.O. Box 883, 1 Corporate Dr., 06484, pg. 1257 **IT**
Industrial Components Group, Two Corporate Dr., Ste. 138, 06484, pg. 127 **IT**
Iroquois Gas Transmission System, One Corporate Dr., Ste. 606, 06484, pg. 1417 **IT**
Iroquois Gas Transmission System, One Corporate Dr., Ste. 606, 06484, pg. 1787 **PB**
LANDSTAR HOLDING, First Shelton Pl., 1000 Bridgeport Ave., 06484, pg. 978 **PB**
Market Data Retrieval, 16 Progress Dr., 06484-1117, pg. 536 **PB**
MatrixOne, Inc., Two Trap Falls, Ste. 503, 06484, pg. 18 **PV**
Moore & Munger Marketing Inc., Two Corporate Dr., Ste. 434, 06484, pg. 1197 **PV**
Olivetti North America, Two Enterprise Dr., 06484, pg. 1002 **PB**
Parker Kalon, 510 River Rd., 06484, pg. 233 **PB**
PEOPLE'S CHOICE TV CORP., Two Corporate Dr., Ste. 249, 06484, pg. 1274 **PB**
Philips Medical Systems North America Company, 710 Bridgeport Ave., 06484-0915, pg. 1055 **IT**
PRECISION RESOURCE INC., 25 Forest Parkway, 06484, pg. 880 **PV**

RAYTECH CORPORATION, One Corporate Dr., Ste. 512, 06484, pg. 1363 **PB**
Rhone-Poulenc Basic Chemicals Co., P.O. Box 881, 06484, pg. 1110 **IT**
RUDEL MACHINERY COMPANY, INC., 3 Enterprise Dr., 06484, pg. 950 **PV**
Spectra-Tech, Two Research Dr., 06484-0869, pg. 1593 **PB**
SWISS ARMY BRANDS, INC., One Research Dr., 06484-0874, pg. 1544 **PB**
Swiss Army Brands Ltd., One Research Dr., 06484-0874, pg. 1544 **PB**
Tetley USA Inc., 100 Commerce Dr., 06484, pg. 1377 **IT**
Turner Construction Company, 2 Trap Falls Dr., 06484, pg. 1645 **PB**
Victorinox, One Research Dr., 06484-0874, pg. 1544 **PB**

Simsbury

Blue Ridge Indemnity Co., 86 Hopmeadow St., 06070, pg. 345 **PB**
Blue Ridge Insurance Co., P.O. Box 519, 86 Hopmeadow St., 06070, pg. 345 **PB**
EXECUTIVE RISK, INC., 82 Hopmeadow St., 06070-7683, pg. 599 **PB**
Veeder-Root Company, 125 Powder Forest Dr., 06070, pg. 482 **PB**

Somersville

P.M.D., 24 Scitico Rd., 06072, pg. 832 **PV**

South Glastonbury

First Federal Savings, 879 Main St., 06073, pg. 632 **PB**
J.T. SLOCOMB COMPANY, 68 Matson Hill Rd., 06073, pg. 1006 **PV**

South Windham

Eclipse Combustion, Inc., 243 Hartford Tpke., Ste. 103, 06066, pg. 360 **PB**
Elastomer Components Unit, 730 Windham Rd., 06266, pg. 1402 **PB**

South Windsor

CLS Laser Systems, P.O. Box 767, 5 Jeffrey Dr., 06074-3460, pg. 1002 **PB**
ELECTRO METHODS INC., 330 Governors Hwy., 06074, pg. 369 **PV**
First Federal Savings, 481 Buckland Rd., 06074, pg. 632 **PB**
Gerber Optical, Inc., 40 Gerber Rd. E., pg. 740 **PB**
GERBER SCIENTIFIC, INC., 83 Gerber Rd. W., 06074, pg. 740 **PB**
JP Foodservice, Inc.-Hartford, 625 Nutmeg Rd., 06074, pg. 918 **PB**
Keystone Pipeline Services, Inc., 37 Sea Pave Rd., 06074, pg. 1271 **PV**
National Service Cleaning Corporation, 260 Ellington Rd., 06074, pg. 1208 **PB**
Waldo Bros. Company, 595 Nutmeg Rd., N., 06074-2461, pg. 1147 **PV**

Southington

GIBBS WIRE & STEEL COMPANY, INC., P.O. Box 520, Metals Dr., 06489-0520, pg. 451 **PV**
IDEAL FORGING CORPORATION, 167 Center St., 06489, pg. 557 **PV**

Southport

Grand Banks Yachts, Ltd., 136 John St., 06490, pg. 531 **IT**
Iggesund Paperboard Inc., 107 John St., 06490, pg. 886 **IT**
Medical Marketing Group, Inc., 2960 Post Rd., 06490, pg. 1091 **PV**
STURM, RUGER & CO., INC., Lacey Pl., 06490, pg. 1526 **PB**
Wassall USA Inc., 107 John St., 06490, pg. 1486 **IT**

Stafford

Tyco Printed Circuit Group, Four Old Monson Rd., 06075, pg. 1648 **PB**

Stafford Springs

Tyco Backplanes, P.O. Box 100, 06076, pg. 1648 **PB**

Stamford

ABB Financial Services Inc., Four Stamford Forum, Tresser Blvd., 06901, pg. 4 **IT**
ABB Investment Management, Four Stamford Forum, Tresser Blvd., 06901, pg. 4 **IT**
ABB Project & Export Finance (USA) Inc., 900 Long Ridge Rd., 06904, pg. 4 **IT**
ABB Treasury Center (USA) Inc., Four Stamford Forum, Tresser Blvd., 06901, pg. 4 **IT**
ADM Cocoa, Inc., 300 First Stamford Place, 06902, pg. 27 **PB**
A.S. MANAGEMENT CORPORATION, 760 Summer St., 06901, pg. 7 **PV**

ASI Market Research, Inc., 263 Tresser Blvd., 06901, pg. 554 **PV**
The Advocate, 75 Tresser Blvd., 06904-9307, pg. 1616 **PB**
AmeriData Technologies, Inc., 700 Canal St., 06902, pg. 711 **PB**
Applied Industrial Materials Corporation, 100 First Stamford Pl., 3rd Fl., 06904, pg. 1736 **PB**
BTR, Inc., 333 Ludlow St., 06902, pg. 127 **IT**
H.J. BAKER & BRO., INC., 595 Summer St., 06901-1407, pg. 112 **PV**
THE F.A. BARTLETT TREE EXPERT CO., 1290 E. Main St., 06902, pg. 119 **PV**
Blue Mountain Consolidated Water Company, High Ridge Pk., 06905, pg. 379 **PB**
BOLLIGER, INC., 88 Viaduct Rd., 06907, pg. 155 **PV**
J. Brown/LMC Group, 1010 Washington Blvd., 8th Fl., 06901, pg. 764 **PB**
CB Commercial Real Estate Group Eastern Division, 177 Broad St., 06901, pg. 272 **PB**
CU CapitalCorp, High Ridge Park, 06905, pg. 380 **PB**
CUC International, Inc., 707 Summer St., 06901, pg. 320 **PB**
CUC Publishing, 707 Summer St., 06901, pg. 320 **PB**
CVC of Ohio, High Ridge Pk., 06905, pg. 380 **PB**
Cadbury Beverages, High Ridge Park, 06905, pg. 248 **IT**
Cadbury Beverages North America, Six High Ridge Park, 06905-0800, pg. 248 **IT**
Career Blazers Learning Center of Stamford, Nine W. Broad St., 06902, pg. 209 **PV**
CENDANT CORPORATION, 707 Summer St., 06901, pg. 320 **PB**
CHAMPION INTERNATIONAL CORP., One Champion Plaza, 06921, pg. 333 **PB**
Champion International Corp., Paper Div., One Champion Plaza, 06921, pg. 334 **PB**
Champion International Corp., Wood Products Div., One Champion Plaza, 06921, pg. 334 **PB**
CHARTWELL RE CORPORATION, Four Stamford Plaza, 107 Elm St., 06902, pg. 336 **PB**
Chartwell Reinsurance Company, Four Stamford Plaza, 107 Elm St., 06912, pg. 336 **PB**
Chrysler Capital Corp., 225 High Ridge Rd., 06905-3032, pg. 354 **PB**
Circon ACMI, 300 Stillwater Ave., 06904, pg. 373 **PB**
Citicorp Information Resources, Inc., Four Stamford, 06901, pg. 377 **PB**
Citizens Communications Services, Inc., High Ridge Park, 06905, pg. 380 **PB**
Citizens Resources Company, High Ridge Pk., 06905, pg. 380 **PB**
Citizens Telecommunications, High Ridge Park, P.O. Box 3801, 06905-1390, pg. 380 **PB**
CITIZENS UTILITIES COMPANY, P.O. Box 3801, High Ridge Pk., 06905-1390, pg. 379 **PB**
Clairol, Inc., One Blachley St., 06922, pg. 254 **PB**
Coats & Clark Inc. (Sales Office), 1266 E. Main St., 06905, pg. 300 **IT**
Coats Patons (North America) Inc., 72 Cummings Pt. Rd., 06902, pg. 300 **IT**
COMMUNICATIONS SUPPLY CORPORATION, 260 West Ave., 06902, pg. 259 **PV**
Comp-U-Card Division, 707 Summer St., 06904, pg. 320 **PB**
CONAIR CORPORATION, One Cummings Point Rd., 06904, pg. 261 **PV**
CONESTOGA CORPORATION, 72 Cummings Point Rd., 06902, pg. 262 **PV**
Corporacion Del Cobre (U.S.A.), Inc., 177 Broad St., 14th Fl., 06901, pg. 303 **IT**
Cowles Business Media, Inc., Six River Bend, 06907, pg. 281 **PV**
Cowles Enthusiast Media, Inc., Four High Ridge Park, 06905, pg. 281 **PV**
CRANE CO., 100 First Stamford Pl., 06902, pg. 456 **PB**
CROMPTON & KNOWLES CORPORATION, One Station Pl., Metro Ctr., 06902, pg. 459 **PB**
Crown Lance, Inc., 88 Viaduct Rd., 06907, pg. 155 **PV**
Crush U.S.A., Six High Ridge Park, 06905, pg. 248 **IT**
Cuisinart Inc., One Cummings Point Rd., 06904, pg. 261 **PV**
Dakota Specialty Insurance Company, Four Stamford Plaza, 107 Elm St., 06912, pg. 337 **PB**
Development and Manufacturing, P.O. Box 1600, 06904, pg. 1784 **PB**
DEVON GROUP, INC., 281 Tresser Blvd., Ste. 501, 06901-3227, pg. 503 **PB**
Electric Energy Export Corp., High Ridge Pk., 06905, pg. 380 **PB**
Enso International, Inc., 281 Tresser Blvd., 15th Fl., 06901, pg. 457 **IT**
Envirosource Treatment & Disposal Services, Inc., P.O. Box 10309, Five High Ridge Park, 06904-2309, pg. 587 **PB**
THE EXCELLENCE GROUP, 1011 High Ridge Rd., 06905, pg. 387 **PV**
FAG Holding Corporation, 911 Hope St., 06907, pg. 469 **IT**
FAG Information Services Inc., 911 Hope St., 06907, pg. 469 **IT**
Facultative Resources, Inc., One Canterbury Green, 06901, pg. 215 **PV**
FIRST MEDICAL GROUP INC., 1055 Washington Blvd., 06901, pg. 636 **PV**
First Union National Bank of Connecticut, 300 Main St., 06904, pg. 640 **PB**
Flowing Wells, Inc., High Ridge Pk., 06905, pg. 380 **PB**
Fraser Paper Limited, Nine W. Broad St., P.O. Box 10055, 06904, pg. 434 **IT**
Fraser Papers, Inc., 70 Seaview Ave., 06902, pg. 434 **IT**
Fuji Medical Systems USA, Inc., P.O. Box 120035, 333 Ludlow St., 06902, pg. 524 **IT**

Geographic Index-U.S.

Fujitsu Networks Industries, 1266 E. Main St., 06902, pg. 529　**IT**

G.E. Capital Commercial Real Estate Financing, 292 Long Ridge Rd., 06902, pg. 712　**PB**

GRC Realty Corp., Financial Ctr., P.O. Box 10353, 06904, pg. 725　**PB**

GTE CORPORATION, One Stamford Forum, 06904, pg. 696　**PB**

GANTOS INC., 1266 E. Main St., Fifth Fl., 06902, pg. 702　**PB**

General Electric Capital Services, Inc., 260 Long Ridge Rd., 06927, pg. 711　**PB**

General Electric Investment Corp., 3003 Summer St., 06905, pg. 712　**PB**

GENERAL HOST CORPORATION, One Station Pl., 06902, pg. 715　**PB**

GENERAL RE CORPORATION, Financial Ctr., 695 E. Main St., 06904-2351, pg. 725　**PB**

General Reinsurance Corp., 695 E. Main St., 06904, pg. 725　**PB**

GENERAL SIGNAL CORPORATION, One High Ridge Pk., 06904, pg. 726　**PB**

General Star Management Company, Financial Ctr., P.O. Box 10354, 06904-2354, pg. 725　**PB**

Genesis Underwriting Management Company, Financial Centre, P.O. Box 10352, 06904, pg. 725　**PB**

GENEVE CORPORATION, 96 Cummings Point Rd., 06902, pg. 446　**PV**

Glen Alsace Water Company, High Ridge Park, 06905, pg. 380　**PB**

GOODWAY TECHNOLOGIES CORPORATION, 420 West Ave., 06902-6384, pg. 464　**PV**

Great Brands of Europe, 208 Harbor Dr., 06902, pg. 381　**IT**

Group W Satellite Communications, 250 Harbor Dr., 06904, pg. 275　**PB**

Guinness Import Company, Six Landmark Sq., 06901, pg. 412　**IT**

HRH/Atlas Construction Inc., 110 Lenox Ave., 06906, pg. 1035　**IT**

HARGRO ENTERPRISES, INC., One Landmark Sq., 06901, pg. 502　**PV**

Hewlett-Packard Company, 4 Stamford Forum, 9th Fl., 06820, pg. 814　**IT**

Home Products. Div., High Ridge Rd., 06904, pg. 1054　**IT**

HYPERION SOFTWARE, 900 Long Ridge Rd., 06902, pg. 851　**PB**

IBM Credit Corporation, 290 Harbor Dr., 06904, pg. 896　**PB**

ICON INTERNATIONAL, Two Stamford Plaza, 8th Fl., 281 Tresser Blvd., 06901, pg. 556　**PV**

Independence Holding Company, 96 Cummings Point Rd., 06902, pg. 446　**PV**

InterLake Papers, Inc., 301 Tresser Blvd., 06901, pg. 436　**PB**

Jefferies & Company, Inc., Metro Center, One Station Pl., Four S., 06902, pg. 925　**PB**

Axel Johnson Inc., 300 Atlantic St., 06901-3522, pg. 709　**IT**

Just Kid, Inc., 300 First Stamford Pl., 06902, pg. 804　**PV**

KeySpan Energy Services Inc., 300 First Stamford Pl., 06902, pg. 259　**PV**

Korn/Ferry International, One Landmark Sq., 06901, pg. 633　**PV**

Kvaerner Energy Development, Inc., 100 First Stamford Pl., 06902, pg. 770　**IT**

Kvaerner Hydro Power, Inc., 100 First Stamford Pl., 06902, pg. 770　**IT**

Kvaerner Inc., 100 First Stamford Pl., 06902, pg. 770　**IT**

Kvaerner Venture Inc., 100 First Stamford Pl., 06902, pg. 770　**IT**

Lake Heritage Utilities, Inc., High Ridge Pk., 06905, pg. 380　**PB**

Leaf River Corp., 75 Prospect St., 06904, pg. 736　**PB**

Learning International, 680 Washington Blvd., 06901, pg. 1617　**PB**

Lincoln Snacks Company, Four High Ridge Park, 06905, pg. 1187　**PB**

LONE STAR INDUSTRIES, INC., 300 First Stamford Pl., 06912, pg. 1012　**PB**

Marketing and Customer Operations, P.O. Box 1600, 06904, pg. 1784　**PB**

Media Networks Inc., P.O. Box 10096, One Station Place, 06904-2096, pg. 1612　**PB**

Metromedia International Telecommunications, Inc., 333 Ludlow St., 06902, pg. 1103　**PB**

Millsport, Stamford Towers, 750 Washington Blvd., 06901, pg. 1224　**PB**

MORMAC MARINE TRANSPORT, INC., Three Landmark Sq., 06901, pg. 762　**PV**

Morton Chemical Div., Viaduct Rd., 06907, pg. 1135　**PB**

Mott's Inc., Six High Ridge Pk., 06905, pg. 248　**IT**

NER Holdings, Inc., One Landmark Sq., 06901, pg. 502　**PV**

Nationwide Papers, One Champion Plaza, 06921, pg. 334　**PB**

Nestle Capital Corporation, Six Landmark Sq., 8th fl., 06901-2705, pg. 916　**IT**

Nestle Holdings, Inc., Five High Ridge Park, 06905, pg. 916　**IT**

A.C. NIELSEN, 177 Broad St., 06901, pg. 1183　**PB**

NINE WEST GROUP, INC., Nine W. Broad St., 06902, pg. 1185　**PB**

Norelco Consumer Products Company, High Ridge Park, P.O. Box 10166, 06904-2166, pg. 1054　**IT**

North Castle Design, 300 First Stamford Pl., 06902, pg. 804　**PV**

North Castle Direct, 300 First Stamford Pl., 06902, pg. 804　**PV**

NORTH CASTLE PARTNERS ADVERTISING, INC., 300 First Stamford Pl., 06902, pg. 804　**PV**

North Castle Public Relations, 300 First Stamford Pl., 06902, pg. 804　**PV**

Northeast Region, 2777 Summer St., Ste. 506, 06905, pg. 1024　**PB**

Nukem, Inc., 300 Atlantic St., 06901, pg. 1081　**IT**

OCG Holdings, Inc., 120 Long Ridge Rd., 06904, pg. 1219　**PB**

Olin-Asahi Interconnect Technologies, 120 Long Ridge Rd., 06904, pg. 1219　**PB**

Olin Electronic Materials, Inc., P.O. Box 1355, 06904, pg. 1218　**PB**

Olin Far East, Limited, 120 Long Ridge Rd., 06904, pg. 1219　**PB**

OMEGA ENGINEERING, INC., One Omega Dr., 06907, pg. 816　**PV**

PCCP, Inc., P.O. Box 7900, 292 Long Ride Rd., 06904, pg. 361　**PB**

Peabody Corporation USA, P.O. Box 2331, 39 Maple Tree Ave., 06906-0331, pg. 1066　**IT**

Peabody Engineering Corp., 39 Maple Tree Ave., 06906, pg. 1065　**IT**

Perkins-Goodwin Co. Inc., 300 Atlantic St., 5th Fl., 06901, pg. 586　**IT**

PETROLEUM HEAT & POWER CO., 2187 Atlantic St., 06902, pg. 1281　**PB**

PIMCO ADVISORS, 2187 Atlantic St., 06902, pg. 1296　**PB**

Pitney Bowes Business Supplies & Services, One Elmcroft Rd., 06926, pg. 1303　**PB**

Pitney Bowes Business Systems-International, One Elmcroft Rd., 06926, pg. 1303　**PB**

Pitney Bowes Business Systems-U.S., One Elmcroft Rd., 06926, pg. 1303　**PB**

PITNEY BOWES INC., One Elmcroft Rd., 06926-0700, pg. 1303　**PB**

Playtex Apparel, Inc., 700 Fairfield Ave., 06904, pg. 1433　**PB**

PRIMEENERGY CORPORATION, One Landmark Sq., 06901, pg. 1328　**PB**

PrimeEnergy Management Corporation, One Landmark Sq., 06901, pg. 1329　**PB**

QFC Holding Company, 300 Atlantic St., Ste. 1001, 06901, pg. 1349　**PB**

Rayonier Forest Resources, 1177 Summer St., 06905-5529, pg. 1363　**PB**

RAYCNIER INC., 1177 Summer St., 06905-5529, pg. 1363　**PB**

Real Decisions Corp., 56 Top Gallant Rd., 06092, pg. 395　**PB**

Resolute Group, Inc., 100 First Stamford Pl., 06902, pg. 220　**PB**

Resolute Management Corp., 100 First Stamford Pl., 06902, pg. 220　**PB**

Resolute Management Corporation, 100 First Stamford Pl., 06902, pg. 220　**PB**

REUNION INDUSTRIES, INC., One Stamford Landing, 62 Southfield Ave., 06902, pg. 1383　**PB**

ROSCO LABORATORIES, INC., 52 Harbor View Ave., 06903, pg. 944　**PV**

SBC Warburg Dillon Read, 677 Washington Blvd., 06901, pg. 1329　**IT**

SLI International Corp., P.O. box 10377, One Circle West, 06904-2377, pg. 1268　**IT**

SVM of Texas, Inc., 100 First Stamford Pl., 06904, pg. 386　**PV**

Sara Lee Intimates, 700 Fairfield Ave., 06904, pg. 1434　**PB**

Savin Corporation, 5th Flr., North Tower, 333 Ludlow St., 06904-2270, pg. 1114　**IT**

Savin Credit Corporation, 5th Flr., N. Tower, 333 Ludlow St., 06904, pg. 1114　**IT**

SERVICE AMERICA CORPORATION, 300 First Stamford Pl., 06904, pg. 986　**PV**

Service America Corporation of Wisconsin, 100 First Stamford Pl., 06904, pg. 986　**PV**

Service America of Texas Inc., 100 First Stamford Pl., 06904, pg. 986　**PV**

Servomation Duchess, Inc., 100 First Stamford Pl., 06904, pg. 986　**PV**

Servomation Inc., 100 First Stamford Pl., 06904, pg. 986　**PV**

Servomation Food Service of Ontario Limited, 100 First Stamford Pl., 06904, pg. 986　**PV**

Signet Star Holdings, Inc., One Canterbury Green, 06901, pg. 216　**PB**

SILGAN CORPORATION, Four Landmark Sq., Ste. 400, 06901, pg. 1473　**PB**

Sonoco Fibre Drum, 1266 Main St., 06902, pg. 1486　**PB**

Southwestern Capital Corporation, High Ridge Pk., 06905, pg. 380　**PB**

Southwestern Investments, Inc., High Ridge Park, 06905, pg. 380　**PB**

Special Services Company, 121 Hamilton Ave., 06906, pg. 229　**PB**

Spectrum Asset Management, Inc., Four High Ridge Pk., 06905, pg. 1674　**PB**

STAMFORD CAPITAL, 1266 E. Main St., 06902, pg. 1029　**PV**

Stamford Superior Drug Co., Inc., 37 Brownhouse Rd., 06902, pg. 229　**PV**

Star Gas Corporation, P.O. Box 120011, 06912-0011, pg. 1281　**PB**

Statoil North America Inc., 225 High Ridge Rd., 06905, pg. 1298　**IT**

Sun City Sewer Company, High Ridge Pk., 06905, pg. 380　**PB**

Sun City West Utilities Company, High Ridge Pk., 06905, pg. 380　**PB**

SUN HILL INDUSTRIES, INC., 48 Union St., 06906, pg. 1051　**PV**

Sundrop, Six High Ridge Pk., 06905, pg. 248　**IT**

TIG Reinsurance, 300 First Stamford Pl., 06902, pg. 1556　**PB**

Temco Building Maintenance, Inc., 463 Fairfield Ave., 06902, pg. 1574　**PB**

Thomson Book/Reference Group, Metro Center, One Station Pl., 06902, pg. 1600　**PB**

THE THOMSON CORPORATION, Metro Ctr., One Station Pl., 6th Fl., 06902, pg. 1599　**PB**

Thomson Financial Services, One Station Pl., 06902, pg. 1601　**PB**

Thomson Holdings Inc., One Station Pl., 06902, pg. 1601　**PB**

Thomson Professional Publishing, Metro Center, One Station Pl., 06902, pg. 1601　**PB**

Thomson U.S. Inc., One Station Pl., 6th Fl., 06902, pg. 1601　**PB**

The Time Warner Cable Group, 300 First Stamford Pl., 06902-6732, pg. 1610　**PB**

TOSCO CORPORATION, 72 Cummings Point Rd., 06902, pg. 1624　**PB**

Trade Dimensions, 263 Tresser Blvd., 5th Fl., 06901, pg. 1447　**IT**

Transportation Controls Sector, One High Ridge Pk., 06904, pg. 727　**IT**

Trelleborg-Boliden, 3 Landmark Square, 06901, pg. 1423　**IT**

Trenwick America Reinsurance Corporation, Metro Center, One Station Place, 06902, pg. 1634　**PB**

TRENWICK GROUP INC., Metro Ctr., One Station Pl., 06902, pg. 1634　**PB**

Tubac Valley Water Company, Inc., High Ridge Pk., 06905, pg. 380　**PB**

United Distillers USA, Inc., Six Landmark Sq., 06901, pg. 412　**IT**

Utilities Advances Corporation, High Ridge Park, 06905, pg. 380　**PB**

Van Ommeren Shipping, Inc., Three Stamford Landing, 46 Southfield Avenue, 06902, pg. 758　**IT**

Van Ommeren USA Inc., 3 Stamford Landing, Ste. 370, 46 Southfield Ave., 06902, pg. 758　**IT**

Vernon Computer Leasing Inc., 77 Selleck Street, 06902, pg. 559　**PB**

Wahlstrom & Company, 1290 Main St., 06902, pg. 1641　**PB**

WARRANTECH CORPORATION, 300 Atlantic St., 06901, pg. 1740　**PB**

Welbilt Corporation, 225 High Ridge Rd., 06905, pg. 188　**PB**

The Wheatley Group, Inc., Stamford Harbor Park, 333 Ludlow St., 06902, pg. 152　**PB**

Willis Faber North America, Inc.-Connecticut, Surety & Fidelity, 2777 Summer St., Sixth Fl., 06905, pg. 1503　**IT**

Wine World Estates, Inc., Two Stamford Landing, Ste. 195, 06902, pg. 917　**IT**

Xerox Business Equipment, Inc., P.O. Box 1600, 06904, pg. 1784　**PB**

Xerox Corporate Research Group, P.O. Box 1600, 06904, pg. 1784　**PB**

XEROX CORPORATION, P.O. Box 1600, 800 Long Ridge Rd., 06904, pg. 1783　**PB**

Xerox Credit Corporate Finance Div., 100 First Stamford Pl., 06904, pg. 1785　**PB**

Xerox Credit Corporation, 100 First Stamford Pl., 06904, pg. 1785　**PB**

Xerox Document Processing, P.O. Box 1600, 06904, pg. 1784　**PB**

Xerox Financial Services Inc., P.O. Box 1600, 06904, pg. 1784　**PB**

The Xerox Foundation Inc., P.O. Box 1600, 06904, pg. 1785　**PB**

Xerox Real Estate & General Services Division, P.O. Box 1600, 06904, pg. 1785　**PB**

Xerox Realty Corporation, P.O. Box 1600, 06904, pg. 1785　**PB**

Stonington

Hubbell Premise Wiring, Inc., P.O. Box 901, 14 Lord's Hill Rd., 06378-0901, pg. 844　**PB**

Kellems Div., Lord's Hill, Rte. No. 1, 06378, pg. 844　**PB**

Stratford

AlliedSignal Aerospace, 550 Main St., 06497-7593, pg. 50　**PB**

AMERICAN FROZEN FOODS, INC., 355 Benton St., 06497, pg. 55　**PV**

BRIDGEPORT FITTINGS, INC., 705 Lordship Blvd., 06497, pg. 168　**PV**

DIANON SYSTEMS, INC., 200 Watson Blvd., 06497, pg. 506　**PB**

Dictaphone Corp., 3191 Broadbridge Ave., 06497-2559, pg. 1045　**PV**

Facsimile Systems/Pitney Bowes Office Systems, 3191 Broadbridge Ave., 06497, pg. 1303　**PB**

IL INTERNATIONAL INC., 400 Long Beach Blvd., 06497, pg. 855　**PB**

IL (Stratford), Inc., 400 Long Beach Blvd., 06497, pg. 856　**PB**

IL USA, Inc., 400 Long Beach Blvd., 06497, pg. 856　**PB**

Jeumont-Schneider of America, 76 Ferry Blvd., 06497, pg. 706　**IT**

Mikron Corp. Stratford, 35 Ontario St., 06497, pg. 867　**IT**

ORIEL INSTRUMENTS CORPORATION, 250 Long Beach Blvd., 06497, pg. 819　**PV**

Sikorsky Aircraft, P.O. Box 9129, 6900 Main St., 06497-9129, pg. 1691　**PB**

THE U.S. BAIRD CORPORATION, P.O. Box 9706, 1700 Stratford Ave., 06497, pg. 1124　**PV**

PB - *U.S. Public Companies Volume*
PV - *U.S. Private Companies Volume*
IT - *International Public & Private Companies Volume*

Geographic Index-U.S.

Suffield

Adams Industries, Inc., 1160 South St., 06078, pg. 187 **PB**
Sweet Life Foods, Inc., 1120 Harvey Ln., 06078, pg. 1541 **PB**
Teleflex Fluid Systems Inc., One Firestone Dr., 06078-2611, pg. 1569 **PB**

Taftville

HELIKON FURNITURE CO., INC., 607 Norwich Ave., 06380, pg. 520 **PV**

Terryville

Iseli Company, Greystone Rd., 06786, pg. 481 **PB**
NAPCO, Inc., Plymouth Indus. Pk., 16 N. Harwinton Ave., 06786, pg. 1592 **PB**

Thomaston

Elometa Corporation, 341 Railroad St., 06787, pg. 1098 **PV**
Minelco, Inc., 135 S. Main St., 06787, pg. 308 **PB**
SUMMIT CORPORATION OF AMERICA, 1430 Waterbury Rd., 06787, pg. 1050 **PV**
Tech Systems Corp., 401 Watertown Rd., 06787, pg. 313 **PV**
TREADWELL CORPORATION, 341 Railroad St., 06787, pg. 1098 **PV**
Vacuum Metalizing Div., 156 N. Main St., 06787, pg. 463 **PB**

Torrington

Adams House Healthcare, 800 Fern Dr., 06790, pg. 1711 **PB**
Fafnir Div. of Torrington Co., 59 Field St., 06790, pg. 877 **PB**
The Register Citizen, 190 Water St., 06790, pg. 935 **PB**
Retconn, 199 W. Pearl Rd., 06790, pg. 1456 **PB**
The Torrington Co., 59 Field St., 06790, pg. 877 **PB**
THE TURNER & SEYMOUR MFG. COMPANY, 100 Lawton St., 06790, pg. 1109 **PV**

Trumbull

American Trading Real Estate Properties, Inc., Trefoil Park, 35 Corporate Dr., 06611, pg. 64 **PV**
Babcock Intl. Inc., 101 Oakview Dr., 06611-4769, pg. 131 **IT**
Chesebrough-Pond's, 75 Merritt Blvd., Trumbull Corp. Pk., 06611, pg. 1436 **IT**
Copier Systems/Pitney Bowes Office Systems, 100 Oakview Dr., 06611, pg. 1303 **PB**
Golf Shop Operations, 5520 Park Ave., 06611, pg. 1174 **PB**
Golf World, 5520 Park Ave., 06611, pg. 1174 **PB**
Hometown Publications, P.O. Box 298, 06611, pg. 601 **PV**
HOWE FURNITURE CORPORATION, 12 Cambridge Dr., 06611, pg. 543 **PV**
ITT Flygt Corporation, P.O. Box 1004, 35 Nutmeg Dr., 06611-0943, pg. 860 **PB**
NYT Event/Sports Marketing, 5520 Park Ave., 06611, pg. 1174 **PB**
The New York Times Magazine Company Group, 5520 Park Ave., 06611, pg. 1174 **PB**
The Pilot Pen Corp. of America, 60 Commerce Dr., 06611, pg. 1057 **IT**
Ragu Foods, Inc., 75 Merritt Blvd., 06611, pg. 1436 **IT**
Snow Country, 5520 Park Ave., 06611, pg. 1174 **PB**
Snow Country Business, 5520 Park Ave., 06611, pg. 1174 **PB**
Sodexho USA Central, Four Trefoil Dr., 06611-0945, pg. 1274 **IT**
Sports/Leisure Magazines Group, 5520 Park Ave., 06611, pg. 1174 **PB**
Tennis, 5520 Park Ave., 06611, pg. 1174 **PB**
Tennis Buyer's Guide, 5520 Park Ave., 06611, pg. 1174 **PB**
Walsh Construction Company, 101 Oakview Dr., 06611-0400, pg. 143 **PB**
Walsh Industrial & Commercial Group, 101 Oakview Dr., 06611, pg. 143 **PB**
Welcome Wagon-Intl., Inc., Seven Cambridge Dr., 06611, pg. 321 **PB**

Unionville

SANFORD & HAWLEY, INC., 1790 Farmington Ave., 06085, pg. 965 **PV**

Vernon Rockville

First Federal Savings, Tri-City Plaza, 06066, pg. 632 **PB**

Wallingford

ALK Laboratories, Inc., Research Center, 27 Village Ln., 06492, pg. 288 **IT**
Allegheny Ludlum-Wallingford, 80 Valley St., 06492, pg. 43 **PB**
Amphenol Corporation, 358 Hall Ave., 06492-0384, pg. 629 **PV**
Arrow/Schweber Electronics, 12 Beaumont Rd., 06492, pg. 134 **PB**

CUSTOMEDIX CORPORATION, 53 N. Plains Industrial Rd., 06492, pg. 298 **PV**
Cyro Industries, South Cherry St., 06492, pg. 1454 **IT**
DNE Systems, Inc., 50 Barnes Park N., 06492, pg. 58 **PB**
Dataproducts New England, Inc., Barnes Park N., 06492, pg. 621 **IT**
Davis Electric, 334 N. Cherry St. Ext., 06492, pg. 1240 **IT**
Dow United Technologies, 15 Sterling Dr., 06492-1843, pg. 523 **PB**
Infra-Metals Corp., Eight Pent Highway, 06492, pg. 1070 **IT**
H.B. Ives, 62 Barnes Park North, 06492, pg. 506 **PV**
Jeneric/Pentron Corp., 53 N. Plains Industrial Rd., 06492, pg. 298 **PV**
LDDS WorldCom, 9A Barnes Industrial Rd., 06492, pg. 1779 **PB**
Lindenmeyr Munroe, P.O. Box 5011, 14 Research Pkwy., 06492, pg. 224 **PB**
NOVAMETRIX MEDICAL SYSTEMS INC., Five Technology Dr., 06492, pg. 1203 **PB**
Times Fiber Communications, Inc., 358 Hall Ave., 06492, pg. 629 **PV**
TRANSACT TECHNOLOGIES INCORPORATED, Seven Laser Ln., 06492, pg. 1629 **PB**
URS Greiner, Inc., 11 Fairfield Blvd., 06492, pg. 1659 **PB**

Waterbury

ABRAMS & CO. PUBLISHING INC., 61 Mattatuck Heights, 06705, pg. 10 **PV**
Allegheny Ludlum-Waterbury, 271 Railroad Hill St., 06708, pg. 43 **PB**
ANAMET INC., 698 S. Main St., 06706, pg. 70 **PV**
Anchor Stampings, 130 Huntington Ave., 06708, pg. 865 **PB**
Bristol Instruments Div., 40 Bristol St., 06708, pg. 472 **IT**
Computer Communication Company, P.O. Box 4340, 27A S. Commons Rd., 06704, pg. 711 **PB**
M.J. DALY & SONS, INC., P.O. Box 2797, 110 Mattatuck Heights, 06723, pg. 309 **PV**
FiberCote Industries, Inc., 172 E. Aurora St., 06725, pg. 1258 **PB**
Graphic Learning, 61 Mattatuck Heights, 06705, pg. 10 **PV**
Greenery Rehab - Waterbury, 177 Whitewood Rd., 06708, pg. 836 **PB**
HSI International, 1500 Meriden Rd., 06705, pg. 513 **PB**
HAYDON SWITCH & INSTRUMENT, INC., 1500 Meriden Rd., 06705, pg. 513 **PB**
High-Lites, Inc., 2142 Thomaston Ave., 06704, pg. 821 **IT**
Highland Manufacturing, 1240 Wolcott St., 06705, pg. 866 **PB**
HUBBARD HALL INC., 563 S. Leonard St., 06708, pg. 544 **PV**
IGC Advanced Superconductors, Inc., 1875 W. Thomaston Ave., 06704, pg. 893 **PB**
ITW Waterbury Buckle, 952 S. Main St., 06721, pg. 867 **PB**
Lindberg Heat Treating Co., 130 Huntington Ave., 06720, pg. 999 **PB**
MACDERMID INCORPORATED, 245 Freight St., 06702, pg. 1029 **PB**
MacDermid Systems, Inc., 245 Freight St., 06702, pg. 1030 **PB**
Mitchell-Bradford International, 563 S. Leonard St., 06708, pg. 544 **PV**
New Dimensions in Education, 61 Mattatuck Heights, 06705, pg. 10 **PV**
Shorewood Packaging Corporation of Connecticut, 155 S. Leonard St., 06720-0110, pg. 1468 **PB**
Teleflex Automotive Manufacturing Corp., 105 Progress Ln., 06705, pg. 1569 **PB**
Time-Mist Div., 835 S. Main St., 06720, pg. 308 **PB**
TRUELOVE & MACLEAN INC., 984 Waterville St., 06704, pg. 1107 **PV**
Waterbury Companies, Inc., P.O. Box 1812, 06722, pg. 308 **PB**
Waterbury Companies, Inc.-Metal & Button Div., 32 Mattatuck Heights, 06705, pg. 308 **PB**
Waterbury Headers, Inc., 217 Interstate Ln., 06705, pg. 984 **PV**
Webster Bank, 145 Bank St., 06702, pg. 1751 **PB**
WEBSTER FINANCIAL CORPORATION, Webster Plaza, 145 Bank St., 06702, pg. 1751 **PB**

Watertown

Barbour Thread Inc., 150 Callender Rd., 06795, pg. 618 **IT**
Bristol Babcock, Inc., 1100 Buckingham St., 06795, pg. 472 **IT**
Helicoid Gauge Div., 1100 Buckingham, 06795, pg. 473 **IT**
Winchester Electronics, 400 Park Rd., 06795, pg. 1003 **PB**

Wauregan

C & M CORPORATION, 51 S. Walnut St., 06387, pg. 191 **PV**

West Hartford

ABBOTT BALL COMPANY, Railroad Place, 06110-0100, pg. 9 **PV**
Chandler Evans Control Systems Division, P.O. Box 330651, Charter Oak Blvd., 06133-0651, pg. 401 **PB**
Curtis 1000, Inc., 150 Vanderbilt Ave., 06110, pg. 70 **PB**
Danaher Tool Group-West Hartford Operations, P.O. Box H, 31 Brook St., 06133, pg. 481 **PB**
Delta America Inc., Ste. 117 Corporate Ctr. W., 433 S. Main St., 06110, pg. 391 **IT**

HEALTH RESOURCES INTERNATIONAL, 433 S. Main St., Ste. 302, 06110-1670, pg. 514 **PV**
ISS Mall Services, Inc., 24 Andover Dr., 06110, pg. 656 **IT**
New England Centerless Grinding, 167 South St., 06110, pg. 391 **IT**
THE WIREMOLD COMPANY, 60 Woodlawn St., 06110, pg. 1184 **PV**

West Haven

Bayer Corporation/Pharmaceutical Division, 400 Morgan Ln., 06516, pg. 173 **IT**
DEITSCH PLASTICS COMPANY, 14 Farwell St., 06516, pg. 320 **PV**
Enthone-OMI, Inc., 350 Frontage Rd., 06516, pg. 138 **PB**
Ethone OMI-West Haven, 350 Frontage Rd., 06516, pg. 138 **PB**
HERLIN PRESS INC., 475 Heffernan Dr., 06516, pg. 524 **PV**

Westbrook

Emergi-Lite, Inc., Emergi Lane, 06498, pg. 725 **IT**
LEE COMPANY, Two Pettipaug Rd., 06498, pg. 657 **PV**

Westport

Allianz of America, Inc., 55 Greens Farms Rd., 06881, pg. 58 **IT**
BASES International Research Division, 55 Greens Farms Rd., 06880, pg. 120 **PV**
Brambles Security Services Inc., 500 Post Rd. E., 06880, pg. 211 **IT**
Caradon (USA) Inc., 33 Riverside Ave., 06880, pg. 267 **IT**
Cash Bases Incorporated, c/o Tridex Corporation, 61 Wilton Rd., 06880, pg. 1637 **PB**
CHESSCO INDUSTRIES, INC., 1300 Post Rd. E., 06880, pg. 234 **PV**
COGNIZANT CORPORATION, 200 Nyala Farms Rd., 06880, pg. 395 **PB**
Cognizant Enterprises, Inc., 200 Nyala farms, 06880, pg. 395 **PB**
DEVLIEG-BULLARD INC., One Gorham Island, 06880, pg. 704 **PB**
Greenwood Publishing Group Inc., 88 Post Rd. W., 06881, pg. 1094 **PV**
LDDS WorldCom, 191 Post Rd. W., 06880, pg. 1779 **PB**
MB America, Inc., 33 Riverside Ave., 06880, pg. 267 **IT**
MB Group Enterprises, Inc., 33 Riverside Ave., 06880, pg. 267 **IT**
Mantrose Bradshaw Zinsser Group, 1175 Post Rd. E., 06880, pg. 1358 **PB**
MARKETING CORP. OF AMERICA, 285 Riverside Ave., 06880, pg. 704 **PV**
Mitsubishi Silicon America-Eastern Regional Sales Office, 191 Post Rd. W., Ste. 33, 06880, pg. 875 **IT**
Joshua Morris Publishing, Inc., 355 Riverside Ave., 06880, pg. 1367 **PB**
NEWMAN'S OWN, INC., 246 Post Road E., 06880, pg. 797 **PV**
Phibro Division of Salomon Inc., 500 Nyala Farms, 06880-6262, pg. 1633 **PB**
Playtex Beauty Care, Inc., 300 Nyala Farms Rd., 06880, pg. 1311 **PB**
Playtex Investment Corp., 300 Nyala Farms Rd., 06880, pg. 1311 **PB**
Playtex Marketing Corporation, 300 Nyala Farms Rd., 06880, pg. 1311 **PB**
Playtex Products Corp., 300 Nyala Farms Rd., 06880, pg. 1311 **PB**
PLAYTEX PRODUCTS INC., 300 Nyala Farms Rd., 06880, pg. 1310 **PB**
Reader's Digest Young Families, Inc., 355 Riverside Ave., 06880, pg. 1367 **PB**
TN Technologies Inc., 228 Saugatuck Ave., 06880, pg. 1641 **PV**
TEREX CORPORATION, 500 Post Rd. E., Ste. 320, 06880, pg. 1581 **PB**
TRIDEX CORPORATION, 61 Wilton Rd., 06880, pg. 1637 **PB**

Wethersfield

The Continuum Company, Inc., 100 Great Meadow Rd., 06109, pg. 422 **PB**

Willimantic

BICC Brand-Rex, 1600 W. Main St., 06226, pg. 120 **IT**
COMPUDYNE CORPORATION, 120 Union St., 06226-3004, pg. 419 **PB**
MicroAssembly Systems, 120 Union St., 06226, pg. 419 **PB**

Wilton

Barry Blau & Partners, Inc., 241 Danbury Rd., 06897, pg. 148 **PV**
Blau Consulting Group, 241 Danbury Rd., 06897, pg. 148 **PV**
Blau Global Network, 241 Danbury Rd., 06897, pg. 148 **PV**
Blau HealthDirect, 241 Danbury Rd., 06897, pg. 148 **PV**
BLAU MARKETING TECHNOLOGIES, INC., 241 Danbury Rd., 06897, pg. 148 **PV**
Blau Media Direct, 241 Danbury Rd., 06897, pg. 149 **PV**
Blau Technology Group, 241 Danbury Rd., 06897, pg. 149 **PV**

Geographic Index-U.S.

Blau Williams Television Time, 241 Danbury Rd., 06897, pg. 149 — PV
D & B Enterprises inc, 187 Danbury Rd., 06897, pg. 535 — PB
DELOITTE & TOUCHE LLP, Ten Westport Rd., 06897-0820, pg. 322 — PV
LOUIS DREYFUS CORPORATION, Ten Westport Rd., 06897-0810, pg. 342 — PV
MGR Performance Media, 372 Danbury Rd., 06897-2530, pg. 1641 — PB
MGR Sports, 372 Danbury Rd., 06897-2530, pg. 1641 — PB
Market Growth Resources, Inc., 372 Danbury Rd., 06897-2530, pg. 1641 — PB
The Pantene Co., Ten Wesport Rd., 06897, pg. 1330 — PB
Perq Research Corporation, 372 Danbury Road, 06897, pg. 1447 — IT
SVG Lithography Systems, 77 Danbury Rd., 06897, pg. 1474 — PB
TLP East, 213 Danbury, 06897, pg. 1224 — PB

Windsor

AAR Engine Component Services, 601 Marshall Phelps Rd., 06095, pg. 1 — PB
ABB AMDATA, 1000 Day Hill Rd., 06095, pg. 3 — IT
ABB C-E Services, 200 Great Pond Rd., 06095, pg. 3 — IT
ABB Combustion Engineering Nuclear Power, 1000 Prospect Hill Rd., 06095, pg. 3 — IT
ABB Combustion Engineering Systems, 1000 Prospect Hill Rd., 06095, pg. 3 — IT
ABB Power Plant Controls, Two Waterside Crossing, 06095, pg. 4 — IT
ABB Power Plant Laboratories, P.O. Box 500, 06095, pg. 4 — IT
ADVO, INC., P.O. Box 755, One Univac Ln., 06095-0755, pg. 23 — PB
Barnes Group Aerospace Components, 169 Kennedy Road, 06095, pg. 190 — PB
BLUE BELL/KING KOIL, INC., 770 Bloomfield Ave., 06095, pg. 150 — PV
Circle Freight International USA, 530-D Hayden Station Rd., 06095, pg. 371 — PB
Culbro Land Resources, Inc., Eight Griffin Rd. North, 06095, pg. 708 — PB
DATRON INCORPORATED, Eight Griffin Rd. N., 06095, pg. 313 — PV
Emhart Corp., 123 Day Hill Rd., 06095, pg. 233 — PB
Konica Business Machines USA, Inc., 500 Day Hill Rd., 06095, pg. 748 — IT
Mountain View Healthcare, 581 Poquonock Ave., 06095, pg. 1714 — PB
THE SPENCER TURBINE CO., 600 Day Hill Rd., 06095, pg. 1025 — PV
TRC COMPANIES, INC., Five Waterside Crossing, 06095, pg. 1557 — PB
Unisource (North East), P.O. Box 740, 100 Helmsford Way, 06095, pg. 1671 — PB
Utimaco Safeware, Inc., Seven Waterside Crossing, 06095, pg. 1444 — IT
Windsor Airmotive, 170 Old Kennedy Rd., 06095, pg. 190 — PB
Windsor Manufacturing, 169 Old Kennedy Rd., 06095, pg. 190 — PB

Windsor Locks

AST Research, Inc., Air Exchange Bldg., 85-159, Bradley Intl. Airport, 06096, pg. 1181 — IT
THE DEXTER CORPORATION, One Elm St., 06096-2334, pg. 504 — PB
Dexter Nonwovens Division, Two Elm St., 06096-2335, pg. 504 — PB
Hamilton Standard, One Hamilton Rd., 06096-1010, pg. 1690 — PB
Jani King of Hartford, Inc., One Corporate Dr., Ste. 103, 06096, pg. 582 — PV
Springfield Sugar & Prod. Co., P.O. Box 385, 06096, pg. 1541 — PB
ThermoTec Inc., 334 Ella Grasso Tpke., 06096, pg. 360 — PV

Winsted

SKF Plain Bearings, 149 Colebrook River Rd., 06098, pg. 1157 — IT
SON CHIEF ELECTRICS, INC., 41 Meadow St., 06098, pg. 1014 — PV
Winsted Precision Ball Co., 249 Rockwell St., 06098, pg. 468 — IT

Woodbridge

Lilly Industries, Inc., 15 Lunar Dr., 06525, pg. 995 — PB
Research Publications, Inc., 12 Lunar Dr., 06525, pg. 1600 — PB
TIE Systems Northeast, 1768 Litchfield Tpike., 06525, pg. 1085 — PV

Woodbury

The Woodbury Telephone Company, 297 Main St. S., 06798, pg. 1491 — PB

Yantic

Arrow Paper Supply Food Co., 237 Otrobando Ave., 06389, pg. 918 — PB

DELAWARE

Bear

Silicone Technologies, 1100 Governor Lea Blvd., 19701, pg. 165 — PB

Bethany Beach

Interstate Realty Inc. T/A Sea Colony Realty, Rt.1 & Pennsylvania Ave., 19930, pg. 426 — PV

Bridgeville

Ralph & Paul Adams, Inc., Market St. & Railroad Ave., 19933, pg. 596 — PV
DELAGRA CORPORATION, P.O. Box 126, Railroad Ave., 19933, pg. 321 — PV
O.A. NEWTON & SON CO., U.S. Rte. 13, 19933, pg. 797 — PV

Camden-Wyoming

Camdel Metals Division, P.O. Box 143, VEPCO Industrial Pk., 19934, pg. 780 — PV

Claymont

Advanta National Bank USA, Brandywine Corporate Center, 650 Naamans Rd., 19703, pg. 22 — PB

Clayton

Hanover Foods Corp., Rt. 6 & Duck Creek Rd., 19938, pg. 499 — PV
METAL MASTERS FOODSERVICE EQUIPMENT, 100 Industrial Blvd., 19938, pg. 734 — PV

Delaware City

VPI Mirrex Corp., 1389 Schoolhouse Rd., 19706, pg. 1141 — PV

Dover

AGIP Petroleum Co., Inc., 229 S. State St., 19901, pg. 428 — IT
Aladdin Holding Company, 32 Loockerman Sq., Ste. L-100, 19901, pg. 31 — PV
CFM International Inc., 306 S. State St., 19901, pg. 1166 — IT
Catalog Resources, Inc., 100 Enterprise Place, 19901, pg. 970 — PB
Chesapeake Investment Co., Cannon Bldg., 861 Silver Lake Blvd., Ste. 200, 19901, pg. 347 — PB
Chesapeake Services Company, 909 Silver Lake Blvd., Ste. 200, 19901, pg. 347 — PB
CHESAPEAKE UTILITIES CORPORATION, 909 Silver Lake Blvd., 19904, pg. 347 — PB
Chubb Custom Insurance Company, 306 S. State St., 19901, pg. 355 — PB
Dover Exploration Company, 350 S. Queen St., 19901, pg. 347 — PB
Eastern Shore Natural Gas Company, 350 S. Queen St., 19901, pg. 347 — PB
Ke-Master, 60 Starlifter Ave., 19901, pg. 1053 — PV
Kredietbank North American Finance Corp., c/o The Prentice Hall Corp., System, Inc., 229 S. State St., 19901, pg. 760 — IT
NFC International Holdings (U.S.A.) Inc., 229 South State St., 19901, pg. 901 — IT
NationsBank/Delaware, 800 Silver Lake Blvd., 19901, pg. 1162 — PB
Parfums Givenchy W.H.D. Inc., 15 E. North West, 19901, pg. 781 — IT
SNECMA Inc., 306 S. State St., 19901, pg. 1166 — IT
Skipjack, Inc., Cannon Bldg., 861 Silver Lake Blvd., Ste. 200, 19901, pg. 347 — PB
Steelworks, Inc. Dover Division, P.O. Box 557, 19903-0557, pg. 1039 — PV
SUNROC CORPORATION, 60 Starlifter Ave., 19901, pg. 1053 — PV
Takeda Finance USA, Inc., Ste. L-100, 32 Loockerman Sq., Kent Cty., 19901, pg. 1350 — IT
Tokio Marine Delaware Corporation, 32 Lookerman Sq., Ste. L-100, 19901, pg. 1392 — IT
The Webb Company, 32 Lockerman Sq., Ste. L-100, 19901, pg. 1078 — IT

Frederica

ILC Dover, Inc., P.O. Box 266, Harrington-Frederica Rd., 19946, pg. 555 — PV

Greenwood

DELAWARE ELECTRIC CO-OP, Rte. 13, 19950, pg. 321 — PV

Harrington

JC Penney National Bank, P.O. Box 27, East & Clark St., 19952, pg. 917 — PB

Hockessin

A. Schulman, Inc., 742 Yorklyn Rd., Ste. 260, 19707, pg. 1441 — PB

Lewes

Barcroft Co., Henlopen Dr., 19958, pg. 1110 — IT

Middletown

AET Specialty Nets & Profiles, Middletown Indus. Pk., P.O. Box 582, 19709, pg. 122 — PB
QUAKER CITY MOTOR PARTS COMPANY, 680 North Broad, 19709, pg. 898 — PV

Milford

BURRIS FOODS, INC., 501 S.E. Fifth St., 19963, pg. 188 — PV
CLOVER YARNS INC., 715 S. Washington St., 19963, pg. 247 — PV
Kent Sussex Tire Service, 914 N. Walnut St., 19963, pg. 987 — PV

Millsboro

First Omni Bank, N.A., 499 Mitchell St., 19966, pg. 65 — IT
Intervet America, Inc., S. State St. & Old Landing Rd., 19966, pg. 48 — IT
Public Water Supply Company, Rte. 4, Box 210, 19966, pg. 1110 — PB
Townsends, P.O. Box 468, 19966, pg. 1094 — PV

New Castle

APEX SPECIALTY MATERIALS, INC., One Corporate Commons, 100 W. Commons Blvd., Ste. 208, 19720, pg. 77 — PV
ATLANTIC AVIATION CORP., 153 N. DuPont Hwy., 19720-5000, pg. 94 — PV
Citibank Delaware, One Penns Way, 19720, pg. 377 — PB
Citicorp Leasing Inc., One Penns Way, 19720, pg. 377 — PB
Community Credit Corporation, 10 Penn Mart Shopping Ctr., 19720, pg. 1729 — PB
EA Engineering, Science & Technology, Inc., New Castle Corporate Commons, 92 Read's Way, Ste. 109, 19720, pg. 541 — PB
Feralloy Eastern Div., 20 Davidson Ln., 19720, pg. 1070 — PB
GEORGE & LYNCH, INC., P.O. Box 471, 113 W. 6th St., 19720, pg. 448 — PV
Greater Philadelphia/Wilmington, New Castle County Airport, 155 N. Dupont Hwy., 19720, pg. 218 — PB
Keen Welding Division, 4063 New Castle Ave., 19720-1492, pg. 611 — PV
MacSaveer Financial Services, New Castle Corp. Commons, Two Reads Way, Ste. 224, 19720, pg. 805 — PB
SPI Polyols, Inc., 321 Cherry La., 19720, pg. 599 — IT
T.L. Smith Delaware, 314 Baywest Blvd., 19720, pg. 1009 — PV
SPACECON, Inc., 292 New Churchmans Rd., 19720, pg. 913 — PB
Specialty Restaurants Corp, 143 N. DuPont Hwy., 19720, pg. 1023 — PV
Sponsor's Plan Asset Management, Inc., 44 Forrester Ave., 19720, pg. 1020 — PB
Tecot Electric Supply Company, 55 Lukens Dr., 19720, pg. 951 — PV
Zenith Products Corp., 400 Lukens Dr., 19720, pg. 1054 — PB

Newark

AMP-AKZO Company, 710 Dawson Dr., 19713, pg. 8 — PB
Aramark Healthcare Support Services, Inc., 2911 Ogletown Rd., 19713, pg. 79 — PV
ARTESIAN RESOURCES CORPORATION, 664 Churchmans Rd., 19702, pg. 135 — PB
Artesian Wastewater Management Inc., 664 Churchmans Rd., 19702, pg. 135 — PB
Artesian Water Company, Inc., 664 Churchmans Rd., 19702, pg. 135 — PB
AUTOTOTE CORPORATION, 100 Bellevue Rd., 19714-6009, pg. 150 — PB
Avon Sales & Distribution Branch, 2100 Ogletown Rd., 19711, pg. 156 — PB
The Bank of New York (Delaware), White Clay Center, Rte. 273, 19711, pg. 178 — PB
Brake Parts, Inc., 111 Lake Dr., 19702, pg. 560 — PB
Campbell Finance Corp., 200 Continental Dr., Ste. 102, 19713, pg. 299 — PB
Charter Rockford Behavioral Health System, Inc., 100 Rockford Dr., 19713, pg. 1035 — PB
Chase Bank International, Commonwealth Bldg., University Plaza, 19702, pg. 338 — PB
Delmarva Energy Company, University Office Plaza, 252 Chapman Rd., 19714-6066, pg. 431 — PB
Delmarva Industries, Inc., University Office Plaza, 252 Chapman Rd., 19714-6066, pg. 431 — PB
Delmarva Services Co., University Office Plaza, 252 Chapman Rd., 19714-6066, pg. 431 — PB
Du Pont Pharmaceuticals, Elkton Rd., 19711, pg. 531 — PB
W.L. GORE & ASSOCIATES, INC., 555 Paper Mill Rd., 19711, pg. 465 — PV
Morgan Guaranty International Finance Corporation, 500 Stanton Christiana Rd., 19713, pg. 1129 — PB

PB - *U.S. Public Companies Volume*
PV - *U.S. Private Companies Volume*
IT - *International Public & Private Companies Volume*

Geographic Index-U.S.

J.P. Morgan Overseas Capital Corporation, 500 Stanton Christiana Rd., 19713, pg. 1129 **PB**
J.P. Morgan Services Inc., 500 Stanton Christiana Rd., 19713, pg. 1129 **PB**
PML Securities Co., Christiana Executive Campus, 300 Continental Dr., 19713, pg. 892 **PV**
Perma-Flex Rollers, Inc., Diamond State Industrial Pk., 375 Bellevue Rd., 19713, pg. 1202 **IT**
Reynolds Aluminum Supply Company, 7000 Pencader Blvd., 19702-3310, pg. 1386 **PB**
The Southwood Company, 664 Churchmans Rd., 19702, pg. 136 **PB**
WSFS Credit Corp., 2400 Philadelphia Pike, 19703, pg. 1729 **PB**

Newport

CIBA Specialty Chemicals-Pigments Division, 205 S. James St., 19804-2490, pg. 291 **IT**

Odessa

Tidewater Utilities, Inc., P.O. Box 1000, 603 Main St., 19730-1000, pg. 1110 **PB**
White Marsh Environmental Systems, Inc., P.O. Box 1000, 603 Main St., 19730-1000, pg. 1110 **PB**

Rehoboth Beach

Outlook, Incorporated, 28 Tidewaters Rd., Henlopen Acres, 19971, pg. 623 **PV**

Seaford

Bio Medic Data Systems, 1 Silas Rd., 19973, pg. 641 **PV**
LAB PRODUCTS, INC., 742 Sussex Ave., 19973, pg. 641 **PV**

Selbyville

Baltimore Trust Company, One W. Church St., 19975, pg. 1088 **PB**

Smyrna

CUSTOM DECOR, INC., 124 Fisher St., 19977, pg. 298 **PV**

Wilmington

AAA Investment Company, 911 Washington St., 19801, pg. 51 **PV**
ABC Holding Company, Inc., 500 W. 2nd St., 19801, pg. 512 **PB**
AET Packaging Films, P.O. Box 8908, 1313 Market St., 19894, pg. 122 **PB**
AFIA, One Beaver Valley Rd., 19850, pg. 366 **PB**
AFIA (Cigna) Corporation, Limited, One Beaver Valley Road, 19850, pg. 364 **PB**
AFIA Finance Corporation, One Beaver Valley Rd., 19850, pg. 363 **PB**
AFIA (INA) Corporation, Limited, One Beaver Valley Rd., 19850, pg. 366 **PB**
Aaron Investment Company, Mellon Bank Bldg., 10th & Market St., 19801, pg. 12 **PB**
AgrEvo USA Company, Little Falls Centre One, 2711 Centerville Rd., 19808, pg. 1203 **IT**
Alamco-Delaware, Inc., 103 Springer Bldg., 3411 Silverside Rd., 19810, pg. 403 **PB**
ALKI Corporation, pg. 1173 **PB**
Allfinco, Inc., 919 N. Market St., 19801, pg. 854 **PV**
Alliant Techsystems (Aerospace Division), Hercules Plaza, 19894-0001, pg. 47 **PB**
Allied Security Inc., 501 Silverside Rd., Ste. 94, 19809, pg. 41 **PV**
American Express Credit Corporation, One Christian Centre, 301 N. Walnut St., Ste. 1002, 19801-2919, pg. 74 **PB**
American Income Holding, Inc., 1105 N. Market, Ste. 1300, 19899, pg. 1622 **PB**
Amfidis, 229 S. State St., 19804, pg. 533 **IT**
Aqualon, Hercules Plaza, P.O. Box 5417, 19850-5417, pg. 810 **PB**
Armstrong Cork Finance Corp., 300 Delaware Ave., 19899, pg. 132 **PB**
Armstrong Ventures, Inc., 300 Delaware Ave., 19899, pg. 132 **PB**
Armstrong World Industries (DE) Inc., 300 Delaware Ave., 19899, pg. 132 **PB**
AtoHaas Mexico Inc., 3411 Silverside Rd., 19810, pg. 1403 **PB**
BC International-Cosmetics and Image Services, Inc., 300 Delaware Ave., Ste. 1704, 19801-1622, pg. 198 **PB**
BMW (US) Holding Corporation, 1100 N. Market St, Ste. 780, 19801, pg. 177 **IT**
Bank of Delaware, 222 Delaware Ave., 19801, pg. 1243 **PB**
Bankers Trust (Delaware), 1001 Jefferson St., 19801, pg. 185 **PB**
BanPonce Financial Corp., 1209 Orange St., 19801, pg. 176 **PB**
Bay Mills (Delaware), Inc., 100 W. 10th St., 19801, pg. 1170 **IT**
Bell Atlantic Capital Funding Corp., 501 Carr Rd., Ste. 201, 19809, pg. 202 **PB**
Bell Atlantic Capital Investments, Inc., 501 Carr Rd., Ste. 201, 19801, pg. 202 **PB**
Bell Atlantic-DE, 901 Tatnall St., 2nd Fl., 19801, pg. 202 **PB**
Bell Atlantic Financial Services, 1001 Jefferson Plz., 5th Fl., 19801, pg. 202 **PB**
Bell Atlantic Investments, Inc., 501 Carr Rd., Ste. 201, 19809, pg. 202 **PB**
Bell Atlantic Network Funding Corporation, 501 Carr Rd., Ste. 201, 19809, pg. 202 **PB**
Bell Atlantic New Zealand Investments, Inc., 501 Carr Rd., Ste. 201, 19801, pg. 203 **PB**
BENEFICIAL CORPORATION, One Christina Ctr., 301 N. Walnut St., 19801, pg. 211 **PB**
Beneficial Credit Services, Inc., One Christina Ctr., 301 N. Walnut St., 19808, pg. 211 **PB**
Beneficial Management Corporation of America & Affiliated Corps., One Christina Ctr., 308 N. Walnut St., 19808, pg. 211 **PB**
Beneficial National Bank, One Christina Ctr., 301 N. Walnut St., 19808, pg. 211 **PB**
Bertelsmann Music Group, 1013 Centre Rd., 19805, pg. 191 **IT**
Brandywine Realty & Development, Inc., 2200 Concord Pike, 19803, pg. 165 **PV**
BRANDYWINE SPORTS, INC., 2200 Concord Pike, 19803, pg. 165 **PV**
CLIC Company I, 902 Market St., 19801-3015, pg. 1164 **PV**
CSC UNITED STATES, 1013 Center Rd., 19805, pg. 197 **PV**
CABRE CORP., 1209 Orange St., 19801, pg. 289 **PB**
Canadian Imperial Holdings, Inc., 100 W. Tenth St., 19801, pg. 257 **IT**
CANISCO RESOURCES, INC., 300 Delaware Ave., Ste. 714, 19801, pg. 301 **PB**
Capitol Outdoor Acquisition Co., Inc., One Beaver Valley Rd., 19850, pg. 361 **PB**
Capitol Outdoor Leasing Co., Inc., One Beaver Valley Rd., 19850, pg. 361 **PB**
Cariplo Finance Inc., c/o Corporation Trust Company, 1209 Orange St., 19801, pg. 275 **IT**
Carpenter Investments, Inc., Baynard Bldg., Room 209F, 3411 Silverside Dr., 19810, pg. 307 **PB**
Central Pennsylvania Investment Co., 1409 Foulk Rd., Ste. 102, 19803, pg. 1222 **PB**
Chase Manhattan Bank Delaware, 222 Delaware Ave., 19801, pg. 338 **PB**
The Chase Manhattan Bank (USA), NA, 802 Delaware Ave., 19801, pg. 338 **PB**
Chase Manhattan Overseas Banking Corporation, 802 Delaware Ave., 13th Fl., P.O. Box 15371, 19850, pg. 338 **PB**
Cigna Guaranty Holdings, Inc., One Beaver Valley Rd., 19850, pg. 357 **PB**
Cigna Healthcare of Delaware, Inc., One Beaver Valley Rd., Ste. CHP, 19803, pg. 359 **PB**
Cigna Healthcare of New Jersey, Inc., One Beaver Valley Rd., Ste. CHP, 19803, pg. 360 **PB**
Cigna Healthcare of Pennsylvania, Inc., One Beaver Valley Rd. Ste. CHP, 19803, pg. 360 **PB**
Cigna Holdings, Inc., One Beaver Valley Rd., 19850, pg. 357 **PB**
Cigna International Holdings, Ltd., P.O. Box 15047, One Beaver Valley Rd., 19850, pg. 363 **PB**
Cigna International Special Investments Inc., One Beaver Valley Rd., 19850, pg. 357 **PB**
Cigna Properties, Inc., P.O. Box 15047, One Beaver Valley Rd., 19850, pg. 358 **PB**
Cigna Real Estate, Inc., One Beaver Valley Rd., 19850, pg. 365 **PB**
Cigna Worldwide Insurance Company, One Beaver Valley Rd., 19850, pg. 365 **PB**
Robert F. Coleman, Inc., One Beaver Valley Rd., 19850, pg. 366 **PB**
Collective Mortgage Services, Inc., 5301 Limestone Rd., Ste. 224, 19808, pg. 1528 **PB**
Colonial Penn Group, Inc., 501 Silverside Rd., 19807, pg. 990 **PB**
Columbia Atlantic Trading Corporation, 20 Montchanin Rd., 19807, pg. 402 **PB**
Columbia Gas System Service Corp., 20 Montchanin Rd., 19807-0020, pg. 403 **PB**
Columbia LNG Corp., 20 Montchanin Rd., 19807, pg. 403 **PB**
Commerz Financial Products USA Inc., pg. 310 **IT**
CONECTIV, 800 King St., 19899, pg. 430 **PB**
CONSOLIDATED FURNITURE CORPORATION, 1201 N. Orange St, Ste. 790, 19801, pg. 265 **PV**
CONSTRUCTION MANAGEMENT SERVICE, 3600 Silverside Rd., 19810, pg. 266 **PV**
CoreStates Bank of Delaware NA, Three Beaver Valley Rd., 19803, pg. 447 **PB**
DCV INC., 3521 Silverside Rd., Ste. 2K, 19810, pg. 301 **PV**
DIMC, Inc., 300 Delaware Ave., STe. 522, 19801, pg. 1465 **PB**
Daimler-Benz Capital Inc., 1201 N. Market St., Ste. 1406, 19801, pg. 368 **IT**
Dawson International Investments (Kinross) Inc, 900 Market St., 19801, pg. 386 **IT**
Del-Prime, Inc., 103 Springer Bldg., 3411 Silverside Rd., 19810, pg. 1326 **PB**
Del-Vest Inc., 222 Delaware Ave., 19801, pg. 1243 **PB**
Delaware American Life Insurance Co., One Alico Plaza, 19801, pg. 84 **PB**
Delaware Charter Guarantee & Trust Co., 1013 Center Rd., 19805, pg. 885 **PV**
Delaware Computing Services Inc., 5700 Kirkwood Hwy., Ste. 205, 19808, pg. 184 **IT**
Delaware Reinsurance Company, One Beaver Valley Rd., 19850, pg. 363 **PB**
Delmarva Capital Investments, Inc., 800 King St., 19899, pg. 431 **PB**
Delmarva Power & Light Company, 800 King St., 19899, pg. 430 **PB**
DELPHI FINANCIAL GROUP, INC., 1105 N. Market St., Ste. 1230, 19899, pg. 496 **PB**
Dicalite Holdings, Inc., 103 Springer Bldg., 3411 Silverside Rd., 19810, pg. 903 **PV**
Disc Manufacturing Cinram, 1409 Foulk Rd., Ste. 102, 19803, pg. 293 **IT**
Du Pont Agricultural Products, 1007 Market St., 19898, pg. 531 **PB**
Du Pont Automotive Products, 1007 Market St., 19898, pg. 531 **PB**
DU PONT (E.I. DU PONT DE NEMOURS & CO.), 1007 Market St., 19898, pg. 530 **PB**
Du Pont Imaging Systems, Barley Mill Plaza, 19898, pg. 531 **PB**
Du Pont International, 1007 Market St., 19898, pg. 531 **PB**
Du Pont International Sales Corp., 1007 Market St., 19898, pg. 531 **PB**
Du Pont Materials & Logistics Division, 1007 Market St., 19898, pg. 531 **PB**
The Du Pont Merck Pharmaceutical Company, Dupont-Merck Plaza, P.O. Box 80723, 19880-0025, pg. 531 **PB**
Du Pont Printing & Publishing, P.O. Box 800300, 19880-0030, pg. 531 **PB**
EA Financial, Inc., 900 Market St., 19801, pg. 541 **PB**
Eaton Administration Corp., P.O. Box 8985, 1105 N. Market St., 19899, pg. 558 **PB**
Eaton International Corp., The Corporation Trust Company, 100 W. Tenth St., 19801, pg. 558 **PB**
Ebasco Corporation, 1209 Orange St., 19801, pg. 1587 **PB**
838 Investment Group, Inc., 838 Market St., 19899, pg. 1729 **PB**
Emcee Cellular, Inc., 103 Springer Bldg., 3411 Silverside Rd., 19810, pg. 571 **PB**
Emons Finance Corporation, Delaware Trust Bldg., 900 Market St., Ste. 200, 19801, pg. 578 **PB**
Encoat-North Arlington, Inc., Corporate Trust Center, 1209 Orange Street, 19801, pg. 1020 **PB**
Enserch Shirley, c/o Corporation Trust Center, 1209 Orange St., 19801, pg. 1587 **PB**
Environmental Financial Services Corp., c/o Gunnip & Co., 2625 Concord Pike, 19803, pg. 1208 **PB**
Equicor-Cigna Corporation, One Beaver Valley Rd., 19850, pg. 362 **PB**
Equicor Holdings, Inc., One Beaver Valley Rd., 19850, pg. 362 **PB**
Europ Assistance U.S. Holdings, Inc., 1209 Orange St., 19801, pg. 90 **IT**
European Catering Services, 1209 Grange St., 19801, pg. 560 **IT**
Executive Park, Inc., One Beaver Valley Rd., 19850, pg. 365 **PB**
F&P Holding, Inc., 222 Delaware Ave., 18974, pg. 449 **IT**
FCC National Bank, 300 N. King St., 19801, pg. 627 **PB**
FWI Holdings Inc., 1209 Orange St., 19801, pg. 519 **IT**
Fan Blade Associates, Inc., 1209 Orange St., 19801, pg. 1166 **IT**
First State Paper, Inc., P.O. Box 10007, 100 Paper Pl., 19720, pg. 223 **PV**
First USA Bank, Three Christina Ctr., 201 N. Walnut St., 19801, pg. 174 **PB**
First USA Federal Savings Bank, Three Christina Ctr., 201 N. Walnut St., 19801, pg. 174 **PB**
Forbo America Inc., 1105 N. Market St., 19801, pg. 497 **IT**
G-I Holdings Inc., 818 Washington St., 19801, pg. 433 **PV**
G Industries Corporation, 818 Washington St., 19801, pg. 433 **PV**
GK Finance Corporation, 900 Market St., 19801, pg. 459 **PV**
GRC Holding, Inc., 103 Springer Bldg., 3411 Silverside Rd., 19810, pg. 903 **PV**
Gamma INAC, Inc., One Beaver Valley Rd., 19850, pg. 365 **PB**
General Portfolios Corp., Mellon Bank Ctr., 10th Market St. S., 2nd Fl., 19801, pg. 695 **PB**
Gist-Brocades, Inc., 1105 N. Market St., Ste. 1300, 19801, pg. 1143 **IT**
Gypsum Wall Board Plant & Plaster Mill, P.O. Box 310, 19899, pg. 737 **PB**
HHH, Inc., Rodney Square North, 19890, pg. 847 **PB**
HSI Corp., 1403 Foulk Rd., Ste. 102, 19803, pg. 847 **PB**
Hard Rock Cafe International Inc., 1105 N. Market St., Ste. 1216, 19801, pg. 1087 **IT**
Hatzel & Buehler, Inc., 2093 Philadelphia Pike, 19810, pg. 266 **PV**
Hercules Credit, Inc., Hercules Plaza, 19894, pg. 810 **PB**
Hercules Food & Functional Products Co., Hercules Plaza, 19894, pg. 810 **PB**
HERCULES INCORPORATED, Hercules Plaza, 1313 N. Market St., 19894-0001, pg. 809 **PB**
Hercules Inc., Absorbent & Textile Products Group, Hercules Plaza, 19894, pg. 810 **PB**
Hercules Inc., Paper Technology Group, Hercules Plaza, 19894, pg. 810 **PB**
Hercules Inc., Resins Group, Hercules Plaza, 19894, pg. 810 **PB**
Hercules-Sanyo, Inc., 1313 N. Market St., 19894, pg. 810 **PB**
Hercules Trading Corp., Hercules Plaza, 19894, pg. 810 **PB**
Hewlett Packard Avondale, 2850 Centerville Rd., 19808-1610, pg. 816 **PB**
Horizon Initiatives, 1001 Jefferson St., Ste. 700, 19801, pg. 423 **PB**
Horizon Investment Corp., N. Market St., 19801, pg. 1205 **IT**
ICI Advanced Materials, Concord Pike & New Murphy Rd., 19897, pg. 663 **IT**

Geographic Index-U.S.

PB - *U.S. Public Companies Volume*
PV - *U.S. Private Companies Volume*
IT - *International Public & Private Companies Volume*

DELAWARE DIRECTORY OF CORPORATE AFFILIATIONS

ICI Agricultural Products, Delaware Corporate Center, Two Righter Pkwy., 19897, pg. 663 **IT**
ICI American Holdings Inc., Concord Plaza, 3411 Silverside Rd., 19850, pg. 663 **IT**
ICI Americas, Inc., Concord Plaza, 3411 Silverside Rd., 19850, pg. 663 **IT**
ICI Chemicals & Polymers, Concord Pike & New Murphy Rd., 19897, pg. 663 **IT**
ICI Colors, Concord Pike & New Murphy Rd., 19897, pg. 663 **IT**
ICI Films, Concord Pike & New Murphy Rd., 19897, pg. 664 **IT**
ICI Polyester Polymer, Concord Pike & New Murphy Rd., 19897, pg. 664 **IT**
ICI Specialties, Concord Pike & New Murphy Rd., 19897, pg. 664 **IT**
ICO, Inc., One Beaver Valley Road, 19850, pg. 361 **PB**
INA Financial Corporation, One Beaver Valley Rd., 19850, pg. 362 **PB**
INA Overseas Properties, Ltd., P.O. Box 15047, One Beaver Valley Rd., 19850, pg. 363 **PB**
IPM Inc., 3513 Concord Pike, Ste. 3000, 19803, pg. 1237 **PB**
ISP Global Technologies Inc., 818 Washington St., 19801, pg. 858 **PB**
ISP International Corp., 818 Washington St., 19801, pg. 858 **PB**
ISP Investments Inc., 818 Washington St., 19801, pg. 858 **PB**
Ikon Capital, 2625 Concord Pike, 19803, pg. 863 **PB**
Imasco Finance L.L.C., Corporate Trust Ctr., 1209 Orange St., 19801, pg. 112 **IT**
Innovative Data Services Inc., 3422 Old Capital Trail, Ste. 968, 19808, pg. 193 **PV**
International Petroleum Corporation of Delaware, 505 S. Market St., 19801, pg. 906 **PB**
Inter-Urban, Inc., 300 Delaware Ave., Ste. 307, 19801-1622, pg. 1700 **PB**
Intracorp, Inc., 1209 Orange St., 19801, pg. 362 **PB**
J & J Snack Foods Investment Corp., Wilmington Bank Bldg., 2nd Fl., Tenth & Market St., 19801, pg. 916 **PB**
Jones Holding Corporation, 300 Delaware Ave., Ste. 534, 19801-1622, pg. 933 **PB**
Jones Investment Co., Inc., 300 Delaware Ave., Ste. 534, 19801-1622, pg. 933 **PB**
Kao Corporation of America (DE), 902 N. Market St., Ste. 404, 19801, pg. 717 **IT**
KEEN COMPRESSED GAS CO., 101 Rogers Rd., 19801, pg. 611 **PV**
KEG Restaurants U.S., Inc., Corporate Trust Centre, 1209 Orange St., 19801, pg. 1499 **IT**
LF Corp., 1403 Foulk Rd., Ste. 102, 19803, pg. 1015 **PB**
L.S. Holding Company, One Beaver Valley Rd., 19850, pg. 358 **PB**
Latina Holdings, Ltd., One Beaver Valley Rd., 19850, pg. 363 **PB**
Legwear Holdings, Inc., 10173 Centre Rd., 19805, pg. 576 **IT**
Life Technologies Investment Holdings, Inc., 1013 Centre Rd., 19805, pg. 505 **PB**
MBNA America Bank N.A., 11th & King, 19884, pg. 1023 **PB**
MBNA Consumer Services, Inc., 11th & King, 19884-0131, pg. 1023 **PB**
MBNA CORPORATION, 1100 N. King St., 19884-0131, pg. 1023 **PB**
MBNA Insurance Services, 11th & King, 19884-0131, pg. 1023 **PB**
MBNA Marketing Systems, Inc., 11th & King, 19884, pg. 1023 **PB**
MEC USA, Inc., 7209 Orange Street, 19801, pg. 873 **IT**
Malrosian, Inc., One Beaver Valley Rd., 19850, pg. 357 **PB**
Mariana Properties, Inc., One Beaver Valley Rd., 19850, pg. 365 **PB**
Matlack (DE), Inc., One Rollins Plaza, Box 1791, 19899, pg. 1057 **PB**
MATLACK SYSTEMS, INC., 2200 Concord Pike, 19803, pg. 1057 **PB**
Mellon Bank (DE) National Association, Tenth & Market Sts., 19801, pg. 1085 **PB**
Merck Holdings, Inc., 902 N. Market St., Ste. 265, 19801, pg. 1091 **PB**
Merona Industries, Inc., 1105 N. Market St. - Ste, 1300, 19801, pg. 1239 **PB**
Modern Equipment Rentals Inc., 24 Brookside Dr., 19804, pg. 754 **PV**
Morgan Holdings Corp., 902 Market St., 19801, pg. 1129 **PB**
J.P. Morgan Delaware, 902 Market St., 19801, pg. 1129 **PB**
J.P. Morgan Trust Company of Delaware, 902 Market St., 19801, pg. 1130 **PB**
NC Builders Inc., 2000 Foulk Rd., Ste. F, 19810, pg. 775 **PV**
NIPA HARDWICKE, INC., 104 Hagley Bldg., 3411 Silverside Rd., 19810, pg. 771 **PV**
Nabisco Music Publishers, Inc., 1105 N. Market St., 19801, pg. 1355 **PB**
Nabisco Music Ventures, Inc., 1105 N. Market St., 19801, pg. 1355 **PB**
National Holding Investment Co., 200 W. Ninth St. Plaza, 19801, pg. 1159 **PB**
The New Galveston Company, 1209 Orange St., 19801, pg. 467 **PB**
New York Life & Health Insurance Company, 300 Delaware Ave., 19801, pg. 795 **PV**
NYLIFE Funding Inc., Ste. 780, 1100 N. Market St., 19801-1281, pg. 795 **PV**
The News-Journal Company, 831 Orange St., P.O. Box 1111, 19899, pg. 699 **PB**
Nippon Paint (USA) Inc., 911 Washington St., 19801-1545, pg. 937 **IT**
Nittany Investment Co., 1409 Foulk Rd., Ste. 102, 19803, pg. 1222 **PB**
Noma Corporation, 1209 Orange St., 19801, pg. 955 **IT**
Old Guard Group, Inc., P.O. Box 8985, 1105 N. Market St., 19899, pg. 1216 **PB**
PNC Bancorp Inc., 300 Delaware Ave., 19810, pg. 1243 **PB**
PNC Bank, Delaware, 222 Delaware Ave., 19801, pg. 1243 **PB**
PNC National Bank, 103 Belleview Pkwy., 19809, pg. 1243 **PB**
PNC National Investment Corporation, 300 Delaware Ave., 19810, pg. 1243 **PB**
Penn Virginia Equities Corp., 1105 N. Market St., Ste. 1300, 19801, pg. 1271 **PB**
Pepper, Hamilton & Scheetz, 1201 Market St., Ste. 1401, 19801-1163, pg. 851 **PV**
Pharos Holdings, Inc., 108 Webster Bldg., 3411 Silverside Rd., 19810, pg. 1289 **IT**
Philadelphia Drilling Company, One Beaver Valley Rd., 19850, pg. 358 **PB**
Philadelphia Eagle Drilling Corporation, P.O. Box 15047, One Beaver Valley Rd., 19850, pg. 358 **PB**
Philadelphia Falcon Drilling Corporation, One Beaver Valley Rd., 19850, pg. 358 **PB**
Philadelphia Investment Corporation of Delaware, One Beaver Valley Rd., 19850, pg. 357 **PB**
Philadelphia Jefferson Corporation, One Beaver Valley Road, 19850, pg. 365 **PB**
Philipp Holzmann USA, Inc., 1105 Market St., Ste. 1300, 19801, pg. 633 **IT**
Philips & Dupont Optical Company, 1409 Foulk Rd., Ste. 200, 19803-0469, pg. 1055 **IT**
Plenum Publishing Facilities, 3202 Kirkwood Hwy., 19808, pg. 1311 **PB**
Primerica Bank, P.O. Box 15069, 19850, pg. 1633 **PB**
Principal Health Care of Delaware, Inc., Little Falls Center #2, 2751 Centerville Rd., Ste. 400, 19808, pg. 885 **PV**
Prodair Corporation, 1105 N. Market St., Ste. 1300, 19801, pg. 31 **PB**
Provestco, Inc., P.O. Box 7048, 19713, pg. 892 **PV**
Prudential Securities Group Inc., 1220 N. Market St., 19801, pg. 893 **PV**
Quaker Chemical Corp., Silverside Carr Exec. Ctr., 501 Silverside Rd., Ste. 34, 19809, pg. 1346 **PB**
Quebecor Printing Corporation, Corporation Trust Center, 1209 Orange St., 19801, pg. 1078 **IT**
RGP HOLDING, INC., P.O. Box 7048, 19803, pg. 903 **PV**
REALCONN, Inc., One Beaver Valley Rd., 19850, pg. 365 **PB**
Redland America Corporation, 1105 N. Market St., Ste. 1300, 19899, pg. 1091 **IT**
Redland, Inc., P.O. Box 8985, 1105 N. Market St., Ste. 1300, 19899, pg. 1091 **IT**
Republic Overseas Banks Holding Corporation, 1201 Market St., 19801, pg. 1380 **PB**
Resource America, Inc., 2317 Pennsylvania Ave., 19806, pg. 1382 **PB**
RIBNY Overseas Investments Holding Corportation, 1201 Market St., Ste. 2200, 19801, pg. 1380 **PB**
John Rich & Sons, 900 Market St., Ste. 200, 19801, pg. 1188 **PV**
Rohm and Haas Capital Corporation, 3411 Silverside Rd., 19810, pg. 1403 **PB**
Rohm and Haas Credit Corporation, 3411 Silverside Rd., 19810, pg. 1403 **PB**
Rohm and Haas Equity Corporation, 3411 Silverside Rd., 19810, pg. 1403 **PB**
Rohm and Haas Latin America, Inc., 3411 Silverside Rd., 19810, pg. 1403 **PB**
Rohm and Haas Performance Plastics Inc., 3411 Silverside Rd., 19810, pg. 1403 **PB**
Rollins Logistics Inc., P.O. Box 1791, 19899, pg. 1405 **PB**
ROLLINS TRUCK LEASING CORP., One Rollins Plaza, 19803, pg. 1405 **PB**
SEI Corporation, 101C Ridgley Bldg., 3519 Silverside Rd., 19810-1921, pg. 1417 **PB**
SEP Inc., Corporation Trust Center, 1209 Orange St., 19801, pg. 1166 **IT**
SMS-Wilmington, 1010 Concord Ave., 19802, pg. 1463 **PB**
SWMIC Inc., 300 Delaware Ave., Ste. 522, 19801, pg. 1465 **PB**
Salem Asset Management Corp., 300 Delaware Ave., Ste. 1704, 19801, pg. 961 **PV**
Sandhills Inc., 913 N. Market St., Ste. 806, 19801, pg. 837 **PV**
Sauer Holdings, 715 King St., Ste. 310, 19801, pg. 968 **PV**
Savannah Investment Company, 300 Delaware Ave., Ste. 1704, 19899, pg. 873 **PB**
Schlumberger Industries, Inc., 100 W. Tenth St., 19801, pg. 1439 **PB**
Schlumberger Malco, Inc., 1209 Orange St., 19801, pg. 1439 **PB**
Schlumberger Technologies, Inc., 1209 Orange St., 19801, pg. 1439 **PB**
The Scottsdale Executive Centre Corporation, One Beaver Valley Rd., 19850, pg. 365 **PB**
Signal Investment & Management Co., Wilmington Trust Ctr., 1100 North Market St., Ste. 780, 19801-1239, pg. 342 **PB**
Skadden, Arps, Slate, Meagher & Flom LLP, One Rodney Sq., P.O. Box 636, 19899, pg. 1004 **PV**
Smurfit Plastic Packaging Div., 1204 East 12th St., 19802, pg. 1271 **IT**
Southern Cross Investment Co., 100 West Tenth St., 19899 pg. 662 **IT**
Southwest Stainless, L.P., 1403 Faulk Rd., Ste 102, 19803, pg. 847 **PB**
Spar Aerospace (U.S.) Limited, P.O. Box 551, One Rodney Sq., 19899, pg. 1288 **IT**
SPEAKMAN COMPANY, 301 E. 30th St., 19802, pg. 1021 **PV**
Spectra-Physics, Inc., 108 Webster Bldg., 3411 Silverside Rd., 19810, pg. 1289 **IT**
Spiegel Acceptance Corporation, 400 W. Ninth St., Ste. 101, 19801, pg. 1499 **PB**
Star States Development Co., 838 Market St., 19899, pg. 1729 **PB**
Stuart Disease Management Services, Inc., Little Falls Ctr. 1, Ste. 100, 2711 Centerville Rd., 19808, pg. 1525 **IT**
TC Capital Management Inc., 913 N. Market St., Ste. 806, 19801, pg. 837 **PV**
TDW Delaware, Inc., 1105 N. Market St., Ste. 1300, 19899, pg. 1180 **PV**
Tate & Lyle Inc., 1403 Foulk Rd., Ste. 19803, 19803, pg. 1357 **IT**
Technitrol International, Inc., 103 Springer Bldg., 19810, pg. 1564 **PB**
Technitrol Investments, Inc., P.O. Box 7048, 19803, pg. 1564 **PB**
Telefonica North America, Inc., 1209 Orange St., 19801, pg. 1372 **IT**
Thorn EMI Inc., Little Falls Center, 2751 Centerville Rd., Ste. 205, 19808, pg. 427 **IT**
The Timberland World Trading Company, Corporation Trust Center, 1209 Orange St., 19801, pg. 1609 **PB**
Times Leasing, Inc., c/o United States Corp. Co., 32 Loockerman Sq., Ste. L-100, 19901, pg. 1176 **PB**
TOWNSENDS, INC., 919 N. Market, Ste 420, 19801, pg. 1094 **PV**
TriStar Ventures Corporation, 20 Montchanin Rd., 19807, pg. 403 **PB**
Tyco Investment Corp., 902 N. Market St., Ste. 270, 19801, pg. 1058 **PB**
U.O.D., Inc., 300 Delaware Ave., Ste. 307, 19801-1622, pg. 1700 **PB**
Universal Technology Corp., 1105 N. Market St., 19801, pg. 1205 **IT**
U.O. Fenwick, Inc., 300 Delaware Ave., Ste. 307, 19801-1622, pg. 1700 **PB**
VIMRX PHARMACEUTICALS, INC., 2751 Centerville Rd., Ste. 210, 19808, pg. 1702 **PB**
VULCAN INTERNATIONAL CORPORATION, 300 Delaware Ave., Ste. 1704, 19801, pg. 1725 **PB**
WSFS FINANCIAL CORPORATION, 838 Market St., 19801, pg. 1728 **PB**
Waslic Company II, 902 Market St., 19801-3341, pg. 1164 **PV**
Waterford Foods USA, Inc., 1013 Center Rd., 19805, pg. 102 **IT**
The West Company of Delaware, Inc., 103 Springer Bldg., 3411 Silverside Rd., 19810, pg. 1755 **PB**
The Whitaker Corporation, 4550 New Linden Hill Rd., Ste. 450, 19808, pg. 8 **PB**
Wilmington Savings Fund Society (FSB), 838 Market St., 19801, pg. 1729 **PB**
WILMINGTON TRUST CORPORATION, Rodney Sq. N., 1100 N. Market St., 19890-0001, pg. 1770 **PB**
Winterthur U.S. Holdings Inc., P.O. Box 25130, 19899, pg. 345 **IT**
Woodward-Clyde, 1200 Philadelphia Pike, 19809, pg. 1657 **PB**
Xamak, 3411 Silverside Rd., 19810, pg. 1403 **PB**
Zeneca Engineering, Bancroft Bldg., Concorde Plaza, 19897, pg. 1525 **IT**
Zeneca Inc., P.O. Box 15438, 19850, pg. 1525 **IT**
Zeneca Plant Science, 1800 Concord Pike, 19897, pg. 1525 **IT**

Yorklyn

NVF COMPANY, 1166 Yorklyn Road, 19736, pg. 772 **PV**

DISTRICT OF COLUMBIA

Washington

ABC/Kane Productions International, Inc., 3333 K St. NW, Ste. 450, 20007, pg. 511 **PB**
Action Pay-Per-View, One BET Plaza, 1900 W Place NE, 20018, pg. 235 **PB**
Acxiom Corporation, 1155 Connecticut Ave. N.W., Ste. 300, 20036-4306, pg. 18 **PB**
Advanced Marketing Concepts, Inc., 1100 H St. N.W., 20080, pg. 1741 **PB**
ADWORKS, INC., 2401 Pennsylvania Ave., N.W., Ste. 200, 20037, pg. 23 **PV**
Aerospatiale Inc., 1101 Fifteenth St., N.W., Ste. 300, 20005, pg. 29 **IT**
Air France (Mid Atlantic Region), Ste. 312, 1120 Connecticut Ave., N.W., 20036, pg. 560 **IT**
Ajinomoto U.S.A., Inc., Washington D.C. Office, 1120 Connecticut Ave., N.W., Ste. 416, 20036, pg. 40 **IT**
Alenia S.p.A., 15th St., N.W., Ste. 610-1101, 20006, pg. 653 **IT**
Allbritton Communications Company, 800 17th St., N.W., Ste. 301, 20006, pg. 854 **PV**
Allbritton Group, Inc., 808 17th St. N.W., Ste. 300, 20006, pg. 854 **PV**
Allbritton News Bureau, Inc., 800 17th St. N.W., Ste. 301, 20006, pg. 854 **PV**
Allbritton Television Productions, Inc., Ste. 301, 800 17th St., N.W., 20006, pg. 854 **PV**
Allied Advertising Agency, Public Relations, 1100 17th St., N.W., Ste. 401, 20036, pg. 38 **PV**
Allied Capital Advisors, Inc., 1666 K St. N.W., 9th, 20006, pg. 47 **PB**

PB - *U.S. Public Companies Volume*
PV - *U.S. Private Companies Volume*
IT - *International Public & Private Companies Volume*

Geographic Index-U.S.

Allied Capital Commercial Corporation, 1666 K St. N.W., 9th Fl., 20006, pg. 47 **PB**

ALLIED CAPITAL CORPORATION, 1666 K St., N.W., Ninth Fl., 20006, pg. 47 **PB**

Allied Capital Corporation II, 1666 K St., 9th Fl., 20006, pg. 47 **PB**

Allied Capital Financial Corporation, 1666 K St., N.W. Ninth Fl., 20006, pg. 48 **PB**

Allied Capital Lending Corporation, 1666 K St. N.W., 9th Fl., 20006, pg. 48 **PB**

Allied Development Corp., 1666 K St. N.W., Ninth Fl., 20006, pg. 48 **PB**

Allied Investment Corp., 1666 K St. N.W., Ninth Fl., 20006, pg. 48 **PB**

Allright Parking Washington, Inc., 104 Irving St., N.W., 20010, pg. 43 **PV**

Alyeska Pipeline Service Company, 1667 K St., N.W., Ste. 450, 20006, pg. 48 **PV**

America Cafe, Union Station, 50 Massachusettes Ave., N.E., 20001, pg. 130

The American Bankers Association Insurance Association, 1120 Connecticut Ave. N.W., 20036, pg. 51 **PV**

The American Bankers Association Learning & Development Incorporated, 1120 Connecticut Ave. N.W., 20036, pg. 51 **PV**

The American Bankers Association Securities Association, 1120 Connecticut Ave., N.W., 20036, pg. 51 **PV**

THE AMERICAN BANKERS ASSOCIATION, 1120 Connecticut Ave., N.W., 20036, pg. 51 **PV**

AMERICAN ENTERPRISE INSTITUTE FOR PUBLIC POLICY RESEARCH, 1150 17th St. N.W., 20036, pg. 53 **PV**

American Financial Skylink Inc., 1120 Connecticut Ave. N.W., 20036, pg. 51 **PV**

American Mathematical Society Washington Office, 1527 18th St., N.W., 20036, pg. 59 **PV**

Amoco Research Center, 1615 M St. N.W., Ste. 200, 20036-3209, pg. 103 **PB**

AMTRAK-NATIONAL RAILROAD PASSENGER CORP., 60 Massachusetts Ave. N.E., 20002, pg. 68 **PV**

Arianespace, Inc., 700 13th St. N.W., Ste. 230, 20005, pg. 81 **IT**

ATLANTIC PLUMBING SUPPLY COMPANY, 807 V St., N.W., 20001, pg. 95 **PV**

BAA Mc Arthur-Glen Europe, 1900 K St. N.W., Ste. 6500, 20036, pg. 604 **PV**

BET Affiliate Marketing - YSB & Emerge Magazines, One BET Plaza, 1900 W Pl. N.E., 20018, pg. 235 **PB**

BET Cable Network Operations, 1899 Ninth St., N.E., 20018, pg. 235 **PB**

BET Direct, One BET Plaza, 1900 W Place NE, 20018, pg. 235 **PB**

BHP Petroleum (Americas) Inc., 1225 Eye Street NW, Ste. 500, 20005, pg. 225 **IT**

BNA Business Information Division, 1231 25th St. N.W., 20037, pg. 181 **PV**

BNA Environment & Safety Services Div., 1231 25th St., N.W., 20037, pg. 182 **PV**

BNA Health Care Information Division, 1231 25th St. N.W., 20037, pg. 182 **PV**

BNA Legal Services Div., 1231 25th St., N.W., 20037, pg. 182 **PV**

BNA PLUS, 1231 25th St. N.W., 20037, pg. 182 **PV**

BNA Software, 1231 25th St. N.W., 20037, pg. 182 **PV**

Banco do Brasil S.A.-Washington, 2020 K St. NW, Ste. 450, 20006, pg. 141 **IT**

Bank Marketing Association, 1120 Connecticut Ave. N.W., 20036, pg. 51 **PV**

BANNER AEROSPACE, INC., Dulles International Airport, 300 W. Service Rd., 20041, pg. 187 **PB**

Baring Asset Management Holdings, Inc., 700 13th St., N.W., Ste. 950, 20005, pg. 647 **IT**

Baring Private Equity Partners, 601 13th Street N.W., Ste. 450 N., 20005-3808, pg. 647 **IT**

Bayer Corporation, 1101 Pennsylvania Ave., N.W., Ste. 515, 20004-2514, pg. 172 **IT**

Bear Stearns Fiduciary Services, Inc., 805 15th St. N.W., Ste. 1120, 20005, pg. 198 **PB**

Bell Atlantic-Washington, D.C., Inc., 1710 H St., N.W., 20006, pg. 203 **PB**

BLACK ENTERTAINMENT TELEVISION HOLDINGS INC., One BET Plaza, 1900 W. Place, N.E., 20018-1211, pg. 235 **PB**

Blue Cross and Blue Shield Assn. Government Relations, Metropolitan Square Building, 655 Fifteenth St., N.W., Ste. 350, 20005, pg. 151 **PV**

Brandywood Estates, Inc., 1100 H St., N.W., 20080, pg. 1741 **PB**

THE BUREAU OF NATIONAL AFFAIRS, INC., 1231 25th St., N.W., 20037, pg. 181 **PV**

Burns & Roe Enterprises, Inc., 1400 'K' St. N.W., Ste. 910, 20005, pg. 187 **PV**

BUSINESS EQUIPMENT CENTER, 1615 M St. N.W., Ste. 100, 20036-3209, pg. 189 **PV**

CAB (Corporation for American Banking), 1120 Connecticut Ave., N.W., 20036, pg. 51 **PV**

California Microwave Navigation Systems, Inc., 2809 N. Glade St. N.W., 20016, pg. 293 **PV**

Calspan SRL Corporation, Ste. 1111, 800 Connecticut Ave., 20006, pg. 1136 **PV**

Canterbury Hotel, 1733 N Street N.W., 20036, pg. 1067 **PV**

Career Blazers of Washington, DC, 1025 Conneticut Ave. N.W., 20036, pg. 209 **PV**

The Carlyle Group, 1001 Pennsylvania Ave. N.W., 20004, pg. 213 **PV**

CARLYLE HOLDING CORPORATION, 1001 Pennsylvania Ave. N.W., Ste. 220 S., 20004, pg. 213 **PV**

Carr Real Estate Services, 1700 Pennsylvania Ave., N.W., 20006, pg. 309 **PB**

CARRAMERICA REALTY, 1700 Pennsylvania Ave. N.W., 20006, pg. 308 **PB**

Center Cafe, Union Station, 50 Massachusettes Ave., N.W., 20002, pg. 130 **PB**

CENTURY BANCSHARES, INC., 1275 Pennsylvania Ave. N.W., 20004, pg. 328 **PB**

Chemonics International-Consulting Div., 2000 M St., N.W., #200, 20036, pg. 591 **PB**

China Airlines Ltd., 1730 K St. N.W., Rm. 712, 20006, pg. 285 **IT**

Chubu Electric Power Co., Inc. (Washington Office), 900 17th St., N.W., Suite 1220, 20006, pg. 290 **IT**

Cineplex Odeon Corporation, 1101 23rd St. N.W., 20037, pg. 293 **IT**

Citicorp Savings of Washington, D.C., 1775 Pennsylvania Ave., N.W., 20006, pg. 377 **PB**

Clark & Weinstock, 888 16th St., NW, 20006, pg. 1223 **PB**

Coe & Clerici, Inc., 1133 Connecticut Ave., N.W., Ste. 1000, 20036, pg. 304 **PV**

Congressional Quarterly, 1414 22nd. St. NW, 20037, pg. 1088 **PV**

Correctional Treatment Facility, 1901 E. Street S.E., 20003, pg. 450 **PV**

Courtyard by Marriott, Marriott Dr., 20058, pg. 1048 **PB**

Crab Run Gas Co., 1100 H St., N.W., 20080, pg. 1740 **PB**

Crain Communications, Washington, D.C., 814 National Press Bldg., 20045-1801, pg. 285 **PV**

Criterion Life Insurance Co., One GEICO Plaza, 20076, pg. 219 **PB**

D.C. Chartered Health Plan, 820 First St. N.E., Ste. LL-100, 20002, pg. 1241 **PV**

DANAHER CORPORATION, 1250 24th St., N.W., Ste. 800, 20037, pg. 480 **PB**

Defense Credit Union Council, 805 15th St. N.W., 20005, pg. 288 **PV**

DeLeuw, Cather & Company, 1133 15th St., N.W., 20005, pg. 841 **PV**

DEMOCRATIC NATIONAL COMMITTEE, 430 S. Capitol St., S.E., 20003, pg. 324 **PV**

THE DONOHOE COMPANIES, INC., 2101 Wisconsin Ave. N.W., 20007, pg. 340 **PV**

EDF International North America, Inc., 1730 Rhode Island Ave., N.W., Ste. 509, 20036, pg. 437 **IT**

Eagle Tech Inc., 2100 Washington Blvd., 20009, pg. 1199 **PB**

Edelman Worldwide, Inc., 1420 K St., NW, 20005, pg. 362 **PV**

Electronic Warfare Systems, 490 L'Enfant Plaza East, S.W. #8206, 20024-2179, pg. 1002 **PB**

Emerge Communications, One BET Plaza, 1800 W Place NE, 20018, pg. 235 **PB**

Equifax Consumer Direct, 801 Pennsylvania Ave. N.W., Ste. 350, 20004, pg. 588 **PB**

Equifax Government & Special Services, 801 Pennsylvania Ave. N.W., Ste. 620, 20004, pg. 588 **PB**

Fairfield Inn, One Marriott Dr., 20058, pg. 1048 **PB**

Fairview Properties, Inc., 1729 H St., N.W., 20006, pg. 623 **PV**

FEDERAL NATIONAL MORTGAGE ASSOCIATION (FANNIE MAE), 3900 Wisconsin Ave. NW, 20016, pg. 615 **PB**

Fiduciary International, Inc., 1750 Pennsylvania Ave. N.W., Ste. 300, 20006, pg. 621 **PB**

First Union National Bank of Washington, 740 15th St. N.W., 20005, pg. 640 **PB**

Fleishman-Hillard, Inc., 1301 Connecticut Ave. N.W., 20036-1816, pg. 411 **PV**

FlightSafety Washington Office, 300 Metropolitan Sq., 655 15th St., N.W., 20005, pg. 219 **PB**

FOLGER NOLAN FLEMING DOUGLAS, 725 15th St., N.W., 20005, pg. 416 **PV**

FORMAN BROTHERS, INC., 4235 Sheriff Rd., N.E., 20019, pg. 418 **PV**

Foster Wheeler International Corporation, Ste. 650, 1667 K St., 20006, pg. 677 **IT**

Four Seasons Washington, 2800 Pennsylvania Ave. N.W., 20007, pg. 502 **IT**

Frontier Communications of the Mid Atlantic, Inc., 2100 M St., N.W., Ste. 306, 20037, pg. 683 **PB**

GEICO Casualty Company, One GEICO Plaza, 20076, pg. 219 **PB**

GEICO Corporation, One GEICO Plaza, 20076-0001, pg. 219 **PB**

GEICO Facilities Corporation, GEICO Plaza, 20076, pg. 219 **PB**

GEICO General Insurance Co., One GEICO Plaza, 20076-0001, pg. 219 **PB**

GEICO Indemnity Company, One GEICO Plaza, 20047-001, pg. 220 **PB**

GEICO Investment Services Co., GEICO Plaza, 20076, pg. 220 **PB**

GEICO Properties, Inc., GEICO Plaza, 20076, pg. 220 **PB**

GEICO Washington Properties, Inc., GEICO Plaza, 20076, pg. 220 **PB**

General Instrument Corporation, 1133 21st St. N.W., Ste. 405, 20036, pg. 716 **PB**

Goldman, Sachs & Co., 1101 Pennsylvania Ave., N.W., Ste. 900, 20004, pg. 462 **PV**

Governing Magazine, 1100 Connecticut Ave. 13th Fl., 20036, pg. 1088 **PV**

Government Employees Financial Corporation, One Geico Plaza, 20076, pg. 220 **PB**

Government Employees Insurance Co. (GEICO), One GEICO Plaza, 20076, pg. 220 **PB**

Grace Washington Inc., 919 18th St. NW, Ste. 400, 20007, pg. 755 **PB**

Hampshire Gas Co., 1100 H St., N.W., 20080, pg. 1740 **PB**

Hampshire Hotel, 1310 New Hampshire Ave., 20036, pg. 1067 **PV**

Hot Shoppes Cafeterias & Restaurants, Marriott Dr., 20058, pg. 1048 **PB**

Howard Johnson, 1430 Rhode Island Ave. N.W., 20005, pg. 1067 **PV**

ICF Kaiser Engineers, Blue Plains Treatment Plant, 5000 Overlook Ave. S.W., 20032, pg. 853 **PB**

ING Real Estate, 601 13th St., Ste. 450 N., 20005-3808, pg. 648 **IT**

Iberia Air Lines of Spain, 1825 K St., 20006, pg. 575 **IT**

The Industrial Bank of Japan, Limited (Washington), 1701 Pennsylvania Ave., N.W., Ste. 960, 20006, pg. 674 **IT**

Information Resources Division, 1231 25th St., N.W., 20037, pg. 182 **PV**

Institute of Certified Bankers, 1120 Connecticut Ave. N.W., 20036, pg. 51 **PV**

INTERAMERICAN DEVELOPMENT BANK, 1300 New York Ave., 20577, pg. 566 **PV**

International Telecommunications Satellite Organization (INTELSAT), 3400 International Dr. N.W., 20008-3098, pg. 223 **IT**

IRON ROAD RAILWAYS INC., 1300 Connecticut Ave. N.W., Ste. 903, 20036, pg. 575 **PV**

The Japan Development Bank-Washington, D.C. Representative Office, 1101-17th St., N.W., Ste. 1001, 20036, pg. 702 **IT**

S.C. Johnson & Son Inc., 900 17th St. N.W. Ste. 506, 20006-2501, pg. 592 **PV**

JOHNSTON, LEMON & CO. INC., 1101 Vermont Ave., N.W., Ste. 800, 20005, pg. 595 **PV**

Judd & Detweiler, Inc., 1500 Eckington Pl., N.E., 20002, pg. 855 **PV**

Judd's Incorporated, 1500 Eckington Pl., N.E., 20002, pg. 855 **PV**

KRT News & Information Services, 790 National Press Bldg., 20045, pg. 965 **PB**

THE KAEMPFER COMPANY, INVESTMENT BUILDERS, 1900 K St. N.W., Ste.650, 20036, pg. 604 **PV**

The Kansai Electric Power Co - Washington Office, 2001 L St. N.W., Ste. 801, 20036, pg. 723 **IT**

Kilborn SNC-Lavalin, 1815 H St. N.W., Ste. 500, 20006, pg. 1152 **IT**

THE KIPLINGER WASHINGTON EDITORS, INC., 1729 H St., N.W., 20006, pg. 623 **PV**

Korn/Ferry International, Presidential Plaza, 900 19th St., N.W., 20006, pg. 633 **PV**

Legi-Slate Inc., 777 N. Capitol St., 20002, pg. 1743 **PB**

Lockheed-Martin W.I.C., 401 M St. S.W., 20024-2610, pg. 1007 **PB**

MCI Telecommunications Corp., 1801 Pennsylvania Ave. N.W., 20006, pg. 1024 **PB**

MRCO, 111 Massachusetts Ave., N.W., 20001, pg. 1116 **PV**

MTel International, 1350 J Street N.W., Ste. 1100, 20005, pg. 1120 **PV**

Marriott Distribution Services (MDS), Marriott Dr., 20058, pg. 1048 **PB**

Marriott Hotels, Resorts, and Suites, Marriott Dr., 20058, pg. 1048 **PB**

MARRIOTT INTERNATIONAL, INC., One Marriott Dr., 20058, pg. 1047 **PB**

Marriott Management Services (MMS), Marriott Dr., 20058, pg. 1048 **PB**

Marriott Ownership Resorts, Marriott Dr., 20058, pg. 1048 **PB**

Marriott Senior Living Services, Marriott Dr., 20058, pg. 1048 **PB**

Martin Marietta Air Traffic Systems, 475 School Street, SW, 20024, pg. 1007 **PB**

Maryland Ventures, Inc., GEICO Plaza, 20076, pg. 220 **PB**

MAURICE ELECTRIC SUPPLY COMPANY, 500 Penn St., N.E., 20002, pg. 715 **PV**

McGraw-Hill Continuing Education Center, 4401 Connecticut Ave., 20008, pg. 1070 **PV**

Merrill/Washington, 06, 1776 I St., N.W., Ste. 225, 20006, pg. 1097 **PV**

Microsoft Federal Systems, 5335 Wisconsin Ave. N. W. 20015-2030, pg. 1108 **PV**

Mitsui & Co. (U.S.A.), Inc., Ste. 400; 1701 Pennsylvania Ave., N.W., 20006, pg. 879 **IT**

J.P. Morgan Securities Inc., 1300 I St. N.W., 10th Fl., 20005, pg. 1129 **PB**

NKK America Inc., 1215 17th St. N.W., 20036, pg. 902 **IT**

NRI Schools, 4401 Connecticut Ave., N.W., 20008, pg. 1071 **PB**

Nacional Financiera, 1615 L St., N.W. Ste. 310, 20036, pg. 904 **IT**

National Bank of Pakistan, 1825 Connecticut Ave. N.W., 20009, pg. 908 **IT**

National Cattlemen's Beef Association, 1301 Pennsylvania Ave. N.W., Ste. 300, 20004, pg. 780 **PV**

NATIONAL GEOGRAPHIC SOCIETY, 1145 17th St. NW, 20036, pg. 783 **PV**

NATIONAL JOURNAL GROUP, 1501 M St. N.W., 3rd Fl., 20005, pg. 785 **PV**

NATION'S BUSINESS, 1615 H St., N. W., 20062-2000, pg. 788 **PV**

NationsBank Metro, 1801 K St., N.W., 20006, pg. 1162 **PB**

NewsEdge Corp., 1129 20th St. N.W., Ste. 410, 20036, pg. 1180 **PV**

Nichimen America, Inc., Washington Office, 1111 19th St. N.W., Ste. 404, 20036, pg. 928 **IT**

North American Representative Office (NARO), 1730 Pennsylvania Ave., N.W. Ste. 975, 20006, pg. 89 **IT**

OCE, 20 Massachusetts Ave. N.W., 20314-0002, pg. 994 **IT**

Olivetti, 1129 N. Hamp Ave., 20037, pg. 1002 **IT**

Paige Publications, One BET Plaza, 1900 W Place NE, 20018, pg. 235 **PB**

Pepper, Hamilton & Scheetz, 1300 Nineteenth St., N.W., 20036-1685, pg. 851 **PV**

Pequod Associates, 611 Pennsylvania Ave., 20003, pg. 590 **PB**

PB - *U.S. Public Companies Volume*
PV - *U.S. Private Companies Volume*
IT - *International Public & Private Companies Volume*

Geographic Index-U.S.

PERPETUAL CORPORATION, 808 17th St. N.W., Ste. 300, 20006, pg. 854 PV
Pitney Bowes Management Services, 901 E. St. N.W., 20004-2037, pg. 1304 PB
Plaza Resources Company, GEICO Plaza, 20076, pg. 220 PB
Portals Confederation Corporation, 1025 Vermont Ave., 20005, pg. 326 IT
POSAM Washington Office, 1800 K St., Ste. 1110, 20006, pg. 1062 IT
Potomac Capital Investment Corporation, 1801 K St., N.W., Ste. 900, 20006-1301, pg. 1319 PB
POTOMAC ELECTRIC POWER COMPANY, 1900 Pennsylvania Ave., N.W., 20068, pg. 1318 PB
QUADRANGLE DEVELOPMENT CORPORATION, 1001 G St., N.W., Ste. 700 W., 20001, pg. 898 PV
Quadrangle Management Company, 1001 G. St., N.W., Ste. 700 W, 20036, pg. 898 PV
Quality Hotel Downtown, 1315 16th St. N.W., 20036, pg. 1067 PV
Quik Park Inc., 1001 G. St., N.W., Ste. 700 W, 20036, pg. 898 PV
RTCdirect, 1055 Thomas Jefferson St. N.W., Ste. 500, 20007, pg. 1483 IT
Reed Travel Publishing-Washington D.C., 1156 15th St. N.W., Ste. 302, 20005, pg. 1097 IT
Residence Inn, Marriott Dr., 20058, pg. 1048 PB
Riggs Bank N.A., 1503 Pennsylvania Ave., N.W., 20005, pg. 1390 PB
Riggs Investment Management Corporation, 808 17th St., N.W., 20006, pg. 1390 PB
RIGGS NATIONAL CORPORATION, 800 17th St. N.W., 20006, pg. 1389 PB
Rosendorf/Evans, 1750 K St. N.W., 20006, pg. 597 PB
Russ Reid Co., 1300 I St. N.W., Ste. 250W, 20005, pg. 952 PV
SGS - Permanent Delegation to the International Financial Institutions, 1800 Massachusetts Ave., N.W., 6th Fl., 20036-1872, pg. 1153 IT
SLM HOLDING CORP., 1050 Thomas Jefferson St. N.W., 20007, pg. 1419 PB
Sandoz Pharmaceuticals Corp., 1615 L St. N.W., Ste. 1320, 20036-5610, pg. 974 IT
Sequoia, Washington Harbour, 20090, pg. 130 PB
SIGAL CONSTRUCTION CORP., 3299 K St. N.W., 20007, pg. 999 PV
Singapore Airlines Ltd., 1050 17th St., N.W., Ste. 480, 20036, pg. 1374 IT
Skadden, Arps, Slate, Meagher & Flom LLP, 1440 New York Ave., N.W., 20005, pg. 1004 PV
SkyTel Corp., 1350 I St., N.W., Ste. 1100, 20005, pg. 1120 PB
B. Smith's (D.C.), Union Station, 50 Massachusetts Ave., N.E., 20002, pg. 130 PB
Super Concrete Corp., 5001 Fort Toten Dr. N.E., 20011, pg. 166 IT
TAJ INTERNATIONAL HOTELS, 1315 16th St., N.W., 20036, pg. 1067 PV
Tax Management, Inc., 1250 23rd St., N.W., 2nd Fl., 20037, pg. 182 PV
Taylor & Francis, 1101 Vermont Ave. N.W., Ste. 200, 20005, pg. 1358 IT
TEMPS & COMPANY, 2000 Pennsylvania Ave. N.W., Ste. 104, 20006, pg. 1075 PV
Thai Airways Intl. Ltd.-Washington, 601 13th St., N.W., Ste. 390, 20005, pg. 1381 IT
Timmons & Company Inc., 1850 K St. N.W., Ste. 850, 20006, pg. 1483 IT
The Tokyo Electric Power Company-Washington, 1901 L St. N.W., Ste. 720, 20036, pg. 1394 IT
Chas. H. Tompkins Co., 1333 H St., N.W., 20005, pg. 633 IT
The Top Five Club, Inc., GEICO Plaza, 20076, pg. 220 PB
Trust Fund Advisors, Inc., 111 Massachusetts Ave., N.W., 20001, pg. 1116 PV
UST Fiduciary Services, Ltd., 1300 Eye St. N.W. #1080 E., 20005, pg. 1688 PB
ULICO Casualty Company, 111 Masachusetts Ave., N.W., 20001, pg. 1116 PV
ULICO Indemnity, 111 Massachusetts Ave., N.W., 20001, pg. 1116 PV
ULLICO INC., 111 Massachusetts Ave., N.W., 20001, pg. 1115 PV
The Union Labor Life Insurance Co., 111 Massachusetts Ave., N.W., 20001, pg. 1116 PV
Union Standard of America Life Insurance Co., 111 Masachusetts Ave., N.W., 20001, pg. 1116 PV
Unioncare, Inc., 111 Massachusetts Ave., N.W., 20001, pg. 1116 PV
UNIRISC, Inc., North Bldg., 1120 20th St., N.W., Ste. 720, 20036, pg. 117 PB
USA FLORAL PRODUCTS, INC., 1025 Thomas Jefferson St., Ste. 600W, 20007, pg. 1685 PB
U.S. OFFICE PRODUCTS COMPANY, 1025 Thomas Jefferson St. N.W. Ste. 600E, 20007, pg. 1686 PB
WJLA-TV, 3307 Tilden Street, N.W., 20008, pg. 854 PV
WMAL, Inc., 4400 Jennifer St., N.W., 20015, pg. 512 PB
WMZQ-AM/FM, 5513 Connecticut Ave., NW, 20015, pg. 779 PV
WRQX-FM, 4400 Jennifer St., N.W., 20015, pg. 512 PB
WTTG, 5151 Wisconsin Ave., N.W., 20016, pg. 926 IT
WUSA-TV, 4100 Wisconsin Ave., N.W., 20015, pg. 702 PB
Washington Analysis Corporation, 1130 Connecticut Ave. NW, Ste. 210, 20036, pg. 911 IT
Washington Gas Energy Systems, Inc., 1100 H St., N.W., 20080, pg. 1741 PB
THE WASHINGTON POST COMPANY, 1150 15th St. N.W., 20071, pg. 1742 PB
The Washington Post National Weekly Edition, 1150 15th St. N.W., 20071, pg. 1743 PB
Washington Post Newspaper Division, 1150 15th St., 20071, pg. 1743 PB
The Washington Post Writers Group, 1150 15th St. N.W., 20071, pg. 1743 PB
Washington Service Bureau, Inc., 655 Fifteenth St., N.W., 20005, pg. 1513 IT
Washington Terminal Company, 50 Massachusetts Ave., N.E., 20002, pg. 69 PV
Westinghouse Government Operations, 600 New Hampshire Ave.,N.W., Ste. 1200, 20037, pg. 273 PB
THE WORLD BANK, 1818 H St., N.W., 20433, pg. 1188 PV
Worldwide Assistance Services Inc., 1133 15th St. NW, Ste. 400, 20005, pg. 90 IT
Zenith Administrators, Inc., 111 Massachusetts Ave., N.W., 20001, pg. 1116 PV

FLORIDA

Alachua

Driltech Inc., P.O. Box 338, Driltech Dr., 32615, pg. 1352 IT
HUNTER MARINE CORPORATION, Rte. 441, 32615, pg. 549 PV

Altamonte

Property Asset Management, 237 S. Westmonte Dr., Ste. 240, 32714, pg. 891 PV

Altamonte Springs

The Crossings Associates, 600 N. Lake Blvd., Ste. 140, 32701, pg. 361 PB
ECI Telecom Inc., 927 Fern St., 32701, pg. 643 IT
EDD-Florida, 650 S. Northlake Blvd., Ste. 400, 32701, pg. 205 PB
Evans Environmental & Geological Science and Management, Inc., 445 Douglas Ave., 32714, pg. 563 PB
Gould Paper of Florida, Inc., 825 Sunshine Ln., 32714, pg. 467 PV
GREATER CONSTRUCTION CORP., 1105 Kensington Park Dr., 32714, pg. 476 PV
Horizon Place Associates, 600 N. Lake Blvd., Ste. 140, 32701, pg. 361 PB
I.V. One, 285 W. Central Pkwy., Ste. 1719, 32714-2554, pg. 229 PB
PCA Solutions, P.O. Box 166007, 32716, pg. 1293 PB
PENCO-Florida, 1180 Spring Centre S. Blvd., 32714, pg. 1508 IT
Priority Healthcare Corporation, 285 W. Central Pkwy., Ste. 1704, 32714-2554, pg. 229 PB
Rauland-Borg Corporation of Florida, 474 S. N. Lake Blvd., Ste. 1016, 32701, pg. 911 PV
Richardson Electronics Ltd.-Southeastern, 283 N. Lake Blvd., 32701, pg. 1388 PB
Security Warranty Association of Florida, 505 Mailland Ave., 32701, pg. 1231 PB
TRI-CITY ELECTRICAL CONTRACTORS INC., 430 West Dr., 32714, pg. 1100 PV
ULLO INTERNATIONAL, INC., 901 Douglas Ave., Ste. 100, 32714, pg. 1116 PV
Vorwerk USA Inc., 973 Sunshine La., 32714, pg. 1481 IT

Apopka

Hydro Conduit Corp., P.O. Box 17008, 2313 Vulcan Rd., 32860, pg. 246 IT
Laser Systems, 2787 S. Orange Blossom Trail, 32703-4397, pg. 1002 PB
Lehigh Utilities Inc., c/o Southern States Utilities, Inc. 100 Color Pl., 32703, pg. 1116 PB
Omega Environmental Inc., 3102 S. Ovarland Rd., 32703, pg. 1222 PB
TPS Technologies Inc., 2070 South Orange Blossom Trail, 32703, pg. 1594 PB
VJ GROWERS, INC., 500 W. Orange Blossom Trail, 32712, pg. 1130 PV

Arcadia

Grove Division, Rte. 1 Box 889, 33821, pg. 1229 PB
The Orchid Center, P.O. Box 1116, 33821, pg. 1050 PV
SUN BULB COMPANY, INC., 1615 S.W. Hwy. 17, 34266, pg. 1050 PV
Sun Chemical Company, Inc., P.O. Box 309, 33821, pg. 1050 PV

Auburndale

Auburndale Star, 213 E. Lake Ave., Box 126, 33823-9998, pg. 995 PV
COLORADO BOXED BEEF CO., 302 Progress Rd., 33823, pg. 25 PV
Fleetwood Homes of Florida, Inc.-Auburndale, 700 S. Bartow Ave., 33823, pg. 651 PB
Sheppard Foodservice, Inc., 601 Page St., 33823, pg. 1529 PV

Aventura

AlliedSignal Fluorocarbons, 20801 Biscayne Blvd., Ste. 435, 33180, pg. 51 PB
Coscan Waterways, Inc., 21169 Yacht Club Dr., 33180, pg. 228 IT
Northern Trust Bank of Florida, N.A., 3001 Aventura Blvd., 33180, pg. 1196 PB
Poe & Brown of Florida, 18305 Biscayne Blvd., Ste. 401, 33160, pg. 1312 PB

Avon Park

Sebring News-Sun, 2227 U.S. 27 S., 33870, pg. 1175 PB
SUNPURE LTD., 1600 W. SunPure Rd., 33825, pg. 1053 PV

Bartow

Concentrate Division, P.O. Box 2158, 33830, pg. 1229 PB
HOMES OF MERIT INC., Bartow Air Base, Bldg. 121, 33830, pg. 537 PV
ORANGE-CO., INC., 2020 U.S. Hwy. 17 S., 33830-2158, pg. 1229 PB

Belle Glade

ATLANTIC SUGAR ASSOCIATION, INC., 26400 State Rd. 880, 33430, pg. 95 PV
SUGAR CANE GROWERS COOPERATIVE OF FLORIDA, Airport Road, P.O. Box 666, 33430, pg. 1049 PV

Big Pine Key

Crain Broadcasting, Rte. 5, Box 183E, 33043-9782, pg. 285 PV

Boca Raton

ADT Security Services, One Boca Pl., P.O. Box 5035, 2255 Glades Rd., 33431-0835, pg. 1648 PB
AiC National Projects Office, 621 N.W. 53rd St., Ste. 140, 33487-8211, pg. 110 PB
Alber Engineering, Inc., 990 S. Rogers Circle, 33487-2813, pg. 126 IT
Alewife Boston Ltd., One Town Center Rd., 33486-1010, pg. 755 PB
Alro Group, Boca Raton, P.O. Box 3031, 6200 Park of Commerce Blvd., 33431-0931, pg. 46 PV
Arvida, 7900 Glades Road, 33429, pg. 578 PV
Bank of America Illinois Trust Company of Florida, N.A., One Boca Pl., 2255 Glades Rd., Ste. 337 W, 33431, pg. 181 PB
BITOR America Corp., 5100 Town Center Cir., Ste. 450, 33486, pg. 1045 IT
Boca Raton Convalescent Center, 755 Meadows Rd., 33432, pg. 1712 PB
Boca Raton News, Inc., Box 580, 33 S.E. Third St., 33432, pg. 259 PV
BOCA RESEARCH INC., 1377 Clint Moore Rd., 33487, pg. 239 PB
BROTHERS GOURMET COFFEES, INC., One Boca Place, 2255 Glades Rd., Ste. 100E, 33431, pg. 259 PB
CASI-RUSCO INC., 1155 Broken Sound Pkwy., N.W., 33487, pg. 218 PV
Chiron Vision, 4800 N. Federal Hwy., 33431, pg. 350 PB
COMPUTER PRODUCTS, INC., 7900 Glades Rd., Ste. 500, 33434, pg. 422 PB
CONCORD ASSETS GROUP, 150 E. Palmentto Park Rd., 4th Fl., 33432, pg. 261 PV
Coscan Florida, Inc., Ste. 400 East Bldg., 1900 Corporate Blvd. N.W., 33431, pg. 228 IT
Darex Puerto Rico, Inc., One Town Center Rd., 33486-1010, pg. 755 PB
Dewey and Almy Company, One Town Center Rd., 33486-1010, pg. 755 PB
Dreamport, Inc., 5801 N. Congress Ave., 33487, pg. 767 PB
Ecarg, Inc., One Town Ctr. Rd., 33486, pg. 755 PB
ENGLE HOMES, INC., 123 N.W. 13th St., Ste. 300, 33432, pg. 583 PB
Fleet Bank, F.S.B., 2255 Glades Rd., 33431, pg. 649 PB
The Fountains, 3800 N. Federal Hwy., 33431, pg. 1256 PB
Gloucester New Communities, One Town Center Rd., 33486-1010, pg. 755 PB
Grace A-B Inc., One Town Center Rd., 33486-1010, pg. 755 PB
Grace Chemical Company of Cuba, One Town Center Rd., 33486-1010, pg. 755 PB
Grace Communications, Inc., One Town Center Rd., 33486-1010, pg. 755 PB
Grace Environmental Inc., One Town Center Rd., 33486-1010, pg. 755 PB
Grace H-G Inc., One Town Center Rd., 33486-1010, pg. 755 PB
Grace PAR Corporation, One Town Center Rd., 33486-1010, pg. 755 PB
W.R. GRACE & CO., One Town Ctr. Rd., 33486-1010, pg. 754 PB
W.R. Grace Capital, One Town Center Rd., 33486-1010, pg. 755 PB
W.R. Grace Land Corporation, One Town Center Rd., 33486-1010, pg. 755 PB
Hampton Lakes Associates, 220 Glades Rd., Ste. 702, 33431, pg. 361 PB
Hanover Square Corporation, One Town Center Rd., 33486-1010, pg. 755 PB
ITW Mima, Inc., 1081 Holland Dr., 33487, pg. 866 PB
Intergraph Corporation, The North 40, Ste. Cw230, 5201 Congress Ave., 33487, pg. 891 PB
INTERNATIONAL SEAWAY TRADING CORPORATION, 7100 W. Camino Real, Ste. 110, 33433, pg. 572 PV
INVESTORS INSURANCE GROUP, INC., 7200 W. Camino Real, 33433, pg. 911 PB

Geographic Index-U.S.

PB - *U.S. Public Companies Volume*
PV - *U.S. Private Companies Volume*
IT - *International Public & Private Companies Volume*

LDDS WorldCom, 1515 S. Federal Hwy., #400, 33432, pg. 1779 **PB**

Leisegang Medical, Inc., 6401 Congress Ave., 33487, pg. 698 **PB**

Levitt Corporation, 7777 Glades Rd., Ste. 440, 33434, pg. 1035 **PV**

Levitz Furniture Corporation, 6111 Broken Sound Pkwy., N.E., 33487-2799, pg. 990 **PV**

LEVITZ FURNITURE INCORPORATED, 6111 Broken Sound Pkwy. N.W., 33487-2799, pg. 990

H. Miller & Sons, Inc., 9033 Glades Road, Ste. A, 33434, pg. 989 **PB**

Monolith Enterprises, Inc., One Town Center Rd., 33486-1010, pg. 755 **PB**

NABI, 5800 Park of Commerce Blvd. N.W., 33487, pg. 1148 **PB**

Northern Trust Bank of Florida, N.A., 301 Yamato Rd., 33431, pg. 1196 **PB**

PURITY WHOLESALE GROCERS, 6413 Congress Ave., Ste. 250, 33487, pg. 896 **PV**

Rexall Inc. Consumer Products Div., 851 Broken Sound Pkwy., N.W., 33487, pg. 1384 **PB**

REXALL SUNDOWN INC., 851 Broken Sound Pkwy. N.W., 33487, pg. 1384 **PB**

SENSORMATIC ELECTRONICS CORPORATION, 951 Yamato Rd., 33431-0700, pg. 1457 **PB**

Sony Professional Products Co., 6500 Congress Ave., 33487-2808, pg. 1284 **IT**

Symbol, 7900 Glades Rd., Ste. 340, 33434, pg. 1546 **PB**

Thompson Nutritional Products, 851 Broken Sound Pkwy, N.W., 33487, pg. 1384 **PB**

Town Colony Associates, 933 Clint Moore Rd., 33431, pg. 362 **PB**

Town Colony II Associates, 2200 Glades Rd., 33431, pg. 362 **PB**

Trans Leasing International, Inc.-Southeast Region, 777 Yamato Rd., Ste. 116, 33431, pg. 1628 **PB**

U.S. Trust Mortgage Service Company, 280 E. Palmetto Park Rd., 33432, pg. 1688 **PB**

W.R.C. Technical Ventures, One Town Center Rd., 33486-1010, pg. 755 **PB**

Water Street Corporation, One Town Center Rd., 33486-1010, pg. 755 **PB**

Woolwich Sewer Company, Inc., One Town Center Rd., 33486-1010, pg. 755 **PB**

Woolwich Water Company, Inc., One Town Center Rd., 33486-1010, pg. 755 **PB**

WORRELL ENTERPRISES, INC., 1450 S. Dixie Hwy., 33432, pg. 1191 **PV**

Bonita Springs

Northern Trust Bank of Florida, N.A., 26790 S. Tamiami Trail, 33923, pg. 1196 **PB**

WCI COMMUNITIES, INC., 24301 Walden Ctr. Dr., 34134, pg. 1144 **PV**

Boynton Beach

Boulevard Manor Nursing Center, 2839 S. Seacrest Blvd., 33435, pg. 1256 **PB**

Contemporary Communications Corporation, 1500 N.W. 22nd Ave., 33426-8292, pg. 1137 **PB**

Contemporary Digital Services, Inc., 1500 N.W. 22nd Ave., 33426-8292, pg. 1137 **PB**

Contemporary Group, Inc., 1500 Gateway Blvd., 33426-8292, pg. 1137 **PB**

Embarc Communication Services, Inc., 1500 N.W. 22nd Ave., 33426-8292, pg. 1137 **PB**

Empire Communications Consultants, Inc., 1500 N.W. 22nd Ave., 33426-8292, pg. 1137 **PB**

MLM Florida Yellow Pages Company, Inc., 1901 S. Congress, 33426, pg. 767 **PV**

Motorola Messaging, Information & Media Inc., 1500 N.W. 22nd Ave., 33426, pg. 1138 **PB**

Motorola North American Paging Subscriber Division, 1500 Gateway Blvd., #110, 33498, pg. 1137 **PB**

Motorola Paging Subscriber Group, 1500 Gateway Blvd., #110, 33498, pg. 1137 **PB**

Sermatech Southeast, 507 Industrial Way, 33426-3644, pg. 1570 **PB**

Bradenton

Beall's Dept. Stores, 1806 38th Ave. E., 34206, pg. 126 **PV**

BEALL'S, INC., 1806 38th Ave. E., 31208, pg. 126 **PV**

Bealls Outlet Inc., 1806 38th Ave. E., 34206, pg. 126 **PV**

The Bradenton Herald, Inc., 102 Manatee Ave. W., 34205, pg. 964 **PB**

Champssports, 311 Manatee Ave. W., 34205, pg. 1777 **PB**

Charter Behavioral Health System at Manatee Adolescent Treatment Services, Inc., 1324 37th Ave., E., 34208, pg. 1033 **PB**

Charter Behavioral Health System of Bradenton, Inc., 4480 51st St., W., 34210, pg. 1033 **PB**

Cook/Sarasota Moving Systems Inc., 4505 30th St., W., 34207, pg. 273 **PV**

Florida Sun Publications, Inc., 717 First St., 34208, pg. 1026 **IT**

NEW ENGLAND MACHINERY, INC., 6204 29th St. E., 34203, pg. 793 **PV**

Northern Trust Bank of Florida, N.A., 233 15th St., W., 34205, pg. 1196 **PB**

TS Publications (Florida), Inc., 717 First St. East, 34206, pg. 1320 **IT**

Team Edition Apparel, Inc., 4208 19th St., Court East, 34208, pg. 1777 **PB**

Thermal Equipment Systems, Inc., P.O. Box 20746, 4024 Murfield Dr. E., 34203, pg. 360 **PV**

Tropicana Dole Beverages North America, 1001 13th Ave. E., 34208, pg. 1217 **IT**

Brandon

Atlantic Works, 524 Grand Regency, 33541, pg. 1017 **PB**

Wehr Constructors, Inc., 917 S. Parsons, 33511, pg. 1159 **PV**

Brooksville

Hernando County Jail, 16425 Spring Hill Dr., 34609, pg. 450 **PB**

Poe & Brown of Florida, 614 E. Jefferson, 34601, pg. 1312 **PB**

SunTrust Bank, Nature Coast, One E. Jefferson St., 34601, pg. 1537 **PB**

Thomas & Betts/Amerace, 16228 Flight Path Dr., 34609, pg. 1598 **PB**

Bushnell

Speedling Incorporated Bushnell Division, P.O. Box 307, 33513, pg. 1024 **PV**

Sumter County Times, 303 E. McCollum Ave., 33513, pg. 648 **PB**

Canal Point

Bryant Sugar House, 111 Ponce de Leon Ave., 33438, pg. 1126 **PB**

Cantonment

Pensacola Mill, Champion International Corporation, 375 Muscogee Rd., 32533, pg. 334 **PB**

Cape Canaveral

Johnson Controls World Services Inc., 7315 N. Atlantic Ave., 32920, pg. 932 **PB**

Kennedy Space Center Operations, Kennedy Space Ctr., 32899, pg. 1597 **PB**

United Technologies Chemical Systems Division, P.O. Box 222, 32920-0222, pg. 1690 **PB**

Cape Coral

BVK/McDonald, 3625 Del Prado Blvd., 33904, pg. 108 **PB**

Cape Coral National Bank, 2724 Del Prado Blvd., 33904, pg. 607 **PB**

Country Club Inn, Inc., 4003 Palm Tree Blvd., 33904, pg. 151 **PV**

Dekoron/Unitherm Division, 1531 Commerce Creek Blvd., 33909, pg. 689 **PV**

Casselberry

Devco of Orlando, Inc., P.O. Box 176, 32707, pg. 988 **PV**

Intergraph Corporation, 950 S. Winter Park Dr., Ste. 325, 32707, pg. 891 **PV**

ROYAL JEEP EAGLE CHRYSLER PLYMOUTH, INC., 485 Cimeron Blvd., 32707, pg. 948 **PV**

Clearwater

AEROSONIC CORPORATION, 1212 N. Hercules Ave., 33765, pg. 25 **PB**

Alro Group, Clearwater, 12490 49th St., 34622, pg. 46 **PV**

AmSouth Bank, 2575 Countryside Blvd., 34621, pg. 105 **PB**

DAYTON ANDREWS INC., 2388 Gulf to Bay Blvd., 33765, pg. 74 **PV**

BWI Inex Vision Systems, 13327 U.S. Hwy. 19N, 33764, pg. 130 **IT**

Baymont Technologies Inc., Rubin Icot Ctr., 14100 58th St. N., 34620-3796, pg. 31 **IT**

BIC Special Mkts. Div., 14421 Myer Lake Circle, 34620, pg. 1273 **IT**

BUFKOR, INC., 13100 56th Court N., Ste. 710, 33760, pg. 179 **PV**

Champion Modular Restaurant Company, 12812 60th St. N., 33760, pg. 343 **PB**

CHECKERS DRIVE-IN RESTAURANTS, INC., 600 Cleveland St., Ste. 1050, 34615, pg. 342 **PB**

Clearwater Auto Auction Inc., 5153 126th Ave. N., 33760, pg. 1648 **PV**

Clearwater Phillies, 800 Phillies Dr., 33515, pg. 861 **PV**

Compass Distribution, 12200 34th St., N, 34622, pg. 838 **PV**

DATAFLEX CORPORATION, 2145 Calumet St., 34625, pg. 313 **PB**

Eckerd Drug Co., P.O. Box 4689, 34618, pg. 917 **PB**

EVA-TONE INC., 4801 Ulmerton Rd., 33762, pg. 384 **PV**

HSN Mail Order, P.O. Box 9090, 34618-9090, pg. 1685 **PB**

Hansen Plastics Division, 2050 Sunnydale Blvd., 34625, pg. 1110 **PV**

C.H. HEIST CORP., 810 N. Belcher Rd., 33765, pg. 807 **PB**

Home Shopping Club, Inc., P.O. Box 9090, 34618, pg. 1685 **PB**

InterVascular, Inc., 16331 Bay Vista Dr., 34620, pg. 487 **IT**

KAYDON CORPORATION, Arbor Shoreline Office Park, 19345 U.S. 19 N., Ste. 500, 33764, pg. 945 **PB**

Klockner-Borsch Tooling Technologies, 211 Sunnydale Blvd., 34625, pg. 737 **IT**

LINCARE HOLDINGS INC., 19337 U.S. Hwy. 19 N., Ste. 500, 33764, pg. 1063 **PB**

MAXXIM MEDICAL, INC., 10300 49th St. N., 33762, pg. 1063 **PB**

Melitta North America, Inc., 13925 58th St. N., 33760, pg. 857 **IT**

Melitta U.S.A., Inc., 17757 US 19N., Ste. 600, 34624, pg. 857 **IT**

Motorola Radius, 13575 58th St. N., Ste. 152, 34620-3704, pg. 1138 **PB**

94th Aero Squadron of Pinellas County, Inc., 94th Fairchild Dr., 34620, pg. 1023 **PV**

Oxford Instruments, Latin America Operations, 13825 Icot Blvd., Ste. 614, 33760, pg. 1018 **IT**

Oxford Instruments-Medical Systems Div., 11526 53rd St. N., 34620, pg. 1018 **IT**

Pinellas Crabcooker, Inc., 16100 Fairchild Dr., 34620, pg. 1023 **PV**

Pinellas Farmhouse, Inc., 15481 49th St., 34622, pg. 1023 **PV**

Porta Holdings Inc., 17755 U.S. S. 19, N., Ste. 150, 34624, pg. 857 **PV**

RehabWorks Inc., 521 S. Greenwood Ave., 34616, pg. 839 **PB**

RISSER OIL CORP., 2865 Executive Dr., 33762, pg. 932 **PV**

St. Pete Auto Auction, 14950 Roosevelt Blvd., 34622, pg. 283 **PV**

Signature Flight Support, St. Petersburg/Clearwater, Airport, 34625, pg. 114 **IT**

Smiths Industries Aerospace & Defense Systems Inc.-Clearwater, 14180 Roosevelt Blvd., 34622, pg. 1268 **IT**

Smiths Industries Aerospace & Defense Systems Inc.-Product Support, P.O. Box 9013, 14180 Roosevelt Blvd., 34622, pg. 1268 **IT**

Square D Co., 1700 Sunshine Dr., 34625, pg. 1208 **PV**

Square D Company-Assembly Operations, 1771 Hercules Ave., 34625, pg. 1208 **PV**

Sun Micro Stamping Inc., 14055 US Highway 19 N., 33764, pg. 1531 **PB**

Tampa Bay Steel, 10551 47th St. N., 34622, pg. 1067 **PV**

TECH DATA CORPORATION, 5350 Tech Data Dr., 34620, pg. 1562 **PB**

Tech Data Education, 5350 Tech Data Dr., 34620, pg. 1562 **PB**

TECHNOLOGY RESEARCH CORPORATION, 5250 140th Ave. N., 34620, pg. 1564 **PB**

U.S. Home Mortgage Corporation, 311 Park Place Blvd., Ste. 500, 34619, pg. 1683 **PB**

Zept Technologies, 5320 140th Ave. N., 33720, pg. 118 **PV**

Clewiston

Clewiston Sugar House, 111 Ponce de Leon Ave., 33440, pg. 1126 **PV**

Everglades Sugar Refinery, Inc., P.O. Box 1268, 33440, pg. 873 **PV**

South Central Florida Express, Inc., 900 S. W.C. Owen, 33440, pg. 1126 **PV**

Southern Garden Citrus Processing, P.O. Box 1207, 33440, pg. 1126 **PV**

United States Corrulite Corporation, P. O. Box 2307, 33440, pg. 1126 **PV**

UNITED STATES SUGAR CORPORATION, 111 Ponce de Leon Ave., 33440, pg. 1126 **PV**

Cocoa Beach

Boeing Aerospace Operations, 1355 N. Atlantic Ave., 32932-0220, pg. 241 **PB**

Boeing Technical Operations, Inc., 1355 N. Atlantic Ave., 32932-0220, pg. 242 **PB**

CSR, 1325 N. Atlantic Ave., Ste. 160, 32931, pg. 1365 **PB**

Coconut Creek

Greenstone Roberts Public Relations, 3730 Coconut Creek Pkwy., 33066, pg. 763 **PB**

Coconut Grove

WATSCO, INC., 2665 S. Bayshore Dr., Ste. 901, 33133, pg. 1745 **PB**

Coral Gables

AERO PERU CORPORATION, 95 Merrick Way, Ste. 700, 33134, pg. 24 **PV**

Alcoa Inter-America, Inc., 396 Alhambra, Ste. 200, 33134, pg. 60 **IT**

Amphion Holdings Inc., Two Columbus Ctr., 55 Alhambra Plaza, 33134, pg. 1257 **IT**

AVATAR HOLDINGS INC., 255 Alhambra Cir., 33134, pg. 151 **PB**

Avatar Realty, Inc., 255 Alhambra Cir., 33134, pg. 151 **PB**

Avatar Utilities, Inc., 255 Alhambra Cir., 33134, pg. 151 **PB**

Avatar Vacation Resorts, Inc., 255 Alhambra Cir., 33134, pg. 151 **PV**

Bacardi Service Corp., (North America), 2100 Biscayne Blvd., 33134, pg. 131 **IT**

Bacardi Services (North America) Corp., 866 Ponce de Leon Blvd., 33134, pg. 131 **IT**

BANACOL MARKETING CORP., 2655 La Jeune Rd., 33134, pg. 113 **PV**

Bank of Tokyo-Mitsubishi Ltd. (Miami Agency), 2100 Ponce de Leon Blvd., Penthouse Ste., 33134, pg. 157 **IT**

Leo Burnett Worldwide, Latin American Hdqtrs., 550 Biltmore, Ste. 870, 33134, pg. 184 **PV**

PB - *U.S. Public Companies Volume*
PV - *U.S. Private Companies Volume*
IT - *International Public & Private Companies Volume*

Geographic Index-U.S.

1179

BUSINESS MENS INSURANCE CORPORATION, 1320 S. Dixie Hwy., 6th Fl., 33146, pg. 189   PV

BUSINESHIP INTERNATIONAL INC., One Al Hambra Plaza, Ste. 1400, 33134, pg. 189   PV

CAC Medical Centers, Inc., 75 Valencia Ave., 33134, pg. 1678   PB

Capital Assurance Company, Inc., Two Columbus Ctr., 55 Alhambra Plaza, 33114, pg. 1257   IT

Central/Southern Division, One Alhambra Plaza, Ste. 1225, 33134, pg. 412   IT

Colonnade Enterprise Corporation, 180 Aragon Ave., 33134, pg. 132   IT

DMB&B/Miami, 1200 Anastasia Ave., 33134, pg. 304   PV

DEL RIVERO MESSIANU ADVERTISING, LTD., 770 S. Dixie Hwy., Ste. 109, 33146, pg. 321   PV

Empresas ICA Sociedad Controladora (Miami), 2655 Lejeune Rd., Ste. 1000, 33134, pg. 454   IT

EQUITRAC CORPORATION, 836 Ponce de Leon Blvd., 33134, pg. 590   PB

Evans & Fitzgerald Advertising, 1320 S. Dixie Hwy., Ste. 385, 33146, pg. 701   PV

Gestetner Regional Services Inc. (USA), 1550 Madruga Ave., Ste. 403, 33146, pg. 1115   IT

Getty Oil (Guatemala), Inc., 150 Alhambra Cir., 33134, pg. 1583   IT

Hilton International Co., 901 Ponce de Leon Ave., 33134, pg. 787   IT

Northern Trust Bank of Florida, N.A., 595 Biltmore Way, 33134, pg. 1196   PB

Phelps Dodge Intl. Corp., 2121 Ponce de Leon Blvd., 33134, pg. 1286   PB

RAMSAY HEALTH CARE, INC., Columbus Ctr., 1 Alhambra Plaza, Ste. 750, 33134, pg. 1360   PB

Reader's Digest Latinoamerica S.A., 2655 Le Jeune Rd., Ste. 301, 33134, pg. 1367   IT

RENEX CORP., 2100 Ponce de Leon Blvd., Ste. 950, 33134, pg. 1377   PB

Rexel, Inc., 150 Alhambra Cir., Ste. 900, 33134, pg. 1107   IT

Sandvik Latin America, Inc., 2801 Pnce De Leon Ave., 33134, pg. 1185   IT

Seagram Latin America, Two Al Hambra Plaza, 33134, pg. 1217   IT

Skandia Direct Operations Corporation, Two Columbus Ctr., 55 Alhambra Plaza, 33134, pg. 1257   IT

Skandia U.S. Insurance Company, Two Columbus Ctr., 55 Alhambra Plaza, 33134, pg. 1257   IT

STIEFEL LABORATORIES, INC., 255 Alhambra Cir., Ste. 1000, 33134, pg. 1043   PV

SUNGLASS HUT INTERNATIONAL, 255 Alhambra Cir., 33134, pg. 1535   PB

United HealthCare of Florida, Inc., 75 Valencia Ave., 33134, pg. 1678   PB

Wackenhut Airline Services, Inc., 1500 San Remo Ave., 33146, pg. 1731   PB

Wackenhut Intl., Inc., 1500 San Remo Ave., 33146, pg. 1731   PB

Wackenhut Nuclear Services, 1500 San Remo Ave., 33146, pg. 1731   PB

Wackenhut Services, Inc., 1500 San Remo Ave., 33146, pg. 1731   PB

WOMETCO ENTERPRISES, INC., 3195 Ponce de Leon Blvd., 33134, pg. 1186   PV

Coral Springs

AQUA CARE SYSTEMS INC., 11820 N.W. 37th St., 33065, pg. 987   PB

Boca Greens Inc., 10181 W. Sample Rd., 33065, pg. 988   PB

CONTINENTAL PLASTIC CARD CO., 3651 N.W. 120th Ave., 33065, pg. 269   PV

Jaco Electronics, Inc., 9900 W. Sample Rd., Ste. 404, 33065, pg. 921   PB

M.A.P. Builders Inc., 10212 W. Sample Rd., 33065, pg. 988   PB

Outpatient Surgery Center of Coral Springs, 967 University Dr., 33071, pg. 405   PB

Plants, Sites & Parks, 10240 W. Sample Rd., 33065, pg. 1446   IT

SAWGRASS ELECTRONICS GROUP INC., 3900 Coral Ridge Dr., 33065, pg. 968   PV

Crestview

Silvercrest Manor, 103 Ruby Ln., 32536, pg. 837   PB

Crystal River

Citrus County Chronicle, 1624 N. Meadowcrest Blvd., 34229, pg. 648   PV

Pro-Line Boats, P.O. Box 1348, 34423, pg. 58   PV

Dade City

Lykes Pasco Inc., P.O. Box 97, 33526, pg. 682   PV

Lykes Transport Inc., 9721 US Hwy 98, 33525, pg. 682   PV

Multi-Line Cans, Inc., P.O. Box 1194, 33526, pg. 682   PV

Dania

Citibank (Florida) N.A., 255 E. Dania Beach Blvd., 33004, pg. 377   PB

PIC N'PAY SUPERMARKETS, INC., 130 S.W. First Ave., 33004, pg. 864   PV

SAI Distributors, 1901 Tigertail Blvd., 33304, pg. 1488   PB

SOUND ADVICE, INC., 1901 Tigertail Blvd., 33004, pg. 1488   PB

TMP Worldwide/Recruitment Division, 1815 Griffin Rd., Ste. 101, 33004, pg. 1065   PV

Tele-Quote, Inc., 499 Sheridan St., 33004, pg. 28   IT

Davie

Global Precision, Inc., 2100 S.W. 71st Ter., pg. 125   PV

Lauderdale-Miami Auto Auction Inc., 5353 S. State Rd. 7, 33314, pg. 1649   PB

Perma-Fix of Ft. Lauderdale, Inc., 3701 SW 47 Ave., Ste. 109, 33314, pg. 1279   PB

SAFE ALARM, INC., 4490 S.W. 64th Ave., 33314, pg. 960   PV

Daytona Beach

ALUMA SHIELD INDUSTRIES, INC., 405 Fentress Blvd., 32114, pg. 47   PV

BUDGET GROUP, INC., 125 Basin St., Ste. 210, 32114, pg. 178   PV

Burns & Wilcox - Daytona Beach Office, 444 Seabreeze Blvd., Ste. 887, 32118, pg. 610   PB

Cognos Corp.-Daytona Sales Office, 444 Seabreeze Blvd., Ste. 887, 32118, pg. 306   IT

CONSOLIDATED-TOMOKA LAND CO., 149 S. Ridgewood Ave., 32114, pg. 437   PB

John Crane Belfab, 305 Fentress Blvd., 32114, pg. 1339   IT

Hilb, Rogal and Hamilton Company of Daytona Beach, Inc., P.O. Drawer 70, 32115-0070, pg. 827   PB

Horizon Healthcare & Specialty Center, 1350 S. Nova Rd., 32114, pg. 836   PB

Indigo Development Inc., 149-C S. Ridgewood Ave., 32114, pg. 437   PB

Indigo Group Inc., 149-C S. Ridgewood Ave., 32114, pg. 437   PB

Indigo Group Ltd., 149-D S. Ridgewood Ave., 32114-0809, pg. 437   PB

MacDuff Underwriters, 220 S. Ridgewood Ave., 32115, pg. 437   PB

Martin Marietta Automations Systems, 1800 International Speedway Blvd., 32114, pg. 1007   PB

Oceans Racquet Club, Inc., 3060 S. Atlantic Ave., 32019, pg. 355   PB

POE & BROWN, INC., 220 S. Ridgewood Ave., 32114, pg. 1312   PB

Reliance Realty, Inc., 444 Seabreeze Blvd., 32018, pg. 355   PB

South Daytona Mfg. Division, 3100 S. Ridgewood Ave., 32119, pg. 518   PB

Southeast Region, 300 Fentress Blvd., 32114, pg. 617   PB

SunTrust Bank, East Central Florida, 120 S. Ridgewood Ave., 32114, pg. 1537   PB

De Funiak Springs

Regions Bank/Walton/Holmes County, P.O. Box 610, 32433, pg. 1373   PB

De Land

Ardmore Farms, 1915 N. USA Highway 17, 32720, pg. 1348   PB

Deland District-Florida Public Utilities, 401 N. Stone St., 32720, pg. 655   PB

KELLER KITCHEN CABINETS, 2526 W. State Rd. 44, 32720, pg. 612   PV

De Leon Springs

Spartor Electronics Florida, Inc., Johnson Lake Rd., 32130, pg. 496   PB

Deerfield Beach

AdultCare, Inc., 858 S. Military Trail, 33442, pg. 499   IT

All American Semiconductor of Florida, Inc., 1400 E. Newport Center Dr., No. 205, 33442, pg. 41   PB

Arrow/Schweber Electronics, 400 Fairway Dr., 33441, pg. 134   PB

DX Communications, Inc., 1143 W. Newport Center Dr., 33442, pg. 694   PB

DEVCON INTERNATIONAL CORP., 1350 E. Newport Ctr. Dr., Ste. 201, 33442, pg. 502   PB

Gemaire Distributors, Inc., 198 Locke Rd., 33442, pg. 1746   PB

Gould Paper of Florida, Inc., 652 S.W. 12th Ave., 33492, pg. 467   PB

JM FAMILY ENTERPRISES INC., 100 N.W. 12th Ave., 33442, pg. 577   PV

KITCHENS OF THE OCEANS, INC., 104 S.E. Fifth Ct., 33441, pg. 625   PV

LIST INDUSTRIES, INC., 401 N.W. 12th Ave., 33442, pg. 669   PV

Medtronic, Inc., 450 Fairway Dr., Ste. 103, 33441, pg. 1083   PB

Micros of South Florida, Inc., 836 Military Trail, 33442, pg. 1106   PB

Mr. Bracket, 1341 W. Newport Ctr. Dr., 33442, pg. 1055   PB

OUTSOURCE INTERNATIONAL, 1144 E. Newport Ctr. Dr., 33442, pg. 1236   PB

Play Systems, One Stainless Plaza, 33441, pg. 1029   PV

Pulte South Florida Division, 1350 E. Newport Center Dr. #200, 33442, pg. 1345   PB

Pylon Manufacturing Corp., 1341 W. Newport Ctr. Dr., 33442, pg. 1055   PB

Service America Systems, Inc., 515 N.W. 12th Ave., 33442, pg. 344   PB

ServiCenter USA, 500 Fairway Dr., Ste. 205, 33441, pg. 1201   PB

STAINLESS INCORPORATED, One Stainless Plaza, 33441-4798, pg. 1029   PV

Tarmac Florida, 455 Fairway Dr., 33605, pg. 1355   IT

Richard Young Office Products, Inc., 508 S. Military Trail, 33442, pg. 450   PB

Deland

SouthTrust Bank of Central Florida, 100 E. New York Ave., 32724, pg. 1492   PB

Delray Beach

Aircraft Products Company, 12807 Lake Dr., 33447, pg. 159   PB

Champion Realty, Inc., 1690 S. Congress Ave., Ste. 200, 33445, pg. 1231   PB

EBI/AOA Division, 1395 N.W. 17th Ave., Ste. 109, 33445, pg. 231   PB

EMPIRE OF CAROLINA, INC., 5150 Linton Blvd., 5th Fl., 33484, pg. 579   PB

OCEAN PROPERTIES, LTD., 1100 Linton Blvd., Ste. C-9, 33444, pg. 811   PV

OFFICE DEPOT INC., 2200 Old Germantown Rd., 33445, pg. 1212   PB

Oriole Enterprises, Inc., 1690 S. Congress Ave., Ste. 200, 33445, pg. 1231   PB

Oriole Golf & Tennis Club, Inc., 1690 S. Congress Ave., Ste. 200, 33445, pg. 1231   PB

ORIOLE HOMES CORP., 1690 S. Congress Ave., Ste. 200, 33445-6327, pg. 1230   PB

Oriole International, 1690 S. Congress Ave., Ste. 200, 33445, pg. 1231   PB

Pier Club, Inc., 1690 S. Congress Ave., 33445, pg. 1231   PB

South Florida Residential Mortgage Co., 1690 S. Congress Ave., Ste. 102, 33445, pg. 1231   PB

SUNBEAM CORPORATION, 1615 S. Congress Ave., 33445, pg. 1533   PB

WESTMARK GROUP HOLDINGS INC., 355 N.E. Fifth Ave. Ste. 4, 33483, pg. 1761   PB

Destin

Force V Corporation, 1225 Airport Rd., 32541, pg. 1447   PB

Sandestin Resort Inc., 5300 Hwy. 98, E. Emerald Coast Pkwy., 32541, pg. 1250   IT

Sime Darby Commodities Inc., 5500 Hwy. 98 E., 32541, pg. 1250   IT

Dover

B & R Foods, 3150 N. Gallagher Rd., 33527, pg. 1278   PB

Dunedin

Curtin & Pease/Peneco, Inc, 1022 Main St., 34698, pg. 1306   PB

Dunnellon

Riverland News, 20491 The Granada, 34432, pg. 648   PV

Edgewater

Boston Whaler, Inc., 4121 S. U.S. Hwy One, 32141, pg. 689   PV

Coronado Paint Company, 308 Old Country Rd., 32132, pg. 1488   IT

Englewood

Englewood Community Hospital, Inc., 700 Medical Blvd., 34223, pg. 404   PB

Eustis

Lake Eustis Care Center, 411 W. Woodward Ave., 32726, pg. 837   PB

Shasta Beverage Inc., P.O. Box 1160, 2221 Hwy. 44 W., 32727-1160, pg. 1153   PB

Fernandina Beach

Fernandina Beach News Leader, Inc., 511 Ash St., 32034, pg. 1175   PB

Fernandina Div.-Florida Public Utilities, 911 S. Eighth St., 32034, pg. 655   PB

First Coast Community Bank & Trust, 1900 S. 14th St., 32034, pg. 1549   PB

Nassau Terminals, 501 North Third Street, 32034, pg. 758   IT

PETROFERM INC., 5415 First Coart Hwy., 32034, pg. 858   PV

Fort Lauderdale

Alamo Rent-A-Car Inc., 110 S.E. Sixth St., 33301, pg. 1379   PB

Allied Security Inc., 2880 W. Oakland Park Blvd., Ste. 111, 33311, pg. 40   PV

AlliedSignal Air Transport Avionics, 2100 N.W. 62nd St., 33309, pg. 50   PB

B&G Electronics, 5801 N. Andrews, 33309, pg. 1462   IT

PB - U.S. Public Companies Volume
PV - U.S. Private Companies Volume
IT - International Public & Private Companies Volume

1180

BVK/McDonald, 1100 Lee Wagener Blvd., Ste. 311, 33315, pg. 108 PV
BANKATLANTIC BANCORP, INC., 1750 E. Sunrise Blvd., 33304, pg. 183 PB
BASIC FOOD INTERNATIONAL INC., 2601 E. Oakpond Park Bend, 33306, pg. 121 PV
BLACK FIN YACHT CORPORATION, 3391 S.E. 14th Ave., 33316, pg. 147 PV
Blockbuster Holding Corp., One Blockbuster Plaza, 33301-1860, pg. 775 PV
Blockbuster Music Holding Corporation, One Blockbuster Plaza, 33301-1860, pg. 775 PV
Blockbuster Pictures Holding Corporation, One Blockbuster Plaza, 33301-1860, pg. 776 PV
Blockbuster Videos Inc., One Blockbuster Plaza, 33301-1860, pg. 776 PV
Blumberg Communications of Florida Inc., 2501 Davie Rd., Ste. 210, 33314, pg. 305 PB
Calgon Interamerican Corp., 1290 Western Rd., Ste. 202, 33326, pg. 455 IT
Capital Factors, Inc., 1799 W. Oakland Park Blvd., 33311, pg. 1669 PB
Cemex, S.A. de C.V. - Fort Lauderdale, 1600 S.E. 17th St., Ste. 418, 33316, pg. 278 IT
Centex-Rooney Construction Co., Inc., 6300 N.W. Fifth Way, 33309, pg. 322 PB
Certified Poultry & Egg Co., Inc., 5545 NW 35th Ave., 33309, pg. 1529 PB
Clear Results Marketing, 1975 E. Sunrise Blvd. #400, 33304, pg. 383 PB
Community Psychiatric Centers of Florida, Inc., 1601 E. Las Olas Blvd., 32216, pg. 1712 PB
CONCURRENT COMPUTER CORPORATION, 2101 W. Cypress Creek Rd., 33309-1892, pg. 430 PB
Consolidated Cigar Corp., 5900 N. Andrews Ave., Ste. 700, 33309, pg. 690 PV
Consolidated Cigar Corporation, 5900 N. Andrews Ave., Ste. 700, 33309, pg. 690 PV
Continental Cement Co. of Florida Inc., P.O. Box 13128, Pt. Everglades Station, 33316, pg. 1201 IT
CYBERGUARD CORPORATION, 2000 W. Commercial Blvd., 33309, pg. 470 PB
Dana South American Operations, 200 E. Las Olas Blvd., Str. 1600, 33301, pg. 480 PB
DaVinci Systems, Inc., 5410 N.W. 33rd Ave., Suite 100, 33309, pg. 539 PB
Domestic Cigars, 5900 N. Andrews Ave., Ste. 700, 33309, pg. 690 PV
Dynalco Controls Corporation, 3690 N.W. 53rd St., 33309, pg. 457 PB
EAC-Embraer Aircraft Corporation, 276 S.W. 34th St., 33315, pg. 452 IT
ECI Telecom Americas Inc., 1201 W. Cypress Creek Rd., 33309, pg. 643 IT
ENCORE COMPUTER CORPORATION, 6901 W. Sunrise Blvd., 33313-4499, pg. 580 PB
Fahlgren, 600 Corporate Dr., Ste. 300, 33334, pg. 391 PV
FINNAIR, 3600 W. Commercial Blvd., Ste. 12, 33309, pg. 486 IT
Flanigan's Enterprises, Inc., 5450 North State Rd. #7, pg. 648 PB
FLANIGAN'S ENTERPRISES, INC., 2841 Cypress Creek Rd., 33309, pg. 648 PB
Flanigan's Enterprises, Inc., 2600 W. Davie Blvd., pg. 648 PB
Flanigan's Enterprises, Inc., 1720 N. Andrews Ave., pg. 648 PB
Florida Heat Pump, 601 N.W. 65th Ct., 33309-6109, pg. 506 PV
Florida Medical Center South, 6701 W. Sunrise Blvd., 33313, pg. 1577 PB
FLORIDA PANTHERS HOLDINGS, INC., 100 N.E. Third Ave., 2nd Fl., 33301, pg. 654 PB
Frontier Insurance Company of New York, Cypress Ct. Corporate Park, 6360 N.W. Fifth Way, Ste. 303, 33309, pg. 685 PB
Global Food Corporation, 1300 S.E. 17th St., Ste. 300, 33335, pg. 121 PV
LEON SHAFFER GOLNICK ADVERTISING, INC., 5401 N. Federal Hwy., 33308, pg. 463 PV
Gribetz International, Inc., 13800 NW 4th St., 33325, pg. 986 PB
HSS Recruiting, Inc., 6245 N. Federal H, Ste. 500, 33308, pg. 840 PB
HSSI Management Company, Inc., 6245 N. Federal Hwy., Ste. 500, 33308, pg. 840 PB
HSSI Medicare Home Office, Inc., 6245 N. Federal Hwy., Ste. 500, 33308, pg. 840 PB
HSSI Travel Nurse Operation, 6245 N. Federal Hwy., Ste. 500, 33308, pg. 840 PB
Ha-Lo Marketing & Promotions, 4101 Ravenswood Rd., Ste. 406, 33312, pg. 773 PB
HARRIS DRURY COHEN, 1901 W. Cypress Creek Rd., 6th Fl., 33309, pg. 505 PV
The Harwood Companies, Inc., 3355 Enterprise Ave., 33331, pg. 1433 PB
HEALTH PROFESSIONALS, INC., 515 E. Las Olas Blvd., Ste. 1600, 33301, pg. 802 PB
Hilb, Rogal and Hamilton Company of Fort Lauderdale, 1000 Corporate Dr., Ste. 100, 33334, pg. 827 PB
Hill, Holiday, Connors, Cosmopulos, Inc., 600 Southeast Two Ct., Second Fl., 33301, pg. 529 PV
HOSPITAL STAFFING SERVICES, INC., 6245 N. Federal Hwy., Ste. 500, 33308-1900, pg. 840 PB
Hunter Douglas Verticals, 6277 N.W. 28th Way, 33309, pg. 639 IT
HVIDE MARINE INCORPORATED, 2200 Eller Dr., 33316, pg. 851 PB
Hyde Park Markets, 6452 N.W. 5th Way, 33309, pg. 653 PB
Incor of Florida, 1001 N.W. 58th Ct., 33309, pg. 309 PV
INTERIM SERVICES INC., 2050 Spectrum Blvd., 33309, pg. 892 PB
Jacobs Asset Management, 200 E. Broward Blvd., Ste. 1920, 33301, pg. 1673 PB
Keller Ladders Inc., 6365 N.W. Sixth Way, Ste. 201, 33309, pg. 1684 PB
LDI Auto Paint, 3621 N.E. 4th Ave., 33310, pg. 639 PV
Lambda Physik, Lakeshore Bus. Ctr., 3201 W. Commercial Blvd., Ste. 110, 33309, pg. 395 PB
Logo of the Americas, 1675 N. Commerce Pkwy., 33326, pg. 462 IT
Maritime Leisure Corporation, 1510 S.E. 17th St., 33316, pg. 21 IT
MIAMI SUBS CORPORATION, 6300 N.W. 31st Ave., 33309, pg. 1103 PB
Microsoft Latin America, Cambridge Executive Ctr., 899 W. Cypress Creek Rd., Ste. 400, 33309, pg. 1108 PB
Milk Products Holdings (Latin America) Ltd., One Financial Plaza, Ste. 2001, 33394, pg. 923 IT
Modcomp, 1650 W. McNab Rd., 33309, pg. 283 PB
ED MORSE AUTOMOTIVE GROUP, 6363 N.W. Sixth Way, Ste. 400, 33309, pg. 763 PV
NationsBank of Florida Corporation, One Financial Plaza, 33394, pg. 1162 PB
94th Aero Squadron Restaurant, Inc., 2500 NW 62nd St., 33309, pg. 1023 PV
NORTH AMERICAN COMPANY, 312 S.E. 17th St., #300, 33316-2524, pg. 803 PV
Northern Trust Bank of Florida, N.A., 1100 E. Las Olas Blvd., 33301, pg. 1196 PB
Northern Trust Bank of Florida, N.A., 2601 E. Oakland Pk. Blvd., 33306, pg. 1196 PB
NuArc Southern Div., 3601 NW 10th Ave., 33309, pg. 809 PV
OCEAN BIO-CHEM INC., 4041 S.W. 47th Ave., 33314, pg. 1211 PB
Office Connection, Inc., 5301 N.W. Ninth Ave., 33309, pg. 1687 PB
Parkson Corporation, 2727 N.W. 62nd St., 33309, pg. 710 IT
PARLUX FRAGRANCES INC., 3725 S.W. 30th Ave., 33312, pg. 1264 PB
Parlux, Ltd., 3725 S.W. 30th Ave., 33312, pg. 1264 PB
Poe & Brown of Florida, 5900 N. Andrews Ave., Ste. 900, 33309, pg. 1312 PB
Precision Resource Florida Div., 6681 N.W. 17th Ave., 33309, pg. 880 PV
Premium Products Division, 5900 N. Andrews Ave., Ste. 700, 33309, pg. 690 PV
RHG Fort Lauderdale, 1509 S.W. 1stAve., 33315, pg. 1151 IT
REPUBLIC INDUSTRIES, INC., 450 E. Las Olas Blvd., 33301, pg. 1378 PB
KENNY ROGERS ROASTERS, 899 W. Cypress Creek Rd., Ste. 500, 33309, pg. 939 PV
SMS-Ft. Lauderdale, 100 W. Cypress Creek Rd., Ste. 1050, 33309, pg. 1463 PB
Sea Ranch Properties, 312 S.E. 12th St., Ste. 300, 33316-2524, pg. 803 PV
Solair, Inc., 3380 S.W. 11th Ave., 33315, pg. 187 PB
Southern Electric Supply Co., Inc., 4700 NW 15th Ave., Bay A, 33309, pg. 1107 IT
THE SPORTS AUTHORITY INC., 3383 N. State Rd. Seven, 33319, pg. 1499 PB
Staff Source, 6245 N. Federal Hwy., Ste. 500, 33308, pg. 841 PB
STARBRITE CORP., 4041 S.W. 47 Ave., 33314, pg. 1510 PB
THE STEPHAN COMPANY, 1850 W. McNab Rd., 33309, pg. 1514 PB
STILES CORPORATION, 6400 N. Andrews Ave., 33309, pg. 1043 PV
Sun City Egg Marketing, Inc., 5545 NW 35th Ave., 33309, pg. 1529 PB
SUN CITY INDUSTRIES, INC., 5545 N.W. 35th Ave., 33309, pg. 1529 PB
SUN INTERNATIONAL HOTELS LIMITED, 1415 E. Sunrise Blvd., 10th Fl., 33304, pg. 1531 PB
Sun-Sentinel Company, 200 E. Las Olas Blvd., 33301, pg. 1636 PB
SunTrust Bank, South Florida, N.A., 501 E. Las Olas Blvd., 33301, pg. 1538 PB
Telematics Inc., 1201 W. Cypress Creek Rd., 33309, pg. 643 IT
Templeton Investment Counsel, Inc., 500 E. Broward Blvd., Ste. 2100, 33394-3091, pg. 680 PB
Triarc Restaurant Group, 1000 Corporate Dr., 33334, pg. 1635 PB
UNC Accessory Services-Florida, 3000 S.W. 4th Ave., 33315, pg. 710 PB
United Foam Plastics Corporation, 4800 NW 15th Ave., 33309-2781, pg. 1112 PV
United Technologies Microelectronics Center, 1405 Springdale Dr., 33326, pg. 1690 PB
Vacation Break USA, Park Plaza Ste. 200, 6400 N. Andrews Ave., 33309, pg. 611 PB
WAXY (FM), 1975 E. Sunrise Blvd., 33304, pg. 925 PB
WHYI-FM, 1975 E. Sunrise Blvd., Ste. 400, 33304, pg. 385 PB
Weatherby Locums Inc., 3230 W. Commercial Blvd., Ste. 240, 33309, pg. 1155 PV
Westinghouse Audio Intelligence Devices, 1400 N.W. 62nd St., 33309, pg. 273 PB
ZIMMERMAN & PARTNERS ADVERTISING, INC., 2200 W. Commercial Blvd., Ste. 300, 33309, pg. 1206 PV

Fort Meade

US Agri-Chemicals Corporation, 3225 State Rd., 630 W., 33841-9799, pg. 1255 IT

Fort Myers

Avac Systems Inc., 15680 Kilmarnock Dr., 33912, pg. 278 IT
Basic American Medical, Inc., One University Park, 12800 University Dr., Ste. 560, 33907-5337, pg. 403 PB
CMSF, Inc., 3550 Colonial Blvd., 33912, pg. 1033 PB
Cape Coral Realty, Inc., 1811 Cape Coral Pkwy., 33904, pg. 151 PB
CHICO'S FAS INC, 11215 Metro Pkwy., 33912, pg. 349 PB
F & E Community Developers of Florida, Inc., 8280 College Pkwy., Ste. 101, 33919-5122, pg. 404 PB
First National Bank of Fort Myers, 7130 College Pkwy., 33912, pg. 608 PB
Fort Myers Branch Office, 10491 Six Mile Cypress Pkwy., Ste. 107, 33912, pg. 1683 PB
Fort Myers Miracle, Lee County Stadium, 14100 Six Mile Cypress Pkwy., 33912, pg. 751 PV
Gulf Coast League Twins, Lee County Stadium, 14200 Six Mile Cypress Pkwy., 33912, pg. 751 PV
HARPER BROS., INC., 14860 Six Mile Cypress Pkwy., 33912, pg. 504 PV
Hilb, Rogal and Hamilton Company of Fort Myers, 1614 Colonial Blvd., 33907, pg. 827 PB
Holiday RV Superstores, Inc.-Ft. Myers, 8050 Bayshore Rd., 33917, pg. 830 PB
Hospital Data Processing, 3955 Fowler Ave., 33901, pg. 405 PB
Miller Brands, Inc., 1699 Gator Rd., 33912, pg. 1289 PB
News-Press Publishing Co., 2442 Anderson Ave., 33902, pg. 701 PB
Northern Trust Bank of Florida, N.A., 8060 College Pkwy., S.W., 33919, pg. 1196 PB
Owen-Ames-Kimball Co., 11941 Fairway Lakes Dr., 33913-8338, pg. 824 PV
Poe & Brown of Florida, 4210 Metro Pkwy., Ste. 300, 33916, pg. 1312 PB
Premier Tropic Staffing, Inc., 2450 Winkler Ave., Ste. 1, 33901, pg. 405 PB
Price/Palmer Wireless Corp., 12800 University Dr., 33907-5337, pg. 1324 PB
Rehabilitative Health Services, Inc., 3945 Fowler St., 33901-2699, pg. 405 PB
Rottlund Homes of Florida, Inc., 17595 S. Tamiami Trail, Ste. 106, 33908, pg. 1406 PB
SIMS Portex Inc., 5100 Tice St., 33905, pg. 1268 IT
Society First Federal Savings Bank, 2201 Second St., 33901, pg. 954 PB
South Florida Land Division, 10491 Six Mile Cypress Pkwy., Ste. 105, 33912, pg. 1683 PB
SouthTrust Bank, Southwest Florida, 1530 Heitman St., 33901, pg. 1492 PB
SunTrust Bank, Southwest Florida, 12730 New Brittany Blvd., 33907, pg. 1538 PB
Tri-City Electrical Contractors Inc., Airport Woods, 12296 Matterhorn Rd., Ste. 3A, 33913, pg. 1100 PV
URS Greiner, Inc., 2891 Center Pointe Dr., Ste. 303, 33916, pg. 1658 PB
WCKT, 4110 Center Pointe Dr., Ste. 212, 33916, pg. 384 PB
WXRM, 4110 Center Pointe Dr., Ste. 212, 33916, pg. 385 PB
WIRELESS ONE NETWORK LP, 2100 Electronics Lane, 33912, pg. 1184 PV
Zellerbach Division, 10231 Metro Pkwy. S.E., Ste. 102, 33912, pg. 1075 PB

Fort Pierce

SunTrust Bank, Treasure Coast, N.A., 111 Orange Ave., 34950, pg. 1538 PB

Fort Walton Beach

Dialysis Service of Florida, 348 Miracle Strip Pkwy., Ste. 16, 32548, pg. 1080 PB
Emerald Coast Cable Television, 320 Racetrack Rd., N.W., 32547, pg. 455 PB
Metric Systems Corp., 645 Anchors St., 32548, pg. 1563 PB
Northwest Florida Daily News, P.O. Drawer 2949, 32549, pg. 425 PV
QMS Circuits, Inc., 40 Hill Ave., 32548, pg. 1346 PB
Regions Bank/Okaloosa/Bay County, P.O. Box 2769, 32549-2769, pg. 1372 PB
TWC Cable Partners, 100 Cable Way, 10303, pg. 455 PB
Vitro Services Corporation, Industrial Park, 557 Mary Esther Cut-off, 32548-4090, pg. 1627 PB
Western Florida Cellular Telephone Corp., 824 North Eglin Pkwy., 32547, pg. 1708 PB

Gainesville

American Eagle, P.O. Box 5669, 32602-5669, pg. 617 PB
Athletic Attic Retail Company, 18 NW 33rd Ct., 32607, pg. 936 PB
Atkins Technical Company, 3401 S.W. 40th Blvd., 32608, pg. 1080 PV
Browning-Ferris Industries of Florida, Inc., P.O. Box 908, 32602, pg. 263 PB
Cox Cable University City, Inc., 1115 N.W. Fourth St., 32601, pg. 455 PB
Cox Communications-Gainesville/Ocala, P.O. Box 147012, 6020 N.W. 43rd St., 32614-7012, pg. 454 PB
Diversitech, Inc., 2411 N.W. 41st St., 32606-6662, pg. 288 IT
Florida Farm Bureau Casualty Insurance Company, 5700 S.W. 34th St., 32602, pg. 1016 PV

PB - *U.S. Public Companies Volume*
PV - *U.S. Private Companies Volume*
IT - *International Public & Private Companies Volume*

Geographic Index-U.S.

Gainesville Sun Publishing Company, 2700 S.W. 13th St., 32608, pg. 1175   PB
Hilb, Rogal and Hamilton Company of Gainesville, Florida, Inc., 2201 N.W. 40th Terrace, 32605, pg. 827   PB
North Central Florida Division, 924 S. Main St., 32602, pg. 656   PB
PERMA-FIX ENVIRONMENTAL SERVICES, INC., 1940 N.W. 67th Pl., Ste. A, 32653, pg. 1279   PB
Perma-Fix Environmental Services, Inc., 1940 N.W. 67th Pl., Ste. A, 32653, pg. 1279   PB
Southern Electric Supply Co., Inc., 3005 SW Williston Rd., 32608, pg. 1107   IT

Green Cove Springs

Pyramid Southern Mouldings, 300 S. Magnolia Ave., 32043, pg. 1335   IT

Gulf Breeze

Bay Breeze Center, 3375 Gulf Breeze Pkwy., 32561, pg. 836   PB

Haines City

HAINES CITY CITRUS GROWERS ASSOCIATION, Eight Railroad Ave., 33844, pg. 494   PV
Haines City Herald & Ridge Shopper, 11 C St., Box 1596, 33844-1596, pg. 995   PV

Hallandale

Flanigan's Enterprises, Inc., 4 N. Federal Hwy., pg. 648   PB
Promark, 3121 W. Hallandale Blvd., 33009, pg. 815   PB

Heathrow

AMERICAN AUTOMOBILE ASSOCIATION, 1000 AAA Dr., 32746-5063, pg. 50   PV
BRITE VOICE SYSTEMS, INC., 250 International Pkwy., Ste 300, 32746, pg. 175   PB
CENTRAL STATES ENTERPRISES, INC., 300 International Pkwy., Ste. 150, 32746, pg. 225   PV
DIXON TICONDEROGA COMPANY, 195 International Pkwy., 32746-5036, pg. 514   PB

Hialeah

Belson Products Div., 5980 Miami Lakes Dr., 33014, pg. 1771   PB
Cam-Stat, Inc., 1800 W. Fourth Ave., 33010, pg. 1746   PB
Chock Full O' Nuts Coffee Company, 590 W. 84th St., 33014, pg. 351   PB
City Gas Company of Florida, 955 E. 25th St., 33013-3498, pg. 1147   PB
Comare Products, 5980 Miami Lakes Dr., 33014, pg. 1771   PB
Dayton Superior Corp., 9745 N.W. 80th Ave., 33015, pg. 932   PV
Dialysis Corporation of America, 2201 W. 76th St., 33016, pg. 1080   PB
Fidelity National Title Insurance Company of Pennsylvania, 14100 Northwest 58 Ct., 33014, pg. 621   PB
Flamingo Products, Inc., 3095 E. 11th Ave., 33013, pg. 382   PV
Flanigan's Enterprises, Inc., 1150 W. 84th St., pg. 648   PB
Fortune Products, Inc., 5980 Miami Lakes Dr., 33014, pg. 1771   PB
GATOR INDUSTRIES INC., 1000 S.E. Eighth St., 33010, pg. 441   PV
General Wig Manufacturers, Inc., 13982 N.W. 58th Ct., 33014, pg. 690   PV
H & D Graphics, 950 S.E. Eighth St., 33010, pg. 68   PB
J.I. KISLAK INC., 7900 Miami Lakes Dr. W., 33016, pg. 624   PV
J.I. Kislak Mortgage Corporation, 7900 Miami Lakes Dr., 33016, pg. 624   PV
J.I. Kislak Mortgage Service Corporation, 7900 Miami Lakes Dr., 33102, pg. 624   PV
Littlemaid, 5980 Miami Lake Dr., 33014, pg. 1771   PB
GUS MACHADO ENTERPRISES, 1200 W. 49th St., 33012, pg. 691   PV
MASON DISTRIBUTORS, INC., 5105 N.W. 159th St., 33014, pg. 712   PV
MED/WASTE, INC., 6175 N.W. Third St., Ste. 324, 33014, pg. 1077   PB
MEDICORE INC., 2337 W. 76th St., 33016, pg. 1080   PB
P.E./Del Mar, Inc., 1800 W. Fourth Ave., 33010, pg. 1746   PB
QUIPP, INC., 4800 N.W. 157th St., 33014, pg. 1353   PB
Quipp Systems, Inc., 4800 N.W. 157th St., 33014, pg. 1353   PB
Rho Sigma, Inc., 1800 W. 4th Ave., 33010, pg. 1746   PB
SECURITY PLASTICS, INC., 14427 N.W. 60th Ave., 33014, pg. 981   PV
Summit Machinery Co., 1095 W. 21st Place, 33010, pg. 971   PB
TIE Systems, Inc. Southeast Florida, 14100 Palmetto Frontage Rd., Ste. 100, 33016, pg. 1085   PV
Techdyne, Inc., 2230 W. 77th St., 33016, pg. 1080   PB
TELEMUNDO GROUP, INC., 2290 W. Eighth St., 33010, pg. 1570   PB
Varon, 1100 E. 41st St., 33013, pg. 233   PB
Watsco Components, Inc., 1800 W. Fourth Ave., 33010, pg. 1746   PB
WINDMERE-DURABLE HOLDINGS, 5980 Miami Lakes Dr., pg. 1771   PB

Windmere Prods. Div., 5980 Miami Lakes Dr., 33014, pg. 1771   PB

High Springs

The Lamson & Sessions Co., Rte. 2, 1405 E. Santa Fe Blvd., 32643, pg. 976   PB

Hollywood

Aircraft Technology, Inc., 3000 Taft St., 33021, pg. 804   PB
ATLAS PEN & PENCIL CORPORATION, 3040 N. 29th Ave., 33022, pg. 96   PV
CONMODORE HOLDINGS, 4000 Hollywood Blvd., Ste. 385 S., 33021, pg. 414   PB
Dun & Bradstreet Latin America & Caribbean, 200 South Park Road, Ste. 300, 33021, pg. 536   PB
ESS-FOOD USA Inc., 4601 Sheridan St., Ste. 420, 33021, pg. 429   IT
Florida Coca-Cola Bottling Company, 3350 Pembroke Rd., 33021, pg. 393   PB
GGR, Inc., 4651 Sheridan St., Suite 355, 33021, pg. 480   PV
HEICO Aerospace Corporation, 3000 Taft St., 33021, pg. 804   PB
HEICO CORPORATION, 3000 Taft St., 33021, pg. 804   PB
Homeowners Marketing Services, Inc., 6365 Taft St., Ste. 2000, 33024, pg. 832   PB
Homeowners Marketing Services International, Inc., 6365 Taft St., Ste. 2000, 33024, pg. 832   PB
Jani King of Miami, Inc., 4000 Hollywood Blvd., Ste. 5155, 33021, pg. 582   PV
Jet Avion Corporation, 3000 Taft St., 33021, pg. 804   PB
LPI Corporation, 3000 Taft St., 33021, pg. 804   PB
Natbank, F.S.B., 4031 Oakwood Blvd., Oakwood Plaza, 33020, pg. 907   IT
New Pier Operating Company, Inc., 4651 Sheridan St., 33021, pg. 480   PV
Reed Travel Publishing-Miami, 3440 Hollywood Blvd., Ste. 460, 33021, pg. 1097   IT
WDZL Channel 39, 2055 Lee St., 33020, pg. 1636   PB
Western International Media Corporation, 4000 Hollywood Blvd., Suite 112-N, 33021, pg. 1167   PV

Howey in the Hills

SILVER SPRINGS CITRUS CO-OP, P.O. Box 155, 25411 Mare Ave., 34737, pg. 1000   PV

Immokalee

Calumet Florida, Inc., Hwy. 846 E., 33934, pg. 1308   PB

Indialantic

Level Five Research Inc., 503 Fifth Ave., 32903, pg. 561   PV

Inverness

Regions Bank/Citrus County, 800 W. Main St., 34450, pg. 1372   PB

Islamorada

Lor-E-Lei, 96 Madiera Rd., Meter Mile 82, 33036, pg. 130   PB

Jacksonville

A&E Reprographic & Supply Co., 3312 Beach Blvd., 32207, pg. 1735   PB
AT&T American Transtech Inc., 8000 Baymeadows Way, 32216, pg. 10   PB
AT&T Universal Card Services Corp., 8775 Baypine Rd., 32256, pg. 11   PB
ACCUSTAFF INCORPORATED, One Independent Dr., 32211, pg. 15   PB
Adcom Wire Company, 925 N. Lane Ave., 32201, pg. 966   PB
Air Land Forwarders, Inc., P.O. Box 37977, 32254, pg. 1049   PV
Aircraft Products Company, 11710 Central Pkwy., 32224, pg. 159   PB
AirKaman of Jacksonville, Inc., Jacksonville Intl. Airport, P.O. Box 18157, 32229, pg. 942   PV
Allbritton Jacksonville, Inc., 7025 A.C. Skinner Pkwy., 32256, pg. 854   PB
Allied Security Inc., 3947 Blvd. Center Dr., #2, 32207, pg. 40   PB
American City Business Journals, Inc., 1200 Gulf Life Dr., Ste. 501, 32207, pg. 19   PB
American Heritage Life Insurance Co., 1776 American Heritage Life Dr., 32224, pg. 79   PB
AMERICAN HERITAGE LIFE INVESTMENT CORP., 1776 American Heritage Life Dr., 32224, pg. 78   PB
American Natl. Can Co., 3331 W. 12th St., 32205, pg. 1029   IT
American Norit Co. Inc., 420 Agmac Ave., 32205, pg. 95E   IT
American Technical Ceramics (Florida), Inc., 2201 Corporate Square Blvd., 32216, pg. 93   PB
Anthem Health Plans of Florida Inc., 10151 Deerwood Park Blvd., Ste. 400, 32256, pg. 76   PV
Apalachicola Northern RR, 1650 Prudential Dr., 32207, pg. 1427   PB
ARTHUR TREACHER'S, INC., 7400 Baymeadows Way, Ste. 300, 32256, pg. 136   PB

Astor Products, 5244 Edgewood Ct., 32254-3601, pg. 1772   PB
Atlantic Coast Asphalt, 5154 Edwards St., 32205, pg. 544   PV
THE AUCHTER COMPANY, 1021 Oak St., 32204, pg. 98   PV
Austill Packaging, P.O. Box 2710, 3389 Powers Ave., 32217, pg. 1269   IT
Bacardi-Martini Product Development Inc., 12200 N. Main St., 32218, pg. 131   IT
Bacardi-Martini Product Quality Americas Inc., 12200 N. Main St., 32218, pg. 131   IT
Baker Distributing Company, 7892 Baymeadows Way, 32256, pg. 1746   PB
Barnett Annuities Corp., 9000 Southside Blvd., 32256, pg. 1162   PB
Barnett Bank N.A., 50 N. Laura St., 32202, pg. 1162   PB
Barnett Banks, Inc., 50 N. Laura St., 32202-3638, pg. 1162   PB
Barnett Banks Services Insurance, Inc., 9000 Southside Blvd., 32256, pg. 1162   PB
Barnett Capital Advisors Inc., 9000 Southside Blvd., 32256, pg. 1162   PB
Barnett Inc., 3333 Lenox Ave., 32205, pg. 1749   PB
Barnett Investments Inc., 9000 Southside Blvd., 32256, pg. 1162   PB
Barnett Merchant Services Corp., 9000 Southside Blvd., 32256, pg. 1162   PB
Barnett Mortgage Company, 9000 Southside Blvd., 32256, pg. 1162   PB
Barnett Recovery Corporation, 9000 Southside Blvd., 32256, pg. 1162   PB
Barnett Technologies, Inc., 9000 Southside Blvd., 32256, pg. 1162   PB
BEACON SALES CORPORATION, 5905 Macy Ave., 32211, pg. 126   PV
BEAVER STREET FISHERIES, INC., 1741 W. Beaver St., 32209, pg. 128   PV
Bergen Brunswig Medical Corporation, 7501 Phillips Hwy., 32216, pg. 214   PB
BetzDearborn Paper Process Group, 7510 Bay Meadows Way, 32256, pg. 226   PB
BODY SHOP OF AMERICA, 6225 Powers Ave., 32217, pg. 154   PV
Browning-Ferris Industries of Florida, Inc., P.O. Box 16996, 32216, pg. 263   PB
CDI Marine Company, 4040 Woodcock Dr., Ste. 200, 32207-2719, pg. 277   PB
CSX Technology, Inc., 500 Water St., 32202, pg. 284   PB
CSX Transportation, Inc., 500 Water St., 32202, pg. 284   PB
CAIN & BULTMAN, 2145 Dennis St., 32204, pg. 199   PV
Cap Gemini America (Jacksonville Branch), 6821 Southpoint Dr. N., Ste. 112, 32216, pg. 264   IT
Capital Credit Corporation, 8000 Arlington Expressway, Ste. 210, 32211, pg. 1667   PB
Caribbean Moving & Storage, Inc., P.O. Box 60069, 32254, pg. 1049   PV
Carolina Casualty Insurance Company, Jackson Bldg., 8381 Dix Ellis Trail, Ste. 400, 32256, pg. 216   PB
Castleton Beverage Corp., 12200 N. Main St., 32218, pg. 132   IT
W.C. Caye & Co., 5409 Broadway Ave., 32254, pg. 220   PV
Chapparal Partners, c/o Foley & Lardner, The Greenleaf Bldg., 32201, pg. 365   PB
Charter Behavioral Health System of Jacksonville, Inc., 3947 Salisbury Rd., 32216, pg. 1034   PB
Chemrock Corporation, 32254, pg. 903   PV
Chesebrough-Pond's Household Products Div., 4880 Bull's Bay Highway, 32219, pg. 1435   IT
COGGIN AUTOMOTIVE GROUP, 4306 Pablo Oaks Ct., 32224, pg. 250   PV
Coggin Pontiac-GMC Inc., 9201 Atlantic Blvd., 32211, pg. 250   PV
Commercial Metals Co., 2038 N. Lane Ave., 32254, pg. 413   PB
Computer Power, Inc., 661 Riverside Ave., 32204, pg. 56   PB
Container Strapping, 6838 Stuart Ave., 32205, pg. 867   PB
THE WILLIAM COOK AGENCY, INC., 225 Water St., Ste. 1600, 32202, pg. 273   PV
William Cook Direct Marketing, Inc., 225 Water St., Ste. 1600, 32202, pg. 273   PV
Corrugated Packaging, P.O. Box 18016, 32229, pg. 737   PB
J.B. COXWELL CONTRACT, INC., 6741 Lloyd Rd. W., 32254-1249, pg. 283   PV
Crane Resistoflex/Defense, 2575 West 5th St., 32205, pg. 457   PB
Customized Transportation, Inc., 10407 Centurion Pkwy. N., Ste. 400, 32256, pg. 284   PV
Data Storage Center, P.O. Box 6367, 32254, pg. 1049   PV
DeLeuw, Cather & Company, 4417 Beach Blvd., Ste. 400, 32207, pg. 841   PB
WALTER DICKINSON INC., One Independent Dr., Ste. 2401, 32202, pg. 331   PV
Dillard, A ResourceNet International Company, P.O. Box 37889, 5595 Commonwealth Ave., 32236, pg. 902   PB
Dillard Paper Co. of Jacksonville, 5955 Commonwealth Ave., 32254, pg. 902   PB
ELKINS CONSTRUCTORS, INC., 4501 Beverly Ave., 32210, pg. 372   PV
EquiCredit Corporation, 1801 Art Museum Dr., 32207, pg. 1162   PB
Evans Environmental & Geological Science and Management, Inc., 8049 Arlington Expressway, 32211, pg. 563   PB
Excel Industries of Florida, 9444 Florida Mining Blvd., 32257, pg. 598   PB

PB - *U.S. Public Companies Volume*
PV - *U.S. Private Companies Volume*
IT - *International Public & Private Companies Volume*

1182

U.S. LOCATED COMPANIES FLORIDA

First Colonial Insurance Company, 1776 American Heritage Life Dr., 32224, pg. 79 **PB**
First Union National Bank of Florida, 225 Water St., 32202, pg. 640 **PB**
Florala Telephone Co., 1550 Prudential Dr., 32207, pg. 1427 **PB**
Florida Associated Services, Inc., 1776 American Heritage Life Dr., 32224, pg. 79 **PB**
Florida Hardware Company, 436 Cassat Ave., 32205, pg. 335 **PV**
FLORIDA ROCK INDUSTRIES, INC., 155 E. 21st St., 32206, pg. 655 **PB**
Flowers Baking Co. of Jacksonville, Inc., 2261 W. 30th St., 32209, pg. 657 **PB**
GATX Logistics, Inc., 1301 Gulf Life Dr., Ste. 1800, 32207, pg. 691 **PB**
GATX Logistics, Inc.-Florida (Honda), 2001 N. Ellis Rd., 32254, pg. 691 **PB**
GATX Logistics NorPack, Inc., 1301 Gulf Life Dr., Ste. 1800, 32207, pg. 691 **PB**
GATX Logistics Properties, Inc., 1301 Gulf Life Dr., Ste. 1800, 32207, pg. 691 **PB**
GATE PETROLEUM COMPANY, 9540 San Jose Blvd., 32257-3627, pg. 441 **PV**
Green Tree Acceptance, Inc., 8659 Bay Pine Rd., Ste. 301, 32256, pg. 762 **PB**
Gulf Telephone Co., 1650 Prudential Dr., 32207, pg. 1427 **PB**
The Hamilton Collection, 4810 Executive Park Ct., 32216, pg. 163 **PV**
The Hamilton Group Limited, Inc., 4810 Executive Park Ct., 32216, pg. 163 **PV**
Hamilton Worldwide Direct Response Group, 4810 Executive Park Ct., 32216, pg. 163 **PV**
JERRY HAMM CHEVROLET INC., 2600 Phillips Hwy., 32207, pg. 497 **PV**
HANDLING SYSTEMS ENGINEERING, 3000 W. 45th St., 32209, pg. 499 **PV**
Harland Bartholomew & Associates Inc., 4417 Beach Blvd., Ste. 400, 32207, pg. 842 **PV**
Harmon Industries-Jacksonville, 6830 Hay Ave., 32254, pg. 788 **PB**
Harris Specialty Chemical, 10245 Centurion Pkwy. N., 32256, pg. 505 **PV**
HealthCare USA, 8705 Perimeter Park Blvd., Ste. 3, 32216, pg. 454 **PB**
Hewlett-Packard Company, 6800 S. Point Pkwy., Ste. 301, 32216, pg. 814 **PB**
Homeside Lending Company, 7301 Baymeadows Way, 32256, pg. 906 **IT**
Humana Medical Plan Inc.-Jacksonville, 4190 Belfort Rd., Ste. 250, 32216, pg. 848 **PB**
Ideon Group, Inc., 7596 Centurion Pkwy., 32256, pg. 320 **PB**
Investors Insurance Corp., 3030 Hartley Rd., 32257, pg. 912 **PB**
Investors Marketing Group, Inc., 3030 Hartley Rd., 32257, pg. 912 **PB**
Jacksonville Crawdaddy Corp., 1643 Prudential Dr., 32207, pg. 1023 **PV**
Jacksonville Properties, Inc., 1550 Prudential Dr., 32207, pg. 1427 **PB**
Jacksonville Welding Supply, Inc., P.O. Box 40787, 32203, pg. 1320 **PB**
Jani King of Florida, Inc., 4417 Beach Blvd., Ste. 202, 32207, pg. 582 **PV**
KOGER EQUITY INC., 3986 Boulevard Center Dr., 32207, pg. 965 **PB**
Laboratory Supply Company, 3069 Mercury Rd., 32207, pg. 642 **PV**
Landstar Gemini, Inc., P.O. Box 19116, 477 Woodcock Dr., 32245, pg. 978 **PB**
Landstar ITCO, Inc., P.O. Box 17701, 4057 Carmichael Ave., 32245, pg. 978 **PB**
Landstar Logistics, Inc., 4057 Carmichael Ave., 32245, pg. 978 **PB**
Landstar Ranger, Inc., P.O. Box 19060, 4057 Carmichael Ave., 32245, pg. 978 **PB**
Leggett Wire Company, 925 N. Lane Ave., 32201, pg. 986 **PB**
Lil'Champ/Food Stores Inc., P.O. Box 23180, 32241-3180, pg. 837 **PV**
Loan America Financial Corp., 9000 Southside Blvd., 32256, pg. 1162 **PB**
Walter Lorenz Surgical, Inc., P.O. Box 18009, 1520 Tradeport Dr., 32229-8009, pg. 231 **PB**
Lydall Southern Products, 500-B.N. Ellis Rd., 32254, pg. 1021 **PB**
MAC PAPERS, INC., 3300 Phillips Hwy., 32207, pg. 689 **PV**
Media General Broadcasting, Inc. (WJWB-TV), 9117 Hogan Rd., 32216, pg. 1078 **PB**
Merrill Lynch Credit Corporation, Building 200, 7751 Belfort Pkwy., 32256, pg. 1098 **PB**
MILLER ELECTRIC COMPANY, 2251 Rosselle St., 32204, pg. 747 **PV**
Monticello Bank, 10601-36 San Jose Blvd., 32257, pg. 759 **PV**
THE MONTICELLO COMPANIES, INC., 1604 Stockton St., 32204, pg. 759 **PV**
Monticello Drug Co., 1604 Stockton St., 32204, pg. 759 **PV**
M.D. MOODY & SONS INC., 4652 Phillips Hwy., 32207, pg. 759 **PV**
Moran Towing of Florida, 1534 E. Adams St., 32202, pg. 761 **PV**
National Distributing Co., Inc., 9423 No. Main St., 32218, pg. 781 **PV**
HARRY PEPPER & ASSOCIATES, 215 Century 21 Dr., 32216, pg. 851 **PV**
PHYSICIAN SALES AND SERVICES INC., 4345 S. Point Blvd., 32216, pg. 1293 **PB**
The Pilot Corporation of America, 3901 Regent Blvd., East Park, 32224, pg. 1057 **IT**
PLOOF TRUCK LINES, INC., 1414 Lindrose St., 32206, pg. 872 **PV**
Poe & Brown of Florida, Bldg. 100, 10151 Deerwood Pk. Blvd., Ste. 100, 32256, pg. 1312 **PB**
Post-Newsweek Stations, Florida, Inc., P.O. Box 5270, Four Broadcast Pl., 32207, pg. 1743 **PB**
Principal Health Care of Florida, Inc., 1200 Riverplace Blvd., Ste. 500, 32207, pg. 885 **PV**
PROGRESSIVE DRIVER SERVICES, INC., 2000 Corporate Sq. Blvd., 32216, pg. 890 **PV**
Pyramid Mouldings, 7406 Fullerton St., Ste. 210, 32256, pg. 1335 **IT**
REGENCY DODGE INC., 9875 Atlantic Blvd., 32225, pg. 918 **PV**
REGENCY GROUP INC., 121 W. Forsyth St., Ste. 200, 32202, pg. 918 **PV**
RehabCare Outpatient Services, Inc., Bldg. B, 8777 San Jose Blvd., Ste. 302A, 32217, pg. 1373 **PB**
Revlon Manufacturing Facilities, 5335 Obermeyer Dr., 32217, pg. 690 **PV**
Rhone Poulenc - Water Treatment Chemicals, 5930 Souter Dr., 32219-3740, pg. 1112 **IT**
RIVERSIDE GROUP, INC., 7800 Belfort Pkwy., Ste. 100, 32256, pg. 1391 **PB**
SCM Glidco Organic, P.O. Box 389, Foot of West 61st St., 32201, pg. 594 **IT**
Safecard Services, Inc., 7596 Centurion Pkwy., 32256, pg. 320 **PB**
St. Joe Container Co., 1550 Prudential Dr., 32207, pg. 1427 **PB**
ST. JOE CORP., DuPont Center, Ste. 400, 1650 Prudential Dr., 32207, pg. 1426 **PB**
St. Joe Industries, Inc., 1650 Prudential Dr., Ste. 1400, 32207, pg. 1427 **PB**
St. Joe Telephone & Telegraph Company, 1650 Prudential Dr., Ste. 800, 32207, pg. 1427 **PB**
St. Joseph Land & Development Company, 1650 Prudential Dr., Ste. 400, 32207, pg. 1427 **PB**
South Pasadena Associates, 121 Jackson Pl., pg. 365 **PB**
Southeast Properties Holding Corporation, Inc., 3986 Boulevard Center Dr., 32207, pg. 965 **PB**
Southeastern Bonded Warehouses, Inc., 1301 Gulf Life Dr., Ste. 1800, 32207, pg. 691 **PB**
Southeastern Metals Manufacturing Co. Inc, 11801 Industry Dr., 32218, pg. 742 **PB**
SouthTrust Bank of Jacksonville, 51 W. Bay St., 32238, pg. 1492 **PB**
STEIN MART, INC., 1200 Riverplace Blvd., 32207, pg. 1514 **PB**
THE STELLAR GROUP INC., 2900 Hartley Rd., 32257, pg. 1040 **PV**
Storage Systems Engineering, 3000 W. 45 St., 32209, pg. 499 **PV**
SUCCESS DEVELOPMENT INTERNATIONAL, 9799 Old St. Augustine Rd., 32257, pg. 1048 **PV**
Sudco Development Co., Inc., P.O. Box 60069, 32254, pg. 1049 **PV**
THE SUDDATH COMPANIES, 815 S. Main St., 32207-8187, pg. 1049 **PV**
Suddath Moving Systems, Inc., P.O. Box 61802, 32254, pg. 1049 **PV**
Suddath Transportation Service, P.O. Box 60069, 32254, pg. 1049 **PV**
Suddath Van Lines, P.O. Box 60069, 32254, pg. 1049 **PV**
Summit Commercial Property, Inc., 6622 Southpoint Dr., S., Ste. 400, 32216, pg. 1049 **PV**
SunTrust Bank, North Florida, N.A., 200 W. Forsyth St., 32202, pg. 1537 **PB**
Sysco Food Services-Jacksonville, 1501 Lewis Industrial Rd., 32236-7045, pg. 1551 **PB**
Talisman Sugar Corp., 1650 Prudential Dr., Ste. 400, 32207, pg. 1427 **PB**
Thoro, 10245 Centurion Pkwy. N., 32256, pg. 505 **PV**
UNISON INDUSTRIES, 7575 Baymeadows Way, 32256, pg. 1120 **PV**
Unisource (S.E. Regional Office), 7785 Baymeadows Way, Ste. 200, 32256, pg. 1671 **PB**
Unit Logistics Inc., 1301 Gulf Life Dr., Ste. 1800, 32207, pg. 691 **PB**
Unit Multi-Pack, Inc., 1301 Gulf Life Dr., 32207, pg. 691 **PB**
United Railway Signal Group Inc., 1387 Cassat Ave., 32205, pg. 2 **PB**
Vistakon Johnson & Johnson Vision Products, Inc., P.O. Box 10157, 4500 Salisbury Rd., 32247, pg. 929 **PB**
Voyager Group, Inc., Voyager Bldg., P.O. Box 2918, 32203, pg. 68 **PB**
Voyager Service Programs, Inc., 4250 Lakeside Dr., Ste. 304, 32210, pg. 68 **PB**
WAWS-TV, 11700 Central Pkwy., 32224-7628, pg. 384 **PB**
WJXT-TV, 1851 Southampton Rd., 32207, pg. 1743 **PB**
WQIK-AM, 5555 Radio Ln., 32205, pg. 923 **PB**
WQIK-FM, 5555 Radio Ln., 32205, pg. 923 **PB**
WTLV-TV, 1070 E. Adams St., 32202, pg. 702 **PB**
Wellspring Resources, LLC, 301 W. Bay St., Suite 2600, 32202, pg. 1154 **PV**
Wellspring Resources, LLC, 301 W. Bay St., Suite 2600, 32202, pg. 1513 **PB**
White Electrical Construction Co., 1873 Everlee Rd., 32216, pg. 1172 **PV**
John Wieland Homes of Jacksonville, Inc., 3901 Monument Rd, 32225, pg. 1175 **PV**
Winn-Dixie, Inc.-Jacksonville Div., 5233 Commonwealth Ave., 32205, pg. 1771 **PB**
WINN-DIXIE STORES, INC., 5050 Edgewood Ct., 32254-3699, pg. 1771 **PB**
WOOLVERTON OLDSMOBILE-G.M.C. TRUCK, INC., 1325 Cassat Ave., 32205, pg. 1188 **PV**
Xomed Surgical Products, 6743 Southpoint Dr. N., 32216, pg. 253 **PB**
Zellerbach Division, 1030 N. Ellis Rd., 32205, pg. 1075 **PB**

Jacksonville Beach

Naturally You, 933 N. Third St., 32250, pg. 1015 **PV**
SOUTHEASTERN MEDEQUIP, INC., 905 N. 3rd St., 32250, pg. 1015 **PV**

Jasper

Jasper Textile, Rte. 2, Box 35, 32052, pg. 542 **PV**

Jupiter

Chartwells Dining Services, 1070 E. Indiantown Rd., 33477, pg. 324 **IT**
The Courier Journal, 800 Indiantown Rd., 33458, pg. 1447 **PB**
Ellison Graphics, 1400 Indiantown Rd., 33468, pg. 524 **PV**
Florida Pneumatic Mfg. Corp., 851 Jupiter Park Lane, 33458-8998, pg. 1240 **PB**
Jonathan's Landing, Inc., 17290 Jonathan Dr., 33477, pg. 61 **PB**
Jupiter Beach Resort, Five North A1A, 33477, pg. 800 **PV**
Philips Components, P.O. Box 689605, 1440 W. Indiantown Rd., 33468, pg. 1054 **IT**
Philips Components, 1440 W. Indiantown Rd., 33458, pg. 1054 **IT**
Senercomm Inc., 3930 RCA Blvd., pg. 1527 **PB**

Kennedy Space Center

EG & G Florida, P.O. Box 21267, 32815, pg. 544 **PB**
Intergraph, John F. Kennedy Space Ctr., 32899, pg. 890 **PB**

Key Biscayne

Corporate Services International, Inc., 104 Crandon Blvd., #307, 33149, pg. 840 **IT**
Northern Trust Bank of Florida, N.A., 328 Crandon Blvd., Ste. 101, 33149, pg. 1196 **PB**

Kissimmee

Fairfield Orlando at Cypruss Palms, 5300 Fairfield Lake Rd., 34746, pg. 611 **PB**
Horizon Specialty & Rehabilitation Center of Kissimmee, 221 Park Place Blvd., 34741, pg. 836 **PB**
KISSIMMEE TOYOTA INC., 2535 N. Orange Blossom Trail, 34744, pg. 624 **PV**
Poe & Brown of Florida, 1637-B E Vine, 34744, pg. 1312 **PB**
Southern Electric Supply Co., Inc., 500 E. Donegan Ave., 34744, pg. 1107 **IT**
United Foam Plastics Corporation, 2175 Partin Settlement Rd., 34744-8697, pg. 1112 **PV**

La Belle

ALICO, INC., 640 S. Main St., 33935, pg. 41 **PB**
Saddlebag Lake Resorts, Inc., 640 S. Main St., 33935, pg. 41 **PB**

Lake Buena Vista

Benihana Orlando Corp., 1751 Hotel Plaza Blvd., 32830, pg. 212 **PB**
Walt Disney Attractions-Walt Disney World, 1675 Buena Vista Dr., Ste. 410, 32830-1000, pg. 513 **PB**
Lake Buena Vista Communities, Inc., P.O. Box 35, 32830, pg. 513 **PB**
Reedy Creek Energy Services, Inc., 5300 Center Dr., 32830-1000, pg. 514 **PB**
URS Greiner, Inc., P.O. Box 22152, 32830, pg. 1658 **PB**
Vista Insurance Services, Inc., P.O. Box 10190, 32830-10190, pg. 514 **PB**

Lake City

Aero Corporation, Lake City Airport, 32055, pg. 1766 **PB**
Lake City Correctional Facility, Rte. 7, Box 1000, 32055, pg. 450 **PB**
Lake City Reporter, Inc., 126 E. Duval St., 32055, pg. 1175 **PB**

Lake Mary

Ambico, 2950 Lake Emma Rd., 32746, pg. 1369 **PB**
Arrow/Schweber Electronics, 37 Skyline Dr., Ste. 3101-3, 32746, pg. 134 **PB**
Calibron, Inc., 2950 Lake Emma Rd., 32746, pg. 1369 **PB**
DiscWasher, 2950 Lake Emma Rd., 32746, pg. 1369 **PB**
Eldeen Manufacturing Corporation, 2950 Lake Emma Rd., 32746, pg. 1369 **PB**
FARO TECHNOLOGIES, INC., 125 Technology Park, 32746, pg. 613 **PB**
Milgray/Florida, Inc., 755 Rinehart Rd., 32746-4876, pg. 206 **PB**
RECOTON CORPORATION, 2950 Lake Emma Rd., 32746, pg. 1369 **PB**
Rembrandt, 2950 Lake Emma Rd., 32746, pg. 1369 **PB**
Scholastic Book Fairs, Inc., 1080 Greenwood Blvd., 32746, pg. 1440 **PB**

PB - U.S. Public Companies Volume
PV - U.S. Private Companies Volume
IT - International Public & Private Companies Volume

Geographic Index-U.S.

Sound Quest, 2950 Lake Emma Rd., 32746, pg. 1369   PB
WOFL-TV, 35 Skyline Dr., 32746, pg. 1094   PB

Lake Placid

Corrugated Packaging, 400 S. Rte. 70 W., 33852, pg. 737   PB
Lake Placid Groves, 600 State Rd. 70 W., 33871, pg. 437   PB
Lykes Agriculture, 7 Lykes Rd., 33852, pg. 682   PV

Lake Wales

CITRUS WORLD INC., 650 US Hwy. 27 N., 33853-1111, pg. 241   PV
EAGER BEAVER, 4425 Hwy 27 S., 33853, pg. 354   PV
Lake Wales Daily Highlander, 33 W. Orange Ave., Box 872, 33859-0872, pg. 995   PV
Liqui-Box Corp., 104 S. Scenic Hwy., 33853, pg. 1001   PB
E.B. Malone Corp., 309 Acuff Rd., 33853, pg. 193   PB

Lake Worth

AMERICAN MEDIA, INC., 600 E. Coast Ave., 33464-0001, pg. 87   PB
Flanigan's Enterprises, Inc., 102 N. Dixie Hwy., pg. 648   PB
Medicana Nursing Center, 1710 Lucerne Ave., 33460, pg. 1257   PV
MIDCOAST MORTGAGE CORPORATION, 5700 Lake Worth Rd., 33463, pg. 744   PV

Lakeland

Advanced Separation Technologies Incorporated, 5315 Great Oak Dr., 33801, pg. 655   PB
Alcosa/Sunwise, 2505 Knights Station Rd., 33809, pg. 499   PV
AMICO-Lakeland, 1033 Pine Chase Ave., 33801, pg. 30   PV
Bodolay/Pratt Div., 5015 N. Frontage Rd., 33809, pg. 832   PV
BREED TECHNOLOGIES, INC., P.O. Box 33050, 5300 Old Tampa Hwy., 33807-3050, pg. 251   PB
CUTLER MANUFACTURING CORPORATION, 3240 Flightline Dr., 33811, pg. 298   PV
DISCOUNT AUTO PARTS, INC., 4900 Frontage Rd. S., 33815, pg. 510   PB
Florida Favorite Fertilizer, P.O. Box 8000, 33802, pg. 1064   IT
Florida Tile Ceramic Centers, Inc., 100 S. Kentucky Ave., # 210, 33801, pg. 1322   PV
Florida Tile Industries, Inc., One Sikes Blvd., 33815 -1575, pg. 1322   PV
Floyd Theatres, Inc., 4226 Old Hwy. 37, 33813, pg. 1056   PB
Food Processing Systems, P.O. Box 1708, Fairway Ave., 33802, pg. 605   PB
Full Circle Transport, Inc., 4355 Drane Field Rd., 33811, pg. 847   PB
Haleyville Drapery Manufacturing Division, 1910 W. Olive St., 33815, pg. 491   PV
Hawthorne Lakeland, Inc., 3470 Dranefield Rd., 33811, pg. 512   PV
Imperial Auto Auction, 310 S. County Line Rd., 33809, pg. 282   PV
JE Merit Constructors, Inc., Hwy. 98S State Rd. 540, 33803, pg. 921   PB
J.I. Services Corp., 4355 Drane Field Rd., 33811, pg. 847   PB
Jacobs Engineering Group Inc., Hwy. 98S State Rd. 540 E., 33813, pg. 921   PB
JuNo Industries, Inc., 4355 Drane Field Rd., 33811, pg. 847   PB
Lakeland Auto Auction, P.O. Box 90007, Interstate 4 & Hwy. 33, 33804, pg. 282   PV
Lakeland Flight Academy, Lakeland Airport, 2949 Medulla Road, 33811, pg. 218   PV
Lakeland Ledger Publishing Corporation, 401 S. Missouri Ave., 33801, pg. 1175   PB
Omega Environmental Services, 20 Lake Wire Dr., 33815, pg. 1222   PB
Precision Die & Engineering, Inc., 400 Kathleen Blvd., 33802, pg. 1322   PB
PUBLIX SUPERMARKETS INC., 1936 George Jenkins Blvd., 33815, pg. 893   PV
QUALITY PETROLEUM CORP., 1625 George Jenkins Blvd., 33815, pg. 899   PV
Shopper Publishing Group, 2901 W. Memorial Blvd., Drawer 1110, 33802-1110, pg. 995   PV
Southern-Owners Insurance Company, 2710 W. Memorial Blvd., 33801-1016, pg. 101   PV
Velda Farms, 402 S. Kentucky, Ste. 500, 33801, pg. 1527   PV

Lantana

Country Weekly, Inc., 600 E. Coast Ave., 33464-0002, pg. 87   PB
Distribution Services, Inc., 600 E. Coast Ave., 33464-0002, pg. 87   PB
Fairview Printing, 600 East Coast Ave., 33464-0002, pg. 87   PB
NDSI, Inc., 600 E. Coast Ave., 33464-0002, pg. 87   PB
Soap Opera Magazine, 600 E. Coast Ave., 33464-0002, pg. 87   PB
Star Editorial, Inc., 600 E. Coast Ave., 33464, pg. 87   PB
Weekly World News, Inc., 600 E. Coast Ave., 33464-0002, pg. 87   PB

Largo

AMF Inc. Lytel Division, 230 Commerce Dr., 34640,   PB
Eckerd Corporation, 8333 Bryan Dairy Rd., 33777, pg. 917   PB
Electromechanical Systems, Inc., 6200 118th Ave. N., 34643, pg. 424   PB
Hit Promotional Products Inc., 7150 Bryan Dairy Rd., 34647, pg. 277   PV
Idex Investor Services, Inc., 201 Highland Ave., 34640, pg. 27   IT
Idex Management, Inc., 201 Highland Ave., 34640, pg. 27   IT
Indian Rocks National Bank, 12360 Indian Rocks Rd., 34644, pg. 608   PB
Intersecurities, Inc., 201 Highland Ave., 34640, pg. 27   IT
KTL Truck Lines, 1501 Lake Ave. S.E., 33771, pg. 66   PV
Kleinert's Inc. of Florida, 2300 S. Belcher Rd., 33771, pg. 625   PB
Linvatec Corp., 11311 Concept Blvd., 34643, pg. 431   PB
Martin Marietta Specialty Components, Inc., P.O. Box 2908, 34349-2908, pg. 1007   PB
Nokia Paging, 12345 Starkey Rd., Ste. K, 34643, pg. 952   IT
Nokia Sourcing, Inc., 2210 Tall Pines Dr., Ste. 200, 33771, pg. 953   IT
OVERSTREET PAVING COMPANY, 1390 Donegan Rd., 33771, pg. 823   PV
PARADYNE, 8545 126th Ave., 33773, pg. 838   PV
Smith & Nephew United Inc., 11775 Starkey Rd., 34649-1970, pg. 1263   PB
SOUTHERN APPAREL CORPORATION, 12420 73rd Court N., 33773, pg. 1015   PV
Test and Colibration Instruments, 8600 Somerset Dr., 33773, pg. 100   PV
Western Reserve Life Assurance Co. of Ohio, 201 Highland Ave., 34640, pg. 27   IT

Lecanto

Citrus County Detention Facility, 1295 S. Lecanto Hwy., 34431, pg. 450   PB

Leesburg

CEM South, 31800 Progress Rd., 34748, pg. 1009   PV
FLORIDA CRUSHED STONE COMPANY, 1616 S. 14th St., 34748, pg. 414   PV
Lake County Cablevision, 1310 Marion St., 34748, pg. 448   PB
Poe & Brown of Florida, 1023 W. Dixie Ave., 34748, pg. 1312   PB
T.L. Smith Florida, P.O. Box 9914, Executive Blvd., 34749-0914, pg. 1009   PV

Live Oak

ALLTEL Florida, Inc., 206 White Ave. S.E., P.O. Box 550, 32060, pg. 56   PB

Longboat Key

Northern Trust Bank of Florida, N.A., 540 Bay Isles Rd., 34228, pg. 1197   PB

Longwood

Auto-trol Technology Corp.-Orlando, 2180 W. State 434, Ste. 2180, 32779, pg. 148   PB
Expansion Valve Division, 777 Bennett Dr., 32750-6353, pg. 1260   PB
S.I. GOLDMAN CO., 799 Bennett Dr., 32750, pg. 461   PV
Lancer USA Inc., 705 J. West Hwy. 434, 32750, pg. 551   IT
QUALITY TOYOTA, 2925 N. Hwy. 17-92, 32750, pg. 899   PV
BILL RAY NISSAN, INC., 2724 N. Hwy. 1792, 32750, pg. 911   PV
Regions Bank/Orlando, 425 U.S. Hwy. 19-92, 32750, pg. 1372   PB
Southeast Fire Sprinkler Company, 799 Bennett Dr., 32750, pg. 462   PV
SPRAY-TECH, INC., 1086 Florida Central Pkwy., 32750, pg. 1026   PV

Lutz

Florida Health Facilities, Inc., 21808 State Rd. 54, 33549, pg. 1035   PB
Upright, 1106 Ballinger Dr., 33549-4415, pg. 1128   PV

Lynn Haven

RHG Panama City (Florida), 504 E. 3rd St., 32444, pg. 1151   IT

Madison

JIMMY DAVIS ENTERPRISES, INC., 420 Lake Shore Dr., 32340, pg. 315   PV
Dixie Packers, P.O. Box 622, State Rd. 53 S., 32340-0622, pg. 1772   PB

Maitland

Arlon, Inc., 2251 Lucien Way, Ste. 300, 32751, pg. 165   PB

BAIRNCO CORPORATION, 2251 Lucien Way, Ste. 300, 32751, pg. 165   PB
Burke, Bales & Mills/HEPY, Inc., 341 N. Maitland Avd., Ste. 130, 32751, pg. 503   PV
CAP Gemini America (Orlando Branch), 2700 Westhall Ln., Ste. 130, 32751, pg. 264   IT
DEL AMERICAN PROPERTIES, INC., 1101 N. Lake Destiny Dr., Ste. 400, 32751, pg. 321   PV
Halcyon Underwriters, 2600 Lake Lucien Dr., Ste. 102, 32781, pg. 1312   PV
Kasco Corporation, 2251 Lucien Way, Ste. 300, 32751, pg. 165   PB
La Amistad Residential Treatment Center, 201 Alpine Drive, 32751, pg. 1697   PB
Poe & Brown of Florida, 2600 Lake Lucien Dr., Ste. 100, 32751-7234, pg. 1312   PB
Premier Insurance Company, P.O. Box 945075, 32794, pg. 681   PB

Marathon

Keynoter Publishing Company, Inc., P.O. Box 500158, 33050, pg. 964   PB

Marco Island

Marco Island Eagle, 579 Elkcam Cir., 33937, pg. 1175   PB

Margate

Continental Cement Co. Inc., P.O. Box 93-9007, 33093-9007, pg. 1201   IT

Marianna

Marianna Div.-Florida Public Utilities, 311 N. Jefferson St., 32446, pg. 655   PB
Regions Bank/Marianna, P.O. Box 340, 32447, pg. 1372   PB
SouthTrust Bank of Northwest Florida, 111 W. Lafayette St., 32446, pg. 1492   PB

Medley

Daher Golden Eagle - Miami, 11700 N.W. 100 Rd., 33178, pg. 749   PB
Dillard Paper Co. of Miami, 9253 N.W. 100th St., 33178, pg. 902   PB
Hydro Conduit Corp., 10401 N.W. 121st. Way, 33178, pg. 246   IT
L. LURIA & SON, INC., 10025 N.W 116 Way, Ste. 18, 33178, pg. 1020   PB

Melbourne

Air Traffic Control Systems Division, P.O. Box 5100, 32902, pg. 792   PB
Atlantic Scientific Corporation, 4300 Fortune Pl., Ste. A, 32904, pg. 208   IT
Cape Publications, Inc., Gannett Plaza, 32936, pg. 700   PB
DBA SYSTEMS, INC., 1200 S. Woody Burke Rd., 32902, pg. 472   PB
Electronics & Systems Integration Division, 2000 W. Nasa Blvd., Box 9650, 32902, pg. 1198   PB
Engineering & Technical Services, Inc., 7100 Technolgy Dr., 32904, pg. 75   PB
Fiber Optic Services, Inc., 100 Rialto Pl., Ste. 500, 32901, pg. 750   PB
G.E. Harris Energy Control Systems, LLC, 407 John Rhodes Blvd., 32901, pg. 712   PB
The Goldfield Consolidated Mines Co., 100 Rialto Pl., Ste. 500, 32901, pg. 750   PB
THE GOLDFIELD CORPORATION, 100 Rialto Pl., Ste. 500, 32901, pg. 750   PB
HARRIS CORPORATION, 1025 W. NASA Blvd., 32919, pg. 791   PB
Harris Publishing Systems Corporation, 505 N. John Rodes Blvd., 32934, pg. 791   PB
Harris Semiconductor, P.O. Box 883, 32901, pg. 792   PB
Hewlett-Packard Company, 255 E. Drive, Ste. B, 32901, pg. 814   PB
The Lordsburg Mining Company, 100 Rialto Place, Ste. 500, 32901, pg. 750   PB
Melbourne Divisions Support Operations, P.O. Box 37, 32902-0037, pg. 791   PB
Nokia Products Corporation, 1801 Penn St., Ste. 3, 32901, pg. 952   IT
Omni Business Systems, Inc., 2725 Center Place, 32940, pg. 864   PB
PARAVANT COMPUTER SYSTEMS, INC., 1615A W. Nasa Blvd., 32901, pg. 1257   PB
Partel Research Corp., 250 East Dr., 32904, pg. 27   IT
Poe & Brown of Florida, 100 Rialto Pl., Ste. 215, 32901, pg. 1312   PB
Relm Communications, Inc., Technology Dr., 32904, pg. 1376   PB
TEC Cellular, 7619 Emerald Dr., 32904, pg. 1430   PB
Targ-It-Tronics Inc., 7100 Technology Dr., 32904, pg. 713   IT
Telecommunications Systems, 1025 W. NASA Blvd., 32919, pg. 792   PB
Transcomm Division, P.O. Box 5100, 32902-5100, pg. 792   PB
The Viera Company, 7380 Murrell Rd., Ste. 201, 32900, pg. 344   PV

PB - *U.S. Public Companies Volume*
PV - *U.S. Private Companies Volume*
IT - *International Public & Private Companies Volume*

1184

Geographic Index-U.S.

Merritt Island

ISLAND LINCOLN-MERCURY, 1850 E. Merritt Island Causeway, 32952, pg. 576 PV

Miami

AAKO Inc., 2875 N.E. 191 St., Ste. 903-A, 33180, pg. 830 IT
AAR Landing Gear Center, 9371 N.W. 100th St., 33178, pg. 1 PB
ABN AMRO Bank, N.V. (Miami), Interterra Bldg., 5th Fl., 1200 Brickell Ave., 33131, pg. 10 IT
ACBJ Business Journals, Inc., 7950 N.W. 53rd St., Ste. 210, 33166, pg. 19 PV
Acer Latin America, 1601 NW 84th Ave., 33126, pg. 22 IT
Ackerley Communications of Florida, Inc., 5800 NW 77th Court, 33166, pg. 16 PB
THE AD TEAM OF FLORIDA INC., 11900 Biscayne Blvd., Ste. 620, 33181, pg. 16 PV
Adaptec - Latin America, 5805 Blue Lagoon Dr., 33131, pg. 19 PB
Adtranz Miami, 8145 N.W. Seventh St., Ste. 518, 33126-8007, pg. 369 IT
AERO SYSTEMS AVIATION CORP., 5415 N.W. 36th St., 33166-5899, pg. 24 PV
Aerolineas Argentinas, 6100 Blue Lagoon Dr., Ste. 210, 33126, pg. 575 IT
AeroThrust Corp., P.O. Box 522236, 33152, pg. 276 IT
Air France (Southeastern Region), 1001 S. Bayshore, 33131, pg. 561 IT
AIR JAMAICA LTD., 9200 S. Dadeland Blvd., Ste. 820, 33156, pg. 28 PV
Aircraft Service International Group, Dawson Bldg., 8240 N.W. 52nd Terrace, Ste. 200, 33166, pg. 1719 PB
Alba Forwarding Co., Inc., 1801 N.W. 82nd Ave., 33126, pg. 32 PV
JOHN ALDEN FINANCIAL CORPORATION, 7300 Corporate Ctr. Dr., 33126, pg. 39 PB
John Alden Life Insurance Company, 7300 Corporate Center Dr., 33126, pg. 39 PB
ALL AMERICAN SEMICONDUCTOR, INC., 16115 N.W. 52nd Ave., 33014, pg. 41 PB
All American Technologies, 16115 N.W. 52nd Ave., 33014, pg. 41 PB
Allright Miami, Inc., 150 S.E. Second Ave., Ste. 900, 33131, pg. 42 PV
Alpha Pay Phones, Ltd. III, 2300 N.W. 89th Pl., 33172, pg. 1275 PB
Alpnet, 280 S.W. 12th Ave., 33442, pg. 58 PB
Americ Disc, 8455 N.W. 30th Ter., 33122, pg. 539 IT
American Bankers Insurance Co. of Florida, 11222 Quail Roost Dr., 33157, pg. 67 PB
AMERICAN BANKERS INSURANCE GROUP, INC., 11222 Quail Roost Dr., 33157-6596, pg. 67 PB
American Bankers Life Agents Services, Inc., 11222 Quail Roost Dr., 33157, pg. 67 PB
American Bankers Life Assurance Co. of Florida, 11222 Quail Roost Dr., 33157, pg. 67 PB
American Communications Corp., 100 S.E. Second St., 33131, pg. 1173 PB
AMERICAN INTERNATIONAL CONTAINER, INC., 11825 N.W. 100th Rd., 33178-1034, pg. 57 PV
American Southern Financial Group, One S.E. Third Ave., 11th Fl., 33131, pg. 618 PV
Amerinsurance, Inc., 3401 N.W. 82nd Ave., #300, 33122, pg. 333 IT
Amstar Insurance Company, 3401 N.W. 82nd Ave., #100, 33122, pg. 333 IT
Amstar Management Company, 3401 N.W. 82nd Ave., #100, 33122, pg. 333 IT
AMTRADE INTERNATIONAL BANK, 1001 S. Bayshore Dr., Ste. 2800, 33131, pg. 68 PV
Angel Station, Inc., 18191 N.W. 68th Ave., 33015, pg. 314 PB
ASSOCIATED GROCERS OF FLORIDA, INC., 7000 N.W. 32nd Ave., 33147, pg. 91 PV
ATLANTIC GULF COMMUNITIES CORPORATION, 2601 S. Bayshore Dr., 33133-5461, pg. 144 PB
Atlantic Pump & Eqipment Co., 3055 N.W. 84th Ave., 33122, pg. 846 PB
AVANTI PRESS INC., 13449 N.W. 42nd Ave., 33054, pg. 101 PV
Avatar Development Corp., 255 Alhambra Cir., 33134, pg. 151 PB
Avatar Properties Inc., 255 Alhambra Cir., 33134, pg. 151 PB
AVIATION SALES COMPANY, 6905 N.W. 25th St., 33122, pg. 154 PB
BCI HOLDING CORPORATION, 3595 N.W. 110th St., 33167, pg. 106 PV
BGLS Inc., 100 S.E. 2nd St., 33131, pg. 259 PB
Bacardi-Martini Promotions, 2075 Biscayne Blvd., 33137, pg. 131 IT
BACARDI-MARTINI, USA, INC., 2100 Biscayne Blvd., 33137, pg. 109 PV
Bacardi-Martini U.S.A., Inc., 2100 Biscayne Blvd., 33137, pg. 131 IT
Baker Norton Pharmaceuticals, Inc., 8800 N.W. 36th St., 33178, pg. 914 PB
Ballast Nedam Construction Inc., Credit Bank Tower, Ste. 730, 2800 Biscayne Blvd., 33137, pg. 134 IT
Banca Nazionale Del Lavoro (Miami), Interterra Bldg., 1200 Brickell Ave., 18th Fl., 33131, pg. 136 IT
Banco de la Nacion Argentina, 777 Brickell Ave., Ste. 802, 33131, pg. 140 IT
Banco do Brasil S.A.-Miami, One Biscayne Tower, 38th Fl., 2 S. Biscayne Blvd., Suite 3870, 33131, pg. 141 IT
Banco Santander International, 1401 Brickell Ave., 33131, pg. 143 IT
Banco Santander International Miami, 14th Floor, 1401 Brickell Ave., 33131, pg. 143 IT
Bank of Boston International, 800 Brickell Ave., Ste. 1500, 33131, pg. 184 PB
The Bank of New York Trust Company of Florida, N.A., 800 Brickell Ave., Ste. 300, 33131, pg. 179 PB
Barclays Bank PLC, 18th fl., 801 Brickell Ave., 33131, pg. 165 IT
BEBER & SILVERSTEIN & PARTNERS, INC., 3361 S.W. Third Ave., 33145, pg. 128 PV
Beckman Coulter, 11800 S.W. 147th Ave., 33196-2500, pg. 199 PB
Geoffrey Beene Fragrances, 15595 N.W. 15th Ave., 33169, pg. 681 PB
BENIHANA, INC., 8685 N.W. 53rd Ter., 33166, pg. 211 PB
Benihana International, Inc., 8685 N.W. 53rd Terrace, 33166, pg. 212 PB
Benihana National Corp., 8685 N.W. 53rd Terr., 33166, pg. 212 PB
Benihana National of Florida Corp., 8685 N.W. 53rd Terrace, 33166, pg. 212 PB
Benihana of Texas, Inc., 8685 N.W. 53rd Ter., 33166, pg. 212 PB
Beverage Canners International Corp., 3595 N.W. 110th St., 33167, pg. 106 PV
Big Splash Kendall Corp., 8727 S. Dixie Hwy., 33143, pg. 212 PB
Biscayne Apparel, Inc., 2665 S. Bayshore Dr., Eighth Fl., 33133, pg. 233 PB
Boston Scientific Symbiosis, 8600 N.W. 41 St., 33166, pg. 247 PB
Brain Power Inc., P.O. Box 559501, 33255-9501, pg. 772 PB
BRAMAN WORLD CAR CENTER, 2044 Biscayne Blvd., 33137, pg. 165 PV
Brock Communications, Inc., 2300 N.W. 89th Pl., 33172, pg. 1275 PB
BROOKE GROUP LTD., 100 S.E. Second St., 33131, pg. 259 PB
Burdines, 22 E. Flagler St., 33131, pg. 618 PB
Burger King Corporation, P.O. Box 020783, 17777 Old Cutler Rd., 33157, pg. 411 IT
Campus Telephone Services, Inc., 2300 N.W. 89th Pl., 33172, pg. 1275 PB
Canon Latin America, Inc., 6505 Blue Lagoon Dr., Ste. 325, 33126, pg. 262 IT
CARFEL, INC., 6900 N.W. 77th Ct., 33166, pg. 210 PV
Caribbean Foreign Trade Corporation, 6300 N.W. 84th Ave., 33166, pg. 279 IT
Caribe Express Latin American Div., 6701 N.W. Seventh St., Ste. 190, 33126, pg. 211 PV
Carifone, 2300 N.W. 89th Pl., 33172, pg. 1275 PB
CARNIVAL CORPORATION, Carnival Pl., 3655 N.W. 87th Ave., 33178-2428, pg. 306 PB
Carnival Hotels & Casinos, 3250 Mary St., 33133, pg. 1265 PB
Carrier Corp. Latin Amer Opers, 2100 N.W. 88th Ct., 33172-2433, pg. 1689 PB
Case Paper Co. of Florida, Inc., 3200 N.W. 119 St., 33167, pg. 218 PV
CATALINA LIGHTING, INC., 18191 N.W. 68th Ave., 33015, pg. 314 PB
Catalina Real Estate Trust, Inc., 18191 N.W. 68th Ave., 33015, pg. 314 PB
Cedars Medical Center Victoria Pavillion, 1400 NW 12th Ave., 33136, pg. 404 PB
Celebrity Cruises, Inc., 5201 Blue Lagoon Dr., 33126, pg. 1410 PB
Central Park South, Inc., 700 N.W. 107th Ave., 33172, pg. 987 PB
Chemwest Corp., 7270 N.W. 12th St., Ste. 350, 33126, pg. 332 IT
Circle Freight International USA - Free Zone Office, Free Zone Facility, 2335 N.W. 107 Ave., C-11, Box 10, 33172, pg. 371 PB
Circle Freight International USA - Latin America, Miami Intl. Commerce Ctr., 2323 N.W. 82nd Ave., 33126, pg. 371 PB
Circle International, Miami Intl. Commerce Ctr., 2323 N.W. 82nd Ave., 33126, pg. 371 PB
Circle International, 2323 N.W. 82nd Ave., 33122, pg. 372 PB
Clinton Machinery and Supply, 5800 Miami Lakes Dr., 33014, pg. 1177 PV
Coastal Fuel Terminals, Inc., 8700 W. Flagler St., 33174, pg. 390 PB
Coastal Fuels Marketing, Inc., 8700 W. Flagler St., 33174, pg. 390 PB
Coastal Fuels of Puerto Rico, Inc., 8700 W. Flagler St., 33174, pg. 390 PB
Coastal Tug & Barge, Inc., 8700 W. Flagler St., 33174, pg. 390 PB
COLUMBIA LABORATORIES, INC., 2665 S. Bayshore Dr., Ste. PH2B, 33133, pg. 405 PB
Commodore Aviation, P.O. Box 661078, 33266-1078, pg. 690 IT
Conso Products Co., Airport Corporate Ctr., 7200 Corporate Center Dr., Ste. 411, 33126, pg. 434 PB
Consolidated Water Co., 255 Alhambra Cir., 33134, pg. 151 PB
Continental Homes of Miami, 8000 Governor's Sq., 33016, pg. 441 PB
Cordis, a Johnson & Johnson Company, 5200 Blue Lagoon Dr., 33126, pg. 928 PB
COSMO COMMUNICATIONS CORPORATION, 16501 N.W. 16th Ct., 33169, pg. 451 PB
COSTA CRUISE LINES, N.V., World Trade Ctr., 80 S.W. Eighth St., Ste. 2700, 33130, pg. 278 PV
Coutts & Co (USA) International Limited, 701 Brickell Ave., Ste. 2400, 33131, pg. 911 IT
CRISPIN PORTER & BOGUSKY, 2699 S. Bayshore Dr., 33133, pg. 290 PV
Crispin Porter & Bogusky Advertising, 2699 S. Bayshore Dr., 9th Fl., 33133, pg. 290 PV
CRUISE HOLDINGS LTD., 901 S. American Way, 33132, pg. 293 PV
DCA at Banyan Tree, Inc., 700 N.W. 107th Ave., 33172, pg. 987 PB
DCA at Boca del Mar Inc., 700 N.W. 107th Ave., 33172, pg. 987 PB
DCA at Boca del Mar No. 5, Inc., 700 N.W. 107th Ave., 33172, pg. 987 PB
DCA at Boca del Mar No. 4, Inc., 700 N.W. 107th Ave., 33172, pg. 987 PB
DCA at Boca del Mar No. 3, Inc., 700 N.W. 107th Ave., 33172, pg. 987 PB
DCA at Boca del Mar No. 2, Inc., 700 N.W. 107th Ave., 33172, pg. 987 PB
DCA at Carmel Place, Inc., 700 N.W. 107th Ave., 33172, pg. 987 PB
DCA at Haciendas, Inc., 700 N.W. 107th Ave., 33172, pg. 987 PB
DCA at Palm Place Inc., 700 N.W. 107th Ave., 33172, pg. 987 PB
DCA at Pembroke Points, Inc., 700 N.W. 107th Ave., 33172, pg. 987 PB
DCA at Pine Lakes, Inc., 700 N.W. 107th Ave., 33172, pg. 987 PB
DCA at the California Club, Inc., 700 N.W. 107th Ave., 33172, pg. 987 PB
DCA at Waterside, Inc., 700 N. W. 107th Ave., 33172, pg. 988 PB
DCA at Waterside No. 2, Inc., 700 N.W. 107th Ave., 33172, pg. 988 PB
DCA at Welleby Inc., 700 N.W. 107th Ave., 33172, pg. 988 PB
DCA at West Kendall, Inc., 700 N.W. 107th Ave., 33172, pg. 988 PB
DCA at Westchester, Inc., 700 N.W. 107th Ave., 33172, pg. 988 PB
DCA Financial Corp., 700 N.W. 107th Ave., 33172, pg. 988 PB
DCA Homes, Inc., 700 N.W. 107th Ave., 33172, pg. 988 PB
DCA Homes West, Inc., 700 N.W. 107th Ave., 33172, pg. 988 PB
DCA of Broward County, Inc., 700 N.W. 107th Ave., 33172, pg. 988 PB
DCA of California, Inc., 700 N.W. 107th Ave., 33172, pg. 988 PB
DCA of Dade City, 700 N.W. 107th Ave., 33172, pg. 988 PB
DCA of Golden Gate, Inc., 700 N.W. 107th Ave., 33172, pg. 988 PB
DCA of Hialeah, Inc., 700 N.W. 107th Ave., 33172, pg. 988 PB
DCA of Homestead Inc., 700 N.W. 107th Ave., 33172, pg. 988 PB
DCA of Kendall Inc., 700 N.W. 107th Ave., 33172, pg. 988 PB
DCA of Lake Worth Inc., 700 N.W. 107th Ave., 33172, pg. 988 PB
DCA of Lakeshore, Inc., 700 N.W. 107th Ave., 33172, pg. 988 PB
DCA of Nevada, Inc., 700 N.W. 107th Ave., 33172, pg. 988 PB
DCA of Palm Beach City, 700 N.W. 107th Ave., 33172, pg. 988 PB
DCA of San Francisco Inc., 700 N.W. 107th Ave., 33172, pg. 988 PB
DCA of the Hammocks, Inc., 700 N.W. 107th Ave., 33172, pg. 988 PB
DCA of West Florida, 700 N.W. 107th Ave., 33172, pg. 988 PB
DCA of West Virginia, Inc., 700 N.W. 107th Ave., 33172, pg. 988 PB
DCA Oil & Gas One, Inc., 700 N.W. 107th Ave., 33172, pg. 988 PB
DCA Properties, Inc., 700 N.W. 107th Ave., 33172, pg. 988 PB
DCA Realty Inc., 700 N.W. 107th Ave., 33172, pg. 988 PB
DCA Services, Inc., 700 N.W. 107th Ave., 33172, pg. 988 PB
Dade Behring, 9750 N.W. 25th St., 33172, pg. 110 PV
Daewoo International America Corp. - Miami, 8390 N.W. 53rd St., Ste. 312, 33166, pg. 357 IT
Daisytek Latin America, 1825 N.W. 87th Ave., 33172, pg. 477 PB
Danzas Management Latin America, Inc., 10813 NW 30th St., Ste. 102, 33172, pg. 382 IT
De La Rue Security Printing, 5200 Blue Lagoon Dr., Ste. 100, 33126, pg. 386 IT
De La Rue Systems (Latin America), 5200 Blue Lagoon Dr., Ste. 100, 33126, pg. 387 IT
Deutsch-Sudamerikanische Bank AG, Miami Agency, 7th Fl., 801 Brickell Ave., 33131, pg. 418 IT
Devco Land Corp., 700 N.W. 107th Ave., 33172, pg. 988 PB
Development Corporation of America, 700 N.W. 107th Ave., 33172, pg. 987 PB
Development Corp. of Delray, Inc., 700 N.W. 107th Ave., 33172, pg. 988 PB
Diamedix Corporation, 2140 N. Miami Ave., 33127, pg. 914 PB
Dispatch Services, Inc., P.O. Box 592036, AMF, 33159, pg. 1719 PB
Dresdner Bank Lateinamerica, 801 Brickell Ave., 6th Fl., 33131, pg. 418 IT
E & G FOODS, 7007 N.W. 37th Ave., 33147, pg. 352 PV

Geographic Index-U.S.

PB - *U.S. Public Companies Volume*
PV - *U.S. Private Companies Volume*
IT - *International Public & Private Companies Volume*

Editorial Caribe Inc., 9200 S. Dade Land Blvd. Ste. 209, 33156, pg. 1168 **PB**

Evans Environmental & Geological Science and Management Inc., 99 S.E. 5th St., 4th Fl., 33131, pg. 563 **PB**

FAG Interamericana AG, 2335 N.W. 107th Ave., 33152, pg. 469 **IT**

FDP CORP., 2140 S. Dixie Hwy., 33133, pg. 603 **PB**

FMS MANAGEMENT SYSTEMS, INC., 2655 N.E. 189th St., 33180, pg. 389 **PB**

FARM STORES, 5800 N.W. 74th Ave., 33166, pg. 394 **PV**

Farrey's Wholesale Hardware Co., Inc., 1850 N.E. 146th St., 33181, pg. 335 **PV**

Fedders International, 7925 N.W. 12th St., Ste. 122, 33126, pg. 614 **PB**

Federal Assist, 9485 Sunset Dr., Ste. A-170, 33173, pg. 334 **IT**

Fiduciary Trust International of the South, International Place Bldg., 100 S.E. Second St., Ste. 2300, 33131-1101, pg. 621 **PB**

Filbert Corp., 7218 N.W. 56th St., 33166, pg. 1140 **PV**

Financial Data Planning Corp., 2140 So. Dixie Hwy., 33133, pg. 603 **PB**

Financial Exchange, Inc., 11222 Quail Roost Dr., 33157, pg. 67 **PB**

First Atlantic Building Corp., 700 N.W. 107th Ave., 33172, pg. 988 **PB**

FIRST FLORIDA EQUITIES, INC., 7740 S.W. 104th St., Ste. 200, 33156, pg. 407 **PV**

First Health Center, 7910 NW 25th St., Ste. 100, 33122, pg. 404 **PV**

Flanigan's Management Services, Inc., 16565 N.W. 15th Ave., 33169, pg. 648 **PV**

Florida Home Finders, 2601 S. Bayshore, 33131, pg. 144 **PB**

Florida Homes Title, 700 N.W. 107th Ave., 33172, pg. 988 **PB**

Flowers Baking Co. of Miami, Inc., 17800 N.W. Miami Ct., 33269-0483, pg. 657 **PB**

FRENCH FRAGRANCES INC., 14100 N.W. 60th Ave., 33014, pg. 681 **PV**

The Gate Development Corp., 700 N.W. 107th Ave., 33172, pg. 988 **PB**

Global Trading Ltd., One Datran Center, Ste. 1101, 9100 S. Dadeland Blvd., 33156, pg. 688 **IT**

Goldman, Sachs & Co., First Union Financial Ctr., 200 S. Biscayne Blvd., Ste. 3700, 33131, pg. 462 **PV**

Goya Foods of Florida, 1900 N.W. 92nd Ave., 33172, pg. 468 **PV**

Grant Center of Deering, 20601 S.W. 157th Ave., 33187, pg. 405 **PB**

Greenwich Air Services, Miami Intl. Airport, 4590 N.W. 36th St., Bldg. 23, 33166, pg. 710 **PB**

Greyhound Leisure Services, Inc., P.O. Box 592355, 33159, pg. 1718 **PV**

HIG CAPITAL MANAGEMENT, 1001 Brickell Bay Dr., Ste. 2708, 33131, pg. 490 **PV**

HARRISON CONSTRUCTION CORP., 1000 N.W. 54th St., 33127, pg. 506 **PV**

Harte-Hanks Shopper Miami, P.O. Box 169003, 33116, pg. 794 **PB**

EDD HELMS ELECTRICAL CONTRACTING, 17850 N.E. Fifth Ave., 33162, pg. 520 **PV**

Edd Helms Electrical Service, Inc., 17830 N.E. Fifth Ave., 33162, pg. 521 **PV**

Ed Helms McDonald Air Conditioning, Inc., 17830 N.E. 5th Ave., 33162, pg. 521 **PV**

Hewlett-Packard Company, Waterford Bldg., 9th Fl., 5200 Blue Lagoon, 33126, pg. 814 **PB**

Honeywell Inc., 14505 Commerce Way, Ste. 500, 33016, pg. 834 **PB**

Iberia Air Lines of Spain, 6100 Blue Lagoon Dr., 2nd Fl., 33126, pg. 575 **IT**

INJECTION FOOTWEAR CORP., 8730 N.W. 36th Ave., 33147, pg. 563 **PB**

Inktel Marketing, 12845 N.W. 45th Ave., 33054, pg. 101 **PV**

INTERACTIVE TELECARD SERVICES, INC. (ITS), 444 Brickell Ave., Ste. 650, 33131, pg. 566 **PB**

Intercontinental Bank, 200 S.E. First St., 33131, pg. 1162 **PB**

International Dessert Partners, 5200 Blue Lagoon Dr., Ste. 790, 33126, pg. 447 **PB**

Interval International Inc., 6262 Sunset Dr., 33143, pg. 320 **PB**

ITOCHU Building Products Co., Inc., 3200 N.W. 125th St., 33167, pg. 694 **IT**

IVAX CORPORATION, 4400 Biscayne Blvd., 33137-3227, pg. 914 **PB**

JL Media Inc., 722 Corporate Center Dr., Ste. 201, 33166, pg. 577 **PV**

Jetro Cash & Carry, 2041 N.W. 12th Ave., 33127, pg. 587 **PV**

Kantel Communications, Inc., 2300 N.W. 89th Pl., 33172, pg. 1275 **PB**

Kendall Regional Medical Center, 11750 Bird Rd., 33175, pg. 405 **PB**

Kendall Therapy Center, Ltd., 6825 SW 87th Ave., 33173, pg. 405 **PB**

Keyes Asset Managemet, One S.E. 3rd Ave., Ste. 1100, 33131, pg. 618 **PV**

THE KEYES COMPANY REALTORS, One S.E. 3rd Ave., Ste. 1100, 33131, pg. 618 **PV**

Keyes Investments, 1 S.E. 3rd Ave., Ste. 1100, 33131, pg. 618 **PV**

Keyes National Referral, 1 S.E. 3rd Ave., Ste 1100, 33131, pg. 618 **PV**

Kintetsu Intermodal Inc., 8551 Kintetsu Way, 33122, pg. 735 **IT**

Kintetsu World Express Inc., 8551 Kintetsu Way, 33122, pg. 735 **IT**

KNIGHT-RIDDER, INC., One Herald Plaza, 33132-1693, pg. 963 **PB**

Korn/Ferry International, 200 S. Biscayne Blvd. # 2790, 33131, pg. 633 **PV**

Ladenburg, Thalmann Group Inc., 100 S.E. Second St., 33131, pg. 1173 **PB**

Lamar Caribbean Sales Div., 2144 N.W. 7th Ave., 33137, pg. 1539 **PB**

LANCHILE AIRLINES, 9700 S. Dixie Hwy., Penthouse, 33156, pg. 645 **PV**

Landis & Staefa Inc., 12370 S.W. 130 St., 33186, pg. 800 **IT**

Latin America Area, 2007 N.W. 84th Ave., 33126, pg. 281 **IT**

Latin American Representative Comdisco, Inc., One Datran Ctr., 9100 S. Dackland Blvd., Ste. 1011, 33156, pg. 408 **PB**

HENRY LEE COMPANY, 3301 N.W. 125 St., 33167, pg. 657 **PV**

Leisure Colony Management Corp., 700 N.W. 107th Ave., 33172, pg. 988 **PB**

Lennar Commercial Properties, Inc., 700 N.W. 107th Ave., 33172, pg. 988 **PB**

LENNAR CORPORATION, 700 N.W. 107th Ave., Ste. 400, 33172, pg. 987 **PB**

Lennar Financial Services, Inc., 730 N.W. 107 Ave., Ste. 400, 33172, pg. 988 **PB**

Lennar Homes Inc., 760 N.W. 107 Ave., Ste. 201, 33172, pg. 988 **PB**

Lennar Management Corp., 700 N.W. 107th Ave., 33172, pg. 988 **PB**

Lennar Realty, Inc., 700 N.W. 107th Ave., 33172, pg. 988 **PB**

LILLIE RUBIN FASHIONS INC., 15705 N.W. 13th Ave., 33169, pg. 667 **PV**

Liuski International Miami, Inc., 2708 N.W. 72nd Ave., 33122, pg. 1005 **PV**

Lucerne Lakes Golf Colony Inc., 700 N.W. 107th Ave., 33172, pg. 988 **PB**

LUMAS REALTY, INC., 9240 S.W. 72nd St., Ste. 216, 33173, pg. 680 **PV**

Frank R. MacNeill & Son, Inc., 9690 NW 41st St., 33178, pg. 705 **IT**

Malone & Hyde, Inc.-Miami, 3400 N.W. 74th Ave., 33152, pg. 653 **PV**

Manatee Towing Company, 8700 W. Flagler St., 33174, pg. 390 **PV**

Map Holding, 3401 N.W. 82nd Ave., # 100, 33122, pg. 333 **IT**

MAPFRE Corporation of Florida, 3401 N.W. 82nd Ave., # 100, 33122, pg. 333 **IT**

MAPFRE Insurance Company of America, Inc., 3401 N.W. 82nd Ave., # 100, 33122, pg. 333 **IT**

Marine Exhibition Corporation, 4400 Richenbacker Causeway, 33149, pg. 1186 **PV**

Mars-South, 9240 SW 72nd St., Ste. 218, 33173, pg. 707 **PV**

Marubeni America Corporation, 8401 N.W. 53rd Terr., Ste. 107, 33166, pg. 845 **IT**

MASTEC, INC., 3155 N.W. 77th Ave., 33122, pg. 1055 **PB**

MED-LAB SUPPLY COMPANY, INC., 923 N.W. 27th Ave., 33125, pg. 726 **PV**

Medical Park Diagnostic Center, 9090 SW 87th Court, 33176, pg. 405 **PB**

Merisel Latin America, 2010 N.W. 84th Ave., 33122, pg. 1096 **PV**

METRO FORD INC., 9000 N.W. Seventh Ave., 33150, pg. 736 **PV**

Miami Elevator, P.O. Box 520217, 33152, pg. 521 **PB**

The Miami Herald, One Herald Plaza, 33132, pg. 964 **PB**

Miami Learning Center, P.O. Box 661198, 4800 N.W. 36th St., 33266, pg. 219 **PB**

Mitsui & Co. (U.S.A.), 6303 Blue Lagoon Dr., Ste. 415, 33126, pg. 879 **IT**

Moran Towing of Miami, PO Box 113239, 33131, pg. 761 **PV**

National Insurance Agency, Inc., 11222 Quail Roost Drive, 33157, pg. 67 **PB**

NationsBank/Miami, 1221 Brickell Ave.: 16th FL., 33131, pg. 1162 **PB**

NEW VALLEY CORPORATION, 100 S.E. Second St., 32nd Fl., 33131, pg. 1173 **PB**

New Valley Realty Corp., 100 S.E. Second St., 32nd Fl., 33131, pg. 1173 **PB**

94th Aero Squadron of Miami, Inc., 1395 NW 57th Ave., 33122, pg. 1023 **PV**

North Miami Beach Surgical Center, 120 NE 167th St., 33162, pg. 405 **PB**

Northern Trust Bank of Florida, N.A., 700 Brickell Ave., 33131, pg. 1196 **PB**

NORTHWESTERN MEATS INC., 2100 N.W. 23rd St., 33142, pg. 807 **PV**

NORWEGIAN CRUISE LINE, 7665 Corp. Center Dr., 33126, pg. 808 **PV**

Oak Hill West, Inc., 700 N.W. 107th Ave., 33172, pg. 988 **PB**

OMEGA RESEARCH INC., 8700 W. Flagler St., 33174, pg. 1222 **PV**

THE PBS&J CORPORATION, 2001 N.W. 107th Ave., 33172, pg. 825 **PV**

PCA Life Reinsurance, 5835 Blue Lagoon Dr., 33126, pg. 1293 **PB**

PTC Corrections, 2300 N.W. 89th Pl., 33172, pg. 1275 **PB**

PTC Services, 2300 N.W. 89th Pl., 33172, pg. 1275 **PB**

Palm Electronics Manufacturing Corp., 16115 N.W. 52nd Ave., 33014, pg. 42 **PV**

Pan American Division, Airport Corp. Ctr., 7400 N.W. Corp. Ctr. Dr., Ste. A, 33126, pg. 1262 **PV**

The Paper House/Southern Paper, 3475 N.W. 60th St., 33142, pg. 467 **PV**

Par Four Development Corp., 700 N.W. 107th Ave., 33172, pg. 988 **PB**

Par One Development Corp., 700 N.W. 107th Ave., 33172, pg. 988 **PB**

Par Two Development Corp., 700 N.W. 107th Ave., 33172, pg. 988 **PB**

Parbel Inc., 5200 Blue Lagoon Dr., Ste. 500, 33126, pg. 818 **IT**

PEOPLES TELEPHONE COMPANY, INC., 2300 N.W. 89th Pl., 33172, pg. 1275 **PB**

PEREZ TRADING CO. INC., 3490 N.W. 125th St., 33167, pg. 852 **PV**

Philadelphia Local Telegraph Company, 100 S.E. Second St., 33131, pg. 1173 **PB**

PHYSICIAN CORPORATION OF AMERICA, 6101 Blue Lagoon Dr., Ste. 200, 33126, pg. 1293 **PB**

Poe & Brown of Florida, 8000 Governors Sq. Blvd., Ste. 400, 33016, pg. 1312 **PB**

Poe & Brown of Florida, 8100 Oak Ln., Ste. 306, 33016, pg. 1312 **PB**

POLLO TROPICAL, INC., 7300 N. Kendall Dr., Ste. 800, 33156, pg. 1315 **PB**

Portable Cellular Communications, 2300 N.W. 89th Pl., 33172, pg. 1276 **PB**

POTAMKIN COMPANY, 4675 S.W. 74th St., 33143, pg. 876 **PB**

Potamkin Toyota, Inc., 19390 N.W. Second Ave., 33169, pg. 877 **PV**

Premier Cruises, 901 S. American Way, 33132, pg. 293 **PV**

Princess Casinos Inc., 1031 Ives Dairy Rd., 33179, pg. 818 **IT**

Prism Integrated Sanitation Management, Inc., 8300 Executive Center Dr., Ste. 400, 33166-4680, pg. 592 **PB**

PURITY PRODUCTS INC., 1800 N.W. 70th Ave., 33126, pg. 896 **PV**

REAL HOLDING MANAGEMENT CORP., 9688 S.W. 24th St., 33165, pg. 913 **PV**

RealCold Storage, 8020 N.W. 60th St., 33166, pg. 1025 **PV**

Region Western Hemisphere Tamrock EJC, 782 N.W. 42nd Ave., Ste. 429, 33126, pg. 1352 **IT**

Rendic International, 10700 Caribbean Blvd., Ste. 204, 33189, pg. 413 **PV**

Republic International Bank of New York, Two S. Biscayne Blvd., 33131, pg. 1380 **PV**

REPUBLIC NATIONAL BANK OF MIAMI, Ten N.W. 42nd Ave., 33126, pg. 924 **PV**

Republic New York Trust Company of Florida, National Association, Two S. Biscayne Blvd., 33131, pg. 1381 **PV**

Riggs International Banking Corporation, 800 Brichell Ave., 33131, pg. 1390 **PB**

Riviera Land Corp., 700 N. W. 107th Ave., 33172, pg. 989 **PB**

Rohm & Haas Co. Research Labs, 2600 S. Douglas Rd., Ste. 1100, 33134-6134, pg. 1403 **PB**

ROYAL CARIBBEAN CRUISES LTD., 1050 Caribbean Way, 33132-3203, pg. 1410 **PB**

Royce Laboratories, 5350 N.W. 165th St., 33014, pg. 1746 **PV**

RYDER SYSTEM, INC., 3600 N.W. 82nd Ave., 33166, pg. 1413 **PB**

SMC Mortgage Corp., 700 N.W. 107th Ave., 33172, pg. 989 **PB**

Samsung Electronics Co., Ltd., 2700 N.W. 87th Ave., 33172, pg. 1183 **IT**

Sea Containers Caribbean Inc., Airport Corporate Center, 7200 NW 19th St., Ste. 305, 33126, pg. 1214 **IT**

Seventh Street Corp., 16565 N.W. 15th Ave., 33169, pg. 648 **PV**

Sharp Electronics Corporation, 6100 Blue Lagoon Drive, Ste. 230, 33126, pg. 1229 **PB**

SiboneyUSA, 1401 Brickell Ave., Ste. 1100, 33131, pg. 1641 **PV**

Silverado Communications Corp., 2300 N.W. 89th Pl., 33172, pg. 1276 **PB**

Sol Melia America, Brickell Ave. 1000, 5th Fl., 33131, pg. 1277 **IT**

South Florida Test Service, 17301 Okeechobee Rd., 33018, pg. 96 **PV**

Southern Diesel Systems, Inc., 244 S.W. 6th St., 33130, pg. 1646 **PV**

Southern Underwriters, Inc., 8600 N.W. 36th St., 33166, pg. 1257 **IT**

SOUTHERN WINE & SPIRITS OF AMERICA INC., 1600 N.W. 163rd St., 33169, pg. 1017 **PV**

SPEC's MUSIC, INC., 1666 N.W. 82nd Ave., 33126, pg. 1497 **PB**

SPIEGEL MEATS, INC., 8020 N.W. 60th St., 33166, pg. 1025 **PV**

Standard Chartered Bank (Miami), 701 Brickell Ave., Ste. 1700, 33131, pg. 1294 **IT**

Standard Communications, 2300 N.W. 89th Pl., 33172, pg. 1276 **PB**

State Home Mortgage Corp., 700 N.W. 107th Ave., 33172, pg. 989 **PB**

Sterling Healthcare Group, Inc., 5835 Blue Lagoon Dr., 33126, pg. 608 **PB**

Stone & Webster Engineering, 20803 Biscayne Blvd., Ste. 303, 33180-1429, pg. 1519 **PB**

Sun Ray Products, Inc., 570 NE 185th St., 33179, pg. 752 **IT**

SunTrust Bank, Miami, N.A., 777 Brickell Ave., 33131, pg. 1537 **PB**

SUPREME INTERNATIONAL CORP., 3000 N.W. 107th Ave., 33172, pg. 1542 **PB**

Supreme Lumber & Millwork Co., 7440 N.W. 79th St., 33176, pg. 989 **PB**

Geographic Index-U.S.

PB - *U.S. Public Companies Volume*
PV - *U.S. Private Companies Volume*
IT - *International Public & Private Companies Volume*

Swiss Bank Corporation, 701 Brickell Ave., Ste. 3250, 33131, pg. 1329 **IT**
Sysco Food Services of South Florida, Inc., 555 N.E. 185th St., 33179, pg. 1552 **PB**
TBAC - Canterbury, Inc., 8490 NW 68th St., 33166, pg. 1560 **PB**
TIC Group Ltd., 700 N.W. 107th Ave., 33172, pg. 989 **PB**
TMP Worldwide/Direct Marketing Services, 2799 Northwest 82nd Ave., 33122, pg. 1064 **PV**
TMP Worldwide, Inc., 3785 N.W. 82nd Ave., Ste. 408, 33166, pg. 1064 **PV**
Taca International Airlines, S.A., 4299 N. W. 36th St., 33166, pg. 1346 **IT**
Tech-Aerofoam Products, Inc., 3551 N.W. 116th St., 33167, pg. 473 **PV**
Tech Data Latin America, 8501 NW 17th St., Ste. 101, 33126, pg. 1562 **PB**
Terumo Medical-Miami, 6161 Blue Lagoon Dr., Ste. 340, 33126, pg. 1376 **IT**
Tiger Direct, Inc., 9100 S. Dadeland Blvd., Ste. 1500, 33156, pg. 747 **PB**
Tiger Direct, Inc. (d/b/a Tiger Software, Inc.), 9100 S. Dadeland Blvd. Ste. 1500, 33156, pg. 747 **PB**
TINSLEY ADVERTISING, 2660 Brickell Ave., 33129, pg. 1088 **PV**
Townhomes of Country Run, Inc., 700 N.W. 107th Ave., 33172, pg. 989 **PB**
Transatlantic Holdings Inc., 8300 N.W. 53rd St., Ste. 101, 33166, pg. 84 **PB**
Transatlantic Holdings, Inc.-Miami (Latin America), 800 N.W. 53rd St., Ste. 101, 33166, pg. 83 **PB**
Transbrasil Airlines, Inc., P.O. Box 520862, Ste. F, 5757 Blue Lagoon Dr., Ste. 400, 33126, pg. 1416 **IT**
TRANSMEDIA NETWORK INC., 11900 Biscayne Blvd., 33181, pg. 1631 **PB**
Travel Channel-Latin America, 5201 Blue Lagoon Dr., Ste. 600, 33126, pg. 647 **PV**
TriVest, 2665 So. Bayshore Drive, Ste. 801, 33133, pg. 233 **PB**
THE TRUMP GROUP, 4000 Island Blvd., 33160, pg. 1107 **PV**
Turner Construction Co., 2500 S.W. Third Ave., 33129, pg. 1645 **PB**
URS Greiner, Inc., 5805 N.W. 11th St., Ste. 340, 33126, pg. 1658 **PB**
URS Greiner, Inc., 5805 N.W. 11th St., Ste. 340, 33126-2032, pg. 1658 **PV**
U.T.A. Cable Corp., 700 N.W. 107th Ave., 33172, pg. 989 **PB**
Union-Transport Corporation-Miami Office, 3028 N.W. 72nd Ave., 33122, pg. 1119 **PV**
U.S. Commercial Telephone Corp., 2300 N.W. 89th Pl., 33172, pg. 1276 **PV**
U.S. Computers, 2127 N.W. 79th Ave., 33126, pg. 815 **PV**
Universal American Mortgage Company, 700 N.W. 107th Ave., 33172, pg. 989 **PB**
Universal American Realty Corp., 700 N.W. 107th Ave., 33172, pg. 989 **PB**
Universal Title Insurors, Inc., 700 N.W. 107th Ave., 33172, pg. 989 **PB**
Utell International-Miami, 6100 Waterford Bldg., Ste. 335, 6100 Blue Lagoon Dr., 33126, pg. 1098 **IT**
VARTA Batterie AG, 2111 N.W. 84th Ave., 33122, pg. 1452 **IT**
Victoria Station Inc., Dadeland Mall, 7541 N. Kendall, 33156, pg. 8 **PV**
Victoria Station Inc., 6301 N.W. 36th St., 33166, pg. 8 **PB**
WBGG-FM, 194 N.W. 187th St., 33169, pg. 384 **PB**
WFOR-TV Channel 4, 8900 N.W. 18th Ter., 33172, pg. 275 **PB**
WIOD, Inc., 194 N.W. 187th St., 33169, pg. 385 **PB**
WMRZ-WLYF-WMXJ, 20450 N. W. Second Ave., 33169, pg. 926 **PB**
WNWS (AM) & WLYF (FM), 20450 N.W. Second Ave., 33169, pg. 926 **PB**
WPLG-TV, 3900 Biscayne Blvd., 33137, pg. 1743 **PB**
Warren Pet Products, 507 N.E. 189th St., 33179, pg. 1142 **PV**
Western Union Data Services Company, Inc., 100 S.E. Second St., 33131, pg. 1173 **PB**
WestWayne - Miami, 2121 Douglas Rd., 2nd Fl., 33145, pg. 1170 **PV**
Willis Faber North America, Inc.-Florida, 1401 Brickell Ave., Ste. 1010, 33131, pg. 1503 **IT**
Withers/Suddath Van Lines, Inc., 6900 N.W. 74th Ave., 33152, pg. 1049 **PV**
Wollard Airport Equipment Co., 6950 N.W. 77th Ct., 33122, pg. 866 **PV**
Young & Rubicam Latam (Miami), Courvoisier Centre II, 601 Brickell Key Dr., Ste. 900, 33131-4330, pg. 1198 **PV**
Zenith Goldline Pharmaceuticals, 4400 Biscayne Blvd., 33137, pg. 915 **PB**

Miami Beach

APL CORPORATION, 6917 Collins Ave., 33141, pg. 7 **PV**
Bank Hapoalim (Miami), 201 S. Biscayne Blvd., Suite 1320, 33131, pg. 149 **IT**
Miami Heart Institute-South, 4701 Meridian Ave., 33140, pg. 405 **PV**
Parfums Givenchy W.H.D. Inc., Ste. 300, 20801 Biscayne Blvd., 33180, pg. 781 **PV**
RIU INTERNATIONAL PAN AMERICAN OCEAN RESORT HOTEL, 17875 Collins Ave., 33160, pg. 904 **PV**
Specialty Restaurants Corp., South Point Pk., #1 Washington Ave., 33139, pg. 1023 **PV**

Miami Springs

ERJ Insurance Group, 208 Park St., 33166, pg. 79 **PB**

INTERNATIONAL RECOVERY CORP., 700 S. Royal Poinciana Blvd., Ste. 800, 33166, pg. 906 **PB**
World Fuel Services of FL, 700 S. Royal Poinciana Blvd., Ste. 800, 33166, pg. 906 **PB**

Milton

Armstrong-Hunt, Inc., One Armstrong Rd., 32583, pg. 83 **PV**
Formweld Fittings, 8118 Progress Dr., 32583, pg. 256 **IT**

Miramar

Asbury Worldwide, 3810 Executive Way, 33025, pg. 1110 **PV**
Asbury Worldwide, Latin America, 3810 Executive Way, 33025, pg. 1110 **PB**
Dillard, A ResourceNet International Company, 3280 Executive Way, 33025, pg. 902 **PB**
Humana Medical Plan Inc.-Miami, 3400 Lakeside Dr., 33027, pg. 848 **PB**
Tasco Sales Inc., 2889 Commerce Pkwy., 33025, pg. 928 **PV**
Zellerbach Division, 10550 Commerce Pkwy., 33025, pg. 1075 **PB**

Mount Dora

Handex of Florida, Inc., 30941 Suneagle Dr., 32757, pg. 499 **PV**
Sundor Brands Inc., 1501 Robie Ave., 32757, pg. 1331 **PB**
Sundor Brands Inc., 19931 Robie Ave., 32757, pg. 1331 **PV**

Mulberry

W.S. BADCOCK CORPORATION, 200 Phosphate Blvd. N.W., 33860, pg. 109 **PV**
Florida Pipe & Supply Company, 600 N. Prairie Industr. Pkwy., 33860, pg. 847 **PB**
Industrial & Specialty Chemicals Plant, P.O. Box 646, Old Hwy. 60 W., 33860, pg. 1062 **PV**

Naples

Brown Brothers Harriman Trust Co. of Florida, Collier Financial Center, 4501 Tamiami Trail North, 33940, pg. 173 **PV**
Cableware Technology Div., 900 Industrial Blvd., 33942, pg. 675 **PV**
Collier County Publishing Company, 1075 Central Ave., 33940, pg. 1447 **PB**
Customer Service Center of F.N.B., L.L.C., 840 Goodlette Rd., N., Ste. 201, 34102, pg. 607 **PB**
Fidelio Technologies, Inc., 2640 Golden Gate Pkwy., 33942, pg. 1106 **PB**
Fifth-Third Trust Co. & Savings Bank, FSB, P.O. Box 413021, 33941-3021, pg. 622 **PB**
First National Bank of Naples, 900 Goodlette Rd., N., 34102, pg. 607 **PB**
Gargiulo Inc., 15000 Old 41 N., 34110, pg. 1124 **PB**
HEALTH MANAGEMENT ASSOCIATES, INC., 5811 Pelican Bay Blvd., Ste. 500, 34108, pg. 802 **PB**
The Huntington Trust Company of Florida, N.A., 600 Fifth Ave. S., Ste. 201, 33940, pg. 850 **PB**
International Automated Energy Systems, Inc., 2600 Goldengate Pkwy., Ste. 105, 33942, pg. 331 **PV**
Key Trust Company of Florida, National Association, 3777 Tamiami Trail N., Ste. 100, 32801-3394, pg. 954 **PB**
Marshall & Ilsley Trust Company of Florida, HMA Corporate Ctr.-Pelican Bay, 800 Laurel Oak Dr., Ste. 101, 33963, pg. 1051 **PB**
Naples Daily News, 1075 Central Ave., 33940, pg. 1448 **PB**
Northern Trust Bank of Florida, N.A., 4001 Tamiami Trail N., 33940, pg. 1196 **PB**
Northern Trust Bank of Florida, N.A., 530 Fifth Ave. S., 33940, pg. 1196 **PB**
Poe & Brown of Florida, 2150 Goodlette Rd. N., Ste. 503, 33940-4811, pg. 1312 **PB**
Quest Futures Group, Inc., 7051 Verde Way, 33963, pg. 909 **PV**
Renaissance, 900 Imperial Golf Course Blvd., 33942, pg. 1257 **PV**
Society National Trust Company, 3777 Tamiami Trail North, Ste. 100, 33940, pg. 955 **PB**
Southwest Banks, Inc., 900 Goodlette Rd., N., 34102, pg. 607 **PB**

New Port Richey

Pall Aerospace, 10540 Ridge Rd., 34653, pg. 1253 **PB**
Sunbelt Newspapers, Inc., 6214 U.S. Hwy. 19, 34652, pg. 1079 **PB**

North Miami

BSA Advertising, Inc., One Turnberry Pl., 19495 Biscayne Blvd., 7th Fl., 33180, pg. 108 **PV**
Flanigan's Enterprises, Inc., 13205 Biscayne Blvd., pg. 648 **PB**
MARIE BRIZARD WINES & SPIRITS USA, 11900 Biscayne Blvd., Ste. 600, 33181-2726, pg. 702 **PV**

North Palm Beach

Alandco Inc., 11770 U.S. Highway One, 33408, pg. 608 **PB**

ESI Energy, Inc., 11760 US Hwy. One, 33408, pg. 608 **PB**
FPL GROUP, INC., 700 Universe Blvd., 33408, pg. 608 **PB**
Florida Power & Light Company, 700 Universe Blvd., 33408, pg. 608 **PB**
Mutual Service Corporation, 701 N. Federal Hwy., Ste. 300, 33418-3799, pg. 831 **PV**
NBD Trust Company of Florida N.A., The Towers, Ste. 101, 11300 U.S. Highway 1, 33408-3224, pg. 628 **PB**
Northern Trust Bank of Florida, N.A., 11780 U.S. Hwy. 1, Bldg. 3, Ste.100, 33408, pg. 1196 **PB**

Ocala

ABB Kent Meters, 953 N.E. Osceola Ave., 34470, pg. 4 **IT**
All American Recycling, 4351 W. Hwy. 40, 34482, pg. 413 **PB**
ALL PRO WINDOW SUPPLY, INC., 2648 N.W. Sixth St., 34475, pg. 35 **PV**
Charter Springs Behavioral Health System, Inc., 3130 S.W. 27th Ave., 32674, pg. 1035 **PB**
Clairson International Corp., 650 S.W. 27th Ave., 34478, pg. 575 **PB**
CompAir Mako, 1634 S.W. 17th St., 34474, pg. 1242 **IT**
Cox Cable Greater Ocala, Inc., P.O. Box 2318, 34478, pg. 455 **PB**
Emergency One, Inc., 1701 S.W. 37th Ave., 32678, pg. 617 **PB**
Flair Corporation, 4647 S.W. 40th Ave., 34474-5799, pg. 1676 **PB**
Hawthorne Ocala, 1200 S.W. 60th Ave., 32674, pg. 512 **PV**
Mako Compressors, Inc., 1634 S. W. 17th St., 34474, pg. 1243 **IT**
MARK III INDUSTRIES, 5401 N.W. 44th Ave., 34482, pg. 704 **PB**
Microdyne Corp., P.O. Box 7213, 491 Oak Rd., 32672, pg. 1105 **PB**
NOBILITY HOMES, INC., 3741 S.W. 7th St., 34474, pg. 1186 **PB**
NOVO Products, 520 S.W. 31st Ave., 34474, pg. 1055 **PB**
Ocala Star-Banner Corporation, 2121 S.W. 19th Ave., 34474, pg. 1175 **PB**
Pneumatic Products Corp., 4647 S.W. 40th Ave., 34474, pg. 1676 **PB**
Quality Computer Forms, Inc., 402 S.W. 33rd Ave., 34474, pg. 947 **PV**
Southern Electric Supply Co., Inc., 111 S.E. Eighth St., 34471, pg. 1107 **IT**
SunTrust Bank, North Central Florida, 203 E. Silver Springs Blvd., 32670, pg. 1537 **PB**
ZENTOX CORP., 2140 N.E. 36th Ave., 34470, pg. 1204 **PV**
Zentox NEPCCO, 2140 N.E. 36th Ave., 32670-3173, pg. 1204 **PV**

Ocoee

Florida Auto Auction of Orlando, Inc., P.O. Box 220, 11801 W. Hwy. 50, 34761, pg. 282 **PV**
Sysco Food Services of Central Florida, Inc., 200 W. Story Rd., 34761-0130, pg. 1551 **PB**

Okahumpka

LESTER COGGINS TRUCKING, Hwy. 33 S., 34762, pg. 250 **PV**

Oldsmar

Godfrey Engineering, 129 Fairfield St., 34677, pg. 751 **PV**

Opa Locka

ALTERMAN TRANSPORT LINES, INC., 12805 N.W. 42nd Ave., 33054, pg. 47 **PV**
W. Braun Co., 13165 N. W. 45th. Avenue, 33054-4305, pg. 166 **PV**
W. Braun International, 13165 N.W. 45th Ave., 33054, pg. 166 **PV**
Safety Disposal System, Inc., 3890 N.W. 132nd St., 33054, pg. 1077 **PV**

Orange Park

Anchor Inc., 50 Industrial Loop North, 32073, pg. 903 **PB**
SUNRISE NISSAN OF ORANGE PARK, 1565 Wells Rd., 32073, pg. 1053 **PV**

Orlando

A - 1 Medical Equipment, Inc., 4506 L.B. McLeod Rd., Ste. F, 32811, pg. 884 **PB**
AP Journals, Inc., 6277 Sea Harbour Dr., 32887, pg. 783 **PB**
Aaron Scrap Metals, P.O. Box 607069, 32860-7069, pg. 413 **PB**
Academic Press International Corp., 6277 Sea Harbour Dr., 32887, pg. 783 **PB**
ACOUSTI ENGINEERING CO. OF FLORIDA, 4656 34th St. S.W., 32811, pg. 14 **PV**
Addison Products Company, 7050 Overland Rd., 32810, pg. 518 **PV**
Airline Equipment Div., 7300 Presidents Dr., 32809, pg. 605 **PB**
Alfa Romeo Distributors of North America, 6220 S. Orange Blossom Trail, Ste. 200, 32809, pg. 481 **IT**
Allied Security Inc., 5151 Adanson St., Ste. 98, 32804, pg. 40 **PV**

PB - U.S. Public Companies Volume
PV - U.S. Private Companies Volume
IT - International Public & Private Companies Volume

Geographic Index-U.S.

ALLIED TIRE SALES, 3320A Maggie Blvd., 32811, pg. 41 **PV**

Alro Group, Orlando, 2505 Forsyth Rd., 32807, pg. 46 **PV**

American City Business Journals of Florida, Inc., 1221 W. Colonial Dr., Ste. 101, 32804, pg. 19 **PV**

American Medical Rentals, Inc., 4506 L.B. McLeod Rd., Ste. F, 32811, pg. 884 **PB**

AmeriSource-Orlando Div., 2100 Directors Row, 32809, pg. 97 **PB**

AMICK CONSTRUCTION, 401 Ferguson Dr., 32805, pg. 66 **PV**

AST Research, Inc., 5955 T.G. Lee Blvd., Ste. 150, 32822, pg. 1181 **PB**

Atlas Roll-Lite Door Corporation, 10407 Rocket Blvd., 32824-8512, pg. 766 **PB**

ATTORNEYS' TITLE INSURANCE FUND, 5955 T. G. Lee Blvd., Ste. 500, 32822, pg. 98 **PV**

Bahama Breeze, 5900 Lake Ellenor Dr., 32809, pg. 484 **PB**

Banco Popular, N.A. (Florida), 5551 Vanguard St., Ste. 100, 32819, pg. 176 **PB**

Bergen Brunswig Drug Company, 2702 Directors Row, 32809, pg. 213 **PB**

Bergen Brunswig Medical Corporation, 2702 Directors Row, 32809, pg. 214 **PB**

Beta Medical Equipment, Inc., 4506 L.B. McLeod Rd., Ste. F, 32811, pg. 884 **PB**

Bindley Western, Orlando Division, 2600 Titan Row, 32809, pg. 228 **PB**

Bindley Western, Southeastern Division, 6950 Presidents Dr., 32809, pg. 228 **PB**

Biocare Medical, Inc., 4506 L.B. McLeod Rd., 32811, pg. 884 **PB**

Breathing and Relief, Inc., 4506 L.B. McLeod Rd., Ste. F, 32811, pg. 884 **PB**

Brister Pharmacy, Inc., 4506 L.B. McLeod Rd., Ste. F, 32811, pg. 884 **PB**

Brister's Medical Associates, Inc., 4506 L.B. McLeod Rd., Ste. F, 32811, pg. 884 **PB**

Broder Bros. Co. Of Florida, Inc., 1255 LaQuinta Dr., Bldg. 130, 32809, pg. 171 **PV**

Brooksville Primary Care Clinic, Inc., 4506 L.B. McLeod Rd., Ste. F, 32811, pg. 884 **PB**

Camden Medical Supply, Inc., 4506 L.B. McLeod Rd., Ste. F, 32811, pg. 884 **PB**

Care Medical Supplies, Inc., 4506 L.B. Mcleod Rd., Ste. F, 32811, pg. 884 **PB**

Carlisle Crane Co, 18351 E. Colonial Dr., 32820, pg. 211 **PV**

CARSE OIL CO. INC., 1700 S. Bumby Ave., 32806, pg. 216 **PV**

Central Florida Press L.C., 4560 L.B. McLead Rd., 32811, pg. 291 **PB**

Certified Food Service of Orlando, Inc., 1273 Central Florida Pkwy., 32809, pg. 1529 **PV**

Charlotte Medical Supply, Inc., 4506 L.B. McLeod Rd., Ste. F, 32811, pg. 884 **PB**

CHEMCENTRAL/Orlando, 8120 S. Orange Ave., 32809, pg. 232 **PV**

Chep USA, The Landmark Bldg., 225 E. Robinson St., 32801-4393, pg. 211 **IT**

CHIP SUPPLY INC., 7725 N. Orange Blossom Trail, 32810, pg. 237 **PV**

Church Street Clinic, Inc., 4506 L.B. McLeod Rd., Ste. F, 32811, pg. 884 **PB**

Classic Nissan, 1983 N. Semoran Blvd., 32807, pg. 8 **PV**

Clinical Laboratory, Inc., 4506 L.B. McLeod Rd., Ste. F, 32811, pg. 884 **PB**

Community Home Oxygen, Inc., 4506 L.B. McLeod Rd., Ste. F, 32811, pg. 884 **PB**

Consolidated Electric Supply, Inc., 480 L.B. McLeod Rd., 32811, pg. 1107 **IT**

Control Laser Corporation, 7503 Chancellor Dr., 32809, pg. 599 **PB**

Cook Composites & Polymers Inc., 10124 Rocket Blvd., 32821, pg. 1409 **IT**

CORRECT CRAFT, INC., 6100 S. Orange Ave., 32809, pg. 276 **PV**

Cramer-Krasselt, 225 E. Robinson St., Ste. 570, 32801, pg. 286 **PV**

Crane Inspection & Certification Bureau, 5874 S. Semoran Blvd., 32812, pg. 1153 **IT**

CRUISES ONLY INC., 1011 E. Colonial Dr., 32803, pg. 293 **PV**

Cues, 3201 Vineland Rd., 32811, pg. 545 **PB**

Cynthiana Home Health Care, Inc., 4506 L.B. McLeod Rd., Ste. F, 32811, pg. 884 **PB**

DANIELS MANUFACTURING CORPORATION, 526 Thorpe Rd., 32824, pg. 310 **PV**

DARDEN RESTAURANTS, INC., 5900 Lake Ellenor Dr., 32809, pg. 483 **PB**

DATAMAX INTERNATIONAL CORPORATION, 4501 Parkway Commerce Blvd., 32808, pg. 313 **PV**

Dayton Superior Corporation, 10101 C General Drive, 32824, pg. 932 **PV**

Dillard, A ResourceNet International Company, 2224 Hazelhurst Ave., 32804, pg. 902 **PV**

Dillard Paper Co. of Orlando, 4141 John Young Pkwy., Ste. 5, 32804, pg. 902 **PB**

Distinct Home Health Care, Inc., 4506 L.B. McLeod Rd., Ste. F, 32811, pg. 884 **PB**

Drew Primary Care Clinic, Inc., 4506 L.B. McLeod Rd., Ste. F, 32811, pg. 884 **PB**

ELXSI CORPORATION, 3600 Rio Vista Ave., Ste. A, 32805, pg. 545 **PB**

Eta Home Health Care, Inc., 4506 L.B. McLeod Rd., Ste. F, 32811, pg. 884 **PB**

ETC Simulation Group, 12443 Research Pkwy., Ste. 405, 32826, pg. 587 **PB**

East Tennessee Infusion & Respiratory, Inc., 4506 L.B. McLeod Rd., Ste. F, 32811, pg. 884 **PB**

E.C. Ernst South East, 3320 Vineland Rd., Ste. B, 32811, pg. 861 **PV**

Encore Home Health Care, Inc., 4506 L.B. McLeod Rd., Ste. F, 32811, pg. 884 **PB**

Epsilon Home Health Care, Inc., 4506 L.B. McLeod Rd., Ste. F, 32811, pg. 884 **PB**

Essential Home Health Care, Inc., 4506 L.B. McLeod Rd., Ste. F, 32811, pg. 884 **PB**

Family Care Specialists, Inc., 4506 L.B. McLeod Rd., Ste. F, 32811, pg. 884 **PB**

Florida Medical Collection Services, Inc., 11183 South Orange Blossom Trail, 32821-0340, pg. 404 **PB**

Furman Wholesale Lumber Branch, 2021 S. Division St., 32805, pg. 431 **PB**

GAI Consultants-Southeast, Inc., 201 E. Pine St., Ste. 200, 32801, pg. 434 **PV**

GCI Orange, Inc/GCI Orlando, Inc., 200 S. Orange Ave., Ste. 2240, 32801, pg. 470 **PV**

GKI Electronic Enclosure Division-Orlando, 11205 Satellite Blvd., 32821, pg. 717 **PB**

GALAXY FOOD COMPANY, 2441 Viscount Row, 32809, pg. 697 **PV**

Gate City Medical Equipment, Inc., 4506 L.B. McLeod Rd., Ste. F, 32811, pg. 884 **PB**

GENCOR INDUSTRIES, INC., 5201 N. Orange Blossom Trail, 32810, pg. 705 **PB**

General Combustion Corporation, 5201 N. Orange Blossom Trail, 32810, pg. 705 **PB**

Government Aerospace Systems Division-Orlando Operations, 12249 Science Dr., 32826, pg. 792 **PB**

GRANTHAM DISTRIBUTING COMPANY, INC., 2685 Hensrob Rd., 32804, pg. 470 **PV**

Graseby Ionics, 12151 Research Parkway, 32826, pg. 1268 **IT**

Greenstone Roberts/Florida, Sunbank Center-Park Bldg., 250 S. Orange Ave., Ste. 700, 32801-3441, pg. 763 **PB**

Greenville Primary Care Clinic, Inc., 4506 L.B. McLeod Rd., Ste. F, 32811, pg. 884 **PB**

Greenwood Multi-Specialty Clinic, Inc., 4506 L.B. McLeod Rd., Ste. F, 32811, pg. 885 **PB**

Grenada Doctors Clinic, Inc., 4506 L.B. McLeod Rd., Ste. F, 32811, pg. 885 **PB**

Grenada Family Doctors, Inc., 4506 L.B. McLeod Rd., Ste. F, 32811, pg. 885 **PB**

Guthrie North America, Inc., 7380 Sandlake Rd., 32819, pg. 113 **IT**

H. Venture Corp., P.O. Box 2273, 32801, pg. 847 **PB**

Hanson Engineers, 200 E. Robinson St. Ste. 730, 32801, pg. 500 **PV**

Harcourt Brace & Company - Elementary Div., 6277 Sea Harbor Dr., 32887, pg. 783 **PB**

Harcourt Brace & Company Farm Publications Inc., 6277 Sea Harbor Dr., 32887, pg. 783 **PB**

Harcourt Brace & Company Intl. Corp., 6277 Sea Harbor Dr., 32887, pg. 783 **PB**

Harcourt Brace & Company Media Systems Corporation, 6277 Sea Harbor Dr., 32887, pg. 783 **PB**

Harcourt Brace & Company Real Properties Corporation, 6277 Sea Harbor Dr., 32887, pg. 783 **PB**

Harmon Glass of Florida, Inc., 535 West Central Blvd., 32801, pg. 120 **PB**

Headache and Pain Management Center, Inc., 4506 L.B. McLeod Rd., Ste. F, 32811, pg. 885 **PB**

Headache Center of the West Coast, 4506 L.B. McLeod Rd., Ste. F, 32811, pg. 885 **PB**

Headache Management of America, Inc., 4506 L.B. McLeod Rd., Ste. F, 32811, pg. 885 **PB**

Health & Medications at Home, Inc., 4506 L.B. McLeod Rd., Ste. F, 32811, pg. 885 **PB**

Health at Home, 4506 L.B. McLeod Rd., Ste. F, 32811, pg. 885 **PB**

Health Care Services of Mississippi, Inc., 4506 L.B. McLeod Rd., Ste. F, 32811, pg. 885 **PB**

Healthcare Business Solutions, Inc., 4506 L.B. McLeod Rd., Ste. F, 32811, pg. 885 **PB**

Healthcare Claims Recovery, Inc., 4506 L.B. McLeod Rd., Ste. F, 32811, pg. 885 **PB**

Heartland Home Care, Inc., 4506 L.B. McLeod Rd., Ste. F, 32811, pg. 885 **PB**

HEINTZELMAN'S TRUCK CENTER INC., 2424 John Young Pkwy., 32804, pg. 519 **PV**

Hewlett-Packard Company, 6177 Lake Ellenor Dr., 32809, pg. 814 **PB**

Hilb, Rogal and Hamilton Company of Orlando, Southeast Bank Bldg., 201 E. Pine St., Ste. 400, 32801, pg. 827 **PB**

Holiday RV Rental/Leasing, Inc., 7851 Greenbrier Pkwy., 32819, pg. 829 **PB**

HOLIDAY RV SUPERSTORES, INC., 7851 Greenbriar Pkwy., 32819, pg. 829 **PB**

Holiday RV Superstores, Inc.-Orlando, 5001 Sand Lake Rd., 32819, pg. 830 **PB**

Holland Medical Services, Inc., 4506 L.B. McLeod Rd., Ste. F, 32811, pg. 885 **PB**

Hollandale Primary Care, Inc., 4506 L.B. McLeod Rd., Ste. F, 32811, pg. 885 **PB**

Holt, Rinehart and Winston, Inc., 6277 Sea Harbor Dr., 32887, pg. 783 **PB**

Home Care Solutions of Murray, Inc., 4506 L.B. McLeod Rd., Ste. F, 32811, pg. 885 **PB**

Home Medical Systems, Inc., 4506 L.B. McLeod Rd., Ste. F, 32811, pg. 885 **PB**

Hughes Acquisition Corp., 20 N. Orange Ave., Ste. 200, 32801, pg. 847 **PB**

HUGHES SUPPLY, INC., 20 N. Orange Ave., Ste. 200, 32801, pg. 846 **PB**

IRT Property Company, 7800 Southland Blvd., Ste. 157, 32809, pg. 858 **PB**

Ikon Office Solutions, 4150 John Young Pkwy., 32804, pg. 863 **PB**

Indianola Primary Care Clinic, Inc., 4506 L.B. McLeod Rd., Ste. F, 32811, pg. 885 **PB**

Integral Home Health Care, Inc., 4506 L.B. McLeod Rd., Ste. F, 32811, pg. 885 **PB**

Intensive Home Care Nurses, Inc., 4506 L.B. McLeod Rd., Ste. F, 32811, pg. 885 **PB**

Intensive Home Care Services, Inc., 4506 L.B. McLeod Rd., Ste. F, 32811, pg. 885 **PB**

Internal Medicine Grand View, Inc., 4506 L.B. McLeod Rd., Ste. F, 32811, pg. 885 **PB**

International Medical Services and Supplies, Inc., 4506 L.B. McLeod Rd., Ste. F, 32811, pg. 885 **PB**

International Therapeutic Services, Inc., 4506 L.B. McLeod Rd., Ste. F, 32811, pg. 885 **PB**

INX Incorporated/Pressroom, 603 Central Florida Pkwy., Bay #3, 32824, pg. 1311 **IT**

Jenks (INMETCO), P.O. Box 592187, 32859-2187, pg. 559 **PV**

KELSEY CONSTRUCTION, INC., 306 E. Princeton St., 32804, pg. 613 **PV**

Kelsey Development, 306 E. Princeton St., 32804, pg. 613 **PV**

LM&S/Orlando, 20 N. Orange Ave. #1209, 32801, pg. 651 **PV**

LAMS, 4506 L.B. McLeod Rd., Ste. F, 32811, pg. 885 **PB**

LANDSTAR DEVELOPMENT COMPANY, 120 Fairway Woods Blvd., 32824, pg. 649 **PV**

Lexington Primary Care, Inc., 4506 L.B. McLeod Rd., Ste. F, 32811, pg. 885 **PB**

Liberty Home Health Care, Inc., 4506 L.B. McLeod Rd., Ste. F, 32811, pg. 885 **PB**

Lovejoy Medical, Inc., 4506 L.B. McLeod Rd., Ste. F, 32811, pg. 885 **PB**

M.A.B. Paints, 720 Central Florida Pkwy., 32824, pg. 175 **PV**

Macon Primary Care Clinic, Inc., 4506 L.B. McLeod Rd., Ste. F, 32811, pg. 885 **PB**

Major Medical Supply, Inc., 4506 L.B. McLeod Rd., Ste. F, 32811, pg. 885 **PB**

Manheim's Greater Orlando Auto Auction, 9800 Bachman Rd., 32824, pg. 282 **PV**

Martin Marietta Electronics & Missiles, P.O. Box 555837, 32855-5837, pg. 1007 **PB**

Massey Cadillac, Inc., 4241 N. John Young Pkwy., 32804, pg. 713 **PV**

MCNAMARA PONTIAC ISUZU INC., 1010 W. Colonial Dr., 32804, pg. 724 **PV**

DON MEALEY CHEVROLET INC., 3707 W. Colonial Dr., 32808, pg. 726 **PV**

MEARS TRANSPORTATION GROUP, 324 W. Gore St., 32806, pg. 726 **PV**

Medic-Aire Medical Equipment, Inc., 4506 L.B. McLeod Rd., Ste. F, 32811, pg. 885 **PB**

Medical Electro-Therapeutics, Inc., 4506 L.B. McLeod Rd., Ste. F, 32811, pg. 885 **PB**

Mitsukoshi (U.S.A.) Inc.-Orlando Branch, First Office Place, 7232 Sandlake Rd., Ste. 303, 32819, pg. 883 **IT**

Motorola Radius, 12424 Research Pkwy., 32826-3249, pg. 1138 **PB**

National Distributing Co., Inc., 3601 Silver Star Rd., 32808, pg. 781 **PV**

NATIONAL HEALTH PRODUCTS, 731 Kirkman Rd., 32811, pg. 784 **PV**

National Medical Equipment Centers, Inc., 4506 L.B. McLeod Rd., Ste. F, 32811, pg. 885 **PB**

National Medicine Center - Groveland, Inc., 4506 L.B. McLeod Rd., Ste. F, 32811, pg. 885 **PB**

Neste Polyester Inc., 11487 Rocket Blvd., 32824, pg. 913 **IT**

Nightingale Home Health Care, Inc., 4506 L.B. McLeod Rd., Ste. F, 32811, pg. 885 **PB**

94th Aero Squadron of Orlando, Inc., 494 Rickenbacker Dr., 32803, pg. 1023 **PV**

North Florida Pain Institute, Inc., 4506 L.B. McLeod Rd., Ste. F, 32811, pg. 885 **PB**

Olive Garden Italian Restaurants, 5900 Lake Ellenor Dr., 32809, pg. 484 **PB**

Orlando Sentinel Communications, 633 N. Orange Ave., 32801, pg. 1636 **PB**

Oxygen Therapy Associates, 4506 L.B. McLeod Rd., Ste. F, 32811, pg. 885 **PB**

P & E, INC., 7482 Presidents Dr., 32809, pg. 825 **PV**

PSI Health Care, Inc., 4506 L.B. McLeod Rd., Ste. F, 32811, pg. 885 **PB**

Perry Family Practice, Inc., 4506 L.B. McLeod Rd., Ste. F, 32811, pg. 885 **PB**

Physician's Formulary Services, Inc., 4506 L.B. McLeod Rd., Ste. F, 32811, pg. 885 **PB**

Pioneer Medical Services, Inc., 4506 L.B. McLeod Rd., Ste. F, 32811, pg. 885 **PB**

Polk City Pharmacy, Inc., 4506 L.B. McLeod Rd., Ste. F, 32811, pg. 885 **PB**

Port City Electrical Supply, Inc., P.O. Box 2273, 32801, pg. 847 **PB**

Primary Home Health Care, Inc., 4506 L.B. McLeod Rd., Ste. F, 32811, pg. 885 **PB**

Pulmo-Dose, Inc., 4506 L.B. McLeod Rd., Ste. F, 32811, pg. 885 **PB**

Quality Home Health Care, Inc., 4506 L.B. McLeod Rd., Ste. F, 32811, pg. 885 **PB**

Quebecor Printing Orlando, 6300 Hazeltine Natl. Dr., 32822, pg. 1076 **IT**

RCG Information Services, Corporation, 4506 L.B. McLeod Rd., Ste. F, 32811, pg. 885 **PB**

RN Home Care Medical Equipment Company, Inc., 4506 L.B. McLeod Rd., Ste. F, 32811, pg. 885 **PB**

Red Lobster USA, 5900 Lake Ellenor Dr., 32809, pg. 484 **PB**

REED MOTORS, INC., 3776 W. Colonial Dr., 32808, pg. 916 **PV**

PB - *U.S. Public Companies Volume*
PV - *U.S. Private Companies Volume*
IT - *International Public & Private Companies Volume*

Geographic Index-U.S.

1188

REGAL MARINE INDUSTRIES INC., 2300 Jetport Dr., 32809, pg. 917 **PV**
Respitech Home Health Care, Inc., 4506 L.B. McLeod Rd., Ste. F, 38211, pg. 885 **PB**
Responsive Home Health Care, Inc., 4506 L.B. McLeod Rd., Ste. F, 38211, pg. 885 **PB**
River Ranch - Orlando, 7492 Chancellor Drive, 32809, pg. 491 **IT**
RoTech Employee Benefits Corporation, 4506 L.B. McLeod Rd., Ste. F, 38211, pg. 885 **PB**
RoTech Home Medical Care, Inc., 4506 L.B. McLeod Rd., Ste. F, 38211, pg. 885 **PB**
RoTech Medical Corporation, 4506 L.B. McLeod Rd., Ste. F, 32811, pg. 884 **PB**
RoTech Oxygen & Medical Equipment, Inc., 4506 L.B. McLeod Rd., Ste. F, 38211, pg. 885 **PB**
Rotech/Texas, Inc., 4506 L.B. McLeod Rd., Ste. F, 32811, pg. 885 **PB**
Rothert's Hospital Equipment, Inc., 4506 L.B.McLeod Rd., Ste. F, 32811, pg. 885 **PB**
Sea World of Florida, 7007 Sea World Dr., 32821, pg. 114 **IT**
Sealy Mattress Company - Orlando, 11220 Space Blvd., 32821, pg. 979 **PB**
Select Home Health Care, Inc., 4506 L.B. McLeod Rd., Ste. F, 32811, pg. 885 **PB**
Senatobia Family Practice, Inc., 4506 L.B. McLeod Rd., Ste. F, 38211, pg. 885 **PB**
Signature Flight Support, Signature Plaza, 201 S. Orange Ave., Ste. 1100, 32801, pg. 114 **IT**
South County Health Care Services, 4506 L.B. McLeod Rd., Ste. F, 32811, pg. 885 **PB**
South County Private Duty Agency, Inc., 4506 L.B. McLeod Rd., Ste. F, 32811, pg. 885 **PB**
Southeast Correct Craft, Inc., P.O. Box 13117, 32859, pg. 277 **PV**
SOUTHEASTERN REALTY GROUP INC., 933 Lee Rd., Ste. 400, 32810, pg. 1015 **PB**
Southern IV Therapy, Inc., 4506 L.B. McLeod Rd., Ste. F, 32811, pg. 885 **PB**
Southern Medical, Inc., 4506 L.B. McLeod Rd., Ste. F, 32811, pg. 885 **PB**
SouthTrust Bank, Orlando, P.O. Box 2166, 135 W. Central Blvd., 32801, pg. 1492 **PB**
Spiralkote, 1200 Central Florida Pkwy., 32837, pg. 411 **PV**
Stat Medical Equipment, Inc., 4506 L.B. McLeod Rd., Ste. F, 32811, pg. 885 **PB**
Stone Packaging Systems, Inc., 4364 S.W. 34th St., 32811, pg. 1521 **PB**
SunBank Capital Management, N.A., 200 S. Orange Ave., 32801, pg. 1537 **PB**
Sunshine Home Health Care, Inc., 4506 L.B. McLeod Rd., Ste. F, 32811, pg. 885 **PB**
SunTrust, 200 S. Orange Ave., 32801, pg. 1537 **PB**
SunTrust Bank, Central Florida, N.A., 200 S. Orange Ave., 32801, pg. 1537 **PB**
Thermotech Systems Corporation, 5201 N. Orange Blossom Trail, 32810, pg. 705 **PB**
Theta Home Health Care, Inc., 4506 L.B. McLeod Rd., Ste. F, 32811, pg. 885 **PB**
The Towne Pharmacy, Inc., 4506 L.B. McLeod Rd., Ste. F., 32811, pg. 885 **PB**
TRANSPO ELECTRONICS, INC., 2150 Brengle Ave., 32808, pg. 1097 **PB**
TRAYLOR CHEMICAL & SUPPLY CO., 1911 Traylor Blvd., 32804, pg. 1098 **PV**
Tupelo Home Health, Inc., 4506 L.B. McLeod Rd., Ste. F, 32811, pg. 885 **PB**
TUPPERWARE CORPORATION, 14901 S. Orange Blossom Trail, 32837, pg. 1644 **PB**
Tupperware U.S., Inc., P.O. Box 2353, 32802-2353, pg. 1644 **PB**
Turbine Engine Components Textron, 2287 Premier Row, 32859, pg. 1589 **PB**
Turner Construction Company, 800 N. Magnolia Ave., Ste. 1301, 32803, pg. 1645 **PB**
Typo-Graphics, Inc., 2602 E. Livingston St., 32803-5850, pg. 503 **PB**
URS Greiner, Inc., 315 E. Robinson St., Ste. 245, 32801, pg. 1658 **PB**
Union-Transport Corporation-Orlando Office, 6300 Hazeltine National Dr., 32822, pg. 1120 **PV**
United Self Insured Services, 5728 Major Blvd., Ste. 450, 32819, pg. 1312 **PB**
Universal Studios Florida, 1000 Universal Studios Plaza, 32819, pg. 1087 **IT**
Valley Medical, Inc., 4506 L.B. McLeod Rd., Ste. F, 32811, pg. 885 **PB**
Value Care, Inc., 4506 L.B. McLeod Rd., Ste. F, 32811, pg. 885 **PB**
Verily Enterprises, Inc., 6277 Sea Harbor Dr., 32887, pg. 783 **PB**
VitalCare Health Services, Inc., 4506 L.B. McLeod Rd., Ste. F, 32811, pg. 885 **PB**
VitalCare of America, Inc., 4506 L.B. McLeod Rd., Ste. F, 32811, pg. 885 **PB**
VitalCare of Florida, Inc., 4506 L.B. McLeod Rd., Ste. F, 32811, pg. 885 **PB**
VitalCare of Nevada, Inc., 4506 L.B. McLeod Rd., Ste. F, 32811, pg. 885 **PB**
VitalCare of Pennsylvania, Inc., 4506 L.B. McLeod Rd., Ste. F, 32811, pg. 885 **PB**
VitalCare of Texas, Inc., 4506 L.B. McLeod Rd., Ste. F, 32811, pg. 885 **PB**
WFTV, Inc., 639 W. Central Blvd., 32801, pg. 282 **PV**
Western International Media Corporation, Signature Plaza, 201 S. Orange Ave., Ste. 870, 32801, pg. 1167 **PV**
Western Waste Industries, Inc. of Florida, 1334 North Goldenrod Rd., 32807, pg. 1686 **PB**
Westinghouse Power Generation, 4350 Alafaya Trail, 32826-2399, pg. 273 **PB**

Wichita Medical Care, Inc., 4506 L.B. McLeod Rd., Ste. F, 32811, pg. 885 **PB**
WILLIAMS COMPANY OF ORLANDO, INC., 2301 Silver Star Rd., 32804, pg. 1177 **PV**
Willis Corroon Administrative Services Corporation, 7041 Grand National Dr., Ste. 200, 32819-1290, pg. 1504 **IT**
Winn-Dixie Stores, Inc.-Orlando Div., 3015 Coastline Dr., 32808, pg. 1771 **PB**
Women's Health Care Services, Inc., 4506 L.B. McLeod Rd., Ste. F, 32811, pg. 885 **PB**
YESAWICH, PEPPERDINE & BROWN, 1900 Summit Tower Blvd., Ste. 600, 32810, pg. 1195 **PV**
Zellerbach Division, 3032 Mercy Dr., 32808, pg. 1075 **PB**
Zeta Home Health Care, Inc., 4506 L.B. McLeod Rd., Ste. F, 32811, pg. 885 **PB**

Ormond Beach

Major Pharmaceuticals, 533 N Nova Rd., Ste 214, 32174, pg. 475 **PV**
Metal Fab Corporation, P.O. Box 2611, 32175, pg. 658 **PB**
TANNING RESEARCH LABS., INC., 1190 U.S. 1 North, 32126-5111, pg. 1068 **PV**

Oviedo

C&D Groves, c/o A. Duda & Sons., Inc., P.O. Box 257, 32765, pg. 365 **PB**
A. DUDA & SONS INC., 1975 W. State Rd. 426, 32765, pg. 344 **PV**

Palatka

PDM Bridge Corp., Barge Port, Rte. Six, Comfort Rd., 32177, pg. 1304 **PB**
PDM Bridge Corp., Box 970, Rte. 6, Comfort Rd., 32177, pg. 1305 **PB**
The Palatka Daily News, Inc., 1825 St. Johns Ave., 32177, pg. 1175 **PB**
Primary Pulp & Paper Plant, P. O. Box 919, State Rd. 216, 32077, pg. 736 **PB**

Palm Bay

DRS Optronics, Inc., 2330 Commerce Park Dr., N.E., 32905, pg. 474 **PB**
Printer Operations-Storage Tek, 340 Kirby Ave., 32905, pg. 1523 **PB**

Palm Beach

Bank of Boston - Florida, N.A., 450 Royal Palm Way, 33480, pg. 184 **PB**
Wally Findlay Galleries, Inc., 165 Worth Ave., 33480, pg. 405 **PV**
J.P. Morgan Florida, FSB, 109 Royal Palm Way, 33480, pg. 1129 **PB**
J.P. Morgan Securities Inc., 109 Royal Palm Way, 33480, pg. 1129 **PB**
Northern Trust Bank of Florida, N.A., 440 Royal Palm Way, 33480, pg. 1196 **PB**
The Quick & Reilly Group Inc., 230 S. County Rd., 33480, pg. 650 **PB**

Palm Beach Gardens

Correctional Foodservices Management, 4200 Wackenhut Dr., #100, 33410, pg. 1731 **PB**
DYCOM INDUSTRIES, INC., First Union Ctr., Ste. 600, 4440 PGA Blvd., 33410-6542, pg. 538 **PB**
Fiber Cable, Inc., First Union Ctr., 4440 P.G.A. Blvd., Ste. 600, 33410, pg. 538 **PB**
Oasis Outsourcing, Inc., 4200 Wackenhut Dr., Ste. 100, 33410, pg. 1731 **PB**
THE WACKENHUT CORPORATION, 4200 Wackenhut Dr., Ste. 100, 33410, pg. 1731 **PB**
Wackenhut Corrections Corporation, 4200 Wackenhut Dr., 33410, pg. 1731 **PB**
Wackenhut Resources, Inc., 4200 Wackenhut Dr., #100, 33410, pg. 1731 **PB**
WEISS GROUP., 4176 Burns Rd., 33410, pg. 1160 **PV**
Weiss Money Management, Inc., 4176 Burns Rd., 33410, pg. 1160 **PV**
Weiss Rating, Inc., 4176 Burns Rd., 33410, pg. 1160 **PV**
Weiss Research, Inc., 4176 Burns Rd., 33410, pg. 1160 **PV**

Palm City

Liberty Medical Supply, Inc., 3595 S.W. Corporate Pkwy., 34990, pg. 1315 **PB**

Palm Coast

ABB CEAG Power Supplies Inc., One Pine Lakes Pkwy., 32137, pg. 4 **IT**

Palm Harbor

ABR INFORMATION SERVICES, INC., 34125 U.S. Hwy. 19 N., 34684-2116, pg. 2 **PB**
CLEANERS HANGER CO., 3055 Reun Dr., 34685, pg. 245 **PV**
Golf Hosts, Inc., 36750 U.S. Hwy. 19 N., 34684, pg. 1036 **PB**
Leviton Telecom, 3442 Eastlake Rd. 318, 34685, pg. 663 **PV**

Palmetto

SOUTHERN AGRICULTURAL INSECTICIDES, INC., 7600 Bayshore Rd., 34221, pg. 1015 **PV**
Sysco Food Services of West Coast Florida, Inc., 3000 69th St. E., 34221, pg. 1552 **PB**

Panama City

Abbeville-Grimes Railway Company, P.O. Box 2775, 32402, pg. 1521 **PB**
Arizona Chemical Div., 1001 E. Business, Hwy. 98, 32401, pg. 450 **PB**
Bay Correctional Facility, 5400 Bayline Dr., 32404, pg. 450 **PB**
Bay County Jail, Bay County Jail, 314 1/2 Harmon, 32401, pg. 450 **PB**
Bay County Jail Annex, 6600 Nehi Rd., 32404, pg. 450 **PB**
E-Z Serve Convenience Stores, Inc.-Panama City Market, 1136 Beck Ave., 32401, pg. 540 **PB**
News Herald, P.O. Box 1940, 32402, pg. 425 **PV**
Panama City Coca-Cola Bottling Co., 300 Fifth St., 32402, pg. 392 **PB**
WJHG-TV, Inc., Channel 7, 8195 Front Beach Rd., 32407, pg. 759 **PB**
Wellstream Company, 1700 C Ave., 32401, pg. 528 **PB**

Pembroke Pines

Claire's Boutiques, Inc., Three S.W. 129th Ave., 33027, pg. 381 **PB**
CLAIRE'S STORES INC., Three S.W. 129th Ave., 33027, pg. 381 **PB**
DECORATOR INDUSTRIES, INC., 10011 Pines Blvd., Ste. #201, 33024-6136, pg. 491 **PB**
Maroone Automotive Group, 8600 Pines Blvd., 33024, pg. 1379 **PB**

Pensacola

Allright Pensacola Parking, 134 W. Government St., 32501, pg. 43 **PV**
Bank of Pensacola, P.O. Box 10885, 32524-0885, pg. 1549 **PB**
THE LEWIS BEAR COMPANY, P.O. Box 13567, 32591-3567, pg. 127 **PV**
Compass Bank of the South, N.A., 33 W. Garden St., 32501, pg. 419 **PB**
Cox Communications-Pensacola/Ft. Walton, 2205 LaVista Ave., 32504, pg. 455 **PB**
EA Engineering, Science & Technology, Inc., 8800 University Pky., Ste. C-1, 32514, pg. 541 **PB**
Gulf Power Company, One Energy Placea, 32520-0601, pg. 1490 **PB**
Hewlett-Packard Company, 4700 Bayou Blvd., Bldg. 6, 32503, pg. 814 **PB**
Horizon Specialty Center of Pensacola, 6984 Pine Forest Rd., 32526, pg. 836 **PB**
Horizon's Bayside Manor, 4343 Langley Ave., 32504, pg. 836 **PB**
Hygeia Coca-Cola Bottling Company, 7330 N. Davis Hwy., 32504, pg. 393 **PB**
National Distributing Co., Inc. 6256 N. W. St., 32505, pg. 781 **PV**
Pacer Industries, Inc., 9101 Ely Street, 32514, pg. 560 **PB**
Pensacola News-Journal, Inc., One News Journal Plaza, 32501, pg. 701 **PB**
Regions Bank/Santa Rosa County, P.O. Box 12089, 32501-5728, pg. 1372 **PB**
SunTrust Bank, West Florida, 220 West Garden St., 32501, pg. 1538 **PB**
Western Florida Cellular Telephone Corp., 401 E. Chase St., Ste. 107, 32501, pg. 1708 **PB**
THE WINDHAM COMPANY, 407 S. Pace Blvd., 32501, pg. 1182 **PV**

Perry

MARTIN ELECTRONICS, INC., 10625 Puckett Rd., 32347, pg. 709 **PV**

Pinellas Park

I.C. Thomasson Ass., 8680 49th St. N., Ste. 201, 33782, pg. 1083 **PV**
Kohler Construction Company, Inc., 6425 53rd St. N., 34665, pg. 538 **PB**
Molex, 4650 62nd Ave. N., 33781, pg. 1122 **PB**
Pall Aero Power, 6301 49th St. N., 34665, pg. 1253 **PB**
Pall Safety Atmospheres, Inc., 6301-49th St. N., 34665, pg. 1254 **PB**
Transitions Optical, Inc., 9251 Belcher Rd., 33782, pg. 1245 **PB**

Plant City

Alumax Extrusions, Inc., Industrial Park, P.O. Box 4709, 33567, pg. 59 **PB**
CEGF (USA) Inc., P.O. Box 3368, 33564, pg. 606 **PB**
Fleetwood Homes of Florida, Inc.-Plant City, 3804 Sydney Rd., 33567, pg. 651 **PB**
International Petroleum Corporation, 105 S. Alexander St., 33566, pg. 906 **PB**
Lykes Meat Group, 4611 Lykes Rd., 33564, pg. 1479 **PB**
MTL INC., 3108 Central Dr., 33567, pg. 1028 **PB**
Montgomery Tank Lines, Inc., 3108 Central Dr., 33567, pg. 1028 **PB**

PB - U.S. Public Companies Volume
PV - U.S. Private Companies Volume
IT - International Public & Private Companies Volume

Geographic Index-U.S.

PARADISE, INC., 1200 Dr. Martin Luther King Blvd., 33566, pg. 1256 **PB**
Plant City Steel Co., P.O. Drawer A, 33564-9001, pg. 793 **PB**
PRESTO FOOD STORES, INC., 607 S. Alexander St., 33566, pg. 882 **PV**
Winn Dixie Superbrand Dairies, 3304 Sydney Rd., 33567-1181, pg. 1771 **PB**

Plantation

Cigna Dental Health, Inc., P.O. Box 189060, 300 N.W. 82nd Ave., Ste. 700, 33318-9060, pg. 358 **PB**
Cigna Dental Health of Colorado, Inc., P.O. Box 189060, 300 N.W. 82nd Ave., Ste. 700, 33318, pg. 358 **PB**
Cigna Dental Health of Delaware, Inc., P.O. Box 189060, 300 N.W. 82nd Ave., Ste. 700, 33318, pg. 358 **PB**
Cigna Dental Health of Florida, Inc., P.O. Box 189060, 300 N.W. 82nd Ave., Ste. 700, 33318, pg. 358 **PB**
Cigna Dental Health of Kansas, Inc., P.O. Box 189060, 300 N.W. 82nd Ave., Ste. 700, 33318, pg. 358 **PB**
Cigna Dental Health of Kentucky, Inc., P.O. Box 189060, 300 N.W. 82nd Ave., Ste. 700, 33318, pg. 358 **PB**
Cigna Dental Health of Maryland, Inc., P.O. Box 189060, 300 N.W. 82nd Ave., Ste. 700, 33318, pg. 358 **PB**
Cigna Dental Health of New Jersey, Inc., P.O. Box 189060, 300 N.W. 82nd Ave., Ste. 700, 33318, pg. 358 **PB**
Cigna Dental Health of Ohio, Inc., P.O. Box 189060, 300 N.W. 82nd Ave., Ste. 700, 33318, pg. 358 **PB**
Cigna Dental Health of Pennsylvania, Inc., P.O. Box 189060, 300 N.W. 82nd Ave., Ste. 700, 33318, pg. 358 **PB**
Cigna Dental Health Plan of North Carolina, Inc., P.O. Box 189060, 300 N.W. 82nd Ave., Ste. 700, 33318, pg. 358 **PB**
DSS Engineers, Inc., 150 Bells Pine Island Rd., 33324, pg. 1519 **PB**
Environmental Construction, Inc. (ECI), 1490 N.W. 65th Ave., 33313, pg. 607 **IT**
Kemper National Services, 1601 S.W. 80th Terrace, 33324, pg. 614 **PV**
NATIONAL BEVERAGE CORP., One N. University Dr., Ste. 400A, 33324, pg. 1153 **PB**
Novo Nordisk Pharmaceuticals, Inc., Ste. 108, 1776 North Pine Island Rd., 33322, pg. 987 **IT**

Plymouth

Eastern Div.-Plymouth, 2823 Orange Ave., 32768, pg. 463 **PB**

Pompano Beach

The Central Press of Miami, Inc., 2901 Gateway Dr., 33069, pg. 1735 **PB**
Central Sprinkler Company, 2209 N.W. 30th Pl., 33069, pg. 327 **PB**
Dyno Merchandise Corp., 1571 W. Copans Rd., Ste. 105, 33604, pg. 428 **PB**
F.A.I. Trading Company, Powder Line, 2500 N.W. 29th Manor, 33069, pg. 686 **PB**
Lambda Novatronics Inc., 500 S.W. 12th Ave., 33061-0878, pg. 1241 **IT**
Marine Air Systems, Inc., 2000 N. Andrews Ave. Ext., 33069, pg. 1071 **PV**
MEDIA PRINTING CORPORATION, 4300 N. Powerline Rd., 33073, pg. 726 **PV**
Process Automation, 2900 Gateway Dr., 33069, pg. 422 **PB**
Pueblo International, Inc., 1300 N.W. 22nd St., 33069, pg. 894 **PB**
PUEBLO XTRA INTERNATIONAL, INC., 1300 N.W. 22nd St., 33069, pg. 894 **PV**
RTP, 2900 Gateway Dr., 33069, pg. 422 **PB**
South Atlantic Tri-City, 3800 Park Central Blvd. N., Ste. 3810, 33064, pg. 1100 **PV**
Sun City Produce, Inc., 1390 Hammondville Rd., 33069, pg. 1529 **PB**
Trimble Navigation Ltd., Florida Sales/Technical Support, 1000 W. McNab Rd., Ste. 233, 33069, pg. 1638 **PB**
Winn-Dixie Stores Inc.-Miami Div., 1141 S.W. 12th Ave., 33069, pg. 1771 **PB**
Xtra Super Food Centers, Inc., 1300 N.W. 22nd St., 33069, pg. 894 **PV**

Ponte Vedra Beach

TBWA Chiat/Day Florida, 202 ATP Tour Blvd., Ste. 300, 32082, pg. 1062 **PV**

Port Charlotte

Fawcett Memorial Hospital, Inc., 21298 Olean Blvd., N.W., 33952, pg. 404 **PB**
First of America - Florida, 1600 Tamiami Tr., 33948-2031, pg. 636 **PB**

Port Richey

Gulf Coast Food Service Inc., 8402 Lemon Rd., 34668, pg. 1529 **PB**
Virgo Optics, Inc., 6736 Commerce Ave., 34668, pg. 1647 **PB**

Port Saint Joe

St. Joe Communications, Inc., P.O. 1007, 32456, pg. 1427 **PB**

St. Joe Forest Products Company, P.O. Box 190, 32456, pg. 1427 **PB**

Port Saint Lucie

First American Title Co. of St. Lucie County, Inc., 201 S.W. Port St. Lucie Blvd., Ste. 205, 34984, pg. 625 **PB**
RIGHT IDEAS INC., 1950 SE Port Saint Lucie Blvd., Ste. 203, 34952, pg. 930 **PV**

Punta Gorda

Industrial Electrical Products, 7474 Utilities Rd., 33982, pg. 1598 **PB**
Turner Foods Corporation, 25450 Airport Rd., 33950, pg. 608 **PB**

Quincy

Engelhard Corp.-Quincy Operations, P.O. Box 410, 32353, pg. 582 **PB**
MacTavish Furniture Industries, Quincy Office Plant, P.O. Box 1079, 32351, pg. 12 **PB**
PRINTING HOUSE, INC., P.O. Box 310, 32353, pg. 886 **PV**
Quincy Corp., Rte. 4, Box 245, 32351, pg. 1545 **PB**
The Quincy State Bank, P.O. Box 700, 32351, pg. 1549 **PB**
Quincy Telephone Company, 107 W. Franklin St., 32351, pg. 1571 **PB**
SuperValu, Inc.-Quincy Div., 32351, pg. 1540 **PB**

Riviera Beach

AMERIPATH, INC., 7289 Garden Rd., Ste. 200, 33404, pg. 96 **PB**
Birdsall, Inc., 821 Ave. E, 33404-1683, pg. 1182 **PB**
Microsemi PPC, Inc., 3680 Investment Ln., 33404, pg. 1107 **PB**
MOHAWK PLASTICS, INC., 2290 Ave. L, 33404, pg. 755 **PV**
Philips Circuit Assemblies, 2001 W. Blue Heron Blvd., 33404-5099, pg. 1054 **IT**
Sysco Food Services of Southeast Florida, Inc., P.O. Box 198509, 33419, pg. 1552 **PB**
Vital Pharma, Inc., 1006 W. 15th St., 33404, pg. 1723 **PB**

Rockledge

Brevard Div., 4180 S. Hwy. One, 32955, pg. 1148 **PB**
Harris Space Systems Corp., 295 Barnes Blvd., 32955, pg. 791 **PB**
Hydro Aluminum Bohn, Inc., 100 Gus Hipp Blvd., 32955-4701, pg. 961 **IT**

Safety Harbor

JACOBSEN MANUFACTURING, INC., 600 Packard Ct., 34695, pg. 580 **PV**

Saint Augustine

American Natural Snacks, 87 Riberia St., 32084, pg. 752 **IT**
Atlantic East Coast Terminal, One Malaga St., 32084, pg. 1427 **PB**
Carlisle Container Manufacturing Company, 4035 Reynolds Blvd., 32092, pg. 305 **PB**
Dade County Land Holding Co., One Malaga St., 32084, pg. 1427 **PB**
Florida East Coast Deliveries, Inc., One Malaga St., 32084, pg. 1427 **PB**
Florida East Coast Highway Dispatch Co., One Malaga St., 32084, pg. 1427 **PB**
Florida East Coast Industries Inc., One Malaga St., 32084, pg. 1427 **PB**
Florida East Coast Inspections, Inc., One Malaga St., 32084, pg. 1427 **PB**
Florida East Coast Railway Co., One Malaga St., 32084, pg. 1427 **PB**
Florida Express Carrier Inc., One Malaga St., 32084, pg. 1427 **PB**
Gran Central Corporation, One Malaga St., 32084, pg. 1427 **PB**
Ideal Division, 3200 Parker Dr., 32095-0897, pg. 1396 **IT**
LUHRS CORPORATION, 255 Diesel Rd., 32086, pg. 680 **PV**
MAINSHIP CORPORATION, 255 Diesel Rd., 32086, pg. 697 **PV**
Operations Unlimited, Inc., One Malaga St., 32084, pg. 1427 **PB**
Railroad Concrete Crosstie Corp., One Malaga St., 32084, pg. 1427 **PB**
Railroad Track Construction Corp., One Malaga St., 32084, pg. 1427 **PB**
Tensolite Company, 100 Tensolite Dr., 32092, pg. 305 **PB**
Tree of Life, Inc., 315 Industrial Dr., 32084, pg. 752 **IT**
VAW of America, Inc., P.O. Box 367, 32084, pg. 1466 **IT**

Saint Cloud

Comtech Antenna Systems, Inc., 3100 Communications Rd., 32769, pg. 425 **PB**
Comtech Systems, Inc., 3100 Communications Rd., 32769, pg. 425 **PB**
Southern Oaks Health Care Center, 2355 Kissimmee Park Rd., 34769, pg. 837 **PB**

Saint Petersburg

Allied Clinical Laboratories, Inc., 9424-44 International Ct., 33716, pg. 973 **PB**
America's Store, 2501 110th Ave. N., 33716-1900, pg. 1685 **PB**
BancTec Payment Systems, 888 Executive Center Dr. W., Ste. 200, 33702, pg. 177 **PB**
BARGER BUILDERS, 5565 Ninth St. N., 33703, pg. 116 **PV**
Barry-Wehmiller Packaging Systems, 4710 28th St. N., 33714, pg. 118 **PV**
CamEra, Inc., 1615 118th Ave. N., 33716, pg. 1457 **PB**
CATALINA MARKETING CORPORATION, 11300 Ninth St. N., 33716-2329, pg. 314 **PB**
Cook Moving Systems, Inc. (Florida Corporation), 10491 Gandy Blvd., 33702, pg. 273 **PV**
COX LUMBER CO., 3300 Fairfield Ave. S., 33712, pg. 283 **PV**
Danka Business Systems, 11201 Danka Cir. N., 33716, pg. 379 **IT**
Dayton Rogers Of Florida, 7205 30th Ave. N., 33710, pg. 318 **PV**
Diamond P Sports, 9675 Fourth St. N., 33702, pg. 544 **PV**
Don Ce Sar Resort Hotel Ltd., 3400 Gulf Blvd., 33706, pg. 361 **PB**
DYWIDAG Systems International, USA, Inc., 3624 Bella Vista Dr. E., 33706, pg. 424 **IT**
E-C Apparatus Corp., 3831 Tyrone Blvd. N., 33709, pg. 1595 **PB**
ECI Div., 1501 72nd St. North, 33733-2248, pg. 1365 **PB**
Eagle Asset Management, Inc., 880 Carillon Pkwy., 33716, pg. 923 **PB**
ECHELON INTERNATIONAL CORPORATION, One Progress Plaza, Ste. 1500, 33701, pg. 560 **PB**
Electric Fuel Corp., One Progress Plaza, 33701, pg. 1685 **PB**
EUROPA CRUISES CORPORATION, 150 153rd Ave., Ste. 200, 33708, pg. 595 **PB**
F & F Productions, Inc., 9675 Fourth St. N., 33702, pg. 544 **PV**
FTSB BROADCASTING, 3839 4th St. N., Ste. 420, 33703, pg. 389 **PV**
Federal Construction Co., P.O. Box 1257, 1355 Snell Island Blvd. N.E., 33731-1257, pg. 774 **IT**
First American Real Estate Information Services, Inc., 150 Second Ave.N., Ste. 1600, 33701, pg. 625 **PB**
Florida Power Corporation, 3201 34th St. S., 33713, pg. 655 **PB**
FLORIDA PROGRESS CORPORATION, Barnett Tower, One Progress Plaza, 33701, pg. 655 **PB**
Florida Trend Magazine, 490 First Ave. S., 33701, pg. 1088 **PV**
Geonex, 8950 Ninth St. N., 33702, pg. 448 **PV**
GEONEX CORPORATION, 8950 Ninth N., 33702, pg. 447 **PV**
HSN Insurance, Inc., 12000 25th Ct. N., 33716-1923, pg. 1685 **PB**
HSN Lifeway Health Products, Inc., 12000 25th Ct. N., 33716-1923, pg. 1685 **PB**
HSN Mail Order, Inc., 12000 25th Ct. N., 33716-1923, pg. 1685 **PB**
Heritage Asset Management, Inc., The Raymond James Fin. Ctr., 880 Carillon Pkwy., 33716, pg. 923 **PB**
Home Shopping Network, Inc., 2501 118th Ave. N., 33716-1900, pg. 1685 **PB**
Hubbard Communications, 9675 Fourth St. N., 33702, pg. 544 **PV**
Investment Management & Research, Inc., The Raymond James Fin. Ctr., 880 Carillon Pkwy., 33716, pg. 923 **PB**
JMI-Daniels Pharmaceuticals, Inc., 2517 25th Ave. N., 33713, pg. 934 **PB**
JABIL CIRCUIT, INC., 10800 Roosevelt Blvd. N., 33716, pg. 919 **PB**
Raymond James & Associates, Inc., The Raymond James Fin. Ctr., 880 Carillon Pkwy., 33716, pg. 923 **PB**
Raymond James Capital, The Raymond James Fin. Ctr., 880 Carillon Pkwy., 33716-2749, pg. 923 **PB**
RAYMOND JAMES FINANCIAL, INC., The Raymond James Fin. Ctr., 880 Carillon Pkwy., 33716-2749, pg. 923 **PB**
Raymond James Partners, Inc., 880 Carillon Pkwy., 33716, pg. 923 **PB**
Raymond James Realty Advisors, Inc., 880 Carillon Pkwy., 33716, pg. 923 **PB**
Northern Trust Bank of Florida, N.A., 100 Second Ave., 33713, pg. 1197 **PB**
Olin Pantex, Inc., 10101 Ninth St. N., 33716, pg. 1219 **PB**
PAYLESS CAR RENTAL SYSTEM, INC., 2350 34th Street N., 33713, pg. 844 **PV**
Planning Corporation of America, The Raymond James Fin. Ctr., 880 Carillon Pkwy., 33716, pg. 923 **PB**
PLASMA-THERM, INC., 10050 16th St. N., 33716, pg. 1308 **PB**
Poe & Brown of Florida, 9800 Fourth St. N., Ste. 303, 33742-2268, pg. 1312 **PB**
PRECISION SYSTEMS, INC., 11800 30th Ct. N., 33716, pg. 1321 **PB**
Precisionaire, Inc., 2399 26th Ave., N., 33734, pg. 648 **PB**
PRIMEX TECHNOLOGIES, INC., 10101 Ninth St., N., 33716, pg. 1329 **PB**
Progress Capital Holdings, Inc., One Progress Plaza, 33701, pg. 655 **PB**
RJ Credit Partners, 880 Carillon Pkwy., 33716, pg. 923 **PB**
RJ Leasing, Inc., The Raymond James Fin. Ctr., 880 Carillon Pkwy., 33716, pg. 923 **PB**
RJ Properties, Inc., The Raymond James Fin. Ctr., 880 Carillon Pkwy., 33716, pg. 923 **PB**
RJ Realty, Inc., 880 Carillon Pkwy., 33716, pg. 923 **PB**

PB - U.S. Public Companies Volume
PV - U.S. Private Companies Volume
IT - International Public & Private Companies Volume

St. Petersburg Times, 490 First Ave. S., 33701, pg. 1088 **PV**
R.P. Scherer North America, 2725 Scherer Dr. North, 33716-1016, pg. 1438 **PB**
Sensor Systems Division, 2800 Anvil St. N., 33710, pg. 158 **PB**
Silor Optical of Florida, 4900 Park St. N., 33709, pg. 462 **IT**
SouthTrust Bank, West Florida, P.O. Box 15708, 150 Second Ave., N., 33733, pg. 1492 **PB**
TWC of Florida, Incorporated, 3101 62nd St., N., 33710, pg. 1755 **PB**
Tape & Label Engineering, 2950 47th Ave. N., 33714, pg. 1157 **PV**
Tecniflo Omega, Inc., 3251 46th Ave. N., 33714, pg. 1222 **PB**
Templeton Funds Management, Inc., 700 Central Ave., 33701-3628, pg. 680 **PB**
Robert Thomas Securities, Inc., The Raymond James Fin. Ctr., 880 Carillon Pkwy., 33716, pg. 923 **PV**
THE TIMES PUBLISHING CO., 490 First Ave. S., 33701, pg. 1087 **PB**
USA NETWORKS, INC., 2501 118th Ave. N., 33716-1900, pg. 1685 **PB**
Vernitron Sensor Systems, 2801 72nd St. N., 33710, pg. 157 **PV**
WWRM, Inc., 877 Executive Ctr. Dr., W., Ste. 300, 33702, pg. 282 **PV**
Yesawich, Pepperdine & Brown, 150 Second Ave. N., 33701, pg. 1196 **PV**

Sanford

Comair Aviation Academy, Inc., 2700 Flight Line Ave., 32773, pg. 406 **PB**
Dealers Auto Auction of Sanford, Inc., 3895 State Rd. 46 E., 32771, pg. 1649 **PB**
Distribution Systems Division, 201 Hickman Dr., 32771, pg. 4 **IT**
Harper Mechanical Corporation, 5401 Benchmark Ln., 32773, pg. 322 **IT**
Lazerdata, 123 Tech Dr., 32771, pg. 127 **IT**
Medium Voltage Equipment, 201 Hickman Dr., 32771, pg. 4 **IT**
Mid-Florida Div.-Florida Public Utilities, 830 W. Sixth St., 32771, pg. 655 **PB**
Southern Electric Supply Co., Inc., 3501 S. Sanford Ave., 32773, pg. 1108 **IT**
SUNNILAND CORPORATION, P.O. Box 8001, 32772-8001, pg. 1053 **PV**

Sanibel

Community Bank of the Islands, 2450 Periwinkle Way, 33957, pg. 1162 **PB**

Sarasota

AMERICAN MARINE HOLDINGS INC., 7110 21st St. E., 34243, pg. 58 **PV**
Bank of America Illinois Trust Company of Florida, N.A. (Sarasota Branch), 1819 Main St., Ste. 1204, 34236-5984, pg. 181 **PB**
Bausch & Lomb Contact Lens Division-FL, 2040 Whitfield Ave., 34243, pg. 194 **PB**
CM Shredder Div., 1920 Whitfield Ave., 34293, pg. 405 **PV**
Chris-Craft Boats, 8161 15th St. E., 34243, pg. 478 **PV**
CORRECTIONAL SERVICES CORPORATION, 1819 Main St., Ste. 1000, 34236, pg. 450 **PB**
Donzi Marine Corporation, 7110 21st St. E., 34243, pg. 58 **PV**
East Manor Medical Care Center, 1524 S. East Ave., 33579, pg. 1712 **PB**
ELCOTEL, INC., 6428 Parkland Dr., 34243, pg. 568 **PB**
Electro Corporation, 1845 57th St., 34243, pg. 127 **IT**
Escast, Automated Equipment & Tooling Div., 2080 Limbus Ave., 34243, pg. 612 **PB**
Florida Cities Water Co., 2112 Gulf Gate Dr., 33579, pg. 151 **PV**
Flowers Baking Co. of Bradenton, Inc., 6490 Parkland Dr., 34243, pg. 657 **PB**
Hewlett-Packard Company, 201 Field End Rd., Ste. B-1, 34240, pg. 814 **PB**
Hillhaven Convalescent Center Sarasota, 1625 S. Osprey Ave., 33579, pg. 1713 **PB**
Hynautic, 1579 Barber Rd., 34240, pg. 857 **PV**
Infresco Corporation, 1741 Main St., 34236, pg. 420 **PB**
Iwerks Entertainment, 3307 Clark Rd., Ste. 204, 34231, pg. 915 **PB**
KALIN ENTERPRISES, INC., 5252 S. Tamiami Trail, 34231, pg. 606 **PV**
Kalin Financial Division, 5252 S. Tamiami Trail, 34231, pg. 606 **PV**
Klockner-Bartelt, Inc., 5501 North Washington Blvd., 34234, pg. 737 **IT**
L3 Communications Advanced Recorders Div., 6000 Fruitville Rd., 34232, pg. 638 **PV**
W.G. MILLS, INC., 3301 Whitfield Ave., 34243, pg. 749 **PV**
94th Aero Squadron of Sarasota, Inc., 8301 N. Tamiami Trail, 34243, pg. 1023 **PV**
Northern Trust Bank of Florida, N.A., 1515 Ringling Blvd., 34236, pg. 1196 **PB**
OFI Technology, Inc., 5696 Pinkney Ave., 31277, pg. 915 **PB**
Octel Messaging Div., Live Oak Ctr., 2201 Cantu Ct., Ste. 116, 34232, pg. 1018 **PB**
Oxford Health Plans (FL), Inc., 1390 Main St., 34236, pg. 1239 **PB**

Poe & Brown of Florida, 1819 Main St., Ste. 315, 34236, pg. 1312 **PB**
Provident Bank of Florida, 1549 Ringling Blvd., 34236, pg. 1338 **PB**
Sarasota Herald-Tribune Company, 801 S. Tamiami Trail, 34236, pg. 1175 **PB**
SouthTrust Bank, Suncoast, 1800 2nd St., 34236, pg. 1492 **PB**
Sun Coast Closures of Florida, Inc., 7350 26th Court E., 34243, pg. 1530 **PB**
SunLite Furniture, 1227 Hardin Ave., 34243, pg. 1684 **PB**
SunTrust Bank, Gulf Coast, 1777 Main St., 34230, pg. 1537 **PB**
Taylor Woodrow Homes Florida Inc., 7120 S. Beneva Rd., 2nd Fl., 34235, pg. 1359 **IT**
Taylor Woodrow Property Co. of America Inc., 1900 Longmeadow, 34235, pg. 1359 **IT**
Teleflex Electrical Systems, 1816 57th St., 34243-2297, pg. 1569 **PB**
TELTRONICS INC., 2150 Whitfield Industrial, 34243, pg. 1573 **PB**
Tropitone Furniture Co., Inc., P.O. Box 3197, 34230, pg. 1105 **PV**
UNIROYAL TECHNOLOGY CORPORATION, Two N. Tamiami Trail, Ste. 900, 34236, pg. 1670 **PB**
Wellcraft Marine Corp., 1651 Whitfield Ave., P.O. Box 13011, 34243, pg. 447 **PV**

Sebastian

eMerge Vision Systems, 10305 102nd St. Ter., 32958, pg. 1425 **PB**
XL Vision Inc., 10305 102nd Ter., 32958, pg. 1424 **PV**

Sebring

Koch Oil Company, P.O. Box 1965, Office Park Rd., 33871-1965, pg. 628 **PV**

Seffner

Diamond Products Company, 435 Canning Plant Rd., 33584, pg. 510 **PV**
LAZY DAYS R V CENTER, INC., 6130 Lazy Days Blvd., 33584, pg. 655 **PB**
RTG FURNITURE CORP., 11540 E. US Hwy. 92, 33584, pg. 905 **PV**

Seminole

Appel Uniforms Div., 10099 Seminole Blvd., 33772, pg. 1539 **PB**
D'Armigene Design Center, 10099 Seminole Blvd., 33772, pg. 1539 **PB**
Shane Uniforms, 10099 Seminole Blvd., 33772, pg. 1539 **PB**
SUPERIOR SURGICAL MFG. CO., INC., 10099 Seminole Blvd., 33772, pg. 1539 **PV**
Universal Laundry Bags Div., 10099 Seminole Blvd., 33772, pg. 1539 **PB**
Worklon Div., 10099 Seminole Blvd., 33772, pg. 1539 **PB**

Spring Hill

North Florida Div., 2368 Fairskies Dr., 34606, pg. 1683 **PB**

Starke

SMI Joist Florida, C-100 A Lincoln City Rd., 32091, pg. 412 **PB**
Windsor Manor, 602 E. Laura St., 32091, pg. 837 **PB**

Stuart

Bank of America Illinois Trust Company of Florida, N.A. (Representative Office), 2363 S.E. Ocean Blvd., 34996, pg. 181 **PB**
Dickerson Realty Florida, Inc., P.O. Box 719, 33494, pg. 331 **PV**
Fleet Trust Co. of Florida, N.A., 819 S. Federal Hwy., Ste. 100, 34994, pg. 649 **PB**
Northern Trust Bank of Florida, N.A., Monterey Commons, 2201 S.E. Kingswood Ter., 34996, pg. 1196 **PB**
Southeastern Printing Company Inc., 3601 SE Dixie Hwy., 34997, pg. 1056 **PV**
Stuart News Company, 1939 S. Federal Hwy., 34994, pg. 1448 **PV**
Village Common Shopping Center, 2300 E. Ocean Blvd., B1, 34996, pg. 1250 **PV**

Sun City

SPEEDLING INCORPORATED, 4300 Old U.S. Hwy 41, 33586-7220, pg. 1024 **PV**
Speedling Incorporated Sun City Nursery Division, P.O. Box 7129, 33586, pg. 1024 **PV**

Sunrise

AIM Electronics Corporation, 4880 N. Hiatus Rd., 33321, pg. 598 **PV**
JAN BELL MARKETING INC., 14051 N.W. 14th St., 33323, pg. 207 **PB**
DCA General Contractors, Inc., 8320 N.W. 27th Pl., 33313, pg. 988 **PB**
Essef Caribbean, Incorporated, 13794 N.W. 4th St., Ste. 204, 33325, pg. 592 **PB**

HOMEOWNERS GROUP, INC., 400 Sawgrass Corp. Pkwy., 33325, pg. 832 **PB**
McArthur Dairy, Inc., 500 Sawgrass, Corporate Pkwy., 33325, pg. 491 **PB**
NaBANCO, 1404 N.W. 136 Ave., 33323, pg. 631 **PB**
Nortel CALA Inc., 1500 Concord Terr., 33323-2815, pg. 969 **IT**
Nurre Caxton, 4615 N.W. 103rd Ave., 33351, pg. 460 **IT**
The Racal Corporation, 1601 N. Harrison Pkwy., 33323, pg. 1082 **IT**
Racal-Datacom, 1601 N. Harrison Pkwy., 33323, pg. 1083 **IT**
W.B. Homes, Inc., 3000 Sunrise Lakes Dr. W., 33322, pg. 989 **PV**

Surfside

Flanigan's Enterprises, Inc., 9494 Harding Ave., pg. 648 **PB**

Tallahassee

Capital Paving Co., Inc., 7118 Beech Ridge Trail, 32312, pg. 956 **PB**
Central Insurance Corp. of Tallahassee, 7118 Beech Ridge Trail, 32312, pg. 956 **PB**
Governor's Square, Inc., 1500 Apalachee Pkwy., 32301, pg. 1408 **PB**
Green Tree Acceptance, Inc., 2011 Delta Blvd., 22303, pg. 762 **PB**
HCA-Florida Group, 1830 Buford Ct., 32308, pg. 403 **PB**
HMS Partners-Tallahassee, 511 Beverly St., 32301, pg. 492 **PV**
Hewlett-Packard Company, Kogerama Bldg., Ste. 101, 1300 Executive Center Dr., 32301, pg. 814 **PB**
Hydro Conduit Corp., P.O. Box 5526, Woodville Hwy. Truck Rte., 32314, pg. 246 **IT**
Killearn Advisers, Inc., 7118 Beech Ridge Trail, 32312, pg. 956 **PB**
Killearn Apartment Management, Inc., 7118 Beech Ridge Trail, 32312, pg. 956 **PB**
Killearn Construction, Inc., 7118 Beech Ridge Trail, 32312, pg. 956 **PB**
Killearn Realty, Inc., 3500 Kinhega Dr., 32312, pg. 956 **PB**
MCKENZIE TANK LINES, INC., P.O. Box 1200, 32302-1200, pg. 723 **PV**
ROSE PRINTING COMPANY, INC., 2503 Jackson Bluff Rd., 32304, pg. 945 **PV**
Simmons Outdoor Corporation, 3520 Thomasville Rd., Ste. 500, 32308, pg. 238 **PB**
SmithKline Beecham Labs, 1892 Professional Park C, 32308-4506, pg. 1265 **IT**
SunTrust Bank, Tallahassee, N.A., 2051 Thomasville Road, 32312, pg. 1538 **PB**
Tallahassee Democrat, Inc., 277 N. Magnolia Dr., 32302, pg. 964 **PB**
The Tallahassee State Bank, P.O. Box 2275, 32316, pg. 1549 **PB**
WTWC-TV, 8440 Dear Lake Rd., 32312, pg. 439 **PV**
Watkins Engineers & Constructors, Inc., P.O. Box 2194, 1238 Airport Ave., 32316, pg. 333 **PV**
Woodward-Clyde, 3676 Hartsfield Rd., 32303, pg. 1657 **PV**

Tallevast

Davis Process Div., 2650 Tallevast Rd., 34270, pg. 1682 **PB**

Tamarac

ARCH ALUMINIUM & GLASS L.C., P.O. Box 25127, 33321, pg. 79 **PV**
GRAPHLINE INC., 5701 N.W. 94th Ave., 33321-4399, pg. 471 **PV**

Tampa

AiC IBM Project Support Office, 600 N. Westshore Blvd., Ste. 304, 33609-1145, pg. 110 **PB**
Achieve Global, 8875 Hidden River Pkwy., 33637, pg. 1617 **PB**
ADVANTAGE LIFE PRODUCTS, INC., 1006 N. Dale Mabry, Ste. 210, 33618, pg. 22 **PB**
Adventure Island, 4500 Bougainvillea Ave., 33617, pg. 114 **PB**
Allied Security, Inc., 1311 N. Westshort Blvd., #303, 33607, pg. 41 **PV**
Allright Florida, Inc., 403 Washington St., 33602, pg. 42 **PV**
Alternative Remedial Technologies, Inc., 14497 N. Dale Mabry Hwy., Ste. 140, 33618, pg. 607 **IT**
AMERISTEEL, 5100 W. Lemon St., Ste. 312, 33609, pg. 65 **PV**
AmSouth Bank, 100 N. Tampa St., Ste. 3400, 33602, pg. 105 **PB**
Anchor Glass Container Corporation, 4343 Anchor Plaza Pkwy., 33634, pg. 327 **IT**
Anicom, 6375 Harney Rd., Suite 104, 33610, pg. 115 **PB**
Aramark Sports & Entertainment Services Group Inc., 600 Ashley Dr., 33602, pg. 79 **PV**
B&B CORPORATE HOLDINGS, INC., 9330 Adamo Dr., 33619, pg. 104 **PV**
B&L Pharmaceuticals, Inc., 8500 Hidden River Pkwy., 33637, pg. 194 **PB**
BPA International - Tampa, 5201 W. Kennedy Blvd., Ste. 730, 33609, pg. 107 **PV**
BSA Advertising, Inc., 1408 Northwestshore Blvd., Ste. 804, 33607, pg. 108 **PV**

Geographic Index-U.S.

BVK/McDonald - Tampa, 238 E. Davis Blvd., Ste. 203, 33606, pg. 108 PV
Bausch & Lomb Pharmaceutical Division, 8500 Hidden River Pkwy., 33637, pg. 194 PB
Bayside Auto Auction of Tampa Inc., 3225 N. 50th St., 33619, pg. 1648 PB
Bayside Underwriters Insurance Agency, Inc., 3802 Coconut Palm Dr., 33619, pg. 1334 PB
Beneficial Savings Bank, FSB, 430 Knights Run Ave., 33602-5714, pg. 211 PB
Benjamin Center Associates, 3030 N. Rocky Point Dr. W., Ste. 550, 33607, pg. 361 PB
BENTLEY PHARMACEUTICALS, INC., 4830 W. Kennedy Blvd., Ste. 548, 33609, pg. 212 PB
Bergen Brunswig Medical Corporation, 5008 Tampa W. Blvd., 33684, pg. 214 PB
Best Insurors, Inc., 1500 N. Dale Mabry Hwy., 33607, pg. 1736 PB
Blazer Financial Services, 8900 Grand Oak Cir., 33637-1050, pg. 1741 PB
BRIGGS INDUSTRIES, INC., 4350 W. Cypress St., Ste. 800, 33607, pg. 168 PV
Burns & Wilcox - Tampa Office, 3820 Northdale Blvd., Ste. 108-B, 33624, pg. 610 PV
Burnup & Sims ComTec, Inc., 7221 Dr. Martin Luther King Blvd., 33619, pg. 1056 PB
Busch Gardens Tampa, 3605 Bougainvillea Ave., 33617, pg. 114 PB
Business Guides Inc., 3922 Coconut Palm Dr., 33619, pg. 656 PV
Business Journal Publications, Inc., 405 N. Reo, Ste. 210, 33609, pg. 19 PV
CAP Gemini America (Tampa Branch), 100 W. Kennedy Blvd., Ste. 801, 33602, pg. 264 IT
Cardem Insurance Co., Ltd., 1500 N. Dale Mabry, 33607, pg. 1736 PB
Carrabba's Italian Grill, Inc., 405 N. Reo St., Ste. 210, 33609, pg. 1235 PB
CELOTEX CORPORATION, 4010 Boy Scout Blvd., 33607-5750, pg. 221 PV
Central Florida Pipeline Corp., 100 GATX Drive, 33605-6860, pg. 692 PB
Century Door U.S.A. Inc., 1 N. Dale Mabry, 33609, pg. 1067 IT
Chase Bank of Florida, N.A., 4915 Independence Pkwy., 33634, pg. 338 PB
Chase Education Finance, 4915 Independence Pkwy., 33634, pg. 338 PB
Chase Home Mortgage Corporation, 4915 Independence Pkwy., 33634, pg. 338 PB
Chili Pepper of Rocky Point, Inc., 2425 Rocky Point Dr., 33607, pg. 1023 PV
Cigna Healthcare of Florida, Inc., 5404 Cypress Center Dr., Ste. 365, 33609, pg. 359 PB
City Finance Company, 8900 Grand Oak Cir., 33637-1050, pg. 1741 PB
CLAYTON GROUP, INC., 9501 U.S. Hwy, 92 E., 33610, pg. 244 PV
Coast RV, Inc., 203A Kelsey Ln., 33619, pg. 388 PB
Commercial Metals Co., P.O. Box 5021, 33675, pg. 413 PB
Comprehensive Behavioral Care, Inc., 9200 W. Cypress, Ste. 300, 33607, pg. 419 PB
ConAgra Seafood Companies, P.O. Box 2819, 33601, pg. 427 PB
ConAgra Shrimp Company, P.O. Box 2819, 33601, pg. 427 PB
Consumer Finance Group, 8900 Grand Oak Cir., 33637-1050, pg. 1741 PB
Benjamin Cooke Associates, 3030 N. Rocky Point Dr. W., Ste. 550, 33607, pg. 361 PB
Cott Corporation - South East Region, 4501 East Acline Drive, 33605, pg. 338 IT
Crown Door Corp., P.O. Box 15277, 5110 W. Clifton Ave., 33614, pg. 1067 IT
DSI Transports, 8515 Palm River Rd., 33619, pg. 1285 IT
Walter Dickinson, Inc., 210 S. Macdill Ave., 33609, pg. 331 PV
Dillard, A ResourceNet International Company, P.O. Box 13567, 4514 S. S. Church Ave., 33681-3567, pg. 902 PB
Dillard Paper Co. of Tampa, 4514 S. Church Ave., 33611, pg. 902 PB
Dixie Building Supplies, Inc., 1500 N. Dale Mabry Hwy., 33607, pg. 1736 PB
Dun & Bradstreet Pension Services, Inc., 3501 Frontage Rd., 33607, pg. 536 PB
Duro Paper Bag Mfg. Co., P.O. Box 5004, 33675, pg. 349 PV
EIS, Inc., 4934 Distribution Dr., 33605, pg. 368 PV
Eagle Tech Inc., 200 S. Hoover Blvd. Ste. 21, 33609-3540, pg. 1199 PB
Edy's Southeast Region, 410 Ware Blvd.; Ste. 612, 33619, pg. 530 PB
Evans Environmental & Geological Science and Management, Inc., 8509D Benjamin Rd., 33634, pg. 563 PB
Fahlgren, 100 N. Tampa St., Ste. 3300, 33602, pg. 391 PV
Farmland Hydro, L.P., 100 N. Tampa St., Ste. 3200, 33614, pg. 961 IT
Feather Fine Services, 7020 Anderson Rd., 33624, pg. 1306 PB
FERMAN OLDSMOBILE, 1307 W. Kennedy Blvd., 33606, pg. 401 PV
First American Title Co. of Florida, Inc., 2802 W. Waters Ave., 33614, pg. 625 PB
First of America Bank Florida, One First America Bank Plz., 33611, pg. 636 PB
FLORIDA CAPITAL PARTNERS, 100 N. Tampa St., Ste. 2410, 33602, pg. 414 PV
Florida Mining & Materials Concrete Corp., 13228 N. Central Ave., 33612, pg. 1489 PB
Florida Outlet Marts, Inc., 101 E. Kennedy Blvd., 2700 Barnett Plaza, 33601-1102, pg. 1164 PV
Fore Line Security, 8419 SunState St., 33634, pg. 917 PV
GTE Florida Incorporated, One Tampa City Ctr., 201 North Franklin St., 33602, pg. 697 PB
GTE Leasing Corporation, One Tampa City Ctr., 201 N. Franklin St., Ste. 1800, 33602-5813, pg. 696 PB
General Employment Enterprises, Inc., 5201 W. Kennedy, Ste. 124, 33609, pg. 714 PB
Gould Paper of Florida, Inc., 5132 Tampa West Blvd., 33634, pg. 467 PV
Gould's Paper House, Inc., 7711 Anderson Rd., 33634, pg. 467 PV
Great Western Consumer Finance Group, 8900 Grand Oak Cir., 33637-1050, pg. 1741 PB
Greater Tampa Bay Auto Auction, 401 S. 50th St., 33619, pg. 282 PV
Green Tree Acceptance, Inc., 4950 W. Kennedy Blvd., 33609, pg. 762 PB
GULF COAST RECYCLING, 1901 N. 66th St., 33619, pg. 487 PV
Gulfstream Leasing Corporation, 600 N. Florida Ave., 33602, pg. 1162 PB
HDR Techserv Inc., 5100 W Kennedy Blvd. Ste. 300, 33609-1824, pg. 206 IT
Harner Properties, Inc., 1500 N. Dale Mabry Hwy., 33607, pg. 1736 PB
Harbour Island, Inc., 424 Knights Run Ave., 33602, pg. 211 PB
HARVARD INDUSTRIES, INC., 2502 N. Rocky Point Dr., Ste. 960, 33607, pg. 796 PB
HAVATAMPA, INC., 3901 Riga Blvd., 33619, pg. 510 PV
Hewlett-Packard Company, 5550 W. Idlewild, #150, 33634, pg. 814 PB
Hilb Rogal and Hamilton Company of Tampa Bay, Inc., 5405 Cypress Cente Dr., Ste. 330, 33609, pg. 827 PB
Holiday RV Superstores, Inc.-Tampa, 2910 Overpass Rd., 33619, pg. 830 PB
Holly Music, 4531 Oak Fair Blvd., 33610, pg. 780 PB
Household Products, 3601 E. Columbus Dr., 33605, pg. 387 PB
Household Products, 3702 E. Columbus Dr., 33605, pg. 387 PB
Hydro Agri North America, 100 N. Tampa St., Ste. 3200, 33602, pg. 961 IT
Hydro Conduit Corp., P.O. Box 5077, 1915 62nd St., 33619, pg. 246 IT
ISS Landscape Management Services, Inc., 1704 N. A St., 33606, pg. 656 IT
Insurance Administration Center., Inc., 401 E. Jackson St., Ste. 1700, 33602, pg. 1312 PB
Intergraph Corporation, 5045 Cypress Ctr. Dr., 33609, pg. 891 PB
International Container Systems, 5401 W. Kennedy Blvd., Ste. 760, 33609, pg. 685 IT
Jay Advertising, Inc.-Tampa, 2701 N. Rocky Point Dr., 33607, pg. 583 PV
JUMBO SPORTS INC., 4701 W. Hillsborough Ave., 33614, pg. 935 PB
Kase International, 8875 Hidden River Pkwy., Ste. 400, 33637, pg. 1617 PB
Kash N Karry Food Stores, Inc., 6422 Harney Rd., 33610, pg. 463 IT
KIMMINS CORP., 1501 Second Ave. E., 33605, pg. 960 PB
Lambert Smith Hampton, 544 S. Mariner St., Ste. 100, 33609, pg. 797 IT
R.G. Laurence Co., Inc., 12501 Telecom Dr., 33637, pg. 1747 PB
Leslie Controls, Inc., 12501 Telecom Dr., 33637-0903, pg. 1746 PB
LYKES BROTHERS INC., 400 N. Tampa St., 33602, pg. 682 PV
LYKES ENERGY, INC., 400 N. Tampa St., 33602, pg. 682 PV
Lykes Insurance Inc., P.O. Box 2879, 33601, pg. 682 PV
Martin's Uniforms Div., 5201 W. Armenia, 33603, pg. 1539 PB
MCNEEL INTERNATIONAL CORP., 5401 W. Kennedy Blvd., Ste. 751, 33609, pg. 724 PV
Meadow Steel Products, 5110 Santa Fe Rd., 33619, pg. 593 IT
Media General Broadcast Group, Inc., 905 E. Jackson St., 33602, pg. 1078 PB
MEDICAL MANAGER CORPORATION, 3001 N. Rocky Point Dr. E., Ste. 100, 33607, pg. 1080 PB
Medicenter, Tampa, 4411 N. Habana, 33614, pg. 1714 PB
Mid-State Homes, Inc., 1500 N. Dale Mabry Hwy., 33607, pg. 1736 PB
MISENER MARINE CONSTRUCTION, 5440 W. Tyson Ave., 33611, pg. 752 PV
National Programs Division, 401 E. Jackson St., Ste. 1700, 33602, pg. 1312 PB
NationsBank Florida, 600 N. Florida Ave., 33602, pg. 1162 PB
Nokia Mobile Phones Inc., 6200 Courtney Campbell Causeway, Ste.900, 33607, pg. 952 IT
Normandale Properties, 4350 W. Cypress, Ste. 701, 33622, pg. 818 PV
Nutmeg Mills Inc., 4408 W. Linebaugh Ave., 33624, pg. 702 PB
O'Donnell-Usen Fisheries Corp., 5024 Uceta Rd., 33619, pg. 427 PB
Opus South Construction Corporation, 4200 W. Cypress, Ste. 444, 33607, pg. 818 PV
OPUS SOUTH CORPORATION, 4200 W. Cypress, Ste. 444, 33607, pg. 818 PV
OUTBACK STEAKHOUSE INC., 550 N. Reo St., Ste. 204, 33609, pg. 1235 PB
PNC Trust Company of Florida, N.A., One Tampa City Center, Ste. 2400, 36602, pg. 1244 PB
PARADIGM COMMUNICATIONS, 5301 W. Cypress St., 3rd Fl., 33607, pg. 838 PV
Paradigm Learning, 5301 W. Cypress St., 3rd Fl., 33607, pg. 838 PV
Paradigm National Yellow Pages Group, 5301 W. Cypress St., 3rd Fl., 33607, pg. 838 PV
Parafax, 5301 W. Cypress St., 3rd Fl., 33607, pg. 838 PV
PENNINSULAR MEAT COMPANY, INC., 4401 N. Westshore Blvd., 33614, pg. 850 PV
Peoples Gas System, Inc., 702 N. Franklin St., 33602, pg. 1565 PB
PHARMERICA, INC., 3611 Queen Palm Dr., 33619, pg. 1286 PB
Phillies Cigar Company, 3901 Riga Blvd., 33619, pg. 510 PV
Premdor, Inc., One N. Dale Mabry, Ste. 950, 33609, pg. 1067 IT
Premdor U.S. Holdings, Inc., 1 N. Dale Mabry, 33609, pg. 1067 IT
Prime Systems Group, 5405 W. Cypress St., Ste. 120, 33607, pg. 1329 PB
Progressive American Insurance Co., 3802 Coconut Palm Dr., 33619, pg. 1334 PB
Progressive Bayside Insurance Co., 3802 Coconut Palm Dr., 33619, pg. 1334 PB
Progressive Southeastern Insurance Co., 3802 Coconut Palm Dr., 33619, pg. 1335 PB
Property Asset Management, 4919 Memorial Hwy., Ste. 100, 33634, pg. 891 PV
Pullman/Holt Corp., 10702 46th St., 33617, pg. 1173 PV
Pulte Southeast Division, 511 Bayshore St., Ste. 305, 33606, pg. 1345 PB
Pulte Tampa Division, 4014 Gunn Hwy., Ste. 200, 33624, pg. 1345 PB
Raybro Electric Supplies, 4910 Adamo Dr., Ste. A, 33605, pg. 265 PV
REEVES SOUTHEASTERN CORPORATION, P.O. Box 1968, 33601, pg. 916 PV
Reflectone Training Systems, Inc., 4908 Tampa W. Blvd., 33634, pg. 218 IT
REPTRON ELECTRONICS, INC., 14401 McCormick Dr., 33626, pg. 1377 PB
Resource, Inc., 3825 Henderson Blvd., Ste. 402, 33629, pg. 896 PB
Reynolds Metals Company-Tampa, 10420 Malcolm McKinley Dr., 33612, pg. 1386 PB
ROBBINS MANUFACTURING COMPANY, 13001 N. Nebraska Ave., 33612, pg. 935 PV
Rocky Point Village Corp., 2500 Rocky Point Dr., 33607, pg. 1023 PV
Sargento Foods, Inc., P.O. Box 151745, 6002 Benjamin, 33384, pg. 966 PV
Savin of Tampa Bay, 207 B Kelsey Ln., 33619, pg. 1114 IT
Sequent Computer Systems, Inc., 3001 N. Rocky Point Dr., Ste. 200, 33607, pg. 1459 PB
Service General Southeast, Ste. 108-B, 3820 Northdale Blvd., 33624, pg. 609 PV
Shaker Advertising Agency, 4920 Cypress St., 33609, pg. 989 PV
Singleton Seafood Co., P.O. Box 2819, 33601, pg. 427 PB
Somerset Pharmaceuticals Inc., 5415 W. Laurel St., 33607, pg. 1143 PB
South State Terminal, 2101 GATX Dr., 33605, pg. 692 PB
Southwest Florida Pipeline Corp., 2101 GATX Dr., 33605-6860, pg. 692 PB
Stewart Smith Southeast, Inc., 601 Bayshore Blvd., Ste. 720, 33606, pg. 1508 IT
Sun Financial Group, Inc., 2502 N. Rocky Pt. Dr., Ste. 375, 33607-1483, pg. 691 PB
SunTrust Bank, Tampa Bay, 401 E. Jackson St., 33602, pg. 1538 PB
Superior Wholesale Drug Co., 7909 Woodland Center Blvd., 33614, pg. 229 PB
TECO Coal Corp., 702 N. Franklin, 33602, pg. 1565 PB
TECO Transport & Trade Corp., 702 N. Franklin St., 33602, pg. 1565 PB
TIE Systems Florida (North), 1911 U.S. Highway 301 N., Ste. 120, 33619, pg. 1085 PV
Tampa Bay Moving Systems Inc., 5105 W. Clifton Ave, 33634, pg. 273 PV
TAMPA BAY SHIP BUILDING & REPAIR CO., 1130 McCloskey Blvd., 33605, pg. 1067 PV
TAMPA BAY STEEL, 6901 E. 6th Ave., 33619, pg. 1067 PV
Tampa Electric Co., 702 N. Franklin St., 33602, pg. 1565 PB
Tampa Intl. Forest Products, Inc., 5401 W. Kennedy Blvd., 33609, pg. 669 PB
Tampa Pump Station, 2101 GATX Dr., 33605-6632, pg. 692 PB
Tampa Retail Division, 401 E. Jackson St., Ste. 1400, 33602, pg. 1312 PB
Tampa Television, Inc., P.O. Box 1410, 33602, pg. 1078 PB
The Tampa Tribune, 202 S. Parker St., 33606, pg. 1079 PB
TECO Coalbed Methane, Inc., 702 N. Franklin St., 33602, pg. 1565 PB
TECO Diversified, Inc., 702 N. Franklin St., 33602, pg. 1565 PB
TECO ENERGY, INC., 702 N. Franklin St., 33602, pg. 1565 PB
TECO Finance, Inc., 702 N. Franklin, 33602, pg. 1565 PB
TECO Investments, Inc., 702 N. Franklin, 33602, pg. 1565 PB
TECO Power Services, Inc., 702 N. Franklin St., 33602, pg. 1565 PB

PB - *U.S. Public Companies Volume*
PV - *U.S. Private Companies Volume*
IT - *International Public & Private Companies Volume*

TECO Properties, Inc., 702 N. Franklin St., 33602, pg. 1565 **PB**
Telecredit Marketing Services, 5301 W. Idlewild Ave., 33634, pg. 588 **PB**
Telecredit Service Corp., 5301 W. Idlewild Ave., 33614, pg. 588 **PB**
Teledigm, Ste. 314, 3rd. Fl., 5301 W. Cypress St., 33607, pg. 838 **PB**
THEOCHEM LABS., INC., 7373 Rowlett Park Dr., 33610-1141, pg. 1079 **PV**
Total Research Corporation, Sunforest Exec. Pk., 5130 Eisenhower Blvd., 33634, pg. 1625 **PB**
TRAK Microwave Corp., 4726 Eisenhower Blvd., 33634-6391, pg. 1563 **PB**
TransCor Waste Service, Inc., 1501 Second Ave., 33605, pg. 960 **PB**
Tri-City Electrical Contractors Inc., 5910 Hartford St., 33619, pg. 1100 **PB**
TROPICAL SPORTSWEAR INTERNATIONAL, 4902 W. Waters Ave., 33634, pg. 1105 **PV**
URS Greiner, Inc., 7650 W. Courtney Campbell Causeway, 33607, pg. 1658 **PB**
URS Greiner, Inc., 5400 W. Spruce St., 33607, pg. 1659 **PB**
Union-Transport Corporation-Tampa Office, 5600 Airport Blvd., Ste. 33634, pg. 1120 **PV**
United Companies Mortgage of Florida, Inc., 4302 El Prado Blvd., 33629, pg. 1675 **PB**
United Foam Plastics Corporation, 4911 Nassau St., 33607-3813, pg. 1113 **PB**
U.S. Chem Resources Inc., 2701 No. Rocky Point Dr., Ste 1030, 33607, pg. 1255 **PB**
Van Leeuwen Pipe & Tube of the Southeast, Inc., 2721 N. 36th St., 33605, pg. 1450 **IT**
Van Leeuwen Pipe & Tube Corp., 2721 N. 36th Street, 33605, pg. 1450 **IT**
WFLA-AM, 4002-A Gandy Blvd., 33611, pg. 922 **PB**
WFLZ-FM, 4002-A Gandy Blvd., 33611, pg. 922 **PB**
WFTS-TV, 4501 Columbus Dr. E., 33605, pg. 1448 **PB**
WMTX-AM, 5510 Gray St., Ste. 130, 33609, pg. 385 **PB**
WMTX-FM, 5510 Gray St., Ste. 130, 33609, pg. 385 **PB**
WRBQ-AM, 5510 Gray St., Ste. 130, 33609, pg. 385 **PB**
WRBQ-FM, 5510 Gray St., Ste. 130, 33609, pg. 385 **PB**
WWWB-TV, 7201 E. Hillsborough Ave., 33610, pg. 516 **PV**
Walbridge Aldinger Company, 410 Ware Blvd., Ste. 900, 33619, pg. 1147 **PV**
WALTER INDUSTRIES, INC., 1500 N. Dale Mabry Hwy., 33607, pg. 1736 **PB**
Jim Walter Computer Services, Inc., 1500 N. Dale Mabry Hwy., 33607, pg. 1737 **PB**
Jim Walter Homes, Inc., 1500 N. Dale Mabry, 33607, pg. 1737 **PB**
J.W. Walter, Inc., 1500 N. Dale Mabry Hwy., 33607, pg. 1736 **PB**
Walter Land Co., 1500 N. Dale Mabry Hwy., 33607, pg. 1737 **PB**
Wattyl/MCI Paints, 5206 N. Dale Mabry Hwy., 33614, pg. 1488 **IT**
WestWayne - Tampa, 401 E. Jackson St., Ste. 3600, 33602, pg. 1170 **PV**
WHITE MOP WRINGER COMPANY, 10702 N. 46th St., 33617, pg. 1172 **PV**
Willis Corroon Construction Svcs. Corp. of Florida, 7650 Courtney Cswy., Ste. 920, 33607, pg. 1504 **IT**
Willis Corroon Corp. of Florida, 7650 Courtney Campbell Cswy., Ste. 920, 33607, pg. 1505 **IT**
Winn-Dixie Stores, Inc.-Tampa Div., 2400 E. Hillsborough Ave., 33610, pg. 1771 **PB**
Woodward-Clyde, 9950 Princess Palm Ave., Ste. 232, 33619, pg. 1657 **PB**
World Trade Center, One Tampa City Center, 33602, pg. 1075 **IT**
Zellerbach Division, 9105 Sabal Industrial Blvd., 33619, pg. 1108 **PB**
Zephyrhills Water Corp., 6403 Harney Rd., 33610, pg. 919 **IT**
Zurn Balke-Durr, Inc., P.O. Box 31718, 33631-3718, pg. 401 **IT**

Tarpon Springs

ABC PACKAGING MACHINE CORP., 811 Live Oak St., 34689, pg. 3 **PV**
Golf Host Resorts, Inc., P.O. Box 1088, 34688-1088, pg. 1036 **PV**
Innisbrook/Hilton Resort, P.O. Drawer 1088, 34688, pg. 1036 **PV**
Lightning Optical Corporation, 431 E. Spruce St., 34689, pg. 1647 **PB**
Vloc, 431 E. Spruce St., 34689, pg. 1647 **PB**

Temple Terrace

GTE Data Services Incorporated, P.O. Box 290152, Telecom Park, 33687-0152, pg. 696 **PB**

Titusville

DAVID BOLAND, INC., 3050 S. Hopkins Ave., 32780, pg. 154 **PV**
Lockheed Space Operations Co., 1100 Lockheed Way, 32780, pg. 1009 **PB**
PATCH COMMUNICATIONS, 5211 S. Washington Ave., 32780, pg. 842 **PV**
Southeast Power Corporation, Jay Jay & Hammock Rds., 32781, pg. 750 **PB**

Umatilla

GOLDEN GEM GROWERS INC., 39017 Golden Gem Dr., 32784, pg. 460 **PV**
Mercer Products Co., 37235 State Road 19, 32784, pg. 802 **IT**

Valparaiso

Vanguard Bank & Trust Company, 23 S. John Sims Pkwy., 32580, pg. 1549 **PB**

Venice

The Cook Bates Division, P.O. Box 1886, 34284-1886, pg. 815 **PB**
NBD Bank FSB, 1320 Venice Ave. E., 34284-0848, pg. 628 **IT**
Northern Trust Bank of Florida, N.A., 901 Venetia Bay Blvd., Ste. 100, 34292, pg. 1196 **PB**

Vero Beach

FlightSafety Academy, P.O. Box 2708, 2805 Airport Blvd., 32961, pg. 218 **PB**
FLORAFAX INTERNATIONAL, INC., 8075 20th St., 32966, pg. 654 **PB**
Maag Agrochemicals Inc, 5690 58th Ave., 32961-6430, pg. 973 **IT**
THE NEW PIPER AIRCRAFT, INC., 2926 Piper Dr., 32960, pg. 794 **PV**
Northern Trust Bank of Florida, N.A., 755 Beachland Blvd., 32963, pg. 1196 **PB**
Northern Trust Bank of Florida, N.A., 1440 S. AIA, 32963, pg. 1196 **PB**
Redgate Communications Corp., 660 Beachland Blvd., 32963, pg. 66 **PB**
SEALED-SWEET GROWERS, INC., 1991 74th Ave., 32966, pg. 1108 **PV**
Southern Electric Supply Co., Inc., 680 Eighth Ct., 32962, pg. 1108 **IT**
Vara Internatonal, 1201 19th Pl., 32960, pg. 293 **PB**
GEORGE E. WARREN CORPORATION, 605 17th St., 32960, pg. 1151 **PV**

Wauchula

PEACE RIVER ELECTRIC COOPERATIVE, INC., 1499 Highway 17 N., 33873, pg. 845 **PV**

Wellington

B/E AEROSPACE, INC., 1400 Corporate Way Ctr., 33414, pg. 159 **PB**

Wesley Chapel

Pittway Real Estate, 26806 SR 54 W., 33543, pg. 1306 **PB**

West Palm Beach

Allright West Palm Beach, Inc., 335 Clematis St., 33402, pg. 43 **PV**
Atlantic Pump & Equipment Co. of West Palm Beach, 4389 West Roads Dr., 33407, pg. 846 **PV**
Bankers Trust Co. of Florida, N.A., 505 S. Flagler Dr., 33401, pg. 185 **PB**
Biztel Corporation, 1655 Palm Beach Lakes Blvd, Ste. 1410, 33404, pg. 1779 **PB**
Burnup & Sims TelCom, Inc., 2269 N. Indian Rd., 33409, pg. 1056 **PB**
CSR Florida, 1501 Belvedere Rd., 33406, pg. 245 **IT**
CV REIT, INC., 100 Century Blvd., 33417, pg. 286 **PB**
Coastal Wholesale, Inc., 1600 Old Okeechobee Rd., 33409, pg. 846 **PB**
Convalescent Center of The Palm Beaches, 300 Fifteenth St., 33401, pg. 1712 **PB**
COOKER RESTAURANT CORPORATION, 5500 Village Blvd., 33407, pg. 442 **PB**
ECOS GROUP, INC., 1000 Southern Blvd., Ste. 200, 33405, pg. 563 **PB**
First Wisconsin Trust Company of Florida, 515 Flager Dr., Ste. 2100, 33401, pg. 643 **PB**
FLORIDA PUBLIC UTILITIES COMPANY, 401 S. Dixie, 33401, pg. 655 **PB**
Florida Residential Treatment Centers, Inc., 1950 Benoist Farms Rd., 33411, pg. 1035 **PB**
Generations Gold, 525 South Flagler Dr., Ste. 401, 33401, pg. 463 **PV**
Green Tree Acceptance, Inc., 2090 Palm Beach Lakes Blvd., 33409, pg. 762 **PB**
Harris Trust Company of Florida, 505 S. Flagler Dr., Ste. 1400, 33401, pg. 155 **IT**
K. Hovnanian Companies of Florida, Inc., 1800 So. Australian Ave., 33409, pg. 843 **PB**
Meditrust Operating Company, 777 S. Flaglar Dr., E. Tower, 33401, pg. 1081 **PB**
Meyer Laminates, Inc., 1900 Australian Ave., 33404, pg. 864 **IT**
National City Trust Company, 1401 Forum Way, Ste. 503, 33401, pg. 1154 **PB**
NICKLAUS GOLF COMPANY, L.C., 7830 Byron Dr., 33404, pg. 799 **PV**
94th Aero Squadron of West Palm Beach, Inc., 3989 Southern Blvd., 33406, pg. 1023 **PV**
OVERSEAS SERVICE CORPORATION, 1100 Northpoint Pkwy., 33407, pg. 823 **PV**
OXBOW CORPORATION, 1601 Forum Pl., 33401, pg. 825 **PV**
Palm Beach Div.-Florida Public Utilites, 401 S. Dixie Hwy., 33401, pg. 655 **PB**
Poe & Brown of Florida, 1401 Forum Way, Ste. 600, 33401-2324, pg. 1312 **PB**
Proudfoot USA Company, 1700 Palm Beach Lake Blvd., Ste. 700, 33401, pg. 1072 **IT**
Republic Security Bank, 4400 Congress Ave., 33407, pg. 1382 **PB**
REPUBLIC SECURITY FINANCIAL CORPORATION, 4400 Congress Ave., 33407-3288, pg. 1381 **PB**
Rinker Materials Corp., 1501 Belvedere Rd., 33406, pg. 246 **IT**
SERVICO, INC., 1601 Belvedere Rd., Ste. 501S, 33406, pg. 1462 **PB**
SLIM-FAST FOODS COMPANY, 777 South Flagler Dr., Ste. 1400, 33401, pg. 1006 **PV**
Steego Corporation, 5114 Okeechobee Blvd., Ste. 112, 33417, pg. 216 **IT**
Subaru Southeast Region, 1685 Florida Mango Rd N., 33402, pg. 523 **IT**
THOMPSON MEDICAL COMPANY, INC., 222 Lakeview Ave., 17th Fl., 33401-6112, pg. 1083 **PB**
TRUMP PLAZA OF THE PALM BEACHES, 525 S. Flagler Dr., 33401, pg. 1108 **PV**
Voltelcon, 1655 Palm Beach Lakes Blvd., 33401, pg. 1724 **PB**
WPTV, 622 N. Flagler Dr., 33401, pg. 1448 **PB**
The Weitz Company, Inc., 560 Village Blvd., Ste. 120, 33409, pg. 1161 **PV**
Wellington Regional Medical Center, 10101 Forest Hill Blvd., 33414, pg. 1697 **PB**
West Palm Beach Auto Auction, Inc., 600 Sansbury Way, 33411, pg. 1649 **PB**
West Palm Beach Training Center, Palm Beach Intl. Airport, 3887 Southern Blvd., 33406, pg. 219 **PB**

White Springs

PCS Phosphate - White Springs, P.O. Box 300, 32096, pg. 1065 **IT**

Whitehouse

SMI Steel Florida, 10483 General Ave., 32220, pg. 412 **PB**
Whitehouse Plant, Wood Products Div., P.O. Box 308, 32220, pg. 334 **PB**

Wildwood

Avesta Sheffield Pipe Co., 1101 N. Main St., 34785, pg. 221 **IT**

Winter Garden

HELLER BROS. PACKING CORP., 288 9th St., 34787, pg. 520 **PV**

Winter Haven

BOWEN BROTHERS FRUIT CO., INC., 305 Ave. E, S.W., 33880, pg. 162 **PV**
INDIAN RIVER TRANSPORT CO., 2580 Executive Rd., 33884, pg. 560 **PV**
Poe & Brown of Florida, 290 Cypress Gardens Blvd., 33880, pg. 1312 **PB**
Winter Haven News Chief, 650 Sixth St., S.W., 33880-3399, pg. 995 **PV**

Winter Park

ASN INCORPORATED, 500 S. Park Ave., Ste. 100, 32789, pg. 8 **PV**
The Creative Services Inc., 3260 University Blvd., No. 175, 32790, pg. 1072 **IT**
Philip Crosby Associates, Inc., 3260 University Blvd., Ste. 175, 32792, pg. 1072 **PV**
DODGE OF WINTER PARK, 1050 N. Orlando Ave., 32789, pg. 337 **PV**
Grizzard, 130 University Park Dr., Ste. 165, 32792, pg. 482 **PV**
ROGER HOLLER CHEVROLET & GEO CO., 860 W. Fairbanks Ave., 32789, pg. 534 **PV**
HUBBARD CONSTRUCTION CO., 1936 Lee Rd., 32789, pg. 544 **PV**
Logicon Eagle Technology, Inc., 950 N. Orlando Ave., 32789, pg. 1199 **PB**
Orlando Branch Office, 3260 University Blvd., Ste. 195, 32792, pg. 1683 **PV**
Orlando Paving Company, 1936 Lee Rd., 32789, pg. 544 **PV**
PALMER ELECTRIC CO., 875 Jackson Ave., 32789, pg. 834 **PV**
Training Systems Division, 1155 S. Semoran Blvd., Ste. 1121, 32792, pg. 219 **PB**
WESH Television, Inc., 1021 N. Wymore Rd., 32789-1782, pg. 1344 **PB**
Wheeled Coach Industries, Inc., 2778 N. Forsyth Rd., 32792, pg. 400 **PB**

Yulee

Sears Logistics Services, One Imeson Park Blvd., Bldg. 200, 32097, pg. 1452 **PB**

Geographic Index-U.S.

Zephyrhills

Vitality Foodservice, Inc., P.O. Box 9006, 4011S Country Rd., 54 E., 33540, pg. 682 PV

GEORGIA

Acworth

AMERICO MANUFACTURING CO., INC., 6224 No. Main St., 30101, pg. 64 PV

Albany

ADDISON STEEL INC., 1920 Ledo Rd., 31707, pg. 17 PV
The Albany Herald Publishing Co., Inc., 126 N. Washington, 31701, pg. 759 PB
Atlas Automotive, Inc., 2800 Phillips Dr., 31707, pg. 444 PV
Cooper Tire & Rubber Company, Albany Plant, 3300 Sylvester Rd., 31703, pg. 445 PB
Corrugated Packaging, 405 Maxwell Dr., 31705, pg. 736 PB
Enco-Georgia, 1425 Industrial Ave., 31707, pg. 375 PV
GRAY COMMUNICATIONS SYSTEMS, INC., 126 N. Washington St., 31701, pg. 759 PB
Gray Real Estate & Development Co., P.O. Box 48, 31702-0048, pg. 759 PB
Miller Brewing Company, 405 Cordele Rd., 31708, pg. 1289 PB
National Distributing Co., Inc., 1105 Albany Ct., 31701, pg. 781 PV
Nut Tree Pecan Company, Inc., P.O. Box 3890, 1316 Oakridge Dr., 31706, pg. 1201 PV
Security Bank and Trust Company, P.O. Box 1088, 700 Pine Ave., 31703, pg. 1549 PB
SunTrust Bank, South Georgia, N.A., 410 W. Broad, 31701, pg. 1538 PB
Tara Foods, 1900 Cowles Ave., 31708-001, pg. 967 PB
WALB-TV, Inc., Channel 10, 1709 Stuart Ave., 31707, pg. 759 PB

Alma

Fleetwood Homes of Georgia, Inc.-Alma, P.O. Box 767, 32 W. Industrial Park, 31510, pg. 651 PB

Alpharetta

ABI National Accounts, 1020 Cambridge Sq., 30201, pg. 70 PB
Academy Insurance Group, Inc., 110 Nobel Ct., Ste.1200, 30202, pg. 27 IT
Academy Life Insurance Co., 110 Nobel Ct., Ste. 1200, 30202, pg. 27 IT
Amoco Performance Products, Inc., 4500 McGinnis Ferry Rd., 30005, pg. 102 PB
BTS Inc., 2001 Westside Pkwy. Ste. 120, 30201-7408, pg. 204 IT
Equifax Information Technology, 1525 Windward Concourse, 30202, pg. 588 PB
FOCAS, 9335 Industrial Trace, 30201, pg. 329 IT
Golden Peanut Company, 100 Northpoint Ctr. E, Ste. 400, 30202, pg. 459 PV
HOOVER GROUP, INC., 2001 Westside Pkwy., Ste. 155, 30004, pg. 538 PV
Industrial Environmental Products, Inc., 914 Curie Dr., 30202, pg. 1215 PB
MacGregor Golf Company, 3025 Windward Pl., Ste. 300, 30005, pg. 72 IT
MacMillan Bloedel Inc., 5895 Windward Pkwy., 30202-4182, pg. 829 IT
PBD, INC., 1650 Bluegrass Lakes Pkwy., 30201, pg. 825 PV
PROTO SYSTEMS OF ATLANTA, 630 Simms Industrial Blvd., 30004, pg. 891 PV
RLI Southeast Regional Office, 2475 Northwinds Pkwy., Ste. 300, 30004, pg. 1356 PB
Siemens Energy & Automation Inc., 3333 Old Milton Pkwy., 30005, pg. 1245 IT
Southeastern Regional Office, 5895 Windward Pkwy., 30201, pg. 224 PV
Telecorp Systems Inc., 605 Buttercup Trace, 30202, pg. 316 IT
Vencare, Incorporated, 1105 Sanctuary Pkwy., 30201, pg. 1715 PB

Alto

Mount Vernon Mills, Inc., Riegel Textile Div. (Alto), P.O. Box 649, 30510, pg. 835 PV
Mount Vernon Textile Group, Hwy. 23 & 441, 30510, pg. 836 PV

Americus

Martin Marietta Assembly Services, 300 Martin Marietta Dr., 31709, pg. 1007 PB
Metalux Lighting, 428 Southerfield Rd., 31709, pg. 443 PB
Myo-Tech Electronics, P.O. Box 725, 31709, pg. 244 PB
N.B.F. Bollinger Industries, 303 Swett Ave., 31709, pg. 243 PB
Sheffield Hardware Company, 314 N. Dudley, 31709, pg. 335 PV
Sumter Bank and Trust Company, P.O. Box 767, 31709, pg. 1549 PB
THE TOG SHOP, Lester Square, 31710, pg. 1090 PV

Athens

Athens First Bank & Trust Co., 124 E. Hancock Ave., 30613-3899, pg. 1549 PB
Carrier Corp. Transicold Division, 700 Olympic Dr., 30601-1631, pg. 1689 PB
Champion Int'l. Corp., 600 Dairy Park Rd., 30607, pg. 334 PB
Charter Behavioral Health System of Athens, Inc., 240 Mitchell Bridge Rd., 30606, pg. 1033 PB
Eaton Corp., Supercharger Div., 695 Indian Hills Rd., 30601, pg. 556 PB
Holiday Inn, P.O. Box 1666, Broad & Lumpkin Sts., 30602, pg. 134 PV
Lectro Products, Inc., 420 Athena Dr., 30601, pg. 126 IT
Noramco, Inc., P.O. Box 800001, 30608-8001, pg. 929 PB
Oliver Rubber Co., 165 Dougherty St., 30601, pg. 1504 PB
Oliver Rubber Co., 215 Oneta St., 30603, pg. 1504 PB
Peterson Spring-Georgia Plant, Old Hull Rd., 30613, pg. 857 PV
Seaboard Farms, 898 Barber St., 30601-2030, pg. 1449 PB
SunTrust Bank, Northeast Georgia, N.A., 101 N. Lumpkin St., 30601, pg. 1538 PB

Atlanta

ABN AMRO Bank, N.V. (Atlanta), One Ravinia Dr., Ste. 1200, 30346-2103, pg. 10 IT
AFC ENTERPRISES, Six Concourse Pkwy., Ste. 1700, 30328-5352, pg. 5 PV
AGA Cookers Inc., 1900 Lake Park Drive, 30080, pg. 555 IT
AGL Energy Services, Inc., 303 Peachtree St., N.E., 30308, pg. 7 PB
AGL RESOURCES, 303 Peachtree St. N.E., 30302-4569, pg. 6 PB
AIG Aviation, Inc., 100 Colony Sq., 30361, pg. 85 PB
AJC INTERNATIONAL, INC., 5188 Roswell Rd., N.W., 30342, pg. 6 PV
AMC, INC., 240 Peachtree St. N.W., Ste. 2200, 30303, pg. 6 PV
APAC Holdings, Inc., 3340 Peachtree Rd. N.E., Ste. 600, 30326, pg. 139 PB
ASI Properties, Inc., 470 E. Paces Ferry Rd., 30305, pg. 91 PB
AST Research, Inc., 47 Perimeter Center E., Ste. 1102, 30346, pg. 1181 IT
ATC HEALTHCARE SERVICES INC., 2675 Paces Ferry Rd. SE, 30339, pg. 8 PV
AVA, 2175 Parklake Dr., N.E., Ste. 200, 30345, pg. 8 PV
AVA Leasing Service Company, 2175 Parklake Dr., N.E., Ste. 200, 30345, pg. 8 PV
Aaron Rents Convention Furnishings, 1100 Aaron Bldg., 309 E. Paces Ferry Rd., 30305, pg. 12 PB
AARON RENTS, INC., 309 E. Paces Ferry Rd. N.E., 30305-2377, pg. 12 PB
Aaron's Rental Purchase, 1100 Aaron Bldg., 309 E. Paces Ferry Rd., 30305, pg. 12 PB
Abrams Construction, Inc., 5775-A Glenridge Dr. N.E., Ste. 200, 30328, pg. 14 PB
Abrams Fixture Corporation, 362 Jones Ave. N.W., 30314, pg. 14 PB
ABRAMS INDUSTRIES, INC., 1945 The Exchange, Ste. 300, 30339, pg. 14 PB
Abrams Properties, Inc., 5775-A Glenridge Dr. N.E., Ste. 200, 30328, pg. 14 PB
AccuScan, 4000 Dekalb Tech. Pkwy., Ste., 30340, pg. 890 IT
Acxiom Corporation, Atlanta Financial Center, 3342 Peachtree Rd., Ste. 200, 30326, pg. 18 PB
ADAIR GREENE ADVERTISING, 200 Atlanta Tech. Ctr., 1575 Northside Dr., 30318, pg. 16 PV
ADAMS WINE CO., 451 Sawtell Ave., S.E., 30315, pg. 17 PV
The Aegis Group, Inc., 15 Dunwoody Pk., 30338, pg. 150 PB
AgraTrade Financing, Inc., 244 Perimeter Center Pkwy., 30346, pg. 459 PV
Agvestments, Inc., 244 Perimeter Center Pkwy. N.E., 30346, pg. 459 PV
AKZO Coatings Inc., 3032 Bankers Industrial Dr., 30360-2717, pg. 46 IT
Alcan Cable Division, Three Ravinia Dr., Ste.1600, 30346-2133, pg. 50 IT
Alchem Plastics Corp.-Georgia, Ten Enterprise Blvd., 30336, pg. 1495 PB
Alimak Elevator Company, 3040 Amwiler Rd., 30360, pg. 34 PV
Alitalia, 223 Perimeter Center Pkwy., Ste. 530, 30346, pg. 652 IT
ALLEGIANT PHYSICIAN SERVICES, 500 Northridge Rd., Ste. 500, 30350, pg. 45 PB
ALLIED FOODS, INC., 1450 Hills Place NW, 30318, pg. 39 PV
Allright Parking of Georgia, 100 Luckie N.W., 30301, pg. 43 PV
ALLTEL Information Services-Healthcare Div., 200 Ashford Center N., 30338, pg. 55 PB
ALTAMA DELTA CORPORATION, 2330 DeFour Hills Rd., 30313, pg. 47 PV
ALUMAX INC., 3424 Peachtree Rd., N.E., Ste. 2100, 30326, pg. 59 PB
Ambulatory Resources, Inc., 3414 Peachtree Rd., N.E., Ste, 1400, 30326, pg. 1033 PB
AMEDIA, Inc., 470 E. Paces Ferry Rd., 30305, pg. 91 PB
Amerford International Corporation, 8010 Roswell Road, 30350, pg. 1388 IT
American Bank Note Company, 127 Peachtree St., Ste. 1700, 30303, pg. 68 PB
AMERICAN BUSINESS PRODUCTS, INC., 2100 River Edge Pkwy., Ste. 1200, 30328, pg. 70 PB
American Cellular Communications Corporation, 1100 Peachtree St., 30309-4599, pg. 208 PB
American Cities Business Journals, Inc., 1801 Peachtree St., Ste. 150, 30309, pg. 19 PV
American Health Consultants, Bldg. 6, Ste. 400, 3525 Piedmont Rd. N.E., 30305, pg. 1601 PB
American Photo Group, 1117 Perimeter Ctr. W., 30346, pg. 551 PB
American Security Group, 3290 Northside Pkwy., N.W., 30327, pg. 499 IT
AMERICAN SOFTWARE, INC., 470 E. Paces Ferry Rd., 30305, pg. 91 PB
American Software, Inc., Southern, 470 E. Paces Ferry Rd., 30305, pg. 91 PB
Amoco Fabrics & Fibers Company, 900 Cir. 75 Pkwy., Ste. 550, 30339-3098, pg. 102 PB
Amoco Foam Products Co., 375 Northridge Rd., Ste. 600, 30350-3297, pg. 102 PB
Amoco Nisseki Claf Inc. (ANCI), 900 Circle 75 Pkwy., Ste. 1400, 30339, pg. 102 PB
AMP Inc. Lytel Division, 2300 Parklake Dr NE Ste 240, 30345-2905, pg. 8 PB
Amquest, Inc., 470 E. Paces Ferry RD., 30305, pg. 91 PB
Anacomp Magnetics, Inc., 2115 Monroe Dr., 30324, pg. 107 PB
Analysts International, Southern Region, Perimeter 400 Ctr., Suite 850, 1100 Johnson Ferry Rd., N.E., 30342-1746, pg. 110 PB
APEX SUPPLY CO., INC., 2500 Button Gwinnett Dr., 30340-1597, pg. 77 PV
ATLANTA BEVERAGE CO., 5000 Fulton Industrial Blvd. SW, 30336, pg. 94 PV
Atlanta Blueprint Company, 1052 W. Peachtree St., N.W., 30309, pg. 1735 PB
Atlanta Braves, Inc., 521 Capital Ave., 30312, pg. 1614 PB
Atlanta Gas Light Company, 1219 Carolina St. N.E., 30302-4569, pg. 7 PB
Atlanta Hawks, Inc., One CNN Center, South Tower, Ste. 405, 30348, pg. 1614 PB
The Atlanta Journal, 72 Marrieta St. N.W., 30303-2804, pg. 281 PV
ATLANTA LIFE INSURANCE COMPANY, 100 Auburn Ave. N.E., 30303, pg. 94 PV
Atlanta MOB, Inc., 3414 Peachtree Rd., N.E., Ste. 1400, 30326, pg. 1033 PB
Atlanta National League Baseball Club, Inc., 521 Capitol Ave., S.W., 30312, pg. 1614 PB
Atlanta Regional Office, Bldg. 400, Ste. 610, 3715 Northside Pkwy., N.W., 30327, pg. 1715 PB
ATLANTIC AMERICAN CORPORATION, 4370 Peachtree Rd., N.E., 30319-3000, pg. 143 PB
Atlantic American Life Insurance Company, 4370 Peachtree Rd., N.E., 3rd Fl., 30319-3000, pg. 143 PB
Atlantic Envelope Co., 1700 Northside Dr. N.W., 30318, pg. 1160 PB
ATLANTIC SOUTHEAST AIRLINES INC., 100 Hartsfield Centre Pkwy., Ste. 800, 30354-1356, pg. 144 PB
Atlantic Steel Industries, Inc., 1300 Mecaslin St., N.W., 30318, pg. 696 IT
Atlantis Plastic Films, Inc., 1870 The Exchange, Ste. 200, 30339, pg. 145 PB
ATLANTIS PLASTIC, INC., 1870 The Exchange, Ste. 200, 30339, pg. 145 PB
ATLAS SUPPLY COMPANY, 1775 The Exchange, Ste. 400, 30339, pg. 96 PV
The Audichron Company, 3605 Clearview Pl., 30340, pg. 570 PB
Aunt Fanny's Bakery, 1039 Grant St., S.E., 30303, pg. 657 PB
AUSTIN KELLEY ADVERTISING, INC., The Palisades, 5901 Peachtree Dunwoody Rd., NE, 30328, pg. 100 PV
Auto Lenders Acceptance Corp., 300 Interstate N. Pkwy., Ste. 800, 30339, pg. 499 IT
Autocomp, Inc., 2161 Monroe Dr. N.E., 30324, pg. 1735 PB
Autodesk, 5901 Peachtree Dunwoody Rd., Ste. 400C, 30328, pg. 149 PB
Automated Wagering International, Inc., 115 Perimeter Center Pl. Ste. 911, 30346, pg. 1319 PB
AUTOMOBILE PROTECTION CORPORATION-APCO, 15 Dunwoody Park, Ste. 100, 30338, pg. 150 PB
Aviation Constructors, Inc., 2690 Cumberland Pkwy., Ste. 200, 30339, pg. 246 PV
B&M Equipment, Inc., 141 Piedmont Ave., N.E., 30303, pg. 127 PV
BBS Holdings, Inc., 4510 Southern Bell Ctr., 675 W. Peachtree St., 30375, pg. 209 PB
BSA Advertising, Inc., 1040 Crown Pointe Pkwy., Ste. 950, 30338, pg. 108 PV
BWAY CORP., 8607 Roberts Dr., Ste. 250, 30350, pg. 164 PB
Banca Nazionale Del Lavoro (Atlanta), Marquis Tower, 245 Peachtree Ctr. Ave., Ste. 2120, 30303, pg. 136 IT
The Bank of Nova Scotia, 600 Peachtree St., N.E., Ste. 2700, 30308, pg. 156 IT
The Bank of Tokyo-Mitsubishi, Ltd. (Atlanta Agency), Georgia-Pacific Ctr., 133 Peachtree St. N.E., Ste. 4970, 30303-1808, pg. 157 IT
Bankers Fidelity Life Insurance Company, 4370 Peachtree Road N.E., 3rd Fl., 30319-3000, pg. 143 PB
BANKHEAD ENTERPRISES INC., 1080 Bankhead Ave., 30318, pg. 114 PV
Barton Brands of Georgia, Inc., 650 Fairburn Rd., S.W., 30331, pg. 300 PB
Basic American Medical Products, Inc., 2935 Bankers Industrial Dr., 30360, pg. 758 PB

PB - *U.S. Public Companies Volume*
PV - *U.S. Private Companies Volume*
IT - *International Public & Private Companies Volume*

U.S. LOCATED COMPANIES GEORGIA

BEAUDRY FORD, INC., 141 Piedmont Ave., N.E., 30303, pg. 127 PV
Beers Construction Company, 70 Ellis St., N.E., 30303, pg. 1261 IT
Behavioral Health Systems of Indiana, Inc., 3414 Peachtree Rd., N.E., Ste. 1400, 30326, pg. 1033 PB
BellSouth Advertising & Publishing Corp., Rm. 420, 59 Executive Pk. Dr., S., 30329, pg. 208 PB
BellSouth Applied Technologies, Inc., 675 W. Peachtree St. N.E., 30375, pg. 209 PB
BellSouth Cellular Corp., 1100 Peachtree St., Ste. 1000, 30309, pg. 208 PB
Bellsouth Cellular National Marketing, Inc., 1100 Peachtree St., Ste. 1000, 30309-4599, pg. 208 PB
BELLSOUTH CORPORATION, 1155 Peachtree St., N.E., Rm. 2001, 30309-3610, pg. 207 PB
BellSouth Enterprises, Inc., 1100 Peachtree St., N.E., Ste. 1000, 30309-4599, pg. 208 PB
BellSouth Financial Services Corporation, Ste. 1400, 1800 Century Blvd., 30345, pg. 209 PB
BellSouth Information Systems, Inc (BIS), 1957 Lakeside Pkwy., Ste. 510, 30084, pg. 208 PB
BellSouth International, Inc., Ste. 1024, 1100 Peachtree St., N.E., 30309-4599, pg. 208 PB
Bellsouth Mobile Data, Inc., 1100 Peachtree St., Ste. 1020, 30309-4599, pg. 208 PB
Bellsouth Mobile Systems Group, 1100 Peachtree St., Ste. 1000, 30309-4599, pg. 208 PB
BellSouth Mobility, Inc., 1100 Peachtree St., 30309-4599, pg. 208 PB
BellSouth Network Solutions, Inc., 1800 Century Blvd., Ste. 170, 30345, pg. 209 PB
Bellsouth Personal Communications, Inc., 3353 Peachtree Rd., Ste. 400, 30326, pg. 208 PB
BellSouth Resources, Inc., 1155 Peachtree St., N.E., Ste. 2008, 30309-3610, pg. 208 PB
BellSouth Telecommunications, Inc., 675 W. Peachtree St., N.E., 30375, pg. 209 PB
Bellsouth Wireless, Inc., 1100 Peachtree St., Ste. 1000, 30309-4599, pg. 208 PB
Beltway Community Hospital, Inc., 3414 Peachtree Rd., N.E., Ste. 1400, 30326, pg. 1033 PB
Bergemann USA, Inc., P. O. Box 941519, 30341-0519, pg. 401 IT
Bergen Brunswig Medical Corporation, 3720 Zip Industrial Blvd., S.E., 30354, pg. 214 PB
BETTER BRANDS OF ATLANTA, INC., 755 Jefferson St. NW, 30318, pg. 141 PV
Big River Industries, 365 Northridge Rd., Ste. 450, 30350, pg. 242 IT
Bindley Western, Mid-South Division, 120 Selig Dr. S.W., 30336, pg. 228 PB
Birmingham Field Office, 115 Perimeter Center Place, Ste. 965, 30346, pg. 840 IT
Bishop Brothers Auto Auction, 2244 Stewart Ave., 30315, pg. 282 PV
BLIMPIE INTERNATIONAL, INC., 1775 The Exchange, Ste. 600, 30339, pg. 236 PB
Blimpie International, Inc., 1775 The Exchange, Ste. 600, 30339, pg. 236 PB
Boge Suspension Systems, Inc., Atlanta Indus. Dr., Ste. E, 30331, pg. 835 IT
Bondo/Mar-Hyde Corporation, 3700 Atlanta Industrial Pkwy. N.W., 30331, pg. 1357 PB
Boral Industries Inc., 2859 Paces Ferry Rd., Ste. 1520, 30339, pg. 203 IT
The Botsford Group, 1 Buckhead Plaza, 3060 Peachtree Rd., Ste. #510, 30305, pg. 409 PV
Bowne of Atlanta, Inc., 1570 Northside Dr., 30325, pg. 248 PB
Broadcast and Video Enterprises Div., 2600 Cumberland Pkwy., 30339, pg. 647 PV
BROCK INTERNATIONAL INC., 2859 Paces Ferry Rd., Ste. 1000, 30339, pg. 258 PB
Browning-Ferris Industries of Georgia, Inc., Two Peachtree St., N.W., 30318, pg. 263 PB
BULL RUN CORPORATION, 4370 Peachtree Rd. NE, 30319, pg. 267 PB
Burnham, 100 Hartsfield Ctr., Ste. 310, 30354, pg. 686 IT
Burnham Service Co., Inc., 100 Hartsfield Ctr. Pkwy., Ste. 310, 30354, pg. 686 IT
Burrell Communications Group, Inc., 100 Colony Sq. Bldg., 1175 Peachtree St., NE, Ste. 502, 30361, pg. 188 PV
Buypass Corporation, 360 Interstate N. Pkwy., Ste. 400, 30339, pg. 446 PB
C.A.C.O. Services, Inc., 3414 Peachtree Rd., N.E., Ste. 1400, 30326, pg. 1033 PB
CCM, Inc., 3414 Peachtree Rd., N.E., Ste. 1400, 30326, pg. 1033 PB
CIBC Inc., 200 Galleria Pkwy., Ste. 650, 30330, pg. 257 IT
CL Capital Management, Inc., Ste. 600, 6201 Powers Ferry Rd. N.W., pg. 255 IT
CL Capital Management Inc., 260 Interstate North Circle, 30339, pg. 326 IT
CMI-Atlanta, 5730 Glen Ridge Dr., Ste. 306, 30328, pg. 287 PV
CMS Tansportation & Distribution, 4200 Northside Pkwy., Bldg. 8, Ste. C, 30327, pg. 66 PV
CNN (Cable News Network), One CNN Ctr., 30348, pg. 1614 PB
CNN Headline News, One CNN Ctr., Box 105366, 30348, pg. 1614 PB
CNN Radio, One CNN Ctr., Box 105366, 30348, pg. 1614 PB
CPS Associates, Inc., 3414 Peachtree St., N.E., Ste. 1400, 30326, pg. 1033 PB
CRSS Strategic Consultants, Two Concourse Pkwy, #125, 30328, pg. 1415 IT
CSR America Inc., Resurgens Plaza, Ste. 2110, 945 East Paces Ferry Road, 30326, pg. 245 IT
CableRep, Inc., 1400 Lake Hearn Dr., N.E., 30319, pg. 455 PB
Cadmus-Atlanta Manufacturing, 2300 Defoor Hills Rd., N.W., 30318, pg. 290 PB
Cadmus Marketing Services, 2300 DeFoor Hills Rd., 30318, pg. 291 PB
Cadmus Marketing Services, 2300 DeFoor Hills Rd., N.W., 30318, pg. 291 PB
CAGLE'S INC., 2000 Hills Ave., N.W., 30318, pg. 291 PB
Canada Life Insurance Company of America, Ste. 600, 6201 Powers Ferry Rd., 30339, pg. 255 IT
Canada Life of America Financial Services, Inc., Ste. 600, 6201 Powers Ferry Rd. N.W., 30339, pg. 255 IT
CAP Gemini America (Atlanta Branch), 1800 Century Blvd., N.E., Ste. 910, 30345, pg. 263 IT
Capitol Outdoor Advertising, Inc., 732 Ashby St., NW, 30318, pg. 361 PB
Carat ICG, 3340 Peachtree Rd. N.E., Ste. 1800, 30326, pg. 207 PV
Carrier Sales, Concourse Corp. Ctr., Six Concourse Pkwy., 6th Fl., 30328, pg. 1024 PB
W.G. Carroll, Inc., 1 Clay Place, 30354, pg. 1071 PB
CARTER & ASSOCIATES, 1275 Peachtree St. N.E., 30367-1801, pg. 216 PV
The Cartoon Network, 1050 Techwood Dr., 30318, pg. 1614 PB
Caye Steel & Wire Co., 787 Windsor St., S.W., 30315, pg. 220 PV
Cerner Corporation -Southeast Region, # 5 Concourse Pkwy., Ste. 410, 30328, pg. 331 PB
Charter Arbor Indy Behavioral Health System, Inc., 3414 Peachtree Rd., N.E., Ste. 1400, 30326, pg. 1033 PB
Charter Bay Harbor Behavioral Health System, Inc., 3414 Peachtree Rd., N.E., Ste. 1400, 30326, pg. 1033 PB
Charter Behavioral Health System at Los Altos, Inc., 3414 Peachtree Rd., N.E., Ste. 1400, 30326, pg. 1033 PB
Charter Behavioral Health System of Baywood, Inc., 3414 Peachtree Rd., N.E., Ste. 1400, 30326, pg. 1033 PB
Charter Behavioral Health System of Chicago, Inc., 3414 Peachtree Rd., N.E., Ste. 1400, 30326, pg. 1033 PB
Charter Behavioral Health System of Chula Vista, Inc., 3414 Peachtree Rd., N.E., Ste. 1400, 30326, pg. 1034 PB
Charter Behavioral Health System of Fort Worth, Inc., 3414 Peachtree Rd., N.E., Ste. 1400, 30326, pg. 1034 PB
Charter Behavioral Health System of Michigan City, Inc., 3414 Peachtree Rd., N.E., Ste. 1400, 30326, pg. 1034 PB
Charter Behavioral Health System of Mobile, Inc., 3414 Peachtree Rd., N.E., Ste. 1400, 30326, pg. 1034 PB
Charter Behavioral Health System of Texarkana, Inc., 3414 Peachtree Rd. N.E., Ste. 1400, 30326, pg. 1034 PB
Charter Behavioral Health System of Tucson, Inc., 3414 Peachtree Rd., N.E., Ste. 1400, 30326, pg. 1034 PB
Charter Behavioral Health System of Visalia, Inc., 3414 Peachtree Rd., N.E., Ste. 1400, 30326, pg. 1034 PB
Charter Behavioral Health System of Yorba Linda, Inc., 3414 Peachtree Rd., N.E., Ste. 1400, 30326, pg. 1034 PB
Charter Behavioral Health Systems of Atlanta, Inc., 811 Juniper St., N.E., 30308, pg. 1034 PB
Charter Brawner Behavioral Health System, Inc., 2414 Peachtree Rd., N.E., Ste. 1400, 30326, pg. 1034 PB
Charter Canyon Behavioral Health Systen, Inc., 3414 Peachtree Rd., N.E., Ste. 1400, 30326, pg. 1034 PB
Charter Contract Services, Inc., 3414 Peachtree Rd., N.E., Ste. 1400, 30326, pg. 1034 PB
Charter Fenwick Hall Behavioral Health System, Inc., 3414 Peachtree Rd., N.E., Ste. 1400, 30326, pg. 1034 PB
Charter Financial Offices, Inc., 3414 Peachtree Rd., N.E., Ste. 1400, 30326, pg. 1034 PB
Charter Hospital of Columbus, Inc., 3414 Peachtree Rd., N.E., Ste. 1400, 30326, pg. 1034 PB
Charter Hospital of Denver, Inc., 3414 Peachtree Rd., N.E., Ste. 1400, 30326, pg. 1034 PB
Charter Hospital of Ft. Collins, Inc., 3414 Peachtree Rd., N.E., Ste. 1400, 30326, pg. 1034 PB
Charter Hospital of Laredo, Inc., 3414 Peachtree Rd., N.E., Ste. 1400, 30326, pg. 1034 PB
Charter Hospital of Miami, Inc., 3414 Peachtree Rd., N.E., Ste. 1400, 30326, pg. 1034 PB
Charter Hospital of St. Louis, Inc., 3414 Peachtree Rd., N.E., Ste. 1400, 30326, pg. 1034 PB
Charter Hospital of Santa Teresa, Inc., 3414 Peachtree Rd., N.E., Ste. 1400, 30326, pg. 1034 PB
Charter Hospital of Torrance, Inc., 3414 Peachtree Rd., N.E., Ste. 1400, 30326, pg. 1034 PB
Charter Indiana BHS Holding, Inc., 3414 Peachtree Rd., N.E., Ste. 1400, 30326, pg. 1034 PB
Charter Lakehurst Behavioral Health System, Inc., 3414 Peachtree Rd., N.E., Ste. 1400, 30326, pg. 1034 PB
Charter Laurel Heights Behavioral Health System, Inc., 3414 Peachtree Rd., N.E., Ste. 1400, 30326, pg. 1034 PB
Charter Meadows Behavioral Health System, Inc., 3414 Peachtree Rd., N.E., Ste. 1400, 30326, pg. 1035 PB
Charter Medical-California, Inc., 3414 Peachtree Rd., N.E., Ste. 1400, 30326, pg. 1035 PB
Charter Medical-Clayton County, Inc., 3414 Peachtree Rd., N.E., Ste. 1400, 30326, pg. 1035 PB
Charter Medical-Cleveland, Inc., 3414 Peachtree Rd., N.E., Ste. 1400, 30326, pg. 1035 PB
Charter Medical-Dallas, Inc., 3414 Peachtree Rd., N.E., Ste. 1400, 30326, pg. 1035 PB
Charter Medical Executive Corporation, 3414 Peachtree Rd., N.E., Ste. 1400, 30326, pg. 1035 PB
Charter Medical Information Services, Inc., 3414 Peachtree Rd., N.E., Ste. 1400, 30326, pg. 1035 PB
Charter Medical International, S.A., Inc., 3414 Peachtree Rd., N.E., Ste. 1400, 30326, pg. 1035 PB
Charter Medical-Long Beach, Inc., 3414 Peachtree Rd., N.E., Ste. 1400, 30326, pg. 1035 PB
Charter Medical Management Company, 3414 Peachtree Rd., N.E., Ste. 1400, 30326, pg. 1035 PB
Charter Medical-New York, Inc., 3414 Peachtree Rd., N.E., Ste. 1400, 30326, pg. 1035 PB
Charter Medical of Florida, Inc., 3414 Peachtree Rd., N.E., Ste. 1400, 30326, pg. 1035 PB
Charter of Alabama, Inc., 3414 Peachtree Rd., N.E., Ste. 1400, 30326, pg. 1035 PB
Charter Peachford Behavioral Health System, Inc., 2151 Peachford Rd., 30338, pg. 1035 PB
Charter Petersburg Behavioral Health System, Inc., 3414 Peachtree Rd., N.E., Ste. 1400, 30326, pg. 1035 PB
Charter Psychiatric Hospitals, Inc., 3414 Peachtree Rd., N.E., Ste. 1400, 30326, pg. 1035 PB
Charter Regional Medical Center, Inc., 3414 Peachtree Rd., N.E., Ste. 1400, 30326, pg. 1035 PB
Charter Suburban Hospital of Mesquite, Inc., 3414 Peachtree Rd., N.E., Ste. 1400, 30326, pg. 1035 PB
Charter Thousand Oaks Behavioral Health System, Inc., 3414 Peachtree Rd., N.E., Ste. 1400, 30326, pg. 1035 PB
Charter Treatment Center of Michigan, Inc., 3414 Peachtree Rd., N.E., Ste. 1400, 30326, pg. 1035 PB
Charter White Oak Behavioral Health System, Inc., 3414 Peachtree Rd., N.E., Ste. 1400, 30326, pg. 1035 PB
Chesapeake Bagel Bakery, Six Concourse Pkwy., Ste 1700, 30328, pg. 5 PV
CHICK-FIL-A, INC., 5200 Buffington Rd., 30349, pg. 236 PV
Church's Chicken, Inc., Six Concourse Pkwy., Ste. 1800, 30328-5352, pg. 5 PV
Cigna Healthcare of Georgia, Inc., Midtown Plaza II, Ste. 1300, 1360 Peachtree St., N.E., 30309, pg. 359 PB
Circuit City Southern Div., 3755 Atlanta Industrial Pkwy., 30331, pg. 374 PB
Citicorp (USA), Inc., 211 Perimeter Ctr. ENE, 30346, pg. 377 PB
Citizens Mortgage Corporation, 900 Circle 75 Pkwy., 30339, pg. 1132 IT
Cleveland Electric Co., 1281 Fulton Industrial Blvd. NW, 30336, pg. 246 PV
Cleveland Electric Co., 3980 Martin Luther King Dr., 30336, pg. 246 PV
CLEVELAND GROUP, INC., 2690 Cumberland Pkwy., Ste. 200, 30339, pg. 246 PV
Coast RV, Inc., 1795 Continental Way, 30316, pg. 388 PB
THE COCA-COLA COMPANY, One Coca-Cola Plaza, 30313, pg. 392 PB
Coca-Cola Enterprises - Eastern Group/Southeast Region, 2500 Wendy Ridge, Ste. 700, 30339, pg. 393 PB
COCA-COLA ENTERPRISES INC., 500 Windy Ridge Pkwy., Ste. 700, 30339, pg. 393 PB
The Coca-Cola Export Corporation, One Coca-Cola Plaza, 30313, pg. 392 PB
Coca-Cola Financial Corporation, One Coca-Cola Plaza, 30313, pg. 392 PB
Coca-Cola Interamerican Corp., One Coca-Cola Plaza, 30313, pg. 392 PB
Coca-Cola USA, One Coca-Cola Plaza N.W., 30313, pg. 392 PB
Cognos Corp.-Atlanta Sales Office, Corporex Ctr., 400 Interstate N. Pkwy., Ste. 1060, 30339-5017, pg. 306 IT
Colonial Pipeline Co., 3390 Peachtree Rd., N.E., 30326, pg. 1584 PB
COLONIAL PIPELINE COMPANY, 945 E. Paces Ferry Rd., N.E., 30326-1125, pg. 254 PV
Columbia Tri-Star Television Distribution - Atlanta, 1201 W. Peachtree St., Ste. 4820, 30309, pg. 1282 IT
Columbian Chemicals Company, 1600 Parkwood Cir., Ste. 400, 30339, pg. 1286 PB
Commercial Cold Storage, Inc., 4300 Pleasantdale Rd., 30340, pg. 1519 PB
Commerzbank Aktiengesellschaft Atlanta Agency, Promenade Two, Ste. 3500, 1230 Peachtree St. N.E., 30309, pg. 310 IT
Confed Admin. Services, Inc., 260 Interstate North Circle, 30348-5103, pg. 326 IT
Confed Managed Healthcare, Inc., 260 Interstate North Circle, 30348, pg. 326 IT
Confederation Financial Holdings, Inc., 260 Interstate North Circle, 30339, pg. 326 IT
Confederation Financial Services (U.S.) Inc., 260 Interstate North Circle, 30339, pg. 326 IT
Confederation Life Insurance and Annuity Company, 260 Interstate North Circle, 30339, pg. 326 IT
Constar International, Inc., P.O. Box 43325, 5375 Drake Dr., 30336, pg. 463 PB
Consultec, Inc., 6065 Roswell Rd., N.E., 30328, pg. 443 PV
Corporate National Accounts Southeast, Five Concourse Pkwy., Ste. 2500, 30328, pg. 1024 PB
Correctional Behavioral Solutions, Inc., 3414 Peachtree Rd., N.E., Ste. 1400, 30326, pg. 1035 PB
Correctional Behavioral Solutions of Indiana, Inc., 3414 Peachtree Rd., N.E., Ste. 1400, 30326, pg. 1035 PB
COUSINS PROPERTIES INCORPORATED, 2500 Windy Ridge Pkwy., Ste. 1600, 30339, pg. 453 PB
COVINGTON INDUSTRIES, 2625 Cumberland Pkwy., 30339, pg. 280 PV
Cox Communications, Inc., 1400 Lake Hearn Dr. N.E., 30319, pg. 282 PV
COX COMMUNICATIONS, INC., 1400 Lake Hearn Dr., N.E., 30319, pg. 454 PB
COX ENTERPRISES, INC., 1400 Lake Hearn Dr., 30319, pg. 281 PV
Cox Texas Publications, Inc., 1400 Lake Hearn Dr., 30319, pg. 281 PV
CRAVEY, GREEN & WAHLEN, INCORPORATED, 12 Piedmont Ctr., Ste. 210, 30305, pg. 287 PV
CRAWFORD & COMPANY, 5620 Glenridge Dr. N.E., 30342, pg. 458 PB

PB - *U.S. Public Companies Volume*
PV - *U.S. Private Companies Volume*
IT - *International Public & Private Companies Volume*

Geographic Index-U.S.

The Credit Bureau, Inc. of Georgia, 1600 Peachtree St., N.W., 30309, pg. 588 **PB**

Creditanstalt-Bankverein, Atlanta Representative Office, Two Ravinia Dr., Ste. 1680, 30346, pg. 347 **IT**

Creditor Resources, Inc., 1100 Johnson Ferry Rd., Ste. 30, 30342, pg. 27 **IT**

Crow Wood Glen Associates, 2849 Pace's Ferry Rd., 30339, pg. 361 **PB**

CROWN CRAFTS, INC., 1600 RiverEdge Pkwy., Ste. 200, 30328, pg. 465 **PB**

Curtis 1000, Inc., 2100 River Edge Pkwy., Ste. 1100, 30328, pg. 70 **PB**

Cushman & Wakefield, Atlanta Office, 1201 W. Peachtree St., Ste. 3200, 30309, pg. 873 **IT**

DG Bank-Atlanta Branch, SunTrust Plaza, Ste. 2900, 303 Peachtree St. N.E., 30308-3252, pg. 352 **IT**

DSM Chemicals North America, Inc., Waterstone Bldg., 4751 Best Rd., Ste. 140, 30337, pg. 354 **IT**

DSM Melamine Americas, Inc., Waterstone, Ste. 140, 4751 Best Rd., 30337, pg. 355 **IT**

Dai-Ichi Kangyo Bank, Ltd.-Atlanta, Marquis Two Tower, Ste. 2400, 285 Peachtree Center Ave. N.E., 30303, pg. 359 **IT**

Delhaize The Lion America, Inc., Atlanta Plaza, Ste. 2160, 950 E. Paces Ferry Rd., 30326, pg. 463 **IT**

Delinvest, Inc., 950 E. Paces Ferry Rd., 30326, pg. 463 **IT**

Delrest, Inc., 950 E. Paces Ferry Rd., 30326, pg. 463 **IT**

DELTA AIR LINES, INC., 1030 Delta Blvd., Dept. 971, 30320-6001, pg. 497 **PB**

Dentsu USA-Atlanta Office, Peachtree Ctr., South Tower, 225 Peachtree St. NE, 12th Fl., 30303, pg. 393 **IT**

Desert Springs Hospital, 3414 Peachtree Rd., N.E., Ste. 1400, 30326, pg. 1035 **PB**

Dettelbach Pesticide Corp., 2170 Piedmont Rd., N.E., 30324, pg. 1405 **PV**

DeVilbiss Spray Booth Div., 520 Wharton Cir., 30336, pg. 866 **PB**

Diagnostic Imaging of Atlanta, L.P., 600 W. Peachtree St., Ste. 130, 30308, pg. 1715 **PV**

Diameter Paper Co., 6200-B Purdue Dr., P.O. Box 43509, 30336, pg. 165 **PV**

Dixie Express, Inc., 3240 Pointe Pkwy., 30092, pg. 1622 **PB**

DORSEY TRAILERS, INC., Bldg. 1, Ste. 1700, 2727 Paces Ferry Rd., 30339, pg. 520 **PB**

Dowty Aerospace North America, 210 Interstate Pkwy. N., Ste. 700, 30339, pg. 1337 **IT**

Dun & Bradstreet Software Services, 66 Perimeter Center E., 30346, pg. 532 **PV**

EA Engineering, Science & Technology, Inc., 1870 The Exchange, Ste. 100, 30339, pg. 541 **PB**

ECC International Inc., Suite 200G, 5775 Peachtree Dunwoody Rd., N.E., 30342, pg. 455 **IT**

Edelman Worldwide, Inc., Eight Peidmont Ctr., 3525 Peidmont Rd., N.E., Ste. 610, pg. 362 **PV**

ELECTRICAL INSULATION SUPPLIERS, 1255 Collier Rd., 30318, pg. 368 **PV**

ELECTROLUX CORPORATION, 2300 Windy Ridge Pkwy., Ste. 900, 30339, pg. 369 **PV**

Electronic Tele-Communications, Inc., 3605 Clearview Pl., 30340, pg. 570 **PB**

Elkay Plastics Co., Inc., Stock Service Center, 5290 Westgate Dr., Unit D, 30336, pg. 372 **PV**

Employee Assistance Services, Inc., 3414 Peachtree Rd., N.E., Ste. 1400, 30326, pg. 1035 **PB**

English China Clays, Inc., Ste. 200G, 5775 Peachtree Dunwoody Rd., N.E., 30342, pg. 455 **IT**

The Enterprise Group, 3343 Peachtree Rd., Ste. 450, 30326, pg. 769 **PV**

Equifax Center for Information Research, 1600 Peachtree St., N.W., 30309, pg. 588 **PB**

Equifax Credit Marketing Services, Inc., Two Ravinia Dr., Ste. 500, 30346, pg. 588 **PB**

EQUIFAX INC., 1600 Peachtree St., N.W., 30309, pg. 588 **PB**

Equifax Insurance Services Inc., 1360 Peachtree St., 30309, pg. 588 **PB**

Ericsson Network Systems, Inc., Two Ravinia Dr., Ste. 1330, 30346, pg. 1365 **IT**

Esix, 1899 Powers Ferry Rd, Ste. 375, 30339-5655, pg. 565 **PV**

Executive Courier, Inc., 120 Ottley Dr., 30324, pg. 1736 **PB**

Expert Systems, Inc., 1301 Hightower Trail, Ste. 201, 30350, pg. 1157 **PB**

Fahlgren, 3060 Peachtree Rd., Ste. 2000, 30305, pg. 391 **PV**

Federal Home Loan Mortgage Corporation (Freddie Mac)-Southeast/Southwest Region, 2839 Paces Ferry Rd., N.W., Ste. 700, 30339, pg. 615 **PB**

The Feldspar Corp., 1040 Crown Pointe Pkwy., Ste. 270, 30338, pg. 1523 **IT**

57th Fighter Group of Atlanta, Inc., 3829 Clairmont Rd., 30341, pg. 1023 **PV**

Financial Collection Agencies (1990) Inc., Paces Cumberland Bldg., 2675 Paces Ferry Rd. N.W., Ste. 320, 30339, pg. 471 **IT**

Financial Life Insurance Co. of Georgia, Two Peachtree St., N.E., 30383, pg. 1730 **PB**

Fireman's Fund Insurance Co. of Georgia, 302 Perimeter Ctr. N., 30346, pg. 59 **IT**

First Family Financial Services, 4362 Peachtree Rd., N.E., 30319, pg. 663 **PB**

First Image Management Co., Three Corporate Sq., Ste. 400, 30329, pg. 631 **PB**

First Union National Bank of Georgia, 999 Peachtree St., Ste. 1200, 30309, pg. 640 **PB**

FISCHBACH & DOUGHERTY, INC., 6065 Barfield Rd., Ste. 210, 30328, pg. 408 **PV**

FITZGERALD & CO., One Buckhead Plaza, 3060 Peachtree Rd. N.W., Ste. 500, 30305, pg. 409 **PV**

Flanigan's Lounge #600, Powers Ferry Landing, pg. 648 **PB**

Flanigan's Enterprises, Inc. of Georgia, 6300 Powers Ferry Rd., 30339, pg. 648 **PB**

Fleet Finance, Inc., 211 Perimeter Ctr. Pkwy., 30346, pg. 650 **PB**

Fleishman-Hillard, Inc., Harris Tower, Ste. 1250, 233 Peachtree St., NE, 30303-1507, pg. 411 **PV**

Foresight Software, Inc., Six Concourse Pkwy., Ste. 2200, 30328, pg. 872 **PV**

Forest Place Associates, 3945 Cumberland Club Dr., 30339, pg. 361 **PB**

Fuji Bank, Atlanta, Marquis One Tower, Ste. 2100, 245 Peachtree Ctr. Ave., N.E., 30303, pg. 519 **IT**

Furman Wholesale Lumber Branch, 1800 D Montreal Cir., 30084, pg. 431 **PV**

G-P Confederation, Inc., 260 Interstate North Circle, 30339, pg. 326 **IT**

GAC Color Graphics, 4540 Frederick Dr., S.W., 30336, pg. 1038 **PV**

GATX Logistics, Inc.-Georgia (Atlas), 5095 Phillip Lee Dr., 30336-2389, pg. 691 **PB**

GATX Logistics, Inc.-Georgia (Public), 1785 Westgate Pkwy., 30336, pg. 691 **PB**

GEC Avionics Inc., 2975 Northwoods Pkwy., 30366, pg. 544 **IT**

GK Stores Inc., 244 Perimeter Ctr. Pkwy., N.E., 30346, pg. 459 **PB**

GNB Technologies, 375 Northridge Rd., Ste. 100, 30350, pg. 1021 **PV**

GTE Mobile Communications Incorporated, 245 Perimeter Center Pkwy., 30346, pg. 696 **PB**

GTE Mobilnet Incorporated, 245 Perimeter Center Pkwy., 30346, pg. 696 **PB**

General Employment Enterprises, Inc., 5780 Peachtree & Dunwoody Rd., Ste. 525, 30342, pg. 714 **PV**

General Shale Products Corp., 2142 James Jackson Rd., 30318, pg. 844 **IT**

General Shale Products Corp., 3195 Brick Plant Rd., N.W., 30318, pg. 844 **IT**

General Trade Associates, 228 Margaret St., S.E., 30315, pg. 448 **PV**

GENERAL WHOLESALE COMPANY, INC., 1271 A Tacoma Dr., 30318, pg. 445 **PV**

GENUINE PARTS COMPANY, 2999 Circle 75 Pkwy., 30339, pg. 732 **PB**

Georgia Casualty & Surety Company, 4370 Peachtree Rd. N.E., 2nd Fl., 30319-3000, pg. 143 **PB**

Georgia Dealers Auto Auction, 7205 Campbellton Rd., 30331, pg. 282 **PB**

Georgia Federal Bank, FSB, 20 Marietta St., 30303, pg. 640 **PB**

GEORGIA GULF CORPORATION, 400 Perimeter Ctr. Ter., Ste. 595, 30346, pg. 734 **PB**

GEORGIA-PACIFIC CORPORATION, 133 Peachtree St. N.E., 30303-5605, pg. 735 **PB**

Georgia-Pacific Industrial Wood Products Div., 133 Peachtree St. N.E., 30303, pg. 735 **PB**

Georgia-Pacific Pulp & Paper Division, Ste. 1800, Harris Tower, 233 Peachtree St. N.E., 30303, pg. 735 **PB**

Georgia Power Co., 333 Piedmont Ave. N.E., 30308, pg. 1490 **IT**

Georgia Television Company, 1601 W. Peachtree St. N.E., 30309, pg. 282 **IT**

GEORGIA TENT & AWNING INC., 228 Margaret St. S.E., 30315, pg. 448 **PV**

Gilman Wallcovering Div., 325 Fulton Indus. Circle, 30336, pg. 596 **PV**

GOLD KIST, INC., 244 Perimeter Ctr. Pkwy., N.E., 30346, pg. 459 **PB**

Graphic Industries, Inc., 2155 Monroe St., N.E., 30324, pg. 1735 **PB**

GRIZZARD, 229 Peachtree St., N.E., Ste. 900, 30303, pg. 482 **PV**

Grolsch Importers Inc., 1985 N. Park Pl., 30339, pg. 559 **IT**

Gulf Coast EAP Services, Inc., 3414 Peachtree Rd., N.E., Ste. 1400, 30326, pg. 1036 **PB**

Gulf State Mortgage, Inc., 900 Circle 75 Pkwy., 30339, pg. 1133 **IT**

Gwinnett Immediate Care Center, Inc., 3414 Peachtree Rd., N.E., Ste. 1400, 30326, pg. 1036 **PB**

HBO & Company of Georgia, 301 Perimeter Ctr. N., 30346, pg. 770 **PB**

HBO & Company (VI), Inc., 301 Perimeter Ctr. N., 30346, pg. 770 **PB**

HBOC, 301 Perimeter Ctr. N., 30346, pg. 770 **PB**

HCS, Inc., 3414 Peachtree Rd., N.E., Ste. 1400, 30326, pg. 1036 **PB**

Hakuhodo Advertising America Inc., 3390 Peachtree Rd. N.E., Ste. 1000, 30326, pg. 588 **IT**

Hamilton, Allen & Associates, Inc, One Buckhead Plaza, Ste. 1550, 3060 Peachtree Rd., N.W., 30305, pg. 1673 **PB**

Harbinger Carpet, 1755 The Exchange, 30339, pg. 1121 **PV**

HARDIN CONSTRUCTION GROUP, INC., 1380 W. Paces Ferry Rd., 30327, pg. 501 **PB**

Harris Protocall, Inc., 3772 Pleasantdale Rd., Ste. 165, 30340, pg. 792 **PB**

HAVERTY FURNITURE COMPANIES, INC., 866 W. Peachtree St. N.W., 30308, pg. 799 **PB**

Hazelwood Farms Bakeries, Inc., 3500 Empire Blvd., 30354, pg. 1541 **PV**

Healthsource Georgia, 1000 Parkwood Circle, Ste. 700, 30339, pg. 360 **PV**

HEERY INTERNATIONAL, INC., 999 Peachtree St., N.E., 30367, pg. 519 **PV**

Hewlett-Packard Company, 1995 N. Park Pl., 30339, pg. 814 **PB**

Hilb, Rogal and Hamilton Company of Atlanta, Inc., 200 Galleria Pkwy., Ste. 1290, 30339, pg. 827 **PB**

Holcomb Bridge Immediate Care Center, Inc., 3414 Peachtree Rd., N.E., Ste. 1400, 30326, pg. 1036 **PB**

Holder Construction Company, 3333 Cumberland Cir., Ste. 400, 30339, pg. 534 **PV**

HOLDER CORPORATION, 3333 Cumberland Cir., Ste. 400, 30339, pg. 533 **PV**

Holiday Inn Worldwide, Three Ravinia Dr., Ste. 2000, 30346-2149, pg. 170 **IT**

Holland Sweetener North America, Inc., 1100 Circle 75 Pkwy., Ste. 690, 30339-3097, pg. 1407 **IT**

Holox Inc., 600 Northside Dr. N.W., 30318, pg. 811 **IT**

THE HOME DEPOT, INC., 2455 Paces Ferry Rd., N.W., 30339, pg. 831 **PB**

Hospital Investors, Inc., 3414 Peachtree Rd., N.E., Ste. 1400, 30326, pg. 1036 **PB**

Howell Industrial Clinic, 730 Peachtree St. N.E., Ste. 100, 30308, pg. 1715 **PB**

IDX Systems Corporation-Atlanta, 11 Peidmont Ctr., Ste. 800, 30305, pg. 854 **PB**

ING Investment Management Inc., 300 Galleria Pkwy, N.W., Ste. 1200, 30339-3149, pg. 648 **IT**

ING (U.S.) Capital Corporation, 200 Galleria Pkwy., N.W., Ste. 950, 30339, pg. 648 **IT**

IRT Management Company, 200 Galleria Pkwy., Ste. 1400, 30339, pg. 858 **PB**

IRT PROPERTY COMPANY, 200 Galleria Pkwy., Ste. 1400, 30339, pg. 858 **PB**

ISS International Service System, Inc., Two Concourse Pkwy., Ste. 270, 30328, pg. 656 **IT**

Imaging Technologies Services, Buckhead Branch, pg. 1736 **PB**

Imaging Technologies Services, Inc., 1052 West Peachtree St., N.W., 30309, pg. 1735 **PB**

Indimac Home Improvement Division, 400 Interstate N. Pkwy., 200 Platinum Towers, 30339, pg. 857 **PV**

The Industrial Bank of Japan Trust Company (Atlanta Agency), 191 Peachtree Tower, Ste. 3600, 191 Peachtree St., N.E., 30303, pg. 675 **IT**

INTEGRATEC, 3003 Chamblee Tucker Rd., 30341, pg. 588 **PB**

Integrated Graphic Services, 560 Monroe Pl., N.E., 30324, pg. 1736 **PV**

Intelligent Media Ventures, Inc., 57 Executive Park Dr. S., 30329, pg. 208 **PV**

Intellimedia Commerce, Inc., Two Piedmont Ctr., Ste. 300, 30305, pg. 91 **PV**

INTERFACE INC., 2859 Paces Ferry Rd., Ste. 2000, 30339, pg. 889 **PB**

INTERNATIONAL AIRLINE SUPPORT GROUP, INC., 1954 Airport Rd., Ste. 200, 30305, pg. 894 **PB**

Invesco Capital Management, 1315 Peachtree St. N.E., Ste. 500, 30309, pg. 685 **IT**

IRT Alamba Inc., 200 Galleria Pkwy., Ste 1400, 30339, pg. 858 **PB**

IRT Capital Corp., 200 Galleria Pkwy., Ste. 1400, 30339, pg. 858 **PB**

Tom James Of Atlanta, Inc., 2800 N. Druid Hills Rd., 30329, pg. 581 **PV**

Jefferies & Company, Inc., 3414 Peachtree Rd. N.E., Ste. 656, 30326, pg. 925 **PB**

The Jim Dandy Co., Inc., 1888 Emery St. N.W., Suite 300, 30318, pg. 918 **IT**

W.B. JOHNSON PROPERTIES, LLC, 3424 Peachtree Rd., N.E. Ste. 2075, 30326, pg. 594 **PV**

Kaiser Permanente, Southeast Division, Bldg. #9, 3495 Piedmont Rd., 30305, pg. 605 **PV**

Karastan Bigelow Commercial, 1755 The Exchange, 30339, pg. 1121 **PV**

H. KESSLER & COMPANY, 87 Peachtree St., S.W., 30303, pg. 616 **PV**

H. Kessler & Company, 2044 Campbellton Rd. S.W., 30303, pg. 616 **PV**

Keystone Southern Warehouse-Atlanta, 777 A Wharton Dr., 30336, pg. 955 **PB**

Kintetsu World Express Inc., 4694 Aviation Pkwy., Ste. E, 30349, pg. 734 **IT**

Korn/Ferry International, 303 Peachtree St., N.E., Ste. 1600, 30308, pg. 633 **PV**

Kragie/Newell, 365 Northridge Rd., Ste. 470, 30350, pg. 635 **PV**

Kredietbank Atlanta Branch, 2 Midtown Plaza, 1349 Peachtree St., Ste. 1750, 30309, pg. 760 **IT**

Kruger Pulp & Paper Sales, Inc., 6445 Powers Ferry Rd., Ste. 205, 30339, pg. 762 **IT**

Krupp Hoesch Steel Products Inc., One Ravinia Dr., Ste. 1100, 30346, pg. 515 **IT**

LDDS WorldCom, 945 E. Paces Ferry Rd. #2100, 30326, pg. 1779 **PB**

LTCB Atlanta, Ste. 2801, Marquis One Tower, 245 Peachtree Center Ave., N.E., 30303, pg. 816 **IT**

Lambert Smith Hampton, 1375 Peachtree St., Ste. 250, 30309, pg. 797 **IT**

Lanham Waste Control, Inc., c/o CT Corporation System, 2 Peachtree St., N.W., 30383, pg. 264 **PB**

Lanier Clothes, 222 Piedmont Ave., N.E., 30308, pg. 1239 **PB**

Lanier Worldwide Inc., 2300 ParkLake Dr. N.E., 30345-2979, pg. 791 **PB**

LAROCHE INDUSTRIES INC., 1100 Johnson Ferry Rd., 30342, pg. 651 **PV**

Law Companies Group, 1000 Abernathy Rd., N.E., 30328, pg. 653 **PV**

LAW ENGINEERING, INC., Three Ravinia Dr., Ste. 1830, 30346, pg. 653 **PV**

LEISURE TECHNOLOGY, INC., 5570 Glennidge Dr., 30342, pg. 659 **PV**

Geographic Index-U.S.

Lender's Single Interest, 2200 Century Pkwy., Ste. 650, 30345, pg. 1356 PB
Leslie - Locke, Inc., 4501 Circle 75 Pkwy., Ste. 4300, 30331, pg. 989 PB
LEVMARK CAPITAL CORPORATION, 2801 Buford Hwy., N.E., 30329, pg. 663 PV
Life Insurance Company of Georgia, 5780 Powers Ferry Road N.W., 30327-4390, pg. 648 IT
Lockheed-Latin America, 2401 Lake Park Dr., Ste. 265, 30080, pg. 1008 PB
Lockheed Martin Information Display Systems, 6765 Peachtree Industrial Blvd., 30360-2289, pg. 1008 PB
Logility, Inc., 470 E. Paces Ferry Rd., 30305, pg. 91 PB
Loher Drive Systems, Inc., 2840 Mt. Wilkinson Pkwy., Ste. 160, 30339, pg. 400 IT
The London Agency, Inc., 6 Concourse Pkwy., Ste. 2700, 30328-5346, pg. 1784 PB
Lotus Word Processing Division, 5600 Glenridge Drive, 30342, pg. 896 PB
MCI Business Markets, MCI Center, Three Ravinia Dr., 30346, pg. 1024 PB
MCI COMMUNICATIONS CORP., 3 Ravinia Dr., 30346, pg. 1023 PB
MCI Systemhouse, Three Ravinia Dr., 30346-2102, pg. 1024 PB
MSC Southeast Office, 100 Galleria Pkwy., Ste. 400, 30339, pg. 1031 PB
MacTavish Furniture Industries, 1100 Aaron Bldg., 309 E. Paces Ferry Rd., 30305, pg. 12 PB
Magellan Colonial Institute, Inc., 3414 Peachtree Rd., N.E. Ste. 1400, 30326, pg. 1036 PB
Magellan Contract Services, Inc., 3414 Peachtree Rd., N.E., Ste. 1400, 30326, pg. 1036 PB
Magellan Financial Offices, 3414 Peachtree Rd., N.E., Ste. 1400, 30326, pg. 1036 PB
MAGELLAN HEALTH SERVICES, INC., 3414 Peachtree Rd., N.E., Ste. 1400, 30326, pg. 1033 PB
Magellan Medical Executive Corporation, 3414 Peachtree Rd., N.E., Ste. 1400, 30326, pg. 1036 PB
Magellan Medical Information Services, Inc., 3414 Peachtree Rd., N.E., Ste. 1400, 30326, pg. 1036 PB
Magellan Mental Health Options, Inc., 3414 Peachtree Rd., N.E., Ste. 1400, 30326, pg. 1036 PB
Magellan Public Network, Inc., 3414 Peachtree Rd., N.E., Ste. 1400, 30326, pg. 1036 PB
Magellan Public Solutions, Inc., 3414 Peachtree Rd., N.E., Ste. 1400, 30326, pg. 1036 PB
Mailtek, Inc., 4080 Shirley Dr. S.W., 30336, pg. 1550 PB
Makita U.S.A. Inc.-Atlanta, 4680 River Green Pkwy., 30136-2566, pg. 831 IT
Mandarin Meadows, Inc., 3414 Peachtree Rd., N.E., Ste. 1400, 30326, pg. 1036 PB
Manheim Auctions, Inc., 1400 Lake Hearn Dr., N.E., 30319, pg. 282 PV
Marcam Corporation, Latin American Headquarters, 5775 D Glenridge Dr., Ste. 150, 30328, pg. 1043 PB
Marine Midland Business Loans, Inc., 200 Galleria Pkwy., Ste. 200, 30339, pg. 581 IT
Market Facts, Inc., 400 Colony Sq., Ste. 200, 1201 Peachtree St., N.E., 30361, pg. 1047 PB
Marshall Erdman & Assoc., Inc., 3097 Presidential Dr., 30340, pg. 380 PV
Mead Coated Board, 950 E. Paces Ferry Rd., Ste. 2075, 30326, pg. 1074 PB
Mead Containerboard, 1100 Circle 75 Pkwy., Ste. 500, 30339, pg. 1074 PB
Mead Packaging, 1040 W. Marietta St., N.W., 30318, pg. 1074 PB
Mead Packaging International, Inc., 1040 W. Marietta St. N.W., 30302, pg. 1076 PB
Mecaslin Street Corporation, 1300 Mecaslin St. N.W., 30301, pg. 696 IT
THE MEDIA INVESTMENT GROUP, One Buckhead Plaza, 3060 Peachtree Rd., NW., Ste. 500, 30305, pg. 726 PV
MedTrac, Inc., Five Concourse Pkwy., Ste. 2600, 30328-5346, pg. 1504 IT
Mercury Air Center, 1200 Hartsfield Dr., 30320, pg. 1093 PB
Mercury Air Center, 1951 Airport Rd., 30341, pg. 1093 PB
Merrill Corporation, 1451 Tower Place, 3340 Peachtree Road, 30326, pg. 1097 PB
Metro Atlanta Properties, 6065 Barfield Rd., Ste. 210, 30328, pg. 408 PV
Meyer Laminates Georgia Inc., 330 Patton Dr., 30336, pg. 864 IT
MicroBilt Corporation, 6190 Powers Ferry Rd., Ste. 400, 30339, pg. 631 PB
Microsoft Consulting Services, 6 Concourse Pkwy NE Ste 200, 30328-5351, pg. 1108 PB
Milton Investments, Inc., 950 E. Paces Ferry Rd., 30326, pg. 463 IT
Mitsui & Co. (U.S.A.), 2500 Windy Ridge Pkwy., 30339, pg. 879 IT
Modern Technologies, 2951 Flowers Rd. S., Ste. 110, 30341, pg. 755 PV
Mohawk Commercial Carpet, 1755 The Exchange, 30339, pg. 1121 PB
THE MONARCH COMPANY, INC., 1100 Johnson Ferry Rd., N.E., Ste. 460, 30342, pg. 756 PV
MORRISON RESTAURANTS, INC., The Hartsfield Collonade, 4893 Riverdale Rd., Ste. 260, 30337, pg. 1134 PB
Motorola AIEG Holding, Inc., pg. 1137 PB
Motorola Radius, 400 Interstate N. Pkwy., Ste. 450, 30339-5000, pg. 1138 PB
Eric Mower & Associates, 3379 Peachtree Rd, NE, Ste. 550, 30326, pg. 765 PV
MRS. WINNER'S CHICKEN & BISCUIT RESTAURANTS, 5995 Barfield Rd., 30328, pg. 766 PV
Munich American Reinsurance Co. (Marc Life), 56 Perimeter Ctr. E., N.E., 30346, pg. 897 IT
NRCTSC, Yale Bldg., Ste. 107, 2945 Flowers Rd. S., 30341, pg. 1182 PB
NYTRNG, Inc., Monarch Plaza, 15th Fl., 3414 Peachtree Rd., 30326, pg. 1174 PB
NAC Reinsurance Corporation-Atlanta, 115 Perimeter Ctr. Pl., Ste 545, 30346, pg. 1144 PB
NATIONAL DATA CORPORATION, National Data Plaza, 30329-2010, pg. 1155 PB
NATIONAL DISTRIBUTING CO., INC., One National Dr., S.W., 30336, pg. 781 PV
National Linen & Uniform Service, 1420 Peachtree St., N.E., 30309, pg. 1160 PB
National Management, Inc., 133 Peachtree St. N.E., 30303, pg. 736 PB
NATIONAL SERVICE INDUSTRIES, INC., 1420 Peachtree St., N.E., 30309, pg. 1160 PB
NationsBank Georgia Corporation, 35 Broad St., 30303, pg. 1162 PB
NationsBank Investment Advisors, Inc., 35 Broad St., 30303, pg. 1165 PB
NationsBank South, 35 Broad St., 30303, pg. 1163 PB
NationsBank Trust, P.O. Box 4899, 30302, pg. 1165 PB
Nedlloyd Holdings (U.S.A.) Inc., 2100 Riveredge Pkwy., Ste 300, 30328, pg. 1145 IT
Nedlloyd Lines (U.S.A.) Corp., 2100 Riveredge Pkwy. N.W., 30328, pg. 1145 IT
Neste Polyester Inc., 4480 Frederick Dr., 30336, pg. 913 IT
New Line Cinema-Atlanta, 4501 Circle 75 Pkwy., 30339, pg. 1614 PB
NEW VISION TELEVISION, 5784 Lake Forrest Dr., Ste. 275, 30328, pg. 794 PV
The New York Times Company Regional Newspaper Group, 1100 Monarch Plaza, 3414 Peachtree Rd., N.E., 30326, pg. 1174 PB
NEWCARE HEALTH CORPORATION, 6000 Lake Forest Dr., Ste.315, 30328, pg. 1176 PB
NewsEdge Corp., 3355 Lennox Rd., 30326, pg. 1180 PB
NORRELL CORPORATION, 3535 Piedmont Rd., N.E.-Bldg. 14, 30305, pg. 1192 PB
North American Sales, National Data Plaza, 30329, pg. 1156 PB
North Bros. Co., 3250 Woodstock Rd., S.E., 30316, pg. 853 PV
NuArc Southeastern Div., 446 Armour Circle N.E., 30324, pg. 809 PV
Numetrix Inc., Bldg. 400, 1000 Abernathy Rd., N.E., Ste. 1535, 30328, pg. 990 IT
Oaks at Baymeadow Associates, 2849 Paces Ferry Rd., Ste. 240, 30339, pg. 361 PB
Oaks at Regency Associates, 2849 Paces Ferry Rd., Ste. 240, 30339, pg. 361 PB
Orkin Exterminating Co., Inc., 2170 Piedmont Rd., N.E., 30324, pg. 1404 PB
Orkin Lawn Care, P.O. Box 647, 2170 Piedmont Rd., N.E., 30324, pg. 1405 PB
Orkin Plantscaping, 2170 Piedmont Rd., N.E., 30324, pg. 1405 PB
Outdoor Services, Eight Piedmont Ctr. #102, 30305, pg. 1166 PV
Outlet Square of Atlanta, Inc., 4166 Buford Hwy., 30345, pg. 1408 PB
Oxford Apparel, Inc., 222 Piedmont Ave., N.E., 30308, pg. 1239 PB
Oxford de Colon, S.A., 222 Piedmont Av., 30308, pg. 1239 PB
OXFORD INDUSTRIES, INC., 222 Piedmont Ave. N.E., 30308, pg. 1239 PB
Oxford International, Inc., 222 Piedmont Ave., N.E., 30308, pg. 1239 PB
Oxford of Luverne, Inc., 222 Piedmont Ave., N.E., 30308, pg. 1239 PB
Pacific-Charter Medical, Inc., 3414 Peachtree Rd., N.E., Ste. 1400, 30326, pg. 1036 PB
PARAGON HEALTH NETWORK, INC., One Ravinia Dr., Ste. 1500, 30346, pg. 1256 PB
Pasta Central, 1775 The Exchange, Ste. 600, 30339, pg. 236 PB
PATTON MANAGEMENT, INC., 1745 Phoenix Blvd., Ste. 430, 30349, pg. 843 PV
Payson Georgia, Inc., 3480 Oakcliff Rd., 30340, pg. 844 PV
Peachford Professional Network, Inc., 3414 Peachtree Rd., N.E., Ste. 1400, 30326, pg. 1036 PB
PENCO-Georgia, 2970 Clairmont Rd., Ste. 205, 30329, pg. 1508 IT
Penn Emblem Co., 5475 Fulton Industrial Pkwy., 30336, pg. 849 PV
Perimeter Center, Inc., 4400 Ashford-Dunwoody Rd., 30346, pg. 1408 PB
Perimeter Mall, Inc., 4400 Ashford-Dunwoody Rd., 30346, pg. 1408 PB
Perimeter Mall Management Corp., 1360 Perimeter Mall, 4400 Ashford-Dunwoody, 30346, pg. 1408 PB
Perma-Fix Environmental Services, Inc., 6075 Roswell Rd., Ste. 602, 30328, pg. 1279 PB
Philips Speech Processing, 64 Perimeter Center E., 6th Fl., 30364, pg. 1055 IT
Piedmont Div., 2999 Circle 75 Pkwy., 30339, pg. 732 PB
PINKERTON & LAWS INC., 1810 Water Pl., Ste.220, 30339, pg. 865 PV
Pitney Bowes Management Services, 1800 Century Pkwy., Ste. 150, 30345, pg. 1304 PB
Plantation Pipe Line Co., 3390 Peachtree Ave. N.E., 30326, pg. 348 PB
Poe & Brown of Georgia, Inc., 1100 Abernathy Rd., Ste. 200, 30328, pg. 1312 PB
Polysius Corp., Ste. 500, 180 E. Interstate North, 30339, pg. 512 IT
Pony Express Delivery Services, Inc, 6165 Barfield Rd., Ste. 200, 30328, pg. 245 PB
Popeye's Chicken & Biscuits, Six Concourse Pkwy., Ste. 1600, 30328, pg. 5 PV
Precision Die & Engineering, Inc., 6160 Boat Rock Rd., 30336, pg. 1322 PB
President Baking Company, 41 Perimeter Ctr. E., Ste. 400, 30346, pg. 1069 IT
Preussag International Steel Corp., 5780 Peachtree-Dunwoody Rd. NE, Ste. 595, 30342, pg. 1070 IT
Principal Health Care of Georgia, Inc., 400 N. Creek, Ste. 300, 3715 Northside Pkwy., 30327, pg. 885 PV
PRINTPACK INC., 4335 Wendell Dr., 30336, pg. 886 PV
Prism Communications LLc, Five Concourse Pkwy., 30328, pg. 209 IT
Prizma Photographics, 1055 Spring St., 30309, pg. 1735 PB
Professional Aviation Associates, Inc., 4694 Aviation Pkwy., 30349, pg. 187 PB
The Proven Method, 3423 Piedmont Rd., Ste. 402, 30305, pg. 91 PB
PsyCare, 5500 Interstate N. Pkwy., 30328, pg. 888 PB
Publix Super Markets, Inc., 2849 Paces Ferry Rd., Ste. 500, 30339-3769, pg. 894 PV
PURITAN/CHURCHILL CHEMICAL COMPANY, 916 Ashby St., N. W., 30318, pg. 895 PV
Quadras, Inc., 3176 Marjan Dr., 30340, pg. 1736 PB
Quest Staffing, 500 Northridge Rd., Ste. 500, 30350, pg. 45 PB
RDM SPORTS GROUP, 250 Spring St. NW, Ste. 3S, 30303, pg. 1354 PB
RET Corp., One CNN Ctr., Box 105366, 30348, pg. 1615 PB
RLI Transportation, 2200 Century Pkwy., Ste. 650, 30345, pg. 1356 PB
RP alpha/Atlanta, 1010 Huntcliff, Ste. 1250, 30350, pg. 950 PV
RPC INCORPORATED, 2170 Piedmont Rd., N.E., 30324, pg. 1356 PB
R.T.M. WINNERS, 5995 Barfield Rd., 30328, pg. 906 PV
Rank America, Inc., Five Concourse Pkwy., Ste. 2400, 30328, pg. 1087 IT
Rank Orlando, Inc., Five Concourse Pkwy., Ste. 2400, 30328, pg. 1087 IT
The Remembrance Institute, 230 John Wesley Dobbs Ave., 30303, pg. 499 IT
Rentokil Initial Plant Services (USA) Inc., 17 Executive Park S., 30329, pg. 1285 IT
Rentokil Initial USA, 10198 Collier Rd. N.W., 30318, pg. 1286 IT
Reprographics Imaging Technologies, 1052 W. Peachtree St., N.W., 30309, pg. 1736 PB
Residential Support Services, Inc., 1950 Sullivan Rd., 30337, pg. 1175 PV
Reynolds Aluminum Supply Company, 1441 Ellsworth Industrial, 30318-4156, pg. 1386 PB
Rhodes, Inc., 4370 Peachtree Rd., N.E., 30319, pg. 805 PB
Rich's/Lazarus/Goldsmith's, 223 Perimeter Center Pkwy., 30346, pg. 618 PB
RIDGEWOOD PROPERTIES, INC., 2859 Paces Ferry Rd., Ste. 700, 30339, pg. 1389 PB
Risk Sciences Group, Inc., 5620 Glenridge Dr., 30342, pg. 458 PB
The Ritz-Carlton Hotel Company LLC, 3414 Peachtree Rd., Ste. 300, 30326, pg. 594 PV
RIVERWOOD INTERNATIONAL CORPORATION, 3350 Cumberland Circle, Ste. 1400, 30339, pg. 1391 PB
Rivoli, Inc., 3414 Peachtree Rd., N.E., Ste. 1400, 30326, pg. 1036 PB
The Robinson-Humphrey Company, Inc., 3333 Peachtree Rd., 30326, pg. 1633 PB
Rogers Bridge Company, Inc., 1800 Briarcliff Rd. N.E., 30329, pg. 993 PV
Rollins Continental Inc., 2170 Piedmont Rd., NE, 30324, pg. 1405 PB
ROLLINS, INC., 2170 Piedmont Rd. N.E., 30324, pg. 1404 PB
Rollins Supply, Inc., 2170 Piedmont Rd., NE, 30324, pg. 1405 PB
ROSS SYSTEMS, INC., Two Concourse Pkwy., Ste. 800, 30328, pg. 1406 PB
ROSSER INTERNATIONAL, INC., 524 W. Peachtree St., 30308, pg. 946 PV
ROYAL OAK ENTERPRISES, INC., 900 Ashwood Pkwy., Ste. 800, 30338, pg. 948 PV
H.J. RUSSELL & CO., 504 Fair St. S.W., 30313, pg. 952 PV
Rust Environment & Infrastructure, 3980 DeKalb Technology Pkwy., 30340-2758, pg. 273 PB
S.Two Systems, Inc., 600 Embassy Row, Ste. 300, pg. 1524 PB
SMS-Atlanta, 400 Northridge Rd., Ste. 700, 30350, pg. 1463 PB
SRA - Atlanta, Two Midtown Plaza, 1360 Peach St. N.E., Suite 1770, 30309, pg. 958 PV
Sakura Bank - Atlanta Agency, Marquis One Tower, Ste. 2703, 245 Peachtree Center Ave., N.E., 30303, pg. 1179 IT
Sales Technologies, 3445 Peachtree Rd., N.E., Ste. 1400, 30326, pg. 395 PB
Sandwell Inc., 300-2690 Cumberland Parkway, 30339, pg. 1188 IT
Sato Kogyo U.S.A. Corporation - Atlanta, 659 Peachtree St., NE, Ste. 900, 30308, pg. 1197 IT
SAWYER RILEY COMPTON INC., 3423 Piedmont Rd., Ste. 400, 30305, pg. 969 PV
SCHERER HEALTHCARE, INC., 2859 Paces Ferry Rd., Ste. 300, 30339, pg. 1437 PB
Selig Chemical Industries, 840 Selig Dr., S.W., 30336, pg. 1160 PB
Sequent Computer Systems, Inc., 1050 Crowne Point Pkwy., N.E., Ste. 1800, 30338, pg. 1459 PB

Geographic Index-U.S.

PB - *U.S. Public Companies Volume*
PV - *U.S. Private Companies Volume*
IT - *International Public & Private Companies Volume*

Service Uniforms Div., 4040 Shirley Dr., 30336, pg. 1539   PB
Servitex Linen, One National Dr. S.W., 30336, pg. 782   PV
Shefco, Inc., 3240 Pointe Pkwy., 30092, pg. 1622   PB
SHEPHERD CONSTRUCTION CO., INC., 1800 Briarcliff Rd., NE, 30329, pg. 993   PV
SIGA, INC., Bldg. 14, Ste. 100, 4200 Northside Pkwy. N.W., 30327, pg. 999   PV
Simmons Company, One Concourse Pkwy., Ste. 600, 30328, pg. 686   IT
Singapore Airlines Ltd., 230 Peachtree St. N.W., 30303, pg. 1374   IT
Sistemas de Terapia Respiratoria S.A., Inc., 3414 Peachtree Rd., N.E., Ste. 1400, 30326, pg. 1036   IT
Sonoco Engraph, Inc., 2635 Century Pkwy. N.E., Ste. 900, 30345, pg. 1486   PB
Sophie Mae Division, 317 North Ave. N.E., 30308, pg. 454   PB
South Trust Bank of Georgia, 2000 Riveredge Pkwy., 30328, pg. 1492   PB
South Trust Bank of Georgia, 1 Georgia Center, 600 W. Peachtree, 30308, pg. 1492   PB
Southcorp U.S.A., Inc., 100 Galleria Pkwy., Ste. 900, 30339, pg. 1287   IT
Southeast Behavioral Systems, Inc., 3414 Peachtree Rd., N.E., Ste. 1400, 30326, pg. 1036   PB
Southeast Kinko's, Inc., Six Concourse Pkwy., Ste. 2300, 30328-5366, pg. 622   PV
Southeast Region, 780 Johnson Ferry Rd., Ste. 800, 30342, pg. 1024   PB
Southern Communications Services, 64 Perimeter Ctr. E., 30346, pg. 1490   PB
SOUTHERN COMPANY, 270 Peachtree St. N.W., 30303, pg. 1489   PB
Southern Company Services, Inc., 64 Perimeter Ctr. E., 30346, pg. 1490   PB
Southern Development and Investment Group, 64 Perimeter Ctr. E., 30346, pg. 1490   PB
Southern Signatures, Inc., 201 Armour Dr., 30324, pg. 1736   PB
Southland Life Insurance Company, 5780 Powers Ferry Road N.W., 30327-4390, pg. 648   IT
SouthTrust Bank of Georgia, 600 W. Peachtree St., 30308, pg. 1492   PB
SPACE MASTER INTERNATIONAL, 1040 Crown Pointe Pkwy., Ste. 900, 30338, pg. 1019   PB
Specialty Restaurants Group, 3300 Northlake Parkway, 30345, pg. 1023   PV
Square D Co., 5000 Westpark, 30336, pg. 1208   IT
Stein Facilities Management, 2161 Monroe Dr., N.E., 30324, pg. 1736   PB
The Stein Printing Company, Inc., 2161 Monroe Dr., N.E., 30324, pg. 1736   PB
Sterilization Services of Georgia, 6005 Boatrock Blvd., 30336, pg. 46   PV
Stevens Graphics, Inc., 713 Glenn St., S.W., 30310, pg. 208   PB
Stuart Circle Hospital Corporation, 3414 Peachtree Rd., N.E. Ste. 1400, 30326, pg. 1036   PB
The Sumitomo Bank, Ltd.-Atlanta Agency, Georgia-Pacific Center, 133 Peachtree St., N.E., Ste. 3210, 30303, pg. 1309   IT
Sunbrand Div., 3900 Green Industrial, 30341, pg. 1177   PV
Sunlink Corporation, Ste. 1100, 1100 Peachtree St. N.E., 30309, pg. 208   PB
SunTrust Bank, Atlanta, 25 Park Place, N.E., 30303, pg. 1538   PB
SUNTRUST BANKS, INC., 303 Peachtree St., N.E., 30308, pg. 1537   PB
SunTrust Banks of Georgia, Inc., One Park Place N.E., 30303, pg. 1538   PB
SunTrust Insurance Company, 303 Peachtree St., 30308, pg. 1538   PB
SunTrust Mortgage Inc., 360 Interstate N. Pkwy., Ste. 600, 30332, pg. 1538   PB
SunTrust Securities, Inc., 25 Park Place, N.E., 30303, pg. 1538   PB
SunTrust Service Corporation, 250 Piedmont Ave., N.E., 30303, pg. 1538   PB
Superior Telecommunications, 150 Interstate North Pkwy., Ste. 300, 30339, pg. 58   PB
SuperStation Inc., 1050 Techwood Dr. N.W., 30318, pg. 1615   PB
Surgical Information Systems, 500 Northridge Rd., Ste. 350, 30350, pg. 45   PB
Swift Textiles, Inc., 5 Concourse Parkway, 30328-5350, pg. 415   IT
Sybra, Inc., 8300 Dunwoody Place, 30350, pg. 270   PV
TBS Productions, Inc., P.O. Box 105366, 1050 Techwood Dr., 30318, pg. 1615   PB
TBS Properties, Inc., 1 CNN Center Plaza, 30335, pg. 1615   PB
TMP Worldwide, Inc., 47 Perimeter Center E., Ste. 500, 30346, pg. 1064   PB
TMP Worldwide/Recruitment Division, 47 Perimeter Ctr. E., Ste. 500, 30346, pg. 1065   PV
Takenaka (U.S.A.) Corporation, Atlanta Office, 4893 Riverdale Rd., Ste. 350, 30337, pg. 1351   IT
Tampella Power Corp., Ste. 1125, 2300 Windy Ridge Pkwy., 30339, pg. 1354   IT
Tamrock EJC USA Inc., P.O. Box 44347, 860 Westlake Pkwy., 30336, pg. 1352   IT
Taracorp Evans, Inc., 740 Lambert Dr., 30324, pg. 1068   PV
TARACORP, INC., 3490 Piedmont Rd. N.E., Ste. 1311, 30305, pg. 1068   PV
TAUSCHE MARTIN LONSDORF, 18 International Blvd., 30303, pg. 1069   PV
Taylor Woodrow Property Company (Georgia) Inc., 2801 Buford Hwy., Ste. 350, The Honeywell Center, 30329, pg. 1359   IT

TELEPHONE DIRECTORY ADVERTISING, 8399 Dunwoody Place, 30350, pg. 1073   PV
Thomson Company, Inc., Century Springs E., 6100 Lake Forrest Dr., Ste. 500, 30328, pg. 1429   PB
Time Products, Inc., 3780 Browns Mill Rd. S.E., 30354, pg. 1079   PB
Todd-AO/Editworks, 3399 Peachtree Rd., N.E., Ste. 200, 30326, pg. 1619   PV
Tokio Marine Management Inc. - Atlanta, One Ravine Dr., Ste. 1130, 30346, pg. 1392   IT
Tosoh America, Inc., 1100 Circle 75 Pkwy., Ste. 600, 30339-3097, pg. 1407   IT
Tosoh USA, Inc., 1100 Circle 75 Pkwy., Ste. 600, 30339-3097, pg. 1408   IT
Total Audio Visual Services, 1990 Defoor Ave., 30318, pg. 305   PV
Toto Industries (Atlanta), Inc., 1800 Murphy Ave., S.W., 30310, pg. 1410   IT
Tower Printing Company, 1201 W. Peachtree St., 30309, pg. 1736   PV
TRAMMELL CROW RESIDENTIAL SERVICES, 2859 Paces Ferry Rd., Ste. 1400, 30339, pg. 1095   PV
Transilwrap Co., Inc., 3616 McCall Pl., 30340, pg. 1097   PV
TRANSUS INTERMODAL L.L.C., 2090 Jonesboro Rd., S.E., 30315-6704, pg. 1097   PB
The Travel Channel, 2690 Cumberland Pkwy., Ste. 500, 30339, pg. 647   PB
TREND LABORATORIES INC., 3397 Rilman Rd., N.W., 30327, pg. 1634   PV
Trend Media, 3397 Rilman Rd., 30339, pg. 1634   PV
Triad Personnel Services, Bldg. 3, Ste. 101, 5825 Glenridge Dr., 30328, pg. 715   PV
TRITON MANUFACTURING, INC., Bldg. 17, Ste. 100, 8255 Dunwoody Pl., 30350, pg. 1104   PV
Trusco Capital Management, 50 Hurt Plaza, Ste. 1400, 30303, pg. 1538   PB
Trust Company Of Georgia, 25 Park Pl. N.E., 30303, pg. 1538   PB
Turner Broadcasting Sales, Inc., One CNN Ctr., Box 105366, 30348, pg. 1615   PB
Turner Broadcasting System Inc., One CNN Ctr., 30303, pg. 1614   PB
Turner Construction Company, 7000 Central Pkwy., Ste. 850, 30328, pg. 1645   PB
Turner Home Entertainment, P.O. Box 105366, One CNN Ctr., 30348, pg. 1615   PB
Turner Marketing, Inc., 1050 Techwood Dr. N.W., 30318, pg. 1615   PV
Turner Music Publishing, Inc., 1050 Techwood Dr., N.W., 30318, pg. 1615   PB
Turner Network Sales, P.O. Box 105366, One CNN Ctr., 30348, pg. 1615   PB
Turner Network Sales, Inc., 100 International Blvd., 30303, pg. 1615   PB
Turner Network Television, Inc., 1050 Techwood Dr. N. W., 30318, pg. 1615   PB
Turner Omni Venture, Inc., 100 International Blvd., 30342, pg. 1615   PB
Turner Private Networks, 100 International Blvd., 30348, pg. 1614   PB
Turner Program Services, Inc., One CNN Center, Box 105366, 30348, pg. 1615   PB
Turner Publishing, Inc., One CNN Center Plaza, 30335, pg. 1615   PB
Turner Reciprocal Advertising Corporation, P.O. Box 105366, 30348, pg. 1615   PB
Turner Sports, Inc., One CNN Center Plaza, 30335, pg. 1615   PB
UCB Pharma Inc., 1950 lake Park Dr., 30080, pg. 1427   IT
URS LOGISTICS, One Concourse Pkwy., Ste. 450, 30328, pg. 1114   PV
Unitec Capitol Insurance Company, 400 Perimeter Ctr. Terrace, Ste. 345, 30346, pg. 303   PV
United Capitol Insurance Company, 400 Perimeter Center Ter., Ste. 345, 30346, pg. 685   PB
United Family Life Insurance Co., 230 Houston St., N.E., 30303, pg. 499   IT
United HealthCare of Georgia, Inc., 3390 Peachtree Rd., Ste. 600, 30326, pg. 1678   PB
UNITED PARCEL SERVICE OF AMERICA, INC., 55 Glenlake Pkwy. N.E., 30328, pg. 1123   PV
UNITED PARKING, INC., 100 Peachtree St., Ste. 335, 30303, pg. 1123   PV
U.S. Healthcare of Georgia, Inc., 3500 Piedmont Rd., Ste. 300 30305, pg. 27   PV
Unitog Rental Facility, 25 C Enterprise Blvd. S.W., 30336, pg. 1693   PV
UNIVEST FINANCIAL SERVICES, LLC, 7000 Central Park Ave., Ste. 970, 30328, pg. 1128   PV
VW Mall, Inc., 200 Galleria Pkwy., Ste. 1400, 30339, pg. 858   IT
Video Service Company, 1400 Lake Hearn Dr. N.E., 30319, pg. 455   PV
VININGS INDUSTRIES INC., 2303 Cumberland Parkway, 30339-4501, pg. 1141   PV
Vitalink Pharmacy Services, Inc., One Ravinia Dr.,Ste. 1240, 30346, pg. 1042   PV
Vulcan Materials Company-Southeast Div., 2299 Perimeter Park Dr., Ste. 200, 30341, pg. 1726   PB
WGNX, Inc., 1810 Briarcliff Rd., N.E., 30329, pg. 1636   PB
WGST-AM, 550 Pharr Rd. N.E., 30305, pg. 923   PB
W.I.N. Systems, Inc., 15 Dunwoody Park, 30338, pg. 150   PB
WKHX-AM/WKHX-FM, 210 Interstate N., Ste. 600, 30339, pg. 512   PB
WPCH-FM, 550 Pharr Rd. N.E., 30363, pg. 923   PB
WQXI-WSTR, One Capital City Plaza, 3350 Peachtree Rd., Ste. 240, 30326, pg. 946   PB
WSB, Inc., 1601 W. Peachtree St., N.E., 30309, pg. 282   PB
WVEE-FM, 1201 Peachtree St., N.E., 30361, pg. 470   PB

WXIA-TV, 1611 W. Peachtree, N.E., 30309, pg. 702   PB
Wachovia Bank of Georgia, N.A., 191 Peachtree St., N.E., 30303, pg. 1730   PB
Wachovia Corporate Services, Inc., 191 Peachtree St., N.E., 30303-1757, pg. 1730   PB
Watkins Associated Developers, 1958 Monroe Dr. NE, 30301, pg. 1153   PV
WATKINS ASSOCIATED INDUSTRIES INC., 1958 Monroe Dr. N.E., 30324, pg. 1153   PV
Wattyl Paint Corporation, 5275 Peachtree Industrial Blvd., 30341, pg. 1488   IT
The Weather Channel, 300 Interstate North Pkwy., 30339, pg. 647   PB
WEST BUILDING MATERIALS, Lakeside Office Pk., Bldg. D, 5775 Glenridge Dr., Ste. 500, 30328, pg. 1163   PB
Western Behavioral Systems, Inc., 3414 Peachtree Rd., N.E., Ste. 1400, 30326, pg. 1036   PB
Western International Media Corporation, 1155 Peachtree St., Ste. 100, 30309, pg. 1167   PV
WESTWAYNE, INC., 1100 Peachtree St. N.E., Ste. 1800, 30309, pg. 1170   PV
WHITE ELECTRICAL CONSTRUCTION CO., 1730 Chattahoochee Ave., 30318, pg. 1172   PV
Wieland Financial Services, Inc., 1950 Sullivan Rd., 30337, pg. 1175   PV
JOHN WIELAND HOMES INC., 1950 Sullivan Rd., 30337, pg. 1175   PV
WILEN MANUFACTURING COMPANY, INC., 3760 Southside Industrial Pkwy., 30354, pg. 1176   PV
Williams Bros., 934 Glenwood Ave S.E., 30316, pg. 198   IT
Williams Detroit Diesel-Allison S.E., Inc., 2849 Moreland Ave. S.E., 30315, pg. 1179   PV
Williams Printing Company, 1240 Spring St., N.W., 30309, pg. 1736   PB
Willis Corroon Administrative Services Corporation, Five Concourse Pkwy., Ste. 2600, 30328, pg. 1504   IT
Willis Corroon Corp. Of Georgia, Five Concourse Pkwy., Ste. 2600, 30328, pg. 1506   IT
Willis Corroon Financial Services Corp., Five Concourse Pkwy., Ste. 2600, 30328, pg. 1507   IT
Willis Faber North America, Inc.-Georgia, 6000 Lake Forrest Dr., Ste. 250, 30328, pg. 1503   IT
Wilsey Foods, Inc., 1630 Huber St. NW, 30318, pg. 879   IT
Windsor Insurance, 2525 Cumberland Pkwy., 30339, pg. 75   PB
Wine World Estates, 1117 Perimeter Ctr. W., Ste. 11-101, 30338, pg. 917   IT
Wink Davis Equipment Company, Inc., 800 Miami Cir., NE, 30324, pg. 1498   PV
Winn-Dixie Atlanta, Inc., 5400 Fulton Industrial Blvd., 30336, pg. 1771   PB
R.E. Wolfe Enterprises of Edinburg, 2849 Paces Ferry Rd., Ste. 370, 30339, pg. 1379   PB
Wood Forest Associates, 3945 Cumberland Club Dr., 30339, pg. 362   PB
Wood Hills Associates, 2849 Paces Ferry Rd., Ste. 120, 30339, pg. 362   PB
Woodward-Clyde, 1117 Perimeter Ctr. W. Ste., 500 E., 30338, pg. 1657   PB
Wright & Lopez, Inc., P.O. Box 491539, 1745 Phoenix Blvd., Ste. 430, 30349, pg. 843   PV
WWF Paper Corporation - Southeast, P.O. Box 44105, 5255 Fulton Industrial Blvd., 30336, pg. 1145   PV
Yokohama Tire Corp., 1820 Independence Sq., Ste. B, 30338, pg. 1521   IT
Zellerbach Division, 2281 DeFoor Hills Rd. N.W., 30318, pg. 1075   PB
Zeneca Pharmaceuticals, 35 Glenlake Pkwy., # 355, 30328-3475, pg. 1525   IT
Zep Manufacturing Company, 1310 Seaboard Industrial Blvd., N.W., 30318, pg. 1160   PB
Zimmerman & Partners Advertising, Inc., 3400 Peachtree Rd. NE, Ste. 939, 30326, pg. 1206   PV

Augusta

Athens Newspapers, Inc., P.O. Box 936, 30903, pg. 996   PV
Augusta Mall, Inc., 3450 Wrightsboro Rd., 30909, pg. 1408   PB
Augusta Mill Supply, P.O. Box 969, 1219 New Savannah Rd., 30901, pg. 91   PV
Azalea Development Company, 725 Broad St., 30901, pg. 994   PV
Blackman Uhler Chemical Co., Glass Factory Ave., 30901, pg. 1548   PB
Boral Bricks Inc., Arthern Rd., 30913, pg. 203   IT
CASTLEBERRY/SNOW'S BRANDS, INC., 1621 15th St., 30901, pg. 219   PB
W.C. CAYE & COMPANY, INC., 923 Broad St., 30901, pg. 220   PV
Charter Augusta Behavioral Health System, Inc., P.O. Box 14939, 3100 Perimeter Pkwy., 30909, pg. 1033   PV
ConAgra Feed Co., 980 Molly Pond Rd., 30901, pg. 428   PB
DSM Resins US, Inc., P.O. Box 2452, 31 Columbia Nitrogen Rd., 30903, pg. 355   IT
Dillard, A ResourceNet International Company, 1427 Marvin Griffin Rd., P.O. Box 1330, 30903, pg. 902   PV
E-Z-GO Textron, 1451 Marvin Griffin Rd., 30903-0388, pg. 1589   PB
Electrical Equipment Company, 1441 Greene St., 30903, pg. 368   PV
Frigidaire Home Products, 104 Warren Rd., 30907, pg. 439   PV
Gary Concrete Products Inc., River Watch Pkwy. at I-20, 30917-4600, pg. 1795   PB
General Wholesale Company, Inc., 813 Fifth St., 30901, pg. 446   PV

PB - U.S. Public Companies Volume
PV - U.S. Private Companies Volume
IT - International Public & Private Companies Volume

1198

Imaging Technologies Services, pg. 1736 **PB**
Luker Inc., 514 National Ave., 30901, pg. 459 **PV**
MARKS & MORGAN JEWELERS INC, 2559 Washington Rd., 30901-3165, pg. 705 **PV**
MERRY LAND & INVESTMENT COMPANY, INC., 624 Ellis St., 30901, pg. 1098 **PB**
Millhaven Company, Inc., 725 Broad St., 30901, pg. 994 **PV**
Morris Communications Corporation, P.O. Box 936, 30903, pg. 995 **PV**
National Distributing Co., Inc., 3316 Perkins Rd., 30906, pg. 781 **PV**
President Baking-Augusta, P.O. Box 2207-13, 1550 Marvin Griffin Rd., 30903-5299, pg. 1069 **IT**
SHIVERS TRADING & OPERATING CO., 725 Broad St., 30901, pg. 994 **PV**
Southeastern Newspapers Corporation, P.O. Box 936, 30903, pg. 996 **PV**
Stauffer Communications, Inc., P.O. Box 936, 30913, pg. 995 **PV**
SunTrust Bank, Augusta, N.A., 801 Broad St., 30901, pg. 1538 **PB**
Thermal Ceramics Inc., 2102 Old Savannah Road, 30903, pg. 894 **IT**
Tranter, Inc., 1054 Claussen Rd., Ste. 314, 30907, pg. 521 **PB**
J.B. White, Regency Mall, Ste. 300, 30904, pg. 1090 **PB**

Austell

Austell Box Board Corporation, 3100 Washington St., 30001, pg. 303 **PB**
Best Wholesale Co., Inc., 5521 Collins Blvd., S.W., 30001, pg. 814 **PV**
Bindley Western, Austell Division, 8055 Troon Cir., 30001, pg. 228 **PB**
CARAUSTAR INDUSTRIES, INC., 3100 Washington St., 30001, pg. 303 **PB**
Caraustar Paper Sales, Inc., P.O. Box 519, 30001, pg. 303 **PB**
OLD FASHION FOODS, INC., 5521 Collins Blvd., SW, 30001, pg. 814 **PV**
Six Flags Over Georgia, 7561 Six Flags Pkwy., 30001, pg. 1612 **PB**
Subaru of America Southeast Region, P.O. Box 278, 220 The Bluff, 30001-0278, pg. 523 **IT**
Sweetwater Paper Board Co., Inc., 5700 Paper Mill Rd., 30001, pg. 304 **PB**

Bainbridge

ELBERTA CRATE & BOX COMPANY, P.O. Box 795, 606 Dorthan Hwy., 31717, pg. 367 **PV**
FLINT RIVER MILLS, 1100 Dothan Rd., 31717, pg. 413 **PV**
Lynch Machinery, Inc., 601 Independent St., 31717, pg. 1022 **PB**
STONES, INC., 531 Calhoun St., 31717, pg. 1045 **PV**

Baldwin

Best Aviation, 555 Broiler Blvd., 30511-0558, pg. 403 **PV**
FIELDALE CORPORATION, 555 Broiler Blvd., 30511-0558, pg. 403 **PV**

Baxley

Akzo Coatings Inc., Hwy. 341 E., P.O. Box 349, 31513, pg. 47 **IT**
Rexam Mulox USA, P.O. Box 245, 515 North Blvd., 31513, pg. 1106 **IT**

Bogart

BENSON'S, INC., 134 Elder St., 30622, pg. 134 **PV**
Benson's Old Home Kitchens, P.O. Box 429, 30622, pg. 134 **PV**
ROPER INDUSTRIES, INC., 160 Ben Burton Rd., 30622, pg. 1405 **PB**
TIE Systems-Athens, 199 Ben Burton Cir., 30622, pg. 1085 **PV**

Bremen

King Packaging Company, Inc., P.O. Drawer, 407 Sangamore Rd., 30110, pg. 872 **PB**

Broxton

Fleetwood Homes of Georgia, Inc.-Broxton, P.O. Box 810, Ambrose Hwy., 31519, pg. 651 **PB**

Brunswick

Barnett Bank of Southeast Georgia, N.A., 700 Gloucester St., 31520, pg. 1162 **PB**
Jered Brown Brothers Inc., P.O. Box 904, 1608 New Castle St., 31520, pg. 1468 **PB**
Brunswick Pulp & Paper Company, P.O. Box 1438, W. 9th St., 31520, pg. 736 **PB**
The Coastal Bank of Georgia, P.O. Box 1024, 31521, pg. 1549 **PB**
Gypsum Wall Board Plant and Plaster Mill, P.O. Box 1397, Foot of Union St., 31521, pg. 737 **PB**
Hercules Inc.-Brunswick, P.O. Drawer 1517, Cook St., 31521, pg. 810 **PB**
KING & PRINCE SEAFOOD CORPORATION, 100 Lanier Blvd., 31520, pg. 620 **PV**

Marine Port Terminals Inc., 225 Newcastle Street, 31520, pg. 758 **IT**
Primary Pulp & Paper Plant, P.O. Box 143 A, 31521, pg. 736 **PB**
Standard Distributing Co. Inc., 1725 T St., 31520, pg. 781 **PV**
SunTrust Bank, Southeast Georgia, N.A., 510 Gloucester St., 31520, pg. 1538 **PB**

Buford

Makita Corporation of America, 2650 Buford Hwy., 30518, pg. 831 **IT**
Rohrer Corporation, 1800 Enterprise Dr., 30518, pg. 940 **PV**

Cairo

Dean Pickles & Specialty Products, 17 First Ave., NE, 31728, pg. 490 **PB**
IRA HIGDON GROCERY, INC., Alton Hall Rd., 31728, pg. 527 **PV**

Calhoun

Bretlin, Inc., 185 S. Industrial Blvd., 30701, pg. 514 **PB**
Carriage Designs, Inc., S. Industrial Blvd., 30703-7010, pg. 514 **PB**
Carriage Industries, Inc., 185 S. Industrial Blvd., 30703, pg. 514 **PB**
Carriage Transport, Inc., P.O. Box 12542, 30703, pg. 514 **PB**
Horizon Carpet, S. Industrial Blvd., 30701, pg. 1121 **PB**
Ismac, Inc., 1155 Marine Dr., 30701, pg. 744 **IT**
Karastan, 160 S. Industrial Blvd., 30701, pg. 1121 **PB**
Mannington Carpet, P.O. Box 281, 30701, pg. 700 **PV**
MOHAWK INDUSTRIES, INC., P.O. Box 12069, 160 S. Industrial Blvd., 30701, pg. 1121 **PB**
OMC Calhoun, 100 Marine Dr., 30701, pg. 478 **PV**
Professional Travel Inc., 1015 B South Wall St., 30701, pg. 408 **PV**

Canton

Evenflo Company, Inc., P.O. Box 709, 1000 Evenflo Dr., 30114, pg. 629 **PB**
Seaboard Farms of Canton, P.O. Box 907, Univerter Rd., 30114, pg. 1449 **PB**

Carrollton

Citizens Bank and Trust of West Georgia, P.O. Box 2127, 30117, pg. 1549 **PB**
Douglas & Lomason Company, 540 Alabama St., 30117, pg. 830 **IT**
Fitel Lucent, 201 Adamson Industrial Blvd., 30117, pg. 530 **IT**
Regions Bank/Carroll County, P.O. Box 2127, 30117, pg. 1372 **PB**
SOUTHWIRE COMPANY, One Southwire Dr., 30119, pg. 1019 **PV**

Cartersville

Birmingham Southeast, 384 Old Grassdale Rd., N.E., 30121, pg. 232 **PV**
Bundy Corporation, Cartersville Plant, Two Swisher Dr., 30120, pg. 1340 **IT**
Dorsey Trailers, Inc., 25 Kincannon Rd., 30120, pg. 520 **PB**
Harley Valve & Instrument, 407 Old Mill Rd., 30120, pg. 880 **PB**
Pandel, Inc., 21 River Dr., 30120, pg. 889 **PB**
Philadelphia Carpet Div., Old Mill Rd., 30120, pg. 1464 **PB**

Cedar Springs

Chattahoochee Industrial Railroad, P.O. Box 253, 31732, pg. 736 **PB**

Cedartown

Henkel Corp.- Process Chemicals, 701 Wissahickon, 30125, pg. 611 **IT**
Regions Bank-Cedartown/Rockmart, 120 N. Main St., 30117, pg. 1372 **PB**

Chamblee

IPD Printing & Distributing, Inc., 5800 Peachtree Rd., 30341, pg. 1735 **PB**
North DeKalb Cable T.V. Company, 3425 Malone Dr., 30341, pg. 1448 **PB**
Northside Blueprint & Supply Company, 5141 New Peachtree Rd., 30341, pg. 1735 **PB**
Table Pride, Inc., 1940 Will Ross Court, 30341, pg. 658 **PB**

Chatsworth

Cohutta Banking Company, P.O. Box 10, 30705, pg. 1549 **PB**
Galaxy Carpet Mills, Inc., 235 Industrial Blvd., 30705, pg. 1121 **PB**
Patcraft Commercial Carpet, Duvall Rd., 30705, pg. 900 **PV**
Playfield Industries Inc., P.O. Box 8, Murray Industrial Park, 30705-0008, pg. 1362 **IT**

Chickamauga

ADC Systems Integration Group, P.O. Box 919, 50 Industrial Dr., 30707, pg. 4 **PB**
Salem Carpet Mills, P.O. Box 138, 30707, pg. 1464 **PB**

Clarkesville

CMI Industries, Inc., Hwy. 441 N., 30523, pg. 195 **PV**

Clarkston

Edward Don & Company-Clarkston Branch, 696 Park N. Blvd., Ste. 100, 30021, pg. 339 **PV**
Freeman Products, Parknorth Business Center, 715 Parknorth Blvd., Ste. 110, 30021, pg. 1105 **PV**
SEROLOGICALS CORPORATION, 780 Park N. Blvd., Ste. 110, 30021, pg. 1460 **PB**

Clayton

Regions Bank/Raybun County, P.O. Box 406, 30525, pg. 1372 **PB**

Cleveland

Regions Bank/White County, P.O. Box 247, 30528, pg. 1373 **PB**

Cochran

The Citizens Bank of Cochran, East Dykes St., 31014, pg. 1549 **PB**

College Park

Atlanta Learning Center, 1804 Hyannis Ct., 30337, pg. 218 **PB**
Circle Freight International USA, 475 Plaza Dr., 30349, pg. 371 **PB**
Circle International, 985 Sullivan Rd., 30349, pg. 371 **PB**
Sysco Food Services of Atlanta, Inc., 2225 Riverdale Rd., 30349, pg. 1551 **PB**

Columbus

AFLAC INCORPORATED, AFLAC Center, 1932 Wynnton Rd., 31999, pg. 28 **PB**
American Family Life Assurance Co. of Columbus, American Family Center, 31999, pg. 28 **PB**
Barnett Bank of Southwest Georgia, P.O. Box 1497, 31902, pg. 1162 **PB**
Bradley Marketing Services, P.O. Box 140, 1001 Front Ave., 31902-0140, pg. 164 **PV**
Bradley Specialty Retailing, 1023 Front Ave., 31902, pg. 164 **PV**
W.C. BRADLEY CO., 1017 Front Ave., 31902, pg. 164 **PV**
W.C. Bradley Farms Inc., P.O. Box 140, 1001 Front Ave., 31902-0140, pg. 164 **PV**
Burnham General Partner, Inc., 5000 Burnham Blvd., 31907, pg. 686 **IT**
Burnham World Forwarding Inc., 5000 Burnham Blvd., 31907, pg. 686 **IT**
Callaway Chemical Company, 6003 Hamilton Rd., 31993, pg. 1726 **PB**
CARMIKE CINEMAS, INC., Carmike Plaza, 1301 First Ave., 31901, pg. 305 **PB**
W.C. Caye & Co., 1016 Virginia St., 31904, pg. 220 **PV**
Columbus Bank and Trust Company, 1148 Broadway, P.O. Box 120, 31902, pg. 1549 **PB**
Columbus Coca-Cola Bottling Co., 6055 Coca-Cola Blvd., 31908, pg. 392 **PB**
The Columbus Ledger & Enquirer, 17 W. 12th St., 31994, pg. 964 **PB**
COLUMBUS MILLS, INC., 4600 River Rd., 31904, pg. 256 **PV**
Columbus Recycling, Inc., 756 Lindsey Dr., 31906, pg. 303 **PB**
Communicorp, Inc., 1001 Lockwood Ave., 31906, pg. 28 **PB**
Developers Investors, Inc., 1001 Front Ave., 31993, pg. 164 **PV**
GEORGIA CROWN DISTRIBUTING, Seven Crown Circle, 31907, pg. 448 **PV**
Greater Washington Investments, Inc., 105 13th St., 31901, pg. 933 **PV**
THE HARDAWAY COMPANY, 945 Broadway, 31901, pg. 501 **PV**
BILL HEARD ENTERPRISES, INC., 200 Brookstone Ctr., Ste. 205, 31904, pg. 515 **PV**
JOHNSTON INDUSTRIES, INC., 105 Thirteenth St., 31901, pg. 933 **PB**
Lincoln Marketing, Inc., 31902, pg. 1550 **PB**
Litho-Krome Company, 1323 11th Ave., 31994, pg. 496 **PV**
Mead Coated Board Division, 1200 Brookstone Center, Ste. 225, 39108-9908, pg. 1074 **PB**
Pace Industries, Inc., 4949 Schatulga Rd., 31908, pg. 986 **PB**
The R.W. Page Corp., 17 W. 12th St., 31901, pg. 964 **PB**
PASCOE BUILDING SYSTEMS, INC., 1724 Northside Industrial Blvd., 31904, pg. 1388 **PV**
Regions Bank/Columbus, P.O. Box 1377, 31902-1377, pg. 1372 **PB**
SouthTrust Bank of Columbus, 1237 First Ave., 31902, pg. 1492 **PB**

Geographic Index-U.S.

SunTrust Bank, West Georgia, N.A., 1246 First Ave., 31901, pg. 1538 **PB**
SYNOVUS FINANCIAL CORP., 901 Front Ave., Ste. 301, 31901, pg. 1548 **PB**
Synovus Securities, Inc., P.O. Box 120, 31902, pg. 1550 **PB**
TOM'S FOODS, INC., 900 Eighth St., 31902, pg. 1090 **PV**
Total System Services, Inc., 1200 Sixth Ave., 31902, pg. 1550 **PB**
United Cities Gas Co., GA/SC Div., 1421 4th Ave., 31993, pg. 146 **PB**
J.H. Williams, P.O. Box 7577, 31908, pg. 1481 **PB**

Commerce

ALLTEL Georgia, Inc., 103 Georgia Ave., P.O. Box 439, 30529, pg. 56 **PB**
Mount Vernon Mills, Inc., 689 S. Elm St., 30529, pg. 835 **PV**

Conley

Central Sprinkler Company, 4350 Old McDonough Rd., 30027, pg. 327 **PB**
Hickson Corporation, 1579 Koppers Rd., 30027, pg. 619 **IT**

Conyers

American Bank Note Company, 2908 S. Park Terrace, 30208, pg. 68 **PB**
Bruno's Inc.-Georgia, 3530 S. Highway 20, 30208, pg. 265 **PB**
Burgmann Seals America, Inc., 3585 Cherry Creek Dr., 30208, pg. 233 **IT**
Conyers, 905 Flat Shoals Rd., 30207, pg. 1715 **PB**
Finishline Industries Inc. of Georgia, 1275 S. Main St., 30207, pg. 428 **PV**
Foamex, 1705 A Rockdale Industrial Blvd., 30207, pg. 1686 **PV**
Hano Document Printers, Inc., P.O. Box 1159, 30207, pg. 1686 **PB**
Kysor/Warren, 1600 Industrial Blvd., 30012, pg. 1445 **PB**
Lithonia Lighting Co., 1335 Indus. Blvd., P.O. Box A, 30207, pg. 1160 **PB**
Madison Industries Inc. of Georgia, 1035 S. Access Rd., S.W., 30207, pg. 428 **PV**
Maxell Corp. of America, 1400 Parker Rd., 30207, pg. 622 **IT**
Pratt Industries USA, 1977 Sarasota Pkwy., 30208, pg. 1066 **IT**
QSP Distribution Services, Inc., 1917 Rockdale Industrial Blvd., 30207, pg. 1367 **PB**
Regions Bank/Rockdale County, P.O. Box 80905, 30143-80905, pg. 1372 **PB**
The Rockdale Citizen Publishing Company, 969 S. Main, 30207, pg. 759 **PB**
Sealy-Stearns & Foster Bedding Co. - Atlanta, 1705 Rockdale Industrial Blvd., 30207, pg. 979 **PV**
Takahashi Works U.S.A., Inc., P.O. Box 80966, 2030 E. Park Dr., 30207, pg. 744 **IT**
Visy Paper Inc., 1800 Sarasota Pkwy., 30208, pg. 1066 **IT**

Coolidge

MacTavish Furniture Industries, Coolidge Factory, 434 N. Pine St., 31738, pg. 12 **PB**

Cordele

Homestead Homes, 501 S. Midway Rd., 31015, pg. 318 **PB**

Cornelia

Regions Bank/Habersham County, P.O. Box 310, 30531, pg. 1372 **PB**
Schnadig Corp., P.O. Box 2000, Clarksville Highway, Rte. 2, 30531, pg. 971 **PV**

Covington

Bard Radiology Div., 8195 Industrial Blvd., 30209-9998, pg. 189 **PB**
Bard Urological Div., 8195 Industrial Blvd., 30209-9998, pg. 189 **PB**
Covington Specialty Print, P.O. Box 72, 30209, pg. 786 **PB**
Hercules Inc.-Oxford, Alcovy Rd., 30209, pg. 810 **PB**

Cumming

Regions Bank/Forsyth County, P.O. Box 1800, 30130, pg. 1372 **PB**

Dacula

GATX Logistics (JmH), Inc., 4125 University Pkwy., 30211, pg. 691 **PB**

Dahlonega

REFRIGIWEAR, INC., P.O. Box 39, 54 Breakstone Dr., 30533, pg. 917 **PV**

Dalton

Aladdin Mills, 2001 Antioch Rd., 30720, pg. 1121 **PB**

American Emulsions Co., Inc., 1202 Dozier St., 30721, pg. 1357 **PB**
AstroTurf Manufacturing, 809 Kenner St., 30720, pg. 1018 **PV**
BEAULIEU GROUP, 1502 Coronet Dr., 30720, pg. 127 **PV**
Beaulieu United, P.O. Box 4329, 30719-4329, pg. 128 **PV**
BROWN INDUSTRIES, INC., Indus. Blvd., P.O. Box 1103, 30720, pg. 174 **PV**
Buchanan Industries, Inc., 3358 Carpet Capital Dr., 30720, pg. 1052 **PB**
CAF HOLDING COMPANY, 311 Smith Industrial Blvd., 30720, pg. 192 **PV**
Cabin Crafts Carpets, P.O. Drawer 2128, 30722-2128, pg. 1464 **PB**
Cagle's Farms Inc., P.O. Box 38, 30722, pg. 292 **PB**
Candlewick Group, Waring Rd., P.O. Box 1368, 30720, pg. 514 **PB**
Collins & Aikman Floorcoverings, Inc., 311 Smith Industrial Blvd., 30720, pg. 192 **PV**
ConAgra Broiler Co., 433 S. Hamilton, 30720, pg. 427 **PB**
Custom Colorants, Inc., 108 Waterworks St., pg. 1052 **PB**
Evans-Black Carpet Mills, 616 E. Walnut Ave., 30720, pg. 1464 **PB**
FIVE STAR FOODS INCORPORATED, 1220 Vendmore Dr., 30721, pg. 409 **PV**
General Latex & Chemical Corporation (Georgia), P.O. Box 709, 30720, pg. 444 **PV**
New York Carpet World, Maildrop 071-01, P.O. Drawer 2128, 30722-2128, pg. 1464 **PB**
Perpetual Machine, 1803 Abutment Rd., 30720, pg. 1079 **PV**
Plastron Dalton, 207 Brookhollow Industrial Blvd., 30720, pg. 15 **PV**
Professional/First Travelcorp, 302 S. Thornton Ave., 30720, pg. 408 **PV**
QUEEN CARPET CORPORATION, 2305 Lakeland Rd., 30721, pg. 900 **PV**
Regions Bank/Dalton/Cartersville/Chattanooga, P.O. Box 1504, 30722, pg. 1372 **PB**
Salem Carpet Mills, 1401 Underwood St., P.O. Box 914, 30720-0914, pg. 1464 **PB**
SHAW INDUSTRIES, INC., 616 E. Walnut Ave., 30721, pg. 1464 **PB**
Star Recycling, Inc., 145 Phelps Rd., 30720, pg. 304 **PB**
Sunrise Carpet Ind. Inc., One World Plaza, 30722, pg. 1190 **PV**
TEXTILE RUBBER & CHEMICAL COMPANY, 1400 Tiarco Dr., 30720, pg. 1079 **PV**
White-Crest Dorsett Inc., One World Plaza, 30722, pg. 1190 **PV**
WORLD CARPETS, INC., One World Plaza, 30722, pg. 1190 **PV**

Dawsonville

TATUM FARMS INT., INC., 6683 Hwy. 136 W., 30534, pg. 1069 **PV**

Decatur

Allied Automotive Group, 160 Clairmont Ave., Ste. 600, 30030, pg. 48 **PB**
ALLIED HOLDINGS, INC., 160 Clairmont Ave., Ste. 600, 30030, pg. 48 **PB**
Axis Group, 160 Clairmont Ave., Ste. 600, 30030, pg. 48 **PB**
Bio-Lab, Inc., 627 E. College Ave., 30030, pg. 760 **PB**
Dairy Queen of Georgia, Inc., 730 DeKalb Industrial Way, 30033, pg. 220 **PB**
DeVry Institute of Technology, 250 N. Arcadia, 30030, pg. 504 **PB**
JOHN H. HARLAND COMPANY, 2939 Miller Rd., 30035, pg. 785 **PB**
H. Kessler & Company, 2014 Candler Rd., 30034, pg. 616 **PV**
RMC Industries Corporation, P.O. Box 728, 30031, pg. 1081 **IT**
Robarb Inc., 5325 Dividend Dr., 30035, pg. 802 **IT**
Schizophrenia Treatment and Rehabilitation, Inc., 209 Church St., 30030, pg. 1036 **PB**
South Dekalb, 72 S. Dekalb Mall, 30034, pg. 1408 **PB**
Spectris Technologies, Inc., 2364 Park Central Blvd., 30035, pg. 14 **IT**
TRONCALLI MOTORS, INC., 1625 Church St., 30033, pg. 1104 **PV**

Doraville

CHEMCENTRAL/Atlanta, One Alchemy Pl., 30360, pg. 232 **PV**
Consilium Bulk - Babcock Atlanta Inc., 2365 Pleasantdale Rd., 30340, pg. 131 **IT**
Corrugated Packaging, 4600 N.E. Expressway, 30340, pg. 737 **PB**
Dillard, A ResourceNet International Company, 50 Best Friend Rd., P.O. Box 620098, 30362, pg. 902 **PB**
GATX Logistics, Inc.-Georgia (Norpack), 2915 N.E. Pkwy., 30360, pg. 691 **PB**
Paper Recycling, Inc., 4069 Winters Chapel Rd., 30360, pg. 304 **PB**
SmithKline Beecham Clinical Laboratories, 3500 McCall Place, 30340, pg. 1265 **IT**
Stanfast, Inc., Northcrest 85 Business Park, 3731 Northcrest Rd., Ste. 19, 30340, pg. 1505 **PB**
Unisource, 3587 Oakcliff Rd., 30340, pg. 1671 **PB**

Douglas

Douglas Products Division, 1545 Kelly Dr., 31533, pg. 1565 **PB**

Elixir Industries, Southside Industrial Park, 31533, pg. 371 **PV**
Fleetwood Homes of Georgia, Inc.-Douglas/Northside Industrial Park, Northside Indus. Pk., 31533, pg. 651 **PB**
Fleetwood Homes of Georgia, Inc. #51, 2122 Broxton Rd., Hwy. 441 N., 31533, pg. 651 **PB**
Fleetwood Homes of Georgia, Inc.-Southwest-Industrial Park, 1515 Kellogg Dr., 31533, pg. 651 **PB**
Nutratech Animal Health, P.O. Box 2425, 1246 Loyce Ln., 31533, pg. 128 **PB**

Douglasville

Atlanta Mfg. Facility, 4155 Scofield Rd., 30134, pg. 976 **PV**
Eclipse Combustion, Inc., 6817 Knollwood Dr., 30135, pg. 360 **PV**
Regions Bank/Douglas County, P.O. Box 1178, 30117, pg. 1372 **PB**
YOUNG REFINING CORP., 7982 Huey Rd., 30134, pg. 1202 **PV**

Dublin

Flexsteel Division, Industrial Park, 31040, pg. 654 **PB**
WAREHOUSE HOME FURNISHINGS DISTRIBUTOR, 1851 Telfair St, 31021, pg. 1150 **PV**

Duluth

AGCO CORPORATION, 4205 River Green Pkwy., 30096-2568, pg. 28 **PB**
Akerlund & Rausing NA Inc., 3450 Corporate Way, 30136, pg. 33 **IT**
Ames Taping Tool Systems Co., 3305 Breckenridge Blvd., Ste. 122, 30136, pg. 103 **PV**
Arrow/Schweber Electronics, Ste. E, 4250 River Green Pkwy., 30136, pg. 133 **PB**
Atlanta Sales, 3360 Satellite Blvd., Ste. 14, 30096, pg. 611 **PV**
BancTec, Inc.-Atlanta, 3483 Satellite Blvd., Ste. 101, 33016, pg. 177 **PB**
Banks Environmental Service Technologies, Inc., 2875 N. Berkeley Lake Rd., Ste. 4, 30136, pg. 114 **PV**
Boeing North America, Tactical Systems Division, 1800 Satellite Blvd., 30136, pg. 241 **PB**
CIBA-Vision Corporation, 11460 John's Creek Pkwy., 30155, pg. 973 **IT**
CIBA Vision Group Management Inc, 11460 Johns Creek Pkwy., 30155, pg. 973 **IT**
Columbia Pictures Southern Division, 3100 Breckenridge Blvd., Ste. 135, 30136, pg. 1281 **IT**
ConAgra Poultry Co., 2475 Meadowbrook Pkwy., 30136, pg. 427 **PB**
Curtis 1000, Inc., 1725 Breckenridge Pkwy., #1000, 30348, pg. 70 **PB**
Delta Apparel, 3355 Breckenridge Blvd., Ste. 100, 30096, pg. 498 **PB**
Deutsche Babcock Technologies, Inc., 2675 Breckenridge Blvd., 30136, pg. 401 **IT**
Ford, Bacon & Davis Companies Inc., 2675 Breckenridge Blvd., 30136, pg. 401 **IT**
Ford, Bacon & Davis Companies Inc., 2675 Breckenridge Blvd., 30136, pg. 401 **IT**
Heraeus Amersil Inc., 3473 Satellite Blvd., 30136-5821, pg. 616 **IT**
Hunter Douglas Architectural Products Inc., 11455 Lakefield Dr., 30136, pg. 639 **IT**
Lucent Technologies Construction Services Inc., 4725 River Green Pkwy., 30136, pg. 1018 **IT**
M.F. Bank Restoration Co., 2875 N. Berkeley Lake Rd., 30136, pg. 114 **PV**
Mary Kay Cosmetics, Inc., 1963 Ashview Ct., 30236, pg. 711 **PV**
NEW HERMES INCORPORATED, 2200 Northmont Pkwy., 30096, pg. 793 **PV**
Nordson North American Div., 11475 Lakefield Dr., 30136, pg. 1188 **PB**
PFS Investments Inc., 3120 Breckenridge Blvd., 30199, pg. 1633 **PB**
Primerica Financial Services, 3120 Breckenridge Blvd., 30199-1000, pg. 1633 **PB**
Primerica Life Insurance Company, 3120 Breckenridge Blvd., 30199-1000, pg. 1633 **PB**
Pulte Georgia Division, 3100 Breckenridge Blvd., Ste. 712, 30136, pg. 1344 **PB**
Rentokil Initial Pest Control, P.O. Box 957149, 30136, pg. 1285 **IT**
Rusch, 2475 Meadowbrook Pkwy., 30136, pg. 1569 **PB**
SatCom Technologies Division, 4825 River Green Pkwy., 30136, pg. 424 **PB**
Southeast Marketing Div., 2400 Pleasant Hill Rd., Ste. 325, 30136, pg. 296 **PV**
Triumph Releasing Corporation - Southeastern Territory, 3100 Breckenridge Blvd., Ste. 135, 30136-4933, pg. 1282 **IT**
Von Roll, Inc., 3025 Breckenridge Blvd., Ste. 170, 30136, pg. 1480 **IT**
WEGENER CORPORATION, 11350 Technology Cir., 30097, pg. 1751 **PB**

Dunwoody

BMW of North America, Inc.-Southeastern Region, 1280 Hightower Trail, 30350, pg. 177 **IT**
Southern Back & Orthopaedic Center-Dunwoody, 4488 N. Shallowford Rd., Ste. 210, 30338, pg. 1716 **PB**

PB - *U.S. Public Companies Volume*
PV - *U.S. Private Companies Volume*
IT - *International Public & Private Companies Volume*

1200

Geographic Index-U.S.

East Point

Air Courier Dispatch, 3130 S. Barton, Ste. 600, 30349, pg. 450 **PB**
Dependable Courier, 3130 S. Martin St., Bldg. 1, Ste. 800, 30344, pg. 450 **PB**
Flo-Pac Southeast, 1120 Oakleigh Dr., 30344, pg. 414 **PV**
Zeneca Specialty Inks, 2247 Lawrence St., 30344, pg. 1525 **IT**

Eastman

Eastman Kodak Health Care Inc., P.O. Box 159, Chester Rd., 31023-0159, pg. 555 **PB**
Reynolds Metals Company-Eastman, # 1 Industrial Dr., 31023, pg. 1385 **PB**

Eastonollee

DeKalb Concrete Products, Inc., Turner Rd., 30538, pg. 417 **PV**

Eatonton

HORTON HOMES, INC., 101 Industrial Blvd., 31024, pg. 540 **PV**

Elberton

C & K Tracking, Inc., 1130 Hartwell Hwy., 30635, pg. 1396 **PB**
DICKSON ELBERTON MILLS INC., 120 Seaboard St. S.E., 30635, pg. 331 **PV**
Georgia Stone Industries, Inc., Hwy. 72 W., 30635, pg. 793 **PV**
Keystone & Childs, Inc., Box 6077 Washington Hwy., 30635, pg. 1396 **PB**
Regions Bank/Elbert County, P.O. Box 190, 30635, pg. 1372 **PB**
Seaboard Farms of Elberton, Old Middleton Rd., 30635, pg. 1449 **PB**

Ellaville

MWS, 601 S. Broad St., Hwy. 19, 31806, pg. 443 **PB**
TCI, Inc., P.O. Box 13, 610 Dixon Dr., 31806, pg. 1358 **PB**

Ellenwood

Bellamy Brothers Contracting Company, 16 Fairview Rd., 30049, pg. 132 **PV**
BELLAMY BROTHERS, INC., 16 Fairview Rd., 30294, pg. 132 **PV**

Ellijay

Regions Bank/Gilmer County, P.O. Drawer T, 30540, pg. 1372 **PB**

Eton

Howard Carpet Mills, Inc., Old Federal Rd., 30724, pg. 1464 **PB**

Evans

Greenfield Industries Inc., 470 Old Evans Rd., 30809, pg. 950 **PB**

Fairburn

Porex Corp., 500 Bohannon Rd., 30213, pg. 1548 **PB**
Porex Technologies Corp. of Georgia, 500 Bohannon Rd., 30213, pg. 1548 **PB**
United Foam Plastics Corporation, 7401 Graham Rd., 30213-2915, pg. 1112 **PV**

Fairmount

Frontier Communications of Fairmount, Inc., P.O. Box 159, 134 North Ave., 30139, pg. 683 **PB**

Fitzgerald

Coachmen Recreational Vehicle Company of Georgia, Northside Industrial Park, 142 Benjamin Hills Dr., 31750, pg. 388 **PB**
Elixir Industries, 31750, pg. 371 **PV**
H. R. KAMINSKY & SONS, INC., 136 Bowens Mill Hwy., 31750, pg. 606 **PV**
LOWELL PACKING COMPANY, P.O. Box 220, 31750, pg. 679 **PV**

Folkston

BHA Group, Rt. 2, Box 1840, 31537, pg. 161 **PB**

Forest Park

American Natl. Can Co., 48 Royal Dr., 30050, pg. 1029 **IT**
Bagcraft Corporation of America, Georgia Div., 18 Royal Dr., 30050, pg. 136 **PB**
Dan-Co Bakery, Inc., 301 Monty Industrial Blvd., 30053, pg. 657 **PB**

Hamworthy USA, Inc., Forest Park, 5690 Southfield Ct., Ste. 100, 30050, pg. 1066 **IT**
Holiday RV Superstores of South Atlanta, Inc., 5814 Frontage Rd., 30050, pg. 830 **PB**
Household Products, 17 Lake Mirror Rd., 30050, pg. 387 **PB**
Union-Transport Corporation-Atlanta, 114 Southfield Pky., Ste. 170, 30050, pg. 1119 **PV**

Fort Oglethorpe

AMERICAN CONSUMERS, INC., 418-A Battlefield Pkwy., 30742, pg. 70 **PB**
Galaxy Carpet Mills, Inc., 217 W. Patterson, 30742, pg. 1121 **PB**

Fort Valley

The Citizens Bank, 302 Vineville St., 31030-1199, pg. 1549 **PB**
Sureco Inc., 310 Hwy. 341 S., 31030, pg. 1390 **PB**

Franklin

Regions Bank/Heard County, P.O. Box 1450, 30217, pg. 1372 **PB**

Gainesville

CWT Farms International, 1180 Airport Industrial Park, 30501, pg. 202 **IT**
Chicopee, P.O. Box 2537, 30503-2537, pg. 113 **IT**
ConAgra Broiler Co., P.O. Box 181, 949 Industrial Blvd., 30501, pg. 427 **PB**
Deep South Products, P.O. Box 2534, 2255 White Sulfer Rd., 30501, pg. 1772 **PB**
Elan Pharmaceutical Research Corp., 1300 Gould Dr., 30501, pg. 436 **IT**
GRESS FOODS INC., 950 Industrial Blvd., 30501, pg. 480 **PV**
Hilb, Rogal and Hamilton Company of Gainesville, Georgia, 100 Brenau Ave., 30501, pg. 827 **PB**
Hydro Conduit Corp., P.O. Box 2493, 978 Davis St., 30503, pg. 246 **IT**
Kubota Manufacturing of America Corporation, Gainesville Industrial Park N., 2715 Ramsey Rd., 30501, pg. 762 **IT**
MANSFIELD OIL COMPANY, 1025 Airport Pkwy. SW, 30501-6813, pg. 700 **PV**
MAR-JAC POULTRY INC., P.O. Box 1017, 30503, pg. 701 **PV**
National Auto Research, P.O. Box 758, Hwy. 129 S. at Barrett Rd., 30503, pg. 516 **PV**
Norton Construction Products, P.O. Box 2898, 30503, pg. 1177 **IT**
Regions Bank, P.O. Drawer 937, 30503, pg. 1371 **PB**
Southland Publishing Co., 345 Green St. N.W., P.O. Box 838, 30503, pg. 701 **PB**

Garden City

Oceanic Shipping Co., 6002 Commerce Blvd., 31408, pg. 1046 **PV**
Pro Shop (Savannah, GA), 5516-B Export Blvd., 31408, pg. 861 **PB**
STRACHAN SHIPPING CO., 6002 Commerce Blvd., 31408, pg. 1045 **PV**
Yokohama Tire Corp., Georgia Port Authority, Hunt Rd., 31408, pg. 1521 **IT**

Griffin

Best Mfg. Inc.-Hospitality Div., 1530 Kell Ln., 30224, pg. 140 **PV**
Osmose Wood Preserving, Inc., 1016 Everee Inn Rd., 30223, pg. 821 **PV**
Southeastern Textile Co. Div., 1530 Kell Ln., 30224, pg. 140 **PV**
Vernay Manufacturing, Inc., P.O. Box 759, 30224, pg. 1137 **PV**

Grovetown

GIW Industries, Inc., 5000 Wrightsboro Rd., 30813, pg. 721 **IT**

Hampton

Atlanta Motor Speedway, Hwy. 19 & 41, 30228, pg. 1498 **PB**
J & J, Inc., 30 Oak St., 30228, pg. 847 **PB**

Hapeville

Center for Comprehensive Examinations, 3578 Altalnta Ave., 30354, pg. 1715 **PB**
Industrial Clinic, 3580 Atlanta Ave., 30354, pg. 1715 **PB**
Orthopaedic Rehabilitation Center of Atlanta, 3578 Atlanta Ave., 30354, pg. 1715 **PB**

Harlem

SOUTHERN BEVERAGE PACKERS, INC., 6341 Natures Way, 30814, pg. 1015 **PV**

Hazlehurst

Bank of Hazlehurst, P.O. Box 128, 31539, pg. 1549 **PB**
Fuel South, Inc., P.O. Box 572, 31539, pg. 596 **PV**

Homer

Regions Bank/Banks County, P.O. Box 247, 30547, pg. 1371 **PB**
Scales Transport Corporation, 507 A Sample Scales Rd., 30547, pg. 66 **PV**

Homerville

Brockway Standard Inc., U.S. Hwy. 84 W., 31634, pg. 164 **PB**

Jasper

Regions Bank/Pickens County, P.O. Box 789, 30143, pg. 1372 **PB**

Jefferson

Regions Bank/Jackson County, P.O. Box 5, 30549, pg. 1372 **PB**

Kennesaw

THE ATHLETE'S FOOT GROUP, INC., 1950 Vaughn Rd., 30144, pg. 94 **PV**
A.M. Castle & Co., 3775 Cobb International, 30144, pg. 313 **PB**
Chemtronics Inc., 8125 Cobb Ctr. Dr., 30144, pg. 892 **IT**
Dornier Medical Systems, Inc., 1155 Roberts Blvd., 30144, pg. 368 **IT**
Engineered Construction-Atlanta, 175 TownPark Dr., Ste. 240, 30144, pg. 442 **PB**
THE GEORGIA MARBLE COMPANY, Bldg. 100, 1201 Roberts Blvd., 30144, pg. 448 **PV**
Heidelberg USA, Inc., 1000 Gutenberg Dr., 30144, pg. 604 **IT**
Interface Research Corporation, 100 Chastain Ctr. Blvd., Ste. 165, 30144, pg. 889 **PB**
Klockner-Moeller, 1000 Cobb Place Blvd., 30144, pg. 736 **IT**
PACESETTER STEEL SERVICE, INC., 3300 Town Point Dr., 30144, pg. 830 **PV**
Rhone-Poulenc Performance Resins & Coatings, 112 Town Park Dr., Ste. 130, 30144, pg. 1110 **IT**
S & J Industries, 2130 Barrett Park Dr., Ste. 103, 30144, pg. 803 **PV**

La Fayette

ROPER Corporation, 1507 Broomton Rd., 30728, pg. 710 **PB**
Salem Carpet Mills, P.O. Box 887, 30728, pg. 1464 **PB**

La Grange

Commercial Bank and Trust Company of Troup County, P.O. Box 250, 30241, pg. 1549 **PB**
Interface Flooring Systems Inc., P.O. Box 1503, 30241, pg. 889 **PB**
Kaydon Corporation, Filtration Division, 1571 Forrest Ave., 30240, pg. 946 **PB**
LaGrange Molded Products, Inc., P.O. Box 1707, 30241, pg. 977 **PB**
McCord Payen, 1641 Lukken Industrial Dr. West, 30240, pg. 1335 **IT**
Mobil Chemical Co.- Film Div., 111 Pegasus Pkwy., 30240-5824, pg. 1118 **PB**
Piedmont Mechanical, Inc., 103 Cooley Industrial Dr., P.O. Box 308, 30241, pg. 865 **PV**
Raytheon Systems Company, 1302 Orchard Hill Rd., 30240, pg. 1365 **PB**
Rinnai America Corp., Lukken Industrial Dr. W., 30240, pg. 1118 **IT**
Safa, LLC, 1621 Lukken Industrial Dr. W., 30240, pg. 1313 **IT**
Shorewood Packaging Corporation of Georgia, 1707 Shorewood Dr., 30240, pg. 1468 **PB**
Sumitomo Rubber Industries - Atlanta, 1710 Shorewood Drive, 30240, pg. 1317 **IT**
WOODBURY BUSINESS FORMS, INC., 101 Lukken Industrial Dr. E., 30240, pg. 1186 **PV**

Lawrenceville

Alfa Laval Celleco Inc., 1000 Laval Blvd., 30243, pg. 1378 **IT**
Avesta ABE Inc., 1800 J. MacLeod Dr., 30243, pg. 221 **IT**
W.C. Caye & Co., 238 Hurricane Shoals Rd., 30243, pg. 220 **PV**
Celleco Hedemora, 1000 Laval Blvd., 30243, pg. 1378 **IT**
Danfoss Automatic Controls, 1775-G Macleod Dr., 30243, pg. 377 **IT**
Dulmison Inc., 1725 Purcell Rd., 30243, pg. 894 **IT**
High Proformance Industrial Doors, 975 Old Norcross Road, 30245, pg. 36 **PB**
Koltex, Inc., 1000 Laval Blvd., Suite 100, 30243, pg. 1378 **IT**
Lotus Cars USA, Inc., 500 Marathon Pkwy., 30045, pg. 1071 **PV**
Motorola Energy Products Division, 1700 Belle Meade Ct., 30243, pg. 1137 **PB**

Geographic Index-U.S.

SMI Georgia Rebar, 251 Hosea Rd., 30045, pg. 412　PB
Sharp Electronics Corporation Southeast Regional Office, 725 Old Norcross Rd., 30245, pg. 1229　IT
Simon Marketing, Inc., 1440 Lakes Pkwy. Ste. 100, 30243, pg. 1001　PV
U.N. Alloy Steel Div., 601 Old Norcross Pl., 30245, pg. 1001　IT
U.N.A. Corp., 601 Old Norcross Rd., Ste. C, 30245, pg. 1001　IT

Lilburn

Trench Electric, 646 Exchange Place, Ste. 202, 30247, pg. 113　IT

Lindale

Lindale Mfg. Inc., Park St., 30147, pg. 479　PV

Lithia Springs

Hyundai Motor America Southern Regional Office, 240 N. Thornton Rd., 30057, pg. 641　IT
Outokumpu Wenmec, Inc., 351 Thornton Rd., Ste. 115, 30122, pg. 1017　IT
Super Discount Markets, Inc., 420 Thornton Road, 30057, pg. 463　IT

Lithonia

Corona Engineering Corporation, 5220 Minola Dr., 30038, pg. 1761　PB
Hydro Conduit Corp., 6890 Chapman Rd., 30058, pg. 245　IT

Loganville

Action Commodities Corporation, P.O. Box 1384, 30249, pg. 1076　PV

Lovejoy

Talmadge Farms, Talmadge Rd., 30250, pg. 292　PB

Lumber City

Amercord Inc., P.O. Box 458, Industrial Park, 31549, pg. 696　IT

Mableton

Nelson Westerberg Atlas, 6701 Discovery Blvd., 30126, pg. 1164　PV

Macon

BLUE BIRD CORPORATION, P.O. Box 7839, 31209, pg. 151　PV
Boeing Georgia Inc., 7979 N.E. Industrial Blvd., 31297, pg. 241　PB
Brown & Williamson Tobacco Corp.-Macon Plant, P.O. Box 1056, 31298, pg. 111　IT
CMCA, Inc., 577 Mulberry St., 31298, pg. 1033　PB
CNL FINANCIAL CORP., 2960 Riverside Dr., 31204, pg. 281　PB
CNL/Resource Marketing Corp., 1122 Gray Hwy., 31208, pg. 282　PB
Celegec Automation Projects Inc., 2871 Avondale Mill Rd., 31206, pg. 53　PB
Charter Behavioral Health System of Central Georgia, Inc., 3500 Riverside Dr., 31210, pg. 1033　PB
CHEROKEE BRICK & TILE CO., 3250 Waterville Rd., 31206, pg. 233　PV
Cherokee National Life Insurance Co., 1122 Gray Hwy., 31208, pg. 282　PB
Commodore National Life, 1122 Gray Hwy., 31208, pg. 282　PB
Cox Communications-Middle Georgia, 6601 Hawkinsville Road, 31297-0278, pg. 455　PB
Dillard, A ResourceNet International Company, 3115 Hillcrest Ave., 31208, pg. 902　PB
Down River Forest Products, Inc., 3271 Franklinton Rd., 31201, pg. 763　PB
J.M. Huber, Clay Div., One Huber Rd., 31298, pg. 545　PV
Ikon Capital, Inc., 1667 Eisenhower Pkwy., 31206, pg. 863　PB
Ikon Office Solutions-Central Georgia, 1667 Eisenhower Pkwy., 31206, pg. 863　PB
Keebler Co./Macon Bakery, 4375 Mead Rd., 31298, pg. 657　PB
LH, Inc., 577 Mulberry St., 31298, pg. 1036　PB
Macon Blue Print Company, 444 Walnut St., 31208, pg. 1735　PB
Macon Recycling, Inc., 3065 Broadway, 31201, pg. 304　PB
Macon Telegraph Publishing Company, 120 Broadway, 31201, pg. 964　PB
Magellan Health Services, Inc., 577 Mulberry St., 31298, pg. 1036　PB
Magellan Imaging, Inc., 577 Mulberry St., 31298, pg. 1036　PB
Magellan Medical International-Arabia, Inc., 577 Mulberry St., 31298, pg. 1036　PB
Magellan Medical International, Inc., 577 Mulberry St., 31298, pg. 1036　PB
Magellan Medical International, S.A., Inc., 577 Mulberry St., 31298, pg. 1036　PB

Magellan Medical Management Company, 577 Mulberry St., 31298, pg. 1036　PB
McClain of Georgia, Inc., 860 Fulton St., 31206, pg. 1065　PB
Rexam Mulox, 7592 NE Industrial Blvd., 31297, pg. 1106　IT
Richmond MOB, Inc., 577 Mulberry St., 31298, pg. 1036　PB
S & S Cafeterias, 2124 Riverside Dr., 31208, pg. 1007　PV
S & S Diversified Food Service, Inc., 2124 Riverside Dr., 31208, pg. 1007　PV
S & S Food Administrators, 2124 Riverside Dr., 31208, pg. 1007　PV
Servitex, Inc., One Servitex Dr., 31217, pg. 781　PV
Shallowford Providers, Inc., 577 Mulberry St., 31298, pg. 1036　PB
SMITH & SONS FOODS, INC., 2124 Riverside Dr., 31208, pg. 1006　PV
Structured Healthcare Systems, Inc., 577 Mulberry St., 31298, pg. 1036　PB
SunTrust Bank, Middle Georgia, N.A., 606 Cherry St., 31201, pg. 1538　PB
T.K.G. International Corp., 2630 Weaver Rd., 31201, pg. 1349　IT
WMAZ-WAYS Radio, 1314 Gray Hwy., 31213, pg. 699　PB
Y.K.K. (U.S.A.) Inc., 4234 Ocmulgee E. Blvd., 31297, pg. 1515　IT

Madison

APPLE SOUTH, INC., Hancock at Washington, 30650-1304, pg. 121　PB
Bank of Morgan County, P.O. Box 917, 30650, pg. 1371　PB
Ivex Packaging Corporation-Madison, P.O. Box 508, 1500 Industrial Blvd., 30650, pg. 915　PB
Preferred Surety Corporation, 286 Hancock St., 30650, pg. 1538　PB
WELLINGTON INDUSTRIES INC., 1140 Monticello Rd., 30650-0244, pg. 1161　PV

Marietta

AFGD, 3200 Austell Rd., 30060, pg. 84　IT
Adaptec - Southern Region, 142 S. Park Sq. N.E., 30060, pg. 19　PB
Aigner Products Division, Bldg. 400, 1395 Marietta Pkwy., Ste. 116, 30067, pg. 152　PB
Atlanta Beverage Company, 1250 Atlanta Industrial Dr., 30066, pg. 94　PV
Atlanta Hill Restaurant Corp., 2239 Powers Ferry Rd., 30067, pg. 1023　PV
Automated Products, Inc. (Leader Systems, Inc.), 814 Livingston Ct., 30067, pg. 1659　PB
Bekaert Associates, Inc., Bldg. 1, Ste. 100, 2440 Sandy Plains Rd., 30066-7207, pg. 184　IT
Bekaert Corporation, 1395 S. Marietta Pkwy., Bldg. 500, Ste. 100, 30067, pg. 184　IT
Blockbuster Music, 1351 Dividend Dr., Ste. K, 30067, pg. 776　PV
Blue Circle Aggregates, Inc., Two Pkwy. Center, 1800 Pkwy. Place, Ste. 1200, 30067, pg. 198　IT
Blue Circle America Inc., Two Pkwy. Center, 1800 Pkwy. Pl., Ste. 1200, 30067, pg. 197　IT
Cadmus Technology Solutions, 2151 Northwest Pkwy., Ste. 200, 30067, pg. 291　PB
Carolina Builders Corporation, 1666 Boswell Rd., 30060, pg. 1512　IT
Ceramic Tile International, 4041 Kingston Ct., 30064, pg. 564　PV
Clinical-Management Systems, Inc., 1850 Parkway Pl., 6th Fl., 30067, pg. 1057　PB
Cobb Reprographics & Office Supply, 799 Roswell St., S.E., 30060, pg. 1735　PB
Comverse Network Systems, 1850 Pkwy. Pl., Ste. 327, 30067, pg. 425　PB
DYWIDAG Systems International, USA, Inc., 1341 Canton Rd., Ste. H1, 30066, pg. 424　IT
ER-WE-PA USA Ltd., 3061-C Kingston Court, 30067, pg. 491　IT
Elec-Tel Supply Company, 863 White Circle Ct., 30060, pg. 847　PB
FLEXIBLE PRODUCTS COMPANY, 1007 Industrial Park Dr., 30061, pg. 412　PV
Fujikura America Inc., 2121 New Market Parkway, S.E., Ste. 100, 30067, pg. 525　IT
Graphic Systems, 3001 Kingston Ct., 30067, pg. 1060　PB
Gypsum Joint Systems Plant, 1466 White Rd. Court, P.O. Box 776, 30060, pg. 737　PB
Hillhaven Rehabilitation & Convalescent Center, 26 Tower Rd., 30060, pg. 1713　PB
IFS Systems, Inc., 1130 N. Chase Pkwy., Ste. 200, 30067, pg. 1165　PV
LEP Profit International, Inc., 1950 Spectrum Cir., Ste. B510, 30067, pg. 571　PV
Lockheed Aeronautical Systems Company, 86 S. Cobb Dr., 30063, pg. 1007　PB
MSC Southern Regional Office, 1850 Parkway Pl., 30067, pg. 1031　PB
Materials Handling Equipment, 560 Webb Industrial Dr., N.E., 30062, pg. 1156　PV
MATRIA HEALTHCARE, INC., 1850 Parkway Pl., 30067, pg. 1057　PB
Nationwide Credit, 2253 Northwest Pkwy., 30067, pg. 631　PB
NATIONWIDE CREDIT INC., 2253 NW Pkwy., Ste. A, 30067, pg. 788　PB
Plastic Suppliers, Inc., 1174 Hayes Industrial Dr., 30062, pg. 871　PV

Quantum Corporation, Bldg. 400, 1395 Marietta Pkwy., Ste. 204, 30060, pg. 1350　PB
Rauma USA, Inc., 1800 Parkway Place, Ste. 230, 30067, pg. 1428　IT
Rhone-Poulenc Specialty Chemicals Div., 1525 Church St. Extension, 30060, pg. 1110　IT
SKW Chemicals Inc., 4651 Olde Towne Pkwy., Ste. 200, 30068, pg. 1465　IT
Shimizu America Corporation-Atlanta Marietta Office, Ste. 100, Bldg., 1470, 1355 Terrell Mill Rd., 30067, pg. 1233　IT
Simkins Carton Div.-Marietta, 1069 Atlanta Industrial Dr., 30066, pg. 1000　PV
Solvay Pharmaceuticals, Inc., 901 Sawyer Rd., 30062, pg. 1278　IT
Sope Creek, 1700 Cumberland Pt. Dr. #5, 30067, pg. 1539　PB
Southern Tea Co., 1267 Cobb Industrial Dr., 30066, pg. 1377　IT
Suntory Water Group, Inc., 2141 Powers Ferry Rd., 30067, pg. 1321　IT
Symbol, 2221 Newmarket Pkwy., Ste. 116, 30067-9311, pg. 1546　PB
Tatung Co. of America, 815 Allgood Rd., 30062, pg. 1357　IT
Terminal Technologies, Inc., 140 Marble Mill Rd., Ste. A, 30060, pg. 1460　PB
Thermal Industries Inc., 2171 C. Kingston Ct., 30067-8927, pg. 491　PV
United Companies Lending Corp. (Georgia), 1950 Spectrum S-B312, 30067, pg. 1675　PB
U.S. Steamservice, Inc., 2300 Windy Ridge Pkwy., Ste. 1125, 30067, pg. 1354　IT
Jervis B. Webb Co. of Georgia, 560 Webb Industrial Dr., N.E., 30062, pg. 1157　PV
YKK (U.S.A.), 1306 Cobb Industrial Dr., 30066, pg. 1515　IT

Martinez

Carole Fabrics Corp., 633 N.W. Frontage Rd., 30907, pg. 639　IT
Club Car, Inc., 4152 Washington Rd., 30907, pg. 877　PB

Mc Donough

DOWLING TEXTILE MANUFACTURING CO., 615 Macon Rd., 30253, pg. 341　PV
Snapper Power Equipment, 535 Macon Rd., 30253, pg. 1103　PB
Toppan Interamerica Inc., 1131 Hwy. 155 S., 30253, pg. 1399　IT

Mc Rae

Frigidaire Home Products, Rte. 23 E., Box 370, 31055, pg. 440　IT

Midland

The Game Inc., 7100 Jamesson Rd., 31820, pg. 1413　PB

Milledgeville

Concord Fabrics Inc., 80 Hwy. 22, 31061, pg. 429　PB
The Union-Recorder, P.O. Box 520, 31061, pg. 259　PV

Millen

Bank of Millen, 836 E. Winthrop Ave., 30442, pg. 1371　PB
Bellcrest Holding Co., Inc., 206 Magnolia St., 30442, pg. 1049　PV

Monroe

AVONDALE INCORPORATED, 506 S. Broad St., 30655, pg. 102　PV
Flambeau Southeast Co., 1533 S. Broad St., 30655, pg. 409　PV
National Bank of Walton County, P.O. Box 729, 30655, pg. 1549　PB
Walton Fabric Division of Avondale Mills, 119 First St., 30655, pg. 103　PV

Montezuma

Southern Frozen Foods, 321 Plant St., 31063, pg. 887　PV

Morrow

E.J. Brach, Inc., 1260 Southern Rd., 30260, pg. 163　PV
THE WILLIAM CARTER COMPANY, 1590 Adamson Pkwy., #400, 30260, pg. 217　PV
Toto Kiki USA, Inc., 1155 Southern Road, 30260, pg. 1410　IT
Toto USA, Inc., 1155 Southern Road, 30260, pg. 1410　IT

Moultrie

BEADLES LUMBER COMPANY, INC., 900 6th St., N.E., 31768, pg. 126　PV
Destiny Industries Inc., Industrial Park, 31768, pg. 1209　PB
Ennis Business Forms of Georgia, Industrial Dr., 31768, pg. 583　PB
Moultrie Container Div., P.O. Box 1299, 31776, pg. 1289　PB
RIVERSIDE MANUFACTURING CO., 301 Riverside Dr., 31768, pg. 934　PV

Turning Point Care Center, 319 E. Bypass, P.O. Box 1177, 31768, pg. 1697 **PB**

Nashville

Chaparral Boats, Industrial Blvd., 31639, pg. 1356 **PB**
J.H. HARVEY COMPANY, 727 S. Davis St., 31639, pg. 508 **PV**
Nashville Textile Corp., 202 Industrial Park, 31639, pg. 542 **PV**

Newnan

Bank of Coweta, P.O. Box 1218, 30264, pg. 1549 **PB**
William L. Bonnell Co., Inc., 25 Bonnell St., 30263, pg. 1634 **PB**
Johnson Yokogawa Corporation, Four Dart Rd., 30265, pg. 1521 **IT**
Kawasaki Loaders Manufacturing Corp., (U.S.A.), 60 Amlajack Blvd., 30265, pg. 725 **IT**
OLSONITE CORPORATION, 25 Dart Rd., 30265, pg. 815 **PV**
Sivaco Georgia, P.O. Box 1194, 24 Herring Rd., 30265, pg. 696 **IT**
Sivaco Wire Group, 24 Herring Road, 30265-1006, pg. 696 **IT**
Southern States Vehicle Auction of Atlanta Inc., 300 Raymond Hill Rd., 30265, pg. 1649 **PB**
U.S. Can Company, 434 Cornith Rd., 30264, pg. 1681 **PB**
Yokogawa Corporation of America, Two Dart Rd., Shenandoah Industrial Pk., 30265, pg. 1521 **IT**

Norcross

AFCO Metals, Inc., 4400 Peachtree Industrial Blvd., 30071, pg. 879 **PB**
AGCO INC., 2782 Simpson Circle, 30071, pg. 26 **PB**
ALLIANCE AMERICA, 4888 S. Old Peachtree Rd., 30071, pg. 37 **PV**
Allied Diagnostic Imaging Resources, Inc., 5440 Oakbrook Pkwy., 30093, pg. 282 **PV**
Allied Security Inc., 5855 Five Oak Pkwy., Ste. A, 30093, pg. 41 **PV**
ALLTEL Supply, Inc., 6625 The Corners Pkwy., Ste. 400, 30092, pg. 55 **PB**
Alumax Primary Aluminum Corporation, 6625 The Corners Pkwy., Ste. 500, 30092, pg. 60 **PB**
American Technical Services Group, Inc., 5680 Oakbrook Pkwy., Ste. 165, 30093, pg. 1523 **PB**
AmeriServe of Norcross, 4101 Blue Ridge Industrial Pkwy., 30071, pg. 533 **PV**
Antec Group, 2100-A Nancy Hanks Dr., 30071, pg. 116 **PV**
Aromat Southeast Sales Office, 5555 Triangle Pkwy., Ste. 450, 30092, pg. 848 **IT**
Atlanta Casualty Company, 3169 Holcomb Ridge Rd., 30071, pg. 75 **PB**
Atlantic States Bank, 1725 Indian Trail Rd., 30091, pg. 629 **PB**
BWI Fords Holmatic, 1750 Corporate Dr., 30093, pg. 130 **IT**
Binks Manufacturing Company, 5575 Spalding Dr., 30092-2559, pg. 229 **PB**
Bostik Inc., 5680 Oakbrook Pkwy., 30093-1809, pg. 1409 **IT**
Bowman Distribution, 1625 Oakbrook Dr., 30093, pg. 190 **PB**
Burnup & Sims Communications Services, 1650 Oakbrook Dr., Ste. 445, 30093, pg. 1056 **PB**
Ceramic Tile International, 5870-C Oakbrook Pkwy., 30093, pg. 564 **PV**
Chem Free Corporation, 8 Meca Way, 30093, pg. 888 **PV**
Chips and Technologies, Inc., 3091 Governors Lake Dr., Ste. 270, 30071, pg. 349 **PB**
Citadel Corporation, 6075 The Corners Pkwy., Ste. 200, 30092, pg. 995 **IT**
CLASSIC MARKETS CORP., 6689-L Peachtree Industrial Blvd., 30092, pg. 244 **PV**
Data General Corp., 1626 Jeurgens Ct., 30093, pg. 485 **PB**
Deutz Corporation, 3883 Steve Reynolds Blvd., 30093, pg. 408 **IT**
Durex Consumer Products, 3585 Engineering Dr., Ste. 200, 30092, pg. 815 **IT**
Durkopp Adler America Inc., 3025 Northwoods Pkwy., 30071, pg. 468 **IT**
EDD-Atlanta, 3850 Holcomb Bridge Rd., Ste. 110, 30092, pg. 204 **PB**
EDWARDS BAKING CO., 6875 Jimmy Garden Blvd., Ste 3200, 30071, pg. 365 **PV**
ELECTROMAGNETIC SCIENCES, INC., P.O. Box 7700, 660 Engineering Dr., Technology Park, 30092, pg. 569 **PB**
Embraco North America, Inc., 1725 Corporate Dr., Ste. 300, 30093, pg. 1765 **PB**
Federated Systems Group, 6801 Governor's Dr., pg. 618 **PB**
FOOD & GAS, INC., 3850 Holcomb Bridge Rd., Ste. 255, 30092, pg. 417 **PV**
L.B. Foster Company-Doraville Yard/Coated Pipe, 6455 Old Peachtree Rd., 30071, pg. 676 **PB**
L.B. Foster Company-Doraville Yard/Fabrication Shop, 6455 Old Peachtree Rd., 30071, pg. 676 **PB**
G.E.-Hitachi HVB Inc., 4258 Communications Dr., 30093, pg. 622 **IT**
GPD/Embraco North America, Inc., 1725 Corporate Dr., Ste. 300, 30093, pg. 1765 **PB**
GENERAL TIME CORP., 520 Guthridge Ct., 30092, pg. 445 **PV**
Gould Southern, 1826 A. Doan Way, 30093, pg. 467 **PB**

Graco Southeast Regional Sales & Distribution Center, 3560 Engineering Dr., 30092-2881, pg. 757 **PB**
Haas Publishing Companies, Inc., 3119 Campus Dr., 30071, pg. 1327 **PB**
Harwick Standard Distribution Corp., 5380 Peachtree Ind., Blvd., Ste. 210, 30071, pg. 509 **PV**
HAYES CORPORATION, 5854 Peachtree Corners E., 30092, pg. 800 **PB**
Hayes Microcomputer Products, Inc., 5854 Peachtree Corners E., 30092, pg. 801 **PB**
Hewlett-Packard Company, 3607 Parkway Ln., Ste. 300, 30092, pg. 814 **PB**
Hitachi Home Electronics, 3890 Steve Reynolds, 30093, pg. 621 **IT**
Hitachi Home Electronics (America) Inc., 3890 Steve Reynolds Blvd., 30093, pg. 622 **IT**
Hitachi Home Electronics, Eastern Region, 3890 Steve Reynolds Blvd., 30093, pg. 622 **IT**
Hitachi Koki U.S.A. Ltd., 3950 Steve Reynolds Blvd., 30093, pg. 620 **IT**
Howell Medical Center, 6475 Jimmy Carter Blvd., Ste. 200, 30071, pg. 1715 **PB**
J.M. Huber, Solem Div., 4940 Peachtree Indus. Blvd., Ste. 340, 30071, pg. 545 **PV**
Humboldt Wedag Division, 3200 Pointe Pkwy., 30092, pg. 408 **IT**
IQ SOFTWARE CORPORATION, 3295 River Exchange Dr., Ste. 550, 30092, pg. 858 **PV**
ITW Fluid Products Group, 4366 Shackelford Rd., 30093, pg. 866 **PB**
Ikon Office Solutions-Atlanta, 6971 Peachtree Industrial Blvd., 30092, pg. 863 **PB**
Intelligent Enclosures Corp., One Meca Way, 30093, pg. 888 **PB**
INTELLIGENT SYSTEMS CORP., 4355 Shackleford Rd., 30093, pg. 888 **PB**
ISOLYSER COMPANY, INC., 650 Engineering Dr., 30092, pg. 914 **PB**
KHD Deutz of America Corporation, 3883 Steve Reynolds Blvd., 30093, pg. 408 **IT**
Kawneer Company, 555 Guthridge Ct., 30092, pg. 60 **PB**
LXE Inc., 303-T Research Dr., 30092, pg. 569 **PB**
Lambent Technologies Inc., 4437 Park Dr., Ste. E, 30093, pg. 858 **PV**
Land Span Inc., 6270 McDonough Dr., 30093, pg. 1153 **PV**
Liuski International Atlanta, Inc., 6585 Crescent Dr., 30071, pg. 1005 **PB**
LIUSKI INTERNATIONAL, INC., 6585 Crescent Dr., 30071, pg. 1005 **PB**
London International, U.S. Holdings Inc., 3585 Engineering Dr., Ste. 200, 30092, pg. 815 **IT**
Marigold Glove Division, 3585 Engineering Dr., Ste. 200, 30092, pg. 815 **IT**
Medaes International, 2850 Colonnades Ct., 30071, pg. 287 **IT**
Media Recovery Inc.-Georgia, 6075 Atlantic Blvd., 30071, pg. 727 **PV**
MIGHTY DISTRIBUTING SYSTEM, 50 Technology Park, 30092, pg. 745 **PV**
Milgray/Atlanta, Inc., 3000 Northwoods Pky., 30071, pg. 206 **IT**
Mizuno Corporation of America, 5125 Peachtree Indus. Blvd., 30092, pg. 885 **IT**
Mizuno Golf Company, 5125 Peachtree Indus. Blvd., 30092, pg. 885 **IT**
Mizuno USA, Inc., 5125 Peachtree Ind. Blvd., 30092, pg. 885 **IT**
Motorola Radius, 330 Research Ct., #200, 30092-2920, pg. 1138 **PB**
National Technical Services, 5680 Oakbrook Pkwy., Ste. 165, 30093-1841, pg. 1523 **PB**
The New York Times Distribution Corp., 6525 The Corners Pkwy., Ste. 110, 30092, pg. 1176 **PB**
North Central Division, 1000 Ctr. Pl., 30093, pg. 1255 **PB**
Notifier Engineered Systems Company, Inc. (NESCO), 1650 Oakbrook Dr., Ste. 435, 30093, pg. 1306 **PB**
Ohmeda Medical Engineering, 2850 Colonnades Ct., 30071, pg. 121 **IT**
PAMECO CORP., 1000 Center Pl., 30093, pg. 1255 **PB**
Paper Recycling International, 5335 Triangle Pkwy., Ste. 400, 30092, pg. 1522 **PB**
Phillips & Jacobs/South, 3905 Steve Reynolds Blvd., Ste. 100, 30093, pg. 1329 **PB**
Plaid Enterprises Inc., P.O. Box 7600, 1649 International Blvd., 30091, pg. 352 **PV**
Plexco/Spirolite, 4094 Blue Ridge Industrial Pkwy., 30071, pg. 348 **PB**
Public Health Software Systems, One Meca Way, 30093, pg. 888 **PV**
Raytheon Engineers & Constructors, 145 Technology Park, 30092-2913, pg. 1366 **PB**
ROCK-TENN COMPANY, 504 Thrasher St., 30071, pg. 1396 **PB**
Rock-Tenn Company, Mill Division, Inc., P.O. Box 4098, 30091, pg. 1397 **PB**
Rock-Tenn Converting Co., P.O. Box 4098, 30091, pg. 1397 **PB**
Saab Cars USA, Inc., 4405-A International Blvd., 30093, pg. 687 **IT**
SAUL BROS. & COMPANY, INC., 6500 Peachtree Industrial Blvd., 30071, pg. 676 **PB**
SCIENTIFIC-ATLANTA, INC., One Technology Pkwy. S., 30092-2967, pg. 1443 **PB**
SmithKline Beecham Labs, 5335 Triangle Pkwy. Ste. 350, 30092-2556, pg. 1265 **IT**
Southern Division, 1000 Ctr. Pl., 30093, pg. 1255 **PB**
Square D Co., 5275 Triangle Pkwy., 30092-2537, pg. 1208 **IT**
Standard Cap & Seal, 3150 Clinton St., 30071, pg. 1486 **PB**

Stanfast, Inc., Northbelt Business Park, 6145 Northbelt Pkwy., Ste. F, 30071, pg. 1505 **PB**
SUN DATA INC., One Sun Court, 30092, pg. 1050 **PV**
Sunds Defibrator, Inc., 2900 Ft. Yards Dr., 30071, pg. 1428 **IT**
Symix Systems Inc., 3500 Pkwy. Ln., Ste. 350, 30092, pg. 1547 **PB**
TIE Systems Georgia, 680 Engineering Dr., Ste. 150, 30092, pg. 1085 **PV**
Taisei America Corp., 6525 The Corners Pkwy., Ste. 411, 30092, pg. 1347 **IT**
TEKGRAF, INC., 2979 Pacific Dr., # 8, 30071, pg. 1073 **PV**
J.M. Tull Metals Co., Inc., 4400 Peachtree Industrial Blvd., 30071, pg. 879 **PB**
Ulbrich of Georgia, Inc., 1465 Beaver Ruin Rd., 30093, pg. 1115 **PB**
Vicon Industries-Southern Inc., 3010 Business Park Dr., Ste. B, 30071, pg. 1719 **PB**
Volt Services Group, 5300 Oakbrook Pkwy., 30093, pg. 1724 **PB**
WAFFLE HOUSE, INCORPORATED, 5986 Financial Dr., 30071, pg. 1146 **PV**
Western Division, 1000 Ctr. Pl., 30093, pg. 1255 **PB**
Winchester Carton Corp., P.O. Box 4098, 30091, pg. 1397 **PB**
Wyle Electronics-Atlanta, 6025 The Corners Pkwy Ste 111, 30092-3328, pg. 1457 **IT**

Ochlocknee

Oil-Dri Corporation of Georgia, P.O. Box 200A, 31773, pg. 1215 **PB**
Oil-Dri Transportation Co., P.O. Box 380, 31773, pg. 1215 **PB**

Peachtree City

Andersen 2000 Inc., 306 Dividend Dr., 30269, pg. 462 **PB**
CROWN ANDERSEN INC., 306 Dividend Dr., 30269, pg. 462 **PB**
Fasson Roll Materials Div., 316 Hwy. 74 S., 30269, pg. 153 **PB**
Furukawa Electric America Inc. (FEA), 200 Westpark Dr., Ste. 190, 30269, pg. 530 **IT**
Goody Products, Inc., 600 Westpark Dr., 30269, pg. 1177 **PB**
Harris Waste Mgmt. Group, Inc., 200 Clover Reach Dr., 30269, pg. 473 **PB**
Megadoor Inc., P.O. Box 2957, 435 Dividend Dr., Ste. B., 30269, pg. 269 **PV**
Oriental Motor U.S.A. Corp., 300 Tivoli Gardens, Ste. 212, 30269, pg. 1008 **IT**
Peachtree National, 2603 Hwy. 54 W., 30269, pg. 1549 **PB**

Pearson

Fleetwood Homes of Georgia, Inc.-Pearson/Railroad Rd., P.O. Box 899, Railroad St., 31642, pg. 651 **PB**

Perry

Georgia Production Site, 200 Thompson Rd., 31069, pg. 1198 **PB**
Hye Precision Co., 745 Carroll St., 31069, pg. 73 **IT**
TOLLESON LUMBER COMPANY, INC., 903 Jernigan St., 31069, pg. 1090 **PV**

Port Wentworth

Aztec Trading Company, S.A., Crossgate Rd., 31407, pg. 736 **PB**
Food Carrier, Inc., P.O. Box 2287, Two Grange Rd., 31407-2287, pg. 872 **PB**

Preston

Prestec, P.O. Box 78, Hwy. 41 S., Industrial Pk., 31824, pg. 444 **PB**

Quitman

Brooks County Sausage, P.O. Box 351, 31643, pg. 1479 **PB**

Red Oak

Atlanta Auto Auction, Inc., 4900 Buffington Rd., 30272, pg. 282 **PV**

Redan

Parex, Inc., 1870 Stone Mountain, Lithonia Rd., 30074, pg. 789 **IT**

Riceboro

Interstate Paper Corporation, One Interstate Rd., 31323, pg. 573 **PV**
Newport Timber, One Interstate Rd., 31323, pg. 573 **PV**

Ringgold

Ashley Carpet, P.O. Box 220, 30736, pg. 1464 **PB**
Majestic Carpet Mills, P.O. Box 220, 30736, pg. 1464 **PB**
Salem Carpet Mills, P.O. Box 10, 30736, pg. 1464 **PB**

PB - *U.S. Public Companies Volume*
PV - *U.S. Private Companies Volume*
IT - *International Public & Private Companies Volume*

Salem Carpet Mills, P.O. Box 220, 30736, pg. 1464   **PB**
Walker Equipment Corp., 4009 Cloud Springs Rd., 30736, pg. 1308   **PB**
Winston Carpet Co., P.O. Box 220, 30736, pg. 1464   **PB**

Rockmart

J.L. LESTER & SON, INC., 326 S. Marble St., 30153, pg. 660   **PV**
Rockland React-Rite, Inc., 327 Industrial Dr., 30153, pg. 889   **PB**

Rome

AmSouth Bank of Georgia, 1400 Turner McCall Blvd., 30161, pg. 105   **PB**
BATTEY MACHINERY COMPANY, 2960 New Calhoun Hwy., N.E., 30161, pg. 123   **PV**
Bekaert Corporation, Darlington Dr., P.O. Box 1205, 30162-1205, pg. 184   **IT**
Citizens First Bank, 701 Broad St., 30162-1313, pg. 1549   **PB**
Katsushiro Rome Corporation, 300 W. Hermitage Rd., N.E., 30161, pg. 744   **IT**
MARGLEN INDUSTRIES, 1748 Ward Mountain Rd., 30161, pg. 702   **PV**
Regions Bank/Rome, P.O. Box 5267, 30163-3801, pg. 1372   **PB**
Scripps Howard Cable of Northwest Georgia, 707 E. First St., 30161, pg. 1448   **PB**
SunTrust Bank, Northwest Georgia, N.A., 100 E. Second Ave., 30161, pg. 1538   **PB**
Todd Advertising Agency, Inc., 531 Broad St., 30162-0553, pg. 1090   **PV**
J.L. TODD AUCTION CO., P.O. Box 553, 30162-0553, pg. 1090   **PV**

Roswell

Advance Security, 200 Mansell Ct., 5th Fl., 30076, pg. 1126   **PV**
Ahlstrom Process Equipment Inc., 1007A Mansell Ct., 30076-4805, pg. 34   **IT**
Ahlstrom Recovery Inc., 30 Mansell Ct., 30076-1580, pg. 34   **IT**
Amano Cincinnati - Atlanta Branch Office, 1005 Mansell Rd., Ste. D, 30076-1507, pg. 70   **IT**
B & R INDUSTRIAL AUTOMATION, 1325 Northmeadow Pkwy., Ste. 130, 30076, pg. 105   **PV**
CAPITAL LENDING SERVICES, INC., 570 Colonial Park Dr., Ste. 304, 30075, pg. 206   **PV**
Cigna Excess & Surplus Insurance Services, Inc. (GA), Bldg. 100, 1080 Holcomb Bridge Rd., Ste. 300, 30076, pg. 362   **PV**
CIVES CORPORATION, 411 Rouse Ln., 30076, pg. 241   **PV**
Emtex Leasing Corp., 910 Holcomb Bridge Rd., 30077, pg. 1177   **PV**
Gate City Equipment Company, Inc., 2000 Northfield Ct., 30076-3825, pg. 1016   **PV**
Health Care and Nonwovens Sector, 1400 Holcomb Bridge Rd., 30076, pg. 958   **PB**
Kimberly-Clark Integrated Services Corp., 1400 Holcomb Bridge, 30076, pg. 959   **PB**
Kimberly-Clark Technical Products, Inc., 1400 Holcomb Bridge Rd., 30076, pg. 959   **PB**
Kvaerner Hymac Corporation, Holcomb Bridge Rd., Bldg. 200, Ste. 350, 30076-4343, pg. 770   **IT**
Logistics Sector, 1400 Holcomb Bridge Rd., 30076, pg. 958   **PB**
Micropolis Corporation, 225 Ivywood Ln., 30076, pg. 742   **PV**
Neenah Paper, 1400 Holcomb Bridge Rd., Ste. 200, 30076, pg. 958   **PB**
North American Pulp & Paper Sector, 1400 Holcomb Bridge Rd., 30076, pg. 958   **PB**
Service & Industrial Sector, Dept. D, 1400 Holcomb Bridge Rd., 30076, pg. 958   **PB**
Specialty Products, 1400 Holcomb Bridge Rd., 30076, pg. 958   **PB**
Stainless Ice-Tainer Co. (SITCO), 1172 Grimes Bridge Rd., Suite 300, 30075, pg. 646   **IT**
Syntellect Technology Corp., 1000 Holcomb Wods Pkwy., Ste. 410A, 30076, pg. 1550   **PB**
TCI Enterprises, LLC, 645-I Hembree Park Dr., 30076, pg. 1148   **PB**
Technical Paper, Dept. M, 1400 Holcomb Bridge Rd., 30076, pg. 958   **PB**
U.S. SECURITY ASSOCIATES, INC., 200 Mansell Ct., 5th Fl., 30076, pg. 1126   **PV**
United TransNet, Inc., 1080 Holcomb Bridge Rd., 30076, pg. 449   **PB**

Saint Marys

Gilman Building Products Co., 1000 Obsborne St., 31558, pg. 454   **PV**
Gilman Paper Co., 1000 Osborne St., 31558, pg. 454   **PV**
Saint Marys Railroad Co., 110 Osborne St., P.O. Box 520, 31558, pg. 454   **PV**

Saint Simons Island

Charter By-The-Sea Behavioral Health System, Inc., 2927 Demere Rd., 31522, pg. 1034   **PB**
Hilb, Rogal and Hamilton Company of St. Simons Island, 225 Marina Dr., 31522, pg. 827   **PB**

Sandersville

BURGESS PIGMENT CO., Beck Blvd., 31082, pg. 182   **PV**
Piedmont Minerals, P.O. Box 1056, 31082, pg. 1081   **PV**
THIELE KAOLIN CO., Kaolin Rd., 31082, pg. 1081   **PV**
Villa South Inc., South Harris St., 31082, pg. 1081   **PV**
WACO Chemical Company, P.O. Box 5069, 31082, pg. 1081   **PV**

Sandy Springs

Regions Bank/Atlanta, 6637 Roswell Rd., 30328, pg. 1371   **PB**

Savannah

Allright Parking of Georgia, Inc., 401 W. Bay St., 31401, pg. 43   **PV**
American Savannah Broadcasting Co., 11 The News Place, 31405, pg. 912   **PV**
The Branigar Organization, Inc., 6555 Abercorn Ext., 31406, pg. 1666   **PV**
Carrier Air Terminal Facility, 101 Coleman Blvd., 31408-9540, pg. 1689   **PB**
CARSON PRODUCTS COMPANY, 64 Ross Rd., 31403-2039, pg. 309   **PV**
CARVER, INC., 115 Coleman Blvd., 31408, pg. 217   **PV**
Charter Behavioral Health System of Savannah, Inc., 1150 Cornell Ave., 31406, pg. 1034   **PB**
Chatham Towing Company, Inc., P.O. Box 576, 31402, pg. 254   **PV**
Colonial Drilling & Exploration Corporation, P.O. Box 576, 31402, pg. 254   **PV**
Colonial Marine Industries, Inc., 26 E. Byron St., 31401, pg. 254   **PV**
COLONIAL OIL INDUSTRIES, 101 N. Lathrop Ave., 31401, pg. 253   **PV**
Colonial Terminals, Inc., P.O. Box 576, 31402, pg. 254   **PV**
DERST BAKING COMPANY, INC., 1311 W. 52nd St. Ext., 31405, pg. 254   **PV**
Dixie Crystals Brands, Inc., P.O. Box 1977, 31402-1977, pg. 872   **PV**
Enmark Stations, Inc., P.O. Box 576, 31402, pg. 254   **PV**
Food Carrier, Inc., P.O. Box 2287, 31402-2287, pg. 872   **PV**
Gulfstream Aerospace Corporation, 500 Gulfstream Rd., 31408, pg. 419   **PV**
Hardwood Plywood Plant, Old Louisville Rd., 31498, pg. 737   **PV**
Harleysville Atlantic Insurance Company, P.O. Box 187, 31402-0187, pg. 786   **PV**
Healthsource Savannah, Inc., 7130 Hodgson Memorial Dr., Ste. 4000, 31416, pg. 360   **PB**
Hercules Inc.-Savannah, Old Louisville Rd., 31408, pg. 810   **PV**
Hewlett-Packard Company, 1000 Business Center Dr., Ste. 40, 31405, pg. 814   **PB**
Hilb, Rogal and Hamilton Company of Savannah, Inc., 7 E. Congress St., Ste. 1002, 31401, pg. 827   **PB**
Hillhaven Convalescent Center Savannah, 11800 Abercorn St., 31406, pg. 1713   **PB**
Intermarine U.S.A. Inc., 301 N. Lathrop Ave., 31402-3045, pg. 324   **IT**
Interstate Stations, Inc., P.O. Box 576, 31402, pg. 254   **PV**
Kemira Chemicals Inc., One Kemira Rd., 31404, pg. 729   **IT**
Kemira Holdings Inc., P.O. Box 368, 31402, pg. 729   **IT**
Kemira Incorporated, P.O. Box 368, 31402, pg. 729   **IT**
Kemira Water Treatment, Inc., P.O. Box 2247, 31402, pg. 729   **IT**
Kockums Cancar Corp., 101 B Cluman Blvd., 31408, pg. 124   **IT**
KUHLMAN CORPORATION, Three Skidaway Village Sq., 31411, pg. 968   **PB**
Morgans, P.O. Box 308, 110 Ann St., 31402, pg. 91   **PV**
MORRIS NEWSPAPER CORPORATION, 27 Abercorn St., 31401, pg. 762   **PV**
National Distributing Co., Inc., 1414 Mills B. Lane Blvd., 31405, pg. 781   **PV**
Quaker Chemical Corp., 1000 Business Center Dr., Ste. 110, 31405, pg. 1346   **PB**
Savannah Convalescent Center, 815 E. 63rd St., 31405, pg. 1714   **PB**
Savannah Electric & Power Co., 600 E. Bay St., 31401, pg. 1490   **PB**
Savannah Foods & Industries, Inc., Two E. Bryan St., 31401, pg. 872   **PV**
Savannah Foods Industrial, Inc., P.O. Box 339, 31402-0339, pg. 873   **PV**
Savannah Learning Center, Travis Field, P.O. Box 2307, 31402, pg. 219   **PV**
Savannah Sugar Refinery, P.O. Box 710, 31498-4710, pg. 873   **PV**
Stone Savannah River Pulp and Paper, P.O. Box 548, 31402, pg. 1520   **PB**
SunTrust Bank, Savannah, N.A., 33 Bull St., 31401, pg. 1538   **PB**
Transtates Properties, Inc., 6555 Abercorn Ext., 31405, pg. 1666   **PV**
Union Camp Woodlands Div., P.O. Box 1391, W. Lathrop Ave., 31402, pg. 1666   **PB**
Vigoro Industries, Southeast Division, P.O. Box 246, 31402, pg. 856   **PB**
White Electrical Construction Co, 1514A Lot 2, Old Dean Forest Rd., 31408, pg. 1172   **PV**

Scottdale

GEORGIA DUCK & CORDAGE MILLS, 21 Laredo Dr., 30079, pg. 448   **PV**

Summit-Beers Construction Company, P.O. Box 866, 30079, pg. 1261   **IT**
Thermo Materials, P.O. Box 925, 30079, pg. 330   **PB**

Screven

Broadhurst Environmental, Inc., 4800 Broadhurst Rd., 31560, pg. 1379   **PB**

Sea Island

The Cloister, 100 Cloister Pl., 31561, pg. 978   **PV**
SEA ISLAND COMPANY, 100 Hudon Pl., 31561, pg. 977   **PV**
Sea Island Properties, Inc., 100 First St., 31561, pg. 978   **PV**
Sea Island Services, Inc., 100 Hudson Pl., 31561, pg. 978   **PV**

Smyrna

BKNT, Inc., 4900 Highland Pkwy., 30080, pg. 1703   **PB**
Graseby Andersen, 500 Technology Ct., 30082-5211, pg. 1268   **IT**
Green Tree Acceptance, Inc., P.O. Box 727, 30080, pg. 762   **PB**
HEAD DISTRIBUTING CO., 4820 N. Church Ln., 30080, pg. 514   **PV**
Hickson Corporation, 1955 Lake Park Dr., Ste. 250, 30080, pg. 619   **IT**
Intergraph Corporation, 3300 Highland Pkwy., Ste. 260, 30082, pg. 891   **PB**
LSI Atlanta, 5000 Highlands Pkwy., 30082, pg. 1437   **PB**
Magnus Software Corporation, 2233 Lake Park Drive, Ste. 400, 30080-8856, pg. 795   **PB**
MORRISON HEALTH CARE INC., 1955 Lake Park Dr., Ste. 400, 30080, pg. 1133   **PB**
Murata Electronics North America, Inc., 2200 Lake Park Dr., 30080-7604, pg. 897   **IT**
RACETRAC PETROLEUM, INC., 300 Technology Ct., 30082, pg. 906   **PV**
Retail Stores, Inc., 4900 Highland Pkwy., 30080, pg. 1703   **PB**
S.P. Richards Co., 6300 Highlands Pkwy., 30082, pg. 732   **PB**
SLJ RETAIL LLC, 400 Technology Court, Ste. F, 30082, pg. 957   **PV**
SHEA COMMUNICATIONS CO., 4770 S. Atlanta, 30080, pg. 990   **PV**
UNITED DISTRIBUTORS, INC., 2627 Collins Springs Dr., 30080, pg. 1121   **PV**

Statesboro

Cooper Tools, 6644 Old River Rd. N., 30458, pg. 444   **PB**
Frontier Communications of Georgia, Inc., P.O. Box 807, 76 E. Girady St., 30458, pg. 683   **PB**
Sea Island Bank, Two East Main St., 30458, pg. 1549   **PB**
Statesboro Plant, 6644 Old River Rd. N., 30458, pg. 444   **PB**
T.J. U.S. Company, 917 Hwy. 301 S., 30458, pg. 1152   **PB**

Stockbridge

Eagle's Landing Country Club, Inc., 600 County Club Dr., 30281, pg. 956   **PB**
KILLEARN PROPERTIES, INC., 385 Country Club Dr., 30281, pg. 956   **PB**
Killearn Properties of Georgia, 100 Eagles Landing Way, 30281, pg. 956   **PB**
Stockbridge, 3584 Hwy. 138, S.E., 30281, pg. 1716   **PB**

Stone Mountain

Albany Engineered Systems, 1707 Stone Ridge Dr., 30083, pg. 1593   **PB**
Atlanta Beverage Company, 1375 Beverage Dr., 30083, pg. 94   **PV**
Self-Insurance Administrators, Inc., 2300 W. Park Pl., Ste. 140, 30087-8676, pg. 144   **PV**
Southwest Vacuum Devices, Inc., 4601 Lewis Rd., 30083, pg. 1720   **PV**

Sugar Valley

American Rug Craftsmen, 3090 Sugar Valley Rd. N.W., 30746, pg. 1121   **PV**

Suwanee

Avon Sales & Distribution Branch, 425 Horizon Dr., 30174, pg. 156   **PB**
Central States Multiplex, P.O. Box 157, Hwy. 23 & 31, 30174, pg. 16   **PV**
Firearms Training Systems, Inc., 7340 McGinnis Ferry Rd., 30174-1247, pg. 222   **PV**
Juki Union Special Inc.-Atlanta Office, 600 Satellite Blvd., 30174, pg. 716   **IT**
Kubota Tractor Corp., 1025 Northbrook Pkwy., 30174-2931, pg. 762   **IT**
M.A. Hanna Color, 800 Satellite Dr., 30174, pg. 781   **PB**
Oki Telecom Group, 437 Old Peachtree Rd., 30174, pg. 1000   **IT**
Pfaff-Pegasus of U.S.A., 7270 McGinnis Ferry Rd., 30174, pg. 1046   **IT**

PB - *U.S. Public Companies Volume*
PV - *U.S. Private Companies Volume*
IT - *International Public & Private Companies Volume*

1204

Geographic Index-U.S.

Swainsboro

American Yard Products Inc., Electric Rd., P.O. Box 1678, 30401, pg. 440 **IT**

Tallapoosa

Hoover Hanes Company, 280 Pequanac Dr., 30176, pg. 56 **PV**

Thomaston

THOMASTON MILLS, INC., 115 E. Main St., 30286-0311, pg. 1599 **PB**

Thomasville

Commercial Bank, P.O. Box 710, 31799, pg. 1549 **PB**
Davco Div., 1828 Metcalf Ave., 31792, pg. 1682 **PB**
Davis Meter & Supply Div., 1820 Metcalf Ave., 31792, pg. 1682 **PB**
Flowers Baking Co. of Thomasville, Inc., 236 S. Madison St., 31792, pg. 657 **PB**
FLOWERS INDUSTRIES, INC., 1919 Flowers Cir., 31757, pg. 656 **PB**
ICI Seeds, P.O. Box 8, 111 Commerce Park Dr., 31799, pg. 1524 **IT**
Mrs. Smith's Bakeries, Inc., P.O. Box 1338, 31799-1338, pg. 657 **PB**
Sunnyland Inc., 603 Cassidy Rd., 31792, pg. 1479 **PB**
Turbine Engine Components Textron, 1211 Old Albany Rd., 31792, pg. 1588 **PB**
U.S. Filter/Davis Water & Waste Industries, Inc., 1820 Metcalf Ave., 31792, pg. 1682 **PB**

Thomson

Allied Bank of Georgia, P.O. Drawer 1020, 30824, pg. 1373 **PB**
Hoover Treated Wood Products, Inc., Knox Shopping Ctr., Main St., 30824, pg. 1193 **PB**
UTA Thompson Plant, 1884 Warrenton Hwy., 30824, pg. 1691 **PB**

Tifton

DIXIE OIL COMPANY, U.S. Hwy. 82 E., 31793-1007, pg. 337 **PV**
First Community Bank of Tifton, 218 Love Ave., Box 8, 31792, pg. 1549 **PB**
Tifton Aluminum Co., Inc., Southwell Blvd., 31794, pg. 61 **PB**

Toccoa

Basic American Wood Products, 202 Elberton St., 30577, pg. 404 **PB**
Dempster Equipment, P.O. Box 1388, 30577, pg. 1089 **PV**
FIRST FRANKLIN FINANCIAL CORP., 213 E. Tugalo St., 30577, pg. 407 **PV**
Frandisco Life Insurance Co., 213 E. Tugalo St., 30577, pg. 407 **PV**
Frandisco Property & Casualty Insurance, 213 E. Tugalo St., 30577, pg. 407 **PV**
GEM INDUSTRIES FINANCE CORPORATION, Highway 123 N., 30577, pg. 442 **PV**
Gem Southeast, Inc., Hwy. 123 N., 30577, pg. 443 **PV**
Gilbert & Bennett, P.O. Box 1205, 30577, pg. 453 **PV**
Patterson Pump Company, P.O. Box 790, U.S. Highway 123 South, 30577, pg. 754 **PB**
Regions Bank/Stephens County, P.O. Box 730, 30577, pg. 1373 **PB**

Trion

Mount Vernon Mills, Inc., Riegel Textile Div. (Trion), P.O. Box 7, 30753, pg. 835 **PV**

Tucker

Bausch & Lomb Oral Care Division, 5243 Royal Woods Pkwy., Ste. 100, 30084, pg. 194 **PB**
Black Diamond Energy, Inc., 2100 E. Exchange Pl., 30085, pg. 812 **PV**
Cadmus Catalogs, 5150 N. Royal Atlanta Dr., 30084, pg. 290 **PB**
Cadmus Interactive, 5203 S. Royal Atlanta Dr., 30084, pg. 291 **PB**
Energy & Process Corp., 2146 Flintstone Dr., 30084, pg. 1512 **IT**
European Bakers, LTD, 5055 S. Royal Atlanta Dr., 30084, pg. 657 **PB**
Gensym Corporation, Southeast Area Office, 100 Crescent Ctr. Pkwy., Ste.1290, 30084, pg. 731 **PB**
GEORGIA TRANSMISSION CORPORATION, P.O. Box 1349, 30085-1349, pg. 448 **PV**
I.P.C., 2191 N. Lake Pkwy., Ste. 116, 30084, pg. 484 **PB**
INDUSTRIAL DISTRIBUTION GROUP, 2500 Royal Pl., 30084, pg. 875 **PB**
Kearney Company, 1928 Montreal Rd., 30084, pg. 444 **PB**
LPS Laboratories Inc., 4647 Hugh Howell Rd., P.O. Box 105052, 30085-5052, pg. 892 **IT**
Lane Limited, 2280 Mountain Industrial Blvd., 30084, pg. 1129 **IT**
M M SYSTEMS CORPORATION, 4520 Elmdale Dr., 30084, pg. 685 **PV**

Morgan Chemical Products Inc., P.O. Box 105052, 4647 Hugh Howell Rd., 30085-5052, pg. 892 **IT**
OGLETHORPE POWER CORP., 2100 E. Exchange Pl., 30084, pg. 812 **PV**
Rhone-Poulenc Rorer, 4660 Hammermill Rd., 30084, pg. 1111 **IT**
Sears Logistics Services, 2301 Mountain Ind. Blvd., 30084-3808, pg. 1452 **IT**
SOUTHERN ELECTRONICS CORPORATION, 4916 N. Royal Atlanta Dr., 30084, pg. 1490 **PB**
Southern Electronics Distributors International, 4916 N. Royal Atlanta Dr., 30084, pg. 1490 **PB**
Sunkist Growers, Inc.-Southern Division, Heritage Place, Ste. 360, 4500 Hugh Howell Rd., 30084, pg. 1052 **PV**
3 Score, Inc., 5150 N. Royal Atlanta Dr., 30084, pg. 291 **PB**
Tobacco Exporters International (USA) Limited, 2280 Mountain Industrial Blvd., 30084, pg. 1129 **IT**
VIDEO DISPLAY CORPORATION, 1868 Tucker Industrial Dr., 30084, pg. 1720 **PB**

Union City

SOUTHERN MILLS, INC., 6501 Mall Blvd., 30291, pg. 1016 **PV**

Union Point

CHIPMAN-UNION, INC., 500 Sibley Ave., 30669, pg. 237 **PV**

Valdosta

Crackin' Good Bakers, 701 N. Forrest St., 31601-4124, pg. 1772 **PB**
Drumheller Bag & Supply, P.O. Box 1846, 31603, pg. 802 **PV**
First State Bank and Trust Company, P.O. Box 1248, 31601, pg. 1549 **PB**
GRIFFIN CORPORATION, 2509 Rocky Ford Rd., 31601, pg. 480 **PV**
Saft America Inc., 711 Industrial Blvd., 31601, pg. 55 **IT**

Vidalia

Standard Distributing Co., Inc., P.O. Box 1305, 30474, pg. 781 **PV**

Vienna

Formaldehyde, P.O. Box 396, 31092, pg. 737 **PB**

Villa Rica

Fairfield Plantation, 1602 Lakeview Pkwy., 30180, pg. 611 **PB**

Warner Robins

CB & T Bank of Middle Georgia, P.O. Box 2107, 31099, pg. 1549 **PB**
NavCom Defense Electronics, Inc., 626 Dunbar Rd., 31093, pg. 789 **PV**
Tampella Power Corp., P.O. Box 905, 31099, pg. 1354 **IT**

Washington

Edison Plastics Co., P.O. Box 609, 199 Edison Dr., 30673, pg. 1179 **PV**
Georgia Woodlands Railroad Co., 210 Depot St., 30673-0549, pg. 171 **PV**

Watkinsville

Dygert Seating, 7920 Macon Hwy., 30677, pg. 654 **PB**

Waycross

Bacon Grocery Co., Inc., 102 Lee Ave., 31501, pg. 596 **PV**
BIG J Super Stores, Inc., 102 Lee Ave., 31501, pg. 596 **PV**
JONES COMPANY, INC., 102 Lee Ave., 31501, pg. 596 **PV**
Kwickie/Flash Foods, Inc., 102 Lee Ave., 31501, pg. 596 **PV**
Scapa Dryer Fabrics, Inc., P.O. Box 1949, 2500 Scapa Rd., 31501, pg. 1202 **IT**
Walker-Jones Cheverolet-Buick-Oldsmobile Inc., 102 Lee Ave., 31501, pg. 596 **PV**
Waycross Molded Products, Inc., P. O. Box 58, 31501, pg. 977 **PB**
Waycross Plant, Wood Products Div., P.O. Box 1299, 31502, pg. 334 **PB**

Waynesboro

PERFECTION-SCHWANK INC., Hwy. 56 N. P.O. Box 749, 30830-0749, pg. 853 **PV**

West Point

BATSON-COOK COMPANY, 817 Fourth Ave., 31833, pg. 123 **PV**
WESTPOINT STEVENS INC., P.O. Box 71, 507 W. Tenth St., 31833, pg. 1762 **PB**

White

Marglen Yarn Plant, 3439 Hwy. 411 NE, 30184, pg. 702 **PV**

Winder

Duck Head Apparel, 220 E. Athens St., 30680, pg. 498 **PB**
Regions Bank/Barrow County, 209 N. Broad St., 30680, pg. 1371 **PB**
Southeastern Metal Processing, 509 Bankhead Hwy., 30680, pg. 1221 **PB**

Winston

Certified Food Service of Ga., Inc., 5253 Post Rd., 30187, pg. 1529 **PB**

Woodbine

Rhone-Poulenc, P.O. Box 428, 31569-0428, pg. 1109 **IT**

Wrens

Glit, P. O. Box 709, 809 Broad St., 30833-0709, pg. 944 **PB**

Zebulon

Pike Div., Route 1, Box 179-B, 30295, pg. 1599 **PB**

GUAM

Agana

Asahi Bank Guam Branch, Ste. 710, Bank of Guam Bldg., 111 Chalan Santo Papa, 96910, pg. 82 **IT**
Asahi Finance (Guam) Inc., Ste. 710, Bank of Guam Bldg., 111 Chalan Santo Papa, 96910, pg. 82 **IT**
Caere FSC Corporation, pg. 291 **PB**
Citicorp Credit, pg. 378 **PB**
Eastman Kodak Company, G.C.I.C. Building, West Soledad Avenue, 9th Fl., Ste. 906, 96910, pg. 551 **PB**
Guam Publications, Inc., P.O. Box DN, 96910, pg. 702 **PB**
Loewe Guam, Inc., 901A Pacific News Bldg., 96910, pg. 781 **IT**
Louis Vuitton Guam, Inc., P.O. Box EB, 901A Pacific News Bldg., 96910, pg. 781 **IT**
Nissan Motor Corporation in Guam, P.O. Box 726, Marine Dr., E. Agana, 96910, pg. 945 **IT**
Pacific Media, Inc., c/o Guam Publications, P.O. Box DN, 96910, pg. 702 **PB**
Shell Company (Pacific Islands) Ltd., Hi-Tech Bldg., 2nd Fl., 545 West Marine Dr., 96912, pg. 1137 **IT**
Shell Guam Inc., Hi-Tech Bldg., 2nd Fl., 545 West Marine Dr., 96910, pg. 1137 **IT**
Tektronix Foreign Sales Corporation, Bank of Hawaii Bldg., Ste. 401, 134 W. Soledad Ave., P.O. Box BF, 96910, pg. 1567 **PB**
Tokio Marine Management Inc. - Guam, P.O. Box 2980, 96910, pg. 1392 **IT**
Zurich Insurance (Guam), Inc., GCIC Bldg., Ste. 900, 414 W. Soledad Ave., 96910, pg. 1532 **IT**

Barrigada

Carrier Guam, P.O. BOX P.O. Box, Mpo, 96921-3847, pg. 1691 **PB**

Tamuning

Atkins Kroll Inc., 433 S. Marine Dr., 96911, pg. 671 **IT**
Pacificare of Guam, 231 Guerrero Dr., 96911, pg. 1251 **PB**

Tumon

Mitsukoshi (Guam) Inc., Hotel Joinus 327, San Vitores Rd., 96911, pg. 883 **IT**
S.C. Properties (Guam), Inc., Pia Resorts Hotel #803, 270 Chichirica St., 96911, pg. 1233 **IT**
United Worldwide Corporation, Young's Professional Bldg., 788 N. Marine Dr., 1st Fl., 96911, pg. 1653 **PB**

HAWAII

Aiea

Bergen Brunswig Drug Company, 99-810 Iwaena St., 96701, pg. 213 **PB**
Carrier Building Systems & Services, 99 1285 Halawa Vally Rd. A 17, 96701, pg. 1689 **PB**
Kenwood Service Corporation-Hawaii Branch, 99-994 Iwaena St., 96701, pg. 730 **IT**
Superior Coffee & Foods/Hawaii, 99-910 Iwaena St., 96701-3248, pg. 191 **PV**

Ewa Beach

Earle M. Jorgensen Company/Honolulu, 91-104 Kalaeloa Blvd., 96707, pg. 600 **PV**

Hilo

HT&T Company, Inc., P.O. Box 4190, 96720, pg. 190 **PV**

Geographic Index-U.S.

Hawaii Electric Light Co., Inc., 1200 Kilauea, 96720-1027, pg. 800 **PB**
ISEMOTO CONTRACTING CO. LTD., 648 Piilani St., 96720, pg. 575 **PV**
Mauna Loa Macadamia Nut Corporation, HC/01 Box 3, 96720, pg. 190 **PV**
Mauna Loa Orchids, Ltd., P.O. Box 4007, 96722, pg. 415 **PV**
PUNA PLANTATION HAWAII LTD., 50 E. Puainako St., 96720, pg. 895 **PV**

Honolulu

A & B Development Co. (California), 822 Bishop St., 96813, pg. 39 **PB**
A & B-Hawaii, Inc., P.O. Box 3440, 822 Bishop, 96801-3440, pg. 39 **PB**
A & B Properties, Inc., 822 Bishop St., 96813, pg. 39 **PB**
Adtech Inc., 3465 Waialae Ave., Ste. 200, 96816, pg. 208 **IT**
Air Engineering Co., Inc., 2308 Pahounui Dr., 96819, pg. 65 **PB**
Ajinomoto U.S.A., Inc., Hawaii Branch, Pacific Tower, P.O. Box 3245, 1001 Bishop St., Ste. 1330, 96801, pg. 40 **IT**
ALEXANDER & BALDWIN, INC., 822 Bishop St., 96813, pg. 39 **PB**
ALOHA AIRGROUP, INC., 371 Aokea St., 96819, pg. 44 **PV**
Aloha Airlines, Inc., Honolulu Intl. Airport, 96820, pg. 44 **PV**
Aloha Auto Auction, P.O. Box 17160, Bldg. 905, Kapalama Military Res., Sand Is. Access, 96819, pg. 1648 **PB**
Aloha Auto Auction, 1600 Kapiolani Blvd., Ste. 620, 96814, pg. 1648 **PB**
Amelco, Inc., 2308 Pahounui Dr., 96819, pg. 65 **PB**
American Electric Co., Ltd., 2308 Pahounui Dr., 96819, pg. 65 **PB**
American Insurance Agency, Inc., 900 Fort St. Mall, Ste. 500, 96813, pg. 986 **PV**
American Savings Bank, F.S.B., 915 Fort St. Mall, 96813, pg. 800 **PB**
American Security Properties, Inc., 999 Bishop St., 96813, pg. 635 **PB**
Amfac Agribusiness, Inc., 700 Bishop St., 96813, pg. 578 **PV**
Amfac/JMB Hawaii, Inc., 700 Bishop Street, 96813, pg. 577 **PV**
Amfac Sugar and Agribusiness, Inc., P.O. Box 3230, 96801, pg. 578 **PV**
ARMSTRONG PRODUCE LTD., 651 Ilalo St., 96813, pg. 83 **PV**
Asahi Breweries U.S.A., Inc., 415 S. St., #3501 Makai, 96813, pg. 83 **IT**
BHP Hawaii, Inc., 733 Bishop St., 96813, pg. 225 **IT**
BHP International Ltd., 733 Bishop St., 96813, pg. 225 **IT**
BHP South Pacific, Inc., 733 Bishop St., 96813, pg. 225 **IT**
Bancorp Investment Group, Ltd., 130 Merchant St., 96813, pg. 1248 **PB**
Bank of Hawaii, 130 Merchant St., 96813, pg. 1248 **PB**
BARNWELL INDUSTRIES, INC., 1100 Alakea, Ste. 2900, 96813, pg. 190 **PB**
C. Brewer & Company, Limited, 827 Fort St., 96813, pg. 190 **PV**
Brewer Environmental Industries, LLC, P.O. Box 48, 96810, pg. 190 **PV**
BUYCO, INC., 827 Fort St. Mall, 96813, pg. 190 **PV**
CB Bancshares, Inc. (City Bank), 201 Merchant St., 96813, pg. 1179 **PB**
CPB INC., 220 S. King St., 96813, pg. 282 **PB**
CPB Properties, Inc., 220 S. King St., 96813, pg. 283 **PB**
Carrier Pidgin, 1890 E. W. Rd., 96822-2318, pg. 1689 **PB**
Central Pacific Bank, 220 S. King St., 96813, pg. 283 **PB**
China Airlines Ltd., Honfed Tower, Ste. 1410, 1357 Kapiolani Blvd., 96814, pg. 285 **IT**
Crossroads Press, Inc., 833 Halekauwila St., 96808, pg. 19 **PV**
Theo. H. Davies & Co., Ltd, Davies Pacific Center, 841 Bishop St., Ste. 2300, 96813, pg. 704 **IT**
Theo Davies Marine Agencies, Inc., 680 Iwelei Rd., Ste. 670, 96817, pg. 704 **IT**
Dillingham Construction Pacific, Ltd., 614 Kapahulu Ave., 96812, pg. 333 **PV**
EA Engineering, Science & Technology, Inc., Hawaii Kai Corporate Plaza, 6600 Kalanianaole Hwy., Ste. 200, 96825, pg. 541 **PB**
Enerco, Inc., 733 Bishop St., 96813, pg. 225 **IT**
FH Center, Inc., 999 Bishop St., 96813, pg. 635 **PB**
FHB Properties, Inc., 999 Bishop St., 96813, pg. 635 **PB**
FHI International, Inc., 999 Bishop St., 96813, pg. 634 **PB**
FHL Lease Holding Company, Inc., Interstate Bldg., 2nd Fl., 1314 S. King St., 96814, pg. 635 **PB**
Fireman's Fund Insurance Co. of Hawaii, Inc., Grosvenor Ctr., 737 Bishop St., 96813, pg. 59 **IT**
First American Title Co. of Hawaii, Inc., 923 Nuuana Ave., 96813, pg. 625 **PB**
First Federal Savings & Loan of America, 851 Fort Street Mall, 96813, pg. 1248 **PB**
First Hawaiian Bank, 999 Bishop St., 96813, pg. 634 **PB**
First Hawaiian Capital 1, 2339 Kamehameha Hwy., 96819, pg. 635 **PB**
First Hawaiian Creditcorp, Inc., Interstate Bldg., 2nd Fl., 1314 S. King St., 96814, pg. 635 **PB**
FIRST HAWAIIAN, INC., 999 Bishop St., 96813, pg. 634 **PB**
First Hawaiian Insurance, Inc., 2339 Kamehameha Hwy., 96819, pg. 635 **PB**
First Hawaiian Leasing, Inc., Interstate Bldg., 2nd Fl., 1314 S. King St., 96814, pg. 635 **PB**

First Insurance Co. of Hawaii, Ltd., 1100 Ward Ave., 96814, pg. 1011 **PB**
Fletcher Pacific Construction Company Limited, Ocean View Centre, 707 Richards St., 96813, pg. 495 **IT**
Fuji Photo Film Hawaii, Inc., 1650 Kalakaua Ave., 96826, pg. 524 **IT**
Gasco, Inc., P.O. Box 3379, 96842, pg. 225 **IT**
HC&D Div., 2344 Pahounui Dr., 96819, pg. 99 **PB**
HEI Diversified, Inc., 900 Richards St., 96813, pg. 800 **PB**
HEI Investment Corp., 900 Richards St., 96813, pg. 800 **PB**
HEI Power Corp., P.O. Box 3160, 96802, pg. 800 **PB**
Haseko (Hawaii) Inc., Ste. 820, 820 Mililani St., 96813, pg. 600 **IT**
Haseko Realty Inc., 820 Mililani St., Ste. 820, 96813, pg. 600 **IT**
Hawaii Independent Refinery, 733 Bishop St., 96813, pg. 225 **IT**
Hawaii Newspaper Agency, Inc., 605 Kapiolani Blvd., 96813, pg. 701 **PB**
Hawaii Pizza Hut Inc., Moanalua Shopping Center, 96818-3908, pg. 704 **PB**
Hawaii Service Center, Brewer Environmental Labs., 311 Pacific St., 96817, pg. 829 **PV**
Hawaiian Advertising & Public Relations, Inc., 900 Fort St. Mall, Ste. 600, 96813, pg. 986 **PV**
HAWAIIAN AIRLINES, INC., 3375 Koapaka St., Ste. G350, 96819, pg. 799 **PB**
Hawaiian Airlines, Inc., 531 Ohohia St., 96819, pg. 799 **PB**
Hawaiian Bitumuls & Paving Company, P.O. Box 2240, 110 Puuhole St., 96804, pg. 333 **PB**
Hawaiian Dredging & Construction Company, 614 Kapahulu Ave., 96815, pg. 333 **PV**
Hawaiian Electric Company, Inc., 900 Richards St., 96813, pg. 800 **PB**
HAWAIIAN ELECTRIC INDUSTRIES, INC., 900 Richards St., 96813, pg. 799 **PB**
Hawaiian Independent Refinery, Inc., 733 Bishop St., 96813, pg. 225 **IT**
Hawaiian Pacific Elevator Company, 1268 Young St., Ste. 300, 96814, pg. 521 **PV**
Hawaiian Tug & Barge Corp., P.O. Box 3288, Pier 24, 96801, pg. 800 **PB**
Hewlett-Packard Company, Pacific Tower, Ste. 2400, 1001 Bishop St., 96813, pg. 814 **PB**
The Honolulu Advertiser, 605 Kapiolani Blvd., 96813, pg. 701 **PB**
Honolulu Fueling Facilities Corp., 1600 Kapiolani Blvd., Ste. 1300, 96814, pg. 700 **IT**
Intergraph Corporation, 2828 Paa St., Ste. 2150, 96819, pg. 891 **PB**
International In-Flight Catering Co. Ltd., Honolulu Intl. Airport, 310 Rodgers Blvd., 96819, pg. 700 **IT**
Island Air, Intl. Airport, 99 Kapalulu Pl., 96819, pg. 44 **PV**
JWG Associates, Inc., 1311 Kapiolani Blvd., Ste. 406, 96814, pg. 579 **PV**
KG (Hawaii) Corporation, 1585 Kapiolani Blvd, Ste. 1404, 96814, pg. 764 **IT**
KGMB-TV, 1534 Kapiolani Blvd., 96814, pg. 983 **PB**
KHON-TV, 1170 Auahi St., 96814, pg. 1685 **PB**
KITV, 1290 Ala Moana Blvd., 96813, pg. 926 **PB**
Kaiser Permanente, Hawaii Division, 711 Kapiolani Blvd., 96813, pg. 605 **PV**
Kanebo Cosmetics of Hawaii, Inc., Ste. 110, 1221 Kapiolani Blvd., 96814, pg. 722 **IT**
Kumagai Gumi Co., Ltd. Hawaii Branch, Ala Mona Pacific Center, 1585 Kapiolani Blvd., Ste. 1404, 96814, pg. 764 **IT**
Kumagai Properties Inc., Ala Moana Pacific Center, 1585 Kapiolani Blvd., Ste. 1404, 96814, pg. 764 **IT**
Kyotaru Restaurant, 2160 Kalakauo Ave., 96826, pg. 777 **IT**
Liberty Bank, 99 North King St., 96817, pg. 1189 **IT**
Loewe Hawaii, Inc., Ala Moana Pacific Center, P.O. Box 2690, 96845, pg. 578 **PV**
Loewe Hawaii Inc., 2255 Kuhio Ave., Ste. 1400, 96815, pg. 781 **IT**
Louis Vuitton Hawaii, Ste. 1400, 2255 Kuhio Ave., 96815, pg. 781 **IT**
Malama Pacific Corp., 915 Fort St Mall, # 702, 96813, pg. 800 **PV**
MAUI DIVERS OF HAWAII, 1520 Liona St., 96814, pg. 715 **PV**
MAUI VARIETIES, LTD., 7192 Kalanianaole Hwy., 96825, pg. 715 **PV**
MAUNA LOA MACADAMIA PARTNERS, L.P., 827 Fort St., 96813, pg. 1060 **PB**
Mauna Loa Resources Inc., 827 Fort Street, 96813, pg. 191 **PV**
Mitsukoshi (U.S.A.) Inc.-Hawaii Branch, Waikiki Trade Center 920, 2255 Kuhio Ave., pg. 883 **IT**
Molokai Ranch Ltd., 55 Merchant St., Ste. 2000, 96813, pg. 216 **IT**
MUTUAL WELDING CO., LTD., 739 Ahua, 96819, pg. 770 **PV**
Nippon Express Hawaii Inc., Waikiki Business Plaza, 2270 Kalakaua Ave., Ste. 1517, 96815-2561, pg. 934 **IT**
Nissan Motor Corporation in Hawaii, Ltd., 2881 Kilihau St., 96819, pg. 945 **IT**
Obayashi Corporation-Honolulu, 725 Kapiolani Blvd., 4th Fl., 96813, pg. 995 **IT**
Obayashi Hawaii Corporation, 725 Kapiolani Blvd., 4th Fl., 96813, pg. 995 **IT**
PACIFIC CENTURY FINANCIAL CORPORATION, 130 Merchant St., 96813, pg. 1248 **PB**
Pacific Energy Conservation Services, Inc., 900 Richards St., 96813, pg. 800 **PV**
Pacific Guardian Life Insurance, 1440 Kapiolani Blvd., Ste. 1700, 96814, pg. 854 **IT**
Pacific Home Furnishings, pg. 1465 **PV**

PENCO-Hawaii, 1164 Bishop St., Ste. 1710, 96813, pg. 1508 **IT**
PERSIS CORPORATION, 605 Kapiolani Blvd., 96813, pg. 855 **PV**
Plumbing Specialties & Supplies, Inc., 925 Kokea St., 96817, pg. 1512 **IT**
RLI/Hawaii Product Lines, Makai Tower, Ste. 1717, 733 Bishop St., 96813, pg. 1356 **PB**
Real Estate Delivery, Inc., 999 Bishop St., 96813, pg. 635 **PB**
Reed Travel Publishing-Hawaii, 1357 Kapiolani Blvd., Ste. 860, 96814, pg. 1097 **PB**
Reynolds Metals Company-Honolulu, 91-320 Komohana St., 96707, pg. 1385 **PB**
Rollins Hudig Hall of Hawaii, Inc., 1221 Kapiolani Blvd., 96814, pg. 117 **IT**
Royal Copenhagen Hawaii, Inc., 2199 Kalia Rd., 96815, pg. 1134 **IT**
SCP (Maui 5), Inc., 1440 Kapiolani Blvd., Ste. 1111, 96814, pg. 1233 **IT**
Schuman Carriage Company, P.O. Box 2420, 1234 S. Berentania St., 96804, pg. 523 **IT**
Servco Insurance Agency, Inc., 500 Fort St. Mall, Ste. 500, 96813, pg. 986 **PV**
Servco Investment Corp., 900 Fort St. Mall, Ste. 600, 96813, pg. 986 **PV**
SERVCO PACIFIC INC., 900 Fort St. Mall, Ste. 600, 96813, pg. 986 **PV**
THE SHIDLER GROUP, 810 Richard St., Ste. 1000, 96813, pg. 994 **PV**
Shiseido Company Ltd., 1516 S. King St., 96826, pg. 1235 **PV**
SunMac Hawaii, Ltd., P.O. Box 2720, 972 So. Queen St., 96803, pg. 1053 **PV**
Taco Aloha, Inc., Moanalua Shopping Center, 96818, pg. 704 **PV**
Taisei Hawaii Corp., 1600 Kapiolani Blvd., 17th Fl., 96814, pg. 1347 **IT**
Takenaka (U.S.A.) Corporation, Honolulu Office, 737 Bishop St., Ste. 1620, 96813, pg. 1351 **IT**
TERUYA BROS., LIMITED, 1276 Young St., 96814, pg. 1077 **PV**
3M Hawaii, 4443 Malaai St., 96818, pg. 1606 **PB**
Times Super Market Ltd., 2153 N. King St., 96819, pg. 1078 **PV**
Tokio Marine Management Inc. - Honolulu, Pacific Tower, 1001 Bishop St., Ste. 2970, 96813, pg. 1392 **IT**
Toshiba Hawaii, Inc., 327 Kamakee St., 96814, pg. 1405 **IT**
Towne Development Of Hawaii, Inc., 220 S. King St., Ste 680, 96813, pg. 1206 **PV**
Woodward-Clyde, 1144 Tenth Ave., Ste. 200, 96816, pg. 1656 **PB**
Y.T. Pacific Enterprises, Inc. (Bistro Icho), 930 Hauoli St., 96826, pg. 1350 **IT**
Young Brothers, Ltd., P.O. Box 3288, Pier 24, 96801, pg. 800 **PB**
Zellerbach Division, 2250 Alahao Pl., 96819-2211, pg. 1076 **PB**

Kahuku

Turtle Bay Hilton Golf & Tennis Resort, 57-091 Kamehameha Hwy., 96731, pg. 829 **PB**

Kahului

Gasco, Inc., 70 Hana Hwy., 96732, pg. 225 **IT**
Kahului Trucking & Storage, Inc., 140 Hobron Ave., 96732, pg. 39 **PB**
Maui Electric Co., Ltd., 210 W. Kamehameha Ave., 96732, pg. 800 **PB**
MAUI LAND & PINEAPPLE CO., INC., 120 Kane St., 96732, pg. 1060 **PB**
Maui Pineapple Co., Ltd., P.O. Box 187, 120 Kane St., 96732, pg. 1060 **PB**
VALLEY ISLE PRODUCE, V.I.P. FOOD SERVICE, 90 Amala Pl., 96732, pg. 1132 **PV**

Kailua

Mintech, Inc., P.O. Box 324, 25 Kaneoha Bay Dr., Ste. 106, 96734, pg. 1279 **PB**

Kailua Kona

Gasco, Inc., 74-5564 Kaiwi St., 96740, pg. 225 **IT**

Kalaheo

Hawaiian Fruit Specialties Co., Ltd., P.O. Box 637, 96741, pg. 190 **PV**

Kapaau

Kohala Joint Venture, pg. 845 **PB**

Kaunakakai

Olokele Sugar Co., Limited, P.O. Box 156, 96747, pg. 191 **PV**

Keaau

Puna Sugar Co., Ltd., P.O. Box 210, 96749, pg. 578 **PV**
SURE SAVE SUPER MARKET LTD., 16-204 Melekahiwa Pl., 96749, pg. 1056 **PV**

PB - *U.S. Public Companies Volume*
PV - *U.S. Private Companies Volume*
IT - *International Public & Private Companies Volume*

1206

Geographic Index-U.S.

Kekaha

Kekaha Sugar Company, Limited, P.O. Box AA, 96752, pg. 578 **PV**

Kihei

Four Seasons Resorts, 3900 Wailea, Alanui Dr., 96753, pg. 502 **IT**
Thermal Electron Tech. Co., 535 Lipoa Pkwy., 96753-6902, pg. 1593 **PB**

Kilauea

Kilauea Agronomics, Inc., P.O. Box 80, 96754, pg. 190 **PV**

Kunia

ICI Seeds, P.O. Box 8, 94-880 Kunia Rd., 96759, pg. 1524 **IT**

Lahaina

Amfac Property Investment Corp., 2530 Kekaa Dr., 96761, pg. 577 **PV**
Kaanapali Water Corporation, 2530 Kekaa Dr., 96761, pg. 578 **PV**
Kapalua Land Co., Ltd., 1000 Kapalua Dr., 96761, pg. 1060 **PB**
Pioneer Mill Company, Ltd., P. O. Box 727, 96761, pg. 578 **PV**

Lanai City

Lanai Co., Ltd., P.O. Box 310, 96763, pg. 313 **PB**

Lihue

The Garden Island, P.O. Box 231, 96766, pg. 1343 **PB**
Gasco, Inc., 3990 Rice St., 96766, pg. 225 **IT**
Kauai Sugar Storage Co., P.O. Box 1743, 96766, pg. 578 **PV**
The Lihue Plantation Company, Limited, P.O. Box 751, 96766, pg. 578 **PV**

Makawao

Maui Fresh Eggs, 198 Makani Rd., 96768, pg. 1132 **PV**

Pahala

Ka'u Agribusiness Co., Inc., P.O. Box 130, 96777, pg. 190 **PV**

Paia

East Maui Irrigation Co., Ltd., P. O. Box 48, 96779, pg. 39 **PB**

Papaikou

Mauna Kea Agribusiness Co., Inc., P.O. Box 15, 96781, pg. 190 **PV**

Princeville

PRINCEVILLE CORPORATION, Princeville Center, 5-4280 Kuhio Hwy., 96722, pg. 885 **PV**
Princeville Corporation, 5-4280 Kuhio Hwy., 96722, pg. 1321 **IT**
Princeville Hotel Corporation, 5520 Ka Haku Rd., 96722, pg. 885 **PV**
Princeville Management Corporation, Princeville Center, 5-4280 Kuhio Hwy., 96722, pg. 885 **PV**
Princeville Realty Corporation, Princeville Center, 5-4280 Kuhio Hwy., 96722, pg. 885 **PV**
Princeville Utilities Company, Inc., Princeville Center, 5-4280 Kuhio Hwy., 96722, pg. 885 **PV**

Puhi

Kauai Commercial Company, Inc., 1811 Leleiona St., 96766, pg. 39 **PB**

Puunene

Hawaiian Commercial & Sugar Co., P.O. Box 266, 96784, pg. 39 **PB**

Wahiawa

Dole Hawaii, 1116 Whitmore, 96786, pg. 515 **PB**

Wailuku

Wailuku Agribusiness Co., Inc., P.O. Box 520, 96793, pg. 191 **PV**

Waipahu

BetterBrands, Ltd., 94-501 Kau St., 96797, pg. 1202 **PV**
Redondo's Inc., 94-140 Leokane St., 96797, pg. 936 **IT**
Waiahole Irrigation Co., Ltd., P.O. Box O, 96797, pg. 578 **PV**

IDAHO

Boise

ALBERTSON'S, INC., 250 Parkcenter Blvd., 83706, pg. 38 **PB**
AMERICAN ECOLOGY CORPORATION, 805 W. Idaho St., Ste. 200, 83702-8916, pg. 71 **PB**
BCC Mexico, S.A. de C.V., P.O. Box 50, 1111 W. Jefferson St., 83728, pg. 243 **PB**
BCT, Inc., One Jefferson Sq., P.O. Box 50, 83728, pg. 243 **PB**
Bank of America Idaho, 208 S. Capitol Blvd., 83701, pg. 180 **PB**
Bergen Brunswig Medical Corporation, 300 N. Sailfish Pl., 83704, pg. 214 **PB**
Boise Cascade Asia Ltd., P.O. Box 50, 1111 W. Jefferson St., 83728, pg. 243 **PB**
Boise Cascade Building Materials Distribution Div., 1111 W. Jefferson St., 83728, pg. 243 **PB**
BOISE CASCADE CORPORATION, P.O. Box 50, 1111 W. Jefferson St., 83728, pg. 242 **PB**
Boise Cascade Paper Div., 1111 W. Jefferson St., 83728-1414, pg. 243 **PB**
Boise Cascade Timber & Wood Products Division, 1111 W. Jefferson St., 83702, pg. 243 **PB**
Boise Park Suites, 424 E. Park Ctr. Blvd., 83706, pg. 1537 **PB**
Browning-Ferris Industries of Idaho, Inc., 117 E. 37th, 83714, pg. 263 **PB**
Clearfield Insurance, Ltd., One Jefferson Sq., P.O. Box 50, 83728, pg. 243 **PB**
Community Psychiatric Centers of Idaho, Inc., 303 N. Allumbaugh St., 83704, pg. 1712 **PB**
Computrol, Inc., 499 E. Corporate Dr., 83642, pg. 83 **PV**
Contractor Equipment Supply Company (CESCO), 2049 Commerce St., pg. 673 **PV**
Cuban Electric Co., One Jefferson Sq., P.O. Box 50, 83728, pg. 243 **PB**
Ebasint International, Inc., One Jefferson Sq., P.O. Box 50, 83728, pg. 243 **PB**
Emmett Power Company, One Jefferson Sq., P.O. Box 50, 83728, pg. 243 **PB**
Environmental/Government Group, P.O. Box 73, 83729, pg. 1134 **PV**
EvansGroup Technology, Union Block Bldg., 720 W. Idaho St., 83702, pg. 385 **PV**
First American Title Co. of Idaho, 7311 Potomac Dr., 83704, pg. 625 **PB**
First Interstate Bank of Idaho, N.A., 877 W. Main St., 83702, pg. 1753 **PB**
First Security Bank of Idaho, N.A., 119 N. Ninth St., 83702, pg. 637 **PB**
Heavy Civil Construction, P.O. Box 22, 83729, pg. 1134 **PV**
Hewlett Packard-Boise, P.O. Box 15, 83707-0015, pg. 816 **PB**
Hillcrest Health Care, Inc., 1093 S. Hilton, 83705, pg. 1713 **PB**
IBP-Boise, P.O. Box 9346, 83707, pg. 852 **PB**
Ida-West Energy Company, 199 Shoreline Ln., Ste. 310, 83702, pg. 862 **PV**
IGI Resources, Inc., 300 Mallard Dr., Ste. 350, 83706, pg. 568 **PV**
IDACORP, INC., P.O. Box 7123, 83707, pg. 862 **PV**
Idaho Energy Resources Co., 1220 W. Idaho St., 83707, pg. 862 **PV**
IDAHO POWER COMPANY, 1221 W. Idaho St., 83702-5627, pg. 861 **PB**
Idaho Power Resources Corp., 1220 W. Idaho St., 83707, pg. 862 **PB**
The Idaho Statesman, 1200 N. Curtis Rd., 83707, pg. 701 **PB**
Idaho Utility Products Company, 1220 W. Idaho St., 83707, pg. 862 **PB**
Intermountain Gas Co., 555 S. Cole Rd., 83709, pg. 568 **PB**
INTERMOUNTAIN INDUSTRIES, INC., 555 S. Cole Rd., 83709, pg. 568 **PV**
International Infrastructure Division, P.O. Box 73, 83729, pg. 1134 **PB**
JPB General Placerville Corporation, P.O. Box 50, 1111 W. Jefferson St., 83728, pg. 243 **PB**
Jefferson Square, Inc., P.O. Box 50, 1111 W. Jefferson St., 83728, pg. 243 **PB**
Kettle Falls Limestone Company, P.O. Box 50, One Jefferson Sq., 83728, pg. 243 **PB**
Key Bank of Idaho, P.O. Box 2557, 702 W. Idaho St., 83701, pg. 954 **PB**
Kuna Corporation, P.O. Box 50, One Jefferson Sq., 83728, pg. 243 **PB**
LB INDUSTRIES INC., 1401 Shoreline Dr., 83701, pg. 639 **PV**
Lamb-Weston, 3100 Vista, Ste. 110, 83706, pg. 427 **PB**
Micron Communications, Inc., 3176 S. Denver Way, 83705, pg. 1105 **PB**
Micron Systems Integration, Inc., 7560 S. Federal Way, 83716, pg. 1105 **PB**
MICRON TECHNOLOGY INC., P.O. Box 6, 8000 S. Federal Way, 83707-0006, pg. 1105 **PB**
MORRISON KNUDSEN CORPORATION, Morrison Knudsen Plaza, 720 Park Blvd., 83712, pg. 1133 **PB**
NASHUA HOMES OF IDAHO INC., 5200 Federal Way, 83707, pg. 774 **PV**
Norco Windows, Inc., 200 E. Mallard Dr., 83706, pg. 1556 **PB**
Ore-Ida Foods, Inc., 220 W. Parkcenter Blvd., 83706, pg. 805 **PB**

Orient Mining Company, One Jefferson Sq., P.O. Box 50, 83728, pg. 243 **PB**
PETERSON MOTOR COMPANY, 9101 W. Fairview, 83704, pg. 857 **PV**
Piper Jaffray Inc., 1161 River St., Ste. 340, 83702-7065, pg. 1301 **PB**
Rogers Brothers Seed Company, 1755 Westgate Dr., #100, 83704, pg. 974 **IT**
Rogers N.K. Seed Co., 900 N. Armstrong Pl., 83704, pg. 974 **IT**
J.R. SIMPLOT COMPANY, 999 Main St., Ste. 1300, 83702, pg. 1002 **PV**
J.R. Simplot Company Food Group, P.O. Box 9386, 83707, pg. 1002 **PV**
Stellar Dynamics, 1220 W. Idaho St., 83707, pg. 862 **PB**
SUNSHINE MINING AND REFINING COMPANY, 877 W. Main St., Ste. 600, 83702, pg. 1536 **PB**
Sysco Food Services of Idaho, Inc., 5710 Pan Am Ave., 83705, pg. 1551 **PB**
TJ INTERNATIONAL, INC., 200 E. Mallard Dr., 83706, pg. 1556 **PB**
III Exploration Co., P.O. Box 7608, 555 S. Cole Rd., 83707, pg. 568 **PV**
Trus Joist MacMillan, 200 E. Mallard, 83706, pg. 1556 **PB**
U.S. Bank Financial Services, Inc., 101 S. Capital Blvd., 83733, pg. 1681 **PB**
U.S. Bank of Idaho, 101 Capitol Blvd., 83702, pg. 1681 **PB**
Voyageur Panel Limited, P.O. Box 50, 1111 W. Jefferson St., 83728, pg. 243 **PB**
WAREMART INC., 8590 Fairview Ave., 83704, pg. 1150 **PV**
Willis Corroon Corp. of Idaho, First Interstate Ctr., 877 Main St., Ste. 700, 83702, pg. 1506 **IT**
Zellerbach Division, 101 N. Cole Rd., 83704, pg. 1075 **PB**

Buhl

CLEAR SPRINGS FOODS, INC., P.O. Box 712, 83316, pg. 245 **PV**
Rangen Aquaculture Research, 115 13th Ave., S., 83316, pg. 909 **PV**
RANGEN, INC., 115 13th Ave., S., 83316, pg. 909 **PV**
Reed Brothers Inc., P.O. Box 472, 83316, pg. 916 **PV**
REED GRAIN & BEAN COMPANY, Ninth & Elm, 83316, pg. 916 **PV**

Burley

Black Pine Mine, P.O. Box 578, 83318, pg. 1269 **PB**

Caldwell

THE CAXTON PRINTERS LTD., 312 Main St., 83605, pg. 220 **PV**
M1 KIT Mfg. Co., P.O. Box 250, 1124 Garber St., 83606, pg. 962 **PV**
Manufactured Housing Div., P.O. Box 990, 412 Kit Ave., 83606, pg. 962 **PV**
R-2 KIT Mfg. Co., P.O. Box 1420, 412 Kit Ave., 83606, pg. 962 **PV**
Recreational Vehicle Div., P.O. Box 990, 412 Kit Ave., 83606, pg. 962 **PV**
J.R. Simplot Co.-Diversified Products Group, 223 Rodeo Ave., 83605, pg. 1002 **PV**

Challis

Grouse Creek Unit, P.O. Box 647, 83226, pg. 804 **PB**

Coeur D'Alene

ADVANCED INPUT DEVICES, INC., W. 250 A I D Dr., 83815, pg. 21 **PV**
Bank of America, 401 Front St., 83814, pg. 180 **PB**
Callahan Mining Corporation, P.O. Box I, 83816, pg. 394 **PB**
COEUR D'ALENE MINES CORPORATION, 505 Front Ave., 83814, pg. 394 **PB**
Coeur Explorations, Inc., 505 Front Ave., 83814, pg. 394 **PB**
Coeur International Inc., 505 Front Ave., 83814, pg. 394 **PB**
EMPIRE AIRLINES, 2115 Government Way, 83814, pg. 374 **PV**
HECLA MINING COMPANY, 6500 Mineral Dr., 83814-8788, pg. 803 **PB**
IDAHO FOREST INDUSTRY, INC., 2850 Seltice Way, 83814, pg. 556 **PV**
Kvaerner EnviroPower, Inc., 2880 Packsaddle Dr., 83814, pg. 770 **IT**
Pinnacle Exploration, Inc., 505 Front Ave., 83814, pg. 394 **PB**

Firth

IDAHO SUPREME COMPANY, 614 E. 800 N. St., 83236, pg. 557 **PV**

Fruitland

WOODGRAIN MILLWORK, P.O. Box 369, 83619, pg. 1187 **PV**

Grand View

J.R. Simplot Company-Agriculture Group, HC85, Box 275, 83624, pg. 1002 **PV**

PB - *U.S. Public Companies Volume*
PV - *U.S. Private Companies Volume*
IT - *International Public & Private Companies Volume*

Geographic Index-U.S.

1207

Geographic Index-U.S.

Hayden Lake

Louisiana Pacific Northern Div., P.O. Box 4000-98, 83835, pg. 1015   **PB**

Hazelton

Conida Farms, P.O. Box 128, 83335, pg. 693   **PV**

Idaho Falls

AmeriSource-Idaho Falls Div., 935 Lincoln Rd., 83401, pg. 97   **PB**
ELECTRICAL WHOLESALE SUPPLY COMPANY, INC., P.O. Box 2147, 1990 Rollandet Ave., 83403, pg. 368   **PV**
Hewlett-Packard Company, 1830 E. 17th St., Ste. A, 83401, pg. 814   **PB**
INDUSTRIAL CONSTRUCTION, INC., 5345 S. Heyrend Cir., 83402, pg. 560   **PV**
Penford Products, 1088 W. Sunnyside Rd., 83402, pg. 1269   **PB**
Piper Jaffray Inc., 506 S. Woodruff Ave., 83401-5298, pg. 1301   **PB**

Inkom

Ash Grove Cement-Western Region Cement Plant, 230 Cement Rd., 83245, pg. 88   **PV**

Kellogg

Sunshine Precious Metals, Inc., P.O. Box 1080, pg. 1536   **PB**

Kendrick

GEORGE F. BROCKE & SONS, INC., First St. & Brown, 83537, pg. 170   **PV**
Potlatch Telephone Company, P.O. Box 138, 702 E. Main, 83537, pg. 1571   **PB**
Troy Telephone Co., Inc., 702 E. Main, 83537, pg. 1572   **PB**

Ketchum

SCOTT SPORTS GROUP, 110 Lewis St., 83340, pg. 977   **PV**
Scott U.S.A., 110 Lewis St., 83340, pg. 977   **PV**
Sun Valley Cablevision, Inc., P.O. Box 537, 83340, pg. 1553   **PB**

Laclede

RILEY CREEK LUMBER COMPANY, Riley Creek Rd., 83841, pg. 931   **PV**

Lewiston

Blount, Inc. Sporting Equipment Group, 2299 Snake River Ave., 83501, pg. 238   **PB**
St. Maries River Railroad, P.O. Box 1016, 83501, pg. 1318   **PB**

Lewisville

IDAHOAN FOODS, One Potato Place, 83431, pg. 557   **PV**

McCall

Stibnite Mine, 114 N. 3rd St., 83638, pg. 477   **PB**

Meridian

Canfor U.S.A. Corporation, P.O. Box 674, 83642, pg. 260   **IT**
Davco Service, Inc., 225 N. Meridian Rd., 83641, pg. 673   **PV**
Ecodyne Cooling Tower Services, 435 E. Washington Ave., 83642-1730, pg. 29   **PB**
Elixir Industries, 501 N. Eagle Rd., 83642, pg. 371   **PV**
Farm Store No. 1, 1626 E. First St., P.O. Box 270, 83642, pg. 1039   **PV**

Mullan

Lucky Friday Unit, Interstate Hwy. 90, 83846, pg. 804   **PB**

Nampa

Amalgamated Sugar Co., P.O. Box 87, 83653, pg. 48   **PV**
Browning-Ferris Industries of Idaho, Inc., P.O. Box Q, 83653, pg. 263   **PB**
Idaho Independent Television, Inc., P.O. Box 1211, 83651, pg. 147   **PV**
Micron Custom Manufacturing Services, Inc., 16399 Franklin Rd., 83687, pg. 1105   **PB**
Micron Electronics, Inc., 900 E. Karcher Rd., 83687, pg. 1105   **PB**
Selkirk Metalbestos N.A., 1820 E. Fargo, 83687, pg. 1794   **PB**
Union Seed Co., Four Ninth Ave. S., 83651, pg. 646   **PV**

Paul

Amalgamated Sugar Co., P.O. Box 700, 83347, pg. 48   **PV**

Payette

American Fine Foods, Inc., 25 N. 6th St., P.O. Box 460, 83661, pg. 349   **PB**

Pocatello

American Microsystems, Inc., 2300 Buckskin Rd., 83201, pg. 702   **IT**
COWBOY OIL COMPANY, 2700 S. Fifth Ave., 83205, pg. 280   **PV**
Medical Innovations Corp., 1999 Alvin Ricken Dr., 83201, pg. 171   **PB**
Piper Jaffray Inc., 353 N. Fourth Ave., Ste. 110, 83201-6391, pg. 1302   **PB**

Post Falls

Harpers Manufacturing, 1500 W. Seltice Way, 83854, pg. 957   **PB**
Harpers Sales, 1500 W. Seltice Way, 83854, pg. 957   **PB**
Hauser Lake Lumber Operation, Inc., W. 4750 Prairie Ave., 83854, pg. 652   **PB**

Rexburg

MWCA, 4212 S. Hwy. 191, 83440, pg. 804   **PB**

Rupert

MAGIC VALLEY FOODS, INC., Hwy. 24 & Hwy. 25, 83350, pg. 695   **PV**

Sandpoint

COLDWATER CREEK, One Coldwater Creek Dr., 83864, pg. 396   **PB**

Shelley

Idaho Potato Opers., 434 S. Emerson, 83274, pg. 411   **IT**

Twin Falls

Amalgamated Sugar Co., P.O. Box 127, 83303, pg. 48   **PV**
Haney Seed Co., 347 S. Park Ave. W., 83303, pg. 428   **PV**
Longview Fibre Co. Western Container Div., 348 S. Park Ave. W., 83303, pg. 1014   **PB**
Piper Jaffray Inc., 233 Second St. N., 83303, pg. 1301   **PB**
ScottPolar Corporation, 502 Madrona St., 83303-0048, pg. 1400   **IT**

Weiser

Tamarack Homes Div., P.O. Box 190, Rte. #3, 83672, pg. 332   **PB**

ILLINOIS

Abbott Park

Abbott Chemical & Agricultural Products Division, One Abbott Park Rd., 60064-3500, pg. 13   **PB**
Abbott International Div., One Abbott Park Rd., 60064-3500, pg. 13   **PB**
ABBOTT LABORATORIES, 100 Abbott Park Rd., 60064-3500, pg. 13   **PB**
Abbott Laboratories, One Abbott Park Rd., 60064-3500, pg. 13   **PB**
Abbott Pharmaceutical Products Division, One Abbott Park Rd., 60064-3500, pg. 13   **PB**
CMM Transportation Inc., One Abbott Park Rd., 60064-3500, pg. 13   **PB**

Addison

Akzo Resins & Vehicles, 150 So. Fairbank St., 60101, pg. 48   **IT**
Avent America Inc., 1765 W. Courtland Ct., Unit L, 60101, pg. 261   **IT**
Citizens Utilities Company of Illinois, 315 S. Stewart Ave., 60101, pg. 380   **PB**
Claire Manufacturing Co., 500 Vista Ave., 60101, pg. 504   **PV**
DeVRY Institute of Technology, 1221 Swift Rd., 60101, pg. 346   **PV**
Dukane CSDIT Div., 780 W. Belden Ave., 60101, pg. 346   **PV**
Escast, Inc., 21 No. Church St., 60101, pg. 612   **PB**
FENTON PRESS, INC., 1544 Wrightwood Ct., 60101, pg. 400   **PV**
Film Products Division, 712 Winthrop, 60101, pg. 707   **PB**
Fischer Imaging Corporation, RMS Manufacturing Division, 2301 Windsor Ct., 60101, pg. 647   **PB**
Gingiss Formalwear, Inc., 2101 Executive Dr., 60101, pg. 455   **PV**
GINGISS INTERNATIONAL, 2101 Executive Dr., 60101, pg. 455   **PV**
Italtractor America Inc., 1208 Capitol Dr., 60101, pg. 654   **IT**
Lawson Products, Inc., pg. 980   **PB**

LeaRonal, Inc., 1717 Armitage Court, 60101, pg. 982   **PB**
Littell, 145 N. Swift Rd., 60101-1447, pg. 862   **IT**
Liuski International Illinois, Inc., 936 Fullerton Ave., 60101, pg. 1005   **PB**
MAGNECO/METREL, INC., 223 Interstate Rd., 60101, pg. 695   **PV**
MINERALLAC CO., 466 Vista Ave., 60101, pg. 750   **PV**
Minuteman International, Inc., 111 S. Rohlwing Rd., 60101, pg. 587   **PB**
Mitsubishi Engine North America Inc. (MENA), 1250 Green Briar Dr., 60101, pg. 874   **IT**
Mulay Plastics Inc., Ten Laura Dr., 60101, pg. 344   **PV**
OVERTON GEAR & TOOL CORP., 530 Westgate Dr., 60101, pg. 823   **PV**
THE PAMPERED CHEF, LTD., 350 S. Rohling Rd., 60101, pg. 835   **PV**
Sprayway, Inc., 484 Vista Ave., 60101, pg. 462   **PV**
Subaru Mid-America, Inc., 301 Mitchell Court, 60101, pg. 523   **IT**
VIL, 145 N. Swift Rd., 60101-1447, pg. 862   **IT**
VICTOR TECHNOLOGY, 780 W. Beldon Ave., 60101, pg. 1139   **PV**
Wing Industries North Central, 775 Belden Ave. #D, 60101, pg. 1183   **PV**

Albion

Champion Laboratories, Inc., 200 S. Fourth St., 62806, pg. 1113   **PV**
Luber-Finer, Inc., S. 4th St., 62806, pg. 1113   **PV**

Alsip

ARDCO, INC., 12400 S. Laramie Ave., 60658, pg. 80   **PV**
Bunzl Packaging Consultants Inc., 6051 W. 115th St., 60482, pg. 233   **IT**
Chisholm, Boyd & White Co., 4101 W. 126th St., 60658, pg. 1136   **PV**
Crown Cork & Seal Company, Inc.-Corporate Technologies, William J. Avery Tech. Ctr., 11535 S. Central Ave., 60482-2523, pg. 463   **PB**
Custom Food Products Inc., 5145 W. 123rd St., 60803, pg. 448   **PV**
Dings Magnetic Co., 4101 W. 126th St., 60658, pg. 1136   **PV**
GRIFFITH LABORATORIES WORLDWIDE, INC., One Griffith Ctr., 60803, pg. 481   **PV**
Ideal School Supply Company, 5623 W. 115th St., 60482, pg. 288   **PV**
Lombard Architectural Precast Prod. Co, 4245 W. 123rd. St., 60803, pg. 673   **PV**
LOMBARD COMPANY, 4245 W. 123rd St., 60803, pg. 673   **PV**
MARTIN EXPLORATION MANAGEMENT COMPANY, 4501 W. 127th St., 60803, pg. 709   **PV**
Scientific Dust Collectors, 4101 W. 126th St., 60658, pg. 1136   **PV**
Thermal Industries Inc., 12559 S. Springfield Ave., 60658-1408, pg. 491   **PV**
Tri-Can International, Ltd., 12828 Ridgeway Ave., 60658, pg. 1022   **PB**
Tuthill Pump, 12500 S. Pulaski Rd., 60658, pg. 1111   **PV**
Ulbrich of Illinois, Inc., 12340 S. Laramie, 60658, pg. 1115   **PV**
Van Leer Containers, Inc., 4300 W. 130th St., 60803, pg. 1146   **IT**

Alton

Alton Telegraph, 111 E. Broadway, 62002, pg. 934   **PB**
Laclede - Alton Plant, P.O. Box 2576, 62002, pg. 974   **PB**
Millers Classified Insurance Company, 111 E. Fourth St., 62002, pg. 748   **PV**
MILLERS MUTUAL INSURANCE ASSN., 111 E. Fourth St., 62002, pg. 748   **PV**
MISSISSIPPI LIME CO., Seven Alby St., 62002, pg. 753   **PV**
D.R. Sparks Insurance Services, Inc., 111 E. Fourth St., 62002-9006, pg. 748   **PV**

Antioch

Quaker Industries, 90 McMillen Rd., 60002-1845, pg. 1259   **PB**

Arcola

Collegiate Cap and Gown, 901 Bob King Dr., 61910, pg. 523   **PV**

Argo

Argo Terminal, 8500 W. 68th St., 60501, pg. 692   **PB**
Corn Products North America Div., 6500 Archer Rd., 60501, pg. 448   **PB**

Arlington Heights

Adams Business Media, 2101 S. Arlington Hgts., Ste. 150, 60005, pg. 16   **PV**
AMCOL INTERNATIONAL CORP., One N. Arlington, 1500 W. Shure Dr., 60004, pg. 63   **PB**
American Business Information Marketing, 2101 S. Arlington Heights Rd., 60005, pg. 70   **PV**
American Colloid Company, 1500 Shure Dr., 60004, pg. 63   **PB**
Amersham Corporation, 2636 S. Clearbrook Dr., 60005, pg. 992   **IT**

PB - *U.S. Public Companies Volume*
PV - *U.S. Private Companies Volume*
IT - *International Public & Private Companies Volume*

1208

Amersham Corporation (Amersham QSA), 2636 S. Clearbrook Dr., 60005, pg. 992   IT

Amersham Healthcare, 2636 S. Clarebrook Dr., 60005, pg. 992   IT

Amersham Life Science, Inc., 2636 S. Clearbrook Dr., 60005, pg. 992   IT

Ampco Metal, Inc., 1117 E. Algonquin Rd., 60005, pg. 67   PV

Barnes & Reinecke, Inc., 425 E. Algonquin Rd., 60005, pg. 49   PB

Celnor, Inc., 1501 W. Shrue Dr., 60004, pg. 1137   PB

Colloid Environmental Technologies Company (CETCO), 1350 W. Shure Dr., 60004, pg. 64   PB

Composites Distribution Corp., 723 W. Algonquin Rd., 60006, pg. 435   PV

Daewoo International America Corp. - Chicago, Sears Towers, 3206 N. Kennicat Ave., 60004, pg. 357   IT

GLS CORPORATION, 723 W. Algonquin Rd., 60006, pg. 435   PV

Hamer Guitars, 835 W. University, 60004, pg. 942   PB

THE HASSINGER COMPANIES HOFFMAN HOMES, 330 East Algonquin, Ste. 3, 2nd Fl., 60005, pg. 510   PV

Intergraph Corporation, 85 W. Algonquin Rd., 60005, pg. 891   PB

Iowa Cellular Communications, Inc., 1501 W. Shure Dr., 60004, pg. 1137   PB

Kuwait Airways, Central USA, Ste. 107, 2015 So. Arlington Heights Rd., 60005, pg. 764   IT

MARKET FACTS, INC., 3040 W. Salt Creek Ln., 60005, pg. 1046   PB

Mitsumi Electronics Corp., 2101 S. Arlington Hts. Rd., Ste. 117, 60005, pg. 884   IT

Modar Communications, Inc., 1501 W. Shure Dr., 60004, pg. 1137   PB

Montana Minerals Development Corp., One North Arlington, 1500 W. Shure Dr., 60004, pg. 64   PB

Motorola Cellular Service, Inc. (California), 1501 W. Shure Dr., 60004, pg. 1138   PB

Motorola Cellular Service, Inc. (Illinois), 1501 W. Shure Dr., 60004, pg. 1138   PB

Motorola Multimedia Group, 3436 N. Kennicott, Ste. 150, 60004, pg. 1137   PB

Motorola PCS, Inc., 1475 W. Shure Dr., 60004, pg. 1138   PB

Motorola Recovery Service, Inc., 1501 W. Shure Dr., 60004, pg. 1138   PB

Nakano Foods Inc., 415 W. Golf Rd., Ste. 55, 60005, pg. 883   IT

Nanocor, Inc., 1500 W. Shore Dr., 60004, pg. 64   PB

Network Ventures Long Distance Mexico Holdings, Inc., 1501 W. Shure Dr., 60004, pg. 1138   PB

Network Ventures I, Inc., 1501 W. Shure Dr., 60004, pg. 1138   PB

Network Ventures Telecom Mexico, Inc., 1501 W. Shure Dr., 60004, pg. 1138   PB

Network Ventures II, Inc., 1501 W. Shure Dr., 60004, pg. 1138   PB

Omni Capital Partners, Inc., 1475 W. Shure Dr., 60004, pg. 1138   PB

Pace, 550 W. Algonquin Rd., 60005, pg. 919   PV

PADDOCK PUBLICATIONS, INC., P.O. Box 280, 60006, pg. 833   PV

Quebecor Printing Arlington Heights, 59 W. Seegers Rd., 60005, pg. 1076   PB

RP alpha/Chicago, 3105 N. Wilke Rd., Ste. U, 60004, pg. 950   PV

Shimizu America Corporation-Chicago Office, 2101 S. Arlington, Heights Rd., Ste. 135, 60005, pg. 1233   IT

Symbol, 709 W. Algonquin Rd., 60005, pg. 1546   PB

TIE Systems, Inc. Illinois, 719 W. Algonquin, 60005, pg. 1085   PV

Wabash National Finance Corp., 9 N. Vail Ave., 60005, pg. 1730   PB

WEBER MARKING SYSTEMS, INC., 711 W. Algonquin Rd., 60008, pg. 1157   PV

Arthur

New Progress, 402 E. Progress St., 61911, pg. 1066   PV

Assumption

THE GSI GROUP, INC., 1004 E. Illinois St., 62510, pg. 436   PV

Aurora

Allsteel, Inc., Allsteel Dr., 60507, pg. 772   PB

Aurora National Bank, Two S. Broadway, 60505, pg. 760   PB

The Beacon-News, 101 S. River St., 60506, pg. 275   PV

Bernina of America Inc., 3500 Thayer Ct., 60504-6182, pg. 189   IT

Change-O-Matic/Wesco, 1266 S. Orchard Rd., 60507, pg. 1039   PV

Eby-Brown Co., 1001 Sullivan Rd., 60506, pg. 359   PV

FIRST ALERT, INC., 3901 Liberty St. Rd., 60504, pg. 406   PV

GREATBANC, INC., 105 East Galena Blvd., 60505, pg. 760   PB

GreatBanc Trust Company, 105 E. Galena Blvd., Ste. 500, 60505, pg. 760   PB

Harper-Wyman Co., 3600 Thayer Ct., Ste. 110, 60504, pg. 1209   PB

Harris Bank Aurora, N.A., 1252 N. Lake St., 60507, pg. 154   IT

KNOMARK, INC., 328 Gale St., 60506, pg. 627   PV

L & D GROUP, 1225 Corporate Blvd., Ste. 103, 60504, pg. 638   PV

Luwa Filter Corp., 401 Hankes Ave., 60505, pg. 617   PV

McKee Door, Inc., 1941 Selmarten Dr., 60507, pg. 69   PB

NICOR Technologies, P.O. Box 3014, 60566-7014, pg. 1183   PB

PENCO-Illinois, 75 Executive Dr., Ste. 106, 60504, pg. 1508   PV

PETCARE PLUS, INC., 700 N. Commerce Dr., 60504-8174, pg. 856   PV

Henry Pratt Co., 401 S. Highland, 60504, pg. 1651   PB

RONEY OTMAN, 735 Prairie St., 60506, pg. 943   PV

Solar Communications, 611 N. Enterprise, 60504, pg. 1012   PV

SPECIALTY EQUIPMENT COMPANIES INC., 1245 Corporate Blvd., Ste. 401, 60504, pg. 1496   PB

SUCCESSORIES, INC., 2520 Deal Rd., 60504, pg. 1049   PV

WIL-FREDS INC., 274 E. Indian Trail, 60505, pg. 1176   PV

Willis Corroon Administrative Services Corporation, 1187 N. Farnsworth, Ste. 1C, 60505, pg. 1504   IT

Willis Corroon Corp. of Illinois, P.O. Box 951, 540 W. Galena Blvd., 60507, pg. 1506   IT

Bannockburn

The Balcor Company, 2355 Waukegan Rd., 60015, pg. 74   PB

Brunswick Bicyles Div., 2275 Half Day Rd., 60015, pg. 265   PB

IMC GLOBAL, 2345 Waukegan Rd., Ste. 200, 60015, pg. 856   PB

Barrington

AETNA PLYWOOD, INC., 104 S. Wynstone Park Dr., 60010, pg. 25   PV

BMW Credit Corp., 600 N. Hard Road, 60010, pg. 177   IT

BMW Leasing Corp., 600 N. Hart Road, 60010, pg. 177   IT

CAI, 550 W. Northwest Hwy., 60010, pg. 914   PV

Harris Bank Barrington, N.A., 201 S. Grove Ave., 60010, pg. 154   IT

National School Bus Service, 18-4 E. Dundee Rd., Ste. 103, 60010, pg. 1213   IT

PARK FOODS L.P., 511 Lake Zurich Rd., 60010, pg. 839   PV

RECON/OPTICAL, INC., 550 W. Northwest Hwy., 60010, pg. 914   PV

ROSE PACKING COMPANY, 65 S. Barrington Rd., 60010, pg. 945   PV

Standard Register-Barrington, 700 W. Main St., 60010, pg. 1505   PB

Bartlett

Flexonics OEM Products, 300 E. Devon Ave., 60103, pg. 1222   IT

Harris Bank Bartlett, 335 S. Main St., 60103, pg. 154   IT

Senior Flexonics Inc., 300 E. Devon Ave., 60103, pg. 1222   IT

Batavia

ALDI FOOD INC., 1200 N. Kirk Rd., 60510, pg. 33   PV

American Natl. Can Co., 475 N. Kirk Rd., 60510, pg. 1029   IT

Ball Publishing, 335 N. River St., 60510, pg. 188   PV

Harris Bank Batavia, N.A., 155 W. Wilson St., 60510, pg. 154   IT

Jiffy Products of America, Inc., 951 Swanson Dr., 60510-4202, pg. 706   PV

Sealy Mattress Company of Illinois, 1030 Fabyan Pkwy., 60510, pg. 979   PB

Watlow Batavia, Inc., 1310 Kingsland Dr., 60510, pg. 1153   PV

Bedford Park

Absorbent Manufacturing & Technology, Inc., 6650 Oak Park Ave., 60638, pg. 546   PB

American Bank Note Company, 5858 W. 73rd St., 60638, pg. 68   PB

American Natl. Can Co., 7300 S. Narragansett, 60638, pg. 1029   IT

Argo Terminal Co., 8800 W. 71st St., 60638, pg. 435   PV

Beaut-Ease Corporation, 5401 W. 65th St., 60638, pg. 551   PV

The Belt Railway Co. of Chicago, 6900 S. Central Ave., 60638, pg. 284   PB

CHEMCENTRAL/Chicago, 7050 W. 71st St., 60638, pg. 232   PV

CHEMCENTRAL CORPORATION, 7050 W. 71st St., 60638, pg. 231   PV

Commercial Forged Products, 5757 W. 65th St., 60638-5584, pg. 1192   PV

CORN PRODUCTS INTERNATIONAL, INC., 6500 S. Archer Rd., 60501, pg. 447   PB

CORRUGATED METALS, INC., 6520 S. Cicero, 60638, pg. 277   PV

GATX Logistics, Inc.-Illinois (Honda), 6220 W. 73rd St., 60638, pg. 691   PB

GOODMAN EQUIPMENT CORP., 5430 W. 70th Pl., 60638, pg. 464   PV

HELLER SEASONINGS & INGREDIENTS, INC., P.O. Box 128, 60499, pg. 520   PV

Improved Blow Molding Equipment Company, Inc., 5430 W. 70th Pl., 60638, pg. 464   PV

Leggett & Platt, Inc., 7200 S. Mason Ave., 60499, pg. 985   PB

Pro Shop (Chicago, IL), 6733 W. 73rd St., 60638, pg. 861   PV

Rexam Release, 5001 W. 66th St., 60638, pg. 1107   IT

United States Aluminum Corp.-Illinois, 6969 W. 73rd St., 60638, pg. 895   PB

Beecher

Dovatech, Ltd., 449 W. Corning Rd., 60401, pg. 520   PB

Belleville

Belleville News-Democrat, P.O. Box 427, 62222-0427, pg. 964   PB

FKG Oil Company, 721 Main, 62220, pg. 764   PV

Illinois-American Water Co., P.O. Box 24040, 300 N. Water Works Dr., 62223-9040, pg. 95   PB

Magna Bank, St. Clair Region, 222 E. Main St., 62222, pg. 1037   PB

MARSH COMPANY, 707 East B, 62221, pg. 707   PV

MOTO, INC., 721 W. Main, 62222, pg. 764   PV

Bellwood

American Natl. Can Co., Graphic Arts Div., 2400 Maywood Dr., 60104, pg. 1029   IT

Berol Inc., 2711 Washington Blvd., 60104, pg. 1177   PB

Handschy Industries, 120 25th Ave., 60104, pg. 403   PV

Lawson Mardon Flexible Packaging, Inc., 5303 St. Charles Rd., 60104, pg. 67   IT

RMT Technology, 435 Eastern Ave., 60104, pg. 927   PV

Sanford Corporation, 2711 Washington Blvd., 60104, pg. 1178   PB

SLEEPECK PRINTING COMPANY, 815 S. 25th Ave., 60104, pg. 1005   PV

Varlen Instruments, Inc., 2777 W. Washington, 60104, pg. 1711   PB

Belvidere

Belvedere Company, One Belvedere Blvd., 61008, pg. 1008   PV

Central Beauty Equipment, One Belvedere Blvd., 61008, pg. 1008   PV

Central Rubber Company, 844 E. Jackson St., 61008, pg. 1776   PB

Champion Dairypak Div., 801 Fifth Ave., 61008, pg. 334   PB

Dean Foods Co., 630 Meadow St., 61008, pg. 491   PB

Bensenville

Advance Thermal Corp., 544 York Rd., pg. 1096   PV

Alliant Foodservice, 800 Supreme Dr., 60106-1889, pg. 244   PV

Almega Corporation, 607C Country Club Dr., 60106, pg. 546   PB

Antec Group, 888 Thomas Dr., 60106, pg. 116   PB

CALUMET PHOTOGRAPHIC, INC., 890 Supreme Dr., 60106, pg. 202   PV

Central Sprinkler Company, 85 O'Leary Dr., 60106, pg. 327   PB

CHICAGO WHITE METAL CASTING, INC., Rt. #83 & Fairway Dr., 60106, pg. 236   PV

Circle Freight International USA, 491 Supreme Dr., 60106, pg. 371   IT

Douwe Egberts Coffee Systems Americas, 950 Supreme Dr., 60106, pg. 1433   PB

Elkay Plastics Co., Inc., Stock Service Center, 200 W. Thorndale Ave., 60106, pg. 372   PV

Max Gruenhut International, Inc., 411 E. Irving Park Rd., 60106, pg. 372   PV

Hyundai Corp., U.S.A., 1000 Tower Ln., Ste. 160, 60106, pg. 641   IT

International Aero-Sea Forwarders Inc., 765 Rte. 83, Ste. 115, 60106, pg. 683   IT

Labauto, Inc., 1000 Tower Ln., Ste. 210, 60106, pg. 785   IT

Labinal Aero & Defense Systems, Inc., 1000 Tower Ln., Ste. 210, 60106, pg. 786   IT

LeFebure, Area North, 1116 N. Tower Ln., 60106, pg. 387   IT

MILLER FLUID POWER CORP., 800 N. York Rd., 60106, pg. 747   PV

Namco Cybertainment Inc., 877 Supreme Dr., 60106-1106, pg. 905   IT

PRECISION EXTRUSIONS, 720 E. Green Ave., 60106, pg. 879   PV

Rhenus Transport International Corp., 110 N. Tower Ln., 60106, pg. 1460   IT

Superior Coffee and Foods, 990 Supreme Dr., 60106, pg. 1434   PV

WEN PRODUCTS, INC., 1088 W. Thomdale, 60106, pg. 1144   PB

Benton

Bombardier Corporation, 451 E. Illinois Ave., 62812, pg. 200   IT

Berwyn

Commercial National Bank of Berwyn, 3322 Oak Park, 60402, pg. 379   PB

Lake River Corporation, 5005 Harlem, 60402, pg. 961   PB

Big Rock

EXECUTIVE CAPITAL CORP., 47 W. 210 Rte. 30, 60511, pg. 388   PV

PB - *U.S. Public Companies Volume*
PV - *U.S. Private Companies Volume*
IT - *International Public & Private Companies Volume*

Geographic Index-U.S.

1209

Bloomingdale

SAMUEL BINGHAM CO., 127 E. Lake St., Ste. 303, 60108-1124, pg. 144 **PV**
Buss (America) Inc., 230 Covington Dr., 60108, pg. 490 **IT**
Buss Waeschle Holding Corp., 230 Covington Dr., 60108-3106, pg. 490 **IT**
California Microwave-TeleCom Transmission Systems, Inc., 171 N. Covington Dr., 60108, pg. 293 **PB**
COMARK, 444 Scott Dr., 60108, pg. 257 **PV**
Georg Fischer Corporation, 230 Covington Dr., 60108-3115, pg. 491 **IT**
Outokumpu Copper Drawn Products Inc., 129 Fairfield Way, 60108, pg. 1016 **IT**
Outokumpu Copper Inc., 129 Fairfield Way, 60108, pg. 1016 **IT**
Outokumpu Copper (U.S.A.) Inc., 129 Fairfield Way, 60108, pg. 1015 **IT**
Outokumpu Metals (USA) Inc., 129 Fairfield Way, Ste. 308, 60108, pg. 1015 **IT**
Precision Products Division, 250 Covington Dr., 60108, pg. 903 **PV**
Waeschle Inc., 230 Covington Dr., 60108-3106, pg. 490 **IT**

Bloomington

ADM/GROWMARK, 1701 Towanda Ave., 61701, pg. 128 **PB**
BEER NUTS, INC., 103 N. Robinson St., 61701, pg. 130 **PV**
Kathryn Beich, Inc., 101 S. Lumber St., 61701, pg. 917 **IT**
Bridgestone/Firestone Off Road Tire Company-Bloomington, Veterans Pkwy. & Fort Jesse Rd., 61701, pg. 213 **PV**
CC Services, 1711 GE Rd., 61704, pg. 279 **PV**
Central Illinois Periodicals, Inc., P.O. Box 3757, 61702, pg. 664 **PV**
Country Casualty Insurance Company, P.O. Box 2100, 1711 GE Rd., 61704, pg. 279 **PV**
Country Investors Life Assurance Company, 1711 GE Rd., 61704, pg. 279 **PV**
COUNTRY LIFE INSURANCE COMPANY, 1711 GE Rd., 61704, pg. 278 **PV**
Country Mutual Insurance Company, 1700 Towanda Ave., 61702-2100, pg. 279 **PV**
Country Preferred Insurance Company, P.O. Box 2100, 1711 GE Rd., 61704, pg. 279 **PV**
The Eureka Company, 1201 E. Bell St., 61701, pg. 440 **IT**
Farm Credit Council Services, 712 I A A Dr., 61702, pg. 398 **PV**
GROWMARK, INC., 1701 Towanda Ave., 61701, pg. 484 **PV**
Hewlett-Packard Company, P.O. Box 1607, 2205 E. Empire St., 61702-1607, pg. 814 **PB**
Magna Bank, Bloomington Region, 1304 E. Empire St., 61701, pg. 1037 **PB**
Mary Kay Cosmetics, Inc., 221 Covington Dr., 60108, pg. 711 **PV**
Olin Fabricated Metals Products, Inc., 2047 Ireland Grand Rd., 61707, pg. 1219 **PB**
State Farm Fire and Casualty Co., One State Farm Plaza, 61701, pg. 1036 **PV**
State Farm General Insurance Co., One State Farm Plaza, 61701, pg. 1036 **PV**
State Farm Life and Accident Assurance Co., One State Farm Plaza, 61710, pg. 1036 **PV**
State Farm Life Insurance Co., One State Farm Plaza, 61710, pg. 1036 **PV**
STATE FARM MUTUAL AUTOMOBILE INSURANCE COMPANY, One State Farm Plaza, 61710, pg. 1036 **PV**
Sugar Creek Packing Co., 410 East St., 61702, pg. 1049 **PV**

Blue Island

Clark Oil & Refining Corporation-Blue Island Refinery, 131st & Kedzie Ave., 60406, pg. 243 **PV**
First National Bank of Blue Island, 13057 S. Western Ave., 60406, pg. 474 **PV**
G & W ELECTRIC CO., 3500 W. 127th St., 60406, pg. 433 **PV**
Gilbert & Bennett, P.O. Box 56, 60406, pg. 453 **PV**
Earle M. Jorgensen Honing Center/Blue Island, 2850 W. 139th St., 60406, pg. 600 **PV**
MODERN DROP FORGE CO., 13810 S. Western Ave., 60406, pg. 754 **PV**

Bolingbrook

Arena Auto Auction Inc., 200 W. Old Chicago Dr., 60440, pg. 1648 **PB**
DYWIDAG Systems International, USA, Inc., 301 Marmon Dr., 60440, pg. 424 **IT**
Tellabs International, Inc., 1000 Remington Blvd., 60440, pg. 1573 **PB**

Bourbonnais

Kankakee, IL Steel Division, 972 E. 4500 N Rd., 60914-4127, pg. 232 **PB**

Bradley

CHICAGO STEEL TAPE, 1159 E. North St., 60915, pg. 235 **PV**

Bridgeport

Plains Illinois, Inc., P.O. Box 318, 62417, pg. 1308 **PB**

Bridgeview

Enthone OMI-Bridgeview, 9809 Industrial Dr., 60455, pg. 138 **PB**
Ivex Packaging Corporation-Bridgeview, 8100 S. 77th Ave., 60455, pg. 915 **PB**
Triumph Industries, 8687 S. 77th Ave., 60455, pg. 1641 **PB**

Broadview

Arrow Fluid Power, 2111 W. 21st St., 60153, pg. 85 **PV**
BEARING HEADQUARTERS CO., P.O. Box 6267, 2550 S. 25th Ave., 60153, pg. 127 **PV**
Robert Bosch Corporation, 2800 S. 25th Ave., 60153, pg. 204 **IT**
Bosch Sales Group, 2800 S. 25th Ave., 60153, pg. 205 **IT**
Elkay Manufacturing, 2700 S. 17th Ave., 60153, pg. 372 **PV**
Gears & Sprockets, Inc., 2625 W. 16th St., 60153, pg. 127 **PV**
Independent Metals, 2107 Gardiner Rd., 60153, pg. 559 **PV**
Industrial Information Headquarters Co., 2601 W. 16th St., 60153, pg. 127 **PV**
Intech Technology Corporation, 2001 W. 16th St., 60153-3952, pg. 490 **IT**
Lehigh Press Cadillac, 25 & Lexington, 60153, pg. 659 **PB**
NATIONAL VAN LINES, INC., 2800 W. Roosevelt Rd., 60153, pg. 788 **PV**
REPLOGLE GLOBES, INC., 2801 S. 25th Ave., 60153, pg. 923 **PV**
TEMPLETON, KENLY & CO., INC., 2525 Gardner Rd., 60153, pg. 1075 **PV**
Unisource (Midwest Region), 2601 S. 25th Ave., 60153, pg. 1671 **PB**

Buffalo Grove

Advantest America, Inc., 1100 Busch Pkwy., 60089-4503, pg. 25 **IT**
ANGUS CHEMICAL COMPANY, 1500 E. Lake Cook Rd., 60089, pg. 75 **PV**
Automotive Energy Controls Group, 887 Deerfield Pkwy., 61237, pg. 1137 **PB**
BT Office Products International, Inc, 2150 Lake Cook Rd., Ste. 590, 60089, pg. 756 **IT**
BT-U.S.A., Inc., 2150 E. Lake Cook Rd., Ste. 590, 60089, pg. 756 **IT**
Bran & Luebbe Inc., 1025 Busch Pkwy., 60089, pg. 1378 **IT**
Bull Data Systems Inc., 2150 E. Lake Cook Rd., 60089, pg. 316 **IT**
Burgess SAIA Inc., 1335 Barclay Blvd., 60089, pg. 1500 **IT**
COLFAX ENVELOPE CORPORATION, 951 Commerce Ct., 60089, pg. 252 **PV**
John Crane Marine USA, 1536 Barclay Blvd., 60089, pg. 1339 **IT**
Indeck Energy Services, Inc., 1130 Lake Cook Rd., 60089, pg. 559 **PV**
Konami Computer Entertainment Chicago Inc., 900 Deerfield Pkwy., 60089-4510, pg. 746 **IT**
Konami Corporation of America Inc., 900 Deerfield Pkwy., 60089, pg. 746 **IT**
Konami of America Inc., 900 Deerfield Pkwy., 60089-4510, pg. 746 **IT**
Landis & Staefa, Inc., 1000 Deerfield Pway., 60089-4547, pg. 800 **IT**
Landis & Staefa Inc., 1000 Deerfield Pkwy., 60089, pg. 800 **IT**
Mid-West Automation Systems, Inc., 1400 Busch Pkwy., 60089, pg. 475 **PB**
Motorola Lighting Inc., 887 Deerfield Pkwy., 60089, pg. 1138 **PB**
Plews/Edelmann, 165 Arlington Heights Rd.; Ste.150, 60089-1974, pg. 1396 **IT**
Sargent-Welch Scientific Company, 911 Commerce Ct., 60089-5229, pg. 1704 **PB**
Video Communication & Info. Systems Div./Lighting Products, 1010 Johnson Dr., 60089, pg. 1405 **IT**
Washington Specialty Metals, 1400 E. Lake Cook Rd., 60089, pg. 1020 **PB**
WOODHEAD INDUSTRIES, INC., 2150 E. Lake Cook Rd., Ste. 400, 60089, pg. 1776 **PB**
Zenith Data Systems International, 2150 E. Lake Cook Rd., 60089, pg. 317 **IT**

Burr Ridge

Assembly Component Systems, Inc., 240 W. 83rd St., 60521, pg. 980 **PB**
Blockbuster Video Limited Partnership, 8320 S. Madison St., 60521, pg. 776 **PV**
GKN Walterscheid Inc., 16 W. 030-83rd St., 60521-5802, pg. 536 **IT**
IMPO Glazile, 7600 County Line Rd., Unit 1, 60521, pg. 1239 **IT**
M&M/Mars, 660 W. 79th St., 60521, pg. 707 **PV**
M-C Power Corporation, 8040 S. Madison St., 60521, pg. 689 **IT**
MARK SHALE, 161 Tower Dr., Unit 6, 60521, pg. 989 **PV**

Mark Shale Direct, 161 Tower Dr., Unit 6, 60521, pg. 989 **PV**
TIMEMED LABELING SYSTEMS, INC., 144 Tower Dr., 60521, pg. 1087 **PV**

Byron

Kysor/Westran, 602 E. Blackhawk Dr., 61010, pg. 968 **PB**

Cairo

ServiceMaster Manufacturing Services, 1210 Commercial Ave., 62914, pg. 1462 **PB**

Calumet City

Cavexsa North America, 1700 167th St., Ste. 10, 60609, pg. 694 **PV**
Cavexsa (U.S.A.) Inc., 1700 167th St., Ste. 10, 60609, pg. 694 **PV**
Evans, Inc., River Oaks Shopping Ctr., 159th & Torrence Ave., 60409, pg. 596 **PB**
LaSalle Bank Madison, 1701 River Oaks Dr., 60409, pg. 10 **IT**

Carbondale

Magna Bank, Carbondale Region, 601 E. Main St., 62901, pg. 1037 **PB**
Southern Illinoisan, 710 N. Illinois Ave., 62901, pg. 984 **PB**
VOGLER MOTOR COMPANY, INC., 1170 E. Main, 62901, pg. 1143 **PV**

Carlinville

CENTRAL ILLINOIS STEEL COMPANY, P.O. Box 78, 62626, pg. 223 **PV**
Farmers and Merchants Bank of Carlinville, 240 E. Main St., 62626, pg. 644 **PB**
PRAIRIE FARMS DAIRY, INC., 1100 N. Broadway, 62626, pg. 878 **PV**
Prairie Farms Dairy Supply Corp., 1100 N. Broadway, 62626, pg. 879 **PV**

Carmi

MARTIN & BAYLEY INC., County Hwy. 1350 N., 62821, pg. 708 **PV**
Trelleborg YSH, Inc.-Carmi Division, 102 Industrial Ave., 62821, pg. 1422 **IT**
Trelleborg YSH, Inc.-Carmi Mixing Division, 1500 E. Main, 62821, pg. 1422 **IT**

Carol Stream

Agricultural Publishing Group, 191 S. Gary Ave., 60188, pg. 512 **PV**
American Flange & Manufacturing Co. Inc., 290 E. Fullerton Ave., 60188-0688, pg. 1146 **IT**
BERLIN INDUSTRIES, INC., 175 Mercedes Dr., 60188, pg. 136 **PV**
CHRISTIANITY TODAY, INC., 465 Gundersen Dr., 60188, pg. 238 **PV**
Davies Molding Co., 350 Kehoe Blvd., 60188, pg. 859 **PV**
Eaton Corporation Automotive Controls Division, 191 E. North Ave., 60188, pg. 557 **PB**
Farm Progress Publications, 191 S. Gary Ave., 60188, pg. 513 **PB**
Fiatallis North America, Inc., 245 E. North Ave., 60188, pg. 483 **IT**
GRAYLINE HOUSEWARES, 455 Kehoe Blvd., Ste. 105, 60188, pg. 472 **PV**
Inland Detroit Diesel-Allison, 210 Alexandra Way, 60188, pg. 564 **PV**
The Meyercord Company, 365 E. North Ave., 60188, pg. 867 **PB**
Shima American Corp., 485 E. Lies Rd., 60188, pg. 1232 **IT**
Thyssen Specialty Steels, Inc., 360 Village Dr., 60188, pg. 1388 **IT**
TYNDALE HOUSE PUBLISHERS, INC., 351 Executive Dr., 60188, pg. 1112 **PV**
Vickers Modular, 423 St. Paul Blvd., 60188-5207, pg. 25 **IT**

Carpentersville

Acme Industrial Company, 441 Maple Ave., 60110, pg. 586 **PV**
MCWHORTER TECHNOLOGIES, INC., 400 E. Cottage Place, 60110, pg. 1074 **PB**
Photo Mechanix Inc., 11 W. Main St., 60110-1706, pg. 891 **PV**
REVCOR, INC., 251 Edwards Ave., 60110, pg. 925 **PV**

Carthage

Electronic Controls Division, 111 E. Buchanan St., 62321, pg. 1101 **PV**
Magnetoelastic Devices Inc. (MDI), 111 E. Buchanan St., 62321, pg. 1101 **PB**

Cary

COILCRAFT, INC., 1102 Silver Lake Rd., 60013, pg. 250 **PV**
Harris Bank Cary-Grove, 122 W. Main St., 60013, pg. 154 **IT**

Hollister Medical Systems Division, 755 Industrial Dr., 60013, pg. 535 PV
SeaquistPerfect Dispensing, 1160 N. Silver Lake Rd., 60013, pg. 125 PB
Tru-Test Mfg. Co., 201 Jandus Rd., 60013, pg. 1108 PV

Centralia

Cambridge Industries, Inc., 2400 S. Wabash, 62801, pg. 202 PV
Magna Bank, Centralia Region, 140 S. Locust St., 62801, pg. 1037 PB

Champaign

Advanced Filtration Systems, Inc., 3206 Farber Dr., 61821, pg. 316 PB
CENTRAL DATA CORPORATION, 1602 Newton Dr., 61821, pg. 223 PV
Collegiate Cap and Gown, 1000 N. Market St., 61820, pg. 523 PV
I.H. FRENCH & CO. INC., 41 E. University, Ste. 2C, 61820, pg. 427 PV
Frontier Communications-Lakeside, Inc., 1400 W. Anthony Dr., 61821, pg. 683 PB
Frontier Communications-Midland, Inc., 1400 W. Anthony Dr., 61821, pg. 683 PB
Frontier Communications of Illinois, Inc., 1400 W. Anthony Dr., 61821, pg. 683 PB
Frontier Communications-Prairie Inc., 1400 W. Anthony Dr., 61821, pg. 684 PB
ICI Seeds, Rte. 48 S. RR1 Box 33, 61821, pg. 1524 IT
Johnson Ross Corporation, 502 S. Kenwood, 61821, pg. 279 PB
Limagrain Genetics Corp., R.R.#1, Box 232A, 61821, pg. 566 IT
REGENCY ASSOCIATES LIMITED PARTNERSHIP, 1701 Broadmoor Dr., Ste. 200, 61821, pg. 918 PV
Regency Management Service L.L.C., 1701 Broadmoor Dr., Ste. 200, 61821, pg. 918 PV
SuperValu, Inc.-JM Jones Div., P.O. Box 9008, 61826, pg. 1540 PB
Vesuvius U.S.A., 1404 Newton Dr., 61821, pg. 329 IT
WICD-TV, 250 S. Country Fair Dr., 61821, pg. 439 PV

Charleston

Consolidated Market Response, 700 W. Lincoln, Ste. 200, 61920, pg. 1073 PB
NationsBank of Charleston, 418 Sixth St., 61920, pg. 1164 PB

Cherry Valley

Ipsen International, Inc., 984 Ipsen Road, 61016, pg. 1149 IT

Chester

GILSTER MARY LEE CORP., 1037 State St., 62233, pg. 455 PV
Party Pac Div., P.O. Box 227, 62233, pg. 455 PV
Py-O-My Div., P.O. Box 227, 62233, pg. 455 PV

Chicago

ABC RAIL PRODUCTS CORP., 200 S. Michigan Ave., 60604, pg. 2 PB
ABD Group Inc., 1100 W. Washington Blvd., 60607, pg. 503 PB
ABN AMRO Chicago Corp., 208 S. La Salle St., Ste. 200, 66004, pg. 10 IT
ABN AMRO Chicago Corp Financial Services, 208 S. La Salle St., 60604, pg. 10 IT
ABN AMRO Chicago Corporation, 208 S. La Salle St., 2nd Fl., 60604, pg. 10 IT
ABN-AMRO North America Inc., Chicago, 135 S. La Salle St., 60603, pg. 10 IT
ABN/LaSalle North America Inc., 135 S. LaSalle St., Rm. 340, 60603, pg. 11 IT
AON Advisors, Inc., 123 N. Wacker Dr., 60606, pg. 117 PB
AON Reinsurance Agency, Inc., 123 N. Wacker Dr., 60606, pg. 117 PB
AON Risk Services, Inc., 123 N. Wacker Dr., 60606, pg. 117 PB
AON Specialty Group, Inc., 123 N. Wacker Dr., 60606, pg. 117 PB
APT, 8410 W. Bryn Mawr, 60631, pg. 1570 PB
ABBELL ASSOCIATES, 332 S. Michigan Ave., Ste. 1260, 60604, pg. 9 PV
Abbyland Illinois, Inc., 1237 Fulton St, 60607, pg. 10 PV
ABELSON-TAYLOR, INC., 35 E. Wacker Dr., Ste. 900, 60601, pg. 10 PV
ACCURATE PERFORATING CO., 3636 S. Kedzie Ave., 60632, pg. 12 PV
ACTIVE ELECTRICAL SUPPLY COMPANY, 4240 W. Lawrence Ave., 60630, pg. 15 PV
Acxiom Corporation, 300 S. Riverside Plaza, Ste. 688 N., 60606-6613, pg. 18 PB
Advance Ross Corporation, 233 S. Wacker Dr., Ste. 9700, 60606-6502, pg. 320 PB
Advance Ross Electronics Corp., 233 S. Wacker Dr., Ste. 9700, 60606, pg. 320 PB
Advance Ross Steel Co., 233 S. Wacker Dr., Ste. 7700, 60606, pg. 320 PB
Advance Transformer Co., 2950 N. Western Ave., 60618, pg. 1054 IT
Advanswers Media/Programming, 211 E. Ontario, 60611, pg. 117 IT
Advertising Age, 740 N. Rush St., 60611, pg. 284 PV
AETNA BEARING COMPANY, 4600 W. Schubert, 60639, pg. 25 PV
Air France (North Central), John Hancock Center, Mezzanine, 975 N. Michigan Ave., 60611, pg. 560 IT
Airtex, 2900 N. Lestern Ave., 60618, pg. 1113 PV
AIRTITE CONTRACTORS INC., 2900 N. Western Ave., 60618-8089, pg. 29 PV
Akzo Nobel Chemicals Inc., 300 S. Riverside Plaza, 60606, pg. 47 IT
Akzo Nobel Inc., 300 S. Riverside Plaza, 60606, pg. 47 IT
ALENITE L.P., 5750 W. Bloomingdale Ave., 60639, pg. 33 PV
Alexander & Alexander Inc., Two Prudential Plaza, 180 N. Stetson Ave., 60601, pg. 117 PB
All American Life Insurance Co., 8501 W. Higgins Rd., 60631, pg. 77 PB
ALLIED PRODUCTS CORPORATION, Ten S. Riverside Plaza, Ste. 400, 60606, pg. 48 PB
Allright Parking Chicago, Inc., 216 N. Jefferson, 2nd Fl., 60661, pg. 43 PV
ALVA/AMCO PHARMACAL COMPANIES, INC., 6625 N. Avondale Ave., 60631, pg. 47 PV
Ambria, 2300 Lincoln Park W., 60614, pg. 661 PV
Ambrosi & Associates, Inc., 1100 W. Washington, 60607-2027, pg. 503 PB
Amco Corporation, 901 N. Kilpatrick Ave., 60651, pg. 985 PB
Amerian Appraisal Property Tax Services, Inc., Ten S. Riverside Plaza, Ste. 300, 60606, pg. 50 PV
American Country Financial Services Corp., 222 N. LaSalle St., Ste. 1600, 60601, pg. 1030 PV
American Country Insurance Co., 222 N. LaSalle St., Ste. 1600, 60601, pg. 1030 PV
AMERICAN DECAL & MFG. CO., 4100 W. Fullerton Ave., 60639, pg. 53 PV
AMERICAN LIBRARY ASSOCIATION, 50 E. Huron St., 60611, pg. 58 PV
The American Meat Packing Corp., 3946 S. Normal Ave., 60609, pg. 575 PV
American National Bank & Trust Co. of Chicago, 33 N. LaSalle St., 60690, pg. 628 PB
American National Bank & Trust of Chicago, 30 N. LaSalle St., 60690, pg. 627 PB
American National Can Company, 8770 W. Bryn Mawr Ave., 60631-3542, pg. 1029 IT
American Natl. Can Co.-Food Plastic N. America, 8770 West Bryn Mawr Ave., 60631-3542, pg. 1029 IT
American Real Estate Investment & Development Co., 401 S. LaSalle, Ste. 608, 60605, pg. 9 IT
American Software, Inc., Mid-America, Riverway, Ste. 680, 6133 N. River Rd., 60018, pg. 91 PB
American Steel Foundries, 10 S. Riverside Plaza, 60606, pg. 68 PV
Ameritech, 225 W. Randolph St., 60606, pg. 97 PB
Ameritech Applied Technologies, Inc., 500 W. Madison St., Ste. 2800, 60606, pg. 98 PB
Ameritech Audiotex Services Inc., 600 S. Federal, 60605, pg. 98 PB
Ameritech Corp., 30 S. Wacker Dr., 60606, pg. 98 PB
AMERITECH CORPORATION, 30 S. Wacker Dr., 60606, pg. 97 PB
Ameritech Custom Business Services, 225 W. Randolph, 60606, pg. 98 PB
Ameritech Development Corporation, 10 S. Wacker Drive, 21st Floor, 60606, pg. 98 PB
Ameritech Enhanced Business Services, 225 W. Randolph, 60606, pg. 98 PB
Ameritech Information Systems Inc., 350 N. Orleans, 3rd Fl., 60654, pg. 98 PB
Ameritech International Inc., 10 So. Wacker, 21st Fl., 60606, pg. 98 PB
Ameritech New Media, 300 S. Riverside Plaza, 18th Fl., 60606, pg. 98 PB
Amfac, Inc., 900 N. Michigan Ave., 20th Fl., 60611, pg. 577 PV
Amli Realty, Inc., 100 So. Wacker Dr., 60606, pg. 169 PB
Amoco Abu Dhabi Exploration Co., 200 E. Randolph Dr., 60601, pg. 103 PB
Amoco Chemical Holding Co., 200 E. Randolph, 60601, pg. 102 PB
Amoco Chemicals, 200 E. Randolph, 60601, pg. 102 PB
Amoco Company, 200 E. Randolph Dr., 60601, pg. 102 PB
AMOCO CORPORATION, 200 E. Randolph Dr., 60601-7125, pg. 101 PB
Amoco Credit Corporation, 200 E. Randolph, 60601, pg. 103 PB
Amoco Development Company, 200 E. Randolph Dr., 60601, pg. 103 PB
Amoco Japan Ltd., 200 E. Randolph Dr., 60601, pg. 102 PB
Amoco Leasing Corporation, 200 E. Randolph Dr., 60601, pg. 102 PB
Amoco Oil Company, 200 E. Randolph Dr., 60601, pg. 102 PB
Amoco Production Company, 200 E. Randolph Dr., 60601-7125, pg. 102 PB
Amoco Properties Incorporated, 200 E. Randolph, 60601, pg. 103 PB
Amoco Realty Company, 200 E. Randolph, 60601, pg. 103 PB
Amoco Supply & Trading Company, 200 E. Randolph, 60601, pg. 103 PB
AmProp Finance Company, 200 E. Randolph Dr., 60601, pg. 103 PB
AMSTED INDUSTRIES INCORPORATED, Blvd. Tower S., 44th Floor, 205 N. Michigan Ave., 60601, pg. 68 PV
AMSTED Industries International, 200 W. Monroe St., 60606, pg. 68 PV
Animal Nutrition Div., 222 S. Riverside Plaza, 60606, pg. 268 PV
ANIXTER INTERNATIONAL, Two N. Riverside Plaza, 60606, pg. 115 PB
AON CORPORATION, 123 N. Wacker Dr., 60606, pg. 117 PB
AON Risk Services Inc. of Illinois, 123 N. Wacker Dr., 60606, pg. 117 PB
Appleton Electric Co., 1701 W. Wellington Ave., 60657, pg. 572 PB
Aramark Food Services, 425 E. McFetridge Dr., 60605, pg. 79 PV
Archibald Candy Company, 1137 W. Jackson Blvd., 60607, pg. 597 PV
ARRINGTON TRAVEL CENTER INC., 55 W. Monroe St., 60603, pg. 85 PV
Arthur Andersen, 225 N. Michigan Ave., 60601, pg. 72 PV
Arvey Paper & Office Products, 3351 W. Addison St., 60618, pg. 903 PB
ASHLEY INTERNATIONAL & PASCHEN, 2739 N. Elston Ave., 60647, pg. 88 PV
Associated Aviation Underwriters, 300 S. Riverside Plaza, Ste. 2160 South, 60606, pg. 355 PB
ATLAS ELECTRIC DEVICES CO., 4114 N. Ravenswood Ave., 60613, pg. 96 PV
AUTO DRIVEAWAY CO., 310 S. Michigan Ave., 60604, pg. 100 PV
Avanzare, 161 E. Huron, 60611, pg. 661 PV
N.W. Ayer & Partners Chicago, 515 N. State St., Ste. 2100, 60610, pg. 104 PV
Azcon Corp., 224 S. Michigan Ave., Ste. 425, 60604, pg. 153 PV
AZTECA FOODS, INCORPORATED, 5005 S. Nagle, 60638, pg. 104 PV
BA Futures, Incorporated, 200 W. Adams St., Ste. 2700, 60606, pg. 180 PB
BDO SEIDMAN, LLP, Two Prudential Plaza, 180 N. Stetson Ave., Ste. 4300, 60601, pg. 106 PV
BET Midwest Media/Affiliate Sales, Two Prudential Plaza, #4350, 60601, pg. 235 PB
BMO Financial, Inc., 111 W. Monroe St., 60603, pg. 154 IT
BPA International - Chicago, Ste. 1550, 120 N. La Salle St., 60602, pg. 107 PV
BSA Advertising, Inc., 225 N. Michigan Ave., Ste. 805, 60601, pg. 108 PV
Bacon's Information, Inc., 332 S. Michigan Ave., Ste. 900, 60604, pg. 1327 PB
Bagcraft Corporation of America, 3900 W. 43rd St., 60632, pg. 136 PB
BAIRD & WARNER INC., 200 W. Madison St., 60606, pg. 111 PV
BAKER & MCKENZIE, ATTORNEYS AT LAW, One Prudential Plaza, 130 E. Randolph Dr., Ste. 2500, 60601, pg. 111 PV
Baker Engineering, Inc., 118 S. Clinton St., 60606, pg. 168 PB
Bally Total Fitness Corporation, 8700 W. Bryn Mawr Ave., 60631, pg. 171 PB
BALLY TOTAL FITNESS HOLDINGS CORPORATION, 8700 W. Bryn Mawr Ave., 60631, pg. 171 PB
Banca Commerciale Italiana, 150 N. Michigan Ave., Ste. 1500, 60601, pg. 652 IT
Banca Nazionale Del Lavoro (Chicago), Xerox Ctr., 55 W. Monroe St., Ste. 600, 60603, pg. 136 IT
Banco di Sicilia, 200 W. Madison St., 60606, pg. 140 IT
Banco do Brasil S.A.-Chicago, Two N. LaSalle St., Ste. 2005, 60602, pg. 141 IT
Banco Popular, Illinois, 4000 W. North Ave., 60639, pg. 176 PB
BancTec, Inc.-Chicago, 8420 W. Bryn Mawr Ave., Ste. 1000, 60631, pg. 177 PB
THE BANK FUNDS COMPANY LLC, 208 S. LaSalle St., Ste. 1680, 60604, pg. 113 PV
Bank Hapoalim (Chicago), 225 N. Michigan Ave., Ste. 900, 60601-7601, pg. 149 IT
Bank Leumi le-Israel B.M., 100 N. LaSalle St., 60602, pg. 150 IT
Bank of America Illinois, 231 S. LaSalle St., 60697, pg. 180 PB
Bank of Montreal - Chicago, 115 S. LaSalle St., 60603, pg. 154 IT
Bank of Montreal Global, Inc., 111 W. Monroe St., 60603, pg. 154 IT
The Bank of Nova Scotia, 181 W. Madison, Ste. 3700, 60602, pg. 156 IT
The Bank of Tokyo-Mitsubishi, Ltd., 227 W. Monroe St., 60606, pg. 157 IT
Bank One, Chicago, 208 So. La Salle, 60604, pg. 173 PB
Bankers Life & Casualty Company, 222 Merchandise Mart Plaza, 60654-2001, pg. 433 PB
Bankers Life Holding Corp., 4444 W. Lawrence Ave., 60630, pg. 433 PB
BANNER WHOLESALE GROCERS, INC., 115 S. Water Market, 60608, pg. 114 PV
Banque Paribas-Chicago, 227 W. Monroe, Ste. 3300, 60606, pg. 319 IT
Barton Beers, Ltd., 55 E. Monroe St., Ste. 1700, 60603, pg. 300 PB
Barton Brands, Ltd., 55 E. Monroe, 17th Fl., 60603, pg. 300 PB
Barton Incorporated, 55 E. Monroe St., Ste. 1700, 60603, pg. 300 PB
Bear, Stearns & Co. Inc., Chicago, Three First National Plaza, 60602, pg. 198 PB
Beardsley & Piper, L.L.C., 5501 W. Grand Ave., 60639, pg. 859 PV
BELTONE ELECTRONICS CORPORATION, 4201 W. Victoria, 60646, pg. 132 PV

Geographic Index-U.S.

PB - *U.S. Public Companies Volume*
PV - *U.S. Private Companies Volume*
IT - *International Public & Private Companies Volume*

BENNETT BROTHERS, INC., 30 E. Adams St., 60603, pg. 133 **PV**
Berkshire Furniture Co., 5950 W. 51st St., 60638, pg. 985 **PB**
Bessin Corporation, 1001 W. Exchange Ave., 60609, pg. 1433 **PB**
BEVERLY BANCORPORATION INC., Tinley Park, 60643, pg. 227 **PB**
Big Bowl Cafe, 159.5 W. Erie St., 60610, pg. 661 **PV**
BIGSBY & KRUTHERS COMPANIES, 1750 N. Clark St., 60614, pg. 143 **PV**
Binswanger Realty Group-Midwest, Sears Tower Ste. 6230, 233 S. Wacker Dr., 60606, pg. 144 **PV**
Bistro Soups, Ltd., 2501 N. Damen, 60647, pg. 1140 **PV**
Blackstone Mfg. Co., Inc., 4630 W. Harrison St., 60644, pg. 560 **PV**
WILLIAM BLAIR & COMPANY L.L.C., 222 W. Adams St., 60606, pg. 148 **PV**
Blau Direct Edge, Inc., 875 N. Michigan Ave., Ste. 2800, 60611, pg. 148 **PV**
M. BLOCK & SONS, INC., 2355 S. Blue Island Ave., 60608, pg. 150 **PV**
BLOMMER CHOCOLATE CO., 600 W. Kinzie St., 60610, pg. 150 **PV**
Blue Crab Lounge, 21 E. Hubbard, 60611, pg. 661 **PV**
BLUE CROSS AND BLUE SHIELD ASSOCIATION, 225 N. Michigan Ave., 60601-7680, pg. 151 **PV**
BLUE CROSS & BLUE SHIELD OF ILLINOIS, 233 N. Michigan Ave., 60601, pg. 151 **PV**
Blue Island Railroad, 636 Michigan Ave., 60638, pg. 865 **PB**
BODINE ELECTRIC COMPANY, 2500 W. Bradley Pl., 60618, pg. 154 **PV**
BORG WARNER AUTOMOTIVE, INC., 200 S. Michigan Ave., 60604, pg. 245 **PB**
BORG-WARNER SECURITY CORPORATION, 200 S. Michigan Ave., 60604, pg. 245 **PB**
Boulevard Bancorp, Inc., 410 N. Michigan Ave., 60611-4181, pg. 1680 **PB**
Bowne of Chicago, Inc., 325 W. Ohio St., 60610, pg. 248 **PB**
Boye Needle, 4343 N. Ravenswood Ave., 60613, pg. 1192 **PV**
BRACH & BROCK CONFECTIONS, INC., 401 N. Cicero Ave., 60644, pg. 163 **PV**
BRADNER CENTRAL COMPANY, 333 S. Des Plaines St., 60661-5596, pg. 164 **PV**
Bradner Smith & Co., 333 S. DesPlaines St., 60661-3596, pg. 164 **PV**
Bradshaw-Praeger Co., 3248 W. 47th Pl., 60632, pg. 1358 **PV**
Brambles USA Inc., The Wrigley Bldg., Ste. 610, 400 N. Michigan Ave., 60611, pg. 211 **IT**
W. BRAUN COMPANY, 300 N. Canal St., 60606, pg. 166 **PV**
BRAWNEY PLASTICS, INC., 2700 N. Palina, 60614, pg. 166 **PV**
BREUER/TORNADO, 7401 W. Lawrence Ave., 60656-3489, pg. 167 **PV**
Bridgford Foods of Illinois, 170 N. Green St., 60607, pg. 252 **PB**
BROWN MARKETING COMMUNICATIONS, 200 S. Wacker Dr., 40th Fl., 60606-5828, pg. 661 **PV**
Bub City Crabshack & Bar-B-Q, 901 W. Weed St., 60622, pg. 661 **PV**
BULLEY & ANDREWS COMPANY, 1755 W. Armitage Ave., 60622, pg. 180 **PV**
LEO BURNETT COMPANY, INC., 35 W. Wacker Dr., 60601, pg. 183 **PV**
Burns & Wilcox - Chicago Office, 300 S. Wacker Dr., Ste. 1150, 60606-6610, pg. 609 **PV**
BURRELL COMMUNICATIONS GROUP INC., 20 N. Michigan Ave., 60602, pg. 188 **PV**
Business Insurance, 740 Rush St., 60611-2590, pg. 285 **PV**
Business Management Personnel, Inc., 150 S. Wacker Dr., Ste. 775, 60606, pg. 714 **PB**
Business Marketing, 740 Rush St., 60611, pg. 285 **PV**
John O. Butler Co., 4635 W. Foster Ave., 60630, pg. 1320 **IT**
CBC-U.S.A Inc., 70 W. Madison St., Ste. 5500, 60602, pg. 337 **PV**
CC INDUSTRIES, INC., 222 N. LaSalle St., Ste. 1000, 60601, pg. 192 **PV**
CCC Information Services, 444 Merchandise Mart, 60654-4636, pg. 562 **PV**
CFB INDUSTRIES, INC., 1467 N. Elston, 60622, pg. 194 **PV**
CG Trust Company, 525 W. Monroe St., Ste. 1800, 60606, pg. 358 **PB**
CNA Financial Corp., CNA Plaza, 60685, pg. 1010 **PB**
CNA Insurance Companies, CNA Plaza, 333 S. Wabash Ave., 60685-0001, pg. 1010 **PB**
CPM, INC., 515 N. State St., Ste. 2200, 60610-4320, pg. 196 **PV**
CRSS Civil Engineers, Inc., 8700 W. Bryn Mawr, 60631, pg. 1415 **IT**
CTC Illinois Trust Company, 209 W. Jackson Blvd., Ste. 700, 60606, pg. 179 **PB**
Cabell Construction Company, 120 S. Riverside Plaza, 60606, pg. 370 **PV**
Cadaco, 4300 W. 47th Ave., 60632-4476, pg. 910 **PV**
Cafe Ba-Ba-Reeba, 2024 N. Halsted, 60614, pg. 661 **PV**
CAPSURE HOLDINGS CORP., Two N. Riverside Plaza, Ste. 600, 60606, pg. 303 **PB**
Car-X Muffler & Brake, 8430 W. Bryn Mawr, 60631, pg. 1578 **PV**
Carat ICG, One E. Erie, Ste. 640, 60611, pg. 207 **PV**
Cardwell-Freight Components, 8400 S. Stewart Ave., 60620, pg. 271 **IT**
Cariplo (Chicago), 190 S. La Salle St., 60603, pg. 275 **IT**

Carr Asset Management Inc., 10 S. Wacker Dr., Ste. 1125, 60606, pg. 313 **IT**
Carrier Building Systems & Services, 215 S. Aberdeen, 60607-2901, pg. 1689 **PB**
Carson Pirie Scott & Company, One S. State St., 60603, pg. 309 **PB**
Carson Pirie Scott & Company-Dept. Stores Div., One S. State St., 60603, pg. 309 **PB**
CARSTENS, 7310 W. Wilson Ave., 60656, pg. 216 **PV**
Case Paper Co. of Illinois, Inc., 900 West 45th St., 60609, pg. 218 **PV**
CASH & CARRY GROCER INC., 2844 W. Armitage Ave., 60647, pg. 218 **PV**
Castrol Industrial, 630 W. Washington, 60606, pg. 235 **IT**
Casualty Insurance Co., 321 N. Clark St., Ste. 600, 60610-4789, pg. 681 **PB**
CBC Bancorp, Ltd., 4801 W. Fullerton Ave., 60639, pg. 337 **PV**
CEBCOR (CONSOLIDATED EMPLOYMENT BENEFITS CORP.), 300 West Adams, Ste. 609, 60606, pg. 220 **PV**
CENTRAL STEEL & WIRE COMPANY, P.O. Box 5100, 3000 W. 51st St., 60632, pg. 327 **PV**
CENTURY AMERICA CORPORATION, 875 N. Michigan Ave., Ste. 3707, 60611, pg. 225 **PV**
CENTURY 21 AGMONT REAL ESTATE, INC., 3405 W. Lawrence Ave., 60625, pg. 226 **PV**
Certified Life Insurance, 222 Merchandise Mart Plaza, 60654-2001, pg. 433 **PV**
Charms Company, 7401 S. Cicero Ave., 60629, pg. 1621 **PV**
Chernin's Shoe Outlet, 1001 S. Clinton, 60607, pg. 233 **PV**
CHERNIN'S SHOES, INC., 1001 S. Clinton, 60607, pg. 233 **PV**
Chicago Asset Management Company, 70 W. Madison St., 56th Fl., 60602, pg. 1672 **PV**
Chicago AutoWerks, Inc., 1157 W. Monroe St., 60607, pg. 1030 **PV**
Chicago Baking Co., 40 E. Garfield Blvd., 60615, pg. 665 **PV**
Chicago Boat Yard, Inc., 1269 W. Lemoyne St., 60622, pg. 194 **PV**
CHICAGO CREATIVE PARTNERSHIP, 230 W. Superior, 60610, pg. 234 **PV**
Chicago Financial Printing Division, 350 E. 22nd St., 60616-1423, pg. 194 **PV**
Chicago Fire Brick Co., 1467 N. Elston, 60622, pg. 194 **PV**
Chicago Fire Brick of Delaware, Inc., 1467 N. Elston Ave., 60622, pg. 194 **PV**
Chicago Intermodal Co., 636 Michigan Ave., 60638, pg. 865 **PB**
Chicago Magazine, 500 N. Dearborn St., Ste. 1200, 60610, pg. 1328 **PV**
CHICAGO MERCANTILE EXCHANGE, 30 S. Wacker Dr., 60606, pg. 235 **PV**
Chicago National League Ball Club, Inc. (Chicago Cubs), 1060 W. Addison, 60613, pg. 1635 **PV**
Chicago Paper Board Corporation, 900 N. Ogden Ave., 60622, pg. 303 **PV**
Chicago Plant, 7300 W. Wilson Ave., 60656-4793, pg. 443 **PV**
Chicago Rail Link, 2728 E. 104th St., 60617-5766, pg. 171 **PB**
CHICAGO READER, INC., 11 E. Illinois, 2nd Fl., 60611, pg. 235 **PV**
Chicago South Financial Center, 7801 S. State St., 60619, pg. 1196 **PV**
Chicago Steel & Wire, 10257 S. Torrence Ave., 60617, pg. 636 **PV**
Chicago Sun Times, 401 N. Wabash Ave., 60611, pg. 632 **PV**
Chicago Title & Trust Co., 171 N. Clark St.-10CC, 60601-3294, pg. 42 **IT**
Chicago Title Insurance Co., 117 N. Clark St., 60601, pg. 42 **IT**
Chicago Transit Authority, Merchandise Mart Plaza, 60654, pg. 919 **PV**
Chicago Tribune Co., 435 N. Michigan Ave., 60611, pg. 1635 **PV**
CHICAGO TUBE & IRON CO., 2531 W. 48th St., 60632, pg. 235 **PV**
Chicago Union Station Company, 210 S. Canal St., 60606, pg. 69 **PV**
Chicago West Pullman & Southern Railroad, 2728 E. 104th St., 60617, pg. 171 **PV**
China Airlines Ltd., 225 N. Michigan Ave., Rm.209, 60601, pg. 285 **PV**
Cho Hung Bank, Ten S. Wacker Dr., Ste. 1850, 60606, pg. 287 **PV**
Chrome Crankshaft of Illinois, 6010 S. New England Ave., 60638, pg. 1710 **PB**
Cigna Excess & Surplus Insurance Services, Inc. (IL), 525 W. Monroe, Ste. 2220, 60606, pg. 363 **PV**
Cigna Insurance Company of Illinois, 8755 W. Higgins Rd., 60631, pg. 366 **PV**
Cineplex Odeon Corporation -Chicago, 70 E. Lake St., Ste. 1600, 60601-5905, pg. 293 **IT**
Citywide Towing, 1157 W. Monroe St., 60607, pg. 1030 **PV**
Clark Distribution Services Company, 7300 S. Cicero, 60629, pg. 876 **PB**
P.J. Clarke's, 1204 No. State Pkwy., 60610, pg. 661 **PV**
Classic Residence by Hyatt, 200 W. Madison, 60606, pg. 551 **PV**
CLOVERHILL BAKERY, 2035 N. Narragansett Ave., 60639-3842, pg. 247 **PV**
CLUNE CONSTRUCTION LIMITED, 11 S. LaSalle St., Ste. 1900, 60603, pg. 247 **PV**
Coastwise Trading Company, Inc., 200 E. Randolph, 60601, pg. 103 **PB**

COBRA ELECTRONICS CORPORATION, 6500 W. Cortland St., 60707, pg. 391 **PB**
CODE, HENNESSY & SIMMONS, INC., Ten S. Wacker, Ste. 3175, 60606, pg. 249 **PV**
Coleman Holding Company, 2500 Commonwealth Ave., 60064, pg. 968 **PB**
COLUMBIA PIPE & SUPPLY COMPANY, 1120 W. Pershing Rd., 60609, pg. 256 **PV**
Columbia Tri-Star Television Distribution - Chicago Office, 645 N. Michigan Ave., Ste. 834, 60611, pg. 1282 **IT**
COLUMBIAN ADVERTISING INC., 201 E. Ohio St., 60611, pg. 256 **PV**
Combined Insurance Company of America, 123 N. Wacker Dr., 60606, pg. 118 **PB**
ComEd, One First Natl. Plaza, 60603, pg. 1664 **PB**
Commerzbank Aktiengesellschaft Chicago Branch, 311 South Wacker Dr., Ste. 5800, 60606, pg. 310 **IT**
Commerzbank Futures Corporation, 311 Wacker Dr., Ste. 5850, 60606, pg. 310 **IT**
Commonwealth Edison Company of Indiana, Inc., One First National Plaza, 60690-0767, pg. 1664 **PB**
Commonwealth Research Corp., One First National Plaza, 60603, pg. 1664 **PB**
Community Finance Corporation, 6700 W. North Ave., 60607, pg. 1428 **PV**
Concomber, Ltd., One First National Plaza, 60603, pg. 1664 **PB**
Consolidated Distilled Products, 3201 S. Kedzie Ave., 60623, pg. 772 **PV**
CONTINENTAL ASSURANCE COMPANY, CNA Plaza, 22 South, 60685, pg. 267 **PB**
Continental Catalina, Inc., 225 W Wacker Dr., Ste. 1800, 60606, pg. 441 **PB**
Continental Community Development Corp., 231 S. Lasalle St., 60697, pg. 181 **PB**
Continental Copper, Inc., 225 W. Wacker Dr., Ste. 1800, 60606, pg. 441 **PB**
Continental Illinois Venture Corp., 231 S. LaSalle St., 60697, pg. 181 **PB**
CONTINENTAL MATERIALS CORPORATION, 225 W. Wacker Dr., 18th Fl., 60606-1229, pg. 441 **PB**
Continental Partners Group, Inc., 231 S. LaSalle St., 60697, pg. 181 **PB**
Continental Quicksilver, Inc., 225 W. Wacker Dr., Ste. 1800, 60606, pg. 441 **PB**
Continental Uranium, Inc., 225 W. Wacker Dr., 60606, pg. 441 **PB**
Copperweld Chicago Division, 7401 S. Linder Ave., 60638, pg. 662 **IT**
Corbett HealthConnect, A Frank J. Corbett, Inc., Company, 211 E. Chicago Ave., 60611-2660, pg. 1223 **PB**
Coregis Group, 181 W. Madison, 60607, pg. 711 **PB**
Coris-Mobium Creative Group, Ste. 2000 The Merchandise Mart, 200 World Trade Ctr., 60610, pg. 518 **PB**
CORNELL FORGE COMPANY, 6666 W. 66th St., 60638, pg. 276 **PV**
Corporate National Accounts Midwest, 8750 W. Bryn Mawr, Ste. 1400, 60631, pg. 1024 **PB**
Costain Holdings, Inc., 30 S. Wacker Dr., Ste. 3920, 60606, pg. 337 **IT**
Cotter Acceptance Co., Inc., 8600 W. Bryn Mawr, 60631-3505, pg. 1108 **PV**
COUGLE COMMISSION COMPANY, INC., 345 N. Aberdeen, 60607, pg. 278 **PV**
Crain Associated Enterprises, 500 N. Dearborn St., 60610-9988, pg. 285 **PV**
CRAIN COMMUNICATIONS, INC., 740 N. Rush St., 60611-2590, pg. 284 **PV**
Crain's Chicago Business, 740 Rush St., 60611, pg. 285 **PV**
Cramer-Krasselt, 225 N. Michigan Ave., 24th Fl., 60601, pg. 285 **PV**
Cravens, Dargan & Company, Pacific Coast of Illinois, Inc., 525 W. Monroe, 60606, pg. 366 **PB**
DAVID CRAVIT & ASSOCIATES ADVERTISING, 737 N. Michigan Ave., 60611, pg. 287 **PV**
Creative Card Co., 4401 W. Cermak Rd., 60623, pg. 89 **PB**
Credit Agricole (CNCA) U.S.A. (Chicago), 55 East Monroe St., Ste. 4700, 60603, pg. 341 **IT**
Credit Lyonnais, 227 West Monroe St., Ste. 3800, 60606, pg. 344 **IT**
Crown Crafts Home Furnishings of Illinois, Inc., Merchandise Mart, Room 1344, 60654, pg. 465 **PB**
Culinary Foods, Inc., 4201 S. Ashland Ave., 60609-2305, pg. 1652 **PB**
CYBORG SYSTEMS, INC., Two N. Riverside Plaza, Ste. 1200, 60606, pg. 299 **PV**
Cyprus Rod Chicago Corporation, 2324 S. Kenneth Ave., 60623, pg. 471 **PB**
D & H Piping, 5051 S. Western Blvd., 60609, pg. 338 **PV**
DFM/TATHAM, 980 N. Michigan Ave. Ste. 800, 60611, pg. 410 **IT**
DG FOODS, LLC, 135 S. LaSalle St., 60603, pg. 301 **PV**
DKB Financial Futures Corp., 10 So. Wacker Dr., Ste. 1835, 60606, pg. 360 **IT**
Dai-Ichi Kangyo Bank, Ltd.-Chicago, 10 South Wacker Dr., 26th Fl., 60606, pg. 359 **IT**
Daily Southtown, 7001 W. 60th St., 60638, pg. 632 **IT**
Daiwa Securities America Inc.-Chicago, 311 S. Wacker Dr., Ste. 1650, 60606, pg. 375 **IT**
Danaher Tool Group, 5200 W. Armstrong Ave., 60646, pg. 481 **IT**
THE DARTNELL CORPORATION, 4660 N. Ravenswood Ave., 60640, pg. 312 **PV**
DataMate Products Group, 7444 West Wilson Ave., 60656, pg. 1101 **PB**
Daubert Chemical Company, Inc., 4700 So. Central Ave., 60638, pg. 313 **PV**
THE DEARBORN GROUP, 33 N. Dearborn St., Ste. 1030, 60602, pg. 319 **PV**

PB - *U.S. Public Companies Volume*
PV - *U.S. Private Companies Volume*
IT - *International Public & Private Companies Volume*

Geographic Index-U.S.

Deutsche Bank AG (Chicago Branch), Three First National Plaza, 227 West Monroe Ave. Ste. 4350, 60606, pg. 403 IT
DeVRY Institute of Technology, 3300 Campbell Ave., 60618, pg. 504 PB
Dext Company of IL, 2300 W. St. Paul Ave., pg. 1444 PB
Diamond Technology Partners, 875 N. Michigan Ave., Ste. 3000, 60611, pg. 1424 PB
Diners Club Inc., 8430 W. Bryn Mawr Ave., 60631, pg. 377 PB
Diosynth, Inc., 3432 W. Henderson St., 60618, pg. 48 IT
Donnelley Business Centers, 77 W. Wacker Dr., 60601-1696, pg. 518 PB
R.R. DONNELLEY & SONS COMPANY, 77 W. Wacker Dr., 60601-1696, pg. 517 PB
DonTech, 205 N. Michigan Ave., 60601, pg. 98 PB
DORMEYER INDUSTRIES, 6585 N. Avondale Ave., 60631, pg. 340 PV
DREIS & KRUMP MANUFACTURING COMPANY, 7400 S. Loomis Blvd., 60636, pg. 342 PV
Dresdner Bank AG, 190 S. LaSalle St., Ste. 2700, 60603, pg. 418 IT
DUDEK & BOCK SPRING MANUFACTURING COMPANY, 5100 W. Roosevelt Rd., 60644, pg. 344 PV
DUFF & PHELPS UTILITIES INCOME INC., 55 E. Monroe St., 60603, pg. 534 PB
Dugan Valva Contess-Chicago, 343 W. Erie, Ste. 430, 60610, pg. 345 PV
EFS/San Diego Service Corporation, 6700 W. North Ave., 60707, pg. 1428 PB
EFS Service Corporation, 6700 W. North Ave., 60707, pg. 1428 PB
EJL Advertising/Chicago, Equitable Bldg., 401 N. Michigan Ave., 60611, pg. 673 PV
ESJ Hotel Corporation, 3401 N. California, 60618, pg. 1265 PB
Eagle Industries, Inc., Two N. Riverside Plaza, Ste. 1100, 60606, pg. 473 PV
Eaglemark Financial Services, Inc., 150 S. Wacker Dr., Ste. 3020, 60606, pg. 786 PB
Ebony Fashions, 820 S. Michigan Ave., 60605, pg. 592 PV
Eclipse Combustion, Inc., 6117 N. Elston Ave., 60646-4799, pg. 360 PV
ECONOMY FOLDING BOX CORP., LaSalle & 26th Sts., 60616, pg. 362 PV
EDELMAN PUBLIC RELATIONS WORLDWIDE, 200 E. Randolph Dr., Ste. 6300, 60601, pg. 362 PV
Edelman Worldwide, 211 E. Ontario, 60611, pg. 588 IT
Edens Industrial Park, Inc., 225 W. Wacker Dr., Ste. 1800, 60606, pg. 441 PB
Edison Development Canada, Inc., One First National Plaza, 60603, pg. 1664 PB
Henry Eisen Adv. Agency, Inc., 4591 W. 72nd St., 60629, pg. 1621 PB
ELECTRO BRAND, INC., 5410 W. Roosevelt Rd., 60644, pg. 368 PV
Electronic Media, 740 Rush St., 60611, pg. 285 PV
ELGIN DAIRY FOODS, INC., 3707 W. Harrison St., 60624, pg. 370 PV
ELI'S CHEESE CAKE COMPANY, 6701 W. Forest Preserve Dr., 60634-1407, pg. 371 PV
Elrick & Lavidge, Inc., Ten S. Riverside Pl., Ste. 1730, 60606, pg. 588 PB
Encyclopaedia Britannica Direct, Inc., 310 S. Michigan Ave., 60604, pg. 375 PV
Encyclopaedia Britannica Educational Corporation, 310 S. Michigan, 60604, pg. 375 PV
ENCYCLOPAEDIA BRITANNICA, INC., 310 S. Michigan Ave., 60604, pg. 375 PV
Energy Absorption Systems, Inc., One E. Wacker Dr., 30th Fl., 60601, pg. 1353 PB
A. EPSTEIN AND SONS, INTL., INC., 600 W. Fulton St., 60661-1199, pg. 379 PV
Epstein Civil Engineering, Inc., 600 W. Fulton, 60606, pg. 379 PV
Epstein Construction Inc., 600 W. Fulton St., 60606, pg. 379 PV
Epstein Engineering Export, Ltd., 600 W. Fulton St., 60606, pg. 379 PV
EQUITY GROUP INVESTMENTS, Two N. Riverside Plaza, Ste. 600, 60606-2639, pg. 380 PV
EQUITY RESIDENTIAL PROPERTIES TRUST, Two N. Riverside Plaza, Ste. 450, 60606, pg. 590 PB
Essex, L.L.C., 401 N. Michigan Ave., 60611, pg. 428 PV
EURO RSCG Tatham, 980 N. Michigan Ave., 60611, pg. 601 IT
Europa Management Inc., 55 E. Jackson Blvd., 60604, pg. 1096 PV
Europe Tax-Free Shopping Ltd., 233 S. Wacker Dr., Ste. 9700, 60606-6502, pg. 320 PB
EVANS, INC., 36 S. State St., 60603, pg. 596 PB
EVEREN SECURITIES, INC., 77 W. Wacker Dr., 60601, pg. 597 PB
Everest, One Financial Place, 440 S. LaSalle, 40th Fl., 60605, pg. 661 PV
Everfresh Beverages Inc., 200 W. Adams, Ste. 2011, 60606, pg. 1153 PB
Everyday Learning/Creative Publications Group, Two Prudential Plaza, Ste. 1200, 60601, pg. 1635 PB
F&F FOODS, 3501 W. 48th Pl., 60632, pg. 388 PV
FMC CORPORATION, 200 E. Randolph Dr., 60601, pg. 604 PB
FMC Food Machinery Group, 200 E. Randolph, 60601, pg. 605 PB
Facom Tools Inc., 3535 W. 47th St., 60632, pg. 570 IT
Fannie May Candy Shops, Inc., 1137 W. Jackson, 60607, pg. 598 PV
Farley Candy Company, 2945 W. 31st St., 60623, pg. 397 PV
FARLEY, INC., 233 S. Wacker Dr., Ste. 5000, 60606, pg. 394 PV
Fashionaire, 716 W. Kinzie St., 60610, pg. 796 PB
Federal Home Loan Mortgage Corporation (Freddie Mac)-North Central Region, 333 W. Wacker Dr., Ste. 3100, 60606, pg. 615 PB
Fenchurch Capital Management Limited, 311 S. Wacker Dr., Ste. 4825, 60606, pg. 420 IT
Feralloy Corp., 8755 W. Higgins Rd., Ste. 970, 60631, pg. 1070 IT
Feralloy Indiana Corp., 8755 W. Higgins Rd., 60631, pg. 1070 IT
Feralloy Midwest Corp., 8755 W. Higgins Rd., 60631, pg. 1070 IT
Feralloy Midwest Div., 12550 S. Stony Island Ave., 60633, pg. 1070 IT
Feralloy North American Steel Corp., 8755 W. Higgins Rd., 60631, pg. 1070 IT
Feralloy West Corp., 8755 W. Higgins Rd., 60631, pg. 1070 IT
FERGUSON PUBLISHING COMPANY, 200 W. Madison, 60606, pg. 401 PV
Fers Personal Financial Services, L.L.C., 401 N. Michigan Ave., 60611, pg. 428 PV
Fers Technology Group, L.L.C., 401 N. Michigan Ave., 60611, pg. 428 PV
Fiber Optic Products Division, 7444 W. Wilson Ave., 60656, pg. 1101 PB
Fiduciary Management Associates, Inc., 55 W. Monroe St., Ste. 2550, 60603, pg. 1673 PB
WALLY FINDLAY GALLERIES INTERNATIONAL, 188 E. Walton Pl., 60611, pg. 405 PV
A. FINKL & SONS CO., 2011 N. Southport Ave., 60614, pg. 405 PV
FINNAIR, P.O. Box 10942, 60610, pg. 486 IT
First Capital Corp. of Chicago, One First National Plaza, 60670, pg. 628 PB
First Chicago Credit Corp., One First National Plaza, 60670, pg. 628 PB
First Chicago Financial Corp., One First National Plaza, 60670, pg. 628 PB
First Chicago Futures, Inc., One First National Plaza, 60670, pg. 628 PB
First Chicago Investment Corp., One First National Plaza, 60670, pg. 628 PB
First Chicago Leasing Corp., One First National Plaza, 60670, pg. 628 PB
FIRST CHICAGO NBD CORPORATION, One First National Plaza, Ste. 91, 60670, pg. 627 PB
First Chicago Trading Co., One First National Plaza, 60670, pg. 628 PB
First National Bank of Chicago, One First National Plaza, 60670, pg. 627 PB
Fleishman-Hillard, Inc., John Hancock Center, Ste. 3300, 875 N. Michigan Ave., 60611-1901, pg. 411 PV
Flex-Kleen Corporation, 165 No. Canal St., 60606, pg. 29 PB
Flex-O-Film Plastic Div., 1100 N. Cicero Ave., 60651, pg. 412 PV
FLEX-O-GLASS, INC., 4647 W. Augusta Blvd., 60651, pg. 412 PV
FLORSHEIM GROUP INC., 200 N. LaSalle St., 60601-1014, pg. 656 PB
FLYING FOOD FARE, INC., 5945 S. Keating Ave., 60629, pg. 415 PV
Follett Educational Services, 5563 S. Archer Ave., 60638, pg. 417 PV
Food Life, Water Tower Place, 835 N. Michigan Ave., Mezzanine Level, 60611, pg. 661 PV
Foote-Jones/Illinois Gear, 2102 N. Natchez Ave., 60707, pg. 1370 PB
Force Imaging Technologies, 3424 Touthy Ave., 60645-2717, pg. 251 PB
Four-Ten Corp., 410 N. Michigan Ave., 60611, pg. 1781 PB
FRANKEL & COMPANY, 111 E. Wacker Dr., 60601, pg. 424 PV
FRIEDMAN, EISENSTEIN, RAEMER AND SCHWARTZ, LLP, 401 N. Michigan Ave., Ste. 2600, 60611, pg. 428 PV
FRUIT OF THE LOOM, INC., 5000 Sears Tower, 233 S. Wacker Dr., Ste. 5000, 60606, pg. 685 PB
Fuji Securities Inc.-Chicago, 311 S. Wacker Dr., Ste. 2000, 60606-6620, pg. 519 IT
GATX CORPORATION, 500 W. Monroe St., 60661-3676, pg. 690 PB
GATX Las Vegas Corporation, 500 W. Monroe, 60661, pg. 692 PB
GATX Pipeline Company, 500 W. Monroe, 60661, pg. 692 PB
GATX Terminals Corporation, 500 W. Monroe, 60661, pg. 692 PB
GCI HOLDINGS CORPORATION, 2141 S. Jefferson St., 60616, pg. 434 PV
GGP/Homart, Inc., 53 West Monroe Rd., Ste.3100, 60603, pg. 715 PB
GMO Land Company, 636 Michigan Ave., 60638, pg. 865 PB
GSC ENTERPRISES, INC., 55 E. Monroe St., Ste. 1600, 60603, pg. 436 PV
GSP MARKETING SERVICES, INC., 320 W. Ohio, 60610, pg. 436 PV
G.Y. Industries, Inc., 30 S. Laflin St., 60607, pg. 89 PB
Gatorade Worldwide Division, 321 N. Clark St., 60610, pg. 1347 PB
General American Transportation Corporation, 500 W. Monroe St., 60661-3676, pg. 692 PB
General Drug Co., 200 N. Fairfield Ave., 60612, pg. 1007 PV
General Electric Capital Railcar Services, 33 W. Monroe St., 60603, pg. 712 PB
General Electric Railcar Repair Services Corp., 33 W. Monroe, 60603, pg. 712 PB
General Employment Enterprises, Inc., 120 S. Riverside Plaza, 60606, pg. 714 PB
General Felt- Central Div., 13-150 Merchandise Mart, 60654, pg. 1095 PV
General Growth Management, Inc., 55 W. Monroe, Ste. 3100, 60603, pg. 715 PB
GENERAL GROWTH PROPERTIES INC., 55 W. Monroe, Ste. 3100, 60603, pg. 715 PB
GERBER PLUMBING FIXTURES CORPORATION, 4600 W. Touhy Ave., 60646, pg. 449 PV
Godwins, Booke & Dickenson, Inc., 123 N. Wacker Dr., Ste. 1000, 60606, pg. 117 PB
GOLD EAGLE COMPANY, 4400 S. Kildare, 60632, pg. 459 PV
Goldblatt's Department Stores, 5630 W. Belmont Ave., 60634, pg. 917 PB
The Golden Touch Division, 4400 S. Kildare, 60632, pg. 459 PV
Goldman, Sachs & Co., 4900 Sears Tower, 60606, pg. 462 PV
Golin/Harris Communications, Inc., 111 E. Wacker Dr., 10th Fl., 60601-3704, pg. 1226 IT
GOLUB & CO., 625 N. Michigan Ave., Ste. 2000, 60611, pg. 463 PV
GONNELLA BAKING CO., 2002-14 W. Erie St., 60612, pg. 463 PV
SHELDON GOOD & CO., 333 W. Wacker Dr., Ste. 450, 60606-1225, pg. 463 PV
Graham Gregory Bozell, Inc., 455 N. City Front Dr., 15th Fl., 60611, pg. 1642 PB
GRAHAM PAINT AND VARNISH COMPANY, 4800 S. Richmond St., 60632, pg. 468 PV
GRANT/JACOBY, INC., 737 N. Michigan Ave., 60611, pg. 470 PV
GRANT THORNTON LLP, 800 One Prudential Plaza, 130 East Randolph Dr., 60601, pg. 470 PV
Graphics Management, Ste. 2000 The Merchandise Mart, 200 World Trade Ctr., 60601, pg. 518 PB
Graycor Blasting Company Inc., 12233 Ave. O, 60633, pg. 472 PV
GRAYMILLS CORP., 3705 N. Lincoln Ave., 60613, pg. 473 PV
GREAT AMERICAN MANAGEMENT & INVESTMENT, INC., Ste. 1100, Two N. Riverside Plaza, 60606, pg. 473 PV
Great Western Steel, 2310 W. 58th St., 60636, pg. 1640 PB
Greater Chicago Auto Auction, 12000 S. Cicero Ave., 60658, pg. 282 PV
Grey Directory Marketing Inc., 350 W. Hubbard St., 60610, pg. 764 PB
Griffin Wheel Co., 200 W. Monroe St., 60606, pg. 68 PV
R.J. Grunts/Chicago, 2056 Lincoln Park W., 60614, pg. 661 PV
HGC Bank, 111 W. Monroe St., 60603, pg. 154 IT
HLB COMMUNICATIONS, INC., 875 N. Michigan Ave., Ste. 1340, 60611, pg. 491 PV
HOH Architects, Inc., 180 N. Wabash Ave., 60601, pg. 492 PV
HOH Engineers, Inc., 180 N. Wabash Ave., 60601, pg. 492 PV
THE HOH ORGANIZATIONS, 180 N. Wabash Ave., 60601, pg. 492 PV
HRR Enterprises, Inc., 2129 W. Pershing Rd., 60609, pg. 607 PV
HSN Telecommunications, Inc., 100 S. Sangamon, 60607, pg. 1685 PB
THE C.P. HALL COMPANY, 311 S. Wacker Dr., Ste. 4700, 60606, pg. 495 PV
HAMILTON COMMUNICATIONS GROUP, INC., 727 N. Hudson, 60610, pg. 497 PV
The Hamilton Communications Group, 727 N. Hudson, 60610, pg. 497 PV
HAMMACHER, SCHLEMMER & CO., INC., 303 W. Erie St., 60610, pg. 497 PV
Hanna Corporation, 1765 N. Elston Ave., 60622, pg. 231 PV
Harcourt Brace & Company Legal and Professional Publications, Inc., 176 W. Adams, Ste. 2100, 60603, pg. 783 PB
HARPO ENTERTAINMENT GROUP, 110 N. Carpenter St., 60607, pg. 504 PV
HARRINGTON & KING, 5655 Fillmore St., 60644, pg. 504 PV
Harris & Bank, 111 W. Monroe St., 60603, pg. 154 IT
Harris Bankcorp, Inc., 111 W. Monroe St., 60603, pg. 154 IT
Harris Building Services Corporation, 111 W. Monroe St., 60603, pg. 154 IT
Harris Futures Corporation, 111 W. Monroe St., 60603, pg. 154 IT
Harris Investment Management, Inc., 111 W. Monroe St., 60603, pg. 154 IT
Harris Investors Direct, Inc., 111 W. Monroe St., 60603, pg. 154 IT
Harris-Nesbitt Thomson Securities, Inc., 111 W. Monroe St., 60603, pg. 155 IT
Harris Trading Advisory Corporation, 111 W. Monroe St., 60603, pg. 154 IT
Harriscorp Capital Corporation, 111 W. Monroe St., 60603, pg. 155 IT
Harriscorp Finance, Inc., 111 W. Monroe St., 60603, pg. 155 IT
Harriscorp Leasing, Inc., 111 W. Monroe St., 60603, pg. 155 IT
Hart Schaffner & Marx Clothes, 101 N. Wacker Dr., 60606, pg. 795 PB
HARTMARX CORPORATION, 101 N. Wacker Dr., 60606, pg. 795 PB
HARZA ENGINEERING CO., Sears Tower, 233 S. Wacker Dr., 60606-6392, pg. 509 PV

PB - *U.S. Public Companies Volume*
PV - *U.S. Private Companies Volume*
IT - *International Public & Private Companies Volume*

Harza Environmental Services, Inc., 233 S. Wacker Dr., 9th Fl., 60606-6392, pg. 509   **PV**

Hat Dance, 325 W. Huron, 60610, pg. 661   **PV**

Harry O. Hefter-Associates, Inc., 180 N. Wabash Ave., 60601, pg. 492   **PV**

Heitman Financial Ltd., 180 N. LaSalle, 60601-2886, pg. 1673   **PB**

Helene Curtis Industries, Inc., 325 N. Wells St., 60610, pg. 1434   **IT**

Helene Curtis North America, 325 N. Wells St., 60610, pg. 1434   **IT**

Heller Financial, Inc., 500 W. Monroe St., 60661, pg. 519   **IT**

HELLER INTERNATIONAL, 500 W. Monroe, 60661, pg. 520   **PB**

Heller International Corporation, 500 W. Monroe St., 60661, pg. 519   **IT**

Heller International Group, Inc., 500 W. Monroe St., 60661, pg. 519   **IT**

Hewlett-Packard Company, 25 W. Monroe, #1308, 60606, pg. 814   **PB**

Hickman, Williams & Company of Kentucky, 13513 S. Calumet Ave., 60627, pg. 525   **PV**

Hickory Furniture Company, 55 E. Monroe St., 60603, pg. 903   **PV**

Hinckley & Schmitt, Inc., 6055 S. Harlem Ave., 60638, pg. 1322   **IT**

Hodges Division, 901 N. Kilpatrick Ave., 60651, pg. 985   **PV**

Hollinger International Inc., 401 N. Wabash Ave., Ste. 740, 60611, pg. 632   **PB**

Home Owners Life Insurance Co., 307 N. Michigan Ave., 60601, pg. 1218   **PB**

HOME PRODUCTS INTERNATIONAL, INC., 4501 W. 47th St., 60632, pg. 832   **PB**

Hospitality Management Systems, Inc., 541 N. Fairbanks, Ste. 1880, 60611, pg. 1527   **PV**

Household Products Co., 5063 S. Merrimac Ave., 60638, pg. 387   **PB**

Howard's Electronics, 4573 Archer St., 60632, pg. 1720   **PV**

H.D. HUDSON MANUFACTURING COMPANY, 500 N. Michigan Ave., 60611, pg. 545   **PV**

Humana Health Chicago, Inc., 30 S. Wacker Dr., 60606, pg. 847   **PB**

Hummingbird Specialized Solutions, 727 N. Hudson, 60610, pg. 497   **PV**

Hy-Alloy Steels Co., 5100 W. 73rd St., 60638, pg. 313   **PV**

Hyatt Air, Inc., 200 W. Madison, 60606, pg. 551   **PV**

HYATT CORPORATION, 200 W. Madison St., 39th Fl., 60606, pg. 551   **PV**

Hyatt Hotels Corporation, 200 W. Madison St., 60606, pg. 551   **PV**

Hyatt International Corporation, 200 W. Madison, 60606, pg. 551   **PV**

I.B. DIFFUSION, LP, 5020 W. Roosevelt Rd., 60650, pg. 553   **PV**

IDC SERVICES, INC., 541 N. Fairbanks Ct., 60611, pg. 554   **PV**

IG Autotrim, Inc., 2639 E. 126th St., 60605, pg. 1117   **PV**

IGA, INC. (INDEPENDENT GROCERS ALLIANCE), 8725 W. Higgins, 60631, pg. 555   **PV**

IIT RESEARCH INSTITUTE, Ten W.35th St., 60616, pg. 555   **PV**

ING Futures & Options, The Sears Tower, 233 Wacker Dr., 52nd Fl., 60606, pg. 647   **IT**

IPC-International Parts Corp., 225 N. Michigan Ave., 60601, pg. 1766   **PB**

ITT Hoffman, 3500 N. Spaulding Ave., 60618, pg. 860   **PB**

ITT McDonnell & Miller, 3500 N. Spalding, 60618, pg. 860   **PB**

ITW Basic Switch Products, 6615 W. Irving Park Rd., 60634, pg. 866   **PB**

ITW Panel Switches and Systems, 6615 W. Irving Park Rd., 60634, pg. 866   **PB**

ITW Switches, 6615 W. Irving Park Rd., 60634, pg. 867   **PV**

Iberia Air Lines of Spain, 205 N. Michigan Ave., Ste. 3317, 60601, pg. 575   **IT**

Illinois Auto Central Div., 4750 S. Central, 60638, pg. 558   **PV**

Illinois Banc One Services, Inc., 120 W. Madison, 60602, pg. 174   **PB**

ILLINOIS CENTRAL CORPORATION, 455 N. Cityfront Plaza Dr., 60611-5504, pg. 864   **PB**

Illinois Union Insurance Company, 8755 W. Higgins Rd., 60631, pg. 365   **IT**

Impact Communications Group, FCB Center, 101 E. Erie St., 10th Fl., 60611-2897, pg. 1641   **PV**

Indiana Financial Investors, Inc., 737 N. Michigan Ave., Ste. 1200, 60611, pg. 903   **PV**

Indosuez Carr Futures Inc., 10 S. Wacker Dr., Ste. 1125, 60606, pg. 314   **IT**

The Industrial Bank of Japan, Limited (Chicago Branch), 227 W. Monroe St., Ste. 2600, 60606, pg. 674   **IT**

Industrial Coatings Group, 2141 S. Jefferson St., 60616, pg. 434   **PV**

INDUSTRIAL STEEL & WIRE COMPANY, 1901 N. Narragansett Ave., 60639, pg. 561   **PV**

INFORMATION RESOURCES, INC., 150 N. Clinton St., 60661, pg. 875   **PB**

INFOVEST, INC., 444 Merchandise Mart, 60654-1105, pg. 562   **PV**

Inland International, Inc., 30 W. Monroe, 18th Fl., 60603, pg. 879   **PV**

INLAND STEEL INDUSTRIES, INC., 30 W. Monroe St., 60603, pg. 879   **PB**

Inso Chicago Corporation, 401 N. Wabash, Ste. 600, 60611, pg. 882   **PB**

Inter-Continental and Forum Hotels, 505 No. Michigan Ave., 60611, pg. 1178   **IT**

Interbrand Schechter, 303 E. Wacker Dr., 60601, pg. 1224   **PB**

INTERCOUNTY TITLE CO. OF ILLINOIS, 120 W. Madison, 60602, pg. 567   **PV**

Intercraph Corporation, 515 N. State St., 60610, pg. 891   **PB**

Interior Space International, 600 W. Fulton St., 60606, pg 379   **PV**

International Business and Mercantile Reassurance Company, 307 N. Michigan Ave., 60601, pg. 1218   **PB**

The International Commercial Bank of China, Two N. La Salle St., Ste. 1803, 60602, pg. 683   **IT**

International Division, 4400 S. Lildare, 60632, pg. 459   **PV**

International Quaker Food Products, 321 N. Clark St., 60610, pg. 1347   **PB**

Interstate National Corp., 55 E. Monroe St., 60603, pg. 59   **IT**

Intervisual Communications Inc., 77 W. Wacker Dr., 60601, pg. 518   **PV**

Investment Leasing Services, Inc., 55 E. Monroe, 60603, pg. 1073   **PV**

J & F Steel Corporation, 3360 W. 43rd St., 60632, pg. 79   **IT**

JG INDUSTRIES, INC., 5630 W. Belmont Ave., 60634, pg. 917   **PB**

JMB REALTY CORPORATION, 900 N. Michigan Ave., 60611, pg. 577   **PV**

Jack Levy Associates, Public Relations Dept., One E. Erie, 60611, pg. 664   **PV**

Jay Acvertising Corp.-Chicago Div., IPC Group, 101 Wacker Dr., Ste. 1600, 60606, pg. 583   **PV**

JAYS FOODS LLC, 825 E. 99th, 60628, pg. 584   **PV**

Jefferies & Company, Inc., 55 W. Monroe St., Ste. 400, 60603, pg. 925   **PB**

Jennings Land Company, 30 S. Wacker Dr., Ste. 2706, 60606, pg. 481   **PB**

JERNEERG INDUSTRIES, INC., 328 W. 40th pl., 60609, pg. 586   **PV**

Johnson Products Co., Inc., 8522 S. Lafayette, 60620, pg. 915   **PB**

JOHNSON PUBLISHING COMPANY, INC., 820 S. Michigan Ave., 60605, pg. 591   **PV**

JOHNSTOWN AMERICA INDUSTRIES, 980 N. Michigan Ave., Ste. 1000, 60611, pg. 933   **PB**

JORDAN TAMRAZ CARUSO ADVERTISING, INC., JTC Bldg., 1419 N. Wells St., 60610-1395, pg. 599   **PV**

Joslyn Corporation, 969 W. 37 Pl., 60609, pg. 481   **PB**

Joslyn Foreign Sales Corporation, 30 S. Wacker Dr., 60606, pg. 481   **PB**

Joslyn Manufacturing Co., 969 W. 37th Pl., 60609, pg. 481   **PB**

Joslyn Manufacturing Co.-Hardware Div., 3700 S. Morgan St., 60609, pg. 481   **PB**

Joslyn Sierra Corporation, 30 S. Wacker Dr., Ste. 2706, 60605, pg. 482   **PB**

Jupiter Energy Corp., 919 N. Michigan Ave., 60611, pg. 602   **PV**

Keebler Cone Co., 10839 S. Langley, 60628, pg. 657   **PV**

KELLY, SCOTT AND MADISON, INC., 35 E. Wacker Dr., Ste. 150, 60601, pg. 613   **PV**

Kensington & Eastern Railroad, 636 Michigan Ave., 60638, pg. 865   **PV**

KENTILE OPERTING CO., 4532 S. Kolin Ave., 60632, pg. 615   **PV**

Keystone Master Warehouse-Chicago, 3327 W. 47th Pl., 60632, pg. 955   **PV**

KEYWELL CORPORATION, 11900 S. Cottage Grove Ave., 60628, pg. 619   **PV**

Keywell Corporation, 11900 S. Cottage Grove Ave., 60628, pg. 619   **PV**

Knight Architects Engineers Planners, Inc., 549 W. Randolph St., 60661, pg. 626   **PV**

LESTER B. KNIGHT & ASSOCIATES, INC., 549 W. Randolph St., 60661, pg. 626   **PV**

Lester B. Knight Facilities Management, Inc., 549 W. Randolph St., 60661, pg. 627   **PV**

Koch Minerals, P.O. Box 17539, 60617-0539, pg. 628   **PV**

Korn/Ferry International, 120 S. Riverside Plaza, Ste. 918, 60606 pg. 633   **PV**

Kuroda Precision Industries, Ste. 108, 9400 W. Foster Ave., 60656 pg. 764   **IT**

L & W Supply Corp., 125 S.Franklin, 60606-4678, pg. 1650   **PB**

LINC Anthem Inc., 303 E. Wacker Dr., 60601, pg. 996   **PB**

LINC Finance Corporations, 303 East Wacker Dr., 60601, pg. 996   **PB**

LINC Financial Services, Inc., 303 E. Wacker Dr., 60601, pg. 996   **PB**

LINC Management Services, 303 E. Wacker Dr., 60601, pg. 996   **PB**

LIT America Inc., 30 S. Wacker, Ste. 1120, 60606, pg. 18   **PB**

LA PREFERIDA, INC., 3400 W. 35th St., 60632, pg. 640   **PV**

Lake Shore Press, Inc., 680 N. Lake Shore Dr., 60611, pg. 1310   **PB**

LAKEWOOD ENGINEERING & MANUFACTURING CO., 501 N. Sacramento Blvd., 60612, pg. 644   **PV**

LAKIN GENERAL CORPORATION, 2044 N. Dominick St., 60614, pg. 644   **PV**

Landau & Heyman Inc., 180 N. LaSalle, Ste. 1420, 60601, pg. 646   **PV**

LAPHAM-HICKEY STEEL CORP., 5500 W. 73rd St., 60638, pg. 651   **PV**

LaSalle Advisors Limited, 11 S. LaSalle St., 60603, pg. 979   **PB**

LaSalle Bank Lake View, 3201 N. Ashland Ave., 60657, pg. 10   **IT**

LaSalle Cragin Bank, 5200 W. Fullerton Ave., 60639, pg. 10   **IT**

LaSalle National Bank, 135 S. LaSalle, 60603, pg. 10   **IT**

LaSalle Northwest National Bank, 4747 W. Irving Park Rd., 60641, pg. 10   **IT**

LASALLE PARTNERS, 200 E. Randolph Dr., 60601, pg. 978   **PB**

LaSalle-Talman Bank, 30 W. Monroe St., 60603, pg. 11   **IT**

LAVA WORLD INTERNATIONAL/HAGGERTY ENTERPRISES, INC., 5921 W. Dickens Ave., 60639, pg. 653   **PV**

THE LEAP PARTNERSHIP, 22 W. Hubbard St., 60610, pg. 653   **PV**

Lease Investment Corporation, 303 East Wacker Dr., 60601, pg. 996   **PB**

LETTUCE ENTERTAIN YOU ENTERPRISES, INC., 5419 N. Sheridan Rd., 60640, pg. 661   **PV**

THE CHAS. LEVY COMPANY, 1200 N. North Branch St., 60622, pg. 664   **PV**

Charles Levy Transportation Inc., 1200 N. North Branch St., 60162, pg. 664   **PV**

JACK LEVY ASSOCIATES, One E. Erie St., 60611, pg. 664   **PV**

THE LEVY ORGANIZATION, 980 N. Michigan Ave., Ste. 400, 60611, pg. 664   **PV**

Levy Real Estate Partners, 980 N. Michigan Ave., Ste. 400, 60611, pg. 664   **PV**

Levy Restaurants, 980 N. Michigan Ave., Ste. 400, 60611, pg. 664   **PV**

LEVY SECURITY CORP., 230 E. Ohio St., 60611, pg. 664   **PV**

Lifestyle Brands, Ltd., 680 N. Lake Shore Dr., 60611, pg. 1310   **PB**

LINC CAPITAL GROUP, 303 E. Wacker Dr., Ste. 1000, 60601, pg. 996   **PB**

LincAm Properties, Inc., 125 S. Wacker Dr., Ste. 3100, 60606, pg. 997   **PB**

LINCOLN PROVISION, INC., 824 W. 38th Place, 60609, pg. 668   **PV**

Lindenmeyr Central, 541 N. Fairbanks Ct., Ste. 1200, 60611, pg. 224   **PV**

Lindenmeyr Paper, 541 N. Fairbanks, Ste. 1200, 60611, pg. 224   **PV**

Arthur D. Little, Inc., 77 W. Wacker Dr., 7thFl., 60601, pg. 670   **PV**

Litton Precision Gear Div., 4545 S. Western Blvd., 60609-3059, pg. 1003   **PV**

LOEBER MOTORS, INC., 1111 N. Clark St., 60610, pg. 672   **PV**

Lois/EJL Advertising/Chicago, Equitable Bldg., 401 N. Michigan Ave., 60611, pg. 1011   **PB**

Lois/EJL Chicago, 2300 Merchandise Mart, 60654, pg. 1011   **PB**

THE LONG COMPANY, 300 W. Washington St., 60606, pg. 674   **PV**

Long-Term Credit Bank of Japan, Limited - Chicago, 190 South La Salle, Suite 800, 60603, pg. 816   **IT**

Longman Group USA Inc., 500 N. Dearborn St., 60605, pg. 1026   **IT**

MHIA Chicago Office, 875 N. Michigan Ave., Ste. 1201, 60611, pg. 874   **IT**

Maggiano's Little Italy, 516 N. Clark, 60610, pg. 661   **PV**

Managed Properties, Inc., 6700 W. North Ave., 60707, pg. 1428   **PB**

Marblehead Lime Co., 222 N. LaSalle St., 60601, pg. 709   **PB**

MARKETING SUPPORT, INCORPORATED, 200 East Randolph St., Ste. 5000, 60601, pg. 705   **PV**

MarketSource Corporation, 445 East Ohio, #3912, 60611, pg. 705   **PV**

THE MARMON GROUP, INC., 225 W. Washington St., 60606, pg. 706   **PV**

Marshall Field, 111 N. State Ave., 60602, pg. 489   **PB**

Marshall Field's, 111 N. State St., 60690, pg. 111   **PB**

The Marvel Group, Inc., 3843 W. 43rd St., 60632, pg. 1053   **PV**

Masonite Corporation, One S. Wacker Dr., 3rd Fl., 60606, pg. 904   **PB**

Material Service Corp., 222 N. LaSalle St., 60601, pg. 709   **PB**

Matra Transit, 8755 W. Higgins, Ste. 900, 60631, pg. 795   **PV**

MAUREY MANUFACTURING CORP., 2907 S. Wabash Ave., 60616, pg. 715   **PV**

Maytag International, Inc., 8700 W. Bryn Mawr Ave., 60631, pg. 1065   **PV**

MCCAIN BINDERY SYSTEMS, INC., 6200 W. 60th St., 60638, pg. 719   **PV**

The McClure Group/American Teledirect, OMNI Offices, 625 N. Michigan Ave., Ste. 500, 60611, pg. 720   **PV**

MCCONNAUGHY STEIN SCHMIDT BROWN, North Pier, 401 E. Illinois St., Ste. 500, 60611, pg. 720   **PV**

JAMES MCHUGH CONSTRUCTION CO., 2222 S. Indiana Ave., 60616, pg. 721   **PV**

Mellon Leasing Corporation, 55 W. Monroe St., Ste 2600, 60603, pg. 1085   **PB**

MERCHANT CAPITAL GROUP LTD., 200 W. Adams, Ste. 2905, 60606, pg. 732   **PV**

Merrill Corporation, 650 W. Washington Blvd., 60661, pg. 1097   **PB**

MESIROW FINANCIAL, 350 N. Clark St., 60610, pg. 733   **PV**

METHODE ELECTRONICS INC., 7444 W. Wilson Ave., 60656, pg. 1101   **PB**

Metra Commuter Rail, 547 N. Jackson, 60661, pg. 919   **PV**

Metra, Commuter Rail Service Board, 547 N. Jackson, 60606, pg. 919   **PV**

Metron Steel, 12900 Metron Dr., 60633, pg. 572   **IT**

METRON STEEL CORP., 12900 S. Metron Dr., 60633, pg. 736   **PV**

Metz Baking Co., 2883 S. Hillock Ave., 60608, pg. 1022   **PV**

PB - *U.S. Public Companies Volume*
PV - *U.S. Private Companies Volume*
IT - *International Public & Private Companies Volume*

Geographic Index-U.S.

The Meyne Company, 1755 W. Armitage Ave., 60622, pg. 180 PV
Michigan Holdings, Inc., 111 W. Monroe St., 60603, pg. 155 IT
MID AMERICAN ELEVATOR CO., INC., 820 Wolcott, 60622, pg. 743 PV
Midas-International Corp., 225 N. Michigan Ave., 60601, pg. 1766 PB
MIDCO INTERNATIONAL INC., 4140 W. Victoria, 60646, pg. 744 PV
Midland Finance Co., 7541 N. Western Ave., 60645, pg. 1093 PB
Midway Games, Inc., 3401 N. California Ave., 60618, pg. 1727 PB
Midwest Mezzanine Fund, 208 S. LaSalle, 60604, pg. 10 IT
Midwestern Holdings, Inc., 111 W. Monroe St., 60603, pg. 155 IT
MARILYN MIGLIN, L.P., 127 W. Huron, 60610, pg. 745 PV
Miller & Co., 55 E. Monroe St., 60603, pg. 1458 IT
Miller Comprehensive CPA Review, Inc., 176 W. Adams, Ste. 2050, 60603, pg. 783 PB
MILTON INDUSTRIES, INC., 4500 W. Cortland St., 60639, pg. 749 PV
MINCE MASTER, 6530 W. Dakin St., 60634, pg. 749 PV
ED MINIAT, INC., 945 W. 38th St., 60609, pg. 750 PV
Mississippi Valley Corp., 636 Michigan Ave., 60638, pg. 865 PB
The Mitsubishi Trust & Banking Corporation, 440 S. LaSalle St., Ste. 3100, 60605, pg. 876 IT
Mitsui & Co. (U.S.A.), Inc., 200 E. Randolph Dr., 60601, pg. 879 IT
The Mitsui Trust and Banking Company - Chicago, 190 S. LaSalle St., Ste. 1000, 60603, pg. 883 IT
Mitsui Trust & Banking Company, Limited, 190 S. LaSalle St., Ste. 1000, 60603, pg. 883 IT
Mity Nice Grill, Water Tower Place, 835 N. Michigan Ave., Mezzanine Level, 60611, pg. 661 PV
Modern Healthcare, 740 Rush St., 60611, pg. 285 PV
Montgomery & Collins, Inc. of Illinois, 525 W. Monroe, Ste. 2221, 60606-3629, pg. 366 PB
MONTGOMERY WARD & CO., INC., Montgomery Ward Plaza, 619 W. Chicago Ave., 60671, pg. 758 PV
E.R. MOORE CO., 1810 W. Grace St., 60613, pg. 759 PV
J.P. Morgan & Co. Incorporated, 227 W. Monroe St., 60606, pg. 1129 PB
J.P. Morgan Futures Inc., 227 W. Monroe St., 60606, pg. 1129 PB
J.P. Morgan Securities Inc., 227 W. Monroe St., 60606, pg. 1129 PB
Morgan Stanley Chicago, 440 S. LaSalle St., 60605, pg. 1132 PB
MORTON INTERNATIONAL INC., Morton Intl. Bldg., 100 N. Riverside Plaza, 60606-1596, pg. 1134 PB
Morton International Inc., 333 W. Wacker Dr., 60606-1292, pg. 1135 PB
Morton Salt, 100 N. Riverside Plaza, 60606-1597, pg. 1135 PB
Morton's of Chicago, Inc., 350 W. Hubbard St., Ste. 350, 60610, pg. 1136 PB
NAC Reinsurance Corporation-Chicago, Ten S. Wacker Dr., Ste. 1915, 60606-7407, pg. 1144 PB
NLI Properties Central, Inc., 190 S. LaSalle St., Ste. 1660, 60603, pg. 935 IT
NRG Energy Mining Company, 55 E. Monroe, 60603, pg. 1073 PV
NRG Incorporated, 55 E. Monroe, 60603, pg. 1073 PV
NRG NuFuel Co., 55 E. Monroe, 60603, pg. 1073 PV
NRG Technology, Inc., 55 E. Monroe, 60633, pg. 1073 PV
NS Sales Inc., c/o Nippon Steel USA, Inc., 900 Michigan Ave. #2810, 60611, pg. 940 IT
NWS INC., 2600 W. 35th St., 60623, pg. 772 PV
NACOLAH Holding Corp. Inc., 222 S. Riverside Plaza, 60606, pg. 963 PV
Nadel Architects Inc. & Marvin Fitch, 819 S. Wabash, 7th Fl., 60605, pg. 773 PV
National Baking, 5001 W. Polk St., 60644, pg. 1022 PV
National Bank of Greece Chicago Branch, 168 N. Michigan Avenue, 60601, pg. 907 IT
National Bank of Pakistan, 39, So. La Salle St., 60603, pg. 908 IT
National-Ben Franklin Insurance Co. of Illinois, 200 S. Wacker Dr., 60606, pg. 1011 PB
National Cattlemen's Beef Association, 444 N. Michigan Ave., 60611, pg. 780 PV
National Surety Corporation, 200 W. Monroe St., 60606, pg. 59 IT
NATIONAL SURGERY CENTERS, INC., 30 S. Wacker Dr., Ste. 2302, 60601, pg. 1161 PB
National Thermal Insulation, 55 E. Jackson Blvd., 60604, pg. 1096 PV
National Waste Services Inc., 2608 S. Damon, 60608, pg. 49 PB
NATIONWIDE BEEF, INC., 219 N. Green St., 60607, pg. 788 PV
NatWest Futures Inc., 175 W. Jackson Blvd., Ste. A1527, 60602, pg. 911 IT
NAVISTAR INTERNATIONAL CORPORATION, 455 N. Cityfront Plaza Dr., 60611, pg. 1167 PB
Navistar International Transportation Corp., 455 N. Cityfront Plaza Dr., 60611, pg. 1167 PB
NAYLOR PIPE COMPANY, 1230 E. 92nd St., 60619, pg. 789 PV
Naz-Dar Company, 1087 N. North Branch St., 60622, pg. 1084 PV
Newark Electronics Corporation, 4801 N. Ravenswood Ave., 60640, pg. 1068 IT
Newberg Perini, 651 W. Washington Blvd., 60661, pg. 1278 PB
NEWLY WEDS FOODS INC., 4140 W. Fullerton Ave., 60639, pg. 796 PV
NewsEdge Corp., 208 S. LaSalle Ste., Ste. 1260, 60604, pg. 1180 PB
Nichimen America, Inc., Chicago Branch, 225 N. Michigan Ave., 60601, pg. 928 IT
Nikko Securities Co., Chicago, One S. Wacker Dr., 27th Fl., 60606, pg. 930 IT
Nippon Steel U.S.A., Inc., 900 North Michigan Ave., Ste. 2810, 60611, pg. 940 IT
Nobart, Inc., 1133 S. Wabash Ave., 60605-2302, pg. 503 PB
NOBART, INC., 1133 S. Wabash Ave., 60605, pg. 800 PV
Noble & Associates/Chicago, 515 N. State St., 29th Fl., 60610, pg. 800 PV
Noble & Associates Public Relations, 515 N. State, 29th Fl., 60610, pg. 800 PV
NorLease, Inc., 50 S. LaSalle St., 60675, pg. 1196 PB
North American Grain Div., 222 S. Riverside Plaza, 60606, pg. 268 PV
Northern Futures Corporation, 50 S. LaSalle St., 60675, pg. 1196 PB
The Northern Trust Company, 8501 W. Higgins Rd., 60631, pg. 1197 PB
The Northern Trust Company, 6401 N. Harlem Ave., 60631, pg. 1197 PB
The Northern Trust Company, 50 S. LaSalle St., 60675, pg. 1197 PB
NORTHERN TRUST CORPORATION, 50 S. LaSalle St., 60675, pg. 1195 PB
Northern Trust Securities, Inc., 50 S. LaSalle St., 60675, pg. 1196 PB
Northridge Industries, Inc., 200 W. Madison St., 60606, pg. 551 PV
The John Nuveen Company, 333 W. Wacker Dr., 60606, pg. 1429 PB
Nystrom Division of Herff Jones, 3333 Elston Ave., 60618, pg. 523 PV
OCE Holding USA, 5450 N. Cumberland, 60656, pg. 994 IT
OCE USA, Inc., 5450 N. Cumberland Ave., 60656, pg. 994 IT
ODG, 6200 W. 51st St., 60638, pg. 1774 PB
OSI, 1034 S. Kostner St., 60624, pg. 1068 PV
O'BRYAN BROTHERS INC., 4220 W. Belmont Ave., 60641, pg. 810 PV
OIL-DRI CORPORATION OF AMERICA, 410 N. Michigan Ave., Ste. 400, 60611, pg. 1214 PB
Old Kent Bank, 233 S. Wacker Dr. LI, 60606-6306, pg. 1216 PB
Old Republic Dealer Service Corporation, 307 N. Michigan Ave., 60601, pg. 1218 PB
OLD REPUBLIC INTERNATIONAL CORPORATION, 307 N. Michigan Ave., 60601, pg. 1218 PB
OLSON RUG COMPANY, 832 S. Central Ave., 60644, pg. 815 PV
OmniTRAX Inc., 2728 E. 104th St., 60617-5766, pg. 171 PV
O'NEIL INDUSTRIES INC., 2751 N. Clybourn Ave., 60614, pg. 817 PV
W.E. O'Neil Construction Company, 2751 N. Clybourn Ave., 60614, pg. 817 PV
Options Clearing Corp., 440 S. LaSalle St., 60605, pg. 62 PV
Optoelectronic Products Division, 7444 W. Wilson Ave., 60656, pg. 1101 PB
ORIX Real Estate Equities, Inc., 100 N. Riverside Plaza, Ste. 1400, 60606, pg. 1009 IT
Oto-Sonic, Inc., 4200 W. Bryn Mawr, 60646, pg. 132 PV
Outdoor Services, 737 N. Michigan Ave. #1210, 60611, pg. 1166 PV
Outdoor Systems, Inc.-Chicago, 444 N. Michigan Ave., 60611, pg. 1235 PB
R.S. OWENS, 5535 N. Lynch Ave., 60630, pg. 824 PV
PC QUOTE, INC., 300 S. Wacker Dr., Ste. 300, 60606, pg. 1240 PB
PCI Investments Inc., 2739 N. Elston Ave., 60647, pg. 89 PV
PLM Railcar Management Services, Inc., 10 S. Riverside Plaza, Ste. 1210, 60606, pg. 1241 PB
PPM America Inc., 225 W. Wacker Dr., Ste. 1200, 60606, pg. 1073 IT
PRC Environmental Management, Inc., 200 E. Randolph Dr., Ste. 4700, 60601, pg. 1582 PB
PS PROMOTIONS, INC., The PS Bldg., 8 E. Huron St., 60611-2706, pg. 828 PV
PVS Chemicals, Inc., 12260 S. Carondolet, 60633, pg. 828 PV
Pacific Wine Co., 2701 S. Western Ave., 60608, pg. 843 PV
Packaging and Material Handling Division, 200 E. Randolph Dr., 60601, pg. 606 PB
Paragus, 620 N. State St., 60610, pg. 661 PV
Parmelee Transportation Co., 1730 S. Indiana Ave., 60616, pg. 1030 PV
Frank Paxton Lumber Company, 5701 W. 66th St., 60638, pg. 585 PV
PEERLESS CONFECTION COMPANY, 1250 W. Schubert Ave., 60614, pg. 847 PV
Pensions & Investments, 740 Rush St., 60611, pg. 285 PV
Peoples District Energy Corporation, 130 Randolph Dr., 60601-6207, pg. 1275 PB
PEOPLES ENERGY CORPORATION, 130 E. Randolph Dr., 24th Fl., 60601-6207, pg. 1274 PB
Peoples Energy Services Corporation, 130 E. Randolph Rd., 60601-6207, pg. 1275 PB
The Peoples Gas Light & Coke Co., 130 E. Randolph Dr., 60601-6207, pg. 1275 PB
Peoples NGV Corp., 130 E. Randolph Dr., 60601-6207, pg. 1275 PB
THE PEPPER COMPANIES, INC., 643 N. Orleans St., 60610, pg. 851 PV
Pepper Environmental Technologies, Inc., 643 North Orleans St., 60610, pg. 851 PV
Peters Machinery Co., 4700 N. Ravenswood, 60640-4493, pg. 944 PB
Pharmaceutical Basics, Inc., 8755 W. Higgins, Ste. 810, 60631, pg. 48 IT
Pie Piper Products, Ltd., 2501 N. Damen, 60647, pg. 1140 PV
Pitney Bowes Management Services, 209 S. Jackson, 60606-6907, pg. 1304 PB
PITTWAY CORPORATION, 200 S. Wacker Dr., Ste. 700, 60606-5802, pg. 1305 PB
Playboy Clubs International, Inc., 680 N. Lake Shore Dr., 60611, pg. 1310 PB
PLAYBOY ENTERPRISES, INC., 680 N. Lake Shore Dr., 60611, pg. 1309 PB
Playboy Franchisings Inc., 680 N. Lake Shore Dr., 60611, pg. 1310 PB
PLIBRICO CO., 1800 N. Kingsbury St., 60614, pg. 872 PV
Plibrico Sales & Service, Inc., 1800 N. Kingsbury, 60614, pg. 872 PV
Postal Systems Inc., 6802 McCormick Rd., 60645-2797, pg. 201 PB
Potentia Healthcare Communications Partners, 211 E. Chicago Ave., Ste. 920, 60611-2660, pg. 1224 PB
Practice Development Institute, 401 N. Michigan Ave., #2600, 60601, pg. 428 PV
Pragmaton, 211 E. Chicago Ave., 60611, pg. 1224 PB
Precision, 1140 Merchandise Mart, 60654, pg. 581 PV
Precision Universal Joint Co., 3440 N. Kedzie, 60618, pg. 443 PB
PRIME GROUP REALTY TRUST, 77 W. Wacker Dr., Ste. 3900, 60601, pg. 1326 PB
Private Brands, 707 N. Western Ave., 60612-1288, pg. 508 PV
Private Label Division, 4400 S. Kildare, 60632, pg. 459 PV
Process Color Plate, 1200 W. Monroe, 60607, pg. 1437 PB
Production Payments, Inc., 541 N. Fairbanks Ct., 60611, pg. 554 PV
PRODUCTION TOOL CORPORATION, 1229-41 E. 74th St., 60619, pg. 889 PV
Promotion Information Management (PIM), 165 N. Canal St., 60606, pg. 649 PV
QST INDUSTRIES, INC., 231 S. Jefferson, 60661, pg. 897 PV
THE QUAKER OATS COMPANY, Quaker Tower, 321 N. Clark St., 60610-4714, pg. 1347 PB
QUALITY CONTROL CORPORATION, 7315 W. Wilson Ave., 60656, pg. 898 PV
Quantum Media International, Inc., 875 N. Michigan Ave., 60611, pg. 899 PV
QUIXOTE CORPORATION, One E. Wacker Dr., Ste. 3000, 60601, pg. 1353 PB
R D I S CORPORATION, 55 E. Monroe St., Ste. 1600, 60603, pg. 903 PV
RLI Chicago Regional Office, 150 S. Wacker Dr., Ste. 1340, 60606, pg. 1356 PB
Ragold, Inc., 20 N. Wacker Dr., Ste. 3100, 60606, pg. 1084 IT
Rahway River Land Co., 500 W. Monroe, 60661, pg. 692 PB
RAPID MOUNTING & FINISHING CO., 4300 W. 47th St., 60632-4476, pg. 910 PV
Reader's Digest, 111 E. Wacker Dr., 60601-4208, pg. 1367 PB
READY METAL MANUFACTURING COMPANY, 4500 W. 47th St., 60632, pg. 913 PV
REFCO GROUP LTD., 111 W. Jackson Blvd., Ste. 1700, 60604, pg. 917 PV
Refco Inc., 111 W. Jackson, 60604, pg. 917 PV
REGIONAL TRANSPORTATION AUTHORITY (RTA), 181 W. Madison, Ste. 1900, 60602, pg. 918 PV
RELIANCE ELEVATOR COMPANY, 1101 W. Adams St., 60607, pg. 921 PV
REVERE ELECTRIC SUPPLY CO., 2501 W. Washington Blvd., 60612, pg. 926 PV
RICHCO INC., 5825 N. Tripp Ave., 60646, pg. 929 PV
Riddell Sports, Inc., 3670 N. Milwaukee Ave., 60641, pg. 1389 PB
Hal Riney & Partners Heartland, 224 S. Michigan Ave, Ste. 700, 60604, pg. 931 PV
The Ritz-Carlton, 160 E. Pearson St., 60611, pg. 502 IT
The Riverside Publishing Co., 3 O'Hare Towers, 8420 W. Bryn Mawr Rd., 60631, pg. 841 PB
RMI Insurance Co., NBC Tower, Ste. 31110, 455 N. Cityfront Plaza Dr., 60611, pg. 741 PV
Roberts & Schaefer Co., 120 S. Riverside Plaza, Ste. 400, 60606, pg. 371 PV
Rohm & Haas Illinois Inc., pg. 1403 PB
Rollins Hudig Hall of Montana, Inc., 123 N. Wacker Dr., 60606, pg. 117 PB
Ryan Insurance Group, Inc., 123 N. Wacker Dr., 60606, pg. 118 PB
Joseph T. Ryerson & Son, Inc., 2621 W. 15th Pl., 60608, pg. 879 PB
Ryerson Tull, 2621 W. 15th Pl., 60608, pg. 879 PB
RYMER FOODS INC., 4600 S. Packers Ave., Ste. 400, 60609, pg. 1414 PB
Rymer International Seafood Inc., 300 W. Washington Blvd., Ste. 1505, 60606, pg. 1414 PB
Rymer Meat Inc., 4600 S. Packers Ave., 60609, pg. 1414 PB
Ryobi North America, Inc., 225 W. Wacker Dr., Ste. 1900, 60606, pg. 1151 IT
S & C ELECTRIC COMPANY, 6601 N. Ridge Blvd., 60626-3997, pg. 954 PV
S-B Power Tool Company, 4300 W. Peterson Ave., 60646-5999, pg. 205 IT

PB - *U.S. Public Companies Volume*
PV - *U.S. Private Companies Volume*
IT - *International Public & Private Companies Volume*

Geographic Index-U.S.

SAS Institute, Inc., Two Prudential Plaza, 180 N. Stetson Ave., Ste. 5200, 60601, pg. 966 — **PV**

SBS Pharmaceuticals, 205 N. Fairfield Ave., 60612, pg. 1007 — **PV**

SEI Corporation, Two N. Riverside Plaza, 5th Fl., 60606-2637, pg. 1417 — **PV**

SEI Corporation, 181 W. Madison, 27th & 28th Fl., 60602, pg. 1417 — **PV**

SK Hand Tool Corp., 3535 W. 47th St., 60632, pg. 570 — **IT**

SPSS INC., 444 N. Michigan Ave., 60611, pg. 1430 — **PV**

Safco Technologies, Inc., 6060 Northwest Hwy., 60631, pg. 1430 — **PV**

SAHARA ENTERPRISES INC., Three First National Plaza, 60602, pg. 960 — **PV**

ST. PAUL BANCORP, INC., 6700 W. North Ave., 60707, pg. 1428 — **PB**

St. Paul Federal Bank for Savings, 6700 W. North Ave., 60707, pg. 1428 — **PB**

Sakura Bank - Chicago Branch, 227 W. Monroe St., Ste. 4700, 60606, pg. 1179 — **IT**

Sakura Dellsher, Inc., 10 S. Wacker Dr., 32nd Fl., 60606, pg. 1179 — **IT**

Sanwa Business Credit Corporation, One S. Wacker Dr., Ste. 3900, 60606, pg. 1189 — **IT**

Sanwa Futures L.L.C., 141 W. Jackson Blvd., Ste. 1755, 60604, pg. 1189 — **IT**

Sanyo Corp., 5432 N. Milwaukee Ave., 60630-1225, pg. 1191 — **IT**

Sara Lee Bakery, 224 S. Michigan Ave., 60604, pg. 1433 — **PB**

Sara Lee Bakery Worldwide, 224 S. Michigan Ave., 60604, pg. 1433 — **PB**

SARA LEE CORPORATION, Three First National Plaza, 70 W. Madison St., 60602-4260, pg. 1432 — **PV**

Sara Lee Corporation, Three First National Plaza, 60602, pg. 1434 — **PB**

SARGENT & LUNDY, 55 E. Monroe St., 60603, pg. 965 — **PV**

Schal Bovis Inc., 200 W. Hubbard St., 60610, pg. 1033 — **PV**

SCHULZE & BURCH BISCUIT COMPANY, 1133 W. 35th St., 60609, pg. 973 — **PV**

Sciaky, Inc., 4915 W. 67th St., 60638, pg. 862 — **PV**

Scoozi, 410 W. Huron, 60610, pg. 661 — **PV**

Searle Chemicals, Inc., P.O. Box 5110, 60680, pg. 1125 — **PV**

Select Canfield, 50 E. 89th Place, 60619, pg. 982 — **PV**

Self-Insurers Service, Inc., 123 N. Wacker Dr., 60601, pg. 117 — **PB**

Selfix, Inc., 4501 W. 47th St., 60632, pg. 832 — **PB**

SERVICE WEB OFFSET CORPORATION, 2500 S. Dearborn St., 60616, pg. 987 — **PV**

Shaw's Crab House/Chicago, 21 E. Hubbard, 60610, pg. 661 — **PV**

JOHN G. SHEDD AQUARIUM, 1200 N. Lake Shore Dr., 60605, pg. 991 — **PV**

Sheldon Good & Company Auctions, 333 W. Wacker Dr., Ste. 450, 60606, pg. 464 — **PV**

J.E. Siebel & Sons Company Inc., 4055 W. Peterson Ave., 60646, pg. 1110 — **IT**

Simmons Airlines, 900 N. Franklin, Ste. 800, 60610, pg. 9 — **PV**

Singapore Airlines Ltd., 122 So. Michigan, # 1710, 60603, pg. 1374 — **IT**

Singapore Tourist Promotion Board - Chicago, Two Prudential Plaza, 180 N. Stetson Ave., Ste. 1450, 60601, pg. 1254 — **IT**

Karl Singer Companies, Inc., 123 N. Wacker Dr., 60606, pg. 118 — **PV**

Skadden, Arps, Slate, Meagher & Flom (Illinois), 333 W. Wacker Dr., 60606, pg. 1004 — **PV**

Societe Generale, 181 W. Madison, Ste. 3400, 60602, pg. 1273 — **IT**

SOFT SHEEN PRODUCTS, INC., 1000 E. 87th St., 60619, pg. 1012 — **PV**

South Chicago Railroad Company, 636 Michigan Ave., 60638, pg. 865 — **PV**

SOUTHSIDE FORD TRUCK SALES INC., 810 W. Pershing Rd., 60609, pg. 1018 — **PV**

SOVEREIGN SPECIALTY CHEMICAL, INC., 225 W. Washington St., Ste. 2200, 60606, pg. 1019 — **PV**

Special Editions, Ltd., 680 N. Lake Shore Drive, 60611, pg. 1310 — **PB**

Special Instruments, 4201 W. Victoria, 60646, pg. 132 — **PV**

Spectra Marketing Systems, 333 W. Wacker Dr., Ste. 650, 60606, pg. 1447 — **PV**

Speedy Brake & Muffler, 8430 W. Bryn Mawr, 60631, pg. 1578 — **PB**

Speedy Car-X, Inc., 8430 W. Bryn Mawr Ave., 4th Fl., 60631, pg. 1578 — **PB**

The Sports Section Inc., 5207 N. Rose St., 60656, pg. 103 — **IT**

STANDARD MANIFOLD COMPANY, INC., 4020 N. Tripp Ave., 60641, pg. 1031 — **PV**

State Advertising Agency, Inc., 36 S. State St., 60603, pg. 597 — **PB**

State Bank of India, 19 South LaSalle Street, Ste. 200, 60603, pg. 1297 — **IT**

Steiner Co., Inc., One E. Superior St., 60611, pg. 1039 — **PV**

Steiner Electric Company, 2415 W. 19th. St., 60608, pg. 1039 — **PV**

STELAR INC., Ten S. Riverside Pl., Ste. 1459, 60606, pg. 1040 — **PV**

Sterling Steel Service Ltd., 13535 S. Torrence Ave., 60633, pg. 345 — **PV**

Stewart Smith Mid America, Inc., 120 S. Riverside Plaza, 60606, pg. 1508 — **IT**

THE STIFFEL COMPANY, 700 N. Kingsbury, 60610, pg. 1043 — **PV**

STOCK YARDS PACKING CO., INC., P.O. Box 12450, 60612 0450, pg. 1043 — **PV**

Stokely-Van Camp, Inc., 321 N. Clark St., 60610, pg. 1348 — **PB**

Stone & Webster Engineering, 120 S. Riverside Plaza, 60606-3913, pg. 1519 — **PB**

STONE CONTAINER CORPORATION, 150 N. Michigan Ave., 60601-7568, pg. 1520 — **PB**

Stone Forest Industries, 150 N. Michigan Ave., 60601, pg. 1521 — **PB**

Storck U.S.A., L.P., 500 N. Michigan Ave., Ste. 1100, 60611, pg. 1304 — **IT**

Strombecker Chemtoy Division, 600 North Pulaski Rd., 60624, pg. 1047 — **PV**

STROMBECKER CORPORATION, 600 N. Pulaski Rd., 60624, pg. 1047 — **PV**

Sula Supply, 837 N. California, 60622, pg. 1140 — **PV**

The Sumitomo Bank, Ltd.-Chicago Branch, Sears Tower, Ste. 4800, 233 S. Wacker, 60606, pg. 1308 — **IT**

Sumitomo Corporation of America, Two Prudential Plaza, 180 N. Stetson, 60601, pg. 1312 — **IT**

Sumitomo Metal U.S.A. Corp., Ste. 1000, 8750 W. Bryn Mawr Ave., 60631, pg. 1316 — **IT**

The Sumitomo Trust & Banking Co., Ltd., 10 South Wacker Dr., Ste. 2975, 60606, pg. 1317 — **IT**

SUPERIOR BANK, One Lincoln Ctr., 60181, pg. 1054 — **PB**

SUPERIOR GRAPHITE CO., 120 S. Riverside Plaza, 60606, pg. 1054 — **PV**

Supreme Beauty Products, 820 S. Michigan Ave., 60605, pg. 592 — **PV**

Sussex Group, Ltd., 5630 W. Belmont Ave., 60634, pg. 918 — **PB**

The Sweets Mix Company, Inc., 7401 S. Cicero Ave., 60629, pg. 1621 — **PB**

Swiss Bank Corporation, 141 W. Jackson Blvd., 60604, pg. 1329 — **IT**

Switchcraft, 5555 N. Elston Ave., 60630, pg. 1366 — **PB**

SYSTEM SOFTWARE ASSOCIATES, INC., 500 W. Madison St., Ste. 3200, 60661, pg. 1552 — **PB**

Systems Capital Corporation, 55 E. Monroe, 60603, pg. 1073 — **PV**

TMP Worldwide, Inc., 420 N. Wabash, Ste. 401, 60611, pg. 1065 — **PV**

TMP Worldwide/Recruitment Division, 420 N. Wabash, Ste. 300, 60611, pg. 1065 — **PV**

TN Media Inc., 101 E. Erie St., 60611, pg. 1641 — **PV**

TRI International Co., 7401 S. Cicero Ave., 60629, pg. 1621 — **PB**

TTX CO., 101 N. Wacker Dr., 60606, pg. 1066 — **PV**

Taisei America Corp., 225 W. Wacker Dr., Ste. 1950, 60606, pg. 1347 — **IT**

Talent Partners, 303 E. Ohio St., 60611, pg. 554 — **PV**

TALK-A-PHONE CO., 5013 N. Kedzie Ave., 60625, pg. 1067 — **PV**

Talman Home Mortgage Corp. & Talman Insurance Services, Inc., 30 W. Monroe St., 60603, pg. 11 — **IT**

Taproot Interactive, Inc., 400 N. State St., 60610, pg. 503 — **PB**

TARGETCOM, INC., The North Pier Terminal, 401 E. Illinois, Ste. 333, 60611, pg. 1069 — **PV**

TECHNOLOGY SOLUTIONS COMPANY (TSC), 205 N. Michigan Ave., Ste. 1500, 60601, pg. 1564 — **PB**

Telco Capital Corp., 737 N. Michigan, Ste. 1200, 60611, pg. 903 — **PB**

TELCO CAPITAL CORPORATION, 55 E. Monroe, 60603, pg. 1073 — **PV**

TELEPHONE AND DATA SYSTEMS, INC., 30 N. LaSalle St., Ste. 4000, 60602, pg. 1570 — **PB**

Thai Airways Intl. Ltd.-Chicago, 444 N. Michigan Ave., 3540, 60611, pg. 1381 — **IT**

Thompson-Starrett Construction Company, Inc., 120 S. Riverside Plaza, 60606, pg. 371 — **PV**

THRALL ENTERPRISES, INC., 181 W. Madison St., Ste. 4750, 60602, pg. 1084 — **PV**

360 DEGREES COMMUNICATIONS COMPANY, 8725 W. Higgins Rd., 60631, pg. 1607 — **PV**

THYBONY WALL COVERINGS CO., 3720 N. Kedzie Ave., 60618, pg. 1084 — **PV**

Tokio Marine Management Inc. - Chicago, 444 N. Michigan Ave., 60601, pg. 1392 — **IT**

Tokyo-Mitsubishi Futures (USA) Inc., Ten S. Wacker Dr., Ste. 1030, 60606, pg. 157 — **IT**

Tool & Engineering Co., 900 W. 18th St., 60608, pg. 394 — **PV**

The Tootsie Roll Company, 7401 S. Cicero Ave., 60629, pg. 1621 — **PB**

TOOTSIE ROLL INDUSTRIES, INC., 7401 S. Cicero Ave., 60629, pg. 1621 — **PB**

Tootsie Roll Management, Inc., 7401 S. Cicero Ave., 60629, pg. 1621 — **PB**

Tootsie Roll Manufacturing Inc., 7401 S. Cicero Ave., 60629, pg. 1621 — **PB**

Tootsie Rolls-Latin America, Inc., 7401 S. Cicero Ave., 60629, pg. 1621 — **PB**

Tootsietoy Division, 600 No. Pulaski Rd., 60624, pg. 1047 — **PV**

Tootsietoy Preschool Products Div., 600 N. Pulaski, 60624, pg. 1047 — **PV**

TORCO OIL CO., 111 E. Wacker Dr., Ste. 1300, 60601, pg. 1092 — **PV**

Toronto Dominion (Illinois), Inc., 70 West Madison, Ste. 5430, 60602, pg. 1401 — **IT**

Total Research Corporation, 625 N. Michigan Ave., Ste. 420, 60611, pg. 1625 — **PB**

Total Security Solutions, 200 S. Michigan Ave., 60604, pg. 245 — **PV**

Toyo Seikan Kaisha, Ltd. (U.S.A.), 444 N. Michigan Ave., Ste. 3658, 60611, pg. 1411 — **IT**

Trace Laboratories Central, 4621 N. Olcott Ave., 60656, pg. 1101 — **PV**

Transamerica Commercial Finance Corp., Inc., Boulevard Towers N., 225 N. Michigan Ave., 60601, pg. 1630 — **PB**

Transatlantic Holdings Inc., 500 W. Madison St., Ste. 2710, 60661, pg. 84 — **PB**

TRANSCO INC., 55 E. Jackson Blvd., 60604, pg. 1096 — **PV**

Transco Products Inc., 55 E. Jackson Blvd., 60604, pg. 1096 — **PV**

Transco Realty Inc., 55 E. Jackson Blvd., 60604, pg. 1097 — **PV**

Transcoat Inc., 55 E. Jackson Blvd., 60604, pg. 1097 — **PV**

TRANSILWRAP COMPANY, INC., 2828 N. Paulina St., 60657, pg. 1097 — **PV**

Transilwrap Manufacturing Division, 2615 N. Paulina St., 60614, pg. 1097 — **PV**

Transportation Division, 150 N. Michigan Ave., 60601, pg. 663 — **PV**

TREASURE ISLAND FOODMARTS INC., 3460 N. Broadway, 60657, pg. 1098 — **PV**

Tribune Broadcasting Company, 435 N. Michigan Ave., 60611, pg. 1636 — **PB**

TRIBUNE COMPANY, 435 N. Michigan Ave., 60611-4001, pg. 1635 — **PB**

Tribune Education, Two Prudential Plaza, Ste. 1175, 60601, pg. 1636 — **PB**

Tribune Media Services, Inc., 435 N. Michigan Ave., 60611, pg. 1636 — **PB**

Tribune Publishing Company, 435 N. Michigan Ave., 60611, pg. 1636 — **PB**

TRIPLE A SPECIALTY COMPANY, 4953 W. 66th St., 60638, pg. 1103 — **PV**

TRIPPE MFG. CO., 500 N. Orleans, 60610-4188, pg. 1104 — **PV**

TRITON INDUSTRIES, INC., 1020 N. Kolmar Ave., 60651, pg. 1104 — **PV**

TrizecHahn Properties Inc., 500 W. Madison St., Ste. 3650, 60661, pg. 1425 — **IT**

TRUE NORTH COMMUNICATIONS INC., Corporate Headquarters, 101 E. Erie St., 60611-2897, pg. 1641 — **PB**

TRUSERV CORPORATION, 8600 W. Bryn Mawr, 60631-3505, pg. 1108 — **PV**

Tucci Benucch, 900 Michigan N., 60611, pg. 661 — **PV**

Tucci Milan, Six W. Hubbard, 60610, pg. 662 — **PV**

Turner Construction Co., 230 S. LaSalle St., Ste.750, 60604, pg. 1645 — **PB**

TURTLE WAX, INC., 5655 W. 73rd St., 60638, pg. 1110 — **PV**

2-Mile Company, 500 W. Monroe, 60661, pg. 692 — **PV**

UIP Engineered Products, Inc., 5401 W. Grand Ave., 60639, pg. 860 — **PV**

Un Grand Cafe', 2300 Lincoln Park W., 60614, pg. 662 — **PV**

UNR-Leavitt Div., 1717 W. 115th St., 60643, pg. 1404 — **PV**

USG CORPORATION, 125 S. Franklin, 60606-4678, pg. 1660 — **PB**

USG Interiors, Inc., 125 S. Franklin, 60606-4678, pg. 1660 — **PB**

USG International, 125 S. Franklin, 60606-4678, pg. 1660 — **PV**

ULTIMO LTD., 48 E. Oak St., 60611, pg. 1116 — **PV**

Unichema U.S.A., 4650 So. Racine Ave., 60609, pg. 1436 — **IT**

UNICOM CORPORATION, One First National Plaza, 10 S. Deerborn St., 60603, pg. 1664 — **PB**

Union Bank of Switzerland, 30 S. Wacker Dr., 60606, pg. 1440 — **IT**

United Casualty Insurance Company of America, One E. Wacker Dr., 60601, pg. 1694 — **PV**

United States Cellular Corporation, 8410 W. Bryn Mawr, Ste. 700, 60631, pg. 1572 — **PB**

United States Gypsum Co., 125 S. Franklin, 60606-4678, pg. 1660 — **PB**

USLIFE Financial Institution Marketing Group, Inc., 8501 W. Higgins Rd., 60631, pg. 77 — **PB**

USA Network, 401 No. Michigan Ave., 60611, pg. 1686 — **PV**

U.S. Yellow Pages, Olympic Center, 737 N. Michigan Ave., 60611, pg. 1167 — **PV**

UNITRIN, INC., One E. Wacker Dr., 60601, pg. 1693 — **PB**

UNITY MANUFACTURING CO., 1260 N. Clybourn Ave., 60610, pg. 1126 — **PV**

UNIVERSAL OVERALL COMPANY, 1060 W. Van Buren St., 60607, pg. 1127 — **PV**

Urban Retail Properties, Inc., 900 N. Michigan Ave., 60611, pg. 1700 — **PB**

URBAN SHOPPING CENTERS, INC., 900 N. Michigan Ave., 60611, pg. 1700 — **PB**

Valley Forge Life Insurance Company, CNA Plaza, 60685, pg. 267 — **PV**

VANCE INDUSTRIES, INC., 7401 W. Wilson Ave., 60656, pg. 1133 — **PV**

Verson Division, 1355 E. 93rd St., 60619, pg. 48 — **PV**

Vienna Beef, Ltd., 2501 N. Damen, 60647, pg. 1140 — **PV**

VIENNA SAUSAGE MFG. CO., 2501 N. Damen, 60647, pg. 1139 — **PV**

The Vigoro Corporation, 225 N. Michigan Ave., Ste. 2500, 60601, pg. 856 — **PB**

Viracon of Illinois, Inc., 1315 N. Branch St., 60622, pg. 120 — **PB**

Virginia Surety Co., Inc., 123 N. Wacker Dr., 60606, pg. 118 — **PV**

Viskase Corporation, 6855 W. 65th St., 60638, pg. 586 — **PB**

VITA FOOD PRODUCTS, INC., 2222 W. Lake St., 60612, pg. 1142 — **PV**

C.J. WITMER CO., 4202 W. 45th St., 60632, pg. 1142 — **PV**

WBBM-TV, 630 N. McClurg Ct., 60611, pg. 275 — **PB**

WCKG, Inc., 150 N. Michigan Ave., Ste. 1040, 60601, pg. 274 — **PB**

WFLD Inc., 205 No. Michigan Ave., 60601, pg. 926 — **IT**

WGCI-AM/FM, 6 N. Michigan Ave., 9th Fl., 60602, pg. 335 — **PB**

WGN Radio, 435 N. Michigan Ave., 1st Fl., 60611, pg. 1636 — **PB**

WGN-TV, 2501 Bradley Place, 60618, pg. 1636 — **PB**

WLIT-FM, 150 N. Michigan Ave., 60611, pg. 779 — **PV**

PB - *U.S. Public Companies Volume*
PV - *U.S. Private Companies Volume*
IT - *International Public & Private Companies Volume*

Geographic Index-U.S.

WLS-AM Holding Company, Inc., 190 N. State St., 60601, pg. 512 **PB**
WLS-FM Radio, Inc., 190 N. State St., 60601, pg. 512 **PB**
WLS, Inc., 190 N. State St., 60601, pg. 512 **PB**
WLS Television, Inc., 190 N. State St., 60601, pg. 512 **PB**
WMS Games Inc., 3401 N. California Ave., 60618, pg. 1727 **PB**
WMS Gaming Inc., 3401 N. California Ave., 60618, pg. 1727 **PB**
WMS INDUSTRIES INC., 3401 N. California Ave., 60618, pg. 1727 **PB**
WTTW (CHANNEL 11), 5400 N. St. Louis, 60625, pg. 1145 **PV**
Wabash Fibre Box Company-Chicago Plant, 6850 W. 62nd St., 60638, pg. 1170 **PV**
Waldom Electronics, Inc., 4301 W. 69th St., 60629-5719, pg. 944 **PB**
Wall Street Deli, Inc., 228 S. Wabash St., Ste. 228, 60604, pg. 1734 **PV**
Walsh Construction Co. of Illinois, 929 W. Adams, 60607, pg. 1148 **PV**
WALSH GROUP, 929 W. Adams, 60607, pg. 1148 **PV**
Waterloo Railway Company, 636 Michigan Ave., 60638, pg. 865 **IT**
Welded Tube, 1855 E. 122nd St., 60633, pg. 101 **IT**
Welded Tube Company, 1855 E. 122nd St., 60633, pg. 101 **IT**
WELLS-GARDNER ELECTRONICS CORP., 2701 N. Kildare Ave., 60639, pg. 1753 **PB**
Western International Media Corporation, Olympia Ctr., 737 N. Michigan Ave., Ste. 1200, 60611, pg. 1501 **PV**
WestLB Chicago, 181 W. Madison St., Ste. 4850, 60602, pg. 1493 **IT**
Wholesale/Retail Division, 4400 S. Kildare, 60632, pg. 459 **PB**
Williams Electronics Games, Inc., 3401 N. California Ave., 60618, pg. 1727 **PB**
Willis Corroon Aerospace-Midwest Region, 135 S. LaSalle St., Ste. 1800, 60603, pg. 1505 **IT**
Willis Corroon Corp. of Illinois, 135 S. La Salle St., Ste. 1800, 60603, pg. 1506 **IT**
Willis Faber North America, Inc.-Illinois, Wrigley Bldg., Ste. 904, 400 N. Michigan Ave., 60611, pg. 73 **IT**
Wilson Sporting Goods Co., 8700 W. Bryn Mawr Ave., 60631, pg. 1621 **PV**
Wilson Steel & Wire Co., 4840 S. Western Ave., 60609, pg. 686 **PV**
WIRTZ CORPORATION, 680 N. Lakeshore Dr., 60611, pg. 1184 **PV**
Woodward-Clyde, 122 S. Michigan Ave., Ste. 1920, 60603, pg. 1656 **PB**
World Book Childcraft Division, 510 Merchandise Mart Plaza, 60654, pg. 218 **PB**
World Book Finance, Inc., 510 Merchandise Mart Plaza, 60654, pg. 218 **PB**
World Book International, 525 W. Monroe, 20th Fl., 60606, pg. 218 **PB**
World Book Publishing, 525 W. Monroe, 20th Fl., 60606, pg. 218 **PB**
World Trade & Marketing, LTD., 7401 S. Cicero Ave., 60629, pg. 1621 **PV**
WORLD'S FINEST CHOCOLATE, INC., 4801 S. Lawndale Ave., 60632, pg. 1191 **PV**
Worldwide Foods, Inc., 3400 W. 35th St., 60632, pg. 640 **PV**
Worldwide Produce, Inc., 70-72 Water Market, 60608, pg. 640 **PV**
Worldwide Quaker Beverages, 321 N. Clark St., 60611, pg. 1347 **PB**
WM. WRIGLEY JR. COMPANY, 410 N. Michigan Ave., 60611, pg. 1781 **PB**
Yamaichi International (America) Inc.-Chicago Branch, 30 S. Wacker Dr., Ste. 3903, 60606, pg. 1517 **IT**
Yates Investment Casting Wax Inc., 1615 W. 15th St., 60608, pg. 234 **IT**
Yellow Cab Co., 1730 So. Indiana Ave., 60616, pg. 1030 **PV**
Young & Rubicam Chicago, One S. Wacker Dr., Ste. 1800, 60606, pg. 1198 **PV**
Z. Cavaricci, 350 N. Orleans Ste. 1225, 60654, pg. 1203 **PV**
Zenith Media Services, Inc., 737 N. Michigan Ave., Ste. 2000, 60611, pg. 1204 **PV**
Ziegler Securities Division, One S. Wacker Dr., Ste 3080, 60606-4617, pg. 1792 **PV**
Zimmerman & Partners Advertising, Inc., 645 N. Michigan Ave., Ste. 800, 60611, pg. 1206 **PV**
Zurich Kemper Investments, Inc., 222 S. Riverside Plaza, 60606, pg. 1530 **IT**

Chicago Heights

CWR Transportation Company, 1020 S. Washington, 60411, pg. 297 **PV**
CHICAGO HEIGHTS STEEL, 211 E. Main, 60411, pg. 234 **PV**
First National Bank in Chicago Heights, 100 First National Plaza, 60411, pg. 760 **PB**
Holland Company, 1020 S. Washington, 60411, pg. 297 **PV**
IMCO Recycling of Illinois, Inc., 100 First National Plaza, Ste. 500, 60411, pg. 871 **PB**
J & J Snack Foods Corp./Midwest, 401 E. Joe Orr Rd., 60411, pg. 916 **PV**
Liquid Colorant Operation, 385 East Joe Orr Rd., 60411, pg. 1134 **PB**
Morgan Marshall Industries, Inc., 383 E. 16th St., 60411, pg. 904 **PV**
Oil Purification Services of America, Inc., 375 E. Joe Orr Rd., 60411, pg. 46 **PV**

Plastic Suppliers Inc., 3330 Holeman Ave., 60411, pg. 871 **PV**
Star Publications, 1526 Otto Blvd., 60411, pg. 632 **IT**
Thrall Car Mfg. Co., 2521 State St., 60411-0218, pg. 344 **PV**
Transportation Corp. of America, 26th & State Sts., 60411, pg. 344 **PV**
UGL, Inc., 1001 State St., 60411, pg. 1117 **IT**
Vacudyne Inc., 375 E. Joe Orr Rd., 60411, pg. 46 **PV**

Chicago Ridge

Methode Technical Components, 6633 W. 99th St., 60415, pg. 1101 **PB**

Cicero

AMD INDUSTRIES INC., 4620 W. 19th St., 60804-2597, pg. 6 **PV**
CHICAGO EXTRUDED METALS CO., 1601 S. 54th Ave., 60804, pg. 234 **PV**
Danly Die Set Division, 2115 S. 54th Ave., 60650, pg. 264 **PV**
BRAD FOOTE GEAR WORKS, INC., 1309 S. Cicero Ave., 60650, pg. 417 **PV**
HARRIS STEEL CO., 1223 S. 55th Ct., 60804, pg. 506 **PV**
Kropp Forge Co., 5301 W. Roosevelt Rd., 60650, pg. 1064 **PV**
Lenc-Smith Inc., 4616 W. 19th St., 60618, pg. 1727 **PV**
Manufacturers' Junction Railroad Company, 2335 S. Cicero Ave., 60650-2451, pg. 1731 **PV**
Pub/Data, Inc., 5615 W. Cermak Rd., 60650, pg. 1076 **IT**
Simkins Carton Div.-Chicago, 5701 W. Ogden Ave., 60804, pg. 1000 **PV**
SOMMER & MACA INDUSTRIES, INC., 5501 W. Ogden Ave., 60804, pg. 1013 **PV**

Clarendon Hills

Woodland Mold & Tool Company, 452 Park Ave., 60514, pg. 694 **PB**

Clinton

Action Clinton, Rte. 10 E., P.O. Box 111, 61727, pg. 15 **PV**
Revere Ware Corporation, 1000 S. Chermain St., 61727, pg. 448 **PB**

Coal City

DEMERT & DOUGHERTY, INC., 1300 E. North St., 60416, pg. 323 **PV**

Collinsville

IMC Agribusiness, 6 Executive Dr., 62234, pg. 856 **PB**
S.A.S.I. CORPORATION, 1700 St. Louis Rd., 62234, pg. 955 **PV**
UMB First National Bank, 201 E. Main St., 62234, pg. 1654 **PB**

Columbia

Magna Bank, Columbia Region, 102 N. Main St., 62236, pg. 1037 **PB**

Colusa

COLUSA ELEVATOR CO., P.O. Box 26, 62329, pg. 257 **PV**

Countryside

HOLLYMATIC CORPORATION, 600 E. Plainfield Rd., 60525, pg. 535 **PV**
People's Choice-TV Corp. Preferred Entertainment, Inc., 6260 Joliet Rd., 60525, pg. 1274 **PB**
SOKOL & COMPANY, 5315 Dansher Rd., 60525, pg. 1012 **PV**

Crestwood

Computers, Etc., 13575 S. Cicero Ave., 60445, pg. 1522 **PB**

Creve Coeur

Peoria & Pekin Union Railway Co., 101 Wesley Rd., 61611, pg. 432 **PB**

Crystal Lake

APTARGROUP, INC., 475 W. Terra Cotta Ave., Ste. E, 60014, pg. 125 **PV**
Black Dot Graphics, Inc., 6115 Official Rd., 60039-9684, pg. 503 **PB**
Colman OEM, Inc., 7510 Virginia Rd., 60014, pg. 1242 **IT**
Curran Contracting Company, 7502 S. Main St., 60014, pg. 297 **PV**
CURRAN GROUP, INC., 7502 S. Main St., 60014, pg. 297 **PV**
Follett Library Resources, 4506 Northwest Hwy., 60014, pg. 417 **PV**
Precision Twist Drill Co., P.O. Box 9000, One Precision Plaza, 60039-9000, pg. 1185 **IT**
Rigby Education, 500 Coventry Lane, 60014, pg. 1094 **IT**

Triumph Twist Drill Co., One Precision Plaza, Box 9000, 60039-9000, pg. 1185 **IT**

Danville

CURT BULLOCK BUILDERS, INC., 720 S. Gilbert St., 61832, pg. 180 **PV**
CCL Custom Manufacturing, One W. Hegeler Ln., 61832-8398, pg. 238 **IT**
Commercial-News, 17 W. North St., 61832, pg. 700 **PB**
Donnelley Logistic Services, P.O. Box 360, 3295 E. Main St., pg. 518 **PB**
Grist Mill Company, 805 N. Griffin, 61832, pg. 766 **PB**
Hurletron Inc., 1938 E. Fairchild St., 61832, pg. 46 **PV**
Hyster International Sales Corporation, P.O. Box 847, 61832, pg. 1149 **PB**
Krupp Gerlach Company, 1000 Lynch Spur, 61834-0214, pg. 508 **IT**
Krupp Gerlach Company, Lynch Spur, 61834, pg. 508 **IT**
Palmer-American National Bank, Two W. Main St., 61852, pg. 1217 **PB**
TMP Worldwide, Inc., P.O. Box 1190, 61834-1190, pg. 1064 **PV**
Vermilion County Division, P.O. Box 1130, 322 N. Gilbert St., 61834-1130, pg. 438 **PB**

Darien

SELECT BEVERAGES, INC., 7955 S. Cass Ave., Ste. 201, 60561, pg. 982 **PV**

De Kalb

Caron International, 200 Gurler Rd., Ste. 1, 60115, pg. 786 **PV**
The Daily Chronicle, P.O. Box 587, 60115, pg. 1343 **PB**
DEKALB GENETICS CORPORATION, 3100 Sycamore Rd., 60115, pg. 493 **PB**
DeKalb Swine Breeders, Inc., 3100 Sycamore Rd., 60115, pg. 493 **PB**
Nehring Electrical Works Company, 813 E. Locust St., 60115, pg. 968 **PV**
A.O. Smith Harvestore Products, Inc., 345 Harvestore Dr., 60115, pg. 1477 **PB**
Stahl Construction Company, P.O. Box 506, 60115, pg. 297 **PV**

Decatur

ADM Corn Processing Division, P.O. Box 1470, 62525, pg. 127 **PB**
ADM Ethanol Sales, P.O. Box 1470, 62525, pg. 127 **PB**
ADM Food Additives Division, P.O. Box 1470, 62525, pg. 127 **PB**
ADM Food Oils, P.O. Box 1470, 62525, pg. 128 **PB**
ADM Lecithins, P.O. Box 1470, 62525, pg. 128 **PB**
ADM Processing Div., P.O. Box 1470, 62525, pg. 127 **PB**
ADM Protein Specialties, P.O. Box 1470, 62525, pg. 128 **PB**
Akorn Manufacturing, Inc., 150 S. Wyckles Rd., 62525, pg. 34 **PB**
American River Transportation Co., 4666 Faries Pkwy., 62525, pg. 128 **PB**
ARCHER DANIELS MIDLAND COMPANY (ADM), 4666 Faries Pkwy., 62526, pg. 127 **PB**
BLACK & CO., 1717 E. Garfield Ave., 62526, pg. 146 **PV**
Bridgestone/Firestone Tire Manufacturing Operations-Decatur, 2500 N. 22nd St., 62525, pg. 213 **IT**
Decatur Herald & Review, 601 E. William St., 62525, pg. 983 **PB**
Hickory Point Bank & Trust, 5525 Hickory Point Rd., 62526, pg. 1128 **PB**
IP Gas Supply Co., 500 S. 27th St., 62525, pg. 869 **PB**
Illinois Power Company, 500 S. 27th St., 62525, pg. 869 **PB**
Illinova Generating Co., 2828 N. Monroe, 62526-3269, pg. 870 **PB**
ILLINOVA INC., 500 S. 27th St., 62525, pg. 869 **PB**
LG Seeds Inc., P.O. Box 950, 62525, pg. 566 **IT**
Magna Bank, Decatur Region, One Millikin Ct., 62523, pg. 1037 **PB**
Mueller Co., 500 W. Eldorado, 62522, pg. 1650 **PB**
Southern Cotton Oil Co., Inc., P.O. Box 1470, 62525, pg. 128 **PB**
A.E. Staley Manufacturing Co., 2200 E. Eldorado St., 62525, pg. 1356 **IT**
WAND Television, Inc., 904 Southside Dr., 62525, pg. 11 **PV**
Wagner Castings Company, 825 N. Lowber, 62521, pg. 894 **PB**
ZEXEL Illinois Inc., 625 Southside Dr., 62521, pg. 1528 **IT**
ZEXEL Inc., 707 Southside Dr., 62521, pg. 1528 **IT**

Deerfield

Alliant Foodservice, Inc., One Parkway N., 60015, pg. 244 **PV**
Baxter Global Business Corporation, One Baxter Pkwy., 60015, pg. 196 **PB**
Baxter Healthcare Corporation, One Baxter Pkwy., 60015, pg. 196 **PB**
BAXTER INTERNATIONAL INC., One Baxter Pkwy., 60015-4633, pg. 196 **PB**
Bourbon Warehouse Receipts, Inc., 510 Lake Cook Rd., 60015, pg. 675 **PV**
Dade Behring, Inc., P.O. Box 778, 1717 Deerfield Rd., 60015-0778, pg. 110 **PV**
Dade Behring Inc., P.O. Box 778, 1717 Deerfield Rd., 60015-0778, pg. 626 **IT**

Geographic Index-U.S.

Deutsche Credit Corporation, 2333 Waukegan Rd., 60015, pg. 403 — IT

EA Engineering, Science & Technology, Inc., 444 Lake Cook Rd., Ste. 18, 60015, pg. 541 — PB

Fujisawa Research Institute of America, Pkwy. North Center, Three Pkwy. N., 60015, pg. 525 — IT

Fujisawa U.S.A., Pkwy. North Center, Three Pkwy. North, 60015, pg. 525 — IT

Fujisawa U.S.A. Inc., Three Pkwy. N. Center, 60015, pg. 525 — IT

GAYLORD CONTAINER CORPORATION, 500 Lake Cook Rd., Ste. 400, 60015, pg. 704 — PB

J&M Company, 400 Lake Cook Rd., Ste. 107, 60015, pg. 770 — PV

J2, Inc., Arborlake Center, 1751 Lake Cook Rd., Ste. 550, 60015, pg. 598 — PV

JBB Worldwide, Inc., 510 Lake Cook Rd., 60015-4916, pg. 675 — PB

JORDAN INDUSTRIES, INC., 1751 Lake Cook Rd., Ste. 550, 60015, pg. 598 — PV

KLEINSCHMIDT INC., 450 Lake-Cook Rd., 60015-4973, pg. 625 — PV

Leica Inc., 111 Deer Lake Rd., 60015, pg. 806 — IT

MMI COMPANIES, INC., 540 Lake Cook Rd., 60015, pg. 1027 — PB

MERIDIAN TECHNOLOGY LEASING SERVICES, 570 Lake Cook Rd., Ste. 300, 60015, pg. 732 — PB

Metz Baking Company, 520 Lake Cook Rd., Ste. 550, 60015, pg. 1022 — PV

MY OWN MEALS, INC., 400 Lake Cook Rd., 60015, pg. 770 — PV

The NutraSweet Company, 1751 Lake Cook Rd., 60015, pg. 1125 — PV

PREMARK INTERNATIONAL, INC., 1717 Deerfield Rd., 60015, pg. 1321 — PB

STS CONSULTANTS, INC., 1415 Lake Cook Rd., 60015, pg. 959 — PV

Shaw's Deerfield, 660 Lake Cook Rd., 60015, pg. 661 — PV

SPECIALTY FOODS CORPORATION, 520 Lake Cook Rd., Ste. 500, 60015, pg. 1022 — PV

TAP Pharmaceuticals, Inc., Bannockburn Lake Office Plaza, 2355 Waukegan Rd., 60015, pg. 1350 — IT

Tenneco Automotive, 111 Pfingsten Rd., 60015, pg. 1577 — PB

Tenneco Packaging, Consumer Products Group, One Pkwy. N., 60015, pg. 1579 — PB

Tenneco Specialty Products, One Parkway North Center, 60015, pg. 1579 — PB

Teradyne Telecommunications Division, 1405 Lake Cook Rd., 60015, pg. 1581 — PB

V. Mueller, 1435 Lake Cook Rd., 60015, pg. 44 — PB

WALGREEN CO., 200 Wilmot Rd., 60015, pg. 1733 — PB

Walker Manufacturing Co., 111 Pfingsten Rd., 60015, pg. 1578 — PV

Zenith Data Systems, 510 Lake Cook Rd., Ste. 100, 60015, pg. 317 — IT

Depue

Frontier Communications of DePue, Inc., P.O. Box 110, Fourth & Lake Sts., 61322, pg. 683 — PB

Des Plaines

Bake-Line Products, Inc., One Bake-Line Plaza, 60016, pg. 657 — PB

Beck/Arnley Worldparts Corp., 29 E. Rawls Rd., 60018, pg. 561 — PB

Bradley Printing Company, 2170 S. Mannheim Rd., 60018, pg. 1778 — PB

Bresler's Industries, Inc., 999 E. Touhy Ave., Ste. 333, 60018, pg. 1520 — IT

C-LINE PRODUCTS, INC., 1530 Birchwood Ave., 60018, pg. 192 — PV

Candle Corporation of America, 999 E. Touhy Ave., 60018, pg. 239 — PB

THE CHICAGO FAUCET CO., 2100 S. Clearwater Dr., 60018-5999, pg. 234 — PV

Chicago Laser Systems, 1798 Sherwin Ave., 60018, pg. 569 — PB

Cigna Healthcare of Illinois, Inc., 1700 Higgins Rd., Ste. 600, 60018, pg. 359 — PB

CLOUD CORPORATION, 424 Howard Ave., 60018, pg. 247 — PV

DSC LOGISTICS, INC., 1750 S. Wolf Rd., 60018, pg. 306 — PV

Dentsply Gendex Division, 901 W. Oakton St., 60018, pg. 499 — PB

DISTRIBUTION AMERICA, 2700 River Rd., Ste. 300, 60018-4107, pg. 335 — PV

DOALL COMPANY, 254 N. Laurel Ave., 60016, pg. 337 — PV

Filtran, 875 Seegers Rd., 60016, pg. 1421 — PB

FRANK CONSOLIDATED ENTERPRISES INC., 666 Garland Place, 60016, pg. 423 — PV

Geonex, 2140 Wolf Rd., 60018, pg. 448 — PV

A.J. GERRARD AND COMPANY, 400 E. Touhy Ave., 60018-2684, pg. 449 — PV

Hausman Bus Sales, Inc., 10 East Golf Rd., 60016, pg. 326 — IT

ITC Flavor & Seasoning Div., 521 Santa Rosa Dr., 60018, pg. 459 — PB

ITW Fastex, 195 Algonquin Rd., 60016, pg. 866 — PB

Interstate Steel Co. Inc., 401 E. Touhy Ave., 60017, pg. 572 — IT

JUNO LIGHTING, INC., 1300 S. Wolf Rd., 60018, pg. 935 — PB

Justrite Manufacturing Company, 2454 Dempster St., 60016, pg. 617 — PV

Kester Solder, 515 E. Touhy Ave., 60018-2675, pg. 1003 — PB

LA MARCHE MFG. CO., 106 Bradrock Dr., 60018, pg. 640 — PV

Larry's Industries, Inc., 999 E. Touhy Ave., 60018, pg. 1520 — IT

LAWSON PRODUCTS, INC., 1666 E. Touhy Ave., 60018, pg. 980 — PB

LITTELFUSE, INC., 800 E. Northwest Hwy., 60016, pg. 1001 — PB

Mark Antenna Products, Inc., 1757 S. Winthrop Dr., 60018, pg. 424 — PV

Micropolis Corporation, 2200 E. Devon, Ste. 114, 60018, pg. 742 — PV

Midwest Dental, 901 W. Oakton St., 60018, pg. 499 — PB

Midwest Litho Arts, 125 E. Oakton, 60018, pg. 1779 — PB

National Lamination Co., 555 Santa Rosa Dr., 60018, pg. 1068 — PV

Nippondenso of Los Angeles (Chicago), 2604 E. Dempster, 60016, pg. 1412 — IT

Omni-One, 2200 E. Devon Ave., Ste. 246, 60018, pg. 715 — PB

PAMCO Printed Tape & Label Company, Inc., 2200 South Wolf Rd., 60018, pg. 598 — PV

Porth Plastic Co., 1630 Birchwood Ave., 60018, pg. 233 — IT

Pro Portion Industries, Inc., 999 E. Touhy Ave., 60018, pg. 1520 — IT

Reed Elsevier Business Information-Des Plaines, 1350 E. Touhy Ave., 60018, pg. 1095 — IT

J.H. ROBERTS INDUSTRIES INC., 3158 Des Plaines Ave., Ste. 115, 60018, pg. 935 — PV

SRDS, 1700 Higgins Rd., 60018, pg. 958 — PV

SAGE ENTERPRISES, INC., 999 E. Touhy Ave., Ste. 200, 60018-2736, pg. 960 — PV

Sandoz Agro, Inc., 1300 E. Touhy Ave., 60018, pg. 974 — IT

SCHAWK, INC., 1695 River Rd., 60018, pg. 1437 — PB

Schawkgraphics, 1600 E. Sherwin Ave., 60018, pg. 1437 — PB

SCHNADIG CORPORATION, 1111 E. Touhy, Ste. 500, 60018, pg. 971 — PV

THE SPRING AIR COMPANY, 2980 River Rd., 60018, pg. 1027 — PV

STEWART WARNER INSTRUMENTS CORPORATION, 200 Howard Ave., Bldg. 250, 60018, pg. 1042 — PV

Subaru of America, Inc., 2250 E. Devon Ave., Ste. 223, 60018, pg. 523 — IT

Sunflower Group In-Store Services, 2340 River Rd., Ste. 213, 60018, pg. 1052 — PV

Symons Corporation, 200 E. Touhy Ave., 60018, pg. 932 — PV

Sysco Food Services Chicago, Inc., 250 Wieboldt Dr., 60016-3192, pg. 1551 — PB

TriStar Pictures Central Division, 2800 River Rd., Ste. 210, 60018, pg. 1283 — IT

Triumph Releasing Corporation - Central Territory, 2800 River Rd., Ste. 230, 60018-4213, pg. 1282 — IT

Triumph Releasing Corporation - Great Lakes Territory, 2800 River Rd., Ste. 230, 60018-4213, pg. 1282 — IT

UOP, 25 E. Algonquin Rd., 60017, pg. 52 — IT

UNITED STATIONERS INC., 2200 E. Golf Rd., 60016-1267, pg. 1689 — PB

United Stationers Supply Co., 2200 E. Golf Rd., 60016, pg. 1689 — PB

Wesley-Jessen, 333 E. Howard Ave., 60018, pg. 111 — PV

West Agro, Inc.-Des Plaines, 1855 S. Mount Prospect, 60018, pg. 1379 — IT

Dixon

Amboy Specialty Foods, 820 Palmyra Ave., 61021, pg. 490 — PV

AMCORE Bank, Rock River Valley, P.O. Box 309, 101 W. First St., 61021-3080, pg. 64 — PB

Dixonweb Printing Company, 1226 W. 7th. St., 60121, pg. 1005 — PV

RAYNOR GARAGE DOORS, 1101 E. River Rd., 61021, pg. 912 — PV

Dolton

American Ingredients Company, 14622 Lakeside Ave., 60419, pg. 244 — IT

Downers Grove

Aetna Life Insurance Company of Illinois, 1020 31st St., 60515, pg. 26 — PB

Aisin World Corp. of America, 2001 Butterfield Rd., Ste. 1450, 60515, pg. 39 — IT

Armour Food Company, 2001 Butterfield Rd., 60515-1049, pg. 427 — PB

Armour Swift Eckrich, 2001 Butterfield Rd., 60515, pg. 426 — PV

ARROW GEAR COMPANY, 2301 Curtiss St., 60515, pg. 85 — PV

BURNSIDE CONSTRUCTION CO., 2400 Wisconsin Ave., 60515, pg. 187 — PV

Butterball Turkey Company, 2001 Butterfield Rd., 60515, pg. 382 — PB

J.L. Clark Tube Div., 2300 Wisconsin Ave., 60515, pg. 382 — PB

Customer Development Corporation, Executive Tower West II, 1411 Opus Pl., Ste. 630, 60515, pg. 298 — PV

DYNAGEAR INC., 2500 Curtiss St., 60515, pg. 350 — PV

ELGIN NATIONAL INDUSTRIES, INC., 2001 Butterfield Rd., Ste. 1020, 60515, pg. 370 — PV

FTD, INC./FLORISTS TRANSWORLD DELIVERY, INC., 3113 Woodcreek Dr., 60515, pg. 389 — PV

FIRST HEALTH GROUP CORP., 3200 Highland Ave., 60515-1223, pg. 635 — PB

FLEXIBLE STEEL LACING COMPANY, 2525 Wisconsin Ave., 60515, pg. 413 — PB

GNWC Wire, Cable & Network Products, 1401 Brook Drive, 60515, pg. 259 — PV

Griffin Pipe Products Co., 1400 Opus Pl., Ste. 700, 60515, pg. 68 — PV

IRD Mechanalysis, Inc., 2600 Warrenville Rd., Ste. 207, 60515, pg. 790 — PB

ITW Norwood Marking Systems, 2538 Wisconsin Ave., 60515, pg. 866 — PB

Kingsley Machine Co., 2538 Wisconsin Ave., 60515, pg. 866 — PB

LOVEJOY INC., 2655 Wisconsin Ave., 60515-4299, pg. 677 — PV

MTI VACATIONS, INC., 2211 Butterfield Rd., 60515, pg. 688 — PV

MAGNETROL INTERNATIONAL, 5300 Belmont Rd., 60515, pg. 696 — PV

MAY & SPEH, INC., 1501 Opus Pl., 60515, pg. 1063 — PV

Novartis Seeds, Inc., 5300 Katrine Ave., 60515, pg. 974 — IT

Processed Meats/Poultry, 2001 Butterfield Rd., 60515, pg. 426 — PB

STI Controls, L.P., 5300 Belmont Rd., 60563, pg. 696 — PV

SENTINEL TECHNOLOGIES INC., 2550 Warrenville Rd., 60515, pg. 984 — PV

ServiceMaster Business & Industry Group, One Service Master Way, 60515, pg. 1462 — PB

THE SERVICEMASTER COMPANY, One ServiceMaster Way, 60515, pg. 1461 — PB

ServiceMaster Food Management Services, One ServiceMaster Way, 60515, pg. 1462 — PB

ServiceMaster Healthcare Management Services, Inc., One Service Master Way, 60515, pg. 1462 — PB

ServiceMaster Home Health Care Services Inc., One ServiceMaster Way, 60515, pg. 1462 — PB

ServiceMaster International, One ServiceMaster Way, 60515, pg. 1462 — PB

ServiceMaster Management Services Corporation, One ServiceMaster Way, 60515, pg. 1462 — PB

John M. Smyth Co., 1013 Butterfield Rd., 60515, pg. 990 — PB

SPIEGEL, INC., 3500 Lacey Rd., 60515-5432, pg. 1498 — PB

Tricon Electromechanical Plant, 5402 Janes Ave., 60515, pg. 1103 — PV

White Cap, Inc., 1101 31st St., 60515, pg. 1207 — IT

Dundee

Colgate-Palmolive IPD, 35 W. 525th Boncosky Rd., 60118, pg. 397 — PB

HAEGER INDUSTRIES, INC., Seven Maiden Ln., 60118, pg. 493 — PV

Haeger Potteries, Inc., Seven Maiden Ln., 60118, pg. 493 — PV

MILK SPECIALTIES COMPANY, P.O. Box 278, 60118, pg. 746 — PV

Dwight

Bank of Dwight, 132 E. Main St., 60420, pg. 1316 — PB

Dwight Mfg. Division, R.R. #1 Box 118, 60420-9607, pg. 518 — PB

East Alton

Defense & Ammunition Segment, Shamrock St., 62024, pg. 1219 — PB

Magna Bank, Riverbend Region, 347 W. Main St., 62024, pg. 1037 — PB

Marine Systems, Inc.-Midwest, 1145 E. Airline Dr., Ste. 1&2, 62024, pg. 961 — PB

Olin Specialty Metals Corporation, 427 N. Shamrock St., 62024, pg. 1219 — PB

East Dubuque

CRESCENT ELECTRIC SUPPLY CO., 7750 Dunleith Dr., 61025, pg. 289 — PV

Phoenix Chemical Company, 16675 Hwy. 20 West, 61025, pg. 856 — PB

East Moline

Case International, 1100 3rd St., 61244-1355, pg. 1579 — PB

John Deere Harvester Works, 1100 13th Ave., 61244, pg. 492 — PB

EAST MOLINE METAL PRODUCTS COMPANY, 1201 Seventh St., 61244-1400, pg. 357 — PV

Upper Rock Island County Landfill, 17201 20th Ave., N., 61244, pg. 49 — PB

East Peoria

fp CameoColor, Inc., 700 Pinecrest Dr., 61611, pg. 411 — PV

Titan Wheel-Peoria, 601 N. Main St., 61611, pg. 1619 — PB

East Saint Louis

Akzo LanChem Corp., 2904 Missouri Ave., 62205, pg. 47 — IT

Edwardsville

CASSENS TRANSPORT COMPANY, 145 N. Kansas St., 62025, pg. 219 — PV
Edwardsville Intelligencer, 117 N. Second St., 62025, pg. 517 — PV
FLORISTS' MUTUAL INSURANCE CO., 500 St. Louis St., 62025, pg. 415 — PV
General Life Insurance Company Of America, 95 N. Research Dr., 62025, pg. 443 — PV

Effingham

JOHN BOOS & COMPANY, 315 S. First St., 62401, pg. 156 — PV
Consolidated Communications Directories, Inc., 1200 Network Ctr. Dr., 62401, pg. 1073 — PV
EFFINGHAM-CLAY SERVICE CO., 410 S. Willow, 62401, pg. 365 — PV
Fedders North America, Inc., 415 Wabash Ave., 62401, pg. 615 — PB
PETTY COMPANY, INC., P.O. Box 250, 62401, pg. 860 — PV

Elgin

AirTronics Co., 516 Slade Ave., 60120-3098, pg. 944 — PB
American Antenna Corp, 1500 Executive Dr., 60120, pg. 207 — PV
ARTISTIC CARTON COMPANY, 1975 Big Timber Rd., 60123, pg. 87 — PV
BUTERA FINER FOODS INC., One Clock Tower Plaza, 60120, pg. 189 — PV
Butler Pharma Pak, Inc., 1300 Abbott Dr., 60120, pg. 1320 — IT
CR Services, 735 Tollgate Rd., 60123-9332, pg. 1157 — PV
CAPSONIC GROUP, INC., 460 S. Second St., 60123, pg. 207 — PV
Chicago Rawhide, 735 Tollgate, 60123-2193, pg. 1157 — IT
DSM Desotech Inc., 1122 St. Charles St., 60120, pg. 354 — IT
Daily Courier-News, 300 Lake St., 60120, pg. 275 — PV
Diamond Forecast, 1600 Fleetwood Dr., 60120, pg. 730 — PB
Digital Media Center, 1275 Davis Rd., 60123, pg. 518 — PB
Dover Industries, Inc., P.O. Box 7428, 60121, pg. 520 — PB
Eby Brown Co., 1313 Timber Dr., 60123, pg. 359 — PV
Elgin Digital Colorgraphic Service Center, 645 Tollgate Rd., 60123, pg. 518 — PB
Elgin Sweeper Company, 1300 W. Bartlett Rd., 60121-0537, pg. 617 — PV
Flender Corporation, 950 Tollgate Rd., 60123, pg. 400 — IT
Harig Grinders, 1875 Big Timber Rd., 60123, pg. 252 — PB
ITW Shakeproof/Automotive Products, St. Charles Rd., 60120, pg. 867 — PB
ITW Shakeproof/Industrial Products, St. Charles Rd., 60120, pg. 867 — PB
ITW Shakeproof/Specialty Products, St Charles Rd., 60120, pg. 867 — PB
Intertron, 158 N. Edison Ave., 60123, pg. 1507 — PB
Johnson Industries, 1424 Davis Rd., 60123, pg. 543 — PV
MASTER MOLDED PRODUCTS CORPORATION, 1000 Davis Rd., 60123, pg. 714 — PV
Matsushita Television Corp., 1707 N. Randall Rd., 60123, pg. 847 — IT
Middleby Marshall/CTX, 1400 Toastmaster Dr., 60120-9272, pg. 1110 — PB
Panasonic Factory Automation Co., 1707 N. Randall Rd., 60123, pg. 847 — IT
Pet Ag Inc., 30 W. 432 Rte. 20, 60120, pg. 746 — PV
Rinn Corporation, 1212 Abbott Dr., 60123, pg. 499 — PB
SAFETY-KLEEN CORP., 1000 N. Randall Rd., 60123, pg. 1425 — PV
SEIGLE'S HOME & BUILDING CENTERS, 1331 Davis Rd., 60123, pg. 981 — PV
SIMPSON ELECTRIC CO., 853 Dundee Ave., 60120, pg. 1002 — PV
W.J. & DENNIS CO., 1111 Davis Rd., 60123-1388, pg. 1144 — PV
Williams Healthcare Systems, 158 N. Edison Ave., 60123, pg. 1507 — PB

Elk Grove Village

AAR Aircraft Turbine Center, 1111 Nicholas Blvd., 60007, pg. 1 — PB
AAR Allen Aircraft, 1111 Nicholas Blvd., 60007, pg. 1 — PB
AAR Cooper Aviation, 2149 E. Pratt Blvd., 60007, pg. 1 — PB
AAR Defense Systems, 2100 Touhy, 60007, pg. 1 — PB
Acme Printing Ink Co., Inc., 651 Bonnie Lane, 60007, pg. 1311 — IT
Ahern Fire Protection, 1100 Howard St., 60007, pg. 27 — PV
Air Wis Services, Inc., 1200 E. Algonquin Rd., 60007, pg. 1653 — PB
Air Wisconsin, Inc., 1200 E. Algonquin Rd., 60007, pg. 1653 — PB
Allied Digital Technologies, 1200 Thorndale Ave., 60007, pg. 48 — PB
Anchor Wire Rope Div., 1150 Howard St., 60007, pg. 1001 — IT
Ansco Photo-Optical Products Corp., 1801 Touhy Ave., 60007, pg. 587 — IT
APPLE VACATIONS WEST INC., 101 Northwest Point Blvd., 60009, pg. 78 — PV
AQUION, 2080 E. Lunt Ave., 60007, pg. 78 — PV
Banta Direct Marketing Group, 2075 Busse Ave., 60007, pg. 188 — PB
Berlin Industries, Inc., 855 Morse Ave., 60007, pg. 136 — PB

CAPCO U.S.A., Inc., 2300 E. Higgins Rd., Ste. 206-A, 60007, pg. 278 — IT
Cardinal EG Saws Corp., 1255 Tonne Rd., 60007, pg. 228 — IT
CHICAGO MACHINE TOOL COMPANY, 2150 Touhy Ave., 60007, pg. 235 — PV
Chicago Magnet Wire Corp., 901 Chase Ave., 60007, pg. 1054 — IT
CIRCUIT SYSTEMS, INC., 2350 E. Lunt Ave., 60007, pg. 374 — PB
CLARK FOODSERVICE, INC., 950 Arthur Ave., 60007, pg. 242 — PV
Commercial Record Center, 1500 Arthur Ave., Unit C, 60007, pg. 1164 — PV
Concord Computing Corp., 1713 Carmen Dr., pg. 429 — PV
Connector Division America and Asia, 1500 Morse Ave., 60007, pg. 786 — IT
Cook Moving Systems, Inc. (Illinois Corporation), 2195 Arthur Ave., 60007, pg. 273 — PV
Cooper Lighting Division, 400 Busse Rd., 60007-2195, pg. 443 — PB
Covia, LLC, 1200 E. Algonquin Rd., 60007, pg. 1653 — PB
Crafts Technology, Inc., 91 Joey Dr., 60007, pg. 307 — PV
Creative Computers, Inc., 2525 Busse Rd., 60007, pg. 458 — PV
Daher Golden Eagle - Chicago, 2311 W. Touhy Ave., 60007, pg. 749 — IT
DENA CORPORATION, 850 Nicholas Blvd., 60007, pg. 324 — PV
Domcor U.S.A., 2701 Lively Blvd., 60007-6732, pg. 415 — IT
Domicile Management Services, Inc., 1200 E. Algonquin Rd., 60007, pg. 1653 — PB
Dupli-Color Products Company, 1601 Nicholas Blvd., 60007, pg. 1466 — PB
Electro Rent Corporation-ESD, Inc., 1820 Elmhurst Rd., 60007, pg. 568 — PB
Fanuc USA Corp., 1331 Greenleaf Ave., 60007, pg. 477 — IT
FIELD CONTAINER COMPANY, L.P., 1500 Nicholas Blvd., 60007, pg. 403 — PV
Freeman Products, 1480 Devon Ave., 60007, pg. 1105 — PV
Frisby P.M.C. Incorporated, 1500 Chase, 60007, pg. 894 — PB
GFI-Genfare, 751 Pratt Blvd., 60007, pg. 727 — PB
Gensym Corporation, Midwestern Regional Office, 25 N.W. Point, 60007, pg. 731 — PB
GLOBE-AMERADA GLASS COMPANY, 2001 Greenleaf Ave., 60007, pg. 458 — PV
Gomiya USA, Inc., 1500-A E. Higgins Rd., 60007, pg. 531 — IT
Groen, A Dover Industries Co., 1900 Pratt Blvd., 60007, pg. 521 — PB
Haking International, 1801 Touhy Ave., 60007, pg. 587 — IT
Halo Lighting, 400 Busse Rd., 60007-2195, pg. 443 — PB
Halogen Insulator & Seal Corp., 150 Gaylord St., 60007, pg. 1174 — PV
Harris Bank Elk Grove, N.A., 500 E. Devon Ave., 60007, pg. 154 — IT
Harwick Standard Distribution Corp., 800 Estes Ave., 60007, pg. 509 — PV
Hobart/McIntosh Paper Company, 1825 Greenleaf Ave., 60007-5596, pg. 72 — IT
INX Corporation, 651 Bonnie Lane, 60007, pg. 1311 — PB
ITW Linx, 201 Scott St., 60007, pg. 866 — PB
InterPost Systems USA Inc., 1851 Howard St., 60007, pg. 720 — IT
L. KARP & SONS, INC., 1301 Estes Ave., 60007, pg. 607 — PV
Kintetsu Intermodal Inc., 2571 Busse Rd., Ste. 301, 60007, pg. 735 — IT
Kintetsu World Express Inc., 2571 Busse Rd., Ste. 302, 60007, pg. 734 — IT
Kintetsu World Express Inc., 955 Arthur Ave., 60007, pg. 735 — IT
Kuraki America Corp., 1831 Howard St., Ste. F, 60007, pg. 764 — IT
LA-CO INDUSTRIES MARKAL COMPANY, 1201 Pratt Blvd., 60007, pg. 640 — PV
Labinal Components & Systems Inc., 1500 Morse Ave., 60007-5783, pg. 786 — IT
Lehigh Press ColorTronics, 361 Bonnie Lane, 60007, pg. 659 — PB
LITTLE LADY FOODS, INC., 2323 Pratt Blvd., 60007, pg. 671 — PV
MATERIAL SCIENCES CORPORATION, 2200 E. Pratt Blvd., 60007-5995, pg. 1056 — PB
A.W. MENDENHALL CO., INC., 2301 Lunt Ave., 60007, pg. 731 — PV
MIDLAND PAPER CO., 1825 Greenleaf Ave., 60007, pg. 744 — PV
Mileage Plus Holdings, Inc., 1200 E. Algonquin Rd., 60007, pg. 1653 — PB
Mileage Plus Marketing, Inc., 1200 E. Algonquin Rd., 60007, pg. 1653 — PB
Mitrans Corporation, 2256-A Landmeier Rd., 60007, pg. 874 — IT
Morton Chemical Div., 2401 E. Pratt Blvd., 60004, pg. 1135 — PB
Nelson Westerberg International Inc., 1500 Arthur Ave., Ste. 100, 60007, pg. 1164 — PV
Neradt Tool & Stamping Company, 2545 American Ln., 60007, pg. 269 — PV
The New Home Sewing Machine Co., 1704 Carmen Dr., 60007, pg. 699 — IT
Nichifu America, Inc., 1681 Elmhurst Rd., 60007, pg. 927 — IT
PETERSEN ALUMINUM CORPORATION, 1005 Tonne Rd., 60007, pg. 856 — PV
PLASTAG CORPORATION, 1800 Greenleaf Ave., 60007, pg. 870 — PV

Portage Tool Company, 2045 Pratt Blvd., 60007, pg. 1075 — PV
Pre Finish Metals Inc., 2111 E. Pratt Blvd., 60007, pg. 1057 — PB
Pre Finish Metals Inc.-Commercial Sales Office, 915 Busse Rd., 60007, pg. 1056 — PB
Pre Finish Metals Incorporated, 2300 E. Pratt Blvd., 60007, pg. 1056 — PB
Premier Coatings, Inc., 2250 Arthur Ave., 60007, pg. 1488 — IT
QA Products, Inc., 1301 Mark St., 60007, pg. 244 — IT
RainSoft Water Treatment Systems, 2080 E. Lunt Ave., 60007, pg. 78 — PV
Re-Mi Foods Inc., 1201 Tonne Rd., 60007, pg. 158 — PV
Reynolds and Reynolds, 901 Busse Rd., 60007, pg. 1385 — PV
ROLLEX CORPORATION, 2001 Lunt Ave., 60007, pg. 941 — PV
Ropak Central Inc., 1350 Arthur Ave., 60007, pg. 811 — IT
Ropak Materials Handling Div., 2601 Allan Dr., 60007, pg. 812 — IT
SNK America, Inc., 1800 Howard St., 60007, pg. 1234 — IT
Sakata Inx USA Corp., 610 Bonnie Lane, 60007, pg. 1311 — IT
Salem Carpet Mills, 2800 Carl Blvd., 60007, pg. 1464 — PB
JOHN B. SANFILIPPO & SON, INC., 2299 Busse Rd., 60007, pg. 1431 — PB
SigmaTron, Inc., 2201 Landmeier Rd., 60007, pg. 374 — PB
STEINER ELECTRIC COMPANY, 1250 Touhy Ave., 60007, pg. 1039 — PV
SUN PROCESS CONVERTING COMPANY, 505 Bonnie Ln., 60007, pg. 1051 — PV
Tech Group Chicago, Inc., 211 Seegers Ave., 60007, pg. 1071 — PV
TECHNICAL IMAGE PRODUCTS, INC./DGI, 1250 Pratt Blvd., 60007, pg. 1072 — PV
Thermal Industries Inc., 568 Crossen Ave., 60007-2006, pg. 1390 — PV
Tigerflex Corporation, 801 Estes Ave., 60007, pg. 1390 — IT
J.J. Tourek Co., 1800 Touhy Ave., 60007, pg. 1111 — PV
UAL CORPORATION, 1200 E. Algonquin Rd., 60007, pg. 1652 — PB
U.N.A. Corporation, 1550 Howard St., 60007, pg. 1001 — IT
U.N. Alloy Steel Div., 1550 Howard St., 60007, pg. 1001 — IT
U.S.S. SEKO WORLDWIDE, 790 Busse St., 60007, pg. 1115 — PV
Union-Transport Corporation-Chicago Office, 2601 Allan Dr., 60007, pg. 1119 — PV
United Air Lines Credit Corporation, 1200 E. Algonquin Rd., 60007, pg. 1653 — PB
United Air Lines, Inc., 1200 E. Algonquin Rd., 60007-0100, pg. 1653 — PB
United Aviation Fuels Corp., 1200 E. Algonquin Rd., 60007, pg. 1653 — PB
United GHS Inc., 1200 E. Algonquin Rd., 60007, pg. 1653 — PB
United Vacations, Inc., 1200 E. Algonquin Rd., 60007, pg. 1653 — PB
WWF Paper Corporation - Midwest, 1150 Lively Blvd., 60007, pg. 1145 — PV
NELSON WESTERBERG, INC., 1500 Arthur Ave., Ste. 200 W, 60007, pg. 1163 — PV
Nelson Westerberg of Illinois, 1201 Arthur Ave., 60007, pg. 1164 — PV
World Book Educational Products, 101 Northwest Pt. Blvd., 60007, pg. 218 — PB
World Color-Chicago Div., 2000 Arthur Ave., 60007, pg. 1778 — PB

Elmhurst

BWD Automotive Corp. (International), 900 N. Church Rd., 60126, pg. 561 — PB
Bell Atlantic Services, 501 W Lake St. Ste. 105, 60126-1419, pg. 203 — PV
Brake Parts, Inc., 900 N. Church Rd., 60126, pg. 560 — PB
CPS Credit Corp., 140 Industrial Dr., 60126, pg. 309 — PB
The Chamberlain Group, Inc., 845 Larch Ave., 60126, pg. 344 — PV
Chamberlain Manufacturing Corp., 845 Larch Ave., 60126, pg. 344 — PV
Duchossois Communications, Inc., 845 Larch Ave., 60126, pg. 344 — PV
DUCHOSSOIS INDUSTRIES, INC., 845 Larch Ave., 60126, pg. 344 — PV
Follett College Stores Corp., 400 W. Grand, 60126, pg. 417 — PV
Graphic Direct, Inc., 185 Industrial Dr., 60126, pg. 1735 — PB
Graphic Direct, Inc.-Illinois, 179 Spangler Ave., 60126, pg. 1735 — PB
ILLINOIS AUTO ELECTRIC CO., 656 County Line Rd., 60126, pg. 557 — PV
Illinois Auto Electric Midwest Engine Warehouse Div., 515 Romans Rd., 60126, pg. 558 — PV
Keebler Company, One Hollow Tree Lane, 60126, pg. 657 — PV
Management Data Service, 655 West Grand, Ste. 220, 60126, pg. 1687 — PV
MCMASTER CARR SUPPLY CO. INC., 600 County Line, 60126, pg. 724 — PV
NORTHWESTERN GOLF COMPANY, 835 N. Church Rd., 60126-1005, pg. 806 — PV
OFFICE EQUIPMENT COMPANY OF CHICAGO, 900 N. Church Rd., 60126, pg. 812 — PV
Old Kent Bank-Illinois, 105 S. York St., 60126, pg. 1216 — PB
Pro-Select, 835 N. Church Rd., 60126-1005, pg. 806 — PV
THE PROTECTOR CORPORATION, 110 Cottage Hill, 60126, pg. 891 — PV

Pyle Inc., 650 W. Grand Ave., 60126, pg. 629 **PV**
SEMBLEX CORPORATION, 199 W. Diversey, 60126, pg. 983 **PV**
TOCCOA METAL TECHNOLOGIES, INC., 310 W. Lake St., Ste. 219, 60126, pg. 1089 **PV**
UB Foods U.S., Inc., 677 Larch Ave., 60126, pg. 1442 **IT**
WHITE HEN PANTRY, INC., 660 Industrial Dr., 60126, pg. 1172 **PV**

Elmwood

Shissler Seed Co., R.R. #3, 61529, pg. 566 **IT**

Elwood

Polymer & Surfactant Plant, R.R. #1, 60421, pg. 1514 **PB**

Evanston

Barton-Aschman Associates, Inc., 820 Davis St., 60204, pg. 841 **PV**
CR LLC, 1235 Hartrey Ave., 60202, pg. 196 **PV**
CENTURY PUBLISHING COMPANY, 990 Grove St., 60201, pg. 226 **PV**
Evanston Bank, 603 Main St., 60202, pg. 760 **PV**
Evanston Insurance Company, Shand Morahan Plaza, Church & Oak, 60201, pg. 1046 **PB**
Illinois Banc One Corporation, 800 Davis St., 60204, pg. 174 **PB**
Illinois Banc One Insurance Services, Inc., 800 Davis St., 60204, pg. 174 **PB**
Illinois Banc One Leasing Corp., 800 Davis St., 60204, pg. 174 **PB**
Illinois Banc One Life Insurance Co., 800 Davis St., 60204, pg. 174 **PB**
Illinois Banc One Title Co., 800 Davis St., 60204, pg. 174 **PB**
Immtech International, Inc., 906 University Place, 60201, pg. 459 **PV**
Industrial Bookstore, 1633 Central St., 60201, pg. 701 **PV**
Inside Sports, Inc., 990 Grove St., 60201, pg. 226 **PV**
MANUFACTURERS' NEWS, INC., 1633 Central St., 60201, pg. 700 **PV**
Markel Insurance Company, Shand Morahan Plaza, Church & Oak, 60201, pg. 1046 **PB**
McDougal/Littell, 1560 Sherman Ave., 60201, pg. 841 **PV**
MEDICUS SYSTEMS CORPORATION, One Rotary Ctr., Ste. 1111, 60201, pg. 1080 **PB**
Mistal, Inc., 1603 Orrington Ave., 60204, pg. 1579 **PB**
PCA West Inc., 1603 Orrington Ave., pg. 1578 **PB**
Pico-Matic Inc., 1011 Pitner Ave., 30202, pg. 813 **PV**
Proof Positive/Farrowlyne Associates, Inc., 1620 Central St., 60201, pg. 503 **PB**
ROBINSON BUS SERVICE, 1528 Emerson St., 60201, pg. 936 **PV**
Robinson Bus Service, 1528 E. Merson St., 60201, pg. 936 **PV**
Robinson Coaches, 1528 E. Emerson St., 60201, pg. 936 **PV**
Shand, Morahan & Co., Inc., Shand Morahan Plaza, Church & Oak, 60201, pg. 1046 **PB**
SHURE BROTHERS INCORPORATED, 222 Hartrey Ave., 60202-3696, pg. 997 **PV**
Sole Control, 820 Davis St., # 444, 60201, pg. 1369 **PV**
T C MANUFACTURING COMPANY, INC., 1527 Lyons St., 60201, pg. 1062 **PV**
Tapecoat Company, 1527 Lyon St., 60201, pg. 1062 **PV**
Tenneco Packaging, 1603 Orrington Ave., 60201-3853, pg. 1579 **PB**
World Book Direct Marketing, One Rotary Center, 1560 Sherman Ave., Ste. 1111, 60201, pg. 218 **PB**
World Publishing Company, 990 Grove St., 60201, pg. 226 **PV**

Fairfield

Airtex Products, 407 W. Main St., 62837, pg. 1113 **PV**

Fairview Heights

Americoal Services Company, 50 Jerome Ln., 62208, pg. 1790 **PB**
Central Bank, One Central Bank Bldg., 6701 N. Illinois, 62208, pg. 643 **PB**
Franklin Coal, 50 Jerome Ln., 62208, pg. 1790 **PB**
Old Ben Coal Co., 50 Jerome Ln., 62208, pg. 1790 **PB**
Phoenix Land Company, 50 Jerome Ln., 62208, pg. 1790 **PB**
SMC Mining Company, 50 Jerome Ln., 62208, pg. 1790 **PB**
SRA - Fairview Heights, 331 Salem Pl., Ste. #200, 62208, pg. 958 **PV**
Turner Electric Corporation, 9510 St. Clair Ave., 62208-1639, pg. 1705 **PB**
ZEIGLER COAL HOLDING COMPANY, 50 Jerome Ln., 62208, pg. 1790 **PB**

Flora

North American Lighting, Inc., #20 Industrial Park, 62839, pg. 743 **IT**
Rexam Containers - US, P.O. Box 639, 2 Industrial Pk., 62839, pg. 1106 **IT**
Sparton Engineered Products, Inc.-Flora Group, P.O. Box 399, 62839, pg. 1496 **PB**

Forest Park

ABELL-HOWE COMPANY, 7747 Van Buren St., 60130, pg. 10 **PV**
Arrow Sintered Products, 7650 Industrial Dr., 60130, pg. 85 **PV**
Roosevelt Paper Company, 7801 W Industrial Dr., 60130, pg. 943 **PV**

Frankfort

Harris Bank Frankfort, 690 N. LaGrange Rd., 60423, pg. 154 **IT**
ITW Deltar-Fasteners, 21555 S. Harlem Ave., 60423, pg. 866 **PB**
ITW Deltar-Special Products, 21555S. Harlem Ave., 60423, pg. 866 **PB**

Franklin Park

AAllied Die Casting Mfg., Inc., 3021 Cullerton Dr., 60131, pg. 903 **PV**
Alkco Lighting Company, 11500 W. Melrose Ave., 60131, pg. 821 **IT**
Annuity Network Inc., 10035 W. Grand Ave., 60131, pg. 1428 **PB**
B.Via International Housewares, Inc., 9234 W. Belmont Ave., 60440, pg. 566 **PB**
BWD Automotive Corp., 11045 Gage Ave., 60131, pg. 560 **PB**
BADGER AIR BRUSH COMPANY, 9128 W. Belmont Ave., 60131, pg. 110 **PV**
BINKS SAMES CORPORATION, 9201 Belmont Ave., 60131-2887, pg. 229 **PB**
Brunner & Lay, Inc., 9300 King, 60131, pg. 176 **PV**
CPC Foodservice Group, 9353 W. Belmont Ave., 60131, pg. 224 **PB**
A.M. CASTLE & CO., 3400 N. Wolf Rd., 60131, pg. 312 **PB**
CENTRAL GROCERS CO-OP, 11100 W. Belmont, 60131, pg. 223 **PV**
CONWAY IMPORT CO. INC., 11051 W. Addison St., 60131, pg. 272 **PV**
DEAN FOODS COMPANY, 3600 N. River Rd., 60131, pg. 489 **PB**
Delta-Unibus Corp., 11323 W. Franklin Ave., 60131-1116, pg. 1319 **PB**
DIVANE BROS. ELECTRIC CO., 2424 N. 25th Ave., 60131-0937, pg. 336 **PV**
Ekco Cleaning, Inc., 9234 W. Belmont Ave., 60440, pg. 566 **PB**
Ekco Housewares, Inc., 9234 W. Belmont Ave., 60131, pg. 566 **PB**
EVERSHARP PEN CO., 9240 W. Belmont, 60131, pg. 386 **PV**
Gaynes Engineering Co., 1091 E. Green St., 28577, pg. 801 **PV**
Gendex-Del Medical Imaging Corp., 11550 W. King St., 60131, pg. 494 **PB**
THE GREAT FRAME UP SYSTEMS, INC., 9335 Belmont Ave., 60131, pg. 473 **PV**
HOUSTON FOODS COMPANY, 3501 Mt. Prospect Rd., 60131-1312, pg. 542 **PV**
Hubbell Steel Corporation, 11305 Franklin Ave., 60131, pg. 742 **PB**
Inktel Marketing, 11241 Melrose St., 60131, pg. 101 **PV**
Investment Network, Inc., 10035 W. Grand Ave., 60131, pg. 1428 **PB**
Joslyn Manufacturing Co.-Apparatus Div., 9200 W. Fullerton, 60131, pg. 481 **PB**
KDC Financial Limited Partnership, 3201 North Wolf Road, 60131, pg. 744 **IT**
MacLean Power Systems, 11411 Addison St., 60131, pg. 692 **PV**
NELSEN STEEL & WIRE CO., 9400 W. Belmont Ave., 60131, pg. 790 **PV**
NOONAN MACHINE CO., 1091 E. Green St., 28577, pg. 801 **PV**
Precision Steel Warehouse, Inc., 3500 Wolf Rd., 60131, pg. 217 **PB**
The Procuto Machine Co., 2950 Hart Dr., P.O. Box 366, 60131, pg. 889 **PV**
Program Water Technologies, 10500 Seymour Ave., 60131, pg. 1006 **PV**
Quality Lighting, Inc., 11530 W. Melrose Ave., 60131-8389, pg. 821 **PV**
RCM INDUSTRIES, 3021 Cullerton Dr., 60131, pg. 902 **PV**
SPF Insurance Agency, 10035 W. Grand Ave., 60131, pg. 1428 **PB**
St. Paul Service, Inc., 10035 W. Grand Ave., 60131, pg. 1428 **PB**
SLOAN VALVE COMPANY, 10500 Seymour Ave., 60131, pg. 1006 **PV**

Freeburg

The Wiegmann Company, 501 W. Apple St., 62243, pg. 845 **PB**

Freeport

Anchor Hocking Corporation, 29 E. Stephenson St., 61032, pg. 1177 **PB**
FURST-McNESS COMPANY, 120 E. Clark St., 61032, pg. 432 **PV**
General Casualty Company of Illinois, 2900 Pearl City Rd., 61032, pg. 346 **IT**

Honeywell's Micro Switch Division, 11 W. Spring St., 61032-4353, pg. 834 **PB**
NEWELL CO., 29 E. Stephenson St., 61032, pg. 1176 **PB**
Newell Operating Company, 29 E. Stephenson St., 61032, pg. 1177 **PB**
Newell Window Furnishings Co., 916 S. Arcade Ave., 61032, pg. 1177 **PB**
Sauer-Sundstrand, P.O. Box 537, 580 N. Henderson Rd., 61032, pg. 1198 **IT**

Galesburg

Maytag Galesburg Refrigeration Products, 1801 Monmouth Blvd., 61401, pg. 1064 **PB**
Norwest Bank Illinois, N.A., 200 E. Main St., 61401, pg. 1202 **PB**
Oak Run Utilities, 1192 Parkview Rd., 61401, pg. 438 **PB**

Galva

ICI Seeds, US Hwy. 34, RR1 Box 191A, 61434, pg. 1524 **IT**
UNIVERSAL BOILERS CORP., 1207 Second St., 61434-8912, pg. 1126 **PV**

Geneseo

IBP-Joslin, P.O. Box 28, 61254, pg. 852 **PB**

Geneva

Burgess-Norton Mfg. Co., 737 Peyton St., 60134, pg. 68 **PV**
Cetron Electronics Manufacturing Division, 715 Hamilton St., 60134, pg. 1388 **PB**
MINER ENTERPRISES INC., 1200 E. State St., 60134, pg. 749 **PV**

Gibson City

M&W, 1020 S. Sangamon Ave., 60936, pg. 35 **PB**

Girard

Thermic Refractories Inc., P.O. Box 128, 62640, pg. 894 **IT**

Glen Ellyn

Augat, Inc., Interconnection Products-Carol Stream, 800 Roosevelt Rd., Ste. B1414, 60137, pg. 1598 **PB**
CHAMPION PARTS, INC., 751 Roosevelt Rd., Bldg. 7, Ste. 110, 60137, pg. 334 **PB**
Donohue Pulp & Paper Sales Corp., P.O. Box 3118, 60138, pg. 1177 **IT**
Pitney Bowes Software Systems, 1200 Roosevelt Road, 60137-7000, pg. 1304 **PB**

Glencoe

Harris Bank Glencoe-Northbrook, N.A., 333 Park Ave., 60022, pg. 154 **IT**

Glendale Heights

CHAMPION BUSINESS FORMS, 1966 Quincy, 60139, pg. 228 **PV**
Champion Direct Mail Printing, P.O. Box 5038, 60139, pg. 228 **PV**
Edy's Midwest Region, 601 Wall St., 60139, pg. 529 **PB**
Nifast Corporation, 701 Regency Dr., 60139, pg. 947 **PB**
Remcor Products Co., 500 Regency Dr., 60139, pg. 646 **IT**
Sumitomo Machinery Corp. of America, 175 W. Lake Dr., 60139, pg. 1314 **IT**

Glenview

Alimak Elevator Company, 2101 John's Ct., 60025, pg. 34 **PV**
Cumberland Leasing Co., 3600 W. Lake Ave., 60025, pg. 865 **PB**
Glenview State Bank, 800 Waukegan Rd., 60025, pg. 295 **PV**
ITW Angleboard, 3610 W. Lake Ave., 60025, pg. 866 **PB**
ITW Components & Tools, 3700 W. Lake Ave., 60025-5811, pg. 866 **PB**
ITW Corporate Technology, 3600 W. Lake Ave., 60025, pg. 866 **PB**
ITW Deltar, 3600 W. Lake Ave., 60025, pg. 866 **PB**
ITW Magnaflux, 3624 W. Lake Ave., 60025, pg. 866 **PB**
ITW Signode, 3610 W. Lake Ave., 60025, pg. 867 **PB**
ILLINOIS TOOL WORKS INC., 3600 W. Lake Ave., 60025-5811, pg. 865 **PB**
Kraft Foods Inc., Kraft Court, 60025, pg. 1288 **PB**
MARCH MANUFACTURING INC., 1819 Pickwick Ave., 60025, pg. 702 **PV**
Pioneer Press Newspapers Inc., 3701 West Lake Ave., 60025, pg. 632 **IT**
Scott Forseman/Addison Wesley, 1900 E. Lake Ave., 60025, pg. 927 **IT**
ZENITH ELECTRONICS CORP., 1000 Milwaukee Ave., 60025, pg. 1790 **PB**
Zenith Sales Co. Div., 1000 Milwaukee Ave., 60025, pg. 1790 **PB**
Zenith Video Tech Corporation, 1000 Milwaukee Ave., 60025, pg. 1790 **PB**

Geographic Index-U.S.

Glenwood

Culligan, 320 W. 194th St., 60425-1502, pg. 467 **PB**
HomeByer's Preferred, Inc., 2 Science Rd., 60425-1586, pg. 977 **PB**
LANDAUER, INC., Two Science Rd., 60425-1586, pg. 977 **PB**
RIVERDALE CHEMICAL CO., 425 W. 194th St., 60425-1584, pg. 934 **PV**
James Walker Mfg. Co., P.O. Box 467, 511 W. 195th St., 60425-0467, pg. 1485 **IT**

Golden

Methode Electrical Products Div., 2400 N. County Rd., 62339, pg. 1101 **PB**

Goodfield

DMI, INC., P.O. Box 65, 61742-0065, pg. 305 **PV**

Granite City

Affiliated Metals Company, 1020 Niedringhaus Ave., 62040, pg. 1100 **PB**
Capri Sun Inc., 2901 Hwy. 3, 62040, pg. 1288 **PB**
Feralloy St. Louis Div., 2500 Nameoki Dr., 62040, pg. 1070 **IT**
Magna Bank, Madison Region, 1960 Edison Ave., 62040, pg. 1037 **PB**
National Steel Corp., Granite City Division, 1951 State St., 62040, pg. 902 **IT**
Taracorp Industries, Inc., 1200 16th St., 62040, pg. 1068 **PB**
Terminal Railroad Association of St. Louis, 2016 Madison Ave., 62040, pg. 1668 **PB**

Grant Park

Ivex Packaging Corporation-Engineering Group, P.O. Box 399, 221 E. Greenwood, 60940, pg. 915 **PB**
Ivex Packaging Corporation-Floral and Nursery Products, P.O. Box 518, 221 E. Greenwood, 60940, pg. 915 **PB**
Ivex Packaging Corporation-Grant Park, P.O. Box G, 304 North E. Main St., 60940, pg. 915 **PB**

Grayslake

LeaseCard Auto Group, P.O. Box 388, 1039 E. North Corporate Cir., 60030, pg. 1628 **PB**
Nuvotron, P.O. Box 388, 1039 E. North Corporate Cir., 60030, pg. 1628 **PB**

Greenville

THE BRADFORD NATIONAL BANK OF GREENVILLE, 100 E. College Ave., 62246, pg. 164 **PV**
Peterson Spring-Greenville Plant, Peterson Industrial Dr., 62246, pg. 857 **PV**

Gurnee

Aeros Instruments, Inc., 1111 Lakeside Dr., 60031, pg. 1028 **PV**
ALRA LABORATORIES, INC., 3850 Clearview Ct., 60031, pg. 45 **PV**
Crown Moving & Storage Inc., of Illinois, 1200 North Estes, 60031, pg. 1171 **PV**
Danaher Corporation, 1675 Delany Rd., 60031, pg. 480 **PB**
JOSEPH J. HENDERSON & SON, INC., 4288 Grand Ave., 60031, pg. 521 **PV**
PARIS PRESENTS, 3800 Swanson Ct., 60031, pg. 839 **PV**
PAYSON CASTERS, INC., 2323 Delaney Rd., 60031, pg. 844 **PV**
Six Flags Great America, Inc., P.O. Box 1776, 542 North Rte. 21, 60031, pg. 1611 **PB**
SQUIRE-COGSWELL COMPANY, 1111 Lakeside Dr., 60031, pg. 1027 **PV**

Harrisburg

First National Bank, Two E. Locust, 62946, pg. 1217 **PB**

Hartford

Clark Oil & Refining Corporation-Wood River Refinery, 201 E. Hawthorne, 62048, pg. 243 **PV**
Hartford-Wood River Terminal, One Piasa Ln., 62048, pg. 864 **PV**
PIASA MOTOR FUELS INC., One Piasa Ln., 62048, pg. 864 **PV**
Piasa Oil Transport Inc., One Piasa Ln., 62048, pg. 864 **PV**

Harvard

Big Foot Cattle Co., 11511 Rte. 14, 60033, pg. 1140 **PV**
Dean Foods Co., 6303 Maxon Rd., 60033, pg. 491 **PB**
Fuel Systems Textron (Harvard Plant), 710 W. Park St., 60033, pg. 1589 **PB**

Harvey

Allied Tube & Conduit Corporation, 16100 So. Lathrop Ave., 60426, pg. 1650 **PB**
Metal Lubricants Co., 17050 Lathrop Ave., 60426, pg. 518 **IT**
WHITING CORPORATION, 15700 Lathrop Ave., 60426-5198, pg. 1173 **PV**

Harwood Heights

F C L GRAPHICS, 4600 N. Olcott, 60656, pg. 389 **PV**
NT DOR-OMATIC, 7350 W. Wilson Ave., 60656, pg. 771 **PV**

Hawthorn Woods

Sunrise Leasing Corporation, 36 Lynn Dr., 60047, pg. 1535 **PB**

Hazel Crest

MI-JACK PRODUCTS, INC., 3111 W. 167th St., 60429, pg. 740 **PV**

Hebron

Filtertek Inc., 11411 Price Rd., 60034-0310, pg. 546 **PB**
Shutters, Inc., 12213 Hwy. 173, 60034, pg. 832 **PB**

Herrin

Maytag/Herrin Laundry Products, 410 E. Lyerla Dr., 62948, pg. 1064 **PB**

Highland

B-Line Systems, Inc., 509 W. Monroe St., 62249, pg. 1471 **PB**
BASLER ELECTRIC COMPANY, Rte. 143, 62249, pg. 111 **PV**
DuCoa L.P., P.O. Box 219, 62249, pg. 301 **PV**
Highland News-Leader, 822 Broadway, 62249, pg. 964 **PB**

Highland Park

Highland Park Financial Center, 579 Central Ave., 60035, pg. 1196 **PB**
P.R. Solo Cup, Inc., 1700 Old Deerfield Rd., 60035, pg. 1013 **PV**
SOLO CUP COMPANY, 1700 Old Deerfield Rd., 60035, pg. 1013 **PV**
Solo Cup Company, 1700 Old Deerfield Road, 60035, pg. 1013 **PV**

Hillsboro

Eagle Zinc Co., P.O. Box 340, Rural Rte. 1, 218 Indus. Park Dr., 62049, pg. 331 **PV**
NationsBank of Central IL, 420 S. Main, 62049, pg. 1164 **PB**

Hillside

COMMERCIAL LIGHT COMPANY, 245 Fencl Ln., 60162-6006, pg. 258 **PV**
EIS, Inc., 300 N. Mannheim Rd., 60162, pg. 368 **PV**
INTERNATIONAL LOGISTICS LIMITED, 330 S. Mannheim Rd., 60162, pg. 571 **PV**
L&J TECHNOLOGIES, 5911 Butterfield Rd., 60162, pg. 638 **PV**
Levy Home Entertainment, 4201 N. Raymond Dr., 60102, pg. 664 **PV**
National Energy Management LLC, 4415 W. Harrison St., 60162-1902, pg. 1033 **PB**
S&H Citadel, Inc., 5999 Butterfield Rd., 60162, pg. 990 **PB**
Zellerbach Division, 125 Fencl Ln., 60162, pg. 1075 **PB**

Hinsdale

AMLINGS FLOWERLAND, 540 W. Ogden Ave., 60521, pg. 66 **PV**
Amlings Landscape Co., 540 W. Ogden Ave., 60521, pg. 66 **PV**
Banta Publications Group, 908 N. Elm Ste. 110, 60521-3606, pg. 188 **PB**
Case International, AGR Engineering, 7 S. 600 Cty Line Rd., 60521, pg. 1579 **PB**
Harris Bank Hinsdale N.A., 50 S. Lincoln St., 60521, pg. 154 **IT**
K & R EXPRESS SYSTEMS INC., 15 W. 460 Frontage Rd., 60521, pg. 602 **PV**
Olivetti Systems & Networks, 1315 W. 22nd St., Ste. 41, 60521-2057, pg. 1002 **PV**
Star Finishing Products, Inc., 360 Shore Dr., 60521-5822, pg. 1358 **PB**
SunGard Investment Systems Inc., 11 Salt Creek Ln., 60521, pg. 1535 **PB**
Sungard Trust & Shareholder Systems Group, 11 Salt Creek Ln., 60521, pg. 1535 **PB**
TUTHILL CORPORATION, 908 N. Elm St., 60521, pg. 1110 **PV**

Hodgkins

CERTIFIED GROCERS MIDWEST, INC., One, Certified Dr., 60525-4894, pg. 226 **PV**
SILBRICO CORPORATION, 6300 River Rd., 60525, pg. 1000 **PV**

Hoffman Estates

AMERICAN TOOL COMPANIES, INC., 2800 W. Higgins Rd., Ste. 805, 60195, pg. 63 **PV**
Ameritech Cellular and Paging Services, 2000 W. Ameritech Ctr. Dr., 60195-5000, pg. 98 **PV**
Ameritech Consumer Services, 2000 W. Ameritech Center Dr., 60195, pg. 98 **PB**
Ameritech Small Business Services, 2000 W. Ameritech Center Dr., 60195, pg. 98 **PB**
CAREER EDUCATION CORPORATION, 2800 W. Higgins Rd., Ste. 790, 60195, pg. 209 **PV**
Central Region Sales, 2200 W. Higgins Rd., 60195, pg. 1572 **PB**
Focus Media, 2800 W. Higgins Rd., Ste. 500, 60195, pg. 415 **PV**
Fraser Paper Limited, 2300 Barrington Rd., Ste.215, 60195, pg. 434 **IT**
National Tire & Battery, 3333 Beverly Rd., 60179, pg. 1452 **PB**
Pulte Illinois Division, 2500 W. Higgins Rd., Ste. 770, 60195, pg. 1344 **PB**
SAFECO Insurance Co. of Illinois, 1900 West Hassell Rd., 60196, pg. 1423 **PB**
Sears Auto Centers, 3333 Beverly Rd., 60179, pg. 1452 **PB**
SEARS, ROEBUCK AND CO., 3333 Beverly Rd., 60179, pg. 1452 **PB**
Sears Tire Group, 3333 Beverly Rd., 60179, pg. 1452 **PB**
TMP Worldwide, Inc., Northwest Corporate Center, 2500 West Higgins Rd., Ste. 900, 60195, pg. 1064 **PV**
THOMAS ENGINEERING INC., 575 W. Central Rd., 60195, pg. 1082 **PV**
Zeneca Pharmaceuticals, 2500 W. Higgins Rd., Ste. 1040, 60195, pg. 1525 **IT**

Homewood

AMERICAN TECHNICAL PUBLISHERS, INC., 1155 W. 175th St., 60430, pg. 63 **PV**
Bank of Homewood, 2034 Ridge Rd., 60430, pg. 474 **PV**
CARL BUDDIG & COMPANY, 950 W. 175th St., 60430-2040, pg. 178 **PV**
Graycor Construction Company Inc., One Graycor Dr., 60430, pg. 472 **PV**
Graycor Industrial Constructors Inc., One Graycor Dr., 60430, pg. 472 **PV**
Graycor International Inc., One Graycor Dr., 60430, pg. 472 **PV**
GRAYCOR OPERATING COMPANIES, One Graycor Dr., 60430, pg. 472 **PV**
Hunter Douglas Metals, 915 W. 175th St., 60430, pg. 639 **IT**

Hoopeston

Environmental Development Corp., Vermillion Country, Rd. 4000, 60942, pg. 189 **PB**
Silgan Containers, 320 W. Main St., 60942, pg. 1473 **PB**

Huntley

H.S. CROCKER CO., INC., 12100 Smith Dr., 60142, pg. 290 **PV**
DFC Transportation Co., 12007 Smith Dr., 60142, pg. 490 **PB**
DUO-FAST CORPORATION, 13951 S. Quality Dr., 60142, pg. 347 **PV**
Harris Bank Huntley, 10604 Rte. 47, 60142, pg. 154 **IT**
Union Special Corp., One Union Special Plaza, 60142, pg. 716 **IT**

Ipava

BADER & CO., P.O. Box 19, 61441, pg. 110 **PV**

Itasca

AST Research, Inc., Ste. 295W, One Pierce Pl., 60143, pg. 1182 **IT**
AMP Inc. Lytel Division, 450 E. Devon Ste. 175, 60143-1261, pg. 8 **PB**
Arrow/Schweber Electronics, 1140 W. Thorndale, 60143, pg. 134 **PB**
Autodesk, 2 Pierce Pl., Ste. 1810, 60143, pg. 149 **PB**
Auto-trol Technology Corp.-Chicago, One Pierce Pl., Ste. 295 E., 60143, pg. 148 **PB**
Bando America, Inc., 1149 W. Bryn Mawr, 60143, pg. 145 **IT**
Bankers Box/Records Storage Systems, 1789 Norwood Ave., 60143, pg. 400 **PV**
Boise Cascade Office Products Corporation, 800 W. Bryn Mawr Ave., 60143, pg. 243 **PB**
BOLER COMPANY, 500 Park Blvd., Ste. 1010, 60143, pg. 155 **PV**
CCL Label Sales & Marketing, 500 Park Blvd., Ste. 776, 60143-3121, pg. 238 **IT**
CORS, One Pierce Place, Ste. 300 E., 60143, pg. 196 **PV**
Capstone Electronics Div., 1100 W. Thorndale Ave., 60143, pg. 134 **PB**

PB - *U.S. Public Companies Volume*
PV - *U.S. Private Companies Volume*
IT - *International Public & Private Companies Volume*

Geographic Index-U.S.

1221

CIMLINC INCORPORATED, 1222 Hamilton Pkwy., 60143, pg. 239 **PV**

Conam Inspection, 1247 W. Norwood Ave., 60143, pg. 1299 **IT**

CONTINENTAL WEB PRESS, INC., 1430 Industrial Dr., 60143, pg. 269 **PV**

Copyholder Division, 1789 Norwood Ave., 60143, pg. 400 **PV**

Critics' Choice Video, Inc., 800 Thorndale, 60143, pg. 1310 **PB**

EMKAY, INC., 805 W. Thorndale, 60143, pg. 374 **PV**

Enesco Corporation, 225 Windsor, 60143, pg. 1508 **PB**

ENVIRONETX, 1351 E. Irving Park Rd., 60143-2300, pg. 378 **PV**

Euroclean, 1151 Bryn Mawr Ave., 60143, pg. 440 **PV**

EXCELSIOR MANUFACTURING & SUPPLY CORP., 1465 E. Industrial Dr., 60143, pg. 387 **PV**

FELLOWES MANUFACTURING CO., 1789 Norwood Ave., 60143-1095, pg. 400 **PV**

FIRST MIDWEST BANCORP, INC., 300 Park Blvd., Ste. 400, 60143, pg. 636 **PB**

First Midwest Bank, N.A., 300 Park Blvd., Ste. 400, 60143, pg. 636 **PB**

Flex-Kleen Corporation, One Pierce Place, Ste. 1500 West, 60143, pg. 29 **PV**

Fuji Graphic Arts Div., 1285 Hamilton Parkway, 60143, pg. 524 **IT**

ARTHUR J. GALLAGHER & CO., Two Gallagher Ctr., Two Pierce Pl., 60143-3141, pg. 698 **PB**

Geotronics of North America, Inc., 911 Hawthorne Dr., 60143, pg. 1289 **IT**

EDWARD HINES LUMBER CO., 550 E. Devon Ave., 60143, pg. 530 **PV**

ITW Buildex, 1349 Bryn Mawr, 60143, pg. 866 **PB**

ITW Hi-Cone, 1140 W. Bryn Mawr, 60143, pg. 866 **PB**

Information Processing Products, 1789 Norwood Ave., 60143, pg. 400 **PV**

Klockner-Moeller, 1003 Hawthorn Dr., 60143, pg. 736 **IT**

KNOWLES ELECTRONICS, INC., 1151 Maplewood Dr., 60143, pg. 627 **PV**

MHIA Machine Tool Division, 907 W. Irving Park Rd., 60143, pg. 874 **IT**

MTI Systems Div., 1140 W. Thorndale Ave., 60143, pg. 135 **PB**

Noma-International, Inc., 450 E. Devon Ave., Ste. 300, 60143, pg. 955 **IT**

OCE-U.S.A., 1800 Bruning Dr. W., 60143, pg. 994 **IT**

OFFICE ELECTRONICS, INC., 865 W. Irving Park Rd., 60143, pg. 812 **PV**

PMP Fermentation Products, Inc., 500 Park Blvd., Ste. 450, 60143, pg. 525 **IT**

Partner Industrial Products Inc., 907 W. Irving Park Rd., 60143, pg. 440 **IT**

Pepsi-Cola Central, 300 Park Blvd., Ste. 500, 60143, pg. 1277 **PB**

Playboy Preferred, Inc., 800 Thorndale, 60143, pg. 1310 **PB**

Power Shred Division, 1789 Norwood Ave., 60143, pg. 400 **PV**

PUTMAN PUBLISHING CO., 555 Pierce Rd. Ste. 301, 60143, pg. 896 **PV**

Quest Inc., 880 W. Thorndale Ave., 60143-1341, pg. 1435 **IT**

THE RESTAURANT COMPANY, One Pierce Pl., Ste. 100E, 60143, pg. 925 **PV**

Serta, Inc., 325 Spring Lake Dr., 60143, pg. 985 **PV**

Tecfor Inc., 907 W. Irving Park Rd., 60143, pg. 440 **IT**

Uddeholm Corporation, 851 Expressway Dr., 60143, pg. 1471 **IT**

Ivesdale

Grand Prairie Co-op, Inc., Sloan Station, R.R. 1, 61851, pg. 469 **PV**

Jacksonville

DAVEL COMMUNICATIONS GROUP, INC., 601 W. Morgan St., 62650, pg. 488 **PB**

Elliott State Bank, 73 Central Bank Plaza, 62651, pg. 643 **PB**

LUNDIA DIV. OF MII, INC., 600 Capitol Way, 62650, pg. 680 **PV**

Jerseyville

U.S. Can Company, P.O. Box 70, County Rd., 62052, pg. 1681 **PB**

Joliet

Barrett Hardware & Industrial Supply Company, 324 Henderson Ave., 60432, pg. 335 **PV**

Crane Valves/North American, 104 N. Chicago St., 60431, pg. 457 **PB**

Crossfield Chemical, 101 England Ave., 60435, pg. 1435 **PV**

DeSoto Inc., P.O. Box 609-60434, 900 E Washington St., 60433, pg. 956 **PB**

First Midwest Mortgage Corporation, 2801 W. Jefferson St., 60435, pg. 636 **PB**

First Midwest Trust Company, N.A., 121 N. Chicago St., 60431-1205, pg. 636 **PB**

Harcros Chemicals Inc., P.O. Box 458, 60434, pg. 598 **IT**

Hendrickson Stamping, P.O. Box 70, One Genstar Ln., 60434, pg. 155 **PV**

Herald-News, 300 Caterpillar Dr., 60436, pg. 275 **PV**

Insta-Foam Products, Inc., 1500 Cedarwood Dr., 60435, pg. 412 **PV**

Ivex Packaging Corporation-Mill Division, P.O. Box 685, 292 Logan Ave., 60434, pg. 915 **PB**

Kernlite Company, 104 No. Chicago St., 60431, pg. 457 **PB**

SHEFFIELD STEEL CORPORATION-JOLIET, One Industry Ave., 60435, pg. 991 **PV**

Joppa

Electric Energy, Inc., P.O. Box 165, 62953, pg. 870 **PB**

Kankakee

Bioproducts, Inc.-Research & Development, 1048 S. Hieland Rd., 60964, pg. 145 **PV**

Consumers Illinois Water Co., P.O. Box 152, 1000 S. Schuyler Ave., 60901, pg. 438 **PB**

DE Brush Company, 1325 Harvard DR., 60901, pg. 370 **PV**

ELECTRON BEAM TECHNOLOGIES, 1275 Harvard Dr., 60901, pg. 370 **PV**

Essette Pendaflex, 1625 Duane Blvd., 60901, pg. 460 **IT**

TTC ILLINOIS INC., 50 Meadowview Ctr., 60901, pg. 1066 **PV**

United Coatings, Inc., 2850 Festival Dr., 60901, pg. 1466 **PB**

Keensburg

Amax Coal Company, 1000 Beall Woods Rd., 62852, pg. 470 **PB**

Kenilworth

INTERMARK WORLD PRODUCTS, LTD., 632 Green Bay Rd., 60043, pg. 567 **PV**

Kewanee

Boss Manufacturing Company, 221 W. First St., 61443, pg. 1142 **PV**

Compaction America, 2000 Kentville Rd., 61443, pg. 1676 **PB**

Empire Clothing, 1700 Burlington, 61443, pg. 387 **PV**

Illinois Star-Courier, 105 E. Central Blvd., 61443, pg. 983 **PB**

Kewanee Boiler Manufacturing Company, Inc., 101 Franklin, 61443, pg. 270 **PB**

VISTA 2000, INC., 221 W. First St., 61443, pg. 1142 **PV**

Kirkland

Limagrain Genetics Corp., P.O. Box 278, Rte. 72W, 60146, pg. 566 **IT**

La Grange

Alamo Group, Inc., 500 Shawnut, 60525, pg. 35 **PB**

Danka Business Systems, 405 E. Shawmut, 60525, pg. 379 **IT**

Electro-Motive Division, 9301 W. 55th St., 60525, pg. 719 **IT**

Funding Services Inc., 405 E. Shawmut, 60525, pg. 379 **IT**

Henkel Corporation Functional Products Div., 5325 S. Ninth Ave., 60525, pg. 610 **IT**

Henkel Corporation Polymers Division, 5325 S. Ninth Ave., 60525, pg. 610 **IT**

Henkel Functional Products Div., 5325 S. 9th Ave., 60525, pg. 610 **IT**

Musser Div., 505 E. Shawmut, 60525, pg. 1054 **IT**

La Salle

Illinois Cement Co., P.O. Box 442, 61301, pg. 322 **PB**

Ladd

Phillips-Joanna, Inc., P.O. Box 425, 61329, pg. 434 **PV**

Lafox

National Electronics Manufacturing Division, 40W267 Keslinger Rd., 60147, pg. 1388 **PB**

RICHARDSON ELECTRONICS, LTD., 40W267 Keslinger Rd., 30147-0393, pg. 1387 **PB**

Richardson Electronics Ltd.-Central, 40W267 Keslinger Rd., 60147, pg. 1388 **PB**

Lake Bluff

Albrecht/Buehler Communications Div., 41 Waukegan Rd., 60044, pg. 574 **PV**

Buehler, Limited, P.O. Box 1, 41 Waukegan Rd., 60044, pg. 574 **PB**

CLARIN, 927 North Shore Dr., 60044, pg. 242 **PV**

ELE International, Inc./Soiltest, 86 Albrecht Dr., 60044-8004, pg. 1287 **IT**

Enfield Industrial Corp., 46 Sherwood Terrace, 60044, pg. 554 **PB**

LIQUID CONTROLS LLC, 105 Albrecht Dr., 60044, pg. 669 **PV**

The Northern Trust Company, 120 E. Scranton Ave., 60044, pg. 1197 **PB**

PATERNO IMPORTS LIMITED, 900 Armour Dr., 60044, pg. 843 **PV**

President Baking-Plantation, 1400 Skokie Hwy., 60044, pg. 1069 **IT**

Lake Forest

BRUNSWICK CORPORATION, One N. Field Ct., 60045-4811, pg. 265 **PB**

Brunswick Indoor Recreation Group, 1 N. Field Ct., 60045-4811, pg. 265 **PB**

MERCURY FINANCE CO., 100 Field Dr., Ste. 340, 60045, pg. 1093 **PB**

Moore Business Forms & Systems Div., 275 Field Dr., 60045, pg. 890 **IT**

Moore Document Solutions, 275 N. Field Dr., 60045, pg. 890 **IT**

The Northern Trust Company, 265 Deerpath Rd., 60045, pg. 1197 **PB**

The Northern Trust Company, 959 S. Waukegan Rd., 60045, pg. 1197 **PB**

PACKAGING RESOURCES, INCORPORATED, One Conway Park, 100 Field Dr., Ste. 300, 60045, pg. 833 **PV**

The Popcorn Factory, 13970 W. Laurel Dr., 60045, pg. 421 **PV**

PORTEC, INC., 100 Field Dr., Ste. 120, 60045, pg. 1317 **PB**

Lake Zurich

ARROW PNEUMATICS CO. INC., 500 N. Oakwood Rd., 60047, pg. 85 **PV**

J.R. Technical, 500 Oakwood Rd., 60047, pg. 85 **PV**

R.A. Briggs & Co., 650 N. Church St., 60047, pg. 536 **PV**

Robinson Nugent, Inc., First Bank Plaza, Ste. 304, 60047, pg. 1394 **PB**

Lansing

The Harry Alter Company, 17725 Volbrecht Rd., 60438, pg. 1075 **PV**

Bryant Mungo Division, 2055 N. Ruby St., 60160, pg. 1075 **PV**

Morton Automotive Coatings, 2701 E. 170th St., 60438, pg. 1135 **PB**

TEMPERATURE EQUIPMENT CORPORATION, 17725 Volbrecht Rd., 60438, pg. 1075 **PV**

Lawrenceville

Peoples National Bank, P.O. Box 495, 909 12th St., 62439, pg. 1217 **PB**

Lemont

Caro Trans Intl., 15700 W. 103rd St., 60439, pg. 130 **PB**

Chicago Consolidated, 20 W. 151, 101st St., 60439, pg. 533 **PB**

Clipper Exxpress, 15700 W. 103rd St., 60439, pg. 130 **PB**

FOLGER ADAM SECURITY INC., 16300 W. 103rd St., 60439, pg. 416 **PV**

M.A. Hanna Resin Distribution, 990 107th St., 60439, pg. 781 **PB**

Libertyville

CORCOM, INC., 844 E. Rockland Rd., 60048-3375, pg. 446 **PB**

FOULDS INC., 520 E. Church St., 60048, pg. 421 **PV**

Harris Bank Libertyville, 354 N. Milwaukee Ave., 60048, pg. 154 **IT**

HOLLISTER INCORPORATED, 2000 Hollister Dr., 60048, pg. 535 **PV**

Howe Scale, 1840 Industrial Dr., Ste. 100, 60048-9400, pg. 1299 **IT**

Isomedix Operations Inc., 1880 Industrial Dr., 60048, pg. 1515 **PB**

LIBERTYVILLE LINCOLN-MERCURY SALES, INC., 941 S. Milwaukee Ave., 60048, pg. 666 **PV**

Motorola Cellular Subscriber Group, 600 N. U.S. Hwy. 45, 60048, pg. 1137 **PB**

Whiteswan/Meta, 14044 W. Petronella, Ste. 1, 60048, pg. 342 **PV**

Lincoln

Lincoln Courier, 601 Pulaski St., 62656, pg. 275 **PV**

Magna Bank, Lincoln Region, 303 S. Kickapoo St., 62656, pg. 1037 **PB**

Lincolnshire

ACCO World Corporation, 300 Tower Pkwy., 60069-3665, pg. 674 **PB**

Advent Loudspeakers, 25 Tri-State Intl. Office Ctr., 60069, pg. 1369 **PB**

AKORN, INC., 100 Tri-State Dr., Ste. 100, 60069, pg. 34 **PB**

ALTAIR CORPORATION, 350 Barclay Blvd., 60069, pg. 46 **PV**

ALTERNATIVE RESOURCES CORPORATION, 100 Tri-State International, Ste. 300, 60069, pg. 59 **PB**

Brake-Pro Systems, Inc., 100 Tri State International, Ste. 300, 60069, pg. 1578 **PB**

Charmilles Technologies Corp., 560 Bond St., 60069-4224, pg. 489 **IT**

Daiichi Fine Chemicals, Lincolnshire Corporate Ctr., One Overlook Pt., Ste. 250, 60069, pg. 879 **IT**

PB - *U.S. Public Companies Volume*
PV - *U.S. Private Companies Volume*
IT - *International Public & Private Companies Volume*

FAVORITE BRANDS INTERNATIONAL, INC., 75 Tri-State Intl., Ste. 222, 60069, pg. 397   **PV**
Grainger, 333 Knightsbridge Pkwy., 60069-3639, pg. 758   **PB**
W.W. GRAINGER, INC., 455 Knightsbridge Pkwy., 60069-3620, pg. 758   **PB**
Harvest Industries, Inc., 350 Barclay Blvd., 60069, pg. 46   **PV**
HEWITT ASSOCIATES LLC, 100 Half Day Rd., 60069, pg. 524   **PV**
IVEX PACKAGING CORPORATION, 100 Tri-State Dr., Ste. 200, 60069, pg. 915   **PB**
Ivex Packaging Corporation-Food Packaging Division, 100 Tri-State Drive, Suite 200, 60069, pg. 915   **PB**
Komatsu America Corp., P.O. Box 1422, 200 Tri-State Intl., 60069-1422, pg. 744   **IT**
LINC Equipment Services, 550 Bond St., 60069, pg. 996   **PV**
MDA Scientific, Inc., 405 Barclay Blvd., 60069, pg. 618   **IT**
MHI Lithograph Printing, 600 Barclay Blvd., 60069, pg. 874   **IT**
MasterBrand Industries, Inc., 300 Tower Pkwy., 60069-3665, pg. 675   **PB**
Motorola ARDIS, 300 Knightsbridge Pkwy., 60069, pg. 1137   **PB**
Nichols Aluminum, 200 Schelter Rd., 60069, pg. 1350   **PB**
Phase Linear, 25 Tri-State Intl. Office Ctr., 60069, pg. 1369   **PB**
Purac America, Inc., 111 Barclay Blvd., 60069, pg. 244   **IT**
QUILL CORP., 100 Schelter Rd., 60069, pg. 901   **PV**
Recoton Auto Corporation, 25 Tri-State Intl. Office Ctr., Ste. 400, 60069, pg. 1369   **PB**
Stella Foods Inc., 25 Tri-State International, Ste. 258, 60069, pg. 1040   **PV**
Sun Electric, 420 Barclay Blvd., 60069, pg. 1480   **PB**
Tenneco Automotive Trading Company, 100 Tri State Intl., pg. 1578   **PB**
VANCE PUBLISHING CORPORATION, 400 Knightsbridge Pkwy., 60069, pg. 1133   **PV**

Lincolnwood

ATF, INC., 3550 W. Pratt Ave., 60645, pg. 8   **PV**
ADMIRAL MAINTENANCE SERVICE L.P., 4343 W. Touhy Ave., 60646, pg. 17   **PV**
Bank of Lincolnwood, 4433 W. Touhy, 60646, pg. 436   **PB**
Bell & Howell Document Management Products Company, 6800 McCormick Blvd., 60645-2797, pg. 201   **PB**
BIG JOE MANUFACTURING CO., 7225 N. Kostner, 60646, pg. 143   **PV**
Bones/Lincolnwood, 7110 N. Lincoln Ave., 60646, pg. 661   **PV**
Hilton Active Apparel, 6850 Central Park, 60645, pg. 940   **PB**
JELMAR COMPANY, 6600 N. Lincoln Ave., 60645, pg. 585   **PV**
Loeber Motors, Inc., 7101 N. Lincoln, 60646, pg. 672   **PV**
LONDON LITHO ALUMINUM CO., INC., 7100 N. Lawndale Ave., 60645, pg. 673   **PV**
MID-CONTINENT SCREW PRODUCTS CO., 3701 W. Lunt Ave., 60645, pg. 1062   **PV**
NTC/Contemporary Publishing Group, 4255 W. Touhy Ave., 60646-1975, pg. 1635   **PB**
Passport Books, 4255 W. Touhy Ave., 60646, pg. 1636   **PB**
VGM Career Horizons, 4255 W. Touhy Ave., 60646, pg. 1636   **PB**

Lisle

Acacia Technologies, 2400 Cabot Dr., 60532, pg. 420   **PB**
All American Technologies of Chicago, Inc., 1989 J University Ln., 60532, pg. 41   **PB**
BOC, 2100 Western Ct., 60532-3900, pg. 121   **IT**
Budget Rent A Car Corporation, 4225 Naperville Rd., 60532, pg. 178   **PV**
Capital Agricultural Property Services, Inc., 801 Warrenville Rd., Ste. 150, 60532, pg. 892   **PV**
Distributed Systems Division, 801 Warrenville Rd., 60532, pg. 1522   **PV**
THE INTERLAKE CORPORATION, 550 Warrenville Rd., 60532-4387, pg. 892   **PB**
LaSalle Bank of Lisle, 4733 Main St., 60532, pg. 10   **IT**
Lisle Corporetum Offices, 750 Warrenville Rd., 60532-4345, pg. 518   **PB**
Lockformer Company, 711 Ogden Ave., 60532, pg. 1100   **PV**
Molex Alin International Incorporated, 2222 Wellington Ct., 60532, pg. 1122   **PB**
Molex Electrical Systems Inc., 2222 Wellington Ct., 60532, pg. 1122   **PB**
Molex Fiber Optic Inc., 2222 Wellington Ct., 60532, pg. 1122   **PB**
MOLEX INCORPORATED, 2222 Wellington Ct., 60532, pg. 1121   **PB**
Molex International, Inc., 2222 Wellington Court, 60532, pg. 1122   **PB**
Molex US Inc., 2222 Wellington Ct., 60532, pg. 1122   **PB**
PETTIBONE CORPORATION, 4225 Naperville Rd., Ste. 200, 60532, pg. 859   **PV**
Porsche Credit Corporation, Inc., 4343 Commerce Ct., Ste. 104, 60532, pg. 1063   **IT**
Ruppman Marketing Technologies, Inc., 1963 University Ln., 60532, pg. 952   **PV**
STERLING SUPPLY COMPANY, INC., 4900 Lincoln Ave., 60532, pg. 1041   **PV**
TELLABS OPERATIONS, INC., 4951 Indiana Ave., 60532, pg. 1572   **PB**
TRICON INDUSTRIES, INC., 1600 Eisenhower Ln., Ste. 200, 60532, pg. 1102   **PV**

Van den Bergh Foods Company, 2200 Cabot Dr., 60532, pg. 1436   **IT**
Victor Products, 1945 Ohio St., 60532-2189, pg. 480   **PB**
VOLVO AND HONDA SALES & SERVICE, 4375 Lincoln Ave., 60532, pg. 1143   **PV**
WALLACE COMPUTER SERVICES, INC., 2275 Cabot Dr., 60532-3630, pg. 1735   **PB**
Wausau General Insurance Company, 901 Warrenville Rd., 60532, pg. 789   **PV**

Litchfield

Hydraulics Inc., 725 McKinley Ave., 62056, pg. 560   **PB**
ROLLER DERBY SKATE CORP., 311 W. Edwards St., 62056, pg. 941   **PV**
Sierra Inc., 725 McKinly Ave., 62056, pg. 560   **PV**

Lockport

KINETICSYSTEMS CORPORATION, 900 N. State St., 60441-2292, pg. 620   **PV**

Lombard

ACI Telecentrics Inc., 2200 S. Main, Ste. 203, 60148, pg. 3   **PB**
Addison Insurance Agency, 2500 Highland Ave., 60148, pg. 1677   **PB**
Addison Insurance Company, 2500 Highland Ave., Ste. 210, 60148, pg. 1677   **PB**
AXIA INCORPORATED, 100 W 22nd St., Ste. 134, 60148-4877, pg. 103   **PV**
Baldwin Web Controls, 1051 N. Main St., Ste. B., 60148, pg. 170   **PV**
Benihana Lombard Corp., 747 E. Butterfield Rd., 60148, pg. 212   **PB**
Bunzl Packaging, 1140 N. Dupage, 60148, pg. 233   **IT**
ComCoTec, Inc., 2505 S. Finley Rd., 60148, pg. 539   **PB**
Commercial Testing & Engineering Co., 1919 S. Highland Ave., Ste. 210 B, 60148, pg. 1153   **PV**
Crabtree Premium Finance, 2500 Highland Ave., Ste. 230, 60148, pg. 1677   **PB**
Eagle Converting Inc., 201 Eisenhower Lane S., 60148, pg. 165   **PV**
Evans, Inc., Yorktown Shopping Ctr., Butterfield Rd. & Highland Ave., 60148, pg. 596   **PB**
Financial Collection Agencies (1990) Inc., Greenbrook Executive Center, 100 W 22nd Ave., Ste. 151, 60148-4863, pg. 471   **IT**
HUB GROUP, INC., 377 E. Butterfield Rd., Ste 700, 60148, pg. 844   **PB**
Hush Puppies Retail, Inc., 330 E. Roosevelt Rd., 60148, pg. 1775   **PB**
IDX Systems Corporation-Chicago, One Imperial Pl., 1 E. 22nd St., Ste. 700, 60148, pg. 854   **PB**
KYB Corporation of America, 901 Oak Creek Dr., 60148, pg. 727   **IT**
LOMBARD LINCOLN-MERCURY & LEASING, INC., 500 E. Roosevelt Rd., 60148, pg. 673   **PV**
MC2 Inc., 701 E. 22nd St., 60148-5072, pg. 1210   **PB**
The Martin-Brower Company, 333 E. Butterfield Rd., 5th Fl., 60148, pg. 1102   **PB**
METROMAIL CORPORATION, 360 E. 22nd St., 60148, pg. 1102   **PB**
MidCon Corp., 701 E. 22nd St., 60148-5072, pg. 1210   **PB**
Natural Gas Pipeline Co. America, 701 E. 22nd St., 60148-5072, pg. 1210   **PB**
Vanguard Financial Services, 1110 Main St., 60148, pg. 1216   **PB**
Vulcan Materials Company-Midwest Div., 747 E. 22nd St., Ste. 200, 60148, pg. 1726   **PB**
Warsteiner Importers Agency, 1148 N. Main St., 60148, pg. 1486   **PB**

Long Grove

American Manufacturers Mutual Insurance Company, One Kemper Dr., 60049, pg. 614   **PV**
American Motorists Insurance Co., One Kemper Dr., 60049, pg. 614   **PV**
American Protection Insurance Co., One Kemper Dr., 60049, pg. 614   **PV**
CF INDUSTRIES, INC., One Salem Lake Dr., 60047, pg. 193   **PV**
Federal Kemper Life Assurance Company, One Kemper Dr., 60049, pg. 1530   **IT**
KEMPER INSURANCE COMPANIES, 1 Kemper Dr., 60049, pg. 614   **PV**
Kemper Investors Life Insurance Company, One Kemper Dr., 60049, pg. 1530   **IT**
Kemper Reinsurance Co., One Kemper Dr., 60049, pg. 614   **PV**
Lumbermen's Mutual Casualty Company, One Kemper Dr., 60049, pg. 614   **PV**
National Loss Control Service Corp., One Kemper Dr., 60049, pg. 614   **PV**

Loves Park

American Pfauter Corp., P.O. Box 2698, 61132, pg. 617   **IT**
Mid-American Financial Services Company, P.O. Box 2685, 5930 N. Second St., 61111, pg. 65   **PB**
Pfauter-Maag Cutting Tools, 61111, pg. 617   **IT**
TD Electronics, Inc., 6815 Elm Dr., pg. 1646   **PB**

Lyons

Berry Bearing Company, 4242 S. First Ave., 60534, pg. 732   **PB**

Machesney Park

C & C Manufacturing Inc., 1330 Anvil Rd., 61115, pg. 646   **IT**

Macomb

Haeger Potteries of Macomb, Inc., 411 Calhoun, 61455, pg. 493   **PV**

Madison

Laclede - Metro-East Processing, Washington Ave. & Race St., 62060, pg. 974   **PB**
SPECTRULITE CONSORTIUM, INC., 1001 College St., 62060-0258, pg. 1024   **PV**

Manteno

Ivex Packaging Corporation-Manteno, 1050 Sycamore Rd., 60950, pg. 915   **PB**

Mapleton

ODG, Rte. 24, Factory Rd., 61547, pg. 1774   **PB**

Marengo

The Arnold Engineering Company, 300 North West St., 60152, pg. 103   **PB**
Harris Bank Marengo, 100 W. Washington St., 60152, pg. 154   **IT**
Nissan Forklift Corporation, North America, 240 N. Prospect St., 60152, pg. 944   **IT**

Marion

Marion 100, Inc., P.O. Box 277, 62959, pg. 708   **PV**

Marshall

First National Bank of Marshall, 215 N. Michigan Ave., 62441, pg. 634   **IT**

Matteson

Bank of Matteson, 4600 W. Lincoln Hwy., 60443, pg. 474   **PV**
GREAT LAKES FINANCIAL RESOURCES, INC., 4600 W. Lincoln Hwy., 60443, pg. 474   **PV**

Mattoon

Blaw-Knox Construction Equipment Corporation, 750 Broadway Ave., E., 61938, pg. 877   **PB**
Central National Bank of Mattoon, 1400 Charleston Ave., 61938, pg. 643   **PB**
Consolidated Communications, 121 S. 17th St., 61938, pg. 1073   **PB**
Consolidated Communications Mobile Services, Inc., 121 S. 17th St., 61938, pg. 1073   **PB**
Consolidated Communications Operator Services, Inc., 1501 Charleston Ave., 61938, pg. 1073   **PB**
Consolidated Communications Public Services, Inc., 1421 Charleston Ave., 61938, pg. 1073   **PB**
Elasco Agency Sales, Inc., 1100 Old State Rd., 61938, pg. 846   **PB**
Electric Laboratories & Sales Corp., P.O. Box 729, 1100 Old State Rd., 61938, pg. 847   **PB**
Justrite Mfg. Co., W. Rte. 121, 61938, pg. 617   **PB**
Mattoon Mfg. Division, P.O. Box 1668, Rte. 45 N., pg. 518   **PB**

Mc Cook

S.A. Healy Company, Box 11, 9600 W. 47th St., 60525, pg. 483   **IT**
Reynolds Metals Company-Illinois, First Ave. & 47th St., 60525, pg. 1385   **PB**

McGaw Park

ALLEGIANCE HEALTHCARE CORP., 1430 Waukegan Rd., 60085, pg. 44   **PB**
Allegiance Healthcare Corp., 1430 Waukegan Rd., 60085, pg. 44   **PB**
Allegiance Healthcare International, 1430 Waukegan Rd., 60085, pg. 45   **PB**
Convertors/Custom Sterile, 1500 Waukegan Rd., Bldg. WM, 60085, pg. 44   **PB**
Cost Management Services, 1430 Waukegan Rd., 60085, pg. 44   **PB**
Distribution, 1450 Waukegan Rd., 60085, pg. 44   **PB**
Medi-Vac/Airlife Respiratory Care, 1500 Waukegan Rd., 60085, pg. 44   **PB**

McHenry

CHROMA CORPORATION, 3900 Dayton St., 60050, pg. 238   **PV**

Geographic Index-U.S.

Follett Software Company, 1391 Corporate Dr., 60050-7041, pg. 417 — PV
Hydraulics Inc., 1600 N. Industrial Dr., 60050, pg. 560 — PB
OMNI Products, Inc., 3911 Dayton St., 60050, pg. 816 — PV
Raybestos/Brake Parts Inc., 4400 Prime Parkway, 60050, pg. 560 — PB

Melrose Park

AGI INC., 1950 N. Ruby St., 60160, pg. 5 — PV
ALBERTO-CULVER COMPANY, 2525 Armitage Ave., 60160-1163, pg. 37 — PB
American Citrus Products Corporation, 2000 N. 15th Ave., 60160-1473, pg. 537 — PV
Anning-Johnson Company, 1959 Anson Dr., 60160, pg. 76 — PV
ANSON INDUSTRIES, INC., 1959 Anson Dr., 60160, pg. 76 — PV
Banco Popular, 1600 W. Lake St., 60160, pg. 176 — PB
Benjamin Moore & Co., North & 25th Aves., 60160, pg. 133 — PV
Dale Foods, 1501 N. 31st Ave., 65801, pg. 301 — PV
Gage Food Products Company, 1501 N. 31st Ave., 60160, pg. 301 — PV
HOME JUICE CO., 2000 N. 15th Ave., 60160-1473, pg. 537 — PV
Jewel-Osco, 1955 W. North Ave., 60160, pg. 93 — PB
KREHER STEEL CO., INC., 1550 N. 25th Ave., 60160, pg. 635 — PV
Lindberg Heat Treating Co., 1975 N. Ruby St., 60160, pg. 999 — PV
Name Saver Company, 2000 N. 15th Ave., 60160-1473, pg. 537 — PV
National Bancorp, Inc., One Winston Plaza, 1600 W. Lake St., 60160, pg. 176 — PB
RHC/SPACEMASTER CORPORATION, 1400 N. 25th Ave., 60160, pg. 904 — PV
RAM GOLF CORPORATION, 2020 Indian Boundary Dr., 60160, pg. 908 — PV
REYNOLDS MACHINE TOOL CORP., 2033 N. 17th Ave., 60160, pg. 926 — PV
Tree Fresh Foods Corp., 2000 N. 15th Ave., 60160, pg. 537 — PV
Tropar Mfg. Co., Inc., 3306 Bloomingdale, 60160, pg. 1105 — PV

Mendota

CCS Mendota, 1501 Washington Rd., 61342, pg. 518 — PB
HCC INC., 1501 1st Ave., 61342, pg. 490 — PV
National Manufacturing Co., S. 14th Ave., 61342, pg. 860 — PV
Spartan Tool, 1506 W. Division St., 61342, pg. 860 — PV

Metamora

Metamora Fixtures Production Center, 501 E. Madison, 61548, pg. 496 — PV

Metropolis

Southern Illinois Riverboat Casino Cruise, Inc., 207 Ferry St., pg. 1310 — PB

Midlothian

ARROW CHEVROLET, INC., 14640 Cicero Ave., 60445, pg. 85 — PV
DOBER CHEMICAL CORP., 14461 Waverly, 60445, pg. 337 — PV
Industrial Laundry Group of Amerclean, 14461 Waverly, 60445, pg. 337 — PV
MORAN INDUSTRIES, INC., 4444 W. 147th St., 60445, pg. 760 — PV
U.S. Transparts, 4444 W. 147th St., 60445, pg. 760 — PV

Milan

EAGLE FOOD CENTERS, INC., Rte. 67 & Knoxville Rd., 61264, pg. 547 — PB
Thomas Lighting-Milan Operations, Quad City Industrial Air Pk., 7300 50th St., 61264, pg. 1599 — PB

Mokena

Cashin Systems Corp., 19747 Wolf Rd., 60448, pg. 1378 — IT
Formax, Inc., 9150 191st St., 60448, pg. 1378 — IT
ITW Deltar-Insert Molded, 9629 W. 197th St., 60448, pg. 866 — PB
North Central Crane & Excavator Sales Corp., 8501 W. 191st Street, 60448, pg. 1041 — PB

Moline

Cox Communications-Quad Cities, 3900 26th Ave., 61265, pg. 455 — PB
DEERE & COMPANY, John Deere Rd., 61265-8098, pg. 491 — PB
Deere Credit, Inc., 400 19th St., 61265, pg. 492 — PB
John Deere Commercial Products, Inc., John Deere Rd., 61265, pg. 492 — PB
John Deere Credit Company, John Deere Rd., 61265, pg. 492 — PB
John Deere Health Care, Inc., 1515 Fifth Ave., Ste. 200, 61265, pg. 492 — PB
John Deere Industrial Equipment Company, John Deere Rd., 61265, pg. 492 — PB

John Deere Insurance Company, 3400 80th St., 61265, pg. 492 — PB
John Deere Technologies International, Inc., 3300 River Dr., 61265, pg. 492 — PB
Deere Marketing Services, Inc., John Deere Rd., 61265, pg. 492 — PB
Hilb Rogal & Hamilton Company of the Quad Cities, 2200 52nd Ave., 61266, pg. 827 — PB
KONE Elevators North America, One Montgomery Ct., 61265, pg. 746 — IT
Lilly Industries, Inc., 5400 23rd Ave., 61265, pg. 994 — PV
Moline Accessories Company, 325 19th St., 61265-1395, pg. 746 — IT
Montgomery Elevator Export Corporation, One Montgomery Ct., 61265, pg. 746 — IT
Montgomery Elevator International Company, One Montgomery Court, 61265, pg. 746 — IT
Montgomery KONE Inc., One Montgomery Ct., 61265, pg. 746 — IT
TIE Systems, Inc. Mississippi Valley, 2316 Fifth Ave., 61265, pg. 1085 — PV
WQAD-TV, 3003 Park 16th St., 61265, pg. 1174 — PB
WILLIAMS, WHITE & CO., 600 River Dr., 61265, pg. 1179 — PV

Momence

Custom Farm Seed, P.O. Box 160, 60954, pg. 1435 — IT
Gilster Mary Lee Corp., 305 E. Washington, 60954, pg. 455 — PV

Montgomery

Aurora Metals Division L.P.C., 1995 Greenfield Rd., 60538, pg. 529 — PV
General American Door Company, 5050 Base Line Rd., 60538, pg. 732 — PV
Lyon Metal Products, Inc., 420 N. Main St., 60538, pg. 638 — PV
PROCESSED PLASTIC COMPANY, 1001 Aucutt Rd., 60538, pg. 888 — PV

Monticello

A.O. Smith/Uppco, Inc., 302 N. Sixth St., 47960, pg. 1477 — PB

Morris

Alumax Mill Products, Inc., 5555 E. Hwy. 6, 60450-0900, pg. 59 — PB
Folding Carton (Morris), 1000 E. Armstrong St., 60450, pg. 1270 — IT

Morrisonville

UMB First State Bank of Morrisonville, 409 Carlin St., 62546, pg. 1654 — PB

Morton Grove

Tommy Armour Golf, 8350 N. Lehigh Ave., 60053, pg. 1683 — PB
Avon Manufacturing Lab., 6901 Golf Rd., 60053, pg. 156 — PB
Avon Sales & Distribution Branch, 6901 Golf Rd., 60053, pg. 156 — PB
CHICAGO SHOW PRINTING CO., 8330 N. Austin Ave., 60053, pg. 235 — PV
John Crane Mechanical Seals, 6400 Oakton St., 60053, pg. 1339 — IT
DIEBEL MANUFACTURING CO., 6505 Oakton St., 60053, pg. 331 — PV
Elastomer Seals - North America, 6400 W. Oakton St., 60053, pg. 1338 — IT
ITT Bell & Gossett, 8200 N. Austin Ave., 60053, pg. 860 — PB
ITT Domestic Pump, 8200 N. Austin Ave., 60053, pg. 860 — PB
ITT Fluid Handling, 8200 N. Austin, 60053, pg. 860 — PB
Ingrid Division of Lawnware, 8220 N. Austin Ave., 60053, pg. 654 — PV
Isomedix Operations Inc., 7838 Nagle Ave., 60053, pg. 1515 — PV
John Crane North America, 6400 W. Oakton St., 60053, pg. 1339 — IT
PAUL J. KREZ COMPANY, 7831 N. Nagle Ave., 60053, pg. 635 — PV
Lapmaster International Ltd., 6400 W. Oakton St., 60053, pg. 1338 — IT
LAWNWARE PRODUCTS, INC., 8220 N. Austin, 60053, pg. 653 — PV
WILLIAM A. RANDOLPH, INC., 6340 Capulina Ave., 60053, pg. 909 — PV
REVELL-MONOGRAM INC., 8601 Waukegan Rd., 60053, pg. 926 — PV
SCHWARZ PAPER COMPANY, 8338 Austin Ave., 60053, pg. 974 — PV

Mount Carmel

Security Bank & Trust Co., 400 Market St., 62863, pg. 1217 — PB

Mount Morris

AMCORE Bank, Rock River Valley, P.O. Box 151, Two W. Main St., 61054-0151, pg. 64 — PB

International Horticulture Publications Company, 122 S. Wesley Ave., 61054-1497, pg. 1154 — PV
Kable News Company, 16 S. Wesley Ave., 61054, pg. 105 — PV
Quebecor Printing Mt. Morris Inc., 404 N. Wesley Ave., 61054, pg. 1076 — IT
WATT PUBLISHING CO., 122 S. Wesley Ave., 61054-1497, pg. 1154 — PV

Mount Olive

Hano Document Printers, Inc., P.O. Box 278, 62069, pg. 1686 — PB

Mount Prospect

ADVANCE MECHANICAL SYSTEMS, INC., 2080 S. Carboy, 60056-5750, pg. 18 — PV
Amano Cincinnati - Chicago Branch Office, 1842 S. Elmhurst Rd., 60056-5711, pg. 70 — IT
CUMMINS-ALLISON CORP., 891 Feehanville Dr., 60056, pg. 295 — PV
ERO, Inc., 585 Slawin Ct., 60056, pg. 526 — PV
ERO Industries, Inc., 585 Slawin Ct., 60056, pg. 526 — PV
Hedstrom Corporation, 585 Slawin Ct., 60056, pg. 526 — PV
Hedstrom Holding Co., 585 Slawin Ct., 60056, pg. 526 — PV
Hitachi Zosen U.S.A. Ltd.-Chicago, 1699 Wall St., Ste. 425, 60056, pg. 623 — IT
Kay Ray Sensall Inc., 1400 Business Center Dr., 60056, pg. 574 — PV
Makita U.S.A. Inc.-Chicago, 1450 Feehanville Dr., 60056-6011, pg. 831 — IT
Mitsubishi Electric Industrial Control, 800 E. Business Center Ave., 60056-2178, pg. 872 — IT
MULTIGRAPHICS INC., 431 Lakeview Ct., 60056, pg. 1141 — PB
National Material Limited Partnership, 1965 Pratt Blvd., Elk Grove Village, 60056-5798, pg. 1068 — PV
NETWORK SERVICES COMPANY, 1550 Bishop Ct., 60056-6039, pg. 791 — PV
Piher International Corporation, 903 Feehanville Dr., 60056, pg. 853 — PV
SALTON/MAXIM HOUSEWARES, INC., 550 Business Ctr. Drive, 60056, pg. 1430 — PV
SCHUMACHER ELECTRIC CORPORATION, 801 Business Center Dr., 60056, pg. 973 — PV
Stenograph Corporation, 1500 Bishop Ct., 60056, pg. 860 — PV
Sumitomo Electric Carbide, Inc., 1001 Business Ctr. Dr., 60056, pg. 1313 — IT
TDK Corporation of America, 1600 Feehanville Dr., Ste. 100, 60056, pg. 1336 — IT
Toko America, Inc., 1250 Feehanville Dr., 60056, pg. 1393 — IT

Mount Pulaski

Frontier Communications of Mt. Pulaski, Inc., 117 W. Jefferson St., 62548, pg. 684 — PB

Mount Vernon

Citizens Bank of Illinois, P.O. Box 369, 117 N. 10th St., 62864, pg. 280 — PB
GTY Tire Co., P.O. Box 1029, 62864, pg. 327 — IT
Hevi-Duty/Dowzer, Industrial Park, P.O. Box 829, 62864, pg. 726 — PB
Mount Vernon Neon, One Neon Dr., 62864, pg. 386 — PV
National Mine Service Company, Mt. Vernon Div., State Rd. 37 N., 62864, pg. 281 — PV
NationsBank of Mount Vernon, Ninth & Main Sts., 62864, pg. 1164 — PB

Muncie

ICI Seeds, P.O. Box 20, Muncie Rd., 61857, pg. 1524 — IT

Mundelein

Accucare Div., One Medline Pl., 60060, pg. 728 — PV
Advanced Polymers Division, 1150 Allanson Rd., 60060, pg. 689 — PB
Bio-Logic FSC International Corp., One Bio-logic Plaza, 60060, pg. 230 — PB
BIO-LOGIC SYSTEMS CORP., One Bio-logic Plaza, 60060, pg. 230 — PB
Biologic 83 Research Corp., One Bio-logic Plaza, 60060, pg. 230 — PB
Circuit Works, 100 Terrace Dr., 60060, pg. 669 — PV
Dermal Management Sys., One Medline Pl., 60060, pg. 728 — PV
Dynacor Div., One Medline Place, 60060, pg. 728 — PV
IMC Fertilizer, Inc., One Nelson C. White Pkwy., 60060, pg. 856 — PB
K&B Mundelein, 675 Tower Rd., 60060, pg. 623 — PV
MACLEAN-FOGG CO., 1000 Allanson Rd., 60060, pg. 692 — PV
Medcrest Div., One Medline Pl., 60060, pg. 728 — PV
MEDLINE INDUSTRIES, INC., One Medline Pl., 60060, pg. 728 — PV
PRINT-O-TAPE, INC., 755 Tower Rd., 60060, pg. 886 — PV
Rexam Medical Packaging, Inc., 1919 Butterfield Rd., 60060-9735, pg. 1106 — IT
Rexam Medical Packaging, Inc., 1919 S. Butterfield Rd., 60060, pg. 1107 — IT

Murphysboro

Curwood, Inc., 19th & Wall Sts., 62966, pg. 210 — PB

PB - U.S. Public Companies Volume
PV - U.S. Private Companies Volume
IT - International Public & Private Companies Volume

1224

Geographic Index-U.S.

Naperville

Alliance Wall Midwest Regional Office, Ste. 258, 1 Enry Ctr., 60563, pg. 38   PV

Allied Van Lines, Inc., 215 W. Diehl Rd., 60563, pg. 901   IT

American Pharmaceutical Services, Inc., 171 W. Diehl Rd., 60563, pg. 1257   PB

Amoco Technology Company, 55 E. Shuman Blvd., 60563-8987, pg. 103   PB

Brake Parts, Inc., 1510 Frontenac, 60563, pg. 560   PB

CATHOLIC ORDER OF FORESTERS, P.O. Box 3012, 355 W. Shuman Blvd., 60566-7012, pg. 220   PB

Charter Linden Oaks Behavioral Health System, Inc., 852 West St., 60540, pg. 1035   PB

CHICAGO RIVET & MACHINE COMPANY, 901 Frontenac Rd., 60563, pg. 348   PB

De La Rue Faraday - Midwest, 2764 Goldview Rd., 60563, pg. 387   IT

Dynasonics, 522 W. 5th Ave., 60563, pg. 906   PV

EMS-Illinois, 1771 W. Diehl Rd., Ste. 120, 60563, pg. 565   PB

EBY-BROWN CO., 280 W. Shuman Blvd., Ste. 280, 60563, pg. 359   PV

General Employment Enterprises, Inc., 280 W. Shuman Blvd., Ste. 185, 60563, pg. 714   PV

HARBOUR CONTRACTORS, INC., 22 E. Chicago Ave., Ste. 200, 60540, pg. 500   PV

Harris Bank Naperville, 503 N. Washington St., 60566, pg. 154   IT

Hewlett-Packard Company, 1200 E. Diehl Rd., 60566, pg. 814   PB

Homeshield Fabricated Products, 1771 W. Diehl Rd., #200, 60566-7038, pg. 1350   PB

Interlake Material Handling Div., 1240 E. Diehl Rd., Ste. 200, 60566, pg. 893   PB

Johnson Moving & Storage, 1811 High Grove La., Unit 167, 60540, pg. 594   PV

Keystone Industries, Inc., 55 E. Shuman Blvd., Ste. 500, 60566, pg. 1711   PB

Laidlaw Transit, 1240 E. Diehl Rd., Ste. 104, 60563, pg. 259   IT

James Martin Insight, Inc., 1751 W. Diehl Rd., 60566, pg. 784   PB

Moroch Associates, Inc., General Motors Building, 387 Shuman Blvd., Ste. 380 E., 60563, pg. 762   PV

NALCO CHEMICAL COMPANY, One Nalco Ctr., 60563-1198, pg. 1150   PB

Nalco Chemical Process Chemicals Division, One Nalco Ctr., 60563, pg. 1150   PB

Nalco Chemical Water and Waste Treatment Div., One Nalco Ctr., 60563, pg. 1150   PB

Nalco Fuel Tech, 1001 Frontenac Rd., 60563-1198, pg. 1150   PB

National Education Training Group, 1751 W. Diehl Rd., 60563, pg. 784   PB

Newspaper Services of America, Inc., 1245 E. Diehl Rd., Ste. 300, 60563, pg. 909   PV

NICOR Energy Services Company, 1844 Ferry Rd., 60563-9600, pg. 1182   PB

NICOR Energy Ventures Company, 1844 Ferry Rd., 60563-9600, pg. 1182   PB

NICOR Gas Exchange Company, 1844 Ferry Rd., 60563-9600, pg. 1182   PB

NICOR Hub, Inc., 1844 Ferry Rd., 60563-9600, pg. 1182   PB

NICOR INC., 1844 Ferry Rd., 60563-9600, pg. 1182   PB

NICOR NGV Corp., 1844 Ferry Rd., 60563-9600, pg. 1183   PB

Northern Illinois Gas Company, 1844 Ferry Rd., 60563-9600, pg. 1183   PB

The Northern Trust Company, 400 E. Diehl Rd., 60563, pg. 1197   PB

Pittway Systems Technology Grp., 1771 Diehl Rd., Ste. 190, 60563, pg. 1306   PB

QUALITY CHEKD DAIRIES, INC., 1733 Park St., 60563, pg. 898   PV

Regency Savings Bank, 24 N. Washington St., 60540, pg. 406   PV

RHEA & KAISER MARKETING COMMUNICATIONS, Naperville Financial Ctr., 400 E. Diehl Rd., 60563-1342, pg. 927   PV

Solar Communications, 1500 Shore Dr., 60563, pg. 1012   PV

SOLAR COMMUNICATIONS, INC., 1120 Frontenac Rd., 60563-1799, pg. 1012   PV

Treated Water Outsourcing, c/o U.S. Filter/HPD, 55 Shuman Blvd., Ste. 900, 60563, pg. 1150   PB

VARLEN CORPORATION, P.O. Box 3089, 55 Shuman Blvd., 60566-7089, pg. 1710   PB

Vitalink Pharmacy Services, Inc., 1250 E. Diehl Rd., Ste. 208, 60563, pg. 1041   PB

Wine World Estates, Inc., 650 Diehl Rd., 60563, pg. 917   IT

Nashville

Morgantown Machine Anderson Mavor, P.O. Box 191, Mine Rd., 62263, pg. 280   IT

National Stock Yards

Swift Independent Packing Co., 62071, pg. 427   PB

Newton

United Technologies, Automotive, P.O. Box 134, Marshall Dr., 62448-0134, pg. 1691   PB

Niles

Adams Elevator Equipment Company, 6310 Howard St., 60714, pg. 1205   IT

Ashton Drake Div., 9200 N. Maryland, 60714, pg. 163   PV

Bekaert Corporation, 6600 Howard St., 60714-5670, pg. 184   IT

BRADFORD EXCHANGE LTD., 9333 N. Milwaukee Ave., 60714, pg. 163   PV

CCL Custom Manufacturing, 6100 W. Howard St., 60714, pg. 238   IT

COCA-COLA BOTTLING CO. OF CHICAGO, 7400 N. Oak Park Ave., 60714, pg. 248   PV

CUSTOM ACCESSORIES INC., 6440 W. Howard St., 60714, pg. 298   PV

DANN DEE DISPLAY FIXTURES, 7555 N. Caldwell Ave., 60714-3807, pg. 310   PV

Design/Craft Fabric Corp., 7227 N. Oak Park Ave., 60714, pg. 1357   PB

A.B. Dick Company, 5700 W. Touhy Ave., 60714-4690, pg. 791   PV

Duncan & Hill Division, 5980 W. Touhy Ave., 60714-4610, pg. 773   PB

FORT DEARBORN COMPANY, 6035 Gross Point Rd., 60714, pg. 419   PV

HA-LO INDUSTRIES, INC., 5980 Touhy Ave., 60714, pg. 773   PB

HEYMAN CORPORATION, 6045 W. Howard St., 60714, pg. 524   PV

Image By Design, 7555 N. Caldwell Ave., 60714-3807, pg. 310   PV

JARKE CORPORATION, 6333 W. Howard, 60714, pg. 583   PV

JOHNSON & QUIN, INC., 7460 N. Lehigh Ave., 60714, pg. 590   PV

MFRI INC., 7720 Lehigh Ave., 60714, pg. 1026   PB

Mid Res Service Div., 7720 Lehigh Ave., 60648, pg. 1026   PB

Midwesco Mechanical Energy, 7720 Lehigh Ave., 60714, pg. 1026   PB

NIGHTINGALE-CONANT CORP., 7300 N. Lehigh Ave., 60714, pg. 799   PV

NORTHWESTERN INDUSTRIAL PIPING, 7475 Oak Park Ave., 60714, pg. 806   PV

NUARC COMPANY, INC., 6200 W. Howard St., 60714-3404, pg. 808   PV

Oshkosh B'Gosh Hosiery Co., 6045 W. Howard St., 60714, pg. 525   PV

Perma-Pipe Div., 7720 Lehigh Ave., 60714, pg. 1026   PB

PRECISION CARBIDE TOOL COMPANY, INC., 7450 Natchez Ave., 60714, pg. 879   PV

Sate-Lite Manufacturing Company, 6220-30 Gross Point Rd., 60648, pg. 598   PV

GEORGE T. SCHMIDT, 6151 W. Howard St., 60714, pg. 970   PV

Sterling Hosiery Co., 6045 W. Howard St., 60714, pg. 525   PV

Synchro-Start Products, Inc., 6250 Howard St., 60714-3433, pg. 627   PV

Thermal-Care Div., 7720 Lehigh Ave., 60714, pg. 1026   PB

Tru-Fit Glove & Headwear Div., 6045 W. Howard St., 60714, pg. 525   PV

Vapor, 6420 W. Howard St., 60714, pg. 1761   PB

WICO, 7847 North Caldwell, 60714, pg. 1144   PV

Normal

Bloomington-Normal Seating Company, 2031 Warehouse Rd., 61761, pg. 830   IT

Bundy Corporation, Bloomington Plant, 1802 Industrial Park Rd., 61761, pg. 1340   IT

Diamond Star Motors, 100 N. Diamond Star Pkwy., 61761, pg. 875   IT

GATX Contract Carriers, Inc., 2601 D. West College, 61761, pg. 691   PB

GATX Logistics, Inc.-Illinois, 2601 W. College Ave., 61761, pg. 691   PB

North Aurora

AURORA PACKING CO., INC., 125 Grant St., 60542, pg. 99   PV

Aurora Pump, 800 Airport Rd., 60542, pg. 726   PB

ServiceMaster Manufacturing Services, 200 Alder Rd., 60542, pg. 1462   PV

North Chicago

Abbott Diagnostic Products, Abbott Park, AP-6C, 60064, pg. 13   PB

Abbott Hospital Products Division, One Abbott Park Rd., 60064, pg. 13   PB

Coleman Cable Systems, Inc., 2500 Commonwealth Ave., 60064, pg. 968   PB

FANSTEEL, INC., One Tantalum Pl., 60064, pg. 612   PB

FEDERAL CHICAGO CORPORATION, 925 Martin Luther King Dr., 60064, pg. 398   PV

KING WIRE INC., One Cable Pl., 60064, pg. 621   PV

KRONE CASTING CORP., 925 M.L. King Dr., 60064, pg. 636   PV

North Riverside

EDWARD DON & COMPANY, 2500 S. Harlem Ave., 60546, pg. 339   PV

Evans, Inc., North Riverside Shopping Ctr., F-9 North Riverside Park, 60546, pg. 596   PB

Northbrook

THE ALLSTATE CORPORATION, 2775 Sanders Rd., 60062-6127, pg. 55   PB

APOLLO COLORS INC., 3000 Dundee Rd. , Suite 415, 60062, pg. 77   PV

BTI AMERICAS, INC., 400 Skokie Blvd., 60062-2887, pg. 108   PV

BELL FLAVORS & FRAGRANCES, 500 Academy Dr., 60062, pg. 131   PV

Borden Italian Foods, 2301 Shermer Rd., 60062, pg. 158   PV

BRADLEY REAL ESTATE, INC., 40 Skokie Blvd. Ste. 600, 60062-1626, pg. 250   PB

Caremark International Inc, 2215 Sanders Rd., 60062, pg. 1082   PB

Carlisle Food Service Products Company, 2100 Sanders, Ste. 120, 60062, pg. 305   PB

Churny Company Inc., 2215 Sanders Rd., Ste. 330, 60062, pg. 1288   PB

Cracker Jack Division, 2301 Shermer Rd., 60062, pg. 157   PV

CRANE CONSTRUCTION CO., 343 Wainwright Dr., 60062, pg. 286   PV

CULLIGAN INTERNATIONAL COMPANY, One Culligan Pkwy., 60062, pg. 467   PB

DMB&B/Yellow Pages, 40 Skokie Blvd., Ste. 210, 60062, pg. 303   PV

Disease Management, 2215 Sanders Rd., 60062, pg. 1082   PB

DONLEN CORP., 2315 Sanders Rd., 60062, pg. 340   PV

ERD Environmental, Inc., 3100 Dundee Rd., 60062, pg. 546   PB

EUROMARKET DESIGNS, INC., 725 Landwehr Rd., 60062, pg. 384   PV

Finnsteel Inc., Five Revere Dr., Ste. 502, 60062, pg. 1089   IT

Fiskars Inc.-Latin America, 3100 Dundee Rd., 60062, pg. 492   IT

FLINN & DREFFEIN ENGINEERING CO., 3520 Commercial Ave., 60062, pg. 413   PV

FluoroScan Imaging Systems, Inc., 650B Anthony Trail, 60062, pg. 831   PV

STEVE FOLEY CADILLAC, 100 Skokie Blvd., 60062, pg. 416   PV

FULLERTON METALS CO., 3000 Shermer Rd., 60065-3002, pg. 431   PV

GENERAL BINDING CORPORATION, One GBC Plaza, 60062-4195, pg. 707   PB

GRUBB & ELLIS COMPANY, 2215 Sanders Rd., 4th Fl., 60062, pg. 767   PB

Grubb & Ellis Management Services, Inc., 2215 Sanders Rd., 60062, pg. 767   PB

H.K. INTERNATIONAL, INC., 3670 Commercial Ave., 60062, pg. 491   PV

HANDGARDS INC., 950 Skokie Blvd., 60062, pg. 499   PV

Heads & Threads, 2727 Shermer Rd., 60062, pg. 42   PB

IDEX CORPORATION, 630 Dundee Rd., Ste. 400, 60062, pg. 862   PB

International Services, 2215 Sanders Rd., 60062, pg. 1082   PB

JMP Newcor Holdings Inc., 3100 Dundee Rd., Ste. 704, 60062, pg. 1025   IT

JMP Newcor International Inc., 3100 Dundee Rd. Ste. 704, 60062, pg. 1025   IT

JAMES BUILDING CORPORATION, 1535 Lake Cook Rd., Ste. 302, 60062, pg. 580   PV

JUPITER INDUSTRIES, INC., 2215 Sanders Rd., 60062, pg. 602   PV

Lane Broadcasting, Inc., One Lane Ctr., 1200 Shermer Rd., 60062, pg. 650   PV

Lane Hospitality, Inc., 1200 Shermer Rd., 60062, pg. 650   PV

LANE INDUSTRIES, INC., One Lane Ctr., 1200 Shermer Rd., 60062, pg. 649   PV

Lane Security, Inc, 1200 Shermer Rd., 60062, pg. 650   PV

LaSalle Bank Northbrook, 1200 Shermer Rd., 60062, pg. 10   IT

Norman Levy Associates, Inc., 400 Skokie Blvd., Ste. 400, 60062, pg. 664   PV

M.D. Industries, Inc., P.O. Box 1355, 5 Revere Dr., 60065-4647, pg. 352   PB

MAGELLAN INTERNATIONAL TRADING, 3701 Commercial Ave., 60062, pg. 694   PV

Miura Boiler Co. Ltd., 350 Pfingsten Rd., Ste. 100, 60062, pg. 884   IT

Motorola Automotive & Industrial Electronics Group, 4000 Commercial Ave., 60062, pg. 1137   PV

Motorola Automotive Products Inc., 4000 Commercial Dr., 60062, pg. 1137   PV

NORTH SHORE MOVERS, 600 Waukegan Rd., 60062, pg. 805   PV

Old World Automotive Products, 4065 Commercial Ave., 60062, pg. 817   PB

OLD WORLD INDUSTRIES, INC., 4065 Commercial Ave., 60062, pg. 817   PV

ON-COR FROZEN FOODS INC., 627 Landwehr Rd., 60062, pg. 817   PV

Parts Company of America, 1657 Shermer Rd., 60062-5362, pg. 758   PV

Pharmaceutical Services, 2215 Sanders Rd., 60062, pg. 1082   PB

Physician Practice Management, 2215 Sanders Rd., 60062, pg. 1082   PB

Rank Video Services America Inc., 555 Huehl Rd., 60062, pg. 1087   IT

S & C Maintenance Corp., 3175 Commercial Ave., Ste. 222, 60062, pg. 1021   PV

SERFILCO, LTD., 1777 Shermer Rd., 60062-5360, pg. 985   PV

PB - *U.S. Public Companies Volume*
PV - *U.S. Private Companies Volume*
IT - *International Public & Private Companies Volume*

Geographic Index-U.S.

Spatz & Co. Development, 3175 Commercial Ave., Ste. 203, 60062, pg. 1021   PV
SPATZ CENTERS INC., 3175 Commercial Ave., Ste. 222, 60062, pg. 1021   PV
Spatz Centers, Inc., 3175 Commercial Ave., Ste. 222, 60062, pg. 1021   PV
Splitfire, Inc., 4065 Commercial Ave., 60062, pg. 814   PV
TEMKIN & TEMKIN, Bldg. 800, 450 Skokie Blvd., 60062, pg. 1074   PV
TRANS LEASING INTERNATIONAL INC., 3000 Dundee Rd., 60062, pg. 1628   PV
Universal Foot Care Products, 300 Wainwright Dr., 60062, pg. 1437   PB
Wood Terminal Company, 899 Skokie Blvd., 60062, pg. 675   PV
Daniel Woodhead Company, 3411 Woodhead Dr., 60062, pg. 1776   PB
Y.K.K. (U.S.A.) Inc., 2165 N. Shermer Rd., 60062, pg. 1515   IT

Northfield

ARTRA GROUP INCORPORATED, 500 Central Ave., 60093, pg. 136   PB
DACOR CORPORATION, 161 Northfield Rd., 60093, pg. 306   PV
Guilford Mills (Apparel, Home & Industrial Fabrics), Two Northfield Plaza, 60093, pg. 769   PB
Kraft Foods, Inc., Three Lakes Dr., 60093-2753, pg. 1287   PB
Richard Lewis Paper Corporation, P.O. Box 8559, 211 N. Waukegan Rd., 60093, pg. 467   PV
MAGNACRAFT, STRUTHERS, DUNN, INC., 211 Waukegan Rd., 60093, pg. 695   PV
McKnight Medical Communications, 2 Northfield Plaza, 60093, pg. 1600   PB
McKnight Medical Communications Company, 2 Northfield Plaza, Ste. 300, 60093, pg. 1601   PB
Miller Advertising Agency Inc.-Chicago, One Northfield Plaza, Ste. 300, 60093, pg. 746   PV
STEPAN COMPANY, 22 W. Frontage Rd., 60093, pg. 1514   PB
Tombstone Pizza Corporation, Kraft Ct., Three Lakes Dr., 60093-2753, pg. 1288   PB

Northlake

Chicago Tribune Direct, 505 Northwest Ave., 60164, pg. 1635   PB
Dominick's Finer Foods, 505 Railroad Ave., 60164, pg. 1202   PV
General Printing Ink, 135 W. Lake St., 60164, pg. 370   IT
OMNI Superstores, 505 Railroad Ave., 60164, pg. 1202   PV
SHURFINE INTERNATIONAL, INC., 2100 N. Mannheim Rd., 60164-1889, pg. 997   PV
Transilwrap Company, Inc., One West Lake St., 60164, pg. 1097   PV

O Fallon

O'Fallon Progress, 612 State St., 62269, pg. 964   PB

Oak Brook

ACE HARDWARE CORPORATION, 2200 Kensington Ct., 60521, pg. 12   PV
ADVOCATE HEALTH CARE, 2025 Windsor Dr., 60521, pg. 23   PV
AirMate, 1200 Jorie Blvd., 60521-9981, pg. 317   PV
American Drug Stores Inc., 1818 Swift Dr., 60521, pg. 93   PB
Aramark Correctional Services, 2000 Spring Ave., Ste. 300, 60523, pg. 79   PV
Bio-Energy Partners, 3003 Butterfield Rd., 60521, pg. 315   PB
BLISTEX, 1800 Swift Dr., 60523, pg. 149   PV
CLTV News, 2000 York Rd., Ste. 114, 60523, pg. 1635   PB
Cabinetry Division, 2222 Camden Ct., 60521, pg. 372   PV
Carrier Building Services, 2803 Butterfield Rd., 60521-1156, pg. 1689   PB
Cordley Temprite, 2222 Camden Ct., 60521, pg. 372   PV
EA Engineering, Science & Technology, Inc., 125 Windsor Dr., Ste. 108, 60521, pg. 541   PV
ELKAY MANUFACTURING COMPANY, 2222 Camden Ct., 60523, pg. 372   PV
ENVIRODYNE INDUSTRIES, INC., 701 Harger Rd., Ste. 190, 60523, pg. 586   PB
FEDERAL SIGNAL CORPORATION, 1415 W. 22nd St., 60523, pg. 616   PB
First of America Bank-Illinois, N.A., 1111 W. 22nd St., 60523, pg. 636   PB
GTE Airfone Incorporated, P.O. Box 9000, 2809 Butterfield Rd., 60522-9000, pg. 696   PB
General Employment Enterprises, Inc., 2803 Butterfield Rd., Ste. 260, 60523, pg. 714   PB
Gibson Electric Co., 2100 South York Rd., 60523-1916, pg. 572   PV
Golden State Foods-Oak Brook, 2211 York Rd., Ste. 208, 60521, pg. 460   PV
Graphics Management, 2122 York Rd., Ste 310, pg. 518   PV
GREAT LAKES DREDGE & DOCK CO., 2122 York Rd., 60523-1981, pg. 474   PV
Griffith Micro Science International Inc., Commerce Plaza, 2001 Spring Rd., Ste. 500, 60521, pg. 481   PV
Illinova Energy Partners, 1420 Kensington Rd., Ste. 305, 60521, pg. 870   PV
THE INLAND GROUP, INC., 2901 Butterfield Rd., 60521, pg. 564   PV

KME Kabelmetal America Inc., 1000 Jorie Blvd., Ste. 111, 60523, pg. 719   IT
Keller Graduate School of Management, One Tower Ln., 60181, pg. 504   PB
MFS Telecom Companies, One Tower Ln., Ste. 1600, 60181, pg. 1779   PB
Maggiano's Little Italy, 240 Oak Brook Ctr., 60521, pg. 661   PV
McCain Citrus Inc., 2905 Butterfield Rd., 60523-1102, pg. 850   IT
McCain Foods Inc., 2905 Butterfield Rd., 60523-1106, pg. 850   IT
McCain U.S.A. Inc., 2905 Butterfield Rd., 60523-1106, pg. 850   IT
MCDONALD'S CORPORATION, One Kroc Dr., 60523, pg. 1068   PB
McDonald's Intl., McDonald's Campus, Kroc Dr., 60521, pg. 1069   PB
McDonald's U.S.A., McDonald's Plaza, 60521, pg. 1069   PB
Natco Limited Partnership, 2122 York Road, 60523, pg. 134   IT
North American Trailing Co., 2122 York Rd., 60521, pg. 474   PV
OAG, 2000 Clearwater Dr., 60523, pg. 1097   IT
THE O'BOISE CORPORATION, 1111 W. 22nd St., Ste. 640, 60521, pg. 810   PV
Principal Health Care of Illinois, Inc., One Lincoln Ctr., Ste. 1040, 60181, pg. 885   PV
R C Freightway, 900 Jorie Blvd., pg. 518   PB
Relocation Consultants, 2210 Camden Ct., 60521, pg. 1635   PV
Rexam Release, Inc., 915 Harger Rd., Ste. 300, 60523, pg. 1107   IT
SPR, INC., 2015 Spring Rd., Ste. 750, 60521, pg. 1419   PB
SecurityLink from Ameritech, Two Mid America Plaza, Ste. 200, 60521, pg. 98   PB
Symix Systems Inc., 1515 W. 22nd St., Ste. 400, 60521, pg. 1547   PB
TBWA Chiat/Day Chicago, AT&T Plaza, 1111 W. 22nd St., 60521, pg. 1062   PV
TCF Bank Illinois, 1420 Kensington Rd., Ste. 320, 60521, pg. 1554   PB
Trase-Miller, 2625 Butterfield Rd., Ste. 217 N, 60521, pg. 688   PV
Tribune Regional Programming Inc., 2000 York Rd., Ste. 114, 60521, pg. 1636   PV
U.S. CAN COMPANY, 900 Commerce Dr., Ste. 302, 60523, pg. 1681   PB
Utell International-Oak Brook, 2000 Clearwater Dr., 60521, pg. 1098   IT
WASTE MANAGEMENT, INC., 3003 Butterfield Rd., 60523-1100, pg. 1744   PB

Oak Brook Terrace

Amoco Pipeline Co., One Mid-America Plz., Ste. 300, 60181-4450, pg. 102   PB
Cara Corporation, 1900 Spring Rd., Ste. 450, 60521, pg. 148   PV
Cova Financial Services Life Insurance Co., One Tower Ln., Ste 3000, 60181-4644, pg. 443   PV
DEVRY INSTITUTES, One Tower Ln., Ste. 1000, 60181, pg. 503   PV
First Penn-Pacific Life Insurance Co., 1801 S. Meyers Rd., 60181, pg. 998   PB
GENERAL EMPLOYMENT ENTERPRISES, INC., Oakbrook Terrace Tower, One Tower Ln., Ste. 2100, 60181, pg. 714   PV
Harris Bank Oakbrook Terrace, 17 W. 695 Roosevelt Rd., 60181, pg. 154   IT
Keller Graduate School of Management, One Tower Ln., Ste. 1000, 60181, pg. 504   PV
NATIONAL TRUCK LEASING SYSTEM, One S. 450 Summit Ave., Ste. 300, 60181, pg. 787   PV
The Northern Trust Company, One Oakbrook Ter., 60181, pg. 1197   PB
PLATINUM TECHNOLOGY, INC., 1815 S. Meyers Rd., 60181, pg. 1309   PB
Simon Marketing, Inc., One Trans Am Plaza Dr., Ste. 120, 60181, pg. 1001   PV
Van Kampen/American Capital Inc., One Parkview Plaza, 60181, pg. 1132   PV
WOZNIAK INDUSTRIES, INC., Two Mid America Plaza, Ste. 706, 60181, pg. 1192   PV
Xerox Financial Services Life Insurance Co., One Tower Ln., Ste. 300, 60181-4644, pg. 1785   PB

Oak Forest

Rhone-Poulenc Rorer, 4325 Frontage Rd., 60452, pg. 1111   IT

Oak Lawn

Beverly Trust Company, 10312 S. Cicero, 60453, pg. 227   PB
Oak Lawn Imaging Center, 4700 W. 95 St., 60453, pg. 1080   PB

Oak Park

THE FIRST BANK OF OAK PARK, 11 W. Madison, 60302, pg. 406   PV
SHAKER ADVERTISING AGENCY, The Shaker Bldg., 1100 Lake St., 60301, pg. 988   PV
Vegetarian Times, P.O. Box 570, 60303, pg. 281   PV

Odell

Odell State Bank, 200 S. Waupansie St., 60460, pg. 1316   PB

Olney

Roadmaster/Brunswick, 4730 E. Radion Tower Rd., 62450, pg. 265   PB

Olympia Fields

DEDERT CORPORATION, 20000 Governors Dr., 60461, pg. 320   PV
Personal Finance Co., 3612 W. Lincoln Hwy., Ste. 23, 60461, pg. 750   PV

Oregon

Dayton Superior Corp., First & Adams, 61061, pg. 932   PV
WOOD EQUIPMENT COMPANY, P.O. Box 1000, 2606 Illinois Ave. Rt. 2 S., 61061-1000, pg. 1186   PV
Woods Equipment Company, 2606 IL Rte. 2 South, 61061, pg. 249   PV

Orion

Frontier Communications of Orion, Inc., P.O. Box 85, 1020 Fourth St., 61273, pg. 684   PB

Orland Park

ANDREW CORPORATION, 10500 W. 153rd St., 60462, pg. 112   PB
Andrew International Corp., 10500 W. 153rd St., 60462, pg. 112   PB
Circle Service Co., 10500 W. 153rd. St., 60462, pg. 112   PB
J.M. PROCESS SYSTEMS INC., 15507 S. 70th Ct., 60462, pg. 577   PV

Oswego

Georg Fischer Disa Inc., 80 Kendall Point Dr., 60543, pg. 488   IT
Junker Inc., 2015B Rte. 34, 60543, pg. 1014   IT

Ottawa

BWD Automotive Corp., 1111 McKinley Rd., 61350, pg. 560   PV
LA SALLE COUNTY FARM SUPPLY, 3107 N. Rte. 23, 61350, pg. 640   PB

Palatine

Chemdal Corporation, 1530 E. Dundee Rd., Ste. 350, 60067, pg. 64   PB
DIETZGEN CORPORATION, 1218 W. N.W. Hwy., 60067, pg. 332   PV
EXAR Corp.-Northcentral, 800 E. Northwest Hwy., 60067, pg. 598   PB
Harris Bank Palatine, N.A., 50 N. Brockway, 60067, pg. 154   IT
Milgray/Chicago, Inc., Kennedy Corporate Ctr. I, 1530 E. Dundee Rd., 60067-8319, pg. 206   PB
SELLSTROM MANUFACTURING CO., One Sellstrom Dr., 60067, pg. 983   PV
Shorewood Packaging Company of Illinois, Inc., Countryside Executive Ctr., 1250 W. Northwest Hwy., Ste. 502, 60067, pg. 1468   PB
Square D Company, 1415 S. Roselle Rd., 60067, pg. 1208   IT
Successories, 750 W. Euclid, 60067, pg. 1049   PV
TEC Incorporated, 315 S. Hicks Rd., 60067, pg. 687   PB
WEBER-STEPHEN PRODUCTS CO., 200 E. Daniels Rd., 60067, pg. 1157   PV
WILTON CORPORATION, 300 S. Hicks, 60067, pg. 1181   PV
Wilton Machinery Div., 300 S. Hicks Rd., 60067, pg. 1181   PV
Wilton Tool Div., 300 S. Hicks Rd., 60067, pg. 1181   PV

Palos Heights

Rust Remedial, 7250 West College Dr., 60463, pg. 1366   PB

Paris

A.C. Humko, 1800 S. Main, 61944, pg. 92   IT
Morgan Food Specialty Inc., 1800 S. Main, 61944, pg. 92   IT

Park Forest

CONTINENTAL/MIDLAND, INC., 24000 S. Western Ave., 60466, pg. 268   PV
International Pin, 24000 S. Western Ave., 60466, pg. 269   PV
PATCO L.P., 24000 S. Western Ave., 60466, pg. 269   PV

Park Ridge

Illinois Banc One Mortgage Corporation, 1440 Renaissance, 60068, pg. 174   PB

Geographic Index-U.S.

Locksmith Publishing Corp., 850 Busse Hwy., 60068, pg. 1432 **IT**
GEORGE S. MAY INTERNATIONAL COMPANY, 303 S. Northwest Hwy., 60068-4255, pg. 717 **PV**
PROTECTION MUTUAL INSURANCE CO., 300 S. Northwest Hwy., 60068, pg. 891 **PV**
Ragnar Benson, Inc., 250 S. N.W. Highway, 60068, pg. 99 **PV**
RITTENHOUSE INC., 250 S. Northwest Hwy., 60068, pg. 933 **PV**
Rittenhouse Paper Co., 250 S. Northwest Hwy., 60068, pg. 933 **PV**

Pecatonia

Dean Foods Co., 215 W. Third St., 61063, pg. 491 **PB**

Pecatonica

Ipsen Ceramics, 325 John St., 61063, pg. 1149 **IT**

Peoria

Advanced Technology Services Inc., 8201 N. University, 61615, pg. 315 **PB**
Agronaut Great Central Insurance Co., P.O. Box 807, 3625 N. Sheridan Rd., 61652-0807, pg. 129 **PB**
Biotechnica International, 40001 War Memorial Dr., 61614, pg. 566 **IT**
Brecks, 6523 N. Galena Rd., 61632, pg. 420 **PV**
Caterpillar Americas Co., 100 N.E. Adams St., 61629, pg. 315 **PB**
Caterpillar Asia Pacific Holding Inc., 100 N.E. Adams St., 61629, pg. 315 **PB**
CATERPILLAR INC., 100 N.E. Adams St., 61629, pg. 315 **PB**
Caterpillar Industrial Products, Inc., 100 N.E. Adams St., 61629, pg. 316 **PB**
Caterpillar Investment Management Ltd., 100 N.E. Adams St., 61629, pg. 316 **PB**
Caterpillar Logistics Services, Inc., 100 N.E. Adams St., 61629-9610, pg. 316 **PB**
Caterpillar of Delaware, Inc., 100 N.E. Adams St., 61629, pg. 316 **PB**
Caterpillar Risk Management Services Ltd., 100 N.E. Adams, 61629-5320, pg. 316 **PB**
Caterpillar Securities Inc., 100 N.E. Adams, 61629-5330, pg. 316 **PB**
Caterpillar Services Limited, 100 N.E. Adams St., 61629, pg. 316 **PB**
Caterpillar World Trading Corporation, 100 N.E. Adams St., 61629, pg. 316 **PB**
Central Illinois Light Company, 300 Liberty St., 61602-1238, pg. 367 **PB**
CILCO Energy Corp., 300 Liberty St., 61602, pg. 367 **PB**
CILCO Exploration & Development Co., 300 Liberty St., 61602, pg. 367 **PB**
CILCORP INC., 300 Hamilton Blvd., Ste. 300, 61602, pg. 367 **PB**
CILCORP Investment Management Inc., 300 Hamilton Blvd., Ste. 300, 61602, pg. 367 **PB**
CILCORP Ventures Inc., 300 Hamilton Blvd., Ste. 300, 61602, pg. 367 **PB**
CUSTOMER DEVELOPMENT CORPORATION, 8600 N. Industrial Rd., 61615, pg. 298 **PV**
ELECSYS INC., 8800 Allen Rd., 61615-1584, pg. 367 **PV**
FLEMING PACKAGING CORP., 1028 S.W. Adams St., 61602, pg. 411 **PV**
Fleming-Potter Co., 1028 S.W. Adams St., 61602, pg. 411 **PV**
Fleming-Potter Fast Printing, 1114 S.W. Jefferson St., 61602, pg. 411 **PV**
Fleming-Potter Webkote, 1016 S.W. Adams, 61602, pg. 411 **PV**
FOSTER & GALLAGHER, INC., 6523 N. Galena Rd., 61632, pg. 420 **PV**
Glencoe/McGraw Hill, 809 W. Detweiller Dr., 61615, pg. 1070 **PV**
International Paper Label Div., 8401 N. University St., 61615-1627, pg. 903 **PB**
INTERSTATE PRODUCERS LIVESTOCK ASSOCIATION, 1705 W. Luthy, 61615, pg. 573 **PV**
Ivex Packaging Corporation-Peoria, P.O. Box 1820, Foot of Sloan St., 61656, pg. 915 **PB**
Keystone Steel & Wire Co., 7000 S.W. Adams St., 61641, pg. 955 **PB**
KLAUS RADIO INC., 8400 N. Allen Rd., 61615, pg. 625 **PV**
Kwikee Illustration Systems, 1720 W. Detweiller Dr., 61615, pg. 766 **PV**
LG Seeds Inc., 4001 N. War Memorial Dr., Ste. 200, 61614, pg. 566 **IT**
Magna Bank, Peoria Region, 107 S.W. Jefferson, 61602, pg. 1037 **PB**
Mt. Hawley Insurance Company, 9025 N. Lindbergh Dr., 61615, pg. 1356 **PB**
MULTI-AD SERVICES, INCORPORATED, 1720 W. Detweiller Dr., 61615, pg. 766 **PV**
L.R. NELSON CORPORATION, One Sprinkler Ln., 61615, pg. 790 **PV**
Nexus International Inc., 100 N.E. Adams St., 61629, pg. 316 **PB**
Peoria Journal Star, Inc., One News Plaza, 61643, pg. 275 **PV**
Peoria Medical Research Corporation, 300 Liberty St., 61602, pg. 316 **PB**
Primedia Inc., #2 News Plaza, 61614, pg. 1328 **PB**
QST Communications, Inc., 300 Hamilton Blvd., Ste. 330, 61602, pg. 367 **PB**

QST Energy, Inc., 300 Hamilton Blvd., Ste. 330, 61602, pg. 367 **PB**
QST Enterprises Inc., 300 Hamilton Blvd., Ste. 330, 61602, pg. 367 **PB**
QST Environmental Inc., 8900 N. Industrial Rd., 61615, pg. 367 **PB**
RLI CORP., 9025 N. Lindbergh Dr., 61615, pg. 1356 **PB**
RR-1 Limited Partnership, Fulton Plaza, 331 Fulton St., Ste. 1133, 61601, pg. 316 **PB**
Re Cas, 1720 W. Detweiller Dr., 61615, pg. 766 **PV**
Redco, Inc., 1619 Luthy Dr., 61615, pg. 926 **PV**
ROHN INDUSTRIES, INC., 6718 W. Plank Rd., 61604, pg. 1404 **PB**
RUPPMAN MARKETING TECHNOLOGIES, INC., 2001 Ruppman Plaza, 61614, pg. 951 **PV**
Ruppman National Yellow Pages Service Inc., 222 N.E. Monroe St., 8th Fl., 61602, pg. 952 **PV**
BEN SCHWARTZ MARKET, INC., 209 W. McClure, 61604, pg. 974 **PV**
Small, Parker & Blossom, 456 Fulton, Ste. 345, 61602, pg. 280 **PV**
Spring Hill Nurseries Co., Reservation Center, 6523 North Galena Road, 61656, pg. 420 **PV**
Stanfast, Inc., 8206 N. University St., 61615, pg. 1505 **PB**
UNR-Rohn Div., P.O. Box 2000, 61656, pg. 1404 **PB**

Peoria Heights

Air Vent Inc., 4801 N. Prospect Rd., 61614, pg. 1170 **IT**
COHEN FURNITURE COMPANY, 1203 E. Marietta, 61614, pg. 250 **PV**

Peotone

Southcorp Packaging USA, Inc., 515 First St., 60468, pg. 1287 **IT**

Peru

Carus Chemical Company, Chemical Div., 315 Fifth St., 61354, pg. 217 **PV**
CARUS CORPORATION, 315 Fifth St., 61354, pg. 217 **PV**
MAZE NAILS, 100 S. Church St., 61354, pg. 718 **PV**

Petersburg

MENARD ELECTRIC COOPERATIVE, 122 S. Sixth St., 62675, pg. 731 **PV**

Philo

Grand Prairie Co-op, Inc., N. Harrison St., 61864, pg. 469 **PV**

Pinckneyville

Universal Studios Mfg., Highway 154, 62274, pg. 1216 **IT**

Plainfield

Coil Plus-Illinois Inc., 2001 Coil Plus Drive, 60544, pg. 872 **IT**
SPRING-GREEN LAWN CARE CORPORATION, 11927 Spaulding School Dr., 60544, pg. 1027 **PV**

Plano

PLANO MOLDING CO., 431 E. South St., 60545, pg. 869 **PV**

Pontiac

Bank of Pontiac, 300 W. Washington St., 61764, pg. 1316 **PB**
Bank of Pontiac-West, 1703 W. Reynolds, 6164, pg. 1316 **PB**
PONTIAC BANCORP, INC., P.O. Box 710, 61764, pg. 1316 **PB**
Pontiac Division, 1600 N. Main St., 61764, pg. 518 **PB**
Ringier America, Pontiac Division, 1600 N. Main St., 61764, pg. 1778 **PB**

Poplar Grove

Candlewick Division, 2021 Candlewick Dr. S.E., 61065, pg. 438 **PB**

Posen

R.J. CORR NATURALS, INC., 14828 McKinley Ave., 60469, pg. 276 **PV**
Down River Forest Products, Inc., P.O. Box 341, 60469, pg. 763 **PB**

Prairie View

Edax International, Inc., 60069, pg. 1053 **IT**

Princeton

CHAMPION PNEUMATIC MACHINERY CO., INC., 1301 N. Euclid Ave., 61356, pg. 228 **PV**

Princeville

H C Products Co., 917 No. Santa Fe Ave., 61559, pg. 61 **PB**
Princeville Canning Co., 61559, pg. 349 **PB**

Prospect Heights

Household Finance Corporation, 2700 Sanders Rd., 60070, pg. 842 **PB**
HOUSEHOLD INTERNATIONAL, INC., 2700 Sanders Rd., 60070, pg. 842 **PB**
Household Retail Services, Inc., 2700 Sanders Rd., 60070, pg. 842 **PB**

Quincy

Broadcast Electronics, Inc., 4100 N. 24th St., 62301, pg. 531 **PV**
Browning-Ferris Industries of Quincy, Illinois, Inc., 2821 Wismann Ln., 62301, pg. 264 **PB**
Corrugated Products Division, 2925 Wisman Ln., 62305-3682, pg. 763 **PB**
GARDNER DENVER MACHINERY INC., 1800 Gardner Expwy., 62301-4024, pg. 703 **PB**
Glenayre Electronics, Inc., One Quintron Way, 62301, pg. 747 **PB**
J.M. Huber, Calcium Carbonate Division, 3150 Gardner Expwy., 62301, pg. 545 **PV**
THE KNAPHEIDE MFG. CO., 18-48 Westphale Strasse, 62301, pg. 626 **PV**
MOORMAN'S INC., 1000 N. 30th St., 62301, pg. 760 **PV**
NationsBank of Quincy, Sixth and Hampshire, 62301, pg. 1164 **PB**
Penn-Daniels, Inc., 505 N. 24th St., 62301, pg. 1467 **PB**
Quincy Compressor Division Coltec Industries, 3501 Wismann Lane, 62301, pg. 402 **PB**
Quincy Design & Manufacturing, 3400 Wisman Ln., 62301, pg. 176 **PV**
TITAN INTERNATIONAL, INC., 2701 Spruce St., 62301, pg. 1618 **PB**
Titan Wheel Corporatio Of Illinois, 2701 Spruce St., 62301, pg. 1618 **PB**

Raleigh

Centrifugal Services, 5595 Highway, 34 N., 62977, pg. 370 **PV**

Rantoul

Caradco, P.O. Box 920, 61866, pg. 61 **PB**
Rantoul Products Textron Inc., 300 Shellhouse Dr., 61866, pg. 1589 **PB**

Richmond

JOHN STERLING CORPORATION, 11600 Sterling Pkwy., 60071, pg. 1041 **PV**
Watlow Gordon, 5710 Kenosha St., 60071, pg. 1153 **PV**

Ridge Farm

First Ridge Farm State Bank, P.O. Box 530, 61870, pg. 634 **PB**

Ringwood

Morton Chemical Div., 5005 Barnard Mill Rd., P.O. Box 238, 60072, pg. 1135 **PB**

River Grove

Follett Campus Resources, 2233 West St., 60171, pg. 417 **PV**
Follett Collegiate Graphics, 2233 West St., 60171, pg. 417 **PV**
FOLLETT CORPORATION, 2233 West St., 60171, pg. 416 **PV**
FORT LOCK CORPORATION, 3000 N. River Rd., 60171, pg. 919 **PV**
Richardson Electronics Security Systems Division, 3030 N. River Rd., 60171, pg. 1388 **PV**

Riverdale

ACME METALS INCORPORATED, 13500 S. Perry Ave., 60827-1182, pg. 16 **PB**
Acme Packaging Corporation, 13500 S. Perry Ave., 60627-1182, pg. 16 **PB**
Acme Steel Co., 13500 S. Perry Ave., 60627-1182, pg. 16 **PB**

Riverwoods

CCH Incorporated, 2700 Lake Cook Rd., 60015-3888, pg. 1513 **IT**
NOVUS Financial Corporation, 2500 Lake Cook Rd., 60015, pg. 1132 **PB**
NOVUS Services, Inc., 2500 Lake Cook Rd., 60015, pg. 1132 **PB**
Riverwoods, 2700 Lake Cook Rd., 60015, pg. 1513 **IT**
SPS Payment Systems, Inc., 2500 Lake Cook Rd., 60015, pg. 1132 **PB**
Wolters Kluwer U.S., 2700 Lake Cook Rd., 60015, pg. 1513 **IT**

PB - *U.S. Public Companies Volume*
PV - *U.S. Private Companies Volume*
IT - *International Public & Private Companies Volume*

Roberts

HICKS OIL-HICKS GAS, INC., U.S. 54 & 115, 60962, pg. 526 PV
Rocket Supply Corp., U.S. 54 & 115, 60962, pg. 527 PV

Robinson

First Crawford State Bank, 108 W. Main St., 62454, pg. 634 PB

Rochelle

Aigner Products Division, One Aigner Pkwy., P.O. Box 376, 60168, pg. 152 PB

Rock Falls

Antec Manufacturing, Route 30 W., 61071, pg. 116 PB

Rock Island

Bituminous Casualty Corp., 320-18th St., 61201, pg. 1218 PB
Bituminous Fire and Marine Insurance Co., 320 18th St., 61201, pg. 1218 PB
JAYDON INCORPORATED, 7800 14th St. West, 61201, pg. 584 PV
MODERN WOODMEN OF AMERICA, 1701 First Ave., 61201, pg. 755 PV
WHBF, Telco Bldg., 231 18th St., 61201, pg. 1021 PB
DON E. WILLIAMS CO., 7920 14th St. W., 61201, pg. 1177 PV

Rockford

A-1 WireTech, Inc., 840 39th Ave., 61109, pg. 672 IT
AMCORE Bank N.A., Rockford, P.O. Box 1537, 501 Seventh St., 61110-0037, pg. 64 PB
AMCORE Capital Management, Inc., P.O. Box 1537, 501 Seventh St., 61110-0037, pg. 64 PB
AMCORE Consumer Finance Company, Inc., 262 N. Phelps Ave., 61108, pg. 64 PB
AMCORE FINANCIAL, INC., 501 Seventh St., 61104, pg. 64 PB
AMCORE Financial Life Insurance Company, P.O. Box 1537, 501 Seventh St., 61104, pg. 64 PB
AMCORE Investment Group, N.A., AMCORE Financial Plaza, 501 Seventh St., 61110-0037, pg. 64 PB
AMCORE Investment Services, Inc., P.O. Box 1537, 501 Seventh St., 61110-0037, pg. 64 PB
AMCORE Mortgage, Inc., P.O. Box 1687, 1021 N. Mulford Rd., 61110-0187, pg. 64 PB
AMCORE Trust Company, P.O. Box 1537, 501 Seventh St., 61110-0037, pg. 65 PB
Amerock Corporation, 4000 Auburn St., 61101, pg. 1177 PB
AQUA-AEROBIC SYSTEMS INC., 6306 Alpine Rd., 61111, pg. 78 PV
AquaMatic, 2412 Grant Ave., 61103-3991, pg. 1234 PV
Association Management Corp., 303 N. Main St., 61101, pg. 433 PB
Atwood Mobile Products, 4750 Hiawatha Dr., 61103-1298, pg. 598 PB
Bank One, Rockford, NA, 6000 E. State St., 61110, pg. 173 PB
Barber-Colman Company, 555 Colman Center Dr., 61108, pg. 1242 IT
JOSEPH BEHR & SONS INC., 1100 Seminary St., 61104, pg. 130 PV
BOURTON GROUP, 5100 E. State St., Ste. 4, 61108, pg. 162 PV
Bowman Distribution, 5052 28th Ave., 61109, pg. 190 PB
Business Information Group, 304 N. Main, 61101, pg. 433 PB
Camcar Textron, 600-18th Ave., 61104-5181, pg. 1589 PB
CLARCOR, INC., 2323 Sixth St., 61104, pg. 381 PB
Color Corp. of America, 200 Sayre, 61101, pg. 1707 PB
Danfoss Electronic Drives, 2995 Eastrock Dr., 61109, pg. 377 IT
Dean Foods Co., 1126 Kilburn Ave., 61101, pg. 491 PB
DELTA POWER CO., 4484 Boeing Dr., 61109, pg. 322 PV
DeVlieg-Bullard Services Group, 10100 Forest Hills Rd., 61111, pg. 502 PB
Eclipse Combustion, Inc., 1665 Elmwood Rd, 61103, pg. 360 PV
ECLIPSE INC., 1665 Elmwood Rd., 61103, pg. 360 PV
Elco Construction Products Division, 111 Samuelson Rd., P.O. Box 7009, 61125, pg. 1590 PB
Elco Consumer Products Corp., 1111 Samuelson Rd., 61125, pg. 1590 PB
Elco International/Synergy Division, 111 Samuelson Rd., P.O. Box 7009, 61125, pg. 1590 PB
Elco Precision Forming Div., 1111 Samuelson Rd., P.O. Box 7009, 61125, pg. 1590 PB
Elco SDD, P.O. Box 5346, 6483 Falcon Rd., 61125, pg. 1590 PB
Elco Textron, 1111 Samuelson Rd., 61125, pg. 1590 PB
Enkel Corporation, 8155 Burden Rd., 61132-2902, pg. 170 PB
Envirovac, Inc., 1260 Turret Dr., 61115, pg. 439 IT
Freeway Rockford, 4701 Boeing Dr., 61109, pg. 426 PV
Greenlee Textron, 4455 Boeing Dr., 61109-2988, pg. 1589 PB
Gunite Corporation, 302 Peoples, 61104-7092, pg. 933 PB
Health & Life Insurance Co. of America, Admin. Office, 304 N. Main St., 61101, pg. 434 PB

Ingersoll Cutting Tool Co., 505 Fulton Ave., 61103, pg. 562 PV
Ingersoll GmbH Inc., 1303 Eddy Ave., 61103, pg. 562 PV
INGERSOLL INTERNATIONAL INC., 707 Fulton Ave., 61103, pg. 562 PV
The Ingersoll Milling Machine Co., 707 Fulton Ave., 61103, pg. 562 PV
Landstar Inway, Inc., P.O. Box 7013, 2330 23rd Ave., 61125-7013, pg. 978 IT
MATTISON TECHNOLOGIES, INC., 545 Blackhawk Park Ave., 61104, pg. 714 PV
Mid-States Forging Die & Tool Co., 2844 E. Rock Dr., 61109, pg. 754 PV
National Group Life Insurance Company, Admin. Office, 304 N. Main St., 61101, pg. 433 PB
Network Air Medical Systems, Inc., 303 N. Main St., 31101, pg. 433 PB
North Safety Products, Health Care Division, 1515 Elmwood Rd., 61103, pg. 1037 IT
Pernovo, Perstorp New Business Development Inc., P.O. Box 117, 3747 N. Meridian Rd., 61105, pg. 1037 IT
Perstorp Inc., 3747 N. Meridian Rd., 61105, pg. 1039 IT
Pierce Chemical Company, P.O. Box 117, 3747 N. Meridian Rd., 61105, pg. 1037 IT
Pioneer Direct Corporation, 303 N. Main St., 61101, pg. 433 PB
Pioneer Life Insurance Co. of Illinois, 304 N. Main St., 61105-0120, pg. 434 PB
PRECISION PRODUCTS CORPORATION, 4205 Galleria Dr., 61111, pg. 879 PV
ROCKFORD ACROMATIC PRODUCT CO., 1500 11th Ave., 61104, pg. 938 PV
Rockford International Group, 612 Harrison Avenue, 61104, pg. 938 PV
Rockford Mercantile Agency, P.O. Box 4629, 2502 S. Alpine Rd., 61108, pg. 65 PB
Rockford Newspapers, Inc., 99 E. State St., 61104, pg. 701 PB
ROCKFORD PRODUCTS CORP., 707 Harrison Ave., 61104-7197, pg. 938 PV
Rocknel Fastener, Inc., 5309 11th St., 61125-7009, pg. 1590 PB
Rodenstock Precision Optics, Inc., 4845 Colt Rd., 61109, pg. 1007 IT
H.A. Schlatter, Inc., 4640 Colt Rd., 61109, pg. 1206 IT
Slick Aircraft Products, 530 Blackhawk Park Ave., 61104, pg. 1120 PV
Sundstrand Aerospace Electronics, P.O. Box 7002, 4450 Kishwaukee St., 61125, pg. 1533 PB
Sundstrand Aerospace Group Operation, P.O. Box 7002, 4747 Harrison Ave., 61125-7002, pg. 1533 PB
Sundstrand Aviation Mechanical, 4747 Harrison Ave., P.O. Box 7002, 61125, pg. 1533 PB
SUNDSTRAND CORPORATION, 4949 Harrison Ave., 61125-7003, pg. 1533 PB
Sundstrand Electric Power Systems, 4747 Harrison Ave., P.O. Box 7002, 61125, pg. 1533 PB
Sundstrand Service Corp., 4747 Harrison Ave., P.O. Box 7002, 61125-7002, pg. 1534 PB
SUNTEC INDUSTRIES INC., 2210 Harrison Ave., 61125, pg. 1054 PV
The Testor Corporation, 620 Buckbee St., 61104, pg. 1358 PV
Textron Logistics Company, 5910 Falcon Rd., 61125-7033, pg. 1590 PB
Truck Components Inc., 302 Peoples Ave., 61104, pg. 933 PB
Union Benefit Life Insurance Co., Admin. Office, 304 N. Main St., 61101, pg. 434 PB
U.S. Filter/Arrowhead Inc., 4669 Sheppard Trail, 61103, pg. 1682 PB
Waldrich Coburg Ingersoll GmbH Inc., 1302 Eddy Ave., 61103, pg. 562 PV
Waldrich Siegen Ingersoll GmbH Inc., 1303 Eddy Ave., 61103, pg. 562 PV
W.A. Whitney Co., 650 Race St., 61101, pg. 594 PV
WOODWARD GOVERNOR COMPANY, 5001 N. Second St., 61125-7001, pg. 1776 PV

Rockton

Beloit Corporation-Blackhawk Plant, 1165 Prarie Hill Rd., 61072, pg. 789 PB
Taylor Company, 750 N. Blackhawk Blvd., 61072, pg. 1496 PB

Rolling Meadows

Ace Fastener, 1100 Hicks Rd., 60008, pg. 845 PV
American Tire & Service Company, 2550 W. Golf Rd., 60008, pg. 213 IT
Ameritech Capital Services, 2550 W. Golf Rd., 60008, pg. 98 IT
Ameritech Credit Corporation, 2550 W. Golf Rd., 60008, pg. 98 PB
Anixter Cable TV, 2850 Golf Rd., 60008, pg. 115 PB
THE ANTEC CORPORATION, 2850 W. Golf Rd., 60008, pg. 116 PB
Aromat North Central Sales Office, 1701 Golf Rd., Ste. 900, 60008, pg. 848 IT
Bohler-Uddeholm Corp., 4902 Tollview Dr., 60008, pg. 1471 IT
Bridgestone/Firestone Inc. Retail Operations, 2550 W. Golf Rd., Ste. 400, 60008, pg. 213 PV
CHR Division, 3660 Edison Place, 60008, pg. 689 PB
CM PARTNERS, INC., 5550 Meadowbrook Dr., 60008, pg. 195 PV
Dewco Chicago, 1861 Hicks Rd., Ste. A, 60006, pg. 1178 PV
Electrodynamics, Inc., 1200 Hicks Rd., 60008, pg. 308 PB

First Source Financial, Inc, 2850 W. Golf Rd., 5th Fl., 60008, pg. 842 PB
Gino's East/Rolling Meadows, Paddock Shopping Center, 1321 W. Golf Rd., 60008, pg. 661 PV
Granplex, Inc., Three Continental Towers, 1701 Golf Rd., Ste. 801, 60008, pg. 927 IT
Great Northern Mortgage Company, 2850 W. Golf Rd., Ste. 403, 60008, pg. 141 PB
Harris Bank Arlington-Meadows, 3250 Kirchoff Rd., 60008, pg. 154 IT
Hewlett-Packard Company, 5201 Tollview Dr., 60008, pg. 814 PB
HOSTMARK MANAGEMENT GROUP, 1600 Golf Rd., Ste. 800, 60008, pg. 541 PV
Interconnect Products Division, 1700 Hicks Rd., 60008, pg. 1101 PB
Just Data, 2850 W. Golf Rd., 60008, pg. 115 PB
KELSO-BURNETT COMPANY, 5200 Newport Dr., 60008, pg. 613 PV
Kelso-Burnett Rolling Meadows Branch, 5200 Newport Dr., 60008, pg. 613 PV
Komori America Corporation, 5520 Meadowbrook Indus. Ct., 60008, pg. 745 IT
MMC Electronics America Inc., 4080 Winnetka Ave., 60008, pg. 875 IT
MYR GROUP INC., 1701 W. Golf Rd., Tower 3, Ste. 1012, 60008, pg. 1029 PB
THE MIDDLEBY CORPORATION, 2850 W. Golf Rd., Ste. 405, 60008, pg. 1109 PB
Milage Plus, Inc., 1600 Golf Rd., Ste. 520, 60008, pg. 1653 PV
MOLON MOTOR & COIL CORP., 3737 Industrial Ave., 60008, pg. 756 PV
Monitor Liability Managers, Inc., 2850 Golf Rd., Ste. 800, 60008, pg. 215 PB
Motorola Pan American Wireless Infrastructure Division, One Continental Tower, 1701 Golf Rd., 60008, pg. 1137 PB
NORDX/CDT, 3701 Algonquin Rd., Ste. 260, 60008, pg. 287 PB
Navistar Financial Corporation, 2850 W. Golf Rd., 60008, pg. 1167 PB
Network Buss Division, 4001 Industrial Ave., 60008, pg. 1101 PB
PEACE INDUSTRIES INC., 1100 Hicks Rd., 60008, pg. 845 PV
Pepsi-Cola General Bottlers, Inc., III Crossroads of Commerce, 3501 Algonquin Rd., 60008, pg. 1277 PB
Rock Falls Technology, 2850 W. Golf Rd., 60008, pg. 115 PB
SMS-Chicago, 1600 Golf Rd., 60008, pg. 1463 PB
Spotnails, 1100 Hicks Rd., 60008, pg. 845 PV
Taylor Hobson Pneumo, 2100 Golf Rd., Ste. 350, 60008-4231, pg. 1087 IT
Wellman Engineering Resins, 1807 Hicks Ave., Ste. D, 60008, pg. 1752 PB
WHITMAN CORPORATION, 3501 Algonquin Rd., 60008, pg. 1766 PB

Romeoville

FLEETWOOD SYSTEMS, INC., 1305 Lakeview Dr., 60446, pg. 410 PV
Sharp Electronics Corporation Midwest Regional Office, 1300 Naperville Dr., 60441, pg. 1229 IT

Roscoe

Mastergear Division, 11447 Second St., 61073, pg. 1370 PB

Roselle

Case International, P.O. Box 40, 60172, pg. 1579 PB
Exhibitgroup/Giltspur, 200 N. Gary Ave., 60172, pg. 1718 PB
Fyrnetics, Inc., 1055 Stevenson Ct. Ste. 102W, 60172, pg. 1499 IT
Globe Fasteners Group, 1000 Stevenson Court, Suite 106, 60172, pg. 694 IT
ROMAN, INC., 555 Lawrence Ave., 60172, pg. 942 PV

Rosemont

APV Crepaco, Inc., 9525 W. Bryn Mawr Ave., 60018, pg. 1240 IT
Advance Transformer Co., O'Hare International Ctr., 10275 W. Higgins Rd., 60018, pg. 1054 IT
Algoma Central Railway Inc., P.O. Box 5062, 60017-5062, pg. 1772 PB
Ameritech Communications, Inc., 9525 W. Bryn Mawr, 60018, pg. 98 IT
ANICOM, INC., 6133 N. River Rd., Ste. 1000, 60018, pg. 115 PB
Aramark Services, Rosemont Horizon, 6920 Mannheim Rd., 60018, pg. 79 PV
Theodore Barry & Associates, 10275 W. Higgins Rd, Suite 480, 60018, pg. 118 PV
Brierley & Partners, 6250 River Rd., Ste. 8030, 60018, pg. 168 PV
CCL Custom Manufacturing, 6133 N. River Rd., Ste. 800, 60018, pg. 238 PB
Cigna Dental Care of Illinois, Inc., 10400 W. Higgins Rd., Ste. 700, 60018, pg. 358 PB
Comdisco Continuity Services, 6111 North River Rd., 60018, pg. 408 PB
COMDISCO, INC., 6111 N. River Rd., 60018, pg. 407 PB
Dean Food Products Division, 10255 W. Higgins Rd., 60018, pg. 490 PB

PB - *U.S. Public Companies Volume*
PV - *U.S. Private Companies Volume*
IT - *International Public & Private Companies Volume*

1228

Dean Foods Specialty Products, 10255 W. Higgins Rd., 60018, pg. 490 **PB**
Fox Valley & Western Ltd., P.O. Box 5081, 60017-5062, pg. 1772 **PB**
Iberia Air Lines of Spain - Reservation Center, 6250 River Rd., 60018, pg. 575 **IT**
International Flavors & Fragrances, Inc., 6400 Shafer Ct., Ste. 760, 60018, pg. 898 **PB**
JEOL (U.S.A.), Inc., 9801 West Higgins, Ste. 220, 60018, pg. 697 **IT**
LINDBERG CORPORATION, 6133 N. River Rd., Ste. 700, 60018, pg. 999 **PB**
London House, 9701 West Higgins Rd., 60018, pg. 1070 **PB**
North & South Railways Limited, P.O. Box 5062, 60017-5062, pg. 1772 **PB**
Olicom Americas - Central, 10275 W. Higgins Rd., Ste. 470, 60018, pg. 1001 **PB**
Oxford Health Plans (IL), Inc., 9801 W. Higgins Rd., Ste. 720, 60018, pg. 1239 **PB**
RESTONIC MATTRESS CORPORATION, 9450 W. Bryn Mawr, 60018, pg. 925 **PB**
Sault Ste. Marie Bridge Co., P.O. Box 5062, 60017-5062, pg. 1772 **PB**
Sequent Computer Systems, Inc., One O'Hare Centre, 6250 River Rd., Ste. 7050, 60018, pg. 1459 **PB**
VELSICOL CHEMICAL CORPORATION, 10400 W. Higgins Rd., Ste. 600, 60018, pg. 1135 **PB**
WCL Railcars, Inc., P.O. Box 5062, 60017-5062, pg. 1773 **PB**
Wisconsin Central International, Inc., P.O. Box 5062, 60017-5062, pg. 1773 **PB**
Wisconsin Central Ltd., P.O. Box 5062, 60017-5062, pg. 1773 **PB**
WISCONSIN CENTRAL TRANSPORTATION CORPORATION, 6250 N. River Rd., Ste. 9000, 60018, pg. 1772 **PB**

Round Lake

Baxter Fenwal Division, P.O. Box 490, 60073, pg. 196 **PB**
THE GRIEVE CORPORATION, 500 Hart Rd., 60073, pg. 480 **PV**
I.V. Systems Division, Rte. 120 & Wilson Rd., 60073, pg. 196 **PB**

Rushville

Frontier Communications-Schuyler, Inc., 127 S. Congress St., 62681, pg. 684 **PB**

Russell

CAMOSY, INC., Rt. 41 & Stateline Rd., 60075, pg. 203 **PV**

Saint Charles

Audible/Visible & Waterflow Division, 3825 Ohio Ave., 60194, pg. 1306 **PB**
Country Sampler Store, 707 Kautz Rd., 60174, pg. 963 **PV**
Custom Source Realty Corporation, 36 W. 965 Ridgewood, 60175, pg. 1429 **PB**
Dukane Audio Visual Div., 2900 Dukane Dr., 60174, pg. 346 **PV**
Dukane Communications Systems Div., 2900 Dukane Dr., 60174, pg. 346 **PV**
DUKANE CORPORATION, 2900 Dukane Dr., 60174, pg. 345 **PV**
Dukane SeaCom Division, 2900 Dukane Dr., 60174, pg. 346 **PV**
Dukane Ultrasonics Div., 2900 Dukane Dr., 60174, pg. 346 **PV**
Garvey International, Inc., One Foxfield Sq., 60174, pg. 440 **PV**
Harris Bank St. Charles, One E. Main St., 60174, pg. 154 **IT**
Jefferson Smurfit Label, 1501 Indiana Ave., 60174, pg. 1270 **IT**
OMRON Manufacturing of America, Inc., 3705 Ohio Ave., 60174, pg. 1005 **IT**
SAMPLER PUBLICATIONS INC., 707 Kautz Rd., 60174, pg. 963 **PV**
System Sensor Division, 3825 Ohio Ave., 60174, pg. 1306 **PB**
UNITED LABORATORIES, INC., 320 37th Ave., 60174, pg. 1122 **PV**

Saint Francisville

Akin Seed Company, R.R. 1, Box 203, 62460-9989, pg. 566 **IT**

Saint Joseph

Grand Prairie Co-op, Inc., Box 330, Fulls Siding, R.R. 1, 61873, pg. 469 **PV**
Grand Prairie Co-op, Inc., 108 N. Main St., 61873, pg. 469 **PV**

Sandwich

CTS Corp. Frequency Controls, 400 Reimann Ave., 60548, pg. 285 **PB**

Savanna

Metform, Inc., 2551 Wacker Rd., 61074, pg. 692 **PV**

Savoy

Grand Prairie Co-op, Inc., P.O. Box 68, 61874, pg. 469 **PV**

Schaumburg

A-OK Delaware Inc., 905 Golf Rd., 60173, pg. 533 **IT**
Air Link Communications, Inc., 1301 E. Algonquin Rd., 60196, pg. 1137 **IT**
Ambassador Office Equipment, Inc., 425 N. Martingale Rd., 60173, pg. 262 **PV**
American Gasket & Rubber, 119 E. Comerce Dr., 60173, pg. 15 **PV**
American Guarantee & Liability Insurance Company, Zurich Towers, 1400 American Ln., 60196, pg. 1530 **IT**
American Xyrofin Inc., 1101 Perimeter Dr., Ste. 475, 60173-5008, pg. 350 **IT**
American Zurich Insurance Company, Zurich Towers, 1400 American Ln., 60196, pg. 1530 **IT**
Aramark Uniform Services, Inc., 1827 Walden Office Sq., Ste. 200, 60173, pg. 79 **PV**
Atlet, Inc., 502 Pratt Ave. N., 60193, pg. 97 **IT**
Avesta Sheffield, Inc., 425 N. Martingale Rd., Ste. 2000, 60173-2218, pg. 221 **IT**
BMW of North America-Central Region, 1002 E. Algonquin Rd., 60195, pg. 177 **IT**
Benihana Schaumburg Corp., 1200 E. Higgins Rd., 60173, pg. 212 **PV**
Brico International Group, 905 E. Golf Rd., 60173, pg. 533 **IT**
British Steel, Inc., 475 N. Martingale Rd., 60173, pg. 221 **IT**
Browning-Ferris Industries of Illinois, Inc., 1827 Walden Office Sq., Ste. 107, 60195, pg. 263 **PB**
Chips and Technologies, Inc., 1002 E. Algonquin Rd., Ste. 108, 60173, pg. 349 **PB**
Cognos Corp.-Chicago Sales Office, 425 N. Martingale Road, Ste. 930, 60173-2207, pg. 306 **PB**
Comdisco Technical Services, Inc., 800 Albion Way, 60193, pg. 408 **PB**
Credit Card Sentinel, 200 N. Martingale, 60173, pg. 759 **PB**
Dawson's Handy Andy Home Improvement Centers, 905 E. Golf Rd., 60173, pg. 533 **IT**
Dun & Bradstreet Software (Schaumberg), 425 North Martingale Rd., 60173-5124, pg. 532 **IT**
EDD-Chicago, 175 W. Central Rd., 60195, pg. 204 **IT**
ESMR, Inc, 1303 E. Algonquin Rd., 60196, pg. 1137 **PB**
ESMR Sub, Inc., 1303 E. Algonquin Rd., 60196, pg. 1137 **PB**
Ferro Rosemar, 1425 S. Wright Blvd., 60193-4537, pg. 619 **PB**
Fidelity & Surety Division, 1901 N. Roselle Rd., Ste. 575, 60195, pg. 215 **PB**
Foster Electric (U.S.A.) Inc., 1751 N. Wilkening Court, 60173, pg. 500 **PB**
Futaba Corporation of America, 711 E. State Pkwy., 60195, pg. 531 **PV**
General Employment Enterprises, Inc., 1101 Perimeter Dr., Ste. 735, 60173, pg. 714 **PB**
Glory USA, Inc., 707 Remington Rd., Ste. 2, 60173, pg. 554 **IT**
Stephen Gould of Illinois, Inc., 1051 Perimeter Dr., Ste. 715, 60173-5055, pg. 467 **PV**
Grand Illusion Sportswear, 1088 National Pkwy., 60173, pg. 1472 **PB**
Handy Andy Helping Hands, 905 E. Golf Rd., 60173, pg. 533 **IT**
Handy Andy Holding Co., 905 E. Golf Rd., 60173, pg. 533 **IT**
Handy Andy Realty Co., 905 E. Golf Rd., 60173, pg. 533 **IT**
Harco Insurance Services, Inc., 600 Woodfield Dr., 60173, pg. 1167 **PB**
Harco Leasing Co., Inc., 600 Woodfield Dr., 60196, pg. 1167 **PB**
Harris Bank Hoffman-Schaumburg, 275 S. Roselle Rd., 60193, pg. 154 **IT**
Hi-Temp Materials, Inc., 509 E. State Pkwy., 60195, pg. 344 **PB**
IPC Holding Corp., 1303 E. Algonquin Rd., 60196, pg. 1137 **PB**
ISI Insortex, 1050 N. National Pkwy., 60173, pg. 428 **PV**
IMPAXX, INC., 999 Plaza Dr., Ste. 830, 60173, pg. 558 **PV**
Jani King of Illinois, Inc., 1701 E. Woodfield Rd., Ste. 680, 60173, pg. 582 **PV**
Earle M. Jorgensen Company/Chicago, 1900 Mitchell Blvd., 60193, pg. 600 **PV**
Kubota Tractor Corp. Engine Division, 1300 Remington Rd., Ste. K, 60173, pg. 762 **IT**
Leo Satellite Services, Inc., 1303 E. Algonquin Rd., 60196, pg. 1137 **PB**
MDI Systems, Inc., 1124 Tower Rd., 60173, pg. 1137 **PB**
MSC Illinois Office, 425 N. Martingale Rd., 60173, pg. 1031 **PB**
Metrocom Trunked Radio Communication Systems, Inc., 1301 E. Algonquin Rd., 60196, pg. 1137 **PB**
Metrolink Communications Corporation, 1301 E. Algonquin Rd., 60196, pg. 1137 **PB**
Mijac Enterprises, Inc., 1301 E. Algonquin Rd., 60196, pg. 1137 **PB**
Mobil Chemical Co., 1900 E. Golf Rd., Ste. 1150, 60173-5036, pg. 1118 **PV**
Motorola Acceptance Corporation, 1303 E. Algonquin Rd., 60196, pg. 1137 **PB**
Motorola Caribe Pacifico Ltd., 18th Floor, 425 Martingale, 60173, pg. 1137 **PB**

Motorola China, Inc., 1303 E. Algonquin Rd., 60196, pg. 1138 **PB**
Motorola Communications & Electronics, Inc., 1301 E. Algonquin Rd., 60196, pg. 1138 **PB**
Motorola Communications International, Inc., 1303 E. Algonquin Rd., 60196, pg. 1138 **PB**
Motorola Credit Corporation, 1303 E. Algonquin Rd., 60196, pg. 1138 **PB**
Motorola Energy Systems, Inc., 1303 Algonquin Rd., 60196, pg. 1137 **PB**
Motorola General Systems Group, 1301 E. Algonquin Rd., 60196, pg. 1137 **PB**
MOTOROLA, INC., 1303 E. Algonquin Rd., 60196, pg. 1136 **PB**
Motorola, Inc., 1303 E. Algonquin Rd., 60195, pg. 1138 **PB**
Motorola International Capital Corp., 1303 E. Algonquin Rd., 60196, pg. 1138 **PB**
Motorola International Development Corp., 1303 E. Algonquin Rd., 60196, pg. 1138 **PB**
Motorola International, Inc., 1303 E. Algonquin Rd., 60196, pg. 1138 **PB**
Motorola International Paging, Inc., 1301 E. Algonquin Rd., 60196, pg. 1137 **PB**
Motorola International Sales, Inc., 1303 E. Algonquin Rd., 60196, pg. 1138 **PB**
Motorola Land Mobile Product Sector, 1301 E. Algonquin Rd., 60196, pg. 1137 **PB**
Motorola Pagetel, Inc., 1303 E. Algonquin Rd., 60196, pg. 1138 **PB**
Motorola Radio Network Solutions Group, 1301 E. Algonquin Rd., 60196, pg. 1138 **PB**
Motorola Radio Products Group, 1301 E. Algonquin Rd., 60196, pg. 1138 **PB**
Motorola Satellite Communications, Inc., 1303 E. Algonquin Rd., 60196, pg. 1138 **PB**
Motorola SF, Inc., 1303 E. Algonquin Rd., 60196, pg. 1138 **PB**
Motorola Wireless Data Group, 50 E. Commerce Dr., Ste. M1, 60173, pg. 1137 **PB**
Motorola Wireless Service, Inc., 1301 E. Algonquin Rd., 60196, pg. 1138 **PB**
MYCOM, Inc., 1303 E. Algonquin Rd., 60196, pg. 1138 **PB**
A.C. Nielsen Company, 150 N. Martingale Rd., 60173, pg. 1183 **PB**
Nippon Sanso U.S.A., Inc., 300 N. Martingale Rd., Ste. 200, 60173, pg. 938 **PB**
The Northern Trust Company, 1501 Woodfield Rd., 60173, pg. 1197 **PB**
Olympic Steel - Chicago Division, 1901 Mitchell Blvd., 60193, pg. 1221 **PB**
OMRON Electronics Inc., One E. Commerce Dr., 60173, pg. 1005 **IT**
OMRON Management Center of America, Inc., 1300 Basswood St., Ste. 100, 60173, pg. 1005 **IT**
OMRON Systems, Inc., 55 E. Commerce Dr., 60173, pg. 1005 **IT**
Oriental Motor U.S.A. Corp., 915 N. Plum Grove Rd., Ste. C, 60173, pg. 1008 **IT**
POWER CONTRACTING & ENGINEERING CORP., 2360 N. Palmer Dr., 60173, pg. 877 **PV**
Renishaw Inc., 623 Cooper Ct., 60173, pg. 1103 **IT**
Rockwell PMC/Baker Perkins, 100 E. Commerce Dr., 60173, pg. 1240 **IT**
A. Schulman, Inc., Embassy Plaza, 1933 Meacham Rd., Ste. 500, 60173, pg. 1441 **PB**
Shoreland Communications, Inc., 1301 E. Algonquin Rd., 60196, pg. 1139 **PB**
The Signature Group, 200 N. Martingale, 60173-2096, pg. 758 **PV**
SmithKline Beecham Clinical Laboratories, 506 E. State Pkwy., 60173, pg. 1265 **IT**
Steadfast Insurance Company, Zurich Towers, 1400 American Ln., 60196, pg. 1530 **IT**
Sterling Electronics, 2050 Algonquin Rd., Ste. 608, 60173, pg. 1051 **PB**
Sumikin Bussan International Corp.-Chicago Branch, 301 E. Commerce Dr., 60173, pg. 1308 **IT**
Sumikin Bussan International Corp. - Food Div., 425 N. Martingale Rd. Ste.1070, 60173, pg. 1308 **IT**
Sunbeam Household Products, 1501 Woodfield Rd., Ste. 400N, 60173, pg. 1533 **PB**
Taiyo Yuden (U.S.A.) Inc., 1930 N. Thoreau Dr., 60173, pg. 1349 **IT**
The Thermos Company, 300 N. Martingale, Ste. 200, 60173, pg. 938 **PV**
Triad Personnel Services, 1821 Walden Office Sq., Ste. 300, 60173, pg. 715 **PB**
USLIFE Agency Services, Inc., One Woodfield Lake, 60173, pg. 77 **PB**
The Yokohama Rubber Co., Ltd., 1325 Remington Rd., Ste. Q, 60195, pg. 1521 **IT**
Zurich American Insurance Company of Illinois, The Zurich Towers, 1400 American Ln., 60196-1056, pg. 1530 **IT**
Zurich American Insurance Company of Illinois, Zurich Towers, 1400 American Ln., 60196, pg. 1530 **IT**
Zurich American Lloyds, Zurich Towers, 1400 American Ln., 60196, pg. 1530 **IT**
Zurich Insurance Company, Zurich Towers, 1400 American Ln., 60196, pg. 1530 **IT**
Zurich Life Insurance Company of America, Zurich Towers, 1400 American Ln., 60173-4987, pg. 1530 **IT**

Schiller Park

ATLAS LIFT TRUCK RENTALS & SALES, INC., 5050 N. River Rd., 60176, pg. 96 **PV**
ATLAS WIRE CORPORATION, 9525 W. River St., 60176, pg. 97 **PV**
ATOLS TOOL AND MOLD CORP., 3828 N. River Rd., 60176, pg. 97 **PV**

Geographic Index-U.S.

Mayfair Molded Products Corporation, 3700 N. Rose St., 60176, pg. 1192 **PV**

Rotary Paper Manifold Co., 4250 United Pkwy., 60176, pg. 165 **PV**

Square D Co., 9522 W. Winona St., 60176-1084, pg. 1208 **IT**

Stewart-Warner Electronics Company, 3701 N. 25th Ave., 60176, pg. 811 **PB**

United Insurance Company of America, 10509 United Pkwy., 60176-1715, pg. 1694 **PV**

WARNER CANDY COMPANY, INC., 10507 Delta Pkwy., 60176-1703, pg. 1150 **PV**

Wilton Tool Corp., 9525 W. Irving Pk., 60176-1923, pg. 1181 **PV**

Seneca

L.B. Foster Company-Seneca Yard, Shipyard Terminal & Indus. Pk., 520 E. Shipyard Rd., Bldg. #8, 61360, pg. 676 **PB**

Sesser

Consolidation Coal Co., Rend Lake Mine, P.O. Box 566, 62884, pg. 531 **PB**

Shelbyville

Warner-Ishi Corporation, Rte. 16 W., R.R. 3, Box 36, 62565, pg. 689 **IT**

Sidney

Grand Prairie Co-op, Inc., Block, R.R. 1, 61877, pg. 469 **PV**

Skokie

Alnor Instrument Company, 7555 N. Linder Ave., 60077, pg. 1559 **PB**

ALstrip, Inc., 4901 Main St., 60077, pg. 43 **PB**

AMERICAN LOUVER CO., 7700 N. Austin Ave., 60077, pg. 58 **PV**

Anixter Inc., 4711 Golf Road, 60076, pg. 115 **PB**

BELL & HOWELL HOLDINGS, 5215 Old Orchard Rd., 60077-1076, pg. 201 **PB**

CASTCRAFT INDUSTRIES, INC., 3649 W. Chase Ave., 60076, pg. 219 **PV**

Castcraft Software Optifont, 3649 W. Chase Ave., 60076, pg. 219 **PV**

Cloud Corporation, 7455 N. St. Louis Ave., 60076, pg. 247 **PV**

CRAFTY BEAVER HOME CENTER, 4810 Oakton, 60077, pg. 284 **PV**

Dussek Campbell, Inc., P.O. Box 549, 3650 Touhy Ave., 60076, pg. 234 **IT**

FEL-PRO INCORPORATED, 7450 N. McCormick Blvd., 60076, pg. 399 **PV**

Florasynth Inc., 3720 Touhy Ave., 60076, pg. 173 **IT**

Hirsh Company, 8051 Central Park Ave., 60076, pg. 963 **PB**

K.W. Power Source, 3555 Howard St., 60076, pg. 127 **PV**

Kingston Marketing Co., 7711 Gross Point Rd., 60076, pg. 1091 **PV**

KLEIN TOOLS INC., 7200 McCormick Blvd., 60076, pg. 625 **PV**

Lambent Technologies Inc., 7274 N. Central Park, 60076, pg. 858 **PV**

NutraSweet International, Ltd., P.O. Box 830, 60076, pg. 1125 **PB**

OHMITE MANUFACTURING COMPANY, 3601 Howard St., 60076, pg. 813 **PV**

Old Orchard Hospital, Inc., 9700 Kenton St., 60076, pg. 1714 **PB**

Panalarm Products, Ametek, Inc., 7401 No. Hamlin Ave., 60076, pg. 100 **PB**

Powers Process Controls, 3400 Oakton St., 60076, pg. 457 **PV**

Quartet Manufacturing Co., 5700 Old Orchard Rd., 60077, pg. 707 **PB**

RAND MCNALLY & COMPANY, 8255 N. Central Park, 60076-2908, pg. 908 **PV**

RAULAND-BORG CORPORATION, 3450 W. Oakton St., 60076-2951, pg. 911 **PV**

SASIB Packaging North America, 7515 N. Linder Ave., 60077, pg. 1194 **IT**

SASIB Packaging North America, 7515 N. Linder Ave., 60077, pg. 1194 **IT**

W.H. Salisbury & Company, 7520 N. Long Ave., 60077, pg. 1244 **IT**

Searle & Co., 5200 Old Orchard Rd., 60077, pg. 1125 **PB**

Searle Laboratories, 4901 Searle Pkwy., 60077, pg. 1125 **PB**

TMP Worldwide, Inc., 8001 N. Lincoln Ave., Ste. 700, 60077, pg. 1064 **PV**

TEMPEL STEEL COMPANY, 5215 Old Orchard Rd., 60077-1076, pg. 1075 **PV**

3Com Corporation, 8100 N. McCormick Blvd., 60076-2999, pg. 1604 **PB**

3Com Personal Communications Div., 7770 N. Frontage Rd., 60076-2690, pg. 1604 **PB**

TOPCO ASSOCIATES, INC., 7711 Gross Point Rd., 60077-2697, pg. 1091 **PV**

Transfertech, Inc., 3649 W. Chase Ave., 60076, pg. 219 **PV**

Type Films of Chicago Co., 3649 W. Chase Ave., 60076, pg. 219 **PV**

Type Founders of Chicago, 3649 W. Chase Ave., 60076, pg. 219 **PV**

Welch/Thomas Vacuum, 7300 N. Linder, 60077, pg. 1599 **PB**

World Brands Inc., 7711 Gross Point Rd., 60077, pg. 1091 **PV**

South Beloit

AMCORE Bank, 640 Blackhawk Blvd., 61080, pg. 64 **PB**

AMCORE Insurance Group, Inc., 640 Blackhawk Blvd., 61080, pg. 64 **PB**

Gardner Abrasives, 481 Gardner St., 61080-1394, 61080, pg. 1699 **PB**

National Twist Drill Div., P.O. Box 307, 5404 East Rockton Rd., 61080-0307, pg. 1370 **PB**

New York Twist Drill Div., P.O. Box 368, 61080, pg. 1370 **PB**

Prime Cast, Inc., 429 Gardner St., 61080, pg. 142 **PB**

South Beloit Water, Gas & Electric Co., 61080, pg. 1728 **PB**

Warner Electric Industrial Products Division, 449 Gardner St., 61080, pg. 480 **PB**

South Elgin

HOEFER PLASTICS CORPORATION, 500 N. Collins St., 60177-1195, pg. 532 **PV**

IHC GROUP, INC., 1797 N. La Fox St., 60177, pg. 555 **PV**

South Holland

Bell Packaging Corporation-South Holland Div., 300 W. 170 S., 60473, pg. 1066 **IT**

CALUMET CARTON COMPANY, 16920 State St., 60473, pg. 201 **PV**

Huls America Inc., 16800 S. Canal St., 60473, pg. 1455 **IT**

Oletex, Inc., 16800 S. Canal St., 60473, pg. 56 **PV**

Van Leeuwen Pipe & Tube Corp., 15555 South LaSalle Street, 60473-1267, pg. 1450 **IT**

H. Wilson Company, 555 W. Taft Dr., 60473, pg. 359 **PV**

Zoll Food Corp., 15600 S. Wentworth Ave., 60473, pg. 426 **PB**

Sparta

Quad County Publishing, Inc., 116 W. Main St., 62286, pg. 964 **PB**

Spring Grove

INTERMATIC INC., Intermatic Plaza, 60081, pg. 567 **PV**

Springfield

Abraham Lincoln Insurance Co., P.O. Box 5147, 5250 S. Sixth St. Rd., 62703, pg. 406 **PV**

Allegiance Insurance Company, One Horace Mann Plaza, 62715, pg. 362 **PB**

Allegiance Life Insurance Company, One Horace Mann Plaza, 62715, pg. 836 **PB**

AmerenCIPS, 607 E. Adams St., 62739, pg. 65 **PB**

The American Franklin Life Insurance Co., Franklin Square, 62713, pg. 76 **PB**

ANDERSON ELECTRIC, INC., 3501 S. Sixth St., 62703-4705, pg. 72 **PV**

BUNN-O-MATIC CORPORATION, 1400 Stevenson Dr., 62703, pg. 180 **PV**

CAPITOL GROUP, 1900 S. Eighth St., 62703, pg. 206 **PV**

CIPSCO Investment Company, 607 East Adams St., 62739, pg. 56 **PB**

Cox Communications-Springfield, 711 S. Dirksen Pkwy., 62703, pg. 455 **PB**

Dirksen House Healthcare, 555 W. Carpenter St., 62702, pg. 1712 **PB**

EGIZII ELECTRIC, INC., 700 N. MacArthur Blvd., 62702, pg. 466 **PV**

FFG Investments, Inc., 205 S. Fifth St., Tenth Fl., 62701, pg. 644 **PB**

FFG Trust, Inc., 205 S. Fifth St., 62701, pg. 644 **PB**

FIRST COMMONWEALTH CORPORATION, 5250 S. Sixth St., 62703, pg. 406 **PV**

First Commonwealth Corporation, 5250 S. 6th St. Rd., P.O. Box 5147, 62703, pg. 406 **PV**

First National Bank of Central Illinois, 205 S. Fifth St., 62701, pg. 644 **PB**

FIRSTBANK OF ILLINOIS CO., 205 S. Fifth St., 62701, pg. 643 **PB**

The Franklin Life Insurance Company, Franklin Sq., 62713, pg. 75 **PB**

Freeman Energy Corporation, 1999 Wabash Ave., Ste. 200B, 62704, pg. 709 **PB**

HANSON ENGINEERS INC., 1525 S. Sixth St., 62703, pg. 530 **PV**

Hobbs Corporation, Yale Blvd. & Ash St., 62703, pg. 127 **IT**

HORACE MANN EDUCATORS CORPORATION, One Horace Mann Plaza, 62715-0001, pg. 835 **PB**

Horace Mann Insurance Company, One Horace Mann Plaza, 62715, pg. 836 **PB**

Horace Mann Life Insurance Company, One Horace Mann Plaza, 62715, pg. 836 **PB**

Legacy Audio Inc., 3023 E. Sangamon Ave., 62702, pg. 45 **PB**

LEXIS Document Services, 801 Adlai Stevenson Dr., 62703, pg. 1096 **IT**

Magna Bank, Springfield Region, 1825 S. 6th St., 62703, pg. 1037 **PB**

ROBERTS FOODS, INC., 1615 W. Jefferson St., 62702, pg. 935 **PV**

The State Journal-Register, One Copley Plaza, 62705, pg. 275 **PV**

Teachers Insurance Company, One Horace Mann Plaza, 62715, pg. 836 **PB**

Universal Guarantee Life Insurance, P.O. Box 5147, 5250 S. Sixth St. Rd., 62703, pg. 406 **PV**

WICS-TV, 2680 East Cook St., 62703, pg. 439 **PV**

Sterling

AMCORE Bank N.A., Rock River Valley, 302 First Ave., 61081-3663, pg. 64 **PB**

NORTHWESTERN STEEL & WIRE CO., 121 Wallace St., 61081, pg. 1201 **PB**

Northwestern Steel & Wire Company-Kentucky, A Delaware Corp., P.O. Box 618, 121 Wallace St., 61081-0618, pg. 1201 **PB**

WAHL CLIPPER CORP., 2900 N. Locust, 61081, pg. 1146 **PV**

Wayne Dalton of Sterling, 301 W. 3rd St., 61081-8200, pg. 1155 **PV**

Stockton

Excel of Stockton, 301 S. Simmons St., 61085, pg. 598 **PB**

Streamwood

DURACO PRODUCTS, INC., 1109 E. Lake St., 60107, pg. 348 **PV**

Streator

Illinois Fruit & Produce Corp., One Quality Ln., 61364, pg. 918 **PB**

Industrial Div., 1621 S. Illinois St., 61634, pg. 617 **PB**

JP Foodservice, Inc.-Streator, One Quality Ln., 61364, pg. 918 **PB**

Vactor Mfg. Inc., 1621 S. Illinois St., 61364, pg. 617 **PB**

Sugar Grove

Oak Grigsby, 84 N. Duggan Rd., 60554, pg. 1209 **PB**

Sullivan

E.J. Brach, Inc., 811 S. Hamilton, 61951, pg. 163 **PV**

Livergood Grain Co., 200 W. Harrison, 61951, pg. 1357 **IT**

Summit

W. Braun Distribution Center, 7224 W. 60th St., 60501, pg. 166 **PV**

Summit Argo

Harris Bank Argo, 7549 W. 63rd St., 60501, pg. 154 **IT**

Sycamore

DRIV-LOK, INC., 1140 Park Ave., 60178, pg. 343 **PV**

IDEAL INDUSTRIES, INC., 1000 Park Ave., 60178, pg. 557 **PV**

SEYMOUR OF SYCAMORE, INC., 917 Crosby Ave., 60178, pg. 988 **PB**

Sycamore Plant, 821 Park Ave., 60178, pg. 444 **PB**

Sycamore Systems, Inc., 449 N. California St., 60178, pg. 638 **PV**

Taylorville

First Trust and Savings Bank of Taylorville, S. Side Sq., 106-111 W. Market St., 62568, pg. 644 **PB**

Primary Pulp & Paper Plant, P.O. Box 369, 1200 Elm St. E., 62568, pg. 736 **PB**

SANGAMON INDUSTRIES, Rt. 48 W., 62568, pg. 965 **PV**

Teutopolis

SIEMER MILLING COMPANY, 111 W. Main St., 62467, pg. 998 **PV**

Thomson

American Xyrofin Inc., West 3, Mile Rd., 61285, pg. 350 **IT**

Tilton

Danville Div., 410 S. 6th St., 61833, pg. 180 **PV**

Tinley Park

Encore Computer Corp., 16335 S. Harlem Ave., Ste. 417, 60477, pg. 580 **PB**

GOODHEART-WILLCOX PUBLISHER, 18604 W. Creek Dr., 60477-6243, pg. 464 **PV**

PANDUIT CORP., 17301 S. Ridgeland Ave., 60477-3091, pg. 836 **PV**

Tolono

GRAND PRAIRIE CO-OP, INC., One S. Calhoun, 61880, pg. 468 **PV**

PB - *U.S. Public Companies Volume*
PV - *U.S. Private Companies Volume*
IT - *International Public & Private Companies Volume*

Grand Prairie Co-op, Inc., Apex, R.R. 1, 61880, pg. 469 — PV

Toluca

Bernardi Italian Foods, 301 W. Third St., 61369, pg. 1182 — PV

Tuscola

Cab-o-Sil Div. Cabot Corp., 700 E. U.S. Hwy. 36, 61953-9643, pg. 289 — PB

University Park

Federal Signal Corporation, Signal Div., 2645 Federal Signal Dr., 60466, pg. 616 — PB
University Park Division, P.O. Box 788, 2500 Federal Signal Dr., 60466, pg. 438 — PB

Urbana

Champaign-Urbana Communications, Inc., 303 Fairlawn Dr., 61801, pg. 1610 — PB
Federal Signal International Ltd., 2645 Federal Signal Dr., 60466, pg. 616 — PB
Hamsvedp Industries, Inc., 80 Kettering Pkwy., 61803, pg. 502 — PV

Vandalia

John Crane Inc., Rte. 51 & Payne Dr., 62471, pg. 1338 — IT
Laclede - Vandalia Branch, 1201 Janette Ave., 62471, pg. 974 — PB
Vandalia Leader-Union, Box 315, 229 So. Fifth St., 62471, pg. 648 — PV

Vernon Hills

CDW COMPUTER CENTERS, INC., 200 N. Milwaukee Ave., 60061, pg. 277 — PB
COSMETIQUE, INC., 200 Corporate Woods Pkwy., 60061, pg. 277 — PV
Drummond American Corporation, 600 Corporate Woods Pkwy., 60061-3108, pg. 980 — PB
Komatsu America International Company, 440 N Fairway Dr., 60061-8112, pg. 744 — IT
LaSalle Bank Northbrook/Vernon Hills, 515 E. Townline Rd., 60061, pg. 10 — IT
Moore Business Products & Services Divisions, One Hawthornde Pl., Ste. 245, 175 E. Hawthorn Pkwy., 60061, pg. 890 — IT
Okabe Company, Inc., 645 Forest Edge Dr., 60061, pg. 999 — IT
OMRON Healthcare, Inc., 300 Lakeview Pkwy., 60061, pg. 1005 — IT
PNC Mortgage Corporation of America, 440 N. Fairway Dr., 60061, pg. 1243 — PB
Paslode, 888 Forest Edge Dr., 60061, pg. 867 — PB
Presstech Controls Inc., 859 West End St., Ste.H, 60061, pg. 790 — PV
Rust-Oleum Corporation, 11 Hawthorn Pkwy., 60061, pg. 1445 — PV
Scotsman Ice Systems, 775 Corporate Woods Pkwy., 60061, pg. 1445 — PV
SCOTSMAN INDUSTRIES, INC., 820 Forest Edge Dr., 60061, pg. 1444 — PV
TIGER ELECTRONICS, INC., 980 Woodlands Pkwy., 60061, pg. 1086 — PV
Wickes Inc., 706 Deerpath Dr., 60061, pg. 1391 — PB
ZEBRA TECHNOLOGIES CORPORATION, 333 Corporate Woods Pkwy., 60061-3109, pg. 1790 — PB

Villa Park

Alro Specialty Metals, Villa Park, 236 E. Sidney Ct., 60181-1198, pg. 46 — PV
ICI Katalco, Two Transam Plaza Dr., Ste. 230, 60181, pg. 664 — IT
KNOGO Regional Office-Chicago, 11 West Park Blvd., 60181, pg. 1458 — PV
Mold-Tech, 621 E. Wildwood Ave., 60181-2762, pg. 1506 — PB
Rawal Engravers, P.O. Box 40, 621 E. Wildwood Rd., 60181, pg. 1506 — PB
Unitog Rental Facility, 1050 N. Villa Ave., 60181, pg. 1693 — PB
Willis Corroon Corp. of Illinois, One Oakbrook Ter., Ste. 700, 60181, pg. 1506 — IT

Warrenville

PLYMOUTH TUBE COMPANY, 29 W. 150 Warrenville Rd., 60555, pg. 873 — PV
Reltec, Inc., 3350 Weaver Pkwy., 60555, pg. 921 — PV
D.A. STUART COMPANY, 4580 Weaver Pkwy., 60555, pg. 1048 — PV

Warsaw

Methode Electrical Products Div., 704 N. 4th St., 62379, pg. 1101 — PB

Wasco

T & D Metal Products, 601 E. Walnut St., 60183, pg. 638 — PV

Waukegan

Aigner Products Division, 2340 Ernie Krueger Cir., 60087, pg. 152 — PB
AMERICAN FLUORESCENT CORPORATION, 2345 Ernie Krueger Cir., 60087, pg. 54 — PV
BEUTLICH, L.P., 1541 Shields Dr., 60085-8304, pg. 141 — PB
Cherry Electrical Products, 3600 Sunset Ave., 60087, pg. 346 — PB
CHERRY ELECTRICAL PRODUCTS CORPORATION, 3600 Sunset Ave., 60087, pg. 346 — PB
Dexter Packaging Products, E. Water St., 60085-5652, pg. 504 — PB
A.L. HANSEN MANUFACTURING CO., 701 Pershing Rd., 60085, pg. 500 — PV
Johnson Outboards Marine Corp., 100 Sea-Horse Dr., 60085, pg. 478 — PV
LAKE COUNTY PRESS, 98 Noll St., 60085, pg. 643 — PV
Luxor, 2245 Delany Rd., 60087, pg. 359 — PV
The News-Sun, 100 W. Madison Ave., 60085, pg. 275 — PV
North Shore Gas Co., 3001 Grand Ave., 60085, pg. 1275 — PB
OMC Marine Power Products Group, 200 Sea Horse Dr., 60085, pg. 478 — PV
Outboard Marine Corporation, 100 Sea-Horse Dr., 60085, pg. 478 — PV
Silgan Containers, 1301 Dugdale Rd., 60085, pg. 1473 — PB
Vanco International, Inc., 1565 Shields Dr., 60085, pg. 1720 — PB

West Chicago

Ball FloraPlant, 622 Town Rd., 60185, pg. 112 — PV
BALL HORTICULTURAL COMPANY, 622 Town Rd., 60185-2698, pg. 112 — PV
Ball Seed Co., 622 Town Rd., 60185-2698, pg. 112 — PV
Belliss & Morcom (USA) Inc., 1275 W. Roosevelt Rd., 60185, pg. 1065 — IT
CREATIVE MARKETING INTERNATIONAL CORP., 31W001 North Ave., 60185, pg. 287 — PV
Dean Foods/McDonald's Sales Division, Bldg. 2, Unit 13, 245 W. Roosevelt Rd., 60185, pg. 490 — PB
THE JEL SERT CO., Rt. 59 & Conde St., 60185-0261, pg. 585 — PV
Microlite Corporation, 1150 Powis Rd., 60185, pg. 1306 — PV
National Controls Corporation, 1725 Western Dr., 60185, pg. 277 — PV
Northwestern Flavors Inc., 120 N. Aurora Ave., 60185, pg. 1781 — PV
Pan-American Seed Co., 622 Town Rd., 60185-2698, pg. 112 — PV
Preferred Millwork, Inc., 980 Hawthorne Ln., 60185, pg. 706 — PB
Rexam Release, Inc., 1400 Harvester Rd., 60185, pg. 1107 — IT
St. Paul Financial Development Corp., 907 Wild Ginger Trail, 60185, pg. 1429 — PB
Xetron, 1150 Powis Rd., 60185, pg. 1306 — PV

West Frankfort

American Publishing Management Services Inc., 107-115 S. Emma St., 62896, pg. 632 — IT

Westchester

Acme Resin Corp., 10330 W. Roosevelt Rd., 60153, pg. 157 — PV
Allied Security Inc., 10001 W. Roosevelt Rd., Ste. 305, 60154, pg. 41 — PV
CAP Gemini America (Chicago Commercial Branch), Two Westbrook Corporate Ctr., 60154, pg. 263 — IT
Daubert Coated Products, Inc., One Westbrook Corp. Center, Ste. 1000, 60154, pg. 313 — PV
DAUBERT INDUSTRIES, INC., One Westbrook Corp. Ctr., Ste. 1000, 60154, pg. 313 — PV
Devro-Teepak, Inc., Three Westbrook Corporate Ctr., 60154, pg. 408 — IT
ECP Incorporated, One Westbrook Corp. Center, Ste. 1000, 60154, pg. 313 — PV
Harris Bank Westchester, 10500 W. Cermak Rd., 60154, pg. 154 — IT
MDL Information Systems-Midwest Sales, 3 Westbrook Corporate Center, Ste.520, 60154, pg. 1100 — IT
Numetrix Inc., One Westbrook Corp. Ctr., Ste. 500, 60154, pg. 990 — IT

Western Springs

Laidlaw Brothers, 4072 Forest Ave., 60558, pg. 191 — IT

Westmont

AFG, Inc., Oakmont Circle One, 601 Oakmont Ln., Ste. 110, 60559-5549, pg. 955 — PB
BVK/McDonald - Chicago, 999 Oakmont Plaza Dr., Ste. 380, 60559, pg. 108 — PV
Claricom, One Oakhill Ctr., 60559, pg. 111 — PV
Everpure Inc., 660 N. Blackhawk Dr., 60559, pg. 467 — PB
Exchange Bank of DuPage, 139 N. Cass, 60559, pg. 10 — IT
Flexonics Hose, 406 E. Plaza Dr., 60559, pg. 1222 — IT
GOSS GRAPHIC SYSTEMS, 700 Oakmont Ln., 6055-5546, pg. 466 — PV
IWI HOLDING LIMITED, 1010 Executive Ct., Ste. 300, 60559, pg. 861 — PB

LaSalle Bank Westmont, 139 N. Cass Ave., 60559, pg. 10 — IT

Wheaton

Plastofilm Industries, Inc., 935 W. Union, 60187, pg. 915 — PB
SPRAYING SYSTEMS CO., North Ave. at Schmale Rd., 60188, pg. 1026 — PV
Torco Automotive Division, 800 E. Roosevelt Rd., 60187, pg. 1092 — PV

Wheeling

ADC L.P., 1720 S. Wolf Rd., 60090, pg. 4 — PV
ACCO Brands, Inc., 770 South ACCO Plaza, 60090, pg. 674 — PV
J.W. ALLEN & COMPANY, 555 Allendale Dr., 60090, pg. 37 — PV
American Millibar Div., 43 W. Hintz Ave., 60090, pg. 1001 — IT
BARR ELECTRIC CORPORATION, 222 E. Marquardt Dr., 60090, pg. 117 — PV
CAPITAL GRAPHICS INC., P.O. Box 216, 60090-9998, pg. 206 — PV
CAPITOL CONSTRUCTION GROUP, INC., 1400 S. Wolf Rd., Bldg. 100, 60090, pg. 206 — PV
Clear Shield National, Inc., 1175 Wheeling Rd., 60090, pg. 586 — PB
Cole Taylor Bank, 350 E. Dundee Rd., 60090, pg. 1070 — PV
Corpak Inc., 100 Chaddick Dr., 60090, pg. 1592 — PB
Economy Mechanical Industries, Inc., 77 S. Wheeling, 60090, pg. 602 — PV
Fluid Management, Inc., 1023 Wheeling Rd., 60090, pg. 862 — PB
The Hidden Valley Ranch Co., 1197 Willis Ave., 60090, pg. 387 — PB
The Illinois Lock Co. Div., 301 W. Hintz Ave., 60090, pg. 548 — PB
INDECK POWER EQUIPMENT COMPANY, 1111 S. Willis, 60090, pg. 559 — PV
Inland Die Casting, 161 Carpenter Ave., 60090, pg. 903 — PV
Masury Paint, 1191 S. Wheeling Rd., 60090, pg. 1707 — PB
Miura Boiler U.S.A., Inc., 600 Northgate Pkwy., Ste. M, 60090, pg. 884 — IT
94th Aero Squadron of Palwaukee, Inc., 1070 S. Milwaukee Ave., 60090, pg. 1023 — PV
ORVAL KENT FOOD CO., 120 W. Palatine Rd., 60090, pg. 820 — PV
THE SEGERDAHL CORP., 1351 S. Wheeling Rd., 60090, pg. 981 — PV
SKOKIE VALLEY BEVERAGE CO., 199 Shepard Ave., 60090, pg. 1005 — PV
SPORT MART, INC., 1400 S. Wolf Rd., Ste. 200, 60090, pg. 1070 — PV
TAYLOR CAPITAL GROUP, 350 E. Dundee Rd., Ste. 300, 60090, pg. 1070 — PV
U.S. Tsubaki, Inc., 301 E. Marquardt Dr., 60090, pg. 1425 — IT
Wheeling Division, 1075 Noel St., 60090, pg. 519 — PB
Wheeling Division, 301 Alice St., 60090, pg. 519 — PB

Willowbrook

Baldwin InLine Finishing, 7001 Adams St., 60521, pg. 170 — PB
Coris-Powerbase Technology Group, 7501 S. Quincy, 60521-5544, pg. 518 — PB
PET LIFE FOODS, INC., 7628 Plaza Ct., 60521, pg. 856 — PV
Viscosity Oil Company, pg. 1579 — PB

Wilmette

Harris Bank Wilmette N.A., 1701 Sheridan Rd., 60091, pg. 154 — IT

Wilmington

Beverly National Bank, 417 S. Water St., 60481, pg. 227 — PB

Winfield

Behavioral Health Services, 27 W. 350 High Lake Rd., 60190, pg. 223 — PV
CENTRAL DUPAGE HEALTH SYSTEM, 27 W. 353 Jewell Rd., 60190, pg. 223 — PV
Central DuPage Hospital Association, 25 N. Winfield Rd., 60190, pg. 223 — PV

Winnetka

Harris Bank Winnetka N.A., 520 Green Bay Rd., 60093, pg. 154 — IT
Winnetka Financial Center, 62 Green Bay Rd., 60093, pg. 1197 — PB

Wood Dale

AAR CORP., One AAR Place, 1100 N. Wood Dale Rd., 60191, pg. 1 — PB
AEC/Application Automation, Inc., 801 AEC Drive, 60191, pg. 1041 — PV
AEC/Application Engineering Corporation, 801 AEC Drive, 60191, pg. 1041 — PV

Geographic Index-U.S.

AEC, Inc., 801 AEC Drive, 60191, pg. 500 **PV**
AEC/Whitlock, Inc., 801 AEC Dr., 60191, pg. 1041 **PV**
AGIE U.S.A. Ltd., 185 Hansen Ct., Ste. 100, 60191-1146, pg. 490 **IT**
Arcadia Shops, Inc., 1501 N. Michael Dr., 60191-1095, pg. 381 **PB**
Cheshire, 1500 Mittel Blvd., 60191-1073, pg. 545 **PB**
Comdisco Medical Exchange, Inc., 1421 N. Wood Dale Rd., 60191, pg. 408 **PB**
Dytel Inc., 160 Hansen Ct., Ste. 100, 60191, pg. 1550 **PB**
Ericsson Network Systems, Inc., 360 Beinoris Dr., 60191, pg. 1365 **IT**
Eskay Screw Corporation, 321 Foster Ave., 60191, pg. 1054 **PV**
Grohe America, Inc., 900 Lively Blvd., 60191, pg. 559 **IT**
ITW Brand Merchandising, 226 Gerry Dr., 60191, pg. 866 **PB**
ITW Nexus, 230 Gerry Dr., 60191, pg. 866 **PB**
ITW Ramset/Red Head, 1300 N. Michael Dr., 60191, pg. 867 **PB**
Komatsu America Industries Corp., 199 E. Thorndale Avenue, 60191, pg. 744 **IT**
Mecatool USA, 165 Hansen Ct. #111E, 60191, pg. 490 **IT**
MIYANO MACHINERY, INC., 940 N. Central Ave., 60191, pg. 754 **PV**
Robin America, Inc., 940 Lively Blvd., 60191, pg. 523 **PV**
GEORGE SOLLITT CONSTRUCTION, 790 North Central Ave., 60191, pg. 1013 **PV**
Videojet Systems International, Inc., 1500 Mittel Blvd., 60191-1073, pg. 545 **IT**

Woodridge

Catellus Development Corporation, 1200 Internationale Pkwy., Ste. 100, 60517, pg. 315 **PB**
Copco, 2240 W. 75th St., 60517, pg. 1182 **PV**
Hendrickson International, 800 Frontage Rd., 60517, pg. 155 **PV**
Rowoco, 2240 W. 75th St., 60517, pg. 1182 **PV**
Weston Gallery, 2240 W. 75th St., 60517, pg. 1182 **PV**
WILTON INDUSTRIES, INC., 2240 W. 75th St., 60517, pg. 1181 **PV**

Woodstock

AMCORE Bank N.A., Northwest, P.O. Box 1547, 225 W. Jackson St., 60098-1547, pg. 64 **PB**
AUTOMATIC LIQUID PACKAGING, INC., 2200 W. Lake Shore Dr., 60098, pg. 101 **PV**
Harris Bank Woodstock, 101 S. Benton St., 60098, pg. 154 **IT**
Morton Chemical Div., 1275 Lake Ave., 60098, pg. 1135 **PB**
North American Professional Products, 1500 McConnell Rd., 60098-7310, pg. 238 **IT**

Yorkville

Amurol Confections Co., 2800 N. Rte. 47, 60560, pg. 1781 **PB**

Zeigler

NationsBank of Franklin County, Circle and Wilcox, 62999, pg. 1164 **PB**

Zion

AKZO Coatings Inc., 1915 Industrial Ave., 60099-1435, pg. 46 **IT**
BAT Office Products, 2501 Deborah Ave., 60099, pg. 1686 **PB**
Kelso-Burnett Zion Branch, 3065 Sheridan Rd., 60099, pg. 613 **PV**
L & M Corrugated Container Corp., 27th & Deborah, 60099, pg. 1521 **PB**

INDIANA

Albion

Albion Wire, Inc., State Rd. 8 E, 46701, pg. 526 **PV**
Lyall Assemblies, Inc., 61 E. 400 S., 46701, pg. 484 **PV**

Alexandria

RAM GRAPHICS, INC., State Rd., Nine S., 46001, pg. 908 **PV**

Anderson

Commercial Service Printing, 1200 E. Fifth St., 46018, pg. 1151 **PV**
Delco Remy America, Inc., 2902 Enterprise Dr., 46013, pg. 495 **PB**
DELCO REMY INTERNATIONAL, INC., 2902 Enterprise Dr., 46013, pg. 495 **PB**
Hoosier Park Ltd., 4500 Dan Patch Circle, pg. 356 **PV**
PAY LESS SUPER MARKETS, INC., First Savings Tower, 33 W. Tenth St., 46015, pg. 844 **PV**
WARNER PRESS, INC., 1200 E. Fifth St., 46018, pg. 1150 **PV**
Warner Press Publishers, 1200 E. Fifth St., 46018, pg. 1151 **PV**

Angola

Day Tech Industries, 319 Pokagon Trail, 46703, pg. 315 **PV**
Micromatic Operations (Angola Plant), 1101 Wohlert St., 46703, pg. 1589 **PB**
Mid West Correct Craft, Inc., P.O. Box 216, 46703, pg. 277 **PV**
Trans-Guard Industries, 903 S. Wayne, 46703, pg. 172 **PV**

Argos

Ristance Corporation, 10590 17th Rd., 46501, pg. 561 **PB**

Ashley

Burndy Corporation, Ashley Plant, P.O. Box 397, 300 HL Thompson, Jr. Dr., 46705-0397, pg. 1340 **IT**

Auburn

The Auburn State Bank, 101 N. Main St., 46706, pg. 674 **PB**
Cooper Tire & Rubber Company, Auburn Plant, 725 W. 11th St., 46706, pg. 445 **PV**
Evans Ball Brass & Aluminum Foundry, 520 Hazel St., 46706, pg. 385 **PV**
KRUSE INTERNATIONAL, 5540 CR 11-A at 69, 46706, pg. 636 **PV**
RANCO Manufacturing Company, 1101 Oren Dr., 46706, pg. 1386 **PV**
Renaissance Publishing Co., Inc., 318 E. Seventh, 46706, pg. 185 **IT**
Rieke Corporation, 500 W. Seventh St., 46706, pg. 1054 **PB**

Aurora

AURORA CASKET COMPANY, U.S. 50 West, 47001, pg. 99 **PV**

Austin

MORGAN FOODS, INC., 90 W. Morgan St., 47102, pg. 761 **PV**

Avilla

Auto Jectors, Inc., 200 Deko Dr., 46710, pg. 484 **PV**
Hoosier Wire, Inc., 302 Progress Way, 46710, pg. 526 **PV**
Insulated Division, 302 Progress Way, 46710, pg. 526 **PV**
Pent Plastics, Inc., 303 E. Fourth St., 46710, pg. 484 **PV**
Wire Tech, Inc., Progress Way, 46710, pg. 526 **PV**

Batesville

Batesville Casket Company, Inc., One Batesville Blvd., 47006-7798, pg. 828 **PB**
The Forethought Group, Inc., 1069 State Rte. 46 E., 47006, pg. 828 **PB**
Hill-Rom Company, Inc., 1069 State Rte. 46 E., 47006-9167, pg. 828 **PB**
HILLENBRAND INDUSTRIES, INC., 700 State Rd. 46 E., 47006-8835, pg. 828 **PB**

Bedford

BRUNNER ENGINEERING & MANUFACTURING, INC., 800-900 X St., 47421, pg. 176 **PV**
IMCO Recycling of Indiana Inc., 1005 4th St., 47421, pg. 871 **PV**

Beech Grove

ADM Milling Co., 854 Bethel P.O. Box 610, 46107, pg. 128 **PB**

Berne

E.P. GRAPHICS, INC., 169 S. Jefferson, 46711, pg. 354 **PV**
HOUSE OF WHITE BIRCHES, INC., 306 E. Parr Rd., 46711, pg. 542 **PV**
Micro-Precision Operations, 525 Berne St., 46711, pg. 1589 **PB**
Resistor Networks, 406 Parr Rd., 46711, pg. 286 **PB**

Bicknell

Beech Coal Company, RR1, Box 129, 47512, pg. 471 **PB**

Bloomington

Citizens Bank of Central Indiana-Bloomington Region, 200 S. Washington, 47401-3537, pg. 280 **PB**
HALL SIGN, INC., 4495 W. Vernal Pike, 47402, pg. 495 **PV**
Medium Voltage Outdoor Equipment, 300 N. Curry Pk., 47404, pg. 4 **IT**
Midwest Natural Foods, P.O. Box 2629, 225 Daniels Way, 47402, pg. 752 **IT**
Motion Control Industries, Inc., 1031 E. Hillside Dr., 47401, pg. 305 **PV**
PTS ELECTRONICS CORPORATION, 5233 S. Hwy. 37, 47401, pg. 828 **PV**

Bluffton

SARKES TARZIAN, 205 N. College Ave., 47404, pg. 966 **PV**

Bluffton

BAIC International, 805 So. Decker Dr., 46714, pg. 478 **IT**
Bluffton Agri/Industrial Corp. d/b/a BAIC, 805 So. Decker Dr., 46714, pg. 478 **IT**
FRANKLIN ELECTRIC CO., INC., 400 E. Spring St., 46714, pg. 679 **PB**
The Fremont Co., 800 S. Dougherty, 46714, pg. 427 **PV**
Old-First National Bank in Bluffton, 304 W. Market St., 46714, pg. 674 **PB**

Boonville

Boonville Mining Services, Inc., 110 W. Division St., 47601, pg. 177 **PV**
Lincoln Industries, Inc., 702 South 7th St., 47601, pg. 1207 **PV**

Borden

Kimball Office Furniture Manufacturing, P.O. Box C, 47106, pg. 957 **PB**

Bourbon

Reynolds Metals Company-Bourbon, 606 W. Center St., 46504, pg. 1385 **PB**

Brazil

First State Bank, Brazil Banking Center, State Road 59 S., 47834, pg. 634 **PB**

Bremen

Ristance Corporation, E. 2nd St., 46506, pg. 561 **PB**

Bristol

BPC Division, State Rd. 15 South, 46507, pg. 618 **IT**
Bristolipe Division, 503 Vistula St., 46507, pg. 618 **IT**
Thor Indiana, Inc., P.O. Box 338, State Rd., 15 N. Stoutco Dr., 46507, pg. 1602 **PB**
Ventline Div., P.O. Box 629, 46507, pg. 1398 **IT**

Brook

Per Pak (Brook), P.O. Box 136, 47922, pg. 1270 **IT**

Brookston

FLUIDRIVE INC., Box 600, 47923, pg. 415 **PV**

Butler

Therma-Tru Indiana Mfg. Opers., 108 Mutzfield Rd., 46721, pg. 1080 **PV**
Universal Tool & Stamping, P.O. Box 100, Main at Commerce, 46721-0100, pg. 17 **PB**

Cambridge City

Dean Foods, P.O. Box 267, 151 S. Green, 47327, pg. 490 **PB**
MEG, P.O. Box 240, 502 S. Green St., 47327-0240, pg. 686 **PV**

Carmel

ADT Security Systems, Inc., 12166 N. Meridian, 46032, pg. 1649 **PB**
Alloy Ring Service, 177 W. Carmel Drive, 46032, pg. 780 **PB**
Bankers National Life Insurance Co., 11815 N. Pennsylvania St., 46032, pg. 433 **PB**
Beneficial Standard Life Insurance Company, 11815 N. Pennsylvania St., 46032, pg. 433 **PB**
CHIC, 1185 N. Pennsylvania St., 46032, pg. 433 **PB**
Conseco Capital Management, Inc., 11825 N. Pennsylvania St., 46032, pg. 433 **PB**
CONSECO INC., 11825 N. Pennsylvania St., 46032, pg. 432 **PB**
Conseco Risk Management, Inc., 11825 N. Pennsylvania St., 46032, pg. 433 **PB**
Firestone Building Products Company, 525 Congressional Blvd., 46032, pg. 214 **IT**
Firestone Industrial Products Co., 12650 Hamilton Crossing Blvd., 46032, pg. 214 **IT**
Fujitsu Ten Corp. of America/Indianapolis, 701 Congressional Blvd., Ste. 260, 46032, pg. 526 **IT**
Great American Reserve Insurance Company, 11815 Pennsylvania St., 46032, pg. 433 **PB**
Halliburton Energy Services, 269 W. Carmel Dr., 46032-2527, pg. 776 **PB**
Hewlett-Packard Company, 11911 N. Meridian St., 46032, pg. 814 **PB**
Integrated Information Services Inc., 11911 N. Meridian St., 46032, pg. 860 **PV**
Intermediate Holdings, Inc., 11825 N. Pennsylvania St., 46032, pg. 433 **PB**
KAUFFMAN PRODUCTS, INC., 1092 Third Ave., S.W., 46032-2575, pg. 609 **PV**
Lincoln American Life Insurance Co., 11825 N. Pennsylvania St., 46032, pg. 433 **PB**

PB - U.S. Public Companies Volume
PV - U.S. Private Companies Volume
IT - International Public & Private Companies Volume

1232

National Fidelity Life Insurance Co., 11815 N. Pennsylvania St., 46032, pg. 433 **PB**
O'MALIA FOOD MARKETS INC., 867 W. Carmel Dr., 46032-5804, pg. 816 **PV**
Skanska E&C, 11590 N. Meridian St., 46032, pg. 1261 **IT**
THD, Inc., 11825 N. Pennsylvania St., 46032, pg. 433 **PB**
Texas Instruments Adc, Semiconductor Div., 550 Congressional Dr., 46032-5609, pg. 1585 **PB**
United Presidential Life Insurance Co., 11815 N. Pennsylvania St., 46032, pg. 434 **PB**
Washington National Insurance Co., 11815 N. Pennsylvania St., 46032, pg. 434 **PB**

Chandler

Indiana Hardwoods, P.O. Box 309, Hwy. 62 West, 47610, pg. 957 **PB**

Chesterton

Bethlehem Steel-Burns Harbor Division, P.O. Box 248, 46304, pg. 226 **PB**
Harley Valve & Instrument, 2100 State Rd. 149, 46304, pg. 880 **PB**
Magnetics International, Inc., 1111 N. State Rd., 46304, pg. 879 **PB**
NBD Banking Company, North, 109 Broadway, 46304, pg. 628 **PB**

Churubusco

Churubusco State Bank, 102 N. Line St., 46723, pg. 674 **PB**

Clarksville

GOHMANN ASPHALT & CONSTRUCTION INC., 1630 Broadway, 47129, pg. 459 **PV**
HUGHES GROUP, 590 Missouri Ave., Ste. 204, 47129, pg. 546 **PV**
Riverton Truckers, Inc., P.O. Box 2602, 47131, pg. 459 **PV**

Clinton

Clinton State Bank, 407 S. Main St., 47842, pg. 1217 **PB**

Columbia City

Columbia Die Mold, 900 W. Connection Way, 46725, pg. 879 **PV**
PRECISION PLASTICS INC., 900 W. Connection Way, 46725, pg. 879 **PV**
Steel Tank & Fabricating Corp., James St., 46725, pg. 615 **PV**

Columbus

Arvin Finance Corp., One Noblitt Plaza, 47201, pg. 137 **PB**
ARVIN INDUSTRIES, INC., One Noblitt Plaza, 47201, pg. 136 **PB**
Arvin International, Inc., One Noblitt Plaza, 47201, pg. 137 **PB**
COSCO, INC., 2525 State St., 47201, pg. 277 **PV**
CUMMINS ENGINE COMPANY, INC., 500 Jackson St., 47202-3005, pg. 467 **PB**
Cummins Engine Company, Inc., 1000 Fifth St., 47201, pg. 468 **PB**
DUNLAP & CO. INC., P.O. Box 328, 47202, pg. 346 **PV**
Enceratec, Inc., 810 Brown St., 47201, pg. 1405 **IT**
Engineering Ceramic Technologies, Inc., 2525 Sandcrest Dr., Ste. C, 47203, pg. 469 **PB**
Flambeau Products-Columbus, 4325 Middle Rd., 47202, pg. 410 **PV**
Reeves Division, 1225 Seventh St., 47201, pg. 1398 **PB**
SYTECH, 635 S. Mapleton, 47201, pg. 468 **PB**
Toyota Industrial Equipment Mfg., Inc., 5555 Inwood Dr., 47202-2487, pg. 1412 **IT**

Connersville

Custom Extrusions, P.O. Box 286, 5120 N. State Rd., 47331, pg. 567 **PV**
Roots Division, 900 W. Mount St., 47331, pg. 528 **PB**
Stant Manufacturing Inc., 1620 Columbia Ave., 47331-1696, pg. 1397 **IT**

Corydon

THE KELLER MANUFACTURING CO., INC., 701 N. Water St., 47112, pg. 612 **PV**

Covington

COVINGTON FOODS, INC., P.O. Box 206, 419 4th. St., 47932, pg. 280 **PV**

Crawfordsville

Crawford Industries, 1414 Crawford Dr., 47933, pg. 64 **PV**
Crawfordsville Documentation Division, State Rd. 32 W., One Documemtaion Dr., pg. 518 **PB**
Crawfordsville Manufacturing Division, 1009 Sloan St., 47933-2741, pg. 518 **PB**
Crawfordsville Telemarketing, 1823 E. Elmore St., 47933-2741, pg. 518 **PB**
GREFCO, Inc., 1489 Concord Rd., 47933, pg. 903 **PB**
H-C Industries, Inc., 1205 E. Elmore St., 47933, pg. 60 **PB**

MCM ENTERPRISES, INC., 510 S. Oak St., 47933, pg. 686 **PV**
Mid-State Wire Company, 510 S. Oak, 47933, pg. 686 **PV**
Nucor Steel-Indiana, R.R. 2, P.O. Box 311, 47933, pg. 1205 **PB**
Precision Plastics, 1001 E. College St., 47933, pg. 879 **PV**
Raybestos Aftermarket Products Co., 964 E. Market St., 47933, pg. 1363 **PB**
Raybestos Products Co., 1204 Darlington Ave., 47933, pg. 1363 **PB**
SOMMER METALCRAFT CORPORATION, 315 Poston Dr., 47933, pg. 1013 **PV**

Cromwell

Dekko Heating Technologies, Inc., 9455 W. Gilbert Lake Rd., 46732, pg. 484 **PV**

Crown Point

Tampella Power Corp., Ste. 209, 10971 Four Seasons Pl., 46307, pg. 1354 **IT**

Dale

Dale Wood Manufacturing, P.O. Box 317, Buffaloville Rd., 47523, pg. 957 **PB**

Daleville

BURLINGTON MOTOR HOLDINGS INC., 14611 W. Commerce Rd., 47334, pg. 183 **PV**

Danville

Long Cooling Systems Inc., 501 Commerce Dr., 46122, pg. 815 **IT**

Decatur

All American Homes, Inc., 1418 S. 13th St., 46733, pg. 388 **PB**
Fleetwood Motor Homes of Indiana, Inc.-Decatur Plant, P.O. Box 1006, 1803 Winchester St., 46733, pg. 651 **PB**
GoldShield Fiberglass of Indiana, Inc., 2004 Patterson St., 46733, pg. 652 **PB**
Motor Home Service Facility-Decatur, Indiana, P.O. Box 1007, 1420 W. Patterson St., 46733, pg. 652 **PB**

Delphi

CHROMCRAFT REVINGTON, INC., P.O. Box 238, 1100 N. Washington St., 46923, pg. 352 **PB**
Globe Valve Corporation, 1200 N. Washington, 46923, pg. 449 **PV**
Peters-Revington Corp., 1100 N. Washington, 46923, pg. 352 **PB**

Dunkirk

Indiana Plant, P.O. Box 222, 47336, pg. 1214 **PB**

East Chicago

Inland Steel Products Company, 3210 Watling St., 46312, pg. 879 **PB**
Safety-Kleen Oil Recovery Co., 601 Riley Rd., 46312, pg. 1426 **PB**
Voest-Alpine Services and Technologies Corp.-East Chicago, 425 W. 151st St., 46312, pg. 1471 **IT**

Eaton

Colony Printing & Labeling, 600 E. Washington, 47338, pg. 976 **PB**

Edinburgh

AMOS-HILL ASSOCIATES, INC., 112 Shelby Ave., 46124, pg. 67 **PV**
Star Container, Co., 2885 W. 800 Rd. N., 46124, pg. 1071 **PV**

Elkhart

ACCRA PAC GROUP, 2730 Middlebury St., 46516, pg. 11 **PV**
Anderson Industries, Inc., 1120 N. Main St., 46514, pg. 599 **PB**
Atwood Better Products, P.O. Box 1927, 57912 Charlotte Ave., 46517, pg. 598 **PB**
Atwood Mobile Products, 27417 County Rd. 6, 46514, pg. 598 **PB**
Automotive Products, 1142 W. Beardsley Ave., 46514, pg. 285 **PB**
Vincent Bach Co., 600 Industrial Pkwy., 46516-5414, pg. 1514 **PB**
Belvedere, 1120 N. Main St., 46514, pg. 598 **PB**
Bock Industries Inc., 57540 State Rd. 19 South, 46515, pg. 265 **IT**
CTS CORPORATION, 905 West Blvd. N., 46514, pg. 285 **PB**
Canida Rubber Company, P.O. Box 4101, 46514, pg. 976 **PB**
Coachmen Automotive, 1520 Mishawaka St., 46514, pg. 388 **PB**

COACHMEN INDUSTRIES, INC., 601 E. Beardsley Ave., 46514, pg. 387 **PB**
Coast RV, Inc., 3002 Coast Ct., 46514, pg. 388 **PB**
CREATION WINDOWS OF INDIANA, INC., 53061 Ada Dr., 46514, pg. 287 **PV**
CROWN INTERNATIONAL, INC., 1718 W. Mishawaka Rd., 46517-9439, pg. 293 **PV**
Dexter Axle Div., 222 Collns Rd., 46515, pg. 1396 **IT**
The Dometic Corporation, 2320 Industrial Pkwy., 46516, pg. 440 **IT**
DOMORE CORPORATION, 2400 Sterling Ave., 46516, pg. 339 **PV**
Dygert Seating, 53381 Marina Dr., 46515, pg. 654 **PB**
Electrocomponents, 1142 W. Beardsley Ave., 46514, pg. 286 **PB**
Elixir Industries, 2040 Industrial Parkway, 46516, pg. 371 **PV**
Elixir Industries, 640 Collins Rd., 46516, pg. 371 **PV**
Elkhart Metals Division, P.O. Box 4537, 1514 W. Lusher, 46514, pg. 1048 **PV**
Elkhart Products Corp.-Plumbing Division, 1255 Oak St., 46515, pg. 63 **PB**
EXCEL INDUSTRIES, INC., 1120 N. Main St., 46514, pg. 598 **PB**
FABWEL INC., 1838 Middlebury St., 46516, pg. 390 **PV**
FASTEC INDUSTRIAL, 23348 County Rd. 6, 46515, pg. 397 **PV**
Fastec SW Corporation, 23348 County Rd. 6, P.O. Box 1048, 46515, pg. 397 **PV**
Fic Trading Corporation, 23348 County Rd. 6, P.O. Box 1048, 46515, pg. 397 **PV**
Four Wind International Corp., 701 County Rd. 15, 46515, pg. 1602 **PB**
General Generic Trucking Div., 2040 Toledo Rd., 46516, pg. 11 **PV**
Haarmann & Reimer Food Ingredients Div., P.O. Box 932, 1884 Miles Ave., 46515, pg. 173 **IT**
Haleyville Manufacturing Of Elkhart, 2936 Lillian St., 46514, pg. 491 **PB**
Health Care, Inc., 2825 Middlebury St., 46516, pg. 11 **PV**
HOMAN LUMBER MART, INC., 1650 W. Lusher, 46517, pg. 536 **PV**
Homette Corporation, 2520 By-Pass Rd., 46514, pg. 1476 **PB**
Indiana Manufacturing Facility, 1722 Mishawaka Rd., 46517, pg. 1123 **PB**
Kem Krest Corp., 2040 Toledo Rd., 46516, pg. 11 **PV**
The Kent Company, 2310 Industrial Pkwy., 46516, pg. 440 **IT**
Klem Supply, Inc., 510 S. 2nd St., 46516, pg. 953 **PB**
LaSalle Bristol Corp., P.O. Box 1900, 601 County Rd. 17, 46516, pg. 618 **IT**
Layton Homes Corp., 2520 By-Pass Rd., 46514, pg. 1476 **PB**
Lilly Industries, 28335 Clay St., 46517, pg. 994 **PB**
The Lux Co., Inc., 2135 Industrial Pkwy, 46516, pg. 388 **PV**
Morgan Drive Away, Inc., 28651 U.S. Hwy. 20 W., 46514, pg. 1022 **PB**
The Morgan Group, Inc., 28651 U.S. 20, W., 46515, pg. 1022 **PB**
NBD Bank, P.O. Box 1686, 121 W. Franklin St., 46516, pg. 628 **PB**
Neste Polyester Inc., 435 Harrison, 46516, pg. 913 **IT**
NIBCO, INC., 1516 Middlebarry St., 46516, pg. 798 **PV**
Nickles Bakery of Indiana Inc., 600 Harrison St., 46516, pg. 799 **PV**
PATRICK INDUSTRIES INC., 1800 S. 14th St., 46515, pg. 1264 **PB**
Plastic Form Inc., 53893 N. Park Ave., 46514, pg. 1055 **PB**
Reese Products, Inc., 51671 State Rd. 19 N., P.O. Box 1706, 46515, pg. 1054 **PB**
Royale Coach, 1330 Wade Dr., 46517, pg. 1123 **PV**
Schuller Intl. Inc., 2730 Industrial Pkwy., 46516-5401, pg. 927 **PB**
The Selmer Co., Inc., 600 Industrial Pkwy., 46516-5414, pg. 1514 **PB**
Shelter Components Corporation, 27217 County Rd. 6, 46514, pg. 952 **PB**
Shelter Components of IN, Inc., 27217 County Rd., Ste. 6C, 46514, pg. 953 **PB**
Shelter Distribution, 21861 Protecta Dr., 46516, pg. 953 **PB**
Shelter Distribution, P.O. Box 30, pg. 953 **PB**
Shelter Products Group, 3221 Magnum Dr., 46516, pg. 1396 **IT**
SICAN CORP., 2400 Sterling Ave., 46516, pg. 997 **PV**
SKYLINE CORPORATION, 2520 By-Pass Rd., 46514-1584, pg. 1476 **PB**
Skyline Homes, Inc., 2520 By-Pass Rd., 46514, pg. 1476 **PB**
Society National Bank, 301 S. Main St., 46515, pg. 955 **PB**
Specialty Window Coverings, 1655 Gateway Ct., 46514, pg. 491 **PV**
Sturgis Iron & Metal, Elkhart Metals Division, P.O. Box 4537, 1514 W. Lusher Ave., 46514-0537, pg. 1048 **PV**
Thetford Corp., Warehouse Div., 55712-B County Rd. 15, 46514, pg. 352 **PV**
Tredit Tire & Wheel Co., 57941 Charlotte St., 46517, pg. 300 **PV**
We Vac Plastics, 2401 S. 17th St., 46517-1415, pg. 352 **PV**
Wilcox Industries, Inc., 21067 Protecta Dr., 46516, pg. 1196 **PB**
YODER OIL COMPANY INC., 2204 California Rd., 46514, pg. 1196 **PV**
HAROLD ZIEGLER FORD-ELKHART, 2525 By Pass Rd., 46514, pg. 1205 **PV**

Geographic Index-U.S.

Evansville

American General Finance, Inc., 601 N.W. Second St., 47704, pg. 76 **PB**
ANCHOR INDUSTRIES INC., 1100 Burch Dr., 47711, pg. 71 **PV**
Atlas Specialized Transportation, 1212 St. George Rd., 47711, pg. 97 **PV**
Atlas Terminal Co., 5959 N. Fares Ave., 47711, pg. 97 **PV**
Atlas Van Lines, Inc., 1212 St. George Rd., 47711, pg. 97 **PV**
Atlas Van Lines Intl., 1212 St. George Rd., 47711, pg. 97 **PV**
Atlas World-Class Travel, 1212 St. George Rd., 47711, pg. 97 **PV**
ATLAS WORLD GROUP, INC., 1212 St. George Rd., 47711, pg. 97 **PV**
BERRY PLASTICS CORPORATION, 101 Oakley St., 47706, pg. 137 **PB**
Brake Supply Co., 1300 W. Lloyd Expwy., 47712, pg. 628 **PV**
Bristol-Myers Oncology Division, 2400 Pennsylvania St., 47712, pg. 254 **PB**
Bristol-Myers Squibb Pharmaceutical Division, 2400 Pennsylvania St., 47712, pg. 254 **PB**
Bristol-Myers Squibb U.S., 2400 W. Lloyd Expwy., 47721, pg. 254 **PB**
Bristol-Myers Squibb U.S. Pharmaceutical Group, 2400 W. Lloyd Expwy., 47721, pg. 254 **PB**
Browning-Ferris Industries of Indiana, Inc., P.O. Box 2269, 47714, pg. 263 **PB**
CNB BANCSHARES, INC., 20 N.W. Third St., 47739-0001, pg. 280 **PB**
Casino Aztar, 421 N.W. Riverside Dr., 47708, pg. 158 **PB**
Charter Behavioral Health System of Evansville, LLC, 7200 East Indiana, 47715, pg. 1034 **PB**
Citizens Insurance of Evansville, 111 S.E. Third St., 47708, pg. 280 **PB**
Citizens Trust Company of Indiana, N.A., 20 N.W. Third St., 47739-0001, pg. 280 **PB**
Coach Label, 1405 W. Missouri St., 47710, pg. 387 **PV**
ComSource, Inc., 20 N.W. Fourth St., 47741-0001, pg. 1471 **PB**
CRESLINE PLASTIC PIPE CO. INC., 955 Diamond Ave., 47711, pg. 289 **PB**
DSM Engineering Plastics Inc., P.O. Box 3333, 2267 W. Mill Rd., 47732-3333, pg. 354 **IT**
Energy Systems Group, Inc., 20 N.W. Fourth St., 47741-0001, pg. 1471 **PB**
ESCALADE SPORTS, 817 Maxwell Ave., 47711, pg. 591 **PB**
Escalade Sports Sales & Marketing, 817 Maxwell Ave., 47717, pg. 591 **PB**
EVANA AUTOMATION SPECIALISTS, 5825 Old Boonville Hwy., 47715, pg. 384 **PV**
The Evansville Courier, 300 E. Walnut St., 47713, pg. 1447 **PV**
Evansville Veneer & Lumber Co., 100 S. Kentucky Ave., 47714, pg. 957 **PB**
Faultless Caster, 1421 N. Garvin St., 47711, pg. 473 **IT**
Guardian Automotive, 601 No. Congress Ave., 47715, pg. 486 **PV**
Hahn Equipment Co., 1625 N. Garvin St., 47711, pg. 1624 **PB**
Hartford Bakery, Inc., 500 N. Fulton, 47710, pg. 665 **PV**
Indiana Tube Corp., 2100 Lexington Ave., 47730, pg. 780 **PB**
THE KARGES FURNITURE COMPANY INC., 1501 W. Maryland, 47710, pg. 607 **PV**
KELLER CRESCENT CO., 1100 E. Louisiana St., 47711, pg. 612 **PV**
Kentucky Indiana Lumber Co., 1700 N. Kentucky, 47711, pg. 615 **PB**
GEORGE KOCH SONS, INC., Ten S. 11th Ave., 47744, pg. 628 **PB**
LEWIS BROTHERS BAKERIES, INC., 500 N. Fulton Ave., 47710, pg. 665 **PV**
Marcy Fitness Products, Inc., 817 Maxwell Ave., 47706, pg. 591 **PB**
Mead Johnson & Co., 2400 W. Lloyd Expwy., 47721-00001, pg. 254 **PB**
Mead Johnson Laboratories, 2400 Pennsylvania St., 47712, pg. 254 **PB**
Mead Johnson Nutritional Group, 2400 W. Lloyd Expressway, 47721-0001, pg. 254 **PB**
Merit Life Insurance Co., P.O. Box 39, 601 N.W. Second St., 47708, pg. 77 **PB**
OLD NATIONAL BANCORP, 420 Main St., 47708, pg. 1217 **PB**
Photoplas Ltd., P.O. Box 418, 47703, pg. 915 **PV**
RED SPOT PAINT & VARNISH CO., 1107 E. Louisiana, 47711, pg. 915 **PV**
Regency Property Services L.L.C., 101 N.W. First St., Ste. 120, 47708, pg. 918 **PV**
Rexam Closures, 3245 Kansas Rd., 47711, pg. 1106 **IT**
A. Schulman, Inc., 122 N. St. Joseph Ave., 47712, pg. 1441 **PB**
SIGCORP, INC., 20 N.W. Fourth St., 47735-3606, pg. 1473 **PB**
Silgan Containers, 2201 W. Maryland St., 47712, pg. 1473 **PB**
Smith & Butterfield, 2800 Lynch Rd., 47733, pg. 333 **PB**
Southern Indiana Gas & Electric Co., 20 N.W. Fourth St., 47741-0001, pg. 1471 **PB**
Southern Indiana Minerals, Inc., 20 N.W. Fourth St., 47741-0001, pg. 1471 **PB**
Southern Indiana Properties, Inc., 100 N.W. Second St., Ste. 310, 47708, pg. 1471 **PB**
TRAYLOR BROTHERS, INC., 835 N. Congress Ave., 47715, pg. 1098 **PV**

Uniseal, Inc., 1800 W. Maryland St., 47712, pg. 628 **PV**
WFIE-TV, 1115 Mt. Auburn Rd., pg. 992 **PB**
Yosemite Insurance Co., P.O. Box 59, 601 N.W. Second St., 47701, pg. 77 **PB**

Fairmount

Frontier Communications of Indiana, Inc., 221 W. Washington St., 46928, pg. 683 **PB**

Ferdinand

DMI Furniture, Inc., 514 W. Eighth St., Box 172, 47532, pg. 473 **PB**

Fishers

INDIANA RECORDS MANAGERS, 10022 Lantern Rd., Ste. 800, 46038, pg. 560 **PV**
Topics Newspapers, 13095 Publishers Pl., 46038, pg. 326 **PB**

Flora

Bright National Bank, P.O. Box 188, Four E. Main St., 46929, pg. 633 **PB**

Folwer

Demeter, Inc., 98 S. & 100 E., Ste. A, 47944, pg. 127 **PB**

Fort Wayne

Agency Media Services, Inc., P.O. Box 988, 46801, pg. 1190 **PB**
Alro Group, Fort Wayne, P.O. Box 10360, 2211 Freeman St., 46851-0360, pg. 46 **PV**
Arco, 1319 Production Rd., 46808, pg. 264 **PV**
Bemrose USA, Inc., 9434 Lima Rd., Ste. C, 46818, pg. 135 **IT**
Bowmar Technologies, 8000 Bluffton Rd., 46809, pg. 248 **PB**
Central Soya Company, Inc., 1400 Fort Wayne Natl. Bank Bldg., 46802, pg. 324 **IT**
Charter Beacon Behavioral Health System, Inc., 1720 Beacon St., 46805, pg. 1033 **PB**
CHEMCENTRAL/Fort Wayne, 7415 Nelson Rd. E., 46803, pg. 232 **PV**
City Storage & Transfer, Inc., P.O. Box 988, 46801, pg. 1191 **PB**
CONNOR CORPORATION, 1319 Production Rd., 46808, pg. 264 **PB**
Connor Plastic Technologies, 1319 Production Rd., 46808, pg. 264 **PB**
The Crown Group-Fort Wayne Plant, 4301 Engle Rd., 46804, pg. 292 **PV**
EDD-Ft. Wayne, 525 Airport N. Office Pk., 46825, pg. 205 **PV**
ESSEX INTERNATIONAL, INC., 1601 Wall St., 46802, pg. 593 **PB**
Fasson Roll Materials Div., 3011 Independence Dr., 46808, pg. 153 **PB**
FEMCO Magnet Wire Corporation, 1601 Wall St., 46801, pg. 530 **IT**
Fill-Rite Division, 4204 Ferguson Rd., 46809, pg. 1110 **PB**
A Five Star Forwarding, Inc., P.O. Box 988, 26801, pg. 1191 **PB**
Fleet Insurance Management, Inc., P.O. Box 988, 46801, pg. 1191 **PB**
Foamex, 3005 Commercial Rd., 46809, pg. 1094 **PV**
Fort Wayne National Bank, 110 W. Berry St., 46801, pg. 674 **PB**
FORT WAYNE NATIONAL CORPORATION, 110 W. Berry St., 46801, pg. 673 **PB**
Fort Wayne Newspapers, Inc., 600 W. Main St., 46802, pg. 964 **PB**
Fort Wayne Vehicle Auction Inc., 3600 E. Washington Blvd., 46803, pg. 1649 **PB**
Fort Wayne Wizards, 4000 Parnell Ave., 46805, pg. 1191 **PB**
GAI Consultants, Inc., 1400 Airports N. Office Pk., Ste A, 46825, pg. 434 **PV**
G.E. Capital Fleet Services, P.O. Box 2204, 46801-2204, pg. 710 **PB**
Great Falls North American, Inc., P.O. Box 988, 46801, pg. 1191 **PB**
HWI Building Corp., 6502 Nelson Rd., 46803, pg. 502 **PV**
HARDWARE WHOLESALERS, INC., 6502 Nelson Rd., 46803, pg. 502 **PV**
HARRIS-KAYOT, INC., 2801 W. State Blvd., 46808, pg. 506 **PV**
Health Care Management Corp., Inc., 1910 St. Joe Center Rd., Ste. 61, 46825, pg. 405 **PB**
Hewlett-Packard Company, 111 E. Ludwig Rd., Ste. 108, 46825, pg. 814 **PB**
Holsum of Fort Wayne, Inc., 156 E. Murray, 46858, pg. 665 **PV**
ITT Aerospace/Communications Div., 1919 W. Cook Rd., 46801, pg. 859 **PB**
Indiana Broadcasting Co. (WANE), 2915 W. State Blvd., 46808, pg. 11 **PB**
Indiana Franklin Realty, Inc., P.O. Box 60, One Summit Sq., 46801, pg. 72 **PB**
Indiana Michigan Power Company, One Summit Sq., 46801, pg. 72 **PB**
JP Foodservice, Inc.-Fort Wayne, 7235 Vicksburg Pike, 46804, pg. 918 **PB**
JTC LLC, 301 Airport North Office Park, 46825, pg. 579 **PV**

KELLEY AUTOMOTIVE GROUP, 811 Ave. of Autos, 46804, pg. 612 **PV**
The Richard Leahy Corporation, 3818 Illinois Rd., Ste. 212, 46804, pg. 997 **PB**
Lincoln Financial Advisors, 3811 Illinois Rd., Ste. 205, 46804, pg. 998 **PB**
Lincoln Financial Group, Inc., 1300 S. Clinton St., 46802, pg. 997 **PB**
Lincoln Foodservice Products, Inc., 1111 N. Hadley Rd., 46804, pg. 188 **IT**
Lincoln Investment Management Inc., 200 E. Berry St., 46802, pg. 998 **PB**
Lincoln National Administrative Services Corp., One Reinsurance Pl., 1700 Magnavox Way, 46804, pg. 998 **PB**
Lincoln National (China) Inc., 200 E. Berry St., 46802, pg. 998 **PB**
LINCOLN NATIONAL CORPORATION, 200 E. Berry St., 46802-2706, pg. 997 **PB**
Lincoln National Health & Casualty Insurance Co., One Reinsurance Pl., 1700 Magnavox Way, 46804, pg. 998 **PB**
Lincoln National Intermediaries, Inc., One Reinsurance Pl., 1700 Magnavox Way, 46804, pg. 998 **PB**
The Lincoln National Life Insurance Co., 1300 S. Clinton St., 46802, pg. 998 **PB**
Lincoln National Management Services, Inc., One Reinsurance Pl., 1700 Magnavox Way, 46804, pg. 998 **PB**
Lincoln National Realty Corporation, 200 E. Berry St., 46802, pg. 998 **PB**
Lincoln National Reinsurance Company (Barbados) Limited, c/o Kenneth J. Clark, 1700 Magnavox Way, 46804, pg. 998 **PB**
Lincoln National Reinsurance Company (Bermuda) Limited, c/o Kenneth J. Clark, 1700 Magnavox Way, 46804, pg. 998 **PB**
Lincoln National Risk Management, Inc., One Reinsurance Pl., 1700 Magnavox Way, 46804, pg. 998 **PB**
Lincoln National Structured Settlement, Inc., One Reinsurance Pl., 1700 Magnavox Way, 46804, pg. 998 **PB**
Mattel Power Wheels, P.O. Box 6700, 3405 Meyer Rd., 46896-0700, pg. 1058 **PB**
THE MEDICAL PROTECTIVE COMPANY, 5814 Reed Rd., 46835, pg. 728 **PV**
NACAL, Inc., P.O. Box 988, 46801, pg. 1191 **PB**
NBD Banking Company, Northeast, 200 East Berry St., 46802, pg. 628 **PB**
NBS Imaging Systems, Inc., 1530 Progress Rd., 46808, pg. 898 **IT**
NAVTRANS Container Lines, Inc., P.O. Box 988, 46801, pg. 1192 **PB**
NAVTRANS International Freight Forwarding, Inc., P.O. Box 988, 46801, pg. 1192 **PB**
News Publishing Company, 600 W. Main St., P.O. Box 100, 46802, pg. 964 **PB**
NorAm Forwarding, Inc., P.O. Box 988, 46801, pg. 1192 **PB**
North American Distribution Systems, Inc., P.O. Box 988, 46801, pg. 1192 **PB**
North American Forwarding, Inc., P.O. Box 988, 46801, pg. 1192 **PB**
North American Moving & Storage, Inc., P.O. Box 988, 46801, pg. 1192 **PB**
North American Transport Insurance Co., P.O. Box 988, 46801, pg. 1192 **PB**
North American Van Lines, Inc., 5001 U.S. 30 W., 46818, pg. 1191 **PB**
North American Van Lines of Texas, Inc., P.O. Box 988, 46801, pg. 1192 **PB**
Norwest Bank Indiana, N.A., 111 E. Wayne St., 46802, pg. 1202 **PB**
OMNISOURCE CORPORATION, 1610 N. Calhoun St., 46808, pg. 817 **PV**
Paramount Tube, 1430 Progress Rd., 46808, pg. 880 **PV**
PERFECTION BAKERIES INC., 350 Pearl St., 46802, pg. 852 **PV**
PETROLEUM TRADERS CORPORATION, 7110 Pointe Inverness Way, 46804, pg. 859 **PV**
Phelps Dodge Magnet Wire Co., One Technology Ctr., 2131 S. Coliseum Blvd., 46803, pg. 1286 **PB**
Poly Hi Solidur, Inc., 2710 American Wy., 46809, pg. 731 **PV**
Price River Coal Co., Inc., P.O. Box 60, One Summit Sq., 46801, pg. 72 **PB**
Raytheon Systems Company Electronics Systems, 1010 Production Rd., 46808-1187, pg. 1365 **PB**
REA MAGNET WIRE COMPANY, INC., 3600 E. Pontiac St., 46803, pg. 913 **PV**
Relocation Management Systems, Inc., P.O. Box 988, 46801, pg. 1192 **PB**
ROGERS MARKETS INC., 528 W. Washington Blvd., 46802, pg. 940 **PV**
A. Schulman, Inc., 9017 Coldwater, Ste. 300A, 46825, pg. 1441 **PV**
Scott's Food Stores Inc., 4118 N. Clinton St., 46805, pg. 1541 **PB**
SEYFERT FOODS, INC., 1001 Paramount Rd., 46808, pg. 988 **PB**
Slater Steels Corporation, P.O. Box 630, 2400 Taylor St. W., 46801, pg. 1263 **IT**
Spicer Axle Div., P.O. Box 1209, 46801, pg. 479 **PB**
Spicer Off-Highway Axle Div., 2424 W. State St., 46808, pg. 479 **PB**
Spicer Trailer Products Div., 2424 W. State Blvd., 46808, pg. 479 **PB**
SuperValu, Inc.-Food Marketing Div., 4815 Executive Blvd., 46808, pg. 1540 **PB**
TMP Worldwide, Inc., 5001 US Hwy. 30 West, Ste. D, 46818, pg. 1064 **PV**

PB - *U.S. Public Companies Volume*
PV - *U.S. Private Companies Volume*
IT - *International Public & Private Companies Volume*

Geographic Index-U.S.

THORNHILL OIL COMPANY, INC., 2920 Connett St., 46802, pg. 1084 **PV**

A Three Rivers Forwarding, Inc., P.O. Box 988, 46801, pg. 1191 **PB**

TOKHEIM CORPORATION, 10501 Corporate Dr., 46845, pg. 1620 **PB**

Triple Crown Services Company, 6920 Point Inverness Way, Ste. 300, 46804, pg. 432 **PB**

Wabash Fibre Box Company-Fort Wayne Plant, Baer Field, Baer Field - Box #9310, 46899, pg. 1170 **PV**

Wayne Home Equipment Div., 801 Glasgow Ave., 46803, pg. 218 **PB**

Weatherhead Brake Div., 9434 Lima Rd., Ste. A, 46815, pg. 480 **PB**

Frankfort

General Seating of America Inc., 2298 W. Clinton State Rd. 28, 46041-8772, pg. 902 **IT**

THE KAY COMPANY, INC., 509 W. Barner St., 46041, pg. 610 **PB**

Zeneca Resins US, 3110 W. State Rd. #28, 46041-8778, pg. 1525 **IT**

Franklin

JOHNSON COUNTY FARM BUREAU CO-OP, 755 Hamilton Ave., 46131, pg. 591 **PV**

KYB Industries Inc., 2625 North Morton, 46131, pg. 727 **IT**

Fremont

Amcast Automotive-Fremont Plant, 3675 E. Depot St., 46737, pg. 63 **PB**

Laclede - Fremont Branch, P.O. Box 629, Feather Valley Rd., 46737, pg. 974 **PB**

Laclede Mid America Inc., P.O. Box 629, Feather Valley Rd., 46737, pg. 974 **PB**

French Lick

French Lick Furniture, 990 S St. Rd. 145, 47432, pg. 957 **PB**

JSI, Beechwood Ave., 47432, pg. 583 **PV**

Garrett

Custom Lights, Inc., 1605 Dekko Dr., 46738, pg. 484 **PV**

Fleetwood Homes of Indiana, Inc., 1119 Fuller Dr., 46738, pg. 651 **PB**

Garrett Products, Inc., 1605 Dekko Dr., 46738, pg. 484 **PV**

Mossberg Industries, Hubbard Division, 2047 N. Second St., 46738, pg. 764 **PV**

Gary

Bivona Inc., 5700 W. 23rd Ave., 46406, pg. 818 **IT**

Blue & Gray Brokerage, 1000 Colfax St., 46406, pg. 1687 **PB**

Blue & Gray Transportation, 1000 Colfax St., 46406, pg. 1687 **PB**

Carolina Logistics, 1000 Colfax St., 46406, pg. 1687 **PB**

Carolina National Transportation, 1000 Colfax St., 46406, pg. 1687 **PB**

Chris-Craft Industrial Products, Inc., Mono-Sol Div., 407 County Line Rd., 46403, pg. 351 **PB**

DIXIE DAIRY COMPANY, 1200 W. 15th Ave., 46407, pg. 337 **PV**

JACK GRAY TRANSPORT, INC., 4600 E. 15th Ave., 46403, pg. 471 **PV**

Gulf Line Brokerage, 1000 Colfax St., 46406, pg. 1687 **PB**

Gulf Line Transportation, 1000 Colfax St., 46406, pg. 1687 **PB**

Inland Detroit Diesel-Allison, 2601 E. 15th Ave., 46402, pg. 564 **PV**

Keystone Lines, 1000 Colfax St., 46406, pg. 1687 **PB**

Post-Tribune, 1065 Broadway, 46402, pg. 632 **IT**

Primary Pulp & Paper Plant, P.O. Box 4326, Second Pl. & Waite Sts., 46404, pg. 736 **PB**

TC Services, 1000 Colfax St., 46406, pg. 1687 **PB**

USX Gary Works, Steel Production, 1 N. Broadway, 46402-3101, pg. 1662 **PB**

US 1 INDUSTRIES INC., 1000 Colfax St., 46406, pg. 1687 **PB**

Gas City

Amcast Automotive-Gas City Plant, P.O. Box 640, 6231 E. 500 S., 46933, pg. 63 **PB**

Geneva

Elkhart Products Corporation-Industrial Division, 700 Rainbow Rd., 46740, pg. 63 **PB**

Goshen

CARLTON MANUFACTURING, INC., 2700 W. Wilden, 46528, pg. 212 **PV**

Dutchmen Manufacturing, Inc., 305 Steury Ave., 46526, pg. 1602 **PB**

GLS of Indiana, 64323 US 33, 46526, pg. 435 **PV**

GOSHEN RUBBER CO., INC., 1525 S. Tenth St., 46526, pg. 465 **PV**

Haleyville Manufacturing, 521 E. Lincoln Ave., 46526, pg. 491 **PB**

LIBERTY HOMES, INC., 1101 Eisenhower Dr., N., 46526, pg. 992 **PB**

Perfection Automotive Products Corporation, 1101 Eisenhower Dr. S., 46526, pg. 1577 **PB**

RIETH-RILEY CONSTRUCTION CO. INC., 3626 Elkhart Rd., 46526, pg. 930 **PV**

Starcraft Automotive Group, Inc., 2703 College Ave., 46526, pg. 1511 **PB**

STARCRAFT CORPORATION, 2703 College Ave., 46526, pg. 1510 **PB**

Supreme Corporation, 16500 Country Rd. 38, 46527-0463, pg. 1542 **PB**

SUPREME INDUSTRIES, INC., 65140 U.S. 33 E., 46526, pg. 1541 **PB**

Troyer Foods, Inc., 17141 State Rd. 4, 46526, pg. 619 **IT**

Unitog Rental Facility, 117 W. Jefferson, 46526, pg. 1693 **PB**

Granger

Charter South Bend Behavioral Health System, Inc., 6704 N. Gumwood Dr., 46530, pg. 1035 **PB**

Greenfield

Roll Coater, Inc., 3398 E. U.S. 40, 46140, pg. 137 **PB**

Greensburg

Fifth Third Bank of Central Indiana, 314 W. Main St., 47240, pg. 621 **PB**

KOVA FERTILIZER INC., 1330 N. Anderson St., 47240, pg. 634 **PV**

Sintering Technologies, Inc., P.O. Box 588, Barachel Lane & Montgomery Rd., 47240, pg. 468 **PB**

Greenwood

Binks Manufacturing Company, 500 Polk St., Ste. 15, 46143-1629, pg. 229 **PB**

Citizens Bank of Central Indiana, P.O. Box 70, 720 Executive Park Dr., Ste. 3000, 46142-0070, pg. 280 **PB**

Citizens Bank of Central Indiana-Central Region, P.O. Box 70, 720 Executive Park Dr., Ste. 3000, 46142-0070, pg. 280 **PB**

Indiana-American Water Co., Inc., P.O. Box 570, 401 Camby Court, 46142, pg. 95 **PB**

Lockhart Cadillac South, 1287 U.S. 31 S., 46143, pg. 672 **PV**

Mark VII Transportation Company, Inc., 201 S. Emerson Ave., Ste. 130, 46143, pg. 1046 **PB**

Saturn of Greenwood, 1287 U.S. 31 S., 46143, pg. 672 **PV**

Takenaka (U.S.A.) Corporation, Indianapolis Office, 43 South Park Blvd., 46143, pg. 1351 **IT**

Griffith

Bird Treatment Services, 1115 East Ridge Rd., Ste. 342, 46319, pg. 166 **PB**

Hammond

AT&T Customer Information, 2855 N. Franklin Rd., 46322-1635, pg. 10 **PB**

CALUMET CONSTRUCTION CORPORATION, 1247 169th St., 46324, pg. 201 **PV**

DOMBROWSKI & HOLMES, INC., Three 141st St., 46327, pg. 338 **PV**

HAMMOND GROUP INC., P.O. Box 6408, 5231 Hohman Ave., 46325, pg. 498 **PV**

Indiana Harbor Belt Railroad Co., 2721 161st St., 46323-1099, pg. 432 **PB**

Keil Chemical Div., 3000 Sheffield Ave., 46320, pg. 619 **PV**

LaSalle Steel Company, 1412 E. 150th St., 46327, pg. 1181 **PB**

MORRISON, INC., 1830 Summer St., 46320, pg. 762 **PV**

NI-TEX, Inc., 5265 Hohman Ave., 46320, pg. 1185 **PB**

NIPSCO Capital Markets, Inc., 5265 Hohman Ave., 46320, pg. 1185 **PB**

NIPSCO Development Company, Inc., 5265 Hohman Ave., 46320, pg. 1185 **PB**

NIPSCO Energy Services, Inc., 5265 Hohman Ave., 46320, pg. 1185 **PB**

NIPSCO Energy Trading Corporation, Inc., 5265 Hohman Ave., 46320, pg. 1185 **PB**

NIPSCO Exploration Co., Inc., 5265 Hohman Ave., 46320, pg. 1185 **PB**

NIPSCO Fuel Company, Inc., 5265 Hohman Ave., 46320, pg. 1185 **PB**

NIPSCO INDUSTRIES, INC., 5265 Hohman Ave., 46320, pg. 1185 **PB**

Northern Indiana Public Service Company, 5265 Hohman Ave., 46320, pg. 1185 **PB**

Ortman Fluid Power Division, 19th W. 143 St., 46327, pg. 402 **PV**

SCREW CONVEYOR CORP., 700 Hoffman St., 46327, pg. 977 **PV**

Shore Line Shops, Inc., 5265 Hohman Ave., 46320, pg. 1185 **PB**

SMITH MOTORS, INC., 6405 Indianapolis Blvd., 46320, pg. 1009 **PV**

Hartford City

Citizens First State Bank, 101 W. Washington St., 47348, pg. 632 **PB**

Zellerbach Division, 1000 E. Grant St., 47348, pg. 1075 **PB**

Highland

Highland Hydraulics, Inc., 9939 Express Dr., 46322, pg. 127 **PV**

Hyre Electric Company of Indiana, Inc., 2655 Garfield Ave., 46322, pg. 572 **PB**

Reed Minerals, 8149C Kennedy Ave., 46322, pg. 793 **PB**

Hobart

Charter Behavioral Health System of Northwest Indiana, Inc., 101 W. 61st Ave., State Rd. 51, 46342, pg. 1034 **PB**

FRESH FOOD, INC., 1901 E. 37th Ave., 46342-2579, pg. 427 **PV**

Howe

Multi-Plex, Inc., State Rd. 9 N., 46746, pg. 315 **PV**

Huntingburg

DMI Furniture, Inc., 611 Eighth St., 47542, pg. 473 **PB**

DMI Furniture, Inc., 703 N. Chestnut, 47542, pg. 473 **PB**

DMI Furniture, Inc., 12 DMI Ln., 47542, pg. 473 **PB**

DMI Furniture, Inc., 213 W. 1st St., 47542, pg. 473 **PB**

Kimball Flight Operations, 2715 W. 900 South Airport Road., 47542-9628, pg. 957 **PV**

Huntington

First National Bank of Huntington, 354 Jefferson Park Mall, 46750, pg. 674 **PB**

Halliburton Energy Services, P.O. Box 444, 46750-0444, pg. 776 **PB**

Memcor Truohm, 1320 Flaxmill Rd., 46750, pg. 813 **PV**

Noll Printing Corporation, 100 Noll Plaza, 46750, pg. 821 **PB**

OUR SUNDAY VISITOR, INC., 200 Noll Plaza, 46750, pg. 821 **PV**

Square D Co., 6 Commercial Rd., 46750, pg. 1208 **IT**

Wabash Magnetics, P.O. Box 829, 1375 Swan St., 46750-0829, pg. 351 **PB**

Indianapolis

AM General Corporation, 1428 W. Henry St., 46221, pg. 922 **PB**

Abelson-Taylor, Inc., Circle Tower Bldg., Monument Cir., Ste. 622, 46204, pg. 10 **PV**

ACORDIA, INC., 111 Monument Circle, Ste. 3200, 46204, pg. 14 **PV**

Adesa Inc., 310 E. 96th St., Ste. 410, 46240, pg. 1116 **PB**

Allied Security Inc., 3901 N. Meridian St., Ste. 15, 46208, pg. 40 **PV**

Allison Engine Company Inc., P.O. Box 420, S-29, 46206-0420, pg. 1127 **IT**

Allison Transmission, P.O. Box 894, 46206-0894, pg. 719 **PB**

Allright Parking of Indianapolis, Inc., 312 Massachusetts Ave., 46204, pg. 43 **PV**

ALLtimate Catering, 9300 Crosspoint Blvd., 46256-3350, pg. 1049 **PB**

Alro Group, Indianapolis, 5620 Churchman Ave., 46203, pg. 46 **PV**

Ambassadair Travel Club, Inc., 7337 W. Washington St., 46231, pg. 106 **PB**

Amber Tours, Inc., 7337 W. Washington St., 46231, pg. 106 **PB**

Amber Travel, Inc., 7337 W. Washington St., 46231, pg. 106 **PB**

American Cablevision of Indianapolis, Inc., 3030 Roosevelt Ave., 46218, pg. 1610 **PB**

AMERICAN PRECAST CONCRETE, INC., 1030 S. Kitley Ave., 46203, pg. 60 **PV**

American Red Ball Transit Co. Inc., 1335 Sadlier Circle, E. Dr., 46239, pg. 97 **PV**

American States Economy Insurance Co., 500 N. Meridian St., 46207, pg. 997 **PB**

American States Insurance Companies, 500 N. Meridian St., 46204-1275, pg. 997 **PB**

American States Insurance Co. of Texas, 500 N. Meridian St., 46207, pg. 997 **PB**

American States Life Insurance Co., 500 N. Meridian St., 46207, pg. 997 **PB**

American Trans Air Execujet, Inc., 7337 W. Washington St., 46231, pg. 106 **PB**

American Trans Air, Inc., 7337 W. Washington St., 46231, pg. 106 **PB**

American Trans Air Training Corp., 7337 W. Washington St., 46231, pg. 106 **PB**

AMERICAN UNITED LIFE INSURANCE COMPANY, One American Sq., 46204, pg. 64 **PV**

AMTRAN, INC., 7337 W. Washington St., 46231, pg. 106 **PV**

ANACOMP, INC., P.O. Box 40888, 11550 N. Meridian St., Ste. 600, 46240-0888, pg. 106 **PB**

Analysts International, Central Region, 7340 Shadeland Station, Ste. 100, 46256-3919, pg. 110 **PB**

Anthem Blue Cross & Blue Shield, 4040 Vincent Cir., 46268, pg. 76 **PV**

Anthem Health Companies, 5451 W. Lakeview Parkway South Dr., 46268, pg. 76 **PV**

ANTHEM, INC., 120 Monument Cir., 46204, pg. 76 **PV**

APEX PRECISION TECHNOLOGY INC., 2060 Yandes, 46202, pg. 77 **PV**

Arrow/Schweber Electronics, 7108 Lakeview Pkwy. W. Drive, 46268, pg. 134 **PB**

PB - *U.S. Public Companies Volume*
PV - *U.S. Private Companies Volume*
IT - *International Public & Private Companies Volume*

Geographic Index-U.S.

1235

Geographic Index-U.S.

Associated Hosts, Inc., 8910 Purdue Rd., 46268, pg. 215 **IT**

Associated Hosts of California, 8910 Purdue Rd., 46268, pg. 215 **IT**

Associated Hosts of Indiana, 8910 Purdue Rd., 46268, pg. 215 **IT**

Associated Hosts of Texas, Inc., 8910 Purdue Rd., 46268, pg. 215 **IT**

BW Transportation Services, Inc., 4212 W. 71st St., 46268, pg. 228 **PB**

BALDWIN & LYONS, INC., 1099 N. Meridian St., 46204, pg. 169 **PB**

Balkamp, Inc., 2601 Holt Rd., 46241, pg. 732 **PB**

Banc One Indiana Corporation, 111 Monument Cir., 46277, pg. 173 **PB**

Banc One Mortgage Corporation, 333 No. Pennsylvania St., 46277, pg. 175 **PB**

BENJAMIN FRANKLIN LITERARY & MEDICAL SOCIETY, INC., 1100 Waterway Blvd., 46202, pg. 133 **PV**

BEST ACCESS SYSTEMS, 6161 E. 75th St., 46250, pg. 223 **PV**

Beveridge Paper Co., 717 W. Washington St., 46204, pg. 1000 **PB**

Bindley Western Drug Company, 4212 W. 71st St., 46268, pg. 228 **PB**

BINDLEY WESTERN INDUSTRIES, INC., 10333 N. Meridian St., Ste. 300, 46290, pg. 228 **PB**

Boehringer Mannheim Biochemicals Div., 9115 Hague Rd., 46250, pg. 331 **IT**

Boehringer Mannheim Corporation, 9115 Hague Rd., 46250, pg. 331 **IT**

Bridgeport Brass Corporation, 1800 S. Holt Rd., 46251, pg. 1219 **IT**

Brougher Agency, Inc., 525 S. Meridian St., 46225, pg. 464 **IT**

THE BRULIN CORPORATION, 2920 Dr. Andrew J. Brown Ave., 46205, pg. 176 **PV**

Burns & Wilcox - Indianapolis Office, 6801 Lake Plaza Dr., Ste. A-108, 46220, pg. 610 **PV**

CALDWELL VANRIPER, INC., 1314 N. Meridian, 46202, pg. 200 **PV**

Calumet Construction Corporation-Indianapolis Division, 5455 W. 86th St., Ste. 123, 46268-1212, pg. 202 **PV**

Capitol Consolidated, 7034 Brookville Rd., 46226, pg. 233 **IT**

Car Brite, Inc., 1910 S. State St., 46203, pg. 352 **PV**

Carlisle Equipment Co, 7255 W. Washington St., 46241, pg. 211 **PV**

Carrier Corp., 7310 W. Morris, 46206, pg. 1690 **PB**

Carrier Corporation, Residential Products, 7310 W. Morris St., 46231, pg. 1689 **PB**

CENTRAL NEWSPAPERS, INC., 135 N. Pennsylvania St., Ste. 1200, 46204-2400, pg. 326 **PB**

CENTRAL SUPPLY CO., INC., 8900 E. 30th St., 46219, pg. 225 **PV**

Charlotte Community Hospital, 4000 E. Southport Rd., 46237, pg. 404 **PV**

Charter Indianapolis Behavioral Health System, Inc., 5602 Caito Dr., 46226, pg. 1034 **PV**

CHEMCENTRAL/Indianapolis, 5850 W. 82nd St., 46278, pg. 232 **PB**

Children's Better Health Institute, 1100 Waterway Blvd., 46202, pg. 133 **PV**

Cigna Insurance Company of the Midwest, 9200 Keystone Crossing, 46240, pg. 365 **PB**

Cinergy Investments, Inc., 251 N. Illinois St., Ste. 1400, 46204, pg. 369 **PB**

Circle Business Credit, Inc., 8720 Castle Creek Pkwy., Ste. 400, 46250, pg. 1785 **PB**

Circle Freight International USA, 5701 W. Progress Rd., 46241, pg. 371 **PV**

Circle International, 5701 W. Progress Rd., 46241, pg. 371 **PV**

CITIZENS GAS & COKE UTILITY, 2020 N. Meridian St., 46202-0906, pg. 241 **PV**

COLLINS OLDSMOBILE INC., 4080 Lafayette Rd., 46254, pg. 253 **PV**

CONSOLIDATED PRODUCTS, INC., 500 Century Bldg., 36 S. Pennsylvania St., 46204, pg. 436 **PB**

Consolidated Specialty Restaurant, 500 Century Bldg., 36 S. Pennsylvania St., 46204, pg. 436 **PB**

Consumer Marketing Services, Inc., One Indiana Sq., Ste. M220, 46266, pg. 628 **PB**

Corange U.S. Holdings, Inc, 9115 Hague Rd., 46250, pg. 331 **IT**

COUNTRYMARK COOPERATIVE, INC., 950 N. Meridian St., 46204-3909, pg. 279 **PV**

Covance Inc., 8211 SciCor Drive, 46214, pg. 454 **PB**

Crawal, 4001 S. High School Rd., 46241, pg. 177 **PV**

Creswell, Munsell, Fultz & Zirbel, 2123 Pamela Dr., 46220, pg. 1197 **PV**

CROSSMANN COMMUNITIES, INC., 9292 N. Meridian St., Ste. 300, 46260, pg. 461 **PB**

Crown Moving & Storage Inc., 8040 Castleton Rd., 46250, pg. 1171 **PV**

Crown Products, 3401 Newton Ave., 46201, pg. 1014 **PV**

CRYSTAL FLASH PETROLEUM CORP., 5221 Ivy Tech Dr., 46268, pg. 294 **PV**

The Curtis Publishing Company, 1000 Waterway Blvd., 46202, pg. 986 **PV**

D-A Lubricant Co., Inc., 1340 W. 29th St., 46208, pg. 1068 **IT**

Delta Faucet Corporation, 55 E. 111th St., 46280, pg. 1053 **PB**

DeMars Program Management, Inc., 1919 N. Meridan St., 46202, pg. 450 **PV**

DeVilbiss Ransburg Industrial Liquid Systems (IN), 3939 West 56th St., Dock 6, 46254-1597, pg. 865 **PB**

Diamond Chain Company, 402 Kentucky Ave., 46207, pg. 68 **PV**

Dista Products Co., Lilly Corporate Center, 46285, pg. 993 **PB**

Dow Elanco, 9330 Zionsville Rd., 46268, pg. 522 **PB**

Dow Elanco, 9002 Purdue Rd., 46268-1189, pg. 523 **PB**

DowBrands, L.P., 9550 Zionsville Rd., 46268, pg. 523 **PB**

DOWNEY DESIGNS INTERNATIONAL, 2265 Executive Dr., 46241, pg. 342 **PV**

James H. Drew Corp., P.O. Box 68935, 5455 W. 86th St., Ste. 204, 46268, pg. 1084 **PB**

DUKE REALTY INVESTMENTS, INC., 8888 Keystone Crossing, Ste. 1200, 46240, pg. 535 **PB**

Duracell Products Co., P.O. Box 68460, 8002 Allison Ave., 46268-1614, pg. 743 **PB**

E & A INDUSTRIES, INC., 101 W. Ohio, Ste. 1350, 46204, pg. 352 **PV**

E & A Investors, L.P., 101 W. Ohio St., Ste. 1350, 46204, pg. 352 **PV**

EDD-Indianapolis, 6982 Hillsdale Ct., 46250-2040, pg. 205 **PV**

ELCO Management Corporation, Lilly Corporate Center, 46285, pg. 993 **PB**

EPIC, Inc., 55 E. 111th St., 46280, pg. 1053 **PB**

Eby Brown Co., 5820 Fortune Circle, 46251, pg. 359 **PV**

Elanco Animal Health, Lilly Corporate Ctr., 46285, pg. 993 **PB**

Endless Vacation, 3502 Woodview Trail, 46268, pg. 322 **PV**

Energy Realty, Inc., 1630 N. Meridian St., 46202, pg. 875 **PB**

ERMCO, INC., 1631 W. Thompson Rd., 46217, pg. 381 **PV**

EvansGroup, 200 S. Meridian, Ste. 500, 46225, pg. 385 **PV**

Farbest Inc., 950 N. Meridian, 46204, pg. 279 **PV**

Financial Protection Marketing Inc., 7440 N. Shadeland Ave. P.O. Box 501670, 46250, pg. 1336 **PB**

FINISH LINE, INC., 3308 N. Mitthoeffer Rd., 46236, pg. 623 **PB**

Firestone Building Products Company-Beech Grove, 3525 S. Arlington, 46203, pg. 214 **PB**

First Indiana Bank, A Federal Savings Bank, First Indiana Plaza, 135 N. Pennsylvania St., 46204, pg. 1484 **PB**

First Indiana Corporation, 135 N. Pennsylvania, 46204, pg. 1484 **PB**

Frontier Transport Corporation, 1560 E. Raymond St., 46203, pg. 1469 **IT**

Gema, P.O. Box 88220, 46208, pg. 866 **PB**

General Employment Enterprises, Inc., 101 W. Ohio St., Ste. 770, 46204, pg. 714 **PB**

General Employment Enterprises, Inc., 8606 Allisonville Rd., 46250, pg. 715 **PB**

GEUPEL DEMARS, INC., 1919 N. Meridian St., 46206, pg. 449 **PV**

Geupel DeMars, Inc., 1919 N. Meridan St., 46202, pg. 450 **PV**

Ghafari Associates, Inc., 6330 E. 75th St., Ste. 118, 46250, pg. 450 **PV**

GLENROY CONSTRUCTION CO. INC., 450 S. Ritter Ave., 46219, pg. 456 **PV**

GENE B. GLICK COMPANY, INC., 8330 Woodfield Crossing Blvd., Ste. 200, 46240, pg. 457 **PV**

Golden Care Inc., 2431 Directors Row, 46241, pg. 1531 **PV**

Stephen Gould of Indiana, Inc., 8606 Allisonville Rd., Ste. 127, 46250, pg. 467 **PV**

THOMAS L. GREEN & CO., INC., 202 N. Miley Ave., 46222, pg. 477 **PV**

Green Tree Acceptance, Inc., 9245 N. Meridian, 46240, pg. 762 **PB**

GREGG APPLIANCES INC., 4151 E. 96th St., 46240, pg. 479 **PV**

GUIDANT CORPORATION, 111 Monument Cir., 29th Fl., 46204-0906, pg. 768 **PB**

HPS, INC., 8020 Zionsville Rd., 46268, pg. 492 **PV**

HAHN SYSTEMS, INC., 2401 Production Dr., 46241, pg. 493 **PV**

Harbour Water Corporation, 1220 Waterway Blvd., 46202, pg. 1185 **PB**

PAUL HARRIS STORES, INC., 6003 Guion Rd., 46254, pg. 792 **PB**

Paul Harris Stores of Virginia, Inc., 6003 Guion Rd., 46254, pg. 792 **PB**

Healthcare Prescription Services, Inc., 3830 E. Southport Rd., 46237, pg. 405 **PV**

Healthsource Indiana, 225 S.E. St., Ste. 240, 46202, pg. 360 **PV**

Healthsource Indiana Managed Care Plan, Inc., 225 S.E. St., Ste. 100, 46202, pg. 360 **PV**

Hebrew National Kosher Foods Div., 602 W. Ray St., 46225, pg. 429 **PB**

Herff Jones, Fine Papers, 4601 W. 62nd St., 46268, pg. 523 **PV**

HERFF JONES INC., 4501 W. 62nd St., 46268, pg. 523 **PV**

Herff Jones, Jewlery, 4719 W. 62nd St., 46268, pg. 523 **PV**

HIGH POINT OIL CO., 3520 East 96th St., Ste. 1L, 46240, pg. 528 **PV**

HOLCOMB & HOKE MFG. COMPANY, INC., 1545 Van Buren, 46203, pg. 533 **PV**

Hoosier Insurance Company, 8500 Keystone Crossing, Ste. 200, 46240, pg. 346 **PV**

Huber, Hunt & Nichols, Inc., P.O. Box 128, 2450 S. Tibbs Ave., 46241, pg. 548 **PV**

HUBLER CHEVROLET INC., 8220 S. U.S. 31, 46227, pg. 545 **PV**

THE HUNT CORPORATION, 250 E. 96th St., Ste. 415, 46240, pg. 548 **PV**

Hunt International, 250 E. 96th St., Ste. 415, 46240, pg. 548 **PV**

The Hunt Paving Company, Inc., P.O. Box 128, S. Tibbs Ave., 46206, pg. 548 **PV**

Hunt Sports, 250 E. 96th St., Ste. 415, 46240, pg. 548 **PV**

Huntington Bancshares Indiana, Inc., Capital Ctr., 201 N. Illinois St., 46204, pg. 868 **PB**

HURCO COMPANIES, INC., One Technology Way, 46268, pg. 850 **PB**

Hurco Manufacturing Company, One Technology Way, 46268, pg. 850 **PB**

IEI Investments, Inc., 1630 N. Meridian St., 46202, pg. 875 **PB**

IGC Energy, Inc., 1630 N. Meridian St., 46202, pg. 875 **PB**

ITT Educational Services, Inc., 5975 Castle Creek Pkwy.-North Dr., 46250, pg. 1512 **PB**

ITW Micro-Poise Division, P.O. Box 88512, 46208, pg. 865 **PB**

ITW Ransburg Electrostatic Systems, 8227 Northwest Blvd., 46278, pg. 867 **PB**

IWC Resources Corporation, 1220 Waterway Blvd., 46202, pg. 1185 **PB**

IWC Services, Inc., 1220 Waterway Blvd., 46202, pg. 1185 **PB**

IEI Services, LLC, 1630 N. Meridian St., 46202, pg. 875 **PB**

Ikon Office Solutions-Indiana, 7330 Woodland Dr., 46278, pg. 863 **PB**

Indiana Bell Telephone Company, Inc., 240 N. Meridian St., 46204, pg. 98 **PB**

Indiana Broadcasting Co. (WISH), 1950 North Meridian, P.O. Box 7088, 46207, pg. 11 **PB**

Indiana Digital Access, 3030 Roosevelt Ave., 46218, pg. 1610 **PB**

INDIANA ENERGY, INC., 1630 N. Meridian St., 46202-1496, pg. 874 **PB**

Indiana Gas Company, Inc., 1630 N. Meridian St., 46202, pg. 875 **PB**

Indiana Insurance Company, 350 E. 96th St., 46240, pg. 648 **IT**

INDIANAPOLIS LIFE INSURANCE CO., 2960 N. Meridian St., 46208, pg. 560 **PV**

Indianapolis Newspapers, Inc., 307 N. Pennsylvania St., 46204, pg. 326 **PB**

Indianapolis Power & Light Company, One Monument Cir., 46204, pg. 913 **PB**

Indianapolis Water Company, 1220 Waterway Blvd., 46202, pg. 1185 **PB**

Indy Lighting, Inc., 8431 Castlewood Drive, 46250, pg. 935 **PV**

Inland Container-Containerboard Division, 4030 Vincennes Rd., 46268-0937, pg. 1575 **PB**

Inland Container Corporation, 4030 Vincennes Rd., 46268-0937, pg. 1575 **PB**

Intercontinental Corporation, 135 N. Pennsylvania St., Ste 770, 46204, pg. 464 **IT**

Intergraph Corporation, 5881 E. 82nd St., Ste. 105, 46250, pg. 891 **PB**

IPALCO ENTERPRISES, INC., One Monument Cir., 46204, pg. 912 **PB**

JWG Associates, Inc., 151 N. Delaware, Ste. 1115, 46211, pg. 579 **PV**

Earle M. Jorgensen Company/Indianapolis, 2300 S. Tibbs Ave., 46241, pg. 600 **PB**

Kennedy Equipment Co., Inc., 801 E. Sumner Ave., 46227, pg. 614 **PV**

KENNEDY TANK & MANUFACTURING CO., INC., 833 E. Sumner Ave., 46227, pg. 614 **PV**

KENWORTH OF INDIANAPOLIS INC., 2929 S. Holt Rd., 46241, pg. 615 **PV**

Keystone Group, Inc., 5121 E. 65th St., 46220, pg. 981 **PV**

LDI, LTD., 54 Monument Circle, 46204, pg. 639 **PV**

LABSCO, 7721 Records St., 46226, pg. 642 **PV**

ELI LILLY AND COMPANY, Lilly Corporate Ctr., 46285, pg. 992 **PB**

Eli Lilly and Company of India, Inc., Lilly Corporate Ctr., 46285, pg. 993 **PB**

Eli Lilly Asia, Inc., Lilly Corporate Center, 46285, pg. 993 **PB**

Eli Lilly International Corporation, Lilly Corporate Ctr., 46285, pg. 993 **PB**

LILLY INDUSTRIES, INC., 733 S. West St., 46225, pg. 994 **PB**

Lilly Industries, Inc., 546 W. Abbott St., 46206, pg. 994 **PB**

Lilly Industries, Inc., 715 E. Maryland St., 46202, pg. 995 **PB**

Lilly Research Laboratories, Lilly Corporate Ctr., 46285, pg. 993 **PB**

LINSCO Reinsurance Company, 500 N. Meridian St., 46204-1275, pg. 998 **PB**

The Liposome Manufacturing Company, Inc., 6925 Guion Rd., 46268, pg. 1000 **PB**

LOCKHART CADILLAC INC., 5550 N. Keystone Ave., 46220, pg. 672 **PV**

Logo 7, Inc., 8677 Logo 7 Ct., 46219, pg. 1644 **PB**

Lone Star Industries, Inc., 3905 Vincennes Rd., Ste. 400, 46268, pg. 1012 **PB**

Loy Instrument Co., Inc., P.O. Box 19426, 2111 N. Kitley Ave., 46219-0426, pg. 360 **PV**

MSC Corporation, 941 N. Meridian Ave., 46204, pg. 110 **PB**

MSC Indiana Office, 6444 Dover Rd., 48220, pg. 1031 **PB**

Macmillan Computer Publishing USA, 201 W. 103rd St., 46290, pg. 777 **PV**

Macmillan Digital USA, 201 W. 103rd St., 46290, pg. 777 **PV**

Macmillan Publishing USA, 201 W. 103rd St., 46290, pg. 777 **PV**

Major Video Concepts, Inc., 7998 Georgetown Rd., 46268, pg. 639 **PV**

PB - *U.S. Public Companies Volume*
PV - *U.S. Private Companies Volume*
IT - *International Public & Private Companies Volume*

1236

Maplehurst Farms, Inc., 3745 Farnsworth St., 46241, pg. 490 **PB**

MARC Promotion, 5948 N. College Ave., 46220-2554, pg. 701 **PB**

MARSH SUPERMARKETS, INC., 9800 Crosspoint Blvd., 46256-3350, pg. 1049 **PV**

Masco Corporation of Indiana, 55 E. 111th St., 46280, pg. 1053 **PB**

Matrix Technologies, Inc., 6964 Corporate Dr., 46278, pg. 714 **PV**

MAYS CHEMICAL COMPANY, 561 E. 71st St., 46220, pg. 718 **PV**

MCFARLING FOODS, INC., 333 W. 14th St., 46206, pg. 721 **PB**

Medical Education and Research Foundation, 1100 Waterway Blvd., 46202, pg. 133

MERIDIAN INSURANCE GROUP, INC., 2955 N. Meridian St., 46208-4788, pg. 1095 **PB**

Meridian Security Insurance Company, 2955 N. Meridian St., 46208-4788, pg. 1095 **PB**

MICRO-MET L CORP., 3419 Roosevelt Ave., 46218, pg. 742 **PB**

Mid-America Capital Resources, Inc., One Monument Cir., P.O. Box 1595, 46206-1595, pg. 913 **PB**

Mid-America Energy Resources, P.O. Box 1595, One Monument Cir., 46206-1595, pg. 913 **PB**

MILESTONE CONTRACTORS INC., 5950 S. Belmont, 46217, pg. 745 **PV**

Milgray/Indiana, Inc., 5226 Elmwood Ave., 46203, pg. 206 **PB**

MITCHEL & SCOTT MACHINE CO., INC., 1841 Ludlow Ave., 46201, pg. 753 **PB**

NBD Bank (Indiana), One Indiana Square, 46266, pg. 628 **PB**

NBD Brokerage Services, Inc., One Indiana Sq., Ste. 109, 46266, pg. 628 **PB**

NBD Credit Insurance Agency, Inc., One Indiana Sq., Ste. M220, 46266, pg. 628 **PB**

NBD Leasing, Inc., One Indiana Square, 46266, pg. 628 **PB**

NBD Life Insurance Company, One Indiana Sq., Ste. M220, 46266, pg. 628 **PB**

NBD Mortgage Corporation, One Indiana Sq., Ste. M910, 46266, pg. 628 **PB**

NBD Neighborhood Revitalization Corp., One Indiana Sq., Ste. 1620, 46266, pg. 628 **PB**

National Associated Design Co., 8910 Purdue Rd., 46268, pg. 215 **IT**

National City Bank, Indiana, One National City Ctr., Ste. 400E, 46255, pg. 1154 **PB**

National Data Center, 2401 Directors Row, Ste. D, 46241-4933, pg. 648 **IT**

National Infusion Services, Inc., 10610 N. Pennsylvania Ave., Ste. A, 46280, pg. 229 **PB**

NATIONAL RETAIL HARDWARE ASSN., 5822 W. 74th St., 46278, pg. 786 **PV**

NATIONAL WINE & SPIRITS CORP., P.O. Box 1602, 46206-1602, pg. 788 **PV**

Newcourt Financial USA, Inc., 111 Monument Circle, Ste. 300, 46204, pg. 924 **IT**

NOBLE ROMAN'S INC., One Virginia Ave., Ste. 800, 46204, pg. 1187 **PB**

NORTH AMERICAN CAPACITOR CO., 7545 Rockville Rd., 46214, pg. 803 **PV**

North American Roofing Systems, Inc., 6151 W. 80th St., 46278, pg. 803 **PB**

One Investment Agency, Inc., First Indiana Plaza, 135 N. Pennsylvania St., 46204, pg. 1484 **PB**

One Investment Corporation, First Indiana Plaza, 135 N. Pennsylvania St., 46204, pg. 1484 **PB**

One Mortgage Corporation, First Indiana Plaza, 135 N. Pennsylvania St., 46204, pg. 1484 **PB**

One Property Corporation, First Indiana Plaza, 135 N. Pennsylvania St., 46204, pg. 1484 **PB**

Overland Transportation System, Inc., 6500 E. 30th St., 46219, pg. 1469 **IT**

PSI Power Resource Development, Inc., 251 N. Illinois St., Ste. 1410, 46204, pg. 369 **PB**

PSI Power Resource Operations, 251 N. Illinois St., Ste. 1410, 46204, pg. 369 **PB**

Peerless Aire Corporation, 55 E. 111th St., 46280, pg. 1053 **PB**

Peerless Faucet Corporation, P.O. Box 40980, 46280, pg. 1053 **PB**

PENCO-Indiana, 3850 Priority Way, South Dr., 46240, pg. 1508 **IT**

Pentek Corporation, 8502 Brookville Rd., 46239-9427, pg. 352 **PB**

Pepper Construction of Indiana, Inc. LLC, 1850 W. 15th St., 46202, pg. 851 **PV**

Physicians Insurance Company of Indiana, 8425 Woodfield Crossing, Ste. 300, 46240, pg. 1080 **PB**

Pioneer Express Inc., 1560 West Raymond St., 46206, pg. 1469 **PV**

Planes Moving & Storage Of Indianapolis, Inc., 2521 Planes Dr., 46219, pg. 869 **PV**

Praxair Surface Technologies, Inc., 1500 Polco St., 46224, pg. 1320 **PB**

Prime Technology, Inc., 9855 Crosspoint Blvd., Ste. 118, 46256, pg. 884 **PV**

Principal Health Care of Indiana, Inc., One North Pennsylvania, Ste. 300, 46204, pg. 885 **PV**

Productive Business Interiors, 6971 Hillsdale Ct., 46250, pg. 560 **PV**

Protective Insurance Company, 1099 N. Meridian St., 46204, pg. 169 **PB**

RCI Travel, 3502 Woodview Trail, 46268, pg. 322 **PB**

Radio Indianapolis, Inc., 8120 Knue Rd., 46250, pg. 860 **PV**

Red Ball Forwarders, Inc., 1335 Sadlier Circle, E. Dr., 46239, pg. 97 **PV**

Red Ball Leasing, Inc., 1347 Sadlier Circle, E. Dr., 46239, pg. 97 **PV**

Rehabilitative Health Services, Inc., 4000 East Southport Road, 46237-3229, pg. 405 **PB**

REILLY INDUSTRIES, INC., 300 N. Meridian St., Ste. 1500, 46204, pg. 919 **PV**

Reilly Industries Inc., 1500 S. Tibbs, 46241, pg. 919 **PV**

Relm Communications, Inc., 7707 Records St., 46226, pg. 1376 **PB**

Relm Demand Side Management Systems, 7707 Record St., 46226, pg. 1376 **PV**

Resort Condominiums International, 3502 Woodview Trace, 46268-1104, pg. 322 **PB**

Roadrunner Distribution Systems, Inc., 217 S. Belmont Ave., Ste. K, 46222, pg. 911 **PV**

Rollins Hudig Hall of Indiana, Inc., 201 N. Illinois, 46204, pg. 117 **PB**

Rottlund Homes of Indiana, Inc., 662 E. 82nd St., Ste. F, 46250, pg. 1406 **PB**

The Rytex Company, 5850 W. 80th St., 46278, pg. 62 **PB**

SNS Investment Company, 500 Century Bldg., 36 S. Pennsylvania, 46204, pg. 436 **PB**

Sagamore Insurance Company, 1099 N. Meridian St., 46204, pg. 169 **PB**

SANISERV MANUFACTURING CORP., 2020 Production Dr., 46241, pg. 965 **PV**

The Saturday Evening Post Society, 1100 Waterway Blvd., 46202, pg. 133 **PV**

Saturn of Indianapolis, 5333 Pike Plaza Rd., 46254, pg. 672 **PV**

Schwitzer, Inc., 6040 W. 62nd St., 46278, pg. 968 **PB**

SECURITY GROUP INC., 5121 E. 65th St., 46220, pg. 981 **PV**

Seradyn, Inc., 1200 Madison Ave., 46225, pg. 871 **IT**

SERVAAS, INC., 1000 Waterway Blvd., 46202, pg. 986 **PV**

SERVICE SUPPLY CO. INC. OF INDIANA, 603 E. Washington St., 46204, pg. 987 **PV**

Shand Mining Inc., 5595 West 74th St., 46278, pg. 281 **IT**

Shook Indiana Division, 5920 Castleway West Dr., Ste. 106, 46250-1931, pg. 996 **PB**

SIGNATURE INNS, INC., 250 E. 96th St., Ste. 450, 46240, pg. 1473 **PB**

SIMON DEBARTOLO GROUP, INC., 115 W. Washington St., 46204, pg. 1474 **PB**

Smugglers Inn of IL, Inc., 8910 Purdue Rd., 46268, pg. 216 **PB**

THE SOMERSET GROUP, INC., 135 N. Pennsylvania St., Ste. 2800, 46204, pg. 1484 **PB**

STANDARD MANAGEMENT CORPORATION, 9100 Keystone Crossing, Ste. 600, 46240, pg. 1502 **PB**

Steak 'n Shake, Inc., 36 S. Pennsylvania St. #500, 46204, pg. 437 **PB**

Stewart-Warner South Wind Corp., 5701 Fortune Circle S., 46241, pg. 127 **PB**

Stratis Corporation, 5653 W. 73rd St., 46278, pg. 862 **PV**

Sunrise Restaurant Inc., 8910 Purdue Rd., 46268, pg. 216 **IT**

SUPERIOR OIL CO. INC., 400 W. Regent St., 46225, pg. 1055 **PV**

Sysco Food Services of Indianapolis, Inc., 4000 W. 62nd St., 46268, pg. 1551 **PB**

TMP Worldwide-Interactive/Medsearch, On Line Career Ctr., 2780 Waterfront Pkwy. E. Dr., Ste. 100, 46214, pg. 1065 **PB**

Tetra-Pak Processing Systems, 757 E. Murry St., 46227, pg. 1379 **IT**

THOMAS & SKINNER, INC., 1120 E. 23rd St., 46205, pg. 1082 **PV**

Trivoli Systems, 9025 N. River Rd., 46240, pg. 896 **PV**

Truevision, Inc., 7340 Shadeland Station, 46256, pg. 1643 **PB**

URS Greiner, Inc., 546 S. Meridian, Ste. 714, 46225, pg. 1658 **PB**

Underwriters & Management Services Inc., 3600 Woodview Trace, Ste. 301, 46268, pg. 998 **PV**

Uniden Corporation, 9340 Castlegate Drive, 46256, pg. 1433 **IT**

United Chemical Products, 1650 Lueft St., 46222, pg. 718 **PV**

UNITED FARM FAMILY LIFE INSURANCE CO., 225 S. East St., 46202, pg. 1122 **PB**

United Standard Asset Growth Corp., 1311 W. 96th St., 46240, pg. 26 **IT**

Universal Flavors Corp., 5600 W. Raymond St., 46241-0167, pg. 1695 **IT**

Utility Data Corporation, 1220 Waterway Blvd., 46202, pg. 1185 **PB**

VASA Brougher, Inc., 525 S. Meridian St., 46225, pg. 464 **IT**

VASA Care, 525 S. Meridian St., 46225, pg. 464 **IT**

VASA Finance Corp., 525 S. Meridian St., 46225, pg. 464 **IT**

VASA Life Insurance Co., 525 S. Meridian St., 46206, pg. 464 **IT**

Vasa North America, 525 S. Meridian St., 46225-1122, pg. 464 **IT**

VASA North Atlantic Insurance Company, 525 S. Meridian St., 46225, pg. 464 **IT**

VASA Properties I, 525 S. Meridian St., 46225, pg. 464 **IT**

VASA Realty, Inc., 525 S. Meridian St, 46225, pg. 464 **IT**

Video Indiana - WTHR, P.O. Box 1313, 46206, pg. 335 **PV**

Village Pantries, Inc., 9800 Crosspoint Blvd., 46256-3350, pg. 1049 **PB**

WRTV, 1330 No. Meridian St., 46202, pg. 1070 **PB**

WXIN, 1440 N. Meridian St., 46202, pg. 1636 **PB**

Waterway Holdings, Inc., 1220 Waterway Blvd., 46202, pg. 1185 **PB**

WHEATON VAN LINES, INC., 8010 Castleton Rd., 46250, pg. 1171 **PV**

R.O. WHITESELL & ASSOCIATES, INC, 3334 Founders Rd., 46268, pg. 1173 **PV**

F.A. WILHELM CONSTRUCTION CO., INC., 3914 Prospect St., 46203, pg. 1176 **PV**

Willis Corroon Administrative Services Corporation, 3850 Priority Way S. Dr., Ste. 214, 46240, pg. 1504 **IT**

Wood Industries, 5125 W. 78th St., 46268, pg. 944 **PB**

Young Automotive Group, 9190 Priority Way W., Ste. 216, 46240, pg. 1095 **PV**

Zellerbach Division, 5620 Dividend Dr., 46241, pg. 1075 **PB**

Zimmer Custom-Made Packaging Co., 1450 E. 20th St., 46218, pg. 802 **PV**

Zionsville Water Corporation, 1220 Waterway Blvd., 46202, pg. 1185 **PB**

Jasper

Aristokraft, Inc., One Aristokraft Square, P.O. Box 420, 47547, pg. 675 **PB**

Artec Manufacturing, 1037 E. 15th St., 47549-1007, pg. 957 **PB**

BR ASSOCIATES, INC., Der Buro Komplex, 4201-A Mannheim Road, 47546-9618, pg. 107 **PV**

Bosendorfer USA, 1600 Royal St., 47549, pg. 957 **PB**

Citizens Bank of Jasper, P.O. Box 151, 47547-0151, pg. 280 **PV**

Community, 932 Mill St., 47546, pg. 583 **PV**

Corporate Logistics Services, 1805 Dispatch Rd., 47549, pg. 957 **PB**

Decora', One Aristokraft Square, 47546, pg. 675 **PB**

Dubois County Bank, One DCB Plaza, 47547, pg. 1217 **PB**

Jasper Corporation, 2407 Newton St., 47549-1002, pg. 957 **PB**

Jasper Furniture Company, 1180 E. 16th St., 47549-1009, pg. 957 **PB**

Jasper Laminates, 1620 Cherry St., 47549-1004, pg. 957 **PB**

Jasper Plastics, Kimball Industrial Park, 1220 Power Dr., 47549-1016, pg. 957 **PB**

JASPER SEATING CO., INC., P.O. Box 231, 932 Mill St., 47546, pg. 583 **PV**

JOFCO INC., 13th & 402 E. Vine St., 47546, pg. 588 **PV**

Kimball Electronics Group, 1038 E. 15th St., 47549-1003, pg. 957 **PB**

KIMBALL INTERNATIONAL, INC., 1600 Royal St., 47549-1001, pg. 956 **PB**

Kimball Lodging Group, 1180 E. 16th St., 47549-1009, pg. 957 **PB**

Kimball Office Furniture Co., 1600 Royal St., 47549, pg. 957 **PB**

Kimball Upholstered Products, 340 E. 11th Ave., 47549-1005, pg. 957 **PB**

Kimball Upholstered Products, 1710 Kimball Blvd., 47549-1006, pg. 957 **PB**

National Office Furniture Co., 1600 Royal St., 47549, pg. 957 **PB**

NORTH AMERICAN PRODUCTS CORP., 1180 Wernsing Rd., 47546, pg. 803 **PV**

ToolPro, Kimball Industrial Park, 1220 Power Dr., 47549-1017, pg. 957 **PB**

Jeffersonville

American Commercial Lines Inc., 1701 E. Market St., 47130, pg. 284 **PB**

Charter Behavioral Health System of Jefferson, Inc., 2700 River City Park Dr., 47130, pg. 1034 **PV**

Colgate-Palmolive Purchasing, P.O. Box 9, 47131-0009, pg. 397 **PB**

KITCHEN KOMPACT, INC., KK Plaza, 47130, pg. 624 **PV**

NBD Banking Company, 460 Spring St., 47130, pg. 628 **PB**

Vessel Management Systems Company, 1701 E. Market St., 47130, pg. 284 **PB**

Waterway Communications Inc., 1701 E. Market St., 47130, pg. 284 **PV**

Wyandot, Inc., 125 Peacely St., 47130, pg. 1193 **PV**

Kendallville

Albion Wire Inc., Kendallville Wire Division, 811 Commerce Dr., 46755, pg. 526 **PV**

Courier Kendallville, Inc., 2500 Marian Dr., 46755, pg. 453 **PB**

Flint & Walling Industries, Inc., 95 N. Oak St., 46755, pg. 1053 **PV**

GROUP DEKKO, Hwy. 6 & County Rd. 400 E., 46755, pg. 484 **PV**

No-Sag Foam Products Company, 2225 Production Rd., 46755, pg. 986 **PB**

PVC Compounders, 6928 N - 400 E, 46755, pg. 484 **PV**

Pent Assemblies, Inc., US 6 & Cr 400 E, 46755, pg. 484 **PV**

Pent Products, Inc., US 6 & Cr 400 E, 46755, pg. 484 **PV**

Reclaimers, Inc., 6928 N - 400 E, 46755, pg. 1050 **IT**

Silicones, Inc., US 6 & Cr 400 E, 46755, pg. 526 **PV**

Taylor Made, Indiana, P.O. Box 157, 46755, pg. 1071 **PV**

Kentland

ICI Seeds, P.O. Box 67, US Hwy. 24 & 41, 47951, pg. 1524 **IT**

Kingsbury

Roll Coater, Inc., P.O. Box 326, 46345, pg. 137 **PB**

Geographic Index-U.S.

Knox

Indiana Fineblanking Division, P.O. Box 409, 1200 Klockner Dr., 46534, pg. 737   IT

Kokomo

Delco Electronics Corporation, P.O. Box 9005, One Corp. Ctr., 46904-9005, pg. 720   PB
HAYNES INTERNATIONAL, INC., 1020 W. Park Ave., 46904, pg. 801   PB
Kokomo Gas & Fuel Company, 900 East Blvd., 46904-9015, pg. 631   PB
KOKOMO GRAIN CO., INC., 1002 W. Morgan St., 46901, pg. 631   PB
Kokomo Sanitary Pottery Corp., 2500 N. Union St., 46903, pg. 449   PV
Motorola Radius, Semiconductor, 2733 S. Albright Rd., 46902-3996, pg. 1138   PB

Kouts

Merit Steel Company, Inc., Rte. 8, P.O. Box 386, 46347, pg. 986   PV

La Porte

Berkel Incorporated, One Berkel Dr., 46350, pg. 545   IT
Bonnie Baking Co., 800 Boyd Blvd., 46350, pg. 665   PV
Commercial Intertech Distribution Services, 500 Harrison, 46350, pg. 411   PB
HILER INDUSTRIES, 118 Kommler, 46350, pg. 529   PV
Silgan Containers, 300 N. Fail Rd., 46530, pg. 1473   PB
Teledyne Casting Service, 300 Philadelphia St., 46350-0488, pg. 43   PB

Lafayette

Charter Lafayette Behavioral Health System, Inc., 3700 Rome Dr., 47905, pg. 1034   PB
Chemrock Corporation, 1451 State Rd. 25 W., 47905, pg. 903   PV
Consolidated Industries Corp., P.O. Box 7800, Brady Ln. & Concord Rd., 47903, pg. 188   IT
Cox Communications-Lafayette, 325 S. Creasy Ln., 47903, pg. 455   PB
Ice Cream Specialties, Inc., 2600 Concord Rd., 47905, pg. 879   PV
Journal & Courier, 217 N. Sixth St., 47901, pg. 701   PB
Landis & Staefa Inc., P.O. Box 7180, 47903, pg. 800   IT
BOB ROHRMAN AUTO GROUP, 701 Sagamore Pkwy. S., 47905, pg. 940   PV
SCHWAB CORP., 3000 Main St., 47904, pg. 974   PV
A.E. Staley Manufacturing Co., 3300 U.S. 52 Bypass, 47904, pg. 1357   IT
Subaru-Isuzu Automotive, Inc., 5500 State Rd. 38 E., 47903, pg. 523   IT
WABASH NATIONAL CORP., 1000 Sagamore Pkwy. S., 47905, pg. 1730   PB
Warren Industries, Inc., 3200 S. St., 47904, pg. 945   PV

Lagrange

Machine-Rite Products, 1775 E. U.S. 20, 46761, pg. 599   PB

Lanesville

Motorola Radius, P.O. Box 8, 47136-0008, pg. 1138   PB

Laotto

Dekko Technical Center, 11913 E. 450 S., 46763, pg. 484   PV

Lebanon

Bayley/Fan Group, 843 Indianapolis Ave., 46052, pg. 1398   IT

Liberty

Farmers State Bank, 310 N. Main St., 47353, pg. 633   PB

Ligonier

Vibration Automobile Division, 1496 Gerber St., 46767, pg. 428   PV

Logansport

Elco Precision Stamping Div., P.O. Box 660, 46947, pg. 1590   PB
Matthew Warren Inc., 500 E. Ottawa, 46947, pg. 500   PB
SMALL PARTS, INC., 600 Humphrey St., 46947, pg. 1006   PV
United Technologies Control Systems, 131 Godfrey St., 46947-1843, pg. 1690   PB

Madison

GROTE INDUSTRIES, 2600 Lanier Dr., 47250, pg. 483   PV
Holset Engineering Company Ltd., 2971 Michigan Rd., 47250, pg. 468   PB
Rotary Lift, 2700 Lanier Dr., 47250, pg. 521   PB

Marion

Banc One Financial Services, Inc., 1614 N. Baldwin Ave., 46952, pg. 173   PB
Bell Packaging Corporation-Marion Div., 3102 So. Boots St., 46953, pg. 1066   IT
Cambridge Industries, Inc., 1700 Factory Ave., 46952, pg. 202   PV
Chronicle-Tribune, 610 So. Adams St., 46952, pg. 700   PB
Fidelity Federal Savings Bank, 116 W. Fourth S., 46952, pg. 632   PB
GenCorp Vehicle Sealing Div., 1700 Factory Ave., 46952, pg. 706   PB
Property-Owners Insurance Co., 3950 W. Delphi Pike, 46952, pg. 101   PV
Structural Products Division, 3102 S. Boots St., 46953, pg. 1066   IT

Martinsville

OEM Group, 1201 S. Ohio St., 46151, pg. 787   PB

Merrillville

Graphics Systems Division, North Tower, 1000 E. 80th Pl., Ste. 629, 46410, pg. 153   PB
JLW Financial Management Systems, Inc., 1000 E. 80th Pl., 46410, pg. 28   IT
Soabar Graphics Division, North Tower, 1000 E. 80th Pl., Ste. 629, 46410, pg. 153   PB

Mexico

The Sherrill Corp., 1 River Ave., 46958, pg. 298   PV

Michigan City

Anco Products, 402 Royal Rd., 46360, pg. 442   PB
W.E. Anderson Div., P.O. Box 358, 46360, pg. 350   PV
DWYER INSTRUMENTS INC., 102 Highway 212, 46361, pg. 350   PV
HBC Insurance Group, 515 Franklin Sq., 46360-3369, pg. 539   PV
HORIZON BANCORP, 515 Franklin Sq., 46360-3369, pg. 538   PB
Horizon Bank, 515 Franklin Square, 46360-3369, pg. 539   PB
JOSAM COMPANY, P.O. Box T-525 W. U.S. 20, 46360, pg. 300   PV
The Loan Store, Inc., 200 W. 80th, 46360-3369, pg. 539   PV
Love Controls Corporation, 102 Hwy. 212, 46361, pg. 350   PV
Mercoid Div., P.O. Box 258, 46360, pg. 350   PV
Paltier Inc., 1701 Kentucky St., 46360, pg. 638   PV
Sprague Devices, Inc., P.O. Box 389, 46361, pg. 561   PB
Sullair Corporation, 3700 E. Michigan Blvd., 46360, pg. 534   PB
Trans-Apparel Group, 5000 S. Ohio St., 46360, pg. 796   PB
Valve Assemblers & Manufactureres, Inc., P.O. Box 358, 46360, pg. 350   PV
Weil-McLain, 500 Blaine St., 46360-2388, pg. 1676   PB

Middlebury

Abtco, Inc., P.O. Box 509, 46540, pg. 20   IT
Elkhart Capital Corporation, 221 US 20 W., 46540, pg. 1442   PV
Harter, 1451 Harter Dr., 46540, pg. 581   PV
JAYCO INC., 903 S. Main St, 46540, pg. 583   PV
JET, Inc., P.O. Box 460, 46540, pg. 584   PV
Kenco, 0758 County Rd. #2, 46540, pg. 1769   PB
Marlette Homes, Inc., 221 U.S. 20 W., 46540, pg. 1442   PB
SCHULT HOMES CORPORATION, 221 U.S. Hwy. 20 W., 46540, pg. 1442   PB
Schult Homes Corporation, P.O. Box 151, 46540, pg. 1442   PB
Shasta Industries, 14489 U.S. 20, 46540, pg. 388   PB
SYNDICATE SYSTEMS, INC., P.O. Box 70, 410 N. Main St., 46540-0070, pg. 1060   PB
Travelmaster Recreational Vehicles, P.O. Box 631, 46540, pg. 388   PB
Viking Formed Products, Yoder Industrial Park, P.O. Box 319, 300 York Dr., 46540, pg. 388   PB

Milford

Brock Manufacturing, P.O. Box 2000, 46542, pg. 285   PB
CTB, Inc. State Rd. 15 N., 46542, pg. 285   PB
CTB INTERNATIONAL CORP., State Rd. 15 N., 46542, pg. 284   PB
Chore-Time/Brock International, P.O. Box 2000, 46542, pg. 285   PB
Chore-Time Cage Systems, P.O. Box 2000, 46542, pg. 285   PB
Chore-Time Equipment, P.O. Box 2000, 46542, pg. 285   PB

Mishawaka

AM General Corporation, 13200 McInley Hwy., 46545, pg. 922   PB
AM General Corporation, 408 S. Byrkit St., 46544, pg. 922   PV
AmeriSource-Mishawaka Div., 1655 E. 12th St., 46544, pg. 97   PB
B&B MOLDERS, 58471 Fir Rd., So., 46544, pg. 105   PV
Dodge Division, 500 S. Union St., 46544-9990, pg. 1398   PB
Elixir Industries, 5201 Lincoln Way E, 46544, pg. 371   PV
Hewlett-Packard Company, 245 W. Edison, Ste. 150, 46545, pg. 814   PB
JORDAN MOTORS, INC., 609 E. Jefferson Blvd., 46545, pg. 599   PV
National Steel Corporation, 4100 Edison Lakes Pkwy., 46545, pg. 902   IT
Nyloncraft, 616 W. McKinley Hwy., 46545, pg. 599   PB
Patrick Metals, 5020 Lincolnway E., 46544, pg. 1265   PB
QUALITY DINING INC., 4220 Edison Lakes Pkwy., 46545, pg. 1349   PB
Ristance Corporation, 14155 Esther Ave., 46545, pg. 561   PB
SOUTH BEND PLASTICS, INC., 1810 Clover Rd., 46545, pg. 1014   PV
Tellabs Research, 3740 Edison Lake #110, 46545, pg. 1573   PB
Thermoplastics, Inc., 1400 S. Industrial Dr., 46544, pg. 1590   PB

Mitchell

Regal Cutting Tools Div., Metric Industrial Park, 5100 S. Meridian, 47446, pg. 1370   PB

Monroe

Strick Corp., 301 N. Polk St., 46772-9703, pg. 1787   PB

Monroeville

ICI Seeds, 2426 Webster Rd. Rte. One, 46773, pg. 1524   IT

Monticello

Bassett Rotary Tool Co., 710 W. Fisher St., 47960, pg. 617   PB
Dean Foods Company, P.O. Box 850, 904 Main St., 47960, pg. 490   PB
EXCEL CO-OP INC., 210 W. Harrison St., 47960, pg. 387   PV
Monticello Exchanger & Manufacturing, 806 N. First St., 47960, pg. 176   PV

Mooresville

General Shale Products Corp., P.O. Box 96, 46158, pg. 844   IT
Nice Pak Products, Inc., Nice Pak Rd., 41658, pg. 798   PV

Mount Summit

Brooks Foods, Rte. 36, 47361, pg. 887   PV

Mount Vernon

Citizens Bank, Posey County Region, 112 E. Third St., 47620, pg. 281   PB
Mount Vernon Democrat, Box 767, 425 Main St., 47620, pg. 648   PV
People's Bank & Trust Co., 402 Main St., 47620, pg. 1217   PB

Muncie

ALLTRISTA CORPORATION, 345 S. High St., Ste. 200, 47305-2398, pg. 56   PB
Alro Group, Muncie, 2301 S. Walnut St., 47302, pg. 46   PB
BALL CORPORATION, 345 S. High St., 47307-0407, pg. 170   PB
CITY MACHINE TOOL & DIE COMPANY, INC., 1302 E. Washington St., 47305, pg. 241   PV
Consumer Products Company, 345 S. High St., Ste. 201, 47305, pg. 56   PB
Duffy Tool & Stamping, Inc., 3224 Meeker Ave., 47302, pg. 169   PV
Feeny Manufacturing Company, State Rd. Three N., 47308, pg. 963   PB
THE GILBERT COMPANIES, INC., 700 S. Council St., 47305, pg. 453   PB
MAXON CORPORATION, 201 E. 18th St., 47302-4124, pg. 716   PV
McQuick's Oilube, Inc., P.O. Box 46, 47308, pg. 1348   PB
Muncie Newspapers, Inc., 125 S. High St., 47302, pg. 326   PB
Plastic Packaging Company, 1401 E. Memorial Dr., 47302, pg. 57   PB
Power Transformer Division, 3500 S. Cowan Rd., 47307-0448, pg. 4   IT
Power Transformers & Components, 3500 Cowan Rd., 47302, pg. 4   IT
Unitog Rental Facility, 601 E. Main St., 47305, pg. 1693   PB
Witt Company, 2415 S. Walnut St., 47302, pg. 1185   PB

Nappanee

FAIRMONT HOMES, INC., 502 S. Oakland, 46550, pg. 391   PV
Sprague Devices, Inc., 1750 Cheyenne, 46550, pg. 561   PB

New Albany

B-Bar-B Flexible Packaging Systems, 30 E. Tenth St., 47150, pg. 1000 **PB**
BEACH MOLD & TOOL INC., 999 Progress Blvd., 47150, pg. 125 **PV**
Discount Labels, Inc., 4100 Earnings Way, 47151, pg. 70 **PB**
EAS Technologies, Inc., 4345 Security Pkwy., 47151, pg. 331 **PB**
FIRE KING INTERNATIONAL, INC., 101 Security, 47150, pg. 406 **PV**
KAISER WHOLESALE, INC., 415 E. Oak St., 47150, pg. 605 **PB**
Liberty National Bank and Trust Company of Indiana, 120 W. Spring St., 47150, pg. 173 **PB**
Liqui-Box Acquisition Corporation, 30 E. Tenth St., 47150, pg. 1000 **PB**
PNC Bank, 400 State St., 47150, pg. 1243 **PB**
ROBINSON NUGENT, INC., 800 E. Eighth St., 47150, pg. 1394 **PB**
Robinson Nugent, Inc., 800 E. Eighth St., 47150, pg. 1394 **PB**
Robinson Nugent, Inc.-Indiana, 800 E. Eighth St., 47150, pg. 1395 **PB**
SAMTEC INC., 810 Progress Blvd., 47150, pg. 963 **PV**

New Carlisle

AlliedSignal Automotive Proving Grounds, 32104 State Rd. 2, 46552, pg. 51 **PB**
Carris Reels, Inc.-Indiana Div., 300 Michigan, 46552, pg. 215 **PV**
I/N Kote, 30755 Edison Rd., 46552, pg. 879 **PB**
I/N Tek, 30755 Edison Rd., 46552, pg. 879 **PB**

New Castle

Allegheny Ludlum-New Castle, P.O. Box 309, 516 W. State Rd. 38, 47362, pg. 43 **PB**
AMERIANA BANCORP, 2118 Bundy Ave., 47362, pg. 66 **PB**
Ameriana Bank, 2118 Bundy Ave., 47362, pg. 66 **PB**
Ameriana Insurance Agency, 2020 S. Memorial Dr., 47362, pg. 66 **PB**
Avesta Sheffield Holding Co., P.O. Box 370, 549 W. St. Rd. 38, 47362, pg. 221 **IT**
Avesta Sheffield Plate Inc., P.O. Box 370, 47362, pg. 221 **IT**
Indiana Title Insurance Company, 1309 Broad St., 47362, pg. 66 **PB**
Linsco/Private Ledger Brokerage Service, 2118 Bundy Ave., 47362, pg. 66 **PV**
MODERNFOLD, INC., 1711 I Ave., 47362, pg. 755 **PV**
New Castle Chassis Systems Div., 1817 I Ave., 47362, pg. 353 **PB**

New Haven

Superior Linkage Division, 2110 Summit St., 46774, pg. 1111 **PV**

New Paris

Flexsteel Division, P.O. Box 129, 46553, pg. 654 **PB**

New Washington

Power Equipment Supply Company, P.O. Box 190, 47162, pg. 369 **PB**

Newport

First Citizens State Bank, Newport Banking Center, Southeast Corner, Market & Main, 47966, pg. 634 **PB**

Noblesville

Firestone Industrial Products Company-Noblesville Plant, 1700 Firestone Blvd., 46060, pg. 214 **IT**
Indiana Seed Co., Inc., P.O. Box 440, 46060, pg. 646 **PV**
INDUSTRIAL DIELECTRICS, INC., 407 S. Seventh St., 46060, pg. 560 **PV**
Power Con, 94 Ashbourne Circle, 46060, pg. 736 **IT**

North Manchester

Indiana Lawrence Bank, 106 N. Market St., 46962, pg. 633 **PB**

North Vernon

Union Bank & Trust Co., 7 N. Fifth St., 47285, pg. 633 **PB**

North Webster

Dekko Heating Technologies, Inc., Rte. 1 Backwater Rd,. Box 337, 46555, pg. 484 **PV**

Orleans

Citizens Bank of Central Indiana-Orleans Region, P.O. Box 224, 200 S. Maple, 47452, pg. 280 **PB**
PAOLI, INC., 201 East Martin St., 47452, pg. 837 **PV**

Peru

AMERICAN STATIONERY CO., INC., 300 N. Park Ave., 46970-1756, pg. 62 **PV**
BRYAN STEAM CORPORATION, P.O. Box 27, 46970, pg. 176 **PV**
David Levin Co., P.O. Box 164, 46970, pg. 1048 **PV**
Square D Co., 252 N. Tippecanoe, 46970, pg. 1208 **IT**

Pittsboro

Home Telephone Co. of Pittsboro, Inc., 17 W. Main, P.O. Box 189, 46167, pg. 1571 **PB**

Plainfield

Cinergy, 1000 E. Main St., 46168, pg. 369 **PB**
Galyan's Trading Co., 2382 E. Main, 46168, pg. 995 **PB**

Plymouth

BOMARKO, INC., N. Oak Rd., 46563, pg. 156 **PV**
Dean Pickles & Specialty Products, 1430 Western Ave., 46563, pg. 490 **PB**
DoorCraft & Challenge, 2526 N. Western, 46563, pg. 585 **PV**
Dura-Vent, 1177 Markley Dr., 46563, pg. 1267 **IT**
Liquid Coatings & Dispersions Division, 1301 N. Flora St., 46563, pg. 619 **PB**

Portage

Feralloy Processing Company, 6600 U.S. Hwy. 12, 46368, pg. 1070 **IT**
GREAT LAKES PETERBILT, GMC, 5900 Southport Rd., 46368, pg. 475 **PV**
HUNTER CORP., 6000 Southport Rd., 46368, pg. 549 **PV**
Indiana Pickling & Processing Corp., 6600 U.S. Highway 12, 46368, pg. 1070 **IT**

Porter

Smith Environmental Technologies Corp., 800 Canonie Dr., 46304, pg. 1477 **PB**
SoilTech, Inc., 800 Canonic Dr., 46304, pg. 1478 **PB**

Portland

Portland Plant, 700 Industrial Dr., 47371, pg. 1044 **PV**
Teledyne Portland Forge, E. Lafayette St., 47371-0905, pg. 43 **PB**

Princeton

Citizens Bank, Gibson County Region, 101 N. Hart St., 47670, pg. 281 **PB**
Gibson County Bank, 225 N. Hart, 47670, pg. 1217 **PB**
Hansen Corporation, South First St., 47670-2369, pg. 868 **IT**
Hurst Manufacturing, 1551 E. Broadway, 47670, pg. 573 **PV**
Rexam Closures, RR1 Box 100A, Country Rd. 100, 47670, pg. 1106 **IT**

Rensselaer

JASPER COUNTY FARM BUREAU CO-OP ASSOCIATION, INC., Hwy. 231, P.O. Box 238, 47978, pg. 583 **PV**
The Ohio Mattress Company Licensing & Componets Group, P.O. Box 258, 1132 N. Cullen, 47978, pg. 979 **PV**

Richmond

Alchem Plastics Corp.-Indiana, 4815 Woodside Dr., 47375, pg. 1495 **PB**
Alcoa Closure Systems, International, 1701 Williamsburg Pike, 47374, pg. 60 **PB**
Amcast Automotive-Richmond Plant, P.O. Box 1607, 1561 N.W. 11th St., 47374, pg. 63 **PB**
Belden Wire & Cable Company, 2200 U.S. Hwy. 27 S., 47374, pg. 201 **PB**
CARPENTER INDUSTRIES, INC., 1100 Industries Rd., 47374, pg. 215 **PB**
Cinram Inc., 1600 Rich Rd., 47374, pg. 293 **IT**
Color-Box Inc., 623 S. G St., 47374, pg. 347 **PB**
Convenience Stores Distributors, 133 N.W. L St., 47374, pg. 1049 **PB**
Harris Broadcast Division, 3712 National Rd., West, 47374, pg. 791 **PB**
HOFFCO/COMET INDUSTRIES, INC., 358 N.W. F St., 47374, pg. 532 **PV**
Palladium Publishing Corp., 1175 N. A St., 47374, pg. 701 **PB**
Perfect Circle Products Div., P.O. Box 1166, 47375, pg. 479 **PV**
SWAYNE ROBINSON & COMPANY, 214 Main St., 47375, pg. 936 **PV**
RODEFELD CO., INC., 96 W. Main St., 47374, pg. 939 **PV**
Schuller Intl. Inc., 814 Richard Ave., 47374, pg. 927 **PB**
TEC Fab Div., 1480 N.W. 11th St., 47374, pg. 868 **PV**

Ridgeville

Champion Homes Div., P.O. Box 57, 700 N. Portland St., 47380, pg. 332 **PB**

Roachdale

Communications Corp. of Indiana, 127 N. Meridian, P.O. Box 248, 46172, pg. 1571 **PB**

Rochester

Airvac Inc., P.O. Box 528, 4217 N. Old U.S. 31, 46975, pg. 431 **IT**

Rockport

Eck Miller Transportation Corporation, P.O. Box 248, 47635, pg. 911 **PB**
PEERLESS POTTERY, INC., N. Lincoln Ave., 47635, pg. 847 **PV**
Spencer County Journal-Democrat, P.O. Box 6, 541 Main St., 47635, pg. 648 **PV**

Rockville

First Parke State Bank, Rockville Banking Center, U.S. 41 North & Anderson St., 47872, pg. 634 **PB**
Rockville National Bank, 128 W. Ohio St., 47872, pg. 1217 **PB**

Rushville

Fujitsu Ten Corp. of America/Rushville, 616 Conrad Harcourt Way, 46173, pg. 526 **IT**
HERITAGE CO-OP, 210 N. Washington, 46173, pg. 524 **PV**

Saint Joe

Nucor Fasteners, 6730 County Rd. 60, 46785, pg. 1205 **PB**

Salem

Kimball Office Furniture Manufacturing, Kimball Blvd., 47167, pg. 957 **PB**
O.P. LINK HANDLE COMPANY, 403 S. Main, 47162, pg. 668 **PV**
Salem Operations, Rte. 1, Box 178, 47167, pg. 1566 **PB**

Santa Claus

Heritage Hills, P.O. Box 199, Hwy. 162, 47579, pg. 957 **PB**
National Office Furniture Manufacturing, P.O. Box 209, Hwy. 162 S., 47579, pg. 957 **PB**

Scottsburg

Holm Industries, Inc., P.O. Box 450, 47170, pg. 1504 **PB**

Sellersburg

INTERLOCK INDUSTRIES, INC., 7800 State Rd. 60, 47172, pg. 567 **PV**
Metal Sales Manufacturing Corporation, 7800 State Rd. 60, 47172, pg. 567 **PV**
Sellersburg Stone Company, Inc., P.O. Box D, 1019 Utica St., 47172, pg. 459 **PV**

Seymour

Aisin U.S.A. Mfg. Inc., 1700 E. Fourth St., 47274, pg. 39 **IT**
Cummins Engine Company, Inc., 800 E. Third St., 47274, pg. 468 **PB**
Cummins Komatsu Engine Company, 800 E. Third St., 47274, pg. 468 **PB**
Cummins Komatsu Engine Company, 800 E. Third St., 47274, pg. 744 **IT**
R.R. Donnelley Seymour Inc., P.O. Box 385, 709A Ave. E., pg. 518 **PB**
THE JOHN C. GROUB COMPANY INC., 900 A Ave. E, Freeman Field, 47274, pg. 484 **PV**
KOCOLENE OIL CORP., 1725 E. Tipton St., 47274, pg. 629 **PV**
ROSE ACRE FARMS, 6874 N. Base Rd., 47274, pg. 944 **PV**
Schwarz Pharma Manufacturing, Inc., 120 E. Third St., 47274, pg. 1211 **IT**
Seymour Housewares, 885 N. Chestnut St., 47274, pg. 832 **PB**
SEYMOUR MANUFACTURING COMPANY, P.O. Box 248, 47274-0248, pg. 988 **PV**
Shadowood Golf Inc., P.O. Box448, 47274, pg. 629 **PV**
Wal Mart Distribution Center, 2100 E. Tipton St., 47274-3570, pg. 1733 **PB**

Shelbyville

Cambridge Industries, Inc., 501 N. Ridge Dr., 46176, pg. 202 **PV**
K-T Corp., 850 Elston Dr., 46176, pg. 1640 **PB**
KCL CORPORATION, 701 Hodell St., 46176, pg. 603 **PB**

PB - U.S. Public Companies Volume
PV - U.S. Private Companies Volume
IT - International Public & Private Companies Volume

Geographic Index-U.S.

Sheridan

UNITED FEEDS, INC., P.O. Box 108, 46069, pg. 1122   PV

South Bend

AM General Corporation, 105 N. Niles Ave., 46634-7025, pg. 922   PB
AlliedSignal Aircraft Landing Systems, 3520 Westmoor St., 46628-1373, pg. 50   PV
AlliedSignal Controls & Accessories, 717 No. Bendix Drive, 46620, pg. 50   PB
AlliedSignal Transportation Inc., 739 N. Sheridan St., 46619-0898, pg. 51   PB
Alro Group, South Bend, P.O. Box 2319, 2025 S. Main St., 46680-2319, pg. 46   PV
BMK Printing, Inc, 3615 McGill St., 46628, pg. 156   PB
BATTEAST CONSTRUCTION COMPANY, INC., 430 E. LaSalle Ave., 46617, pg. 123   PB
Bosch Braking Systems-North America, 401 N. Bendix Dr., 46634-4001, pg. 204   IT
Calumet Construction Corporation-South Bend Division, 3215 Sugar Maple Ct., Ste. A, 46628, pg. 202   PV
Datalink Systems, LLC, 1818 Commerce Dr., 46624, pg. 647   PB
EWI/South Bend Stamping Division, 601 W. Broadway, 46624, pg. 1014   PV
Environmental Services of America-IN, Inc., 604 S. Scott St., 46601, pg. 546   PV
1ST SOURCE CORPORATION, 100 N. Michigan St., 46634, pg. 638   PB
1st Source Leasing, 100 N. Michigan, 46601, pg. 638   PB
Heraeus/Kulzer, Inc. - Dental Products Div., 4315 South Lafayette Blvd., 46614-2517, pg. 616   IT
Interplastic Molding Products Div., 1545 S. Olive St., 46619, pg. 572   PV
Interstate Glass Co. Inc., 3801 S. Main, 46614, pg. 120   PV
J & B Products, Inc., 755 W. Chippewa Ave., 46614, pg. 399   PV
Key Trust Company of Indiana, National Association, 202 S. Michigan Ave., 46601, pg. 955   PB
Mohawk Flush Doors, Inc.-Commerical Door Plant, 402 N. Sheridan St., 46619, pg. 1067   IT
PETERSEN GRAPHICS GROUP, 2920 W. Sample St., 46619, pg. 856   PB
Raco, Inc., 3902 W. Sample St., 46619, pg. 845   PB
SCHURZ COMMUNICATIONS, INC., 225 W. Colfax Ave., 46626, pg. 973   PV
Society National Bank, Indiana, 202 S. Michigan Blvd., 46601, pg. 954   PB
South Bend Perishables Division, 2107 Western Ave., 46634, pg. 948   PV
South Bend Scrap & Processing, 1305 Prairie Ave., 46613, pg. 1048   PV
SOUTH BEND STAMPING, 601 W. Broadway St., 46601, pg. 1014   PV
Spin-Cast Plastics, Inc., 3300 N. Kenmore St., 46628, pg. 1353   PB
Toro-Wheel Horse, 515 W. Ireland Rd., 46614, pg. 1624   PB
TrustCorp Mortgage Company, 100 E. Wayne St., 46601, pg. 638   PB
Valley American Bank, P.O. Box 328, 101 N. Main St., 46624-0324, pg. 674   PB
Wells Electronics Inc., 1701 S. Main St., 46613, pg. 1241   IT

Speed

ESSROC CEMENT, CORP., Highway 31, 47172, pg. 384   PV

Sullivan

Allomatic Products Company, 609 E. Chaney St., 47882, pg. 1363   PB
Ayrshire Land Company, P.O. Box 490, 47882, pg. 471   PV
First Farmers State Bank, Sullivan Banking Center, 15 S. Main St., 47842, pg. 634   PB

Sunman

Peoples Bank & Trust Company, Hwy. 101 N., 47041, pg. 633   PB

Syracuse

Aero Manufacturing, Inc., 1018 W. Brooklyn St., 46567, pg. 1602   PB
Dutchmen Fold Down Camper Division, 813 W. Brooklyn St., 46567-1432, pg. 1602   PB
RLI Program Underwriters, 12225 State Rd., Ste. 7, 46567, pg. 1356   PV

Tell City

Perry County News, Box 309, 537 Main St., 47586, pg. 648   PV

Terre Haute

Bemis Polyethylene Packaging Div., P.O. Box 905, 47808, pg. 210   PB
Charter Terre Haute Behavioral Health System, Inc., 1400 Crossing Blvd., 47802, pg. 1035   PB
Chicago Cutlery, Inc., 1536 Beech St., 47804, pg. 716   PB
Citizens Bank of Western Indiana, 350 Wabash Ave., 47808, pg. 280   PB
Digital Audio Disc Corp., 1800 N. Fruitridge, 47804-1780, pg. 1284   IT
FIRST FINANCIAL CORPORATION, One Financial Plaza, 47807, pg. 633   PB
GENERAL HOUSEWARES CORP., 1536 Beech St., 47804, pg. 715   PB
HULMAN & COMPANY, 900 Wabash Ave., 47808, pg. 547   PV
Merchants National Bank, 701 Wabash Ave., 47807, pg. 1217   PB
Root Dry Goods Company, Inc., 1 W. Honey Creek Dr. A, 47802, pg. 1090   PB
SHENANGO INDUSTRIES, 1200 College Ave., 47802, pg. 992   PV
Terre Haute First National Bank, One First Financial Plaza, 47807, pg. 634   PB
Tri-Manufacturing, 333 S. 3rd St., 47807, pg. 710   PB
Tri-Remanufacturing, 3390 Locust St., 47803, pg. 710   PB
Wabash Fibre Box Company-Terre Haute Plant, 2000 N. 19th St., 47804, pg. 1170   PV
WESTON PAPER & MANUFACTURING CO., 2001 N. 19th St., 47804, pg. 1169   PV
Weston Paper & Mfg. Co. Mill Div., P.O. Box 539, 2401 Praireton Ave., 47808, pg. 1170   PV

Thorntown

Frontier Communications of Thorntown, Inc., P.O. Box 37, 115 E. Bow St., 46071, pg. 684   PV

Tipton

Steel Parts Corp., Berryman Pike, 46072, pg. 881   PB

Topeka

ALLIED CARBI-TECH, INC., 827 W. Lake St., 46571, pg. 38   PV

Union City

Centennial Transportation Industries, L.P., 350 Deerfield Road, 47390, pg. 1119   PV
UNION CITY BODY COMPANY, L.P., 350 W. Deerfield Rd., 47390, pg. 1118   PV
Union Trust Bank, 211 W. Pearl St., 47390, pg. 633   PB

Upland

AVIS INDUSTRIAL CORPORATION, 1909 S. Main St., 46989, pg. 102   PV
The Pierce Co., Inc., 201 N. 8th St., 46989, pg. 102   PV

Valparaiso

MB Manufacturing, 213 State Rd. 49 South, 46383, pg. 300   PV
McGill Mfg. Co. Bearing Division, 909 No. Lafayette, 46383, pg. 573   PV
McGill Manufacturing Company, Inc., 909 N. Lafayette St., 46383, pg. 573   PV
McGill Mfg. Co., Inc. Electrical Division, 1002 No. Campbell St., 46383, pg. 573   PB
Pinnacle Bank, 56 S. Washington St., 46383-5598, pg. 1297   PB
PowderTech Corporation, 5103 Evans Ave., 46383, pg. 878   IT
Ugimag Inc., 405 Elm St., 46383, pg. 1029   IT
Union Electric Steel Corp., 3702 Montdale Park Dr., 46383, pg. 104   PB
URSCHEL LABS INCORPORATED, P.O. Box 2200, 46384, pg. 1129   PV

Van Buren

WEAVER POPCORN COMPANY, INC., 130 E. Main St., 46991, pg. 1156   PV

Versailles

Ohio Rod Products Company, Inc., 1415 S. Benham Rd., 47042, pg. 370   PV

Vevay

National Attorneys' Title Assurance Fund, Inc., 306 W. Pike St., 47043-1136, pg. 98   PV
Vevay Deposit Bank, 102 W. Main St., 47043, pg. 633   PB

Vincennes

Citizens Bank, Vincennes Region, 2400 Hart St., 47591, pg. 281   PB
Gemtron Corporation, 2000 Chestnut St., 47591, pg. 1523   IT
Lewis Vincennes, Inc., 3114 Old Decker Rd., 47591, pg. 665   PV
Security Bank & Trust Co., 20 N. Third St., 47591, pg. 1217   PB
Southwest IN Regional Youth Village, Vincennes Industrial Pk., 1700 Theobald Ln., 47591, pg. 451   PB
Vincennes Newspapers, Inc., 702 Main St., 47911, pg. 326   PB
VINCENNES STEEL CORP., P.O. Box 236, 47591, pg. 1141   PV

Wabash

Diehl Machines, 981 S. Wabash St., 46992-0465, pg. 944   PB
FORD METER BOX COMPANY, 775 Manchester Ave., 46992-0443, pg. 418   PV
Markhon Industries, Inc, 200 Bond St., 46992, pg. 614   PV
Martin-Yale Industries, Inc., 251 Wedcor Dr., 46992, pg. 591   PB
Wabash Alloys Division, P.O. Box 466, 46992, pg. 264   PV
Wabash Magnetics, 1450 First St., 46992, pg. 351   PV
Wabash Valley Landfill Company Ltd., 1151 Manchester Ave., 46992, pg. 1380   PB

Wakarusa

Holiday Rambler, 606 Nelson's Pkwy., 46573, pg. 1123   PV
UTILIMASTER CORP., 65266 State Rd. 19, 46573, pg. 1130   PV

Waldron

Home Telephone Co., Inc., P.O. Box 68, 46182, pg. 1571   PB

Walkerton

American Door Company of Michigan, Inc., P.O. Box 1, 111 Muskin Ave., 46574, pg. 1067   IT
Walkerton, 104 Industrial Pk. Rd., 46574, pg. 1176   PB

Wanatah

Wanatah Trucking Co., US Hwy. 30 W., 46390, pg. 1726   PB

Warsaw

BIOMET, INC., Airport Industrial Pk., 46580, pg. 231   PB
DA-LITE SCREEN COMPANY, INC., 3100 N. Detroit St., 46580-0137, pg. 306   PV
DePuy, Inc., 700 Orthopedic Dr., 46581, pg. 331   IT
First National Bank of Warsaw, 102 S. Buffalo St., 46580, pg. 674   PB
The Flexaust Co., Boggs Indus. Park, 46580, pg. 394   PB
Stephen Gould of Indiana, Inc., 2176 Biomet, Ste. 3, 46580, pg. 467   PV
LAKELAND FINANCIAL CORPORATION, 202 E. Center St., 46580, pg. 975   PB
Warsaw Mfg. Division, P.O. Box 837, 2801 W. Old Rte. 30, pg. 519   PB
Zimmer, Inc., Boggs Industrial Park, 46580, pg. 254   PB
Zimmer Orthopaedic Implant Division, 715-727 N. Detroit St., 46580, pg. 254   PB

Washington

United Southwest Bank, 204 E. Main St., 47501, pg. 1217   PB
Washington Plant, 227 Front St., P.O. Box 108, 47501, pg. 1620   PB

Waterloo

Nucor Building Systems, 305 Industrial Pkwy., 46793, pg. 1205   PB

West Baden Springs

Springs Valley Mfg., 8331 W. St. Rd. 56, 47469, pg. 957   PB

West Lafayette

GREAT LAKES CHEMICAL CORPORATION, One Great Lakes Blvd., 47906, pg. 760   PB
Microelectronics, 1201 Cumberland Ave., 47906, pg. 286   PB
WLFI-TV, P.O. Box 2618, 47906-2618, pg. 148   PV

Westfield

Callahan Enterprises, P.O. Box 367, 1122 E. 169th St., 46074, pg. 566   IT
STANDARD LOCKNUT, INC., 1045 E. 169th St., 46074, pg. 1031   PV

Whiting

Amoco Oil Refinery, 2815 Indianapolis Blvd., 46394-2197, pg. 103   PB

Williamsport

The Citizens State Bank, 106 N. Monroe St., 47993, pg. 1217   PB

Winchester

SILVER TOWNE L.P., 120 E. Union City Pike, 47394, pg. 1000   PV

PB - U.S. Public Companies Volume
PV - U.S. Private Companies Volume
IT - International Public & Private Companies Volume

1240

Winona Lake

Warsaw Orthopedic Inc., 100 Publishers Dr., 46590, pg. 1482   **PB**

Yorktown

YORKTOWN TOOL & DIE CORPORATION, 2101 S. West St., 47396, pg. 1196   **PV**

IOWA

Adair

ADAIR FEED & GRAIN COMPANY, 1200 Broad St., 50002-3855, pg. 16   **PV**
Crawford & Crawford, Inc., 1200 Broad St., 50002, pg. 16   **PV**

Afton

Dekko Heating Technologies, Inc., 1924 High School Dr., 50830, pg. 484   **PV**

Albia

A.Y.M. Inc., 1701 Hwy. 5 S., 52531, pg. 721   **PV**

Algona

Algona Food Equipment Co., P.O. Box 280, 50511, pg. 840   **PB**

Amana

Amana Farms, Inc., P.O. Box 189, 52203, pg. 48   **PV**
Amana-Nordstrom Motel Co., P.O. Box 189, 52203, pg. 48   **PV**
AMANA SOCIETY, INC., 506 39th Ave., 52203, pg. 48   **PV**
Amana Society Service Co., 708 49th Ave., 52203, pg. 48   **PV**

Ames

Brenton Savings Bank, FSB, 424 Main St., 50010, pg. 251   **PB**
PMI, 620 Arrasmith Tr., 50010, pg. 1089   **PV**
Piper Jaffray Inc., 402 Main St., 50010-6150, pg. 1301   **PB**
Sargent Metal Fabricating, 650 Arrasmith Tr., 50010, pg. 1089   **PV**
Sauer-Sundstrand Company, 2800 E. 13th St., 50010, pg. 1198   **IT**
TODD & SARGENT, INC., 620 Arrasmith Tr., 50010-9022, pg. 1089   **PV**
U.S. Filter Co., Ames, 600 Arrasmith Trail, 50010-9710, pg. 61   **PB**

Anamosa

LeFebure Electronic Assembly, P.O. Box 1, Old Dubuque Rd., 52205, pg. 387   **IT**

Ankeny

CASEY'S GENERAL STORES, INC., P.O. Box 3001, One Convenience Blvd., 50021-8045, pg. 312   **PB**
John Deere Des Moines Works, P.O. Box 1595, 50021, pg. 492   **PB**
Mercantile Bank of Ankeny, P.O. Box 17, 305 S. Ankeny Blvd., 50021, pg. 1087   **PB**
Perishable Distributors of IA, 2741 PDI Place, 50021, pg. 551   **PV**
Sunrise Dairy, 1440 S.E. Cortina, 50021, pg. 551   **PV**
Tone Brothers Inc., 2301 S.E. Tone's Dr., 50021-8888, pg. 237   **IT**

Aplington

O's Gold Seed Co., Rte. Two, 50604, pg. 1048   **IT**

Armstrong

ART'S-WAY MANUFACTURING CO., INC., P.O. Box 288, Hwy. 9 W., 50514, pg. 136   **PB**

Atlantic

The Clarinda Company, 1209 Sunnyside Lane, 50022, pg. 206   **PV**

Bettendorf

BEE LINE COMPANY, 2700 62nd St., 52722, pg. 129   **PV**
Fireman's Fund Insurance Co. of Iowa, 3740 Utica Ridge Rd., 52722, pg. 59   **IT**
Indeco, Inc., 630 E. River Dr., 52722, pg. 591   **PV**
Riverside Products Div., 225 33rd St., 52722, pg. 1008   **PV**
The Schebler Co., Hwy. 67 & Fenno Rd., 52722, pg. 366   **PV**
Sivyer Steel Corporation, 225 33rd. St., 52722, pg. 1008   **PV**
Willis Corroon Administrative Services Corporation, Alpine Office Centre, 2435 E. Kimberly Rd., Ste. 270-S, 52722, pg. 1504   **IT**

Boone

FAREWAY STORES, INC., 2300 E. Eighth St., 50036, pg. 393   **PV**
Mercantile Bank, P. O. Box 519, 724 Story St., 50036, pg. 1087   **PB**
Quinn Machine & Foundry, 1518 E. 12th St., 50036, pg. 571   **PV**

Burlington

Antennacraft Co., P.O. Box 1005, 52601, pg. 1560   **PB**
BURLINGTON BASKET CO., 922 Bluff Rd., 52601, pg. 183   **PV**
Burlington Timber Co., 922 Bluff Rd., 52601, pg. 183   **PV**
CHITTENDEN & EASTMAN CO., 401 S. Roosevelt, 52601, pg. 237   **PV**
Eastman House Of Alabama, Inc., 401 S. Roosevelt, 52601, pg. 238   **PV**
Eastman House Of California, Inc., 401 S. Roosevelt, 52601, pg. 238   **PV**
Iowa Industries Inc., P.O. Box 768, 3009 Sylvania Dr., 52601, pg. 442   **PB**
Mason & Hanger, P.O. Box 63, 52535-0063, pg. 711   **PV**
Murray Turbomachinery Corporation, 1106 Washington St., 52601, pg. 1110   **PV**
Vista Bakery, Inc., 3000 Mt. Pleasant, 52601, pg. 977   **PB**

Carroll

ICI Seeds, Rte. Two, Box 92A, 51401, pg. 1524   **IT**

Carter Lake

OWEN INDUSTRIES, INC., Fifth & Ave. H, 51510, pg. 824   **PV**
USSI, 2200 Abbott Dr., 51510, pg. 1629   **PB**

Cedar Falls

AG SERVICES OF AMERICA, INC., 2302 W. First St., 50613, pg. 6   **PB**
Blackhawk, 118 Blackhawk Ln., 50613, pg. 1176   **PB**
CMI Metro Pave, 115 E. 19th St., 50613, pg. 279   **PB**
TOP AIR MANUFACTURING, INC., 317 Savannah Park Rd., 50613, pg. 1621   **PB**
Viking Pump, Inc., 406 State St., 50613, pg. 862   **PB**

Cedar Rapids

AEGON USA, Inc., 4333 Edgewood Rd., N.E., 52499-0010, pg. 26   **IT**
APACHE HOSE & BELTING COMPANY, INC., 4805 Bowling St., S.W., 52404, pg. 76   **PV**
Arrow/Schweber Electronics, 375 Collins Rd., N.E., 52402, pg. 134   **PB**
Avionics & Communications, 350 Collins Rd. N.E., 52498, pg. 1397   **PB**
Cedarapids, Inc., 916 16th St., N.E., 52402, pg. 1365   **PB**
Cox Communications-Cedar Rapids, 6300 Council St., N.E., 52402, pg. 454   **PB**
Creswell, Munsell, Fultz & Zirbel, L.P., 4211 Signal Ridge Rd., N.E., 52402, pg. 1197   **PV**
DecisionMark, 200 Second Ave. S.E., Ste. 300, 52401, pg. 442   **PV**
THE GAZETTE COMPANY, 500 Third Ave. S.E., 52401, pg. 442   **PV**
The Gazette Marketing, 621 Fourth Ave. S.E., 52401, pg. 442   **PV**
Genencor International, Inc., 1000 41st Avenue Dr., S.W., 52404, pg. 349   **IT**
Hawkeye Holding, Inc., 4333 Edgewood Rd. N.E., 52499, pg. 27   **IT**
Hewlett-Packard Company, 4050 River Center Ct., 52402, pg. 442   **PB**
HIGHWAY EQUIPMENT COMPANY, 616 D Ave., N.W., 52405, pg. 529   **PV**
IES INDUSTRIES INC., 200 First St. S.E., 52401, pg. 855   **PB**
IES Investments Inc., P.O. Box 351, 200 First St. S.E., 52401, pg. 855   **PB**
IES Transportation, Inc., P.O. Box 351, 200 First St. S.E., 52406, pg. 855   **PB**
IES Utilities Inc., P.O. Box 351, 200 First St. S.E., 52406, pg. 855   **PB**
Industrial Energy Applications, P.O. Box 351, 200 First St. S.E., 52406, pg. 855   **PB**
Interactive Media, Inc., 500 Third Ave. S.E., 52401, pg. 442   **PV**
Iowa Farmer Today, 500 Third Ave. S.E., 52401, pg. 442   **PV**
Iowa Precision Industries, 5480 Sixth St. S.W., 52404, pg. 1100   **PB**
KCRG Radio & TV Stations, Second Ave. at 5th St., 52401, pg. 442   **PV**
KGAN-TV, 600-602 Old Marion Rd., N.E., 52406, pg. 439   **PV**
LARKEN INC., 3330 Southgate Ct. S.W., 52404, pg. 651   **PV**
LeFebure Corp., 308 29th St. N.E., 52402, pg. 387   **IT**
LinkUSA Corporation, 230 Second Ave. S.E. Ste. 400, 52401, pg. 684   **PB**
Longview Fibre Co. Central Container Div., 1601 Blair's Ferry Rd. N.E., 52406, pg. 1014   **PB**
LOOMIS BROTHERS, INC., 1619 F. Ave., N.E., 52406, pg. 675   **PV**
MCLEODUSA INCORPORATED, Town Center, 221 3rd Ave., S.E., Ste. 500, 52401, pg. 1073   **PB**

Mercantile Bank of Cedar Rapids, 129 16th Ave. S.W., 52406, pg. 1088   **PB**
MET-COIL SYSTEMS CORP., 5486 Sixth St. S.W., 52404, pg. 1099   **PB**
Midland Forge Division, 101 50th Ave. S.W., 52404, pg. 406   **PB**
National Propane Corp., 200 First St., Ste. 700, 52401, pg. 1635   **PB**
Norand Mobile Systems Div., 550 Second St., S.E., 52401, pg. 1699   **PB**
PDM Steel Service Center-Cedar Rapids, 155 50th Ave. S.W., 52404, pg. 1305   **PB**
Penford Products Co., 1001 First St., S.W., 52404, pg. 1269   **PB**
Penny Saver, 621 Fourth Ave. S.E., 52401, pg. 442   **PV**
Roush Products Co., Inc., 1000 Wenig Rd., NE, 52402, pg. 411   **IT**
Square D Company, 3700 Sixth St. S.W., 52406, pg. 1208   **IT**
Svedala Industries-Universal Engineering, 800 First Ave. N.W., 52405, pg. 1326   **IT**
D.C. TAYLOR CO., 312 29th St., N.E., 52402, pg. 1070   **PV**
UNITED FIRE & CASUALTY COMPANY, 118 Second Ave. S.E., 52407, pg. 1677   **PB**
United Life Insurance Company, P.O. Box 73909, 52401, pg. 1677   **PB**
Vigortone AG Products, Inc., 5264 Council St. N.E., 52406-1230, pg. 1357   **IT**
Williams Fastener & Supply Co., P.O. Box 74678, 52407, pg. 1178   **PV**

Charles City

Salsbury Chemicals, Inc., 1205 11th St., 50616-0486, pg. 297   **PB**
Salsbury Laboratories, Inc., 2000 Rockford Rd., 50616, pg. 1277   **IT**
Solvay Animal Health, Inc., 2000 Rockford Rd., 50616, pg. 1278   **IT**

Chariton

Mercantile Bank of Chariton, 917 Braden Ave., 50049, pg. 1088   **PB**

Clarence

Cenex/Land O'Lakes, Inc., P.O. Box 248, 1655 140th St., 52216-0248, pg. 646   **PV**

Clarinda

The Clarinda Company, 220 No. 1st St., 51632, pg. 206   **PV**
NSK-AKS Precision Ball Company, 1100 N. First St., 51632, pg. 903   **IT**

Clarion

HAGIE MANUFACTURING CO., 721 Central Ave. W., 50525, pg. 493   **PV**
Palco MFG., Hwy. 3 E., 50525, pg. 493   **PV**

Clinton

Champion Int'l. Corp., P.O. Box 859, 52732, pg. 334   **PB**
CUSTOM PAK, INC., 86 16th Ave. N., 52732, pg. 298   **PV**
Mercantile Bank of Clinton County N.A., 405 S. Third St., 52732, pg. 1088   **PB**
Midwest Poly, PO Box 3023, 52732, pg. 298   **PV**
The Lamson & Sessions Co., 1001 S. Second St. & Tenth Ave., 52733, pg. 976   **PB**

Clive

Graphic Arts Supply Division, 10730 Hickman Rd., 50325, pg. 205   **PB**
PDM Water, 9550 Hickman Rd., 50325, pg. 1304   **PB**
Reames Foods Inc., 8665 Harbach, 50053, pg. 977   **PB**

Columbus Junction

IBP-Louisa County, 52738, pg. 852   **PB**

Conrad

RITCHIE INDUSTRIES, INC., 120 S. Main, 50621, pg. 933   **PV**

Coon Rapids

ICI Seeds, P.O. Box 300, 615 Main St., 50058, pg. 1524   **IT**

Coralville

Advertiser, 106 First Ave., 52242, pg. 442   **PV**
HEARTLAND EXPRESS, INC., 2777 Heartland Dr., 52241-7321, pg. 803   **PB**
Stanley Enviromental, Inc., 2656 Crosspark Rd., 52241, pg. 1033   **PV**

Council Bluffs

ConAgra Frozen Foods, 1023 Fourth St., 51501, pg. 427   **PB**

PB - *U.S. Public Companies Volume*
PV - *U.S. Private Companies Volume*
IT - *International Public & Private Companies Volume*

Geographic Index-U.S.

FUTURE FOAM, INC., 1610 Avenue N, 51501, pg. 433   **PV**
IBP-Council Bluffs, 2700 23rd Ave., 51501, pg. 852   **PB**
Mercantile Bank of Council Bluffs, P.O. Box 68, 333 W. Broadway, 51501, pg. 1088   **PB**
STUART ENTERTAINMENT INC., 3211 Nebraska Ave., 51501, pg. 1526   **PB**
Timpte, Inc., 2801 23rd Ave., 51501, pg. 1088   **PV**

Cresco

Donaldson Co., Inc., P.O. Box 429, 111 Donaldson Ct., 52136, pg. 517   **PB**

Creston

Gits Manufacturing Company, Inc., R.R. 2, Box 47, Highway 34 E., 50801-8900, pg. 1705   **PB**
Wellman Dynamics Corp., P.O. Box 147, U.S. Rte. 34 E., 50801, pg. 612   **PB**

Davenport

BWI Kartridg Pak, 807 W. Kimberly Rd., 52806, pg. 130   **IT**
Big A Auto Parts, 225 W. 35th St., 52804, pg. 10   **PB**
E.J. Brach, Inc., 4371 Boies Ave., 52808, pg. 163   **PV**
John Deere Davenport Works, P.O. Box 4198, 52808, pg. 492   **PB**
Green Tree Acceptance, Inc., P.O. Box 8081, 52809, pg. 762   **PB**
Hewlett-Packard Company, 4440 Brady St., Ste. #103, 52806, pg. 814   **PB**
Iowa-American Water Co., P.O. Box 979, 230 E. Second St., 52805, pg. 95   **PB**
Earle M. Jorgensen-Specialty Tubing Div., 3116 W. 73rd St., 52806, pg. 600   **PV**
Lafarge Corp, Davenport, 220 Emerson Pl., Ste. 300, 52801, pg. 788   **IT**
LEE ENTERPRISES, INCORPORATED, 215 N. Main St., Ste. 400, 52801-1924, pg. 983   **PB**
Litton Instruments & Life Support, 2734 Hickory Grove Rd., 52804-1299, pg. 1003   **PB**
Missouri Portland Cement Holding, 220 Emerson Pl., Ste. 300, 52801, pg. 788   **IT**
Nichols Aluminum, 1725 S. Rockingham Rd., 52808, pg. 1350   **PB**
Nichols-Homeshield, 201 W. 2nd St., Ste. 420, 52801-0186, pg. 1350   **PB**
Nichols-Homeshield Casting, 2101 J.M. Morris Blvd., 52802, pg. 1350   **PB**
Piper Jaffray Inc., 1409 E. Kimberly Rd., 52807-1923, pg. 1303   **PB**
Quad-City Times, 124 E. Second St., 52801, pg. 984   **PB**
Republic Automotive Parts Sales, Inc., 220 W. 53rd St., 52806, pg. 1378   **PB**
Solar Plastics-Quad Cities, 1924 Comenitz Dr., 52802, pg. 1129   **PV**
The Walling Co., Inc., 4122 W. Rusholme, 52804, pg. 360   **PV**

De Witt

Ennis Midwest Div., P.O. Box 30, 52742, pg. 583   **PB**

Decorah

DECO PRODUCTS CO., 506 Sanford St., 52101, pg. 320   **PV**
Watlow Infrared Company, Freeport Industrial Pk., 52101, pg. 1153   **PV**

Denison

IBP-Denison, P.O. Box 397, 51442, pg. 852   **PB**

Des Moines

AE Farms, Inc., 700 Corning, 50313, pg. 72   **PV**
ADVENTURE LANDS OF AMERICA, INC., Interstate 80 & Hwy. 65, 50316, pg. 22   **PV**
AID Finance, 701 5th Ave., pg. 39   **PV**
ALLIED MUTUAL INSURANCE COMPANY, 701 Fifth Ave., 50391-2000, pg. 39   **PV**
Allied Tire, 5201 N.E. 15th St., 50313, pg. 39   **PV**
American Life & Casualty Insurance Co., 405 Sixth Ave., 50309, pg. 433   **PV**
American Life Holding Corp., 1400 Des Moines Bldg., 50309, pg. 432   **PV**
AMERICAN MUTUAL LIFE HOLDING CO., 611 Fifth Ave., 50309, pg. 59   **PV**
American Natl. Can Co., 1500 E. Aurora, 50313, pg. 1029   **IT**
AMERICAN REPUBLIC INSURANCE CO., 601 Sixth Ave., 50301, pg. 61   **PV**
AmerUS Life, 611 Fifth Ave., 50309, pg. 59   **PV**
ANDERSON ERICKSON DAIRY COMPANY, 2229 Hubbell Ave., 50317, pg. 72   **PV**
Better Homes and Gardens Books, 1716 Locust St., 50309-3400, pg. 1094   **PB**
Better Homes and Gardens Magazine, 1716 Locust St., 50309-3023, pg. 1094   **PB**
Better Homes and Gardens Real Estate Service, 2000 Grand Ave., 50309-3379, pg. 1094   **PB**
Better Homes and Gardens Special Interest Publications, 1716 Locust St., 50309-3023, pg. 1094   **PB**
Better Homes and Gardens Wood Magazine, 1912 Grand Ave., 50309-3023, pg. 1094   **PB**

Brenton Bank, 400 Locust St., Ste. 200, 50309, pg. 251   **PB**
BRENTON BANKS, INC., Capital Square, 400 Locust St., Ste. 200, 50309, pg. 251   **PB**
Browning-Ferris Industries of Iowa, Inc., 4487 Delaware St., 50313, pg. 263   **PB**
BUDGET MARKETING, INC., 1171 Seventh St., 50306, pg. 178   **PV**
CMF&Z Public Relations, P.O. Box 4807, 50306, pg. 1197   **PV**
Cablevision VII, Inc., 2300 Center Sq., 50309, pg. 1555   **PB**
Cablevision II, Inc., 2300 Center Sq., 50309, pg. 1161   **PB**
Capital Resources Group, Ltd., 400 Locust St., Ste 300, 50309, pg. 1161   **PV**
Central Tractor Farm & Country, Inc., 3915 Delaware Ave., 50313, pg. 237   **PV**
Communications Data Services, Inc., 1901 Bell Ave., 50315, pg. 517   **PV**
Corn States Hybrid Service, Inc., 2505 McKinley Ave., 50321, pg. 1124   **PB**
COUNTEC Recycling Systems Division, 443 S.W. 6th St., 50309, pg. 1318   **PB**
Country America Magazine, 1716 Locust St., 50309, pg. 1094   **PB**
Country Home Magazine, 1716 Locust St., 50309-3023, pg. 1094   **PB**
Craftways Corp., 1716 Locust St., 50309, pg. 1094   **PB**
Cybus Capital Markets, 520 Walnut St., 50309, pg. 769   **PV**
Dee Zee Mfg., Inc., 1572 N.E. 58th Ave., 50313, pg. 976   **PV**
Des Moines Mfg. Division, 5701 S.W. Park Ave., 50321-1250, pg. 518   **PV**
Des Moines Register & Tribune Co., 715 Locust St., 50304, pg. 700   **PB**
Des Moines Tire, 120 S.W. Fifth St., 50309, pg. 947   **PB**
EMC Insurance Companies, P.O. Box 712, 717 Mulberry Street, 50303, pg. 545   **PB**
EMC INSURANCE GROUP, INC., 717 Mulberry St., 50309, pg. 545   **PB**
EAGLE IRON WORKS, 129 E. Holcomb Ave., 50313, pg. 354   **PV**
Equitable Life Insurance Company of Iowa, 604 Locust St., 50309, pg. 647   **IT**
Equitable of Iowa Companies, 909 Locust St., 50309-2899, pg. 647   **IT**
Equity FC, Ltd., 711 High St., 50392, pg. 885   **PV**
FARMERS MUTUAL HAIL INSURANCE CO. OF IOWA, 2323 Grand Ave., 50312, pg. 395   **PV**
Farmland Mutual Insurance Company, 1963 Bell Ave., 50315, pg. 789   **PV**
Firestone Agricultural Tire Company, 730 E. Second St., 50309, pg. 214   **IT**
Firestone Agricultural Tire Company-Des Moines, 2nd Ave. & Hoffman Ln., 50315, pg. 214   **IT**
Firstar Corporation-Iowa, 520 Walnut St., 50306, pg. 643   **PB**
Florist Distributing, 2403 Bell Ave., 50321, pg. 551   **PV**
FRYETECH, INC., 10550 New York Ave., 50322, pg. 430   **PV**
Golf for Women, 1716 Locust St., 50309, pg. 1094   **PB**
Graham Construction Corp., 500 Locust St., 50309, pg. 468   **PV**
GRAHAM GROUP, INC., 500 Locust St., 50309, pg. 468   **PV**
Heritage Cablevision, Inc., 2300 Financial Ctr., 50312, pg. 1555   **PB**
Insta-Pro International, Ltd., 10301 Dennis Dr., 50322, pg. 1104   **PV**
International Travel Associates Corp., 400 Locust, Ste. 400, 50309, pg. 555   **PV**
Invista Capital Management Inc., Hub Tower, 699 Walnut St., 50309, pg. 885   **PV**
THE IOWA PACKING CO., 1800 Maury St., 50317, pg. 575   **PV**
IOWA PAINT MFG. COMPANY, INC., 17th St. & Grand Ave., 50309, pg. 575   **PV**
JP Foodservice, Inc.-Des Moines, 2500 Dixon St., 50316, pg. 918   **PB**
KCCI Television, Inc., 888 Ninth St., 50309-1288, pg. 1343   **PB**
KRAGIE/NEWELL, 2633 Fleur Drive, 50321, pg. 634   **PV**
Laboratory Supply Company, 6390 N.E. 14th St., 50313, pg. 642   **PV**
Locust Street Securities, Inc., 909 Locust St., 50306, pg. 885   **PV**
Lomar Distributing, P.O. Box 1800, 50301, pg. 551   **PV**
MWR Telecom Inc., 201 S.E. 1st St., 50309, pg. 1073   **PB**
Mail Order Book Sales, 1716 Locust St., 50336, pg. 1094   **PB**
Mercantile Bank of Iowa, 222 Equitable Bldg., 604 Locust St., 50309-3723, pg. 1087   **PB**
Mercantile Investment & Trust Services, 431 E. Locust St., 50309, pg. 1088   **PB**
Merck Medco Managed Care, 6109 Willowmere Dr., 50321-1230, pg. 1091   **PB**
MEREDITH CORPORATION, 1716 Locust St., 50309-3023, pg. 1094   **PB**
Meredith List Marketing, 1716 Locust St., 50309, pg. 1094   **PB**
Meredith Publishing Group, 1716 Locust St., 50309, pg. 1094   **PB**
Meredith Publishing Services, 1716 Locust St., 50309, pg. 1094   **PB**
Meredith Video Publishing, 1716 Locust St., 50309, pg. 1094   **PB**
Meta Farm, 10215 Dennis Dr., 50322, pg. 1104   **PV**
MidAmerican Capital Company, 666 Grand Ave., 50309, pg. 1109   **PB**
MIDAMERICAN ENERGY HOLDINGS, 666 Grand Ave., 50309, pg. 1109   **PB**

Midwest Capital Group, 666 Grand Ave., 50309, pg. 1109   **PB**
Midwest Living Magazine, 1716 Locust St., 50309-3023, pg. 1094   **PB**
Mothers Back Issues, Inc., P.O. Box 10941, 50340, pg. 1056   **PV**
Mother's Bookshelf, P.O. Box 10941, 50340, pg. 1056   **PV**
Norwest Bank Iowa, N.A., Seventh & Walnuts Sts., 50309-4012, pg. 1202   **PB**
Norwest Financial Business Credit, Inc., 219 Eighth St., 50309, pg. 1202   **PB**
Norwest Financial, Inc., 206 Eighth St., 50309, pg. 1202   **PB**
Norwest Financial Leasing, Inc., 206 Eighth St., 50309, pg. 1202   **PB**
Norwest Mortgage, Inc., 450 S.W. Fifth St., 50322, pg. 1202   **PB**
Optimage Interactive Services Co., 1900 N.W. 114th St., 50322, pg. 1054   **IT**
PHI Marketing Services, P.O. Box 1111, 7100 N.W. 62nd Ave., 50131-98111, pg. 1299   **PB**
Patrician Associates, Inc., 711 High St., 50309, pg. 885   **PV**
Frank Paxton Lumber Company, 1400 Market Street, 50303, pg. 585   **PV**
Peoples Abstract Co., 510 Locust St., 50309, pg. 626   **PV**
Petula Associates, Ltd., 711 High St., 50309, pg. 885   **PV**
PIONEER HI-BRED INTERNATIONAL, INC., 800 Capital Sq., 400 Locust St., 50309-2340, pg. 1298   **PB**
Pioneer International Operations Division, 800 Capital Sq., 400 Locust St., 50309-2340, pg. 1299   **PB**
Piper Jaffray Inc., 700 Walnut St., Ste. 1300, 50309-3800, pg. 1301   **PB**
Pirelli Armstrong Midwest Division, P.O. Box 1616, 2345 E. Market St., 50306, pg. 1058   **IT**
Principal Development Associates, Inc., 711 High St., 50309, pg. 885   **PV**
Principal Financial Advisors, Inc., 711 High St., 50392-3480, pg. 885   **PV**
THE PRINCIPAL FINANCIAL GROUP, 711 High St., 50392-0150, pg. 885   **PV**
Principal International, Inc., 50392-0001, pg. 886   **PV**
Principal Investors Corporation, 711 High St., 50392, pg. 886   **PV**
Principal Marketing Services, Inc., 711 High St., 50309, pg. 886   **PV**
Principal Mutual Life Insurance Co., 711 High St., 50309-0001, pg. 886   **PV**
Principal Residential Mortgage, Inc., 711 High St., 50392-0820, pg. 886   **PV**
Principal Spectrum Associates, Inc., 711 High St., 50392, pg. 886   **PV**
Princor Financial Services Corporation, 711 High St., 50309, pg. 886   **PV**
Princor Management Corporation, 711 High St., 50309, pg. 886   **PV**
Rain and Hail Insurance Services Inc., Regency West 1, 1501 50th St., Ste. 200, 50265, pg. 365   **PV**
Republic Automotive Parts Sales, Inc., P.O. Box 3349, 1685 E. Euclid, 50316-0349, pg. 1378   **PB**
SofTechnics Retail Management Systems, 10550 New York Ave., Suite C, 50322-3775, pg. 1012   **PV**
STEELWORKS, INCORPORATED, 1500 Delaware Ave., 50317, pg. 1039   **PV**
Successful Farming Magazine, 1716 Locust St., 50309, pg. 1094   **PB**
SuperValu, Inc.-Des Moines Div., 3900 N.W., 106th St., 50322, pg. 1540   **PB**
Titan Tire Corporation, P.O. Box 1616, 2345 E. Market St., 50317, pg. 1618   **PB**
TOWNSEND ENGINEERING CO., 2425 Hubbell Ave., 50317, pg. 1094   **PV**
Traditional Home, 1716 Locust St., 50309, pg. 1094   **PB**
TRIPLE F, INC., 10104 Douglas Ave., 50322, pg. 1104   **PV**
USG Annuity & Life Company, P.O. Box 617, 50303, pg. 647   **IT**
Uniroyal Chemical Co., Inc., 1701 48th St., Ste. 102, 50265, pg. 460   **PB**
Village Distributors, Inc., 800 Second Ave., Ste. 300, 50309, pg. 1161   **PV**
Vulcan Construction Company, 400 Locust St., Ste. 300, 50309, pg. 1161   **PV**
WHO-TV, 1801 Grand Ave., 50309, pg. 1174   **PB**
WEEKS AND LEO CO., INC., 4000 N. W. 100th, 50322, pg. 1158   **PV**
THE WEITZ COMPANY, INC., Capital Square, 400 Locust St., Ste. 300, 50309, pg. 1160   **PV**
The Weitz Company, Inc., 800 2nd Ave., 50309, pg. 1161   **PV**
Younkers, Inc., 701 Walnut St., 50397, pg. 1334   **PB**

Dubuque

Antique Trader Publications, 100 Bryant St., 52003, pg. 649   **PV**
Barnstead/Thermolyne Corporation, 2555 Kerper Blvd., 52001, pg. 1545   **PB**
Corrugated Packaging, 2150 Kerper Blvd., 52001, pg. 737   **PB**
Eagle Window & Door, Inc., 375 E. Ninth St., 52001, pg. 67   **PB**
FDL Foods, Inc., 701 E. 16th St., 52001, pg. 396   **PV**
Flexsteel Division, Jackson & Ruby Sts., 52001, pg. 654   **PB**
FLEXSTEEL INDUSTRIES, INC., Brunswick Ind. Block, 52001, pg. 653   **PB**
Frommelt Industries, 4343 Chavenelle Rd., 52004-1200, pg. 933   **PV**
IPC Development Co., 1000 Main St., 52001, pg. 910   **PB**
INTERSTATE POWER COMPANY, 1000 Main St., 52001-0769, pg. 910   **PB**

PB - *U.S. Public Companies Volume*
PV - *U.S. Private Companies Volume*
IT - *International Public & Private Companies Volume*

1242

Geographic Index-U.S.

A.Y. MCDONALD INDUSTRIES, INC., 4800 Chavenelle Rd., 52002, pg. 721 **PV**
A.Y. McDonald Mfg. Co., 4800 Chavenelle Rd., P.O. Box 508, 52004-0508, pg. 721 **PV**
A.Y. McDonald Supply Co. Inc., 4800 Chavenelle Rd., 52002, pg. 721 **PV**
Mercantile Bank of Dubuque, N.A., 270 W. Seventh St., 52004, pg. 1088 **PB**
Metz Baking Co., 25 Main St., P.O. Box 446, 52001, pg. 1022 **PV**
VALLET FOOD SERV INC., 1230 E. 12th St., 52001, pg. 1131 **PV**

Dyersville

All American Homes of Iowa Inc., 1551 15th Ave., S.E., 52040, pg. 388 **PB**
The Ertl Company, Inc, P.O. Box 500, Hwy. 136 & 20, 52040, pg. 1684 **PB**

Eddyville

Ajinomoto U.S.A., Inc., Iowa Plant, One Ajinomoto Dr., 52553, pg. 40 **IT**
Heartland Lysine, Inc., Heartland Dr., 52553, pg. 40 **IT**

Eldridge

BAWDEN CORPORATION, 400 S. 14th Ave., 52748, pg. 124 **PV**
Bawden Printing, Inc., 400 S. 14th Ave., 52748, pg. 124 **PV**

Ellsworth

UNCLE B'S BAKERY, INC., 441 Dubuque St., 50075, pg. 1664 **PB**

Estherville

Golden Sun Feeds, Inc., Box 517, Hwy. Four S., 51334-0517, pg. 895 **PV**

Fairfield

DEXTER COMPANY, 2211 W. Grimes, 52556, pg. 329 **PV**
HAWTHORNE COMMUNICATIONS, INC., 300 N. 16th St., 52556, pg. 512 **PV**

Forest City

Winnebago Acceptance Corp., 605 W. Crystal Lake Rd., 50436, pg. 1772 **PB**
Winnebago Health Care Management Company, 605 W. Crystal Lake Rd., 50436, pg. 1772 **PB**
WINNEBAGO INDUSTRIES, INC., 605 W. Crystal Lake Rd., 50436, pg. 1772 **PB**
Winnebago International Corp., 605 W., 50436, pg. 1772 **PB**
Winnebago R.V., Inc., 605 W. Crystal Lake Rd., 50436, pg. 1772 **PB**

Fort Dodge

Cenex/Land O'Lakes, Inc., 2827 Eighth Ave. S., 50501, pg. 646 **PV**
Frontier Communications of Iowa, Inc., 600 First Ave., 50501, pg. 683 **PB**
Gypsum Board & Gypsum Joint Systems, R. R. 4, P.O. Box 758, 50501, pg. 737 **PB**
NEW COOPERATIVE INC., 2626 First Ave. S., 50501, pg. 792 **PV**
Sanofi, 2116 Eighth Ave. S., 50501-5427, pg. 446 **IT**

Fort Madison

Sheaffer Inc., 301 Ave. H, 52627, pg. 542 **IT**
Sheaffer Inc., 301 Avenue H, 52627, pg. 542 **IT**

Garner

Iowa Mold Tooling Co., 500 Highway 18 W., 50438, pg. 894 **PB**

Glenwood

Opinion-Tribune, P.O. Box 191, 116 So. Walnut St., 51534, pg. 648 **PV**
Unitog Rental Facility, 505 Nuckolls Rd., 51534, pg. 1693 **PB**

Greene

Iowa Northern Railroad, 17177 N. Laurel Pike Dr., Ste. 423, 50636, pg. 575 **PV**

Grimes

Heartland Pantry, 11500 N.W. 54th Ave., 50111, pg. 551 **PV**
Mrs. Grimes Foods, 512 N. Main St., 55435, pg. 394 **PV**

Grinnell

Donaldson Co., Inc., P.O. Box 717, South East St., 50112, pg. 517 **PB**

Golden Sun Feeds, Inc., 1006 Industrial Ave., 50112, pg. 895 **PV**
Wolverine Technologies Inc., P.O. Box 685, 50112, pg. 1171 **IT**

Hamburg

Vogel Popcorn Company, P.O. Box 69, 2301 Washington St., 51640, pg. 427 **PB**

Harlan

Wilson Seeds Inc., 1408 Hwy. 44, 51537, pg. 646 **PV**

Houghton

Brower Equipment, Hwy. 16 West, 52631, pg. 511 **PV**
HAWKEYE STEEL PRODUCTS, INC., 609 Main, 52631, pg. 511 **PV**

Hull

THE FOREIGN CANDY CO., INC., 451 Black Forest Rd., 51239, pg. 418 **PV**

Humboldt

The Chantland Company Division, P.O. Box 69, Hwy. 169, 50548, pg. 830 **IT**
Mercantile Bank of Humboldt County, 701 Sumner Ave., 50548, pg. 1088 **PB**

Ida Grove

MIDWEST INDUSTRIES, INC., Hwy. 59 & 175, 51445, pg. 744 **PV**

Indianola

Herschel Adams, 1301 N. 14th St., 50125, pg. 35 **PB**

Iowa City

Iowa Service Center, 1165 S. Riverside Dr., 52246, pg. 829 **PV**
NCS Information Technology & Measurements Division, 2510 N. Dodge St., 52240-4448, pg. 1155 **PB**
Press-Citizen Company, Inc., 319 E. Washington St., 52244, pg. 701 **PB**
Protein Blenders, 2420 Old Hwy., 218 S., 52244, pg. 1116 **IT**
Rexam Release, 2000 Industrial Park Rd., 52240, pg. 1107 **IT**

Iowa Falls

Riverside Book & Bible House, Inc., 1500 Riverside Dr., 50126, pg. 598 **PV**

Jefferson

The Jefferson Division, 208 E. Central St., 50129, pg. 349 **PB**

Johnston

Green Meadows, Ltd., 5608 Merle Hay Rd., 50131, pg. 1299 **PB**

Keokuk

Headco Machine Works, Inc., Box 969, Main Street Rd., 52632, pg. 127 **PV**
Midwest Carbide Corporation, P.O. Box 607, 365 Carbide Lane, 52632, pg. 33 **PB**
Nitrous Oxide Corp. (Donora), P.O. Box 607, 365 Carbide Ln., 52632, pg. 33 **PB**
ROQUETTE AMERICA INC., P.O. Box 6647, 52632, pg. 944 **PV**
Schlegel Naao, 3200 Main St., 52632-2259, pg. 128 **IT**
United Cities Gas Co., Great River Div., 10th & Johnson St., 52632, pg. 146 **PB**

Lake Mills

Fleetguard Inc., 311 N. Park, 50450, pg. 468 **PB**

Lansing

Blumenthal/Lansing Company, 1929 Main St., 52151, pg. 1187 **PB**

Laurens

Positech Corporation, Rush Lake Rd., 50554, pg. 406 **PB**

Le Mars

HARKER'S DISTRIBUTION, INC., 801 Sixth St., S.W., 51031, pg. 502 **PV**

Maquoketa

Dynagear Oil Pumps, Inc., 140 Jacobson Rd., 52060-3208, pg. 350 **PV**

Golden Sun Feeds, Inc., 305 Pershing Rd., 50260, pg. 895 **PV**
Mercantile Bank of Maquoketa, 120 S. Main, 52060, pg. 1088 **PB**

Marquette

Bituma Corporation, 508 Hwy. 18 W., 52158, pg. 705 **PB**

Marshalltown

Fisher Controls International, Inc., 205 S. Center St., 50158, pg. 573 **PB**
Mercantile Bank of Marshalltown, P.O. Box 717, 123 W. Main, 50158, pg. 1088 **PB**
Swift Independent Packing Co., 402 N. 10th Ave., 50158, pg. 427 **PB**

Mason City

Cenex/Land O'Lakes, Inc., 1609 19th St. S.W., 50401, pg. 646 **PV**
Curries Company, 525 Ninth St. S.E., 50401, pg. 18 **IT**
Curtis 1000, Inc., 1319 18th St., 50401, pg. 70 **PB**
David Manufacturing Company (DMC), 1600 12th St., N.E., 50401, pg. 436 **PV**
Globe-Gazette, 300 N. Washington, 50401, pg. 983 **PB**
IMI Cornelius, Inc. (IA), 2421 15th St. S. W., 50401, pg. 646 **IT**
Northwestern States Portland Cement, 1840 N. Federal, 50401, pg. 628 **IT**
Piper Jaffray Inc., 20 E. State St., 50401-3318, pg. 1302 **PB**

Monticello

Corrugated Packaging, 823 N. Cedar St., P.O. Box 266, 52310, pg. 736 **PB**
Energy Mfg. Co., 204 Plastic Lane, 52310, pg. 194 **PV**
Star Building Systems, 101 W. South St., 52310, pg. 1394 **PB**

Mount Ayr

Mercantile Bank of Mount Ayr, P.O. Box 426, 101 S. Fillmore, 50854, pg. 1088 **PB**

Mount Pleasant

Ceco Building Systems-Midwestern Region, P.O. Box 72, Iris Rd., 52641, pg. 221 **PV**
Garretson Equipment Co., Inc., P.O. Box 111, 52641, pg. 1300 **PV**
Heatilator Inc., 1915 W. Saunders Rd., 52641, pg. 772 **PB**
Wal Mart Distribution Center, 1501 Maple Leaf Dr., 52641-1482, pg. 1733 **PB**
XLM Company, 1917 W. Saunders Rd., 52641, pg. 772 **PB**

Muscatine

BANDAG, INCORPORATED, 2905 N. Hwy. 61, 52761-5886, pg. 177 **PB**
Equipment Manufacturing Plant, 6501 49th St. S., Muscatine Indus. Park, 52761, pg. 177 **PB**
Grain Processing Corp., 1600 Oregon St., 52761, pg. 1134 **PV**
The HON Co., 200 Oak St., 52761, pg. 772 **PB**
The HON Co. Systems Furniture Plant, Hwy. 61 North, 52761, pg. 772 **PB**
HON INDUSTRIES INC., 414 E. Third St., 52761-7109, pg. 772 **PB**
Kent Feeds Inc., 1600 Oregon St., 52761, pg. 1134 **PV**
Muscatine Holdings, Inc., 2905 N. Hwy. 61, Bandag Ctr., 52761, pg. 177 **PB**
Muscatine Journal, 301 E. Third St., 52761, pg. 984 **PB**
NAC Inc., 2905 N. Hwy. 61, Bandag Ctr., 52761, pg. 177 **PB**
Ring King Visibles, Inc., P.O. Box 599, 52761, pg. 460 **IT**
THE STANLEY CONSULTANTS GROUP, Stanley Bldg., 225 Iowa Ave., 52761, pg. 1032 **PV**
Stanley Consultants, Inc., Stanley Bldg., 225 Iowa Ave, 52761, pg. 1033 **PV**
Stanley Design-Build, Inc., Stanley Bldg., 225 Iowa Ave., 52761, pg. 1033 **PV**
Thermice Corporation, P.O. Box 356, 52761, pg. 1341 **PB**
Vakuum Vulk, Inc. U.S., 2905 N. Hwy. 61, Bandag Ctr., 52761, pg. 177 **PB**
VARIED INVESTMENTS, INC., 1600 Oregon St., 52761, pg. 1134 **PV**

Newton

Jenn-Air, 403 W. Fourth St. N., 50208, pg. 1064 **PB**
Maytag Company, One Dependability Sq., 50208, pg. 1064 **PB**
MAYTAG CORPORATION, 403 W. Fourth St. N., 50208, pg. 1064 **PB**
Maytag Financial Services Corp., 403 W. 4th St., N., 50208, pg. 1065 **PB**
Mercantile Bank of Jasper County, P.O. Box 1166, 112 W. Second St. S., 50208, pg. 1088 **PB**
THE VERNON COMPANY, One Promotion Pl., 50208-0600, pg. 1137 **PV**

Northwood

Fieldstone Cabinetry Inc., P.O. Box 109, Hwy. 105 E., 50459, pg. 1053 **PB**

PB - *U.S. Public Companies Volume*
PV - *U.S. Private Companies Volume*
IT - *International Public & Private Companies Volume*

Geographic Index-U.S.

1243

Fieldstone Transportation Company, P.O. Box 109, Hwy. 105 E., 50459, pg. 1053   **PB**

Oelwein

Donaldson Co., Inc., 301 Fifth Ave., S.W., 50662, pg. 517   **PB**

Onawa

Mercantile Bank of Onawa, P.O. Box 319, 1030 Tenth St., 51040, pg. 1088   **PB**

Osceola

Dekko Automotive Technologies Iowa Assemblies Div., Hwy. 34 W., 3330 W. McLane, 50213, pg. 484   **PV**

Oskaloosa

Clow Valve Div., S. Second St., 52577, pg. 725   **PV**
Piper, Jaffray & Hopwood, Inc., 716 A Ave. W., 52577-2032, pg. 1300   **PB**

Ottumwa

Ottumwa Courier, 213 E. Second St., 52501, pg. 984   **PB**

Pella

Mercantile Bank of Pella, P.O. Box 147, Broadway at Franklin, 50219, pg. 1088   **PB**
PELLA CORPORATION, 102 Main St., 50219, pg. 848   **PV**
Pella Travel Inc., 701 Main St., 50219, pg. 555   **PB**
Van Gorp Corp., 1410 W. Washington St., 50219, pg. 573   **PB**
VERMEER MANUFACTURING COMPANY, 2411 Hwy. 102, 50219, pg. 1137   **PV**

Perry

IBP-Perry, RR 2, Box 7, 50220, pg. 852   **PV**

Postville

AlliedSignal Laminate Systems, N.E. Cty Rd., 52162, pg. 51   **PB**

Ralston

WEST CENTRAL COOPERATIVE, P.O. Box 68, 51459, pg. 1163   **PV**

Red Oak

Douglas & Lomason Company, 2700 N. Broadway, 51566, pg. 830   **IT**
Red Oak Express, P.O. Box 377, 2012 Commerce Dr., 51566, pg. 648   **PV**

Rock Rapids

Mercantile Bank of Lyon County, P.O. Box 631, 203 S. Second Ave., 51246, pg. 1088   **PB**

Shenandoah

EARL MAY SEED & NURSERY L.C., 208 N. Elm St., 51603, pg. 356   **PV**

Sibley

Mercantile Bank of Osceola County, N.A., 248 Ninth St., 51249, pg. 1088   **PB**

Sioux Center

Groschopp, Inc., 420 15th St. NE, 51250, pg. 559   **IT**

Sioux City

BC Hydrotile Machinery Co., 111 S. George St., 51102, pg. 571   **PV**
INTERNATIONAL PIPE MACHINERY CORP., 111 S. George St., 51102, pg. 571   **PV**
IRVING F. JENSEN CO., INC., 2220 Hawkeye Dr., 51102, pg. 586   **PV**
McCracken, 111 S. George St., 51102, pg. 571   **PV**
Missouri Valley Steel Co., 1300 Division St., 51105, pg. 824   **PV**
Piper Jaffray Inc., 700 Fourth St., Ste. 100, 51101-1743, pg. 1302   **PB**
SIOUX HONEY ASSOCIATION, 301 Lewis Blvd., 51101, pg. 1003   **PV**
Sioux Tools, Inc., 2901 Floyd Blvd., 51102, pg. 1480   **PB**
Siouxland Galvanizing Corp., 2301 Bridgeport Dr., 51111, pg. 656   **PV**
Solar Plastics-Sioux City Division, 1658 Riverside Blvd., 55109, pg. 1129   **PV**
TERMINAL GRAIN CORP., 518 8th St., 51101, pg. 1077   **PV**
TERRA INDUSTRIES, INC., Terra Centre, 600 Fourth St., 51102, pg. 1581   **PB**
Terra International, Terra Centre, 600 Fourth St., 51102, pg. 1581   **PB**

Slater

Garst Seed Company, 2369 330th St., 50244, pg. 1524   **IT**
ICI Seeds, P.O. Box 500, 300 30th St., 50244, pg. 1524   **IT**

South Amana

Limagrain Genetics Corp., P.O. Box 29A, Rte. 1, 52334, pg. 566   **IT**

Spencer

Piper Jaffray Inc., Four E. Fourth St., 51301, pg. 1303   **PB**

Spirit Lake

Abu Garcia Inc., 1900 18th St., 51360-1099, pg. 822   **PV**
Berkley, Inc., 1900 18th St., 51360-1099, pg. 822   **PV**
OUTDOOR TECHNOLOGIES GROUP, 1900 18th St., 51360-1099, pg. 822   **PV**

Storm Lake

IBP-Storm Lake, P.O. Box 669, 50588, pg. 852   **PV**
Piper Jaffray Inc., 304 E. Fifth St., Ste. 2312, 50588-2312, pg. 1302   **PB**
Vigorena Feeds, Inc., P.O. Box 1205, West Hwy. #7, 50588, pg. 1116   **IT**

Tipton

Mercantile Bank of Tipton, P.O. Box 70, 52772, pg. 1088   **PB**

Urbandale

Continental Western Insurance Company, 11201 Douglas Ave., 50322, pg. 215   **PB**
Rottlund Homes of Iowa, Inc., 2928 104th St., 50322, pg. 1406   **PB**

Vinton

Mercantile Bank of Vinton, P.O. Box 112, 110 W. Fourth, 52349, pg. 1088   **PB**

Washington

Mercantile Bank of Washington County, N.A., P.O. Box 7, 300 S. Iowa Ave., 52353, pg. 1088   **PB**
Washington Manufacturing Company, Inc., P.O. Box 486, 800 E. Seventh St., 52353, pg. 612   **PB**

Waterloo

John Deere Engine Works, 400 Westfield Ave., 50701, pg. 492   **PB**
John Deere Waterloo Works, 400 Westfield Ave., 50701, pg. 492   **PB**
GMAC Mortgage Corporation of Iowa, 3451 Hammond Ave., 50702-5345, pg. 720   **PB**
IBP-Waterloo, 501 N. Elk Run Rd., 50703, pg. 852   **PB**
KWWL-TV, 500 E. 4th St., 50703, pg. 912   **PV**
PETERS CONSTRUCTION CORP., 901 Blackhawk Rd., 50701, pg. 856   **PV**
Piper Jaffray Inc., 173 W. Fourth St., 50701-5401, pg. 1302   **PB**
Waterloo Industries, Inc., 300 Ansborough Ave., 50701, pg. 675   **PB**
WATERLOO SERVICE COMPANY, 1402 Logan St., 50703, pg. 1152   **PV**

Waukee

DOWNEY PRINTING, 400 Deming Ave., 50263, pg. 342   **PV**

Waverly

CUNA Mutual Life Insurance Co., 2000 Heritage Way, 50677-9202, pg. 296   **PV**
Members Life Insurance Company, 2000 Heritage Way, 50677, pg. 296   **PV**

Webster City

Beam Industries, P.O. Box 788, 1700 Second St., 50595, pg. 440   **IT**
Frigidaire Home Products-Laundry Products, 400 Des Moines St., 50595, pg. 440   **IT**
Harris Metals-Arrow Acme Co., East Highway 20, P.O. Box 218, 50595, pg. 999   **PB**

West Burlington

Joanne Plastics, 1418 W. Mt. Pleasant St., 52655, pg. 183   **PV**
Thompson Machines, 1406 W. Mt. Pleasant St., 52655, pg. 183   **PV**

West Des Moines

ALC Incorporated, 2829 Westown Pkwy., Ste. 100, 50266, pg. 55   **PV**
AgCast, Regency W. 2, Ste. 105, 1401 50th St., 50266, pg. 484   **PB**
Agri Financial Services Inc., 2829 Westown Pkwy., Ste. 100, 50266, pg. 55   **PV**
Agri Terminal Corporation, 2829 Westown Pkwy., Ste. 100, 50266, pg. 55   **PV**
Agrifutures Incorporated, 2829 Westown Pkwy., Ste. 100, 50266, pg. 55   **PV**
AMERICAN GRAIN & RELATED INDUSTRIES, 2829 Westown Pkwy., Ste. 100, 50266, pg. 55   **PV**
Ansvar America Life Insurance Company, 1111 Ashworth Rd., 50265-3538, pg. 880   **PV**
Central Property & Casualty Insurance Company, 1111 Ashworth Rd., 50265-3538, pg. 880   **PV**
Deere Credit Services, Inc., 1415 28th St., 50265, pg. 492   **PB**
Delavan Gas Turbine Products Division, 811 Fourth St., 50265, pg. 401   **PB**
Delavan, Inc., 811 Fourth St., 50265, pg. 401   **PB**
Equity Fire & Casualty Insurance Company, 1111 Ashworth Rd., 50265-3538, pg. 881   **PV**
Hawkeye Leasing Corporation, 1200 35th St., Ste. 300, 50266, pg. 1087   **PB**
Hawkeye Quality Service Corporation, 4400 Westown Pkwy., Ste. 303, 50266, pg. 1087   **PB**
Hawkeye-Security Insurance Co., 4200 University Ave., 50265-5945, pg. 543   **IT**
Hawkeye Security Insurance Company, 4200 University Ave., 50265, pg. 543   **IT**
Hewlett-Packard Company, 4445 Corporate Dr., Ste. 100, 50265, pg. 814   **PV**
HY-VEE FOOD STORES INCORPORATED, 5820 Westown Pkwy., 50266, pg. 550   **PV**
Hy Vee Weitz Construction, L.C., 1501 50th St., Ste. 325, 50266, pg. 1161   **PV**
ITA GROUP INC., 4800 Westown Pkwy., Ste. 300, 50266, pg. 555   **PV**
Industrial & Transportation Equipment Co., 2829 Westown Pkwy., Ste. 100, 50266, pg. 55   **PV**
Integrated Business Systems, 4949 Pleasant St., 50266, pg. 565   **PV**
Mid Continent Bottlers, Inc, 4500 Westown Pkwy., Ste. 277, 50266, pg. 142   **PV**
Midwest Mutual Insurance Co., 1111 Ashworth Rd., 50265-3538, pg. 881   **PV**
Mrs. Clarks Food Inc, 2829 Westown Pkwy., Ste. 100, 50266, pg. 55   **PV**
NATIONAL TRAVELERS LIFE CO., 5700 Westown Pkwy., 50266-8221, pg. 787   **PV**
Preferred Abstainers Insurance Compan, 1111 Ashworth Rd., 50265-5088, pg. 880   **PV**
Preferred America Insurance Company, 1111 Ashworth Rd., 50265-3538, pg. 880   **PV**
Preferred Risk Life Insurance Co., 1111 Ashworth Rd., 50265-3538, pg. 880   **PV**
Preferred Risk Lloyd's Insurance Company, 1111 Ashworth Rd., 50265-3538, pg. 880   **PV**
PREFERRED RISK MUTUAL INSURANCE, 1111 Ashworth Rd., 50265-3538, pg. 880   **PV**
Principal Health Care of Iowa, Inc., 4600 Westown Pkwy., Regency 6, Ste. 301, 50266, pg. 885   **PV**
ProFormance Awards Inc., 4800 Westown Pkwy., Ste. 100, 50266, pg. 555   **PV**
ReliaStar Mortgage Company, 7015 Vista Dr., 50266, pg. 1376   **PB**
Sysco Food Services of Iowa, Inc., 2420 W. Grand Ave., 50265, pg. 1551   **PB**

West Union

H & H DISTRIBUTING COMPANY, INC., 304 S. Vine, 52175, pg. 489   **PV**

Winnsboro

Mastercraft Corporation, Rt. 3, Box 333, 71295, pg. 447   **PV**

KANSAS

Abilene

DUCKWALL-ALCO STORES, INC., 401 Cottage St., 67410, pg. 533   **PB**
Farmers National Bank, P.O. Box 399, 400 N. Broadway, 67410, pg. 1654   **PB**

Andover

INTERNATIONAL COLD STORAGE CO., INC., 215 E. 13th St., 67002, pg. 568   **PV**

Arkansas City

The Arkansas City Daily Traveler, P.O. Box 988, 5th Ave. & A St., 67005-0988, pg. 995   **PV**
Montgomery Elevator Architectural Products Division, Strother Field Industrial Park, P.O. Box 987, 67005, pg. 746   **IT**
Total Petroleum, Inc., 1400 S. M St., 67005, pg. 1663   **PB**

PB - *U.S. Public Companies Volume*
PV - *U.S. Private Companies Volume*
IT - *International Public & Private Companies Volume*

1244

Assaria

Great Plains Grain Drills, 108 W. Second, 67416, pg. 475   **PV**

Atchison

ATCHISON CASTING CORPORATION, 400 S. Fourth St., P.O. Box 188, 66002-0188, pg. 142   **PB**
Atchison/St. Joe Division, 400 S. Fourth St., 66002, pg. 142   **PB**
Blish-Mize Co., 223 S. Fifth St., 66002, pg. 335   **PV**
City National Bank, P.O. Box 309, 626 Commercial, 66002, pg. 1654   **PB**
MIDWEST GRAIN PRODUCTS, INC., 1300 Main St., 66002, pg. 1111   **PB**
Unit Rail Anchor Company, 2604 Industrial St., 66002, pg. 1711   **PB**

Baxter Springs

Bagcraft Corporation of America, Midwest Div., 100 Bagcraft Blvd., 66713, pg. 136   **PB**
Liebherr Mining Truck, Inc., P.O. Box 269, 1000 W. 5th St., 66713, pg. 808   **IT**
Waterjet Cutting Systems Div., 635 W. 12th, 66713, pg. 877   **PB**

Beloit

FARMWAY CO-OP INC., 204 E. Court St., 67420, pg. 396   **PV**
Sunflower Mfg. Co., Inc., P.O. Drawer 628, 67420, pg. 1676   **PB**

Blue Rapids

Gypsum Wall Board Plant & Plaster Mill, P.O. Box 187, 66411, pg. 737   **PB**

Burlington

Wolf Creek Nuclear Operating Corp., P.O. Box 411, 66839, pg. 943   **PB**
Wolf Creek Nuclear Operating Corp., P.O. Box 411, 1550 Oren Rd., N.E., 66893, pg. 1759   **PB**

Chanute

Ash Grove Cement Plant, P.O. Box 519, 66720, pg. 88   **PV**

Coffeyville

ACME FOUNDRY, INC., 1502 Spruce, 67337, pg. 13   **PV**
Dixon Industries, Inc., Airport Industrial Pk., 67337-0945, pg. 238   **PB**
Funk Manufacturing Co., P.O. Box 577, Hwy. 169 N., Industrial Park, 67337, pg. 492   **PB**
Magic Circle Manufacturing Div., 1209 Buckey, 67337, pg. 13   **PV**
MEDICALODGES, INC., 201 W. Eighth St., 67337, pg. 728   **PV**
Medicalodges, Inc., P.O. Box 509, 201 W. 8th St., 67337-0509, pg. 728   **PV**

Concordia

First Bank & Trust, P.O. Box 329, 130 E. 7th, 66901, pg. 1654   **PB**

De Soto

SEALRIGHT COMPANY, INC., 9201 Packaging Dr., 66018, pg. 1451   **PB**
Sealright Mfg. West, Inc., 9201 Packaging Dr., 66018, pg. 1452   **PB**

Dodge City

CRUSTBUSTER, INC., P.O. Box 1438, 67801, pg. 293   **PV**
Dodge City Daily Globe, 705 Second St., Box 820, 67801-0820, pg. 995   **PV**
Dodge City Shopper's Weekly, 316 W. Wyatt Earp, 67801, pg. 995   **PV**
Farmland National Beef Packing Company, LP, 2000 E. Trail, 67801, pg. 396   **PV**
GIBSON'S DISCOUNT CENTERS INC., 100 Chaffin Industrial Pk., 67801, pg. 452   **PV**

Edwardsville

Champ/Pik-A-Nut Service Line, 845 S. Ninth St., 66113, pg. 1503   **PB**
GILLIAM CANDY BRANDS, 207 S. Ninth St., 66113, pg. 454   **PV**

El Dorado

Texaco USA, P.O. Box 1121, 67042-1121, pg. 1583   **PB**

Ellsworth

CASHCO, INC., 607 W. 15th, 67439, pg. 218   **PV**

Emporia

Didde Web Press, 1200 Graphic Arts Rd., 66801, pg. 331   **PV**
IBP-Emporia, 2101 W. Sixth Ave., 66801, pg. 852   **PB**
Kansa Corporation, P.O. Box 668, 3700 Oaks Dr., 66801-0668, pg. 170   **PB**

Fairway

KCTV, 4500 Shawnee Mission Pkwy., 66205, pg. 1094   **PB**

Fort Scott

Ennis Business Forms of Kansas, Inc., P.O. Box 310, 66701, pg. 583   **PB**
KEY INDUSTRIES, INC., 400 Marble Rd., 66701, pg. 618   **PV**
WARD KRAFT, INC., 2401 S. Cooper St., 66701, pg. 634   **PV**

Frontenac

Sugar Creek Packing Co., 1600 W. McKay St., 66762, pg. 1049   **PV**

Garden City

Garden City Complex, P.O. Box 1649, 67846, pg. 1052   **PV**
Target, 204 E. Fulton Plaza, 67846, pg. 984   **PB**

Girard

PRODUCERS CO-OP ASSOCIATION, INC., 300 Buffalo St., 66743, pg. 888   **PV**

Goddard

Atlas Alchem Plastics, Inc., 431 Industrial Rd., 67052, pg. 1496   **PB**

Great Bend

DOONAN & SONS, INC., Jct. Hwy. 56 & 156, 67530, pg. 340   **PV**
The Fuller Brush Company, One Fuller Way, 67530, pg. 282   **PB**
KSNC, N. Hwy. 281, P.O. Box 689, 67530, pg. 984   **PB**
Security State Bank, P.O. Box 909, 1623 Main St., 67530, pg. 1654   **PB**
West Plains Energy, Broadway at Morton, 67530, pg. 1701   **PB**

Haviland

Haviland Telephone Company, Inc., 106 N. Main St., 67059, pg. 1021   **PB**

Hays

Commerce Bank, N.A., 718 Main, 67601, pg. 410   **PB**
SUNFLOWER ELECTRIC POWER CORPORATION, 301 W. 13th St., 67601, pg. 1052   **PV**

Hesston

EXCEL INDUSTRIES, INC., 200 S. Ridge Rd., 67062, pg. 387   **PV**

Hiawatha

Piper Jaffray Inc., 105 S. Sixth St., 66434-2306, pg. 1303   **PB**

Holcomb

Holcomb Station, #1 Holcomb Lane, 67851, pg. 1052   **PV**
IBP-Finney County, P.O. Box 149, 67851, pg. 852   **PB**

Holton

BMB Company, N. Vermont at 9th, 66436, pg. 35   **PB**

Humboldt

MONARCH CEMENT CO., P.O. Box 1000, 66748, pg. 1123   **PB**

Hutchinson

Collingwood Grain, Inc., 1600 N. Lorraine; Ste. 200, 67501, pg. 128   **PB**
COLLINS INDUSTRIES, INC., 15 Compound Dr., 67502, pg. 399   **PV**
Deluxe Specialties Mfg. Co., 1908 E. Lexington, 67501, pg. 1640   **PB**
Dillon Companies, Inc., 700 E. 30th, 67501, pg. 967   **PB**
Golden Plains Care Center, 1202 E. 23rd St., 67502, pg. 837   **PB**
HARRIS ENTERPRISES INC., One N. Main, Ste. 616, 67501, pg. 505   **PV**
KRAUSE PLOW CORP., 305 S. Monroe St., 67501, pg. 635   **PV**
Mobile-Tech Corp., P.O. Box 2326, Rt. 2, HABIT, 67504, pg. 400   **PB**

Republic Group Incorporated

REPUBLIC GROUP INCORPORATED, 811 E. 30th Ave., 67502-4341, pg. 1378   **PB**
Republic Paperboard Co.-Hutchinson Mill, P.O. Box 1267, First & Halstead, 67504-1267, pg. 1378   **PB**
Wheeled Coach Industries, Inc., Habit, Rt. 2, 67505, pg. 400   **PB**

Independence

Tubular & Equipment Services, LLC (TES), 201 No. Penn, Ste. 401, 67301, pg. 162   **PV**

Industrial Airport

Toro Kansas, P.O. Box 1, 100 Industrial Pky., 66031, pg. 1624   **PB**

Iola

Herff Jones, Fine Papers, Hwy. 169 N. & Miller Rd., 66749, pg. 523   **PV**
Midland Brake, Inc., 2702 N. State St., 66749, pg. 561   **PB**

Kanopolis

Acme Brick Co., P.O. Box 98, 67454, pg. 936   **PB**

Kansas City

American Beauty Macaroni, 501 Funston Rd., 66115, pg. 812   **PB**
American Ingredients Company, 550 So. 18th St., 66109, pg. 244   **IT**
ASSOCIATED WHOLESALE GROCERS, INC., 5000 Kansas Ave., 66106, pg. 93   **PV**
Browning-Ferris Industries of Kansas City, Inc., 3150 N. Seventh, 66115, pg. 263   **PB**
Central Plains Steel Co., 201 Donovan Rd., 66115, pg. 824   **PV**
Century Labs, Inc., 3200 S. 24th St., 66106, pg. 975   **PB**
Century Lubricants Co., 2140 S. 88th St., 66111-8701, pg. 518   **IT**
Commercial National Bank, 601 Minnesota Ave., 66101, pg. 1654   **PB**
CRAMER INC., 625 Adams St., 66105, pg. 285   **PV**
EARP DISTRIBUTION CENTER, 6550 Kansas Ave., 66111, pg. 356   **PV**
Galamba Metals, Inc., Second & Riverview, 66118, pg. 437   **PV**
Garsite, Inc., 539 S. 10th St., 66104, pg. 1066   **PV**
Gear Headquarters Inc., 3012 S. 24th St., 66106, pg. 127   **PV**
H.E.S. International, Inc., 1851 Merriman Ln., 66106, pg. 1209   **PB**
Harcros Chemicals Inc., 5200 Speaker Rd., 66106-2930, pg. 598   **IT**
International Tank, Inc, 636 Adams St., 66105, pg. 1066   **PV**
LADY BALTIMORE FOODS, INC., 1601 Fairfax Trafficway, 66115, pg. 975   **PB**
Landfill, Inc., P.O. Box 15200, 66115, pg. 264   **PB**
Mid-West Conveyor Co., Inc., 2601 Mid West Drive, 66112, pg. 1398   **PV**
NRL Financial Corp., 636 Adams St., 66105, pg. 1066   **PV**
Sealy Mattress Company of Kansas City, Inc., 3100 Fairfax Traffic Way, 66115, pg. 979   **PV**
Sericol Inc., P.O. Box 2914, 1101 Cambridge Circle Dr., 66110, pg. 235   **IT**
SPANGLER INC., 2930 S. 44th St., 66106, pg. 1020   **PV**
Stone Southwest Corp., 5050 Kansas Ave., 66106-1135, pg. 1521   **PB**
Sunflower Racing Inc., P.O. Box 12036, 9700 Leavenworth Rd., 66109, pg. 831   **PB**
T H Agriculture & Nutrition Co. Inc., 8907 State Ave., 66112-1645, pg. 1055   **IT**
TSI HOLDINGS, INC., 636 Adams St., 66104, pg. 1066   **PV**
Tri State Tank Corp., 636 Adams St., 66105, pg. 1066   **PV**
UNIVERSAL CONSTRUCTION COMPANY, INC., 29 Greystone Ave., 66103, pg. 1127   **PV**
VILE-GOLLER, FINE ART PRINTING & LITHOGRAPHY, 101 Greystone, 66103, pg. 1140   **PV**
Waste Disposal, Inc., P.O. Box 15200, 66115, pg. 264   **PB**

Lawrence

FARMER'S COOPERATIVE ASSOCIATION, P.O. Box 687, 2121 Moody Rd., 66044, pg. 395   **PV**
Interx Research Corp., 2201 W. 21st St., 66047, pg. 1091   **PB**
Kansas Public Service, 110 E. 9th St., 66044, pg. 1701   **PB**
LAWRENCE PAPER COMPANY, 2801 Lakeview Rd., 66044, pg. 654   **PV**
Lawrence Production Center, P.O. Box 99, 101 McDonald Dr., 66044-0099, pg. 496   **PV**
Lawrence Technology, 2400 Packer Rd., 66044, pg. 298   **PB**
NCS Information Technology, 1421 Research Park Dr., 66049-3858, pg. 1155   **PB**
Piper Jaffray Inc., 901 Vermont St., Ste. B, 66044-8658, pg. 1302   **PB**

Leavenworth

Leavenworth Detention Center, 100 Highway Ter., 66048, pg. 450   **PB**
Leavenworth Production Center, 450 Eisenhower Rd., 66048-5091, pg. 496   **PV**

PB - *U.S. Public Companies Volume*
PV - *U.S. Private Companies Volume*
IT - *International Public & Private Companies Volume*

Geographic Index-U.S.

Logicon Technical Services Inc., P.O. Box 681, 66048-1098, pg. 1199   **PB**

Leawood

MMC CORP., 11100 Ash St., Ste. 100, 66211, pg. 687   **PV**

Lecompton

BARANCORP, Northern Cross Ranch, Rte. 1, 66050, pg. 115   **PV**
Baranski & Associates, Northern Cross Ranch, Rte. 1, 66050, pg. 115   **PV**
D.A. Baranski & Co., Northern Cross Ranch, 66050, pg. 115   **PV**
Joseph A. Baranski Literary Agency, Northern Cross Ranch, Rte. 1, 66050, pg. 115   **PV**
Baranski Publishing Company, Northern Cross Ranch, Rte. 1, 66050, pg. 115   **PV**
Northern Cross, Ltd., Northern Cross Ranch, Rte. 1, 66050, pg. 115   **PV**

Lenexa

American Camper, 14760 Santa Fe Trail Dr., 66215, pg. 265   **PB**
Arrow/Schweber Electronics, 8208 Melrose Dr., 66214, pg. 134   **PV**
Bremson Data Systems, Inc., 11691 W. Eighth St., 66214, pg. 551   **PB**
Chemdex, Inc., 12340 Santa Fe Dr., 66215, pg. 1063   **IT**
Intergraph Corporation, 14839 W. 95th St., 66215, pg. 891   **PB**
Kansas City Laboratory, 9608 Loiret Blvd., 66219, pg. 829   **PV**
Lab One, 10310 W. 84th Ter., 66204, pg. 1449   **PB**
Marketing Communications, 10605 W. 84th Ter., 66214-1697, pg. 794   **PB**
Nellcor Puritan Bennett, 11150 Thompson Ave., 66219, pg. 1040   **PB**
PERFORMANCE CONTRACTING GROUP, 16047 W. 110th St., 66219, pg. 853   **PV**
Perkins Industries, Inc., 10453 W. 84th Terr., 66214, pg. 158   **PV**
Puritan-Bennett Aero Systems Co., 10800 Pflumm Rd., 66215, pg. 1040   **PV**
SOR INC., 14685 W. 105th St., 66215, pg. 957   **PV**
Sterling Electronics, 14635 W. 95th St., 66215, pg. 1052   **PB**
TMP Worldwide, Inc., 8325 Lenexa Dr., Ste. 201, 66214-1695, pg. 1064   **PV**
U.S. SAFETY, 8101 Lenexa Dr., 66214, pg. 1125   **PV**
Veterinary Laboratories, Inc., 12340 Santa Fe Dr., 66215, pg. 1063   **IT**
Veterinary Medicine Publishing Co., Inc., 9073 Lenexa Dr., 66215, pg. 1600   **PV**
WESTLAKE HARDWARE, INC., 15501 W. 99th St., 66219, pg. 1169   **PV**
WILLIAMS FOODS INC., 13301 W. 99th St., 66215, pg. 1178   **PV**
Wolferman's, Inc., 8900 Marshall Dr., 66215, pg. 1434   **PB**

Liberal

Farmland National Beef Packing Company, L.P., P.O. Box 978, 67905-0978, pg. 396   **PV**
National Carriers, Inc., P.O. Box 978, 67905-0978, pg. 396   **PV**
National Helium Corporation, P.O. Box 2079, 67905, pg. 534   **PB**

Manhattan

Citizens Bank & Trust, P.O. Box 218, 6th & Humboldt, 66502-0032, pg. 1654   **PB**

Maple Hill

HOTEL CORPORATION OF AMERICA, Rte. 10, 66507, pg. 541   **PV**

Mc Pherson

American Maplan Corporation, 823 S. By-Pass, P.O. Box 832, 67460, pg. 825   **IT**
Jayhawk Pipeline, L.L.C., 1391 Iron Horse Rd., 67460, pg. 781   **PV**
NATIONAL COOPERATIVE REFINERY ASSOCIATION, 1391 Iron Horse Rd., 67460, pg. 781   **PV**
R-4 KIT Mfg. Co., P.O. Box 586, 1000 Kit Ave., 67460, pg. 962   **PB**
VANGUARD PLASTICS, INC., 831 N. Vanguard St., 67460, pg. 1134   **PV**

Merriam

IBT, INC., 9400 W. 55th St., 66203, pg. 553   **PV**
V.T. INC., 8500 Shawnee Mission Pkwy., Ste. 200, 66202, pg. 1131   **PV**
Zenith Construction Co, Inc., 5600 Merriam Dr., 66205, pg. 585   **PV**

Mission

The Pyramid Life Insurance Co., 6201 Johnson Dr., 66202-0772, pg. 1694   **PB**

Mission Woods

LAYNE CHRISTENSON CO., 1900 Shawnee Mission Pkwy., 66205-2001, pg. 981   **PB**
Layne-Western Co., Inc., 1900 Shawnee Mission Pkwy., 66205, pg. 981   **PB**

Moundridge

BRADBURY COMPANY, INC., Air Industrial Pk., 67107, pg. 163   **PV**
Haven Commodities LLC, P.O. Box D, 67107, pg. 743   **PV**
Lubrication Consultants, L.L.C., 307 W. Cole, 67107, pg. 743   **PV**
MID-KANSAS CO-OP ASSOCIATION, 307 W. Cole, 67107, pg. 743   **PV**

New Century

Danisco Ingredients USA, Inc., 201 New Century Pkwy., 66031, pg. 378   **IT**
Graphic Technology, Inc., 301 Gardner Dr., 66031, pg. 950   **IT**
Sprint North Supply, 600 New Century Pkwy., 66031, pg. 1501   **PB**

Newton

The Newton Kansan, P.O. Box 268, 121 W. 6th St., 67114-0268, pg. 995   **PV**
Norcraft Companies, 900 S. Meridian Ave., 67114, pg. 802   **PV**

Oberlin

KSNK, P.O. Box 238, 67749, pg. 984   **PB**

Olathe

ADM Arkady, 100 Paniplus Rd., 66061, pg. 127   **PB**
AlliedSignal Commercial Avionic Systems, 400 N. Rogers Rd., 66062-1212, pg. 50   **PB**
Cedar Creek Properties Inc., 66061, pg. 88   **PV**
Cedar Creek Realty Co., Inc., 66061, pg. 88   **PV**
INLAND ASSOCIATES, 15021 W. 117th St., 66062, pg. 563   **PV**
JcAir, Inc., 400 Industrial Pkwy., 66031, pg. 751   **PB**
KELTATIM PUBLISHING COMPANY, 514 S. Canvas Ave., 66061, pg. 613   **PV**
Lister-Fetter Inc., 815 E. 56 Hwy., 66061, pg. 127   **PV**
Mid-Central/Sysco Food Services, Inc., 1915 Kansas City Rd., 66061-0820, pg. 1551   **PB**
Olathe Daily News, 514 S. Canvas Ave., 66061, pg. 613   **PV**
Osillatex Corporation, 620 N. Lindenwood Dr., 66062, pg. 521   **PB**
Simon Aviation Ground Equipment Inc., P.O. Box 2110, 550 Old Highway 56, 66061-2110, pg. 1252   **PB**
Simon-R O Corp., P.O. Box 2110, 550 Old Highway 56, 66051-211C, pg. 1252   **IT**

Oswego

Labette Cor Conservation Camp, 2501 Seventh St., 67358, pg. 450   **PV**

Overland Park

ADM Milling Co., 8000 W. 110th St., 66210, pg. 128   **PB**
ADM Milling Co. - Valley Grain, 8000 West 110th St., 66210, pg. 128   **PB**
ADM Milling Co., 8000 W. 110th St., 66210, pg. 128   **PB**
AST Research, Inc., Ste. 200, 35 Corporate Woods, 66210, pg. 1182   **IT**
APPLEEEE'S INTERNATIONAL, INC., 4551 W. 107th St., Ste. 100, 66207, pg. 122   **PB**
Associated Directory Services, 7500 W. 110th. St., 66210, pg. 1415   **PB**
Black & Veatch Pritchard, Inc., 10950 Grandview Dr., 66210, pg. 146   **PV**
Bridge, 10975 Grandview Dr., Ste. 200, 66210, pg. 1162   **PV**
Business Markets Organization, 5454 W. 110th St., 66211, pg. 1500   **PB**
Carrier Markets, 5454 W. 110th St., 66211, pg. 1500   **PB**
Charter Behavioral Health System of Kansas City, Inc., 8000 W. 127th St., 66213, pg. 1034   **PB**
Consumer and Small Business Markets, 5454 W. 110th St., 66211, pg. 1501   **PB**
Crop Growers Insurance, P.O. Box 25951, 10895 Lowell, Ste. 300, 66225-5951, pg. 328   **IT**
DIDDE CORPORATION, 10875 Benson Dr., Ste. 200, 66210 pg. 331   **PV**
E For M Corp., 9221 Corvera Rd., 66215, pg. 1047   **PB**
ELECTRO DYNAMICS CRYSTAL CORPORATION, 9075 Cody, 66214, pg. 368   **PB**
Emery Expedite!, 10881 Lowell, 66210, pg. 281   **PB**
Employers Reinsurance Corp., 5200 Metcalf Ave., 66201, pg. 711   **PB**
Ericsson, Inc., P.O. Box 4405, 11200 W. 93rd St., 66204, pg. 1364   **IT**
FINANCIAL ASSOCIATES, 10977 Granada Ln., 66211, pg. 404   **PV**
Garnac Grain Co., Inc., 7101 College Blvd., 66210-2315, pg. 802   **PV**
Great Salt Lake Minerals Corp., 8300 College Blvd., 66210, pg. 505   **PV**

Hawk Management & Financial Services Inc., 6800 College Blvd., Ste. 600, 66211, pg. 511   **PV**
HAWK MANAGEMENT CORPORATION, 6800 College Blvd., Suite 600, 66211, pg. 511   **PV**
Help USA Inc., 6800 College Blvd., Ste. 600, 66211, pg. 511   **PV**
Higher Education Loan Program of Kansas, 6800 College Blvd., Suite 600, 66211, pg. 511   **PV**
Horizon Specialty Hospital - Kansas City, 6509 W. 103rd, 66212, pg. 837   **PB**
Indian Creek Nursing Center, 6515 W. 103rd St., 66212, pg. 837   **PB**
Indian Meadows Nursing Center, 6505 W. 103rd St., 66212, pg. 837   **PB**
Innovative Health Alliances, 10727 El Monte, 66211, pg. 839   **PB**
Intertec Publishing, 9800 Metcalf, 66212-2215, pg. 1327   **PB**
Jani King of Kansas City, Inc., 10561 Barkley Ste. 610, 66212, pg. 582   **PV**
Jostens Sportswear, Freeway Industrial Park, 66204, pg. 686   **PB**
K.W. Sales, 3855 W. 95th St., 66206, pg. 736   **IT**
Kansas Gas Service, 7421 W. 129th St., 66213, pg. 1226   **PB**
Ketchum Directory Advertising/Kansas City, 7015 College Blvd., Ste. 700, 66211, pg. 616   **PV**
LA PETITE ACADEMY INC., 14 Corporate Woods, 8717 W. 110th St., Ste. 300, 66210, pg. 640   **PV**
MRA, AN INTEGRATED MARKETING COMMUNICATIONS AGENCY, 10551 Barkley, 66212, pg. 687   **PV**
The Marley Cooling Tower Co., 7401 W. 129th St., 66213, pg. 1676   **PB**
Marley Pump, 7401 W. 129 St., 66213, pg. 1676   **PB**
Midwest Mechanical Contractors Inc., 4550 W. 109th St., Ste. 100, 66211, pg. 687   **PV**
Milgray/Kansas City, Inc., 6400 Glenwood, 66202, pg. 206   **PB**
Mission Supply Co., 14609 W. 106th St., 66214, pg. 1788   **PB**
Moroch & Associates, Inc., 6400 W. 110th St., Ste. 206, 66211, pg. 762   **PV**
National Integrated Services, 7301 College Blvd., 66210, pg. 1500   **PV**
NORFOODS, INC., 7101 College Blvd., Ste. 800, 66210, pg. 802   **PV**
North American Salt Company, 8300 College Blvd., 66210, pg. 505   **PV**
Overland Energy, Inc., 10990 Roe Ave., 66207, pg. 1788   **PB**
Overland Park State Bank & Trust, P.O. Box 4368, 7109 W. 80th St., 66204, pg. 1654   **PB**
PASSPORT TRAVEL, INC., 6340 Glenwood #7, 66202-4099, pg. 842   **PV**
Principal Commercial Advisors, Inc., 11050 Roe Ave., Ste. 200, 66211, pg. 885   **PV**
RLI Heartland Regional Office, 7400 College Blvd., Ste. 330, 66210, pg. 1356   **PB**
Sprint Publishing & Advertising, y, 7015 College Blvd., Ste. 400, 66211, pg. 1501   **PB**
Summit Telemarketing, 7500 W. 110th St., 66210, pg. 1415   **PB**
THE SUNFLOWER GROUP, 10561 Barkley, Ste. 300, 66212, pg. 1052   **PV**
Technology Services, 9350 Metcalf, 66212, pg. 1501   **PV**
TIE/COMMUNICATIONS, INC., 10975 Grandview Dr., Bldg. 27, 66210, pg. 1085   **PV**
United Cities Gas Co., KS/IA/MO Div., 9401 Indian Creek Pkwy., Ste 450, 66210, pg. 146   **PV**
U.S. Central Credit Union, 7300 College Boulevard, Ste.600, 66210, pg. 288   **PV**
Universal Underwriters Insurance Co., 6363 College Blvd., 66211, pg. 1530   **IT**
Universal Underwriters of Texas, 6363 College Blvd., 66211, pg. 1530   **IT**
UTLAS International, 8300 College Blvd., 66210, pg. 1600   **PB**
Woodward-Clyde, 10975 El Monte St., Ste. 100, 66211, pg. 1656   **PV**
YELLOW CORPORATION, 10990 Roe Ave., 66211, pg. 1788   **PB**
Yellow Freight System, Inc., 10990 Roe Ave., 66211, pg. 1788   **PB**
Yellow Redevelopment Corp., 10990 Roe Ave., 66207, pg. 1788   **PB**
Yellow Services, Inc., 10990 Roe Ave., 66211, pg. 1788   **PB**

Parsons

Day & Zimmermann Kansas Division, 23018 Rooks Rd., Ste. A, 67357-9106, pg. 317   **PV**
Dayton Superior Corp., 1900 Wilson, 67537, pg. 932   **PV**
Parsons Precision Products, Inc., P.O. Box 320, 3333 Main St., 67357, pg. 598   **PV**
Peabody TecTank, Inc., P.O. Box 996, 67357, pg. 1477   **PB**

Pittsburg

Agri-Graphics, Box 46, 66762, pg. 46   **PV**
Atkinson Industries, Inc., P.O. Box 268, 66762, pg. 159   **PB**
Castlegate Inc., 911 E. Jefferson St., 66762, pg. 1067   **IT**
Harvest Brands, Inc., Box 46, 66762, pg. 46   **PV**
McNally Manufacturing, 1308 N. Walnut, 66762, pg. 1326   **IT**
McNally Wellman Kansas Div., 1201 N. Walnut, 66762, pg. 1326   **IT**

Geographic Index-U.S.

NPC INTERNATIONAL, INC., 720 W. 20th St., 66762, pg. 1146 **PB**
Pittsburg Morning Sun, P.O. Box H, 701 N. Locust, 66762-4038, pg. 995 **PV**
Pizza Hut Division, 720 W. 20th St., 66762, pg. 1147 **PB**
Superior Industries-Pittsburg, 1500 E. 27th St. Terrace, 66762, pg. 1539 **PB**

Plainville

Schult Homes Corporation, Hwy. K-18 Rd., 67663, pg. 1442 **PB**

Prairie Village

Heat Process & Control, 4518 W. 89th St., 66207, pg. 360 **PV**

Pratt

Kansas Gas Supply, P.O. Box 8548, 30317 N. U.S. Hwy. 281, 67124, pg. 1146 **PB**

Russell

King of the Road, P.O. Box 553, 67665, pg. 236 **PV**
Russell State Bank, P.O. Box 713, 507 Main, 67665, pg. 1654 **PB**

Salina

Application Systems, P.O. Box 5060, 67402-5060, pg. 475 **PV**
Asherman, P.O. Box 5060, 67402-5060, pg. 475 **PV**
El Dorado National, 304 Avenue B, 67401, pg. 1602 **PB**
GREAT PLAINS MANUFACTURING, INC., P.O. Box 5060, 67402-5060, pg. 475 **PV**
Land Pride, P.O. Box 5060, 67402-5060, pg. 475 **PV**
The National Bank of America, P.O. Box 560, 100 S. Santa Fe, 67402-0560, pg. 1654 **PB**
Rema Bakeware, 625 E. North St., 67401, pg. 1177 **PB**

Shawnee Mission

ADM Milling Co. - Rice Division, P.O. Box 7007, 66207, pg. 128 **PB**
Amoco Research Center, 8700 Indian Creek Pkwy. Ste. 1, 66210-1506, pg. 103 **PB**
ASH GROVE CEMENT COMPANY, 8900 Indian Creek Pkwy., 66210, pg. 87 **PV**
Ash Grove Cement Company Sales Office, 8900 Indian Creek Pkwy., 66210, pg. 87 **PV**
Ash Grove Materials Corp., 8900 Indian Creek Pkwy., 66210, pg. 87 **PV**
Batesco Quarries Division, 8900 Indian Creek Pkwy., 66210, pg. 88 **PV**
Benchmark Insurance Company, 6701 W. 64th St., Ste. 125 Bldg. 5, 66202, pg. 93 **PV**
Century Concrete, Inc., 8900 Indian Creek Pkwy., 66210, pg. 88 **PV**
DARLING ENVELOPE CORPORATION, 5400 Antioch Dr., 66202, pg. 311 **PV**
Fordyce Concrete Co., Inc., 8900 Indian Creek Pkwy., 66210, pg. 88 **PV**
Herff Jones Yearbooks, P.O. Box 10, 6015 Travis Lane, 66202, pg. 524 **PV**
JAMI, INC., Commerce Plaza 1, Ste. 210, 7300 W. 110th St., 66210, pg. 581 **PV**
JENKINS & ASSOCIATES, 5602 Merriam Dr., 66203, pg. 585 **PV**
MRP Midwest, Inc., P.O. Box 2982, 66201, pg. 553 **PV**
Material Transport Co., 8900 Indian Creek Pkwy., 66210, pg. 88 **PV**
Quikrete Materials, Inc., 8900 Indian Creek Pkwy., 66210, pg. 88 **PV**
ResourceNet International, P.O. Box 2967, 66201, pg. 903 **PB**
SMS-Kansas City, 4350 Shawnee Mission Pkwy., 66205, pg. 1463 **PB**
SEABOARD CORPORATION, 9000 W. 67th St., 66202, pg. 1448 **PB**
Shamrock Aggregates, Inc., 8900 Indian Creek Pkwy., 66210, pg. 88 **PV**
Subsurface Development Company, 8900 Indian Creek Pkwy., 66210, pg. 88 **PV**
Sunrise Industrial Automation & Design, P.O. Box 2982, 66201, pg. 553 **PV**
Supermarket Insurance Agency, Inc., 6701 W. 64th St., Ste. 125 Bldg. 5, 66202, pg. 93 **PV**
Union Quarries, Inc., P.O. Box 25348, 66225, pg. 88 **PV**
Waddell & Reed, Inc., 6300 Lamar, 66202, pg. 1623 **PB**
Waddell and Reed, Inc., 6300 LaMar Ave., 66202, pg. 1623 **PB**

South Hutchinson

Collins Bus Corp., 415 W. Sixth St., 67505, pg. 400 **PB**

Topeka

ADAMS BUSINESS FORMS, 200 SW Jackson, 66603, pg. 16 **PV**
American Bindry-Midwest, 914 Jefferson, 66607, pg. 52 **PV**
THE AMERICAN COMPANIES, INC., 2101 N. Topeka, 66608, pg. 52 **PV**
American Investors Life Insurance Company, 555 S. Kansas Ave., 66601, pg. 59 **PB**

American Investors Sales Group, Inc., 555 S. Kansas Ave., 66603, pg. 59 **PV**
AmVestors Acquisition Subsidiary, Inc., 555 S. Kansas Ave., 66601, pg. 59 **PV**
Amvestors Financial Corporation, 555 S. Kansas Ave., 66601, pg. 59 **PB**
AmVestors Investment Group, Inc., 555 S. Kansas Ave., 66601, pg. 59 **PV**
CGF INDUSTRIES, 800 NationsBank Tower, 66603, pg. 194 **PV**
Cash & Carry Div., Two Townsite Plaza, 66601, pg. 652 **PB**
Econo-Clad Books, 2101 N. Topeka, 66608, pg. 52 **PV**
Falley's Inc., 3120 S. Kansas Ave., 66611, pg. 1202 **PV**
General Merchandise Distributors, Inc., 7215 S. Topeka Blvd., 66601, pg. 653 **PB**
Green Tree Acceptance, Inc., 2945 Wanamaker Dr., 66614, pg. 762 **PB**
Highland Park Bank & Trust, P.O. Box 5228, 2100 S.E. 29th St., 66605, pg. 1654 **PB**
Hillhaven Topeka, 711 Garfield, 66606, pg. 1714 **PV**
Hill's Pet Nutrition, 400 W. 8th St., S.W., 66603, pg. 397 **PV**
IMA of Topeka Inc., 1631 S. Topeka Blvd., 66601-1537, pg. 565 **PV**
KPL, 818 Kansas Ave., 66612, pg. 1759 **PB**
KSNT-TV, 6835 S.W. Blue Inn Rd., 66614, pg. 983 **PB**
Kansas Fire & Casualty Co., 400 Kansas Ave., 66603, pg. 221 **PB**
Kansas Information Network, 5600 W. 6th St., 66606, pg. 995 **PV**
ED MARLING STORES, INC., 2950 McClure Rd., 66614, pg. 705 **PV**
Mid Continent Market Center, 818 Kansas Ave., 66612, pg. 1759 **PB**
North Plaza State Bank, 2014 N. Topeka Blvd., 66608, pg. 1654 **PB**
Ogden Publishing, 1503 S.W. 42nd St., 66609-1265, pg. 812 **PV**
Ohse Foods Inc., P.O. Box 750200, 66675-0200, pg. 396 **PV**
PAYLESS SHOESOURCE, INC., 3231 S.E. Sixth St., 66607, pg. 1268 **PB**
PENCO-Kansas, 3601 SW 29th St., Ste. 125, 66614, pg. 1508 **IT**
Piper Jaffray Inc., 2445 S.W. Wanamaker Rd., Ste. 100, 66614-5435, pg. 1301 **PB**
Prebound Periodicals, Inc., 914 Jefferson, 66607, pg. 52 **PV**
The Topeka Capital-Journal, 616 Jefferson St., 66607-1197, pg. 995 **PV**
Topeka Production Center, 240 Madison, 66607-1147, pg. 496 **PV**
Topeka Recycling Center, 834 Adams St., 66607, pg. 1378 **PV**
Topeka Television, Corp., 6835 N.W. U.S. Hwy. 24, 66618, pg. 984 **PV**
Veterinary Companies of America, 400 W. Eighth S., 66603, pg. 397 **PV**
Werner & Pfleiderer Inc., P.O. Box 8250, 1701 N. Topeka Blvd., 66608-0220, pg. 510 **IT**
Westar Energy, 818 Kansas Ave., 66612, pg. 1759 **PB**
Westar Security, 818 Kansas Ave., 66612, pg. 1760 **PB**
WESTERN RESOURCES, INC., 818 Kansas Ave., 66612-1217, pg. 1759 **PB**

Valley Center

B&D Instruments and Avionics, Inc., 209 W. Main, 67147, pg. 208 **IT**
Penny & Giles Aerospace Inc., P.O. Box 318, 67147-0318, pg. 208 **IT**

Wa Keeney

WESTERN COOPERATIVE ELECTRIC ASSOCIATION, INC., P.O. Box 278, 67672, pg. 1165 **PV**

Wamego

Balderson Inc., 600 Balderson Blvd., 66547, pg. 315 **PB**

Weir

Acme Brick Co., P.O. Box 247, 66781, pg. 936 **PB**

Wellington

GEC Precision Corp., 1515 N. Hwy. 81, 67152, pg. 545 **IT**

Westwood

BMA Financial Services, Inc., 1901 W. 47th Pl., Ste. 210, 66205, pg. 90 **IT**
FISCA OIL CO., INC., 4830 Rainbow Blvd., 66205, pg. 408 **PV**
Meta Oil Inc., 4830 Rainbow Blvd., 66205, pg. 408 **PV**
SPRINT CORPORATION, 2330 Shawnee Mission Pkwy., 66205, pg. 1500 **PB**
Sprint International, 2330 Shawnee Mission Pkwy, 66205, pg. 1500 **PB**

Wetmore

J.B.N. Telephone Co., Second & Kansas, 66550, pg. 1021 **PB**

Wichita

ADVANTAGE COMPANIES, INC., 8200 Thorn Dr., 67226, pg. 22 **PV**
Air Midwest, Inc., 2230 Air Cargo Rd., 67209, pg. 1099 **PB**
Allen's Concrete, Inc., 2020 N. Amidon, 67203, pg. 933 **PV**
Ameritech, 3040 N Meridian St 3038 N Meri, 67204-4100, pg. 97 **PB**
Ark Valley Concrete, Inc., P.O. Box 4048, 2020 N. Amidon, 67203, pg. 933 **PV**
ASSOCIATED COMPANY, INC., 1501 S. McLean Blvd., 67213, pg. 89 **PV**
Atlas Alchem Plastics, Inc., 1444 S. Tyler Rd., 67277, pg. 1495 **PV**
Beech Acceptance Corp., Inc., P.O. Box 85, 67201, pg. 1365 **PB**
Beech Holdings, Inc., P.O. Box 85, 67201, pg. 1365 **PB**
BERRY COMPANIES, INC., 3223 N. Hydraulic, 67219, pg. 137 **PV**
Boeing Military Airplanes, 3801 S. Oliver, 67210, pg. 241 **PB**
Bombardier, Learjet Inc., One Learjet Way, 67277, pg. 200 **IT**
Brite Voice Systems, Inc., 7309 E. 21stSt., N., 67206, pg. 257 **PB**
Browning-Ferris Industries of Kansas, Inc., 2745 N. Ohio, 67219, pg. 263 **PB**
M. BRUENGER & CO., INC., 6250 N. Broadway, 67219, pg. 175 **PV**
Builders Development Inc., 1081 S. Glendale, 67218, pg. 440 **PV**
Builders Inc., 1081 S. Glendale, 37218, pg. 440 **PV**
Case CE Wichita Div., 1500 S. McLean Blvd., 67277, pg. 311 **PB**
A.M. Castle & Co., 1874 Florence Ct., 67277, pg. 313 **PB**
Central Plains Steel Co., 3900 Comatara Dr., 67226, pg. 824 **PV**
Certified Bakers, 3500 N. Santa Fe, 67219, pg. 653 **PV**
The Cessna Aircraft Co., One Cessna Boulevard, 67215-8716, pg. 1589 **PB**
Cessna Finance Corp., 5800 E. Pawnee, 67218, pg. 1589 **PB**
Chance Coach, Inc., 4219 Irving, 67209, pg. 228 **PV**
CHANCE INDUSTRIES, INC., 4219 Irving, 67209, pg. 228 **PV**
Charter Wichita Behavioral Health System, Inc., 8901 E. Orme, 67207, pg. 1035 **PV**
Cherry Creek Village Nursing Center, 8100 E. Pawnee, 67207, pg. 837 **PV**
Cherry Creek Village Retirement Center, 8200 E. Pawnee, 67207, pg. 837 **PV**
Cigna Healthcare of Kansas City/Missouri, Inc., 101 S. Webb Rd., Ste. 200, 67207, pg. 359 **PB**
Coastal Refining & Marketing, 1100 E. 21st St., 67214, pg. 390 **PB**
Coleman Worldwide, 250 N. St. Francis St., 67202, pg. 416 **PB**
Community Psychiatric Centers of Kansas, Inc., 5111 E. 21st, 67208, pg. 1712 **PV**
Concrete Accessories Company, Inc., 2020 N. Amidon, 67204, pg. 933 **PV**
CONTINENTAL AMERICAN CORP., 5000 E. 29th St. N., 67220, pg. 267 **PV**
DAVIS-MOORE OLDSMOBILE, INC., 6215 E. Kellogg, 67218, pg. 315 **PV**
Dold Foods, 2929 N. Ohio, 66204, pg. 840 **PV**
EBY CORPORATION, 610 N. Main St., 67203, pg. 359 **PV**
Martin K. Eby Construction Company, Inc., 610 Main St., 67201, pg. 359 **PV**
Electromech Technologies, 2600 S. Custer, 67217, pg. 1168 **PV**
EVCON Industries, 3110 N. Mead, 67219, pg. 1788 **PV**
Evcon Industries, Inc., 250 N. St. Francis Ave., 67202, pg. 1788 **PV**
Excel Corp., 151 N. Main, 67202, pg. 210 **PB**
Farm Credit Bank of Wichita, Farm Credit Bank Bldg., 245 N. Waco, 67202, pg. 398 **PV**
FOLEY HOLDING COMPANY, INC., 1550 S. West St., 67213, pg. 416 **PV**
Foley Tractor Company, Inc., 1550 S. West St., 67213, pg. 416 **PV**
Full Service Beverage Company, 2901 S. Kansas, 67216, pg. 34 **PV**
GARVEY INDUSTRIES, INC., 300 W. Douglas, Ste. 1000, 67202, pg. 440 **PV**
GOLDSMITHS, INC., 151 N. Main St., 67202, pg. 462 **PV**
Hart Machinery Sales Co., 1205 N. Mosley St., 67214, pg. 970 **PB**
Hewlett-Packard Company, North Rock Business Pk., 3450 N. Rock Rd., Ste. 300, 67226, pg. 814 **PB**
HIGH PLAINS CORPORATION, O.W. Garvey Bldg., 200 W. Douglas, Ste. 820, 67202, pg. 825 **PB**
Hilland Dairy Company, 700 E. Central, 67202, pg. 879 **PV**
Hillhaven Wichita, 932 N. Topeka, 67214, pg. 1714 **PB**
Horizon Specialty Hospital - Wichita, 8080 East Pawnee, 67207, pg. 837 **PV**
IMA of Wichita Inc., 250 N. Water, Ste. 600, 67202, pg. 565 **PV**
Insituform Plains, Inc., 4421 W. Harry, 67209, pg. 882 **PV**
INSURANCE MANAGEMENT ASSOCIATES, 250 N. Water, Ste. 600, 67202, pg. 565 **PV**
KGE, 120 E. First, 67202, pg. 1759 **PB**
KSAS-TV, 316 N. West St., 67203, pg. 384 **PB**
KSNW-TV, 833 N. Main St., 67203, pg. 983 **PB**
Kaneb Pipe Line Co., 100 N. Broadway, Ste. 550, 67202, pg. 942 **PB**
Koch Engineering Co., Inc., 4111 E. 37th St., N., 67204, pg. 628 **PV**

PB - *U.S. Public Companies Volume*
PV - *U.S. Private Companies Volume*
IT - *International Public & Private Companies Volume*

Geographic Index-U.S.

KOCH INDUSTRIES, INCORPORATED, 4111 E. 37th St. N., 67220, pg. 628 **PV**
Kragie/Newell, 3500 N. Rock Rd., Bldg. 400, 67226, pg. 635 **PV**
KREONITE, INC., 715 E. Tenth St., 67201, pg. 635 **PV**
L&S Machine Company, Inc., 2019 Southwest Blvd., 67277, pg. 157 **PB**
Lario Enterprises, Inc., 301 S. Market, 67202, pg. 651 **PV**
LARIO OIL & GAS COMPANY, 301 S. Market, 67202, pg. 651 **PV**
LATSHAW ENTERPRISES, INC., 2533 S. West St., 67277, pg. 979 **PB**
THE LAW COMPANY, INC., 345 Riverview, 67203, pg. 653 **PB**
Lindberg Heat Treating Company, Batson Div., 1009 S. West, 67213, pg. 999 **PB**
LINDER & ASSOCIATES, INC., 840 N. Main, 67203, pg. 668 **PV**
LOVE PACKAGING GROUP, 700 E. 37th St., 67219, pg. 677 **PV**
Marble Products Div., 4645 Palisade, 67217, pg. 1349 **IT**
Matrix Aviation, Inc., 1701 S. Hoover, 67209, pg. 187 **PB**
MedTrac, Inc., 300 W. Douglas, Eighth Fl., 67201-2697, pg. 1504 **IT**
MISCO INDUSTRIES, 257 N. Broadway, Ste. 200, 67202, pg. 752 **PV**
MOUNTAIN IRON & SUPPLY COMPANY, Ste. 200, 257 N. Broadway, 67202, pg. 764 **PV**
Multimedia Cablevision, Co., 701 E. Douglas Ave., 67202, pg. 699 **PV**
Multimedia Security Service, 800 E. Waterman St., 67202, pg. 699 **PV**
New Coleman Holdings Inc., 250 N. St. Francis St., 67202-2610, pg. 690 **PV**
North American Recreation Products Company, 250 N. St. Francis Ave., 67202, pg. 691 **PV**
Pennypower Shopping News, Inc., 650 N. Carriage Pkwy., #60, 67208, pg. 794 **PB**
PETROLEUM INC., 301 N. Main, Ste. 1300, 67202, pg. 858 **PV**
Pharmacists Public Relations Bureau, 4969 South Lulu Court, Ste. 10, 67216, pg. 295 **PV**
Product Support Division, P.O. Box 7730, K12-12, 67277, pg. 241 **PB**
Quik Print Inc., 9415 E. Harry, Ste. 203, 67207, pg. 421 **PV**
Raytheon Aircraft Company, 10511 E. Central, 67206, pg. 1365 **PB**
Remco America, Inc., 8200 E. Thorn Dr., 67226, pg. 1385 **IT**
Rent-A-Center, Inc., 8200 E. Rent-A-Center Dr., 67226, pg. 1385 **IT**
Rich-Mix Products, 2020 N. Amidon, 67204, pg. 933 **PV**
Risk Management Associates Inc., 250 N. Water, Ste. 600, 67202, pg. 565 **PV**
RITCHIE CORPORATION, 2020 N. Amidon, 67203, pg. 933 **PV**
Ritchie Paving, Inc., 2020 N. Amidon, 67203, pg. 933 **PV**
Ritchie Sand Company, Inc., 2020 N. Amidon, 67203, pg. 933 **PV**
SJL of Kansas Corp., 833 N. Main, 67203, pg. 984 **PV**
SHEPLERS, INC., 6501 W. Kellogg, 67209, pg. 993 **PV**
Smith Fiberglass Products, Inc., 2501 S. West St., 67217, pg. 1477 **PB**
STAR LUMBER & SUPPLY COMPANY, INC., 325 S. West St., 67213, pg. 1034 **PV**
THORN Americas, 8200 E. Thorn Dr., 67226, pg. 1385 **IT**
Total Petroleum, Inc., 2040 S. Rock Rd., Ste. 50, 67027, pg. 1663 **PB**
Unisource, 2904 S. Spruce St., 67216, pg. 1671 **PB**
Wescon Products Company, 2533 S. West, P.O. Box 7710, 67277, pg. 979 **PB**
WESTERN GRAIN, INC., 107 N. Market St., Ste. 703, 67202, pg. 1165 **PV**
Western Mobile Kansas Inc., 3511 S.W. St., 67217-1043, pg. 1091 **PV**
Wichita Business Journal, Inc., 110 S. Main St., STe. 200, 67202, pg. 20 **PV**
Wichita Cessna Learning Center, 1951 Airport Rd., P.O. Box 12304, 67277, pg. 219 **PB**
Wichita Cessna Maintenance Learning Center, P.O. Box 12263, 1962 Midfield Road, 67277, pg. 219 **PB**
The Wichita Eagle and Beacon Publishing Co., Inc., 825 E. Douglas St., 67202, pg. 964 **PB**
Wichita Learjet Learning Center, Two Learjet Way, 67209, pg. 219 **PB**
Wichita Raytheon Learning Center, 9720 E. Central Ave., 67206, pg. 219 **PB**
Wichita Raytheon Maintenance Learning Center, 9525 E. Central Ave., 67206, pg. 219 **PB**
Wichita Service Center, 1638 Calvert St., 67217, pg. 829 **PV**
Willis Corroon Administrative Services Corporation, P.O. Box 2697, 300 W. Douglas, Eighth Fl., 67201-2697, pg. 1504 **IT**
Willis Corroon Corp. of Kansas, P.O. Box 2697, 300 W. Douglas, Eighth Fl., 67201-2697, pg. 1506 **IT**

KENTUCKY

Ashland

Addington Holding Co., 1500 N. Big Run Rd., 41102, pg. 1379 **PB**
Broughton Foods Company, 2516 Carter Ave., 41105, pg. 260 **PB**
Columbia Coal Gasification Corp., 336-338 14th St., 41101, pg. 402 **PB**
Columbus Showcase, Ashland Division, P.O. Box 1387, 41105, pg. 257 **PV**

Cox Communications-Ashland, 225 Russell Rd., U.S. 23 N., 41101, pg. 454 **PB**
Green Valley Environmental, Inc., 1500 N. Big Run Rd., 41102, pg. 1379 **PB**
Kentucky Power Co., 1701 Central Ave., P.O. Box 1428, 41101, pg. 72 **PB**
Kentucky West Virginia Gas Co., 525 N. Lake Dr., 41653, pg. 590 **PB**
West Virginia Cellular Telephone Corp., 238 Russel Rd., 41101, pg. 1708 **PB**

Auburn

AUBURN HOSIERY MILLS, INC., 113 E. Main St., 42206, pg. 98 **PV**

Bardstown

Bird Vinyl, 1010 Winthrow Ct., 40004, pg. 699 **IT**
Kentucky Standard, P.O. Box 639, 110 W. Stephen Foster Ave., 40004, pg. 648 **PV**

Beaver Dam

Ohio County Balefill, Inc., 100 Landfill Ln., 42320, pg. 1379 **PB**

Bedford

Trimble Banner Democrat, P.O. Box 289, West St., 40006, pg. 648 **PV**

Benton

Lake Haven Health Care Center, Rte. 8, Box 110, 42025, pg. 1714 **PB**

Berea

Churchill Weavers, Inc., 100 Churchill Dr., 40403, pg. 465 **PB**
Tokico (USA) Inc., 301 Mayde Rd., 40403, pg. 1391 **IT**

Bowling Green

Bando Manufacturing of America, Inc., 2720 Pioneer Dr., 42101, pg. 145 **IT**
Bowling Green Health Care Center, 4079 Scottsville Rd., 42101, pg. 1712 **PB**
CAMPING WORLD, INC., 650 Three Springs Rd., 42102, pg. 204 **PV**
DESA INTERNATIONAL, 2701 Industrial Dr., 42101, pg. 326 **PV**
Detrex Equipment Div., 401 Emmett Ave., 42101, pg. 501 **PB**
First American National Bank, 551 E. 10th Street, 42102, pg. 624 **PB**
Gitano Fashions Ltd., P.O. Box 90015, 10018, pg. 686 **PB**
Holley Replacement Parts Division, P.O. Box 10360, 42102-7360 pg. 402 **PB**
HOUCHENS INDUSTRIES INC., 900 Church St., 42101, pg. 541 **PV**
Houchens Markets, 900 Church St., 42101, pg. 541 **PV**
Lilly Industries, Inc., 347 Central Ave., 42101, pg. 994 **PB**
Lord Corporation, P.O. Box 8500, 2800 Pioneer Dr., 42102-8500, pg. 676 **PV**
NHK-Associated Spring Suspension Components Inc., 3251 Nashville Rd., 42101, pg. 902 **IT**
Nyloncraft, 100 N. Graham Dr., 42101, pg. 599 **PB**
Save-A-Lot, 900 Church St., 42101, pg. 541 **PB**
Scott Tobacco, 939 Adams, P.O. Box 658, 42102-0658, pg. 272 **PB**
Sumitomo Electric Wiring Systems, Inc., P.O. Box 90031, 604 Three Springs Rd., 42102-9031, pg. 1313 **IT**
Trans Financial Bank, N.A., P.O. Box 90001, 500 E. Main, 42101, pg. 1628 **PB**
TRANS FINANCIAL, INC., 500 E. Main St., 42101, pg. 1628 **PB**
Union Underwear Co., Inc., 1 Fruit of the Loom Dr., 42103, pg. 685 **PB**

Bulan

Cyprus Mountain Coals Corporation, P.O. Box 423, 41722, pg. 471 **PB**

Burgin

Keystone Brush & Contact Co., 440 Burgin Danville Rd., P.O. Box 478, 40310, pg. 623 **PV**

Burnside

The Kingsford Products Co., S. U.S. Hwy. 27, P.O. Box 487, 42519, pg. 387 **PB**

Calvert City

ISP Chemicals Inc., P.O. Box 37, Rt. 95 Industrial Area, 42029, pg. 858 **PB**

Campbellsville

Central Kentucky News-Journal, 428 Woodlawn Ave., 42718, pg. 648 **PV**

Carrollton

The News-Democrat, 422 Main St., 41008, pg. 648 **PV**

Catlettsburg

Calgon Carbon Corp., Catlettsburg, P.O. Box 664, 41129, pg. 293 **PB**

Cave City

Cave City Chevrolet, I-65 & Hwy. 90 E., 42127, pg. 712 **PV**

Cold Spring

Graphic Resources, Inc., 300 Industrial Rd., 41076, pg. 1486 **PB**
GRIFFIN INDUSTRIES, INC., 4221 Alexandria Pike, 41076, pg. 480 **PV**

Columbia

IMO Pump, 476 Industrial Way, 42728, pg. 857 **PB**

Corbin

General Shale Products Corp., P.O. Box 720, 30318, pg. 844 **IT**

Covington

BASES International, 50 E. River Center Blvd., Suite 1000, 41011, pg. 120 **PV**
BASES WORLDWIDE, 50 E. River Center Blvd., Ste. 1000, 41011, pg. 120 **PV**
BASES Worldwide, 50 E. River Center Blvd., Suite 1000, 41011, pg. 120 **PV**
The Burke Institute, 50 E. River Center Blvd., Suite 1000, 41011, pg. 120 **PV**
CPX Constructors, Inc., 50 E. Rivercenter Blvd., Ste. 1200, 41011, pg. 276 **PV**
Corporex Development, 50 E. Rivercenter Blvd., Ste. 1200, 41011, pg. 276 **PV**
Corporex Properties Inc., 50 E. Rivercenter Blvd., Ste. 1200, 41011, pg. 276 **PV**
Duro Paper Bag Mfg. Co., 1301 Madison Ave., 41011, pg. 349 **PV**
E & D Grain Marketing Co, P.O. Box 175735, 41011-5735, pg. 353 **PV**
International Paper-Distribution Group, 50 E. River Center, Ste. 700, 41011, pg. 902 **PB**
JACOR COMMUNICATIONS, INC., 50 E. Rivercenter Blvd., 12th Fl., 41011, pg. 922 **PB**
R.A. JONES & CO. INC., 2701 Crescent Springs Rd., 41017, pg. 597 **PV**
The Kentucky Post, 421 Madison Ave., 41011, pg. 1447 **PB**
Loewen Group International, Inc., 50 E. River Center Blvd., 41011, pg. 814 **IT**
Matrix Building Co., Inc., 1650 Russell St., 41011, pg. 694 **PV**
OMNICARE, INC., 50 E. River Ctr. Blvd., 41011, pg. 1223 **PB**
Quality Hotel Riverview, 668 W. 5th St., 41011, pg. 682 **PB**

Crescent Springs

BLUE GRASS QUALITY MEATS, 2645 Commerce Dr., 41017, pg. 152 **PV**

Cynthiana

E.D. BULLARD COMPANY, 1898 Safety Way, 41031-9303, pg. 180 **PV**
Bundy Corporation, Cynthiana Plant, Hwy. 356 White Oak Pike, P.O. Box 100, 41031, pg. 1340 **IT**
Cynthiana Democrat, P.O. Box 160, 412 Webster at Springdale, 41031, pg. 648 **PV**

Danville

ATR Wire & Cable Co., Inc., P.O. Box 908, 40422, pg. 694 **IT**
Danville Mfg. Division, P.O. Box 140, Lebanon Rd., pg. 518 **PB**
GemStone Gasket Co., P.O. Box 907, 40422, pg. 480 **PB**
Jannock Steel Fabricating, Inc., 160 Stewarts Ln., 40422, pg. 699 **IT**

Dry Ridge

GUSHER PUMPS, INC., 22 Ruthman Dr., 41035, pg. 488 **PV**

Edmonton

SPD Magnet Wire Co., 909 Industrial Dr., 42129, pg. 1313 **IT**

Elizabethtown

AP Techno Glass Company, P.O. Box 5000, 42702, pg. 84 **IT**
Ambrake Corporation, 300 Ring Rd., 42701, pg. 721 **PB**

PB - *U.S. Public Companies Volume*
PV - *U.S. Private Companies Volume*
IT - *International Public & Private Companies Volume*

1248

Bowman Distribution, 873 W. Park Dr., 42701, pg. 190 **PB**
CDR Pigments & Dispersions, 305 Ring Rd., 42701-8747, pg. 413 **PV**
COCA-COLA BOTTLING CO. OF ELIZABETHTOWN, 1201 N. Dixie, 42701, pg. 248 **PV**
Liberty National Bank and Trust Company of Central Kentucky, 1200 N. Dixie, 42701, pg. 173 **PB**
Magna Division, 1001 West Park Rd., 42701, pg. 575 **PB**
News-Enterprise, 408 W. Dixie Ave., 42701, pg. 648 **PV**
Rock of Ages Memorials LLC, P.O. Box 370, 42701, pg. 1396 **PB**
Tele Scripps Cable, 2919 Ring Rd., 42701, pg. 1448 **PB**

Eminence

Henry County Local, 1378 Eminence Rd., 40019, pg. 648 **PV**

Erlanger

Ancra Cincinnati, 3300 Turfway Rd., Ste. 110, 41018, pg. 71 **PV**
Aquionics Inc., P.O. Box 18395, 41018, pg. 590 **IT**
Castell Interlocks Inc., 21 Kenton Lands Rd., 41018, pg. 590 **IT**
Cincinatti Learning Center, 1600 W. Dolwick Dr., 41018, pg. 218 **PB**
Cinti Fab, 2835 Crescent Springs Rd., 41018, pg. 240 **PV**
COMAIR HOLDINGS, INC., 2258 Tower Dr., 41018, pg. 406 **PB**
Comair, Inc., 2258 Tower Dr., 41018, pg. 406 **PB**
Design Performance Group, 1895 Airport Exchange Blvd., 41018, pg. 1309 **PV**
Kintetsu World Express Inc., 1420 Jamike Ave., 41018, pg. 734 **IT**
Liberty National Bank of Northern Kentucky, 3414 Dixie Hwy., 41018, pg. 173 **PB**
Post Glover Resistors Inc., 167 Gap Way, 41018, pg. 590 **IT**
TRESSA, INC., 2711 Circleport Dr., 41018, pg. 1100 **PV**
Van Melle USA, Inc., 1 Van Melle Lane, 41018, pg. 1451 **IT**

Florence

ALL PRO BUMPER TO BUMPER INC., 7300 Turf Rd. Ste. 410, 41042, pg. 35 **PV**
American Inks & Coatings Corp., Ink Division, 7880 Foundation Dr., 41042, pg. 56 **PV**
American Sign & Marketing Services, Inc., 7430 Industrial Rd., 41042, pg. 1309 **PB**
Emerald Industries Inc., 8060 Bluegrass Dr., 41042, pg. 657 **PB**
EQUITABLE BAG COMPANY, INC., 7600 Empire Dr., 41042, pg. 380 **PV**
The Fifth Third Bank of Northern Kentucky, 8100 Burlington Pike, 41012, pg. 621 **PB**
Florence Deposit Bank, 7000 Dixie Hwy., 41042, pg. 173 **PB**
THE HENNEGAN COMPANY, 7455 Empire Dr., 41042, pg. 522 **PV**
HOPPLE PLASTICS, INC., 7430 Empire Dr., 41042, pg. 538 **PV**
IPC Power Resistors International Inc., 7453 Empire Dr., Unit #105, 41042-2990, pg. 590 **IT**
KECO INDUSTRY, INC., 7375 Industrial Rd., 41042, pg. 611 **PV**
Krauss-Maffei Corp., 7095 Industrial Rd., P.O. Box 6270, 41042-6270, pg. 836 **IT**
LASCO Panel Products, 8015 Dixon Dr., 41042, pg. 1398 **IT**
LITTLEFORD DAY INC., 7451 Empire Dr., 41042, pg. 671 **PV**
Mackay, Inc., 7435 Empire Dr., 41042, pg. 210 **PB**
THE NIELSEN COMPANY, 7405 Industrial Rd., 41042, pg. 799 **PV**
Senior Engineering Co.-Central Region, 7067 Production Court, 41042, pg. 1222 **IT**
A.O. Smith Water Products Division, 8160 Holton Dr., 41042, pg. 1477 **PB**
Sweco, 8029 Dixie Hwy., 41042, pg. 574 **PB**
Van Nostrand Reinhold, 7625 Empire Dr., 41042, pg. 1600 **PB**

Fordsville

National Office Furniture Manufacturing, Hwy. 69 South, 42343, pg. 957 **PB**

Fort Mitchell

PAUL HEMMER CONSTRUCTION COMPANY, 250 Grandview Dr., 41017, pg. 521 **PV**
PNC Bank, Ohio National Assoc., 2216 Dixie Hwy., 41017, pg. 1243 **PB**

Fort Wright

Silmar Resins, 3535 Latonia Ave., 40105, pg. 572 **PV**

Frankfort

Centria, 1099 U.S. Hwy. 421 South, 40601-8821, pg. 225 **PV**
Investors Heritage Life Insurance Co., P.O. Box 717, 200 Capital Ave., 40602, pg. 952 **PB**
KENTUCKY INVESTORS, INC., 200 Capital Ave., 40601, pg. 951 **PB**

Porritts & Spencer (Western), Inc., P.O. Box 755, 40602, pg. 1202 **IT**

Franklin

Brown Printing Central, P.O. Box 451, 42134, pg. 190 **IT**
Outokumpu Copper Franklin, Inc., 4720 Bowling Green Rd., 42135, pg. 1016 **IT**
PREP - STAT/SPECTRUM, 765 Industrial By-Pass, 42134, pg. 882 **PV**
Simpson County Bank, 117 W. Cedar St., 42134, pg. 1669 **PB**

Fulton

Advance Seed Company, P.O. Box 488, 600 Stephen Beale Dr., 42041, pg. 566 **IT**
Excel Manufacturing of Kentucky, 800 N. College St., 42041, pg. 598 **PB**

Georgetown

Berol Corp., Bourbon & Chambers St., 40324, pg. 1178 **PB**
Celtite Inc., 150 Carley Ct., P.O. Box 2600, 40324, pg. 234 **IT**
Federal Packaging Corporation, Lexington Rd., 40324, pg. 303 **PB**
Toyota Motor Manufacturing, U.S.A., Inc., 1001 Cherry Blossom Way, 40324, pg. 1412 **IT**
Vascor, Ltd., P.O. Box 555, 40324, pg. 912 **IT**

Ghent

Gallatin Steel Company, Rte. 1, Box 320, 41045, pg. 414 **IT**

Gilbertsville

BRT Transfer Terminal, Inc., P.O. Box 35, 42044, pg. 1726 **PB**
Reco Transportation Inc., 42044, pg. 1726 **PB**

Glasgow

Glasgow Mfg. Division, Donnelley Dr., 42141-9799, pg. 518 **PB**
UNITED FARM TOOLS, INC., 113 W. Public Sq., 4th Fl., 42141, pg. 1122 **PV**

Greensburg

Greensburg Manufacturing, P.O. Box 169, 42743, pg. 957 **PB**

Greenville

First State Bank, 131 E. Main Croff, 42345, pg. 1217 **PB**
SuperValu, Inc.-Greenville Div., Box 427, Green Dr., 42345, pg. 1540 **PB**

Hardinsburg

Indiana Hardwoods, Cloverport Mill, RR 2 Hwy. 60, 40143, pg. 957 **PB**

Harlan

The Harlan Daily Enterprise, Hwy. 421 S., PO Drawer E, 40831, pg. 632 **IT**

Harold

Big Sandy Wholesale Co., P.O. Box 249, 41635, pg. 493 **PV**

Harrodsburg

Bay West Paper Corporation, 1150 Industry Rd., 40330, pg. 1747 **PB**
Cor Sam Glass Tec Research & Development Center, 680 E. Office St., 40330, pg. 449 **PB**
Harrodsburg Health Care, Hwy. 68 & Eminent Ave., 40330, pg. 1713 **PB**

Hazard

Herald Voice, 380 Main St., 41701, pg. 1343 **PB**
WYMT-TV, Four Black Gold Blvd., 41702, pg. 759 **PB**

Hebron

Hutch Sports USA, Inc., 2850 Earhart Ct., 41048, pg. 1354 **PB**
POMEROY COMPUTER RESOURCES, 1020 Petersburg Rd., 41048, pg. 1315 **PB**

Henderson

Accuride Corp., P.O. Box 40, 2315 Adams Ln., 42420, pg. 1286 **PB**
Atlantis Molded Plastics, Inc., Indus. Pk., US Hwy. 60 W., P.O. Box 3, 42420, pg. 145 **PB**
Citizens Bank of Kentucky, P.O. Box 32, 42420, pg. 280 **PB**
Ellis Grain River Terminal, Box 332, 42420, pg. 824 **PV**

James C. Ellis Grain Co., Box 332, 42420, pg. 824 **PV**
Farmers Bank & Trust Co., 301 Second St., 42420, pg. 1217 **PB**
Gamco Products Co., P.O. Box 318, 1105 Fifth St., 42420, pg. 1053 **PB**
Gibbs Die Casting Corp., 369 Community Dr., 42420, pg. 628 **PV**
P.B. & S. Chemical Co., P.O. Box 20, 42420, pg. 1458 **IT**

Highland Heights

General Cable Co., 4 Tesseneer Dr., 41076, pg. 1487 **IT**
General Cable Corporation, Four Tesseneer Dr., 41076, pg. 1486 **IT**
General Cable Guardian Products Division, Four Tessineer Dr., 41076, pg. 1487 **IT**
Guardian Products/Capital Wire, Four Tesseneer Dr., 41076, pg. 1487 **IT**
Harris Allied Systems, #4 Tesseneer Dr., 41076, pg. 791 **PB**

Hodgenville

Larue County Herald News, 40 Shawnee Dr., 42748, pg. 648 **PV**

Hopkinsville

HOPKINSVILLE ELEVATOR COMPANY, INC., Skyline Dr., 42241, pg. 538 **PV**
HOPKINSVILLE MILLING CO., 2001 S. Walnut St., 42240, pg. 538 **PV**
Liberty National Bank of Western Kentucky, 1101 S. Main, 42241, pg. 173 **PB**
MHI Machine Tool U.S.A. Inc., 330 Bill Bryan Blvd., 42240, pg. 874 **IT**
NationsBank of Kentucky, 712 S. Main St., 42240, pg. 1163 **PB**

Horse Cave

BALE OF KENTUCKY, INC., 1288 E. Main St., 42749, pg. 112 **PV**
Farmers Investment Company, Inc., 1288 E. Main St., 42749, pg. 112 **PV**

Hyden

Leslie County Telephone Company, Inc., P.O. Box 969, Main St., 41749, pg. 1571 **PB**

Jeffersontown

Waukesha Cherry-Burrell, 10300 Bunsen Way, 40299, pg. 1677 **PB**

Jenkins

National Mine Service Company, Jenkins Div., P.O. Box 872, Main St., 41537, pg. 281 **IT**

Kimper

Jesse Branch Coal Co., 8259 Upper Johns Creek Rd., 41539, pg. 139 **PV**
Kyber Coal Co., 8259 Upper Johns Creek Rd., 41539, pg. 138 **PV**

La Grange

The Oldham Era, P.O. Box 5, 204 S. First St., 40031, pg. 648 **PV**
PNC Bank Kentucky, Inc., 415 S. First, 40031, pg. 1243 **PB**

Lambric

Consol of Kentucky, Inc., 15345 Kentucky Hwy. 542, 41340, pg. 531 **PB**

Langley

Kentucky Hydrocarbon Division, Old Road 80, Floyd County, 41645, pg. 589 **PB**

Lawrenceburg

The Anderson News, Box 116, 133 S. Main St., 40342, pg. 648 **PV**
Boulevard Distillers and Importers Inc., 1525 Tyrone Rd., 40342, pg. 567 **IT**
Austin Nichols & Co. Inc., 1525 Tyrone Rd., 40342, pg. 567 **IT**
Universal Fasteners Inc., 302 Factory Ave., 40342, pg. 1515 **IT**

Lebanon

The Lebanon Enterprise, Box 679, 119 So. Proctor Knott Ave., 40033, pg. 648 **PV**

Lewisport

Commonwealth Aluminum-Lewisport, P.O. Box 480, 42351, pg. 415 **PB**

Geographic Index-U.S.

Lexington

Addington Environmental, Inc., 771 Corporate Dr., Ste. 1000, 40503, pg. 1379 PB
Addington Resources, Inc., 2343 Alexandria Dr., Ste. 400, 40504, pg. 1379 PB
Aichi Steel Works, Ltd., 771 Corporate Dr., Ste. 460, 40503, pg. 36 IT
Ashland Services Company, 3475 Dabney Dr., 40509, pg. 139 PB
Athens Paper Co., Inc., 2061 Buck Ln., 40511, pg. 94 PV
BIZZACK INC., 2265 Executive Dr., 40505, pg. 146 PV
BLUE GRASS CHRYSLER-PLYMOUTH INC., 1651 N. Broadway, 40505, pg. 152 PV
Blue Grass Physician Management Group, Inc., 3050 Rio Dosa Dr., 40509, pg. 1033 PB
Charter Ridge Behavioral Health System, Inc., 3050 Rio Dosa Dr., 40509, pg. 1035 PB
Circle International, 4000 Versailles Rd., Blue Grass Airport, 40510, pg. 371 PB
CLARK MATERIAL HANDLING COMPANY, 742 Short St., 40508, pg. 243 PV
Collection Services, Inc., 2343 Alexandria Dr., 40504, pg. 1379 PB
COMMUNITY NEWSPAPER HOLDINGS INC., 269 W. Main St., 6th Fl., 40507, pg. 259 PV
Costain Coal Inc., 249 E. Main St., Ste. 400, 40507, pg. 337 IT
D & K Healthcare Resources-Lexington Division, 516 W. Fourth St., 40508, pg. 472 PB
DAWAHARES, INC., 1845 Alexandria Dr., 40504, pg. 316 PV
Fansteel VR/Wesson-Lexington, P.O. Box 11399, Lisle Rd., 40575, pg. 612 PB
First Recovery, 3499 Dabney Dr., 40509, pg. 139 PB
JAMES N. GRAY CONSTRUCTION CO., INC., 10 Quality St., 40507, pg. 472 PV
Green Tree Acceptance of Kentucky, Inc., 2525 Harrodsburg Rd., Ste. 400, 40504, pg. 762 PB
K.I.M Coal Co., 600 Kincaid Tower, 40508, pg. 1359 IT
KU Capital Corporation, One Quality St., 40507, pg. 941 PB
KU ENERGY, One Quality St., 40507, pg. 940 PB
KEENELAND ASSOC., INC., 4201 Versailles Rd., 40510, pg. 611 PV
Kentucky-American Water Co., 2300 Richmond Rd., 40502, pg. 95 PB
Kentucky Indiana Lumber Co., P.O. Box 5506, 40555, pg. 615 PV
Kentucky Utilities Company, One Quality St., 40507, pg. 941 PB
Lexington Division, 890 Russell Cave Rd., 40583, pg. 333 PB
LEXMARK INTERNATIONAL GROUP, INC., 740 New Circle Rd., 40550, pg. 991 PB
Lexmark International, Inc., 740 New Circle Rd., 40550, pg. 991 PB
LODESTAR ENERGY INC., 333 W. Vine St., 40507, pg. 672 PV
LONG JOHN SILVER'S, INC., 300 W. Vine St., 40507, pg. 674 PV
Mahco, Inc., 2355 Harrodsburg Rd., 40504, pg. 711 PV
MASON & HANGER CORPORATION, INC., 2355 Harrodsburg Rd., 40504-3363, pg. 711 PV
Mason & Hanger Corporation, Inc., 2355 Harrodsburg Rd., 40504, pg. 711 PV
Mason & Hanger Engineering Inc., 2355 Harrodsburg Rd., 40504-3363, pg. 711 PV
McAlpin's, 2301 Richmond Rd., 40502, pg. 1090 PB
Mitsui & Co. (U.S.A.), Inc., 771 Corporate Dr., Ste. 450, 40503, pg. 879 IT
National Mines Corp., 333 W. Vine St., Ste. 1000, 40507, pg. 903 IT
O-Ring Div., 2360 Palumbo Dr., 40512-1751, pg. 1262 PB
PNC Bank, P.O. Box 400, 101 E. Vine St., 40507, pg. 1243 PB
SCT Government Systems, 1733 Harrodsburg Rd., Ste. 100, 40504-3617, pg. 1552 PB
Sakura Bank - Lexington Representative Office, 771 Corporate Drive, 4th Fl., Ste. 430, 40503, pg. 1179 IT
SEED RESTAURANT GROUP, INC., 2470 Polombo Dr., 40509, pg. 981 PV
Semicon Associates, 1801 Old Frankfort Pike, 40504, pg. 330 PB
Square D Company, 1601 Mercer, 40511, pg. 1208 IT
Stearns Company Limited, 410 W. Vine St., 40507, pg. 1037 PV
STEARNS ENTERPRISES, INC., 410 W. Vine St., 40507, pg. 1037 PV
Stearns Phoenix Broadway, 410 W. Vine St., 40507, pg. 1037 PV
Toyota Motor Corporation, Supplier Support Center, 771 Corporate Dr., Ste. 700, 40503, pg. 1412 IT
Valvoline Company, 3499 Dabney Dr., 40509, pg. 139 PB
The Valvoline Company, 3499 Dabney Dr., 40509, pg. 139 PB
Valvoline Instant Oil Change, Inc., P.O. Box 14000, 40512-4046, pg. 139 PB
Versatech Engineering, 835 Porter Pl., 40504, pg. 712 PV
WKYT-TV, 2851 Winchester Rd., 40555, pg. 759 PB
WTVQ-TV (ABC) Channel 36, 2940 Bryant Rd., 40509, pg. 1078 PB
Wabash Fibre Box Company-Lexington Plant, 2575 Palumbo Dr., 40509, pg. 1170 PV
Willis Corroon Corporation of Lexington, 870 Corporate Dr., Ste. 401, 40503, pg. 1505 IT
Zellerbach Division, 1700 Fortune Ct., 40505, pg. 1075 PB
Zerec Corp., 3499 Dabrey Dr., 40509, pg. 139 PB

Liberty

The Casey County News, P.O. Box 40, Campbellsville St., 42539, pg. 648 PV

London

Mrs. Smith's Bakeries of Pennsylvania, Inc., 501 E. Fourth St., 40741, pg. 658 PB

Louisville

AAF-International, 215 Central Ave., 40208, pg. 3 PV
A.C. Medical, Inc., The Humana Bldg., 500 W. Main St., 40202, pg. 403 PB
ACBJ Business Publications, Inc., Business First Bldg., 111 W. Washington St., 40202, pg. 19 PV
Ademco Sensor Company, 10170 Lin Station Rd., Ste. 505, 40223, pg. 1306 PB
AEGON USA, Inc., 400 W. Market St., 40232, pg. 26 IT
Airguard Industries Inc., 3807 Bishop Ln., 40218, pg. 382 PB
ALGOOD FOOD COMPANY, 2440 S. Floyd St., 40209, pg. 34 PV
All-State Ford Truck Sales, 1357 Gardiner Ln., 40232, pg. 524 PV
ALLIED SPORTING GOODS INC., 3401 Bashford Ave. Ct., 40218, pg. 41 PV
AlliedSignal Turbocharging & Truck Brake Systems Aftermarket Distribution Center, 12740 Westport Rd., Ste. B, 40223, pg. 51 PB
Allright Louisville Co., Inc., 321 W. Chestnut St., 40202, pg. 42 PV
Alro Group, Louisville, P.O. Box 17349, 310 Baxley Ave., 40217-0349, pg. 46 PV
American Medicorp Development Co., The Humana Bldg., 500 W. Main St., 40201, pg. 403 PB
AmeriSource-Louisville Div., 244 E. Woodlawn Ave., 40214, pg. 97 PB
Anderson Park, Inc., 700 Central Ave., 40208, pg. 356 PB
THE APPAREL GROUP, LTD., P.O. Box 32100, 40232, pg. 78 PV
Athens Paper Co., Inc., 7855 National Turnpike, 40214, pg. 94 PV
J. Bacon & Sons, 3600 Bardstown Rd., 40218, pg. 1090 PB
Banc One Kentucky Corporation, 416 W. Jefferson St., 40202-3244, pg. 173 PB
Bank One, Kentucky, NA, 416 W. Jefferson St., 40202, pg. 173 PB
BARGAIN SUPPLY COMPANY, 844 E. Jefferson St., 40206, pg. 116 PV
Bergen Brunswig Drug Company, 7841 National Tpke., 40214, pg. 214 PB
Bioproducts, Inc., 4820 Jennings Lane, 40218, pg. 145 PV
BLUE BOAR CAFETERIA CO., 106 Bauer Ave., 40207, pg. 151 PV
Blue Grass Cooperage Co., Egan Ave., 40221, pg. 261 PB
Bluegrass Coca-Cola Bottling Company, 1661 W. Hill St., 40210-1749, pg. 393 PB
BROADWAY CHEVROLET, 717 W. Broadway, 40202, pg. 170 PV
Brown & Williamson Tobacco Corp., Louisville Galleria, 1500 Brown & Williamson Tower, 40202, pg. 111 IT
Brown-Forman Beverages Worldwide, 850 Dixie Hwy., 40210, pg. 261 PB
BROWN-FORMAN CORPORATION, 850 Dixie Hwy., 40210, pg. 261 PB
BROWN WOOD PRESERVING COMPANY, 6201 Camp Ground Rd., 40216, pg. 174 PV
Bunton Division, 4601 E. Indian Trail, 40213, pg. 1589 PB
BYERLY FORD-NISSAN INC., 4041 Dixie Hwy., 40216, pg. 191 PV
CALDWELL TANKS, INC., 4000 Tower Rd., 40219, pg. 200 PV
Capital Liberty, L.P., 680 Fourth Ave., 40202, pg. 26 IT
Carbide Products, P.O. Box 3727, 40201, pg. 304 PB
CARDINAL ALUMINUM CO., 6910 Preston Hwy., 40219, pg. 208 PV
Carlisle Equipment Company, 3800 Crittenden Dr., 40209, pg. 211 PV
CARRIER VIBRATING EQUIPMENT, INC., 3400 Fern Valley Rd., 40213, pg. 215 PV
Charter Louisville Behavioral Health System, Inc., 1405 Browns Ln., 40207, pg. 1035 PB
CHEMCENTRAL/Louisville, 1825 Appleton Ln., 40216, pg. 232 PV
Chesapeake Packaging Co./Louisville, 1344 Beech St., 40211, pg. 346 PB
Chi-Chi's Inc., Triad East, 10200 Linn Station Rd., 40223, pg. 393 PV
Chicago Medical School Hospital, Inc., The Humana Bldg., 500 W. Main St., 40202, pg. 404 PB
CHURCHILL DOWNS, INC., 700 Central Ave., 40208, pg. 356 PB
Churchill Downs Management Co., 700 Central Ave., 40208, pg. 356 PB
Citizens Banc Leasing, 4040 Dixie Hwy., 40216, pg. 280 PB
The Cobb Group, 9420 Bunsen Pkwy. #300, 40220, pg. 1276 IT
BILL COLLINS FORD INC., 4220 Bargetown Rd., 40218, pg. 253 PV
COMMONWEALTH INDUSTRIES, INC., Citizens Plaza, Ste. 1900, 500 W. Jefferson St., 40202, pg. 415 PB
Community Hospitals of Galen, Inc., The Humana Bldg., 500 W. Main St., 40202, pg. 404 PB
C. Lee Cook Div., P.O. Box 1038, 40201, pg. 521 PB
Corporate Engineering, 2105 Production Dr., 40299, pg. 575 PB
The Courier-Journal Louisville Times Co., 525 W. Broadway, 40201-7431, pg. 700 PB
Courtaulds Coatings Inc., 400 S. 13th St., 40203, pg. 338 IT
CREATIVE ALLIANCE, INC., 437 W. Jefferson St., 40202, pg. 287 PV
CROSS MOTORS CORP., P.O. Box 34067, 40232, pg. 291 PV
CUMMINS CUMBERLAND INC., 304 Whittington Pkwy., Ste. 200, 40222, pg. 295 PV
DMI FURNITURE INC., 101 Bullitt Ln., Ste. 205, 40222, pg. 473 PB
DAHLEM COMPANY, INC., 6200 Dutchman Ln., Ste. LL2, 40205-3285, pg. 306 PV
Dairy Mart Southeast, 10300 Linn Station Rd., 40223, pg. 476 PB
Dairy Queen Corporate Store, 9656 Bluegrass Pkwy. #200, 40299-1902, pg. 220 PB
Dealers Truck Equipment, 12000 Westport Rd., 40223, pg. 700 PV
Delmonico Foods, 2501 S. Floyd St., 40217, pg. 812 PB
Devoe Coatings Co., 4000 Dupont Circle, 40207, pg. 663 IT
Down River Forest Products, Inc., 1391 Dixie Hwy., 40210, pg. 763 PB
Dynacraft, 7010 Riverport Dr., 40258, pg. 1246 PB
ERD Environmental, Inc., 410 W. Chestnut St., Ste. 200, 40202, pg. 546 PB
Early Times Distillers Co., 850 Dixie Hwy., 40210, pg. 261 PB
Edison Homes-Southeast, Inc., The Humana Bldg., 500 W. Main St., 40201, pg. 404 PB
Extendicare Properties, Inc., The Humana Bldg., 500 W. Main St., 40202, pg. 404 PB
FASHION SHOP OF KENTUCKY INC., 11008 Decimal Dr., 40299, pg. 397 PV
The Fifth Third Bank of Kentucky, Louisville, 200 West Broadway, 40201-1110, pg. 621 PB
Fischer Packing Co., 1860 Mellwood Ave., 40206, pg. 201 IT
G.E. Appliances, Appliance Park, 40225, pg. 710 PB
Galen Alaska Realty, Inc., The Humana Bldg., 500 W. Main St., 40202, pg. 404 PB
Galen Hospital Corporation, Inc., The Humana Bldg., 500 W. Main St., 40202, pg. 404 PB
Galen Hospital Illinois, Inc., The Humana Bldg., 500 W. Main St., 40202, pg. 404 PB
Galen Hospital of Baytown, Inc., The Humana Bldg., 500 W. Main St., 40202, pg. 404 PB
Galen International Holdings, Inc., The Humana Bldg., 500 W. Main St., 40202, pg. 404 PB
Galen Medical Corporation, The Humana Bldg., 500 W. Main St., 40202, pg. 404 PB
Galen of Florida, Inc., The Humana Bldg., 500 W. Main St., 40202, pg. 404 PB
Galen of Illinois, Inc., The Humana Bldg., 500 W. Main St., 40202, pg. 404 PB
Galen of Kansas, Inc., The Humana Bldg., 500 W. Main, 40202, pg. 404 PB
Galen of Kentucky, Inc., The Humana Bldg., 500 W. Main St., 40202, pg. 404 PB
Galen of Louisiana, Inc., The Humana Bldg., 500 W. Main St., 40202, pg. 404 PB
Galen of Mississippi, Inc., The Humana Bldg., 500 W. Main St., 40202, pg. 404 PB
Galen of North Carolina, Inc., The Humana Bldg., 500 W. Main St., 40202, pg. 404 PB
Galen of Tennessee, Inc., The Humana Bldg., 500 W. Main St., 40202, pg. 404 PB
Galen of West Virginia, Inc., The Humana Bldg., 500 W. Main St., 40202, pg. 404 PB
Galen Virginia Hospital Corporation, The Humana Bldg., 500 W. Main St., 40202, pg. 404 PB
Gannett Direct Marketing Services, 3400 Robards Ct., 40218, pg. 699 PB
GATEWAY PRESS, INC., 4500 Robards Lane, 40218, pg. 441 PV
General Hospitals of Galen, Inc., The Humana Bldg., 500 W. Main St., 40202, pg. 404 PB
Gohmann Asphalt & Construction of KY., Inc., P.O. Box 19257, 2001 Outer Loop, 40219, pg. 459 PV
GREAT FINANCIAL BANK FSB, One Financial Sq., 40202, pg. 473 PV
GREENBULL INC., 11225 Bluegrass Pkwy., 40299, pg. 477 PV
GRINDMASTER CORPORATION, 4003 Collins Ln., 40245-1643, pg. 482 PV
GRISANTI, INC., 9300 Shelbyville Rd., Ste. 508, 40222, pg. 482 PV
H.H.U.K., Inc., The Humana Bldg., 500 W. Main St., 40202, pg. 405 PB
HALL CONTRACTING CORP., 3800 Crittenden Dr., 40209, pg. 495 PV
Healthsource Kentucky, 100 Mallard Creek Rd., Ste. 300, 40207, pg. 360 PB
HENDERSON ELECTRIC CO., INC., 4502 Poplar Level Rd., 40213, pg. 521 PV
HESCO PARTS CORPORATION, Ten Station Pk., 40210, pg. 524 PV
Hewlett-Packard Company, 305 N. Hurstborune Ln., Ste. 100, 40222, pg. 814 PB
HILLERICH & BRADSBY CO., 800 W. Main St., 40202, pg. 530 PV
Neil Huffman Chrysler Plymouth Dodge, 4126 Shelbyville Rd., 40207, pg. 546 PV
NEIL HUFFMAN NISSAN INC., 3922 Dutchmans Lane, 40207, pg. 546 PV
Neil Huffman Volkswagon Mazda Suburu, 4926 Dixi Highway, 40216, pg. 546 PV

PB - *U.S. Public Companies Volume*
PV - *U.S. Private Companies Volume*
IT - *International Public & Private Companies Volume*

Humana Health Plan, Inc., 101 E. Main St., 40202, pg. 848 **PB**
Humana Health Plan of Louisiana, Inc., 500 W. Main St., 40202, pg. 848 **PB**
Humana Health Plan of Georgia, Inc., 500 W. Main St., 40202, pg. 848 **PB**
HUMANA INC., The Humana Bldg., 500 W. Main St., 40202, pg. 847 **PB**
Hydro Aluminium Louisville, 9400 Williamsburg Plaza, Ste. 120, 40222, pg. 961 **IT**
Ikon Office Solutions-Kentucky, 11401 Bluegrass Pkwy., 40299, pg. 863 **PB**
Independence Television Co., Independence Square, 624 W. Muhammad Ali Blvd., 40203, pg. 147 **PV**
Jenisys Engineered Products, Inc., 9000 Wessex Pl., Ste. 201, 40222, pg. 698 **IT**
K.C.I. Coatings, Inc., 201 E. Market St., 40202, pg. 890 **PV**
KMA Insurance Agency, Inc., 303 N. Hurstbourne Pkwy., 40222, pg. 741 **PB**
KMIC Investment Company, 303 N. Hurstbourne Pkwy., 40222, pg. 741 **PB**
Kentucky Fried Chicken Corporation (KFC), 1441 Gardiner Ln., 40213, pg. 1636 **PB**
KENTUCKY INDIANA LUMBER CO. INC., 227 E. Lee St., 40208, pg. 615 **PV**
Kentucky Insurance Co., One Riverfront Plaza, 19th Fl., 40202, pg. 1454 **PB**
KENTUCKY MANUFACTURING CO., 2601 S. Third St., 40208, pg. 615 **PV**
Kentucky Medical Insurance Company (KMIC), Forum Two, 303 N. Hurstbourne Pkwy., Ste. 200, 40222-5143, pg. 741 **PV**
Kosmos Cement Company, 15301 Dixie Hwy., 40272, pg. 1012 **PB**
LDDS WorldCom, 9300 Shelbyville Rd., Ste. 1000, 40222, pg. 1779 **PB**
LG & E ENERGY CORP., 220 W. Main St., 40202, pg. 970 **PB**
LG & E Energy Systems Inc., 220 West Main St., 40202, pg. 970 **PB**
LABORATORY SUPPLY COMPANY, INC., 250 Ottawa Ave., 40209, pg. 641 **PV**
LANTECH INC., 11000 Bluegrass Pkwy., 40299, pg. 650 **PV**
JACOB LEVY & BROS., INC., 1126 W. Breckinridge St., 40210, pg. 664 **PV**
Liberty Investment Services, Inc., 416 W. Jefferson St., 40202, pg. 173 **PV**
Liqui-Dri Foods, Inc., 12730 H. Westport Rd., 40223, pg. 1348 **PV**
Liquid Transporters, Inc., 1292 Fern Valley Rd. 40219, 40233, pg. 1424 **IT**
Louisville Airline Learning Center, 4528 Bishop Ln., 40218, pg. 219 **PB**
LOUISVILLE BEDDING COMPANY, 10400 Bunsen Way, 40299, pg. 677 **PV**
Louisville Gas and Electric Company, 220 W. Main St., 40202, pg. 970 **PB**
Louisville Ladder Div., 1163 Algonquin Parkway, 40208, pg. 574 **PB**
LOUISVILLE SCRAP MATERIAL CO., INC., 301 E. Main St., 40202, pg. 677 **PV**
Louisville Shopping Center, Inc., 50 The Mall in St. Matthews, 40207, pg. 1407 **PB**
Louisville Transportation, 1601 S. Preston St., 40217, pg. 567 **PV**
MGH Medical, Inc., The Humana Bldg., 500 W. Main St., 40202, pg. 405 **PB**
Maker's Mark Distillery, Inc., 6200 Dutchmans Ln., Ste. 103, 40205, pg. 63 **IT**
Mall St. Matthews Corporation, 50 The Mall, 5000 Shelbyville Rd., 40207, pg. 1408 **PB**
MANNING EQUIPMENT, INC., 12000 Westport Rd., 40223, pg. 700 **PV**
Manning Light Truck Equipment, 3709 Bishop Ln., 40218, pg. 700 **PV**
Manning Truck Modification, 12000 Westport Rd., 40223, pg. 700 **PV**
Medicenter, Louisville, 432 E. Jefferson St., 40402, pg. 1714 **PB**
MERCER TRANSPORTATION CO., 1128 W. Main St., 40203, pg. 732 **PV**
Mid-America Auto Auction, 3515 Newburg Rd., 40218, pg. 1649 **PB**
BOB MONTGOMERY CHEVROLET/HONDA, 5340 Dixie Hwy., 40216, pg. 758 **PV**
NTS DEVELOPMENT COMPANY, 10172 Linn Station Rd., 40223, pg. 772 **PV**
National Asset Management Corporation, 101 S. Fifth St., 40202, pg. 1154 **PB**
National City Bank, Kentucky, 101 S. Fifth St., 40202, pg. 1154 **PB**
National City Leasing Corporation, 101 S. Fifth St., 40202-3101, pg. 1154 **PB**
National City Processing, Inc., 101 Bullitt Ln., Ste. 450, 70222, pg. 1154 **PB**
NEILL-LAVIELLE SUPPLY CO., 1711 S. Floyd St., 40208, pg. 790 **PV**
Notifier Network Technologies Company, pg. 1306 **PV**
ORR SAFETY COMPANY, 2360 Millers Lane, 40216, pg. 820 **PV**
PMM, Inc., The Humana Bldg., 500 W. Main St., 40202, pg. 405 **PB**
PNC Bank, Citizens Plaza, 500 W. Jefferson, 40202, pg. 1242 **PB**
PNC Community Development Corp., 500 W. Jefferson St., 40296, pg. 1243 **PB**
PNC Financial Services, Inc., 500 West Jefferson St., 40296, pg. 1243 **PB**
PNC Florida, Inc., 500 W. Jefferson St., 40296, pg. 1243 **PB**

PNC Leasing Corp., 500 W. Jefferson St., 40296, pg. 1243 **PB**
PNC Realty Corporation, 500 W. Jefferson St., 40296, pg. 1243 **PB**
PAPA JOHN'S INTERNATIONAL INC., 11492 Bluegrass Pkwy., 40299, pg. 1255 **PB**
Frank Paxton Lumber Company, 4990 South Crittenden Drive, 40233, pg. 585 **PV**
PENCO-Kentucky, Watterson Tower, 1930 Bishop Ln., Ste. 415, 40218, pg. 1508 **IT**
Penn Locomotive Gear, 470 Roberts Ave., 40214, pg. 261 **IT**
PORCELAIN METALS CORP., 1400 S. 13th St., 40210, pg. 876 **PV**
President Baking-Louisville, 2287 Ralph Ave., 40216, pg. 1069 **IT**
Primark Tool Group, 1350 S. 15th St., 40210, pg. 575 **PV**
Primary Medical Management, Inc., The Humana Bldg., 500 W. Main St., 40202, pg. 405 **PB**
PROGRESS PAINT MFG. CO., 201 E. Market St., 40202, pg. 890 **PV**
Providan Agency Group, 680 Fourth Ave., 40202, pg. 27 **PB**
Providan Property & Casualty Insurance Co., 323 W. Broadway, 40202, pg. 27 **PB**
Prudential Service Co., 11405 Bluegrass Pkwy., 40299-2394, pg. 893 **PV**
Quality Bearing Service of Kentucky, Inc., Watterson Warehouse-Section 20, 5899 Produce Rd., 40218, pg. 1711 **PV**
Queens Group Kentucky, Inc., 4501 Allmond Ave., 40209, pg. 900 **PV**
RALLY'S HAMBURGERS, INC., 10002 Shelbyville Rd., Ste.150, 40223, pg. 1359 **PB**
RAPID INDUSTRIES, INC., 4003 Oaklawn Dr., 40219, pg. 910 **PV**
Remote Services, Inc., 10300 Linn Station Rd., 40223, pg. 477 **PB**
RES-CARE INCORPORATED, 10140 Linn Station Rd., 40223, pg. 1382 **PB**
REV-A-SHELF, 2409 Plantside Dr., 40299, pg. 925 **PV**
Rhone-Poulenc, 1515 S. 11th St., 40210-2319, pg. 1109 **IT**
Rigo/Black Leaf, 8011 New Lagrange Rd. # 1, 40222, pg. 1390 **PV**
Saint-Gobain Advanced Materials Corporation, 1600 W. Lee St., 40201, pg. 1173 **IT**
Sandvik Sorting Systems, 500 E. Burnett Ave., 40217, pg. 1186 **IT**
Shandwick USA, 950 Breckenridge Lane, 40207, pg. 1227 **IT**
Sociede Anonyme de l'Exploitation de L'Hopital de la Tour, The Humana Bldg., 500 W. Main St., 40202, pg. 405 **PB**
Southern Graphics Systems, 2823 S. Floyd St., 40213, pg. 1386 **IT**
STEEL TECHNOLOGIES INC., 15415 Shelbyville Rd., 40245, pg. 1513 **PB**
SULLIVAN & COZART INC., 822 W. Kentucky St., 40203, pg. 1049 **PV**
SAM SWOPE AUTO GROUP, INC., Swope Auto Ctr., 40299, pg. 1059 **PV**
Sysco/Louisville Food Services Co., 7705 National Turnpike, 40214, pg. 1552 **PB**
TARRANT SERVICE, INC., 1830 Cargo Ct., 40299, pg. 1069 **PV**
Taywood Minerals Inc., 2600 Citizens Plaza, 40202, pg. 1359 **IT**
Taywood Mining Inc., 2600 Citizens Plaza, 40202, pg. 1359 **IT**
THOMAS INDUSTRIES INC., 4360 Brownsboro Rd., Ste. 300, 40232, pg. 1598 **PB**
THORNTON OIL CORP., 10101 Linn Station Rd., Ste. 200, 40223, pg. 1084 **PV**
Thorobred Containers Incorporated, 1400 Southwestern Pkwy., 40211, pg. 567 **PV**
Thoroughbred Plastics Corp., 11601 Electron Dr., 40299, pg. 261 **PB**
Thriftway, Inc., 720 Locust Ln., 40217, pg. 1771 **PB**
TOWN & COUNTRY FORD INC., 6015 Preston Hwy., 40219, pg. 1093 **PV**
TRI-CITY OLDSMOBILE INC., 3920 Dutchmans Ln., 40207, pg. 1100 **PV**
TRICON GLOBAL RESTAURANTS, INC., 1441 Gardiner Lane, 40213, pg. 1636 **PB**
Trimac Bulk Transportation, Inc., 1292 Fern Valley Rd. 40219, 40233, pg. 1424 **IT**
Trimac Transportation, Inc.-Eastern Division, c/o Liquid Transporters, Inc., pg. 1424 **IT**
UMI Data Courier, 620 S. Third St., 40202, pg. 201 **PB**
United Leasing Company, The Summit II, Ste. 105, 4360 Brownsboro Rd., 40207-1642, pg. 741 **PV**
VAC Data Management, Inc., 100 E. Liberty St., 40202, pg. 575 **PB**
VALU DISCOUNT, INCORPORATED, 3916 Dupont Square S., 40207, pg. 1132 **PV**
VENCOR, INC., 400 W. Market St., Ste. 3300, 40202, pg. 1711 **PB**
Vermont American Tool Corp., 101 S. 5th St., Ste. 2300, 40202, pg. 575 **PB**
HENRY VOGT MACHINE CO., 1000 W. Ormsby Ave., 40210, pg. 1143 **PV**
Vulcan-Hart Corp., 2006 N. Western Pkwy., 40203, pg. 1322 **PB**
WAMZ-FM, 520 W. Chestnut, 40202, pg. 384 **PB**
WAVE-TV, 725 S. Floyd, 40203, pg. 992 **PB**
WHAS-AM, 520 W. Chestnut, 40202, pg. 385 **PB**
WHKW-FM, 520 W. Chestnut, 40202, pg. 385 **PB**
WKJK-AM, 520 W. Chestnut, 40202, pg. 385 **PB**
WLKY-AM, 1918 Mellwood Ave., 40206, pg. 1344 **PB**
WLKY-TV, 1918 Mellwood Ave., 40206-1035, pg. 1344 **PB**

WEHR CONSTRUCTORS INC., 2517 Plantside Dr., 40299, pg. 1159 **PV**
Western Pioneer Life Insurance Co., 100 Mallard Creek Rd., Ste. 400, 40207, pg. 853 **PV**
WHITTENBERG CONSTRUCTION CO., 4774 Allmond Ave., 40209, pg. 1174 **PV**
Willis Corroon Administrative Services Corporation, 2300 Greene Way, 40220, pg. 1504 **IT**
Willis Corroon Corporation of Louisville, 2303 Greene Way, Ste. 100, 40220, pg. 1505 **IT**
Windsor Health Care Center, 9600 Lamburne Blvd., 40272, pg. 1715 **PB**
Winn-Dixie Louisville, Inc., 720 Locust Ln., 40213, pg. 1771 **PB**
Wireless Data Group, 3899 Produce Rd., #208, 40218-3096, pg. 1139 **PB**
Yokohama Tire Corporation, 6101 Cane Run Rd., 40258, pg. 1521 **IT**
Zellerbach Division, 1001 Industrial Blvd., 40219, pg. 1075 **PB**
ZINIZ INC., 3955 E. Blue Lick Rd., 40229, pg. 1206 **PV**
ZOELLER CO., 3280 Old Millers Lane, 40216, pg. 1207 **PV**

Ludlow

DURO BAG MANUFACTURING CO., Davies & Oak Sts., 41016, pg. 348 **PV**

Madisonville

Ahlstrom Filtration, Inc.-Madisonville Mill, 215 Nebo Rd., 42431, pg. 35 **IT**
Citizens Bank of Kentucky, 149 S. Main St., 42431, pg. 280 **PB**
Farmers Bank & Trust Co., 77 N. Main St., 42431, pg. 1217 **PB**
Landstar Ligon, Inc., 2911A Anton Rd., 42431, pg. 978 **PB**
National Mine Service Company, Madisonville Div., P.O. Box 497, Natl. Mine Dr., 42431, pg. 281 **IT**
Peoples Security Finance Company, Inc., P.O. Box 76, 42431, pg. 280 **PB**

Mayfield

Kentucky-Tennessee Clay Co., P.O. Box 6002, 5080 State St., Rt. 45 S., 42066, pg. 804 **PB**

Maysville

Emerson Power Transmission Co., 1248 E. Second St., 41056, pg. 573 **PB**

Middlesboro

Cyprus Cumberland Coal Corporation, 501 North 19th St., 40965, pg. 471 **PB**
Daily News, PO Box 579, 120 N. 11th. Street, 40965, pg. 632 **IT**
Dura-Line Corp., South 23rd St., 40965, pg. 598 **PV**

Millersburg

Stamler Corporation, Main & Stamler Sts., 40348, pg. 814 **PV**

Morganfield

Citizens Bank of Kentucky, 101 E. Main St., 42437, pg. 280 **PB**
Morganfield National Bank, P.O. Box 390, 42437, pg. 1217 **PB**
Trelleborg YSH, Inc.-Western Kentucky Division, P.O. Box 329, U.S. Hwy. 60 N. Industrial Pk., 42437, pg. 1422 **IT**

Morgantown

Morgantown Plastics Company, 825 Rochester Rd., 42261, pg. 1054 **PB**

Mount Sterling

Cooper Tire & Rubber Company, Mt. Sterling Plant, 250 Oak Grove Dr., 40353, pg. 445 **PB**
Precision Resource-Kentucky Div., 171 Oak Grove Dr., pg. 880 **PV**

Murray

Kenlake Foods, 300 N. L.P. Miller St., 42071-2102, pg. 967 **PV**
Major Pharmaceuticals, 415 S. Fourth St., 42071, pg. 475 **PV**
Ryan Foods, 100 E. Chestnut St., 42071, pg. 491 **PB**

Newport

L.B. Foster Company-Newport Plant, 910 Lowell St., 41071, pg. 676 **PB**
Heinz Pet Products Company, One Riverfront Pl., 41071, pg. 806 **PB**
NS GROUP, INC., Ninth & Lowell Sts., 41072, pg. 1147 **PB**
NATIONAL BAND & TAG CO., 721 York, 41071, pg. 780 **PV**

PB - *U.S. Public Companies Volume*
PV - *U.S. Private Companies Volume*
IT - *International Public & Private Companies Volume*

Geographic Index-U.S.

1251

Newport Steel Corporation, Ninth & Lowell Sts., 41072, pg. 1147 — **PB**
SENCORP, One Riverfront Pl., 41071, pg. 983 — **PV**
Star-Kist Foods Inc., One Riverfront Pl., 41071, pg. 805 — **PB**
Star-Kist Foods, Inc., One Riverfront Pl., 41071, pg. 806 — **PB**
TRAUTH DAIRY INC., 16 E. 11th St., 41071, pg. 1098 — **PV**

Nicholasville

SARGENT & GREENLEAF, INC., One Security Dr., 40356, pg. 965 — **PV**
Sargent and Greenleaf, One Security Dr., 40356, pg. 981 — **PV**

Owensboro

Farmers Elevators, Inc., 719 E. 2nd Street, 42301, pg. 824 — **PV**
FIELD PACKING COMPANY, Six Dublin Ln., 42304, pg. 403 — **PV**
The HON Co., Owensboro Plant, 931 Wing Ave., 42301, pg. 772 — **PB**
Liberty National Bank of Owensboro, 200 E. Third, 42301, pg. 173 — **PB**
MPD, INC., 316 E. 9th St., 42303, pg. 687 — **PV**
MPH & CMI, 316 E. Ninth St., 42301, pg. 687 — **PV**
MODERN WELDING CO., INC., P.O. Box 1450, 2880 New Hartford Rd., 42303, pg. 755 — **PV**
OWENSBORO GRAIN CO., INC., 719 E. Second St., 42301, pg. 824 — **PV**
Smith & Butterfield, 115 E. 3rd St., 42301, pg. 333 — **PB**
Southern Petroleum Equipment Co., Inc., 1610 Haynes Ave., 42303, pg. 614 — **PV**
Southern Tank & Manufacturing, Inc., 1501 Haynes Ave., 42303, pg. 614 — **PV**
Texas Gas Transmission, 3800 Frederica St., 42301, pg. 1769 — **PB**
Western Kentucky Gas Co., P.O. Box 866, 2401 New Hartford Rd., 42302, pg. 146 — **PB**
Willis Corroon Corporation of Owensboro, 401 Frederica St., Ste. 201A, 42301, pg. 1505 — **IT**

Owenton

Schlumberger Industries, 970 Hwy. 127 N., 40359-9805, pg. 1439 — **PB**

Paducah

AmeriSource-Paducah Div., 322 N. Third St., 42001, pg. 97 — **PB**
Charter Behavioral Health System of Paducah, Inc., 435 Berger RD., 42002-7609, pg. 1034 — **PB**
Grocery Supply of Paducah, 911 Joe Clifton Dr., 42002-7703, pg. 436 — **PV**
Pressure Pak Container, Inc., 3200 Bullard St., 42001, pg. 300 — **PV**

Paris

The Fifth Third Bank of Kentucky, 41 Main St., 40361, pg. 621 — **PB**
Weatherly Consumer Products, 1750 17th St., 40361, pg. 1682 — **PB**

Pikeville

Eastern Division, P.O. Box, Tollage Creek Rd., 41501, pg. 337 — **IT**
Willis Corroon Administrative Services Corporation, 548 S. Mayo Trail, 41501, pg. 1504 — **IT**

Pineville

Pineville Health Care Center, Inc., Rte. 1, Box 102, 40977, pg. 1714 — **PB**

Richmond

Lectrodryer Div., Ajax Magnethermic Corp., P.O. Box 2500, 40476-2602, pg. 113 — **IT**
MADISON GROCERY CO., INC., P.O. Box 580, 40476-0580, pg. 694 — **PV**
Roosevelt Paper Company, 11001 Paper Blvd., 41094, pg. 943 — **PV**

Russell

ASHLAND, INC., 1000 Ashland Dr., 41169, pg. 138 — **PB**

Russellville

ARCO Aluminum, P.O. Box 3000, 42276, pg. 144 — **PB**
BTR Precision Die Casting, Inc., Hwy. 68 West, P.O. Box 440, 42276, pg. 127 — **IT**
Trans Financial Bank, F.S.B., 135 W. Fourth St., 42276, pg. 1628 — **PB**

Scottsville

Dade Lease Management, Inc., 427 Beech St., 42164, pg. 515 — **PB**
Dolgencorp, Inc., 427 Beech St., 42164, pg. 515 — **PB**
DOLLAR GENERAL CORP., 427 Bee St., 42164, pg. 338 — **PV**

Shelbyville

Alcoa Fujikura Inc., 421 Haven Hill Rd., 40065, pg. 61 — **PB**
Bekaert Corporation, 2000 Isaac Shelby Dr., 40065, pg. 184 — **IT**
Landmark Community Newspapers, Inc., 601 Taylorsville Rd., 40065, pg. 648 — **PV**
Liberty National Bank of Shelbyville, 544 Main, 40065, pg. 173 — **PB**
Ohio Valley Aluminum Company, 1100 Brooks Industrial Park, 40065, pg. 567 — **PV**
Plastic Parts, Inc., 545 Pierce Industrial Rd., 40065, pg. 1143 — **PB**
ROLL FORMING CORPORATION, Industrial Park, 1070 Brooks Industrial Rd., 40065, pg. 941 — **PV**
Sentinel-News, P.O. Box 399, 703 Taylorsville Rd., 40066, pg. 648 — **PV**
Soltech, Inc, 400 Issac Shelby Dr., 400065, pg. 1237 — **PB**

Shepherdsville

ALLTEL Kentucky, Inc., 229 Lees Valley Rd., P.O. Box 68, 40165, pg. 56 — **PB**
Pioneer News, P.O. Box 98, 455 N. Buckman, 40165, pg. 648 — **PV**

Shively

Citizens Bank of Kentucky, 4040 Dixie Hwy., 40216, pg. 280 — **PB**

Somerset

Alumitech, 1278 Hwy. 461, 42501, pg. 513 — **PV**
SOMERSET REFINERY INC., 600 Monticello St., 42501, pg. 1013 — **PV**
SOUTHERN BELLE DAIRY COMPANY, P.O. Box 1020, 607 E. Bourne Ave., 42502-1020, pg. 1015 — **PV**

Springfield

The Springfield Sun, P.O. Box 31, 117 Cross Main, 40069, pg. 648 — **PV**

Stanford

Tri-K Landfill, Inc., 1905 Kentucky Hwy. 324, 40484, pg. 1379 — **IT**

Stanton

U.S. Brick, Inc.-Sipple Brick Division, P.O. Box 567, Hwy. 213 No., 40380, pg. 699 — **IT**

Stearns

OUTDOOR VENTURE CORP., Hwy. 92, 42653, pg. 822 — **PV**

Sturgis

Pyro Mining Co., P.O. Box 267, 42459, pg. 337 — **IT**
West Kentucky Division, P.O. Box 289, 42459, pg. 337 — **IT**

Taylorsville

Spencer Magnet, P.O. Box 219, 306 Main St., 40071, pg. 648 — **PV**

Union

PNC Bank, Northern Kentucky, 9990 U.S. 42, 41091, pg. 1243 — **PB**

Versailles

Carolina Steel Service Center Plant, 107 Fieldview Dr., 40383, pg. 214 — **PV**
Kuhlman Electric Corporation, 101 Kuhlman Blvd., 40383, pg. 368 — **PB**

Walton

Clarion Manufacturing Corp. of America, P.O. Box 240, 237 Beaver Rd., 41094, pg. 296 — **IT**
Continental Web Press Of Kentucky, 125 Richwood Dr., 41094, pg. 269 — **PV**
Duro Paper Bag Mfg. Co., Richwood Industrial Pk., Shoreland Dr., 41094, pg. 349 — **PV**
Dynamec, International Industrial Park, 12209 Chandler Dr., 41094, pg. 193 — **IT**

West Prestonburg

ICI Explosives, P.O. Box 307, 41668, pg. 664 — **IT**

Wilder

CARLISLE EQUIPMENT COMPANY, 840 Licking Pike, 41076, pg. 211 — **PV**
Circle Freight International USA, 9 Beacon Dr., 41076, pg. 371 — **PB**
Circle International, 9 Beacon Dr., 41076, pg. 371 — **PB**
Max Gruenhut International Inc. USA, 9 Beacon Dr., 41076, pg. 372 — **PB**

Williamsburg

Firestone Industrial Products Company-Williamsburg, One Firestone Blvd., 40769-0509, pg. 214 — **IT**

Williamstown

Epperson Waste Disposal, Inc., 2260 Cynthiana Rd., 41097, pg. 1379 — **PB**
Grant County News, P.O. Box 247, 146 N. Main, 41097, pg. 648 — **PV**

Winchester

Bundy Corporation, Winchester Tool Plant, P.O. Box 515, 40392-0515, pg. 1341 — **IT**
Charleston Bottoms Rural Electric, 4775 Lexington Rd., 40391, pg. 357 — **PV**
Corrugated Products Division, P.O. Box 533, 400 Mt. Sterling Rd., 40391, pg. 763 — **PB**
Delgasco, Inc., 3617 Lexington Rd., 40391, pg. 497 — **PB**
DELTA NATURAL GAS COMPANY, INC., 3617 Lexington Rd., 40391, pg. 497 — **PB**
Delta Resources, Inc., 3617 Lexington Rd., 430391, pg. 497 — **PB**
Deltran, Inc., 3617 Lexington Rd., 40391, pg. 497 — **PB**
EAST KENTUCKY POWER CO-OP, 4775 Lexington Rd., 40391, pg. 356 — **PV**
Enpro, Inc., 3617 Lexington Rd., 40391, pg. 497 — **PB**
Structural Foam Plastics, Inc., 5555 Rockwell Rd., 40391, pg. 1048 — **PB**
Wright & Lopez, Inc., 129 Hud Rd., 40391, pg. 843 — **PV**

LOUISIANA

Abbeville

Zapata Haynie Corp., P.O. Box 369, 70510, pg. 1790 — **PB**

Alexandria

Alexandria Daily Town Talk, 1201 Third St., 71306, pg. 326 — **PB**
Century Telephone Enterprises, Inc., 6501 Coliseum, 71303-3735, pg. 329 — **PB**
Century Telephone, Region I, P.O. Drawer 6117, Government St., 71307-6117, pg. 329 — **PB**
Dolphin Construction Co., 4600 Lee St., 71301, pg. 1585 — **PB**
Louisiana Industries Div., 4600 Lee St., 71301, pg. 1585 — **PB**
PETRON, INC., 1600 Harris St., 71301, pg. 859 — **PV**
Rapides Bank & Trust Company of Alexandria, 400 Murray St., 71301, pg. 630 — **PB**
Southern Electric Supply Co., Inc., 3008 Broadway, 71301, pg. 1108 — **IT**
Surplus Warehouse-Alexandria, Hwy. 28 W., 5614 Coliseum Blvd., 71303, pg. 119 — **PV**

Amelia

Tidewater Marine, Inc., P.O. Box 1519, 70340, pg. 1608 — **PB**

Amite

Amite Foundry and Machine, Inc., 13040 Foulks Ln., 70422, pg. 142 — **PB**

Arcadia

ConAgra Feed Mill, Hwy. 80 E., 71001, pg. 427 — **PB**

Avery Island

MCILHENNY COMPANY, 70513, pg. 722 — **PV**
McIlhenny Resources, 70513, pg. 722 — **PV**

Avondale

American Melamine Industries Inc., 70094, pg. 355 — **IT**
AVONDALE INDUSTRIES, INC., 5100 River Rd., 70094, pg. 156 — **PB**

Bastrop

Rhone Poulenc - Basic Chemical Division, P.O. Box 551, 71221-0551, pg. 1112 — **IT**

Baton Rouge

A-G Safety Sales, Inc., 5830 McCann Dr., 70809, pg. 1650 — **PB**
ACME REFRIGERATION OF BATON ROUGE INC., 11844 S. Choctaw Dr., 70815, pg. 13 — **PV**
Ahlstrom Process Equipment Inc., 1301 Industriplex Blvd., Ste. 5, 70809, pg. 34 — **IT**
AIRTROL, INC., 3960 North St., 70806, pg. 29 — **PV**
Allright Baton Rouge, Inc., 218 Laurel, 70801, pg. 42 — **PV**
ANCO INSULATIONS, INC., 15981 Airline Hwy., 70817, pg. 71 — **PV**
Ascension Water Co., 8755 Goodwood Blvd., 70806, pg. 123 — **PV**
ASSOCIATED GROCERS, INC., 8686 Anselmo Ln., 70810, pg. 90 — **PV**

PB - *U.S. Public Companies Volume*
PV - *U.S. Private Companies Volume*
IT - *International Public & Private Companies Volume*

1252

Geographic Index-U.S.

Bank One, Louisiana, 451 Florida St., 70801, pg. 173 **PB**
BARBER BROTHERS CONTRACTING COMPANY, 2636 Dougherty Dr., 70805, pg. 115 **PV**
Baton Rouge Machine Works Inc., 12612 Ronaldson Rd., 70807, pg. 1489 **IT**
BATON ROUGE WATER WORKS COMPANY, 8755 Goodwood Blvd., 70806, pg. 122 **PV**
Block Plant, P.O. Box 1107, 4747 Choctaw Dr., 70821, pg. 936 **PB**
Bourque Printing, 13112 S. Choctaw Dr., 70815, pg. 333 **PB**
BUQUET & LE BLANC INC., 18145 Petroleum Rd., 70809, pg. 181 **PV**
Cajun Bayou Distributors & Management, Inc., 7110 Airline Hwy., 70806, pg. 1294 **PV**
CAJUN ELECTRIC POWER CO-OP, 10719 Airline Hwy., 70816, pg. 199 **PV**
Capitol Steel, Inc., 2655 N. Foster Dr., 70805, pg. 412 **PV**
CARTER CHAMBERS SUPPLY, INC., 6800 S. Choctaw Dr., 70806, pg. 216 **PV**
Chotin Carriers, Inc., 7747 Tom Drive, 70806, pg. 962 **PB**
Cigna Healthcare of Louisiana, Inc., 4354 S. Sherwood Forest Blvd., Ste. D240, 70816, pg. 360 **PB**
City National Bank of Baton Rouge, 445 North Blvd., 70821, pg. 629 **PB**
COLEMAN OLDSMOBILE, INC., P.O. Box 3315, 70821, pg. 252 **PV**
DSM Copolymer, Inc., 5955 Scenic Hwy., 70821, pg. 354 **IT**
Delta Insurance Services Corp., P.O. Box 261748, 70826-1748, pg. 91 **PV**
DIAMOND MOTORS INC., 12422 Florida Blvd., 70815, pg. 330 **PV**
DISTRIBUTORS OIL COMPANY, INC., 4085 Florida Blvd., 70806, pg. 336 **PV**
Dixie Linehaul Group, 7747 Tom Dr., 70806, pg. 961 **PB**
Dixie River Tow Group, 7747 Tom Dr., 70806, pg. 961 **PB**
A.K. DURNIN CHRYSLER PLYMOUTH, INC., 6815 Florida Blvd., 70806, pg. 348 **PV**
Express 1 Stop, 2773 N. Flannery Rd., 70814, pg. 1050 **PV**
Flowers Baking Co. of Baton Rouge, Inc., 1504 Florida Blvd., 70821, pg. 657 **PB**
FRAENKEL COMPANY, 10600 S. Choctaw Dr., 70815, pg. 423 **PV**
Green Tree Acceptance of Louisiana, Inc., 3232 Sherwood Forest Blvd., Ste. 225, 70816-2218, pg. 762 **PB**
GROUP INSURANCE INC. OF LOUISIANA, Sherwood Tower, 3636 Sherwood Forest Blvd. Ste. 111, 70816, pg. 484 **PV**
Guaranty Broadcasting, 929 Government St., 70802, pg. 485 **PV**
GUARANTY CORPORATION, 929 Government St., 70802, pg. 485 **PV**
Guaranty Income Life Insurance Co., 929 Government St., 70802, pg. 485 **PV**
HECK INDUSTRIES, 5415 Choctaw, 70805, pg. 519 **PV**
Hewlett-Packard Company, 4334 S. Sherwood Forrest Blvd., Ste. 185, 70816, pg. 814 **IT**
HI NABOR SUPERMARKET INC., 7201 Winbourne Ave., 70805, pg. 525 **PV**
Institutional Equipment & Interiors, Inc., P.O. Box 2467, 70821, pg. 1294 **PB**
JE Merit Constructors, Inc., 4949 Essen Ln., 70809, pg. 921 **PB**
Jacobs Engineering Group Inc., 4949 Essen Ln., 70809, pg. 921 **PB**
Jacobs Maintenance, Inc., 4949 Essen Lane, 70809, pg. 921 **PB**
LAMAR CORPORATION, 5551 Corporate Blvd., 70808, pg. 644 **PV**
LaRoche Air Systems Inc., 10132 Mammoth Dr., 70814-4420, pg. 652 **PV**
Lincoln Big Three, Inc., P.O. Box 3274, 70821, pg. 37 **IT**
Louisiana Farm Bureau Casualty Insurance Company, 9516 Airline Hwy., 70815, pg. 1016 **PV**
Louisiana Reference Laboratory, 6746 Goya Ave., Ste. A, 70806, pg. 1265 **IT**
Louisiana Utilities Supply Company, 2056 Sorrel, 70821, pg. 245 **PV**
M.O.V. of Louisiana, Inc., 5801 McCann Dr., 70809, pg. 162 **PV**
Maison Blanche, Inc., 1500 Main St., pg. 1090 **PB**
Medical Center of Baton Rouge, 17000 Medical Center Dr., 70816, pg. 405 **PB**
Mercantile Credit Corp., 1500 Main St., 70802, pg. 1090 **PB**
Network Acquisition Corp., 525 Florida St., 70801, pg. 1169 **PB**
NETWORK LONG DISTANCE, INC., 525 Florida St., 70801, pg. 1169 **PB**
THE NEWTRON GROUP INC., 8183 W. El Cajon Dr., 70815, pg. 797 **PV**
Norton Process Services Inc., 4137 S. Sherwood Forest Blvd., Ste. 220, 70816, pg. 1176 **IT**
OLINDE HARDWARE & SUPPLY CO., 9536 Airline Hwy., 70815, pg. 814 **PV**
PALA GROUP, INC., 16347 Old Hammond Hwy., 70816, pg. 834 **PV**
Pala Interstate, 16347 Old Hammond Hwy., 70816, pg. 834 **PV**
Parish Water Company, Inc., 8755 Goodwood Blvd., 70806, pg. 123 **PV**
Payne & Keller Company, Inc., 4949 Essen Ln., 70809, pg. 921 **PV**
PENCO-Louisiana, 8676 Goodwood Blvd., Ste. 401, 70806, pg. 1508 **IT**
PERFORMANCE CONTRACTORS INC., 9865 Pecue Lane, 70810, pg. 853 **PV**
PICCADILLY CAFETERIAS, INC., 3232 Sherwood Forest Blvd., 70816, pg. 1294 **PB**

Piccadilly Restaurants, Inc., P.O. Box 2467, 70821, pg. 1294 **PB**
Premier Bank N.A., 451 Florida St., 70821, pg. 173 **PB**
Premier Securities Corporation, 451 Florida St., 70801, pg. 173 **PB**
Reynolds Metals Company-Baton Rouge, P.O. Box 4448, Brooklawn Dr., 70821, pg. 1385 **PB**
Southern Electric Supply Co., Inc., 8536 S. Choctaw Dr., 70815, pg. 1108 **IT**
Southern Instruments, Inc., 4949 Essen Ln., 70809, pg. 921 **PB**
Southern Manufacturers Rep., Inc., P.O. Box 15621, 70895, pg. 736 **IT**
Southern Mortgage Company, Inc., 4041 Essen Ln., 70809, pg. 1675 **PB**
Stupp Corporation, 12555 Ronaldson Rd., 70807, pg. 1048 **PB**
SULLIVAN OIL COMPANY, 1785 Wooddale Ct., 70806-1523, pg. 1050 **PV**
TPT Transportation Company, 7747 Tom Drive, 70806, pg. 962 **PB**
Thomas Pipe & Steel, Inc., P.O. Box 53187, 70892, pg. 508 **PV**
TURNER INDUSTRIES, 8687 United Plaza Blvd., 70809, pg. 1109 **PV**
UPB of Louisiana, 8440 Jefferson Hwy., 70809, pg. 1669 **PB**
United Communications Corporation of Louisiana, Inc., 8550 United Plaza Blvd., 70809, pg. 1675 **PB**
UNITED COMPANIES FINANCIAL CORPORATION, One United Plaza, 4041 Essen Ln., 70809, pg. 1675 **PB**
United Companies Investor Services, Inc., 4041 Essen Laneza Blvd., 70809, pg. 1675 **PB**
United Companies Lending Corporation, 4041 Essen Ln., 70809, pg. 1675 **PB**
United Companies Life Insurance Co., 4041 Essen Lane, 70809, pg. 1271 **PB**
United Companies Realty & Development Co., Inc., P. O. Box 1591, One United Plaza, 70821, pg. 1675 **PB**
United General Title Insurance Company, 4041 Essen Ln., 70821, pg. 1675 **PB**
United General Title Insurance Company-Baton Rouge, Two United Plaza, 8550 United Plaza Blvd., Ste. 502, 70809, pg. 1675 **PB**
United Plan Insurance Agency, Inc., 4041 Essen Ln., 70821, pg. 1675 **PB**
WOODFIN PONTIAC-ISUZU, 300 Wooddale Blvd., pg. 1187 **PV**
Woodward-Clyde, 2822 O'Neal Ln., 70816, pg. 1656 **PV**

Belle Chasse

Dixie Carriers, Inc., 33 W.P.A. Rd., 70037, pg. 962 **PB**
Dixie Fuels Limited, 33 W.P.A. Rd., 70037, pg. 962 **PB**
Dixie Fuels II, Limited, 33 W.P.A. Rd., 70037, pg. 962 **PB**

Bogalusa

American Fabrics Co., 215 Industrial Pkwy., 70427, pg. 53 **PV**

Bossier City

Charter Louisiana Behavioral Health System, Inc., 1514 Doctor's Dr., 71111, pg. 1035 **PB**
Liberia Mfg. Co., 4300 Viking Rd., 71111, pg. 491 **PB**
Louisiana Downs, 8000 E. Texas, 71111, pg. 319 **PV**

Breaux Bridge

Coastal Telephone & Electronics, P.O. Drawer 340, 151 Domengeaux, 70517, pg. 329 **PB**

Broussard

Chem-Tech, Inc., 200 N. Morgan, 70518, pg. 1478 **PB**
Cliffs Drilling Co., 3735 Hwy. 90 E., 70518, pg. 386 **PB**
ENSCO Marine Co., 620 Moulin Rd., 70518, pg. 585 **PB**

Cade

BRUCE FOODS CORP., Hwy 182 W., 70519, pg. 175 **PV**

Carville

Cos-Mar, Inc., 6235 Louisiana Hwy. 75, 70721, pg. 1044 **IT**

Chalmette

Chalmette Medical Center, 9001 Patricia St., 70043, pg. 1697 **PB**
Domino Sugar Corporation-Chalmette, 7417 N. Peters St., 70032, pg. 1356 **IT**
Laboratory Supply Company, 401 E. Magistrate St., 70043, pg. 642 **PV**

Cotton Valley

Hunt Oil Cotton Valley District, P.O. Box 38, 71018-0038, pg. 548 **PV**

Covington

Fritz Culver, Inc., P.O. Box 569, 70434-0569, pg. 778 **PB**
IRT Property Company, 19267 Slemmer Rd., Ste. 100, 70433, pg. 858 **PB**

De Quincy

KARTS INTERNATIONAL INC., 109 Northpark Blvd., Ste. 210, 70433, pg. 944 **PB**
SCP Pool Corporation, 128 Northpark Blvd., 70433-5070, pg. 249 **PV**

Asbury Louisiana, Inc., P.O. Box 876, 70633, pg. 87 **PV**

Denham Springs

Pro Shop (Baton Rouge, LA), P.O. Box 964, 70727-0964, pg. 861 **PB**

Donaldsonville

Melamine Chemicals, Inc., P.O. Box 748, 70346, pg. 344 **PB**
Security Industrial Insurance Co., Inc., P.O. Box 609, 70346, pg. 814 **IT**
Triad Chemical, P.O. Box 310, 39041 Hwy. 18W., 70346-0310, pg. 1117 **PB**
Triad Nitrogen, Inc., P.O. Box 310, 70346-0310, pg. 1117 **PB**

Dubach

Dubach Gas Company, P.O. Box 68, Hwy. 167 S., Rt. 2, Box 1-3, 71235, pg. 567 **PB**

Erath

Texaco USA, P.O. Box 356, 70533-0356, pg. 1583 **PB**

Geismar

Monochem, Inc., 70734, pg. 158 **PV**
Rubicon Inc., P.O. Box 517, 70734, pg. 460 **PV**
Uniroyal Chemical Co., Inc., P.O. Box 397, Highway 30, 70734, pg. 460 **PB**
Uniroyal Chemical Co., Inc., P.O. Box 118, 70734, pg. 460 **PB**

Gonzales

Advanced Tel, Inc., 913 S. Burnside Ave., 70737, pg. 358 **PV**
East Ascension Telephone Company, 913 S. Burnside Ave., 70737, pg. 358 **PV**
Eatel Construction Co., Inc., 913 S. Burnside Ave., 70737, pg. 358 **PV**
Eatel Publishing Inc., 913 S. Burnside Ave., 70737, pg. 358 **PV**
Eatel Technology Outlet, 913 S. Burnside Ave., 70737, pg. 358 **PV**
EATELCORP INC., 913 S. Burnside Ave., 70737, pg. 358 **PV**

Gramercy

Colonial Sugar, Inc. Refinery, P.O. Box 3360, 1230 S. Fifth Ave., 70052, pg. 872 **PB**

Gretna

ANF Partners # 1, 701 Madison St., 70053, pg. 361 **PB**
BCP TECHNICAL SERVICE, INC., 401 Whitney Ave., Ste. 314, 70056, pg. 106 **PV**
PSG, P.O. Box 308, 70054, pg. 1774 **PB**
REAGAN EQUIPMENT COMPANY, INC., 2550 Belle Chase Hwy., 70053, pg. 913 **PV**

Hammond

Deposit Guaranty National Bank of Louisiana, 201 N.W. Railroad Ave., 70401, pg. 500 **PB**
Zapata Haynie Corp., P.O. Box 2868, 70404, pg. 1789 **PB**

Harahan

Arrow-Sysco Food Services, Inc., 1451 River Oaks W., 70123-2176, pg. 1551 **PB**
Atlas Steel & Wire, 221 Hord St., 70123, pg. 65 **PV**
Cox Communications-Jefferson Parish Office, 338 Edwards Ave., 70123, pg. 455 **PB**
DigiCourse, Inc., 5200 Toler St., 70123, pg. 643 **PV**
DIVERSIFIED GROUP, INC., 5801 Citrus Blvd., 70123, pg. 336 **PV**
Intralox, Inc., 201 Laitram Ln., 70123, pg. 643 **PV**
THE LAITRAM CORPORATION, 220 Laitram Ln., 70123, pg. 643 **PV**
Laitram Machinery Inc., 220 Laitram Ln., 70123, pg. 643 **PV**
Lapeyre Stair, Inc., 220 Laitram Ln., 70123, pg. 643 **PV**
ODG, 1320 Sams Ave., 70123, pg. 1774 **PB**
RHG New Orleans, 5515 Pepsi St., Suite C, 70123, pg. 1151 **IT**
Southern Electric Supply Co., Inc., 5712 Jarvis St., 70123, pg. 1108 **IT**
Tano Automation, Inc., 5700 Citrus Blvd., Ste. E, 70123, pg. 1763 **PB**
Video Services, Inc., 520 Elmwood Park Blvd., 70123, pg. 47 **PB**
WALLE CORPORATION, 600 Elmwood Park Blvd., 70123, pg. 1771 **PV**
Winn-Dixie Louisiana, Inc., 600 Edwards Ave., 70123, pg. 1771 **PB**

Geographic Index-U.S.

Geographic Index-U.S.

Harvey

ACME TRUCK LINE, INC., 1105 Peters Rd., 70059, pg. 14   PV

EVANS INDUSTRIES, INC., 1255 Peters Rd., 70058, pg. 385   PV

INTREPID ENTERPRISES, INC., 1848 Industrial Blvd., 70058, pg. 574   PV

LGS Concord Corp., 1233 Westbank Expwy., 70059, pg. 380   PB

LGS Energy Corp., 1233 Westbank Expwy., 70058, pg. 380   PB

LGS Exploration, Inc., 1233 Westbank Expwy., 70058, pg. 380   PB

LGS Financial Services, Inc., 1233 Westbank Expwy., 70058, pg. 380   PB

LGS Pipeline, Inc., 1233 Westbank Expwy., 70058, pg. 380   PB

LGS Securities, Inc., P.O. Box 433, 70059, pg. 380   PB

LESON CHEVROLET COMPANY, INC., 1501 Westbank Expwy., 70058, pg. 660   PV

Pool Company, 3640 Peters Rd., 70058, pg. 1316   PB

PRODUCTION MANAGEMENT COMPANIES, INC., 2439 Manhattan Blvd., Ste. 500, 70058, pg. 888   PV

Production Management Industries, Inc., 2804 Peters Rd., 70058, pg. 889   PV

Sigma Coatings, Inc., P.O. Box 816, 70059, pg. 1044   IT

Van Leeuwen Pipe & Tube Corp., 2439 Manhattan Blvd., Ste. 300, 70767, pg. 1449   IT

Homer

Ludlow Laminating & Coating Div., 1 Minden Rd., Box 749, 71040, pg. 1647   PB

Houma

Caro Produce & Institutional Foods, 2324 Bayou Blue Rd., 70364, pg. 1278   PV

Cudd Pressure Control, Inc., Station 1, Box 10128, 70363, pg. 1356   PB

The Houma Courier Newspaper Corporation, 3030 Barrow St., 70360, pg. 1175   PB

Marine Systems, Inc., 116 Capital Blvd., 70360, pg. 961   PB

Marine Systems, Inc.-Gulf Coast, 116 Capital Blvd., 70360, pg. 961   PB

Patterson Services, Inc., Station 1, Box 10128, 70363, pg. 1356   PB

Patterson Truck Line, Station 1, Box 10128, 70363, pg. 1356   PB

Pride Offshore, Inc., 410 S. Van Ave., 70363, pg. 1325   PB

Rail Systems, Inc., 116 Capital Blvd., 70360, pg. 961   PB

SAIA Motor Freight Lines, 104 Woodlawn Ranch Rd., 70363, pg. 1788   PB

Sunset P&A Services, Inc., 298 Prospect Ave., 70363, pg. 1149   PB

Independence

Waterbury Companies, Inc.-Independence Div., 129 Calhoun St., 70443, pg. 308   PB

Jamestown

Acme Brick Co., P.O. Box 5044, Highway 792, 71045, pg. 936   PB

Jeanerette

M.A. PATOUT & SON, 3512 J. Patout Burns Rd., 70544, pg. 843   PV

Jefferson

CHEMCENTRAL/New Orleans, 333 River Rd., 70121, pg. 232   PV

Jena

Century Telephone of Central Louisiana, Inc., P.O. Box 1386, 211 Second St., 71342-1386, pg. 329   PB

JUSTISS OIL CO., INC., 1810 E. Oak St., 71342, pg. 602   PV

Kenner

ADVANCED REMEDIATION INC. (ARM), 711 Oxley St., 70062, pg. 22   PV

Chemfix International, Inc., 711 Oxley St., 70062, pg. 22   PV

GEO. H. LEHLEITNER & CO., INC., 202 Crofton Rd., 70062, pg. 659   PV

Martin's Uniforms Div.- New Orleans, 2708 Delaware Ave., 70062, pg. 1539   PB

La Place

BAYOU STEEL CORPORATION, 138 Hwy. 3217, 70068, pg. 197   PB

River Parishes Hospital, 500 Rue de Sante, 70068, pg. 1697   PB

Lafayette

ABDALLA'S LAFAYETTE, INC., 900 E. St. Mary, 70503, pg. 10   PV

Ambar, Inc., 221 Rue de Jean, Ste. 301, 70508, pg. 126   PV

AMEAR Marine, Inc., 221 Rue de Jean, Ste. 301, 70508, pg. 126   PV

Bateman Food & Nutrition for Healthcare, 710 Robley, Ste. 210, 70503, pg. 324   IT

Campbell Wells Corporation, 2014 W. Pinhook Rd., Ste. 900, 70508, pg. 1686   PB

Charter Behavioral Health System of Lafayette, Inc., 302 Dulles Dr., 70506, pg. 1034   PB

Chemrich, Inc., 101 La Rue France. Ste. 300, 70508, pg. 49   IT

Evangeline Airmotive, Inc., P.O. Box 91073, 70509, pg. 1281   PV

The First National Bank of Lafayette, 600 Jefferson St., 70501, pg. 630   PB

Forest Oil Offshore Production Office, 900 S. College Rd., 70503, pg. 670   PB

GLOBAL INDUSTRIES, LTD., 107 Global Cir., 70593-1936, pg. 748   PB

Gulf Offshore Marine, 221 Rue De Jean, #117, 70508, pg. 769   PB

Hunt Oil Lafayette Land Office, Bldg. 14, 106 Oil Center Dr., Ste. 103, 70508, pg. 548   PB

Huval Bakery, Inc., 720 W. Simcoe St., 70502, pg. 657   PB

International Petroleum Corporation of Lafayette, 238 Jerome Rd., 70507, pg. 906   PB

Marsnland Energy, Inc., P.O. Box 53316, 70505, pc. 158   PV

Newpark Environmental Services, Inc., 4023 Ambassador Caffery Pkwy., 4th Fl., 70503, pg. 1179   PB

OSCA, P.O. Box 80627, 70508-0627, pg. 760   PB

OFFSHORE LOGISTICS, INC., 224 Rue de Jean, 70508, pc. 1212   PB

Offshore Logistics International, Inc., P.O. Box 5C, 900 E. University, 70503, pg. 1213   PB

Offshore Logistics Services, Inc., P.O. Box 5C, 900 E. University, 70503, pg. 1213   PB

Oil Mop, Inc., 221 Rue de Jean, Ste. 301, 70508, pg. 126   PV

PERFORMANCE MEDICAL GROUP, 803 Cajun Dome Blvd., 70506, pg. 853   PV

Production Operators, Inc. (Lafayette Office), P.O. Box 53776, 70505-3776, pg. 298   PV

SOLOCO, Inc., 4023 Ambassador Caffery Pkwy., 5th Fl., 70503, pg. 1179   PB

Trans Louisiana Gas Co., P.O. Box 4331, 420 W. Pinhook Rc., 70502, pg. 145   PB

Weatherford Enterra U.S., L.P., P.O. Box 80889, 770598-0839, pg. 1749   PB

Lake Charles

Boeing Louisiana, Inc., 330 Broad St., 70501-1397, pg 242   PB

Charter Behavioral Health System of Lake Charles, Inc, 4250 Fifth Ave., S., 70605, pg. 1034   PB

Cit-Con Oil Corporation, P.O. Box 1578, 70602, pg 1045   IT

Citgo Petroleum, P.O. Box 1562, 70602, pg. 1045   IT

ERA Aviation, Inc., P.O. Box 6550, Lake Charles Municipal Airport, 70606-6550, pg. 1410   PB

The First National Bank of Lake Charles, One Lakeside Plaza, 70601, pg. 630   PB

KPLC-TV, P.O. Box 1488, 320 Division St., 70602, pg. 992   PB

The Lake Charles Group, 6102 Common St., 70605, pg. 74   IT

Players Lake Charles, Inc., 800 Bilbo St., 70601, pg. 1310   PB

Reynolds Metals Company-Lake Charles, P.O. Box LL70602, Granger Rd., 70605, pg. 1385   PB

Serv-Tech, Inc., Eastern Area, 330 Walcot, 70669, pg. 1460   PB

SHEARMAN CORPORATION, 4900 Hwy. 90 E., 70601, pg. 991   PV

Surplus Warehouse-Lake Charles, 339 Martin Luther King Blvd., 70616, pg. 119   PV

Woodward-Clyde, 3519 Patrick St., Ste. 247, 70605, pg. 1656   PB

Lake Providence

TERRAL SEED CO., INC., 604 Ninth St., 71254, pg. 1077   PV

Leesville

Southern Electric Supply Co., Hyw. 171 S., 71446, pg. 1108   IT

Livingston

Henderson Auctions, 13340 Florida Blvd., 70754, pg. 577   PV

JAH ENTERPRISES, INC., 13340 Florida Blvd., 70754, pg. 577   PV

Lockport

BOLLINGER SHIPYARDS, INC., P.O. Box 250, Highway 308, 70374, pg. 155   PV

Mansfield

Dolet Hills Mining Venture, P.O. Box 291-C, Rte. 2, 71052, pg. 337   IT

Marksville

Gulfco Investment, Inc., 613 N. Main St., 71351, pg. 1093   PB

Metairie

BENSON MOTORS CORPORATION, 5800 Airline Hwy., 70003, pg. 134   PV

Browning-Ferris Industries of Louisiana, Inc., P.O. Box 1435, 70004, pg. 263   PB

Burns & Wilcox - Metairie Office, 2424 Edenborn, #620, 70001, pg. 610   PV

CONSOLIDATED COMPANIES INC. (CONCO), 2450 Severn, Ste. 514, 70004, pg. 265   PV

CROWN BUICK, INC., 2121 Clearview Pkwy., 70001, pg. 292   PV

E-Z Serve Convenience Stores, Inc.-Central Zone Office, 4621 W. Napoleon, Ste. 108, 70001, pg. 540   PV

Fireman's Fund Insurance Co. of Louisiana, 110 Veterans Blvd., Ste. 260, 70005, pg. 59   IT

First Louisiana Acceptance Corp., Security Homestead Bldg., 4900 Veteran's Blvd., Ste. 1010, 70002, pg. 184   PB

Global Special Risks, Inc. Holdings, 2610 Edenborn Ave., 70002, pg. 1503   IT

Hilb, Rogal and Hamilton Company of Louisiana, 3545 N. I-10 Service Rd., Ste. 300, 70002, pg. 827   PB

Intergraph Corporation, Ste. 100, 3545 N. Interstate, 10 Serv Rd., 70002-3516, pg. 891   PB

L & L Environmental Services, 3421 N. Causeway Blvd., Ste. 502, 70009, pg. 638   PV

L & L Maintenance & Repair, 3421 N. Causeway Blvd., Ste. 502, 70009, pg. 638   PV

L & L OIL COMPANY, INC., 3421 N. Causway Blvd., Ste. 502, 70002, pg. 638   PV

LOUISIANA GAMING MANAGEMENT, INC., 4441 Utica St., Ste. 206, 70006, pg. 677   PV

MCC GROUP, L.L.C., 3001 17th St., 70002, pg. 686   PV

Machinery Sales & Supply Co., P.O. Box 73783, 70003, pg. 971   PB

Moroch & Associates, Inc., 3500 N. Causeway #1516, 70006, pg. 762   PV

NEWPARK RESOURCES, INC., II Lakeway Ctr., 3850 N. Causeway Blvd., Ste. 1770, 70002, pg. 1179   PB

PETROLEUM HELICOPTERS, INC., 2121 Airline Highway, Ste. 400, 70004-0578, pg. 1281   PB

Principal Health Care of Louisiana, Inc., 3421 N. Causeway Blvd., Ste. 600, 70002, pg. 885   PV

REILY ELECTRICAL SUPPLY, INC., 3011 Lausat, 70001, pg. 919   PV

ROYAL OLDSMOBILE MAZDA, INC., 3400 Veterans Blvd., 70002, pg. 948   PV

SECO Industries, Inc., 2800 Veterans Blvd., Ste. 300, 70002, pg. 1460   PB

SMS-New Orleans, 3850 N. Causeway Blvd., 70002, pg. 1463   PB

Service General South, 2424 Edenborn, #620, 70001, pg. 609   PV

STEWART ENTERPRISES, INC., 110 Veterans Memorial Blvd., 70005, pg. 1518   PB

Trans-American Steamship Agency, 3525 N. Causeway Blvd., 70002-3629, pg. 1418   IT

VICTORY FINANCIAL GROUP, INC., 3115 6th St., 70002, pg. 1139   PV

Floyd West & Company, 2424 Edenborn, #620, 70001, pg. 609   PV

Minden

FIBREBOND CORPORATION, P.O. Box 5001, 1300 Davenport Ave., 71055, pg. 402   PV

KRC (Southern) Inc., P.O. Box 779, 1200 Davenport Dr., 71058-1035, pg. 1202   IT

Mister Twister, Drawer 996, 71055, pg. 992   PV

Monroe

Central Bank of Monroe, 300 DeSiard St., 71211, pg. 629   PB

Century Cellularnet, P.O. Box 4065, 71211, pg. 330   PB

Century Cellunet, Inc., 100 Century Park Dr., 71203, pg. 330   PB

Century Printing & Publishing Co., 3000 Cameron St., 71201, pg. 330   PB

CENTURY TELEPHONE ENTERPRISES, INC., 100 Century Park Dr., 71203, pg. 329   PB

Foresthill Telephone, Inc., P.O. Box 4065, 71211, pg. 330   PB

Larsen-Readfield Telephone Company, P.O. Box 4065, 71211, pg. 330   PB

News-Star Publishing Company, 411 N. Fourth St., 71201, pg. 700   PB

Ouachita Coca-Cola Bottling Company, P.O. Box 1571, 71210, pg. 393   PB

Regions Bank/North Louisiana, P.O. Box 7232, 71211, pg. 1372   PB

Rio Linda Chemical Co., Inc., 355 Harmon McDonald Rd., 71202, pg. 49   IT

Solon Springs Telephone Co., P.O. Box 4065, 71211, pg. 330   PB

Surplus Warehouse-Monroe, 3032 DeSiard St., 71201-7210, pg. 120   PV

PB - *U.S. Public Companies Volume*
PV - *U.S. Private Companies Volume*
IT - *International Public & Private Companies Volume*

1254

Universal Telephone, Inc., P.O. Box 4065, 71211, pg. 330 **PB**

Morgan City

BERWICK BAY OIL CO. INC., 3205 Youngs Rd., 70380, pg. 138 **PV**
Fabrication & Offshore Operations, P.O. Box 188, 70381, pg. 1068 **PB**
Marine Systems, Inc.-Gulf Coast, 323 Chennault St., 70380, pg. 961 **PB**
Oceaneering International, Inc., 931 Hwy. 90 E., 70380, pg. 1211 **PB**
Oilfield Marine Services-Americas Region, 931 Hwy. 90 E., 70380, pg. 1211 **PB**

Natchitoches

ConAgra Broiler Co., P.O. Box 108, Hwy. One, S. Bypass, 71457, pg. 427 **PB**

New Iberia

Mallard Bay Drilling, Inc., P.O. Box 13530, 70562-3530, pg. 1259 **PB**
Regions Bank/New Iberia, P.O. Box 11240, 70562-1240, pg. 1372 **PB**
Trappey's Fine Foods, Inc., 900 E. Main St., 70560, pg. 105 **PB**
UNIFAB INTERNATIONAL INC., 5007 Port Rd., 70562, pg. 1665 **PB**
Varco BJ Drilling Systems, 8404 W. Hwy. 90, 70560, pg. 1709 **PB**
Varco BJ Oil Tools, 8404 W. Hwy. 90, 70518, pg. 1709 **PB**

New Orleans

Acme Brick Co., 11201 Old Gentilly Hwy., 70129, pg. 936 **PB**
Allright New Orleans, Inc., 150 Barrone St., Ste. 301, 70112, pg. 43 **PV**
American Classic Voyagers Company, Robin Street Wharf, 1380 Port of New Orleans Pl., 70130-1890, pg. 380 **PV**
Aqua Power Marine Products Div., 500-B Edwards Ave., 70183, pg. 857 **PB**
Aquatrol Corporation, 3501 Jourdon Rd., 70126, pg. 577 **PV**
Aramark Sports & Entertainment Services Inc., 900 Convention Ctr. Blvd., 70130, pg. 79 **PV**
BVK/McDonald - New Orleans, 7801 Maple St., 70118, pg. 108 **PV**
Belarus Machinery of U.S.A., Inc., 6101 Chef Menteur Hwy., 70126, pg. 101 **IT**
BELLWETHER TECHNOLOGY CORPORATION, 203 Carondelet St., Ste. 250, 70130, pg. 132 **PV**
BLUMENTHAL PRINT WORKS, INC., 905 S. Broad St., 70125, pg. 153 **PV**
Boeing Petroleum Services, Inc., 850 S. Clearview Pkwy., 70123, pg. 242 **PB**
BOH BROS. CONSTRUCTION CO., LLC, 730 S. Tonti St., 70153, pg. 154 **PV**
Bollinger Algiers Inc., 434 Powder St., 70114, pg. 155 **PB**
Brock Exploration Corporation, 1340 Poydras St., Ste. 1700, 70112, pg. 953 **PB**
Bunny Bread Co., Inc., 5646 Lewis Rd., 70126, pg. 657 **PB**
CNG Coal Co., CNG Tower, 1450 Poydras St., 70112-6000, pg. 435 **PB**
CNG Producing Co., CNG Tower, 1450 Poydras St., 70112-6000, pg. 435 **PB**
CPC of Louisiana, Inc., 3601 Coliseum St., 70015, pg. 1712 **PB**
Central Gulf Lines, Inc., Poydras Center, 650 Poydras St., Ste. 1700, 70130, pg. 907 **PB**
Cox Communications-New Orleans, 2120 Canal St., 70112, pg. 455 **PB**
DIXIE BREWING CO., INC., 2537 Tulane Ave., 70119, pg. 336 **PV**
Doussan Inc., 2525 St. Bernard Ave., 70119, pg. 938 **IT**
DRUMM & ASSOCIATES, INC., 233 Okeefe Ave., Ste. 1450A, 70112, pg. 343 **PV**
ENTERGY CORPORATION, 639 Loyola Ave., 70113, pg. 585 **PB**
Entergy Louisiana, Inc., 639 Loyola Ave., 70113, pg. 586 **PB**
Entergy New Orleans, Inc., 639 Loyola Ave., 70113, pg. 586 **PB**
FAIR GROUNDS CORPORATION, 1751 Gentilly Blvd., 70119, pg. 609 **PB**
Family Inns of New Orleans, Inc., 6303 Chef Menteur, 70126, pg. 392 **PV**
FIRST COMMERCE CORPORATION, 201 St. Charles Ave., 70160-0279, pg. 629 **PB**
First National Bank of Commerce, 210 Baronne St., 70112, pg. 629 **PB**
Forest Lines Inc., 1700 Poydras Ctr., 650 Poydras St., 70130, pg. 907 **PB**
Freeport-McMoRan Copper & Gold, Inc., 1615 Poydras St., 70112, pg. 680 **PB**
FREEPORT-McMORAN INC., 1615 Poydras St., 70112, pg. 680 **PB**
Freeport-McMoRan Resource Partners, Ltd., 1615 Poydras St., 70112, pg. 681 **PB**
P.T. Freeport Indonesia Co., 1615 Poydras St., 70112, pg. 681 **PB**
Getty Gas Gathering, Inc., 400 Poydras St., 70130, pg. 1583 **PB**
Kenneth Gordon IAG, Inc., 1008 Elmwood Park Blvd., 70123, pg. 581 **PV**

Great River Oil & Gas Corp., CNG Tower, 1450 Poydras St., Ste. 1520, 70112, pg. 735 **PB**
HIBERNIA CORPORATION, 313 Carondelet St., 70130, pg. 825 **PB**
Hibernia National Bank, 313 Carondelet St., 70130, pg. 825 **PB**
Howard Weil Labouisse Friedrichs, Inc., 1100 Poydress St., Ste. 900, 70163, pg. 985 **PB**
INDUSTRIAL METALS OF THE SOUTH, 401 N. Roman St., 70112, pg. 561 **PV**
Inexco Oil Company, 909 Poydras St., 70112, pg. 269 **PB**
Insurance Brokers & Managers, Inc., 2626 Canal St., 70119, pg. 1677 **PV**
International-Matex Tank Terminals, 9th Fl., Ste. 321, St. Charles Ave., 70130, pg. 758 **IT**
International Paint Gulf Div., 3915 Louisa St., P.O. Box 26069, 70186, pg. 339 **PB**
International Petroleum Corporation of Louisiana, 14890 Intracoastal Dr., 70129, pg. 906 **PB**
INTERNATIONAL SHIPHOLDING CORPORATION, Poydras Ctr., Ste. 1700, 650 Poydras St., 70130, pg. 907 **PB**
Jefferies & Company, Inc., 400 Poydras St., Ste. 1850, 70130, pg. 925 **PB**
KKND, 929 Howard Ave., 70113, pg. 384 **PB**
MORRIS KIRSCHMAN & COMPANY, INC., 5050 Almonaster, 70126, pg. 623 **PV**
Kvaerner Ships Equipment Inc., 1418 Edwards Ave., Ste. B, 70123, pg. 770 **IT**
LL&E Colombia, Inc., 909 Poydras St., 70112, pg. 269 **PB**
LL&E Europe-Africa-Middle East, Inc., 909 Poydras St., 70112, pg. 269 **PB**
LL&E, Inc., 909 Poydras St., 70112, pg. 269 **PB**
LL&E (Netherlands), Inc., 909 Poydras St., 70112, pg. 269 **PB**
LL&E Netherlands Petroleum Company, 909 Poydras St., 70112, pg. 269 **PB**
LL&E Petroleum Marketing, Inc., 909 Poydras St., 70112, pg. 1136 **IT**
LL&E Petroleum Resources Marketing, L.P., 909 Poydras St., Ste. 3600, 70112, pg. 269 **PB**
LL&E Pipeline Corp., 909 Poydras St., 70112, pg. 269 **PB**
LL&E Properties, Inc., 909 Poydras St., 70112, pg. 269 **PB**
Lafayette Insurance Company, 2626 Canal St., 70119, pg. 1677 **PV**
The Louisiana Coca-Cola Bottling Company Limited, 1050 S. Jefferson Davis Pkwy., 70125, pg. 393 **PV**
The Louisiana Land and Exploration Company, 909 Poydras St., 70112, pg. 269 **PB**
LUNDY ENTERPRISES, INC., 10555 Lake Forest Blvd., Ste. 1J, 70127, pg. 681 **PV**
Magnolia Chemicals & Solvents, 1020 Sams Ave., 70123, pg. 1071 **IT**
MariTrend, Inc., 3001 Tchoupitoulas St., 70115-1039, pg. 1135 **PV**
Marquis Investments, P.O. Box 61239, 70161, pg. 629 **PV**
Martin Marietta Manned Space Systems, P.O. Box 29304, 70189, pg. 1007 **PB**
Maurin-Ogden Management Corporation, 615 Baronne St., Ste. 100, 70113, pg. 715 **PV**
MAURIN-OGDEN PROPERTIES, 460 Broadway St., 70118, pg. 715 **PV**
MCDERMOTT INTERNATIONAL, INC., 1450 Poydras St., Ste. 1871, 70112-6050, pg. 1067 **PB**
Murphy Exploration & Production Co., 131 S. Robertson, 70112, pg. 1142 **PB**
National Marine, Inc., 1515 Poydras St., Ste. 1500, 70130, pg. 1135 **PV**
Nestle Beverage Company, 5500 Chef Menteur Hwy., 70126, pg. 917 **IT**
New Orleans Waterfront Rest. Corp., Bermuda St. Wharf, 2 Bermuda St., 70114, pg. 1023 **PV**
ORECK CORPORATION, 100 Plantation Rd., 70123, pg. 819 **PV**
ORLEANS MATERIALS & EQUIPMENT CO., INC., 5501 France Rd., 70126, pg. 820 **PV**
PAN-AMERICAN LIFE INSURANCE COMPANY, 601 Poydras St., 70130, pg. 836 **PV**
Pan-Marine International, Inc., 1440 Canal St., Ste. 2100, 70112, pg. 1608 **PB**
Paxton Beautiful Woods, 14200 Chef Menteur Hwy., 70189, pg. 585 **PB**
Pental Insurance Co., Ltd., 1440 Canal St., Ste. 2100, 70112, pg. 1608 **PB**
Petroleum Helicopters Inc., P.O. Box 23502, 5728 Jefferson Hwy., 70183, pg. 1281 **PB**
Point Marine, Inc., 1440 Canal St., Ste. 2100, 70112, pg. 1608 **PB**
Premier Investment Advisors, L.C., 4318 Place St. Charles, 70170, pg. 173 **PB**
Regions Bank/Southern Louisiana, P.O. Box 30208, 70130, pg. 1373 **PB**
Reily Foods Company, 640 Magazine St., 70130, pg. 919 **PV**
WILLIAM B. REILY & CO., INC., 640 Magazine St., 70130, pg. 919 **PV**
Riedel-Smith Environmental Services, 14101 Old Gentilly Rd., 70129, pg. 1478 **PV**
River Oaks Hospital, 1525 River Oaks Rd. W., 70123, pg. 1697 **PB**
Riverwalk, P.O. Box 52709, 70152, pg. 1408 **PB**
ROBINSON LUMBER & EXPORT COMPANY, 4000 Tchoupitoulas St., 70115, pg. 936 **PV**
Robinson Lumber Company, 4000 Tchoupitoulas St., 70115, pg. 936 **PV**
Schwegmann Giant Super Markets, 5300 Gentilly Rd., 70126, pg. 629 **PV**
Seafarer Boat Corporation, 1440 Canal St., Ste. 2100, 70112, pg. 1608 **PB**
Spectrum Control Technology Inc., 4100 Michaud Blvd., 70129, pg. 1497 **PB**

Standard Coffee Service, 640 Magazine St., 70130, pg. 919 **PV**
STANDARD SUPPLY & HARDWARE CO., 832 Tchoupitoulas St., 70130, pg. 1032 **PV**
Stirling Properties, Inc., 615 Baronne St., Ste. 100, 70113, pg. 715 **PV**
Textron Marine & Land Systems, 6600 Plaza Dr., 70127, pg. 1589 **PB**
TIDEWATER INC., 1440 Canal St., Ste. 2100, 70112, pg. 1608 **PB**
Tidewater Marine International, Inc., 1440 Canal St., Ste. 2100, 70112, pg. 1608 **PB**
Tidewater Marine Service, Inc., 1440 Canal St., Ste. 2100, 70112, pg. 1608 **PB**
Tidewater Marine Western, Inc., 1440 Canal St., Ste. 2100, 70112, pg. 1608 **PB**
Tidewater Offshore Services, Inc., 1440 Canal St., Ste. 2100, 70112, pg. 1608 **PB**
Tidex (Malaysia) Sdn. Bhd., 1440 Canal St., Ste. 2100, 70112, pg. 1608 **PB**
Tidex Nigeria Ltd., 1440 Canal St., Ste. 2100, 70112, pg. 1608 **PB**
THE TIMES-PICAYUNE PUBLISHING CORP., 3800 Howard Ave., 70140, pg. 1087 **PV**
Twenty Grand Offshore, 1440 Canal St., Ste. 2100, 70112, pg. 1608 **PB**
Upton Printing Co., 746 Carondelet St., 70130, pg. 333 **PB**
VECTURA GROUP, INC., 1515 Poydras St. 1500, 70112, pg. 1135 **PV**
WDSU Television, Inc., 846 Howard Ave., 70113-1134, pg. 1344 **PB**
WGNO Inc., 2 S. Canal St., Ste. 2800, 70130, pg. 1636 **PB**
WNOE, 929 Howard Ave., 70113, pg. 385 **PB**
WODT-AM, 2228 Gravier St., 70119, pg. 385 **PB**
WQUE-FM, 2228 Gravier St., 70119, pg. 385 **PB**
WVUE-TV, 1025 S. Jefferson Davis Pkwy., 70125, pg. 1685 **PB**
WYLD-AM/FM, 2228 Gravier St., 70119, pg. 386 **PB**
Walk, Haydel & Associates, Inc., 600 Carondelet St., 70130, pg. 624 **IT**
Waterman Steamship Corporation, Poydras Ctr., 650 Poydras St., Ste. 1700, 70130, pg. 907 **PB**
Weatherford Enterra U.S., L.P., 925 Common St., Ste. 1425, 70112, pg. 1749 **PB**
Wemco, Inc., 966 S. White St., 70125, pg. 909 **PV**
WHITNEY HOLDING CORPORATION, 228 St. Charles Ave., 70130, pg. 1766 **PB**
Whitney National Bank, 228 St. Charles Ave., 70130, pg. 1766 **PB**
Willis Corroon Corp. of Louisiana, The Poydras Ctr., Ste. 1600, 650 Poydras St., 70130, pg. 1506 **IT**
Wilson Brothers Drilling Co., 909 Poydras St., 70112, pg. 269 **PB**
Windsor Court Hotel L.P., 300 Gravier St., 70140, pg. 1214 **IT**

New Roads

Regions Bank/Central Louisiana, P.O. Box 250, 70760, pg. 1372 **PB**

New Sarpy

TransAmerican Refining Corp., 14902 River Rd., 70078, pg. 1096 **PV**

Norco

Norco Terminal, 15272 River Rd., 70079, pg. 692 **PB**

Oak Grove

RUFFIN BUILDING SYSTEMS, INC., 6914 Hwy. 2, 71263-8930, pg. 950 **PV**

Opelousas

The Daily World, I-49 S. Service Rd., 70571, pg. 1175 **PB**
Lou Ana Foods, Inc., 731 N. Railroad, 70571, pg. 879 **IT**

Pineville

CENTRAL LOUISIANA ELECTRIC COMPANY, INC., 2030 Donahue Ferry Rd., 71360, pg. 325 **PB**

Plain Dealing

Century Telephone of North LA, Inc., P.O. Box 428, 122 N. Lynch, 71064-0428, pg. 329 **PB**
ChipMill, Hwy. 3 N., 71604, pg. 76 **PV**

Port Allen

Van Leeuwen Pipe & Tube Corp., 1123 Highway 190 West, 70767, pg. 1449 **IT**
WESTGATE INC., 1355 Beaulieu Ln., 70767, pg. 1169 **PV**

Prairieville

Hamco, Inc., 16131 Hwy. 44 N., 70769, pg. 465 **PB**

Raceland

Raceland Raw Sugar Corp., P.O. Box 159, Hwy. 3199 & Mill St., 70394-0159, pg. 843 **PV**

PB - *U.S. Public Companies Volume*
PV - *U.S. Private Companies Volume*
IT - *International Public & Private Companies Volume*

Rayville

Continental/Murray, Hwy. 80 E., 71269, pg. 268 **PV**
Williamson-Dickie, 108 Ollie St., 71869, pg. 1179 **PV**

Ruston

T.L. JAMES & COMPANY, 106 W. Mississippi Ave., 71270, pg. 580 **PV**
UNR Home Products Div., 600 Jonesboro St., 71273, pg. 1404 **PB**

Saint Rose

Circle International, 125 Mallard, Ste. D, 70087, pg. 371 **PB**
Hewlett-Packard Company, 160 James Dr., E., 70087, pg. 814 **PB**
T.L. James & Co., Inc., James Business Park, 100 James Dr., 70087, pg. 580 **PV**
New Orleans Laboratory, 161 James Dr. W., Ste. 100, 70087, pg. 829 **PV**

Shreveport

Allright Shreveport, Inc., 729 Travis St., 71162, pg. 43 **PV**
BAYOU STATE OIL CORPORATION, 1115 Hawn Ave., 71107, pg. 125 **PV**
Beaird Industries, Inc., 601 Benton Kelly St., 71106, pg. 1639 **PV**
Braswell Concrete Products, Inc., 6731 Lindwood, 71106, pg. 628 **IT**
Braswell Industries, 6731 Lindwood, 71106, pg. 628 **IT**
Cablevision of Shreveport, 6529 Quilen Rd., 71108, pg. 1610 **PB**
Cand Investments Inc., P.O. Box 21119, 71101, pg. 501 **PB**
Charter Forest Behavioral Health System, Inc., 9320 Linwood Ave., 71106, pg. 1034 **PB**
Cigna Healthplan of North Louisiana, One Bellemead Ctr., 6425 Youree Dr., Ste. 200, 71105-4625, pg. 360 **PB**
Cigna Healthplan of Shreveport, Inc., One Bellemead Centre, 6425 Youree Dr., Ste. 200, 71105-4625, pg. 360 **PB**
Coca-Cola Bottling Co. of Shreveport, 305 Stoner, 71101, pg. 393 **PB**
Commercial National Bank, Commercial National Tower, P.O. Box 21119, 71101, pg. 500 **PB**
Cornerstone Natural Gas, Inc.-Shreveport, 400 Travis St., Ste. 503, 71101, pg. 567 **PB**
Crystal Eurasia Oil Co., 229 Milan St., 71101, pg. 466 **PB**
Crystal Exploration & Production Co., 229 Milam St., 71120, pg. 466 **PB**
CRYSTAL OIL COMPANY, 229 Milam St., 71101, pg. 466 **PB**
Crystal Program Ltd., Inc., 229 Milam St., 71120, pg. 466 **PB**
Doctors Hospital of Shreveport, 1130 Louisiana Ave., 71101, pg. 1697 **PB**
Eclipse Combustion, Inc., 202 Martha Anne Dr., 71115, pg. 360 **PV**
Frigidaire Home Products-Specialty Power Equipment, P.O. Box 91329, 5020 Flournoy-Lucas Rd., 71129, pg. 440 **IT**
The Frymaster Corp., P.O. Box 5100, 8700 Line Ave., 71135-1000, pg. 188 **IT**
Galen BH, Inc., 1800 Irving Place, 71101, pg. 404 **PB**
GATX Logistics, Inc.-Louisiana, 7540 W. Bert Kouns Industrial Loop, 71129, pg. 691 **PB**
Group Insurance of Shreveport, 1700 Centenary Blvd., 71101, pg. 484 **PV**
HDW, Incorporated, 6900 Woolworth Rd., 71129, pg. 335 **PV**
Hattiesburg Gas Storage, Inc., 229 Milam St., 71101, pg. 466 **PB**
KSLA-TV, P.O. Box 41812, 77134, pg. 912 **PV**
NorAm Energy Corp., 525 Milam St., 71101, pg. 843 **PB**
NorAm Field Services Corp., P.O. Box 21734, 71151, pg. 843 **PB**
NorAm Gas Transmission, P.O. Box 21734, 525 Milam St., 71151, pg. 843 **PB**
ROUNDTREE AUTOMOTIVE GROUP, 8660 Fern Ave., Ste. 200, 71105, pg. 947 **PV**
SMITH MANAGEMENT CO., INC., 800 Spring St., Ste. 120, 71101, pg. 1009 **PV**
Southwestern Electric Power Co., 428 Travis St., 71156, pg. 324 **PB**
The Times, 222 Lake St., 71130, pg. 700 **PB**
Trans-Serve, Inc., 4365 Blanchard Rd., 71107, pg. 944 **PV**
Uniform Inc., 7133 W. Park Rd., 71129, pg. 1202 **IT**
Welbilt Varimixer, 8700 Line Ave., 71135-1000, pg. 189 **IT**

Slidell

AmClyde Gulf Coast Division, 60036 Cabiran Rd., 70460, pg. 778 **PB**
Capitol Steel-Slidell, P.O. Box 3219, 70459, pg. 412 **PB**
Gaylord Chemical Corporation, 106 Galeria Blvd., 70458, pg. 704 **PB**
Greenery Neurological Rehabilitation, 1400 Lindberg Dr., 70458, pg. 837 **PB**
Utility Steel Fabrication, Inc., 60042 Cabiran Rd., 70460, pg. 778 **PB**

Springhill

Citizens First Bank, 124 N. Main, 71075, pg. 630 **PB**

Sterlington

Koch Nitrogen Division, P.O. Box 626, 71280-0626, pg. 628 **PV**

Sulphur

Firestone Synthetic Rubber & Latex Company-Lake Charles, 1801 Hwy. 108 E., 70663, pg. 214 **IT**

Thibodaux

Comet-Press Newspapers, Inc., 705 W. 5th St., 70301, pg. 1175 **PB**
The Daily Comet, 705 W. 5th St., 70301, pg. 1175 **PB**
Stark Candy Company, 109 Candy Ln., 70301, pg. 1113 **PV**

Welsh

Century Telephone of Evangeline, Inc., P.O. Box 827, 106 E. South St., 70591, pg. 329 **PB**

West Monroe

Coated & Laminated Products, Jonesboro Hwy., 71294, pg. 927 **PB**
Corrugated Packaging, 400 Central, 71291, pg. 737 **PB**
Wood Products/Forest Resources/Energy Resource Div., P.O. Box 488, 71294, pg. 1311 **PB**
Zeneca Specialty Inks, 108 Enterprise Dr., 71292, pg. 1525 **IT**

Westlake

Conoco Oil Refinery, P.O. Box 37, 37 Old Spanish Trail, 70669-0037, pg. 531 **PB**
PUMPELLY OIL, INC., Old Spanish Trail, 70669, pg. 895 **PV**

Westwego

Automatic Power, Inc., P.O. Box 414, 1340 Westbank Expwy., 70096-0414, pg. 1289 **IT**
Cyro Industries, 10800 River Rd., 70094, pg. 1454 **IT**
Methanex Fortier Inc., 10800 River Rd., 70094, pg. 862 **IT**

White Castle

CORA TEXAS MANUFACTURING CO., INC., 32505 Hwy. Ore., 70788, pg. 275 **PV**

Winnfield

Neste Resins Corporation, Hwy. 167, P.O. Box 1010, 71483, pg. 913 **IT**
Winn Correctional Center, Gum Springs Rd., Hwy. 560, 71483, pg. 451 **PB**

Zachary

Grant Chemical Div., Hwy. 61 N. & Irene Rd., 70791, pg. 618 **PV**
Port Hudson Pulp Mill, Mount Pleasant Rd., P.O. Box 430, 70791, pg. 737 **PB**
Primary Pulp & Paper Plant, P.O. Box 430, 70791, pg. 736 **PB**

MAINE

Ashland

Fraser Paper Limited, Maine Timberlands, P.O. Box P, 04732, pg. 434 **IT**
J. Pau Levesque & Sons Inc, P.O. Box X, 04732, pg. 434 **IT**
Pinkham Lumber, 04732, pg. 248 **PB**

Auburn

Gates Formed-Fibre Products, P.O. Box 1300, 04210-9156, pg. 1396 **PB**
LEPAGE BAKERY, INC., 60 Second St., 04210, pg. 360 **PV**
PIONEER PLASTICS CORPORATION, One Pionite Rd., 04211-1014, pg. 867 **PV**
S.P.C. TRANSPORT, P.O. Box 1718, 04211, pg. 957 **PV**

Augusta

Central Maine Newspapers, 274 Western Ave., 04330, pg. 439 **PV**
CENTRAL MAINE POWER COMPANY, 83 Edison Dr., 04336, pg. 325 **PB**
Central Securities Corp., Edison Dr., 04336, pg. 325 **PB**
Cumberland Securities Corp., Edison Drive, 04336, pg. 325 **PB**
Joseph Kirschner Co., Riverside Dr., 04330, pg. 599 **PV**
Maine Electric Power Co., Inc., Edison Dr., 04336, pg. 325 **PB**
Maine Yankee Atomic Power Co., Edison Dr., 04330, pg. 1038 **PB**
Pine State Beverage, Eight Ellis Ave., 04330, pg. 865 **PV**

PINE STATE TRADING COMPANY, Eight Ellis Ave., 04330, pg. 865 **PV**
Pine State Vending, Eight Ellis Ave., 04330, pg. 865 **PV**

Bangor

Bangor & Aroostook Railroad Co., Northern Maine Junction Pk., RR2, Box 45, 04401-9602, pg. 575 **PV**
BANGOR HYDRO-ELECTRIC COMPANY, 33 State St., 04401, pg. 178 **PB**
Bangor-Pacific Hydro Associates, 33 State St., 04401, pg. 178 **PB**
Bangor VAR Company, Inc., 33 State St., 04401, pg. 178 **PB**
Canadian American Railroad Company, Northern Maine Junction Park, R.R. 2, Box 45, 04401-9602, pg. 575 **PV**
DARLING'S, 153 Perry Rd., 04401, pg. 311 **PV**
Dead River Petroleum Co., 55 Broadway, 04401, pg. 318 **PV**
Dead River Transport, 55 Broadway, 04401, pg. 318 **PV**
East Branch Improvement Company, 33 State St., 04401, pg. 178 **PB**
THE ERIN COMPANY, 500 Main St., 04401, pg. 381 **PV**
Jordan's Foods-Bangor Division, 216 Thatcher St., 04401, pg. 599 **PV**
Penobscot Hydro Company, Inc., 33 State St., 04401, pg. 178 **PB**
Superior Paper Products, Inc., 120 Rice St., 04401, pg. 864 **PV**
VILLAGE CAR COMPANY, 40 Summer St., 04401, pg. 1140 **PV**

Bath

Bath Iron Works Corporation, 700 Washington St., 04530, pg. 709 **PB**
Stinson Seafood, Company, One Edwards St., 04530, pg. 1043 **PV**

Belfast

PENOBSCOT FROZEN FOODS, INC., 28 Pierce St., 04915, pg. 850 **PV**

Berwick

Prime Tanning Co., Inc., Sullivan St., 03901, pg. 884 **PV**

Bethel

AMERICAN SKIING COMPANY, P.O. Box 450, 04217, pg. 61 **PV**

Biddeford

AVX Tantalum Div., One Components Dr., 04005, pg. 775 **IT**
FIBER MATERIALS, INC., Biddeford Industrial Park, 5 Morin St., 04005, pg. 402 **PV**
Intermat, 389 Hill St., 04005, pg. 402 **PV**
Sermatech Maine, 24 Landry St., 04005-4310, pg. 1570 **PB**
Valmet Inc.- Honeycomb Division, Alfred Rd., 04005, pg. 1448 **IT**
Waterbury Companies, Inc., Biddeford Indus. Pk., 04005, pg. 308 **PB**

Brewer

EASTERN FINE PAPER, 517 S. Main St., 04412-0517, pg. 357 **PV**

Brunswick

Casco Cable Television Inc., 336 Bath Rd., 04011, pg. 709 **PV**
Maine Yankee, 329 Bath Rd., 04011, pg. 325 **PB**

Bucksport

Bucksport Mill, Champion International Corp., P.O. Box 1200, River Rd., 04416, pg. 334 **PB**

Burlington

Hewlett-Packard (New England), 29 Burlington Mall, 01803-4182, pg. 815 **PB**

Caribou

Jordan's Foods-Caribou Division, Bennett Dr., 04736, pg. 599 **PV**

Casco

HANCOCK LUMBER, INC., Rte. 121, 04015, pg. 498 **PV**

Corinna

West Penobscot Telegraph & Telephone Co., P.O. Box 0, Spring St., 04928, pg. 1572 **PB**

Costigan

Costigan Plant, Wood Products Div., P.O. Box 159, Greenfield Rd., 04423, pg. 334 **PB**

Geographic Index-U.S.

Dexter

Dexter Shoe Company, 114 Railroad Ave., 04930, pg. 217   **PB**

East Wilton

Forster, Inc., Mill St., 04234, pg. 330   **PV**

Ellsworth

Atlantic Cellular Telephone Corp., 180B High St., 04605, pg. 1708   **PB**

Farmington

Franklin Shoe Co., R.R. 4, Box 5010, 04938, pg. 988   **PV**

Fort Kent

DAIGLE OIL CO., 44 W. Main St., 04743, pg. 307   **PV**

Freeport

EASTLAND SHOE MANUFACTURING CORPORATION, Five Park St., 04032, pg. 357   **PV**
Healthsource Maine, Inc., Two Stonewood Dr., 04032, pg. 360   **PB**
L.L. BEAN, INC., Casco St., 04033, pg. 639   **PV**

Fryeburg

Carpenter Steel Div., 82 Portland St., 04037, pg. 307   **PB**
Forest Industries, Inc., 18 Fair St., 04037, pg. 968   **PV**

Gorham

Hill-Loma, Inc., Gorham Industrial Pk., 04038, pg. 461   **PV**
SEBAGO, INC., 55 Hutcherson Dr., 04038, pg. 980   **PV**

Gray

Kassbohrer North America, P.O. Box 1277, 32 Lewiston Rd., 04039, pg. 368   **IT**

Greenville

Greenville Division, P.O. Box 592, Norris St., 04441, pg. 438   **PB**

Guilford

Guilford of Maine, Inc., Oak St., 04443, pg. 889   **PB**

Hartland

Hartland & St. Albans Telephone Co., Elm St., 04943, pg. 1572   **PB**
IRVING TANNING CO., Three Main St., 04943, pg. 575   **PV**

Jay

Otis Specialty Papers, P.O. Box 10, One Mill St., 04239, pg. 1107   **IT**

Kennebunk

SHAPE INC., Seven Shape Dr., 04043, pg. 990   **PV**

Kingfield

Sugarloaf/USA, RR 1, Box 5000, 04947, pg. 62   **PV**

Kittery

Johnson Printing Co., 84 Government St., 03904-1654, pg. 592   **PV**
Watts Fluidair, 9 Cutts Rd., 03904, pg. 1243   **IT**

Lewiston

ANDROSCOGGIN SAVINGS BANK, 30 Lisbon St., 04240, pg. 74   **PV**
Fairview Wine Co., 21 Saratoga St., 04240, pg. 1173   **PV**
Federal Distillers, 21 Saratoga St., 04240, pg. 1173   **PV**
GEIGER BROTHERS, Mt. Hope Ave., 04240, pg. 442   **PV**
Lawrence & Company, 21 Saratoga St., 04240, pg. 1173   **PV**
Maine Bottlers, 21 Saratoga St., 04240, pg. 1173   **PV**
Philips Elmet Corporation, 1560 Lisbon Rd., 04240, pg. 1055   **IT**
The Union Water-Power Co., 150 Main St., P.O. Box 1225, 04240, pg. 325   **PB**
WHITE ROCK DISTILLERIES INC., 21 Saratoga St., 04241, pg. 1173   **PV**

Machias

Ischua Creek Holding Company, Inc., 9450 Very Rd., pg. 1137   **PB**

Madawaska

Fraser Paper Limited, 25 Bridge St., 04756, pg. 434   **IT**

Madison

Madison Paper Industries, P.O. Box 129, 04950, pg. 1174   **PB**

Millinocket

Great Northern Paper, Inc., One Katahdin Ave., 04462-1398, pg. 248   **PB**
Millinocket Division, Rte. #11 HC-74, Box 2, 04462, pg. 438   **PB**

Newport

Maine/Sysco, Inc., Industrial Park, P.O. Box 100, 04953-0100, pg. 1551   **PB**

North Anson

Somerset Telephone Co., Elm St., 04958, pg. 1572   **PB**

North Berwick

HUSSEY CORPORATION, Dyer St., 03906, pg. 550   **PV**

Old Town

Fort James Timber Corp., 970 S. Main St., 04458, pg. 672   **PB**
Kagan Lown, Gilman Falls Ave., 04468, pg. 1273   **PB**
Old Town Canoe, 58 Middle Street, 04468, pg. 933   **PB**
PENOBSCOT SHOE COMPANY, 450 N. Main St., 04468, pg. 1273   **PB**

Oxford

National Wood Products, Co., 822 Main St., 04270, pg. 968   **PV**
PARK MANUFACTURING, INC., P.O. Box 263, Rte. 26, 04270, pg. 840   **PV**

Portland

ABB Environmental Services Inc., 261 Commercial St., 04101, pg. 4   **IT**
Casco-Northern Corporation, One Monument Sq., 04104, pg. 184   **PB**
Claims Service International, Inc., 2211 Congress St., 04122, pg. 1699   **PB**
CONSUMERS WATER COMPANY, Three Canal Plaza, 04112, pg. 438   **PB**
DEAD RIVER COMPANY, One Dana St., 04101, pg. 318   **PV**
Deering Ice Cream, Inc., 135 Walton St., 04103, pg. 403   **PV**
DIVERSIFIED COMMUNICATIONS, 121 Free St., 04101, pg. 336   **PV**
EPX, P.O. Box 3878, 04104, pg. 354   **PV**
EMERY WATERHOUSE COMPANY, Rand Rd., 04102, pg. 373   **PV**
Fleet Bank of Maine, 2 Porter Sq., 04101, pg. 649   **PB**
GUY GANNETT COMMUNICATIONS, One City Ctr., 11th Floor, 04101, pg. 439   **PV**
J.E. Goold & Company, Riverside Industrial Pkwy., 04104, pg. 229   **PV**
Ikon Office Solutions-North New England, 122 Pinetree Industrial Pkwy., 04102, pg. 864   **PV**
JORDAN'S MEATS, 38 India St., 04112, pg. 599   **PV**
Key Bank of Maine, One Canal Plaza, 04112, pg. 954   **PB**
Key Trust Company of Maine, One Canal Plaza, 04112, pg. 954   **PB**
NELSON & SMALL INC., 212 Canco Rd., 04103, pg. 790   **PV**
Nichols Portland Div., 2400 Congress St., 04102-0603, pg. 1260   **PB**
NORTHEASTERN GRAPHIC SUPPLY, INC., 14 Industrial Way, 04104, pg. 805   **PV**
OAKHURST DAIRY, 364 Forest Ave., 04101, pg. 809   **PV**
PEOPLES HERITAGE FINANCIAL GROUP, INC., One Portland Sq., 04101, pg. 1275   **PB**
Peoples Heritage Savings Bank, P.O. Box 9540, One Portland Sq., 04112, pg. 1275   **PB**
The Portland Newspapers, 390 Congress St., 04104, pg. 439   **PV**
Select Robinson Inc., 160 Fox St., 04101, pg. 274   **IT**
SuperValu, Inc.-Maine Div., 56 Milliken St., 04104, pg. 1540   **PB**
UNUM, Tower B, 100 Middle St., Fourth Fl., 04101, pg. 1699   **PB**
UNUM CORPORATION, 2211 Congress St., 04122, pg. 1699   **PB**
UNUM Development Corp., 2211 Congress St., 04122, pg. 1699   **PB**
UNUM Holding Company, 2211 Congress St., 04122, pg. 1699   **PB**
UNUM Life Insurance Company of America, 2211 Congress St., 04122, pg. 1699   **PB**
UNUM Sales Corp., 2211 Congress St., 04122, pg. 1700   **PB**
WGME-TV, 1335 Washington Ave., 04104, pg. 439   **PV**
XTRA, Inc., 222 St. John St., 04102, pg. 1787   **PB**

Presque Isle

Maine and New Brunswick Electrical Power Company, Ltd., 209 State St., 04769, pg. 1038   **PB**
MAINE POTATO GROWERS, INC., 56 Parsons St., 04769, pg. 697   **PV**
MAINE PUBLIC SERVICE COMPANY, 209 State St., 04769, pg. 1038   **PB**
SuperValu, Inc.-Maine Div., P.O. Box 191, 370 Airport Dr., 04769, pg. 1540   **PB**

Prospect Harbor

STINSON SEAFOOD COMPANY, Rte. 186, 04669, pg. 1043   **PV**

Raymond

Dielectric Communications, Tower Hill Rd., 04071, pg. 727   **PB**

Rockland

FMC Marine Colloids Div., 5 Maple St., 04841-2915, pg. 605   **PB**

Rockport

Camden/Rockland Division, 855 Rockland St., 04856, pg. 438   **PB**
Consumers Maine Water, 855 Rockland St., 04856, pg. 438   **PB**

Sanford

Augat, Inc., Interconnection Products-Sanford Plant, Sanford Industrial Estates, 04073, pg. 1598   **PB**
Sprague, 678 Main St., 04073, pg. 1722   **PB**
WASCO PRODUCTS, INC., 26 Pioneer Ave., 04073, pg. 1152   **PV**

Scarborough

HANNAFORD BROS. CO., 145 Pleasant Hill Rd., 04074, pg. 781   **PB**
Martin's Foods of South Burlington, Inc., 145 Pleasant Hill Rd., 04074, pg. 782   **PB**
Plain Street Properties, Inc., 145 Pleasant Hill Rd., 04074, pg. 782   **PB**
POLLACK CORPORATION, 600 Roundwood Dr., 04070, pg. 874   **PV**
Shop 'n Save-Mass., Inc., 145 Pleasant Hill Rd., 04074, pg. 782   **PB**

Searsport

General Alum - New England, Kidder Point Rd., 04974, pg. 443   **PV**

Skowhegan

Hartland Division, One Waterworks Dr., 04976, pg. 438   **PB**
Skowhegan Division, RR #1, Box 780, One Waterworks Dr., 04976, pg. 438   **PB**
Somerset Mill, RR #3, Box 1600, 04976, pg. 1193   **IT**

Solon

SOLON MANUFACTURING COMPANY, Ferry St., 04979, pg. 1013   **PV**

South Gardiner

Newark Paperboard Products Mercer Div., River Rd., 04345, pg. 796   **PV**

South Portland

G.H. Bass & Co., 600 Sable Oaks Dr., 04116, pg. 1291   **PB**
Bass Retail Div., 600 Sable Oaks Dr., 04116, pg. 1291   **PB**
Citibank (Maine) N.A., 100 Foden Rd., 04106, pg. 377   **PB**
CONNORS BRUNSWICK, INC., 778 Main St., 04106, pg. 264   **PV**
Dead River Properties, 49 Atlantic Place, 04106, pg. 318   **PV**
Wright Express Corporation, 97 Darling Ave., 04106, pg. 321   **PB**

Stillwater

H.E. SARGENT, INC., 101 Bennoch Rd., 04489, pg. 966   **PV**

Thomaston

Chemrock Corporation, 04861, pg. 903   **PV**

Thorndike

Thorndike Press, Box 159, 04986, pg. 777   **PV**

PB - *U.S. Public Companies Volume*
PV - *U.S. Private Companies Volume*
IT - *International Public & Private Companies Volume*

Geographic Index-U.S.

Warren

Warren Telephone Co., Union St., P.O. Box 273, 04864, pg. 1572 **PB**

Waterville

CROWE ROPE INDUSTRIES L.L.C., P.O. Box 600, 04901, pg. 291 **PV**
C.F. HATHAWAY, Ten Water St., 04901, pg. 510 **PV**

Wells

SPENCER PRESS, INC., 90 Spencer Dr., 04090, pg. 1025 **PV**

Westbrook

Acadia Insurance Company, One Acadia Commons, 04092, pg. 215 **PB**
Atlantic Cellular Telephone Corp., Two Thomas Dr., 04092, pg. 1708 **PB**
Jordan's Foods-Westbrook Division, Thomas Dr., 04092, pg. 599 **PV**
Lindenmeyr Munroe, 510 County Rd., 04092, pg. 224 **PV**
PG VINYL WINDOWS/PG PROGLASS CONSTRUCTION, 865 Spring St., 04092, pg. 826 **PV**
SAUNDERS BROTHERS, 170 Forest St., 04098, pg. 968 **PV**
H.A. Stiles Co., 170 Forest St., 04092, pg. 968 **PV**

Wilton

G.H. Bass & Co., P.O. 659, Weld Road, 04294, pg. 1291 **PB**

Windham

Atlantic Antibodies, Inc., 52 Anderson Rd., 04062, pg. 483 **IT**
Charles River Laboratories-ME, 43 Anderson Rd., 04062, pg. 194 **PB**

Winslow

Kimberly-Clark, Winslow, 14 Benton Ave., 04901, pg. 958 **PB**

Winthrop

Progressive Distributors, Inc., 04364, pg. 782 **PB**

Woodland

Eastern Softwood Sawmill, P. O. Box 667, 04694, pg. 738 **PB**
Georgia Pacific, Maine St., 04694, pg. 736 **PB**
Primary Pulp & Paper Plant, Main St., 04694, pg. 736 **PB**
St. Croix Water Power Co., Main St., 04694, pg. 736 **PB**

Yarmouth

Cole-Haan, One Cole Haan Dr., 04096, pg. 1184 **PB**
Custom Builder, 38 Lafayette St., 04096, pg. 190 **IT**

MARIANA PACIFIC

Saipan

Loewe Saipan Inc., 209 Fiesta II, Shopping Plaza, La Fiesta San Roque, San Roque, 96950, pg. 781 **IT**
Louis Vuitton Saipan Ltd, 207 Fiesta II, La Fiesta San, Roque, Shopping Plaza, San Roque, 96950, pg. 781 **IT**
Mobil Oil Micronesia, Inc., P.O. Box 367, 96950, pg. 1119 **PB**

MARYLAND

Aberdeen

Harford Systems, Inc., P.O. Box 700, 21001, pg. 641 **PV**
Household Products, 1319 Perryman Rd., 21001-4026, pg. 387 **PB**

Accokeek

Beretta U.S.A. Corp., 17601 Beretta Dr., 20607, pg. 188 **IT**

Adamstown

Trans-Tech, Inc., 5520 Adamstown Rd., 21710, pg. 57 **PB**

Adelphi

DSC, 7411 Riggs Rd. Ste. 216, 20783-4246, pg. 475 **PB**

Annapolis

Aeronautical Radio, Inc., 2551 Riva Rd., 21401, pg. 81 **PV**
The Annapolis Banking & Trust Co., Main St. & Church Cir., P.O. Box 311, 21404, pg. 1088 **PB**

ARINC INC. (CONSOLIDATED), 2551 Riva Rd., 21401-7465, pg. 81 **PV**
Capital-Gazette Communications, Inc., 200 Capital Dr., 21401, pg. 649 **PB**
Farmers Bank of Maryland, Five Church Cir., 21401-1973, pg. 641 **PB**
Intercap Graphics Systems, 116 Defense Hwy., 21401, pg. 890 **PB**
Kvaerner Masa Marine Inc., Power Technology Center, 201 Defense Hwy., Ste. 202, 21401, pg. 770 **IT**
The McClure Group, 1319 Blackwalnut Ct., 21403, pg. 720 **PV**
C. Plath North American Div., 222 Severn Ave., 21403-2569, pg. 1002 **PV**
UNC Accessory Services, 175 Admiral Cochrane Dr., 21401, pg. 710 **PB**
UNC Aviation Services, Inc., 175 Admiral Cochrane Dr., 21401, pg. 710 **PB**
WWF Paper Corporation - Mid Atlantic, 9055 Junction Dr., 20701, pg. 1145 **PV**

Annapolis Junction

Government Communications Systems Division, 108-20 Guilford Rd., 20701, pg. 293 **PB**
Osicom Technologies Inc., 9020 Junction Dr., 20701, pg. 1233 **PB**

Baltimore

AAF MCQUAY, INC., 111 S. Calvert, Ste. 2800, 21202, pg. 2 **PV**
ACI Holding Inc., 100 E. Pratt St., 5th Fl., 21202, pg. 464 **IT**
AUSA Holding Company, 1111 N. Charles St., 21201, pg. 27 **IT**
AUSA Life Insurance Co., 1111 North Charles St., 21201, pg. 27 **IT**
Adams Express Co., Seven St. Paul St., Ste. 1140, 21202, pg 1280 **PV**
AEGON USA, Inc., 1111 N. Charles St., 21201-4571, pg. 26 **IT**
Airborne Systems Integration Division, pg. 293 **PV**
ALBAN TRACTOR CO. INC., 8531 Pulaski Hwy., 21237, pg. 32 **PV**
Allmetal Screw Products Corp., 3700 Copper St., Ste 114, 21227, pg. 41 **PV**
Allright Baltimore, Inc., Five N. Liberty St., 21201, pg. 42 **PV**
AMERICAN TRADING AND PRODUCTION CORPORATION, One N. Charles St., 21201, pg. 63 **PV**
American Trading Real Estate Properties, Inc., P.O. Box 238, 21203, pg. 64 **PV**
Amoco Research Center, One N. Charles St., Ste. 1500, 21201-3723, pg. 103 **PV**
Assurance Company of America, 3910 Keswick Rd., 21211, pg. 1530 **PV**
ATLANTIC BUILDERS GROUP INC., 23 Fontana Lane, 21237, pg. 95 **PV**
Atlantic Federal Savings Bank, 100 West Rd., 21204, pg. 1543 **PB**
The Avalon Hill Game Company, 4517 Harford, 21214, pg. 1123 **PV**
Avesta Sheffield East, Inc., 7700 Rolling Mill Rd., 21224, pg. 221 **IT**
BT Alex. Brown Inc., One South St., 21202, pg. 185 **PB**
BAINES MANAGEMENT CO., 200 S. Arlington Ave., Ste. 300, 21223, pg. 111 **PV**
Baltimore Business Publications, Inc., 117 Water St., 21202, pg. 19 **PV**
BALTIMORE GAS AND ELECTRIC COMPANY, Gas & Electric Bldg., Charles Ctr., 21201, pg. 172 **PB**
BALTIMORE STATIONERY CO./TOTAL OFFICE, 2524 Kirk Ave., 21218, pg. 113 **PV**
The Baltimore Sun Newspapers, 501 N. Calvert St., 21278-0001, pg. 1616 **PB**
Baltimore-Washington Auto Exchange Inc., 7151 Brookdale Dr., 21244, pg. 1648 **PB**
Baumgarten Stamp Co., 342 N. Charles St., 21203, pg. 58 **PV**
Bell Atlantic-MD, 1 E. Pratt St., 21202, pg. 202 **PB**
Beltsville Distribution Point, 6925 San Tomas Rd., 21227, pg. 247 **PB**
Benelli Moto Guzzi North America, 1501 Caton Ave., 21227, pg. 482 **IT**
Better Homes Insurance Associates, Inc., 1111 N. Charles St., 21202, pg. 27 **IT**
BRUNING PAINT COMPANY, 601 S. Haven St., 21224, pg. 76 **PV**
WM. T. BURNETT & CO., INC., 1500 Bush St., 21230, pg. 86 **PV**
CSX Technology, 100 N. Charles St. # C, 21201-3812, pg. 284 **PB**
Cadmus Financial Communications, Two N. Charles St., Ste. 940, 21201, pg. 291 **PB**
CAP Gemini America (Baltimore Branch), World Trade Center, 401 E. Pratt St., Ste. 545, 21202, pg. 263 **IT**
Carey Division, 9108 Yelllow Brick Rd., Ste. B, 21237, pg. 399 **PV**
CATHOLIC RELIEF SERVICES, 209 W. Fayette St., 21201, pg. 220 **PV**
Central Maryland Surgery Center, 1500 Joh Ave., 21227, pg. 803 **PV**
Chase Bank of Maryland, Ten E. Baltimore St., 21202, pg. 338 **PB**
Chemical Specialties Manufacturing Corp., 901 N. Newkirk St., 21205, pg. 1357 **PB**
Chesapeake Packaging Co./Baltimore, 725 Pittman Rd., 21226, pg. 346 **PB**

COLLMAN GRAPHICS, INC., 1820 Portal St., 21224, pg. 253 **PV**
Colonial American Casualty and Surety Company, 300 Saint Paul Pl., 21203, pg. 1530 **IT**
Commercial Credit Company, 300 St. Paul Pl., 21202, pg. 1633 **PB**
Constellation Energy Projects & Services, Inc., 7225 Windsor Blvd., 21244, pg. 172 **PB**
Constellation Energy Source, Inc., P.O. Box 1475, Spring Gardens Complex, 21203, pg. 172 **PB**
Constellation Holdings, Inc., 250 W. Pratt St., 21201, pg. 172 **PB**
Constellation Investments, Inc., 250 W. Pratt St., 23rd Floor, 21201, pg. 172 **PB**
Constellation Power, Inc., 250 W. Pratt St., 21201, pg. 172 **PB**
Constellation Real Estate Group Inc., 250 W. Pratt St., 21201, pg. 172 **PB**
Credit & Risk Management Associates, 100 E. Pratt St., 16th Fl., 21202, pg. 610 **PB**
Crown Central Holding Corp., P.O. Box 1168, 21203, pg. 462 **PB**
CROWN CENTRAL PETROLEUM CORPORATION, One N. Charles St., 21203, pg. 462 **PB**
Crown Central Petroleum Foundation, P.O. Box 1168, 21203, pg. 462 **PB**
Crown Gold, Inc., P.O. Box 1168, 21203, pg. 462 **PB**
Crown Nigeria, Inc., P.O. Box 1168, 21203, pg. 462 **PB**
The Crown Oil & Gas Co., P.O. Box 1168, 21203, pg. 462 **PB**
Crown Stations, Inc., P. O. Box 1168, 21203, pg. 462 **PB**
Delsey Luggage Inc., Meadow Ridge, Industrial Pk., 6375 Business Pkwy., Ste. A, 21227, pg. 192 **IT**
Dext Company of MD, 3220 Sun St., 21226, pg. 1444 **PB**
Domino Sugar Corporation-Baltimore, 1100 Key Hwy. E., 21230, pg. 1356 **IT**
Dryden Oil Company, Inc., 9300 Pulaski Hwy., 21220, pg. 235 **IT**
DURRETT-SHEPPARD STEEL CO., INC., 6800 E. Baltimore, 21224, pg. 349 **PV**
DYWIDAG Systems International, USA, Inc., 1740 E. Joppa Rd., 21234, pg. 424 **IT**
EISNER & ASSOCIATES, INC., 12 W. Madison St., 21201, pg. 366 **PV**
Eisner, Petrou & Associates, Inc., 12 W. Madison St., 21201, pg. 366 **PV**
ELLICOTT MACHINE CORPORATION INTERNATIONAL, 1611 Bush St., 21230, pg. 372 **PV**
ENVIRONMENTAL ELEMENTS CORPORATION, 3700 Koppers St., 21227, pg. 586 **PB**
Executive Management and Consultant Services, Inc., 1111 N. Charles St., 21201, pg. 27 **IT**
FZ Corporation, P. O. Box 1168, 21203, pg. 462 **PB**
Fairfax Savings Bank, P.O. Box 17119, 17 Light St., 21203, pg. 1543 **PB**
Fast Fare, Inc., P.O. Box 1168, 21203, pg. 462 **PB**
Ferguson Lyon Conklin & Company Inc., 2101 Race & McComas Sts., 21230, pg. 1512 **IT**
Fidelity & Deposit Company of Maryland, 300 Saint Paul Pl., 21203, pg. 1530 **IT**
Fidelity & Guaranty Life Insurance Co., 100 Light St., 21202, pg. 1659 **PB**
First Maryland Annuities Agency Corporation, 25 S. Charles St., 21201, pg. 64 **IT**
First Maryland Bancorp, First Maryland Bldg., 25 S. Charles St., 21201, pg. 64 **IT**
First Maryland Brokerage Corporation, 25 S. Charles St., 21201, pg. 64 **IT**
First Maryland Credit Corp., 25 S. Charles St., 21201, pg. 64 **IT**
First Maryland Leasecorp, 25 S. Charles St., 21201, pg. 64 **IT**
First Maryland Life Insurance Company, 25 S. Charles St., 21201, pg. 64 **IT**
First National Bank of Maryland, 25 S. Charles St., 21201, pg. 64 **IT**
First-Re Life Insurance Company, 1111 N. Charles St., 21201, pg. 27 **IT**
Fuchs Lubricants, Midlantic Div., 1700 S. Caton Ave., 21227, pg. 518 **IT**
FUTURES PERSONNEL SERVICES, Maryland Exec. Park, 8600 LaSalle Rd. #315, 21286, pg. 433 **PV**
GCI Lowell Inc/WZYZ F.M., 1829 Reistertown Rd., 21208, pg. 470 **PV**
Grace Davison, 10 E. Baltimore St., 21202, pg. 755 **PB**
GRAY KIRK/VANSANT ADVERTISING, INC., The World Trade Center, 21202, pg. 472 **PV**
GREEN SEED CO., 4764 Hollins Ferry Rd., 21227, pg. 477 **PV**
JOHN GROSS & CO., 1521-M S. Edgewood St., 21227, pg. 483 **PV**
Harborplace, 200 E. Pratt St., 21202, pg. 1407 **PB**
Harte-Hanks Direct Marketing Maryland, Lansdowne Industrial Pk., 100 Alco Pl., 21227, pg. 794 **PB**
Hedwin Corporation, 1600 Roland Heights Ave., 21211, pg. 1278 **IT**
Hewlett-Packard Company, 3701 Koppers St., 21227, pg. 814 **PB**
Hilb, Rogal and Hamilton Company of Baltimore, 1104 Kenilworth Dr., Ste. 500, 21204, pg. 827 **PB**
Hinkle Easter Products, 1600 Union Ave., 21211, pg. 666 **PV**
Hudson Aviation Services Inc., Delaware, P.O. Box 18568, 21240, pg. 845 **PB**
Hydro Conduit Corp., P.O. Box 26046, 6411 Eastern Ave., 21224, pg. 245 **IT**
Ikon Office Solutions-Baltimore, 7140 Windsor Blvd., 21207, pg. 863 **PB**
Incor, Inc., 4601 N. Point Blvd., 21219, pg. 308 **PB**
Insect Control & Research Corp., 1330 Dillon Heights Ave., 21228, pg. 724 **PV**

International Petroleum Corporation of Maryland, 6305 E. Lombard St., 21224, pg. 906 PB
Interstate Steel Supply Co. of Maryland, 1600 Cherry Hill Rd., 21230-0165, pg. 1100 PB
Investment Counselors of Maryland, Inc., 803 Cathedral St., 21201, pg. 1673 PB
Kaydon Ring & Seal, Inc., P.O. Box 626, 21203, pg. 946 PB
Kidde Systems, Inc., 4971 Mercantile Rd., 21236, pg. 1341 PB
Krafcor Unlimited, 6301 Seaforth St., 21224, pg. 1022 PV
The Lakefront Dock & Railroad Terminal Co., Two N. Charles St., 21201, pg. 432 PB
C.J. LANGENFELDER & SON, INC., 8427 Pulaski Hwy., 21237, pg. 650 PV
LaSalle Advisors Limited, 100 E. Pratt St., 21202, pg. 979 PB
Legg Mason Capital Management Inc., 111 S. Calvert St., 21203, pg. 985 PB
LEGG MASON, INC., 111 S. Calvert St., 21203, pg. 984 PB
Legg Mason Wood Walker, Incorporated, 111 S. Calvert St., 21203, pg. 985 PB
Lever, 5300 Holabird Ave., 21224-6010, pg. 1435 IT
LIFE-LIKE PRODUCTS, INC., 1600 Union Ave., 21211, pg. 666 PV
Lincoln National Income Fund, Inc., c/o The Prentice Hall Corp., 929 N. Howard St., 21201, pg. 998 PB
Liuski International Maryland, Inc., 6605 Selnick Dr., 21227, pg. 1005 PB
Lockheed Martin Aerostructure, 103 Chesapeake Park Plaza, 21220, pg. 1006 PB
Logicon Technical Services Inc., 1119 Wilson Dr., 21223-3230, pg. 1199 PB
John D. Lucas Printing Company, 1820 Portal St., 21224, pg. 253 PV
MBC Agency, Inc., Two Hopkins Plaza, 21201, pg. 1089 PB
MBC Leasing, Two Hopkins Plaza, 21201, pg. 1089 PB
MBC Realty, Inc., Two Hopkins Plaza, 21201, pg. 1089 PB
MLIG, Inc., Two E. Chase St., 21202, pg. 27 IT
MNC Financial, Inc., 111 Market St., Ste. 700, 21202, pg. 639 PB
MNC Mortgage Corporation, 111 Market Pl., 21203, pg. 639 PB
Maine Bonding & Casualty Company, 3910 Keswick Rd., 21211, pg. 1530 IT
MAMMA ILARDO'S CORP., 3600 Clipper Mill Rd., Ste. 260, 21211, pg. 699 PV
MARS SUPER MARKETS, INC., 7183 Holabird Ave., 21222, pg. 707 PV
Martin Marietta Software Services, 3102 Timanus Ln., 21207, pg. 1007 PB
Maryland Casualty Co., 3910 Keswick Rd., 21211, pg. 1530 IT
Maryland Commercial Insurance Group, 3910 Keswick Rd., 21211, pg. 1530 IT
Maryland Insurance Company, 3910 Keswick Rd., 21211, pg. 1530 IT
Maryland Lloyds, 3910 Keswick Rd., 21211, pg. 1530 IT
Maryland Netherlands Credit Insurance Company, 210 N. Charles St., Rm. 713, 21201, pg. 1530 IT
Maryland Personal Insurance Group, 3910 Keswick Rd., 21211, pg. 1530 IT
Maserati Automobiles, Incorporated, 1501 Caton Ave., 21227, pg. 482 IT
MERCANTILE BANKSHARES CORPORATION, Two Hopkins Plaza, 21201, pg. 1088 PB
Mercantile Mortgage Corp., 20 S. Charles St., 3rd Fl., 21201, pg. 1089 PB
Mercantile-Safe Deposit & Trust Co., Two Hopkins Plaza, 21201, pg. 1089 PB
Metro/Basics, 5483 Baltimore Pike, 21229, pg. 1388 PB
MONARCH AVALON, INC., 4517 Harford, 21214, pg. 1123 PB
Mondawmin Corporation, 1200 Mondawmin Concourse, 21215, pg. 1407 PB
MONTEBELLO BRANDS INC., 1919 Willow Spring Rd., 21222, pg. 758 PV
Monumental General Administrators, Inc., Two E. Chase St., 21202, pg. 27 IT
Monumental General Casualty Company, 1111 N. Charles St., 21202, pg. 27 IT
Monumental General Insurance Company, 1111 N. Charles St., 21202, pg. 27 IT
Monumental General Insurance Group, Inc., 1111 N. Charles St., 21202, pg. 27 IT
Monumental General Mass Marketing, Inc., 1111 N. Charles St., 21201, pg. 27 IT
Monumental Life Insurance Company, Two E. Chase St., 21202, pg. 27 IT
Moran Towing of Maryland, 1615 Thames St., 21231, pg. 761 PV
National Standard Insurance Company, 3910 Keswick Rd., 21211, pg. 1530 IT
Nicholas, Fayette & Greenbrier RR Co., 100 N. Charles St., 21201, pg. 432 PB
Northern Insurance Company of New York, 3910 Keswick Rd., 21211, pg. 1530 IT
THE ORIOLES, INC., Oriole Park at Camden Yards, 21201, pg. 819 PV
Orsan Corp., c/o Corporation Trust Inc., 32 South St., 21202, pg. 791 IT
THE PARK CIRCLE MOTOR CO., 1829 Reisterstown Rd., 21208, pg. 839 PV
Park Fast of Maryland, 100 W. Fayette St., 21201, pg. 364 PV
PARKS LLC, 3330 Henry G. Parks Jr. Circle, 21215, pg. 840 PV
PETROLEUM & RESOURCES CORP., Seven St. Paul St., Ste. 1140, 21202, pg. 1280 PB
PHARMAKINETICS LABORATORIES, INC., 302 W. Fayette St., 21201, pg. 1285 PB
POLK AUDIO, INC., 5601 Metro Dr., 21215, pg. 1315 PB
POLY-SEAL CORPORATION, 1810 Portal St., 21224, pg. 875 PV
POMPEIIAN, INC., 4201 Pulaski Hwy., 21224, pg. 875 PV
T. ROWE PRICE ASSOCIATES, INC., 100 E. Pratt St., 21202, pg. 1324 PB
T. Rowe Price Investment Services Inc., 100 E. Pratt St., 21202, pg. 1324 PB
Professional Learning Systems, 351 W. Camden St., 21201, pg. 1748 PB
Provident Bank of Maryland, 114 E. Lexington St., 22201, pg. 1337 PB
PROVIDENT BANKSHARES CORPORATION, 114 E. Lexington St., 21202, pg. 1337 PB
RTKL ASSOCIATES INC., One South St., 10th Fl., 21202, pg. 906 PV
Radio One of Maryland, 100 Saint Paul St., 21202, pg. 906 PV
Rammer Inc., 7391 Washington Blvd., Ste. 101-102, 21227, pg. 1352 IT
Reisterstown Federal Savings Bank, 11817 Reisterstown Rd., 21136, pg. 1543 PB
Rhone-Poulenc Alcolac, 3440 Fairfield Rd., 21226, pg. 1110 IT
Rita-Ann Distributors, 901 Curtain Ave., 21218, pg. 97 PB
The Roost, Inc., Gatehouse, 5100 Falls Rd., 21210, pg. 1409 PB
Rothschild/Pell, Rudman & Co., Inc., 32 South St., 21202, pg. 1674 PB
Rowe Price-Fleming International Inc., 100 E. Pratt St., 21202, pg. 493 IT
Sandoz Consumer Pharmaceutical, 2601 Madison Ave., 21217-4072, pg. 974 IT
SCHMIDT BAKING CO., INC., 7801 Fitch Ln., 21236, pg. 970 PV
SCOTSMAN HOLDING INC., 8211 Town Center Dr., 21236, pg. 976 PV
SEED CORPORATION OF AMERICA, 4764 Hollins Ferry Rd., 21227, pg. 981 PV
Sevenson Industrial Services, Inc., 7112 Garden View, 21220, pg. 1463 PB
Shandwick Baltimore, 1629 Thames St., Ste. 204, 21231, pg. 1227 IT
Sheridan Electronic Systems, 400 E. Pratt St., 21202, pg. 993 PV
SHILLCRAFT, INC., 8899 Kelso Dr., 21221, pg. 994 PV
Simkins Maryland Board, P.O. Box 3249, 21228, pg. 1000 PV
Snavely Forest Products, Inc., 2901 Chalbs St., 21226, pg. 1010 PV
SO-LO-FOOD, INC., 4701 O'Donnell St., 21224, pg. 1011 PV
Stanfast, Inc., 3741 Commerce Dr., Ste. 309, 21227, pg. 1505 PB
Survey Research Associates, 6115 Falls Rd., 21209, pg. 123 PV
SYLVAN LEARNING SYSTEMS INC., 1000 Lancaster St., 21202, pg. 1545 PB
TBC Direct, Inc., 1030 N. Charles St., 21201-5402, pg. 1095 PV
TWD Baltimore, 3630 Commerce Dr., 21227, pg. 229 PB
Tencarva Machinery Co., 1766 Sulphur Spring Rd., 21227, pg. 1076 PV
Textron Compressor Components, 6401 Chemical Rd., 21226-1705, pg. 1590 PB
Thermal Industries, Inc., 2668 Merchant Dr., 21230, pg. 491 PV
Titan Steel Corp., 2500-B Broening Hwy., 21224, pg. 1089 PV
TRAHAN, BURDEN & CHARLES, INC., 1030 N. Charles St., 21201-5402, pg. 1095 PV
Trahan, Burden & Charles, Inc., Public Relations, 1030 N. Charles St., 21201-5402, pg. 1095 PV
TURNBULL ENTERPRISES, INC., 3501 Marmenco Ct., 21230, pg. 1109 PV
USF&G CORPORATION, 6225 Smith Ave. LA 0303, 21209, pg. 1659 PB
Union-Transport Corporation-Baltimore Office, Dunmar Bldg., 2700 Broening Hwy., Ste. 211B, 21222, pg. 1119 PV
United Financial Services, Inc., Two E. Chase St., 21202, pg. 27 IT
United States Fidelity & Guaranty Company, 6225 Centennial Way, 21209, pg. 1659 PB
U.S. Pharmaceuticals, 7205 Windsor Blvd., 21244, pg. 58 PB
U.S. Tag, 2217 Robb St., 21218, pg. 333 PB
Valiant Insurance Company, 3910 Keswick Rd., 21211, pg. 1530 IT
The Valspar Corp. Protective Coatings Div., 1401 Severyn St., 21230, pg. 1707 PB
Valu Foods Inc., 4701 Odonnell St., 21224, pg. 1012 PV
The Village of Cross Keys, Inc., 5100 Falls Rd., 21210, pg. 1409 PB
Voest-Alpine Industries, Inc.-Continuous Casting, 4611 N. Point Blvd., 21219, pg. 1470 IT
Voest-Alpine Services and Technologies Corp.-Baltimore, 4611 N. Poin Blvd., 21219, pg. 1471 IT
WBAL-AM, 3800 Hooper Ave., 21211, pg. 516 PV
WBAL Division, 3800 Hooper Ave., 21211, pg. 516 PV
WBAL-TV, 3800 Hooper Ave., 21211, pg. 516 PV
WIYY-FM, 3800 Hooper Ave., 21211, pg. 516 PV
WJZ-TV, 3725 Malden Ave., 21211, pg. 275 PB
WMAR-TV, 6400 York Rd., 21212, pg. 1448 PB
WAVERLY, INC., 351 W. Camden St., 21201-2436, pg. 1748 PB
Waverly International, 351 W. Camden St., 21201, pg. 1748 PB
WELLS ALUMINUM CORP., 809 Gleneagles Ct., Ste. 300, 21286, pg. 1161 PV
White Marsh Equities Corp., 8200 Perry Hall Blvd., 21236, pg. 1409 PB
The Whitestone Corporation, 1111 N. Charles, 21202, pg. 27 IT
THE WHITING-TURNER CONTRACTING CO., 300 E. Joppa Rd., 21286, pg. 1174 PV
Williams & Wilkins Book Publishing, 351 W. Camden St., 21201, pg. 1748 PB
Williams & Wilkins Periodical Publishing, 351 W. Camden St., 21201, pg. 1748 PB
Williams Scotsman, Inc., 8211 Town Ctr. Dr., 21236, pg. 976 PV
THE ZAMOISKI CO., 3000 Waterview Ave., 21230, pg. 1203 PV
Zippy Mart, Inc., P.O. Box 1168, 21203, pg. 462 PB

Bel Air

Charter Behavioral Health System at Hidden Brook, Inc., 522 Thomas Run Rd., 21014, pg. 1033 PB
The Forest Hill State Bank, 130 S. Bond St., 21014-7307, pg. 1089 PB
Homestead Publishing, Ten Hays St., 21014, pg. 1616 PB
Maryland-American Water Co., 126 S. Main St., 21014, pg. 95 PB

Belcamp

Airborne Systems Integration Division, 1362 Brass Mill Rd., 21017, pg. 293 PB
Bata Shoe Co., Inc., 4501 Pulaski Hwy., 21017, pg. 195 PV
CHB CORP., P.O. Box 479, 4501 Pulaski Hwy., 21017, pg. 194 PV
INDEPENDENT CAN COMPANY, P.O. Box 370, 1300 Brass Mill Rd., 21017-0370, pg. 559 PV

Beltsville

BIOSPHERICS INCORPORATED, 12051 Indian Creek Ct., 20705, pg. 232 PB
DURON, INC., 10406 Tucker St., 20705, pg. 349 PV
EG & G Aerospace & Engineered Products, 11642 Old Baltimore Pike, 20705, pg. 542 PB
Fidelio Software Corporation, 12000 Baltimore Ave., 20705, pg. 1106 PB
MICROS SYSTEMS INC., 12000 Baltimore Ave., 20705-1384, pg. 1106 PB
TEXTILEASE CORPORATION, 10733 Tucker St, 20705, pg. 1079 PV
Thermal Industries Inc., 12110 Conway Rd., 20705-1302, pg. 491 PV

Bethesda

AMI Capital Inc., 7200 Wisconsin Ave., 20814, pg. 1116 PV
Acacia Financial Corporation, 7315 Wisconsin Ave., 20814, pg. 11 PV
THE ACACIA GROUP - ACACIA LIFE INSURANCE CO., 7315 Wisconsin Ave., 20814, pg. 10 PV
Acacia National Life Ins. Co., 7315 Wiscounsin Ave., 20814, pg. 11 PV
Advisor's Group, 7315 Wisconsin Ave., 20814, pg. 11 PV
Bell Atlantic Specialty Guides, 6701 Democracy Blvd. 9th Flr., 20817-1572, pg. 203 PB
Benihana of Bethesda Corp., 7315 Wisconsin Ave., 20814, pg. 212 PB
Bernard Johnson Young Inc., 6705 Rockledge Dr., 3rd Fl., 20817, pg. 136 PV
Earle Palmer Brown Public Relations, 6935 Arlington Rd., 20814, pg. 174 PV
Calvert Group, Ltd., 4550 Montgomery Ave., Ste. 1000 N, 20814, pg. 11 PV
CHEVY CHASE CARS & GEO, 7725 Wisconsin Ave., 20814, pg. 234 PV
Clark Construction Group, Inc., 7500 Old Georgetown Rd., 20814, pg. 242 PV
CLARK ENTERPRISES, INC., 7500 Old Georgetown Rd., 15th Fl., 20814, pg. 242 PV
Cogema Inc., 7401 Wisconsin Ave., 20814-3416, pg. 305 IT
COLEMAN CADILLAC INC., 10400 Auto Park Ave., 20817, pg. 251 PV
COMSAT CORPORATION, 6560 Rock Spring Dr., 20817, pg. 424 PB
COMSAT International Ventures, 6560 Rock Spring Dr., 20817-1146, pg. 425 PB
COMSAT World Systems, 6560 Rock Spring Dr., 20817-1146, pg. 424 PB
Comstream, A Spar Company, 6701 Democracy Blvd., Ste. 300, 20817, pg. 1288 IT
Congressional Information Service (CIS), 4520 East-West Hwy., 20814, pg. 1096 IT
Disclosure Incorporated, 5161 River Rd., 20816, pg. 1325 PB
DISCOVERY COMMUNICATIONS, INC., 7700 Wisconsin Ave., 20814, pg. 334 PV
Discovery Networks, Inc., 7700 Wisconsin Ave., 20814, pg. 334 PV
EDS, Government Systems Group, 6430 Rockledge Dr., Ste. 600, 20817, pg. 570 PB
FEDERAL DATA CORPORATION, 4800 Hampton Ln., 20814, pg. 398 PV
Firemen's Insurance Company of Washington, D.C., P.O. Box 31130, 7315 Wisconsin Ave, Ste. 300W, 20814, pg. 215 PB

Geographic Index-U.S.

PB - *U.S. Public Companies Volume*
PV - *U.S. Private Companies Volume*
IT - *International Public & Private Companies Volume*

GOODWILL INDUSTRIES INTERNATIONAL, 9200 Rockville Pike, 20814, pg. 464 **PV**
Gwynedd Partners, 7316 Wisconsin Ave., 20814, pg. 361 **PB**
Host International, Inc., 10400 Fernwood Rd., 20817, pg. 841 **PB**
HOST MARRIOTT CORPORATION, 10400 Fernwood Rd., 20817-1109, pg. 841 **PB**
HOST MARRIOTT SERVICES CORPORATION, 10400 Fernwood Rd., 20817, pg. 841 **PB**
I-NET, Inc., 6700 Rockledge Dr., Ste. 100, 20817, pg. 1737 **PB**
IBM Systems Integration Div., 6600 Rockledge Dr., 20817, pg. 896 **PB**
INFORMATION SYSTEMS & NETWORK CORPORATION, 10411 Motor City Dr., 20817, pg. 561 **PV**
INTEC, 4800 Montgomery Ln., 11th Fl., 20814, pg. 19 **IT**
LOCKHEED MARTIN CORPORATION, 6801 Rockledge Dr., 20817, pg. 1006 **PB**
Lockheed Martin Electronics Group, 6801 Rockledge Dr., 20817, pg. 1006 **PB**
Martin Marietta Information Group, 6801 Rockledge Dr., 20817, pg. 1007 **PB**
Martin Marietta Information Systems, 6801 Rockledge Dr., 20817, pg. 1007 **PB**
Martin Marietta International, Inc., 6801 Rockledge Dr., 20817, pg. 1009 **PB**
Martin Marietta Space Group, 6801 Rockledge Dr., 20817, pg. 1007 **PB**
MILLER & LONG CO. INC., 4824 Rugby Ave., 20814, pg. 746 **PV**
National Information Services (NIS), 4520 East-West Hwy., 20814, pg. 1096 **IT**
NationsBank/Maryland, 6610 Rockledge Dr., 20817, pg. 1162 **PB**
Numatec Inc., 7401 Wisconsin Ave., 20814-3416, pg. 305 **IT**
OXFORD REALTY FINANCIAL GROUP, 7200 Wisconsin Ave., 11 Fl., 20814, pg. 825 **PV**
Pathfinder Mines Corporation, 7401 Wisconsin Ave., 20814-3416, pg. 305 **IT**
PennCorp Financial, Inc., 3 Bethesda Metro Center, Ste. 1600, 20814, pg. 1271 **PB**
Pike & Fischer, 4600 East-West Hwy. Ste. 200, 20814-1438, pg. 182 **PB**
Rosendorf/Evans, 125 Montgomery Mall, 7101 Democracy, 20817, pg. 597 **PB**
SNYDER COMMUNICATIONS, INC., 6903 Rockledge Dr., Two Democracy Ctr., Ste. 1400, 20817, pg. 1481 **PB**
STARTEC GLOBAL COMMUNICATIONS CORPORATION, 10411 Motor City Dr., 20817, pg. 1511 **PB**
UNITED BROADCASTING L.P., 7200 Wisconson Ave., Ste. 212, 20814, pg. 1121 **PB**
U.S. Generating Company, 7500 Old Georgetown Rd., Ste. 1300, 20814-6161, pg. 1241 **PB**
WATSON WYATT WORLDWIDE, 6707 Democracy Blvd., Ste. 800, 20817, pg. 1154 **PV**
Weichert Realtors, Inc., 6410 Rockledge Dr., 20817, pg. 1159 **PV**
Willis Corroon Corp. of Wash. D.C., Three Bethesda Metro Ctr., Ste. 400, 20814, pg. 1507 **IT**
Willis Corroon Inspace, Inc., Three Bethesda Metro Ctr., Ste. 450, 20814, pg. 1507 **IT**
Worldscope/Disclosure, LLC, 5161 River Rd., 20816, pg. 1325 **PB**
Xerox Research, 4340 E. W. Hwy., 20814-4411, pg. 1784 **PB**

California

Electronic Systems Division, 23481 Cottonwood Pkwy., 20619-9517, pg. 1627 **PB**
Veda Systems, Incorporated, 6A Pecan Ct., 20619, pg. 1136 **PV**

Calverton

Encore Computer Corp., 4061 Powder Mill Rd., Ste. 400, 20705, pg. 580 **PB**
Winchester Homes, Inc., 4061 Powder Mill Rd., Ste. 500, 20705, pg. 1764 **PB**

Cambridge

Coldwater Seafood Corp., Woods Rd., 21613, pg. 251 **PV**
Interstate Core Pack, 903 Woods Rd., 21613, pg. 573 **PV**

Capital Heights

E.C. Ernst, Inc., P.O. Box 4040, 20791-4040, pg. 861 **PV**

Chestertown

DAVID A. BRAMBLE, INC., 705 Morgnec Rd., 21620, pg. 165 **PV**
The Chestertown Bank of Maryland, P.O. Box 60, 211 High St., 21620, pg. 1088 **PB**
Huls America Inc., Rte. 297, 21620, pg. 1455 **IT**
Schlegel Maryland, Bldg. 115 Lynchburg Dr., 21620, pg. 128 **IT**

Cheverly

PEAKE PRINTERS, INC., 2500 Schuster Dr., 20781, pg. 845 **PV**

Chevy Chase

FDC Reports Inc., 5550 Friendship Blvd., Ste. 1, 20815-7278, pg. 1100 **IT**
Franklin Property Co., 8401 Connecticut Ave., 20815, pg. 1435 **PB**
B.F. Saul Advisory Co., 8401 Connecticut Ave., 20815, pg. 1435 **PB**
SAUL CENTERS INC., 8401 Connecticut Ave., 20815, pg. 1435 **PB**
Victor O. Schinnerer & Co., Ltd., Two Wisconsin Cir., 20815, pg. 1049 **PB**
Sharonville Hotel Corporation, 8401 Connecticut Ave., 20815, pg. 1435 **PB**
STEUART INVESTMENT COMPANY, 5454 Wisconsin Ave., Ste. 1600, 20815, pg. 1042 **PV**
Sullyfield Corporation, 8401 Connecticut Ave., 20815, pg. 1435 **PB**

Clarksburg

CTel Corporation (North America), 22240 Comsat Dr., 20871, pg. 643 **IT**
COMSAT Laboratories, 22300 COMSAT Dr., 20871, pg. 424 **PB**
COMSAT Mobile Communications, 22300 Comsat Dr., 20871-9475, pg. 424 **PB**
Microwave Signal, Inc., 22300 Comsat Dr., 20871, pg. 8 **PB**

College Park

Amecom Div., 5115 Calvert Rd., 20740-3898, pg. 1002 **PB**
Commerce Bank, 9658 Baltimore Ave., Ste. 207, 20740, pg. 1038 **PB**
94th of College Park, Inc., 5240 Calvert Rd., 20740, pg. 1023 **PV**
Stone Industrial, 9207 51st Av. & Cree Rd., 20740, pg. 880 **PV**

Columbia

AlliedSignal Microelectronics & Technology Center, 9140 Old Annapolis Rd., 21045, pg. 50 **PB**
AlliedSignal Technical Service, One Bendix Rd., 21045-1897, pg. 50 **PB**
The American City Corp., American City Bldg., 21044, pg. 1407 **PB**
American Environmental Network, Inc., 9151 Rumsey Rd., Ste. 150, 21045, pg. 1587 **PB**
Aoki Corporation, 10500 Little Patuxelt Pkwy., Ste. 650, 21044, pg. 78 **IT**
Arnold Advertising, Amdahl Bldg., 10420 Little Patuxent Pkwy., 21044, pg. 84 **PV**
Arrow/Schweber Electronics, 9800 Patuxent Woods Dr., Ste. J., 21046, pg. 133 **PB**
B&L Jewelry Store, 6301 Stevens Forest Rd., 21045, pg. 921 **PV**
Baltimore Center, Inc., Hdqtrs. Bldg., 21044, pg. 1407 **PB**
Barclay & Sons, 6301 Stevens Forest Rd., 21045, pg. 921 **PV**
Barlow & Eaton, 6301 Stevens Forest Rd., 21045, pg. 921 **PV**
Benchmark Appraisal Group, 10440 Shaker Dr., Ste. 105, 21046, pg. 1089 **PB**
BOWLES FLUIDICS CORPORATION, 6625 Dobbin Rd., 21045, pg. 248 **PB**
Owen Brown B Development Co., Headquarters Bldg., 21044, pg. 1409 **PB**
Burns & Wilcox - Columbia Office, 9841 Brokenland Pkwy., #314, 21046, pg. 609 **PV**
CSSI Corporation, 10260 Old Columbia Rd., 21046, pg. 1182 **PB**
Carpentry & Hardware Services, 8925-9 McGaw Ct., 21045, pg. 503 **PV**
Castleberg's, 6301 Stevens Forest Rd., 21045, pg. 921 **PV**
Cigna Healthcare Mid-Atlantic, Inc., 9700 Patuxent Woods Dr., 21046, pg. 359 **PB**
Columbia Mall, Inc., 10300 Little Patuxent Pkwy., 21044, pg. 1407 **PB**
Columbus Square Shopping Center Company, c/o The Rouse Company, 10275 Little Patuxent Pkwy., 21044-3456, pg. 361 **PB**
Community Research & Development, Inc., Headquarters Bldg., 21044, pg. 1407 **PB**
Cornerstone Title Company, 11000 Broken Land Pkwy., 21044, pg. 1414 **PB**
Coscan Adler Limited Partnership, The Parkview Bldg., Ste. 400, 10480 Little Pautuxtent Pkwy., 21044-3502, pg. 228 **IT**
The Cosmetic Center Inc., 8700 Robert Fulton Dr., 21046, pg. 689 **PV**
Dataproducts Corp., 8990 Old Annapolis Rd., 21045, pg. 620 **IT**
Deerfield Homes, Inc., Headquarters Bldg., 21044, pg. 1409 **PB**
Delaware Coca-Cola Bottling Company, Inc., 9770 Patuxent Woods Dr., 21046, pg. 393 **PB**
Duratek Corporation, 8955 Guilford Rd., Ste. 200, 21046, pg. 694 **PB**
EDD-Maryland, 8945 Guilford, Ste. 130, 21046, pg. 205 **PB**
ESL Inc., 6724 Alexander Bell Dr., 21046-2100, pg. 1558 **PB**
Echo Farms Golf & Country Club, Inc., Headquarters Bldg., 21044, pg. 1409 **PB**
Entrust Home Financing, 8910 Rte. 108, 21045, pg. 1013 **PB**

ESSEX CORPORATION, 9150 Guilford Rd., 21046, pg. 593 **PB**
GTCO CORPORATION, 7125 Riverwood Dr., 21046, pg. 436 **PV**
General Physics Corporation, 6700 Alexander Bell Dr., 21046, pg. 694 **PB**
General Physics Finance Inc., 6700 Alexander Bell Dr., 21046, pg. 694 **PB**
General Physics Mohawk Corporation, 6700 Alexander Bell Dr., 21046, pg. 694 **PB**
General Physics Niagara Corporation, 6700 Alexander Bell Dr., 21046, pg. 694 **PB**
General Physics Ohio Corporation, 6700 Alexander Bell Dr., 21046, pg. 694 **PB**
General Physics Philadelphia Corporation, 6700 Alexander Bell Dr., 21046, pg. 694 **PB**
General Technical Services, Inc., 6700 Alexander Bell Dr., 21046, pg. 695 **PB**
HEAD USA, INC., 9189 Red Branch Rd., 21045, pg. 514 **PV**
Henebrys, 6301 Stevens Forest Rd., 21046, pg. 921 **PV**
Hub Furniture Store, 6301 Stevens Forest Rd., 21045, pg. 920 **PV**
IceLandAir, 5950 Symphony Woods Rd., Ste. 410, 21044, pg. 658 **IT**
Inventory Management Corp., 6700 Alexander Bell Dr., 21046, pg. 694 **PB**
JP Foodservice Distributors, Inc., 9830 Patuxent Woods Dr., 21046, pg. 918 **PB**
JP FOODSERVICE, INC., 9830 Patuxent Woods Dr, 21046, pg. 918 **PB**
Jaco Electronics, Inc., Rivers Ctr., 10270 Old Columbia Rd., 21046, pg. 920 **PB**
The Kline Furniture Co., 6301 Stevens Forest Rd., 21045, pg. 920 **PV**
LUSKIN'S, INC., 7125 Columbia Gateway, 21046, pg. 681 **PV**
MERIDIAN MEDICAL TECHNOLOGY, INC., 10240 Old Columbia Rd., 21046, pg. 1095 **PB**
Milgray/Washington, Inc., 6460 Dobbin Rd., 21045, pg. 207 **PB**
Morton's Jewelry Co., 6301 Stevens Forest Rd., 21045, pg. 921 **PV**
NAI Systems Division, 7125 Riverwood Dr., 21046, pg. 1144 **PB**
New Business, Rouse Co. Bldg., 21044, pg. 1407 **PB**
New Orleans Riverwalk Associates, 10275 Little Patuxent Pkwy., 21044, pg. 361 **PB**
Norbury Construction Co., Headquarters Bldg., 21044, pg. 1409 **PB**
Nucletron Corporation, 7080 Columbia Gateway Dr., 21046-2133, pg. 389 **IT**
Oldelft Corp. of America, 9108 Guilford Road, 21046, pg. 389 **IT**
PPD Pharmaco, Inc., Woodmere Bldg. 1, Ste. 100, 9881 Broden Land Pkwy., 21046, pg. 1285 **PB**
Paramus Park Shopping Center Limited Partnership, c/o The Rouse Company, 10275 Little Patuxent Pkwy., 21044, pg. 365 **PB**
Power Management Associates, Inc., 6700 Alexander Bell Dr., 21046, pg. 695 **PB**
RII Holding, Inc., Headquarters Bldg., 21044, pg. 1407 **PB**
Relco, 6301 Stevens Forest Rd., 21045, pg. 921 **PV**
RELIABLE STORES, INC., 6301 Stevens Forest Rd., 21046, pg. 920 **PB**
Rouse Commerce, Inc., Headquarters Bldg., 21044, pg. 1407 **PB**
Rouse Commercial Development Div., Rouse Co. Bldg., 21044, pg. 1407 **PB**
THE ROUSE COMPANY, Rouse Co. Headquarters Bldg., 10275 Little Patuxent Parkway, 21044-3456, pg. 1407 **PB**
The Rouse Co. Financial Services, Inc., Headquarters Bldg., 21044, pg. 1407 **PB**
The Rouse Company of Arkansas, Inc., Headquarters Bldg., 21044, pg. 1407 **PB**
The Rouse Company of California, Inc., 10275 Little Patuxent Pkwy., 21044, pg. 1407 **PB**
The Rouse Company of Florida, Inc., Headquarters Bldg., 21044, pg. 1408 **PB**
The Rouse Company of Iowa, Inc., Headquarters Bldg., 21044, pg. 1408 **PB**
The Rouse Company of Kentucky, Inc., Headquarters Bldg., 21044, pg. 1408 **PB**
The Rouse Company of Louisiana, Headquarters Bldg., 21044, pg. 1408 **PB**
The Rouse Company of New York, Inc., Rouse Co. Headquarters Bldg., 10275 Little Patuxent Pkwy., 21044, pg. 1408 **PB**
The Rouse Company of Oregon, Inc., Headquarters Bldg., 21044, pg. 1408 **PB**
The Rouse Company of Virginia, Inc., Headquarters Bldg., 21044, pg. 1408 **PB**
Rouse Controllers Div., Rouse Co. Bldg., 21044, pg. 1407 **PB**
Rouse Finance Div., Rouse Co. Bldg., 21044, pg. 1407 **PB**
Rouse Legal Div., Rouse Co. Bldg., 21044, pg. 1407 **PB**
Rouse Management, Inc., Headquarters Bldg., 21044, pg. 1409 **PB**
Rouse Office & Community Development Div., Rouse Co. Bldg., 21044, pg. 1407 **PB**
Rouse Operating Properties Div., Rouse Co. Bldg., 21044, pg. 1407 **PB**
Rouse Personnel & Administrative Services Div., Rouse Co. Bldg., 21044, pg. 1407 **PB**
Rouse Research & Site Strategy Div., Rouse Co. Bldg., 21044, pg. 1407 **PB**
Rouse Retail Leasing Div., Rouse Co. Bldg., 21044, pg. 1407 **PB**
THE RYLAND GROUP, INC., 11000 Broken Land Pkwy., 21044, pg. 1414 **PB**

Geographic Index-U.S.

S&N Katz Jewelers, 6301 Stevens Forest Rd., 21045, pg. 921 **PV**

The Saratoga Equip. Corp., Headquarters Bldg., 21044, pg. 1409 **PB**

Scott Jewelers, 6301 Stevens Forest Rd., 21045, pg. 921 **PV**

Shimadzu Scientific Instruments, Inc., 7102 Riverwood Dr., 21046, pg. 1232 **IT**

Sienna Biotech, Inc., 9115 Guilford Rd., Ste. 180, 21046, pg. 92 **PB**

STANDARD MEDICAL IMAGING, INC., 9002 Red Branch Rd., 21045, pg. 1032 **PV**

Sterling Electronics, 6304 Woodside Ct., #115, 21046-1071, pg. 1051 **PB**

Symbol, 8990 Old Annapolis Rd., 21045, pg. 1546 **PB**

TIE Systems Mid-Atlantic, 8310 Guilford Rd., Ste. B, 21046, pg. 1085 **PB**

TRC Holding Co. of Washington, D.C., Headquarters Bldg., 21044, pg. 1409 **PB**

The Apex Group, Inc., 7151 Columbia Gateway Dr., Ste. F., 21046, pg. 4 **PB**

Tuchenhagen North America, Inc., 9165 Rumsey Rd., 21045, pg. 1426 **IT**

Weiss Jewelers, 6301 Stevens Forest Rd., 21045, pg. 921 **PV**

Wilmington Homes, Inc., Headquarters Bldg., 21044, pg. 1409 **PB**

Crisfield

Carvel Hall, 4251 Crisfield Hwy., P.O. Box 271, 21817, pg. 1061 **PV**

Crofton

Branch Data Comm, 2127 Espey Ct., Ste. 110, 21114, pg. 165 **PV**

DAVCO RESTAURANTS INC., 1657 Crofton Blvd., 21114, pg. 488 **PB**

Cumberland

The Kelly-Springfield Tire Company, 12501 Willowbrook Rd., 21502, pg. 753 **PB**

S. SCHWAB COMPANY, 12101 Upper Potomac Industrial Pk., 21502, pg. 974 **PV**

Denton

The Peoples Bank of Maryland, 205 Market St., 21629, pg. 1089 **PB**

East New Market

Charter Behavioral Health System of Delmarva, 3680 Warwick Rd., Rte. 1, 21631, pg. 1034 **PB**

Easton

Cadmus-Easton Manufacturing, 500 Cadmus Ln., 21601, pg. 290 **PB**

Cadmus Journal Services, Inc., 500 Cadmus Ln., 21601-0969, pg. 291 **PB**

Sea Watch International, Ltd., 8978 Glebe Park Dr., 21601, pg. 928 **IT**

Elkton

County Banking & Trust Company, 123 North St., 21921, pg. 1089 **PB**

Elkon Gas Service, 241 S. Bridge St., 21921-0129, pg. 1148 **PB**

Elkton DLV Operations, P.O. Box 241, 21922-0241, pg. 1597 **PB**

Konica Supplies Manufacturing U.S.A., Inc., Upper Chesapeake Corp. Ctr., 1000 Konica Dr., 21921, pg. 749 **IT**

Liqui-Box Corp., 505 Blue Ball Rd., 21921, pg. 1000 **PB**

Schult Homes Corporation, Trinco Indus. Pk., Rte. 545 Blue Ball Rd., 21921, pg. 1442 **PB**

Terumo Medical Factory, 950 Elkton Blvd., 21921, pg. 1376 **IT**

Ellicott City

C.R. DANIELS, INC., 3451 Ellicott Ctr. Dr., 21043, pg. 310 **PV**

WILKINS-ROGERS INCORPORATED, 27 Frederick Rd., 21043, pg. 1176 **PV**

Federalsburg

Maryland Plastics, Inc., 251 E. Central Ave., 21632, pg. 641 **PV**

Frederick

AUSHERMAN CONSTRUCTION COMPANY, 8031 Reichs Ford Rd., 21701, pg. 99 **PV**

AVEMCO CORPORATION, Frederick Municipal Airport, 411 Aviation Way, 21701, pg. 151 **PB**

AVEMCO Insurance Co., 411 Aviation Way, 21701, pg. 152 **PB**

Builders Supply and Lumber Co., Inc., 7490 New Technology Way, 21703, pg. 1344 **PB**

Eastalco Aluminum Company, 5601 Manor Woods Rd., 21703, pg. 60 **PB**

Frederick Gas Co., Inc., 1800 N. Market St., 21701, pg. 1740 **PB**

Frederick Manufacturing Co., 20 S. Wisnet St., 21701, pg. 956 **PV**

Frederick Trading Company, 7901 Trading Ln., 21701, pg. 335 **PV**

Fredericktown Bank & Trust Co., 30 N. Market St., P.O. Box 510, 21701-0510, pg. 1089 **PB**

Loss Management Services, Inc., 411 Aviation Way, 21701, pg. 152 **PB**

Pathology Associates International Corporation, 15 Worman's Mill Ct., Ste. I, 21701, pg. 976 **PB**

Racal Health & Safety, Inc., 7305 Executive Way, 21704, pg. 1083 **IT**

SFA Datacomm Inc., 7450 New Technology Way, 21701, pg. 956 **PB**

SACOM, 5716B Industry Ln., 21701, pg. 956 **PV**

Solarex Corporation, 630 Solarex Ct., 21701, pg. 103 **PB**

Talent Tree Personnel Services Inc., 7470 New Technology Way, 21703, pg. 1286 **IT**

Frostburg

The Fidelity Bank, 59 E. Main St., 21532, pg. 1089 **PB**

Gaithersburg

Arrow/Schweber Electronics, 200 Perry Pkwy., 20877, pg. 134 **PB**

Aspen Publishers, Inc., 200 Orchard Ridge Dr., 20878, pg. 1513 **IT**

Bechtel Power Corporation, 9801 Washingtonian Blvd., 20878, pg. 128 **PB**

Comprint, Inc., 9030 Comprint Court, 20877, pg. 1743 **PB**

DRS Electronic Systems, Inc., 200 Professional Dr., 20879, pg. 474 **PB**

Data Control Systems, 211 Perry Pkwy., 20877, pg. 420 **PB**

Edy's Mid-Atlantic Region, 7820 Cessna Ave., 20879, pg. 529 **PB**

ELECTRO MECHANICAL DESIGN SERVICES, INC., 16618 Oakmont Ave., 20877, pg. 369 **PV**

Electronic Systems Group, 200 Professional Dr., 20879, pg. 474 **PB**

The Gazette Newspapers, Inc., 1200 Quince Orchard Blvd., 20878, pg. 1743 **PB**

Genetic Therapy, Inc., 938 Copper Rd., 20878, pg. 973 **IT**

Hayes Corporation, Regional Office, 1300 Quince Orchard Blvd., 20878, pg. 801 **PB**

LCTI, Inc., 205 Perry Pkwy., Ste. One, 20877, pg. 406 **PB**

Lockheed Martin Federal Systems-Gaithersburg, 700 North Frederick Ave., 20879, pg. 1008 **PB**

MANOR CARE, INC., 11555 Darnestown Rd., 20878, pg. 1041 **PB**

Manor Healthcare Corp., 11555 Darnestown Rd., 20878, pg. 1041 **PB**

MASTERS INC., 7891 Beechcraft Ave., 20879, pg. 714 **PV**

MEDIMMUNE, INC., 35 W. Watkins Mill Rd., 20878, pg. 1081 **PB**

NVR Building Products, Quince Diamond Exec. Ctr., 555 Quince Orchard Rd., Ste. 300, 20878, pg. 1148 **PB**

NVR Homes, Inc., Quince Diamond Exec. Ctr., 555 Quince Orchard Rd., Ste. 300, 20878, pg. 1148 **PB**

NationsBank Insurance Inc., 10010 Montgomery Village Ave., 20879, pg. 1162 **PB**

Paul Revere Insurance Group, 903 Russell Ave., Ste. 300, 20879, pg. 1338 **PB**

Pioneer Standard of Maryland, Inc., 9100 Gaither Rd., 20877, pg. 1300 **PB**

Potomac Digital, Inc./Scott Data, 45 W. Watkins Mill Rd., Ste. C, 20878, pg. 711 **PB**

Potomac Valley Bank, 702 Russell Ave., 20877, pg. 1089 **PB**

Printer Systems Corporation, 207 Perry Parkway, 20877, pg. 729 **PB**

Quanta Systems Corporation, 213 Perry Pkwy., 20877, pg. 420 **PB**

TMP Worldwide, Inc., 317 E. Diamond Ave., 2nd Fl., 20877, pg. 1064 **PV**

Telecommunications Group, 700 Quince Orchard Rd., 20878, pg. 1745 **PB**

Tetra Tech NUS, Inc., 910 Clopper Rd., 20878, pg. 1582 **PB**

Woodward-Clyde, 200 Orchard Ridge Dr., Ste. 101, 20878, pg. 1656 **PB**

Germantown

Fairchild Controls, 20305 Century Blvd., 20874-1182, pg. 794 **IT**

GEOMET Technologies, Inc., 20251 Century Blvd., 20874, pg. 1717 **PB**

Germantown, 20305 Century Blvd., 20874-1182, pg. 794 **IT**

MICROLOG CORPORATION, 20270 Goldenrod Ln., 20876, pg. 1105 **PB**

N Base Communications, 12401 Middlebrook Rd., Ste. 160, 20874, pg. 1027 **PB**

Old Dominion Systems of Maryland, 20270 Goldenrod Ln., 20876, pg. 1105 **PB**

Optim Electronics Corporation, Middlebrook Technology Park, 12401 Middlebrook Rd., 20874, pg. 208 **IT**

SAIC, 20201 Century Blvd., 2nd Flr., 20874, pg. 976 **PV**

Telecommunications Techniques Corp., 20410 Observation Dr., 20876, pg. 539 **PB**

Glen Burnie

First National Mortgage Corporation, 6704 Curtis Ct., 21061, pg. 64 **IT**

Harundale Mall, P.O. Box 1027, 21061, pg. 1407 **PB**

Holmatro, Inc., 505 McCormick Dr., 21061, pg. 632 **IT**

Samuel Meisel & Company, Inc., 6691 Baymeadow Dr., 21060, pg. 103 **IT**

OPTIC GRAPHICS, INC., 101 Dover Rd., 21060, pg. 818 **PV**

Quebecor Printing Glen Burnie, 7364 Baltimore & Annapolis Blvd., 21061, pg. 1076 **IT**

Greenbelt

ARGOSystems, Inc., 7474 Greenway Center Dr., Ste. 400, 20770, pg. 240 **PB**

Bardon USA Inc., 6401 Golden Triangle Dr., Ste. 400, 20770, pg. 166 **IT**

GREENHORNE & O'MARA, INC., 9001 Edmonston Rd., 20770, pg. 477 **PV**

OAO Technology Solutions, Inc., 7500 Greenway Ctr. Dr., 16th Fl., 20770-3585, pg. 1425 **PB**

Greensboro

Technitrol Component Division, P.O. Box 119, 21639, pg. 1564 **PB**

Hagerstown

ALLEGHENY POWER SYSTEM, INC., 10435 Downsville Pike, 21740-1766, pg. 42 **PB**

Angstrohm Precision, Inc., P.O. Box 1827, 21740, pg. 1722 **PB**

Danzer Industries Inc., 17500 York Rd., 21740, pg. 747 **PB**

Farmers and Merchants Bank and Trust, 59 W. Washington St., 21740, pg. 1542 **PB**

GLOBAL ENVIRONMENTAL CORP., 17500 York Rd., 21740, pg. 747 **PB**

Hagerstown Cement Plant Independent Cement Corp., P.O. Box 655, Security Road Extended, 21740, pg. 629 **PB**

Hydro Conduit Corp., 1000 Sherman Ave., 21740, pg. 246 **IT**

ISP Mineral Products Inc., 34 Charles St., 21740, pg. 858 **PB**

JAMISON DOOR COMPANY, JV Jamison Dr., 21740, pg. 581 **PV**

Maryland Ribbon Company, 857 Willow Cir., 21740, pg. 812 **PV**

National Book Distributors, 100 Western Maryland Parkway, 21740, pg. 780 **PB**

The Potomac Edison Co., 10435 Downsville Pike, 21740-1766, pg. 42 **PB**

Powertrain Div., 13302 Pennsylvania Ave., 21742, pg. 1103 **IT**

Rohr Industries, Hagerstown Plant, 18238 Showalter Rd., 21740, pg. 751 **PB**

Stationery House, Inc., 1000 Florida Ave., 21740, pg. 89 **PB**

TFX Marine, 101 W. Maryland Pkwy., 21740, pg. 1570 **PB**

TRISTATE ELECTRICAL SUPPLY CO., INC., 1741 Dual Hwy., 21740, pg. 1104 **PB**

Hanover

Browning-Ferris, Inc., 1800 Parkway Dr., 21076, pg. 263 **PB**

Land Mobile Products Sector, Mid Atlantic, 7230 Pkwy. Dr., 21076-1307, pg. 1137 **PB**

Quanta SecurSystems, Inc., 7255 Standard Dr., 21076, pg. 420 **PB**

Shorrock Military Systems Inc., 7255 Standard Dr., 21076, pg. 1286 **IT**

Havre De Grace

Cleaning Solutions Group/Cello, 1354 Old Post Rd., 21078, pg. 1466 **PB**

J.M. Huber, Chemicals Division, 907 Revolution St., 21078, pg. 545 **PV**

Hunt Valley

AAI Corporation, York Rd. & Industry Ln., 21030, pg. 1679 **PB**

CSX Intermodal, Inc., 200 International Cir., 21030, pg. 284 **PB**

Clarion Cosmetics, 11050 York Rd., 21030, pg. 1330 **PB**

Condiment Plant, 10950 Beaver Dam at Gilroy Rd., 21031, pg. 1066 **PB**

Cover Girl Cosmetics, 11050 York Rd., 21030, pg. 1330 **PB**

EA ENGINEERING, SCIENCE & TECHNOLOGY, INC., 11019 McCormick Rd., 21031, pg. 540 **PB**

EA Global, Inc., 11019 McCormick Rd., 21031, pg. 541 **PB**

FAWN INDUSTRIES, INC., 311 International Cir., Ste. 140, 21030, pg. 397 **PV**

Government Components Division, 10713 Gilroy Rd., 21030, pg. 8 **PB**

Interact Accessories, Inc., 10945 McCormick Rd., 21030, pg. 389 **PB**

MHI Corrugating Machinery Company (MCMC), 11204 McCormick Rd., 21031-1076, pg. 874 **PB**

Maryland Specialty Wire, Inc., 100 Cockeysville Rd., 21030, pg. 780 **PB**

McCormick Flavor Division-U.S.A., 226 Schilling Cir., 21031, pg. 1066 **PB**

Geographic Index-U.S.

MARYLAND DIRECTORY OF CORPORATE AFFILIATIONS

McCormick Ingredients, 10901 Gilroy Rd., 21031, pg. 1066 PB
McCormick/Schilling, 211 Schilling Circle, 21031, pg. 1066 PB
Millennium Inorganic Chemicals, 200 International Circle Ste. 5000, 21030, pg. 593 IT
Millennium Inorganic Chemicals, 200 International Cir., Ste. 5000, 21030, pg. 1111 PB
PHH Corporation, 307 International Circle, 21030, pg. 321 PB
PHH Financial Services, Inc., 11333 McCormick Rd., 21031-1000, pg. 321 PB
Procter & Gamble Cosmetics Co., 11050 York Rd., 21030, pg. 1330 PB
Redland Genstar Stone Products Company, Executive Plaza IV, 21031, pg. 1091 IT
Spice Plant, 350 Club House Ln., 21031, pg. 1066 PB
THE WARD MACHINERY COMPANY, 10615 Beaver Dam Rd., 21030, pg. 1149 PV
Willis Corroon Administrative Services Corporation, Five N. Park Dr., 21030, pg. 1504 IT
Willis Corroon Corp. of Maryland, Five N. Park Dr., 21030, pg. 1506 IT

Hyattsville

Bayside Traffic Services of Maryland, 6300 Sheriff Rd., 20785, pg. 741 PB
Bursil, Inc., 6300 Sheriff Rd., 20785, pg. 741 PB
Chantilly Partners, 4351 Garden City Dr., 20785, pg. 361 PB
Dutton Partners, 8181 Professional Pl., Ste. 236, 20785, pg. 361 PB
Editors Press, Inc., 3401 East West Hwy., 20782, pg. 623 PV
Eight O'Clock Coffee, 3300 Pennsy Dr., 20785, pg. 1375 IT
Friendship Macomb SC, Inc., 6300 Sheriff Rd., 20785, pg. 741 PB
GF McLean Shopping Center, 6300 Sheriff Rd., 20785, pg. 741 PB
GFS Realty, Inc., 6300 Sheriff Rd., 20785, pg. 741 PB
Giant Construction Co., Inc., 6300 Sheriff Rd., 20785, pg. 741 PB
Giant of Cherry Hill, Inc., 6300 Sheriff Rd., 20785, pg. 741 PB
Giant of Maryland, Inc., 6300 Sheriff Rd., 20785, pg. 741 PB
Giant of Salisbury, Inc., 6300 Sheriff Rd., 20785, pg. 741 PB
Giant of Talbot County, Inc., 6300 Sherriff Rd., 20785, pg. 741 PB
Insituform East, Inc., 3421 Pennsy Dr., 20785, pg. 330 PB
Leco Inc., 6300 Sheriff Rd., 20785, pg. 741 PB
LUSTINE OLDSMOBILE & BUICK, INC., 5323 Baltimore Ave., 20781, pg. 681 PV
Martin Marietta Space & Aeronautics Services, 8000 Corporate Dr., 20785, pg. 1007 PB
Maryland Concession & Vending Company, 6300 Sheriff Rd., 20785, pg. 741 PB
Montrosse Crossing Inc., 6300 Sheriff Rd., 20785, pg. 741 PB
The Mudge Paper Co., 2003 Beaver Rd., 20785, pg. 902 PB
SFA, INC., 1401 McCormick Dr., 20785, pg. 956 PV
Shaw Community Supermarket, 6300 Sheriff Rd., 20785, pg. 741 PB
Specialties Bindery, Inc., 4815 Laurence St., 20781, pg. 1078 IT
Super G Inc., 6300 Sheriff Rd., 20785, pg. 741 PB
Warex-Jessup, Inc., 6300 Sheriff Rd., 20785, pg. 741 PB
Washington Area Distribution Center, 3400 Pennsy Dr., 20785, pg. 921 PV
Washington Homes, Inc. of Virginia, 1802 Brightseat Rd., 20785-4235, pg. 1741 PB
Windgate Partners, 4351 Garden City Dr., Ste. 300, 20785, pg. 362 PB

Jarrettsville

Intergraph Corporation, 802 Stone Haven Dr., 21084, pg. 890 PB

Jessup

Baltimore Aircoil Company, 7595 Montevideo Rd., 20794, pg. 68 PV
Central Sprinkler Company, 8230 Preston Court, 20794, pg. 327 PB
Commercial Interior Builders, Inc., 8265-A Patuxent Range Rd., 20794, pg. 913 PB
Greenway Corporation, 7201 Montevideo Rd., 20794, pg. 1770 PB
Lancaster Foods, Inc., 7825-A Rappahanock Ave., 20794, pg. 487 PV
Lindenmeyr Munroe, 8240 Preston Ct., 20794, pg. 224 PV
Smelkinson Sysco Food Services, Inc., 8000 Dorsey Run Rd., 20794, pg. 1550 PB
TATE ACCESS FLOORS, INC., 7510 Montevideo Rd., 20794, pg. 1069 PV

Joppa

Reynolds Aluminum Recycling Company, 710 C Pulaski Hwy., 21085-3926, pg. 1386 PB

Kensington

WASHINGTON REAL ESTATE INVESTMENT TRUST, 10400 Connecticut Ave., Concourse Level, 20895, pg. 1743 PB

La Plata

Bank of Southern Maryland, 304 Charles St., 20646, pg. 1088 PB
WILLS GROUP, INC., 6355 Crain Hwy., 20646, pg. 1180 PV

Landover

CEILING & PARTITIONS, INC., 8812 Spectrum Dr., 20785, pg. 221 PV
CERBCO, INC., 3421 Pennsy Dr., 20785, pg. 330 PB
Crown Books Corporation, 3300 75th Ave., 20785, pg. 484 PB
Crown Books East Corporation, 3301 Pennsy Dr., 20785, pg. 484 PB
DART GROUP CORPORATION, 3300 75th Ave., 20785, pg. 484 PB
Dart Group Financial Corp., 3300 75th Ave., 20785, pg. 484 PB
S. FREEDMAN & SONS, INC., 3322 Pennsy Dr., 20785, pg. 425 PV
GIANT FOOD INC., 6300 Sheriff Rd., 20785, pg. 741 PB
Homebuyer's Mortgage, Inc., 1802 Brightseat Rd., 20785, pg. 1741 PB
New Homebuyer's Title, 1802 Brightseat Rd., 20785, pg. 1741 PB
Total Beverage Corporation, 3300 75th Ave., 20785, pg. 484 PB
Trak Auto Corporation, 3300 75th Ave., 20785, pg. 484 PB
Trak Auto West, Inc., 3300 75th Ave., 20785, pg. 484 PB
WASHINGTON HOMES, INC., 1802 Brightseat Rd., 6th Fl., 20785-4235, pg. 1741 PB

Lanham

AMI GROUP, INC., 4855 Walden Lane, 20706, pg. 7 PV
Biblic Distribution Ctr., 4720 Boston Way, pg. 1128 PV
COMNET CORPORATION, 4200 Parliament Pl., Ste. 600, 20706-1860, pg. 416 PB
DARCARS LTD., 9020 Lanham Severn Rd., 20706, pg. 311 PV
DAYCON PRODUCTS COMPANY, INC., 4901 Forbes Blvd., 20706, pg. 317 PV
E.M.I. Travel Center, Inc., 4501 Forbes Blvd., 20706, pg. 580 PB
Encore Clubs, Inc., 4501 Forbes Blvd., 20706, pg. 580 PB
Encore Group, Inc., 4501 Forbes Blvd., 20706, pg. 580 PB
ENCORE MARKETING INTERNATIONAL, INC., 4501 Forbes Blvd., 20706, pg. 580 PB
Group 1 Software, Inc., 4200 Parliament Pl., #600, 20706-1844, pg. 417 PB
Integral Marketing, Inc., 5000 Philadelphia Way, Ste. C, 20706, pg. 883 PB
INTEGRAL SYSTEMS, INC., 5000 Philadelphia Way, Ste. A, 20706-4417, pg. 883 PB
Intersys, Inc., 5000 Philadelphia Way, Ste. A., 20706-4417, pg. 883 PB
Land Rover North America, 4371 Parliament Pl., 20706, pg. 177 IT
THE MAXIMA CORPORATION, 4200 Parliament Pl., Ste. 300, 20706, pg. 716 PV
PANTECH CONSTRUCTION CO., 4372 Lottsford Vista Rd., 20706, pg. 837 PV
THE PHILADELPHIA BOURSE, INC., 4601 Forbes Blvd., 20706, pg. 861 PB
Quality Services International, Inc., 4501 Forbes Blvd., 20706, pg. 580 PB
RJO ENTERPRISES, INC., 4640 Forbes Blvd., 20706, pg. 904 PV
RMS Information Systems, Inc., 4221 Forbes Blvd., 20706, pg. 1425 PB
RMS TECHS, INC., 4221 Forbes Blvd., 20706, pg. 905 PV
RADIO ONE INC., 5900 Princess Garden Pkwy., Ste 800, 20706, pg. 906 PV
Rohde & Schwarz, Inc., 4425 Nicole Dr., 20706, pg. 1124 IT
Rowman & Littlefield Publishers, Inc., 4720 Boston Way, 20706, pg. 1128 PV
Sensenich Wood Propeller Co., Inc., 4601 Forbes Blvd., 20706, pg. 861 PV
Shoppers Food Warehouse, 4600 Forbes Blvd., 20706, pg. 484 PB
UNIVERSITY PRESS OF AMERICA, INC., 4720 Boston Way, 20706, pg. 1127 PV
Zellerbach Division, Eastpoint Metro Business Ctr., 4451 Parliament Pl., 20706, pg. 1075 PB

Largo

Hechinger Company Investors II, L.P., 1801 McCormick Dr., 20774, pg. 477 PV

Laurel

The Citizens National Bank, 517 Main St., 20707, pg. 089 PB
General Sciences Corp., 6100 Chevy Chase Dr., 20707-2929, pg. 976 PV
Gould Paper Corporatioin-Baltimore/Washington, 14502 Greenview Dr., Ste. 204, 20708, pg. 467 PV
Maurexco Exporters, 13 C St., Ste. D, 20707, pg. 715 PV
S & S GRAPHICS, INC., 14880 Sweitzer Ln., 20707, pg. 955 PV

Leonardtown

The First National Bank of St. Mary's, 41615 Park Ave., 20650, pg. 1089 PB

Linthicum Heights

Cadmus Journal Services, 940 Elk Ridge Landing Rd., 21090-2908, pg. 290 PB
Cadmus Journal Services, Inc., Airport Sq. Seven, 940 Elkridge Landing Rd., 21090-2908, pg. 291 PB
Circle Freight International USA, 810-R Oregon Ave., 21090, pg. 371 PB
Circle International, 810-R Oregon Ave., 21090, pg. 371 PB
Electronic Sensors & Systems Division, 1580-A W. Nursery Rd., 21290-2202, pg. 1198 PB
Goldwell Cosmetics (USA) Inc., 981 Corporate Blvd., 21090, pg. 718 IT
Roy Rogers Restaurants, 1099 Winterson Rd., Ste. 200, 21090, pg. 1069 PB
TNT Logistics North America, 1306 Concourse Dr., Ste. 401, 21090-1032, pg. 1343 IT
Trace Laboratories East, 1190 Winterson Rd., Ste. 100, 21090, pg. 1101 PB
Westinghouse Wireless Services, 930 International Dr., 21090, pg. 273 PB

Lutherville

Stephen Gould of Maryland, Inc., 9480 Deereco Rd., 21093, pg. 467 PV
Oriole Homes Corp. of Maryland, 204 Heaver Plaza, 1301 York Rd., 21093, pg. 1231 PB
Seabreeze Properties, Inc., 204 Heaver Plaza, 1301 York Rd., 21093, pg. 1231 PB
SUNBELT BEVERAGES, 2330 W. Joppa Rd., Ste. 330, 21093, pg. 1051 PV

Marlow Heights

OURISMAN CHEVROLET, 4400 Branch Ave., 20748, pg. 821 PV

Millersville

Gould Electronics Inc., Fiber Optics, 1121 Benfield Blvd., 21108, pg. 1592 PB

Mitchellville

AT&T Communications, 11512 Lottsford Ter., 20721-2290, pg. 10 PB

Montgomery Village

KETTLER BROTHERS, INC., 9426 Stewartown Rd., 20879, pg. 617 PV

Oakland

Bausch & Lomb Eyewear Division-MD, Rte. 135, 21550, pg. 194 PB

Ocean City

Atlantic Bank, 4604 Coastal Hwy., 21842-3291, pg. 642 PB

Odenton

AT&T Image Solution, 2445 Blue Spring Ct., 21113-2525, pg. 11 PB
Encore Computer, 1413 Annapolis Rd., Ste. 400, 21113, pg. 580 PB
Handex of Maryland, Inc., 360 Morgan Rd., 21113, pg. 499 PV
Nevamar Division, 8339 Telegraph Rd., 21130-1397, pg. 903 PB
Special Filaments Odenton, 8335 Telegraph Rd., 21113, pg. 77 PV

Owings Mills

CMG Health, 25 Crossroads Dr., 21117, pg. 1036 PB
B. GREEN & CO., 10075 Red Run Blvd., 21117, pg. 476 PV
Hathaway Industrial Automation, Inc., 11431 Crown Hill Rd., 21117, pg. 799 PB
INTEGRATED HEALTH SERVICES, INC., 10065 Red Run Blvd., 21117, pg. 884 PB
Kvaerner EnviroPower Inc., 10055 Red Run Blvd., 21117, pg. 770 IT
LION BROTHERS COMPANY, INC., 10246 Reisterstown Rd., 21117, pg. 669 PV
Quest International Flavors & Foods Inc., 10 Painters Mill Rd., 21117, pg. 1436 IT
Schlumberger Malco Inc., 9800 Reisterstown Rd., 21117, pg. 1206 IT
SWEETHEART CUP COMPANY INC., 10100 Reisterstown Rd., 21117, pg. 1058 PV
Sweetheart Cup Company Inc., 10100 Reisterstown Rd., 21117, pg. 1058 PV

Geographic Index-U.S.

PB - *U.S. Public Companies Volume*
PV - *U.S. Private Companies Volume*
IT - *International Public & Private Companies Volume*
1262

UNIVERSAL SECURITY INSTRUMENTS INC., 10324 S. Dolfield Rd., 21117, pg. 1697 **PB**

Parkville

White Marsh Mall, Inc., 8200 Perry Hall Blvd., 21236, pg. 1409 **PB**

Pasadena

Bendix Security Systems, 1803 Wye Cliffe Ct., 21122-3540, pg. 51 **PB**

Pikesville

Port City Press, Inc., 1323 Greenwood Rd., 21208, pg. 855 **PV**

Pocomoke City

Lankford-Sysco Food Services, Inc., U.S. Rte. 13, 21851, pg. 1551 **PB**
Sharp Energy, Inc., Rte. 13 & Stockton Rd., 21851, pg. 347 **PB**
Sharpgas, Inc., Rte. 13 & Stockton Rd., 21851, pg. 347 **PB**

Pomfret

Xerox Research, Rte. Two, 20675, pg. 1784 **PB**

Potomac

Carl M. Freeman Mgmt Co, 11325 Seven Locks Rd., 20854, pg. 426 **PV**
CARL M. FREEMAN ASSOCIATES, INC., 11325 Seven Locks Rd., 20854, pg. 426 **PV**
PHILLIPS PUBLISHING INTERNATIONAL, INC., 7811 Montrose Rd., 20854, pg. 862 **PV**
Serino Coyne Public Relations, 9468 Copenhaver Dr., 20854, pg. 985 **PV**

Preston

Preston Trucking Company, Inc., 151 Easton Blvd., 21655, pg. 1788 **PB**

Prince Frederick

Calvert Bank & Trust Co., Calvert Village Shopping Ctr., P.O. Box 590, 20678, pg. 1088 **PB**

Princess Anne

Peninsula Bank, 11738 Somerset Ave., 21853, pg. 1089 **PB**

Riderwood

Esskay, P.O. Box 587, 21139-0587, pg. 1479 **PB**

Rockville

AECL Technologies Inc., 9210 Corporate Blvd., Ste. 410, 20850, pg. 97 **IT**
All American Semiconductor of Rockville, Inc., 14636 Rothgeb Dr., 20850, pg. 41 **PB**
AMERICAN HEALTH ASSISTANCE FOUNDATION, 15825 Shady Grove Rd., Ste. 140, 20850, pg. 56 **PV**
American Trading Real Estate Properties, Inc., Research Blvd. Ctr., Ste. 304, 1803 Research Blvd., 20850, pg. 64 **PV**
Aspen Systems Corp., 2277 Research Blvd., 20850-3172, pg. 1513 **IT**
AXENT TECHNOLOGIES, 2400 Research Blvd., Ste. 200, 20850, pg. 157 **PB**
BNA Communications, Inc., 9439 Key West Ave., 20850, pg. 182 **PV**
Banner Life Insurance Co., 1701 Research Blvd., 20850, pg. 805 **IT**
Boehringer Mannheim Pharmaceuticals Corp., 15204 Omega Dr., 20850, pg. 331 **IT**
British Telecom Tymnet, 1201 Seven Locks Rd., 20854-2931, pg. 223 **IT**
CDA Investment Technologies, Inc., 1355 Picard Dr., Ste.220, 20850, pg. 1600 **PB**
CRI Liquidating REIT, Inc., CRI Bldg., 11200 Rockville Pike, 20852, pg. 459 **PB**
CAPITAL BANK, N.A., One Church St., Ste. 100, 20850, pg. 205 **PV**
Charter Behavioral Health System at Potomac Ridge, Inc., 14901 Broschart Rd., 20850, pg. 1033 **PB**
Computer Center-Maryland, 15245 Shady Grove Rd., Ste. 370, 20850, pg. 204 **PB**
Computer Data Systems, Inc., One Curie Ct., 20850, pg. 28 **PB**
CRIIMI MAE, 11200 Rockville Pike, 20852, pg. 459 **PB**
EG & G Washington Analytical Services Center, 1396 Piccard Dr., 20850, pg. 543 **PB**
Eaton Corporation, Semi-Conductor, 7600 Standish Pl., 20855, pg. 557 **PB**
FEDERAL REALTY INVESTMENT TRUST, 1626 E. Jefferson St., 20852-4041, pg. 616 **PB**
First Union National Bank of Maryland, Congressional Plaza Branch, 110 Congressional Plaza Branch, 20852, pg. 640 **PB**

Geo-Centers, Inc., 1801 Rockville Pike, Ste. 405, 20852, pg. 447 **PV**
Health Care Institutional Services, 1300 Piccard Dr., 20850, pg. 1156 **PB**
Hekimian Laboratories, Inc., 15200 Omega Dr., 20850-3240, pg. 709 **IT**
Hewlett-Packard Company, Four Choke Cherry Rd., 20850, pg. 814 **PB**
Hilb, Rogal and Hamilton Company of the District of Columbia, 2275 Research Blvd., Ste. 300, 20850, pg. 827 **PB**
Institute for Human Resources, 1700 Rockville Pike, Ste. 500, 20852, pg. 1678 **PB**
JTC Environmental Consultants, Inc., Four Research Pl., Ste. L10, 20850, pg. 694 **PB**
Kaiser Permanente, Central East Division, 2101 E. Jefferson St., 20852, pg. 605 **PV**
Keane Federal Systems, 1375 Piccard Dr., Ste. 200, 20850, pg. 946 **PB**
Legal & General America, Inc., 1701 Research Blvd., 20850, pg. 805 **IT**
Life Technologies, Inc., 9800 Medical Center Dr., 20849-6482, pg. 504 **PB**
Lockheed Martin Air Traffic Management, 9211 Corporate Blvd., 20850, pg. 1008 **PB**
MSC Eastern Engineering Services Office, 7529 Standish Place, Ste. 105, 20855, pg. 1031 **PB**
MANUGISTICS GROUP, INC., 2115 E. Jefferson St., 20852, pg. 1042 **PB**
Manugistics Inc., 2115 E. Jefferson St., 20852, pg. 1042 **PB**
McCORMICK PAINT WORKS COMPANY, 2355 Lewis Ave., 20851, pg. 720 **PV**
Mellon Bank (MD), 1901 Research Blvd., 20850, pg. 1085 **PB**
MID ATLANTIC MEDICAL SERVICES, INC., Four Taft Ct., 20850, pg. 1109 **PB**
Montgomery Surgery Center, 46 W. Gude Dr., 20850, pg. 803 **PB**
Moore Response Graphics, 6116 Executive Blvd., Ste. 415, 20852-4920, pg. 890 **IT**
NatVest, Inc., 51 Monroe St., Ste. 1500, 20850, pg. 647 **PB**
Novavax Inc., 12111 Parklawn Dr., 20852, pg. 855 **PB**
Orion Network Systems Incorporated, 1350 Piccard Dr., Ste. 400, 20850, pg. 218 **IT**
Otsuka America Pharmaceutical, Inc., 2440 Research Blvd., Ste. 250, 20850, pg. 1013 **IT**
Principal Behavioral Health Care, Inc., 1801 Rockville Pike, Ste. 601, 20852, pg. 885 **PB**
Principal Health Care, Inc., 1801 Rockville Pike, Ste. 601, 20852, pg. 885 **PV**
Principal Health Care of the Mid-Atlantic, Inc., 1801 Rockville Pike, Ste. 110, 20852, pg. 886 **PV**
Pulse Electronics, Inc., 5706 Frederick Ave., 20852, pg. 1761 **PB**
Racal Communications, Inc., Five Research Pl., 20850, pg. 1083 **IT**
The Riggs National Bank of Maryland, 2400 Research Blvd., 20850, pg. 1390 **PB**
Rockville Crushed Stone, Inc., 13900 Piney Meeting House Rd., 20850, pg. 166 **IT**
SRA - Rockville, 5635 Fishers Ln., 20852, pg. 958 **PV**
SAS Consulting Services, Inc., 1700 Rockville Pike, Ste. 330, 20852, pg. 966 **PB**
Street Retail, Inc., 1626 E. Jefferson St., 20852-4041, pg. 616 **PB**
Systems Design Division, 1601 Research Blvd., 20850-3173, pg. 1627 **PB**
Systems Integration Division, 1601 Research Blvd., 20850-3173, pg. 1627 **PB**
TSI Washington Laboratories, Two Taft Ct., 20850, pg. 733 **PB**
Taft Group, 12300 Twinbrook Pkwy., Ste. 450, 20852-1606, pg. 1601 **PB**
Tracor Integrated Solutions, 1601 Research Blvd., 20850-3173, pg. 1627 **PB**
Tracor Systems Technologies, Inc., 1601 Research Blvd., 20850-3173, pg. 1627 **PB**
WESTAT, 1650 Research Blvd., 20850, pg. 1163 **PV**
Western International Media Corporation, 11921 Rockville Pike, Ste. 405, 20852, pg. 1167 **PV**

Saint Leonard

Aeroflex Systems Corp., pg. 24 **PB**

Saint Michaels

St. Michaels Bank, P.O. Box 70, 213 Talbot St., 21663, pg. 1089 **PB**

Salisbury

CASE FOODS, INC., 1325 Mt. Herman Rd., Ste. 9B, 21801, pg. 217 **PV**
Eaton Corporation-Heinemann Products, Commercial Controls Division, 2300 Northwood Dr., 21801-7807, pg. 557 **PB**
K & L Microwave Div., 408 Coles Cir., 21801, pg. 521 **PB**
PERDUE FARMS INCORPORATED, Old Ocean City Rd., 21802, pg. 852 **PV**
Perdue Transportation Inc., P.O. Box 1537, 21802-1537, pg. 852 **PV**
Piedmont Airlines, Inc., Salisbury Wicomico County Airport, 21801, pg. 1680 **PB**

Savage

Subaru of America, Inc., 8611 Larkin Rd., P.O. Box 427, 20763, pg. 523 **IT**

Severn

JP Foodservice, Inc.-Baltimore, 8024 Telegraph Rd., 21144, pg. 918 **PB**

Showell

Perdue Farms, Inc., Pitts Rd., 21862, pg. 852 **PV**

Silver Spring

CHOICE HOTELS INTERNATIONAL, INC., 10750 Columbia Pike, 20901, pg. 351 **PB**
D.C. Branch Office, 10230 New Hampshire Ave., Ste. 304, 20903, pg. 1683 **PB**
EA Engineering, Science & Technology, Inc., Box 21, 8401 Colesville Rd., Ste. 500, 20910, pg. 541 **PB**
EA Engineering, Science & Technology, Inc., 8401 Colesville Rd., Ste. 500, 20910, pg. 541 **PB**
HIAC/ROYCO Division, 11801 Tech Rd., 20904, pg. 1250 **PB**
HARKINS BUILDERS, INC., 12301 Old Columbia Pike, 20904, pg. 502 **PV**
Lucent Technologies, 8403 Colesville Rd. 14th Flr., 20910-3314, pg. 1017 **PB**
Perstorp Analytical Inc., 12101 Tech Rd., 20904, pg. 1039 **IT**
Perstorp Analytical Inc. Division NIRSystems, 12101 Tech Rd., 20904, pg. 1039 **IT**
Pulte Chesapeake Division, 11120 New Hampshire, Ste. 208, 20904, pg. 1344 **PB**
Racal Avionics, Inc., 8851 Monard Dr., 20910, pg. 1082 **IT**

Sparks

The Arundel Corporation, 34 Loveton Cir., Ste. 102, 21152-5000, pg. 656 **PB**
Arundel Sand & Gravel Co., 34 Loveton Cir., 21152-5000, pg. 656 **PB**
Becton Dickinson Microbiology Systems, Seven Loveton Cir., 21152, pg. 199 **PB**
Becton Dickinson Primary Care Diagnostics, Seven Loveton Cir., 21152-0370, pg. 199 **PB**
EA Engineering, Science & Technology, Inc., 15 Loveton Cir., 21152, pg. 541 **PB**
EA Engineering, Science & Technology, Inc., 19 Loveton Cir., 21152, pg. 541 **PB**
EA Laboratories, 19 Loveton Cir., 21152, pg. 541 **PB**
Fila USA, 14114 York Rd. P.O. Box 3000, 21152-3000, pg. 484 **IT**
Maryland Rock Industries, Inc., 34 Loveton Cir., 21152-5000, pg. 656 **PB**
Maryland Stone Inc., 34 Loveton Cir., 21152, pg. 656 **PB**
McCORMICK & COMPANY, INCORPORATED, 18 Loveton Cir., 21152-6000, pg. 1066 **PB**
Sparks State Bank, 14804 York Rd., 21152, pg. 1089 **PB**
TESSCO TECHNOLOGIES, INC., 34 Loveton Cir., 21152, pg. 1582 **PB**

Sparrows Point

Automatic Metal Blanking, Inc., 1440 Grays Rd., 21219, pg. 300 **PV**
Bethlehem Steel-Sparrows Point Division, Main Office Bldg., Rte. 151, 21219, pg. 226 **PB**

Stevensville

Ross-McNatt Naval Architects, 301 Pier One Rd., Ste. 200, 21666, pg. 110 **PB**

Taneytown

THE TANEY CORPORATION, 5130 Allendale Lane, 21787, pg. 1067 **PV**

Timonium

Brooks-Shettle Co., Timonium Corp. Ctr., 9515 Deereco Rd., 21093, pg. 152 **PB**
Claster Television, 9630 Deerco Rd., 21093, pg. 797 **PB**
DIAMOND COMIC DISTRIBUTORS, INC., 1966 Greenspring Dr., Ste. 300, 21093, pg. 330 **PV**
GROTECH CAPITAL GROUP, INC., 9690 Deereco Rd., Ste. 800, 21093, pg. 483 **PV**
Matterhorn Bank Programs, Inc., Timonium Corp. Ctr., 9515 Deereco Rd., 21093, pg. 152 **PB**
MEDEX Assistance Corporation, Timonium Corp. Ctr., 9515 Deereco Rd., 21093, pg. 152 **PB**
Romper Room Enterprises, Inc., 9630 Deerco Rd., 21093, pg. 797 **PB**
URS Greiner, Inc., 2219 York Rd., Ste. 200, 21093, pg. 1658 **PB**

Towson

Allied Security Inc., 1055 Taylor Ave., #303, 21286, pg. 40 **PV**
AMERICAN STONE-MIX, INC., 8320 Bellona Ave., 21204, pg. 62 **PV**

PB - *U.S. Public Companies Volume*
PV - *U.S. Private Companies Volume*
IT - *International Public & Private Companies Volume*

Barry Blau & Partners of Maryland, Inc., 849 Fairmont Ave., Ste. 200, 21286, pg. 148 — PV
THE BLACK & DECKER CORPORATION, 701 E. Joppa Rd., 21286, pg. 233 — PB
Black & Decker Inc., 701 E. Joppa Rd., 21286, pg. 234 — PB
Intergraph Corporation, 8600 Lasalle Rd., 21286, pg. 890 — PB
Sanwa General Equipment Leasing, 502 Washington Ave., Ste. 800, 21204, pg. 1189 — IT

Upper Marlboro

BRANCH GROUP INC., 1049 Prince George Blvd., 20774, pg. 165 — PV
DAVENPORT INSULATION, INC, 15445 Depot Lane, 20772, pg. 314 — PV
First Virginia Bank-Maryland, 9420 Pennsylvania Ave., 20772-2698, pg. 642 — PB
McArdle Printing Co., Inc., 800 Commerce Dr., 20772, pg. 182 — PV
MURRY'S, INC., 8300 Pennsylvania Ave., 20772, pg. 768 — PV
Oceaneering Technologies, 501 Prince George's Blvd., 20774, pg. 1211 — PB

Waldorf

BESCHE OIL COMPANY, INC., 3045 Old Washington Rd., 20601, pg. 139 — PV

Walkersville

BioWhittaker, Inc., 8830 Biggs Ford Rd., 21793-0127, pg. 297 — PB
Clonetics, Inc., 8830 Biggs Ford Rd., 21793-0127, pg. 297 — PB
Rotorex Company, Inc., 8301 B Retreat Rd., 21793, pg. 615 — PB

Westminster

Carroll County Times, P.O. Box 346, 201 Railroad Ave., 21157, pg. 648 — PV
Knorr Brake Corporation, P.O. Box 9300, 21157, pg. 738 — IT
MONUMENTAL MILLWORK, INC., 344 Manchester Rd., 21157, pg. 759 — PV
Westminster Bank & Trust Co. of Carroll County, 71 E. Main St., 21157, pg. 1089 — PB

White Marsh

J. GIBSON MCILVAIN CO., P.O. Box 222, 21162, pg. 722 — PV

Whiteford

McCorquodale ColorCard, Inc., 2737 Whiteford Rd., 21160, pg. 1106 — IT

Williamsport

Sealy of Maryland & Virginia, Inc., 70-81 Industrial Park, 21795, pg. 979 — PV
SuperValu, Inc.-Maryland Div., P.O. Box 109, Interstate Industrial Park, 21795-0109, pg. 1540 — PB

Woodbine

Universal Insulation, Inc., Woodbine Rd., 21797, pg. 314 — PV

MASSACHUSETTS

Abington

Colony House Healthcare, 277 Washington St., 02351, pg. 1712 — PB

Acton

Acorn Structures, 930 Main St., 01720, pg. 320 — PV
Acton Environmental Testing, 533 Main St., 07120, pg. 1161 — PB
Ascom Nexion Inc., 289 Great Rd., 01720-4739, pg. 86 — IT
CML GROUP, INC., 524 Main St., 01720-3993, pg. 279 — PB
Corning Costar Corporation, 45 Nagog Pk., 01720, pg. 448 — PB
DATA INSTRUMENTS, INC., 100 Discovery Way, 01720, pg. 312 — PV
DECK HOUSE INC., 930 Main St., 01720, pg. 320 — PV
ENSR, 35 Nagog Park, 01720, pg. 354 — PV
Field Effects, Inc., Six Eastern Rd., 01720, pg. 893 — PB
REX LUMBER COMPANY, 840 Main St., 01720-5804, pg. 926 — PV

Adams

BUTLER WHOLESALE PRODUCTS, INC., 37 Pleasant St., 01220, pg. 190 — PV

Agawam

Ebtec Corporation, P.O. Box 465, 120 Shoemaker Ln., 01001, pg. 1337 — IT
Wentgate Dynaweld Inc., P.O. Box 465, 120 Shoemaker Ln., 01001, pg. 1337 — IT

Allston

CAMBRIDGE STREET METAL CO., 500 Lincoln St., 02134, pg. 203 — PV

Amesbury

CRAIG SYSTEMS, Ten Industrial Way, 01913, pg. 284 — PV
ESSEX COUNTY GAS COMPANY, Seven N. Hunt Rd., 01913, pg. 593 — PB
The Flexaust Co., 11 Chestnut St., 01913, pg. 394 — PB
LNG Storage Inc., P.O. Box 500, Seven N. Hunt Rd., 01913-0800, pg. 593 — PB
Northern Energy, Seven N. Hunt Rd., 01913, pg. 593 — PB

Amherst

Cox Communications-Amherst, 160 Old Farm Rd., 01002, pg. 454 — PB

Andover

AMP Inc. Lytel Division, Industrial, 2 Alonesos Way, 01810, pg. 8 — PB
ANDOVER BANCORP, INC., 61 Main St., 01810, pg. 111 — PB
ANDOVER CONTROLS, 300 Brickstone Sq., 01810, pg. 73 — PV
Andover Controls Corp., 300 Brickstone Sq., 01810, pg. 120 — IT
Andover Controls International Inc., 300 Brickstone Sq., 01810, pg. 73 — PV
Andover Controls Securities, 300 Brickstone Sq., 01810, pg. 73 — PV
DYNAMICS RESEARCH CORPORATION, 60 Frontage Rd., 01810-5498, pg. 539 — PB
EDD-Boston, 100 Burtt Rd. G-01, 01810, pg. 204 — PB
Enterprise Networks Business Unit, One Riverside Dr., 01810, pg. 1503 — PB
FTP SOFTWARE INC., 100 Brickstone Sq., 01810, pg. 609 — PB
Genetics Institute, Inc., One Burtt Rd., 01810, pg. 80 — PB
Hewlett-Packard Company, 1775 Minuteman Rd., 01810, pg. 814 — PB
ISI Systems Inc., Two Tech Dr., 01810, pg. 1373 — IT
Inchcape Testing Services, One Tech Dr., 01810, pg. 672 — PB
Lawrence Savings Bank, 342 North Main Street, 01810, pg. 980 — PB
Mast Industries, 100 Old River Rd., 01810, pg. 996 — PB
Peter Gray Corporation, 66 Lowell Junction Rd., 08180-5916, pg. 1763 — PB
PICTURETEL, 100 Minuteman Rd., 01810, pg. 1294 — PB
REAL WORLD, 206 Andover St., 01810, pg. 913 — PV
Smith & Nephew Endoscopy, 160 Dascomb Rd., 01810, pg. 1263 — IT
Specialty Filaments Inc., Two Dundee Park, Ste. 103, 01810, pg. 77 — PV
STANDARD DUPLICATING MACHINES CORP., 10 Connector Rd., 01810, pg. 1031 — PV
SuperValu, Inc.-Andover Div, 340 Ballardvale Rd., 01810, pg. 1540 — PB
Taras Valve Company, Inc., 815 Chestnut St., 01845, pg. 1747 — PB
VLT Corporation, 23 Frontage Rd., 01810, pg. 1719 — PB
VICOR CORPORATION, 400 Federal St., 01810, pg. 1719 — PB
Vicor International, 23 Frontage Rd., 01810, pg. 1719 — PB
Watts Regulator Co., 815 Chestnut St., 01845, pg. 747 — PB
Xerox Research, Oak St., 01810, pg. 1784 — PB

Arlington

Brigham's, Inc., 30 Mill St., 02174, pg. 483 — PV
SIMPSON GUMPERTZ & HEGER INC., 297 Broadway, 02174, pg. 1002 — PV

Ashland

Kidde-Fenwal, Inc., 400 Main St., 01721, pg. 1500 — IT
Nyacol Products, Inc., P.O. Box 349, Megunco Rd., 01721, pg. 827 — PB
Rexam Medical Packaging, P.O. Box 27, 150 Homer Ave., 01721, pg. 1107 — IT

Athol

Duall Plastics, Inc., 764 S. Athol Rd., 01331, pg. 233 — IT
THE L.S. STARRETT COMPANY, 121 Crescent St., 01331, pg. 1511 — PB
WHIPPS, 38 S. Main St., 01331, pg. 1171 — PV

Attleboro

AUTOMATIC MACHINE PRODUCTS COMPANY, 17 Wall St., 02703, pg. 101 — PV
John Brown Plastics Machinery, 100 Roddy Ave., 02703-7974, pg. 773 — IT
Cumberland Eng. Div., 100 Roddy Ave., 02703, pg. 773 — IT
Cumberland Engineering, 100 Roddy Ave., 02703, pg. 774 — IT
GLINES & RHODES, INC., 189 East St., 02703, pg. 457 — PV
Penny & Giles Controls Inc., 163 Pleasant St., 02703, pg. 208 — IT
Stern-Leach Company, 49 Pearl St., 02703, pg. 329 — IT
SWANK, INC., 6 Hazel St., 02703, pg. 1543 — PB
Texas Instruments Materials & Controls Group, 34 Forest St., 02703, pg. 1586 — PB
Trafalgar House Inc., 116 Roddy Ave., 02703-7974, pg. 774 — IT

Auburn

CONSOLIDATED BEVERAGES, INC., 12 St. Mark St., 01501, pg. 264 — PV
Liqui-Box Corp., Ten Millbury St., 01601, pg. 1001 — PB
Montrose/CDT, Auburn Indus. Pk., 28 Sword St., 01501, pg. 287 — PB

Avon

Central Sprinkler Company, 27R Doherty Ave., 02322, pg. 327 — PB
THE FIRST YEARS INC., One Kiddie Dr., 02322-1171, pg. 642 — PB
T.W. Kutter, Inc., 91 Wales Ave., 02322, pg. 1378 — IT
Trace Optical LLC, Avon Industrial Pk., 40 Robbie Rd., 02322, pg. 293 — PV
WESTERBEKE CORPORATION, Avon Indus. Park, 41 Ledin Dr., 02322, pg. 1757 — PB

Ayer

Associated Environmental Systems, P.O. Box 564, 19 Willow Rd., 01432, pg. 284 — PV
CAINS FOODS, L.P., 114 E. Main St., 01432, pg. 199 — PV
HORN PACKAGING CORPORATION, 11 Westford Rd., 01432, pg. 539 — PV
M.A. Hanna Resin Distribution, Molumco Industrial Park, 01932, pg. 781 — PB

Baldwinville

Data General Corp. Travel, 34 Winchester St., 01436-1434, pg. 485 — PB

Bedford

A.C. Scanning, Inc., One DeAngelo Dr., 01730, pg. 1735 — PB
All American Semiconductor of Massachusetts, Inc., 19 Crosby Dr., 01730, pg. 41 — PB
AMRAY, INC., 160 Middlesex Turnpike, 01730, pg. 67 — PV
W.E. Andrews Co., Inc., 140 South Rd., 01730, pg. 1735 — PB
EA Engineering, Science & Technology, Inc., 175 Middlesex Tpke., 3rd Fl., 01730, pg. 541 — PB
Electronic Printing Systems, 23 Crosby Dr., 01730, pg. 551 — PB
EMTEC Magnetics DataSource Media Inc., Nine Oak Park Dr., 01730-1471, pg. 743 — IT
Enterprising Service Solutions Corporation, Two Crosby Dr., 01730, pg. 729 — PB
FUJIFILM Microdisks U.S.A., Inc., 35 Crosby Dr., 01730, pg. 524 — IT
GIESECKE & DEVRIENT ENGINEERING, INC., 23 Crosby Dr., 01730-1401, pg. 452 — IT
IDEA CORPORATION, 7 Oak Park, 01730, pg. 557 — PB
Iris Graphics Inc., 6 Crosby Dr., 01730, pg. 644 — IT
Kaye Instruments, Inc., 15 De Angelo Dr., 01730, pg. 208 — IT
MIE, Inc., Seven Oak Pk., 01730, pg. 1558 — PB
MEGAPULSE, INC., Eight Preston Ct., 01730, pg. 729 — PV
MILLIPORE CORPORATION, 80 Ashby Rd., 01730, pg. 1112 — PB
MITRE CORPORATION, Burlington Rd., 01730, pg. 753 — PV
PSDI, 100 Crosby Dr., 01730, pg. 828 — PV
Parametric Technology Corporation, 100 Crosby Dr., 01730, pg. 1257 — PB
PROGRESS SOFTWARE CORPORATION, 14 Oak Park Dr., 01730, pg. 1334 — PB
Raytheon Electronics Systems, Hartwell Rd., 01730, pg. 1364 — PB
Scitex America Corp., 8 Oak Park Drive, 01730, pg. 644 — IT
SECURITY DYNAMICS TECHNOLOGIES, 20 Crosby Dr., 01730, pg. 1453 — PB
SPIRE CORPORATION, One Patriots Pk., 01730-2396, pg. 1499 — PB
Spire International Sales Corporation, One Patriots Pk., 01730-2396, pg. 1499 — PB
Sterimatics Corporation, Patriot Park, 01730, pg. 1113 — PB

Bernardston

Mohawk Plastics, Inc., P.O. Box 181, 01337, pg. 755 — PV

Beverly

Amicon, Inc., 72 Cherry Hill Drive, 01915, pg. 1113 — PB
Blueberry Hill Healthcare, 75 Brimbal Ave., 01915, pg. 1712 — PB
C.P. CLARE CORPORATION, 78 Cherry Hill Dr., 01915, pg. 382 — PB

DynaPert Inc., 71 Cherry Hill Dr., 01915, pg. 522 **PB**
ELECTRIC INSURANCE CO., 152 Conant St., 01915, pg. 368 **PV**
Fisons Instruments USA, 55 Cherry Hill Dr., 01915, pg. 1111 **IT**
Frequency and Time Systems, Inc., 34 Tozer Rd., 01915, pg. 488 **PB**
Greenery Extended Care Center of Beverly, 40 Heather St., 01915, pg. 836 **PB**
JOHNNY APPLESEED'S, INC., 30 Tozer Road, 01915, pg. 590 **PV**
Parker Brothers, 50 Dunham Rd., 01915, pg. 797 **PB**
Tonka International Division, 50 Dunham Rd., 01915, pg. 797 **PB**

Billerica

Advanced Automation Associates, Inc., 43 Manning Rd., 01821, pg. 1435 **PB**
AMERICAN SCIENCE & ENGINEERING, INC., 829 Middlesex Tpke., 01821, pg. 90 **PB**
Azonix, 900 Middlesex Tpke., 01821, pg. 457 **PB**
Bard Vascular Systems Div., 129 Concord Rd., 01821-0566, pg. 189 **PB**
Bay Networks, Inc., Eight Federal St., 01821, pg. 196 **PB**
Bull HN Information Systems (Asia) Inc., Technology Pk., 2 Wall St., 01821, pg. 316 **IT**
Bull HN Information Systems Inc., 300 Concord Rd., 01821-4199, pg. 316 **IT**
CSO Service CO. Inc., Technology Pk., 2 Wall St., 01821, pg. 316 **IT**
CSP INC., 40 Linnell Cir., 01821, pg. 283 **PB**
Eurotherm Gauging Systems Inc., 900 Middlesex Tpke., Bldg. 6, 01821, pg. 466 **IT**
FURMAN LUMBER COMPANY, INC., 32 Manning Rd., 01821, pg. 431 **PV**
General Microcircuits Corporation, 780 Boston Rd., 01821, pg. 717 **PB**
Harte-Hanks Data Technologies, 25 Linnell Circle, 01821, pg. 794 **PB**
Kodak Electronic Printing Systems, 164 Lexington Rd., 01821, pg. 551 **PB**
Mobil Solar Energy Corporation, Four Suburban Park Dr., 01821-3980, pg. 1119 **PB**
Nipson Printing Systems Inc., Technology Pk. MA02-413-N, 2 Wall St., 01821, pg. 316 **IT**
Orbotech Inc., 44 Manning Rd., 01821, pg. 1007 **IT**
PACER INFOTEC INC., 900 Technology Park, 01821, pg. 830 **PV**
POLYFIBRON TECHNOLOGIES CORP., Bldg. 2, 900 Middlesex Tpke., 01821-3946, pg. 875 **PV**
PREPRESS SOLUTIONS, INC., 29 Dunham Rd., 01821, pg. 882 **PB**
SAZTEC INTERNATIONAL, INC., 43 Manning Rd., 01821, pg. 1435 **PB**
Scanalytics, 40 Linnell Cir., 01821, pg. 283 **PB**
Select Robinson Inc., 17 Progress Rd., 01821, pg. 274 **IT**
Sipex Corporation, 22 Linnell Cir., 01821, pg. 1415 **PB**
USCI, 1200 Technology Park Dr., 01821-0566, pg. 189 **PB**
Unidesk Inc., Technology Park, 2 Wall St., 01821, pg. 316 **IT**
Visions Systems, 40 Linneu Cir., 01821, pg. 283 **PB**
WSI Corporation, Four Federal St., 01821, pg. 1325 **PB**
WANG LABORATORIES, INC., 600 Technology Park Dr., 01821, pg. 1737 **PB**

Bolton

Yankee Atomic Electric Co., 580 Main St., 01740, pg. 325 **PB**

Boston

ABM AMRO Bank, N.V. (Boston), Exchange Pl., 53 State St., 19th Flr., 02109, pg. 10 **IT**
AEW Capital Management, L.P., 225 Franklin St., 02110, pg. 737 **PV**
AEW PARTNERS, L.P., 225 Franklin St., 02110, pg. 5 **PV**
AFA Protective Systems, Inc., 61 Batterymarch St., 02110, pg. 5 **PB**
AFA Mass., Inc., 61 Batterymarch St., 02110, pg. 6 **PB**
M. Abelman Company, Inc., 84 Stonely Rd., 02130, pg. 694 **PB**
Acadian Asset Management, Tow International Pl., 02110, pg. 1672 **PB**
Acordia Northeast, 88 Broad St., 02110, pg. 671 **IT**
ADVENT INTERNATIONAL, 101 Federal St., 02110, pg. 22 **PV**
AEARO COMPANY, One Washington Mall, 8th Fl., 02108-2610, pg. 23 **PV**
Affiliated Publications, Inc., 135 Morrissey Blvd., 02107-2378, pg. 1174 **PB**
Algonquin Gas Transmission Corporation, 1284 Soldiers Field Rd., 02135, pg. 534 **PB**
ALLIED ADVERTISING AGENCY, PUBLIC RELATIONS, 545 Boylston St., 11th Fl., 02116, pg. 38 **PV**
Allright Boston Parking, Inc., 59 Temple Pl., Ste. 402, 02111, pg. 42 **PV**
Alpnet, 945 Concord St., Ste. 134, 01701, pg. 58 **PV**
American Council for International Studies, 19 Bay State Rd., 02215, pg. 57 **PV**
American Finance Group, Inc., 24 School St., 02108, pg. 1241 **PB**
American Financial Group Securities Corp., 88 Broad St., 02110, pg. 380 **PV**
The Arbour Hospital, 49 Robinwood Ave., P.O. Box 9, 02130, pg. 1696 **PB**
ARNOLD COMMUNICATIONS, INC., 101 Arch St., 02110, pg. 83 **PV**

Arnold Direct, 101 Arch St., 02110, pg. 84 **PV**
Arnold Information Technology, 101 Arch St., 02110, pg. 84 **PV**
Arnold Interactive, 101 Arch St., 02110, pg. 84 **PV**
Arnold Public Relations, 101 Huntington Ave., 02199, pg. 84 **PV**
ART TECHNOLOGY GROUP, 101 Huntington Ave., 02199, pg. 86 **PV**
THE ATLANTIC MONTHLY MAGAZINE, 77 N. Washington St., 02114, pg. 95 **PV**
AU BON PAIN CO., INC., 19 Fid Kennedy Ave., 02210, pg. 146 **PB**
BSA Advertising, Inc., 31 St. James Ave., 9th Fl., 02116, pg. 108 **PV**
Back Bay Advisors, Inc., 399 Boylston St., 02116, pg. 737 **PV**
BAIN CAPITAL, Two Copley Pl., 02116, pg. 110 **PV**
Balco, Inc., 306 Northern Ave., 02205, pg. 376 **PV**
BancBoston Brokerage Inc., 100 Federal St., 02110, pg. 184 **PB**
BancBoston Capital, Inc., 100 Federal St., 02110, pg. 184 **PB**
BancBoston Financial Co., 100 Federal St., 02110, pg. 184 **PB**
BancBoston Investment Inc., 100 Federal St., 02110, pg. 184 **PB**
BancBoston Leasing Inc., 100 Federal St., 02100, pg. 184 **PB**
BancBoston Real Estate Capitol Corporation, 100 Federal St., 02110, pg. 184 **PB**
BancBoston Ventures Inc., 100 Federal St., 02110, pg. 184 **PB**
Bancireland/First Financial Inc., One Financial Ctr., 16th Fl., 02111, pg. 152 **IT**
The Bank of Nova Scotia, 101 Federal St., 02110, pg. 156 **IT**
BANKBOSTON CORPORATION, 100 Federal St., 02110, pg. 183 **PB**
Banta Integrated Media, 651 Beacon St., 02215-3278, pg. 188 **PB**
Baring Asset Management Inc., High Street Tower, 125 High St., Ste. 2700, 02110-2713, pg. 647 **IT**
Batterymarch Financial Management, 200 Clarendon St., 02116, pg. 985 **PV**
Bay State Cruise Company, 184 High St., Ste. 501, 02110, pg. 1274 **PB**
BayBank, N.A., 175 Federal St., 02110, pg. 184 **PB**
BayBanks, Inc., 175 Federal St., 02110, pg. 184 **PB**
Bear, Stearns & Co. Inc., Boston, One Federal St., 02110, pg. 198 **IT**
BECKWITH ELEVATOR CO., 274 Southampton St., 02118, pg. 128 **PV**
Bell Atlantic New England, 125 High St., Room 1237, 02110, pg. 202 **PB**
Berkeley Financial Group, 101 Huntington Ave., 02199-7603, pg. 589 **PV**
BERKSHIRE REALTY COMPANY, INC., Harbor Plaza, 470 Atlantic Ave., 02210, pg. 221 **PV**
BLAUER MANUFACTURING CO., INC., 20 Aberdeen St., 02215, pg. 149 **PV**
BLUE CROSS AND BLUE SHIELD OF MASSACHUSETTS, 100 Summer St., 02110, pg. 151 **PV**
BOSTON BEER COMPANY, 75 Arlington St., 02116, pg. 246 **PB**
BOSTON CELTICS LIMITED PARTNERSHIP, 151 Merrimac St., 02114, pg. 246 **PB**
The Boston Company, Inc., One Boston Pl., 9th Fl., 02108, pg. 1085 **PB**
BOSTON EDISON COMPANY, 800 Boylston St., 02199-9119, pg. 247 **PB**
Boston Energy Technology Group, Inc., 800 Boylston St., 02179, pg. 247 **PB**
Boston Gas Company, One Beacon St., 02108, pg. 549 **PB**
The Boston Globe, 135 Morrissey Blvd., 02107, pg. 1175 **PB**
Boston Globe Electronic Publishing, Inc., One Exeter Plaza, 699 Boylston St., 02116, pg. 1175 **PB**
Boston Globe Investments, 135 Morrissey Blvd., 02107-2378, pg. 1175 **PB**
The Boston Herald, One Herald Square, 02106, pg. 926 **IT**
Boston International Data Services, Inc., 100 Federal St., 02110, pg. 184 **PB**
Boston Overseas Holding Corp., 100 Federal St., 02110, pg. 184 **PB**
Boston Safe Deposit & Trust Co., One Boston Pl., 9th Fl., 02108, pg. 1085 **PB**
Boston Security Counsellors, Inc., 100 Federal St., 02110, pg. 23 **PB**
Boston Trade Bank, Ten Post Office Sq., 02109, pg. 184 **PB**
Boston Wharf Company, 253 Summer, 02210, pg. 1035 **IT**
Bowne of Boston, Inc., 411 D St., 02210, pg. 248 **PB**
Branch Electric Supply Co., Inc., 817 Albany St., 02119, pg. 165 **PV**
The Brewskeller, Faneuil Hall Market, 02109, pg. 130 **PB**
Brewster Wholesaler Company, 200 Clarendon St., 02116, pg. 1485 **PB**
BRONNER SLOSBERG HUMPHREY/STRATEGIC INTERACTIVE GROUP, The Prudential Tower, 800 Boylston St., 02199, pg. 171 **PV**
Brown & Company Securities Corporation, One Beacon St., 02108, pg. 337 **PB**
Browning-Ferris Industries, Inc., 100 Hallet St., 02124, pg. 263 **PB**
Building Technologies Engineering, 306 Northern Ave., 02205, pg. 376 **PV**

Burns & Wilcox - Boston Office, 60 State St., 36th Fl., 02109, pg. 609 **PV**
C.B.E Technologies Inc., 50 Redfield Rd., 02109, pg. 1389 **PV**
Cablevision of Boston, 28 Travis St., 02134, pg. 288 **PB**
CABOT CORPORATION, 75 State St., 02109-1806, pg. 288 **PB**
Cadmus Custom Publishing, 101 Huntington Ave., 13th Fl., 02199-7603, pg. 290 **PB**
Cadmus Custom Publishing, 101 Hunington Ave. 13th, 02199, pg. 291 **PB**
CAMBRIDGE-LEE INDUSTRIES, INC., 500 Lincoln St., Allston Station, 02134, pg. 202 **PV**
Candela Skin Care Center of Boston, 28 Arlington St., 02116, pg. 300 **PB**
Candela Skin Care Centers, Inc., 31 St. James Ave., Ste. 818, 02116, pg. 300 **PB**
Carbon Black Div., 75 State, 02109, pg. 289 **PB**
Carter Rice, 273 Summer, 02101, pg. 903 **PB**
Chancellor Asset Corporation, 745 Atlantic Ave., 02111, pg. 335 **PB**
CHANCELLOR CORPORATION, 745 Atlantic Ave., 02111, pg. 335 **PB**
Chancellor DataComm, Inc., 745 Atlantic Ave., 02111, pg. 335 **PB**
Chancellor Financial Sales & Services, Inc., 745 Atlantic Ave., 02111, pg. 335 **PB**
Chancellor Fleet Corporation, 745 Atlantic Ave., 02111, pg. 335 **PB**
Chancellor Management Corporation, 745 Atlantic Ave., 02111, pg. 335 **PB**
CHARLES RIVER FOODS, INC., One Widett Circle, 02118, pg. 230 **PV**
Chase Global Funds Service Company, 73 Tremont St., 02101-2108, pg. 308 **PB**
J.W. CHILDS ASSOCIATES, L.P., One Federal St., 21st. Fl., 02110, pg. 237 **PV**
Cipriani Kremer Design, 101 Huntington Ave., 02199, pg. 84 **PV**
Citicorp (USA), Inc., 1 Boston Place, 02108, pg. 377 **PB**
Clarendon Insurance Agency Inc., 500 Boylston St., 02116, pg. 1319 **IT**
COLE HERSEE COMPANY, 20 Old Colony Ave., 02127-2467, pg. 251 **PV**
Commercial Union Corporation, One Beacon St., 02108, pg. 308 **IT**
Commercial Union Insurance Company, One Beacon St., 02108, pg. 308 **IT**
CONNELL LIMITED PARTNERSHIP, Fort Hill Sq., One International Pl., 31st Fl., 02110-2635, pg. 264 **PV**
Dewey Square Investors Corporation, One Financial Ctr., 24th Fl., 02111, pg. 1673 **PB**
Distrigas Corp., 200 State St., 02109, pg. 289 **PB**
Distrigas of Massachusetts Corporation, 200 State St., 02109, pg. 289 **PB**
Diversified Group, Prudential Tower Bldg., 02199, pg. 743 **PB**
Diversified Insurance Agency, Inc., 101 Federal St. 18th Fl., 02110, pg. 366 **PB**
Dynabilt Products, 31 Industrial Dr., 02136, pg. 188 **PV**
EUA Bioten, Inc., P.O. Box 2333, 02107-2333, pg. 549 **PB**
EUA Energy Investment Corporation, One Liberty Sq., 02109, pg. 549 **PB**
EUA Ocean State Corporation, One Liberty Sq., 02109, pg. 549 **PB**
EASTERN UTILITIES ASSOCIATES, One Liberty Sq., 02109, pg. 549 **PB**
EATON VANCE CORP., 24 Federal St., 02110, pg. 559 **PB**
EDWARDS AND KELCEY, INC., The Schrafft Center, 529 Main St., Ste. 203, 02129, pg. 364 **PV**
Energex Corp., 24 Federal St., 02110, pg. 559 **PB**
Energy Investors Management, Inc., John Hancock Place, P.O. Box 111, 02117, pg. 589 **PV**
ENERGY SYSTEMS INDUSTRIES, INC., 306 Northern Ave., Bldg. 53, 02205, pg. 376 **PV**
EQUIS FINANCIAL GROUP, 88 Broad St., 02110, pg. 379 **PV**
Evans, Inc. (MA), 426 Washington, 02101, pg. 596 **PB**
FMR Corp., 82 Devonshire St., 02109, pg. 403 **PV**
Faneuil Hall Marketplace, Inc., Core 1, Third Fl. S. Market, Bldg., 1 Faneuil Hall MarketPlace, 02109, pg. 1408 **PV**
Fast Company Magazine, 77 N. Washington St., 02114, pg. 95 **PV**
Fidelity Capital, 82 Devonshire St., 02109, pg. 403 **PV**
FIDELITY INVESTMENTS (FMR CORP.), 82 Devonshire St., 02109, pg. 402 **PV**
Filene's, 426 Washington St., 02108, pg. 1063 **PB**
Financial Collection Agencies (1990) Inc., 529 Main St., Ste. 606, 02129, pg. 471 **IT**
FINNAIR, 20 Park Plaza, 02116, pg. 485 **IT**
First Mutual of Boston, 800 Boylston St., 02199, pg. 184 **PB**
First Source Yellow Pages, 420 Boylston St., 02116, pg. 84 **PV**
First State Insurance Company, 150 Federal St., 02110-1753, pg. 794 **PB**
Fleet Bank, 30 Winter St., 02105, pg. 649 **PB**
Fleet Bank of Massachusetts, N.A., One Federal St., 02110, pg. 649 **PB**
FLEET FINANCIAL GROUP, INC., One Federal St., 02110-2010, pg. 648 **PB**
Fleet Investment Advisors, Inc., 75 State St., 02109, pg. 650 **PB**
Fleet National Bank of Massachusetts, 75 State St., 02109, pg. 649 **PB**
THE FORUM CORPORATION, One Exchange Pl., 02109, pg. 499 **PV**
Four Seasons Hotel, 200 Boylston St., 02116, pg. 502 **IT**
Franklin Portfolio Associates Trust, One Post Office Sq., 02109, pg. 1085 **PB**

Geographic Index-U.S.

GCI Boston, Inc., 1200 Soldiers Field Rd., 02134, pg. 470 — PV

Gillette Co.-Parker Pen USA, Gillette Company, Prudential Tower Bldg., 02199, pg. 745 — PB

THE GILLETTE COMPANY, Prudential Tower Bldg., 02199, pg. 743 — PB

The Gillette Company, Gillette Grooming Products, USA, One Gillette Pk., 02127, pg. 744 — PB

The Gillette Company, Personal Care Group, One Gillette Park, 02127-1096, pg. 744 — PB

Globe Newspaper Company, 135 Morrissey Blvd., 02107, pg. 1175 — PB

THE GOLDHIRSH GROUP, 38 Commercial Wharf, 02110, pg. 461 — PV

GOLDMAN FINANCIAL GROUP, One Post Office Sq. #41, 02109-2103, pg. 461 — PV

Goldman, Sachs & Co., 125 High St., Ste. 1700, 02110, pg. 462 — PV

GORDON BROTHERS PARTNERS INC., 40 Broad St., 02109, pg. 465 — PV

HCW Oil Income Fund (Devonian), 101 Summer St., 02110, pg. 361 — PB

Hagler, Mastrovita & Hewitt, Inc., 225 Franklin St., 02110, pg. 1673 — PB

Harbor Electric Energy Company, 800 Boylston St., 02199, pg. 247 — PB

Hellman, Jordan Management Company, Inc., 75 State St., 02109, pg. 1673 — PB

Helmsman Management Services, Inc., 175 Berkeley St., 02117, pg. 666 — PV

HILL, HOLLIDAY, CONNORS, COSMOPULOS, INC., John Hancock Tower, 200 Clarendon St., 02116, pg. 529 — PV

HOLLAND MARK MARTIN, 312 Stuart St., 02116, pg. 534 — PV

Houghton Mifflin College Div., 222 Berkeley St., 02116-3764, pg. 841 — PB

HOUGHTON MIFFLIN COMPANY, 222 Berkeley St., 02116, pg. 841 — PB

Houghton Mifflin School Division, 222 Berkeley St., 02116, pg. 841 — PB

Houghton Mifflin Trade & Reference Div., 222 Berkeley St., 02116-3764, pg. 841 — PB

HOUSTON HERSTEK FAVAT, 360 Newbury St., 02115, pg. 542 — PV

IDG Communications, One Exeter Plaza, 02116, pg. 569 — PV

IDG International News Group, 31 Milk St., Ste. 210, 02109, pg. 569 — PV

IDX Systems Corporation-Boston, 116 Huntington Ave., 02116, pg. 854 — PB

ITT Sheraton Corporation, 60 State St., 02109, pg. 1512 — PB

Iberia Air Lines of Spain, 20 Providence St., 02116, pg. 575 — IT

Illinois Mentor, Inc., 313 Congress St., 02210, pg. 1036 — PB

The Impex Group Limited, One Post Office Sq., 02109, pg. 1036 — PV

Independence Investment Associates, Inc., 53 State St., 02109, pg. 589 — PV

Information Services Division, Ten City Square, 02129, pg. 946 — PB

INGALLS, One Design Center Pl., 02210, pg. 562 — PV

Inner City, Inc., 120 Southampton St., 02118, pg. 1313 — PB

INSO CORPORATION, 31 St. James Ave., 11th Flr., 02116-4101, pg. 882 — PB

Interactive Solutions, 855 Boylston St., 02116, pg. 1224 — PB

INTERNATIONAL DATA GROUP, One Exeter Plaza, 02116-2851, pg. 569 — PV

Invesco Inc., 101 Federal St., 02110, pg. 685 — IT

Investors Services Group, One Exchange Place, 02109, pg. 631 — PB

Jefferies & Company, Inc., One Post Office Sq., Ste. 4000, 02109, pg. 925 — PB

JILLIAN'S ENTERTAINMENT CORPORATION, 727 Atlantic Ave., Ste. 600, 02111, pg. 587 — PV

John Hancock Advisers, Inc., 101 Huntington Ave., 02199, pg. 589 — PV

John Hancock Capital Corporation, John Hancock Place, 02117, pg. 590 — PV

John Hancock Leasing Corporation, John Hancock Pl., 02117, pg. 590 — PV

JOHN HANCOCK MUTUAL LIFE INSURANCE COMPANY, John Hancock Pl., 200 Clarendon St., 02116, pg. 589 — PV

John Hancock Subsidiaries, Inc., John Hancock Pl., 02117, pg. 589 — PV

KEANE, INC., Ten City Sq., 02129, pg. 946 — PV

Keyport Life Insurance Company, 125 High St., 02110-2712, pg. 666 — PV

Korn/Ferry International, 101 Federal St., 24th Flr., 02110, pg. 633 — PV

Korn/Ferry Organizational Consulting, 75 Federal St., 02110, pg. 633 — PV

Laura Ashley (USA) Inc., Six St. James Ave., 10th Fl., 02116, pg. 804 — IT

THOMAS H. LEE CO., 75 State St., 02109, pg. 658 — PV

Lexington Insurance Co., 100 Summer St., 02112, pg. 84 — PB

Liberty Distributors Inc., 600 Atlantic Ave., 02210, pg. 666 — PB

Liberty Financial Companies, 600 Atlantic Ave., 02210, pg. 666 — PV

Liberty Insurance Corporation, 175 Berkeley St., 02117, pg. 666 — PV

Liberty Mutual Fire Insurance Co., 175 Berkeley St., 02117, pg. 666 — PV

LIBERTY MUTUAL INSURANCE CO., 175 Berkeley St., 02117, pg. 666 — PV

Lifetime Advisers Inc., Boylston St., 02116, pg. 1319 — IT

Liquid Paper Corp., Prudential Tower Bldg., 02199, pg. 744 — PB

Loomis, Sayles & Co., One Financial Center, 02111, pg. 737 — PV

MFS Financial Services Inc., 500 Boylston St., 02116, pg. 1319 — IT

MFS Service Center Inc., 50 Milk St., 02109, pg. 1319 — IT

Marblehead Energy Corp., 24 Federal St., 02110, pg. 559 — PB

The Marketplace Cafe, 301 Faneuil Hall, 02109, pg. 130 — PB

Marlborough Capital Advisors, Inc., 399 Boylston St., 02116, pg. 737 — PV

Massachusetts Caring for Children Foundation, Inc., 100 Summer St., 02110, pg. 151 — PV

Massachusetts Casualty Insurance Company, 711 Atlantic Ave., P.O. Box 9099, 02205-9099, pg. 1319 — IT

Massachusetts Financial Services Company (MFS), 500 Boylston St., 02116, pg. 1319 — IT

Massachusetts Mentor, Inc., 313 Congress St., 02210, pg. 1036 — PB

MediaOne, The Pilot House, Lewis Wharf, 02110, pg. 1688 — PB

Merrill/Boston, 121 High St., 02110, pg. 1097 — PB

Miller Shandwick Technologies, Four Copley Pl., Ste. 605, 02116, pg. 1227 — IT

Montaup Electric Co., One Liberty Sq., P.O. Box 2333, 02110, pg. 550 — PB

J.P. Morgan Securities Inc., Two International Pl., 18th Fl., 02110, pg. 1129 — PB

NS Invest II, Inc., c/o Nippon Steel U.S.A., Inc., 101 Federal St., 5th fl., 02110, pg. 913 — IT

National Bank of Greece, 33 State, 02109, pg. 907 — IT

National Employee Benefits Corporation, 101 Federal St., 18th Fl., 02110, pg. 366 — PB

National Leisure Group, 1249 Boylston St., 02215, pg. 320 — PB

National Mentor Healthcare, Inc., 313 Congress St., 02210, pg. 1036 — PB

National Mentor, Inc, 313 Congress St., 02210, pg. 1036 — PB

NEW BALANCE ATHLETIC SHOE, INC., 61 N. Beacon St. 02134, pg. 792 — PV

The New England, 501 Boylston St., 02116-3700, pg. 737 — PV

New England Insurance Company, 150 Federal St., 02110-1753, pg. 794 — PB

New England Investment Associates, 399 Boylston St., 7th Fl., 02116, pg. 737 — PV

New England Investment Companies, Inc., 399 Boylston St., Ste. 13, 02117, pg. 737 — PV

New England Life Insurance Co, 501 Boylston St., 02117, pg. 738 — PV

New England Life Mortgage Funding Corp., 501 Boylston St., 02117, pg. 738 — PV

New England Pension & Annuity Co., 501 Boylston St., 02117, pg. 738 — PV

New England Reinsurance Corporation, 150 Federal St., 02110-1753, pg. 794 — PB

New England Securities Corp., 399 Boylston St., 02116, pg. 738 — PV

New Ventures Division, 100 Summer St., 02110, pg. 51 — PV

Newport, 501 Boylston Street, 02117, pg. 738 — PV

Nissin Molecular Biology Institute, Inc., 20 Overland St., 02115, pg. 950 — IT

Noptek c/o Advent International, 101 Federal St., 5th Fl., 02110, pg. 913 — PV

North Castle Partners Advertising, 419 Boylston St., 02116, pg. 604 — PV

Northeast Properties, Inc., 24 Federal St., 02110, pg. 559 — PB

Oar Bar & Grill, Faneuil Hall Market, 02109, pg. 130 — PB

Oechsle International Advisors L.P., One International Pl., 02110, pg. 418 — IT

Ohio Mentor, Inc., 313 Congress St., 02210, pg. 1036 — PB

Orion Intl. Sales, Inc., 529 Main St., 02129, pg. 1592 — PB

Orion Research Inc., The Schrafft Center, 529 Main St., 02129, pg. 1592 — PB

PNC Bank New England, 99 High Street, 02110, pg. 1243 — PB

PWS-Kent Publishing Co., Statler Office Bldg., 20 Park Plaza, 02116, pg. 1600 — PB

PanAgora Asset Managment, Inc., 260 Franklin St., 22nd Fl., 02110, pg. 987 — PV

PEABODY OFFICE FURNITURE CORPORATION, 234 Congress St., 02110, pg. 844 — PV

Pell, Rudman & Company, 100 Federal St., 37th Fl., 02110, pg. 1673 — PB

Physician Partners of New England, Inc., 100 Summer St., 02110, pg. 151 — PV

Pioneer Associates Inc., 60 State St., 02109, pg. 1298 — PB

Pioneer Capital Corporation, 60 State St., 02109, pg. 1298 — PB

Pioneer First Polish Trust, 60 State St., 02109, pg. 1298 — PB

Pioneer Funds Distributor, Inc., 60 State St., 02109, pg. 1298 — PB

Pioneer Funds Marketing GmbH, 60 State St., 02109, pg. 1298 — PB

Pioneer Goldfields Limited, 60 State St., 02109, pg. 1298 — PB

THE PIONEER GROUP, INC., 60 State St., 02109, pg. 1298 — PB

Pioneer International Corporation, 60 State St., 02109, pg. 1298 — PB

Pioneer Investments Corporation, 60 State St., 02109, pg. 1298 — PB

Pioneer Investments Poland Ltd., 60 State St., 02114, pg. 1298 — PB

Pioneer Management (Ireland) Limited, 60 State St., 02109, pg. 1298 — PB

Pioneer Metals & Technology, Inc., 60 State St., 02109, pg. 1298 — PB

Pioneer Plans Corporation, 60 State St., 02109, pg. 1298 — PB

Pioneer SBIC Corp., 60 State St., 02109, pg. 1298 — PB

Pioneering Management Corporation, 60 State St., 02109, pg. 1298 — PB

Pioneering Services Corporation, 60 State St., 02109, pg. 1298 — PB

Pollak-Actuation, 195 Freeport St., 02122, pg. 1045 — PV

Pollak Division, 195 Freeport St., 02122, pg. 1045 — PV

Power Conversion, Seven Elkins St., 02127, pg. 422 — PB

Power Conversion North America, 7 Elkins St., 02127, pg. 422 — PB

Primark Decision Economics, INc., 260 Franklin St., Ste. 1510, 02110, pg. 1325 — PB

Profesco Corporation, John Hancock Place, 02117, pg. 590 — PV

Professional Economic Services, Inc., John Hancock Place, 02117, pg. 590 — PV

PROPERTY CAPITAL TRUST, 101 Federal St., 02110-1817, pg. 1335 — PB

Putnam Investments, Inc., One Post Office Square, 02109, pg. 1049 — PB

Quebecor Printing (USA) Corp., 125 High St., 02110, pg. 1076 — IT

RLI Boston, 28 State St., Ste. 1100, 02109, pg. 1356 — PB

Randolph Computer Corporation, 100 Federal St., 02110, pg. 184 — PB

Raytheon Engineers & Constructors, Inc., 100 Summer St., 02110, pg. 1366 — PB

Recoll Management Corp., 245 Summer St., 02209, pg. 650 — PB

Rockton Associates, Incorporated, 245 Summer St., 02107, pg. 1519 — PB

Rollins Hudig Hall of Massachusetts, Inc., 99 High St., 02110, pg. 117 — PB

SBC Warburg Dillon Read Inc., 31 Milk St., 02109, pg. 1329 — IT

SEI Corporation, 101 Federal St., 14th Fl., 02110, pg. 1417 — PB

Salt Water Sportsman, 77 Franklin St., 02110, pg. 1617 — PB

Self-Insurers' Management Corporation, 101 Federal St., 18th Fl., 02110, pg. 366 — PB

Senior Markets Division, 100 Summer St., 02110, pg. 151 — PV

Shreve, Crump & Low Co., 330 Boylston St., 02116, pg. 197 — IT

Shuwa Trust of Boston, 265 Franklin St., 02110, pg. 1237 — IT

Skadden, Arps, Slate, Meagher & Flom LLP, One Beacon St., 02108, pg. 1004 — PV

SONESTA INTERNATIONAL HOTELS CORPORATION, 200 Clarendon St., 02116, pg. 1485 — PB

South Carolina Mentor, Inc., 313 Congress St., 02210, pg. 1036 — PB

SPAULDING & SLYE, 125 High St., 02110, pg. 1021 — PV

SPORTO CORP., Two Midway St., 02210, pg. 1026 — PV

Spring Lane Assocs., Inc., 24 Federal St., 02110, pg. 559 — PV

State Street Bank & Trust Co., 225 Franklin St., 02110, pg. 1513 — PB

STATE STREET CORPORATION, 225 Franklin St., 02110, pg. 1513 — PB

State Street Research & Management Company, One Financial Ctr., 30th Fl., 02111, pg. 738 — PV

State Street Research Investment Services, Inc., One Financial Ctr., 31st Fl., 02111-2690, pg. 738 — PV

Stationery Products Division, One Gillette Pk., 02127, pg. 744 — PB

Sterling Office Services, 75 State St., 10th Fl., 02109, pg. 1221 — PB

Stone & Webster Civil & Transportation Services, Inc., 245 Summer St., 02107, pg. 1519 — PB

Stone & Webster Construction Company, Inc., 245 Summer St., 02107, pg. 1519 — PB

Stone & Webster Engineering & Constructors Corp., 245 Summer St., 02210, pg. 1519 — PB

STONE & WEBSTER, INCORPORATED, 245 Summer St., 02210, pg. 1519 — PB

Stride Rite Footwear, Inc., 960 Harrison Ave., 02118, pg. 1525 — PV

Sun Capital Advisers, Inc., 185 Devonshire St., Ste. 1075, 02110, pg. 1319 — IT

TNE Advisors, Inc., 501 Boylston St., 02116, pg. 738 — PV

TNE Funding Corporation, 501 Boylston St., 02117, pg. 738 — PV

TNE Information Services, 501 Boylston St., 02116, pg. 738 — PV

TNE Investment Services Corp., 399 Boylston St., 02116, pg. 737 — PV

TNT VACATIONS, Two Charlesgate W., 02215-3552, pg. 1065 — PV

Teberebie Goldfields, Ltd., 60 State St., 02109, pg. 1298 — PB

TECH/OPS SEVCON, INC., One Beacon St., 02108-3106, pg. 1563 — PB

Technology Solutions Inc., 2 Oliver St., 9th Fl., 02109, pg. 1157 — PV

Teradyne Assembly Test/East Division, 321 Harrison Avenue, 02118, pg. 1581 — PB

TERADYNE, INC., 321 Harrison Ave., 02118, pg. 1580 — PB

Teradyne Industrial/Consumer Division, 321 Harrison Avenue, 02118, pg. 1581 — PB

Thomson Financial Services, Inc., 11 Farnsworth St., 02210, pg. 1600 — PB

Triumph Releasing Corporation - New England Territory, 535 Boylston St., 6th Fl., 02116-3720, pg. 1282 — IT

PB - *U.S. Public Companies Volume*
PV - *U.S. Private Companies Volume*
IT - *International Public & Private Companies Volume*

Geographic Index-U.S.

Turner Construction Co., 855 Boylston St., 02116, pg. 1645 — PB

UAM Fund Services Inc., 211 Congress St., 02110, pg. 1674 — PB

UAM Investment Services, Inc., 211 Congress St., 02110, pg. 1674 — PB

URS Greiner, Inc., 31 Saint James Ave., 02116, pg. 1658 — PB

UST Capital Corp., 40 Court St., 02108, pg. 1660 — PB

UST CORPORATION, 40 Court St., 02108, pg. 1660 — PB

UST Leasing Corporation, 55 Court St., 02108, pg. 1660 — PB

UNICCO SERVICE COMPANY, Four Copley Pl., 07116, pg. 1117 — PV

UNITED ASSET MANAGEMENT CORPORATION, One International Pl., 44th Fl., 02110, pg. 1672 — PB

USTrust, 30 Court St., 02108, pg. 1660 — PB

United States Trust Company, 40 Court St., 02108, pg. 1660 — PB

Vicorp Interactive Systems, Inc., 399 Boylston St., 02116, pg. 1321 — PV

WBZ Radio & WBZ-TV, 1170 Soldiers Field Rd., 02134, pg. 275 — PB

WCVB Division, Five TV Place, Needham Br., 02192, pg. 516 — PV

WCVB-TV, Five TV Place, Needham Br., 02192, pg. 516 — PV

WLVI-TV, 75 Morrissey Blvd., 02125, pg. 1636 — PB

WWF National, 529 Main St., 02129, pg. 1145 — PV

WALDO BROS. COMPANY, 202 Southampton St., 02118, pg. 1147 — PV

S.D. Warren Co., 225 Franklin St., 28th Fl., 02110, pg. 1193 — IT

Western International Media Corporation, 1 Exeter Plaza, 699 Boylston St., 02116, pg. 1167 — PV

Wickersham Hunt Schwantner, The Berkeley Building, 420 Boylston St., 02116, pg. 84 — PV

THE WILDER COMPANIES, 101 Huntington Ave., 13th Fl., 02199, pg. 1176 — PV

Willis Corroon Corp. of Massachusetts, One Exeter Plaza, 11th Fl., 02116-2855, pg. 1506 — PV

WINTHROP PRINTING COMPANY, INC., 235 Old Colony Ave., 02127, pg. 1184 — PV

Woolf Associates, 101 Huntington Ave., 02199, pg. 84 — PV

WORK/FAMILY DIRECTIONS, 930 Commonwealth Ave., 02215-1212, pg. 1188 — PV

X-L-CO, Inc., 60 State St., 02109, pg. 1787 — PB

XTRA CORPORATION, 60 State St., 11th Fl., 02109, pg. 1786 — PB

Yankee Group Research, Inc., 31 St. James Ave., 02116, pg. 1325 — PV

ZOOM TELEPHONICS, INC., 207 South St., 02111, pg. 1794 — PB

Boxboro

NEC Technologies, Inc., 1414 Massachusetts Ave., 01719-2298, pg. 900 — IT

Boxford

EG & G Venture Management, P.O. Box 220, 01921, pg. 544 — PB

Braintree

ALL SEASONS SERVICES, INC., 100 Grandview Rd., 02184-2624, pg. 35 — PV

Berger Instruments, 50 Messina Dr., 02184, pg. 235 — PV

BRADLEES INC., One Bradlees Cir., 02184, pg. 249 — PB

CHASE CORPORATION, 50 Braintree Hill Park, Ste. 220, 02184, pg. 337 — PB

Chase Export Corporation, 50 Braintree Hill Park, Ste. 220, 02184, pg. 337 — PB

CLEAN HARBORS, INC., P.O. Box 850327, 1501 Washington St., 02185-0327, pg. 383 — PB

WARREN E. COLLINS, INC., 220 Wood Rd., 02184, pg. 253 — PV

THE FLATLEY COMPANY, 50 Braintree Hill Office Park, 02184, pg. 410 — PV

GROUND ROUND INC., 35 Braintree Hill Office Park, 02184-9078, pg. 766 — PB

HAEMONETICS CORPORATION, 400 Wood Rd., 02184, pg. 773 — PB

J.L. HAMMETT COMPANY, One Hammett Pl., 02184, pg. 498 — PV

Hazeltine Ocean Systems, 115 Bay State Dr., 02184, pg. 544 — IT

Quebecor Printing Semline Inc., 180 Wood Rd., 02184, pg. 1078 — IT

Bridgewater

Keith Highlanders Shoes, 31 Perkins St., 02324, pg. 612 — PV

Brighton

Barry Controls, 40 Guest St., 02135, pg. 124 — PB

Barry Controls Industrial/Defense, 40 Guest St., 02135, pg. 124 — PB

Bickford's Family Restaurants, 1330 Soldier's Field Rd., 02135, pg. 545 — PB

Boston Operations, 145 N. Beacon, 02135, pg. 443 — PB

Dooley Equipment Corp., 164 Market St., 02135, pg. 264 — PB

Greenery Rehabilitation Center, 99 Chestnut Hill Ave., 02135, pg. 837 — PV

Vlier Engineering, 40 Guests St., 02135, pg. 124 — PB

Barry Wright Intl. Corp., 40 Guest St., 02135, pg. 124 — PB

Brockton

ADAP INC., 525 Campanella Dr., 02401, pg. 4 — PV

CHRISTY'S MARKETS, INC., 22 Christy's Drive, 02401, pg. 238 — PV

Eastern Edison Company, 110 Mulberry St., 02401, pg. 550 — PB

Embassy House Healthcare, 2 Beaumont Ave., 02402, pg. 1712 — PV

Etonic Tretorn, 147 Centre St., 02402-2787, pg. 629 — PV

GZA Drilling, Inc., 1215 W. Chestnut St., 02401, pg. 697 — PB

Goodman Knitting Company, P.O. Box 1100, 300 Manley St., 02403, pg. 948 — PB

GEO. E. KEITH COMPANY, 135 Oak Hill Way, 02401, pg. 611 — PV

Knapp Shoes-Wholesale Division, One Knapp Center, 02401, pg. 401 — PV

New England Wholesale Drug Company, 1150 W. Chestnut St., 02401, pg. 229 — PB

Northern Isles, 300 Manley St., 02403, pg. 948 — PB

Puma North America, 147 Centre St., 02402-2787, pg. 1072 — IT

Tretorn, 147 Centre St., 02402, pg. 1072 — IT

Brookline

BROOKLINE SAVINGS BANK, 160 Washington St., 02146, pg. 171 — PV

HRI Hospital, 227 Babcock St., 02146, pg. 1697 — PB

Burlington

Allied Security Inc., 41 Third Ave., 01803, pg. 40 — PV

Associated Testing Laboratories, Inc., 53 Second Ave., 01803, pg. 1341 — PB

Cerner Corporation -Northeast Region, One New England Executive Pk., 01803, pg. 331 — PB

Cognos Corp., 67 S. Bedford St., Ste. 200 W., 01803-5164, pg. 306 — IT

Cognos Corp.-Boston Sales Office, One Burlington Business Ctr., 67 S. Bedford St., 01803-5164, pg. 306 — IT

DYNATECH CORPORATION, Three New England Executive Pk., 01803-5087, pg. 539 — PB

Epsilon, 50 Cambridge St., 01803, pg. 74 — PB

FAY, SPOFFORD & THORNDIKE, INC., Five Burlington Woods, 01803, pg. 397 — PV

INTERMETRICS, INC., 23 Fourth Ave., 01803-3303, pg. 567 — PV

Intermetrics Securities, Inc., 23 Fourth Ave., 01803-3303, pg. 568 — PV

M/A-Com, Inc. Components Group, 43 South Ave., 01803, pg. 8 — PB

Microwave Semiconductor Group, 43 South Ave., 01803, pg. 8 — PB

NEWSEDGE CORPORATION, 80 Blanchard Rd., 01803, pg. 1180 — PB

OPEN MARKET, INC., One Wayside Rd., 01803, pg. 1226 — PB

ORGANIZATIONAL DYNAMICS INC., 15 New England Executive Pk., 01803, pg. 819 — PV

Polaroid Corp.- Camera Division, One Upland Rd., 01803-1406, pg. 1313 — PB

Raytheon Service Co., Two Wayside Rd., 01803, pg. 1366 — PB

SQA, Inc., One Burlington Woods, 01803, pg. 1361 — PB

Sequent Computer Systems, Inc., 25 Burlington Mall Rd., 01803, pg. 1459 — PB

Sevcon, Inc., 40 North Ave., 01803-3391, pg. 1563 — PB

Sharp Electronics Corporation, 14 Second Avenue, 01803, pg. 1229 — IT

Siemens Nixdorf Information Systems Inc., 200 Wheeler Rd., 01803, pg. 1245 — IT

SuperValu, Inc.-Northeastern Reg., 99 S. Bedford St., Suite 116, 01803, pg. 1540 — PB

Sybase Professional Services, 77 S. Bedford St., 01803, pg. 1544 — PB

Systems Group, 43 South Ave., 01803, pg. 8 — PB

Tellabs Wireless Systems, 30 North Ave., 01803, pg. 1573 — PB

THINKING MACHINES CORPORATION, 16 New England Executive Pk., 01803, pg. 1081 — PV

U.S. Healthcare, Inc. (Massachusetts), Three Burlington Woods Dr., 01803, pg. 26 — PB

U.S. Healthcare of New Hampshire, Inc., Three Burlington Woods Dr., 01803, pg. 27 — PB

Victoria Station Inc., 128 Middlesex Turnpike, 01803, pg. 8 — PV

Videoserver Connections, 63 Third Ave., 01803, pg. 1720 — PB

VIDEOSERVER, INC., 63 3rd Ave., 01803, pg. 1720 — PB

ZOLL MEDICAL CORPORATION, 32 Second Ave., 01803-4420, pg. 1207 — PV

Buzzards Bay

H.L. BOUTON COMPANY INC., 320 Main St., 02532, pg. 162 — PV

Lensclean, Inc., 320 Main St., 02532, pg. 162 — PV

Cambridge

ADVANCED MAGNETICS, INC., 61 Mooney St., 02138-1038, pg. 20 — PB

ALKERMES, 64 Sidney St., 02139, pg. 41 — PB

ALLAIRE CORPORATION, OneAlewife Ctr., 02140, pg. 36 — PB

Ballinger Publishing Co., 54 Church St., 02138, pg. 927 — IT

Banta Integrated Media, 222 Third St., Ste. 174, 02142, pg. 188 — PB

Bio-Rad Digilab Div., 237 Putnam Ave., 02139, pg. 230 — PB

Bio-Rad Semiconductor Systems Div., 237 Putman Ave., 02139, pg. 230 — PB

BIOGEN, INC., 14 Cambridge Ctr., 02142, pg. 230 — PB

Blackwell Publishers, Inc., 238 Main St., 02142, pg. 197 — PB

Blackwell Scientific Publications, Inc., 3 Cambridge Center, Ste. 208, 02142, pg. 197 — IT

CDM Engineers & Constructors Inc., Ten Cambridge Center, 02142, pg. 204 — PV

COM/Energy Acushnet Realty, One Main St., 02142, pg. 414 — PB

COM/Energy Cambridge Realty, One Main St., 02142-9150, pg. 414 — PB

COM/Energy Enterprises, One Main St., 02142-9150, pg. 414 — PB

COM/Energy Freetown Realty, One Main St., 02142-9150, pg. 414 — PB

COM/Energy Research Park Realty, One Main St., 02142-9150, pg. 414 — PB

COM/Energy Resources Inc., One Main St., 02142-9150, pg. 414 — PB

COM/Energy Services Co., One Main St., 02142-9150, pg. 414 — PB

COM/Energy Steam Co., One Main St., 02142-9150, pg. 414 — PB

CSC Index, Inc., 5 Cambridge Center, 02142, pg. 422 — PB

CALIFORNIA PRODUCTS CORP., 169 Waverly, 02139, pg. 201 — PV

Cambridge Electric Light Co., One Main St., 02142-9150, pg. 414 — PB

Cambridge Technology Partners, 304 Vassar St., 02139, pg. 1424 — PB

CAMP DRESSER & MCKEE INC., One Cambridge Ctr., 02142, pg. 203 — PV

Camp Dresser & McKee International Inc., Ten Cambridge Ctr., 02142, pg. 204 — PV

Canal Electric Co., One Main St., 02142-9150, pg. 415 — PB

Cetia Inc., 58 Charles St., 02141, pg. 1383 — IT

Commonwealth Electric Co., One Main St., 02142-9150, pg. 415 — PB

COMMONWEALTH ENERGY SYSTEM, One Main St., 02142-9150, pg. 414 — PB

Commonwealth Energy System, Electric Division, One Main St., 02142-9150, pg. 414 — PB

Commonwealth Energy System, Gas Division, One Main St., 02142-9150, pg. 414 — PB

Commonwealth Gas Co., One Main St., 02142, pg. 415 — PB

Darvel Realty Trust, One Main St., 02142-9150, pg. 415 — PB

Fiberlock Technologies, Inc., 630 Putnam Ave., 02139, pg. 201 — PV

GTE Internetworking, 150 CambridgePark Dr., 02140, pg. 696 — PB

GTE Internetworking, 70 Fawcett St., 01238, pg. 696 — PB

GENERAL LATEX & CHEMICAL CORPORATION, 675 Massachusetts Ave., 02139, pg. 444 — PV

Genetics Institute, Inc., 87 Cambridge Park Dr., 02140, pg. 79 — PB

GENSYM CORPORATION, 125 Cambridge Park Dr., 02140, pg. 731 — PB

GENZYME CORPORATION, One Kendall Sq., 02139-1562, pg. 733 — PB

Grace Construction Products, 62 Whittemore Ave., 02140, pg. 755 — PB

Haviland Candy Inc., 134 Cambridge Ave., 02139, pg. 1113 — PV

Hopkinton LNG Corp., One Main St., 02142-9140, pg. 415 — PB

ISYS Corp., 55 Cambridge Pkwy., 02142, pg. 896 — PB

International Polaroid Corp., 575 Technology Square, 8th Fl., 02139, pg. 1313 — PB

THE LEARNING CO., INC., One Athenaeum St., 02142, pg. 982 — PB

LIFELINE SYSTEMS, INC., 640 Memorial Dr., 02139-4851, pg. 992 — PB

Arthur D. Little Enterprises, Inc., Acorn Park, 02140-2390, pg. 670 — PV

ARTHUR D. LITTLE, INC., 25 Acorn Park, 02140-2390, pg. 670 — PV

Arthur D. Little School of Management, Acorn Park, 02140-2390, pg. 670 — PV

Lotus Business Products Div., 55 Cambridge Pkwy., 02142, pg. 896 — PB

Lotus Development Corporation, 55 Cambridge Pkwy., 02142, pg. 896 — PB

Lotus Engineering & Scientific Products Div., 55 Cambridge Pkwy., 02142, pg. 896 — PB

Lotus Information Center Group, 55 Cambridge Pkwy., 02142, pg. 896 — PB

Lotus Information Network Corporation, 55 Cambridge Pkwy., 02142, pg. 896 — PB

Lotus Information Services Div., 55 Cambridge Pkwy., 02142, pg. 896 — PB

Lotus International Div., 55 Cambridge Pkwy., 02142, pg. 896 — PB

Lotus Research & Development Group, 55 Cambridge, 02142, pg. 896 — PB

MAC-GRAY CORPORATION, 22 Water St., 02141, pg. 1029 — PB

The Net Market Company, 155 Second St., 02141, pg. 321 — PB

New England Confectionery Co., 254 Massachusetts Ave., 02139, pg. 1113 — PV

PB - *U.S. Public Companies Volume*
PV - *U.S. Private Companies Volume*
IT - *International Public & Private Companies Volume*

Geographic Index-U.S.

NEW ENGLAND TECHNOLOGY GROUP, INC., 101 Rogers St., 02142, pg. 793 **PV**
Omega Performance Group, 44 R Brattle St., 02138, pg. 816 **PV**
ON TECHNOLOGY CORPORATION, One Cambridge Ctr., 02142, pg. 1225 **PB**
PMC, Inc., 549 Technology Sq., 02139, pg. 1313 **PB**
Pilot Software, One Canal Pk., 02141, pg. 872 **PV**
Polaroid Asia Pacific Limited, 549 Technology Sq., 02139, pg. 1313 **PB**
Polaroid Caribbean Corp., 549 Technology Sq., 02139, pg. 1313 **PB**
POLAROID CORPORATION, 549 Technology Sq., 02139, pg. 1313 **PB**
Polaroid Foundation, 549 Technology Sq., 02139, pg. 1314 **PB**
PROGRAMART CORPORATION, 124 Mount Auburn St., 02138, pg. 890 **PB**
Recreational Products Div., 169 Waverly, 02139, pg. 201 **PV**
Redgate Communications Corp., Davenport Bldg., 3rd Fl., 25 First St., 02141, pg. 66 **PB**
SEXTON CAN CO., INC., 23 E. St., Ste. 301, 02141, pg. 988 **PB**
Sperry Top-Sider, Inc., Five Cambridge Ctr., 02142, pg. 1525 **PB**
STAR MARKETS COMPANY, INC., 625 Mt. Auburn St., 02138, pg. 1035 **PB**
Stark Candy Company, 254 Massachusetts Ave., 02139, pg. 1113 **PB**
Stride-Rite International, Five Cambridge Ctr., 02142, pg. 1525 **PB**
TAD RESOURCES INTERNATIONAL, INC., 639 Massachusetts Ave., 02139, pg. 1062 **PV**
The Weber Group, 101 Main St., 02142, pg. 1157 **PV**
WEBER PUBLIC RELATIONS WORLDWIDE, 101 Main St., 02142, pg. 1157 **PV**

Canton

BLH Electronics, Inc., 75 Shawmut Rd., 02021, pg. 1289 **IT**
J. BAKER, INC., 555 Turnpike St., 02021, pg. 167 **PB**
BOSTON MUTUAL LIFE INSURANCE CO., 120 Royall St., 02021, pg. 161 **PV**
Brite Voice Systems, 40 Shawmut Road, 02021-1409, pg. 257 **PB**
BUTLER AUTOMATIC, INC., 480 Neponset St., 02021, pg. 189 **PV**
CMI HOLDING CORP., 120 Pequot Way, 02021, pg. 195 **PV**
C.R.H International, Inc., 15 Dan Rd., 02021, pg. 828 **PB**
Chadwick-Miller Inc., Ten Pequot Way, 02021, pg. 195 **PB**
CiMatrix L.L.C., Five Shawmut Rd., 02021, pg. 1395 **PB**
Colgate Oral Pharmaceutical, One Colgate Way, 02021-1597, pg. 397 **PV**
Comdisco Laboratory & Scientific Group, 50 Shawmut Rd., 02021, pg. 408 **PB**
COPLEY PHARMACEUTICALS, INC., 25 John Rd., 02021, pg. 446 **PB**
CUMBERLAND FARMS, INC., 777 Dedham St., 02021, pg. 295 **PV**
DeWolfe & Fiske Inc., P. O. Box 510, Pequot Industrial Pk, 02021, pg. 195 **PV**
JAMES FERRERA & SONS, INC., 135 Will Dr., 02021, pg. 401 **PV**
First United Small Business Investment Co., 135 Will Dr., 02021, pg. 402 **PV**
Great Scott Food Markets, Inc., 135 Will Dr., 02021, pg. 402 **PV**
Hills Department Store Company, 15 Dan Rd., 02021, pg. 828 **PB**
HILLS STORES CO., 15 Dan Rd., 02021, pg. 828 **PB**
Instron Asia, Ltd., 100 Royall St., 02021, pg. 882 **PB**
INSTRON CORPORATION, 100 Royall St., 02021, pg. 882 **PB**
Instron Export Corp., 100 Royall St., 02021, pg. 882 **PB**
Instron Japan Co., Ltd., 100 Royall St., 02021, pg. 882 **PB**
Instron Realty Trust, 100 Royall St., 02021, pg. 883 **PB**
Kinney Vacuum Company, 495 Turnpike St., 02021, pg. 1110 **PV**
Lauriat Inc., Pequot Industrial Pk, 02021, pg. 195 **PV**
Media Recovery Inc.-Massachusetts, 480 Neponset St., 02021, pg. 727 **PV**
Morris Merchants, Inc., 425 Turnpike St., 02021, pg. 1706 **PV**
Morse Shoe, Inc., 555 Turnpike St., 02021, pg. 168 **PB**
Morse Shoe Leased Div., 555 Turnpike St., 02021, pg. 168 **PB**
NIDEC, 152 Will Dr., 02021, pg. 933 **IT**
NIDEC Power General, 152 Will Dr., 02021, pg. 933 **IT**
THE PASTENE COMPANIES LTD., 275 Turnpike St., 02021, pg. 842 **PV**
PLYMOUTH RUBBER COMPANY, INC., 104 Revere St., 02021, pg. 1311 **PB**
Pollak-Switching, 300 Dan Rd., 02021, pg. 1045 **PV**
S.W.B. & Company, P.O. Box 264, 28 Cedar St., 02021, pg. 941 **PV**
Stream International Holdings Inc., 275 Dan Rd., 02021, pg. 518 **PB**
THOMPSON STEEL CO., INC., 120 Royall St., 02021, pg. 1083 **PV**
Wilson/Shore Instruments, 100 Royall St., 02021-1089, pg. 883 **PB**
XRL Corporation, 150 Dan Rd., 02021-2849, pg. 569 **PB**

Chelmsford

ADRA SYSTEMS, INC., Two Executive Dr., 01824, pg. 18 **PV**

ESA, INC., 22 Alpha Rd., 01824, pg. 354 **PV**
ESA Laboratories, 22 Alpha Rd., 01824, pg. 354 **PV**
Freudenberg Nonwovens Limited Partnership, 20 Industrial Ave., 01824, pg. 505 **PV**
Freudenberg Pellon Corporation, 20 Industrial Ave., 01824, pg. 507 **PV**
ITK INTERNATIONAL, INC., One Executive Dr., 01824, pg. 556 **PB**
ITK Telecommunications, Inc., One Executive Dr., 01824, pg. 556 **PB**
Intergraph Corporation, Optronics Div., Seven Stuart Rd., 01824, pg. 891 **PB**
Intergraph Corporation, Optronics Div., 21 Alpha Rd., 01824, pg. 891 **PB**
Lockheed Martin Microwave-FSI, 16 Maple Rd., 01824, pg. 1008 **PB**
MERCURY COMPUTER SYSTEMS, INC., 199 Riverneck Rd., 01824-2820, pg. 732 **PB**
Microwave Radio Communications, 20 Alpha Rd., 01824, pg. 294 **PB**
NEPA-Massachusetts, Inc., #6 Courthouse Ln., 01863, pg. 1036 **PB**
New England CRInc., 12 Elizabeth Dr., 01824, pg. 1753 **PB**
Semtech Northeast Region, 221 Chelmsford St., Ste. #3, 01824, pg. 1456 **PB**
SKY Computers, Inc., 27 Industrial Ave., 01824, pg. 109 **PB**

Chelsea

CATAMOUNT PETROLEUM, P.O. Box 9151, 90 Everett Ave., 02150-2337, pg. 220 **PV**
DAV-EL WORLDWIDE, 200 Second St., 02150, pg. 314 **PV**
Gulf Oil, P.O. Box 9151, 90 Everett Ave., 02150-2337, pg. 295 **PV**
GULF OIL LIMITED PARTNERSHIP, 90 Everett Ave., 02150, pg. 487 **PV**
KAYEM FOODS, INC., 75 Arlington St., 02150, pg. 610 **PV**
TTS Corporation, 100 Everett Ave., 02150-2328, pg. 262 **PV**
TOWN & COUNTRY CORPORATION, 25 Union St., 02150, pg. 1625 **PB**
Town & Country Fine Jewelry Group, Inc., 25 Union St., 02150, pg. 1625 **PB**

Chestnut Hill

GC COMPANIES, INC., 1300 Boylston St., 02167, pg. 593 **PB**
GC International, Inc., 1280 Boylston St., 02167, pg. 593 **PB**
GCC Investments, Inc., 1300 Boylston St., 02167, pg. 593 **PB**
General Cinema Theatres, Inc., 1280 Boylston St., 02167, pg. 593 **PB**
HARCOURT GENERAL, INC., 27 Boylston St., 02167, pg. 784 **PB**
Maine Associates, 1330 Boylston St., 02167, pg. 361 **PB**
The Neiman-Marcus Group, Inc., 27 Boylston St., 02167, pg. 784 **PB**
SAFETY 1ST, INC., 210 Boylston St., 02167, pg. 1425 **PB**

Chicopee

COLLINS ELECTRIC COMPANY, INC., 53 Second Ave., 01020, pg. 253 **PV**
DHP LIMITED PARTNERSHIP, 45 Plainfield, 01013, pg. 302 **PV**
Dudley Sports Co. Division, P.O. Box 7053, 521 Meadow St., 01021-7053, pg. 629 **PV**
FACEMATE CORPORATION, Five W. Main St., 01020, pg. 391 **PV**
Ludlow Technical Products Div., Two Ludlow Park, 01021, pg. 1347 **PV**
Lym-Tech Scientific, P.O. Box 157, 01014, pg. 683 **PV**
JOHN R. LYMAN COMPANY, 60 Depot St., 01013, pg. 683 **PV**
Mullen Testers, 939 Chicopee St., 01013-2797, pg. 1506 **PV**
Newark Paperboard Products Mercer Div., 70 Better Way, 01022, pg. 796 **PV**
Raytheon Engineers & Constructors, One Broadway, 0102C, pg. 1366 **PB**
Spalding P.O. Box 901, 425 Meadow St., 01013, pg. 629 **PV**
Spalding & Evenflo Companies, Inc., 425 Meadow St., 01021, pg. 629 **PV**
Spalding Sports Worldwide, 425 Meadow Street, 01021, pg. 630 **PV**
Sundor Brands Inc./Lincoln, 106 Longzak, 01022, pg. 1331 **PB**

Clinton

Delta Suprenant Wire & Cable Inc., 172 Sterling St., 01510, pg. 391 **IT**
LFE Industrial Systems Corporation, 55 Green St., 01510, pg. 1045 **PB**
LFE Traffic Control, 55 Green St., 01510, pg. 1045 **PB**
ROCKBESTOS-SUPRENANT CABLE CORP., 172 Sterling St., 01510, pg. 938 **PV**
The Weetabix Company, Inc., 20 Cameron St., 01510, pg. 1488 **IT**

Concord

Allied Plywood Corporation, 200 Baker Ave., Suite 210, 01742-2112, pg. 1193 **PB**
MANUFACTURERS' SERVICES LTD., 200 Baker Ave., 01742, pg. 701 **PV**
Oxford Instruments, 130A Baker Ave. Ext., 01742, pg. 1018 **IT**
STARMET CORPORATION, 2229 Main St., 01742, pg. 1511 **PB**
Sybase Inc., 561 Virginia Rd., 01742, pg. 1544 **PB**
TOTH DESIGN, 30 Monument Sq., 01742, pg. 1093 **PV**
Walden House Healthcare, 785 Main St., 01742, pg. 1715 **PB**
Welch Foods Inc., A Cooperative, Three Concord Farms, 555 Virginia Rd., 01742, pg. 784 **PV**

Dalton

CRANE & CO., INC., 30 South St., 01226, pg. 286 **PV**
Radar Companies, Inc., 401 South St., 01226, pg. 789 **PB**

Danvers

Ahlstrom Inc., One Corporate Plaza, 55 Ferncroft Rd, Ste. 200, 01923, pg. 35 **IT**
Fishery Products International USA, 18 Electronics Ave., 01923, pg. 492 **IT**
Fuddruckers, Inc., One Corporate Pl., 55 Ferncroft Rd., 01923, pg. 325 **IT**
Greenery Extended Care Center at Danvers, 56 Liberty St., 01923, pg. 836 **PB**
ITW Adhesives, 30 Endicott St., 01923, pg. 866 **PB**
ITW Devcon Industrial, 30 Endicott St., 01923, pg. 866 **PB**
ITW Engineered Polymers Businesses, 30 Endicott St., 01923, pg. 866 **PB**
Medtronic Interventional Vascular, 37A Cherry Hill Dr., 01923-5186, pg. 1083 **PB**
PENCO-New England States, 311 Liberty Sq., 01923, pg. 1508 **IT**
PictureTel Corporation-World Headquarters, The Tower at Northwoods, 222 Rosewood Dr., 01923, pg. 1295 **PB**
PictureTel International Corp.-Asia Pacific/Americas Headquarters, The Tower at Northwoods, 222 Rosewood Dr., 01923, pg. 1295 **PB**
Signal Capital Corporation, 55 Ferncroft Rd., 01923, pg. 115 **PB**
Turbine Engine Components Textron, P.O. Box 30, 54 Cherry Hill Dr., 01923-0030, pg. 1588 **PB**
Unique Casual Restaurants, inc., One Corporate Pl., 55 Ferncroft Rd., 01923, pg. 324 **IT**
VG Instruments Inc., 32 Commerce, Cherry Hill Dr., 01923, pg. 1594 **PB**
Ventron Div., 150 Andover St., 01923, pg. 1135 **PB**

Dedham

ALIMED, INC., 297 High St., 02026, pg. 34 **PV**
Bell Atlantic North, 990 Washington St. # 332, 02026-6714, pg. 203 **PB**
Lindenmeyr Central, 990 Washington St., 02026, pg. 224 **PV**
Lindenmeyr Paper, 990 Washington St., Ste 205s, 02026, pg. 224 **PV**
LOJACK CORPORATION, 333 Elm St., 02026, pg. 1012 **PB**
NATIONAL AMUSEMENTS, INC., 200 Elm St., 02027, pg. 775 **PV**
PAPA GINO'S INC., 600 Providence Hwy., 02026, pg. 837 **PV**
Robert Scott/David Brooks, 122 Allied Dr., 02026, pg. 948 **PB**

Dorchester

SWIFT INSTRUMENTS, INC., 952 Dorchester Ave., 02125, pg. 1058 **PV**

Dracut

Keating Materials, 2140 Bridge St., 01826, pg. 611 **PV**

Dudley

Gentex Optics, Inc., P.O. Box 307, 183 W. Main St., 01571, pg. 462 **IT**

East Boston

Circle Frieght International USA, 160 McClellan Hwy., 02128, pg. 371 **PB**
Circle International, 160 McClellan Hwy., 02128, pg. 371 **PB**
Leonard Florence Associates, 175 McClellan Hwy., pg. 1061 **PV**
GODDESS BRA COMPANY, 156 Porter St., 02128, pg. 458 **PV**
Max Gruenhut International Inc. USA, 160 McClelland Hwy., 02128, pg. 372 **PB**
SYRATECH CORPORATION, 175 McClellan Hwy., 02128-9114, pg. 1060 **PV**
Towle Manufacturing Corporation, 175 McClellan Hwy., 02128, pg. 1061 **PV**

PB - *U.S. Public Companies Volume*
PV - *U.S. Private Companies Volume*
IT - *International Public & Private Companies Volume*

Geographic Index-U.S.

1268

East Bridgewater

The Foxboro Company, 600 N. Bedford St., 02333, pg. 1243   IT

Shaw's Supermarkets, Inc., 140 Laurel St., 02333, pg. 1170   IT

East Dedham

PRUDENTIAL METAL SUPPLY CORP., 171 Milton St., 02026, pg. 893   PV

East Longmeadow

AMERICAN SAW & MFG. COMPANY, 301 Chestnut St., 01028, pg. 61   PV

Milton Bradley Company, 443 Shaker Rd., 01028, pg. 797   PB

East Walpole

Ciba Corning Diagnostics Corporation, 333 Coney St., 02032, pg. 973   IT

HOLLINGSWORTH & VOSE CO., 112 Washington St., 02032, pg. 534   PV

East Weymouth

BRADY ENTERPRISES, INC., 167 Moore Rd., 02189, pg. 165   PV

Easthampton

Stanley Home Products, 50 Payson Ave., 01027, pg. 282   PB

Tubed Products, Inc., 44 O'Neill St., 01027, pg. 1066   PB

Easton

Dana Lighting, Inc., 55 Norfolk Ave., 02375, pg. 314   PB

Erving

Erseco, Inc., 45 E. Main St., 01344-0248, pg. 382   PV

ERVING INDUSTRIES, INC., 120 E. Main St., 01344, pg. 382   PV

Erving Paper Mills, Inc., 97 E. Main St., 01344-0038, pg. 382   PV

Everett

Coldwater Seafood Corp., 60 Commercial St., 02149, pg. 251   PV

DANIELS PRINTING COMPANY, 40 Commercial St., 02149, pg. 310   PV

JP Foodservice, Inc.-Boston, 201 Beacham St., 02149, pg. 918   PB

Joan & David Helpern, Inc., 1935 Revere Beach Pkwy., 02149, pg. 521   PV

Prolerized New England Co., 60 Rover St., 02149, pg. 1440   PB

Fairhaven

Acushnet Company, 333 Bridge St., 02719-0965, pg. 675   PB

Acushnet International Inc., 333 Bridge St., 02719-0965, pg. 675   PB

Citizens Bank of Massachusetts, 215 Washington St., 02719, pg. 1132   IT

Titleist & Foot-Joy Worldwide, 333 Bridge St., 02719-0965, pg. 675   PB

Fall River

Aberdeen Mfg. Corp. Louis Hand Plant, 847 Pleasant St., 02722, pg. 1094   PV

ASHWORTH BROS., INC., 89 Globe Mills Ave., 02724, pg. 89   PV

Fall River Gas Appliance Co., Inc., 155 N. Main St., 02720, pg. 612   PB

FALL RIVER GAS COMPANY, 155 N. Main St., 02722, pg. 611   PB

J & J Corrugated Box, P.O. Box 1231, 350 N. Main St., 02720-1231, pg. 736   PB

Lightolier Division, 631 Airport Rd., 02720, pg. 730   PB

MOLTEN METAL TECHNOLOGY, INC., 421 Currant Rd., 02720, pg. 1123   PB

Northeast Publishing, Inc.-The Herald News, 207 Pocasset Street, 02722-3010, pg. 935   PB

PARKS CORPORATION, One West St., 02720-1311, pg. 840   PV

PRIORITY FINISHING CORP., 160 Stevens St., 02722, pg. 887   PV

QUAKER FABRIC CORPORATION, 941 Grinnell St., 02722, pg. 1347   PB

The Richman Brothers Co., 502 Bedford St., 02720, pg. 1777   PB

WHALING INDUSTRIES, INC., 387 Quarry St., 02723, pg. 1170   PV

Whaling Manufacturing Company, Inc., 387 Quarry St., 02732, pg. 1170   PV

Fitchburg

CheMarketing International, Inc., 99 Development Rd., 01420, pg. 173   IT

ChemDesign Corporation, 99 Development Rd., 01420, pg. 173   IT

Fitchburg Gas and Electric Light Co., 285 John Fitch Hwy., 01420-8207, pg. 1692   PB

NICHOLAS PAPER, INC., 435 Main St., 01420, pg. 798   PV

PWA Rolland Decor Inc., 642 River St., 01420, pg. 274   IT

Safety Fund National Bank, 470 Main St., 01420, pg. 278   PB

SIMONDS INDUSTRIES INC., 135 Intervale Rd., 01420-0500, pg. 1001   PV

Technical Specialties Division, 44 Old Princeton Rd., 01420, pg. 620   PV

Florence

Perstorp Compounds Inc., 238 Nonotuck St., 01060, pg. 1037   IT

Perstorp Inc., 92 Main St., 01060, pg. 1039   IT

SUMMIT PLASTIC SOLUTIONS, INC., 296 Nonotuck St., 01062, pg. 1050   PV

Foxboro

EMS Eastern Regional Office, 100 Foxboro Blvd., 02035, pg. 565   PB

Equipment Sales Co., 34 School St., Ste. 209, 02035, pg. 594   PB

The Foxboro Company, 33 Commercial St., 02035, pg. 1243   PB

MAGUIRE GROUP INC., 225 Foxborough Blvd., 02035, pg. 696   PV

New England Tap Corporation (NETCO), 132 Central St., Ste. 16, 02035, pg. 368   PB

Siebe North Inc., 33 Commercial St., 02035, pg. 1242   IT

Framingham

Allcom, Inc., 139 Newbury St., 01701, pg. 711   PB

ARROW AUTOMOTIVE INDUSTRIES, INC., Three Speen St., 01701, pg. 133   PB

BOSE CORPORATION, The Mountain, 01701-9168, pg. 160   PV

CIO Publishing Corp., 492 Old Connecticut Path, 01701, pg. 569   PV

CHARLES RIVER DATA SYSTEMS, INC., 46 Park St., 01702, pg. 230   PV

Cigna Healthcare of Massachusetts, Inc., 20 Speen St., 01701, pg. 360   PB

COMPUTER CORPORATION OF AMERICA, 500 Old Connecticut Path, 01701-9378, pg. 260   PV

Computerworld, Inc., 500 Old Connecticut Park, 01701, pg. 569   PV

Consolidated Group, Inc., 15 Pleasant St., 01701, pg. 351   PV

CREATIVE PLAYTHINGS LTD., 33 Loring Dr., 01701, pg. 287   PV

Customer Development Corporation, 492 Old Connecticut Path, 3rd Fl., 01701, pg. 298   PV

Dennison Data Systems Div., 300 Howard St., 01701, pg. 152   PB

Dennison Fastener Div., 300 Howard St., 01701, pg. 152   PB

Dennison Imaging Systems Div., 300 Howard St., 01701, pg. 152   PB

Dennison International Co., 300 Howard St., 01701, pg. 153   PB

Dennison Panamericana, Inc., 300 Howard St., 01701, pg. 152   PB

Dennison Specialty Products Div., 300 Howard St., 01701, pg. 152   PB

Dennison Therimage Div., 300 Howard St., 01701, pg. 152   PB

Dennison Transoceanic Corporation, 300 Howard, 01701, pg. 152   PB

Dun & Bradstreet Software (Framingham), 550 Cochituate Rd., 01701-9324, pg. 532   IT

Ericsson Network Systems, Inc., 1661 Worcester Rd., Ste. 202, 01701, pg. 1364   IT

Genzyme Transgenics, 5 Mountain Rd., 01701, pg. 733   PB

HomeGoods, 492 Old Connecticut Pass, 01701, pg. 1557   PB

IDG Communications Research, 492 Old Conneticut Path, 01701, pg. 569   PV

IDG List Services, 492 Old Conneticut Path, 01701, pg. 569   PV

IG Laboratories, Inc., One Mountain Road, 01701, pg. 733   PB

IMS/International, 500 Old Conneticut Path, 01701, pg. 569   PV

International Data Corp., 5 Speen St., 01701, pg. 570   PV

MarketPulse, 500 Old Connecticut Pass, 01701-9378, pg. 260   PV

The Marmax Group, 770 Cochituate Rd., 01701, pg. 1557   PB

Marshalls, Inc., 770 Cochituate Rd., 01701, pg. 1557   PB

The Middlesex News, 33 New York Ave., 01701, pg. 794   PB

Network World, Inc., Five Speen St., 01701, pg. 569   PV

Paramount Development Assocs., Inc., Box 9160, 73 Mt. Wayte Ave., 01701, pg. 1278   PB

Perini Building Co., Inc. U.S. Heavy Division, Box 9160, 73 Mt. Wayte Ave., 01701, pg. 1278   PB

PERINI CORPORATION, 73 Mt. Wayte Ave., 01701, pg. 1278   PB

Perini Land and Development Co., Box 9160, 73 Mt. Wayte Ave., 01701, pg. 1278   PB

Perini Management Services, Inc., Box 9160, 73 Mt. Wayte Ave., 01701, pg. 1278   PB

PerSeptive Biosystems, Inc., 500 Old Connecticut Path, 01701, pg. 1279   PB

Symbol, 205 Newbury St., Ste. 410, 01701, pg. 1546   PB

T.J. Maxx, 770 Cochituate Rd., 01701, pg. 1557   PB

THE TJX COMPANIES, INC., 770 Cochituate Rd., 01701, pg. 1556   PB

TMP Worldwide/Interactive Division, Two Kendall St., Ste. 301, 01701, pg. 1065   PV

Therimage Products Div., 300 Howard St., 01701, pg. 152   PB

World Expo Corporation, P.O. Box 9107, 111 Speen St., 01701-9107, pg. 571   PV

Zeneca Pharmaceuticals, 205 Newbury St., Ste. 407, 01701, pg. 1525   IT

Franklin

AI/FOCS, Inc., 130 Constitution Blvd., 02038, pg. 1776   PB

BIW Cable Systems, Inc., 20 Forge Pk., 02038, pg. 417   IT

Chromatic Technologies, Inc., Nine Forge Pkwy., 02038, pg. 417   IT

Coastal Marketing Inc., 430 Frankin Village Dr., Ste. 178, 02038-4020, pg. 390   PB

Draka U.S.A., Nine Forge Pkwy., 02038, pg. 417   IT

Franklin House Healthcare, 130 Chestnut St., 02038, pg. 1712   PB

Garelick Farms, Inc., 1199 W. Central St., 02038, pg. 1527   PB

Helix/Hi-Temp Cables, Inc., 9 Forge Parkway, 02038, pg. 417   IT

Klockner-Moeller Corp., 25 Forge Pkwy., 02038, pg. 736   IT

Thermo Environmental Instrument Inc., 8 West Forge Pkwy., 02038, pg. 1593   PB

Thermo Jarrell Ash Corporation, 27 Forge Pkwy., 02038-3148, pg. 1594   PB

Van Leer Metallized Products (USA) Ltd., 24 Forge Pkwy., 02038, pg. 1146   IT

WWF Paper Corp.-New England, 290 Beaver St., 02038, pg. 1145   PV

Gardner

S. BENT & BROTHERS, INC., 85 Winter St., 01440, pg. 134   PV

Collier-Keyworth Company, One Tuttle Pl., 01440, pg. 985   PB

Gem Industries NE Inc., 525 Parker St., 01440, pg. 442   PV

SIMPLEX TIME RECORDER CO., Simplex Plaza, 01441, pg. 1002   PV

Georgetown

Salomon-North America Inc., 400 E. Main St., 01833, pg. 1181   IT

UFP TECHNOLOGY, 172 E. Main St., 01833, pg. 1112   PV

Gloucester

BATTENFELD GLOUCESTER ENGINEERING CO. INC., P.O. Box 900, Blackburn Industrial Park, 01930, pg. 123   PV

Battenfeld Gloucester Engineering Co., Inc., P.O. Box 900, Blackburn Industrial Park, 01930, pg. 825   IT

Flex-Key Corporation, 18 Sargent St., 01930, pg. 142   PB

The Gorton Group, 128 Rogers St., 01930, pg. 1434   IT

Ion Implant Systems, Blackburn Industrial Park, 35 Dory Rd., 01930, pg. 1710   IT

Kona Corporation, P.O. Box 1227, 35 Emerson Ave., 01930, pg. 138   PV

Musician Magazine, P.O. Box 701, 31 Commercial St., 01930, pg. 1446   IT

NUTRAMAX PRODUCTS, INC., Nine Blackburn Dr., 01930-2237, pg. 1206   PB

Rule Industries, Inc., Cape Ann Industrial Park, 01930, pg. 950   PB

Great Barrington

Great Barrington Healthcare, 148 Maple Ave., 01230, pg. 1712   PB

Greenfield

ROGERS, LUNT & BOWLEN CO., 298 Federal St., 01301, pg. 939   PV

RUGG MANUFACTURING COMPANY, 105 Newton St., 01302, pg. 950   PV

Groton

NEW ENGLAND BUSINESS SERVICE, INC., 500 Main St., 01471, pg. 1170   PB

Hanson

LITECONTROL CORPORATION, 100 Hawks Ave., 02341, pg. 669   PV

Geographic Index-U.S.

Haverhill

Conmed Andover Medical, Inc., 60 Newark St., 01832, pg. 431 **PB**
The Haverhill Gazette, 447 W. Lowell Ave., 01831, pg. 1343 **PB**
PLASTIC ENGINEERING CO. INC., 35 Walnut St., 01830, pg. 871 **PV**
United Foam Plastics Corporation, 175 Ward Hill Ave., 01835, pg. 1112 **PV**

Hingham

DM MANAGEMENT COMPANY, 25 Recreation Park Dr., 02043, pg. 473 **PB**
DynaVac, 110 Industrial Pk. Rd., 02043, pg. 1076 **PV**
Harris Rebar Boston, Inc., 295 Lincoln St., 02043, pg. 598 **IT**
Massachusetts-American Water Co., P.O. Box 9112, 75 Sargent Wm. B. Terry Dr., Ste. 170, 02043-1545, pg. 95 **PB**
Massachusetts Capital Resources Company, 75 Sargent Wm. B. Terry Dr., Ste. 170, 02043-1545, pg. 95 **PB**
Talbots, Inc., 175 Beal St., 02043, pg. 28 **IT**

Holbrook

S-N Bedding Co. Inc., 12 Mear Road, 02343, pg. 1249 **IT**

Holden

Reedspectrum, Holden Industrial Park, 01520, pg. 624 **IT**

Holliston

EASY DAY MANUFACTURING COMPANY, P.O. Box 8000, 01746-8000, pg. 358 **PV**
Lista International Corporation, 106 Lowland St., 01746, pg. 812 **IT**
TMP Worldwide, Inc., The TMP Bldg., 125 Hopping Brook Rd., 01746, pg. 1064 **PV**

Holyoke

Atlas Copco Berema, Inc., 161 Lower Westfield Rd., 01040, pg. 96 **IT**
Atlas Copco Compressors, Inc., 161 Lower Westfield Rd., 01040, pg. 96 **IT**
Autron Incorporated, P.O. Box 350, 01040, pg. 845 **PV**
CDI Managed Services, 150 Lower Westfield Rd., 01040, pg. 277 **PB**
Dennison Stationery Products Company, Sullivan Rd., 01040, pg. 1258 **PB**
Dielectric Polymers, Inc., 218 Race St., 01040, pg. 1258 **PB**
Dual Manufacturing & Engineering, Inc., 80 Bigelow St., 01040, pg. 432 **PV**
HAZEN PAPER COMPANY, 240 S. Water St., 01040, pg. 514 **PV**
Holyoke Food Mart, Inc., 2215 N. Hampton St., 01040, pg. 1375 **IT**
Holyoke Power and Electric Co., One Canal St., 01040, pg. 1195 **PB**
Holyoke Water Power Co., One Canal St., 01040, pg. 1195 **PB**
JPS Elastomerics Corp., 9 Sullivan Rd., 01040-2800, pg. 578 **PV**
Parsons Paper Div. of NVF Co., 84 Sargeant St., 01040, pg. 772 **PV**
TOTSY MANUFACTURING COMPANY, INC., One Bigelow St., 01040, pg. 1093 **PV**

Hopedale

MKRD-Laser Service, Five Airport Dr., 01747, pg. 685 **PV**

Hopkinton

Dennison Imaging Systems Div., 86 South Street, 01748, pg. 152 **PB**
EMC CORPORATION, 171 South St., 01748-9103, pg. 545 **PB**
INTERFACE ELECTRONICS CORPORATION, 228 South St., 01748, pg. 567 **PB**
Earle M. Jorgensen Company/Boston, 59 South St., 01748, pg. 600 **PV**
Matec Applied Sciences, Inc., 75 South St., 01748, pg. 1056 **PB**
MATEC CORPORATION, 75 South St., 01748, pg. 1056 **PB**
SierraCom, 99 South St., 01748, pg. 999 **PV**
Valpey-Fisher Corporation, 75 South St., 01748, pg. 1056 **PB**
Valpey-Fisher Frequency Control Div., 75 South St., 01748, pg. 1056 **PB**
Valpey-Fisher Ultrasound Div., 75 South St., 01748, pg. 1056 **PB**
Zymark Corporation, Zymark Center, 68 Elm St., 01748, pg. 139 **PV**

Hudson

ACT MANUFACTURING, 108 Forest Ave., 01749, pg. 3 **PB**
AMERICAN TECHNOLOGY CORPORATION, 428 Main St., 01749, pg. 63 **PV**

THE ENTWISTLE COMPANY, Bigelow St., 01749, pg. 378 **PV**
Hudson Demand Services, 36 Parmenter Rd., 01749, pg. 518 **PB**
Hudson Mfg. Division, 555 Main St., 01749-2912, pg. 518 **PB**
Hypertronics Corporation, 16 Brent Dr., 01749, pg. 1268 **IT**
Kaman Electromagnetics Corp., Two Fox Rd., 01749, pg. 942 **PB**

Hyannis

CAPE COD POTATO CHIP COMPANY, 100 Breed's Hill Rd., 02601, pg. 205 **PB**
Educational Finance Group, One Financial Pl., Ste. 2-2, 297 North St., 02601, pg. 1679 **PV**
Greenery Rehabilitation & Skilled Nursing Center, 89 Lewis Bay Rd., 02601, pg. 837 **PB**

Hyde Park

Howden Sirocco, Inc., One Westinghouse Plaza, 02136, pg. 636 **IT**
Work 'n Gear, 65 Sprague St., 02136, pg. 168 **PB**

Indian Orchard

HEAT BATH PARK METALLURGICAL CORP., 107 Front St., 01151, pg. 518 **PV**
JANLYNN CORPORATION, 34 Front St., 01151, pg. 582 **PV**

Ipswich

Converter Power, Inc., Locust Rd., 01938, pg. 856 **PB**
Micro-Mech. Inc., 33 Newburyport Tpke., 01938, pg. 578 **IT**

Lakeville

Ocean Spray International Inc., One Ocean Spray Dr., 02349, pg. 811 **PV**
Ocean Spray International Services, Inc., One Ocean Spray Dr., 02349, pg. 811 **PV**
SAIC Engineering, Inc., Ten Riverside Dr., 02347, pg. 376 **PV**

Lancaster

River Terrace Healthcare, Ballard Hill Rd., 01523, pg. 714 **PB**

Lawrence

AGRI-MARK, INC., P.O. Box 5800, 100 Milk St., 01842, pg. 26 **PV**
Cerplex Mass, Inc., 270 Merimack St., 01843, pg. 332 **PB**
Freudenberg Building Systems, Inc., 94 Glenn St., 01843, pg. 506 **IT**
Lawrence Division, 360 Merrimack St., Bldg. #1, 01843, pg. 27 **PV**
LAWRENCE PUMPS, INC., 371 Market St., 01843, pg. 654 **PV**
Lawrence Savings Bank, 255 Essex Street, 01842, pg. 930 **PB**
MALDEN MILLS INDUSTRIES, INC., 46 Stafford St., 01844, pg. 698 **PV**
OOMPHIES, INC., 350 Merry Mack St., 01843, pg. 817 **PV**
Stride Rite Footwear, Inc., Five Franklin St., 01840, pg. 1525 **PB**

Lenox

Beloit Lenox, Div., Crystal St., 01240, pg. 789 **PB**

Leominster

Alphagary Corporation, P.O. Box 808, 170 Pioneer Dr., 01453, pg. 802 **IT**
Claremont Flock, Scott Dr., 01453, pg. 242 **PV**
Costech, 111 Crawford St., 01453, pg. 870 **PV**
DSM Thermoplastic Elastomers Inc., 690 Mechanic St., 01453-4451, pg. 355 **IT**
Imaging Services, 27 Nashua St., 01453, pg. 1076 **IT**
Lakso Div., 44 Mead St., 01453, pg. 832 **PV**
Mohawk/CDT, 9 Mohawk Dr., 01453, pg. 287 **PB**
Omnirel Corporation, 205 Crawford St., 01453, pg. 1792 **PB**
Pferd, Inc., 30 Jytek Dr., 01453, pg. 1046 **IT**
Polaroid Corp. Research & Development - General Scanning, P.O. Box 1263, 01453-8263, pg. 1313 **PB**
Quebecor Printing Eusey Press Inc., 27 Nashua St., 01453, pg. 1078 **PB**
Tamor Corp., 20 Mohawk Dr., 01453, pg. 832 **PB**
Tucker Housewares, 25 Tucker Dr., 01453, pg. 1118 **PB**

Lexington

Chase Access Services Corp., 95 Haydon Ave., 02173, pg. 337 **PB**
DRI/McGraw-Hill, 24 Hartwell Ave., 02173, pg. 1071 **PB**
Thomas K. Dyer, Inc., 1762 Massachusetts Ave., 02173, pg. 492 **PV**
Emerson & Cuming Specialty Polymers, 55 Hayden Ave., 02173, pg. 1435 **IT**
Fresenius Medical Care, Inc., Two Ledgemont Ctr., 92 Hayden Ave., 02173, pg. 505 **IT**

Fresenius Medical Care (North America), 95 Hayden Ave., 2 Ledgemont Ctr., 02173, pg. 505 **IT**
HAMPSHIRE CHEMICAL CORP., 55 Hayden Ave., 02173, pg. 498 **PV**
Hospital Staffing Services of Massachusetts, Inc., 430 Beford St., Ste. 325, 02173, pg. 840 **PB**
Interactive Data Corporation, Two Ledgemont Center, 95 Hayden Ave., 02173-9144, pg. 1025 **IT**
The Keds Corporation, 191 Spring St., 02173, pg. 1525 **PB**
Lockheed Martin Infared Imaging Systems, Two Forbes Rd., 02173, pg. 1008 **PB**
Logica, Inc., 32 Hartwell Ave., 02173, pg. 814 **IT**
NUMBER NINE VISUAL TECHNOLOGY, 18 Hartwell Ave., 02173-3103, pg. 1206 **PB**
PALOMAR MEDICAL TECHNOLOGIES, 45 Hartwell Ave., 02173, pg. 1255 **PB**
RAYTHEON COMPANY, 141 Spring St., 02173, pg. 1364 **PB**
Raytheon Engineers & Constructors International, Inc., 125 Spring St., 02173, pg. 1366 **PB**
SRA - Boston, Lexington Office Pk., 430 Bedford St., Ste. 175, 02173, pg. 958 **PV**
Seratronics, Inc., Two Ledgemont Ctr., 95 Hayden Ave., 02173, pg. 505 **IT**
Stride Rite Children's Group, Inc.-Retail Div., 191 Spring St., 02173, pg. 1525 **PB**
THE STRIDE RITE CORPORATION, 191 Spring St., 02173, pg. 1524 **PB**
Woodward-Clyde, One Cranberry Hill, 02173, pg. 1657 **PB**

Littleton

Angiographic Devices, P.O. Box 1154, 300 Foster St., pg. 1596 **PB**
Borden Foods Co., 119 Russell St., Ste. 30, 01460, pg. 158 **PV**
Whittaker Xyplex, 295 Foster St., 01460, pg. 1767 **PB**
XRE Corporation, 300 Foster St., 01460, pg. 1595 **PB**

Lowell

ACACIA NETWORKS, INC., 650 Suffolk St., 01854, pg. 11 **PV**
BRADFORD INDUSTRIES, INC., 1857 Middlesex St., 01851, pg. 163 **PV**
Bull Electronics, 1001 Pawtucket Blvd., 01854, pg. 316 **IT**
COLONIAL GAS COMPANY, 40 Market St., 01852-1806, pg. 400 **PB**
Courier Companies, Inc., 165 Jackson St., 01852, pg. 453 **PB**
EUA Citizens Conservation Services, Inc., Boott Mills South, 100 Foot of John St., 01852, pg. 549 **PB**
EUA Cogenex Corporation, Boott Mills S., 100 Foot of John St., 01852, pg. 549 **PB**
Healthcare Staffing Solutions, Inc., Cross Point Towers II, pg. 1373 **PB**
Ideal Tape Company, 1400 Middlesex St., 01851, pg. 69 **PB**
Interstate Container Corporation, Industrial Ave. E., 01853, pg. 573 **PV**
M/A-COM Inc., 1011 Pawtucket Blvd., 01853, pg. 8 **PB**
MSC Aries, 600 Suffolk St., 01854, pg. 1031 **PB**
MSC Lowell Office, 600 Suffolk St., 01854, pg. 1031 **PB**
Network Systems Integration, 246 Market St., 01853, pg. 711 **PB**
Northeast Energy Management, Boott Mills S., 100 Foot of John St., 01852, pg. 549 **PB**
Prince Foods Div., Prince Ave., 01853, pg. 158 **PV**
Textron Systems Corporation, Two Industrial Ave., 01851-5199, pg. 1589 **PB**
Transgas Inc., 87 Industrial Ave., 01852, pg. 401 **PB**
U.S. Filter, Ten Technology Dr., 01851, pg. 1682 **PB**

Ludlow

LUDLOW TEXTILES CO., INC., State St., 01056, pg. 680 **PV**

Lunenburg

P.J. KEATING COMPANY, Reservoir Rd., 01462, pg. 610 **PV**
MAKI CORPORATION, 160 Mass Ave., 01462, pg. 697 **PV**
Maki Home Center, Inc., 160 Mass Ave., 01462, pg. 698 **PV**

Lynn

EASTERN SMELTING & REFINING CORPORATION, 37-39 Bubier St., 01901, pg. 357 **PV**
Richdale Dairy Stores, Inc., 626 Lynnway, 01905, pg. 969 **PV**
SCANGAS BROTHERS HOLDINGS, INC., 626 Lynway, 01905, pg. 969 **PV**
West Lynn Creamery, Inc., 626 Lynnway, 01905, pg. 969 **PV**
West Lynn Creamery Realty Corporation, 626 Lynnway, 01905, pg. 969 **PV**

Lynnfield

Boston Acoustics Foreign Sales Corp., 70 Broadway, 01940, pg. 246 **PB**

Malden

ACME CANVAS CO., INC., 171 Medford St., 02148, pg. 13 — PV
ASAHI/AMERICA, INC., 35 Green St., P.O. Box 653, 02148, pg. 137 — PB
James Brudnick Company, 219 Medford St., 02148, pg. 1007 — PV
Century Products Inc., 171 Medford St., 02148, pg. 13 — PV
HealthGate Data Corp., 380 Pleasant St., Ste. 230, 02148, pg. 1182 — PB
NEW ENGLAND COFFEE COMPANY, 100 Charles St., 02148, pg. 792 — PV
PALMER MANUFACTURING COMPANY, 243 Medford St., 02148, pg. 835 — PV
Toromont Process Systems Inc., 200 Maplewood St., 02148, pg. 1401 — IT

Mansfield

Albany International Research Co., 777 West St., 02048-9114, pg. 36 — PB
Robert Allen Ametek, 55 Cabot Blvd., 02048, pg. 432 — PV
Ametex Fabrics, Inc., 120 Forbes Blvd., 02048, pg. 432 — PV
Augat, Inc., P.O. Box 448, 89 Forbes Blvd., 02048, pg. 1597 — PB
CTI Cryogenics Div., Mansfield Corp. Ctr., Nine Hampshire St., 02048, pg. 808 — PB
Ceramtec North America Applications, Inc., 171 Forbes Blvd., 02048-1148, pg. 860 — IT
F.H. CHASE, INC., 120 Forbes Blvd., 02048, pg. 230 — PV
Grace Cocoa/Merckens, 150 Oakland St., 02048, pg. 128 — PB
HELIX TECHNOLOGY CORP., Mansfield Corp. Ctr., Nine Hampshire St., 02048-9171, pg. 808 — PB
The Kendall Company, 15 Hampshire St., 02048, pg. 1647 — PB
Kendall Healthcare Products Company, One Mansfield Corp. Center, 15 Hampshire St., 02048, pg. 1647 — PB
Lindenmeyr Munroe, 240 Forbes Blvd., 02048, pg. 224 — PV
Polyken Technologies, 15 Hampshire St., 02048, pg. 1647 — PB

Marblehead

Beringer Division, P.O. Box 485, 01945, pg. 774 — IT
Berlinger Div., P.O. Box 485, Berligner Way, 01945, pg. 773 — PV
Norman Levy Associates, Inc., Two Catherine Lane, 01945, pg. 664 — PV

Marlborough

Aromat New England Sales Office, 5 Mount Royal Ave., 01752, pg. 848 — IT
ARTEL VIDEO SYSTEMS, INC., 237 Cedar Hill St., 01752, pg. 86 — PV
THE BUTCHER COMPANY, 67 Forest St., 01752-3012, pg. 189 — PV
CONCORD COMMUNICATIONS, INC., 33 Boston Post Rd. W., 01752, pg. 429 — PB
Encore Computer Corporation, 300 Nickerson Rd., 2nd Fl., 02370, pg. 580 — PV
Handex of New England, Inc., 398 Cedar Hill St., 01752, pg. 499 — PV
Isis Distributed Systems, Inc., 55 Fairbanks Blvd., 01752, pg. 1524 — PB
Kidde Technologies Inc., 700 Nickerson Rd., 01752, pg. 1500 — IT
Koehler Manufacturing Company, 123 Felton St., 01752, pg. 706 — PV
Massachusetts Container Corporation, 300 Cedar Hill St., 01752, pg. 263 — PV
MEDIA 100, INC., 290 Donald Lynch Blvd., 01752-4748, pg. 1079 — PB
Merisel, 293 Boston Post Rd. W., 01752, pg. 1096 — PB
Olicom, Inc., 450 Donald Lynch Blvd., 01752-4728, pg. 1001 — IT
The Ramsey Company, 120 Bartlett St., 01752, pg. 189 — PV
Raytheon Electronics Systems, 1001 Boston Post Rd., 01752, pg. 1364 — PB
The Rockport Company, 220 Donald J. Lynch Blvd., 01752, pg. 1370 — PB
Shipley Co., LLC, 455 Forest St., 01752, pg. 1403 — PB
STRATUS COMPUTER, INC., 55 Fairbanks Blvd., 01752, pg. 1524 — PB
Viewlogic Systems Group, 293 Boston Post Rd. W., 01752-4615, pg. 1548 — PB
Worcester Controls Corp., 33 Locke Dr., 01752, pg. 128 — IT

Marshfield

Abington-Rockland Mariner, 165 Enterprise Dr., P.O. Box 682, 02050, pg. 700 — PB
Braintree Forum, 165 Enterprise Dr., P.O. Box 682, 02050, pg. 700 — PB
Canton News, 165 Enterprise Dr., P.O. Box 682, 02050, pg. 700 — PB
Cohasset Mariner, 165 Enterprise Dr., P.O. Box 682, 02050, pg. 700 — PB
Hanover Mariner, 165 Enterprise Ave., P.O. Box 682, 02050, pg. 701 — PB
Hingham Mariner, 165 Enterprise Dr., P.O. Box 682, 02050, pg. 701 — PB

The Holbrook Sun, 165 Enterprise Dr., P.O. Box 682, 02050, pg. 701 — PB
Kingston Independent Voice, 165 Enterprise Dr., P.O. Box 682, 02050, pg. 701 — PB
Mariner Newspapers, Inc., 165 Enterprise Dr., 02050, pg. 701 — PB
Marshfield Mariner, 165 Enterprise Dr., P.O. Box 682, 02050, pg. 701 — PB
Norwell Mariner, 165 Enterprise Dr., P.O. Box 682, 02050, pg. 701 — PB
Pembroke Mariner, 165 Enterprise Dr., P.O. Box 682, 02050, pg. 701 — PB
Randolph Mariner, 165 Enterprise Dr., P.O. Box 682, 02050, pg. 701 — PB
Scituate Mariner, 165 Enterprise Dr., P.O. Box 682, 02050, pg. 701 — PB
Weymouth News, 165 Enterprise Dr., P.O. Box 682, 02050, pg. 702 — PB

Mashpee

Augat, Inc., Interconnection Products-Mashpee, 106 Salmouth Rd., 02649, pg. 1598 — PB

Mattapoisett

Loga Athletic/Headwear Inc., Five Industrial Dr., 02739-0961, pg. 1644 — PB

Maynard

DIGITAL EQUIPMENT CORPORATION, 111 Powdermill Rd., 01754-1499, pg. 507 — PB

Medfield

CIBA Corning Diagnostics Corp., 63 North St., 02052-1688, pg. 973 — IT

Medford

August A. Busch & Co. of Massachusetts, Inc., 440 Riverside Ave., 02155, pg. 114 — PB
HOUSE OF BIANCHI, INC., One Brainard Ave., 02155, pg. 541 — PV
PC Week, Ten Presidents Landing, 02155, pg. 1276 — IT
Rowenta (USA), Inc., 196 Boston Ave., 4th Fl., 02155, pg. 569 — IT
Ziff Information Services, Ten Presidents Landing, 02155, pg. 1276 — IT
Ziff Technologies, Ten Presidents Landing, 02155, pg. 1276 — IT

Medway

Cybex International, Inc., Ten Trotter Dr., 02053, pg. 1114 — PV

Melrose

ARMATRON INTERNATIONAL, INC., Two Main St., 02176, pg. 131 — PB
Automatic Radio International, Two Main St., 02176, pg. 131 — PB
Echovision Division, Two Main St., 02176, pg. 131 — PB
Flowtron/Galaxie Division, Two Main St., 02176, pg. 131 — PB

Merrimac

WOLVERINE MASSACHUSETTS CORPORATION, 51 E. Main St., 01860, pg. 1186 — PV

Methuen

Flexible Circuit Products Division, 145 Milk St., 01844, pg. 1264 — PB
Lawrence Savings Bank, 20 Jackson Street, 01844, pg. 980 — PB
Lawrence Savings Bank, 148 Lowell Street, 01844, pg. 980 — PB
MICROTOUCH SYSTEMS, INC., 300 Griffin Pk., 01844, pg. 1108 — PB
NSC Corporation, 49 Danton Dr., 01844, pg. 1208 — PB
National Surface Cleaning, Inc., 49 Danton Dr., 01844, pg. 1208 — PB
PARLEX CORPORATION, 145 Milk St., 01844, pg. 1264 — PB

Middleboro

ALDEN SHOE CO., INC., One Taunton St., 02346, pg. 33 — PV
Greenery Rehabilitation & Skilled Nursing Center, P.O. Box 1330, Isaac St., 02346, pg. 837 — PB
Nordberg-Read, Inc., 25 Wareham St., 02346, pg. 1428 — IT
OCEAN SPRAY CRANBERRIES, INC., One Ocean Spray Dr., 02349, pg. 811 — PV
SAIC Engineering, Inc., 101 E. Grove St., 02346, pg. 976 — PV
Thermo Consulting Engineers Inc., 101 East Grove St., 02346, pg. 1594 — PB
WINTHROP-ATKINS CO., INC., 35 E. Main St., 02346, pg. 1183 — PV

Middleton

AUTOROLL MACHINE CO., LLC, 11 River St., 01949, pg. 101 — PV
Bell Atlantic Yellow Pages, 35 Village Rd., 01949, pg. 203 — PB
Bostik, Inc., Boston Street, 01949, pg. 1409 — IT
Middleton Aerospace Corporation, 206 S. Main St., 01949, pg. 124 — IT

Milford

BOSTON DIGITAL CORP., Granite Park, 125 Fortune Blvd., 01757, pg. 161 — PV
CLEARPOINT ENTERPRISES, 25 Birch St., Unit B41, 01757, pg. 245 — PV
Fenwal Electronics, Inc., 450 Fortune Blvd., 01757, pg. 1341 — PB
Intergen Center for Diagnostic Products, 25 Birch St., 01757, pg. 567 — PB
Millipore Intertech, 34 Maple St., 01757, pg. 1113 — PB
PC CONNECTION, INC., 528 Rte. 13, 03055, pg. 826 — PV
STRAWBERRIES INC., 205 Fortune Blvd., 01757, pg. 1046 — PV
TSI Corporation, 25 Birch St., 01757-3574, pg. 733 — PB
WATERS CORPORATION, 34 Maple St., 01757, pg. 1745 — PB
Waxie Maxie Quality Music Co., 205 Fortune Blvd., 01757, pg. 1047 — PV

Millbury

Coppus Murray Group, Tuthill Corporation, Millbury Park, P.O. Box 8000, 01527-8000, pg. 1110 — PV
NEW ENGLAND NEWSPAPER SUPPLY COMPANY, INC., 9 Railroad Ave., 01527, pg. 793 — PV

Monson

Zero Plastics, 288 Main St., 01057, pg. 1791 — PB

Natick

Alpine American, Five Michigan Dr., 01760, pg. 635 — IT
BJ'S WHOLESALE CLUB, INC., One Mercer Rd., 01760, pg. 162 — PB
BOSTON SCIENTIFIC CORP., One Boston Scientific Pl., 01760, pg. 247 — PB
COGNEX CORPORATION, One Vision Dr., 01760, pg. 394 — PB
HEC, Inc., 24 Prime Pkwy., 01760, pg. 1194 — PB
Market Facts, Inc., One Apple Hill, 01760, pg. 1047 — PB
PAINE FURNITURE CO., 323 Speen St., 01760, pg. 834 — PV

Needham

AIRONET Wireless Communications, Inc., 160 Gould St., Ste. 130, 02194-2300, pg. 1573 — PB
Allyn & Bacon, 160 Gould St., 02194-2310, pg. 778 — PV
American Bank Note Company, 75 Second Ave., Ste. 430, 02194, pg. 68 — PB
AST Research, Inc, 6th Floor, 75 Second Ave., 02194, pg. 188 — IT
Banta Digital Group, 114 First Ave., 02194-2805, pg. 188 — PB
CARE MATRIX CORP., 197 First Ave., 02194, pg. 305 — PB
Coca-Cola Bottling Co. of New England, Nine B St., 02194, pg. 393 — PB
DESIGNS, INC., 66 B St., 02194, pg. 501 — PB
The Designs/OLS Partnership, c/o Designs, Inc., 66 B St., 02194, pg. 501 — PB
Dreyer's New England Division, 629 Highland Ave., 02194, pg. 529 — PB
Duracell Inc. Environmental, 37 A St., 02194-2806, pg. 743 — PB
GTE Government Systems Corporation, 77-A Street, 02194-2892, pg. 696 — PB
Ginn Division, 160 Gould St., 02194-2310, pg. 778 — PV
LILY TRANSPORTATION CORP., 145 Rosemary St., 02194, pg. 667 — PV
MEDITRUST CORPORATION, 197 First Ave., Ste. 300, 02194-9127, pg. 1081 — PB
TIE Systems, Inc. New England, 10 Kearney Rd., 02194, pg. 1085 — PB
WFXT-TV, 100 Second Ave., 02194, pg. 926 — IT

New Bedford

Aegis, Inc., 50 Welby Rd., 02745, pg. 1219 — PB
AEROVOX INC., 740 Bellville Ave., 02745, pg. 25 — PB
Alberox Corporation, Industrial Park, 02745, pg. 893 — IT
BRITTANY DYEING & PRINTING CORPORATION, 1357 E. Rodney French Blvd., 02741, pg. 170 — PV
Cliftex, 194 Riverside Ave., 02746, pg. 1777 — PB
EPEC, INC., 174 Duchaine Blvd., 02745, pg. 379 — PB
Frionor U.S.A. Inc., 40 Herman Melville Blvd., 02741, pg. 516 — IT
Rodney Metals, 1357 E. Rodney French Blvd., 02744-2124, pg. 43 — PB
SHEPARD CLOTHING COMPANY, 800 Acushnet Ave., 02740, pg. 992 — PV
U.S. Ring Binder Corp., 429 Church St., 02745, pg. 707 — PB
Velvet Drive Transmissions, 200 Theodore Rice Blvd., 02745-1290, pg. 1370 — PB

Geographic Index-U.S.

Newburyport

Alfa Laval Contherm Inc., 111 Parker St., 01950, pg. 1378   **IT**
BIXBY INTERNATIONAL CORP., One Preble Rd., 01950, pg. 146   **PV**
SAMUEL CABOT, INC., 100 Hale St., 01950, pg. 198   **PV**
Genus Inc.-Ion Technology Products, Four Stanley Tucker Dr., 01950, pg. 732   **PB**
Gould Electronics Inc., Shawmut Circuit Protection Division, 374 Merrimac St., 01950 -1998, pg. 1592   **PB**
Henschel Corp., Nine Hoyt Dr., 01950, pg. 957   **PV**

Newton

Bostonian Shoe Co., 156 Oak St., 02164, pg. 297   **IT**
Butterworth-Heinemann USA, 313 Washington St., 02158, pg. 1094   **IT**
CAMBRIDGE SOUNDWORKS, INC., 311 Needham St., 02164, pg. 202   **PB**
Cellcor, 200 Wells Ave., 02159, pg. 471   **PB**
Clarks Cos. N.A., Upper Falls, 156 Oak St., 02164, pg. 297   **IT**
Computer Enterprises, Inc., 109 Oak St., 02164, pg. 1072   **PV**
EDP/TEMPS Inc., 109 Oak St., 02164, pg. 1072   **PV**
Firestone Financial, 38 Glen Ave., 02159, pg. 1660   **PB**
FRED V. FOWLER COMPANY, INC., 66 Rowe St., 02166, pg. 422   **PV**
GZA GeoEnvironmental, Inc., 320 Needham St., 02164, pg. 697   **PB**
GZA GEOENVIRONMENTAL TECHNOLOGIES, INC., 320 Needham St., 02164, pg. 697   **PB**
GEO-CENTERS, INC., Seven Wells Ave., 02159, pg. 447   **PV**
Hanover Stores, 156 Oak St., Upper Falls, 02164, pg. 297   **IT**
HEALTH AND RETIREMENT PROPERTIES TRUST, 400 Centre St., 02158, pg. 801   **PB**
Home Care p.r.n., Inc., 109 Oak St., 02164, pg. 1072   **PV**
Hygeia Sciences, Inc., 330 Nevada St., 02160-1432, pg. 310   **PB**
Ivex Packaging Corporation-Industrial Products Division, 55 Tower Rd., 02164, pg. 915   **PB**
Mall of New Hampshire, One Wells Ave., 02159, pg. 361   **PB**
Manchester Mall Joint Venture, One Wells Ave., Ste. 300, 02159, pg. 361   **PB**
Marcam Corporation, North American Operations, 95 Wells Ave., 02159, pg. 1043   **PB**
MARCAM SOLUTIONS, INC., 95 Wells Ave., 02159, pg. 1042   **PB**
Micromet Instruments, Inc., Seven Wells Ave., 02159, pg. 447   **PV**
MicroTemps Systems & Programming, 109 Oak St., 02164, pg. 1072   **PV**
NRC Inc., 45 Industrial Pl., 02164, pg. 173   **IT**
Reed Elsevier Business Information, 275 Washington St., 02158, pg. 1095   **IT**
Regalite Plastic Corp., 300 Needham St., 02164, pg. 1234   **PV**
SRI-Soil & Rock Instrumentation, 320 Needham St., 02164, pg. 697   **PB**
Seaboard Flour Corporation, 200 Boylston St., 02167, pg. 1449   **PB**
Softbank Holdings Inc., 10 Langley Rd., Ste. 403, 02159, pg. 1276   **IT**
STACKPOLE LTD., 85 Wells Ave., 02159, pg. 1028   **IT**
Sunrise Healthcare Corporation, 2101 Washington St., 02162, pg. 1531   **PB**
Systems Management & Development, 109 Oak St., 02164, pg. 1072   **PV**
TAC/Medical Services Inc., 109 Oak St., 02164, pg. 1072   **PV**
TAC/TEMPS Inc., 109 Oak St., 02164, pg. 1072   **PV**
TECHNICAL AID CORPORATION, 109 Oak St., 02164, pg. 1072   **PV**
Worcester Center, One Wells Ave., 02159, pg. 362   **PB**

North Adams

Excelsior Printing Co., 60 Roberts Dr., 01247, pg. 286   **PV**
Excelsior Process & Engraving Inc., Curan Hwy., Rte. 8, 02147, pg. 286   **PV**
Morrison Berkshire Inc., 865 S. Church St., 01247, pg. 762   **PV**

North Andover

Greenery Extended Care Center of North Andover, 75 Park St., 01845, pg. 837   **PV**
LAWRENCE SAVINGS BANK, 30 Massachussetts Ave., 01845, pg. 980   **PB**
Lawrence Savings Bank, 30 Massachussetts Ave., 01845, pg. 980   **PB**
MIC Technology Corporation, 797 Turnpike St., 01845, pg. 24   **PB**
Manotec Communications, 40 High St., 01845, pg. 1373   **IT**
Schneider Automation, Inc., One High St., 01845, pg. 980   **PB**
WATTS INDUSTRIES, INC., 815 Chestnut St., 01845-6098, pg. 1746   **PB**

North Attleboro

APV Crepaco, Inc., Dryer Div., 165 John L. Dietsch Sq., 02763, pg. 1240   **IT**

General Findings, 57 John L. Dietsch Sq., 02761, pg. 655   **PV**
Handy & Harman Electronic Materials Corp., 72 Elm St., 02761, pg. 780   **PB**
LEACH & GARNER COMPANY, 57 John L. Dietsch Sq., 02761, pg. 655   **PV**
North Attleboro Gas Company, 62 Reed Ave., 02760, pg. 1337   **PV**
Thomas & Betts, P.O. Box 2510, 452 John Dietsch Blvd., 02763, pg. 1598   **PB**

North Billerica

BTU Engineering Corporation, 23 Esquire Rd., 01862, pg. 164   **PB**
BTU INTERNATIONAL, INC., 23 Esquire Rd., 01862, pg. 164   **PB**
General Latex & Chemical Corporation, 200 Iron Horse Pk., 01862, pg. 444   **PV**
Guilford Rail System, Iron Horse Park, High Street, 01862, pg. 487   **PV**
IEA, Inc.-Massachusetts, 149 Rangeway Rd., 01862, pg. 126   **PB**
Spincraft Massachusetts, 67 High St., 01862, pg. 1506   **PB**

North Chelmsford

COURIER CORPORATION, 15 Wellman Ave., 01863, pg. 453   **PB**

North Dighton

American Auto Auction, Inc., 123 Williams St., 02764, pg. 282   **PV**
BIW Cable Manufacturing Plant, 22 Joseph E. Warner Blvd., 02764, pg. 417   **IT**
THE HARODITE FINISHING COMPANY INC., 66 South St., 02764, pg. 503   **PV**
Princess House, Inc., 455 Somerset Ave., 02754, pg. 399   **PB**

North Falmouth

BENTHOS, INC., 49 Edgerton Dr., 02556, pg. 212   **PB**
TapTone Container Inspection Systems, 49 Edgerton Dr., 02556, pg. 212   **PB**

North Grafton

WYMAN-GORDON, 244 Worcester St., 01536, pg. 1782   **PB**
Wyman-Gordon Forgings, P.O. Box 8001, 244 Worcester St., 01536, pg. 1782   **PB**

North Oxford

Standard Wool, Inc., P.O. Box 760, 627 Main St., 01537, pg. 1502   **PV**

North Reading

CONVERSE INC., One Fordham Rd., 01864, pg. 441   **PB**
Lindenmeyr Munroe, 200 Riverpack Dr., 01864, pg. 224   **PV**

North Uxbridge

Nelmor Co., Inc., Rivulet St., 01538, pg. 1041   **PV**

Northampton

DataViews, 47 Pleasant St., 01060, pg. 539   **PB**
Electro Optical Div., 347 King St., 01060, pg. 965   **PB**

Northborough

Crystal Biotech, Inc., 56 Hudson St., 01532, pg. 1056   **PB**
Diamond Film Division, Goddard Rd., 01532, pg. 1171   **PV**
Ericsson Business Communications, Inc., 50 Bearfoot Rd., 01532, pg. 1364   **IT**
Isomedix Operations Inc., 435 Whitney St., 01532, pg. 1515   **PB**
Matec Instruments, Inc., 56 Hudson St., 01532, pg. 1056   **PB**

Northbridge

Coz Plastics Inc., P.O. Box 940, Providence Rd., 01534, pg. 827   **PV**

Norton

Eureka Manufacturing Co., Inc., 47 Elm St., 02766, pg. 913   **PV**
Hallsmith-Sysco Food Services, 380 S. Worcester St., 02766, pg. 1550   **PB**

Norwell

Chicago Rivet & Machine Co.-Automated Assembly Systems, 74 Accord Park Dr., 02061, pg. 349   **PB**
Kluwer Academic Publishers, 101 Philip Dr., 02061, pg. 1513   **IT**
Richardson Electronics Ltd.-Northeastern, 167 Washington St., 02061, pg. 1388   **PB**
Wearguard Corp., Longwater Dr., 02061, pg. 79   **PV**

AVEDIS ZILDJIAN COMPANY, 22 Longwater Dr., 02061, pg. 1206   **PV**

Norwood

ADVANCED INSTRUMENTS, INC., Two Technology Way, 02062, pg. 22   **PV**
ANALOG DEVICES, INC., One Technology Way, 02062-9106, pg. 107   **PB**
Bandwidth Optimization Business Unit, 63 Nahatan St., 02062, pg. 1568   **PB**
Bird Incorporated, 1077 Pleasant St., 02062, pg. 1170   **IT**
Bird Roofing Products, Inc., 1077 Pleasant St., 02062, pg. 1171   **IT**
Broadband Business Unit, 63 Nahatan St., 02062, pg. 1568   **PB**
Compdata Services Corp., 320 Norwood Park S., 02062-5702, pg. 277   **PB**
Computer Products Division, One Technology Way, 02062, pg. 108   **PB**
Fluor Daniel GTI, Inc., 100 River Ridge Rd., 02062, pg. 660   **PB**
GAGGENAU USA CORPORATION, 425 University Ave., 02062, pg. 437   **PV**
Innovative Membrane Systems, Inc., 189 Dean St., 02062, pg. 1320   **PB**
JET SPRAY CORP., 825 University Ave., 02062, pg. 586   **PV**
Jet Spray International, 825 University Ave., 02062, pg. 587   **PV**
Keystone New England Warehouse-Norwood, 117 Lenox St., 02062, pg. 955   **PB**
Microcom, 500 River Ridge Dr., 02062-5028, pg. 417   **PB**
Phoenix Technologies Ltd., 846 University Ave., 02062-3950, pg. 1292   **PB**
THE SAVOGRAN COMPANY, 259 Lenox St., 02062, pg. 968   **PV**
Strato/Infusaid, Inc., 1400 Providence Hwy., 02062-9998, pg. 1284   **PB**
Subaru of New England, Inc., 95 Morse St., 02062, pg. 523   **IT**
TELCO SYSTEMS, INC., 63 Nahatan St., 02062, pg. 1568   **PB**

Orange

RODNEY HUNT COMPANY, 46 Mill St., 01364-1268, pg. 549   **PV**
KRH Rolls Inc., P.O. Box 422, Orange Industrial Airpark, 01364-0422, pg. 1202   **IT**

Orleans

NICKERSON LUMBER COMPANY, 15 Main St., 02653, pg. 798   **PV**

Oxford

Dart Trucking Company, Inc., 200 Old Webster Rd., 01540, pg. 94   **PB**
Webster Spring Co., Inc., 430 Main St., 01540, pg. 986   **PB**

Palmer

Jarvis (East), 127 S. Main St., 01069, pg. 1506   **PB**
Palmer House Healthcare, P.O. Box 566, Shearer St., 01609, pg. 1714   **PB**
Rathbone Precision Metals, 1241 Parker St., 01069, pg. 307   **PB**

Peabody

Anadventure II Corporation, Three Centennial Dr., 01960, pg. 109   **PB**
ANALOGIC CORPORATION, Eight Centennial Dr., 01960, pg. 109   **PB**
Analogic Scientific, Eight Centennial Dr., 01961, pg. 109   **PB**
APPLIED EXTRUSION TECHNOLOGIES, INC., Three Centennial Dr., 01960, pg. 122   **PB**
BOSTON ACOUSTICS, INC., 300 Jubilee Dr., 01960, pg. 246   **PB**
CHELSEA INDUSTRIES, INC., 58 Palasky St., 01960, pg. 231   **PV**
Coltec Peabody Division, Fifth St., 01960, pg. 402   **PB**
Eastman Gelatine Corp., 227 Washington St., 01960, pg. 551   **PB**
HYDE ATHLETIC INDUSTRIES, INC., 13 Centennial Dr., 01960, pg. 851   **PB**
JEOL (U.S.A.), Inc., 11 Dearborn Road, 01960, pg. 697   **IT**
Medical Imaging Products Group, Eight Centennial Dr., 01960, pg. 109   **PB**
METAPOINT PARTNERS, Three Centennial Dr., 01960-7931, pg. 735   **PV**
Snell Acoustics, 300 Jubilee Dr., 01960, pg. 246   **PB**
TransCapacity, L.P., 83 Pine St., Ste. 101, 01960, pg. 550   **PB**
Walbar Inc., Peabody Industrial Center, 01960, pg. 402   **PB**
Walbar Turbine Components Division, P.O. Box 3369, Peabody Industrial Ctr., 01960, pg. 402   **PB**
Webster Industries Div., 58 Pulaski St., 01960, pg. 231   **PV**
Xerox Imaging Systems, Inc., Nine Centennial Dr., 01960, pg. 1785   **PB**

Pembroke

HYER INDUSTRIES INC./THAYER SCALE, Rte. 139, 02359, pg. 552   **PV**

PB - *U.S. Public Companies Volume*
PV - *U.S. Private Companies Volume*
IT - *International Public & Private Companies Volume*

1272

Pittsfield

THE BERKSHIRE GAS COMPANY, 115 Cheshire Rd.,
01201, pg. 216 — **PB**
BERKSHIRE LIFE INSURANCE COMPANY, 700 South St.,
01201, pg. 136 — **PV**
G.E. Plastics, One Plastics Ave., 01201, pg. 710 — **PB**
General Dynamics, 100 Plastics Ave., 01201, pg. 1006 — **PB**
General Dynamics Defense Systems, 100 Plastics Ave.,
01201, pg. 709 — **PB**
Kay-Bee Toy & Hobby Shops, Inc., 100 West St., 01201,
pg. 437
PETRICCA INDUSTRIES, INC., 550 Chesire Rd., 01201,
pg. 858 — **PV**

Plainville

THE HILSINGER CO. L.P., 33 W. Bacon St., 02762,
pg. 530 — **PV**
PLAINVILLE STOCK COMPANY, INC., 104 South St.,
02762, pg. 868 — **PV**

Plymouth

BVA Cogen, Inc., 33 Christa McAuliffe Blvd., 02360,
pg. 1787 — **PB**
Kao Infosystems Company (MA), 40 Grissom Rd., 02360,
pg. 717 — **IT**
PartyLite Gifts, Inc., 59 Armstrong Rd., 02360, pg. 239 — **PB**
Richards Micro-Tool, Inc., 250 Nicks Rock Rd., 02360,
pg. 1054 — **PB**

Pocasset

Data Industrial Corporation, 53 Portside Dr., 02559,
pg. 487 — **PB**

Quincy

American Overseas Marine Corp., 116 E. Howard St.,
02169, pg. 709 — **PB**
BAY STATE MILLING CO., 100 Congress St., 02169,
pg. 124 — **PV**
Boston Financial Data Services, Inc., Two Heritage Dr.,
02171, pg. 1513 — **PB**
Boston Gear, 14 Hayward St., 02171, pg. 857 — **PB**
Commercial Union Life Insurance Company of America,
Newport Office Park, 108 Myrtle St., 02171-1753,
pg. 308 — **IT**
Compu-Mark, 500 Victory Rd., 02171, pg. 1601 — **PB**
NFPA Research Foundation, One Batterymarch Pk.,
pg. 783 — **PV**
NATIONAL FIRE PROTECTION ASSOCIATION, One
Batterymarch Park, 02269, pg. 782 — **PV**
GEORGE W. PRESCOTT PUBLISHING CO., 400 Crown
Colony Dr., 02169, pg. 882 — **PV**
QUINCY MUTUAL FIRE INSURANCE COMPANY, 57
Washington, 02169-9155, pg. 901 — **PV**
The Stop & Shop Companies, Inc., 1385 Hancock St.,
02169, pg. 750 — **IT**
Superior Brands, Inc., 122 Quincy Shore Dr., 02171,
pg. 917 — **IT**
Thomson & Thomson, 500 Victory Rd., 02171-1545,
pg. 1601 — **PB**

Randolph

BMS On-Line Services, Inc., 31 West St., 02368,
pg. 647 — **PB**
Chase & Sons Division, 19 Highland Ave., 02368,
pg. 337 — **PB**
Delphax Systems, 35 Pacella Park Dr., 02368, pg. 153 — **PB**
Dunkin' Donuts Incorporated, 14 Pacella Park Dr., 02368,
pg. 63 — **IT**
Louis Kmito & Son, Inc., P.O. Box 199, 02368, pg. 264 — **PB**
Ohio-Sealy Mattress Manufacturing Co., Inc., One
Posturepedic Dr., 02368, pg. 979 — **PV**

Raynham

Johnson & Johnson Professional, Inc., 325 Paramount Dr.,
02767, pg. 928 — **PB**
TRUCCHIS MARKETS, 1062 Broadway, 02767,
pg. 1107 — **PV**

Reading

Addison-Wesley Higher Education, Jacob Way, 01867,
pg. 1026 — **IT**
Addison-Wesley Longman, Inc., One Jacob Way, 01867,
pg. 1026 — **IT**
The Education Publishing Group, Jacob Way, 01867,
pg. 1026 — **IT**
The General Publishing Group, Jacob Way, 01867,
pg. 1026 — **IT**
The International Publishing Group, Jacob Way, 01867,
pg. 1027 — **IT**
TASC, Inc., 55 Walkers Brook Dr., 01867, pg. 1325 — **PB**
Triad Personnel Services, 23 Walkers Brook Dr., Ste. 46,
01867, pg. 715 — **PB**

Readville

BURTMAN IRON WORKS, INC., 31 Industrial Dr., 02137,
pg. 188 — **PV**

Rehoboth

WNAC, 33 Pine St., 02769, pg. 926 — **IT**

Revere

Coastal Oil New England, Inc., 222 Lee Burbank Hwy.,
02151, pg. 390 — **PB**
IDB WorldCom, 300 Ocean Ave., 02151, pg. 1779 — **PB**
LDDS/WorldCom Communications, 300 Ocean Ave.,
02151, pg. 1779 — **PB**
TREND-LINES INC., 135 American Legion Hwy., 02151,
pg. 1099 — **PV**
Union-Transport Corporation-Boston, 30 Railroad Ave.,
02151, pg. 1119 — **PV**

Rockland

SIMS Level 1 Inc., 160 Weymouth St., 02370,
pg. 1268 — **IT**
Vaponics Inc., 20 Reservoir Park Dr., 02370, pg. 1234 — **PB**

Russell

TEXON MATERIALS INC., 1190 Huntington Rd., 01071,
pg. 1079 — **PV**

Salem

Atwood & Morrill Co., Inc., 285 Canal St., 01970,
pg. 1489 — **IT**
EG & G Optoelectronics-Salem, 35 Congress St., 01970,
pg. 543 — **PB**
Victoria Station Inc., Pickering Wharf, 01970, pg. 8 — **PV**

Saugus

Henkel Leather Chemicals Div., P.O. Box 1151, 222 Central
St., 01906, pg. 610 — **IT**

Sharon

Dynisco, Inc., Four Commercial St., 02067, pg. 138 — **PV**
EA Engineering, Science & Technology, Inc., Sharon
Commerce Center, 2 Commercial St., Ste. 106, 02067,
pg. 541 — **PB**

Sheffield

DSM Sheffield Plastics, 119 Salisbury Rd., 01257,
pg. 354 — **IT**

Shelburne Falls

Lamson and Goodnow Mfg. Co., 45 Conway St., 01370,
pg. 940 — **PV**

Shrewsbury

ELKAY PRODUCTS, INC., 800 Boston Turnpike, 01545,
pg. 372 — **PV**
Quantum, 333 S. St., 01545-4112, pg. 1350 — **PB**

Somerset

ALDEN AUTO PARTS WAREHOUSE, INC., 535 Grand
Army Hwy., 02725, pg. 33 — **PV**

Somerville

AMES SAFETY ENVELOPE COMPANY, INC., 21 Properzi
Way, 02143, pg. 66 — **PV**
HERB CHAMBERS COS., 259 McGrath Hwy., 02145,
pg. 227 — **PV**
Houghton Mifflin Interactive Corp., 120 Beacon St., 02143,
pg. 841 — **PB**
MASSACHUSETTS ENVELOPE CO., 30 Cobble Hill Rd.,
02143, pg. 712 — **PV**
SSB Leeway Corp., Davis Sq., 212 Elm St., 02144,
pg. 1484 — **PB**
JOHN SOLOMON, INC., 515 Somerville Ave., 02143,
pg. 1013 — **PV**
SOMERSET SAVINGS BANK, 212 Elm St., 02144,
pg. 1484 — **PB**
Somerville Lumber & Supply Co., 779 McGrath Hwy.,
02145, pg. 1268 — **PB**
M.S. WALKER, INC., 20 Third Ave., 02143, pg. 1147 — **PV**

South Dartmouth

Concordia Custom Yachts, 300 Gulf Rd., 02748,
pg. 968 — **PV**

South Deerfield

CHANNING L. BETE CO., INC., 200 State Rd., 01373,
pg. 140 — **PV**
Deerfield Urethane, Inc., Rtes. 5 and 10, 01373,
pg. 173 — **IT**
Rule Cutting Tools, Inc., Deerfield Industrial Park, 01373,
pg. 951 — **PB**

South Easton

Pharmosol Corporation, One Norfolk Rd., P.O. Box 326,
02375, pg. 446 — **IT**
Pitney Bowes Direct, P.O. Box 1000, 63 Norfolk Ave.,
02375-1190, pg. 1304 — **PB**

South Hadley

Electronic Internconnect Systems Inc., 775 New Ludlow
Rd., 01075, pg. 955 — **IT**
Rexam DSI, One Canal St., 01075, pg. 1106 — **IT**
Rexam Graphics, 28 Gaylord St., 01075, pg. 1107 — **IT**

South Lee

Mead Specialty Paper, Willow St., Rte. 102, 01260,
pg. 1074 — **PB**

South Walpole

Bird Machine Company, 100 Neponset St., 02071-9103,
pg. 166 — **PB**

Southborough

Data General Customer Service Division, Coslin Dr., 01772,
pg. 485 — **PB**
NEW ENGLAND FROZEN FOODS, INC., One Harvest Ln.,
01772, pg. 793 — **PV**
3Com Corporation, 118 Turnpike Rd., 01772, pg. 1604 — **PB**

Southbridge

AOTEC, 14 Mechanic, 01550, pg. 60 — **PV**
American Optical Corp., 14 Mechanic St., 01550,
pg. 60 — **PV**
American Optical-Safety Division, 14 Mechanic St., 01550,
pg. 289 — **PB**
HYDE MANUFACTURING CO., 54 Eastford Rd., 01550,
pg. 551 — **PV**

Southwick

Comark Communications Inc., 104 Feeding Hills Rd.,
01077, pg. 1383 — **IT**
Thomson Tubes, Rte. 57, 104 Feeding Hills Rd., P.O. Box
1088, 01077, pg. 1384 — **IT**

Spencer

FLEXCON CO., INC., Flexcon Industrial Pk., 01562,
pg. 412 — **PV**

Springfield

A&P / Waldbaum's Food Mart, 112 Industry Ave., 01104,
pg. 1375 — **IT**
AmeriSource-Springfield, 570 Cottage St., 01104,
pg. 97 — **PB**
Bank of Western Massachusettes, 29 State St., 01103,
pg. 351 — **PB**
BIG Y FOODS INC., 280 Chestnut St., 01102-7840,
pg. 143 — **PV**
Eastfield Mall, Inc., 1655 Boston Rd., 01129, pg. 1408 — **PB**
Hano Document Printers, Inc., 99 Guion St., 01104,
pg. 1686 — **PB**
Hasbro International, Inc., P. O. Box 3400, 01101,
pg. 797 — **PB**
Holyoke Lithograph Co., Inc., 655 Page Blvd., 01104,
pg. 1078 — **IT**
Jahn Foundry Corp., 115 Stevens St., 01104, pg. 142 — **PB**
Longview Fibre Co. Eastern Container Div., Palmer Ave.,
01101, pg. 1014 — **PB**
MML Investors Services, Inc., 1414 Main St., 01144-1013,
pg. 712 — **PV**
MASSACHUSETTS MUTUAL LIFE INSURANCE CO., 1295
State St., 01111, pg. 712 — **PB**
MASSMUTUAL CORPORATE INVESTORS, 1295 State
St., 01111, pg. 1055 — **PB**
Merriam-Webster, Inc., 47 Federal St., 01102, pg. 375 — **PV**
Nu Visions Manufacturing Corp., 225 Carando Dr., 01104,
pg. 1205 — **PB**
PACKAGE MACHINERY CO., 380 Union St., 01089-4123,
pg. 832 — **PV**
PETER PAN BUS LINES, INC., P.O. Box 1776, Main St.,
01102-1776, pg. 856 — **PV**
Polysar, 950 Worcester St., 01151-1043, pg. 174 — **IT**
F.L. ROBERTS & CO. INC., 93 W. Broad St., 01105,
pg. 935 — **PV**
Smith & Wesson Corp., 2100 Roosevelt Ave., 01102,
pg. 1397 — **IT**
Titeflex Corporation, 603 Hendee St., 01109, pg. 1340 — **IT**
Titeflex Industrial Americas, 170 Tapley St., 01104-2893,
pg. 1340 — **IT**
WGGB-TV, 1300 Liberty St., 01102-0040, pg. 439 — **PV**
WHYN, 1331 Main St., 01103, pg. 385 — **PB**
Westvaco Corporation-Envelope Div., 2001 Roosevelt Ave.,
01104, pg. 1762 — **PB**

Sterling

Anderson Power Products Div., P.O. Box 5079, Pratt's
Junction Rd., 01564, pg. 528 — **PV**
Carbolon Division, P.O. Box 5079, Pratt's Junction Rd.,
01564, pg. 528 — **PV**

PB - *U.S. Public Companies Volume*
PV - *U.S. Private Companies Volume*
IT - *International Public & Private Companies Volume*

Geographic Index-U.S.

Stoneham

A.W. CHESTERTON COMPANY, Middlesex Industrial Park, 225 Fallon Rd., 02180, pg. 234   **PV**
Kintetsu World Express Inc., 200 Fallon Rd., 02180, pg. 734   **IT**

Stoughton

ARK-LES CORPORATION, 95 Mill St., 02072, pg. 82   **PV**
Branch Electric Supply Co., 179 Campanelli Pkwy., 02072, pg. 165
BROOKFIELD ENGINEERING LABORATORIES, INC., 240 Cushing St., 02072, pg. 171   **PV**
Courier Stoughton, Inc., 100 Alpine Cir., 02072, pg. 453   **PB**
E & A Environmental Consultants, Inc., 1613 Central St., 02072, pg. 571   **PB**
FABREEKA INTERNATIONAL, INC., 1023 Turnpike St., 02072, pg. 390   **PV**
FRANKLIN SPORTS, INC., 17 Campanelli Pkwy., 02072, pg. 424   **PV**
Gould Paper Corporation-New England, 532 Page St., 02072, pg. 467   **PV**
Grossman's, Inc., 90 Hawes Way, 02072, pg. 585   **PV**
J.C. Higgins Corp., 70 Hawes Way, 02072, pg. 572   **PB**
HIT OR MISS, INC., 100 Campanelli Pkwy., 02072-9112, pg. 531   **PV**
Hoboken Floors-New England Division, 181 Campanelli Pkwy., 07072-3703, pg. 532   **PV**
MARSON/CREATIVE FASTENER, INC., 44 Campanelli Pkwy., 02072, pg. 708   **PV**
NHD Hardware, 365 Washington St., 02072, pg. 3   **PV**
REEBOK INTERNATIONAL LTD., 100 Technology Ctr. Dr., 02072, pg. 1369   **PB**
SEMCO INDUSTRIES INC., 80 Hawes Way, 02072, pg. 983   **PV**
Spaulding Company, Inc., 80 Hawes Way, 02072, pg. 983   **PV**

Sturbridge

GALILEO CORP., Galileo Park, 01566, pg. 698   **PB**
SPECTRAN CORPORATION, 50 Hall Rd., 01566, pg. 1497   **PB**

Sudbury

CHISWICK TRADING INC., 33 Union Ave., 01776, pg. 237   **PV**

Sutton

POLYVINYL FILMS, INC., 19 Depot St., 01590, pg. 875   **PV**

Taunton

Arley Corporation, 540 Myles Standish Blvd., 02780, pg. 1130   **PV**
Independent Nail Company, 30 Mozzone Blvd., 02780, pg. 718   **PV**
REED & BARTON CORPORATION, 144 W. Britannia, 02780, pg. 916   **PV**
Reed & Barton Housewares, 144 W. Britannia, 02780, pg. 916   **PV**
Reed & Barton Silversmiths, 144 W. Britannia, 02780, pg. 916   **PV**
ROBERTSON FACTORIES, INC., 33 Chandler Ave., 02780, pg. 936   **PV**
Sheffield Silver Co., 144 W. Britannia St., 02780, pg. 916   **PV**
Taunton Daily Gazette, Five Cohannet St., 02780, pg. 935   **PB**
VKO, INC., 540 Myles Standish Blvd., 02780, pg. 1130   **PV**

Tewksbury

AVID TECHNOLOGY, INC., Metropolitan Technology Park, One Park W., 01876, pg. 154   **PB**
Bard Interventional Products, 200 Ames Pond Dr., 01876-1200, pg. 189   **PB**
DEMOULAS MARKET BASKET, 875 East St., 01876, pg. 324   **PV**
ECRM, 554 Clark Rd., 01876, pg. 353   **PV**
Stephen Gould of New England, Inc., 30 Commerce Way, 01876, pg. 467   **PV**
Jaco Electronics, Inc., 1053 East St., 01876, pg. 921   **PB**
MURO PHARMACEUTICAL, INC., 890 East St., 01876-1496, pg. 767   **PV**

Thorndike

Cascade Diamond, P.O. Box 627, Church St., 01079, pg. 274   **IT**

Townsend

STERILITE CORPORATION, 30 Scales Lane, 01469, pg. 1040   **PV**

Turners Falls

Judd Wire, Inc., 55 Turnpike Rd., 01376-2699, pg. 1313   **IT**

Tyngsboro

Field Effects, 300 Vesper Executive Pk., Ste. E, 01879, pg. 894   **PB**
Hussey Plastics Co., 65 Middlesex Rd., 01879, pg. 550   **PB**
JOAN FABRICS CORP., 100 Vesper Executive Pk., 01879, pg. 588   **PV**

Wakefield

Converse Network Systems, 100 Quannapowitt Pkwy., 01880, pg. 425   **PB**
Contex Prepress Systems, 101 Edgewater Dr., 01880, pg. 1787   **PB**
Data Conversion Products, 360 Audubon Rd., 01880, pg. 109   **PB**
HIGH VOLTAGE ENGINEERING CORPORATION, 401 Edgewater Place, 01880, pg. 528   **PB**
SMS-Boston, 301 Edgewater Pl., 01880, pg. 1463   **PB**
XYVISION, INC., 101 Edgewater Dr., 01880, pg. 1787   **PB**

Walpole

Bird-Johnson Company, 110 Norfolk St., 02081, pg. 709   **IT**
EXAR Corp.-Northeast, 11 Cyprus Ln., pg. 598   **PB**
Ingersoll Rand Tool & Hoist, 50 School St., 02081-3532, pg. 877   **PB**
Seabeam Instruments, Inc., 141 Washington E., 02032, pg. 228   **PV**
Veratec Division, 95 West St., 02081, pg. 904   **PV**
WALPOLE WOODWORKERS, INC., 767 East St., 02081, pg. 1148   **PV**

Waltham

AllEnergy Marketing Company, L.L.C., Three University Park, 95 Sawyer Rd., 02154, pg. 549   **PB**
BGS SYSTEMS, INC., One First Ave., 02254-9111, pg. 161   **PB**
Becton Dickinson & Co., Massachusetts Div., 411 Waverley Oaks Rd., 02154, pg. 199   **PB**
THE BILTRITE CORPORATION, Two University Office Park, 51 Sawyer Rd., 02254-9045, pg. 144   **PV**
CBL & Associates Properties, Inc., Watermill Ctr., 800 S. St., Ste. 395, 02154-1439, pg. 273   **PB**
CSC Consulting Group, One University Office Park, 29 Sawyer Rd., 02154, pg. 422   **PB**
California Agriwaste Corporation, P.O. Box 9046, 02254, pg. 1591   **PB**
CAMBEX CORPORATION, 360 Second Ave., 02154, pg. 296   **PB**
Community Newsdealers, Inc., 60 First Ave., 02254, pg. 1175   **PB**
Consulting & Systems Integration, One University Office Park, 29 Sawyer Rd., 02154, pg. 422   **PB**
DMR Group, Inc., 404 Wyman St., Ste. 150, 02154, pg. 528   **IT**
Delano Energy Company, Inc., P.O. Box 9046, 02254, pg. 1591   **PB**
Dynaray Incorporated, 411 Waverly Oaks Rd., 02154, pg. 725   **IT**
FIRE CONTROL INSTRUMENTS, INC., 301 Second Ave., 02205, pg. 406   **PV**
Fire Controls Instruments, 301 2nd Ave., 02154-1133, pg. 1306   **PV**
FOSTER-MILLER, INC., 350 2nd Ave., 02154, pg. 421   **PV**
GTE Laboratories Incorporated, 40 Sylvan Rd., 02254, pg. 697   **PB**
GENOME THERAPEUTICS CORPORATION, 100 Beaver St., 02154, pg. 730   **PB**
GLOBAL PETROLEUM CORP., 800 South St., 02254, pg. 457   **PV**
H M K ENTERPRISES, INC., 800 South St., 02154, pg. 489   **PV**
HARVEY INDUSTRIES, INC., 43 Emerson Rd., 02154, pg. 508   **PV**
HOLOGIC, INC., 590 Lincoln St., 02154, pg. 831   **PB**
IRI Software, 1601 Trapelo Rd., 02154, pg. 876   **PB**
INTEGRA TECHNOLOGIES CORP., 132 Calvary St., 02154, pg. 565   **PV**
INTERLEAF, INC., 62 4th Ave., 02154, pg. 893   **PB**
Jeepers! Inc., 60 Hickory Dr., 02154, pg. 222   **PV**
KOLLMORGEN CORPORATION, Reservoir Place, 1601 Trapelo Rd., Bldg. A, 02154-7333, pg. 965   **PB**
KRONOS INCORPORATED, 400 5th Ave., 02154, pg. 967   **PB**
Money Management Systems, Inc., 1000 Winter St., 02154, pg. 1535   **PB**
Motorola Radius, Northeast Division, 45 Rumford Ave., 02154-3844, pg. 1138   **PB**
N.A.P. Commercial Electronic Corp., 580 Winter St., 02254, pg. 1054   **PB**
Nichimen America, Inc., Boston Office, Bay Colony Corp. Ctr., 1000 Winter St., Ste. 3400, 02154, pg. 928   **IT**
Nichols Aircraft Div., 48 Woerd Ave., 02254-9115, pg. 1262   **PB**
Northeastern Regional Office, P.O. Box 9124, 404 Wyman Street, 02254-9124, pg. 224   **PV**
OAK INDUSTRIES INC., 1000 Winter St., 02154, pg. 1209   **PB**
PARAMETRIC TECHNOLOGY CORPORATION, 128 Technology Dr., 02154, pg. 1257   **PB**
PAREXEL INTERNATIONAL CORPORATION, 195 West St., 02154, pg. 1257   **PB**
PAREXEL International Corporation, 1601 Trapelo Rd., 02154, pg. 1258   **PB**
Phase3 Systems Inc., 504 Totten Pond Rd., 02154, pg. 1535   **PB**

Philips E.C.G., 100 First Ave., 02254, pg. 1054   **IT**
Polaroid Corp. Research & Development, 1265 Main St., 02254, pg. 1313   **PB**
PRIMARK CORPORATION, 100 Winter St., Ste. 4300, 02154, pg. 1325   **PB**
RP alpha/Boston, 300 5th Ave., 5th Fl., 02154, pg. 950   **PV**
Raytheon, P.O. Box 139, 02254-0139, pg. 1365   **PB**
Refractive Centers International, 21 Hickory Dr., 02154, pg. 1529   **PB**
Risk Management Solutions, Inc., 800 South St., 02154, pg. 489   **PV**
Sodexho USA, 153 Second Ave., 02254-1164, pg. 1274   **IT**
Standard-Thomson Corporation, 152 Grove St., 02254-91009, pg. 1396   **IT**
STEINWAY MUSICAL INSTRUMENTS, INC., 800 South St., Ste. 425, 02154, pg. 1514   **PB**
SUMMIT TECHNOLOGY, INC., 21 Hickory Dr., 02154, pg. 1528   **PB**
TE Energy Systems, Inc., P.O. Box 9046, 91 Wyman St., 02254-9046, pg. 1592   **PB**
TEC Energy Corporation, 02254, pg. 1592   **PB**
TECO Generation Inc., 45 First Ave., 02254, pg. 1592   **PB**
TGM Detectors Inc., 160 Bear Hill Rd., 02154-1075, pg. 892   **IT**
TMP Worldwide/Recruitment Division, 170 Tracer Ln., 02154, pg. 1065   **PV**
Tecogen Inc., 45 First Ave., Box 9046, 02254, pg. 1592   **PB**
Thermedota, Inc., P.O. Box 9046, 02254, pg. 1592   **PB**
THERMO ELECTRON CORPORATION, 81 Wyman St., 02254, pg. 1591   **PB**
Thermo Electron of Maine, Inc., P.O. Box 9046, 02254, pg. 1592   **PB**
Thermo Electron of New Hampshire, Inc., P.O. Box 9046, 02254, pg. 1592   **PB**
Thermo Electron of Whitefield, Inc., P.O. Box 9046, 02254, pg. 1593   **PB**
Thermo Energy Systems Corporation, 81 Wyman St., 02254-9046, pg. 1593   **PB**
Thermo Fibertek, Inc., P.O. Box 9046, 81 Wyman St., 02254-9046, pg. 1593   **PB**
Thermo Instrument Systems Inc., 101 First Ave., 02254, pg. 1593   **PB**
Woodland Biomass Power, Inc., P.O. Box 9046, 02254, pg. 1596   **PB**

Ward Hill

EASTERN CANVAS PRODUCTS, INC., 50 Rogers Rd., 01835, pg. 357   **PV**
Johnson Matthey Catalog Co., 30 Bond Street, 01835, pg. 713   **IT**

Ware

Kanzaki Specialty Papers Inc., Cummings St., 01082, pg. 998   **IT**

Wareham

Robertsons Auto Body, P.O. Box 231, 02571, pg. 936   **PV**
ROBERTSON'S AUTO SALVAGE, 2680 Cranberry Hwy., 02571, pg. 936   **PV**
Tremont Nail Co., P.O. Box 111, 02571, pg. 718   **PV**

Warren

Warren Pumps Inc., 82 Bridges Avenue, 01083, pg. 857   **PB**

Watertown

AMCEL CORP., One Galen St., 02172, pg. 48   **PV**
Haartz-Mason, Inc., 270 Pleasant St., 02172, pg. 1358   **PB**
IONICS, INCORPORATED, 65 Grove St., 02172, pg. 912   **PB**
Micro USPD Inc., 580 Pleasant St., 02172, pg. 1107   **PB**
Sertech Laboratories, Inc./SSI, 580 Pleasant St., 02172, pg. 1107   **PB**
United Electronics Industries, Inc., 110 Dexter Ave., 02172-4202, pg. 1690   **PB**

Wayland

CANDELA CORPORATION, 530 Boston Post Rd., 01778, pg. 300   **PB**
Kruger Pulp & Paper Sales, Inc., 266 Pelham Island Road, 01778-2515, pg. 762   **IT**

Webster

Chase & Sons-Webster Branch, Goya Industrial Park, Cudworth Rd., 01570, pg. 337   **PB**

Wellesley

EG & G, INC., 45 William St., 02181, pg. 542   **PB**
FILENE'S BASEMENT, INC., 40 Walnut St., 02181, pg. 622   **PB**
FREEMAN ASSOCIATES, INC., 20 William St., 02181, pg. 425   **PV**
JWG ASSOCIATES, INC., 888 Worcester Rd., 02181, pg. 579   **PV**

PB - *U.S. Public Companies Volume*
PV - *U.S. Private Companies Volume*
IT - *International Public & Private Companies Volume*

1274

Geographic Index-U.S.

Wellesley Hills

AMERICAN BILTRITE INC., 57 River St., 02181-2097, pg. 68 **PB**
BTR Paper Group, 60 Williams St., Ste. 300, 02181, pg. 127 **IT**
Logica Technology Systems, Inc., 327 Washington St., 02181, pg. 814 **IT**
Sun Benefit Services Company, Inc., One Sun Life Executive Park, 02181, pg. 1319 **IT**
Sun Investment Services Company, One Sun Life Executive Park, 02181, pg. 1319 **IT**
Sun Life Assurance Company of Canada (U.S.), One Sun Life Executive Park, 02181, pg. 1319 **IT**
Sun Life Finance Corporation, One Sun Life Executive Park, 02181, pg. 1319 **IT**
Sun Life of Canada, One Sun Life Executive Park, 02181, pg. 1319 **IT**
Tri-Mass., Inc., 32 Monadnock Rd., 02181, pg. 1621 **PB**

Wenham

MULLEN ADVERTISING, INC., 36 Essex St., 01984-1799, pg. 766 **PV**
Mullen Advertising, Inc., Public Relations Div., 36 Essex St., 01984-1799, pg. 766 **PV**

West Bridgewater

Chadwick's of Boston, 35 United Dr., 02379, pg. 996 **PB**
Cricket Lane, 400 Manley St., 02379, pg. 948 **PB**
EUA Service Corporation, 750 W. Center St., 02379, pg. 549 **PB**
Quebecor Printing Semline Inc., 90 Pleasant St., 02379, pg. 1077 **IT**

West Roxbury

Armstrong Labs., 423 La Grange St., 02132, pg. 852 **IT**
UNO RESTAURANT CORPORATION, 100 Charles Park Rd., 02132, pg. 1698 **PB**
West Roxbury Crushed Stone Co., 10 Grove St., 02132, pg. 265 **PB**

West Springfield

Connecticut Driveshaft, 59 Kelso Ave., 01089, pg. 263 **PV**
T.F. Cushing, Inc., 126 Myron St., 01089, pg. 141 **PB**
K & M Electronics, Inc., 11 Interstate Dr., 01089, pg. 395 **IT**
MANUFACTURERS TECHNOLOGIES, INC., 59 Interstate Dr., 01089, pg. 701 **PV**
MassWest Insurance Company, 123 Interstate Dr., 01089, pg. 345 **IT**
National Metal Industries, 203 Circuit Ave., 01090-1776, pg. 1506 **PB**
SULLIVAN PAPER COMPANY, 61 Progress Ave., 01089, pg. 1050 **PV**
United Technologies Diesel Systems, 103 Myron St., 01089-1474, pg. 1690 **PB**

West Warren

EZ International, 85 South St., 01092, pg. 1192 **PV**
WM. E. WRIGHT LIMITED PARTNERSHIP, 85 South St., 01092, pg. 1192 **PV**

Westborough

AMP Inc. Lytel Division, 110 Turnpike Rd., 01581-2808, pg. 8 **PB**
Alden Electronics, Inc., 40 Washington St., 01581-0500, pg. 872 **PV**
ARCH COMMUNICATIONS GROUP, INC., 1800 W. Park Dr., Ste. 250, 01581, pg. 127 **PB**
ARDENT SOFTWARE, INC., 50 Washington St., 01581, pg. 129 **PB**
Astra USA, Inc., 50 Otis St., 01581, pg. 93 **IT**
BANYAN SYSTEMS INC., 115 & 120 Flanders Rd., 01581, pg. 189 **PB**
Bay State Energy Development, Inc., 300 Friberg Pkwy., 01581-5039, pg. 197 **PB**
BAY STATE GAS COMPANY, 300 Friberg Pkwy., 01581-5039, pg. 196 **PB**
Bay State Gas Company, 300 Friberg Pkwy., 01581-5039, pg. 197 **PB**
Bytex Corporation, Westborough Technology Park, Four Technology Dr., 01581, pg. 1522 **PB**
Concentric Data Systems, 110 Turnpike Rd., 01581, pg. 1734 **PB**
Daewoo Telecom Co. (Newton), 117 Flanders Rd., 01581, pg. 357 **IT**
DANAFILMS, INC., Five Otis St., 01581, pg. 309 **PV**
DATA GENERAL CORPORATION, 4400 Computer Dr., 01580, pg. 485 **PB**
Data General International, Inc., 4400 Computer Dr., 01580, pg. 485 **PB**
Data General Manufacturing Division, 4400 Computer Dr., 01580, pg. 485 **PB**
Data General Sales & Marketing Division, 4400 Computer Dr., 01580, pg. 485 **PB**
Data General Systems Development Division, 4400 Computer Drive, 01580, pg. 485 **PB**
Datagen, Inc., 4400 Computer Dr., 01580, pg. 485 **PB**
Design Data, Inc., 4400 Computer Dr., 01580, pg. 485 **PB**
Digital Computer Controls, Inc., 4400 Computer Dr., 01580, pg. 485 **PB**

Energy USA, 2000 W. Park Dr., Ste. 300, 01581-5039, pg. 197 **PB**
Globe Specialty Products, Inc., 27 Otis St., 04581, pg. 1175 **PB**
Intergraph Corporation, Westborough Office Park, 1800 W. Park Drive, 01581-3901, pg. 891 **PB**
Long Island Communications Corp., 4400 Computer Dr., 01580, pg. 485 **PB**
Massachusetts Electric Co., 25 Research Dr., 01582, pg. 1171 **PB**
MICRON SEPARATIONS, INC., 135 Flanders Rd., 01581, pg. 742 **PB**
N.D.T. Engineering Inc., P.O. Box 128, 01581, pg. 989 **PV**
NEES Energy, Inc., 25 Research Dr., 01582, pg. 1171 **PB**
Nantucket Electric Company, 25 Research Dr., 01582, pg. 1171 **PB**
Natural Gas Development Inc., 300 Friberg Pkwy., 01581, pg. 197 **PB**
New England Electric Resources, Inc., 25 Research Dr., 01582, pg. 1171 **PB**
NEW ENGLAND ELECTRIC SYSTEM, 25 Research Dr., 01582, pg. 1171 **PB**
New England Energy, Inc., 25 Research Dr., 01582, pg. 1171 **PB**
New England Hydro Finance Company, Inc., 25 Research Dr., 01582, pg. 1171 **PB**
New England Hydro-Transmission Electric Company, Inc., 25 Research Dr., 01582, pg. 1171 **PB**
New England Power Co., 25 Research Dr., 01582, pg. 1171 **PB**
New England Power Service Co., 25 Research Dr., 01582, pg. 1171 **PB**
PROTEON, INC., Nine Technology Dr., 01581, pg. 1336 **PB**
Sentry Technology Group, One Research Dr., 01581, pg. 1425 **PB**
STAPLES, INC., One Research Dr., 01581, pg. 1509 **PB**
TBV, Inc., P.O. Box 1210, 121 Flanders Rd., 01581-6210, pg. 1138 **PV**
Tekra Corp., East Coast Div., 23 Bridle Ln., 05181, pg. 1073 **PV**
WSA Systems & Services, Inc., 4400 Computer Dr., 01580, pg. 485 **PB**

Westfield

BERKSHIRE INDUSTRIES, INC., 109 Apremont Way, 01085, pg. 136 **PV**
COLUMBIA MANUFACTURING INC., One Cycle St., 01085, pg. 255 **PV**
Jen-Coat Inc., 132 N. Elm St., 01086, pg. 70 **PB**
MESTEK, INC., 260 N. Elm St., 01085, pg. 1099 **PB**
SPC Company of New York, Inc., 57 N. Elm St., 01085-1619, pg. 1468 **PB**
SAVAGE ARMS INC., 100 Springdale Rd., 01085, pg. 968 **PB**
H.B. SMITH CO., INC., 47 Westfield Industrial Pk. Rd., 01085, pg. 1008 **PB**
STANHOME INC., 333 Western Ave., 01085, pg. 1508 **PB**

Westford

Courier Connection, Inc., One Pleasant St., 01886, pg. 453 **PB**
Courier Westford, Inc., One Pleasant St., 01886, pg. 453 **PB**
Dataproducts Corp., One Technology Park Dr., 01886-3139, pg. 620 **IT**
DAVOX CORP., Six Technology Park Dr., 01886, pg. 488 **PB**
GENRAD, INC., 7 Technology Park Dr., 01886-0033, pg. 731 **PB**
Middlesex Insurance, Three Carlisle Rd., 01886, pg. 985 **PV**
Patriot General Insurance Co., 3 Carlisle Rd., 01886, pg. 985 **PV**
Tau-tron, 10 Liberty Way, 01886, pg. 727 **PB**
VERYFINE PRODUCTS, INC., 210 Littleton Rd., 01886-0670, pg. 1137 **PV**

Westminster

W.E. AUBUCHON CO., INC., 95 Aubuchon Dr., 01473, pg. 98 **PV**

Weston

EASTERN ENTERPRISES, Nine Riverside Rd., 02193, pg. 548 **PB**

Westwood

Dade Behring Inc., 151 University Ave., 02090, pg. 110 **PV**
The Faxon Company, Inc., 15 Southwest Park, 02090, pg. 385 **IT**
Federal Information Services, 15 Southwood Pk., 02090, pg. 385 **IT**
LTX Asia International, Inc., LTX Park at University Ave., 02090, pg. 972 **PB**
LTX CORPORATION, LTX Park at University Ave., 02090, pg. 972 **PB**
LTX International, Inc., LTX Park at University Ave., 02090, pg. 972 **PB**
LTX Test Systems Corporation, LTX Park at University Ave., 02090, pg. 972 **PB**
Linear Division, LTX Park at University Ave., 02090, pg. 972 **PB**
Quebecor Printing Semline Inc., 270 University Ave., 02090, pg. 1077 **IT**

Solion, 400 Blue Hill Dr., 02090, pg. 1293 **PB**

Weymouth

Anchor Wire Rope Division, 106 Finnell Dr., 02188, pg. 1001 **IT**
Fisher Pierce Division, 90 Libbey Pkwy., 02189, pg. 1250 **PB**
U.N. Alloy Steel Div., 106 Finnell Dr., 02188, pg. 1001 **IT**
U.N. Alloy Steel Sales, Inc., 106 Finnell Dr., 02188, pg. 1001 **IT**
U.N.A. Corp., 106 Finnell Dr., 02188, pg. 1001 **IT**

Whitinsville

Smith Valve Corporation, One Main St., 01588, pg. 1651 **PB**

Wilbraham

FRIENDLY ICE CREAM CORP., 1855 Boston Rd., 01095, pg. 682 **PB**

Williamstown

LITCHFIELD FINANCIAL CORPORATION, 430 Main St., 01267, pg. 1001 **PB**

Wilmington

APV Gaulin Inc., Wilmington Technology Pk., 500 Research Dr., 01887, pg. 1241 **IT**
APV Vent-Axia Inc., 230 Ballardvale St., 01887, pg. 1241 **IT**
Aerospace Products, Inc., 50 Fordham Rd., 01887, pg. 100 **PB**
AGFA EPS Division, 200 Ballardvale St., 01887, pg. 172 **IT**
ALTRON INCORPORATED, One Jewel Dr., 01887-3390, pg. 75 **PB**
Analog Devices Semiconductor, 804 Woburn St., 01887, pg. 108 **PB**
Arrow Commercial Systems Div., 25 Upton Dr., 01887, pg. 133 **PB**
Arrow/Schweber Electronics, 25 Upton Dr., 01887, pg. 133 **PB**
Bewleys Coffee USA, 892 Main St., 01887, pg. 254 **IT**
CAPRIUS, INC., 46 Janspin Rd., 01887, pg. 303 **PB**
Capstone Electronics Div., 25 Upton Dr., 01887, pg. 134 **PB**
CENTENNIAL TECHNOLOGIES, INC., Seven Lopez Rd., 01887, pg. 322 **PB**
Charles River Biotechnical Services, Inc., 251 Ballardvale St., 01887, pg. 194 **PB**
Charles River Laboratories, Inc., 251 Ballardvale St., 01887, pg. 194 **PB**
DATAWATCH CORPORATION, 234 Ballardvale St., 01887, pg. 488 **PB**
DIAMOND CRYSTAL SPECIALTY FOODS, INC., Ten Burlington Ave., 01887, pg. 330 **PV**
Edwards High Vacuum International, 301 Ballardvale St., 01887, pg. 121 **IT**
Great Source Education Group, 181 Ballardvale St., 01887, pg. 841 **PB**
Ingold Electrodes Inc., 261 Ballardvale St., 01887, pg. 973 **IT**
KEVLIN CORPORATION, Five Cornell Pl., 01887, pg. 953 **PB**
Keytek Instrument Corporation, 260 Fordham Rd., 01887, pg. 1592 **PB**
Koch Membrane Systems, 850 Main St., 01887, pg. 628 **PV**
Lightolier, Industrial Way, 01887, pg. 730 **PB**
MAST Microwave Division, 240 Ballardvale St., 01887, pg. 953 **PB**
Mettler-Toledo Process Analytical, Inc., 261 Ballardvale St., 01887, pg. 4 **PV**
Milgray/New England, Inc., Ballardvale Park, 187 Ballardvale St., 01887, pg. 206 **PB**
Omni-Flow, Inc., 317 New Boston St., 01887, pg. 13 **PB**
Polymer Technology Corporation, 100 Research Dr., 01887, pg. 195 **PB**
QC OPTICS, INC., 46 Jonspin Rd., 01887, pg. 1345 **PB**
RAFFI & SWANSON, INC., 100 Eames St., 01887, pg. 907 **PV**
Swix Sport USA Inc., 261 Ballardvale St., 01887-1013, pg. 1390 **IT**
Tecomet, Inc., 115 Eames St., 01887, pg. 1591 **PB**
Texas Industrial Services, Inc., 68 Jonspin Rd., 01887, pg. 1665 **PB**
Textron Systems, 201 Lowell Street, 01887, pg. 1589 **PB**
Transplantation & Industrial Products Div., 829 Woburn St., 01887, pg. 108 **PB**
U Two Corporation, 68 Jonspin Rd., 01887, pg. 1665 **PB**
UNIFIRST CORPORATION, 68 Jonspin Rd., 01887, pg. 1665 **PB**
Vent-Axia Inc., 230 Ballardvale St., Bldg. B, 01887, pg. 1268 **IT**
Zeneca Resins, 730 Main St., 01887, pg. 1525 **IT**

Winchester

Metrica Systems, 8 Winchester Pl., 01890, pg. 4 **PB**

Woburn

ALPHA INDUSTRIES, INC., 20 Sylvan Rd., 01801, pg. 57 **PB**

Geographic Index-U.S.

Ampex Corporation, 400 W. Cummings Pk., #3900, 01801, pg. 104 **PB**

Braun, North America, 400 Unicorn Park Dr., 01801, pg. 743 **PB**

CPS DIRECT, INC., 20 Cabot Rd., 01801, pg. 196 **PV**

CVD Incorporated, 185 New Boston St., 01801, pg. 1135 **PB**

Chomerics Inc., 77 Dragon Ct., 01888-4014, pg. 1262 **PB**

Eldim Inc., 55 Sixth Rd., 01801, pg. 673 **IT**

General Employment Enterprises, Inc., 444 Washington St., Ste. 303, 01801, pg. 714 **PB**

Herley-MDI, Ten Sonar Dr., 01801, pg. 811 **PB**

L3 Communications Hycor Div., 10 Gill St., 01801, pg. 638 **PB**

LYTRON INCORPORATED, 55 Dragon Ct., 01801, pg. 684 **PB**

Matra Datavision U.S.A., 30 Commerce Way, 01801, pg. 795 **IT**

Northern Research & Engineering Corp., 39 Olympia Ave., 01801, pg. 877 **PB**

POLYMEDICA INDUSTRIES, INC., 11 State St., 01801, pg. 1315 **PB**

PolyMedica Pharmaceuticals (U.S.A.), Inc., 11 State St., 01801, pg. 1315 **PB**

PRINTED CIRCUIT CORPORATION, Ten Micro Dr., 01801, pg. 886 **PV**

Sterling Electronics, 15D Constitution Way, 01801, pg. 1051 **PB**

Synex Corp., Six Gill St., 01801, pg. 138 **PV**

Thermedics Inc., 470 Wildwood St., 01888-1799, pg. 1592 **PB**

Thermo Cardiosystems Inc., P.O. Box 2697, 470 Wildwood St., 01888, pg. 1592 **PB**

Worcester

AMI LEASING CORPORATION, 46 West Boylston St., 01605, pg. 7 **PV**

Allegro MicroSystems Inc., 363 Plantation St., 01605, pg. 1188 **IT**

ALLMERICA FINANCIAL CORPORATION, 440 Lincoln St., 01653, pg. 54 **PB**

ALLMERICA SECURITIES TRUST, 440 Lincoln St., 01605, pg. 54 **PB**

AMGRO, Inc., 472 Lincoln St., 01605, pg. 54 **PB**

AQUILA BIOPHARMACEUTICALS, INC., 365 Plantation St., 01605, pg. 126 **PB**

AUGUST WEST SYSTEMS, 38 Austin St., 01609, pg. 98 **PV**

Bancroft House Healthcare, 835 Main St., 01610, pg. 1711 **PB**

Bassett Printers, 40 Rockdale St., 01606, pg. 616 **PV**

BLOCH/NEW ENGLAND, INC., 53 Northborough St., 01604, pg. 149 **PB**

A.M. Castle & Co., 70 Quinsigamond Ave., 01610, pg. 313 **PB**

DAVID CLARK COMPANY INCORPORATED, Box 15054, 360 Franklin St., 01615-0054, pg. 242 **PV**

Deutsche Babcock-Riley International Inc., P.O. Box 15040, 01615-0040, pg. 401 **IT**

Dryden Oil of New England, 692 Millbury St., 01607, pg. 235 **IT**

FALLON COMMUNITY HEALTH PLAN, Ten Chestnut St., 01608, pg. 392 **PV**

First Allmerica Financial Life Insurance Company, 440 Lincoln St., 01605, pg. 54 **PB**

First Massachusettes Bank, N.A., 295 Park Ave., 01609, pg. 187 **PB**

Flagship Bank & Trust Company, 306 Main St., 01613, pg. 351 **PB**

GHM INDUSTRIES, INC., 41 Fremont St., 01603-2360, pg. 435 **PV**

Gessner/Miller Corporation, 41 Fremont St., 01603, pg. 435 **PV**

Greenery Extended Care Center, 59 Acton St., 01604, pg. 837 **PB**

The Hanover American Insurance Company, 100 N. Parkway, 01653, pg. 54 **PB**

The Hanover Insurance Company, 100 N. Pkwy., 01605, pg. 54 **PB**

KERVICK ENTERPRISES, INC., 40 Rockdale St., 01606, pg. 616 **PB**

Komtek, 40 Rockdale St., 01606, pg. 616 **PV**

Lindberg Heat Treating Co., 284 Grove St., 01605, pg. 999 **PB**

Massachusetts Bay Insurance Co., 100 N. Parkway, 01653, pg. 54 **PB**

Massachusetts Steel Treating, 112 Harding St., 01604, pg. 882 **PV**

Micro Networks Corp., 324 Clark St., 01606, pg. 969 **PV**

MORGAN CONSTRUCTION CO., 15 Belmont St., 01605, pg. 761 **PV**

N E D CORP., 18 Grafton St., 01604, pg. 771 **PV**

Neles-Jamesbury Corp., 640 Lincoln St., 01615, pg. 1428 **IT**

New England Research, Inc., 15 Sagamore Rd., 01605, pg. 724 **PV**

Norton Company, P.O. Box 15008, One New Bond St., 01615-0008, pg. 1173 **IT**

Norton Foreign Affiliates Holding Corporation, One New Bond St., 01615-0008, pg. 1174 **IT**

Norton International Inc., One New Bond St., 01606, pg. 1174 **IT**

Norton Proppants Inc., One New Bond St., 01615-0008, pg. 1176 **IT**

PCC Specialty Products, Inc., 255 Park Ave., Ste. 508, 01609-1946, pg. 1321 **PB**

Pace Power Constructors, Inc., P.O. Box 2758, 01613-2758, pg. 401 **IT**

The Paul Revere Corporation, 18 Chestnut St., 01608, pg. 1338 **PB**

Peterson Spring-Commonwealth Plant, 42 Harlow St., 01605, pg. 857 **PV**

POLAR BEVERAGES, 40 Walcott St., 01603, pg. 873 **PV**

THE PRESMET CORP., 112 Harding St., 01604, pg. 882 **PV**

PROVIDENCE AND WORCESTER RAILROAD COMPANY, 75 Hammond St., 01610, pg. 1336 **PB**

RCI Riley Construction, Inc., P.O. Box 488, 01613-0488, pg. 401 **IT**

Riley Consolidated, Inc., 45 McKeon, 01615, pg. 401 **IT**

Riley Stoker Corporation, 45 McKeon, 01615, pg. 401 **IT**

Sanken Electric U.S.A. Corp., 363 Plantation St., 01605, pg. 1188 **IT**

TSI Mason Laboratories, 57 Union St., 01608, pg. 733 **PB**

WALKER MAGNETICS GROUP, INC., 17 Rockdale St., 01606, pg. 1147 **PV**

O.S. Walker Co. Inc., 17 Rockdale St., 01606, pg. 1147 **PV**

The Worcester Insurance Co., 120 Front St., Ste. 500, 01608-1408, pg. 787 **PB**

G.F. WRIGHT STEEL & WIRE COMPANY, 243 Stafford, 01603, pg. 1192 **PV**

Youngstown Miller Corp., 41 Fremont St., 01613, pg. 435 **PV**

Wrentham

FMC-Crosby Valve, Inc., 43 Kendrick St., 02093, pg. 605 **PB**

MICHIGAN

Ada

AMWAY CORPORATION, 7575 Fulton St. E., 49355-0001, pg. 69 **PV**

Adrian

Citizens Gas Fuel Company, 127 N. Main St., 49221, pg. 1025 **PB**

Dura Convertible Systems, Inc., 1365 East Beecher St., 49221, pg. 399 **PB**

Ervin Amasteel Div., 915 Tabor, 49221, pg. 382 **PB**

Hillhaven Convalescent Center Adrian, 730 Kimole Lane, 49221, pg. 1713 **PB**

Hydro Aluminum Bohn, Inc., 1607 E. Maumee St., 49221, pg. 361 **IT**

InterAmerican Zinc, Inc., 401 Gulf St., 49221, pg. 871 **PV**

Lynwood Manor, 730 Kimole Ln., 49221, pg. 837 **PB**

Merillat Corporation, P.O. Box 1946, 5353 W. U.S. 2257, 49221, pg. 1054 **PV**

Merillat Industries Inc., P.O. Box 1946, 5353 W. U.S. 2237, 49221, pg. 1053 **PV**

Merillat Transportation Company, P.O. Box 1946, 5353 W. U.S. 2257, 49221, pg. 1054 **PB**

Simplex Products, 1801 W. U.S. 223, 49221, pg. 940 **PB**

VENCHURS PACKAGING, INC., 800 Liberty St., 49221, pg. 135 **PV**

Wacker Silicones Corporation, 3301 Sutton Rd., 49221, pg. 625 **IT**

Albion

Reed Plastics (MI), Albion Industrial Park, 49224, pg. 974 **IT**

Allegan

Allegan County Cablevision Inc., 1169 26th St., 49010, pg. 237 **PB**

L. PERRIGO COMPANY, 117 Water St., 49010, pg. 1280 **PB**

Allen Park

BELLE TIRE DISTRIBUTOR INC., 3500 Enterprise Dr., 4810 , pg. 132 **PV**

THE VIRTUAL GROUP, 17333 Federal Dr., Ste. 220, 4810 , pg. 1141 **PV**

Alma

Lippert Components, Inc., P.O. Box 9, 48801, pg. 529 **PB**

Total Petroleum, Inc., E. Superior St., 48801, pg. 1663 **PB**

Alpena

Abtco, Inc., P.O. Box 425, 49707, pg. 20 **IT**

Alro Group, Alpena, 815 W. Miller St., 49707, pg. 46 **PV**

BESSER COMPANY, 801 Johnson St., 49707, pg. 139 **PV**

PANEL PROCESSING, INC., 120 N. Industrial Hwy., 49707, pg. 835 **PV**

Anchorville

ISI Robotics II, 6100 Titan Dr., 48004, pg. 646 **PB**

Ann Arbor

A E Clevite, Inc., 325 E. Eisenhower Pkwy., 48104, pg. 1334 **IT**

Ann Arbor Computer, 1201 E. Ellsworth, 48104, pg. 1156 **PV**

Applicon Inc., P.O. Box 986, 4251 Plymouth Rd., 48106-0986, pg. 465 **PV**

Applied Intelligence Systems, Inc., 3923 Ranchero Dr., 48108, pg. 569 **PV**

ASIA flxible Automotive Tech. Corp., 3800 Packard Ste. 240, 48108, pg. 444 **PV**

Automobile Magazine, 120 E. Liberty, 48104, pg. 1328 **PB**

BioImage Products, 777 Eisenhower Pkwy., Ste. 950, 48108, pg. 1112 **PV**

BORDERS GROUP, INC., 500 E. Washington St., 48104, pg. 245 **PB**

Borders, Inc., 311 Maynard St., 48108, pg. 245 **PB**

Braun-Brumfield, Inc., 100 N. Staebler Rd., 48103, pg. 993 **PV**

CableData Telecommunications, Inc., 2929 Plymouth Rd., Ste. 300, 48105, pg. 1659 **PB**

Chi Systems Division, 130 S. First St., 48104, pg. 1539 **PB**

COMSHARE, INCORPORATED, 555 Briarwood Cir., 48108-3302, pg. 425 **PB**

Con-Way Central Express, Inc., 4880 Venture Dr., 48108, pg. 281 **PB**

Con-Way NOW, 4880 Venture Dr., 48108, pg. 281 **PB**

Distributor Concepts, 2460 S. Industrial Hwy., 48104, pg. 620 **PV**

Domino's Pizza Distribution Corp., P.O. Box 990, 48106, pg. 339 **PV**

DOMINO'S PIZZA INC., 30 Frank Lloyd Wright Dr., 48106, pg. 339 **PV**

Domino's Pizza International, Inc., P.O. Box 997, 48106, pg. 339 **PV**

EDWARDS BROTHERS, INC., 2500 S. State St., 48106, pg. 365 **PV**

ERVIN INDUSTRIES, INC., 3893 Research Park Dr., 48108, pg. 382 **PV**

FINGERLE LUMBER CO., 617 S. Fifth Ave., 48106, pg. 405 **PV**

Fujitsu Ten Corp. of America/Michigan, 3915 Research Park Dr., Ste. A-9, 48108, pg. 526 **IT**

Gal Corp., 2141 So. State St., 48106, pg. 1249 **IT**

Gelman Sciences, Inc., 600 S. Wagner Rd., 48103-9019, pg. 1253 **PB**

GENERAL AUTOMOTIVE CORPORATION, 3800 Packard, Ste. 240, 48108, pg. 443 **PV**

Great Lakes Bancorp, 401 E. Liberty, 48107, pg. 1554 **PB**

H-D Michigan, Inc., 315 W. Huron St., Ste. 400, 48103, pg. 786 **PV**

Hop-In Michigan, Inc., 2141 South State St., 48106, pg. 1249 **IT**

INTERFACE SYSTEMS, INC., 5855 Interface Dr., 48103, pg. 889 **PB**

JPE, INC., 775 Technology Dr., Ste. 200, 48108, pg. 919 **PB**

KING GROUP, INC., 2460 S. Industrial Hwy., 48104, pg. 620 **PV**

Lynn Arthur Associates, 2929 Plymouth Rd., Ste 300, 48105, pg. 1659 **PB**

M.A.R.C.O., 1254 North Main St., 48104, pg. 355 **PV**

MALLOY LITHOGRAPHING INC., 5411 Jackson Rd., 48103, pg. 698 **PV**

Mathematical Reviews, 416 4th St., 48107, pg. 59 **PV**

NSK Corporation, 3861 Research Park Dr., 48108, pg. 903 **IT**

NEMATRON CORP., 5840 Inerface Dr., 48103, pg. 791 **PV**

Philips Display Components, 1600 Huron Pkwy., 48106-0963, pg. 1055 **IT**

Planet Music, Inc., 311 Maynard St., 48108, pg. 245 **PB**

REINALT-THOMAS CORP., 903 Airport Dr., 48108, pg. 919 **PV**

Society Bank, Michigan, 100 S. Main St., 48107, pg. 954 **PB**

Stamptech, 727 W. Ellsworth Rd., 48104, pg. 692 **PV**

SYMPLEX COMMUNICATIONS CORP., 35 Research Dr., 48103, pg. 1060 **PB**

T & N Industries, Inc., 777 E. Eisenhower Pkwy., Ste. 600, 48108, pg. 1334 **PB**

Tecumseh Products Research Lab., 3869 Research Park Dr., 48108, pg. 1566 **PB**

Thetford Corporation, P.O. Box 1285, 48106, pg. 352 **PV**

Townsend & Bottum, Inc., 2245 S. State St., 48104, pg. 146 **PV**

Toyota Technical Center, U.S.A., Inc., 1555 Woodridge Ave., 48105, pg. 1413 **IT**

Transportation Group, 795 Highland Dr., 48108, pg. 475 **PB**

TriMas Corporation, 315 E. Eisenhower Pkwy., 48108, pg. 1054 **PB**

UBE Machinery, Inc., 5700 S. State St., 48108, pg. 1427 **IT**

UMI, 300 N. Zeeb Rd., 48106, pg. 201 **PB**

Walden Book Company, 100 Phoenix Dr., 48108, pg. 245 **PB**

Auburn Hills

ABB Paint Finishing, 1250 Brown Rd., 48326, pg. 5 **IT**

APX INTERNATIONAL, 275 Rex Blvd., 48326, pg. 7 **PV**

ALARON INC., 1026 Doris Rd., 48326, pg. 31 **PV**

Auburn Hills, 1187 Center Rd., 48326, pg. 1176 **PB**

Audi of America, 3800 Hamlin Rd., 48326, pg. 1474 **IT**

Automotive Original Equipment Div., P.O. Box 21-5190, 48321-5590, pg. 1045 **PB**

Automotive Systems Division, 1250 Brown Rd., 48326, pg. 4 **IT**

Automotive Welding Center, 1250 Brown Rd., 48326, pg. 4 **IT**

Behr Systems, Inc., 2469 Executive Hills Blvd., 48326, pg. 421 **IT**

Budd Technical Center, 1515 Atlantic Blvd., 48055, pg. 1388 **IT**

CHAMPION ENTERPRISES, INC., 2701 University Dr., Ste. 300, 48326, pg. 332 **PB**

PB - *U.S. Public Companies Volume*
PV - *U.S. Private Companies Volume*
IT - *International Public & Private Companies Volume*

1276

Champion Home Builders Co., 2701 University Dr., Ste. 300, 48326-2566, pg. 332 **PB**
CHRYSLER CORPORATION, 1000 Chrysler Dr., 48326-2766, pg. 352 **PB**
CHURCH & CHURCH INC., 70 S. Cray Rd., 48326, pg. 239 **PV**
D & S Plastics International, 1200 Harmon Rd., 48326-1550, pg. 1277 **IT**
Dodge Car/Truck Division, 1000 Chrysler Dr., 48326, pg. 353 **PB**
Emitec Inc., c/o GKN Automotive Inc., 3300 University Dr., 48326-2362, pg. 535 **IT**
Epic Technical Group, 1900 Updike Ct., 48326, pg. 560 **PB**
FAIRVIEW CONSTRUCTION, INC, 1080 Opdyke Rd., 48326, pg. 392 **PV**
GKN Automotive Inc., 3300 University Dr., 48326-2362, pg. 535 **IT**
GKN Technology US, 3300 University Dr., 48326-2362, pg. 535 **IT**
GUARDIAN INDUSTRIES CORP., 2300 Harman Rd., 48326-1714, pg. 485 **PV**
Haden Environmental Corporation, 1399 Pacific Dr., 48326, pg. 586 **PV**
Haden, Inc., 1399 Pacific Dr., 48326, pg. 586 **IT**
Haden Research & Development Corporation, 1399 Pacific Dr., 48326, pg. 586 **IT**
Haden Schweitzer Corporation, 1399 Pacific Dr., 48326, pg. 586 **IT**
HEIGHTS HEATING & COOLING, 2005 Pontiac Rd., 48326, pg. 519 **PV**
Jabil Circuit, Inc./North, Metro N. Technology Park, 1700 Atlantic Blvd., 48326, pg. 920 **PB**
Jeep, 1000 Chrysler Dr., 48326-2766, pg. 353 **PB**
Liberty Paper & Bag Co., 111 Corporate Dr., 48326, pg. 233 **IT**
MHIA Turbocharger Division, 1140 Centre Rd., 48326, pg. 874 **IT**
Major Pharmaceuticals Corp., 3720 Lapeer Rd., 48326, pg. 475 **PV**
Nim-Cor, Inc., 1399 Pacific Dr., 48326, pg. 586 **IT**
NORTH ELECTRIC SUPPLY, INC., 1290 N. Opdyke Rd., 48326, pg. 805 **PV**
Paint Application Division, 1250 Brown Rd., 48326, pg. 4 **IT**
Ramsay-Havenwyck, Inc., 1525 University Dr., 48057, pg. 1361 **PB**
Siemens Automotive Corporation, 2400 Executive Hills Dr., 48326-2980, pg. 1245 **IT**
Takatta Inc., 2500 Tatta Dr., 48326-2636, pg. 528 **PV**
VW Credit, Inc., 3800 Hamlin Rd., 48326, pg. 1474 **IT**
Volkswagen of America, Inc., 3800 Hamlin Rd., 48326, pg. 1474 **IT**
Walbro Automotive Corp., 1227 Centre Rd., 48326, pg. 1733 **PB**

Bad Axe

Huron-Daily Tribune, 211 N. Heisterman St., 48413, pg. 517 **PV**
NEEB CORPORATION, 136 W. Huron, 48413, pg. 790 **PV**

Baraga

Pettibone Michigan Div., Superior Ave., P.O. Box 368, 49908, pg. 860 **PV**

Battle Creek

Alro Group, Battle Creek, P.O. Box 20, 801 N. 20th St., 49016-0020, pg. 46 **PV**
ARCHWAY COOKIES, INC., 5451 W. Dickman Rd., 49015, pg. 80 **PV**
Battle Creek Enquirer, 155 W. Van Buren, 49016, pg. 700 **PB**
Battle Creek Gas Company, 55 Hamblin Rd., 49017, pg. 1489 **PB**
Kal Grafx Imaging, 549 Admiral Ave., 49015, pg. 387 **PV**
KELLOGG COMPANY, One Kellogg Sq., 49016-3599, pg. 947 **PB**
Kellogg North America Division, One Kellogg Square, 49016, pg. 947 **PB**
Kellogg Sales Company, One Kellogg Square, 49016, pg. 947 **PB**
Kellogg USA Convenience Foods Division, One Kellogg Sq., 49016-3599, pg. 947 **PB**
Kellogg USA Inc., One Kellogg Square, 49016, pg. 947 **PB**
Lotte U.S.A., Inc., 5243 Wayne Rd., 49015, pg. 819 **IT**
Triple S Plastics, Battle Creek, 150 McQuiston Dr., 49015, pg. 1640 **PV**
UNION PUMP COMPANY, 4600 W. Dickman Rd., 49015, pg. 1119 **PV**
UNITED STEEL & WIRE CO., 4909 Wayne Rd., 49015, pg. 1126 **PV**

Bay City

Carbone of America, Ultra Carbon Div., 900 Harrison St., 48708, pg. 1028 **IT**
Chemical Bank Bay Area, 213 Center Ave., 48708, pg. 345 **PB**
Newcor Bay City Division, 1846 Trumbull Dr., 48707, pg. 1176 **PB**
Second National Bank of Bay City, 701 Washington, 48706, pg. 379 **PB**
UNITED PROPERTIES, P.O. Box 903, 48707-0903, pg. 1123 **PV**

Beaverton

Brown Machine, 330 N. Ross Street, 48612, pg. 774 **IT**
Brown Machine Div., 330 North Ross St., 48612, pg. 773 **IT**

Belding

Falcon-Belding, 815 S. Front St., 48890, pg. 611 **PB**

Bellaire

Lamina Inc., Bellaire Plant, 100 Fairgrounds Rd., 49615, pg. 75 **IT**

Belleville

Automotive Opers., 12950 Haggerty Rd., 48111, pg. 1134 **PB**
HURON VALLEY STEEL CORP., 41000 Huron River Dr., 48111, pg. 549 **PV**
MURRAY'S DISCOUNT AUTO STORES, 8080 Haggerty Rd., 48111, pg. 768 **PV**
Olympic Laser Processing, LLC, 6331 Schooner Dr., 44811, pg. 1221 **PB**
REPUBLIC DIE & TOOL COMPANY, 45000 Van Born Rd., 48111, pg. 923 **PV**
Spring Arbor Distributors, 10885 Textile Rd., 48111, pg. 563 **PB**
Thompson-McCully Asphalt Paving Co., 5905 Belleville Rd., 48111, pg. 1083 **PV**
THOMPSON-McCULLY CO., 5905 Belleville Rd., 48111, pg. 1083 **PV**

Benton Harbor

ALL-PHASE ELECTRIC SUPPLY CO., 875 Riverview Dr., 49022, pg. 35 **PV**
Alro Group, Benton Harbor, 1860 Yore Ave., 49022-9610, pg. 46 **PV**
Ausco Products, Inc., 2245 Pipestone Rd., 49020, pg. 299 **PV**
GAST MFG. CORP., 2300 M-139, 49022, pg. 440 **PV**
Heath Company, 455 Riverview Dr., 49022, pg. 317 **IT**
QUALITY PACKAGING PRODUCTS, INC., 352 W. Britain Ave., 49022, pg. 899 **PV**
Shoreline Bank, 823 Riverview Dr., 49022, pg. 1468 **PB**
SHORELINE FINANCIAL CORP., 823 Riverview Dr., 49022, pg. 1467 **PV**
WHIRLPOOL CORPORATION, Administrative Ctr., 2000 N. M63, 49022, pg. 1764 **PB**
Whirlpool Financial Corp., Administrative Center, 49022, pg. 1765 **PB**

Big Rapids

Chemical Bank Central, 125 N. Michigan Ave., 49307, pg. 345 **PB**
Old Kent Bank of Big Rapids, 101 No. Michigan, 49307, pg. 1216 **PB**

Bingham Farms

Cumis General Insurance Company, 30200 Telegraph Rd., 48025-4502, pg. 296 **PV**
Frontier Communications Services, 30300 Telegraph Rd., 48025, pg. 684 **PB**
League General Insurance Company, 30200 Telegraph Rd., 48025-4502, pg. 296 **PV**
Pro-Therapy of America, 30150 Telegraph Rd., Ste. 235, 48025, pg. 839 **PB**
TRERICE TOSTO COLLIERS INTERNATIONAL, 32100 Telegraph Rd., Ste. 100, 48025-2453, pg. 1099 **PV**

Birch Run

Tay-Ban Corporation, P.O. Box 343, 4532 E. Rathbun, 48415, pg. 1380 **PB**

Birmingham

ALC Communications, 30300 Telegraph Rd., 48010, pg. 556 **PV**
CMI-Detroit, 555 S. Old Woodward Ave., Ste. 613, 48009, pg. 287 **PV**
Pre Finish Metal Inc.-Detroit Sales Office, 1010 Bowers St., 48009, pg. 1056 **PB**
A. Schulman, Inc., 2100 E. Maple Rd., 48009, pg. 1441 **PB**

Blissfield

BLISSFIELD MANUFACTURING COMPANY, 626 Depot St., 49228, pg. 149 **PV**

Bloomfield Hills

A J M PACKAGING CORPORATION, E-4111 Andover Rd., Ste 100, 48032, pg. 2 **PV**
CMI Holding Co., 2600 S. Telegraph, 48013, pg. 1623 **PB**
Detroit Division, 1577 North Woodward, Ste. 200, 48304, pg. 1613 **PB**
Georg Fischer Automotive Products Inc., 2655 Woodward Ave., Ste. 300, 48304, pg. 488 **IT**
NSK-Autoliv, Inc., 281 Enterprise Ct., 48302, pg. 439 **IT**
NEWCOR, INC., 1825 S. Woodward, Ste. 240, 48302, pg. 1176 **PB**
NOBLE INTERNATIONAL LTD., 33 Bloomfield Hills Pkwy., Ste. 155, 48304, pg. 1187 **PB**
ORLEANS INTERNATIONAL, INC., 6441 Inkster Rd., Ste. 140, 48301, pg. 820 **PV**
PULTE CORPORATION, 33 Bloomfield Hills Pkwy., Ste. 200, 48304-2946, pg. 1344 **PB**
Pulte Diversified Companies, Inc., 33 Bloomfield Hills Pkwy., Ste. 200, 48304, pg. 1344 **PB**
Pulte Home Corporation, 33 Bloomfield Hills Pkwy., Ste. 200, 48304, pg. 1344 **PB**
ROSS ROY COMMUNICATIONS, INC., 100 Bloomfield Hills Pkwy., 48304, pg. 946 **PV**
TAUBMAN CENTERS, INC., 200 E. Long Lake Rd., Ste. 300, 48303-0200, pg. 1561 **PB**
VSI HOLDINGS, INC., 2100 N. Woodward Ave., 48304-2263, pg. 1703 **PB**
Visual Services Inc., 2100 N. Woodward Ave., W. 201, 48304-2263, pg. 1703 **PB**
Wellman Engineering Resins, 1100 Woodward Ave., Ste. 222, 48304, pg. 1752 **PB**

Boyne City

AlliedSignal Guidance Systems Div., 375 N. Lake St., 49712, pg. 50 **PB**
Augat, Inc., Automotive Components Division-Boyne City, One Augat Dr., 49712, pg. 1598 **PB**

Breckenridge

B&W CO-OP, INC., 216 Eastman St., 48615, pg. 105 **PV**
B & W Farm Center, 7581 E. Monroe, 48615, pg. 105 **PV**

Bridgeport

Great Lakes-Eglinton, 6950 Junction Rd., 48722, pg. 1676 **PB**

Bridgman

PEMCO DIE CASTING CORPORATION, 9864 Church St., 49106, pg. 848 **PV**
Weldun International, Inc., 9850 Red Arrow Hwy., 49106, pg. 205 **IT**

Brighton

Cognos Corp.-Detroit Sales Office, 10315 E. Grand River, Ste. 305, 48116, pg. 306 **IT**
LK Tool USA, Inc., 12701 Grand River, 48116, pg. 1418 **IT**
Novex Tool Div., 777 Advance St., 48116, pg. 616 **PB**
Old Kent Bank of Brighton, 300 W. North St., 48116, pg. 1216 **PB**
Wyman-Gordon Forgings, Inc, 7250 Whitmore Lake Rd., 48116, pg. 1782 **PB**

Bronson

Bronson Specialties, Inc., 404 Union St., 49028, pg. 1277 **IT**

Brown City

El Dorado National, 6892 Maple Valley Rd., 48416, pg. 1602 **PB**
FRANK INDUSTRIES, INC., 3950 Burnsline Rd., 48416, pg. 423 **PV**
Xplorer Motor Home Div., 3950 Burnsline Rd., 48416, pg. 423 **PV**

Buchanan

Altec Lansing Corp., 600 Cecil St., 49107, pg. 479 **PV**
E.V. International, Inc., 602 Cecil St., 49107, pg. 479 **PV**
Electro-Voice, Inc., 600 Cecil St., 49107, pg. 479 **PV**

Burr Oak

Bleyco Paper Co. of Michigan, 951 Front St., 49030, pg. 731 **PV**

Burton

FLINT MANUFACTURING CO., G-3084 E. Hemphill Rd., 48529, pg. 413 **PV**

Byron Center

Falcon Foam Corporation, 8240 Byron Center Rd., 49315, pg. 1237 **PB**

Cadillac

AAR Cadillac Manufacturing Div., 201 Haynes St., 49601, pg. 1 **PB**
B & P MANUFACTURING, 8052 E. Boon Rd., 49601, pg. 105 **PV**
Cadillac Pipe, 5305 Hwy. M-115, 49601, pg. 881 **PV**
Chemical Bank West, 115 N. Mitchell, 49601, pg. 345 **PB**
Fiamm Technologies Inc., 1550 Leeson Dr., 49601, pg. 480 **IT**
Four Winns, Inc., 925 Frisbie, 49601, pg. 478 **PV**
Kysor Cooling Systems, 1100 Wright St., 49601, pg. 968 **PB**

PB - *U.S. Public Companies Volume*
PV - *U.S. Private Companies Volume*
IT - *International Public & Private Companies Volume*

Old Kent Bank of Cadillac, 123 S. Mitchell, 49601, pg. 1216   **PB**

Caledonia

FOREMOST CORPORATION OF AMERICA, 5600 Beech Tree Ln., 49316, pg. 667   **PB**
Foremost Insurance Co., 5600 Beech Tree Lane, 49316, pg. 667   **PB**

Calumet

Michigan-American Water Company, 311 Fifth St., 49913, pg. 95   **PB**

Canton

American Yazaki Corp., Inc., 6700 Haggerty Rd., 48187, pg. 1520   **IT**
Draw-Tite, Inc., 40500 Van Born Rd., 48188, pg. 1054   **PB**
MascoTech Tubular Products, Inc., 7444 Haggerty Rd., 48187, pg. 1055   **PB**
Miesel/Sysco Food Service Co., 41600 Van Born Rd., 48188, pg. 1551   **PB**

Carney

Gilbert & Bennett, P.O. Box 38, 49812, pg. 453   **PV**

Caro

Chemical Bank Thumb Area, P.O. Box 146, 240 N. State St., 48723, pg. 345   **PB**
Independent Bank-East Michigan, 1111 W. Caro Rd., 48723, pg. 874   **PB**

Cass City

WALBRO CORPORATION, 6242 Garfield St., 48726-1325, pg. 1733   **PB**

Center Line

AETNA INDUSTRIES, INC., 24331 Sherwood, 48015, pg. 25   **PV**

Centreville

Viking Recreational Vehicles, Inc., 580 W. Burr Oak St., 49032, pg. 388   **PB**

Charlevoix

LexaLite International Corporation, 10163 U.S. 31 N., 49720, pg. 1527   **PB**

Charlotte

CFA HOLDING COMPANY, 1023 Reynolds Rd., 48813, pg. 194   **PV**
Care Free Aluminum Products, Inc., 1023 Reynolds Rd., 48813, pg. 194   **PV**
Eaton County Abstract & Title Company, 121 W. Lawrence Ave., 48813, pg. 625   **PV**
LINN PRODUCTS, INC., 1700 E. Packard Hwy., 48813, pg. 669   **PV**
SPARTAN MOTORS, INC., 1000 Reynolds Rd., 48813, pg. 1495   **PB**

Chatham

Chatham Telephone Co., P.O. Box 197, 49816, pg. 1571   **PB**

Chelsea

BookCrafters U.S.A. Inc., 140 Buchanan St., 48118, pg. 70   **PB**
CHELSEA MILLING CO., 201 North St., 48118, pg. 231   **PV**
CHELSEA STATE BANK, 1010 S. Main St., 48118, pg. 231   **PV**

Chesterfield

Bundy Corporation, Phoenix Center, 26950 - 23 Mile Rd., 48051-1911, pg. 1340   **IT**
Bundy Corporation, Russell Schmidt Tool Plant, 50751 E. Russell Schmidt, 48051-2498, pg. 1341   **IT**
LIONEL LLC, 50625 Richard W. Blvd., 48051-2493, pg. 669   **PV**
ST. CLAIRE PLASTICS CO., 30855 Teton Pl., 48047, pg. 960   **PV**

Clare

Alchem Plastics Corp.-Michigan, 314 E. Fourth St., 48617, pg. 1495   **PV**
Chemical Bank Michigan, 807 McEwan St., P.O. Box 710, 48617, pg. 345   **PB**
Mitchell Corporation, Clare Div., 528 Holly St., 48617, pg. 753   **PV**

Clarkston

Greenery Health Care Center at Clarkston, 4800 Clintonville Rd., 48346, pg. 837   **PB**
Sheldahl, Inc. (Clarkston), 6060 Dixie Hwy., Ste. E, 48346, pg. 1465   **PB**

Clawson

CARGILL DETROIT CORP., 1250 N. Crooks Rd., 48017, pg. 210   **PV**
RECARO NORTH AMERICA, INC., 905 W. Maple Rd., 48017, pg. 914   **PV**
TMP Worldwide, Inc., 1250 Fourteen Mile Rd., Ste. 100, 48017, pg. 1064   **PV**

Clinton

HARDWOODS OF MICHIGAN, INC., 430 Division St., 49236, pg. 502   **PV**

Clinton Township

JOHN CARLO INC., 21570 Hall Rd., 48038, pg. 211   **PV**
JIM CAUSLEY PONTIAC GMC INC., 38111 Gratiot Ave., 48036, pg. 220   **PV**
JAMES CHEVROLET INC., 35500 S. Gratiot Way, 48035, pg. 580   **PV**
Nippon Paint Research Institute (America) Inc., 44382 Macomb Industrial Dr., 48036, pg. 937   **IT**
TWEDDLE LITHO COMPANY, 24700 Maplehurst, 48036, pg. 1111   **PV**

Clio

WEYI, Inc., Box 250, 2225 W. Willard Rd., 48420, pg. 389   **PV**

Coldwater

Bundy Corporation, Coldwater Plant, 421 Race St., 49036, pg. 1340   **IT**
Coldwater Cablevision Inc., 623 E. Chicago Rd., 49036, pg. 287   **PB**
Coldwater Reporter, Inc., 15 W. Pearl St., 49036, pg. 1077   **PB**
Emtec Products Corporation, 200 Jay St., 49036, pg. 968   **PB**

Comstock Park

RAPID ENGINEERING INC., 1100 Seven Mile Rd., 49321, pg. 910   **PV**
Zin-Plas Corporation, 25 N. Park St., 49321, pg. 1258   **PB**

Corunna

U.S. Brick, Inc.-Michigan Division, 3820 Serr Rd., Box 66, 48817, pg. 699   **IT**

Croswell

Dean Pickle & Specialty Products, 55 E. Sanborn St., 48422, pg. 490   **PB**

Davison

GENOVA PRODUCTS, INC., 7034 E. Court St., 48423, pg. 447   **PV**
Wiltic Chemical Manufacturing, 422 Rising St., 48423, pg. 447   **PV**

Dearborn

ADRAY APPLIANCE & PHOTO CENTER, INC., 20219 Carlysle, 48124, pg. 18   **PV**
Alcoa Fujikura, 17000 Executive Plaza Dr., 48126, pg. 60   **PB**
American Renaissance Insurance Company, The American Rd., 48121, pg. 664   **PB**
The American Road Insurance Company, The American Rd., 48121, pg. 664   **PB**
BILL WINK CHEVROLET, 10700 Ford Rd., 48126, pg. 144   **PV**
CMS ENERGY CORPORATION, Fairlane Plaza S., Ste. 1100, 330 Town Center Dr., 48126, pg. 279   **PB**
CMS Engineering Co., 330 Town Center Dr., Ste. 1000, 48126, pg. 280   **PB**
CMS Enterprises, Inc., 330 Town Center Dr., Ste. 1000, 48126, pg. 279   **PB**
CMS Generation Co., 330 Town Center Dr., Ste. 1000, 48126, pg. 280   **PB**
CMS Midland, Inc., 330 Town Center Dr., Ste. 1000, 48126, pg. 280   **PB**
Cambridge Industries, Inc., 5433 Miller Rd., 48126, pg. 202   **PV**
Car Product Development, The American Rd., 48121, pg. 662   **PB**
Car Programs Management, The American Rd., 48121, pg. 662   **PB**
Cardinal Redevelopment Corporation, The American Rd., 48121, pg. 663   **PB**
CARHARTT, INC., Three Parklane Blvd., Ste. 1600W, 48126-0600, pg. 210   **PV**
DALE INDUSTRIES INC., 6455 Kingsley Ave., 48126, pg. 308   **PV**

Dearborn Capital Corporation, The American Rd., 48121, pg. 663   **PB**
Detroit Downtown Development Corporation, The American Rd., 48121, pg. 664   **PB**
Environ, Inc., The American Rd., 48121, pg. 664   **PB**
Fairlane Life Insurance Company, The American Road, 48121, pg. 664   **PB**
Ford Asia-Pacific, Inc., The American Rd., 48121, pg. 664   **PB**
Ford Auto Club, Inc., The American Rd., 48121, pg. 663   **PB**
Ford Body & Assembly Operations, The American Rd., 48121, pg. 662   **PB**
Ford Body Engineering, The American Rd., 48121, pg. 662   **PB**
Ford Casting Division, The American Rd., 48121, pg. 662   **PB**
Ford Climate Control Division, The American Way, 48121, pg. 662   **PB**
Ford Colorado Properties, Inc., The American Rd., 48121, pg. 663   **PB**
Ford Communications, Inc., The American Rd., 48121, pg. 664   **PB**
Ford Consumer Discount Company, The American Rd., 48121, pg. 664   **PB**
Ford Credit Auto Receivables Corporation, The American Rd., 48121-1899, pg. 663   **PB**
Ford Design Staff, The American Rd., 48121, pg. 663   **PB**
Ford Direct Markets, Incorporated, The American Rd., 48121, pg. 664   **PB**
Ford Electronics & Refrigeration Corp., The American Rd., 48121, pg. 664   **PB**
Ford Electronics Division, The American Rd., 48121, pg. 662   **PB**
Ford Engine Division, The American Rd., 48121, pg. 662   **PB**
Ford Environmental & Safety Engineering Staff, The American Rd., 48121, pg. 663   **PB**
Ford Financial Services Inc., The American Rd., 48121, pg. 663   **PB**
Ford Glass & Metal, Inc., The American Rd., 48121, pg. 664   **PB**
Ford Holdings Inc., The American Rd., 48121, pg. 663   **PB**
Ford International Export Sales (Asia-Pacific Region) Incorporated, The American Rd., 48121, pg. 664   **PB**
Ford International Services, Inc., The American Rd., 48121, pg. 664   **PB**
Ford Investment Partnership, The American Rd., 48121-1899, pg. 664   **PB**
Ford Leasing Development Co., The American Road, 48121, pg. 664   **PB**
Ford Manufacturing Operations, The American Rd., 48121, pg. 662   **PB**
Ford Marketing Staff, The American Rd., 48121, pg. 662   **PB**
FORD MOTOR COMPANY, The American Rd., 48126, pg. 661   **PB**
Ford Motor Credit Company, The American Rd., 48121, pg. 663   **PB**
Ford Motor Credit Company of Puerto Rico Inc., The American Rd., 48121-1899, pg. 664   **PB**
Ford Motor Dealership Facilities Co., The American Rd., 48121, pg. 664   **PB**
Ford Motor Land Development Corporation, The American Rd., 48121, pg. 663   **PB**
Ford New Holland Credit Company, The American Rd., 48121-1899, pg. 664   **PB**
Ford North American Automotive Operation, The American Rd., 48121, pg. 662   **PB**
Ford North American Design, The American Rd., 48121, pg. 662   **PB**
Ford of Europe, Incorporated, The American Rd., 48121, pg. 662   **PB**
Ford Parts and Service Div., Schaeffer Rd., 48121, pg. 662   **PB**
Ford Plastic & Trim Products International, Inc., The American Rd., 48121, pg. 662   **PB**
Ford Product Assurance, The American Road, 48121, pg. 662   **PB**
Ford Purchasing & Supply Staff, The American Rd., 48121, pg. 664   **PB**
Ford Research Staff, The American Rd., 48121, pg. 664   **PB**
Ford Sales Operations, The American Rd., 48121, pg. 662   **PB**
Ford Technical Affairs & Operating Staffs, The American Rd., 48121, pg. 662   **PB**
Ford Transmission and Chassis Div., The American Rd., 48121, pg. 662   **PB**
Ford Truck Operations, The American Rd., 48121, pg. 662   **PB**
Fordson Coal Company, The American Rd., 48121, pg. 664   **PB**
GHAFARI ASSOCIATES, INC., 17101 Michigan Ave., 48126, pg. 450   **PV**
Ghia, Inc., The American Rd., 48121, pg. 664   **PB**
Greenfield Properties, Inc., The American Rd., 48121, pg. 663   **PB**
Howden Sirocco, Fluid Drive Department, 811 Tireman Ave., 48126, pg. 636   **IT**
KASLE STEEL CORPORATION, 4343 Wyoming St., 48126, pg. 608   **PV**
KENWAL PRODUCTS CORP., 8223 W. Warren Ave., 78126, pg. 615   **PV**
EDWARD C. LEVY CO., 9300 Dix Ave., 48120, pg. 664   **PV**
LIVERNOIS ENGINEERING COMPANY, 25315 Keen, 48124, pg. 672   **PV**
Livernois Vehicle Co., 25241 Trowbridge St., 48124, pg. 672   **PV**

PB - *U.S. Public Companies Volume*
PV - *U.S. Private Companies Volume*
IT - *International Public & Private Companies Volume*

U.S. LOCATED COMPANIES MICHIGAN

MSC Dearborn Office, One Parklane Blvd., 48126, pg. 1031 PB
NAAO Marketing, The American Rd., 48121, pg. 662 PB
NAAO Production Purchasing, The American Rd., 48121, pg. 662 PB
Parklane Insurance Co., The American Road, 48121, pg. 664 PB
Philco Finance Corporation, The American Rd., 48121, pg. 663 PB
Predelivery Service Corporation, The American Rd., 48121, pg. 664 PB
Renaissance Center Venture, The American Rd., 48121, pg. 663 PB
ROUGE STEEL COMPANY, 3001 Miller Rd., 48121, pg. 1406 PB
The Standard Products Co., 2401 S. Gulley Rd., 48124, pg. 1504 PB
THE STANDARD PRODUCTS COMPANY, 2401 S. Gulley Rd., 48124, pg. 1504 PB
Union Trucking Co., 2401 S. Gully Rd., 48124, pg. 1505 PB
United Technologies Automotive, 5200 Auto Club Dr., 48126, pg. 1691 PB
VILLAGE FORD INC., 23535 Michigan Ave., 48124, pg. 1140 PV
Vista Insurance Company, The American Rd., 48121, pg. 664 PB
Westborn Service Center, Inc., 2401 S. Gully Rd., 48124, pg. 1505 PB
Worldwide Automotive Industry, One Parklane Blvd., 48126, pg. 1031 PB
F.B. WRIGHT CO., 9999 Mercier Ave., 48121, pg. 1192 PV

Deckerville

Midwest Rubber, 3525 Range Line Rd., 48427-0098, pg. 1176 PB

Detroit

AC Rochester Overseas Corporation, 3044 W. Grand Blvd., 48202, pg. 722 PB
AJM Packaging Corporation, 6910 Dix, 48209, pg. 2 PV
ANR Atlantic Pipeline Co., 500 Renaissance Ctr., 48243, pg. 389 PB
ANR Blue Lake Company, One Woodward Ave., 48226, pg. 389 PB
ANR Eaton Company, One Woodward Ave., 48226, pg. 389 PB
ANR Gasification Properties Co., 500 Renaissance Center, 48243, pg. 389 PB
ANR Iroquois, Inc., 500 Renaissance Ctr., 48243, pg. 389 PB
ANR Jackson Company, One Woodward Ave., 48226, pg. 389 PB
ANR Northeastern Gas Storage Company, One Woodward Ave., 48226, pg. 389 PB
ANR Pipeline Co., 500 Renaissance Ctr., 48243, pg. 389 PB
ANR Ren-Cen, Inc., One Woodward Ave., 48226, pg. 389 PB
ANR Southern Pipeline Company, 500 Renaissance Ctr., 48243, pg. 389 PB
ANR Storage Co., One Woodward Ave., 48226, pg. 389 PB
ANR Western Storage Co., One Woodward Ave., 48226, pg. 389 PB
ANRFS Holdings, Inc., One Woodward Ave., 48226, pg. 389 PB
ACME MILLS CO. INC., 5151 Loraine St., 48208, pg. 13 PV
ADVANCE STEEL CO., 9635 French Rd., 48213, pg. 21 PV
Ajax Metal Processing, 4651 Bellevue Ave., 48207, pg. 250 PV
Alro Group, Detroit, 18695 Sherwood Ave., 48234, pg. 46 PV
AMERICAN AXLE & MANUFACTURING, 1840 Holbrook Ave., 48212, pg. 51 PV
American Natural Offshore Co., 500 Renaissance Ctr., 48243, pg. 389 PB
American Steel Corp., 7170 E. McNichols, 48212, pg. 903 IT
Ameritech, 444 Michigan Ave., 48226, pg. 97 PB
APEX BROACH & MACHINE CO., 6401 E. Seven Mile Rd., 48234, pg. 77 PV
Applied Industrial Technologies, 1450 Howard St., 48216, pg. 122 PB
ARMADA CORPORATION, 600 Buhl Bldg., 48226, pg. 82 PV
ARROW METAL PRODUCTS CORPORATION, 1200 Mt. Elliott Ave., 48207, pg. 85 PV
Automotive Financial Services, Inc., 12000 Chrysler Dr., 48288, pg. 354 PB
Automotive News, 1400 Woodbridge Ave., 48207-3187, pg. 284 PV
AutoWeek, 1400 Woodbridge Ave., 48207-3187, pg. 284 PV
N.W. Ayer & Partners Detroit, 2000 Fisher Bldg., 48202, pg. 104 PV
BING STEEL INC., 6349 Strong, 48211, pg. 144 PV
BLUE CROSS & BLUE SHIELD OF MICHIGAN, 600 Lafayette E. Blvd., 48226, pg. 151 PV
BOOTH AMERICAN, 333 W. Fort St., Ste. 1230, 48226-3134, pg. 156 PV
Bowlerama Lanes, Inc., 21630 W. Seven Mile Rd., 48219, pg. 475 PV
Brencal Contractors Inc., 6686 E. McNichols Rd., 48212, pg. 106 PV
BRIAN UNLIMITED DISTRIBUTION COMPANY, INC., 13131 Lyndon, 48227, pg. 167 PV
Broad Rack Structures, 601 Washington Blvd., 48226, pg. 170 PV
BROAD, VOGT & CONANT, INC., 601 Washington Blvd., 48226, pg. 170 PV
C.F. BURGER CREAMERY COMPANY, 8101 Greenfield, 48228, pg. 182 PV
CATTLEMAN'S, INC., 1825 Scott St., 48207, pg. 318 PB
Central Steel & Wire Company, 13400 Mt. Elliott Ave., 48212, pg. 327 PB
Chassis Overseas Corp., 3044 W. Grand Blvd., 48202, pg. 723 PB
Chrysler Advance Manufacturing Operations, P.O. Box 353, 48288, pg. 353 PB
Chrysler/Plymouth Division, 12000 Chrysler Dr., 48288-0857, pg. 353 PB
Chrysler Sales Group, 12000 Chrysler Dr., 48288, pg. 353 PB
Coastal Great Lakes, Inc., 500 Rennaissance Ctr., 48243, pg. 390 PB
Comerica Acceptance Corporation, P.O. Box 4707, 48226, pg. 409 PB
Comerica Bank Michigan, 500 Woodward Ave., 48226, pg. 409 PB
COMERICA INCORPORATED, Comerica Tower at Detroit Ctr., 500 Woodward Ave., 48226, pg. 408 PB
Commonwealth Industries, 5900 Commonwealth, 48208, pg. 1054 PB
CONTINENTAL PAPER & SUPPLY CO., 6400 E. Eight Mile Rd., 48234, pg. 269 PV
Continental Wood Preservers, Inc., 7500 E. Davison Ave., 48212, pg. 1193 PB
Crain's Detroit Business, 1400 Woodbridge Ave., 48207-3187, pg. 285 PV
CROWLEY, MILNER & COMPANY, 2301 W. Lafayette, 48216, pg. 461 PB
The Crown Group-Detroit Plant, 6300 E. Seven Mile Rd., 48234, pg. 292 PV
Cummings-Moore Graphite Co., 1646 N. Green Ave., 48209, pg. 87 PV
DTE ENERGY COMPANY, 2000 Second Ave., 48226, pg. 475 PB
Davis Tool & Engineering Co., 19250 Plymouth Rd., 48228, pg. 315 PV
Dearborn Fabricating & Engineering Co., 19440 Glendale Ave., 48223, pg. 1397 IT
Defabco Installation, 12900 Auburn, 48223, pg. 1397 IT
Delco Chassis Overseas Corporation, 3044 W. Grand Blvd., 48202, pg. 723 PB
Delco Electronics Overseas Corporation, 3044 W. Grand Blvd., 48202, pg. 721 PB
DETROIT CITY DAIRY, INC., 15004 Third Ave., 48203, pg. 328 PV
Detroit Diesel Corp., 13400 W. Outer Dr., 48239, pg. 850 PV
DETROIT ELECTRO-COATINGS CO. LLC, 2599 22nd St., 48216, pg. 328 PV
Detroit Free Press, 321 W. Lafayette St., 48226, pg. 965 PB
THE DETROIT MEDICAL CENTER, 663 Woodward Ave., Ste. 200, 48201, pg. 328 PV
Detroit Monthly, 1400 Woodbridge Ave., 48207-3187, pg. 285 PV
The Detroit News, 615 W. Lafayette Blvd., 48226, pg. 700 PB
Detroit Newspapers, 615 W. Lafayette Blvd., 48226, pg. 965 PB
Domestic Uniform Rental, 3800 18th St., 48208, pg. 338 PV
Dynecol, Inc., 6520 Georgia, 48211, pg. 828 PV
The Edison Illuminating Co. of Detroit, 2000 Second Ave., 48226, pg. 476 PB
Empire State Pipeline Company, 500 Rennaissance Ctr., 48243, pg. 390 PB
Eonic Inc., 464 E. Hollywood, 48203, pg. 1176 PB
EVANS INDUSTRIES, INC., 200 Renaissance Center, 48243, pg. 385 PV
Farmer Jack Supermarkets, 18718 Borman Ave., 48228, pg. 1375 IT
Faygo Beverages, Inc., 3579 Gratiot Ave., 48207, pg. 1153 PB
FEDERAL SCREW WORKS, 535 Griswold St., Ste. 2400, 48226, pg. 616 PB
FERROUS PROCESSING & TRADING CO., 9100 John Kronk Ave., 48210, pg. 402 PV
First Federal of Michigan, 1001 Woodward Ave., 48226-1967, pg. 336 PB
FIRST INDEPENDENCE NATIONAL BANK, 44 Michigan Ave., 48226, pg. 635 PB
First of America Community Development Corporation, Penobscott Bldg., 645 Griswold, 48226, pg. 637 PB
Fitzsimons Manufacturing Co., 3775 E. Outer Dr., 48234, pg. 1045 PB
FLINT INK CORP., 25111 Glendale Ave., 48239, pg. 413 PV
Ford Division, 300 Renaissance Ctr., 48243, pg. 662 PB
Frankel Metal Company, 19300 Filer Ave., 48234, pg. 735 PV
Frank's Nursery & Crafts, Inc., 6501 E. Nevada, 48234, pg. 715 PB
Gale Research Inc., 835 Penobscot Bldg., 48226-4094, pg. 1600 PB
GALLAGHER-KAISER CORP., 13710 Mt. Elliot, 48212, pg. 438 PV
GAYLORD PRINTING, INC., 15500 Woodrow Wilson, 48238, pg. 441 PV
General Motors Acceptance Corporation (GMAC), 3044 W. Grand Blvd., 48202, pg. 719 PB
GENERAL MOTORS CORPORATION, General Motors Bldg., 3044 W. Grand Blvd., 48202, pg. 718 PB
General Motors Corporation-Automotive Components Grp. Worldwide, 3044 W. Grand Blvd., 48202, pg. 719 PB
Ghafari Associates, Inc., 407 E. Fort St., Ste. 303, 48226, pg. 450 PV
GMAC Insurance Holdings, 3044 W. Grand Blvd., 48202, pg. 719 PB
Grand Trunk Corporation (GTC), 1333 Brewery Park Blvd., 48207-2699, pg. 258 IT
Grand Trunk Western Railroad, Inc., 1333 Brewery Park Blvd., 48207, pg. 258 IT
Great Lakes Filter, 5151 Loraine St., 48208, pg. 13 PV
Great Lakes Gas Transmission Co., 2100 Buhl Bldg., Ste. 16, 1 Woodward Ave., 48226, pg. 1417 IT
JOHN E. GREEN CO., 220 Victor Ave., 48203, pg. 477 PV
Heat Bath Park Metallurgical Products, 8074 Military Ave., 48204, pg. 518 PV
HELM, INC., 14310 Hamilton, 48203, pg. 520 PV
HOBAN FOODS, INC., 1599 E. Warren Ave., 48207, pg. 531 PV
Hoskins Mfg. Co., 600 Buhl Bldg., 48226, pg. 83 PV
Hoskins Thermal Systems, Inc., 600 Buhl Bldg., 48226, pg. 83 PV
IDEA ENGINEERING & FABRICATING, 13881 Elmira Rd., 48227, pg. 557 PV
Ivex Packaging Corporation-Detroit, 9125 W. Jefferson, 48209, pg. 915 PB
Jeep/Eagle Division, 12000 Chrysler Dr., 48288, pg. 353 PB
JEFFERSON CHEVROLET CO., 2130 E. Jefferson, 48207, pg. 584 PV
THE JOHN JOHNSON CO., 1481 14th St., 48216, pg. 591 PV
ALBERT KAHN ASSOCIATES, INC., Albert Kahn Bldg., 7430 Second Ave., 48202-2798, pg. 604 PV
The Albert Kahn Collaborative, Inc., 277 Gratiot Ave., Ste. 700, 48226-2247, pg. 604 PV
Keywell Co., 3075 Lonyo St., 48209, pg. 619 PV
L-ZOS OPTICS, LTD., 23600 Grand River Ave., 48219, pg. 639 PV
RAY LAETHEM PONTIAC-BUICK-GMC-TRUCK, INC., 17677 Mack Ave., 48224, pg. 642 PV
Lafayette Steel, 3600 N. Military St., 48210, pg. 1221 PB
LETTS INDUSTRIES, INC., 1111 Bellevue Ave., 48207, pg. 661 PV
Lincoln-Mercury Division, 300 Renaissance Ctr., 48243, pg. 662 PB
LITTLE CAESAR ENTERPRISES, INC., Fox Office Ctr., 2211 Woodward Ave., 48201-3400, pg. 671 PV
LUDINGTON NEWS CO. INC., 1600 E. Grand Blvd., 48211-3195, pg. 679 PV
MCN ENERGY GROUP, INC., Guardian Bldg., 500 Griswold St., 48226, pg. 1024 PB
MCN Investment, 500 Griswold St., 48243, pg. 1025 PB
MARTIN UNIVERSAL DESIGN, INC., 4444 Lawton Ave., 48208, pg. 709 PV
Massey Cadillac, Inc., 24600 Grand River, 48219, pg. 713 PV
McGraw Glass Div., 9400 McGraw Ave., 48288, pg. 353 PB
MCINERNEY-MILLER BROTHERS INC., 2001 Brewster St., 48207, pg. 722 PV
Meridian Environmental Services, Inc., 312 S. West End St., 48209, pg. 1095 PB
MEXICAN INDUSTRIES IN MICHIGAN, 1801 Howard, 48216, pg. 739 PV
MichCon, 500 Griswold St., 48226, pg. 1025 PB
Midwest Energy Resources Co., 2000 Second Ave., 48226, pg. 476 PB
Milford Fabricating Co., 19200 Glendale Ave., 48223, pg. 1388 IT
Motors Trading Corporation, 3044 W. Grand Blvd., 48202, pg. 721 PB
C.A. MUER CORP., 1548 Porter St., 48216, pg. 766 PV
NBD Community Development Corporation, 611 Woodward Ave., 48226, pg. 628 PB
NBD Financial Services of Michigan, Inc., 611 Woodward Ave., 48226, pg. 628 PB
NBD Securities, Inc., 611 Woodward Ave., 48226, pg. 628 PB
NTH Consultants, Ltd., 277 Gratiot, Ste. 600, 48226, pg. 772 PV
NTS Detroit, 12601 Southfield Rd., 48223, pg. 1161 PB
North American Passenger Car Platforms, 3044 W. Grand Blvd., 48202, pg. 719 PB
Office Depot, 151 W. Fort St., 48226, pg. 1212 PB
Outdoor Systems, Inc.-Michigan, 88 Custer Ave., 48202, pg. 1235 PB
Outer Drive Manufacturing Technical Center, 3675 E. Outer Dr., 48288, pg. 353 PB
PVS CHEMICALS, INC., 10900 Harper Ave., 48213, pg. 828 PV
PVS-Nolwood Chemicals, Inc., 10900 Harper Ave., 48213, pg. 828 PV
PVS Technologies, Inc., 10900 Harper Ave., 48213, pg. 828 PV
Packer Security Patrol, Inc., 1487 Farnsworth St., 48211, pg. 1603 PB
Palm Pool Products, 22520 Grand River Ave., 48219, pg. 847 PB
PARK MOTOR SALES COMPANY, 18100 Woodward Ave., 48203, pg. 840 PV
PATTERSON LABORATORIES, INC., 11930 Pleasant Ave., 48217, pg. 843 PV
PENSKE CORPORATION, 13400 Outer Dr. W., 48239-4001, pg. 850 PV
Penske Performance, Inc., 13400 Outer Dr. W., 48239, pg. 850 PV
Pepper, Hamilton & Scheetz, 100 Renaissance Center, 36th Fl., 48243-1157, pg. 851 PV
Polk Automotive Data Services Div., 1155 Brewery Park Blvd., 48207-2697, pg. 874 PV

Geographic Index-U.S.

PB - *U.S. Public Companies Volume*
PV - *U.S. Private Companies Volume*
IT - *International Public & Private Companies Volume*

Geographic Index-U.S.

Polk City Directory Div., 1155 Brewery Park Blvd., 48207-2697, pg. 874 **PV**
Pontiac-GMC Division, P.O. Box 43130, 100 Renaissance Ctr., 48265, pg. 720 **PV**
Post-Newsweek Stations, Michigan, Inc., 550 W. Lafayette Blvd., 48231, pg. 1743 **PB**
PVS Transportation, 11001 Harper, 48213, pg. 828 **PV**
Quaker Chemical Corp., 14301 Birwood Ave., 48238, pg. 1346 **PB**
RenTco Trailer Corporation, 11148 Harper, 48232, pg. 1787 **PB**
RONEY & CO., One Griswold St., 48226, pg. 943 **PV**
Saginaw Overseas Corporation, 3044 W. Grand Blvd., 48202, pg. 723 **PV**
SEAMAN-PATRICK PAPER COMPANY, 2000 Howard St., 48216, pg. 979 **PV**
Seibert-Oxidermo, Inc., 6455 Strong, 48211, pg. 502 **PV**
Service Steel Division, 13700 Sherwood, 48212, pg. 1133 **PV**
SHERWOOD FOOD DISTRIBUTORS, 18615 Sherwood, 48234, pg. 993 **PV**
Smith Hinchman Grylls Associates, Inc., 150 W. Jefferson Ave., Ste. 100, 48226, pg. 1010 **PV**
SMITHGROUP, INC., 150 W. Jefferson, Ste. 100, 48226, pg. 1010 **PV**
Specialty Restaurants Corp., 201 W. Atwater St., 48226, pg. 1023 **PV**
Steinbach Stores, Inc., 2301 W. Lafayette, 48216, pg. 461 **PB**
THE STROH BREWERY COMPANY, 100 River Pl., 48207, pg. 1047 **PV**
Syndeco Realty, 660 Plaza Dr., Ste. 2300, 48226, pg. 476 **PB**
TWB, 5151 Wesson St., 48210, pg. 1780 **PB**
Texas Offshore Pipeline System, Inc., 500 Renaissance Ctr., 48243, pg. 389 **PB**
Thorn Apple Valley-Deli & Smoked Meats Division, 3925 Tillman, 48208, pg. 1603 **PB**
Thorn Apple Valley-Frederick Division, 1487 Farnsworth, 48211, pg. 1603 **PB**
Thyssen Inc., 400 Rennaissance Ctr., Ste. 1700, 48243, pg. 1389 **IT**
Thyssen Specialty Steels, Inc., 8837 Lyndon St., 48238, pg. 1388 **IT**
Turner Construction Co., 150 W. Jefferson, Ste.1300, 48226, pg. 1645 **PV**
Unisys Finance Corporation, One Unisys Dr., 43232, pg. 1671 **PB**
Unitex Offshore Transmission Company, 500 Renaissance Ctr., 48243, pg. 389 **PB**
VAN PELT CORPORATION, 13700 Sherwood, 48212, pg. 1133 **PV**
VULCAN IRON WORKS, INC., 12700 Lyndon, 48227, pg. 1144 **PV**
WDIV-TV, 550 W. LaFayette Blvd., 48231, pg. 1743 **PB**
WJR-AM, 2100 Fisher Bldg., 48202, pg. 512 **PB**
WPLT-FM, 2100 Fisher Bldg., 48202, pg. 512 **PB**
WALBRIDGE ALDINGER COMPANY, 613 Abbott St., 48226-2521, pg. 1146 **PV**
Wesley's Quaker Maid Ice Cream, 18940 Weaver, 48228, pg. 1375 **IT**
RALPH C. WILSON ENTERPRISES, 400 Renaissance Center, Ste. 2140, 48243, pg. 1181 **PV**
WINSTON STEEL PRODUCTS CO., 2700 W. Warren Ave., 48208, pg. 1183 **PV**
WOLVERINE PACKING CO., 1340 Winder, 48207, pg. 1186 **PV**
Young & Rubicam Detroit, 200 Renaissance Ctr., Ste. 1000, 48243, pg. 1198 **PV**
YOUNG SUPPLY COMPANY, 888 W. Baltimore Ave., 48202, pg. 1202 **PV**

Dexter

Thetford Corp. Mfg. Facility, 800 Baker Rd., 48130, pg. 352 **PV**

Dowagiac

Autocam-Pax, Inc., 201 Percy St., 49047, pg. 148 **PB**
Rospatch Jessco, Inc., 202 Spaulding St., 49047, pg. 98 **PB**

Dundee

Dundee Cement Co., 6211 Ann Arbor Rd., 48131, pg. 628 **IT**
Holnam Inc., P.O. Box 122, 6211 Ann Arbor Rd., 48131, pg. 628 **IT**

Durand

Marsh Products Co., 7505 E. M-71, 48429, pg. 881 **PV**
PREMARC CORPORATION, 7505 Hwy. M-71, 48429, pg. 881 **PV**
Simplicity Engineering, Inc., 212 South Oak St., 48429, pg. 1066 **PV**

East Jordan

EAST JORDAN IRON WORKS, 301 Spring St., 49727, pg. 356 **PV**

East Lansing

CIBA Specialty Chemicals, Formulated Materials Group, 4917 Dawn Ave., 48823, pg. 291 **IT**
MICHIGAN PHYSICIANS MUTUAL LIABILITY INC., 1301 N. Hagadorn Rd., 48826, pg. 741 **PV**

East Tawas

Starboard Industries, Inc., 935 N. Aulerich, 48730, pg. 919 **PB**

Eastpointe

COLONIAL DODGE, INC., 24200 Gratiot, 48021, pg. 253 **PV**
Copper & Brass Sales, Inc., 17401 Ten Mile Rd., 48021, pg. 1389 **IT**
THE MONAHAN COMPANY, 21321 Kelly Rd., 48021, pg. 756 **PV**

Eaton Rapids

Akemi Plastics, Inc., 5265 S. Clinton Trail, 48827, pg. 1061 **PB**
Dean Pickles & Specialty Products, P.O. Box 70, 502 Marlin St., 48827, pg. 490 **PB**
Eaton Technologies Inc., 402 Haven St., 48827-1832, pg. 558 **PB**
Michigan Packaging Company, P.O. Box 99, 223 N. Main St., 48827, pg. 763 **PB**

Eau Claire

Michigan Tube Co., 45 Love Rd., P.O. Box 157, 49111, pg. 533 **PV**

Ecorse

The Crown Group Ecorse Plant, 100 Mill St., 48229, pg. 292 **PV**
National Steel Corp., Great Lakes Division, One Quality Dr., 48229, pg. 903 **IT**

Edwardsburg

Better Bath Components, Inc., 69836 Krause Rd., 49112, pg. 953 **PB**
Duo-form of Michigan, Inc., 69836 Kraus, 49112, pg. 953 **PB**
Georgie Boy Manufacturing, Inc., 69950 M 62, 49112, pg. 388 **PB**

Elkton

Active Industries, Inc., 81 Drettmann Dr., 48731, pg. 16 **PV**

Escanaba

Escanaba Paper Co., P.O. Box 757, 49829, pg. 1076 **PB**
Mead Publishing Paper, P.O. Box 757, 49829, pg. 1074 **PB**
National Pipe Line Co., 49829, pg. 1259 **PB**

Evart

Evart Products Co., 601 W. Seventh St., 49631, pg. 353 **PB**
Liberty Dairy, 530 N. River St., 49631, pg. 490 **PB**

Farmington

Autocon Technologies, Inc., 38455 Hills Tech Dr., 48331-5751 pg. 850 **PB**
Automation Software, Inc., 27300 Haggerty Rd., Ste. F20, 48331, pg. 110 **PB**
Automotive Worldwide Sector, 24175 Research Dr., 48335-2634, pg. 1558 **PV**
Blue Line Distributing, 24120 Haggerty Rd., 48024, pg. 671 **PV**
Bosch Automotive Group, 38000 Hills Tech Dr., 48331-3417, pg. 204 **IT**
Burns & Wilcox Ltd., 30833 Northwestern Hwy., Ste. 220, 48334, pg. 609 **PV**
Burns & Wilcox - Southfield Office, 30833 Northwestern Hwy., Ste. 120, 48334, pg. 610 **PV**
CSC Healthcare Systems, 34505 W. Twelve Mile Rd., 48018, pg. 423 **PB**
ELECTRO-MATIC PRODUCTS INC., 23409 Industrial Park Ct., 48335, pg. 369 **PV**
Elwell-Parker, Inc., 23944 Freeway Park Dr., 48335, pg. 373 **PV**
A.J. Etkin Construction Co., P.O. Box 9061, 30445 Northwestern Hwy., Ste. 250, 48018, pg. 384 **PV**
ALEX J. ETKIN, INC., 30445 Northwestern Hwy., Ste. 250, 48334-2533, pg. 384 **PV**
FARMINGTON HILLS HOLDING COMPANY, 35200 Grand River Ave., 48335, pg. 395 **PV**
Federal APD, Inc., 24700 Crestview Ct., 48335, pg. 616 **PB**
Futaba Corporation of America, 34115 W. 12 Mile Rd., Ste. 180, 48334, pg. 531 **PV**
GA Insurance Services, 30833 Northwestern Hwy., #220, 48334, pg. 609 **PV**
GKK Automotive, 34975 West Twelve Mile Rd., 48333-9067, pg. 706 **PB**
GSE, Inc., 26340 Research Dr., 48024, pg. 1676 **PB**
Greenery Extended Care Center at Farmington, 34225 Grand River Ave., 48335, pg. 837 **PB**
J. LEE HACKETT CO., 23550 Haggerty Rd., 48335, pg. 492 **PV**
Household Life Insurance Co., 32991 Hamilton Ct., 48334-3358, pg. 842 **PV**

East Tawas

PAUL INMAN ASSOCIATES INC., 30095 Northwestern Hwy., 48334, pg. 564 **PV**
H.W. KAUFMAN FINANCIAL GROUP, INC., 30833 Northwestern Hwy., Ste. 220, 48334, pg. 609 **PV**
Kawasaki Robotics (U.S.A.), Inc., 24402 Sinacola Ct., 48335, pg. 725 **IT**
LIFETIME DOORS INC., 30700 Northwestern Hwy., 48334, pg. 666 **PV**
NPR of America Inc., 32985 Hamilton Ct., Ste. 122, 48334, pg. 938 **IT**
NTH CONSULTANTS, LTD., 38955 Hills Tech Dr., 48331, pg. 772 **PV**
Nichimen America, Inc., Detroit Office, 32000 Northwestern Hwy., Ste. 155, 48334, pg. 928 **IT**
Optech S.A.R.L., Northwestern Hwy., 48334, pg. 1005 **IT**
Royal Premium Budget, Inc., 30833 Northwestern Hwy.-Ste. 220, 48334, pg. 609 **PV**
Bob Saks Jeep-Eagle, 35200 Grand River, 48335, pg. 395 **PV**
Bob Saks Oldsmobile Inc., 35200 Grand River, 48335, pg. 395 **PV**
Bob Saks Toyota, 35200 Grand River, 48335, pg. 395 **PV**
Saturn of Farmington, 24730 Haggerty Rd., 48335, pg. 713 **PV**
BOB SELLERS PONTIAC GMC TRUCK INC., 38000 Grand River, 48335, pg. 983 **PV**
STAR CUTTER CO., 23461 Industrial Park Dr., 48335, pg. 1034 **PV**
TIE Systems-Farmington Hills, 24701 Halsted Rd., 48331, pg. 1085 **PV**
Teksid, Inc., 39300 Country Club Dr., 48331, pg. 483 **IT**
Waterjet Cutting Systems Division, 203400 Halstead Rd., 48335, pg. 877 **PB**

Farmington Hills

ACO INC., 23333 Commerce Dr., 48335-2764, pg. 3 **PV**
AMERISURE COMPANIES, 26777 Halsted Rd., 48331-3586, pg. 65 **PV**
Atlas Copco Tools Inc., 37735 Enterprise Ct., Ste. 300, 48331, pg. 96 **IT**
CAPCO U.S.A., Inc. (Detroit), 2760 Farmington Rd., Ste. 201, 48334, pg. 279 **IT**
A.M. Castle & Co., 38555 Hill Tech. Dr., Ste. 300, 48331, pg. 313 **PB**
COMPUWARE CORPORATION, 31440 Northwestern Hwy., 48334, pg. 423 **PB**
CUNNINGHAM-LIMP DEVELOPMENT CO., 38799 W. 12 Mile Rd., Ste. 100, 48331, pg. 297 **PV**
Desoutter, Inc., 24415 Halsted Rd., 48335, pg. 96 **IT**
DOMESTIC UNIFORM RENTAL CO., 30555 Northwestern Hwy., Ste. 300, 48334, pg. 338 **PV**
EXOTIC RUBBER & PLASTICS CORP., 34700 Grand River Ave., 48332-0395, pg. 388 **PV**
Fiat Auto R&D, 39300 Country Club Dr., 48331-3473, pg. 483 **IT**
Stephen Gould of Michigan, Inc., 37678 Enterprise Ct., 48331, pg. 467 **PV**
HDS SERVICES, 33469 W. 14 Mile Rd., 48331, pg. 490 **PV**
Harman Automotive, 30665 N.W. Hwy., 48334, pg. 796 **PB**
Hydro Aluminum Bohn, Inc., 30230 Orchard Lake Rd., Ste. 150, 48334, pg. 961 **IT**
Magna Lomason Corp., 24600 Hallwood Ct., 48335-1671, pg. 830 **PV**
MARKETING DISPLAYS INTERNATIONAL, 38271 W. 12 Mile Rd., 48331, pg. 705 **PV**
Mechanical Heat & Cold, Inc., 24535 Hallwood Ct., 48335-1667, pg. 322 **PV**
MELODY FOODS, INC., 30777 Northwestern Hwy., 48334, pg. 730 **PV**
Michigan National Bank, N.A., 27777 Inkster Rd., 48334, pg. 906 **PV**
Michigan National Corporation, 27777 Inkster Rd., 48333-9065, pg. 906 **IT**
Nissan CR Corporation, 39001 Sunrise Dr., 48331, pg. 944 **PV**
Nissan Research & Development Corp., 39001 Sunrise Dr., 48331, pg. 945 **IT**
OMRON Automotive Electronics Inc., 30600 Northwestern Hwy., Ste. 250, 48334, pg. 1005 **IT**
Pioneer Snacks, 30777 Northwestern Hwy., Ste 300, 48334, pg. 730 **PV**
Rieter Automotive North America Inc, 38555 Hills Tech Dr., 48331, pg. 1117 **IT**
Symbol, 33533 W. 12 Mile Rd., Ste. 134, 48331, pg. 1546 **PB**
URS Greiner, Inc., 34405 W. 12 Mile Rd., 48331, pg. 1658 **PB**
Waling Tool & Die Co., 23850 Freeway Park Dr., 48335, pg. 172 **PV**
Webb Electric Co., 34375 W. Twelve Mile Rd., 48331, pg. 1156 **PV**
JERVIS B. WEBB COMPANY, 34375 W. 12 Mile Rd., 48331, pg. 1156 **PV**
Jervis B. Webb Worldwide Co., 34375 W. Twelve Mile Rd., 48331, pg. 1156 **PV**
ZEXEL USA Corporation, 37735 Enterprise Ct., Ste. 600, 48331, pg. 1528 **IT**

Ferndale

DETROIT COIL COMPANY, 2435 Hilton Rd., 48220, pg. 328 **PV**
Greer Steel Company Ferndale Michigan Service Center, 1530 E. Nine Mile Rd., 48220, pg. 479 **PV**
HENNELLS, INC., 1200 Woodward Hts., 48220, pg. 522 **PV**
ITW Woodworth, 1300 E. Nine Mile Rd., 48220, pg. 867 **PB**

PB - *U.S. Public Companies Volume*
PV - *U.S. Private Companies Volume*
IT - *International Public & Private Companies Volume*

H.W. Jencks, Inc., 2435 Hilton Rd., 48220, pg. 328   **PV**
OVERHEAD CONVEYOR CO., 1330 Hilton Rd., 48220-2898, pg. 822   **PV**
WALKER WIRE & STEEL COMPANY, 660 E. Ten Mile Rd., 48220, pg. 1147   **PV**

Flat Rock

AutoAlliance International Inc., One International Dr., 48134, pg. 849   **IT**
Mazda Systems of North America, Inc., 27200 International Dr., 48134, pg. 849   **IT**

Flint

AVC/NU-VISION, INC., 2284 S. Ballenger Hwy., 48503, pg. 9   **PV**
Alro Group, Flint, P.O. Box 496, 3501 Western Rd., 48501-0496, pg. 46   **PV**
AUSTIN GROUP, 2300 Austin Pky., 48507, pg. 99   **PV**
Auto Blankers, 1301 Alabama, 48505, pg. 608   **PV**
Buick Motor Div. General Motors Corp., 902 E. Hamilton Ave., 48550-0176, pg. 720   **PB**
CITIZENS BANKING CORPORATION, 328 South Saginaw St., 48502, pg. 379   **PB**
Citizens Commercial & Savings Bank, One Citizens Banking Ctr., 48502, pg. 379   **PB**
DWF of Flint, Inc., 5100 Exchange Dr., 48507, pg. 326   **PV**
Delphi Energy & Engine Management Systems, 4800 S. Saginaw St., 48501-1360, pg. 719   **PB**
Hewlett-Packard Company, 2348 Stone Bridge Dr., Bldg. H, 48504, pg. 814   **PB**
Service Parts Operations, 6060 W. Bristol Rd., 48554, pg. 720   **PB**
WJRT-TV, 2302 Lapeer Rd., 48502, pg. 984   **PB**
Willowbrook Manor, 4436 Beecher Rd., 48532, pg. 837   **PB**
Young Environmental Clean Up, G 5305 N. Dort Hwy., 48505, pg. 1202   **PV**
R.S. YOUNG EXCAVATING, INC., G-5305 N. Dort Hwy., 48505, pg. 1202   **PV**
Zellerbach Division, G-4488 W. Bristol Rd., 48507, pg. 1075   **PB**

Fowlerville

BENT TUBE, INC., 9649 W. Van Buren Rd., 48836, pg. 134   **PV**

Frankenmuth

DeVlieg-Bullard Tooling Systems Division, 126 North Main St., 48734, pg. 502   **PB**

Fraser

AMERICAN AIRCRAFT PARTS MANUFACTURING CO., 17917 Masonic Blvd., 48026, pg. 49   **PV**
Cross Huller, 17801 E. Fourteen Mile Rd., 48026, pg. 1389   **IT**
ISI Norgren, Inc., 31915 Groesbeck Hwy., 48026, pg. 646   **IT**
LOGGHE STAMPING COMPANY, 16711 13 Mile Rd., 48026, pg. 672   **PV**
MP Pumps, Inc., 34800 Bennett Dr., 48026, pg. 1566   **PV**
OAKLAND TOOL & MANUFACTURING COMPANY, 34700 Commerce Dr., 48026, pg. 809   **PV**
U.S. MANUFACTURING CORP., 17717 Masonic Blvd., 48026, pg. 1125   **PV**

Fremont

Gerber Finance Co., 445 State St., 49412, pg. 973   **PV**
Gerber Products Company, 445 State St., 49413, pg. 973   **IT**
Gerber Products Overseas, 445 State St., 49413, pg. 973   **IT**
Lilly Industries, Inc., 411 Darling St., 49412, pg. 994   **PB**
Sundor Brands Inc., 502 Connie Ave., 49412, pg. 1331   **PB**

Galesburg

Eaton Corporation, Truck Components Operations-North America, 13100 E. Michigan Ave., 49053, pg. 557   **PB**

Galien

Carris Reels, Inc.-Michigan Div., 205 W. Southeastern Ave., 49113, pg. 215   **PV**

Garden City

DEARBORN GAGE COMPANY, 32330 Ford Rd., 48135, pg. 319   **PV**

Gaylord

DWF of Gaylord, 1370 Milbocker Rd., 49735, pg. 326   **PV**
Old Kent Bank of Gaylord, 123 W. Main, 49735, pg. 1217   **PB**
Ward Lake Drilling, Inc., P.O. Box 1663, 685 E. M32, 49735, pg. 1078   **PV**

Gladstone

NORTHERN MICHIGAN VENEERS, INC., 933 N. 8th St., 49837, pg. 805   **PV**

Grand Haven

THE CHALLENGE MACHINERY CO., 1433 Fulton Ave., 49417, pg. 227   **PV**
Eagle-Ottawa Leather Co., 200 Beachtree St., 49417, pg. 1105   **PV**
Old Kent Bank of Grand Haven, 233 Washington St., 49417, pg. 1217   **PB**
STANCO METAL PRODUCTS, INC., 2101 168th Ave., 49417-0307, pg. 1030   **PV**
Weyburn Bartel, Inc., U.S. 31 at M 45, 49417, pg. 1334   **IT**

Grand Junction

MICHIGAN BLUEBERRY GROWERS ASSN., Drawer B, 04726 County Rd. 215, 49056, pg. 740   **PV**

Grand Rapids

APV Baker Inc., 3200 Fruit Ridge Ave., N.W., 49504, pg. 1240   **IT**
Abrasives, Inc., 4936 Kendrick St., 49512, pg. 884   **PV**
ADVANCE PACKAGING CORPORATION, 4450 36th St., S.E., 49512, pg. 18   **PV**
Alro Group, Grand Rapids, P.O. Box 1846, 1033 Freeman S.W., 49501-1846, pg. 46   **PV**
Alvey Of Michigan, 2680 Horizon Dr. S.E., 49546-7580, pg. 47   **PV**
American Federation Insurance Co., P.O. Box 2450, 49501, pg. 667   **PB**
AMERICAN METAL & PLASTICS INC., 450 32nd St. SW, 49518, pg. 59   **PV**
AMERICAN SEATING COMPANY, 401 American Seating Ctr., N.W., 49504, pg. 61   **PV**
AmeriServe of Grand Rapids, 435 Ionia Ave. S.W., 49503, pg. 533   **PB**
AMERIWOOD INDUSTRIES INTERNATIONAL INC., Park Century Bldg., 168 Louis Campau Promenade, Ste. 400, 49503, pg. 98   **PV**
Amway Hotel Corporation, 187 Monroe NW, 49503, pg. 69   **PV**
April Hill, Inc., 190 28th St. S.E., 49508, pg. 483   **PV**
AUTOCAM CORPORATION, 4070 E. Paris Ave. S.E., 49512, pg. 148   **PV**
Bell Packaging Corporation-Grand Rapids Div., 2000 Beverly St., S.W., 49509, pg. 1066   **IT**
BISSELL INC., 2345 Walker N.W., 49544, pg. 145   **PV**
Blackmer Pump/Dover Resources Co., 1809 Century Ave. S.W., 49509, pg. 521   **PV**
BOOTH NEWSPAPERS, INC., 155 Michigan N.W., 49503, pg. 238   **PV**
CCL Labeling Equipment, 4460 40th St. S.E., 49512, pg. 371   **IT**
Circle Freight International USA, 4457-40th St. S.E., 49508, pg. 751   **IT**
Clipper Belt Lacer Company, 1995 Oak Industrial Dr., N.E., 49505, pg. 413   **PV**
Comp-Aire, 4185 44th St., 49508, pg. 569   **IT**
Comp-Aire Systems Inc., 4185 44th St. S.E., 49508, pg. 126   **IT**
Computer Design Inc., 2880 E. Beltline, N.E., 49505, pg. 465   **PV**
Computer Design, Inc., 2880 E. Beltline N.E., 49505, pg. 1053   **PB**
L.G. Cook Distributor, Inc., 5400 33rd St. S.E., 49512, pg. 335   **PV**
Country Fresh, Inc., 2555 Buchanan Ave., S.W., 49518, pg. 1526   **PB**
Crown Coat, Inc., 700 Wealthy St., S.W., 49504, pg. 1024   **PV**
D & W FOOD CENTERS, INC., 3001 Orchard Vista Dr., S.E., 49546, pg. 300   **PV**
DICKINSON PRESS, INC., 5100 33rd St. S.E., 49512, pg. 331   **PV**
Dielink, 2066 Bristol N.W., 49504, pg. 1060   **PV**
Earth Technology Corp., 5555 Glenwood Hills Pkwy. S.E., 49512, pg. 1648   **IT**
Evans Tempcon Inc., 701 Ann St. N.W., 49504, pg. 7   **PV**
Foremost Financial Services Corp., P.O. Box 2450, 49501, pg. 667   **PB**
Foremost Property & Casualty Insurance Company, P.O. Box 2450, 49501, pg. 667   **PB**
Foremost Signature Insurance Co., P.O. Box 2450, 49501, pg. 667   **PB**
Forest View Psychiatric Hospital, 1055 Medical Park Dr. SE, 49546, pg. 1697   **PB**
FROST INC., 2020 Bristol NW, 49504, pg. 430   **PV**
Gantos, Inc., 3260 Patterson S.E., 49512, pg. 702   **PB**
Gear Research Incorporated, 4329 Eastern Ave., SE, 49508, pg. 598   **PV**
BF Goodrich Avionic Systems, Inc., 5353 52nd St., S.E., 49588-0873, pg. 751   **PB**
GORDON FOOD SERVICE INC., 333 50th St., 49548, pg. 465   **PV**
Grace Broadcasting Limited Partnership, 180 N. Division, 49503, pg. 362   **PV**
Grand Rapids Die Casting Corp., P.O. Box Q, 25 N. Park St., 49501, pg. 1258   **PV**
Grand River Infrastructure, Inc., 2701 Chicago Dr., S.W., 45909, pg. 881   **PV**
Green Tree Acceptance, Inc., 3835 28th St. SE, 49508, pg. 762   **PB**
GROCERS BAKING CO., 210 28th St. S.E., 49508, pg. 482   **PV**
Guardsman Consumer Products Div., P.O. Box 88010, 2960 Lucerne, S.E., 49518, pg. 995   **PB**
Gypsum Wall Board Plant, 2228 Butterworth Rd., S.W., 49504, pg. 737   **PB**

H S DIE & ENGINEERING, INC., 0-215 Lake Michigan Dr., NW, 49544, pg. 489   **PV**
HARROW INDUSTRIES, 2627 E. Beltline, S.E., 49546, pg. 506   **PV**
Hartger & Willard Mortgage Associates, Inc., 141 Ionia Avenue, 49503, pg. 1216   **PB**
Haviland Consumer Products, Inc., 421 Ann St., N.W., 49504, pg. 511   **PV**
HAVILAND ENTERPRISES, 421 Ann St., N.W., 49504, pg. 511   **PV**
Haviland Products, 421 Ann St., N.W., 49504, pg. 511   **PV**
Hewlett-Packard Company, 3033 Orchard Vista, S.E., Ste. 100, 49506, pg. 814   **PB**
Hilb, Rogal and Hamilton Company of Grand Rapids, 3196 Kraft S.E., 49512, pg. 827   **PB**
HOLLY'S INC., 3033 Orchard Vista Dr. S.E., Ste. 306, 49546, pg. 535   **PV**
Ikon Office Solutions-Michigan, 2780 44th S.W., 49509, pg. 863   **PB**
Instructional Fair, Inc., 2400 Turner Ave., 49501, pg. 288   **PV**
Jet Electronics & Technology, Inc., 5353 52nd St., S.E., 49508, pg. 751   **PB**
Keebler Co./Grand Rapids Bakery, 310 28th St. S.E., 49508, pg. 657   **PB**
Keeler Brass Company, 955 Godfrey Ave., 49503, pg. 473   **IT**
KINDEL FURNITURE COMPANY, 100 Garden S.E., 49507, pg. 620   **PV**
KNAPE & VOGT MFG. CO., 2700 Oak Industrial Dr. N.E., 49505, pg. 963   **PB**
Knoll Grand Rapids, 4300 36th St., S.E., 49508, pg. 627   **PV**
Kysor/Michigan Fleet, 1988 Alpine Ave., N.W., 49544, pg. 968   **PB**
Leon Plastics, Inc., 4901 Clay Ave., S.W., 49548, pg. 1684   **PV**
LESLIE METAL ARTS CO., INC., 3225 32nd St., S.E., 49512, pg. 660   **PV**
Lilly Industries, Inc., 4999 36th St. S.E., 49518, pg. 994   **PB**
MAGHIELSE TOOL CORPORATION, 731 Broadway, N.W., 49504, pg. 694   **PV**
Mazda Distributors (Great Lakes), Inc., 618 Kenmoor, 49546, pg. 849   **IT**
McAlear Associates, Inc., P.O. Box 111, 5303 28th St. Pl. S.E., 49501-0111, pg. 1508   **IT**
Medtronic DLP, 620 Watson SW, 49504, pg. 1083   **PB**
MEIJER, INC., 2929 Walker Ave. N.W., 49544, pg. 729   **PV**
J.W. MESSNER, INC., Waters Bldg., 161 Ottawa, N.W., Ste. 403, 49503-2705, pg. 734   **PV**
MICHIGAN WHEEL CORPORATION, 1501 Buchanan Ave., S.W., 49507-1697, pg. 741   **PV**
MOSS TELECOMMUNICATIONS SERVICES, 561 Century Ave., 49503, pg. 763   **PV**
NTH Consultants, Ltd., 4635 44th St., Ste. C-180, 49512, pg. 772   **PB**
National Food Express, Inc., 2000 Oak Industrial Dr., 49505, pg. 1603   **PB**
Old Kent Bank, One Vandenberg Ctr., 49503, pg. 1216   **PB**
Old Kent Brokerage Services, Inc., One Vanderberg Center, 49503, pg. 1216   **PB**
OLD KENT FINANCIAL CORPORATION, One Vandenberg Ctr., 111 Lyon N.W., 49503-2414, pg. 1216   **PB**
Old Kent Financial Life Insurance Company, One Vandenberg Center, 49503, pg. 1217   **PB**
Old Kent Mortgage Company, 49503, pg. 1216   **PB**
OLIVER PRODUCTS COMPANY, 445 Sixth St., N.W., 49504, pg. 815   **PV**
OWEN-AMES-KIMBALL CO., 300 Ionia Ave. N.W., 49503, pg. 823   **PV**
Owen-Ames-Kimball Engineering, Inc., 300 Ionia Ave. N.W., 49503, pg. 824   **PV**
Parmalat White Knight, 5252 Clay Ave., S.W., 49548, pg. 1023   **IT**
Paulstra CRC Corporation, 460 Fuller St., 49503, pg. 1410   **IT**
PRIDGEON & CLAY, INC., 50 Cottage Grove SW, 49507, pg. 883   **PV**
Prime Technology Imports, Ltd., 4936 Kendrick St., 49512, pg. 884   **PV**
PRIME TECHNOLOGY, INC., 4936 Kendrick St., 49512, pg. 884   **PV**
RI HOLDINGS, 1500 Union Ave., S.E., 49507, pg. 904   **PV**
RANIR CORPORATION/DCP, 4701 E. Paris Ave. S.E., 49512-5353, pg. 909   **PV**
Rapidparts Inc., 1940 Turner N.W., 49504, pg. 315   **PB**
Rapistan Demag Corp., 507 Plymouth Ave. N.E., 49505, pg. 837   **IT**
Recreational Products Div., 4674 Clay Ave., 49548, pg. 205   **PB**
Rowe International, Inc., 1500 Union Ave. S.E., 49507, pg. 904   **PB**
Sackner-Central, 2700 Patterson Ave., 49546, pg. 924   **PB**
Sackner Products, 2700 Patterson Ave., S.E., 49546, pg. 924   **PB**
A. Schulman, Inc., 500 Cascade W. Pkwy., S.E., 49546, pg. 1441   **PB**
Shield Insurance, 3900 Sparks Dr., S.E., 49518, pg. 1021   **PV**
Smiths Industries Aerospace & Defense Systems Inc.-Grand Rapids Operation, 4141 Eastern Ave. S.E., 49518-8727, pg. 1268   **IT**
SOFTECH, INC., 3260 Eagle Park Dr., N.E., 49525, pg. 1482   **PB**
SPARTAN STORES INC., 850 76th St., S.W., 49518, pg. 1021   **PV**
SPECTRUM INDUSTRIES, 522 Plymouth N.E., 49505, pg. 1024   **PV**
Steelcase Financial Services, Inc., 901 44th St. S.E., 49508, pg. 1038   **PV**
STEELCASE INC., P.O. Box 1967, 49501, pg. 1038   **PV**

PB - U.S. Public Companies Volume
PV - U.S. Private Companies Volume
IT - International Public & Private Companies Volume

Steelcase, Inc./Athens Plant, One Vandenburgh Pl., 49503, pg. 1038 **PV**
Steelcase Inc./International Div., 901 44th St. S.E., 49508, pg. 1038 **PV**
Steketee Paul & Sons Company, Inc., 86 Monroe Center, 49503-3215, pg. 346 **PV**
Suspa, Inc., 3970 Roger B. Chaffee Dr. SE, 49548, pg. 1322 **IT**
SYNERGIS TECHNOLOGIES GROUP, 795 36th St. S.E., 49548, pg. 1060 **PV**
Sysco Food Services of Grand Rapids, Inc., 3700 Sysco Court, S.E., 49512, pg. 1551 **PV**
TCH INDUSTRIES INC., 3040 Charlevoix Dr. S.E., 49546, pg. 1063 **PV**
Thorn Apple Valley-Grand Rapids Division, 2000 Oak Industrial Dr., N.E., 49505, pg. 1603 **PB**
Thorn Apple Valley-Transportation Division, 2000 Oak Industrial Dr., 49505, pg. 1603 **PB**
TOWER AUTOMOTIVE, INC., 6303 28th St., S.E., 49546, pg. 1625 **PB**
TRANSNATIONAL MOTORS INC., 618 Kenmoor Ave. S.E., 49546, pg. 1097 **PV**
URS Greiner, Inc., 3950 Sparks Dr. S.E., 49546, pg. 1658 **PB**
United Wholesale Inc., 850 76th St., S.W., 49518, pg. 1021 **PV**
UNIVERSAL FOREST PRODUCTS, INC., 2801 E. Beltline, N.E., 49505, pg. 1696 **PV**
WBCT-FM, 77 Munroe Ctr., Ste. 1000, 49503, pg. 384 **PB**
WOOD-AM/FM, 77 Monroe Ctr., N.W., Ste. 1000, 49503, pg. 385 **PB**
WZZM, 645 Three Mile Rd., 49504, pg. 926 **IT**
WILLIAMS DISTRIBUTING COMPANY, 658 Richmond N.W., 49504, pg. 1177 **PV**
Willis Corroon Corp. of Western Michigan, 678 Front Ave. N.W., 49504, pg. 1507 **IT**
Zellerbach Division, 4855 52nd St. S.E., Ste. E, 49508, pg. 1076 **PB**
The Zondervan Corporation, 5300 Patterson, S.E., 49503, pg. 927 **IT**

Grandville

GRANDVILLE PRINTING COMPANY, 4719 Ivanrest Ave. SW, 49418, pg. 469 **PV**
Milcare, Inc., 4545 Canal Ave., S.W., 49418-9724, pg. 1112 **PB**
X-RITE, INCORPORATED, 3100 44th St., S.W., 49418, pg. 1783 **PB**

Grayling

Chemical Bank North, 2500 I-75 Business Loop, P.O. Box 686, 49738, pg. 345 **PB**
Grayling State Bank, 305 Michigan Ave., 49738, pg. 379 **PB**

Greenville

Frigidaire Home Products-Refrigerator Products, 635 W. Charles St., 48838, pg. 440 **IT**
Printco Group, 1321 Van Deinse, 48838, pg. 228 **PB**

Grosse Ile

Business Air, 9505 Groh Rd. # 100, Hanger # 2, 48138, pg. 539 **PV**

Grosse Pointe Park

Jefferson Chevrolet, 15175 E. Jefferson, 48230, pg. 584 **PV**

Grosse Pointe Woods

Denton Concrete Services Inc., 20415 Mack Ave., 48236, pg. 325 **PV**
DENTON ENTERPRISES INC., 20415 Mack Ave., 48236, pg. 325 **PV**

Hamtramck

KOWALSKI SAUSAGE CO., INC., 2270 Holbrook Ave., 48212, pg. 634 **PV**

Hancock

D & N Bank, 400 Quincy St., 49930, pg. 472 **PB**
D & N Capital Corporation, 400 Quincy St., 49930, pg. 472 **PB**
D & N FINANCIAL CORPORATION, 400 Quincy St., 49930, pg. 472 **PB**
D & N Mortgage Corporation, 400 Quincy St., 49930, pg. 472 **PB**
Quincy Insurance Agency, Inc., 400 Quincy St., 49930, pg. 472 **PB**

Harbor Springs

Control Engineering Co., 8212 Harbor Springs Rd., 49740, pg. 1156 **PV**
Webb Heavy-Duty Roller Conveyor Systems, 8212 Harbor Springs Rd., 49740, pg. 1156 **PV**

Hastings

Bliss, 1004 E. State St., 49058, pg. 196 **PV**
Flex-Fab, 1843 Gun Lake Rd., 49058, pg. 412 **PV**

FLEXFAB HORIZONS INTERNATIONAL, INC., 1843 Gun Lake Rd., 49058, pg. 412 **PV**
HASTINGS MANUFACTURING COMPANY, 325 N. Hanover, 49058-1598, pg. 798 **PB**
National Bank of Hastings, 241 W. State St., 49058, pg. 633 **PB**

Hazel Park

Meier Metal Service Centers, Inc., 1471 E. Nine Mile Rd., 48030, pg. 1100 **PB**

Hemlock

Hemlock Semiconductor Co., 12334 Gedes Rd., 48626, pg. 523 **PB**

Hillsdale

Alsons Corporation, 42 Union St., 42942, pg. 1053 **PB**
Bundy Corporation, Hillsdale Plant, 200 Arch St., 49242, pg. 1340 **IT**
Hillsdale Daily News, P.O. Box 287, 33 McCollum, 49242, pg. 995 **PB**
Hillsdale Tool & Mfg. Co., 135 E. South St., 49242, pg. 355 **PV**
Old Kent Bank of Hillsdale, Ten S. Broad St., 49242, pg. 1217 **PB**
THE SHANE GROUP INC., 250 Industrial Dr., 49242, pg. 989 **PV**
Teleflex Automotive, 266 Industrial Drive, 49242, pg. 1569 **PB**

Holland

BLD Products, Ltd., 534 East 48th St., 49423, pg. 1055 **PB**
BEVERAGE AMERICA, INC., 545 E. 32nd St., 49423, pg. 141 **PV**
BRADFORD COMPANY, 13500 Quincy St., 49424, pg. 163 **PV**
Castex Incorporated, 12875 Ransom St., 49424, pg. 1577 **PB**
Charter House Incorporated, 4660 136th Ave., 49424, pg. 1029 **PV**
DONNELLY CORPORATION, 414 E. 40th St., 49423-5368, pg. 519 **PV**
HAWORTH, INC., One Haworth Ctr., 49423, pg. 511 **PV**
THE HOLLAND HITCH COMPANY, 467 Ottawa Ave., 49423, pg. 534 **PV**
The Holland Sentinel, 54-56 W. 8th St., 49423-9953, pg. 995 **PV**
Hydro Aluminum Bohn, Inc., 365 W. 24th St., 49423, pg. 961 **IT**
Information Products, Inc., 414 E. 40th St., 49423, pg. 519 **PB**
J B LABS, INC., 13295 Reflections Dr., 49424, pg. 576 **PV**
LaBarge Mirrors, Inc., 300 E. 40th St., 49422-1769, pg. 432 **PV**
Micromatic Textron, 345 E. 48th St., 49423, pg. 1589 **PB**
Old Kent Bank of Holland, 36 E. Eighth, 49423, pg. 1217 **PB**
LOUIS PADNOS IRON & METAL CO., 185 W. Eighth, 49423, pg. 834 **PV**
Prince Corporation, One Prince Ctr., 49423, pg. 932 **PB**
Thermotron Industries, 291 Kollen Park Dr., 49423, pg. 1136 **PV**
TRENDWAY CORPORATION, 13467 Quincy St., 49424, pg. 1099 **PV**
UTA Holland Plant, 50 W. Third St., 49423, pg. 1691 **PB**

Holly

Donnelly Electronics, 1410 N. Holly Rd., 48442, pg. 519 **PB**
Georg Fischer Disa Holding Corp., P.O. Box 40, 407 Hadley St., 48442-0040, pg. 488 **IT**
Georg Fischer Disa Inc., P.O. Box 40, 407 Hadley St., 48442-0040, pg. 488 **IT**
Georg Fischer Disa, Inc., P.O. Box 40, 407 Hadley St., 48442-0040, pg. 490 **IT**

Holt

Hose Products Div. Plant, 1355 S. Cedar Rd., 48842, pg. 1260 **PB**
SPARTAN INTERNATIONAL INC., 1845 Cedar St., 48842, pg. 1020 **PV**

Homer

Tru-Turn Corporation, 29991 M-60 E., 49245, pg. 513 **PV**

Howell

Chem-Trend Incorporated, 1445 W. McPherson Park Dr., 48844, pg. 235 **IT**
Citizens Insurance Company of America, 645 W. Grand River, 48843, pg. 54 **PB**
Citizen's Management, Inc., 645 W. Grand River, 44843, pg. 54 **PB**
Greenery Health Care Center, 3003 W. Grand River Ave., 48843, pg. 837 **PB**

Hudson

Day Industries, 3991 Munson Hwy., 49247, pg. 878 **PV**

METALLOY CORPORATION, 103 W. Main St., 49247, pg. 735 **PV**

Imlay City

Champion Motor Coach, Inc., 275 Graham Rd., 48444, pg. 332 **PB**

Inkster

Wolverine Gasket & Manufacturing Co., 2638 Princess St., 48141, pg. 355 **PV**

Ionia

INDEPENDENT BANK CORPORATION, 230 W. Main St., 48846, pg. 874 **PB**

Iron Mountain

BACCO CONSTRUCTION CO., P.O. Box 458, 3660 N. U.S. 2, 49801, pg. 109 **PV**
CABLE CONSTRUCTORS, INC., P.O. Box 190, 105 Kent St., 49801, pg. 197 **PV**
CHAMPION, INC., 105 East A St., 49801, pg. 228 **PV**
Inland Detroit Diesel-Allison, 600 Industrial Park Dr., 49801, pg. 564 **PV**
Klungess Electronic supply, P.O. Box 885, 105 Kent St., 49801, pg. 197 **PV**

Jackson

Advance Packaging Corporation-Jackson Facility, 2400 E. High St., 49204, pg. 18 **PV**
ALLIED CHUCKER & ENGINEERING COMPANY, 3529 Scheele Dr., 49202, pg. 38 **PV**
ALRO GROUP, 3100 E. High St., 49204, pg. 45 **PV**
Alro Group, Jackson, P.O. Box 927, 3100 E. High St., 49204-0927, pg. 46 **PV**
Alro Group, Jackson Plastics, 903 Baldan Rd., 49203, pg. 46 **PV**
Alro Industrial Supply Group, 3100 E. High St., 49204, pg. 46 **PV**
Britains Petite Inc., P.O. Box 1069, 2922 Wildwood Ave., 49204, pg. 789 **PB**
CMS Nomeco, One Jackson Sq., 49201, pg. 280 **PB**
Camp Healthcare, 2010 E. High St., 49203, pg. 1425 **IT**
Consumers Energy, 212 W. Michigan Ave., 49201, pg. 280 **PB**
Crankshaft Machine Group, 314 N. Jackson St., P.O. Box 1127, 49201, pg. 102 **PV**
DAWN FOOD PRODUCTS, INC., 2021 Micor Dr., 49203, pg. 316 **PV**
Engineered Systems Group, 300 S. East Ave., 49203, pg. 24 **PB**
Frontier Communications of Michigan, Inc., Two North Plaza, P.O. Box 3005, 49204, pg. 683 **PB**
Hayes-Albion, 1999 Wildwood Ave., 49202, pg. 796 **PB**
HEAT CONTROLLER, INC., 1900 Wellworth Ave., 49203, pg. 518 **PV**
Horizon Technology Group - Jackson Division, 825 Carroll St., 49202, pg. 539 **PV**
Jacobson Credit Corporation, 3333 Sargent Rd., 49201-8847, pg. 922 **PB**
JACOBSON STORES INC., 3333 Sargent Rd., 49201-8847, pg. 922 **PB**
Jacobson Stores Realty Company, 3333 Sargent Rd., 49201-8847, pg. 922 **PB**
MacSteel Div., 3100 Brooklyn Rd., 49203, pg. 1349 **PB**
Michigan Gas Storage Co., 212 W. Michigan Ave., 49201, pg. 280 **PB**
PLASTIGAGE CORPORATION, 2917 Wildwood Ave., 49202, pg. 871 **PV**
SPARTON CORPORATION, 2400 E. Ganson, 49202, pg. 1496 **PB**
Vickers Actuator Products, 2425 W. Michigan, 49202, pg. 1780 **PB**
WSP, 4905 S. Meridian, 49201, pg. 1780 **PB**
Wolverine Technologies Inc., 701 Liberty St., 49204, pg. 1171 **IT**

Jonesville

Mark I Molded Plastics, Inc., P.O. Box 35, U.S. 12 East, 49250, pg. 599 **PB**

Kalamazoo

The Acorn, 143 S. Kalamazoo Mall, 49007, pg. 454 **PV**
Adel Medical Limited, 2725 Fairfield Rd., 49002, pg. 1526 **PB**
Aero-Motive Company, 5688 ML Ave. E., 49003, pg. 1776 **PB**
Alro Group, Kalamazoo, 5139 Wynn Rd., 49003-3537, pg. 46 **PV**
Asgrow International Corp., 7000 Portage Rd., 49001, pg. 1048 **IT**
Asgrow Seed Company, 2605 E. Kilgore Rd., 49002-1782, pg. 1048 **IT**
BIGGS GILMORE COMMUNICATIONS, 100 W. Michigan Ave., Ste. 300, 49007, pg. 143 **PV**
CMC Kalamazoo Inc., 2016 N. Pitcher St., 49007, pg. 1030 **PV**
C.R.A. Holdings Inc., 2016 N. Pitcher St., 49007, pg. 1029 **PV**
CONTEMPO COLORS, One Paper Pl., 49001, pg. 267 **PV**
Doubleday Bros. & Co., 1919 E. Kilgore Rd., 49002, pg. 1506 **PB**
Dunkley Intl., 1910 Lake St., pg. 234 **PV**

PB - *U.S. Public Companies Volume*
PV - *U.S. Private Companies Volume*
IT - *International Public & Private Companies Volume*

1282

Geographic Index-U.S.

Durametallic Corp., 2100 Factory St., 49001, pg. 658 **PB**
FIRST OF AMERICA BANK CORPORATION, 211 S. Rose St., 49007-5264, pg. 636 **PB**
First of America Bank, N.A., 108 E. Michigan Ave., 49007, pg. 636 **PB**
First of America Brokerage Services, Inc., 211 S. Rose St., 49007, pg. 636 **PB**
First of America Insurance Company, One First of America Pkwy., 49009-8002, pg. 637 **PB**
First of America Investment Corp., 303 N. Rose St., Ste. 500, 49003, pg. 637 **PB**
First of America Securities, Inc., 157 S. Kalamazoo Mall, 49007, pg. 637 **PB**
First of America Trust Company, 211 S. Rose St., 49007, pg. 637 **PB**
GILMORE BROS., INC., 143 S. Kalamazoo Mall, 49007, pg. 454 **PV**
Glassmaster Controls Company, Inc., 831 Cobb Ave., pg. 746 **PV**
GREAT LAKES TECHNOLOGIES CORP., 300 S. Kalamazoo Mall, Ste. 210, 49007, pg. 475 **PV**
Hercules Inc.-Kalamazoo, 411 Hercules Av., 49004, pg. 810 **PB**
Hewlett-Packard Company, 5360 Holiday Ter., 49009, pg. 814 **PB**
HUMPHREY PRODUCTS COMPANY, Kilgore at Sprinkle Rd., 49001, pg. 547 **PV**
Interkal, Inc., 5981 E. Cork St., 49003, pg. 759 **IT**
Jarvis-Pemco, P.O. Box 1068, 1872 Ravine Rd., 49005, pg. 1506 **PB**
KALAMAZOO HOLDINGS, INC., 3713 W. Main St., 49006, pg. 606 **PV**
Kalamazoo Scrap & Processing, 2730 Millcork, 49001, pg. 1048 **PV**
Kalsec, Inc., 3713 W. Main St., 49006, pg. 606 **PV**
LSI/KALA, 2325 Burdick St., 49007, pg. 1437 **PB**
MANATRON, INC., 2970 S. Ninth St., 49009, pg. 1040 **PB**
Master Craft Corp., 831 Cobb Ave., 49007, pg. 267 **IT**
MEDICAL SURGICAL SPECIALTIES, LTD., 3310 Miller Rd., 49001, pg. 728 **PV**
MERCHANTS PUBLISHING CO., 20 Mills St., 49001, pg. 732 **PV**
MIDWEST FASTENERS CORPORATION, 9031 Shaver Rd., 49002, pg. 744 **PV**
Old Kent Bank-Southwest, 136 E. Michigan Ave., 49007, pg. 1217 **PB**
PEC Michigan, 1821 Vanderbilt Rd., 49024, pg. 871 **PB**
PEC Mid West Technical Center, 1811 Vanderbilt Rd., 49024, pg. 871 **PB**
Pharmacia & Upjohn, 7000 Portage Rd., 49001, pg. 1048 **IT**
Pharmacia & Upjohn Adria Laboratories, 7000 Portage Rd., 49001, pg. 1049 **IT**
Pharmacia & Upjohn Central American Management Company, 7000 Portage Rd., 49001, pg. 1048 **IT**
Pharmacia & Upjohn Inter-American Corp., 7000 Portage Rd., 49001, pg. 1048 **IT**
Pharmacia & Upjohn Intl. Inc., 7000 Portage Rd., 49001, pg. 1048 **IT**
Pharmacia & Upjohn Pharmaceutical Div., 7000 Portage Rd., 49001, pg. 1048 **IT**
Physiotherapy Associates, Inc., 2725 Fairfield Rd., 49002, pg. 1526 **PB**
PRAB, INC., 5944 E. Kilgore Rd., 49003, pg. 1319 **PB**
Primary Pulp & Paper Plant, 2425 King Hwy., 49001, pg. 736 **PB**
STRYKER CORPORATION, 2725 Fairfield Rd., 49002, pg. 1525 **PB**
Stryker Far East, Inc., 2725 Fairfield Rd., 49002, pg. 1526 **PB**
Stryker Puerto Rico, Inc, 2725 Fairfield Rd., 49002, pg. 1526 **PB**
Stryker Sales Corporation, 2725 Fairfield Rd., 49002, pg. 1526 **PB**
TIE Systems-Kalamazoo, 2912 Business One Dr., 49001, pg. 1085 **PV**
TUCO Animal Health, 7000 Portage Rd., 49001, pg. 1048 **IT**
A.M. TODD COMPANY, 1717 Douglas Ave., 49007, pg. 1089 **PV**
Todd Juice Products, P.O. Box 50711, 49005, pg. 1090 **PV**
Total Plastic Inc., 2927 Milcork, 49001, pg. 313 **PV**
Zellerbach Division, 8132 Merchants Pl., 49002, pg. 1075 **PB**

Kalkaska

ITW Coding Products, 111 W. Park Dr., 49646, pg. 867 **PB**
Trim Division, 829 U.S. 131 N., 49646, pg. 355 **PB**
WAYNE WIRE CLOTH PRODUCTS, INC., 10 Dresden St., 49646, pg. 1155 **PV**

Kentwood

Bananza Air Management Systems, Inc., 5320 52nd St., S.E., 49508, pg. 910 **PV**
Kal Grafx, 4617 E. Paris, 49512, pg. 387 **PV**
Market Development Co., 5296 Eastern Ave., 49508, pg. 1021 **PV**
Steelcase Design Partnership, 4300 44th St. S.E., 49508, pg. 1038 **PV**
Sterling Color Process, 4617 E. Paris Ave., N.E., 49512, pg. 387 **PV**
Stow Davis Furniture Co., 4300 44th St., S.E., 49508, pg. 1038 **PV**

Kingsford

Lake Shore, Inc., 900 W. Breitung Ave., 49801, pg. 814 **PV**
LODAL, INC., 620 N. Hooper St., 49802, pg. 672 **PV**

Lake Orion

Harry S. Peterson Co., Inc., 3340 S. Lapeer Rd., 48360, pg. 1465 **IT**

Lansing

Alro Group, Lansing, 1800 W. Willow St., 48915, pg. 46 **PV**
Auto-Air Composites, Inc., 5640 Enterprise Dr., 48911, pg. 290 **PV**
AUTO-OWNERS INSURANCE, 6101 Anacapri Blvd., 48917, pg. 100 **PV**
Auto-Owners Life Insurance Co., 6101 Anacapri Blvd., 48917, pg. 100 **PV**
CADE INDUSTRIES, INC., 5640 Enterprise Dr., 48911, pg. 289 **PV**
Cade International, Inc., 5640 Enterprise Dr., 48911, pg. 290 **PV**
Capitol Cadillac, Corp., 5901 S. Pennsylvania Ave., 48911, pg. 712 **PV**
DOUGLAS STEEL FABRICATING CORPORATION, 1312 S. Waverly Rd., 48917, pg. 341 **PV**
GRANGER COMPANIES, 16980 Wood Rd., 48906, pg. 469 **PV**
GRANGER CONSTRUCTION CO., 6267 Aurelius Rd., 48911, pg. 469 **PV**
Granger Container Service, 16980 Wood Rd., 48906, pg. 469 **PV**
Granger Land Development Co., 16980 Wood Rd., 48906, pg. 469 **PV**
Granger Waste Management Co., 16980 Wood Rd., 48906, pg. 469 **PV**
Home-Owners Insurance Co., 6101 Anacapri Blvd., 48917, pg. 100 **PV**
Intergraph Corporation, 7402 Westshire Dr., Ste. 115, 48917, pg. 890 **PV**
Jackson National Life Insurance Company, 5901 Executive Dr., 48911, pg. 1073 **IT**
JEPSON-MURRAY ADVERTISING, 1116 N. Washington Ave., 48906, pg. 586 **PV**
Jet Die, 5300 Aurelius Rd., 48909, pg. 190 **PB**
Lansing State Journal, 120 E. Lenawee St., 48919, pg. 701 **PV**
Lindberg Heat Treating Co., 2127 W. Willow St., 48917, pg. 999 **PB**
MAXCO, INC., P.O. Box 80737, 1118 Centennial Way, 48908, pg. 1061 **PV**
Maxco Inc.-Painters Supply Division, 325 River St., 48933, pg. 1061 **PV**
Meijer Wholesale Inc., 3309 S. Creyts Rd., 48917-8508, pg. 729 **PV**
Melling Forging Company, 1709 Thompson St., 48906, pg. 102 **PV**
NTH Consultants, Ltd., 520 Creyts Rd., Ste. A, 48917, pg. 772 **PV**
Old Kent Bank-Lansing, pg. 1216 **PB**
Oldsmobile Div. General Motors Corp., 920 Townsend St., 48921, pg. 720 **PB**
Padnos-Summit, P.O. Box 13070, 48901, pg. 834 **PV**
PENCO-Michigan, 913 W. Holmes Rd., Ste. 205, 48910, pg. 1508 **IT**
SPARTAN OIL CORP., 419 Spring St., 48912, pg. 1021 **PV**
WSYM-TV, 600 W. St. Joseph St., 48933, pg. 601 **PV**
WOHLERT CORP., 708-12 E. Grand River Ave., 48906, pg. 1185 **PV**

Lapeer

Cambridge Industries, Inc., 1455 Inlay City, 48446, pg. 202 **PV**
DURAKON INDUSTRIES, INC., 2101 N. Lapeer Rd., 48446-8799, pg. 537 **PB**
Duraliner U.S.A., 2101 N. Lapeer Rd., 48446, pg. 537 **PB**
Trayco, Inc., P.O. Box 398, 693 S. Court St., 48446, pg. 1054 **PB**

Leslie

Independent Bank-South Michigan, 144 S. Main St., 49251, pg. 874 **PB**

Lexington

Huron Manufacturing Div., 6554 Lake Shore Rd., 48450, pg. 1684 **PV**

Litchfield

Simpson Mfg. Div., 917 Anderson Rd., 49252, pg. 1475 **PB**

Livonia

A&W RESTAURANTS, INC., 17197 N. Laurel Pk. Dr., Ste. 500, 48152, pg. 1 **PV**
AAR Advanced Structures Div., 12633 Inkster Rd., 48150, pg. 1 **PV**
AM General Corporation, 31744 Enterprise Dr., 48151, pg. 922 **PV**
Air Gage Company, 12170 Globe, 48150, pg. 1676 **PB**
Alpha Coatings, 32711 Glendale Ave., 48150, pg. 1152 **PV**
Ashland-Davis Company, 17199 Laurel Park Rd., 48152, pg. 1171 **IT**
AWREY BAKERIES, INC., 12301 Farmington Rd., 48150, pg. 103 **PV**
BASF Corporation Polymers Division, 13000 Levan St., 48150, pg. 105 **IT**
PETER A. BASILE SONS INC., 13000 Newburgh Rd., 48151, pg. 121 **PV**
Binks Manufacturing Company, 11996 Merriman Rd., 48150-1991, pg. 229 **PB**
BILL BROWN FORD INC., 32222 Plymouth Rd., 48150, pg. 173 **PV**
Cloverlanes, Inc., 28900 Schoolcraft, 48150, pg. 475 **PV**
Clyde Corporation, 11900 Mayfield St., 48150, pg. 862 **PV**
COMPUTER METHODS CORPORATION, 13740 Merriman St., 48150, pg. 260 **PV**
CONTRACTORS STEEL COMPANY, 36555 Amrhein Rd., 48150-1182, pg. 270 **PV**
Copco Steel Co., 17199 N. Laurel Park Dr., Ste. 300, 48152, pg. 1150 **IT**
The Crown Group-Livonia Plant, 31774 Enterprise Dr., 48150, pg. 292 **PV**
Engineered Systems Inc., 11900 Mayfield St., 48150, pg. 862 **PV**
Fluid Recycling Services Company, L.L.C., 31690 Glendale Rd., 48150, pg. 1346 **PB**
Foodland Distributors, 12701 Middlebelt Rd., 48150, pg. 1541 **PV**
Fox Video Company, 39000 Seven Mile Rd., 48152, pg. 926 **IT**
Froude Consine Inc., Ste. B16, 39201 Schoolcraft Rd., 48150, pg. 473 **IT**
GREAT LAKES REALTY CORP., 28900 Schoolcraft Rd., 48150, pg. 475 **PV**
GREAT LAKES WHOLESALE DRUGS, 31778 Enterprise Dr., 48150, pg. 475 **PV**
HOMETOWN COMMUNICATIONS NETWORK, INC., 36251 Schoolcraft Rd., 48150, pg. 537 **PV**
Hy-Form Products, Inc., 35588 Veronica Dr., 48150, pg. 493 **PV**
JLK America Inc., PO Box 3359, 31800 Industrial Rd., 48151-3359, pg. 951 **PB**
LANDMARK SYSTEMS INC., 30777 School Craft Rd., 48150, pg. 649 **PV**
Leone Food Service Corp., 30660 Plymouth Rd., 48150, pg. 244 **PV**
Livonia-Rubber & Plastics Div., 32975 Industrial Rd., 48150, pg. 1176 **PB**
Lumonics Corp., 19776 Haggerty Rd., 48152, pg. 1315 **IT**
MSC Livonia Office, 38777 Six Mile Rd., 48152, pg. 1031 **PB**
Melody Farms, 3111 IndustrialDr., 48150, pg. 730 **PV**
Metropolitan Asphalt, Inc., 13000 Newburgh Rd., 48151, pg. 121 **PV**
THE MILLGARD CORP., 12822 Stark Rd., 48150, pg. 748 **PV**
NHK International Corp., 13961 Farmington Rd., 48154, pg. 902 **IT**
Norgren/Detroit, 36740 Commerce, 48150, pg. 647 **IT**
PHILLIPS SERVICE INDUSTRIES, INC., 11900 Mayfield St., 48150, pg. 862 **PV**
PLASTOMER CORP., 37819 Schoolcraft Rd., 48150, pg. 872 **PV**
PSI Repair Services, Inc., 11900 Mayfield St., 48150, pg. 862 **PV**
RS ELECTRONICS, 34443 Schoolcraft Rd., 48150, pg. 905 **PV**
RTI Laboratories Division, 31628 Glendale, 48050, pg. 1542 **PB**
Rancare Inc., 31742 Enterprise Dr., 48150, pg. 1073 **PB**
ROUSH INDUSTRIES INC., 11916 Market St., 48150, pg. 948 **PV**
Sames Electrostatic, Inc., 11998 Merriman Rd., 48150-1919, pg. 229 **PB**
Triangle Special Products, 13015 Fairlane, 48250, pg. 147 **PB**
VALASSIS COMMUNICATIONS, INC., 19975 Victor Pkwy., 48152, pg. 1704 **PB**
Valassis Inserts, 36111 Schoolcraft Rd., 48150, pg. 1704 **PB**
Valeo/Acustar Thermal Systems, 37564 Amrhein St., 48150, pg. 354 **PB**
Varity Kelsey Hayes, 12025 Tech Center Dr., 48150, pg. 820 **IT**
VISPAC Inc., 3500 Industrial, 48150, pg. 1703 **PB**
WASHERS, INCORPORATED, 33375 Glendale Ave., 48150, pg. 1152 **PV**
Willis Corroon Administrative Services Corporation, 38777 W. Six Mile Rd., Ste. 400, 48153, pg. 1504 **IT**
Willis Corroon Corp. of Michigan, 38777 W. Six Mile Rd., Ste. 400, 48151, pg. 1506 **IT**
Woodward-Clyde, 38777 W. Six Mile Rd., Ste. 200, 49152, pg. 1656 **PB**

Lowell

KING MILLING COMPANY, 115 S. Broadway St., 49331, pg. 621 **PV**

Ludington

Great Lakes Castings Corporation, 800 N. Washington, 49431, pg. 169 **PV**
Old Kent Bank of Ludington, 124 S. James St., 49431, pg. 1217 **PB**
Pandrol Jackson, Inc., 200 S. Jackson Rd., 49431, pg. 280 **IT**

PB - *U.S. Public Companies Volume*
PV - *U.S. Private Companies Volume*
IT - *International Public & Private Companies Volume*

Macomb Township

ACR INDUSTRIES INC., 15375 23 Mile Rd., 48042, pg. 3 — PV

Madison Heights

AJAX PAVING INDUSTRIES INC., One Ajax Dr. Ste. 200, 48071, pg. 29 — PV
Alpha Bolt Company, 1524 E. Fourteen Mile Rd., 48071, pg. 1152 — PB
CAMBRIDGE INDUSTRIES INC., 555 Horace Brown Dr., 48071, pg. 202 — PV
Century Supply Corp., 31691 DeQuindra, 48071, pg. 1389 — PB
Chapman Security Systems, Inc., 950 E. Whitcomb, 48071, pg. 394 — PB
CIBA-GEIGY Formulated Systems Group (Automotive Center), 31601 Research Park Dr., 48071, pg. 973 — IT
CODE-ALARM, INC., 950 E. Whitcomb, 48071, pg. 393 — PB
Code Alarm Security Systems, 950 E. Whitcomb, 48071, pg. 394 — PB
D-M-E Company, 29111 Stephenson Hwy., 48071, pg. 368 — PB
Fairlanes Bowl, Inc., 29600 Stephenson Hwy., 48071, pg. 475 — PV
H.B. Fuller Automotive Products, 31601 Research Park Dr., 48071, pg. 687 — PB
H & L Tool Co., 32701 Dequindre Rd., 48071, pg. 349 — PB
Haden Management Corporation, 32450 N. Avis Dr., 48071, pg. 586 — IT
Haden Technical Services Corporation, 1521 E. Avis Dr., 48071, pg. 586 — IT
Henkel Surface Technologies, 32100 Stephenson Hwy., 48071, pg. 610 — IT
James Steel & Tube Company, 29774 Stephenson Hwy., P.O. Box 71545, 48071, pg. 102 — PV
KASPER MACHINE COMPANY, 29275 Stephenson Hwy., 48071, pg. 608 — PV
Lason, Inc., 29400 Stephenson Hwy., 48071, pg. 979 — PB
MCNAUGHTON-MCKAY ELECTRIC CO., 1357 E. Lincoln Ave., 48071, pg. 724 — PV
Peterson Spring-Madison Heights Plant, 32601 Industrial Dr., 48071, pg. 857 — PB
Printing Service Incorporated, 1451 E. Lincoln Rd., 48071, pg. 1736 — PB
RING SCREW WORKS, 31550 Stephenson Hwy., 48071, pg. 931 — PV
Sanko Peterson Corporation, 32399 Milton, 48071, pg. 857 — PB
Schlegel North American Automotive Operations, 31791 Sherman Dr., P.O. Box 71367, 48071, pg. 128 — IT
TRIANGLE ELECTRIC COMPANY, 29787 Stephenson Hwy., 48071, pg. 1102 — PV
WALL COLMONOY CORP., 30261 Stephenson Hwy., 48071, pg. 1148 — PV

Manchester

Johnson Controls, Inc. (Engineered Plastics Div.), 912 City Rd., 48158, pg. 932 — PV
Johnson Controls, Inc., Plastics Technology Group, P.O. Box 129, 912 City Rd., 48158, pg. 932 — PB
Manchester Plastics, 500 W. Madison, 48158, pg. 399 — PB

Manistee

Akzo Salt Inc., 1501 Main St., 49660, pg. 48 — IT

Manistique

Manistique Papers, Inc., 453 South Mackinac, 49854, pg. 762 — IT

Marine City

Bundy Corporation, Marine City Plant, 6100 King Rd., 48039-0510, pg. 1340 — IT

Marlette

Active Homes Corp., 7939 S. Van Dyke, 48453, pg. 16 — PV

Marne

Birchwood Care Center, 15140 16th Ave., 49435, pg. 837 — PB

Marquette

Republic Automotive Parts Sales, Inc., 211 S. Fifth St., 49855, pg. 1378 — PB
Taystee Bakeries, 855 W. Washington St., 49855, pg. 1022 — PV

Marshall

Chemical Bank South, 115 West Drive S., 49068, pg. 345 — PB
Eaton Corporation, Engine Components Division, 19218 B Drive S., 49068-9790, pg. 556 — PB
Eaton Corporation, Tort Control Division, 1101 W. Hanover St., 49068, pg. 557 — PB
Midwest Metallurgical Lab., Inc., 15290 Fifteen Mile Rd., 49068, pg. 1679 — PB

Perstorp Components Inc.-Marshall, 905 Industrial Rd., 49068, pg. 1040 — IT

Marysville

Bundy Corporation, Marysville Plant, P.O. Box 328, 184 Grtatiot Blvd., 48040-0328, pg. 1340 — IT
Evans St. Clair, 2541 Mills St., 48040, pg. 385 — PV

Mason

DART CONTAINER CORP., 500 Hogsback Rd., 48854, pg. 311 — PV

Melvindale

Feralloy North American Steel Co. Ltd. Partnership, 18030 Riatto, 48122, pg. 1070 — IT
North American Steel Management Corp., 18030 Rialto, 48122, pg. 1070 — IT

Mendon

Lear Plastics Corp., 236 W. Clark St., 49072, pg. 982 — PB

Menominee

Anchor Coupling Inc., 5520 Thirteenth St., 49858, pg. 315 — PB
Bell Packaging Corporation-Menominee Div., P.O. Box 310, 49858, pg. 1066 — IT
Giddings & Lewis Casting Technology, 1610 15th St., 49858, pg. 1389 — IT

Michigan Center

AIRMASTER FAN CO., 1300 Falahee Rd., 49203, pg. 29 — PV

Midland

CFC Data Corp., 127 Townsed St., 48640, pg. 345 — PB
CPI Engineering Services, Inc., 2300 James Savage Rd., 48641-1666, pg. 1016 — PB
Chemical Bank & Trust Company, 333 E. Main St., P.O. Box 231, 48640, pg. 345 — PB
CHEMICAL FINANCIAL CORPORATION, 333 E. Main St., 48640-0569, pg. 345 — PB
Dorinco Reinsurance Co., 2030 Dow Ctr., 48640, pg. 522 — PB
THE DOW CHEMICAL COMPANY, 2030 Dow Ctr., 48674, pg. 522 — PB
Dow Chemical North America, 2020 Dow Center, 48640, pg. 522 — PB
Dow Corning Corporation, 2200 W. Salzburg Rd., 48611, pg. 523 — PB
Dow Credit Corporation, 2030 Willard H. Dow Ctr., 48674, pg. 522 — PB
Ingersoll CM Systems Inc., 3505 Centennial Dr., 48640, pg. 562 — PV
Liquid Molding Systems, Inc., , 800 S. Jefferson, 48640, pg. 125 — PB
Midland Daily News, 124 S. McDonald St., 48640, pg. 517 — PV
Quebecor Printing Pendell Inc., 1700 James Savage Rd., 48642, pg. 1077 — IT
Quebecor Printing Pendell Inc., 1700 James Savage Rd., 48640, pg. 1078 — IT

Milan

Cresive Milan Division, 555 Platt, 48160, pg. 289 — PV

Milford

Parks Omega, Inc., 4901 McCarthy Dr., 48381, pg. 1222 — PB

Millington

Wolverine Telephone Company, 4712 E. Main St., P.O. Box 292, 48746, pg. 1572 — PB

Monroe

Communications & CableVision, Inc., 899 S. Telegraph Rd., 48161, pg. 287 — PB
Detroit Stoker Co., 1510 E. First St., 48161, pg. 1679 — PB
LA-Z-BOY INCORPORATED, 1284 N. Telegraph Rd., 48162-3390, pg. 972 — PB
McPherson Strut Company Inc., One Intl. Dr., pg. 1578 — PB
Michigan Gas Utilities, 899 S. Telegraph, 48161, pg. 1701 — PB
MIDWAY PRODUCTS CORPORATION, 523 Detroit Ave., 48161, pg. 744 — PV
Monroe Auto Equipment Co., One International Dr., 48161, pg. 1577 — PB
Monroe Cablevision Inc., P.O. Box 808, 48161, pg. 147 — PV
River Raisin Cablevision Inc., 1070 S. Telegraph Rd., 48161, pg. 287 — PB

Mount Clemens

Admore Inc., 24707 Wood Ct., 48045, pg. 583 — PB
Aeroquip Inoac Company, 19700 Hall Road, 40843, pg. 24 — PB

Mount Pleasant

Delfield Company, 980 South Isabella Rd., 48858, pg. 1445 — PB

Muskegon

The Access Works, Inc., 1800 E. Keating Ave., 49442, pg. 410 — PV
AMSTORE CORPORATION, 1221 E. Keating St., 49442, pg. 68 — PV
Bekaert Corporation, 2121 Latimer Dr., 49442, pg. 184 — IT
Brunswick Bowling & Billiards Corp., P.O. Box 329, 525 W. Laketon, 49443, pg. 265 — PB
CWC Castings Textron, 1085 W. Sherman Blvd., 49441, pg. 1590 — PB
CWC Textron Company, 1085 W. Sherman Blvd., 49441, pg. 1590 — PB
Cannon-Muskegon Corp., Box 506, 2875 Lincoln St., 49441, pg. 1420 — PV
ESCO, P.O. Box 448, 49443-0448, pg. 383 — PV
Finishmaster Inc., 3610 Airline Rd., 49444, pg. 639 — PV
FLEET ENGINEERS, INC., 1800 E. Keating Ave., 49442, pg. 410 — PV
General Dynamics Land Systems Div., 76 Getty St., 49442-1238, pg. 709 — PB
Goetze Corp. of America, 1839 Sixth St., 49441, pg. 1335 — IT
Hasper Equipment Co., 3662 Airline Rd., 49444, pg. 247 — PB
Kaydon Corporation, Bearings Division, 2860 McCracken, 49441, pg. 946 — PB
KURDZIEL INDUSTRIES, INC., 801 W. Norton Ave., Ste. 300, 49441, pg. 637 — PV
Lee Industries, 1800 E. Keating Ave., 49442, pg. 410 — PV
Lift Tech International, P.O. Box 769, 414 W. Broadway Ave., 49443-0769, pg. 406 — PB
Michigan Spring Company, 2700 Wickham Dr., 49443, pg. 880 — PB
Midland Grocery of Michigan, Inc., 1764 Creston St., 49443, pg. 948 — PV
Muskegon Construction Company, 425 Catawba Ave., 49443, pg. 824 — PV
NEWAY ANCHORLOK INTERNATIONAL INC., 1950 Industrial Blvd., 49442, pg. 796 — PV
QUALITY STORES INC., 455 E. Ellis Rd., 49441, pg. 899 — PV
SPX CORPORATION, 700 Terrace Point Dr., 49443, pg. 1420 — PB
Sun Chemical Corp. of Michigan, 4925 Evanston Ave., 49443, pg. 370 — IT
UNC Johnson Technology, 2034 Latimer Dr., 49442, pg. 710 — PB
ZEPHYR INC., P.O. Box 5069, 49445, pg. 1204 — PV

New Haven

Bundy Corporation, New Haven Plant, P.O. Box 481000, 30600 Commerce Blvd., 48048-1000, pg. 1340 — IT

New Hudson

Elopak, Inc., 30000 S. Hill Rd., 48165, pg. 1390 — IT

New Troy

STANLEY KNIGHT CORPORATION, 3604 Glendora Rd., 49119, pg. 1033 — PV

Niles

ABB Garden City Fan, 1701 Terminal Rd., 49120, pg. 4 — IT
AgTec, Inc., 1420 S. 11th St., 49120, pg. 6 — PB
Capitol Hardware, Inc., 601 N. Eighth St., 49120, pg. 904 — PV
HESS ENGINEERING INC., 191 Fir Rd., 49120-9766, pg. 524 — PV
NATIONAL-STANDARD CO., 1618 Terminal Rd., 49120, pg. 1160 — PB
Rubber Group, 1618 Terminal Rd., 49120, pg. 1160 — PB
Silverbrook Manor, 911 S. Third St., 49120, pg. 837 — PB
Specialty Products Group, 1618 Terminal Rd., 49120, pg. 1160 — PB
Welding Products Group, 1618 Terminal Rd., 49120, pg. 1161 — PB

Northville

MascoTech Industrial Components, Inc., 21800 Haggerty Rd., Ste. 110, 48167, pg. 1055 — PB

Norway

North Star/Norway, 512 9th Ave., 49870, pg. 602 — PV

Novi

Autodesk Mechanical Division, 26200 Town Center Dr., 48375, pg. 149 — PB
Borel & Dunner, Inc., 22530 Heslip Dr., 48050, pg. 260 — PB

PB - *U.S. Public Companies Volume*
PV - *U.S. Private Companies Volume*
IT - *International Public & Private Companies Volume*

1284

Geographic Index-U.S.

Clarion Corporation of America, Detroit Engineering Office, 41140 Bridge St., 48375, pg. 296 **IT**
DEMARIA BUILDING CO. INC., 45500 Grand River Ave., 48376, pg. 323 **PV**
GENERAL FILTERS, INC., 43800 Grand River Ave., 48375, pg. 444 **PV**
Hewlett-Packard Company, 39550 Orchard Hill Place Dr., 48050, pg. 814 **PB**
KEY PLASTICS, INC., 21333 Haggerty Rd., Ste. 200, 48375, pg. 618 **PV**
Klockner-Moeller, 39830 Grand River Ave., Ste. B, 48375, pg. 736 **IT**
Micanol, Inc., P.O. Box 881, 46001 Grand River Ave., 48376, pg. 1453 **PB**
MICHIGAN CAT, 24800 Novi Rd., 48375, pg. 740 **PV**
MICHIGAN MILK PRODUCERS ASSOCIATION, 41310 Bridge St., 48375, pg. 741 **PV**
NBD Equipment Finance, Inc., 39555 Orchard Hill Pl., Ste. 340, 48375, pg. 628 **IT**
SMS-Ann Arbor, 39555 Orchard Hill Pl., Ste. 450, 48375, pg. 1463 **PB**
SECOM GENERAL CORPORATION, 46035 Grand River Ave., 48374, pg. 1453 **PB**
Uniflow Corporation, P.O. Box 705, 26600 Heyn Dr., 48376, pg. 1453 **PB**
Zellerbach Division, 41581 Eleven Mile Rd., 48375, pg. 1075 **PB**

Oak Park

Barton-Malow Rigging Co., 21090 Fern Ave., 48237, pg. 120 **PV**
Cadillac Electric, 20700 Hubbell Ave., 48237, pg. 1068 **IT**
The Robert Carter Corp., 13305 Capital, 48237, pg. 1676 **PB**
CLOVERDALE EQUIPMENT CO., 13133 Cloverdale, 48237, pg. 247 **PV**
F/N Group, Inc., P.O. Box 47160, 48237, pg. 84 **PB**
ICEE-USA Corp., 13050 Northend St., 48237, pg. 916 **PB**
Lamina Inc., 14925 W. Eleven Mile Rd., 48237, pg. 75 **PV**
MCINERNEY INC., 14100 W. Eight Mile Rd., 48237, pg. 722 **PV**
MEL FARR AUTOMOTIVE GROUP, INC., 24750 Greenfield Rd., 48237, pg. 723 **PV**
H.O. TRERICE COMPANY, 12950 W. Eight Mile Rd., 48237, pg. 1099 **PV**
THE WICKMAN CORP., 10325 Capital Ave., 48237, pg. 1175 **PV**

Okemos

Saturn of Okemos, 1728 Grand River, 48864, pg. 713 **PV**

Owosso

Charmilles Technologies Manufacturing Corp., 1550 E. South St., 48867, pg. 489 **IT**
Chemical Bank Key State, 100 E. Main St., 48867, pg. 345 **PB**
Corrugated Packaging, 465 S. Delaney Rd., 48867, pg. 737 **PB**
Insituform North, Inc., P.O. Box 250, 1950 Sequoia Trail, 48867, pg. 882 **PB**
MITCHELL CORPORATION OF OWOSSO, 123 N. Chipman St., 48867, pg. 753 **PV**
Old Kent Bank-Central, 123 N. Washington, 48867, pg. 1216 **PB**
Real Brick Products, Inc., 106 North Washington St., 48867, pg. 699 **IT**
Woodard Inc., 317 S. Elm St., 48867, pg. 192 **PV**

Oxford

Finite Filter Div., P.O. Box 599, 500 Glaspie St., 48371-5132, pg. 1260 **PB**

Paw Paw

WARNER VINEYARDS, 706 S. Kalamazoo St, 49079, pg. 1151 **PV**

Perry

Shiawassee Telephone Company, P.O. Box 167, 129 S. Main St., 48872, pg. 1572 **PB**

Petoskey

Old Kent Bank of Petoskey, 300 E. Mitchell, 49770, pg. 1217 **PB**
URS Greiner, Inc., 601 Ingalls, 49770, pg. 1658 **PB**

Pinconning

Century Telephone of Michigan, Inc., 4399 N. Huron Rd., 48650, pg. 329 **PB**
Century Telephone, Region IV, 4399 N. Huron Rd., 48650, pg. 329 **PB**
MAGLINE, INC., 503 S. Mercer St., 48650, pg. 695 **PV**
Northern Tube, 401 E. Fifth St., 48650, pg. 230 **PV**

Plainwell

Concept Manufacturing Company, Inc., 928 Industrial Pkwy., 49080, pg. 548 **PV**

Plymouth

AE Goetze-North America, 47001 Port St., 48170, pg. 1334 **IT**
Aisin World Corp.-Detroit, 14933 Keel St., 48170, pg. 39 **IT**
Arrow/Schweber Electronics, 494720 Helm St., 48170, pg. 133 **PB**
BRODER BROS. CO., 45555 Port St., 48170, pg. 170 **PV**
DAVIS INDUSTRIES INC., 14500 Sheldon Rd., Ste. 140, 48170, pg. 315 **PV**
Diversey Lever, 14496 Sheldon Rd., STe. 210, 48170, pg. 1437 **IT**
Dow Corning S.T.I., 47799 Hayard, Ste. 99, 48170, pg. 523 **PV**
Durr Industries, Inc., 40600 Plymouth Rd., P.O. Box 2129, 48170-4297, pg. 421 **IT**
FREUDENBERG-NOK, 47690 E. Anchor Ct., 48170, pg. 427 **PV**
Futaba Corporation of America, 14492 Sheldon Rd., Ste. 350, 48170, pg. 531 **IT**
Gage Adistra Corp., 101 Union St., 48107, pg. 437 **PV**
Graco Industrial/Automotive Equipment Division, 47700 Halyard Dr., 48170-2412, pg. 757 **PB**
Isuzu Motors America Inc., 46401 Commerce Center Dr., 48170, pg. 692 **IT**
Johnson Controls, Inc., 49200 Halyard Dr., 48170, pg. 932 **PB**
LOU LARICHE CHEVROLET INC., 40875 Plymouth Rd., 48170, pg. 651 **PV**
DON MASSEY CADILLAC INC., 40475 Ann Arbor Rd., 48170, pg. 712 **PV**
NATIONAL CONCRETE PRODUCTS COMPANY, 939 S. Mill St., 48170, pg. 781 **PV**
National Riggers & Erectors, 14650 Jib St., 48170, pg. 511 **PV**
Optrex Glass, 44160 Plymouth Oaks Dr., 48170, pg. 84 **IT**
Perstorp Components Inc., 47785 Anchor Ct., 48170, pg. 1040 **IT**
PLASTIPAK PACKAGING INC., 9135 General Ct., 48170, pg. 872 **PV**
POWER PROCESS PIPING, INC., 45780 Port St., 48170, pg. 878 **PV**
Saturn of Plymouth, 4301 Massey Dr., 48170, pg. 713 **PV**
SIMPSON INDUSTRIES, INC., 47603 Halyard Dr., 48170-2429, pg. 1474 **PB**
Sumitomo Electric Automotive Inc., 45300 Polaris Ct., 48170, pg. 1313 **IT**
TAPCO INTERNATIONAL CORPORATION, 45657 Port St., 48170-6010, pg. 1068 **PV**
VICTORY PACKAGING, 9070 General Dr., 48170, pg. 1139 **PV**
Winkelman Stores Credit Corp., 45000 Helm St., 48170, pg. 858 **PV**
Winkelman Stores, Inc., 45000 Helm St., 48170, pg. 858 **PV**

Pontiac

A B C APPLIANCE INC., One Silverdome Industrial Pk., 48343, pg. 2 **PV**
Armada Times, 48 W. Huron St., P.O. Box 9, 48056, pg. 513 **PB**
GEORGE W. AUCH CO., 735 S. Paddock, 48341, pg. 98 **PB**
Brown City Banner, 48 W. Huron St., P.O. Box 9, 48056, pg. 513 **PB**
GM Powertrain Group, 895 Joslyn Rd., Room 2B25, 48340-2920, pg. 719 **PB**
GSW Thermoplastics - Michigan, 1735 Highwood East, Bldg. J, 48340, pg. 538 **IT**
GenCon Services, Inc., 735 S. Paddock, 48341, pg. 98 **PV**
Great Lakes Media, Inc., 48 W. Huron St., 48343, pg. 513 **PB**
Limbach Co., P.O. Box 420728, 48342-0728, pg. 322 **IT**
Midwest Management Co., 3300 Countryside Circle, 48057, pg. 988 **PB**
Pontiac-GMC Truck Division, 31 Judson St., 48341, pg. 720 **PB**
Bert L. Smokler & Co., 3300 Countryside Circle, 48057, pg. 989 **PB**

Port Huron

Acheson Colloids Company, 1600 Washington Ave., 48060, pg. 12 **PV**
ACHESON INDUSTRIES, INC., 511 Fort St., Rm. 315, 48061, pg. 12 **PV**
Bindicator Company, 1915 Dove St., P.O. Box 610009, 48061, pg. 138 **PV**
The Crown Group Port Huron Plant, 1631 Dove St., 48060, pg. 292 **PV**
E.B. Eddy Paper, Inc., 1700 Washington Ave., 48060, pg. 1495 **IT**
Hilb, Rogal and Hamilton Company of Port Huron, 1923 Holland Ave., 48061, pg. 827 **PB**
MARY MAXIM, INC., 2001 Holland Ave., 48060, pg. 716 **PV**
SEMCO Energy Services, Inc., P.O. Box 5026, 405 Water St., 48060, pg. 1489 **PB**
Southeastern Development Company, P.O. Box 5026, 405 Water St., 48060, pg. 1489 **PB**
Southeastern Financial Services, Inc., P.O. Box 5026, 405 Water St., 48060, pg. 1489 **PB**
Southeastern Michigan Gas Company, 2915 Lapeer Rd., 48060, pg. 1489 **PB**

SOUTHEASTERN MICHIGAN GAS ENTERPRISES, INC., 405 Water St., 48060, pg. 1489 **PB**
The Times Herald Co., 911 Military St., 48060, pg. 701 **PB**
Waltec American Forgings, Inc., 2440 20th St., 48060, pg. 453 **IT**

Portage

Charles River Laboratories-MI, P.O. Box 176, 49081, pg. 194 **PB**
Contech Div. (Kalamazoo), 8080 Moorsbridge Rd., Ste. 200, 49024, pg. 1421 **PB**
Buck Forkardt, Inc., 4169 Commercial Ave., 49002-9701, pg. 1484 **IT**
Ronningen-Petter Div., P.O. Box 188, 49081, pg. 521 **PB**
Spring Tools Company, 9718 Portage Rd., 49002, pg. 857 **PV**

Pullman

PULLMAN INDUSTRIES, INC., 5576 109th Ave., 49450, pg. 894 **PV**

Quincy

Acorn Window Systems, 42 Cole St., 49082, pg. 14 **PV**
ACORN WINDOW SYSTEMS INC., 42 Cole St., 49082, pg. 14 **PV**
Actex, Inc., 1146 E. Chicago Rd., 49082, pg. 13 **PV**

Quinnesec

Quinnesec Mill, Champion International Corp., U.S. Hwy. 2, 49876, pg. 334 **PB**

Redford

Detrex Industrial Chemical Specialties Div., 26000 Capitol Ave., 48239-2499, pg. 502 **PB**

Redford Township

Alro Specialty Metals, Redford, 24800 Plymouth Rd., 48239, pg. 46 **PV**

Richland

Pneumatic Div., 8676 E. M-89, 49083-0901, pg. 1259 **PV**

Richmond

BEC INC., 37601 Logg Rd., 48062, pg. 106 **PV**
Wellington Manufacturing, Inc., 69620 Lowe Plank Rd., 48062, pg. 1117 **IT**

River Rouge

Fabricon Products, 1721 W. Pleasant Ave., 48218, pg. 355 **PV**
Shelby Steel Processing Co., 40 Haltiner, 48218, pg. 1065 **PB**
Texaco USA, P.O. Box 18028, 48218-0028, pg. 1583 **PB**

Riverside

MPH Industries, P.O. Box 131, 49084, pg. 726 **PB**

Rochester

LETICA CORPORATION, 52585 Dequidnre, 48307, pg. 661 **PV**
Rochester Gear, Inc., 4483 Orion Rd., 48064, pg. 1176 **PB**
Sackner-Automotive Sales Office, 2573 S. Rochester Rd., Ste. 100, 48307-4475, pg. 924 **PB**
Vickers Inc., 2730 Research Dr., 48309-3574, pg. 25 **PB**

Rochester Hills

Bernal Division, 2960 Technology Dr., 48309, pg. 1517 **PB**
CHRISTIAN MEMORIAL CULTURAL CENTER, 521 E. Hamlin Rd., 48307, pg. 238 **PV**
FANUC Robotics North America, Inc., 3900 W. Hamlin Rd., 48309-3253, pg. 477 **IT**
Harlan Electric Co., 2695 Crooks Rd., 48309, pg. 1029 **PB**
Lear Corporation, 2998 Waterview Dr., 48309, pg. 982 **PB**
Long Manufacturing Ltd., 1885 Enterprise Dr., 48309, pg. 815 **IT**
MPI International, Inc., P.O. Box 090040, 2129 Austin Ave., 48309-0040, pg. 737 **IT**
MACRO COMPUTER PRODUCTS INC., 2523 Product Ct., 48309, pg. 693 **PV**
Macro Soft, 2523 Product Ct., 48309, pg. 693 **PV**
Maui Cup, 1700 W. Hamlin Rd., 48309, pg. 661 **PV**
Spar Marketing Force, Inc., 1757 Northfield Dr., 48309, pg. 23 **PB**
Speedring Systems, Inc., 2909 Waterview Dr., 48309, pg. 158 **PB**
TOC, 1885 Enterprise Dr., 48309, pg. 815 **IT**

Rockford

B & L Plastics Inc., One Industrial Dr., 49341, pg. 867 **PB**
Bates Div., 9341 Courtland Dr., 49351, pg. 1775 **PB**
Domestic Licensing, 9341 Courtland Dr., 49351, pg. 1775 **PB**
Hush Puppies Company, 9341 Courtland Dr., 49351, pg. 1775 **PB**

Geographic Index-U.S.

Independent Bank-West Michigan, 78 S. Main St., 49341, pg. 874 **PB**
WWW Retail, Inc., 9341 Courtland Dr., 49351, pg. 1775 **PB**
Wolverine Brand Div., 9341 Courtland Dr., 49351, pg. 1775 **PB**
Wolverine Leather Div., 9341 Courtland Dr., 49351, pg. 1775 **PB**
WOLVERINE WORLD WIDE, INC., 9345 Courtland Dr., 49351, pg. 1775 **PV**

Romeo

Romeo Rim Inc., 74000 Van Dyke Rd., 49065, pg. 300 **PV**

Romulus

CHEMCENTRAL/Detroit, 13395 Huron River Dr., 48174-0906, pg. 232 **PV**
Circle Freight International, 6760 Metroplex Dr., Metroplex Industrial Dr., 48174, pg. 370 **PB**
Circle International, 6930 Metroplex Dr., 49508, pg. 371 **PV**
Form Flow, Inc., 6901 Cogswell, 48184, pg. 1453 **PV**
HAYES WHEELS INTERNATIONAL, INC., 38481 Huron River Dr., 48174, pg. 513 **PB**
HEADER PRODUCTS INC., 11850 S. Wayne Rd., 48174-0188, pg. 514 **PV**
Horizon Technology Group - Romulus Division, 27991 Northline Rd., 48174, pg. 539 **PV**
L & H Die, Inc., P.O. Box 157, 38200 Ecorse Rd., 48174, pg. 1453 **PV**
RamaTech LLC, 28111 Northline, 48174, pg. 539 **PV**
Seibert-Oxidermo, Inc., 16255 Wahrman, 48174, pg. 502 **PB**
VCST Inc., 11677 South Wayne Rd. Ste. 10, 48174, pg. 1134 **IT**
Voest-Alpine Services and Technologies Corp.-Romulus, 28975 Smith Rd., 48174, pg. 1471 **IT**

Roseville

ACTIVE TOOL & MANUFACTURING CO., INC., 32901 Gratiot Ave., 48066, pg. 16 **PV**
ATLAS TOOL INC., 29880 Groesbeck Hwy., 48066, pg. 97 **PV**
Corrugated Products Division, 20101 Cornillie Dr., 48066-1766, pg. 763 **PB**
Direct Tool Inc., 15300 Martin Rd., 48066, pg. 250 **PV**
HOFLEY MANUFACTURING COMPANY, 15500 12 Mile Rd., 48066, pg. 532 **PV**
JEFFREY BUICK-NISSAN INC., 30800 Gratiot Ave., 48066, pg. 585 **PV**
Mill & Abrasive Supply, Inc., 27690 Groesbeck Hwy., 48066, pg. 951 **PV**
ROSEVILLE CHRYSLER PLYMOUTH JEEP INC., 25800 Gratiot Ave., 48066, pg. 946 **PV**

Rothbury

Kurdziel Iron of Rothbury, Inc., 2625 Winston Rd., 49452, pg. 637 **PV**

Royal Oak

THE COON-DE VISSER CO., P.O. Box 81, 1500 N. Stephenson Hwy., 48068, pg. 273 **PV**
JIM FRESARD PONTIAC BUICK, INC., 400 N. Main St., 48067, pg. 427 **PV**
Industrial & Automotive Fasteners, Inc., 3200 W. 14 Mile Rd., 48073, pg. 919 **PV**
MascoTech Forming Technologies, 2727 W. 14 Mile Road, 48073, pg. 1055 **PB**
Pulte Homes of Michigan, 315 S. Woodward Ave., Ste. 110, 48067-2488, pg. 1344 **PB**
ROYAL OAK FORD INC., 27550 Woodward, 48067, pg. 948 **PV**
Warrick Controls, Inc., 4237 Normandy Ct., 48073, pg. 482 **PB**

Saginaw

APV Chemical Machinery, Inc., Process Systems Div., 1000 Hess St., 48601, pg. 1240 **IT**
Cox Communications-Saginaw, 720 N. Bates St., 48602, pg. 455 **PB**
DURO-LAST ROOFING, INC., 525 W. Morley Dr., 48601, pg. 349 **PV**
Means Industries, Inc., 1860 S. Jefferson, 48601, pg. 1711 **PB**
Michigan Sugar Company, P.O. Box 1348, 48605, pg. 873 **PB**
SBS HOLDINGS, INC., 302 Waller St., 48602, pg. 955 **PV**
SBS Products, Inc., 302 Waller St., 48602, pg. 955 **PV**
Second National Bank of Saginaw, 101 N. Washington, 48607, pg. 379 **PB**
WNEM-TV, 107 N. Franklin St., 48606, pg. 1094 **PB**
WOLOHAN LUMBER CO., 1740 Midland Rd., 48603, pg. 1774 **PB**

Saint Clair

Long Manufacturing Inc., 2020 Christian B. Haas, 48079, pg. 815 **IT**
MascoTech Coatings, 4662 Puttygut Rd., 48039, pg. 1055 **PB**

Saint Clair Shores

Binderline Development, Inc./Draftline Engineering Co., Inc., 33100 Freeway Dr., 48082, pg. 493 **PB**
Breed Technologies, 23001 Industrial Dr. W., 48080, pg. 251 **PB**
ROY O'BRIEN INC., 22201 E. Nine Mile Rd., 48080, pg. 810 **PV**
JOHN M. OLSON COMPANY, 26210 Harper, 48081, pg. 815 **PV**

Saint Johns

Old Kent Bank of St. Johns, 201 E. Walker, 48879, pg. 1217 **PB**

Saint Joseph

Bosch Braking Systems-North America, St. Joseph Plant, 3737 Red Arrow Way., 49085-9217, pg. 204 **IT**
IPC Communication Services, 501 Colonial Dr., 49085, pg. 601 **PV**
Industrial Rubber Goods, 1776 Hilltop Rd., 49085, pg. 229 **PV**
KitchenAid Co., Sparks Administrative Ctr., 701 Main St., 49085, pg. 1765 **PV**
Pinnacle Bank, 830 Pleasant St., 49085, pg. 1297 **PB**
PINNACLE FINANCIAL SERVICES INC., 830 Pleasant St., 49085, pg. 1297 **PV**
Swan Technologies Corporation, P.O. Box 167, Hilltop Rd., 49085, pg. 317 **IT**

Saline

Associated Spring, 1445 Barnes Ct., 48176, pg. 190 **PB**
CRESCIVE DIE & TOOL, INC., 905 Woodland Dr., 48176, pg. 289 **PV**
MCNAUGHTON & GUNN, INC., 960 Woodland Dr., 48176-9058, pg. 724 **PV**
R & B MACHINE TOOL CO., 1705 Woodland Dr., 48176, pg. 901 **PV**
RENOSOL CORP., 1512 Woodland Dr., 48176, pg. 922 **PV**
Saline Investment Co., P.O. Box 100, 48176, pg. 902 **PV**
SENSORS, INC., 6812 So. State Rd., 48176, pg. 984 **PV**

Sandusky

Trelleborg YSH, Inc.-Sandusky Division, 180 Dawson St., 48471-1099, pg. 1422 **IT**

Sault Sainte Marie

Edison Sault Electric Company, 725 E. Portage Ave., 49783, pg. 592 **PB**
ESELCO, INC., 725 E. Portage Ave., 49783, pg. 591 **PB**
Northern Tree Service, Inc., 725 E. Portage Ave., 49783, pg. 592 **PB**
Wohlert Special Products, 1415 Industrial Park Dr., 49783, pg. 1185 **PV**

Shelby

Oceana Foods, P.O. Box 156, 97 W. Second St., 49455, pg. 234 **PV**
TRI-MARK METAL CORP., P.O. Box 182035, 48318, pg. 1100 **PV**

Sheridan

Happy Holiday Tree Farms, 3819 E. Sidney Rd., 48884, pg. 254 **PV**
Wright Plastic Products, Inc., 201 Condensery Rd., 48884, pg. 1061 **PB**

South Haven

South Haven Coil Inc., P.O. Box 409, 49090, pg. 548 **PV**
Trelleborg YSH, Inc., 400 Aylworth Ave., 49090, pg. 1422 **IT**

Southfield

ALL NATION INSURANCE COMPANY, 29621 Northwestern Hwy., 48034, pg. 35 **PV**
Allied Security Inc., 104 Northland Towers West, 15565 Northland Dr., 48075, pg. 41 **PV**
AlliedSignal Inc., AlliedSignal Automotive, 20650 Civic Center Dr., 48086-5029, pg. 51 **PB**
Altek, 21624 Melrose, 48075, pg. 483 **PV**
Amcast Automotive, 300 Galleria Officentre, Ste. 208, 48034, pg. 63 **PB**
AMERICAN DENTAL TECHNOLOGIES, 28411 Northwestern Hwy., Ste. 1100, 48034-5541, pg. 70 **PB**
AMURCON CORPORATION, 30215 Southfield Rd., Ste 200, 48076, pg. 69 **PV**
Amurcon Equities, 30215 Southfield Rd., Ste. 200, 48076, pg. 69 **PV**
The ARGOS Group, American Center Bldg., Ste 675, 27777 Franklin Rd., 48034, pg. 120 **PV**
Arnold Advertising, 26555 Evergreen Rd., Ste. 1700, 48076, pg. 84 **PV**
AST Research, Inc., 26677 W. Twelve Mile, 48034, pg. 1181 **IT**
AVIS FORD INC., 29200 Telegraph Rd., 48034, pg. 101 **PV**

BET Media Sales, 2000 Town Ctr., Ste. 1900, 48075, pg. 235 **PB**
Barton Malow Co., American Center Bldg., 27777 Franklin Rd., Ste 800, 48034, pg. 120 **PV**
BARTON MALOW ENTERPRISES, INC., American Ctr. Bldg., 27777 Franklin Rd., Ste. 800, 48034, pg. 120 **PV**
Brass-Craft Manufacturing Company, 100 Galleria Office Ctr., 48034, pg. 1053 **PB**
Bridgestone/Firestone Original Equipment Tire Sales Company, 26777 Central Park Blvd., Ste. 250, 48076, pg. 213 **IT**
CMI INTERNATIONAL INC., 30333 Southfield Rd., 48076, pg. 195 **PV**
Celegec Automation Projects Inc., 27301 W. Eleven Mile Rd., 48034, pg. 53 **IT**
Cerner Corporation -Great Lakes Region, 2833 Telegraph Rd., Ste. 500, 48034-1903, pg. 331 **PB**
Chrysler Credit Corp., 27777 Franklin Rd., 48034, pg. 354 **PB**
Chrysler Financial Corporation, 27777 Franklin Rd., 48034-8286, pg. 354 **PB**
Chrysler Insurance Co., 27777 Franklin Rd., 48034, pg. 354 **PB**
Chrysler Life Insurance Co., 27777 Franklin Rd., 48034, pg. 354 **PB**
Chrysler Overseas Capital Corporation, 27777 Franklin Rd., 48034, pg. 354 **PB**
DON COLEMAN ADVERTISING, INC., 26555 Evergreen Rd., 18th Fl., 48076, pg. 251 **PV**
D.O.C. OPTICS CORPORATION, 19800 W. Eight Mile Rd., 48075, pg. 305 **PV**
Dataproducts Corp., 24275 W. 12 Mile Rd., 48034, pg. 620 **IT**
Detrex Automation Div., P.O. Box 5111, 48086-5111, pg. 501 **PB**
DETREX CORPORATION, 24901 Northwestern Hwy., Ste. 500, 48075, pg. 501 **PB**
Dofasco USA Inc., 26877 N.W. Hwy., Ste. 104, 48034-8431, pg. 414 **IT**
EDS, Business Operations Group, P.O. Box 511, 26533 Evergreen Rd., 48086, pg. 570 **PB**
ENGINEERING SERVICE, INC., 21556 Telegraph Rd., 48034, pg. 376 **PV**
Excel Automotive Systems, 27335 W. Eleven Mile Rd., 48034, pg. 599 **PV**
Fasco Industries, Inc., 23800 W. Ten Mile Rd., Ste. 208, 48034, pg. 125 **IT**
FEDERAL-MOGUL CORPORATION, 26555 Northwestern Hwy., 48034, pg. 615 **PB**
General Employment Enterprises, Inc., 17117 W. Nine Mile Rd., Ste. 1039, 48075, pg. 714 **PB**
GIFFELS ASSOCIATES, INC., 25200 Telegraph Rd., 48034-2599, pg. 452 **PV**
Giffels Strategic Consultants, L.L.C., 25200 Telegraph Rd., Ste. 201, 48034-7412, pg. 452 **PV**
Giffels Technologies, Inc., P.O. Box 5063, 25200 Telegraph Rd., Ste. 101, 48086-5063, pg. 452 **PV**
GUARDIAN ALARM CO., 20800 Southfield Rd., 48075, pg. 485 **PV**
Guilford Mills (Automotive & Upholstery Fabrics), 26899 Northwestern Hwy., Ste. 200, 48034, pg. 769 **PB**
HARLEY ELLINGTON DESIGN, 26913 Northwestern Hwy., Ste. 200, 48034, pg. 503 **PV**
Hiram Walker, 3000 Town Ctr., Ste. 3200, 48075, pg. 63 **IT**
Hygrade Food Products Corporation, 40 Oak Hollow Rd. #355, 48034, pg. 1433 **PB**
Intergraph Corporation, 28411 Northwestern Hwy., Ste. 600, 48034, pg. 890 **PB**
JOY SERVICE, 21700 Northwest Hwy., 48075, pg. 602 **PV**
Kobe Steel USA Inc., 1000 Town Center, Ste. 2450, 48075, pg. 740 **IT**
LEAR CORPORATION, 21557 Telegraph Rd., 48086, pg. 981 **PB**
NORMAN LEVY ASSOCIATES, INC., 21415 Civic Ctr. Dr., Ste. 306, 48076, pg. 664 **PV**
MHIA Air-Conditioning & Refrigeration Machinery Division, 3000 Town Center, Ste. 1960, 48075, pg. 874 **IT**
Magna International of America, Inc., 26200 Lahser Rd., Ste. 300, 48034, pg. 830 **IT**
Marketing Information Group, 26955 Northwestern Hwy., 48034, pg. 874 **PV**
MARS ADVERTISING CO., 24209 Northwestern Hwy., 48075, pg. 706 **PV**
Mars Public Relations Group, 24209 Northwestern Hwy., 48075, pg. 707 **PV**
THE R.J. MARSHALL CO., 26776 W. 12 Mile Rd., 48034, pg. 708 **PV**
Master Data Center, 29100 Northwestern Hwy., Ste. 300, 48034, pg. 778 **PV**
MAXITROL CO., 23555 Telegraph Rd., 48037, pg. 716 **PV**
Mid-States Mortgage Corp., One Town Sq., Ste. 1913, 48076, pg. 982 **PV**
Mitsubishi Motors America, Inc., 3000 Town Ctr., Ste. 1960, 48075, pg. 876 **IT**
Mitsui & Co. (U.S.A.), 1000 Town Ctr., 48075, pg. 879 **IT**
ART MORAN PONTIAC-GMC INC., 29300 Telegraph Rd., 48034, pg. 760 **PV**
NYK Bulkship-Detroit, 3000 Town Center, Ste. 1340, 48075, pg. 941 **IT**
Nippon Steel Corporation, 1000 Town Center, #2840, 48075, pg. 940 **IT**
Nissan Trading Corp., USA, 3000 Town Center, Ste. 2939, 48075, pg. 945 **IT**
Norsk Magnesium Market Development Center, 21644 Melrose Ave., 48075-7905, pg. 961 **IT**
Old Kent Bank-East, 32500 Telegraph, 48075, pg. 1216 **PB**
Outdoor Services, Travelers Tower, 26555 Evergreen, Ste. 1210, 48076, pg. 1166 **PV**
PARLIAMENT COMPANY, 26911 Northwestern Hwy., Ste. 105, 48034, pg. 840 **PV**

PB - U.S. Public Companies Volume
PV - U.S. Private Companies Volume
IT - International Public & Private Companies Volume

PEERLESS DISTRIBUTING CO., 21700 Northwestern Hwy., Ste. 1160, 48075, pg. 847 **PV**
PEREGRINE INCORPORATED, 25200 Telegraph Rd., 48086, pg. 852 **PV**
Perini Building Company-Central U.S. Division, 2000 Town Ctr., Ste. 1600, 48075, pg. 1278 **PB**
PETERSON AMERICAN CORP., 21200 Telegraph Rd., 48034, pg. 857 **PV**
Plumbers Quality Tool Manufacturing Co., Inc., 27700 Northwestern Hwy., 48034, pg. 1053 **PB**
R.L. POLK & CO., 26955 Northwestern Hwy., 48034, pg. 874 **PV**
Prime Technology, Inc., 21670 Melrose Ave., Bldg. 15, 48075, pg. 884 **PV**
Professional Information Managment, One Town Sq., Ste. 1913, 48075, pg. 982 **PV**
PROGRESSIVE TOOL & INDUSTRIES CO., 21000 Telegraph Rd., 48034, pg. 890 **PV**
Renault USA, 4000 Town Center Dr., #480, 48075, pg. 1102 **IT**
Royal Financial Services Inc., 25800 Northwestern Hwy., 48037, pg. 1130 **IT**
Sakura Bank - Detroit Representative Office, 3000 Town Center, Ste. 2555, 48075, pg. 1179 **IT**
SELIGMAN & ASSOCIATES, INC., One Town Sq., Ste. 1913, 48076, pg. 982 **PV**
Sequent Computer Systems, Inc., 26999 Central Park Blvd., Ste. 150, 48076, pg. 1459 **PB**
Shandwick Detroit, 25800 N.W. Hwy., Ste. 800, 48075, pg. 1227 **IT**
Solvents & Environmental Services Div., 24901 Northwestern Hwy., Ste. 512, 48075, pg. 502 **PV**
Stewart Smith Specialty Risks, Inc., 26899 N.W. Hwy., Ste. 207, 48034, pg. 1508 **IT**
Sumitomo Corporation of America, The American Center Bldg., 27777 Franklin Rd., Ste. 1410, 48034, pg. 1312 **IT**
Superior Consultant Company, Inc., 400 Town Center, Ste. 1100, 48075, pg. 1539 **PB**
SUPERIOR CONSULTANT HOLDINGS CORP., 4000 Town Center, Ste. 1100, 48075, pg. 1538 **PB**
TAV Foods Service, 18700 W. Ten Mile Rd., 48075, pg. 1603 **PB**
TAMAROFF BUICK INC., 28585 Telegraph Rd., 48034, pg. 1067 **PV**
Tamaroff Leasing Co., 28585 Telegraph Rd., 48034, pg. 1067 **PV**
THORN APPLE VALLEY, INC., 26999 Central Park Blvd., Ste. 300, 48076, pg. 1602 **PB**
Toyota Motor Corporation, Detroit Branch, 4000 Town Center, Ste. 800, 48075, pg. 1412 **IT**
Unique Concepts International, 24209 Northwestern Hwy., 48075, pg. 707 **PV**
UNIVERSAL STANDARD HEALTHCARE, INC., 26500 North Western Hwy., 48076, pg. 1697 **PB**
Universal Standard HealthCare of Delaware, Inc., 21705 Evergreen Rd., 48075, pg. 1698 **PB**
Universal Standard HealthCare of Michigan, Inc., 21705 Evergreen Rd., 48075, pg. 1698 **PB**
Universal Standard HealthCare of Ohio Inc., 21705 Evergreen Rd., 48075, pg. 1698 **PB**
VESCO OIL CORP., 16055 W. 12 Mile Rd., 48076, pg. 1138 **PV**
WLTI-FM, 28411 Northwestern Hwy., Ste. 1000, 48034, pg. 779 **PV**
WXYZ TV - Channel 7 of Detroit, Inc., 20777 W. Ten Mile Rd., 48037, pg. 1448 **PB**
Western International Media Corporation-Detroit, Travelers Tower, 26555 Evergreen, Ste. 1210, 48076, pg. 1167 **PV**
Western Marketing Div., 20800 Civic Ctr. Dr., 48076, pg. 296 **PV**
WINDPOINT PARTNERS, One Towne Sq., Ste. 780, 48076, pg. 1182 **PV**
YAFFE & COMPANY, First Center Office Plaza, 26913 Northwestern Hwy., Ste. 500, 48034, pg. 1195 **PV**
Young Spring & Wire Company, P.O. Box 999, 48075, pg. 987 **PB**

Southgate

ASC INCORPORATED, One Sunroof Ctr., 48195, pg. 8 **PV**
Aeromotive Services Co., One Sunroof Center, 48195, pg. 8 **PV**
American Sunroof Company, One Sunroof Center, 48195, pg. 8 **PV**
Amoco Research Center, One Heritage Dr., Ste. 220, 48195-3048, pg. 103 **PB**
Automobile Specialty Co., One Sunroof Ctr., 48195, pg. 8 **PV**
STU EVANS LINCOLN-MERCURY INC., 16800 Fort St., 48195, pg. 385 **PV**
SOUTHGATE FORD INC., 16501 Fort St., 48195, pg. 1018 **PV**

Sparta

Pak-Sak Industries, Inc., 122 S. Aspen St., 49345, pg. 1061 **PB**
SPEEDRACK PRODUCTS GROUP, LTD., 7903 Venture Ave., 49345, pg. 1024 **PV**
Tesa Tuck Inc., 324 S. Union Ave., 49345, pg. 182 **IT**
Wilbur-Ellis Agricultural, 4160 Ten Mile N.W., 49345, pg. 1176 **PV**

Spring Lake

Integrated Metal Technologies, Inc., 17155 Van Wagoner Rd., 49456, pg. 1112 **PB**

Kysor/Medallion, 17150 Hickory, 49456, pg. 968 **PB**
Meridian Inc., 18558 171st. Ave., 49456, pg. 1112 **PB**

Springport

Specialty Castings, 211 Mill St., P.O. Box 129, 49284, pg. 591 **PV**

Standish

State Bank of Standish, 120 N. Forest St., 48658, pg. 379 **PB**

Stanton

Chemical Bank Montcalm, 110 E. Main, P.O. Box 277, 48888, pg. 345 **PB**

Sterling Heights

AFM, 44650 Merill Rd., 48314, pg. 1363 **PB**
ADVANCED ACCESSORIES SYSTEMS, LLC., Sterling Town Ctr., 12900 Hall Rd., Ste. 200, 48313, pg. 21 **PV**
Atlas Copco AFS Inc., 5500 18 Mile Rd., 48314, pg. 96 **IT**
Automotive Products USA Inc., 6515 Cobb, 48312, pg. 113 **IT**
Breed Technologies, 7000 Nineteen Mile Rd., 48314, pg. 251 **PB**
CHIVAS PRODUCTS LTD., 42555 Merrill Rd., 48314-3266, pg. 238 **PV**
Crusader Marine Engines, 7100 E. 15 Mile Rd., 48312, pg. 1591 **PB**
Ghafari Associates, Inc., 41150 Technology Pky. Dr., Ste. 106, 48314, pg. 450 **PV**
JEROME-DUNCAN FORD, 8000 Ford Country Ln., 48313, pg. 586 **PV**
MCCLAIN INDUSTRIES, INC., 6200 Elmridge Rd., 48310, pg. 1065 **PB**
Metro Cell, Inc., 5963 E. 14 Mile Rd., 48312, pg. 910 **PV**
Metro 25 Tire Centers, 5963 E. 14 Mile Rd., 48312, pg. 910 **PV**
Micro Processor Systems, Inc., 6405 19 Mile Rd., 48314, pg. 558 **PB**
THE RAO GROUP INC., 5977 E. 14-Mile Rd., 48312, pg. 910 **PV**
STERLING HEIGHTS DODGE, INC., 40111 Van Dyke, 48313, pg. 1041 **PV**
Volvo Automated Systems of North America, 7000 Nineteen Mile Rd., 48314, pg. 1477 **IT**
BUFF WHELAN CHEVROLET & GEO, INC., 40445 Van Dyke Ave., 48313, pg. 1171 **PV**

Stevensville

Cast-Matic Corporation, 2800 Yasdick Dr., 49127, pg. 894 **PB**

Sturgis

Grumman Olson Division, 1801 S. Nottawa Rd., 49091, pg. 1198 **PB**
Kirsch, 309 N. Prospect St., 49091, pg. 1176 **PB**
Michigan CA-TV Company, 120 1/2 W. Chicago Rd., 49091, pg. 287 **PV**
Northrop Grumman Allied Industries, Inc., 1801 S. Nottawa Rd., 49091, pg. 1198 **PV**
Sturgis Foundry Corp., 1000 W. West, 49091, pg. 83 **PV**
STURGIS IRON & METAL COMPANY, INC., 70675 Centerville Rd., 49091, pg. 1048 **PV**

Suttons Bay

Sprague Devices, Inc., P.O. Box 250, 49682, pg. 561 **PB**

Swartz Creek

HOUGEN MANUFACTURING INC., 3001 Hougen Dr., 48473, pg. 541 **PV**

Taylor

B.G. INDUSTRIES, 6835 Monroe Blvd., 48180, pg. 106 **PV**
CONTRACT INTERIORS INC., 14716 Allen Rd., # 101, 48180-5383, pg. 270 **PV**
F.X. COUGHLIN CO., 27050 Wick Rd., 48180, pg. 278 **PV**
EMS-Togo, 20600 Eureka Rd., Ste. 414, 48180, pg. 981 **IT**
HORIZON ENTERPRISES GROUP LLC, 20400 Superior Rd., 48180, pg. 539 **PV**
Horizon Investment Group, 20400 Superior Rd., 48180, pg. 539 **PV**
Horizon Properties, 20400 Superior Rd., 48180, pg. 539 **PV**
Horizon Technology Group - Link Tool & Mfg. Div., 9495 Inkster Rd., 48180, pg. 539 **PV**
Horizon Technology Group LLC, 20400 Superior Rd., 48180, pg. 539 **PV**
Horizon Technology Group - Taylor Division, 24518 Ecorse Rd., 48180, pg. 539 **PV**
KARP'S BAKERY SUPPLY, 21740 Trolley, 48180, pg. 608 **PV**
Kintetsu World Express Inc., 27247 N. Line Rd., 48180, pg. 735 **IT**
MASCO CORPORATION, 21001 Van Born Rd., 48180, pg. 1052 **PB**

MASCOTECH, INC., 21001 Van Born Rd., 48180, pg. 1055 **PB**
MEYER JEWELERS, 20500 Eureka Rd., Ste. 200, 48180, pg. 739 **PV**
Sealy Mattress Company of Michigan, Inc., 21450 Trolley Industrial Dr., 48180, pg. 979 **PV**
21st Vision, 20400 Superior Rd., 48180, pg. 539 **PV**
Union-Transport Corporation-Detroit Office, 27209 Northline Rd., 48180, pg. 1119 **IT**

Tecumseh

Faraday, Inc., 805 S. Maumee, 49286, pg. 1246 **IT**
Refrigeration Aftermarket Division, 100 E. Patterson, 49286, pg. 1566 **PB**
TECUMSEH PRODUCTS COMPANY, 100 E. Patterson St., 49286, pg. 1565 **PB**
Tecumseh Products Co. Compressor & Refrigeration Group of Divisions, 100 East Patterson St., 49286, pg. 1566 **PB**

Tekonsha

Tekonsha Engineering Co., 537 N. Church St., 43286, pg. 560 **PB**

Temperance

ROLLED ALLOYS, INC., 125 W. Sterns Rd., 48182, pg. 941 **PV**

Three Rivers

Armstrong Fluid Handling, 211 Armstrong Blvd., 49093, pg. 83 **PV**
ARMSTRONG INTERNATIONAL, INC., 816 Maple St., 49093, pg. 83 **PV**
Armstrong-Yoshitake, Inc., 221 Armstrong Blvd., 49093, pg. 83 **PV**
DOCK FOUNDRY COMPANY, 428 Fourth St., 49093, pg. 337 **PV**
THE JOHNSON CORPORATION, 805 Wood St., 49093, pg. 591 **PV**
Michigan Gas Company, 16587 Enterprise Dr., 49093, pg. 1489 **PB**
Peterson Spring-CIMA Plant, 16805 Heimbach Rd., 49093, pg. 857 **PV**
Peterson Spring-Packaging & Distribution, 16805-1 Heimbach Rd., 49093, pg. 857 **PV**
Peterson Spring-Three Rivers Plant, 800 W. Broadway, 49093, pg. 857 **PV**
Three Rivers Iron & Metal, P.O. Box 247, 206 E. Broadway, 49093, pg. 1048 **PV**

Traverse City

CHERRY CENTRAL COOPERATIVE, 1771 N. US 31 S., 49684, pg. 233 **PV**
Cone Drive Textron, 240 E. 12th St., 49685-0272, pg. 1589 **PB**
EMPIRE NATIONAL BANK, 1227 E. Front St., 49686, pg. 374 **PV**
Guyot-Hicks-Anderson & Associates, pg. 1217 **PV**
Lake States Insurance Co., P.O. Box 352, 12935 S. West Bay Shore Dr., 49685-0352, pg. 787 **PV**
Old Kent Bank-Grand Traverse, 102 W. Front St., 49685, pg. 1216 **PB**
Shell West Exploration & Production Inc., Continental Purchasing, Grandview Bldg., 49684, pg. 1142 **IT**
VENTURI INC., P.O. Box 6348, 49685-6348, pg. 1136 **PV**

Trenton

DSC LTD., 1491 W. Jefferson Ave., 48183, pg. 305 **PV**
Old Kent Bank-Southeast, 2674 W. Jefferson, 48183, pg. 1217 **PB**

Troy

AST Research, Inc., 200 East Big Beaver, 48083, pg. 1182 **IT**
Acustar, Inc., 1850 Research Dr., 48083, pg. 353 **PB**
Acustar, Inc., Electronics Group, 1850 Research Dr., 48083, pg. 353 **PB**
Acustar, Inc., Engineered Products Group, 1850 Research Dr., 48083, pg. 353 **PB**
Adaptive Technologies Corp., 985 Troy Ct., 48083, pg. 950 **PB**
ROBERT B. AIKENS & ASSOCIATES LLC., 2690 Crooks Rd., 48084, pg. 28 **PV**
Akzo Coatings Inc. (MI), 1845 Maxwell St., 48084, pg. 46 **IT**
Alcoa Fujikura, 1200 Stevenson Hwy., 48083, pg. 61 **PB**
AMERICAN SPEEDY PRINTING CENTERS, INC., 1800 W. Maple Rd., 48084, pg. 62 **PV**
Ameritech Advertising Services, 100 E. Big Beaver, 15th Fl., 48083, pg. 97 **PB**
Ameritech Publishing, Inc., 100 E. Big Beaver Rd., 48083, pg. 98 **PB**
Anicom, 1902 Northwood, 48084, pg. 115 **PB**
ARBOR DRUGS, INC., 3331 W. Big Beaver Rd., 48084, pg. 126 **PB**
Auto-trol Technology Sales, Troy Office Ctr., Bldg. B, 320 E. Big Beaver Rd., Ste. 160, 48083, pg. 148 **PB**
Balance Engineering Corp., 1731 Thorncroft, 48084-4613, pg. 865 **PB**
Bertrand Faure Technical Center Inc., 2380 Meijer Dr., Ste. B, 48084-7146, pg. 193 **IT**

Bosch Braking Systems-North America, Engineering Center, 900 W. Maple Rd., 48084, pg. 205   IT
The Budd Company, P.O. Box 2601, 3155 W. Big Beaver Rd., 48007-2601, pg. 1388   IT
Budd Plastics Design Center, 1850 Research Dr., 48083, pg. 1388   IT
Budd Plastics Research & Development Center, 1850 Research Dr., 48084, pg. 1388   IT
CNB International, 900 Wilshire, Ste. 205, 48084, pg. 196   PV
Cadillac Plastic & Chemical Co., 2855 Coolidge Hwy., Ste. 300, 48084, pg. 781   PV
CADILLAC PRODUCTS, INC., 5800 Crooks Rd., 48098-2830, pg. 198   PV
Chrysler Realty Corp., 1450 W. Long Lake Rd., Ste. 280, 48098, pg. 354   PB
Cimlinc, Incorporated, 1699 Stutz Dr., 48084, pg. 239   PV
Coltec Automotive Division, 1748 Northwood Dr., 48084, pg. 401   PB
Comau Productivity Systems, Inc., 754 W. Maple, 48084, pg. 483   PV
DMB&B Central And Regional IT Services, P.O. Box 5012, 3310 W. Big Beaver, 48007-5012, pg. 302   PV
DMB&B Public Relations, 3310 W. Big Beaver, P.O. Box 5012, 48007-5012, pg. 303   PV
DMB&B Detroit, P.O. Box 5012, 48007-5012, pg. 302   PV
Daewoo International America Corp. - Detroit, 2855 Coolidge Hwy., Ste. 224, 48084, pg. 357   IT
Dana Commercial Credit Corporation, 201 W. Big Beaver Rd., 48084, pg. 479   PB
Dana Commercial Credit Small Tkt., 201 W. Big Beaver, 48084, pg. 480   PB
De-Sta-Co, A Dover Resources Co., P.O. Box 2800, 48007, pg. 521   PB
Defiance Testing & Engineering Services, 1960 Ring Dr., 48083, pg. 493   PB
Delco-Electronics Customer Support, 750 Chicago Rd., 48083, pg. 720   PB
Delphi Automotive Systems, 5725 Delphi Dr., 48098-2815, pg. 719   PB
Du Pont-Kansai Automotive Coatings, Inc., P.O. Box 7013, 950 Stephenson Hwy., 48007, pg. 544   IT
EG & G Structural Kinematics, 950 Maplelawn, 48084, pg. 544   PB
Eaton Corp. Div., 1728 Maplelawn Rd., 48099, pg. 556   PB
Eaton Corporation, Specialties Division, 1728 Maplelawn Rd., 48084, pg. 557   PB
EFFICIENT ENGINEERING CO., 130 Town Center Dr., 48084, pg. 365   PV
El Dorado Tire Co., 1120 E. Long Lake Rd., 48098, pg. 1312   PV
ENERGY CONVERSION DEVICES, INC., 1675 W. Maple Rd., 48084, pg. 581   PB
ENGINEERING TECHNOLOGY LTD. (E.T.), Chicago Rd., 48083-4223, pg. 377   PV
Entertainment Publications, Inc., 2125 Butterfield Rd., 48084, pg. 320   PB
Farnam Sealing Systems Division, 1707 Northwood Dr., 48084, pg. 401   PB
Fastcut Tool Corporation, 1830 Stephenson Hwy., 48083, pg. 368   PV
Fayette Tubular Products, 1835 Technology Dr., 48083, pg. 481   PB
First Capital Financial Corp., P.O. Box 7090, 48007, pg. 473   PV
General Dynamics Services Co., P.O. Box 760, 295 Kirts Blvd., 48099-0760, pg. 709   PB
Giffels Hoyem Basso, Inc., 3150 Livernois, Ste. 300, 48083-5028, pg. 452   PV
Glacier Vandervell, Inc., 50 W. Big Beaver Rd., Ste. 450, 48084, pg. 1334   IT
HANDLEMAN COMPANY, 500 Kirts Blvd., 48084-4142, pg. 779   PB
HARMONY HOUSE RECORDS & TAPES, 1755 E. Maple, 48083-4287, pg. 503   PB
Hewlett-Packard Company, 560 Kirts Rd., Ste. 101, 48084, pg. 814   PB
Home Computer Software Div., 500 Kirts, 48084, pg. 779   PB
Hueller Hille Corporation, 1740 E. Maple Rd., 48083, pg. 1387   IT
Huntington Bancshares Michigan, Inc., 801 W. Big Beaver Rd., 48084, pg. 850   PB
IHI International Inc., Top of Troy Bldg., Ste. 1110, 755 W. Big Beaver Rd., 48084, pg. 689   IT
Ingersoll Milling Machine Co., Timberland Office Park, 5455 Corporate Dr., Ste. 200, 48098, pg. 562   PV
INTERMET CORPORATION, 5445 Corporate Dr., Ste. 200, 48098, pg. 894   PB
Jani King of Michigan, Inc., 27777 Franklin Rd., 48098, pg. 582   PV
KAMAX-G.B. DUPONT L.P., 500 W. Long Lake Rd., 48098, pg. 606   PV
Kelly Assisted Living Services, Inc., 999 W. Big Beaver, 48084, pg. 949   PB
Kelly Marketing, 999 W. Big Beaver, 48084, pg. 949   PB
Kelly Professional Services, Inc., 999 W. Big Beaver, 48084, pg. 949   PB
Kelly Properties, Inc., 999 W. Big Beaver, 48084, pg. 949   PB
Kelly Services (Australia), Ltd., 999 W. Big Beaver, 48084, pg. 949   PB
KELLY SERVICES, INC., 999 W. Big Beaver Rd., 48084, pg. 949   PB
Kelly Technical, 999 W. Big Beaver, 48084, pg. 949   PB
Kelly Temporary Services, Ltd., 999 W. Big Beaver, 48084, pg. 949   PB
KMART CORPORATION, 3100 W. Big Beaver Rd., 48084, pg. 963   PB
Kragie/Newell, 2690 Crooks Rd., Ste. 200, 48084, pg. 635   PV

LASON, INC., 1305 Stephenson Hwy., 48083, pg. 979   PB
Leslie-Michigan, 3155 W. Big Beaver Rd., Ste. 205, 48084, pg. 903   PB
Lois/EJL Detroit, 201 W. Big Beaver Rd., #490, 48084, pg. 1011   PB
Manchester Plastics, 201 W. Big Beaver Rd., Ste. 1040, 48084, pg. 399   PB
Meridian Retail, Inc., 888 W. Big Beaver Rd., 48084, pg. 503   PB
MERITOR AUTOMOTIVE, INC., 2135 W. Maple Rd., 48084, pg. 1096   PB
Meritor Wabco Vehicle Control Systems, 2135 W. Maple Rd., 48084, pg. 1096   PB
Modern Prototype Company, 2927 Elliott St., 48084, pg. 277   PV
Motion & Control Sales Div., 651 Robbins Dr., 48007-3500, pg. 1261   PV
Motor Crash Estimating Guide, 5600 Crooks Rd., 48098, pg. 516   PB
NBD Bank (Michigan), 900 Tower Dr., Ste. 8312, 48098, pg. 628   PB
NBD Insurance Agency, Inc., 900 Tower Dr., 48098, pg. 628   PB
NBD Mortgage Company, 900 Tower Dr., 48098, pg. 628   PB
National Book Distributors, 500 Kirts, 48084, pg. 780   PB
O/E AUTOMATION, INC., 3290 W. Big Beaver, Ste. 116, 48084, pg. 809   PB
Ovonic Battery Company, Inc., 1826 Northwood Rd., 48084, pg. 581   PB
OXFORD AUTOMOTIVE, INC., 1250 Stevenson Hwy., 48083, pg. 825   PV
PMI Motion Technologies, 1985 W. Big Beaver, 48084, pg. 965   PB
PALMER MOVING & STORAGE CO., 1900 Stevenson Hwy., 48083, pg. 835   PV
Polytech Netting Industries, 1280 E. Big Beaver, 48084, pg. 1362   PV
Porsche-Delta Engineering Co., 1807 E. Maple Rd., 48083, pg. 1590   IT
Randall Textron, 750 Stephenson Hwy., 48083, pg. 1590   PB
Rexair, Inc., P.O. Box 3610, 3221 W. Big Beaver, Ste. 200, 48084, pg. 1684   PB
Rockwell Clutch Company, 2135 W. Maple Rd., 48084, pg. 1096   PB
Rockwell Heavy Vehicle Suspension Systems Company, Inc., 2135 W. Maple Rd., 48084, pg. 1096   PB
Sachs Automotive Corp.-North American OEM Operations, 2002 Stephenson Hwy., 48083, pg. 835   IT
Sanwa Leasing Corp., Somerset Place Tower II, Ste. 400, 2401 W. Big Weaver Rd., 48084, pg. 1189   IT
The Saturn Corporation, P.O. Box 7025, 48007-7025, pg. 721   PB
MIKE SAVOIE CHEVROLET INC., 1900 W. Maple Rd., 48099, pg. 968   PV
R.P. SCHERER CORPORATION, 2301 W. Big Beaver, 48084, pg. 1437   PB
DEAN SELLERS FORD INC., 2600 W. Maple, 48084, pg. 983   PV
Societe Services Kelly, 999 W. Big Beaver, 48084, pg. 949   PB
Solvay Automotive Inc., 2565 W. Maple Rd., 48084, pg. 1277   IT
SOMERSET PONTIAC GMC INC., 1850 W. Maple Rd., 48084, pg. 1013   PV
SpeedChoice, 1017 Naughton, 48083, pg. 1274   PV
Standard Brokerage Services, Inc., 2600 W. Big Beaver Rd., 48084, pg. 11   IT
Standard Federal Bank, 2600 W. Big Beaver Rd., 48084, pg. 10   IT
Stanley Door Systems, 1225 E. Maple Rd., 48083, pg. 1509   PB
Stelco USA, Inc., 2855 Coolidge Hwy., Ste. 203, 48084-3202, pg. 1300   IT
Strelinger Company, 1402 Rankin St., 48083, pg. 951   PB
Sulzer Plasma Technik, Inc., 1972 Meijer Dr., 48084, pg. 1307   IT
TKD, N.A., 1205   PV
TMP Worldwide/Recruitment Division, 3001 Big Beaver Rd., Ste. 602, 48084, pg. 1065   PV
Teleflex Automotive, 700 Stephenson Hwy., 48083-1122, pg. 1569   PB
Textron Automotive Company, 750 Stephenson Hwy., 48083, pg. 1590   PB
Textron Automotive Interiors Company, 750 Stephenson Hwy., 48083, pg. 1590   PB
Tidy Car International, Inc., 1290 E. Maple, 48084, pg. 1205   PV
TROY MOTORS, 777 John R Rd., 48083, pg. 1106   PV
United Solar Systems Corp., 1100 West Maple Rd., 48084, pg. 581   PB
USA Network, 3250 W. Big Beaver, 48084, pg. 1686   PB
Video Treasures, 500 Kirts, 48084, pg. 780   PB
Vorelco, Inc., 888 W. Big Beaver Rd., 48084, pg. 1474   IT
ZIEBART INTERNATIONAL CORPORATION, 1290 E. Maple Rd., 48083, pg. 1205   PV

Utica

MNP CORP., 44225 Utica Rd., 48317, pg. 687   PV
MEADE GROUP, INC., P.O. Box 18901, 48318, pg. 725   PV
TASTEE FREEZ INTERNATIONAL INC., 48380 Van Dyke, 48317, pg. 1069   PV

Vanderbilt

H & H TUBE & MANUFACTURING CO., 108 Garfield St., 49795, pg. 489   PV

Vicksburg

TRIPLE S PLASTICS, INC., 14320 Portage Rd., 49097, pg. 1639   PB
Triple S Plastics Tooling & Technology Centre, 14300 Portage Rd., 49097, pg. 1640   PB

Wakefield

Connor Forest Industries, Inc., 601 Sunday Lake St., 49968, pg. 168   PV

Walker

Thorn Apple Valley-Walker Division, 49504, pg. 1603   PB

Walled Lake

AMERICAN PLASTIC TOYS INC., 799 Ladd Rd., 48390, pg. 60   PV
GKN Drivetech Inc., 1164 Ladd Rd., 48390, pg. 535   IT
Industrial Burner Systems, 4165 Martin Rd., 48390, pg. 360   PV
WILLIAMS INTERNATIONAL, 2280 W. Maple Rd., 48390, pg. 1178   PV
Williams-Rolls, Inc., 2280 W. Maple Rd., 48390, pg. 1178   PV

Warren

Acco Systems Div., 12755 E. Nine Mile Rd., 48089, pg. 472   IT
ART VAN FURNITURE INC., 6500 E. Fourteen Mile Rd., 48092, pg. 86   PV
ATREX INCORPORATED, 24060 Hoover Rd., 48089, pg. 97   PV
Automotive Moulding Company, 23751 Amber, 48089, pg. 485   PV
Bundy Corporation, Warren Plant, 12345 E. Nine Mile Rd., 48090-2001, pg. 1341   IT
Bundy International, 12345 E. Nine Mile Rd., 48090, pg. 1340   IT
Bundy North America, 12345 E. Nine Mile Rd., 48090, pg. 1340   IT
Cadillac Motor Car Division, Cadillac World Headquarters, 30009 Van Dyke, Bldg. 2-6, 48090-9020, pg. 720   PB
Campbell-Ewald Advertising, 30400 Van Dyke Ave., 48093, pg. 908   PB
Chevrolet Motor Div. General Motors Corp., 30007 Van Dyke Ave., 48090-9065, pg. 720   PB
Chevrolet, Pontiac, GM of Canada Group, 30001 Van Dyke Ave., 48090, pg. 720   PB
COLD HEADING CO., 2177 Hoover Rd., 48089, pg. 250   PV
Component Operations, 6565 E. 8 Mile Rd., 48091-2090, pg. 353   PV
THE CROWN GROUP, INC., 2111 Walter Reuther Dr., 48091, pg. 292   PV
ELIAS BROTHERS RESTAURANTS, INC., 4199 Marcy Rd., 48091, pg. 371   PV
Ervins Group, 6655 Chicago Rd., 48092, pg. 13   PV
Ethone OMI-Warren, 21441 Hoover Rd., 48089, pg. 138   PV
FOLAND'S JEWELRY BROKERS, 4100 E. 14 Mile Rd., 48092, pg. 416   PV
General Dynamics Land Systems Div., P.O. Box 2074, 48090-2074, pg. 709   PB
GROESBECK LUMBER & SUPPLY, INC., 23155 Groesbeck Hwy., 48089, pg. 483   PV
IROQUOIS DIE & MFG. CO., 24400 Hoover, 48089, pg. 575   PV
Kee Cutters, 25040 Easy St., 48089, pg. 1054   PB
Kee Services, 25120 Easy St., 48089, pg. 1054   PB
Knurlet Tool Co., 24807 Romano St., 48091, pg. 608   PB
Lamb Technicon, 5663 E. Nine Mile Rd., 48091-2593, pg. 1699   PV
Machining and Assembly Systems, 5663 E. Nine Mile Rd., 48091-2593, pg. 1699   PV
MACHINING ENTERPRISES INC., 11400 Toepfer, 48089, pg. 691   PV
MADISON ELECTRIC CO., 31855 Van Dyke St., 48093-1047, pg. 694   PV
MANUFACTURERS PRODUCTS COMPANY, 26020 Sherwood Ave., 48091, pg. 701   PV
Modern Engineering, Inc., 28000 Dequindre Rd., 48092, pg. 277   PV
NATIONAL LUMBER CO., 24595 Groesbeck Hwy., 48089, pg. 785   PV
PRESTIGE STAMPING, INC., 23513 Groesbeck Hwy., 48090, pg. 882   PV
The Prince Co. of Michigan, 26155 Groesbeck Hwy., 48089, pg. 158   PV
PRODUCTION TOOL SUPPLY CO., 8655 E. Eight Mile Rd., 48089, pg. 889   PV
Punchcraft Company, 30500 Ryan Rd., 48092, pg. 1054   PB
Reska Spline Products Inc., 22225 Easy St., 48089, pg. 1054   PB
RING TECHNOLOGIES, INC., 12901 Stephens Dr., 48089, pg. 931   PV
RINKE PONTIAC-GMC CO., P.O. Box 749, 48090, pg. 931   PV
ROTARY MULTIFORMS, INC., 2160 E. Eleven Mile Rd., 48091, pg. 947   PV
Sandvik Hard Materials, 21551 Mullin Avenue, 48089-3091, pg. 1186   IT
Service Solution, 28635 Mound Rd., 48092, pg. 1421   PB

PB - *U.S. Public Companies Volume*
PV - *U.S. Private Companies Volume*
IT - *International Public & Private Companies Volume*

Geographic Index-U.S.

1288

VARI-FORM, 12341 E. Nine Mile Rd., 48089-2614, pg. 1340 **IT**

Waterford

DUNHAM'S ATHLEISURE CORPORATION, 5000 Dixie Hwy., 48329, pg. 346 **PV**

Wayland

WINDEMULLER ELECTRIC INC., 1176 Electric Ave., 49348, pg. 1182 **PV**

Wayne

Browning-Ferris Industries of Michigan, Inc., 5400 Cogswell Rd., 48184, pg. 263 **PV**
JACK DEMMER FORD, INC., 37300 Michigan Ave., 48184, pg. 323 **PV**
MARK CHEVROLET INC., 33200 Michigan Ave., 48184, pg. 704 **PV**
Unistrut Corporation, 35660 Clinton St., 48184, pg. 1651 **PB**

Weidman

Randell, 0520 Coldwater Rd., 48893, pg. 520 **PB**

West Bloomfield

Iberia Air Lines of Spain, 5600 W. Maple Rd., Ste. 303, 48033, pg. 575 **IT**

West Branch

Taylor Building Products Company, 631 N. First St., 48661, pg. 67 **PB**

West Olive

Northland Evergreens, Inc., 11161 120th Ave., 49460, pg. 60 **PV**

Westland

Horizon Technology Group - Westland Division, 6140 Hix Rd., 48185, pg. 539 **PV**
Nederman Inc., 6100 Hix Rd., 48185, pg. 281 **IT**
Pace Mechanical Services, Inc, 38568 Webb Dr., 48185, pg. 572 **PB**
Red Spot Westland Inc., 555 S. Edwin, 48185, pg. 915 **PV**
Textron Automotive Trim Operations, 1515 Newburgh Rd., 48185, pg. 1590 **PB**

White Cloud

LUBECON SYSTEMS, INC., 201 N. Webster St., 49349, pg. 679 **PV**

White Pigeon

The Andersons White Pigeon Terminal, 13600 Anderson Rd., 49099, pg. 111 **PB**
Dutch Housing, Inc., P.O. Box 687, 68956 U.S. 131, 49099, pg. 333 **PB**
White Pigeon Paper Company, River St., 49099, pg. 87 **PV**

White Pine

Copper Range Company, Wilcox Rd., 49971-0100, pg. 862 **IT**

Whitehall

Acutex Division, 2001 Peach St., 49461, pg. 1421 **PB**

Williamston

Bergen Brunswig Drug Company, One Industrial Pk., 48895, pg. 214 **PB**
Keck Instruments, Inc., 1099 W. Grand River Ave., 48895, pg. 367 **PB**

Wixom

CCL Custom Manufacturing Corp., 50000 W. Pontiac Trail, 48393, pg. 239 **IT**
Digital Fuel Injection, Inc., 29387 Lorie Lane, 48393, pg. 560 **PB**
Durr Automation, Inc., P.O. Box 1014, 50055 Pontiac Trail, 48393, pg. 421 **IT**
Sloan Flushmate, 1155 Grand River Ave., 48303, pg. 1006 **PV**

Woodhaven

Quality Coil Processing, 25225 Hall Rd., 48183, pg. 608 **PV**

Woodland

Your Staff, Inc., 20300 Ventura Blvd., Ste. 150, 48897, pg. 949 **PB**

Wyandotte

Atochem, 17168 W. Jefferson, 48192-4206, pg. 445 **IT**
BASF Corporation, Wyandotte Site, 1609 Biddle Avenue, 48192, pg. 105 **IT**
Chelsea Group, 2944 Biddle Ave., 48192, pg. 539 **PV**
Horizon Technology Group - Wyandotte Division, 4261 13th St., 48192, pg. 539 **PV**
McCord Payen Inc., 191 Labadie St., 48192, pg. 1334 **IT**

Wyoming

Capital Concept & Engineering, 781 36th St., S.E., 49548, pg. 1060 **PV**
CHEMCENTRAL/Grand Rapids, 2940 Stafford Ave., S.W., 49548, pg. 232 **PV**
Diesel Technology Company, 2300 Burlingame Ave., S.W., 49509-0919, pg. 205 **IT**
Frames Unlimited Inc., 3343 Lousma Drive S.E., 49548, pg. 1206 **PV**
L & L/Jiroch Distributing Co., 1180 58th St. S.W., 49509, pg. 1021 **PV**
Q-Check Systems, 795 36th St., S.E., 49548, pg. 1060 **PV**
ZIMDAR ENTERPRISES/FRAMES UNLIMITED, 3343 Lousma Dr. S.E., 49548, pg. 1206 **PV**

Ypsilanti

AMERICAN INTERNATIONAL AIRWAYS, 842 Willow Run Airport, 84198-0899, pg. 57 **PV**
Eby Brown Co., Eight Michigan Ave., 20850, pg. 359 **PV**
Kalitta Flying Service, 872 Willow Run Airport, 48198, pg. 57 **PV**
Pentastar Aviation, Inc., 824 Willow Run Airport, 48198, pg. 354 **PV**
Ypsi-Arbor Lanes, 2985 Washtenaw, 48197, pg. 475 **PV**
ZANTOP INTERNATIONAL AIRLINES, INC., 840 Willow Run Airport, 48198-0840, pg. 1204 **PV**

Zeeland

Bell & Howell Mailmobile Co., 411 E. Roosevelt St., 49464, pg. 201 **PB**
Bil Mar Foods, Inc., 8300 96th Ave., 49464, pg. 1433 **PB**
Fuel Systems Textron Inc., 700 N. Centennial, 49464, pg. 1589 **PB**
GENTEX CORPORATION, 600 N. Centennial St., 49464, pg. 731 **PB**
Milcare, Inc., 8500 Byron Rd., 49464, pg. 1112 **PV**
HERMAN MILLER, INC., P.O. Box 302, 855 E. Main Ave., 49464, pg. 1111 **PB**
HOWARD MILLER, 860 E. Main Ave., 49464, pg. 747 **PV**
ODL INCORPORATED, 215 E. Roosevelt Ave., 49464, pg. 809 **PV**
Office Pavilion Division (Sls. & Mktg. Div.), 8500 Byron Road, 49464, pg. 1112 **PB**
TLC Group, Inc., 8300 Logistic Dr., 49464, pg. 352 **PB**
Zeeland Chemicals, Inc., 215 N. Centennial St., 49464, pg. 297 **PB**

MINNESOTA

Albert Lea

Bridon Cordage Inc., 909 16th St., 56007, pg. 215 **IT**
Farmstead, 1000 E. Main St., 56007, pg. 396 **PV**
Piper Jaffray Inc., 1425 St. John Ave., 56007, pg. 1302 **PB**
DAVE SYVERSON LINCOLN MERCURY, P.O. Box 251, 1410 E. Main, 56007, pg. 1061 **PV**
Ventura Foods, 919-14th St., 56007, pg. 508 **PV**

Alexandria

APV Douglas Machine Corp., 3404-T Iowa St., 56308, pg. 1240 **IT**
Brenton Engineering Company, 4750 County Rd. 13, N.E., 56308, pg. 395 **PV**
First American Bank, P.O. Box 309, 720 Broadway, 56308, pg. 167 **PV**
ITW Heartland Components, 1601 36th Ave. South, 56308, pg. 866 **IT**
KSAX-TV, 415 Fillmore, 56308, pg. 544 **PV**
Piper Jaffray Inc., Midway Mall, 2904 S. Broadway, 56308-3474, pg. 1301 **PB**

Anoka

The Cornelius Company, One Cornelius Place, Hwy. 10 W., 55303, pg. 646 **IT**
Eley Americas Inc., One Cornelius Place, 55303-6234, pg. 646 **IT**
Federal Cartridge Co., 900 Ehlen Dr., 55303, pg. 239 **PB**
FIRST TEAM SPORTS INC., 1201 Lund Blvd., 55303, pg. 638 **PV**
Hoffman Engineering Company, 900 Ehlen Dr., 55303-7504, pg. 1273 **PV**
IMI Cornelius Inc. (MN), One Cornelius Pl., 55303-6234, pg. 646 **IT**
Lund Industries Inc., 911 Lund Blvd., 55303, pg. 1020 **PB**
LUND INTERNATIONAL HOLDINGS, INC., 911 Lund Blvd., 55303, pg. 1020 **PB**

Apple Valley

Adaptec - Midwestern Region, 7493 W. 147th St., Ste. 204, 55124, pg. 19 **PB**

Arden Hills

Alpo Pet Foods, 4251 Fernwood Ave., 55112, pg. 917 **IT**
CONTROL DATA SYSTEMS, INC., 4201 Lexington Ave. N., 55126, pg. 441 **PB**
Corporate Express Office Products, 1233 W. County Rd. E., 55112, pg. 449 **PB**
INX International, 3750 N. Dunlap, 55112, pg. 1311 **IT**
LAND O'LAKES, INC., 4001 Lexington Ave. N., 55126-2998, pg. 645 **PV**
MSI INSURANCE COMPANIES, Two Pine Tree Dr., 55112-3793, pg. 688 **PV**
Metaphase Technology, Inc., 4201 Lexington Ave., North, 55126, pg. 1525 **PB**
Pension Solutions, Inc., Two Pine Tree Dr., 55112-3793, pg. 688 **PV**
Pharmacia & Upjohn Deltec, Inc., 1265 Grey Fox Rd., 55112, pg. 1049 **IT**
RTI Export, Inc. (Barbados), 1260 Red Fox Rd., 55115, pg. 1455 **PB**
Resistance Technology Inc., 1260 Red Fox Rd., 55112, pg. 1455 **PB**
SCHOLLS INC., 4440 Round Lake Rd., 55112, pg. 972 **PV**

Austin

ASTRUP DRUGS, INC., 905 N. Main, Box 658, 55912, pg. 93 **PV**
HORMEL FOODS CORP., One Hormel Pl., 55912-3680, pg. 840 **PB**
Hormel Frozen Foods Div., One Hormel Pl., 55912, pg. 840 **PB**
Hormel International Corporation, One Hormel Pl., 55912, pg. 840 **PB**
Piper Jaffray Inc., Town Ctr. Bldg., 329 N. Main St., Ste. 104, 55912-3407, pg. 1302 **PB**
Terra International, 109 N. Main St., 55912, pg. 1581 **PB**

Avon

D.H. BLATTNER & SONS, INC., P.O. Box 37, 56310, pg. 148 **PV**

Bayport

ANDERSEN CORPORATION, 100 Fourth Ave. N., 55003-1096, pg. 71 **PV**
Andersen Windows, Inc., 100 4th Ave. N., 55003, pg. 72 **PV**

Benson

Lor Al Products Inc, 2200 Hall Ave., 56215, pg. 6 **PB**
TYLER INDUSTRIES, P.O. Box 249, East Hwy. 12, 56215, pg. 1112 **PV**

Blaine

DAYTON ROGERS MFG. CO., 8401 West 35 W. Service Dr., 55449, pg. 318 **PV**
Earle M. Jorgensen Company/Minneapolis, 1775 101st Ave. N.E., 55434, pg. 600 **PV**

Blooming Prairie

Atochem, 157 W. Hwy. N., 55917, pg. 445 **IT**

Bloomington

AST Research, Inc., 8400 Normandale Lake Blvd., Ste. 920, 55437, pg. 1181 **IT**
Century Manufacturing, 9231 Penn Ave. S., 55431, pg. 1273 **PB**
CERIDIAN CORPORATION, 8100 34th Avenue S., 55425, pg. 330 **PB**
Ceridian Employer Services, 8100 34th Ave., S., 55425, pg. 331 **PB**
Chase Manhattan Financial Center, Inc., 8300 Norman Ctr. Dr., Ste. 190, 55437, pg. 338 **PB**
CLARKLIFT OF MINNESOTA, INC., 501 W. 78th St., 55420, pg. 243 **PV**
COMPLAST, INC., 321 W. 83rd St., 55420, pg. 259 **PV**
Computing Devices International, 8800 Queen Ave. S., 55431, pg. 331 **PB**
Design Concepts Integration, Inc., 10740-BW Lyndale Ave. S., 55420, pg. 572 **PV**
EDD-Minnesota, 9401 James Ave. S., #142, 55431, pg. 205 **PB**
Encara, 7803 Glenroy Rd., 55439, pg. 97 **PB**
Firstaff, Inc., Northland Plaza Bldg., 3800 W. 80th St., Ste. 1155, 55431-4426, pg. 15 **PB**
Firstar Bank of Minnesota, 1550 E. 79th St., Ste. 880, 55425, pg. 643 **PB**
Gander Mountain Retail, 4567 W. 80th St., 55437, pg. 534 **PV**
HITCHCOCK INDUSTRIES, INC., 8701 Harriet Ave. S., 55420, pg. 531 **PV**
HOLIDAY COMPANIES, 4567 W. 80th St., 55437, pg. 534 **PV**
HOYT HOME IMPROVEMENT, 9057 Lindale Ave. S., 55420, pg. 543 **PV**
IKOS Systems, Inc., One Appletree Sq, Ste. 201-D, 55425, pg. 864 **PB**
Iconovex Corporation, 7448 W. 78th St., 55439, pg. 880 **PB**
Innomedica, 7452 W. 78th ST., 55439, pg. 880 **PB**

PB - U.S. Public Companies Volume
PV - U.S. Private Companies Volume
IT - International Public & Private Companies Volume

1289

Geographic Index-U.S.

Jesco Company, 2626 E. 82nd St., Ste. 300, 55425, pg. 590 **PV**

AL JOHNSON CONSTRUCTION CO., 2626 E. 82nd St., Ste. 300, 55425, pg. 590 **PV**

Kraus-Anderson Realty Company, 4220 W. Old Shakopee Rd., Ste. 200, 55437-2995, pg. 635 **PV**

Lawn-Boy Inc., 8111 Lyndale Ave. So., 55420, pg. 1624 **PB**

Lifetouch Portrait Studios Inc., 7831 Glenroy Rd., 55437, pg. 667 **PB**

Lifetouch Senior Portraits Inc., 7831 Glenroy Rd., 55439, pg. 667 **PB**

Lifetouch Video Creations, Inc., 7831 Glenroy Rd., 55439, pg. 667 **PB**

Lucht, Inc., 11201 Hampshire Ave. S., 55438, pg. 1201 **PB**

Metropolis General Partnership, 3500 W. 80th St., 55431, pg. 361 **PB**

MINNESOTA VALLEY ENGINEERING/CRYOGENIC ASSOCIATION, 8011 34th Ave. S., Ste. 100, 55425, pg. 751 **PV**

North Central Marketing Div., 2780 E. 82nd St., 55425, pg. 296 **PV**

Piper Jaffray Inc., 8500 Normandale Lake Blvd., Ste. 210, 55437-3815, pg. 1301 **PB**

RINGER CORPORATION, 9555 James Ave. S., Ste. 200, 55431-2543, pg. 1390 **PB**

Seagate Magnetics, 7801 Computer Ave., S., 55435-5412, pg. 1450 **PB**

THE TORO COMPANY, 8111 Lyndale Ave. S., 55420, pg. 1623 **PB**

Toro Credit, 111 Lyndale Ave. S., 55420-1196, pg. 1624 **PB**

Toro Probiotic Products, Inc., 811 Lyndale Ave. S., 55420, pg. 1624 **PB**

Tucci Benucch, Mall of America, Ste. W114 W. Market, 55425, pg. 661 **PV**

Twin City Diner, Mall of America, Space N-130, Level 1, North Garden, 55425, pg. 662 **PV**

United Sugars Corp., 7801 E. Bush Lake Rd., Ste. 100, 55439, pg. 52 **PV**

ViaTech Development Laboratory, Two Appletree Sq., Ste. 141, 55425, pg. 1309 **PV**

WALSER AUTOMOTIVE GROUP, 1309 Clover Dr., 55420, pg. 1148 **PV**

Brainerd

ANDERSON BROTHERS CONSTRUCTION BRAINERD, 1500 Highway 210 E., 56401, pg. 72 **PV**

Brainerd Daily Dispatch, 506 James St. Box D, 56401-2942, pg. 995 **PV**

First American Bank, 321 S. Seventh St., 56401, pg. 167 **PV**

Piper Jaffray Inc., 517 N.W. Fourth St., 56401-2972, pg. 1302 **PB**

Recreational Products Div., 1123 S. 6th St., 56401, pg. 205 **PB**

Breckenridge

First American Bank, 225 N. Fifth St., 56520, pg. 167 **PV**

Brooklyn Center

Medtronic Promeon, 6700 Shingle Creek Pkwy., 55430, pg. 1083 **PB**

Vision-Ease Lens, 6800 Shingle Creek Pkwy., 55430, pg. 162 **PB**

Brooklyn Park

Varitronic Systems, Inc., 6835 Winnetka Cir., 55428, pg. 250 **PB**

Vision-Ease Lens Inc., 7100 Northland Cir., Ste. 312, 55428, pg. 162 **PB**

WILSONS THE LEATHER EXPERTS INC., 7401 Boone Ave., N., 55428, pg. 1181 **PV**

Brooten

Crow River Industries Incorporated, 850 Hwy. 55, 56316, pg. 1040 **PB**

Burnsville

CAIRE, Inc., 3505 County Rd. 42, 55300, pg. 751 **PV**

Frontier Communications of Minnesota, Inc., 14450 Burnhaven Dr., 55337, pg. 684 **PB**

Herff Jones Photography, 12222 Riverwood Dr., 55337, pg. 524 **PV**

Kraus-Anderson Insurance, 1935 W. Burnsville Parkway, 55437, pg. 635 **PV**

Piper Jaffray Inc., Professional Plaza, 1601 E. Hwy. 13, Ste. 200, 55337-6848, pg. 1302 **PB**

Vital Signs MN, Inc., 12250 Nicollet Ave. S., 55337, pg. 1723 **PB**

XATA CORPORATION, 151 E. Cliff Rd., Ste. 10, 55337, pg. 1783 **PB**

Byron

AGRILAND COMPANY, 302 Byron Ave. N., 55920, pg. 26 **PV**

Cambridge

Blue Fox Tackle Co., 645 N. Emerson, 55008, pg. 802 **PV**

MOTEK ENGINEERING & MANUFACTURING COMPANY, 625 Second Ave., S.E., 55008, pg. 764 **PV**

Cannon Falls

Cannon Equipment Co., 324 W. Washington, 55009, pg. 646 **IT**

Champlin

McLean Midwest, 11611 Business Park Blvd. N., 55316, pg. 1791 **PB**

Chanhassen

Banta Digital Group, 18790 W. 78th St., 55317-0426, pg. 188 **PB**

Banta Direct Marketing Group, 18780 West 78th St., 55317-0426, pg. 188 **PB**

Dataserv Computer Maintenance, Inc., 19011 E. Lake Dr., 55317, pg. 1737 **PB**

THE INSTANT WEB COMPANIES, 7951 Powers Blvd., 55317, pg. 565 **PB**

Redmond Products, Inc., 18930 W. 78th St., 55317, pg. 254 **PB**

United Mailing, Inc., 1001 Park Rd., 55317, pg. 565 **PV**

Victory Envelope, Inc., 1000 Park Rd., 55317, pg. 565 **PV**

Chaska

Commercial Environmental Systems Group, Inc., 101 W. 82nd St., 55318, pg. 1193 **PB**

LAKE REGION MANUFACTURING, INC., 340 Lake Hazeltine Dr., 55318, pg. 643 **PV**

Mammoth, Inc., 101 W. 82nd St., 55318, pg. 1193 **PB**

Nesco Ameican Harvest Inc., 4064 Peavey Rd., 55318, pg. 735 **PV**

NordicTrack, Inc., 104 Peavey Rd., 55318, pg. 279 **PB**

Pies, Inc., 300 Lake Hazleton Dr., 55318, pg. 658 **PB**

Sanofi, Diagnostias Pasteur, 1000 Lake Hazeltine Dr., 55318-1037, pg. 446 **IT**

Softsoap Enterprises, Inc., 134 Columbia Ct. S., 55318, pg. 397 **PB**

Softsoap Enterprises, Inc., 1107 Hazeltine Blvd., 55318, pg. 397 **PB**

Circle Pines

BERMO, INC., 4501 Ball Rd., N.E., 55014, pg. 136 **PV**

Orbex Inc., 4444 Ban Rd., NE, 55014, pg. 238 **PB**

Cloquet

DIAMOND BRANDS, INC., 1800 Cloquet Ave., 55720, pg. 330 **PV**

Duluth & Northeastern Railroad Co., Ave. C & Arch St., 55720, pg. 1318 **PB**

Northern Minnesota Utilities, 910 Cloquet Ave., 55720, pg. 1701 **PB**

Cokato

CTS Corporation-Connector Division, 400 Cokato St., 55321, pg. 285 **PB**

CAM Manufacturing, Inc., 13369 60th St., S.W., 55321, pg. 293 **PV**

Cold Spring

Cold Spring Granite (Canada) Ltd., 202 S. Third Ave., 56320, pg. 251 **PV**

COLD SPRING GRANITE COMPANY, 202 S. Third Ave., 56320, pg. 250 **PV**

Granit-Bronz, Inc., 202 S. Third Ave., 56320, pg. 251 **PV**

Royal Melrose Granites, 202 S. Third Ave., 56320, pg. 251 **PV**

Coon Rapids

North American Metals Distribution Group, 455 85th Ave. N.W., 55433, pg. 1118 **IT**

Vincent Metal Goods-Northern Division, 455 85th Ave. NW, 55433, pg. 1118 **IT**

Vincent Metal Goods-Southern Division, 455 85th Ave. NW, 55433, pg. 1118 **IT**

Crookston

First American Bank N.A., P.O. Box 613, 201 N. Broadway, 56716, pg. 167 **PV**

Crystal

TIMESAVERS INC., 5270 Hamson Ct., 55429, pg. 1088 **PV**

Detroit Lakes

DYNAMIC HOMES, INC., 525 Roosevelt Ave., 56501, pg. 538 **PB**

First American Bank, P.O. Box 827, 56502, pg. 167 **PV**

Snappy Air Distribution Products, P.O. Box 1168, 1011 11th Ave., S.E., 56501, pg. 1506 **PB**

Dodge Center

MCNEILUS COMPANIES, Hwy. #14 East, 55927, pg. 725 **PV**

Duluth

Corporate Express Office Products, 4424 Haines Rd., 55811, pg. 449 **PB**

DAVIDSON PRINTING COMPANY, 4444 Haines Road, 55811-1524, pg. 314 **PV**

Duluth News-Tribune, 424 W. First St., 55802, pg. 964 **PB**

Georgia Pacific Hardboard, 1320 W. Railroad St., 55802, pg. 736 **PB**

Glass Block, 1600 Miller Trunk Hwy., 55811, pg. 1090 **PB**

Lake Superior Paper Industries, 100 N. Central Ave., 55807, pg. 436 **PB**

MINNESOTA POWER, 30 W. Superior St., 55802-2093, pg. 1116 **PB**

MONSON TRUCKING, INC., 5102 S. Cant Rd., 55804, pg. 758 **PV**

Norwest Bank Minnesota North, N.A., 230 W. Superior St., 55802-3500, pg. 1202 **PB**

Piper Jaffray Inc., Lake Superior Pl., 21 W. Superior St., 55802-2075, pg. 1301 **PB**

Rainy River Energy Corporation, 30 W. Superior St., 55802, pg. 1116 **PB**

Republic Automotive Parts Sales, Inc., 1730 W. Michigan St., 55806, pg. 1378 **PB**

Superwood Corp., 14th Ave., West at Waterfront, 55802, pg. 736 **PB**

Synertec, Incorporated, 30 W. Superior St., 55802, pg. 1116 **PB**

Unitog Rental Facility, 17 N. 20th Ave. W., 55806, pg. 1693 **PB**

UtilEquip, Incorporated, 30 W. Superior St., 55802, pg. 1116 **PB**

WDIO-TV, Ten Observation Rd., 55811, pg. 544 **PV**

Dunnell

Glasstite, Inc., Highway 4, North, 56127, pg. 1361 **PB**

Eagan

Brown-Minneapolis Tank & Fabricating Co., 2875 Hwy. #55, 55121, pg. 914 **PB**

Cray Research, 655-A Lone Oak Dr., 55121, pg. 1473 **PB**

DART TRANSIT COMPANY, 800 Lone Oak Rd., 55121, pg. 311 **PV**

INTERNATIONAL RESEARCH & EVALUATION, 21098 IRE Control Ctr., 55121-0098, pg. 571 **PV**

MediVators, Inc., 2995 Lone Oak Cir., Ste. 10, 55121-0387, pg. 301 **PB**

NCS Charles W. Oswald Technology Center, 1313 Lone Oak Rd., 55121-1334, pg. 1155 **PB**

Marshall W. Nelson & Assoc., 4155 Sibley Memorial Hwy., 55122-1904, pg. 360 **PV**

Northwest Aerospace Training Corporation, 2600 Lone Oak Pt., 55121, pg. 1200 **PB**

A. Schulman, Inc., 1380 Corp. Center Curve, Ste. 316, 55121, pg. 1441 **PB**

Unitog Rental Facility, 3375 Mike Collins Drive, 55121, pg. 1693 **PB**

East Grand Forks

First National Bank of East Grand Forks, 303 Third St. N.W., 56721, pg. 1681 **PV**

Eden Prairie

AeroMet Corporation, 7623 Anagram Dr., 55334, pg. 1029 **PB**

All American Semiconductor of Minnesota, Inc., 7716 Golden Triangle Dr., 55344, pg. 41 **PB**

Americable, Inc., 7450 Flying Cloud Dr., 55344, pg. 585 **PB**

AmeriSource-Minneapolis, 6810 Shady Oak Rd., 55344, pg. 97 **PB**

APERTUS TECHNOLOGIES INCORPORATED, 7275 Flying Cloud Dr., 55344, pg. 119 **PB**

ARGOSY ELECTRONICS, INC., 10300 W. 70th St., 55344, pg. 81 **PV**

Arrow/Schweber Electronics, 1012A West 76th St., 55344, pg. 134 **PB**

Automatic Assembly, 6425 Flying Cloud Dr., 55424-0064, pg. 1382 **PB**

Banta Information Services Group, 7000 Washington Ave., S., 55344-3580, pg. 188 **PB**

Banta Information Services Group, 7530 Washington Ave., S., 55344-3580, pg. 188 **PB**

Banta Information Services Group, 7000 Washington Ave. S., 55344-3580, pg. 188 **PB**

BEST BUY CO., INC., 7075 Flying Cloud Drive, 55344, pg. 223 **PB**

Browning-Ferris Industries of Minnesota, Inc., 9813 Flying Cloud Dr., 55347, pg. 267 **PB**

BUFFETS, INC., 10260 Viking Dr., 55344-7229, pg. 267 **PB**

DEPARTMENT 56 INC., One Village Pl, 6436 City W. Pkwy., 55344, pg. 500 **PB**

Design Services Group, 6533 Flying Cloud Dr., Ste. 100, 55344, pg. 1541 **PB**

Digital Typeface Corporation, 9955 W. 69th St., 55344, pg. 799 **PB**

Eaton Corporation, Hydraulics Division, 15151 Hwy. 5, 55344, pg. 557 **PB**

PB - *U.S. Public Companies Volume*
PV - *U.S. Private Companies Volume*
IT - *International Public & Private Companies Volume*

1290

Geographic Index-U.S.

ENSTAR, INC., 6479 City West Pike, 55344, pg. 585 **PB**
ENStar Networking Corp., 7450 Flying Cloud Dr., 55344, pg. 585 **PB**
Evergreen Buffets, Inc., 10260 Viking Dr., Ste. 100, 55344, pg. 267 **PB**
FUNCO, INC., 10120 W. 76th St., 55344, pg. 688 **PB**
G.E. Capital Fleet Services, Three Capital Dr., 55344, pg. 712 **PB**
GELCO INFORMATION NETWORK, INC., 10700 Prairie Lakes Dr., 55344-3886, pg. 442 **PV**
Holaday Industries, Inc., 14825 Martin Dr., 55344, pg. 208 **IT**
ITT Cannon Switch Products, Inc., 8081 Wallace Rd., 55344, pg. 859 **PB**
Jaco Electronics, Inc., 6458 City W. Pkwy., 55344, pg. 921 **PB**
KMSP Television, Inc., 11358 Viking Dr., 55344, pg. 352 **PB**
LaserMaster Export Corporation, 9955 W. 69th St., 55344, pg. 979 **PB**
LASERMASTER TECHNOLOGIES, INC., 9955 W. 69th St., 55344, pg. 979 **PB**
LIFETOUCH, PORTRAIT STUDIOS, 1100 Viking Dr., 55344, pg. 667 **PV**
MCC Behavioral Care, Inc., 11095 Viking Dr., Ste. 350, 55344, pg. 362 **PB**
MCC Independent Practice Association of Greater New York, 11095 Viking Dr., Ste. 350, 55344, pg. 362 **PV**
MTS SYSTEMS CORPORATION, 14000 Technology Dr., 55344-2290, pg. 1028 **PB**
Magnetics Data, Inc., 6754 Shady Oak Rd., 55344, pg. 696 **PV**
Medtronic Bio-Medicus, 9600 W. 76th St., 55344-3790, pg. 1083 **PB**
Medtronic In Stent, Inc., 6271 Burg Dr., 55346, pg. 1083 **PB**
NATIONAL COMPUTER SYSTEMS, 11000 Prairie Lakes Dr., 55344, pg. 1155 **PB**
PLUM, 11095 Viking Dr., Ste. 480, 55344, pg. 1504 **IT**
PPT VISION, INC., 10821 W. 70th St., 55344, pg. 1245 **PB**
Perkin Elmer Physical Electronics Div., 6509 Flying Cloud Dr., 55344, pg. 1279 **PB**
Phillips & Temro Industries Inc., 9700 W. 74th St., 55344, pg. 1388 **IT**
Preferred Products, Inc., 11095 Viking Dr., 55344, pg. 1541 **PB**
Reliance Motion Control, Inc., 6950 Washington Ave. S., 55344, pg. 1398 **PB**
RESEARCH, INCORPORATED, 6425 Flying Cloud Dr., 55344, pg. 1382 **PB**
C.H. ROBINSON CO., 8100 Mitchell Rd., Ste. 200, 55344, pg. 1394 **PB**
Rosemount Measurement Division, 12001 Technology Dr., 55344, pg. 574 **PB**
STARKEY LABORATORIES, INC., 6700 Washington Ave. S., 55344, pg. 1035 **PV**
Sterling Electronics, 9675 W. 76th St., Ste. 100, 55344, pg. 1051 **PB**
STERNER LIGHTING SYSTEMS INCORPORATED, 7575 Corporate Way, 55344, pg. 1042 **PV**
Studio 70, 6533 Flying Cloud Dr., Ste. 100, 55344, pg. 1541 **PV**
SUPERVALU, INC., 11840 Valley View Rd., 55344-3691, pg. 1540 **PB**
E.A. SWEEN COMPANY, 16101 W. 78th St., 55344, pg. 1058 **PV**
TIE Systems, Inc. Minnesota, 11445 Valley View Rd., 55344, pg. 1085 **PV**
Thermo Solutions, 6425 Flying Cloud Dr., 55424-0064, pg. 1382 **PB**
WESTERN PETROLEUM COMPANY, 9531 W. 78th St., Ste. 102, 55344, pg. 1168 **PV**
Witcher Construction Company, 9855 W. 78th, Ste 270, 55344, pg. 347 **PV**
Woodlake Sanitary Service, Inc., 9813 Flying Cloud Dr., 55344, pg. 265 **PB**

Edina

Archco Inc., 7101 York Ave. S., pg. 331 **PB**
Byerly's Inc., 7171 France Ave. S., 55435, pg. 680 **PV**
CAP Gemini America (Minneapolis Branch), 7300 France Ave. S., Ste. 412, 55435, pg. 264 **IT**
Community Credit Co., 3101 W. 69th St., 55435, pg. 1201 **PB**
Diversified Pharmaceutical Services, Inc., 7760 France Ave. S., Ste. 500, 55435, pg. 1265 **IT**
Golden Valley Microwave Foods, Inc., 7450 Metro Blvd., 55439, pg. 427 **PB**
GRAND HOLDINGS, INC., 5101 Vernon Ave., South, 55436, pg. 468 **PV**
C.F. HAGLIN & SONS, 4005 W. 65th St., 55435, pg. 493 **PV**
Insituform Central, Inc., 4510 W. 77th St., 55435, pg. 882 **PB**
KEY CADILLAC, INC., 6825 York Ave. S., 55435, pg. 617 **PV**
LUND FOOD HOLDINGS, INC., 4100 W. 50th St., 55424, pg. 680 **PV**
Lund's Inc., 4100 W. 50th St., Ste. 2100, 55424, pg. 680 **PV**
NCS Data Collection Systems, 4401 W. 76th St., 55435-5192, pg. 1155 **PB**
NASH FINCH COMPANY, 7600 France Ave. S., 55435, pg. 1151 **PB**
Orange Julius of America, 7505 Metro Blvd., 55439, pg. 220 **PB**
PARANATAL CARE OF AMERICA, INC., 4930 W. 77th St., Ste. 360, 55436, pg. 839 **PV**

PREMIER SALONS INTERNATIONAL, 6800 France Ave. S., Ste. 300, 55435, pg. 881 **PV**
SICO INCORPORATED, 7525 Cahill Rd., 55439, pg. 997 **PV**
Y.K.K. (U.S.A.) Inc., 7151 Metro Blvd., 55439, pg. 1515 **IT**

Elk River

THE CRETEX COMPANIES, 311 Lowell Ave., 55330, pg. 289 **PV**
UNITED POWER ASSOCIATION, P.O. Box 800, 55330, pg. 1123 **PV**

Eveleth

Eveleth Mines, P.O. Box 180, 55734, pg. 1213 **PB**

Excelsior

LYMAN LUMBER COMPANY, P.O. Box 40, 300 Morse Ave., 55331, pg. 683 **PV**

Fairfax

SOUTH CENTRAL CO-OP, Hwy. 4, S., 55332, pg. 1014 **PV**

Fairmont

ROSENS DIVERSIFIED, INC., 1120 Lake Ave., 56031, pg. 945 **PV**
Rosens, Inc., P.O. Box 933, 1120 Lake Ave., 56031, pg. 945 **PV**
Weigh-Tronix, Inc., 1000 Armstrong Dr., 56031, pg. 1299 **IT**

Faribault

Butter Kernel Products, P.O. Box 598, 55021, pg. 393 **PV**
FARIBAULT WOOLEN MILL CO., 1500 Second Ave., N.W., 55021, pg. 394 **PV**
Faribo Woolens, Inc., 1819 N.W. Second Ave., 55021, pg. 394 **PV**
McQuay Int'l, 300 24th St. N.W., 55021-2301, pg. 3 **PV**
Norwest Bank Faribault, N.A., 25 N.W. Fourth St., 55021, pg. 1202 **PB**

Farmington

DAKOTA ELECTRIC ASSOCIATION, 4300 220th St. W., 55024, pg. 308 **PV**
Dakota Energy Alternatives, Inc., 4300 220th St. W., 55024, pg. 308 **PV**

Fergus Falls

Minnesota-Dakota Generating Co., 215 Cascade St. S., 56537, pg. 1235 **PB**
OTTER TAIL POWER COMPANY, 215 Cascade St. S., 56537, pg. 1234 **PB**
Piper Jaffray Inc., 125 S. Mill St., 56537, pg. 1303 **PB**
Proximity Controls Corp., P.O. Box 386, Route 6, 56537, pg. 350 **PV**

Forest Lake

Century Fence Co., P.O. Box 277, 55025, pg. 226 **PV**
PLASTECH CORPORATION, 20 N. Lake St., Ste. 210, 55025, pg. 870 **PV**

Fridley

FURNITURE GROUP INDUSTRIES, 5900 Main St. N.E., 55432, pg. 432 **PB**
KURT MANUFACTURING CO. INC., 5280 Main St. N.E., 55421, pg. 637 **PV**
Tower Electronics, Inc., 281 S. Commerce, 55432, pg. 20 **PB**

Golden Valley

Audiotone, Inc., 4101 Dahlberg Dr., 55422, pg. 194 **PB**
Bausch & Lomb Hearing Systems Division, 4120 Olson Memorial Hwy., 55422, pg. 194 **PB**
CYBEROPTICS CORPORATION, 5900 Golden Hills Dr., 55416, pg. 470 **PB**
Dahlberg, Inc., 4101 Dahlberg Dr., 55422, pg. 194 **PB**
Dahlberg Inc. Retail Stores Div., 4101 Dahlberg Dr., 55422, pg. 194 **PB**
Fredonia Seed Co., 7500 Olson Memorial Hwy., 55427, pg. 974 **IT**
GRACO INC., 4050 Olson Memorial Hwy., 55422, pg. 756 **PB**
J.H. LARSON ELECTRICAL COMPANY, 700 Colorado Ave., S., 55416, pg. 652 **PV**
JIM LUPIENT ENTERPRISES, 7100 Wayzata Blvd., 55426, pg. 681 **PV**
NK Lawn & Garden, 7500 Olson Memorial Hwy., 55427, pg. 974 **IT**
Northrup King Co., 7500 Olson Memorial Hwy., 55427, pg. 974 **IT**
Pedigree Seed Co., 7500 Olson Memorial Hwy., 55427, pg. 974 **IT**
Red Line Healthcare Corp., 3121 10th Ave. N., 55427, pg. 974 **IT**
SUNRISE LEASING CORPORATION, 5500 Wayzata Blvd., Ste. 725, 55416, pg. 1535 **PB**

Thompson Division, 8421 Wayzata Blvd., Ste. 300, 55426, pg. 1683 **PB**

Grand Rapids

Blandin Paper Company, 115 S.W. First St., 55744, pg. 495 **IT**

Harris

ARCON CONSTRUCTION CO., INC., 43425 Frontage Rd., 55032, pg. 80 **PV**

Hastings

HASTINGS CO-OP CREAMERY COMPANY, 1701 Vermillion St., 55033, pg. 510 **PV**
Polka Dot Dairy/Tom Thumb Food Markets, 110 E. 17th St., 55033, pg. 874 **PV**
POLKA DOT DAIRY/TOM THUMB, INC., 110 E. 17th St., 55033, pg. 874 **PV**
SMEAD MANUFACTURING COMPANY, 600 E. Smead Blvd., 55033, pg. 1006 **PV**

Hector

COMMUNICATIONS SYSTEMS, INC., 213 S. Main St., 55342, pg. 415 **PB**
Suttle Apparatus Corporation, 1001 Hwy. 212E, 55342, pg. 416 **PB**

Hibbing

Great Northern Iron Ore, 801 E. Howard St., 55746, pg. 760 **PB**
ITW Irathane, P.O. Box 276, 55746, pg. 866 **PB**
Kahler Park Hotel, 1402 E. Howard St., 55746, pg. 1537 **PB**
Ryan Construction Company Of Minnesota, Ryan Bldg., 55746, pg. 953 **PV**
Viking Explosives & Supply Inc., 4469 Hwy. 5, 55746, pg. 1115 **PB**

Hopkins

ATIO Corporation USA, Inc., 10801 Excelsior Blvd., 55343, pg. 1716 **PB**
Advance Circuits, Commercial Div. Plant, 560 16th Ave., So., 55343, pg. 713 **IT**
ALLIANT TECHSYSTEMS, 600 Second St., N.E., 55343-8367, pg. 47 **PB**
FBS Life Insurance Company, First Bank Hopkins, 16 Ninth Ave. N., 55343, pg. 1681 **PB**
INNOVEX, INC., 1313 Fifth St. S., 55343, pg. 880 **PB**
Innovex Precision Products, 1313 Fifth St. S., 55343, pg. 880 **PB**
Marshall Labs Inc., 201 3rd St. S., 55343-7770, pg. 531 **PB**
Motorola Radius, 5620 Smetana Dr. Ste. 100, 55343-9611, pg. 1138 **PB**
Napco International, Inc., 11111 Excelsior Blvd., 55343, pg. 1716 **PB**
REUTER MANUFACTURING INC., 410 11th Ave. S., 55343, pg. 1383 **PB**
Risk Planners, Inc., 215 E. Excelsior Blvd., 55343, pg. 1541 **PB**
Spantek Division, 1520 S. Fifth St., 55343, pg. 1129 **PB**
VENTURIAN CORP., 11111 Excelsior Blvd., 55343, pg. 1716 **PB**
Walser Leasing Inc., 317 Main St., 55343, pg. 1148 **PV**
Warrington Financial Systems Inc., 601 2nd Ave. S., 55343, pg. 1535 **PB**

Hutchinson

ADC Solitra Oy, P.O. Box 157, 1065 Fifth Ave., S.E., 55350, pg. 4 **PB**
FSF FINANCIAL CORP., 201 Main St. S., 55350-2573, pg. 608 **PB**
First Federal FSB, 201 Main St., S., 55350-2573, pg. 608 **PB**
Firstate Services, Inc., 201 Main St., S., 55350-2573, pg. 608 **PB**
Hutchinson Technology Asia, Inc., 40 W. Highland Park, 55350, pg. 850 **PB**
HUTCHINSON TECHNOLOGY INC., 40 W. Highland Park, 55350-9784, pg. 850 **PB**

International Falls

First American Bank, P.O. Box 511, 56649, pg. 167 **PV**
International Falls Power Company, 523 Third Ave., 56649, pg. 243 **PB**
Minnesota, Dakota & Western Railway Co., 56649, pg. 243 **PB**

Inver Grove Heights

BITUMINOUS ROADWAYS, INC., 9050 Jefferson Trail W., 55077, pg. 146 **PV**
CENEX, INC., 5500 Cenex Dr., 55075, pg. 221 **PV**
Cenex/Land O'Lakes, Inc., 5500 Cenex Dr., 55077, pg. 222 **PV**
Pine Bend Landfill, Inc., 2495 E. 117th St., 55075, pg. 264 **PV**

PB - *U.S. Public Companies Volume*
PV - *U.S. Private Companies Volume*
IT - *International Public & Private Companies Volume*

Jordan

Theradyne Corporation, 395 Ervin Indus. Dr., 55352, pg. 637   PV

Lakeville

Arden Foods, Inc., 21150 Hamburg Ave., 55044, pg. 972   PV
Arden International Kitchens, Inc., 21150 Hamburg Ave., 55044, pg. 972   PV
CHEMCENTRAL/Minnesota, 21675 Hamburg Ave., 55044, pg. 232   PV
Despatch Industries, 8860 207th St. W., 55044, pg. 327   PV
GRIST MILL COMPANY, 21340 Hayes Ave., 55044, pg. 766   PB
Rexam Medical Packaging Lakeville, 8235 220th St. W., 55044, pg. 1106   IT

Le Center

DYNA TECHNOLOGY INCORPORATED, 225 S. Cordova Ave., 56057, pg. 350   PV
WINCO, 225 S. Cordova Ave., 56057, pg. 350   PV

Lester Prairie

Lester Buildings Division, 111 2nd Ave. S., 55354, pg. 271   PB

Lewiston

Herff Jones Photography, Box 100, 135 Rice St., 55952, pg. 523   PV

Litchfield

FIRST DISTRICT ASSOCIATION, P.O. Box 842, 216 W. Commercial St., 55355, pg. 406   PV
JOHNSON BROS. CORPORATION, 23577 Minnesota Hwy. 22, 55355, pg. 590   PV
Litchfield Precision Components, One Precision Dr., 55355, pg. 880   PV

Little Falls

Crestliner, Inc., 609 13th Ave. NE, 55345, pg. 447   PV
Glastron Boats, 700 W. River Rd., 56345, pg. 447   PV
Larson Boats, Paul Larson Memorial Dr., 56345, pg. 447   PV

Long Lake

WASHINGTON SCIENTIFIC INDUSTRIES, INC., 2605 W. Wayzata Blvd., 55356, pg. 1744   PB

Long Prairie

Banta Publications Group, 100 Banta Rd., 56347-1903, pg. 188   PB
Long Prairie Packing Co., 10 Riverside Dr., 56347, pg. 945   PV

Luverne

Berkley Information Services, P.O. Box 657, 10 Roundwind Rd., 56156, pg. 216   PB
IBP-Luverne, P.O. Box 210 W. Hwy. 17, 56156, pg. 852   PB
Tri-State Insurance Company of Minnesota, One Roundwind Rd., 56156, pg. 215   PB

Mankato

Atlas-Alchem Plastics-Minnesota, 480 Industrial Rd., 56001, pg. 1496   PV
HINIKER COMPANY, Box 3407, Airport Rd., 56002-3407, pg. 530   PV
HONEYMEAD PRODUCTS CO., 2020 S. Riverfront Dr., 56001, pg. 537   PV
Hubbard Feeds Inc., 424 N. Riverfront Dr., 56002, pg. 1116   IT
Hubbard Milling Company, P.O. Box 8500, 56002, pg. 1182   PV
Lewis Drug Mankato, 1351 Madison Ave., 56001, pg. 665   PV
NSP-Southeast Region, 210 Lime St., 56002, pg. 1195   PB
Perfecseal, Inc., 1301 Third Ave., 56001, pg. 210   PB
Piper Jaffray Inc., Union Depot, 112 S. Riverfront Dr., 56001-3619, pg. 1301   PB
TAYLOR CORPORATION, 1725 Roe Crest Dr., 56003, pg. 1070   PV

Maple Grove

Banta Catalog Group, 7401 Kilmer Ln., 55369-5699, pg. 188   PB
Minneapolis Auto Auction, 8001 Jefferson Hwy., 55369, pg. 282   PV
Norstan Financial Services, Inc., 6900 Wedgwood Rd., Ste. 150, 55311, pg. 1192   PB
Rolm Resale Systems, 6490 Sycamore Ct., 55369, pg. 1192   PV
WORLD AEROSPACE CORPORATION, 8625 Monticello Ln., N., 55369, pg. 1188   PV

Maplewood

KSTP-AM, Inc., 2792 Maplewood Dr., 55109, pg. 544   PV

Marcell

Valley Forest Resources Co., P.O. Box 27, 56657, pg. 1140   PV

Marshall

First American Bank Southwest, 208 E. College Dr., 56258, pg. 167   PV
LYON COUNTY CO-OP OIL CO., 1100 E. Main, 56258, pg. 684   PV
Norwest Bank Minnesota Southwest, N.A., 400 W. Main St., 56258, pg. 1202   PB
SCHWAN'S SALES ENTERPRISES, 115 W. College Dr., 56258, pg. 974   PV

Mendota Heights

Circle Freight International USA, 1450 Northland Dr., 55120, pg. 371   PB
Circle International, 1450 Northland Dr., 55120, pg. 371   PB
Farmers Insurance Group, 880 Sibley Mem. Hwy., 55118-1736, pg. 111   IT
Ikon Office Solutions/D.C. Hey, 1031 Mendota Heights Rd., 55120, pg. 863   PB
Solvay Animal Health, Inc., 1201 Northland Dr., 55120, pg. 1277   IT

Milaca

Medtronic Milaca, Inc., 900 Sixth Ave. N.E., 56353, pg. 1083   PB

Minneapolis

A&W Restaurants, Inc.-Carousel Div., 9549 Penn Ave., 55431, pg. 2   PV
ACI TELECENTRICS, INC., 3100 W. Lake St., Ste. 300, 55416, pg. 3   PB
AIC-FSS ADVERTISING, 8200 Normandale Blvd., Ste. 330, 55437, pg. 5   PV
AIC-FSS Advertising, 8200 Normandale Blvd., Ste. 400, 55437-1074, pg. 6   PV
APG Division, 5250 N.E. Industrial Blvd., 55421, pg. 1129   PV
ADOLFSON & PETERSON, INC., 6701 W. 23rd St., 55426, pg. 17   PV
Allianz Life Insurance Company of North America, 1750 Hennepin Ave., 55403-2195, pg. 18   IT
Allied Security Inc., 430 First Ave. N., Ste. 280, 55401, pg. 40   PV
Allright Parking Minnesota, Inc., 320 Young-Quinlan Bldg., 81 S. Ninth St., 55402, pg. 43   PV
American Dairy Queen Corporation, 7505 Metro Blvd., 55439, pg. 220   PV
American Enterprise Investment Services, Inc., IDS Tower, 55402, pg. 73   PB
American Express Financial Advisor, IDS Tower 10, 55440, pg. 73   PB
American Natl. Can Co., 150 26th St., S.E., 55414, pg. 1029   PV
American Paging, Inc., 1300 Godward St. N.E., Ste. 3100, 55413, pg. 1570   PB
AMERIPRIDE SERVICE COMPANY, 47 S. Ninth St., 55402, pg. 65   PV
ANALYSTS INTERNATIONAL CORPORATION, 7615 Metro Blvd., 55439, pg. 110   PB
Animal Fair, 7664 W. 78th St., 55439, pg. 885   PV
APOGEE ENTERPRISES, INC., 7900 Xerxes Ave. S., Ste. 1800, 55431-1159, pg. 120   PB
Arnold Advertising, 8300 Norman Ctr. Drive, Ste. 510, 55437, pg. 84   PV
ARROW TANK & ENGINEERING CO., 8950 Evergreen Blvd., 55433, pg. 85   PV
Atlas Manufacturing Division, 2950 Weeks Ave., S.E., 55414, pg. 1129   PV
Audio King Midwest, 3501 S. Hwy. 100, 55416, pg. 1662   PV
AUGSBURG FORTRESS, PUBLISHERS, 100 S. Fifth St., Ste. 700, 55402, pg. 98   PV
AULT INCORPORATED, 7300 Boone Ave. N., 55428-1028, pg. 147   PV
BKG Finishing Systems, Inc., 4131 Pheasant Ridge Dr., N.E., 55434, pg. 865   PB
BMC INDUSTRIES, INC., Two Appletree Sq., Ste.400, 55425, pg. 162   PV
BPMC, Inc., 315 27th Ave. N.E., 55418, pg. 118   PV
BRW, INC., 700 Third St., S., 55415, pg. 107   PV
BACHMAN'S, INC., 6010 Lyndale Ave. S., 55419, pg. 109   PV
M.F. BANK & COMPANY, INC., 615 First Ave. N., 55413, pg. 113   PV
The Bank of Tokyo-Mitsubishi, Ltd. (Minnesota Corporate Banking), 90 S. Seventh St., Ste. 5100, 55402, pg. 157   IT
BANNER ENGINEERING CORP., 9714 Tenth Ave. N., 55441, pg. 114   PV
THE BARBERS, HAIRSTYLING FOR MEN & WOMEN, INC., 300 Industrial Blvd. N.E., 55413, pg. 115   PV
BEMIS COMPANY, INC., 222 S. Ninth St., Ste. 2300, 55402, pg. 210   PB
Bepex Corporation, 333 N.E. Taft St., 55413, pg. 636   IT

THE BERGQUIST COMPANY, 5300 Edina Industrial Blvd., 55439, pg. 135   PV
Berkley Administrators, 8441 Wayzata Blvd., Ste. 100, 55459-0143, pg. 216   PB
Berkley Risk Services, Inc., 920 2nd Ave. S., Ste. 700, 55402, pg. 215   PB
Betty Crocker Products, Number One General Mills Blvd., 55426, pg. 718   PB
Big 'G' Div., Number One General Mills Blvd., 55426, pg. 718   PB
Henry Birks Jewelers, Inc., Ste. 900, Butler Sq., 100 No. 6th St., 55403, pg. 197   IT
E.W. Blanch Capital Risk Solutions, Inc., 3500 W. 80th St., 55431, pg. 236   PB
E.W. BLANCH HOLDINGS, INC., 3500 W. 80th St., 55431, pg. 236   PB
E.W. Blanch International, Inc., 3500 W. 80th St., 55431, pg. 236   PB
E.W. Blanch Wholesale Insurance Services Inc., 3500 W. 80th St., 55431, pg. 236   PB
Blumberg Communications Inc., 525 N. Washington Ave., 55401, pg. 305   PB
J. Brown & Associates Minneapolis/St. Paul, Two Appletree Sq., Ste. 301, 55425, pg. 764   PB
BUHLER INC., 1100 Xenium Ln., 55441, pg. 179   PV
BUREAU OF ENGRAVING, 3400 Technology Dr., 55418, pg. 181   PV
CAE Vanguard, Inc., 3500 W. 80th St., Ste. 100, 55431, pg. 237   IT
Camerz Photo Products, 4800 Quebec Ave. N., 55428, pg. 1292   PB
CAMPBELL MITHUN ESTY, 222 S. Ninth St., 55402, pg. 204   PV
Canadian Pacific Railway, 105 S. Fifth St., 55402, pg. 259   IT
Cargill Animal Nutrition Div., P.O. Box 5614, 55440-5614, pg. 210   PV
Cargill Citro-America, Inc., P.O. Box 9300, 55440, pg. 210   PV
Cargill Flour Div., Mail Stop 61, P.O. Box 9300, 55440-9300, pg. 210   PV
Cargill Salt Inc., P.O. Box 5621, 55440, pg. 48   IT
Cargill Seed Div., P.O. Box 5645, 55440, pg. 210   PV
Carlson Acquisition Group, Carlson Parkway, 55459, pg. 212   PV
Carlson International Division, P.O. Box 59159, Carlson Parkway, 55459, pg. 212   PV
Carlson Learning Company, Carlson Parkway, 55459, pg. 212   PV
Carlson Leasing, Inc., P.O. Box 59159, Carlson Parkway, 55459-8215, pg. 212   PV
Carlson Marketing Group, Inc., P.O. Box 59159, Carlson Parkway, 55459, pg. 212   PV
Carlson Promotion Division, P.O. Box 59159, Carlson Parkway, 55459, pg. 212   PV
Carlson Retail Marketing, Carlson Parkway, 55459-8289, pg. 212   PV
Carlson Travel Group, Inc., P.O. Box 59159, Carlson Pkwy., 55459, pg. 212   PV
Carlson Travel Network International, P.O. Box 59159, Carlson Pkwy., 55459, pg. 212   PV
Carlson Wagonlit Travel, Carlson Parkway, 55459, pg. 212   PV
CARMICHAEL LYNCH, INC., 800 Hennepin Ave., 55403, pg. 213   PV
CARTER DAY INTERNATIONAL, 500 73rd Ave., N.E., 55432, pg. 216   PV
Carter Day International, Inc., 500 73rd Ave., N.E., 55432, pg. 217   PV
CASH PLUS, INC., 222 S. Ninth St., Ste. 2200, 55402, pg. 218   PV
Cat Pumps Corporation, 1681 94th Lane N.E., 55434, pg. 336   PV
Caterpillar Paving Products Inc., 9401 85th Ave. N., 55440, pg. 316   PV
Century Leasing & Liquidating, Inc., 5500 Norwest Ctr., 90 S. 7th St., 55402, pg. 1159   PB
Ceridian Performance Partners, 8100 34th Ave. S., 55425, pg. 331   PB
ChexSystems, Inc., 1550 E. 79th St., Ste. 700, 55420, pg. 498   PB
THE CHURCHILL COMPANIES, 333 S. 7th St., Ste. 3100, 55402, pg. 239   PV
City Looks Salons, 300 Industrial Blvd., N.E., 55413, pg. 115   PV
CLARITY COVERDALE FURY ADVERTISING, 120 South Sixth St., Ste. 1300, 55402, pg. 242   PV
Clear Channel Television, Inc., c/o WFTC-TV, 1701 Broadway St., N.E., 55413, pg. 383   PB
COLLE & MCVOY, INC., 8500 Normandale Lake Blvd., Ste. 2400, 55437, pg. 252   PV
COLWELL INDUSTRIES, INC., 123 N. Third St., 55401, pg. 257   PV
COMPUTER NETWORK TECHNOLOGY CORPORATION, 605 N. Hwy. 169 Ste. 800, 55441, pg. 421   PB
ConAgra Grain Companies, 730 Second Ave. So., 14th Fl., 55402, pg. 426   PB
Connect Computer, 7101 Metro Blvd., pg. 1192   PB
Conwed Plastics, 2810 Weeks Ave. S.E., 55414, pg. 990   PB
Corrugated Packaging, 4300 Olson Hwy., 55422, pg. 737   PB
Cost Cutters, 300 Industrial Blvd., N.E., 55413, pg. 115   PV
Courier Dispatch Division, 620 Olson Memorial Hwy., 55411, pg. 450   PB
COWLES MEDIA COMPANY, 329 Portland Ave., 55415, pg. 280   PV
Creo International, 60 S. Sixth St., Ste. 2600, 55402, pg. 710   PV
D & K Healthcare Resources-Minneapolis Division, 800 N. Third St., 55401, pg. 472   PB

PB - U.S. Public Companies Volume
PV - U.S. Private Companies Volume
IT - International Public & Private Companies Volume

Geographic Index-U.S.

D.Q.F., Inc., 7505 Metro Blvd., 55439, pg. 220 **PB**
DAIN RAUSCHER CORPORATION, Dain Bosworth Plaza, 60 S. Sixth St., 19th Fl., 55402-4422, pg. 476 **PB**
Dain Rauscher Incorporated, Dain Rauscher Plaza, 60 S. Sixth St., 55402-4422, pg. 476 **PB**
Damark Financial Services, Inc., 7101 Winnetka Ave. N., 55428, pg. 478 **PB**
DAMARK INTERNATIONAL, INC., 7101 Winnetka Ave., N., 55428, pg. 478 **PB**
Danaher Controls, 4601 Excelsior Blvd., 55416-4960, pg. 480 **PB**
DAYTON HUDSON CORPORATION, 777 Nicollet Mall, 13th Fl., 55402, pg. 489 **PB**
DEALERS MANUFACTURING COMPANY, 7120 Northland Ter., 55428, pg. 318 **PV**
John Deere Company, P.O. Box 855, 55440, pg. 492 **PB**
T.S. Denison & Company, 9601 Newton Ave., S., 55431, pg. 288 **PV**
The Department Store Division of Dayton Hudson Corporation, 700 Nicollet Mall, 55402, pg. 489 **PB**
DESPATCH INDUSTRIES, 63 St. Anthony Pkwy., 55418, pg. 327 **PV**
Detector Electronics Corporation, 6901 W. 110th St., 55438, pg. 1500 **IT**
Diversified Business Credit, Inc., 3970 Multifoods Tower, 33 S. Sixth St., 55402, pg. 1154 **PV**
DIVERSIFIED DYNAMICS CORPORATION, 1681 94th Ln. N.E., 55449, pg. 336 **PV**
f. Dohmen Company, 2001 Kennedy St., N.E., 55413, pg. 338 **PV**
DONALDSON COMPANY, INC., 1400 W. 94th St., 55431, pg. 517 **PB**
DURA AUTOMOTIVE SYSTEMS, INC., 4508 IDS Ctr., 55402, pg. 537 **PB**
E&S Insulation, 7100 Medicine Lake Rd., 55427, pg. 366 **PV**
EBP Life Insurnace Co., 600 S. Hwy. 169, Ste. 500, 55426, pg. 635 **PB**
The Edison Group, 60 S. Sixth St., Ste. 2600, 55402, pg. 710 **PV**
EGAN COS., 7100 Medicine Lake Rd., 55427, pg. 365 **PV**
Egan McKay Electrical Contractors, 7100 Medicine Lake Rd., 55427, pg. 366 **PV**
Egan Mechanical Contractors Inc., 7100 Medicine Lake Rd., 55427, pg. 366 **PV**
Fairway Foods, Inc., 4567 W. 80th St., 55437, pg. 534 **PV**
FAME, 60 S. Sixth St., Ste. 2600, 55402, pg. 710 **PV**
FARIBAULT FOODS INC., Baker Bldg., Ste. 1000, 706 2nd Ave. S., 55402-3010, pg. 393 **PV**
Farm Credit Leasing Services Corporation, 1600 Colonnade, 5500 Wayzata Blvd., 55416-1252, pg. 398 **PV**
FilmTec Corporation, 7200 Ohms Lane, 55435, pg. 523 **PV**
First Bank National Association, Sixth & Marquette, 55480, pg. 1681 **PB**
First Midwest Auto Park, Inc., 414 Nicollet Mall, 55401, pg. 1195 **PB**
Fleischmann Malting Company, Inc., P.O. Box 15245, 55414, pg. 128 **PB**
FLO-PAC CORPORATION, 700 N. Washington Ave., Ste. 400, 55401, pg. 414 **PV**
Flo-Pac Midwest, 918 N. 3rd St., 55401, pg. 414 **PV**
FOLEY-BELSAW COMPANY, 3300 5th St., NE, 55418, pg. 416 **PV**
Foley Martens Company, 3300 E. Fifth St., 55418, pg. 416 **PV**
Food Ingredients, P.O. Box 116, 55440, pg. 646 **PV**
Foster Products Corporation, 3900 Jackson St., 55421, pg. 686 **PB**
Frontier Communications North Central, Inc., 1300 Nicollet Mail, Ste. 218, 55443, pg. 683 **PB**
GE Capital/IT Solutions, 10200-51st Ave. N., 55442, pg. 711 **PB**
GFI AMERICA, 2815 Blaisdell Ave., S., 55408, pg. 435 **PV**
GABBERT'S, INC., 3501 Galleria, 55435, pg. 437 **PV**
GAGE MARKETING GROUP, 10000 Highway 55, 55441-6365, pg. 437 **PV**
General Mills, Consumer Foods Sales Div., Number One General Mills Blvd., 55426, pg. 718 **PV**
GENERAL MILLS, INC., One General Mills Blvd., 55426, pg. 717 **PB**
General Mills, Marketing Services Div., Number One General Mills Blvd., 55426, pg. 718 **PV**
General Mills Operations, Inc., Number One General Mills Blvd., 55426, pg. 718 **PB**
General Mills Sales, Inc., Number One General Mills Blvd., 55426, pg. 718 **PB**
GENMAR HOLDINGS, INC., 100 S. Fifth St., Ste. 2400, 55402, pg. 447 **PV**
The Glass Depot, Inc., 2450 Minnehaha Ave. S., 55404, pg. 120 **PV**
Gold Medal Div., Number One General Mills Blvd., 55426, pg. 718 **PV**
Gold Medal Insurance Co., Number One General Mills Blvd., 55426, pg. 718 **PB**
GOLDNER HAWN JOHNSONS & MORRISON INCORPORATED, 5250 Norwest Ctr., 90 S. 7th St., 55402-4123, pg. 462 **PV**
Graco Communications Center, 3110 Washington Ave. N., 55411, pg. 757 **PV**
Grand Metropolitan Foodservice Inc., 200 S. Sixth St., 55402, pg. 408 **IT**
Graystone Corporation, 1221 Nicollet Mall, 55401, pg. 1195 **PV**
GREAT CLIPS, INC., 3800 W. 80th St., Ste. 400, 55431, pg. 473 **PV**
Great Northern Insurance Co., 1000 Pillsbury Ctr., 55402, pg. 355 **PB**
Green Giant International, Inc., Pillsbury Center, 55402, pg. 411 **IT**

Grinnell Supply Sales Division, 1201 W. 96th St., 55431-2605, pg. 1648 **PB**
Grow Biz Games, Inc., 4200 Dahlberg Dr., 55422, pg. 767 **PB**
GROW BIZ INTERNATIONAL, INC., 4200 Dahlberg Dr., 55422, pg. 767 **PB**
The Haagen-Dazs Company Inc., 200 South Sixth St., 55402-1464, pg. 411 **IT**
HAMMEL, GREEN & ABRAHAMSON, INC., 1201 Harmon Pl., 55403, pg. 497 **PV**
Harmon Contract Glazing, Inc., 660 Kasota Ave., 55414, pg. 120 **PV**
Harmon Glass Company, 4000 Olson Memorial Hwy., Ste. 600, 55422, pg. 120 **PV**
HARMONY ENGINEERING CORPORATION, 460 Hoover St., N.E., 55413, pg. 503 **PV**
HAUENSTEIN & BURMEISTER, INC., 2629 30th Ave., S., 55406, pg. 510 **PV**
HAWKINS CHEMICAL, INC., 3100 E. Hennepin Ave., 55413, pg. 800 **PB**
Hawkins Water Treatment Group, Inc., 3000 E. Hennepin Ave., 55413, pg. 800 **PV**
HAWORTH GROUP INC., TCF Tower, 10th Fl., 121 S. Eighth St., 55402, pg. 511 **PV**
D.C. Hey Company, 7399 Bush Lake Rd., 55435, pg. 863 **PV**
Holiday Station Stores, Inc., 4567 W. 80th St., 55437, pg. 534 **PV**
HONEYWELL INC., Honeywell Plaza, 2701 4th Ave., S., 55408, pg. 833 **PB**
Hospitality Procurement Division, Carlson Pkwy., P.O. Box 59159, 55459-8202, pg. 212 **PV**
IDS Certificate Company, IDS Tower, 55402, pg. 73 **PB**
IDS Financial Services, Inc., 2900 IDS Tower, 55402, pg. 73 **PB**
IDS Property Casualty Insurance Company, Ten IDS Tower, 55440, pg. 73 **PB**
IDS Trust Co., 33 S. Sixth St., Ste. 2800, 55402, pg. 73 **PB**
IFG Asset Management Services, Inc., Dain Bosworth Plaza, 60 S. Sixth St., 20th Fl., 55402-7957, pg. 476 **PB**
ITT Hartford Life & Annuity Insurance Corporation, Waterford Park, 505 N. Hwy. 169, 55441, pg. 795 **PB**
Industrial Chemical & Equipment, 3230 E. Hennepin Ave., 55413, pg. 800 **PB**
Industrial Custom Products L.L.C., 2801 37th. Ave., NE, 55421, pg. 352 **PV**
International Dairy Queen, Inc., 7505 Metro Blvd., 55439, pg. 220 **PB**
INTERNATIONAL MULTIFOODS CORPORATION, 33 S. Sixth St., 55402-0942, pg. 900 **PB**
Interplastic Commercial Resins Division, 2015 N.E. Broadway, 55413, pg. 572 **PV**
Investment Advisers, Inc., 1100 Dain Tower, P.O. Box 1160, 55440, pg. 813 **IT**
Jani King of Minnesota, Inc., 3033 Excelsior Blvd., Ste. 325, 55416, pg. 582 **PV**
JAPS-OLSON COMPANY, 7500 Excelsior Blvd., 55411-1694, pg. 582 **PV**
JEWELMONT CORPORATION, 800 Boone Ave., N., 55427, pg. 587 **PV**
Jones Lumber, 722 Kasota Cir., 55414, pg. 585 **PV**
JOSTENS, 5501 Norman Center Dr., 55437-1088, pg. 934 **PB**
The Jostens Foundation, Inc., 5501 Norman Center Dr., 55437, pg. 934 **PB**
K-Tel Consumer Products, Inc., 2605 Fernbrook Ln. N., 55447, pg. 938 **PB**
K-Tel Direct, Inc., 2605 Fernbrook Ln. N., 55447, pg. 938 **PB**
K-TEL INTERNATIONAL, INC., 2605 Fernbrook Lane North, 55447-1480, pg. 937 **PB**
KARE-TV, 8811 Olson Memorial Hwy., 55427, pg. 702 **PB**
KQRS-AM/FM, 917 N. Lilac Dr., 55422, pg. 512 **PB**
KQRS, Inc., 917 N. Lilac Dr., 55422, pg. 512 **PB**
Karmelkorn Shoppes, 7505 Metro Blvd., 55439, pg. 220 **PB**
Karwoski & Courage, 60 S. Sixth St., Ste. 2800, 55402, pg. 710 **PV**
Kinko's Service Corp., 612 Washington Ave. S.E., 55414-2916, pg. 622 **PV**
Kintetsu World Express Inc., 7550 23rd Ave. S., Ste. 126, 55450, pg. 734 **IT**
KNUTSON CONSTRUCTION CO., 5500 Wayzata Blvd., Ste. 300, 55416-1216, pg. 627 **PV**
Korn/Ferry International, 4816 IDS Ctr., 55402, pg. 633 **PV**
Kraus-Anderson Construction Company, 525 S. Eighth St., 55404, pg. 635 **PV**
KRAUS-ANDERSON INCORPORATED, 523 S. 8th St., 55404, pg. 635 **PV**
Kraus-Anderson, Incorporated, 523 S. Eighth St., 55404-1078, pg. 635 **PV**
Kraus-Anderson Mortgage Company, 523 S. Eighth St., 55404, pg. 635 **PV**
Lagerquist Corporation, P.O. Box 9510, 55440, pg. 521 **PB**
Land O'Lakes Finance Co., P.O. Box 116, 55420, pg. 646 **PV**
Land O'Lakes International Division, P.O. Box 116, 55440, pg. 646 **PV**
LaPaz, 414 Nicollet Mall, 55401, pg. 1195 **PB**
LAWSON SOFTWARE, 1300 Godward St., 55413, pg. 654 **PV**
Leslie Paper, Interchange Tower, Ste. 1414, 600 S. Hwy. 55436, pg. 903 **PV**
Lifetouch National School Studios Inc., 7800 Picture Dr., 55436, pg. 667 **PV**
Lifetouch Publishing Inc., 400 Paramount Plaza, 7831 Glenroy Rd., 55435, pg. 667 **PV**
Litho Colorplate, 2626 2nd St. N.E., Ste. 100, 55418, pg. 1437 **PB**

Longview Fibre Co. Central Container Div., 5851 E. River Rd., 55421, pg. 1014 **PB**
Lowry Hill Investment Advisors, Inc., Norwest Ctr., Sixth & Marquette, 55479-1026, pg. 1201 **PB**
Lupient Automotive Group, 750 Pennsylvania Ave., 55426, pg. 681 **PV**
LUTHERAN BROTHERHOOD, 625 Fourth Ave. S., 55415, pg. 681 **PV**
Lutheran Brotherhood Family for Mutual Funds, 625 Fourth Ave. S., 55415, pg. 682 **PV**
Lutheran Brotherhood Financial Corporation, 625 Fourth Ave. S., 55415, pg. 682 **PV**
Lutheran Brotherhood Foundation, 625 Fourth Ave. S., 55415, pg. 682 **PV**
Lutheran Brotherhood Real Estate Products Company, 625 Fouth Ave. S., 55415, pg. 682 **PV**
Lutheran Brotherhood Research Corp., 625 Fourth Ave. S., 55145, pg. 682 **PV**
Lutheran Brotherhood Securities Corp., 625 Fourth Ave. S., 55415, pg. 682 **PV**
Lutheran Brotherhood Variable Insurance Products Company, 625 Fouth Ave. S., 55415, pg. 682 **PV**
MGI PHARMA INC., Opus Center, 9900 Bren Rd. E., Ste. 300E, 55343-9667, pg. 1026 **PB**
MPC Minneapolis, 7309 W. 27th St., 55426, pg. 851 **IT**
E.F. MacDonald Motivation Div., P.O. Box 59159, 55459, pg. 212 **PV**
MALT-O-MEAL COMPANY, 80 S. Eighth St., Ste. 2600, 55402-2297, pg. 699 **PV**
Marigold Foods, Inc., 2929 University Ave. S.E., 55414, pg. 752 **IT**
MARQUETTE BANCSHARES INC., P.O. Box 1000, 55480-1000, pg. 706 **PV**
MARTIN/WILLIAMS ADVERTISING INC., 60 South Sixth St., Ste. 2800, 55402, pg. 710 **PV**
MCGLYNN BAKERIES INC., 7350 Commerce La., 55432, pg. 721 **PV**
McGraw-Hill Healthcare Publications Group, 4530 W. 77th St., 55435, pg. 1071 **PV**
MCLAUGHLIN GORMLEY KING COMPANY, 8810 Tenth Ave., N., 55427, pg. 723 **PV**
McQuay International, 13600 Industrial Park Blvd., 55441, pg. 3 **PV**
MedTrac, Inc., 200 S. Sixth St., Ste. 1600, 55402-1436, pg. 1504 **IT**
Medtronic Heart Valve Division, 7000 Central Ave. N.E., 55432-1350, pg. 1083 **PB**
MEDTRONIC, INC., 7000 Central Ave. N.E., 55432-3576, pg. 1082 **PB**
Medtronic Neurological Div., 800 53rd Ave. N.E., 55421-1200, pg. 1083 **PB**
Mesaba Aviation, Inc., 7501 26th Ave. S., 55450, pg. 1099 **PV**
MESABA HOLDINGS, INC., 7501 26th Ave. S., 55450, pg. 1099 **PV**
Metallurgical, Inc., 900 E. Hennepin Ave., 55414, pg. 1594 **PV**
MICHAEL FOODS, INC., 5353 Wayzata Blvd., 55416, pg. 1103 **PV**
Miki Holding Company, 2845 Harriet Ave. So., 55408, pg. 866 **IT**
Military Avionics Division, 2600 Ridgway Pkwy., 55413-1719, pg. 834 **PB**
MILLER MEESTER ADVERTISING INC., 17 N. Washington, 55401, pg. 747 **PV**
MINCO PRODUCTS, INC., 7300 Commerce Ln., 55432, pg. 749 **PV**
Minneapolis Milling, 480 Grain Exchange Blvd., 55415, pg. 128 **PB**
Minnegasco, 800 Lasalle Ave., 55402, pg. 843 **PB**
Minnesota Laboratory, 1710 Douglas Dr. N., 55422, pg. 829 **PV**
MINNESOTA TWINS BASEBALL CLUB, 34 Kirby Pucket Pl., 55415, pg. 750 **PV**
Mocon FSC Corporation, 7500 Boone Ave. N., 55428, pg. 1121 **PB**
MODERN CONTROLS, INC., 7500 Boone Ave. N., 55428, pg. 1120 **PB**
M.A. MORTENSON COMPANY, 700 Meadow Ln. N., 55422, pg. 763 **PV**
NRG Energy, Inc., 1221 Nicollet Mall, 55401, pg. 1195 **PB**
NRG Group, Inc., 1221 Nicollet Mall, 55401, pg. 1195 **PB**
NRG Resource Recovery, Inc., 1221 Nicollet Mall, 55401, pg. 1195 **PB**
NRG Thermal Corporation, 1221 Nicollet Mall, 55401, pg. 1195 **PB**
NWNL Benefits Corp., 20 Washington Ave. S., 55401, pg. 1375 **PB**
NWNL Health Management Corp., 20 Washington Ave., S., 55401, pg. 1375 **PB**
NWNL Management Corp., 20 Washington Ave. S., 55401, pg. 1375 **PB**
Narco Medical Services Inc., 7667 Cahill Rd., 55435, pg. 1468 **IT**
National Car Rental System, Inc., 7700 France Ave., S., 55435, pg. 1379 **PB**
NATIONAL CITY BANCORP, Sixth On The Mall, 651 Nicollet Mall, 55402-1611, pg. 1153 **PB**
National Hotel Corp., P.O. Box 59159, Carlson Pkwy., 55459, pg. 212 **PV**
Neste Polyester Inc., 8290 Main St., N.E., 55432, pg. 913 **IT**
Network Systems Corporation, 7600 Boone Ave. N., 55428, pg. 1522 **PB**
Network Systems Credit Corp., 7600 Boone Ave. N., 55428, pg. 1522 **PB**
NORCOSTCO, INC., 3203 N. Hwy. 100, 55422, pg. 801 **PV**
Nord Photo Engineering, Inc., 4800 Quebec Ave. N., 55428, pg. 1292 **PB**
Nordic Ware, Hwy. 7 at 100, 55416, pg. 806 **PV**

PB - *U.S. Public Companies Volume*
PV - *U.S. Private Companies Volume*
IT - *International Public & Private Companies Volume*

1293

Geographic Index-U.S.

Norenco Corp., 1221 Nicollet Mall, 55401, pg. 1195 **PB**
North American Financial Corp., Carlson Parkway, 55459, pg. 212 **PV**
North Star Title, 5075 Wayzata Blvd., 55416, pg. 1554 **PB**
NORTHERN STATES POWER COMPANY, 414 Nicollet Mall, 55401, pg. 1195 **PB**
NORTHLAND ALUMINUM PRODUCTS, INC., 5005 Hwy. 7, 55416, pg. 805 **PV**
NORTHLAND ELECTRIC SUPPLY COMPANY, 521 S. Tenth St., 55404, pg. 806 **PV**
Northwestern National Life Insurance Co., 20 Washington Ave. S., 55401, pg. 1375 **PB**
Norwest Audit Services, Inc., Sixth & Marquette, 55479, pg. 1201 **PB**
Norwest Bank International, Norwest Ctr., Sixth & Marquette, 55479-1026, pg. 1202 **PB**
Norwest Bank Minnesota N.A., Norwest Ctr., Sixth & Marquette, 55479, pg. 1202 **PB**
Norwest Business Credit, Inc., Sixth & Marquette, 55479-2058, pg. 1202 **PB**
NORWEST CORPORATION, Norwest Center, Sixth & Marquette, 55479, pg. 1201 **PB**
Norwest Equipment Finance, Inc., 733 Marquette Ave., Ste. 300, 55479-2048, pg. 1202 **PB**
Norwest Insurance, Inc., Norwest Ctr., Sixth & Marquette, 55479-1026, pg. 1202 **PB**
Norwest Investment Services, Inc., Norwest Ctr., Sixth & Marquette, 55479-0030, pg. 1202 **PB**
Norwest Properties, Inc., Sixth & Marquette, 55479, pg. 1202 **PB**
Norwest Services, Inc., 255 Second Ave. S., 55479-2004, pg. 1202 **PB**
Norwest Venture Capital Management, Inc., 2800 Piper Jeffrey Tower, 222 S. 9th St., 55402, pg. 1202 **PB**
Oildyne, 4301 Quebec Ave. No., 55428, pg. 411 **PV**
Oildyne ASG Group, 4301 Quebec Ave., N., 55428, pg. 411 **PV**
Onan Corporation, 1400 73rd Ave., N.E., 55432-3796, pg. 468 **PB**
Option One, 60 S. Sixth St., Ste. 2800, 55402, pg. 710 **PV**
Orr-Schelen-Mayeron & Assoc., Inc., 2021 E. Hennepin Ave., 55413, pg. 1341 **PV**
PACE ANALYTICAL SERVICES, 17100 Elm St., Ste. 200, 55414, pg. 829 **PV**
Pacing Business Unit, 7000 Central Ave. N.E., 55432, pg. 1083 **PV**
PADILLA SPEER BEARDSLEY INC., 224 Franklin Ave., W., 55404, pg. 833 **PV**
PALM BEACH BEAUTY PRODUCTS CO., 950 Xenia Ave., S., 55416, pg. 834 **PV**
Parachute, Inc., 120 South Sixth St., Ste. 1475, 55402, pg. 242 **PV**
Paragon Reinsurance Risk Management Services, Inc., 3500 W. 80th St., 55431, pg. 236 **PV**
PARK CONSTRUCTION COMPANY, 7900 Beech St., N.E., 55432, pg. 839 **PV**
Peregrine Capital Management, Inc., 800 La Salle Ave., Ste. 1850, 55492-2018, pg. 1202 **PV**
PERISCOPE MARKETING COMMUNICATIONS, 921 Washington Ave. S., 55415, pg. 853 **PV**
PHOTO CONTROL CORPORATION, 4800 Quebec Ave. N., 55428, pg. 1292 **PB**
Photo Mechanical Services Inc., 333 W. 78th St., 55420-1113, pg. 891 **PV**
The Physician and Sportsmedicine, 4530 W. 77th St., 55435, pg. 1071 **PV**
Piggly Wiggly Northland Corp., P.O. Box 355, 7600 France Ave. S., 55440-0355, pg. 1152 **PV**
Pillsbury Bakeries and Foodservice, Inc., 200 S. Sixth St., 55402, pg. 411 **IT**
Pillsbury Co., 200 S. 6th St., 55402-1464, pg. 411 **IT**
The Pillsbury Company, 200 S. Sixth St., 55402-1464, pg. 411 **IT**
Pillsbury Grain Export, Inc., Pillsbury Center, 55402, pg. 411 **IT**
Piper Capital Management, Incorporated, 222 S. Ninth St., 55402-3804, pg. 1303 **PB**
PIPER JAFFRAY COMPANIES, INC., Piper Jaffray Tower, 222 S. Ninth St., 55402-3804, pg. 1300 **PB**
Piper Jaffray Inc., 222 S. Ninth St., Ste. 400, 55402-3804, pg. 1302 **PB**
Piper Jaffray, Inc., 222 S. Ninth St., 55402-3804, pg. 1303 **PB**
Piper Jaffray Inc., 222 S. Ninth St., 55402-3354, pg. 1303 **PB**
Piper Jaffray Ventures Inc., 222 S. Ninth St., 55406, pg. 1303 **PB**
Piper Trust Company, 222 S. Ninth St., 55402-3804, pg. 1303 **PB**
POLARIS INDUSTRIES, INC., 1225 Hwy. 169 N., 55441, pg. 1313 **PB**
Postgraduate Medicine, 4530 W. 77th St., 55435, pg. 1071 **PV**
PREMIUMWEAR, INC., 7566 Market Pl. Dr., 55344-3629, pg. 1323 **PB**
President Homes, 4808 N. Lilac Dr., 55429, pg. 970 **PV**
PRINCESS SOFT TOYS, 7664 W. 78th St., 55439-2518, pg. 884 **PV**
Prospect Foundry, Inc., 1225 Winter St., N.E., 55413, pg. 142 **PV**
QUADION CORPORATION, 3630 Wooddale Ave., 55416, pg. 898 **PV**
R&D Systems Inc., 614 McKinley Pl. N.E., 55413, pg. 1564 **PB**
RTS Systems, 9600 Aldrich Ave., S., 55420, pg. 1074 **PV**
Radisson Hotel Corporation, Carlson Pkwy., 55459-8204, pg. 212 **PV**
Radisson Hotels International Inc., P.O. Box 59159, Carlson Pkwy., 55459, pg. 212 **PV**
Ramsey Technology, Inc., 501 Nineth Ave. N.W., 55433, pg. 1592 **PB**

REGIS CORPORATION, 7201 Metro Blvd., 55439, pg. 1373 **PB**
Reinsurance Alternatives, 7900 Zeroxes Ave. S., Ste. 2030, 55431, pg. 1503 **IT**
Reinsurance Alternatives, Inc., 7900 Xerxes Ave. S., Ste. 2030, 55431, pg. 1503 **IT**
RELIASTAR FINANCIAL CORP., 20 Washington Ave. S., 55401, pg. 1375 **PB**
ReliaStar Investment Research, Inc., 100 Washington Ave. S., Ste. 800, 55401, pg. 1376 **PB**
RISCOMP INDUSTRIES, INC., 2905 Northwest Blvd., #30, 55441-2644, pg. 932 **PV**
JOHN ROBERTS COMPANY, 9687 E. River Rd., 55433, pg. 935 **PV**
Roll Source, Inc., 560 Kasota Ave SE, 55414, pg. 1671 **PV**
Ryan Construction Company, 700 International Center, 900 Second Ave. S., 55402, pg. 953 **PV**
RYAN CONSTRUCTION COMPANY OF MINNESOTA, INC., 700 International Center, 900 Second Ave. S., 55402, pg. 953 **PV**
SKW Natures Inc., 7711 Computer Ave., 55435, pg. 1465 **IT**
Safe-ran Systems Corporation, 4650 Main St. N.E., 55421, pg. 127 **IT**
Sancoz Clinical & Nutrition Div., 5320 W. 23rd St., 55416, pg. 974 **IT**
Sancoz Food Service & Industrial Division, 5320 W. 23rd St., P.O. Box 370, 55416, pg. 974 **IT**
Sanin Learning, P.O. Box 5614, 55440-5614, pg. 210 **PV**
SCHERER BROS. LUMBER COMPANY, Nine Ninth Ave., N.E., 55413, pg. 970 **PV**
PAUL A. SCHMITT MUSIC COMPANY, 88 S. 10th St., 55403, pg. 971 **PV**
SCHOENECKERS, INC., 7630 Bush Lake Rd., 55439, pg. 971 **PV**
School Products Group, 5501 Norman Center Dr., 55437, pg. 934 **PB**
Scoria Incorporated, 1221 Nicollet Mall, 55401, pg. 1195 **PB**
SCOVILLE PRESS, INC., 14505 27th Ave., N., 55447, pg. 977 **PV**
Sequent Computer Systems, Inc., 8400 Normandale Lake Blvd., 55437, pg. 1459 **PV**
Shandwick Minneapolis, 8400 Normandale Lake Blvd., Ste. 500, 55437, pg. 1227 **IT**
Sico North America Inc., 7525 Cahill Rd., 55440, pg. 997 **PV**
SIFCO Custom Machining, 2430 N. Winnetka Ave., 55427, pg. 1471 **PV**
Snacks Unlimited Division, One General Mills Blvd., 55426, pg. 718 **PB**
Solar Plastics-Minneapolis, 732 30th Ave. S.E., 55414, pg. 1129 **PV**
L.H. SOWLES COMPANY, INC., 2813 Bryant Ave. S., 55408, pg. 1019 **PV**
Star Tribune, Minneapolis-St. Paul, 425 Portland Ave., 55488, pg. 281 **PV**
STEVENS-LEE COMPANY, 1600 Xenium Lane N., 55441, pg. 1042 **PV**
StorageTek Network Systems Group, 7600 Boone Ave. N., 55428, pg. 1522 **PB**
SuperValu, Inc.-Minneapolis Div., 55343, pg. 1540 **PB**
TCF Agency, 801 Marquette Ave., 55402, pg. 1554 **PB**
TCF Bank Minnesota FSB, 801 Marquette Ave., 55402, pg. 1554 **PB**
TCF FINANCIAL CORP., 801 Marquette Ave., Ste. 302, 55402, pg. 1554 **PB**
TCF Financial Services Inc., 801 Marquette Ave., 55402, pg. 1554 **PB**
TCF Mortgage Corporation, 801 Marquette Ave., 12th Fl., 55402, pg. 1554 **PB**
TCR Corporation, 1600 67th Ave., 55430, pg. 1632 **PB**
TK Gray, 2812 S. Anthony Ln., 55418, pg. 1329 **PB**
TL Systems Corporation, 8700 Wyoming Ave. N., 55445-4840, pg. 205 **IT**
TMP Worldwide, Inc., 7825 Washington Ave. South, Ste. 800, 55439, pg. 1064 **PV**
T O PLASTICS, INC., 2901 E. 78th St., 55425, pg. 1065 **PV**
Target Stores, 33 S. Sixth St., 55402, pg. 469 **PB**
TECHNE CORPORATION, 614 McKinley Pl. N.E., 55413, pg. 1563 **PB**
TELEX COMMUNICATIONS, INC., 9600 Aldrich Ave. S., 55420, pg. 1074 **PV**
TENNANT COMPANY, 701 N. Lilac Dr., 55440, pg. 1577 **PB**
Texas Telemarketing, Inc., 7101 Winnetka Ave. N., 55428, pg. 478 **PB**
Thermo King Corporation, 314 W. 90th St., 55420, pg. 877 **PB**
Thielle Engineering, 7225 Bush Lake Rd., 55439, pg. 118 **PV**
Title Insurance Company of Minnesota, 400 Second Ave. S., 55401, pg. 1218 **PB**
Total Research Corporation, Carlson Pkwy., 55459, pg. 1625 **PV**
Tri-State Land Company, Box 530, Soo Line Bldg., 55440, pg. 259 **IT**
Turner Construction Company, 310 S. Fourth Ave., Ste. 200, 55415, pg. 1645 **PB**
TWIN CITY DIE CASTINGS CO., 1070 33rd Ave. S.E., 55414, pg. 1111 **PV**
Tyson's Corner Hotel Associates, 1300 Nicollet Mall, 55101, pg. 362 **PV**
Union-Transport Corporation-Minneapolis Office, 7700 22nd Ave. S., Ste. 171, 55450, pg. 1120 **PV**
Unisource, 560 Kasota Ave., S.E., 55414, pg. 1671 **PV**
United Power & Land Co., 414 Nicollet Mall, 55401, pg. 1195 **PB**

U.S. BANCORP, First Bank Pl., 601 Second Ave. S., 55402-4302, pg. 1680 **PB**
Unitog Rental Facility, 2306 Washington Ave. N., 55411, pg. 1693 **PB**
UNIVERSAL COOPERATIVES, INC., 7801 Metro Pkwy., 55425, pg. 1127 **PV**
UPPER MIDWEST INDUSTRIES, INCORPORATED, 2940 Weeks Ave. S.E., 55414, pg. 1129 **PV**
THE VALSPAR CORPORATION, 1101 S. Third St., 55415, pg. 1707 **PB**
Valspar Paints, 1101 S. Third, 55440, pg. 1707 **PB**
Vehicle Systems Division, 4301 Quebec Ave. N., 55428, pg. 411 **PV**
Ventures Group, P.O. Box 116, 55440, pg. 646 **PV**
VIDEOLABS, INC., 5960 Golden Hills Dr., 55416, pg. 1720 **PB**
Viking Computer Services, 2021 E. Hennepin Ave., Ste. 250, 55413-2724, pg. 472 **PV**
Viking Forest Products, Inc., 7716 W. 78th St., 55435, pg. 669 **PB**
Vincent Metals Division, 724 24th Ave., S.E., 55414, pg. 1118 **IT**
WCCO-TV, 90 S. 11th St., 55403, pg. 275 **PB**
WFTC-TV, 1701 Broadway St., N.E., 55413, pg. 385 **PV**
WALMAN OPTICAL COMPANY, 801 12th Ave. N., 55411, pg. 1148 **PV**
Washington Square Advisors, Inc., 100 Washington Ave. S., Ste. 700, 55401, pg. 1376 **PB**
WAYCROSSE INC., P.O. Box 9300, Dept. 28, 55440, pg. 1155 **PV**
We Care Hair, 300 Industrial Blvd. N.E., 55413, pg. 115 **PV**
Weinstein International Seafood, 5738 Olson Hwy., 55422, pg. 54 **PV**
WELLENS & CO., INC., P.O. Box 24656, 55424, pg. 1161 **PV**
Western International Media Corporation, 10 S. Fifth St., Ste. 315, 55402, pg. 1167 **PV**
Weston Engraving, 2626 2nd St. N.E., 55418, pg. 1437 **PB**
WILLIAMS STEEL & HARDWARE COMPANY, 60 28th Ave., N., 55440-0540, pg. 1178 **PV**
Willis Corroon Corp. of Minnesota, 200 S. Sixth St., Ste. 1600, 55402-1436, pg. 1506 **IT**
Willis Corroon International/Americas, 200 S. Sixth St., Ste. 1600, 55402-1436, pg. 1507 **IT**
WITCHER CONSTRUCTION CO., 9855 W. 78th St., Ste. 270, 55344, pg. 1185 **PB**
Woodward-Clyde, Park Place W. Bldg., Ste. 660, 6465 Wayzata Blvd., 55426, pg. 1656 **PB**
XERXES CORPORATION, 7901 Xerxes Ave. S., 55431, pg. 1194 **PB**
Yoplait USA, One General Mills Blvd., 55426, pg. 718 **PB**
Zero-Max, Inc., 13200 Sixth Ave. No., 55441-5509, pg. 866 **IT**
ZIEGLER INC., 901 W. 94th St., 55420, pg. 1205 **PV**
Ziegler Thrift Trading, Inc., 733 Marquette Ave., Ste. 106, 55402-2340, pg. 1792 **PV**

Minnetonka

ADC TELECOMMUNICATIONS, INC., 12501 Whitewater Dr., 55343, pg. 4 **PB**
AG-CHEM EQUIPMENT CO., INC., 5720 Smetana Dr., 55343-9688, pg. 6 **PB**
Advance Circuits, Inc., 5929 Baker Rd., Ste. 476, 55345, pg. 713 **IT**
Advance Circuits, Specialty Products, 15102 Minnetonka Indus. Road, 55343, pg. 713 **IT**
AgTec Inc., 5720 Smetana Dr., 55343, pg. 6 **PB**
BRIDGEMAN'S RESTAURANTS INC., 5700 Smetana Dr., Ste. 110, 55343, pg. 167 **PV**
CARLSON COMPANIES, INC., 701 Carlson Pkwy., 55305, pg. 211 **PV**
Carlson Real Estate Company, 111 Chesire Ln., Ste. 700, 55305, pg. 212 **PV**
CHECK TECHNOLOGY CORPORATION, 12500 White Water Dr., 55343, pg. 342 **PB**
CHRONIMED INC., 13911 Ridgedale Dr., 55305, pg. 352 **PB**
Comdisco Integrated Services, 5500 Feltl Rd., 55343-7920, pg. 408 **PV**
Congress Life Insurance Company, 10901 Red Circle Dr., 55343, pg. 980 **PV**
Daig Corporation, 14901 DeVea Pl., 55345, pg. 1428 **PV**
DATACARD CORPORATION, 11111 Bren Rd. W., 55343, pg. 312 **PV**
DataCard Corporation, 11111 Bren Rd. W., 55343, pg. 312 **PV**
DataCard Equipment, 11111 Bren Rd. W., 55343, pg. 312 **PV**
DataCard Plastic Card Services, 11111 Bren Rd. W., 55343, pg. 312 **PV**
DataCard Service, 11111 Bren Rd. W., 55343, pg. 312 **PV**
Datatrol Transaction Terminals, 11111 Bren Rd. W., 55343, pg. 312 **PV**
DIGI INTERNATIONAL INC., 11001 Bren Rd. E., 55343, pg. 506 **PB**
ELA Medical Inc., 15245 Minnetonka Blvd., 55345, pg. 818 **IT**
FINGERHUT CORP., 4400 Baker Rd., 55343, pg. 623 **PB**
Flexmedics Corporation, 12400 Whitewater Dr., Ste. 2040, 55343, pg. 862 **PV**
G&K SERVICES, INC., 5995 Opus Pky., Ste. 500, 55343, pg. 690 **PB**
GRAND CASINOS, INC., 130 Cheshire Ln., 55305, pg. 758 **PB**
INSIGNIA SYSTEMS, INC., 10801 Red Circle Dr., 55343, pg. 881 **PB**
Lindenmeyr Central, 5100 Thimsen Ave., 55345, pg. 224 **PV**
MLT Vacations, Inc., 5130 Hwy. 101, 55345, pg. 1200 **PB**

Geographic Index-U.S.

MSC Tradenames, 10400 Yellow Circle Dr., 55343, pg. 1142 **PB**
Media Play, Inc., 10400 Yellow Circle Dr., 55343, pg. 1142 **PB**
Merrill Custom Communications, 5400 Feltl Rd., 55343, pg. 1097 **PB**
Miller Publishing Co., 12400 Whitewater Dr., Ste. 160, 55343, pg. 513 **PB**
Minnesota Fire & Casualty Company, 10225 Yellow Cir. Dr., 55343, pg. 787 **PB**
MUSICLAND GROUP INC., 10400 Yellow Circle Dr., 55343, pg. 1142 **PB**
The Musicland Group, Inc., 10400 Yellow Circle Dr., 55343, pg. 1142 **PB**
Musicland Retail, Inc., 10400 Yellow Circle Dr., 55343, pg. 1142 **PB**
NORMARK CORPORATION, 10395 Yellow Circle Dr., 55343, pg. 802 **PV**
North American Outdoor Group, Inc., 12301 Whitewater D., 55343, pg. 321 **PB**
On Cue, Inc., 10400 Yellow Circle Dr., 55343, pg. 1142 **PB**
OPUS CORP., 800 OPUS Ctr., 9900 Bren Rd. E., 55343, pg. 818 **PV**
OSMONICS, INC., 5951 Clearwater Dr., 55343-8995, pg. 1233 **PB**
Pentax Vision Inc., 11545 Encore Cir., 55343, pg. 85 **IT**
Quantum Corporation, 5101 Thimsen Ave., 55345, pg. 1350 **PB**
Request, 10400 Yellow Circle Dr., 55343, pg. 1142 **PB**
Ridgedale Center, 12401 Wayzata Blvd., 55403, pg. 1407 **PB**
ROLLERBLADE, INC., 5101 Shady Oak Rd., 55343, pg. 941 **PV**
Roth Corporation, 11300 W. 47th St., 55343, pg. 1099 **PV**
SCICOM DATA SERVICES, LTD., 10101 Bren Rd. E., 55343, pg. 975 **PV**
SECURITY AMERICAN FINANCIAL ENTERPRISES, INC., 10901 Red Circle Dr., 55343, pg. 980 **PV**
Security Life Insurance Company of America, 10901 Red Circle Dr., 55343, pg. 980 **PV**
Smart Cards & Systems, 11111 Bren Rd. W., 55343, pg. 312 **PV**
SNYDER'S DRUG STORES, INC., 14525 Hwy. 7, 55345, pg. 1011 **PV**
Soil Teq, Inc., 5720 Smetana Dr., 55343, pg. 6 **PB**
Suncoast Motion Picture Co., 10400 Yellow Circle Dr., 55343, pg. 1142 **PB**
TMG Caribbean, Inc., 10400 Yellow Circle Dr., 55343, pg. 1142 **PB**
TMG UK Delaware, Inc., 10400 Yellow Circle Dr., 55343, pg. 1142 **PB**
Tonka Products Division, Minnetonka Corporate Ctr., 6000 Clearwater Dr., 55343, pg. 797 **PB**
UNITED HEALTHCARE CORPORATION, 300 Opus Ctr., 9900 Bren Rd. E., 55343, pg. 1677 **PB**
United HealthCare of Oregon, Inc., 300 Opus Ctr., 9900 Bren Rd., E., 55343, pg. 1678 **PB**
United HealthCare Services, Inc., 300 Opus Ctr., 9900 Bren Rd., E., 55343, pg. 1678 **PB**

Montevideo

Innovex Prairie West Manufacturing, Airport Indus. Park, 1633 N. 9th St., 56265, pg. 880 **PB**
SL Montevideo Technology, Inc., 2002 Black Oak Ave., 56265, pg. 1419 **PB**

Monticello

Sunny Fresh Foods, 206 W. Fourth St., 55362, pg. 210 **PV**

Moorhead

AMERICAN CRYSTAL SUGAR COMPANY, 101 N. Third St., 56560, pg. 52 **PV**
Norwest Bank Minnesota West, N.A., 730 Center Ave., 56560, pg. 1202 **PB**

Mora

BLUEWATER, 811 E. Maple, 55051, pg. 153 **PV**
Engineered Polymers Corporation, 1020 E. Maple Ave., 55051, pg. 328 **IT**

Mound

Lunalite, Inc., 5300 Shoreline Blvd., 55364, pg. 1624 **PB**
Solarium Systems, Inc., 5340 Shoreline Blvd., 55364, pg. 120 **PB**

New Brighton

DOTRONIX, INC., 160 First St. SE, 55112-7894, pg. 520 **PB**
Hypro Corporation, 375 Fifth Ave. N.W., 55112, pg. 1767 **PB**
REMMELE ENGINEERING, INC., 10 Old Highway 8 S.W., 55112, pg. 921 **PV**

New Hope

CTS Corporation-Connector Division, 9210 Science Ctr. Dr., 55428, pg. 285 **PB**
Connector Products, 9210 Science Ctr. Dr., 55428, pg. 285 **PB**
Independent Metals, 5701 International Pkwy., 55426-3097, pg. 559 **PV**
Labinal Components & Systems Inc., 8821 Science Center Dr., 55428-3619, pg. 786 **IT**

Only Deals, Inc., 5000 Winnetka Ave. N., 55428, pg. 1697 **PB**
UNIVERSAL INTERNATIONAL, INC., 5000 Winnetka Ave. N., 55428, pg. 1697 **PB**

New London

CABLE SPINNING EQUIPMENT INC., P.O. Box 308, 100 West Central, 56273, pg. 197 **PV**
Mid-State Telephone Co., P.O. Box 609, 56273, pg. 1571 **PB**
VIDAR, INC., P.O. Box 287, 56273-0287, pg. 1139 **PV**

New Ulm

Custom Servo Motors, 2121 Bridge St., 56073, pg. **PB**
NORTH CENTRAL AMPI, INC., P.O. Box 455, 56073, pg. 804 **PV**
Piper Jaffray Inc., 9 1/2 N. Minnesota St., 56073, pg. 1303 **PB**

New York Mills

Lund Boats, W. Front St., 56567, pg. 447 **PV**

Newport

FRITZ CO. INC., 1912 Hastings Ave., 55055, pg. 429 **PV**

North Mankato

Kato Engineering Div., 2075 Howard Dr., 56003, pg. 1398 **PB**
MICO INC., 1911 Lee Blvd., 56003, pg. 741 **PV**

Northfield

Malt-O-Meal Co., 701 W. Fifth St., 55057, pg. 699 **PV**
Northfield East Operation, 805 N. Hwy. Three, 55057-0170, pg. 1465 **PB**
Northfield West Operation, 1150 Sheldahl Rd., 55057-0170, pg. 1465 **PB**
SHELDAHL, INC., 1150 Sheldahl Rd., 55057-9444, pg. 1465 **PB**
Sheldahl Intl., Inc., 1150 Sheldahl Rd., 55057, pg. 1465 **PB**

Norwood

BONGARDS CREAMERIES INC., 13200 County Rd. 51, 55368, pg. 156 **PV**

Oakdale

IMATION CORPORATION, One Imation Place, 55128-3414, pg. 870 **PB**

Owatonna

FEDERATED MUTUAL INSURANCE COMPANY, 121 E. Park Sq., 55060, pg. 399 **PV**
King Company, 1001 N.W. 21st Ave., 55060, pg. 1676 **PB**
Mustang Manufacturing Company, Inc., County Rd. 45 N., 55060, pg. 704 **PB**
Owatonna Canning Company, 900 N. Cedar Ave., 55060, pg. 349 **PB**
Power Team Division, 2121 W. Bridge St., 55060, pg. 1421 **PB**
Viracon/Curvlite, Inc., 800 Park Dr., 55060, pg. 120 **PB**
Viracon, Inc., 800 Park Dr., 55060, pg. 120 **PB**
WENGER CORPORATION, P.O. Box 448, 555 Park Dr., 55060, pg. 1162 **PV**

Perham

BARREL O'FUN SNACK FOODS CO., 800 4th St. N.W., 56573, pg. 118 **PV**
Land O'Lakes Dairy Foods, 110 Third Ave. N.E., 56573-1831, pg. 646 **PV**
Windy Hill Pet Food Co., P.O. Box 190, 145 1st Ave. N., 56573, pg. 1182 **PV**

Pine Island

Land O'Lakes Inc., 206 Second Ave. N.W., 55963-9161, pg. 646 **PV**

Plainview

Lakeside Packing Co., 1055 W. Broadway, 55964-1059, pg. 644 **PV**

Plymouth

Accraply, Inc., 3580 Holly Ln. N., 55447-1269, pg. 118 **PV**
ACROMETAL COMPANIES, INC., 2600 Niagara Ln. N., 55447, pg. 14 **PV**
Advance Machine Company, 14600 21st Ave. N., 55447, pg. 932 **IT**
Baldor Electric Company, 12955 State Hwy. 55, 55441, pg. 169 **PB**
BRAUNS FASHIONS CORPORATION, 2400 Xenium Ln. N., 55441, pg. 251 **PB**
CIPRICO, INC., 2800 Campus Dr., 55441, pg. 370 **PB**
Crow River Industries Incorporated, 2800 Northwest Blvd., 55441, pg. 1040 **PB**

Deltak Inc., 13330 12th Ave. N., 55441, pg. 924 **PB**
Fiskars Inc.-Power Sentry Division, 3555 Holly Ln., Ste. 30, 55447, pg. 492 **IT**
GORDON & FERGUSON OF DELAWARE, INC., 2915 Niagara Ln., 55447, pg. 465 **PV**
HOYT DEVELOPMENT, 13400 15th Ave., Ste. F, 55441, pg. 543 **PV**
JP Foodservice, Inc.-Minneapolis, 9605 54th Ave. N., 55442, pg. 918 **PB**
Juno, Inc., 14755 27th Ave. N., Ste. C1, 55447, pg. 909 **PV**
MikroPrecision Instruments, Inc., 5480 Nathan Lane N., 55442-3939, pg. 1179 **PB**
A.C. Nielsen Company, 14505 21st Ave. N., Ste. 226, 55447, pg. 1183 **PB**
A.C. Nielsen Company (Minneapolis), 14505 21st Ave. N., Ste. 226, 55447, pg. 1183 **PB**
Norstan Communications, Inc., 605 North Hwy. 169, 55441, pg. 1192 **PB**
NORSTAN, INC., 605 North Hwy. 169, 12th Fl., 55441, pg. 1192 **PB**
Novel Biomedical, 13845 Industrial Park Blvd., 55441, pg. 401 **PB**
Olympic Steel - Minneapolis Division, 625 Xenium Lane N., 55441, pg. 1221 **PB**
George Peltier & Assocs., 3025 Harbor La., Ste. 235, 55447, pg. 736 **IT**
PROGRESS CASTING GROUP, INC., 2600 Niagara Ln. N., 55447, pg. 890 **PV**
RJ Associates, 2905 N.W. Blvd., Ste. 30, 55441-3832, pg. 932 **PV**
Sauer-Sundstrand, 3900 Annapolis Ln. N., 55441, pg. 1198 **IT**
Schneider (USA) Inc., 5905 Nathan Ln., 55442-1656, pg. 1284 **PB**
TRICORD SYSTEMS, INC., 2905 Northwest Blvd., Ste. 20, 55441, pg. 1637 **PB**
United Hardware Distributing Co., 5005 Nathan Ln., 55442, pg. 335 **PV**
WAGNER SPRAY TECH CORP., 1770 Fernbrook Ln., 55447, pg. 1146 **PV**

Princeton

CRYSTAL CABINET WORKS, INC., 1100 Crystal Dr., 55371, pg. 293 **PV**

Ramsey

ANOKA ELECTRIC COOPERATIVE, 14601 Ramsey Blvd. N.W., 55303, pg. 75 **PV**

Red Wing

Central Research Laboratories, 250 Hwy 19, 55066, pg. 521 **PB**
Citizens Security Mutual Insurance, P.O. Box 3500, 406 Main St., 55066-3500, pg. 1095 **PB**
Dayco PTI, Inc., 4079 Pepin Ave., 55066, pg. 1045 **PB**
S.B. Foot Tanning Co., P.O. Box 73, 55066, pg. 915 **PV**
Insurance Company of Ohio, P.O. Box 3500, 55066-3500, pg. 1095 **PB**
Norwest Bank Red Wing, N.A., Fourth & Plum, 55066-3155, pg. 1202 **PB**
RED WING PUBLISHING COMPANY, 2760 N. Service Dr., 55066, pg. 915 **PV**
RED WING SHOE CO., INC., 314 Main St., 55066-2337, pg. 915 **PV**
Red Wing Shoe Vasque Div., 314 Main St., Riverfront Center, 55066, pg. 915 **PV**

Redwood Falls

FARMERS UNION MARKETING & PROCESSING ASSOCIATION, Box 319, 56283, pg. 395 **PV**
Schult Homes Corporation, 201 Industrial Dr., 56283, pg. 1442 **PB**

Renville

SOUTHERN MINNESOTA BEET SUGAR COOPERATIVE, E. Hwy 212, 56284, pg. 1016 **PV**

Rochester

Browning-Ferris Industries of Rochester, Inc., P.O. Box 6423, 55903, pg. 264 **PB**
CRENLO, INC., 1600 Fourth Ave., N.W., 55901, pg. 288 **PB**
GREENWAY CO-OP SERVICE, 3520 E. River Rd., N.E., 55906, pg. 478 **PV**
Holiday Inn Downtown, 220 S. Broadway, 55904, pg. 1537 **PB**
The Kahler Hotel, 20 S.W. Second Ave., 55902, pg. 1537 **PB**
Kahler Inn & Suites, Nine N.W. Third Ave., 55901, pg. 1537 **PB**
Kahler Plaza Hotel, 101 S.W. First Ave., 55902, pg. 1537 **PB**
Lawler's, Inc., 225 Woodlake Dr., S.E., 55904, pg. 1537 **PB**
Marquette Bank Rochester, P.O. Box 4800, 55903, pg. 706 **PV**
Norwest Bank Minnesota South, N.A., 21 First St. S.W., 55903-3300, pg. 1202 **PB**
Pace Dairy Foods, P.O. Box 6818, 55903-6818, pg. 967 **PB**
Piper Jaffray Inc., 102 S. Broadway, Ste. 300, 55904-6522, pg. 1302 **PB**

PB - U.S. Public Companies Volume
PV - U.S. Private Companies Volume
IT - International Public & Private Companies Volume

1295

Geographic Index-U.S.

Dave Syverson Truck Center, Inc., 6300 S. 63 Highway, 55904, pg. 1061   PV
WATERS INSTRUMENTS, INC., 2411-7 St. N.W., 55901, pg. 1745   PB

Rogers

ULTRA PAC, INC., 21925 Industrial Blvd., 55374, pg. 1662   PB

Rosemount

REESE ENTERPRISES, INC., 16350 Asher Ave., 55068, pg. 916   PV

Roseville

Advance Circuits, Commercial Div., 1633 Terrace Drive, 55343, pg. 713   IT
A.M. Castle & Co., 2500 W. Country Rd. B., Ste. 140, 55113, pg. 313   PB
CROWN HOLDINGS, INC., 2500 W. County Rd. C, 55113, pg. 293   PV
Crown Iron Works Company, 2500 W. County Rd. C, 55113, pg. 293   PV
Eclipse-Dungs Controls, L.P., 2740 Patton Rd., 55113, pg. 360   PV
GREAT PLAINS COMPANIES, INC., 3030 Centre Pointe Dr., Ste 900, 55113, pg. 475   PV
Metz Baking Co., 2745 Long Lake Rd., 55113, pg. 1022   PV
MUSKA ELECTRIC COMPANY, 1985 Oakcrest Ave., 55113, pg. 768   PV
North Coast Mortgage, Inc., 2679 Long Lake Rd., 55113, pg. 1406   PV
OLD DUTCH FOODS, INC., 2375 Terminal Rd., 55113, pg. 814   PV
Plum Building Systems, Inc., 3030 Centre Pointe Dr., Ste. 900, 55113, pg. 475   PV
THE ROTTLUND COMPANY, INC., 2681 Long Lake Rd., 55113, pg. 1406   PB

Round Lake

Sathers Inc., Sather Plaza, 56167-0028, pg. 397   PV

Rushford

Lucas SEI Electronics, LLC, P.O. Box 607, Hwy. 43 N., 55971-0607, pg. 1313   IT

Saint Bonifacius

NORWESCO, INC., 4365 Steiner St., 55375, pg. 808   PV

Saint Cloud

ANDERSON TRUCKING SERVICE INC., 203 Cooper Ave. N., 56303, pg. 72   PV
BANKERS SYSTEMS INCORPORATED, 6815 Sauk View Dr., 56303, pg. 114   PV
BRUTGER EQUITIES, INC., One Sunwood Dr., 56301, pg. 176   PV
D.C.I., INC., 600 N. Fifth Ave, 56303, pg. 301   PV
First American Bank N.A., 1100 W. St. Germain St., 56301, pg. 167   PV
First American Trust Company of Minnesota, Cold Spring Ctr., 4150 Second St. S., Ste. 150, 56301, pg. 167   PV
Frigidaire Home Products-Freezer Products, 701 33rd Ave. N, 56303, pg. 440   IT
Gold'n Plump Poultry, 4150 Second St. S., Ste. 200, 56301, pg. 577   PV
G.R. Herberger's, Inc., 600 Mall Germain, 56301, pg. 1333   PB
JFC INC., 4150 Second St. S., Ste. 200, 56301, pg. 577   PV
NSP-Northwest Area, 3515 Third St., N., 56301, pg. 1195   PB
Piper Jaffray Inc., 4150 Second St. S., Ste. 500, 56301-7319, pg. 1302   PB
PrimeVest Financial Services, Inc., 400 First St. S., Ste. 300, 56301, pg. 1376   PB
St. Cloud Daily Times, Inc., 3000 N. Seventh St., 56302, pg. 701   PB
Vision-Ease Lens, 700 N. 54th Ave., 56301, pg. 162   PB
WOODCRAFT INDUSTRIES, INC., 525 Lincoln Ave. S.E., 56304, pg. 1187   PV

Saint James

TONY DOWNS FOODS COMPANY, 400 Armstrong Blvd. N., 56081, pg. 342   PV

Saint Joseph

Jannock Steel Fabricating, Inc., 31084 Joseph St., 56374, pg. 699   IT

Saint Louis Park

Montgomery Ward Direct, 600 S. Hwy. 169, 55426, pg. 623   PB
Moore Data Management Services Div., 1660 S. Hwy. 100, 400 Parkdale Plaza E., 55416, pg. 890   IT
Nordic Ware Direct, Inc., 5005 Hwy. 7, 55416, pg. 806   PV
Novartis Nutrition Corporation, 5100 Gamble Dr., 55416, pg. 974   IT

Repligen Sandoz Research Corp., 5100 Gamble Dr., 55416, pg. 974   IT
Travelers Express Company, Inc., 1550 Utica Ave. S., 55416, pg. 1718   PB
Walser Ford Inc., 3555 S. Hwy. 100, 55416, pg. 1148   PV

Saint Paul

AP Technology Management Inc., 600 W. County Rd. D, 55112, pg. 18   PV
API GROUP INC., 2366 Rose Pl., 55113, pg. 7   PV
Aero Systems Engineering Inc., 358 E. Fillmore Ave., 55107, pg. 276   IT
AETRIUM INC., 2350 Helen St., 55109, pg. 27   PB
Agribank, FCB, 375 Jackson St., 55101, pg. 398   PV
All Nation Insurance Co., 155 Aurora Ave., 55103, pg. 35   PV
AmClyde Engineered Products Co., 240 E. Plato Blvd., 55107, pg. 778   PB
American Natl. Can Co., 755 N. Prior, 55104, pg. 1029   PB
American Natl. Can Co., 139 Eva St., 55107, pg. 1029   IT
Anchor Hocking Plastics, 224 Ryan Ave., 55164, pg. 1177   PB
Artist Graphics, 900 Long Lake Rd., 55112, pg. 271   PV
Ascend Financial Services, 400 Robert St. N., 55101, pg. 750   PV
Autocon Industries Inc., 995 University Ave. W., 55104-4705, pg. 1026   IT
Banta Catalog Group, 655 Fairview Ave. N., 55104, pg. 188   PB
Banta Catalog Group, 655 Fairview Ave. N., 55104-1792, pg. 188   PB
BERGER TRANSFER & STORAGE, INC., 2950 Long Lake Rd., 55113, pg. 135   PV
Best Brands, 1765 Yankee Doodle Rd., 55121, pg. 617   PV
BlueLine Software Inc., pg. 120   PB
W. Braun Co., 1 W. Water St., 55107, pg. 166   PV
BREMER FINANCIAL CORPORATION, 445 Minnesota St., Ste. 2000, 55101, pg. 167   PV
Bremer Financial Services, Inc., 445 Minnesota St., Ste. 2000, 55101, pg. 167   PV
BROWN & BIGELOW, INC., 345 Plato Blvd. E., 55107, pg. 172   PV
BUERKLE BUICK-HONDA CO., 3350 Hwy. #61 N., 55110, pg. 178   PV
Burns & Wilcox, 1740 Rice St., Ste. 300, 55113, pg. 609   PV
CATHOLIC DIGEST, P.O. Box 64090, 55164, pg. 220   PV
Chicago Tube & Iron Company of Minnesota, 2940 Eagandale Blvd., 55121, pg. 235   PV
Clarinda Color L.L.C., 1780 W. 7th St., 55116, pg. 206   PV
Commercial Care Division, 3M Center, Bldg. 223-3N-05, 55144-1000, pg. 1605   PB
Consolidated Acceptance Corp., Inc., 1100 Landmark Towers, 345 Saint Peter St., 55102, pg. 762   PV
Construction & Home Improvement Markets Division, 3M Center, Bldg. 225-4S-08, 55144-1000, pg. 1605   PB
CONTROL SYSTEMS INC., 900 Long Lake Rd., Ste. 200, 55112, pg. 271   PV
CONUS Communication Company Limited Partnership, 3415 University Ave., 55114, pg. 544   PV
The Cooperage, 551 Barge Channel Rd., 55107-2441, pg. 763   PV
Cross Pointe Paper Corporation, 1295 Bandana Blvd. N., Ste. 335, 55108, pg. 434   IT
Curtis 1000, Inc., 707 W. County Rd. E., 55126, pg. 70   PV
Dental Products Division, 3M Center, Bldg. 275-2E-03, 55144-1000, pg. 1605   PB
Design Systems Inc., 3M Ctr. Bldg. 2, 55144, pg. 13   IT
DynaMark, Inc., 4295 Lexington Ave., 55126, pg. 610   PV
EFG Technologies Inc., 85 E. Seventh Pl., Ste. 400, 55101, pg. 1679   PV
EMPI, INC., P.O. Box 26500, 599 Cardigan Rd., 55126-3965, pg. 545   PV
ECOLAB INC., Ecolab Center, 370 N. Wabasha St., 55102, pg. 562   PB
FBS Information Services Corporation, 1200 Energy Park Dr., 55108, pg. 1681   PB
FINANCIAL LIFE COMPANIES, INC., 445 Minnesota St., 55101, pg. 404   PV
First American Insurance Agencies, Inc., 445 Minnesota St., Ste. 2000, 55101, pg. 167   PV
First Trust National Association, 180 E. 5th St., 55101, pg. 1681   PB
Food & Beverage, Ecolab Center, 55102, pg. 562   PB
Full Circle, P.O. Box 64089, 55164, pg. 222   PV
H.B. FULLER COMPANY, 1200 Willow Lake Blvd., 55164-0683, pg. 686   PB
H.B. Fuller International Inc., 1200 County Rd. E., 55112, pg. 687   PV
GTA Agency, Inc., 1100 Landmark Towers, 345 St. Peter Street, 55102, pg. 762   PV
Gourmet Foods, Inc., 860 Vandalia St., 55114, pg. 752   IT
Graphic Arts Supply Division, 2446 University Ave., 55114, pg. 205   PB
Great Lakes Coal and Dock Company, 1031 Childs Rd., 55106, pg. 139   PB
GREAT NORTHERN IRON ORE PROPERTIES, W-1290 First National Bank, 332 Minnesota St., 55101-1361, pg. 760   PB
Green Tree Acceptance, Inc., Landmark Towers, 345 St. Peter St., Ste. 600, 55102, pg. 762   PB
Green Tree Agency, Inc., 1100 Landmark Towers, 345 Saint Peter St., 55102, pg. 763   PB
Green Tree Agency of Nevada, Inc., 1100 Landmark Towers, 345 St. Peter Street, 55102, pg. 763   PB
Green Tree Consumer Discount Company, 1100 Landmark Towers, 345 St. Peter St., 55102, pg. 763   PB

Green Tree Credit Corp., 1100 Landmark Towers, 345 St. Peter Street, 55102, pg. 763   PB
Green Tree Finance Corp.-One, 1100 Landmark Towers, 345 St. Peter St., 55102, pg. 763   PB
GREEN TREE FINANCIAL CORPORATION, 1100 Landmark Towers, 345 St. Peter St., 55102-1639, pg. 761   PB
Green Tree Life Insurance Co., 1100 Landmark Towers, 345 St. Peter St., 55102, pg. 763   PB
Guidant Corporation-Cardiac Rhythm Management Group, 4100 Hamline Ave. N., 55112-5798, pg. 768   PV
Harris Air Systems Company, 2300 Territorial Rd., 55114, pg. 505   PV
HARRIS CONTRACTING CO., y, 909 Montreal Cir., 55102, pg. 505   PV
HARVEST STATES COOPERATIVES, 1667 N. Snelling Ave., 55108, pg. 508   PV
Hawkins Terminal I, 1125 Childs Road, 55106, pg. 800   PB
Hewlett-Packard Company, 2025 W. Larpenteur Ave., 55113, pg. 814   PB
Hoyle Products, 345 Plato Blvd. E., 55107, pg. 172   PV
HUBBARD BROADCASTING, INC., 3415 University Ave., 55114, pg. 543   PV
INTERACTIVE TECHNOLOGIES, INC., 2266 N. Second St., 55109, pg. 888   PB
Intergraph Corporation, 1355 Mendota Heights Rd., Ste. 130, 55120, pg. 890   PV
INTERPLASTIC CORP., 1225 Willow Lake Blvd., 55110-5145, pg. 572   PB
Jareen Co., 224 Ryan Ave., 55164, pg. 1177   PB
JOHNSON BROTHERS WHOLESALE LIQUOR, 2285 University Ave. W., 55114, pg. 591   PV
KSTP-FM, Inc., 3415 University Ave., 55114, pg. 544   PV
KSTP-TV, 3415 University Ave., 55114-2099, pg. 544   PV
KING KOIL LICENSING COMPANY INC., 770 Transfer Rd., Ste. 13, 55114, pg. 621   PV
LAMPERT YARDS, INC., 1850 Como Ave., 55108, pg. 645   PV
LAN-O-SHEEN, INC., 1021 Bandana Blvd. E., Ste 122, 55108, pg. 645   PV
Liv-A-Snaps, Inc., 4251 Fernwood, 55164, pg. 917   IT
Lockheed Martin Tactical Defense Systems-Eagan, P.O. Box 64525, 55164-0525, pg. 1009   PB
MIMLIC Corp., 400 Robert St. N., 55101, pg. 750   PV
McNeil (Ohio) Corporation, 1700 W. Hwy. 36, 55113, pg. 1273   PB
MEDICAL GRAPHICS CORP., 350 Oak Grove Pkwy., 55127, pg. 1080   PB
Medical Products Technology, 3M Ctr., Bldg. 275-5W-05, 55144-1000, pg. 1605   PB
Medical-Surgical Division, 3M Center, Bldg. 275-4W-02, 55144-1000, pg. 1605   PB
MERRILL CORPORATION, One Merrill Cir., 55108, pg. 1097   PB
MICRO COMPONENT TECHNOLOGY INC., 2340 W. County Rd., 55513, pg. 1104   PB
MIDWEST AUTO PARTS DISTRIBUTORS, INC., 2565 Kasota Ave., 55108, pg. 744   PV
MIMLIC Asset Management Company, 400 Robert St. N., 55101, pg. 750   PV
Ministers Life Insurance Co, 400 Robert St. N., 55101, pg. 750   PV
Ministers Life Resources, 400 N. Robert St., 55416, pg. 750   PV
MINNESOTA BREWING COMPANY, 882 W. Seventh St., 55102, pg. 1115   PB
THE MINNESOTA MUTUAL LIFE INSURANCE COMPANY, 400 Robert St. N., 55101, pg. 750   PV
Mycogen Seeds, 1340 Corporate Ctr. Curve, 55121, pg. 1142   PB
Nesota Co., 400 Robert St. N., 55101, pg. 750   PV
NEW MECH COMPANIES, INC., 1633 Eustis St., 55108, pg. 794   PV
NORCRAFT COMPANIES, INC., 30 E. Plato Blvd., 55107, pg. 801   PV
North Central Life Insurance Company, 445 Minnesota St., 55101, pg. 404   PV
Northwest Aircraft Inc., Minneapolis-St. Paul Intl. Airport, 55111, pg. 1200   PB
NORTHWEST AIRLINES CORP., 5101 Northwest Dr., 55111-3034, pg. 1199   PB
Northwest Airlines, Inc., 5101 Northwest Dr., 55111-3034, pg. 1200   PB
OLD HOME FOODS, INC., 370 University Ave., 55103, pg. 814   PV
Packaging Systems Division, 3M Center, Bldg. 220-8W-01, 55144-1000, pg. 1605   PB
PAPER CALMENSON & CO., P.O. Box 64432, 55164-0432, pg. 837   PV
PATTERSON DENTAL COMPANY, 1031 Mendota Heights Rd., 55120, pg. 1265   PB
Patterson Dental Supply, Inc., 1031 Mendota Heights Rd., 55120, pg. 1265   PV
PENTAIR, INC., Water's Edge Plaza, 1500 W. County Rd. B2, Ste. 400, 55113-3105, pg. 1273   PB
Peoples Communications System, 277 E. Fillmore Ave., 55107, pg. 851   PV
PEOPLES ELECTRIC CONTRACTOR, INC., 277 E. Fillmore Ave., 55107, pg. 851   PV
Pharmaceuticals Division, 3M Center, Bldg. 275-3W-01, 55144-1000, pg. 1605   PB
Piper Jaffray Inc., Piper Jaffray Plaza, 444 Cedar St., Ste. 2200, 55101-2108, pg. 1302   PB
Plastics, Inc., 224 Ryan Ave., P.O. Box 43610, 55164, pg. 1177   PB
PrimeNet Marketing Services, P.O. Box 21800, 2250 Pilot Knob Rd., 55120-0800, pg. 602   PV
Quality Park Products, 2520 Como Ave., 55108, pg. 1038   PB
Quebecor List Services, 1999 Shepard Rd., 55116, pg. 1078   IT

PB - U.S. Public Companies Volume
PV - U.S. Private Companies Volume
IT - International Public & Private Companies Volume

1296

Geographic Index-U.S.

Quebecor Printing St. Paul Inc., 1999 Shepard Rd., 55116, pg. 1078   IT

RLI Midwest Regional Office, 445 Minnesota St., 55101, pg. 1356   PB

Recreational Products Div., 500 Hardman Ave. S., 55075, pg. 205   PB

Rice Park Properties, 1100 Landmark Towers, 345 St. Peter Street, 55102, pg. 763   PB

RIHM MOTOR COMPANY, 2108 University Ave., 55114, pg. 931   PV

Rock-Tenn Co., 2250 Wabash Ave., 55114, pg. 1397   PB

SCM Specialty Chemicals Inc., 3M Center, 55144, pg. 594   IT

St. Jude International Sales Corp., One Lillehei Plaza, 55117, pg. 1428   PB

ST. JUDE MEDICAL, INC., One Lillehei Plaza, 55117-9983, pg. 1427   PB

St. Paul Bank for Cooperatives, 375 Jackson St., 55164-0949, pg. 398   PV

THE ST. PAUL COMPANIES, INC., 385 Washington St., 55102, pg. 1429   PB

St. Paul Fire and Marine Insurance Co., 385 Washington St., 55102, pg. 1429   PB

ST. PAUL METALCRAFT, INC., 3737 N. Lexington Ave., 55126, pg. 961   PV

Saint Paul Pioneer Press Division, 345 Cedar St., 55101, pg. 964   PB

RON SAXON FORD, INC., 225 University Ave., 55103, pg. 969   PV

Schwing America Inc., 5900 Centerville Rd., 55127, pg. 1211   IT

Sealy of Minnesota, Inc., 825 Transfer Rd., 55114, pg. 979   PV

SIMS Deltec, 1265 Grey Fox Rd., 55112, pg. 1268   IT

SMYTH, CO., 1085 Snelling Ave., N., 55108, pg. 1010   PV

THE SPORTSMAN'S GUIDE, INC., 411 Farwell Ave., 55075, pg. 1499   PV

F.H. STOLTZE LAND & LUMBER COMPANY, 2497 7th Ave. E., Ste. 105, 55109, pg. 1044   PV

Super Cycle, Inc., 775 Race St., 55117, pg. 914   PV

Sysco Food Services of Minnesota, Inc., 2400 Country Rd. J, 55112, pg. 1551   PB

System One Control, 277 E. Fillmore Ave., 55107, pg. 851   PV

TCF Foundation, 405 N. Robert St., 55101, pg. 1554   PB

TCF Insurance, 405 N. Robert St., 55101, pg. 1554   PB

TCF Securities, 405 N. Robert St., 55101, pg. 1554   PB

Tape Manufacturing Division, 3M Center, Bldg. 220-3E-02, 55144-1000, pg. 1605   PB

TAPEMARK, 150 E. Marie Ave., 55118, pg. 1068   PV

3M, Product Information Ctr., 3M Center, Bldg. 304-1-01, 55144-1000, pg. 1604   PB

TRADEHOME SHOE STORES, INC., 429 Prior Ave., 55104, pg. 1095   PV

Unisys Midwest, P.O. Box 64942, 55164-0942, pg. 1671   PB

U.S. Filters Control Systems, 141 S. Lafayette Freeway, 55107, pg. 61   PB

United States Satellite Broadcasting, Co., 3415 University Ave., 55114, pg. 544   PV

VILLAUME INDUSTRIES, INC., 2926 Lone Oak Circle, 55121, pg. 1140   PV

West Information Publishing Group, 610 Opperman Dr., 55123-1308, pg. 1602   PB

WINTZ COMPANIES, 2323 Terminal Rd., 55113, pg. 1184   PV

Woodgate Consolidated Incorporated, 1100 Landmark Towers, 345 St. Peter Street, 55102, pg. 763   PB

Woodgate Utilities Incorporated, 1100 Landmark Towers, 345 St. Peter Street, 55102, pg. 763   PB

Zellerbach Division, 2930 Long Lake Rd., 55113, pg. 1075   PB

Saint Peter

Alumacraft Boat Co., 315 W. St. Julien St., 56082, pg. 1088   PV

Onan Power Electronics, 922 N. Swift St., 56082, pg. 468   PB

Winpower Inc., P.O. Box 495, 56082, pg. 350   PV

Sartell

DEZurik, 250 Riverside Ave. N., 56377, pg. 726   PB

Sartell Mill, Champion International Corp., 100 E. Sartell St., 56377, pg. 334   PB

Sauk Rapids

MIDWEST VISION CENTERS, 2672 Hwy. 23 N.E., 56379, pg. 745   PV

Stearns Manufacturing Company, 1100 Stearns Dr., 56379, pg. 940   PB

Savage

CONTINENTAL MACHINES, INC., 5505 W. 123rd St., 55378-1299, pg. 268   PV

ROAD MACHINERY & SUPPLIES CO., 5633 W. Hwy. 13, 55378, pg. 934   PV

Shakopee

Broadband Connectivity Group, 1187-1087 Park Pl., 55379, pg. 4   PB

ChemRex Inc., 889 Valley Park Dr., 55379, pg. 1465   IT

CONKLIN CO. INC., 551 Valley Park Dr., 55379, pg. 263   PV

Northstar Auto Auction Inc., 4908 Valley Ind. Blvd. N, 55379, pg. 1649   PB

Valleyfair, One Valleyfair Dr., 55379, pg. 319   PB

Shoreview

Deluxe Business Systems Division, 3660 Victoria St. N., 55126-2906, pg. 498   PB

DELUXE CORPORATION, 3680 Victoria St. N., 55126-2966, pg. 498   PB

Multi-Clean Inc., 600 Cardigan Rd., 55126, pg. 587   IT

TSI INCORPORATED, 500 Cardigan Rd., 55126-3996, pg. 1559   PB

South Saint Paul

First American Bank Metro, 633 S. Concord St., 55075, pg. 167   PV

Waterous Company, 300 John E. Carroll Ave. E, 55075, pg. 52   PV

Springfield

Coleman Powermate Compressors, 118 W. Rock St., 56087, pg. 691   PV

Staples

MPC Staples, Airport Industrial Park, 56479, pg. 851   IT

Stillwater

Arrow Building Centers, 2000 W. Tower Dr., 55082, pg. 265   PV

CONSOLIDATED LUMBER CO., 808 N. Fourth St., 55082, pg. 265   PV

Cub Foods Stores, P.O. Box 9, 421 S. Third St., 55082-0009, pg. 1541   PB

INCSTAR Corporation, 1990 Industrial Blvd., 55082, pg. 483   IT

Piper Jaffray Inc., 106 E. Chestnut St., 55082-5116, pg. 1302   PB

UFE INCORPORATED, 1850 S. Greeley St., 55082-0007, pg. 1112   PV

Thief River Falls

ARCTIC CAT INC., 600 Brooks Ave. S., 56701, pg. 128   PB

Two Harbors

Piper Jaffray Inc., 626 First Ave., Ste. 1506, 55616-1506, pg. 1301   PB

Vadnais Heights

I.C. SYSTEM, INC., 444 E. Hwy. 96, 55127, pg. 553   PV

John Rickson Properties, 444 E. Hwy. 96, 55127, pg. 553   PV

Victoria

HEI, INC., P.O. Box 5000, 1495 Steiger Lake Ln., 55386, pg. 770   PB

Virginia

Inland Steel Mining Co., 5950 Old Hwy. 53, 55792, pg. 879   PB

Warroad

MARVIN LUMBER & CEDAR COMPANY, Hwy. #11, 56763, pg. 710   PV

Waseca

Brown Printing Co., Inc., U.S. Hwy. 14 W., 56093, pg. 190   IT

Waverly

Charter Behavioral Health System of Waverly, Inc., 109 North Shore Dr., 55390, pg. 1034   PB

Wayzata

CARGILL, 15407 McGinty Rd. W., 55391-2399, pg. 210   PV

Champps Entertainment, Inc., 153 E. Lake St., 55391, pg. 325   IT

North Star Steel Co., 15407 McGinty Road, Dept. 51, 55391, pg. 210   PV

Piper Jaffray Inc., 319 Barry Ave. S., 55391-1660, pg. 1302   PB

SCHOTT CORPORATION, 1000 Parkers Lake Rd., 55391, pg. 972   PV

White Bear Lake

MICROPURE MEDICAL, INC., 1839 Buerkle Rd., 55110, pg. 743   PV

Microvena Corporation, 1861 Buerkle Rd., 55110, pg. 862   PV

Willmar

First American Bank & Trust, P.O. Box 1018, 302 S.W. Fifth St., 56201, pg. 167   PV

Jennie-O Foods, Inc., 2505 Willmar Ave. S.W., 56201, pg. 840   PB

Limagrain Genetics Corp., P.O. Box 1033, 56201, pg. 566   IT

MINNESOTA ELECTRIC SUPPLY COMPANY, 1209 E. Hwy. 12, 56201, pg. 750   PB

Winona

Badger Crane Co., 217 Patennaude Dr., 55987, pg. 102   PV

Badger Equipment Co., 217 Patenaude Dr., 55987, pg. 102   PV

Benchmark Electronics, Inc.-Winona Division, 4245 Theurer Blvd., 55987, pg. 211   PB

FASTENAL COMPANY, 2001 Theurer Blvd., 55987-1500, pg. 614   PB

ICI Fiberite, 501-559 W. Third Ave., 55987, pg. 664   IT

Lucas Body Systems - Lake Center Industries, Winona, 5752 Industrial Park Rd., 55987, pg. 820   IT

Lucas Body Systems - North America, P.O. Box 5649, 5676 Industrial Park Rd., 55987, pg. 820   IT

Peerless Chain Company, 1416 E. Sanborn St., 55987, pg. 1268   PB

PEERLESS INDUSTRIAL GROUP, INC., 1416 E. Sanborn St., 55987, pg. 1268   PB

Polymer Composites Inc., 4610 Theurer Blvd., 55987, pg. 624   IT

WATKINS INCORPORATED, 150 Liberty St., 55987, pg. 1153   PV

Watlow Winona, Inc., 1241 Bundy Blvd., 55987, pg. 1153   PV

Winona Daily News, 601 Franklin St., 55987, pg. 984   PB

WINONA KNITS, 1200 Storr's Pond Rd., 55987, pg. 1183   PV

Winona Knitting Mills, Inc., 902 E. Second St., 55987, pg. 779   PB

Winsted

LITTFIN LUMBER COMPANY, 555 Baker Ave., 55395, pg. 670   PV

Woodbury

Fortis Financial Group, 500 Bielenberg Dr., 55125, pg. 499   IT

Worthington

BEDFORD INDUSTRIES, INC., 1659 Rowe Ave., 56187-8700, pg. 129   PV

GORDY'S, INC., 1131 Oxford St., 56187, pg. 465   PV

Swift & Company, P.O. Box 369, Hwy. 60 N.E., 56187, pg. 427   PB

MISSISSIPPI

Artesia

United Cement Co., P.O. Box 185, 39736, pg. 628   IT

Baldwyn

Catalina Industries, One Catalina Way, 38824, pg. 314   PB

Batesville

Batesville American Mfg., P.O. Box 838, Hwy. 51 South, 38606, pg. 957   PB

Belmont

Falcon-Belmont, 22 Falcon Dr., 38827, pg. 611   PB

Belzoni

NBC Bank, FSB (Belzoni), 111 Church St., 39038, pg. 1155   PB

Biloxi

Boomtown-Biloxi, P.O. Box 369, 39533, pg. 831   PB

Gulf Publishing Company, Inc., P.O. Box 4567, 39535, pg. 964   PB

Blue Mountain

Bench Craft, Inc., P.O. Box 86, State Hwy. 15 N., 38610, pg. 432   PV

Blue Mountain Production Co., 31 County Rd. #827, 38610, pg. 1215   PB

Booneville

Heartland Building Products, Inc., 200 Park Pl., 38829, pg. 699   IT

PB - *U.S. Public Companies Volume*
PV - *U.S. Private Companies Volume*
IT - *International Public & Private Companies Volume*

Brandon

Shell West Exploration & Production Inc., 300 Shell Oil Rd., 39042-8430, pg. 1142   **IT**

Byhalia

Gem, 2 Gem Blvd., 38611, pg. 510   **PV**

Calhoun City

Calhoun City Telephone Company, P.O. Box 578, Main St., 38916, pg. 1571   **PB**

Canton

Canton Sales & Storage Co., 555 Mathews Dr., 39046, pg. 1159   **PB**
Madison Furniture Industries, P.O. Drawer 111, 39046, pg. 1465   **PB**

Charleston

Charleston Industries, One Industrial Park, 38921, pg. 856   **PV**

Clarksdale

Cooper Tire & Rubber Company, Clarksdale Plant, P.O. Box 130, 2205 Dr. Martin Luther King Blvd., 38614, pg. 445   **PB**
Farm Press, 14920 U.S. Highway 61, 38614, pg. 1328   **PB**
United Southern Bank, 211 E. Second St., 38614, pg. 1669   **PB**

Cleveland

Brandywine Foods, Inc., Pearman Rd., 38732, pg. 1652   **PB**
Duo-Fast Corporation, 800 N. Pearman, 38732, pg. 348   **PV**

Clinton

AKZO Coatings Inc., 1000 Industrial Pk. Dr., 39056-3210, pg. 46   **IT**

Columbus

AIRLINE MANUFACTURING COMPANY, INC., 104 Williamson Rd., 39704, pg. 29   **PV**
AMERICAN TROUSER, INC., 605 17th St. S., 39701, pg. 64   **PV**
Baldor Electric Company, P.O. Box 2443, 311 Yorkville Park, 39702, pg. 169   **PB**
Beneke, Tuffy Lane, 39701, pg. 964   **PV**
CECO BUILDING SYSTEMS, Hwy. 45 N., P.O. Box 6500, 39701-6500, pg. 221   **PV**
Ceco Building Systems-Southern Region, Hwy. 45 N., P.O. Box 911, 39801, pg. 221   **PV**
Ikon Office Solutions-Mississippi, 3602 Highway 45 N., 39701, pg. 863   **PB**
J and O Diesel, Hwy 45 S. & Hwy 82 W., 39701, pg. 1101   **PV**
Magnolia Division, Tuffy Lane, 39701, pg. 964   **PV**
Manufactured Home, Tuffy Ln., 39701, pg. 964   **PV**
Microtek Medical, Inc., 512 Lehmberg Rd., 39702, pg. 914   **PB**
Newell Paper Co. of Columbus, 1616 Seventh Ave. S., 39708, pg. 579   **PV**
SANDERSON PLUMBING PRODUCTS INC., Tuffy Ln., 39701, pg. 964   **PV**
Sani-Med, Tuffy Ln., 39701, pg. 964   **PV**
SanTran Inc., P.O. Box 1367, 39703, pg. 964   **PV**
Southern Electric Supply Co., Inc., 1121 Gardner Blvd., 39704, pg. 1108   **IT**
United Technologies Motor Systems, P.O. Box 2228, 39704-2228, pg. 1690   **PB**

Corinth

Intex Plastics Corporation, P.O. Box 957, 38834, pg. 574   **PV**
Kimberly-Clark Hospital Service Products, RT 8 Kendrick Rd., 38834-9808, pg. 959   **PB**
OUTDOOR COMMUNICATIONS, INC., 512 Taylor St., 38834, pg. 822   **PV**
Ringier America, Corinth Division, One Golding Dr., 38834, pg. 1778   **PB**

Diamondhead

PURCELL CO., INC., 4401 E. Aloha Dr., 39525, pg. 895   **PV**

Elliott

HANKINS LUMBER COMPANY, INC., Camp McCain Rd., 38926, pg. 499   **PV**

Ellisville

Detrick Refractory Fibers, Inc., P.O. Box 340, S.E. Mississippi Industry Park, 39437, pg. 761   **PB**

Fayette

Fayette Enterprises, Inc., P.O. Box 188, 39069, pg. 688   **PB**

Florence

ALLTEL Mississippi, Inc., 101 Lewis St., P.O. Box 7, 39073, pg. 56   **PB**

Forest

Raytheon Systems Mississippi, Rte. 5, Hwy. 80 E., 39074, pg. 1365   **PB**

Gautier

National American Corporation, 2012 Hwy. 90, 39553, pg. 1688   **PB**

Greenville

Brent Transportation Co., 716 Hwy. One N., 38701, pg. 961   **PV**
MOELLER PRODUCTS CO., INC., 1281 Pickett St., 38703, pg. 755   **PV**
Nicholson, 1825 N. Theobald St., 38703, pg. 444   **PV**
Southern Electric Supply Co., Inc., 601 Kentucky St., 38701, pg. 1108   **IT**
Surplus Warehouse-Greenville, 541 S. Theobald, 38701, pg. 119   **PV**

Greenwood

Delta Correctional Facility, 3800 Baldwin Rd., 38930, pg. 450   **PB**
HDW, Incorporated, 1100 Sycamore St, 38930, pg. 335   **PV**
Southern Electric Supply Co., Inc., 1407 Main St., 38930, pg. 1108   **IT**
STAPLE COTTON COOPERATIVE ASSOCIATION, 214 W. Market St., 38930, pg. 1033   **PV**
Staple Cotton Cooperative Association/Itta Bena, P.O. Box 547, 38930, pg. 1033   **PV**
Staple Cotton Discount Corporation, P.O. Box 547, 38930, pg. 1033   **PV**
Supreme Electronics Corp., 1714 Carrollton Ave., 38930-5818, pg. 825   **PB**
VIKING RANGE CORP., 111 Front St, 38930, pg. 1140   **PV**

Grenada

Heatcraft Inc., Hwy. 51 South, 38901, pg. 659   **PB**
Union Planters Bank of Mississippi, 2000 Gateway, 38901, pg. 1669   **PB**

Gulfport

ROY ANDERSON CORP., 11400 Reichold Rd., 39503, pg. 72   **PV**
Avondale Gulfport Marine Inc., 11367 Reichhold Rd., 39503, pg. 157   **PB**
Community Psychiatric Centers of Mississippi, Inc., 11150 Hwy. 49, 39503, pg. 1712   **PB**
Gulfport Convalescent Center Manor, 1530 Broad Ave., 39501, pg. 1713   **PB**
HALTER MARINE GROUP, INC., 13085 Industrial Seaway Rd., 39503, pg. 778   **PB**
Mississippi Power Co., 2992 W. Beach Blvd., 39501, pg. 1490   **PB**
BUTCH OUSTALET FORD SAAB, INC., 9274 Hwy. 49, 39503, pg. 821   **PV**
Southern Electric Supply Co., Inc., 1270 28th St., 39501, pg. 1108   **IT**
STRUTHERS INDUSTRIES INC., 1500 34th St., 39501, pg. 1048   **PV**
Sun Herald, 205 DeBuys Rd., 39507, pg. 964   **PV**
VR/Wesson Hydro Carbide-Gulfport, P.O. Box 2368, 39503, pg. 512   **PB**

Guntown

COLUMBIAN ROPE COMPANY, 145 Towery St., 38849-0270, pg. 256   **PB**

Hattiesburg

Hattiesburg American, 825 N. Main St., 39401, pg. 701   **PB**
Hercules Inc.-Hattiesburg, P.O. Drawer 1937, 39403-1937, pg. 810   **PB**
Magna Mortgage, 100 W. Front St., 39401-3460, pg. 1669   **PB**
Mississippi Auto Auction Inc., 7510 U.S. Hwy. 49 N., 39402, pg. 1649   **PV**
Newell Paper Co. of Hattiesburg, 125 Newman St., 39483, pg. 579   **PV**
UPB of Southern Mississippi, 110 S. 40th Ave., 39402, pg. 1669   **PB**
WHLT, 990 Hardy St., 39401, pg. 1078   **PB**

Hernando

Valvoline, Inc., 720 Vaiden Dr., 38632, pg. 139   **PB**

Holly Springs

Holly Springs Brick and Tile, Inc., P.O. Box 310, 38635, pg. 699   **IT**
The Wurlitzer Company, 805 Northwest Street, 38635, pg. 169   **PB**

Horn Lake

Dover Elevator Systems, Inc., 6266 Hurt Rd., 38637, pg. 521   **PB**
Flavorite Laboratories, 5980 Hurt Rd., 38671, pg. 1090   **PV**

Houston

Masterblend, Inc., 602 Dulaney St., 38851, pg. 986   **PB**

Indianola

DELTA PRIDE CATFISH, INC., Industrial Park, 38751, pg. 322   **PV**
SOUTH FRESH FARMS, P.O. Box 848, 38751, pg. 1014   **PV**
SuperValu, Inc.-Lewis Grocer Div., Hwy. 49 South, 38751, pg. 1540   **PB**

Isola

Country Skillet Catfish Co., Box 271, 38754, pg. 428   **PB**

Jackson

Allen & Hoshall, 3000 Old Canton Rd., 39216, pg. 36   **PV**
Aztec Industries, Inc., 125 Aztec Dr., 39218, pg. 159   **PB**
Brambles Div. of Brambles Equipment Services Inc., 3880 Lynch St., 39209, pg. 211   **IT**
Browning-Ferris Industries of Mississippi, Inc., P.O. Box 1638, 39205, pg. 263   **PB**
CCG, 6360 Interstate 55 N., Ste. 300, 39211, pg. 1182   **PB**
Cal-Maine Egg Products Inc., 3330 Woodrow Wilson Blvd., 39209, pg. 292   **PB**
Cal-Maine Farms, 3320 Woodrow Wilson Blvd., 39209, pg. 292   **PB**
CAL-MAINE FOODS, INC., 3320 W. Woodrow Wilson Blvd., 39209, pg. 292   **PB**
CAPITOL STREET CORP., 711 W. Capitol St., 39203, pg. 207   **PV**
Charter Behavioral Health System of Jackson, Inc., 3531 Lakeland DR., 39208, pg. 1034   **PB**
CHEMFIRST INC., 700 North St., 39202-3095, pg. 344   **PB**
The Clarion-Ledger, 311 E. Pear St., P.O. Box 40, 39205, pg. 700   **PB**
Cochran/Sysco Food Services, 4400 Milwaukee St., 39209-2683, pg. 1550   **PB**
Dallas Printing, 323 E. Hamiton St., 39205, pg. 333   **PB**
DEPOSIT GUARANTY CORP., 210 E. Capitol St., 39205, pg. 500   **PB**
Deposit Guaranty Investments, Inc., 210 E. Capitol St., 39205, pg. 501   **PB**
Deposit Guaranty Mortgage Co., 210 E. Capitol St., 39205, pg. 501   **PB**
Deposit Guaranty National Bank, 210 E. Capitol St., 39205, pg. 500   **PB**
The Deviney Company Inc., Springridge Rd., 39212, pg. 1056   **PB**
DEWEY CORPORATION, 5500 U.S. Hwy. 80 W., 39209, pg. 329   **PV**
Doublecoat, L.L.C., 951 Prisock Rd., 39212, pg. 266   **PV**
Dynapower/Stratopower, 5353 Highland Dr., 39206, pg. 24   **PB**
Entergy Mississippi, Inc., 308 E. Pearl St., 39201, pg. 586   **PB**
Entergy Operations, Inc., 1340 Echelon Pkwy., 39213, pg. 586   **PB**
ERGON, INC., 2829 Lakeland Dr., 39208, pg. 380   **PV**
G & W Life Insurance Co., P.O. Box 1200, 39215, pg. 501   **PB**
GO Manufacturing, 1420 Ridgeway St., 39213, pg. 1632   **PB**
Green Tree Acceptance of Mississippi, Inc., 409 Briarwood Dr., Ste. 303, 39236, pg. 762   **PB**
Group Insurance of Jackson, 519 E. Amite, 32901, pg. 484   **PV**
Hewlett-Packard Company, 1675 Lakeland Dr., Ste. 102, 39216, pg. 814   **PB**
Interstate Jitney Jungle Stores, Inc., 1770 Ellis Ave., Ste. 200, 39204, pg. 588   **PV**
Jackson MS Steel Division, 3630 Fourth St., 39208-2003, pg. 232   **PB**
JACKSON PAPER COMPANY, 197 N. Gallatin St., 39207, pg. 579   **PV**
Jackson Sales & Storage Co., P.O. Box 68361, 39286, pg. 1159   **PB**
Jitney-Jungle Bakery, Inc., 1770 Ellis Ave., Ste. 200, 39204, pg. 588   **PV**
JITNEY-JUNGLE STORES OF AMERICA, INC., 1770 Ellis Ave., Ste. 200, 39204, pg. 588   **PV**
KLLM TRANSPORT SERVICES, INC., 3475 Lakeland Dr., 39208, pg. 939   **PB**
MTel Space Technologies Corp., Security Center, S. Bldg., 200 S. Lamar, 39225, pg. 1120   **PB**
McCarty Foods, Inc., P.O. Box 2718, 39207, pg. 1652   **PB**
McRae's, Inc., 3455 Hwy. 80 W., 39209, pg. 1333   **PB**
Miller Intermodal Logistics Services Inc., S 500 Hwy. 80 W., 39209, pg. 329   **PV**
Miller Transporters, Inc., 5500 U.S. Hwy. 80 W., 39209, pg. 329   **PV**

Geographic Index-U.S.

Mississippi Energies, Inc., 711 W. Capitol St., P.O. Box 3348, 39203, pg. 753 **PV**

Mississippi Farm Bureau Casualty Insurance Company, 6310 I 55 N., 39211, pg. 1016 **PV**

MISSISSIPPI VALLEY GAS CO., 711 W. Capital St., 39203, pg. 753 **PV**

MOBILE TELECOMMUNICATIONS TECHNOLOGIES CORP., MTel Ctr., S. Bldg., 200 S. Lamar, 39201, pg. 1120 **PB**

Mosinee Converted Products Div., 3915 Beasley Rd., 39213, pg. 1747 **PB**

NEWSPRINT SOUTH, INC., 460 Briarwood Dr., Ste. 505, 39206, pg. 797 **PV**

PENCO-Mississippi, Four River Bend Pl., Ste. 204, 39208, pg. 1508 **IT**

Premium Tank Line Inc., 6033 I-55 S., pg. 329 **PV**

Presto Manufacturing Company, 109 Presto Ln., 39286, pg. 1159 **PB**

Pump and Save, Inc., 1770 Ellis Ave., Ste. 200, 39204, pg. 588 **PV**

Quikrete Materials, Inc., P.O. Box 8098, 39284, pg. 88 **PV**

Riedel-Smith Environmental Services, 133 Commerce Park Dr., 39213, pg. 1478 **PB**

Sanderson Farms Foods Div., P.O. Box 97149, 39288, pg. 1431 **PB**

Soterra Inc., P.O. Box 18, 39205, pg. 763 **PB**

Southern Jitney-Jungle, Inc., 1770 Ellis Ave., Ste. 200, 39204, pg. 588 **PV**

SOUTHLAND OIL COMPANY, 5170 Galaxie Dr., 39206, pg. 1018 **PV**

Surplus Warehouse-Jackson, 440 Hwy. 80 E., 39284, pg. 119 **PV**

System Energy Resources, Inc., Echelon One, 1340 Echelon Pkwy., 39213, pg. 586 **PV**

Tencarva Machinery Company, 854 Foley St., 39207-3710, pg. 1076 **PV**

Tower Loan of Mississippi, Inc., P.O. Box 6482, 131 Channel 16 Way, 39212, pg. 207 **PV**

TREND LINE CORPORATION, 4400 River Oaks Dr., 39208, pg. 1099 **PV**

Truck Center South, 412 Hwy. 49 S., 39288, pg. 1101 **PV**

TRUSTMARK CORPORATION, P.O. Box 291, 248 E. Capital St., 39205-0291, pg. 1643 **PB**

Trustmark National Bank, P.O. Box 291, 39205-0291, pg. 1643 **PB**

UAD Laboratories, 8339 Hwy. 18 West, 39209, pg. 670 **PB**

UPB of Central Mississippi, 329 E. Capitol St., 39201, pg. 1669 **PB**

United Companies Lending Corp. (Mississippi), 1414 Ellis Ave., 39204, pg. 1675 **PB**

Valley Innovative Management Service, 4400 River Oaks Dr., 39208, pg. 1099 **PV**

Veritas DGC INC, P.O. Box 98159, 39298-8159, pg. 1137 **PV**

Vickers AMD, 5353 Highland Dr., 39206-3449, pg. 25 **PV**

WJTV, 1820 TV Road, 39204, pg. 1078 **PB**

WAPT, 7616 Channel 16 Way, 39209, pg. 926 **IT**

Willis Corroon Administrative Services Corporation, Four River Bend Pl., Ste. 201, 39208, pg. 1504 **IT**

Woodward-Clyde, 1553 E. Countyline Rd., Ste. 203, 39211, pg. 1656 **PV**

WORLDCOM, INC., 515 E. Amite St., 39201-2702, pg. 1779 **PB**

YAZOO POWER EQUIPMENT, LLC, 3650 Bay St., 39213-5509, pg. 1195 **PV**

Laurel

SANDERSON FARMS, INC., 225 N. 13th Ave., 39441-0988, pg. 1430 **PB**

Sanderson Farms Processing Div., P.O. Box 988, 39941, pg. 1431 **PB**

Sanderson Farms Production Div., P.O. Box 988, 39941, pg. 1431 **PB**

Southern Electric Supply Co., Inc., 215 S. Magnolia St., 39440, pg. 1108 **IT**

Leland

La-Z-Boy Leland, Rte. 2, Box 500, 38756, pg. 973 **PB**

Liberty

Liberty Distribution Center, 2101 N. Lightburne St., 64068, pg. 496 **PV**

Long Beach

Oreck Manufacturing Company, 21180 Johnson Rd., 39560, pg. 819 **PV**

Louisville

TAYLOR MACHINE WORKS, INC., 650 N. Church Ave., 39339, pg. 1070 **PV**

Lucedale

Lucedale Industries, 110 Virginia St., 39452, pg. 501 **PV**

Madison

Beech Aerospace Services, Inc., 555 Industrial Dr. S., 39110, pg. 1365 **PB**

Fluidex Div., 147 West Hoy Rd., 39110-0130, pg. 1260 **PB**

SOUTHERN BAG CORPORATION, 25 Wood Green Place, 39110, pg. 1015 **PV**

Magee

Tyson Foods, Inc., P.O. Box 366, 39111, pg. 1652 **PB**

McComb

CROFT METALS, INC., 124 24th St., 39648, pg. 290 **PV**

Meridian

ATLAS ROOFING CORP., 802 Hwy. 19 N., Ste. 190, 39307, pg. 96 **PV**

Bergen Brunswig Medical Corporation, 6300 St. Louis St., 39301, pg. 214 **PV**

Great River Insurance Company, 4909 Great River Dr., 39305, pg. 215 **PV**

Meridian Lamps, Inc., 6604-A Old Hwy., 80 West, 39304, pg. 314 **PB**

Meridian Machine Works, Inc., P.O. Box 5393, Spector St., 39302, pg. 378 **PV**

Newell Paper Co. of Meridian, 2501 Front St., 39302, pg. 579 **PV**

PEAVEY ELECTRONICS CORP., 711 A St., 39301, pg. 845 **PV**

Southern Electric Supply Co., Inc., 301 46th Ct., 39301, pg. 1107 **IT**

Southern Electric Supply Co., Inc., 912 13th St., 39301, pg. 1108 **IT**

Tri-State Mack Inc., Cellers Dr., 39301, pg. 1101 **PV**

Webster-Portalloy Chains, Inc., P.O. Box 1747, 3800 Second St., 39302, pg. 1158 **PV**

Monticello

Primary Pulp & Paper Plant, P.O. Box 608, Sandifer Rd., 39654, pg. 736 **PB**

Morton

Craft-Co Enterprises Inc., P.O. Box 289, Highway 80 W., 39117, pg. 955 **IT**

Moss Point

Automatic Processing, Inc., 4212 Dutch Bayou Rd., 39563, pg. 159 **PB**

Natchez

Callon Offshore Production, 200 N. Canal St., 39121, pg. 295 **PB**

CALLON PETROLEUM COMPANY, 200 N. Canal St., 39121, pg. 295 **PB**

CONDERE CORPORATION, 89 Kelly St, 31920, pg. 262 **PV**

Fidelity Tire Mfg. Co., P.O. Box 927, 39121-0927, pg. 262 **PV**

Mississippi Marketing, Inc., 200 N. Canal St., 39120, pg. 295 **PB**

Wilcox Energy Company, 304 Franklin St., 39120, pg. 295 **PB**

New Albany

Davis Wood Products, Inc.-Mississippi Div., P.O. Box 146, 102 Industrial Dr., 38652, pg. 316 **PV**

Master-Bilt Products, Hwy. 15 N., 38652, pg. 1506 **PB**

New Albany Gazette, P.O. Box 300, 713 Carter Ave., 38652, pg. 648 **PV**

Piper Impact, Inc., 922 State Rd. 15N., 38652, pg. 1349 **PB**

Stratolounger, Highway West 178, 38652, pg. 265 **PV**

UPB of Northeast MS, 112 E. Bankhead St., 38652, pg. 1669 **PB**

New Augusta

Leaf River Forest Products, Inc., P.O. Box 329, 39462-0329, pg. 736 **PB**

Newton

La-Z-Boy South, 133 Scanlan, 39345, pg. 973 **PB**

Ocean Springs

Browning-Ferris Industries of Mississippi, Inc., P.O. Box 550, 39564, pg. 263 **PB**

Lips USA Inc., 300 Washington Ave., 39564-4640, pg. 812 **IT**

Olive Branch

American Metal Products, 8601 Hacks Cross, 38654, pg. 1053 **PB**

Fraenkel Company, 8300 Industrial Dr., 38654, pg. 423 **PV**

Marietta, Inc., 11170 Green Valley Dr., 38654, pg. 703 **PV**

METRO FOODS, INC., 10635 Marina Dr., 38654, pg. 736 **PV**

Oxford

Southern Electric Supply Co., Inc., 2651 W. Oxford Loop, 38655, pg. 1108 **IT**

Pascagoula

Bird-Johnson Company-Gulf Coast Operations, P.O. Box 1528, 3719 Industrial Rd., 39567, pg. 709 **IT**

First Chemical Corp., P.O. Box 7005, 39568-7005, pg. 344 **PB**

Ingalls Shipbuilding, 1000 Access Rd., P.O. Box 149, 39567-0149, pg. 1003 **PB**

Mississippi Phosphates Corp., 601 Industrial Rd., 39568-0804, pg. 1117 **PB**

Pearl

Paine Supply of Jackson, Inc., 220 One Stop Pl., 39208, pg. 847 **PB**

Pearlington

Star Export Services Inc., P.O. Box 74, 39572, pg. 664 **IT**

Philadelphia

Connor Corporation, 931 Hwy. 19 N., 39350, pg. 264 **PV**

Pontotoc

HANSBERGER PRECISION GOLF INC., 238 Industrial Circle, 38863, pg. 499 **PV**

Poplarville

Movie Star Factory Outlet Stores, 217 Hwy. 11 S., 39470, pg. 1141 **PB**

Port Gibson

National Plastics Corporation, Industrial Ave., 39150, pg. 1037 **IT**

Puckett

Hydro Aluminum Bohn, Inc., P.O. Box 306, Hwy. 18, 39151, pg. 961 **IT**

Richland

The Calvert Co., 120 Aztec Dr., 39218, pg. 159 **PB**

Dixie National Life Insurance Company, 855 S. Pear Orchard Rd., Ste. 305, 39157, pg. 1502 **PB**

Wabash Fibre Box Co.-Jackson, 127 Interstate Dr., 39218, pg. 1170 **PV**

Ridgeland

BILL'S DOLLAR STORES, INC., 1025 N. Park Dr., 39157, pg. 144 **PV**

Gulf South Medical Supply, Inc., 426 Christine Dr., 39157, pg. 1294 **PB**

Hewlett-Packard Company, 800 Woodland Pkwy., Ste. 101, 39157, pg. 814 **PB**

Mobile Communications Corporation of America, Ste. 300, 1800 East County Line Rd., 39157, pg. 1120 **PB**

SOUTHERN FARM BUREAU CASUALTY INSURANCE COMPANY, 1800 E. County Line Rd., Ste. 400, 39157-1800, pg. 1016 **PV**

Rienzi

Frontier Communications of Mississippi, Inc., Hwy. 356, 38865, pg. 684 **PB**

Ripley

Oil-Dri Production Co., P.O. Box 476, 38663, pg. 1215 **PB**

Saltillo

Bassett Motion Division, Turner Industrial Park, P.O. Box 1210, 38866, pg. 193 **PB**

Sardis

Armor Bond Building Products, Inc., Industrial Rd., 38666, pg. 699 **IT**

INCA Presswood Pallets, Ltd., Sardis Indus. Park, P.O. Box 129, 38666, pg. 678 **IT**

Scott

DELTA & PINE LAND COMPANY, P.O. Box 157, 38772, pg. 497 **PB**

Senatobia

Chromcraft Corporation, One Quality Ln., 38668, pg. 352 **PB**

Peoples Bank, Hwy. 51, 38668, pg. 639 **PB**

Ringier America, Senatobia Division, 121 Matthews Dr., 38668, pg. 1778 **PB**

Senatobia Division, 121 Matthews Dr., 38668, pg. 518 **PB**

PB - U.S. Public Companies Volume
PV - U.S. Private Companies Volume
IT - International Public & Private Companies Volume

Sherman

Barclay Furniture Company, P.O. Box 399, 38869, pg. 974 **PB**

Southaven

First Tennessee Bank National Association Mississippi, 615 Goodman Rd. E., 38671, pg. 639 **PB**
Malone & Hyde, Inc.-Southaven, 2929 State Line Rd., 38671, pg. 653 **PB**

Starkville

Commercial Seating Division, P.O. Box 825, 39760, pg. 654 **PB**
Garan Manufacturing Corp., Hwy. 12 W., 39759, pg. 703 **PB**
Gulf States Manufacturers, Inc., 101 Airport Rd., 39759, pg. 699 **IT**

Stoneville

Stoneville Pedigreed Seed Co., P.O. Box 167, 4852 Old Leland Rd., 38776, pg. 1124 **PB**

Summit

Kellwood Lingerie/Active Group, 1401 Old Highway 51N, 39666, pg. 948 **PB**

Taylorsville

Formaldehyde, P.O. Box 556, 39168, pg. 737 **PB**

Tishomingo

Heil Environmental Industries (H.E.I.L.), Hwy. 25 N., 38873, pg. 520 **PB**

Tunica

Planters Bank, 1202 E. Edwards Ave., 38676, pg. 639 **PB**

Tupelo

Action Industries, Inc., 5380 Hwy. 145, 38801, pg. 688 **PB**
BANCORP SOUTH INC., One Mississippi Plaza, 38801, pg. 176 **PB**
Bank of Mississippi, One Mississippi Plaza, 38801, pg. 176 **PB**
Century Credit Life Insurance Company, One Mississippi Plaza, 38801, pg. 176 **PB**
Cooper Tire & Rubber Company, Tupelo Plant, P.O. Box 170, 1689 S. Green St., 38802, pg. 445 **PB**
Delta International Machinery Corp. (Tupelo), P.O. Box 1508, 1200 S. Gloster, 38802, pg. 1273 **PB**
FMC Material Handling Systems Division, P.O. Box 1370, 38802, pg. 605 **PB**
HANCOCK FABRICS, INC., 3406 W. Main St., 38803-2400, pg. 779 **PB**
Jesco, 353 N. Gloster St., 38801, pg. 1676 **PB**
Personal Finance Corp., 211 Court St., 38801, pg. 176 **PB**
Shannon Division, P.O. Box 527, 38802, pg. 1566 **PB**
Stone Container Corp.-Tupelo, P.O. Drawer 1769, 38801, pg. 1521 **PB**
Super Sagless Corp., S. Green St., 38801, pg. 986 **PB**
Thomas Lighting-C&I Indoor Division, 1015 S. Green St., 38801, pg. 1599 **PB**
Tri-State Mack Inc., 2193 S. Eason Blvd., 38801, pg. 1101 **PV**

Verona

Aircap Industries Corp., Hwy. 45 S., 38879, pg. 688 **PV**
Gibson Container Division, Industrial Park S., 38879, pg. 1170 **PV**
Sackner-South Div., 220 Midway Ave., 38879, pg. 924 **PB**

Vicksburg

OMR Transportation Company, Port Terminal Cir. 477, P.O. Box 1859, 39181-1859, pg. 962 **PV**
Rainbow Casino, 1444 Rawnton Rd., 39180, pg. 47 **PB**
Rainbow Casino Vicksburg L.P., 1380 Rawnton Rd., pg. 47 **PB**
Southern Electric Supply Co., Inc., 520 Depot St., 39180, pg. 1108 **IT**
Vicksburg Plant, 5035 Hwy. 61 S., P.O. Box 820824, 39180, pg. 444 **PB**

Water Valley

Valley Fresh, Inc., 190 Lafayette St., 38965, pg. 1132 **PV**

West Point

Bryan Foods, 100 Churchill Rd., 39773, pg. 1433 **PB**
FLEXIBLE FLYER TOYS, 100 Tubb Ave., 39773, pg. 412 **PV**

Yazoo City

MISSISSIPPI CHEMICAL CORPORATION, U.S. Hwy. 49 E., 39194, pg. 1117 **PB**

Mississippi Phosphates Corp., P.O. Box 388, 39194, pg. 1117 **PB**
Mississippi Potash. Inc., P.O. Box 388, 39194, pg. 1117 **PB**

MISSOURI

Antonia

Masterchem Industries, P.O. Box 368, 3135 Hwy. M., 63052, pg. 1501 **IT**

Arnold

WK Mfg. Company, Tenbrook Rd., 63010, pg. 603 **PV**

Aurora

Bioproducts, Inc., 117 N. Morgan St., 65605, pg. 145 **PV**

Ballwin

Fru-Con Construction Corporation, 15933 Clayton Rd. W., 63022-0100, pg. 196 **IT**

Belle

The Kingsford Products Co., Hwy. 28, Star Rte. 3, 65013, pg. 387 **PB**

Belton

Quik N Tasty Foods, 822 Quiktrip Way, 64012, pg. 901 **PV**

Berger

GenCorp Vehicle Sealing Div., P.O. Box 135, Bailey Rd., 63014, pg. 706 **PB**

Berkeley

Brake Fluid Operations, 9151 Latty Ave., 63134, pg. 443 **PB**
McDonnell Aircraft & Missile Systems Div., McDonnell Blvd. & Airport Rd., 63134, pg. 241 **PB**
ReCon Services, Inc., 6647 Romiss Ct., 63134, pg. 260 **PV**

Blue Springs

Blue Springs Examiner, P.O. Box 1057, 500 W. R.D. Mize Rd., 64013-2421, pg. 995 **PV**
FIKE CORPORATION, 704 S. Tenth St., 64015, pg. 404 **PV**
HARMON INDUSTRIES, INC., 1300 Jefferson Ct., 64015, pg. 788 **PB**

Bolivar

Alltel Missouri, Inc., 218 East Broadway, 65613, pg. 56 **PB**

Bonne Terre

Resco Products Of Missouri, P.O. Box 440, Old Bonne Terre Rd., pg. 924 **PV**

Boonville

NationsBank of Boonville, 412 Main St., 65233, pg. 1164 **PB**

Branson

Fairfield Branson, 110 Willow Bend Blvd., 65616, pg. 610 **PB**
SILVER DOLLAR CITY, INC., Box 791 HCI, 65616-9602, pg. 1000 **PV**

Bridgeton

Beta Raven Inc., P.O. Box 633, 4372 Green Ash Dr., 63042, pg. 1361 **PB**
GRAMEX CORPORATION, 11966 St. Charles Rock Rd., 63044, pg. 468 **PV**
Hewlett-Packard Company, 13001 Hollenberg Dr., 63044, pg. 814 **PB**
Hussmann Corp., 12999 St. Charles Rock Rd., 63044, pg. 1766 **PB**
Materials Research Corp., 3450 Bridgeland Dr., Ste. E, 63044, pg. 1283 **IT**
National Vendors, 12955 Enterprise Way, 63044, pg. 457 **PB**
St. Louis Auto Auction, 13813 St. Charles Rock Rd., 63045, pg. 283 **PV**
The Trane Company-International, 20 Corporate Woods Dr., 63044-4419, pg. 92 **PB**
URS Greiner, Inc., 4610 N. Lindbergh, Ste. 104, 63044, pg. 1658 **PB**

Buffalo

Batesco Quarries Div., 65622, pg. 88 **PV**

Butler

Batesco Quarries Div., Hwy. 52, 64730, pg. 88 **PV**

Cape Girardeau

Atlas-Alchem Plastics-Missouri, 2500 Spartech Ave., 63701, pg. 1496 **PB**
BioKyowa Inc., P.O. Box 1550, 5469 Nash Rd., 63701, pg. 778 **IT**
D & K Healthcare Resources Division, P.O. Box 2108, 63702, pg. 472 **PB**
The Resin Exchange, 4753 Nash Rd., 63701, pg. 1496 **PB**
UPB of Girardeau Co., 407 N. Kingshighway, 60702, pg. 1669 **PB**

Carthage

Administradora Soal S.A. de C.V., P.O. Box 757, 64838, pg. 987 **PB**
Carreiro Holdings S.A. de C.V., P.O. Box 757, 64838, pg. 987 **PB**
Comercializadora S.A. de C.V., P.O. Box 757, 64836, pg. 987 **PB**
ConAgra Turkey Company, P.O. Box 697, 411 Main St., 64836, pg. 427 **PB**
Display Technologies Electrohome Inc., 1001 N. Francis St., 64836, pg. 438 **IT**
Doerner Products Ltd., P.O. Box 757, 64836, pg. 986 **PB**
Dream Makers, Inc., One Leggett Rd., 64836, pg. 986 **PB**
Dresher, Inc., One Leggett Rd., 64836, pg. 986 **PB**
EST Company of Tennessee, Inc., 1 Leggett Rd., 64836, pg. 986 **PB**
Fibras Acolchables S.A. de C.V., P.O. Box 757, 64836, pg. 987 **PB**
Gribetz Threads, Inc., P.O. Box 757, 64836, pg. 986 **PB**
Hanes Fabrics Company, Inc., P.O. Box 757, 64836, pg. 986 **PB**
Hanes Holding Company, P.O. Box 757, 64836, pg. 986 **PB**
L&P Acquisition Company-8, P.O. Box 757, 64838, pg. 986 **PB**
L&P Acquisition Company-9, P.O. Box 757, 64838, pg. 986 **PB**
L&P Acquisition Company-7, P.O. Box 757, 64838, pg. 986 **PB**
L&P Acquisition Company-10, P.O. Box 757, 64838, pg. 986 **PB**
L&P Aluminum Smelting Acquisition Company, 1 Leggett Rd., 64836, pg. 986 **PB**
L&P Automotive Europe GmbH, P.O. Box 757, 64836, pg. 987 **PB**
L&P Automotive Holdings Company, P.O. Box 757, 64836, pg. 986 **PB**
L&P International Holdings Company, P.O. Box 757, 64836, pg. 986 **PB**
L&P Mexico, S.A. de C.V., P.O. Box 757, 64836, pg. 986 **PB**
L&P Property Management Company, P.O. Box 757, 64836, pg. 986 **PB**
L&P Transportation Co., 1 Leggett Rd., P.O. Box 757, 64836, pg. 986 **PB**
L&P Western Spring Co., P.O. Box 757, 64836, pg. 986 **PB**
Leggett & Platt Foreign Sales Corporation, P.O. Box 757, 64836, pg. 986 **PB**
LEGGETT & PLATT, INCORPORATED, One Leggett Rd., 64836, pg. 985 **PB**
Leggett and Platt International Corporation, 1 Leggett Rd., P.O. Box 757, 64836, pg. 986 **PB**
Leggett & Platt International Development Co., P.O. Box 757, 64836, pg. 986 **PB**
MG Loan Company, 1 Leggett Rd., 64836, pg. 986 **PB**
National Frame Company, P.O. Box 757, 64836, pg. 986 **PB**
NationsBank of Southwest Missouri, 231 So. Main St., 64836, pg. 1164 **PB**
OTT FOOD PRODUCTS, 705 W. Fairview, 64836, pg. 821 **PV**
Steadly Company, 2530 Grand Ave, 64836, pg. 986 **PV**
Stylelander Metal Stamping, Inc., P.O. Box 757, 64836, pg. 986 **PB**
VWR Textiles & Supplies, Inc., P.O. Box 757, 64836, pg. 986 **PB**
Webster Wire, Inc., No. 1 Leggett Rd., 64836, pg. 986 **PB**
H.E. WILLIAMS, INC., 831 W. Fairview Ave., 64836, pg. 1178 **PV**

Cassville

Justin Boot Company, 11th & Presley, 65625, pg. 937 **PB**
NationsBank of Cassville, 503 Main St., 65625, pg. 1164 **PB**

Charleston

Gates Rubber Co. Inc., 1300 Plant Rd., 63834-2375, pg. 1396 **IT**

Chesterfield

Affholder, Inc., 17988 Edison Ave., 63005-3700, pg. 881 **PB**
ANGELICA CORPORATION, 424 S. Woods Mill Rd., 63017-3406, pg. 113 **PB**
Biokyowa Inc., 1400 Elbridge Payne, Ste. 110, 63017, pg. 778 **IT**

Geographic Index-U.S.

PB - *U.S. Public Companies Volume*
PV - *U.S. Private Companies Volume*
IT - *International Public & Private Companies Volume*

1300

Bull Moose Tube Company, 1819 Clarkson Rd., Ste. 100, 63017, pg. 265   IT
Champion Ignition Products, 901 Roosevelt Parkway, 63017, pg. 442   PB
Cooper Automotive Division, 901 Roosevelt Pkwy., 63017, pg. 443   PB
Countrywide Services Corp., 400 S. Woodsmill Rd., 63017-3400, pg. 789   PV
DIERBERGS MARKETS INC., 1422 Elbridge Payne Rd., 63017, pg. 332   PV
Fasco DC Motors, 500 Chesterfield Ctr., Ste. 200, 63017, pg. 125   IT
HCI CHEMTECH, 424 S. Woods Mill Rd., #325, 63017, pg. 490   PV
Harland Bartholomew & Associates Inc., 425 Woodsmill Rd. S., Ste. 150, 63017, pg. 842   PV
Huttig Sash & Door Co., 14500 S. Outer Forty Rd., Ste. 400, 63017, pg. 457   PB
Insituform Missouri, Inc., 17988 Edison Ave., 63005-3700, pg. 882   PB
INSITUFORM TECHNOLOGIES, INC., 702 Spirit 40 Park Dr., 63005, pg. 881   PB
Invacare Health Care Furnishings, 739 Goddard Ave., 63005, pg. 911   PB
KELLWOOD COMPANY, 600 Kellwood Pkwy., 63017, pg. 948   PB
Mark Andy, Inc., 18081 Chesterfield Airport Rd., 63005, pg. 521   PB
MAVERICK TUBE CORPORATION, 400 Chesterfield Ctr., 2nd Fl., 63017, pg. 1060   PB
MiTek, Inc., 14515 N. Outer Forty Rd., Ste. 300, 63017, pg. 1106   PB
Nutri-Quest, Inc., 1400 Elbridge Payne, Ste. 110, 63017, pg. 778   IT
Pactem Systems, Inc., 17988 Edison Ave., 63005-3700, pg. 882   PB
Paradata Financial Systems, 18102 Chesterfield Airport Rd., Ste. J., 63005, pg. 1778   PB
Riedel-Smith Environmental Services, 18207 Edison Ave., 63005, pg. 1478   PB
SACHS HOLDING COMPANY, 400 Chesterfield Ctr., Ste. 600, 63017, pg. 959   PV
Sachs Properties, 400 Chesterfield Ctr., Ste. 600, 63017, pg. 959   PV
St. Louis Sales, 390 S. Woods Mill Rd., Ste. 125, 63017, pg. 611   PV
Silgan Plastic Corp., Bldg. 14515, Westland Pl. N. Outer 40, Ste. 210, 63017, pg. 1473   PB
Sunrise Leasing Corporation, 400 Chesterfield Ctr., Ste. 400, 63017, pg. 1535   PB
Symbol, 1415 Elbridge Payne Rd., 63017-8522, pg. 1546   PB
Tetra Plastics, 620 Spirit of St. Louise Blvd., 63005, pg. 1184   PB
Torin Engineered Blowers, 500 Chesterfield Ctr., Ste. 200, 63017, pg. 125   IT
Wagner Brake Subsidiary, 930 Roosevelt Pkwy., 63017, pg. 443   PB
Wagner Lighting Products, 901 Roosevelt Pkwy., 63017, pg. 442   PB

Chillicothe

R.A. Sales, Inc., P.O. Box 350, 411 S. Brunswick St., 64601, pg. 1377   PB
Rupp Automotive, P.O. Box 350, 411 S. Brunswick St., 64601, pg. 1378   PB

Clarence

Maytag Clarence Component Parts, P.O. Box 70, Old Hwy. 36, 63437, pg. 1064   PB

Clayton

Busch Entertainment Corp., 231 S. Bemiston, Ste. 600, 63105, pg. 114   PB
Commerce Bank, N.A., 8000 Forsyth, 63105, pg. 409   PB
County Realty Corp., 8000 Forsyth, 63105, pg. 409   PB
THE EARTHGRAINS COMPANY, 8400 Maryland Ave., 63105, pg. 547   PB
FIRST BANKS AMERICA, INC., 135 N. Meramec, 63105, pg. 626   PB
GRAYBAR ELECTRIC COMPANY, INC., 34 N. Meramec Ave., 63105, pg. 472   PV
St. Louis Countian, 7777 Bonhomme, Ste. 1205, 63105, pg. 513   PV
SITE OIL COMPANY OF MISSOURI, 50 S. Bemiston Ave., 63105, pg. 1004   PV
SPARTECH CORPORATION, 7733 Forsyth Blvd., Ste. 1450, 63105, pg. 1495   PB
TOBERMAN, 230 S. Bestien, Ste. 1440, 63105, pg. 1089   PV
Western International Media Corporation, The Sevens Bldg., 7777 Bonhomme Ave., Ste. 1720, 63105, pg. 1167   PV

Columbia

Charter Behavioral Health System of Columbia, Inc., 200 Portland St., 65201, pg. 1034   PB
Columbia House Healthcare, 1801 Towne Dr., 65202, pg. 1712   PB
MFA INCORPORATED, 201 Ray Young Dr., 65201, pg. 686   PV
MFA OIL COMPANY, One Ray Young Dr., 65201, pg. 687   PV
SHELTER MUTUAL INSURANCE COMPANY, 1817 W. Broadway, 65218, pg. 992   PV
Silvey Corporation, 3301 W. Broadway, 65201, pg. 543   IT

Square D Co., 4800 Paris Rd., 65202, pg. 1208   IT
TOASTMASTER, INC., 1801 N. Stadium Blvd., 65202, pg. 1619   PB
UPB of Mid-Missouri, 3111 S. Providence Rd., 65203, pg. 1669   PB
Watlow Columbia, Inc., 2101 Pennsylvania Dr., 65202, pg. 1153   PV

Concordia

T&W Disposal Co., RR 3 Box 111, 64020, pg. 49   PB

Creve Coeur

American Automobile Insurance Co., 727 Craig Rd., 63141, pg. 59   IT
Browning-Ferris Industries of St. Louis, Inc., 11506 Bowling Green, 63146, pg. 264   PB
ELDER MANUFACTURING COMPANY, 12747 Olive Rd., Ste. 300, 63141, pg. 367   PV
Hydro Conduit Corp., 11433 Bowling Green, 63146, pg. 245   PB
Intergraph Corporation, 701 Emerson Rd., Ste. 445, 63141, pg. 890   PB
Jeffco Land Reclamation, Inc., 11506 Bowling Green, 63141, pg. 264   PB

Cuba

Gypsum Firedoor Core Plant, Hwy. 19 So., P.O. Box N, 65453, pg. 737   PB
Midland Brake, Inc., 65453, pg. 561   PB

Des Peres

Colonial Bank, 12230 Manchester Rd., 63131, pg. 643   PB
Edison Fuse Gear, 11939 Manchester Rd., 63131, pg. 443   PB
Land Title Insurance Co. of St. Louis, 12360 Manchester, Ste. 100, 63131, pg. 626   PB

Desloge

SuperValu, Inc.-Desloge Div., 701 S. Main St., 63601, pg. 1540   PB

Dexter

Lemons Waste Systems Inc., Star Rte. Box 115, Hwy. 25, N., 63841, pg. 49   PB
Poplar Bluff Companies, Star Rte. Box 115, Hwy. 25, N., 63841, pg. 49   PB

Dixon

ALLTEL Missouri, Inc., 205 E. High School Dr., P.O. Box 250, 65459, pg. 56   PB

Earth City

DIAGRAPH CORPORATION, 3401 Rider Trail S., 63045-1110, pg. 330   PV
Everest & Jennings, Inc., 3601 Ridge Trail S., 63045, pg. 758   PB
Express Scripts Vision, 3801 Ultra Comp Dr., 63045, pg. 601   PB
Green Tree Acceptance, Inc., 502 Earth City Expwy., Ste. 139, 63045, pg. 762   PB
Earle M. Jorgensen Company/St. Louis, 3701 Rider Trail S., 63045, pg. 600   PV
National General Insurance Co., One National General Plaza, 63045, pg. 721   PB
National General Insurance Company, One National General Plaza, 63045, pg. 720   PB
Suntel Corp., 4203 Earth City Expwy., 63045, pg. 814   PB
YOUNG DENTAL MANUFACTURING, 13705 Shoreline E. Court, 63045, pg. 1201   PV

Ellisville

Bussmann Division, 114 Old State Rd., 63021-5942, pg. 443   PB
Gould Midwest, Inc., 1302 Clarkson/Clayton Ctr., Ste. 101, 63011, pg. 467   PB

Eureka

Six Flags St. Louis, I-44 & Allenton Rd., 63025, pg. 1612   PB

Excelsior Springs

AMERICAN ITALIAN PASTA COMPANY, 1000 Italian Way, 64024, pg. 85   PB
Douglas & Lomason Company, P.O. Box 187, 301 S. McCleary, 64024, pg. 830   IT
Gilmour Hose Company, 140 Corum Road, 64024, pg. 575   PB

Farmington

Daily Press Leader, 218 N. Washington, 63640, pg. 1343   PB
Iron Mountain Forge Corporation, P.O. Box 897, 63640, pg. 1411   PB
LeFebure Manufacturing Corporation, 1901 Progress Dr., 63640, pg. 387   IT

Trimfoot Company, 115 Trimfoot, 63640, pg. 1684   PB

Fenton

Atlas/Soundolier, 1859 Intertech Dr., 63026, pg. 64   PB
Binks Manufacturing Company, 1725 Larkin Williams Rd., 63026-2082, pg. 229   PB
Cardinal Systems, 100 Sun Valley Cir., 63026, pg. 1379   IT
CLAYTON CORPORATION, 866 Horan Dr., 63026-2416, pg. 244   PV
Clayton Metals Corp., 866 Horan Dr., 63026-2416, pg. 244   PV
Clayton Plastics Corp., 866 Horan Dr., 63026-2416, pg. 244   PV
Convenience Products, Inc., 866 Horan Dr., 63026-2416, pg. 244   PV
Fabick & Company, One Fabick Dr., 63026, pg. 390   PV
Fabick Brothers Equipment, One Fabick Dr., 63026, pg. 390   PV
JOHN FABICK TRACTOR COMPANY, One Fabick Dr., 63026, pg. 390   PV
Fabick Machinery, One Fabick Dr., 63026, pg. 390   PV
Fabick Tractor, One Fabick Dr., 63026, pg. 390   PV
Fleischmann's Yeast, 206 Fabricator Dr., 63026, pg. 237   IT
Industrial Waste Management,Inc., 271 Wolfner Dr., 63026, pg. 1279   PB
KOLLER ENTERPRISES, INC., 1400 S. Hwy. 141, 63026, pg. 631   PV
MARITZ INC., 1375 N. Highway Dr., 63099, pg. 703   PV
Maritz Marketing Research, Inc., 1297 N. Highway Dr., 63099, pg. 704   PV
Maritz Performance Improvement Company, 1400 S. Highway Dr., 63099, pg. 704   PV
Maritz Travel Co., 1395 N. Highway Dr., 63099, pg. 704   PV
Mayflower Transit, Inc., One Mayflower Dr., 63026, pg. 1117   PV
People's Choice-TV of St. Louis, Inc., 818 Horan Dr., 63026, pg. 1274   PB
RAWLINGS SPORTING GOODS COMPANY, 1859 Intertech Dr., 63026, pg. 1361   PB
Schreiber, Yonley & Associates, 271 Wolfner Dr., 63026, pg. 1280   PB
TACONY CORPORATION, 1760 Gilsinn Lane, 63026, pg. 1066   PV
UNIGROUP, INC., One United Dr., 63026, pg. 1117   PV
UniGroup Worldwide, Inc., P.O. Box 26150, 63026, pg. 1117   PV
United Leasing, Inc., One United Dr., 63026, pg. 1117   PV
United Van Lines, Inc., One United Dr., 63026, pg. 1117   PV
Vanliner Group, Inc., One United Dr., 63026, pg. 1117   PV
Vanliner Insurance Co., One United Dr., 63026, pg. 1117   PV

Festus

CENTRAL VALLEY PUBLISHING, 1400 W. Main St., 63028, pg. 225   PV
USMEDIA Group, 1400 W. Main St., 63028, pg. 225   PV

Florissant

DYWIDAG Systems International, USA, Inc., 5421 Trail Bend Dr., 63033, pg. 424   IT

Forsyth

NationsBank Tri-Lakes, Hwy. 160, 65653, pg. 1165   PB

Fredericktown

Democrat News, 131 S. Main, 63645, pg. 1343   PB

Fulton

DANUSER MACHINE CO., 500 E. Third, 65251, pg. 310   PV
Stride Rite Footwear, Inc., 820 State St., 65251, pg. 1525   PB

Gainesville

Hodgson Mill, Inc., HCR 1, Box 32-5, 65655, pg. 998   PV

Gladstone

Ceco Concrete Construction LLC, 2900 Brooktree Ln., Ste. 200, 64119, pg. 859   PV

Grain Valley

Harmon Industries-Grain Valley, Argo & Dillingham, 64029, pg. 788   PB

Grandview

ACCESS INDUSTRIES, 4001 E. 138th St., 64030, pg. 11   PV
American Ingredients Company, 13830 Botts Rd., 64030, pg. 244   IT
KING LOUIE INTERNATIONAL, 13500 15th St., 64030, pg. 621   PV
Metcraft, Inc., 13910 Kessler Dr., 64030, pg. 453   IT
Ruskin Div., 3900 Dr. Greaves Road, 64030, pg. 1398   IT

PB - *U.S. Public Companies Volume*
PV - *U.S. Private Companies Volume*
IT - *International Public & Private Companies Volume*

Geographic Index-U.S.

Swartwout Industries, 3900 Dr. Greaves Rd., 64030, pg. 1398 **IT**
TOROTEL, INC., 13402 S. 71 Hwy., 64030, pg. 1624 **PB**
Torotel Products, Inc., 13402 S. 71 Hwy., 64030, pg. 1624 **PB**

Grant City

Adcom of Iowa, Inc., Old Hwy. 169 N., 64456, pg. 1137 **PV**

Hamilton

Stride Rite Footwear, Inc., North Fram St., P.O. Box 188., 64644, pg. 1525 **PB**

Hannibal

Buckhorn Rubber Products Inc., P.O. Box 998, 5157 Industrial Dr., 63401, pg. 1143 **PB**
Cosmoflex, Inc., 4142 Industrial Ave., 63401, pg. 753 **PB**
The Hannibal Courier-Post, P.O. Box A, 200 N. 3rd St., 63401-3504, pg. 995 **PV**
Watlow Industries, Inc., Six Industrial Loop Dr., 63401, pg. 1153 **PV**

Hazelwood

Distribution Control Systems, Inc. (DCS), 5657 Campus Pkwy., 63045, pg. 546 **PV**
Hazelwood Farms Bakeries, Inc. 8840 Pershall Rd., 63042, pg. 1541 **PB**
Hunter/Krey Foods, 6038 N. Lindburgh Blvd., 63042, pg. 75 **PB**
Seven-Up Bottling Co. of St. Louis, 555 McDonell Blvd., 63042, pg. 142 **PV**
SuperValu, Inc.-Hazelwood Div., 7100 Hazelwood Ave., 63042, pg. 1540 **PB**
SuperValu, Inc.-St. Louis Div., 63042, pg. 1541 **PB**

Herculaneum

The Doe Run Company, 881 Main St., 63408, pg. 922 **PV**

Hermann

STEVEN MANUFACTURING CO., P.O. Box 170, 104 Industrial Dr., 65041, pg. 1042 **PV**

Independence

Atlas Systems, 3114 Weatherford Rd., 64055, pg. 511 **PV**
The Independence Examiner, P.O. Box 458, 410 S. Liberty, 64051-0458, pg. 995 **PV**
T.L. Smith Midwest, P.O. Box 1954, 3916 S. Lynn Ct., Ste. B, 60455, pg. 1009 **PV**

Jefferson City

Grocery Supply of Jefferson City, 2732 Merchants Dr., 65109, pg. 436 **PV**
Ikon Office Solutions-Jefferson City, 2211 St. Mary's Blvd., 65101, pg. 863 **PB**
Maytag/Jefferson City Component Parts, 1535 Fairground Rd., 65109, pg. 1064 **PB**
PENCO-Missouri, 1907 William St., 65109, pg. 1508 **IT**
Scholastic Inc. National Distribution Center, 2931 E. McCarthy Rd., 65101, pg. 1440 **PB**

Joplin

Allied Oil & Supply, P.O. 2247, I44 & Hwy 43- South 1 Mile, 64804, pg. 39 **PV**
AmeriSource-Joplin Div., 5th St. & Grand Ave., 64801, pg. 97 **PV**
The Counter Patch of Joplin, 3316 E. 32nd, Box 1330, 64802-1330, pg. 995 **PV**
CONTRACT FREIGHTERS, INC., 4701 E. 32nd St., 64804, pg. 270 **PV**
DOANE PRODUCTS CO., W. 20th & State Line Rd., 64804, pg. 337 **PV**
THE EMPIRE DISTRICT ELECTRIC COMPANY, 602 Joplin St., 64801, pg. 579 **PB**
Explo-Midwest, Inc., 2803 S. Rangeline, 64801, pg. 663 **IT**
Farmers Chemical Co., P.O. Box 225, 64802, pg. 396 **PV**
Fleming Foods of Missouri, Inc., 3001 Davis Blvd., 64801, pg. 653 **PB**
King Press Corporation, 13th & Maiden Ln., 64801, pg. 1341 **PB**
LaBarge, P.O. Box 1210, 64802-1210, pg. 973 **PB**
Midcon Cables Co., 2500 Davis Blvd., 64804, pg. 594 **PB**
Senior Engineering Co.-Joplin, P.O. Box 1385, 2702 W. 9th St., 64801, pg. 1222 **IT**
Stauffer Media Systems, Inc., 3316 East 32nd Street, 64802-1330, pg. 995 **PV**
TM Freight Brokers, P.O. Box 113, 64802, pg. 1101 **PV**
TRI-STATE MOTOR TRANSIT CO., E. Seventh St. Rd. & Business I-44, 64802, pg. 1101 **PV**

Kansas City

ACBJ Business Journals, Inc., 324 E. 11th St., Ste. 800, 64106, pg. 19 **PV**
AMC ENTERTAINMENT, INC., 106 W. 14th St., 64105, pg. 6 **PV**
AMF Bowling Centers Inc., 4555 E. Red Bridge Rd., 64131, pg. 7 **PV**

Alfa-Laval Agri, Inc., 11100 N. Congress Ave., 64153, pg. 1378 **IT**
Allied Oil & Supply, Inc., 200 E. 14th Ave., 64116, pg. 39 **PV**
Allied Security Inc., 3515 Broadway, Ste. 203, 64111, pg. 40 **PV**
Allright Carpark, Inc., 1221 Baltimore, Ste. 300, 64105, pg. 42 **PV**
American Cablevision of Kansas City, Inc., P.O. Box 5454, 64131, pg. 1610 **PB**
AMERICAN CENTURY COMPANIES, INC., 4500 Main St., 64111, pg. 52 **PV**
American Century Investments, 4500 Main St., Ste. 1500, 64111, pg. 52 **PV**
American Ingredients Company, 3947 Broadway, 64111, pg. 244 **IT**
AMERICAN MARKETING INDUSTRIES, INC., 10450 Holmes Rd., 64131, pg. 58 **PV**
American Multi-Cinema, Inc., 106 W. 14th St., 64105, pg. 6 **PV**
AMICO-Riverside, 601 N.W. Business Park Lane, 64150, pg. 30 **PV**
Arrowhead Containers Inc., 5301 E. Front St., 64120, pg. 1017 **PV**
BHA Company, Inc., 8800 E. 63rd St., 64133, pg. 161 **PV**
BHA GROUP HOLDINGS INC., 8800 E. 63rd St., 64133, pg. 161 **PV**
BMA Resources, Inc., One Penn Valley Park, BMA Tower, P.O. Box 419949, 64141, pg. 1449 **PB**
BMA Selectcare, Inc., BMA Tower, One Penn Valley Park, 64108, pg. 90 **IT**
BMC Real Estate, Inc., 31st & Southwest Trafficway, 64108, pg. 271 **PB**
BV&K Direct, The Congress Bldg., 3535 Broadway #200, 64111, pg. 108 **PV**
BARKLEY & EVERGREEN ADVERTISING, INC., 423 W. Eighth, 64105, pg. 116 **PV**
Barkley Evergreen & Partners Public Relations, 423 W. 8th St., Ste. 700, 64105, pg. 116 **PV**
BARTLETT AND COMPANY, 4800 Main St., Ste. 600, 64112, pg. 118 **PV**
BARTON NELSON INC., 13700 Wyandotte, 64145, pg. 120 **PV**
Bayer Corporation/Agriculture Division, 8400 Hawthorn Rd., 64120-2306, pg. 173 **IT**
Bergen Brunswig Drug Company, 1501 Southern Rd., P.O. Box 34311, 64120, pg. 214 **PB**
BERNSTEIN-REIN ADVERTISING, INC., 4600 Madison, Ste. 1500, 64112, pg. 137 **PV**
BLACK & VEATCH, 8400 Ward Pkwy., 64114-2031, pg. 146 **PV**
Black & Veatch International-Energy, P.O. Box 8405, 64114, pg. 146 **PV**
Bucon, Inc., 7400 E. 13th St., 64126, pg. 271 **PV**
Buildings Division, P.O. Box 8405, 64114, pg. 146 **PV**
BURD & FLETCHER COMPANY, 321 W. Seventh St., 64105, pg. 181 **PV**
BURNS & MCDONNELL ENGINEERS-ARCHITECTS-CONSULTANTS, 9400 Ward Pkwy., 64114, pg. 187 **PV**
Burns & McDonnell Waste Consultants, Inc., 9400 Ward Pkwy., 64114, pg. 187 **PV**
Business Men's Assurance Company of America, BMA Tower, One Penn Valley Park, 64108, pg. 90 **IT**
Butler Buildings Division, BMA Tower, Penn Valley Park, 64108, pg. 271 **PB**
BUTLER MANUFACTURING COMPANY, BMA Tower, Penn Valley Park, 64141-0917, pg. 271 **PB**
Butler Real Estate, P.O. Box 419917, 64141, pg. 271 **PB**
CBI Insurance Co., 1000 Walnut, 64106, pg. 410 **PB**
Capital for Business, Inc., 1000 Walnut, 64106, pg. 410 **PB**
Carland, Inc., 1055 Broadway, Ste. 990, 64105, pg. 944 **PB**
CARTER COMPANIES, 100 Northwest Pkwy., 64150, pg. 216 **PV**
A.M. Castle & Co., 6100 Stilwell Ave., 64120, pg. 313 **PB**
CERNER CORPORATION, 2800 Rockcreek Pkwy., 64117, pg. 331 **PB**
Cerner Corporation -Midwest Region, 2702 Rockcreek Pkwy., Ste. 200, 64117-2534, pg. 331 **PB**
CHEMCENTRAL/Kansas City, 910 No. Prospect Ave., 64120-1685, pg. 232 **PV**
Circle Freight International USA, 9701 N. Conant Ave., 64153, pg. 371 **PB**
CLARKSON CONSTRUCTION COMPANIES, 4133 Gardner Ave., 64120, pg. 244 **PV**
Colony Paints, 912 Baltimore, Ste. 1000, 64105, pg. 1707 **PB**
COMMERCE BANCSHARES, INC., 1000 Walnut St., 64106, pg. 409 **PB**
Commerce Bank N.A., 1000 Walnut, 64106, pg. 409 **PB**
Commerce Brokerage Services, Inc., 1000 Walnut, 64106, pg. 410 **PB**
Commerce Property & Casualty Agency, Inc., 1000 Walnut, 64106, pg. 410 **PB**
CONCORDE CAREER COLLEGES, INC., City Center Sq., 12th & Baltimore, 64196, pg. 430 **PB**
Consumer Services Group, 8140 Ward Pkwy., 64114, pg. 1501 **PB**
The Continuum Company, Inc., 301 W. 11th, 64105, pg. 422 **PB**
CONTRACTORS SUPPLY COMPANY, INC., 800 E. 18th St., 64108, pg. 270 **PV**
Cook Composites & Polymers Inc., 820 E. 14th Ave., 64116-6389, pg. 1409 **IT**
The Cooperative Finance Assn., Inc., 10100 N. Executive Hilla Blvd., Ste. 100, 64153, pg. 396 **PV**
Cottons Bread Bakeries, 12 E. Armour Blvd., 64141, pg. 909 **PB**
Crown Power & Redevelopment Corp., 2405 Grand, Ste. 200, 64108, pg. 496 **PV**
DST Realty, Inc., 104 Baltimore Ave., 64105, pg. 943 **PB**

DST Securities, Inc., 1055 Broadway St., 64105, pg. 943 **PB**
DST Systems, Inc., 1055 Broadway St., 64105, pg. 943 **PB**
DAVIS PAINT COMPANY, 1311 Iron St., 64116, pg. 315 **PV**
DEAN OPERATIONS INC., 1201 W. 31st St., 64108, pg. 318 **PV**
DEBRUCE GRAIN INC., 2702 Rockcreek Pkwy., Ste. 400, 64117, pg. 319 **PV**
DeVRY Institute of Technology, 11224 Holmes Rd., 64131, pg. 504 **PB**
DODSON GROUP, 9201 State Line Rd., 64114, pg. 338 **PV**
Dolly Madison Bakeries, 12 E. Armour Blvd., 64141, pg. 909 **PB**
DUNN INDUSTRIES INC., 929 Holmes, 64106, pg. 347 **PV**
J.E. Dunn Construction Co., 929 Holmes, 64106, pg. 347 **PV**
J.E. Dunn Equities, Inc., 929 Holmes, 64106, pg. 347 **PV**
Dunn Realty, Inc., 929 Holmes, 64106, pg. 347 **PV**
Empire Candle, Inc., 2100 Broadway, 67108, pg. 330 **PV**
Environmental Specialists, Inc., 3001 E. 83rd St., 641321, pg. 1379 **PV**
FARMLAND INDUSTRIES, INC., 3315 N. Oak Trafficway, 64116, pg. 395 **PV**
Farmland Industries U.K. Ltd., 3315 N. Oak Trafficway, 64116, pg. 396 **PV**
Fiduciary Trust Co. of New Hampshire, 2400 Pershing Rd., 64018, pg. 1623 **PB**
Fixtures Furniture, 1642 Crystal, 64126, pg. 581 **PV**
Fleishman-Hillard, Inc., 2405 Grand Blvd., #700, 64108-2522, pg. 411 **PV**
Fortis Benefits Insurance Company, 2323 Grand Blvd., 64108, pg. 499 **IT**
Frederick Manufacturing Corporation, 4840 E. 12th St., 64127, pg. 238 **PB**
Funeral Security Plans, Inc., 1331 Brush Creek Blvd., 64110, pg. 796 **PV**
GALAMET, INC., 3005 Manchester, 64129, pg. 437 **PV**
Garney Companies, Inc., 1331 N.W. Vivion Rd., 64118-4554, pg. 440 **PV**
GARNEY HOLDING COMPANY, INC., 1331 N.W. Vivion Rd., 64118-4554, pg. 440 **PV**
GOLDEN STAR INC., 400 E. Tenth Ave., 64116, pg. 460 **PV**
Grain Systems Division, 7400 E. 13th St., 64126, pg. 271 **PB**
H & R BLOCK, INC., 4400 Main St., 64111, pg. 770 **PB**
HNTB CORPORATION, 1201 Walnut, Ste. 700, 64106, pg. 492 **PV**
HALLMARK CARDS, INC., 2501 McGee, 64108, pg. 495 **PV**
Hallmark International, P.O. Box 419580, 2501 McGee, 64141-6580, pg. 496 **PV**
Halls Merchandising Inc., 200 E. 25th St., 64108, pg. 496 **PV**
Havens Erectors, 7219 E. 17th St., 64126, pg. 511 **PV**
HAVENS STEEL CO., 7219 E. 17th St., 64126, pg. 510 **PV**
Helzberg's Diamond Shops, Inc., 1825 Swift Ave., 64116-3606, pg. 220 **PB**
Hewlett-Packard Company, 6601 Westchester Ave., 64133, pg. 814 **PB**
Hoechst-Marion-Rousell, Marion Park Drive, 64137, pg. 625 **IT**
Hoechst Marion Roussel North America, P.O. Box 9627, 10236 Marion Park Dr., 64134-0627, pg. 625 **IT**
Holsum Bread Bakeries, 12 E. Armour Blvd., 64141, pg. 909 **PB**
HOULIHAN'S RESTAURANT GROUP, Two Brush Creek Blvd., 64112, pg. 841 **PV**
Humana Insurance Company, 10450 Holmes St., Ste. 330, 64131, pg. 848 **PV**
Hydro Conduit Corp., P.O. Box 9187, N.W. Rte. 9 & Van de Populaire Rd., 64168, pg. 245 **IT**
Infrastructure Business, P.O. Box 8405, 64114, pg. 146 **PV**
INTERSTATE BAKERIES CORPORATION, P.O. Box 409627, 64141-6627, pg. 909 **PB**
Interstate Brands Corporation, 12 E. Armour Blvd., 64111, pg. 909 **PB**
Interstate Corp., 12 E. Armour Blvd., 64141, pg. 909 **PB**
Investors Fiduciary Trust Company, 127 W. 10th St., 64105-1716, pg. 1513 **PB**
Jones & Babson, Inc., 2440 Pershing Rd., 64108, pg. 90 **IT**
The Jones Store Co., 1201 Main, 64105, pg. 1090 **PV**
Earle M. Jorgensen Company/Kansas City, 1701 W. 25th, 64108, pg. 600 **PV**
KLT Energy Services Inc., P.O. Box 410192, 64141, pg. 943 **PB**
KLT Gas, Inc., P.O. Box 410225, 64141, pg. 943 **PB**
KLT Inc., P.O. Box 410233, 64141, pg. 943 **PB**
KLT Investments, P.O. Box 410225, 64141, pg. 943 **PB**
KLT Power Inc., P.O. Box 410225, 64141, pg. 943 **PB**
KLT Telecom Inc., P.O. Box 410225, 64141, pg. 943 **PB**
KMBC Division, 1049 Central St., 64105, pg. 516 **PV**
KMBC-TV, 1049 Central St., 64105, pg. 516 **PV**
KSHB-TV, 4720 Oak St., 64112, pg. 1448 **PV**
Kansas City Auto Auction, 3901 N. Great Midwest Dr., 64161, pg. 282 **PV**
KANSAS CITY CHIEFS FOOTBALL CLUB, INC., One Arrowhead Dr., 64129, pg. 607 **PV**
KANSAS CITY LIFE INSURANCE CO., 3520 Broadway, 64111-2565, pg. 942 **PB**
KANSAS CITY POWER & LIGHT COMPANY, 1201 Walnut St., 64106-2124, pg. 943 **PB**
Kansas City Recycling Center, 136 Main St., 64105, pg. 1378 **PB**
Kansas City Royals Radio Network, P.O. Box 419969, 64141, pg. 995 **PV**

PB - *U.S. Public Companies Volume*
PV - *U.S. Private Companies Volume*
IT - *International Public & Private Companies Volume*

1302

Geographic Index-U.S.

KANSAS CITY SOUTHERN INDUSTRIES, INC., 114 W. 11th St., 64105-1804, pg. 943
The Kansas City Southern Railway Co., Marketing Dept., 114 W. 11th St., 64105, pg. 944 **PB**
The Kansas City Star Company, 1729 Grand Blvd., 64108, pg. 964 **PB**
Kansas City Terminal Railway Co., 3435 Broadway, 64111, pg. 1668 **PB**
Keller Graduate School of Management, City Center Sq., 1100 Main St., Ste. 303, 64105, pg. 504 **PB**
KOCH SUPPLIES INC., 1411 W. 29th St., 64108, pg. 628 **PV**
Landa Motor Lines, 114 W. 11th St., 64105, pg. 944 **PB**
Lilly Industries, Inc., 1136 Fayette St., 64116, pg. 995 **PB**
Long Distance International, 8140 Ward Pkwy., 64114, pg. 1501 **PB**
Mangum Mfg. Co. of Missouri, Inc., 1137 Salin, 64116, pg. 46 **PB**
Mark Risk Management, Inc., Ste. 200, 10100 N.W. Executive Hills Blvd., pg. 1046 **PB**
Mark VII Transportation Solutions, Inc., Ste. 200, 10100 N.W. Executive Hills Blvd., 64153, pg. 1046 **PB**
MASSMAN CONSTRUCTION COMPANY, 8901 State Line Rd., 64114, pg. 713 **PV**
Media Recovery Inc.-Missouri, 8511 Hillcrest, Suite 230, 64138, pg. 727 **PV**
Merita Bread Bakeries, 12 E. Armour Blvd., 64141, pg. 909 **PB**
MicroAge Solutions, Inc. (MAS), 452 Ward Pkwy., 64112, pg. 1105 **PB**
Mid-America Financial Corp., 1000 Walnut, 64106, pg. 410 **PB**
Mid-South Microwave, Inc., 114 W. 11th St., 64105, pg. 944 **PB**
Midland Brake, Inc., 8600 N.E. Underground Dr., Ste. 200, 64161, pg. 561 **PB**
Midland Color Company, 6455 Universal Ave., 64120, pg. 1311 **IT**
MIDWAY FORD TRUCK CENTER INC., 7601 N.E. 38th St., 64161, pg. 744 **PV**
Millbrook Bread Bakeries, 12 E. Armour Blvd., 64141, pg. 909 **PB**
Miller Automation, Inc. (MO), 3950 N.E. 33rd Terr., Ste. One, 64117, pg. 867 **PB**
Missouri Gas Energy, 3420 Broadway, 64111, pg. 1491 **PB**
Missouri Public Service, 10700 E. 350 Hwy., 64138, pg. 1701 **PB**
Moline Accessories Corporation, 430 W. Seventh St., 64105, pg. 746 **IT**
Monark Egg Corporation, 601 E. Third St., 64106, pg. 1104 **PB**
NATIONAL FARMS INC., 1600 Genessee St., 64102, pg. 782 **PV**
NationsBank of Kansas City, 10th & Baltimore, 64183, pg. 1164 **PB**
The Network of City Business Journals, Inc., 3535 Broadway, 64111, pg. 19 **PB**
D.W. NEWCOMER'S SONS, INC., 1331 Brush Creek Blvd., 64110, pg. 796 **PV**
Nofsinger, Inc., 9400 Ward Pkwy., 64114, pg. 187 **PV**
Northwest PARS, Inc., 7300 Tiffany Springs Pkwy., 64153, pg. 1200 **PB**
NuArc Co., 301 W. Armour Blvd., 64111, pg. 809 **PV**
Old American Insurance Co., 3520 Broadway, 64111, pg. 943 **PB**
Outdoor Systems, Inc.-Kansas City, 2459 Summit St., 64108, pg. 1235 **PB**
Output Technologies SRI Group, Inc., 2450 Summit, 64108, pg. 944 **PB**
Pabtex, Inc., 1055 Broadway. Ste. 990, 64105, pg. 944 **PB**
PACKAGE SERVICE COMPANY, LLC., 851 N.W. 45th St., Ste. 310, 64116, pg. 833 **PV**
PANACO, INC., 1050 W. Blue Ridge Blvd., 64145-1216, pg. 1255 **PV**
Frank Paxton Company, 6311 St. John Ave., 64123, pg. 585 **PV**
Frank Paxton Lumber Company, 6311 St. John Ave., 64123, pg. 585 **PV**
PAYLESS CASHWAYS, INC., 2300 Main St., P.O. Box 419466, 64108, pg. 1267 **PB**
Perma-Fix of Kansas City, 5951 Manchester Trafficway, 64130, pg. 1280 **PB**
Piper Jaffray Inc., 4600 Madison Ave., Ste. 1200, 64112-3025, pg. 1301 **PB**
Pollenex, 800 E. 101 Ter., 64131, pg. 1391 **PB**
Power Business, P.O. Box 8405, 64114, pg. 146 **PV**
PrecipTech, Inc., 8800 E. 63rd St., 64133, pg. 161 **PB**
Principal Health Care of Kansas City, Inc., 1001 E. 101st Terr., Ste. 300, 64143, pg. 885 **PV**
Red Hill Coal Co., 1201 Walnut, 64105, pg. 943 **PB**
revolution, inc., 911 Main St., Ste. 1000, 64105, pg. 1131 **PV**
Reynolds Metals Company-Kansas City, Executive Park, 1800 Reynolds Ave., 64120, pg. 1385 **PB**
Rice-Carden Corp., 114 W. 11th St., 64105, pg. 944 **PB**
THE RIVAL COMPANY, 800 E. 101 Ter., Ste. 100, 64131, pg. 1391 **PB**
RUSSELL STOVER CANDIES, INC., 1000 Walnut St., 64106, pg. 953 **PV**
SCHUTTE LUMBER COMPANY, 3001 Southwest Blvd., 64108, pg. 973 **PV**
SEAFIELD CAPITAL CORPORATION, 2600 Grand Ave., Ste. 500, 64141, pg. 1449 **PB**
Shared Services Division, 8400 Ward Pkwy, 64114-2031, pg. 146 **PV**
Shawver Price, Inc., 1423 Swift, 64116, pg. 511 **PV**
Signboard Hill Productions, 2501 McGee, 64108, pg. 496 **PV**
SIMONDS-SHIELDS-THEIS GRAIN CO., 4800 Main St., Ste. 401, 64112, pg. 1001 **PV**

Southern Development Co., 114 W. 11th St., 64105, pg. 944 **PB**
Southern Group, Inc., 1055 Broadway, Ste. 990, 64105, pg. 944 **PB**
Southern Leasing of Kansas City, Inc., 1055 Broadway, Ste. 990, 64105, pg. 944 **PB**
Sprint PCS, 4900 Main St., 64112, pg. 1501 **PB**
Standard Havens, 8800 E. 63rd St., 64133, pg. 1365 **PB**
Stuart Hall Co., Inc., 5414 Front St., 64120, pg. 1178 **PB**
SUTHERLAND LUMBER CO., 4000 Main St., 64111, pg. 1057 **PB**
Swingster Company, 10450 Holmes Rd., 64131, pg. 58 **PV**
Tanabe-Marion Laboratories, 9300 Ward Pkwy., 64114, pg. 1354 **IT**
TENSION ENVELOPE CORP., 819 E. 19th St., 64108-1781, pg. 1077 **PV**
Titan Sales Corp., 800 E. 101 Ter., 64131, pg. 1391 **PB**
Tolmak, Inc., 114 W. 11th St., 64105, pg. 944 **PB**
TOPSY'S INTERNATIONAL INC., 221 W. 74th Terrace, 64114, pg. 1092 **PV**
Transilwrap Co., Inc., 4231 E. 75th Terrace, 64132, pg. 1097 **PB**
Turner Construction Company, 1627 Main St., Ste. 400, 64108, pg. 1645 **PB**
Two Rivers Psychiatric Hospital, 5121 Raytown Rd., 64133, pg. 1697 **PB**
UMB FINANCIAL CORPORATION, 1010 Grand Ave., 64106, pg. 1653 **PB**
UMB Properties, Inc., 1010 Grand Ave., 64141, pg. 1655 **PB**
THE UHLMANN CO., 1009 Central, 64105, pg. 1115 **PV**
United Brake Systems, Inc., 8600 N.E. Underground Dr., Pillar #203, 64161, pg. 561 **PB**
United Investors Management Company, 2400 Pershing Rd., 64141, pg. 1623 **PB**
United Missouri Brokerage Services, P.O. Box 419232, 64161, pg. 1655 **PB**
United Missouri Capital Corporation, 1010 Grand Ave., 64106, pg. 1655 **PB**
United Missouri Insurance Co., 1010 Grand Ave., 64141, pg. 1655 **PB**
United Missouri Leasing Corporation, 1010 Grand Ave., 64106, pg. 1655 **PB**
United Missouri Mortgage Company, 1010 Grand Ave., 64106, pg. 1655 **PB**
UNITOG COMPANY, 101 W. 11th St., 64105, pg. 1693 **PB**
Unitog Rental Facility, 1735 Cherry St., 64105, pg. 1693 **PB**
Universal Dairy Equipment, Inc., 11100 N. Congress Ave., 64153, pg. 1379 **IT**
UTILICORP UNITED INC., 20 W. 9th St., 64105, pg. 1700 **PV**
VALENTINE RADFORD, INC., 911 Main St., Ste. 1000, 64105, pg. 1131 **PV**
W & R Insurance Agency, Inc. of Alabama, Inc., 2400 Pershing Rd., 64108, pg. 1623 **PB**
W & R Insurance Agency, Inc. of Massachusetts, Inc., 2400 Pershing Rd., 64108, pg. 1623 **PB**
W & R Insurance Agency, Inc. of Montana, Inc., 2400 Pershing Rd., 64108, pg. 1623 **PB**
W & R Insurance Agency, Inc. of Nevada, Inc., 2400 Pershing Rd., 64108, pg. 1623 **PB**
W & R Insurance Agency, Inc. of Utah. Inc., 2400 Pershing Rd., 64108, pg. 1623 **PB**
W & R Insurance Agency, Inc. of Wyoming, Inc., 2400 Pershing Rd., 64108, pg. 1623 **PB**
Wabash Fibre Box Company, 4343 Clary Blvd., 64130, pg. 1170 **PV**
Waddell & Reed Asset Mngmt. Co., 2400 Pershing Rd., 64108, pg. 1623 **PB**
Waddell & Reed Investment Mngmt. Co., 2400 Pershing Rd., 64018, pg. 1623 **PB**
Waddell & Reed Services Co., 2400 Pershing Rd., 64108, pg. 1623 **PB**
Waverly Products Co., 800 E. 101 Ter., 64131, pg. 1391 **PB**
Waverly Products Co., Ltd., 800 E. 101 Ter., 64131, pg. 1391 **PB**
Weber's Bread Bakeries, 12 E. Armour Blvd., 64141, pg. 909 **PB**
West Agro, Inc., 11110 N. Congress Ave., 64153, pg. 1379 **PV**
Western Auto Supply Company, 2107 Grand Bldv., 64108, pg. 1452 **PB**
Western International Media Corporation, 1 Ward Parkway Bldg., 1 Ward Pkwy., Ste. 106, 64112, pg. 1167 **PV**
WESTFALL GMC TRUCK INC., 3915 N.E. Randolph Rd., 64161, pg. 1169 **PV**
Whitman's Candies, Inc., 1000 Walnut St., Ste. 700, 64106, pg. 953 **PV**
Wholesale Services Group, 8140 Ward Pkwy., 64114, pg. 247 **IT**
Wholesale Services Group, 8140 Ward Pkwy., 64114, pg. 1501 **PB**
Wilcox Electric, Inc., 2001 N.E. 46th St., 64116, pg. 1384 **IT**
H.R. Williams Inc., pg. 1078 **PV**
WOLCOTT & LINCOLN, INC., 4800 Main St., Ste. 565, 64112, pg. 1185 **PV**
Worlds of Fun & Oceans of Fun, 4545 Worlds of Fun Ave., 64161, pg. 319 **PB**
Wymo Fuels Inc., 1201 Walnut, 64106-2124, pg. 943 **PB**
XEBEC CORPORATION, 5612 Brighton Ter., 64130, pg. 1194 **PV**

Kearney

Variform, Inc., 303 W. Major, 64060, pg. 1193 **PB**

Kennett

Barton's of Kennett, South By-Pass, 63857, pg. 119 **PV**
Kelley Electric Company, P.O. Box 428, 63857, pg. 453 **PV**

Kingsville

STAHL SPECIALTY COMPANY, 111 E. Pacific St., 64061, pg. 1029 **PV**

Kirkwood

METALTECH, INC., 206 Prospect Ave., 63122, pg. 735 **PV**
Shop 'n Save Warehouse Foods, Inc., 10461 Manchester Rd., 63122, pg. 1541 **PB**

La Grange

La Grange Foundry Inc., 700 N. Main, 63448, pg. 142 **PB**

Lamar

O'SULLIVAN INDUSTRIES HOLDINGS, 1900 Gulf St., 64759, pg. 1234 **PB**

Lebanon

ALL STAR GAS CORPORATION, 1700 S. Jefferson St., 65536, pg. 35 **PV**
All Star Gas Field Services, P.O. Box 303, 65536, pg. 35 **PV**
All Star Gas, Inc., 1700 S. Jefferson St., 65536, pg. 35 **PV**
All Star Gas Transports (MO), P.O. Box 303, 65536, pg. 36 **PV**
Carl A. Lowe Industries, Inc., Interstate 44, P.O. Box 989, 65536, pg. 478 **PV**
NationsBank of Lebanon, 104 N. Jefferson, 65536, pg. 1164 **PB**
Sea Nymph Inc., 2900 Industrial Dr., 65536, pg. 478 **PV**

Lees Summit

Aichelin-Stalh, Inc., 810 C N.W. Main St., 64086, pg. 1029 **PV**
Auction Transport Inc., 1100 S.E. Hamblen Rd., 64081, pg. 1648 **PB**
Farmers Insurance Group, 401 S.W. Oldham Pkwy. Ste. 202, 64081-2700, pg. 111 **IT**
Harmon Industries-Lees Summit, Lakewood Bus. Ctr., 624 N.E. Jones Industrial Dr., 64064, pg. 788 **PB**
Laboratory Supply Company, 1009A N.E. Jib Ct., 64064, pg. 642 **PV**
Metro Auto Auction of Kansas City, Inc., 101 SW Oldham Pkwy., 64081, pg. 1649 **PB**
Piper Jaffray Inc., 609 N.E. Hwy. 291, Ste. 230, 64086-2548, pg. 1301 **PB**

Lexington

NationsBank River Valley, 1016 Main St., 64067, pg. 1164 **PB**

Liberty

Banta Publications Group, 3401 Heartland Dr., 64068-0298, pg. 188 **PB**
FAMILY SMACKS, INC., 405 S. Leonard St., 64068, pg. 393 **PV**
FERRELLGAS PARTNERS, L.P., One Liberty Plaza, 64068, pg. 618 **PV**
XTRA-Intermodal Division, 8 Victory Ln., 64068, pg. 1787 **PB**

Louisiana

Allparts, Inc., 20151 Hwy. UU, 63353, pg. 919 **PB**
Aqualon-Louisiana, Hwy. 79 at County Rd. D, 63353-0429, pg. 810 **PB**

Malden

Barton's of Malden, 802 N. Douglas, 63863, pg. 119 **PV**

Manchester

Bank Building, 13537 Barrett Parkway Dr., Ste. 215, 63021, pg. 407 **PV**
Clayton House Healthcare, 1251 E. Clayton Rd., 63011, pg. 1712 **PB**
Financial Research Associates, 13537 Barrett Pkwy. Dr., Ste. 215, 63021, pg. 407 **PV**
FIRST FINANCIAL BUILDING CORPORATION, 13537 Barrett Pkwy. Dr., Ste. 215, 63021, pg. 407 **PV**

Mansfield

Mans-Steel Div., P.O. Box 137, 65704, pg. 550 **PV**
Mans-Steel Foundry, P.O. Box 137, 65704, pg. 550 **PV**

Marceline

Herff Jones Yearbooks, 726 E. Gracia, 64658, pg. 524 **PV**

PB - *U.S. Public Companies Volume*
PV - *U.S. Private Companies Volume*
IT - *International Public & Private Companies Volume*

Geographic Index-U.S.

Geographic Index-U.S.

WALSWORTH PUBLISHING COMPANY, INC., 306 N. Kansas, 64658, pg. 1148   PV

Marshall

NationsBank of Marshall, 102 E. Arrow St., 65340, pg. 1164   PB

Maryland Heights

Accent Furniture, Inc., 2440 Adie Rd., 63043, pg. 949   PV
Alco Controls Div., 11911 Adie Rd., 63141, pg. 572   PB
Boyd Flotation, Inc, 2440 Adie Rd., 63043, pg. 949   PV
CHEMCENTRAL/St. Louis, 2646 Metro Blvd., 63043, pg. 232   PV
CLARK DOOR CO., INC., 2564 Metro Blvd., 63043, pg. 242   PV
Cott Corporation - North Central Region, 2525 Schuetz Road, 63043, pg. 337   IT
Cott Vending, 11558 Rock Island Road, 63043, pg. 338   IT
EXPRESS SCRIPTS, INC., 14000 Riverport Dr., 63043, pg. 600   PB
FORD STEEL CO., INC., 2475 Rock Island Blvd., 63043, pg. 418   PV
Forest Pharmaceuticals, Inc., 2510 Metro Blvd., 63043, pg. 670   PV
FRED WEBER, INC., 2320 Creve Coeur Mill Rd., 63043, pg. 424   PV
GREY EAGLE DISTRIBUTORS INC., 2340 Millpark Dr., 63043, pg. 480   PV
IVTx, 14000 Riverport Dr., 63043, pg. 601   PB
Jani King of St. Louis, Inc., 2337 Welding Pkwy., 63043, pg. 582   PV
Midwest Employer's Casualty Company, 13801 Riverport Dr., Ste. 200, 63043-4810, pg. 215   PB
Practice Patterns Science, 14000 Riverport Dr., 63043, pg. 601   PB
RS Electronics, 2555 Metro Blvd., 63043, pg. 905   PV
ROYAL WATERBEDS, 2440 Adie Rd., 63043, pg. 949   PV
J.D. STREETT & CO., INC., 144 Weldon Pkwy., 63043, pg. 1047   PV
Sverdrup Civil, Inc., 13723 Riverport Dr., 63043, pg. 1057   PV
SVERDRUP CORPORATION, 13723 Riverport Dr., 63043, pg. 1057   PV
Sverdrup Environmental Inc., 13723 Riverport Dr., 63043, pg. 1057   PV
Sverdrup Investments, Inc., 13723 Riverport Dr., 63043, pg. 1057   PV

Maryville

Laclede Chain Manufacturing Plant, 2500 E. First St., 64468, pg. 974   PB
New England Business Service, 200 E. South Ave., 64468, pg. 1171   PB

Mexico

Biocraft Bulk Manufacturing, 5000 Christopher Dr., 65265, pg. 1381   IT
A.P. GREEN INDUSTRIES, INC., Green Blvd., 65265, pg. 761   PB
Lefebure Manufacturing Corporation, 1600 Bassford Dr., 65265, pg. 387   IT

Moberly

MID-AM BUILDING SUPPLY, INC., 1615 Oman Bradley Dr., 65270, pg. 743   PV

Monett

BankVision Software, Ltd., 6663 Hwy. 60, 65708, pg. 809   PB
EFCO CORPORATION, 1000 County Rd., 65708, pg. 353   PV
JACK HENRY & ASSOCIATES, INC., P.O. Box 807, 663 Hwy. 60, 65708, pg. 808   PB
Jack Henry International, 663 Hwy. 60, 65708, pg. 809   PB
Jumping Jacks, 601 13th St., 65708, pg. 767   PV
MIRACLE RECREATION EQUIPMENT COMPANY, Hwy. 60 & Bridal Ln., 65708, pg. 752   PV

Monroe City

DIEMAKERS, INC., 801 Second St., 63456, pg. 332   PV
Monroe City Division, 135 Front St., 63456, pg. 986   PB
United Missouri Bank Northeast, 201 N. Main St., 63456, pg. 1654   PB

Montgomery City

Alliance Heater Company, 1040 Industrial Park Dr., 63361, pg. 1153   PV

Mountain Grove

NationsBank Mountain Grove, 111 Maple St., 65711, pg. 1164   PB
RICHARDS BROTHERS OF MOUNTAIN GROVE, P.O. Box 866, 65711, pg. 928   PV

Neosho

La-Z-Boy Midwest, 4301 Howard Bush Dr., 64850, pg. 973   PB

Pace Industries Inc., 3700 Howard Bush Dr., 64850, pg. 986   PB

Nevada

NationsBank of Nevada, Cherry & Main Sts., 64772, pg. 1164   PB

New London

New London Telephone Company, 501 S. Main St., 63459, pg. 1571   PB

North Kansas City

DWF o North Kansas City, 21 W. 13th Ave., 64116, pg. 926   PV
Ensley Tool Co. Inc., 420 E. 10th Ave., 64116, pg. 129   IT
Folding Carton (Kansas City), 110 E. 10th Ave., 64116, pg. 270   IT
Hamilton Lamp Corp., 1836 Levee Rd., 64116, pg. 354   PB
THERMAL TECHNOLOGY INDUSTRIES, 1321 Burlington, 64116, pg. 1080   PV
Zellerbach Division, 1307 Vernon St., 64116, pg. 1075   PB

O Fallon

Hitchiner Mfg. Co., Inc., E. Terra & Cannonball Lane, P.O. Box 220, 63366, pg. 531   PV
VENTURE STORES, INC., 2001 E. Terra Ln., 63366-0110, pg. 1716   PB

Oak Grove

Oak Grove Publications, Inc., 1218 Broadway, 64075, pg. 995   PV

Overland

UtilCo Group, 7400 W. 110th St., Ste. 320, 66210, pg. 1701   PB

Pacific

Folding Carton (Pacific), 1101 S. Denton, 63069, pg. 270   IT
Pacific Heater Corporation, 115 Flier Dr., 63069, pg. 1153   PV

Park Hills

The Daily Journal, 1513 St. Joe Dr., 63601, pg. 1343   PB

Perryville

Solar Communications, 1205 Corporation La., 63775, pg. 1012   PV

Pevely

Silgan Containers, 8750 Pevely Industrial Dr., 63070, pg. 1473   PB

Pleasant Hill

Chucks Disposal Company, 209 Cedar, 64080, pg. 49   PB

Poplar Bluff

Gates Rubber Co. Inc., 1650 Rowe Pkwy., 63901-7014, pg. 1395   IT
PEC Moark, Rt. 13, Box 1, 63901, pg. 871   PV

Portageville

Barton's o Portageville, 712 Hwy. 61 N., 63873, pg. 119   PV

Richland

NationsBank of Pulaski County, 65556, pg. 1164   PB

Richmond

NationsBank of River Valley, Thornton & Main Sts., 64085, pg. 1164   PB
RAY-CARROLL COUNTY GRAIN CO-OP, 807 W. Main St., 64085, pg. 911   PV

Saint Ann

Union-Transport Corporation-Saint Louis Office, 500 NW Plaza, Ste. 322, 63074, pg. 1120   PV

Saint Charles

ACF Industries, Inc., 620 N. Second St., 63301-2081, pg. 556   PV
American Railcar Industries, 100 Clark St., 63301-0275, pg. 556   PV
Community Psychiatric Centers of Missouri, Inc., 5931 Hwy. 94 S., 63301, pg. 1712   PB

Magna Bank, St. Charles Region, 2216 W. Elm St., 63301, pg. 1037   PB
Orchard Farm Telephone Company, 5065 N. Hwy. 94, 63301, pg. 1571   PB
Penn Emblem Co., P.O. Box 1157, 63302, pg. 849   PV
Unitog Company, 1754 Scherer Pkwy., 63301, pg. 1693   PB

Saint Clair

Landstar T.L.C., Inc., P.O. Box 310, #1 TLC Pkwy., 63077, pg. 978   PB
SPORTSMAN SUPPLY, P.O. Box 500, 63077, pg. 1026   PV

Saint Genevieve

Biltbest Windows, 175 Tenth St., 63670, pg. 1683   PB

Saint James

USA Vacuum Ind. Inc. LLC, 321 Hardy St., 65559, pg. 1067   PV

Saint Joseph

Boehringer Ingelheim Animal Health Inc., 2621 N. Belt Hwy., 64506-2002, pg. 199   IT
MNX Carriers, Inc., 5310 St. Joseph Ave., 64505, pg. 1046   PV
MNX Transport, Inc., 5310 St. Joseph Ave., 64505, pg. 1046   PB
MNX Trucking, Inc., 5310 St. Joseph Ave., 64505, pg. 1046   PV
Missouri-American Water Co., P.O. Box 6276, 1003 E. Maartens Dr., 64506, pg. 95   PB
Missouri-Nebraska Express, Inc., 5310 St. Joseph Ave., 64505, pg. 1046   PV
NEWS-PRESS & GAZETTE COMPANY, 825 Edmond St., 64501, pg. 797   PV
Prime Tanning Corp., 205 Florence Rd., 64504, pg. 884   PV
Research Seeds, Inc., 225 Florence Rd., 64504, pg. 646   PV
SJLP Inc., P.O. Box 998, 520 Francis St., 64502-0998, pg. 1427   PB
ST. JOSEPH LIGHT & POWER CO., P.O. Box 998, 64502-4562, pg. 1427   PB
Seitz Foods Inc., P.O. Box 247, Lower Lake Rd. & Packers Ave., 64502, pg. 1434   PB
C.D. SMITH DRUG COMPANY, 3907 S. 48th Terrace, 64503, pg. 1007   PV
Snorkel, 400 Jules St., 64501, pg. 500   PV
Stetson Hat Co., 4500 Stetson Trail, 64502, pg. 510   PV
Uniland Mfg. Co., Inc., 7002 King Hill Ave., 64504, pg. 975   PV
United Missouri Bank Northwest, Tenth & Penn, 64503, pg. 1654   PB
Urbana Laboratories, 310 S. Third St., 64501, pg. 646   PV
Wilsey Foods, Inc., 6000 Industrial Rd., 64504, pg. 879   IT
WIRE ROPE CORPORATION OF AMERICA, INC., 609 N. 2nd St., 64501, pg. 1184   PV

Saint Louis

ACI Gateway, 1701 Convention Plaza, 63103, pg. 891   IT
Adam's Mark Hotels & Resorts, 11330 Olive St. Rd., 63141, pg. 489   PV
Advanswers Media/Programming, 10 Broadway, 63102, pg. 117   IT
The Agricultural Group, Monsanto Company, 800 N. Lindbergh Blvd., 63167, pg. 1125   PB
Ahern Fire Protection, 1539 S. Kingshighway, 63110-2227, pg. 27   PV
J.S. ALBERICI CONSTRUCTION CO., INC., 2150 Kienlen Ave., 63121-5592, pg. 32   PV
ALLEN FOODS, INC., 8543 Page Ave., 63114, pg. 37   PV
ALLIED HEALTHCARE PRODUCTS, INC., 1720 Sublette Ave., 63110-1968, pg. 48   PB
ALLIED INDUSTRIAL GROUP, INC., Chromalloy Plaza, 120 S. Central, Ste. 1500, 63105, pg. 39   PV
Allied Security Inc., 1900 Stanton Plaza, #400, 1910 Pine St., 63103, pg. 41   PV
Allright Missouri, Inc., 915 Olive St., Ste. 953C, 63101, pg. 42   PV
The Alton & Southern Railway Co., 210 N. 13th St., 63103, pg. 1668   PB
Alumax Engineered Metal Processes, Inc., 1277 N. Warson Rd., 63132, pg. 60   PB
Alumax Foils, Inc., 6100 S. Broadway, 63111, pg. 60   PB
ALVEY SYSTEMS, INC, 9301 Olive Blvd., 63132, pg. 47   PV
AMEREN CORPORATION, 1901 Chouteau Ave., 63103, pg. 65   PB
AmerenUE, 1901 Chouteau Ave., 63103, pg. 66   PB
American Bank Note Company, 314 N. Broadway, Ste. 1239, 63102, pg. 68   PB
American Cablevision of St. Louis, Inc., 9231 W. Florissant, 63136, pg. 1610   PV
American Natl. Can Co., 3200 S. Kingshighway Blvd., 63139, pg. 1029   IT
American Recreation Products, Inc., 1224 Fern Ridge Office Park, 63141, pg. 948   PV
Analysts International, Midwest Region, 600 Emerson Rd., Ste. 200, 63141-6708, pg. 110   PB
Angelica Image Apparel, 700 Rosedale Ave., 63112, pg. 113   PV
ANHEUSER-BUSCH COMPANIES, INC., One Busch Pl., 63118, pg. 113   PB

PB - *U.S. Public Companies Volume*
PV - *U.S. Private Companies Volume*
IT - *International Public & Private Companies Volume*

1304

Anheuser-Busch, Inc., One Busch Pl., 63118, pg. 114 PB
Anheuser-Busch International, Inc., One Busch Pl., 63118, pg. 114 PB
Anheuser-Busch Investment Capital Corporation, One Busch Pl., 63118, pg. 114 PB
Anheuser-Busch Recycling Corporation, 10733 Sunset Office Dr., 63127-1087, pg. 114 PB
BENJAMIN ANSEHL COMPANY, 1555 Page Industrial Blvd., 63132, pg. 75 PV
APEX OIL COMPANY, INC., 8182 Maryland Ave., 63105, pg. 77 PV
Arch Coal, Inc., City Place One, Third Flr., 63141, pg. 139 PB
Arrow/Schweber Electronics, 2380 Schuetz Rd., 63146, pg. 134 PB
ATAPCO Office Products Group, 12312 Olive Blvd., Ste. 400, 63141, pg. 64 PV
BDC, Inc., 1353 Baur Blvd., 63132, pg. 360 PV
Bakers/Leeds Shoe Stores, 501 N. Broadway, 63102, pg. 563 PB
Baldor Electric Company, 3560 Scarlet Oak Blvd., 63122, pg. 169 PB
Baring Venture Partners Limited, P.O. Box 12491, 63132, pg. 647 IT
BARRY-WEHMILLER COMPANY, 8020 Forsyth Blvd., 63105, pg. 118 PV
Beech-Nut Nutrition Corporation, 800 Market St., 63101, pg. 1359 PB
Bekins Distribution Services Co., 7711 Bonhomme Ave., Ste. 410, 63105-1809, pg. 841 PB
BELDEN INC., 7701 Forsyth Blvd., Ste. 800, 63105, pg. 200 PB
BENTLEY INTERNATIONAL, INC., 9719 Conway Rd., 63124, pg. 212 PB
BERG ELECTRONICS, 101 S. Hanley Rd., Ste. 400, 63105, pg. 212 PB
BFA Educational Media, 2349 Chaffee Dr., 63146, pg. 863 PV
Biltwell Company, Inc., 2005 Walton Rd., 63114, pg. 795 PB
Bondex Intl., Inc., 3616 Scarlet Oak Blvd., 63122, pg. 1357 PB
Borden Decorative Products, 1154 Reco Ave., 63126, pg. 158 PV
BRECKENRIDGE MATERIAL COMPANY, 2833 Breckenridge Industrial Ct., 63144, pg. 166 PV
Bremner, Inc., 800 Market St., 63102, pg. 1359 PB
Bridge, 717 Office Pkwy., 63141, pg. 1162 PV
BROWN GROUP, INC., 8300 Maryland Ave., 63105, pg. 262 PB
Brown Retail Development Co., P.O. Box 29, 63166, pg. 262 PB
Brown Shoe Company, 8300 Maryland Ave., 63105, pg. 262 PB
Broyhill Furniture Industries, Inc., 101 S. Hanley Rd., 63105, pg. 688 PB
Bunzl Distribution USA Inc., 701 Emerson, Ste. 410, 63141, pg. 233 IT
Bunzl USA Inc., 701 Emerson Rd., 63141, pg. 233 IT
Burns & Wilcox-St. Louis Office, 655 Craig Rd., #348, 63141, pg. 610 PV
Busch Agricultural Resources, Inc., 1010 Market St., 20th Fl., 63101, pg. 114 PB
Busch Creative Services Corporation, 1881 Pine St., 63103, pg. 114 PB
Busch Properties, Inc., One Busch Pl., 63118, pg. 114 PB
CCT Holdings Corp., 12444 Powerscourt Dr., 63131, pg. 230 PV
CPI CORP., 1706 Washington Ave., 63103, pg. 283 PB
CAP Gemini America (St. Louis Branch), 1034 S. Brentwood Blvd., Ste. 1780, 63117, pg. 264 IT
Carat ICG, 1001 Craig Rd., Ste. 330, 63146, pg. 207 PV
Carboline Co., 350 Hanley Industrial Court, 63144-1599, pg. 1357 PB
CENTRAL STATES DIVERSIFIED, INC., 5221 Natural Bridge Rd., 63115, pg. 224 PV
Centrifugal & Mechanical Industries, 201 President St., 63118, pg. 370 PV
CHARTER COMMUNICATIONS, INC., 12444 Powerscourt Dr., Ste. 400, 63131, pg. 230 PV
Charter National Life Insurance Co., 8301 Maryland Ave., 63105-3644, pg. 990 PB
CHECKMARK COMMUNICATIONS, 1111 Chouteau, 63102, pg. 231 PV
Chemtech Products Inc., 1633 Des Peres Rd., Ste. 210, 63131, pg. 39 PV
Chesterfield Industrial Park, Inc., 12001 Lackland Rd., 63146, pg. 1153 PV
Chiron, 4777 Le Bourget Dr., 63134-3120, pg. 350 PB
Chiron Corporation, 4766 La Guardia, 63134, pg. 350 PB
Cigna Healthcare of St. Louis, Inc., 8182 Maryland, Ste. 301, 63105, pg. 360 PB
Citicorp Acceptance Co., Inc., 666 Mason Ridge Center Dr., 63141, pg. 378 PB
Citicorp Mortgage, Inc., 670 Mason Ridge Center Dr., 63141, pg. 378 PB
Civic Center Corporation, 300 Stadium Plaza, 63102, pg. 114 PB
Clark Detroit-Diesel Allison, 1424 Ashby Rd., 63132, pg. 242 PV
Clark Oil Trading Company, 8182 Maryland Ave, 63105, pg. 77 PV
CLARK REFINING & MARKETING INC., 8182 Maryland Ave., 63105-3721, pg. 243 PV
Coda, 501 N. Broadway, 63102, pg. 563 PB
COMPUTER SALES INTERNATIONAL INC., 10845 Olive St., Ste 301, 63141, pg. 260 PV
COMPUTERIZED MEDICAL SYSTEMS, INC., 1195 Corporate Lake Dr., 63132, pg. 260 PV
CONCORDIA PUBLISHING HOUSE, 3558 S. Jefferson, 63118, pg. 261 PV
Consolidated Network, Inc., 540 Maryville Ctr. Dr., Ste. 400, 63141-5833, pg. 1073 PB
Consolidation Coal Co.-Mid-Continent Region, 12755 Olive Blvd., 63141, pg. 531 PB
CONTICO INTERNATIONAL, INC., 1101 N. Warson Rd., 63132, pg. 267 PV
CONTINENTAL WATER COMPANY, 535 N. New Ballas Rd., 63141, pg. 269 PV
Coronet/MTI, 2349 Chaffee Dr., 63146, pg. 863 PV
CORRIGAN BROS., INC., 3545 Gratiot, 63103, pg. 277 PV
Corrigan Company Mechanical Contractors, 3545 Gratiot, 63103, pg. 277 PV
CROWN FOODS INC., 5243 Manchester, 63110, pg. 292 PV
Crown Shoe Company, L.L.C., 1520 Washington Ave., 63103, pg. 1089 PV
CUPPLES PRODUCTS, INC., 10733 Sunset Office Dr., # 200, 63127, pg. 297 PV
CURTIS-TOLEDO, INC., 1905 Kienlen Ave., 63133, pg. 298 PV
D & K HEALTHCARE RESOURCES, INC., 8000 Maryland, Ste. 920, 63105, pg. 471 PB
DMB&B St. Louis, Gateway Tower, One Memorial Dr., 63102, pg. 303 PV
DWF of Saint Louis, Inc., 2715 LaSalle St., 63104, pg. 326 PV
Dataproducts Corp., 130 S. Bemiston, Ste. 300, 63105-1913, pg. 620 IT
David & Sons, 8064 Chivvas Drive, 63123, pg. 917 IT
Delfia, Inc., C3ND, 800 N. Lindburgh Blvd., 63167, pg. 1124 PB
DENNIS CHEMICAL CO., INC., 2700 Papin St., 63103, pg. 324 PV
Deutsche Financial Services Corporation, 655 Maryville Ctr. Dr., 63141-5832, pg. 403 IT
DIRECTORY DISTRIBUTING ASSOCIATES, INC., 4363 Woodson Rd., 63134, pg. 334 PV
The Doe Run Company, 1801 Park 270 Dr., Ste. 300, 63146, pg. 922 PV
Du Pont Protein Technologies International, 1034 Danforth Dr., 63102, pg. 531 PB
DUKE MANUFACTURING CO., INC., 2305 N. Broadway, 63102, pg. 346 PV
Dykem Company, 8501 Delport Dr., 63114, pg. 866 PB
EAC CORPORATION, 347 N. Lindbergh Blvd., 63141, pg. 353 PV
EG & G Missouri Metals, 9970 Page Blvd., 63132, pg. 544 PB
EG & G Optoelectronics-St. Louis, 10900 Page Ave., 63132, pg. 543 PB
EDISON BROTHERS STORES, INC., 501 N. Broadway, 63102, pg. 563 PB
A.G. Edwards & Sons, Inc., One N. Jefferson Ave., 63103, pg. 565 PB
A.G. EDWARDS, INC., One N. Jefferson Ave., 63103, pg. 565 PB
A.G. Edwards Trust Company, One N. Jefferson Ave., 63103, pg. 565 PB
Elf Aquitaine Asphalt, Inc., 1000 Executive Pkwy., 63141, pg. 445 IT
EMERSON ELECTRIC CO., 8000 W. Florissant Ave., 63136-8506, pg. 572 PB
ENGINEERED SUPPORT SYSTEMS INC., 1270 N. Price Rd., 63132, pg. 583 PB
ENTERPRISE RENT-A-CAR COMPANY, 600 Corporate Pk. Dr., 63105, pg. 377 PV
ESCO ELECTRONICS CORPORATION, 8888 Ladue Rd., Ste. 200, 63124, pg. 546 PB
Eveready Battery Co., Checkerboard Sq., 63164, pg. 1360 PB
FALCON PRODUCTS, INC., 9387 Dielman Industrial Dr., 63132, pg. 611 PB
Famous-Barr, 601 Olive St., 63101, pg. 1063 PB
Ferguson Machine Co., 11820 Lackland Rd., 63141, pg. 457 PB
Fleishman-Hillard, 200 N. Broadway, 63102, pg. 411 PV
FLEISHMAN-HILLARD INC., 200 N. Broadway, 63102, pg. 411 PV
Foamex International-Consumer Products Division, 101 S. Hanley, Ste. 1225, 63105, pg. 1094 PV
Fox Photo, Inc., 1706 Washington Ave., 63103, pg. 283 PB
FURNITURE BRANDS INTERNATIONAL INC., 101 S. Hanley Rd., 63105-3493, pg. 688 PB
LOU FUSZ AUTOMOTIVE NETWORK, 925 N. Lindbergh, 63141, pg. 432 PV
Lou Fusz Motor Company, 925 N. Lindbergh, 63141, pg. 432 PV
GSW Jackes-Evans Manufacturing Co., 4427 Geraldine Ave., 63115, pg. 538 IT
Gared Sports Inc., 1107 Mullanphy, 63106, pg. 799 PV
GATEWAY APPAREL, INC., 8500 Valcour, 63123, pg. 441 PV
Genelco, Inc., 1600 S. Brentwood., Ste. 500, 63144, pg. 443 PV
GENERAL AMERICAN LIFE INSURANCE CO., 700 Market St., 63101, pg. 443 PV
General Metal Products, 3883 Delor St., 63116-3327, pg. 1192 PV
GenMark, Inc., 670 Mason Ridge Center Dr., 63141, pg. 443 PV
Golden Cat Corporation, Checkerboard Sq., 6T, 63164-0001, pg. 1360 PB
Graphic Systems, 10866 Indian Head Ind. Blvd., 63106, pg. 1060 PB
Graybar International, Inc., 8170 Lackland Rd., 63114, pg. 472 PV
GROSSMAN IRON & STEEL COMPANY, Five N. Market, 63102, pg. 483 PV
Group Health Plan, Inc., 940 West Port Plaza, Ste. 300, 63146, pg. 454 PB
GUARANTEE ELECTRICAL COMPANY, 3405 Bent Ave., 63116, pg. 485 PV
Guth Lighting Company, 2615 Washington Blvd., 63103, pg. 821 IT
H&K America Inc., 11756 Borman Dr., Ste. 100, 63146, pg. 737 IT
HBE Adam's Rib, 11330 Olive St. Rd., 63141, pg. 489 PV
HBE Bank Facilities, 11330 Olive St. Rd., 63141, pg. 489 PV
HBE CORPORATION/DESIGN BUILD DIVISIONS, 11330 Olive Street Rd., 63141, pg. 489 PV
HBE Medical Buildings, 11330 Olive St. Rd., 63141, pg. 489 PV
Hanwa American Corp., 3401 Morganford Rd., 63116, pg. 595 IT
HARBOUR GROUP LTD., 7701 Forsyth Blvd., Ste. 600, 63105, pg. 500 PV
Harness Division, 101 S. Henley Rd., 63105, pg. 526 PV
Harvard Interiors Manufacturing Co., 4321 Semple Ave., 63120, pg. 796 PB
HELLMUTH, OBATA & KASSABAUM, INC., 211 N. Broadway, Ste. 600, 63102, pg. 520 PV
Hewlett-Packard Company, 530 Maryville Centre Dr., 63141, pg. 814 PB
HILL-BEHAN LUMBER COMPANY, 6515 Page Blvd., 63133, pg. 529 PV
Hospital Building & Equipment Co., 11330 Olive St. Rd., 63141, pg. 489 PV
Ice Cream Specialties, Inc., 8419 Hanley Industrial Dr., 63144, pg. 879 PV
Ikon Office Solutions-St. Louis, 5317 Mirex Drive, 63119-5200, pg. 864 PB
InnerVision Studios Inc., 11783 Borman Dr., 63146, pg. 114 PB
Intergraph Corporation, 11116 South Town Sq., Ste. 201, 63123, pg. 890 PB
International Wire Group Inc., 101 S. Hanley Rd., 63105, pg. 526 PV
Interstate Bakeries Corporation-Central Division, 1217 Gratiot, 63103, pg. 909 PB
Jeans West, Inc., 501 N. Broadway, 63102, pg. 563 PB
EDWARD JONES, 12555 Manchester Rd., 63131, pg. 597 PV
JONES MEDICAL INDUSTRIES INC., 1945 Craig Rd., 63146, pg. 933 PB
KSDK, Inc., 1000 Market St., 63101, pg. 702 PB
KTVI-TV, Inc., 5915 Berthold St., 63110, pg. 926 IT
KV PHARMACEUTICAL COMPANY, 2503 S. Hanley Rd., 63144, pg. 941 PB
Killark Electric Manufacturing Co., 3940 Martin Luther King Dr., 63115, pg. 844 PB
Koch Materials Division, 1000 Executive Parkway Dr., 63141-6325, pg. 628 PV
Koken Mfg. Co. Inc., 1631 Dr. M.L. King Dr., 63106, pg. 1349 IT
Kragie/Newell, 11720 Borman Dr., Ste. 101, 63146, pg. 635 PV
KUPPER PARKER COMMUNICATIONS INC., 8301 Maryland Ave., 63105, pg. 637 PV
LaBarge Clayco Wireless, 2199 Innerbelt Bus. Ctr. Dr., 63114, pg. 973 PB
LaBarge Electronics, P.O. Box 14499, 707 N. Second St., 63178, pg. 973 PB
LABARGE, INC., 9900-A Clayton Rd., 63124, pg. 973 PB
LABARGE PIPE & STEEL COMPANY, 901 N. Tenth St., 63101, pg. 641 PV
Laclede Chain Manufacturing Company, One Metropolitan Sq., 211 North Broadway, 63102, pg. 974 PB
Laclede Development Co., 720 Olive St., 63101, pg. 974 PB
Laclede Energy Resources, Inc., 720 Olive St., 63101, pg. 974 PB
LACLEDE GAS COMPANY, 720 Olive St., 63101, pg. 973 PB
Laclede Gas Family Services, Inc., 720 Olive St., 63101, pg. 974 PB
Laclede Investment Corp., 720 Olive St., 63101, pg. 974 PB
Laclede Pipeline Co., 720 Olive St., 63101, pg. 974 PB
LACLEDE STEEL COMPANY, One Metropolitan Sq., 211 N. Broadway, 63102, pg. 974 PB
Laclede Venture Co., 720 Olive St., 63101, pg. 974 PB
Lapham-Hickey Steel Corp., 500 S. Spring Ave., 63110, pg. 651 PV
LASERSIGHT INC., 12161 Lackland Rd., 36146, pg. 979 PB
Lee-Rowan Company, 6333 Etzel Ave., 63133, pg. 1177 PB
Legal Communications Corporation, 612 N. 2nd St., 63102, pg. 513 PB
Lever, 1400 N. Pennsylvania Ave., 63133-1226, pg. 1435 IT
Charles S. Lewis & Co., Inc., 8625 Grant Rd., 63123, pg. 1489 IT
Life Uniform & Shoe Shops, 700 Rosedale Ave., 63112, pg. 113 PB
Light Helicopter Turbine Engine Company (LHTEC), 12400 Olive Blvd., Ste. 400, 63141, pg. 51 PB
Lincoln Automotive, One Lincoln Way, 63120-1576, pg. 1273 PB
Lincoln Industrial, One Lincoln Way, 63120, pg. 1273 PB
Lindberg Heat Treating Co., 650 E. Taylor Ave., 63147, pg. 999 PB
LOUIS LONDON ADVERTISING & SALES PROMOTION, 6665 Delmar, Ste. 300, 63130, pg. 674 PV
Lyndon Property Insurance Company, 645 Maryville Ctr. Dr., Ste. 200, 63141, pg. 685 PB
MCC Div., P.O. Box 5840, 675 McDonnell Blvd., 63134, pg. 1039 PB

Geographic Index-U.S.

PB - *U.S. Public Companies Volume*
PV - *U.S. Private Companies Volume*
IT - *International Public & Private Companies Volume*

Magna Bank, 1401 S. Brentwood Blvd., 63144, pg. 1037 **PB**
MAGNA GROUP, INC., One Magna Pl., 1401 S. Brentwood Blvd., 63144-1401, pg. 1037 **PB**
Magnetek Motors & Generators, 1145 Corporate Lake Dr., 63132, pg. 1037 **PB**
MALLINCKRODT INC., 7733 Forsyth Blvd., 63105-1820, pg. 1039 **PB**
Mallinckrodt Inc., 675 McDonnell Blvd., 63042, pg. 1039 **PB**
MANNA PRO CORPORATION, 7711 Carondelet Ave., Ste 800, 63128, pg. 700 **PV**
Manufacturers Railway Company, 2850 So. Broadway, 63118, pg. 114 **PV**
Marco Sales Co., 1100 Macklind Ave., 63110, pg. 628 **PV**
MasterCard International, Inc., 12115 Lackland Rd., 63146, pg. 714 **PV**
THE MAY DEPARTMENT STORES COMPANY, 611 Olive St., 63101-1799, pg. 1063 **PB**
May Department Stores International, Inc., 615 Olive St., 63101, pg. 1064 **PB**
May Design & Construction Co., 611 Olive St., 63101, pg. 1064 **PB**
May Merchandising Company, 615 Olive St., 63101, pg. 1064 **PB**
McCarthy Brothers Co., 1341 N. Rock Hill Rd., 63124, pg. 719 **PB**
MCCARTHY BUILDING COMPANIES, 1341 N. Rock Hill Rd., 63052, pg. 719 **PB**
Medicine Shoppe International, Inc., 1100 N. Lindbergh, 63132, pg. 304 **PB**
MERCANTILE BANCORPORATION INC., One Mercantile Ctr., 63101, pg. 1087 **PB**
Mercantile Bank of St. Louis N.A., 721 Locust St., 63101, pg. 1087 **PB**
Mercantile Business Credit, Inc., 100 S. Brentwood, Ste. 500, 63105, pg. 1087 **PB**
Mercantile Insurance Services, Inc., Eighth & Locust & Mercantile Tower, 63101, pg. 1088 **PB**
Mercantile Investment Services, Inc., Mercantile Tower, 63101, pg. 1087 **PB**
Mercantile Trust Company N.A., Mercantile Tower, 63101, pg. 1088 **PB**
Messier-Dowty International Marketing, 841 Braefield Ct., Ste. 100, 63107, pg. 1340 **IT**
Metal Container Corporation, 3636 S. Geyer Rd., Ste. 400, 63127, pg. 114 **PB**
Midcoast Aviation, Inc., P.O. Box 10056, 63145, pg. 959 **PV**
Midland Color Company, 5215 Manchester, 63110, pg. 1311 **IT**
MIDWEST PETROLEUM CO., 6760 S.W. Ave, 63143, pg. 745 **PV**
Mills & Partners, 101 S. Hanley Rd., 63105, pg. 526 **PV**
THE MILNOT COMPANY, 100 S. Fourth St., Ste. 1010, 63102, pg. 749 **PV**
MISS ELAINE INC., 1717 Olive St., 63103, pg. 752 **PV**
Mississippi River Transmission, P.O. Box 14521, 9900 Clayton Rd., 63124-14521, pg. 843 **PB**
Mississippi Valley Advisors Inc., One Mercantile Ctr., 63101, pg. 1087 **PB**
Mississippi Valley Life Insurance Company, Mercantile Tower, 63101, pg. 1087 **PB**
Missouri Medical Insurance Company, 8630 Delmar Blvd., Ste. 100, 63124, pg. 1080 **PB**
Mitek Industries, 4203 Shoreline Dr., 63045, pg. 1106 **PV**
MONSANTO COMPANY, 800 N. Lindbergh Blvd., 63167, pg. 1124 **PB**
Monsanto Enviro-Chem. Systems, Inc., 14522 S. Outer Rd., P.O. Box 14547, 63178, pg. 1125 **PV**
Monsanto Environmental Health Redevelopment Corp., C/ O: EHL, 800 N. Lindburgh Blvd., 63167, pg. 1125 **PB**
Moog Automotive, Inc., 6565 Wells Ave., 63133, pg. 443 **PV**
Moran Foods, Inc./Save-A-Lot Ltd., 8474 Delport Dr., 63114, pg. 1541 **PV**
Mosby-Year Book, Inc., 11830 Westline Industrial Dr., 63146, pg. 1616 **PV**
Motorola Manufacturing Technology Division, 12977 N. Forty Dr., Ste. 210, 63141, pg. 1138 **PV**
MRS. ALISON'S COOKIE COMPANY, 1780 Burns, 63132, pg. 765 **PV**
Gunther Nash Mining Construction, 2150 Kienlen, 63121, pg. 32 **PV**
NationsBank of St. Louis, 100 N. Broadway, 63166, pg. 1164 **PB**
NationsBank West, 100 N. Broadway, Ste. 1575, 63102, pg. 1164 **PB**
94th of St. Louis, Inc., 5933 McDonnel Blvd., 63134, pg. 1023 **PV**
NIXDORFF KREIN INDUSTRIES INC., 760 Office Pkwy., Ste. 48, 63141, pg. 799 **PV**
Nooter Construction Co., 1400 So. Third St., 63104, pg. 801 **PV**
Nooter Consulting Services, Inc., 1400 S. Third St., 63104, pg. 801 **PV**
NOOTER CORPORATION, 1400 S. Third St., 63104, pg. 801 **PV**
Nooter/Eriksen, Inc., 5000 Cedar Plaza Pkwy., 63128, pg. 801 **PV**
Nooter Fabricators, Inc., P.O. Box451, 63166, pg. 801 **PV**
Nordyne Inc., 1801 Park 270 Dr., Ste. 600, 63146, pg. 1193 **PB**
Northeast Marketing-St. Louis Business Center, 7777 Bonhomme, Ste. 1410, 63105, pg. 649 **PB**
Oaktree, 501 N. Broadway, 63102, pg. 564 **PB**
Outdoor Systems, Inc.-St. Louis, 6767 N. Hanley Rd., 63134, pg. 1235 **PB**
Pagoda, 8300 Maryland Ave., 63105, pg. 262 **PB**
Paragon Life Insurance Co., 100 S. Brentwood, 63105, pg. 443 **PV**

Particle Dynamics, Inc., 2503 S. Hanley Rd., 63144, pg. 941 **PB**
Peabody COALSALES Company, 701 Market St., Ste. 830, 63101-1826, pg. 594 **IT**
Peabody Development Company, Ste. 310, 301 N. Memorial Dr., 63102, pg. 594 **IT**
Peabody Holding Company, Inc., 701 Market St., Ste. 700, 63101-1826, pg. 594 **IT**
Permea, 11444 Lackland Rd., 63146, pg. 31 **PB**
Personal Performance Consultants, 1401 S. Brentwood Blvd., Ste. 400, 63144, pg. 1036 **PB**
Petroleum Fuel & Terminal, 8182 Maryland Ave., 63105, pg. 77 **PV**
Pevely Dairy Company, 1001 S. Grand Blvd., 63104-1084, pg. 879 **PV**
Phoenix Films & Video, 2349 Chaffee Dr., 63146, pg. 863 **PV**
THE PHOENIX LEARNING GROUP, INC., 2349 Chaffee Dr., 63146, pg. 863 **PV**
PINNACLE AUTOMATION INC., 9301 Olive Blvd., 63132, pg. 866 **PV**
Piper Jaffray Inc., Pierre Laclede Ctr., Ste. 580, 7733 Forsyth Blvd., 63105-1817, pg. 1301 **PB**
Precision Foods, Inc., 11457 Olde Cabin Rd., 63141, pg. 1134 **PV**
PRESIDENT CASINOS, INC., 800 N. First St., 63102, pg. 1323 **PB**
Providian Auto & Home Insurance Group, 11975 Westline Dr., 63146-3290, pg. 27 **IT**
PULITZER PUBLISHING COMPANY, 900 N. Tucker Blvd., 63101, pg. 1343 **PB**
Purina Grocery Products Group, Checkerboard Sq., 63164, pg. 1360 **PV**
PURINA MILLS, INC., 1401 S. Hanley Rd., 63144, pg. 895 **PV**
RPR Correspondant Clearing, 515 Olive St., 63101, pg. 476 **PB**
RALCORP HOLDINGS INC., 800 Market St., Ste. 2900, 63101, pg. 1359 **PB**
Ralston Foods, Inc., 800 Market St., 63102, pg. 1359 **PB**
RALSTON PURINA COMPANY, Checkerboard Sq., 63164, pg. 1359 **PB**
Ralston Purina International, Checkerboard Square, 63164, pg. 1360 **PB**
Ravarino & Freschi, Inc., 611 E. Marceau St., 63111-3839, pg. 158 **PV**
REHABCARE GROUP, INC., 7733 Forsyth Blvd., Ste. 1700, 63105, pg. 1373 **PB**
Reinsurance Group Of America, 660 Mason Ridge Center Dr., 63141, pg. 443 **PB**
REPP Ltd. Big and Tall, 501 N. Broadway, 63102, pg. 564 **PB**
Revertex-Americas, 2700 Papin St., 63103, pg. 324 **IT**
J. Riggings, 501 N. Broadway, 63102, pg. 564 **PB**
The Right Shoe Only, Inc., 8300 Maryland Ave., 63105, pg. 262 **PB**
SBC-Asset Management Inc., 12140 Woodcrest Executive Dr., Suite 300, 63141, pg. 1416 **PB**
SLM Electronics, 11880 Borman Dr., 63146, pg. 961 **PV**
SMS-St. Louis, 1801 Park 270 Dr., Ste. 200, 63146, pg. 1463 **PV**
SABRELINER CORPORATION, 7733 Forsyth Blvd., Ste. 1500, 63105-1821, pg. 959 **PV**
Safety National Casualty Corp., 2043 Woodland Pkwy., Ste. 200, 63146, pg. 496 **PB**
St. Louis Airline Learning Center, 4619 Le Bourget Dr., 63134, pg. 219 **PB**
St. Louis Business Journal Corp., One Metropolitan Sq., Ste. 2170, 63102, pg. 20 **PV**
St. Louis Daily Record, 612 N. Second St., 63188, pg. 513 **PV**
St. Louis Metallizing Co., 4123 Sarpy Ave., 63110, pg. 801 **PV**
ST. LOUIS MUSIC, INC., 1400 Ferguson, 63133, pg. 960 **PV**
ST. LOUIS NATIONAL BASEBALL CLUB L.P., 250 Stadium Plaza, 63102, pg. 961 **PV**
St. Louis Post-Dispatch, 900 N. Tucker Blvd., 63101, pg. 1343 **PB**
St. Louis Refrigerator Car Company, 2850 S. Broadway, 63118, pg. 114 **PB**
St. Louis Sabreliner Learning Center, 6185 Aviation Dr., 63134, pg. 219 **PB**
Save-A-Lot, Inc., 8474 Delport Dr., 63114, pg. 1541 **PB**
SCHNUCK MARKETS, INC., 11420 Lackland Rd., 63146-6928, pg. 971 **PV**
A. Schulman, Inc., 514 Earth City Expwy., Ste. 351, 63045-1303, pg. 1441 **PB**
Sherwood-Davis & Geck, 1915 Olive St., 63103, pg. 80 **PB**
Sidney Rich & Associates, 8300 Maryland Ave., 63105, pg. 262 **PB**
SIGMA-ALDRICH CORPORATION, 3050 Spruce St., 63103, pg. 1471 **PB**
Sigma-Aldrich FS Corp., P.O. Box 14508, 63178, pg. 1472 **PB**
Sigma Chemical Co., 3050 Spruce St., 63103, pg. 1472 **PB**
Sigma Diagnostics Div., 3300 S. Second St., 63141, pg. 1472 **PB**
Sigma Redevelopment Corp., 3050 Spruce St., 63103, pg. 1472 **PB**
Sigma Second Street Redevelopment Corp., 3050 Spruce St., 14508, pg. 1472 **PB**
SIMMONS, DURHAM & ASSOCIATES, 701 Market, Ste. 200, 63101, pg. 1000 **PV**
Size 5-7-9 Shops, Inc., 501 N. Broadway, 63102, pg. 564 **PB**
SmithKline Beecham Clinical Laboratories, 2040 Concourse Dr., 63146, pg. 1265 **IT**
Jefferson Smurfit Corporation, 8182 Maryland Ave., 63105, pg. 1269 **IT**

Jefferson Smurfit Corporation, 8182 Maryland Avenue, 63105, pg. 1271 **IT**
Jefferson Smurfit Corporation (U.S.), 8182 Maryland Ave., 63105, pg. 1271 **IT**
Jefferson Smurfit Folding Carton & Boxboard Mills Div., 8182 Maryland, 63105, pg. 1270 **IT**
Smurfit Packaging Corporation, 8182 Maryland Ave., 63105, pg. 1271 **IT**
SOLUTIA INC., 10300 Olive Blvd., P.O. Box 66760, 63166-6760, pg. 1483 **PB**
Southern Illinois and Missouri Bridge Co., 210 N. 13th St., 63103, pg. 1668 **PB**
Southwestern Bell Technology Resources, 550 Maryville Centre Dr., 63141, pg. 1416 **PB**
Southwestern Bell Telephone Co., One Bell Center, 63101-3099, pg. 1416 **PB**
Southwestern Bell Yellow Pages Inc., P.O. Box 31907, 12800 Publications Dr., 63131, pg. 1415 **PB**
Spirolox Division, 29 Cassens Court, 63026, pg. 946 **PB**
The Sporting News Publishing Company, 10176 Corporate Sq., Ste. 200, 63132, pg. 1616 **PV**
Steering and Suspension Division, 6565 Wells Ave., 63133, pg. 443 **PV**
STIFEL FINANCIAL CORP., 500 N. Broadway, 63102, pg. 1518 **PB**
Storz Instrument Co., 3365 Tree Court Industrial Blvd., 63122, pg. 79 **PB**
STUPP BROS., INC., 120 S. Central Ave., Ste. 1650, 63105, pg. 1048 **PV**
Suburban Newspapers of Greater St. Louis, 1714 Deer Tracks Trail, 63131, pg. 935 **PV**
Sunbelt Footwear, Ltd., 8300 Maryland Ave., 63105, pg. 262 **PV**
Sunmark Inc., 3660 S. Geyer Rd., 63127-1238, pg. 917 **IT**
SUNNEN PRODUCTS COMPANY, 7910 Manchester Ave., 63143, pg. 1053 **PV**
Sverdrup Facilities, Inc., 400 S. 4th St., 63102-1826, pg. 1057 **PV**
Systems & Electronics Inc., 201 Evans Ln., 63121-1126, pg. 547 **PB**
TBWA Chiat/Day St. Louis, 22 N. Euclid Ave., 63103, pg. 1062 **PV**
TIE Systems Missouri, 1858 Craig Park Ct., 63146, pg. 1085 **PV**
TMP Worldwide, Inc., 12825 Flushing Meadow Dr., 63131, pg. 1064 **PV**
TARLTON CORPORATION, 5500 W. Park Ave., 63110-1898, pg. 1069 **PV**
TAYLOR-MORLEY, INC., 1224 Fern Ridge Pkwy., 3rd Flr., 63141, pg. 1071 **PV**
Taylor - Morley Management Company, 1224 Fern Ridge Pkwy., 3rd Fl., 63141, pg. 1071 **PV**
Team Rehab, Inc., 141 N. Meramec Ave., 63105, pg. 1373 **PB**
Thermal Industries, Inc., 1570 Page Industrial Ct., 63132-1347, pg. 491 **PV**
TOBER INDUSTRIES, INC., 1520 Washington Ave., 63103, pg. 1089 **PV**
TRANS WORLD AIRLINES, INC., One City Center, 515 N. Sixth St., 63101, pg. 1629 **PB**
Trebla Chemical Company, 8417 Chaplin Industrial Dr., 63114, pg. 282 **PB**
TUBULAR STEEL INC., 1031 Executive Pkwy., 63141, pg. 1108 **PV**
UPB of Missouri, 8182 Maryland Ave., 63105, pg. 1669 **PB**
Union Electric Development Corporation, 1901 Chouteau Ave., 63103, pg. 66 **PB**
Union Pacific Technologies, 7930 Clayton Rd., 63117, pg. 1668 **PB**
U.S. Electrical Motor Division, 8100 W. Florissant Ave., 63136-1491, pg. 573 **PB**
U.S. Ring-St. Louis, 6800 Arsenal, 63139, pg. 707 **PB**
Upright, 10665 Kahlmeyer Dr., 63132-1619, pg. 1128 **PV**
The Valley Line Company, 120 S. Central Ave., 63105, pg. 284 **PV**
Visual Simulation Systems Division, 5695 Campus Pkwy., 63042-2338, pg. 218 **PV**
Walnut Street Securities, Inc., 670 Mason Ridge Center Dr., 63141, pg. 443 **PV**
Warner-Jenkinson Co., 2526 Baldwin, 63106, pg. 1696 **PB**
Watlow Electric Company of California, 12001 Lackland Rd., 63146, pg. 1153 **PV**
Watlow Electric Foreign Sales Corporation, 12001 Lackland Rd., 63146, pg. 1153 **PV**
WATLOW ELECTRIC MANUFACTURING COMPANY, 12001 Lackland Rd., 63146, pg. 1153 **PV**
Watlow St. Louis, Inc., 12001 Lackland Rd., 63146, pg. 1153 **PV**
THE WESTERN GROUP, 1637 N. Warson Rd., 63132, pg. 1165 **PV**
Western Waterproofing Company of America, Inc., 1637 N. Warson, 63132, pg. 1165 **PV**
White-Rodgers Div., Emerson Electric Co., 9797 Reavis Rd., 63123, pg. 573 **PB**
Whitmire Micro-gen Research Laboratories Inc., 3568 Tree Court Indus. Blvd., 63122, pg. 592 **PV**
The Wild Pair, 501 N. Broadway, 63102, pg. 564 **PB**
WILLERT HOME PRODUCTS, INC., 4044 Park Ave., 63110, pg. 1177 **PV**
WILLIAMS PATENT CRUSHER AND PULVERIZER CO., 2701 N. Broadway, 63102, pg. 1178 **PV**
Willis Corroon Administrative Services Corporation, 8112 Maryland Ave., 63105-3721, pg. 1504 **IT**
Willis Corroon Corp. of Missouri, 8112 Maryland Ave., 63105-3721, pg. 1506 **IT**
Woodward-Clyde, 2318 Millpark Dr., 63043, pg. 1656 **PB**
World Import Co., 1520 Washington Ave., 63103, pg. 1089 **PV**
Worldwide Directory Product Sales, 1000 Des Peres, Ste. 220, 63131-2041, pg. 1415 **PB**

Geographic Index-U.S.

PB - *U.S. Public Companies Volume*
PV - *U.S. Private Companies Volume*
IT - *International Public & Private Companies Volume*

XTRA Lease, Inc., 1801 Park 270 Dr., Ste. 400, 63146, pg. 1786 **PB**

Y.K.K. (U.S.A.) Inc., 10820 Ambassador Blvd., 63132, 1515 **IT**

Zellerbach Division, 10805 Sunset Office Dr., Ste. L-110, 63127, pg. 1075 **PB**

Zemenick & Walker, Inc., 100 S. Brentwood Blvd., Ste. 450, pg. 644 **PB**

ZOLTEK COMPANIES, INC., 3101 McKelvey Rd., 63044, pg. 1794 **PB**

Saint Peters

Duchesne Bank, 5500 Mexico Rd., 63376, pg. 643 **PB**

MEMC Electronic Materials, Inc., 501 Pearl Drive, 63376, pg. 1455 **IT**

Specialty Insurance Underwriters, Inc., 195 Spencer Rd., 63376, pg. 152 **PB**

U.S. Specialty Insurance Co., 195 Spencer Rd., 63376, pg. 152 **PB**

Sarcoxie

Justin Boot Company, P.O. Box 609, 12th & Clarence, 64862, pg. 937 **PB**

Scott City

Environmental Services of America-MO, Inc., 3100 Industrial Fuels Dr., 63781, pg. 546 **PB**

SuperValu, Inc.-Scott City Div., Daugherty St., 63780, pg. 1541 **PB**

Sedalia

Broderick & Bascom Rope Co., 24150 Oakgrove Ln., 65301, pg. 68 **PV**

Seymour

Steel Processors Div., P.O. Box 496, 65746, pg. 550 **PV**

Sikeston

Barton's of Sikeston, 309-15 E. Malone, 63801, pg. 119 **PV**

Cott Corporation - North Central Region (Sikeston), 310 Larcel Drive, 63801, pg. 337 **IT**

Lewis Bros. Bakeries (MO), 504 Kendall, 63801, pg. 665 **PV**

Springfield

American National General Insurance Company, Corporate Center, 1949 E. Sunshine, 65899, pg. 88 **PB**

American National Insurance Service Co., Corporate Center, 1949 E. Sunshine, 65899, pg. 88 **PB**

American National Property & Casualty Co., Corporate Center, 1949 E. Sunshine, 65899, pg. 87 **PB**

Ash Grove Lime Plant, P.O. Box 323, Rte. 3, 65803, pg. 88 **PV**

ASSOCIATED ELECTRIC CO-OP INC., 2814 S. Golden, 65801, pg. 89 **PV**

BancTec Financial Systems, 1949 E. Sunshine, 65804, pg. 177 **PB**

BASS PRO SHOPS, INC., 2500 E. Kearney St., 65898, pg. 122 **PV**

Browning-Ferris Industries of Springfield, Inc., 2115 W. Bennett, 65807, pg. 264 **PB**

Burns & Wilcox - Springfield Office, 1949 E. Sunshine, Ste. 2-310, 65804, pg. 610 **PV**

Consumers Markets Inc., 639 W. Chestnut Expwy., 65802, pg. 653 **PV**

DT INDUSTRIES INC., 1949 Sunshine, Ste. 2-300, 65804, pg. 475 **PB**

J.L. DeGraffenreid & Sons, Inc., 2848 N. LeCompte Rd., 65803, pg. 301 **PV**

ERICKSON TRANSPORT CORPORATION, 2255 N. Packer Rd., 65803, pg. 381 **PV**

Greene County Realty Company, 233 S. Patterson, 65801, pg. 1230 **PB**

HSI Aviation, Inc., 1200 E. Woodhurst, Bldg. J, 65804, pg. 849 **PB**

Hiland Dairy Company, 1133 E. Kearney, 65803, pg. 879 **PV**

Huntco Steel Co., 1200 E. Woodhurst, Bldg. J, 65804, pg. 849 **PB**

HUTCHENS INDUSTRIES INC., 215 N. Patterson, 65802-2206, pg. 550 **PV**

Inter-Pak Electronics, 2500 Airport Commerce Ave., P.O. Box 2847, 65803-0847, pg. 1003 **PB**

Karchmer Iron & Metal Company, 634 E. Phelps, 65806, pg. 413 **PB**

Lady Baltimore of Missouri, Inc., 4550 W. Maple Dr., 65807, pg. 975 **PB**

Litton Systems, Inc. Advanced Circuitry Div., 4811 W. Kearney, 65803-0847, pg. 1003 **PB**

MD Pneumatics, 4840 W. Kearney, 65803, pg. 1111 **PV**

Medicenter, Springfield, 1911 S. National, 65804, pg. 1714 **PB**

MID-AMERICA DAIRYMEN, INC., 3253 E. Chestnut Expwy., 65802-2584, pg. 743 **PV**

Missouri Auction Services Corp., 2944 W. Sunshine, 65807, pg. 282 **PB**

Modern American Life Insurance Company, 1000 W. Sunshine St., 65807, pg. 853 **PB**

Mueller International Sales Corp., 1600 W. Phelps, 65802, pg. 1141 **PB**

PAUL MUELLER COMPANY, 1600 W. Phelps, 65802, pg. 1141 **PB**

NationsBank of Southern Missouri, 117 Park Central Sq., 65806, pg. 1164 **PB**

NOBLE & ASSOCIATES, 336 S. Barnes, 65802, pg. 800 **PV**

Noble & Associates Promotion Group, 336 S. Barnes, 65802, pg. 800 **PV**

O'REILLY AUTOMOTIVE INC., 233 S. Patterson, 65802, pg. 1230 **PB**

O'Reilly Aviation, 233 S. Patterson, 65801, pg. 1230 **PB**

Ozark Automotive Distributors, Inc., 233 S. Patterson, 65801, pg. 1230 **PB**

POSITRONIC INDUSTRIES, INC., 423 N. Campbell, 65803, pg. 876 **PV**

REYCO INDUSTRIES, INC., 600 N. Prospect St., 65802, pg. 926 **PV**

Earl Scheib Automotive Paint Finishes, Inc., 1940 E. Trafficway, 65802, pg. 1437 **PB**

SOUTHERN MISSOURI CONTAINERS INC., 900 N. Belcrest St., 65802, pg. 1017 **PV**

The Springfield News Leader, 651 Boonville Ave., 65801, pg. 701 **PB**

Springfield Relay Systems, Inc., 2115 W. Bennett, 65807, pg. 264 **PB**

UPB of Southwest Missouri, 2045 S. Glenstone, 65808, pg. 1669 **PB**

Western International Media Corporation, 1949 E. Sunshine, Corp. Center One, Ste. 1-112, 65804, pg. 1167 **PV**

Stoutland

Stoutland Telephone Company, P.O. Box 97, Highway T, 65567, pg. 1572 **PB**

Stover

Benjamin Sheridan, 400 S. Walnut, 65078, pg. 291 **PV**

Strafford

Midwest Products, Inc., R.R. 1, Box 417, 65757, pg. 849 **PB**

Sullivan

Paramount Metalizing Div., 1008 W. North Service Rd., 63080, pg. 631 **PV**

Tipton

Stride Rite Footwear, Inc., 300 Monittau, 65081, pg. 1525 **PB**

Town and Country

HUNTCO INC., 14323 S. Outer Forty Dr., #600N, 63017, pg. 849 **PB**

Trenton

Contadina/Libby/Trenton Div., 1401 Harris Ave., 64683, pg. 916 **IT**

Troy

Douglas & Lomason Company, 1403 S. Third St., 63379, pg. 830 **IT**

NationsBank of Troy, 200 Main St., 63379, pg. 1165 **PB**

Watlow Process Systems, 300-A Industrial Dr., 63379, pg. 1153 **PV**

Union

Esselte Pendaflex, W. Park Ave., 63084, pg. 460 **IT**

Rexam Containers - US, P.O. Box 469, West Park Rd., 63084, pg. 1106 **IT**

Spartan Showcase, Inc., P.O. Box 470, 63084, pg. 904 **PV**

Unionville

Dunlap Manufacturing Co., P.O. Box 248, 63665, pg. 1137 **PV**

University City

Unitog Rental Facility, 6200 Olive Blvd., 63130, pg. 1693 **PB**

Warrensburg

Autoshred Inc., P.O. Box 866, Rt. 3, 64093, pg. 49 **PB**

Unitog Company, Hwy. 50 E., 64093, pg. 1693 **PB**

Warrenton

Binkley Company, 101 S. Elm St., 63383, pg. 534 **PV**

Ludlow-Saylor Inc., 1402 E. Old Highway 40, 63383, pg. 1066 **IT**

Warsaw

Unitog Company, P.O. Box 145, 65355, pg. 1693 **PB**

Washington

AEROLYTE SYSTEMS, One Cable Car Dr., 63090, pg. 24 **PV**

Pacer Industries, Inc., 1901 W. Main St., 63090, pg. 561 **PB**

SPORLAN VALVE COMPANY, 206 Lange Dr., 63090, pg. 1026 **PV**

Webb City

CARDINAL SCALE MANUFACTURING COMPANY, 203 E. Dogherty, 64870, pg. 209 **PV**

Detecto Scale Company, 203 E. Daugherty, 64870, pg. 209 **PV**

Webster Groves

Clayton Reinsurance, Ltd., 231 W. Lockwood Ave., 63119, pg. 1374 **PB**

Old Reliable Casualty Co., 231 W. Lockwood Ave., 63119, pg. 1374 **PB**

THE RELIABLE LIFE INSURANCE COMPANY, 231 W. Lockwood Ave., 63119, pg. 1374 **PB**

Wellsville

Wellsville Fire Brick Company, P.O. Box 71, West Hwy. 19, 63384, pg. 194 **PV**

Weston

MCCORMICK DISTILLING CO., One McCormick Ln., 64098, pg. 720 **PV**

MONTANA

Anaconda

Beal Mountain Mining Inc., 1800 Fairmont Rd., 59711, pg. 1269 **PB**

Billings

Automatic Music Service of Billings, Inc., 1327 Weil St., 59101, pg. 1319 **PB**

Balcron Oil Division, 1601 Lewis Ave. Bldg., 59102, pg. 589 **PB**

The Billings Gazette, 401 N. Broadway, 59101, pg. 983 **PB**

CNJ DISTRIBUTING, P.O. Box 20878, 59102, pg. 196 **PV**

Coluson Technologies, 12 Garden Ave., 59107, pg. 1523 **PB**

CORCORAN TRUCKING COMPANY, 221 Lomond Ln., 59101, pg. 275 **PV**

DENNY MENHOLT FRONTIER CHEVROLET, 1617 First Ave., N., 59101, pg. 324 **PV**

Fargo Glass & Paint Co., 4211 First Ave., S., 59101, pg. 393 **PV**

First Bank Montana, National Association, 303 N. Broadway, 59101, pg. 1680 **PB**

First Trust Company of Montana, National Association, P.O. Box 30678, 303 N. Broadway, 59101, pg. 1681 **PB**

Henneseys, Rimrock Mall, 59102, pg. 1090 **PB**

Hewlett-Packard Company, 710 Grand Ave., Ste. 12, 59101, pg. 814 **PB**

Montana Power Billings Div., P.O. Box 80330, 59103, pg. 1126 **PB**

NORTHWEST PIPE FITTINGS, INC., 33 S. Eighth St. W., 59102-5840, pg. 806 **PV**

Norwest Bank Montana, N.A., P.O. Box 30058, 59117, pg. 1202 **PB**

Piper Jaffray Inc., 224 N. Broadway, 59101-1935, pg. 1301 **PB**

RYAN OLDSMOBILE, 324 S. 24th St., W., 59102, pg. 953 **PV**

SafetyMaster Corporation, 12 Garden Ave., 59101, pg. 1523 **PB**

SELOVER BUICK, INC., 523 N. 29th St., 59101, pg. 983 **PV**

L.H. Sowles Company, Inc., 302 S. 24th St., 59101, pg. 1019 **PV**

SuperValu, Inc.-Ryans Div., 1629 King Ave. W., 59102, pg. 1541 **PB**

Sysco Food Services of Montana, Inc., 1509 Monad Rd., 59101, pg. 1551 **PB**

West Advertising/Public Relations, Inc., Transwestern 3 Bldg., 4th Fl., 59103, pg. 603 **PV**

Western Syncoal Company, P.O. BOx 7137, 59103-7137, pg. 1127 **PB**

Westmoreland Resources, Inc., 401 N. 31st St., Ste. 1620, 59103, pg. 1761 **PB**

Black Eagle

Montana Refining Co., 1900 10th St., 59414, pg. 830 **PB**

Bozeman

Bozeman Care Center, 321 N. Fifth Ave., 59715, pg. 1712 **PB**

COUNTRY CLASSIC DAIRIES, INC., P.O. Box 968, 59771, pg. 278 **PV**

Dana Design, 333 Simmetal Way, 59715, pg. 940 **PB**

HAMILTON STORES, INC., 1709 W. College St., 59715, pg. 497 **PV**

Geographic Index-U.S.

Montana Power Bozeman Div., P.O. Box 490, 59715, pg. 1126 — PB
Piper Jaffray Inc., 215 W. Mendenhall, Ste. C-3, 59715-3993, pg. 1301 — PB
POWER HOUSE TECHNOLOGIES, INC., 2311 S. Seventh Ave., 59715, pg. 1319 — PB
Skyland Scientific Services, Inc., 900 Technology Blvd., 59715, pg. 1515 — PB
Video Lottery Consultants, Inc., 2311 S. 7th Ave., 59715, pg. 1319 — PB

Butte

Altana Exploration Company, 16 E. Granite St., 59701, pg. 1127 — PB
Butte Convalescent Center, 2400 Continental Dr., 59701, pg. 837 — PB
Butte Park Royal, 3251 Nettie St., 59701, pg. 837 — PB
Canadian-Montana Gas Co., Ltd., 40 E. Broadway, 59701, pg. 1127 — PB
Canadian-Montana Pipeline Co., 40 E. Broadway, 59701, pg. 1127 — PB
Colstrip Community Services Company, 40 E. Broadway, 59701, pg. 1127 — PB
Continental Energy Services, Inc., 40 E. Broadway, 59701, pg. 1127 — PB
Entech, Inc., 16 E. Granite, 59701, pg. 1127 — PB
Glacier Gas Company, 40 E. Broadway, 59701, pg. 1127 — PB
Horizon Coal Services, Inc., 16 E. Granite, 59701, pg. 1127 — PB
MONTANA POWER COMPANY, 40 E. Broadway, 59701-9394, pg. 1126 — PB
The Montana Standard, 25 W. Granite St., 59701, pg. 984 — PB
North American Resources Co., 16 E. Granite, 59701, pg. 1127 — PB
Piper Jaffray Inc., First National Financial Ctr., 1940 Dewey Blvd., Ste. D, 59701-3724, pg. 1302 — PB
Rhone Poulenc Inc., P.O. Box 3146, 59702-3146, pg. 1112 — IT
Tetragenics, Inc., Hennessy Bldg., 130 N. Main St., 59701, pg. 1127 — PB
TOWN PUMP, INC., 600 S. Main St., 59701, pg. 1093 — PV
TRI Touch America, Hennessy Bldg., 130 N. Main St., 59701, pg. 1127 — PB

Clancy

Ash Grove Cement-Western Region Cement Plant, 100 Montana Hwy. 518, 59634, pg. 88 — PV

Colstrip

Western Energy Company, P.O. Box 99, 59323-0099, pg. 1127 — PB

Columbia Falls

COLUMBIA FALLS ALUMINUM COMPANY, 2000 Aluminum Dr., 59912, pg. 255 — PV

Deer Lodge

Colonial Manor of Deer Lodge, 1100 Texas Ave., 59722, pg. 837 — PB

Dillon

Parkview Acres, 200 Oregon St., 59725, pg. 1714 — PB

Gardiner

Mineral Hill Mine, P.O. Box 92, 13 Crevice Mountain Rd., 59030, pg. 1345 — IT

Glendive

F.T. REYNOLDS COMPANY, 1014 W. Towne St., 59330, pg. 926 — PV

Great Falls

BUTTREY FOOD & DRUG COMPANY, 601 Sixth St., S.W., 59404, pg. 271 — PB
D.A. DAVIDSON & CO., Davidson Bldg., 59401, pg. 314 — PV
ENERGY WEST INC., One First Ave. S., 59403, pg. 581 — PB
Energy West Resources, One First Ave. S., 59401, pg. 581 — PB
Financial Aims Corporation, Davidson Bldg., 59401, pg. 314 — PV
Great Falls Tribune, 205 River Dr. S., 59403, pg. 700 — PB
Missouri River Manor, 1130 17th Ave., S., 59405, pg. 837 — PB
Montana Power Great Falls Div., P.O. Box 589, 59401, pg. 1126 — PB
Montana Sun, Inc., One First Ave. S., 59401, pg. 581 — PB
National-General Supply, Inc., P.O. Box 2288, 410 14th St. S.W., 59403, pg. 1160 — PV
Northwest Fence Products Co., P.O. Box 1204, 226 2nd Ave., So., 59403, pg. 1160 — PV
PACIFIC HIDE & FUR DEPOT, 1401 3rd St.N.W., 59404, pg. 831 — PB
Piper Jaffray Inc., 26 Fourth St. N., 59401-4072, pg. 1301 — PB
TrustCorp., Davidson Bldg., 59403-2309, pg. 314 — PV

Hamilton

CARL WEISSMAN & SONS, INC., P.O. Box 1609, 59403, pg. 1160 — PV

Ravalli Republic, 232 Main St., 59840, pg. 1343 — PB

Helena

Basin Creek Mine, 5944 Hwy. 12, W., 59601, pg. 1269 — PB
Cormorant Corp., 406 Fuller Ave., 59601, pg. 1195 — PB
Hydrometrics, Inc., 2727 Airport Rd., 59601, pg. 138 — PB
The Independent Record, 317 Cruse Ave., 59604, pg. 983 — PB
Montana Power Helena Div., P.O. Box 5329, 59601, pg. 1126 — PB
Piper Jaffray Inc., 1414 Knight St., 59601-2350, pg. 1303 — PB
Western Care Nursing Home No. 439, 2475 Winne Ave., 59601, pg. 1715 — PB
Willis Corroon Administrative Services Corporation, 314 N. Last Chance Gulch, Ste. 200, 59601, pg. 1504 — IT

Hilger

CR Kendall Corporation, Kendall Mine, P.O. Box 799, 59451, pg. 302 — PB

Jefferson City

Montana Tunnels Mining, Inc., P.O. Box 176, 59638, pg. 1269 — PB

Kalispell

EQUITY SUPPLY COMPANY, P.O. Box 579, 59903, pg. 380 — PV
First Interstate Bank of Montana, N.A., Two Main St., 59901, pg. 1753 — PB
SEMITOOL, INC., 655 W. Reserve Dr., 59901, pg. 1456 — PB

Livingston

Livingston Convalescent Center No. 434, 510 S. 14th St., 59047, pg. 1714 — PB

Missoula

Browning-Ferris Industries of Montana, Inc., P.O. Box 8449, 59801, pg. 263 — PB
Green Tree Acceptance of Montana, Inc., 619 S.W. Higgins, Ste. B, 59801, pg. 762 — PB
IGT-Montana, Incorporated, 2118 S. Reserve St., 59801, pg. 300 — PB
The Missoulian, 500 S. Higgins Ave., 59801, pg. 984 — PB
Piper Jaffray Inc., 127 E. Front St., 59802-4489, pg. 1302 — PB

Poplar

A & S TRIBAL INDUSTRIES, Industrial Park Rd., 59255, pg. - — PV

Seeley Lake

PYRAMID MOUNTAIN LUMBER, Boy Scout Rd., 59868, pg. 896 — PV

Whitefish

Colonial Manor of Whitefish, 1305 E. Seventh St., 59937, pg. 837 — PB

Zortman

Zortman Mining Inc., P.O. Box 313, 59546, pg. 1269 — PB

NEBRASKA

Alliance

Woolrich Store Co., E. Hwy. #2, 69301, pg. 1188 — PV

Auburn

Auburn Consolidated Industries, Inc., 2100 S. J St., 68305-0350, pg. 762 — IT

Aurora

Chief Industries - Housing Div., P.O. Box 127, 68818, pg. 236 — PV

Beatrice

DEMPSTER INDUSTRIES INC., 711 So. 6th, 68310, pg. 324 — PV
F. D. Kees Power Equipment, 700 Park Ave. 68310, pg. 1195 — PB
Land O'Lakes Inc., 2020 S. Sixth St., Ste. 908, 68310-5103, pg. 646 — PV

Bellevue

Information Technology Division, 1404 Fort Crook Rd. S., 68005-2969, pg. 1516 — PB

Blair

D.L. Blair Inc., 1548 Front St., 68008, pg. 148 — PV

Central City

Atlantic Homes Div., P.O. Box 148, Hwy. 14 N., 68826, pg. 332 — PB

Clay Center

DAHLSTEN TRUCK LINE, INC., 101 W. Edgar St., 68933, pg. 306 — PV

Columbus

BEHLEN MFG. CO., 4025 E. 23rd St., 68601, pg. 130 — PV
Dale Electronics, Inc., 1122 23rd St., 68601-3647, pg. 1722 — PB
Douglas & Lomason Company, 1851 E. 32nd Ave., 68601, pg. 830 — IT
FLEISCHER MANUFACTURING, INC., 2281 16th Ave., 68601, pg. 410 — PV
NEBRASKA PUBLIC POWER DISTRICT, 1414 15th St., 68602-0499, pg. 789 — PV

Dakota City

IBP-Dakota City, P.O. Box 515, 68731, pg. 852 — PB
IBP, INC., IBP Ave., 68731, pg. 852 — PB

Deshler

REINKE MANUFACTURING CO., INC., 101 Reinke Rd., 68340, pg. 920 — PV

Elkhorn

Brumko Magnetics, 150 Binfield St., 68022, pg. 696 — PV

Fremont

CRX Inc., 1200 Hamilton, 68025, pg. 49 — PB
Fremont Mfg., 700 S. Downing, 68025, pg. 1215 — PB
Magnus Metals, S. Bell & Viaduct, 68025, pg. 394 — PV
Shade Pasta, Inc., 805 S. Union, 68025, pg. 802 — PV

Gering

AGROMAC INTERNATIONAL, INC., 220757 E. Hwy. 92, 69341, pg. 27 — PV
MASEK DISTRIBUTING INC., 1100 Rundell Rd., 69341, pg. 711 — PV

Gothenburg

GRN Corp., 1000 12th Street, 69138, pg. 466 — PV

Grand Island

Chief Construction, 2107 S. North Rd., P.O. Box 2078, 68802-2078, pg. 236 — PV
Chief E-Z Breaker, Inc., 2809 E. Hwy. 30, 68801, pg. 236 — PV
Chief Financial Services, 1811 W. Second St., Ste. 425, 68803, pg. 236 — PV
Chief Industries - Agri/Industrial Products Div., P.O. Box 2078, 68802, pg. 236 — PV
Chief Industries - Buildings Div., P.O. Box 2078, 68802, pg. 236 — PV
CHIEF INDUSTRIES, INC., 3942 W. Old Hwy. 30, 68803, pg. 236 — PV
Chief Industries Inc.- Fabrication Div., 119 S. Adams St., 68801, pg. 236 — PV
Country General Stores, 123 S. Webb Rd., 68803, pg. 237 — PV
Ecology System Dept., P.O. Box 2078, 68802, pg. 236 — PV
Electronic Display Systems (Kallego), 2809 E. Hwy. 30, 68801, pg. 236 — PV
Grand Island Contract Carriers & Brokerage, Inc., P.O. Box 2078, 68802-2078, pg. 236 — PV
The Grand Island Daily Independent, P.O. Box 1208, 1st & Cedar Sts., 68802-1208, pg. 995 — PB
Hornady Ammunition, 3625 Old Potash Hwy., 68801, pg. 540 — PV
HORNADY MANUFACTURING COMPANY, 3625 Old Potash Hwy., 68803, pg. 539 — PV
The Overland National Bank, 21st & First Ave., 68848, pg. 629 — PB

Hastings

ALLENS OF HASTINGS, INC., 1115 W. Second St., 68901, pg. 37 — PV
Chief Ethanol Fuels, Inc., P.O. Box 488, 68902-0488, pg. 236 — PV
City National Bank, Third & Lincoln Ave., 68901, pg. 629 — PB
DUTTON-LAINSON CO., 451 W. Second, 68902, pg. 350 — PV

PB - U.S. Public Companies Volume
PV - U.S. Private Companies Volume
IT - International Public & Private Companies Volume

1308

Kearney

Baldwin Filters, P.O. Box 6010, 4400 E. Hwy. 30, 68848-6010, pg. 381 — **PB**
THE BUCKLE, INC., P.O. Box 1480, 2407 W. 24th St., 68847, pg. 267 — **PB**
Chief Agri/Industrial Division, P.O. Box 848, 68848, pg. 236 — **PV**
Engine Components Div., 4200 Highway 30 East, 68848, pg. 557 — **PV**
First National Bank, 21st & First Ave., 68848, pg. 629 — **PB**

Lexington

IBP-Lexington, P.O. Box 920, 68850, pg. 852 — **PB**
LEXINGTON CO-OP OIL CO., P.O. Box A, 68850, pg. 666 — **PV**

Lincoln

Aliant Cellular Telephone Company, 1440 M St., 68508, pg. 40 — **PB**
Aliant Communications Co., 1440 M St., 68508, pg. 40 — **PB**
ALIANT COMMUNICATIONS INC., 1440 M St., 68508, pg. 40 — **PB**
Aliant Systems Inc., 2201 Winthrop Rd., 68502, pg. 41 — **PB**
American Tool Companies, Inc., 301 S. 13th St., Ste. 600, 68508, pg. 63 — **PV**
AMERITAS LIFE INSURANCE CORP., 5900 O St., 68510, pg. 65 — **PV**
Ameritas Variable Life Insurance Company, 5900 O St., 68510, pg. 65 — **PV**
Assurity Life Inc., 1526 K St., 68501, pg. 1187 — **PV**
Bader Rutter & Assoc. Inc., 825 M St., Ste. 200, 68508, pg. 110 — **PV**
Cook Family Foods, Ltd., 200 S. Second St., 68508, pg. 428 — **PV**
Cooperative Service Co., 1001 S. 70th St., Ste. 210, 68510, pg. 789 — **PV**
CRETE CARRIER CORP., 400 N.W. 56th, 68528, pg. 289 — **PV**
EA Engineering, Science & Technology, Inc., 121 S. 13th St., Ste. 701, 68508, pg. 541 — **PB**
FIRST COMMERCE BANCSHARES, INC., 1248 O St., 68508-1423, pg. 629 — **PB**
First Commerce Investors, 13th & O, 68508, pg. 629 — **PB**
First Commerce Mortgage Company, 13th & O, 68508, pg. 629 — **PB**
First Commerce Technologies, 500 NBC Ctr., 68508, pg. 629 — **PB**
Fleming Co. of Nebraska, Inc., 1601 Pioneer Blvd., 68501, pg. 653 — **PB**
Gooch Foods, Inc., 510 South St., 68502, pg. 128 — **PB**
Information Technology, Inc., 1345 Old Cherry Rd., 68512, pg. 647 — **PB**
Isco Environmental Division, 531 Westgate Blvd., 68528, pg. 914 — **PB**
ISCO, INC., 4700 Superior St., 68505, pg. 913 — **PB**
Isco Separation Instruments Division, 4700 Superior St., 68504, pg. 914 — **PB**
E.F. Johnson Radio Systems, 4800 NW 1st St., 68521, pg. 1630 — **PB**
Johnson Gear, 1401 W. Bond Cir., 68521, pg. 85 — **PV**
Journal Star Lincoln, 926 P St., 68501, pg. 983 — **PB**
Kawasaki Motors Manufacturing Corp., U.S.A., 6600 N.W. 27th St., 68524, pg. 725 — **IT**
LINCOLN ELECTRIC SYSTEMS, 1040 O St., 68508, pg. 668 — **PV**
Lincoln Graphics Inc., 2000 Judson St., 68521-1322, pg. 503 — **PB**
LINCOLN INDUSTRIES, 10001 S. 70th St., Ste. 102, 68501, pg. 668 — **PB**
National Bank of Commerce, 13th & O, 68508, pg. 629 — **PB**
NATIONAL RESEARCH CORPORATION, 1033 O St., 68508, pg. 1159 — **PB**
NEBRASKA BOOK CO., INC., 4700 S. 19th, 68512, pg. 789 — **PV**
Pegler-Sysco Food Services Co., 1700 Center Park Rd., 68512, pg. 1550 — **PB**
Piper Jaffray Inc., 200 Cornhusker Plaza, 301 S. 13th St., Ste. 200, 68508-2500, pg. 1301 — **PB**
Prairie Communications, Inc., P.O. Box 81309, 68508, pg. 41 — **PB**
Ransomes-Cushman-Ryan, 900 N. 21st St., 68503, pg. 1088 — **IT**
SCHNIEBER FINE FOODS, INC., 2500 State Fair Park Dr., 68504, pg. 971 — **PV**
SmithKline Beecham Labs, 601 W. Cornhusker Hwy., 68521-3577, pg. 1265 — **IT**
SNYDER INDUSTRIES, INC., 4700 Fremont St., 68504, pg. 1011 — **PV**
Square D Co., 1717 Centerpark Rd., 68512, pg. 1208 — **IT**
TRANSCRYPT INTERNATIONAL, 4800 N.W. 1st St., 68521, pg. 1630 — **PB**
Union Insurance Company, 3641 Village Dr., 68516, pg. 216 — **PV**
WOODMEN ACCIDENT & LIFE CO., 1526 K St., 68508, pg. 1187 — **PV**

Lindsay

LINDSAY MANUFACTURING COMPANY, E. Hwy. 91, Box 156, 68644, pg. 999 — **PB**
Lindsay Transportation Inc., Box 156, 68644, pg. 1000 — **PB**

Louisville

Ash Grove Cement Plant, P.O. Box 609, 68037, pg. 88 — **PV**

Madison

IBP-Madison, P.O. Box 1010, 68748, pg. 852 — **PB**

McCook

First National Bank, P.O. Box 1388, 108 W. P St., 69001, pg. 629 — **PB**

Minden

Royal Plastic, P.O. Box 380, 68959, pg. 453 — **PV**

Morrill

KELLEY BEAN CO., INC., Bean Blvd., 69358, pg. 612 — **PV**

Norfolk

Affiliated Carriers, Inc., P.O. Box 1067, 68702-1067, pg. 25 — **PV**
AFFILIATED FOODS COOPERATIVE INC., 13th St. & Omaha Ave., 68701, pg. 25 — **PV**
Affiliated Independent Development, P.O. Box 1067, 67802-1067, pg. 25 — **PV**
Affiliated Insurance Services, Inc., P.O. Box 1067, 67802-1067, pg. 25 — **PV**
BeefAmerica, 1500 S. Logan, 68701, pg. 130 — **PV**
GTL Truck Lines, Inc., P.O. Box 769, 1200 S. 13th St., 68702-0769, pg. 1152 — **PV**
Nebraska Dairies, Inc., P.O. Box 769, 1200 S. Johnny Carson Blvd., 68702-0769, pg. 1152 — **PV**
Nucor Cold Finish-Nebraska, P.O. Box 59, 68702, pg. 1205 — **PB**
R.X.D., Inc., 806 Cluster Ave., 68702, pg. 1376 — **PB**

North Platte

American Door Company of Michigan, Inc.-Flush Door Plant, P.O. Box 218, 69101, pg. 1067 — **IT**
Western Nebraska National Bank, Third & Dewey, 69101, pg. 629 — **PB**

Oakland

HOLMQUIST GRAIN & LUMBER CO., 200 N. Logan Ave., 68045-0127, pg. 535 — **PV**

Ogallala

ASC, 301 W. O St., 69153, pg. 1236 — **IT**
Ogallala Electronics, 601 W. First St., 69153, pg. 1420 — **PB**

Ohiowa

FEED SERVICE CORP., R.R. Two, Box 31, 68416, pg. 399 — **PV**
Mid-America Feed Yard, Rte. Two, Box 31, 68416, pg. 399 — **PV**

Omaha

ACCEPTANCE INSURANCE CO., INC., 222 S. 15th St., Ste. 600 N., 68102-1628, pg. 14 — **PB**
Acceptance Insurance Companies, Inc., 222 S. 15th St., Ste. 600 N., 68102, pg. 15 — **PB**
AG PROCESSING INC., A COOPERATIVE, 12700 W. Dodge Rd., 68154, pg. 26 — **PV**
Ahern Fire Protection, 4428 S. 139th St., 68137, pg. 27 — **PV**
Allied Construction Specialities, 2200 S. 21st St., 68108, pg. 39 — **PV**
Allied Oil & Supply, 2209 S. 24th St., 68108, pg. 39 — **PV**
ALLIED OIL & SUPPLY, INC., 2209 S. 24th St., 68108, pg. 39 — **PV**
Allied Tire Co., 2209 S. 24th St., 68108, pg. 39 — **PV**
Allright Corporation, 202 N. 19th St., 68102, pg. 42 — **PV**
Allright Parking - Omaha, 202 North 19th St., 68102, pg. 43 — **PV**
AMERICAN BUSINESS ADVERTISING, 5711 S. 86th Cir., 68127, pg. 51 — **PV**
AMERICAN BUSINESS INFORMATION, INC., 5711 S. 86th Circle, 68127, pg. 69 — **PB**
American Business Information Marketing, 5711 S. 86 Cir., 68127, pg. 70 — **PB**
Applied Communications, Inc., 330 S. 108th Ave., 68154, pg. 1629 — **PB**
Aquila Energy Corp., 2533 N. 117th Ave., Ste. 200, 68164, pg. 1701 — **PB**
Aquila Energy Marketing, 2533 N. 117th Ave. Ste. 300, 68164, pg. 1701 — **PB**
Aquila Energy Resources, 2533 N. 117th St., Ste. 300, 68164, pg. 1701 — **PB**
Baker's Supermarkets, Inc., 8420 W. Dodge, 68114, pg. 652 — **PB**
Ballantyne of Omaha, Inc., Strong International, 4350 McKinley Rd., 68112, pg. 17 — **IT**
BEEFAMERICA OPERATING CO., INC., 14748 W. Center Rd., 68144, pg. 130 — **PV**
BERKSHIRE HATHAWAY INC., 3555 Farnam St., Ste. 1440, 68131, pg. 217 — **PB**
Browning-Ferris Industries of Nebraska, Inc., 2121 S. 24th St., 68108, pg. 263 — **PB**
CD-Rom Technologies, 5711 S. 86 Cir., 68124, pg. 70 — **PB**
Cable Services Group, 2525 N. 117th Ave., 68164, pg. 283 — **PB**
CALENERGY CO., 302 S. 36th St., Ste. 400, 68131-3845, pg. 292 — **PB**
Call Interactive, 2121 N. 117th St., 68164, pg. 631 — **PB**
CARLSON SYSTEMS, 8990 F St., 68127, pg. 212 — **PV**
Coleman Powermate, Inc., 7202 World Communications Dr., 68122, pg. 691 — **PV**
Coleman Powermate Inc., 1 Landmark Ctr., 14748 W. Center Rd., 68144, pg. 691 — **PV**
Commercial Federal Bank, 2120 S. 72nd St., 68124, pg. 411 — **PB**
COMMERCIAL FEDERAL CORPORATION, 2120 S. 72nd St., 68124, pg. 411 — **PB**
ConAgra Broiler Co., One ConAgra Dr., 68102, pg. 427 — **PB**
ConAgra Dairy & Food Oils, One ConAgra Dr., 68102, pg. 427 — **PB**
ConAgra Diversified Products Companies, One ConAgri Dr., 68102, pg. 428 — **PB**
ConAgra Feed Ingredient Merchandising Company, One ConAgra Dr., 68102, pg. 428 — **PB**
ConAgra Frozen Food Company, 5 Conagra Dr., 68102, pg. 427 — **PB**
ConAgra Fruen Milling Co., 1 Conagra Dr., 68102, pg. 428 — **PB**
ConAgra Grocery Products Packaging Company, One ConAgra Dr., 68102, pg. 426 — **PB**
CONAGRA, INC., One ConAgra Dr., 68102-5001, pg. 425 — **PB**
ConAgra International, One Central Park Plaza, 68102, pg. 426 — **PB**
ConAgra Poultry Foodservice Co., One ConAgra Dr., 68102, pg. 427 — **PB**
ConAgra Prepared Food Companies, Five ConAgra Drive, 68102-5005, pg. 427 — **PB**
ConAgra Retail Companies, One ConAgra Dr., 68102, pg. 426 — **PB**
ConAgra Specialty Grain Products Co., One ConAgra Dr., 68102, pg. 427 — **PB**
ConAgra Trading Companies (CTC), One Central Park Plaza, 68102, pg. 428 — **PB**
ConAgra Trading & Processing Companies, Nine Conagra Dr., 68102, pg. 428 — **PB**
Continental General Corporation, 8901 Indian Hills Dr., 68114, pg. 1164 — **PV**
Continental General Insurance Company, 8901 Indian Hills Dr., 68114, pg. 1164 — **PV**
Continental Print & Photo Co., 8901 Indian Hills Dr., 68114, pg. 1164 — **PV**
Cornhusker Casualty Co., 9140 W. Dodge Rd., 68114, pg. 221 — **PB**
Cox Communications-Omaha, 11505 W. Dodge Rd., 68154, pg. 455 — **PB**
D & D Salads, 9425 N 48th St., 68152, pg. 551 — **PV**
DWF of Omaha, 9312 G Street, 68127, pg. 326 — **PV**
LEO A. DALY COMPANY, 8600 Indian Hills Dr., 68114, pg. 309 — **PV**
Data Documents Holdings, Inc., 4205 S. 96th St., 68127, pg. 449 — **PB**
Data Documents, Inc., 9503 F St., 68127, pg. 449 — **PB**
DATA TRANSMISSION NETWORK CORPORATION, 9110 W. Dodge Rd., Ste. 200, 68114, pg. 486 — **PB**
Empire Fire & Marine Insurance Co., 1624 Douglas St., 68102, pg. 1530 — **IT**
Empire Indemnity Insurance Company, 1624 Douglas St., 68102, pg. 1530 — **IT**
Exclusive Healthcare, Inc., Mutual of Omaha Plaza, 68175, pg. 770 — **PV**
F. C. Banks, 206 S. 19th St., 68102-1704, pg. 398 — **PV**
Farmers National Company, 11516 Nicholas St., Ste. 100, 68154-4427, pg. 738 — **PV**
Farmers Union Co-Operative Insurance Company of Nebraska, 407 N. 117th St., 68154, pg. 395 — **PV**
First Data Resources, 10825 Farnham Dr., 68154, pg. 631 — **PB**
First Mortgage Corporation, P.O. Box 2158, 68103-2158, pg. 501 — **PB**
Freedom Investment, 11422 Miracle Hills Dr., Ste. 501, 68154, pg. 476 — **IT**
Fruen Oat Milling Co., One ConAgra Dr., 68102, pg. 428 — **PB**
GODFATHER'S PIZZA, INC., 9140 W. Dodge Rd., 68114, pg. 458 — **PV**
Gourmet Popping Corn Co., 11213 E. Circle-Ste. B, 68137, pg. 977 — **PV**
Gra-Gar Inc., 14507 Frontier Rd., 68138, pg. 1755 — **PB**
Grain Flour Milling Co., One Central Park Plaza, 68102, pg. 428 — **PB**
Graphic Arts Supply Division, 4110 S. 52nd St., 68117, pg. 205 — **PB**
Guarantee American Life Company, 8801 Indian Hills Dr., 68114, pg. 768 — **PB**
GUARANTEE LIFE INSURANCE CO., 8801 Indian Hills Dr., 68114, pg. 768 — **PB**
HDR Engineering, Inc., 8404 Indian Hills Dr., 68114, pg. 207 — **IT**
HDR Inc., 8404 Indian Hills Dr., 68114, pg. 206 — **IT**
Henningsen Foods, Inc., 14334 Industrial Rd., 68137, pg. 1074 — **PV**
Henningson, Durham & Richardson Inc., 8404 Indian Hills Dr., 68114, pg. 207 — **IT**
Hewlett-Packard Company, 11626 Nicholas St., 68154, pg. 814 — **PB**
Hillhaven Omaha, 7410 Mercy Rd., 68124, pg. 1713 — **PB**
Hydro Conduit Corp., P.O. Box 318, Hwy. 275 W. Valley, 68064, pg. 245 — **IT**
ITI MARKETING SERVICES, INC., 902 N. 91 Plaza, 68114, pg. 555 — **PV**
Imperial Casualty & Indemnity Co., Grain Exchange Bldg., 1905 Harney St., Ste. 300, 68102, pg. 103 — **PB**
INACOM CORP., 10810 Farnam Dr., 68154, pg. 873 — **PB**
Integrated Marketing Services, 3250 N. 93rd St., 68134, pg. 631 — **PB**

PB - *U.S. Public Companies Volume*
PV - *U.S. Private Companies Volume*
IT - *International Public & Private Companies Volume*

Geographic Index-U.S.

1309

KETV, 2665 Douglas St., 68131-2699, pg. 1343   **PB**
KHR, 3030 L St., 68107, pg. 603   **PV**
KMTV-3, 10714 Mockingbird Drive, 68127, pg. 983   **PV**
Kiewit Construction Group, Inc., 1000 Kiewit Plaza, 68131, pg. 619   **PV**
Kiewit Mining Group, Inc., 1000 Kiewit Plaza, 68131, pg. 619   **PV**
PETER KIEWIT SONS INC., 1000 Kiewit Plaza, 68131, pg. 619   **PV**
Kirkpatrick Pettis Smith Polian, Inc., 10250 Regency Cir., Ste. 200, 68114, pg. 770   **PV**
LOZIER CORPORATION, 6336 Pershing Dr., 68110, pg. 679   **PV**
MFS Network Technologies, Inc., pg. 1779   **PB**
MFS WorldCom, Inc., P.O. Box 542020, 11808 Miracle Hills Dr., 68154-8000, pg. 1779   **PB**
Major Group Inc., 222 S. 15th St., St. 600 N., 68102, pg. 15   **PV**
MASTERCRAFT FURNITURE CORP., 1111 N. 13th St., 68102, pg. 714   **PV**
MUTUAL OF OMAHA INSURANCE COMPANY, Mutual of Omaha Plaza, 68175, pg. 769   **PV**
Mutual of Omaha Investor Services, Inc., 10235 Regency Cir., 68114, pg. 770   **PV**
Nash Finch Co., 7401 F St., 68127, pg. 1152   **PB**
National Disposal Service of Nebraska, Inc., 212 S. 24th St., 68108, pg. 264   **PB**
National Indemnity Co., 3024 Harney St., 68131, pg. 221   **PB**
National Indemnity Company of Mid-America, 3024 Harney St., 68131, pg. 221   **PB**
Nebraska Engineering Co., P.O. Box 12277, 68112, pg. 1064   **PV**
Nebraska Furniture Mart, Inc., 700 So. 72nd St., 68103, pg. 221   **PV**
Northern Natural Gas Co., P.O. Box 3330, 68103-0330, pg. 584   **PB**
Northern Plains Natural Gas Co., P.O. Box 3330, 68103-0330, pg. 584   **PB**
Norwest Bank Nebraska, N.A., P.O. Box 3408, 68103, pg. 1202   **PB**
Omaha Auto Auction Inc., 9201 S. 144th St., 68138, pg. 1649   **PB**
Omaha Div., 4417 Q St., 68107, pg. 180   **PV**
Omaha Plant-Kellogg USA, P.O. Box 3866, 68103, pg. 947   **PB**
Omaha Property and Casualty Insurance Co., 3102 Farnam St., 68131, pg. 770   **PV**
OMAHA PUBLIC POWER DISTRICT, OPPD Energy Plaza, 444 S. 16th St. Mall, 68102-2247, pg. 815   **PV**
OMAHA STEAKS, P.O. Box 3300, 68103, pg. 815   **PV**
Omaha Steaks-Retail Stores, 10909 John Galt Blvd., 68103, pg. 816   **PV**
Omaha Vaccine Company, 3030 L St., 68107, pg. 603   **PV**
Orent GraphicArts, Inc., 4805 G St., 68117-1414, pg. 503   **PB**
PACESETTER CORPORATION, 4343 S. 96th St., 68127, pg. 830   **PV**
PAMIDA HOLDINGS CORPORATION, 8800 F St., 68127, pg. 1255   **PB**
Pamida, Inc., 8800 F St., 68127, pg. 1255   **PB**
Pamida Transportation Co., 8800 F St., 68127, pg. 1255   **PB**
Paxton & Vierling, P.O. Box 1085, 68101, pg. 824   **PV**
PENCO-Nebraska, 11128 John Galt Blvd., Ste. 585, 68137, pg. 1508   **IT**
PHYSICIANS MUTUAL INSURANCE CO., 2600 Dodge, 68131-2671, pg. 864   **PV**
Piper, Jaffray & Hopwood, Inc., 910 N. 96th St., Ste. 200, 68114-2548, pg. 1300   **PB**
PRECISION INDUSTRIES, 4611 S. 96th St., 68127, pg. 879   **PV**
Principal Health Care of Nebraska, Inc., P.O. Box 541210, 330 N. 117th St., 68154, pg. 886   **PV**
PROGRESS WEST CORPORATION, 10180 L Street, 68127, pg. 890   **PV**
Railway Educational Bureau, 1809 Capitol Ave., 68102, pg. 1000   **PV**
Reed Travel Publishing-Omaha, 810 N. 96th St., Ste. 007, 68114, pg. 1097   **IT**
Rochester-Midland ICL, 1015 N. 14th St., 68102, pg. 937   **PV**
THE SCOULAR COMPANY, The Scoular Bldg., 2027 Dodge St., 68102, pg. 977   **PV**
Scoular Properties, Inc., 2027 Dodge St., 68102, pg. 977   **PV**
Seaway Importing Company, 8800 F St., 68127, pg. 1255   **PB**
Sergeant's Pet Products Company, 15th & Douglas, 68102-5009, pg. 427   **PB**
Skinner Macaroni, 6848 F St., 68117, pg. 812   **PB**
SUPERIOR INDUSTRIES OF NEBRASKA, INC., 11218 John Galt Blvd., 68137, pg. 1055   **PV**
TIE Systems-Omaha/Des Moines, 1501 Y St., 68107, pg. 1085   **PV**
TN Services Inc., 800 Blackstone Centre, 302 S. 36th St., 68134-2453, pg. 1642   **PV**
Tele-Trip Company, Mutual of Omaha Plaza, 68175, pg. 770   **PV**
TRANSACTION SYSTEMS ARCHITECTS, INC., 330 S. 108th Ave., 68154, pg. 1629   **PB**
Union Pacific Railroad Company, 1416 Dodge St., 68179, pg. 1668   **PB**
Unisource, 5220 F St., 68117, pg. 1671   **PB**
United HealthCare of the Midlands, Inc., 2717 N. 118th Cir., 68164-9672, pg. 1678   **PB**
United of Omaha Life Insurance Company, Mutual of Omaha Plaza, 68175, pg. 770   **PV**
United World Life Insurance Company, Mutual of Omaha Plaza, 68175, pg. 770   **PV**

Utell International-Omaha, 810 N. 96th St., 68114-2594, pg. 1098   **IT**
Valmont Financial Corporation, 11213 Davenport, Ste. 303, 68154, pg. 335   **PB**
Valmont Indemnity Co. Ltd., 11213 Davenport, Ste. 303, 68154, pg. 335   **PB**
Ventura Foods, 1604 Fort St., 68110, pg. 508   **PV**
The Walling Co., Inc., 6103 N. 90th St., 68134, pg. 360   **PV**
WARREN DISTRIBUTION, INC., 727 S. 13th St., 68102, pg. 1151   **PV**
The Weitz Company, Inc., Executive Plaza, 6818 Grover St., Ste. 201, 68106, pg. 1161   **PV**
WERNER ENTERPRISES, INC., 14507 Frontier Rd., 68138, pg. 1754   **PB**
WESTIN, INC., 11808 W. Center Rd., 68144, pg. 1169   **PV**
Woodward-Clyde, One Old Mill Bldg., 101 S. 108th Ave., 68154, pg. 1656   **PV**
Wright & Wilhelmy Co., 11005 E St., 68137, pg. 335   **PV**
Zeneca Ag Products, 4111 Gibson Rd., 68107, pg. 1525   **IT**
Ziegler Medical Equipment Group, Inc., 9305 H Ct., 68127, pg. 1792   **PB**

Pender

AUTOMATIC EQUIPMENT MFG. CO., Industrial Park, One Mill Road, 68047, pg. 101   **PV**

Schuyler

WAGNER MILLS INC., P.O. Box 545, 68661, pg. 1146   **PV**

Scottsbluff

Ameri-Co Carriers, Inc., 1702 E. Overland, 69361, pg. 63   **PB**
Nationwide Freight Services, Inc., 1702 E. Overland, 69361, pg. 64   **PB**

South Sioux City

Great West Casualty Company, 1100 W. 29th St., 68776, pg. 1218   **PB**

Valley

VALMONT INDUSTRIES, INC., W. Hwy. 275, 68064, pg. 1706   **PB**
Valmont Irrigation Division, W. Hwy. 275, 68064, pg. 1707   **PB**

Waverly

National Crane, 11200 N. 148th St., 68462, pg. 593   **IT**

Wayne

Great Dane Trailers-Nebraska, Inc., 1200 Centennial Rd., 68787, pg. 1030   **PV**

West Point

First National Bank, P.O. Box 187, 142 S. Main, 68788, pg. 629   **PB**
IBP-West Point, RR 3, Box 57, 68788, pg. 852   **PB**

York

Champion Home Builders Co., Box 585, 68467, pg. 332   **PB**
Sundstrand Aviation Operations, 2800 Division Ave., P.O. Box 523, 68467, pg. 1533   **PV**
Sunflower Carriers, P.O. Box 9, 68467, pg. 289   **PV**
The York News-Times, P.O. Box 279, 327 Platte Ave., 68467-0279, pg. 995   **PV**

NEVADA

Battle Mountain

McCoy/Cove Mines, One McCoy Rd.-Box 1658, 89820, pg. 562   **PB**

Boulder City

Boulder City Care Center, 601 Adams Blvd., 89005, pg. 837   **PB**
Computer Sports World, 1005 Elm St., 89005, pg. 484   **PV**

Carlin

Cominco American Resources Incorporated, Buckhorn Operations, P.O. Box 847, 89822, pg. 307   **IT**

Carson City

Carson Convalescent Center, 2898 Hwy. 50 E., 89701, pg. 837   **PB**
Joan Cook, 2500 Arrowhead Dr., 89706, pg. 879   **PB**
CUBIX CORPORATION, 2800 Lockheed Way, 89706, pg. 294   **PV**
Harrah's Reno Holding Company, 502 E. John St., Rm. E, 89701, pg. 791   **PB**
INITIO, INC., 2500 Arrowhead Dr., 89706, pg. 879   **PB**
MALLORY, INC., 550 Mallory Way, 89701, pg. 698   **PV**
R&R Advertising, 102 S. Nevada St., 89701, pg. 902   **PV**

Sierra Cast Inc., 2727 Lockheed, 89701, pg. 1782   **PB**
Sierra Convalescent Center, 201 Koontz Ln., 89701, pg. 837   **PB**
UNITED ENGINE & MACHINE COMPANY, 4909 Goni Rd., 89706, pg. 1121   **PV**

Dayton

BRUCE INDUSTRIES, INC., 101 Evans Ave., 89403, pg. 175   **PV**
CIMCO, 80 Airport Vist Blvd., 89403, pg. 574   **PV**

Elko

Bullfrog Mine, P.O. Box 519, 89803, pg. 169   **IT**
Dee Gold Mining Co., P.O. Box 1193, 89801, pg. 1089   **IT**
Goldstrike Mine, P.O. Box 29, 89801, pg. 169   **IT**
Meikle Mine Project, P.O. Box 29, 89801, pg. 169   **IT**

Ely

Magma-Robinson Mining District, P.O. Box 37, 89319, pg. 224   **IT**

Fallon

Fallon Convalescent Center, 365 W. A St., 89406, pg. 837   **PB**
SMI Joist Nevada, 2121 Trento Ln., 89406, pg. 413   **PB**

Fernley

CR Minerals Corporation, Operations Office, 100 Front St., 89408, pg. 302   **PB**
Nevada Cement Co., P.O. Box 895, 89408, pg. 323   **PB**

Hawthorne

Day & Zimmermann Hawthorne Corporation, P.O. Box 15, 89415-0015, pg. 317   **PV**

Henderson

ALTA GOLD CO., 601 Whitney Ranch Dr., Ste 10, 89014, pg. 58   **PB**
Ethel M Chocolates, P.O. Box 98505, 89193, pg. 707   **PV**
Henderson Convalescent Hospital, 1180 E. Lake Mead, 89015, pg. 837   **PB**
Hydro Conduit Corp., 2100 Burns Rd., 89015, pg. 245   **IT**
KVVU Broadcasting Corporation, 25 TV5 Dr., 89014, pg. 1094   **PB**
Oakwood Financial Corporation, P.O. Box 50401, 89016, pg. 1209   **PB**
Oakwood Funding Corp., P.O. Box 50401, 89016, pg. 1209   **PB**
Railroad Pass Casino, 2800 S. Boulder Hwy., 89105, pg. 375   **PB**
Sun City MacDonald Ranch, 2055 W. Horizon Ridge Pkwy., 89012, pg. 495   **PB**

Incline Village

FORTIFIBER CORPORATION, 1001 Tahoe Blvd., 89451, pg. 419   **PB**
Hyatt Regency Lake Tahoe Resort & Casino, Country Club Dr. at Lakeshore, 89450, pg. 551   **PV**

Jean

Goldstrike Hotel, One Main St., 89109, pg. 375   **PB**
Nevada Landing, Two Goodsprings Rd., 89109, pg. 375   **PB**

Las Vegas

APT Coin Machines, Inc., 4380 Boulder Hwy., 89109, pg. 47   **PB**
ATC Healthcare, 4045 Spencer St., 89119, pg. 8   **PV**
AGRIBIOTECH, INC., 2700 Sunset Rd., C-25, 89120, pg. 28   **PB**
ALADDIN HOTEL & CASINO, 3667 Las Vegas Blvd. S., 89193-3958, pg. 30   **PV**
ALLIANCE GAMING CORPORATION, 6601 S. Bermuda Rd., 89119, pg. 46   **PB**
Allied Security Inc., Executive Ctr. E., 1515 E. Tropicana Ave., Ste. 395, 89119, pg. 40   **PV**
Allright Sierra Parking Inc., 222 E. Carson Ave., 89101, pg. 43   **PV**
AMERICAN PACIFIC CORPORATION, 3770 Howard Hughes Pkwy., Ste. 300, 89109, pg. 88   **PB**
AMPAC Development Company, 3770 Howard Hughes Pkwy., Ste. 300, 89109, pg. 88   **PB**
Anicom, 4545 Cameron St., Ste. A, 89103, pg. 115   **PB**
Asher/Gould Advertising, Inc. - Las Vegas, 3900 Paradise Rd., Ste. 109, 89109, pg. 88   **PV**
Associated Business Products, 3095 E. Patrick Ave., 89120, pg. 863   **PB**
Atlandia Design & Furnishings, Inc., 3260 S. Industrial Rd., 89109, pg. 1116   **PB**
BFD Productions, Inc., 1221 S. Casino Ctr., 89104, pg. 1321   **PB**
Bally Gaming Inc., 6601 S. Bermuda Rd., 89119, pg. 47   **PB**
Bally's Grand Inc. (Las Vegas), 3645 Las Vegas Blvd. S., 89109, pg. 829   **PB**
Behavioral Healthcare Options, Inc., 2801 S. Valley View Blvd., 89102, pg. 1469   **PB**

PB - U.S. Public Companies Volume
PV - U.S. Private Companies Volume
IT - International Public & Private Companies Volume

1310

Geographic Index-U.S.

Bio Dermis Corporation, 3753 Howard Hughes Pkwy., Ste. 310, 89109, pg. 873 — PB
Bioplexus Corporation, 3753 Howard Hughes Pkwy., Ste. 310, 89109, pg. 874 — PB
BOYD GAMING CORPORATION, 2950 S. Industrial Rd., 89109, pg. 249 — PB
CMCI, Inc., 1061 E. Falmingo Rd., Ste. One, 89119, pg. 1033 — PB
CMFC, Inc., 1061 E. Flamingo Rd., Ste. 1, 89119, pg. 1033 — PB
CSR West, 6075 E. Eastern Ave., Ste. 10, 89119, pg. 245 — IT
Caesars World, Inc., 3570 Las Vegas Blvd. S., 89109, pg. 1512 — PB
Caesars World Merchandising, Inc., 4325 Aldebaron Ave., 89103, pg. 1512 — PB
Calnev Pipeline Company, 5049 N. Sloan Ln., 89115, pg. 692 — PB
Cardivan Co., 1110 Palms Airport Dr., 89119, pg. 920 — PB
Carson Water Co., 5241 Spring Mountain Rd., 89102, pg. 1493 — PB
Casino Electronics, Inc., 4380 Boulder Hwy., 89121, pg. 47 — PB
Casino Properties, Inc., 4949 N. Rancho Dr., 89130, pg. 1432 — PB
Charter Behavioral Health System of Nevada, Inc., 7000 W. Spring Mountain Rd., 89117, pg. 1034 — PB
Circus Circus Hotel Casinos, Inc., 2880 Las Vegas Blvd. S., 89109, pg. 374 — PB
CIRCUS CIRCUS - LAS VEGAS, 2880 Las Vegas Blvd. S., 89109-1120, pg. 374 — PB
Circus Circus-Las Vegas Hotel & Casino, 2880 Las Vegas Blvd. S., 89109, pg. 375 — PB
Citibank (Nevada) N.A., 8725 W. Sahara Ave., 89163, pg. 377 — PB
COMMERICAL ROOFERS INC., 3430 S. Valley View Blvd., 89102, pg. 258 — PV
Corral Coin, Inc., 1110 Palms Airport Dr., 89119, pg. 920 — PB
Corral United, Inc., 1110 Palms Airport Dr., 89119, pg. 920 — PB
Coventry Homes of Las Vegas, 7330 Smoke Ranch Rd., Ste. B, 89128, pg. 495 — PB
Coventry Homes of Nevada, Inc., 7320 Smoke Ranch Rd., Ste. C, 89128, pg. 495 — PB
DBT ONLINE, INC., 5550 W. Flamingo Rd., Ste. B Five, 89103, pg. 472 — PB
Daher Golden Eagle - Las Vegas, 2595 Chandler Ave., Ste. 1, 89120, pg. 749 — PB
Desert Lane Care Center, 660 Desert Ln., 89106, pg. 837 — PB
Disposal Urban Maintenance Procession Co., Inc., 7900 Vegas Valley Rd., 89122, pg. 1380 — PB
Dolisos, 3014 Rigel Ave., 89102, pg. 566 — IT
Dunn Reber Glenn Marz/Las Vegas, 1221 Town Center Dr., Ste. B, 89134, pg. 347 — PV
EG & G Special Projects, P.O. Box 93747, 821 Grier Dr., 89193-3747, pg. 543 — PB
ELSINORE CORPORATION, 202 E. Fremont St., 89101, pg. 570 — PB
Elsub Corporation, 202 Fremont St., 89101, pg. 570 — PB
Ever-Ski Properties, Inc., 4949 N. Rancho Dr., 89130, pg. 1432 — PB
Family Healthcare Services, Inc., 1701 W. Charleston Blvd., 89102, pg. 1469 — PB
Family Home Hospice, Inc., 1701 W. Charleston Blvd., 89102, pg. 1469 — PB
Financial Collection Agencies (1990) Inc., 4045 S. Spencer St., Ste. 401-A, 89119, pg. 471 — IT
First American Title Co. of Nevada, 3760 Pecos-McLeod Interconnect, Ste. 7, 89121, pg. 625 — PB
First Security Bank of Nevada, 530 Las Vegas Blvd., 89101, pg. 637 — PB
Firstar Capital Markets Group, 3800 Howard Hughes Pkwy., Ste. 1120, 89109, pg. 643 — PB
Flowmatrix Corporation, 860 Grier Dr., Ste. B-2, 89120, pg. 874 — PB
Foothill Investment Company, P.O. Box 10297, 19297, pg. 665 — PV
Four Queens Inc., 202 Fremont St., 89101, pg. 570 — PB
GES Exposition Services, Inc., 950 Grier Dr., 89119, pg. 1718 — PB
GNLV, Corp., 129 E. Fremont St., 89101, pg. 1117 — PB
GRADCO SYSTEMS, INC., 3753 Howard Hughes Pkwy., Ste. 200, 89109, pg. 757 — PB
Graphic Arts Supply Division, 3620 W. Reno, Unit J, 89118, pg. 205 — PB
Green Tree Acceptance, Inc., 1830 E. Sahara Ave., Ste. 220, 89104, pg. 762 — PB
Hacienda Hawaiian Properties, Inc., 4949 N. Rancho Dr., 89130, pg. 1432 — PB
Hacienda Hotel Inc., 4949 N. Rancho Dr., 89130, pg. 1432 — PB
Hansen Mechanical Contractors, Inc., 6325 S. Valley View Blvd., 89118, pg. 572 — PB
Health Plan of Nevada, Inc., 2720 N. Tenaya Way, 89128-0424, pg. 1469 — PB
Hewlett-Packard Company, 4570 S. Eastern, Ste. 22 & 23, 89119, pg. 814 — PB
Higgins Las Vegas Operations, 4030 Industrial Ctr., Ste. 503, 89109, pg. 527 — PB
Hillhaven Convalescent Center Las Vegas, 5659 Duncan Dr., 89106, pg. 1713 — PB
Hilton Hotels, Gaming Div., 3930 Howard Hughes Pkwy., 89109, pg. 829 — PB
Horizon Specialty Hospital - Las Vegas, 640 Desert Lane, 89106, pg. 837 — PB
Howard Hughes Corporation, 3800 Howard Hughes Pkwy., 89109, pg. 1407 — PB
Humana Health Insurance of Nevada, Inc., 9900 Covington Cross Dr., 89134, pg. 847 — PB

Huntco Nevada, Inc., 2437 E. Cheyenne, 89030, pg. 849 — PB
INAMED CORPORATION, 3800 Howard Hughes Pkwy., Ste. 900, 89109, pg. 873 — PB
JS&A GROUP, INC., 3350 Palms Center Dr., 89103, pg. 578 — PV
Jackpot Casino, Inc., 1110 Palms Airport Dr., 89119, pg. 920 — PB
Jackpot City, Inc., 1110 Palms Airport Dr., 89119, pg. 920 — PB
JACKPOT ENTERPRISES, INC., 1110 Palm Airport Dr., 89119, pg. 920 — PB
Jackpot Gaming, Inc., 1110 Palms Airport Dr., 89119, pg. 920 — PB
FLETCHER JONES MANAGEMENT GROUP, 175 E. Reno Ave., Ste. C6, 89119, pg. 597 — PV
KLAS, 3228 Channel 8 Dr., 89109, pg. 647 — PB
Kaufman and Broad of Nevada, Inc., 4755 Industrial Rd., 89103, pg. 945 — PB
Las Vegas Convalescent Center, 2832 Maryland Pkwy., 89109, pg. 1714 — PB
Las Vegas Sports Consultants, 675 Grier Dr., Ste. 201, 89119, pg. 484 — PB
LAS VEGAS SUN, 800 S. Valley View Blvd., 89107, pg. 652 — PV
Lawry's The Prime Rib, 4043 Howard Hughes Pkwy., 89109, pg. 654 — PV
Lewis Building Co., Inc., 3325 Alibaba Lane, Ste. 603, 89132, pg. 665 — PV
Lewis Homes of Nevada, 3325 Ali Baba Ln., 89132, pg. 665 — PV
Lewis Properties, P.O. Box 19297, 5420 S. Polaris, 89132, pg. 665 — PV
Luxor Hotel, P.O. Box 98640, 89113, pg. 375 — PB
MGM Grand Development, Inc., 3799 Las Vegas Blvd. S., 89109, pg. 1027 — PB
MGM Grand Hotel, Inc., 3799 Las Vegas Blvd. S., 89109, pg. 1027 — PB
MGM GRAND, INC., 3799 Las Vegas Blvd. S., 89109, pg. 1026 — PB
MGM Grand Merchandising, Inc., 3799 Las Vegas Blvd. S., 89019, pg. 1027 — PB
MarCor Development Co., 3700 W. Flamingo, 89103, pg. 1390 — PB
MarCor Resort Properties, Inc., 3700 W. Flamingo, 89103, pg. 1390 — PB
Maxpro, 2545 Ontario Dr., 89128, pg. 1663 — PB
MEDI-MAIL, INC., 871-C Grier Dr., 89119-3717, pg. 726 — PV
MEDNET, MPC CORPORATION, 871C Grier Dr., 89119, pg. 1082 — PB
MESA AIR GROUP, Hughes Ctr., Ste. 200, 3753 Howard Hughes Pkwy., 89109, pg. 1098 — PB
MIKOHN GAMING CORPORATION, 1045 Palms Airport Dr., 89193, pg. 1111 — PB
The Mirage Casino/Hotel, 3400 Las Vegas Blvd. S., 89109, pg. 1117 — PB
MIRAGE RESORTS INCORPORATED, 3400 Las Vegas Blvd., S., 89109, pg. 1116 — PB
MISSION INDUSTRIES, 1100 Foremaster Ln., 89101, pg. 752 — PV
Nadel Architects, PC Nevada, 444 E. Warm Springs Rd., Ste. 102, 89119, pg. 773 — PB
Nevada National Bancorporation, 2300 West Sahara Blvd., 89102, pg. 181 — PB
NEVADA POWER COMPANY, 6226 W. Sahara Ave., 89102, pg. 1469 — PB
Nevada State Bank, 4th & Carson St., 89101, pg. 1793 — PB
New Castle Corp., 3850 Las Vegas Blvd. S., 89109, pg. 375 — PB
North Las Vegas Care Center, 3215 E. Cheyenne, 89030, pg. 837 — PB
Norwest Bank Nevada, N.A., 3300 W. Sahara Ave., 89102, pg. 1202 — PB
Pacificare of Nevada, 700 E. Warm Springs, 89119, pg. 1251 — PB
Paiute Pipeline Co., 5241 Spring Mountain Rd., 89193-8510, pg. 1493 — PB
PAUL-SON GAMING CORPORATION, 2121 Industrial Rd., 89102, pg. 1265 — PB
PEPCON Systems, Inc., 3770 Howard Hughes Pkwy., Ste. 300, 89109, pg. 88 — PB
Pioneer Finance Corp., 4949 N. Rancho Dr., 89130, pg. 1432 — PB
Poe & Brown of Nevada, 6550 S. Pecos Blvd., Ste. 103, 89120, pg. 1312 — PB
R&R ADVERTISING, 8076 W. Sahara Ave., 89117, pg. 902 — PV
Resort Marketing International, 4949 N. Rancho Dr., 89130, pg. 1432 — PB
Richmond American Homes of Nevada, Inc., 400 S. Eastern Ave., #18, 89119, pg. 1025 — PB
RIO HOTEL & CASINO INC., 3700 W. Flamingo Rd., 89103, pg. 1390 — PB
Rio Properties, Inc., 3700 W. Flamingo, 89103, pg. 1390 — PB
Sahara Illinois Corp., 4949 N. Rancho Dr., 89130, pg. 1432 — PB
Sahara Las Vegas Corp., 4949 N. Rancho Dr., 89130, pg. 1432 — PB
Sahara Mississippi Management Company, Inc., 4949 N. Rancho Dr., 89130, pg. 1432 — PB
Sahara Nevada Corp., 4949 N. Rancho Dr., 89130, pg. 1432 — PB
Sahara Parkville, Inc., 4949 N. Rancho Dr., 89130, pg. 1432 — PB
Sahara Resorts, 4949 N. Rancho Dr., 89130, pg. 1432 — PB
Santa Fe Coffee Company, 4949 N. Rancho Dr., 89130, pg. 1432 — PB
SANTA FE GAMING CORPORATION, 4949 N. Rancho Dr., 89130, pg. 1432 — PB

Santa Fe Hotel Inc., 4949 N. Rancho Dr., 89130, pg. 1432 — PB
Santa Fe Valley, Inc., 4949 N. Rancho Dr., 89130, pg. 1432 — PB
Scenic Air Lines, 241 E. Reno Way, 89119, pg. 1476 — PB
SHOWBOAT, INCORPORATED, 2800 Fremont St., 89104, pg. 1469 — PB
Showboat Operating Co., 2800 E. Fremont St., 89104, pg. 1469 — PB
Sierra Health and Life Insurance Company, Inc., 2720 N. Tenaya Way, 89128-0424, pg. 1469 — PB
SIERRA HEALTH SERVICES, INC., 2724 N. Tenaya Way, 89128-0424, pg. 1469 — PB
Sierra Healthcare Options, Inc., 2720 N. Tenaya Way, 89128-0424, pg. 1469 — PB
Silver City Casino, 3001 Las Vegas Blvd. S., 89109, pg. 375 — PB
Silver State Disposal Service, Inc., 770 E. Sahara, 89104, pg. 1380 — PB
Slots-A-Fun, Inc., 2890 Las Vegas Blvd. S., 89109, pg. 375 — PB
SOUTHWEST GAS CORPORATION, 5241 Spring Mountain Rd., 89102, pg. 1493 — PB
Southwest Gas Transmission Company, 5241 Spring Mountain Rd., 89102, pg. 1493 — PB
Southwest Medical Associates, Inc., 2350 W. Charleston Blvd., 89102, pg. 1470 — PB
Southwestern Reprographics Inc., 1025 S. Main, 89107, pg. 1176 — PB
Standard Restaurant Equipment Co., 5675 S. Valley View Dr., 89118-2411, pg. 1031 — PB
Sun City Las Vegas, 9555 Del Webb Blvd., 89134, pg. 495 — PB
Sun City Summerlin, 9555 Del Webb Blvd., 89134, pg. 495 — PB
Sun Microsystems, R&D, 3690 S. Eastern Ave., 89109-3319, pg. 1531 — PB
TAL Financial Corporation, 4570 S.E. Ave., 89119, pg. 1553 — PB
Talavera at Peccole Ranch, 2251 S. Fort Apache, 89117, pg. 163 — PB
TANG INDUSTRIES INC., 3773 Howard Hughes Pkwy., Ste. 350 N., 89019, pg. 1068 — PV
Tempo Advertising, Inc., 4949 N. Rancho Dr., 89130, pg. 1432 — PB
Torrey Pines Care Center, 1701 S. Torrey Pines, Dr., 89102, pg. 1715 — PB
TRACINDA CORPORATION, 4835 Kovall Ln., 89109, pg. 1095 — PV
Treasure Island, Corp., 3300 Las Vegas Blvd. S., 89109, pg. 1117 — PB
Tropicana Resort & Casino, 3801 Las Vegas Blvd. S., 89109, pg. 159 — PB
United Coin Machine Co., 4380 Boulder Hwy., 89121, pg. 47 — PB
United HealthCare of Nevada, Inc., 200 Hughes Ctr., 3753 Howard Hughes Pkwy., 89109, pg. 1678 — PB
US Bank, 2300 West Sahara Blvd., 89102, pg. 181 — PB
Utility Financial Corp., 5241 Spring Mountain Rd., 89102, pg. 1493 — PB
Valley Food Distributors of Nevada, 300 W. Bonanza Rd., 89106, pg. 919 — PB
Valley Hospital Medical Center, 620 Shadow Ln., 89106, pg. 1697 — PB
Vegas Electric Supply, 3700 Regulus Ave., 89102, pg. 265 — PV
Vegas Valley Convalescent Center, 2945 Casa Vegas, 89109, pg. 837 — PB
Westco Food Service, 2570 Kielway, 89030, pg. 244 — IT
Western International Media Corporation, Hughes Center, 3753 Howard Hughes Pkwy., Ste. 101, 89109, pg. 1167 — PV
WILCO REPROGRAPHIC, INC., 1025 S. Main, 89101, pg. 1176 — PB
Willis Corroon Administrative Services Corporation, 2001 E. Flamingo Rd., Ste. 100F, 89119, pg. 1504 — IT
Young Electric Signs Las Vegas Div., 5119 S. Cameron St., 89118, pg. 1201 — PV
Zellerbach Division, 3250 W. Harmon Ave., 89103, pg. 1076 — PB

Laughlin

Colorado Belle, 2100 S. Casino Dr., 89028, pg. 375 — PB
Edgewater Hotel Corp., 2020 S. Casino Dr., 89029, pg. 375 — PB
GNL, Corp., 2300 S. Casino Dr., 89029, pg. 1116 — PB
Harrah's Laughlin, Inc., 2900 S. Casino Dr., 89029, pg. 790 — PB
Pioneer Hotel Inc., 2200 Casino Dr., 89029, pg. 1432 — PB
Ramada Express, 2121 S. Casino Dr., 89029, pg. 158 — PB

Lovelock

Coeur Rochester, Inc., P.O. Box 1057, 89419, pg. 394 — PB

Minden

BENTLY NEVADA CORPORATION, 1617 Water St., 89423, pg. 134 — PV
Bently Rotor Dynamics Research Corp., P.O. Box 2529, 89423, pg. 134 — PV
PolyPhaser Corporation, 2225 Park Pl., 89423, pg. 1268 — IT

North Las Vegas

FREHNER CONSTRUCTION COMPANY, INC., 4040 Frehner Rd., 89030, pg. 426 — PV

PB - *U.S. Public Companies Volume*
PV - *U.S. Private Companies Volume*
IT - *International Public & Private Companies Volume*

Geographic Index-U.S.

1311

Reno

Allright Sierra Parking, Inc., 220 S. Center, 89501, pg. 43 **PV**
AMERCO, 1325 Airmotive Way, Ste. 100, 89502, pg. 48 **PV**
BHP Minerals Laboratory, 204 Edison Way, 89502, pg. 227 **IT**
Bank of America Nevada, 5190 NeilRd., 89502, pg. 180 **PB**
Battle Mountain Exploration Company, 220 S. Rock Blvd., Ste. 15, 89502, pg. 193 **PB**
Battle Mountain Exploration Company, 4967 Energy Way, 89502, pg. 193 **PB**
Circus Circus-Reno Hotel & Casino, 500 N. Sierra St., 89503, pg. 375 **PB**
Cordex Exploration Co., 573 East Second St., 89502, pg. 1089 **IT**
John Deere Capital Corporation, One E. First St., Ste. 600, 89501, pg. 492 **PB**
John Deere Receivables, Inc., One E. First St., Ste. 600, 89501, pg. 492 **PB**
DUNN REBER GLENN MARZ, 50 Washington St., 89503, pg. 347 **PV**
Echo Bay Mining Company, 5401 Longley Ln., Ste. 5, 89511, pg. 562 **PB**
FMC Gold Co., 5011 Meadowwood Way, 89502, pg. 605 **PB**
Farmers Insurance Group, 100 W Grove St. Ste. 200, 89509-4027, pg. 111 **IT**
First American Title Co. of Nevada, 241 Ridge St., 89501, pg. 625 **PB**
First Interstate Bank of Nevada, N.A., One E. First St., 89501, pg. 1753 **PB**
The HVR Company, 12150 Moya Blvd., 89506, pg. 387 **PB**
HAMILTON CO., INC., P.O. Box 10030, 89520-0012, pg. 497 **PV**
Harrah's Arizona Corporation, 206 N. Virginia St., 89501, pg. 790 **PB**
Harrah's California Corporation, 206 N. Virginia St., 89501, pg. 790 **PB**
Harrah's California SSR Corporation, 206 N. Virginia St., 89501, pg. 790 **PB**
Harrah's Colorado Investment Corporation, 206 N. Virginia St., 89501, pg. 790 **PB**
Harrah's Las Vegas, 206 N. Virginia St., 89501, pg. 790 **PB**
Harrah's Management Co., 206 N. Virginia Dr., 89501, pg. 790 **PB**
Harrah's South Shore Corp., 300 E. Second St., 89501, pg. 791 **PB**
Hewlett-Packard Company, 1000 Bible Way, Ste. 47, 89502, pg. 814 **PB**
Higgins Reno Operations, 4975 Energy Way, 89510, pg. 527 **PV**
Hydro Conduit Corp., P.O. Box 798, 999 Marietta Way, 89432, pg. 245 **IT**
IGT-International Corp. Development, P.O. Box 10120, 6110 Plumas St., 89510-0120, pg. 900 **PB**
IGT North America, P.O. Box 10580, 520 S. Rock Blvd., 89510-0580, pg. 900 **PB**
INTERNATIONAL GAME TECHNOLOGY, P.O. Box 10580, 9295 Prototype Dr., 89510-0580, pg. 900 **PB**
International Rotex, Inc., P.O. Box 20697, 89515, pg. 460 **IT**
Lands of Sierra, 294 E. Moana Ln., Ste. 18, 89520, pg. 1470 **PB**
Lawson Products, Inc., 1381 Capital Blvd., 89502, pg. 980 **PB**
Mercury Air Center, 655 S. Rock Blvd., 89502, pg. 1093 **PB**
The Minerals Laboratory, 204 Edison Way, 89502, pg. 224 **IT**
Model Dairy, P.O. Box 3017, 500 Gould St., 89505, pg. 1527 **PB**
MountainGate Data Systems, Inc., 9393 Gateway, 89511, pg. 1008 **PB**
Nevada Bell, 645 E. Plumb Ln., 89520, pg. 1416 **PB**
Nevada Holding Co., 401 Ryland St., Ste. 401, 89502, pg. 1721 **PB**
PENCO-Nevada, 1755 E. Plumb Ln., Ste. 269, 89502, pg. 1508 **IT**
Phillips Investment Company, 85 Keystone, 89513, pg. 1291 **PB**
Phillips Petroleum International Investment Company, 85 Keystone Ave., P.O. Box 6256, 89513, pg. 1291 **PB**
Physicians Hospital for Extended Care, 2045 Silverada Blvd., 89512, pg. 837 **PB**
Porsche Cars North America, Inc., 100 W. Liberty, 89501, pg. 1063 **IT**
Porsche Enterprises Inc., 200 S. Virginia St., 89501, pg. 1063 **IT**
R&R Advertising, 615 Riverside Dr., 89503, pg. 902 **PV**
Reno Convalescent Center, 1300 Mill St., 89502, pg. 1714 **PB**
Reno Gazette Journal, 955 Kuenzli, 89520, pg. 701 **PB**
Reno Mfg. Division, 14100 Lear Blvd., 89506-1657, pg. 518 **PB**
RENOAIR INC., 220 Edison Way, 89502, pg. 922 **PV**
THE SANDS REGENT, 345 N. Arlington Ave., 89501, pg. 1431 **PB**
Sierra Pacific Power Co., 6100 Neil Rd., 89511, pg. 1470 **PB**
SIERRA PACIFIC RESOURCES, 6100 Neil Rd., 89511, pg. 1470 **PB**
Sotheby's Financial Services, Inc., 1400 S. Virginia St., 89502, pg. 1487 **PB**
Trahan, Burden & Charles, Inc., 300 South Wells Ave., Ste. 16, 89502, pg. 1095 **PV**

Tuscarora Gas Pipeline Co., P.O. Box 30057, 6100 Neil Rd., 89520, pg. 1470 **PB**
URS Greiner, Inc., 1755 E. Plumb Ln., Ste. 145, 89502, pg. 1659 **PB**
Western International Media Corporation, 1325 Airmotive Way, Ste. 175, 89502, pg. 1167 **PV**
Willis Corroon Administrative Services Corporation, 1755 E. Plumb Ln., Ste. 267, 89502, pg. 1504 **IT**
Wooster Magikoter West Division, 4960 Joule St., 89502, pg. 1188 **PV**
Zante, Inc., 345 N. Arlington Ave., 89501, pg. 1431 **PB**

Round Mountain

Round Mountain Gold Corporation, P.O. Box 480, 1 Smoky Valley Mine Rd., Hwy. 376, 89045, pg. 562 **PB**

Sparks

Barrick Gold, 1395 Greg St., Ste. 107, 89431, pg. 169 **IT**
Barrier Films Corp., 555 Dermody Way, pg. 1190 **PV**
Diebold of Nevada, Inc., 1220 E. Greg St., #2, 89431, pg. 506 **PB**
Direct Dental Supply Co., 1267 Spice Island Dr., 89431, pg. 1265 **PB**
Ebara International Corp., 350 Salomon Circle, 89434, pg. 431 **IT**
GBC/Veloblind, 850 Spice Island, 89431, pg. 707 **PV**
Genova-Nevada, 1150 Southern Way, 89431, pg. 447 **PV**
Granite Construction Inc.-Nevada Div., 1900 Glendale Ave., 89431, pg. 759 **PB**
GRIFFIN TRANSPORT SERVICES, INC., 1095 Spice Island Dr., Ste. 100, 89431, pg. 481 **PV**
Hearthstone of Northern Nevada, 1950 Baring Blvd., 89431, pg. 837 **PB**
Homestake Mining Company, 1375 Greg St., Ste. 105, 89431, pg. 833 **PB**
Kassbohrer North America, 310A Coney Island Dr., 89431, pg. 368 **IT**
Knape & Vogt Mfg. Co., 725 Greg St., 89431, pg. 963 **PB**
J.R. Michaels, Inc., 1605 Greg Street, 89431, pg. 372 **PB**
Mount Vernon Plastics Company, 1420 Kleppe Ln., 89431, pg. 1386 **PB**
PDM Steel Service Center-Sparks, 1250 Kleppe Lane, 89431, pg. 1305 **PB**
Quality Bearing Service of Nevada, Inc., 1415 Greg St., Ste. 103, 89431, pg. 1711 **PB**
Real City Casino, 2121 Victorian Ave., 89431, pg. 47 **PB**
Snugl Mfg. Co. Inc., 1498 Kleppe Ln., 89431, pg. 138 **PV**
Sparks Family Hospital, 2375 E. Prater Way, 89434, pg. 1697 **PB**
SWIFT TRANSPORTATION CO., 1455 Hulda Way, 89431, pg. 1543 **PB**
Washoe Care Center, 1375 Baring Blvd., 89431, pg. 838 **PB**
Westco Products, 1277 Spice Islands Dr., 89431, pg. 244 **IT**
Young Electric Signs Reno Division, 775 E. Glendale Ave., 89431-7215, pg. 1201 **PV**
Zellerbach Division, 950 United Cir., 89431, pg. 1076 **PB**

Stateline

Desert Palace, Inc., 55 Hwy. 50, 89449, pg. 1512 **PB**

Tonopah

BenguetCorp U.S.A., Inc., 1202 Globemallow Ln., 89049, pg. 187 **IT**

Valmy

Marigold Mining Company, P.O. Box 9, 89438, pg. 1089 **IT**

Verdi

Boomtown-Reno, P.O. Box 399, 89439, pg. 831 **PB**
Firth-Rixson Viking, P.O. Box 339, One Erik Circle, 89439, pg. 488 **IT**
Viking Metallurgical Corporation, One Erik Circle, 89439, pg. 488 **IT**

Winnemucca

Cyanco, 9000 Jungo Rd., 89445, pg. 1115 **PB**
Hycroft Resources & Development, P.O. Box 3030, Drawer M, 89446, pg. 1723 **PB**
Pinson Mine, P.O. Box 192, 89445, pg. 169 **IT**
Pinson Mining Company, P.O. Box 129, 89446, pg. 833 **PB**
Rayrock Mines, Inc., P.O. Box 2100, 89446, pg. 1089 **IT**
The Rosebud Mining Company, L.L.C., P.O. Box 2610, 89446, pg. 804 **PB**

Yerington

O'Sullivan Plastics Corp., 270 US Hwy. 95A N., 89447, pg. 1234 **PB**

NEW HAMPSHIRE

Amherst

Atomic Ski USA Inc., Nine Columbia Dr., 03031, pg. 72 **IT**

Bartlett

Attitash Bear Peak, P.O. Box 308, 03812, pg. 61 **PV**

Bedford

Bull Finance Corporation, 3 Executive Park Dr., 03110, pg. 316 **IT**
Coca-Cola Northern New England, Inc., One Executive Park Dr., 03110, pg. 736 **IT**
DYWIDAG Systems International, USA, Inc., Office 19, Pine Tree Pl., 360-1002 Route 101, 03110, pg. 424 **IT**
ECKMAN CONSTRUCTION COMPANY, 84 Palomino Ln., 03110, pg. 359 **PV**
Green Tree Acceptance, Inc., Three Executive Park Dr., 03102, pg. 762 **PB**
Ikon Office Solutions-North New England, 207 Meetinghouse Rd., 03102-4031, pg. 863 **PB**
Normandeau Associates, Inc., 25 Nashua Rd., 03102, pg. 1594 **PB**
SHAER SHOE CORPORATION, Ten Commerce Pk. N., 03110, pg. 988 **PV**

Belmont

Fleet Bank NH, Jct. Rtes. 3 & 11, 03220, pg. 649 **PB**
KRC (Northern) Inc., P.O. Box 779, Belknap Business & Industrial Pk., 03220-0779, pg. 1202 **IT**

Berlin

Berlin-Gorham Operations, 650 Main St., 03570, pg. 465 **PB**

Bow

Pitco Frialator Inc., 509-512 Rte 3A, 03304, pg. 1065 **PB**

Bretton Woods

Bretton Woods Telephone Company, Mount Washington Place, 03575, pg. 1021 **PB**

Bristol

Freudenberg NOK, Ragged Mountain Hwy., P.O. Box B, 03222, pg. 507 **IT**
Freudenberg North America Limited Partnership, RR 104 Ragged Mountain Hwy., 03222, pg. 507 **IT**

Candia

AC Leasing Corporation, 17 Old Manchester Rd., 03034-0736, pg. 15 **PV**
ACTION EQUIPMENT, 17 Old Manchester Rd., 03034-0736, pg. 14 **PV**
Action Supply, 17 Old Manchester Rd., 03034-0736, pg. 15 **PV**
Action Tire, 17 Old Manchester Rd., 03034-0736, pg. 15 **PV**
JJJ Realty Trust, 17 Old Manchester Rd., 03034-0736, pg. 15 **PV**

Center Barnstead

Timco, Inc., P.O. Box 27, 03225, pg. 126 **PB**

Claremont

CLAREMONT FLOCK CORPORATION, 169 Main St., 03743, pg. 241 **PV**
EAST COAST STEEL, INC., Grissom River Rd., 03743, pg. 356 **PV**

Concord

AUTOMOTIVE SUPPLY ASSOCIATES, INC., 129 Manchester St., 03301, pg. 101 **PV**
Capital Plumbing & Heating Supply Co. Inc., Six Storrs St., 03301, pg. 469 **PV**
Concord General Life Insurance Company, One Pillsbury St., 03301, pg. 79 **PB**
CONCORD LITHO CO., INC., P.O. Box 288, 92 Old Turnpike Rd., 03302, pg. 261 **PV**
Concord Savings Bank, 43 N. Main St., 03301, pg. 278 **PB**
EnergyNorth Natural Gas, Inc., 62 N. Main St., 03301, pg. 582 **PB**
EnergyNorth Propane, Inc., 75 Regional Dr., 03301, pg. 582 **PB**
Granite State Energy, Inc., Four Park St., 03301, pg. 1171 **PB**
Healthsource New Hampshire, Inc., 54 Regional Dr., 03301, pg. 360 **PB**
Merchants Nissan, 175 Manchester St., 03301, pg. 732 **PV**
New England Electric Transmission Corp., Four Park St., 03301, pg. 1171 **PB**
Normandeau Engineers Inc., 10 Ferry St., No. 7, 03301, pg. 1593 **PB**
PATSY'S, INC., 24 Hall St., 03301, pg. 843 **PV**
Pitco Mastermatic Inc., P.O. Box 2272, 03301, pg. 518 **PV**
Sanel Auto Parts Co., 219 S. Main St., 03301, pg. 101 **PV**
Tafa Incorporated, 146 Pembroke Rd., 03301, pg. 866 **PB**
URS Greiner, Inc., Concord Ctr., Ste. 321, Ten Ferry St., Unit 12, 03301, pg. 1658 **PB**

PB - U.S. Public Companies Volume
PV - U.S. Private Companies Volume
IT - International Public & Private Companies Volume

1312

Weeks Dairy Foods, Inc., 330 North State St., 03301, pg. 752 — IT

Conway

THE RENOVATOR'S SUPPLY, INC., P.O. Box 2525, 03818, pg. 923 — PV

Derry

Fireye, Inc., Three Manchester Rd., 03038, pg. 1500 — IT
SAGEM Corporation, 31 So. Main St., 03038, pg. 1273 — IT

Dover

Dover House Healthcare, 307 Plaza Dr., 03820, pg. 1712 — PB
EASTERN AIR DEVICES, INC., One Progress Dr., 03820, pg. 357 — PB
Heidelberg Web Press, Inc., 121 Broadway, 03820-3290, pg. 604 — PV
Liberty Life Assurance Company of Boston, 100 Main St., 03820, pg. 666 — PV
Moore Business Equipment Div., 279 Locust St., 03820-1229, pg. 890 — IT
ROBBINS AUTO PARTS, INC., 110-116 Washington St., 03820, pg. 934 — PV
SMS-Dover, 15 Old Rollingsford Rd., 03820, pg. 1463 — PB
Textron Automotive Interiors Company, Industrial Park, 03820, pg. 1590 — PB

Dublin

Eclipse Combustion, Inc., P.O. Box 303, Boulder Dr., 03444, pg. 360 — PV
YANKEE PUBLISHING INCORPORATED, P.O. Box 520, 03444, pg. 1195 — PV

Exeter

Grinnell Corporation, Three Tyco Park, 03833, pg. 1651 — PB
Grinnell Flow Control, Three Tyco Pk., 03833, pg. 1650 — PB
Keystone International, Inc., Three Tyco Park, 03833, pg. 1650 — PB
Ludlow Corporation, One Tyco Park, 03833, pg. 1651 — PB
SIGARMS Inc., Corporate Park, 03833, pg. 1156 — IT
TYCO INTERNATIONAL LTD., One Tyco Park, 03833-1108, pg. 1647 — PB

Farmington

Farmington National Bank, Eight Central St., 03835, pg. 187 — PB

Franklin

APV Franklin Inc., Griffin Rd. at Rte. 3A, 03235, pg. 1240 — IT

Gilford

BEAU Interconnect Systems, Four Aviation Dr., 03246, pg. 157 — PB

Hampton

Concord Electric Company, Six Liberty Ln., W., 03842-1720, pg. 1692 — PB
Employee Benefit Plan Administration, Inc., 263 Drakeside Rd., 03842, pg. 360 — PB
Exeter & Hampton Electric Co., Six Liberty Ln., W., 03842-1720, pg. 1692 — PB
Fisher Scientific International, Liberty Ln., 03842, pg. 658 — PV
FOSS MANUFACTURING COMPANY INCORPORATED, 380 Lafayette Rd., 03842, pg. 420 — PV
THE GENERAL CHEMICAL GROUP, INC., Liberty Ln., 03842, pg. 707 — PB
The Hampton Water Works Co., One Merrill Industrial Dr., 03842, pg. 95 — PB
Millipore of New Hampshire, Inc., P.O. Box 4778, 03842, pg. 1113 — PB
UNITIL CORPORATION, Six Liberty Ln., W., 03842-1720, pg. 1692 — PB
UNITIL Power Corporation, Six Liberty Ln., W., 03842-1720, pg. 1692 — PB
UNITIL Realty Corporation, Six Liberty Ln., W., 03842-1720, pg. 1692 — PB
UNITIL Resources, Inc., Six Liberty Ln., W., 03842-1720, pg. 1692 — PB
UNITIL Service Corporation, Six Liberty Ln., W., 03842-1720, pg. 1693 — PB
Wheelabrator Technologies Inc., 4 Liberty Lane West, 03842, pg. 1745 — PB

Hanover

Fleet Bank NH, 40 South Main St., 03755, pg. 649 — PB
FUND AMERICAN ENTERPRISES HOLDINGS, INC., 80 S. Main St., 03755, pg. 688 — PB
Hanover Terrace Healthcare, Lyme Rd., 03755, pg. 1713 — PB

Hollis

Pneutronics Div., 26 Clinton Drive, Unit 103, 03049-6593, pg. 1262 — PB

Hooksett

First NH Mortgage Corp., 28 W. River Rd., 03106, pg. 153 — IT
Fleet Bank NH, Two College Park Dr., 03106, pg. 649 — PB
Healthsource, Inc., Two College Park Dr., 03106, pg. 360 — PB
MERCHANTS RENT A CAR, INC., 1278 Hooksett Rd., 03106, pg. 732 — PV

Hudson

Balzers Process Systems, Inc., 8 Sagamore Park Rd., 03051, pg. 997 — IT
Benchmark Electronics, Inc., Pope Technical Park 2, 65 River Rd., CS907, 03051, pg. 211 — PB
Delta Education, Inc., Five Hudson Park Dr., 03051, pg. 1402 — IT
HOWTEK, INC., 21 Park Ave., 03051, pg. 844 — PB
Lowell Shoe, Inc., 8 Hampshire Dr., 03051, pg. 217 — PB
National Telegraph, 17 Executive Dr., 03051, pg. 559 — PV
PRESSTEK, INC., 8-9 Commercial St., 03051, pg. 1324 — PB
Salem Sportswear, 15 Hudson Park Dr., 03051-3995, pg. 686 — PB
Semikron Inc., P.O. Box 66, 11 Executive Dr., 03051, pg. 1220 — IT
Surveillance Systems Div., 65 River Rd., 03051, pg. 1008 — PB

Jaffrey

D.D. BEAN & SONS CO., 207 Peterborough St., 03452, pg. 126 — PV
W.W. Cross, Inc., 77 Webster St., 03452, pg. 127 — PV
Jaffrey Fire Protection Co., 10 Main St., 03452, pg. 127 — PV
TFX Medical Inc., Tall Pines Park, 03452, pg. 1570 — PB

Keene

CFX, 194 West St., 03431, pg. 278 — PB
CFX BANK, 102 Main St., 03431, pg. 277 — PB
CFX Funding, L.L.C., 102 Main St., 03431, pg. 278 — PB
CFX Mortgage, Inc., 194 West St., 03431, pg. 278 — PB
GENERAL TOURS INC., 53 Summer St., 03431, pg. 445 — PB
Kingsbury Assembly Machine Div., 80 Laurel St., 03431, pg. 622 — PV
KINGSBURY CORPORATION, 80 Laurel St., 03431, pg. 621 — PV
Kingsbury Machining Center, Div., 80 Laurel St., 03431, pg. 622 — PV
Kingsbury Service Corp., 80 Laurel St., P.O. Box 2020, 03431, pg. 622 — PV
Kingsbury World Sales, 80 Laurel St., P.O. Box 2020, 03431, pg. 622 — PV
MPB Corporation, Precision Park, Optical Ave., 03431-0547, pg. 1617 — PB
MARKEM CORPORATION, P.O. Box 2100, 150 Congress St., 03431, pg. 704 — PV
The Netherlands Insurance Companies, 62 Maple Avenue, 03431, pg. 648 — IT
Peerless Insurance Company, 62 Maple Avenue, 03431, pg. 648 — IT
Schleicher & Schuell, Inc., P.O. Box 2012, 10 Optical Ave., 03431, pg. 1206 — IT
SIMS Portex Inc., Bowman Dr., 03431-5911, pg. 1268 — IT
SuperValu, Inc.-Keene Div., 350 Marlboro St., 03431, pg. 1540 — PB
VISION FINANCIAL CORPORATION, P.O. Box 506, 55 West St., 03431, pg. 1141 — PV

Laconia

Allen-Rogers Co., 54 Water St., 03246, pg. 315 — PV
Franklin Brush Division, 24 Lexington Dr., 03246, pg. 463 — PV
Lewis & Saunders Inc., O'Shea Industrial Park, P.O. Box 678, 03247, pg. 1337 — IT
M & E Manufacturing Co., 266 Union Ave., 03246, pg. 870 — PV
Wilcom Products, Inc., Rte. Three Daniel Webster Hwy., 03248, pg. 1144 — PB

Lebanon

Allen Bradley Creonics, Etna Rd., 03766, pg. 1397 — PB
Granite State Electric Co., 407 Miracle Mile, Ste. 1, 03766, pg. 1171 — PB
New England Hydro-Transmission Corporation, 407 Miracle Mile, Ste. 1, 03766, pg. 1171 — PB

Littleton

Fleet Bank NH, 85 Main St., 03561, pg. 649 — PB
LITTLETON COIN CO., INC., 646 Union St, 03561, pg. 671 — PV
Norton Pike Division, Highland Ave., 03561, pg. 1176 — IT

Londonderry

Autodesk, 25 Orchard View Dr., 03053, pg. 149 — PB
Blue Seal Feeds, Inc., 15 Buttrick Rd., 03053, pg. 1134 — PV
CADEC Systems Inc., 8 E. Perimeter Rd., 03053, pg. 468 — PB
Consumers New Hampshire Water Co., 322 Nashua Rd., 03053, pg. 438 — PB
JENKINS SPIRITS CORP. LTD., 21 S. Perimeter Rd., 03053, pg. 585 — PV
Kluber Lubrication N. America Inc., 54 N. Wentworth Ave., 03053, pg. 505 — IT
Unicast, 11 Industrial Dr., 03053, pg. 1526 — PB

Manchester

AG Supermarkets Inc., P.O. Box 5200, 725 Gold St., 03108, pg. 91 — PV
ALLARD INDUSTRIES, 124 Joliette St., 03102, pg. 36 — PV
Allied Security Inc., 319 Lincoln St., Ste. 101, 03103, pg. 40 — PV
ASSOCIATED GROCERS OF NEW ENGLAND, INC., 725 Gold St., 03108, pg. 91 — PV
Associated Lease Corp., P.O. Box 5200, 03108, pg. 91 — PV
Capital Plumbing & Heating Supply Co., 25 Union St., 03103, pg. 469 — PV
Central Goulet Supply, 341 Elm St., 03101, pg. 469 — PV
Certified Wholesalers Inc., P.O. Box 5200, 03108, pg. 91 — PV
Crompton Modutec Inc., 920 Candia Rd., 03103, pg. 125 — IT
ENERGYNORTH, INC., 1260 Elm St., 03105, pg. 581 — PB
EnergyNorth Natural Gas, Inc., 1260 Elm St., 03105, pg. 582 — PB
FELTON BRUSH INC., 315 Wilson St., 03103, pg. 400 — PV
First NH Investment Services Corporation, 1000 Elm St., 03101, pg. 153 — IT
Fleet Bank NH, 156 Hanover St., 03101, pg. 649 — PB
Fleet Bank NH, 1155 Elm St., 03101, pg. 649 — PB
French & Bean, P.O. Box 5200, 03108, pg. 91 — PV
Freudenberg NOK, Grenier Industrial Air Park, 03103, pg. 505 — IT
GRANITE GROUP WHOLESALE LLC, 314 Elm St., 03101, pg. 469 — PV
Granite State Insurance Co., 1750 Elm St., 03104, pg. 84 — PB
Granite State Manufacturing Co., 124 Joliette St., 03102, pg. 36 — PV
Hilco, Inc., 1000 Elm St., 03101, pg. 153 — IT
Illinois National Insurance Co., 1750 Elm St., 03104, pg. 84 — PB
Inland National Ins. Co., 1750 Elm St., 03104, pg. 84 — PB
International Computer Services, Inc., 1750 Elm St., 03104, pg. 84 — PB
JAC PAC FOODS, LTD., 163 Hancock St., 03101, pg. 579 — PV
Lindenmeyr Munroe, 468 Pepsi Dr., 03109, pg. 224 — PV
McCord Winn Textron Company, 645 Harvey Rd., 03103, pg. 1590 — PB
Meggitt Avionics Inc., 10 Ammon Dr., 03103-7406, pg. 853 — IT
Meggitt USA, Inc., 540 North Commercial St., 03101, pg. 853 — IT
North American Specialty Insurance Company, 650 Elm St., 03101-2524, pg. 1332 — IT
North Atlantic Energy Corp., 1000 Elm St., 03105, pg. 1195 — PB
Nylon Corporation of America, Inc., 333 Sundial Ave., 03103, pg. 483 — PV
Nyltech North America Inc., 333 Sundial Ave., 03103, pg. 482 — IT
Public Service Company of New Hampshire, 1000 Elm St., 03105, pg. 1195 — PB
Raytheon Marine, 676 Island Pond Rd., 03079, pg. 1366 — PB
Sanmina Corporation-Manchester Plant, 140 Abby Rd., 03103, pg. 1431 — PB
SUMMA FOUR, INC., 25 Sundial Ave., 03103-7251, pg. 1527 — PB
Sweetheart Cup Company Inc., 400 Gay St., 03103, pg. 1058 — PV
Velcro Group Corporation, 406 Brown Ave., 03108, pg. 1462 — IT
Velcro Laminates Inc., 406 Brown Ave., 03108, pg. 1462 — IT
Velcro USA Inc., 406 Brown Ave., 03108, pg. 1462 — IT
Woven Classic Throws, Inc., 41 Dow St., 03101, pg. 465 — PB

Meriden

Meriden Telephone Co., Inc., Main St., 03770, pg. 1571 — PB

Merrimack

CHEMFAB CORPORATION, 701 Daniel Webster Hwy., 03054, pg. 344 — PB
Harcros Chemicals Inc., Daniel Webster Hwy., 03054, pg. 598 — IT
UNITRODE CORPORATION, Seven Continental Blvd., 03054, pg. 1694 — PB

Milford

Dataproducts Corp., Rte. 13 S., 03055, pg. 620 — IT

Hendrix Wire & Cable, 53 Old Wilton Rd., 03055, pg. 1598 **PB**
HITCHINER MANUFACTURING COMPANY, INC., Elm St., 03055, pg. 531 **PV**

Nashua

Adaptec - New England Region, 11 Trafalgar Sq., 03063, pg. 19 **PB**
ADVANCED CIRCUIT TECHNOLOGY, 100 N. Eastern Blvd., 03062, pg. 21 **PV**
Avionics, 95 Canal St.NCA1-6244, 03061, pg. 1008 **PB**
Beebe Rubber Company, 20-22 Marshall St., 03060, pg. 229 **PV**
BROOKSTONE COMPANY, INC., 17 Riverside St., 03062, pg. 259 **PB**
CPM, 150 Burke St., 03061, pg. 705 **PB**
Charter Behavioral Health System of Nashua, Inc., 29 Northwest Blvd., 03063, pg. 1034 **PB**
DTC COMMUNICATIONS, INC., 75 Northeastern Blvd., 03062, pg. 306 **PV**
DARCOM TECHNOLOGIES, INC., 77 Northeastern Blvd., 03062, pg. 311 **PV**
Data Media Corporation, 20 Trafalgar Sq., 03063, pg. 157 **PB**
Edgcomb Metals of New England, 385 W. Hollis St., 03060, pg. 572 **PB**
EKCO GROUP, INC., 98 Spit Brook Rd., Ste. 102, 03062, pg. 566 **PB**
Ekco International, Inc., 98 Spit Brook Rd., 03062, pg. 566 **PB**
EnergyNorth Natural Gas, Inc., 97 Main St., 03060, pg. 582 **PB**
FERROFLUIDICS CORPORATION, 40 Simon St., 03061-2009, pg. 620 **PB**
Fleet Bank-NH, P.O. Box 647, 223 Main St., 03061, pg. 649 **PB**
Greenbriar Terrace Healthcare, 55 Harris Rd., 03060, pg. 1712 **PB**
GUILFORD TRANSPORTATION INDUSTRIES INC., 402 Amherst St., Ste. 300, 03063, pg. 487 **PV**
IKOS Systems, Inc., One Tara Blvd., Ste. 100, 03062, pg. 864 **PB**
INTERNATIONAL SHOE MACHINE CORP., Simon & Ledge Sts., 03060, pg. 572 **PV**
Micro Vesicular Systems, Inc., 20 Cotton Rd., 03063, pg. 855 **PB**
NASHUA CORPORATION, 44 Franklin St., 03060, pg. 1152 **PB**
NEPA-New Hampshire, Inc., 29 Northwest Blvd., 03063, pg. 1036 **PB**
Sanders, A Lockheed Martin Company, 65 Spit Brook Rd., 03061, pg. 1008 **PB**
Seaboard International Forest Products, Inc., 102 Perimeter Rd., 03063, pg. 669 **PB**
Teradyne Circuits Operation, 44 Simon St., 03060, pg. 1581 **PB**
Teradyne Connection Systems, Inc., 44 Simon St., 03060, pg. 1581 **PB**
WHITE PINE SOFTWARE, 542 Amherst St., 03063, pg. 1173 **PV**

New London

Kearsarge Telephone Co., P.O. Box 296, Main St., 03257, pg. 1571 **PB**
The New London Trust Company, Main St., 03257, pg. 1319 **IT**

Newfields

Kingston-Warren Corporation, Rte. 85, 03856, pg. 796 **PB**

Newington

ABB Newington Operations, Old Dover Rd., 03801, pg. 4 **IT**
NESLAB Instruments, Inc., 25 Nimble Hill Rd., 03801, pg. 1595 **PB**

Newport

Pine Tree Castings Div., 411 Sunapee St., 03773, pg. 1526 **PB**
Sturm, Ruger-Newport Plant, 411 Sunapee St., 03773, pg. 1526 **PB**

North Hampton

The Salisbury Water Supply Co., P.O. Box 633, One Merrill Industrial Park Dr., 03862, pg. 95 **PB**

North Haverhill

P&H Transportation, P.O. Box 458, 03774-0458, pg. 164 **PV**

Penacook

RIVERSIDE MILLWORK COMPANY, INC., 77 Merrimack St., 03303, pg. 934 **PV**

Peterborough

BYTE Publications, One Phoenix Mill Ln., 03458, pg. 1070 **PB**
Connell Communications, 86 Elm St., 03458, pg. 569 **PV**

New England Business Service Inc., Vose Farm Rd., 03458, pg. 1171 **PB**
New Hampshire Ball Bearings, Inc., Route 202, 03458, pg. 868 **IT**

Pittsfield

Charles River Laboratories-NH, Eaton Rd., 03263, pg. 194 **PB**

Plaistow

Three Branches, Inc., P.O. Box 1556, 03865, pg. 215 **PV**

Portsmouth

Browning-Ferris Industries of New Hampshire, Inc., P.O. Box 466, 03802, pg. 263 **PB**
Erie Scientific Co., Portsmouth Industrial Pk., Post Rd., 03801, pg. 1545 **PB**
First Signature Bank & Trust Co., 190 Commerce Way, 03801, pg. 589 **PV**
Granite State Gas Transmission, Inc., 325 West Rd., 03801, pg. 197 **PB**
Heinemann USA, 361 Hanover St., 03801-3959, pg. 1094 **IT**
Hussey Products Co., 20 Ladd St., 03801, pg. 550 **PV**
Moran Towing of New Hampshire, 34 Ceres St., 03802-0448, pg. 761 **PV**
National Sea Products Incorporated, One High Liner Ave., 03802-0839, pg. 909 **IT**
Northern Utilities, Inc., 325 West Rd., 03801, pg. 197 **PB**
PAX WORLD FUND FAMILY, 222 State St., 03801-3853, pg. 1466 **PB**
Portsmouth Savings Bank, 333 State St., 03801, pg. 278 **PB**
Pronova Biopolymer Inc., 135 Commerce Way, Ste. 201, 03801, pg. 961 **IT**
Retail Sales, Inc., 170 West Rd., 03801, pg. 1175 **PB**
S&S-Hartwell Co., Inc., One Parade Mall, 03801, pg. 710 **IT**
Sprague Energy Corp., One Parade Mall, 03801, pg. 710 **PB**
Sprague Energy Corp. Northeast Operation, One Parade Mall, 03801, pg. 710 **IT**

Rochester

CABLETRON SYSTEMS, INC., 35 Industrial Way, 03867, pg. 288 **PB**
ENCORE SHOE CORPORATION, 51 Wakefield St., 03867, pg. 375 **PV**
New England Correct Craft, Inc., 142 Flagg Rd., 03867, pg. 277 **PV**
PRIME TANNING CO., INC., 216 Airport Dr., 03867, pg. 884 **PV**
Willis Corroon Corp. of New Hampshire, P.O. Box 5003, 95 S. Main St., 03867, pg. 1506 **IT**

Rollinsford

Damart, Three Front St., 03805, pg. 376 **IT**

Salem

Andover Bank NH, 130 Main St., 03079, pg. 112 **PB**
First USA Paymentech, Inc., 54 Stiles Rd., 03079, pg. 174 **PB**
Geophysical Survey Systems, Inc., Klein Dr., 03079, pg. 1019 **IT**
HADCO CORPORATION, 12A Manor Pkwy., 03079, pg. 773 **PB**
KLEIN Associates, Inc., Klein Dr., 03079, pg. 1019 **IT**
Micropolis Corporation, One Stiles Rd., Ste. 303, 03079, pg. 742 **PV**
Parlex Laminated Cable, Seven Industrial Way, 03079, pg. 1264 **PB**
Quantum Corporation, Seven Stiles Rd., 03079, pg. 1350 **PB**
Salemhaven, 23 Geremonty Dr., 03079, pg. 1714 **PB**
STANDEX INTERNATIONAL CORPORATION, Six Manor Pkwy., 03079, pg. 1505 **PB**
STOCKER & YALE, INC., 32 Hampshire Rd., 03079, pg. 1518 **PB**
UNIVEX CORPORATION, Three Old Rockingham Rd., 03079, pg. 1128 **PV**

Seabrook

North Atlantic Energy Service Corp., Rte 1, Lafayette Rd., 03874, pg. 1195 **PB**

Somersworth

Dowty Palmer-Chenard, 366 Rte. 16, 03878, pg. 1338 **IT**
FaceMate Corp., 200 Main St., 03878, pg. 391 **PV**
Fedco Omega, Inc., P.O. Box 431, 358 Rte. 108, 03676, pg. 1222 **PB**

Stratham

THE TIMBERLAND COMPANY, 200 Domain Dr., 03885, pg. 1609 **PB**
Timberland GmbH c/o The Timberland Company, P.O. Box 5050, 43842-5050, pg. 1609 **PB**

Tilton

EnergyNorth Natural Gas, Inc., Rte. 140, 03276, pg. 582 **PB**
First Deposit National Bank, 295 Main St., 03276, pg. 1338 **PB**
Pike Industries Inc., Rte. 3 at Interstate 93, 03276, pg. 242 **IT**
Wyman-Gordon Investment Castings, Inc., Granite St., 03276, pg. 1782 **PB**

Troy

TROY MILLS, INC., 30 Monadnock St., 03465, pg. 1106 **PV**

Walpole

Hubbard Farms, Inc., Turnpike St., 03608, pg. 1092 **PB**

Waterville Valley

Waterville Valley Ski Area Ltd., P.O. Box 540, One Ski Area Rd., 03215, pg. 62 **PV**

Whitefield

Whitefield Power & Lighting, Whitefield Industrial Pk., Airport Rd., 03598, pg. 1593 **PB**

Wilton

Label Art, Inc., One Riverside Way, 03086, pg. 782 **PV**

NEW JERSEY

Allendale

BLACK MILLWORK CO., INC., 230 W. Crescent Ave., 07401, pg. 147 **PV**
Clarion Corporation of America (Eastern Division), 25 Commerce Dr., 07401, pg. 296 **IT**
Komori America Corporation, Allendale Pk. Eastern Office:, Six Pearl Ct., 07401, pg. 745 **IT**
Marubeni Citizens Cincom Inc., 90 Boroline Rd., 07401, pg. 845 **IT**
Osteonics Corp., 59 Rte. 17, 07401, pg. 1526 **PB**
Recordati Corporation, 110 Commerce Dr., 07401, pg. 1090 **IT**
Sanyo Semiconductor Corporation, 80 Commerce Dr., 07401, pg. 1191 **IT**
Sharplan Lasers, Inc., One Pearl Ct., 07401, pg. 429 **IT**

Andover

Universal Suspension System, P.O. Box 1010, Linecrest Road, Long Pond Farm, 07821, pg. 1545 **PB**
Valley National Bank, 57 Decor Pond Rd., 07821, pg. 1706 **PB**

Annandale

Immunobiology Research Institute, P.O. Box 999, 08801-0999, pg. 928 **PB**

Asbury

ASBURY CARBONS, INC., P.O. Box 144, 405 Old Main St., 08802, pg. 87 **PB**
Asbury Graphite Mills, Inc., P.O. Box 144, 405 Old Main St., 08802, pg. 87 **PV**

Atlantic City

Atlantic City Hilton, Boston Ave. & The Boardwalk, 08404, pg. 829 **PB**
Atlantic City Showboat, P.O. Box 840, 08404, pg. 1469 **PB**
Bally's Park Place, Inc., Park Place & The Boardwalk, 08401, pg. 829 **PB**
Boardwalk Regency Corporation, 2100 Pacific Ave., 08401, pg. 1512 **PB**
Elsinore Shore Associates, 2500 Boardwalk, 08401, pg. 570 **PB**
GREATE BAY CASINO CORPORATION, 136 S. Kentucky Ave., 08401, pg. 760 **PB**
Greate Bay Hotel & Casino, 136 S. Kentucky Ave., 08401, pg. 761 **PB**
Greate Bay Property Funding, 136 S. Kentucky Ave., 08401, pg. 761 **PB**
Harrah's Atlantic City, Inc., 1725 Brigantine Blvd., 08401, pg. 790 **PB**
Harrah's Holiday Inns of New Jersey Inc., 1725 N. Brigantine Blvd., 08401, pg. 790 **PB**
Harrah's New Jersey, Inc., 1725 Brigantine Blvd., 08401, pg. 790 **PB**
HOLLYWOOD CASINO CORP., 136 S. Kentucky Ave., 08401, pg. 830 **PB**
Ireland Gourmet Shop, P.O. Box 59, 08401, pg. 351 **PB**
Ocean Showboat, Inc., 801 Boardwalk, 08401, pg. 1469 **PB**
PLAYERS INTERNATIONAL, INC., 1300 Atlantic Ave., Ste. 800, 08401, pg. 1310 **PB**
Resorts Casino Hotel, 1133 Boardwalk, 08401, pg. 1531 **PB**
Resorts International Hotel Financing, Inc., 1133 Boardwalk, 08404, pg. 480 **PV**

Tropicana Casino & Resort, Brighton and the Boardwalk, 08401-6390, pg. 159
Trump's Marina Casino Resort, Huron & Brigantine, 08401, pg. 1108 **PV**

Avenel

CONCORD CAMERA CORPORATION, 35 Mileed Way, 07001-2403, pg. 429 **PB**
Ivex Packaging Corporation-Avenel, 30 Production Way, 07001, pg. 915 **PB**
SANSONE AUTO MALL, 100 Rte. One, 07001, pg. 965 **PV**
Wall Trends, Inc., P.O. Box 10, 17 Mileed Way, 07001, pg. 1278 **IT**

Barrington

Anchor Optical Co., Inc., 97 E. Gloucester Pike, 08007, pg. 364 **PV**
Crescent Genlyte, 120 E. Gloucester Pike, 08007, pg. 730 **PB**
EDMUND SCIENTIFIC COMPANY, 101 E. Gloucester Pike, 08007-1380, pg. 364 **PV**

Basking Ridge

AT&T Consumer Communications Services, 295 N. Maple Ave., 07920, pg. 10 **PB**
AT&T CORPORATION, Corporate Headquarters, 295 N. Maple Ave., 07920, pg. 10 **PB**
Agile Networks, Inc., 211 Mount Airy Rd., 07920, pg. 1018 **PB**
Douglas Elliman-Gibbons & Ives, Inc., 19 Morristown Rd., 07920, pg. 341 **PV**
HOOPER HOLMES CORPORATION, 170 Mt. Airy Rd., 07920, pg. 835 **PB**
Lucent Technologies, Business Communications Systems Div., 36 Mt. Bethel Rd., 07920, pg. 1017 **PB**
Lucent Technologies Realty Inc., 222 Mt. Airy Rd., 07920, pg. 1019 **PB**
Telecommunications Technology Middle East Inc., 295 N. Maple Ave., 07920, pg. 1018 **PB**

Bayonne

BOOKAZINE COMPANY, INC., 75 Hook Rd., 07002, pg. 156 **PV**
CasChem Inc., 40 Ave. A, 07002, pg. 297 **PB**
International Matex Tank Terminals, Bayonne, Foot of East 22nd St., P.O. Box 67, 07002, pg. 758 **IT**
MURALO CO., INC., 148 E. Fifth St., 07002, pg. 767 **PV**

Bedminster

Bell Atlantic Cellular Consulting Group, Inc., 180 Washington Valley Rd., 07921, pg. 202 **PB**
Bell Atlantic International Wireless Services, Inc., 180 Washington Valley Rd., 07921, pg. 202 **PB**
Bell Atlantic Mobile, 180 Washington Valley Rd., 07921, pg. 202 **PB**
Bell Atlantic Ventures XX, Inc., 180 Washington Valley Rd., 07921, pg. 203 **PB**
NUI Capital Corp., 550 Rte. 202-206, 07921, pg. 1148 **PB**
NUI CORPORATION, 550 Rte. 202-206, 07921, pg. 1147 **PB**
NUI Energy Brokers, Inc., P.O. Box 760, 550 Rte. 202-206, 07921-0760, pg. 1148 **PB**
NUI Energy, Inc., P.O. Box 760, 550 Rte. 202-206, 07921-0760, pg. 1148 **PB**

Belle Mead

Excerpta Medica Inc., 105 Raider Blvd., 08502, pg. 1100 **IT**

Belleville

Hardman Division of Harcros Chemicals, Inc., 600 Cortlandt St., 07109, pg. 598 **IT**
Metro Label Corp., 357 Cortlandt St., 07109, pg. 736 **PV**

Belmar

Air Cruisers Co., P.O. Box 180, 07719, pg. 572 **IT**
Puritan Oil Company, Inc., One S. Black Horse Pike, 08030, pg. 1151 **PV**

Belvidere

Valley National Bank, Rte. 46 & Rte. 519, 07823, pg. 1706 **PB**

Bergenfield

Nova Electric Mfg. Co., 100 School Street, 07621, pg. 866 **PB**

Berkeley Heights

CM Chemical, 50 Valley Rd., 07922, pg. 861 **IT**
EA Engineering, Science & Technology, Inc., Twin Oak Way, 07922, pg. 541 **PB**
Lucent Technologies, Microelectronics Div., Two Oak Way, 07922, pg. 1017 **PB**
Lucent Technologies Opto Inc., Two Oak Way, 07922, pg. 1018 **PB**

Oakite Products, Inc., 50 Valley Rd., 07922, pg. 861 **IT**
Sillcocks Plastics, Inc., 310 Snyder Ave., 07922, pg. 63 **PV**

Berlin

Schuller Intl. Inc., P.O. Box Cn 130, 08009, pg. 927 **PB**
Voest-Alpine International Corp.-Hydro Division, Bldg. #47, Ste. 1, 439 Commerce Ln., 08009, pg. 1470 **IT**

Beverly

Chicopee, 2651 Rte. 130, 08010-2709, pg. 113 **IT**

Birmingham

SYBRON CHEMICALS INC., Birmingham Rd., 08011, pg. 1544 **PB**

Blackwood

K-Tron Electronics, VPR Commerce Center, Ste. 601, 08012, pg. 938 **PB**
METROLOGIC INSTRUMENTS, INC., Coles Rd. Rte. 42, 08012, pg. 1102 **PB**

Blairstown

Valley National Bank, Blairstown Shopping Ctr., 128 Rte. 94, 07825, pg. 1706 **PB**

Bloomfield

ABB Lummus Global Inc., 1515 Broad St., 07003-3096, pg. 4 **IT**
ABB Lummus Heat Transfer, 1515 Broad St., 07003, pg. 5 **IT**
ABB Simcon, Inc., 1515 Broad St., Bldg. A, 07003, pg. 5 **IT**
ENERGY BROKERS GUILD, 50 Franklin St., 07003, pg. 376 **PV**
Kent Paper Co., Inc., 27 Federal Plaza, 07044, pg. 89 **PV**
MINOR RUBBER CO., INC., 70 Ackerman St., 07003, pg. 751 **PV**
PEERLESS TUBE COMPANY, 58 Locust Ave., 07003, pg. 1269 **PB**
Williamhouse Sales Corp., 27 Federal Plaza, 07044, pg. 89 **PB**
WORLD FINER FOODS, INC., 300 Broad Acres Dr., 07003, pg. 1190 **PV**

Bloomingdale

CENTRAL/SHIPPEE, INC., 46 Star Lake Rd., 07403, pg. 224 **PV**
Vibration Mountings & Controls, Inc., 113 Main St., P.O. Box 37, 07403, pg. 24 **PB**

Bloomsbury

KOH-I-NOOR, INC., P.O. Box 68, 100 North St., 08804-0068, pg. 629 **PV**
Mid-Atlantic Correct Craft, Inc., P.O. Box 403, Rte. 173, 08804, pg. 277 **PV**
Wedco, Inc., P.O. Box 397, 08804, pg. 854 **PB**
Wedco Technology, P.O. Box 397, 08804, pg. 854 **PB**

Boonton

Bio-Chem Valve Inc., 85 Fulton St., 07005, pg. 590 **IT**
Carbone of America, Carbon Brush Div., 400 Myrtle Ave., 07005, pg. 1028 **IT**
Drew Industrial, One Drew Plaza, 07005, pg. 139 **PB**
JOHANSON MANUFACTURING CORPORATION, 301 Rockaway Valley Rd., 07005, pg. 589 **PV**
RFL ELECTRONICS, INC., 353 Powerville Rd., 07005, pg. 903 **PV**

Bordentown

B.M.J. Financial Corp., P.O. Box 1001, 243 Rte. 130, 08505, pg. 1528 **PB**
The Bank of Mid-Jersey, 243 Rte. 130, 08505, pg. 1528 **PB**
Circuit Foil USA Inc., 88 U.S. Hwy. 130, 08505-2279, pg. 80 **IT**
Ektelon, One Sportsystem Plaza, 08505-9630, pg. 884 **PV**
National Auto Dealers Exchange, P.O. Box 188, Rte. 206 S., 08505, pg. 282 **PB**
Ocean Spray Cranberries-Bordentown Plant, 104 E. Park St., 08505-1424, pg. 811 **PV**
Prince Golf International, One Sportsystem Plaza, 08505-9630, pg. 884 **PV**
PRINCE SPORTS GROUP INC., One Sportsystem Plaza, 08505-9630, pg. 884 **PV**

Bound Brook

IFC Non Wovens, C/O P.O. Box 387, 08805, pg. 1782 **PB**
Nippon Silica Glass USA, Inc., 1952 Rte. 22 E., 08805, pg. 1407 **IT**
RBH Dispersions, Inc., L-5 Factory Ln., 08805, pg. 370 **IT**
Tosoh USA, Inc.-New Jersey Office, 1952 Rte. 22 E., 08805, pg. 1407 **IT**

Branchburg

AIR & WATER TECHNOLOGIES CORPORATION, U.S. Hwy. 22 W. & Station Rd., 08876, pg. 29 **PB**
Huber, Hunt & Nichols, Inc., 3421 Rte. 22, 08876, pg. 548 **PV**

Branchville

HIGH POINT FINANCIAL CORP., Branchville Sq., Three Broad St., 07826, pg. 826 **PB**
NBSC Holdings Inc., P.O. Box 460, 07826, pg. 826 **PB**
NBSC Investment Advisory Services, Three Broad St., 07826, pg. 826 **PB**
NBSC Investment Co., Three Broad St., 07826, pg. 826 **PB**
NBSC Properties Inc., P.O. Box 460, 07826, pg. 826 **PB**
NBSC Real Estate Company Inc., P.O. Box 460, 07826, pg. 826 **PB**
The National Bank of Sussex County, Three Broad St., 07826, pg. 826 **PB**
Route 206 Development Corp., P.O. Box 460, 07826, pg. 826 **PB**
Selective Insurance Company-Northern New Jersey Branch, 40 Wantage Ave., 07890, pg. 1455 **PB**
Selective Insurance Company of America, 40 Wantage Ave., 07890, pg. 1455 **PB**
SELECTIVE INSURANCE GROUP, INC, 40 Wantage Ave., 07890, pg. 1455 **PB**
Selective Technical Administrative Services, Inc., 40 Wantage Ave., 07890-100, pg. 1456 **PB**
Selective Way Insurance Company, 40 Wantage Ave., 07890, pg. 1456 **PB**
Valley National Bank, Branchville Sq., 07826, pg. 1706 **PB**
Wantage Avenue Holding Company, Inc., 40 Wantage Ave., 07890, pg. 1456 **PB**

Bridgeport

CADDY CORP. OF AMERICA, 509 Sharptown Rd., 08014, pg. 198 **PV**
Forbo Wallcoverings, Inc., P.O. Box 457, 3 Killdeer Court, 08014-0457, pg. 497 **IT**
Heinkel Filtering Systems Inc., 520 Sharptown Rd., 08014, pg. 609 **IT**
Mitsubishi Fuso Truck of America, Inc., 100 Center Sq. Rd., 08014, pg. 875 **IT**
Wellman Day Products Div., Pedricktown Rd., 08014, pg. 1753 **PV**
WWF Paper Corporation - Mid Atlantic, 520 Pedricktown Rd., 08014, pg. 1145 **PV**
Yokohama Tire Corporation, 510 Center Square Rd., 08014, pg. 1521 **IT**

Bridgeton

WHIBCO, INC., 87 E. Commerce St., 08302, pg. 1171 **PV**

Bridgewater

AT&T Business Communications Services, 55 Corporate Dr., 08807, pg. 10 **PB**
Auto-trol Technology Corp.-Bridgewater, 991 U.S. Highway 22, Ste. 200, 08807, pg. 148 **PB**
Geoffrey Beene Retail, 1001 Frontier Rd., 08807, pg. 1291 **PB**
Courier-News Co., 1201 U.S. Hwy. 22 W., 08807, pg. 700 **PB**
Gant Retail, 1001 Frontier Rd., 08807, pg. 1292 **PB**
Ground Water Associates, Inc., 1011 Rte. 22 W., 08807, pg. 552 **PV**
HAMAMATSU CORP., 360 Foothill Rd., 08807-0910, pg. 497 **PV**
Hoechst Marion Roussel, Inc., P.O. Box 6800, 08807, pg. 624 **IT**
HYDRO GROUP, INC., US Hwy. 22W., Ste. 201, 08807, pg. 552 **PV**
National Starch and Chemical Company, Ten Finderne Ave., 08807, pg. 1435 **IT**
RARITAN BANCORP INC., P.O. Box 6909, 454 Rte. 45, 08807, pg. 1361 **PB**
Royal Consumer Business Products, P.O. Box 6945, 08807-0945, pg. 1002 **IT**
Science Management Corporation, 721 Rt. 202-206, 08807, pg. 1717 **PB**
Transax Data, 721 Rte. 202/206, 08807, pg. 1026 **IT**
UNITED NATIONAL BANCORP, 1130 Rte. 22E., 08807, pg. 1679 **PB**
Van Heusen Retail Division, 1001 Frontier Rd., 08807, pg. 1291 **PB**

Broadway

Pinelands Water & Wastewater Co., 117 Newbolds Rd., 08088, pg. 1110 **PB**

Budd Lake

DuPont Merck Pharm Co., 12 Winchester Ave., 07828-2200, pg. 1091 **PB**
Quest International Fragrances Inc., 400 International Dr., 07828, pg. 1436 **IT**
Valley National Bank, 202 Rte. 46, 07828, pg. 1706 **PB**

PB - *U.S. Public Companies Volume*
PV - *U.S. Private Companies Volume*
IT - *International Public & Private Companies Volume*

Buena

EVSCO Pharmaceuticals, Harding Hwy., P.O. Box 209, 08310, pg. 855 **PB**
IGI, INC., Wheat Rd. & Lincoln Ave., P.O. Box 687, 08310, pg. 855 **PB**

Burlington

BURLINGTON COAT FACTORY WAREHOUSE CORPORATION, 1830 Rte. 130, 08016, pg. 268 **PB**
Burlington Woods Convalescent Home, 115 Sunset Rd., 08016, pg. 728 **PB**
Burns & Wilcox, 505 High St., 08016, pg. 609 **PV**
Canon Financial Services, Inc., 250 Commerce Sq. Blvd., 08016, pg. 262 **IT**
DENTSPLY Ceramco, Six Terri Ln., 08016, pg. 499 **PB**
Dupli-fax, Inc., 300 Commerce Sq. Blvd., 08016, pg. 262 **IT**
FRANKLIN ELECTRONIC PUBLISHERS, INC., One Franklin Plaza, 08016-4907, pg. 679 **PB**
Gould Paper Corporation-Mid Atlantic, Two Campus Dr., 08016, pg. 467 **PV**
J.G. Hook Enterprises, Inc., 460 Veterans Dr., 08016, pg. 538 **PB**
Penn Fashions, Inc., Rte. 130, 08016, pg. 268 **PB**
Sharon Sez, Inc., Rte. 130, 08016, pg. 268 **PB**

Caldwell

Carrier Building Systems & Services, 1430 Madison Rd., 07006, pg. 1689 **PB**

Camden

Bakery & Confectionary Division, Campbell Pl., 08103, pg. 299 **PB**
Boam Chemicals Co., Inc., 3rd St. & Jefferson Ave., 08104, pg. 689 **PV**
Boam Produce (Overseas) Ltd., Third St. & Jefferson Ave., 08104, pg. 689 **PV**
Camden Paperboard Corporation, 267 Jefferson Ave., 08104, pg. 303 **PB**
Joseph Campbell Company, Campbell Pl., 08103, pg. 299 **PB**
Campbell Sales Company, Campbell Pl., 08103, pg. 299 **PB**
CAMPBELL SOUP COMPANY, Campbell Pl., 08103-1799, pg. 298 **PB**
Campbell USA, Campbell Pl., 08103, pg. 299 **PB**
Garlock Valves & Industrial Plastics, 602 N. Tenth St., 08101, pg. 402 **PB**
Herider Farms, Inc., Campbell Pl., 08103, pg. 299 **PB**
L3 Communications, 1 Federal St., 08102, pg. 638 **PB**
Mafco Worldwide Corp., Third St. & Jefferson Ave., 08104, pg. 690 **PB**
Magnetic Metals Corp., Hayes Ave. at 21st Street, 08101, pg. 560 **PV**
PARIS FOODS CORP., 1632 Carman St., 08105, pg. 839 **PV**
SL Surface Technology, Inc., 1416 S. Sixth St., 08104, pg. 1419 **PB**
Swanson, Campbell Pl., 08103, pg. 299 **PB**

Cape May

Snow's/Doxee Inc., 994 Ocean Dr., pg. 219 **PV**

Carlstadt

ALDINE TECHNOLOGIES INDUSTRIES INC., 585 Industrial Rd., 07072-1611, pg. 33 **PV**
Applied Graphics Technology, 463 Barell Ave., 07072, pg. 1125 **PV**
Beta Plastics, 120 Amor Ave., 07072, pg. 45 **PV**
Carlyle Industries, Inc., One Palmer Terrace, 07072, pg. 1187 **PB**
Cosan Chemical Corp., 400 13th St., 07072, pg. 297 **PB**
Deer Park Spring Water, Inc., 190 Jony Dr., 07072, pg. 919 **IT**
EAGLE BUTTON CO., INC., 415 14th St., 07072, pg. 354 **PV**
Food Oils Corporation, 145 Grant St., 07072, pg. 1103 **PV**
GENERAL TRADING CO., 455 16th St., 07072, pg. 445 **PV**
J & R Interfacing, 455 Oehler Pl., 07072, pg. 1499 **IT**
Lalique North America, 400 Veterans Blvd., 07072, pg. 797 **PV**
NAMES FOR DAMES, INC., 820 Washington Ave., 07072-3008, pg. 773 **PV**
PIONEER PAPER CORPORATION, 50 Triangle Blvd., 07072, pg. 867 **PV**
Rosenthal U.S.A. Limited, 355 Michele Pl., 07072, pg. 1127 **IT**
STANBEE COMPANY, INC., 70 Broad St., 07072, pg. 1030 **PV**
Stocko Corp., 495 Industrial Rd., 07072, pg. 1301 **IT**
Tho-Ro Products, Inc., 335 Paterson Plank Rd., 07072, pg. 354 **PV**
US Ink Corp., 651 Garden St., 07072, pg. 370 **PV**
Yoo Hoo Chocolate Beverage Corp., 600 Commercial Ave., 07072, pg. 567 **IT**

Carteret

Bagcraft Corporation of America, Eastern Div., Ten Minue St., 07008, pg. 136 **PB**
Carteret Terminal, 78 LaFayette, 07008, pg. 692 **PB**

DI GIORGIO CORPORATION, 380 Middlesex Ave., 07008, pg. 330 **PV**
Karl Koch Erecting Co. Inc., 400 Roosevelt Ave., 07008, pg. 1261 **IT**
NOBODY BEATS THE WIZ, 1300 Federal Blvd., 07008, pg. 800 **PV**
Oxford Instruments-Superconducting Technology, 600 Milik St., 07008-0429, pg. 1018 **IT**
Staflex Products, 50 Middlesex Ave., 07008, pg. 495 **PV**
TAWIL ASSOCIATES INC., 100 Wesley White Dr., 07008, pg. 1070 **PV**
Unity Sewing Supply Div., 900 Milik St., 07008-1117, pg. 1177 **PV**
White Rose Food, 380 Middlesex Ave., 07008, pg. 330 **PV**
WILLCOX & GIBBS, INC., 900 Milik St., 07008, pg. 1177 **PV**

Cedar Grove

Hudson United Bank-Cedar Grove, 85-107 Pompton Ave., 07009, pg. 845 **PB**

Cedar Knolls

Advanced Conversion Products, 85 Horsehill Rd, 07927, pg. 1097 **PV**
Angar Scientific Co., Inc., 52 Horsehill Rd., 07927, pg. 574 **PB**
The Body Shop, Hanover Technical Ctr., 45 Horsehill Rd., 07927-2003, pg. 199 **IT**
Carnrick Laboratories, Inc., 65 Horsehill Rd., 07927, pg. 436 **PV**
Cerberus Pyrotronics Inc., Eight Ridgedale Ave., 07927, pg. 1246 **IT**
Diamonair, 54 Horsehill Rd, 07927, pg. 1003 **PB**
GWC HEALTH, INC., 65 Horsehill Rd., 07927, pg. 436 **PV**
RANJIT CORPORATION, Six Saddle Rd., 07927, pg. 909 **PV**
Schering Berlin Inc., 110 East Hanover Avenue, 07927, pg. 1204 **IT**
Stewart Smith East, Inc., Three Wing Dr., 07927, pg. 1508 **IT**
TRANSISTOR DEVICES, INC., 85 Horsehill Rd., 07927, pg. 1097 **PV**

Chatham

Beechwood Insurance Agency, Inc., One Main St., 07928, pg. 1528 **PB**
INFINICOM, 127 Main St., 07928, pg. 561 **PV**
Summit Bank, One Main St., 07928, pg. 1528 **PB**
TSP Inc., Two Main St., 07928, pg. 457 **IT**

Cherry Hill

Admiral Insurance Company, 1255 Caldwell Rd., 08034, pg. 216 **PB**
CCW Stamp Co., 2324 W. Rte. 70, 08002, pg. 58 **PV**
CM Graphics, 112 Haddontowne Ct., Ste. 204, 08034-3663, pg. 1329 **PB**
Cherry Hill Center, Inc., 514 Cherry Hill Mall, 08034, pg. 1408 **PB**
Courier-Post, 301 Cuthbert Blvd., 08002, pg. 700 **PB**
Data Sources, 20 Brace Rd., 08034, pg. 1600 **PB**
European Coffee Classics, 1401 Berlin Rd., 08034, pg. 857 **IT**
Fuji Heavy Industries USA, Inc., Subaru Plaza, 2235 Rte. 70 W., 08002, pg. 523 **IT**
Garden State Cable, 1250 Hddonfield-Berlin Rd., 08034, pg. 407 **PB**
Garden State Race Track, Inc., P.O. Box 4274, 08034, pg. 908 **PB**
Hemostatix, 26 Olney Ave., 08034, pg. 1073 **PV**
INTERNATIONAL THOROUGHBRED BREEDERS, INC., Rte. 70 & Haddonfield Rd., 08034, pg. 908 **PB**
THE LEHIGH PRESS, INC., 51 Haddonfield Rd., Ste. 210, 08002, pg. 658 **PV**
Lincoln Graphics, 1110 Cornell Ave., 08002, pg. 1437 **PB**
Marsam Pharmaceuticals, Building 31, 24 Olney Ave., 08034, pg. 969 **PV**
Martin Marietta Services Group, Rte. 38, 08358, pg. 1007 **PB**
Martin Marietta Technical Support Services, Rte. 38, 08358, pg. 1007 **PB**
The Media & Marketing Group, Cherry Tree Corp. Ctr., Rt. 38, 08002, pg. 902 **PV**
Melitta Foodservice Corp., 1401 Berlin Rd., 08003, pg. 857 **IT**
PENNY PLATE, INC., 603 Kresson Rd., 08034, pg. 850 **PV**
RBT/STRUM, Cherry Tree Corp. Ctr., Rte. 38, 08002-2957, pg. 902 **PV**
THE SCORE BOARD, INC., 1951 Old Cuthbert Rd., 08034, pg. 1444 **PB**
Sonex, 26 Olney Ave., 08034, pg. 1073 **PV**
Subaru Credit Corporation, Subaru Plaza, P.O. Box 6660, 08034, pg. 523 **IT**
Subaru Financial Services, Inc., Subaru Plaza, P.O. Box 6000, 08034-6000, pg. 523 **IT**
Subaru Leasing Corporation, P.O. Box 6000, Subaru Plaza, 08034-6000, pg. 523 **IT**
Subaru of America, Inc., P.O. Box 6000., 08034-6000, pg. 523 **IT**
Suburban Newspaper Group, 1111 Union Ave., P.O. Box 180, 08034, pg. 700 **PB**
TELEGENIX INC., 26 Olney Ave., 08034, pg. 1073 **PV**
TRINKLE SALES, INC., 1010 Haddonfield-Berlin Rd., 08034, pg. 1103 **PV**
UNITED STATES COLD STORAGE, INC., 100 Dobbs Ln., Ste. 102, 08034, pg. 1124 **PV**

VICTORY REFRIGERATION CO. LC, 110 Woodcrest Road, 08003, pg. 1139 **PV**
Western International Media Corporation, 1930 E. Marlton Pike, Ste. A-7, 08003, pg. 1167 **PV**

Chester

Christy Halsey Oil Co., 65 Maple Ave., 07930, pg. 729 **PV**
C.M. OFFRAY & SON INC., P.O. Box 601, Rte. 24, 07930, pg. 812 **PV**
Valley National Bank, Chester Springs Mall, 07930, pg. 1706 **PB**

Cinnaminson

AFG Industries, Inc., 2600 River Rd., 08077, pg. 84 **IT**
JCI DATA PROCESSING, INC., 200 Rte. 130, 08077, pg. 577 **PV**

Clark

HARCREST INTERNATIONAL, LTD., 136 Central Ave., 07066-1142, pg. 500 **PV**
Harper Industries, Inc., 16 Central Ave., 07066-1142, pg. 501 **PV**
IKG Industries, 270 Terminal Ave., 07066, pg. 793 **PB**
KARNAK CORPORATION, 330 Central Ave., 07066, pg. 607 **PV**
Olicom Americas - East, 57 Brant Ave., Ste. 100, 07066, pg. 1001 **IT**
Poe & Brown of New Jersey, 67 Walnut Ave., 07066, pg. 1312 **PB**

Clayton

Republic Environmental Recycling (New Jersey), Inc., Cenco Blvd., 08312, pg. 1050 **IT**

Cliffside Park

Hudson United Bank-Cliffside Park, 732 Anderson Ave., 07010, pg. 845 **PB**

Clifton

AMERICAN MARKING SYSTEMS, 1015 Paulson Ave., 07015, pg. 58 **PV**
American Roche Intl. Inc., 100 Delawanna Ave., 07015-5034, pg. 1120 **IT**
Avcron Incorporated, P.O. Box 1075, 07114-1075, pg. 859 **PB**
Bensons International Systems Inc., 777 Passaic Ave. - 5th Fl., 07012, pg. 460 **IT**
BISCAYNE APPAREL INC., 1373 Broad St., 3rd Fl., 07013, pg. 232 **PV**
CANTEL INDUSTRIES, INC., 1135 Broad St., Ste. 203, 07013, pg. 301 **PB**
Essex Chemical Corporation, 1401 Broad St., 07015, pg. 523 **PB**
Essex Industrial Chemicals, Inc., 1333 Broad St., 07015, pg. 523 **PB**
Essex Specialty Products, Inc., 1333 Broad St., 07015, pg. 523 **PB**
FEDERAL BUSINESS PRODUCTS, INC., 95 Main St., 07014, pg. 398 **PV**
FRAGRANCE RESOURCES, INC., 620 Route 3 W., 07014, pg. 423 **PV**
Givaudan-Roure Corporation, 100 Delawanna Ave., 07014, pg. 1120 **IT**
Givaudan-Roure Corporation-Flavors Division, 100 Delawanna Ave., 07015, pg. 1119 **IT**
GREATER NEW YORK BOX CO., 149 Entin Rd., 07014, pg. 476 **PV**
Hudson United Bank-Clifton, 295 Clifton Ave., 07011, pg. 845 **PB**
ITT Avionics Division, 100 Kingsland Rd., 07014, pg. 859 **PB**
International Chempack Inc., 1401 Broad St., 07015, pg. 523 **PB**
LCS INDUSTRIES, INC., 120 Brighton Rd., 07012, pg. 970 **PB**
LINENS 'N THINGS, INC., Six Brighton Rd., 07015, pg. 668 **PV**
Paterson Stamp Works, 1015 Paulson Ave., 07015, pg. 59 **PV**
SmithKline Beecham Products Western Hemisphere Div., Intl., 65 Industrial So., 07012, pg. 1264 **IT**
SWEPCO TUBE CORPORATION, One Clifton Blvd., 07015, pg. 1058 **PV**
Whatman Inc., Nine Bridewell Pl., 07014, pg. 1498 **IT**

Clinton

Foster Wheeler Arabia, Ltd., Perryville Corporate Park, 08809, pg. 677 **PB**
Foster Wheeler Constructors, Inc., Perryville Corporate Park, 08809, pg. 677 **PB**
FOSTER WHEELER CORPORATION, Perryville Corporate Park, 08809-4000, pg. 676 **PB**
Foster Wheeler Energy Corporation, Perryville Corporate Park, 08809, pg. 676 **PB**
Foster Wheeler Energy International, Inc., Perryville Corporate Park, 08809, pg. 676 **PB**
Foster Wheeler Facilities Management, Inc., Perryville Corporate Park, 08809, pg. 677 **PB**
Foster Wheeler Power Systems, Inc., Perryville Corporate Park, 08809, pg. 677 **PB**
Foster Wheeler Real Estate Development Corp., Perryville Corporate Park, 08809, pg. 677 **PB**

PB - *U.S. Public Companies Volume*
PV - *U.S. Private Companies Volume*
IT - *International Public & Private Companies Volume*

Geographic Index-U.S.

Foster Wheeler USA Corporation, Perryville Corporate Park, 08809, pg. 677 — PB
Foster Wheeler World Services Corp., Perryville Corporate Park, 08809, pg. 677 — PB
Foster Wheeler Zack, Inc., Pennyville Corp. Pk., 08809-4000, pg. 677 — PB
Meenan Oil Div., 108 W. Main St., 08809, pg. 729 — PV

Closter

Krups North America, Seven Reuten Dr., 07624, pg. 896 — IT
Moulinex Appliances, Inc., Seven Reuten Dr., 07624, pg. 896 — IT
Pavailler U.S.A. Inc., Ten Rnton Dr., 07624, pg. 485 — IT
THE PROMOTION IN MOTION COMPANIES, #3 Reuten Dr., 07624, pg. 890 — PV

Collingswood

Vickers Tedeco Div., 103 E. Linden Ave., 08108-2025, pg. 25 — PV
WHEATLAND TUBE COMPANY, 900 Haddon Ave., 08108, pg. 1170 — PV

Cologne

Collective Bank, 716 W. White Horse Pike, 08213, pg. 1528 — PB

Cranbury

Bohlin Instruments Inc., 2540 Route 130, Ste. 114, 08512, pg. 208 — IT
Bronwing-Ferris Industries of South Jersey, Inc., Cranbury Station, R.D. #4, Box 74A, 08512, pg. 264 — PB
Carter Products Div., Half Acre Road, P.O. Box 1001, 08512 0181, pg. 310 — PB
Carter-Wallace Manufacturing Div., Half Acre Rd., 08512, pg. 310 — PB
MARKETSOURCE CORPORATION, 10 Abeel Road, 08512, pg. 705 — PV
Nielsen & Bainbridge, 17 South Middlesex Ave., 08512, pg. 460 — IT
Rhone-Poulenc Alcolac, CN 7500, 08512-7500, pg. 1110 — IT
Somfy Systems Inc., 47 Commerce Dr., 08512, pg. 376 — PV
United States Protection and Indemnity Agency, Inc., One Continental Dr., 08570, pg. 1011 — PB
Wallace Laboratories, Half Acre Rd., 08512, pg. 310 — PB
Wampole Laboratories, Half Acre Rd., 08512, pg. 310 — PB

Cranford

Ampex Corporation, Six Commerce Dr., #2000, 07016, pg. 104 — PB
CAP Gemini (New Jersey Technologies), 25 Commerce Dr., 07016, pg. 264 — IT
CONSTRUCTION SPECIALTIES, INC., 49 Meeker Ave., 07016, pg. 266 — PV
Construction Specialties of California, 49 Meeker Ave., 07016, pg. 266 — PV
Datasphere, Inc., 49 Meeker Ave., 07016, pg. 266 — PV
GRABER-ROGG, INC., 22 Jackson Dr., 07016, pg. 468 — PV
THE NEWARK GROUP, INC., 20 Jackson Dr., 07016, pg. 796 — PV
Special Erection Services, Inc., 49 Meeker Ave., 07016, pg. 266 — PV
The Summit Mortgage Company, Inc., 750 Walnut Ave., pg. 1528 — PB
TECKNIT INCORPORATED, 129 Dermody St., 07016, pg. 1072 — PV
Wilson USA Inc., 750 Walnut Avenue, 07016, pg. 124 — IT

Cresskill

GFA BRANDS, INC., 211 Knickerbocker Rd., 07626, pg. 435 — PV

Dayton

Chicopee Inc., P.O. Box 1004, 08810, pg. 113 — IT
Makita U.S.A. Inc.-New Jersey, 251 Herrod Blvd., South Brunswick Industrial Pk., 08810-1539, pg. 831 — IT
Ropak Atlantic Inc., 2B Corn Rd., 08810, pg. 811 — IT
Villares Corporation of America, P.O. Box 911, 08810-0911, pg. 23 — IT
Zeneca Specialty Inks, 65 Stults Rd., 08810, pg. 1525 — IT

Deepwater

Du Pont Chambers Works, Rte. 130, 08023, pg. 531 — PB

Delair

ALUMINUM SHAPES, LLC, 9000 River Rd., 08110, pg. 47 — PV
Delair Group, L.L.C., 8600 River Rd., 08110, pg. 47 — PV
Primary Pulp & Paper Plant, Foot of DeRousse Ave., P.O. Box 338, 08110, pg. 736 — PB

Delanco

JEVIC TRANSPORTATION, INC., P.O. Box 5157, 08075, pg. 927 — PB

Delran

Datapro Information Services Grp., 600 Delran Pkwy., 08075-1252, pg. 1070 — PB
Gandalf Systems Corporation, 501 Delran Pkwy., 08075, pg. 540 — IT

Denville

Cigna Healthcare of Northern New Jersey, Inc., Three Stewart Ct., 07834, pg. 360 — PB
Kenwood Service Corporation-New Jersey Branch, 400 Morris Ave., Ste. 102, 07834, pg. 730 — IT

Deptford

Catalysts & Chemicals, 2001 Nolte Dr., 08066-1727, pg. 713 — IT
ICI Polyurethanes Group, Mantua Grove Rd., 08096, pg. 664 — IT
Johnson Matthey Pharmaceuticals Materials, 2001 Nolte Dr., 08066, pg. 713 — IT

Dover

Casio, Inc., 570 Mt. Pleasant Ave., 07801, pg. 274 — IT
Valley National Bank, 100 E. Blackwell St., 07801, pg. 1706 — PB

Dunellen

Hudson United Bank-Dunellen, 324 North Ave., 08812, pg. 845 — PB

East Brunswick

Agro Dynamics, Inc., 10 Alvin Ct., 08816, pg. 563 — PB
ECOSCIENCE CORPORATION, 10 Alvin Ct., 08816, pg. 563 — PB
KEY ENERGY GROUP INC., Two Tower Center, 10th Fl., 08816, pg. 953 — PB
Pall Trincor Corporation, One Kimberly Rd., 08816, pg. 1254 — PB
Princeton Bank & Trust Company National Association, Two Tower Ctr., 08816, pg. 338 — PB
Shaker Advertising Agency, 190 State Hwy. 18, 08816, pg. 989 — PV
The Trump Group, P.O. Box. 186, 08816, pg. 1108 — PV
Whitney Corr-Pak International, Inc., 19 Kimberly Rd., 08816, pg. 249 — PV

East Hanover

Five Star Group, Inc., 903 Murray Road, 07936, pg. 694 — PB
KEYES MARTIN, 100 Eagle Rock Ave., 07936-1946, pg. 618 — PV
Nabisco Biscuit Company, 100 DeForest Ave., 07936, pg. 1355 — PB
Novartis Pharmaceuticals, 59 Route 10, 07936-1080, pg. 973 — IT
Planters Company, 100 DeForest Ave., 07936, pg. 1355 — PB
Sandoz Pharmaceuticals Corp., Bldg. 701, 59 Rte. 10, 07936-1080, pg. 974 — IT
Sandoz Research Institute, Bldg. 404, Rm. 442, Rte. 10, 07936, pg. 974 — IT

East Orange

LOUIS BERGER INTERNATIONAL INC., 100 Halsted Str., 07019, pg. 135 — PV
Broad National Bank-East Orange, 554 Central Ave., 07018, pg. 257 — PB

East Rutherford

ALLIED BUILDING PRODUCTS CORPORATION, 15 E. Union Ave., 07073, pg. 38 — PV
CCA INDUSTRIES, INC., 200 Murray Hill Pkwy., 07073, pg. 276 — PB
CAMBREX CORPORATION, One Meadowlands Plaza, 07073, pg. 297 — PB
Cushman & Wakefield, One Meadowlands Plaza, Ste. 1100, 07073, pg. 873 — PV
DIAMOND CHEMICAL CO., INC., P.O. Box 7428, 07073, pg. 330 — PV
Intergraph Corporation, One Meadowlands Plaza, 07073, pg. 890 — PB
LDDS WorldCom Inc., One Meadowlands Plaza, 07073, pg. 1779 — PB
METROMEDIA COMPANY, One Meadowlands Plaza, 07073, pg. 736 — PV
METROMEDIA INTERNATIONAL GROUP, INC., One Meadowlands Plaza, 07073, pg. 1102 — PB
Sequa Can Machinery, 401 Central Ave., 07073, pg. 1458 — PB
Spartan Security Services, Inc., One Madison St., 07073, pg. 873 — PB
Temco Building Maintenance, Inc., One Madison St., 07073, pg. 1574 — PB
Value Line, 125 E. Union Ave., 07073, pg. 137 — PV

East Windsor

Cultor Food Service, 20 Lake Dr., 08520-5398, pg. 349 — IT

Eatontown

Adamatic, 607 Industrial Way W., 07724, pg. 1322 — PB
AlliedSignal Aerospace Systems & Equipment, 118 Hwy. 35, 07724, pg. 50 — PB
InterDigital Telecom, Inc., 615 Hope Rd., Bldg. 1, 07724, pg. 889 — PB
LAIRD & COMPANY, One Laird Rd., 07724, pg. 642 — PV
Roberts Laboratories, Inc., Four Industrial Way W., 07724, pg. 1393 — PB
ROBERTS PHARMACEUTICAL CORPORATION, Four Industrial Way W., 07724, pg. 1393 — PB
SAIC Technology, One Industrial Way W., 07724-2255, pg. 976 — PV
Telecom Analysis Systems, 34 Industrial Way East, 07724-3319, pg. 208 — IT
VRG International, Inc., 81 Corbett Way, 07724, pg. 1393 — PB

Edgewater

OCTAGON PROCESS INC., 596 River Rd., 07020-1192, pg. 811 — PV
Unilever Research & Development Co., 45 River Road, 07020, pg. 1436 — IT

Edison

AFP Transformers, Inc., 206 Talmadge Rd., 08818, pg. 1674 — PB
Amerchol Corporation, 136 Talmadge Rd., 08818, pg. 1667 — PB
Architectural Wall Systems, LLC, 20 Truman Dr. S., 08817, pg. 403 — PV
Auxilec, Inc., 3920 Park Ave., P.O. Box 989, 08818-0989, pg. 1383 — PB
Baccarat, Inc., 36 Mayfield Ave., 08837, pg. 132 — IT
James Bliss & Co., Inc., 201 Meadow Rd., 08818, pg. 1756 — PB
Bowman Distribution, 220 Meadow Rd., 08817, pg. 190 — PB
CAP Gemini America (NJ Commercial Branch), Raritan Plaza III, Raritan Center, 08837, pg. 264 — IT
CASWELL-MASSEY CO. LTD., 121 Fieldcrest Ave., 08837, pg. 219 — PV
DMR Consulting Group, Inc., 333 Thornall St., 08837-2220, pg. 527 — IT
DYD Co., 180 Raritan Center Pkwy., 08818, pg. 132 — IT
Direct Script, Raritan Ctr., 300 Columbus Cir., 08837-9998, pg. 1239 — PB
Dranetz-BMI, 1000 New Durham Rd., 08818-4019, pg. 1144 — PV
E & B Marine Incorporated, 201 Meadow Rd., 08818, pg. 1756 — PB
E & B Marine Supply, Inc., 201 Meadow Rd., 08818, pg. 1756 — PB
Edison Foam Processing Corp., 521 Sunfield Ave., 08817, pg. 986 — PB
Edison Operation, 55 Mayfield Ave., 08837, pg. 990 — PB
Energis Resources Incorporated, 499 Thornall St., 08837, pg. 1340 — PB
Frigidaire Home Products-Home Comfort Products, 2170 Hwy. 27, 08818, pg. 440 — PB
Goldbergs Marine Distributors, 201 Meadow Rd., 08818, pg. 1756 — PB
Gould Paper Corporation-NJ, 100 Executive Ave., 08817, pg. 467 — PB
HERITAGE INKS INTERNATIONAL, 100 Pershing Ave., 08837, pg. 524 — PV
Holmes Protection of New Jersey, Inc., 21 Northfield Ave., 08818, pg. 1649 — PB
K. Hovnanian Companies Northeast, Inc., 110 Fieldcrest Ave., 08818, pg. 843 — PB
J.M. HUBER CORPORATION, 333 Thornall St., 08818, pg. 544 — PV
Huls America Inc., 40 Nixon Ln., 08837, pg. 1455 — IT
KCS ENERGY INC., 379 Thornall St., 08837, pg. 938 — PB
KCS Energy Marketing Inc., 379 Thornall St., 08837, pg. 938 — PB
KCS Energy Risk Management, 379 Thornall St., 08837, pg. 939 — PB
KCS Power Marketing, Inc., 379 Thornall St., 08837, pg. 939 — PB
Krupp Plastics & Rubber Machinery Inc., P.O. 619, 330 Talmadge Rd., 08818-0619, pg. 510 — IT
MARK LIGHTING FIXTURE CO., INC., Three Kilmer Rd., 08818, pg. 704 — PV
Metex Corporation, 970 New Durham Rd., 08818, pg. 1674 — PB
Metex Export Corp., 970 New Durham Rd., 08818, pg. 1675 — PB
Midlantic Bank, N.A., 499 Thornall St., 08837, pg. 1242 — PB
Modern Handling Equipment of N.J., Inc., 75 New St., 08837, pg. 755 — PV
National Enerdrill, 379 Thornall St., 08837, pg. 939 — PB
NATIONAL FOOD STORES, INC., 76 National Rd., 08817, pg. 783 — PV
NEW BRUNSWICK SCIENTIFIC CO., INC., 44 Talmadge Rd., 08818, pg. 1169 — PB
New Brunswick Scientific Co., Inc., 44 Talmadge Rd., 08818-4005, pg. 1170 — IT
PENTECH INTERNATIONAL, INC., 195 Carter Dr., 08817, pg. 1274 — PB
PHARMACEUTICAL FORMULATIONS, INC., 460 Plainfield Ave., 08818-1904, pg. 1284 — PB
Plenum Publishing Distribution, Raritan Ctr., 200 McGraw Dr., 08837, pg. 1311 — PB
Proliq, Inc., 379 Thornall St., 08837, pg. 939 — PB

PB - U.S. Public Companies Volume
PV - U.S. Private Companies Volume
IT - International Public & Private Companies Volume

Geographic Index-U.S.

1317

Queens Group New Jersey, Inc., 180 Talmadge Rd., 08817, pg. 900 **PB**
Quest Diagnostic, 3537 Progress St., 08820, pg. 1351 **PB**
Revlon Research Center, Inc., Rte. #27 & Talmadge Rd., 08817, pg. 690 **PB**
SGS Control Services Inc., 333 Thornall St., 08818, pg. 1153 **IT**
SMS-New Jersey, 343 Thornall St., 08818, pg. 1463 **PB**
Sea Ranger Products, 201 Meadow Rd., 08818, pg. 1756 **PB**
SHAW CREATIONS, INC., 32 Brunswick Ave., 08817-2578, pg. 990 **PV**
Sterling Davis Standard - Blow Molding Division, 38 Brunswick Ave., 08817, pg. 459 **PB**
Strober New Jersey Building Supply Centers, Inc., 20 Truman Dr. S., 08817, pg. 403 **PV**
Thermometrics, Inc., 808 US Hwy. 1, 08817, pg. 208 **IT**
TOPS APPLIANCE CITY, 45 Brunswick Ave., 08818-1907, pg. 1622 **PB**
TURNKEY TECHNOLOGIES, INC., Ten Parsonage Rd., 08837, pg. 1110 **PV**
TWIN COUNTY GROCERS, INC., 145 Talmadge Rd., 08818, pg. 1111 **PV**
Twinco Graphics, 145 Talmadge Rd., 08818, pg. 1111 **PV**
Twinco Services, Inc., 145 Talmadge Rd., 08818, pg. 1111 **PV**
Twinco Trucking Co., Inc., 145 Talmadge Rd., 08818, pg. 1111 **PV**
WPT, INC., 1000 New Durham Rd., 08818, pg. 1144 **PV**

Egg Harbor Township

Spencer Gifts, Inc., 6826 Blackhorse Pike, 08234-4197, pg. 1216 **IT**

Elizabeth

Alpha Wire Company, 711 Lidgerwood Ave., 07207, pg. 201 **PB**
ATALANTA CORPORATION, Atalanta Plaza, 07206, pg. 93 **PV**
Broad National Bank-Bayway, 1000 S. Elmora Ave., 07202, pg. 257 **PB**
Broad National Bank-Elizabeth, 826 Elizabeth Ave., 07206, pg. 257 **PB**
Browning-Ferris Industries of New Jersey, Inc., P.O. Box 508, 07207, pg. 263 **PB**
Browning-Ferris of Elizabeth, N.J., Inc., 714 Division St., 07207, pg. 264 **PB**
DanTransport International Corporation, Port Authority Indus. Pk., 850 Center Dr., 07201, pg. 476 **IT**
Elizabeth Detention Center, 625 Evans St., 07201, pg. 450 **PB**
Food Haulers, Inc., 600 York St., 07207, pg. 1146 **PV**
Hayward Industrial Products, 900 Fairmount Ave., 07207, pg. 513 **PV**
HAYWARD INDUSTRIES, INC., 900 Fairmount Ave., 07207, pg. 513 **PV**
Hayward Pool Products, Inc., 900 Fairmount Ave., 07207, pg. 513 **PV**
Huls America Inc., Miplom Division, 830 Magnolia Ave., 07201, pg. 1455 **IT**
MAGRUDER COLOR COMPANY, INC., 1029 Newark Ave., 07208, pg. 696 **PV**
MILTON CAN CO., INC., 580 Division St., 07201, pg. 749 **PV**
National Transport Services Co., 600 York St., 07207, pg. 1146 **PV**
Papetti Hygrade Egg Products, One Papetti Pl., 07206, pg. 1104 **PB**
Pittra, Atlanta Plaza, 07206, pg. 94 **PV**
PRIDE PRODUCTS, INC., Five Slater Dr., 07206, pg. 883 **PV**
RSI, 600 York St., 07207, pg. 1146 **PV**
Shop-Rite Beverages, Inc., 600 York St., 07207, pg. 1146 **PV**
Shop-Rite Cigarettes (CT), 600 York St., 07207, pg. 1146 **PV**
Shop-Rite of Bensalem Inc., 600 York St., 07207, pg. 1146 **PV**
Shop-Rite Supermarkets, Inc., 600 York St., 07207, pg. 1146 **PV**
TRR Carriers, Inc., 600 York St., 07207, pg. 1146 **PV**
The Toy Factory, Five Slater Dr., 07206, pg. 883 **PV**
WAKEFERN FOOD CORPORATION, 600 York St., 07207, pg. 1146 **PV**

Elmwood Park

Biocraft Penicillin Dosage Plant, 92 Rte. 46, 07407, pg. 1381 **IT**
Freeman Products, 487 Edward H. Ross Drive, 07407, pg. 1105 **PV**
Garden State Paper Co., Inc., River Dr. Ctr. Two, 07407, pg. 1078 **PB**
JVC Company of America, 41 Slater Dr., 07407, pg. 846 **IT**
JVC Manufacturing Company, 41 Slater Dr., 07407, pg. 847 **IT**
JVC Professional Products Company, 41 Slater Dr., 07407, pg. 847 **IT**
MARCAL PAPER MILLS, INC., One Market St., 07407, pg. 701 **PV**
National Pharmacies, Inc., 491 Edward H. Ross Dr., 07407, pg. 1091 **PB**
National Surface Cleaning-New Jersey Div., 475 Boulevard, 07407, pg. 1208 **PB**
Power Conversion, Inc., 495 Boulevard, 07407-2029, pg. 127 **IT**

SYNETIC, INC., 669 River Dr., Bldg. 2, 07407, pg. 1548 **PB**
TROPHY HOLDINGS INC., 487 Edward H. Ross Dr., 07407, pg. 1105 **PV**
Zimmerman & Partners Advertising, Inc., River Dr. Ctr. 2, 669 River Dr., 07407, pg. 1206 **PV**

Englewood

Custom Health Care, Inc., P.O. Box 9610, 106 Grand Ave., 07631-9610, pg. 647 **PV**
Health & Sciences Research, Inc., 401 S. Van Brunt St., 07631, pg. 733 **PV**
LANDER CO., INC., 106 Grand Ave., 07631, pg. 647 **PV**
Lucas Aerospace Customer Support, 30 Van Mostrand Ave., 07631-4310, pg. 819 **IT**
Permabond International, 480 S. Dean St., 07631, pg. 1455 **IT**
SMS Systems Maintenance Inc., 475 S. Dean St., 07652, pg. 1463 **PB**
Salor Division, 524 Grand Ave., 07631, pg. 1489 **IT**
SPIRE INDUSTRIES, INC., 150 S. Dean St., 07631, pg. 1026 **PV**
STILLMAN & HOAG, INC., 386 Grand Ave., 07631, pg. 1043 **PV**
Technimat/TDS, 180 S. Van Brunt St., 07631, pg. 711 **PV**
Thomson Broadcast Systems, Inc., 49 Smith St., P.O. Box 5236, 07631, pg. 1383 **IT**

Englewood Cliffs

ADVERTISING DISPLAY CO., 570 Sylvan Ave., 07632, pg. 23 **PV**
Best Foods, Box 8000, International Plaza, 07632, pg. 224 **PB**
Best Foods Exports, International Plaza, P.O. Box 8000, 07632, pg. 224 **PB**
Best Foods Grocery Products Group, International Plaza, P.O. Box 8000, 07632, pg. 224 **PB**
BESTFOODS, 700 Sylvan Ave., 07632-9976, pg. 223 **PB**
E.T. BROWNE DRUG CO., INC., 140 Sylvan Ave., 07632, pg. 175 **PV**
CPC Cooperative Management Group, International Plaza, P.C. Box 8000, 07632, pg. 447 **PB**
CPC Latin America Corn Refining Division, P.O. Box 8000, 07632, pg. 448 **PB**
CPC Latin American Consumer Foods Division, P.O. Box 8000, International Plaza, 07632, pg. 447 **PB**
CPC Specialty Markets Group, International Plaza, P.O. Box 8000, 07632, pg. 224 **PB**
Commonwealth Metal, 560 Sylvan Ave., 07632, pg. 412 **PB**
CompreMedx, Inc., 910 Sylvan Ave., 07632, pg. 440 **PB**
CONTINENTAL HEALTH AFFILIATES, INC., 910 Sylvan Ave., 07632, pg. 440 **PB**
Creations Aromatiques, Inc., 400 Sylvan Ave., 07632, pg. 173 **IT**
Ferrari North America, Inc., 250 Sylvan Ave., 07632, pg. 483 **IT**
Ferrarr Financial Services, Inc., 250 Sylvan Ave., 07632, pg. 483 **IT**
Fiat Avio, 250 Sylvan Ave., 07632, pg. 483 **IT**
Fiat Services, Inc., 250 Sylvan Ave., 07632, pg. 483 **IT**
HAZEL BISHOP INTERNATIONAL, 910 Sylvan Ave., 07632, pg. 514 **PV**
Infu-Tech, 910 Sylvan Ave., 07632, pg. 440 **PB**
JT International U.S.A. Inc., 901 Sylvan Ave., 07632, pg. 703 **IT**
Kajima International, Inc., 900 Sylvan Ave., 07632, pg. 722 **IT**
KEPCC - New York Office, Englewood Cliffs Plaza, 270 Sylvan Ave., 07632, pg. 758 **IT**
Konica Headquarters North America, Inc., 440 Sylvan Ave., 07632, pg. 748 **IT**
LG Group Inc., 1000 Sylvan Ave., 07632, pg. 779 **IT**
Thomas J. Lipton Company, 800 Sylvan Ave., 07632, pg. 1435 **PB**
Lucky-Goldstar International (America), 1000 Sylvan Ave., 07632, pg. 779 **IT**
Maxwell Macmillan Professional & Business Reference Publishing, 910 Sylvan Ave., 07632, pg. 1602 **PB**

Englishtown

Countrywide Corporation, 198 RT 9-North Ste-105, 07726-3073, pg. 453 **PB**
WNY GROUP, P.O. Box 655, 07726, pg. 1144 **PV**

Ewing

Goodall Rubber Company, 100 Ludlow Dr., 08638, pg. 1423 **IT**

Ewing Township

Ewing Township-New Jersey Div., 1600 N. Olden Ave., 08638, pg. 353 **PV**

Fair Lawn

BORON LEPORE GROUP, 17-17 Rte. 208 N., 07410, pg. 246 **PB**
Consumer Audio & Video Sales, 2208 Rte. 208 South, 07410, pg. 622 **IT**
ERI Laboratories, 17-10 Willow St., 07410, pg. 574 **PV**
INVERNESS CORP., 17-10 Willow St., 07410, pg. 574 **PV**
Lea & Perrins, Inc., 15-01 Pollitt Dr., 07410, pg. 380 **IT**
Lonza, 17-17 Rte. 208, 07410, pg. 67 **IT**

MACNAUGHTON EINSON GRAPHICS, 20-10 Maple Ave., 07410, pg. 692 **PV**
Maxell Corp. Of America, 22-08 Rte. 208, 07410, pg. 621 **IT**
Onyx Technologies Ltd., 1903 Maple Ave., 07410, pg. 1007 **IT**
PAID Prescriptions, Inc., 1900 Pollitt Dr., 07410, pg. 1091 **PB**
Professional Industrial Sales, 2208 Rte. 208 So., 07410, pg. 622 **IT**
Sandoz Chemical Corp., Purchasing, Fairlawn Ave. & Third St., 07410, pg. 974 **IT**
Sandvik Coromant Company, 1702 Nevins Rd., 07410, pg. 1185 **IT**
Sandvik, Inc., 1702 Nevins Rd., 07410, pg. 1185 **IT**
Symtron Systems, Inc., 17-01 Pollitt Dr., 07410-9980, pg. 1679 **PB**
Teva USA - Biocraft, 18-01 River Rd., 07410, pg. 1381 **PB**
Voest-Alpine International Corp.-Machine Tools Div., 1710 Nevine Rd., 07410, pg. 1471 **IT**
A. ZEREGAS SONS, INC., 20-01 Broadway, 07410, pg. 1204 **PV**

Fairfield

Anco International, 149 New Dutch Lane, 07006, pg. 1287 **PB**
Atlas Copco Rental Inc., 285 Eldridge Rd., 07004-2508, pg. 96 **IT**
Biocraft Cephalosporin Dosage Plant, 8-10 Gloria Ln., 07004, pg. 1381 **IT**
BRADLEY PHARMACEUTICALS, 383 Rte. 46 West, 07004, pg. 249 **PB**
Browning-Ferris Industries of North Jersey, Inc., 54 Montesano Rd., 07004, pg. 264 **PB**
Browning-Ferris Industries of Paterson, N.J., Inc., 54 Montesano Rd., 07004, pg. 264 **PB**
Chronos Richardson, 15 Gardner Rd., 07004, pg. 1299 **IT**
Curtiss-Wright Flight Systems, Inc., 300 Fairfield Rd., 07004, pg. 469 **PB**
Datascope Cardiac Assist Division, 15 Law Dr., 07004, pg. 487 **PB**
DURO-LITE INTERNATIONAL, Nine Law Dr., 07004, pg. 349 **PV**
Duro-Test Corporation, Nine Law Dr., 07004, pg. 349 **PV**
Duro-Test Intl. Corp., Nine Law Dr., 07004, pg. 349 **PV**
EDD-New Jersey, 271 Rte. 46 W., 07004, pg. 205 **PB**
THE ECONOMICS PRESS, INC., 12 Daniel Rd., 07004, pg. 362 **PV**
Fujitsu General America Corp., 353 Route 46 West, 07004, pg. 526 **IT**
General Valve, P.O. Box 1333, 19 Gloria Ln., 07004-3392, pg. 1262 **PB**
Hasselblad USA, Inc., 10 Madison Rd., 07004, pg. 1468 **IT**
Hasselblad USA Inc., 10 Madison Rd., 07004, pg. 1468 **IT**
Health Maintenance Organization of New Jersey, Inc., 55 Land Rd., 07004, pg. 26 **PB**
JVC Service & Engineering Company of America, 107 Little Falls Rd., 07004, pg. 847 **IT**
JASON INDUSTRIAL, INC., 340 Kaplan Dr., 07004, pg. 583 **PV**
Lorentzen & Wettre USA, Inc., 10 Madison Rd., 07004, pg. 271 **IT**
Mita Copystar America Inc., 225 Sand Road, 07004-0008, pg. 870 **IT**
Motorola Radius, 100 Passaic Ave., 07004-3508, pg. 1138 **PB**
Ogden Energy Group, Inc., 40 Lane Rd., 07007-2615, pg. 1213 **PB**
Outdoor Systems, Inc. of New Jersey, 185 U.S. Hwy. 46, 07006, pg. 1235 **PB**
PRIME HOSPITALITY CORP., 700 Route 46 E., 07004, pg. 1326 **PB**
Pro Shop (Fairfield, NJ), 22 Madison Rd., 07004, pg. 861 **PB**
SGS U.S. Testing Company, Inc., 291 Fairfield Ave., 07004, pg. 1153 **IT**
Schiapparelli Biosystems Inc., 368 Passaic Ave., 07004, pg. 1204 **IT**
Skyline Auto Exchange, 100 Rte. 46, 07004, pg. 1649 **PB**
SOFTWARE PUBLISHING CORPORATION, Three A Oak Rd., 07004, pg. 1483 **PB**
Solkatronic Chemicals, Inc., 30 Two Bridges Rd., 07004, pg. 31 **PB**
Specialty Restaurants Corp., 195 Passaic Ave., 07006, pg. 1023 **PV**
SQUARE TWO GOLF INCORPORATED, 18 Gloria Ln., 07004, pg. 1501 **PB**
Titanium Industries, 110 Lehigh Dr., 07004-3044, pg. 34 **IT**
Uddeholm Corporation, 13 Daniel Rd., 07004, pg. 1471 **IT**
United Properties Group, 30 Two Bridges Rd., Ste. 280, 07004, pg. 1692 **PV**
Wilmor Warehouse & Shipping Co., Inc., 39 Plymouth St., 07006, pg. 516 **PV**
Winstar Global Products, Inc., 12 Gardner Rd., 07004, pg. 1772 **PB**

Fairview

Hudson United Bank-Fairview, 410 Fairview Ave., 07022, pg. 845 **PB**

Farmingdale

BEL-RAY COMPANY, INC., Bowman Ave., 07727, pg. 130 **PV**

PB - U.S. Public Companies Volume
PV - U.S. Private Companies Volume
IT - International Public & Private Companies Volume

Geographic Index-U.S.

1318

FREQUENCY ENGINEERING LABORATORIES, Central Ave., 07727, pg. 427   **PV**
Synergistics Industries (NJ) Inc., Ten Ruckle Ave., 07727, pg. 734   **PB**

Flanders

Technical Coatings Co., P.O. Box 4000, 360 Rte. 206, 07836, pg. 133   **PV**

Flemington

JOHANNA FOODS INC., Johanna Farms Rd., 08822, pg. 589   **PV**
Tekni-Plex, Inc., P.O. Box 111, 08822, pg. 1073   **PV**
UNITED STATES BRONZE POWDERS, INC., 408 Route 202, 08822, pg. 1124   **PV**

Florence

Super Fresh Company, 707 Railroad Ave., 08518, pg. 1375   **IT**

Florham Park

Autodesk, 100 Campus Dr., Ste. 220, 07932, pg. 149   **PB**
Automatic Switch Co., 50-60 Hanover Rd., 07932-1595, pg. 573   **PB**
Computer Products, 256 Columbia Turnpike, Ste. 210, 07932-1212, pg. 1002   **PB**
Enserch Development Corporation, 325 Columbia Tpke., 07932, pg. 1587   **PB**
Enserch Development Inc., 325 Columbia Tpke., 07932, pg. 1587   **PB**
Esso International Shipping (Bahamas) Co. Limited, 200 Park Ave., 07932, pg. 601   **PB**
Exxon Company International, 200 Park Ave., 07932, pg. 601   **PB**
First Quadrant Corporation, P.O. Box 939, 100 Campus Dr., 2nd Fl. W., 07932-0939, pg. 1784   **PV**
Heraeus Investment Corporation, 11 Hancock Dr., 07932, pg. 616   **IT**
Ohaus Corporation, P.O. Box 900, 29 Hanover Rd., 07932-0900, pg. 974   **PV**
Pirelli Cable Corporation, 325 Columbia Tpk., 07932, pg. 1059   **IT**
Prudential Defined Contribution Services, 71 Hanover Road, 07932, pg. 892   **PV**
SCHEIN PHARMACEUTICAL, INC., 100 Campus Dr., 07932, pg. 969   **PV**
Signet Star Reinsurance Company, 160 Campus Dr., 07932, pg. 216   **PB**
Signet Star Reinsurance Company, 100 Campus Dr. CN853, 07932-0853, pg. 216   **PB**
Smiths Industries Aerospace & Defense Systems Inc.-Florham Park Operation, 7-11 Vreeland Rd., 07932, pg. 1268   **IT**
STRAHMAN VALVES, INC., Three Vreeland Rd., 07932-1590, pg. 1046   **PV**
TROPAR MFG. CO., INC., Five Vreeland Rd., 07932, pg. 1105   **PV**
TROY CORPORATION, Eight Vreeland Rd., 07932, pg. 1105   **PV**

Folsom

Energy & Minerals, Inc., N. One S. Jersey Plaza, Rte. 54, 08037, pg. 1488   **PB**
SJ EnerTrade, One S. Jersey Plaza, Rt. 54, 08037, pg. 1488   **PB**
SOUTH JERSEY INDUSTRIES, INC., One S. Jersey Plaza, Rte. 54, 08037, pg. 1488   **PB**

Forked River

DCA of New Jersey, Inc., Clearwater Dr. & Rte. 9, 08731, pg. 988   **PB**

Fort Lee

ALPHARMA INC., One Executive Dr., 4th Fl., 07024, pg. 57   **PB**
Animal Health, One Executive Dr., 4th Fl., 07024, pg. 58   **PB**
C&C Associates, Two Executive Dr., 07024, pg. 279   **PV**
CBM AMERICA CORP., Two Executive Dr., 07024, pg. 192   **PV**
CNBC, 2200 Fletcher Ave., 07024, pg. 712   **PB**
CNTIC Representative Office in USA, 2200 Fletcher Ave., 5th Fl., 07024, pg. 285   **IT**
Carillon Importers, Ltd., One Parker Plaza, 07024, pg. 409   **IT**
Couri Carpet Co., Two Executive Dr., 07024, pg. 279   **PV**
Couri-Murad & Co., Two Executive Dr., 07024, pg. 279   **PV**
COURISTAN INC., Two Executive Dr., 07024, pg. 279   **PV**
Courtaulds U.S. Developments Inc., 400 Kelbey St., 07024, pg. 339   **IT**
DIC Americas, Inc., 222 Bridge Plz. S., 07024, pg. 369   **IT**
DIC Trading (USA) Inc., 222 Bridge Plaza S., 07024, pg. 369   **IT**
Donohue Pulp & Paper Sales Corp., One Parker Plaza, 400 Kelby St., 07024, pg. 1076   **PB**
Franklin Advisers, Inc., One Parker Plaza, 16th Fl., 07024, pg. 680   **PB**
IDV North America, One Parker Plaza, 07024, pg. 411   **IT**
Kansai Paint (America), Inc., Two Executive Dr., Ste. 785, 07024, pg. 723   **IT**
Kawasho International (U.S.A.) Inc., One Parker Plaza, 12th Fl., 07024, pg. 726   **IT**

Kohl & Madden Printing Ink Corp. Div., 222 Bridge Plaza South, 07024, pg. 370   **IT**
Lewis Gace Bozell Healthcare Worldwide, One Bridge Plaza, 07024, pg. 1642   **IT**
New York Switch Corporation, One Bridge Plaza N., 07024, pg. 339   **IT**
Nippon Kaiji Kyokai, One Parker Plaza, 07024, pg. 934   **IT**
Nissin Foods (U.S.A.) Eastern Division, 2125 Center Ave., 07024, pg. 949   **IT**
Nissin International Corp., 2125 Center Ave., 07024, pg. 950   **IT**
Okaya (U.S.A.), Inc., 16th Fl., Parker Plz., 400 Kelly St., 07024, pg. 999   **IT**
PHILIPP BROTHERS CHEMICALS, INC., One Parker Plaza, 07024, pg. 861   **PV**
Polychrome Corp. Div., 222 Bridge Plaza South, 07024, pg. 370   **IT**
Republic New York Mortgage Corporation, 222 Bridge Plaza S., 07024, pg. 1381   **PB**
Sullivan Systems Div., 2115 Linwood Ave., 07024, pg. 1379   **PB**
Summit Specialty Chemicals Corporation, 400 Kelby St., 18th Fl., 07024, pg. 1312   **IT**
Sun Chemical Corp., 222 Bridge Plaza South, 07024, pg. 370   **PB**
Sun Chemical Group B.V., 222 Bridge Plz. S., 07024, pg. 370   **IT**

Franklin

Morley Shirt Company, Rte. 23, 07416, pg. 490   **PV**
Valley National Bank, Shop-Rite Shopping Ctr., Rte. 23, 07416, pg. 1706   **PB**

Franklin Lakes

BECTON DICKINSON & COMPANY, One Becton Dr., 07417-1880, pg. 199   **PB**
Becton Dickinson Consumer Prods., One Becton Dr., 07417, pg. 199   **PB**
Becton Dickinson Labware, One Becton Dr., 07417, pg. 199   **PB**
Becton Dickinson Pharmaceutical Systems, One Becton Dr., 07417, pg. 199   **PB**
Becton Dickinson VACUTAINER Systems, One Becton Dr., 07417, pg. 199   **PB**

Freehold

FOODARAMA SUPERMARKETS, INC., Bldg. 6, Ste. I, 922 Hwy. 33, 07728, pg. 661   **PB**
Nestle Beverage Company, 61 Jerseyville Ave., 07728, pg. 918   **IT**
New Linden Price Rite, Inc., 922 Hwy. 33, 07728, pg. 661   **PB**
Regal Drugs, Inc., 922 Hwy. 33, 07728, pg. 661   **PB**
Shop Rite of Malverne, Inc., 922 Hwy. 33, 07728, pg. 661   **PB**

Garfield

Finkel Outdoor Products, Inc., 141 Lanza Ave., 07026, pg. 1094   **PV**
Garden State Paper Mill/Garfield Mill, 950 River Dr., 07026, pg. 1078   **PB**
Nevco Housewares, Inc., 174 Passaic St., 07026, pg. 1341   **PB**
Popular Club Plan, 22 Lincoln Place, 07026, pg. 1078   **PV**
Primex Plastics Corp., 65 River Drive, 07026, pg. 553   **PV**

Garwood

ACCURATE BUSHING CO., INC., 443 North Ave., 07027, pg. 11   **PV**

Glen Rock

Motorola A.C., Inc., 85 Harristown Rd., 07452, pg. 1137   **PB**
Motorola Nortel Communication, 85 Harristown Rd., 07452-3307, pg. 1138   **PB**

Gloucester City

AMSPEC CHEMICAL CORPORATION, 751 Water St., 08030, pg. 67   **PV**

Grenloch

A.L. Hyde Company, One Main St., 08032, pg. 481   **PV**

Guttenberg

KTI, INC., 7000 Blvd. East, 07093, pg. 939   **PV**

Hackensack

Automated Wagering, 401 Hackensack Ave., 07601, pg. 1319   **PB**
BEI MEDICAL SYSTEMS COMPANY, 83 Hobart St., 07601, pg. 106   **PV**
Bergen Record Corp., 150 River St., 07601, pg. 693   **PV**
Bettigole, Andrews & Clark, Inc., 1 University Plaza, 07601, pg. 1593   **PB**
Blue Circle Materials, Inc., P.O. Box 505, 07601, pg. 198   **PV**
Clermont Specialty Managers, Ltd., Three University Plaza, 07601, pg. 215   **PB**

Elscint Inc., 505 Main St., 07601, pg. 450   **IT**
FIRST DATA CORPORATION, 401 Hackensack Ave., 7th Fl., 07601, pg. 630   **PV**
Gremac Inc., 150 River St., 07601, pg. 693   **PV**
Kruger Recycling, Inc.-Hackensack, 75 Essex St., Ste. 202, 07601, pg. 762   **IT**
LOSURDO FOODS, INC., 20 Owens Rd., 07601, pg. 677   **PV**
MACROMEDIA INCORPORATED, 150 River St., 07601, pg. 693   **PV**
Macromedia Leasing, 150 River St., 07601, pg. 693   **PV**
Magna Media Inc., 150 River St., 07601, pg. 693   **PV**
MEDICAL RESOURCES INC., 155 State St., 07601, pg. 1080   **PB**
The Multicare Companies, Inc., 433 Hackensack Ave., 07601, pg. 729   **PB**
National Restoration Contractors, Inc., 221 Hudson St., 07601, pg. 1165   **PV**
Nova Promotion Group Inc., Continental Plaza, 411 Hackensack Ave., 10th Fl., 07601, pg. 393   **IT**
Oki America Inc., Three University Plaza, 07601, pg. 1000   **IT**
SAR U.S.A. Incorporated, 401 Hackensack Ave., Fifth Fl., 07601, pg. 125   **PB**
Safeguards Technology, Inc., 300 Hudson St., 07601-6700, pg. 1286   **IT**
Shionogi & Co., Ltd. - New Jersey, 433 Hackensack Ave., 8th Fl., 07601, pg. 1235   **IT**
SUPERIOR DRAPERY COMPANY, 385 Prospect Ave., 07601, pg. 1054   **PV**
Symbol, 401 Hackensack Ave., 07601-6411, pg. 1546   **PB**
Tanabe Seiyaku Co., Ltd.-U.S. Liasion Office, 07601, pg. 1354   **IT**

Hackettstown

Buchanan Construction Products, Inc., Hackettstown Commerce Park, 101 Bilby Rd., 07840, pg. 557   **PV**
Dynapac Mfg. Inc., 699 Washington Ave., 07840, pg. 1420   **IT**
Elastimold Co., Elastimold, Rte. 24, 07840, pg. 1598   **PB**
M&M/Mars, 800 High St., 07840, pg. 707   **PV**
Modular Power Systems, 36 Newburgh Rd., 07840, pg. 1097   **PV**
Triumph Machine Co., P.O. Box 610, 07840, pg. 35   **PB**
Valley National Bank, 105 Mill St., 07840, pg. 1706   **PB**

Haddon Heights

New Jersey-American Resources Company, 500 Grove St., 08035, pg. 95   **PB**
New Jersey-American Water Co., 500 Grove St., 08035, pg. 95   **PB**
Ply-Gem Manufacturing, 201 Black Horse Pike, 08035, pg. 1193   **PV**

Haddonfield

Cardio Data Services, 89 Haddon Ave., P.O. Box 117, 08033, pg. 1114   **PV**
Mediacomm National, Inc., 132 Kings Hwy. E., Ste. 210, 08033, pg. 384   **PB**
Research Data Corp, 56 Haddon Ave., 08033, pg. 1114   **PV**
U.M. HOLDING LIMITED, 56 Haddon Ave., 08033, pg. 1113   **PV**

Hainesport

PERRY MACHINERY CORPORATION, 25 Mt. Laurel Rd., 08036, pg. 855   **PV**

Hamilton

Consumers New Jersey Water Company, Ten Black Forest Rd., 08691, pg. 438   **PB**

Hammonton

Kellogg Convenience Food Plant, Rte. 461, 08037, pg. 947   **PB**

Harrington Park

United Water Management & Services, 200 Old Hook Rd., 07640, pg. 1692   **PB**
United Water New Jersey, Inc., 200 Old Hook Rd., 07640, pg. 1692   **PB**
UNITED WATER RESOURCES, 200 Old Hook Rd., 07640-1799, pg. 1691   **PB**
United Water Works, 200 Old Hook Rd., 07640, pg. 1692   **PB**

Harrison

Allegria Inc., 1000 First St., 07029, pg. 565   **PV**
Driver-Harris Alloys, Inc., 308 Middlesex St., 07029, pg. 530   **PB**
DRIVER-HARRIS COMPANY, 308 Middlesex St., 07029, pg. 530   **PB**
Eagle Affiliates, Inc., 505 Manor Ave., 07029, pg. 7   **PV**
Harrison Baking Co., 840 Jersey Ave., 07029, pg. 65   **PV**
INNER SECRETS, INC., 1000 First St., 07029, pg. 564   **PV**
LECHTERS, INC., One Cape May St., 07029, pg. 983   **PB**
PEERLESS UMBRELLA CO., INC., 600 7th St., 07029, pg. 847   **PV**
Precision Technology, 1000 S. Frank Rodgers Blvd., 07029, pg. 17   **IT**

PB - *U.S. Public Companies Volume*
PV - *U.S. Private Companies Volume*
IT - *International Public & Private Companies Volume*

Geographic Index-U.S.

Secretly Yours Inc., 1000 First St., 07029, pg. 565 **PV**
TRI-CHEM, INC., One Cape May St., 07029, pg. 1100 **PV**
Worthington, 401 Worthington Ave., 07029-2039, pg. 1780 **PB**

Hasbrouck Heights

ALLIED OFFICE SUPPLIES, 75 Rte. 17 S., 07604, pg. 39 **PV**
Coastal Oil New York, Inc., P.O. Box 818, 611 Rte. 46 W., 07604, pg. 390 **PV**
Ferrari North America, 777 Terrace Ave., 07604, pg. 483 **IT**
JM COMPANY, 777 Terrace Ave., 07604, pg. 577 **PV**

Haskell

General Ceramics, Inc., Greenwood Ave., 07420, pg. 1394 **IT**
National Beryllia Div., 716 First Ave., 07420, pg. 1394 **IT**

Hawthorne

NEXUS PLASTICS, INC., One Loretto Ave., 07506, pg. 797 **PV**
RAG SHOPS, INC., 111 Wagaraw Rd., 07506, pg. 1358 **PB**

Hazlet

IFF FSC, Inc., 07730, pg. 899 **PB**

High Bridge

COMPUTER POWER INCORPORATED, 124 W. Main St., 08829, pg. 421 **PB**

Hightstown

Mettler-Toledo, Inc., 69 Princeton-Hightstown Rd., 08520-0071, pg. 4 **PV**
Primedia Information Inc., 10 Lake Dr., 08520, pg. 1328 **PB**

Hillsborough

Ajax Manufacturing Company, Inc., 321 Valley Rd., 08876, pg. 1030 **PV**
STANDARD AUTOMOTIVE CORPORATION, 321 Valley Rd., 08876-4056, pg. 1030 **PV**

Hillside

Ariston, 485 Bloy St., 07205, pg. 1486 **PB**
Bristol-Myers Research, 1350 Ciberty Ave., 07205, pg. 254 **PB**
DEECO INDUSTRIES, 600 Ramsey Ave., 07205, pg. 320 **PV**
E.C.D., INC., P.O. Box 798, 171 Central Ave., 07205, pg. 353 **PV**
Siltin Industries, Inc., 600 Ramsey Ave., 07205, pg. 320 **PV**

Hoboken

JOSHUA L. BAILY CO., INC., Baker Waterfront Plaza, Two Hudson Place, 07030, pg. 110 **PV**
Hudson United Bank-Hoboken, 60-68 14th St., 07030, pg. 845 **PB**
Instrument Marketing Services, Inc., 1415 Park Ave., 07030, pg. 1153 **IT**
LEON-FERENBACH INC., 95 River St., 07030, pg. 660 **PV**
Nationwide Consumer Testing Institute, Inc., 1415 Park Ave., 07030, pg. 1153 **IT**
Piper Jaffray Inc., Five Marine View Plaza, 07030-5788, pg. 1301 **PB**
TMP Worldwide, Inc., Five Marineview Plaza, 5th Fl., 07030, pg. 1064 **PV**
UNIVERSAL FOLDING BOX COMPANY, INC., Madison & 13th Sts., 07030-3021, pg. 1127 **PV**

Holmdel

LAWN DOCTOR INC., P.O. Box 401, 142 Hwy. 34, 07733-0401, pg. 653 **PV**
Prudential Commercial Insurance Co., 23 Main St., 07733, pg. 892 **PV**
Prudential General Insurance Co., 23 Main St., 07733, pg. 892 **PV**
Prudential Property & Casualty Insurance Company, 23 Main St., 07733, pg. 892 **PV**
Quest Diagnostic-Holmdel, 733 N. Beers St., 07733, pg. 1351 **PB**

Irvington

Industrial Retaining Ring Company, 57 Cordier St., 07111, pg. 1632 **PB**
JABEL, INC., 365 Coit St., 07111, pg. 579 **PV**

Iselin

Automotive Emission Systems, 101 Wood Ave., 08830-0770, pg. 582 **PB**
Chemical Catalysts, 101 Wood Ave., 08830-6000, pg. 582 **PB**

ENGELHARD CORPORATION, 101 Wood Ave., 08830-0770, pg. 582 **PB**
Engelhard Corp. Engineered Materials and Precious Metals Management, 101 Wood Ave., S., 08830-0770, pg. 582 **PB**
Merck Consumer Healthcare Group, Parkway Towers-Bldg. A, Rte. 1 S., 4th Fl., 08830, pg. 1090 **PB**
Merial Ltd., 21000 Ronson Rd., 08830-3077, pg. 1092 **PB**
MIDDLESEX WATER COMPANY, 1500 Ronson Rd., 08830-0452, pg. 1110 **PB**
MILLENNIUM CHEMICALS INC., 99 Wood Ave. S., 08830, pg. 1111 **PB**
NewsEdge Corp., Bldg. A, Ste. 340, 485 Rte. 1, 08830, pg. 1180 **PB**
Petroleum Catalysts, 101 Wood Ave., 08830-0770, pg. 582 **PB**
Pigments & Additives, 101 Wood Ave., 08830, pg. 582 **PB**
Precious Metals Management, 101 Wood Ave., S., 08830, pg. 582 **PB**
SGS Industrial Services, 120 Wood Ave., S., Ste. 505, 08830, pg. 1153 **IT**
Sand Technology Systems Inc., 555 Woodbridge Towers, Route 1 South, 08830, pg. 1183 **IT**
Sequent Computer Systems, Inc., 70 S. Wood Ave., 1st Fl., 08830, pg. 1459 **PB**
Siemens Medical Systems, Inc., 186 Wood Ave. S., 08830, pg. 1246 **IT**
Siemens Transportation Systems, Inc., 186 Wood Ave. S., 08830, pg. 1246 **IT**
U.S. INDUSTRIES, INC., 101 Wood Ave., S., 08830, pg. 1683 **PB**
Utility Service Affiliates, Inc., P.O. Box 500, 08830, pg. 1110 **PB**

Jackson

Six Flags Great Adventure Theme Park & Wild Safari Animal Park, P.O. Box 120, 08527, pg. 1611 **PB**
Span-Track, 50 Progress Rd., 08527, pg. 1117 **PV**
UNEX CONVEYING SYSTEMS, INC., 50 Progress Rd., 08527, pg. 1117 **PV**

Jamesburg

Hyundai Motor America Eastern Regional Office, 1100 Cranbury S. River Road, 08831, pg. 641 **IT**

Jersey City

ALBA FORWARDING CO., INC., One Exchange Place, Ste. 501, 07302, pg. 32 **PV**
Alpha Metals, Inc., 600 Route 440, 07304, pg. 328 **IT**
American Institute of C.P.A.'s Inc.-Harborside Fin. Ctr., 201 Plaza Three, 07311-3881, pg. 57 **PV**
Ameriford Intl. Corp., 66 York St., 07302, pg. 1388 **IT**
Armin Plastics Division, 301 W. Side Ave., 07305, pg. 1647 **PV**
Baldwin Steel Company, Rte. 440, 07306, pg. 345 **PV**
Baldwin Steel Company, P.O. Box A-38, 07304, pg. 401 **IT**
BEL FUSE INC., 198 Van Vorst St., 07302, pg. 200 **PB**
BLOCK DRUG COMPANY, INC., 257 Cornelison Ave., 07302, pg. 236 **PB**
Block Drug Corporation, 105 Academy St., 07302, pg. 237 **PB**
Block Drug Corporation Dental Products Co., 105 Academy St., 07302, pg. 237 **PB**
DKB Data Services (USA) Inc., CALI IFT Bldg., 18th Fl., 95 Christopher Columbus Dr., 07302, pg. 360 **IT**
Daiwa Securities Trust Company, One Evertrust Plaza, 07302, pg. 375 **IT**
DiFeo Automotive Network, 585 Rte. 440, 07304, pg. 1095 **PB**
Dow Jones Markets, Harborside Financial Center, 600 Plaza Two, 07311, pg. 525 **PB**
Dow Jones Telerate Holdings, Inc., Harborside Financial Ctr., 600 Plaza Two, 07311, pg. 525 **PB**
FEDERAL FARM CREDIT BANKS FUNDING CORPORATION, Ten Exchange Pl., Ste. 1401, 07302, pg. 398 **PV**
First Marathon (U.S.A.) Inc., 101 Hudson St., Ste. 3715, 07302, pg. 487 **IT**
Fleet Bank, N.A., Ten Exchange Pl., 07302, pg. 649 **PB**
Hartz Mountain Industries, 2 Journal Sq. Plz., 07306-4000, pg. 508 **PV**
Ivaran Agencies Inc., 111 Pavonia Ave., 07310, pg. 696 **IT**
Jefferies & Company, Inc., Harborside Fin. Center, Plaza III, Ste. 705, 07311, pg. 925 **PB**
Jefferson Insurance Company of New York, Newport Tower, 525 Washington Blvd., 07310-1693, pg. 59 **IT**
Kuehne & Nagel Inc., Ten Exchange Pl., 19th Fl., 07302, pg. 763 **IT**
MFS Intelenet Companies, 101 Hudson St., Ste. 2200, 07302, pg. 1779 **IT**
MAHER TERMINALS INC., Journal Square Plaza, 07306, pg. 697 **PV**
THE B. MANISCHEWITZ COMPANY, One Manischewitz Plaza, 07302, pg. 699 **PV**
Mayer & Schweitzer, Inc., 111 Pavonia Ave. E., 07310, pg. 1443 **PB**
MXNet, Inc., 10 Exchange Pl., pg. 1467 **PB**
Nomura International Trust Company, Exchange Place Center, Ten Exchange Pl., 16th Fl., 07302, pg. 956 **IT**
Panalpina, Inc., 300 Plaza 2, 07311, pg. 1022 **IT**
Pavey Envelope & Tag Corp., 25 Linden Ave. E., 07305, pg. 1036 **PB**
POLAROME INTERNATIONAL, 200 Theodore Conrad Dr., 07305, pg. 874 **PV**

Prolerized Schiabo-Neu Co., One Linden Ave., 07305, pg. 1440 **PB**
RAPID INDUSTRIAL PLASTICS COMPANY, 13 Linden Ave., E., 07305, pg. 910 **PV**
REPUBLIC CONTAINER CORP., 1561 Kennedy Blvd., 07305, pg. 923 **PB**
Ritter Sysco Food Service, Inc., Liberty Industrial Park, 20 Theodore Concord, 07305, pg. 1550 **PB**
FRANK B. ROSS CO. INC., P.O. Box 4085, 07304, pg. 946 **PV**
SCHENKERS International Forwarders, Inc., Ten Exchange Pl., Ste. 1500, 07302-3998, pg. 1459 **IT**
THE SHERWOOD GROUP, INC., Ten Exchange Plaza, 15th Fl., 07302, pg. 1466 **PB**
Sherwood Securities Corp., 10 Exchange Pl., pg. 1467 **PB**
Special Program Management, Inc., Newport Tower, 525 Washington Blvd., 07310, pg. 1504 **IT**
Square Industries, Inc., 921 Bergen Ave., 07306, pg. 326 **PV**
Square Plus Operating Corporation, 921 Bergen Ave., 07306, pg. 326 **PV**
Stafford-Miller Intl., Inc., 257 Cornelison Ave., 07302, pg. 237 **PB**
Standard Tag Mfg. Co., 25 Linden Ave. E., 07305, pg. 1038 **PB**
Star Video Entertainment, L.P., 550 Grand St., 07302, pg. 1132 **PV**
The Trust Company of New Jersey, 35 Journal Square, 07306, pg. 1643 **PB**
THE TRUSTCOMPANY BANCORPORATION, 35 Journal Sq., 07306, pg. 1643 **PB**
UIS, INC., 15 Exchange Pl., Ste. 1120, 07302-3912, pg. 1113 **PV**
USA Network Control Center, 525 Washington Blvd., 07310, pg. 1686 **PB**
W & D Securities, Inc., Harborside Financial Center, Plaza III, Ste. 705, 07311, pg. 925 **PV**
WILSHIRE OIL CO. OF TEXAS, 921 Bergen Ave., 07306-4204, pg. 1770 **PB**

Kearny

AMERICAN STRIP STEEL INC., 55 Passaic Ave., 07032, pg. 62 **PV**
Broad National Bank-Kearny, 180 Schuyler Ave., 07032, pg. 258 **PB**
Duray, Inc., 969 Newark Turnpike, 07032, pg. 1177 **PB**
Franklin-Burlington Plastics, 113 Passaic Ave., 07032, pg. 1496 **PB**
L&R MANUFACTURING CO., 577 Elm St., 07032, pg. 638 **PV**
Mebane Packaging Group., 300 Hoyt St., 07032, pg. 726 **PV**
Pretty Neat Products, 969 Newark Tpke., 07032, pg. 1177 **PB**
Randy International, 590 Belleville Tpke., Bldg. 26, 07032, pg. 909 **PV**
STANDARD CHLORINE CLOROBEN CHEMICAL CORPORATION, 1035 Belleville Tpke., 07032, pg. 1031 **PV**
Universal Flavors, 265 Harrison Ave., 07032, pg. 1695 **PB**

Kenilworth

FRANK BRISCOE CO. INC., 730 Kenilworth Blvd., 07033, pg. 169 **PV**
Flexi-Van Leasing, Inc., 251 Monroe Ave., 07033, pg. 413 **IT**
Flexi-Van United Kingdom, 251 Monroe Ave., 07033, pg. 413 **PV**
FLEXI-VAN LEASING, INC., 251 Monroe Ave., 07033, pg. 413 **PV**
Key Pharmaceuticals, 2000 Galloping Hill Rd., 07033, pg. 1438 **PB**
NATIONAL TOOL & MANUFACTURING COMPANY, 100-124 N. 12th St., 07033, pg. 787 **PV**
RHG New York, 500 South 31 St., 07033, pg. 1151 **IT**
Schering Laboratories, Galloping Hill Rd., 07033, pg. 1438 **PB**
Schering-Plough International, Galloping Hill Rd., 07033, pg. 1438 **PB**
Schering-Plough Research Institute, Galloping Hill Rd., 07033, pg. 1438 **PB**
Ullrich Copper, Inc., Two Mark Rd., 07033, pg. 677 **PB**
White Systems, Incorporated, 30 Boright Ave., 07033, pg. 866 **PV**

Lafayette

NorVal, Inc., P.O. Box 307A, 07848, pg. 1201 **IT**
Sani-Tech Inc., 29 Brookfield Dr., 07848, pg. 1545 **PB**

Lakehurst

American Graphite Co., Ridgeway Blvd., 08733, pg. 515 **PB**

Lakewood

ARNOLD STEEL COMPANY, INC., P.O. Box 739, 08701, pg. 84 **PV**
Bekaert Engineering of North America, 1000 Bennett Blvd., 08701, pg. 184 **IT**
Cucina Classica Italiana, Inc., 1835 Swarthmore Ave., 08701, pg. 1435 **PB**
Cucina Classica Italiana Inc., 1935 Swarthmore Ave, 08701, pg. 1435 **PB**
First American Field Services, 1125 Ocean Ave., 08701, pg. 625 **PB**

PB - *U.S. Public Companies Volume*
PV - *U.S. Private Companies Volume*
IT - *International Public & Private Companies Volume*

1320

Geographic Index-U.S.

Getinge International Inc., 1100 Towbin Ave., 08701, pg. 551 — **IT**
Glasseal Products, Inc., P.O. Box 978, 485 Oberlin, 08701, pg. 490 — **PV**
Hermetite Corp., 485 Oberlin, 08701, pg. 490 — **PV**
Merco/Savory Inc., 725 Vassar Ave., 08701-3100, pg. 189 — **IT**
Micro Warehouse, Inc. of New Jersey, 1720 Oak St., 08701, pg. 1104 — **PB**
MISTER COOKIE FACE, INC., 170 N. Oberlin Ave., 08701, pg. 753 — **PV**
Paco Pharmaceutical Services, Inc., 1200 Paco Way, 08701, pg. 1755 — **PB**
Rhone-Poulenc Specialty Plastics Div., 1665 Corporate Rd. W., 08701, pg. 1110 — **IT**
SARATOGA BRANDS, INC., 1835 Swarthmore Ave., 08701, pg. 1435 — **PB**
STAPO HOLLANDER INDUSTRIES, 200 Syracuse Ct., 08701, pg. 1033 — **PV**

Landing

Valley National Bank, 115 Center St., 07850, pg. 1706 — **PB**

Laurence Harbor

DUFERCO STEEL INC., 100 Metro Park S., 08879, pg. 345 — **PV**

Lawrenceville

DKM Properties Corporation, 1009 Lenox Dr., 08648, pg. 351 — **PV**
GILLESPIE, 3450 Princeton Pike, 08648, pg. 453 — **PV**
IMO INDUSTRIES INC., Bldg. Four W., 1009 Lenox Dr., 08648, pg. 856 — **PB**
Lenox Brands, 100 Lenox Dr., 08648, pg. 261 — **PB**
Lenox, Incorporated, 100 Lenox Dr., 08648, pg. 261 — **PB**
Lenox Products Group, 100 Lenox Dr., 08648, pg. 261 — **PB**
Lenox Retail, 100 Lenox Dr., 08648, pg. 261 — **PB**
Wings Luggage, 100 Lenox Dr., 08648, pg. 262 — **PB**

Lebanon

Pumpex Inc., 103 A Molasses Hill Rd., 08833, pg. 270 — **IT**

Leonia

KULITE SEMICONDUCTOR PRODUCTS, INC., One Willow Tree Rd., 07605, pg. 636 — **PV**

Liberty Corner

Everest Indemnity Insurance Company, 477 Martinsville Rd., 07938-0830, pg. 597 — **PB**
Everest National Insurance Co., 477 Martinsville Rd., 07938-0830, pg. 597 — **PB**
Everest Reinsurance Co., 477 Martinsville Rd., 07938-0830, pg. 597 — **PB**
EVEREST REINSURANCE HOLDINGS, 477 Martinsville Rd., 07938-0830, pg. 597 — **PB**
FEDDERS CORP., P.O. Box 813, 505 Martinsville Rd., 07938, pg. 614 — **PB**
Fedders International, Inc., Westgate Corporate Ctr., 505 Martinsville Rd., P.O. Box 821, 07938, pg. 614 — **PB**
Ingersoll-Dresser Pump Company, 150 Allen Rd., Ste. 102, 07938-0810, pg. 529 — **PB**
Ohmeda, 110 Allen Rd., 07938, pg. 121 — **IT**
Ohmeda, Inc., P.O. Box 804, 110 Allen Rd., 07938-0804, pg. 121 — **IT**
Schering-Plough Healthcare Products Inc., 110 Allen Rd., 07938, pg. 1438 — **PB**
TRANSTECHNOLOGY CORPORATION, 150 Allen Rd., 07938, pg. 1632 — **PB**

Lincoln Park

D & W Capital Corp., 107 Beaver Brook, 07035, pg. 424 — **IT**
DYWIDAG Systems International, USA, Inc., Eastern Div., P.O. Box 488, 107 Beaver Brook, 07035, pg. 424 — **IT**
DYWIDAG-Systems International, USA Inc., 107 Beaver Brook Rd., 07035, pg. 424 — **IT**
Klockner-Moeller, 600 M. Ryerson Rd., 07035-2094, pg. 736 — **PB**
Raynor Distribution Center, 550 Ryerson Rd., 07035, pg. 912 — **PV**

Linden

CARNIVAL CREATIONS, 1050 Edward St., 07036, pg. 213 — **PV**
Celegec Automation, 1418 E. Linden Ave., 07036, pg. 53 — **IT**
COLIVITA USA, INC., 2537 Brunswick Ave., 07036, pg. 252 — **PV**
GENERAL MAGNAPLATE CORPORATION, 1331 U.S. Rte. One, 07036, pg. 717 — **PB**
Gomar Manufacturing Co., Inc., 1501 W. Blancke St., 07036, pg. 51 — **PV**
ICI Packaging Inks, 1301 S. Park Ave., P.O. Box 263, 07036, pg. 664 — **IT**
Shofar Kosher Foods, 2365 E. Linden Ave., 07036, pg. 1433 — **PB**
Tosco Refining Company, 1400 Park Ave., 07036, pg. 1625 — **PB**
TURTLE & HUGHES, INC., 1900 Lower Rd., 07036, pg. 1110 — **PV**

Zeneca Specialty Inks, 1301 S. Park Ave., 07036, pg. 1525 — **IT**

Little Falls

HLS Corp., P.O. Box 422, 150 Clove Rd., 07424, pg. 1483 — **IT**
Peugeot Motors of America Inc., 150 Clove Road, 07424, pg. 1020 — **IT**
Rystan Company, Inc., 47 Center Ave., 07424-0214, pg. 436 — **PV**

Little Ferry

Norel Paper Corporation, 223 Gates Rd., 07643, pg. 1671 — **PB**
Sanyo Fisher Home Appliance & Consumer Products Div., 200 Riser Rd., 07643, pg. 1191 — **IT**
Sanyo Office Machines Div., 210 Riser Rd., 07643, pg. 1191 — **IT**
Scientific Design Co., Inc., 49 Industrial Ave., 07643, pg. 811 — **PV**

Livingston

ALLISON CORPORATION, 15 Okner Pkwy., 07039, pg. 41 — **PV**
Allison Corporation, 15 Okner Pkwy., 07039, pg. 41 — **PV**
American International Adjustment Company, Two Peach Tree Hill Rd., 07039, pg. 85 — **PB**
Broad National Bank-Livingston, 30 W. Mount Pleasant Ave., 07039, pg. 258 — **PB**
Formosa Plastics Corp., U.S.A., Nine Peach Tree Hill Road, 07039, pg. 498 — **IT**
Foster Wheeler Development Corp., 12 Peachtree Hill Rd., 07039, pg. 676 — **PB**
Foster Wheeler Environmental Corporation, Eight Peach Tree Hill Rd., 07039, pg. 677 — **PB**
J-M Manufacturing Co., Inc., Nine Peach Tree Hill Rd., 07039, pg. 498 — **IT**
ROSE ART INDUSTRIES, Six Regent St., 07039, pg. 945 — **PV**

Lodi

Bergen Cable Technologies, Inc., Gregg St., 07644, pg. 1056 — **PB**
INTERPLAST UNIVERSAL INDUSTRIES, INC., 199 Garibaldi Ave., 07644, pg. 571 — **PV**
McCain-Ellios Food Inc., 11 Gregg St., 07644, pg. 850 — **IT**
Mul-T-Lock Ltd., 300-1 Rte. 17 So., 07644, pg. 644 — **IT**
STANLEY ROBERTS, INC., 65 Industrial Rd., 07644, pg. 936 — **PV**

Long Branch

WHEELOCK INC., 273 Branchport Ave., 07740, pg. 1171 — **PV**

Long Valley

WELSH FARMS, INC., 55 Fairview Ave., 07853, pg. 1162 — **PV**

Lyndhurst

The Alexander Consulting Group Inc., 125 Chubb Ave., 5th Fl., 07071, pg. 117 — **PB**
ALPHA INDUSTRIES, Page Ave. & Schuyler Ave., 07071, pg. 45 — **PV**
Atlantic Paper Group, 1100 Valley Brook Ave., Ste. 204, 07071, pg. 467 — **PV**
W. Braun Co., 1050 Wall St. W., 07071, pg. 166 — **PV**
Citizen Watch Co. of America, Inc., 1200 Wall St. W., 07071, pg. 294 — **IT**
CURTISS-WRIGHT CORP., 1200 Wall St. W., Ste. 501, 07071, pg. 469 — **PB**
Fashions Outlet of America, Nine Polito Ave., 07071, pg. 875 — **PV**
HARVEY ELECTRONICS, INC., 205 Chubb Ave., 07071, pg. 796 — **PV**
MOVADO GROUP, INC., 125 Chubb Ave., 07071, pg. 1140 — **PB**
Omega Plastics, P.O. Box 808, Page Ave. & Schuyler Ave., 07071, pg. 45 — **PV**
PLASTIC REEL CORP. OF AMERICA, 745 Brisbin Ave., 07071, pg. 871 — **PV**
Polo/Ralph Lauren, Nine Polito Ave., 07071, pg. 875 — **PV**
Scholastic Inc. Information Center, 1290 Wall St. West, 07071, pg. 1440 — **PB**
Sika Corporation, 201 Polito Avenue, 07071, pg. 1249 — **IT**
SwissAm Inc., 125 Chubb Ave., 07071, pg. 1140 — **PB**
Toshiba America Venture Capital, Inc., 1099 Wall St. W., Ste. 391, 07071, pg. 1405 — **IT**
YKK Corporation of America, 1251 Valley Brook Ave., 07071, pg. 1515 — **IT**

Madison

AMERICAN HOME PRODUCTS CORPORATION, Five Giralda Farms, 07940, pg. 79 — **PB**
Grizzard (Sales Office), 14 Main St., Ste. 302, 07940, pg. 482 — **PV**
Language Institute for English (L.I.F.E.), C/O FDU, Kingsland House, 07940, pg. 221 — **PV**
RICHTON INTERNATIONAL CORPORATION, 340 Main St., 07940, pg. 1389 — **PB**

SCHERING-PLOUGH CORPORATION, One Giralda Farms, 07940-1000, pg. 1438 — **PB**
Whitehall-Robins Healthcare, Five Giralda Farms, 07940-0871, pg. 80 — **PB**
Whitehall-Robins International, Inc., Five Giralda Farms, 07940, pg. 80 — **PB**

Mahwah

AT INFORMATION PRODUCTS, 575 Corporate Dr., 07430-2330, pg. 8 — **PV**
Aiwa America, Inc., 800 Corporate Dr., 07430, pg. 1280 — **IT**
Aston Martin Lagonda of North America, Inc., 533 MacArthur Blvd., 07430-2326, pg. 664 — **PB**
Bennett Brothers, Inc., 211 Island Rd., 07430, pg. 133 — **PV**
DRS Medical Systems, 31 Industrial Ave., 07430, pg. 475 — **PB**
Danfoss Inc., 16 McKee Dr., 07430-2138, pg. 377 — **IT**
FOOTSTAR INC., 933 MacArthur Blvd., 07430, pg. 661 — **PB**
HUBCO, INC., 1000 Mac Arthur Blvd., 07430, pg. 845 — **PB**
INSERRA SHOPRITE, 20 Ridge Rd., 07430, pg. 565 — **PV**
Jaguar Cars, 555 MacArthur Blvd., 07430-2327, pg. 664 — **PB**
Meldisco, 933 MacArthur Blvd., 07430, pg. 661 — **PB**
The New Home Sewing Machine Co., 10 Industrial Ave., 07430, pg. 699 — **IT**
Philips Electronics Instruments Company, 85 McKee Dr., 07430, pg. 1054 — **IT**
Primedia Inc., One Intl. Blvd., Ste. 444, 07495, pg. 1328 — **PB**
SEIKO Corporation of America, 1111 MacArthur Blvd., 07430, pg. 1218 — **IT**
SEIKO Time Corp., 1111 Macarthur Blvd., 07430, pg. 1218 — **IT**
Sharp Electronics Corporation, Sharp Plaza, 07430-2135, pg. 1228 — **IT**
Techalloy Co., Inc., 370 Franklin Turnpike, 07430, pg. 572 — **IT**
The World Almanac, One International Blvd., Ste. 444, 07495, pg. 1328 — **PB**

Manalapan

Calton Homes, Inc., 500 Craig Rd., 07726-8790, pg. 296 — **PB**
CALTON, INC., 500 Craig Rd., 07726-8790, pg. 296 — **PB**
STRATUS SERVICES GROUP, INC., 500 Craig Rd., 07726, pg. 1046 — **PV**

Manasquan

Dialight Corporation, 1913 Atlantic Ave., 08736, pg. 1130 — **IT**

Maple Shade

Stonhard, Inc., One Park Ave., 08052, pg. 1358 — **PB**

Maplewood

Alpine Lace Brands, Inc., 111 Dunnell Rd., 07040, pg. 646 — **PV**
MCT Dairies, Inc., 111 Dunnell Rd., 07040, pg. 646 — **PV**
New Jersey Transit Bus Operations, 180 Boyden Ave., 07040, pg. 794 — **PV**

Marlton

Arrow/Schweber Electronics, Four E. Stow Rd., Ste. 11, 08053, pg. 134 — **PB**
Atlas Building Systems, Inc., P.O. Box 245, 08053, pg. 1201 — **PV**
Stephen Gould of Pennsylvania Corp., Six Eves Dr., 08053, pg. 467 — **PV**
Harleysville-Garden State Insurance Co., 30 Lake Center Exec. Park, 401 Rte. 73 N., Ste. 100, 08053, pg. 787 — **PB**
Harleysville Insurance Company of New Jersey, P.O. Box 967, 08053-0967, pg. 787 — **PB**
MICHAEL'S DEVELOPMENT COMPANY, One E. Stow Rd., 08053, pg. 740 — **PV**
Vineland Transit Mix Concrete Co., Inc., P.O. Box 957, 08053, pg. 1201 — **IT**
Xerox Research, 10 Lake Ctr. Exec. Pk. # 300, 08053, pg. 1784 — **PB**

Mays Landing

Wheaton Plastic Products, 6115 Old Harding Hwy., 08330, pg. 68 — **IT**

Maywood

Ikegami Electronics (U.S.A.), Inc., 37 Brook Ave., 07607, pg. 660 — **IT**
MYRON MANUFACTURING CORPORATION, 205 Maywood Ave., 07607, pg. 771 — **PV**

Medford

CANTERBURY CORPORATE SERVICES, INC., 1600 Medford Plaza, 08055, pg. 301 — **PB**

PB - U.S. Public Companies Volume
PV - U.S. Private Companies Volume
IT - International Public & Private Companies Volume

Mercerville

Congoleum Corporation, P.O. Box 3127, 3705 Quakerbridge Rd., 08619, pg. 69   PB

Merchantville

CLOVER FINANCIAL CORPORATION, 23 W. Park Ave., 08109, pg. 247   PV
Prince Foods Canning Div., P.O. Box 1298, 08109, pg. 158   PV

Metuchen

Scarecrow Press, Inc., 52 Liberty St., P.O. Box 4167, 08840, pg. 794   IT

Mickleton

Bunnell Plastics Division, I-295 & Harmony Rd., 08056, pg. 689   PB

Middlesex

Mason Candlelight, 820 Lincoln Blvd., 08846, pg. 1506   PB
Mason Metals Co., 554 Lincoln Blvd., 08846, pg. 1506   PB
Micro-Tube Fabricators Inc., 250 Lackland Dr., 08846, pg. 780   PB
THERAPEDIC ASSOCIATES, INC., 601 Bound Brook Rd., 08846, pg. 1079   PV

Midland Park

ITT Controls & Instruments Division, 445 Goodwin Ave., 07432, pg. 860   PB
ITT Fluid Technology Corporation, 445 Godwin Ave., 07432, pg. 860   PB
ITT Fluid Transfer Division, 445 Godwin Ave., 07432, pg. 860   PB
F.G. MONTABERT, 175 Paterson Ave., 07432, pg. 758   PV

Millburn

Broad National Bank-Millburn, 225 Millburn Ave., 07041, pg. 258   PB
Dorchester, 16 Bleeker St., 07041, pg. 584   PV
Hoffman Import and Distribution Company, 16 Bleeker St., 07041, pg. 584   PV
Int. Vintners, 16 Bleeker St., 07041, pg. 584   PV
INTERET CORPORATION, 374 Millburn Ave., Ste. 301E, 07041, pg. 567   PV
J&J Distribution Company, 16 Bleeker St., 07041, pg. 584   PV
THE JAYDOR CORPORATION, 16 Bleeker St., 07041, pg. 584   PV
Newmarket Company, 16 Bleeker St., 07041, pg. 584   PV
Rodgers Warehouse and Transport Company, 16 Bleeker St., 07041, pg. 584   PV
SHARON CONCEPTS, 67 E. Willow St., 07041, pg. 990   PV

Millville

ABB K-Flow Inc., P.O. Box 849, Millville Airport, 08332, pg. 4   IT
Decora, 1101 Wheaton Ave., 08332, pg. 67   IT
General Machinery Co., N. Tenth St., 08332, pg. 68   IT
SILVERTON MARINE CORPORATION, 301 Riverside Dr., 08332, pg. 1000   PV
UNC Airwork, Municipal Airport, 08332, pg. 710   PB
Wheaton Coated Products, 1101 Wheaton Ave., 08332, pg. 67   IT
Wheaton do Brazil, 1101 Wheaton Ave., 08332, pg. 68   IT
Wheaton Glass Co., 1101 Wheaton Ave., 08332, pg. 68   IT
Wheaton Glass Products, 3rd & G Sts., 08332, pg. 67   IT
Wheaton Inc., 1101 Wheaton Ave., 08332, pg. 67   IT
Wheaton Injection Molding, 1101 Wheaton Ave., 08332, pg. 68   IT
Wheaton Instruments, 1101 Wheaton Ave., 08332, pg. 68   IT
Wheaton Plastic Containers, 1101 Wheaton Ave., 08332, pg. 68   IT
Wheaton Scientific, 1101 Wheaton Ave., 08332, pg. 68   IT
Wheaton Scientific Products, N. Tenth St., 08332, pg. 68   IT
Wheaton Tubing Products, 1101 Wheaton Ave., 08332, pg. 68   IT

Monmouth Junction

American Natl. Can Co., P.O. Box 1600, 08852, pg. 1029   IT
Communication Group, Black Horse Ln., P.O. Box 125, 08852, pg. 1109   IT
Films for the Humanities & Sciences, Inc., 11 Perrine Rd., 08852, pg. 1327   PB
GUEST SUPPLY, INC., P.O. Box 902, 4301 U.S. Hwy. One, 08852-0902, pg. 768   PB
Rhone-Poulenc, Chemical Division, Black Horse Ln., P.O. Box 125, 08852, pg. 1109   IT
Rhone-Poulenc Inc., Fine Inorganic Chemical Division, Black Horse Ln., P.O. Box 125, 08852, pg. 1110   IT
Rhone-Poulenc, Specialty Plastics Division, P.O. Box 125, Black Horse Ln., 08852, pg. 1110   IT

Montclair

Budde & Westermann, P.O. Box 177, 07042, pg. 411   PV

Montvale

BENJAMIN MOORE & CO., 51 Chestnut Ridge Rd., 07645, pg. 133   PV
Bioplex Corp., 14 Philips Pkwy., 07645, pg. 487   PV
Bush Boake Allen, Inc, 7 Mercedes Drive, 07645, pg. 1666   PB
Butler Design Services, Inc., 110 Summit Ave., 07458, pg. 271   PB
Butler Fleet Services, Inc., 110 Summit Ave., 07645, pg. 271   PB
BUTLER INTERNATIONAL, INC., 110 Summit Ave., 07645, pg. 270   PB
Butler Service Group, Inc., 110 Summit Ave., 07645, pg. 271   PB
Butler Service Group - U.K. Ltd., 110 Summit Ave., 07645, pg. 271   PB
Butler Services, Inc., 110 Summit Ave., 07645, pg. 271   PB
Butler Technology Solutions, Inc., 110 Summit Ave., 07645, pg. 271   PB
Butler Telecom, Inc., 110 Summit Ave., 07645, pg. 271   PB
Butler Utilities Services, Inc., 110 Summit Ave., 07645, pg. 271   PB
Chase Manhattan Leasing, 1 Paragon Dr., Ste. 261, 07645, pg. 338   IT
Compass Foods, Inc., Two Paragon Dr., 07645, pg. 1375   IT
Compilers Plus Inc., 100 Paragon Dr., 07645, pg. 70   PB
Database America Companies, 100 Paragon Dr., 07645, pg. 70   PB
DATABASE AMERICA COMPANIES, 100 Paragon Dr., 07645-0419, pg. 312   PV
Datascope Collagen Products Division, 14 PhilipsPkwy., 07645, pg. 487   PB
DATASCOPE CORP., 14 Philips Pkwy., 07645, pg. 487   PB
Federal Paper Board Company, Inc., 75 Chestnut Ridge Rd., 07645, pg. 903   PB
FEROLIE GROUP, P.O Box 409, Two Van Riper Rd., 07645-0409, pg. 401   PV
GEOTEK COMMUNICATIONS, 102 Chestnut Ridge Rd., 07645, pg. 739   PB
Geotek USA/PowerSpectrum, 102 Chestnut Ridge Rd., 07645, pg. 740   PB
The Great Atlantic & Pacific Tea Company, Inc., 2 Paragon Dr., 07645, pg. 1375   IT
Imperial Bondware Corp., 75 Chestnut Ridge Rd., 07645, pg. 903   PB
Incentive Group Inc., 50 Chestnut Ridge Rd., 07645, pg. 669   IT
MEDCO Containment Services, Inc., 100 Summit Ave., 07645, pg. 1091   PB
Medical Device Register, Five Paragon Dr., 07645, pg. 1600   PB
Medical Economics Company Inc., Five Paragon Dr., 07645, pg. 1601   PB
Mercedes-Benz of North America, Inc., One Mercedes Dr., 07645-0350, pg. 368   IT
Patient Care Communications, Inc., Five Paragon Dr., 07645, pg. 1601   PB
R & C Inc., 225 Summit Ave., 07645, pg. 1090   IT
Reckitt & Colman Inc., 225 Summit Ave., 07645, pg. 1090   IT
Roussel Corporation, 95 Chestnut Ridge Rd., 07645, pg. 625   IT
Thomas Tait & Sons, Ltd., 75 Chestnut Ridge Rd., 07645, pg. 904   PB
Volvo Finance North America, Inc., 25 Phillips Pkwy., 07645, pg. 1477   IT
The Wella Corporation, 12 Mercedes Dr., 07645, pg. 1489   PV
Zeneca Pharmaceuticals, One Paragon Dr., Ste. 230, 07645-1725, pg. 1525   IT

Montville

AST Bearings Division, 115 Main Rd., 07045, pg. 157   PB
Business & Professional Products Group, Three Paragon Dr., 07045, pg. 1284   PV
CONSTRUCTION COUNSELLORS, INC., P.O. Box 617, 07645, pg. 266   PV
MAROTTA SCIENTIFIC CONTROLS, INC., 78 Boonton Ave., 07045, pg. 706   PV
SSD&W INTEGRATED MARKETING COMMUNICATIONS, 350 Main Rd., 07045, pg. 958   PV
Titan Global Ltd., P.O. Box 617, 07645, pg. 266   PV

Moonachie

ACRISON, INC., 20 Empire Blvd., 07074, pg. 14   PV
Allied Your Coffee Partner, 62 Joseph St., 07074, pg. 39   PV
Crest-Foam Corporation, 100 Carol Pl., 07074, pg. 986   PV
Crest-Hood Foam Company, Inc., 100 Carol Place, 07074, pg. 986   PB
KEY HANDLING SYSTEMS, INC., 137 W. Commercial Ave., 07074-1704, pg. 618   PV
Oxford Furniture, Ten Caesar Pl., 07074, pg. 460   IT
PACE PRESS, INC., 1 Caesar Pl., 07074, pg. 829   PV
Richheimer Food, Ten Empire Blvd., 07074, pg. 1158   PV
Sanyo, 51 Joseph St., 07074-1013, pg. 1191   IT
Swissrose International, Inc., 14 Empire Blvd., 07074-1303, pg. 426   PV
Teterboro Learning Center, 100 Moonachie Ave., 07074, pg. 219   PB

WECHSLER COFFEE CORP., Ten Empire Blvd., 07074, pg. 1158   PV

Moorestown

AXIOM INC., 351 New Albany Rd., 08057, pg. 157   PB
Barclay Travel Agency, 308 Harper Dr., Ste. 101, 08057-3245, pg. 317   PV
Eastern Research, Inc., 225 Executive Dr., 08057, pg. 45   PB
FORMATION, INC., 121 Whittendale Dr., 08057, pg. 419   PV
Halliburton Energy Services, 858 N. Lenola Rd., 08057-1041, pg. 776   PB
Linear Switch Corporation, 225 Executive Way, 08057, pg. 45   PB
Martin Marietta Government Electronic Systems, P.O. Box 1027, 08057-3075, pg. 1007   PB
Patton, 390 New Albany Rd., 08057, pg. 1486   PB
Quest Diagnostic-Moorestown, Victoria Medical Arts Bldg., 701 E. Main St., 08057, pg. 1351   PB
RP alpha/New Jersey, 302 Harper Pl., Ste. 203, 08057, pg. 950   PV
THE ROYAL CHINA & PORCELAIN COMPANIES INC., 1265 Glen Ave., 08057-0912, pg. 948   PV
Subaru of America, Inc., P.O. Box P, Glen Ave. & Foster Rd., 08057, pg. 523   IT
TODAY'S MAN, INC., 835 Lancer Dr., 08057, pg. 1619   PB

Morganville

HANDEX ENVIRONMENT INC., 500 Campus Dr., 07751, pg. 498   PV
Handex Environmental Inc., 500 Campus Dr., 07751, pg. 499   PV
Handex of New Jersey, Inc., 500 Campus Dr., 07751, pg. 499   PV

Morris Plains

Adams U.S.A., 201 Tabor Rd., 07950, pg. 1739   PB
Airtron, 200 E. Hanover Ave., 07950, pg. 1003   PB
Alimenterics, Inc., 301 American Rd., 07950, pg. 92   PB
Capsugel, 201 Tabor Rd., 07950, pg. 1739   PB
Esselte Meto, 1200 The American Rd., 07950-2453, pg. 460   IT
Esselte Meto Kimball Systems, 1200 The American Rd., 07950-2453, pg. 460   IT
Gordon Publications, Inc., P.O. Box 650, 301 Gibraltar Dr., 07950-0650, pg. 1096   IT
MET Solutions, LLC, 201 Littleton Rd., 07950, pg. 1642   PB
Meto, USA, 1200 The American Road, 07950, pg. 460   IT
MONROE SYSTEMS FOR BUSINESS, INC., 1000 The American Rd., 07950, pg. 757   PV
Parke Davis Company, Inc., 201 Tabor Rd., 07950, pg. 1739   PB
Parke-Davis Group, 201 Tabor Rd., 07950, pg. 1739   PB
PHYSICIAN COMPUTER NETWORK, INC., 1200 The American Rd., Fl. 2, 07950, pg. 1293   PB
Reed Elsevier Business Information-Morris Plains, 301 Gibraltar Dr., 07950, pg. 1095   IT
Times On-Line Services, Inc., 520 Speedwell Ave., 07950, pg. 1174   PB
WARNER-LAMBERT COMPANY, 201 Tabor Rd., 07950, pg. 1738   PB
Warner-Lambert International Operations, 201 Tabor Rd., 07950, pg. 1739   PB
WEICHERT COMPANY, 1625 State Hwy. 10, 07950, pg. 1159   PV
Willis Corroon Corp. of New Jersey, 201 Littleton Rd., 07950, pg. 1506   IT

Morristown

AT&T Capital Corporation, 44 Whippany Rd., 07960, pg. 924   IT
ATOR Corporation, 475 South St., 07962, pg. 1018   PB
Account Specific Marketing, Inc. (ASM), 10 Park Ave., 07960, pg. 345   PV
ALLIEDSIGNAL INC., 101 Columbia Rd., 07962, pg. 49   PB
AlliedSignal Inc., AlliedSignal Plastic, 101 Columbia Rd., 07962-2332, pg. 51   PB
AlliedSignal Inc., AlliedSignal Specialty Films, 101 Columbia Rd., 07962, pg. 51   PB
AlliedSignal Inc., Chemical Intermediates, 101 Columbia Rd., 07962, pg. 51   PB
AlliedSignal Inc., Fluorocarbons, 101 Columbia Rd., 07962-1139, pg. 51   PB
AlliedSignal, Industrial Fibers, 101 Columbia Rd., 07962-1087, pg. 51   PB
Bayer Corporation/Consumer Care Division, 36 Columbia Rd., 07960, pg. 173   IT
Bell Telephone Laboratories Inc., 475 South St., 07962, pg. 1018   PB
Bellcore, 445 South St., 07960, pg. 976   PV
Champion Int'l. Corp., 155 E. Hanover Ave., 07960, pg. 334   PB
DKB & PARTNERS, INC., 67 East Park Pl., 1776 on the Green, 07960, pg. 302   PV
Danaher Controls, 999 Mount Kemble Ave., 07960-6623, pg. 490   PB
DUGAN VALVA CONTESS INC., 10 Park Ave., 07960, pg. 345   PV
Eastern Region Sales, P.O. Box 362, 07960, pg. 1572   PB
Eastman Kodak Co., 10 Madison Ave., 07960-7303, pg. 555   PB

PB - *U.S. Public Companies Volume*
PV - *U.S. Private Companies Volume*
IT - *International Public & Private Companies Volume*

1322

Edwards & Kelcey Construction, Inc., P.O. Box 1989, 299 Madison Ave., 07962-1989, pg. 364 — PV
Edwards & Kelcey Wireless, P.O. Box 1989, 299 Madison Ave., 07962-1989, pg. 364 — PV
Engineered Construction-New Jersey, 35 Airport Rd., 07960, pg. 1304 — PB
F&G Re, Inc., 55 Madison Ave., 07960, pg. 1659 — PB
GPU, INC., 300 Madison Ave., 07962, pg. 695 — PB
Gemini Consulting, 25 Airport Rd., 07960, pg. 264 — IT
Jersey Central Power & Light Co., 300 Madison Ave., 07962-1911, pg. 695 — PB
Loose Tube Inc., 475 South St., 07962, pg. 1018 — PB
Lucent Technologies Americas Inc., 475 South St., 07962, pg. 1018 — PB
Lucent Technologies Asia/Pacific Inc., 475 South St., 07962, pg. 1018 — PB
Lucent Technologies de Honduras S.A., 475 South St., 07962, pg. 1018 — PB
Lucent Technologies Eastern Ventures Inc., 475 South St., 07962, pg. 1018 — PB
Lucent Technologies Engineering Inc., 475 South St., 07962, pg. 1018 — PB
Lucent Technologies Eurasia Ltd., 475 South St., 07962, pg. 1018 — PB
Lucent Technologies Holdings Inc., 475 South St., 07962, pg. 1018 — PB
Lucent Technologies International Inc., 475 South St., 07962, pg. 1018 — PB
Lucent Technologies Management Services Inc., 475 South St., 07962, pg. 1018 — PB
Lucent Technologies Nicaragua S.A., 475 South St., 07962, pg. 1018 — PB
Lucent Technologies Western Investments Inc., 475 South St., 07962, pg. 1018 — PB
Lucent Technologies World Services Inc., 475 South St., 07962, pg. 1018 — PB
MAGLA PRODUCTS, P.O. Box 1934, 07962, pg. 695 — PV
Market Facts, Inc., 65 Madison Ave., 07960, pg. 1047 — PB
MODERN MEDICAL MODALITIES CORP., 95 Madison Ave., 07960, pg. 1121 — PB
NCS Ventures, Inc., 4½ Mt. Kemble Ave., 07960, pg. 1019 — PB
Schindler Elevator Company, 20 Whippany Road, 07960, pg. 1205 — IT
Titanium Industries, Inc., 48 South St., 07960, pg. 43 — PB
UF6 Flourine Specialties, P.O. Box 1139, 101 Columbia Rd., 07962-1139, pg. 51 — PB
Value Engineering & Management, Inc., P.O. Box 1936, 299 Madison Ave., 07962-1936, pg. 365 — PV
Western Electric Company, 412 Mt. Kemble Ave., 07960, pg. 1019 — PB

Mount Holly

Mount Holly Water Co., 84 Mill St., 08060, pg. 540 — PB
Rexam Medical Packaging, Inc., P.O. Box 158, Shreve St., 08060-0158, pg. 1106 — IT

Mount Laurel

AFA Protective Systems, Inc., 520 Fellowship Rd., Ste. D-404, 08054, pg. 6 — PB
Automotive Rentals, Inc. (ARI), 9000 Midlantic Dr., 08054, pg. 535 — PV
CCL Labeling Equipment, 717 C-E Fellowship Rd., 08054, pg. 238 — IT
Correctional Behavioral Solutions of New Jersey, Inc., 3000 Atrium Way, 08054, pg. 1035 — PB
EDD-Philadelphia, 158 Gaither Dr., Ste. 110, 08054, pg. 205 — PB
Engraph Machine Group, 824A E. Gate Dr., 08054, pg. 1486 — PB
Equity One, Inc., 523 Fellowship Rd., Ste. 220, 08054, pg. 176 — PB
Fleer-Skybox International Inc., Executive Plaza, Ste. 300, 1120 Rte. 73, 08054, pg. 1052 — PB
JOHNSON & TOWERS, INC., 2021 Briggs Rd., 08054, pg. 590 — PB
MSC Northeast Office, 1000 Howard Blvd., Ste. 105, 08054, pg. 1031 — PB
Milgray/Delaware Valley, Inc., 523 Fellowship Rd., 08054, pg. 206 — PB
Okidata Group, 532 Fellowship Rd., 08054, pg. 1000 — IT
PHH Mortgage Services Corporation, 6000 Atrium Way, 08054, pg. 321 — PB
PNC-NJ N.A., 1000 Crawford Pl., Ste. 300, 08054, pg. 1243 — PB
Plastic Suppliers, Inc., 106 Gaither Dr., 08054, pg. 871 — PV
SL INDUSTRIES, INC., 520 Fellowship Rd., Ste. A-114, 08054, pg. 1418 — PB
SL Waber, Inc., 520 Fellowship Rd., Ste. 306, 08054, pg. 1419 — PB
Spring Financial Services, 523 Fellowship Rd., Suite 220, 08054, pg. 176 — PB
TNI, Inc., 6000 Midlantic Dr., 08054, pg. 1058 — PB
Telenex, 13000 Midlantic, 08050, pg. 727 — PB
Tyco Acquisitions, 6000 Midlantic Dr., 08054, pg. 1058 — PB
Tyco Holdings Corporation, 6000 Midlantic Dr., 08054, pg. 1058 — PB
Tyco Industries, Inc., 6000 Midlantic Dr., 08054, pg. 1058 — PB
Tyco Toys, Inc., 6000 Midlantic Dr., 08054, pg. 1058 — PB
Universal Matchbox Group, 6000 Midlantic Dr., 08054, pg. 1058 — PB
View-Master, Inc., 6000 Midlantic Dr., 08054, pg. 1058 — PB

Mount Olive

SPORTCRAFT LTD., 313 Waterloo Valley Rd., 07828, pg. 1026 — PV

TMP Worldwide/Direct Marketing Services, 600 International Drive, 07828, pg. 1064 — PV

Mountain Lakes

COMPUTER HORIZONS CORP., 49 Old Bloomfield Ave., 07046-1495, pg. 421 — PB
Computer Knowledge, 49 Old Bloomfield Ave., 07046-1495, pg. 421 — PB
Unified Systems Solutions Inc., 49 Old Bloomfield Ave., 07046-1495, pg. 421 — PB

Mountainside

Charlie Brown's & The Office Restaurant Group, 1450 Rt. 22 W, 07092, pg. 219 — PV
DURST CORPORATION, 1115 Globe Ave., 07092, pg. 349 — PV
Jaclo Inc., 1115 Globe Ave., 07092, pg. 349 — PV
The Palnut Company, 152 Glen Rd., 07092, pg. 1632 — PB

Murray Hill

The BOC Group Inc. (Delaware), 575 Mountain Ave., 07974, pg. 121 — IT
C.R. BARD, INC., 730 Central Ave., 07974-1199, pg. 189 — PB
Barringer Instruments, Inc., 219 South St., 07974, pg. 192 — PB
Bell Labs, 600 Mountain Ave., 07974, pg. 1018 — PB
Corporate Marketing and Services, 730 Central Ave., 07974, pg. 189 — PB
Dun & Bradstreet, One Diamond Hill Rd., 07974-0027, pg. 535 — PB
THE DUN & BRADSTREET CORPORATION, One Diamond Hill Rd., 07974, pg. 535 — PB
LUCENT TECHNOLOGIES INC., 600 Mountain Ave., 07974, pg. 1017 — PB
Medical Resources Inc., 430 Mountain Ave., 07974-2732, pg. 1080 — PV

Neptune

Asbury Park Press, Inc., 3601 Hwy. 66, 07754, pg. 699 — PB
Container Tooling Corporation, Pkwy. 100, Rte. 66, 07753, pg. 617 — PB
Continental Data Center, 3501 RT 66, 07753-2602, pg. 1011 — PB
Cornerstone Construction & Materials, Inc., Monmouth Shores Corp. Park, 1350 Campus Pkwy., Ste. 302, 07753, pg. 593 — IT
Electronic Measurements, Inc., 405 Essex Rd., 07753, pg. 138 — PV

Neshanic Station

Akzo Engineering Plastics, Inc., P.O. Box 625, Wooden Rd., 08853, pg. 47 — IT

Netcong

Compac Corporation, Old Flanders Rd., 07857, pg. 1054 — PB

New Brunswick

AFA New Jersey, Inc., 961 Joyce Kilmer Ave., 08902, pg. 6 — PB
Akzo Chemical, Inc., 500 Jersey Ave., 08901, pg. 47 — IT
AMCAN Specialty Steels, 330 Milltown Rd., 08816, pg. 308 — PB
Garry Precision Screw Machine, 1010 Jersey Ave., 08903, pg. 1184 — PB
Hydro-Med Sciences, 783 Jersey Ave., 08901, pg. 695 — PB
Interferon Sciences Development Corp., 783 Jersey Ave., 08901, pg. 694 — PB
Interferon Sciences, Inc., 783 Jersey Ave., 08901, pg. 694 — PB
JOHNSON & JOHNSON, One Johnson & Johnson Plaza, 08901, pg. 927 — PB
Johnson & Johnson Development Corporation, One Johnson & Johnson Plaza, 08933, pg. 928 — PB
Johnson & Johnson Finance Corporation, P.O. Box 2660, 08903-2660, pg. 928 — PB
KVK (USA) Inc., 19A Home News Rd., 08901, pg. 370 — IT
Laser Diode Products, 1130 Somerset St., 08901, pg. 892 — IT
McNeil Specialty Products Company, P.O. Box 2400, 501 George St., 08903-2400, pg. 928 — PB
NPDC-AS101, Inc., 783 Jersey Ave., 08901, pg. 694 — PB
Permacel, U.S. Hwy. #1, 08903, pg. 950 — IT
Pressman Toy Corp., Joyce Kilmer Ave., 08901, pg. 882 — PV
VALUE PROPERTY TRUST, 120 Albany St. Plaza, 8th Fl., 08901, pg. 1707 — PB

New Gretna

VIKING YACHT CO., Rte. 9, 08224, pg. 1140 — PV

New Providence

ALPHA ONE EXCHANGE, 121 Chanlon Rd., 07974, pg. 45 — PV
Aromat Corporation, 629 Central Ave., 07974, pg. 847 — IT
Aromat Mid Atlantic Sales, 629 Central Ave., 07974, pg. 848 — IT

BARRINGER TECHNOLOGIES INC., 219 South St., 07974, pg. 191 — PB
R.R. Bowker, 121 Chanlon Rd., 07974, pg. 1096 — IT
CD PRODUCTS, INC., 121 Chanlon Rd., 07974, pg. 276 — PB
Communications Equipment Co., 121 Chanlon Rd., 07974, pg. 276 — PB
Datascan Services Co., 121 Chanlon Rd., 07974, pg. 45 — PV
The Dun & Bradstreet Corporate Foundation, One Diamond Hill Rd., 07974, pg. 535 — PB
General Management Co., 121 Chanlon Rd., 07974, pg. 1040 — PB
HOLLISTER ADVERTISING, 121 Chanlon Rd., 07974, pg. 830 — PB
Hollister Media, 121 Chanlon Rd., 07974, pg. 830 — PB
Keppel Marine Agencies Inc., 571 Central Ave., Ste. 112, 07974, pg. 731 — IT
MANAGEMENT DYNAMICS, 121 Chanlon Rd., 07974, pg. 1040 — PB
Marquis Who's Who, 121 Chanlon Rd., 07974, pg. 1096 — IT
Martindale-Hubbell, 121 Chanlon Rd., 07974, pg. 1096 — IT
NAIS Products Sales Office, 629 Central Ave., 07974, pg. 848 — IT
National Register Publishing, 121 Chanlon Rd., 07974, pg. 1096 — IT
PAMARCO TECHNOLOGIES, INC., 571 Central Ave., 07974, pg. 835 — PV
SCOTT PRINTING CORPORATION, 700 Central Ave., 07974, pg. 977 — PV
SIMON & ASSOCIATES, 121 Chanlon Rd., 07974, pg. 1001 — PV
THE W.B. WOOD COMPANY, 150 Floral Ave., 07974, pg. 1186 — PV

Newark

American Family Publishers, Four Gateway Ctr., Ste. 100, 07102, pg. 1612 — PB
ATLAS REFINERY, 142 Lockwood St., 07105, pg. 96 — PV
BNB Investment Corporation, 905 Broad St., 07102, pg. 258 — PB
Banco Popular, FSB, 500 Bloomfield Ave., 07107, pg. 176 — PB
Banco Totta & Acores, 46 Ferry St., 07105, pg. 145 — IT
Bell Atlantic-NJ, 540 Broad St., 07101, pg. 202 — PB
BEST PROVISION CO., INC., 144 Avon Ave., 07108, pg. 140 — PV
BROAD NATIONAL BANCORPORATION, 905 Broad St., 07102, pg. 257 — PB
Broad National Bank, 905 Broad St., 07102, pg. 257 — PB
Broad National Bank-Ironbound, 7 Wheeler Point Rd., 07105, pg. 257 — PB
Broad National Bank-Jackson, 133 Jackson St., 07105, pg. 258 — PB
Broad National Bank-North Newark, 466 Bloomfield Ave., 07107, pg. 258 — PB
Broad National Bank-Prudential Plaza, 745 Broad St., 07102, pg. 258 — PB
Broad National Realty Corporation, 905 Broad St., 07102, pg. 258 — PB
Bronatoreo, 905 Broad St., 07102, pg. 258 — PB
E.J. BROOKS COMPANY, N. 13th St., 07107, pg. 172 — PV
Canrad Inc., 100 Chestnut St., 07105, pg. 17 — IT
CENTRAL LEWMAR, 60 McClellan St., 07114, pg. 223 — PV
DAIDONE ELECTRICAL INC., 200 Raymond Blvd., 07105, pg. 307 — PV
EDISON PARKING PROPERTIES, LLC, 100 Washington St., 07102, pg. 364 — PV
Enterprise Diversified Holdings Incorporated, 80 Park Plaza, 07101, pg. 1340 — PB
Enterprise Group Development Corporation, 80 Park Plaza, 07101, pg. 1340 — PB
Federal Bronze Products Inc., 50 Wheeler Point Rd., 07105, pg. 1100 — PV
The Fifth & Race Company Limited Partnership, 58 Park Pl., 07102, pg. 361 — PV
First Union Insurance Group, Inc., 550 Broad St., 07102, pg. 640 — PB
FISKE BROTHERS REFINING COMPANY, 129 Lockwood St., 07105, pg. 408 — PB
GEORGIA-BONDED FIBERS, INC., 15 Nutman St., 07103, pg. 734 — PB
Gibraltar Casualty Co., 751 Broad St., 07102, pg. 892 — PV
HANDY STORE FIXTURES, INC., 337 Sherman Ave., 07114, pg. 499 — PV
Hertz Corporation, Newark Intl. Airport, Bldg. 23, 07114, pg. 664 — PB
Janeway Properties, Inc., 100 Washington St., 07102, pg. 364 — PV
JARCHEM INDUSTRIES, INC., 414 Wilson Ave., 07105, pg. 582 — PV
Jarchem Specialty Chemical Division, 40 Ball St., 07105, pg. 583 — PV
Kalmar Inc., 186 Tyler St., 07114, pg. 1421 — PB
Kintetsu World Express Inc., Hemisphere Center Ste. 508, Rte. 1 & 9 S., 07114, pg. 734 — IT
MBL LIFE ASSURANCE CORPORATION, 520 Broad St., 07102-3184, pg. 685 — PV
NAPORANO IRON & METAL, Hawkins St., 07105, pg. 774 — PV
New Jersey Sign Company Inc., 100 Washington St., 07102, pg. 364 — PV
NJ TRANSIT, One Penn Plaza E., 07105-2246, pg. 794 — PV
New Jersey Transit Rail Operations, One Penn Plaza East, 07105, pg. 794 — PV
PSEG Capital Corporation, 80 Park Plaza, 07101, pg. 1340 — PB

PB - *U.S. Public Companies Volume*
PV - *U.S. Private Companies Volume*
IT - *International Public & Private Companies Volume*

Pick Quick Papers, Inc., 60 McClellan St., 07114, pg. 223 — PV

Prometcor Inc., 45-65 Manufacturers Pl., 07105, pg. 1405 — PV

Prudential Agricultural Credit, Inc., Prudential Plaza, 07102, pg. 892 — PV

Prudential Capital & Investment Services, Inc., 100 Mulberry St., 07102, pg. 892 — PV

THE PRUDENTIAL INSURANCE COMPANY OF AMERICA, 751 Broad St., 07102-3777, pg. 892 — PV

The Prudential Investment Corp., 751 Broad St., 07102-3777, pg. 892 — PV

The Prudential Realty Group, 751 Broad St., 07102-3777, pg. 892 — PV

Public Service Electric & Gas Co., 80 Park Plaza, 07101, pg. 1340 — PB

PUBLIC SERVICE ENTERPRISE GROUP INCORPORATED, P.O. Box 1171, 80 Park Plaza, 07101-1171, pg. 1340 — PB

Public Service Resources Corporation, 80 Park Plaza, 07101, pg. 1340 — PB

Rhone-Poulenc Specialty Chemicals, 394 Ferlinghuysen, 07114, pg. 1110 — IT

ROKEACH FOOD DISTRIBUTING INC., 80 Ave. K, 07105, pg. 940 — PV

Rubbermaid Healthcare Products, 39 Tompkins Point Rd., 07114, pg. 1411 — PB

Securities Data Company, Inc., 2 Gateway Ct., 11th Fl., 07102, pg. 1600 — PB

Seton Co., 849 Broadway, 07104, pg. 987 — PV

Skadden, Arps, Slate, Meagher & Flom LLP, One Newark Ctr., 07102, pg. 1004 — PV

Skyline Port Newark Facility, 296 Marlin St., 07114-3011, pg. 1648 — PB

TAP Air Portugal, 399 Market St., 07105, pg. 1418 — IT

Richard E. Thibaut, Inc., 480 Frelinghuysen Ave., 07114, pg. 1358 — PB

Newfield

Charles River Laboratories-NJ, 2569 W. Weymouth Rd., 08344, pg. 194 — PB

Shieldalloy Metallurgical Corportation, P.O. Box 768, 08344, pg. 735 — PV

Newton

E.J. Brooks, 1 Brooks Plz., 07860, pg. 172 — PV

ICI Explosives, 238 Spring St., 07860, pg. 663 — IT

Valley National Bank, 410 Rte. 94, 07860, pg. 1706 — PB

North Arlington

Broad National Bank-North Arlington, 65 River Rd., 07031, pg. 258 — PB

North Bergen

A-P-A TRANSPORT CORP., 2100 88th St., 07047, pg. 2 — PV

Balanced Foods, Inc., 2501 71st St., 07047, pg. 752 — IT

COLONNA BROS., INC., 4102 Bergen Tpke., 07047, pg. 254 — PV

Deerskin Trading Post, Inc., 2001 Tonnelle Ave., 07047, pg. 879 — PB

Frutarom Meer Corporation, 9500 Railroad Ave., 07047-1206, pg. 554 — PV

HUDSON COUNTY NEWS COMPANY, 1305 Paterson Plank Rd., 07047, pg. 545 — PV

Hudson United Bank-North Bergen, 1707 69th St., 07047, pg. 845 — PB

MILLER PRODUCTS COMPANY, INC., 2220 91st St., 07047, pg. 747 — PV

WESTCHESTER LACE, INC., 3901 Liberty Ave., 07047, pg. 1163 — PV

North Brunswick

ABB Turbocharger Company, 1460 Livingston Ave., 08902, pg. 5 — IT

AFA Protective Systems, Inc., 961 Joyce Kilmer Ave., 08902, pg. 5 — PB

BWD Automotive, P.O. Box 6010, Rtes. 1 & 130, 08902, pg. 560 — PB

DeVRY Technical Institute, 630 U.S. Hwy. One, 08902, pg. 504 — PV

E.C.D. Inc., 1201 Jersey Ave., 08902, pg. 353 — PV

Metallurgy, 1460 Livingston Ave., 08902, pg. 4 — IT

Miller Personnel, Inc., 720 Rte. 1 North, 08902, pg. 748 — PV

MILLER RESOURCES INTERNATIONAL, INC., 720 Rte. 1 N., 08902, pg. 748 — PV

Miller Scientific, Inc., 720 Rte. One N., 08902, pg. 748 — PV

Miller Temporaries, Inc., 720 Rte. One N., 08902, pg. 748 — PV

Permacel Tape, Rte. 1, P.O. Box 671, 08902, pg. 153 — PB

USA DETERGENTS, INC., 1735 Jersey Ave., 08902, pg. 1685 — PB

WARD PRODUCTS CORPORATION, 633 Nassau St., 08902, pg. 1149 — PV

Webcraft Games, Inc., 205 N. Center Dr., 08902, pg. 228 — PB

Webcraft Technologies, Inc., Rte. 1 & Adams Station Rd., 08902, pg. 228 — PB

Northvale

AERCO INTERNATIONAL INC., 159 Paris Ave., 07647, pg. 23 — PV

Balsa Development Corporation, Ten Fairway Ct., 07647, pg. 171 — PB

Balsa Ecuador Lumber Corporation, Ten Fairway Ct., 07647, pg. 171 — PB

BALTEK CORPORATION, Ten Fairway Ct., 07647, pg. 171 — PB

Baltek Foreign Sales Corporation, Ten Fairway Ct., 07647, pg. 172 — PB

C.K. Trading Corp., Ten Fairway Ct., 07647, pg. 172 — PB

Crustacea Corporation, Ten Fairway Ct., 07647, pg. 172 — PB

Cryogenic Structures Corporation, Ten Fairway Ct., 07647, pg. 172 — PB

G. JCANNOU CYCLE CO. INC., 151 Ludlow Ave., 07647, pg. 588 — PV

LEONARD KREUSCH, INC., 200 LeGrand Ave., 07647-2406, pg. 635 — PV

MULTIMATIC CORPORATION, 162 Veteran Dr., 07647, pg. 767 — PV

Sanlam Corporation, Ten Fairway Ct., 07647, pg. 172 — PB

TRI-K INDUSTRIES, INC., 151 Veterans Dr., 07647, pg. 1100 — PV

Norwood

Mitsui Foods, Inc., 35 Maple St., 07648-0409, pg. 879 — IT

Northfield Foods, 375 Chestnut St., 07648, pg. 646 — PV

Sanyo Semiconductor Distribution (USA) Corporation, 49 Walnut St., 07648, pg. 1191 — IT

Schunmag-Kieserling Machinery, Inc., P.O. Box 419, 07648, pg. 399 — IT

Sellers & Josephson, 335 Chestnut St., 07648, pg. 1465 — PB

Nutley

A/CD-East, 492 River Rd., 07110, pg. 859 — PB

Hoffmann-La Roche Inc., 340 Kingsland St., 07110, pg. 1120 — IT

Oakland

RUSS BERRIE AND COMPANY, INC., 111 Bauer Dr., 07436, pg. 222 — PB

DRS Photronics, Inc., 138 Bauer Dr., 07436, pg. 474 — PB

Electro-Optical Systems Group, 138 Bauer Dr., 07436, pg. 474 — PB

Meadox Medicals, Inc., 112 Bauer Dr., 07436, pg. 247 — PB

MULHERN BELTING, INC., 148 Bauer Dr., 07436, pg. 766 — PV

Robertet Fragrance, Inc., 125 Bauer Dr., 07436, pg. 1119 — IT

Robertet, Inc., 125 Bauer Dr., 07436, pg. 1119 — IT

Shiseido Cosmetics (America) Ltd., 178 Bauer Dr., 07436, pg. 235 — IT

Titan Tool, Inc., 107 Bauer Dr., 07436, pg. 500 — PV

Oceanport

Concurrent Computer Corporation, 2 Crescent Pl., 07757, pg. 430 — PB

Ogdensburg

Barenbrug Northeast, 150 Main St., 07439, pg. 167 — IT

Old Bridge

BLONDER-TONGUE LABORATORIES, INC., One Jake Brown Rd., 08857, pg. 237 — PB

Oldwick

A.M. BEST COMPANY, Ambest Rd., 08858, pg. 139 — PV

Oradell

Burns & Roe Construction Group Inc., 700 Kinderkamack Rd., 07649, pg. 187 — PV

BURNS & ROE ENTERPRISES, INC., 800 Kinderkamack Rd., 07649, pg. 187 — PV

Burns & Roe Services Corp., 700 Kinderkamack Rd., 07649, pg. 187 — PV

Wyle-Ginsbury Electronics, 660 Kinderkamack Rd., 07649, pg. 1458 — IT

Palmyra

PHILADELPHIA SIGN COMPANY, 707 W. Spring Garden St., 08065, pg. 861 — PV

Paramus

AT&T Wireless Services, 15 E. Midland Ave., 07652, pg. 11 — PB

BATCL-1987-I, Inc., 95 N. Route 17 S., 07653, pg. 202 — PB

BATCL-1987-III, Inc., 95 N. Route 17 S., 07653, pg. 202 — PB

BATCL-1987-II, Inc., 95 N. Route 17 S., 07653, pg. 202 — PB

BATCO-1989-II, Inc., 95 N. Route 17 S., 07653, pg. 202 — PB

Babies "R" Us, 461 From Rd., 07652, pg. 1626 — PB

Bell Atlantic Capital Corporation, 95 N. Rt. 17 South & Century Rd., 07653, pg. 202 — PB

Bell Atlantic Vehicle Management, Inc., 95 N. Route 17 S., 07653 pg. 203 — PB

Camerican International, 45 Eisenhower Dr., 07652, pg. 426 — PB

Card Technology Corp., 70 Eisenhower Dr., 07652, pg. 898 — IT

Consumer Sales Products Co., 15 Essex Rd., 07652, pg. 1281 — IT

Datascope FSC, Ltd., 580 Winters Ave., P.O. Box 5, 07653-0005, pg. 487 — PB

Datascope Holding Corp., 580 Winters Ave., 07653-0005, pg. 487 — PB

Datascope Investment Corp., 580 Winters Ave., P.O. Box 5, 07653-0005, pg. 487 — PB

Datascope Patient Monitoring Division, 580 Winters Ave., 07653, pg. 487 — PB

Dun & Bradstreet Software (Paramus), Mac Centre IV, 61 S. Paramus Rd., 07652, pg. 532 — IT

Einson Freeman Inc., 305 Rte. 17, 07652-2922, pg. 1483 — IT

Ericsson GE Mobile Communications Holding Inc., 15 E. Midland Ave., 07652, pg. 1365 — IT

Ericsson Mobile Data Inc., 15 E. Midland Ave., 07652, pg. 1365 — IT

Fuji Hunt Photographic Chemicals, Inc., Country Club Plaza, Bldg. 1F, W. 115 Century Road, 07652, pg. 524 — IT

Grosvenor Marketing Ltd., E. 210 Rte. 4, Ste. 102, 07652, pg. 92 — PV

Hanjin Co., Ltd., 80 E. Rte. 4 S., Ste. 490, 07652, pg. 592 — IT

Harvey Electronics, 556 Rt. 17N, 07652, pg. 797 — PB

Hewlett-Packard Company, 120 W. Century Rd., 07652, pg. 814 — PB

Ilford Inc., 70 W. Century Rd., 07652, pg. 904 — PB

Kids "R" Us, 461 From Road, 07652, pg. 1626 — PB

LEE MYLES ASSOCIATES CORPORATION, 140 Rte. 17 N., 07652, pg. 657 — PV

Letraset Nielsen & Bainbridge, 40 Eisenhower Dr., 07652, pg. 460 — IT

Lurgi Corporation, Country Club Plaza, W. 115 Century Rd., 07652, pg. 861 — IT

Metal Improvement Co., Ten Forest Ave., 07652, pg. 469 — PB

NCS Operations Center, Atrium E. 80 Rte. 4, 07652-2622, pg. 1155 — PB

Nielsen & Bainbridge, 40 Eisenhower Dr., 07653, pg. 460 — IT

Paramus Park, Inc., 700 Paramus Pk., 07652, pg. 1408 — PB

Patent Construction Systems, One Mack Centre Dr., 07652, pg. 793 — PB

Pfaff American Sales Corp., 610 Winters Ave., 07653, pg. 1046 — IT

Polaroid Corp. Research & Development - Technical & Industrial, W. 95 Century Rd., 07652-1407, pg. 1313 — PB

Roche Professional Service Centers, Inc., 685 N. State Rte. 17, 07652, pg. 1120 — IT

Simon & Schuster International & Business & Professional Group, 240 Frisch Ct., 07652, pg. 778 — PV

Ssangyong (U.S.A.) Inc., 115 W. Century Rd., 07652, pg. 1291 — IT

Stern's, Bergen Mall Shopping Ctr., Rte. 4, 07652, pg. 618 — PB

TOYS "R" US, INC., 461 From Rd., 07652, pg. 1626 — PB

Toys "R" Us International, 461 From Rd., 07652, pg. 1626 — PB

Toys "R" Us United States, 461 From Rd., 07652, pg. 1626 — PB

UJB Investor Services Company, 305 Rte. 17 S., 07652, pg. 1528 — PB

GEORGE UHE CO., INC., 12 Rte. 17 N., 07652, pg. 1115 — PV

United Jersey Bank Services Co, 295 Rte. 17 S., 07652, pg. 1528 — PB

Western Union Financial Services, Inc., One Mack Centre Dr., 07652, pg. 631 — PB

WIRELESS TELECOM GROUP, INC., E. 64 Midland Ave., 07652, pg. 1772 — PB

Yellow Book of New Jersey, Mack Center IV, S. 61 Paramus Rd., 07652, pg. 767 — PV

Park Ridge

Consumer Audio Products Co., Sony Dr., 07657, pg. 1281 — IT

Consumer Display Products Co., Sony Dr., 07656, pg. 1281 — IT

Consumer Video Products Co., Sony Dr., 07656, pg. 1281 — IT

Hertz Claim Management, 225 Brae Blvd., 07656, pg. 664 — PB

The Hertz Corporation, 225 Brae Blvd., 07656, pg. 664 — PB

Hertz Equipment Rental Corp., 225 Brae Blvd., 07656, pg. 664 — PB

Hertz Rent-A-Car, 225 Brae Blvd., 07656, pg. 664 — PB

Information Systems Co., Sony Dr., 07656, pg. 1281 — IT

International Paper Realty Corp., One Maynard Dr., 07656, pg. 904 — PB

Merit Behavioral Care Corp., One Maynard Dr., 07656, pg. 1036 — PB

NATIONAL UTILITY SERVICE, INC., One Maynard Dr., 07656, pg. 787 — PV

Sony Communications Products Co., Sony Dr., 07656, pg. 1281 — IT

Sony Electronics, One Sony Dr., 07656, pg. 1281 — IT

Sony Magnetic Products Co., Sony Dr., 07656, pg. 1281 — IT

Sony Service Co., Sony Dr., 07656, pg. 1281 — IT

Parsippany

ADT Diversified Services, Inc., 300 Interpace Pkwy., 07054, pg. 1649 — PB

Geographic Index-U.S.

ADT Security Systems Manufacturing, 300 Interpace Pkwy., 07054, pg. 1649 **PB**

ADT Security Systems Mid-South, 300 Interpace Pkwy., 07054, pg. 1649 **PB**

ADT Security Systems Mountain West, 300 Interpace Pkwy., 07054, pg. 1649 **PB**

ADT Security Systems Northeast, 300 Interpace Pkwy., 07054, pg. 1649 **PB**

ADT Security Systems West, 300 Interpace Pkwy., 07054, pg. 1649 **PB**

AT&T Networked Commerce Services, Morris Corp. Ctr. III, Bldg. 2, 400 Interpace Pkwy., 07054, pg. 11 **IT**

AT&T Strategy & New Service Innovations, Morris Corp. Ctr. III, Bldg. 2, 400 Interpace Pkwy., 07054, pg. 11 **PB**

AlliedSignal Amorphous Metals, 6 Eastmans Rd., 07054, pg. 51 **PB**

ALLSTATE CAN CORPORATION, One Wood Hallow Rd., 07054, pg. 44 **PB**

Artisan Electronics Corporation, Five Eastmans Rd., 07054, pg. 892 **IT**

Bayer Corporation, 99 Cherry Hill Rd., 07054, pg. 172 **IT**

Bell Atlantic Paging, 1719A Rte. 10,Ste.300, 07054, pg. 203 **PB**

Borg-Warner Protective Services Corporation, Two Campus Dr., 07054, pg. 245 **PB**

BUFFALO COLOR CORPORATION, 959 Rt. 46 E., Ste. 201, 07054, pg. 178 **PV**

Carbone-Lorraine North America, 14 Eastmans Road, 07054, pg. 1028 **IT**

Carbone of America, 14 Eastmans Road, 07054, pg. 1028 **IT**

Central Security Guards, Inc., 300 Interpace Pkwy., 07054, pg. 1649 **PB**

Century 21 Real Estate Corp., Six Sylvan Way, 07054, pg. 321 **PB**

The Chubb Institute, Eight Sylvan Way, 07054, pg. 355 **PB**

Citicorp Info Systems Research, 4 Sylvan Way, 07054-3801, pg. 378 **PB**

Coldwell Banker Real Estate Corporation, Six Sylvan Way, 07054, pg. 321 **PB**

CommonHealth USA, 30 Lanidex Plaza W., 07054, pg. 1483 **IT**

Constructive Communications, Inc., 300 Interpace Pkwy., 07054, pg. 1649 **PB**

Cyanamid International, One Campus Dr., 07054, pg. 79 **PB**

DRS TECHNOLOGIES, INC., Five Sylvan Way, 07054, pg. 474 **PB**

Days Inns of America, Inc., 339 Jefferson Rd., 07054, pg. 321 **PB**

EBI Medical Systems, Inc., P.O. Box 346, Six Upper Pond Rd., 07054-0346, pg. 231 **PB**

EBI Medical Systems, Inc., 3 Entin Rd., 07054, pg. 231 **PB**

EI Energy, Inc., One Upper Pond Rd., 07054-1149, pg. 695 **PB**

EI Power, Inc., One Upper Pond Rd., 07054-1149, pg. 695 **PB**

ERA Real Estate, Six Sylvan Way, 07054, pg. 321 **PB**

ELECTRONIC DRIVES AND CONTROLS, 17 Eastmans Rd., 07054, pg. 370 **PV**

EMERSON RADIO CORP., Nine Entin Rd., 07054, pg. 578 **PB**

Energy Initiatives, Inc., One Upper Pond Rd., 07054-1050, pg. 695 **PB**

Thomas G. Ferguson Associates, Inc., 30 Lanidex Plaza W., 07054-2792, pg. 1483 **IT**

Ferraz Corporation, 14 Eastmans Rd., 07054, pg. 1028 **IT**

Fireman's Fund Indemnity Corporation, 35 Waterview Blvd., 4th Fl., 07054, pg. 59 **IT**

Fireman's Fund Insurance Co. of New Jersey, 35 Waterview Blvd., 4th Fl., 07054, pg. 59 **IT**

Fleischmann Company, Seven Sylvan Way, 07054, pg. 1355 **PB**

GAB Robins North America, Inc., Nine Campus Dr., Ste. 7, 07054, pg. 1153 **IT**

GPU Electric, Inc., One Upper Pond Rd., 07054-1050, pg. 695 **PB**

GPU International, Inc., One Upper Pond Rd., 07054-1050, pg. 695 **PB**

GPU Nuclear Corp., One Upper Pond Rd., 07054-1050, pg. 695 **PB**

GPU Power, Inc., One Upper Pond Rd., 07054-1050, pg. 695 **PB**

GPU Service Corp., 100 Interpace Pkwy., 07054-1149, pg. 695 **PB**

General Chemical Corporation, 90 E. Halsey Rd., 07054, pg. 707 **PB**

General Chemical (Soda Ash) Partners, 90 E. Halsey Rd., 07054, pg. 1407 **IT**

GLOBAL TURNKEY SYSTEMS INC., 20 Waterview Blvd., 3rd Fl., 07054, pg. 457 **PV**

M.H. GREENEBAUM, INC., Ste. 303, Seven Century Dr., 07054, pg. 477 **PV**

HFS, Incorporated, Six Sylvan Way, 07054, pg. 321 **PB**

Harrison Wilson & Associates, Morris Corporate Ctr. 111, 400 Interpace Pkwy., 07054, pg. 1224 **PB**

Hewlett-Packard Company, Ten Sylvan Way, 07054, pg. 814 **PB**

Horizons Consulting Inc., 119 Cherry Hill Rd., 07054, pg. 421 **PB**

INS Investigations Bureau, Inc., Nine Campus Dr., 07054, pg. 1153 **IT**

Intermodal Transportation Services, Inc., Nine Campus Dr., 07054, pg. 1153 **PB**

International Home Foods Inc., 1633 Littleton Rd., 07054, pg. 526 **PV**

International Marine Underwriters of New England, Inc., Six Sylvan Way, 07054, pg. 1784 **PB**

Jani King of New Jersey, Inc., 32 Rte. 46W., 07054, pg. 582 **PB**

Knights Franchise Systems, Inc., 339 Jefferson Rd., 07054, pg. 321 **PB**

Koch Otto H. York Co., Inc., 42 Intervale Rd., 07054-0918, pg. 628 **PB**

LifeSavers Company, Four Gatehall Dr., 07054, pg. 1355 **PB**

LINEAR DYNAMICS INC., 400 Lanidex Plaza 07054, pg. 668 **PV**

MDL Information Systems-Eastern Sales, One Sylvan Way, Ste. 120, 07054, pg. 1100 **IT**

MCBEE SYSTEMS, INC., 299 Cherry Hill Rd., 07054, pg. 718 **PV**

Milgray/New Jersey, 3799 Rte. 46 E., 07054, pg. 206 **PB**

Nabisco Inc., Seven Campus Dr., 07054, pg. 1355 **PB**

The North River Insurance Company, 6 Sylvan Way, 07054, pg. 1784 **PB**

Oriental Motor U.S.A. Corp, 9 Sylvan Way, Ste. 275, 07054, pg. 1008 **IT**

Owens Corning/Foamular, Three Century Dr., 07054, pg. 1237 **PB**

PNY TECHNOLOGIES, INC., 299 Webro Rd.Ave., 07054, pg. 827 **PV**

Polypure Rhone-Poulenc, 1 Gatehall Dr., 07054, pg. 1110 **IT**

SAMUEL SPECIALTY METALS, 600 Parsippany Rd., 07054, pg. 964 **PV**

Silver Burdett Division, 299 Jefferson Rd., 07054, pg. 778 **PB**

Silver Burdett Ginn, P.O. Box 480, 299 Jefferson Rd., 07054-0480, pg. 778 **PB**

Simon & Schuster Elementary Division, 299 Jefferson Rd., 07054-0480, pg. 778 **PB**

Six Flags Theme Parks Inc., 400 Interpace Pkwy., Bldg. C, 3rd Fl., 07054, pg. 1611 **PB**

Sordoni Skanska Construction Co., Morris Corp. Center, Bldg. C, 400 Interpace Pkwy., 07054, pg. 1261 **IT**

Specialty Products Co., Seven Sylvan Way, 07054, pg. 1355 **PB**

Sterling Electronics, 1259 Rte. 46 E., Bldg. 3, 07054, pg. 1052 **PB**

Strategic Outsourcing Services Inc., 119 Cherry Hill Rd., 07054, pg. 421 **PB**

Tenney Environmental, 1719 Rte. 10 E., Ste. 301, 07054, pg. 1077 **PV**

Torre Lazur/Weber Healthcare Public Relations, 20 Waterview Blvd., 07054, pg. 1157 **IT**

UC Industries, Inc., Three Century Dr., 07054, pg. 1237 **PB**

VDM Technologies Corp., P.O. Box 362, Ten Sylvan Way, 07054, pg. 509 **IT**

Valley National Bank, 800 Rte. 46, Arlington Shopping Plaza, 07054, pg. 1705 **PB**

Wise Foods, Inc., Eight Campus Dr., 07054, pg. 157 **PV**

Passaic

Apex International, Inc., 100 Eighth St., 07055, pg. 1720 **PB**

M. GROSSMAN & SON, INC., 245 Fourth St., 07055, pg. 483 **PV**

HERCULES CHEMICAL CO., INC., 111 South St., 07055-9100, pg. 523 **PV**

MELARD MANUFACTURING CORPORATION, 153 Linden St., 07055, pg. 729 **PV**

UNIFOIL CORPORATION, 217 Brook Ave., 07055, pg. 1117 **PV**

Paterson

ACCURATE BOX CO., INC., 86 Fifth Ave., 07509, pg. 11 **PV**

Axelrod Foods, Inc., 104 Thomas St., 07509, pg. 752 **IT**

Biocraft Non-Penicillin Plant, 209 McLean Blvd., 07504, pg. 1381 **PB**

Daicolor-Pope, Inc., 33 Sixth Ave., 07524, pg. 369 **IT**

DOUGLAS STEPHEN PLASTICS, INC., 22-36 Green St., 07501, pg. 341 **PV**

Filmco Industries Inc., 100 5th Ave., 07524, pg. 1081 **PV**

MMG North America Inc., 126 Pennsylvania Ave., 07503-2512, pg. 1344 **IT**

MONA INDUSTRIES, INC., 76 E. 24th St., 07544-0425, pg. 756 **PV**

Morton Chemical Div., 335 McLean Blvd., 07510, pg. 1135 **PB**

PAXAR Woven Labels, 500 E. 35 St., 07509, pg. 1266 **PB**

Power Plastics Inc., 155 Sherman Ave., 07502, pg. 1086 **PV**

SUPREMA SPECIALTIES, INC., 510 E. 35th St., 07543, pg. 1541 **PB**

THERMWELL PRODUCTS CO., INC., 150 E. Seventh St., 07524, pg. 1081 **PV**

TIFFANY EXTRUDERS, INC., 155 Sherman Ave., 07502, pg. 1085 **PV**

Paulsboro

Lilly Industries, Inc., Mid Atlantic Park, 1991 Nolte Dr., RD # 1, 08066, pg. 994 **PB**

Paulsboro Terminal, Third St. & Billingsport Rd., 08066, pg. 692 **PB**

Peapack

Beneficial Insurance Group, Inc., 400 Beneficial Ctr., 07977, pg. 211 **PB**

Beneficial Management Corporation, 200 Beneficial Ctr., 07977, pg. 211 **PB**

Beneficial Tax Masters Inc., 200 Beneficial Ctr., 07977, pg. 211 **PB**

Beneficial Technology Corporation, 500 Beneficial Ctr., 07977, pg. 211 **PB**

The Central National Life Insurance Co. of Omaha, Inc., 400 Beneficial Ctr., 07977, pg. 211 **PB**

KOMLINE-SANDERSON ENGINEERING CORP., 12 Holland Ave., 07977, pg. 631 **PV**

Pennington

Eclipse Combustion, Inc., 320 Sked St., 08534, pg. 360 **PV**

New Jersey National Bank, 370 Scotch Rd., 08650, pg. 447 **PB**

Pegasus International Corporation, Straube Center, 114 W. Franklin Ave., 08534, pg. 1046 **PV**

STRAUBE REGIONAL CENTER LLC, F-106 W. Franklin Ave., 08534, pg. 1046 **PV**

Penns Grove

Van Leeuwen Pipe & Tube Corp., 130 N. Virginia Avenue, 08069, pg. 1450 **IT**

Pennsauken

ADR, Inc., 9285 Commerce Hwy., 08110, pg. 1627 **PB**

Cooper River Convalescent Center, 5101 N. Park Dr., 08109, pg. 729 **PB**

Copelco Financial Services Group Inc., 1700 Suckle Plaza, 08110, pg. 694 **IT**

Curtis Circulation Company, 2500 McClellan Ave., 08109, pg. 794 **IT**

Hachette Distribution Inc., 2500 McClellan Ave., 08109, pg. 794 **IT**

HOLMAN ENTERPRISES, 7411 Maple Ave., 08109, pg. 535 **PV**

HONICKMAN AFFILIATES, 8275 Rte. 130, 08110, pg. 537 **PV**

J & J Snack Foods Corp., 6000 Central Hwy., 08109, pg. 916 **PB**

J & J Snack Foods Corp. of New Jersey, 6000 Central Hwy., 08109, pg. 916 **PB**

J & J Snack Foods Corp. of Pennsylvania, 6000 Central Hwy., 08109, pg. 916 **PB**

J & J SNACK FOODS CORPORATION, 6000 Central Hwy., 08109, pg. 916 **PB**

J & J Snack Foods Sales Corp., 6000 Central Hwy., 08109, pg. 916 **PB**

J & J Snack Foods Transport Corp., 6000 Central Hwy., 08109, pg. 916 **PB**

Lehigh Press Lithographers, 7001 N. Park Dr., 08109, pg. 659 **PB**

MEDIQ Diagnostic Centers, One Mediq Plaza, 08110, pg. 1081 **PB**

MEDIQ INCORPORATED, One MEDIQ Plaza, 08110-1460, pg. 1081 **PB**

MEDIQ Management Services, Inc., One Mediq Plaza, 08110, pg. 1081 **PB**

MEDIQ Management Services, Inc., One MEDIQ Plaza, 08110, pg. 1081 **PB**

MEDIQ/PRN Life Support Services, Inc., One MEDIQ Plaza, 08110, pg. 1081 **PB**

MENU FOODS, INC., 9130 Griffith Morgan Ln., 08110, pg. 731 **PV**

PHOTOTYPE COLOR GRAPHICS, INC., 7890 Airport Hwy., 08109, pg. 864 **PV**

PRIMESOURCE CORPORATION, 4350 Haddonfield Rd., Ste. 222, 08109, pg. 1329 **PB**

Pennsville

Polar Material Inc., Industrial Hwy., 08070, pg. 68 **IT**

Pequannock

BEL-ART PRODUCTS, Six Industrial Rd., 07440-1992, pg. 130 **PV**

D & S Marketing, 6 Industrial Rd., 07440-1992, pg. 130 **PV**

Maddak Inc., 6 Industrial Rd., 07440, pg. 130 **PV**

Perth Amboy

Broad National Bank-Perth Amboy, 365 Convery Plaza, 08861, pg. 258 **PB**

PSG, 1000 Convery Blvd., 08862, pg. 1774 **PB**

SCHOTT BROTHERS, INC., 358 Lehigh Ave., 08861, pg. 972 **PV**

Phillipsburg

Care Center of Lopatcong, 390 Red School Ln., 08865, pg. 729 **PB**

Care Center of Phillipsburg, 843 Wilbur Ave., 08865, pg. 729 **PB**

Mallinckrodt Baker Inc., 222 Red School Ln., 08865, pg. 1039 **PB**

Northern Division, 1099 River Rd., 08865, pg. 438 **PB**

OPT Industries, Inc., 300 Red School Ln., 08865, pg. 1624 **PB**

ORBEL CORPORATION, 150 Anderson St., 08865, pg. 819 **PV**

Pump Repair Centers, 942 Memorial Pkwy., 08865, pg. 877 **PB**

Zappa Plastics, 165 Howard St., 08865, pg. 172 **PV**

Pine Brook

Arrow/Schweber Electronics, 43 Route 46 East, 07058, pg. 134 **PB**

Geographic Index-U.S.

Bergen Brunswig Drug Company, Rte. 80 at Hook Mountain Rd., 07056, pg. 214 **PB**

Binks Manufacturing Company, One Chapin Rd., 07058-9719, pg. 229 **PB**

EINSTEIN MOOMJY INC., I-80 And New Maple Ave., 07058, pg. 366 **PV**

MacGREGOR (USA) Inc., P.O. Box 708, 07058, pg. 670 **IT**

MiniData Services, Inc., P.O. Box 2021, 34 Maple Ave., 07058, pg. 331 **PB**

T-Fal Corporation, 25 Riverside Dr., 07058, pg. 568 **IT**

Villeroy & Boch (USA) Inc., P.O. Box 249, 07058, pg. 1468 **IT**

Piscataway

Allied Security Inc., 501 Hoe Lane, Ste. 105, 08854, pg. 40 **PV**

American Natl. Can Co., 287 S. Randolphville Rd., 08854, pg. 1029 **IT**

AMERICAN STANDARD INC., One Centennial Ave., P.O. Box 6820, 08855-6820, pg. 91 **PB**

CSD, Inc., 55 Knightsbridge Rd., 08854, pg. 1053 **IT**

CAPTIVE PLASTICS, 251 Circle Dr., N., 08854, pg. 207 **PV**

Continental International Life Insurance Co., 15 Corporate Pl. S., 08854, pg. 1700 **PB**

Continental National Life Insurance Co., 15 Corporate Pl. S., 08854, pg. 1700 **PB**

DAQ ELECTRONICS INC., 262-B Old New Brunswick Road, 08854-3756, pg. 300 **PV**

ENZON, INC., 20 Kingsbridge Rd., 08854-3998, pg. 587 **PB**

Enzon, Inc., 20 Kingsbridge Rd., 08854, pg. 588 **PB**

Hapag-Lloyd (America), Inc., 399 Hoes Lane, 08854, pg. 596 **IT**

Hewlett-Packard Company, 20 New England Ave., W., 08854, pg. 814 **PB**

Hoxan America Incorporated, One Centennial Plaza, 3rd Fl., 08854, pg. 363 **IT**

ITW Thielex Plastics Corp., 201 11th St., 08854, pg. 867 **PB**

Johnson & Johnson Health Care Systems Inc., P.O. Box 6800, 425 Hoes Ln., 08855-6800, pg. 928 **PB**

The Kendall-Betham Division, 201 Circle Dr., 08854, pg. 1647 **PB**

New York Representative Office, One Centennial Plaza, 08854, pg. 363 **IT**

Pharmacia & Upjohn Biotech Inc., 800 Centennial Ave., 08854, pg. 1047 **PB**

Pharmacia & Upjohn Corporate Services, 800 Centennial Ave., 08855-1327, pg. 1049 **PB**

Pharmacia & Upjohn U.S. Inc., 800 Centennial Ave., 08855, pg. 1049 **PB**

RHEOMETRIC SCIENTIFIC, One Possumtown Rd., 08854, pg. 1387 **PB**

A. Schulman, Inc., 144B Carlton Ave., 08854, pg. 1441 **PB**

U.S. Fuji Electric, Inc., 240 Circle Dr. N., 08854, pg. 522 **IT**

WELDOTRON CORPORATION, 1532 S. Washington Ave., 08855, pg. 1752 **PB**

Western Union International, Inc., 201 Cenntennial Ave., 08854, pg. 1024 **PB**

Pitman

K-Tron America, Inc., Routes 55 & 553, 08071, pg. 938 **PB**

K-Tron Institute, Routes 55 & 553, 08071, pg. 938 **PB**

K-TRON INTERNATIONAL, INC., P.O. Box 888, Rtes. 55 & 553, 08071-0888, pg. 938 **PB**

Plainfield

INJECTRON CORPORATION, 1000 S. Second St., 07063, pg. 563 **PV**

Plainsboro

Bristol-Myers Squibb U.S. Pharmaceutical Group, 777 Scudder's Mill Rd., 08536, pg. 255 **PB**

Firmenich Incorporated, Plainsboro Rd., 08536, pg. 486 **IT**

Merrill Lynch Bank & Trust Co., 800 Scudders Mill Rd., 08536, pg. 1097 **PB**

Merrill Lynch Business Financial Services Inc., 800 Scudders Mill Rd., 08536, pg. 1098 **PB**

Merrill Lynch Insurance Group, Inc., 800 Scudders Mill Rd., 08536, pg. 1098 **PB**

Merrill Lynch Investment Management, Inc., 800 Scudders Mill Rd., 08536, pg. 1098 **PB**

Merrill Lynch Life Agency Inc., 800 Scudder Mill Rd., 08536, pg. 1098 **PB**

Pleasantville

ATE Investment, Inc., 6801 Black Horse Pike, 08232, pg. 430 **PB**

Atlantic Electric Co., 6801 Black Horse Pike, 08232, pg. 430 **PB**

Atlantic Energy Technology, Inc., 1199 Black Horse Pike, 08232, pg. 430 **PB**

Atlantic Generation, Inc., 6801 Blackhorse Pike, 08232, pg. 430 **PB**

Atlantic Southern Properties, Inc., 1199 Black Horse Pike, 08232, pg. 430 **PB**

Atlantic Thermal Systems, Inc., 6801 Black Horse Pike, 08232, pg. 430 **PB**

Citation Plastics, Co., 1130 Black Horse Pike, 08232, pg. 1755 **PB**

Deepwater Operating Co., 6801 Black Horse Pike, 08232, pg. 430 **PB**

Ireland Coffee Tea, Inc., Eight Canale Dr., 08232, pg. 351 **PB**

PETER LUMBER COMPANY, E. Washington Ave. & Lyons Ct., 08232, pg. 856 **PV**

Point Pleasant Beach

CHEFS INTERNATIONAL, INC., 62 Broadway, 08742, pg. 343 **PB**

Pompton Lakes

ROYLE SYSTEMS GROUP, 1000 Cannonball Rd., 07442, pg. 949 **PV**

Pompton Plains

Cutter Biologicals, 933 Rte. 23, 07444-1039, pg. 174 **IT**

EDWARDS ENGINEERING CORPORATION, 101 Alexander Ave., 07444, pg. 365 **PV**

Port Reading

ALLIED OLD ENGLISH, INC., 100 Markley St., 07064, pg. 39 **PV**

Princeton

ABB Energy Ventures Inc., 202 Carnegie Ctr., Ste. 100, 08540, pg. 4 **IT**

Advanced Television Technology Center, 202 Carnegie Ctr., Ste. 102, 08540, pg. 1405 **IT**

American Re Corporation, 555 College Rd. East, 08543, pg. 897 **IT**

American Re-Insurance Company, 555 College Rd. East, 08543, pg. 897 **IT**

Arm & Hammer Consumer Products, 469 N. Harrison St., CN 5297, 08543-5297, pg. 356 **PB**

Armand Products Company, 469 N. Harrison St., 08543-5297, pg. 356 **PB**

Bell Atlantic Education Services, Inc., 104 Carnegie Center, 08540, pg. 202 **PB**

Bell Atlanticom Systems, Inc., 105 Carnegie Center, Alexander Rd. & U.S. Rt. 1, 08540, pg. 203 **PB**

BERLITZ INTERNATIONAL, INC., 400 Alexander Park, 08540, pg. 221 **PB**

Bracco Diagnostics, Inc., 107 College Rd., E., 08540, pg. 210 **IT**

Bracco Research, Inc., 305 College Rd., E., 08540, pg. 210 **IT**

Bristol-Myers Pharmaceutical Research & Development Division, Rte. 206 Province Line Rd., 08540, pg. 254 **PB**

Bristol-Myers Squibb International, Rte. 206 Province Line Rd., 08540, pg. 254 **PB**

CABLE MICHIGAN, INC., 105 Carnegie Ctr., 08540, pg. 287 **PB**

Carter-Wallace International Div., Two Research Way, 08540-6628, pg. 310 **PB**

CHURCH & DWIGHT CO., INC., 469 N. Harrison St., 08543-5297, pg. 355 **PB**

Church & Dwight Specialty Products Division, 469 N. Harrison St., CN 5297, 08540 -5297, pg. 356 **PB**

Commonwealth Communications, 105 Carnegie Ctr., 08540, pg. 1354 **PB**

ComVideo Systems, Inc./N.J., 105 Carnegie Ctr., 08540, pg. 1354 **PB**

COVANCE, INC., 210 Carnegie Ctr., 08540, pg. 453 **PB**

Custodial Trust Company, 101 Carnegie Center, 08540, pg. 198 **PB**

CYTOGEN CORPORATION, 600 College Rd., E., 08540, pg. 471 **PB**

DATARAM CORPORATION, P.O. Box 7528, 08543-7528, pg. 487 **PB**

Dataram International Sales Corp., Rte. 571, Princeton Rd., 08543-7528, pg. 487 **PB**

Dow Jones Financial News Services, P.O. Box 300, 08543, pg. 524 **PB**

Dow Jones Interactive, Box 300, 08540, pg. 524 **PB**

Dow Jones Interactive Publishing, P.O. Box 300, 08540, pg. 524 **PB**

ENVIRON Corporation, 214 Carnegie Center, 08540, pg. 1285 **PB**

G.E. American Communications, Inc., Four Research Way, 08540, pg. 711 **PB**

Gillespie Public Relations, P.O. Box 3333, 08543, pg. 454 **PV**

INTERPOOL, INC., 211 College Rd. E., 08540, pg. 908 **PB**

Korn/Ferry International, 1 Palmer Square, Ste. 330, 08542, pg. 633 **PV**

Korn/Ferry International, One Palmer Sq., Ste. 330, 08542, pg. 633 **PV**

Lambert-Kay Div., Research Way, P.O. Box 1418, 08512 0187, pg. 310 **PB**

Laporte Inc., 22 Chambers St., 08542, pg. 802 **IT**

THE LIPOSOME COMPANY, INC., One Research Way, 08540, pg. 1000 **PB**

Lucent Technologies Engineering Research Center, P.O. Box 900, 08542-0900, pg. 1018 **IT**

Manchem Inc., Princeton Forrestal Center, 105 College Rd. E., 08540, pg. 1110 **IT**

Martin Marietta Astro Space, P.O. Box 800, 08543, pg. 1007 **PB**

Mobil Research and Development Corporation, P.O. Box 1031, 08543-1031, pg. 1118 **PB**

Monitor Capital Advisors Inc., 504 Carnegie Center, 08540, pg. 795 **PV**

NEC Research Institute, Inc., 4 Independence Way, 08540, pg. 900 **IT**

National Business Employment Weekly, P.O. Box 300, 08543-0300, pg. 524 **PB**

Novo Nordisk Pharmaceuticals, Inc., 100 Overlook Center, Ste. 200, 08540-7810, pg. 987 **IT**

Nycomed Amersham, 101 Carnegie Ctr., 08540, pg. 993 **IT**

PETERSON'S GUIDES, INC., 202 Carnegie Ctr., 08540, pg. 858 **PV**

Pfeiffer of America, Inc., 12 Roszel Rd., Ste. C104, 08540, pg. 125 **PB**

Princeton Gamma-Tech, Inc., 1200 State Rd., 08540, pg. 1015 **PB**

PRINCETON UNIVERSITY PRESS, 41 William St., 08540-5237, pg. 885 **PV**

RCN CORPORATION, 105 Carnegie Ctr., 08540, pg. 1354 **PB**

RCN Long Distance, 105 Carnegie Ctr., 08540, pg. 1354 **PB**

Rhone-Poulenc Inc., CN 5266, 08543-5266, pg. 1112 **IT**

Sarnoff Corporation, 201 Washington Rd., P.O. Box 5300, 08543, pg. 958 **IT**

Singapore Airlines Ltd., Five Independence Way, Ste. 310, 08540, pg. 1374 **IT**

Sovereign Bank of Princeton, 188 Nassau St., 08542, pg. 1494 **PB**

THE SPENCER GROUP INC., 104 Carnegie Ctr., Ste. 210 CN5320, 08540, pg. 1025 **PV**

The Squibb Institute for Medical Research, Rte. 206 Province Line Rd., 08540, pg. 254 **PB**

SUMMIT BANCORP, 301 Carnegie Ctr., 08543, pg. 1527 **PB**

Takeda America, Inc., Ste. 207, 101 Carnegie Ctr., 08540, pg. 1350 **IT**

TOTAL RESEARCH CORPORATION, Five Independence Way - CN5305, 08543-5305, pg. 1625 **PV**

UST Securities Corp., Five Vaughn Dr., CN 5209, 08543, pg. 1688 **PB**

United Jersey Credit Life Insurance Company, 301 Carnegie Ctr., 08543, pg. 1528 **PB**

United Jersey Leasing Company, 301 Carnegie Ctr., 08543-2066, pg. 1528 **PB**

United Jersey Venture Capital, Inc., 301 Carnegie Center, 08543, pg. 1528 **PB**

Villeroy & Boch Tableware, Ltd., Five Vaughn Dr., Ste. 303, 08540, pg. 1468 **IT**

WECHCO, INC., 1000 Herrontown Rd., 08540, pg. 1158 **PV**

West Chemical Products, Inc., 1000 Herrontown Rd., 08540, pg. 1158 **PV**

Princeton Junction

McLean Engineering, 70 Washington Rd., 08550, pg. 1791 **PB**

Prospect Park

THE HABAND CO., 100 Fairview Ave., 07530, pg. 492 **PB**

Rahway

Astra/Merck Group, 126 E. Lincoln Ave., 07065, pg. 1091 **PB**

CARDINAL INC., 1421 Pinewood St., 07065, pg. 208 **PV**

Concord Miniatures, 1421 Pinewood Street, 07065, pg. 209 **PB**

DRI-PRINT FOILS INC., 329 New Brunswick Ave., 07065, pg. 343 **PV**

ENSI, Inc., 937 E. Hazelwood Ave., Bldg. 2, 07065, pg. 546 **PB**

Environmental Services of America, Inc., 937 E. Hazelwood Ave., Bldg. 2, 07065, pg. 546 **PB**

GAFFNEY-KROESE ELECTRICAL SUPPLY CORP., 1697 Elizabeth Ave., 07065, pg. 437 **PV**

Gaffney-Kroese Electrical Supply Corp., 1697 Elizabeth Ave., 07065, pg. 437 **PV**

ISFEL COMPANY, INC., 900 Hart St., 07065, pg. 576 **PV**

Laminaire Corporation, 960 E. Hazelwood Ave., 07065, pg. 1596 **PB**

Merck Human Health Division, P.O. Box 2000, 07065, pg. 1090 **PB**

Merck Manufacturing Div., 126 E. Lincoln Ave., 07065, pg. 1091 **PB**

Merck Research Laboratories, 126 E. Lincoln Ave., 07065, pg. 1091 **PB**

Merck Sharp & Dohme (Argentina), Inc., 126 E. Lincoln Ave., 07065, pg. 1091 **PB**

Merck Sharp & Dohme (Europe), Inc., 126 E. Lincoln Ave., 07065, pg. 1091 **PB**

Merck Sharp & Dohme (Greece) Inc., 126 E. Lincoln Ave., 07065, pg. 1091 **PB**

Merck Sharp & Dohme (I.A.) Corp., 126 E. Lincoln Ave., 07065, pg. 1091 **PB**

Merck Sharp & Dohme Scientific & Management Corp., 126 E. Lincoln Ave., 07065, pg. 1091 **PB**

Merck Vaccine Division, 126 E. Lincoln Ave., 07065, pg. 1091 **PB**

SDI TECHNOLOGIES INC., 1299 Main St., 07065-0901, pg. 956 **PV**

THERMO-MIZER ENVIRONMENTAL CORP., 960 E. Hazelwood Ave., 07065, pg. 1596 **PB**

Ramsey

BMW of North America, Inc.-Eastern Region, 535 E. Crescent Ave., 07446, pg. 177 IT
Bogen Communications, Inc., 50 Spring St., 07446, pg. 739 PB
CAPINTEC INC., Six Arrow Rd., 07446, pg. 205 PV
Colorforms, 133 Williams Dr., 07446, pg. 1625 PB
Melru Corporation, 19 Specor Rd., Ste. 303, 07446, pg. 933 PB
Minolta Corporation, 101 Williams Dr., 07446, pg. 869 IT
THE OKONITE COMPANY, 102 Hilltop Rd., 07446, pg. 813 PV
Werner & Pfleiderer Corporation, 663 E. Crescent Ave., 07446, pg. 511 IT

Rancocas

Inductotherm Corp., 10 Indel Ave., 08073, pg. 560 PV
INDUCTOTHERM INDUSTRIES, INC., Ten Indel Ave., 08073-0157, pg. 560 PV
Tech-Tran Corporation, 50 Indel Ave., 08073, pg. 560 PV

Randolph

Cirrus Diagnostics Inc., 111 Canfield Ave., 07869, pg. 505 PB
JOHN DUSENBERY CO., INC., 220 Franklin Rd., 07869, pg. 349 PV

Raritan

R.W. Johnson Pharmaceutical Research Institute, P.O. Box 300, 920 U.S. Rte. 202, 08869-0602, pg. 928 PB
Ortho Biotech Inc., P.O. Box 670, 700 U.S. Rte. 202 S., 08869-0670, pg. 929 PB
Ortho Clinical Diagnostic Systems Inc., P.O. Box 350, 1001 U.S. Rte. 202, 08869-0606, pg. 929 PB
United Foam Plastics Corporation, One Johnson Dr., 08869-1651, pg. 1112 PV

Red Bank

Carlisle Insurance Company, 200 Schulz Dr., 07701, pg. 1046 PB
GRANUM COMMUNICATIONS, 125 Half Mile Rd., Ste. 200, 07701, pg. 470 PV
HOVNANIAN ENTERPRISES, INC., 10 Hwy. 35, P.O. Box 500, 07701, pg. 843 PB
K. Hovnanian Investment Properties, Inc., 225 Hwy. 35, 07701, pg. 843 PB
Investors Insurance Company of America, 12 Schulz Dr., 07701, pg. 1046 PB
Quest Diagnostic-Red Bank, 11 Globe Ct., 07701, pg. 1351 PB
RUSSELL-STANLEY CORPORATION, 230 Half Mile Rd., 07701, pg. 953 PV
Stinnes Interoil Inc., 151 Bodman Pl., 07701, pg. 1459 IT

Ridgefield

Amalgamet, Inc., Hudson Ave., P.O. Box 296, 07657, pg. 1071 IT
ChaseMellon Shareholder Services, L.L.C., 85 Challenger Rd., 07660, pg. 1085 PB
Lowe Paper Co., 1050 River Rd., 07657, pg. 1000 PV
McHutchinson Div., 695 Grand Ave., 07657, pg. 973 IT
Monarch Industries, Inc., 686 Grand Ave., 07657, pg. 153 PB
NEUMAN DISTRIBUTORS, INC., 175 Railroad Ave., 07657, pg. 1169 PB
TR-Metro Chem, Inc., P.O. Box 376, Hudson Ave., 07657-0376, pg. 1071 IT
Western Waterproofing Co. of America, Inc., 720 Grand Ave., 07657, pg. 1165 PV

Ridgefield Park

CRYSTAL CLEAR INDUSTRIES, P.O. Box 60, 07660, pg. 293 PV
DSM Chemie Linz North America Inc., 65 Challenger Rd., 07660, pg. 356 IT
Daewoo International America Corp. - Ridgefield, 85 Challenger Rd., 07660-2114, pg. 357 IT
Degussa Corporation, 65 Challenger Rd., 07660, pg. 388 IT
MOBILECOMM, 65 Challenger Rd., 07660, pg. 1120 PB
Samsung Electronics America, Inc., 105 Challenger Road, 07660, pg. 1183 PB
Samsung Electronics North America Inc., 105 Challenger Rd., 07660, pg. 1183 IT
UJB Discount Brokerage, 55 Challenger Rd., 07660, pg. 1528 PB

Ridgewood

BolsWessanen USA, Inc., Third Floor E., 1200 East Ridgewood Ave., 07450, pg. 752 IT
CHIPWICH INC., 215 Chestnut St., Ste. C, 07450, pg. 237 PV
Community Energy Alternatives Incorporated, 1200 E. Ridgewood Ave., 07450, pg. 1340 PB
Swiss Life International Services, 1200 E. Ridgewood Ave., 07450, pg. 1332 IT

River Edge

Det Norske Veritas-North & Central America, 70 Grand Ave., 07661, pg. 396 IT
GLOBE MORTGAGE AMERICA, LLC., 70 Grand Ave., 07661-1935, pg. 458 PV
HALOCARBON PRODUCTS CORP., 887 Kinderkamack Rd., 07661, pg. 496 PV
Harte-Hanks Marketing Services, 65 Rte. 4, 07661, pg. 794 PB
HUFFMAN KOOS, 1001 Main St., 07661, pg. 546 PV

Riverdale

Richard Hirschmann of America, Inc., Industrial Row, P.O. Box 229, 07457, pg. 1108 IT

Riverton

Hoeganaes Corp., River Rd. & Taylors Lane, 08077, pg. 893 PB

Robbinsville

Polaris Packaging Inc., 15 Marlen Dr., 08691, pg. 1486 PB

Rochelle Park

Alco Gravure Industries, Inc., 50 Essex St., 07662, pg. 1076 IT
GENERAL OFFICE ENVIRONMENTS INC., 18 Railroad Ave., 07662, pg. 445 PV
Saab Systems, Inc., 201 West Passaic St., 07662, pg. 687 PB
UNITED RETAIL GROUP, INC., 365 W. Passaic St., 07662, pg. 1679 PB

Rockaway

Action Rockaway, 18-32 Green Pond Rd., 07866, pg. 15 PB
ACTION TECHNOLOGY COMPANY, 18 Green Pond Rd., 07866, pg. 15 PV
Edy's Northeast Region, 301 Roundhill Dr., 07866, pg. 529 PB
MCWILLIAMS FORGE CO., Franklin Ave., 07866, pg. 725 PV
Multi-Arc Inc., 200 Roundhill Dr., 07866, pg. 1198 IT
Warner-Chilcott Laboratories, Inc., Rockaway Corporate Center 80, 100 Enterprise Dr., 07866, pg. 436 PB

Rockleigh

Barnes & Noble Direct, One Pond Rd., 07647, pg. 189 PB
Huls America Plastics Division, 10 Link Drive, 07647, pg. 1455 IT
OPTIMAXX INTERNATIONAL, 10 Volvo Dr., 07647, pg. 818 PV
Volvo Cars of North America, Inc., Bldg. A, Volvo Dr., 07647, pg. 1477 IT
Volvo North America Parts Operations Div., P. O. Box 930, Bldg. D, 07647, pg. 1477 IT

Roseland

Amano Cincinnati, Inc., 140 Harrison Ave., 07068, pg. 70 IT
Amano Partners U.S.A. Inc. (A.P.U.), 140 Harrison Ave., 07068, pg. 71 IT
American Bobst Holdings, Inc., 07068, pg. 198 IT
American Safety Technologies, Inc., 655 Eagle Rock Ave., 07068, pg. 892 IT
ANNIN & COMPANY, One Annin Dr., 07068, pg. 73 PV
AUTOMATIC DATA PROCESSING, INC., One ADP Blvd., 07068, pg. 150 PB
B&G FOODS, INC., 426 Eagle Rock Ave., 07068, pg. 105 PB
Bellemead Development Corp., 280 Corporate Ctr., Four Becker Farm Rd., 07068, pg. 355 PB
Bobst Equipment Finance Co., 146 Harrison Ave., 07068, pg. 198 IT
Bobst Group Inc., 146 Harrison Ave., 07068, pg. 198 IT
Trutrac, Inc., 140 Harrison Ave., 07068-1239, pg. 71 IT

Roselle

ROSELLE PAPER CO., INC., 615 E. First Ave., 07203, pg. 945 PV

Rutherford

F-M Tower Company, 201 Rt. 17 N., 07070, pg. 1180 PB
FC New York, Inc., 201 Rt. 17 N., 07070, pg. 1180 PB
FCI 900, Inc., 201 Rt. 17 N., 07070, pg. 1180 PB
FCI SMR Company, 201 Rt. 17 N., 07070, pg. 1180 PB
Fleet Call Corporation, 201 Rt. 17 N., 07070, pg. 1180 PB
Fleet Call of Texas, Inc., 201 Rt. 17 N., 07070, pg. 1180 PB
Fort Worth Communications, Inc., 201 Rt. 17 N., 07070, pg. 1180 PB
Goodkind & O'Dea, Inc., 60 Feronia Way, 07070, pg. 329 PV
Howmedica, Inc., 359 Veterans Blvd., 07070, pg. 1282 PB
LEATHER WAREHOUSE, INC., 225 Highland Cross Rd., 07070, pg. 656 PV
Lindenmeyr Munroe, 301 Veterans Blvd., 07070-2564, pg. 224 PV

River Edge

Mobile Communications of Florida, Inc., 201 Rt. 17 N., 07070, pg. 1180 PB
Mobile Radio of Illinois, Inc., 201 Rt. 17 N., 07070, pg. 1180 PB
SGS International Certification Services, Inc., Meadows Office Complex, 301 Rte. 17, N., 07070, pg. 1153 IT
Safety Net, Inc., 201 Rt. 17 N., 07070, pg. 1181 PB
SIMMONS JUVENILE PRODUCTS, 301 Rte. 17 N., 07070, pg. 1001 PV
Smart SMR, Inc., 201 Rt. 17 N., 07070, pg. 1181 PB
Smart SMR of California, Inc., 201 Rt. 17 N., 07070, pg. 1181 PB
Smart SMR of Illinois, Inc., 201 Rt. 17 N., 07070, pg. 1181 PB
Smart SMR of New York, Inc., 201 Rt. 17 N., 07070, pg. 1181 PB
Smart SMR of Texas, Inc., 201 Rt. 17 N., 07070, pg. 1181 PB
SOFTWARE PLUS INC., 301 Rte. 17 N., 5th Fl., 07070, pg. 1012 PV

Saddle Brook

Alexander's, Inc., Park 80 W., Plaza II, 10th Fl., 07663, pg. 1725 PB
AMLOID CORPORATION, 81 Fifth St., 07662, pg. 66 PV
ARROW FASTENER CO., INC., 271 Mayhill St., 07663, pg. 85 PV
DSM Fine Chemicals USA Inc., 217 Rte. West, 07662, pg. 355 IT
Fuji Electric Corp. of America, Park 80W-Plaza 2, 07663, pg. 522 IT
International Nickel, Inc., Park 80 West-Plaza Two, 07662, pg. 672 IT
Perugina Brands of America, 299 Market St., 07662, pg. 917 IT
SEALED AIR CORPORATION, Park 80 E., 07663, pg. 1450 PB
Sealed Air Packaging Products Division, 301 Mayhill St., 07663, pg. 1451 PB
THERMO ELECTRIC CO., INC., 109 N. Fifth St., 07663-6167, pg. 1080 PV
VORNADO REALTY TRUST, Park 80 W., Plaza II, 07663, pg. 1725 PB

Saddle River

Rockland Electric Co., The Commons, 82 E. Allendale Rd., 07458, pg. 1229 PB

Salem

Garry Electronics, 23 Front St., 08079, pg. 1184 PV
General Connector, 23 Front St., 08079, pg. 1184 PV
MANNINGTON MILLS, INC., Mannington Mills Rd., 08079, pg. 700 PV
WIRE-PRO INC., 23 Front St., 08079, pg. 1184 PV

Sayreville

Co-Steel Sayreville Inc., P.O. Box 249, N. Crossman Rd., 08872, pg. 298 IT
MICHAEL STEVENS LTD., P.O. Box 998, 08871-0998, pg. 1042 PV

Scotch Plains

Financial Collection Agencies (1990) Inc., 1812 Front Street, 07076-1103, pg. 471 IT
Morgan Matroc Inc.-East Coast Sales Division, 1812 Front St., 07076-1103, pg. 893 IT

Seabrook

SEABROOK BROTHERS & SONS, INC., 85 Finley Rd., 08302, pg. 978 PV

Secaucus

AST Research, Inc, 6th Floor, 300 Harmon Meadow Blvd., 07094, pg. 1182 IT
AGEMA Infrared Systems, Inc., 550 County Ave., 07094, pg. 1289 IT
American Tape Co., 300 Lighting Way, 1st Fl., 07094, pg. 685 IT
ANDREW SPORTS CLUB INC., 30 Enterprise Ave., 07094, pg. 73 PV
Bertolli USA, Inc., 300 Harmon Meadow Blvd., 07094, pg. 655 IT
Bowne Insurance Division, 215 Country Ave., 07094, pg. 248 PB
Bernard Chaus, Inc., 800 Secaucus Rd., 07094, pg. 342 PB
Chemgraphics Systems, Inc., 100 Electric Ave., 07094, pg. 338 PB
Chock Full O' Nuts - Food Service Div., 520 Secaucus Rd., 07096-2355, pg. 351 PB
Cognos Corp.-New York Sales Office, 300 Lighting Way, 07094-3695, pg. 306 IT
Command Web Offset Co., 100 Castle Rd., 07096, pg. 693 PV
Dext Company of NJ, 900 Castle Rd., 07094, pg. 1444 PB
Drug Guild Div., 350 Meadowland Pkwy., 07096, pg. 1169 PB
Eppens Smith Co., 520 Secaucus Rd., 07094, pg. 351 PB
Equitable Holding Corporation, 200 Plaza Dr., 07096-1583, pg. 589 PB
Ericsson Business Communications, Inc., 450 Harmon Meadow Blvd., 07094, pg. 1364 IT

Geographic Index-U.S.

Europe Craft Imports, 15 Enterprise Ave., 07094, pg. 129 **PB**
FABER, COE & GREGG, INC., Ten Enterprise Ave. N., 07094, pg. 390 **PV**
Federated Logistics, 500 Meadowlands Pkwy., 07094, pg. 618 **PB**
GOYA FOODS, INC., 100 Seaview Dr., 07096, pg. 468 **PV**
Gucci America Inc., 50 Heartsway, 07094, pg. 686 **IT**
THE HARTZ MOUNTAIN CORP., 400 Plaza Dr., 07094, pg. 508 **PV**
Hartz Mountain Industries, 400 Plaza Dr., 07094-3688, pg. 508 **PV**
HARVE BENARD LTD., 225 Meadowland Pkwy., 07096, pg. 508 **PV**
Hoogovens Aluminium Corp., 101 Venture Way, 07096, pg. 755 **IT**
Internut, 505 Jefferson Ave., 07094, pg. 1010 **PV**
La Touraine Coffee Company, 520 Secaucus Rd., 07096-2355, pg. 351 **PB**
Liz Claiborne Outlet Division, Two Emerson Ln., 07094, pg. 1006 **PV**
Matheson Gas Products, Inc., 30 Seaview Dr., 07096, pg. 938 **PB**
Matsushita Electric Corporation of America, One Panasonic Way, 07094, pg. 847 **IT**
Matsushita Services Co. Div., One Panasonic Way, 07094, pg. 847 **IT**
NYK Line (North America) Inc., 300 Lighting Way, 5th Fl., 07094, pg. 941 **IT**
Noritake Co., Inc., 75 Seaview Dr., 07094, pg. 959 **IT**
Noritake Co., Inc.-Abrasive Division, 75 Seaview Dr., 07094, pg. 959 **IT**
Noritake Co., Inc.-Table Top Division, 75 Seaview Dr., 07094, pg. 959 **IT**
ORIX Commercial Alliance Corporation, 300 Lighting Way, 07096-1525, pg. 1009 **IT**
Panasonic Broadcast Systems Co., Two Panasonic Way, 07094, pg. 847 **IT**
Panasonic Broadcast & Television Systems Company, One Panasonic Way, 07094, pg. 847 **IT**
Panasonic Consumer Electric Co., One Panasonic Way, 07094, pg. 847 **IT**
Panasonic Industrial Co., Two Panasonic Way, 07094, pg. 847 **IT**
PaperDirect, Inc., 100 Plaza Dr., 07094, pg. 498 **PB**
PETRIE RETAIL, INC., 70 Enterprise Ave., 07094, pg. 858 **PV**
Pinelands, Inc., 9 Broadcast Plaza, 07096, pg. 352 **PB**
Reed Travel Group, 500 Plaza Dr., 07096, pg. 1097 **IT**
Reed Travel Publishing, 500 Plaza Dr., 07096, pg. 1097 **IT**
RIBBON NARROW FABRIC COMPANY, 565 Winsor Dr., 07094, pg. 927 **PV**
SCHIAVONE CONSTRUCTION CO., 1600 Patterson Plank Rd., 07096, pg. 970 **PV**
Square D Co., 215 County Ave., 07094, pg. 1208 **IT**
SYMS CORPORATION, Syms Way, 07094, pg. 1547 **PB**
Tsumura International, 300 Lighting Way, 6th Fl., 07096-1578, pg. 1426 **IT**
Utell International-Secaucus, 500 Plaza Dr., 07096-3819, pg. 1098 **IT**
Wayne Coffee Company, 520 Secaucus Rd., 07096-2355, pg. 351 **PB**

Short Hills

AEGON Reinsurance Company of America, 51, JFK Pkwy., 07078, pg. 26 **IT**
AEGON U.S. Holding Corp., 51 JFK Pkwy., 07078, pg. 26 **IT**
Associated Aviation, Inc., 51 John F. Kennedy Pkwy., 07078, pg. 355 **PB**
CORPA Reinsurance Company, c/o Short Hills Management Co., 51 JFK Pkwy., 07078, pg. 28 **IT**
GIANETTINO & MEREDITH ADVERTISING, 788 Morris-Essex Tpke., 07078, pg. 450 **PV**
Hoechst Celanese Advanced Materials, Mack SH Bldg., 150 JFK Parkway, 07078, pg. 624 **IT**
Hoechst Celanese Advanced Technology, Mack SH Building, 150 JFK Parkway, 07078, pg. 625 **IT**
Jefferies & Company, Inc., 51 JFK Pkwy., 3rd Fl., 07078, pg. 925 **PB**

Shrewsbury

WELLMAN, INC., 1040 Broad St., Ste. 302, 07702, pg. 1752 **PB**

Skillman

Advanced Care Products, 199 Grandview Rd., 08558, pg. 928 **PB**
Johnson & Johnson Consumer Products, Grandview Rd., 08558-9418, pg. 928 **PB**
Johnson & Johnson Worldwide Absorbent Products & Materials Research, 199 Grandview Rd., 08558, pg. 928 **PB**
Kepner-Tregoe, Inc., 17 Research Rd., 08558, pg. 1659 **PB**
Personal Products Co., 199 Grandview Rd., 08558-9418, pg. 929 **PB**

Somerset

ACME TUBE INC., One Howard Ave., 08873, pg. 14 **PV**
Berkley Risk Managers, 270 Davidson Ave., 08875, pg. 215 **PB**
Brother International Corporation, Vantage Ct., 200 Cottontail Ln., 08875-6714, pg. 229 **IT**

Digital Insurance Services, 300 Atrium Dr., 07783, pg. 508 **PB**
DIGITAL SOLUTIONS, INC., 300 Atrium Dr., 08873, pg. 508 **PB**
Digital Staff ConnXions, 300 Atrium Rd., 07783, pg. 508 **PB**
Exxon Biomedical Sciences Inc., P.O. Box 235, 08875-0235, pg. 601 **PB**
Ferrero U.S.A., Inc., 600 Cottontail Lane, 08873, pg. 480 **IT**
General Office Environments Inc., 65 Clyde Rd., 08875, pg. 445 **PV**
Huls America Inc., 220 Davidson Ave., 08873-6821, pg. 1455 **IT**
IT Corp., 2200 Cottontail Ln., 08873, pg. 908 **PB**
KATHABAR INCORPORATED, 370 Campus Dr., 08873, pg. 609 **PV**
Kyocera Electronics, Inc., P.O. Box 6727, 100 Randolph Rd., 08873, pg. 776 **IT**
M.A. Hanna Color, 789 New Brunswick Rd., 08873, pg. 781 **PB**
Mary Kay Cosmetics, Inc., 1600 Cottontail Ln., 08873, pg. 711 **PV**
Merrill Lynch Trust Company (New Jersey), 500 Atrium Dr., 08873, pg. 1098 **PB**
Miele Appliances, Inc., 22D Worlds Fair Dr., 08873, pg. 865 **IT**
Philips Lighting, 200 Franklin Square Dr., 08875-6800, pg. 1055 **IT**
Plastics Color Corp., 371 Campus Dr., 08873, pg. 827 **PV**
Radiant Lamp, 200 Franklin Square Dr., 08875-6810, pg. 1055 **IT**
RONSON CORPORATION, Corporate Park III, Campus Dr., 08875, pg. 1405 **PB**
Royal Doulton USA Inc., 701 Cottontail Ln., 08873, pg. 1135 **IT**
SMC, 248 World's Fair Dr., 08873, pg. 898 **PV**
SMS-Somerset, II Executive Dr., 08873, pg. 1463 **PB**
Terumo Medical Corporation, 2100 Cottontail Lane, 08873, pg. 1376 **IT**
Toppan Printing Co. (America) Inc.-New Jersey, 1100 Randolph Rd., 08873, pg. 1399 **IT**
TRIDENT ROWAND GROUP, INC., Two Worlds Fair Dr., 08873, pg. 1103 **PV**
Turner Construction Company, 265 Davidson Ave., 08873, pg. 1645 **PB**
V-L Service Lighting, 200 Franklin Square Dr., 08875, pg. 1055 **IT**
Waldes Truarc/Industrial Retaining Ring, 500 Memorial Dr., 08875, pg. 1632 **PV**
John Wiley & Sons, Inc., One Wiley Dr., 08875, pg. 1768 **PB**
Yashica, Inc., 2301-200 Cottontail Lane, 08873, pg. 776 **IT**
Wm. Zinsser & Co., Inc., 173 Belmont Dr., 08875, pg. 1358 **PV**

Somerville

Air Pollution Control, P.O. Box 1500, 08876, pg. 29 **PB**
AMP Inc. Lytel Division, 61 Chubb Way, 08876-3903, pg. 8 **PB**
William B. Bliss Div., 25 Chubb Way, 08876-1299, pg. 392 **PV**
Custodis-Cottrell, Inc., P.O. Box 1500, 08876, pg. 29 **PB**
Edwal Scientific Products Div., 25 Chubb Way, 08876-1299, pg. 392 **PV**
Egan Machinery Division, South Adamsville Rd., 08876, pg. 774 **IT**
Ethicon, Inc., U.S. Rte. 22, 08876, pg. 928 **PB**
FALCON SAFETY PRODUCTS INC., 25 Chubb Way, 08876-1299, pg. 392 **PV**
Hoechst Celanese Life Sciences Group, Rte. 202-206 North, 08876-1258, pg. 626 **IT**
Hoechst Specialty Products Group, 3070 Highway 22 West, 08876, pg. 625 **IT**
Metcalf & Eddy Companies Inc., P.O. Box 1500, 08876, pg. 29 **PB**
Nelson Westerberg, 180 Meister Ave., 08876, pg. 1164 **PV**
Research-Cottrell, P.O. Box 1500, 08876, pg. 29 **PB**
Research Cottrell, Europe, P.O. Box 1500, 08876, pg. 29 **PB**
Roche Diagnostic Systems, Inc., 1080 U.S. Hwy. 202/206 S., 08876, pg. 1120 **IT**
Roche Molecular Systems, Inc., 1080 U.S. Hwy. 202/206 S., 08876, pg. 1120 **IT**
STRUCTURAL FOAM PLASTICS, INC., 68 County Line Rd., 08876, pg. 1047 **PV**
TEKNI-PLEX, INC., 021 Industrial Pkwy., 08876, pg. 1073 **PV**
TRANSNET CORPORATION, 45 Columbia Rd., 08876, pg. 1631 **PB**
WYANT COPORATION, 100 Readington Rd., 08876, pg. 1781 **PB**

South Amboy

Amboy Aggregates, 415 Main St., 08879, pg. 474 **PV**

South Hackensack

AEP INDUSTRIES, INC., 125 Phillips Ave., 07606-1546, pg. 4 **PB**
AEP Industries, Inc., 125 Phillips Ave., 07606, pg. 5 **PB**
Barbour Thread, 30 Ruta Ct., 07606, pg. 618 **IT**
Dassault Falcon Jet Corp., Teterboro Airport, P.O. Box 2000, 07606, pg. 383 **IT**
J. JOSEPHSON, INC., 35 Horizon Blvd., 07606, pg. 601 **PV**

Georgette Klinger Laboratories, 19 Empire Blvd., 07606, pg. 626 **PV**
NOVILLE, Three Empire Blvd., 07606-1806, pg. 808 **PV**
Share Technologies - Fairchild, Two University Plaza, 07601, pg. 1568 **PB**
SPINNERIN INC., 30 Wesley St., 07606, pg. 1025 **PV**
Ultra Building Systems, Inc., 450 Huyler St., 07606, pg. 194 **PV**
Waltech Inc., 96 Vreeland Ave., 07606, pg. 1241 **IT**

South Plainfield

Bosch Packaging Machinery Division, 121 Corp. Blvd., 07080, pg. 204 **IT**
Chemap, Inc., 901 Hadley Rd., 07080, pg. 1378 **IT**
Degussa Corp., Dental Dept., 3950 S. Clinton Ave., 07080, pg. 388 **IT**
L.A. Dreyfus Co., P.O. Box 500, 07080, pg. 1781 **PB**
Everlasting Valve Co., 108 Somogyi Court, 07080, pg. 83 **PV**
GE Capital/IT Solutions, 109 Corporate Blvd., Ste. J, 07080, pg. 711 **PB**
Heraeus Instruments Inc., 111A Corporate Blvd., 07080, pg. 616 **IT**
Italian Line, 50 Crogwood Rd., 07080, pg. 653 **IT**
Medi-Physics Inc., 900 Durham Ave., 07080, pg. 992 **IT**
NBS Card Services, Inc., 800 Montrose Ave., 07080, pg. 898 **PV**
Robertet Flavors, P.O. Box 247, 640 Montrose Ave., 07080, pg. 1119 **IT**
Sterling Davis Standard, 901 Durham Ave., 07080, pg. 1240 **IT**
Tempil Inc., 2901 Hamilton Blvd., 07080, pg. 90 **PV**
TINGLEY RUBBER CORPORATION, 200 South Ave., 07080, pg. 1088 **PV**
Van Leeuwen Pipe & Tube Corp., 20 Harmich Road, 07080, pg. 1450 **IT**
Warner-Jenkinson, 3615 Kennedy Rd., 07080, pg. 1696 **PB**
Warner-Jenkinson Cosmetic Colors, P.O. Box 705, 107 Wade Ave., 07080, pg. 1696 **PB**
WHITTAKER, CLARK & DANIELS, INC., 1000 Coolidge St., 07080, pg. 1174 **PV**

South River

PULSE BANCORP, INC., Six Jackson St., 08882, pg. 1344 **PB**
Pulse Savings Bank, Six Jackson St., 08882, pg. 1344 **PB**
STRAUSS DISCOUNT AUTO, 9A Brick Plant Rd., 08882-1098, pg. 1046 **PV**

Sparta

Valley National Bank, Seven Woodport Rd., 07871, pg. 1706 **PB**

Springfield

WM. BLANCHARD CO., 199 Mountain Ave., 07081, pg. 148 **PV**
ELECTROID CO., 45 Fadem Rd., 07081, pg. 369 **PV**
Electroid Corp., 45 Fadem Rd., 07081, pg. 1131 **PV**
Greif Division, 140 Mountain Ave., 07081, pg. 763 **PB**
Haarmann & Reimer Corp., 70 Diamond Rd., 07081, pg. 173 **IT**
LEONARD WHOLESALE, INC., 25 Rte. 22, 07081, pg. 660 **PV**
MD Foods USA Inc., P.O. Box 536, 07081-1423, pg. 826 **IT**
QEI, INC., 60 Fadem Rd., 07081-3186, pg. 897 **PV**
SIXTH AVENUE ELECTRONICS CITY, 22 Rte. 22 W., 07081, pg. 1004 **PV**
TORESCO ENTERPRISES, 170 Rte. 22 E., 07081, pg. 1092 **PV**
VALCOR ENGINEERING CORP., Two Lawrence Rd., 07081, pg. 1131 **PV**
VILLAGE SUPER MARKET INC., 733 Mountain Ave., 07081, pg. 1721 **PB**
WESTWOOD COMPUTER CORPORATION, 11 Diamond Rd., 07081, pg. 1170 **PV**
Xanadu Div., 45 Fadem Rd., 07081, pg. 369 **PV**

Stewartsville

Apex Galvanizing Corp., New Village, 119 Edison Rd., 08886, pg. 1138 **PV**

Stirling

Eastern Engraving, 355 Warren Ave., 07980, pg. 1506 **PV**

Succasunna

United Water Mid-Atlantic, 22 Rt. 10, Ste. 102, 07876, pg. 1692 **PB**
Valley National Bank, 230 State Hwy. 10, 07876, pg. 1706 **PB**

Summit

BOURAS INDUSTRIES, 475 Springfield Ave., 07901, pg. 161 **PV**
Charter Behavioral Health System at Fair Oaks, Inc., 19 Prospect St., 07901, pg. 1033 **PB**
Hosokawa Micron Powder Systems, 10 Chatham Rd., 07901, pg. 636 **IT**

PB - *U.S. Public Companies Volume*
PV - *U.S. Private Companies Volume*
IT - *International Public & Private Companies Volume*

Geographic Index-U.S.

LEAR SIEGLER DIVERSIFIED HOLDINGS CORP., 469 Morris Ave., 07902, pg. 655 **PV**
Mikropul Environmental Systems Div., 20 Chatham Rd., 07901, pg. 636 **IT**

Teaneck

Aji Pharma U.S.A., Inc., Glenpointe Ctr. W., 500 Frank W. Burr Blvd., 07666-6894, pg. 40 **IT**
Ajinomoto U.S.A., Inc., Glenpointe Ctr. W., 500 Frank W. Burr Blvd., 07666, pg. 40 **IT**
BNY Information Services, Inc., 1500 Palisade Ave., 07666, pg. 178 **PB**
DIC Digital Supply COrp., Glenpointe Centre W., 500 Frank W. Burr Blvd., 07666, pg. 369 **IT**
Dynaric, Inc., Glenpoint Centre W., 500 Frank W. Burr Blvd., 07666, pg. 369 **IT**
Eisai U.S.A., Inc., Glenpointe Ctr. E., 4th Fl., 300 Frank W. Burr Blvd., 07666, pg. 435 **IT**
Givaudan-Roure, Corporation-Fragrances Div., 1775 Windsor Rd., 07666, pg. 1120 **IT**
Haagen-Dazs, Glenpointe Ctr. E., 0766-6782, pg. 411 **IT**
Lockheed Information Management Services Co., GlennPointe Centre E., 300 Frank W. Burr Blvd., 07666, pg. 1009 **PB**
Parmalat USA Corporation, 400 Frank W. Burr Blvd., 07666, pg. 1023 **IT**
PRIMEPAK COMPANY, 133 Cedar Ln., 07666, pg. 884 **PV**

Tenafly

Colgate-Palmolive Co., Institutional Products Div., 101 N. Summit St., 07670, pg. 397 **PB**
FOCUS2020, INC., 132 Westervelt Ave., 07670, pg. 415 **PV**
West Penetone Corporation, 74 Hudson Ave., 07670, pg. 1158 **PV**

Teterboro

A&E STORES, INC., 1000 Huyler St., 07608, pg. 1 **PV**
AlliedSignal Computer-Aided Engineering Center, Rte. 46, 07608-1173, pg. 50 **PB**
AlliedSignal Guidance & Control Systems, Route 46, 07608-1173, pg. 50 **PB**
Florasynth Inc., 300 North St., 07608, pg. 173 **IT**
Funai Corporation, 100 North St., 07608, pg. 530 **IT**
Hesco, Inc., 200 Green St., 07608, pg. 524 **PV**
Mars Aircraft Services Co. of New Jersey, Teterboro Airport, B Hangar No. 3, 07608, pg. 1 **PB**
QUEST DIAGNOSTICS, INC., One Malcolm Ave., 07608, pg. 1351 **PB**
Sumitomo Heavy Machinery Corporation of America, Seven Malcolm Ave., 07608, pg. 1314 **IT**

Thorofare

AmeriSource-Thorofare, 100 Friars Ln., 08086, pg. 97 **PB**
CHECKPOINT SYSTEMS INC., 101 Wolf Dr., 08086, pg. 343 **PB**
Garlock Bearings Division, 060 Mid-Atlantic Ave., 08086, pg. 402 **PB**
Rapidforms, Inc., Mid Atlantic Corporate Ctr., 301 Grove Rd., 08086, pg. 1171 **PB**
Thermice Corporation, 650 Grove Rd., Ste. 105, 08086, pg. 1341 **PB**

Titusville

Janssen Pharmaceutica, Inc., P.O. Box 200, 1125 Trenton-Harbourton Rd., 08560-0200, pg. 928 **PB**

Toms River

Getinge Disinfection Inc., 1415 Hooper Av., Box H, 08753, pg. 551 **IT**
OCEAN CHEVROLET, INC., Rte. 37 & Peter Ave., 08753, pg. 810 **PV**
Perma Pure Inc., Eight Executive Dr., 08754, pg. 590 **IT**
Rocking Horse One, One Stockton Ct., 08755, pg. 1186 **PB**

Totowa

BIG M, INC., 12 Vreeland Ave., 07512, pg. 143 **PV**
CAPEZIO BALLET MAKERS INC., One Campus Rd., 07512, pg. 205 **PV**
Caravan Brokay, 100 Adams Dr., 07511, pg. 208 **PV**
CARAVAN PRODUCTS COMPANY, INC., 100 Adams Dr., 07511, pg. 208 **PV**
Ferrulmatic, 11 Jackson Rd., 07046, pg. 47 **PB**
HAROLD M. PITMAN CO., INC., 721 Union Blvd., 07512, pg. 867 **PV**
Sandvik Process Systems, Inc., 21 Campus Rd., 07512, pg. 1185 **IT**
Thomson Components, 40G Commerce Way, P.O. Box 540, 07511, pg. 1384 **IT**
VIBRA SCREW INC., 755 Union Blvd., 07511, pg. 1138 **PV**
VITAL SIGNS, INC., 20 Campus Rd., 07512, pg. 1723 **PB**
Woodward-Clyde, 45J Commerce Way, 07512, pg. 1656 **PB**

Towaco

AMCO FOLDING CARTONS, INC., Two Como CT., 07082, pg. 48 **PV**

Trenton

Capitol City Publishing Co., Inc.-The Trentonian, The Trentonian, 600 Perry St., 08602, pg. 934 **PB**
Central Lewmar Trenton Division, 1004 Whitehead Rd., 08638, pg. 223 **PV**
Chessco Process Research Products Div., 1013 Whitehead Rd. Ext., 08638, pg. 234 **PV**
Chris-Craft Industrial Products, Inc., 1980 E. State St., 08619, pg. 351 **PB**
Congoleum Corporation, 861 Sloan Ave., 08619, pg. 69 **PB**
DKB & Partners, 196 W. State St., 08608, pg. 302 **PV**
Delroyd Worm Gear, 121 First Ave., 08619, pg. 857 **IT**
Demag Delaval Turbine, 840 Nottingham Way, 08638, pg. 837 **IT**
Goodall Transportation Co., Box 8237, 08650, pg. 1423 **IT**
Harwick Chemical Corp., 1230 Parkway Ave., Ste. 204, 08628, pg. 509 **PV**
Hertz Corporation, 60 Wallenburg Ave., 06809, pg. 664 **PB**
THE HIBBERT COMPANY, P.O. Box 8116, 400 Pennington Ave., 08650-0116, pg. 525 **PV**
HOMASOTE COMPANY, Off Lower Ferry Rd., 08628-0240, pg. 831 **PB**
JOURNAL REGISTER COMPANY, 50 W. State St., 12th Fl., 08608, pg. 934 **PB**
Melcor Corporation, 1040 Spruce St., 08648, pg. 615 **PV**
Rhein Chemie Corporation, 1008 Whitehead Rd. Extension, 08638, pg. 173 **IT**
Ronson Aviation, Inc., F.B.O. Mercer County Airport, 08607, pg. 1405 **PB**
Rubberhide Company, 493 Whitehead Rd., 08604, pg. 1423 **IT**
TH Property, Inc., 300 Phillips Blvd., 08618, pg. 774 **IT**
Tab Electric Supply Co. Inc., 1601 Greenwood Ave., 08609, pg. 951 **PV**
Trafalgar House Property, Inc., Princeton Crossroads at Ewing, 300 Phillips Blvd., 08618, pg. 774 **IT**

Turnersville

WATSON'S QUALITY TURKEY PRODUCTS, INC., Black Horse Pike, Rte. 168, 08012, pg. 1154 **PV**

Union

Adam Technology Co., 909 Rahway Ave., 07083, pg. 1101 **PB**
Alcan Powders & Pigments Division, 901 Lehigh Ave., 07083, pg. 50 **IT**
American Air Filters, 2204 Morris Ave., 07083-5914, pg. 3 **PB**
Ardell Industries Inc., 555 Lehigh Ave., 07083, pg. 597 **PV**
BED BATH & BEYOND INC., 650 Liberty Ave., 07083, pg. 200 **PB**
Breeze Eastern, 700 Liberty Ave., 07083-4115, pg. 1632 **PB**
Bulkley Dunton JB Papers, P.O. Box 560, 1121 Springfield Rd., 07083, pg. 901 **PB**
CE DE CANDY, INC., 1091 Lousons Rd., 07083, pg. 220 **PV**
ELECTROCATALYTIC, INC., Two Milltown Ct., 07083, pg. 369 **PV**
Elizabethtown Gas Co., P.O. Box 3175, One Elizabethtown Plaza, 07083-1975, pg. 1147 **PB**
THE GENLYTE GROUP INCORPORATED, 2345 Vauxhall Rd., 07083-1948, pg. 729 **PB**
GILETTE FOOD FLAVORINGS, INC., 751 Rahway Ave., 07083, pg. 453 **PV**
Hanovia Colight, 825 Lehigh Ave., 07083, pg. 17 **IT**
Heraeus De Nora Inc., 2655 Rte. 22 West, 07083, pg. 616 **IT**
International Paint Co., Inc., 2270 Morris Ave., 07083, pg. 338 **IT**
International Paint Eastern Div., 2270 Morris Ave., 07083, pg. 339 **IT**
JL MEDIA, INC., 1600 Rte. 22, 07083, pg. 577 **PV**
HAROLD LEONARD & COMPANY, INC., 600 Green Ln., 07083, pg. 700 **PV**
MANNING & LEWIS ENGINEERING CO., 675 Rahway Ave., 07083, pg. 700 **PV**
MULBERRY METAL PRODUCTS, INC., 2199 Stanley Terrace, 07083, pg. 766 **PV**
Murray Tube, P.O. Box 2065, 07083, pg. 1222 **IT**
NUI Environmental Group, Inc., P.O. Box 3175, 07083, pg. 1148 **PB**
RED DEVIL INC., 2400 Vauxhall Rd., 07083, pg. 915 **PV**
Schering-Plough Animal Health, 1095 Morris Ave., 07083, pg. 1438 **PV**
Senior Engineering Co.-Economiser Div., P.O. Box 749, 650 Green Lane, 07083, pg. 1222 **IT**
Senior TIFT, Inc., P.O. Box 2065, 07083, pg. 1222 **IT**
Sperber-Peterman Company, 2333 Morris Ave., Ste. A16, 07083, pg. 107 **PV**
Stonco Genlyte, 2345 Vauxhall Rd., 07083, pg. 730 **PB**
TUSCAN/LEHIGH DAIRIES LP, 750 Union Ave., 07083, pg. 1110 **PV**
Utility Business Services, Inc., 1085 Morris Ave., 07083, pg. 1148 **PB**

Union City

Hudson United Bank-Union City, 3100 Bergenline Ave., 07087, pg. 845 **PB**
Lafayette American Bank, 3100 Bergenline Ave., 07087, pg. 845 **PB**

Upper Saddle River

CAMPMOR INC., 28 Parkway, 07458, pg. 204 **PV**
CLIFFORD PAPER INC., Sherbrook Office Center, 600 E. Crescent Ave., 07458, pg. 246 **PV**
Dugan/Farley Communications, 600 E. Crescent Ave., 07458-1850, pg. 1642 **PB**
Higher Education Division, One Lake St., 07428, pg. 778 **PV**
Hunter Douglas, Inc., Two Pkwy., 07458, pg. 639 **IT**
Minwax Company Div., 10 Mountanview Rd., 07458, pg. 1466 **PB**
Prentice Hall Business Publishing, One Lake St., 07428, pg. 778 **PV**
Prentice Hall Education, Career & Technology, One Lake St., 07428, pg. 778 **PV**
Prentice Hall Engineering, Science & Math, One Lake St., 07428, pg. 778 **PV**
Prentice Hall Humanities & Social Sciences, One Lake St., 07428, pg. 778 **PV**
Prentice Hall Regents/ESL, One Lake St., 07428, pg. 778 **PV**
Prentice Hall School, One Lake St., 07458, pg. 778 **PV**
Simon & Schuster Education Group, One Lake St., 07428, pg. 778 **PV**
Simon & Schuster International, One Lake St., 07428, pg. 778 **PV**
THE TEXWIPE CO., INC., P.O. Box 575, 650 E. Crescent Ave., 07458, pg. 1079 **PV**
The Thompson-Minwax Company, 10 Mountview Rd., 07458, pg. 1466 **PB**
VILLAZON COMPANY INC., P.O. Box 720, 25 Park Way, 07458, pg. 1140 **PV**

Vernon

Valley National Bank, Vernon Plaza, 538 Rte. 515, 07462, pg. 1706 **PB**

Verona

CELENTANO BROS. INC., 225 Bloomfield Ave., 07044, pg. 221 **PV**
MSC New Jersey Technical Office, 59 Grove Ave., 07044, pg. 1031 **PB**

Vineland

ACE GLASS INCORPORATED, 1430 N.W. Blvd., 08360, pg. 12 **PV**
Casa Di Bertacchi, 1910 Gallagher Dr., 08360, pg. 928 **PV**
Chatas Glass Co., Inc., 570 Broadlawn Ter., 08360, pg. 1341 **PB**
The Daily Journal (NJ), 891 E. Oak Rd., 08360, pg. 700 **PB**
Kimble Glass Inc., 537 Crystal Ave., 08360, pg. 1464 **IT**
Kontes Glass Company, Spruce St., P.O. Box 729, 08360, pg. 1464 **IT**
Manischewitz Food Products Corp., 214 N. Delsea Dr., 08360, pg. 699 **PV**
Molecular Packaging Systems, Inc., 2285 East Landis Avenue, 08360, pg. 855 **PV**
Quest Diagnostic-Vineland, 24 W. Landis Ave., 08360, pg. 1352 **PB**
RENNOC CORPORATION, 3501 Southeast Blvd., 08360-7789, pg. 922 **PV**
Vineland Laboratories Inc., 2285 E. Landis Ave., 08360, pg. 855 **PB**
Wallace & Tiernan Inc., 1901 W. Garden Rd., 08360, pg. 61 **PB**

Voorhees

Abetong America Inc., P.O. Box 317, 08043, pg. 1199 **IT**
Advanta Business Services, 1020 Laurel Oak Rd., 08043, pg. 22 **PV**
American Commonwealth Company, P.O. Box 1770, 1025 Laurel Oak Rd., 08043, pg. 95 **PB**
American International Water Services Company, P.O. Box 1770, 1025 Laurel Oak Rd., 08043, pg. 95 **PB**
AMERICAN WATER WORKS COMPANY, INC., P.O. Box 1770, 1025 Laurel Oak Rd., 08043, pg. 95 **PB**
American Water Works Service Company, Inc., P.O. Box 1770, 1025 Laurel Oak Rd., 08043, pg. 95 **PB**
AmericanAnglian Environmental Technologies, Inc., 1025 Laurel Oak Rd., 08043, pg. 95 **PB**
Atlantic Employers Insurance Company, 401 White Horse Rd., 08043, pg. 366 **PB**
Cigna Information Services, Inc., 401 White Horse Rd., 08043, pg. 357 **PB**
Echelon Mall, Inc., Two Echelon Mall, 08043, pg. 1408 **PB**
Echelon Urban Center, Inc., 183 Echelon Rd., 08043, pg. 1408 **PB**
Geo-Con, Inc., 1000 White Horse Rd., Ste. 302, 08043, pg. 1657 **PB**
Greenwich Water System, Inc., P.O. Box 1770, 1025 Laurel Oak Rd., 08043, pg. 95 **PB**
Kresson View Center, 2601 Evesham Rd., 08043, pg. 729 **PB**
Motorola Nortel Communication, Rte. 73 & S. Dutchtown Rd., 08043, pg. 1138 **PB**
Occoquan Land Corporation, P.O. Box 1770, 1025 Laurel Oak Rd., 08043, pg. 95 **PB**
Sungard Computer Services Group, 600 Laurel Oak Rd., 08043, pg. 1534 **PB**
SunGard Financial Systems, 200 Laurel Oak Rd., 08043, pg. 1535 **PB**

PB - U.S. Public Companies Volume
PV - U.S. Private Companies Volume
IT - International Public & Private Companies Volume

Geographic Index-U.S.

1329

Waldwick

Biocraft Bulk Manufacturing, 12 Industrial Park, 07463, pg. 1381 — IT
IKOS Systems, Inc., 4 North St., 07463, pg. 864 — PB
Miller-Friedman Advertising, Four North St., 07463, pg. 746 — PV

Wall

Commercial Realty & Resources Corp., 1415 Wyckoff Rd., 07719, pg. 1172 — PB
DSI, Wedgewood Professional Bldg., 1725 Rte. 35, 07719, pg. 221 — IT
New Jersey Natural Gas Co., 1415 Wyckoff Rd., 07719, pg. 1172 — PB
NEW JERSEY RESOURCES CORPORATION, 1415 Wyckoff Rd., 07719, pg. 1172 — PB
NJR Energy Services Corporation, 1415 Wykoff Rd., 07719, pg. 1172 — PB
PRESS COMMUNICATIONS, LLC, 1350 Campus Pkwy., Ste. 106, 07753, pg. 882 — PV
Seely Equipment & Supply Co., Inc., 1325 Hwy. 34, 07719, pg. 755 — PV
Waterford Crystal, Inc., 1330 Campus Pkwy., 07719, pg. 1487 — IT
Waterford Crystal U.S.A., 1300 Campus Pkwy., 07719, pg. 1487 — IT
Wedgwood U.S.A., 1330 Campus Pkwy., 07719, pg. 1487 — IT

Wallington

FARMLAND DAIRIES, 520 Main Ave., 07057, pg. 395 — PV
Maintech, 39 Patterson Ave., Bldg. E, 07057, pg. 1724 — PB

Warren

Chubb & Son, Inc., 15 Mountain View Rd., 07060, pg. 355 — PB
THE CHUBB CORPORATION, 15 Mountain View Rd., 07059, pg. 354 — PB
Chubb Custom Market, Inc., 21 Mountain View Rd., 07060, pg. 355 — PB
Chubb Insurance Company of New Jersey, 15 Mountain View Rd., 07061-1615, pg. 355 — PB
Cordis, a Johnson & Johnson Company, P.O. Box 4917, 07059-0917, pg. 928 — PB
Federal Insurance Co., 15 Mountain View Rd., 07061-1615, pg. 355 — PB
Lucent Technologies, Network Systems Div., 283 King George Rd., 07059, pg. 1017 — IT
McLaren/Hart Environmental Engineering Corp., 25 Independence Blvd., 07059, pg. 1465 — IT
Pony International Inc., 15 Independence Blvd., 07059, pg. 1036 — IT
Sumitomo Marine Mgmt Services, 15 Independence Blvd., 07059-6747, pg. 1314 — PB
U.S. Filter/Permutit, 30 Technology Dr., CN 4920, 07059, pg. 1682 — PB

Washington

Treitler-Owens, Inc., Box 47B, Brass Castle Rd., 07882, pg. 1238 — PB

Wayne

Applied Coatings, 661 Rt. 23, 07470, pg. 130 — PV
Arrow Group Industries, Inc., 1680 Rte. 23 N, 07474, pg. 477 — PV
Associated Testing Laboratories, Inc., 1133 Rte. 23 S., 07470, pg. 1341 — PB
Atlas Copco North America Inc., 1211 Hamburg Tpk., Ste. 214, 07470, pg. 96 — IT
Berlex Laboratories Inc., 300 Fairfield Rd., 07470, pg. 1204 — IT
BONLAND INDUSTRIES, INC., 50 Newark Pompton Tpke., 07470, pg. 156 — PV
Building Materials Corporation of America, 1361 Alps Rd., 07470, pg. 433 — PV
Castrol North America, 1500 Valley Rd., 07470, pg. 235 — IT
CHEMPLAST, Inc., 150 Dey Rd., 07470, pg. 1174 — IT
Cornell Dubilier Electronics, 1700 Rt. 23 N., 07470, pg. 607 — PV
DIAMOND PRODUCTIONS, INC., 443 Newark Pompton Tpke., 07470, pg. 330 — PV
Drake Bakeries, Inc., 100 Demarest Dr., 07470, pg. 349 — IT
Formica Corporation, Oak Hill Park, 1680 Rte. 23 N., 07474, pg. 129 — IT
GAF CORPORATION, 1361 Alps Rd., 07470, pg. 433 — PV
GAF Materials Corporation, 1361 Alps Rd., 07470, pg. 433 — PV
GAF Premium Products, Inc., 1361 Alps Rd., 07470, pg. 433 — PV
GEC-Marconi Electronic Systems Corp., 164 Totowa Rd., 07474-0975, pg. 544 — IT
THE GRAND UNION COMPANY, 201 Willowbrook Blvd., 07470, pg. 758 — PB
Hanson Engineers, 30 Galesi Dr., 07470, pg. 500 — PV
HOBOKEN WOOD FLOORING CORPORATION, 70 Demarest Dr., 07470, pg. 532 — PV
ISP Environmental Services Inc., 1361 Alps Rd., 07470, pg. 858 — PB
ISP HOLDINGS, INC., 1361 Alps Rd., 07470, pg. 858 — PB

ISP Management Company, Inc., 1361 Alps Rd., 07470, pg. 858 — PB
ISP Real Estate Company, Inc., 1361 Alps Rd., 07470, pg. 858 — PB
ISP Realty Corporation, 1361 Alps Rd., 07470, pg. 859 — PB
International Specialty Products, Inc., 1361 Alps Rd., 07470, pg. 858 — PB
Jacuzzi Whirlpool Bath Inc., 1680 Rte. 23, Ste. 150, 07470-7501, pg. 1684 — PB
Juki Latin America Inc., c/o Juki Union Special Inc., 5 Haul Rd., 07470, pg. 716 — IT
Juki Union Special, Inc., 5 Haul Rd., 07470, pg. 716 — IT
KAPLAN ELECTRONICS, 1700 RT. 23 N, 07470, pg. 607 — PV
Kearfott Guidance & Navigation Corp., 150 Totowa Rd., 07474-0946, pg. 93 — PV
Konica Medical Corporation, 411 Newark-Pompton Tpke., 07470, pg. 749 — IT
MAYER/BERKSHIRE CORPORATION, 25 Edison Dr., 07470, pg. 717 — PV
Mosler Electronic Systems Div., 415 Paterson-Hamburg Tpke., 07470, pg. 763 — PV
Norton Performance Plastics, 150 Dey Rd., 07470, pg. 1174 — IT
Ques Diagnostic-Wayne, 1777 Hamburg Tpke., 07470, pg. 1352 — PV
RAMAPO FINANCIAL CORPORATION, 64 Mountain View Blvd., 07470, pg. 1360 — PB
Sherwood & James Advertising, Inc., 1600 Valley Rd., 07470, pg. 1666 — PB
Toshiba America Consumer Products, Inc., 82 Totowa Rd., 07470, pg. 1405 — IT
UNION CAMP CORPORATION, 1600 Valley Rd., 07470-2066, pg. 1665 — PB
VALLEY NATIONAL BANCORP, 1455 Valley Rd., 07470, pg. 1705 — PB
The Willowbrook Corp., 1400 Willowbrook Mall, 07470, pg. 1408 — PB
Woodward-Clyde, 201 Willowbrook Blvd., 07470, pg. 1657 — PB

Weehawken

Aegis Safety Holdings, Inc., 1500 Harbor Blvd., 07087, pg. 782 — PB
HANOVER DIRECT, INC., 1500 Harbor Blvd., 07087, pg. 782 — PB
MARINE TRANSPORT LINES, INC., 1200 Harbour Blvd., Ninth Fl., 07087, pg. 703 — PV
Maruzen International Co., Ltd., 1220 Harbor Blvd., 10th Fl., 07087, pg. 846 — IT
SMH (U.S.) Inc., 4200 Harbor Blvd., 07087, pg. 1161 — IT
The Specialists Ltd., 1200 Harbor Blvd., 07087, pg. 970 — PB
Tweeds, Inc., 1500 Harbor Blvd., 07087, pg. 782 — PB

West Berlin

All American Technologies of Philadelphia, Inc., 245-D Clifton Ave., 08091, pg. 41 — PB

West Caldwell

THE CHILDREN'S PLACE RETAIL STORES, INC., One Dodge Dr., 07006, pg. 237 — PV
GESTRA, Inc., 10 York Ave., 07006, pg. 549 — IT
Glory USA, Inc., 10A York Ave., 07006, pg. 554 — IT
Kings Super Markets Inc., Two Dedrick Pl., 07006, pg. 643 — IT
MERRIMAC INDUSTRIES, INC., 41 Fairfield Pl., 07006, pg. 1098 — PB
R & R MARKETING, Ten Patton Dr., 07006, pg. 902 — PV
Raritan Display Division, Ten Patton Dr., 07006, pg. 902 — PV
Reitman Division, Ten Patton Dr., 07006, pg. 902 — PV
Ricoh Corporation, Five Dedrick Pl., 07006, pg. 1114 — IT
Road Champs, Inc., Seven Patton Dr., 07006, pg. 923 — PB
Royal Division, Ten Patton Dr., 07006, pg. 902 — PV
Spectrum Division, 10 Patton Dr., 07006, pg. 902 — PV

West Long Branch

EA INDUSTRIES, 185 Monmouth Pkwy., 07764-9989, pg. 541 — PB
Tanon Express, 185 Monmouth Pkwy., 07764, pg. 541 — PB
Tanon Manufacturing, Inc., 185 Monmouth Pkwy., 07764, pg. 541 — PB

West New York

Aetna Handbags, 635 59th St., 07093, pg. 920 — PB
Bonnie International, 5801 Jefferson St., 07093, pg. 920 — PB
Empress Handbags, 635 59th St., 07093, pg. 920 — PB
Hudson United Bank-West New York, 6137 Bergenline Ave., 07093, pg. 845 — PB
JLN, 635 59th St., 07093, pg. 920 — PB
JACLYN, INC., 5801 Jefferson St., 07093, pg. 920 — PB

West Orange

BARTON PRESS, INC., 55 Lakeside Ave., 07052, pg. 128 — PV
Co-Jac Finishers, Inc., 55 Lakeside Ave., 07052, pg. 128 — PV
Organon Inc., 375 Mt. Pleasant Ave., 07052, pg. 48 — IT
Patient Care, Inc., 100 Executive Dr., Ste. 130, 07052, pg. 348 — PB

SELECTO-FLASH, INC., 18 Central Ave., 07052, pg. 982 — PV
US SERVIS, 414 Eagle Rock Ave., 07052, pg. 1687 — PB

West Paterson

BNY Holdings (New Jersey) Corp., 385 Rifle Camp Rd., 07024, pg. 178 — PB
CYTEC INDUSTRIES INC., Five Garret Mountain Plaza, 07424, pg. 471 — PB
Hunt Foreign Investment Corp., Five Garret Mountain Plaza, 07424, pg. 1219 — PB
Midlantic Commercial Co., Inc., One Garret Mountain Plaza, 07424, pg. 1242 — PB
Olin Hunt Sub. I Corp., Five Garret Mountain Plaza, 07424, pg. 1219 — PB
Ruppman Marketing Technologies, Inc., 1130 McBride Ave., 07424, pg. 952 — PV

Westfield

CONNELL CO., 45 Cardinal Dr., 07090-1099, pg. 264 — PV
CROLL-REYNOLDS COMPANY, INC., 751 Central Ave., 07091, pg. 290 — PV
E'TOWN CORPORATION, P.O. Box 788, 600 South Ave., 07090-0788, pg. 540 — PB
E'town Properties Inc., 600 South Ave., 07090, pg. 540 — PB
Elizabethtown Water Company, 600 South Ave., 07090, pg. 540 — PB
Merrill Corporation, 425 North Ave., E., 07090, pg. 1097 — PB
Rice & Sugar Div., 45 Cardinal Dr., 07090-1099, pg. 264 — PV
TORCON, INC., 214 E. Grove St., 07091, pg. 1092 — PV

Westmont

Pepper, Hamilton & Scheetz, Sentry Office Plaza, 216 Haddon Ave., Ste. 321, 08108-2811, pg. 851 — PV

Westville

J.E. BERKOWITZ, LP, Delsea Dr. & Harvard Ave., 08093, pg. 135 — PV
Mars Graphics, Inc., One Deadline Dr., 08093, pg. 793 — PB

Wharton

Antec Group, 321 Richard Mine Rd., 07885, pg. 117 — PB
DIMENSIONAL MERCHANDISING, INC., 86 N. Main St., 07885, pg. 333 — PV
Pneu-Hydro Products, Inc., 353 Richard Mine Rd., 07885, pg. 1593 — PB

Whippany

Communication Techniques, Inc., Nine Whippany Rd., 07981, pg. 521 — PB
THE CORPORATE COMMUNICATIONS GROUP, 26 Parsippany Rd., 07981, pg. 276 — PV
PHILIP FRITZE & SONS, INC., Ten School St., 07981, pg. 429 — PB
GEC (UK) Aerospace Inc., 110 Algonquin Pkwy., 07981-1640, pg. 545 — IT
STEPHEN GOULD PAPER CO., INC., 35 S. Jefferson Rd., 07981, pg. 467 — PV
Isomedix Inc., 11 Apollo Dr., 07981, pg. 1515 — PB
Isomedix Investments, Inc., 11 Apollo Dr., 07981, pg. 1515 — PB
Isomedix Management Inc., 11 Apollo Dr., 07981, pg. 1515 — PB
Isomedix Operations Inc., Nine Apollo Dr., 07981, pg. 1515 — PB
Isomedix Operations Inc., 11 Apollo Dr., 07981, pg. 1515 — PB
Kemira Paper Chemicals, Inc., 16, S. Jefferson Rd., 07981, pg. 729 — IT
Knoll Pharmaceutical Company, 30 N. Jefferson Rd., 07981, pg. 105 — IT

Whitehouse

Fedders North America, Inc., P.O. Box 498, 3421 Rte. 22 E., 08888, pg. 614 — PB
FIMBEL DOOR CORPORATION, 12 Coddington Rd., 08888, pg. 404 — PV

Whitehouse Station

Johnson & Johnson/Merck Consumer Pharmaceuticals Co., One Merck Dr., 08889, pg. 929 — PB
MERCK & CO., INC., P.O. Box 100, One Merck Dr., 08889-0100, pg. 1090 — PB

Willingboro

HILL INTERNATIONAL INC., One Levitt Pkwy., 08046, pg. 529 — PV
Methode Electronics Inc.-East, 10 Industrial Dr., 08046, pg. 1101 — PB
Willing B Wire Corporation, Ironside Ct., 08046, pg. 780 — PB

Wood Ridge

Certech, Inc., One Park Place W., 07075, pg. 307 — PB
SPRINGFIELD PRECISION INSTRUMENTS, INC., P.O. Box 4003, 76 Passaic St., 07075-1004, pg. 1027 — PV

PB - *U.S. Public Companies Volume*
PV - *U.S. Private Companies Volume*
IT - *International Public & Private Companies Volume*

Geographic Index-U.S.

Woodbridge

ALPHA ASSOCIATES, INC., Two Amboy Ave., 07095, pg. 44   PV
Amerada Hess Corp., One Hess Plaza, 07095, pg. 65   PB
Amerada Hess Pipeline Corp., One Hess Plaza, 07095, pg. 65   PB
CPS CHEMICAL COMPANY INC., 900 Rt. 9 N., 07095, pg. 196   PV
Centric Clutch Co., Main St. at U.S. Rt. 9, 07095, pg. 1794   PB
CIBA Self-Medication, Inc., Mack Woodbridge II, 581 Main St., 07095, pg. 973   IT
Hanson North America, 581 Main St., 07095, pg. 593   IT
J.I. Kislak Agency, Inc., 1000 Rte. 9, 07095, pg. 624   PV
MariFarms, Inc., Ten Woodbridge Center Dr., 07095, pg. 593   IT
PATHMARK STORES INCORPORATED, 301 Blair Rd., 07095-0915, pg. 843   PV
Ronson Consumer Products Corp., Three Ronson Rd., 07095, pg. 1405   PV
Royal Foods Distributors, Inc., 215 Blair Rd., 07095, pg. 653   PB
THE SAWTOOTH GROUP, Aspen Corporate Park Two, 1460 Rte. 9 N., 07095, pg. 969   PV
Sunshine Biscuits, Inc., 100 Woodbridge Center Dr., 07095-1196, pg. 434   PB
Sunshine Biscuits, Inc., 100 Woodbridge Center Dr., 07095-1196, pg. 657   PB
White Rose Dairy, 215 Blair Rd., pg. 330   PV
Woodbridge Center, Inc., 250 Woodbridge Ctr. Dr., 07095, pg. 1408   PB
Woodbridge Sanitary Pottery Corp., 500 Green St., 07095, pg. 449   PV

Woodbury

E.D. Collier & Son, Reid & Namoni Sts., 08096, pg. 122   PV
E.P. HENRY CORPORATION, 201 Park Ave., 08096, pg. 522   PV
MediaNews Group, Eastern Operations, 309 So. Broad St., 08096, pg. 727   PV

Woodcliff Lake

Ascom Timeplex, 400 Chestnut Ridge Rd., 07675, pg. 86   IT
BMW (US) Holding Corporation, 300 Chestnut Ridge Rd., 07675, pg. 177   IT
Citicorp International Trade Indemnity Co., Inc., 50 Tice Blvd., 07675, pg. 377   PB
Construction Equipment Group, 200 Chestnut Ridge Rd., 07675, pg. 876   PB
INGERSOLL-RAND COMPANY, 200 Chestnut Ridge Rd., 07675, pg. 876   PB
Ingersoll-Rand Sales Co., Ltd., 200 Chestnut Ridge Rd., 07675, pg. 877   PB
Tanabe U.S.A. Inc., 50 Tice Blvd., 07675, pg. 1354   IT

Wyckoff

Dutch Mill Baking Company, 500 Braen Ave., 07481, pg. 1561   PB
Novamet Specialty Products, 07481, pg. 672   IT

NEW MEXICO

Alamogordo

Casa Arena Blanca, P.O. Box 1906, 205 Moonglow, 88310, pg. 838   PB
Presto Products Manufacturing Co., 1301 LaVelle Rd., 88310, pg. 1159   PB
The Scott Motors Company, 1117 LaVelle Rd., 88310, pg. 598   PV

Albuquerque

AGRA Earth & Environmental, Inc., 4700 Lincoln Rd. N.E., 87109, pg. 31   IT
Albuquerque Auto Auction Inc., 3411 Broadway Blvd., S.E., 87105-0405, pg. 1648   PB
The Albuquerque Tribune, 7777 Jefferson N.E., P.O. Drawer T, 87103, pg. 1447   PB
AMERICAN FURNITURE COMPANY, P.O. Box 3685, 87190-3685, pg. 55   PV
Amtech Systems Corporation, 8600 Jefferson St. N.E., 87113-1629, pg. 105   PB
Bank of America New Mexico, P.O. Box 25000, 87125-9989, pg. 180   PB
Business Machine Center, Inc. (NSL), 4860 Pan American Fwy., N.E., 87109, pg. 863   PB
CEI Enterprises, P.O. Box 9156, 87119, pg. 141   PB
Centex American Gypsum Co., 8001 Jefferson, 87113, pg. 322   PB
Charter Behavioral Health System of New Mexico, Inc., 5901 Zuni Rd., S.E., 87108, pg. 1034   PB
Cigna Dental Health Plan of New Mexico, Inc., 5301 Central Ave. N.E., Ste. 1500, 87108, pg. 358   PB
Creamland Dairies, Inc., 010 Indian School Rd. N.W., 87102, pg. 490   PB
CUTTER AVIATION ALBUQUERQUE, INC, 2502 Clark Carr, Loop S.E., 87106, pg. 298   PV
DWF of Albuquerque, 4717 Lumber Ave., N.E., 87109, pg. 326   PV

EG & G Management Systems, 2450 Alamo Ave., S.E., Ste. 102, 87106, pg. 543   PB
EG & G Management Systems Inc.- Albuquerque Operations, 2450 Alamo Ave., S.E., 87106, pg. 543   PB
Envirco Corporation, 6701 Jefferson N.E., 87109, pg. 1639   PB
First American Title Co. of New Mexico, 2601 Louisiana Blvd. N.E., 87110, pg. 625   PB
First Security Bank of New Mexico, 40 First Plaza, N.W., 87102, pg. 637   PB
FURR'S SUPERMARKETS, 1730 Montano Rd. NW, 87107, pg. 432   PV
GALLES CHEVROLET, 1601 Lomis N.E., 87102, pg. 438   PV
Green Tree Acceptance, Inc., 6400 Uptown Blvd. NE, Ste. 400E, 87110, pg. 762   PB
Hewlett-Packard Company, 5130 Masthead, N.E., 87109, pg. 814   PB
Honeywell Defense Avionics Systems, 9201 San Mateo Blvd. N.E., 87113-2227, pg. 834   PB
HORIZON/CMS HEALTHCARE CORPORATION, 8801 Horizon Blvd. N.E., 87113, pg. 836   PB
Horizon Healthcare Nursing Center, 239 Elm St. NE, 87102, pg. 838   PB
Horizon Specialty Hospital - Albuquerque, 235 Elm St. NE, 87102, pg. 838   PB
Hydro Conduit Corp., P.O. Box 1609, 2800 Second St. S.W., 87103, pg. 245   IT
Jacobs Engineering Group Inc., 2155 Louisiana Blvd., N.E., 87110, pg. 921   PB
Jewel Osco Southwest, Inc., 2500 Louisiana Blvd. N.E., Ste. 400, 87110, pg. 93   PB
KOAT-TV, 3801 Carlisle Blvd. N.E., 87107, pg. 1344   PB
KOB-TV, Inc., Four Broadcast Pl., S.W., 87103, pg. 544   PV
KPMG Peat Marwick LLP, 6565 Americas Pkwy. N.E., 87190, pg. 604   PV
KRQE-TV, 13 Broadcasting Plaza S.W., 87104, pg. 984   PB
Kaufman and Broad New Mexico Division, 7870 Jefferson N.E., 87109, pg. 945   PB
J. KORBER & COMPANY, 2400 Menaul, 87107, pg. 632   PV
Leedshill-Herkenhoff, Inc., 500 Cooper Ave., N.W., Ste. 500, 87102, pg. 80   PV
Lovelace Health Systems, Inc., 5301 Central Ave. N.E., Stes. 400 & 500, 87108, pg. 360   PB
MCBRIDE AND ASSOCIATES, INC., 5555 McLeod, N.E., 87109, pg. 719   PV
Meadows Resources, Inc., Alvarado Sq., 87158, pg. 1339   PB
MELLOY BROS. ENTERPRISES, 7707 Lomas N.E., 87110, pg. 730   PB
Melloy Brothers Inc., 7707 Lomas N.E., 87110, pg. 730   PV
MOUNTAIN STATES CONSTRUCTORS, INC., P.O. BOX 6325, 87197, pg. 764   PV
NZU, Inc., 6100 Indian School Ave., 87110, pg. 1172   PB
NationsBank Sunwest, Inc., 303 Roma N.W., 87125, pg. 1165   PB
New Mexico Broadcasting Co., 13 Broadcast Plaza S.W., 87104, pg. 984   PB
New Mexico Star Tribune Company, 7777 Jefferson St., NE, 87109, pg. 1448   PB
New Mexico Utilities, Inc., Ste. 201, 4700 Irving Blvd., N.W., 87114, pg. 1494   PB
Nobel/Sysco Food Services Co.-Albequerque, 601 Comanche, N.E., 87107, pg. 1551   PB
Nord Pacific Limited, 201 Third St. N.W., #1750, 07102, pg. 1188   PB
NORD RESOURCES CORPORATION, 201 Third Street N.W., #1750, 87102, pg. 1188   PB
Nord Rutile Corp., 201 Third St. N.W., #1750, 87102, pg. 1188   PB
Norwest Bank New Mexico, N.A., 200 Lomas Blvd. N.W., 87102, pg. 1202   PB
Paragon Resources, Inc., Alvarado Sq., 87158, pg. 1339   PB
Frank Paxton Lumber Company, 1909 Bellamah N.W., P.O. Box. 25152, 87125, pg. 585   PV
PENCO-New Mexico, 11000 Candelaria, N.E., Ste. 101E, 87112, pg. 1508   IT
Perma-Fix of New Mexico, 7928 Ranchitos Loop N.E., 87113, pg. 1280   PB
PLAINS ELECTRIC GENERATION TRANSMISSION CO-OP, INC., 2401 Aztec, N.E., 87107, pg. 868   PV
PUBLIC SERVICE COMPANY OF NEW MEXICO, 414 Silver S.W., 87102, pg. 1339   PB
QUALITY PONTIAC GMC BUICK, 1300 Lomas NE, 87102, pg. 899   PV
QualMed Plans for Health-New Mexico, 6100 Uptown Blvd., 87110, pg. 678   PB
Roadrunner Trucking, Inc., 10605 Central Ave. N.W., 87121, pg. 911   PV
Sagebrush Sales Company, 6300 State Rd., 303 S.E., 87105, pg. 1193   PB
SCIENCE & ENGINEERING ASSOCIATES, 6100 Uptown Blvd., N.E., Ste. 700, 87110, pg. 975   PV
Silmax, Inc., 5031 San Diego Ave., NE, 87113, pg. 1317   IT
Sterling Electronics, 3540-D Pan American Fwy., 87107, pg. 1051   PB
SUN HEALTHCARE GROUP INC., 101 Sun Ln. N.E., 87109, pg. 1530   PB
Sunbelt Mining Co., Inc., Alvarado Sq., 87158, pg. 1340   PB
SunBridge Assisted Living, 5131 Masthead St. N.E., 87109, pg. 1531   PB
Sunsoft Corporation, 6815 Academy Pkwy. West N.E., 87109, pg. 462   IT
Sunterra Gas Gathering Company, Alvarado Sq., 87158, pg. 1340   PB

Sunterra Gas Processing Company, Alvarado Sq., 87158, pg. 1340   PB
TIE Systems New Mexico, 2416 Candelaria N.E., 87107, pg. 1085   PV
Talbot Financial Corporation, 7770 Jefferson, N.E., Ste. 200, 87109, pg. 1423   PB
Tecomet-Albuquerque, 4800 Hawkins, N.E., 87109, pg. 1592   PB
Thunderbird Steel Corporation, 4300 Second N.W., 87107, pg. 298   PB
URS Greiner, Inc., 5971 Jefferson Blvd., N.E., Ste. 101, 87109, pg. 1658   PB
Valle Norte Caring Center, 8820 Horizon Blvd. N.E., 87113, pg. 838   PB
Valley National Financial Services Company, Bldg. 5, 2400 Louisiana N.E., Ste. 160, 87110, pg. 173   PB
Wellborn - DE Corp., 215 Rossmoor Rd., S.W., 87125, pg. 347   PV
Willis Corroon Administrative Services Corporation, 11000 Candelaria N.E., Ste. 102 E, 87112, pg. 1505   IT

Anthony

SHARP OIL COMPANY, 217 N. Main, 88021, pg. 990   PV

Artesia

BREWER OIL CO., 1301 W. Main St., 88210, pg. 167   PV
Navajo Corp., 501 E. Main St., 88210, pg. 830   PB
Navajo Pipeline Co., 501 E. Main St., 88210, pg. 830   PB
Navajo Refining Co., P.O. Drawer 159, 501 E. Main, 88210, pg. 830   PB

Bloomfield

Hacienda de Salud - Bloomfield, 803 Hacienda Ln., 87413, pg. 838   PB

Carlsbad

Western Ag-Minerals Company (Mine Office), P.O. Box 511, 5516 Hobbs Hwy., 88220, pg. 856   PB

Chamberino

Alpo Pet Foods, P.O. Box 259, 88027, pg. 917   IT

Clovis

ALLSUPS CONVENIENCE STORES INC., 2112 Thornton, 88101, pg. 44   PV
Cummins Natural Gas Engines, Inc., 409 S. Norris Dr., 88101, pg. 468   PB
New Mexico-American Water Co., 1005 Norris St., 88102, pg. 95   PB
Sunwest Bank of Clovis, N.A., P.O. Drawer 1509, 88101, pg. 1165   PB

Espanola

Hacienda de Salud - Espanola, 720 Hacienda St., 87532, pg. 838   PB
Sunwest Bank of Rio Arriba, N.A., P.O. Box 8, 87532, pg. 1165   PB

Estancia

Torrance County Detention Facility, 209 County Rd. A049, 87016, pg. 451   PB

Farmington

Atomi Corp., P.O. Box 208, 87401, pg. 345   PV
Desert Turbine Services, Inc., 1140 W. Navajo, Hangar 13, 87401, pg. 1099   PB
DUGAN PRODUCTION CORP., 709 E. Murray Dr., 87401, pg. 345   PV
Four Corners Aviation, Inc., 1260 W. Navajo St., 87401, pg. 1099   PB
Giant Exploration & Production Co., 2200 Bloomfield Hwy., 87401, pg. 742   PB
Mesa Airlines, Inc., 2325 E. 30th, 87401, pg. 1099   PB
Mesa Airlines Pilot Development, Inc., 1296 W. Navajo St., 87401, pg. 1099   PB
San Juan Manor, 806 W. Maple, 87401, pg. 838   PB
Sunwest Bank of Farmington, P.O. Box 1560, 87499, pg. 1165   PB
Western Coal Development, 300 W. Arrington, Ste. 200, 87401, pg. 224   IT
Y & S Candies, One Twizzler Way, 87401, pg. 812   PV

Fort Sumner

Pecos Valley Care Center, P.O. Drawer L, 519 N. Tenth, 88119, pg. 838   PB

Gallup

Giant Refining Company, Rte. 3, Box 7, 87301, pg. 742   PB
GURLEY MOTOR COMPANY, 701 W. Coal Ave., 87301, pg. 488   PV
McKinley Manor, 224 Nizhoni Blvd., 87301, pg. 838   PB
Red Rocks Care Center, P.O. Box 1778, 3720 Churchrock Rd., 87301, pg. 838   PB
RICO MOTOR COMPANY, 501-23 W. Coal, 87301, pg. 930   PV

Geographic Index-U.S.

Sunwest Bank of Gallup, P.O. Box 339, 87305,
pg. 1165 **PB**

Grants

Lee Ranch Coal Company, P.O. Box 757, 87020,
pg. 594 **IT**
New Mexico Womens Correctional Facility, 1700 E. Old
Hwy. 66, 87020, pg. 450 **PB**
Quivera Mining Company, 5 Mi. North Junction 53 & 509,
87020, pg. 1118 **IT**

Hobbs

Hobbs Healthcare Center, 5715 Lovington Hwy., 88240,
pg. 838 **PB**
Lea Refining Company, P.O. Box 980, 88241, pg. 830 **PB**
LOREFCO, Inc., P.O. Box 980, 88241, pg. 830 **PB**
Sunwest Bank of Hobbs, N.A., P.O. Box 5310, 88241,
pg. 1165 **PB**

Hurley

Chino Mines Company, 210 Cortez St., 88043,
pg. 1287 **PB**

La Mesa

STAHMANN FARMS, INC., 22500 Hwy. 28, 88044,
pg. 1029 **PV**

La Plata

La Plata Mine, P.O. Box 210, 87418, pg. 224 **IT**

Las Cruces

Block Plant, 1020 E. Kansas, P.O. Drawer FF, 88001,
pg. 936 **PB**
Casa Del Sol, 2905 E. Missouri Ave., 88001, pg. 838 **PB**
Holiday RV Superstores of New Mexico Inc., 1285 Avenida
de Mesilla, 88005, pg. 830 **PB**
KMAZ, First National Bank Tower, 500 S. Main St., Ste.
150, 88001, pg. 983 **PB**
Las Cruces Nursing Center, 2029 Sagecrest Ct., 88001,
pg. 838 **PB**
Sunwest Bank of Las Cruces, N.A., P.O. Box 2047, 88004,
pg. 1165 **PB**

Las Vegas

Southwest Senior Care Center, 2301 Collins Dr., 87701,
pg. 838 **PB**

Lordsburg

Sunshine Haven, W. Railway Ave., 88045, pg. 838 **PB**

Los Alamos

Hewlett-Packard Company, 1362-C Trinity Dr., 87544,
pg. 814 **PB**
Los Alamos Monitor, P.O. Box 1268, 256 DP Rd., 87544,
pg. 648 **PV**
LOS ALAMOS TECHNICAL ASSOCIATES, INC., 1200
Trinity Dr., 87544, pg. 676 **PV**

Pecos

Universal Telephone Southwest-Pecos, P.O. Drawer 488,
New Mexico State Rd. 63, 87552, pg. 330 **PB**

Playas

Phelps Dodge Hidalgo, P.O. Box 67, One Smelter Rd.,
88009, pg. 1287 **PB**

Raton

Sunwest Bank of Raton, N.A., P.O. Drawer 1108, 87740,
pg. 1165 **PB**

Rio Rancho

AMREP Financial Corporation, 333 Rio Rancho Dr., N.E.,
87124, pg. 105 **PB**
AMREP Southwest, Inc., 333 Rio Rancho Dr., N.E.,
87124, pg. 104 **PB**
Bergen Brunswig Drug Company, 510 Laser Rd., 87124,
pg. 214 **PB**
Rio Rancho, 333 Rio Rancho Dr., N.E., 87124, pg. 105 **PB**
Sparton Technology, Inc., 4901 Rockaway S.E., 87124,
pg. 1496 **PB**
Sunwest Bank of Sandoval County, N.A., P.O. Box 15760,
87175, pg. 1165 **PB**

Roswell

BELL GAS, INC., 1811 S.E. Main St., 88201, pg. 131 **PV**
Block Plant, Poe Ave. at Railroad, P.O. Box 1633, 88201,
pg. 936 **PB**
Casa Maria Health Care Center, 1601 S. Main, 88201,
pg. 838 **PB**
The Hondo Company, P.O. Box 2208, 88202, pg. 818 **IT**
Hondo Oil & Gas Company, 410 E. College Blvd., 88201,
pg. 818 **IT**

Hundo Magdelena Oil & Gas Ltd., 410 E. College, 88201,
pg. 818 **IT**
KBIM-TV, 214 N. Main, 88201, pg. 984 **PB**
Roswell Nursing Center, 3200 Mission Arch, 88201,
pg. 838 **PB**
Sunset Villa Nursing Home, 1515 S. Sunset Dr., 88201,
pg. 838 **PB**
Sunwest Bank of Roswell, N.A., P.O. Box 1858, 88201,
pg. 1165 **PB**
Transportation Manufacturing Corporation, P.O. Box 5670
(R.I.A.C.), 88202-5670, pg. 326 **IT**

Ruidoso

Ruidoso Care Center, P.O. Box 2214, Fifth & D St., 88345,
pg. 838 **PB**

Santa Fe

Casa Real Health Care Center, 1650 Galisteo St., 87501,
pg. 838 **PB**
DAVIS SELECTED ADVISORS, L.P., 124 E. Marcy St.,
87501, pg. 315 **PV**
Eberline Instrument Corporation, 504 Airport Rd., 87504-
2108, pg. 1593 **PB**
Eldorado at Santa Fe, Rte. 3, P.O. Box 1, 87501,
pg. 105 **PB**
Environmental Control Inc., Rt. 20, Box 29-EC1, 87501,
pg. 49 **PB**
First Interstate Bank of New Mexico N.A., 124 Washington
Ave., 87501, pg. 1753 **PB**
Genzyme Genetics Div., 2000 Vivigen Way, 87505,
pg. 733 **PB**
Horizon Healthcare Nursing Center, 635 Harkle Rd., 87501,
pg. 838 **PB**
Johnson Storage & Moving, Santa Fe, Rte. 20, Box 2911,
(Corner of Airport Rd. & Colony Dr.), 87501,
pg. 594 **PV**
PE Molecular Informatics, 1800 Old Pecos Trail, Ste. M,
87505, pg. 1279 **PB**
Santa Fe Detention Center, 4250 Airport Rd., 87505,
pg. 451 **PB**
SECURITY CAPITAL GROUP INCORPORATED, 125
Lincoln Ave., 87501, pg. 980 **PV**
Sunwest Bank of Santa Fe, P.O. Box 5375, 87502,
pg. 1165 **PB**
Symbol, 369 Montezuma Ave., Ste. 113, 87501-2626,
pg. 1546 **PV**
Trans-Lux Cocteau Corporation, P.O. Box 22040, 87502,
pg. 1629 **PB**

Silver City

Sunwest Bank of Grant County, P.O. Box 1449, 88062,
pg. 1165 **PB**
TNP Enterprises, Inc.-Mountain Div., 3815 N. Swan St.,
88062, pg. 1557 **PB**
Western New Mexico Telephone Co., 314 Yankee St.,
88062, pg. 1022 **PB**

Taos

Sanco Inc., 24603 Hwy. 64, W., 87571, pg. 49 **PB**

Truth Or Consequences

St. Cloud Mining Co., P.O. Box 1670, 87901, pg. 750 **PB**

Tucumcari

Van Ark Care Center, P.O. Box 1028, 1005 S. Monroe,
88401, pg. 838 **PB**

Tyrone

Phelps Dodge Tyrone, Hwy. 90 S., Tyrone Mine Rd., 88065,
pg. 1287 **PB**

Waterflow

San Juan Mine, P.O. Box 561, 87421, pg. 224 **IT**

NEW YORK

Adams

Great Lakes Cheese of New York, Inc., 23 Phelps Rd.,
13605, pg. 474 **PV**

Akron

Gypsum Joint Systems Plant, Bloomingdale Road, 14001,
pg. 737 **PB**
PERRY'S ICE CREAM CO., INC., One Ice Cream Plaza,
14001, pg. 855 **PV**
Strippit, Inc., 12975 Clarence Ctr. Rd., 14001, pg. 862 **PB**

Albany

A Greenhouse Inc., 4294 Albany St., 12204, pg. 752 **IT**
ALBANK FINANCIAL CORPORATION, Ten N. Pearl St.,
P.O. Box 70, 12207, pg. 36 **PB**
ALBANY INTERNATIONAL CORP., 1373 Broadway,
12204-1907, pg. 36 **PB**
Albany International/Press Fabrics Division, P.O. Box 1109,
12201, pg. 36 **PB**

Albany Port Railroad Co., 40 Beaver St., 12207,
pg. 432 **PB**
Albany Savings Bank, Ten N. Pearl St., 12207, pg. 36 **PB**
Albany Times Union, News Plaza, Box 15000, 12212,
pg. 517 **PV**
American Family Life Assurance Company of New York,
38-40 State St., 12207, pg. 28 **PB**
Arnold Advertising, One Columbia Cir., 12203, pg. 84 **PV**
Broder Bros. Co. of Albany, Bldg. 11, Northeastern
Industrial Pk., 12085, pg. 171 **PV**
Business First of New York, Inc., Two Computer Dr. W.,
12210, pg. 19 **PV**
CT & E Environmental Services Inc., 12 Walker Way,
12205-4946, pg. 1153 **IT**
Callanan Industries, Inc., South St., 12204, pg. 242 **IT**
Combined Life Insurance Co. of New York, Seven
Washington Sq., 12205, pg. 118 **PB**
DE NOOYER CHEVROLET INC., 127 Wolf Rd., 12205,
pg. 318 **PV**
Delmar Publishers Inc., Box 15015, 3 Columbia Cir., 12212,
pg. 1600 **PB**
Fleet Bank, Peter Kiernan Plaza, 12207, pg. 649 **PB**
Gould Paper Corporation-Albany, 4292 Albany St., 12205,
pg. 467 **PV**
Hewlett-Packard Company, Five Computer Dr., S., 12205,
pg. 814 **PB**
HOLBROOK LUMBER COMPANY, 70 Fuller Rd., 12205,
pg. 533 **PV**
HUDSON VALLEY PAPER COMPANY, 981 Broadway,
12207-1315, pg. 543 **PV**
IDS Life Insurance Co. of New York, P.O. Box 5144, 12205,
pg. 73 **PB**
Independent Cement Corporation, 187 Wolf Rd., 12205,
pg. 629 **IT**
Information Integrators, Inc., 915 Broadway, 12207,
pg. 711 **PB**
Intergraph Corporation, 234 Hudson Ave., 12210,
pg. 890 **PB**
Key Bank of New York, 66 S. Pearl St., 12207,
pg. 954 **PB**
Key Trust Company, Key Trust Tower, 54 State St., 12207,
pg. 954 **PB**
KeyCorp Leasing Ltd., Key Trust Tower, 54 State St.,
12201-0655, pg. 954 **PB**
Kruger Recycling Inc., 877 S. Pearl St., 12202, pg. 762 **IT**
MAIN BROTHERS OIL COMPANY, INC., P.O. Box 11029,
12211, pg. 697 **PV**
Eric Mower & Associates, 18 Corporate Woods Blvd.,
12211, pg. 765 **PV**
NCB Properties, Inc., Key Trust Tower, 54 State St., 12207,
pg. 955 **PB**
Northeast Marketing Div., Two Wall St., 12206, pg. 296 **PV**
ORANGE MOTOR COMPANY INC., 799 Central Ave.,
12206, pg. 818 **PV**
PENCO-New York, 421 New Kaner Rd., Ste. One, 12205,
pg. 1508 **IT**
Quest Diagnostic-Albany, 62 Hackett Blvd., 12209,
pg. 1351 **PB**
Sealy Mattress Company of Albany, Inc., P.O. Box 5288, 99
Railroad Ave. & Brown Rd., 12205, pg. 979 **PB**
Southtec, Inc., 1750 N. Broadway, 12204, pg. 1015 **PV**
Sysco Food Services-Albany, 71 Fuller Rd., 12205,
pg. 1551 **PB**
Testcom, Inc., 12 Walker Way, 12205-4946, pg. 1154 **IT**
TRADING PORT, INC., North Manning Blvd. & Prospect
Ave., 12206, pg. 1095 **PB**
TRANS WORLD ENTERTAINMENT CORPORATION, 38
Corporate Cir., 12203, pg. 1626 **PB**
J. TREFFILETTI & SONS, INC., Four N. Ferry St., 12207,
pg. 1099 **PV**
Troy Savings Bank-Albany, 120 States St., 12207,
pg. 1106 **PV**
Troy Savings Bank-Colonie, 103 Wolf Rd., 12205,
pg. 1106 **PV**
Turner Construction Company, 100 State St., 12207,
pg. 1645 **PB**
URS Greiner, Inc., Three Marcus Blvd., 12205,
pg. 1658 **PB**
United Alliant Food Service, 875 Broadway, 12207,
pg. 244 **PV**
WNYT-TV, 15 N. Pearl, 12204, pg. 544 **PV**
WXXA-TV, 28 Corporate Cir., 12203, pg. 385 **PB**
Willis Corroon Administrative Services Corporation, 18
Computer Dr. W., Suite B, 12205, pg. 1505 **IT**

Albion

Bayex Incorporated, P.O. Box 390, 14770 E. Ave., 14411,
pg. 1170 **IT**
Ontario Foods, Inc., 111-117 West Ave., 14411,
pg. 728 **PB**

Alden

Vibratech, Inc., 11980 Walden Ave., 14004-9790,
pg. 862 **PB**

Amherst

Birdair, Inc., 65 Lawrence Bell Dr., 14221, pg. 1348 **IT**
CM Mechanical Handling Systems, 140 J.J. Audubon Pkwy.,
14228-1197, pg. 405 **PB**
COLUMBUS MCKINNON CORP., 140 John James
Audubon Pkwy., 14228-1197, pg. 405 **PB**
Deltran Div., 45 Hazelwood Dr., pg. 90 **PB**
EATON OFFICE SUPPLY CO., INC., 180 John Glenn Dr.,
14228-2292, pg. 358 **PV**
Graseby Goring Kerr Inc., 221 Commerce Dr., 14228,
pg. 1268 **IT**

Geographic Index-U.S.

PB - *U.S. Public Companies Volume*
PV - *U.S. Private Companies Volume*
IT - *International Public & Private Companies Volume*

1332

Hewlett-Packard Company, 130 John Muir Dr., 14228-1179, pg. 814 **PB**
International Imaging Materials, Inc., 310 Commerce Dr., 14228-2396, pg. 1266 **PB**
M&T Financial Corporation, 4925 Main St., 14226, pg. 631 **PB**
MARK IV INDUSTRIES INC., One Towne Centre, 501 John James Audubon Pkwy., 14228, pg. 1044 **PB**
NIAGARA CUTTER, INC., 200 John James Audobon Pkwy., 14228, pg. 798 **PV**
Northstar Life Ins. Company, 100 Corporate PKwy., Ste. 424, 14226, pg. 750 **PV**
Quest Diagnostic-Amherst, 4955 N. Bailey Ave., 14226, pg. 1351 **PB**
STANDARD ELECTRONICS, INC., 215 John Glenn Dr., 14228, pg. 1031 **PB**
Stern Advertising, Inc., 6265 Sheridan Dr., Ste. 216, 14221, pg. 1041 **PV**
Tops Markets, Inc., 6363 Main St., 14221, pg. 750 **IT**
ULTRA TOOL & PLASTICS, INC., 155 Pineview Dr., 14228, pg. 1116 **PV**
Watson Bowman Acme Corp., 95 Pineview Drive, 14228, pg. 505 **PV**

Amityville

GENERAL MICROWAVE CORPORATION, 5500 New Horizons Blvd., 11701, pg. 717 **PB**
HI-TECH PHARMACAL CO., INC., 369 Bayview Ave., 11701, pg. 825 **PB**
Math Associates, 5500 New Horizons Blvd., 11701, pg. 717 **PB**
MONITOR AEROSPACE CORPORATION, 1000 New Horizons Blvd., 11701, pg. 757 **PB**
NIC Components Corp., 6000 New Horizons Blvd., 11701, pg. 1205 **PB**
NAPCO SECURITY SYSTEMS, INC., 333 Bayview Ave., 11701, pg. 1151 **PB**
Nu Horizons International Corp., 6000 New Horizons Blvd., 11701, pg. 1205 **PB**

Amsterdam

Esquire Novelty Co., Forest Ave., 12010, pg. 1047 **PV**
Floquil-Polly S Color Corp., 4517 State Hwy. 30, 12010, pg. 1357 **PB**
Longview Fiber Co. Eastern Container Div., 365 E. Main St., 12010, pg. 1014 **PV**
Mohawk Finishing Products, Inc., 4715 State Hwy. 30, 12010, pg. 1357 **PB**
NOTEWORTHY INDUSTRIES INC., 100 Church St., 12010, pg. 808 **PB**
Pacesetter Products Inc., 14 Park Dr., 12010, pg. 603 **PB**

Ancramdale

Clear Channel Communications International, Shorthorn Farm, 3580 Rte. 82, 12503, pg. 383 **PB**

Angola

Bison Canning Co., Inc., South Main St., 14006, pg. 468 **PV**
Filtration Systems Division, 9542 Hardpan Rd., 14006, pg. 126 **PB**

Armonk

CINE MAGNETICS, INC., 100 Business Park Dr., 10504, pg. 240 **PV**
Color Data East, Five N. Greenwich Rd., 10504, pg. 1437 **PB**
JOS. M. HERMAN SHOE CO., 200 Business Park Dr., 10504, pg. 524 **PV**
INTERNATIONAL BUSINESS MACHINES CORPORATION, One Old Orchard Rd., 10504, pg. 895 **PB**
Y.F. Jelenko & Co., 99 Business Park Drive, 10504, pg. 616 **IT**
MBIA Assurance S.A., 113 King St., 10504, pg. 1023 **PB**
MBIA INC., 113 King St., 10504, pg. 1023 **PB**
MBIA Municipal Investors Service Corporation, 113 King St., 10504, pg. 1023 **PB**
Municipal Bond Investors Assurance Corporation, 113 King St., 10504, pg. 1023 **PB**
Security Equity Life Insurance Company, 84 Business Park Dr., Ste 303, 10504, pg. 443 **PV**
SEMICONDUCTOR PACKAGING MATERIALS CO., INC., One Labriola Ct., 10504, pg. 1456 **PB**

Ashville

Resource America, Inc., P.O. Box 130, 14710, pg. 1382 **PB**

Astoria

CHARMER INDUSTRIES, 1950 48th St., 11105, pg. 230 **PV**

Au Sable Forks

Lake Placid Granite Co., P.O. Box I, 12912, pg. 251 **PV**

Auburn

Auburn Technology, Inc., 100 Orchard St., 13021, pg. 200 **IT**

Carrier Corp. RCD, Carrier Pkwy. TR 2, 13021, pg. 1689 **PB**
Central New York Bottle Co., P.O. Box 696, Rural Rte. 6, 13021, pg. 1289 **PB**
Monorail, Inc., 23 N. Division St., 13021, pg. 256 **PV**
Quest Diagnostic-Auburn, The Carr Bldg., 188 Genesee St., Ste. 217, 13021, pg. 1351 **PB**
SL Auburn, Inc., 89 York St., 13021, pg. 443 **PB**

Avon

XLM Company, Avon Plant, 1150 E. River Rd., 14414, pg. 772 **PB**

Baldwin

Kaufel America Inc., 1170 Atlantic Ave., 11510, pg. 725 **IT**
Lightalarms Electronics Corporation, 1170 Atlantic Ave., 11510, pg. 725 **IT**

Baldwinsville

Municipal Business Unit, 31 E. Genesee, 13027, pg. 861 **PB**

Ballston Spa

CURTIS LUMBER COMPANY, 885 Rte. 67, 12020, pg. 297 **PV**
Mechanical Technology Inc.-Technology Grp.(Malta), 20 Plains Rd., 12020, pg. 1077 **PB**

Batavia

Batavia Wine Cellars, School St., 14020, pg. 300 **PB**
GRAHAM CORPORATION, 20 Florence Ave., 14020, pg. 757 **PB**
Graham Manufacturing Co., Inc., 20 Florence Ave., 14020, pg. 757 **PB**
P.W. MINOR & SON, INC., Three Treadeasy Ave., 14020, pg. 751 **PV**
WESTERN REGIONAL OFF TRACK BETTING, 700 Ellicott St., 14020, pg. 1168 **PV**

Bay Shore

CPC Baking Business, 55 Paradise Ln., 11706, pg. 224 **PB**
Eagle Performance Systems, 100 Spence St., 11706, pg. 758 **PB**
Fox-Knapp, 90 Spence St., 11717, pg. 860 **PV**
General Medical Equipment, 100 Spence St., 11706, pg. 758 **PB**
LAWRENCE METAL PRODUCTS, INC., 260 Spur Dr., S., 11706, pg. 654 **PV**
Lumex Medical Products, 100 Spence St., 11706-2290, pg. 758 **PB**
DAVID PEYSER SPORTSWEAR INC., 90 Spence St., 11717, pg. 860 **PV**
RFI Corp., 100 Pine Aire Dr., 11706, pg. 494 **PB**
UNC Accessory Services-New York, 86 Cleveland Ave., 11706, pg. 710 **PB**
VIA TECH PUBLISHING SOLUTIONS, 1440 Fifth Ave., 11706, pg. 1138 **PV**

Bayport

EDWIN B. STIMPSON COMPANY, INC., 900 Sylvan Ave., 11705, pg. 1043 **PV**

Beacon

Texaco Research Center, P.O. Box 509, 12508-0509, pg. 1583 **PB**

Bedford Hills

Medical Professional Liability Agency, Ltd., Two Depot Plaza, 3rd Fl., 10507, pg. 685 **PB**

Bethpage

Electronics and Systems Integration Division, S. Oyster Bay Rd., 11714-3582, pg. 1198 **PB**
SLEEPY'S THE MATTRESS PROFESSIONALS, 175 Central Ave. S., 11714, pg. 1005 **PV**

Big Flats

SCHWEIZER AIRCRAFT CORPORATION, 1250 Schweizer Rd., 14814, pg. 975 **PV**

Binghamton

Binghamton Cel Tel Co., 206 State St., 2nd Fl., 13901, pg. 1708 **PB**
Chesapeake Packaging Co./Binghamton, 1240 Conklin Rd., 13902, pg. 346 **PB**
Columbian Life Insurance Company, P.O. Box 1381, 13902, pg. 256 **PV**
COLUMBIAN MUTUAL LIFE INSURANCE CO., P.O. Box 1381, 13902, pg. 256 **PV**
Crowley Foods, Inc., 49 Court St. Metro Centre, 13902, pg. 752 **IT**
DORON PRECISION SYSTEMS, INC., 174 Court St., 13902, pg. 341 **PV**

Dover Technologies, One Marine Midland Plaza, 6th Fl., East Tower, 13901, pg. 521 **PB**
Foron International Sales Corp., P.O. Box 400, 13902, pg. 341 **PV**
Imaging Products Division, 40 Charles St., 13902, pg. 902 **PB**
Klockner-Moeller Corp., RR 5, 104J Airport Rd., 13905, pg. 736 **IT**
McIntosh Laboratory Inc., 2 Chambers St., 13903-2699, pg. 296 **IT**
Multiple Parking Services, Inc., Collier Street Ramp Garage, P.O. Box 1569, 13902, pg. 43 **PV**
NGE Enterprises, Inc., P.O. Box 5231-C, 4500 Vestal Pkwy. E., 13902-5231, pg. 1173 **PB**
NEW YORK STATE ELECTRIC & GAS CORPORATION, P.O. Box 5224, 13902-5224, pg. 1173 **PB**
Press & Sun-Bulletin, Vestal Pkwy. E., 13903, pg. 700 **PB**
Quest Diagnostic-Binghamton, 1159 Vestal Ave., 13909, pg. 1351 **PB**
Quest Diagnostic-Binghamton, 159 Front St., 13905, pg. 1351 **PB**
SECURITY MUTUAL LIFE INSURANCE CO. OF NEW YORK, 100 Court St., 13901, pg. 981 **PV**
E.H. TITCHENER & COMPANY, One Titchener Pl., 13905, pg. 1089 **PV**
Universal Instruments Corporation, P.O. Box 825, 13902, pg. 522 **PB**

Blasdell

Grassland Equipment & Irrigation Corp., 250 Lake Ave., 14219, pg. 471 **PV**
Grassland Equipment & Irrigation Corp., 250 Lake Ave., 14209, pg. 471 **PV**
Krepe-Kraft, Inc., 4199 Bay View Rd., 14219, pg. 142 **PB**

Bohemia

Aerospace Avionics Inc., 1000 MacArthur Memorial Hwy., 11716, pg. 126 **IT**
Antenna Systems, 2950 Veterans Memorial Hwy., 11716, pg. 1674 **PB**
Beta Transformers, 40 Orville Dr., 11716, pg. 555 **PV**
Car-lac Electronics, 75 Orville Dr., 11716, pg. 1068 **IT**
Dorne & Margolin, Inc., 2950 Veterans Memorial Hwy., 11716, pg. 1675 **PB**
Enraf-Nonius Company (Ltd Pts), 390 Central Ave., 11716, pg. 389 **IT**
Fasco Sensors & Controls Division, 1000 MacArthur Memorial Hwy., 11716, pg. 127 **IT**
Genco Distributing Div., 100 Orville Dr., 11716, pg. 730 **PB**
The Hudson Corporation, 90 Orville Dr., 11716, pg. 1166 **PB**
ILC Data Device, 105 Wilbur Pl., 11716, pg. 555 **PV**
ILC INDUSTRIES, INC., 105 Wilbur Pl., 11716, pg. 555 **PV**
Link Tech, Inc., 30 Orville Dr., 11716, pg. 555 **PV**
NATURE'S BOUNTY INC., 90 Orville Dr., 11716, pg. 1166 **PB**
PERIPHONICS CORP., 4000 Veterans Memorial Hwy., 11716, pg. 1278 **PB**
Vitamin World, 105 Orville Dr., 11716, pg. 1166 **PB**

Bolivar

Heritage Cutlery, Inc., 7971 Refinery Rd., 14715, pg. 940 **PV**

Brentwood

Allou Distributors Inc., 50 Emjay Blvd., 11717, pg. 55 **PB**
ALLOU HEALTH & BEAUTY CARE, INC., 50 Emjay Blvd., 11717, pg. 55 **PB**
M. Sobol Inc., 50 Emjay Blvd., 11717, pg. 55 **PB**
U.S. Lock, 77 Rodeo Dr., 11717, pg. 1748 **PB**

Brewerton

Quest Diagnostic-Brewerton, Brewerton Plaza, Bartell Rd., 13029, pg. 1351 **PB**

Brewster

CIBA Specialty Chemicals-Performance Polymers Division, 281 Fields Ln., 10509, pg. 291 **IT**
Dunmore Corporation/Brewster, Rte. 6, 10509, pg. 347 **PV**
Hipotronics, Inc., P.O. Box 414, Rte. 22, 10509, pg. 844 **PB**

Briarcliff Manor

Godwins Booke & Dickenson, Inc., 549 Pleasantville Rd., 10510, pg. 118 **PB**
Philips Laboratories, 345 Scarborough Rd., 10510, pg. 1054 **IT**
TETKO, INC., 333 S. Highland Ave., 10510, pg. 1078 **PV**

Broadalbin

Mohawk Furniture, Inc., Five Mill St., 12025, pg. 443 **PV**

Bronx

A & P COAT, APRON & LINEN SUPPLY, 40 W. 170th St., 10452, pg. 1 **PV**
Bustelo Coffee Roasting Co., 733 Brush Ave., 10465, pg. 1377 **PB**
Clay-Park Labs, Inc., Bathgate Industrial Pk, 1700 Bathgate Ave., 10457, pg. 30 **IT**

PB - *U.S. Public Companies Volume*
PV - *U.S. Private Companies Volume*
IT - *International Public & Private Companies Volume*

1333

Geographic Index-U.S.

CONDAL DISTRIBUTORS INC., 531 Dupont St., 10474, pg. 262 **PV**
Consolidated Paper Co., 271 Walnut Ave., 10454, pg. 838 **PV**
DEXTER CHEMICAL CORP., 845 Edgewater Rd., 10474, pg. 329 **PV**
Everlast Sports Manufacturing Corp., 750 E. 132nd St., 10454, pg. 386 **PV**
EVERLAST WORLD BOXING CORP., 750 E. 132nd. St., 10454, pg. 386 **PV**
The Food Emporium, 1400 Food Center Dr., 10474, pg. 1375 **IT**
GATX Logistics, Inc.-New York, 586 River Ave., 10451, pg. 691 **PB**
GATX Logistics, Inc.-N.Y., 586 River Ave., 10451, pg. 691 **PB**
INDUSTRIAL ACOUSTICS COMPANY, INC., 1160 Commerce Ave., 10462, pg. 875 **PB**
LOEHMANN'S, INC., 2500 Halsey St., 10461, pg. 1010 **PB**
National Foods Inc., 600 Food Ctr. Dr., 10474, pg. 429 **PB**
PAPER ENTERPRISES, INC., 850 E. 140th St., 10454, pg. 837 **PB**
Peter Pak Company, 271 Walnut Ave., 10454, pg. 838 **PV**
THE H.W. WILSON CO., 950 University Ave., 10452, pg. 1180 **PV**

Bronxville

Coronet Communications, 17 Kraft Ave., 10708, pg. 1021 **PB**

Brooklyn

BAROUH EATON ALLEN CORPORATION, 67 Kent Ave., 11211, pg. 117 **PV**
Bayside Fuel Oil Corp., 1810 Shore Pkwy., 11214, pg. 125 **PV**
BAYSIDE FUEL OIL DEPOT CORP., 1776 Shore Pkwy., 11214, pg. 125 **PV**
BELMONT METALS, INC., 314-30 Belmont Ave., 11207-4000, pg. 132 **PV**
BLUE RIDGE FARMS, INC., 3301 Atlantic Ave., 11208, pg. 153 **PV**
BROOKLYN UNION, One MetroTech Ctr., 11201-3850, pg. 259 **PB**
Chase Institutional Trust Sys., 4 Metro Tech Ctr. 3 Fl., 11201-3849, pg. 338 **PB**
Chase Securities, Inc., 4 Chase Metrotech Center, 11245, pg. 338 **PB**
CUMBERLAND PACKING CORP., Two Cumberland St., 11205, pg. 295 **PV**
Domino Sugar Corporation-Brooklyn, 49 S. 2nd St., 11211, pg. 1356 **IT**
ESQUIRE RADIO & ELECTRONICS INC., 4100 First Ave., 11232-3321, pg. 383 **PV**
4C FOODS CORPORATION, 580 Fountain Ave., 11208, pg. 421 **PV**
GANIN TIRE CO., INC., 1421-38th St., 11218, pg. 439 **PV**
Gas Energy Inc., 111 Livingston St., 11201, pg. 296 **PB**
GOLDBERGER DOLL MFG. COMPANY, INC., 538 Johnson Ave., 11237, pg. 459 **PV**
Governale Co., Inc., 788 Williams Ave., 11234, pg. 270 **PB**
Greenwald Industries, Inc., 1340 Metropolitan Ave., 11237, pg. 1341 **PV**
GUSSCO MANUFACTURING, INC., 5112 Second Ave., 11232, pg. 488 **PV**
HALSEY DRUG COMPANY, 1827 Pacific St., 11233, pg. 496 **PV**
HAYWIN TEXTILE PRODUCTS, INC., 106 Bayard St., 11222, pg. 514 **PV**
Intergrated Corporation, 2478 86th St., 2nd Fl., 11214, pg. 890 **PB**
J.M.P. BAKERY CO., INC., 508 Junius St., 11212, pg. 578 **PV**
KEY FOOD STORES CO-OPERATIVE, INC., 8925 Ave. D, 11236, pg. 617 **PV**
Ko-Rec-Type, 67 Kent Ave., 11211, pg. 117 **PV**
Lee Spring Company, 1462 62nd St., 11219, pg. 1118 **PV**
Manhattan and Bronx Surface Transit Operating Authority, 370 Jay St., 11201, pg. 739 **PV**
MANHATTAN STORE INTERIORS, INC., 17 Moultrie St., 11222, pg. 699 **PV**
MONARCH LUGGAGE CO. INC., Five Delavan St., 11231, pg. 757 **PV**
New York City Transit Authority, 370 Jay St., 11201, pg. 739 **PV**
OPG INDUSTRIES, 140 58th St., Bldg. 5B, 11220, pg. 809 **PV**
PEERLESS IMPORTERS, INC., 16 Bridgewater St., 11222, pg. 847 **PV**
Penguin Air Conditioning Corp., 26 West St., 11222, pg. 572 **PB**
Polymer Chemicals Group, 700 Court St., 11231, pg. 1774 **PV**
RAINBOW APPAREL DISTRIBUTION CENTER, 1000 Pennsylvania Ave., 11207, pg. 907 **PV**
Reynolds Tire & Rubber, 1421-38th St., 11218, pg. 439 **PV**
Rose Fuel Corporation, 8301 Third Ave., 11209, pg. 125 **PV**
ROYAL FARMS INC., 2101 Ave. X, 11235, pg. 948 **PV**
SALON & FITNESS SYSTEMS, 1535 McDonald Ave., 11230, pg. 962 **PV**
Strober Bros., Inc. Building Supply Centers, Pier Three, Furman St., 11201, pg. 403 **PV**
The Strober Organization, Inc., Pier Three, Furman St., 11201, pg. 403 **PV**
SUNNYDALE FARMS, 400 Stanley Ave., 11207, pg. 1053 **PV**

Tangent Industries Ltd., 4100 First Ave., 11232-3321, pg. 383 **PV**
VTA Management Services, Inc., 1270 E. 19th St., Ste. 1M, 11230, pg. 839 **PV**
VICTORIA PACKING CORPORATION, 443 E. 100th St., 11236, pg. 1139 **PV**

Brownville

Brownville Power Company, Bridge St., 13615, pg. 243 **PB**

Buchanan

Gypsum Wall Board Plant, P.O. Box 128, Off Broadway, 10511, pg. 737 **PB**

Buffalo

API Development Corp., 2777 Walden Ave., 14225, pg. 90 **PB**
AMERICAN PRECISION INDUSTRIES INC., 2777 Walden Ave., 14225, pg. 90 **PB**
ASTRONICS CORPORATION, 1801 Elmwood Ave., 14207, pg. 142 **PB**
B.R. Guest, Ltd., One West Ferry, 14213, pg. 928 **PV**
BARRISTER INFORMATION SYSTEMS CORPORATION, 465 Main St., 7th Fl., 14203, pg. 192 **PB**
Basco Div., 2777 Walden Ave., 14225, pg. 90 **PB**
BENDERSON DEVELOPMENT CO., INC., 570 Delaware Ave., 14202, pg. 132 **PV**
Bison Baseball Inc., 275 Washington St., 14203, pg. 928 **PV**
Buffalo China, Inc., 658 Baily Ave., 14204, pg. 1226 **PV**
Buffalo Color Corporation, 100 Lee St., 14210, pg. 179 **PV**
Buffalo Evening News, Inc., One News Plaza, 14210, pg. 217 **PB**
BUFFALO HOSPITAL SUPPLY CO., INC., 4034 Genesee St., 14225, pg. 179 **PB**
Buffalo Law Journal, 472 Delaware Ave., 14202, pg. 19 **PB**
BUFFALO TRUCK CENTER, 271 Dingens St., 14206, pg. 179 **PV**
Buffalo Waterfront Restaurant Corp., 2 Templeton Terrace, 14202, pg. 1023 **PV**
F.N. BURT COMPANY, INC., 2345 Walden Ave., 14225, pg. 188 **PV**
Business First of New York, LLC, 472 Delaware Ave., 14202, pg. 19 **PB**
CA-1 Services, One Delaware North Place, 438 Main St., 14202, pg. 322 **PV**
C.J. Tower Inc., 128 Dearborn St., 14207, pg. 1071 **PV**
Calspan Operations, 4455 Genesee St., 14225, pg. 1136 **PV**
CARTON-CRAFT CORPORATION, 115 Ash St., 14204, pg. 217 **PV**
CECOS International, Inc., 2321 Kenmore Ave., 14207, pg. 264 **PB**
Charleston Insurance Company, 741 Delaware Ave., 14209-1072, pg. 1455 **PB**
LOUIS P. CIMINELLI CONSTRUCTION CO. INC., 369 Franklin St., 14202, pg. 239 **PV**
Citibank (New York State), 409 Main St., 14203, pg. 377 **PB**
CLARK GUM COMPANY, 1100 Military Rd., 14217, pg. 243 **PV**
Clearing-Niagara, P. O. Box 475, 14240-0475, pg. 196 **PV**
COLAD GROUP INC., 801 Exchange St., 14210, pg. 250 **PV**
Comptek Federal Systems, Inc., 110 Broadway, 14203, pg. 419 **PB**
COMPTEK RESEARCH, INC., 2732 Transit Rd., 14224, pg. 419 **PB**
COMPUTER TASK GROUP, INC. (CTG), 800 Delaware Ave., 14209-2094, pg. 423 **PB**
Conax Buffalo Corporation, 2300 Walden Ave., 14225, pg. 646 **PV**
COOK MOVING SYSTEMS, INC., 1845 Dale Rd., 14225, pg. 272 **PV**
Corrugated Packaging, 1110 Military Road, 14217, pg. 737 **PB**
CURTIS SCREW CO., INC., 1130 Niagara St., 14213, pg. 298 **PV**
JOHN W. DANFORTH CO., 1940 Fillmore Ave., 14214, pg. 309 **PV**
Data Track Account Services, Inc., Ten Lafayette Sq., 14203, pg. 1156 **PB**
JOSEPH DAVIS, INC., 120 W. Tupper St., 14201, pg. 315 **PV**
DELAWARE NORTH COMPANIES, INC., 438 Main St., 14202, pg. 321 **PV**
DeLeuw Cather & Co., Engineering Div., 37 Franklin St., 14204-4107, pg. 841 **PV**
DINAIRE CORP., 145 Gruner Rd., 14227, pg. 334 **PV**
Dunlop Tire Corporation, 200 John James Audubon Pkwy., 14228, pg. 1317 **IT**
EASTMAN WORLDWIDE, 779 Washington St., 14203, pg. 358 **PV**
Elan Foods, 28 Church Street, Ste. 206, 14202, pg. 484 **PV**
Elf Atochem Organic Peroxides Plant, P.O. Box 1048, 14240, pg. 446 **IT**
Exchange Insurance Company, 741 Delaware Ave., 14209-1072, pg. 1455 **PB**
Fedco Automotive Components Company, Inc., 57 Tonawanda St., 14207, pg. 1396 **IT**
FERGUSON ELECTRIC CONSTRUCTION CO., INC., 333 Ellicott St., 14203, pg. 401 **PV**
Ferguson Electric Equipment Corporation, 333 Ellicott St., 14203, pg. 401 **PV**

Ferguson Electric Service Co., Inc., 321 Ellicott St., 14203, pg. 401 **PV**
FIRST EMPIRE STATE CORPORATION, c/o Corporate Reporting, One M&T Plaza, 5th Fl., 14240, pg. 631 **PB**
Freezer Queen Foods Inc., 975 Fuhrmann Blvd., 14203, pg. 340 **IT**
GIT, LTD., P.O. Box 2078, 14219-0278, pg. 742 **PB**
GIBRALTAR STEEL CORP., P.O. Box 2028, 3556 Lake Shore Rd., 14219-0228, pg. 742 **PB**
GRAPHIC CONTROLS CORPORATION, 189 Van Rensselaer St., 14210, pg. 470 **PV**
Gunther Mele Packaging, Inc., 175 Rano St., 14207, pg. 578 **PB**
HL-NIW, Inc., 2321 Kenmore Ave., 14207, pg. 264 **PB**
HSBC Americas, One Marine Midland Ctr., 14203, pg. 580 **IT**
HSC Controls, 390 Youngs Rd., 14221, pg. 1776 **PV**
Habistat Globe Inc., 1400 Clinton St., 14206, pg. 585 **IT**
Highland Land Minerals, Inc., Ten Lafayette Sq., 14203, pg. 1156 **PB**
THE HOWDEN FAN CO., 110 Broadway, 14203, pg. 543 **PV**
Information Systems Div., 685 Howard St., 14240, pg. 152 **PB**
INTEGRATED WASTE SERVICES, INC., 201 Ganson St., 14203, pg. 886 **PB**
Intercontinental Branded Apparel, 2020 Elmwood Ave., 14207, pg. 796 **PB**
Jewett International Corp., 750 Grant St., 14213-1000, pg. 952 **PV**
The Jewett Refrigerator Co., Inc., 750 Grant St., 14213-1000, pg. 952 **PV**
Johnny Carson Apparel, Inc., 2020 Elmwood Ave., 14207, pg. 796 **PB**
Kamro Champion Lighting Products Inc., 45 Comet Ave., 14216, pg. 725 **IT**
Keystone Buffalo Warehouse, 485 Ludwig Ave., 14227, pg. 955 **PB**
Lucas Industries Inc., 672 Delaware Ave., 14209, pg. 820 **IT**
LucasVarity Inc., 672 Delaware Ave., 14209, pg. 820 **IT**
M&T Real Estate, One M&T Ctr., 14240, pg. 631 **PB**
M&T Capital Corporation, M&T Center, One Fountain Plaza, Ninth Fl., 14203, pg. 631 **PB**
M&T Credit Corporation, One M&T Plaza, 14240, pg. 631 **PB**
M&T Mortgage Corp., M&T Center, One Fountain Plaza, 14203-2399, pg. 631 **PB**
M&T Securities, Inc., P.O. Box 1357, 14240, pg. 631 **PB**
Manufacturers & Traders Trust Company, One M&T Plaza, 14240, pg. 631 **PB**
Marine Midland Bank, One Marine Midland Ctr., 14240, pg. 581 **IT**
Marine Midland Leasing Corporation, One Marine Midland Ctr., 14203, pg. 581 **IT**
Marine Midland Mortgage Corporation, One Marine Midland Ctr., 14203, pg. 581 **IT**
Marine Midland Mortgage (USA), Inc., One Marine Midland Ctr., 14203, pg. 581 **IT**
Marine Midland Realty Credit Corporation, 15/F, One Marine Midland Ctr., 14203, pg. 581 **IT**
Marine Midland Securities, Inc., One Marine Midland Ctr., 14203, pg. 581 **IT**
McDonald Products Company, 304 Sonwil Dr., 14225, pg. 1009 **PV**
MCLEAN-THOMAS INC., 266 Broadway, 14204, pg. 724 **PV**
Mentholatum Company, 1360 Niagara St., 14213, pg. 1126 **IT**
MERCHANTS GROUP, INC., 250 Main St., 14202, pg. 1090 **PB**
Miracle Adhesives, 75 Tonawanda St., 14207, pg. 1466 **PB**
MOD-PAC CORP., 873 Hertel Ave., 14216, pg. 142 **PB**
Mokon, 2150 Elmwood Ave., 14207, pg. 1045 **PB**
MOLIN AUTO PARTS INC., 3896 Union Rd., 14225, pg. 756 **PV**
MOLLENBERG-BETZ INC., 300 Scott St., 14204, pg. 756 **PV**
Mosler Counter Systems Div., 200 Race St., 14027, pg. 763 **PV**
Eric Mower and Associates/Buffalo, Inc., 360 Delaware Ave., 14202, pg. 765 **PV**
Multiple Parking Services, Inc., 335 Statler Tower, 107 Delaware Ave., 14202, pg. 43 **PV**
NATIONAL FUEL GAS COMPANY, Ten Lafayette Sq., 14203, pg. 1156 **PB**
National Fuel Gas Distribution Corp., Ten Lafayette Sq., 14203, pg. 1156 **PB**
National Fuel Resources, 10 Lafayette Sq., 14203, pg. 1156 **PB**
NATIONAL HEALTH CARE AFFILIATES, INC., 651 Delaware Ave., 14202, pg. 784 **PV**
Niagara Asset Corporation, 60 Lakefront Blvd., 14202, pg. 955 **PB**
NIAGARA BLOWER COMPANY, 673 Ontario, 14207, pg. 798 **PV**
Niagara Cold Drawn Corp., 110 Hopkins St., 14220, pg. 1181 **PV**
Niagara Exchange Corporation, 741 Delaware Ave., 14209, pg. 1455 **PB**
NIAGARA FRONTIER HOCKEY, L.P., Marine Midland Arena, 1 Seymour Knox III Plaza, 14203, pg. 798 **PV**
Niagara Frontier Transit & Metro System, 181 Ellicott St., 14205, pg. 798 **PV**
NIAGARA FRONTIER TRANSPORTATION AUTHORITY, 181 Ellicott St., 14203, pg. 798 **PV**
Niagara Recycling, Inc., 2321 Kenmore Ave., 14207, pg. 264 **PB**
NIAGARA TRANSFORMER CORP., 1747 Dale Rd., 14225, pg. 798 **PV**

Geographic Index-U.S.

Old Republic Life Insurance Co. of New York, 560
Delaware Ave., 14202, pg. 1218 **PB**
OSMOSE WOOD PRESERVING, INC., 980 Ellicott St.,
14209, pg. 821 **PV**
Outokumpu American Brass Co., 70 Sayre St., 14240-0981,
pg. 1016 **IT**
PVS Chemicals, Inc., 55 Lee St., 14210, pg. 828 **PB**
Pierce & Stevens Corp., 710 Ohio St., 14203, pg. 1019 **PV**
PLYWOOD PLASTICS INC., 111 Tonawanda St., 14207,
pg. 873 **PV**
Pratt & Lambert Paints, 75 Tonawanda St., 14207,
pg. 1466 **PB**
Pratt & Lambert Specialty Products, 75 Tonawanda St.,
14207, pg. 1466 **PB**
Protective Closures Co., Inc., 2150 Elmwood Ave., 14207,
pg. 1045 **PB**
QUACKENBUSH CO. INC., 505 Franklin St., 14202,
pg. 897 **PV**
Regency Thermographers of Buffalo, Inc., 830 Hertel Ave.,
14216, pg. 89 **PB**
Reichhold Chemicals Div., 4201 Genesee St., 14225,
pg. 370 **IT**
RICH PRODUCTS CORP., 1150 Niagara St., 14213,
pg. 928 **PV**
River Ranch - Northeast, 25 Hardwood Place, 14210,
pg. 491 **PV**
RIVER RANCH NORTHEAST, INC., P.O. Box 832, 14240-
0832, pg. 934 **PV**
ROBERT JAMES SALES INC., 269 Hinman Ave., 14216,
pg. 935 **PV**
Rodgard Corporation, 1355 Clinton St., 14206, pg. 142 **PV**
RUSLANDER & SONS, INC., 750 Grant St., 14213-1000,
pg. 952 **PV**
Russer Foods, 665 Perry St., 14210, pg. 1204 **PV**
Santo Tours & Travel, Inc., 354 Cayuga Rd., 14225-1940,
pg. 23 **PV**
SIERRA TECHNOLOGIES INC., 485 Cayuga Rd., 14225,
pg. 999 **PV**
SMITH MCDONALD CORP., 304 Sonwil Dr., 14225,
pg. 1009 **PV**
Smith Metal Arts Company, Inc., 304 Sonwil Dr., 14225,
pg. 1009 **PV**
SNYDER TANK CORP., S-3774 Lakeshore Rd., 14219,
pg. 1011 **PV**
Sorrento Cheese Company, Inc., 2375 S. Park Ave., 14220,
pg. 323 **IT**
Spencer Kellogg, 120 Delaware Ave., 14202, pg. 370 **IT**
Sportservice Corporation, One Delaware North Place, 438
Main St., 14202, pg. 322 **PV**
Trico Products Corporation, 60 Lakefront Blvd., 14202,
pg. 1397 **IT**
TUNMORE OLDSMOBILE INC., 2677 Delaware Ave.,
14216, pg. 1109 **PV**
Turner Construction Company, Firstmark Bldg., 135
Delaware Ave., Ste. 214, 14202, pg. 1646 **PB**
WGRV, 259 Delaware Ave., 14201, pg. 926 **IT**
Waste Stream Technology, Inc., 302 Grote St., 14207,
pg. 1463 **PV**
Wehle Electric Co., Inc., 475 Ellicott St., 14203,
pg. 1492 **IT**
Westwood-Squibb Pharmaceuticals Inc., 100 Forest Ave.,
14213, pg. 255 **PB**
Williams Advanced Materials, Inc., 2978 Main St., 14214,
pg. 266 **PB**
Wiper Check, Inc., 78521, pg. 1397 **IT**
Wolf Group Direct, 40 Fountain Plaza, 14202, pg. 1185 **PV**
WOLF MANSFIELD BOLLING ADVERTISING INC., 40
Fountain Plaza, 14202, pg. 1185 **PV**
Wolf Mansfield Bolling Advertising Inc., 40 Fountain Plaza,
14202, pg. 1186 **PV**
ZEMCO INDUSTRIES, INC., 665 Perry St., 14210,
pg. 1204 **PV**

Burt

Akzo Chemicals Inc., 2153 Lockport & Olcott Rd., 14028,
pg. 47 **IT**

Caledonia

Chloride Power Electronics Inc., One Technology Place,
14423, pg. 287 **IT**

Camden

Camden Wire Co., Inc., 12 Masonic Ave., 13316,
pg. 526 **PV**
Mystic Stamp Company, 24 Mill St., 13316, pg. 671 **PV**
Non-Insulated Division, 12 Masonic Ave., 13316,
pg. 526 **PV**

Camillus

CAMILLUS CUTLERY CO., 54 Main St., 13031,
pg. 203 **PV**

Campbell Hall

Ottaway Newspapers, Inc., P.O. Box 401, 10916,
pg. 525 **PB**

Canajoharie

Beech-Nut Nutrition Corporation, Two Church St., 13317,
pg. 1359 **PB**
La Salle Labs Div., 99 Creek St., 13317, pg. 494 **PB**

Canandaigua

Canandaigua Plastics Div., 203 North St., 14424,
pg. 202 **PV**
Canandaigua Wine Co., 116 Buffalo St., 14424,
pg. 300 **PB**
Canandaigua Wine Company Div., 116 Buffalo St., 93639,
pg. 300 **PB**
CANANDAIGUA WINE COMPANY, INC., 116 Buffalo St.,
14424, pg. 300 **PB**
LABELON CORPORATION, 10 Chapin St., 14424,
pg. 641 **PV**
Manaschewitz Wine Company, 116 Buffalo St., 14424,
pg. 300 **PB**
Roberts Trading Corp., P.O. Box 401, 14424, pg. 300 **PB**

Canastota

DIEMOLDING CORP., 125 Rasbach St., 13032,
pg. 332 **PV**
ERD Environmental, Inc., Marguerite Dr. W., 13032,
pg. 546 **PB**
Northeast Environmental Services, Inc., Marguerite Dr. W.,
RR 3, Box 8B, 13032, pg. 546 **PB**

Carle Place

SABBETH INDUSTRIES LTD, One Old Country, Ste. 565,
11514, pg. 959 **PV**
Takashimaya Enterprises, Inc. (Shiro of Japan), 401 Old
Country Rd., 11514, pg. 1350 **IT**

Carmel

Acxiom Corporation, 39 Seminary Hill Rd., 10512-3681,
pg. 18 **PV**
Danbury Pharmacal Inc., 12 Stoneleigh Ave., 10512,
pg. 969 **PV**
GUIDEPOSTS ASSOCIATES, INC., 39 Seminary Hill Rd.,
10512, pg. 487 **PV**

Castile

Robeson Appliances, Robeson Park, 14427, pg. 1394 **PB**

Castleton on Hudson

Fort Orange Paper Co., Inc., 1900 River Rd., 12033,
pg. 1376 **PB**

Catskill

CATSKILL SAVINGS BANK, 341 Main St., 12414,
pg. 318 **PB**

Cattaraugus

TODCO Engineered Products Div., Rte. 353, 14719,
pg. 823 **PV**

Cazenovia

Dielectric Laboratories, P.O. Box 321, Rte. 20 E., 13035,
pg. 521 **PB**

Centerpont

Vengroff Williams Realty Management, 109 Centerline Rd.,
11721, pg. 1135 **PV**

Central Islip

NORTH AMERICAN ENCLOSURES, INC., 85 Jetson Ln.,
11722, pg. 803 **PV**
Waldbaum's Supermarkets, Inc., One Hemlock St., 11722,
pg. 1375 **IT**

Cheektowaga

Cellular One Buffalo, AppleTree Business Park, 2875 Union
Rd., Ste. 35U, 14227, pg. 1415 **PB**
MIKEN COMPANIES, INC., 75 Boxwood Ln., 14227,
pg. 745 **PV**
RAMA GROUP OF COMPANIES, 25 Boxwood Lane,
14227, pg. 908 **PV**
Research Environmental Management, Inc., 3729 Union
Rd., 14225, pg. 924 **PV**
Specialty Restaurants Corp., 100 Amherst Villa Rd., 14229,
pg. 1023 **PV**
Thermal Industries Inc., 3248 Union Rd., 14227-1044,
pg. 491 **PV**

Chester

Isomedix Operations, Inc., 23 Elizabeth Dr., 10918,
pg. 1515 **PB**

Churchville

Varity Zecal, 456 N. Sanford Rd., 14428, pg. 820 **IT**

Clarence

A.M. Castle & Co., 9530 Main St., 14031, pg. 313 **PB**

D. J. Martin Equipment Co., Inc., 10189 Main St., 14031-
2077, pg. 360 **PV**
Mennen Medical Inc., 10123 Main St., 14031, pg. 858 **IT**

Clifton Park

Jack Byrne Minuteman Lube, 1768 Rte. 9, 12065,
pg. 191 **PV**
Merck Medco Managed Care, LLC, 110 Clifton Corp. Pkwy.,
Bldg. 100, 12065, pg. 1090 **PB**
MICHAELS DEVELOPMENT GROUP, INC., 282 Ushers
Rd., 12065, pg. 740 **PV**
Troy Savings Bank-Clifton Park, Rtes. 9 & 146, 12065,
pg. 1106 **PV**
Troy Savings Bank-Clifton Park Hannaford Office, Clifton
County Rd., 12065, pg. 1106 **PV**

Cobleskill

Hoffman Laces, Ltd., 104 N. Grand St., 12043, pg. 769 **PB**

Cohoes

Cohoes Fashions, Inc., 43 Mohawk St., 12047, pg. 268 **PB**
Financial Collection Agencies (1990) Inc., One Mustang
Drive, 12047, pg. 471 **IT**
MOHAWK PAPER MILLS, INC., 465 Saratoga St., 12047,
pg. 755 **PV**

College Point

EDO Marine & Aircraft Systems, 14-04 111th St., 11356-
1434, pg. 542 **PB**
EDO Marine and Aircraft Systems, 14-04 111th St., 11356-
1434, pg. 542 **PB**
JETRO HOLDINGS, INC., 15-24 132nd St., 11356-2440,
pg. 587 **PV**
Welsbach Electric Corp., 111-01 14th Ave., 11356,
pg. 572 **PB**

Colonie

Cellular One Albany Telephone Company, 1762 Central
Ave., 12205, pg. 1415 **PB**

Commack

Chugai Boyeki (America) Corp., 55 Mall Dr., 11725,
pg. 290 **IT**
ERD WASTE CORP., 356 Veterans Memorial Hwy., 11725,
pg. 546 **PB**
Melville Advertising Inc., 763 Larkfield Rd., 11725,
pg. 1436 **PB**
PMI Motion Technologies Div., 49 Mall Dr., 11725,
pg. 965 **PB**
Protimeter, Inc., 87 Modular Ave., 11725, pg. 208 **IT**
SBARRO, INC., 763 Larkfield Rd., 11725, pg. 1435 **PB**
Sbarro of Roosevelt Field Inc., 763 Larkfield Rd., 11725,
pg. 1436 **PB**
Tempo Instrument Inc., 87 Modular Ave., 11725,
pg. 208 **IT**
VENGROFF WILLIAMS & ASSOCIATES, INC., 777 Lark
Fields Rd., 11725, pg. 1135 **PV**

Congers

ERD Environmental, Inc., 331 Rte. 9W, 10920, pg. 546 **PB**
Materials Research Corp., Route 303, 10920, pg. 1283 **IT**
Process Equipment, Rte. 303, 10920, pg. 1283 **IT**
Strober King Building Supply Centers, Inc., 102 North Rt.
9W, 10920, pg. 403 **PV**

Conklin

Canron Fabrication Corporation - Eastern Division, P.O. Box
421, Shaw Road, 13748, pg. 695 **IT**

Copiague

W.A. BAUM COMPANY, INC., 620 Oak St., 11726,
pg. 124 **PV**
Circa Pharmaceuticals, Inc., 33 Ralph Ave., 11726,
pg. 1746 **PB**
Intercom Systems, Inc., 1385 Akron St., 11726,
pg. 1556 **PB**
TII Corp., 1385 Akron St., 11726, pg. 1556 **PB**
TII Electronics, Inc., 1385 Akron St., 11726, pg. 1556 **PB**
TII INDUSTRIES, INC., 1385 Akron St., 11726,
pg. 1556 **PB**

Corning

Corning Asahi Video Products Company, Houghton Park,
14831, pg. 449 **PB**
Corning Consumer Products Company, Houghton Park,
14831, pg. 448 **PB**
Corning Enterprises Inc., Houghton Park, 14831,
pg. 448 **PB**
CORNING INCORPORATED, One Riverfront Plaza, 14831,
pg. 448 **PB**
Corning International Corporation, Houghton Park, 14830,
pg. 448 **IT**
Dresser-Rand Co., One Baron-Steuben Pl., Ste. 600,
14830, pg. 529 **PB**
Dutch Parking Inc., Centerway Parking Facility, One
Centerway Sq., 14830, pg. 43 **PV**

PB - *U.S. Public Companies Volume*
PV - *U.S. Private Companies Volume*
IT - *International Public & Private Companies Volume*

Cortland

CORTLAND LINE CO., INC., 3736 Kellogg Rd., 13045, pg. 277 **PV**
Cortland Plant, 45 Cleveland St., 13045, pg. 444 **PB**
MARIETTA CORPORATION, P.O. Box 5250, 37 Huntington St., 13045-5250, pg. 702 **PV**
Monarch Cortland Div., 641 NYS Rte. 13, P.O. Box 749, 13045, pg. 1124 **PB**
NCC Industries, Inc., 165 Main St., 13045, pg. 697 **PV**
Pall Trinity Micro Corp., Rte. 281, 13045, pg. 1254 **PB**
SMITH CORONA CORP., 839 Rt. 13 S., 13045, pg. 1007 **PV**
Smith Corona Financial Division, P.O. Box 2020, 839 RT 13 S., 13045, pg. 1007 **PV**

Cuba

Acme Electronics Division, 9963 Rte. 446, 14727, pg. 16 **PB**
Empire Cheese, Inc., 4520 Haskell Rd., 14727, pg. 474 **PV**

De Witt

AGWAY, INC., 333 Butternut Dr., 13214, pg. 27 **PV**
Community Bank N.A., 5790 Widewaters Pkwy., 13214, pg. 416 **PB**
COMMUNITY BANK SYSTEM, INC., 5790 Widewaters Pkwy., 13214, pg. 416 **PB**
Healthsource New York, 5784 Widewaters Pkwy., 13214, pg. 360 **PB**
Patient's Choice, Inc., 5784 Widewaters Pkwy., 13214, pg. 360 **PB**
Stern Advertising, Inc., 5788 Widewaters Pkwy., 13214-2815, pg. 1041 **PV**

Deer Park

AIL Systems Inc., 455 Commack Rd., 11729, pg. 556 **PB**
ALLMETAL SCREW PRODUCTS CORP., 94A E. Jefryn Blvd., 11729, pg. 41 **PV**
Dynarad Corporation, 19 Jefryn Blvd. W., 11729, pg. 494 **PB**
First Choice, Bldg. 2, 450 Commack Rd., 11729, pg. 978 **PB**
GLOBAL STEEL PRODUCTS CORPORATION, 95 Marcus Blvd., 11729, pg. 457 **PV**
A. Goodman & Sons, Inc., 325 Marcus Blvd., 11729, pg. 158 **PV**
Heritage Air Systems, Inc., 305 Suburban Ave., 11729, pg. 572 **PB**
THE LANGER BIOMECHANICS GROUP, INC., 450 Commack Rd., 11729, pg. 978 **PB**

Deferiet

Deferiet Mill, Champion International Corp., 400 Anderson Ave., 13628, pg. 334 **PB**

Delmar

Quest Diagnostic-Delmar, 785 Delaware Ave., 12054, pg. 1351 **PB**

Depew

Leica, Inc., 3362 Walden Ave., 14043, pg. 806 **IT**
D.J. Mead-Hubbs & Howe, 3366 Walden Ave., 14043, pg. 1012 **PV**
Quebecor Printing Buffalo Inc., 2475 George Urban Blvd., 14043, pg. 1078 **IT**

Derby

NEW ERA CAP. CO., 8061 Erie Rd., 14047, pg. 793 **PV**

Dolgeville

DANIEL GREEN CO., One Main St., 13329, pg. 477 **PV**

Dunkirk

FIELDBROOK FARMS, INC., One Ice Cream Dr., 14048, pg. 403 **PV**

East Aurora

ACME ELECTRIC CORPORATION, 400 Quaker Rd., 14052, pg. 16 **PB**
Delevan Div., 270 Quaker Rd., 14052, pg. 90 **PB**
E-L Products Company, 77 Olean St., 14052, pg. 142 **PB**
Fisher-Price, Inc., 636 Girard Ave., 14052, pg. 1058 **PB**
Moog Aircraft Controls Div., Seneca St. at Jamison Rd., 14052, pg. 1127 **PB**
Moog Engine Controls Div., Seneca St. at Jamison Rd., 14052, pg. 1127 **PB**
MOOG INCORPORATED, Seneca St. at Jamison Rd., 14052-0018, pg. 1127 **PB**
Moog Industrial Controls Corp., Seneca St. at Jamison Rd., 14052, pg. 1127 **PB**
Moog International Group, Plant 20, Jamison Rd., 14052, pg. 1127 **PB**
Moog Motion Systems Div., Seneca St. at Jamison Rd., 14052, pg. 1127 **PB**
Moog Space Products Div., Seneca St. at Jamison, 14052-0018, pg. 1127 **PB**

East Bloomfield

Benjamin Sheridan Co., Rtes. 5 & 20, 14443, pg. 291 **PV**
Crosman Airguns, Rts. 5 & 20, 14443, pg. 291 **PV**
CROSMAN CORP., Rtes. 5 & 20, 14443, pg. 291 **PV**
Visible Impact Targets, Rtes. 5 & 20, 14443, pg. 291 **PV**

East Greenbush

Troy Savings Bank-East Greenbush, 615 Columbia Tpke., 12061, pg. 1106 **PV**

East Meadow

STERLING VISION, INC., 1500 Hempsted Tpk., 11554, pg. 1516 **PB**

East Rochester

Allcity Insurance Co., Rochester, P.O. Box 560, 349 W. Commercial St., Ste. 3200, 14445, pg. 990 **PB**
Xerox Technigraphic Products Division, 300 Main St., 14445, pg. 1784 **PB**

East Setauket

CURATIVE HEALTH SERVICES, Box 9052, 14 Research Way, 11733-9052, pg. 469 **PB**

East Syracuse

ANAREN MICROWAVE INC., 6635 Kirkville Rd., 13057, pg. 110 **PB**
DAIRYLEA COOPERATIVE INC., 5001 Brittonfield Pkwy., 13057, pg. 307 **PV**
First SAFECO National Life Insurance Company of New York, 6700 Old Collamer Rd., 13057, pg. 1423 **PB**
Hewlett-Packard Company, 5010 Campuswood Dr., 13057, pg. 814 **PB**
NEC Business Communication Systems (East), Inc., 5890 Enterprise Pkwy., 13057, pg. 900 **IT**
New Process Gear Div., 6600 Chrysler Dr., 13057, pg. 353 **PB**
Pandrol Jackson, Inc., P.O. Box 309, 13057, pg. 280 **IT**
Thermal Industries Inc., 6500 Joy Rd., 13057-1106, pg. 491 **PV**
WIXT-TV, 5904 Bridge St., 13057, pg. 16 **PB**

Edgewood

Introtek International, 150 Executive Dr., 11717, pg. 696 **PV**
Lepel Corporation, 50 Heartland Blvd., 11717, pg. 560 **PV**

Edwards

Edwards Telephone Co., Inc., P.O. Box 36, Main St., 13635, pg. 1571 **PB**

Ellenville

IMPERIAL SCHRADE CORP., Seven Schrade Ct., 12428, pg. 559 **PB**
Imperial Schrade Corp., P.O. Box 7000, Seven Schrade Ct., 12428, pg. 559 **PV**
VAW of America, Inc., P.O. Box 667, 12428, pg. 1466 **IT**

Ellicottville

FITZPATRICK & WELLER, INC., 12 Mill St., 14731-0490, pg. 409 **PV**

Elma

MADER CONSTRUCTION CORP., 970 Bullis Rd., 14059, pg. 693 **PV**
SERVOTRONICS, INC., 1110 Maple Rd., 14059, pg. 1462 **PB**

Elmira

ABB Traction Inc., E. 18th St., 14903, pg. 5 **IT**
ARTISTIC GREETINGS, INC., One Komer Ctr., 14902, pg. 136 **PB**
CHEMUNG FORD, INC., Box 687, 14902, pg. 233 **PV**
Dutch Parking Inc., Clemens Sq., One W. Gray St., 14901, pg. 43 **PV**
Elmira Star-Gazette, 201 Baldwin, 14902, pg. 700 **PB**
HARDINGS, INC., P.O. Box 1507, One Harding Dr., 14902-1507, pg. 502 **PV**
HILLIARD CORPORATION, 100 W. Fourth St., 14902, pg. 530 **PV**
Kennedy Valve, 1021 E. Water St., 14901, pg. 725 **PV**
TRAYER PRODUCTS, INC., 541 E. Clinton St., 14902, pg. 1098 **PV**
Vanguard Binghamton, Inc., 1421 College Ave., 14901, pg. 1708 **PV**

Elmsford

AFP IMAGING CORPORATION, 250 Clearbrook Rd., 10523, pg. 6 **PB**
AFP Imaging Corporation, 250 Clearbrook Rd., 10523, pg. 6 **PB**
American Bank Note Company, 399 Executive Blvd., 10523, pg. 68 **PB**

American Banknote Holographics, 399 Executive Blvd., 10523, pg. 68 **PB**
Baker Engineering, NY, Inc., 400 Executive Blvd., 10523, pg. 168 **PB**
Conway Import Co. Inc., Five Warehouse Ln., 10523, pg. 272 **PV**
Dent-X Division, 250 Clearbrook Rd., 10523, pg. 6 **PB**
Fuji Computer Media Div., 555 Taxter Rd., 10523, pg. 524 **IT**
Fuji Industrial Photo Products Div., 555 Taxter Rd., 10523, pg. 524 **IT**
Fuji Magnetic Products Div., 555 Taxter Rd., 10523, pg. 524 **IT**
Fuji Micrographics Div., 555 Taxter Rd., 10523, pg. 524 **IT**
Fuji Photo Film U.S.A., Inc., 555 Taxter Road, 10523, pg. 524 **IT**
Fuji Photographic Products Div., 555 Taxter Rd., 10523, pg. 524 **IT**
Elof Hansson Inc., 565 Taxter Rd., 10523, pg. 595 **IT**
Elof Hansson Paper & Board, Inc., 565 Taxter Rd., 10523, pg. 595 **IT**
Elof Hansson Pulp, Inc., 565 Taxter Rd., 10523, pg. 864 **IT**
Ikon Office Systems, 350 Executive Blvd., 10523, pg. 595 **IT**
Judel Products Corp., Elmsford Exec. Park, Bldg. 4D 2269 Sawmill River Rd., 10523, pg. 1609 **PB**
KLM Royal Dutch Airlines, 565 Taxter Rd., 10523-0903, pg. 719 **IT**
M. KAMENSTEIN, INC., 565 Taxter Rd., 10523, pg. 606 **PV**
Pitney Bowes Management Services, Five W. Main St., 10523-2416, pg. 1304 **PB**
V-BAND CORPORATION, 565 Taxter Rd., 10523, pg. 1701 **PB**
VARTA Batteries Inc., 300 Executive Blvd., 10523-1202, pg. 1452 **IT**

Endicott

E.J. Footwear Corp., 1100 East Main St., 13760, pg. 1684 **PB**
Empire Division, 1100 E. Main St., 13760, pg. 1684 **PB**
Lehigh Safety Shoe Co., 1100 E. Main St., 13760, pg. 1684 **PB**

Fairport

Atlantic Auto Finance Corp., 800 Perinton RD., 14450, pg. 1095 **PV**
DETECTION SYSTEMS, INC., 130 Perinton Pkwy., 14450, pg. 501 **PB**
Global Van & Storage Co., 400 Mason Rd., 14450, pg. 458 **PV**
Goulds Pumps, Incorporated, 300 WillowBrook Office Pk., 14450-4285, pg. 860 **PB**
Hewlett-Packard Company, 290 Woodcliff Dr., 14450, pg. 814 **PB**
Qualitrol Corp., 1385 Fairport Rd., 14450, pg. 482 **PB**
Silgan Containers, 111 Parce Ave., 14450, pg. 1473 **PB**

Falconer

Sysco Food Services-Jamestown, 800 Allen St. Extension, 14733, pg. 1551 **PB**

Farmingdale

AMERICAN LAUBSCHER CORP., 80 Finn Ct., 11735, pg. 58 **PV**
B.H. AIRCRAFT CO., INC., 441 Eastern Parkway, 11735, pg. 107 **PV**
Birnbach Company, Inc., 81 Schmitt Blvd., 11735, pg. 207 **PB**
COLORADO PRIME CORPORATION, One Michael Ave., 11735, pg. 255 **PV**
Del International, 565 Broad Hollow Rd., 11735, pg. 494 **PB**
DEL LABORATORIES, INC., 565 Broad Hollow Rd., 11735, pg. 494 **PB**
Del Pharmaceuticals, Inc., 565 Broad Hollow Rd., 11735, pg. 494 **PB**
Durakut International Corp., 145 Sherwood Ave., 11735, pg. 740 **IT**
DURO DYNE CORPORATION, P.O. Box 117, 11735, pg. 349 **PV**
Embassy Industries, Inc., 300 Smith St., 11735-1114, pg. 1240 **PV**
56th Fighter Group of Long Island, Inc., Republic Airport-Gate 1, Route 110, 11735, pg. 1023 **PV**
Hoffman Products, 170 Allen Blvd., 11735, pg. 1068 **IT**
La Cross, 565 Broad Hollow Rd., 11735, pg. 494 **PB**
LEATHERS BEST, 500 Bi-County Rd., Ste. 115, 11735, pg. 656 **PV**
Milgray Electronics, Inc., 77 Schmitt Blvd., 11735, pg. 205 **PB**
Milgray/International, Inc., 77 Schmitt Blvd., 11735, pg. 206 **PB**
Milgray/New York, Inc., 77 Schmitt Blvd., 11735, pg. 206 **PB**
MINUTEMAN PRESS INTERNATIONAL, 1640 New Hwy., 11735, pg. 752 **PV**
Naturistics, 565 Broad Hollow Rd., 11735, pg. 494 **PB**
Nutri-Tonic Div., 565 Broad Hollow Rd., 11735, pg. 494 **PB**
Orlandi Inc., 85 Bi-County Blvd., 11735, pg. 1269 **IT**
P & F INDUSTRIES, INC., 300 Smith St., 11735, pg. 1239 **PB**
Parfums Schiaparelli Div., 565 Broad Hollow Rd., 11735, pg. 494 **PB**

PB - *U.S. Public Companies Volume*
PV - *U.S. Private Companies Volume*
IT - *International Public & Private Companies Volume*

1336

PLASCAL CORPORATION, 361 Eastern Pkwy., 11735, pg. 870 · PV

Quencher Div., 565 Broad Hollow Rd., 11735, pg. 494 · PB

Rejuvia Prod. Group, 565 Broad Hollow Rd., 11735, pg. 494 · PB

P.C. RICHARD & SON, 150 Price Pkwy., 11735, pg. 928 · PV

ROSS BICYCLES USA LTD., 51 Executive Blvd., 11735, pg. 946 · PB

Sally Hansen, 565 Broad Hollow Rd., 11735, pg. 494 · PB

Savant Instruments Inc., 110113 Bi County Blvd., 11735, pg. 1595 · PB

Target Rock Corp., 1966 E. Broadhollow Rd., 11735, pg. 470 · PB

Temco Building Maintenance, Inc., 171 Allen Blvd., 11735, pg. 1574 · PB

VERTEX COMPUTER CABLE PRODUCTS, 920 Conklin St., 11735, pg. 1718 · PB

WMF/USA, 85 Price Pkwy., 11735, pg. 1144 · PV

D. WALDNER COMPANY, INC., 125 Rte. 110, 11735, pg. 1147 · PV

Farmington

Griffin Technology Incorporated, 1133 Corporate Dr., 14425, pg. 506 · PB

Telephonics Corp., 815 Broadhollow Rd., 11735, pg. 766 · PB

Ferndale

Time Warner Cable Liberty Division, One Cablevision Ctr., Ste. 2, 12734, pg. 1611 · PB

Fishers

Scientific Calculations, Inc., P.O. Box H, 7796 Victor-Mendon Rd., 14453, pg. 792 · PB

Fishkill

Gould Paper Inc/Midhudson Div., 1123 Rte. 52, 12524, pg. 467 · PV

PROGRESSIVE BANK, INC., 1301 Rte. 52, 12524, pg. 1334 · PB

Floral Park

AMP Inc. Lytel Division, 1995 Linden Blvd., 11003, pg. 8 · PB

PRENTISS INCORPORATED, 21 Vernon St., 11001, pg. 882 · PV

Florida

BIG V SUPERMARKETS, INC., 176 N. Main St., 10921, pg. 143 · PV

Flushing

American Cablevision of Brooklyn, Inc., 41-61 Kissena Blvd., 11355, pg. 1610 · PV

ANGLERS ROSLYN GROUP LTD., 45-25 162nd St., 11358, pg. 74 · PV

BMW, 30-50 Whitestone Express, 11354-8000, pg. 107 · PV

British Airways, 75-20 Astoria Blvd., 11370, pg. 219 · IT

The Chinese American Bank, 38-05 Union St., 11354, pg. 683 · IT

Cho Hung Bank of New York - Flushing Branch, 136-68 Roosevelt Ave., 11354, pg. 288 · IT

FlightSafety International Inc., Marine Air Terminal, LaGuardia Airport, 11371, pg. 218 · PV

LaGuardia Learning Center, Marine Air Terminal, LaGuardia Airport, 11371, pg. 218 · PB

LINZER PRODUCTS CORP., 13330 37th Ave., 11354, pg. 669 · PV

MarineSafety International, Marine Air Terminal-LaGuardia Airport, 11371, pg. 218 · PB

US AIRWAYS SHUTTLE, La Guardia Airport, P.O. Box 710616, 11371, pg. 1124 · PV

Yamato Transport USA, Inc., 1926 Hazen St., 11370, pg. 1519 · IT

Fonda

Kasson & Keller, Main St., 12068, pg. 618 · PV

KEYMARK CORPORATION, Rte. 334, Cayadutta St., 12068, pg. 618 · PV

Forest Hills

Auto-trol Technology Corp., 7161 Austin St., 2nd Fl., 11375, pg. 148 · PB

ENTRON INDUSTRIES LIMITED PARTNERSHIP, 112-41 Queens Blvd., Ste. 100, 11375, pg. 378 · PV

Fort Plain

Beech-Nut Nutrition Corporation, Willett St., 13339, pg. 1359 · PB

Frankfort

AAR Engine Component Services, One W. Frankfort Industrial Park Dr., 13340, pg. 1 · PB

Franklinville

Ontario Knife Co., Empire St., 14737, pg. 1462 · PB

Fredonia

Red Wing Co. Inc., 196 Newton St., 14063, pg. 1398 · IT

Red Wings Inc., 196 Newton St., 14063, pg. 1398 · IT

Freeport

Columbia Cement Co. Inc., 159 Hanse Ave., 11520, pg. 235 · IT

LEARONAL, INC., 272 Buffalo Ave., 11520, pg. 982 · PB

Phipps Press, Inc., 11 Atlantic Ave., 11520, pg. 699 · IT

Friendship

Friendship Dairies, Inc., 701 County Rd 20, 14739, pg. 429 · PV

Fulton

Black Clawson Converting Machinery Company, 46 N. First St., 13069, pg. 147 · PV

Miller Brewing Company, P.O. Box 200, 13069, pg. 1289 · PB

The Morrill Press, Six Morrill Pl., 13069, pg. 1486 · PB

Nestle Chocolate & Confections Company, 555 S. Fourth St., 13069, pg. 917 · IT

Quest Diagnostic-Fulton, AMI Professional Bldg., 98 N. Second St., 13069, pg. 1351 · PB

Sealright Mfg. Fulton, Inc., 100 State St., 13069-2599, pg. 1452 · PB

Fultonville

White Mop Wringer Co., 182 Riverside Dr., 12072, pg. 1173 · PV

Garden City

AAR Technical Service Center, 747 Zeckendorf Blvd., 11530, pg. 1 · PB

AMERICAN FUND ADVISORS, INC., 1415 Kellum Pl., 11530, pg. 55 · PV

Avis Car Leasing, 900 Old Country Rd., 11530, pg. 321 · PB

Avis Rent A Car System, Inc., 900 Old Country Rd., 11530, pg. 321 · PB

D.L. BLAIR INC., 1051 Franklin Ave., 11530, pg. 148 · PV

CHARAN INDUSTRIES, INC., 370 Old Country Rd., 11530, pg. 229 · PV

Charan Realty Group, 370 Old Country Rd., 11530, pg. 229 · PV

Dale Carnegie & Associates, 1475 Franklin Ave., 11530, pg. 308 · PV

Doubleday Book Club, 401 Franklin Ave., 11530, pg. 191 · IT

Doubleday Direct, 401 Franklin Ave., 11530, pg. 191 · IT

DuPont Merck Pharm, 1000 Stewart Ave., 11530-4814, pg. 1091 · PB

Edwards Super Food Stores, Long Island Div., 99 Quentin Roosevelt Blvd., 11530, pg. 750 · PV

Electronic Engineers Master, 645 Stewart Ave., 11530, pg. 516 · PV

Esselte Corporation, 71 Clinton Rd., 11530, pg. 460 · PV

Floor Covering Weekly, 645 Stewart Ave., 11530, pg. 516 · PV

Hearst Business Publishing, Inc./UTP Division, 645 Stewart Ave., 11530, pg. 515 · PV

HUGHES-TREITLER MANUFACTURING CORPORATION, 300 Endo Blvd., 11530, pg. 547 · PV

Integrated Circuits Master Catalog, 645 Stewart Ave., 11530, pg. 516 · PV

Metropolitan Suburban Bus Authority, 700 Commercial Ave., 11530, pg. 739 · PV

Military Book Club, 401 Franklin Ave., 11530, pg. 191 · IT

Motor Magazine, 645 Stewart Ave., 11530, pg. 516 · PV

Motor Publications, 645 Stewart Ave., 11530, pg. 516 · PV

Mystery Guild, 401 Franklin Ave., 11530, pg. 191 · IT

Retirement Advisors, Inc., 645 Stewart Ave., 11530, pg. 516 · PV

Science Fiction Book Club, 401 Franklin Ave., 11530, pg. 191 · IT

Seaway Shopping Centers, Inc., 370 Old Country Rd., 11530, pg. 229 · PV

UTP (United Technical Publications) Division, 645 Stewart Ave., 11530, pg. 516 · PV

White Rose Frozen Food, 700 Dibblee Dr., 11530, pg. 330 · PV

Garden City Park

Nestle Beverage Company, 250 Fulton Ave., 11410, pg. 918 · PV

Geneseo

Quest Diagnostic-Geneseo, 4241 Lakeville Rd., 14454, pg. 1351 · PB

Geneva

Finger Lakes Printing Company, 218 Genesce St., 14456, pg. 559 · PV

Getzville

J.M. JAYSON & CO., INC., 2350 N. Forest Rd., Ste. 12A, 14068, pg. 584 · PV

Glen Cove

Acclaim Distribution, Inc., One Acclaim Plaza, 11542, pg. 15 · PB

ACCLAIM ENTERTAINMENT, INC., One Acclaim Plaza, 11542, pg. 15 · PB

Continental Microwave Technology, Inc., Seven Alexander Pl., 11542-3796, pg. 1289 · IT

Living Color Div., 199 Glen St., 11542, pg. 730 · PB

Micronics Technology, Inc., Seven Alexander Pl., 11542-3796, pg. 1289 · IT

Pall Industrial Hydraulics Corp., 30 Sea Cliff Ave., 11542, pg. 1254 · PB

Pall Mobile Aftermarket Division, 30 Sea Cliff Ave.d., 11542, pg. 1254 · PB

Pall Well Technology Company, 30 Sea Cliff Ave., 11542, pg. 1254 · PB

Glen Head

Essilor of America, 262 Glen Head Rd., 11545, pg. 462 · IT

Flo-Lite Optical Corp., 262 Glen Head Rd., 11545, pg. 462 · IT

HALM INDUSTRIES COMPANY, INCORPORATED, 180 Glen Head Rd., 11545, pg. 496 · PV

Silor Optical Inc., 262 Glen Head Rd., 11545, pg. 462 · IT

Glendale

GEORGE KOVACS LIGHTING, INC., 67-25 Otto Rd., 11385, pg. 634 · PV

CHARLES LEONARD, INC., 79-11 Cooper Ave., 11385, pg. 660 · PV

Glenmont

FARM FAMILY CASUALTY INSURANCE CO., 344 Rte. 9W., 12077, pg. 394 · PV

Glens Falls

Ahlstrom Kamyr Inc., Ridge Ctr., 12801, pg. 34 · IT

Ahlstrom Machinery, Ridge Ctr., 12801, pg. 34 · IT

Albany Engineered Systems, P.O. Box 310, 12801, pg. 1593 · PB

ARROW FINANCIAL CORPORATION, 250 Glen St., 12801, pg. 135 · PB

Astro-Valcour Inc., 18 Peck Ave., 12801, pg. 756 · IT

Butler Wholesale Products, Inc., 56 Boulevard, 12801, pg. 190 · PV

FINCH, PRUYN & CO., INC., One Glen St., 12801, pg. 405 · PV

Flomatic Corporation, 145 Murray St., 12801-4424, pg. 377 · IT

Glen Falls National Bank & Trust Company, 250 Glen St., P.O. Box 307, 12801, pg. 135 · PB

Glens Falls Cement Co., 313 Warren St., 12801, pg. 423 · IT

Kamtech Inc., 11 Pearl St., 12801, pg. 34 · IT

Web Graphics, Inc., Corinth Rd., 12801, pg. 89 · PB

Gloversville

THE GRANDOE CORP., 74 Bleecker St., 12078, pg. 469 · PV

TAYLOR MADE GROUP, INC., P.O. Box 1190, 66 Kingsboro Ave., 12078, pg. 1070 · PV

Taylor Made-New York, 93 S. Blvd., 12078, pg. 1070 · PV

Universal Studios Mfg., Rte. 30A, 12078, pg. 1216 · IT

Grand Island

CANNON, 2170 Whitehaven Rd., 14072, pg. 205 · PV

Edwards High Vacuum, International, 3279 Grand Island Blvd., 14072, pg. 121 · IT

NRD, 2937 Alt Bvld., 14072, pg. 1045 · IT

SIHI Pumps Inc., P.O. Box 460, 303 Industrial Blvd., 14072, pg. 1156 · IT

Granville

Mettowee Lumber & Plastic Co., Inc., 85 Church St., 12832, pg. 1074 · PV

Norton Performance Plastics Co., One Sealants Park, 12832-1652, pg. 1176 · IT

Telegraphics Printing, 85 Church St., 12832, pg. 1074 · PV

TELESCOPE CASUAL FURNITURE, INC., 85 Church St., 12832, pg. 1074 · PV

Great Neck

Adler Shoe Shops, 300 Northern Blvd., 11021, pg. 1764 · PB

AVNET, INC., 80 Cutter Mill Rd., 11021-3108, pg. 155 · PB

Cigna Healthcare of New York, Inc., 1010 Northern Blvd., Ste. 324, 11021, pg. 360 · PB

DuPont Merck, 30 Melbourne Rd., 11021-4638, pg. 1091 · PB

FRESH JUICE COMPANY, 350 Northern Blvd., 11021, pg. 427 · PV

PB - *U.S. Public Companies Volume*
PV - *U.S. Private Companies Volume*
IT - *International Public & Private Companies Volume*

Geographic Index-U.S.

1337

THE FRYE COMPANY, 160 Greatneck Rd., 11021, pg. 430   PV

Georgetown Partners, Inc., 60 Cutter Mill Rd., 11021, pg. 466   PV

GOULD INVESTORS, L.P., 60 Cutter Mill Rd., 11021, pg. 466   PV

HASK TOILETRIES, 277 Northern Blvd., 11021, pg. 509   PV

HUDSON GENERAL CORPORATION, 111 Great Neck Rd., 11021, pg. 845   PB

Hudson Kohala Inc., 111 Great Neck Rd., 11021, pg. 845   PB

InterDigital Communications Corp., 833 Northern Blvd., Ste. 220, 11021, pg. 889   PB

JIMLAR CORPORATION, 160 Great Neck Rd., 11021, pg. 587   PV

The Liquidating Company, Inc., 1010 Northern Blvd., Ste. 324, 11021, pg. 360   PV

UNITED CAPITAL CORP., United Capital Bldg., 9 Park Place, 11021, pg. 1674   PB

United Capital Corp., 111 Great Neck Rd., 11021, pg. 1675   PB

Greene

The Raymond Corporation, S. Canal St., 13778-0130, pg. 123   IT

Raymond Leasing Corporation, South Canal St., 13778, pg. 123   IT

Raymond Sales Corporation, S. Canal St., 13778, pg. 123   IT

Raymond Transportation Corporation, South Canal St., 13778, pg. 123   IT

Greenlawn

GEC-Marconi Hazeltine Corporation, 450 E. Pulaski Rd., 11740, pg. 544   IT

Greenvale

Pall Biomedical Products Corp., 2200 Northern Blvd., 11548, pg. 1254   PB

Pall Biosupport Division, 2200 Northern Blvd., 11548, pg. 1254   PB

PALL CORPORATION, 2200 Northern Blvd., 11548, pg. 1253   PB

Pall East Hills Manufacturing Corp., 2200 Northern Blvd., 11548, pg. 1254   PB

Pall Power Generation Division, 2200 Nothern Blvd., 11548, pg. 1254   PB

Pall Process Filtration Company, 2200 Northern Blvd., 11548, pg. 1254   PB

Pall Ultrafine Filtration Company, 2200 Northern Blvd., 11548, pg. 1254   PB

Russell Associates Inc., 2200 Northern Blvd., 11548, pg. 1254   PB

SLANT/FIN CORPORATION, 100 Forest Dr., 11548, pg. 1005   PV

Guilderland

Troy Savings Bank-Guilderland, 1704 Western Ave., 12203, pg. 1106   PV

Guilderland Center

Colonie Ventures, Inc., P.O. Box 98, 12085, pg. 438   PV

Columbia Executive Associates, P.O. Box 98, 12085, pg. 438   PV

Distribution Unlimited, Inc., P.O. Box 98, 12085, pg. 438   PV

Flint River, P.O. Box 98, 12085, pg. 437   PV

Galesi Enterprises, P.O. Box 98, 12085, pg. 437   PV

Mercer Forge, P.O. Box 98, 12085, pg. 438   PV

Rotterdam Industrial Park, P.O. Box 98, 12085, pg. 437   PV

Rotterdam Ventures Inc., P.O. Box 98, 12085, pg. 437   PV

Scotia Industrial Park, Inc., P.O. Box 98, 12085, pg. 438   PV

Top Of The World Ventures, Inc, P.O. Box 98, 12085, pg. 438   PV

TOW Water Co., Inc., P.O. Box 98, 12085, pg. 438   PV

Walden Residential Operating Partnership, L.P., P.O. Box 98, 12085, pg. 438   PV

Hamburg

Alcor Envelope Co., 160 Elmview Ave., 14075, pg. 1666   PB

Hammondsport

CLARK SPECIALTY CO., INC., 8440 St. Rte. 54, 14840, pg. 243   PV

Hancock

Mallery Lumber Corp.-NY, 36 LaBarre St., 13783, pg. 698   PV

Harriman

Nepera Inc., Rte. 17, 10926, pg. 297   PB

Harrison

Asahi Breweries U.S.A., Inc., 114 Second St., 10528, pg. 83   IT

BNY Mortgage Company, Inc., 440 Mamaroneck Ave., 10528, pg. 178   PB

Canada Life Insurance Company of New York, 500 Mamaroneck Ave., 10528, pg. 255   IT

CASTLE OIL CORPORATION, 500 Mamaroneck Ave., 10528, pg. 219   PV

Citicorp Industrial Credit, Inc., 450 Mamaroneck Ave., 10528, pg. 378   PB

Citicorp, N.A., 450 Mamaroneck Ave., 10528, pg. 377   PB

IMG Communications, 260 Park Ave., 10528, pg. 566   PV

IMG International, 260 Park Ave., 10528, pg. 566   PV

IMG Services, 260 Park Ave., 10528, pg. 566   PV

INTEGRATED MARKETING GROUP, 260 Park Ave., 10528, pg. 566   PV

Rail Europe Inc., 500 Mamaroneck Ave., #314, 10528, pg. 1165   IT

S & P Comstock, 600 Mamaroneck Ave., 5th Fl., 10528, pg. 1071   PB

Hauppauge

AAA Division, 150 Marcus Blvd., 11788, pg. 147   PB

AV Division, 150 Marcus Blvd., 11788, pg. 147   PB

All American Semiconductor of New York, Inc., 275-B Marcus Blvd., 11788, pg. 41   PB

ALLIED DIGITAL TECHNOLOGIES, 140 Fell Ct., Ste. 300, 11788, pg. 48   PB

Allied Digital Technologies Corporation, 15 Gilpin Ave., 11788, pg. 48   PB

AMER CAN TISSUE CORPORATION, 135 Engineers Rd., 11738, pg. 63   PV

ANORAD CORPORATION, 110 Oser Ave., 11788, pg. 75   PV

ARKAY PACKAGING CORPORATION, 22 Arkay Dr., 11788, pg. 82   PV

Arrow/Schweber Electronics, 20 Oser Ave., 11788, pg. 133   PB

AUDIOVOX CORPORATION, 150 Marcus Blvd., 11788, pg. 147   PB

BancTec, Inc.-New York, 888 Veterans Memorial Highway, Ste. 320, 11788-2919, pg. 177   PB

Cellular Mobile Communication Division, 185 Oser Ave., 11788, pg. 147   PB

Component Products Division, 300 Kennedy Dr., 11788, pg. 1503   PB

Daihatsu Diesel (U.S.A.), Inc., 180 Adams Ave., 11788, pg. 364   IT

Dunhill Personnel System, Inc., 150 Motor Pkwy., 11788, pg. 430   PB

Dunstor Leathers, Inc., 400 Wireless Blvd., 11788, pg. 1125   PV

EDD-Long Island, 300 Vanderbilt Motor Pkwy., Ste. 217, 11783, pg. 205   PB

Festo Corporation, 395 Moreland Road, 11788, pg. 430   IT

FLORAL GLASS & MIRROR, INC., 895 Motor Pkwy., 11788, pg. 414   PV

GENERATION METALS CORP., 888 Veterans Memorial Hwy. Ste. 430, 11788-5248, pg. 446   PV

GRAHAM-FIELD HEALTH PRODUCTS, INC., 400 Rabro Dr. E. 11788, pg. 757   PB

HIRSCH INTERNATIONAL CORP., 200 Wireless Blvd., 11788, pg. 829   PB

JACO ELECTRONICS, INC., 145 Oser Ave., 11788, pg. 920   PB

Jani King of New York, Inc., Woodland I, 800 Veterans Memorial Hwy., Ste Two, 11788, pg. 582   PV

Janus Elevator Products Inc., 125 Ricefield Lane, 11788, pg. 590   IT

Koyo International Inc. of America, 325 Marcu Blvd., 11788, pg. 760   IT

L3 Communications Narda-Microwave Div., 435 Moreland Rd., 11788, pg. 638   PV

LNR COMMUNICATIONS, 180 Marcus Blvd., 11788, pg. 639   PV

LEADER INSTRUMENTS CORPORATION, 380 Oser Ave., 11788, pg. 655   PV

Linotype-Hell Company, 425 Oser Ave., 11788, pg. 604   IT

MAHARAM, 45 Rasons Ct., 11788, pg. 696   PV

MANCHESTER EQUIPMENT CO., 50 Market Blvd., 11788, pg. 699   PB

MEDICAL ACTION INDUSTRIES INC., 150 Motor Pkwy., Ste. 205, 11788, pg. 1079   PB

Micro Slides Div., 135 Ricefield Ln., 11788, pg. 125   PB

Pall Rai, Inc., 225 Marcus Blvd., 11788, pg. 1254   PB

POLYMER PLASTICS CORPORATION, 65 Davids Dr., 11788, pg. 875   PV

RS Electronics, 295 Oser Ave., 11788, pg. 905   PV

ROBOTIC VISION SYSTEMS, INC., 425 Rabro Dr. E., 11788, pg. 1395   PB

Sensall, Div. of Rosemount, Inc., 250 Marcus Blvd., 11788, pg. 574   PB

SENTRY TECHNOLOGY CORP., 350 Wireless Blvd., 11788, pg. 1458   PB

SOUTHERN CONTAINER CORPORATION, 115 Engineers Rd., 11788, pg. 1016   PV

STANDARD MICROSYSTEMS CORP., 80 Arkay Dr., 11788, pg. 1502   PB

SUPPORT SYSTEMS ASSOCIATES, INC., 1300 Veterans Memorial Hwy., 11788, pg. 1056   PV

System Products Division, 350 Kennedy Dr., 11788, pg. 1503   PB

TSR INC., 400 Oser Ave., 11788, pg. 1559   PB

Time Electronics, 70 Marcus Blvd., 11788, pg. 155   PB

UNITED STATES LUGGAGE COMPANY, 400 Wireless Blvd., 11788, pg. 1125   PV

Vanguard Instrument Corp., 55 Cabot Ct., 11788, pg. 551   PB

VICON INDUSTRIES, INC., 89 Arkay Dr., 11788, pg. 1719   PB

Hawthorne

Burke Fuel & Heating Co., 475 Commerce St., 10532, pg. 729   PV

The Coca-Cola Bottling Co. of New York, Inc., Three Skyline Dr., 10532, pg. 393   PV

Enterprises Media Group, Three Skyline Dr., 10532, pg. 393   PV

METRIC & MULTISTANDARD COMPONENTS, 120 Old Saw Mill River Rd., 10532, pg. 736   PV

Perini-Metropolitan New York Div., Two Skyline Dr., Fl. 1, 10532, pg. 1278   PB

Hempstead

DAN'S SUPREME SUPER MARKETS INC., 474 Fulton Ave., 11550, pg. 310   PV

Henrietta

Branson Plastic Joining, 1001 Lehigh Station Rd., 14467-9389, pg. 574   PB

Onondaga Litho Supply Co., Inc., 535 Summit Point Dr., Ste. 4, 14467, pg. 1329   PB

Hicksville

AIR TECHNIQUES, INC., 70 Cantiague Rock Rd, 11801, pg. 28   PV

All-Pro Imaging, 70 Cantiague Rock Rd., 11801, pg. 28   PV

SAM ASH MUSIC CORP., 278 Duffy Ave., 11801, pg. 88   PV

Bertan High Voltage, 121 New South Rd., 11801, pg. 494   PB

Cantrock Realty Corp., P.O. Box 12, 11802, pg. 509   PV

EVERGOOD PRODUCTS CORPORATION, 140 Lauman Ln., 11801, pg. 386   PV

Great Earth Distribution, 140 Lauman Ln., 11801, pg. 386   PV

Jelrus International, 70 Cantiague Rock Rd., 11801, pg. 28   PV

LONG ISLAND LIGHTING COMPANY, 175 E. Old Country Rd., 11801, pg. 1013   PB

Speizman Industries, Inc., 59 Tec St., 11801, pg. 1498   PB

STAR MULTI CARE SERVICES INC., 99 Railroad Plaza, Ste. 208, 11801, pg. 1510   PB

STRUCTURAL INDUSTRIES, INC., 96 New South Rd., 11801, pg. 1048   PV

UNIFLEX, INC., 383 W. John St., 11802, pg. 1665   PB

UNIVERSAL PHOTONICS, INC., 495 W. John St., 11801, pg. 1127   PV

Hilton

Quest Diagnostic-Hilton, 1026 Hilton Parma Corners, 14668, pg. 1351   PB

Holbrook

AUSTIN PRODUCTIONS, INC., 815 Grundy Ave., 11741, pg. 100   PV

FISHER SKYLIGHTS, INC., 5005 Veterans Memorial Pkwy., 11741, pg. 408   PV

FOUR SEASONS SOLAR PRODUCTS CORP., 5005 Veterans Memorial Hwy., 11741, pg. 422   PV

Holcomb

Frontier Communications of Seneca Gorham, Inc., 71 Main St., 14469, pg. 684   PB

Rhone-Poulenc Inc., Films Division, 2754 West Park Dr., 14469, pg. 1110   IT

Holtsville

SYMBOL TECHNOLOGIES, INC., One Symbol Plaza, 11742-1300, pg. 1546   PB

Homer

Albany International/Monofilament Plant, 156 So. Main St., 13077, pg. 37   PB

Hoosick Falls

Furon Fluorglas Products, 14 McCaffrey St., P.O. Box 320, 12090-0320, pg. 689   PB

Lydall Composite Materials, P.O. Box 400, 12 Davis St., 12090-0400, pg. 1021   PB

Hopewell Junction

Frontier Communications of Sylvan Lake, Inc., P.O. Box 338, Rt. 82, 12533, pg. 684   PB

TOLLMAN/HUNDLEY HOTELS, 1886 Rt. 52, 12533, pg. 1090   PV

PB - U.S. Public Companies Volume
PV - U.S. Private Companies Volume
IT - International Public & Private Companies Volume

Hornell

General Marble Corporation, One Vanity Ln., 14843, pg. 990 **PB**
Quest Diagnostic-North Hornell, Bethesda Medical Arts Bldg., Bethesda Dr., 14843, pg. 1351 **PB**

Horseheads

Augat, LRC., Communications Division-Horseheads Plant, P.O. Box 111, 14845, pg. 1598 **PB**
Sysco Food Services of Horseheads, 140 Wygant Rd., 14845, pg. 1551 **PB**

Hudson

FOSTER REFRIGERATOR CORPORATION, 6 Aitkin Ave., 12534, pg. 421 **PB**
GINSBERG'S INSTITUTIONAL FOODS, INC., P.O. Box 17, Rte. 66, 12534, pg. 455 **PV**
W.B. McGuire Co., One Hudson Ave., 12534, pg. 823 **PV**
The Register, Inc., P.O. Box 634, 12534, pg. 1079 **PB**

Hudson Falls

POLYCOAT SYSTEMS, INC., Five Depot St., 12839, pg. 875 **PV**
Valmet Inc., Hudson Falls Division, 27 Allen St., 12839-1958, pg. 1449 **IT**

Huntington

FLORENCE CORPORATION, 1647 E. Jericho Tpke., 11743, pg. 414 **PV**
Klockner INA Industrial Installations, Inc., 775 Park Ave., Ste. 320, 11743, pg. 1081 **IT**
NAI TECHNOLOGIES, INC., 282 New York Ave., 11743, pg. 1144 **PB**

Huntington Station

ATC International Technical Ceramics, Inc., One Norden Ln., 11746-2102, pg. 93 **PB**
AMERICAN TECHNICAL CERAMICS CORP., One Norden Ln., 11746-2142, pg. 93 **PB**
DIRECT PRESS MODERN LITHO CORPORATION, 386 Oakwood Rd., 11746, pg. 334 **PV**
Eastco Glove Technologies, 130 W. 10th St., 11746, pg. 548 **PB**
EASTCO INDUSTRIAL SAFETY CORP., 130 W. Tenth St., 11746, pg. 548 **PB**
Safety Wear Corp., 130 W. Tenth St., 11746, pg. 548 **PB**
Worksafe, Inc., 130 W. Tenth St., 11746, pg. 548 **PB**

Inwood

APEX MILLS CORPORATION, 168 Doughty Blvd., 11096, pg. 77 **PV**
BERMIL INDUSTRIES CORP., 461 Doughty Blvd., 11696, pg. 136 **PV**
Inwood Laboratories, Inc., 300 Prospect St., 11696, pg. 670 **PB**
Kintetsu World Express Inc., 45 Rason Rd., 11696, pg. 734 **IT**
MGR EQUIPMENT CORP., 22 Gates Ave., 11696, pg. 687 **PV**
Signal Transformer Co., Inc., 500 Bayview Ave., 11696, pg. 881 **PB**
Studley Products Co., 95 Inip Dr., 11096, pg. 1193 **PB**

Irvington

Berner Bros. Inc., Three Blueberry Hill Rd., 10533, pg. 189 **IT**
CARRAFIELLO, DIEHL & ASSOCIATES, INC., 90 N. Broadway, 10533, pg. 215 **PV**
The Voyager Company, One Bridge St., 10533, pg. 1479 **IT**

Islandia

COMPUTER ASSOCIATES INTERNATIONAL, INC., One Computer Associates Plaza, 11788-7000, pg. 420 **PB**
Computer Associates International, Inc., One Computer Associates Plaza, 11788-7000, pg. 420 **PB**
Enterprise Financial Management Group, One Computer Associates Plaza, 11788-7000, pg. 420 **PB**
Holmes Protection of Long Island, Inc., 3116 Expressway Dr. S., 11722, pg. 1649 **PB**
MK Group, One Computer Associates Plaza, 11788, pg. 420 **PB**
NetHaven, One Computer Associates Plaza, 11788-7000, pg. 420 **PB**
SHERWOOD LUMBER CORPORATION, 300 Corporate Plaza, 11722, pg. 994 **PV**
TIE Systems-Plainview, 3124 Expreeway Dr., 11722, pg. 1085 **PV**

Ithaca

American Demographics, Inc., P.O. Box 68, 14851, pg. 281 **PV**
COURTESY CHEVROLET & IMPORTS INC., 370 Elmira Rd., 14850, pg. 279 **PV**
Emerson Power Transmission Corporation, 620 South Aurora St., 14850, pg. 573 **PB**

Hi-Speed Checkweigher Co., Inc., Five Barr Rd., 14850-9117, pg. 973 **IT**
Ithaca Journal, 123 W. State St., 14850, pg. 700 **PB**
ITHACO INC., 950 Danby Foad, Suite 100, 14850-5720, pg. 576 **PV**
Somerset Railroad Corp., Rte. 13 Ithaca-Dryden Rd., 14850, pg. 1173 **PB**
THERM, INC., P.O. Box 220, 14851, pg. 1079 **PB**
TOMPKINS COUNTY TRUST COMPANY, The Commons, P.O. Box 460, 14851, pg. 1621 **PB**

Jamaica

Alba Forwarding Co., Inc., 147-39 175th St., 11434, pg. 32 **PV**
Amoco Research Center, 11828 Springfield Blvd., 11411-1922, pg. 103 **PV**
ASSOCIATED FOOD STORES, INC., 122-20 Merrick Blvd., 11434, pg. 90 **PV**
Brambles Security Services Inc., Cargo Bldg. 261, JFK Airport, 11430, pg. 211 **PV**
Daher Golden Eagle - New York, 149-23 182nd St., 11413, pg. 749 **PV**
Eon Labs, 227-15 N. Conduit Ave., 11413, pg. 379 **PV**
Green Bus Holding, 16525 147th Ave., 11434, pg. 477 **PV**
GREEN BUS LINES, INC., 165-25 147th Ave., 11434, pg. 476 **PV**
Health Acquisition Corp., 175-20 Hillside Ave., 11432, pg. 1157 **PB**
Kuwait Airways, Northeast Region, Cargo Bldg. 261, JFK International Airport, 11430, pg. 764 **IT**
MTA Long Island Rail Road, Jamaica Station, 11435, pg. 739 **PV**
NEW YORK RACING ASSOCIATION, 110-00 Rockaway Blvd., 11417, pg. 795 **PV**
PICK QUICK FOODS, 83-10 Rockaway Blvd., 11416, pg. 864 **PV**
RANDY INTERNATIONAL, 18208 149th Ave., 11434, pg. 909 **PV**
Spartan Security Services, JFK Airport/Intl. Arrivals, West Wing, Bldg. 52, 11430, pg. 1574 **IT**
Sun Dew Corp., 110-20 Dunkirk St., 11412, pg. 686 **IT**
WORLDWIDE FOOD PRODUCTS INC., 147-07 94th Ave., 11435, pg. 1191 **PV**

Jamestown

THE AARQUE COMPANIES, 111 W. Second St., 14701-0310, pg. 9 **PV**
Aarque Management Corp., 111 W. Second St., 14701, pg. 9 **PV**
Aarque Steel Corporation, 111 W. Second St., 14701, pg. 9 **PV**
ALLTEL New York, Inc., 201 East Fourth St., 14702, pg. 56 **PB**
American Locker Co., Inc., 15 W. 2nd St., 14701, pg. 86 **PB**
AMERICAN LOCKER GROUP, INC., 608 Allen St., 14701, pg. 85 **PB**
American Locker Security Systems, Inc., 608 Allen St., 14701, pg. 86 **PB**
BUSH INDUSTRIES INC., One Mason Dr., 14702, pg. 270 **PB**
Clarke Container Company, Inc., 45 Norwood Ave., 14702, pg. 1045 **PV**
HOPE'S ARCHITECTURAL PRODUCTS INC., 84 Hopkins Ave., 14701, pg. 538 **PV**
Jamestown Metal Products, Inc., 178 Blackstone Ave., 14701, pg. 169 **PV**
Jamestown Perforators Inc., 1914 Washington St., 14701, pg. 617 **PV**
MRC Bearings, 402 Chandler St., 14702-0280, pg. 1157 **IT**
Producto Machine Co. Ring Division, Turner Rd., 14702-0490, pg. 889 **PV**
Quality Markets, Inc., 101 Jackson Ave., W.E., 14701, pg. 1270 **PB**
Weber-Knapp Company, 441 Chandler St., 14702-0518, pg. 473 **IT**

Jericho

Donohue Paper Sales Corporation, 100 Jericho Quadrangle, 11753, pg. 1075 **IT**
FRIENDSHIP DAIRIES, INC., One Jericho Plaza, 11753-1668, pg. 428 **PV**
GETTY PETROLEUM MARKETING INC., 125 Jericho Tpke., 11753, pg. 740 **PV**
Getty Terminals, Inc., 125 Jericho Tpke., 11753, pg. 741 **PB**
GRIFFON CORP., 100 Jericho Quadrangle, 11753, pg. 766 **PB**
KeySpan Energy Management Inc., Center Wing, 30 Jericho Executive Plaza, 11753, pg. 259 **PV**
Leemilts Petroleum, Inc., 125 Jericho Tpke., 11753, pg. 741 **PB**
P.T. Petro Corp., 125 Jericho Tpke., 11753, pg. 741 **PB**
ROSEN ASSOCIATES MANAGEMENT CORP., 33 S. Service Rd., 11753, pg. 945 **PV**
ZIEGLER CHEMICAL & MINERAL CORP., 100 Jericho Quad, Ste. 140, 11753, pg. 1205 **PV**

Johnson City

AZON CORPORATION, 720 Azon Rd., 13790, pg. 104 **PV**
Gateway Communications, 12 Gateway Plaza, Columbia Dr., 13790-0012, pg. 693 **PV**
Martin Marietta Control Systems, 600 Main St., 13790, pg. 1006 **PB**

Johnstown

ELECTRO METRICS, INC., 231 Enterprise Rd., Johnstown Indus. Pk., 12095, pg. 369 **PV**
JOHNSTOWN KNITTING MILL CO., 309 W. Montgomery St., 12095, pg. 595 **PV**

Keeseville

Frontier Communications of AuSable Valley, 310 Front St., 12944, pg. 683 **PB**

Kingston

COLONY LIQUOR DISTRIBUTORS, INC., 132 Flatbush Ave., 12401, pg. 254 **PV**
Huck International Installation Systems Division, P.O. Box 2270, 85 Grand St., 12401, pg. 1597 **PB**
National Micronetics, Inc., 71 Smith Ave., 12401, pg. 1347 **PV**

Kirkwood

Raytheon Systems Co., 265 Industrial Park Dr., 13795, pg. 1364 **PB**

Lackawanna

Integrated Terminals, P.O. Box 24, 1951 Hamburg Tpke., 14218, pg. 742 **PB**

Lagrangeville

COMMAND SECURITY CORPORATION, Rte. 55, Lexington Park, 12540, pg. 409 **PB**
Paragon, 341 Rte. 55 West Wing, 12540-5105, pg. 593 **PB**

Lake Ronkonkoma

MSC Eastern Regional Office, 4175 Veterans Memorial Hwy., 11779, pg. 1031 **PB**

Lake Success

Aceto Agricultural Chemicals Corp., One Hollow Ln., 11042, pg. 15 **PB**
ACETO CORPORATION, One Hollow Ln., Ste. 201, 11042, pg. 15 **PB**
ASTORIA FINANCIAL CORPORATION, One Astoria Federal Plaza, 11042, pg. 141 **PB**
Bergall Corporation, 1981 Marcus Ave., Ste. C115, 11042, pg. 1501 **PB**
Canon U.S.A., Inc., One Canon Plaza, 11042, pg. 262 **IT**
Careco, Inc., 1981 Marcus Ave., Ste. C115, 11042, pg. 1501 **PB**
COMFORCE CORPORATION, 2001 Marcus Ave., 11042, pg. 409 **PB**
FRIENDLY HOLIDAYS INC., 1983 Marcus Ave., 11042, pg. 428 **PV**
Kokusai Electric Co., Ltd. America, 3000 Marcus Ave., Ste. 2E5, 11042, pg. 743 **IT**
PGL Industries, Inc., 1981 Marcus Ave., Ste. C115, 11042, pg. 1501 **PB**
PARK ELECTROCHEMICAL CORPORATION, Five Dakota Dr., 11042, pg. 1258 **PB**
Professional Detail Services, Inc., 1981 Marcus Ave., Ste. C115, 11042, pg. 1501 **PB**
ROCKBOTTOM STORES, INC., One Delaware Dr., 11042, pg. 938 **PV**
STAFF BUILDERS INC., 1983 Marcus Ave. Ste. 200, 11042, pg. 1501 **PB**
Sumitrans Corporation, 1981 Marcus Ave., E-102, 11042, pg. 1312 **IT**
Tender Loving Care Home Care Services, Inc., 1981 Marcus Ave., Ste. C115, 11042, pg. 1501 **PB**
VGF Corporation, One Hollow Ln., 11042, pg. 15 **PB**

Lakewood

Cummins Engine Company, Inc., P.O. Box 1279, 4720 Baker St. Ext., 14750, pg. 468 **PB**

Lancaster

Airtex, 4087 Walden Ave., 14086, pg. 1113 **PV**
DEPEW DEVELOPMENT INC., 4429 Walden Ave., 14086, pg. 409 **PV**
Ecology and Environment Engineering, Inc., Buffalo Corporate Center, 368 Pleasantview Drive, 14086, pg. 563 **PB**
ECOLOGY AND ENVIRONMENT, INC., Buffalo Corporate Center, 368 Pleasant View Dr., 14086-1397, pg. 562 **PV**
Henry & Henry, Inc., 3765 Walden Ave., 14086-1494, pg. 244 **IT**
Scott Aviation, 225 Erie St., 14086-9502, pg. 622 **PB**
SEALING DEVICES INC., 4400 Walden Ave., 14086, pg. 978 **PV**
Tetko Inc., Depew Operations, P.O. Box 346, 14086, pg. 1078 **PV**

Larchmont

D'AGOSTINO SUPERMARKETS INC., 1385 Boston Post Rd., 10538, pg. 306 **PV**
I.C.E. International Capital Equipment, Inc., 1890 Palmer Ave., 10538, pg. 683 **IT**

PB - *U.S. Public Companies Volume*
PV - *U.S. Private Companies Volume*
IT - *International Public & Private Companies Volume*

1339

Geographic Index-U.S.

Latham

Browning-Ferris Industries of New York, Inc., 136 Sicker Rd., 12110, pg. 264   **PB**
Control Network Communications, Inc., Airport Park, 21 British American Blvd., 12110, pg. 711   **PB**
GRASSLAND EQUIPMENT & IRRIGATION CORP., 892-898 Troy Schnectedy Rd., 12110-1698, pg. 471   **PV**
IMPERIAL POOLS, INC., 33 Wade Rd., 12110, pg. 558   **PV**
Intercool Energy Corporation, P.O. Box 461, 12110-0461, pg. 894   **PV**
INTERMAGNETICS GENERAL CORPORATION, 450 Old Niskayuna Rd., 12110, pg. 893   **PB**
KEELER MOTOR CAR COMPANY, INC., 1111 Troy-Schenectady Rd., 12110, pg. 611   **PV**
Magstream Corporation, 451 Old Niskayuna Rd., 12110-0461, pg. 894   **PV**
MECHANICAL TECHNOLOGY INC., 968 Albany-Shaker Rd., 12110, pg. 1077   **PB**
Mechanical Technology Inc.-Technology Grp.(Latham), 968 Albany-Shaker Rd., 12110, pg. 1077   **PB**
NORTHWAY MOTORCAR CORPORATION, 727 New Loudon Rd., 12110, pg. 806   **PV**
PEPSI-COLA ALBANY BOTTLING CO., INC., One Pepsi-Cola Dr., 12110, pg. 852   **PV**
Republic Automotive Parts Sales, Inc., 881 Albany Shaker Rd., 12110, pg. 1378   **PB**
Troy Savings Bank-Latham, Troy-Schenectady Rd. & Sunset Dr., 12110, pg. 1106   **PV**
Turbonetics Energy, Inc., 968 Albany-Shaker Rd., 12110, pg. 1077   **PB**

Laurelton

EON LABS MANUFACTURING, INC., 227-15 N. Conduit Ave., 11413, pg. 379   **PV**

Lawrence

Circle Freight International USA, One Johnson Rd., 11559, pg. 370   **PB**
Circle Freight International USA, One Johnson Rd., 11559, pg. 371   **PB**
Circle International, One Johnson Rd., 11559, pg. 372   **PB**

Le Roy

Chesapeake Packaging Co./LeRoy, 57 N. St., 14482, pg. 346   **PB**
JONES CHEMICALS, INC., 80 Munson St., 14482, pg. 596   **PV**
Lapp Insulator Company, Gilbert St., 14482, pg. 473   **PV**
UPSTATE MILK COOPERATIVES INC., 7115 W. Main St., 14482, pg. 1129   **PV**

Leicester

CPAC, INC., 2364 Leicester Rd., 14481-0175, pg. 282   **PB**

Levittown

COLONIAL COMMERCIAL CORP., 3601 Hempstead Tpke., Ste. 121 I, 11756-1315, pg. 400   **PB**
Devon Capital Corp., 3601 Hempstead Tpke., 11780, pg. 400   **PB**
Sals Investors Partnership, 3601 Hempstead Tpke., 11756, pg. 400   **PB**
Southern Mortgage Associates, Inc., 3601 Hempstead Tpke., 11780, pg. 400   **PB**
Wel-Com Financial Services, Inc., 3601 Hempstead Tpke., 11780, pg. 400   **PB**

Lima

INDUSTRIAL CERAMICS, INC., 7574 E. Main St., 14485, pg. 560   **PV**

Little Falls

BURROWS PAPER CORPORATION, 501 W. Main St., 13365, pg. 188   **PV**
Little Falls Color Print, Riverside Industrial Park, 13365, pg. 1050   **PV**

Little Neck

LEVITON MFG. CO., INC., 59-25 Little Neck Pkwy., 11362, pg. 663   **PV**

Liverpool

AMERICAN GRANBY, INC., 7645 Henry Clay Blvd., 13088, pg. 55   **PV**
First United American Life Insurance Company, 990 Seventh North St., 13088, pg. 1623   **PB**
Grassland Equipment & Irrigation Corp., 315 Commerce Blvd., 13008, pg. 471   **PV**
Hewlett-Packard Company, 7641 Henry Clay Blvd., 13088, pg. 814   **PB**
JOS. J. PIETRAFESA CO., 7400 Morgan Rd., 13090, pg. 865   **PV**
Quest Diagnostic, 4820 W. Taft Rd., 13088, pg. 1351   **PB**
RAYMOUR AND FLANIGAN FURNITURE CO., 7248 Morgan Rd., 13088, pg. 912   **PV**
Tactair Fluid Controls Corp., 4806 W. Taft Rd., 13088, pg. 1196   **PV**

WILL & BAUMER INCORPORATED, Old Liverpool & Buckley Rd., 13088, pg. 1176   **PV**
YOUNG & FRANKLIN, INC., 942 Old Liverpool Rd., 13088, pg. 1196   **PV**

Lockport

Allegheny Ludlum-Lockport, 695 Ohio Street, 14094, pg. 43   **PB**
Buffalo Paperboard Corporation, 470 Ohio St., 14094, pg. 303   **PB**
Delphi Harrison Thermal Systems, 200 Upper Mountain Rd., 14094, pg. 719   **PB**
Lockport Union Sun & Journal, 459-491 S. Transit St., 14094, pg. 1078   **PB**
Sherwood, 120 Church St., 14094, pg. 793   **PB**

Locust Valley

Douglas Elliman-Jane Hayes, Inc., 71 Forest Ave., 11560, pg. 341   **PV**

Long Island City

Aigner Products Division, 4-20 47th Ave., 11101, pg. 152   **PB**
The Allan & Gray Co., 27-17 Jackson Ave., 11101, pg. 1666   **PB**
ANDREA ELECTRONICS CORPORATION, 11-40 45th Rd., 11101, pg. 112   **PB**
B & E MOTOR & CONTROL CORPORATION, 39-40 Crescent St., 11101, pg. 105   **PV**
BESTFORM FOUNDATIONS, INC., 38-01 47th Ave., 11101, pg. 140   **PV**
Boston Piano Company, One Steinway Pl., 11105, pg. 1514   **PB**
CGS INDUSTRIES, INC., 34-09 Queens Blvd., 11101, pg. 194   **PV**
CASE PAPER CO., INC., 23-30 Borden Ave., 11101, pg. 218   **PV**
Citibank Credit Card Marketing, One Court Sq., 29th Fl., 11120, pg. 377   **PB**
Citibank N.A., One Court Sq., 40th Fl., 11120, pg. 377   **PB**
Citicorp Credit Services, Inc., One Court Sq., 11120, pg. 377   **PB**
City & Suburban Delivery Systems, Inc., 47-25 34th St., 11101, pg. 1175   **PB**
COSMOS COMMUNICATIONS, INC., 11-05 44th Dr., 11101, pg. 278   **PV**
Dav-El Services, Inc., 42-05 Tenth St., 11101, pg. 314   **PV**
Dav-El Washington DC Inc., P.O. Box 7151, 11101, pg. 314   **PV**
Dentex Research Development, Inc., 27-07 43rd Ave., 11101, pg. 510   **IT**
Dentsply Cavitron Plant, 1140 Borden Ave., 11101, pg. 499   **PB**
DIAL A MATTRESS USA, 31-10 48th Ave., 11101-3035, pg. 330   **PV**
DURLACHER & CO., INC., 47-11 Van Dam St., 11101, pg. 348   **PV**
EAGLE ELECTRIC MFG. CO., INC., 45-31 Court Sq., 11101, pg. 354   **PV**
ELGIN WATCH COMPANY, 33-00 Northern Blvd., 11101, pg. 371   **PV**
FHE Services, Inc., 47-36 36th St., 11101-1800, pg. 746   **IT**
MAINCO Elevator Services Co., 31-10 41st Ave., 11101, pg. 656   **IT**
MAJOR AUTOMOTIVE GROUP, 43-40 Northern Blvd., 11101, pg. 697   **PB**
Mardevco Credit Corp., 37-18 Northern Blvd., 11101, pg. 1503   **PB**
NEW AGE INTIMATES INC., 29-10 Thomson, 11101, pg. 792   **PV**
NEW YORK ENVELOPE CORP., 29-10 Hunters Point Ave., 11101, pg. 794   **PV**
THE PACE COLLECTION, 11-11 34th Ave., 11106, pg. 829   **PV**
PARAGON PAINT & VARNISH CORP., 5-49 46th Ave., 11101, pg. 838   **PV**
Peerless Paint & Varnish Corp., 5-49 46th Ave., 11101, pg. 838   **PV**
Pepsi-Cola Bottling Co. of Long Island City, 46-00 Fifth St., 11101, pg. 1276   **PB**
Posterloid Corporation, 4862 36th St., 11101, pg. 1315   **PB**
PROPPER MANUFACTURING CO., INC., 36-04 Skillman Ave., 11101, pg. 891   **PV**
QUEENS GROUP, INC., 52-35 Barnett Ave., 11104-1017, pg. 900   **PV**
RIS PAPER COMPANY, 45-11 33rd St., 11101, pg. 932   **PV**
M. RUBIN & SONS INC., 34-01 38th Ave., 11101, pg. 949   **PV**
SCALAMANDRE, INC., 37-24 24th St., 11101, pg. 969   **PV**
Splendor Form Brassiere, Inc., 29-10 Thomson Ave., 11101, pg. 792   **PV**
Standard Division, 37-18 Northern Blvd., 11101, pg. 1503   **PB**
STANDARD MOTOR PRODUCTS INC., 37-18 Northern Blvd., 11101, pg. 1503   **PB**
Steinway & Sons, One Steinway Pl., 11105, pg. 1514   **PB**
United Metering Inc., 10-15 45th Ave., 11101, pg. 1692   **PB**

Lynbrook

Amprobe Instrument, 630 Merrick Rd., 11563, pg. 1676   **PV**
FIRST CENTRAL FINANCIAL CORPORATION, 266 Merrick Rd., 11563, pg. 406   **PV**

First Central Insurance Co., 266 Merrick Rd., 11563, pg. 406   **PV**
Imperial Equities, 211 Broadway, 11563, pg. 674   **PV**
JSB FINANCIAL, 303 Merrick Rd., 11563-2574, pg. 919   **PB**
LONE STAR EQUITIES INC., 211 Broadway, Ste. 302, 11563, pg. 674   **PV**
LONG ISLAND WATER CORPORATION, 733 Sunrise Hwy., 11563, pg. 674   **PV**
Mercury Adjustment Bureau, Inc., 266 Merrick Rd., 11563, pg. 406   **PV**

Macedon

Nance's Food Products, Inc., 3268 Blue Heron View, 14502, pg. 1347   **PB**
Richardson Foods Corporation, 3268 Blue Heron View, 14502, pg. 1347   **PB**

Malone

Tru-Stitch Footwear Div., 123 Catherine St., 12953, pg. 1775   **PB**

Mamaroneck

d'ac, 420 Railroad Way, 10543, pg. 821   **IT**
EDELSON & SONS CORPORATION, 540 W. Boston Post Rd., 10543, pg. 363   **PV**
MARVAL INDUSTRIES, INC., 315 Hoyt Ave., 10543, pg. 710   **PV**
Nessen Lamps, Inc., 420 Railroad Way, 10543, pg. 821   **IT**
ROPER STARCH WORLDWIDE, 566 E. Boston Post Rd., 10543, pg. 944   **PV**
ROSENSHEIN ASSOCIATES, 555 S. Barry Ave., 10543, pg. 945   **PV**

Manhasset

CMP MEDIA, INC., 600 Community Dr., 11030, pg. 279   **PB**
Sabena Belgian World Airlines, 1155 Northern Blvd., 11030, pg. 1168   **IT**

Manlius

Philips Broadband Networks, 100 Fairgrounds Dr., 13104-9990, pg. 1054   **IT**

Maspeth

Atlite Lighting Equip, Inc., 5747 47th St., 11378, pg. 443   **PB**
MANHATTAN BRASS & COPPER CO., 5671 49th Pl., 11378, pg. 705   **PV**
RICHTER & RATNER CONTRACTING CORPORATION, 55-05 Flushing Ave., 11378, pg. 930   **PV**

Massena

Reynolds Metals Company-Massena, P.O. Box 500, 13662, pg. 1385   **PB**

Mattituck

North Fork Bank, 245 Love Ln., 11952, pg. 1194   **PB**

McConnellsville

HARDEN FURNITURE COMPANY, 8535 Mill Pond Way, 13401, pg. 501   **PV**

Mechanicville

American Tissue, Inc., P.O. Box 630, 148 Hudson River Rd, 12118, pg. 63   **PV**
JACK BYRNE FORD & MERCURY, INC., S. Main St., 12118, pg. 191   **PV**

Medina

BernzOmatic, One BernzOmatic Dr., 14103, pg. 1177   **PB**
Medina Journal-Register, 409-13 Main St., 14103, pg. 1079   **PB**
Park Newspapers of Medina, Inc., 409-13 Main St., 14103, pg. 1078   **PB**

Melville

Aer Lingus, 538 Broad Hollow Rd., 11747, pg. 28   **IT**
Altana, Inc., 60 Baylis Rd., 11747, pg. 66   **IT**
ARROW ELECTRONICS, INC., 25 Hub Dr., 11747, pg. 133   **PB**
Arrow/Schweber Electronics Group, 25 Hub Dr., 11747, pg. 133   **PB**
CES/Card Establishment Services Inc., 265 Broadhollow Rd., 11747, pg. 631   **PB**
Career Blazers Learning Center of Melville, 445 Broadhollow Rd., 11747, pg. 209   **PV**
Chyron Corp., Five Hub Dr., 11747, pg. 1372   **IT**
Citicorp Retail Services, Inc., 245 Old Country Rd., 11747, pg. 377   **PB**
Comtech PST Corp., 105 Baylis Rd., 11747, pg. 425   **PB**
COMTECH TELECOMMUNICATIONS CORP., 105 Baylis Rd., 11747, pg. 425   **PB**

PB - *U.S. Public Companies Volume*
PV - *U.S. Private Companies Volume*
IT - *International Public & Private Companies Volume*

1340

Geographic Index-U.S.

Estee Lauder, 350 S. Service Rd., 11747-3230, pg. 594 **PB**
FONAR CORPORATION, 110 Marcus Dr., 11747-4292, pg. 661 **PB**
Gates/Arrow Commercial Systems Div., 25 Hub Dr., 11747, pg. 133 **PV**
General Assurance Company, 201 N. Service Rd., 11747, pg. 543 **IT**
General Assurance Insurance Company of New York, 201 N. Service Rd., 11747, pg. 543 **IT**
GENERAL SEMICONDUCTOR, INC., Ten Melville Park Rd., 11747, pg. 726 **PB**
GENOVESE DRUG STORES, INC., 80 Marcus Dr., 11747, pg. 730 **PB**
GREENSTONE ROBERTS ADVERTISING, One Huntington Quadrangle, 11747, pg. 763 **PB**
A.D. Herman Construction Co., 555 Broad Hallow Rd., 11747, pg. 1035 **PV**
Hewlett-Packard Company, Seven Old Sod Farm Rd., 11747, pg. 814 **PB**
IMI Systems Inc., 290 Broad Hollow Rd., 11747, pg. 1221 **PB**
INTERNATIONAL COMPONENTS CORPORATION, 107 Maxess Rd., 11747, pg. 569 **PV**
Lambda Electronics Inc., 515 Broad Hollow Rd., 11747-3700, pg. 1241 **IT**
Lex Electronics, 25 Hub Dr., 11747, pg. 134 **IT**
Lindenmeyr Munroe, P.O. Box 9082, 30 Hub Dr., 11747-9082, pg. 224 **PV**
LONG ISLAND BANCORP, INC., 201 Old Country Rd., 11747, pg. 1013 **PB**
MTI Systems Corp., 25 Hub Dr., 11747, pg. 134 **PB**
MARCHON EYEWEAR, 35 Hub Dr., 11747, pg. 702 **PV**
NEC America, Inc., 8 Corporate Center Dr., 11747, pg. 900 **IT**
NEC USA, Inc., Eight Corporate Center Dr., 11747, pg. 900 **IT**
NANTUCKET INDUSTRIES, INC., 510 Broadhollow Rd., Ste. 300, 11747, pg. 1151 **PB**
New York Systems Exchange Corp., 150 Broad Hollow Rd., 11747, pg. 1060 **PV**
Newsday, 235 Pinelawn Rd., 11747, pg. 1616 **PB**
Nikon Inc., 1300 Walt Whitman Rd., 11747-3064, pg. 931 **IT**
Nikon Inc., Instrument Group, 1300 Walt Whitman Rd., 11747, pg. 931 **IT**
NORTH FORK BANCORPORATION, INC., 275 BroadHollow Rd., 11747, pg. 1194 **PB**
NORTHVILLE INDUSTRIES CORP., P.O. Box 2937, 25 Melville Pk. Rd., 11747-0398, pg. 806 **PV**
NU HORIZONS ELECTRONICS CORP., 70 Maxess Rd., 11747, pg. 1205 **PB**
OLSTEN CORPORATION, 175 Broad Hollow Rd., 11747, pg. 1220 **PB**
Olsten Financial Services, 175 Broad Hollow Rd., 11747, pg. 1221 **PB**
Olsten Health Services, 175 Broad Hollow Rd., 11590, pg. 1221 **PB**
Olsten Kimberly Qualitycare, 175 Broad Hollow Rd., 11747, pg. 1221 **PB**
Olsten Staffing Services, 175 Broad Hollow Rd., 11747, pg. 1221 **PB**
Olsten Technical Services, 175 Broad Hollow Rd., 11747, pg. 1221 **PB**
Olympus America Inc., Two Corporate Center Dr., 11747-3157, pg. 1005 **IT**
Pennsylvania General Insurance Company of New York, 201 N. Service Rd., 11747, pg. 543 **IT**
PERGAMENT HOME CENTERS, INC., 101 Marcus Dr., 11747, pg. 853 **PV**
RECKSON ASSOCIATES REALTY CORP., 225 Broadhollow Rd., 11747, pg. 1368 **PB**
HENRY SCHEIN, INC., 135 Duryea Rd., 11747, pg. 1437 **PB**
Union-Transport Corporation-Melville Office, 1660 Walt Whitman Rd., 11747, pg. 1119 **PV**
United Technologies, Norden Systems Long Island, 275 Maxess Rd., 11747-3151, pg. 1691 **PB**

Merrick

New York Water Service Corp., 60 Brooklyn Ave., 11566, pg. 993 **PV**

Middle Falls

American Tissue Mills of Greenwich, 192 Country Rte. 53, 12848, pg. 63 **PV**

Middleport

BARDEN & ROBESON CORPORATION, 103 Kelly Ave., 14105, pg. 116 **PV**

Middletown

Bell Flavors & Fragrances, 12 Sprague Ave., 10940, pg. 131 **PV**
Guild Molders Division, Industrial Place, 10940, pg. 463 **PB**

Milton

BROOKLYN BOTTLING CO. OF MILTON, NY, P.O. Box 808, 12547, pg. 171 **PV**

Mineola

Allcity Insurance Co., Mineola, 114 Old Country Rd., 11508, pg. 990 **PB**

American List Corporation, 330 Old Country Rd., 11501, pg. 1481 **PB**
Compass Investment Services, 330 Old Country Rd., 11501, pg. 1194 **PV**
GREAT NECK SAW MANUFACTURERS, INC., 165 E. Second St., 11501, pg. 475 **PV**
Pollio Dairy Products, 120 Mineola Blvd., 11501, pg. 1288 **PB**
Pollio Dairy Products Company, 120 Mineola Blvd., 11501, pg. 1288 **PB**
Robeson Sales Corporation, 49 Windsor Ave., 11501, pg. 1394 **PB**
VAN SON HOLLAND INK CORP. OF AMERICA, 92 Union St., 11501, pg. 1133 **PV**

Monroe

Frontier Communications of New York, Inc., P.O. Box 657, 145 N. Main St., 10950, pg. 684 **PB**
Pittsburgh Tube Co.-Monroe Div., 326 State Hwy.208, 10950, pg. 868 **PV**

Montour Falls

SHEPARD NILES, INC., 250 N. Genesee St., 14865, pg. 992 **PV**

Mount Kisco

KOHLBERG & COMPANY, LLC, 111 Rodeo Circle, 10549, pg. 629 **PV**
Universal Voltronics Corporation, 27 Radio Circle Dr., 10549, pg. 1596 **PB**

Mount Vernon

Ain Plastics, Inc., 249 E. Sandford Blvd., 10550, pg. 1388 **IT**
SIGMUND COHN CORP., 121 S. Columbus Ave., 10553, pg. 250 **PV**
Labelon/Noesting Company, LLC, 603 S. 3rd Ave., 10553, pg. 641 **PV**
MAGNETIC ANALYSIS CORP., 535 S. Fourth Ave., 10550-4499, pg. 695 **PV**
Medwire, 121 S. Columbus Ave., 10553, pg. 250 **PV**
MICHAEL ANTHONY JEWELERS, INC., 115 S. MacQuesten Pkwy., 10550, pg. 1103 **PB**
Potentiometer Div., 750 S. Fulton Av., 10550, pg. 1003 **PB**
Pyrofuse, 121 S. Columbus Ave., 10553, pg. 250 **PV**
RELIABLE AUTOMATIC SPRINKLER CO., INC., 525 N. MacQuesten Pkwy., 10552, pg. 920 **PV**
TORK, INC., One Grove St., 10550, pg. 1092 **PV**
UNIVERSAL BUILDERS SUPPLY, INC., 216 S. Terrace Ave., 10550, pg. 1126 **PV**
Ward Leonard Electric Company, Inc., 31 South St., 10550, pg. 1118 **PV**

Mountainville

STAR ANCHORS & FASTENERS, P.O. Box #1, 20 Industry Dr., 10953-0001, pg. 1033 **PV**

Naples

Widmer's Wine Cellars, Inc., One Lake Niagara Ln., 14512, pg. 300 **PB**

New Hartford

PAR Government Systems Corporation, 8383 Seneca Tpke., 13413-4991, pg. 1256 **PB**
PAR Microsystems Corporation, 8383 Seneca Tpke., 13413-4991, pg. 1256 **PB**
PAR TECHNOLOGY CORPORATION, 8383 Seneca Tpke., 13413-4991, pg. 1256 **PB**
PAR Vision Systems Corporation, 8383 Seneca Tpke., 13413-4991, pg. 1256 **PB**
Partlow Corporation, Two Campion Rd., 13413, pg. 482 **PV**
Rome Research Corporation, 8383 Seneca Tpke., 13413-4991, pg. 1256 **PB**
UTICA MUTUAL INSURANCE COMPANY, 180 Genesee St., 13413, pg. 1129 **PV**
Utica National Insurance Group, 180 Genesee St., 13413, pg. 1130 **PV**

New Hyde Park

Asher Candy Company, 1815 Gilford Ave., 11040, pg. 1052 **PB**
ASSOCIATED GLOBAL SYSTEMS, 3333 New Hyde Park Rd., 11042, pg. 90 **PV**
Chase Auto Finance Corporation, 2000 Marcus Ave., 11040, pg. 337 **PB**
DESIGNATRONICS, INC., Box 5416, 2101 Jericho Tpke., 11042-5416, pg. 327 **PV**
HI-SHEAR INDUSTRIES INC., 3333 New Hyde Park Rd., 11042, pg. 824 **PB**
KIMCO REALTY CORPORATION, 3333 New Hyde Park Rd., 11042-0020, pg. 960 **PB**
MARISA CHRISTINA INC., 415 Second Ave., 11040, pg. 1044 **PB**
McPherson's America, Inc., 3333 New Hyde Park Rd., Ste. 409, 11040, pg. 852 **IT**
MORTON'S RESTAURANT GROUP, INC., 3333 New Hyde Park Rd., Ste. 210, 11042, pg. 1136 **PB**
Regent-Sheffield Ltd., 3333 New Hyde Park Rd., Ste. 409, 11040, pg. 852 **IT**

Sterling Instrument Div., 2101 Jericho Tpke., 11040, pg. 327 **PV**
Stock Drive Products Div., 2101 Jericho Tpke., 11040, pg. 327 **PV**
Stock Model Parts Div., 2101 Jericho Tpke., 11040, pg. 327 **PV**
Techno Div., 2101 Jericho Tpke., 11040, pg. 327 **PV**
Vendor Funding Co., Inc., 3333 New Hyde Park Rd., 11042, pg. 153 **IT**
William Penn Life Insurance Co. of New York, 3003 New Hyde Park Blvd., 11042, pg. 805 **PV**
Willis Corroon Construction Services Corp., P.O. Box 5450, 3333 New Hyde Park Rd., 11040, pg. 1504 **IT**

New Rochelle

ABI National Accounts, 466 Main St., 10801, pg. 70 **PB**
Bakers Pride Oven Company, 30 Pine st., 10801, pg. 1193 **PV**
Bally, Inc., One Bally Pl., 10801, pg. 997 **IT**
Bally Management, One Bally Pl., 10801, pg. 998 **IT**
THE P.J. CARLIN CONSTRUCTION COMPANY, 271 North Ave., Ste. 915, 10801, pg. 211 **PV**
PLUNKETT-WEBSTER, INC., Two Clinton Pl., 10801-0251, pg. 872 **PV**
Polyflon Company, 35 River St., 10801, pg. 457 **PB**
POWERS FASTENING, INC., Two F.B. Powers Square, 10801, pg. 878 **PV**
LILLIAN VERNON CORPORATION, 543 Main St., 10801, pg. 1716 **PB**
JOSEPH VICTORI WINES, INC., 2525 Palmer Ave., 10801, pg. 1139 **PV**
Wittnauer International, Inc., 145 Huguenot St., 10802, pg. 273 **PB**

New Windsor

GretagMacbeth LLC, 617 Little Britain Rd., 12553, pg. 965 **PB**
Macbeth Div., 405 Little Britian Rd., 12553, pg. 965 **PB**
Mid-Valley Oil Company, Inc., One S. Water St., 12550, pg. 1151 **PV**

New York

A&E Television Networks, 235 E. 45th St., 10017, pg. 515 **PV**
A/S/M Communications, Inc., 1515 Broadway, 10036, pg. 1446 **IT**
ABC Cable & International Broadcast, Inc., 77 W. 66th St., 10023, pg. 512 **PB**
ABC, Inc., 77 W. 66th St., 10023-6298, pg. 511 **PB**
ABC News & Sports, 47 W. 66th St., 10023, pg. 511 **PB**
ABC News Holding Company, Inc., 77 W. 66th St., 10023, pg. 511 **PB**
ABC News, Inc., 77 W. 66th St., 10023, pg. 511 **PB**
ABC News Intercontinental, Inc., 77 W. 66th St., 10023, pg. 511 **PB**
ABC Radio Network, Inc., 77 W. 66th St., 10023, pg. 512 **PB**
ABC Sports Holding Company, Inc., 77 W. 66th St., 10023, pg. 511 **PB**
ABC Sports, Inc., 47 W. 66th St., 10023, pg. 511 **PB**
ABC Television Network, 77 W. 66th St., 10023, pg. 511 **PB**
ABC Television Network Group, 77 W. 66th St., 10023, pg. 511 **PB**
ABN AMRO Bank, N.V. (New York), 335 Madison Ave., 16th & 17th Fl., 10017, pg. 10 **IT**
ABN-AMRO Securities (USA) Inc., 335 Madison Ave., 14th Fl., 10017, pg. 11 **IT**
ABP Interactive LLC, 35 W. 35th St., 11th Fl., 10001, pg. 17 **PV**
AEA INVESTORS INC., 65 E. 55th St., 27th Fl., 10022, pg. 4 **PV**
AFA Protective Systems, Inc., 519 Eighth Ave., 10018, pg. 5 **PV**
AFCO Credit Corp., Seven Hanover Sq., 10005, pg. 1085 **PV**
AFD CONTRACT FURNITURE, 1926 Broadway, 10023, pg. 5 **PV**
AGA CATALOG MARKETING & DESIGN, Two Park Ave., 4th Fl., 10016, pg. 5 **PV**
AGA Catalog Marketing & Design, Two Park Ave., 10016, pg. 295 **PV**
A.I. Credit Corp., 70 Pine St., 10270, pg. 85 **PB**
AIB plc, 405 Park Ave., 10022, pg. 64 **IT**
AIC INTERNATIONAL, INC., 117 E. 57th St., Ste. 21H, 10022, pg. 6 **PV**
AIG Consultants, Inc., 70 Pine St., 10270, pg. 85 **PB**
AIG Marketing, Inc., 70 Pine St., 10270, pg. 85 **PB**
AIG Risk Management, Inc., 70 Pine St., 10270, pg. 85 **PB**
AIU Insurance Company, 70 Pine St., 10270, pg. 84 **PB**
AM Entertainment, 1500 Broadway, Ste. 1915, 10036, pg. 38 **PV**
ANZ McCaughan Securities, 1177 Avenue of the Americas, 10036, pg. 98 **IT**
AOC Ladies, 512 Seventh Ave., 9th Fl., 10018, pg. 49 **PV**
AOLP Acquisition Corp., c/o Morgan Stanley, 1251 Avenue of the Americas, 10020, pg. 357 **PB**
AOLP Mezzanine Acquisition Corp., 1251 Avenue of the Americas, 10020, pg. 357 **PB**
AP-Dow Jones News Service, 200 Liberty St., 10281, pg. 524 **PB**
AVC/Nu-Vision, 90 John St., 26th Fl., 10038, pg. 9 **PV**
AXA Re United States, 17 State St., 29th & 30th Fls., 10004-1501, pg. 19 **IT**
Aberdeen Mfg. Corporation, 16 E. 34th St., 10016, pg. 1094 **PV**

PB - *U.S. Public Companies Volume*
PV - *U.S. Private Companies Volume*
IT - *International Public & Private Companies Volume*

1341

Geographic Index-U.S.

Geographic Index-U.S.

Accecones Ricci U.S.A., Inc., Four West 58th St.; Ste. 1150, 10019, pg. 445 **IT**
Accelerated Claims Processing, Inc., 401 Park Ave. South, 10016, pg. 802 **PB**
Acclaim Comics, 275 Seventh Ave., 10001, pg. 15 **PV**
Active Quilting Div., 225 W. 34th St., 10122, pg. 938 **PV**
Acxiom Corporation, 441 Lexington Ave., 18th Fl., 10017-3910, pg. 18 **PB**
Addison-Wesley Longman, Ten E. 53rd St., 10022, pg. 1026 **PB**
ADLER BOSCHETTO PEEBLES & PARTNERS, INC., 136 Madison Ave., 14th Fl., 10016, pg. 17 **PV**
Advanced Risk Management Services, Seven Hanover Sq., 11th Fl., 10004, pg. 1505 **IT**
Advertising Age, 220 E. 42nd St., 10017, pg. 284 **PB**
ADVERTISING CHECKING BUREAU INCORPORATED, 221 W. 41st St., 10036, pg. 23 **PB**
ADVISERS CAPITAL MANAGEMENT INC., 110 E. 42nd St., Ste. 1704, 10017, pg. 23 **PV**
Adweek, 1515 Broadway, 10036, pg. 1446 **PB**
AEGIS Corporate Training, Inc., 290 Madison Ave., 10017, pg. 209 **PV**
Aero Peru, 500 5th Ave., Ste. 2620, 10110, pg. 24 **IT**
Aeropostale/Charter Club, 11 Penn Plaza, 10001, pg. 618 **PB**
Affiliated Fund, Inc., 767 Fifth Ave., 10153-0203, pg. 675 **PV**
Agency and Rep Services Div., 919 Third Ave., Fifth Fl., 10022, pg. 925 **PV**
Agency.Com, 665 Broadway, 9th Fl., 10012, pg. 1223 **PB**
Air Canada, 1166 Ave. of the Americas, 10036, pg. 36 **IT**
Air France, 142 W. 57th St., 18th Fl., 10019, pg. 560 **IT**
Air France (Northeast Region), 142 W. 57th St., 10019, pg. 560 **IT**
Air France (U.S. Region), 142 W. 57th St., 10019, pg. 561 **IT**
Air-India, 345 Park Ave., 10154, pg. 37 **IT**
Air Malta - New York, 630 Fifth Ave., Ste. 2662, 10111, pg. 37 **IT**
Airplay Monitor, 1515 Broadway, 10036, pg. 1446 **PB**
Aladdin Paperbacks, 1230 Ave. of the Americas, 10020, pg. 777 **PV**
Albuquerque Capital Management, Inc., 277 Park Ave., 10172, pg. 337 **PV**
Alcatel USA Corp, 45 Rockefeller Plaza, Rm. 3055, 10111, pg. 55 **IT**
Alexander & Alexander Inc., 1185 Ave. of the Americas, 10036, pg. 117 **PB**
Alexander & Alexander Services Inc., 1185 Ave. of the Americas, 10036, pg. 117 **PB**
ALEXANDER DOLL COMPANY, INC., 615 W. 131st St., 10027, pg. 33 **PV**
ALFIN, INC., 720 Fifth Ave., 8th Fl., 10019, pg. 40 **PB**
Alias Wavefront, One Pennsylvania Plaza, Ste. 1918, 10119, pg. 1474 **PB**
Alitalia Airlines, 666 Fifth Ave., 10103, pg. 652 **IT**
All American Television, Inc., 1325 Avenue of the Americas, 10019, pg. 41 **PV**
All Nippon Airways-New York, 630 Fifth Ave., Ste. 537, 10111, pg. 57 **IT**
All Nippon Management Service Inc., 303 Fifth Ave., 10016, pg. 57 **IT**
All Nippon Travel Service Inc., 303 Fifth Ave., 10016, pg. 57 **IT**
Allcity Insurance Co., 122 Fifth Ave., 10011, pg. 990 **PB**
ALLEGHANY CORPORATION, 375 Park Ave., 10152, pg. 42 **PB**
Alleghany Generating Co., 12 E. 49th St., 10017, pg. 42 **PB**
ALLEN & COMPANY INCORPORATED, 711 Fifth Ave., 10022, pg. 36 **PV**
Alliance Capital Management Corp., 1345 Avenue of the Americas, 10105, pg. 589 **PB**
Allied Communications Group, 1271 Ave. of the Americas, 44th Fl., 10020, pg. 908 **PB**
Allied Impex Corp., 117 E 57th St., Ste. 21H, 10022, pg. 6 **PV**
Allied Security Inc., 322 Eighth Ave., #1702, 10001, pg. 41 **PV**
Allomatic Industries, 737 Park Ave., 10021-4256, pg. 1363 **PB**
Allure, 360 Madison Ave., 10017, pg. 20 **PV**
Almay, Inc., 625 Madison Ave., 10022, pg. 689 **PV**
Alpha Wave Healthcare Communications, 220 E. 42 St., 10017, pg. 617 **PV**
THE ALPINE GROUP, INC., 1790 Broadway, 15th Fl., 10019-1412, pg. 58 **PB**
Alusuisse-Lonza America Inc., 750 Lexington Ave., 22nd. Fl., 10022, pg. 67 **IT**
AMBAC Capital Corp., One State St Plaza, 10004, pg. 63 **PB**
AMBAC FINANCIAL GROUP, INC., One State Street Plaza, 10004, pg. 62 **PB**
AMERADA HESS CORPORATION, 1185 Ave. of the Americas, 10036, pg. 65 **PB**
Amerex Children, 112 W. 34th St., Ste. 2405, 10001, pg. 49 **PV**
Amerex Men's, 350 Fifth Ave, Ste. 1435, 10118, pg. 49 **PV**
AMEREX USA, INC., 350 Fifth Ave., Ste. 1401, 10118, pg. 49 **PV**
America, 9-13 E. 18th St., 10003, pg. 130 **PV**
AMERICAN ARBITRATION ASSOCIATION, 140 W. 51st St., 10020-1203, pg. 50 **PV**
American Artist, 1515 Broadway, 10036, pg. 1446 **IT**
American Baby Magazine, 717 5th Ave., 10022, pg. 1328 **PB**
American Bank Note Company, 200 Park Ave., 49th Fl., 10166-4999, pg. 68 **PB**
American Banker Bond Buyer, One State St Plaza, 10004, pg. 1600 **PB**

AMERICAN BANKNOTE CORP., 200 Park Ave., 49th Fl., 10166-4999, pg. 68 **PB**
AMERICAN BIBLE SOCIETY, 1865 Broadway, 10023, pg. 51 **PV**
American Bio Corporation, 53 Wall St., 10005-2815, pg. 566 **PV**
American Broadcasting Companies, Inc., 77 W. 66th St., 10023, pg. 511 **IT**
AMERICAN BUREAU OF SHIPPING, Two World Trade Ctr., 106th Fl., 10048, pg. 51 **PV**
American Color & Chemical Corporation, 100 E. 42nd St., 10017, pg. 1054 **IT**
American Export Register, Five Penn Plaza, 10001, pg. 1082 **PV**
American Express Bank Ltd., Three World Financial Ctr., Tower C - 200 Vesey St., 10285-2300, pg. 73 **PB**
AMERICAN EXPRESS COMPANY, American Express Tower C, 3 World Financial Center/200 Vesey St., 10285-4805, pg. 73 **PB**
American Express Publishing Corporation, 1120 Ave. of the Americas, 10036, pg. 74 **PB**
American Express Travel Related Services Co., Inc., American Express Tower, World Financial Center, 1C285, pg. 73 **PB**
AMERICAN FABRICS COMPANY, 1359 Broadway, 16th Fl., 10018, pg. 53 **PV**
American Heritage Magazine, 60 Fifth Ave., 10011, pg. 417 **PV**
American Home Assurance Co., 70 Pine St., 10270, pg. 84 **PB**
American Home Entertainment, 1107 Broadway, Ste. 808, 10010, pg. 923 **PB**
American Home Style, 110 Fifth Ave., 10011, pg. 190 **PB**
AMERICAN INDUSTRIAL PARTNERS, 551 Fifth Ave., Ste. 3800, 10176, pg. 56 **PV**
AMERICAN INSTITUTE OF C.P.A.'S INC., 1211 Ave. of the Americas, 10036, pg. 57 **PV**
AMERICAN INTERNATIONAL GROUP, INC., 70 Pine St., 10270, pg. 83 **PB**
American International Life Assurance Company of New York, 70 Pine St., 10270, pg. 84 **PV**
American International Recovery, Inc., 70 Pine St., 10270, pg. 85 **PB**
American International Underwriters Corp., 70 Pine St., 10270, pg. 85 **PV**
American Journal of Nursing Company, 555 W. 57th St., 10019-2961, pg. 1513 **IT**
AMERICAN KENNEL CLUB, INC., 51 Madison Ave., 10010, pg. 58 **PV**
American Life Insurance Company of New York, 320 Park Ave., 10022, pg. 769 **PV**
American Literature Review, Five Penn Plaza, 10001, pg. 1082 **PV**
American Medical Systems, Inc., 235 E. 42nd St., 10017, pg. 1281 **PB**
American Photo, 1633 Broadway, 43rd Fl., 10019, pg. 795 **IT**
American Place, Two Park Ave., 10016, pg. 130 **PB**
AMERICAN RETAIL GROUP, 1114 Ave. of the Americas, 28th Fl., 10036, pg. 61 **PV**
American Scandinavian Banking Corporation, 437 Madison Ave., 10022, pg. 859 **IT**
THE AMERICAN STOCK EXCHANGE, 86 Trinity Pl., 10006-1881, pg. 62 **PV**
American Stock Exchange Clearing Corp., 86 Trinity Place, 10006, pg. 62 **PV**
American Stock Exchange Realty Associates Inc., 86 Trinity Place, 10006, pg. 62 **PV**
American Tractebel Corporation, 12 E. 49th St., 17th Fl., Ste. 1704, 10017, pg. 1415 **PB**
Ameriscribe Corporation, 75 Varick St., 17th Fl., 10013, pg. 1303 **PB**
Amex Commodities Corporation, 86 Trinity Place, 10006, pg. 62 **PV**
AMICALE INDUSTRIES, INC., 1375 Broadway, 10018, pg. 66 **PV**
AMMIRATI, PURIS & LINTAS, INC., 885 2nd Ave., 10017, pg. 66 **PV**
Ammirati Puris Lintas Worldwide, One Dag Hammarskjold Plaza, 10017, pg. 908 **PV**
AMRAIL, Ste. 601-805 Third Ave., 10022, pg. 706 **IT**
AMREP CORPORATION, 641 Lexington Ave., 6th Fl., 10022, pg. 104 **PB**
AMREP Solutions, Inc., 10 Columbus Cir., 10019, pg. 104 **PB**
AMSCO SCHOOL PUBLICATIONS, INC., 315 Hudson St., 10013, pg. 67 **PV**
Amsterdam-Rotterdam Bank N.V. New York, 500 Park Ave., 10022, pg. 9 **IT**
Anaderm Research Corp., 235 E. 42nd St., 10017, pg. 1281 **PB**
Analysts International, Eastern Region, One Penn Plaza, Ste. 1910, 10119-0002, pg. 110 **PB**
ANDAL CORP., 909 Third Ave., 10022, pg. 111 **PB**
The Andean Fund, Inc., 277 Park Ave., 10172, pg. 338 **PB**
ANDERSEN WORLDWIDE, 1345 Ave. of the Americas, 10105, pg. 72 **PB**
ANDERSON & LEMBKE INC., 320 W. 13th St., 9th Fl., 10014, pg. 72 **PV**
Gavin Anderson & Company, 1633 Broadway, 26th Fl., 10019, pg. 1223 **PB**
ANDIN INTERNATIONAL INC., 609 Greenwich St., 10014, pg. 73 **PV**
ANDOVER TOGS, INC., 1333 Broadway, 10118, pg. 112 **PB**
Andrews & Clark, Inc., 49 West 37th St., 10018, pg. 1593 **PB**
Andrews Group, Incorporated, 625 Madison Ave., 11th Fl., 10022, pg. 689 **PB**
ANGLO FABRICS COMPANY, INC., 561 Seventh Ave., 16th Fl., 10018, pg. 74 **PV**

Animal Planet, 641 Lexington Ave., 10022, pg. 334 **PV**
Anjou International Company, 800 Third Ave., 10022, pg. 321 **IT**
AnnTaylor, Inc., 142 W. 57th St., 10019, pg. 116 **PB**
ANNTAYLOR STORES CORPORATION, 142 W. 57th St., 10019, pg. 116 **PB**
AnnTaylor Travel, Inc., 142 W. 57th St., 10019, pg. 116 **PB**
Ansaldo North America, 425 Park Ave., 27th Fl., 10022, pg. 653 **IT**
Anspach Grossman Enterprise, 711 Third Ave., 10017, pg. 1483 **IT**
ANTWERP DIAMOND DISTRIBUTORS INC., 587 Fifth Ave., 10017, pg. 76 **PV**
Aoki Construction (NY) Co., Ltd., 40 W. 57th St., 20th Fl., 10019, pg. 78 **IT**
Apparal America, Inc., 1411 Broadway, Fl. 30, 10018, pg. 120 **PB**
I. APPEL CORPORATION, 149 Madison Ave., 4th Fl., 10016, pg. 78 **PV**
Arabian Oil Company, Ltd. (New York), 535 Madison Ave., 10022, pg. 78 **IT**
The Arbitron Company, 142 W. 57th St., 10019, pg. 331 **PB**
Architectural Record, 1221 Ave. of the Americas, 10020, pg. 1070 **PB**
Area Headquarters-THE AMERICAS, 30th Fl., Grace Bldg., 1114 Ave. of the Americas, 10036, pg. 393 **IT**
Argo International Corp., 140 Franklin St., 10013, pg. 322 **PV**
ARIS INDUSTRIES, INC., 475 5th Ave., 3rd Fl., 10017, pg. 129 **PB**
Arista Records Inc., Six W. 57th St., 10019-3913, pg. 192 **IT**
ARK RESTAURANTS CORP., 85 Fifth Ave., 14th Fl., 10003, pg. 129 **PB**
THE ARLEN CORPORATION, 505 Eighth Ave., 10018, pg. 131 **PB**
Arlen Management Corp., 505 Eighth Ave., 10018, pg. 131 **PB**
Arlen Metals Corporation, 505 Eighth Ave., 10018, pg. 131 **PB**
ARNAV INDUSTRIES, INC., 31 W. 27th St., 10001, pg. 83 **PV**
ARNHOLD AND S. BLEICHROEDER, INC., 1345 Ave. of Americas, 10105-4300, pg. 83 **PV**
Arnold Advertising, 437 Madison Ave., 10022, pg. 84 **PV**
Adrien Arpel, 720 5th Ave., 10019, pg. 40 **PB**
Arrow Shirt Company, 48 W. 38th St., 12th Fl., 10018, pg. 194 **IT**
The Arrow Shirt Company, 575 Fifth Ave., 10017, pg. 194 **IT**
Arts & Entertainment Network/ABC/NBC, 235 E. 45th St., 10019, pg. 512 **PB**
Asahi America Inc., 400 Park Ave., 10022, pg. 85 **IT**
Asahi Chemical Industry America, Inc., Empire State Bldg., 350 Fifth Ave., Ste. 7412, 10118, pg. 84 **IT**
Asahi Glass America, Inc., 450 Lexington Ave., Ste. 1920, 10017-3911, pg. 84 **IT**
Asahi International Ltd., 400 Park Ave., 10022, pg. 85 **IT**
Asarco Exploration Co., 180 Maiden Ln., 10038, pg. 138 **PB**
ASARCO INCORPORATED, 180 Maiden Ln., 10038, pg. 137 **PB**
Asarco International Corp., 180 Maiden Ln., 10038, pg. 138 **PB**
Asarco Santa Cruz, 180 Maiden Lane, 10038, pg. 138 **PB**
Ashikaga Bank-New York Branch, One World Trade Center, Ste. 8151, 10048, pg. 88 **IT**
The Asian Wall Street Journal Weekly, 200 Liberty St., 10281, pg. 524 **PB**
Asiaweek Ltd., Time & Life Bldg., Rockefeller Center, 10020, pg. 613 **PB**
Associated Engineers & Consultants, Inc., 250 W. 34th St., 10119, pg. 1519 **IT**
ASSOCIATED MERCHANDISING CORP. (AMC), 1440 Broadway, 10018, pg. 91 **PV**
Associated Music Publishers, 257 Park Ave. S., 10010, pg. 768 **PV**
THE ASSOCIATED PRESS, 50 Rockefeller Plaza, 10020, pg. 92 **PV**
Associated Press, 50 Rockefeller Plaza, 10020, pg. 92 **PV**
Atco/East-West Records, 75 Rockefeller Plaza, 10019, pg. 1611 **PB**
Athena Venture Partners L.P., 375 Park Ave., Ste. 3303, 10152, pg. 644 **IT**
Atheneum Books for Young Readers, 1230 Ave. of the Americas, 10020, pg. 777 **PV**
Athletic Express, 233 Broadway, 10279, pg. 1777 **PB**
FREDERICK ATKINS, 1515 Broadway, 10036, pg. 94 **PV**
Atlantic Bank of New York Inc., 960 Ave. of the Americas, 10001, pg. 907 **IT**
Atlantic Hardware & Supply Co., 601 W. 26th St., 10001, pg. 400 **PB**
ATLANTIC MUTUAL COMPANIES, 100 Wall St., 26th Fl., 10005-3701, pg. 95 **PV**
Atlantic Mutual Insurance Co., 100 Wall St., 10005, pg. 95 **PV**
Atlantic Recording Corporation, 1290 Sixth Ave., 10104, pg. 1611 **PB**
AUDITS & SURVEYS WORLDWIDE, 650 Sixth Ave., 10011, pg. 147 **PB**
Australia and New Zealand Banking Group Limited, New York, 1177 Avenue of the Americas, 10036, pg. 98 **IT**
Authentic Fitness Corp. East Coast Region, 90 Park Ave., 13th Floor, 10016, pg. 148 **PB**
Autranet, Inc., 140 Broadway, 10005, pg. 589 **PB**
Avon Books, 1350 Ave. of the Americas, 10019, pg. 515 **PV**
AVON PRODUCTS, INC., 1345 Ave. of the Americas, 10105-0196, pg. 155 **PB**

PB - *U.S. Public Companies Volume*
PV - *U.S. Private Companies Volume*
IT - *International Public & Private Companies Volume*

Avon Products, Inc., Nine W. 57th St., 10019, pg. 156 **PB**
Avon Retail Group, Nine W. 57th St., 10019, pg. 156 **PB**
AVRETT, FREE & GINSBERG, INC., 800 Third Ave., 10022, pg. 103 **PV**
AXSYS TECHNOLOGIES, INC., 645 Madison Ave., 9th Fl., 10022, pg. 157 **PB**
Ayer International, Worldwide Plaza, 825 Eighth Ave., 10019, pg. 104 **PV**
N.W. AYER & PARTNERS, Worldwide Plaza, 825 Eighth Ave., 10019-7498, pg. 103 **PV**
Ayer Public Relations, Worldwide Plaza, 825 Eighth Ave., 10019-7498, pg. 104 **PV**
AyerDirect, Worldwide Plaza, 825 Eighth Ave., 10019, pg. 104 **PV**
B. Dalton Bookseller, Inc., 122 Fifth Ave., 10011, pg. 189 **PB**
BBC Warrant Acquisition Corp., c/o Morgan Stanley Lev. Mez. F, 1251 Avenue of the Americas, 10020, pg. 357 **PB**
BBDO Worldwide Inc., 1285 Ave. of the Americas, 10019-6095, pg. 1223 **PB**
BDDP North America, Inc., 11 Madison Ave., 12th Fl., 10010, pg. 117 **IT**
BET New York Media Sales, 380 Madison Ave., 20th Fl., 10017, pg. 235 **PB**
BFCE New York, 645 Fifth Ave., 10022, pg. 161 **IT**
BHC Communications, Inc., 767 Fifth Ave., 10153, pg. 352 **PB**
BHF-Bank, 590 Madison Ave., 10022-2540, pg. 119 **IT**
BHF Securities Corp., 590 Madison Ave., 28th Fl., 10022-2540, pg. 119 **IT**
BJK&E Media Group, 40 W. 23rd St., 10010, pg. 1642 **PB**
BK&S Direct Marketing, 475 Park Ave. S., 15th Fl., 10016, pg. 143 **PV**
BMCG (Business Marketing Communications), 130 5th Ave., 10011, pg. 480 **PV**
BMG/Music, 1540 Broadway, 10036, pg. 191 **IT**
B.M.G. Music Service, 1540 Broadway, 10036, pg. 1383 **IT**
B.M.G. Records, 1540 Broadway, 10036, pg. 1383 **IT**
BNL US Corporation, 25 W. 51st St., 10019, pg. 136 **IT**
BNY Brokerage, Inc., 101 Barclay St., 12W, 10286, pg. 178 **PB**
BNY Capital Markets, One Wall St., 10286, pg. 178 **PB**
BNY Financial Corporation, 1290 Ave. of the Americas, 10104, pg. 178 **PB**
BNY International Financing Corporation, One Wall St., 9th Fl., 10286, pg. 178 **PB**
BPA INTERNATIONAL, 270 Madison Ave., 10016-0699, pg. 107 **PV**
BPI Communications Inc., 1515 Broadway, 10036-8986, pg. 1446 **IT**
BSA ADVERTISING, INC., 360 Lexington Ave., 10017, pg. 107 **PV**
BSA Advertising, Inc., 360 Lexington Ave., 10017, pg. 108 **PV**
BSMG Worldwide, 640 Fifth Ave., 8th Fl., 10019, pg. 1642 **PB**
BT Brokerage Corporation, 529 Fifth Ave., 10017, pg. 185 **PB**
BT Capital Partners, 280 Park Ave., 10017, pg. 185 **PB**
BT Commercial Corporation, 28 Park Ave., 10017, pg. 185 **PB**
BT Equipment Leasing, Inc., 280 Park Ave., 10017, pg. 185 **PB**
BT Futures Corp., 130 Liberty St., 10015, pg. 185 **PB**
B.T. Inc., 783 Fifth Ave., 10018, pg. 1349 **IT**
BT International Trading Corp., 280 Park Ave., 10017, pg. 185 **PB**
BT Investment Managers, Inc., 280 Park Ave., 10017, pg. 185 **PB**
BT North America, Inc., 100 Park Ave., 10017, pg. 223 **IT**
BT Private Clients Group, 280 Park Ave., pg. 185 **PB**
BT Securities Corp., 130 Liberty St., 10006, pg. 185 **PB**
BTM Leasing & Finance, Inc., 1251 Ave. of the Americas, 10020, pg. 157 **IT**
B.U.S. Environmental Services, Inc., 520 Madison Ave., 10022, pg. 860 **IT**
BV Capital Management, Inc., 575 Fifth Ave., 10017, pg. 180 **IT**
BV Capital Markets, Inc., 575 5th Ave., 10017, pg. 180 **IT**
Baar & Beards, 350 5th Ave., 8th Fl., 10118, pg. 839 **PV**
BABY TOGS, INC., 460 W. 34th St., 10001, pg. 108 **PV**
Back Stage/Shoot, 1515 Broadway, 10036, pg. 1446 **IT**
Backstage, 1515 Broadway, 10036, pg. 1446 **IT**
Bain Securities, Inc., 31 W. 52nd St. 4th Fl., 10019, pg. 406 **IT**
BAIRD, PATRICK & CO., INC., 20 Exchange Pl., 10005, pg. 111 **PV**
BALDI, BLOOM & WHELAN ADVERTISING, 41 Madison Ave., 36th Fl., 10010, pg. 112 **PV**
Ballantine Books, 201 E. 50th St., 10022, pg. 21 **PV**
Balson-Hercules Ltd., 1040 Sixth Ave., 10018, pg. 326 **IT**
Banca Commerciale Italiana, One William St., 10004, pg. 652 **IT**
Banca Monte dei Paschi di Siena, 245 Park Avenue, 26th Fl., 10167, pg. 136 **IT**
Banca Nazionale Del Lavoro (New York), 25 W. 51st St., 10019, pg. 136 **IT**
Banca Popolare di Milano, 375 Park Ave, 10152, pg. 137 **IT**
Banca Serfin, S.A., New York Agency, 399 Park Ave., 37th Fl., 10022, pg. 137 **IT**
Banco Central Hispano-U.S.A., 50 Broadway, 10004, pg. 139 **IT**
Banco de la Nacion Argentina, 299 Park Ave., 2nd Fl., 10171, pg. 140 **IT**
Banco de la Provincia de Buenos Aires, 609 5th Ave., 3rd Fl., 10017, pg. 140 **IT**
Banco di Napoli-New York, Four E. 54th St., 10022, pg. 140 **IT**
Banco di Sicilia, 250 Park Ave., 10177, pg. 140 **IT**
Banco do Brasil S.A.-New York, P.O. Box 4449, 550 Fifth Ave., 10036, pg. 141 **IT**
Banco Itau S.A., 540 Madison Ave., 24th Fl., 10022, pg. 142 **IT**
Banco Nacional de Mexico, S.A., 767 5th Ave., 8th F., 10153, pg. 574 **IT**
Banco Santander, 45 E. 53rd St., Fl. 9-10, 10022, pg. 143 **IT**
Banco Santander Puerto Rico, New York Branch, 45 E. 53rd St., 10022, pg. 143 **IT**
Bancomer New York Agency, 115 E. 54th St., 10022, pg. 145 **IT**
Banexi International Financial Services (North America) Corp., 499 Park Ave., 7th Fl., 10022, pg. 163 **IT**
Bank Brussels Lambert, New York Branch, 630 Fifth Ave., 10111-0020, pg. 147 **IT**
Bank Hapoalim B.M., 1177 Avenue of the Americas, 14th Fl., 10036-2790, pg. 149 **IT**
Bank Leumi Trust Company of New York, 579 Fifth Ave., 10017, pg. 150 **IT**
Bank of America, 40 E. 52nd St., 10022, pg. 180 **PB**
Bank of America-The Sequor Group, 127 John St., 10038, pg. 181 **PB**
Bank of Bermuda (New York) Limited, 350 Park Ave., 23rd Fl., 10022, pg. 151 **IT**
Bank of Boston International, 152 W. 57th St., 10019, pg. 184 **PB**
Bank of China, 410 Madison Ave., 10017, pg. 152 **IT**
Bank of China, 42-44 E. Broadway, 10002, pg. 152 **IT**
Bank of Hawaii International Corporation, New York, One Whitehall St., 16th Fl., 10004, pg. 1248 **PB**
Bank of Ireland (U.S.A.), 640 Fifth Ave., 10019, pg. 152 **IT**
Bank of Montreal - New York, 430 Park Ave., 10022, pg. 154 **IT**
Bank of Montreal Trust Company, 77 Water St., 4th Fl., 10005, pg. 154 **IT**
The Bank of New York, 48 Wall St., 10286, pg. 178 **PB**
THE BANK OF NEW YORK COMPANY, INC., 48 Wall St., 10286, pg. 178 **PB**
The Bank of Nova Scotia, One Liberty Plaza, 10006, pg. 156 **IT**
The Bank of Nova Scotia Trust Company of New York, One Liberty Plaza, 23rd Fl., 165 Broadway, 10006, pg. 156 **IT**
The Bank of Tokyo-Mitsubishi, Ltd. (New York Branch), 1251 Ave. of the Americas, 10020-1104, pg. 157 **IT**
Bank of Tokyo-Mitsubishi Trust Company, 1251 Ave. of Americas, 10020-1104, pg. 157 **IT**
Bank of Yokohama New York, One World Trade Center, Ste. 8067, 10048, pg. 159 **IT**
BankAmerica International, 335 Madison Ave., 10007, pg. 181 **PB**
BankAmerica Trust Co. of New York, 335 Madison Ave., 10017, pg. 181 **PB**
Bankers Trust Company, 280 Park Ave., 10017, pg. 185 **PB**
BANKERS TRUST NEW YORK CORPORATION, One Bankers Trust Plaza, 130 Liberty St., 10006, pg. 185 **PB**
Bankmont Financial Corp., 430 Park Ave., 10022, pg. 154 **IT**
Banque Indosuez, 1211 Ave. of the Americas, 7th Fl., 10036-8701, pg. 313 **IT**
Banque International a Luxembourg S.A., 32nd Fl., Chrysler Bldg., 405 Lexington Ave., 33rd Fl., 10174, pg. 162 **IT**
Banque Paribas-New York, The Equitable Tower, 787 Seventh Ave., 10019, pg. 319 **IT**
Bantam Doubleday Dell Publishing Group, Inc., 1540 Broadway, 10036-4094, pg. 191 **IT**
Barclays Bank PLC, USA, 75 Wall St., 10265, pg. 165 **IT**
Baring Brothers International, 535 Madison Ave., 10022, pg. 647 **IT**
Baring Houston & Saunders Inc., 667 Madison Ave., 4th Floor, 10021, pg. 647 **IT**
BARIS SHOE COMPANY, INC., 29 W. 57th St., Ste. 302, 10019, pg. 116 **PV**
BARNES & NOBLE INC., 122 Fifth Ave., 10011, pg. 189 **PB**
BARNEYS INC., 575 5th Ave., 10017, pg. 116 **PV**
BARR & BARR, INC., 330 W. 42nd St., 10036, pg. 117 **PV**
BARR BROTHERS & CO., INC., 90 Washington St., 26th Fl., 10006, pg. 117 **PV**
Barron's The Dow Jones Business & Financial Weekly, 1155 Avenue of the Americas, 8th Fl., 10036, pg. 524 **PB**
Barry Blau & Partners of New York, 767 Third Ave., 15th Fl., 10017, pg. 148 **PV**
Theodore Barry & Associates, 50 Rockefeller Plaza, Suite 1035, 10020, pg. 118 **PV**
Baseline Financial Services, Inc., 61 Broadway, 7th Fl., 10006, pg. 1325 **PB**
Basic Books, Inc., 10 E. 53rd St., 10022, pg. 927 **IT**
BAUME MERCIER, INC., 663 Fifth Ave., 10022, pg. 124 **PV**
BAYER CLOTHING GROUP, 1350 Ave. of the Americas, Ste. 2300, 10019, pg. 124 **PV**
Bayerische Hypotheken-und Wechsel-Bank Aktiengesellschaft New York Branch, Financial Sq., 32 Old Slip, 32nd Fl., 10005, pg. 176 **IT**
Bayerische Landesbank - New York Branch, 560 Lexington Ave., 10022, pg. 176 **IT**
THE BEACON GROUP, 399 Park Ave., 17th Fl., 10022, pg. 125 **PV**
Bear, Stearns & Co. Inc., New York, 245 Park Ave., 10167, pg. 198 **PB**
THE BEAR STEARNS COMPANIES INC., 245 Park Ave., 10167, pg. 197 **PB**
Bear Stearns Mortgage Capital Corporation, 245 Park Ave., 10167, pg. 198 **PB**
Bear Stearns Real Estate Group Inc., 245 Park Ave., 10167, pg. 198 **PB**
Robert A. Becker, 1633 Broadway, 27th Fl., 10019, pg. 601 **IT**
Beech Tree Books, 1350 Ave. of the Americas, 10019, pg. 515 **PV**
Beginner Books, 201 E. 50th St., 10022, pg. 21 **PV**
Bekaert Northeast Sales Company, 11 Penn Plz., 10001-2057, pg. 184 **IT**
Beldoch Industries, 1411 Broadway, 10018, pg. 520 **PB**
Beldoch Popper Division, 1411 Broadway, 10018, pg. 520 **PB**
BELL ATLANTIC CORPORATION, 1095 Avenue of the Americas, 10036, pg. 201 **PB**
Bell Atlantic Credit Company, 1095 Ave. of the Americas, 10036, pg. 202 **PB**
Bell Atlantic Funding Company, 1095 Ave. of the Americas, 10036, pg. 202 **PB**
Matthew Bender & Company, Incorporated, Two Park Ave., 7th Fl., 10016-5675, pg. 1616 **PB**
Benetton U.S.A. Corp., 55 E. 59th St., 24th Fl., 10022, pg. 186 **IT**
Benetton U.S.A. Corporation, 597 5th Ave., 11th Fl., 10017, pg. 186 **IT**
BENTEX KIDDIE CORPORATION, 100 W. 33rd St., Rm. 130, 10001, pg. 134 **PV**
BERENTER GREENHOUSE & WEBSTER, INC., 233 Park Ave. S., 10003, pg. 135 **PV**
Bergdorf Goodman, 754 Fifth Ave., 10019, pg. 785 **PB**
The Berkeley Publishing Group, 200 Madison Ave., 10016, pg. 1215 **IT**
Berkley Publishing Corp., 200 Madison Ave., 10016, pg. 1027 **IT**
BERKLIFF CORPORATION, 180 Madison Ave., 10016, pg. 135 **PV**
Berlitz Publishing Company Inc., 257 Park Ave. S., 10010, pg. 221 **PB**
Berlitz Translation Services, Inc., 257 Park Ave. So., 10010, pg. 221 **PB**
Bermco Paper Company, 315 Park Ave., S., 10010, pg. 467 **PV**
ARNOLD BERNHARD & CO., 220 E. 42nd St., 6th Fl., 10017, pg. 137 **PV**
SANFORD C. BERNSTEIN & CO., INC., 767 Fifth Ave., 10153-0185, pg. 137 **PV**
Bertelsmann Inc., 1540 Broadway, 10036-4094, pg. 191 **IT**
Besnier USA, 950 Third Ave., 22nd Flr., 10022, pg. 323 **IT**
BESSEMER GROUP, INC., 630 Fifth Ave., 10111, pg. 139 **PV**
Best Hospital Supply Div., 1633 Broadway, 10019, pg. 140 **PV**
BEST MANUFACTURING, INC., 1633 Broadway, 18th Fl., 10019, pg. 139 **PV**
Best Mfg. Inc.-Service Apparel Div., 1633 Broadway, 10019, pg. 140 **PV**
Best Textile Co. Div., 1633 Broadway, 10019, pg. 140 **PV**
BESTMED, Inc., 375 Hudson St., 10014-3620, pg. 1422 **PB**
Betmar Hats, Inc., 411 Fifth Ave., 10016, pg. 483 **PV**
BIDDLE SAWYER CORPORATION, Two Penn Plaza, 10121, pg. 142 **PV**
Bidermann Shirt Group, 575 Fifth Ave., 10017, pg. 194 **IT**
BIEDERMAN, KELLY & SHAFFER, INC., 475 Park Ave. S., 15th Fl., 10016, pg. 142 **PV**
BIG FLOWER PRESS HOLDINGS, INC., Three E. 54th St., 17th Fl., 10022, pg. 228 **PB**
Bill Blass, Inc., 625 Madison Ave., 10022, pg. 689 **PV**
Bill Communications, Inc., 355 Park Ave. S., 10010, pg. 1446 **IT**
Billboard Magazine, 1515 Broadway, 10036, pg. 1446 **IT**
Billiton Metals, Inc., 120 W. 45th St., 10036, pg. 1136 **IT**
Birmingham Fire Insurance Co. of Pennsylvania, 70 Pine St., 10270, pg. 84 **PB**
Black Bag Communications, Inc., 100 Ave. of the Americas, 10013, pg. 1152 **PV**
THE BLACK CLAWSON COMPANY, 405 Lexington Ave., 61st Fl., 10174, pg. 147 **PV**
STANLEY BLACKER, INC., 200 W. 57th St., Ste. 507, 10019, pg. 147 **PV**
THE BLACKSTONE GROUP, 345 Park Ave. 31st Fl., 10154, pg. 147 **PV**
BLAIR TELEVISION, 1290 Ave. of the Americas, 10104, pg. 148 **PV**
Blimpie Subs & Salads, 740 Broadway, 10003, pg. 236 **PB**
BLOOMBERG L.P., 499 Park Ave., 10022, pg. 150 **PV**
Bloomingdale's, 1000 Third Ave., 10022, pg. 617 **PB**
BLOOMSBURG MILLS INC., 111 W. 40th St., 10th Fl., 10018, pg. 150 **PV**
Blue Marble Advanced Communications Group, 825 Eighth Ave., 10019-7498, pg. 104 **PV**
BLUE TEE CORPORATION, 250 Park Ave. S., 10003, pg. 153 **PV**
BON JOUR INTERNATIONAL LTD., 1411 Broadway, 10018, pg. 156 **PV**
Bonanza Books, 201 E. 50th St., 10022, pg. 21 **PV**
Bonhomme, 350 Fifth Ave., 10118, pg. 909 **PV**
Book of the Month Club, Time Life Bldg., 3rd Fl., 1271 Avenue of the Americas, 10020-9991, pg. 1612 **PB**
Bookstop, Inc., 122 Fifth Ave., 10011, pg. 189 **PB**
BOOZ, ALLEN & HAMILTON INC., 101 Park Ave., 10178, pg. 157 **PV**
BOSCARALE/TOM TOGS, 106 W. 32nd St., 10001, pg. 160 **PV**
Boston Old Colony Insurance Co., 180 Maiden Ln., 10038, pg. 1010 **PB**
Bovis Inc., 387 Park Ave., 10016, pg. 1033 **IT**
BOWNE & CO., INC., 345 Hudson St., 10014, pg. 248 **PB**

PB - *U.S. Public Companies Volume*
PV - *U.S. Private Companies Volume*
IT - *International Public & Private Companies Volume*

Bowne Business Communications, Inc., 345 Hudson St., 10014, pg. 248 **PB**
Bowne International Inc., 345 Hudson St., 10014, pg. 248 **PB**
Bowne of New York City, Inc., 345 Hudson St., 10014, pg. 249 **PB**
BOX HILL SYSTEMS CORPORATION, 161 Ave. of the Americas, 10013, pg. 249 **PB**
Bozell Worldwide, Inc., 40 W. 23rd St., 10010, pg. 1642 **PB**
Brandweek, 1515 Broadway, 10036, pg. 1446 **IT**
The Bravo Group, 230 Park Ave. S., 9th Fl., 10003, pg. 1197 **PV**
Bride's, 304 E. 45th St., 14th Flr., 10017, pg. 20 **IT**
Bridge, Three World Financial Ctr., 27th Fl., 10281, pg. 1162 **PV**
The Bridgeford Group, 5th Fl., East Bldg., 280 Park Ave., 10017, pg. 674 **PV**
Bristol-Myers Health Care Group, 345 Park Ave., 10154, pg. 253 **PB**
Bristol-Myers International Group, 345 Park Ave., 10154, pg. 254 **PB**
Bristol-Myers Products, 345 Park Ave., 10154, pg. 254 **PB**
BRISTOL-MYERS SQUIBB COMPANY, 345 Park Ave., 10154-0037, pg. 253 **PB**
Bristol-Myers Squibb Consumer Products Group, 345 Park Ave., 10154, pg. 254 **PB**
Bristol-Myers Squibb Pharmaceutical & Nutritional Group, 345 Park Ave., 10154, pg. 254 **PB**
Britrail Travel International Inc., 1500 Broadway, 10th Fl., 10036-4015, pg. 1165 **IT**
Broadcast Operations & Engineering, 47 W. 66th St., 10023, pg. 511 **PB**
Broadcort Capital Corp., 100 Church St., 10007, pg. 1097 **PB**
Brooks Brothers, 346 Madison Ave., 10017, pg. 843 **IT**
Brookwood Companies Inc., 232 Madison Ave., 10th Flr., 10016, pg. 777 **PB**
BROWN BROTHERS HARRIMAN & CO., 59 Wall St., 10005, pg. 173 **PV**
Brown Brothers Harriman Trust Co. of New York, 63 Wall St., 10005, pg. 173 **PV**
EARLE PALMER BROWN, 345 Hudson St., 10014, pg. 173 **PV**
Earle Palmer Brown/New York, 345 Hudson St., 10014-4502, pg. 174 **PV**
Earle Palmer Brown Public Relations, 685 5rd Ave., 23rd Fl., 10017, pg. 174 **PV**
BROWN, HARRIS, STEVENS, INC., 770 Lexington Ave., 10021, pg. 174 **PV**
BrownStone Development Laboratory, 261 Madison Ave., 24th Fl., 10016, pg. 1309 **PB**
Bryant Park Grill, 25 W. 40th St., 10018, pg. 130 **PB**
Brylane L.P., 463 Seventh Ave., 10018, pg. 996 **PB**
Building Maintenance Products, Inc., One Park Ave., 10016, pg. 1574 **PB**
Bulgari Corporation of America, 730 Fifth Ave., 10019, pg. 232 **IT**
Burberrys Shirts, 597 Fifth Ave., 10017, pg. 194 **IT**
Burda Publications, Inc., 1270 Ave. of the Americas, Ste. 1918, 10020, pg. 233 **IT**
Burlington House Area Rugs, 1345 Ave. of The Americas, 10105, pg. 268 **PB**
Burlington Menswear, 1345 Ave. of the Americas, 10105, pg. 268 **PB**
Burmah Castrol USA Inc., 1185 Ave. of the Americas, Ste. 2400, 10036, pg. 235 **IT**
Burmah LNG Shipping, Inc., 1185 Sixth Ave., 24th Fl., 10036, pg. 235 **IT**
Leo Burnett Company, 520 Madison Ave., 10022, pg. 184 **PV**
Burrell/DFA Advertising, 161 W. 54th St., 10019, pg. 188 **PV**
Burson-Marsteller, 230 Park Ave. S., 10003-1566, pg. 1197 **PV**
Business Week, 1221 Ave. of the Americas, 10020, pg. 1069 **PB**
BUTLER CAPITAL CORP., 767 Fifth Ave., 6th Fl., 10153, pg. 190 **PV**
BUTTERICK COMPANY, INC., 161 Sixth Ave., 10013, pg. 190 **PV**
Byer & McGuggart, Inc., 11 Madison Ave., 10010, pg. 117 **IT**
Carl Byoir & Associates, Inc., 466 Lexington Ave., 10017, pg. 1483 **IT**
C & D Distributing Co. Inc., 277 Park Avenue, 10172, pg. 158 **PV**
CAP Gemini America (New York Banking & Insurance), 369 Lexington Ave., 11th Fl., 10017, pg. 264 **IT**
CB Commercial Real Estate Group, New York, 560 Lexington Ave., 10022, pg. 273 **PB**
CBS, 51 W. 52nd St., 10019, pg. 273 **PB**
CBS Affiliate Relations Division, 51 W. 52 St., 10019, pg. 274 **PB**
CBS Broadcast Group, 51 W. 52nd St., 10019, pg. 274 **PB**
CBS Enterprises Division, 51 W. 52 St., 10019, pg. 274 **PB**
CBS Marketing Division, 51 W. 52nd St., 10019, pg. 274 **PB**
CBS News, 524 W. 57th St., 10019, pg. 274 **PB**
CBS Operations & Administration Div., 51 W. 52nd St., 10019, pg. 274 **PB**
CBS Radio, 40 W. 57th St., 14th Fl., 10019, pg. 274 **PB**
CBS Radio Div., 51 W. 52nd St., 10019, pg. 274 **PB**
CBS Sports Div., 51 W. 52nd St., 10019, pg. 274 **PB**
CBS Television Network, 51 W. 52nd St., 10019, pg. 274 **PB**
CBS Television Stations Div., 51 W. 52nd St., 10019, pg. 275 **PB**
CCF International Finance Corp., 590 Park Avenue, 25th Fl., 10022, pg. 342 **IT**

CCF New York, 590 Park Avenue, 25th Fl., 10022-2540, pg. 342 **IT**
CCH Legal Information Services, Inc., 1633 Broadway, 10019, pg. 1513 **IT**
CHF Industries, Inc., One Park Ave., 9th Fl., 10016, pg. 1094 **PB**
CIBC Aviation, Inc., 425 Lexington Ave., Flrs. 2-9, 10017, pg. 257 **IT**
CIBC Capital Corporation, 425 Lexington Ave., 10017, pg. 257 **IT**
CIBC Inc., 425 Lexington Ave., 10017, pg. 257 **IT**
CIBC Oppenheimer Corp., Oppenheimer Tower, World Financial Center, 10281, pg. 257 **IT**
CIC Financial, 180 Maiden Ln., 10038, pg. 1011 **PB**
CIECO (America), Inc., 335 Madison Ave., 10017, pg 694 **IT**
CMI Industries, Inc., 111 W. 40th St., 11th Fl., 10018, pg. 195 **PB**
CPI Group, 180 Maiden Ln., 10038, pg. 1011 **PB**
CSC Healthcare Group, 1675 Broadway, 10019, pg. 423 **PB**
CSC Pinnacle Alliance, c/o J.P. Morgan, 600 Wall St., 10260, pg. 423 **PB**
CSI INTERNATIONAL CORPORATION, 800 Second Ave., 10017, pg. 197 **PV**
CSS USA, 40 W. 23rd St., 10010, pg. 1642 **PB**
CT Corporation System, 1633 Broadway, 10019, pg. 1513 **IT**
Cable & Wireless (N.Y.) Inc., 777 Third 35th, 10017, pg. 247 **IT**
CACHE, INC., 1460 Broadway, 15th Fl., 10036, pg. 289 **PB**
Cadmus Custom Publishing, 12 E. 49th St., 10017, pg. 290 **PB**
Cadmus Financial Communications, 12 E. 49th St., 10017, pg. 291 **PB**
Cadmus Magazines, 12 E. 49th St., 10017, pg. 291 **PB**
Calvin Klein Cosmetics Company, 725 5th Ave., 10022, pg. 1435 **IT**
CALVIN KLEIN, INC., 205 W. 39th St., 10018, pg. 202 **PV**
Calvin Klein Sport, Inc., 205 W. 39th St., 10018, pg. 202 **PV**
Cameo Window Furnishings, One Park Ave., 10016, pg. 1094 **PB**
Campbell Media Alliance, 101 Park Ave., 10178-0065, pg. 1641 **PV**
Campbell Mithun Esty, 1841 Broadway, Ste. 901, 10020, pg. 204 **PV**
Canadian Imperial Bank of Commerce (New York), 425 Lexington Ave., 6th Fl., 10017, pg. 257 **IT**
Canadian Imperial Service Co., 425 Lexington Ave., Flrs. 2-9, 10017, pg. 257 **IT**
Canyon Roads, 1460 First Ave., 10021, pg. 130 **PB**
CAP Gemini America, 1114 Ave. of the Americas, 29th Fl., 10036, pg. 263 **IT**
Capezio Ballet Makers, Inc., 1460 Broadway & 17th St., 10018, pg. 205 **PV**
Capital Cities/ABC Broadcast Group, 77 W. 66th St., 10023, pg. 511 **PB**
Capital Cities/ABC National Television Sales, Inc., 77 W. 66th St., 10023, pg. 511 **PB**
Capital Cities/ABC Owned Radio Stations, 77 W. 66th St., 10023, pg. 512 **PB**
Capital Cities/ABC Publishing Group, 77 W. 66th St., 10002, pg. 512 **PB**
Capital Cities/ABC Radio, 77 W. 66th St., 10023, pg. 512 **PB**
Capital Cities Media, Inc., 77 W. 66th St., 10023, pg. 5·1 **PB**
Capital Markets Assurance Corporation, 885 Third Ave., 14th Fl., 10022, pg. 1023 **PB**
CAPITAL MERCURY SHIRT, 1372 Broadway, 10018, pg. 206 **PB**
Capital Fe Corporation, 787 Seventh Ave., 27th Fl., 10019, pg. 1116 **PB**
Capstar Partners, Inc., 40 E. 52nd St., 12th Fl., 10022, pg. 816 **IT**
Car and Driver, 1633 Broadway, 43rd Fl., 10019, pg. 795 **IT**
CARAT MBS, Three Park Ave., 34th Fl., 10016, pg. 208 **PV**
Cardio-Fitness Corporation, 345 Park Ave., 10154, pg. 806 **PV**
THE CARE GROUP, INC., 257 Park Ave., S., Ste. 12A, 10010, pg. 305 **PB**
The Care Group of New York, Inc., 257 Park Ave. S., 10010, pg. 305 **PB**
Career Blazers Agency, Inc., 590 Fifth Ave., 10036, pg. 209 **PV**
CAREER BLAZERS INC., 590 Fifth Ave., 7th Fl., 10036, pg. 209 **PV**
Career Blazers Learning Center, 290 Madison Avenue, 10169, pg. 209 **PV**
Career Blazers Service Company, Inc., 590 Fifth Ave., 10036, pg. 209 **PV**
Career Blazers Temporary Personnel, 590 Fifth Ave., 10036, pg. 209 **PV**
W.P. CAREY & CO., INC., 50 Rockefeller Plaza, 2nd Fl., 10020, pg. 209 **PV**
CARIBINER INTERNATIONAL, INC., 16 W. 61st St., 10023-7604, pg. 305 **PB**
Cariplo Grand Cayman, 10 East 53rd St., 10022, pg. 275 **IT**
Cariplo New York, 10 E. 53rd St., 10022, pg. 275 **IT**
CARLSON & PARTNERS, INC., 950 Third Ave., 10022, pg. 211 **PV**
Carnegie Inc., 20 W. 55th St., 10019, pg. 272 **IT**
Guy Carpenter & Co., Inc, Two World Trade Ctr., 10048, pg. 1043 **PB**
W.I. Carr (America) Ltd., 1211 Ave. of the Americas, 8th Fl., 10036-8701, pg. 314 **IT**

Carrington Parfums Ltd., 625 Madison Ave., 10022-1801, pg. 689 **PV**
Carter-Wallace Drugs, Inc., 1345 Ave. of the Americas, 10022, pg. 310 **PB**
CARTER-WALLACE, INC., 1345 Ave. of the Americas, 10105, pg. 309 **PB**
CARVER FEDERAL SAVINGS BANK, 75 W.125th St., 10027-4404, pg. 310 **PB**
Castle & Overton, One Rockefeller Plaza, 10020, pg. 586 **IT**
CASTLE CONVERTIBLE FUND, INC., 75 Maiden Ln., 10038, pg. 313 **PV**
CASTLE-HARLAN, INC., 150 E. 58th St., 37th Fl., 10155, pg. 219 **PV**
Castle Harlan Partners III, L.P., 150 E. 58th St., 10155, pg. 219 **PV**
Castle Harlan Partners II, L.P., 150 E. 58th St., 10155, pg. 219 **PV**
Castleberry Knits, Ltd., 530 Seventh Ave., 10018, pg. 989 **PB**
Cella's Confections, Inc., 327 W. Broadway, 10013, pg. 1621 **PB**
Centennial Insurance Co., 100 Wall St., 26th Fl., 10005-3701, pg. 95 **PB**
CENTER PARTNERS MANAGEMENT LLC, 30 Rockefeller Plaza, Ste. 5050, 10020, pg. 222 **PV**
Central Lewmar International, 155 Spring St., 10012, pg. 223 **PV**
CENTRAL SECURITIES CORPORATION, 375 Park Ave., 10152, pg. 326 **PB**
Centre Reinsurance Company of New York, One Chase Manhattan Plaza, 10005, pg. 1530 **IT**
CENTURY BUSINESS CREDIT CORPORATION, 119 W. 40th St., 10018, pg. 225 **PV**
Century Data Services, Inc., 119 W. 40th St., 10018, pg. 226 **PV**
Champs, 233 Broadway, 10279, pg. 1777 **PB**
Channel One Communications, 600 Madison Ave., 10022, pg. 1328 **PB**
The Chapman Agency, 230 Park Ave., S., 10003, pg. 1197 **PV**
Chaps By Ralph Lauren, 90 Park Ave., 12th Fl., 10016, pg. 1738 **PV**
CHARLES ATLAS, LTD., P.O. Box D, Madison Sq. Station, 10159, pg. 229 **PV**
Charles of the Ritz Group Ltd., 625 Madison Ave., 10022, pg. 689 **PV**
Charles Scribner's Sons Reference, 1633 Broadway, 10019, pg. 777 **PB**
Charlio's, 218 W.45th St., 10036, pg. 786 **PB**
CHARTERHOUSE GROUP INTERNATIONAL, INC., 535 Madison Ave., 28th Fl., 10022, pg. 230 **PV**
Charterhouse Inc., 590 Madison Avenue, 27th Floor, 10022, pg. 342 **IT**
Chase Automated Clearing House, Inc., One New York Plaza, 10081, pg. 337 **PB**
Chase Equipment Leasing, Inc., 55 Water St., 10015, pg. 338 **PB**
Chase Equity Incorporated, 885 Third Ave., 10022, pg. 338 **PB**
The Chase Manhattan Bank, 270 Park Ave., 10017, pg. 338 **PB**
THE CHASE MANHATTAN CORPORATION, 270 Park Ave., 10017-2036, pg. 337 **PB**
Chase Manhattan Financial Services, Inc., One World Trade Ctr., 46th Fl., 10081, pg. 338 **PB**
Chase Manhattan Investment Holdings, Inc., One Chase Manhattan Plaza, 10081, pg. 338 **PB**
Chase Manhattan Service Corporation, One Chase Manhattan Plaza, 10018, pg. 338 **PB**
Chase National Corporate Services, Inc., 101 Park Ave., 27th Fl., 10081, pg. 338 **PB**
Chase Trade, Inc., One World Trade Ctr., 78th Fl., 10048, pg. 338 **PB**
Chase U.S. Consumer Services, One World Trade Ctr., 46th Fl., 10081, pg. 338 **PB**
Chatham Imports, Inc., 257 Park Ave. S., 67th Fl., 10010, pg. 847 **PV**
Chatham Ventures, Inc., 277 Park Ave., 10172, pg. 338 **PB**
BERNARD CHAUS, INC., 1410 Broadway, 10018, pg. 342 **PB**
Chemical Engineering, 1221 Ave. of the Americas, 10020, pg. 1071 **PB**
Chemtex Engineering, 560 Lexington Ave., 10022, pg. 872 **IT**
Chemtex Fibers Export, Inc., 560 Lexington Ave., 10022, pg. 872 **IT**
Chemtex Fibers Inc., 560 Lexington Ave., 10022, pg. 872 **IT**
Chemtex International, Inc., 560 Lexington Ave., 10022, pg. 872 **IT**
Chemtex Overseas, Inc., 560 Lexington Ave., 10022, pg. 872 **IT**
Chevy Chase, Inc., 277 Park Ave., 10172, pg. 158 **IT**
The Chiba Bank, Ltd.-New York Branch, 1133 Ave. of the Americas, 10036, pg. 283 **IT**
Chiba Kogyo-New York, East Bldg., 20th Fl., 280 Park Ave., 10017, pg. 284 **IT**
Child Magazine, 110 Fifth Ave., 10011, pg. 190 **PB**
Children's Business, Seven W. 34th St., 4th Fl., 10001, pg. 513 **PB**
China Airlines Ltd., 630 Fifth Avenue, Ste. 1468, 10111, pg. 285 **IT**
The Chinese American Bank, 77 Bowery, 10002-4998, pg. 683 **IT**
The Chinese American Bank, 225 Park Row, 10038-1199, pg. 683 **IT**
THE CHISHOLM-MINGO GROUP, 228 E. 45th St., 10017, pg. 237 **PV**

PB - *U.S. Public Companies Volume*
PV - *U.S. Private Companies Volume*
IT - *International Public & Private Companies Volume*

1344

Chiyoda Life Asset Management of America Inc., Swiss Bank Tower, 25th Fl., Ten E. 50th St., 10022, pg. 287 **IT**

Chiyoda Life Realty of America, Inc., Swiss Bank Tower, 25th Fl., Ten E. 50th St., 10022, pg. 287 **IT**

Cho Hung Bank, 320 Park Avenue, 27th Fl., 10022-6815, pg. 287 **IT**

Cho Hung Bank of New York, 241 5th Ave., 10001, pg. 287 **IT**

CHOCK FULL O' NUTS CORPORATION, 370 Lexington Ave., 10017, pg. 351 **PB**

Chori America, Inc., One Penn Plaza, Ste. 5440, 10119, pg. 288 **IT**

CHRIS-CRAFT INDUSTRIES, INC., 767 Fifth Ave., 46th Fl., 10153, pg. 351 **PB**

Christal Radio, 125 W. 55th St., 10019, pg. 335 **PB**

Christian Dior Perfumes Inc., Nine W. 57th St., 39th Fl., 10019, pg. 781 **IT**

Christian Lacroix Inc., 712 Fifth Ave., 10019, pg. 781 **IT**

Christiania Bank-New York Branch, 11 West 42nd St., 7th Fl., 10036, pg. 289 **IT**

Christiansburg Garment Co. Inc., 1411 Broadway, 10018, pg. 520 **PB**

Christie's East, 219 E. 67th St., 10021, pg. 290 **IT**

Christie's Inc., 502 Park Ave., 10022, pg. 290 **IT**

ChubbHealth New York/New Jersey, 380 Madison Ave., 20th Fl., 10017, pg. 360 **PB**

Chugai Boyeki (America) Corp., 500 Fifth Ave., 57th Fl., 10110, pg. 290 **IT**

Chugai Pharma U.S.A., Inc., 520 Madison Ave., 10022, pg. 291 **IT**

The Chuo Trust & Banking Co., Ltd., Two World Trade Center, Ste. 8322, 10048, pg. 291 **IT**

CineBooks, Inc., 620 Ave. of the Americas, 6th Fl., 10011, pg. 925 **PB**

Cinema Etoile Division, 136 Madison Ave., 10016, pg. 1141 **PB**

Cineplex Odeon Corporation -New York, 241 E. 34th St., 10016, pg. 293 **IT**

CITICORP, 399 Park Ave., 10043, pg. 376 **PB**

Citicorp Business Credit, Inc., 399 Park Ave., 10043, pg. 378 **PB**

Citicorp Capital Investors Ltd., 399 Park Ave., 10043, pg. 378 **PB**

Citicorp Community Development, Inc., 399 Park Ave., 10022, pg. 377 **PB**

Citicorp Real Estate, Inc., 5929 Lexington Ave., 25th Fl., 10022, pg. 378 **PB**

Citicorp Securities Markets, Inc., 399 Park Ave., 10043, pg. 377 **PB**

Citicorp Select Investments, One Court Sq., 11120, pg. 377 **PB**

Citicorp Venture Capital Ltd., 399 Park Ave., 10043, pg. 377 **PB**

CITY POSTAL, INC., 421 Seventh Ave., 10001, pg. 241 **PV**

Claiborne Menswear Div., 1441 Broadway, 10018, pg. 1006 **PB**

Clairol's Consumer Products Division, 345 Park Ave., 10154, pg. 254 **PB**

Clarins USA Inc., 135 E. 57th St., 10022, pg. 295 **IT**

Clarion Books, 215 Park Avenue South, 10003, pg. 841 **PB**

Clark & Weinstock, 52 Vanderbilt Ave., 10017, pg. 1223 **PB**

CYRUS CLARK CO., INC., 267 Fifth Ave., 10016, pg. 242 **PV**

Clay Finlay Inc., 200 Park Ave., 10166, pg. 1673 **PB**

CLAYTON, DUBILIER & RICE, INC, 375 Park Ave., 18th Fl., 10152, pg. 244 **PV**

Clicquot, Inc., 717 Fifth Ave., 10022, pg. 781 **IT**

CLINE, DAVIS & MANN, INC., 450 Lexington Ave., 10022, pg. 246 **PV**

Herbert Clough, Inc., 120 Broadway, 10271-0067, pg. 726 **PB**

Club Med Boutique, Three E. 54th St., 10022, pg. 298 **IT**

Club Med Sales, Inc., 40 W. 57th St., 10019, pg. 298 **IT**

Cluett International Group, 575 Fifth Ave., 10036, pg. 194 **PB**

Clupak, Inc., 299 Park Ave., 10110, pg. 1762 **PB**

Coach, 516 W. 34th St., 10001, pg. 1433 **PB**

Coach/Mark Cross, 516 W. 34th St., 12th Fl., 10001, pg. 1433 **PB**

Cogeneration Technologies Inc., 280 Park Ave. #2700 W, 10017-1216, pg. 1789 **PB**

Cognizant Technology Solutions Corp., 1700 Broadway, 10019, pg. 395 **PB**

Cohn & Wells, 375 Hudson Ave., 8th Fl., 10014, pg. 601 **IT**

COLGATE-PALMOLIVE COMPANY, 300 Park Ave., 10022-7499, pg. 397 **PB**

Colgate U.S.A., 300 Park Ave., 10022, pg. 397 **PB**

P.F. Collier LP, 919 Third Ave., 10022, pg. 433 **IT**

Colonial Homes, 1790 Broadway, 10019, pg. 517 **PV**

Colony Glass, 1115 Broadway, 10010, pg. 976 **PB**

Columbia House Music Club, 19th Floor, 1221 Ave. of the Americas, 10020, pg. 1281 **IT**

Columbia Pictures Eastern Division, 711 5th Ave., 10022, pg. 1281 **IT**

Columbia Pictures Merchandising, 711 Fifth Ave., 10022, pg. 1281 **IT**

Columbia Tri-Star Television Distribution - New York Office, 711 Fifth Ave., 10022, pg. 1282 **IT**

Columbus Bakery, 474 Columbus Ave., 10024, pg. 130 **PB**

Cometals, One Penn Plaza, Ste. 4330, 10119, pg. 412 **IT**

Command Security Corporation, 386 Park Ave. S., 10016, pg. 409 **PB**

Commerce & Industry Insurance Co., 70 Pine St., 10270, pg. 84 **PB**

Commercial Union Capital Corporation, 115 E. 57th St., 10022, pg. 308 **IT**

Commerzbank Aktiengesellschaft New York Branch, Two World Fin. Ctr., 10281-1050, pg. 310 **IT**

Commerzbank Capital Markets Corporation, Two World Financial Ctr., 10281-1050, pg. 310 **IT**

Commodity Information Services Group, 1221 Ave. of the Americas, 42nd Fl., 10020, pg. 1071 **PB**

Commonwealth Bank of Australia, 599 Lexington Ave., 18th Fl., 10022, pg. 313 **IT**

COMMONWEALTH TOY & NOVELTY COMPANY, 45 W. 25th St., 5th Fl., 10010, pg. 258 **PV**

Communicade, 437 Madison Ave., 10022, pg. 1223 **PB**

COMMUNICATIONS DIVERSIFIED, 440 Park Ave., S., 10016, pg. 259 **PV**

COMMUNICATIONS INTERNATIONAL (NY), 645 5th Ave., 17th Fl., 10022, pg. 259 **PV**

Community Care Health Solutions Inc., 235 E. 42nd St., 10017, pg. 1282 **PB**

Owen Comora Associates, 1515 Broadway, 10036, pg. 985 **PV**

Compar, 70 E. 55th St., 10022, pg. 1073 **PV**

Competitive Media Reporting, 11 W. 42nd St., 10036-8088, pg. 1447 **IT**

Component Products Co., Nine W. 57th St., 10019, pg. 1281 **IT**

Compton Partners, 375 Hudson St., 10014, pg. 1422 **PV**

Computer Intelligence InfoCorp, One Park Ave., 10016, pg. 1276 **PB**

Computer Science Press, Inc., 41 Madison Ave., 10010, pg. 1479 **PB**

Computer Shopper, One Park Ave., 10016, pg. 1276 **IT**

CONCORD FABRICS INC., 1359 Broadway, 10018, pg. 429 **PB**

Concord Foreign Sales Corp., Inc., 1359 Broadway, 10018, pg. 430 **PB**

Concord House Division, 1359 Broadway, 10018, pg. 430 **PB**

CONCURRENT INDUSTRIES GROUP, INC., 375 Park Ave., Ste. 1507, 10152, pg. 262 **PV**

The Conde Nast Publications Inc., 350 Madison Ave., 10017, pg. 20 **PV**

Conde Nast Traveler, 360 Madison Ave., 10017, pg. 20 **PV**

Cone Decorative Fabrics, 261 Fifth Ave., 10016, pg. 430 **PB**

Congress Financial Corp., 1133 Ave. of the Americas, 10019, pg. 447 **PB**

Conseco Capital Partners II, L.P., 745 5th Ave., Ste. 2700, 10151, pg. 432 **PB**

Conso Products Co., 261 Fifth Ave., Ste. 1001, 10016, pg. 434 **PV**

CONSOLIDATED EDISON COMPANY OF NEW YORK, INC., Four Irving Pl., Rm. 1624, 10003, pg. 434 **PB**

Constitution Holding Inc., 110 William St., 7th Fl., 10038, pg. 467 **IT**

Constitution Re Corp., 110 William St., 7th Fl., 10038, pg. 467 **IT**

Constitution Reinsurance Corporation, 110 William St., 7th Fl., 10038, pg. 467 **IT**

Consumer Group Special Markets, 1230 Ave. of the Americas, 10020, pg. 777 **PV**

Consumers Mining Company, 110 E. 59th St., 30th Fl., 10022, pg. 1726 **PV**

CONTIFINANCIAL CORPORATION, 277 Park Ave., 10172, pg. 439 **PB**

ContiFinancial Services Corporation, 277 Park Ave., 10172, pg. 439 **PB**

Continental Bank New York Trust Company, 520 Madison Ave., 10022, pg. 181 **IT**

The Continental Corporation, 180 Maiden Ln., 10038, pg. 1011 **PB**

CONTINENTAL GRAIN COMPANY, 277 Park Ave., 10172, pg. 268 **PV**

The Continental Insurance Co., 180 Maiden Ln., 10038, pg. 1011 **PB**

Continental Reinsurance Corp., 180 Maiden Ln., 10038, pg. 1011 **PB**

ContiTrade Services L.L.C., 277 Park Ave., 10172, pg. 439 **PB**

COOPERS & LYBRAND, 1301 Ave. of the Americas, 10019, pg. 274 **PV**

Coppee Industries Inc., 599 Lexington Ave., 10022, pg. 788 **IT**

Copperweld, 555 Madison Ave., 10th Fl., 10022, pg. 662 **IT**

COREQ, Inc., 277 Park Ave., 10172, pg. 338 **PB**

CoreStates Bank International, 180 Maiden Ln., 18th Fl., 10038, pg. 446 **PB**

CORINTHIAN MEDIA, INC., 600 Madison Ave., 10022, pg. 405 **PV**

Corporate Finance Magazine, 1328 Broadway, 10001, pg. 405 **PV**

Corporate National Accounts Northeast, 757 Third Ave., 10th & 11th Fls., 10017, pg. 1024 **PB**

CORTEC GROUP, 200 Park Ave., 20th Fl., 10166, pg. 277 **PV**

Corvita Corporation, 235 E. 42nd St., 10017, pg. 1281 **PB**

Cosmair, Inc., 575 Fifth Ave., 10017, pg. 818 **IT**

Cosmo Oil of U.S.A. Inc., 150 E. 52nd St., 22nd Fl., 10017, pg. 335 **IT**

Cosmo Securities (America) Inc., 165 Broadway, 10006, pg. 335 **IT**

Cosmopolitan, 224 W. 57th St., 10019, pg. 517 **PV**

Coty Inc., 237 Park Ave., 10017, pg. 185 **IT**

Country Living, 224 W. 57th St., 10019, pg. 517 **PV**

Courtaulds Fibers Inc., 104 W. 40th St., 10018, pg. 339 **IT**

Coward-McCann, Inc., 200 Madison Ave., 10016, pg. 1027 **IT**

COWEN & COMPANY, Financial Sq., 10005-3597, pg. 280 **PV**

Cowles Syndicate, Inc., 235 E. 45th St., 10017, pg. 518 **PV**

COX & COMPANY, INC., 200 Varick St., 4th Fl., 10014, pg. 281 **PV**

Coyne Beahm Inc., 440 Park Ave., S., Ste. 1300, 10016, pg. 283 **PV**

Crain's New York Business, 220 E. 42nd St., 10017, pg. 285 **PV**

Credit Agricole (CNCA) U.S.A. (New York), 520 Madison Ave., 10022, pg. 341 **IT**

Credit Lyonnais Americas, 1301 Ave. of the Americas, 10019, pg. 344 **IT**

Credit Nationale, 520 Madison Ave., 34th Fl., 10022, pg. 345 **IT**

Credit Suisse First Boston, Inc., 11 Madison Ave., 10010, pg. 345 **IT**

Creditanstalt American Corporation, 245 Park Ave., 10167, pg. 347 **IT**

Creditanstalt Finance Inc.- New York, 245 Park Ave., 10167, pg. 347 **IT**

CROSCILL, INC., 261 Fifth Ave., 10016, pg. 290 **PV**

Croscill Outlet Store Corp., 261 Fifth Ave., 10016, pg. 291 **PV**

CROTON WATCH COMPANY & NATIONWIDE TIME, 15 W. 37th St., 10018, pg. 291 **PV**

Crown Crafts Home Furnishings, Inc., 339 Fifth Ave., 10016, pg. 465 **PB**

Crown Publishers, Inc., 201 E. 50th St., 10003, pg. 21 **PB**

Crowntuft Manufacturing Co., 180 Madison Ave., Rm. 602, 10016, pg. 948 **PB**

Crum & Forster Managers Corporation (NY), 110 William St., 10038, pg. 1784 **PB**

Culligan, 208 E. 73rd St., 10021-4306, pg. 467 **PB**

Cullman Ventures, Inc., 767 Third Ave., 36th Fl., 10017, pg. 345 **PV**

Cultor Food Science Inc., 205 E. 42nd St., 10017-5706, pg. 349 **IT**

Cunard Line Ltd., 555 Fifth Ave., 10017, pg. 773 **IT**

Cushman & Wakefield, Inc., 51 W. 52nd St., 10019, pg. 873 **IT**

Custom Shop Shirtmakers Inc., 18 E. 50th St., 10th Fl., 10022, pg. 490 **PB**

Cyclops Communications (Interactive), 230 Park Ave., Ste. 16000, 10169, pg. 942 **PV**

THE CYPRESS GROUP LLC., 65 E. 55th St., 10022, pg. 300 **PV**

DC Comics, Inc., 1700 Broadway, 10019, pg. 1614 **PB**

DCA Advertising, Inc., 666 Fifth Ave., 9th Fl., 10103, pg. 393 **IT**

DCI Kids, 392 Fifth Ave., 10016, pg. 348 **PV**

DDB Needham Worldwide Inc., 437 Madison Ave., 10022, pg. 357 **IT**

DDB Needham Worldwide Inc., 437 Madison Ave., 10022, pg. 1223 **PB**

DG Bank-New York, DG Bank Bldg., 609 Fifth Ave., 10017-1021, pg. 352 **IT**

DG European Securities Corporation, DG Bank Bldg., 609 Fifth Ave., 10017-1021, pg. 352 **IT**

DK Publishing, 95 Madison Ave., 10016, pg. 417 **IT**

DKB Financial Products, Inc., One World Trade Center, Ste. 5027, 10048, pg. 360 **IT**

DKB Securities Corporation, One World Trade Center, Suite 5047, 10048, pg. 360 **IT**

DLJ Capital Corp., 140 Broadway, 10005, pg. 589 **PB**

DLJ Merchant Banking Partners, L.P., 277 Park Ave., 10172, pg. 589 **PB**

DMB&B COMMUNICATIONS, 1675 Broadway, 10019-5865, pg. 302 **PV**

DNP (AMERICA), Inc., 2 Park Ave., Suite 1405, 10016, pg. 363 **IT**

D.V.F. Inc., 625 Madison Ave., 10022, pg. 690 **IT**

Da Capo Press, Inc., 233 Spring St., 10013, pg. 1311 **PB**

Daewoo International America Corp. - New York, 104 W. 40th St., 10th Fl., 10018, pg. 357 **IT**

Daewoo Securities (America) Inc., Manhattan Tower, 28th Floor, 101 E. 52nd St., 10022, pg. 359 **IT**

Dai-Ichi Kangyo Bank, Ltd.-New York, One World Trade Center, Ste. 4911, 10048, pg. 359 **IT**

Dai-Ichi Kangyo Trust Company of New York, One World Trade Ctr., Ste. 5031, 10048, pg. 360 **IT**

Dai-Ichi Life Insurance Agency (U.S.A.) Inc., 399 Park Ave., 24th Fl., 10022, pg. 362 **IT**

Dai-Ichi Life Investment Management (U.S.A.), Inc., 399 Park Ave., 24th Fl., 10022, pg. 362 **IT**

Dai-ichi Life (U.S.A.) Inc., 399 Park Ave., 24th Fl., 10022, pg. 362 **IT**

Dai-Ichi Seimei America Corp., 399 Park Ave., 24th Fl., 10022, pg. 362 **IT**

Daido International Inc., 150 E. 52nd St., 7th Fl., 10022, pg. 364 **IT**

Daikin U.S. Corporation, 375 Park Ave., Ste. 3308, 10152, pg. 365 **IT**

Daily News Record, Seven W. 34th St., 10001, pg. 513 **PB**

Daimler-Benz North America Corporation, 375 Park Ave., Ste. 3001, 10152, pg. 368 **IT**

The Daishi Bank, Ltd., 40 E. 52nd St., 20th Fl., 10022, pg. 373 **IT**

Daiwa Asset Management (America) Ltd., Financial Sq., 10th Fl., 32 Old Slip, 10005-3538, pg. 374 **IT**

Daiwa Institute of Research America Inc., Financial Sq., 10th Fl., 32 Old Slip, 10005-3538, pg. 375 **IT**

Daiwa International Capital Management Corp., 380 Madison Ave., 23rd Fl., 10017, pg. 375 **IT**

Daiwa Securities America Inc., Financial Sq., 32 Old Slip, 10005-3538, pg. 375 **IT**

DALE CARNEGIE TRAINING, 780 3rd Ave., 22nd Fl., 10017, pg. 308 **PV**

Dan River, Inc., 1325 Ave. of the Americas, 10019, pg. 479 **PB**

Dana Buchman Div., 1441 Broadway, 10018, pg. 1006 **PB**

Geographic Index-U.S.

Dana Perfumes Corp., 635 Madison Ave., 10022, pg. 922 **PV**
DANCKER, SELLEW & DOUGLAS, INC., 53 Park Pl., 11th Fl., 10007, pg. 309 **PV**
DANI MICHAELS, INC., 462 Seventh Ave., 6th Fl., 10018, pg. 309 **PV**
Dani Michaels, Inc., 1400 Broadway, 2nd Fl., 10018, pg. 309 **PV**
DANIEL CARON SPORTSWEAR, 205 W. 39th St., 16th Fl., 10018, pg. 309 **PV**
DANIELSON HOLDING CORPORATION, 767 Third Ave., 5th Fl., 10017-2023, pg. 483 **PB**
DANSKIN INC., 111 W. 40th St., 10018, pg. 483 **PB**
D'Arcy Masius Benton & Bowles, 1675 Broadway, 10019-5865, pg. 303 **PV**
D'Arcy Masius Benton & Bowles Communications, 1675 Broadway, 10019-5865, pg. 303 **PV**
Darwin Digital, 375 Hudson St., 10024, pg. 1422
Data Communications, 1221 Ave. of the Americas, 10020, pg. 1070 **PB**
Datastream International, Inc., 120 Wall St., 10005, pg. 1325 **PB**
Dauman Displays, Inc., 527 W. 34th St., 10001, pg. 268 **PV**
DAWN JOY FASHIONS, INC., 501 Seventh Ave., 10018, pg. 316 **PV**
J.L. de Ball of America Ind. Apparel Div., 111 W. 40th St., Ste. 414, 10018, pg. 552 **IT**
Dean Witter, Discover & Co., Two World Trade Ctr., 10048, pg. 1132 **PB**
Deitsch Plastic Export Co., 535 Broadway, 10012, pg. 321 **PV**
MARCEL DEKKER, INC., 270 Madison Ave., 10016, pg. 321 **PV**
DELCAL ENTERPRISES, INC., 140 Franklin St., 10013, pg. 322 **PV**
Delcar Digital, 40 W. 23rd St., 10010, pg. 1642 **PV**
Dell Publishing, 1540 Broadway, 10036, pg. 191 **PB**
Delphi Capital Management, Inc., 650 Madison Ave., Ste. 2600, 10022, pg. 496 **PB**
Delta Mills Marketing Company, 1071 Ave. of the Americas, 10018, pg. 498 **PB**
Den norske Bank, New York Branch, 200 Park Ave., 31st Fl., 10166-0396, pg. 392 **IT**
Dental Health Alliance, L.L.C., 462 7th Ave., Ste. 1100, 10018, pg. 499 **IT**
Dentsu Burson Marsteller, Inc., 230 Park Ave. S., 10003, pg. 393 **PV**
Dentsu Communications, 666 Fifth Ave., 9th Fl., 10103, pg. 393 **PV**
Dentsu USA Inc.-New York, 30th Fl., Grace Bldg., 1114 Ave. of the Americas, 10036, pg. 393 **PV**
DENTSU YOUNG & RUBICAM PARTNERSHIPS, 285 Madison Ave., 10017, pg. 325 **PV**
Departures, 1120 Ave. of the Americas, 10036, pg. 74 **PV**
DESAI CAPITAL MANAGEMENT INCORPORATED, 540 Madison Ave., 36th Fl., 10022, pg. 326 **PV**
Designers Knitting Mills, 119 W. 40th St., 22nd Fl., 10018, pg. 778 **PB**
Details, 379 W. Broadway, 10012, pg. 1038 **PV**
Details Magazine, 632 Broadway, 12th Fl., 10012, pg. 20 **PV**
DEUTSCH, INC., 215 Park Ave. S., 10003, pg. 328 **PV**
Deutsche Bank AG (New York Branch), 31 W. 52nd St., 10019, pg. 403 **IT**
Deutsche Bank Capital Corporation, 31 W. 52nd St., 10019, pg. 403 **IT**
Deutsche Bank Government Securities, Inc., 31 W. 52nd St., 10019, pg. 403 **IT**
DEWITT MEDIA, INC., 450 Park Ave. S., 10016, pg. 329 **PV**
The DIALOG Corporation, 75 Wall St., 20th Fl., 10005, pg. 412 **IT**
T.L. DIAMOND COMPANY, 30 Rockefeller Plaza, 10112, pg. 330 **PV**
Diamond Vision, Inc., 430 Park Ave., 10022, pg. 873 **IT**
Digital Station, 130 Fifth Ave., 10011, pg. 480 **PV**
THE DIME SAVINGS BANK OF NEW YORK, 589 Fifth Ave., 10017, pg. 509 **PB**
Discover, 114 5th Ave., 10011, pg. 513 **PB**
Disease Management Sciences Inc., 235 E. 42nd St., 10017, pg. 1282 **PB**
Distribution Services, 1230 Ave. of the Americas, 10020, pg. 777 **PV**
Diversion, 1790 Broadway, 10019, pg. 516 **PV**
F.W. Dodge Group, 1221 Avenue of the Americas, 10020, pg. 1070 **PB**
Dominick & Dominick Futures, Inc., 90 Broad St., 10th Fl., 10004, pg. 339 **PV**
DOMINICK & DOMINICK, INCORPORATED, 32 Old Slip Financial Sq., 34th Fl., 10005, pg. 338 **PV**
Dominion Textile (USA) Inc., 120 W. 44th Street, Suite 503, 10036, pg. 415 **IT**
Domino Sugar Corporation, 1114 Ave. of the Americas, 10036, pg. 1356 **IT**
Don Juan Sportswear, Inc., 350 Fifth Ave., 10118, pg. 845 **IT**
Donaldson, Lufkin, & Jenrette, Inc., 277 Park Ave., 10172, pg. 589 **PB**
Donaldson, Lufkin & Jenrette Securities Corp., 140 Broadway, 10005, pg. 589 **PB**
Donkenny Apparel, Inc., 1411 Broadway, 10018, pg. 520 **PB**
DONNA KARAN, 550 Seventh Ave., 10018, pg. 517 **PV**
DONNKENNY, INC., 1411 Broadway, 10018, pg. 519 **PB**
Door Store, Inc., 116 E. 38th St., 10016, pg. 432 **PV**
DORAL HOTEL & RESORTS MANAGEMENT CO., 90 Park Ave., 28th Fl., 10016, pg. 340 **PV**
Doremus & Company, 200 Varick St., 10014, pg. 1223 **PV**
Dothan Apparel, Inc., 1359 Broadway, 10118, pg. 540 **PV**

Doubleday Book Shops, Inc., 122 Fifth Ave., 10011, pg. 189 **PB**
Doubleday Publishing Company, 1540 Broadway, 10036, pg. 191 **IT**
DOUGLAS ELLIMAN, 575 Madison Ave., 10022, pg. 341 **PV**
DOVER CORPORATION, 280 Park Ave., 10017, pg. 520 **PB**
Dover Handbag Co., Inc., 20 W. 33rd St., Eighth Flr., 10001, pg. 1042 **PV**
DOW JONES & COMPANY, INC., World Financial Center, 200 Liberty St., 10281, pg. 524 **PB**
Drake Beam Morin, Inc., 100 Park Ave., 10017, pg. 783 **PB**
Dresdner Bank AG, 75 Broad St., 10005-2889, pg. 418 **IT**
Dresdner-NY Inc., 75 Wall St., 10005-2889, pg. 418 **IT**
Dresdner Securities (USA) Inc., 75 Wall St., 10005-2889, pg. 418 **IT**
The Dreyfus Corporation, 200 Park Ave., 10166, pg. 1085 **PB**
Dreyfus Retirement Services, 200 Park Ave., 10166, pg. 1085 **PB**
Dreyfus Service Corp., 200 Park Ave., 10166, pg. 1085 **PB**
Duferco Steel Inc., 712 Fifth Ave., 10019, pg. 345 **IT**
Dun & Bradstreet Business Education Services, 711 Third Ave., 5th Fl., 10017, pg. 536 **PB**
Dunavant Commodity Corp., 114 Liberty St., 10006, pg. 346 **PV**
Duncanson & Holt, One Liberty Plaza, 45th Fl., 10006, pg. 1699 **PB**
DunsGate, 711 Third Ave., 10017, pg. 535 **PB**
THE DYSON-KISSNER-MORAN CORPORATION, 565 5th Ave., 4th Fl., 10017, pg. 351 **PV**
EDO CORPORATION, 60 E. 42nd St., Ste. 5010, 10165, pg. 541 **PB**
EFC Property Management, Inc., c/o Orion Capital Corp., 600 5th Ave., 24th Fl., 10020, pg. 1231 **PB**
EMI-Manhattan Records, 810 Seventh Ave., 10019, pg. 428 **IT**
EMI Music, Carnegie Hall Tower, 152 W. 57th St., 10019, pg. 427 **IT**
EMI Music Publishing, 1290 Avenue of the Americas, 10104, pg. 427 **IT**
ESPN Holding Company, Inc., 77 W. 66th St., 10023, pg. 512 **PB**
East Japan Railway Company - New York Office, One Rockefeller Pl., 10020, pg. 431 **IT**
Eastbridge Asset Management Inc., 135 E. 57th St., 10022, pg. 933 **IT**
Eastbridge Capital Inc., 135 E. 57th St., 10022, pg. 933 **IT**
Eastbridge Holdings Inc., 135 E. 57th St., 10022, pg. 933 **IT**
Eastern News Distributors, Inc., 250 W. 55th St., 10019, pg. 517 **PV**
Eastman Radio, Inc., 125 W. 55th St., 10019, pg. 335 **PV**
Eastman Software N.Y., Inc., 622 Third Ave., 30th Fl., 10017, pg. 555 **PB**
THE ECHO DESIGN GROUP, INC., Ten E. 40th St., 10016-0296, pg. 359 **PV**
Edelman Worldwide, Inc., 1500 Broadway, 25th Fl., 10036, pg. 352 **PV**
Educational & Professional Publishing Group, 1221 Ave. of the Americas, 10020, pg. 1070 **PB**
Edwards & Kelcey Engineers, Inc., 90 W. St., Ste. 1700, 10006-1039, pg. 364 **PV**
EDWARDSTONE & COMPANY, INC., 600 Madison Ave., 26th Fl., 10022, pg. 365 **PV**
El Al Israel Airlines, Ltd., 120 W. 45th St., 10036, pg. 435 **IT**
El Rio Grande, 160 E. 38th, 10021, pg. 130 **PV**
Electrical World, 11 W. 19th St., 10011, pg. 1071 **PB**
Electronic Products Magazine, 645 Stewart Ave., 11530, pg. 576 **PV**
Electronic Voting Systems, Inc., 475 Tenth Ave., 10018, pg. 771 **PB**
Elektra Entertainment, 75 Rockefeller Plaza, 10019, pg. 1612 **PB**
Elf Aquitaine, Inc., 280 Park Ave., 36th Fl. W, 10017, pg. 445 **IT**
Elf Sanofi Inc., 90 Park Ave., 10016, pg. 445 **IT**
Elisabeth Division, 1441 Broadway, 10018, pg. 1006 **PB**
Elite Information Systems, Inc., 122 E. 42nd St, Ste. 1700, 10168, pg. 258 **PB**
Elite Parfums, Ltd., 551 Fifth Ave., 10176, pg. 924 **PB**
Elizabeth Arden Company, 1345 Ave. of the Americas, 10105, pg. 1435 **IT**
Elle Publishing, L.P., 1633 Broadway, 44th Fl., 10019, pg. 795 **PV**
ELLEN TRACY INC., 575 Seventh Ave., 10018, pg. 372 **PV**
Douglas Elliman, 2112 Broadway, 10023, pg. 341 **PV**
Elron Technologies Inc., 855 Third Ave., 10022, pg. 64 **IT**
ELSAG Inc., 375 Park Ave., Ste. 3805, 10152, pg. 653 **IT**
Elsevier Science Inc., 655 Ave. of the Americas, 10010, pg. 373 **IT**
EMAP Business Communications USA, 1133 Broadway, #1025 10010, pg. 451 **PV**
EMIGRANT SAVINGS BANK, Five E. 42nd St., 10017, pg. 373 **PV**
EMMERLING POST, INC., 415 Madison Ave., 10017-1163, pg. 374 **PV**
EMPIRE BLUE CROSS & BLUE SHIELD, 622 Third Ave., 10017, pg. 374 **PV**
EMPIRE DIAMOND CORPORATION, 350 Fifth Ave., 10001, pg. 374 **PV**
Empire Insurance Group, 122 Fifth Ave., 10011-5697, pg. 990 **PB**
EMPIRE OFFICE EQUIPMENT, INC., 33 Maiden Ln., 14th Fl., 10038, pg. 374 **PV**

Engineering News-Record Magazine, 1221 Avenue of the Americas, 10020, pg. 1070 **PB**
Enprotech Corp., 335 Madison Ave., 10017, pg. 694 **IT**
Enskilda Securities Inc., New York, 245 Park Ave., 42nd Fl., 10167, pg. 1259 **IT**
ENTERPRISE, 627 Greenwich St., 10014, pg. 377 **PV**
Entertainment Weekly Inc., 1675 Broadway, 10019, pg. 1613 **PB**
Environmental Fragrance Technologies, Ltd., 767 Fifth Ave., 10153, pg. 689 **PV**
A. Epstein & Sons (New York), 245 Fifth Ave., Ste. 1701, 10016, pg. 379 **PV**
THE EQUITABLE COMPANIES INCORPORATED, 1290 Ave. of the Americas, 10104, pg. 588 **PB**
Equitable Financial Consultants, Inc., 1755 Broadway, 3rd Fl., 10019, pg. 589 **PB**
Equitable Investment Corporation, 787 Seventh Ave., 10019, pg. 589 **PB**
The Ericsson Corporation, 100 Park Ave., Ste. 2705, 10017, pg. 1364 **IT**
Erisco, Inc., 1700 Broadway, 10019, pg. 395 **PB**
Ernie's, 2150 Broadway, 10023, pg. 130 **PB**
ERNST & YOUNG, LLP, 787 7th Ave., 10019, pg. 381 **PV**
Erste Bank - New York Branch, 280 Park Ave., 10017, pg. 459 **IT**
ESCO Pest Control Services, 375 Hudson St., 10014, pg. 656 **IT**
Esquire, 250 W. 55th St., 10019, pg. 517 **PV**
ESSENCE COMMUNICATIONS INC., 1500 Broadway, 10036, pg. 383 **PV**
Essex Corporation, 825 Third Ave., 37th Fl., 10022, pg. 320 **PB**
ESTEE LAUDER COMPANIES INC., 767 Fifth Ave., 10153, pg. 594 **PB**
ETIENNE AIGNER, 712 Fifth Ave., 10019, pg. 384 **PV**
Euro-Lloyd Travel, 350 5th Ave., Ste. 1326, 10118, pg. 596 **IT**
European Reinsurance Corporation of America, 380 Madison Ave., 10017, pg. 1332 **IT**
EXCEL TECHNOLOGY, INC., 780 3rd Ave., 10th Fl., 10017, pg. 599 **PB**
EXCELLED SHEEPSKIN & LEATHER COAT CORPORATION, 350 5th Ave., 10018, pg. 387 **PV**
Execution Services Incorporated, 1221 Avenue of the Americas, 10020, pg. 675 **PV**
Exor America, 375 Park Ave., Ste. 2107, 10152, pg. 467 **IT**
Expecting, 685 Third Ave., 10017, pg. 190 **IT**
The Export-Import Bank of Korea, 20th Fl. Hahn Kook Ctr. Bldg., 460 Park Ave., 10022, pg. 467 **IT**
F&S Incorporated, 605 Third Ave., 10158, pg. 1458 **IT**
FCB, 150 E. 42nd St., 10017, pg. 389 **PV**
FAB INDUSTRIES, INC., 200 Madison Ave., 10016, pg. 603 **PB**
FABC (New York) Grp., 499 Park Ave., 10022, pg. 163 **PB**
F.A.O. Schwarz, 767 Fifth Ave., 10153-0199, pg. 750 **IT**
FGI New York, 295 Madison Ave., 10017, pg. 389 **PB**
F.T. Publications Inc., 14 E. 60th St., 10022, pg. 1026 **PV**
Fab International, Ltd., 200 Madison Ave., 10016, pg. 603 **PB**
NEIL FABER MEDIA INC., 157 W. 57th St., 10019, pg. 390 **PV**
M. FABRIKANT & SONS, INC., One Rockefeller Plaza, 10020, pg. 390 **PV**
Facts on File News Services, 11 Penn Plaza, 15th Fl., 10001-2006, pg. 1327 **PB**
Fahlgren, 501 Fifth Ave., Ste. 2103, 10017, pg. 391 **PV**
Fahnestock & Co., Inc., 110 Wall St., 10005, pg. 476 **IT**
Fairchild Publications, Seven W. 34th St., 10001, pg. 513 **PB**
FAIRFIELD MAXWELL LTD., 277 Park Ave., 10172, pg. 391 **PV**
The Family Circle, Inc., 375 Lexington Ave., 10017, pg. 190 **PB**
Family Reading Program Corp., 28 W. 23rd St., 10010, pg. 1367 **PV**
Famous Music Corporation, 1633 Broadway, 11th Fl., 10019, pg. 777 **PV**
Farrar, Straus & Giroux, Inc., 19 Union Sq. W., 10003, pg. 1479 **IT**
FARRELL LINES INCORPORATED, One Whitehall St., 10004, pg. 397 **PV**
Farrell Wako Global Investment Management, Inc., 780 Third Ave., 38th Fl., 10017, pg. 1485 **IT**
Fawcett Books, 201 E. 50th St., 10030, pg. 21 **PV**
FEDERAL HOME LOAN BANK OF NEW YORK, Seven World Trade Center, 22nd Fl., 10048, pg. 399 **PV**
Federated Corporate, 151 W. 34th St., 10001, pg. 618 **PB**
Federated Merchandising, 1440 Broadway, 10018, pg. 618 **PB**
Federated Metals Corp., 180 Maiden Ln., 10038, pg. 138 **PB**
FENWAY PARTNERS INC., 152 W. 57th St., 59th Fl., 10019, pg. 401 **PV**
FERRELLCALVILLO COMMUNICATIONS, INC., 250 Park Ave. S., 10003, pg. 401 **PV**
Fiat Finance U.S.A., Inc., 375 Park Ave., 10152, pg. 483 **IT**
Fiat USA Inc., 375 Park Ave., 27th Fl., 10152, pg. 483 **IT**
Fidelity and Casualty Co. of New York, 180 Maiden Ln., 10038, pg. 1011 **PB**
Fiduciary Financial Services Corp., Two World Trade Center, 10048-0772, pg. 621 **PB**
Fiduciary International, Inc., Two World Trade Ctr., 10048-0772, pg. 621 **PB**
Fiduciary Special Services, Inc., Two World Trade Ctr., 10048-0772, pg. 621 **PB**
FIDUCIARY TRUST COMPANY INTERNATIONAL, Two World Trade Center, Ste. 9400, 10048, pg. 621 **PB**
Field & Stream, Two Park Ave., 10016, pg. 1617 **PB**

Fieldcrest/Cannon Bed Fashions Division, 1271 Ave. of the Americas, 10020, pg. 1296 **PB**
Fila Fitness Ltd., 625 Madison Ave., 10022-1801, pg. 690 **PB**
FINANCIAL SECURITY ASSURANCE HOLDINGS LTD., 350 Park Ave., 10022, pg. 622 **PB**
FINANCIAL WORLD PARTNERS, 1328 Broadway, 10001, pg. 404 **PV**
Financiere Indosuez Inc., 345 Park Ave., 31st Fl., 10154, pg. 314 **IT**
Find/SVP Published Products, Inc., 625 Ave. of the Americas, 10011, pg. 623 **PB**
Wally Findlay Galleries, Inc., 14 E. 60th St., 10022, pg. 405 **PV**
FIND/SVP, INC., 625 Avenue of the Americas, 10011, pg. 623 **PB**
Fine Line Features, 575 Eighth Ave., 16th Fl., 10018, pg. 1615 **PB**
M. FINE & SONS MANUFACTURING CO., INC., 350 Fifth Ave., 10118, pg. 405 **PV**
FINLAY ENTERPRISES, INC., 521 5th Ave., 10175, pg. 623 **PB**
Finlay Fine Jewelry Corporation, 529 Fifth Ave., 10017, pg. 624 **PB**
Finmeccanica S.p.A., 425 Park Ave., 10022, pg. 654 **IT**
FINNAIR, 228 E. 45th St., 10017, pg. 485 **IT**
FINNAIR, 10 E. 40th St., 10016, pg. 486 **IT**
Fiotec, Inc., 335 Madison Ave., 10017, pg. 694 **IT**
Firemen's Insurance Co. of Newark, N.J., 180 Maiden Ln., 10038, pg. 1011 **PB**
Fireside Books, 1230 Ave. of the Americas, 10020, pg. 777 **PV**
First American Title Insurance Co. of N.Y., 228 E. 45th St., 10017, pg. 626 **PB**
First International Reinsurance Company, 485 Madison Ave., 10022, pg. 446 **PV**
The First Republic Building Corp., 302 Fifth Ave., 10001, pg. 637 **PB**
THE FIRST REPUBLIC CORPORATION OF AMERICA, 302 Fifth Ave., 10001, pg. 637 **PB**
First SunAmerica Life Insurance Company, 733 Third Ave., 10017, pg. 1533 **PB**
First Transamerica Life Insurance Company, 575 Fifth Ave., 10017, pg. 1630 **PB**
Fischbach & Moore, Inc., Seven Hanover Sq., 10004, pg. 84 **PB**
Fischbach & Moore International Corp., Seven Hanover Sq., 10004, pg. 84 **PB**
Fitness, 110 Fifth Ave., 10011, pg. 190 **IT**
Fleet Brokerage Securities Corp., 67 Wall St., 10005, pg. 649 **PB**
Fleet Securities, Inc., 14 Wall St., 27th Fl., 10005, pg. 650 **PB**
Fleishman-Hillard, Inc., 1330 Ave. of the Americas, 10019-5422, pg. 411 **PV**
Fleming Capital Management, 1285 Ave. of the Americas, 16th Fl., 10019, pg. 493 **PB**
Fleming Martin Inc., 1285 Ave. of the Americas, 16th Fl., 10019, pg. 493 **IT**
Robert Fleming, Inc., 320 Park Ave., 10022, pg. 493 **IT**
Fodor's Travel Publications, Inc., 201 E. 50th St., 10022, pg. 21 **PV**
Food & Wine, 1120 Ave. of the Americas, 10036, pg. 74 **PB**
Foodservice Director, 355 Park Ave. South, 10010, pg. 1446 **IT**
Foot Locker, 233 Broadway, 10279, pg. 1777 **PB**
Footquarters, 233 Broadway, 10279, pg. 1777 **PB**
Footwear News, Seven W. 34th St., 10001, pg. 513 **PB**
FORBES, INC., 60 Fifth Ave., 10011, pg. 417 **PV**
Forbes Investors Advisory Institute, Inc., 60 Fifth Ave., 10011, pg. 418 **PV**
Forbes Magazine Division, 60 Fifth Ave., 10011, pg. 417 **PV**
Forest City Pierrepont, Inc., 300 Cadman Plaza West, 11201, pg. 669 **PB**
Forest Electric Corp., Two Penn Plaza, 4th Fl., 10121, pg. 571 **PB**
FOREST LABORATORIES, INC., 909 Third Ave., 10022, pg. 670 **PB**
FORSTMANN & COMPANY, INC., 1155 Ave. of the Americas, 10036, pg. 670 **PB**
FORSTMANN LITTLE & CO., 767 Fifth Ave., 44th Fl., 10153, pg. 419 **PV**
Fortis Advisers, Inc., One Chase Manhattan Plaza, 10005, pg. 499 **IT**
Fortis, Inc., One Chase Manhattan Plaza, 41st Fl., 10005, pg. 499 **IT**
Fortune, Time & Life Bldg., Rockefeller Center, 10020, pg. 1613 **PB**
Foster Wheeler International Corporation, 666 Fifth Ave., 10103, pg. 677 **PB**
Fova, Inc., 149 Madison Ave., 10016, pg. 764 **PB**
FOWNES BROTHERS & CO., INC., 411 Fifth Ave., 10016, pg. 422 **PV**
France Telecom Inc., 1270 Ave. of the Americas, 10020, pg. 504 **IT**
Francosteel Corporation, 345 Hudson, 10014, pg. 572 **IT**
FRANK IX & SONS, INC., 469 7th Ave., 11th Fl., 10018, pg. 423 **PV**
Frank Smythson Inc., 138 Lexinton Avenue, 10016, pg. 707 **IT**
FRANKFURT BALKIND PARTNERS, 244 E. 58th St., 10022, pg. 424 **PV**
The Free Press, 1230 Ave. of the Americas, 10020, pg. 777 **PV**
Cliff Freeman & Partners, 375 Hudson St., 10014, pg. 1422 **PB**
W.H. Freeman & Co., 41 Madison Ave., 10010, pg. 1479 **IT**
Lewis Frimel, 1411 Broadway, 10018, pg. 519 **PB**

FUGAZY INTERNATIONAL CORPORATION, 555 Madison Ave., 12 Fl., 10022, pg. 430 **PV**
Fugazy Limousines, 200 Park Ave., 10022, pg. 430 **PV**
Fugazy Travel, 708 3rd Ave., 29th Fl., 10017, pg. 430 **PV**
The Fuji Bank & Trust Co., Two World Trade Center, 79th-81st Fls., 10048, pg. 519 **IT**
Fuji Capital Holdings Inc., Two World Trade Ctr., 82nd Fl., 10048, pg. 519 **IT**
Fuji Capital Markets Corporation, Two World Trade Center, 8oth Fl., 10048, pg. 519 **IT**
Fuji Securities Inc.-New York, Two World Financial Ctr., South Tower, 26th Fl., 10281, pg. 519 **IT**
Fujilease Corporation, Two World Trade Ctr., 79-81st Fls., 10048, pg. 519 **IT**
Fujitsu Limited, 680 Fifth Ave., 10019, pg. 526 **IT**
Fuji-Wolfensohn International, One Bankers Trust Plaza, 130 Liberty St., 10006, pg. 519 **IT**
Furman Selz Holding Corporation, 230 Park Ave., 13th Fl., 10169, pg. 1785 **PB**
Furniture Consultants, 11 W. 19th St., Ninth Fl., 10011, pg. 1686 **PV**
FURNITURE IN PARTS, INC., 116 E. 38th St., 10016, pg. 432 **PV**
G & G Shops, Inc., 520 Eighth Ave., 10018, pg. 858 **PV**
G-B Miller, 71 Fifth Ave., 10003, pg. 746 **PV**
G-III APPAREL GROUP, LTD., 345 W. 37th St., 10018, pg. 690 **PB**
GBI Griffin Bacal Promotions, 130 Fifth Ave., 10011, pg. 480 **PV**
GCI Group Inc., 777 Third Ave., 10017, pg. 764 **PB**
G.E. Information Services, 570 Lexington Ave., 10022, pg. 710 **PB**
GP STRATEGIES CORPORATION, Nine W. 57th St., Ste. 4170, 10019, pg. 694 **PB**
GRP Records, 555 W. 57th St., 10019, pg. 1215 **IT**
GSI Exim America Inc., 461 Fifth Ave., 10017, pg. 578 **IT**
G.T. Global, Inc., 375 Park Ave., Ste. 3401, 10152, pg. 809 **IT**
GT INTERACTIVE SOFTWARE CORP., 417 5th Ave., 8th Fl., 10016, pg. 696 **PB**
Galavision, 605 Third Ave., 12th Fl., 10158, pg. 230 **PV**
W. GAMBY & CO., 1071 Ave. of the Americas, 10018-3704, pg. 439 **PV**
Gan National Insurance Co., 120 Wall St., 10005, pg. 564 **IT**
Gan North America Inc., 120 Wall St., 10005, pg. 564 **IT**
Gant, 404 Fifth Ave., 5th Fl., 10018, pg. 1291 **PB**
GARAN, INCORPORATED, 350 Fifth Ave., 10118, pg. 703 **PB**
Garanimals, 350 Fifth Ave., 10118, pg. 703 **PB**
Garden State Converters, 171 Madison Ave., Rm. 1101, 10016-5110, pg. 1102 **PV**
Gefinor U.S.A., Inc., 375 Park Ave., Ste. 2401, 10152, pg. 542 **IT**
Gem Tech, 450 Westbury Ave., 11514, pg. 944 **PB**
Genamerica Management Corporation, One Liberty Plaza, 10006, pg. 90 **IT**
GenCorp Printworld, 1431 Broadway, 10018, pg. 706 **PB**
GENERAL AMERICAN INVESTORS COMPANY, INC., 450 Lexington Ave., Ste. 3300, 10017, pg. 706 **PB**
GENERAL CIGAR HOLDINGS INC 387 Park Ave., S., 10016, pg. 707 **PB**
General Employment Enterprises, 630 Fifth Ave., Ste. 2000, 10111, pg. 714 **PB**
General Media Automotive Group Inc., 277 Park Ave., 4th Fl., 10172-0003, pg. 444 **PV**
General Media Communications Group Inc., 277 Park Ave., 4th Fl., 10172-0003, pg. 444 **PV**
General Media Entertainment Group Inc., 277 Park Ave., 4th Fl., 10172-0003, pg. 444 **PV**
General Media Films Group Inc., 277 Park Ave., 4th Fl., 10172-0003, pg. 444 **PV**
The General Media Group Inc., 277 Park Ave., 4th Fl., 10172-0003, pg. 444 **PV**
GENERAL MEDIA INTERNATIONAL INC., 277 Park Ave., 4th Fl., 10172-0003, pg. 444 **PV**
General Securities Corporation of North America, One Liberty Plaza, 10006, pg. 90 **IT**
GENERAL TOOLS MFG., CO. INC., 80 White St., 10013, pg. 445 **PV**
Generale Bank, 41st. Floor, 520 Madison Ave., 10022, pg. 547 **IT**
Generale Investment Banking Corporation, 520 Madison Ave. 41st Fl., 10022, pg. 547 **IT**
Generali Underwriters, Inc., One Liberty Plaza, 10006, pg. 90 **IT**
Geneve Capital Group Inc., 485 Madison Ave., 10022, pg. 446 **PV**
Gentlemen's Quarterly, 350 Madison Ave., 10017, pg. 20 **PV**
Geominerals Insurance Company, Inc. (NY), 180 Maiden Ln., 10038, pg. 138 **PB**
Gerber Agri Inc., 11 Penn Plz., Ste. 1020, 10001, pg. 449 **PV**
GERBER INTERNATIONAL INC., 11 Penn Plaza, Ste. 1020, 10001, pg. 448 **PV**
J. Gerber & Co. Inc., 11 Penn Plaza, Ste. 1020, 10001, pg. 449 **PV**
GERSON & GERSON, INC., 112 W. 34th St., 20th Fl., 10120, pg. 449 **PV**
GEYER-MCALLISTER PUBLICATIONS, INC., 51 Madison Ave., 10010-1675, pg. 450 **PV**
Gibraltar Corp. of America, 350 Fifth Ave., 10118, pg. 1528 **PB**
GILMAN INVESTMENT COMPANY, INC., 111 W. 50th St., 10020, pg. 454 **PV**
GIRGENTI, HUGHES, BUTLER & MCDOWELL, 100 Avenue of the Americas, 10013, pg. 455 **PV**
Girl's Division, 1411 Broadway, 10018, pg. 686 **PB**
Gitano Men's Division, 1411 Broadway, 10018, pg. 686 **PB**

Givenchy Corp. (USA), 21 East 75th St., 10021, pg. 780 **IT**
GLAMORISE FOUNDATIONS, INC., 135 Madison Ave., 10016, pg. 455 **PV**
Glamour, 350 Madison Ave., 10017, pg. 20 **PV**
Gleacher Morgan Grenfell Inc., 667 Madison Ave., 10021, pg. 405 **IT**
GLEN OAKS INDUSTRIES, INC., 720 Fifth Avenue, 10019, pg. 456 **PV**
Glen Raven Marketing Corporation, 1350 Broadway, 10018, pg. 456 **PV**
GLENCRAFT LINGERIE, INC., 38 E. 32nd St., 10016, pg. 456 **PV**
Global Advanced Technology Corp., 40 Wall St., 10005, pg. 1517 **IT**
GLOBAL MARKETING RESOURCES (GMR), 360 Madison Ave., 10017, pg. 457 **PV**
Global Sourcing, Inc., 1411 Broadway, 10018, pg. 686 **PB**
Global Special Risks, Inc. of New York, 114 W. 47th St., Rm. 1712, 10036, pg. 1503 **PB**
Globalstar, 600 Third Ave., 36th Fl., 10016, pg. 1014 **PB**
Godiva Chocolatier, Inc., 355 Lexington Ave., 10017, pg. 299 **IT**
GOLDEN BOOKS FAMILY ENTERTAINMENT INC., 888 Seventh Ave., 10106, pg. 749 **PB**
Golden Books Publishing, 888 Seventh Ave., 10106, pg. 749 **PB**
Golden Fleece Outerwear Co., 505 8th Ave., 10018, pg. 1025 **PV**
GOLDMAN, SACHS & CO., 85 Broad St., 10004, pg. 462 **PB**
GOLDSMITH/JEFFREY INC., 235 Park Ave., S., 10003, pg. 462 **PB**
Golf Magazine, Two Park Ave., 10016, pg. 1617 **PB**
Gonzalez y Gonzalez, 625 Broadway, 10012, pg. 130 **PB**
Good Food Magazine, 850 Third Ave., 10022, pg. 925 **IT**
Good Housekeeping, 959 Eighth Ave., 10019, pg. 517 **PV**
GOODTIMES ENTERTAINMENT CO., 16 E. 40th St., 10016, pg. 464 **PV**
Gotham Incorporated, 260 Madison Ave., 10016, pg. 677 **PV**
GOULD PAPER CORPORATION, 11 Madison Ave., 10010, pg. 466 **PV**
Gourmet, 560 Lexington Ave., 18th Fl., 10022, pg. 20 **PV**
GRACE & ROTHSCHILD, 114 Fifth Ave., 10011, pg. 468 **PV**
Grace Hotel Services Corp., 303 Lexington Ave., 10016, pg. 755 **PB**
W.R. Grace & Co.-Conn., 1114 Ave. of the Americas, 10036-7794, pg. 755 **PB**
Graham Gregory Bozell, Inc., 40 W. 23rd St., 10010, pg. 1642 **PB**
Gramercy Assets Corporation, Four Irving Pl., 10003, pg. 435 **PV**
Grand Metropolitan Community Services-USA, 712 Fifth Ave., Ste. 4600, 10019, pg. 408 **IT**
GRANITE BROADCASTING CORPORATION, 767 Third Ave., 34th Fl., 10017, pg. 759 **PB**
EARL G. GRAVES, LTD., 130 Fifth Ave., 10011, pg. 471 **PV**
Earl G. Graves Publishing Co., 130 Fifth Ave., 10011, pg. 471 **PV**
Great American Knitting Mills, 597 Fifth Ave., 10036, pg. 194 **IT**
GREAT! Communications, 114 Fifth Ave., 10011, pg. 764 **PB**
GREAT SCOTT ADVERTISING CO. INC., 1185 Ave. of the Americas, 10036, pg. 475 **PV**
Great Universal Capital Corp., 645 Fifth Ave., 8th Fl., 10022, pg. 658 **PV**
GREATER NEW YORK MUTUAL INSURANCE COMPANY, 200 Madison Ave., 10016, pg. 476 **PB**
The Green Cross Corp.-New York Representative Office, 150 E. 52nd St., 10022, pg. 558 **IT**
GREENWAY PARTNERS, L.P., 277 Park Ave., 27th Fl., 10172, pg. 478 **PV**
GREENWICH STREET CAPITAL PARTNERS, INC., 388 Greenwich St., 36th Fl., 10013, pg. 479 **PV**
Greenwillow Books, 1350 Ave. of the Americas, 10019, pg. 515 **PV**
Grenadier Realty Corp., 909 Third Ave., 10022, pg. 1035 **PV**
GREY ADVERTISING INC., 777 Third Ave., 10017, pg. 764 **PB**
Grey Design & Promotion, 777 Third Ave., 34th Fl., 10017, pg. 764 **PB**
Grey Direct, c/o Grey Advertising, 777 Third Ave., 10017, pg. 764 **PB**
Grey Entertainment Inc., c/o Grey Advertising, 777 Third Ave., 10017, pg. 764 **PB**
Grey Healthcare Group, 114 Fifth Ave., 5th Fl., 10011, pg. 765 **PB**
Grey Interactive, 114 Fifth Ave., 10011, pg. 764 **PB**
GRIFFIN BACAL INC., 130 Fifth Ave., 10011, pg. 480 **PV**
GRIFFIN GROUP, INC., 780 3rd Ave., 10017, pg. 480 **PV**
Grosset & Dunlap, 200 Madison Ave., 10016, pg. 1027 **PV**
Grove's Dictionaries of Music Inc., 345 Park Ave. S., 10th Fl., 10010-1707, pg. 1479 **PB**
Gruner + Jahr International Marketing- and Media Services, Inc., 685 Third Ave., 23rd fl., 10017, pg. 190 **IT**
Gruner + Jahr USA Publishing, 375 Lexington Ave., 10017, pg. 190 **IT**
GRYBAUSKAS BEATRICE, 665 Broadway, 10012-2300, pg. 485 **PV**
The Guardian Insurance & Annuity Co. (GIAC), 201 Park Ave., S., 10003, pg. 486 **PV**
Guardian Investor Services Corp., 201 Park Ave. S., 10003, pg. 486 **PV**

Geographic Index-U.S.

THE GUARDIAN LIFE INSURANCE COMPANY OF AMERICA, 201 Park Ave. S., 10003, pg. 486　PV
The Guber Peters Entertainment Company (New York), 950 Third Ave., 29th Fl., 10022, pg. 1283　IT
Guerlain, Inc., 444 Madison Ave., 10022, pg. 780　IT
Guilford Mills (Apparel, Home & Industrial Fabrics), 469 Seventh Ave., 10018, pg. 769　PB
HBC Informational and Instructional Services, Inc., 111 Fifth Ave., 10003, pg. 783　PB
HBO Film Management, Inc., 1100 Ave. of the Americas, 10036, pg. 1612　PB
HBO Pictures, Inc., 1100 Ave. of Americas, 10036, pg. 1612　PB
HBO Satellites, Inc., 1100 Ave. of the Americas, 10036, pg. 1612　PB
HBO Video, Inc., 1100 Ave. of the Americas, 10036, pg. 1612　PB
HLW INTERNATIONAL LLP, 115 Fifth Ave., 10003, pg. 491　PV
HLW International Services Corporation, 115 Fifth Ave., 10003, pg. 491　PV
HLW Services Corporation, 115 Fifth Ave., 10003, pg. 491　PV
HMG Instore Marketing Inc., 475 10th Ave., 10018, pg. 771　PB
HMG Intermark Manufacturing Inc., 475 10th Ave., 10018, pg. 771　PB
H.M.G. WORLDWIDE CORP., 475 Tenth Ave., 10018, pg. 771　PB
HRH Construction Corp., 909 3rd Ave., 10022, pg. 1035　PV
HRH Construction Interiors, Inc., 909 3rd Ave., 10022, pg. 1035　PV
HSBC Asset Management Americas, Inc., 250 Park Ave., 10177, pg. 581　IT
HSBC Asset Management Americas Inc., 3/F, 250 Park Ave., 10177, pg. 581　IT
HSBC Futures, Inc., 19th Fl., 140 Broadway, 10005, pg. 581　IT
HSBC Holdings Inc., 3/F, 140 Broadway, 10015, pg. 581　IT
HSBC Securities, Inc., 140 Broadway, 10005, pg. 581　IT
Habib Bank Ltd., 44 Wall St., 10005, pg. 584　IT
Habits, Inc., 463 Seventh Ave., Room 1311, 10018, pg. 968　PV
Hachette Filipacchi Magazines Inc., 1633 Broadway, 10019, pg. 794　IT
Hachette Filipacchi USA, 1633 Broadway, 45th Fl., 10019, pg. 794　IT
Hakuhodo Advertising America Inc., 475 Park Ave. S., 18th Fl., 10016, pg. 588　IT
Hall & Cederquist, Inc., 206 East 63rd St., 10021, pg. 1197　PV
Hallmark Entertainment, Inc., 1325 Avenue of the Americas, 21st Fl., 10019, pg. 496　PV
Halmode Apparel, Inc., 501 Seventh Ave., 14th Fl., 10018, pg. 948　PB
Halston Enterprises, Inc., 625 Madison Ave., 10022, pg. 690　PV
HAMPEL/STEFANIDES, 111 Fifth Ave., 10003, pg. 498　PV
Louis Hand Div., 16 E. 34th St., 10016, pg. 1094　PV
HANDY & HARMAN, 250 Park Ave., 10177, pg. 780　PB
HANFT BYRNE RABOY ABRAMS & PARTNERS, INC., 111 Fifth Ave., 10003, pg. 499　PV
Hanwa American Corp., 750 Third Ave., 34th Fl., 10017, pg. 595　IT
Harcourt-Brace, 15 E. 26th St., 10010, pg. 783　PB
Harmag, Inc., 235 E. 42nd St., 10017, pg. 1282　PB
Harmony Books, 201 E. 50th St., 10022, pg. 21　PV
Harper Audio, Ten E. 53rd St., 10022, pg. 926　IT
Harper Reference, Ten E. 53rd St., 10022, pg. 927　IT
HarperCollins Adult Trade Division, Ten E. 53rd St., 10022, pg. 926　IT
HarperCollins Junior Books Division, Ten E. 53rd St., 10022, pg. 927　IT
HarperCollins Publishers, Ten E. 53rd St., 10022, pg. 926　IT
Harper's Bazaar, 1700 Broadway, 10019, pg. 517　PV
Harris Bank International Corp., 430 Park Ave., 10022, pg. 154　IT
HARRIS CHEMICAL GROUP, INC., 399 Park Ave., 10022, pg. 505　PV
Harris Trust Company of New York, 77 Water St., 4th Fl., 10005, pg. 155　IT
Harrison & Star, 16 W. 22nd St., 12th Fl., 10010, pg. 506　PV
HARRISON & STAR, INC., 16 W. 22nd St., 12th Fl., 10010, pg. 506　PV
HARTOG RAHIL FOODS, INC., 529 Fifth Ave., Ste. 1800, 10017, pg. 508　PV
Hartz Group, 667 Madison Ave., 10021, pg. 508　PV
Harve Benard Ltd., 205 W. 39th St., 6th Fl., 10018, pg. 508　PV
HARVEST PARTNERS INC., 767 3rd Ave., 7th Fl., 10017, pg. 508　PV
Harvey Electronics, 2 W. 45th St., 10036, pg. 796　PB
Harvey Electronics, 888 Broadway, 10003, pg. 796　PB
Haseko (New York) Inc., 99 Park Ave., 17th Fl., 10016, pg. 600　IT
HAZEN & SAWYER, 730 Broadway, 10003, pg. 514　PV
THE HE-RO GROUP, LTD., 530 Seventh Ave., 10018, pg. 801　PB
Health Care Ventures Inc., 235 E. 42nd St., 10017, pg. 1282　PB
HEALTH-CHEM CORPORATION, 1212 Ave. of the Americas, 10036, pg. 802　PB
Health Education Technologies (HET) Div., 220 E. 42 St., 10017, pg. 1224　PB
HEALTH MANAGEMENT SYSTEMS, INC., 401 Park Ave. S., 10016, pg. 802　PB

Health Management Systems, Inc., 401 Park Ave. S., 10016, pg. 802　PB
Health Science Communications, 130 5th Ave., 10010, pg. 1422　PV
The Healthcare Connection, 375 Hudson St., 10014, pg. 1422　PB
Healthcare Group, 1790 Broadway, 10019, pg. 515　PV
Healthcare Management Group, 1221 Ave. of the Americas, 10020, pg. 1071　PB
Hearst-Argyle Television Incorporated, 888 Seventh Ave., 10106, pg. 516　PV
Hearst Book Group, 1350 Ave. of the Americas, 10019, pg. 515　PV
Hearst Books/Business Publishing Group, 959 Eighth Ave., 10019, pg. 515　PV
THE HEARST CORPORATION, 959 Eighth Ave., 10019, pg. 515　PV
Hearst Enterprises Division, 224 W. 57th St., 10019, pg. 516　PV
Hearst Entertainment, 235 E. 45th St., 10017, pg. 516　PV
Hearst Entertainment & Syndication, 959 Eighth Ave., 10019, pg. 516　PV
Hearst Magazines Division, 959 Eighth Ave., 10019, pg. 516　PV
Hearst Magazines International, 959 Eighth Ave., 10019, pg. 517　PV
Hearst Marine Books, 1350 Ave. of the Americas, 10019, pg. 515　PV
Hearst New Media & Technology, 959 Eighth Ave., 10019, pg. 517　PV
Hearst Newspapers, 959 Eighth Ave., 10019, pg. 517　PV
Hearst Realty Development Co., Inc., 959 Eighth Ave., 10019, pg. 515　PV
HELMSLEY ENTERPRISES, INC., 230 Park Ave., 10169, pg. 521　PV
Helmsley-Noyes Co., Inc., 22 Cortland St., 10007, pg. 521　PV
Helmsley-Spear Inc., 60 E. 42nd St., 10165, pg. 521　PV
JOAN & DAVID HELPERN, INC., Four W. 58th. St., 10019, pg. 521　PV
Henri Bendel, 11 W. 42nd St., Ninth Fl., 10036, pg. 395　PB
Heraeus Inc., 540 Madison Ave., 10022, pg. 616　IT
Heraeus Precious Metals Management Inc., 540 Madison Ave., 10022, pg. 616　IT
Hercor Laboratories Corp., 1212 Ave. of the Americas, 10036, pg. 802　PB
Hesco Supply Co., Inc., 959 Eighth Ave., 10019, pg. 518　PV
Hewlett-Packard Company, One Pennsylvania Plaza, 34th St. & Eighth Ave., 55th Fl., 10119, pg. 814　PV
Hill and Knowlton, Inc., 466 Lexington Ave., 3rd Fl., 10017, pg. 483　IT
Hill & Wang, 19 Union Sq. W., 10003, pg. 1479　IT
Hill, Holliday/Altschiller, 1740 Broadway, 21st Fl., 10019, pg. 529　PV
Hill Samuel Inc., 527 Madison Ave., 16th Fl., 10022, pg. 813　IT
Hill Samuel International Banking Corp., 527 Madison Ave., 16th Fl., 10022, pg. 813　IT
HILLSIDE CAPITAL INCORPORATED, 405 Park Ave., 10022, pg. 530　PV
Hillside Industries, Inc., 405 Park Ave., 10022, pg. 530　PV
History Book Club, Inc., 485 Lexington Ave., 10017, pg. 1512　PB
The History Channel, 235 E. 45th St., 10017, pg. 512　PB
Hitachi Zosen U.S.A. Ltd., 150 E. 52nd St., 20th Fl., 10022, pg. 623　IT
Hoboken Floors-Capitol Division, c/o D&D Bldg., 979 3rd Ave., 10022, pg. 532　PV
Hoboken Floors-Eastern Flooring Division, c/o D&D Bldg., 979 3rd Ave., 10022, pg. 532　PV
Bernard Hodes Group, 555 Madison Ave., 10022, pg. 1224　PB
The Hokkaido Takushoku Bank, Ltd., New York Branch, Two World Trade Center, 99th Floor, 10048, pg. 626　IT
The Hokuriku Bank, Ltd.-New York, 17 State St., 10th Fl., 1000-, pg. 627　IT
Holmes Protection Group, Inc., 440 Ninth Ave., 10001, pg. 1649　PB
Holmes Protection of New York, Incorporated, 440 Ninth Ave., 10001, pg. 1649　PB
Henry Holt & Co. Publishing, 115 W. 18th St., 10011, pg. 1479　IT
Home Box Office Communications, Inc., 1100 Avenue of Americas, 10036, pg. 1612　PB
Home Box Office, Inc., 1100 Sixth Avenue, 10036, pg. 1612　PB
Home Box Office International, Inc., 1100 Ave. of the Americas, 10036, pg. 1612　PB
Home Box Office Services, Inc., 1100 Ave. of Americas, 10036, pg. 1612　PB
Home Curtain Corporation, 295 Fifth Ave., 10016, pg. 535　PV
Home Fashions, Seven W. 34th St., 10003, pg. 513　PB
Home Furnishings Daily, Seven W. 34th St., 10001, pg. 513　PB
HOME INNOVATIONS, INC., 295 Fifth Ave., 10016, pg. 535　PV
Home Magazine Publishing Corp., 1633 Broadway, 10019, pg. 795　PB
Home Service Publications, Inc., 28 W. 23rd St., 10010, pg. 1367　PV
HONEY FASHIONS LTD., 417 Fifth Ave., 4th Fl., 10016, pg. 537　PV
J.G. HOOK, INC., 498 Seventh Ave., 23rd Fl., 10018, pg. 538　PV
HORIZON PAPER CO., INC., 230 Park Ave., Ste. 840, 10169, pg. 539　PV

HORSEHEAD INDUSTRIES, INC., 110 E. 59th St., 34th Fl., 10022, pg. 540　PB
Horsehead Resource Development Co., Inc., 110 E. 59th St., 10022, pg. 540　PB
Hosokawa Micron International Inc., 780 Third Ave., 10017, pg. 635　IT
Hospitality Design, 355 Park Ave. South, 10010, pg. 1446　PV
HOSPITALITY WORLDWIDE SERVICES, INC., 450 Park Ave., Ste. 2603, 10022, pg. 841　PB
HOST APPAREL, INC., 1430 Broadway, 10018, pg. 540　PV
Host for Her, 1430 Broadway, 10018, pg. 540　PV
Hotel Inter-Continental, 111 E. 48th St., Park & Lexington, 10017, pg. 1178　IT
House Beautiful, 1700 Broadway, 10019, pg. 517　PV
HOUSE OF PERFECTION, INC., 131 W. 33rd St., 10001, pg. 542　PV
HOUSE OF RONNIE, INC., 1372 Broadway, 11th FL., 10018, pg. 542　PV
The House of Seagram, 800 Third Ave., 10022, pg. 1217　IT
Howmedica International, Inc., 235 E. 42nd St., 10017, pg. 1282　PB
Hudson Insurance Company, One Liberty Plaza, 10006, pg. 1258　IT
Hudson Street Partners, 375 Hudson St., 10014, pg. 1422　PV
Hugo Boss Fashions Inc., 645 5th Ave., #21, 10022, pg. 637　IT
Hugo Boss, Inc., 645 5th Ave., 22nd Fl., 10022, pg. 637　IT
Hugo Boss USA, Inc., 49 W. 57th St., 10019, pg. 637　IT
Human Sciences Press, Inc., 233 Spring St., 10013, pg. 1311　IT
Hyosung America, Inc., 250 W. 34th St., Ste. 2020, 10119, pg. 641　IT
Hypo Securities Inc., 32 Old Slip, 33rd Fl., 10005, pg. 176　IT
I/B/E/S International Inc., 345 Hudson St., 10014, pg. 1446　PV
IBJ Schroder Bank & Trust Company, One State St., 10004, pg. 674　IT
IBJ Schroder Bank & Trust Company (Midtown Branch), 126 E. 56th St., 10022, pg. 675　IT
IBJ Schroder Banking Corporation, One State St., 10004, pg. 675　IT
IBJ Schroder International Bank, One State St., 10004, pg. 675　IT
IBJ Schroder Leasing Corporation, One State St., 10004, pg. 675　IT
ICC INDUSTRIES, INC., 460 Park Ave., 10022-1906, pg. 553　PV
ICC Trading, Inc., 460 Park Ave., 10022, pg. 553　PV
ICD GROUP INTERNATIONAL INC., 600 Madison Ave., 10022, pg. 554　PV
ICM Artists, Ltd., 40 W. 57th St., 10019, pg. 554　PV
ICM HOLDINGS INC., 40 W. 57th St, 10019, pg. 554　PV
IDB WorldCom, 380 Madison Ave., Eighth Fl., 10017, pg. 1779　PB
IHI Inc., 280 Park Ave., West Bldg. 30th fl., 10017, pg. 689　IT
ILX Systems, Inc., 111 Fulton St., 10038, pg. 1601　PB
IMG, 22 E. 71st St., 10021, pg. 555　PV
INA Life Insurance Company of New York, 195 Broadway, 11th Fl., 10003, pg. 362　PB
ING Baring (U.S.) Holdings, 667 Madison Ave., 10021, pg. 647　IT
ING (U.S.) Capital Holdings, 135 E. 57th St., 10022, pg. 648　IT
ING (U.S.) Securities Corp., 135 E. 57th St., 10022, pg. 648　IT
ING (U.S.) Financial Services kk, 135 E. 57th St., 10022, pg. 648　IT
ISS Building Maintenance, Inc., 375 Hudson St., 5th Fl., 10014, pg. 656　IT
ISS Cleaning Services Group, Inc., 375 Hudson St., 5th Fl., 10014, pg. 656　IT
ISS Energy Services, Inc., 375 Hudson St., 5th Fl., 10014, pg. 656　IT
ITOCHU Shoe Co., Inc., 19 West 34th St., 10001, pg. 695　IT
ITOCHU Takuma Resource Systems, Inc., 335 Madison Ave., 10017, pg. 695　IT
ITT Corporation, 1330 Ave. of the Americas, 10019, pg. 1512　PB
ITT Information Services, Inc., 1330 Avenue of the Americas, 10019, pg. 1512　PB
Iberia Air Lines of Spain, 655 Madison, 20th Fl., 10021, pg. 575　IT
ICAHN & CO., INC., 767 5th Ave., 47th Fl., 10153, pg. 556　PV
Idmatics Inc., 561 Broadway, #10 A, 10012, pg. 1384　IT
Iffland Kavanagh Waterbury, PLLC, 1501 Broadway, Ste. 606, 10036, pg. 364　PV
Ikon Office Solutions New York, 11 E. 36th St., 10066, pg. 863　PB
Incentive, 355 Park Ave. South, 10010, pg. 1446　IT
Inco United States Inc., One New York Pl., 10004, pg. 672　IT
Independent Financial Planners Corp., 600 Fifth Ave., 10020-2302, pg. 1231　PB
Indosuez Capital (US), 1211 Ave. of the Americas, 10036-8701, pg. 314　IT
The Industrial Bank of Japan, Limited (New York Branch), 245 Park Ave., 10167, pg. 674　IT
The Industrial Bank of Japan Trust Company, 245 Park Ave., 10167, pg. 675　IT
Industrial Equipment News, Five Penn Plaza, 10001, pg. 1082　PV

PB - *U.S. Public Companies Volume*
PV - *U.S. Private Companies Volume*
IT - *International Public & Private Companies Volume*

Industrias La Famosa, Inc., 277 Park Ave., 10172, pg. 158 **PV**
INFORMATION BUILDERS, 1250 Broadway, 10001, pg. 561 **PV**
Innovir Laboratories, Inc., 510 E. 73rd St., 10021, pg. 1702 **PB**
Instinet Corporation, 857 Third Ave., 10022, pg. 1106 **IT**
Institutional Brokers Estimate System Inc. (IBIS), One World Trade Ctr., 18th Fl., 10048, pg. 1325 **PB**
Institutional Investor, Inc., 488 Madison Ave., 10022, pg. 513 **PV**
Insurance Company of Greater New York, 200 Madison Ave., 10016, pg. 476 **PB**
Insurance Company of the State of Pennsylvania, 70 Pine St., 10270, pg. 84 **PB**
The Insurance Corp. of New York, 500 N. Broadway, Ste. 142, 11753, pg. 336 **PB**
Intalcable USA Inc., 499 Park Ave., 23rd Fl., 10022, pg. 655 **PV**
Inter-Continental Hotels & Resorts Corporation, 1120 Ave. of the Americas, 19th Fl., 10036-6700, pg. 1178 **IT**
Interactive Deutsch, 215 Park Ave. S., 10003, pg. 329 **PV**
Interactive Market Systems, Inc., 11 W. 42nd Street, 10036-8088, pg. 1447 **PB**
Interbrand Schechter, 437 Madison Ave., 10017, pg. 1224 **PB**
Intercontinental Apparel, 1330 Ave. of the Americas, 10002, pg. 796 **PV**
Intercosmetics, Inc., 655 Madison Ave., 18th Fl., 10021, pg. 1489 **IT**
Interiors, 1515 Broadway, 10036, pg. 1446 **IT**
Intermark Corp., 475 Tenth Ave., 10018, pg. 771 **PB**
International Apparel Marketing Corp., 80 W. 40th St., 10018, pg. 498 **PB**
International Circulation Distributors, 250 W. 55th St., 10019, pg. 517 **PV**
The International Commercial Bank of China, 65 Liberty St., 10005, pg. 683 **IT**
INTERNATIONAL CUTLERY, LTD, 127 W. 25th St., 10001, pg. 569 **PV**
INTERNATIONAL FLAVORS & FRAGRANCES, INC., 521 W. 57th St., 10019, pg. 898 **PV**
International Life Investors Insurance Company, 335 Madison Ave., 18th Fl., 10017-4683, pg. 27 **IT**
International Media, 101 Park Ave., 10178-0065, pg. 1641 **PB**
INTERNATIONAL PLASTICS COMPANY, 1950 Third Ave., 10029, pg. 571 **PV**
International Typeface Corporation (ITC), Two Hammarskjold Plaza, 10017, pg. 460 **IT**
THE INTERPUBLIC GROUP OF COMPANIES, INC., 1271 Ave. of the Americas, 44th Fl., 10020, pg. 908 **PV**
Interstate Broadcasting Company, Inc., 122 5th Ave., 10011, pg. 1173 **PV**
Interstate Photo Supply Corp., 117 E. 57th St., Ste. 21H, 10022, pg. 6 **PB**
Investment Technology Group, Inc., 900 Third Ave., Second Fl., 10022, pg. 924 **PB**
Ipanema Shoe Corporation, 350 Fifth Ave., Ste. 7100, 1011B, pg. 1312 **PV**
Island Entertainment Group, Inc., 400 Lafayette St., 5th Fl., 10003, pg. 1052 **PV**
Israel Aircraft Industries International Inc., 50 W. 23rd St., 10010, pg. 690 **IT**
Israel Discount Bank of New York, 511 Fifth Ave., 10017, pg. 645 **IT**
ITOCHU International Inc., 335 Madison Ave., 10017, pg. 694 **IT**
Ivy Hill Corporation, 375 Hudson St., 10014, pg. 1611 **PB**
Izod, 404 Fifth Ave., 10018, pg. 1292 **PB**
J&H Marsh & McLennan, Inc., 1166 Ave. of Americas, 10036, pg. 1049 **PB**
J & R MUSIC WORLD, 23 Park Row, 10038, pg. 576 **PV**
J. Crew Group, Inc., 770 Broadway 12th Fl., 10003, pg. 1078 **PV**
JAFCO America Ventures Inc., 17th Fl., Bldg. B, Two World Fin. Ctr., 225 Liberty St., 10281-1196, pg. 955 **PV**
JAL International Services, Third Park Ave. 28th Fl., 10016, pg. 700 **IT**
JBQ SPORT LLC, 70 W. 36th St., Ste. 1004, 10018, pg. 577 **PV**
JBS Productions Holding Company, Inc., 77 W. 66th St., 10023, pg. 511 **PB**
JCB International Credit Card Co., Ltd.-USA, 60 Rockefeller Plaza, 10020, pg. 696 **IT**
JJC Specialist Corp., 26 Broadway, 10004, pg. 650 **PV**
JMCT/Direct, 445 Park Ave., 10022, pg. 599 **PV**
JMCT Publicidad, 445 Park Ave., 10022, pg. 599 **PV**
JMCTtouch, 445 Park Ave., 10022, pg. 599 **PV**
JWG Associates, Inc., 599 Lexington Ave. Ste. 2300, 10022, pg. 579 **PV**
Jabawwat, Inc., 600 Fifth Ave., 10020-2302, pg. 1231 **PB**
JACOBY & MEYERS LAW OFFICES, 10 E. 40th St., 22nd Fl., 10016, pg. 580 **PV**
JACQUES MORET, INC., 1350 Broadway, 10018, pg. 580 **PV**
Jaeger Sportswear Ltd., 818 Madison Ave., 10021, pg. 299 **IT**
Jakson-A CHF Company, One Park Ave., 10016, pg. 1094 **PV**
Japan Airlines American Region, 655 Fifth Ave., JAL Bldg., 10022, pg. 700 **IT**
Japan Energy (U.S.A.), Inc., 12 E. 49th St., Ste. 1710, 10017, pg. 702 **IT**
JAPAN TRAVEL BUREAU INTERNATIONAL, INC., 787 Seventh Ave., 10019, pg. 582 **PV**
JEAN PHILIPPE FRAGRANCES, INC., 551 Fifth Ave., Ste. 1500, 10176, pg. 924 **PB**
Jefferies & Company, Inc., 650 Fifth Ave., 4th Fl., 10019, pg. 925 **PB**

Jefferson Adams Corp., 1221 Ave. of the Americas, 17th Fl., pg. 1724 **PB**
Jerry & Ketchum, 640 Fifth Ave., 10019, pg. 616 **PV**
Jet Vacation, 888 7th Ave., 10106, pg. 560 **IT**
Andy Johns Fashions, Inc., 463 Seventh Ave., 10018, pg. 233 **PB**
Andy Johns MacKintosh, 463 Seventh Ave., 16th Fl., 10018, pg. 233 **PB**
Axel Johnson Ore & Metals, Inc., 110 E. 40th St., 10022, pg. 710 **IT**
Jones New York Outerwear, 512 Seventh Ave., 8th Fl., 10018, pg. 49 **PV**
JORDACHE ENTERPRISES, INC., 1411 Broadway, 10018, pg. 597 **PV**
Jordache Fragrances & Cosmetics, 551 Fifth Ave., 10176, pg. 597 **PB**
THE JORDAN COMPANY, Nine W. 57th St., Ste. 4000, 10019, pg. 597 **PV**
JORDAN, MCGRATH, CASE & TAYLOR INC., 445 Park Ave., 10022, pg. 598 **PV**
JOSEPH, LITTLEJOHN & LEVY, 450 Lexington Ave., Ste. 3350, 10017, pg. 601 **PV**
Journal of Commerce, Inc., Two World Trade Center, 27th Fl., 10048, pg. 1026 **PV**
Jove Publications, Inc., 200 Madison Ave., 10016, pg. 1027 **IT**
Joy Toy, Co., 200 5th Ave., 10010, pg. 1047 **PV**
JOYCE INTERNATIONAL, INC., 156 W. 56th St., 10011, pg. 602 **PV**
Julian Press, 201 E. 50th St., 10022, pg. 21 **PV**
JUNIOR GALLERY LTD., 463 7th Ave., 5th Fl., 10018, pg. 602 **PV**
Jusco USA, Inc., 525 Madison Ave. 4th Fl., 10022, pg. 28 **IT**
Just Toys, 50 W. 23rd St., 10010, pg. 903 **PV**
K & F INDUSTRIES INC., 600 Third Ave., 10016, pg. 602 **PV**
K-III Media Group, 717 Fifth Ave., 10022, pg. 1328 **PB**
KG Land New York Corporation, Four Columbus Cr., Third Fl., 10019, pg. 764 **IT**
KM Construction Co., Four Columbus Circle, 3rd Fl., 10019, pg. 764 **IT**
KOA HOLDINGS, 600 Fifth Ave., 8th Fl., 10020, pg. 603 **IT**
KPMG LLP, 345 Park Ave., 10154, pg. 603 **PV**
KPR, 333 E. 38th St., 10016, pg. 1224 **PB**
KQRS Holding Corporation, 77 W. 66th St., 10023, pg. 512 **IT**
Kable News Co., Inc., 641 Lexington Ave., 10022, pg. 105 **PB**
MAX KAHAN INC., 20 W. 47th St., 10036, pg. 604 **PV**
Kajima U.S.A., Inc., 320 Park Ave., 26th Fl., 10022, pg. 722 **IT**
Kanebo, Ltd., 693 Fifth Ave., 17th Fl., 10022, pg. 722 **IT**
The Kansai Electric Power Co. - New York Office, 375 Park Ave., Ste. 2607, 10152, pg. 723 **IT**
Kansas City Fire and Marine Insurance Co., 180 Maiden Ln., 10038, pg. 1011 **PB**
Kaplan Educational Centers Ltd., 888 Seventh Ave., 23rd Fl., 10106, pg. 1743 **PB**
Katharine Gibbs School, Inc., 52 Vanderbilt Ave., 10017, pg. 209 **PV**
Katz American Television, 125 W. 55th St., 10019, pg. 335 **PB**
Katz Continental Television, 125 W. 55th St., 10019, pg. 335 **PB**
Katz Dimensions, 125 W. 55th St., 10019, pg. 335 **PB**
Katz Hispanic Media, 125 W. 55th St., 10019, pg. 335 **PB**
Katz Media Group, Inc., 125 W. 55th St., 10019, pg. 335 **PB**
Katz Millennium, 125 W. 55th St., 10019, pg. 335 **PB**
Katz National Television, 125 W. 55th St., 10019, pg. 335 **PB**
Katz Radio, 125 W. 55th St., 10019, pg. 335 **PB**
Kawasaki Heavy Industries (U.S.A.), Inc., 599 Lexington Ave., Ste. 2705, 10022, pg. 725 **IT**
Kawasaki Steel America, Park Ave. Plaza, 55 E. 52nd St., 10055, pg. 726 **IT**
KAZ, INC., Ten Columbus Cir., Ste. 1620, 10019, pg. 610 **PV**
Robert Keeshan Associates, Inc., 40 W. 57th St., 10019, pg. 554 **PV**
Kendrick Bay Mining Co., c/o Standard Metals Corp., 156 W. 56th St., 10020, pg. 1502 **PB**
KENNETH COLE PRODUCTIONS, 152 W. 57th St., 10019, pg. 951 **PB**
J.J. Kenny Co., Inc., 65 Broadway, 10006, pg. 1070 **PB**
Ketchum Directory Advertising/New York, 1250 Broadway, 15th Fl., 10001, pg. 616 **PV**
Ketchum Public Relations Worldwide, 292 Madison Ave., 10017, pg. 617 **PV**
Kid Think Inc., 130 Fifth Ave., 10011, pg. 480 **PV**
Kim Eng Securities USA Inc., 406 E. 50th St., 10022, pg. 733 **IT**
King Features Licensing, 235 E. 45th St., 10017, pg. 515 **PV**
King Features Syndicate Division, 235 E. 45th St., 10017, pg. 518 **PV**
KING WORLD PRODUCTIONS, INC., 1700 Broadway 32 Fl. & 33 Fl., 10019, pg. 961 **PB**
Kinney Shoe Corporation, 233 Broadway, 10279, pg. 1777 **PB**
KINNEY SYSTEM, INC., 60 Madison Ave., 7th Fl., 10010, pg. 622 **PV**
Kintetsu World Express Inc., 424 Madison Ave., 10017, pg. 734 **IT**
Kirin USA, Inc., 600 Third Ave., 10016, pg. 736 **IT**
KIRSHENBAUM, BOND & PARTNERS, 145 Ave. of the Americas, 10013, pg. 624 **PV**
Kleinwort Benson, 200 Park Ave., 25th Fl., 10166, pg. 420 **IT**

Kleinwort Benson Investment Management Americas Inc., 200 Park Ave., 25th Fl., 10166, pg. 420 **IT**
Kleinwort Benson North America Inc., 200 Park Ave., 25th Fl., 10166, pg. 420 **IT**
Kleinwort Benson (U.S.A.) Inc., 200 Park Ave., 25th Fl., 10166, pg. 420 **IT**
Klemtner Advertising Inc., 375 Hudson St., 10014-3620, pg. 1422 **PB**
GEORGETTE KLINGER, INC., 501 Madison Ave., 10022, pg. 626 **PV**
Knoll International, 105 Wooster St., 10012, pg. 627 **PV**
Alfred A. Knopf, Inc., 201 E. 50th St., 10022, pg. 21 **PV**
Kobe Steel International (USA) Inc., 34F Dillon Read Bldg., 535 Madison Ave., 10022, pg. 740 **IT**
Kobe Steel U.S.A. Inc. (New York), 535 Madison Ave., 10022, pg. 740 **IT**
KOBRA INTERNATIONAL LTD., 525 7th Ave., 20th Fl., 10018, pg. 628 **PV**
Kodansha America, Inc., 114 Fifth Ave., 18th Fl., 10011, pg. 742 **IT**
KOHLBERG KRAVIS ROBERTS & CO., Nine W. 57th St., 42nd Fl., Ste. 4200, 10019, pg. 629 **PV**
CHARLES KOMAR & SONS, INC., 16 E. 34th St., 10th Fl., 10016, pg. 631 **PV**
PERRY H. KOPLIK & SONS, 505 Park Ave., 10022, pg. 632 **PV**
KORET PIERRE CARDIN, 136 Madison Ave., 10016, pg. 632 **PV**
KOREY, KAY & PARTNERS, 130 Fifth Ave., 10011, pg. 632 **PV**
Korn/Ferry International, 237 Park Ave., 10017, pg. 633 **PV**
KRAFT HARDWARE, INC., 306 E. 61st St., 10021, pg. 634 **PV**
Krazy Glue Inc., 277 Park Ave., 10172, pg. 158 **PV**
Kredietbank New York Branch, 125 W. 55th St.-10th Fl., 10019, pg. 760 **IT**
Kruger Pulp & Paper Sales, Inc., 489 Fifth Ave., 10017, pg. 762 **IT**
KRXY Holding Corporation, 77 W. 66th St., 10023, pg. 512 **IT**
Kubota America Corp., The Chrysler Bldg., 59th Fl., 405 Lexington Ave., 10174, pg. 762 **IT**
Kubota Corp.-New York Office, The Chrysler Bldg., 59th Fl., 405 Lexington Ave., 10174, pg. 762 **IT**
Kubota Finance (U.S.A.), Inc., The Chrysler Bldg., 59th Fl., 405 Lexington Ave., 10174, pg. 762 **IT**
Kuwait Airways Corp., 350 Park Ave., 10022, pg. 764 **IT**
Kvaerner Fjellstrand c/o Finanshuset, 336 Madison Ave., Ste. 1101, 10017, pg. 768 **IT**
Kvaerner Inc., 150 E. 52nd St., 28th Floor, 10022, pg. 770 **IT**
Kvaerner Moss, Inc., 150 E. 52nd St., 28th Fl., 10022, pg. 770 **IT**
The Kyoei Life America Co., Ltd., 375 Fifth Ave., 20th Fl., 10017, pg. 776 **IT**
The Kyoei Life Insurance Co., Ltd.-New York Office, 575 Fifth Ave., 10017, pg. 776 **IT**
The Kyoei Mutual Fire & Marine Insurance Company, New York Representative Office, Graybar Bldg., Ste. 2058, 420 Lexington Ave., 10170, pg. 777 **IT**
Kyowa Hakko U.S.A., Inc., 599 Lexington Ave., Ste. 4103, 10022, pg. 778 **IT**
Kyowa Pharmaceutical Inc., 599 Lexington Ave., Ste. 4103, 10022, pg. 778 **IT**
L3 COMMUNICATIONS, 600 Third Ave., 10016, pg. 638 **PV**
LGT Asset Management, Inc., 375 Park Ave., Ste. 3401, 10152, pg. 809 **PV**
LTCB Latin America, Inc. (LLA), 527 Madison Ave., 26th Fl., 10022, pg. 816 **IT**
LTCB Trust Company, 165 Broadway, 10006, pg. 816 **IT**
LVMH Moet Hennessy Louis Vuitton, Ste. 1830, Two Park Ave., 10016, pg. 781 **IT**
Ladies' Home Journal, 125 Park Ave., 10017, pg. 1094 **PB**
Lady Footlocker, 233 Broadway, 10279, pg. 1777 **PB**
LADY MARLENE SALES CORP., 183 Madison Ave., 10016, pg. 642 **PV**
Lagardere Groupe North America, 1633 Broadway, 45th Fl., 10019, pg. 794 **IT**
Lalique North America, 41 Madison Ave., 8th Fl., 10010, pg. 797 **IT**
Lally, McFarland & Pantello Inc., 60 Madison Ave., 10010, pg. 601 **PV**
TONY LAMBERT COMPANY, 1450 Broadway, 39th Fl., 10018, pg. 644 **PV**
Lambesis, 885 Third Ave., Ste. 2900, 10022, pg. 644 **PV**
Lancaster Group Worldwide, 1325 Ave. of the Americas, 10020, pg. 185 **IT**
Lancaster Inc., 767 Fifth Ave., 10153, pg. 690 **PV**
LAND N SEA, INC., 1375 Broadway, 2nd Fl., 10018, pg. 645 **PV**
Landesbank Hessen-Thuringen Girozentrale New York Branch, 499 Park Ave., 10022, pg. 799 **IT**
Landesgirokasse Bank, 560 Lexington Ave., 5th Fl., 10022, pg. 800 **IT**
Aubrey G. Lanston & Co. Inc., One Chase Manhattan Plz., 53rd Fl., 10005, pg. 675 **IT**
JACK LENOR LARSEN, INC., 233 Spring St., 10013, pg. 652 **PV**
C.J. Lawrence, Morgan Grenfell Inc., Fl. 12/12M, 1290 Ave. of the Americas, 10104-0101, pg. 405 **IT**
Lazard Freres & Co., 30 Rockefeller Plaza, 10112, pg. 1027 **PV**
LAZARE KAPLAN INTL., INC., 529 Fifth Ave., 10017, pg. 981 **PV**
LEBHAR-FRIEDMAN, INC., 425 Park Ave., 10022-3556, pg. 656 **PV**
Lectorum Publications, 111 8th Ave., Ste. 804, 10011, pg. 1440 **PB**

Geographic Index-U.S.

LEE NATIONAL CORPORATION, 645 Fifth Ave., 8th Fl., 10022, pg. 658 — PV
Leff & Wolf Sportswear, Inc., 75 Ninth Ave., 3rd Fl., 10011, pg. 1192 — PV
Legend Capital Group, L.P., 150 E. 58th St., 10155, pg. 219 — PV
Legion Paper Corporation, 315 Park Ave. S., 10010-3680, pg. 467 — PV
Lehman Associates, Inc., 450 Seventh Ave., 45th. Fl., 10123, pg. 1125 — PV
Lehman Brothers, Three World Financial Center, 10285, pg. 987 — PB
LEHMAN BROTHERS HOLDINGS INC., Three World Financial Center, 10285, pg. 987 — PB
Lehman Brothers, Inc., 625 Madison Ave., 10022, pg. 987 — PB
Lehman Brothers International Limited, Three World Financial Center, 10285, pg. 987 — PB
Lehman Commercial Paper Inc., Three World Financial Center, 10285, pg. 987 — PB
Lehrer McGovern Bovis Inc., 387 Park Ave. South, 10016, pg. 1035 — IT
Lerner New York, 460 W. 33rd St., 5th Fl., 10001, pg. 995 — PB
THE LESLIE FAY COMPANIES, INC., 1412 Broadway, 10018, pg. 989 — PB
Leslie Fay Dress, 1412 Broadway, 10018, pg. 989 — PB
Leslie Fay Sportswear, 1412 Broadway, 10018, pg. 989 — PB
Leslie Fay II, 1412 Broadway, 10018, pg. 989 — PB
LEUCADIA NATIONAL CORPORATION, 315 Park Ave. S., 10010-3607, pg. 989 — PB
LEVEL EXPORT SALES CORP., 1460 Broadway, 10036, pg. 662 — PV
Lever Brothers Co., 390 Park Ave., 10022, pg. 1435 — IT
Lever Brothers Household Products Div., 390 Park Ave., 10022, pg. 1436 — IT
Lever Brothers Industrial Division, 390 Park Ave., 10022, pg. 1436 — IT
Larry Levine, 500 7th Ave., 10018, pg. 947 — PV
LEXINGTON PRECISION CORPORATION, 767 Third Ave., 10017, pg. 991 — PB
Liberty Fabrics, 295 Fifth Ave., 10016, pg. 340 — IT
Licensing Works!, 130 Fifth Ave., 10011, pg. 480 — PV
Life Extension Institute, 437 Madison Ave., 10022, pg. 1114 — PV
Life Magazine, Time & Life Bldg., Rockefeller Ctr., 10020, pg. 1613 — PB
Lifetime Television/ABC, 309 W. 49th St., 10019, pg. 512 — PB
Lifetime Television/ABC, 309 W. 49th St., 10019, pg. 516 — PB
Eli Lilly Interamerica, Inc., 691 Fifth Ave., 10022, pg. 993 — PB
Lilyette Brassiere Co., 200 Madison Ave., 10016, pg. 697 — PV
Lindenmeyr Book Publishing, 100 Park Ave., 10017, pg. 224 — PV
LINK Resources, 79 Fifth Ave., 10003, pg. 570 — PV
LION BRAND YARN CO., 34 W. 15th St., 10011, pg. 669 — PV
Lipha Pharmaceuticals, Inc., Nine W. 57th St., Ste. 3825, 10019-2701, pg. 812 — IT
Lippincott & Margulies, Inc., 499 Park Ave., 10022, pg. 1048 — PB
Lippincott-Raven Publishing, 1185 Ave. of the Americas, 10036, pg. 1513 — IT
Arthur D. Little, Inc., 237 Park Ave., 10017, pg. 670 — PV
Little, Brown & Co., 1271 Ave. of the Americas, 10020, pg. 1612 — PB
Little Simon, 1230 Ave. of the Americas, 10020, pg. 777 — PV
Liveright Publishing Corp., 500 Fifth Ave., 10110, pg. 807 — PV
LiveWire: Today's Families Online, 130 Fifth Ave., 10011, pg. 480 — PV
Liz & Co., 1441 Broadway, 10018, pg. 1006 — PB
Liz Claiborne Collection Division, 1441 Broadway, 10018, pg. 1006 — PB
Liz Claiborne Cosmetics, Inc., 1441 Broadway, 10018, pg. 1006 — PB
Liz Claiborne Dress Division, 1441 Broadway, 10018, pg. 1006 — PB
LIZ CLAIBORNE, INC., 1441 Broadway, 10018, pg. 1005 — PB
Liz Claiborne Retail Division, 1441 Broadway, 10081, pg. 1006 — PB
Liz Claiborne Shoe Division, 1441 Broadway, 10018, pg. 1006 — PB
Liz Claiborne Suit Division, 1441 Broadway, 10018, pg. 1006 — PB
Lizsport Division, 1441 Broadway, 10018, pg. 1006 — PB
Lizwear Division, 1441 Broadway, 10018, pg. 1006 — PB
Lloyds Bank Plc., 575 Fifth Ave., 10017, pg. 813 — IT
Loewe Fashions Incorporated, 49 E. 57th St., 10022, pg. 781 — IT
LOEWS CORPORATION, 667 Madison Ave., 10021-8087, pg. 1010 — PB
Loews Hotels, 667 Madison Ave., 10021-8087, pg. 1011 — PB
Loews New York, Lexington Ave. & 51st St., 10017, pg. 1011 — PB
Loews Theatre Management Corp., 711 Fifth Ave., 10022, pg. 1282 — IT
Logica Inc., 5 Penn Plaza, 21st Fl., 10001, pg. 814 — IT
Lois/EJL Direct, 40 W. 57th St., 10019, pg. 1011 — PB
Lois/EJL New York, 40 W. 57th St., 10019, pg. 1011 — PB
LOIS/USA INC., 40 W. 57th St., 6th Fl., 10019, pg. 1011 — PB
London & Leeds (USA) Corporation, One Wall St. Court, 11th Floor, 82 Beaver St., 10005, pg. 788 — IT

LONDON FOG INDUSTRIES, INC., 8 W. 40th St., 10018, pg 673 — PV
London Records, 810 Seventh Ave., 10019, pg. 1052 — IT
Long-Term Credit Bank of Japan - Americas Division, 165 Broadway, 10006, pg. 816 — IT
Long-Term Credit Bank of Japan, Limited - New York, One Liberty Plaza, 165 Broadway, 10006, pg. 816 — IT
Longevity International, Ltd., 277 Park Ave., 4th Fl., 10172-0003, pg. 444 — PV
LORAL SPACE & COMMUNICATIONS, 600 Third Ave., 36th Fl., 10016, pg. 1014 — PB
LORD ABBETT & CO., The General Motors Bldg., 767 Fifth Ave., 10153-0203, pg. 675 — PV
Lord Abbett Bond-Debenture Fund, Inc., 767 Fifth Ave., 10153-0203, pg. 675 — PV
Lord Abbett Developing Growth Fund, Inc., 767 Fifth Ave., 10153-0203, pg. 675 — PV
Lord Abbett Global Fund, Inc., 767 Fifth Ave., 10153-0203, pg. 675 — PV
Lord Abbett Securities Trust, 767 Fifth Ave., 10153-0203, pg. 675 — PV
Lord Abbett Tax-Free Income Fund, Inc., 767 Fifth Ave., 10153-0203, pg. 675 — PV
Lord Abbett U.S. Government Securities Fund, Inc., 767 Fifth Ave., 10153-0203, pg. 675 — PV
Lord & Taylor, 424 Fifth Ave., 10018, pg. 1064 — PV
The Lord Group, 810 Seventh Ave., 10019, pg. 325 — PV
LOT Polish Airlines SA, 500 Fifth Ave., Ste. 408, 10110-0068, pg. 1062 — IT
LOTAS MINARD PATTON MCGIVER, 152 W. 57th St., 10019, pg. 677 — PV
Lothrop, Lee & Shepard Books, 1350 Ave. of the Americas, 10019, pg. 515 — PV
Louis Vuitton North America, Inc., 130 East 59th St., 10022, pg. 781 — IT
Louisiana Community Bar & Grill, 622 Broadway, 10012, pg. 130 — PB
Lowe & Partners/SMS, 1114 Ave. of the Americas, 10036-7796, pg. 678 — PV
Lowe Direct, c/o The Lowe Group, 1114 Ave. of the Americas, 21st Fl., 10036-7796, pg. 678 — PV
THE LOWE GROUP, 1114 Ave. of the Americas, 10036-7796, pg. 677 — PV
LOWE MCADAMS HEALTHCARE, 1740 Broadway, 10019, pg. 678 — PV
Lucky Goldstar International America, Inc., 1385 Broadway, Ste. 606, 10018, pg. 779 — IT
LUCKY WINNER, INC., 525 Seventh Ave., 10018, pg. 379 — PV
Ludgate Communications, Inc., 830 Third Ave., 10022, pg. 1157 — PV
LUKENHEIMER ENERGO VALVES INC., 767 Third Ave., 14th Fl., 10017, pg. 680 — PV
Lutece, 249 East 50th St., 10022, pg. 130 — PB
Lynch & Mayer, Inc, 520 Madison Ave., 10022, pg. 998 — PB
Lyons Lavey Nickel Swift, Inc., 220 E. 42 St., 10017, pg. 1224 — PB
MAN Capital Corporation, 17 State St., 10004, pg. 826 — IT
M/B Interactive, 122 E. 25th St., 10016, pg. 740 — PV
MC2 Adams, 1740 Broadway, 10019, pg. 679 — PV
MCS Business Solutions, Inc., 633 Third Ave., 10017, pg. 262 — PV
MG Electric Power, Inc., 520 Madison Ave., 10022, pg. 862 — PV
MH Leasing International, 270 Park Ave., 31 Fl., 10017, pg. 338 — PV
MIC-USA Inc., 153 E. 53rd St., Ste. 5900, 10022, pg. 867 — PV
MRB Group, Inc., 380 Madison Ave., 10017, pg. 1483 — IT
MTBC, Finance, 520 Madison Ave., 39th Fl., 10022, pg. 876 — IT
MTI/THE IMAGE GROUP, INC., One Dag Hammarskjold Plaza, 10016, pg. 688 — PV
MTI Systems Div., One Pennsylvania Plaza, 250 West 34th St., Ste. 2127, 10119, pg. 135 — PB
MTV: Music Television, 1515 Broadway, 10036, pg. 779 — PV
MTV Networks, 1515 Broadway, 10036, pg. 779 — PV
MacAndrews & Forbes Group, Inc., 36 E. 63rd St., 10021, pg. 689 — PV
MACANDREWS & FORBES HOLDINGS INC., 38 E. 63rd St., 10021, pg. 689 — PV
MACDONALD COMMUNICATIONS, 135 W. 50th St., 60th Fl., 10020, pg. 691 — PV
MacKay-Shields Financial Corp., Nine W. 57th St., 10019, pg. 795 — PV
Mackintosh of New England, Co., 463 Seventh Ave., 10013, pg. 233 — PB
THE MACMANUS GROUP, INC., 1675 Broadway, 10019-5865, pg. 692 — PV
Macmillan General Reference USA, 1633 Broadway, 10019, pg. 777 — PV
Macmillan Library Reference USA, 1633 Broadway, 10019, pg. 777 — PV
Macmillan/McGraw-Hill School Publishing Company, 1221 Ave. of the Americas, 10020-1095, pg. 1070 — PB
Macmillan Reference USA, 1633 Broadway, 10019, pg. 777 — PV
MACNAMARA, STEWART & SAPERSTEIN, 369 Lexington Ave., 10017, pg. 692 — PV
Macy's East, 17th Fl., 151 W. 34th St., 10001, pg. 618 — PB
Mad Magazine, E. C. Creations, Inc., 1700 Broadway, 10019, pg. 1614 — PB
Mademoiselle, 350 Madison Ave., 10017, pg. 20 — PB
Madison Square Garden Center Inc., Two Pennsylvania Plaza 10121, pg. 288 — PB
Madison Square Garden Corporation, Two Pennsylvania Plaza 14th Fl., 10121, pg. 288 — PB
Madison Square Garden Network, Four Pennsylvania Plaza, 4th Fl, 10001, pg. 288 — PB

Mafco Consolidated Group Inc., 35 E. 62nd St., 10021, pg. 690 — PV
Magazine Group, 555 Broadway, 10012, pg. 1440 — PB
Magazine Services Inc., 15 W. 44th St., 10036, pg. 623 — PV
MAIDENFORM WORLDWIDE, 200 Madison Ave., 24th Fl., 10016, pg. 697 — PV
MAJORICA JEWELRY LTD., 366 Fifth Ave., Ste. 507, 10001, pg. 697 — PV
Makhteshim Agan of North America Inc., 551 Fifth Ave., Ste. 1100, 10176, pg. 830 — IT
Malev Hungarian Airlines, U.S. Office, Rockefeller Center, 630 Fifth Ave., Rm. 1900, 10111, pg. 834 — IT
Managing Automation, Five Penn Plaza, 10001, pg. 1082 — PV
Manchester Guardian, 19 W. 44th St.; Ste. 1613, 10036, pg. 577 — IT
Manhattan Accessories Div., 1114 Ave. of the Americas, 10036, pg. 1429 — PB
Manhattan Factory, 417 Fifth Ave., 10016, pg. 1429 — PB
Manhattan Industries Intl. Div., 1114 Ave. of the Americas, 10036, pg. 1429 — PB
The Manhattan Shirt Co., 1114 Ave. of the Americas, 10036, pg. 1429 — PB
MARCUS BROTHERS TEXTILES, INC., 1460 Broadway, 10036, pg. 702 — PV
Mardev, 475 Park Ave. South, 2nd Fl., 10016-6901, pg. 1094 — IT
MARGEOTES/FERTITTA & PARTNERS INC., 411 Lafayette St., 10003, pg. 702 — PV
Margeotes Interactive, 411 Lafayette St., 10003, pg. 702 — PV
Marie Claire, 250 W. 55th St., 10019, pg. 518 — PV
Marine Midland Capital Markets Corporation, 140 Broadway, 10th Floor, 10015, pg. 581 — IT
Market Facts-New York, Inc., 902 Broadway, 10010, pg. 1047 — PB
Market Statistics, 355 Park Ave. South, 10010, pg. 1446 — PV
Marketing Computers, 1515 Broadway, 10036, pg. 1446 — PV
Marks & Spencer Finance Inc., 14th Fl., 346 Madison Ave., 10017, pg. 843 — IT
Marks & Spencer US Holdings Inc., 346 Madison Ave., 10017, pg. 843 — IT
Marquardt & Co., 161 6th Ave., 10013, pg. 223 — PV
MARSH & MCLENNAN COMPANIES, INC., 1166 Ave. of the Americas, 10036, pg. 1048 — PB
MARSHALL JACCOMA MITCHELL ADVERTISING, 41 Madison Ave., 10010, pg. 708 — PV
J.B. MARTIN COMPANY, Ten E. 53rd St., Ste. 3100, 10022, pg. 709 — PV
Sherri Martin, 1400 Broadway, 10018, pg. 316 — PV
Martinair Holland, Ste. 6411, 5 World Trade Center, 10090, pg. 719 — IT
Marubeni America Corporation, 450 Lexington Ave., 10017-3904, pg. 844 — IT
MARVEL ENTERTAINMENT GROUP, 387 Park Ave. S., 10016, pg. 1052 — PB
Marvella Inc., 16 E. 34th St., 10016, pg. 757 — PV
MASTER INDUSTRIES CORP., 350 Fifth Ave., 10118, pg. 713 — PV
Master Trouser/ Master Apparel/ Botany 500 Slacks Ltd., 350 Fifth Ave., 10118, pg. 713 — PV
Maybelline, Inc., 575 Fifth Ave., 10017, pg. 819 — IT
MCCABE & COMPANY, 655 Madison Ave., 15th Fl., 10021, pg. 719 — PV
McCall's Magazine, 375 Lexington Ave., 10017, pg. 190 — PV
McCann-Erickson Worldwide, 750 Third Ave., 10017, pg. 909 — PV
MCCRORY CORPORATION, 1700 Broadway, Ste. 1403, 10019, pg. 720 — PV
Margaret K. McElderry Books, 1230 Ave. of the Americas, 10020, pg. 777 — PV
Wm. H. McGee & Co., Inc., Four World Trade Ctr., Ste. 6274, 10048, pg. 1231 — PB
McGraw-Hill Aviation Week Group, 1221 Ave. of the Americas, 10020, pg. 1070 — PB
McGraw-Hill Broadcasting Co., Inc., 1221 Ave. of the Americas, 10020, pg. 1070 — PB
McGraw-Hill College Division, 1221 Ave. of the Americas, 10020, pg. 1070 — PB
THE MCGRAW-HILL COMPANIES, 1221 Ave. of the Americas, 10020, pg. 1069 — PB
McGraw-Hill Computers & Communications Information Group, 1221 Ave. of the Americas, 10020, pg. 1070 — PB
McGraw-Hill Construction Information Group, 1221 Ave. of the Americas, 10020, pg. 1070 — PB
McGraw-Hill Financial Information Services Group, 65 Broadway, 10004, pg. 1071 — PB
McGraw-Hill Professional Publishing Group, 1221 Ave. of the Americas, 10020, pg. 1070 — PB
McGraw-Hill Publications Services Group, 1221 Ave. of the Americas, 10020, pg. 1071 — PB
McGraw-Hill Securities Trading, Inc., 25 Broadway, 10004, pg. 1071 — PB
MCKINSEY & COMPANY, INC., 55 E. 52nd St., 10022, pg. 723 — PV
John J. McMullen Associates, One World Trade Center, 10048, pg. 308 — PV
Media Direct Partners, Incorporated, 650 Fifth Ave., 10019, pg. 726 — PV
MEDIA FIRST INTERNATIONAL, INC., 205 Lexington Ave., 11th Fl., 10016, pg. 726 — PV
MEDIA INCORPORATED, 650 Fifth Ave., 10019, pg. 726 — PV
MEDIA RESOURCES INTERNATIONAL, 275 Madison Ave., 4th Fl., 10016, pg. 727 — PV
Mediaweek, 1515 Broadway, 10036, pg. 1446 — IT

PB - U.S. Public Companies Volume
PV - U.S. Private Companies Volume
IT - International Public & Private Companies Volume

Geographic Index-U.S.

Meiji Seika (U.S.A.) Inc., 733 Third Ave., Ste. 1910, 10017, pg. 855 — **IT**

The Meijiseimei Asset Management of America, Ltd., 630 Fifth Ave., Ste. 2650, 10111, pg. 854 — **IT**

The Meijiseimei Insurance Agency of New York, Inc., 630 Fifth Ave., 26th-Fl., 10111, pg. 854 — **IT**

The Meijiseimei Realty of America, Inc., 630 Fifth Ave., 26th Fl., 10111, pg. 854 — **IT**

MELLON CORPORATION, 351 W. 35th St., 10001, pg. 730 — **PV**

Mellon Securities Trust Co., 120 Broadway, Ste. 3333, 10271, pg. 1086 — **PB**

Members Only By Europe Craft, 475 Fifth Ave., 3rd Fl., 10017, pg. 129 — **PB**

MENDIK MANAGEMENT CO., INC., 330 Madison Ave., 10017, pg. 731 — **PV**

Men's Journal, 1290 Ave. of the Americas, 10104, pg. 1162 — **PV**

Mercer Consulting Group, Inc., 1166 Ave. of Americas, 10036, pg. 1049 — **PB**

Mercer Management Consulting, Inc., 1166 Ave. of Americas, 10036, pg. 1049 — **PB**

William M. Mercer Companies, Inc., 1166 Ave. of the Americas, 10036, pg. 1049 — **PB**

Meridian Hotels, 420 Lexington Ave., Ste. 1718, 10170, pg. 556 — **IT**

Meridian Sports/Water Sports Group, 625 Madison Ave., 10022, pg. 689 — **PV**

Merita Bank Ltd. New York Branch, 437 Madison Ave., 10022, pg. 859 — **IT**

Merkley Newman Harty, 200 Varick St., 10014, pg. 1224 — **PB**

Merrill Corporation, 200 N. Hudson St., 10013, pg. 1097 — **PB**

MERRILL LYNCH & CO., INC., World Fin. Ctr., N. Tower, 250 Vesey St., 10281, pg. 1097 — **PB**

Merrill Lynch Capital Services, Inc., World Fin. Ctr. N. Tower, 7th Fl., 10281, pg. 1097 — **PB**

Merrill Lynch Derivative Products, Inc., World Fin. Ctr., N. Tower, 10081-1323, pg. 1097 — **PB**

Merrill Lynch Fiduciary Services, Inc., 717 Fifth Ave., 16th Fl., 10022, pg. 1098 — **PB**

Merrill Lynch Futures Inc., Two Broadway, 21st Fl., 10004, pg. 1098 — **PB**

Merrill Lynch Government Securities, Inc., World Fin. Center N. Tower, 10281, pg. 1097 — **PB**

Merrill Lynch Group, Inc., World Fin. Ctr. N. Tower, 10281, pg. 1097 — **PB**

Merrill Lynch, Hubbard, Inc., World Financial Ctr., 225 Liberty St., 10080, pg. 1098 — **PB**

Merrill Lynch International Bank, N. Tower World Fin. Center, 10281, pg. 1097 — **PB**

Merrill Lynch International, Inc., Merrill Lynch Headquarters, 250 Vesey St., 10081-1212, pg. 1098 — **PB**

Merrill Lynch Investment Partners, Inc., ML World Headquarters, WFC S. Tower-6th Fl., 10080-0601, pg. 1098 — **PB**

Merrill Lynch, Pierce, Fenner & Smith, Inc., World Fin. Ctr., 250 Vesey St., 10281, pg. 1098 — **PB**

Merrill Lynch Specialists Inc., World Fin. Ctr., N. Tower, 250 Vesey St., 10281, pg. 1098 — **PB**

Messner Vetere Berger McNamee Schmetterer/EURO RSCG, 350 Hudson St., 10014, pg. 602 — **IT**

Metallbank Capital Corporation, 520 Madison Ave., 10022, pg. 861 — **IT**

Metallgesellschaft Capital Corp., 520 Madison Ave., 10022, pg. 861 — **IT**

Metallgesellschaft Corp., 520 Madison Ave., 27th Fl., 10022, pg. 861 — **IT**

Metallgesellschaft Emerging Markets, Inc., 520 Madison Ave., 10022, pg. 862 — **IT**

Metallgesellschaft Trade Services Co., 520 Madison Ave., 27th Fl., 10022, pg. 862 — **IT**

Metallgesellschaft Trading Corp., 520 Madison Ave., 27th Fl., 10022, pg. 862 — **IT**

METALLURG, INC., Six E. 43rd St., 10017, pg. 735 — **PV**

MetLife Securities, Inc., One Madison Ave., 10010, pg. 738 — **PV**

Metro Color ROP Buy, Ten E. 38th St., 10016, pg. 739 — **PV**

Metro-North Commuter Railroad Company, 347 Madison Ave., 10017, pg. 739 — **PV**

Metropolitan Cafe, 959 1st Ave., 10022, pg. 130 — **PB**

Metropolitan Home Magazine, 1633 Broadway, 10019, pg. 795 — **PV**

Metropolitan Insurance & Annuity Co., One Madison Ave., 10010, pg. 737 — **PV**

Metropolitan Life Holdings, Ltd., One Madison Ave., 10010-3690, pg. 737 — **PV**

METROPOLITAN LIFE INSURANCE CO., One Madison Ave., 10010-3690, pg. 737 — **PV**

METROPOLITAN SUNDAY NEWSPAPERS, INC., Ten E. 38th St., 10016, pg. 739 — **PV**

Metropolitan Tower Life Insurance Co., One Madison Ave., 10010, pg. 737 — **PV**

METROPOLITAN TRANSPORTATION AUTHORITY, 347 Madison Ave., 10017, pg. 739 — **PV**

MEZZINA/BROWN INC., 401 Park Ave. S., 10016, pg. 739 — **PV**

Michelin Corporation, 515 Madison Ave., 40th Floor, 10022, pg. 322 — **IT**

MICKELBERRY COMMUNICATIONS, INC., 405 Park Ave., 10022, pg. 741 — **PV**

Mickey & Company, 1411 Broadway, 10018, pg. 519 — **PB**

Mid Pacific Air Corporation, 100 Park Ave., 10017, pg. 603 — **PV**

Midland International Trade Services (USA) Corporation, 5th Fl., 140 Broadway, 10005, pg. 581 — **IT**

Midland Walwyn Capital Corporation, 712 Fifth Avenue, Ste. 8D, 19919, pg. 865 — **IT**

Mikimoto (America) Co. Ltd., 40 W.57th St., 24th Fl., 10019-4001, pg. 866 — **IT**

MILLER ADVERTISING AGENCY INC., 71 Fifth Ave., 10003, pg. 746 — **PV**

Miller Freeman, 1515 Broadway, 10036, pg. 1443 — **IT**

Monroe G. Milstein, Inc., 263 W. 38th St., 10018, pg. 268 — **PB**

MINERALS TECHNOLOGIES, INC., 405 Lexington Ave., 20th Fl., 10174, pg. 1115 — **PB**

Minet, Inc., 1114 Ave. of the Americas, 10036, pg. 118 — **IT**

Mingo Oxygen Company, 110 E. 59th St., 30th Fl., 10022, pg. 1726 — **PV**

Mining Development Co., 180 Maiden Ln., 10038, pg. 138 — **PB**

Minitel USA, 888 Seventh Ave., 10106, pg. 504 — **IT**

Mirabella, 1633 Broadway, 10019, pg. 795 — **IT**

Miramax Films, Inc., 375 Greenwich St., 10013, pg. 514 — **PB**

Mission Exploration Co., 180 Maiden Ln., 10038, pg. 138 — **PB**

Misty Harbor, 512 Seventh Ave., 9th Fl., 10018, pg. 49 — **PV**

Mitchell Hutchins Asset Management Inc., 1285 Avenue of the Americas, 10019, pg. 1253 — **PB**

Mitchell Hutchins Institutional Investors Inc., 1285 Ave. of the Americas, 10019, pg. 1253 — **PB**

Mitrans Corporation, Ste. 1908, One Penn Plaza, 10119, pg. 874 — **IT**

Mitsubishi Cable America, Inc., 520 Madison Ave., 17th Fl., 10022, pg. 870 — **PB**

Mitsubishi Estate New York, Inc., 30 Rockefeller Plaza, Ste. 4325, 10112, pg. 873 — **IT**

Mitsubishi Heavy Industries America, Inc. (MHIA), 630 Fifth Ave., 10111, pg. 874 — **IT**

Mitsubishi International Corporation, 520 Madison Ave., 10022, pg. 871 — **IT**

Mitsubishi Materials, 399 Park Ave., 38th Fl., 10022, pg. 875 — **IT**

Mitsubishi Oil America, 1270 Ave. of the Americas, 10020, pg. 876 — **IT**

Mitsubishi Rayon America, Inc., 520 Madison Ave., 10022, pg. 876 — **IT**

Mitsubishi Trust & Banking Corporation (U.S.A.), 520 Madison Ave., 39th Fl., 10022, pg. 876 — **IT**

Mitsui & Co. (U.S.A.), Inc., Pan American Bldg., 200 Park Ave., 10166, pg. 879 — **IT**

Mitsui Fudosan (USA), Inc., 1251 Avenue of the Americas, 10020-1104, pg. 882 — **IT**

Mitsui T & B Futures, Two World Financial Center, 41st Fl., 225 Liberty St., 10281, pg. 883 — **IT**

Mitsui T & B Options Inc., Two World Financial Center, 41st Fl., 225 Liberty St., 10281, pg. 883 — **IT**

The Mitsui Trust and Banking Company - New York, 1251 Ave. of the Americas, 39th Fl., 10020-1104, pg. 883 — **IT**

Mitsui Trust Bank (U.S.A.), Two World Financial Center, 41st Floor, 225 Liberty St., 10281, pg. 883 — **IT**

Mitsui Trust & Banking Company, Limited, One World Fin. Ctr., 21st Fl., 200 Liberty St., 10281, pg. 883 — **IT**

Mitsukoshi (U.S.A.) Inc., 12 E. 49th St., 17th Fl., 10017, pg. 883 — **IT**

HENRY MODELL & COMPANY, INC., 498 7th Ave., 10018, pg. 754 — **PV**

Modem Media New York, 150 E. 42nd St., 10017-5612, pg. 1641 — **IT**

Modern Bride Magazine, 717 5th Ave., 10022, pg. 1328 — **PB**

Modern Plastics, 1221 Ave. of the Americas, 10020, pg. 1071 — **PB**

Modern Publishing, 155 E. 55th St., 10022, pg. 1120 — **PV**

Monarch Crown Corporation, 345 Park Ave., 10154, pg. 254 — **PB**

THE MONET GROUP, INC., 350 Fifth Ave., 16th Fl., 10118, pg. 757 — **PV**

Monet Jewelers, 350 5th ave., 16th Fl., 10118, pg. 757 — **PV**

Money, Time & Life Bldg., Rockefeller Center, 10020, pg. 1613 — **PB**

Monitor Surety Managers, Inc., 122 E. 42nd St., Ste. 1518, 10168, pg. 215 — **PB**

Samuel Montagu Inc., 250 Park Ave., 10177, pg. 580 — **IT**

MONY Advisers, Inc., 1740 Broadway, 10019, pg. 769 — **PV**

MONY Credit Corporation, 1740 Broadway, 10019, pg. 769 — **PV**

MONY Funding, Inc., 1740 Broadway, 10019, pg. 769 — **PV**

MONY Life Insurance Co. of America, 1740 Broadway, 10019, pg. 769 — **PV**

MONY Realty Partners, Inc., 1740 Broadway, 10019, pg. 769 — **PV**

MONY Securities Corp., 1740 Broadway, 10019, pg. 769 — **PV**

MONY Ventures, Inc., 1740 Broadway, 10019, pg. 769 — **PV**

Moody's Investors Service, Inc., 99 Church St., 10007, pg. 536 — **PV**

Morgan Futures Corp., 60 Wall St., 10260, pg. 1129 — **PB**

Morgan Grenfell Capital Management Incorporated, 885 Third Ave. 32nd Fl., 10022, pg. 405 — **IT**

Morgan Guaranty Trust Company, 9 W. 57th St., 10019, pg. 1129 — **PB**

Morgan Guaranty Trust Company, 522 Fifth Ave., 10036, pg. 1129 — **PB**

Morgan Guaranty Trust Company, 616 Madison Ave., 10153, pg. 1129 — **PB**

Morgan Guaranty Trust Company of New York, 60 Wall St., 10260, pg. 1129 — **PB**

J.P. Morgan Capital Corporation, 60 Wall St., 10260-0060, pg. 1129 — **PB**

J.P. MORGAN CO. INCORPORATED, 60 Wall St., 10260-0060, pg. 1129 — **PB**

J.P. Morgan Investment Management Inc., 522 Fifth Ave., 10036, pg. 1129 — **PB**

J.P. Morgan Securities Inc., 60 Wall St., 10260, pg. 1129 — **PB**

Morgan Stanley & Co. Incorporated, 1585 Broadway, 10036, pg. 1132 — **PB**

Morgan Stanley Asset Management, Inc., 1585 Broadway, 10036, pg. 1132 — **PB**

Morgan Stanley Capital Group Inc., 1585 Broadway, 10036, pg. 1132 — **PB**

Morgan Stanley Capital I Inc., 1585 Broadway, 10036, pg. 1132 — **PB**

Morgan Stanley Capital Services Inc., 1585 Broadway, 10036, pg. 1132 — **PB**

MORGAN STANLEY DEAN WITTER & CO., 1585 Broadway, 10036, pg. 1132 — **PB**

Morgan Stanley Group Inc., 1585 Broadway, 10036, pg. 1132 — **PB**

Morgan Stanley International Inc., 1585 Broadway, 10036, pg. 1132 — **PB**

The Morgan Stanley Leveraged Equity Fund L.P., 1251 Avenue of the Americas, 10020, pg. 357 — **PB**

The Morgan Stanley Leveraged Mezzanine Fund L.P., 1251 Avenue of the Americas, 10020, pg. 357 — **PB**

The Morgan Stanley Leveraged Senior Debt Fund L.P., 1251 Avenue of the Americas, 10020, pg. 357 — **PB**

Morgan Stanley Realty, Inc., 1585 Broadway, 10036, pg. 1132 — **PB**

Morrow Junior Books, 1350 Ave. of the Americas, 10019, pg. 515 — **PV**

William Morrow & Co., Inc., 1350 Ave. of the Americas, 10019, pg. 515 — **PV**

MORSE DIESEL INTERNATIONAL, INC., 1633 Broadway, 24th Fl., 10019, pg. 762 — **PV**

Moss/Dragoti, 11 Madison Ave., 10010, pg. 117 — **IT**

Mother Earth News, 49 E. 21st St., 11th Fl., 10010, pg. 1056 — **PV**

Motor Boating & Sailing, 250 W. 55th St., 10019, pg. 517 — **PV**

Motorola SMR, Inc., 110 E. 59th St., 10022, pg. 1138 — **PB**

Motown Record Company, J.P., 825 Eighth Ave., 10019, pg. 1052 — **PV**

Mount Vernon Mills Sales Corp., 1450 Broadway 24th fl., 10018, pg. 836 — **PV**

MOVIE STAR, INC., 136 Madison Ave., 10016, pg. 1140 — **PV**

Moygashel USA Inc., 80 W. 40th St., Third Fl., 10018, pg. 798 — **IT**

MR. CHRISTMAS INC., 41 Madison Ave., 10010, pg. 765 — **PV**

MUDD JEANS, INC., 1407 Broadway, Rm. 1107, 10018, pg. 49 — **PV**

Mulberry Street Casuals Ltd., 512 Seventh Ave., 9th Fl, 10018, pg. 49 — **PB**

Muller Data Corp., 90 5th Ave., 10011, pg. 1600 — **PB**

Munich American Reinsurance Co. (Marc), 560 Lexington Ave., 10017, pg. 897 — **IT**

Murdoch Magazines, 755 Second Ave., 10017, pg. 925 — **PV**

MUSEUM BOUTIQUE INTERCONTINENTAL, LTD., 26 E. 64th St., 10021, pg. 768 — **PV**

MUSIC SALES CORPORATION, 257 Park Ave. S., 20th Fl., 10010, pg. 768 — **PV**

THE MUTUAL LIFE INSURANCE COMPANY OF NEW YORK, 1740 Broadway, 10019, pg. 769 — **PV**

MUTUAL OF AMERICA LIFE INSURANCE COMPANY, 320 Park Ave., 10022, pg. 769 — **PV**

NAL/Penguin Inc., 1633 Broadway, 10019, pg. 1027 — **IT**

NAT Capital Corp., 114 West 47th St., Ste. 2400, 10036, pg. 1347 — **IT**

NBC Holdings USA, Inc., 125 W. 55th St., 10019, pg. 907 — **PB**

NEC Industries, Inc., 10 E. 50th St., 25th Fl., 10022, pg. 900 — **IT**

NKK America Inc., 450 Park Ave., 10022, pg. 902 — **IT**

NLI Asset Management Corporation, Ste. 5220, 1251 Ave. of the Americas, 10020-1195, pg. 935 — **IT**

NLI Properties, Ste. 5230, 1251 Ave. of the Americas, 10020-1191, pg. 935 — **IT**

NLI Research Institute, Ste. 5240, 1251 Ave. of the Americas, 10020-1186, pg. 935 — **IT**

NM Funds Management (North America) Inc., 135 W. 50th St., 6th Fl., 10020, pg. 908 — **IT**

NMU Marketing Information Services, 11 W. 42 St., 10036-8088, pg. 1446 — **IT**

NS Finance, Inc., c/o Nippon Steel U.S.A., Inc., Ten E. 50th St., 29th Fl., 10022, pg. 940 — **IT**

NS Finance III, Inc., c/o Nippon Steel U.S.A., Inc., Ten E. 50th St., 29th Fl., 10022, pg. 940 — **IT**

NS Invest, Inc., c/o Nippon Steel U.S.A., Inc., Ten E. 50th St., 29th Fl., 10022, pg. 940 — **IT**

NS Kote, Inc., c/o Nippon Steel U.S.A., Inc., Ten E. 50th St., 29th Fl., 10022, pg. 940 — **IT**

NS Tek, c/o Nippon Steel U.S.A., Inc., Ten E. 50th St., 29th Fl., 10022, pg. 940 — **IT**

NTT America, Inc., 101 Park Avenue, 41st Fl., 10178, pg. 941 — **IT**

NYK Bulkship (USA) Inc., 150 E. 52nd St., 9th Floor, 10022, pg. 941 — **IT**

NYK International (USA) Inc., 666 Fifth Ave., 12th Fl., 10103, pg. 941 — **IT**

NYT Broadcast Holdings, Inc., 229 W. 43rd St., 10036, pg. 1175 — **PB**

NYT Custom Publishing, 122 E. 42nd St., 10168, pg. 1174 — **PB**

Nabisco International Incorporated, 345 Park Ave., 10154, pg. 1355 — **PB**

Namic Caribe, Inc., c/o Schneider/Namic, 235 E. 42nd St., 10017, pg. 1284 — **PB**

Namic Eireann B.V., c/o Schneider/Namic, 235 E. 42nd St., 10017, pg. 1284 — **PB**

Namic Eireann Limited, c/o Schneider/Namic, 235 E. 42nd St., 10017, pg. 1284 — **PB**

Namic International, Inc., c/o Schneider/Namic, 235 E. 42nd St., 10017, pg. 1284 — **PB**

Namic Worldwide B.V., c/o Schneider/Namic, 235 E. 42nd St., 10017, pg. 1284 — **PB**

PB - *U.S. Public Companies Volume*
PV - *U.S. Private Companies Volume*
IT - *International Public & Private Companies Volume*

Geographic Index-U.S.

NEW YORK DIRECTORY OF CORPORATE AFFILIATIONS

Nanto Bank-New York Representative Office, Two World Financial Center, 225 Liberty St., 36th Floor, 10281, pg. 906 **IT**
Nasinsa Securities, 21 E. 63rd St., 10021, pg. 904 **IT**
The National Association for Female Executives, Inc., 135 W. 50th St., 16th Fl., 10020, pg. 691 **PV**
National Bank of Pakistan, P.O. Box 500, 100 Wall Street, 10005, pg. 908 **IT**
National Bank of Pakistan, One United Nations Plaza, 44 E. First Ave., 10017, pg. 908 **IT**
NATIONAL BASKETBALL ASSOCIATION, Olympic Tower, 645 Fifth Ave., 10022, pg. 780 **PV**
National Benefit Life Insurance Co., Two Park Ave., 10016, pg. 1633 **PB**
National Broadcast Unit, 101 Park Ave., 3rd Fl., 10178-0065, pg. 1641 **PB**
National Broadcasting Co., Inc., 30 Rockefeller Plaza, 10112, pg. 712 **PB**
NATIONAL BULK CARRIERS, INC., 1345 Ave. of the Americas, 34th Fl., 10105, pg. 780 **PV**
National Cable, 125 W. 55th St., 10019, pg. 335 **PB**
National Canada Business Corp., 125 W. 55th St., 10019, pg. 907 **IT**
National Canada Corporation, 125 W. 55th St., 10019, pg. 907 **IT**
National Canada Finance Corporation, 125 W. 55th St., 10019, pg. 907 **IT**
National Discount Brokers, Seven Hanover Sq., 10004, pg. 1467 **PB**
National Dynamics, 1120 Park Ave., 10128, pg. 1025 **PV**
The National Enquirer, 600 E. Coast Ave., 10170, pg. 87 **PB**
National Federation of Community Development Credit Unions, 120 Wall St., 10th Fl., 10005, pg. 288 **PV**
NATIONAL FOOTBALL LEAGUE PROPERTIES, INC., 280 Park Ave., 10017, pg. 783 **PV**
NATIONAL INCOME REALTY TRUST, 280 Park Ave., 20th Fl., E., 10017-1216, pg. 1157 **PB**
National Law Publishing Co., 345 Park Ave. S., 10010, pg. 956 **IT**
NATIONAL RESTAURANT MANAGEMENT, INC., 162 W.34th St., 10001, pg. 786 **PV**
NATIONAL SPINNING CO., INC., 111 W. 40th St., 10018, pg. 786 **PV**
National Union Fire Ins. Co. of Pittsburgh, Pa., 70 Pine St., 10270, pg. 84 **PB**
National Yarn Crafts, 111 W. 40th St., 10018, pg. 787 **PV**
NationsBank International, 44 Wall St., 10005, pg. 1165 **PB**
Native Textiles, 16 E. 34th St., 10016, pg. 1684 **PB**
NatWest Markets Group Inc., 175 Water St., 10038, pg. 911 **IT**
NAUTICA ENTERPRISES, INC., 40 W. 57th St., 10019, pg. 1167 **PB**
NedShip International, Inc., The Chrysler Bldg., 405 Lexington Ave., Ste. 31-02, 10174, pg. 1082 **IT**
New Brook Paper, 171 Madison Ave., Rm. 1101, 10016-5110, pg. 1102 **PV**
New Frontiers, 12 E. 33rd St., 11th Fl., 10016, pg. 971 **IT**
New Hampshire Insurance Group, 70 Pine St., 10270, pg. 84 **PB**
New Line Cinema Corporation, 888 Seventh Ave., 20th Fl., 10106, pg. 1614 **PB**
New Line Distribution, Inc., 575 Eighth Ave., 16th Fl., 10018, pg. 1615 **PB**
New Line Home Video, Inc., 575 Eighth Ave., 16th Fl., 10018, pg. 1615 **PB**
New Line International Releasing, Inc., 575 Eighth Ave., 16th Fl., 10018, pg. 1615 **PB**
New Line Marketing, Inc., 575 Eighth Ave., 16th Fl., 10018, pg. 1615 **PB**
New Line Productions, Inc., 575 Eighth Ave., 16th Fl., 10018, pg. 1615 **PB**
NEW PLAN REALTY TRUST, 1120 Ave. of the Americas, 10036, pg. 1172 **PB**
New Plan Securities Corp., 1120 Avenue of the Americas, 10036, pg. 1173 **PB**
New Woman Magazine, Two Park Ave., 11th Fl., 10016, pg. 939 **PV**
NEW YORK CITY OFF-TRACK BETTING CORP., 1501 Broadway, 10036, pg. 794 **PV**
New York Financial Corp., 54 E. 64th St., 10021, pg. 993 **PV**
New York Institiue of Finance, Two Broadway, 5th Fl., 10004-2207, pg. 778 **PV**
New York Knickerbockers, Madison Square Garden, Two Pennsylvania Plaza, 10121-0091, pg. 288 **PB**
New York Law Journal, 345 Park Ave. S., 10010, pg. 956 **IT**
NYLIFE Care, 1 Liberty Plaza, 10006, pg. 795 **PV**
NYLIFE Depositary Corporation, 51 Madison Ave., 10010, pg. 795 **PV**
NYLIFE Equity Inc., 51 Madison Ave., 10010, pg. 795 **PV**
New York Life Foundation, 51 Madison Ave., 10010, pg. 795 **PV**
NYLIFE Inc., 372 Park Ave. S., 10010, pg. 795 **PV**
New York Life Insurance and Annuity Corporation, 51 Madison Ave., 10010, pg. 795 **PV**
NEW YORK LIFE INSURANCE COMPANY, 51 Madison Ave., 10010, pg. 794 **PV**
New York Life International Investment, 51 Madison Ave., 10010, pg. 795 **PV**
NYLIFE Realty Inc., 51 Madison Ave., 10010, pg. 795 **PV**
NYLIFE Securities Inc., 51 Madison Ave., 10010, pg. 795 **PV**
New York Life Worldwide Holding, Inc., 51 Madison Ave., 10010, pg. 795 **PV**
New York Magazine, 444 Madison Ave., 10022, pg. 1328 **PB**
The New York Observer, 54 E. 64th St., 10021, pg. 993 **PV**
New York Office, Two World Trade Ctr., Ste. 9846, 10048, pg. 1517 **IT**
The New York Post, 1211 Ave. of the Americas, 10036-8790, pg. 927 **IT**
New York Rangers Hockey Club, Two Pennsylvania Plaza, 14th Fl., 10121, pg. 288 **PB**
New York Revenue Automation, 111 8th Ave., Ste. 700, 10011, pg. 466 **PB**
The New York Times, 229 W. 43rd St., 10036, pg. 1174 **PB**
THE NEW YORK TIMES COMPANY, 229 W. 43rd St., 10036, pg. 1173 **PB**
New York Times Company Forest Products Group, 229 W. 43rd St., 10036, pg. 1174 **PB**
The New York Times Electronic Media Co., 1120 Ave. of The Americas, 6th Fl., 10036, pg. 1176 **PB**
The New York Times Index, 229 W. 43rd St., 10036, pg. 1174 **PB**
The New York Times Information Services Group, 122 E. 42nd St., 10168, pg. 1174 **PB**
The New York Times News Service, 229 W. 43rd St., 10036, pg. 1174 **PB**
New York Times Newspaper Group, 229 W. 43rd St., 10036, pg. 1174 **PB**
The New York Times Sales, Inc., 229 W. 43rd St., 10036, pg. 1176 **PB**
The New York Times Syndicate, 122 E. 42nd St., 10011, pg. 1174 **PB**
The New York Times Syndication Sales Corporation, 122 E. 42nd St., 10168, pg. 1174 **PB**
THE NEW YORKER MAGAZINE, 20 W. 43rd St., 10036-7440, pg. 795 **PV**
Newbridge Communications, Inc., 333 E. 38th St., 10 Fl., 10016, pg. 191 **IT**
Newbridge Securities, Inc., 120 Wall St., 12th Fl., 10005, pg. 378 **PB**
Newcom Publications Inc., 1633 Broadway, 10019, pg. 795 **IT**
Newhouse Newspapers Metro-Suburbia, Inc., 140 E. 45th, 36th Fl., 10017, pg. 20 **PV**
Newport News, Inc., 711 Third Ave., 10017, pg. 1499 **PB**
News America Holdings Inc., 1211 6th Ave., 10036, pg. 925 **IT**
News America Publishing Inc., 1211 Ave. of the Americas, 10036, pg. 925 **IT**
NewsEdge Corp., 275 Madison Ave., Ste. 500, 10016, pg. 1180 **PB**
Newspaper Enterprise Assoc., c/o United Media, 200 Madison Ave., 10016, pg. 1448 **PB**
Newspaper Enterprise Association, 200 Park Ave., 10166-0079, pg. 1448 **PB**
Newspapers First, 711 Third Ave., 10017, pg. 964 **PB**
Newsweek, Inc., 251 W. 57th St., 10019-1894, pg. 1743 **PB**
Next Day Apparel, 570 Seventh Ave., 20th Fl., 10018, pg. 989 **PB**
NIAGARA CORPORATION, 667 Madison Ave., 10021, pg. 1181 **PB**
Niagara Fire Insurance Co., 180 Maiden Ln., 10038, pg. 1011 **PB**
Nichimen America, Inc., 23rd Fl., 1345 Ave. of the Americas, 10105-0302, pg. 927 **IT**
Austin Nichols & Co. Inc., 156 E. 46th St., 10017, pg. 566 **IT**
Nickelodeon/Nick At Nite, 1515 Broadway, 10036, pg. 779 **PV**
A.C. Nielsen Company (New York), 299 Park Ave., 10171, pg. 1183 **PB**
Nielsen Media Research, 299 Park Ave., 10171, pg. 995 **PB**
Nihon Keizai Shimbun America, Inc., 1325 Ave. of the Americas, Ste. 2500, 10019, pg. 929 **IT**
Nikkan Kogyo Shimbun, Rm. 1411, Lincoln Bldg., 60 E. 42nd St., 10165, pg. 930 **IT**
Nikko Hotels International-USA, 1700 Broadway, 38th fl., 10019, pg. 700 **IT**
Nikko International Capital Management Co., Ltd., 489 5th Ave. 4th Fl., 10017, pg. 930 **IT**
The Nikko Securities Co. International Inc., One World Financial Center, 200 Liberty St., 22nd Fl., 10281, pg. 930 **IT**
Nippon Credit Bank Ltd., New York, 245 Park Ave., 31st Fl., 10167, pg. 932 **IT**
Nippon Credit Trust Company, 245 Park Ave., 25th Fl., 10167, pg. 933 **IT**
Nippon Express U.S.A. Inc., 590 Madison Ave., Ste. 2401, 10022, pg. 934 **IT**
Nippon Life Insurance Company of America, 450 Lexington Ave., Ste. 3200, 10017, pg. 935 **IT**
Nippon Oil (U.S.A.) Limited - New York Office, 280 Park Ave.-W. Bldg., 35th Fl., 10017, pg. 937 **IT**
Nippon Paint (America) Corp., Tower 49, 12 E. 49th St., Ste. 1805, 10017, pg. 937 **IT**
Nippon Steel U.S.A., Inc., Ten East 50th St., 29th Fl., 10022, pg. 939 **IT**
Nissan Capital of America, Inc., 399 Park Ave., 10022, pg. 944 **IT**
Nissan Finance of America, Inc., 399 Park Ave., 10022, pg. 944 **IT**
Nisshin Steel USA, Inc., 375 Park Ave., 10152, pg. 946 **IT**
Nissho Iwai Aerospace (America) Corp., Rockefeller Center, 1211 Ave. of the Americas, 10036, pg. 947 **IT**
NLI International, Ste. 5210, 1251 Ave. of the Americas, 10020-1198, pg. 935 **IT**
NOEL GROUP, INC., 667 Madison Ave., 10021-8029, pg. 1187 **PB**
Noma Showroom, 200 Fifth Ave., Rm. 734, 10010, pg. 955 **IT**
Nomura Asset Capital Corporation, Building B, Two World Financial Ctr., 10281-1198, pg. 956 **IT**
Nomura Asset Management (U.S.A.) Inc., 180 Maiden Ln., 10038, pg. 955 **IT**
Nomura Automation Management Inc., Building B, Two World Financial Ctr., 10281-1198, pg. 956 **IT**
Nomura Capital Services, Inc., Buiding B, Two World Financial Ctr., 10281, pg. 956 **IT**
Nomura Corporate Research & Asset Management Inc., Building B, Two World Financial Ctr., 10281-1198, pg. 956 **IT**
Nomura Holding America, Inc., Building B, Two World Financial Ctr., 10281-1198, pg. 956 **IT**
Nomura Mortgage Capital Corporation, Building B, Two World Financial Ctr., 10281-1198, pg. 956 **IT**
Nomura Mortgage Fund Management Corporation, Two World Financial Ctr., 10281, pg. 956 **IT**
Nomura Real Estate U.S.A., Inc., 150 E. 53nd St., 23rd Fl., 10022-6017, pg. 956 **IT**
Nomura Realty Advisors Inc., 399 Park Ave., 25th Fl., 10022, pg. 956 **IT**
Nomura Research Institute America, Inc., Building B, Two World Finacial Ctr., 10281-1197, pg. 956 **IT**
Nomura Securities International, Inc., Building B, Two World Financial Ctr., 10281-1198, pg. 956 **IT**
Non Ferrous International Corp., 545 Madison Ave., 10022, pg. 872 **IT**
Noonday Press, 19 Union Sq. W., 10003, pg. 1479 **IT**
NORD/LB New York, 1270 Ave. of the Americas, 10022, pg. 958 **IT**
Norell Perfumes, Inc., 767 Fifth Ave., 10153, pg. 690 **PV**
The Norinchukin Bank, 245 Park Ave., 29th Fl., 10167-0104, pg. 958 **IT**
Norsk Hydro USA Inc., 800 Third Ave., 10022, pg. 961 **IT**
North America Syndicate, Inc., 235 E. 45th St., 10017, pg. 515 **PV**
North American Underwear Company, Inc., 180 Madison Ave., Ste. 700, 10016, pg. 686 **PB**
North Coal, Inc., 110 East 59th St., 10022-1385, pg. 709 **IT**
North Coast Investment Corporation, 730 Third Ave., 10017, pg. 361 **PB**
North Point Press, 19 Union Sq. W., 10003, pg. 1479 **IT**
Northern SC Paper Corporation, 229 W. 43rd St., 10036, pg. 1174 **PB**
The Northern Trust Company of New York, 80 Broad St., 19th Floor, 10004, pg. 1197 **PB**
The Northern Trust International Banking Corporation, One World Trade Ctr., Ste. 3941, 10048, pg. 1197 **PB**
W.W. NORTON & COMPANY, INC., 500 Fifth Ave., 10110, pg. 807 **PV**
Norvista Ltd., 228 East 45th Street, 10017, pg. 486 **IT**
Novo Nordisk of North America, Inc., 405 Lexington Ave., Ste. 6400, 10117, pg. 987 **IT**
Noxell Corporation, 200 Park Ave., 10166, pg. 1330 **PB**
Nozaki America, Inc., 1325 Ave. of the Americas, 26th Fl., 10019, pg. 990 **IT**
OCE, One Penn Plaza, 33rd Flr., 10119-0002, pg. 994 **IT**
OMI Bulk Management Co., 90 Park Ave., 10016-1302, pg. 1208 **PB**
OMI CORP., 90 Park Ave., 10016-1302, pg. 1208 **PB**
OXO International, 230 Fifth Ave., Ste. 1100, 10036, pg. 716 **PB**
Obayashi Corporation-New York, 666 5th Ave., 12th Fl., 10103, pg. 995 **IT**
Obion Company, Inc., 1114 Ave. of the Americas, 10036, pg. 1429 **PB**
Object Technology Group - Northeast Region, 885 Third Ave., 25th Fl., 10022-4834, pg. 1154 **IT**
October Films, Inc., 65 Bleeker St., 10012, pg. 1216 **IT**
Odyssey Reinsurance Corporation, One Liberty Plaza, 10006, pg. 1258 **IT**
Oerlikon Buhrle USA, Inc., One Penn Plaza, Ste. 4828, 10119, pg. 998 **IT**
Office of Communications, 77 W. 66th St., 10023, pg. 511 **PB**
Offshore Equities, Inc., 277 Park Ave., 10172, pg. 338 **PB**
Ogden Aviation Services, Two Pennsylvania Plaza, 10121, pg. 1213 **PB**
OGDEN CORPORATION, Two Pennsylvania Plaza, 10121, pg. 1213 **PB**
Ogden Entertainment, Inc., Two Pennsylvania Plaza, 10121, pg. 1213 **PB**
Ogilvy & Mather Worldwide, Inc., Head Office: Worldwide Plaza, 309 W. 49th St., 10019, pg. 1483 **IT**
The Ohio Art Co., 200 Fifth Ave., Ste. 850, 10010, pg. 1214 **PB**
Okura & Co. (America) Inc., 450 Lexington Ave., Ste.1460, 10017, pg. 1001 **IT**
Olivetti Management of America, Inc., 237 Park Ave., 10017-3140, pg. 1002 **IT**
Olympic Airways, 645 Fifth Ave., 10022, pg. 1004 **IT**
Omni Publications International Ltd., 277 Park Ave., 4th Fl., 10172-003, pg. 444 **PV**
OMNICOM GROUP INC., 437 Madison Ave., 9th Fl., 10022, pg. 1223 **PB**
Oppenheimer Capital, One New York Plaza, 10004, pg. 257 **IT**
Oppenheimer Funds, Inc., Two World Trade Ctr., 10048-0203, pg. 712 **PV**
OPPENHEIMERFUNDS DISTRIBUTOR, INC., Oppenheimer **Tower**, World Financial Center, 10281, pg. 818 **PV**
Orangina International, 1290 6th Ave., 10104, pg. 567 **IT**
Orchard Yarn & Thread Co., Inc., 34 W. 15th St., 10011, pg. 669 **PV**
Ord Minnett Group, 26th Fl., 355 Madison Ave., 10017-4681, pg. 1496 **IT**
The Ore & Chemical Corp., 520 Madison Ave., 27th Fl., 10022, pg. 862 **IT**
Oremco Inc., 261 Madison Ave., 14th Fl., 10016, pg. 754 **IT**
Orient-Express Hotels Inc., 1155 Ave. of the Americas, 10036, pg. 1213 **IT**

Geographic Index-U.S.

PB - *U.S. Public Companies Volume*
PV - *U.S. Private Companies Volume*
IT - *International Public & Private Companies Volume*

ORION CAPITAL CORPORATION, 600 Fifth Ave., 10020-2302, pg. 1231 — PB
Orion Properties Corp., 600 Fifth Ave., 10020-2302, pg. 1231 — PB
ORIX USA Corporation-New York, 780 Third Ave., 48th Fl., 10017, pg. 1009 — IT
Orlane, Inc., 555 Madison Ave., 20th Fl., 10022, pg. 1011 — IT
O'Ryan Books, 201 E. 50th St., 10022, pg. 21 — PV
Osaka Gas Co.-New York, 375 Park Ave., Ste. 2109, 10152, pg. 1012 — IT
OshKosh B'Gosh, Inc.-New York, 350 Fifth Ave., 10118, pg. 1233 — PB
Outdoor Life, Two Park Ave., 10016, pg. 1617 — PB
Outdoor Services, 137 Fifth Ave., 10010, pg. 1166 — PB
Outdoor Systems, Inc., 535 Madison Ave., 10022, pg. 1235 — PB
Outdoor Systems, Inc.-New York, 666 Third Ave., 10017, pg. 1235 — PB
Outdoor Systems, Inc. Sales, 666 Third Ave., 10022, pg. 1235 — PB
Outlander, 1412 Broadway, 10018, pg. 989 — PB
OVERSEAS SHIPHOLDING GROUP, INC., 1114 Ave. of the Americas, 10036, pg. 1236 — PB
Owned Television Stations, 1290 Avenue of the Americas, 10104, pg. 148 — PV
Oxford Collection, 1001 Ave. of the Americas, 10018, pg. 1239 — PB
Oxford Men's Wear Division, 350 Fifth Ave., 10118, pg. 1239 — PB
Oxford Separates, 1001 Ave. of the Americas, 10018, pg. 1239 — PB
Oxford Shirts, 350 Fifth Ave., 10018, pg. 1239 — PB
Oxford Slacks Division, 350 Fifth Ave., 10018, pg. 1239 — PB
Oxford University Press, Inc., 198 Madison Ave., 10016, pg. 1019 — IT
PC Magazine, One Park Ave., 10016, pg. 1276 — IT
PDV America Corp., 750 Lexington Ave., 10th Fl., 10022, pg. 1045 — IT
PEC Israel Economic Corporation, 511 Fifth Avenue, 10017, pg. 644 — IT
P.R. Newswire Association Inc., 810 Seventh Ave., 35th Fl., 10019, pg. 1443 — IT
Pace Advertising, 485 Fifth Ave., 10017, pg. 1483 — PV
Pacific Union Assurance Company, 70 Pine St., 10270, pg. 84 — PB
Paco Rabanne Compar, 70 E. 55th St., 17th Fl., 10022, pg. 1073 — IT
Pago Fabrics, Inc., 48 W. 38th St. 8th Fl., 10018, pg. 695 — IT
PaineWebber Capital Inc., 1285 Ave. of the Americas, 10019, pg. 1252 — PB
PAINEWEBBER GROUP INCORPORATED, The PaineWebber Bldg., 1285 Ave. of the Americas, 10019, pg. 1252 — PB
PaineWebber Incorporated, 1285 Ave. of the Americas, 10019, pg. 1252 — PB
PaineWebber Properties Incorporated, 1285 Ave. of the Americas, 10019, pg. 1253 — PB
Pakistan International Airlines Corporation, 521 Fifth Ave., 10175, pg. 1022 — IT
R.J. PALMER, INC., 156 W. 56th St., 10019, pg. 835 — PV
Panel Publishers, Inc., 36 W. 44th St., 10036, pg. 1513 — IT
Pantheon Books, Inc., 201 E. 50th St., 10022, pg. 21 — PV
Paper Corporation of United States, 161 Ave. of the Americas, 4th Fl., 10013, pg. 1671 — PB
PARACORE COMPANY, 660 Madison Ave., 10021, pg. 838 — PV
Parade Publications Inc., 711 Third Ave., 10017, pg. 20 — PV
Parenting Magazine Partners, 25 W. 43rd St., 10036, pg. 1614 — PB
Parents Magazine, 375 Lexington Ave., 10017, pg. 191 — IT
Parfums Givenchy Inc., 717 Fifth Ave., 10022, pg. 781 — IT
Parfums International Ltd., 1345 Ave. of the Americas, 10105, pg. 1435 — IT
Parfums Van Cleef & Arpels, 40 E. 52nd St., 10022, pg. 445 — IT
Paribas North America, The Equitable Tower, 787 Seventh Ave., 10019, pg. 319 — IT
PARIS ACCESSORIES, 350 5th Ave., 8th Fl., 10118, pg. 839 — PV
Paris Securities, Four World Trade Center, Ste. 9184, 10048, pg. 839 — PV
Parsons Brinckerhoff Energy Services Inc., One Penn Plaza, 10119, pg. 841 — PV
PARSONS BRINCKERHOFF INC., One Penn Plaza, 2nd Fl., 10119, pg. 841 — PV
Parsons Brinckerhoff Quade & Douglas, Inc., One Penn Plaza, 2nd Fl., 10119, pg. 841 — PV
Partners & Shevack Design, 1211 Ave. of the Americas, 10036, pg. 842 — PV
Partners & Shevack Direct, 1211 Ave. of the Americas, 10036, pg. 842 — PV
PARTNERS & SHEVACK, INC., 1211 Ave. of the Americas, 10036, pg. 842 — PV
Partners & Shevack Public Relations, 1211 Ave. of the Americas, 10036, pg. 842 — PV
PAUL STUART, INC., Madison Ave. & 45th St., 10017, pg. 844 — PV
Peak Technologies Group, Inc., 600 Madison Ave., 26th Fl., 10022, pg. 890 — PV
Pearson, Inc., 30 Rockefeller Plaza, 50th Fl., 10112-5095, pg. 1026 — IT
PEDONE & PARTNERS ADV., INC., 100 Fifth Ave., 4th Fl., 10011, pg. 846 — PV
Peers & Co., 560 Lexington Ave., 10th Fl., 10022, pg. 816 — IT
DAVID L. PEISTER CO., INC., 29 W. 38th St., 10018, pg. 848 — PV
Penguin Putnam Inc., 375 Hudson St., 10014, pg. 1027 — IT

Pennaco Hosiery, 111 W. 40th St., 10018, pg. 483 — PB
PENNCORP FINANCIAL GROUP, INC., 590 Madison Ave., 10022, pg. 1271 — PB
People, Time & Life Bldg., Rockefeller Ctr., 10020, pg. 1613 — PB
Pepper, Hamilton & Scheetz, 450 Lexington Ave., Ste. 1600, 10017-3904, pg. 851 — PV
PERFECT PEARL COMPANY, INC., 104 W. 29th St., 3rd Fl., 10001, pg. 852 — PV
Performance Products Division, 787 Seventh Ave., 10019, pg. 1500 — PB
Perretti, 270 Columbus Ave., 10023, pg. 130 — PB
Perry Ellis, 1114 Ave. of the Americas, 10036, pg. 1429 — PB
The Peterson Group, 666 3rd Ave., Ste. 21, 10064, pg. 1642 — PB
PETRO CHEM DEVELOPMENT COMPANY, 122 E. 42nd St., Ste. 2308, 10017, pg. 858 — PB
Pfizer Chemical Corp. Ltd., c/o Pfizer International Inc., 235 E. 42nd St., 10017, pg. 1282 — PB
Pfizer Enterprises, 235 E. 42nd. St., 10017, pg. 1282 — PB
Pfizer H.C.P. Corporation, 235 E. 42nd St., 10017, pg. 1282 — PB
Pfizer Health Solutions Inc., 235 E. 42nd St., 10017, pg. 1282 — PB
PFIZER INC., 235 E. 42nd St., 10017-5755, pg. 1281 — PB
Pfizer International, Inc., 235 E. 42nd St., 10017, pg. 1282 — PB
Pfizer International Properties, LLC, 235 E. 42nd St., 10017, pg. 1284 — PB
Pfizer Medical Systems, Inc., 235 E. 42nd St., 10017, pg. 1284 — PB
Pfizer Overseas Inc., 235 E. 42nd St., 10017, pg. 1282 — PB
Pfizer Pharmaceuticals, Inc., 235 E. 42nd St., 10017, pg. 1284 — PB
Pfizer Pharmaceuticals Production Corporation, 235 E. 42nd St., 10017, pg. 1282 — PB
Pfizer Pigments Inc., 235 E. 42nd St., 10017, pg. 1284 — PB
Pharmacists Public Relations Bureau, Two Park Ave. 4th Fl., 10016, pg. 295 — PV
PHARMHOUSE, INC., 860 Broadway, 10003, pg. 1286 — PB
Phelps Dodge Sales Company, 780 Third Ave., 31st Fl., 10017, pg. 1287 — PB
PHILIP MORRIS COMPANIES INC., 120 Park Ave., 10017-5592, pg. 1287 — PB
Philip Morris Management Corp., 120 Park Ave., 10017-5592, pg. 1289 — PB
Philip Morris U.S.A., 120 Park Ave., 10017, pg. 1289 — PB
Philips Credit Corporation, 100 E. 42nd St., 10017-5699, pg. 1055 — IT
Philips Electronics North America Corporation, 100 E. 42nd St., 10017, pg. 1053 — IT
PHILLIPS FINE ART AUCTIONEERS, 406 E. 79th St., 10021, pg. 861 — PV
PHILLIPS-VAN HEUSEN CORPORATION, 1290 Ave. of the Americas, 10104, pg. 1291 — PB
Phoenix Assurance of New York, Inc., Ten E. 50th St., 10022, pg. 1130 — IT
Phoenix Learning Resources, 12 W. 31st St., 100001, pg. 863 — PV
Photo Design, 1515 Broadway, 10036, pg. 1446 — IT
Photo District News, 1515 Broadway, 10036, pg. 1446 — IT
The Pierre, Fifth Ave. & 61st St., 10021, pg. 502 — IT
Pierre Cardin Knits, 1411 Broadway, 10018, pg. 520 — PB
PIERS, 110 Wall St., 10005, pg. 1026 — IT
Pignone, 666 Fifth Ave., 10103, pg. 991 — IT
Piper Jaffray Inc., 333 E. 49th St., Ste. PH A, 10017, pg. 1302 — PB
Plaid Clothing Company, 730 Fifth Ave., 5th Fl., 10104, pg. 796 — PB
Plastics Technology, 355 Park Ave. South, 10010, pg. 1446 — IT
Plenum International Sales Corporation, 233 Spring St., 10013, pg. 1311 — PB
PLENUM PUBLISHING CORPORATION, 233 Spring St., 10013, pg. 1311 — PB
Pocket Books, 1230 Ave. of the Americas, 10020, pg. 777 — PV
Polaroid Education Program, 95 Christopher St., 10014-6605, pg. 1314 — PB
POLO/RALPH LAUREN CORPORATION, 650 Madison Ave., 10022, pg. 874 — PV
Polydor Inc., 810 Seventh Ave., 10019, pg. 1052 — IT
PolyGram Classics, Inc., 810 Seventh Ave., 10019, pg. 1052 — IT
PolyGram Holding, Inc., Worldwide Plaza, 825 Eighth Ave., 10019, pg. 1052 — IT
PolyGram Music Publishing, Inc., 810 Seventh Ave., 10019, pg. 1052 — IT
Polygram Records, Inc., 825 Eighth Ave., 10019, pg. 1052 — IT
POLYVISION CORP., 1790 Broadway, 15th Fl., 10019, pg. 1315 — PB
Poppe Tyson, 40 W. 23rd St., 10010, pg. 1642 — PB
Popular Mechanics, 224 W. 57th St., 10019, pg. 517 — PV
Popular Science, Two Park Ave., 10016, pg. 1617 — PB
Porter Novelli International, 220 E. 42 St., 10017, pg. 1224 — PB
The Portfolio Group, Inc., 30 Rockefeller Plaza, 10017, pg. 338 — PB
Portland House, 201 E. 50th St., 10022, pg. 21 — PV
POSAM New York Office, 375 Park Ave., Ste. 1606, 10152, pg. 1062 — IT
POSNICK & KOLKER, INC., 49 W. 27th St., 10001, pg. 876 — PV
Potamkin Manhattan, 798 Eleventh Ave., 10019, pg. 876 — PV
Potomac Graphic Industries, Inc., 508 West 26th St., 10001, pg. 699 — PV
Clarkson N. Potter, Inc., 201 E. 50th St., 10022, pg. 21 — PV
Power, 11 W. 19th St., 10011, pg. 1071 — PB

Power & Motoryacht Magazine, 249 W. 17th St., 10011, pg. 1328 — PB
Premier Brands, Inc., 488 Seventh Ave., Ste. 11A, 10018, pg. 1068 — IT
PRESSMAN TOY CORP., 200 Fifth Ave., Rm. 1052, 10010, pg. 882 — PV
Prestige Fragrance & Cosmetics, Inc., 767 Fifth Ave., 10153, pg. 690 — PV
Prestige Fragrances, Ltd., 625 Madison Ave., 4th Fl., 10022, pg. 690 — PV
Prestige Perfumes Ltd., 767 Fifth Ave., 10153, pg. 690 — PV
PRICE COMMUNICATIONS CORPORATION, 45 Rockefeller Plaza, Ste. 3200, 10020, pg. 1324 — PB
PRICE WATERHOUSE L.L.P. - U.S., 1177 Ave. of the Americas, 10036, pg. 883 — PV
PRIMEDIA INC., 745 Fifth Ave., 10151, pg. 1327 — PB
Primedia Informatin Group, 717 Fifth Ave., 10022, pg. 1328 — PB
Primedia Magazine Corporation, 1717 Fifth Ave., 10th Fl., 10022, pg. 1328 — PB
Princess Hotels Internacional Inc., 805 Third Ave., 10022, pg. 818 — IT
The Princess Marcella Borghese, Inc., 767 Fifth Ave., 10153, pg. 690 — PV
Pringle of Scotland, 499 Seventh Ave., 10018, pg. 386 — IT
PRISM International, 220 E. 42 St., 10017, pg. 1224 — PB
Producers Masterguide, 330 W. 42nd St., 10036, pg. 1446 — IT
Productos Borden, Inc., 420 Lexington Ave., 10170, pg. 158 — PV
Productos DelTropico C. Par A., 277 Park Ave., 10172, pg. 158 — PV
Professional Book Group, 11 W. 19th St., 10011, pg. 1071 — PB
The Professional Products Division, 345 Park Ave., 10154, pg. 254 — PB
The Program Exchange, 375 Hudson St., 10014, pg. 1422 — PB
Promotional Broadcast Services, 1270 Ave. of the Americas, 10020, pg. 1166 — PV
Pronto, Inc., 277 Park Ave., 10172, pg. 338 — PB
Prudential Securities Inc. One Seaport Plaza, 10292, pg. 892 — PB
Psychology Today, 24 E. 23rd St., 15th Fl., 10010, pg. 1056 — PV
Publicis/Bloom, 304 East 45th St., 10017, pg. 470 — IT
Publicis/Bloom Inc., 304 East 45th St., 10017, pg. 470 — IT
Puerto Rico Tourism Company, 575 Fifth Ave., 10017, pg. 894 — PV
The Putnam & Grosset Group, 200 Madison Ave., 10016, pg. 1027 — IT
The Putnam Berkley Group, Inc., 200 Madison Ave., 10016, pg. 1027 — IT
G.P. Putnam Sons, 200 Madison Ave., 10016, pg. 1215 — IT
Putnam Reinsurance Co., 80 Pine St., 10270, pg. 84 — PB
PYRAMID HANDBAGS INC., 100 W. 33rd St., Ste. 808, 10001, pg. 896 — PV
Quantum Computer Systems, 1370 Broadway, 4th Flr., 10018-7302, pg. 1350 — PV
QUANTUM MEDIA INTERNATIONAL, INC., 41 Madison Avenue, 10010, pg. 899 — PV
Quantum Plus, 1250 Broadway, 18th Fl., 10001, pg. 1224 — PV
Quantum Sport, 70 W. 36th St., Ste. 1004, 10018, pg. 577 — PV
QUANTUM SPORT, 70 W. 36 St., Ste. 1004, 10018, pg. 900 — PV
Quick Nikkei News, Inc., Broad Financial Ctr., 33 Whitehall St., 10004, pg. 929 — IT
Quick & Reilly, Inc., 26 Broadway, 10004, pg. 650 — PB
Quigley Co., Inc., 235 E. 42nd St., 10017, pg. 1284 — PB
Quill Trade Paperbacks, 1350 Ave. of the Americas, 10019, pg. 515 — PV
R/GA Interactive, 350 W. 39th St., 10018, pg. 1641 — PB
RC Communications, Inc., 1633 Broadway, 10019, pg. 1224 — PB
RCA Records U.S., 1540 Broadway, 10036, pg. 192 — IT
RCG International Inc., RCG West, 40th St., 10018, pg. 1374 — PB
RCM Design, 500 7th Ave., 10018, pg. 947 — PV
R.D. Member Services, Inc., 28 W. 23rd St., 10010, pg. 1368 — PB
RD Publications, Inc., 28 W. 23rd St., 10010, pg. 1367 — PB
RGA AND EAST END ACCESSORIES, 350 Fifth Ave., 10001, pg. 903 — PV
RJR NABISCO HOLDINGS CORP., 1301 Ave. of The Americas, 10019, pg. 1354 — PB
RZB New York, DG Bank House, 609 Fifth Ave., 10017-1021, pg. 1084 — IT
Rabbit Ears Book & Audio, 1230 Ave. of the Americas, 10020, pg. 777 — PV
The Racal Corporation, 11 Penn Plaza, 10001, pg. 1083 — IT
Radio City Productions, 1260 Ave. of the Americas, 10020, pg. 873 — PV
Radiologic Sciences, Inc., 235 E. 42nd St., 10017, pg. 1284 — PB
RAI Corporations, 1350 Ave. of the Americas, 10019, pg. 655 — IT
Ralph Lauren Womenswear Co., L.P., 550 Seventh Ave., 10018, pg. 875 — PV
Ramerica, The Empire State Building, 350 Fifth Ave., Ste. 4719, 10118, pg. 741 — IT
Random House Adult Trade Books, 201 E. 50 St., 10022, pg. 21 — PV
Random House, Inc., 201 E. 50th St., 10022, pg. 20 — PV
Rapp Collins Worldwide, 488 Madison Ave., 10022, pg. 1444 — PB
Raval Lace Division, 200 Madison Ave., 10016, pg. 603 — PB

Geographic Index-U.S.

Raytheon Infrastructure Incorporated, Two World Trade Center, 10048, pg. 1366 **PB**
React Magazine, 711 Third Ave., 10017, pg. 20 **PV**
Reader's Digest Publications-US Sales Div., 28 W. 23rd St., 10010, pg. 1367 **IT**
Reader's Digest Sales & Services, Inc., 261 Madison Ave., 10016, pg. 1367 **IT**
Readmore Publications Inc., 22 Portlandt St., 3rd Fl., 10007, pg. 197 **IT**
The Really Useful Company, Inc., 1633 Broadway, Ste. 3801, 10019, pg. 1089 **IT**
RED APPLE COMPANIES, 823 11th Ave., 10019, pg. 914 **PV**
Red Apple Companies Food Group, 823 11th Ave., 10019, pg. 915 **PV**
Redbook, 224 West 57th, 10019, pg. 517 **PV**
Reed Business Information (USA), 475 Park Ave. S., 2nd Fl., 10016, pg. 1094
Reed Elsevier Business Information-New York, 245 W. 17th St., 10011, pg. 1095 **IT**
Reed Elsevier Inc., MetLife Bldg., 17th Fl., 200 Park Ave., 10166, pg. 1095 **IT**
Reed MIDEM Organisation Inc., 475 Park Ave. S., 30th Fl., 10016, pg. 1096 **IT**
Regal, 350 Fifth Ave., Ste. 1430, 10118, pg. 49 **PV**
REGENCY CRUISES INC., 989 6th Ave., 10018, pg. 918 **PV**
Regency Hotel, 540 Park Ave., 10021, pg. 1011 **PV**
Regency Maritime Corp./Regsun Holding Corp., LTD, c/o RCI, 989 6th Ave., 10018, pg. 918 **PV**
REGENT INTERNATIONAL, 1411 Broadway, 7th Fl., 10018, pg. 918 **PV**
Reich & Tang, 600 5th Ave., 10020, pg. 737 **PV**
Reliance Consulting Group, 111 W. 40th St., 10018, pg. 1374 **PB**
Reliance Development Group Inc., Park Ave. Plaza, 55 E. 52nd St., 10055, pg. 1374 **PB**
RELIANCE GROUP HOLDINGS, INC., Park Ave. Plaza, 55 E. 52nd St., 10055, pg. 1374 **PB**
Reliance National Insurance Company, 22, 77 Water St., 10005, pg. 1374 **PB**
Remco Baby, 1107 Broadway, Ste. 808, 10010, pg. 923 **PV**
Remco Toys, 1107 Broadway, Ste. 808, 10010, pg. 923 **PV**
Remy Amerique Inc., 1350 Ave. of the Americas, 10019, pg. 1102 **IT**
RENAISSANCE COSMETICS, INC., 635 Madison Ave., Fifth Fl., 10022, pg. 922 **PV**
RENCO GROUP, 30 Rockefeller Plaza, 10112, pg. 922 **PV**
Republic Bank for Savings, One Hanson Pl., 11243, pg. 1380 **PB**
Republic Factors Corp., 452 Fifth Ave., 10018, pg. 1380 **PB**
Republic National Bank of New York, 452 Fifth Ave., 10018, pg. 1380 **PB**
REPUBLIC NEW YORK CORPORATION, 452 Fifth Ave., 10018, pg. 1380 **PB**
Republic New York Securities Corporation, 452 Fifth Ave., 10018, pg. 1381 **PB**
Republic Services Corporation, 452 Fifth Ave., 10018, pg. 1381 **PB**
Research Institute of America, 90 Fifth Ave., 10011, pg. 1602 **PV**
Resource Net International, 1115 Broadway, 10010, pg. 903 **PV**
Restaurant Associates Catering, 36 W. 44th St., 10036, pg. 925 **PV**
RESTAURANT ASSOCIATES CORPORATION, 120 West 45th St., 16th Fl., 10036, pg. 924 **PV**
Restaurant Business, 355 Park Ave. South, 10010, pg. 1446 **IT**
Retirement Living Publishing Company, Inc., 28 W. 23rd St., 10010, pg. 1367 **PB**
Reuters America Inc., 1700 Broadway, 10019, pg. 1106 **IT**
Revlon, Inc., 625 Madison Ave., 10022, pg. 689 **PV**
Revlon International Corporation, 625 Madison Ave., 10022-1801, pg. 690 **PV**
Revlon-Realistic Professional Products, Inc., 625 Madison Ave., 10022-1801, pg. 690 **PV**
Revlon Service, Inc., 625 Madison Ave., 10022-1801, pg. 690 **PV**
Charles Revson, Inc., 625 Madison Ave., 10022-1801, pg. 690 **PV**
REXX ENVIRONMENTAL CORP., 350 Park Ave., 10022, pg. 1384 **PB**
Rheem Manufacturing Co., 405 Lexington Ave., 22nd Fl., 10174-0307, pg. 1022 **IT**
RIDDELL SPORTS, INC., 900 Third Ave., 10022, pg. 1389 **PB**
RIPPLEWOOD HOLDINGS L.L.C., 712 5th Ave., 49th Fl., 10019, pg. 931 **PV**
Ritz Corporation, 625 Madison Ave., 10022-1801, pg. 690 **PV**
Rizzoli International Publications, Inc., 300 Park Ave. S., 10010, pg. 1078 **IT**
Robby Len Fashions, 1411 Broadway, 10018, pg. 121 **PB**
Rockefeller Center Development Corporation, 1230 Ave. of the Americas, 10020, pg. 873 **IT**
Rockefeller Center Management Corporation, 1230 Ave. of the Americas, 10020, pg. 873 **IT**
Rockefeller Group, Inc., 1221 Avenue of the Americas, 10112, pg. 873 **IT**
Rockefeller Group Telecommunications Services, Inc., 1230 Ave. of the Americas, 10020, pg. 873 **IT**
Rockton Technical Services Corporation, 250 W. 34th St., 10119, pg. 1519 **PV**
ROCKVILLE FABRICS CORPORATION, 225 W. 34th St., 10122, pg. 938 **PV**

The Rodd Group, 15th Fl., 1250 Broadway, 10001, pg. 1224 **PB**
Rolex Industries, Inc., 665 5th Ave., 10022, pg. 1126 **IT**
Rolex Watch U.S.A., Inc., 665 5th Ave., 10022, pg. 1126 **IT**
Rolling Stone Magazine, 1290 Ave. of the Americas, 10104, pg. 1162 **PV**
ROMANN & TANNENHOLZ ADVERTISING, INC., 230 Park Ave., Ste. 16000, 10169, pg. 942 **PV**
Rothchild Asset Management Inc., 1251 Ave. of the Americas, 10020, pg. 947 **PV**
Rothchild Realty Inc., 1251 Avenue of the Americas, 10020, pg. 947 **PV**
S. ROTHCHILD & CO., INC., 500 7th. Ave., 10018, pg. 947 **PV**
Rothchild's Larry L., 500 7th. Ave., 10018, pg. 947 **PV**
Rothschild Inc., 1251 Avenue of the Americas, 10020, pg. 947 **PV**
ROTHSCHILD NORTH AMERICA INC., 1251 Avenue of the Americas, 10020, pg. 947 **PV**
Royal Alliance Associates, Inc., 733 Third Ave., 10017, pg. 1533 **PB**
Royal Bank of Canada, One Financial Sq., 10005-3531, pg. 1131 **IT**
The Royal Bank of Scotland plc, 63 Wall St., 10005, pg. 1133 **IT**
Royal Copenhagen Porcelain Corporation, 683 Madison Ave., 10021, pg. 1134 **IT**
ROYAL OLYMPIC CRUISES, c/o Sun Line Cruises, Inc., One Rockefeller Plaza, Ste. 315, 10020, pg. 1411 **PB**
ROYTEX, INC., 16 E. 34th St., 17th Fl., 10016, pg. 949 **PV**
RUBIN EHRENTHAL & ASSOCIATES, 100 Sixth Ave., 10013, pg. 949 **PV**
RUMS OF PUERTO RICO, 666 Fifth Ave., 15th Fl., 10103, pg. 951 **PV**
RYAN DROSSMAN & PARTNERS, 100 Fifth Ave., 10011, pg. 953 **PV**
SAS Institute, Inc., 34th Floor, 520 Madison Ave., 10022, pg. 966 **IT**
SBC Capital Markets Inc., 222 Broadway, 10036, pg. 1329 **IT**
SBC Portfolio Management International, Inc., Swiss Bank Tower, Ten E. 50th St., 10022, pg. 1329 **IT**
SBC Warburg Dillon Read Inc., 535 Madison Ave., 15th Fl., 10022, pg. 1329 **IT**
SC Suites Corp., 1251 Ave. of the Americas, 22nd Fl., 10020, pg. 1233 **IT**
SCOF U.S. Corporation, Two World Trade Center, 23rd Fl., 10048-0178, pg. 1152 **IT**
SCP Direct Inc., 655 Third Ave., 10017, pg. 1224 **PB**
SEI Corporation, 110 Maiden Ln., 36th Fl., 10005-1702, pg. 1417 **PB**
SFM Entertainment, 1180 Ave. of the Americas, 10036, pg. 957 **PV**
SFM MEDIA CORPORATION, 1180 Ave. of the Americas, 10th Fl., 10036, pg. 956 **PV**
SFM Political Advisory, 1180 Ave. of the Americas, 10036, pg. 957 **PV**
SFM Retail Advisory, 1180 Ave. of the Americas, 10036, pg. 957 **PV**
SFX BROADCASTING INCORPORATED, 150 E. 58th St., 10155, pg. 1417 **PB**
SGS Government Programs Inc., 42 Broadway, 10004, pg. 1153 **IT**
SGS North America Inc., 42 Broadway, 10004-1639, pg. 1153 **IT**
SKI, Two Park Ave., 10016, pg. 1617 **PV**
SMS-New York, Two Penn Plaza, 10121, pg. 1463 **PB**
SRA - New York, 509 Madison Ave., Suite 1004, 10022, pg. 958 **PV**
STV Incorporated, 225 Park Ave. S., 10003, pg. 1421 **PB**
STV International, 225 Park Ave. S., 10003, pg. 1421 **PB**
STV/Silver & Ziskind, 233 Park Ave. S., 10003, pg. 1421 **PB**
SAATCHI & SAATCHI ADVERTISING WORLDWIDE, 375 Hudson St., 9th Fl., 10014-3620, pg. 1422 **PB**
Saatchi & Saatchi Kid Connection, 375 Hudson St., 10016, pg. 1422 **PB**
WILLIAM H. SADLIER, INC., Nine Pine St., 10005-1002, pg. 1422 **PB**
Sag Harbor, 1407 Broadway, Ste. 605, 10018, pg. 948 **PV**
Sail Magazine, 717 5th Ave., 10022, pg. 1328 **PV**
St. Martins Press, Inc., 175 Fifth Ave., 10010, pg. 1479 **IT**
SAKS FIFTH AVENUE, 611 Fifth Ave., 10022, pg. 1429 **PB**
Sakura Bank - New York Branch, 277 Park Ave., 10172-0098, pg. 1179 **IT**
Sakura Global Capital, Inc., Park Avenue Tower, 65 E. 55th St., 10022, pg. 1179 **IT**
Sakura Securities, 350 Park Ave., 9th Fl., 10022, pg. 1179 **IT**
Sakura Trust Company, 350 Park Ave., 10022, pg. 1179 **IT**
Salant Childrens Apparel Group, 1114 Ave. of the Americas, 16th Fl., 10036, pg. 1429 **PB**
SALANT CORPORATION, 1114 Ave. of the Americas, 10036, pg. 1429 **PB**
Sales and Marketing Management, 355 Park Ave. South, 10010, pg. 1446 **IT**
SALLY LOU FASHIONS CORPORATION, 1400 Broadway, 14th Fl., 10018, pg. 962 **PV**
Salomon Smith Barney Holdings, Inc., 388 Greenwich St., 10013, pg. 1633
Samsung America Apparel Showroom, 1359 Broadway Ste. 900, 10018, pg. 1183 **IT**
Sandoz Corporation, 608 Fifth Ave., 10020, pg. 974 **IT**
Sangre de Cristos Ranches Inc., 60 Fifth Ave., 10011, pg. 418 **PV**
Sanmark Group, 136 Madison Ave., 10016, pg. 1141 **PB**
Sanofi Beaute, Inc., 90 Park Ave., 10019, pg. 445 **IT**

Sanofi Pharmaceuticals Inc., 101 Park Ave., 10178, pg. 445 **IT**
Sanofi Pharmaceuticals, Inc., 90 Park Ave., 10016, pg. 445 **IT**
Sanofi Research Co. Inc., 101 Park Ave., 10178, pg. 445 **IT**
Sanpaolo-Nassau, 245 Park Ave., Ste. 3500, 10167, pg. 691 **IT**
Sanpaolo-New York Branch, 245 Park Ave., 35th Fl., 10167, pg. 691 **IT**
SANTEE PRINT WORKS, INC., 58 W. 40th St., 10018, pg. 965 **PV**
Sanwa Bank-New York, Park Ave. Plaza, 55 E. 52nd St., 10055, pg. 1189 **IT**
Sanwa Bank Trust Company of New York, Financial Square, 32 Old Slip, 21st Fl., 10005, pg. 1189 **IT**
Sanwa Financial Products Co., L.P., Park Ave. Plaza, 55 E. 52nd St., 26th fl., 10055, pg. 1189 **IT**
Sanwa Securities (USA) Co., L.P., 599 Lexington Ave., 19th Fl., 10022, pg. 1189 **IT**
Sanyo Corp., 522 Fifth Ave., 10036-7601, pg. 1191 **IT**
Sanyo North American Corporation, 666 Fifth Ave., 10103, pg. 1191 **IT**
Sapporo U.S.A., Inc., New York, 666 3rd Ave. 18th St., 10017, pg. 1193 **IT**
SASSON LICENSING CORP., 1500 Broadway, 22nd Fl., 10036, pg. 967 **PV**
SaTellite Data Broadcast Networks, Inc. (SATNET), 50 Rockefeller Plaza, 10020, pg. 92 **PV**
Savoy Drapery Div., 16 E. 34th St., 10016, pg. 1094 **PV**
Scarborough Research Corporation, 11 W. 42nd Street, 10036-8088, pg. 1447 **PV**
Schieffelin & Somerset Co., 17th Fl., 2 Park Ave., 10016, pg. 412 **IT**
Schirmer Books, 1633 Broadway, 10019, pg. 777 **PV**
G. Schirmer, Inc., 257 Park Ave. S., 10010, pg. 768 **PV**
SCHLUMBERGER LIMITED, 277 Park Ave., 10172, pg. 1439 **PB**
SCHNEIDER MILLS, INC., 462 7th Ave., 10018, pg. 971 **PV**
Schneider/Namic, 235 E. 42nd St., 10017, pg. 1284 **PB**
Schocken Books, 201 E. 50th St., 10022, pg. 21 **PV**
SCHOLASTIC CORPORATION, 555 Broadway, 10012, pg. 1440 **PB**
Scholastic Inc., 555 Broadway, 10012-3999, pg. 1440 **PB**
Scholastic Productions Inc., 524 Broadway, 10003, pg. 1440 **PB**
Schroder & Co. Inc., 787 7th Avenue, 10019, pg. 1210 **IT**
Paul Schulman Co., 11 Madison Ave., 10010, pg. 117 **IT**
F. SCHUMACHER & CO., 79 Madison Ave., 10016-7878, pg. 973 **PV**
SCHWARTZ & BENJAMIN, INC., 1370 Ave. of the Americas, 10019, pg. 974 **PV**
JACK SCHWARTZ SHOES, INC., 155 Ave. of the Americas, 9th Fl., 10013, pg. 974 **PV**
F.J. SCIAME CONSTRUCTION CO. INC., 80 South St., 10038, pg. 975 **PV**
Science & Technology Group, 1221 Ave. of the Americas, 10020, pg. 1071 **PB**
Scientific American, Inc., 415 Madison Ave., 10017, pg. 1479 **PV**
Scientific American Magazine, 415 Madison Ave., 10010, pg. 1479 **PV**
Scientific American Medicine, 415 Madison Ave., 10017, pg. 1479 **PV**
ScotiaMocatta, 26 Broadway, 10004, pg. 156 **IT**
ScotiaMocatta, One Liberty Plaza, 10006, pg. 156 **IT**
Scribner's Bookstores, 122 Fifth Ave., 10011, pg. 189 **PB**
Scudder Kemper Investments, Inc., 345 Park Ave., 10154, pg. 1530 **PV**
Sea Containers Agencies Inc., 1155 Avenue of the Americas, 10036, pg. 1214 **PV**
Sea Containers America Inc., 1155 Ave. of the Americas, 10036, pg. 1213 **PV**
Seabury & Smith, Inc., 1166 Ave. of Americas, 10036, pg. 1049 **PB**
Seagram Asia Pacific/Global Duty Free, 300 Third Ave., 10022, pg. 1217 **IT**
Seagram Beverage Co., 800 3rd Ave., 10022, pg. 1215 **PB**
The Seagram Beverage Group, 375 Park Ave., 10152, pg. 1217 **PB**
Seagram Chateau & Estate Wines Co., 375 Park Ave., 10152, pg. 1215 **PB**
Joseph E. Seagram & Sons, Inc., 375 Park Ave., 10152, pg. 1215 **PB**
The Seagram Spirits and Wine Group, 375 Park Ave., 10152, pg. 1217 **PB**
Seaport Marketplace, Inc., 19 Fulton St., 10038, pg. 1408 **PB**
Seaport Marketplace Theatre, Inc., 19 Fulton St., 10038, pg. 1408 **PB**
Seaport Theatre Management Corporation, 19 Fulton St., 10038, pg. 1408 **PB**
SEIBEL & STERN CORP., 112 W. 33rd St., 10001, pg. 981 **PV**
Gray Seifart & Co., 380 Madison Ave., 10017, pg. 985 **PB**
SELECT COMMUNICATIONS, L.P., 131 Varick St., 11th Fl., 10013, pg. 982 **PV**
Self, 350 Madison Ave., 10017, pg. 20 **PV**
Seligman Financial Services, Inc., 100 Park Ave., 10017, pg. 982 **PV**
Seligman Henderson Co., 100 Park Ave., 10017, pg. 609 **IT**
Seligman Henderson Co., 100 Park Ave., 10017, pg. 982 **PV**
J. & W. SELIGMAN & CO., 100 Park Ave., 10017, pg. 982 **PV**
Seltel, Inc., 125 W. 55th St., 10019, pg. 335 **PB**
Sentry Radio, 125 W. 55th St., 10019, pg. 335 **PB**
SEQUA CORPORATION, 200 Park Ave., 10166, pg. 1458 **PB**

Sequent Computer Systems, Inc., 757 Third Ave., 2nd Fl., 10017, pg. 1459 **PB**

Sequoia (NY), Pier 17, South St. Seaport, 10038, pg. 130 **PB**

SERINO COYNE INC., 1515 Broadway, 36th Fl., 10036, pg. 985 **PV**

Serino Coyne Public Relations, 1515 Broadway, 10036, pg. 985 **PV**

Seventeen Magazine, 850 Third Ave., 10022, pg. 1328 **PB**

Shandwick Americas, The Chrysler Bldg., 405 Lexington Ave., 10174, pg. 1226 **IT**

Shandwick USA, 111 Fifth Ave., 10003, pg. 1227 **IT**

Shane Handbags, 330 Fifth Ave.-Room 1305, 10001, pg. 920 **PB**

Sharps Pixley Brokers Incorporated, 200 Park Ave., 25th Fl., 10166, pg. 403 **IT**

Sharps Pixley Inc., 200 Park Ave., 25th Fl., 10166, pg. 403 **IT**

Shaw Data Services, 122 E. 42nd St., 10168, pg. 1534 **PB**

SHAYKIN & COMPANY, 375 Park Ave., 10152, pg. 990 **PV**

Sheldon Good & Company Auctions NE, 18 E. 41st St., Ste. 1600, 10017-6222, pg. 464 **PV**

SHEPAUG CORPORATION, 54 E. 64th St., 10021, pg. 993 **PV**

Sherle Wagner International, Inc., 60 E. 57th St., 10022, pg. 1054 **PB**

Shieffelin Somerset Co., Two Park Ave., 10016, pg. 412 **IT**

Shimizu America Corporation, 1251 Ave. of the Americas, 22nd Fl., 10020, pg. 1233 **IT**

Shimizu Development (NY), Inc., 1251 Ave. of the Americas, 22nd Fl., 10020, pg. 1233 **IT**

Shimizu Equities (U.S.A.), Inc., 1251 Ave. of the Americas, 22nd Fl., 10020, pg. 1233 **IT**

Shimizu International Finance (U.S.A.), Inc.-New York Office, 1251 Ave. of the Americas, 22nd Fl., 10020, pg. 1233 **IT**

Shimizu Land Corporation, 1251 Ave. of the Americas, 22nd Fl., 10020, pg. 1233 **IT**

Shiseido Cosmetics (America) Ltd., 15th Fl., 900 Third Ave., 10022, pg. 1235 **IT**

Shoko Chukin Bank, 666 5th Ave., 9th Fl., 10103, pg. 1236 **IT**

SHOREWOOD PACKAGING CORPORATION, 277 Park Ave., 10172, pg. 1468 **PB**

Shorewood Packaging Corporation, 277 Park Ave., 10172-0124, pg. 1468 **PB**

Showa Denko America, Inc., 280 Park Ave., 27th Fl. West Bldg., 10017, pg. 1236 **IT**

Showtime Networks Inc., 1633 Broadway, 10019, pg. 779 **PV**

Showtime Satellite Networks, Inc., 1633 Broadway, 10019, pg. 779 **PV**

Showtime/The Movie Channel Inc. (U.K.), 1633 Broadway, 10019, pg. 779 **PV**

Shuwa Corp. of New York, 1330 Ave. of Americas, 10019, pg. 1237 **IT**

HENRY I. SIEGEL COMPANY, INC., 1372 Broadway, 10018, pg. 998 **PV**

Siemens Corporation, 1301 Ave. of the Americas, 10019, pg. 1245 **IT**

Silhouette Books, 300 E. 42nd St., 10017, pg. 1402 **PB**

Simmons, Worldwide Plaza, 14th Fl., 309 W. 49th St., 10019, pg. 1483 **PB**

SIMMONS-BOARDMAN PUBLISHING CORP., 345 Hudson St., 10014, pg. 1000 **PV**

Simon & Schuster, 1230 Ave. of the Americas, 10020, pg. 777 **PV**

Simon & Schuster Audio, 1230 Ave. of the Americas, 10020, pg. 778 **PV**

Simon & Schuster Children's Publishing, 1230 Ave. of the Americas, 4th Fl., 10020, pg. 777 **PV**

Simon & Schuster Consumer Group, 1230 Ave. of the Americas, 10020, pg. 777 **PV**

Simon & Schuster Education Technology Group, Simon & Schuster Bldg., 1230 Ave. of the Americas, 10020, pg. 778 **PV**

Simon & Schuster General Reference USA, 1633 Broadway, 10019, pg. 777 **PV**

Simon & Schuster Interactive, 1230 Ave. of the Americas, 10020, pg. 778 **PV**

Simon & Schuster Trade Division, 1230 Ave. of the Americas, 10020, pg. 777 **PV**

Simon & Schuster's Children's Publishing Div., 1230 Ave. of the Americas, 10020, pg. 777 **PV**

SIMPLICITY HOLDINGS INC., Two Park Ave., 10016, pg. 1002 **PV**

Singapore Airlines Ltd., 55 E. 59th St., Ste. 20B, 10022, pg. 1374 **IT**

Singapore Tourist Promotion Board - New York, 590 Fifth Ave., 12th Fl., 10036, pg. 1254 **IT**

Singer Retail Division, 200 Madison Ave., 10016, pg. 603 **PB**

Sinochem American Holdings Inc., Two World Trade Center, Ste. 2222, 10048, pg. 1255 **IT**

Sinochem Pacific Inc., Two World Trade Center, Ste. 2222, 10048, pg. 1255 **IT**

Sinochem (U.S.A.) Inc., Two World Trade Center, Ste. 2222, 10048, pg. 1255 **IT**

Sirius Reinsurance Corporation, 110 William St., 10038, pg. 4 **IT**

Sirrine BEK Environmental Co. (SBE), Five Penn Plaza, 16th Fl., 10001, pg. 1415 **PV**

Site Realty, Inc., 235 E. 42nd St., 10017, pg. 1284 **PB**

SITHE ENERGIES, INC., 450 Lexington Ave., 37th Fl., 10017, pg. 1004 **PV**

SKADDEN, ARPS, SLATE, MEAGHER & FLOM LLP, 919 Third Ave., 10022, pg. 1004 **PV**

Skandia America Reinsurance Corporation, One Liberty Plaza, 34th Fl., 10006, pg. 1257 **IT**

Skandia Investment Management, Inc., One Exchange Plaza, 28th Fl., 10006, pg. 1257 **IT**

Skandia U.S. Holding Corporation, One Exchange Plaza, 28th Fl., 10006, pg. 1257 **IT**

Skandinaviska Enskilda Banken Corporation, 245 Park Ave., 42nd Fl., 10167, pg. 1259 **IT**

Skiing, Two Park Ave., 10016, pg. 1617 **PB**

Sloan's Supermarkets, Inc., 823 11th Ave., 3rd Fl., 10019-3535, pg. 915 **PV**

Smart Money, 1790 Broadway, 10019, pg. 518 **PV**

B. Smith's, 771-773 8th Ave., 10036, pg. 130 **PB**

SMITH'S PERSONNEL SERVICE, INC., 317 Madison Ave., 10017, pg. 1010 **PV**

Snia U.S.A., Inc., 40 E. 34th St., 10016, pg. 483 **IT**

Soap Opera Digest, 45 W. 25th St., 10010, pg. 1328 **PB**

Soap Opera Weekly, 41 W. 25th St., 10010, pg. 1328 **PB**

Societe Generale, 1221 Ave. of the Americas, 10020, pg. 1273 **IT**

Soligor U.S.A., Inc., 117 E. 57th St., Ste.21H, 10022, pg. 6 **PV**

Solvay Technologies Inc. 500 Fifth Ave. 10110, pg. 1277 **IT**

Somerset Knitting Mills, 1290 Ave. of the Americas, 10104, pg. 1291 **IT**

Sony Music Entertainment, P.O. Box 970, 10274-0970, pg. 1284 **IT**

Sony Music Entertainment, Inc., 550 Madison Ave., 10022, pg. 1281 **IT**

Sony U.S.A., Nine W. 57th St., 10019, pg. 1281 **IT**

SOTHEBY'S HOLDINGS INC., 1334 York Ave., 10021, pg. 1487 **PB**

Sotheby's Inc., 1334 York Ave., 10021, pg. 1487 **PB**

Sotheby's International Realty, 980 Madison Ave., 10021, pg. 1487 **PB**

Southern Peru Copper Corp., 180 Maiden Ln., 10038, pg. 138 **PB**

SOUTHWESTERN FINANCIAL CORPORATION, 590 Madison Ave., 10022, pg. 1018 **PV**

Spartan Security Services, One Park Ave., 10016, pg. 1574 **PV**

Special Markets (RTVCH), 1450 Broadway, 16th Fl., 10018, pg. 1006 **PV**

The Sperry & Hutchinson Company, Inc., 315 Park Ave. S., 10010-3607, pg. 990 **PB**

SPERRY OWENS, INC., 1120 Park Ave., 10128, pg. 1025 **PV**

I. SPIEWAK & SONS, INC., 469 7th Ave, 10th Fl., 10018, pg. 1025 **PV**

Sports Afield, 250 W. 55th St., 10019, pg. 517 **PV**

Sports Illustrated, Time & Life Bldg., Rockefeller Ctr., 10020, pg. 1613 **PB**

SportStyle, Seven W. 34th St., 10003, pg. 513 **PB**

Spot Broadcasting Unit, 101 Park Ave., 10178-0065, pg. 1641 **PV**

Springer-Verlag New York Inc., 175 Fifth Ave., 10010, pg. 1291 **IT**

Square Plus Garage Inc., 13-17 E. 54th, 10022, pg. 326 **IT**

Stagebill, 144 E. 44th St., 10017, pg. 1328 **PB**

Standard & Poor's Ratings Services, 25 Broadway, 10004, pg. 1071 **PB**

The Standard Bank of South Africa, 153 E. 53rd St., 38th Fl., 10022, pg. 1293 **IT**

Standard Chartered Bank, Seven World Trade Center, 10048, pg. 1294 **IT**

Standard Chartered Bank (New York), 160 Water St., 10038-4995, pg. 1294 **IT**

STANDARD METALS CORPORATION, 156 W. 56th St., 10020, pg. 1502 **PB**

Standard New York Inc., 153 E. 53rd St., 38th Fl., 10022, pg. 1293 **IT**

Standard Research Consultants, 420 Lexington Ave., 10170, pg. 50 **PV**

Standard Security Life Insurance Company of New York, 485 Madison Ave., 10022, pg. 446 **PV**

STAR CHILDREN'S DRESS COMPANY, INC., 100 W. 33rd St., 10001, pg. 1034 **PV**

H.C. Starck Inc., 280 Park Ave., 10017, pg. 174 **IT**

Hermann C. Starck, Inc., 280 Park Ave., 10017, pg. 175 **IT**

STARRETT HRH, One Park Ave., 10016, pg. 1035 **PV**

State Bank of India, 460 Park Ave, 2nd Floor, 10022, pg. 1297 **IT**

Stawasz & Partners/Health Care Communications, 445 Park Ave., 10022, pg. 599 **PV**

Steinman, Boynton, Gronquist & Birdsall Inc., 110 William St., 10038, pg. 842 **PV**

Stendhal, 40 E. 52nd Ave., 10022, pg. 445 **PV**

STERN & STERN INDUSTRIES INC., 708 Third Ave., 10017, pg. 1041 **PV**

Sterno, Inc., 300 Park Ave., 10022, pg. 397 **PB**

STET North American, 400 Park Ave., 21st Fl., 10022, pg. 655 **IT**

Stewart Smith East, Inc., 88 Pine St., 17th Fl., 10005, pg. 1508 **IT**

Stone & Webster Management Consultants, Inc., One Penn Plza., 250 W. 34th St., 10119, pg. 1519 **PB**

Stone & Webster Overseas Consultants, Inc., One Penn Plaza, 250 W. 34th St., 10119, pg. 1519 **PB**

Stone & Webster Overseas Group, Inc., 250 W. 34th St., 10119, pg. 1519 **PB**

Stone & Webster Worldwide, Inc., 250 W. 34th St., 10119, pg. 1519 **PB**

STONINGTON PARTNERS INC., General Motors Bldg., 767 Fifth Ave.-48th Fl., 10153, pg. 1045 **PV**

Stora Feldmuhle North America Comp, 230 Park Ave., Ste. 15 14, 10169, pg. 1304 **IT**

Strategy XXI, 515 Madison Ave., 34th Fl., 10022, pg. 1642 **PB**

Successful Meetings, 355 Park Ave. South, 10010, pg. 1446 **IT**

Sudler & Hennessey, 1633 Broadway, 25th Fl., 10019, pg. 1197 **PV**

Suffolk Capital Management, 250 W. 57th ST., Ste. 420, 10107, pg. 1674 **PB**

SUGAR FOODS CORP, 950 Third Ave., 10022, pg. 1049 **PV**

Sulzer, Inc., 200 Park Ave., 10166-0068, pg. 1306 **IT**

Sulzer USA Inc., 200 Park Ave., 16th Fl., 10166, pg. 1306 **IT**

Sumitomo Bank Capital Markets, Inc., 277 Park Ave., 10172, pg. 1308 **IT**

Sumitomo Bank Financial Services, Inc., 277 Park Ave., 10172, pg. 1308 **IT**

Sumitomo Bank Investment Management (New York), Inc., 277 Park Ave., 10172, pg. 1308 **IT**

Sumitomo Bank Leasing & Finance, Inc., 277 Park Ave., 10172, pg. 1308 **IT**

The Sumitomo Bank, Ltd.-New York Branch, 277 Park Ave., 10172, pg. 1309 **IT**

Sumitomo Bank of New York Trust Company, Two World Financial Ctr., Fl. 35, 225 Liberty St., 10281, pg. 1309 **IT**

Sumitomo Bank Securities, Inc., 277 Park Ave., 10172, pg. 1309 **IT**

Sumitomo Chemical America, Inc., 345 Park Ave., 10154, pg. 1311 **IT**

Sumitomo Corporation of America, 345 Park Ave., 10154, pg. 1312 **IT**

Sumitomo Electric Finance U.S.A., Inc., Park Ave. Tower, 65 E. 55th St., 16th Fl., 10022-3219, pg. 1313 **IT**

Sumitomo Electric U.S.A., Inc., Park Ave. Tower, 65 E. 55th St., 16th Fl., 10022-3219, pg. 1313 **IT**

Sumitomo Life America, Inc., 245 Park Ave., 34th Fl., 10167, pg. 1315 **IT**

Sumitomo Life Insurance Agency America, Inc., 245 Park Ave., 34F, 10167, pg. 1315 **IT**

Sumitomo Life Realty (N.Y.), Inc., 245 Park Ave., 34F, 10167, pg. 1315 **IT**

Sumitomo Metal Mining U.S.A. Inc., 345 Park Ave., 10154, pg. 1316 **IT**

The Sumitomo Trust & Banking Co., Ltd., 527 Madison Ave., 10022, pg. 1317 **IT**

The Sumitomo Trust & Banking Co. (U.S.A.), 527 Madison Ave., 10022, pg. 1317 **IT**

THE SUMMIT MEDIA GROUP, 1414 Avenue of the Americas, 3rd. Fl., 10019, pg. 1050 **PV**

Sun Alliance USA, Inc., Ten E. 50th St., 27th Fl., 10022, pg. 1131 **IT**

Sun Insurance Co. of New York, Ten E. 50th St., 10022, pg. 1131 **IT**

Sun Life Insurance and Annuity Company of New York, 67 Broad St., 10004, pg. 1319 **IT**

SunAmerica Asset Management Corporation, 733 Third Ave., 10017, pg. 1533 **PB**

Sunburst, 19 Union Sq. W., 10003, pg. 1479 **IT**

Sunday Magazine Network, 10 East 38 St., 10016, pg. 739 **PV**

SunGard Trading Systems Group, 560 Lexington Ave., 10th Fl., 10022, pg. 1535 **PB**

Sunkyong America, Inc., 110 East 55th St., 10022, pg. 1320 **IT**

Suntory International Corp., 1211 Ave. of the Americas, 10036, pg. 1321 **IT**

Supermarket News, Seven W. 34th St., 10003, pg. 513 **PB**

Surfside Vermont Real Estate Corporation, 10017, pg. 180 **IT**

SUSSEX PUBLISHERS, INC., 49 E. 21st St. 11th Fl., 10010, pg. 1056 **PV**

Svenska Handelsbanken, New York, 153 E. 53rd St., 37th Fl., 10022-4678, pg. 1327 **IT**

Swatch Watch U.S.A., 35 E. 21st St., 10010, pg. 1161 **IT**

Swedbank New York, 12 E. 49th St., 20th Fl., 10017, pg. 1328 **IT**

Sweet's Div., 1221 Ave. of the Americas, 10020, pg. 1070 **PB**

SWIRL, II LTD, Eight W. 38th St. 8th Fl., 10018, pg. 1059 **PV**

Swiss-Am Reassurance Company, 237 Park Ave., 10017, pg. 1333 **IT**

Swiss Bank Corporation, Swiss Bank Tower, 10 E. 50th St., 10022, pg. 1329 **IT**

Swiss Re America Corporation, 237 Park Ave., 10017, pg. 1333 **IT**

Swiss Re Atrium Corporation, 12 E. 49th St., 10017, pg. 1333 **IT**

Swiss Re Capital Markets Corporations, Tower 49, 12th E. 49th St., 10017, pg. 1332 **IT**

Swiss Re Financial Products, 12th E. 49th St., 10017, pg. 1333 **IT**

Swiss Re Life Company America, 237 Park Ave., 10017, pg. 1333 **IT**

Swiss Reinsurance America Corporation, 237 Park Ave., 10017, pg. 1333 **IT**

SwissRe Advisers, Inc., 200 Park Ave., 10166, pg. 1333 **IT**

SwissRe Finance (US) Inc., 237 Park Ave., 10017, pg. 1333 **IT**

Systems Strategies, Inc., One Penn Plaza, 43rd Fl., 10001, pg. 120 **PB**

TAUSA - Trasatlantica Agency USA Inc., 99 Hudson St., 6th Fl., 10013, pg. 1224 **IT**

TBG Services, Inc., 565 5th Ave., 17th Fl., 10017, pg. 1335 **IT**

TBWA CHIAT/DAY, 180 Maiden Ln., 38th Fl., 10038, pg. 1062 **PV**

TBWA Chiat/Day New York, 180 Maiden Ln., 10038, pg. 1062 **PV**

TDC: The Design Center, 130 Fifth Ave., 10011, pg. 1062 **PV**

TDS Ventures, Inc., Time & Life Bldg., Rockefeller Center, 10020, pg. 1614 **PB**

Geographic Index-U.S.

TIE Systems-Manhattan, 70 W. 40th St., 5th Fl., 10018, pg. 1085 **PV**

T.I.E.C.-The Italian Economic Corporation, 25 W. 51st St., 10019, pg. 136 **IT**

TIG HOLDINGS, INC., 65 E. 55th St., 10022, pg. 1555 **PB**

TLC BEATRICE INTERNATIONAL HOLDINGS INC., Nine W. 57th St., 39th Fl., 10019, pg. 1064 **PV**

TM Claims Service, Inc., 101 Park Ave., 10178-0095, pg. 1392 **IT**

TMP WORLDWIDE, INC., 1633 Broadway, 33rd Fl., 10019, pg. 1064 **PV**

TMP Worldwide Recruitment Division, 1633 Broadway, 33rd Fl., 10019, pg. 1065 **PV**

TMP Worldwide/Recruitment Division, 1633 Broadway, 33rd Fl., 10019, pg. 1065 **PV**

TN Entertainment, 101 Park Ave., 10178-0065, pg. 1641 **PB**

TSE Leasing Co., 469 Seventh Ave., 10018, pg. 1025 **PV**

TSL, 50 Broad St., 14th Fl., 10004, pg. 257 **PB**

TSR Consulting Services, Inc., 655 Third Ave., 10017, pg. 1559 **PB**

Taisei America Capital Funding Corp., 114 W. 47th St., Ste. 2400, 10036, pg. 1347 **IT**

Taisei America Corp., 114 W. 47th St., Ste. 2400, 10036, pg. 1347 **IT**

Taiyo Asset Management of America, Inc., 450 Lexington Ave., 38th Fl., 10017, pg. 1349 **IT**

Taiyo Life Realty of America, Inc., 450 Lexington Ave., 38th Fl., 10017, pg. 1349 **IT**

The Taiyo Mutual Life Insurance Co., 277 Park Ave., 43rd Fl., 10172, pg. 1349 **IT**

Takara Belmont U.S.A., Inc., 17 W. 56th St., 10019, pg. 1349 **IT**

Takashimaya Fifth Avenue Corporation, 693 Fifth Ave., 10022, pg. 1350 **IT**

Takashimaya Madison Avenue Corporation, 693 Fifth Ave., 10022, pg. 1350 **IT**

Takashimaya New York, Inc., 693 Fifth Ave., 10022, pg. 1350 **IT**

Takenaka (U.S.A.) Corporation, New York Office, Plaza 57, 145 W. 57th St., 10019, pg. 1351 **IT**

Talbots, 525 Madison Ave. 5th Fl., 10022, pg. 28 **IT**

Tambourine Books, 1350 Ave. of the Americas, 10019, pg. 515 **PV**

Tata Inc., 101 Park Ave., 10178, pg. 1356 **IT**

Taylor Woodrow Construction Corp., 250 Park Ave., 10177, pg. 1359 **IT**

TEACHERS INSURANCE AND ANNUITY ASSOCIATION, 730 Third Ave., 10017, pg. 1071 **PV**

Technip Inc., 225 W. 34th St., Ste. 612, 10001, pg. 1361 **IT**

Technology Solutions Inc., 475 Park Ave. S., 10016, pg. 1157 **PV**

Teenform, Inc., 136 Madison Ave., 10016, pg. 1484 **IT**

Teijin America, Inc., 10 E. 50th St., 23rd Fl., 10022, pg. 1362 **IT**

Telefonica, 535 Madison Ave. 35th Flr., 10022-4212, pg. 1372 **IT**

TeleRep, Incorporated, One Dag Hammarskjold Plaza, 885 Second Ave., 10017, pg. 282 **PV**

Temco Mechanical Maintenance, One Park Ave., 10016, pg. 1574 **PB**

TEMCO SERVICE INDUSTRIES, One Park Ave., 10016, pg. 1574 **PB**

Templeton Quantitative Advisors, 31 W. 52nd St., 10th Fl., 10019, pg. 680 **PB**

TEXAS PACIFIC LAND TRUST, 80 Broadway, Ste. 2700, 10004, pg. 1586 **PB**

Textile Impressions, Inc., 48 W. 38th St., 10018, pg. 695 **IT**

THACKERAY CORPORATION, 400 Madison Ave., Ste. 1508, 10017, pg. 1590 **PB**

Thai Airways Intl. Ltd.-New York, 630 Fifth Ave., Ste. 351, 10111, pg. 1381 **IT**

The Goldhirsh Group, 477 Madison Ave., 10022-5702, pg. 461 **PV**

THE MEDIA EDGE, 1180 Ave. of the Americas, 10036, pg. 1079 **PV**

Think New Ideas, Inc., Onramp, 45 W. 36th St., 12th Fl., 10018, pg. 1224 **PB**

THOMAS PUBLISHING COMPANY, Five Penn Plaza, 10001, pg. 1082 **PV**

Thomas Regional, Five Penn Plaza, 10001, pg. 1082 **PV**

Thomas Register, Five Penn Plaza, 10001, pg. 1082 **PV**

Thompson Bankwatch, Inc., 61 Broadway, 3rd. Fl., 10006, pg. 1600 **PB**

J. Walter Thompson Company, 466 Lexington Ave., 10017, pg. 1483 **PV**

Thomson Bank Watch, Inc., 61 Broadway, 3rd. Fl., 10006, pg. 1600 **PB**

Thyssen Specialty Steels, Inc., 1114 Ave. of the Americas, 10036, pg. 1388 **IT**

TIFFANY & CO., 727 Fifth Ave., 10022, pg. 1608 **PB**

Tiffany & Company, 727 Fifth Ave., 10022, pg. 1609 **PB**

Tiffany & Co. ICT, Inc., 727 Fifth Ave., 10022, pg. 1609 **PB**

Tiffany & Co. International, 727 Fifth Ave., 10022, pg. 1609 **PB**

Tiffany & Co. Japan Inc., 727 Fifth Ave., 10022, pg. 1609 **PB**

Tiffany & Co. Japan Inc. - Japan Branch, 727 Fifth Ave., 10022, pg. 1609 **PB**

Tiffco Jewelery & Chain Crafts, Inc., 727 Fifth Ave., 10022, pg. 1609 **PB**

Tillinghast-Towers Penn, 335 Madison Ave., 10167, pg. 1093 **PV**

Time, Time & Life Bldg., Rockefeller Ctr., 10020, pg. 1613 **PB**

Time Distribution Services, Time & Life Bldg., Rockefeller Center, 10020, pg. 1614 **PB**

Time Inc., Time & Life Bldg., Rockefeller Ctr., 10020, pg. 1612 **PB**

The Time Inc. Book Company, Time & Life Bldg., Rockefeller Center, 10020, pg. 1613 **PB**

Time Inc. Health, 60 E. 42nd St., Ste. 3710, 10065, pg. 1613 **PB**

Time-Life Libraries, Inc., Time & Life Bldg., Rockefeller Center, 10020, pg. 1613 **PB**

Time Warner Cable of New York City, 120 E. 23rd St., 10010, pg. 1611 **PB**

Time Warner Enterprises, 75 Rockefeller Plaza, 10019, pg. 1611 **PB**

TIME WARNER INC., 75 Rockefeller Plaza, 14th Fl., 10019, pg. 1610 **PV**

Time Warner Publishing Inc., Time & Life Building, Rockefeller Center, 10020, pg. 1614 **PV**

Time Warner Sports, 1100 Ave. of the Americas, 10036, pg. 1611 **PV**

Time Warner Trade Publishing, 666 Fifth Ave., 10103, pg. 1614 **PV**

Time Women's Publications Inc., Time & Life Bldg., Rockefeller Center, 10020, pg. 1614 **PV**

Times Books, 201 E. 50th St., 10022, pg. 21 **PV**

Times Mirror Magazines, Inc., Two Park Ave., 10016, pg. 1616 **PB**

TimesFax, 122 E. 42nd St., 10168, pg. 1174 **PB**

TISHMAN REALTY & CONSTRUCTION CO., INC., 666 Fifth Ave., 10103, pg. 1089 **PV**

Tishman Urban Development, 666 Fifth Ave., 10103, pg. 1089 **PV**

THE TITAN INDUSTRIAL CORP., 555 Madison Ave., 10th Fl., 10022, pg. 1089 **PV**

Today's Homeowner, Two Park Ave., 10016, pg. 1617 **PB**

Todd-AO Studios/East, 259 W. 54th St., 10019, pg. 1619 **PB**

TOHC America International Inc., 540 Madison Ave., 37th Fl., 10022, pg. 1390 **IT**

TOHO America Realty Inc., 540 Madison Ave., 37th Fl., 10022, pg. 1390 **IT**

Tohoku Electric Power Co., Inc., Park Avenue Tower, 65 E. 55th St., Ste. 2304, 10022, pg. 1391 **IT**

Tokai Securities, Inc., Park Ave. Plaza, 12th Fl., 55 E. 52nd St., 10055, pg. 1391 **IT**

Tokai Trust Company of New York, Park Ave. Plaza, 55 E. 52nd St., 10055, pg. 1391 **IT**

Tokio Marine Asset Management New York Co., Ltd., 101 Park Ave., 10178-0095, pg. 1392 **IT**

Tokio Marine Management Inc., 101 Park Ave., 10178-0095, pg. 1392 **IT**

Tokio Marine Realty Co., Ltd., 101 Park Ave., 10178-0095, pg. 1392 **IT**

The Tokio (New York) Corporation, 101 Park Ave., 10178-0095, pg. 1392 **IT**

Tokio Re Corporation, 36th Fl., 1 Liberty Plaza, 10006-1404, pg. 1392 **IT**

Tokyo-Mitsubishi Derivative Products (USA), Inc., 1251 Ave. of the Americas, 10020, pg. 157 **IT**

Tokyo-Mitsubishi Securities (U.S.A.), Inc., 1251 Ave. of the Americas, 10020-1104, pg. 157 **IT**

Tomen America Inc., 1285 Ave. of the Americas, 10019, pg. 1395 **IT**

Tomen Energy International Corp., 630 Fifth Ave., 10111, pg. 1399 **IT**

Top Value Media, 535 Fifth Ave., 10016, pg. 739 **PV**

Toppan Printing Co. (America), Inc., 666 Fifth Ave., 10103, pg. 1399 **IT**

THE TOPPS COMPANY, INC., One Whitehall St., 10004-2109, pg. 1621 **PB**

Toray Industries (America) Inc., 5th Fl., 600 Third Ave., 10016, pg. 1400 **IT**

Toronto Dominion Bank Trust Co., 31 W. 52nd St., 19th Fl., 10019-6101, pg. 1401 **IT**

Toronto Dominion Securities (U.S.A.) Inc., 31 W. 52nd St., 10019-6101, pg. 1401 **IT**

Toshiba America Capital Corporation, 1251 Avenue of the Americas, 10020, pg. 1405 **IT**

Toshiba America Inc., 1251 Ave. of the Americas, Ste. 4100 10020, pg. 1405 **IT**

Toshoku America, Inc., 780 Third Ave., 37th Fl., 10017-2024, pg. 1407 **IT**

Totes/Isotoner, Inc., 417 Fifth Ave., 10016, pg. 1433 **PB**

Toth Design & Advertising, 520 Broadway, 10012, pg. 1093 **PV**

Tourism Malaysia - N.Y. Office, 595 Madision Ave., Ste. 1800, 10022, pg. 833 **IT**

TOURNEAU INC., 3 E. 54th St., 10022, pg. 1093 **PV**

Tower Group International, 1221 Ave. of the Americas, 10020, pg. 1071 **PB**

TOWER REALTY TRUST, INC., 120 W. 45th St., 24th Fl., 10036, pg. 1625 **PB**

TOWERS PERRIN, 335 Madison Ave., 10017-4605, pg. 1093 **PV**

Town & Country, 1700 Broadway, 10019, pg. 517 **PV**

TOWNE, SILVERSTEIN, ROTTER INC., 11 Lafayette St., 10003, pg. 1093 **PV**

TOY BIZ, INC., 685 Third Ave., 30th Fl., 10017, pg. 1625 **PB**

Toy Biz, International, 685 Third Ave., 30th Fl., 10017, pg. 1626 **PB**

Toyo Trust Company of New York, 666 5th Ave., 33rd Fl., 10103-3395, pg. 1411 **IT**

Toyobo America Inc., 40 E. 52nd St., 20th Fl., 10022, pg. 1411 **IT**

Toyota Motor Corporate Services of North America, 9 W. 57th St., 10019, pg. 1412 **IT**

TRACE INTERNATIONAL HOLDINGS, INC., 375 Park Ave., 11th Fl., 10152, pg. 1094 **PV**

Trade Show Enterprises, 469 Seventh Ave., 10018, pg. 1025 **PV**

Trademark Research Corporation, 300 Park Ave. S., 10010, pg. 1573 **IT**

Traffic World, Two World Trade Center, 27th Fl., 10048, pg. 1026 **IT**

TRAINER WORTHAM & COMPANY INCORPORATED, 845 Third Ave., 6th Fl., 10022, pg. 1095 **PV**

The Trane Company, 1114 Ave. of the Americas, 10036, pg. 92 **PB**

Trans Pacific Insurance Company, 101 Park Ave., 10178-0095, pg. 1392 **IT**

TRANS RESOURCES, INC., Nine W. 57th St., Ste. 3900, 10019, pg. 1096 **PV**

TRANSAMMONIA INC., 350 Park Ave., 10022, pg. 1096 **PV**

Transatlantic Holdings Inc., 80 Pine St., 10005, pg. 84 **PB**

Transatlantic Holdings, Inc.-New York, 80 Pine St., 10005, pg. 83 **PB**

Transatlantic Reinsurance Co., 80 Pine St., 10005, pg. 84 **PB**

Transderm Laboratories Corporation, 1212 Ave. of the Americas, 10036, pg. 802 **PB**

Transocean Holding Corporation, One Liberty Plaza, 10006, pg. 90 **IT**

TRANSWORLD HOME HEALTHCARE, INC., 555 Madison Ave. 30th Fl., 10222, pg. 1632 **PB**

Transworld Snowboarding, Two Park Ave., 10016, pg. 1617 **PB**

Trappings Co., 469 Seventh Ave., 10018, pg. 1025 **PV**

Travel & Leisure, 1120 Ave. of the Americas, 10036, pg. 74 **PV**

Travel Publications, Inc., 28 W. 23rd St., 10010, pg. 1368 **PV**

TRAVELERS GROUP, 388 Greenwich St., 10013, pg. 1632 **PB**

TrefilARBED Inc., 825 Third Ave., 10022, pg. 79 **IT**

Tri-Continental Corporation, 100 Park Ave., 10017, pg. 982 **PV**

TRIANGLE MARKETING CORP., 171 Madison Ave., Room 1101, 10016-5110, pg. 1102 **PV**

TRIARC COMPANIES, INC., 280 Park Ave., 10017, pg. 1634 **PB**

Triborough Bridge & Tunnel Authority, Randall's Island, 10035, pg. 739 **PV**

Triclinica Inc., 1740 Broadway, 10019, pg. 679 **PV**

Trifari Jewelers, 350 Fifth Ave., 16th Fl., 10118, pg. 757 **PV**

TriStar Pictures Eastern Division, 711 5th Ave., 10022, pg. 1283 **PV**

Triumph Releasing Corporation - New York Territory, 711 5th Ave., 7th Fl., 10022, pg. 1282 **PV**

TRUE NORTH DIVERSIFIED COMPANIES, 40 W. 23rd St., 10010, pg. 1642 **PB**

TRUMP ORGANIZATION, 725 Fifth Ave., 10022, pg. 1108 **PV**

Trump Towers, 725 Fifth Ave., 10022, pg. 1108 **PV**

Trumpet Book Clubs, 555 Broadway, 10012, pg. 1440 **PB**

The Trumpet Club, 666 Fifth Ave., 10103, pg. 191 **IT**

Turner Construction Co., 375 Hudson St., 10014, pg. 1645 **PB**

Turner Construction Company, 375 Hudson St., 10014, pg. 1645 **PB**

THE TURNER CORPORATION, 375 Hudson St., 10014, pg. 1645 **PB**

Turner Development Corporation, 375 Hudson St., 10014, pg. 1646 **PB**

Turner International Industries, Inc., 375 Hudson St., 10014, pg. 1646 **PB**

Turner Steiner International, 375 Hudson St., 10014, pg. 1646 **PB**

Twayne Publishers, 1633 Broadway, 10019, pg. 777 **PV**

Tyco Playtime Inc., 200 Fifth Ave., 10010, pg. 1058 **PB**

Tyco Preschool, 200 5th Ave., 10010, pg. 1058 **PB**

Tyco Toys, Inc., 200 Fifth Ave., 11th Fl., 10010, pg. 1058 **PB**

UAM Retirement Plan Services, Inc., 1133 Ave. of the Americas, 28th Fl., 10036, pg. 1574 **PV**

UBE Industries (America) Inc., 666 Fifth Ave., 10103, pg. 1427 **IT**

UBS Asset Management (New York) Inc., 1211 Ave. of the Americas, 10105, pg. 1440 **IT**

UBS Management North America, 299 Park Ave., 10171-0026, pg. 1440 **IT**

UBS Securities LLC, 299 Park Ave., Fls. 4-7, 10171-0026, pg. 1440 **IT**

UIS Export Corporation, 600 Fifth Ave., 10020, pg. 1113 **PV**

URS Greiner, One Penn Plaza, Ste. 610, 10199, pg. 1659 **PB**

UNAPIX ENTERTAINMENT INC., 200 Madison Ave., 10016, pg. 1664 **PB**

Uniao de Bancos Brasileiros (Unibanco) (Brazil), 555 Madison Ave., 19th Fl., 10022, pg. 1431 **IT**

Uniblend Spinners, 10 E. 40th St., 10016, pg. 1117 **PV**

Unicorp American Corporation, 99 Park Ave., 10016, pg. 1433 **IT**

Unidigital/Cardinal Corp., 545 W. 45th St., 10036, pg. 1664 **PB**

UNIDIGITAL INC., 20 W. 20th St., 10011, pg. 1664 **PB**

Unilever United States Inc., Lever House, 390 Park Ave., 10022, pg. 1435 **IT**

Unimax Corp., 54 E. 64th St., 10021, pg. 993 **PV**

THE UNIMAX CORPORATION, 54 E. 64th St., 10021, pg. 1118 **PV**

Unisource, 161 Ave. of the Americas, 10013-1205, pg. 1671 **PB**

UNISYSTEMS, INC., 155 E. 55th St., 10022, pg. 1120 **PV**

United Acquisition Corporation, 823 11th Ave., 10019, pg. 915 **PV**

United Auto Group, Inc., 375 Park Ave., Ste. 2201, 10152, pg. 1095 **PV**

UNITED CREDIT CORP. & PATRIOT FUNDING, 15 W 44th St., 5th Fl., 10036, pg. 1121 **PV**

U.S. LOCATED COMPANIES NEW YORK

UNITED INDUSTRIAL CORPORATION, 18 E. 48th St., 10017, pg. 1679 PB
United Media, 200 Madison Ave., 10016, pg. 1448 PB
United Missouri Trust Company of New York, One Battery Park Plaza, Eighth Fl., 10004, pg. 1655 PB
UNITED PIECE DYE WORKS, LP, 111 W. 40th St., Rm. 410, 10018, pg. 1123 PV
U.S. Aviation Underwriters, Inc., 199 Water St., 10038, pg. 726 PB
U.S. Clearing Corp., 26 Broadway, 10004, pg. 650 PB
U.S. Direct Selling Division, Nine W. 57th St., 10019, pg. 156 PB
United States Fire Insurance Company, World Financial Ctr., 225 Liberty St., 28th Fl., 10281, pg. 1784 PB
USLIFE Advisers, Inc., 125 Maiden Ln., 10038, pg. 77 PB
USLIFE Corporation, 125 Maiden Ln., 10038, pg. 77 PB
USLIFE Equity Sales Corp., 125 Maiden Ln., 10038, pg. 77 PB
The United States Life Ins. Co. In the City of New York, 125 Maiden Ln., 10038, pg. 77 PB
U.S. NEWS & WORLD REPORT, 450 W. 33rd St., 10001, pg. 1125 PV
USA Networks, 1230 Ave. of the Americas, 10020, pg. 1686 PB
USA Weekend, 535 Madison Ave., 21st Fl., 10022, pg. 701 PB
UNITED STATES REALTY & INVESTMENT CO., 450 7th Ave., 45th Fl., 10123, pg. 1125 PV
U.S. TRUST CORPORATION, 114 W. 47th St., 10036-1532, pg. 1688 PB
U.S. Woolworth Div., 233 Broadway, 10279, pg. 1778 PB
U.S. Yellow Pages, 1270 Ave. of the Americas, 10020, pg. 1167 PV
United World Films Div., 445 Park Ave., 10022, pg. 1216 IT
UNITEL VIDEO, INC., 515 W. 57th, 10019, pg. 1692 PB
Unitel Video, Inc. - Studio & Production Facilities, 8 West 38th St., pg. 1692 PB
Unitel Video, Inc. - Studio Facilities, 508-510 West 57th St., pg. 1692 PB
Unitel Video, Inc. - Studio Facilities, 841 Ninth Ave., pg. 1692 PB
Unitel Video, Inc. - Studio Facilities, 503 West 33rd St., pg. 1692 PB
Unitel Video, Inc. - Studio Facilities, 402 East 76th St., pg. 1692 PB
Unitel Video, Inc. - Studio Facilities, 433-435 West 53rd St., pg. 1692 PB
Unitika America Corp., 666 Fifth Ave., 10103, pg. 1444 IT
Universal Film Exchanges, Inc., 445 Park Ave., 10022, pg. 1216 IT
Universal Studios Distributing Corp., 445 Park Ave., 10022, pg. 1216 IT
Univision Ltd. Partnership, 605 Third Ave., 12th Floor, 10158, pg. 230 PV
UNIWORLD GROUP, INC., 100 Ave. of the Americas, 10013, pg. 1128 PV
UniWorld Hispanic, 100 Ave. of the Americas, 10013, pg. 1128 PV
Urban Outfitters, Inc., 209 W. 38th St., 7th Fl., 10018, pg. 1700 PB
Us Magazine, 1290 Ave. of the Americas, 10104, pg. 1162 PV
USA Broadcasting, 152 W. 57th St., 10019, pg. 1686 PB
Utilities & Industries Management Corp., 54 E. 64th St., 10021, pg. 993 PV
VH-1/Video Hits One, 1515 Broadway, 10036, pg. 779 PV
VNU USA, Inc., 1515 Broadway, 10036-8986, pg. 1447 IT
VSM, INC., 307 E. 53rd St., 10022, pg. 1130 PV
VV PUBLISHING CORP., 36 Cooper Sq., 10003, pg. 1131 PV
Value Line, Inc., 220 E. 42nd St., 6th Flr., 10017, pg. 137 PV
Value Line Publishing, 220 E. 42nd St., 6th Fl., 10017, pg. 137 PV
Value Line Securities, Inc., 220 E. 42nd St., 10017-5891, pg. 137 PV
VAN CLEEF & ARPELS, INC., 744 Fifth Ave., 10019, pg. 1132 PV
The Van Heusen Group of Companies, 1290 Ave. of the Americas, 10104, pg. 1291 PB
Van Nostrand Reinhold Co., 115 Fifth Ave., 10003, pg. 1600 PB
Vanity Fair, 350 Madison Ave., 10017, pg. 20 PV
Vanity Fair, Eight W. 38th St., 10018, pg. 1702 PB
Vantage Global Advisors, Inc., 630 Fifth Ave., 10111, pg. 998 PB
Varig Brazilian Airlines, 380 Madison Ave., 10017, pg. 1451 IT
VEBA Corporation, 605 Third Ave., 10158, pg. 1461 IT
Viacom Broadcasting Inc., 1515 Broadway, 40th Fl., 10036, pg. 778 PV
Viacom Enterprises, 1515 Broadway, 10036, pg. 779 PV
Viacom Inc., 1515 Broadway, 10036, pg. 775 PV
Viacom International Inc., 1515 Broadway, 10036, pg. 778 PV
Viacom Networks Inc., 1515 Broadway, 10036, pg. 779 PV
Viacom Satellite Networks Inc., 1633 Broadway, 10036, pg. 779 PV
Victoria, 224 W. 57th St., 10019, pg. 517 PV
Vigilant Insurance Co., 100 William St., 10038, pg. 355 PB
Villard Books, 201 E. 50th St., 10022, pg. 21 PV
Visage Beaute' Cosmetics, Inc., 767 Fifth Ave., 10153, pg. 690 PV
Vitt Media-Corporate Trade, 90 Park Ave., 10016, pg. 1142 PV
VITT MEDIA INTERNATIONAL, INC., 90 Park Ave., 10016-1301, pg. 1142 PV
Vitt Media-New Media, 1114 Ave. of the Americas, 10036, pg. 1142 PV
Voest-Alpine Industries, Inc., Lincoln Bldg., 60 E. 42nd St., 10165, pg. 1470 IT
Voest-Alpine Industries, Inc.-Continuous Casting, 60 E. 42nd St., 10165, pg. 1470 IT
Voest-Alpine Industries, Inc.-Steelmaking, 60 E. 42nd St., 10165, pg. 1470 IT
Voest-Alpine International Corp.-Purchasing Service, Lincoln Bldg., 60 E. 42nd St., 10165, pg. 1471 IT
Voest-Alpine International Corp.-Railroad Products Div., Lincoln Bldg., 60 E. 42nd St., 10165, pg. 1471 IT
Voest-Alpine International Corporation, Lincoln Bldg., 60 E. 42nd St., 46th Fl., 10165, pg. 1470 IT
Voest-Alpine Services and Technologies Corp., Lincoln Bldg., 60 E. 42nd St., Ste. 1320, 10165, pg. 1471 IT
Voest-Alpine Steel Corp., Lincoln Bldg., 60 E. 42nd St., 10165, pg. 1471 IT
Voest-Alpine Steel Corp.-Forgings & Castings, 60 E. 42nd St., 10165, pg. 1471 IT
Voest-Alpine Steel Corp.-Rolled Steel Products, 60 E. 42nd St., 10165, pg. 1471 IT
Vogue Magazine, 350 Madison Ave., 10017, pg. 20 PV
Volt Delta Resources, Inc., 1221 Ave. of the Americas, 47th Fl., 10020, pg. 1724 PB
VOLT INFORMATION SCIENCES, INC., 1221 Ave. of the Americas, 47th Fl., 10020, pg. 1724 PB
Volt Management Corp., 1221 Ave. of the Americas, 10020, pg. 1724 PB
Volt Technical Services-East, 1221 Ave. of the Americas, 10020, pg. 1724 PB
WABC-AM Radio, Inc., 77 W. 66th St., 10023, pg. 512 PB
WABC T.V., 77 W. 66th St., 10023, pg. 512 PB
WCBS-TV, 524 West 57th St., 10019, pg. 275 PB
WEA Intl., Inc., 75 Rockefeller Plaza, 10019, pg. 1612 PB
WHX CORPORATION, 110 E. 59th St., 30th Fl., 10022, pg. 1726 PB
WHX Entertainment Corporation, 110 E. 59th St., 30th Fl., 10022, pg. 1726 PB
WINS Radio, 888 Seventh Ave., 10106, pg. 274 PB
WLTW-FM, 1515 Broadway, 10036, pg. 779 PV
WNYW, 205 E. 67th St., 10021, pg. 926 IT
WP Coal Company, 110 E. 59th St., 30th Fl., 10022, pg. 1726 PB
WP Steel Venture Company, 110 E. 59th St., 30th Fl., 10022, pg. 1726 PB
WPC Land Company, 110 E. 59th St., 30th Fl., 10022, pg. 1726 PB
WPIX, Inc., 11 WPIX Plaza, 220 E. 42nd St., 10017, pg. 1636 PB
WPLJ-FM Radio, Inc., 77 W. 66th St., 10023, pg. 512 PB
WPP Group USA Inc., Worldwide Plaza, 309 W. 49th St., 10019-7399, pg. 1483 IT
WQXR/FM, WQEW/AM, 122 Fifth Ave., 10011, pg. 1174 PB
WWF Paper Corp.-New York, 185 Madison Ave., 9th & 12th Fls., 10016, pg. 1145 PV
WWT Partnership, Time & Life Bldg., Rockefeller Center, 10020, pg. 1614 PB
Wacoal America Inc., 136 Madison Ave., 10016, pg. 1484 IT
Wagner Stott Clearing Corp., 20 Broad St., 10005, pg. 1097 PB
Wako Securities (America), Inc., One World Trade Ctr., Ste. 8369, 10048, pg. 1485 IT
Walker Group/CNI Inc., 320 W. 13th St., 10014, pg. 1483 IT
WALKER-PIONEER GRAPHICS, 233 Spring St., 9th Fl., 10013, pg. 1147 PV
The Wall Street Journal, 200 Liberty St., 10281, pg. 524 PB
Wallingford Property Holdings Co., 54 E. 64th St., 10021, pg. 1118 PV
WARING & LAROSA, INC., 909 Third Ave., 10022, pg. 1150 PV
Waring & LaRosa Direct, 909 Third Ave., 10022, pg. 1150 PV
Waring LaRosa Gordon Public Relations, 909 Third Ave., 10022, pg. 1150 PV
WARNACO INC., 90 Park Ave., 10016, pg. 1738 PB
Warnaco Inc.-International Div., 90 Park Ave., 12th Fl., 10016, pg. 1738 PB
Warnaco Inc.-Menswear Div., 90 Park Ave., 12th Fl., 10016, pg. 1738 PB
Warner Audio Publishing, 599 Broadway, 10012, pg. 1614 PB
Warner Books, Inc., 1271 Ave. of the Americas, 10020, pg. 1614 PB
Warner Bros. Inc., 75 Rockefeller Plaza, 10019, pg. 1611 PB
Warner Communications Inc., 75 Rockefeller Plaza, 10019, pg. 1611 PB
Warner Music Group, Inc., 75 Rockefeller Plaza, 10019, pg. 1612 PB
Warner Publisher Services, Inc., 666 Fifth Ave., 10019, pg. 1614 PB
Warren Gorham Lamont, 395 Hudson St., 4th Fl., 10014, pg. 1602 PB
Warren Press, Inc., 245 5th Ave., 10016, pg. 89 PB
WARWICK BAKER O'NEILL, 100 Ave. of the Americas, 10013, pg. 1152 PV
Washington National Life Insurance Co. of New York, 120 W. 45th St., 10036, pg. 256 PV
Wasserstein Perella Group, Inc., 31 W. 52nd. St., 10019, pg. 956 IT
Waterhouse Investor Services, 100 Wall St., 29th Fl., 10005, pg. 1401 IT
Waverly Fabrics, 79 Madison Ave., 10016-7878, pg. 973 PV
Weatherall Green & Smith (New York) Inc., 570 Lexington Ave., 10022, pg. 1488 IT
WEATHERLY PRIVATE CAPITAL, INC., 20 Exchange Place, 19th Fl., 10005, pg. 1156 PV
Weatherly Securities Corp., 20 Exchange Pl, 19th Fl., 10005, pg. 1156 PV
Websource, 161 Ave. of the Americas, 10013, pg. 1671 PB
Weilwood Industries, Inc., 119 W. 40th St., 10018, pg. 965 PV
WEISS, WHITTEN, STAGLIANO INC., 96 Morton St., 10014, pg. 1160 PV
WELLMADE INDUSTRIES, INCORPORATED, 131 W. 33rd St., 10001, pg. 1161 PV
Wellman Man-Made Fibers Div., 1133 Ave. of the Americas, 34th Fl., 10036, pg. 1752 PB
Wells BDDP, Inc., 11 Madison Ave., 12th Fl., 10010, pg. 117 IT
WELSH CARSON ANDERSON & STOWE, 320 Park Ave., 25th Fl., 10022, pg. 1162 PV
WENNER MEDIA, 1290 Ave. of the Americas, 2nd Fl., 10104, pg. 1162 PV
West Japan Railway Company, One Rockerfeller Plaza, 10020, pg. 1491 IT
West Merchant Bank Limited, 300 Park Ave., 23rd Fl., 10022, pg. 1493 IT
WEST SHORE ENVELOPE COMPANY, INC., 525 W. 52nd St., 10019, pg. 1163 PV
Westchester Fire Insurance Company, World Financial Ctr., 225 Liberty St., 28th Fl., 10281, pg. 1784 PB
Western Direct, 1270 Avenue of the Americas, 10020, pg. 1166 PV
Western International Media Corporation, 1270 Ave. of the Americas, 10020, pg. 1166 PV
WestLB New York Branch, 23rd & 24th Fl., 1211 Avenue of the Americas, 10036, pg. 1493 IT
Roy F. Weston of New York, 130 W. 30th St., 13th Fl., 10001, pg. 1761 PB
Westpac Banking Corporation, 27th Fl., 335 Madison Ave., 10017-4681, pg. 1496 IT
WESTVACO CORPORATION, 299 Park Ave., 10171, pg. 1762 PB
Westwood One Entertainment, 1675 Broadway, 17th Fl., 10019, pg. 1763 PB
WESTWOOD ONE, INC., 1675 Broadway, 17th Fl., 10019, pg. 1763 PB
Westwood One Radio Networks, 1675 Broadway, 17th Fl., 10019, pg. 1763 PB
Wheeling Construction Products, Inc., 110 E. 59th St., 30th Fl., 10022, pg. 1726 PB
Wheeling-Empire Company, 110 E. 59th St., 30th Fl., 10022, pg. 1727 PB
Wheeling-Pittsburgh Capital Corporation, 110 E. 59th St., 30th Fl., 10022, pg. 1727 PB
Wheeling-Pittsburgh Corporation, 110 E. 59th St., 30th Fl., 10022, pg. 1727 PB
Wheeling-Pittsburgh Funding, Inc., 110 E. 59th St., 30th Fl., 10022, pg. 1727 PB
Wheeling-Pittsburgh Radio Corporation, 110 E. 59th St., 30 Fl., 10022, pg. 1727 PB
Whitehall Stree Real Estate L.P., 85 Broad St., 10004, pg. 462 PV
Wide World Photos, Inc., 50 Rockefeller Plaza, 10020, pg. 92 PV
Wieden & Kennedy-New York, 100 Fifth Ave., 11th Fl., 10011, pg. 1175 PV
WILDER DEEM, INC., 417 Park Ave. Ste. 3 E., 10022, pg. 1176 PV
FREDERICK WILDMAN & SONS LTD., 311 E. 53rd St., 10022, pg. 1176 PV
JOHN WILEY & SONS, INC., 605 Third Ave., 10158, pg. 1768 PB
Williamhouse-Regency, Inc., 245 5th Ave., Rm. 502, 10016, pg. 89 PB
Williams Worldwide, 767 Third Ave., 15th Fl., 10017, pg. 1179 PV
Willis Corroon Aerospace, Wall St. Plaza, 88 Pine St., 10005-1843, pg. 1505 IT
Willis Corroon Corp. of New York, Seven Hanover Sq., 10038, pg. 1506 IT
Willis Corroon Financial Services Corp., Seven Hanover Sq., 10004-2594, pg. 1507 IT
Willis Corroon Financial Services Corp., Wall St. Plaza, 88 Pine St., 10005-1843, pg. 1507 IT
Willis Corroon International/Americas, Seven Hanover Sq., Seventh Fl., 10004-2594, pg. 1507 IT
Willis Corroon Marine & Energy, Seven Hanover Sq., Tenth Fl., 10004, pg. 1508 IT
Willis Faber, Inc., Seven Hanover Sq., 10004, pg. 1503 IT
Willis Faber North America, Inc.-New York, Wall St. Plaza, 28th Fl., 10005-1843, pg. 1503 IT
WILLOUGHBY'S, 136 W. 32nd St., 10001, pg. 1180 PV
WINNER COMMUNICATIONS, INC., 37 Union Sq. W., 10003, pg. 1183 PV
WINSTAR COMMUNICATIONS, 230 Park Ave., Ste. 2700, 10169, pg. 1772 PB
HARRY WINSTON, INC., 718 5th Ave., 10019, pg. 1183 PV
WINSTON RESOURCES, INC., 535 Fifth Ave., 7th Fl., 10017, pg. 1772 PB
Winterthur Reinsurance Corporation of America, Two World Financial Ctr., 225 Liberty St., 42nd Fl., 10281, pg. 346 IT
Woman's Day, 1633 Broadway, 10019, pg. 795 IT
Women's Magazines Group, 110 Fifth Ave., 10011, pg. 190 IT
Women's Sports and Event Marketing, 110 Fifth Ave., 10011, pg. 190 IT
Women's Wear Daily, Seven W. 34th Ave., 10003, pg. 513 PB
Wood, Struthers & Winthrop Management Corp., 140 Broadway, 42nd Fl., 10005, pg. 589 PB
Woodward-Clyde, 363 Seventh Ave., 11th Fl., 10001, pg. 1656 PB
Woody's, 140 7th Ave. S., 10014, pg. 130 PB

PB - *U.S. Public Companies Volume*
PV - *U.S. Private Companies Volume*
IT - *International Public & Private Companies Volume*

Geographic Index-U.S.

WOOLWORTH CORPORATION, Woolworth Bldg., 233
Broadway, 10279-0003, pg. 1777   **PB**
F.W. Woolworth Co., 233 Broadway, 10279, pg. 1777   **PB**
Woolworth Overseas Corp., 233 Broadway, 10279,
pg. 1778   **PB**
Woolworth World Trade Corp., 233 Broadway, 10279,
pg. 1778   **PB**
The World Bank Mission to the United Nations, 809 United
Nations Plaza, Ste. 900, 10017, pg. 1189   **PB**
World Financial Properties, Inc., One Liberty Plaza, 6th Fl.,
10006, pg. 1004
Worldvision Enterprises, 1700 Broadway, 10019-5992,
pg. 776   **PB**
Worldwide Media Research, 101 Park Ave., 10178-0065,
pg. 1641   **PB**
Worldwide Television News, 1995 Broadway, 10023,
pg. 513   **PB**
Worth Publisher Inc., 33 Irving Pl., 10003, pg. 1479   **IT**
CAROLE WREN, INC., 75 Ninth Ave., 3rd Fl., 10011,
pg. 1192   **PV**
Wunderman Cato Johnson, 675 Ave. of the Americas,
10010-5104, pg. 1197   **PV**
Y&R New Technologies, 285 Madison Ave., 10017,
pg. 1198   **PV**
Y.K.K. (U.S.A.) Inc., 45 W. 36th St., 10018, pg. 1515   **IT**
Yamaichi (America) Finance, Inc., Two World Trade Center,
Suite 9650, 10048, pg. 1517   **IT**
Yamaichi (America) Holdings, Inc., Two World Trade Ctr.,
Ste. 9650, 10048, pg. 1517   **IT**
Yamaichi Asset Management (America) Inc., Two World
Trade Ctr., Ste. 9852, 10048, pg. 1517   **IT**
Yamaichi Capital Management, Inc., Two World Trade Ctr.,
Ste. 9828, 10048, pg. 1516   **IT**
Yamaichi Financial Services Inc., Two World Trade Ctr.,
Ste. 9600, 10048, pg. 1517   **IT**
Yamaichi Information Systems Co., Ltd., Two World Trade
Ctr., Ste. 9864, 10048, pg. 1516   **IT**
Yamaichi International (America) Inc., Two World Trade
Ctr., Ste. 9650, 10048, pg. 1517   **IT**
Yamazaki USA Inc., 342 Madison Ave., Ste. 604, 10173,
pg. 1195   **IT**
YAR COMMUNICATIONS, 220 Fifth Ave., 10001,
pg. 1195   **PV**
Yasuda Bank and Trust Company (U.S.A.), 666 Fifth Ave.,
Ste. 802, 10103, pg. 1520   **IT**
The Yasuda Fire & Marine Insurance Co. of America, Two
World Financial Ctr., 225 Liberty St., 43rd Fl., 10281-
1058, pg. 1519   **IT**
Yasuda Life America Agency Inc., 575 Fifth Ave., 10017,
pg. 1520   **IT**
Yasuda Life America Capital Management, Ltd., 575 Fifth
Ave., 28th Fl., 10017, pg. 1520   **IT**
Yasuda Realty America Corporation, 575 Fifth Ave., 10017,
Ste. 9650, 10048, pg. 1520   **IT**
Yesawich, Moss & Brown, 685 Third Ave., 10017,
pg. 1196   **PV**
YORK RESEARCH CORPORATION, 280 Park Ave., Ste.
2700 W., 10017, pg. 1789   **PB**
YOUNG & RUBICAM INC., 285 Madison Ave., 10017,
pg. 1196   **PV**
Young & Rubicam New York, 285 Madison Ave., 10017-
6486, pg. 1198   **PV**
DANIEL F. YOUNG, INC., 17 Battery Pl., Eighth Fl., 10004,
pg. 1200   **PV**
YOUNG STUFF APPAREL GROUP, INC., 1407 Broadway,
6th Fl., 10018, pg. 1202   **PV**
Z. Cavaricci, 1466 Broadway, 10036, pg. 1203   **PV**
ZENITH MEDIA SERVICES, INC., 299 W. Houston St.,
10014, pg. 1204   **PV**
ZICCARDI & PARTNERS, INC., 221 W. 41st St., 10036,
pg. 1205   **PV**
Ziff-Davis Business Media Group, One Park Ave., 10016,
pg. 1276   **IT**
Ziff-Davis Consumer Media Group, One Park Ave., 10016,
pg. 1276   **IT**
Ziff-Davis Interactive, One Park Ave., 10016, pg. 1276   **IT**
Ziff-Davis International Media Group, One Park Ave.,
10016, pg. 1276   **IT**
Ziff-Davis Marketing & Development, One Park Ave.,
10016, pg. 1276   **IT**
Ziff-Davis Publishing Company, One Park Ave., 10016,
pg. 1276   **IT**
ZIM-AMERICAN ISRAELI SHIPPING CO., One World
Trade Ctr., 10048, pg. 1206   **PV**
Zim Container Service, One World Trade Ctr., 10048,
pg. 1206   **PV**
Zomba Group of Companies, 137-139 W. 25th St., 10001,
pg. 1529   **PV**
Zurich Reinsurance Centre, One Chase Manhattan Plaza,
10005, pg. 1530   **IT**

New York Mills

C. WEAVER CHEVROLET, INC., 5036 Commercial Dr.,
13417, pg. 1156   **PV**

Newark

IEC ELECTRONICS CORP., 105 Norton St., 14513,
pg. 854   **PB**
Ultra Technologies, Inc., Rt. 88 S., 14513, pg. 551   **PB**

Newburgh

AMERICAN FELT & FILTER, 311 First St., 12550,
pg. 54   **PV**
EA Engineering, Science & Technology, Inc., 3 Washington
Ctr., 12550, pg. 541   **PB**
Newburgh Auto Auction, Route 17K, P.O. Box 2426, 12550,
pg. 282   **PV**

Noma Intl. Inc., 840 Broadway, 12550, pg. 955   **IT**

Niagara Falls

Affival Inc., 3801 Highland Ave., Box 368, 14302,
pg. 1465   **IT**
Alox Corporation, P.O. Box 517, 3943 Buffalo Ave., 14302,
pg. 1357   **PB**
The Carborundum Corporation, 1625 Buffalo Ave., 14303,
pg. 1173   **IT**
Cascades Niagara Falls, P.O. Box 1830, 4001 Packard Rd.,
11302, pg. 274   **IT**
Clipper Abrasives Inc., 6600 Walmore Rd., 14304,
pg. 1174   **IT**
ESM II, Inc., 3801 Highland Ave., Box 368, 14302,
pg. 1465   **IT**
IPAC, INC., 2107 Liberty Dr., 14304, pg. 555   **PV**
Niacalor, P.O. Box 787, Bufflao Ave. & Chemcial Rd.,
1-302, pg. 1219   **PB**
NUTTALL GEAR CORPORATION, 2221 Niagara Falls
Blvd., 14302, pg. 809   **PV**
Pyron Corp., P.O. Box 310, 5950 Packard Rd., 14304,
pg. 1524   **IT**
Quest Diagnostic-Niagara Falls, 550 Main St., 14302,
pg. 1351   **PB**
SKW Alloys, Inc., 3801 Highland Ave., 14305, pg. 1465   **IT**
SKW Metals & Alloys, Inc., P.O. Box 368, 3801 Highland
Ave., 14305-0368, pg. 1465   **IT**
SCRUFARI CONSTRUCTION CO. INC., 3925 Hyde Park
Blvd., 14305, pg. 977   **PV**
Sevenson Environmental, Ltd., 2749 Lockport Rd., 14302-
0396, pg. 1463   **IT**
SEVENSON ENVIRONMENTAL SERVICES, INC., 2749
Lockport Rd., 14302-0396, pg. 1462   **PB**
Sevenson Industrial Services, Inc., 2749 Lockport Rd.,
14302-0396, pg. 1463   **PB**
Stollberg Inc., P.O. Box 368, 4111 Witmer Rd., 14302,
pg. 1465   **IT**
Tam Ceramics Inc., 4511 Hyde Park Blvd., 14305,
pg. 329   **IT**
TREIBACHER SCHLEIFMITTEL CORP., 2000 College
Ave., 14305, pg. 1099   **IT**
Tulip Corp., Niagara Falls Div., 3125 Highland Ave., 14305,
pg. 1109   **PV**

Niskayuna

ENVIRONMENT/ONE CORPORATION, 2773 Balltown Rd.,
12309-1090, pg. 586   **PB**

North Babylon

CHEM-TAINER INDUSTRIES, 361 Neptune Ave., 11704,
pg. 231   **PV**

North Tarrytown

IBM World Trade Americas/Far East Corporation, Rte. 9,
Town of Mount Pleasant, 10591, pg. 896   **PB**

North Tonawanda

Balzers Tool Coating, Inc., 901 Erie Ave., 14120,
pg. 997   **IT**
Buffalo Pumps, Inc., 874 Oliver St., 14120, pg. 103   **PB**
Chesapeake Packaging Co./North Tonawanda, 51
Robinson St., 14120, pg. 347   **PB**
THRUWAY FASTENERS INC., 2910 Niagara Falls Blvd.,
14120, pg. 1084   **PV**

Norwich

NBT BANCORP INC., 52 S. Broad St., 13815,
pg. 1144   **PB**

Nyack

AM COSMETICS INC., 60 Cedar Hill Ave., 10960,
pg. 3   **PV**
PRESIDENTIAL LIFE CORPORATION, 69 Lydecker St.,
10960, pg. 1323   **PB**

Oceanside

Applied Graphics Technologies, 15 Neil Ct., 11572,
pg. 1125   **PV**

Ogdensburg

American Computer Assembly/Compas, 100 Chimney Point
Dr., 13669, pg. 36   **IT**
Suprema Specialties Northeast, Inc., 30 Main St., 13669,
pg. 541   **PB**

Old Brookville

Banfi Product Corp, 1111 Cedar Swamp Rd., 11545,
pg. 113   **PV**
BANFI VINTNERS, 1111 Cedar Swamp Rd., 11545,
pg. 113   **PV**
House of Banfi, 1111 Cedar Swamp Rd., 11545,
pg. 113   **PV**
Villadoc Inc., 1111 Cedar Swamp Rd., 11545, pg. 113   **PV**
Vinum Inc., 1111 Cedar Swamp Rd., 11545, pg. 113   **PV**

Olean

AVX Corp., P.O. Box 493, 14760, pg. 775   **IT**
BLUE BIRD COACH LINES INC., One Blue Bird Sq.,
14760, pg. 150   **PV**
CONAP INC., 1405 Buffalo St., 14760-1139, pg. 261   **PV**
Dresser-Rand Co. (Olean), N. Fifth St., 14760, pg. 529   **PB**
Olean Advanced Products Division, P.O. Box 493, 14760,
pg. 775   **IT**
Quest Diagnostic-Olean, 2636 W. State St., 14760,
pg. 1351   **PB**

Oneida

D.J. Tableware, Inc., Kenwood Ave., 13421, pg. 1226   **PB**
Oneida Foodservice Division, Kenwood Ave., 13421,
pg. 1226   **PB**
ONEIDA LTD., Administration Bldg., Kenwood Ave., 13421-
2829, pg. 1225   **PB**
Oneida Rostone Corporation, 104 S. Warner St., 13421,
pg. 1383   **PB**
Oneida Silversmiths Div., Kenwood Ave., 13421,
pg. 1226   **PB**
Quest Diagnostic, 238 Main St., 13421, pg. 1351   **PB**
SMITH-LEE CO., INC., 537 Fitch, 13421, pg. 1009   **PV**

Orangeburg

American Dynamics, Ten Corporate Dr., 10962,
pg. 1457   **PB**
Conseco Life of New York, 9-11 Ramland Rd., 10962,
pg. 433   **IT**
Cornell Manufacturing Company, 25 Ramland Rd., 10962,
pg. 602   **PV**
Daikin America, Inc., 20 Olympic Dr., 10962, pg. 365   **IT**
Hino Diesel Trucks (U.S.A.), Inc., 25 Corporate Dr., 10962,
pg. 620   **IT**
INNOVATIVE PLASTICS CORPORATION, 400 Rte. 303,
10962, pg. 565   **PV**
Minigrip Zip-Pak, Route 303, 10962, pg. 867   **IT**
NICE-PAK PRODUCTS, INC., Two Nice Pak Pk., 10962-
1376, pg. 798   **PV**
PAXAR Apparel Identification Systems, 524 Rte. 303,
10962, pg. 1266   **PB**
Pentax Precision Instrument Corp., 30 Ramland Rd., 10962-
2699, pg. 85   **IT**
Quality Metals, Rte. 303, 10962, pg. 1283   **IT**
Subaru Distributor Corp., 6 Ramland Rd., 10962,
pg. 523   **IT**
Takeda USA Inc., Eight Corporate Dr., 10962-2614,
pg. 1350   **IT**
Volkswagen of America, Inc., 39 N. Greenbush Rd., 10962,
pg. 1474   **IT**

Orchard Park

Allegheny Gear Corporation, c/o Astronics Corporation,
P.O. Box 587, 14127, pg. 142   **PB**
Avesta Welding Products Inc., 3176 Abbott Rd., 14127,
pg. 221   **IT**
Azerty Incorporated, 13 Centre Dr., 14127, pg. 20   **IT**
Clinicare Systems, Inc., Ten Centre Dr., 14127,
pg. 442   **PV**
ENIDINE INCORPORATED, Seven Centre Dr., 14127,
pg. 442   **PV**
GAYMAR INDUSTRIES, INC., Ten Centre Dr., 14127,
pg. 442   **PV**
NITRAM ENERGY INC., 227 Thorn Ave., 14127,
pg. 799   **PV**

Oriskany

Strandflex Division, Sutliff Road, 13424, pg. 780   **PB**

Oswego

Quest Diagnostic, 102 W. Utica St., 13126, pg. 1351   **PB**

Owego

Lockheed Martin Federal Systems-Owego, 1801 State
Route 17C, 13827-3998, pg. 1008   **PB**
STAKMORE INC., Elm St., 13827, pg. 1029   **PV**

Oyster Bay

COMMANDER OIL CORPORATION, One Commander Sq.,
11771, pg. 257   **PV**

Ozone Park

Ozone Industries Inc., 101-32 101st St., 11416,
pg. 113   **IT**

Painted Post

Dresser-Rand Co. (Painted Post), 100 Chemung St., 14870,
pg. 529   **PB**

Palmyra

Garlock Sealing Technologies, 1666 Division St., 14522,
pg. 402   **PB**

PB - *U.S. Public Companies Volume*
PV - *U.S. Private Companies Volume*
IT - *International Public & Private Companies Volume*

Patchogue

CLARE ROSE INC./CLARE ROSE OF NASSAU, 72 West Ave., 11772, pg. 945 **PV**

Patterson

Penwest Pharm. Co., 2981 Rte. 22, 12563, pg. 1269 **PB**

Pawling

PAWLING CORPORATION, 157 Charles Colman Blvd., 12564, pg. 844 **PB**
Pawling Savings Bank, 86 Rte. 22, 12564, pg. 1334 **PB**
Presray Corp., 159 Charles Colman Blvd., 12564, pg. 844 **PV**

Pearl River

ACTIVE INTERNATIONAL, One Blue Hill Plaza, 10965, pg. 15 **PV**
Bankers American Life Assurance Company, One Blue Hill Plaza, #1565, 10965-3104, pg. 68 **PB**
Clove Development Corp., One Blue Hill Plaza, 10965, pg. 1229 **PB**
Glen Raven Marketing Corporation, One Blue Hill Plaza, 4th Fl., 10965, pg. 456 **PV**
Hybrid Products, 35 Jefferson Ave., 10965, pg. 1283 **IT**
Imasco Holdings, Inc., Two Blue Hill Plz., 10965-8588, pg. 112 **IT**
O & R Development, Inc., One Blue Hill Plaza, 10965, pg. 1229 **PB**
ORANGE AND ROCKLAND UTILITIES, INC., One Blue Hill Plaza, 10965, pg. 1229 **PB**
Palisades Energy Services, One Blue Hill Plaza, 10965, pg. 1229 **PB**
Saddle River Holdings Corp., One Blue Hill Plaza, 10965, pg. 1229 **PB**

Peekskill

S.M. FRANK & CO., INC., 1000 N. Division St., 10566, pg. 423 **PV**
Kaywoodie, 1000 N. Division St., 10566, pg. 424 **PV**
Medico, Inc., 1000 N. Division St., 10566, pg. 424 **PV**
SHOKAI FAR EAST LTD., Nine Elena Ct., 10566, pg. 996 **PV**
Yello-Bole, 1000 N. Division St., 10566, pg. 424 **PV**

Pelham Manor

IMPERIA BROS., INC., 57 Canal Rd., 10803, pg. 558 **PV**

Penn Yan

Knapp Shoes Inc., One Kenka Business Park, 14527-8895, pg. 401 **PV**
Seneca Flight Oper., 2521 Bath Rd., 14527, pg. 1456 **PV**
Transelco Div., P.O. Box 217, 1789 Transelco Dr., 14527, pg. 619 **PB**

Phelps

EG & G Wright Components, Rte. 96, P.O. Box 160, 14532, pg. 542 **PB**

Philmont

McKechnie Packaging-Philmont, 4562 Martindale Rd., 12565, pg. 851 **IT**

Pittsford

Auto-trol Technology Corp., 1000 Pittsford Victor Rd., 14534, pg. 148 **PB**
MSC Rochester Office, Four Tobey Village Office Park, 14534, pg. 1031 **PB**
Milgray/Upstate New York, Inc., One Corporate Pl., 1170 Pittsford-Victor Rd., 14534, pg. 207 **PB**
Mobil Films and Packaging, 1150 Pittsford-Victor Rd., 14534-3897, pg. 1118 **PB**
MOSCOM CORPORATION, 3750 Monroe Ave., 14534, pg. 1136 **PB**
SENECA FOODS CORPORATION, 1162 Pittsford-Victor Rd., 14534, pg. 1456 **PB**
THE WESTERFELDS, INC., 40A Grove St., 14534, pg. 1164 **PV**

Plainview

AEROFLEX INCORPORATED, 35 S. Service Rd., 11803, pg. 23 **PB**
Aeroflex International, Inc., 35 S. Service Rd., 11803, pg. 24 **PB**
Aeroflex Laboratories Inc., 35 So. Service Rd., 11803, pg. 24 **PB**
ASTREX, INC., 205 Express St., 11803, pg. 141 **PB**
Avest, Inc., 205 Express St., 11803, pg. 141 **PB**
Comstron Division, 35 S. Service Rd., 11803, pg. 24 **PB**
Fosroc Inc., 55 Skyline Dr., 11803, pg. 234 **IT**
MSC Industrial Supply Co., 151 Sunnyside Blvd., 11803, pg. 998 **PV**
Progress International Limited, 205 Express St., 11803, pg. 141 **PB**
Red Wing Products, Inc., 190 Express St., 11803, pg. 480 **IT**

SHOGYO INTERNATIONAL CORPORATION, 45 Executive Dr., 11803, pg. 996 **PV**
SID TOOL CO. INC., 151 Sunnyside Blvd., 11803, pg. 998 **PV**
TOYMAX INTERNATIONAL INC., 125 E. Bethpage Rd., 11803, pg. 1626 **PV**
VEECO INSTRUMENTS, INC., Terminal Dr., 11803, pg. 1711 **PV**

Plattsburgh

Ilco Unican Corp., 32 Veterans Ln., 12901, pg. 1432 **IT**

Pleasant Valley

CONKLIN INSTRUMENT CORPORATION, West Rd., 12569, pg. 263 **PV**
DUTCHESS QUARRY & SUPPLY CO. INC., Arborio Rd., 12569, pg. 350 **PV**

Pleasantville

Ardee Music Publishing, Inc., Reader's Digest Rd., pg. 1367 **PB**
Books & Home Entertainment Div., Reader's Digest Rd., 10570-7000, pg. 1367 **PB**
Looksmart, Inc., Reader's Digest Rd., 10570-7000, pg. 1367 **PB**
MEDICAL LABORATORY AUTOMATION, INC., 270 Marble Ave., 10570, pg. 727 **PV**
Pegasus Investment, Inc., Reader's Digest Rd., 10570-7000, pg. 1367 **PB**
Pegasus Sales, Inc., Reader's Digest Rd., 10570-7000, pg. 1367 **PB**
Pleasantville Music Publishing, Inc., Reader's Digest Rd., 10570, pg. 1367 **PB**
RD Manufacturing Corporation, Reader's Digest Rd., 10570, pg. 1367 **PB**
THE READER'S DIGEST ASSOCIATION, INC., Reader's Digest Rd., 10570-7000, pg. 1367 **PB**
The Reader's Digest Association (Russia) Incorporated, Reader's Digest Rd., 10570, pg. 1367 **PB**
Reader's Digest Entertainment, Inc., Reader's Digest Rd., 10570-7000, pg. 1367 **PB**
Reader's Digest Peru, Reader's Digest Rd., 10570-7000, pg. 1367 **PB**
Reader's Digest Services, Inc., Reader's Digest Rd., 10570-7000, pg. 1367 **PB**
Reader's Digest Sub Eight, Reader's Digest Rd., 10570-7000, pg. 1367 **PB**
Reader's Digest Sub Seven, Reader's Digest Rd., 10570, pg. 1367 **PB**
Reader's Digest Sub Six, Inc., Reader's Digest Rd., 10570, pg. 1367 **PB**
SMDDMS, Inc., Reader's Digest Rd., 10570-7000, pg. 1367 **PB**
Teca Corporation, Three Campus Dr., 10570, pg. 1468 **IT**
VideoVation, Inc., Reader's Digest Rd., 10570, pg. 1368 **PB**
W.A. Publications, Inc., Reader's Digest Rd., 10570, pg. 1368 **PB**

Pomona

BARR LABORATORIES INC., P.O. Box 2900, Two Quaker Rd., 10970-0519, pg. 191 **PB**

Port Chester

Luxo Lamp Corporation, 36 Midland Ave., 10573, pg. 821 **IT**
Nelson Publications, One Gateway Plaza, 10573, pg. 1328 **PB**
New York-American Water Co., Inc., 25 Willett Ave., 10573, pg. 95 **PB**

Port Ewen

Kingston Oil Supply Corp., P.O. Box 788, 12466, pg. 741 **PB**

Port Jefferson

AMP Inc. Lytel Division, 1303 Main St. Unit # 5, 11777-2217, pg. 8 **PB**

Port Jervis

THE FINALS, INC., 21 Minisink Ave., 12771, pg. 404 **PV**
Kolmar Laboratories, Inc., P.O. Box 1111, King St. & Skyline Dr., 12771, pg. 239 **IT**
Skydyne Div., River Rd., 12771, pg. 1 **PB**

Port Washington

Avant Garde Optics Inc., 44 Harbor Park Dr., 11050, pg. 822 **IT**
BAYSIDE MOTION GROUP, 27 Seaview Blvd., 11050, pg. 125 **PV**
BRUCKNER MACHINE & TOOL CORP., 36 Harbor Pk. Dr., 11050, pg. 175 **PV**
Center Laboratories, Inc., 35 Channel Dr., 11050, pg. 813 **PB**
DRI MARK PRODUCTS, INC., 15 Harbor Park Dr., 11050, pg. 342 **PV**
EMPRESS INTERNATIONAL LTD., Ten Harbor Pk. Dr., 11050, pg. 375 **PV**

GLOBAL DIRECT MAIL CORP, 22 Harbor Park Dr., 11050, pg. 747 **PB**
E.W. Howell Company, Inc., P.O. Box 2000, Two Seaview Blvd., 11050, pg. 995 **IT**
Kleinsleep, Two Tri-Harbour Ct., 11050, pg. 1006 **PV**
The Power Line, 382 Channel Dr., 11050, pg. 893 **PV**
PUBLISHERS CLEARING HOUSE, 382 Channel Dr., 11050, pg. 893 **PV**
Scott's Miracle-Gro Products, Inc., 800 Port Washington Blvd., 11050, pg. 1447 **PB**
TDK Electronics Corporation, 12 Harbor Park Dr., 11050, pg. 1336 **IT**
TDK U.S.A. Corporation, 12 Harbor Park Drive, 11050, pg. 1336 **IT**

Poughkeepsie

Bank of the Hudson, 249 Main Mall, 12601, pg. 1319 **PB**
James Burn Intl., 205 Cottage St., 12602, pg. 1506 **PB**
C H Resources, Inc., 284 South Ave., 12601, pg. 325 **PB**
Central Hudson Cogeneration, Inc., 80 Washington St., 12602, pg. 325 **PB**
Central Hudson Enterprises, 80 Washington St., 12602, pg. 325 **PB**
CENTRAL HUDSON GAS & ELECTRIC CORPORATION, 284 South Ave., 12601-4879, pg. 324 **PB**
Central Hudson Resources Inc., 284 South Ave., 12601-4879, pg. 325 **PB**
Effron Fuel Oil Co., Inc., 154 Garden St., 12682, pg. 729 **PV**
Greene Point Development Corp., 284 South Ave., 12602, pg. 325 **PB**
H.O. PENN MACHINERY CO. INC., 54 Noxon Rd., 12603, pg. 849 **PV**
Phoenix Development Co., Inc., 284 South Ave., 12601, pg. 325 **PB**
POUGHKEEPSIE FINANCIAL CORP., 249 Main Mall, 12601, pg. 1319 **PB**
Poughkeepsie Newspapers, 85 Civic Ctr. Plaza, 12602, pg. 700 **PB**
Total Research Corporation, 11 Raymond Ave., Ste. 21, 12603, pg. 1625 **PB**

Purchase

CENTRAL NATIONAL-GOTTESMAN INC., Three Manhattanville Rd., 10577-2110, pg. 224 **PV**
The Reuben H. Donnelley Corporation, One Manhattanville Rd., 10577, pg. 535 **PB**
Fiberlux, Inc., 3010 Westchester Ave., 10577, pg. 1634 **PV**
Hewlett-Packard Company, 2975 Westchester Ave., 10577, pg. 814 **PB**
IBM Programming Systems, 2000 Purchase St., 10577, pg. 895 **PB**
IP Forest Resources Company, Two Manhattanville Rd., 10577, pg. 904 **PB**
IP Timberlands, Ltd., Two Manhattanville Rd., 10577, pg. 904 **PB**
INTEGRAMED AMERICA, One Manhattanville Rd., 10577-2100, pg. 883 **PB**
INTERGEN COMPANY, Two Manhattanville Rd., 10577, pg. 567 **PV**
INTERNATIONAL PAPER COMPANY, Two Manhattanville Rd., 10577, pg. 901 **PB**
Lindenmeyr Central, Three Manhattanville Rd., 10577-2100, pg. 224 **PV**
Lindenmeyr Munroe, Corporate Headquarters, Three Manhattanville Rd., 10577-2110, pg. 224 **PV**
Lindenmeyr Paper Company, Three Manhattanville Rd., 10577, pg. 224 **PV**
MasterCard International-Cirrus Brand, 2000 Purchase St., 10577, pg. 714 **PV**
MASTERCARD INTERNATIONAL, INC., 2000 Purchase St., 10577, pg. 714 **PV**
Mitsubishi Motors Credit of America Inc., 2700 Westchester Ave., 10577-2554, pg. 875 **IT**
Oce-Credit Corporation, 2975 Westchester Ave., 10577, pg. 994 **IT**
PEPSICO, INC., 700 Anderson Hill Rd., 10577, pg. 1276 **PB**
PepsiCo Wines & Spirits International, 700 Anderson Hill Rd., 10577-1444, pg. 1277 **PB**
Thomas Jefferson Life Insurance Co., 2500 Westchester Ave., 10577, pg. 1659 **PV**
Transamerica Leasing Inc., 100 Manhattanville Rd., 2nd Fl., 10577, pg. 1630 **PB**

Queensbury

AngioDynamics, 603 Queensbury Ave., 12804, pg. 540 **PB**
Troy Savings Bank-Glens Falls, 739 Upper Glen St., 12804, pg. 1106 **PV**
Troy Savings Bank-Quaker Road, Quaker & Country Club Rd., 12804, pg. 1106 **PV**

Rego Park

GERALD GROUP INC., 9524 63rd Rd., # NBO, 11374-1142, pg. 448 **PV**
LEFRAK ORGANIZATION INC., 97-77 Queens Blvd., 11374, pg. 658 **PV**

Rensselaer

Allied Security Inc. (NY), 63 Washington St., Ste. 9, 12144, pg. 40 **PV**

PB - *U.S. Public Companies Volume*
PV - *U.S. Private Companies Volume*
IT - *International Public & Private Companies Volume*

Rhinebeck

Beekman 1766 Tavern, Beekman Arms Hotel, Route 9, 4 Mills St., 12572, pg. 130   **PB**

Richmond Hill

COMMERCIAL PLASTICS & SUPPLIES CORP., 98-31 Jamaica Ave., 11418, pg. 258   **PV**

Ridgewood

WESTERN BEEF, INC., 47-05 Metropolitan Ave., 11385, pg. 1758   **PB**

Riverdale

SGD INTERNATIONAL CORP., 360 W. 253rd St., 10471, pg. 957   **PV**

Rochester

ACC CORP., 400 West Ave., 14611, pg. 2   **PB**
ACC TeleCom, 400 West Ave., 14611, pg. 3   **PB**
Agrilink Foods, Inc., 90 Linden Oaks, 14625, pg. 887   **PV**
The Ailing & Cory Company, 1059 W. Ridge Rd., 14615-2731, pg. 1666   **PB**
ALLIANCE AUTOMATED, 400 Trabold Rd., 14624, pg. 38   **PB**
Allright New York Parking, Inc., P.O. Box 40310 Midtown, One Lincoln First Tower-Concourse Level, 14603, pg. 43   **PB**
American Credit Services Inc., Sipley's Bldg., 228 E. Main St., Ste. 300, 14604, pg. 336   **PB**
Arnold Advertising, Southview Commons, 100 White Spruce Blvd., 14623, pg. 84   **PV**
Arrow/Schweber Electronics, 3375 Brighton Henriatta Town Line Rd., 14623, pg. 134   **PB**
Astra Arcus USA, 755 Jevfferson Rd., 14623, pg. 93   **IT**
Bausch & Lomb Inc., One Bausch & Lomb Pl., 14603, pg. 194   **PB**
BAUSCH & LOMB INCORPORATED, One Bausch & Lomb Pl., 14604, pg. 194   **PB**
Bausch & Lomb Insurance Company, 1400 N. Goodman, 14692, pg. 194   **PB**
Bausch & Lomb Opticare, Inc., 1400 N. Goodman St., 14692, pg. 194   **PB**
CVC PRODUCTS, INC., 525 Lee Rd., 14606, pg. 197   **PV**
CALDWELL MANUFACTURING COMPANY, 2605 Manitour Rd., 14624, pg. 200   **PV**
The Case-Hoyt Corporation, 100 Beaver Rd., 14624, pg. 101   **PV**
Cellular One Genesee Telephone Company, 3144 Winton Road South, 14623, pg. 1415   **PB**
Comstock Foods, 90 Linden Oaks Pk., 14625, pg. 887   **PV**
Comstock Michigan Fruit, 90 Linden Oaks Pkwy., 14625, pg. 887   **PV**
Consumer Imaging Division, 343 State St., 14650, pg. 555   **PB**
Curtice Burns Foods, 90 Linden Oaks, 14625, pg. 887   **PV**
Danka Office Imaging, 901 Elmgrove Rd., 14653, pg. 551   **PB**
Davenport Machine Tool Div., 167 Ames St., 14601, pg. 520   **PB**
Dayton Rogers of New York, 1455 Emerson St., 14606, pg. 318   **PV**
Democrat & Chronicle, 55 Exchange Blvd., 14614, pg. 699   **PB**
Digital Link Corporation, 10 Carlson Rd., 14610, pg. 508   **PB**
Discus Electronic Training, 343 State St., 14550, pg. 551   **PB**
Distillation Products Industries, 2255 Mt. Read Blvd., 14603, pg. 551   **PB**
DON ALLESON, INC., 2921 Brighton-Henrietta T.L. Rd., 14623, pg. 339   **PV**
ENI, 100 Highpower Rd., 14623, pg. 354   **PV**
ENI Power Systems, High Power Rd., 14623, pg. 574   **PV**
Eastman Fine Chemicals, 343 State St., 14650, pg. 550   **PB**
EASTMAN KODAK COMPANY, 343 State St., 14650, pg. 550   **PB**
Eastman Kodak Life Sciences Div., 343 State St., 14650, pg. 551   **PB**
Eastman Savings & Loan Association, 377 State St., 14650, pg. 551   **PB**
Eastman Technology Inc., 343 State St., 14550, pg. 551   **PB**
Edicon Systems, 300 Canal View Blvd., 14623, pg. 551   **PB**
Electronic Navigation Industries, 100 Highpower Rd., 14623, pg. 574   **PB**
Energyline Corporation, 89 E. Ave., 14649, pg. 1396   **PB**
ERDLE PERFORATING CO., 100 Pixley Indus. Pkwy., 14624, pg. 380   **PV**
Firth-Rixson Monroe, P.O. Box 1111, McKee Rd., 14603, pg. 488   **IT**
Foley-PLP Company, 1920 Lyell Ave., 14604, pg. 416   **PV**
Frontier Cellular, 161 Chestnut St., 14604, pg. 683   **PV**
FRONTIER CORPORATION, Frontier Ctr., 180 S. Clinton Ave., 14646-0700, pg. 683   **PB**
Frontier Information Technologies, 180 S. Clinton Ave., 14646-0700, pg. 684   **PB**
Frontier InfoServices, 180 S. Clinton Ave., 14646, pg. 684   **PB**
Frontier Network Systems, Inc., 95 N. Fitzhugh St., 14614, pg. 684   **PB**
Genencor International, Four Cambridge Pl., 1870 S. Winton Rd., 14618-3916, pg. 349   **IT**

General Railway Signal Corp., 150 Sawgrass Ave., 14620-2609, pg. 1194   **IT**
The Genesee Brewing Company, Inc., 445 St. Paul St., 14605, pg. 728   **PB**
GENESEE CORPORATION, 445 St. Paul St., 14605, pg. 728   **PB**
Genesee Ventures, Inc., 445 St. Paul St., 14605, pg. 728   **PB**
GETINGE/CASTLE, INC., 1777 E. Henrietta Rd., 14623, pg. 449   **PV**
Getinge/Castle Inc., 1777 E. Henrietta Rd., 14623-3133, pg. 551   **IT**
GLEASON CORPORATION, 1000 University Ave., 14692, pg. 746   **PB**
Gleason Corporation Sales, 1000 University Ave., 14692, pg. 746   **PB**
The Gleason Works, P.O. Box 22970, 14692-2970, pg. 746   **PB**
GLOBAL BEVERAGE CO., 130 Linden Oakes Dr., Ste. C, 14625, pg. 457   **PV**
Gould Paper Corporation of New York, Inc., 1200-C Scottsville Rd., 14624, pg. 467   **PV**
Great Lakes Kraut Co., L.L.C., 90 Linden Oaks, 14625, pg. 887   **PV**
HAHN AUTOMOTIVE WAREHOUSE, INC., 415 W. Main S., 14608, pg. 774   **PB**
Harris Corp., RF Communications Group Marketing Division, 1680 University Ave., 14610, pg. 792   **PV**
Hickey-Freeman/Bobby Jones, 1155 Clinton Ave. N., 1-621, pg. 795   **PB**
Hutchins/Young & Rubicam, 400 Midtown Tower, 14604-2069, pg. 1197   **PV**
Image Acquisition Products Division, 343 State St., pg. 555   **PB**
Integration and Systems Products Div., 343 State St., 14650, pg. 555   **PB**
Intergraph Corporation, 120 Corporate Woods, 14623, pg. 890   **PB**
JAY ADVERTISING, INC., 170 Linden Oaks, 14625, pg. 583   **PV**
Kayex Corp., 1000 Millstead Way, 14624, pg. 727   **PB**
Kodak Bio-Products Division, 343 State St., 14650, pg. 551   **PB**
Kodak Bioscience / Emerging Business Division, 343 State St., 14650, pg. 551   **PB**
Kodak Business Imaging Systems Division, 343 State St., 14350, pg. 555   **PB**
Kodak Business Information Services K.K. (KBISKK), 901 Elm Grove Rd., 14653, pg. 551   **PB**
Kodak Clinical Products Division, 343 State St., 14650, pg. 551   **PB**
Kodak Federal Systems Division, 343 State St., 14650, pg. 555   **PB**
Kodak Graphics Imaging Systems Division, 343 State St., 14650, pg. 551   **PB**
Kodak Health Sciences Division, 343 State St., 14650, pg. 555   **PB**
Kodak Mass Memory Division, 343 State St., 14650, pg. 555   **PB**
Kodak Motion Picture & Audiovisual Products Division, 343 State St., 14650, pg. 555   **PB**
Kodak Printer Products Div., 343 State St., 14650, pg. 555   **PB**
Kodak Processing Laboratories, 343 State St., 14560, pg. 551   **PB**
Kodak Professional Photography Division, 343 State St., 14650, pg. 555   **PB**
Kodak Software Systems Division, 343 State St., 14650, pg. 555   **PB**
LVT, Eldg. 952, 100 Kings Hwy., Ste. 1400, 14617, pg. 551   **PB**
Lawyers Cooperative Publishing Co., 50 Broad St. East, 14694, pg. 1602   **PB**
LIBERTY PRECISION INDUSTRIES, 350 Buell Rd., 14692-2785, pg. 666   **PV**
Light Valve Technology, 343 State St., 14550, pg. 551   **PB**
Lightnin Mixers, P.O. Box 1370, 14603, pg. 726   **PB**
Lindberg Heat Treating Co., 620 Buffalo Rd., 14611, pg. 999   **PB**
Logical Operations, 500 Canal View Blvd., 14623, pg. 1276   **IT**
Magneic Technologies Corporation, 770 Linden Ave., 14625, pg. 1420   **PB**
MATHEWS & BOUCHER, P.O. Box 18528, 14618-0528, pg. 714   **PV**
Medeva Pharmaceuticals, 755 Jefferson Rd., 14623, pg. 852   **IT**
Metrosonics Inc., P.O. Box 23075, 14692, pg. 208   **IT**
Microwave Data Systems, Inc., 300 Main St., 14445, pg. 293   **PB**
MONRO MUFFLER/BRAKE, INC., 200 Holleder Pkwy., 14615, pg. 1124   **PB**
Monroe Forgings Inc., 181 McKee Rd., 14611, pg. 488   **IT**
Monroe Litho Inc., 39 Delevan St., 14605, pg. 1736   **PV**
Eric Mower and Associates, 350 Linden Oaks Dr., 14625, pg. 765   **PV**
Northern Telecom Inc., 97 Humboldt St., 14609-7493, pg. 970   **PV**
Outdoor Systems, Inc.-New York, 1029 Sibley Tower Bldg., 14604, pg. 1235   **PB**
Panalpina Inc., 45 Wells St., 14611, pg. 1022   **PV**
Pathetex, 343 State St., 14550, pg. 551   **PB**
PAYCHEX, INC., 911 Panorama Trail S., 14625, pg. 1267   **PB**
Pfaudler, Inc., 1000 West Ave., 14611, pg. 1393   **PB**
Plywood Plastics, Inc., 279 Burrows St., 14606, pg. 873   **PV**
PRO-FAC COOPERATIVE, INC., 90 Linden Oaks, 14625, pg. 837   **PV**
The Producto Machine Co., 305 Mt. Read Blvd., 14611, pg. 839   **PV**

Professional Auto Warehouse, 415 W. Main St., 14608, pg. 774   **PB**
Pulsafeeder Inc., 2883 Brighton-Henrietta Town Line Rd., 14623, pg. 862   **PB**
Quest Diagnostic, 625 Panorama Trail, 14625, pg. 1351   **PB**
Quest Diagnostic, 1650 Elmwood Ave., 14620, pg. 1351   **PB**
Quest Diagnostic-Rochester, 2024 W. Henrietta Rd., 14623, pg. 1351   **PB**
Rochester Community Savings Bank, 40 Franklin St., 14604, pg. 336   **PB**
ROCHESTER FUND MUNICIPALS, 350 Linden Oaks, 14625-2804, pg. 937   **PB**
ROCHESTER GAS AND ELECTRIC CORPORATION, 89 East Ave., 14649, pg. 1395   **PB**
ROCHESTER MIDLAND CORPORATION, 333 Hollenbeck St., 14621, pg. 937   **PV**
Rochester Telephone Corp., 180 S. Clinton Ave., 14646, pg. 684   **PB**
Roehlen Engraving, 701 Jefferson Rd., 14623, pg. 1506   **PB**
SCT, 3000 Ridge Rd. E., 14622, pg. 1552   **PB**
Schlegel Building Products Div., 1555 Jefferson Rd., P.O. Box 23197, 14692, pg. 128   **IT**
Schlegel Corporation, 1555 Jefferson Rd., 14623-3107, pg. 128   **IT**
Schlegel Industrial Products Div., 1555 Jefferson Rd., P.O. Box 23197, 14692, pg. 128   **IT**
Schlegel Retrofit Corporation, 1555 Jefferson Rd., P.O. Box 23197, 14692, pg. 128   **IT**
Schlegel Rochester Div., 1555 Jefferson Rd., P.O. Box 23197, 14692, pg. 128   **IT**
SENTRY GROUP, 900 Linden Ave., 14625, pg. 984   **PV**
Snowmax Technologies, 343 State St., 14650, pg. 551   **PB**
Thin Film Technology Division, 1400 N. Goodman St., 14609, pg. 194   **PB**
TRAVEL PORTS OF AMERICA INC., 3495 Winton Place, Bldg. C, 14623, pg. 1632   **PB**
Videk, 2200 Brighton-Henrietta Town Line Rd., 14623, pg. 551   **PB**
WHEC-TV, 191 East Ave., 14604, pg. 544   **PV**
WOKR-TV, 4225 W. Henrietta Rd., 14602-0555, pg. 439   **PV**
WROC, Inc., 201 Humboldt St., 14610, pg. 389   **PV**
WEGMANS FOOD MARKETS, INC., 1500 Brooks Ave., 14692, pg. 1158   **PV**
WILMORITE, INC., 1265 Scottsville Rd., 14624, pg. 1180   **PV**
Wolf Group Public Relations, Midtown Plaza, 400 Euclid Bldg., 14604, pg. 1186   **PV**
Xerox Business Services, 70 Linden Oaks, 14625, pg. 1784   **PB**
Xerox Engineering Systems Division, 300 Main Ste. 4-102, 14445, pg. 1784   **PB**
Xerox Installment Sales Div., Xerox Sq., Fl. 026, 100 Clinton Ave., S., 14644, pg. 1785   **PB**
Xerox U.S. Marketing Group, 100 Clinton Ave., S., 14644, pg. 1784   **PB**
Xertronix, 343 State St., 14550, pg. 551   **PB**
3kon Office Solutions-Upstate New York, 350 S. Ave., 14620, pg. 864   **PB**

Rock Hill

Frontier Insurance Company, 195 Lake Louise Marie Rd., 12775-8000, pg. 685   **PB**
FRONTIER INSURANCE GROUP, INC., 195 Lake Louise Marie Rd., 12775-8000, pg. 684   **PB**
Pioneer Claim Management, Inc., 195 Lake Louise Marie Rd., 12775-8000, pg. 685   **PB**

Rockville Center

Barton Distillers Import Corp., 265 Sunrise Hwy., 11570, pg. 300   **PB**
FUTTER LUMBER CORPORATION, 100 Merrick Rd., 11570, pg. 432   **PV**

Rockville Centre

A&M Instruments Inc., Five Nassau St., 11571, pg. 125   **IT**
Allcity Insurance Co., Rockville Centre, 371 Merrick Rd., 11570, pg. 990   **PB**
MULTI-LOCAL MEDIA CORPORATION, 100 N. Central Ave., 11570, pg. 767   **PV**
The Rugby Group, Inc., 100 Banks Ave., 11570, pg. 625   **IT**
URS Greiner, Inc., 66 North Village Ave., 11570, pg. 1659   **PB**
Yellow Book Co., Inc., 100 N. Centre Ave., 11570, pg. 767   **PV**

Rome

Quest Diagnostic-Rome, 1617 N. James St., 13440, pg. 1351   **PB**
ROME CABLE CORPORATION, 421 Ridge St., 13440, pg. 942   **PV**
ROME STRIP STEEL CO., INC., 530 Henry St., 13440, pg. 942   **PV**

Ronkonkoma

AERO DATA METAL CRAFTERS, 2085 Fifth Ave., 11779, pg. 23   **PV**
Air Crafters Inc., 2085 Fifth Ave., 11779, pg. 24   **PV**
American Glace, 4175 Veterans Hwy., Third Fl., 11779, pg. 883   **PB**

Geographic Index-U.S.

PB - *U.S. Public Companies Volume*
PV - *U.S. Private Companies Volume*
IT - *International Public & Private Companies Volume*

Beck/Arnley Worldparts Corp., 2150 Fifth Ave., 11779, pg. 561 **PB**

Health Management, Inc., 80 Air Park Dr., 11779, pg. 338 **IT**

INTEGRATED BRANDS INC., 4175 Veterans Hwy., 3rd Fl., 11779, pg. 883 **PB**

Lab Crafters Inc., 2085 Fifth Ave., 11779, pg. 24 **PV**

LAKELAND INDUSTRIES, INC., 711-2 Koehler Ave., 11779, pg. 975 **PB**

QUALITY KING DISTRIBUTORS INC., 2060 Ninth Ave., 11779, pg. 899 **PV**

Richardson Electronics Ltd.-Eastern, 701-1 Koehler Ave., 11779, pg. 1388 **PB**

Swensen's Ice Cream Co., 4175 Veterans Memorial Highway, 11779, pg. 883 **PB**

Roslyn Heights

Cheyenne, Three Expressway Plaza, 11577, pg. 420 **PV**

Kintetsu World Express (U.S.A.), Inc., 66 Powerhouse Rd., 11577, pg. 734 **IT**

Rouses Point

F.W. Myers & Co., Inc., Myers Bldg., 72 Lake St., 12979, pg. 771 **PV**

F.W. MYERS & CO., INC., Myers Bldg., 72 Lake St., 12979-1091, pg. 770 **PV**

F.W. Myers & Co., Myers Bldg., 72 Lake St., 12979, pg. 771 **PV**

Rye

BEC GROUP, INC., 555 Theodore Fremd Ave., Ste. 302, 10580, pg. 160 **PB**

Companion Life Insurance Co., 401 Theodore Fremd Ave., 10580-8072, pg. 770 **PV**

TIE Systems, Inc. New York, Two Clinton Ave., 10580, pg. 1085 **PV**

Rye Brook

ENTEX INFORMATION SERVICES, Six International Dr., 10573, pg. 378 **PV**

Flik International, Three International Dr., 10573, pg. 324 **IT**

IBM World Trade Europe/Middle East/Africa Corp., 900 King St., 10573, pg. 896 **PB**

Kraft Foods Inc., 800 Westchester Ave., 10573, pg. 1288 **PB**

Kraft Foods International, 800 Westchester Ave., 10573, pg. 1288 **PB**

MCI International Inc., Two International Dr., 10573, pg. 1024 **PB**

PARSONS & WHITTEMORE, INC., Four International Dr., 10573, pg. 840 **PV**

Philip Morris Capital Corporation, 800 Westchester Ave., 10573-1301, pg. 1289 **PB**

Philip Morris International Inc., 800 Westchester Ave., 10573-1301, pg. 1289 **PB**

Sanborn

VOYAGER EMBLEMS, INC., 3707 Lockport Rd., 14132-9705, pg. 1143 **PV**

Sangerfield

Titan Homes, Inc., P.O. Box 56, Hwy. 12, 13455, pg. 332 **PB**

Saratoga Springs

CB NORTH AMERICA, INC., 490 Broadway, 12866, pg. 192 **PV**

CB Sports Inc., 490 Broadway, 12866, pg. 192 **PV**

ESPEY MFG. & ELECTRONICS CORP., 233 Ballston Ave., 12866, pg. 592 **PB**

SARATOGA EQUINE SPORTS CENTER, Nelson Ave., 12866, pg. 965 **PV**

Saratoga Industries, P.O. Box 422, 233 Ballston Ave., 12866, pg. 592 **PB**

The Saratogian, 20 Lake Ave., 12866, pg. 700 **PB**

Sartoga National Bank & Trust Company, 137 S. Broadway, 12866, pg. 135 **PB**

STEWART'S ICE CREAM CO., INC., P.O. Box 435, 12866, pg. 1043 **PV**

Saugerties

EG & G Rotron Industrial Division, North Street, 12477, pg. 543 **PB**

Scarsdale

Accor North America, Two Overhill Rd., 10583, pg. 21 **IT**

Allcity Insurance Co., Scarsdale, 1088 Central Ave., 10583, pg. 990 **PB**

THE CURRY CORPORATION, 727 Central Ave., 10583, pg. 297 **PV**

IBL Limited, Inc., Two Overhill Rd., Ste. 420, 10583, pg. 21 **IT**

NVW (USA) Inc., 700 White Plains Rd., 10583, pg. 754 **IT**

NATIONAL HOME HEALTH CARE CORP., 700 White Plains Rd., 10583, pg. 1157 **PB**

J.A. Sexauer, Inc., 531 Central Park Ave., 10583, pg. 352 **PV**

Schenectady

Campbell Plastics Div., 2900 Campbell Ave., 12306, pg. 1504 **PB**

Cantex Corp., Rotterdam Indus. Park, Bldg. 1, 12306, pg. 113 **IT**

Cengo Construction Corporation, 501 Duanesburg Rd., 12306, pg. 463 **PV**

Central Distributors, Inc., 501 Duanesburg Rd., 12306, pg. 463 **PV**

Coast RV, Inc., 397 Anthony St., 12309, pg. 388 **PB**

ConTec Limited Partnership, 1023 State St., 12307, pg. 699 **PV**

Corrugated Packaging, Bldg. 801, Corporations Pk., 12302, pg. 737 **PB**

DZIC, 120 Erie Blvd., 12305, pg. 317 **PV**

G.E. Power Systems, One River Rd., 12345, pg. 711 **PB**

GALESI GROUP, Rotterdam Industrial Park, 12306, pg. 437 **PV**

GOLUB CORPORATION, 501 Duanesburg Rd., 12306, pg. 463 **PV**

Golub Service Stations, Inc., 501 Duanesburg Rd., 12306, pg. 463 **PV**

INSULATING MATERIALS, INC., One W. Campbell Rd., 12306, pg. 565 **PV**

KAPL, Inc., P.O. Box 1072, 12301-1072, pg. 1007 **PB**

METRO FORD SALES, INC., 3601 State St., 12304, pg. 736 **PB**

O.R.E. Subsidiary Corp., P.O. Box 1082, 12301-1082, pg. 1643 **PB**

Price Chopper Operating Co. in Vt., Inc., 501 Duanesburg Rd., 12306, pg. 463 **PV**

Price Chopper Operating Co., Inc., 501 Duanesburg Rd., 12306, pg. 463 **PV**

Price Chopper Operating Co. of Mass., Inc., 501 Duanesburg Rd., 12306, pg. 463 **PV**

Price Chopper Operating Co. of PA, Inc., 501 Duanesburg Rd., 12306, pg. 463 **PV**

SCHENECTADY INTERNATIONAL, INC., Tenth & Congress St., 12303, pg. 969 **PV**

Troy Savings Bank-Schenectady, 1626 Union St., 12309, pg. 1106 **PV**

TRUSTCO BANK CORP., NY, 320 State St., 12305, pg. 1643 **PB**

Trustco Bank, N.A., 320 State St., 12305, pg. 1643 **PB**

Twin Rivers Textile Printing and Finishing, 301 Nott St., Bldg. 316, 12305, pg. 769 **PB**

WRGB-TV, 1400 Balltown Rd., 12309, pg. 425 **PB**

Scotia

Adirondack Beverages, 701 Corporations Pk., 12302, pg. 873 **PV**

Chesapeake Packaging Co./Scotia, Corporation Park, Bldg. 803, 12302, pg. 347 **PB**

SOFCO-MEAD, INC., 702 Potential Pkwy., 12302, pg. 1012 **PV**

Sea Cliff

Sea Cliff Water Company, 325 Prospect Ave., 11579, pg. 126 **PB**

Seaford

BAST CHEVROLET INC., 3660 Sunrise Hwy., 11783, pg. 122 **PV**

Seneca Falls

Identification Systems, 25 Chestnut St., 13148, pg. 1059 **PB**

SENECA FALLS TECHNOLOGY GROUP, 314 Fall St., 13148, pg. 984 **PV**

Setauket

GMB Sales, 140 Terminal Rd., 11733, pg. 1720 **PV**

Sidney

The At-A-Glance Group, 101 O'Neil Rd., 13838, pg. 295 **PV**

Bendix Connector, Operations, 40-60 Delaware Ave., 13838-1304, pg. 51 **PB**

Skaneateles

L.A.B. Equipment, 1326 New Seneca Turnpike, 13152, pg. 801 **PV**

Skaneateles Falls

P&S Filtration Inc., 4563 Jordan Rd., 13153, pg. 1202 **IT**

Smithtown

BANK OF SMITHTOWN, One E. Main St., 11787, pg. 114 **PV**

Gull Electronic Systems Div., P.O. Box 9400, 300 Marcus Blvd., 11787-9400, pg. 1262 **PB**

SMITHTOWN BANCORP, INC., One E. Main St., 11787, pg. 1479 **PB**

Sodus

Heluva Good Cheese Inc., 6551 Pratt Rd., 14551, pg. 752 **IT**

Solvay

CRUCIBLE MATERIALS CORP., 575 State Fair Blvd., 13209, pg. 293 **PV**

Frazer & Jones Div., 3000 Milton Ave., 13209, pg. 548 **PB**

Somers

IBM Enterprise Systems, P.O. Box 100, Rte. 100, 10589, pg. 895 **PB**

IBM Personal Computer Company, P.O. Box 100, 10589, pg. 896 **PB**

Pepsi-Cola Company, One Pepsi Way, 10589, pg. 1277 **PB**

PepsiCo Foods & Beverages International, One Pepsi Way, 10589, pg. 1277 **PB**

South Otselic

Gladding Braided Products LLC, P.O. Box 164, One Gladding St., 13155-0164, pg. 291 **PV**

Southampton

ALLAN SCHNEIDER ASSOCIATES, 99 Job's Ln., 11968, pg. 971 **PV**

Allan Schneider Associates, 99 Job's Ln., 11968, pg. 971 **PV**

Spring Valley

COSCO INDUSTRIES, 56 Church St., 10977, pg. 277 **PV**

PHARMACEUTICAL RESOURCES, One Ram Ridge Rd., 10977, pg. 1285 **PB**

Springville

T.L. SMITH MACHINE, 7020 Henrietta Rd., 14141, pg. 1009 **PV**

Staten Island

ADVANCE PUBLICATIONS INC., 950 Finger Board Rd., 10305, pg. 18 **PV**

Nassau Metals Corporation, 286 Richmond Valley Rd., 10309, pg. 1019 **PB**

Quest Diagnostic-Staten Island, Todt Hill Medical Ctr., 78 Todt Hill Rd., Ste. 109, 10314, pg. 1351 **PB**

Quest Diagnostic-Staten Island, 1361 Hylan Blvd., 10305, pg. 1352 **PB**

Rouse SI Shopping Management, Inc., Staten Island Mall, 2655 Richmond Ave., 10314, pg. 1408 **PB**

Staten Island Property Inc., 350 Saint Marks Pl., 10301, pg. 180 **IT**

Staten Island Terminal, 500 Western Ave., 10303-1106, pg. 692 **PB**

TELEPORT COMMUNICATIONS GROUP, One Teleport Dr., 10311, pg. 1572 **PB**

Stone Ridge

Charles River Breeding Labs, Rte. 209, 12484, pg. 194 **PB**

Suffern

Avon Manufacturing Lab., Division St., 10901, pg. 156 **PB**

CIBA-GEIGY Pharmaceutical Production, P.O. Box 100, Old Mill Rd., 10901, pg. 973 **IT**

THE DRESS BARN, INC., 30 Dunnigan Dr., 10901, pg. 528 **PB**

First Ameritas Life Insurance Corp. of New York, 400 Rella Blvd., Ste. 214, 10901, pg. 65 **PV**

Syosset

ADI (Ademco Distribution, Inc.), 180 Michael Dr., 11791, pg. 1306 **PB**

AFA PROTECTIVE SYSTEMS, INC., 155 Michael Dr., 11791, pg. 5 **PB**

AFA Protective Systems, Inc., 170 Eileen Way, 11791, pg. 5 **PB**

Ademco Security Group, 165 Eileen Way, 11791, pg. 1306 **PB**

Alarm Device Manufacturing Company, 165 Eileen Way, 11791, pg. 1306 **PB**

AlarmNet/Radscan, 160 Eileen Way, 11791, pg. 1306 **PB**

CHAMPION ALUMINUM WINDOW CORPORATION, 140 Eileen Way, 11791, pg. 227 **PV**

CUTCO INDUSTRIES, INC., P.O. Box 265, 6900 Jericho Tpke., 11791, pg. 470 **PB**

Designed & Engineered Systems, 170 Eileen Way, 11791, pg. 6 **PB**

Fire Burglary Instruments, Inc., 165 Eileen Way, 11791, pg. 1306 **PB**

First Alert Professional, 765 Eileen Way, 11791, pg. 1306 **PB**

Javelin Systems, 165 Eileen Way, 11791, pg. 1306 **PB**

KRANTOR CORPORATION, P.O. Box 996, 11791, pg. 966 **PB**

Lockheed Martin Fairchild Systems, 300 Robbins Lane, 11791, pg. 1008 **PB**

PB - U.S. Public Companies Volume
PV - U.S. Private Companies Volume
IT - International Public & Private Companies Volume

Geographic Index-U.S.

1361

Lockwood Kessler & Bartlett, Inc., One Aerial Way, 11791, pg. 440 **PB**
MEENAN OIL CO. L.P., 6900 Jericho Tpke., 11791, pg. 729 **PV**
NOODLE KIDOODLE INC., 6801 Jericho Tpke., Ste. 100, 11791, pg. 1188 **PB**
Nuyens Liquor Importing, Inc., 40 Underhill Blvd., 11791, pg. 1173 **PV**
PORTA SYSTEMS CORP., 575 Underhill Blvd., 11791, pg. 1317 **PB**
SmithKline Beecham Clinical Laboratories, 575 Underhill Blvd., 11791, pg. 1265 **IT**
STAR INDUSTRIES INC., 345 Underhill Blvd., 11791, pg. 1034 **PV**

Syracuse

Agri-Financial Services, P.O. Box 4910, 13221, pg. 308 **PV**
Agri-Service Agencies, Inc., P.O. Box 4910, 13221, pg. 308 **PV**
Agway Agricultural Products (AAP), P.O. Box 4933, 13221, pg. 27 **PV**
Agway Energy Products (AEP), P.O. Box 4852, 13221, pg. 27 **PV**
Agway General Agency, P.O. Box 4851, 13221, pg. 27 **PV**
Agway Insurance Co., P.O. Box 4851, 13221, pg. 27 **PV**
Agway Retail Services, Salina Meadows Office Park, 301 Plainfield Rd., 13212-4540, pg. 27 **PV**
Allied Advertising Agency, Public Relations, 6311 Fly Rd., Ste. E, 13057, pg. 38 **PV**
American General Life Insurance Company of New York, 300 So. State St., 13201, pg. 76 **PV**
Arrow Hart Wiring Devices, Wolfe & 7th North St., 13221, pg. 444 **PB**
Associated Spring, 1225 State Fair Blvd., 13209, pg. 190 **PB**
CARLISLE COMPANIES INCORPORATED, 250 S. Clinton St., Ste. 201, 13202, pg. 305 **PB**
Carlyle Compressor Co., Inc., 6500 Chrysler Dr., 13657, pg. 1690 **PB**
CARROLS CORPORATION, 968 James St., 13203, pg. 216 **PB**
Cleanroom Technology, Performance Dr., 13212-3448, pg. 569 **IT**
Country Products Group, P.O. Box 4933, 13221, pg. 27 **PV**
Crouse-Hinds, Wolf & Seventh North Sts., 13221, pg. 444 **PB**
Dutch Parking, Inc., 345 S. Warren St., 13202, pg. 43 **PV**
EA Engineering, Science & Technology, Inc., 115 Twin Oaks Dr., 13206, pg. 541 **PB**
EMA Public Relations Services, Inc., 500 Plum St., 13204, pg. 765 **PV**
Empire Livestock Marketing Inc., P.O Box 4844, 13221-4844, pg. 308 **PV**
Esselte Pendaflex, 128 Spencer St., 13221, pg. 460 **IT**
FARMERS AND TRADERS LIFE INSURANCE CO., 960 James St., 13201-1056, pg. 394 **PV**
Green Tree Acceptance, Inc., P.O. Box 514, 5790 Wide Waters Pkwy., 13214, pg. 762 **PB**
Martin Marietta Ocean, Radar & Sensor Systems, PO Box 4840, Electronics Parkway, 13221, pg. 1007 **PB**
ERIC MOWER AND ASSOCIATES, INC., 500 Plum St., 13204, pg. 765 **PV**
MUENCH-KREUZER CANDLE COMPANY, 617 E. Hiawatha Blvd., 13208, pg. 766 **PV**
NIAGARA MOHAWK POWER CORPORATION, 300 Erie Blvd. W., 13202, pg. 1181 **PB**
North American Energy Conservation, Inc., 100 Clinton Sq., Ste. 400, pg. 1789 **PB**
OBERDORFER INDUSTRIES, INC., 6259 Thompson Rd., 13206-1405, pg. 810 **PV**
ONBANCorp, Inc., 101 S. Salina St., 13202, pg. 631 **PB**
OnBank, 101 S. Salina St., 13202, pg. 632 **PB**
OnBank & Trust Co., 101 South Salina Street, 133221, pg. 632 **PB**
P & C Food Markets, Inc., State Fair Blvd. & Van Vleck Rd., 13221, pg. 1270 **PV**
Pass & Seymour/Legrand, 50 Boyd Ave., 13209, pg. 806 **IT**
Paul Revere Insurance Group, 5795 Widewaters Pkwy., 13214-1846, pg. 1338 **PV**
THE PENN TRAFFIC COMPANY, 1200 State Fair Blvd., P.O. Box 4737, 13221-4737, pg. 1270 **PB**
THE PYRAMID COMPANIES, The Clinton Exchange, Four Clinton Sq., 13202, pg. 896 **PV**
Quanta Advertising Corporation, 968 James St., 13203, pg. 216 **PV**
Quest Diagnostic-Syracuse, 600 E. Genesee St., 13202, pg. 1352 **PV**
SYRACUSE SUPPLY COMPANY, 5921 Court St. Rd., 13221, pg. 1060 **PV**
Syracuse Supply Construction & Equipment Division, Colvin Station 294, P.O. Box 37, 13205, pg. 1060 **PV**
Syracuse Supply Leasing Co., Inc., 5921 Court St. Rd., P.O. Box 4945, 13221, pg. 1060 **PV**
Telmark, Inc., P.O. Box 4943, 13221, pg. 27 **PV**
VENTRE PACKING COMPANY, INC., 6050 Court St. Rd., 13206-1730, pg. 1135 **PV**

Tallman

Eastern U.S., P.O. Box 368, 321 Rte. 59, Ste. W1, 10982, pg. 1540 **PB**

Tappan

VITS-BLAVA Technologies Corporation, 30 Rockland Ave., 10983, pg. 399 **IT**

Tarrytown

AMBI INC., 771 Old Saw Mill Rd., 10591, pg. 7 **PB**
AMPACET CORPORATION, 660 White Plains Rd., 10591, pg. 67 **PV**
Bayer Corporation/Diagnostics Division, 511 Benedict Ave., 10591, pg. 173 **IT**
Ciba Specialty Chemicals, P.O. Box 2005, 560 White Plains Rd., 10591, pg. 291 **IT**
The Dannon Co., 120 White Plains Rd., 10591, pg. 379 **IT**
First UNUM Life Insurance Company, Christiania Bldg., Third Fl., 120 White Plains Rd., 10591, pg. 1699 **PB**
Hitachi America, Ltd., 50 Prospect Ave., 10591-4698, pg. 622 **IT**
KANE-MILLER CORP., 555 White Plains Rd., 10591, pg. 607 **PV**
Kymmene USA, 120 White Plains Rd., 10591, pg. 1430 **IT**
SAU-SEA FOODS, INC., 303 S. Broadway, Ste. 224, 10591, pg. 967 **PV**
Stinnes Corporation, 120 White Plains Rd., 10591, pg. 1460 **IT**
Sylamerica, 660 White Plains Rd., 10591, pg. 818 **IT**

Thornwood

Carl Zeiss, Inc., One Zeiss Dr., 10594, pg. 1523 **IT**

Tonawanda

R.P. ADAMS COMPANY, INC., 225 E. Park Dr., 14150, pg. 19 **PB**
Alro Specialty Metals, Tonawanda, 50 Ensminger Rd., 14150-6793, pg. 46 **PV**
BRIMMS INC., 425 Fillmore Ave., 14150, pg. 169 **PB**
Cady Lifters, 1 Fremont St., 14150, pg. 405 **PB**
CHEMCENTRAL/Buffalo, 3709 River Rd., 14150, pg. 232 **PV**
Conco, 1 Fremont St., 14150, pg. 405 **PB**
Electrohome U.S.A. (1989), Inc., 181 Cooper Ave., 14150, pg. 438 **IT**
EXOLON-ESK COMPANY, 1000 E. Niagara St., 14150, pg. 600 **PB**
Niagara Landfill, Inc., River Rd., 14150, pg. 264 **PB**
RONCO COMMUNICATIONS & ELECTRONICS INC., 595 Sheridan St., 14150, pg. 943 **PV**
Sivaco New York, Inc., 3937 River Rd., 14151-0646, pg. 696 **IT**

Troy

Bendix Friction Materials Division, P.O. Box 238, 12181-0238, pg. 1106 **PV**
The Family Investment Services Co., Inc., Second & State Streets, 12180, pg. 1106 **PV**
The Family Mortgage Banking Co., Inc., 433 River St., 12180, pg. 1106 **PV**
GARDEN WAY, INC., 1 Garden Way, 12180, pg. 440 **PV**
INTERSTATE COMMODITIES INC., Seven Madison St., 12181, pg. 573 **PV**
KING FUELS INC., Foot of Main St., 12181, pg. 620 **PV**
LEVONIAN BROTHERS INC., 27 River St., 12180, pg. 663 **PV**
Lydall Manning-Green Island Operation, P.O. Box 328, 12181-0328, pg. 1021 **PV**
MAPINFO CORP., One Global View, 12180, pg. 1042 **PB**
Specialty Restaurants Corp., 377 River St., 12180, pg. 1023 **PV**
STANDARD MANUFACTURING CO., INC., 750 Second Ave., 12182, pg. 1031 **PV**
TS Capital Corp., Second & State Streets, 12180, pg. 1106 **PV**
Troy Publishing Company, Inc., 501 Broadway, 12181, pg. 935 **PV**
THE TROY SAVINGS BANK, Second & State Streets, 12180, pg. 1106 **PV**
Troy Savings Bank-Hudson Valley Plaza, 75 Vandenburgh Ave., 12180, pg. 1106 **PV**
Troy Savings Bank-Main Office, Second & States Streets, 12180, pg. 1106 **PV**
Troy SB Real Estate Co., Inc., Second & State, 12180, pg. 1106 **PV**
Visilox Systems, Inc. (VSI), 405 Jordan Rd., 12180, pg. 611 **IT**

Tuxedo Park

International Paper Co., Long Meadow Rd., 10987, pg. 902 **PB**

Uniondale

European American Bank, EAB Plaza, 11555, pg. 9 **IT**
European American Bank & Trust Co., One EAB Plaza, 11555, pg. 9 **IT**
FLOWERS USA, 165 EAB Plaza, West Twr., 11556, pg. 415 **PV**
FORTUNOFF, 70 Charles Lindberg Blvd., 11553, pg. 420 **PV**
FREQUENCY ELECTRONICS, INC., 55 Charles Lindbergh Blvd., 11553, pg. 681 **PB**
THE HAIN FOOD GROUP INC., 50 Charles Lindberg Blvd., 11553, pg. 774 **PB**
NEW YORK ISLANDERS HOCKEY CLUB, Nassau Coliseum, 11553, pg. 794 **PV**
U.S. Healthcare (New York), Nassau Omni W., 333 Earle Ovington Blvd., Ste. 502, 11553, pg. 26 **PB**

Utica

Bendix Fluid Power Division, P.O. Box 457, 13503-0457, pg. 51 **PB**
Benefit Plans Administrative Services, Inc., 1500 Genesee St., 13502, pg. 416 **PV**
COMMERCIAL TRAVELERS MUTUAL INSURANCE COMPANY, 70 Genesee, 13502, pg. 258 **PV**
CONMED CORPORATION, 310 Broad St., 13501, pg. 431 **PB**
Consolidated Medical Equipment International, Inc., 310 Broad St., 13501, pg. 431 **PB**
GN Nettest Fiber Optic Division, 109 N. Genesee St., 13502, pg. 536 **IT**
Graphic Arts Mutual Insurance Co., P.O. Box 530, 13503, pg. 1130 **PV**
Harza Northeast, Inc., 181 Genesee St., 13501-2168, pg. 509 **PV**
Lucas Aerospace Power Transmission, P.O. Box 457, 211 Seward Ave., 13503, pg. 820 **IT**
THE F.X. MATT BREWING CO., 811 Edward, 13502, pg. 714 **PV**
MELE MANUFACTURING CO., INC., 1712 Erie St., 13503, pg. 730 **PV**
Monitor Life Insurance Company of New York, 70 Genesee St., 13502, pg. 258 **PV**
UNI-Service Operations Corporation, P.O. Box 530, 13503, pg. 1130 **PV**
UTICA BOILERS INC., 2201 Dwyer Ave., 13501, pg. 1129 **PV**
Utica National Life Insurance Company, P.O. Box 530, 13503, pg. 1130 **PV**
Utica Observer-Dispatch, 221 Oriskany Plaza, 13503, pg. 700 **PB**
WUTR-TV, Smith Hill Road, 13502, pg. 1078 **PB**

Valhalla

Bell Atlantic Systems Marketing, 500 Summit Lake Dr. 4th Fl., 10595-1340, pg. 203 **PB**
DEL GLOBAL TECHNOLOGIES, One Commerce Park, 10595, pg. 493 **PB**
Farrand Controls, 99 Wall St., 10595, pg. 951 **PV**
FOUR M CORPORATION, INC., 115 Stevens Ave., 10595, pg. 421 **PV**
Lotepro Corporation, 115 Stevens Ave., 10595, pg. 811 **IT**
RUHLE COMPANIES, INC., 99 Wall St., 10595, pg. 950 **PV**
ZING TECHNOLOGIES, INC., 115 Stevens Ave., 10595, pg. 1792 **PB**

Valley Cottage

Switzerland Cheese Association, Inc., 704 Executive Blvd., 10989, pg. 1211 **IT**

Valley Stream

BALTIC LINEN COMPANY, INC., 260 W. Sunrise Hwy., 11582, pg. 113 **PV**
Circle Freight International USA, 540 Rockaway Ave., 11581, pg. 370 **PV**
Dachser Transport of America Inc., 20 W. Lincoln Ave., 11580, pg. 357 **PV**
Fenton Hill American Limited, B-3 E., Airport Indus. Office, 145 Hook Creek Blvd., 11581, pg. 103 **IT**
Ferre Export Corp., 210 Sunrise Hwy., 11581, pg. 1342 **PB**
Hallman & Lorber, Inc., 70 E. Sunrise Hwy., Ste. 411, 11581-1263, pg. 783 **PV**
International Aero-Sea Forwarders, Inc., Hook Creek Blvd., 145th Ave., Unit C-1A, 11581, pg. 683 **IT**
Marcon Shipping/A.N. Deringer, 11 E. Hawthorne Ave., 11580, pg. 326 **PV**
SID HARVEY INDUSTRIES, 100 E. Mineola Ave., 11580, pg. 998 **PV**
Strober Long Island Building Materials Centers, Inc., 370 W. Merrick Rd., 11580, pg. 403 **PV**
Tamura Corp. of America, Microtran Div., 145 E. Mineola Ave., 11582, pg. 1067 **PV**
TRIANGLE SERVICES, INC., 71 S. Central Ave., 11580, pg. 1110 **PV**
Gary Wood Associates, Inc., 70 E. Sunrise Hwy., Ste. 411, 11581-1263, pg. 783 **PB**

Vestal

BEN ARNOLD CO., INC., 300 Plaza Dr., 13850, pg. 83 **PV**
GREAT AMERICAN INDUSTRIES, INC., 300 Plaza Dr., 13850-3646, pg. 473 **PV**
ITALIAN FOOD MANUFACTURERS, INC., 2317 Vestal Pkwy., E., 13850, pg. 576 **PV**
Quest Diagnostic-Vestal, Vestal Professional Bldg., 300 Main St., 13850, pg. 1352 **PV**
Wholesale Electric Supply Co., 3013 Old Vestal Rd., 13850, pg. 847 **PB**

Victor

EUA Day, 7931 Rae Blvd., 14564, pg. 549 **PB**
HORIZON AEROSPACE LLC, 1290 Atwal Dr., 14564, pg. 538 **PV**
Koch Container, 777 Old Dutch Rd., 14564, pg. 177 **PV**
Ultimate Technology Corporation, 100 Rawson Rd., Ste. 210, 14564, pg. 1637 **PB**

PB - *U.S. Public Companies Volume*
PV - *U.S. Private Companies Volume*
IT - *International Public & Private Companies Volume*

Voorheesville

Atlas Copco Comptec Inc., 46 School Rd., 12186, pg. 96   IT

Walden

New England Laminates Co., Inc., Three Elm St., 12586, pg. 1258   PB
Nicholson Steam Trap, 150 Coldenham Rd., 12586, pg. 1747   PB
Spence Engineering Co., 150 Coldenham Rd., Box 230, 12586, pg. 1747   PB

Wantagh

Meenan LI Div., 3020 Burns Ave., 11793, pg. 729   PV

Wappingers Falls

Hewlett-Packard Company, Executive Sq. Office Bldg., 66 Middlebush Rd., 12590, pg. 814   PB

Warners

Sysco Food Services-Syracuse, Rte. 173 N., Warners Rd., 13164, pg. 1552   PB

Warwick

Genesys Combustion, 87 Sleepy Valley Rd., 10990, pg. 360   PV
TRIUMPH PET INDUSTRIES, INC., 160 Lake Station Rd., 10990, pg. 1104   PV

Waterford

G.E. Silicones, 260 Hudson River Rd., 12188, pg. 711   PB

Watertown

CAR-FRESHNER CORPORATION, 203 N. Hamilton St., 13601, pg. 1   PV
Fisher Gauge Inc./Fishercast Div., P.O. Box 837, 13601, pg. 492   IT
JOHNSON NEWSPAPER CORPORATION, 260 Washington St., 13601, pg. 591   PV
Knorr Brake Holding Corp., 748 Starbuck Ave., 13601, pg. 738   PB
Knorr Brake Truck Systems Company, 748 Starbuck Ave., 13601, pg. 738   IT
Logicon Technical Services Inc., P.O. Box 517, 13603-0517, pg. 1199   PB
New York Air Brake Corporation, 748 Starbuck Ave., 13601, pg. 738   IT
New York Casualty Insurance Co., 120 Washington St., 13601-3352, pg. 787   PB
STEBBINS ENGINEERING & MFG. CO., 363 Eastern Blvd., 13601, pg. 1037   PV

Watervliet

Crestline Distribution Facility, 1801 Ave B, 12189, pg. 1193   PB
The Family Insurance Agency, Inc., 1601 Broadway, 12189, pg. 1106   PV
Hoboken Floors-A.S.T. Division, 1397 Broadway, 12189-3324, pg. 532   PV
Hoboken Floors-Adirondack Division, 1397 Broadway, 12189-3324, pg. 532   PV
Troy Savings Bank, Broadway & 16th St., 12189, pg. 1106   PV

Waverly

Atlantic Lumber Company, State Rt. 34N #352, 14892, pg. 959   PV

Wayland

The Gunlocke Company, One Gunlocke Dr., 14572, pg. 772   PB

Webster

A.D. Data Systems, 765 Basket Rd., 14580, pg. 1246   PB
PSC INC., 675 Basket Rd., 14580-9764, pg. 1245   PB
Webster Research Center, 800 Phillips Rd., Bldg. 230, 14580, pg. 1784   PB

Wellsville

ABB Air Preheater Inc., Andover Rd., P.O. Box 372, 14895, pg. 3   IT
Dresser-Rand Co. (Wellsville), 37 Coats St., 14895, pg. 529   PB

West Hempstead

Beldoch Industries, 44 Cherry Valley Ave., 11552, pg. 519   PB

West Henrietta

GENESEE METAL STAMPINGS, INC., 975 John St., 14586, pg. 446   PV

West Nyack

ALLOY TECHNOLOGY INTERNATIONAL INC., 169 Western Hwy., 10994, pg. 42   PV
BICC Cables Corporation, One Crosfield Ave., 10994, pg. 120   IT
Douglaston Electric, P.O. Box 348, Rte. 303, 10994, pg. 1110   PV
GENERAL BEARING CORP., 44 High St., 10994, pg. 706   PB
United Water New York, 360 W. Nyack Rd., 10994, pg. 1692   PB

West Sayville

BluePoints Co., Inc., Atlantic Ave., 11796, pg. 637   PB

West Seneca

GILLOGLY CHEVROLET & GEO, INC., 1777 Union Rd., 14224, pg. 454   PV

West Valley

West Valley Nuclear Services, P.O. Box 191, 14171-0191, pg. 273   PB

Westbury

AID AUTO STORES, INC., P.O. Box 281, 275 Grand Blvd., 11590-0281, pg. 29   PB
Ames Automotive Warehouse, 275 Grand Blvd., 11590, pg. 29   PB
BRINKMANN INSTRUMENTS, INC., One Cantiague Rd., 11590-0207, pg. 169   PV
DARBY GROUP OF COS., 865 Merrick Ave., 11590, pg. 311   PV
Doak Dermatologics, 67 Sylvester St., 11590, pg. 250   PV
E-Z-EM Imaging Products Division, 717 Main St., 11590, pg. 540   PB
E-Z-EM, INC., 717 Main St., 11590-5021, pg. 540   PB
800-FLOWERS, INC., 1600 Stewart Ave., 11590, pg. 366   PV
Enteric Products, Inc., 717 Main St., 11590, pg. 540   PB
Getko Group Inc., 115 South Service Rd., 11590, pg. 320   PB
JOHN HASSALL, INC., P.O. Box 698, Cantiague Rock Rd., 11590, pg. 509   PV
HITCO, P.O. Box 885, Cantiague Rock Rd., 11590, pg. 509   PV
KING KULLEN GROCERY CO., INC., 1194 Prospect Ave., 11590, pg. 621   PV
Lady Rose Div., 725 Summa Ave., 11590, pg. 714   PV
LIFETIME HOAN CORP., One Merrick Ave., 11590, pg. 992   PB
Lord Bibb Div., 725 Summa Ave., 11590, pg. 714   PV
MASTERS, INC., 1400 Country Rd., 11590, pg. 714   PV
METPAR CORP., 95 State St., 11590, pg. 735   PV
NATHAN'S FAMOUS, INC., 1400 Old Country Rd., Ste. 400, 11590, pg. 1152   PB
H. Sand & Co., Inc., 88 Urban Ave., 11590, pg. 1261   IT
SERVO CORPORATION OF AMERICA, 111 New South Rd., 11590-5026, pg. 987   PV
SPECTRONICS CORPORATION, 956 Brush Hollow Rd., 11590, pg. 1024   PV
Sulzer Metco (Westbury) Inc., 1101 Prospect Ave., 11590, pg. 1307   IT
Susan Terry Div., 725 Summa Ave., 11590, pg. 714   PV
Tracer Products, 956 Brush Hollow Rd., 11590, pg. 1024   PV

Westerlo

HANNAY REELS, P.O. Box 159, 553 SR 143, 12193-0159, pg. 499   PV

Westfield

Mogen David Wine Corp., P.O. Box I, 85 Bourne St., 14787, pg. 1183   PV
NATIONAL GRAPE CO-OP ASSOCIATION, INC., Two S. Portage St., 14787, pg. 784   PV
Renold, Inc., P.O. Box A, 14787, pg. 1104   IT

White Plains

AT&T Communications, One N. Lexington Ave. 12th Fl., 10601-1712, pg. 10   PB
ASOMA CORPORATION, 105 Corporate Park Dr., 10604, pg. 89   PV
Bell Atlantic International, Four W. Red Oak Lane, 10604, pg. 202   PB
BROWNING CHEMICAL CORPORATION, 707 Westchester Ave., 10604, pg. 175   PV
BRUNSCHWIG & FILS, INC., 75 Virginia Rd., 10603, pg. 176   PV
Career Blazers of White Plains, Inc., 202 Mamaroneck Ave., 10601, pg. 209   PV
COLIN SERVICE SYSTEMS, INC., One Brockway Pl., 10601, pg. 252   PV
COMBE INCORPORATED, 1101 Westchester Ave., 10604, pg. 257   PV
Dansk International Designs Ltd., 108 Corporate Park Dr., 10604, pg. 261   PB
Dorman & Wilson, Inc., One N. Lexington Ave., 10601, pg. 985   PB
DREW INDUSTRIES INCORPORATED, 200 Mamaroneck Ave., 10601, pg. 529   PB
Feintool Equipment Corp., One Holland Ave., 10603, pg. 479   IT
Feintool New York Inc., One Holland Ave., 10603, pg. 479   IT
Feintool U.S. Operations Inc., One Holland Ave., 10603, pg. 479   IT
FIDCO, 4 Gannet Dr., 10604, pg. 916   IT
Gannett Suburban Newspapers, One Gannett Dr., 10604, pg. 700   PB
Gerber Life Insurance Co., 66 Church St., 10601, pg. 973   IT
Getty Petroleum Ireland, Ltd., 2000 Westchester Ave., 10650, pg. 1583   PB
Heineken USA Inc., 50 Main St., 10606, pg. 608   IT
Henningsen Foods, Inc., Two Corporate Park Dr., 10604, pg. 1074   IT
IBM Application Solutions, 1133 Westchester Ave., 10604, pg. 895   PB
IBM Personal Systems, 44 S. Broadway, 10601, pg. 895   PB
IBM Real Estate & Construction Div., 1133 Westchester Ave., 10604, pg. 896   PB
IBM Technology Products, 1000 Westchester Ave., 10604, pg. 896   PB
ITT INDUSTRIES, INC., Four W. Red Oak Ln., 10604, pg. 859   PB
Interlaken Capital Aviation Services, Inc., Westchester County Airport, Hangar E, 10604, pg. 216   PB
Kearney-National, Inc., 108 Corporate Park Dr., 10604-3805, pg. 351   PV
KRASDALE FOODS INC., 65 W. Red Oak Ln., 10604, pg. 635   PV
Lender's Bagel Bakery, 250 North St., 10625, pg. 1288   PB
LESLIE BUILDING PRODUCTS, INC., 200 Mamaroneck Ave., 10601, pg. 989   PB
Mistic Brands, Inc., 709 Westchester Ave., 10604, pg. 1635   PB
Mitsubishi Chemical America, Inc., 81 Main St., Ste. 401, 10601, pg. 871   IT
National Economic Research Associates (NERA), 123 Main St., 10601, pg. 1049   PB
NEW ZEALAND LAMB CO., INC., 106 Corporate Park Dr., Ste. 113, 10604, pg. 796   PV
PDL, Inc., 180 S. Broadway, 10605, pg. 1323   PB
PAXAR CORPORATION, 105 Corporate Park Dr., 10604, pg. 1266   PB
PECKHAM INDUSTRIES, INC., 20 Haarlem Ave., 10603, pg. 846   PV
PETALS, 300 Central Ave., 10606, pg. 856   PV
MALCOLM PIRNIE, INC., 104 Corporate Pk. Dr., 10602, pg. 867   PV
Presidential Continental Gardens Corp., 180 S. Broadway, 10605, pg. 1323   PB
PRESIDENTIAL REALTY CORPORATION, 180 S. Broadway, 10605, pg. 1324   PB
Presidential Realty of Iowa, Inc., 180 S. Broadway, 10605, pg. 1324   PB
PRICELLULAR CORPORATION, 711 Westchester Ave., 10604, pg. 1324   PB
PRODIGY INC., 44 S. Broadway, 10601, pg. 888   PV
Royal Copenhagen Porcelain Corporation, 27 Holland Ave., 10603, pg. 1134   IT
Royal Crown Company, Inc., 709 Westchester Ave., 10604, pg. 1635   PB
Saudi Arabian Texaco Inc., 2000 Westchester Ave., 10650, pg. 1583   PB
Seagram's Corp. Research and Development, 3 S. Corporate Park Dr., 10604, pg. 1217   IT
Separation Materials Division, 81 Main St., Ste. 401, 10601, pg. 871   IT
Snapple Beverage Company, 709 Westchester Ave., 10604, pg. 1635   PB
The Sunflower Group, 106 Corporate Park Dr., Ste. 317, 10604, pg. 1052   PV
Texaco Capital Inc., 2000 Westchester Ave., 10604, pg. 1583   PB
Texaco Development Corp., 2000 Westchester Ave., 10650, pg. 1583   PB
TEXACO INC., 2000 Westchester Ave., 10650, pg. 1582   PB
Texaco Indonesia Corp., 2000 Westchester Ave., 10650, pg. 1583   PB
Texaco International Financial Corp., 2000 Westchester Ave., 10650, pg. 1583   PB
Texaco International Trader Inc., 2000 Westchester Ave., 10650, pg. 1583   PB
Texaco Overseas Holdings Inc., 2000 Westchester Ave., 10604, pg. 1583   PB
Texaco Overseas Petroleum Co., 2000 Westchester Ave., 10650, pg. 1583   PB
The Bank of New York Trust Company, 123 Main St., 10602, pg. 179   PB
Triarc Beverage Group, 709 Westchester Ave., 10604, pg. 1635   PB
TRIGEN ENERGY CORPORATION, One Water St., 10601, pg. 1637   PB
WHITE RIVER CORPORATION, Two Gannett Dr., Ste. 200, 10604-4506, pg. 1765   PB
Yamanouchi U.S.A. Inc., 10 Bank St., Ste. 790, 10606, pg. 1519   IT

Whitehall

Troy Savings Bank-Whitehall, 184 Broadway, 12887, pg. 1106   PV

Geographic Index-U.S.

Whitestone

Austrian Airlines, 17-20 White Stone Expwy., 11357, pg. 101 — **IT**
KINRAY INC., 152-35 Tenth Ave., 11537, pg. 622 — **PV**
Slattery Associates Inc., 16-16 Whitestone Expwy., 11357, pg. 1261 — **IT**
WHITE ROCK PRODUCTS CORP., 16-16 White Stone Expwy., 11357, pg. 1173 — **PV**

Williamsville

American Steamship Company, Centerpointe Corp. Park, 500 Essjay Rd., 14221, pg. 690 — **PB**
CIMINELLI DEVELOPMENT COMPANY, INC., 350 Essjay Rd., Ste. 101, 14221, pg. 239 — **PV**
SCIEX, Inc., 395 S. Youngs Road, 14221, pg. 827 — **IT**

Willsboro

NYCO Minerals, P.O. Box 368, 124 Mountainview Dr., 12996-0368, pg. 259 — **IT**

Wilson

Pfeiffer Foods, Inc., 683 Lake Street, 14172, pg. 977 — **PB**

Woodbury

Bankers Life Insurance Co. of New York, 65 Froehlich Farm Blvd., 11797, pg. 560 — **PV**
Bankers Security Life Insurance Society, 1000 Woodbury Rd., Ste. 102, 11797, pg. 1375 — **PB**
Bravo Network, 150 Crossways Park W., 11797, pg. 288 — **PB**
Cablevision, One Media Crossways, 11797, pg. 288 — **PB**
CABLEVISION SYSTEMS CORPORATION, One Media Crossways, 11797, pg. 288 — **PB**
Comforce/Uniforce Staffing Services, 415 Crossways Park Dr., 11797, pg. 409 — **PB**
COMVERSE TECHNOLOGY, INC., 170 Crossways Park Dr., 11797, pg. 425 — **PB**
Ericsson Messaging Systems Inc., 45 Crossways Park Dr. W., 11797, pg. 1365 — **IT**
Harman Consumer Group, 80 Crossways Park W., 11797, pg. 787 — **PB**
HARMAN INTERNATIONAL INDUSTRIES, INC., 80 Crossways Park West, 11797, pg. 787 — **PB**
Hewlett-Packard Company, Three Crossways Pk., W., 11797, pg. 814 — **PB**
JBL Consumer, 80 Crossways Park W., 11797, pg. 787 — **PB**
JENNIFER CONVERTIBLES INC., 419 Crossways Park Dr., 11797, pg. 926 — **PB**
LACKMAN FOOD SERVICE, 303 Crossways Park Dr., 11797, pg. 642 — **PV**
Miller-Mitchell Division & REA Group, 195 Froehlich Farm Blvd., 11797, pg. 746 — **PV**
OVERSEAS MILITARY SALES CORPORATION, 100 Crossways Park W., 11797, pg. 823 — **PV**
PRO, 415 Crossway Parks Dr., 11797, pg. 409 — **PB**
Rainbow Advertising Sales Corporation (RASCO), One Media Crossways, 11797, pg. 288 — **PB**
Rainbow Programming Holdings, Inc., 150 Crossways Park W., 11797, pg. 288 — **PB**
SEAMAN FURNITURE COMPANY, INC., 300 Crossways Pk. Dr., 11797, pg. 1452 — **PB**
Son Cine Optique Photo S.A., 105 Crossways Park, 11797-2016, pg. 1005 — **IT**
THISCO, 415 Crossways Park Dr., 11797, pg. 409 — **PB**
Uniforce Information Services, 415 Crossways Park Dr., 11797, pg. 409 — **PB**
Weight Watchers International, Inc., 175 Crossways Park W., 11797, pg. 806 — **PB**

Woodside

American Cablevision of Queens, Inc., 25-20 Brooklyn-Queens Expwy., 11377, pg. 1610 — **PB**
Bulova Corporation, One Bulova Ave., 11377-7874, pg. 1010 — **PB**
Classic Moments Company, One Bulova Ave., 11377, pg. 1010 — **PB**
Humiseal Div., 26-60 Brooklyn-Queens Expwy. W., 11377, pg. 337 — **PB**
Managistics Incorporated, 32-31 57th St., 11377, pg. 181 — **PB**
Pierre Cardin Formal Wear, 57-07 31st Ave., 11377, pg. 1163 — **PV**
West Mill Clothes, H.M.C. Div., 57-07 31st Ave., 11377, pg. 1163 — **PV**
WEST MILL CLOTHES, INC., 57-07 31st Ave., 11377, pg. 1163 — **PV**

Woodstock

EG & G Rotron, Nine Hasbrouck Ln., 12498, pg. 543 — **PB**

Wyoming

MARKIN TUBING, INC., Pearl Creek Rd., 14591, pg. 705 — **PV**

Yaphank

Steering Wheel Systems North America, 445 County Rd., Ste. 101, 11980, pg. 1558 — **PB**

Yonkers

Aeroclo Metal Products, 700 Nepperham Ave., 10703, pg. 880 — **PV**
AMERICAN SPECIALTIES INC., 441 Saw Mill River Rd., 10701, pg. 62 — **PV**
COAST MANUFACTURING COMPANY, 200 Corporate Blvd., 10701, pg. 248 — **PB**
HEALTH PRODUCTS CORPORATION, 1060 Nepperham Ave., 10703, pg. 514 — **PV**
Kawasaki Rail Car, Inc., One Larkin Plaza, 10701, pg. 725 — **IT**
LKI, 495 S. Broadway, 10705, pg. 635 — **PV**
Lockheed Martin-Fairchild, Ridge Hill, 10710-0800, pg. 1008 — **PB**
Motorola USA, 311 Lee Ave., 10705-2719, pg. 1138 — **PB**
PRECISION VALVE CORPORATION, 700 Nepperham Ave., 10703, pg. 880 — **PV**
Refined Sugars, Inc., One Federal St., 10702, pg. 699 — **IT**
Stewart Stamping Corp., 630 Central Park Ave., 10704, pg. 881 — **PV**
WORLD CLASS FILM CORPORATION, 78 Furnbrook St., 10705, pg. 1190 — **PV**

Yorktown Heights

Dynacast, 1401 Front St., 10598, pg. 300 — **IT**
IBM Research Div., P.O. Box 218, 10598, pg. 896 — **PB**

NORTH CAROLINA

Aberdeen

AAR Power Boss, P.O. Box 1227, Anderson & Taylor Sts., 28315, pg. 1
Aberdeen Citizen News-Record, P.O. Box 336, 202 Sandhills Dr., 28315, pg. 1079 — **PB**
Park Newspapers of Moore County, Inc., P.O. Box 336, 202 Sandhills Dr., 28315, pg. 1079 — **PB**

Ahoskie

Guardian Care of Ahoskie, Stoke St. Extension, 27910, pg. 1712 — **PB**

Albemarle

Hydrolabs Inc., 2028 Kingsley Dr., 28001, pg. 62 — **IT**
Piedmont Nursing Center, Inc., Corner of Salisbury & Bethany Church Rd., 28001, pg. 1714 — **PB**

Alexander

East Carolina Environmental, Inc., 1922 Republican Rd., 27805, pg. 1379 — **PB**

Altamahaw

Glen Raven Mills, Inc.-Glen Touch Plant, P.O. Box 278, 3726 Altamahaw-Union Ridge Rd., 27202, pg. 456 — **PV**

Andrews

OMC Andrews, 1000 Hwy. 19-129 W., 28901, pg. 478 — **PV**

Angier

Angus Fire Armour Corp., Angier Kennebec Rd., 27501, pg. 1500 — **IT**

Apex

Lufkin, P.O. Box 728, Lufkin Rd., 27502, pg. 444 — **PB**
Tipper Tie, Inc., P.O. Box 866, 2000 Lufkin Rd., 27502, pg. 520 — **PB**

Archdale

CENTRAL TRANSPORT, 2829 Uwharrie Rd., 27263, pg. 225 — **PV**
Packrite Packaging, Inc., 3900 Comanche Rd., 27263, pg. 304 — **PB**
U.S. FURNITURE INDUSTRIES, INC., 537 Archdale Blvd., 27263, pg. 1125 — **PV**
Woodmark Originals Inc., 4015 Cheyenne Dr., 27263, pg. 747 — **PV**

Arden

Asheville Industries, Inc., P.O. Box 1157, 28704, pg. 1180 — **PB**
Associated Spring, P.O. Box 746, Underwood Rd., 28704, pg. 190 — **PB**
Coca-Cola Bottling Co. Consolidated of Arden, Rt. 1, Clayton Rd., 28704, pg. 391 — **PB**
NORTH AMERICAN ROOFING SYSTEMS, INC., Three Winner Cir., 28704, pg. 803 — **PV**
Tencarva Machinery Co.-Asheville, 15 F Glen Bridge Rd., 28704, pg. 1076 — **PV**

Asheboro

Corrugated Packaging, P.O. Box 1108, 200 McDowell Rd., 27204, pg. 736 — **PB**

KLAUSSNER CORPORATION, Lewallen St., 27203, pg. 625 — **PV**
Klaussner Furniture Industry, Lewallen St., 27203, pg. 625 — **PV**
Oliver Rubber Co., 408 Telephone Ave., 27203, pg. 1504 — **PB**
Vesture Corporation, 120 E. Pritchard St., 27202, pg. 192 — **PB**
B.B. WALKER COMPANY, 414 E. Dixie Dr., 27203, pg. 1734 — **PB**

Asheville

Akzo Nobel Fibers, Inc., Ridgefield Business Ctr., Ste. 318, 28806, pg. 48 — **IT**
Arco Blueprinters, 524 McDowell St., 28802, pg. 1735 — **PB**
Asheville Citizen Times, 14 O'Henry Ave., 28802, pg. 699 — **PB**
Asheville Laboratory, 54 Ravenscroft Dr., 28801, pg. 829 — **PV**
Blue Ridge Printing, 544 Haywood Rd., 28806, pg. 333 — **PB**
Charter Appalachian Hall Behavioral Health System, Inc., 60 Caledonia Rd., 28803, pg. 1033 — **PB**
Hillhaven Rehabilitation Convalescent Center, Asheville, 91 Victoria Rd., 28801, pg. 1714 — **PB**
MCGUFFEY'S RESTAURANTS, INC., 13 Kenilworth Knoll, 28805, pg. 721 — **PV**
Milkco, Inc., 220 Deaverview Rd., 28816, pg. 878 — **PB**
Multimedia Publishing of North Carolina, Inc., 14 O'Henry Ave., 28802, pg. 699 — **PB**
NCI, 401 Sweeten Creek Industrial Pk., 28803, pg. 1338 — **IT**
Price/McNabb, Inc., One North Pack Sq., 28801, pg. 883 — **PV**
Revco Scientific, 275 Aiken Rd., 28804, pg. 727 — **PB**
Dr. T.C. Smith Co. Inc., 280 N. Hanover St., 28806, pg. 214 — **PB**
Square D Co., 128 Bingham Rd., 28806, pg. 1208 — **IT**

Aurora

A&W Company, P.O. Box 48, 27806, pg. 49 — **IT**
PCS Phosphate - Aurora, P.O. Box 48, Hickory Point Rd., 27806, pg. 1064 — **IT**

Ayden

ICI Seeds, Rte 2, P.O. Box 140, 28513, pg. 1524 — **IT**

Badin

Yadkin, Inc., P.O. Box 576, 28009, pg. 61 — **PB**

Barnardsville

Barnardsville Telephone Co., 1599 Barnardsville Hwy., 28709, pg. 1571 — **PB**

Bath

Flanders CSC Corp., 7013 NC 92, Hwy. E., 27808, pg. 648 — **PB**

Belmont

Belmont Dyers Company, Ten Linestowe Dr., 28012, pg. 732 — **PV**

Benson

Nan Woven, P.O. Box 308, 27504-0308, pg. 113 — **IT**

Beulaville

National Spinning Co., P.O. Box 497, 28518, pg. 787 — **PV**

Biscoe

MYRICK CONSTRUCTION INC., 101 Shady Oak Dr., 27209, pg. 771 — **PV**

Black Mountain

Black Mountain Plant, 1000 Craigmont Rd., 28711-2574, pg. 443 — **PB**
INGLES MARKETS, INCORPORATED, U.S. Hwy. 70 E., 28711, pg. 878 — **PB**

Blowing Rock

Goodwin Weavers, Inc., P.O. Box 408, 28605, pg. 465 — **PB**

Boone

International Resistive Company Inc., P.O. Box 1860, Greenway Rd., 28607, pg. 1344 — **IT**
Southern Agricultural Insecticides, P.O. Box 85, 28607, pg. 1015 — **PV**

Bryson City

Nantahala Power and Light Company, P.O. Drawer 0, 28713, pg. 534 — **PB**

PB - U.S. Public Companies Volume
PV - U.S. Private Companies Volume
IT - International Public & Private Companies Volume

1364

Geographic Index-U.S.

U.S. LOCATED COMPANIES NORTH CAROLINA

Burgaw

Carlisle Poultry & Egg Associates, P.O. Box 854, Hwy 117, S., 28425, pg. 1529 PB
Chloride Power Electronics Inc., 126 Chloride Way, 28425, pg. 287 IT
Guardian Care of Burgaw, Hwy. 117-A, P.O. Box 874, 28425, pg. 1712 PB
U P Systems Inc., 126 Chloride Way, 28425, pg. 287 IT

Burlington

B.I. Transportation, Inc., P.O. Box 691, 27215, pg. 268 PB
BROWN WOOTEN MILLS, INC., 119 E. Holt St., 27217, pg. 174 PV
CAROLINA BIOLOGICAL SUPPLY CO., 2700 York Rd., 27215, pg. 213 PV
Carolina Paper Box Company, Inc., 332 W. Fonville St., 27215, pg. 303 PB
Commercial-Levin, 2600 Park Rd. Extension, 27216, pg. 413 PB
COPLAND FABRICS, INC., P.O. Box 1208, 27216, pg. 274 PV
HOLT HOSIERY MILLS, INC., 2119 W. Webb Ave., 27216, pg. 536 PV
LABORATORY CORP. OF AMERICA HOLDINGS, P.O. Box 2230, 27215, pg. 973 PB
Leesona Corp., Rte. 8, 27215, pg. 774 IT
Roche Biomedical Laboratories, 231 Maple Ave., 27215, pg. 1120 IT
Seaboard Underwriters Agency, Inc., 338 Holly Hill Ln., 27215, pg. 681 PB
Seaboard Underwriters, Inc., 338 Holly Hill Ln., 27215, pg. 681 PB
STAR FOOD PRODUCTS, INC., 727 S. Spring St., 27215, pg. 1034 PV
WBBB, Box 1119, 1109 Tower Dr., 27216, pg. 297 PV
WPCM, Box 1119, 1109 Tower Dr., 27216, pg. 298 PV

Burnsville

Glen Raven Mills, Inc.-Filament Fabrics Division, Drawer 100, Hwy. 19 E., 28714, pg. 456 PV
OMC Burnsville, P.O. Box 10, Highway 19 E., 28714, pg. 478 PV

Butner

ATHOL CORPORATION, 100 22nd. St., 27509, pg. 94 PV

Canton

Canton Mill, Champion International Corporation, Main St., 28716, pg. 334 PB
PAXAR Woven Labels, 100 Service Rd., 28176, pg. 1266 PB

Cary

ASI Landmark, Inc., 1903 N. Harrison Ave., 27513, pg. 110 PB
AEROGLIDE CORPORATION, 100 Aeroglide Dr., 27511, pg. 24 PV
AUSTIN QUALITY FOODS, One Quality Ln., 27513, pg. 100 PV
Capital Data Systems, Inc., 125 Edinburgh South, Ste. 310, 27511, pg. 347 PB
CONTAINER GRAPHICS CORPORATION, 200 Mackenan St., 27511-6447, pg. 267 PV
Currin & Associates, Inc., 125 Edinburgh South, Ste. 300, 27511, pg. 347 PB
Heater Utilities, Incorporated, 202 Mackenan Ct., 27511, pg. 1116 PB
Hewlett-Packard Company, 305 Gregson Dr., 27511, pg. 815 PB
Intergraph Corporation, 200 Regency Pkwy., Ste. 370, 27511, pg. 890 PB
LORD CORPORATION, Crossroads Corporate Park, 110 Corning Rd., Ste.100, 27511, pg. 675 PV
Lord Research & Development, 407-T Gregson Dr., 27511, pg. 676 PV
Oxford University Press, 2001 Evans Rd., 27513, pg. 1019 IT
Pulte Carolina Division, 401 Harrison Oaks Blvd., Ste. 250, 27513-2412, pg. 1344 PB
C.G. Sargents Sons, 100 Aeroglide Dr., 27511, pg. 24 PV
SAS INSTITUTE INC., SAS Campus Dr., 27513-2414, pg. 966 PV
SEER TECHNOLOGIES, INC., 8000 Regency Pkwy., 27511, pg. 1453 PB
Separation Technologies Inc., 118 MacKenan Dr., Ste. 200, 27511, pg. 468 PB
Sintech Division, 1001 Sheldon Dr., 27513, pg. 1029 PB
Tangram Enterprise Solutions, Inc., 11000 Regency Pkwy., Ste. 401, 27511-8504, pg. 1424 PB
Willis Corroon Administrative Services Corporation, 113 Edinburgh S., Ste. 204, 27511, pg. 1505 IT

Catawba

Alumax Extrusions, Inc., P.O. Box 100, Rte. 1, Rd. 1848, 28609, pg. 59 PB

Chapel Hill

DIVI HOTELS, INC., 6340 Quadrangle Dr., Ste. 300, 27514, pg. 336 PV
FGI INC., 206 W. Franklin St., 27516, pg. 389 PV
KENAN TRANSPORT COMPANY, University Square-W., 143 W. Franklin St., 27515, pg. 949 PB
Lakeview Manor, 1716 Legion Rd., 27514, pg. 1714 PB
Willis Corroon & Associates, Inc., Europa Center, Ste. 571, 100 Europa Dr., 27514, pg. 1505 IT

Charlotte

ACC Services, Inc., P.O. Box 669328, 28266, pg. 303 PB
AEA Inc./Auto Parts, 700 W. 28th St., 28206, pg. 1377 PB
Admiration Hosiery Mills, Inc., 340 E. 16th St., 28206, pg. 528 PV
Alemite Corporation, 7725 Little Ave., 28226, pg. 127 IT
Allied Security Inc., 5801 Executive Ctr. Dr., Ste. 226, 28212, pg. 40 PV
ALLISON-ERWIN CO. INC., 2920 N. Tryon St., 28206, pg. 41 PV
Allright Parking Charlotte, Inc., 129 W. Trade St., Suite 1101, 28202, pg. 43 PV
Alro Specialty Metals, Charlotte, 2300 Distribution St., 28203, pg. 46 PV
American and Foreign Insurance Co., 9300 Arrowpoint Blvd., 28217, pg. 1130 IT
AMERICAN BARMAG CO., P.O. Box 7046, 28241, pg. 51 PV
American City Business Journals, Inc., 128 S. Tryon St., Ste. 2300, 28202, pg. 19 PV
American Suessen, P.O. Box 7147, 28217, pg. 1290 IT
Atlantic Coast Carton Company, 528 Turner St., 28208, pg. 303 PB
BASF Corporation Dispersions, 11501 Steele Creek Road, 28273, pg. 105 IT
BASF Corporation Fiber Products Division, 4824 Parkway Plaza Blvd., Ste. 300, 28217, pg. 105 IT
BB&T International, 200 S. College St., 28690, pg. 160 PB
BB&T Leasing Corp., 5130 Parkway Plaza Blvd., 28217, pg. 160 PB
BAKER & TAYLOR, INC., 2709 Water Ridge Pkwy., Ste. 500, 28217, pg. 111 PV
Banta Digital Group, 3101 Stafford Dr., 28208-9556, pg. 188 PB
Barclays American/Mortgage Corp., 5032 Parkway Plaza Blvd., Bldg. 8, 28217, pg. 165 IT
Barclays Bank Commercial Group, 201 S. Tryon St., 28202, pg. 165 IT
BARNHARDT MANUFACTURING CO., 1100 Hawthorne Ln., 28205, pg. 116 PV
BELK STORES SERVICES INC., 2801 W. Tyvola Rd., 28217-4500, pg. 131 PV
Bindley Western, Carolina Division, 10900A S. Commerce Blvd., 28273, pg. 228 PB
Binswanger Realty Group-South, 230 S. Tryon St., Ste. 1200, 28202, pg. 144 PV
BOJANGLES' RESTARAUNTS, INC., 9432 Southern Pine Blvd., 28273, pg. 154 PV
Boston Gear, 3900 Westinghouse Blvd., P.O. Box 7007, 28217, pg. 857 PB
BROADWAY & SEYMOUR, INC., 128 S. Tryon St., 28202, pg. 258 PB
Burns & Wilcox - Charlotte Office, 6135 Park Dr., #200, 28210, pg. 609 PV
Business Journals of North Carolina, LLC, 128 S. Tryon St., Ste. 2250, 28202, pg. 19 PV
C C Beverage Packing Inc., 1900 Rexford Rd., 28211, pg. 391 PB
CCAIR, INC., 4700 Yorkmont Rd., Second Fl., 28208, pg. 276 PB
CCX, INC., 1901 Roxborough Rd., Ste. 205, 28211, pg. 193 PV
CMS Therapies, Inc., 4235 S. Stream Blvd., Ste. 300, 28217, pg. 839 PB
Cadmus Direct Marketing, Inc., 1123 S. Church St., Ste. 1000, 28203, pg. 290 PB
Cadmus Financial, 324 N. MacDowell St., 28204, pg. 290 PB
Cadmus Financial, P.O. Box 30364, 324 N. Mc Dowell St., 28230, pg. 291 PB
Cadmus Financial Communications, 801 S. McDowell St., 28204, pg. 290 PB
Cadmus Promotional Printing, 801 S. McDowell St., 28204, pg. 291 PB
Cadmus Specialty Packaging, 801 S. McDowell St., 28204, pg. 291 PB
Canteen Corporation, 2400 Yorkmont Rd., 28217, pg. 324 IT
Capitol Finance Group, Inc., One First Union Ctr., 28288, pg. 640 PB
Carolina Absorbent Cotton Co., 1100 Hawthorne Ave., 28205, pg. 117 PV
Carolina Commercial Heat Treating, Inc., 6313 Old Pineville Rd., 28224, pg. 742 PB
Carolina Mailing Service, 2700 Westinghouse Blvd., 28210, pg. 1735 PB
Carolina Paper Board Company, Inc., 443 S. Gardner Ave., 28208, pg. 303 PB
Carolina Pump & Supply Corp., P.O. Box 34305, 300 E. 9th St., 28234, pg. 846 PB
Carolina Recycling, Inc., 2426 Chamberlain Ave., 28208, pg. 303 PB
CAROLINA TRACTOR & EQUIPMENT CO., 9000 Stateville Rd., 28269, pg. 214 PV
Case Advertising, Inc., 1900 Rexford Rd., 28211, pg. 391 PB
Case Paper Co. of North Carolina, 1401 Tar Heel Rd., 28208, pg. 218 PV
A.M. Castle & Co., 4040 Chesapeake Dr., 28216, pg. 313 PB
THE CATO CORPORATION, 8100 Denmark Rd., 28273-5975, pg. 318 PB
Central All Pro, 1323 Central Ave., 28206, pg. 1377 PB
Chambers USA Waste, Inc., 4200 Joe St., 28206, pg. 1686 PB
The Charlotte Observer, 600 S. Tryon St., 28202, pg. 964 PB
Charlottetown, Inc., 401 S. Independence Blvd., 28204, pg. 1407 PB
Charlottetown North, Inc., 401 Independence Blvd., 28204, pg. 1407 PB
Charter Pines Behavioral Health System, Inc., 3621 Randolph Rd., 28211, pg. 1035 PB
Chemical Specialties, Inc., One Woodlawn Green, Ste. 250, 28217, pg. 802 IT
Cigna Healthcare of North Carolina, Inc., 7400 Carmel Executive Park, 28226, pg. 360 PB
Circle Freight International USA, 3308 Oak Lake Blvd., 28208, pg. 370 PB
Circle Freight International USA, 4800 A Sirus Ln., 28208, pg. 371 PB
Circle International, 4800 A Sirus Ln., 28208, pg. 371 PB
Clariant Corporation, 4000 Monroe Rd., 28205, pg. 624 IT
Coats North America, 4135 S. Stream Blvd., 28217, pg. 300 IT
COCA-COLA BOTTLING CO. CONSOLIDATED, 1900 Rexford Rd., 28211, pg. 391 PB
Coca-Cola Consolidated, 1900 Rexford Rd., 28211, pg. 392 PB
COGENTRIX INCORPORATED, 9405 Arrowpoint Blvd., 28273-8110, pg. 249 PV
COLLINS & AIKMAN CORPORATION, 701 McCullough Dr., 28262, pg. 399 PB
COLTEC HOLDINGS INC, Three Coliseum Ctr., 2550 W. Tyvola Rd., 28217, pg. 401 PB
Coltec Industries Inc., Threee Coliseum Ctr., 2550 W. Tyvola Rd., 28217, pg. 401 PB
Comfortable Mortgages, Inc., One NCB Plaza, 28231, pg. 1163 PB
Commercial Marketing Systems, 9300 Arrowpoint Blvd., 28217, pg. 1131 IT
Compass Group-USA Division, 2400 Yorkmont Rd., 28217, pg. 324 IT
Consolidated Engravers-East, Inc., P.O. Box 28233, 28233, pg. 351 PV
Consolidated Group, Inc., 311 E. 12th St., 28206, pg. 351 PV
Consolidated Screen-Makers, Inc., 311 E. 12th St., 28206, pg. 351 PV
Constar International, Inc., 4945 Hovis Rd., 28208, pg. 463 PB
Continental General Tire, Inc., 1800 Continental Blvd., 28273-6311, pg. 327 IT
Craftsman Printing Company, 2700 Westinghouse Blvd., 28217, pg. 1735 PB
Crescent Resources, Inc., 400 S. Tryon St., Ste. 1300, 28201, pg. 534 PB
Cronatron Welding Systems, Inc., 6510 Northpark Blvd., 28216-2367, pg. 980 PB
CROWDER CONSTRUCTION CO., 1123 E. Tenth St., 28204, pg. 291 PV
DG Trim Products Div., 8530 Cliff Cameron Dr., 28269-9786, pg. 560 PV
Datasouth Computer Corporation, 4216 Stuart Andrew Blvd., 28217, pg. 267 PB
Delmar, P.O. Box 1013, 28201-1013, pg. 523 PV
Delmar Photographic and Printing Company, 9601 Monroe Rd., 28212, pg. 268 PV
Delmar Studios, 9555 Monroe Rd., 28270, pg. 268 PV
Delta/Cyklop Strapping, 1440-G Westinghouse Blvd., 28217, pg. 865 PB
Detroit Gasket, 8530 Cliff Cameron Dr., 28269-9786, pg. 560 PV
Dillard, A ResourceNet International Company, 3100 Parkside Dr., P.O. Box 668966, 28266, pg. 902 PB
Dixie Reel & Box Co., 10901 Carpet St., 28273, pg. 674 PV
Duff-Norton, 9415 Pioneer Ave., 28273, pg. 406 PB
DUKE ENERGY CORPORATION, 422 S. Church St., 28202-1904, pg. 534 PB
Duke Engineering & Services, Inc., P.O. Box 1004, 28201-1004, pg. 534 PB
Duke/Fluor Daniel, One Coliseum Ctr., 2300 Yorkmont Rd., 28201, pg. 535 PB
Eckerd Drug Co., 1776 Statesville Ave., 28231, pg. 917 PB
Eclipse Combustion, Inc., Key Man Bldg., 1409 E. Blvd., 28203, pg. 360 PV
Erdle Perforating of Carolina, 10721 John Price Rd., 28217, pg. 380 PV
Eurest Dining Services, 2400 Yorkmont Rd., 28217, pg. 324 IT
Fahlgren, 5016 Parkway Plaza, Ste. 270, 28217-1962, pg. 391 PV
First Union Brokerage Services, Inc., One First Union Ctr., 28288, pg. 640 PB
First Union Commercial Corp., One First Union Ctr., 28288, pg. 640 PB
FIRST UNION CORPORATION, One First Union Ctr. Ste. 4000, 28288-0011, pg. 639 PB
First Union Home Equity Corporation, 128 S. Tryon St., 28202, pg. 640 PB
First Union Mortgage Corporation, Two First Union Ctr., 28288, pg. 640 PB
First Union National Bank of North Carolina, One First Union Ctr., 28288, pg. 640 PB
First Union Securities Inc., One First Union Ctr., 28288, pg. 640 PB
FORMS & SUPPLY, INC., 1733 University Commercial Pl., 28213, pg. 419 PV
Freedom Textiles Chemicals Co., 8309 Wilkinson Blvd., 28214, pg. 425 PV
Frito-Lay Inc., 2911 Nevada Blvd., 28273, pg. 1277 PB

PB - *U.S. Public Companies Volume*
PV - *U.S. Private Companies Volume*
IT - *International Public & Private Companies Volume*

Geographic Index-U.S.

GS INDUSTRIES, INC., 1901 Roxborough Rd., Ste. 200, 28211, pg. 435 **PV**

GAS-FIRED PRODUCTS, INC., 305 Doggett St., 28203, pg. 440 **PV**

General Latex & Chemical Corp (N.C.), P.O. Box 5487, 28225, pg. 444 **PV**

GLENAYRE TECHNOLOGIES, INC., 5935 Carnegie Blvd., 28209, pg. 746 **PB**

Globe Indemnity Co., 9300 Arrowpoint Blvd., 28217, pg. 1130 **IT**

Gotaverken Energy Systems Inc., 8008 Corporate Center Dr., 28226, pg. 770 **IT**

Stephen Gould of Carolina, Inc./Charlotte Div., 9800-I Southern Pine Blvd., 28273, pg. 467 **PV**

Harris Teeter, Inc., P.O. Box 33129, 28233, pg. 1412 **PV**

HENDRICK AUTOMOTIVE GROUP, 6000 Monroe Rd., Ste. 100, 28212, pg. 522 **PV**

Hendrick Imports, 6950 E. Independence Blvd., 28212, pg. 528 **PV**

Henkel Corporation Textile Chemicals, 600 Sugar Creek Road E., 28213, pg. 610 **IT**

Hewlett-Packard Company, 9401 Arrow Point Blvd., Ste. 100, 28210, pg. 815 **PB**

Hewlett-Packard Company, 3042 Berkmar Dr., Ste. D, 22901, pg. 815 **PB**

HIGHLAND MILLS INC., 340 E. 16th St., 28206, pg. 528 **PV**

Hoechst Celanese Film & Fiber Intermediates Group, 6000 Carnegie Blvd., 28209, pg. 626 **IT**

Holz-Her U.S. Inc., 5120 Westinghouse Blvd., 28273, pg. 1101 **IT**

Philipp Holzmann USA, Ltd., J.A. Jones Dr., 28287, pg. 633 **IT**

J.M. Huber, Wood Products Div., Mallard Creek Ctr. III-Ste.175, 8604 Cliff Cameron Dr., 28269, pg. 545 **PV**

Husqvarna Forest & Garden Products, 9006 Perimeter Woods Dr., 28216, pg. 440 **IT**

IRT Property Company, 5672-D International Dr., 28270, pg. 858 **PB**

ISC Futures Corporation, Interstate Tower, P.O. Box 1012, 28201-1012, pg. 910 **PB**

ISC Realty Corporation, Interstate Tower, P.O. Box 1012, 28201-1012, pg. 910 **PB**

INDIAN HEAD INDUSTRIES INC., 8530 Cliff Cameron Dr., 28269-9786, pg. 559 **PV**

Industrial Maintenance Corp., 3520 Tryclan, 28217, pg. 562 **PV**

Intergraph Corporation, 9731-J Southern Pine Blvd., 28273, pg. 890 **PB**

Interstate Bakeries Corporation-Eastern Division, 140 Dupree St., 28208, pg. 909 **PB**

Interstate/Johnson Lane Corporation, Interstate Tower, P.O. Box 1012, 28201-1012, pg. 910 **PB**

INTERSTATE/JOHNSON LANE, INC., 121 W. Trade St., Ste. 1100, 28202, pg. 909 **PB**

Jefferson-Pilot Communications, One Julian Price Pl., 28208, pg. 925 **PB**

Jefferson-Pilot Teleproductions, One Julian Price Pl., 28208, pg. 926 **PB**

Jones Capital Corporation, J.A. Jones Dr., 28287, pg. 633 **IT**

J.A. Jones, Inc., J.A. Jones Dr., 28287, pg. 633 **IT**

Jones Management Services, Inc., 6135 Park Ave. South Dr., Ste. 250, 28210, pg. 633 **IT**

Earle M. Jorgensen Company/Charlotte, 4015 Westinghouse Blvd., 28273, pg. 600 **PV**

Joy Energy Systems Inc., P.O. Box 410647, 28241, pg. 789 **PB**

KELLER BUILDING PRODUCTS OF CHARLOTTE, INC., 5901 N. Hill Cir., 28256-0308, pg. 612 **PV**

Kloeckner Ionon of America, Inc., 3501 Asbury Ave., 28206, pg. 737 **IT**

The Knight Publishing Co., Box 32188, 600 S. Tryon St., 28232, pg. 964 **PB**

Kobe Development Corp., 2400 Charlotte Plaza, 28244, pg. 740 **IT**

Krantz America, Inc., 11024 Nations Ford Rd., 28210, pg. 401 **IT**

Kvaerner Pulping Inc., 8008 Corporate Center Dr., 28226, pg. 770 **IT**

LANCE, INC., 8600 South Blvd., 28273, pg. 977 **PB**

Landstar Express America, Inc., P.O. Box 19509, 3411 Oak Lake Blvd., 28219, pg. 978 **PB**

Laporte America Inc., One Woodlawn Green, Ste. 240, 28217, pg. 802 **PV**

Lee Construction Co., P.O. Box 240927, 28224-0927, pg. 782 **PV**

Lilly Industries, Inc., 10300 Claude Freeman Dr., 28262, pg. 994 **PB**

MAR, Inc., One NBC Plaza, 28255, pg. 1163 **PB**

MGM Brakes Div., 8530 Cliff Cameron Dr., 28269-9786, pg. 560 **PV**

MRM Properties, Inc., One NCB Plaza, 28255, pg. 1163 **PB**

Marine Midland Mortgage Servicing Corporation, 7415 Pineville-Matthews Rd., 28226, pg. 581 **IT**

Matthews-Morse Supply, P.O. Box 34308, 2100 Suttle Ave., 28208, pg. 91 **PV**

Meineke Discount Muffler Shops, Inc., 128 S. Tryon St., Ste. 900, 28202, pg. 535 **PB**

Metric Constructors, Inc., J.A. Jones Dr., 28287, pg. 633 **IT**

Michelin Aircraft Tire Corporation, 9700 Research Dr., 28262, pg. 322 **IT**

Mid Atlantic Construction, Inc., 5701 N. Sharon Amity Rd., 28215, pg. 939 **PV**

Midrex Corp., Charlotte Plaza, 28244, pg. 740 **IT**

Mineral Research & Development Corp., One Woodlawn Green, Ste. 240, 28217, pg. 802 **PV**

Moody's FIS, 5250 77 Center Dr., 28217, pg. 536 **PB**

Moore Electric Supply, Inc., 118 Winona St., 28203, pg. 847 **PB**

Morcardshammar Inc., 9800 Southern Pines Blvd., Ste. 6, 28273, pg. 378 **IT**

Murata of America, Inc., P.O. Box 667609, 2120 I-85 South, 28208, pg. 897 **IT**

National Gypsum Company, 2001 Rexford Rd., 28211, pg. 790 **IT**

NATIONAL WELDERS SUPPLY CO. INC., 810 Gesco St., 28208, pg. 788 **PV**

NationsBank Community Development Corp., One NCNB Plaza, 28255, pg. 1165 **PB**

NATIONSBANK CORPORATION, Nationsbank Corporate Ctr., 100 N. Tryon St., 18th Fl., 28255, pg. 1162 **PB**

NationsBank Futures Corp., One NCNB Plaza, 28255, pg. 1165 **PB**

NationsBank Lease Investments, Inc., One NCNB Plaza, 28255, pg. 1165 **PB**

NationsBank Leasing Corp., One NCNB Plaza, 28255, pg. 1165 **PB**

NationsBank Overseas Corp., 2300 NCNB Plaza, 28255, pg. 1165 **PB**

NationsBank Plaza Charlotte, Inc., One NCNB Plaza, 28255, pg. 1165 **PB**

NationsBank Properties, Inc., One NCNB Plaza, 28255, pg. 1165 **PB**

NationsBank Securities, Inc., One NationsBank Plaza, 28255, pg. 1165 **PB**

Neumag USA Corporation, 13504 S. Point Blvd., Ste. H, 28273, pg. 399 **IT**

Newark Insurance Co., 9300 Arrowpoint Blvd., 28217, pg. 1131 **IT**

Nissan Textile Machinery Corp. in U.S.A., P.O. Box 240803, 8300 Arrowridge Blvd., 28224, pg. 945 **IT**

NUCOR CORPORATION, 2100 Rexford Rd., 28211, pg. 1205 **PB**

Okuma America Corporation, 12200 Steel Creek Rd., 28273, pg. 1001 **IT**

On Track, 128 S. Tyron St., Ste. 2275, 28202, pg. 19 **PV**

Package Products Specialty, 8800 South Blvd., 28232, pg. 1486 **PB**

Package Products Specialty-Labels Div., 8800 South Blvd., 28232, pg. 1486 **PB**

Package Products Specialty-Paperboard Div., 8800 S. Blvd., 28210, pg. 1486 **PB**

Arnold Palmer Cadillac Inc., 501 S. Caldwell St., 28202, pg. 713 **PV**

Paramount Carowinds, 14523 Carowinds Blvd., 28273, pg. 776 **PV**

Paramount Parks, 8720 Red Oak Blvd., Ste. 375, 28217, pg. 776 **PV**

PEPSI-COLA BOTTLING COMPANY OF CHARLOTTE INC., 2820 South Blvd., 28209, pg. 852 **PV**

Performance Contracting, Inc., 208 E. Woodlawn, 28217, pg. 353 **PV**

Piedmont Auto Exchange, 406 W. 6th St., 28206, pg. 1377 **PV**

Piedmont Energy Company, 1915 Rexford Rd., 28211, pg. 295 **PB**

Piedmont Interstate Pipeline Company, 1915 Rexford Rd., 28211, pg. 1295 **PB**

Piedmont Intrastate Pipeline Company, 1915 Rexford Rd., 28211, pg. 1295 **PB**

PIEDMONT NATURAL GAS CO., INC., 1915 Rexford Rd., 28211, pg. 1295 **PB**

PNEUMAFIL CORPORATION, 4404 Chesapeake Dr., 28216, pg. 873 **PV**

Poe & Brown of North Carolina, 9144 Arrowpoint Blvd., Ste. 140, 28273, pg. 1312 **PB**

Porta Systems Co., 3 Parkway Plaza Blvd., 28217, pg. 1317 **PB**

Power Sources, Inc., 9140 Arrow Point Blvd., Ste. 370, 28217-8210, pg. 344 **PB**

President Baking-Charlotte, 933 Louise Ave., 28204, pg. 1069 **IT**

PRICE/MCNABB, INC., 2800 Nationsbank Corp. Ctr., 100 N. Tryon St., 28202, pg. 883 **PV**

Principa Health Care of the Carolinas, Inc., 2300 Yorkmont Rd., Ste. 710, 28217, pg. 885 **PV**

Process & Industrial Division-S.E., 6324 Fairview Rd., 28210, pg. 317 **PV**

LAT PURSER & ASSOCIATES, 4530 Park Rd., Ste. 300, 28209, pg. 896 **PV**

Queens Properties, J.A. Jones Dr., 28287, pg. 633 **IT**

RMI Educational Services, 803 Presley Rd., Ste. 104, 28217-0971, pg. 936 **PV**

RADIATOR SPECIALTY COMPANY, 1900 Wilkinson Blvd., 28208, pg. 906 **PV**

Brad Ragan, Inc., 4404 G. Stuart Andrew Blvd., 28217, pg. 753 **PV**

Rea Construction Co., 6135 Park South Dr., Ste. 600, 28210, pg. 633 **IT**

Regency Insurance Company, 3711 Latrobe Drive, 28222, pg. 665 **PB**

Reliance Standard Life Insurance Company, 521 E. Morehead St., Ste. 170, 28202, pg. 496 **PB**

REPUBLIC ALLOYS, INC., 419 Atando Ave., 28206, pg. 923 **PV**

Republic Automotive-AEA Division, 700 W. 28th St., 28206, pg. 1377 **PB**

Republic Automotive Parts Sales, Inc., 700 W. 28th St., 28232, pg. 1378 **PB**

Republic Factors Corp., 2101 W. Rexford Rd., 28211, pg. 1380 **PB**

Rexam Inc., 4201 Congress St., Ste. 340, 28209, pg. 1106 **IT**

Richmond Dental, 1100 Hawthorne Ln., 28205, pg. 117 **PV**

Ringier America, Charlotte Division, 8700 Red Oak Blvd., Ste. J, 28717, pg. 1778 **PB**

Roberts Systems, Inc., 8500 South Tryon Street, 28273, pg. 395 **IT**

ROBERTSON MARKETING INC., 803 Pressley Rd., Ste. 104, 28217-0971, pg. 936 **PV**

RODGERS BUILDERS, INC., 5701 N. Sharon Amity Rd., 28215, pg. 939 **PV**

THE ROWE CORPORATION, 5200-77 Center Dr., Ste. 100, 28217, pg. 948 **PV**

Royal Indemnity Co., 9300 Arrowpoint Blvd., 28217, pg. 1131 **IT**

Royal Insurance, 9300 Arrowpoint Blvd., 28273-8135, pg. 1130 **IT**

Royal Insurance Company of America, 9300 Arrowpoint Blvd., 28217, pg. 1131 **IT**

Royal Life Insurance Company of America, 9300 Arrowpoint Blvd., 28217, pg. 1131 **IT**

Royal Life Insurance Company of New York, 9300 Arrowpoint Blvd., 28217, pg. 1131 **IT**

RUDDICK CORPORATION, 2000 Two First Union Ctr., 28282, pg. 1412 **PB**

SMS-Concast, 2901 Colsgate Rd., Ste. 200, 28211, pg. 1463 **PB**

Safeguard Insurance Co., 9300 Arrowpoint Blvd., 28217, pg. 1131 **IT**

Sandoz Chemical Corporation, 4000 Monroe Rd., 28205, pg. 974 **IT**

Scandura Inc., 1801 N. Tryon St., 28230-0606, pg. 113 **IT**

Scott & Stringfellow, Inc., 4500 Cameron Valley Pkwy., Ste. 250, 28211, pg. 1446 **PB**

Sea-Land Service, Inc., 6000 Carnegie Blvd., 28209, pg. 284 **PV**

Selective Insurance Company of South Carolina, 2550 W. Tyvola Rd., Ste. 40, 28217, pg. 1455 **PB**

Selective Insurance Company of the Southeast, 2550 W. Tyvola Rd., Ste. 40, 28217, pg. 1456 **PB**

Service General East, Ste. 200, 6135 Park Drive S., 28201, pg. 609 **PV**

Shannon Properties, 7520 E. Independence Blvd., Ste. 240, 28227, pg. 488 **PB**

Shorewood Packaging of North Carolina, Inc., 7506 E. Independence Blvd., 28227-9405, pg. 1468 **PB**

6100 Fairview Associates, c/o Queens Properties, 6100 Fairview Rd., 28210, pg. 362 **PV**

Smith & Nephew Casting, Inc., 2500 Distribution St., 28203, pg. 1263 **IT**

Soabar Products Group, 5500 N. Sharon Amity Rd., 28215, pg. 153 **PB**

Solectron Technology, Inc., 6900 Mallard Creek Rd., 28256-2148, pg. 1483 **PB**

SONIC AUTOMOTIVE, INC., 5401 E. Independence Blvd., 28218, pg. 1485 **PB**

SOUTHERN PUMP & TANK COMPANY, 4800 N. Graham St., 28269, pg. 1017 **PV**

SPEIZMAN INDUSTRIES, INC., 508 W. Fifth St., 28202, pg. 1498 **PB**

Sterling Capital Management Company, One First Union Ctr., 301 S. College St., Ste. 3200, 28202-6005, pg. 1674 **PB**

SunGard Trust Systems Inc., 5510 77 Center Dr., 28224, pg. 1535 **PB**

Superior Life Insurance Company, 28255, pg. 1165 **PB**

Supratech Systems Inc., 3801 Westinghouse Commons Dr., 28273, pg. 937 **IT**

TIE Systems North Carolina, 9741-L Southern Pines Blvd., 28273, pg. 1085 **PV**

TIM, Inc., One NCNB Plz., 28255, pg. 1165 **PB**

Tekmatex, Inc., 3601 Performance Rd., 28266, pg. 845 **IT**

Tekra Corp., Southeast Div., 10900-D S. Commerce Blvd., 28273, pg. 1073 **PV**

Tencarva Machinery Co., 4108 Park Rd., Ste. 215, 28209, pg. 1076 **PV**

Tesa Tape, 5825 Carnegie Blvd., 28209, pg. 182 **IT**

Texmac, Inc., 3001 Stafford Dr., 28208, pg. 695 **IT**

Thermal Industries Inc., 3308 C. Oak Lake Blvd., 28208-7707, pg. 491 **PV**

THERMO INDUSTRIES INC., 4300 Golf Acres Dr., 28208, pg. 1080 **PV**

Thomson-CSF Passive Components Inc., 2211 H Distribution Center Dr., 28269, pg. 1384 **IT**

Trevira, 2300 Archdale Dr., 28210, pg. 626 **IT**

Union Special Corp., 13900-F South Lakes Dr., 28217, pg. 716 **IT**

Union-Transport Corporation-Charlotte Office, 1900-G Center Park Dr., 28217, pg. 1119 **IT**

UNITED DOMINION INDUSTRIES, LTD., 2300 One First Union Ctr., 28202-6039, pg. 1675 **PB**

U.S. BOTTLERS MACHINERY CO., 11911 Steele Creek Rd., 28273, pg. 1124 **PV**

Valmet Inc., P.O. Box 7467, 28241, pg. 1448 **IT**

Valmet Inc., Charlotte Division, P.O. Box 7467, 28241, pg. 1448 **IT**

Venture Packaging, Inc., 1600 Westinghouse Blvd., 28273, pg. 138 **PV**

WBT AM & WBCY FM, One Julian Price Pl., 28208, pg. 926 **PB**

WBTV/WBT-AM & FM, One Julian Price Pl., 28208, pg. 926 **PB**

WSOC Television, Inc., 1901 N. Tryon St., 28206, pg. 282 **PB**

Washburn Direct Marketing, Inc., P.O. Box 34688, 1123 S. Church St., 28234-4688, pg. 291 **PV**

Washburn Graphics, Inc., P.O. Box 31517, 801 S. McDowell St., 28231-1517, pg. 291 **PB**

Water Systems (NC), 4302 Raleigh St., 28213, pg. 1037 **PV**

Wattyl/Carolina Coatings, P.O. Box 240415, 711 Pressley Rd., 23217, pg. 1488 **IT**

Wellman Bonded Fibers Div., 10801 Nations Ford Rd., 28273, pg. 1753 **PB**

Wellman Engineering Resins, P.O. Box 7223, 10801 Nations Ford Rd., 28241, pg. 1752 **PB**

PB - *U.S. Public Companies Volume*
PV - *U.S. Private Companies Volume*
IT - *International Public & Private Companies Volume*

Wellman Man-Made Fibers Div., 5146 Parkway Plaza Blvd., 28217, pg. 1752 **PB**

Wellman Man-Made Fibers Div., P.O. Box 31331, 28231, pg. 1752 **PB**

Wesleyan Nursing Home, Inc., 2623 Cranbrook Lane, 28211, pg. 1715 **PB**

John Wieland Homes of North Carolina, Inc., 8325-D Arrowridge Blvd., 28273, pg. 1175 **PV**

Willis Corroon Administrative Services Corporation, Two First Union Center, 301 S. Tryon St., Ste. 2600, 28282-0001, pg. 1505 **IT**

Willis Corroon Corp. of North Carolina, 2 First Union Ctr., Ste. 2600, 301 S. Tryon St., 28202-0001, pg. 1506 **IT**

Winn-Dixie Charlotte, Inc., 2401 Nevada Blvd., 28273, pg. 1771 **PB**

Winston Cup Illustrated, 128 S. Tyron St., Ste. 2275, 28202, pg. 20 **PV**

Winston Cup Scene, 128 S. Tryon St., Ste. 2275, 28202, pg. 20 **PV**

Yale Security, Inc., P.O. Box 25288, 28229, pg. 1499 **IT**

Zellerbach Division, 4021 Rose Lake Dr., 28217, pg. 1075 **PB**

Zellweger Energy Systems, 2200 Executive St., 28208, pg. 618 **IT**

Zeneca Colours, P.O. Box 411609, 9129 Southern Pine Blvd., 28241-1609, pg. 1525 **IT**

Zeneca Specialties, 6601 I-85 N., 28262, pg. 1525 **IT**

Cherryville

P/M Bearing Div., Sunbeam Indus. Park, 28021, pg. 619 **PV**

PPC, Inc., P.O. Box 459, 900 W. Academy St., 28021, pg. 1168 **PB**

Claremont

Alcatel Cable Systems Group, 2512 Penny Rd., 28610, pg. 55 **IT**

Elloree Foods, Inc. (South Carolina), WSMP Dr., 28610, pg. 1729 **PB**

Georgia WSMP, Inc. (Georgia), WSMP Dr., 28610, pg. 1729 **PB**

Greenville Food Systems, Inc., WSMP Dr., 28610, pg. 1729 **PB**

Matthews Prime Sirloin, Inc., P.O. Box 399, 28610, pg. 1729 **PB**

Naples Foods, Inc., P.O. Box 399, 28610, pg. 1729 **PB**

Prime Sirloin, Inc. (Tennessee), WSMP Dr., 28610, pg. 1729 **PB**

Saint Augustine Foods, Inc., P.O. Box 399, 28610, pg. 1729 **PB**

Seven Stars, Inc., WSMP Dr., 28610, pg. 1729 **PB**

South Carolina WSMP, Inc. (South Carolina), WSMP Dr., 28610, pg. 1729 **PB**

Sunshine WSMP, Inc. (Florida), WSMP Dr., 28610, pg. 1729 **PB**

Tennessee WSMP, Inc. (Tennessee), WSMP Dr., 28610, pg. 1729 **PB**

Virginia WSMP, Inc. (Virginia), WSMP Dr., 28610, pg. 1729 **PB**

WSMP, INC., P.O. Box 399, 1 WSMP Dr., 28610, pg. 1729 **PB**

Clarkton

Mount Vernon Mills, Inc., Clarkton, NC, 28433, pg. 835 **PV**

Clayton

Cutter Laboratories Inc., Hwy. 70 E., 27520, pg. 174 **IT**

Data General Corporation, Hwy. 42 East, 27520, pg. 485 **PB**

Novo Nordisk Pharmaceuticals Industries, Inc., 2231 Powhattan Td., 27520, pg. 987 **IT**

Clemmons

YOUNG-PHILLIPS SALES CO., P.O. Box 70, 6399 Amp Dr., 27102, pg. 1201 **PV**

Cliffside

CLEVELAND CAPITAL HOLDINGS, P.O. Box 307, 28024, pg. 246 **PV**

Petroleum World, P.O. Box 307, 28024, pg. 246 **PV**

Clinton

Alcatel Network System, Inc., P.O. Box 140, 28328-0140, pg. 55 **IT**

Fujicone, 100 Industrial Pk., 28328, pg. 1369 **PB**

LUNDY PACKING CO., P.O. Box 49, 28329, pg. 681 **PV**

Park Newspapers of Clinton, Inc., Box 110, 303 Elizabeth St., 28328, pg. 1078 **PB**

Samson Independent, Inc., Box 110, 303 Elizabeth St., 28328, pg. 1078 **PB**

Colfax

COYNE BEAHM INC., 8518 Triad Dr., 27235, pg. 283 **PV**

Concord

Central Carolina Bank, 31 Union St., N., 28025, pg. 276 **PB**

Charlotte Motor Speedway, P.O. Box 600, 28026, pg. 1498 **PB**

The Concord Tribune, Inc., Union St. S., P.O. Box 68, 28025, pg. 1078 **PB**

FIRST CHARTER CORPORATION, P.O. Box 228, 28026-0228, pg. 627 **PB**

First Charter National Bank, 22 Union St. N., 28025, pg. 627 **PB**

Park Newspapers of Concord, Inc., Box 147, Union St., 28025, pg. 1078 **PB**

Philip Morris U.S.A., Cabarrus Mfg. Center, 3321 Hwy. 29 South, 28025, pg. 1290 **PB**

S&D COFFEE INC., 300 U.S. Hwy. 29 Pkwy. S., 28025, pg. 954 **PV**

THE SHOE SHOW OF ROCKY MT., INC., 776 Florence Pl., 28025, pg. 996 **PV**

SPEEDWAY MOTORSPORTS, INC., 5555 Hwy. 29N., 28026, pg. 1498 **PB**

Sysco Food Services of Charlotte, Inc., P.O. Box 96, 28026, pg. 1551 **PB**

Conover

HICKORY PRINTING GROUP, INC., 725 Reese Dr. S.W., 28613-2935, pg. 525 **PV**

JacksonLea, P.O. Box 699, 28613, pg. 924 **PB**

Lane Upholstery, P.O. Box 729, 28613, pg. 688 **PB**

PolyMask Corporation, 500 Thornburg Dr., 28613, pg. 1451 **PB**

Venture Furniture Div., P.O. Box 849, 28613, pg. 688 **PB**

W & L Motor Lines, Inc., 1515 4th St. S.W., 28613, pg. 66 **PV**

Conway

Formaldehyde, P.O. Box 368, 27820, pg. 737 **PB**

Cornelius

Foamex, P.O. Box 188, 28031, pg. 1094 **PV**

Cramerton

Cramerton Automotive Products, L.P., Eagle Rd., 28032, pg. 1095 **PV**

Dallas

Hays Fluid Controls-Division of Romac Industries, 114 Eason Rd., 28034-0580, pg. 942 **PV**

JEWELL BUILDING SYSTEMS, Old Hwy. 321 N., 28034, pg. 587 **PV**

Davidson

AGIE USA Ltd., Griffith St., 28036, pg. 490 **IT**

Dimetrics, Inc., 404 Armour St. W., 28036, pg. 308 **PB**

ELOX Corporation, 565 Griffith St., 28036, pg. 490 **IT**

Ingersoll-Rand Air Centers, 800-D Beaty St., 28036, pg. 876 **PB**

Drexel

Drexel Heritage Furnishings Inc., 101 N. Main St., 28619, pg. 432 **PV**

Dudley

Oriented Strandboard Plant, P. O. Box 308, Old. Mt. Olive Hwy., 28333, pg. 737 **PB**

Dunn

Dunn Nutratech, 1600 S. Wilson Ave., 28334, pg. 128 **PB**

Morganite Environmental Services Inc., P.O. Box 1867, 504 N. Ashe Ave., 28334, pg. 894 **IT**

Morganite Inc., 54 N. Ache Ave., 28334, pg. 893 **IT**

Morganite Inc., One Morganite Dr., 28334, pg. 891 **IT**

Morganite North America Inc., P.O. Box 1867, 504 N. Ashe Ave., 28334, pg. 894 **IT**

Tomahawk Farms, Inc., 603 S. Wilson Ave., 28334, pg. 681 **PV**

Durham

Acurex Environmental Corp., 4915 Prospectus Dr., 27713, pg. 607 **PV**

Angelica Textile Services, Inc., 4020 Stirrup Creek Dr., 27703, pg. 113 **PV**

CCB FINANCIAL CORPORATION, 111 Corcoran St., 27701, pg. 276 **PB**

Cablevision of Durham, Inc., 706 Rigsbee Ave., 22701, pg. 1610 **PV**

COASTAL PHYSICIAN GROUP, INC., 2828 Croasdaile Dr., 27705, pg. 391 **PB**

Cormetech, 5000 Internation Dr., 27712, pg. 449 **PB**

Craftique, 201 N. Maple St., 27703, pg. 1343 **PB**

Freudenberg Nonwovens, Eno Industrial Park, 3440 Industrial Dr., 27704, pg. 505 **IT**

Freudenberg Spunweb Co., P.O. Box 15910 Industrial Dr., 27704, pg. 505 **IT**

Hillhaven-LaSalle Nursing Center, 411 S. LaSalle St., 27705, pg. 1713 **PB**

Hillhaven-Orange Nursing Center, Rte. Box 155, 27705, pg. 1713 **PB**

Hillhaven Rehabilitation Convalescent Center, Durham, 1515 W. Pettigrew, 27705, pg. 1714 **PB**

Hillhaven-Rose Manor Convalescent Center, 4230 N. Rosboro Rd., 27704, pg. 1714 **PB**

Liggett Group Inc., 700 W. Main St., 27701, pg. 259 **PB**

Mail Processing Systems, P.O. Box 14986, 27709, pg. 201 **PB**

Mitsubishi Semiconductor America, Three Diamond Ln., 27704, pg. 872 **IT**

NORTH CAROLINA MUTUAL LIFE INSURANCE CO., 411 W. Chapel Hill St., 27701, pg. 804 **PV**

NORTH CAROLINA MUTUAL WHOLESALE DRUG CO., 816 Ellis Rd., 27703, pg. 804 **PV**

Organon Teknika Corp., 100 Akzo Ave., 27704, pg. 46 **IT**

P.S. INTERNATIONAL INC., 2605 Meridian Pkwy., Ste. 215, 27713, pg. 827 **PV**

PAREXEL International Corporation, 1000 Park 40 Plaza, Ste. 400, 27713, pg. 1258 **IT**

Peoples Security Insurance Company, P.O. Box 61, 27701, pg. 27 **IT**

People's Security Life Insurance, 300 W. Morgan St., 27701, pg. 27 **IT**

Potomac Digital, Inc./Scott Data, 4117 Roxboro Rd., Ste. 110, 27704, pg. 711 **PB**

Qualex Inc., 3404 N. Duke Rd., 27704, pg. 551 **PB**

Quantum Corporation, 1000 Pk. 40 Plaza, Ste. 300, 27713, pg. 1350 **PB**

Reichhold Chemicals, Inc., 2400 Ellis Rd., 27703-5543, pg. 370 **IT**

Reliability Incorporated, North Carolina Operations, 2810 Meridian Pkwy., #134, 27713, pg. 1374 **PB**

Sanmina Corporation-Durham Plant, Triangle Business Ctr., 4022 Stirrup Creek Dr., 27713, pg. 1431 **PB**

Sapiens USA, Inc., 2525 Meridian Pkwy., 27713, pg. 1193 **IT**

Servitex, Inc., 1720 Lawson, 27702, pg. 782 **PV**

SkyBox International Inc., P.O. Box 30009, 300 N. Duke St., 27702-8009, pg. 1052 **PB**

Software Plus Inc., 2605 Meridian Pkwy., Ste 105, 27713, pg. 1012 **PV**

SOUTHCHEM, 2000 E. Pettigrew St., 27702, pg. 1014 **PV**

Surface Technologies, Inc., 1500 E. Club Blvd., 27704, pg. 370 **IT**

WTVD-TV, 411 Liberty St., 27702, pg. 512 **PB**

Eden

Eden News, P.O. Box 308, 804 Washington St, 27288, pg. 1078 **PB**

Miller Brewing Company, 863 East Meadow Rd., 27288, pg. 1289 **PB**

Edenton

MORVEN PARTNERS LP, P.O. Box 465, 27932, pg. 763 **PV**

Elizabeth City

Guardian Care of Elizabeth City, 901 S. Halstead Blvd., 27909, pg. 1712 **PB**

NationsBank Credit Corporation, 410 E. Main St., 27909, pg. 1163 **PB**

Ray Sports Network, 179 Lovers Ln., 27909, pg. 911 **PV**

Elizabethtown

Danaher Controls, P.O. Box 368, 28337-0368, pg. 480 **PB**

Elkin

BB&T Savings Bank, 201 W. Main St., 28621, pg. 160 **PB**

CMI Industries, Inc., 304 E. Main St., 28621, pg. 195 **PB**

Guardian Care of Elkin, 560 Johnson Ridge Rd., 28621, pg. 1712 **PB**

Elon College

ENGINEER CONTROL INTL., Hwy. 100 at Rego Dr., 27244, pg. 376 **PV**

Fair Bluff

Service Telephone Co., Inc., P.O. Box 307, 100 Academy St., 28439, pg. 1572 **PB**

Fairview

COMMUNICATIONS INSTRUMENTS INC., 1396 Charlotte Hwy., 28730, pg. 259 **PV**

Faison

Dean Pickle & Specialty Products, Box 158, 221 W. Center St., 28341, pg. 490 **PB**

Farmville

DIMON, International, Inc., 1200 W. Marlboro Rd., 27828-0166, pg. 510 **PB**

Guardian Care of Farmville, Rte. 1 Box 96, 27828, pg. 1712 **PB**

Fayetteville

CBP Resources, P.O. Box 1659, 28302, pg. 192 **PV**

Concrete Service Co., P.O. Drawer 3129, 1200 1/2 Ramsay St., 28302, pg. 166 **IT**

NORTH CAROLINA NATURAL GAS CORPORATION, 150 Rowan St., 28302, pg. 1194 **PB**

Professional Putters Association, 3007 Fort Bragg Rd., 28303, pg. 896 **PV**

PB - *U.S. Public Companies Volume*
PV - *U.S. Private Companies Volume*
IT - *International Public & Private Companies Volume*

Geographic Index-U.S.

PUTT PUTT GOLF COURSES OF AMERICA, INC., Putt Putt Bldg., 3007 Ft. Bragg Rd., 28303, pg. 896   PV
Southern Golf Distributors, Inc., 2913 Ft. Bragg Rd., 28303, pg. 896   PV
Wellman Man-Made Fibers Div., P.O. Box 20, Cedar Creek Rd., 28302, pg. 1752   PB

Fletcher

Eaton Corp., Fluid Power Div., Cane Creek Industrial Park, 28732, pg. 556   PB
INDUSTRIAL MAINTENANCE OVERFLOW CORPORATION, 6675 Hendersonville Rd., 28732, pg. 561   PV

Forest City

Henson Timber Products Corp., Duke Street, 28043, pg. 1044   PV
Waste Handling Systems, Inc., P.O. Box 215, 28043, pg. 1380   PB

Fort Bragg

Logicon Technical Services Inc., P.O. Box 72739, 28307-2739, pg. 1199   PB

Franklinton

Novo Nordisk BioChem, Inc., P.O. Box 576, State Rd. 1003, 27525, pg. 987   IT

Fuquay Varina

Flexline Hose Inc., 121 Dickens Rd., 27526, pg. 1500   IT
Guilford Mills (Fibers), 200 Dickens Rd., 27526, pg. 769   PB
Southbend, 100 Old Honeycutt Rd., 27526, pg. 1110   PB

Gastonia

AMP Inc. Lytel Division, 3120 N.W. Blvd., 28052-1167, pg. 8   PB
CBP Resources-Gastonia Division, 5533 S. York Rd., 28052, pg. 192   PV
Clean Energy Enterprise, Inc., 400 Cox Rd., 28053, pg. 1340   PV
Dixie Synthetic Yarn Group, 40 Rex Ave., 28054, pg. 514   PB
FMC Corp., Lithium Division, 449 N. Cox Rd., 28054-0020, pg. 605   PB
Firestone Fibers & Textiles Company-Gastonia, P.O. Box 1278, 28053, pg. 214   IT
Guardian Care of Gastonia, 416 N. Highland St., 28052, pg. 1712   PV
Hunter Douglas Pleated Shade Corp., 1924 Chespark Dr., 28052, pg. 639   IT
PSNC Blue Ridge Corp., 400 Cox Rd., 28053, pg. 1340   PB
PSNC Cardinal Pipeline Company, 400 Cox Rd., 28053, pg. 1340   PB
PSNC Production Corp., 400 Cox Rd., 28053, pg. 1340   PB
PARKDALE MILLS, 1630 W. Garrison Blvd., 28053, pg. 840   PV
PUBLIC SERVICE COMPANY OF NORTH CAROLINA, INC., 400 Cox Rd., 28054, pg. 1340   PB
Rauch Industries, Inc., 6048 S. York Rd., 28053, pg. 1061   PV
Rhone-Poulenc Walsh, 207 Telegraph Dr., 28054, pg. 1110   IT
SMI Rebar North Carolina, 2528 N. Chester St., 28052, pg. 412   PB
Scott Mills, 2222 Plastic Dr., 28054, pg. 625   PV
Uniroyal Chemical Co., Inc., 214 West Ruby St., 28054, pg. 460   PB
Wix Div., P.O. Box 1967, 28053, pg. 479   PB

Glade Valley

Topaka Scientific Safety Co., P.O. Box 486, 28627, pg. 71   IT

Glen Raven

GLEN RAVEN MILLS, INC., 1831 N. Park Ave., 27217, pg. 456   PV
Glen Raven Mills, Inc.-Custom Fabrics Division, 1831 North Park Ave., 27217-1100, pg. 456   PV
Glen Raven Mills, Inc.-Glenspun Division, 142 Glen Raven Rd., 27217-1100, pg. 456   PV
Glen Raven Mills, Inc.-Textured Mills Group, Glen Touch Div., 1831 North Park Ave., 27217-1100, pg. 456   PV
Glen Raven Mills, Inc.-Textured Yarn Group-Glen Touch Division, 1831 North Park Ave., 27217-1100, pg. 456   PV
Glen Raven Mills, Inc.-Transportation Division, (Highway 87 N. at Ossipee), 1831 North Park Ave., 27217-1100, pg. 456   PV
Glen Raven Mills, Inc.-Ultraspun Plant, 232 Glen Raven Rd., 27217-1100, pg. 456   PV
Glen Raven Mills, Inc.-Park Ave. Division, PO Box 4268, 1821 North Park Ave., 27215, pg. 456   PV

Goldsboro

AP North American Aftermarket Division, 300 Dixie Trail, 27530, pg. 230   PV

APV Baker Inc., Food Machinery Div., 1200 W. Ash St., 27533-1718, pg. 1240   IT
FRANKLIN BAKING CO., INC., 500 W. Grantham St., 27530, pg. 462   PV
GOLDSBORO MILLING COMPANY, 938 Miller Chapel Rd., 27534, pg. 462   PV
Guardian Care of Goldsboro, 501 Forest Hill Dr., 27530, pg. 1712   PB
Hevi-Duty Electric, P.O. Box 268, 27530, pg. 726   PB
T.A. LOVING COMPANY, 400 Patetown Rd., 27530, pg. 677   PV
Smith Hardware Company, 515 North George St., 27530, pg. 335   PV
SOUTHCO DISTRIBUTING COMPANY, 701 Patetown Rd., 27530, pg. 1014   PV
WGBR, 914 W. Grantham St., 27530, pg. 297   PV
WKTC, 914 W. Grantham St., 27530, pg. 297   PV

Graham

Permatech, Inc., 911 E. Elm St., 27253, pg. 61   PB

Greensboro

AC CORPORATION, 301 Creek Ridge Rd., 27406, pg. 3   PV
American Drew, One Plaza Ctr., 4620 Grandover Pkwy., 27417, pg. 974   PB
Analog Devices, 7910 Triad Center Dr., 27409, pg. 108   PB
Arnold Omega, P.O. Box 18207, 205 Stage Coach Trail, 27419, pg. 1222   PB
BGF INDUSTRIES INC., 3802 Robert Porcher Way, 27410, pg. 106   PB
Berkley Care Network, Inc., Oak Branch Business Park, 5-E Oak Branch Dr., 27407, pg. 216   PV
BLACK CADILLAC OLDS, INC., 601 E. Bessemer Ave., 27405, pg. 146   PV
Burlington Denim, P.O. Box 21207, 27420, pg. 268   PB
BURLINGTON INDUSTRIES, INC., 3330 W. Friendly Ave., 27410, pg. 268   PB
Burlington Madison Yarn, P.O. Box 21207, 27420, pg. 268   PB
CBP RESOURCES, INC., 2410 Randolph Ave., 27406, pg. 192   PV
CMI Industries Inc.-Finished Fabrics Division, P.O. Box 21986, 27420, pg. 195   PV
CARLYLE & CO. JEWELERS, 4615 Dundas Dr., 27407, pg. 192   PV
Carolina By-Products Co. Greensboro Division, 2410 Randolph Ave., 27420, pg. 192   PV
CAROLINA STEEL CORPORATION, 1451 S. Elm St., 27406, pg. 214   PB
Central Sprinkler Company, 156 Industrial Ave., 27406, pg. 327   PB
Charter Greensboro Behavioral Health System, Inc., 700 Walter Reed Dr., 27403, pg. 1034   PB
Chemcl Co., Inc., 2300 Randolph Ave., 27406, pg. 999   PB
CIBA Seeds, Ashville Bldg., 1500 Pinecroft Rd., Ste. 400, 27407, pg. 973   IT
Cone Apparel Products, 3101 N. Elm St., 27408, pg. 430   PB
CONE MILLS CORPORATION, P.O. Box 26540, 3101 N. Elm St., 27415-6540, pg. 430   PB
Dillard, A ResourceNet International Company, 3900 Spring Garden St., 27407, pg. 901   PV
Dillard Paper Co. of Greensboro, 3900 Spring Garden St., 27407, pg. 902   PV
The Disston Co., 7345 G. West Friendly Ave., 27410, pg. 350   PV
ENVIRONMENTAL AIR SYSTEMS, INC., 521 Banner Ave., 27401, pg. 378   PV
Envirotrol Inc., 521 Bonner Ave., 22401, pg. 378   PV
Fluidtec Engineer Products, 408E Gallimore Dairy Rd., 27409, pg. 401   PV
Genetic Design Inc., 7017 Albert Pick Rd., 27409, pg. 733   PV
GENEVA CORPORATION, 300 N. Greene St., Ste. 2100, 27401, pg. 446   PV
Gilbarco Inc., 7300 W. Friendly Ave., 27420, pg. 545   IT
Gilbarco USA, 7300 W. Friendly Ave., 27420, pg. 545   IT
Marithe and Francois Girbaud N.A., 1801 Stanley Rd., 27407, pg. 1702   PB
Greensboro Sales, 7615 Business Park Dr., 27409, pg. 611   PB
Guilford Mills (Apparel, Home & Industrial Fabrics), 4925 W. Market St., 27407, pg. 769   PB
GUILFORD MILLS, INC., 4925 W. Market St., 27407, pg. 768   PB
HALSTEAD INDUSTRIES, INC., 300 N. Green St., Ste. 170C, 27401, pg. 496   PV
Healthtex, Kinston Bldg., Ste. 200, 2303 W. Meadowview Rd., 27407, pg. 1702   PB
HENLEY PAPER COMPANY, 8400 Triad Dr., 27409, pg. 622   PV
Hewlett-Packard Company, 7029 Albert Pick Rd., Ste. 100, 27409, pg. 814   PB
Hewlett-Packard Company, 5605 Roanne Way, 27420, pg. 815   PB
HIGHLAND INDUSTRIES INC., 629 Greenvalley Rd., Ste. 300, 27408, pg. 528   PV
Ikon Office Solutions-Carolinas, 7009 Albert Pick Rd., 27409, pg. 863   PB
JP Investment Management Co., P.O. Box 20407, 27420, pg. 925   PV
Jefferson-Pilot Communications Company, P.O. Box 21008, 27420, pg. 925   PB
JEFFERSON-PILOT CORPORATION, 100 N. Greene St., 27401, pg. 925   PB
Jefferson-Pilot Investor Services, Inc., 100 N. Greene St., 27401, pg. 926   PB

Jefferson-Pilot Life Insurance Co., 100 N. Greene St., 27401, pg. 926   PB
Jefferson-Pilot Property Insurance Company, P.O. Box 20967, 27420, pg. 926   PB
Jefferson-Pilot Title Insurance Co., P.O. Box 22035, 27420, pg. 926   PB
Kayser-Roth Corporation, Inc., 4905 Koger Blvd., 27407, pg. 576   IT
Key Risk Management Services, Inc., 202 Centreport Dr., Ste. 200, 27409, pg. 216   PB
Klopman Fabrics Div., P.O. Box 21207, 27420, pg. 268   PB
LADD FURNITURE, INC., One Plaza Ctr., 4620 Grandover Pkwy., 27417, pg. 974   PB
Ladd International, 4620 Grandover Pkwy., 27417, pg. 975   PB
LADD Transportation, Inc., One Plaza Center, 4620 Grandover Pkwy., 27261, pg. 974   PB
Lea Industries, One Plaza Center, 4620 Grandover Pkwy., 27417, pg. 974   PB
Lees Carpets, 3330 W. Friendly Ave., 27420, pg. 268   PB
Levolor, 7614 Business Park Dr., 27409, pg. 1177   PB
Liberty Systems, 7029 Albert Pick Rd. #101, 27409, pg. 97   PB
Lorillard Tobacco Company, 714 Green Valley Rd., 27408-7018, pg. 1011   PB
Lucent Technologies Advanced Technology Systems, P.O. Box 25000, 27420, pg. 1017   PB
Macpherson Meistergram, 3517 W. Wendover Ave., 27407, pg. 1177   PV
Mann & Hummel Filter Technology Inc., 241 Burgess Road, Suite C, 27409, pg. 484   IT
Mars-North Carolina, 2311 W. Cone Blvd., Ste. 233, 27408, pg. 706   PB
Mass Market Division, 400 N. Elm St., 27401, pg. 1702   PB
Morflex, Inc., 2110 Highpoint Rd., 27403, pg. 919   PV
News & Record, 200 E. Market St., P.O. Box 20848, 27420, pg. 649   PV
Oakwood Acceptance Corp., 7800 McCloud Rd., 27409-9634, pg. 1209   PB
OAKWOOD HOMES CORPORATION, P.O. Box 27081, 27425-7081, pg. 1209   PB
Oakwood Mobile Homes, Inc., 7800 McCloud Rd., 27409-9634, pg. 1209   PB
Perstorp Unidur, Inc., 7343-L W. Friendly Ave., 27410, pg. 1038   IT
Pilliod Furniture, 4620 Grandover Pkwy., 27417, pg. 974   PB
Reed Elsevier Business Information-Greensboro, 7025 Albert Pick Rd., 27409, pg. 1095   IT
Republic Automotive Parts Sales, Inc., 2448 Battleground Ave., 27408, pg. 1378   PB
Rexam Flexible Packaging, P.O. Box 5466, 2600 Phoenix Dr., 27406, pg. 1106   IT
ROLANE FACTORY OUTLETS, 1010 Howard St., 27435, pg. 941   PV
Scott & Stringfellow, Inc., 701 Green Valley Rd., Ste. 102, 27408, pg. 1446   PB
Servitex, Inc., 318 Village Green Dr., 27406, pg. 782   PV
Soabar Graphics Division, 2305 Soabar Dr., 27406, pg. 153   PB
SOUTHERN FOODS, INC., 3500 Old Battleground Rd., 27410, pg. 1016   PV
Southern Pilot Insurance Company, P.O. Box 20967, 27420, pg. 346   IT
Stockhausen Inc., 2401 Doyle St., 27406, pg. 1455   IT
T B Wood's Volkmann Controls, 100 Bonita Dr., 27405, pg. 1562   PB
TENCARVA MACHINERY CO., INC., 7921 Industrial Village Rd., 27409-9691, pg. 1075   PV
Triad International Maintenance Corporation, 623 Radar Rd., 27410, pg. 1325   PB
TRONE ADVERTISING, INC., P.O. Box 35565, 27425, pg. 1104   PV
Trone Public Relations, P.O. Box 35565, 27425-5565, pg. 1105   PV
UNIFI INC., 7201 W. Friendly Ave., 27410, pg. 1665   PB
Unifi International Service, Inc., 7201 W. Friendly Ave., 27410, pg. 1665   PB
United Guaranty Corp., 201 N. Elm St., 27401, pg. 84   PB
United HealthCare of North Carolina, Inc., 2307 W. Cone Blvd., 27408, pg. 1678   IT
VANGUARD CELLULAR SYSTEMS, INC., 2002 Pisgah Church Rd., Ste. 300, 27455-3314, pg. 1707   PV
Volvo Truck North America, Inc., 7825 National Service Rd., Air Park W., 27409-6115, pg. 1477   IT
WFMY-TV, 1615 Phillips St., 27405, pg. 702   PB
Wadkin USA, 7910 Industrial Village Rd., 27409, pg. 231   IT
WEAVER CONSTRUCTION, LLC, P.O. Box 26030, 27420, pg. 1156   PV
Westminster Homes of North Carolina, Inc., P.O. Box 26565, 2706 N. Church St., 27415, pg. 1741   PB
Willis Faber North America, Inc.-North Carolina, 940 Golf House Rd. W., 27377, pg. 1503   IT
Y.K.K. (U.S.A.) Inc., 405 Regional Rd. S., 27409, pg. 1515   IT

Greenville

American Equipment Company, Inc., 2106 Anderson Rd., 29611, pg. 660   PB
University Nursing Center, Rte. 1, Box 21, 27834, pg. 1715   PV
WNCT-TV, 3221 Evans St. Extension, 27834, pg. 1078   PB

Harrisburg

Hendrick Motorsports, P.O. Box 9, 5315 Stowe Lane, 28075, pg. 522   PV
600 Racing Inc., 5245 NC Hwy. 49 S., 28075, pg. 1498   PB

PB - *U.S. Public Companies Volume*
PV - *U.S. Private Companies Volume*
IT - *International Public & Private Companies Volume*

Southeastern Packaging Company, P.O. Box 429, 28075-0429, pg. 764 **PB**

Hayesville

Intercomp (ICM), P.O. Box 206, 28904, pg. 968 **PB**

Hazelwood

Ro-Search, Inc., 133 N. Pine St., 28738, pg. 1752 **PB**

Henderson

AMERICAL CORPORATION, 389 Americal Rd., 27536, pg. 49 **PV**
General Prods. Div., P.O. Box 1637, 27536, pg. 1272 **PV**
Guardian Care of Henderson, 519 Roanoke Ave., 27536, pg. 1712 **PB**
HARRIET & HENDERSON YARNS, INC., 1724 Graham Ave., 27536, pg. 504 **PV**
ROSE'S STORES, INC., 218 S. Garnett St., 27536, pg. 1405 **PB**
J.P. Taylor Co., Inc., P.O. Box 380, 27536, pg. 1695 **PB**

Hendersonville

Hendersonville Newspaper Corporation, 1717 Four Seasons Blvd., 28792, pg. 1175 **PB**
Southern Agricultural Insecticides, P.O. Box 429, 28793, pg. 1015 **PV**
Times-News, 1717 Four Seasons Blvd., 28792, pg. 1175 **PB**

Hickory

Alcatel N.A. Inc., 39 Second St. N.W., 28601, pg. 55 **IT**
Capital Resources, Inc., 120 4th St., S.E., 28602, pg. 657 **PV**
Carolina Steel-Hickory Plant, 1115 3rd Ave. N.W., 28601, pg. 214 **PV**
CENTURY FURNITURE INDUSTRIES, 401 11th St., N.W., 28601, pg. 226 **PV**
Clayton-Marcus Company, Inc., P.O. Box 100, 166 Teaguetown Rd., 28601, pg. 975 **PV**
COMMSCOPE, INC., 1375 Lenoir Rhyne Blvd., 28603, pg. 415 **PB**
DML Products, 620 23rd N.W., 28601, pg. 575 **PB**
Hickory Chair Div., P.O. Box 3147, 28603, pg. 688 **PB**
HICKORY CONSTRUCTION COMPANY, 1728 Ninth Ave., N.W., 28601, pg. 525 **PV**
Hickory Furniture Mart, 2220 Hwy. 70E., Ste. 358B, 28602, pg. 434 **PB**
Institution Food House, Inc., 700 12th St., N.W., 28601, pg. 657 **PV**
Kroehler Furniture Manufacturing Company, Inc., P.O. Box 3740., 28603, pg. 972 **PV**
ALEX LEE, INC., 120 Fourth St., S.W., 28601, pg. 657 **PV**
Merchants Distributors, Inc., P.O. Box 2148, 28601, pg. 657 **PV**
Merchants Transport of Hickory, 543 12th Drive., N.W., 28601, pg. 657 **PV**
PLASTIC PACKAGING, INC., 1246 Main Ave. S.E., 28602, pg. 871 **PV**
Sentrol Controls Group, 1510 Tate Blvd. S.E., 28603, pg. 139 **PV**
SHUFORD MILLS, INC., P.O. Box 2228, 28603, pg. 996 **PV**
Siecor Corporation, P.O. Box 489, 28603, pg. 1245 **IT**
TII-Ditel, P.O. Box 3386, 441 19th St. S.E., 28603, pg. 1556 **PB**
Thomasville Upholstery, Inc., P.O. Box 500, 28603, pg. 688 **PB**

High Point

AIR POWER, INC., 1430 Trinity Ave., 27260, pg. 28 **PV**
Banner Pharmacaps Inc., P.O. Box 2210, 27261-2210, pg. 1272 **IT**
Brayton International Inc., 255 Swathmore Ave., 27264, pg. 1038 **PV**
BRYANT ELECTRIC COMPANY, INC., 215 Balfour Dr., 27263, pg. 176 **PV**
Carborundum Abrasives North America, 2041 Brevard Rd., 27263, pg. 1174 **IT**
CULP, INC., P.O. Box 2686, 101 S. Main St., 27261, pg. 467 **PB**
Directional Furniture, P.O. Box 2005, 27261, pg. 193 **PV**
ELECTRONIC DATA MAGNETICS, INC., 210 Old Thomasville Rd., 27260, pg. 370 **PV**
HARRISS & COVINGTON HOSIERY MILLS, 2525 E. Green Dr., 27261, pg. 504 **PV**
Henredon Upholstery, 641 Ward, 27260, pg. 432 **PV**
High Point Chemical Corporation, 243 Woodbine St., 27261, pg. 717 **IT**
LifeStyle Contract Furnishings, Inc., 1515 W. Green Dr., 27260-1657, pg. 431 **PV**
Lilly Industries, Inc., 1717 English Rd., 27262, pg. 994 **PB**
Lilly Industries, Inc., 2147 Brevard Rd., 27216, pg. 995 **PB**
Maitland-Smith U.S., Inc., 4000 Lineage Ct., Ste. 201, 27265, pg. 432 **PV**
MARSH FURNITURE COMPANY, 1001 S. Centennial St., 27260, pg. 708 **PV**
McEwen Lumber Company, P.O. Box 950, 27261, pg. 903 **PB**
Myrtle/Mueller, A Haworth Co., 801 Millis St., 27261, pg. 512 **PV**
OLD DOMINION FREIGHT LINE, INC., 1730 Westchester Dr., 27260, pg. 1216 **PB**

Clyde Pearson Div., 1420 Progress Ave., 27261, pg. 688 **PB**
Royal Development Co., Inc., 1417 Courtesy Rd., 27261, pg. 688 **PB**
Sara Lee Sock Company, 1823 Eastchester Dr., 27265, pg. 1434 **PB**
SLANE HOSIERY MILLS, INC., 313 S. Centennial St., 27260, pg. 1005 **PV**
THOMAS BUILT BUSES, INC., 1408 Courtesy Rd., 27260, pg. 1082 **PV**
United Eco Systems, 1108 Old Thomasville Rd., 27260, pg. 74 **IT**
Universal Furniture Industries, Inc., 2622 Unwharrie Rd., 27263, pg. 432 **PV**

Hildebran

Impact Furniture Co. Inc., Tex's Fishcamp Rd., 28637, pg. 193 **PB**

Hillsborough

Nameplate, 346 Elizabeth Brady Rd., 27278, pg. 595 **PV**
Piedmont Minerals Division, P.O. Box 566, 27278, pg. 924 **PV**

Holly Ridge

Coast Refrigerated Trucking Co., Inc., One Bacon Pl., 28445, pg. 1603 **PB**
Thorn Apple Valley-Carolina Division, One Bacon Pl., 28445, pg. 1603 **PB**

Hope Mills

Automatic Service Co., P.O. Box 114D, Hwy. 301 So., 28348, pg. 8 **PV**

Hudson

Chemical Coatings, Inc., Hwy 321 Bypass, 28638, pg. 1357 **PB**
DAVIS WOOD PRODUCTS, INC., One Davis St., 28638, pg. 315 **PV**
Kincaid Furniture Co., Inc., 168 E. Main St., 28638, pg. 972 **PB**

Huntersville

Duke Power Co. McGuire Nuclear, 12700 Hagers Ferry Rd., 28078-9340, pg. 534 **PB**
Siegling America Inc., 12201 Van Story Rd., 28078, pg. 497 **IT**
Vickers Tedeco Div., 9801 Kincey Ave. 130, 28078-9168, pg. 25 **PB**

Jacksonville

Automatic Service Co., 1596 Catherine Lake Rd., 28540, pg. 8 **PV**
Onslow Wholesale, Inc., 222 Ellis Blvd., 28540, pg. 8 **PV**

Jamestown

CHEMCENTRAL/Greensboro, 108 Oakdale Rd., 27282-0100, pg. 232 **PB**
Flowers Baking Co. of Jamestown, Inc., 801 W. Main St., 27282, pg. 657 **PB**

Jamesville

Liberty-Penn Div., P.O. Box 279, Hwy. 64, 27846, pg. 340 **IT**

Kannapolis

Fieldcrest Cannon, Inc., One Lake Circle Dr., 28081, pg. 1296 **PB**
Fieldcrest Cannon, Inc., P.O. Box 107, 28081, pg. 1296 **PB**
Kannapolis Rest Home, Inc., 1808 N. Cannon Blvd., 28081, pg. 1714 **PB**

Kenansville

Guardian Care of Kenansville, Beasley St., P.O. Box 478, 28349, pg. 1712 **PB**
Guilford Mills (Automotive & Upholstery Fabrics), 1754 NC 903, 28349, pg. 769 **PB**

Kenly

Aycock Auto Auction, I-95 S. Bagley Rd., Exit 105, 27542, pg. 1648 **PB**

Kernersville

Willowbrook Care Center, Inc., 738 Piney Grove Rd., 27284, pg. 1715 **PB**

Kill Devil Hills

Agrinet Farm Radio Network, P.O. Box 3810, 27948, pg. 911 **PV**
RAY COMMUNICATIONS, INC., 1500 S. Croatan Hwy., 27948, pg. 911 **PV**

Ray Satellite Network, P.O. Box 3810, 27948, pg. 911 **PV**

King

New Fortis Corp., 151 Jefferson Church Rd., 27021, pg. 843 **PB**

Kings Mountain

Cablelink, Incorporated, 311 Childers St., 28086, pg. 1394 **PB**
Central Carolina Bank, 700 W. King St., 28086, pg. 276 **PB**
Cyprus Foote Mineral Co., 348 Holiday Inn Dr., 28086, pg. 471 **IT**
Firestone Fibers & Textiles Co., 100 Firestone Ln., 28086, pg. 214 **IT**
Firestone Fibers & Textiles Company-Kings Mountain, 100 Firestone Ln., 28086-1369, pg. 214 **IT**
Kings Mountain Manufacturing, 1755 S. Battleground Ave., 28086, pg. 3 **IT**
MAUNEY HOSIERY MILLS, INC., 20 Pine St., 28086, pg. 715 **PV**

Kinston

COASTAL WHOLESALE, INC., 500 E. Grainger, 28501, pg. 248 **PV**
Field Controls Co., 2330 Airport Rd., 28504, pg. 860 **PV**
Frigidaire Company Dishwasher Products, 4411 W. Vernon Ave., 28501, pg. 439 **IT**
Glen Raven Mills, Inc.-Kinston Plant, 800 Manning St., P.O. Box 3485, 28502-3485, pg. 456 **PV**
Guardian Care of Kinston, Cunningham Rd., P.O. Box 1438, 28501, pg. 1712 **PB**
HAMPTON INDUSTRIES, INC., 2000 Greenville Hwy., 28502-0614, pg. 779 **PB**
Kinston Die Cutting Corp., 2000 Greenville Hwy., 28501, pg. 779 **PB**
RANDA CORP., 3801 Commerce Dr., 28504, pg. 909 **PV**
Scott & Stringfellow, Inc., 514 Plaza Blvd., 28501, pg. 1446 **PB**
Servitex, Inc., 717 Summit Ave., 28501, pg. 781 **PV**

Knightdale

Square D Co.- Control Products Hqtrs., Hwy. 64 E., 27545, pg. 1208 **IT**

La Grange

Crouse-Hinds Molded Products, Rte. Four, Old Hwy. 70 E., 28551, pg. 444 **PB**

Lake Lure

Fairfield Mountains, 201 Blvd. of the Mountains, 28746, pg. 610 **PB**

Laurel Hill

Richmond Converters, Inc., P.O. Box 338, 28351, pg. 1059 **IT**

Laurinburg

Carolmet Division, P.O. Box 1329, Tinker Dr., 28352, pg. 1442 **IT**
Commercial Products Inc., Rte. 3, Box 171A, 28352, pg. 166 **IT**
Electrical Equipment Company, 226 N. Wilkinson Dr., 28353, pg. 368 **PV**
Railroad Friction Products and Others, P.O. Box 1349, 28352, pg. 1761 **PB**
Railroad Friction Products Corporation, P.O. Box 1349, 28352, pg. 271 **IT**

Leland

TELECHRON OF NORTH CAROLINA, INC., 2025 Trade St., 28451, pg. 1073 **PV**

Lenoir

BERNHARDT FURNITURE CO., 1839 Morganton Blvd., S.W., 28645, pg. 137 **PV**
BLUE RIDGE ELECTRIC MEMBERSHIP CORP., 1216 Blowing Rock Blvd., N.E., 28645, pg. 153 **PV**
Cambridge Industries, Inc., 601 Hibriton Dr., S.W., 28645, pg. 202 **PV**
Hammary Furniture Co., 2464 Norwood St. S.W., 28645, pg. 973 **PB**
PAXAR Printed Labels, P.O. Box 735, 950 German St., 28645, pg. 1266 **PB**
Rockwell Plastic Products, 601 Hibriten Blvd., S.W., 28645, pg. 113 **IT**

Lexington

Auto-Graph Computer Designing Systems, Inc., 651 Perimeter Dr., 40502, pg. 1053 **PB**
Binning's Building Products, Inc., Walser Rd., 27292, pg. 67 **PB**
The Dispatch Publishing Company, Inc., 30 E. First Ave., 27292, pg. 1175 **PB**
Frank IX & Sons, Inc., Bicycle Rd., 27295, pg. 423 **PV**

Lexington Furniture Industries, 411 S. Salisbury St., 27292, pg. 432 **PV**
Porcelanite, Inc., 20 Victor St., 27292, pg. 573 **PV**
Sealy Mattress Company - Lexington, 700 South State St., 27293, pg. 979 **PV**

Liberty

American Modular Technologies, 6306 Old 421 Rd., 27298, pg. 69 **PB**
Collier-Keyworth, Inc., 330 N. Greensborough St., 27298, pg. 985 **PB**

Lillington

Champion Home Builders Co., P.O. Box 1148, Old River Rd., 27546, pg. 332 **PB**
Edwards Brothers - Carolina, 800 Edwards Dr., 27546, pg. 365 **PV**
Titan Homes Div., P.O. Box 1389, Hwy. 401 S., 27546, pg. 332 **PB**

Lincolnton

Cochrane Furniture Co., Inc., 190 Cochrane Rd., 28092, pg. 352 **PV**
General Marble Corporation, 350 N. Generals Blvd., 28092, pg. 990 **PB**
J.H. HEAFNER CO. INC., 814 E. Main St., 28092, pg. 514 **PV**
Hof Textiles Inc., P.O. Box 816, 28093, pg. 923 **IT**
Kawai America Mfg. Inc., 2001 Kawai Rd., 28092, pg. 725 **IT**
Leucadia Inc. Manufacturing Division, 350 N. Generals Blvd., 28092-3557, pg. 990 **PB**
Lincoln Nursing Center, Inc., 1419 Gaston St. Extended, 28092, pg. 1714 **PB**
Mohican Mills Division, P.O. Box 190, 28093, pg. 603 **PB**
Vermont American Tool Group, Indian Creek Rd., 28092, pg. 575 **PB**

Louisburg

Boston Gear, P.O. Box 709, 27594, pg. 857 **PB**
The HON Co., Louisburg Plant, R.R. 7, Box 576, Hwy. 56, 27549, pg. 772 **PB**

Lowell

BRYANT ELECTRIC SUPPLY COMPANY, INC., 825 Groves St., 28098, pg. 177 **PV**

Lumber Bridge

Croft Metals, Inc. of NC, Hwy. 71, 28357, pg. 290 **PV**

Lumberton

Fleetwood Homes of North Carolina, Inc.-Lumberton, P.O. Box 1187, Hwy. 74 W., Rte. 6, 28359, pg. 651 **PB**
Mueller Steam Specialty, 901 Carolina Ave., P.O. Box 1569, 28358, pg. 1676 **PB**
THE OSTERNECK CO. INC., Hwy. 72 E. Business, 28358, pg. 821 **PV**
Park Newspapers of Lumberton, Inc., Box 1028, 121 W. Fifth St., 28358, pg. 1078 **PB**
Robesonian, Box 1028, 121 W. Fifth St., 28358, pg. 1078 **PB**

Madison

GEM-DANDY, INC., P.O. Box 657, 200 W. Academy St., 27025, pg. 442 **PV**
REMINGTON ARMS COMPANY, INC., P.O. Box 700, 870 Remington Dr., 27025, pg. 921 **PV**
Rockingham Nursing Center, Rte. 2, Box 381, 27025, pg. 1714 **PB**

Maiden

Carolina Maiden Corp., P.O. Box 157, 28650, pg. 214 **PV**
CAROLINA MILLS, INC., 618 Carolina Ave., 28650, pg. 214 **PV**

Marion

Calico Printers Assn. (U.S.A. Ltd.), 28752, pg. 300 **IT**
Crane Resistoflex/Industrial, Old Highway #10, 28752, pg. 457 **PB**
Hardwood Drying Operation, P. O. Box 340, 28752, pg. 737 **PB**
Marion Machine Company Division, P.O. Box 1169, Hwy. 70 W., 28752, pg. 1055 **PB**
McDowell News, P.O. Box 810, 28752, pg. 1078 **PB**
Midland Brake, Inc., Hwy. 221 S., P.O. Box 1129, 28752, pg. 561 **PB**
Park Newspapers of Marion, Inc., P.O. Box 610, 28752, pg. 1078 **PB**

Matthews

ALLTEL Carolina, Inc., 131 W. Matthews St., P.O. Box 428, 28106-0428, pg. 55 **PB**
CEM CORPORATION, 3100 Smith Farm Rd., 28106, pg. 277 **PV**
CONBRACO INDUSTRIES INC., 701 Matthews-Mint Hill Rd., 28105, pg. 261 **PV**

FAMILY DOLLAR STORES, INC., 10401 Old Monroe Rd., 28101-1017, pg. 612 **PB**
PCA INTERNATIONAL, INC., 815 Matthews-Mint Hill Rd., 28105, pg. 1240 **PB**
PIC'N PAY STORES, INC., 10301 Old Monroe Rd., 28261, pg. 864 **PV**
RP & C, 701 Matthews-Mint Hill Rd., 28105, pg. 261 **PV**
Rexam Custom, 700 Crestdale Rd., 28106, pg. 1106 **IT**
Rexam Custom, P.O. Box 368, 700 Crestdale St., 28106, pg. 1106 **IT**
Stretch Film, P.O. Box 1354, Stallings Industrial Park, 28107-1354, pg. 5 **PB**

Maxton

COX FURNITURE, Hwy. 74 W., 28364, pg. 283 **PV**

Mc Adenville

STOWE-PHARR MILLS, INC., 100 Main St., 28101, pg. 1045 **PV**

Mc Leansville

REPLACEMENTS, LTD., 1089 Knox Rd., 27301, pg. 923 **PV**

Mebane

Craftique, P.O. Box 428, 27302, pg. 1343 **PB**
Dayco Molded Products, 2312 S. Hwy. 19, 27302, pg. 1045 **PB**
Walter Kidde Portable Equipment Inc., 1394 S. Third St., 27302-9711, pg. 1500 **IT**
KINGSDOWN, INC., 126 W. Holt St., 27302, pg. 622 **PV**
THE MAY APPAREL GROUP, INC., 7412 Oakwood St., 27302, pg. 717 **PV**
MEBANE PACKAGING GROUP, P.O. Box 408, 27302, pg. 726 **PV**
Mebane Plant, 1400 Dogwood Way, 27302, pg. 1044 **PV**

Minot

Power Fuels, Inc., 1801 Burdick Expwy. W., 58701, pg. 203 **PB**
Vision Energy Florida, Inc., 1801 Burdick Expwy. W., 58701, pg. 203 **PB**
Vision Energy North Dakota, Inc., 1801 Burdick Expwy. W., 58701, pg. 203 **PB**
Vision Energy Resources, Inc., 1801 Burdick Expwy. West, 58701, pg. 203 **PB**

Moncure

Neste Resins Corporation, State Rd. 1916, P.O. Box 259, 27559, pg. 913 **IT**

Monroe

Allvac, 2020 Ashcraft Ave., 28110-0531, pg. 43 **PB**
Bank of Union, 201 N. Charlotte Ave., 28112, pg. 627 **PB**
CTB, Inc., P.O. Box 5011, 28111, pg. 331 **PV**
Commercial Products, Inc., P.O. Box 400, 28110, pg. 331 **PV**
Dickerson Carolina, Inc., P.O. Box 400, 28110, pg. 331 **PV**
THE DICKERSON GROUP, INC., 1501 Charlotte Ave., 28110, pg. 331 **PV**
Dickerson, Inc., P.O. Box 400, 28110, pg. 331 **PV**
Dickerson Realty Corp., P.O. Box 400, 28110, pg. 331 **PV**
GenCorp Printworld, 2011 Rocky River Rd. N., 28110, pg. 706 **PB**
Guardian Care of Monroe, 1212 Sunset Dr., 28110, pg. 1712 **PB**
IMO Pump, P.O. Box 5020, 28111-5020, pg. 857 **PB**
Ludwig Industries, 2806 Mason St., 28110, pg. 1514 **PV**
Manetta Home Fashions, 505 Miller, 28110, pg. 1296 **PB**
Monroe Hardware Co., 101 N. Sutherland Ave., 28110, pg. 335 **PV**
PERFECT FIT INDUSTRIES, INC., 201 Cuthbertson St., 28110, pg. 852 **PV**
South Atlantic Equipment, Inc., P.O. Box 5011, 28111, pg. 331 **PV**
Square D Company, 1809 Airport Rd., 28210, pg. 1208 **IT**
USCO, Incorporated, P.O. Box 1160, 115 Henderson St., 28110, pg. 847 **PB**

Mooresville

Fleetwood Homes of North Carolina, Inc./Mooresville, U.S. Hwy. 115 at Timber Rd., 28115, pg. 651 **PB**
General Microcircuits, Inc., 1133 N. Main St., 28115, pg. 1107 **PB**
Mooresville Tribune Inc., P.O. Box 300, 28115, pg. 1079 **PB**
Park Newspapers of Mooresville, Inc., P.O. Box 300, 28115, pg. 1079 **PB**

Morehead City

Burns & Wilcox Ltd., 225 Professional Cir., 28557, pg. 609 **PV**

Morganton

Carolina Shoe Company, P.O. Box 1079, 28680, pg. 217 **PB**
Case Farms, Inc., P.O. Box 308, 28655, pg. 218 **PV**

Henredon Furniture Industries, Inc., P.O. Box 70, 400 Henredon Rd., 28655, pg. 432 **PV**
Molded Fiber/North Carolina, 513 Reed Rd., 28655, pg. 756 **PV**
Morganton News-Herald, P.O. Box 280, 301 Collett St., 28655, pg. 1079 **PB**
Park Newspapers of Morganton, Inc., P.O. Box 280, 301 Collett St., 28655, pg. 1079 **PB**

Morrisville

Adams Products Company, Hwy. 54 West, 27560, pg. 242 **IT**
Dillard, A ResourceNet International Company, 1201 Cross Timbers Pkwy., 27560, pg. 902 **PB**
ESCOD Industries, 4709 Creekstone Dr., 27560, pg. 881 **PV**
FRONT ROYAL, INC., 2200 Gateway Blvd., Ste. 205, 27560, pg. 430 **PV**
Stephen Gould of Carolina, Inc., 2500 Gateway Centre Blvd., 27560, pg. 467 **PV**
Healthsource North Carolina, Inc., 4000 Aerial Center Pkwy., 27560, pg. 360 **PB**
Northern Telecom Switching Networks, 4400 Emperor Blvd., 27560-9768, pg. 970 **IT**
The Redwoods Group, 2200 Gateway Blvd., 27560, pg. 430 **PV**

Mount Airy

Brown Wooten/Ballston Plant, P.O. Box 825, 1546 Carter St., 27030, pg. 175 **PV**
Coordinate Measuring Machine Div., 1372 Boggs Dr., 27030, pg. 1511 **PB**
Cross Creek Apparel, Inc., U.S. Hwy. 52 S., 27030, pg. 1413 **PB**
Ground Flat Stock Div., 1372 Boggs Dr., 27030, pg. 1511 **PB**
INSTEEL INDUSTRIES, INC., 1373 Boggs Dr., 27030, pg. 882 **PB**
Insteel Wire Products, 1373 Boggs Dr., 27030, pg. 882 **PB**
North Carolina Foam Industries, Inc., P.O. Box 1528, 27030, pg. 117 **PV**
PAGE HOLDINGS, INC., 100 Woltz St., 27030, pg. 834 **PV**
Perry Mfg. Co., P.O. Box 1027, 100 Woltz St., 27030, pg. 834 **PV**
Proctor-Silex, Mt. Airy Operations, 561 Hay St., 27030, pg. 1149 **PB**
RENFRO CORP., 661 Linville Rd., 27030, pg. 922 **PV**
SPENCER'S INC., 238 Willow St., 27030, pg. 1025 **PV**
Starrett Granite Surface Plate Division, P.O. Box 1268, 1372 Boggs Dr., 27030, pg. 1511 **PB**

Mount Gilead

Compsee, Inc., 402 N. Main St., 27306, pg. 1073 **PB**
McRae Financial and Leasing Div., 400 N. Main St., 27306, pg. 1073 **PB**
McRae Footwear Div., 402 N. Main St., 27306, pg. 1073 **PB**
McRae Graphics, Inc., 400 N. Main St., 27306, pg. 1074 **PB**
MCRAE INDUSTRIES, INC., 400 N. Main St., 27306, pg. 1073 **PB**
Rae-Print Printing & Packaging, N. Main St., 27306, pg. 1074 **PB**
Uwharrie Environmental, Inc., 500 Landfill Rd., 27306, pg. 1379 **PB**

Mount Holly

American & Efird, Inc., 22 American St., 28120, pg. 1412 **PV**
Freightliner Truck Mfg. Plant, 1800 N. Main St., 28120-9141, pg. 368 **IT**
GASTON COUNTY DYEING MACHINE CO., Hwy. 27 W., 28120, pg. 441 **PV**

Mount Pleasant

TUSCARORA YARNS INC., 8760 E. Franklin St., 28124, pg. 1110 **PV**

Murphy

Litton Clifton Precision South, Slow Creek Road, Hwy. 141, P.O. Box 160, 28906-0160, pg. 1003 **PB**

Nashville

Brigadier Homes of North Carolina, P.O. Box 1007, 27856, pg. 318 **PB**
Carolina Steel-Nash County Plant, 341 Corbett Rd., 27856, pg. 214 **PV**

New Bern

Fairfield Harbour, 750 Broad Creek Rd., 28560, pg. 610 **PB**
Guardian Care of New Bern, 836 Hospital Dr., 28560, pg. 1713 **PB**
Hatteras Yachts, 110 N. Glenburnie Rd., 28560, pg. 447 **PV**
Mack Remanufacturing Center, 701 Industrial Dr., 28562-5447, pg. 1102 **IT**

PB - U.S. Public Companies Volume
PV - U.S. Private Companies Volume
IT - International Public & Private Companies Volume

1370

Newton

Bassett Upholstery Division, East 20th St., 28658, pg. 193 — PB
Cambridge Industries, Inc., 1400B Urris Rd., 28658, pg. 202 — PV
CAROLINA GLOVE CO., Drawer 820, 28658, pg. 214 — PV
Newton-Southeastern Mfg. Div., P.O. Box 289, 28658, pg. 518 — PB
RIDGEVIEW, INC., 2101 N. Main St., 28658, pg. 930 — PV

Norlina

Glen Raven Mills, Inc.-Norlina Plant, P.O. Box 518, Highway U.S. 1 South, 27563, pg. 456 — PV

North Wilkesboro

CAROLINA MIRROR COMPANY, 201 Elkin Hwy., 28659, pg. 214 — PV
Crown Fine Arts, 201 Elkin Hwy., 28659, pg. 214 — PV
LOWE'S COMPANIES, INC., Elkin Hwy. 268 E., 28659, pg. 1015 — PB
Lowe's Home Centers, Inc., Hwy. 268 E., 28659, pg. 1015 — PB
Scott & Stringfellow, Inc., 311 Ninth St., 28659, pg. 1446 — PB
Sterling Advertising Ltd., Hwy. 268 E., 28659, pg. 1015 — PB

Oxford

General Processors, Inc., Industry Dr., 27565, pg. 1502 — PB

Patterson

Sealed Air Food Packaging Division, River Rd., 28613, pg. 1451 — PB

Pembroke

Fleetwood Homes of North Carolina, Inc./Pembroke, P.O. Box 818, E. Railroad Ave., 28372, pg. 651 — PB

Pendleton

Agrotec, Williams Inc., Hwy. 35 N., 27862, pg. 1769 — PB

Pinetops

Instrument Transformer Division, Hwy. 43 N., 27864, pg. 4 — IT
Lucas Body Systems, 100 Hwy. 43, Rte. One, Box 2K, 27864, pg. 820 — IT

Pineville

Baumann Springs USA, Inc., 10710 Southern Loop Blvd., 28134, pg. 171 — IT
Community Psychiatric Centers of North Carolina, Inc., 9600 Pineville-Matthews Rd., 28134, pg. 1712 — PB
Rexam Cartons, P.O. Box 240007, 10500 Industrial Dr., 28134, pg. 1106 — IT
Rutland Plastic Technologies, Inc., 10021 Rodney St., 28134, pg. 414 — PV

Pisgah Forest

ECUSTA Division, P.O. Box 200, 28768, pg. 746 — PB

Pleasant Garden

Boren Clay Products Company, 1410 Forest Acres Circle, 27313, pg. 699 — IT

Raeford

HOUSE OF RAEFORD FARMS, INC., 520 E. Central Ave., 28376, pg. 542 — PV

Raleigh

ABB Power T & D Company Inc., 1021 Main Campus Dr., 27606, pg. 4 — IT
AEA of Raleigh, 1115 New Hope Rd., 27610, pg. 1377 — PB
AVX Raleigh Plant, 3900 Electronics Dr., 27604, pg. 775 — IT
Aeroglide Americas International, Inc., P.O. Box 29505, 27626, pg. 24 — PV
Ajinomoto U.S.A., Inc., North Carolina Plant, 4020 Ajinomoto Dr., 27610, pg. 40 — IT
Allied Security Inc., 100 E. Six Forks Rd., #303, 27609, pg. 41 — PV
American Guarantee Insurance Company, P.O. Box 151, 27602, pg. 629 — PB
Amerimark Inc., 3101 Poplarwood Ct., Ste. 200, 27604, pg. 1237 — PB
AMP Inc. Lytel Division, 6040A Six Forks Rd. Ste. 412, 27609-8601, pg. 8 — PB
Apex, 3510 Spring Forest Rd., pg. 1306 — PB
Aracruz Celulose (USA) Inc., 140 Windchime Ct., 27615, pg. 78 — IT
Ark Les Corp., 3400 Yonkers Rd., 27604-3656, pg. 82 — PV
Arrow/Schweber Electronics, 5240 Greers Dairy Rd., 27604, pg. 134 — PB
Athey Products-Sweeper Div., P.O. Box 669, 27602, pg. 143 — PB

Athey Products-Waste Control Div., P.O. Box 669, 27602, pg. 143 — PB
Boatwright Insulation Company, Inc., P.O. Box 25516, 1515 Sunrise Ave., 27611, pg. 913 — PB
Business Journals of North Carolina, LLC, 3125 Poplarwood Ct., Ste. 304, 27604, pg. 19 — PV
Cablevision of Raleigh, Inc., 2505 Atlantic Ave., 27604, pg. 1610 — PB
Cadmus Financial Communications, Two Hannover Sq., Ste. 1500, 27601, pg. 291 — PB
Capital Equipment Div., P.O. Box 669, 27602, pg. 143 — PB
CAPITOL BROADCASTING CO., INC., 711 Hillsborough St., 27603, pg. 206 — PV
Capstone Electronics Div., 5230 Greens Dairy Rd., 27604, pg. 134 — PB
Carat ICG, 6200 Falls of the Neuse, # 200, 27609, pg. 207 — PV
CaroHome LLC, P.O. Box 1551, 27602, pg. 307 — PB
Carolina Builders Corporation, 3227 Wellington Ct., 27615, pg. 1512 — IT
Carolina Builders Corporation, 3000 Yonkers Rd., 27604, pg. 1512 — IT
Carolina Holdings, Inc., 3227 Wellington Ct., 27615, pg. 1512 — IT
CAROLINA POWER & LIGHT COMPANY, P.O. Box 1551, 27602, pg. 306 — PB
Caronet LLC, P.O. Box 1551, 27602, pg. 307 — PB
CENTURY DATA SYSTEMS, INCORPORATED, 506 N. Harrington St., 27603, pg. 226 — PV
Charles River Laboratories-NC, 41 S. Newhope Rd., 27610, pg. 194 — PB
Charter Northridge Behavioral Health Systems, Inc., 400 Newton St., 27615, pg. 1035 — PB
Cooper Hand Tools, 3535 Glenwood Ave., 27612, pg. 444 — PB
CURTIS MEDIA GROUP, 3012 Highwoods Blvd., Ste. 200, 27604, pg. 297 — PV
Data General Corp., 3120 Highwoods Blvd., 27625, pg. 485 — PB
Delta Consolidated Industries, Inc., 2728 Capital Blvd., 27604, pg. 481 — PB
DurCo Agency, Inc., 2610 Wycliff Rd., 27607, pg. 27 — PB
EDD-North Carolina, 3100 Smoktree Ct. Ste. 800, 27604, pg. 205 — PB
Edward Don & Company-North Carolina Branch, 2321 Blue Ridge Rd., Ste. B, 27607, pg. 339 — PB
Edwards & Broughton Company, 1821 North Blvd., 27604, pg. 1735 — PB
ELECTRICAL EQUIPMENT COMPANY, 1440 Diggs Dr., 27603-2755, pg. 368 — PV
Exide Electronics Group, Inc., 8609 Six Forks Rd., 27615, pg. 126 — IT
FIRST CITIZENS BANC SHARES, INC., 3128 Smoketree Ct., 27604, pg. 628 — PB
First Citizens Bank & Trust Co., P.O. Box 151, 27602, pg. 629 — PB
First Citizens Investor Services, Inc., P.O. Box 151, 27602, pg. 629 — PB
FIRST TRAVELCORP INC., 4513 Creedmoor Rd., Ste. 200, 27612, pg. 408 — PV
Fujitsu Network Switching of America, Inc., 4403 Bland Rd., 27609, pg. 526 — IT
GAI Consultants-NC, Inc., 3812-H Tarheel Dr., 27609, pg. 434 — PB
General Employment Enterprises, 4601 Six Forks Rd., Ste. 500, 27609, pg. 714 — PB
GENERAL PARTS, INC., 2635 Millbrook Rd., 27604, pg. 445 — PV
GLOBAL SOFTWARE, INC., 3200 Atlantic Ave., 27604, pg. 457 — PV
Golden Corral Corporation, 5151 Glenwood Ave., 27612, pg. 575 — PV
GOODMARK FOODS, INC., 6131 Falls of Neuse Rd., 27609, pg. 751 — PB
Green Tree Acceptance of North Carolina, Inc., 3101 Poplar Wood Ct., Ste. 127, 27629, pg. 762 — PB
Gulf South Medical Supply, 3215 Wellington Ct., 27615-4132, pg. 1294 — PB
Hillhaven Convalescent Center Raleigh, 616 Wade Ave., 27605, pg. 1713 — PB
Hillhaven-Sunnybrook Convalescent Center, 25 Sunnybrook Rd., 27610, pg. 1714 — PB
HOWARD, MERRELL & PARTNERS, INC., 8521 Six Forks Rd., Ste. 500, 27615, pg. 542 — PV
IPM-Elyria Operations, 8609 Six Forks Rd., 27615, pg. 126 — IT
IPM Federal Opers. Group, 8609 Six Forks Rd., 27615, pg. 126 — IT
IPM New York, 8609 Six Forks Rd., 27615, pg. 126 — IT
IPM West Coast, 8609 Six Forks Rd., 97615, pg. 126 — IT
INVESTORS MANAGEMENT CORP., 5151 Glenwood Ave., 27612, pg. 574 — PV
Jaco Electronics, Inc., 5206 Greens Dairy Rd., 27604, pg. 920 — PB
W.H. King Drug Co., 8005 Ebenezer Church Rd., 27613, pg. 214 — PB
Large Systems Group, 8609 Six Forks Rd., 276515, pg. 126 — IT
Louis London Advertising & Sales Promotion, 7200 Falls of Neuse Rd., Ste. 304, 27615, pg. 674 — PV
Mackay Radio Systems Inc., P.O. Box 58649, 2121 Discovery Dr., 27658, pg. 1384 — IT
Martin Marietta Aggregates, P.O. Box 30013, 27622, pg. 1007 — PB
Martin Marietta Magnesia Specialties, Inc., P.O. Box 30013, 27622, pg. 1007 — PB
Martin Marietta Materials, Inc., P.O. Box 30013, 27622, pg. 1007 — PB
MCKINNEY & SILVER, 333 Corporate Plaza, 27601, pg. 723 — PV

Measurements Group, Inc., P.O. Box 27777, Dept. TR, 27611-7777, pg. 1722 — PB
Medic Computer Systems, Inc., 8601 Six Forks Rd., Ste. 300, 27615, pg. 870 — IT
Merrell/Chisholm, 4505 Falls of neuse Rd., 27609, pg. 543 — PV
MET Solutions, LLC, Two Hannover Sq., Ste. 1720, 27601, pg. 1642 — PB
Milgray/Raleigh, Inc., 2925 Huntleigh Dr., 27604, pg. 207 — PB
Motorola Radius, 8601 Six Forks Rd., Ste. 201, 27615-2965, pg. 1138 — PB
N.C. Products Corp., 632 Pershing Rd., 27608, pg. 242 — IT
NES HOLDINGS, INC., 3724 National Dr., Ste. 105, 27612, pg. 771 — PV
National Development Co., Inc., 4600 Marriott Dr., Ste. 200, 27612, pg. 1536 — PB
The News & Observer, P.O. Box 191, 27602, pg. 1065 — PB
NORTH CAROLINA EQUIPMENT CO., 3101 Hillsboro St., 27607, pg. 804 — IT
PCS Phosphate - Raleigh, P.O. Box 30321, 3101 Glenwood Ave., 27622, pg. 1064 — IT
PENCO-North Carolina, 4900 N. Park Bldg., 4900 Falls of the Neuse Rd., Ste. 115, 27609, pg. 1508 — IT
PennCorp Financial, Inc., 150 Fayetteville Street Mall, 27601, pg. 1271 — PB
Pepcom Industries, Inc., Six Forks Center II, 4700 Homewood Ct., Ste. 380, 27609-5711, pg. 1321 — IT
Perstorp Flooring, 2809 Highwoods Blvd., Ste. 100, 27604, pg. 1039 — IT
Perstorp Flooring Inc., 2809 Highwoods Blvd., Ste. 100, 27604, pg. 1039 — IT
Plasma Energy Corporation, 7516 Precision Dr., 27613, pg. 344 — PB
Quick 10, 5151 Glenwood Ave., 27612, pg. 575 — PV
Ragazzis, Inc., 5151 Glenwood Ave., 27612, pg. 575 — PV
Republic Automotive Parts Sales, Inc., 1115 New Hope Rd., 27610, pg. 1378 — PB
ROCKETT, BURKHEAD, LEWIS & WINSLOW, 8601 Six Forks Rd., 7th Fl., 27615-8189, pg. 938 — PV
SRS, P.O. Box 1551, 27602, pg. 307 — PB
Scapa Group Inc., 5400 Glenwood Ave., Ste. 218, 27612, pg. 1202 — PB
Scott & Stringfellow, Inc., 2626 Glenwood Ave., Ste. 100, 27608, pg. 1446 — PB
Servitex, Inc., 3301 Hillsborough St., 27607, pg. 781 — PV
Small Systems Group, 8609 Six Forks Rd., 27615, pg. 126 — IT
SouthTrust Bank of North Carolina, 4505 Falls of the Neuse Rd., Ste. 150, 27609, pg. 1492 — PB
Styrotech Corp., 831 Purser, 27603, pg. 1452 — PB
SUNSTATES CORPORATION, 4600 Marriott Dr., Ste. 200, 27612, pg. 1536 — PB
Sunstates Realty Group Inc., 4600 Marriott Dr., Ste. 200, 27612, pg. 1536 — PB
TMP Worldwide/Recruitment Division, 3803B Computer Dr., Ste. 106, 27609, pg. 1065 — PV
TEXFI INDUSTRIES, INC., 5400 Glenwood Ave., Ste. 215, 27612-3228, pg. 1588 — PB
Triangle Life Insurance, P.O. Box 151, 27602, pg. 629 — PB
TRIDENT FINANCIAL CORPORATION, 4601 Six Forks Rd., 27609, pg. 1103 — PV
Turner Construction Company, 628 Hutton St., Ste. 106, 27606, pg. 1646 — PB
URS Greiner, Inc., 4630 Paragon Pk. Rd., 27604, pg. 1658 — PB
Uniroyal Chemical Co., Inc., 158 Wind Chime Ct., 27609, pg. 460 — PB
VARIETY WHOLESALERS, INCORPORATED, 3401 Gresham Lake Rd., 27615, pg. 1134 — PV
WPTF, 3012 Highwoods Blvd., 27604, pg. 298 — PV
WQDR, 3012 Highwoods Blvd., 27604, pg. 298 — PV
WQQK-FM, 8601 Six Forks Rd., Ste. 609, 27615, pg. 385 — PB
WRAL-TV, 2619 Western Blvd., 27606, pg. 206 — PV
WARREN DISTRIBUTING CORP., 226 Glenwood Ave., 27603, pg. 1151 — PB
Western International Media Corporation, 4300 Six Forks Rd., Ste. 350, 27609, pg. 1167 — PV
Winn-Dixie Raleigh, Inc., 2201 S. Wilmington St., 27603, pg. 1771 — PB
Woodward-Clyde, 3109 Poplarwood Ct., Ste. 120, 27604, pg. 1656 — PB
Worldwide Services Group, 8609 Six Forks Rd., 27615, pg. 126 — IT
Xerox Research, 4601 Six Forks Rd. Ste. 300, 27609-5210, pg. 1784 — IT
Zellerbach Division, 3600 Tarheel Dr., 27609, pg. 1075 — PB

Randleman

Mid-State Paper Box Company, Rte. 1, Hwy. 311, 27317, pg. 304 — PB

Reidsville

Boehme Filatex Inc., 209 Watlington Industrial Dr., 27320, pg. 199 — IT
Chace Precision Metals, Inc., 1704 Barnes Street, 27323, pg. 1564 — PB
Elixir Industries, 1203 Freeway Dr., 27320, pg. 371 — PB
North Carolina Gas Service, 140 South Scales St., 27320-0779, pg. 1148 — PB
Reidsville Container Div., P.O. Box 1170, 27320, pg. 1289 — PB

Research Triangle Park

Allen & Hanburys, Five Moore Dr., 27709, pg. 552 — IT
ATCOM, INC., 4920 S. Alston Ave., 27713, pg. 94 — PV

PB - *U.S. Public Companies Volume*
PV - *U.S. Private Companies Volume*
IT - *International Public & Private Companies Volume*

BNR, Inc., 35 Davis Dr., 27709, pg. 969　IT
Becton Dickinson Research Center, 21 Davis Dr., 27709, pg. 199　PB
Bekaert Fibre Technologies:, P.O. Box 13159, 12 T.W. Alexander Drive, 27709-3759, pg. 184　IT
Cerenex Pharmaceuticals, Five Moore Dr., 27709, pg. 553　IT
DMS-10 Div., P.O. Box 13010, 22709, pg. 969　IT
Data General Corp., 62 Alexander Dr., 27709, pg. 485　PB
Digital Switching Div., 4001 E. Chapel Hill-Nelson Hwy., 27709, pg. 969　IT
Ericsson GE Mobile Communications Inc., One Triangle Dr., 27009, pg. 1365　IT
ESCOD Industries, P.O. Box 12138, 27709, pg. 881　PB
Glaxo Dermatology, Five Moore Dr., 27709, pg. 553　IT
Glaxo Pharmaceuticals, Five Moore Dr., 27709, pg. 552　IT
Glaxo Technical Operations, Five Moore Dr., 27709, pg. 552　IT
Glaxo Wellcome Inc., P.O. Box 13398, Five Moore Dr., 27709, pg. 552　IT
Glaxo Wellcome PLC, 3030 Cornwallis Rd., 27709-4498, pg. 553　IT
Harris Semiconductor Microelectronics Center, P.O. Box 13049, 3026 Cornwallis Rd., 27709, pg. 792　PB
IEA, Inc., P.O. Box 12846, 27709, pg. 126　PB
JWG Associates, Inc., 100 Park Dr., Ste. 105, 27709, pg. 579　PV
Kobe-Midrex Research, Pamilco Bldg., 3306 East Chapel Hill Rd., 27709, pg. 740　IT
LITESPEC, Inc., P.O. Box 13367, 76 Alexander Dr., 27709, pg. 1313　IT
Martin Marietta EPA National Computer Center, P.O. Box 14365, 27709-4365, pg. 1007　PB
OMG Americas, 2601 Weck Dr., 27709, pg. 594　PB
Pilling Weck, P.O. Box 12600, One Weck Dr., 27709, pg. 1569　PB
RESEARCH TRIANGLE INSTITUTE, 3040 Cornwallis Rd., 27709, pg. 924　PV
Rhone-Poulenc, Agrochemical Division, T.W. Alexander Dr., 27709, pg. 1109　IT
Sani-Tech Southeast, P.O. Box 13236, 07709, pg. 1545　PB
Sumitomo Electric Lightwave Corp., P.O. Box 13145, 27709, pg. 1313　IT
Wandel & Goltermann Inc., Imperial Ctr., 1030 Swabia Ct., 27709, pg. 1486　IT
Wandel & Goltermann Technologies, Inc., Imperial Ctr., 1030 Swabia Ct., 27709, pg. 1486　IT

Roanoke Rapids

Flambeau Airmold Corporation, 100 Grace Dr., 27870, pg. 409　PV
Guardian Care of Roanoke Rapids, 305 14th St., 27870, pg. 1713　PB
Patch Rubber Company, Becker Farms Indus. Pk., 27870, pg. 1143　PB
Roanoke Rapids Mill, Champion International Corporation, P.O. Box 580, 27870, pg. 334　PB

Roaring River

Abtco, Inc., P.O. Box 98, Hwy. 268, 28669, pg. 20　IT

Robbins

Mansion Homes, P.O. Box 39, 27325, pg. 318　PB

Rockingham

American Cablevision of Carolina, Inc., P.O. Box 668, 801 Broad Ave., 28379, pg. 1610　PV
Cascades Industries Inc., P.O. Box 578, 805 Midway Rd., 28379, pg. 274　PV
Cascades Moulded Pulp, Inc., P.O. Box 578, 805 Midway Rd., 28379, pg. 274　IT
Park Newspapers of Rockingham, Inc., P.O. Box 1888, 28379, pg. 1079　PV
Rockingham-Hamlet Cablevision, Inc., P.O. Box 668, 801 E. Broad Ave., 28379, pg. 1610　PB
Rockingham-Hamlet, Inc., P.O. Box 668, 801 E. Broad Ave., 28379, pg. 1610　PB

Rockwell

Lydall Westex, 711 Palmer Rd., 28138, pg. 1021　PB

Rocky Mount

BNE Land & Development Co., P.O. Box 1908, 27802-1908, pg. 154　PV
BarcaLounger Company, 1450 Atlantic Ave., 27802, pg. 265　PV
BODDIE-NOELL ENTERPRISES INC., 1021 Noell Ln., 27801, pg. 154　PV
Ceco Building Systems-Eastern Region, P.O. Drawer 2387, Hwy. 301 N., 27802, pg. 221　PV
CENTURA BANKS, INC., P.O. Box 1220, 134 N. Church St., 27802, pg. 328　PB
Fast Food Merchandisers Inc., 1233 N. Church St., 27802, pg. 278　PV
Guardian Care of Rocky Mount, 160 Winstead Ave., 27801, pg. 1713　PB
Hardee's Equipment Department, 321 Jeffreys Rd., 27804, pg. 278　PV
Hardee's Food Systems, Inc., 1233 Hardee's Blvd., 27804-2815, pg. 278　PV
Ilco Unican Corp., 400 Jeffreys Rd., 27804, pg. 1432　IT

MBM, 2641 Meadowbrook Rd., 27801, pg. 685　PV
Overseas Commodex Corp., 109 So. Main St., 27801, pg. 1390　IT
Rocky Mount Instruments, Inc., P.O. Box 1358, 27801, pg. 45　PB
Tar River Communications, Inc., P.O. Box 2548, 27801, pg. 701　PB
Texfi Blends Division, 400 English Rd., 27804, pg. 1588　PB

Rocky Point

Cincinnati Thermal Spray South, 11766 Hwy. 210, 28457, pg. 240　PV

Rose Hill

MURPHY FAMILY FARMS, 4134 Hwy. 117, 28458, pg. 768　PV

Roxboro

Air Control Products, 2564 Durham Rd., 27573, pg. 556　PB
Collins & Aikman Products Co., 1803 Main St., 27573, pg. 399　PB
Fleetwood Homes of North Carolina, Inc.-Roxboro, P.O. Box 1223, State Rte. 1703, 600 Lucy Garrett Rd., 27573, pg. 651　PB

Rutherfordton

AAlliec Die Casting Mfg., Inc., P.O. Box 1178, 401 Aallied Drive, 28139, pg. 903　PV
All American Homes of North Carolina, Inc., P.O. Box 929, Hwy. 2215 & 71 W., 28139, pg. 388　PB
Reeves-Industrial Coated Fabrics Plant, Railroad Ave. & U.S. Hwy. 74, 28139, pg. 507　PV
TANNER CO., Oak Springs Rd., 28139, pg. 1068　PV

Saint Pauls

Rocco Quality Foods, Inc., P.O. Box 9, 28384, pg. 937　PV

Salisbury

BPI Inc., Salisbury Plant, 2200 Old Wilkesboro Rd., 28144, pg. 72　PB
Carolina Quarries, Inc., 805 Harris Granite Rd., 28146, pg. 396　PV
Cental Carolina Bank & Trust Company, 507 W. Innes St., 28144, pg. 276　PB
Central Carolina Bank, 215-217 S. Main St., 28144, pg. 276　PB
Central Carolina Bank, 507 Innes St., 28144, pg. 276　PB
Central Carolina Bank, 315 Webb Rd., 28147, pg. 276　PB
Food Lion, Inc., 2110 Executive Dr., 28145-1330, pg. 463　IT
KRC Inc., P.O. Box 1618, 1415 Jake Aalexander Blvd. S., 28145-1618, pg. 1202　IT
Perma-Flex (Southern) Inc., P.O. Box 2389, 1415 Jake Alexander Blvd. S., 28145-2389, pg. 1202　IT
Southern Alloy of America, 770 Cedar Springs Rd., 28147, pg. 1101　PV
STANBACK COMPANY, 1500 S. Main, 28144, pg. 1030　PV

Sanford

Communication Cable, Inc., 1378 Charleston Dr., 27330, pg. 968　PB
DAMSMITH CORP., 109 N. McNeil Rd., 27330, pg. 309　PV
J.T. DAVENPORT & SONS, INC., Hwy. 42 E., 27330, pg. 314　PV
Heins Telephone Company, 106 Gordon St., 27330, pg. 55　PB
LEE-MOORE OIL CO., INC., 1807 Douglas Dr., 27331, pg. 657　PV
Magneti Marelli U.S.A., Inc., P.O. Box 548, 2101 Nash St., 27330, pg. 483　IT
Mart Corporation, 202 Maple Ave., 27330, pg. 309　PV
PH Holding, 1801 Douglas Dr., 27330, pg. 837　PV
Pac-Fab Inc./East, 1620 Hawkins Ave., 27330, pg. 593　PB
THE PANTRY, INC., 1801 Douglas Dr., 27330, pg. 837　PV
Precision Forming Facility, 4901 Womack Rd., 27330, pg. 535　IT
Saxton, P.O. Box 2878, 27330, pg. 968　PB
Securall, Inc., 109 McNeil Rd. N., 27330, pg. 309　PB
TRION, NC., 101 McNeil Rd., 27330, pg. 1639　PB
Whitin Roberts Co., 109 N. McNeil Rd., 27330, pg. 309　PV
Zenith Pumps Div., 5910 Elwin Buchanan Rd., 27330-9551, pg. 1261　PB

Sapphire

Fairfield Sapphire Valley, 4000 Hwy. 64 W., 28774, pg. 611　PV

Scotland Neck

Gilbert & Bennett, P.O. Box 310, 27874, pg. 453　PV
Guardian Care of Scotland Neck, 1400 Junior High School Rd., 27874, pg. 1713　PB

Selma

Eaton Corporation Commercial Controls Division, 1100 E. Preston St., 27576, pg. 556　PB
Flanders Airpure Products Co., LLC, 100 Oak Tree Dr., 27576, pg. 648　PB

Severn

MEHERRIN AGRICULTURE & CHEMICAL CO., 1 Main St., 27877, pg. 729　PV

Shelby

Bindley Western, Kendall Division, 1305 Frederick St., 28150, pg. 228　PB
Cleveland Container Service, Inc., 1160 Bridges Airport Rd., 28150, pg. 1379　PB
Fasco Controls Corporation, 1100 Airport Rd., 28150, pg. 125　IT
SHELBY YARN COMPANY, Hwy. 226, 28151-9000, pg. 991　PV
Specialty Lighting, Washburn Switch Rd., 28151-1680, pg. 821　IT

Siler City

Communication Cable (CCI)-Siler City, P.O. Box 729, 27344, pg. 968　PB
Palm Harbor Homes, 45 Industrial Pkwy., 27344, pg. 1255　PB

Smithfield

Casa Export Limited, P.O. Box 1334, 27577, pg. 1695　PV
CHANNEL MASTER, 1315 Industrial Park Dr., 27577, pg. 228　PB
K.R. Edwards Leaf Tobacco Co., Inc., P.O. Box 1337, 27577, pg. 1694　PB
Flanders Precisionaire, P.O. Box 22, 27577, pg. 648　PB
Universal Woods, Incorporated, P.O. Box 1337, 27577, pg. 1695　PB

Snow Hill

GSH Corp., 310 Kinggold Blvd., 28580, pg. 466　PV

Southern Pines

CF GROUP, P.O. Box 117, 28388, pg. 193　PV
Proctor-Silex, Southern Pines Operations, 575 Yadkin Rd., 28387, pg. 1149　PB

Sparta

Pioneer/Eclipse Corp., 3882 Chestnut Grove Church Rd., 28675, pg. 71　IT

Spencer

Tyco, 28159-0201, pg. 1058　PB

Spindale

Dan River Spindale Inc., 100 Spindale St., 28160, pg. 479　PB
Jameco Industries, Inc., 100 Watts Rd., 28160, pg. 1746　PB
Mitchell Co., 400 Spindale, 28160, pg. 1044　PV
Rutherford Warehouse Corp., Dallas St., 28160, pg. 1044　PV
STONECUTTER MILLS CORP., Dallas Street, 28160, pg. 1044　PV
Stonecutter Trucking Co., Dallas St., 28160, pg. 1044　PV

Spruce Pine

Hampshire Hosiery, Inc., P.O. Box 528, 103 Cross St., 28777, pg. 778　PB
OMC Spruce Pine, 1025 Greenwood Rd., 28777, pg. 478　PV
Suzorite Mineral Products, Inc., 790 Hwy. 226 S., 28777, pg. 1524　IT

Stanley

Dollinger/Technolab, Stanley Industrial Park, 1000 Hwy. 27, 28164, pg. 1676　PB
Queens Group North Carolina, Inc., 1101 Hwy. 27 S., 28164, pg. 900　PV

Star

CLAYSON KNITTING CO. INC., Hwy. 220 S., 27356, pg. 244　PV

Statesville

Bassett Furniture Industries of North Carolina Inc., 1010 S. Bury Rd., 28677, pg. 193　PB
Carris Reels, Inc.-North Carolina Plastics Div., 173 Orbit Rd., 28677, pg. 215　PV
Carris Reels, Inc.-North Carolina Wood Div., 1475 Winston Ave., 28677, pg. 215　PV
Eastern Region, Fanjoy Rd., #1820, 28677, pg. 687　PV

PB - *U.S. Public Companies Volume*
PV - *U.S. Private Companies Volume*
IT - *International Public & Private Companies Volume*

Fischbein Co., 151 Walker Rd., 28687, pg. 103 **PV**
KEWAUNEE SCIENTIFIC CORPORATION, 2700 W. Front St., 28677, pg. 953 **PB**
King Arthur Inc., P.O. Box 6040, 401 Meacham Rd., 28677, pg. 1465 **PB**
Motorola Radius, Rte. 1, 28677-9801, pg. 1138 **PB**
Paper Stock Dealers, Inc., P.O. Box 428, 28677, pg. 1486 **PB**
Park Newspapers of Iredell, Inc., P.O. Box 1071, 222 E. Broad St., 28677, pg. 1078 **PB**
Park Newspapers of Statesville, Inc., P.O. Box 1071, 222 E. Broad St., 28677, pg. 1078 **PB**
Rubbermaid-Statesville Inc., 3330 Taylorsville Rd., 28677, pg. 1411 **PB**
Sackner-Southeast Div., Rte. 16, Box 348, 28667, pg. 924 **PB**
Spicer Clark-Hurth, 1293 Glenway Dr., 28677, pg. 479 **PB**
Statesville Auto Auction, I-77 and Hwy. 21N, 28677, pg. 283 **PV**
Statesville Record and Landmark, P.O. Box 1071, 222 E. Broad St., 28677, pg. 1078 **PB**
Thonet, P.O. Box 5909, 28687, pg. 1465 **PB**
TOTER INCORPORATED, 841 Meacham Rd., 28687, pg. 1092 **PV**
Uniwood Div., Hwy. 90 & Taylorsville Rd., 28677, pg. 903 **PB**
Michael Weinig, Inc., P.O. Box 5009, 1931 Weinig St., 28677, pg. 1488 **IT**
Zimmer Patient Care Systems Division, 5601 Old Mountain Rd., 28677, pg. 254 **PB**

Stoneville

STONEVILLE FURNITURE CO. INC., 525 S. Henry St., 27048, pg. 1045 **PV**

Swannanoa

Beacon Mfg. Co., P.O. Box 395, 28778, pg. 1296 **PB**
Micromatic Operations (Swannanoa Plant), P.O. Box 548, U.S. 70 at Lytle Cove Rd., 28778, pg. 1590 **PB**

Swepsonville

Honda Power Equipment Manufacturing, Inc., Honda Drive, Hwy. 119, 27359, pg. 635 **IT**

Tabor City

Aberdeen Mfg. Corp. Savoy Plant, 8th & Wall St., 28463, pg. 1094 **PV**

Tarboro

BARNHILL CONTRACTING COMPANY, 2311 N. Main St., 27886, pg. 117 **PV**
CLR Corporation, P.O. Box 4000, 501 Daniel St., 27886-4000, pg. 579 **PB**
Caldwell Button Company, 501 Daniel St., 27886-4000, pg. 579 **PB**
Empire Industries, Inc., P.O. Box 4000, 501 Daniel St., 27886-4000, pg. 579 **PB**
GLENOIT MILLS, INC., 3001 N. Main St., 27886, pg. 456 **PV**
Long Equipment Co., 1201 Northern Blvd., 27886, pg. 675 **PV**
LONG MFG. NC, INC., 111 Fairview St., 27886, pg. 674 **PV**
ROYSTER-CLARK, INC., 409 Main St., 27886, pg. 949 **PV**
WCPS, 3403 Main St. N., 27886, pg. 297 **PV**

Thomasville

Davidson Nursing Center, Inc., 706 Pineywood Rd., 27360, pg. 1712 **PB**
FURNISHINGS INTERNATIONAL, INC., 1300 National Hwy., 27360, pg. 431 **PV**
Hydro Conduit Corp., P.O. Box 818, 208 Randolph St., 27361, pg. 246 **PV**
SHELBA D. JOHNSON TRUCKING, 1640 Blair St., 27361, pg. 594 **PV**
LifeStyle Furnishings International, Ltd., 1300 National Hwy., 27360, pg. 431 **PV**
Thomas Manufacturing Co., Inc. of Thomasville, 1024 Randolph St., 27360, pg. 1053 **PB**
Thomasville Furniture Industries, Inc., P.O. Box 339, 401 E. Main St., 27361-0339, pg. 688 **PB**

Timberlake

Roxboro Assembly Facility, 6400 Durham Rd., 27583, pg. 535 **IT**

Troutman

Engineered Sintered Components Company, 250 Old Murdock Rd., 28166, pg. 558 **PB**

Union Grove

CTR Manufacturing, Inc., 774 Zeb Rd., 28689, pg. 238 **PB**

Valdese

AWI Retail, 201 St. Germain St. SW., 28690, pg. 36 **PB**
Alba-Waldensian Export Corp., 201 St. Germain Ave. S.W., 28690, pg. 36 **PB**

ALBA-WALDENSIAN, INC., 201 St. Germain Ave. S.W., 28690, pg. 35 **PB**
BB&T Savings Bank, SSB, 224 Main St., 28690, pg. 160 **PB**
BURKE MILLS, INC., 191 Sterling St., 28690, pg. 267 **PB**
Hickory Hill Furniture Corporation, 501 Hoyle St., 28690, pg. 808 **PV**
Pilot Research Corp., P.O. Box 100, 28690, pg. 36 **PB**

Wake Forest

ATHEY PRODUCTS CORPORATION, 1839 South Main St., 27587, pg. 142 **PB**
The Body Shop Inc., 5036 Walter Kidde Rd., 27587, pg. 199 **IT**

Walnut Cove

Guardian Care of Walnut Cove, 508 Windmill St., 27052, pg. 1713 **PB**

Warsaw

CARROLL'S FOODS, INC., Hwy. 24 W., 28398, pg. 215 **PV**
National Spinning Co., P. O. Box 545, 28398, pg. 787 **PV**

Washington

FLANDERS CORP., 531 Flanders Filters Rd., 27889, pg. 648 **PB**
Flanders Filters, Inc., 531 Flanders Filters Rd., 27889, pg. 648 **PB**
FOUNTAIN POWERBOAT INDUSTRIES, INC., Whichards Beach Road, 27889-0457, pg. 678 **PB**
Fountain Sportswear, P.O. Box Drawer 457, Whichards Beach Rd., 27889-0457, pg. 679 **PB**
Hackney and Sons, Inc., 400 Hackney Ave., 27889, pg. 1097 **PV**
Hackney International, 400 Hackney Ave., 27889, pg. 1097 **PV**
National Spinning Co., P. O. Box 191, 27889, pg. 787 **PV**
Samson Apparel Corp., 418 Brown St., 27889, pg. 779 **PB**
TRANSPORTATION TECHNOLOGIES, INC., 400 Hackney Ave., 27889, pg. 1097 **PV**

Waynesville

WELLCO ENTERPRISES, INC., 150 Westwood Cir., 28786, pg. 1752 **PB**

Weaverville

A-B EMBLEM DIV. OF CONRAD INDUSTRIES, INC., P. O. Box 695, 28787, pg. 2 **PV**
A-B Emblems and Caps, P.O. Box 695, 28787, pg. 2 **PV**
Balcrank Products, One Balcrank Way, 38787, pg. 707 **PB**
Mount Vernon Mills, Inc., Mount Vernon Forming Fabrics, P.O. Box 607, 28787, pg. 835 **PV**
Sonopress, Inc., 108 Monticello Rd., 28787-9442, pg. 191 **IT**

Welcome

WALKER & ASSOCIATES, INC., 7129 Old Hwy. 52, 27374, pg. 1147 **PV**

Weldon

COASTAL LUMBER COMPANY, Green St. Extension, 27890, pg. 248 **PV**

Wendell

Micro Measurements Div., U.S. Hwy. 64, 27611, pg. 1722 **PB**
Photolastic Division, U.S. Hwy. 64, 27611, pg. 1722 **PB**
Vishay Instruments Div., U.S. Hwy. 64, 27611, pg. 1722 **PB**

Whiteville

BB&T Regional Headquarters, 127 W. Webster St., 28472, pg. 160 **PB**
National Spinning Co., P.O. Box 547, 28472, pg. 787 **PV**
Whiteville Apparel Corp., 800 Jefferson St., 28472, pg. 796 **PB**

Whitsett

Focke & Co., Inc., 5730 Millstream Rd., 27377, pg. 496 **IT**
Konica Manufacturing USA, Inc., 6900 Konica Dr., 27377, pg. 749 **IT**
Shionogi Qualicaps, Inc., 6505 Frank Warner Pkwy., 27377-9215, pg. 1235 **IT**

Wilkesboro

DML Industrial Div., 151 Lineberry, 28697, pg. 575 **PB**
ITHACA INDUSTRIES, INC., Hwy. 268 W., 28697, pg. 576 **PV**
Olympic Manufacturing Co., 314A Cothren St., 28697, pg. 200 **PV**

Wilmington

BLOCK INDUSTRIES, INC., 525 N. College Rd., 28405, pg. 150 **PV**
Concrete Service Co., P.O. Box 2176, 28402, pg. 166 **IT**
Dillard, A ResourceNet International Company, 4102 Emerson St., 28403, pg. 902 **PB**
Entrepreneur, Inc., Ten S. Cardinal Dr., 28403, pg. 1191 **PV**
Hillhaven Convalescent Center Wilmington, 2006 S. 16th St., 28401, pg. 1713 **PB**
IFI/Plenum Data Corporation, 102 Eastwood Rd., Ste. D6F, 28405, pg. 1311 **PB**
Mill & Contractors Supply, 410 Smith St., 28401, pg. 91 **PV**
MILLER BUILDING CORP., 1410 Commonwealth Dr., 28403, pg. 746 **PV**
PPD Pharmaco, 3151 S. 17th St., 28414, pg. 1285 **PB**
PHARMACEUTICAL PRODUCT DEVELOPMENT, INC., 3151 17th St. Ext., 28412, pg. 1285 **PB**
Queensboro Steel Corporation, 2925 U.S. Hwy. 421 N., 28401, pg. 1101 **PV**
Reeds Financial Services, Inc., 2515 S. 17th St., 28401, pg. 1370 **PB**
REEDS JEWELERS, INC., 2525 S. 7th St., 28401, pg. 1370 **PB**
Reeds Jewelers of North Carolina, Inc., 2525 S. 17th St., 28401, pg. 1370 **PB**
S&G Prestress Co., P.O. Box 540, 28402, pg. 656 **PB**
Scott & Stringfellow, Inc., 2425 S. 17th St., Ste. 100, 28401, pg. 1446 **PB**
Sprauge Energy Corp. Southeast Operations, 2250 Shipyard Blvd., Ste. 8, 28403-6070, pg. 710 **IT**
Takeda Chemical Products USA, Inc., 101 Takeda Dr., 28401, pg. 1350 **IT**
Tencarva Machinery Co., 108 N. Kerr Ave., Ste. K3, 28405, pg. 1076 **PV**
Welcome Home, Inc., 309D Raleigh St., 28412, pg. 598 **PV**
Wholesale Glass Fabricators Inc., 1380 N. Kerr Ave., 28405, pg. 616 **IT**
Wilmington Morning Star, 1003 S. 17th St., 28401, pg. 1175 **PB**
Wilmington Star-News, Inc., 1003 S. 17th St., 28401, pg. 1175 **PB**
WORSLEY COMPANIES INC., Ten S. Cardinal Dr., 28406, pg. 1191 **PV**

Wilson

W.A. Adams, Inc., 2201 Miller Rd., 27893, pg. 1502 **PB**
Bridgestone/Firestone Tire Manufacturing Operations-Wilson, Firestone Pkwy., 27893, pg. 213 **IT**
Cott Corporation - Mid-Atlantic Region, 4843 Novopharm Boulevard, 27893, pg. 338 **IT**
GNC Corp, 2600 Wilco Blvd., 27893, pg. 466 **PV**
Hydro Conduit Corp., P.O. Box 759, 1509 South Ward Blvd., 27894, pg. 246 **IT**
Kidde Technologies, Inc., 2500 Airport Dr., 27893, pg. 1500 **IT**
Kidde Technologies Inc. (Walter Kidde Aerospace), 2500 Airport Dr., 27893, pg. 1500 **IT**
MELLOBUTTERCUP ICE CREAM INC., 400 S. Douglas St., 27893-4918, pg. 730 **PV**
Nucor Bearing Products, Inc., 2401 Stantonsburg Rd., 27893, pg. 1206 **PB**
Porritts & Spencer Inc., P.O. Box 1411, 3040 Black Creek Rd., 27893, pg. 1202 **IT**
Samson Manufacturing Corp., 1007 Herring Ave., 27822, pg. 779 **PB**
Stancom Home Center, Inc., P.O. Box 1929, 605 S. Tarboro St., 27893, pg. 1502 **PB**
STANDARD COMMERCIAL CORPORATION, 2201 Miller Rd., 27893, pg. 1501 **PB**
Supreme Murphy Corp., 4000 Airport Dr., N.W., 27893, pg. 1542 **PB**
Wilson Convalescent Center, 403 Crestview Ave., 27893, pg. 1715 **PB**
Wilson Service Center, 2711 Commerce Rd., 27893, pg. 214 **PV**

Windsor

LEA LUMBER & PLYWOOD LLC, 412 Hoggard Mill Rd., 27983-8092, pg. 655 **PV**

Winston Salem

Alliance Display & Packaging, 5921 Grassy Creek Blvd., 27105, pg. 1397 **PB**
American Inks & Coatings Corp., Ink Division, 3755 Kimwell Dr., 27103, pg. 56 **PB**
AMP Inc. Lytel Division, 3441 Myer Lee Dr., 27101-6209, pg. 8 **PV**
Arjay Equipment Corporation, Plaza Bldg., 401 N. Main St., 14th Fl., 27102, pg. 1355 **PV**
Arjay Holdings, Inc., Plaza Bldg., 401 N. 14th St., 14th Fl., 27102, pg. 1355 **PB**
BB&T CORPORATION, 200 W. Second St., 27101, pg. 159 **PB**
B/E Aerospace Seating Products, 1455 Fairchild Rd., 27105-4588, pg. 159 **PB**
Bali Company, 3330 Healy Dr., 27103, pg. 1433 **PB**
D.D. Bean & Sons (N.C.) Inc., P.O. Box N93, 27115, pg. 127 **PV**
BEPCO, INC., 2475 S. Stratford Rd., 27103, pg. 134 **PV**
Branch Banking & Trust, 200 W. 2nd St., 27101, pg. 160 **PB**

PB - *U.S. Public Companies Volume*
PV - *U.S. Private Companies Volume*
IT - *International Public & Private Companies Volume*

1373

Geographic Index-U.S.

Carolina Steel-Salem Plant, 1725 Vargrave St., 27107, pg. 214 **PV**
Champion Products, 475 Corporate Square Dr., 27105, pg. 1433 **PB**
Champion Products Inc., 475 Corporate Sq. Dr., 27105, pg. 1433 **PB**
Charter Behavioral Health System of Winston-Salem, Inc., 3637 Old Vinyard Rd., 27104, pg. 1034 **PB**
Chesapeake Display and Packaging Co., 555 Aureole St., 27117, pg. 346 **PB**
Dairy Fresh, Inc., 2221 Patterson Ave., 27015, pg. 1527 **PV**
Dillard, A ResourceNet International Company, 3840 Kimwell Dr., 27114, pg. 902 **PB**
EFG Technologies, Inc., 240 Reynolds Blvd., 27102, pg. 1679 **PB**
GATX Logistics (LWD), Inc., 3334 Healey Dr., Ste. 202, 27103, pg. 691 **PB**
Hanes Companies, Inc., 2000 W. First St., 27104, pg. 986 **PB**
Hanes Hosiery, Inc., 5650 University Pkwy., 27105, pg. 1434 **PB**
Ilco Unican Corp., Safelock Division, 2941 Indiana Ave., 27105, pg. 1432 **IT**
Ilco Unican Corp., Simplex Access Controls Division, 2941 Indiana Ave., 27105, pg. 1432 **IT**
The Innovative Company, P.O. Box 25687, 27107, pg. 1454 **PB**
Integon Casualty Insurance Company, 500 W. Fifth, 27152, pg. 720 **PB**
Integon Corporation, 500 W. Fifth St., 27152, pg. 719 **PB**
Integon General Insurance Corporation, 500 W. Fifth St., 27152, pg. 720 **PB**
Integon Indemnity Corporation, 500 W. Fifth St., 27152, pg. 720 **PB**
Integon National Insurance Co., 500 W. Fifth St., 27152, pg. 720 **PB**
Integon Preferred Insurance Company, 500 W. Fifth St., 27152, pg. 720 **PB**
Integon Specialty Insurance Company, 500 W. Fifth St., 27152, pg. 720 **PB**
Knollwood Hall, 5755 Shattalon Dr., P.O. Box 11907, 27106, pg. 1714 **PB**
Laboratory Supply Company, 112 Griffith Plaza Dr., 27103, pg. 642 **PV**
L'eggs Products, Inc., 5660 University Pkwy., 27105, pg. 1434 **PB**
Lofts Seed, Inc., P.O. Box 26223, 2325 S. Stratford Rd., 27114, pg. 29 **PB**
Long Haymes Carr, Inc., 140 Charlois Blvd., 27103, pg. 909 **PB**
Lowe's Food Stores, Inc., 1381 Old Mill Cir., Ste. 200, 14908, pg. 657 **PV**
LUWA BAHNSON, INC., 3901 West Point Blvd., 27103, pg. 682 **PV**
New South Insurance Company, 500 W. Fifth St., 27152, pg. 720 **PB**
PACE OIL CO., INC., 150 Stratford Court SW, 27103, pg. 829 **PV**
PARRISH TIRE COMPANY, INC., 5130 Indiana Ave., 27102, pg. 840 **PV**
Penn Engineering & Manufacturing Corp. North Carolina Div., 1000 Kapp, 27105, pg. 1270 **PB**
Piedmont Publishing Co., Inc., 418 N. Marshall St., 27102, pg. 1079 **PB**
Premium Budget Plan, Inc., P.O. Box 25687, 27107, pg. 1453 **PB**
RJR Tobacco Company, Inc., P.O. Box 2959, 27102, pg. 1355 **PB**
R.J. Reynolds, Inc., 401 N. Main St., 27102, pg. 1355 **PB**
R.J. Reynolds Tobacco Company, 401 N. Main St., 27102, pg. 1355 **PB**
R.J. Reynolds Tobacco International (Mexico) Inc., P.O. Box 2959, 27102, pg. 1355 **PB**
Salem Carpet Mills, Inc., NCNB Plaza, Ste. 1100, 27102, pg. 1464 **PV**
Salem Carriers. Inc., 245 Charlois Blvd., 27103, pg. 962 **PV**
Salem Leasing Corp., 245 Charlois Blvd., 27103, pg. 962 **PV**
SALEM NATIONAL CORPORATION, 245 Charlois Blvd., 27103, pg. 962 **PV**
Sara Lee Direct, 450 W. Hanes Mill Rd., 27105, pg. 1434 **PB**
Sara Lee Hosiery, 5660 University Pkwy., 27105, pg. 1434 **PB**
Sara Lee Intimates, 3330 Healy Dr., 27103, pg. 1434 **PB**
Sara Lee Knit Products, 1000 E. Hanes Mill Rd., 27105, pg. 1434 **PB**
Sara Lee Personal Products, 470 W. Hanes Mill Rd., 27105, pg. 1434 **PB**
Scott & Stringfellow, Inc., 514 S. Stratford Rd., 27103, pg. 1446 **PB**
Shorewood Packaging Corporation of Virginia, 230 Town Run Ln., 27101-3911, pg. 1468 **PB**
Silas Creek Manor, 3350 Silas Creek Pkwy., 27103, pg. 1714 **PB**
Taracorp Imaco, Inc., 1690 Lowery St., 27101, pg. 1068 **PV**
Taylor Bros., 2415 Stratford Rd., S.W., 27103-0597, pg. 272 **PV**
TAYLOR OIL CO. INC., 110 Oakwood Dr., 27103, pg. 1071 **PV**
Universal Insurance Co., 595 Wallingtown St., 21107-2270, pg. 1454 **PB**
Vulcan Materials Company-Mideast Div., 4401 N. Patterson Ave., 27105, pg. 1725 **PB**
WSJS, 875 W. 5th St., 27101, pg. 385 **PB**
WTQR, 875 W. 5th St., 27101, pg. 385 **PB**
WXII-AM, 700 Coliseum Dr., 27116, pg. 1344 **PB**
WXII-TV, 700 Coliseum Dr., 27116-5356, pg. 1344 **PB**

WXRA, 875 W. 5th St., 27101, pg. 385 **PB**
Wachovia Bank of North Carolina, N.A., 100 N. Main St., 27101, pg. 1730 **PB**
WACHOVIA CORPORATION, 100 N. Main St., 27150, pg. 1730 **PB**
Wachovia International Banking Corp., 100 N. Main St., 27101, pg. 1730 **PB**
Wachovia Investments, Inc., 100 N. Main St., 27101, pg. 1730 **PB**
Wachovia Leasing Corporation, 100 N. Main St., 27101, pg. 1731 **PB**
Wachovia Mortgage Co., 301 N. Main St., 27101, pg. 1731 **PB**
Winston Leaf Tobacco Co., P.O. Box 2499, 27102, pg. 1695 **PB**
Winston-Salem Convalescent Center, 1900 W. First St., 27104, pg. 1715 **PB**
Zeneca Specialty Inks, 120 Regent Dr., 27103, pg. 1525 **IT**

Wrightsville Beach

LaQue Center for Corrosion Technology, Inc., P.O. Box 656 28480, pg. 672 **IT**

Youngsville

CAPTIVE-AIRE SYSTEMS, INC., 112 Wheaton Dr., 27596, pg. 207 **PV**

Zebulon

Glaxo Wellcome Inc., P.O. Box 1217, 1011 No. Arendell Ave., 27597, pg. 552 **IT**
Guardian Care of Zebulon, 509 W. Gannon Ave., 27597, pg. 713 **PB**
NOMACO, INC., 501 NMC Dr., 27597, pg. 801 **PV**

NORTH DAKOTA

Beulah

The Coteau Properties Co., HC3, Box 49, 58523, pg. 149 **PB**

Bismarck

BNI Coal, Ltd., 1126 W. Divide, 58501, pg. 1116 **PB**
BANK OF NORTH DAKOTA, 700 E. Main Ave., 58502, pg. 114 **PV**
Basin Co-Operative Services, 1717 E. Interstate Ave., 585C1-0564, pg. 121 **PV**
BASIN ELECTRIC POWER COOPERATIVE, 1717 E. Interstate Ave., 58501-0564, pg. 121 **PV**
Basin Telecommunication, Inc., 1717 E. Interstate Ave., 585C1-0564, pg. 121 **PV**
The Bismarck Tribune, 707 E. Front Ave., 58501, pg. 983 **PB**
Centennial Energy Holdings, Inc., 400 N. Fourth St., 58501-4092, pg. 1025 **PB**
Dakota Coal Company, 1717 E. Interstate Ave., 58501-0564, pg. 121 **PV**
Dakota Gasification Co., 1600 E. Interstate Ave., 58501-0564, pg. 121 **PV**
Fargo Glass & Paint Co, 1202 Airport Rd., 58504, pg. 393 **PV**
Fidelity Oil Co., 3333 E. Broadway., Ste. 1212, 58501, pg. 1025 **PB**
Fidelity Oil Holdings, Inc., 3333 E. Broadway., Ste. 1212, 58501, pg. 1025 **PB**
Knife River Coal Mining Company, 1915 N. Kavaney Dr., 58501-1698, pg. 1025 **PB**
MDU RESOURCES GROUP, INC., 400 N. Fourth St., 5850 -4092, pg. 1025 **PB**
MEYER BROADCASTING COMPANY, 200 Fourth St. N., 58502, pg. 739 **PV**
Montana-Dakota Utilities Co., 400 N. Fourth St., 58501-4092, pg. 1025 **PB**
Piper Jaffray Inc., Norwest Bank Bldg., 400 E. Broadway Ave., 58501-4038, pg. 1301 **PB**
Prairielands Energy Marketing, Inc., 3333 E. Broadway., Ste. -215, 58501-3395, pg. 1025 **PV**
SuperValu, Inc.-Bismarck Div., 707 Airport Rd., 58501, pg. 1540 **PB**
Williston Basin Interstate Pipeline Company, 200 N. Third St., Ste. 300, 58501-3875, pg. 1026 **PV**

Devils Lake

Devils Lake Journal, 516 4th St., 58301, pg. 1078 **PB**
Midwest Sanitation, Inc., Hwy. 2 West, 58301, pg. 1686 **PB**

Dickinson

Williams Steel & Supply, 124 East 24th St., 58601, pg. 1178 **PV**

Fargo

BORDER STATES INDUSTRIES, INC., 105 25th St. N., 58102-4030, pg. 160 **PV**
BORDER STATES PAVING, INC., Cass County Rd. 20, 58108, pg. 160 **PV**
CASS-CLAY CREAMERY, 1220 Main Ave., 58108, pg. 219 **PV**
COLE PAPERS INC., 1300 38th St., N., 58108, pg. 251 **PV**

COMMUNITY FIRST BANKSHARES, INC., 520 Main Ave., 58124-0001, pg. 416 **PB**
de Lendrecie's, West Acres, 58103, pg. 1090 **PB**
FARGO GLASS & PAINT COMPANY, 1801 Seventh Ave. N., 58102, pg. 393 **PV**
Farm Credit Council Services, 1749 38th St. S.W., 58103-4442, pg. 398 **PV**
First Trust Company of North Dakota, National Association, P.O. Box 1980, 505 Second Ave. N., 58102, pg. 1681 **PB**
FORUM COMMUNICATIONS COMPANY, P.O. Box 2020, 58107, pg. 420 **PV**
ROBERT GIBB & SONS, INC., 205 40th St. S.W., 58103, pg. 451 **PV**
Health Ventures, 737 Broadway, 58123, pg. 733 **PV**
HealthCare Accessories, 737 Broadway, 58124, pg. 733 **PV**
Hornbachers, 2510 Broadway N., 58102, pg. 1541 **PB**
ICI Seeds, P.O. Box 307, 20 Fourth Ave., S., 58103, pg. 1524 **IT**
Melroe Company, 112 N. University Dr., 58102, pg. 877 **PB**
MeritCare Foundation, 737 Broadway, 58123, pg. 733 **PV**
MERITCARE HEALTH SYSTEM, 737 Broadway, 58123, pg. 733 **PV**
MeritCare Hospital, 737 Broadway, 58123, pg. 733 **PV**
MeritCare Medical Group, 737 Broadway, 58123, pg. 733 **PV**
MID AMERICA STEEL, INC., 92 N.P. Ave., 58102, pg. 743 **PV**
NODAK MUTUAL INSURANCE COMPANY, 1101 First Ave., N., 58102, pg. 800 **PV**
Northern Plains Steel Co., 3801 15th Ave. N., pg. 824 **PV**
Norwest Bank North Dakota, N.A., Fourth & Main, 58126, pg. 1202 **PB**
R.D. OFFIT COMPANY, P.O. Box 7160, 58109, pg. 812 **PV**
PIONEER MUTUAL LIFE INSURANCE COMPANY, 203 10th St., N., 58102, pg. 866 **PV**
Piper Jaffray Inc., 51 Broadway, 58102-4970, pg. 1301 **PB**
RCB BAKING COMPANY, 1301 39th St. N., 58102, pg. 1354 **PV**
ROTT-KELLER SUPPLY CO., 65 28th St. S., 58103-0390, pg. 947 **PV**
Steiger Tractor, 3401 1st Ave. No., 58102, pg. 311 **PV**
SuperValu, Inc.-Fargo Div., 3501 12th Ave. N., 58102, pg. 1540 **PB**
Valley Imports, 4001 W. Main, 58107, pg. 1148 **PV**
W.W. WALLWORK, INC., 4001 W. Main, 58103, pg. 1148 **PV**
Wallwork Lease, P.O. Box 1819, 58107, pg. 1148 **PV**

Finley

FINLEY FARMERS GRAIN & ELEVATOR COMPANY, Burlington Northern Right-of-Way, 58230, pg. 405 **PV**

Fort Totten

SIOUX MANUFACTURING CORP., P.O. Box 400, 58335, pg. 1003 **PV**

Grand Forks

AGSCO, INC., 2600 Mill Rd., 58203, pg. 27 **PV**
American West Insurance Company, 2100 Library Cir., 58208, pg. 216 **PV**
Farm Credit Council Services, 2424 32nd Ave. S., 58201-6545, pg. 398 **PV**
First American Bank Valley, P.O. Box 13118, 31 S. Columbia Rd., 58208, pg. 167 **PV**
Grand Forks Herald, Incorporated, 303 Second Ave. N., 58201, pg. 964 **PB**
MINN-DAK GROWERS, LTD., P.O. Box 13276, 58208-3276, pg. 750 **PV**
MINNKOTA POWER COOPERATIVE, INC., 1822 Mill Rd., 58203, pg. 751 **PV**
NSP-North Debate Region, 1206 Fifth Ave., 58201, pg. 1195 **PB**
NODAK ELECTRIC CO-OP, 4000 32 Ave. N., 58208-3000, pg. 800 **PV**
NORTH DAKOTA MILL & ELEVATOR ASSOCIATION, 1823 Mill Rd., 58208, pg. 804 **PV**
Pest Elimination, P.O. Box 1718, 58201, pg. 562 **PB**
Piper Jaffray Inc., 1515 S. Washington St., 58201, pg. 1301 **PB**
Square Butte Electric Cooperative, 1822 Mill Rd., 58203, pg. 751 **PV**

Jamestown

Lucas Aerospace Cargo Systems, 2604 Hwy. 20 N., 58401, pg. 820 **IT**

Lisbon

First American Bank North Dakota, P.O. Box 273, 58054, pg. 167 **PV**

Minot

DAKCO DISTRIBUTORS, INC., 101 E. Central, 58701, pg. 308 **PV**
Dakota Drug, Inc., 28 N. Main St., 58701, pg. 308 **PV**
Fargo Glass & Paint Co., 1811 20th Ave., S.E., 58701, pg. 393 **PV**
First American Bank West, 21st S.W., 58701, pg. 167 **PV**
MINOT BUILDERS SUPPLY ASSOCIATION, 2626 Burdick Expwy., W., 58701, pg. 751 **PV**

PB - *U.S. Public Companies Volume*
PV - *U.S. Private Companies Volume*
IT - *International Public & Private Companies Volume*

1374

Geographic Index-U.S.

Northland Sports Inc., 308 8th St. NE, 58701, pg. 1026 **PV**
Southern Gas Company, 1801 Burdick Expwy. West, 58701, pg. 203 **PB**
Vision Energy Minnesota, Inc., 1801 Burdick Expwy. W., 58701, pg. 203 **PB**
Vision Energy Wisconsin, Inc., 1801 Burdick Expwy. W., 58701, pg. 203 **PB**
Werners, Inc., 1801 Burdick Expwy. W., 58701, pg. 203 **PB**
WESTLIE MOTOR COMPANY, 500 S. Broadway, 58702, pg. 1169 **PV**
WHOLESALE SUPPLY COMPANY, INC., P.O. Box 1948, 3500 Burdick Expwy., E., 58701, pg. 1174 **PV**

Nome

Inter-Community Telephone Company, P.O. Box A, 58062, pg. 1022 **PB**

Oakes

KBC Trading & Processes, 524 S. 7th St., 58474, pg. 428 **PB**

Richardton

Richardton Mfg. Co., First St., S., P.O. Box 290, 58652, pg. 1676 **PB**

Rugby

RUGBY FARMERS UNION ELEVATOR COMPANY, Box 286, 105 E. Dewey St., 58368, pg. 950 **PV**

Underwood

The Falkirk Mining Co., P.O. Box 1087, 58576, pg. 1149 **PB**

Valley City

Integrated Technical Systems (ITS), Valley City Industrial Park, P.O. Box 577, 58072, pg. 311 **PB**

Wahpeton

Blumhardt Manufacturing Company, W. Hwy. 13, 58075, pg. 1063 **PV**
ProGold, 18049 City Rd. 8E, 58075, pg. 53 **PV**
Wil-Rich Noble Company, W. Hwy 13, 58075, pg. 1064 **PV**

West Fargo

Clarklift of North Dakota, 1734 E. Main, 58078, pg. 244 **PV**
Federal Beef Processors North, 750 9th St. N.W., 58074, pg. 435 **PV**
INTERSTATE PAYCO SEED COMPANY, 1215 Prairie Pkwy., 58078, pg. 573 **PV**

OHIO

Ada

Wilson Sporting Goods Co., 217 N. Liberty St., 45810, pg. 73 **IT**

Akron

ASI Investments Holding Co., 3550 W. Market St., 44333, pg. 1441 **PB**
AT&T Communications, 48 W. Bowery St., 44308-1102, pg. 10 **PB**
Admiral Equipment Co., 307 W. North St., 44303, pg. 522 **PB**
AKROCHEM CORPORATION, 255 Fountain St., 44304-1991, pg. 30 **PV**
Akron Standard Division, 1624 Englewood, 44305, pg. 865 **PB**
Akzo Salt Inc., 2065 Manchester Rd., 44314, pg. 48 **IT**
THE FRED W. ALBRECHT GROCERY CO., 2700 Gilchrest Rd., 44305, pg. 32 **PV**
Albrecht Inc., 2850 Gilcrest Rd., 44305, pg. 32 **PV**
American Beverage Corp. Inc., 68 West Waterloo Rd., 44314, pg. 752 **IT**
The Beacon Journal Publishing Company, 44 E. Exchange St., 44328, pg. 963 **PB**
Bekaert Corporation, 3200 W. Market St., Ste. 303, 44313, pg. 184 **IT**
BillCom Akron, 341 White Pond Rd., 44320, pg. 1446 **IT**
Bridgestone/Firestone Information Services Company, 1655 S. Main St., 44317, pg. 213 **IT**
Bridgestone/Firestone Research Laboratories, S. Main St. & Wilbeth, 44317, pg. 213 **IT**
Bridgestone/Firestone Technology Company, 1200 Firestone Pkwy., 44317, pg. 213 **IT**
Caliber System, Inc., 3569 Embassy Pkwy., 44333, pg. 604 **PB**
THE CEDARWOOD CONSTRUCTION COMPANY, 1765 Merriman Rd., 44313, pg. 221 **PV**
Chempower, Inc., 807 E. Turkeyfoot Lake Rd., 44319, pg. 74 **IT**
The Coca-Cola Bottling Co. of Northern Ohio, 1560 Triplett Blvd., 44306, pg. 393 **PB**
Com Alloy International Company, 3550 W. Market St., 44333, pg. 1441 **PB**

COMMAND PLASTIC CORPORATION, 674 Carroll St., 44304, pg. 257 **PV**
THE CYPRESS COMPANIES, 670 W. Market St., 44303, pg. 299 **PV**
Diet Center Worldwide, Inc., The Franchise Support Center, 395 Springside Dr., 44333-2496, pg. 864 **PV**
Diet Center Worldwide, Inc., 395 Springside Dr., 44333, pg. 864 **PV**
Earth Sciences Consultants, Inc. (Ohio Opers.), 190 N. Union St., Ste. 301, 44304, pg. 94 **PB**
FBOH Credit Life Insurance Co., 106 S. Main St., 44308, pg. 647 **PB**
Firestone Synthetic Rubber & Latex Co., 381 W. Wilbeth Rd., 44301, pg. 214 **IT**
First National Bank of Ohio, 106 S. Main St., 44308, pg. 646 **PB**
FIRSTENERGY CORP., 76 S. Main St., 18th Fl., 44308-1890, pg. 644 **PB**
FIRSTMERIT CORPORATION, III Cascade Plaza, 5th Fl., 44308-1103, pg. 646 **PB**
FORM-YOU-3 INTERNATIONAL, INC., 395 Springside Dr., 44333, pg. 418 **PV**
General Tire Intl. Co., One General St., 44329, pg. 327 **IT**
Gilcrest Storage, 2700 Gilcrest Rd., 44305, pg. 32 **PV**
Global Erectors, 807 State Rte. 619, 44319, pg. 74 **IT**
B.F. Goodrich Aerospace, P.O. Box 5501, 250 N. Cleveland-Massillon Rd., 44334, pg. 751 **PB**
Goodyear Rubber Plantations, 1144 E. Market St., Ste. 956, 44316, pg. 753 **PB**
THE GOODYEAR TIRE & RUBBER COMPANY, 1144 E. Market St., 44316-0001, pg. 752 **PB**
Hamlin Steel Products, 2471 Wingate Ave., 44314, pg. 299 **PV**
HARWICK STANDARD DISTRIBUTION CORPORATION, 60 S. Seiberling St., 44305, pg. 509 **PV**
Hewlett-Packard Company, 2717 S. Arlington Rd., 44312, pg. 815 **PB**
Hillhaven Convalescent Center Akron, 145 Olive St., 44310, pg. 1713 **PB**
The Imperial Electric Company, P.O. Box 309, 84 Ira Ave., 44309, pg. 598 **PV**
Jobber Retailer, 341 White Pond Rd., 44320, pg. 1446 **IT**
Ken Tool, 768 E. North St., pg. 1050 **PV**
Koch Engineering Company, Inc., 171 Kelly Ave., 44306, pg. 628 **PV**
Lockheed Martin Tactical Defense Systems (Akron), 1210 Massillon Rd., 44315, pg. 1009 **PB**
MALONE ADVERTISING, INC., 209 S. Main St., 44308, pg. 698 **PV**
Manchester Tool Company, 5142 Manchester Rd., 44319, pg. 617 **PB**
MCNEIL & NRM., INC., 96 E. Crosier St., 44311, pg. 725 **PV**
Modern Tire Dealer, 341 White Pond Rd., 44320, pg. 1446 **IT**
MYERS INDUSTRIES, INC., 1293 S. Main St., 44301, pg. 1143 **PB**
Myers International, Inc., 1293 S. Main St., 44301, pg. 1143 **PB**
Myers Tire Supply Company, 1293 S. Main St., 44301, pg. 1143 **PB**
OES Capital, Inc., 76 S. Main St., 44308, pg. 645 **PB**
OES Fuel, Incorporated, 76 S. Main St., 44308, pg. 645 **PB**
Ohio Edison Company, 76 S. Main St., 18th Fl., 44308-1890, pg. 645 **PB**
Osterman's Inc., 375 Ghent Rd., 44313, pg. 1248 **IT**
PHYSICIANS WEIGHT LOSS CENTERS, INC., 395 Springside Dr., 44333-2496, pg. 864 **PV**
Plastics News, 1725 Merriman Rd., Ste. 300, 44313-5251, pg. 285 **PV**
Pneumatic Scale-Akron, Ten Ascot Pkwy., 44223, pg. 118 **PV**
RAV Construction Company, 1063 S. Broadway St., 44311, pg. 586 **PV**
R.C.A. RUBBER COMPANY, 1833 E. Market St., 44305, pg. 902 **PV**
Reiter Dairy, Inc., 1415 W. Waterloo Rd., 44314, pg. 491 **PB**
Republic Chemical Company, 60 S. Seiberling St., 44305, pg. 509 **PV**
THE RESERVE GROUP, 3560 W. Market St., Ste. 300, 44333, pg. 924 **PV**
Resource America Field & Accounting Operations Headquarters, 2876 South Arlington Rd., 44312, pg. 1382 **PB**
ROADWAY EXPRESS, INC., 1077 Gorge Blvd., 44310, pg. 1392 **PB**
Roberts Express, Inc., 2096 S. Arlington, 44306, pg. 604 **PB**
J.B. Robinson Jewelers, Inc., 375 Ghent Rd., 44333, pg. 1248 **IT**
Rubber & Plastics News, 1725 Merriman Rd., Ste. 300, 44313-5251, pg. 285 **PV**
SCHUBERT INDUSTRIES INC., 1510 Bauer Rd., 44305, pg. 973 **PV**
A. SCHULMAN, INC., 3550 W. Market St., 44333, pg. 1441 **PB**
Sealright Mfg. East, Inc., 1972 Akron Peninsula Rd., 44313, pg. 1452 **PB**
Sovereign Engineered Adhesive, 123 W. Bartges St., 44311-1081, pg. 1019 **PV**
The Springwall Mattress Co., 1510 Bauer Blvd., 44305, pg. 973 **PV**
Steelastic Co., 1557 Industrial Pkwy., 44319, pg. 860 **PV**
Sterling Inc., 375 Ghent Rd., 44333, pg. 1248 **IT**
Sterling Jewelers, Inc., 375 Ghent Rd., 44333, pg. 1248 **IT**
SUMMIT TOOL COMPANY, P.O. Box 9320, 44305, pg. 1050 **PV**

TLT-Babcock, Inc., 3480 W. Market St., 44333, pg. 401 **IT**
TELXON CORPORATION, 3330 W. Market St., 44333, pg. 1573 **PB**
Tire Business, 1725 Merriman Rd., Ste. 300, 44313-5251, pg. 285 **PV**
Uniroyal Chemical Co., Inc., 1745 Merriman Rd., 44313, pg. 460 **PB**
The Westhall Co., 375 Ghent Rd., 44313, pg. 1248 **IT**
Yokohama Corporation of North America, 3560 W. Market St., 44333, pg. 1521 **IT**
Zellerbach Division, 760 Killian Rd., 44319, pg. 1075 **PB**

Alliance

Canterbury Villa of Alliance, 1785 S. Freshley Ave., 44601, pg. 838 **PB**
The Genie Company, 22790 Lakepark Blvd., 44601, pg. 823 **PV**
Horizon Meadows, 1495 Freshley Ave., 44601, pg. 838 **PB**
A.J. Oster Foils, Inc., 2081 McCrea St., 44601, pg. 1219 **PB**
STAR BRONZE COMPANY, 803 S. Mahoning St., 44601, pg. 1034 **PV**
U.S. Can Company, P.O. Box 2906, 44601, pg. 1681 **PB**

Amelia

American Family Home Insurance Co., 7000 Midland Blvd., 45102, pg. 1110 **PB**
American Modern Home Insurance Co., 7000 Midland Blvd., 45102, pg. 1110 **PB**
American Modern Home Insurance Group, 7000 Midland Blvd., 45102, pg. 1110 **PB**
M/G Transportation Services, Inc., 7000 Midland Blvd., 45102, pg. 1111 **PB**
Main Life Insurance Co., 7000 Midland Blvd., 45102, pg. 1111 **PB**
Midland Guardian Co., 7000 Midland Blvd., 45102, pg. 1111 **PB**

Amherst

Amherst Metal Products, Inc., Box 123, Oberlin Rd., 44001, pg. 169 **PV**
Ed Mullinax Ford, Inc., P.O. Box 280, 44001, pg. 1379 **PB**
Nordson Corporation, 555 Jackson St., 44001, pg. 1188 **PB**
Nordson Pacific South Div., 100 Nordson Dr., 44001, pg. 1188 **PB**

Arcadia

Arcadia Telephone Co., 102 W. Freemont St., P.O. Box 157, 44804, pg. 1571 **PB**

Archbold

ARROW TRU-LINE, INC., Route 66 South, 43502, pg. 85 **PV**
Bil-Jax Inc., 125 Taylor Pkwy., 43502, pg. 1061 **IT**
Frozen Specialties, Inc., 720 Barre Rd., 43502, pg. 378 **PV**
SAUDER MANUFACTURING CORPORATION, 930 W. Barre Rd., 43502, pg. 967 **PV**
SAUDER WOODWORKING CO., 502 Middle St., 43502, pg. 967 **PV**

Ashland

Abbott Laboratories/Ashland, 268 E. Fourth St., 44805, pg. 13 **PB**
Aplex Industries Inc., 1101 Myers Pkwy., 44805-1969, pg. 1273 **PB**
The Garber Company, 600 Union St., 44805, pg. 303 **PB**
General Latex & Chemical Corp (Ohio), P.O. Box 498, 44805, pg. 444 **PV**
Hedstrom Corp., 710 Orange St., 44805, pg. 526 **PV**
Hess & Clark Company, 10 E. 7th St., 44805, pg. 426 **PB**
Hydromatic Pumps, 1840 Baney Rd., 44805, pg. 726 **PB**
Liqui-Box Corp., 1817 Masters Ave., 44805, pg. 1000 **PB**
F.E. Myers, 1101 Myers Pkwy., 44805-1969, pg. 1273 **PB**
THE NATIONAL LATEX PRODUCTS CO., 246 E. Fourth St., 44805, pg. 785 **PV**
PHILWAY PRODUCTS, INC., 701 Virginia Ave., 44805, pg. 862 **PV**
WIL Research Laboratories, Inc., 44805, pg. 760 **PB**

Ashtabula

Dart Trucking Company, Inc., 615 E. Sixth St., 44004, pg. 94 **PB**
Detrex General Chemicals & Solvents Div., P.O. Box 1398, 44004, pg. 501 **PB**
Elkem-American Carbide Company (Ashtabula), P.O. Box 1040, 2700 Lake Rd. E., 44004-1040, pg. 33 **PB**
Elkem Ashtabula (Calcium Carbides), P.O. Box 40, 44004, pg. 447 **IT**
MOLDED FIBER GLASS COMPANIES, 1601 W. 29th St., 44005-0675, pg. 755 **PV**
Peoples Savings Bank of Ashtabula, 4200 Park Ave., 44004, pg. 647 **PB**
SCM CHEM Colors & Silica Div., P.O. Box 160, 2426 Middle Rd., 44004-3918, pg. 594 **IT**

Ashville

Reynolds Metals Company-Ashville, 1 Reynolds Rd., 43103, pg. 1385 **PB**

PB - *U.S. Public Companies Volume*
PV - *U.S. Private Companies Volume*
IT - *International Public & Private Companies Volume*

Aurora

Defontaine/Inc., 1400 South Chillicothe Rd., 44202, pg. 509   **IT**
Dekoron Division, 1199 S. Chillicothe Rd., 44202, pg. 689   **IT**
Krupp Hoesch Stahlexport GmbH, 1400 S. Chillicothe Rd., 44202, pg. 515   **IT**
Macromeric Division, 1395 Danner Dr., 44202, pg. 689   **PB**
Rotek Incorporated, 1400 South Chillicothe Rd., 44202, pg. 509   **IT**
Sea World of Ohio, 1100 Sea World Dr., 44202, pg. 114   **PB**

Avon

Aircraft Wheel & Brake Div., 1160 Center Rd., 44011-1297, pg. 1262   **PB**
FREEMAN MANUFACTURING & SUPPLY COMPANY, 1101 Moore Rd., 44011, pg. 426   **PV**

Avon Lake

DIWIDAG Systems International, USA, Inc., 376 Creekside Dr., 44012, pg. 424   **IT**
GL Direct, 33625 Pin Oak Pkwy., 44012-2320, pg. 475   **PV**
THE GEON COMPANY, One Geon Center, 44012, pg. 733   **PB**

Baltic

Baltic Country Manor, 130 Buena Vista St., 43804, pg. 838   **PB**

Barberton

Babcock & Wilcox Co., 120 S. Van Buren Ave., 44203-0351, pg. 1068   **PB**
Leasing Services Corp., 24 Brown St., 44203, pg. 808   **PV**
MALCO PRODUCTS, INC., 361 Fairview Ave., 44203, pg. 698   **PV**
Midwest Rubber Co., 745 Norton Ave., 44203, pg. 56   **PV**
Novar Controls Corp., 24 Brown St., 44203, pg. 808   **PV**
NOVAR ELECTRONICS, 24 Brown St., 44203, pg. 808   **PV**
Whiz Automotive Chemicals Div., 361 Fairview Ave., 44203, pg. 698   **PV**

Batavia

C S Crable Sportswear, Inc., 4101 Founders Blvd., 45103, pg. 1111   **PB**
Cincinnati Milacron Plastics Machinery Group, 4165 Half Acre Rd., 45103, pg. 368   **PB**
Crable Sportswear, Inc., 4101 Founders Blvd., 45103, pg. 1111   **PB**
Ellis & Watts Div., 4400 Glen Willow Lake Ln., 45103-2356, pg. 286   **PB**
Jeff Wyler Buick, Pontiac, Inc., 1117 State Rte. 32, 45103, pg. 1193   **PB**
Jeff Wyler Chevrolet, Inc., 1117 Rte. 32, 45103, pg. 1193   **PB**
SOUTHERN OHIO FABRICATORS, INC., 2565 Batavia-Williamsburg Pike, 45103, pg. 1017   **PV**

Beachwood

ALLEN TELECOM, INC., 25101 Chagrin Blvd., Ste. 350, 44122-5687, pg. 45   **PB**
Beachwood Place, Inc., 23600 Cedar Rd., 44122, pg. 1408   **PB**
Creative Data Systems Divisions, 25101 Chagrin Blvd., Ste 260, 44122, pg. 1516   **PB**
Delphi Packard Electric Systems, 23550 Commerce Park Rd., 44122, pg. 719   **PB**
Forest City Auto Parts, Signature Sq., 25201 Chagrin Blvd., Ste. 350, 44122, pg. 1652   **PB**
MTI Systems Div., 23200 Chagrin Blvd., 44122, pg. 135   **PB**
MORGAN'S FOODS, INC., 24200 Chagrin Blvd., Ste.126, 44122, pg. 1133   **PB**
National Continental Insurance Co., 3401 Enterprise Pkwy., 44122, pg. 1335   **PB**
PCC Airfoils, Inc., 25201 Chagrin Blvd, 44122-5633, pg. 1320   **PB**
Progressive Premium Budget, Inc., 3401 Enterprise Pkwy., 44122, pg. 1335   **PB**
Tremco, Inc., 3735 Green Rd., 44122, pg. 1358   **PB**

Beavercreek

Intergraph Corporation, 4141 Colonel Glenn Hwy., Ste. 275, 45431, pg. 890   **PB**

Bedford

ASF Transport, Inc., 5300 Richmond Rd., 44146, pg. 451   **PV**
Cap Toys, Inc., 26201 Richmond Rd., 44146-1439, pg. 797   **PV**
Franklin Oil Corp., 40 S. Park St., 44146, pg. 892   **IT**
Halex Div., 23901 Aurora Rd., 44146, pg. 217   **PB**
Morgan Matroc Inc.-Electro Ceramics Division, 232 Forbes Rd., 44146, pg. 893   **IT**
Republic Environmental Systems (Cleveland), 33 Industry Dr., 44146, pg. 1380   **PB**
Riser Foods, Inc., 5300 Richmond Rd., 44146, pg. 450   **PV**

Ben Venue Laboratories

BEN VENUE LABORATORIES, INC., 300 Northfield Rd., 44146, pg. 1136   **PV**
WOC Inc., 24460 Aurora Rd., 44146, pg. 1748   **PV**
WAXMAN INDUSTRIES, INC., 24460 Aurora Rd., 44146, pg. 1748   **PB**
Waxman USA Inc., 24460 Aurora Rd., 44146, pg. 1749   **PB**

Bellefontaine

AP Techno Glass Company, 1465 W. Sandusky Ave., P.O. Box 819, 43311, pg. 84   **IT**
BMY Co., 587 Rd. 57 E., 43311-9252, pg. 793   **PV**
Belletech Corp., P.O. Box 790, 700 W. Lake St., 43311, pg. 84   **IT**
HBD INDUSTRIES, INC., 1301 W. Sandusky, 43311, pg. 489   **PV**

Bellevue

American Baler Co., P.O. Box 29, 800 E. Center St., 44811, pg. 102   **PV**
Armstrong Air Conditioning Inc., 421 Monroe St., 44813, pg. 659   **PV**
A. Schulman, Inc., 350 N. Buckeye St., 44811, pg. 1441   **PB**
Sunprene Co., 350 No. Buckeye St., 44811, pg. 1441   **PB**

Bellville

Gormar-Rupp Industries Div., 180 Hines Ave., 44813, pg. 754   **PB**

Belpre

Garrison Brewer, 214 Stone Rd., 45714, pg. 333   **PB**

Berea

Ceilcote Company, 140 Sheldon Rd., 44017, pg. 1465   **IT**
Fosbel, Inc., 640 N. Rocky River Dr., 44017-1628, pg. 234   **IT**
Hansen Coupling Division, 1000 W. Bagley Rd., 44017, pg. 1110   **PV**

Big Prairie

SeaLand Technology, 9030 Township Rd. 1043, 4th St., 44611, pg. 1071   **PB**

Blacklick

Columbus Steel Drum, Inc., 1385 Blatt Blvd., 43004, pg. 385   **PV**

Blanchester

Fulflo Specialties, 414 Fancy St., 45107, pg. 488   **PV**

Blue Ash

Crum & Forster Underwriters Co. of Ohio, 4445 Lake Forest Dr., Ste. 700, 45242, pg. 1784   **PB**

Bluffton

TRIPLETT CORPORATION, One Triplett Dr., 45817, pg. 1104   **PV**

Boardman

Consumers Ohio Water Company, 6650 South Ave., 44512, pg. 458   **PB**
Consumers Service Company, 6650 South Ave., 44512, pg. 459   **PB**

Bowerston

L.J. Smith, Inc., 35280 Scio-Bowerston Rd., 44695, pg. 706   **PV**

Bowling Green

Cooper Tire & Rubber Company, Bowling Green Plant, P.O. Box 1108, 1175 N. Main St., 43402, pg. 445   **PB**
Cooper Tire & Rubber Company, Bowling Green Plant, 400 Van Camp Rd., 43402, pg. 445   **PB**
Hill's Pet Products, P.O. Box 30309, 42101, pg. 397   **PB**
The Lamson & Sessions Co., 501 E. Poe Rd., 43402, pg. 975   **PB**
Marathon Special Prods., 13300 Van Camp Rd., 43402-9391, pg. 1371   **PB**
Sevenson Industrial Services, Inc., 745 Haskins Rd., 43402, pg. 1463   **PB**
Tru-Space, 18515 N. Dixie Hwy., 43402, pg. 1080   **PV**

Brecksville

ARROWHEAD HOLDING CORPORATION, Two Brecksville Commons, 8221 Brecksville Rd., Ste 100, 44141, pg. 86   **PV**
Shook Northern Ohio Division, P.O. Box 41020, 10245 Brecksville Rd., 44141-0420, pg. 996   **PV**
Teledyne Fluid Systems, 10376 Brecksville Rd., 44141, pg. 43   **PB**
Vesper Corporation, 8223 Brecksville Rd, Ste 100, 44141, pg. 86   **PV**

Bridgeport

SCOTT LUMBER COMPANY, 54382 National Rd., 43912, pg. 977   **PV**

Brilliant

Cardinal Operating Co., Cardinal Gen. Station, P.O. Box B, 43913, pg. 72   **PB**

Broadview Heights

Battenfeld of America, Inc., Ken Mar Dr., 44147, pg. 825   **IT**
Greif Division, P.O. Box 391, 44147, pg. 764   **PB**
Jani King of Cleveland, Inc., 9150 S. Hills Blvd., Ste. 15, 44147, pg. 581   **PV**
Ohio Engine Power, 900 KenMar Industrial Pkwy., 44147, pg. 813   **PV**

Brook Park

Bettcher Manufacturing Corporation, 16000 Commerce Park Dr., 44142, pg. 169   **PV**
Bridgestone/Firestone Credit Services Company, 6275 Eastland Rd., 44142, pg. 213   **IT**
NCS Customer Support & Services, 6410 Eastland Rd., Ste. F, 44142-1304, pg. 1155   **PB**
Travaux Construction, Inc., 15587 Snow Rd. #200, 44142, pg. 670   **PB**

Brooklyn

Key Clearing Corp., 4900 Tiedeman Rd., 44144, pg. 955   **PB**

Brookville

BENCHMARK INDUSTRIES, 630 Hay Ave., 45309, pg. 132   **PV**
Stanhope Products Company, 379 Albert St., 45309, pg. 169   **PV**

Brunswick

Consolidated Coatings Corp., P.O. Box 10, 2614 Pearl Rd., 44212, pg. 1357   **PB**
Eaton Corporation, Engineered Fasteners Division, 1060 W. 130th St., 44212, pg. 556   **PB**
Williams Detroit Diesel-Allison Midwest, Inc., 1176 Industrial Pkwy. N., P.O. Box 10, 44212, pg. 1179   **PV**

Bryan

Aro Fluid Products Division, One Aro Center, 43506, pg. 877   **PB**
BARD MFG. CO., 1914 Randolph Dr., 43506, pg. 116   **PB**
Bryan Metals, Inc., 1103 Main St., 43506, pg. 1219   **PB**
Challenge Industries, P.O. Box 547, 633 Commerce Dr., 43506-0547, pg. 438   **IT**
THE OHIO ART COMPANY, INC., One Toy St., 43506, pg. 1214   **PB**
OHIO GAS COMPANY, 200 W. High, 43506, pg. 812   **PV**
SPANGLER CANDY COMPANY, 400 N. Portland, 43506, pg. 1020   **PV**
Trinc Company, 727 E. Wilson St., 43506, pg. 1214   **PB**

Bucyrus

Bucyrus Blades Inc., 260 E. Beal Ave., 44820, pg. 383   **PV**
Hebco Products, P.O. Box 46, 44820, pg. 1055   **PB**
Special Packaging, Inc., 1375 Isaac Beal Rd., 44832, pg. 304   **PB**
Transco Railway Products Inc., 820 Hopley St., 44820, pg. 1096   **PV**

Burton

M.A. Hanna Rubber Compounding, 14330 Kinsman Rd., 44021, pg. 781   **PB**

Byesville

THE FABRI-FORM COMPANY, 10501 Burt St., 43723, pg. 390   **PV**

Cambridge

Marks Transfer & Storage, 300 Gomber Ave., 43725, pg. 390   **PV**

Canal Fulton

VALLEY SYSTEMS, INC., 11580 Lafayette Dr., N.W., 44614, pg. 1706   **PB**

Canal Winchester

Teledyne Specialty Equipment, 955 W. Walnut St., 43110-9436, pg. 44   **PB**

Canfield

Dart Trucking Company, Inc., 61 Railroad St., 44406, pg. 94   **PB**

DartAmerica, Inc., 61 Railroad St., 44406, pg. 94 **PB**

Envirco Transportation, Inc., 61 1/2 Railroad St., 44406, pg. 94 **PB**

GF Office Furniture, 6655 Seville Dr., 44406-9143, pg. 435 **PV**

Lafarge Construction Materials, 6715 Tippecanoe Rd., 44406, pg. 788 **IT**

Linde Hydraulics Corporation, 5089 W. Western Reserve Rd., P.O. Box 82, 44406, pg. 810 **IT**

Pittsburgh-Canfield Corp., 460 W. Main St., 44406, pg. 1726 **PB**

RAINBOW RENTALS, INC., 3711 Starr Ctr. Dr., 44406, pg. 907 **PV**

Seaway Transportation, Inc., 61 Railroad St., 44406, pg. 94 **PB**

TRB National Systems, Inc., 61 Railroad St., 44406, pg. 94 **PB**

Canton

A-E Division, 1243 Raff Rd., S.W., 44710, pg. 222 **PV**

ATM Finance, Inc., 818 Mulberry Rd., S.E., 44707-3256, pg. 506 **PB**

The Akro Corporation, 1212 Seventh St., S.W., 44707, pg. 399 **PV**

Arrow Oilfield Service Company, 1821 Moore Rd. S.E., 44706, pg. 1078 **PV**

Belden & Blake Corporation, 5200 Stoneham Rd., 44720-1543, pg. 1078 **PV**

CAMELOT MUSIC, INC., 8000 Freedom Ave. N.W., 44720, pg. 203 **PB**

Canton Aggregate Division, 1243 Raff Rd., S.W., 44710, pg. 222 **PV**

CANTON DROP FORGE, 4575 Southway St., S.W., 44706, pg. 205 **PV**

CENTRAL ALLIED ENTERPRISES, 1243 Raff Rd., S.W., 44710, pg. 222 **PV**

Central Ohio Coal Co., 301 Cleveland Ave., S.W., 44702, pg. 73 **PB**

Connecting Point Computer Services, 4218 Hills & Dales Rd. N.W., 44708, pg. 471 **PV**

Controlled Power (CPC), 1501 Raff Rd. SW, 44710, pg. 74 **IT**

Corrugated Packaging, 2820 Winfield Way, N.E., 44705, pg. 737 **PV**

Corrugated Products Division, 1250 Bedford Ave. S.W., 44710, pg. 763 **PV**

Crescent Brick Division-East Canton, P.O. Box 3019, pg. 924 **PV**

DIEBOLD, INCORPORATED, 5995 Mayfair Rd., 44720-8077, pg. 506 **PB**

Diebold Latin America Holding Company, Inc., 818 Mulberry Rd., S.E., 44707-3256, pg. 506 **PB**

Diebold Mexico Holding Company, Inc., 818 Mulberry Rd., S.E., 44707-3256, pg. 506 **PB**

FRESH MARK, INC., 1600 Harmont Ave. NE, 44705, pg. 427 **PV**

GRAPHIC ENTERPRISES OF OHIO, INC., 3874 Highland Pk., N.W., 44720, pg. 471 **PV**

HAINES & CO., INC., 8050 Freedom Ave., N.W., Box #2117, 44720, pg. 494 **PV**

HARRISON PAINT CORP., 1329 Harrison Ave., S.W., 44706, pg. 506 **PV**

HERCULES ENGINE COMPANY, 101 Eleventh St. S.E., 44707-3802, pg. 523 **PV**

Hoover Company, 101 E. Maple St. N., 44720, pg. 1065 **PV**

Ikon Office Solutions-North Ohio, 5701 Mayfair Rd., 44720, pg. 864 **PB**

InterBold, P.O. Box 3091, 44720, pg. 897 **PB**

Isler's Refuse Service, Inc., P.O. Box R, Sta. C, 44708, pg. 264 **PV**

JMI-Canton Pharmaceuticals, Inc., 119 Schroyer Ave., S.W., 44702, pg. 934 **PV**

LUNTZ CORPORATION, 237 Tuscarawas St., E., 44702, pg. 681 **PV**

Meter Devices Co, 1000 Prospect Ave., S.W., 44706, pg. 172 **PV**

Ohio Power Company, 301 Cleveland Ave., S.W., 44702, pg. 72 **PV**

Ohio Tar Asphalt, 1243 Raff Rd., S.W., 44710, pg. 222 **PV**

Paumier Company Inc., 5325 Southway St. S.W., 44706, pg. 300 **PV**

REPUBLIC STORAGE SYSTEMS COMPANY INC., 1038 Belden Ave., N.E., 44705, pg. 924 **PV**

Southern Ohio Coal Co., P.O. Box 400, 301 Cleveland Ave., 44701, pg. 73 **PB**

SUAREZ CORPORATION INDUSTRIES, 7800 Whipple Ave. N.W., 44720, pg. 1048 **PV**

Sugardale Foods Inc., 1600 Harmont Ave., N.E., 44705, pg. 427 **PV**

SUPERIOR DAIRY, INC., 4719 Navarre Rd. S.W., 44706, pg. 1054 **PV**

Target Oilfield Pipe & Supply Company (TOPS), 2149 Moore Ave., S.E., 44707, pg. 1078 **PV**

356th Fighter Group, Akron-Canton Airport, 2787 Mt. Pleasant Rd., 44720, pg. 1023 **PV**

THE TIMKEN COMPANY, 1835 Dueber Ave. S.W., 44706-2798, pg. 1617 **PB**

VDM Holding Co., 818 Mulberry Rd., S.E., 44707-3256, pg. 506 **PB**

Windsor Coal Co., 301 Cleveland Ave., S.W., 44701, pg. 73 **PV**

Youngstown Tire & Supply Company, 4900 Navarre Rd., S.W., 44707, pg. 1205 **PV**

ZIEGLER TIRE & SUPPLY COMPANY, INC., 4900 Navarre Rd., S.W., 44706, pg. 1205 **PV**

Carey

Porcelain Products, 225 N. Patterson, 43316, pg. 308 **PB**

Carroll

Diamond Electronics, Inc., P.O. Box 200, 4465 Coon Path, 43112, pg. 1663 **PB**

Carrollton

M & M Precision Systems Corporation, 300 Progress Rd., 45449, pg. 482 **PB**

ROBERDS, INC., 1100 E. Central Ave., 45449-1888, pg. 1393 **PB**

Celina

Community First Bank & Trust, 225 N. Main St., 45822, pg. 633 **PB**

The L.J. Minor Corporation, 1800 Industrial Dr., 45822, pg. 917 **IT**

Centerville

Arrow/Schweber Electronics, 8200 Washington Village Dr., Ste. A, 45458, pg. 133 **PB**

DIMCO-GRAY COMPANY, 8200 S. Suburban Rd., 45458-2709, pg. 333 **PV**

MCM Electronics Inc., 858 E. Congress Park Dr., 45459, pg. 1068 **IT**

Planes Moving & Storage Of Dayton, Inc., 440 Congress Park Dr., 45459, pg. 869 **PV**

Chagrin Falls

Diversey Water Technologies, Inc., 7145 Pine St., 44022, pg. 1150 **PB**

Scot Laboratories, 16841 Park Circle Dr., 44022, pg. 218 **PB**

Stock Equipment Co., 16490 Chillicothe Rd., 44022, pg. 727 **PB**

Chardon

Carlisle Engineered Products, 100 Seventh Ave., Ste. 100, 44024, pg. 305 **PV**

THE CHARDON RUBBER CO., 373 Washington St., 44024, pg. 229 **PV**

ESSEF CORPORATION, 220 Park Dr., 44024, pg. 592 **PB**

First County Bank, 540 Water St., 44024, pg. 607 **PB**

Structural North America, 220 Park Dr., 44024, pg. 593 **PB**

Webb-Triax Company, 215 Fifth Ave., 44024, pg. 1157 **PV**

Chesterland

Channel Products, 7100 Wilson Mills Rd., 44026, pg. 228 **PV**

LFE Instruments, 11655 Chillicothe Rd., 44026, pg. 482 **PB**

Chillicothe

Chillicothe Newspapers, 50 W. Main St., 45601, pg. 700 **PV**

Fine Paper Div., 401 S. Paint St., 45601-0997, pg. 1074 **PB**

Kenworth Truck Co., 65 Kenworth Dr., 45601, pg. 1246 **PV**

The Kitchen Collection Inc., 71 Water St., 45601, pg. 1149 **PB**

State Electric Supply Company, P.O. Box 6198, 13 Renick Ave., 45601, pg. 1036 **PV**

Cincinnati

ABC Rail Cogifer Industries, 5038 Beech St., 45212, pg 2 **PV**

ACBJ Business Publications, Inc., 35 E. Seventh St., Ste. 700, 45202, pg. 19 **PV**

AM Concepts Inc., 400 Broadway, 45202-3341, pg. 1164 **PV**

AST Research, Inc., 8044 Montgomery Rd., Ste. 700, 45236, pg. 1181 **IT**

Abolite Lighting Inc., 10000 Alliance Rd., 45242, pg. 971 **PV**

Access Corporation, 1011 Glendale-Milford Rd., 45215, pg. 994 **IT**

Accord Controls, Inc., 11420 Deerfield Rd., 45242, pg. 658 **PB**

Ace Doran Brokerage, 1601 Blue Rock St., 45223, pg. 340 **PV**

Agricultural Insurance Company, 515 Main St., 45202, pg. 74 **PV**

Airfoil Technologies International LLC, 298 Crescentville Rd., 45246, pg. 1569 **PB**

MIKE ALBERT LEASING, INC., 10340 Evendale Dr., 45241, pg. 32 **PV**

Albright & Wilson Company, P.O. Box 53066, 45253, pg. 49 **IT**

Alex Fries, 10311 Chester Rd., 45215, pg. 646 **PV**

Allied Clinical Laboratory, Inc., 1737 Tennesse Ave., 45229, pg. 973 **PB**

Allied Crescent, c/o The Owens Group, Inc., 2306 W. Galbraith St., 45239, pg. 38 **PV**

Allied Security Inc., 110 Boggs Ln., #140, 45246, pg. 40 **PV**

Allright Cincinnati, Inc., 435 Elm St., Room 530, 45202, pg. 42 **PV**

American Annuity Group, 250 E. Fifth St., 45202, pg. 74 **PB**

American Empire Surplus Lines Insurance Company, 515 Main St., 45202, pg. 74 **PB**

American Financial Enterprises, Inc., One E. Fourth St., 45202, pg. 74 **PB**

American Financial Group, One E. Fourth St., 45202, pg. 75 **PB**

AMERICAN FINANCIAL GROUP, One E. Fourth St., 45202, pg. 74 **PB**

American Money Management Corporation, One E. Fourth St., 45202, pg. 74 **PB**

American National Fire Insurance Company, 580 Walnut St., 45202, pg. 74 **PB**

Autodesk, 4555 Lake Forest Dr., Ste. 650, 45242, pg. 149 **PB**

Automax, Inc., 11444 Deerfield Dr., 45242, pg. 658 **PB**

AVON WORKSHOP FICKS REED, 6245 Creek Rd., 45242, pg. 102 **PV**

Bank One, Cincinnati, 8044 Montgomery, 45236, pg. 173 **PV**

Bardes Corp., 4730 Madison Rd., 45227, pg. 558 **PV**

Bartlett & Co., 36 E. 4th St., 45202, pg. 985 **PB**

BAXTER HODELL DONNELLY PRESTON INC., 3500 Red Bank Rd., 45227-4188, pg. 124 **PV**

Baxter/Peas, 4460 Carver Woods Rd., 45242, pg. 124 **PV**

Beech Isuzu, 7636 Beechmont Ave., 45255, pg. 129 **PV**

Beechmont Chevrolet, Inc, 7600 Beechmont Ave., 45255, pg. 129 **PV**

Beechmont Hyundai, 7636 Beechmont Ave., 45254, pg. 129 **PV**

BEECHMONT INVESTMENTS INC., 8639 Beechmont Ave., 45255, pg. 129 **PV**

Beechmont Porsche Audi Inc., 8639 Beechmont Ave., 45255, pg. 129 **PV**

BELCAN CORPORATION, 10200 Anderson Way, 45242, pg. 131 **PV**

Berean Christian Stores, 8121 Hamilton Ave., 45231, pg. 1506 **PV**

Bettis Electric Actuator Company, 2660 Commerce Blvd., 45241, pg. 483 **IT**

Borden Graphics Division, P.O. Box 15947, 630 Glendale Milford, 45215-0947, pg. 157 **PV**

Bowling Products Div., 30 Garfield Pl., Ste. 1040, 45202, pg. 1725 **PV**

BRAZOS SPORTSWEAR INC., 3860 Virginia Ave., 45227, pg. 251 **PB**

Brody Co. Div., P.O. Box 428707, 45242, pg. 976 **PB**

BROWER PRODUCTS, 3301 Colerain Ave., 45225, pg. 172 **PV**

The Buckeye Oilseed Products Co., One Procter & Gamble Plaza, 45202, pg. 1331 **PB**

BUDCO GROUP INC., 1100 Gest St., 45203, pg. 178 **PV**

THE BUSCHMAN CO., 10045 International Blvd., 45246, pg. 188 **PV**

The Buschman Company, 10045 International Blvd., 45246, pg. 866 **PV**

CAE Ransohoff Inc., 4933 Provident Dr., 45246, pg. 237 **IT**

CAI Holding Company, Inc., 400 E. 4th, 45202, pg. 1164 **PV**

CCL Label, 3642 Muddy Creek Rd., 45238, pg. 238 **IT**

CG&E Resource Marketing, Inc., 139 E. Fourth St., 45202, pg. 369 **PB**

CGE Corporation, 139 E. Fourth St., 45202, pg. 369 **PB**

CGE Eck, Inc., 139 E. Fourth St., 45202, pg. 369 **PB**

CVG Aviation, P.O. Box 75021, 45275, pg. 406 **PB**

Candle-Lite, A Lancaster Colony Co., 4460 Lake Forest Dr., Ste. 200, 45242, pg. 976 **PV**

Canusa-EMI, 7820 Palace Dr., 45249, pg. 1221 **IT**

Cartwright Communications Co., 7812 Red Sky Dr., 45249-1696, pg. 1582 **PB**

A.M. Castle & Co., 675 Renda Ter., 45215, pg. 313 **PV**

Central Steel & Wire Company, 525 Township Ave., 45216, pg. 327 **PB**

CHEMED CORPORATION, 2600 Chemed Ctr., 255 E. Fifth St., 45202-4726, pg. 343 **PB**

CHICAGO WEST PULLMAN CORPORATION, 2300 Star Bank Center, 45202, pg. 235 **PV**

Chicago West Pullman Financial Corporation, 2300 Star Bank Ctr., 45202, pg. 236 **PV**

Chicago West Pullman Heavy Industries, 2300 Star Bank Ctr., 45202, pg. 236 **PV**

Chiquita Banana North America, 250 East Fifth St., 45202, pg. 349 **PB**

CHIQUITA BRANDS INTERNATIONAL, INC., 250 E. Fifth St., 45202, pg. 349 **PB**

Cincinnati Bell Directory Inc., 201 E. Fourth St., 45202, pg. 367 **PV**

Cincinnati Bell Information Systems Inc., 600 Vine St., 45202, pg. 367 **PV**

Cincinnati Bell Long Distance Inc., 201 E. Fourth St., 45202, pg. 367 **PV**

Cincinnati Bell Supply Company, 1022 Kenner St., 45214, pg. 367 **PV**

CINCINNATI BELL TELEPHONE, 201 E. Fourth St., 45202, pg. 367 **PV**

Cincinnati Bell Telephone Company, 201 E. Fourth St., 45202, pg. 367 **PV**

THE CINCINNATI CORDAGE & PAPER COMPANY, 800 E. Ross Ave., 45217, pg. 239 **PV**

Cincinnati Electronics Corp., 2630 Glendale-Milford Rd., 45241-3187, pg. 545 **IT**

The Cincinnati Enquirer, Inc., 312 Elm St., 45202, pg. 700 **PB**

CINCINNATI GEAR COMPANY, 5657 Wooster Pike, 45227, pg. 240 **PV**

Cincinnati Industrial Machinery Div., Hageman Ave., P.O. Box 62027, 45262, pg. 355 **PV**

PB - *U.S. Public Companies Volume*
PV - *U.S. Private Companies Volume*
IT - *International Public & Private Companies Volume*

Geographic Index-U.S.

1377

Cincinnati Limousine Service Inc., 8667 Beechmont Ave., 45255, pg. 129 — PV

CINCINNATI MILACRON INC., 4701 Marburg Ave., 45209, pg. 368 — PB

Cincinnati Milacron Industrial Systems Division, 4701 Marburg Ave., 45209, pg. 368 — PB

Cincinnati Paperboard Corporation, 5500 Wooster Rd., 45226, pg. 303 — PB

The Cincinnati Post, 125 E. Court St., 45202, pg. 1447 — PB

CINCINNATI SUB-ZERO PRODUCTS, INC., 12011 Mosteller Rd., 45241-1528, pg. 240 — PV

CINCINNATI THERMAL SPRAY, INC., 5901 Creek Road, 45242, pg. 240 — PV

CINCOM SYSTEMS, INC., 55 Merchants St., 55246, pg. 240 — PV

CINERGY CORP., 139 East Fourth St., 45202, pg. 368 — PB

Cinergy Corp., 139 E. Fourth St., 45202, pg. 369 — PB

CINergy Services, Inc., 139 E. Fourth St., 45202, pg. 369 — PB

CLARK DETROIT-DIESEL ALLISON, 3133 E. Kemper Rd., 45241, pg. 242 — PV

Clopay Corporation, 312 Walnut St., Ste. 1600, 45202, pg. 766 — PB

Colmain Properties, Inc., 400 E. 4th St., 45202, pg. 1164 — PV

Colpick, Inc., 400 Broadway, 45202-3341, pg. 1164 — PV

Columbus Life Insurance Co., 400 E. Fourth St., 45202-3302, pg. 1164 — PV

Comair Investment Company, P.O. Box 75021, 45275, pg. 406 — PB

Comair Services, Inc., P.O. Box 75021, 45275, pg. 406 — PB

CONSOLIDATED METAL PRODUCTS, INC., 1028 Depot St., 45204, pg. 265 — PV

CORPOREX COMPANIES, INC., 655 Eden Park Dr., 45202, pg. 276 — PV

Corrugated Packaging, 220 W. North Bend Rd., P.O. Box 16058, 45216, pg. 737 — PB

Courtyard Nursing Care, Inc., 400 Broadway, 45202, pg. 1165 — PV

Curtis 1000, Inc., 4690 S. Interstate Dr., Bldg. 6, 45246, pg. 70 — PB

Custom Direct Inc., 4752 River Rd., 45233, pg. 1076 — IT

D H Food Co., One Procter & Gamble Plaza, 45202, pg. 1331 — PB

DWF of Cincinnati, Inc., 1220 Findley St., 45214, pg. 326 — PV

Deer Park Federal Savings and Loan Association, 7200 Blue Ash Rd., 45236, pg. 66 — PB

Dempsey & Siders Insurance Agency, 7840 Montgomery Rd., 45236, pg. 75 — PB

Dinagraphics, Inc., Beech & Robertson, 45212, pg. 1270 — IT

ACE DORAN HAULING & RIGGING COMPANY, 1601 Blue Rock St., 45223, pg. 340 — PV

Dosimeter Corporation of America, 11286 Grooms Rd., 45242-1416, pg. 892 — IT

DuBois Chemicals, 255 E. Fifth St.-Suite 1200, 45202, pg. 1437 — IT

Dugan & Meyers Construction Co., 11110 Kenwood Rd., 45242, pg. 345 — PV

DUGAN & MEYERS INTERESTS, INC., 11110 Kenwood Rd., 45242, pg. 345 — PV

EDI INTERNATIONAL, INC., 1135 Belvedere, Ste. 2A, 45242-1701, pg. 353 — PV

EAGLE-PICHER INDUSTRIES, INC., 580 Walnut St., 45202, pg. 355 — PV

Eagle Properties, Inc., 400 Broadway, 45202, pg. 1164 — PV

Eastside Lincoln Mercury, 429 Ohio Pike, 45255, pg. 129 — PV

ENERFAB INC., 4955 Spring Grove Ave., 45232, pg. 376 — PV

Ethicon Endo-Surgery, Inc., 4545 Creek Rd., 45242-2839, pg. 928 — PB

Evans, Inc., Seventh & Race Sts., 45202, pg. 596 — PB

F & W PUBLICATIONS, INC., 1507 Dana Ave., 45207, pg. 388 — PV

Fahlgren, 414 Walnut St., Ste. 515, 45202, pg. 391 — PV

Fechheimer Bros. Co., 4545 Malsbary Rd., 45242, pg. 217 — PB

Federated Corporate, Seven W. Seventh St., 45202, pg. 618 — PB

FEDERATED DEPARTMENT STORES, INC., Seven W. Seventh St., 45202, pg. 617 — PB

Feintool Cincinnati Inc., 11280 Cornell Pk. Dr., 45242, pg. 479 — IT

George E. Fern Company, 1100 Gest St., 45203, pg. 178 — PV

Fibre Glass-Evercoat Company, 6600 Cornell Rd., 45242, pg. 866 — PB

FIFTH THIRD BANCORP, Fifth Third Center, 45263, pg. 621 — PB

Finnigan MAT Institute, 4450 Carver Woods Dr., 45242, pg. 1591 — PB

Fireman's Fund Insurance Co. of Ohio, 312 Walnut St., Ste. 1100, 45201, pg. 59 — IT

First National Cincinnati Corporation, P.O. Box 1038, 425 Walnut St., 45201, pg. 1510 — PB

Fluor Daniel Inc., 134 Merchant St., 45246, pg. 660 — PB

The Folger Coffee Company, One Procter & Gamble Plaza, 45201, pg. 1331 — PB

FORD DEVELOPMENT CORPORATION, 11148 Woodward Ln., 45241, pg. 418 — PV

Formica Corp., 10155 Reading, 45241, pg. 129 — IT

Fort Washington Investment Advisors, Inc., 420 E. Fourth St., 45202, pg. 1164 — PV

Frisch Florida, Inc., 2800 Gilbert Ave., 45206, pg. 682 — PB

Frisch Germantown Road, Inc., 2800 Gilbert Ave., 45206, pg. 682 — PB

Frisch Indiana, Inc., 2800 Gilbert Ave., 45206, pg. 682 — PB

Frisch Kentucky, Inc., 2800 Gilbert Ave., 45206, pg. 682 — PB

Frisch Ohio, Inc., 2800 Gilbert Ave., 45206, pg. 682 — PB

FRISCH'S RESTAURANTS, INC., 2800 Gilbert Ave., 45206, pg. 682 — PB

GACC Holding Company, One E. Fourth St., 45202, pg. 75 — PB

G.E. Aircraft Engines, One Neumann Way, P.O. Box 156301, 45215, pg. 710 — PB

Gannett Media Technologies International, 151 W. Fourth St., 45202, pg. 699 — PB

GARDNER PUBLICATIONS, INC., 6915 Valley Ave., 45244-3029, pg. 440 — PV

GIBSON GREETINGS, INC., 2100 Section Rd., 45237, pg. 742 — PB

Gibson Greetings International Limited, 2100 Section Rd., 45237, pg. 742 — PB

THE GIBSON GROUP INC., 2985 Madison Rd., 45209, pg. 451 — PV

GLOBE FURNITURE RENTALS, 1925 Greenwood Ave., 45246, pg. 458 — PV

GOLD MEDAL PRODUCTS CO., 10700 Medallion Dr., 45241, pg. 459 — PV

Stephen Gould of Ohio, Corp., 10227 Alliance Rd., 45242, pg. 467 — PV

Gradison Division, 580 Walnut St., 45202, pg. 1068 — PB

Great American Holding Corporation, 580 Walnut St., 45202, pg. 74 — PB

Great American Insurance Company, 580 Walnut St., 45202, pg. 74 — PB

Great American Management Services, Inc., One E. Fourth St., 45202, pg. 75 — PB

GUARANTEE TITLE & TRUST CO., 8280 Montgomery Rd., Ste. 201, 45236, pg. 485 — PV

HMS/Cincinnati, 4750 Creek Rd., 45242, pg. 492 — PV

HMS Direct, 4750 Creek Rd., 45242, pg. 492 — PV

H.P.E., 2985 Madison Rd., Ste. 201, 45209, pg. 451 — PV

THE HABEGGER CORPORATION, 4995 Winton Rd., 45232, pg. 492 — PV

Halma Holdings Inc., 3100 E. Kemper Rd., 45241, pg. 590 — IT

HAMILTON MUTUAL INSURANCE COMPANY OF CINCINNATI, 1520 Madison Rd., 45206, pg. 497 — PV

Harte-Hanks Direct Marketing Cincinnati, 2950 Robertson Ave., 45209, pg. 794 — PB

Hasbro, 615 Elsinore Pl., 45202, pg. 797 — PB

Henkel Corporation - Chemicals Group, 5051 Estecreek Dr., 45232-1647, pg. 610 — IT

Hewlett-Packard Company, 4501 Erskine Rd., 45242, pg. 815 — PV

HICKMAN, WILLIAMS & CO. INC., Chiquita Ctr., 250 E. Fifth St., Ste. 600, 45202, pg. 525 — PV

HILL & GRIFFITH COMPANY, 1262 State Ave., 45204, pg. 529 — PV

Hillshire Farm & Kahn's, 3241 Spring Grove Ave., 45225, pg. 1433 — PB

Hines-Park Foods, Inc., One Procter & Gamble Plaza, 45202, pg. 1331 — PB

Hoechst Marion Roussel Research, 2110 E. Galbrath Rd., 45237-1625, pg. 625 — IT

Holset Engineering Co. Inc., 1320 Kemper Meadow Dr., Ste. 500, 45240, pg. 468 — PB

Honda East, 529 Ohio Pike, 45255, pg. 129 — PV

Honeywell-Measurex Management Systems Division (MSD), 1280 Kemper Meadow Dr., 45240, pg. 833 — PB

HUDEPOHL-SCHOENLING BREWING COMPANY, 1599 Central Pkwy., 45214-2863, pg. 545 — PV

HUGHES-PETERS, INC., 5030 Oaklawn Dr., 45227-1044, pg. 546 — PV

Huls America Inc., 620 Shepherd Dr., 45215, pg. 1455 — IT

Humana Health Plan of Ohio, Inc., 8044 Montgomery Rd., Ste. 460, 45236, pg. 848 — PB

Husman Snack Foods, Co., 1621 Moore St., 45210, pg. 887 — PB

IFS Agency Services, Inc., 311 Pike St., 45202, pg. 1165 — PV

IFS Financial Services, Inc., 311 Pike St., 45202, pg. 1165 — PV

IFS Insurance Agency, Inc., 311 Pike St., 45202, pg. 1165 — PV

IPD Marketing Services, Inc., Seven W. Seventh St., Ste. 1650, 45202, pg. 1336 — PB

ITT A-C Pump/ITT Marlow, 1150 Tennessee Ave., 45229, pg. 860 — PB

ILSCO, 4730 Madison Rd., 45227, pg. 558 — PV

Imperial Adhesives & Chemicals, Inc., 6315 Wiehe Rd., 45237, pg. 1147 — PB

Indiana Glass Company, P.O. Box 42364, 4460 Lake Forest Dr., Ste. 200, 45242-0364, pg. 976 — PB

Industrial Material Distributors, 2985 Madison Rd., 45209, pg. 903 — PB

Information Leasing Corporation, One E. 4th St., 45202, pg. 1338 — PV

Insight Graphic Systems, 10000 Alliance Rd., 45242, pg. 971 — PV

Intergraph Corporation, Get Center, 134 Merchant St., 45246, pg. 890 — PV

Intergraph Corporation, 110 Boggs Ln., Ste. 250, 45246, pg. 890 — PV

Intertek, 8361 Broadwell Rd., 45244, pg. 803 — PV

Jacobs Engineering Group Inc., P.O. Box 465600, 1880 Waycross Rd., 45240, pg. 921 — PB

Jani King of Cincinnati, Inc., 144 Merchant St., 45246, pg. 581 — PB

JAY INSTRUMENT & SPECIALTY CO., 555 N. Wayne Ave., 45215, pg. 583 — PV

The Andrew Jergens Company, 2535 Spring Grove Ave., 45214, pg. 717 — IT

Jetcom, 1650 Magnolia Dr., 45215, pg. 1329 — PB

DAVID JOSEPH CO., 300 Pike St., 45202, pg. 601 — PB

The David J. Joseph Company, 300 Pike St., 45202, pg. 1155 — IT

John R. Jurgensen Co., 11641 Mosteller Rd., 45241, pg. 1131 — PV

K-D LAMP COMPANY, 1910 Elm St., 45210, pg. 603 — PV

KDI PRECISION PRODUCTS, INC., 3975 McMann Rd., 45245, pg. 603 — PV

KO Transmission Company, 139 E. Fourth St., 45202, pg. 369 — PB

Keebler Co./Cincinnati Bakery, 1 Trade St., 45227, pg. 657 — PB

KINGS TOYOTA SUZUKI, 9500 Kings Automall Rd., 45249, pg. 621 — PV

Kip's of Oklahoma, Inc., 2800 Gilbert Ave., 45206, pg. 682 — PB

THE KIRK & BLUM MFG. CO., 3120 Forrer St., 45209, pg. 623 — PV

KLOSTERMAN BAKING COMPANY, INC., 4760 Paddock Rd., 45229, pg. 626 — PV

THE KROGER CO., 1014 Vine St., 45202-1100, pg. 967 — PB

LSI INDUSTRIES, INC., 10000 Alliance Rd., 45242, pg. 971 — PB

LSI Industries, Inc., 10000 Alliance Rd., 45242, pg. 971 — PB

LA ROSA'S, INC., 2334 Boudinot, 45238, pg. 640 — PV

THE F.D. LAWRENCE ELECTRIC CO., 3450 Beekman St., 45223, pg. 645 — PV

Lawrenceburg Gas Co., 139 E. Fourth St., 45202, pg. 369 — PB

Lenscrafters, 8650 Governor's Hill Dr., 45249, pg. 822 — IT

Life Equipment Rebuilders, 1100 Gest St., 45203, pg. 178 — PV

Chas. V. Maescher & Co., Inc., 2106 Florence Ave., 45206, pg. 694 — PV

Maescher Construction Co., 2106 Florence Ave., 45206, pg. 694 — PV

MAESCHER INDUSTRIES, INC., 2106 Florence Ave., 45206, pg. 694 — PV

Manhattan Life Insurance Company, 1876 Waycross Rd., 45240, pg. 1118 — PV

Manhattan National Life Insurance Company, 205 W. Fourth St., 45202, pg. 434 — PB

Mar-Hyde Corporation, 4677 Devitt Dr., 45246, pg. 1357 — PB

Marathon Monitors Incorporated, 3100 E. Kemper Rd., 45241, pg. 590 — IT

Marine & Industrial Engines & Service Div., One Neumann Way, Box 156301, 45215, pg. 710 — PB

Market Facts, Inc., 201 E. Fifth St., 45202, pg. 1047 — PB

Master Fleet Inc., 1601 Blue Rock St., 45223, pg. 340 — PV

MATRIXX Marketing Inc., P.O. Bpx 2301, 201 E. Fourth St., 45201, pg. 368 — PB

McAlpin's, 7913 Montgomery Rd., 45236, pg. 1090 — PB

MCSWAIN CARPETS INC., 2430 E. Kemper Rd., 45241, pg. 725 — PV

MEDIA THAT WORKS, 455 Delta Ave., 45226, pg. 727 — PV

MERIDIAN DIAGNOSTICS, INC., 3471 River Hills Dr., 45244, pg. 1094 — PB

The Merten Company, 1515 Central Pkwy., 45215, pg. 333 — PV

FRANK MESSER & SONS CONSTRUCTION CO. 4612 Paddock R., 45229, pg. 734 — PB

J.W. Messner, Inc., 625 Eden Park Drive, Ste. 300, 45202-6005, pg. 734 — PV

THE MIAMI MARGARINE CO., 6872 Drake Dr., 45243, pg. 740 — PV

Miami Power Corp., 139 E. Fourth St., 45202, pg. 369 — PB

MIAMI SYSTEMS CORPORATION, 10150 Alliance Rd., 45242, pg. 740 — PV

The Miami Valley Insurance Co., 425 Walnut St., 45202, pg. 1510 — PB

THE MIDLAND COMPANY, 7000 Midland Blvd., 45205, pg. 1110 — PB

Midland Enterprises Inc., 300 Pike St., 45202, pg. 549 — PB

Millennium Petrochemicals, Inc., 11500 Northlake Dr., 45249-1694, pg. 594 — IT

Millennium Petrochemicals Inc., 11500 Northlake Dr., 45249, pg. 1111 — PB

MONARCH CONSTRUCTION COMPANY, 1654 Sherman Ave., 45212, pg. 757 — PV

John Morrell & Co., 805 E. Kemper Rd., 45246, pg. 1479 — PB

R.A. MUELLER, INC., 11270 Cornell Park Dr., 45242, pg. 766 — PV

Multimedia Radio, Inc., 140 W. Ninth St., 45202, pg. 699 — PB

MUTUAL MANUFACTURING & SUPPLY CO., 3300 Spring Grove Ave., 45225, pg. 769 — PV

NEW HORIZONS LLC, 2842 Massachusetts Ave., 45225, pg. 794 — PV

AL NEYER, INC., 3800 Red Bank Rd., 45227, pg. 797 — PV

Nielsen Logistics Co, 2940 Highland Ave., 45212, pg. 799 — PV

NORTHLICH STOLLEY LAWARRE, 151 W. 4th St., 45202, pg. 806 — PV

Northlich Stolley LaWarre Public Relations, 151 W. Fourth St., 45202, pg. 806 — PV

NuTone, Inc., Madison & Red Bank Rds., 45227, pg. 1499 — IT

O/B Leasing Company, 1100 Gest St., 45203, pg. 178 — PV

OPW Fueling Components, P.O. Box 405003, 45240-5003, pg. 521 — PB

The Ohio River Company, 580 Walnut St., Ste. 1400, 45202, pg. 549 — PB

Omnicare Pharmacy Services, 2800 Chemed Center, 45202, pg. 1223 — PB

Orgulf Transport Co., 580 Walnut St., Ste. 1400, 45202, pg. 549 — PB

PCC Technical Industries, Inc., One E. Fourth St., 45202, pg. 75 — PB

PNC Bank, Central Trust Ctr., 201 E. Fifth & Main Sts., 45202, pg. 1242 — PB

PB - *U.S. Public Companies Volume*
PV - *U.S. Private Companies Volume*
IT - *International Public & Private Companies Volume*

1378

Geographic Index-U.S.

PNC Bank, Central Trust Ctr., 201 E., Fifth & Main Sts., 45202, pg. 1242 **PB**

PNC Realty Co., Ohio, Central Trust Center, 45402, pg. 1243 **PB**

PNC Realty Mortgage Co., 1000 Central Trust Center, 45202, pg. 1243 **PB**

PSS, 10848 Kentwood Rd., 45242, pg. 1294 **PB**

Pacificare of Ohio, 11260 Chester Rd., # 800, 45246, pg. 1251 **PV**

Parsec, 1100 Gest St., 45203, pg. 178 **PV**

Parsec/Dotson, Inc., 1100 Gest St., 45203, pg. 178 **PV**

Partridge Meats, Inc., 250 E. Fifth St., 45202, pg. 75 **PB**

Frank Paxton Lumber Company, 7455 Dawson, Box 43334, 45243, pg. 585 **PV**

Penn Central Real Estate Group, One East Fouth St., 45202, pg. 178 **PB**

PERRY & DERRICK CO., 2510 Highland Ave., Ste. 510, 45212, pg. 854 **PV**

Piggyback Services, Inc., 1100 Gest St., 45203, pg. 178 **PV**

PLANES MOVING AND STORAGE, INC., 10115 Transportation Way, 45246, pg. 869 **PV**

PLANET PRODUCTS CORP., 4200 Malsbary Rd., 45242, pg. 869 **PV**

PLASTIC MOLDINGS CORP., 2181 Grand Ave., 45214, pg. 871 **PV**

POLYMET CORP., 10073 Commerce Park Dr., 45246, pg. 875 **PV**

THE WM. POWELL COMPANY, 2503 Spring Grove Ave., 45214-1771, pg. 877 **PV**

Processed Products Division, 10825 Kenwood Rd., 45242, pg. 1191 **PV**

Procter & Gamble Commercial Co., One Procter & Gamble Plaza, 45202, pg. 1331 **PB**

THE PROCTER & GAMBLE COMPANY, One Procter & Gamble Plaza, 45202, pg. 1330 **PB**

Procter & Gamble Distr. Co., One Procter & Gamble Plaza, 45202, pg. 1331 **PB**

Procter & Gamble Mfg. Co., One Procter & Gamble Plaza, 45202, pg. 1331 **PB**

Procter & Gamble Pharmaceuticals, Inc., P.O. Box 599, 45201, pg. 1331 **PB**

The Provident Bank, 1 E. 4th St., 45202, pg. 1338 **PB**

The Provident Bank of Kentucky, One E. Fourth St., 45202, pg. 1338 **PB**

Provident Commercial Group, Inc., One E. Fourth St., 45202, pg. 1338 **PB**

Provident Consumer Financial Services, One E. 4th St., 45202, pg. 1338 **PB**

PROVIDENT FINANCIAL GROUP, INC., One E. 4th St., 45202, pg. 1338 **PB**

Provident Securities & Investment Company, One E. 4th St., 45202, pg. 1338 **PB**

Quality Hotel Central, 4747 Montgomery Rd., 45212, pg. 682 **PB**

Rath Black Hawk, 250 E. Fifth St., 45202, pg. 75 **PB**

Red Circle Transport Co., 580 Walnut St., Ste. 1400, 45202, pg. 549 **PB**

REECE-CAMPBELL, INC., 1718 Ralston Ave., 45223, pg. 916 **PV**

RELIABLE CASTINGS CORPORATION, 3530 Spring Grove Ave., 45232, pg. 920 **PV**

RICHARDS INDUSTRIES, INC., 3170 Wasson Rd., 45209, pg. 929 **PV**

Richards Industries Metalworking Group, 9070 Pippin Rd., 45251-3174, pg. 929 **PV**

Richards Industries Valve Group, 3170 Wasson Rd., 45209-0271, pg. 929 **PV**

Richardson-Vicks, Inc., One Procter & Gamble Plaza, 45202, pg. 1331 **PB**

Richardson-Vicks, Inc., Health Care Products, One Procter & Gamble Plaza, 45202, pg. 1331 **PB**

Richardson-Vicks, Inc. Personal Care Products Div., One Procter & Gamble Plaza, 45202, pg. 1331 **PB**

RIEMEIER LUMBER COMPANY, INC., 1528 Gest St., 45203, pg. 930 **PV**

ROBBINS, INC., 4777 Eastern Ave., 45226, pg. 934 **PV**

Rolled Alloys/Atek Metals Division, 9944 Princeton Glendale Rd., 45246, pg. 941 **PV**

Roto-Rooter, 2500 Chemed Ctr., 255 E. Fifth St., 45202-4725, pg. 344 **PB**

ROUGH BROTHERS, INC., 5513 Vine St., 45217, pg. 947 **PV**

SABIN ROBBINS PAPER CO., 106 Circle Freeway Dr., 45246, pg. 959 **PV**

SAKRETE, INC., Fischer Ave. & B&O RR, 45217, pg. 961 **PV**

THE E.W. SCRIPPS COMPANY, 312 Walnut St., 45202, pg. 1447 **PB**

Scripps Howard Broadcasting, 312 Walnut, 45201, pg. 1447 **PB**

Scripps Howard Broadcasting Co., 312 Walnut, 45202, pg. 1448 **PB**

Sealtron, Inc., 9705 Redding Rd., 45215, pg. 490 **PV**

Seasons Congregate Living, Inc., 400 Broadway, 45202, pg. 1164 **PV**

Seasons Management Company, 400 Broadway, 45202, pg. 1164 **PV**

Senco Products, Inc., 8485 Broadwell Rd., 45244, pg. 984 **PV**

SETCO, 5880 Hillside Ave., 45233, pg. 987 **PV**

Simon United States Holdings, Inc., 8044 Montgomery Rd., Ste. 270, 45236, pg. 1252 **IT**

Sive/Young & Rubicam L.P., 36 E. Seventh St., Ste. 2500, 45202, pg. 1197 **PV**

South-Western Publishing Company, 5101 Madison Rd., 45227, pg. 1600 **PB**

Specialty Envelope, 4890 Spring Grove Ave., 45232, pg. 740 **PV**

Specialty Underwriters, Inc., 122 Main St., 45242, pg. 75 **PB**

Spfco Erectors, Inc., 10360 Wayne Ave., 45215, pg. 1017 **PV**

Spur U.S.A. Inc., 11258 Cornell Park Dr., Ste. 612, 45242-1833, pg. 851 **IT**

Squeri Foodservice, 619 Linn St., 45203, pg. 918 **PV**

Stacey Moving & Storage, 5416 Duff Dr., 45246, pg. 869 **PV**

Standard Publishing, 8121 Hamilton Ave., 45231, pg. 1506 **PB**

STANDARD TEXTILE CO., INC., One Knollcrest Dr., 45222, pg. 1032 **PV**

Standex Electronics, 4538 Camberwell Rd., 45209, pg. 1507 **PB**

Star Bank, N.A., P.O. Box 1038, 425 Walnut St., 45201, pg. 1510 **PB**

STARBANC CORPORATION, 425 Walnut St., 45202, pg. 1510 **PB**

Steelcraft Manufacturing Company, 9017 Blue Ash Rd., 45242, pg. 877 **PV**

STEGNER FOOD PRODUCTS CO., 3640 Muddy Creek Rd., 45238, pg. 1039 **PV**

RALPH J. STOLLE CO., 6990 Cornell Rd., 45242, pg. 1044 **PV**

SURGICAL APPLIANCE INDUSTRIES, INC., 3960 Rosslyn Dr., 45209, pg. 1056 **PV**

Jake Sweeney Auto Leasing, Inc., 8276 Vine St., 45216, pg. 1058 **PV**

JAKE SWEENEY AUTOMOTIVE INC., 33 W. Kemper Rd., 45246, pg. 1058 **PV**

Jake Sweeney Jeep Eagle, Inc., 11535 McGillard St., 45246, pg. 1058 **PV**

Sysco Food Services, 10510 Evendale Dr., 45241, pg. 1551 **PB**

TMP Worldwide, Inc., 705 Central Ave., Ste. 300, 45202, pg. 1065 **PV**

Tambrands Inc., One Procter & Gamble Plaza, 45202, pg. 1331 **PB**

Thermal Industries Inc., 4884 Duff Dr., 45246-1124, pg. 491 **PV**

THOMSON MACCONNELL CADILLAC, INC., 2820 Gilbert Ave., 45206, pg. 1084 **PV**

Touchstone Securities, Inc., 311 Pike St., 45202, pg. 1165 **PV**

TOWNE PROPERTIES, 1055 St. Paul Pl., 45202, pg. 1093 **PV**

Tri-State Improvement Co., 139 E. Fourth St., 45202, pg. 369 **PB**

Turner Construction Co., 600 Vine St., Suite 2600, 45202, pg. 1645 **PB**

THE UNION CENTRAL LIFE INSURANCE CO., 1876 Waycross Rd., 45240, pg. 1118 **PV**

Union Light, Heat and Power Co., 139 E. Fourth St., 45202, pg. 369 **PB**

United Air Specialists, Inc., 4440 Creek Rd., 45242, pg. 382 **PV**

UNITED DAIRY FARMERS, INC., 3955 Montgomery Rd., 45212, pg. 1121 **PV**

THE UNITED STATES PLAYING CARD COMPANY, 4590 Beech St., 45212-3497, pg. 1125 **PV**

U.S. Frecision Lens Inc., 3997 McMann Rd., 45245, pg. 448 **PB**

Upright, 644 Linn St. 704, 45203-1739, pg. 1128 **PB**

VALLEY ASPHALT CORPORATION, 11641 Mosteller Rd., 45241, pg. 1131 **PV**

Vidal Sassoon, P.O. Box 599, 45201, pg. 1330 **PB**

Vortec, 10125 Carver Rd., 45242-9976, pg. 865 **PV**

Vulcan Brunswick Bowling Pin Company, 30 Garfield Pl., 45202-4322, pg. 266 **PB**

WCI Machine Tools & Systems, 720 E. Pete Rose Way, 45202, pg. 440 **IT**

WCPO-TV, 500 Central Ave., 45202, pg. 1448 **PB**

WEBN-FM, 1111 St. Gregory, 45202, pg. 922 **PB**

WLW-AM, 1111 St. Gregory, 45202, pg. 922 **PB**

WARM BROTHERS CONSTRUCTION COMPANY, 2335 Florence Ave., 45206, pg. 1150 **PV**

The West Harrison Gas and Electric Co., 139 E. Fourth St., 45202, pg. 369 **PB**

WestAd Inc., 400 Broadway, 45202-3341, pg. 1164 **PV**

THE WESTERN AND SOUTHERN LIFE INSURANCE COMPANY, 400 Broadway, 45202-3302, pg. 1164 **PV**

Western International Media Corporation, 312 Walnut St., Ste. 2550, 45202, pg. 1167 **PV**

Western-Southern Agency, Inc., 400 Broadway, 45202, pg. 1165 **PV**

Western-Southern Life Assurance Co., 400 Broadway, 45202, pg. 1164 **PV**

WestTax, Inc., 400 Broadway, 45202, pg. 1165 **PV**

White Castle Bakery Division, 3126 Exon Ave., 45241-2548, pg. 1172 **PV**

WHITING MANUFACTURING CO., INC., 9999 Carver Rd., 45242, pg. 1174 **PV**

WITT COMPANY, 4454 Steel Pl., 45209, pg. 1185 **PV**

Witt Galvanizing Division, 4454 Steel Pl., 45209, pg. 1185 **PV**

Witt Products Division, 4454 Steel Pl., 45209, pg. 1185 **PV**

JEFF WYLER DEALER GROUP, INC., 829 Eastgate South Dr., 45245, pg. 1193 **PV**

XTEK, INC., 11451 Reading Rd., 45241, pg. 1194 **PV**

Xetron Corp., 460 W. Cresentville Rd., 45246, pg. 1198 **PB**

Xomox Corp., 4444 Cooper Rd., 45242, pg. 574 **PB**

Y.K.K. (U.S.A.) Inc., 4700 Ashwood Dr., 45241, pg. 1515 **IT**

Zeneca Specialties, 10370 Julian Dr., 45215, pg. 1525 **IT**

Circleville

CIRCLE PLASTICS PRODUCTS, INC., 200 Pittsburgh Rd., 43113, pg. 240 **PV**

Du Pont Electronics Information Storage Division, Rt. 23 S. Du Pont Rd., 43113, pg. 531 **PB**

Cleveland

A.G. Industries Inc., One American Rd., 44144, pg. 78 **PB**

AT Acceptance Corporation, 127 Public Sq., 44114, pg. 955 **PB**

AT Financial Corporation, 127 Public Sq., 44114, pg. 955 **PB**

Acme Frame Products, Inc., One American Rd., 44144, pg. 78 **PB**

ACTRON MANUFACTURING COMPANY, 9999 Walford Ave., 44102, pg. 16 **PV**

Adalet Div., 4801 W. 150th St., 44135, pg. 217 **PB**

Adaptive Electronics, 1360 W. Ninth St., Ste. 210, 44113, pg. 17 **PV**

Adec Automation, 1360 W. Ninth St., Ste. 210, 44113, pg. 17 **PV**

ADEC INTERNATIONAL AUTOMATION CORP., 1360 W. Ninth St., Ste. 210, 44113, pg. 17 **PV**

ADVANSTAR COMMUNICATIONS, 7500 Old Oak Blvd., 44130, pg. 22 **PB**

Airflex Div. Eaton Corp., 9919 Clinton Rd., 44144, pg. 556 **PB**

The Ajax Manufacturing Company, 1441 Chardon Rd. N., 44117, pg. 1258 **PV**

Alcan Aluminum Corporation, 6060 Parkland Blvd., 44124, pg. 50 **IT**

Alcan Recycling, 100 Erieview Plaza, 44114, pg. 50 **IT**

Alcan Rolled Products Division, 6060 Parkland Blvd., 44124, pg. 50 **IT**

Alcan Rolled Products Recycling, 100 Erieview, 44114-1878, pg. 50 **IT**

Alcoa Forged Products, 1600 Harvard Ave., 44105-3092, pg. 60 **PB**

Allied Advertising, 1846 Coventry Rd., Ste. 300, 44118-1682, pg. 38 **PV**

Allied Construction Products, Inc., 3900 Kelley Ave., 44114, pg. 1339 **PB**

Allied Insurance Agency, 6300 Wilson Mills Rd., 44143, pg. 1334 **PB**

Allied Security Inc., 7123 Pearl Rd., Ste. 309, 44130, pg. 40 **PV**

Allmetal Screw Products Corp, 672-D Alpha Park Dr., 44143, pg. 41 **PV**

Allright Parking of Cleveland, Inc., 1500 Payne Ave., 44114, pg. 43 **PV**

AMERICAN GREETINGS CORPORATION, One American Rd., 44144-2398, pg. 77 **PB**

American Greetings U.S. Greeting Card Division, One American Rd., 44144, pg. 78 **PB**

American Natl. Can Co., 5300 Dobeckmun S.W., 44102, pg. 1029 **PB**

American Seaway Foods, Inc., 5300 Richmond Rd., 44146, pg. 451 **PV**

AMERICAN TANK & FABRICATING CO., 12314 Elmwood Ave., 44111, pg. 63 **PV**

Ameritech Phone Company, 45 Erieview Plaza, 44114, pg. 98 **PV**

Anchor Fasteners, 26101 Fargo Ave., 44146, pg. 865 **PB**

Anchor Metal Processing, 11830 Brookpark Rd., 44130, pg. 71 **PV**

ANCHOR TOOL & DIE COMPANY, 11830 Brookpark Rd., 44130, pg. 71 **PV**

ANTARES GROUP INC., 4950 Harvard Ave., 44105, pg. 76 **PV**

Apcoa, Inc., McDonald Investment Center, 800 Superior Ave., 10th Floor, 44114, pg. 533 **PV**

APPLIED INDUSTRIAL TECHNOLOGIES, One Applied Plaza, 44115, pg. 122 **PB**

ARGO-TECH CORPORATION, 23555 Euclid Ave., 44117, pg. 81 **PV**

Arocom Marketing Group, Inc., 1350 Euclid Ave., 44115, pg. 730 **PV**

ARROW INTERNATIONAL, 9900 Clinton Rd., 44144, pg. 85 **PV**

Artus, Inc., 10800 Brookpark Rd., 44130, pg. 668 **PB**

Aspen Imaging International, Inc., 3830 Kelley Ave., 44114, pg. 1339 **PB**

Atlas Lederer Co., P.O. Box 20190, 44120, pg. 256 **PB**

THE AUSTIN COMPANY, 3650 Mayfield Rd., 44121, pg. 99 **PB**

AUSTIN POWDER CO., 25800 Science Park Dr., 3rd Fl., 44122, pg. 100 **PV**

Auto Insurance Solutions Inc., 6300 Wilson Mills Rd., 44143, pg. 1334 **PB**

Automation Finishing Inc., 5240 Smith Rd., 44142, pg. 426 **PV**

Automation Group, 6035 Parkland Blvd., 44124-4141, pg. 1259 **PB**

BF Goodrich Landing Systems Division, 3781 E. 77th St., 44105, pg. 751 **PB**

BP America Inc., 200 Public Sq., 44114-2375, pg. 220 **IT**

BP Chemicals, Inc., 4440 Warrensville Ctr. Rd., 44114, pg. 220 **IT**

BP North America Petroleum Inc., 200 Public Sq., 44114, pg. 220 **IT**

BP Oil Co., 200 Public Sq., 44114, pg. 220 **IT**

BP Oil Pipeline Company, 200 Public Sq., 44114, pg. 220 **IT**

BP Pipelines (Alaska) Inc., 200 Public Sq., 44114, pg. 220 **IT**

BV Construction, Inc., 10800 Brookpark Rd., 44130, pg. 668 **PB**

Ballston Development Corporation, 10800 Brookpark Rd., 44130, pg. 668 **PB**

Bankers' Acceptance Corporation, Inc., P.O. Box 94638, 44101-4638, pg. 1153 **PB**

Banks-Baldwin, P.O. Box 318063, 611 Oak Tree Blvd., 44131, pg. 1602 **PB**

Bear Valley, Inc., 10800 Brookpark Rd., 44130, pg. 668 **PB**

Geographic Index-U.S.

Bettcher Manufacturing Corp., 16000 Commerce Park Dr., 44142, pg. 169 PV
Binks Manufacturing Company, Bldg. C, Units 31 & 32, 6909 Engle Rd., 44130-3421, pg. 229 PB
Birmingham Steel Corp., Cleveland Div., 4300 E. 49th St., 44125, pg. 232 PB
Blue Coral/Slick 50, 1215 Valley Belt Rd., 44131-1451, pg. 1348 PB
Bondo/Mar-Hyde Corporation, 4475 E. 175th St., 44128, pg. 1357 PB
Bowman Distribution, 850 E. 72nd St., 44103, pg. 190 PB
Bowne of Cleveland, Inc., 1241 Superior Ave., 44114, pg. 249 PB
BOYKIN LODGING CO., Guildhall Bldg., 45 W. Prospect Ave., Ste. 1500, 44115, pg. 249 PB
BOYKIN MANAGEMENT CO., 50 Public Sq., Ste. 1500, 44113, pg. 162 PV
BRITTANY CORPORATION, 1770 Huntington Bldg., 925 Euclid Ave., 44115, pg. 169 PV
Bronze Headquarters, 1022-30 Berea Rd., 44102, pg. 127 PV
Brooks Technology, 3304 E. 87th St., 44127, pg. 1068 IT
Bruening Bearings, Inc., 3600 Euclid Ave., 44115, pg. 122 PB
BRUSH WELLMAN INC., 17876 St. Clair Ave., 44110, pg. 266 PB
Buxton & Skinner Printing Company, 3830 Kelley Ave., 44114, pg. 1339 PB
C-T Engineering, 4500 Euclid Ave., 44103, pg. 1068 IT
Cambium Corporation, 10800 Brookpark Road, 44130, pg. 668 PB
Canton L.D. Corporation, 10800 Brookpark Rd., 44130, pg. 668 PB
Capital American Finance, 1001 Lakeside Ave., 44114-1195, pg. 433 PB
CARD PAK, INC., 19220 Miles Ave., 44128, pg. 208 PV
Carlon Chimes Co., 25701 Science Park Dr., 44122, pg. 976 PB
Carlton Cards Division, One American Rd., 44144, pg. 78 PB
Carothers Road, Inc., 10800 Brookpark Rd., 44130, pg. 668 PB
Carpenter Reserve Printing Company, 7100 Euclid Ave., 44103, pg. 1735 PB
A.M. Castle & Co., 26800 Miles Rd., 44146, pg. 313 PB
Cement Transit Co., Lee Rd. & Monticello Blvds., 44118, pg. 1084 PB
Certanium Alloys & Research, 4500 Euclid Ave., 44103, pg. 1068 IT
Chagrin Beachwood Inc., 10800 Brookpark Rd., 44130, pg. 668 PB
Champion Int'l. Corp., 7920 Mapleway Dr., 44138, pg. 334 PB
Chandler Products, Inc., 1491 Chardon Rd., 44117, pg. 370 PV
CHART INDUSTRIES, INC., 5885 Landerbrooks Dr., Ste. 150, 44124, pg. 336 PB
Charter One Bank, 1215 Superior Ave., 44114, pg. 336 PB
CHARTER ONE FINANCIAL, INC., Charter One Bank Bldg., 1215 Superior Ave., 44114, pg. 336 PB
Chase Financial Management Corp., 1015 Euclid Ave., 44115, pg. 338 PB
Chase Financial Services Corp., 1015 Euclid Ave., 44115, pg. 338 PB
Chocoamerican Inc., 5885 Grant Ave., 44105, pg. 865 IT
Circle Freight International USA, 17901 Sheldon Rd., 44130, pg. 371 PB
Circle International, 17901 Sheldon Rd., 44130, pg. 371 PB
Cleveland City Forge, 777 E. 79th St., 44103, pg. 1258 PB
CLEVELAND-CLIFFS INC, 1100 Superior Ave., 44114-2589, pg. 386 PB
The Cleveland-Cliffs Iron Company, 1100 Superior Ave., 44114, pg. 386 PB
Cleveland District Cooling Corp., 1801 12th St., Ste. 201, 44114, pg. 913 PB
Cleveland Range, 1333 E. 179th St., 44110, pg. 188 IT
Cleveland Shiprepair Company, 1898 Carter Rd., 44113, pg. 1041 PB
Cleveland Thermal Energy Corporation, 1801 12th St., Ste. 201, 44114, pg. 913 PB
Cleveland Wood Products, 3881 West 150th St., 44111, pg. 217 PB
Cliffs Mining Company, 1100 Superior Ave., 44114, pg. 386 PB
Coaxial Dynamics Inc., 15210 Industrial Pkwy., 44135, pg. 623 PV
Cole Gift Centers, Inc., 5340 Avion Park Dr., 44143, pg. 396 PB
COLE NATIONAL CORPORATION, 5915 Landerbrook Dr., 44124, pg. 396 PB
COLEJON CORPORATION, 1775 E. 45th St., 44103, pg. 251 PV
Columbia Iron & Metal Co., 6600 Grant Ave., 44105, pg. 256 PV
COLUMBIA NATIONAL GROUP, INC., 6600 Grant Ave., 44105, pg. 255 PV
Concourse Development, Inc., 10800 Brookpark Rd., 44130, pg. 668 PB
Condor Tool & Die, Inc., 4541 Industrial Pkwy., 44135, pg. 71 PV
Container Port Group, 1340 Depot St., Ste. 103, 44116, pg. 1191 PV
Corrugated Packaging, 4600 Brookpark Rd., 44134, pg. 737 PB
Coshocton L.D. Corp., 10800 Brookpark Rd., 44130, pg. 668 PB
Cowell's Bingo, 9900 Clinton Rd., 44144, pg. 85 PV
Cox Communications-Cleveland, 12221 Plaza Dr., 44130, pg. 454 PB

Crain's Cleveland Business, 700 W. St. Clair Ave., Ste. 310, 44113-1230, pg. 285 PV
THE CRAWFORD GROUP, 2300 Euclid Ave., 44117, pg. 287 PV
CRES-COR, 12825 Taft Ave., 44108-1683, pg. 288 PB
DCM Manufacturing, Inc., 4540 W. 160th St., 44135, pg. 342 PV
Day-Glo Color Corp., 4515 St. Clair Ave., 44103, pg. 1357 PB
DEFIANCE, INC., 1111 Chester Ave., Ste. 750, 44114-3576, pg. 493 PB
Devoe Paint, 925 Euclid Ave., 44139, pg. 663 IT
Directory Services Group, 1228 Euclid Ave., 44115, pg. 667 PV
DIX & EATON INCORPORATED, 1301 E. 9th St., Ste. 1300, 44114, pg. 336 PB
Dixie Bearings, Inc., 3600 Euclid Ave., 44115, pg. 122 PB
DONLEY'S, INC., 5430 Warner Rd., 44125, pg. 340 PV
DREISON INTERNATIONAL, INC., 6501 Barberton Ave., 44102, pg. 342 PV
Duellman Electric Supply, Inc., 3465 W. 140th St., 44111, pg. 1107 PB
ECC Financial Group, Galleria and Tower at Erieview, 1301 E. Ninth St. 3400, 44114-1817, pg. 558 PB
Eagle Engineering & Manufacturing, Inc., 4560 W. 160th St., 44135, pg. 342 PV
Eagle Ice Cream Div., 90 Broadway, 44146, pg. 451 PV
The East Ohio Gas Co., 1717 E. Ninth St., 44114, pg. 435 PB
EATON CORPORATION, 1111 Superior Eaton Ctr., 44114-2584, pg. 555 PB
Eaton Leasing Corp., Eaton Center, 44114, pg. 558 PB
The Elco Corp., 1000 Belt Line St., 44109, pg. 502 PB
ELWELL-PARKER LIMITED, 4205 St. Clair Ave., 44103, pg. 373 PV
Emery Customs Brokers, 6940A Engle Rd., 44130, pg. 281 PB
The Euclid Chemical Company, 19218 Redwood Rd., 44110, pg. 1358 PB
Euclid Hitachi, 22221 St. Clair Ave., 44117, pg. 622 IT
F.C. Burton L.D. Corp., 10800 Brookpark Rd., 44130, pg. 568 PB
F.C. Hedged Mortgage Co., 10800 Brookpark Rd., 44130, pg. 568 PB
F.C. Laurel, Inc., 10800 Brookpark Rd., 44130, pg. 668 PB
F.C. Parklabrea Towers, Inc., 10800 Brookpark Rd., 44130, pg. 368 PB
F.C. Southridge Corp., 10800 Brookpark Rd., 44130, pg. 368 PB
F.C. Teaneck, Inc., 10800 Brookpark Rd., 44130, pg. 368 PB
F.C.D. Parma Limited Dividend Corp., 10800 Brookpark Rd., 44130, pg. 668 PB
FATA Production Machinery, P.O. Box 43487, 44143, pg. 474 IT
FEDERAL PROCESS CORP., 4620 Richmond Rd., 44128, pg. 399 PV
Ferallow Cleveland Div., 4650 Johnston Pkwy., 44128, pg. 1070 IT
FERRO CORPORATION, 1000 Lakeside Ave., 44114, pg. 618 PB
The Fifth Third Bank of Northeastern Ohio, 1404 E. 9th St., 44114, pg. 621 PB
5300 Richmond Road Corporation, 5300 Richmond Road, 44146, pg. 451 PV
FIGGIE INTERNATIONAL INC., 5875 Landerbrook Dr., Ste. 250, 44124, pg. 622 PB
Figgie Properties Inc., 5875 Landerbrook Dr., Ste. 250, 44124, pg. 622 PB
Filtration Group, 6035 Parkland Blvd., 44124-4141, pg. 1260 PB
Financial Recovery Corporation of America, 6001 Cochran Rd., Rm. 203, 44139-0428, pg. 1153 PB
First American Equity Loan Services, One Erieview Plaza, 5th Fl., 44114-1721, pg. 625 PB
First Union Management, Inc., 55 Public Sq., Ste. 1910, 44113, pg. 641 PV
FIRST UNION REAL ESTATE INVESTMENTS, 55 Public Square, Ste. 1900, 44113-1937, pg. 640 PV
Fisher Properties, Inc., 5300 Richmond Rd., 44146, pg. 451 PV
THE FLORISTS ASSN. OF GREATER CLEVELAND, INC., 21010 Center Ridge Rd., Ste. 300, 44116, pg. 415 PV
Fluid Connectors Group, 6035 Parkland Blvd., 44124-4141, pg. 1260 PB
Forest Bay, Inc., 10800 Brookpark Rd., 44130, pg. 668 PB
Forest City Antelope Valley, Inc., 10800 Brookpark Rd., 44130, pg. 668 PB
Forest City Apartment Mngmt. Div., Terminal Tower, 44113, pg. 668 PB
Forest City Bayside Corporation, 10800 Brookpark Rd., 44130, pg. 668 PB
Forest City Burbank, Inc., 10800 Brookpark Rd., 44130, pg. 668 PB
Forest City Cambridge Inc., 10800 Brookpark Road, 44130, pg. 668 PB
Forest City Capital Corporation, 555 Terminal Tower, 50 Public Square, 44113, pg. 668 PB
Forest City Commercial Construction Company, Inc., 10800 Brookpark Rd., 44130, pg. 668 PB
Forest City Commercial Mngmt. Div., 5745 Chevrolet Blvd., 44130, pg. 668 PB
Forest City Contract Lumber, Inc., 10800 Brookpark Rd., 44130, pg. 668 PB
Forest City Credit Corporation, 10800 Brookpark Rd., 44130, pg. 668 PB
FOREST CITY ENTERPRISES, INC., 10800 Brookpark Rd., 44130-1199, pg. 667 PB
Forest City Eureka, Inc., 10800 Brookpark Rd., 44130, pg. 668 PB

Forest City Grand Terrace, Inc., 10800 Brookpark Rd., 44130, pg. 668 PB
Forest City International Plaza Corporation, 10800 Brookpark Rd., 44130, pg. 668 PB
Forest City Kent, Inc., 10800 Brookpark Rd., 44130, pg. 668 PB
Forest City Land Group, 10800 Brookpark Rd., 44130, pg. 668 PB
Forest City MetroTech Corp., 10800 Brookpark Rd., 44130, pg. 668 PB
Forest City Palmdale, Inc., 10800 Brookpark Rd., 44130, pg. 668 PB
Forest City Park Manor, Inc., 10800 Brookpark Rd., 44130, pg. 668 PB
Forest City Parklabrea, Inc., 10800 Brookpark Rd., 44130, pg. 668 PB
Forest City Rental Properties Corporation, 10800 Brookpark Rd., 44130, pg. 668 PB
Forest City Rental Properties of Nevada, Inc., 10800 Brookpark Rd., 44130, pg. 668 PB
Forest City Residential Development Inc., 10800 Brookpark Rd., 44130, pg. 669 PB
Forest City Rolling Acres, Inc., 10800 Brookpark Rd., 44130, pg. 669 PB
Forest City San Vicente Corp., 10800 Brookpark Rd., 44130, pg. 669 PB
Forest City S.I.A.C. Building, Inc., 10800 Brookpark Rd., 44130, pg. 668 PB
Forest City Southpark Corp., 10800 Brookpark Rd., 44130, pg. 668 PB
Forest City Southpark Two, Inc., 10800 Brookpark Rd., 44130, pg. 669 PB
Forest City 38 Sidney Street, Inc., 10800 Brookpark Rd., 44130, pg. 669 PB
Forest City Vineyard Village, Inc., 10800 Brookpark Rd., 44130, pg. 669 PB
Foseco Holding Inc., 20200 Sheldon Road, 44142, pg. 234 IT
Foseco Inc., P.O. Box 81227, 44181, pg. 234 IT
Fox International Ltd., Inc., 23600 Aurora Rd., 44146, pg. 1720 PV
FREEWAY CORPORATION, 9301 Allen Dr., 44125, pg. 426 PV
G.E. Lighting Division, 1975 Noble Rd., 44112, pg. 710 PB
G.E. Toshiba Lighting Corporation, c/o GE Lighting, Nela Park, 1975 Noble Rd., 44112, pg. 710 PB
GKN Sinter Metals Inc., 50 Public Sq., Ste. 3200, 44113, pg. 535 IT
Gibraltar Strip Steel, Inc., 4300 E. 49th St., 44125, pg. 742 PB
Glastic Corporation, 4321 Glenridge Rd., 44121, pg. 740 IT
Gold Key Insurance Agency, 6300 Wilson Mills Rd., 44143, pg. 1334 PB
Stephen Gould of Ohio, Corp., 4350 Emery Industrial Pkwy., 44128, pg. 467 PV
Great Lakes Confectionery, 5885 Grant Ave., 44105, pg. 865 IT
Great Lakes Environmental Services, Inc., 2777 Broadway Ave., 44115, pg. 924 PV
GREAT LAKES LITHOGRAPH CO., 4005 Clark Ave., 44109-1186, pg. 474 PV
Greenfield Industries, 12985 Snow Rd., 44129, pg. 950 PB
Grow Group, Inc., 925 Euclid Ave., 44115, pg. 663 IT
Guardian Alarm of Cleveland, 1507 Brookpark Rd., 44109, pg. 485 PV
H & D STEEL SERVICE, INC., 9960 York-Alpha Dr., 44133, pg. 489 PV
HMI INDUSTRIES, 3631 Perkins Ave., 44114, pg. 771 PV
Halcyon Insurance Co., 6300 Wilson Mills Rd., 44143, pg. 1335 PB
Hall Systems, Inc., 24400 Sperry Dr., 44145, pg. 1447 PB
Hanna Hamilton Holdings Co., 100 Erieview Plaza, 44114, pg. 781 PB
Hanna Insurance Services Division, 200 Public Sq., Ste. 365000, 44114, pg. 781 PB
M.A. Hanna Color, 800 Kenmar Industrial Pkwy., 44147, pg. 781 PB
M.A. HANNA COMPANY, 200 Public Sq., Ste. 36-5000, 44114, pg. 780 PB
Hanna Marine Services, 200 Public Sq., Ste. 365000, 44114, pg. 781 PB
HAWK CORP., 200 Public Sq., 44114, pg. 511 PV
Health-Mor Acceptance Corp., 3500 Payne Ave., 44114, pg. 771 PB
HEINEN'S INC., 20601 Aurora Rd., 44146, pg. 519 PV
HICKOK INCORPORATED, 10514 Dupont Ave., 44108-1399, pg. 825 PB
HINKLEY LIGHTING INC., 12600 Berea Rd., 44111, pg. 530 PV
J.I. Holcomb Mfg., 4500 Euclid Ave., 44103, pg. 1068 IT
Household Products Co., 13501 Enterprise Ave., 44135, pg. 387 PB
Hower Corp., 10800 Brookpark Rd., 44130, pg. 669 PB
Howmet-Tempcraft, Inc., 3960 S. Marginal Rd., 44114, pg. 213 PV
Hudson Precast Properties, Inc., 10800 Brookpark Rd., 44130, pg. 669 PB
Hydraulics Group, 6035 Parkland Blvd., 44124-4141, pg. 1261 PB
ICI Paints, 925 Euclid Ave., Ste. 900, 44115, pg. 664 IT
ICI Paints, 925 Euclid Ave., 44115, pg. 663 IT
IMG, One Erieview Plaza, Ste. 1300, 44114, pg. 555 PV
ITW Produx, 4910 Commerce Pkwy., 44128, pg. 867 PB
iCatcher, 25 Prospect West, 44115, pg. 1194 PV
Ideal/Mrs. Weiss Noodle Co., 31313 Aurora Rd., 44139-2705, pg. 812 PB
In Town Hotels, Inc., 10800 Brookpark Rd., 44130, pg. 669 PB
In Town Parking, Inc., 10800 Brookpark Rd., 44130, pg. 669 PB

PB - U.S. Public Companies Volume
PV - U.S. Private Companies Volume
IT - International Public & Private Companies Volume

Geographic Index-U.S.

In Town Shopping Center, Inc., 10800 Brookpark Rd., 44130, pg. 669 **PB**
Industrial/Process Division, 1500 W. Third St., 44113-1406, pg. 1134 **PB**
Institutional Trust & Investment Services, 1900 E. Ninth St., 44114, pg. 1154 **PB**
Instrumentation Group, 6035 Parkland Blvd., 44124-4141, pg. 1261 **PB**
Insurance Automation Systems, 3737 Park East Dr., 44122, pg. 1660 **PB**
Insurance Conformation Services, 6300 Wilson Mills Rd., 44143, pg. 1334 **PB**
INTOOL ROTOR COMPANY, 26300 Lakeland Blvd., 44132, pg. 574 **PV**
Iochpe-Maxion Ohio, Inc., 10615 Madison Ave., 44102, pg. 688 **IT**
JERGENS INC., 19520 Nottingham Rd., 44110, pg. 586 **PV**
JONES, DAY, REAVIS & POGUE, North Point, 901 Lakeside Ave., 44114, pg. 596 **PV**
Karas Trucking Co., Inc., 16200 Brookpark Rd., 44135, pg. 264 **PB**
Kay Home Products, Inc., 1971 W. 85th St., 44102, pg. 1258 **PB**
W. H. Kay Company, 17727 S. Miles Rd., 44128, pg. 360 **PV**
KEITHLEY INSTRUMENTS, INC., 28775 Aurora Rd., 44139, pg. 946 **PV**
Keithley Instruments, Inc., 30500 Bainbridge Rd., 44139, pg. 946 **PV**
Keithley Instruments Inc.-Radiation Measurements Div., 6045 Cochran Rd., 44139, pg. 946 **PV**
Keithley International Investment Corp., 28775 Aurora Rd., 44139, pg. 947 **PV**
Ken-Mac Metals, Inc., 17901 Englewood Dr., 44130, pg. 1388 **IT**
Kent Industries, 4500 Euclid Ave., 44103, pg. 1068 **IT**
Key Bank Life Insurance, Ltd., 127 Public Sq., 44114, pg. 954 **PB**
Key Bank USA N.A., 127 Public Sq., 8th Fl., 44114-1306, pg. 954 **PB**
Key Community Development Corporation, 127 Public Square, 44114, pg. 954 **PB**
Key Equity Capital Corp., 127 Public Sq., 44114, pg. 955 **PB**
Key Investments, Inc., 127 Public Sq., 44114, pg. 954 **PB**
Key Mortgage Services, Inc., 127 Public Sq., 44114, pg. 954 **PB**
Key Services Corporation, 2025 Ontario St., 44114, pg. 954 **PB**
Key Trust Company of Ohio, National Association, 127 Public Sq., 44114-1306, pg. 955 **PB**
KEYCORP, 127 Public Sq., 44114-1306, pg. 954 **PB**
KeyCorp Shareholder Services, Inc., 127 Public Square, 44114, pg. 955 **PB**
Kilroy Structural Steel, 8500 Union Ave., 44105, pg. 1640 **PB**
King Bearing, Inc., 3960 Euclid Ave., 44115, pg. 122 **PB**
Kintetsu World Express Inc., 17830 Englewood Dr., Unit 6, 44130, pg. 735 **IT**
Kirby Company, 1920 W. 114th St., 44102, pg. 217 **PB**
Kirkwood Carbon, 4855 W. 130th St., 44135, pg. 623 **PV**
Kirkwood Commutator, 4855 W. 130th St., 44135, pg. 623 **PV**
Kirkwood Foreign Sales Corp., 4855 W. 130th St., 44135, pg. 623 **PV**
KIRKWOOD INDUSTRIES, INC., 4855 W. 130th St., 44135, pg. 623 **PV**
The Otto Konigslow Mfg. Co., 13300 Coit Rd., 44110, pg. 1640 **PB**
L.D. Toledo Corp., 10800 Brookpark Rd., 44130, pg. 669 **PB**
THE LTV CORPORATION, 200 Public Sq., 44114-2308, pg. 971 **PB**
LWI Holdings Inc., 4944 Commerce Pkwy., 44128, pg. 782 **PB**
Lake Erie Screw Corporation, 13001 Athens Ave., 44107, pg. 1054 **PB**
Lakeside Insurance Agency, Inc., 6300 Wilson Mills Rd., 44143, pg. 1334 **PB**
THE LAMSON & SESSIONS CO., 25701 Science Park Dr., 44122-7313, pg. 976 **PB**
Latin American Group, 6035 Parkland Blvd., 44124-4141, pg. 1262 **PB**
LIGGETT-STASHOWER, INC., 1228 Euclid Ave., 44115, pg. 667 **PV**
Liggett-Stashower Public Relations, 1228 Euclid Ave., 44115, pg. 667 **PV**
Lima Limited Dividend Corp., 10800 Brookpark Rd., 44130, pg. 669 **PB**
THE LINCOLN ELECTRIC COMPANY, 22801 St. Clair Ave., 44117-1199, pg. 996 **PB**
Lubriquip, Inc., 18901 Cranwood Pkwy., 44128, pg. 862 **PB**
The Machine Tool Group, 170 E. 131st St., 44108, pg. 503 **PB**
MAGIC AMERICAN CORPORATION, 23700 Mercantile Rd., 44122, pg. 695 **PV**
MAGVS, INC., 4899 Commerce Pkwy., 44060, pg. 696 **PV**
MALRITE COMMUNICATIONS GROUP, INC., 800 Skylight Office Tower, 1660 W. Second St., 44113, pg. 698 **PV**
MAN-GILL CHEMICAL COMPANY, 23000 St. Clair Ave., 44117, pg. 699 **PB**
Management Recruiters International, Inc., 200 Public Sq., 31st Fl., 44114-2301, pg. 277 **PB**
Mannesmann Demag Corporation, 29201 Aurora Rd., 44139, pg. 837 **IT**
Maradyne Corporation, 6501 Barberton Ave., 44102, pg. 342 **PV**
Marine Transportation, 1100 Superior Ave., 44114, pg. 1213 **PB**

Marion Manufacturing, 6501 Barberton Ave., 44102, pg. 342 **PV**
Marshallan Industries, 1971 W. 85th St., 44102, pg. 1259 **PB**
Martin Merkel Inc., 5375 Naiman Pkwy. Ste. B, 44139, pg. 859 **IT**
Master Builders Inc., 23700 Chagrin Blvd., 44122, pg. 1465 **IT**
Matt Construction Services, Inc., 3732 Broadway, 44115, pg. 256 **PV**
Mayfran International, Inc., 6650 Beta Drive, 44143, pg. 1397 **IT**
MCDONALD & COMPANY INVESTMENTS, INC., 800 Superior Ave., Ste. 2100, 44114, pg. 1068 **PB**
MCGEAN-ROHCO, INC., 2910 Harvard Ave., 44105-3010, pg. 721 **PV**
Medusa Aggregate Co., P.O. Box 5668, 3008 Monticello Blvd., 44101, pg. 1084 **PB**
MEDUSA CORPORATION, 3008 Monticello Blvd., 44118, pg. 1084 **PB**
MEGAS BEAUTY CARE, INC., 15501 Industrial Pkwy., 44135, pg. 729 **PV**
MELDRUM & FEWSMITH COMMUNICATIONS INC., 1350 Euclid Ave., 44115, pg. 730 **PV**
Meldrum & Fewsmith Directory Marketing, 1350 Euclid Ave., 44115, pg. 730 **PV**
Meldrum & Fewsmith Interactive, 1350 Euclid Ave., 44115, pg. 730 **PV**
Meldrum & Fewsmith Retail Services Group, 1350 Euclid Ave., 44115, pg. 730 **PV**
Mellon Mortgage Company, 1422 Euclid Ave. Ste. 900, 44115, pg. 1085 **PB**
Meriam Instrument, 10920 Madison Ave., 44102, pg. 218 **PB**
Mesaba-Cliffs Mining Co., Diamond Bldg., 1100 Superior Ave., 44144, pg. 903 **IT**
Metro Parking Systems, 1476 Davenport, 44114, pg. 739 **PV**
METROPOLITAN PROPERTIES SYSTEMS, 1476 Davenport, 44114, pg. 739 **PV**
Mid-Corp, Inc., 10800 Brookpark Rd., 44130, pg. 669 **PB**
Midland Title Security, Inc., One Erieview Plaza, 44114, pg. 626 **PB**
Midwest Mica, 4855 W. 130th St., 44135, pg. 623 **PV**
Milgray/Cleveland, Inc., 6155 Rockside Rd., 44131, pg. 206 **PB**
Mitsui & Co. (U.S.A.), 200 Public Sq., 44114, pg. 879 **IT**
Montgomery Watson, 2000 Bond Court Bldg., 1300 E. Ninth St., 44114, pg. 759 **PV**
Mooney Chemicals, 2301 Scranton Rd., 44113, pg. 1208 **PV**
Morgan's Foods of Missouri, Inc., 24200 Chagrin Blvd., Ste. 126, 44122, pg. 1133 **PB**
Morgan's Restaurants of New Jersey, Inc., 24200 Chagrin Blvd., Ste. 126, 44122, pg. 1133 **PB**
Morgan's Restaurants of Ohio, Inc., 24200 Chagrin Blvd., Ste. 126, 44122, pg. 1133 **PB**
Morgan's Restaurants of PA., Inc., 24200 Chagrin Blvd., Ste. 126, 44122, pg. 1133 **PB**
Morgan's Weirton Foods, Inc., 24200 Chagrin Blvd., Ste. 126, 44122, pg. 1133 **PB**
Morrison Knudsen Corp.-Engineering & Construction, MK-Ferguson Plaza, 1500 W. Third, 44113, pg. 1134 **PB**
Motch Corporation, 1250 E. 222nd St., 44117, pg. 1128 **IT**
Mr. Gasket Inc., 8700 Brookpark Rd., 44129, pg. 560 **PB**
NPA Coatings Inc., 11110 Berea Rd., 44102, pg. 937 **IT**
NACCO INDUSTRIES, INC., 5875 Landerbrook Dr., Ste. 300, 44124-4017, pg. 1149 **PB**
NatCity Investments, Inc., National City Ctr., 1965 E. Sixth St., 44114-3484, pg. 1154 **PB**
National City Bank, 1900 E. Ninth St., 44114, pg. 1154 **PB**
National City Capital Corp., 1965 E. Sixth St., 44114, pg. 1154 **PB**
National City Commercial Finance, Inc., 1965 E. 6th St., Ste. 400, 44114-2214, pg. 1154 **PB**
National City Community Development Corp., 1900 E. Ninth St., 44114-3484, pg. 1154 **PB**
NATIONAL CITY CORPORATION, National City Ctr., 1900 E. Ninth St., 44114-3484, pg. 1154 **PB**
National City Venture Corp., 1965 E. Sixth St., 44114, pg. 1154 **PB**
National Union Electric Corp., 11770 Berea Rd., 44111, pg. 440 **IT**
NationsCredit Commercial Corporation, 4770 Hinkley Industrial Pkwy., 44109, pg. 1165 **PB**
NESCO, INC., 6140 Parkland Blvd., 44124, pg. 791 **PV**
Nestaway, 9501 Granger Rd., 44125, pg. 103 **PV**
New York Frozen Foods, Inc., 25900 Fargo Ave., 44146, pg. 977 **PB**
Newburgh & South Shore Railroad Company, 4200 E. 71st St., 44105-5726, pg. 171 **PV**
NICSAND, INC., P.O. Box 29480, 44129, pg. 799 **PV**
THE NORTH AMERICAN MANUFACTURING CO., 4455 E. 71st St., 44105, pg. 803 **PV**
NORTH AMERICAN REFRACTORIES COMPANY, 1228 Euclid, 44115, pg. 803 **PV**
North Coast Behavioral Research Group, 25 Prospect West, 44115, pg. 1194 **PV**
Northeast Marketing-Cleveland Business Center, 600 Superior Ave., Ste. 1300, 44114, pg. 649 **PB**
OM GROUP, 2301 Scranton Road, 44113, pg. 1208 **PB**
OGLEBAY NORTON COMPANY, 1100 Superior Ave., 44114-2598, pg. 1213 **PB**
Oglebay Norton Industrial Sands, Inc., 1100 Superior Ave., 44114, pg. 1213 **PB**
Oglebay Norton Refractories & Minerals, Inc., 1100 Superior Ave., 44114, pg. 1214 **PB**
Ohio Crankshaft Div., 3800 Harvard Ave., 44105, pg. 1258 **PB**

OHIO MACHINERY CO., 3993 E. Royalton Rd., 44147, pg. 812 **PV**
The Ohio Mattress Company Licensing & Components Group, 10th Fl., Halle Bldg., 1228 Euclid Ave., 44115, pg. 979 **PV**
OLYMPIC STEEL INC., 5096 Richmond Rd., 44146, pg. 1221 **PB**
Operations & Maintenance Division, 1500 W. Third St., 44113-1406, pg. 1134 **PB**
OREO Corporation, 127 Public Sq., 44114, pg. 955 **PB**
Oro Grande, Inc., 10800 Brookpark Rd., 44130, pg. 669 **PB**
Osborn Manufacturing, 5401 Hamilton Ave., 44114, pg. 924 **PB**
PC Investment Company, 6300 Wilson Mills Rd., 44143, pg. 1335 **PB**
PSI-Process Systems International, Inc., 35555 Curtis Blvd., 44095, pg. 336 **PV**
PARK CORP., International Exposition Ctr., 6200 Riverside Dr., 44135, pg. 839 **PV**
Park Drop Forge Div., 777 E. 79th St., 44103, pg. 1258 **PB**
PARK-OHIO INDUSTRIES, INC., 23000 Euclid Ave., 44117, pg. 1258 **PB**
PARKER HANNIFIN CORPORATION, 6035 Parkland Blvd., 44124-4141, pg. 1259 **PB**
Parklabrea Finance Corp., 10800 Brookpark Rd., 44130, pg. 669 **PB**
The Payne Investment Company, 1770 Huntington Bldg., 925 Euclid Ave., 44115, pg. 169 **PV**
Penton Publishing, Inc., 1100 Superior Ave., 44114, pg. 1306 **PV**
Perlmuter Printing Company, 4437 E. 49th St., 44125, pg. 1177 **IT**
Philip Metals Inc., 20521 Chagrin Blvd., 44122, pg. 1050 **PV**
Picker International, Inc., 595 Miner Rd., 44143, pg. 545 **IT**
PinnAcle Media, 25 Prospect West, 44115, pg. 1194 **PV**
PIONEER-STANDARD ELECTRONICS, INC., 4800 E. 131st St., 44105, pg. 1300 **PB**
Playhouse Square Investments, Inc., 10800 Brookpark Rd., 44130, pg. 669 **PB**
Plus Mark, Inc., One American Rd., 44144, pg. 78 **PB**
Portage Development, Inc., 10800 Brookpark Rd., 44130, pg. 669 **PB**
Post Office Building Co., 10800 Brookpark Rd., 44130, pg. 669 **PB**
Power Division, 1500 W. Third St., 44113-1406, pg. 1134 **PB**
Pratt & Lambert United, Inc., 101 Prospect Ave., 44115, pg. 1466 **PB**
Predicasts, 11001 Cedar Ave., 44106, pg. 1600 **PB**
PREFORMED LINE PRODUCTS, 660 Beta Dr., 44143, pg. 1321 **PB**
Premier Autoware, 4500 Euclid Ave., 44103, pg. 1068 **IT**
Premier Energy Corporation, 4500 Euclid Ave., 44103, pg. 1068 **IT**
Premier Farnell, 4500 Euclid Ave., 44103, pg. 1068 **IT**
Premier Fastener, 4500 Euclid Ave., 44103, pg. 1068 **IT**
Premier Foreign Sales Corporation, 4500 Euclid Ave., 44103, pg. 1068 **IT**
Premierco Service Corp., 4415 Euclid Ave., 44103, pg. 1068 **PV**
PREPLINK, 4005 Clark Ave., 44109-1186, pg. 475 **PV**
The Producto Machine Company, 13620 Enterprise Ave., 44135, pg. 889 **PV**
Progressive Casualty Insurance Co., 6300 Wilson Mills Rd., 44143, pg. 1334 **PB**
THE PROGRESSIVE CORPORATION, 6300 Wilson Mills Rd., 44124, pg. 1334 **PB**
Progressive Corp., Agency Group, 6300 Wilson Mills Rd., 44122, pg. 1334 **PB**
Progressive Corp., Financial Services Div., 730 SOM Center Rd., 44143, pg. 1334 **PB**
Progressive County Mutual Insurance Co., 6300 Wilson Mills Rd., 44143, pg. 1335 **PB**
Progressive Gulf Insurance Co., 6300 Wilson Mills Rd., 44143, pg. 1334 **PB**
Progressive Insurance Agency, Inc., 6300 Wilson Mills Rd., 44143, pg. 1335 **PB**
Progressive Investment Company, Inc., 6300 Wilson Mills Rd., 44143, pg. 1335 **PB**
Progressive Max Insurance Co., 6300 Wilson Mills Rd., 44143, pg. 1335 **PB**
Progressive Northern Insurance Co., 6300 Wilson Mills Rd., 44143, pg. 1335 **PB**
Progressive Northwestern Insurance Co., 6300 Wilson Mills Rd., 44143, pg. 1335 **PB**
Progressive Preferred Insurance Co., 6300 Wilson Mills Rd., 44143, pg. 1335 **PB**
Progressive Specialty Insurance Co., 6300 Wilson Mills Rd., 44143, pg. 1335 **PB**
PUBCO CORPORATION, 3830 Kelley Ave., 44114, pg. 1339 **PV**
R & R Homes, Inc., 10800 Brookpark Rd., 44130, pg. 669 **PB**
RB&W Corporation, 23000 Euclid Ave., 44117, pg. 1258 **PB**
RADIX WIRE COMPANY, 26260 Lakeland Blvd., 44132, pg. 907 **PV**
Ramada International Hotels & Resorts, 29800 Bainbridge Rd., 44139, pg. 1048 **PB**
REALTY ONE, 6000 Rockside Woods Blvd., 44131-2350, pg. 914 **PV**
Reliance Electric, 25001 Tungsten Rd., 44117, pg. 1397 **PB**
Reliance Electric Company, 24701 Euclid Ave., 44117, pg. 1398 **PB**
RELTEC CORPORATION, 5875 Landerbrook Dr., Ste. 250, 44124, pg. 921 **PV**

PB - *U.S. Public Companies Volume*
PV - *U.S. Private Companies Volume*
IT - *International Public & Private Companies Volume*

Geographic Index-U.S.

Renaissance International Hotels, 29800 Bainbridge Rd., 44139, pg. 1048 **PB**
RESEARCH ENVIRONMENTAL INDUSTRIES, INC., 2777 Rockefeller Ave., 44115, pg. 924 **PV**
Research Oil Co., 2777 Broadway Ave., 44115, pg. 924 **PV**
Research Trucking Company, Inc., 2777 Broadway Ave., 44115, pg. 924 **PV**
Rini-Rego Supermarkets, Inc., 5300 Richmond Rd., 44146, pg. 451 **PV**
Rolero Omega Operations, 4933 NEO Pkwy., 44128, pg. 443 **PB**
Rollins Hudig Hall of Ohio, Inc., 1300 E. 9th St., 44114, pg. 117 **PB**
Rotanium Products, 4500 Euclid Ave., 44103, pg. 1068 **IT**
ROYAL APPLIANCE MFG. CO., 650 Alpha Dr., 44143-2172, pg. 1410 **PB**
SEI Corporation, 1120 Chester Ave., Ste. 450, 44114, pg. 1417 **PB**
SFZ Transportation Inc., 4750 W. 160th St., 44135, pg. 218 **PB**
SRDC, Inc., 10800 Brookpark Rd., 44130, pg. 670 **PB**
SEALY CORPORATION, Halle Bldg., 10th Fl., 1228 Euclid Ave., 44115, pg. 978 **PV**
Sealy, Inc., 1228 Euclid Ave., 10th Fl., 44115, pg. 979 **PV**
SELECT RESTAURANTS, INC., 30050 Chagrin Blvd., 44124, pg. 982 **PV**
Sequent Computer Systems, Inc., 6450 Rickside Woods Blvd., S., 44131, pg. 1459 **PB**
THE SHERWIN-WILLIAMS COMPANY, 101 Prospect Ave., N.W., 44115-1075, pg. 1465 **PB**
Sherwin-Williams Paint Stores Group, 101 Prospect Ave., N.W., 44115, pg. 1466 **PB**
SIFCO Forge Group, 970 E. 64th St., 44103, pg. 1471 **PB**
SIFCO INDUSTRIES, INC., 970 E. 64th St., 44103, pg. 1470 **PB**
SIFCO Selective Plating, 7908 Schaaf Rd., 44131, pg. 1471 **PB**
Simkins Carton Div.-Cleveland, 7275 Wentworth Ave., 44102, pg. 1000 **PV**
Society Asset Mgmt., Inc., 127 Public Square, 44114, pg. 955 **PB**
Society Equipment Leasing Corporation, 127 Public Square, 44114, pg. 955 **PB**
Society Investments, Inc., 127 Public Square, 44114, pg. 955 **PB**
Society Mortgage Company, 127 Public Square, 44114, pg. 955 **PB**
Society National Bank, 127 Public Sq., 44114, pg. 954 **PB**
South Bay Galleria, Inc., 10800 Brookpark Rd., 44130, pg. 669 **PB**
Specialty Management Co., 9900 Clinton Rd., 44144, pg. 85 **PV**
Specialty Polymers & Chemicals Division, 6100 Oaktree Blvd., 44131, pg. 751 **PV**
Specialty Restaurants Corp., 20000 Brookpark Rd., 44135, pg. 1023 **PV**
Springfield L.D. Corp., 10800 Brookpark Rd., 44130, pg. 669 **PB**
Stanley Air Tools Div., 700 Beta Dr., 44143, pg. 1509 **PB**
The Stearns & Foster Bedding Company, 1228 Euclid Ave., 10th Fl., 44115, pg. 979 **PV**
STERN ADVERTISING, INC., 29125 Chagrin Blvd., 44122, pg. 1041 **PV**
Sunrise Development Co., 10800 Brookpark Rd., 44130, pg. 669 **PB**
Sunrise Land Co., 10800 Brookpark Rd., 44130, pg. 670 **PB**
SuperTrapp Industries, 4540 W. 160th St., 44135, pg. 342 **PB**
Surfside Towers II, Inc., 10800 Brookpark Rd., 44130, pg. 669 **PB**
The Syracuse Adhesives Company, 14500 Darley Ave., 44110, pg. 803 **IT**
TMP Worldwide, Inc., 1382 W. Ninth St., Ste. 300, 44113-1398, pg. 1064 **PV**
TPC Wire & Cable, 4614 Prospect Ave., 44103, pg. 1068 **IT**
TRW Automotive Electronics Group, 1900 Richmond Rd., 44124-3760, pg. 1558 **PB**
TRW INC., 1900 Richmond Rd., 44124-3760, pg. 1558 **PB**
TRW Occupant Restraints Systems, 1900 Richmond Rd., 44124-3760, pg. 1558 **PB**
TRW Steering, Suspension & Engine Group, 1900 Richmond Rd., 44124-3760, pg. 1558 **PB**
TWI International, Inc., 24460 Aurora Rd., 44146, pg. 1559 **PB**
Technicomp, Inc., 1111 Chester Ave., Ste. 300, 44114, pg. 260 **PB**
Terminal Investments, Inc., 10800 Brookpark Rd., 44130, pg. 669 **PB**
Terminal Management, Inc., 10800 Brookpark Rd., 44130, pg. 669 **PB**
Thermal Industries Inc., 4920 Commerce Pkwy., 44128-5981, pg. 491 **PB**
Those Characters From Cleveland, Inc., One American Rd., 44144, pg. 78 **PV**
Tower City Development, Inc., 10800 Brookpark Rd., 44130, pg. 669 **PB**
Tower City Land Corporation, 10800 Brookpark Rd., 44130, pg. 669 **PB**
Tower City Properties, 10800 Brookpark Rd., 44130, pg. 668 **PB**
Tower City Valet Parking, 10800 Brookpark Rd., 44130, pg. 669 **PB**
Tower Hotels, Inc., 10800 Brookpark Rd., 44130, pg. 669 **PB**
Transilwrap Co., Inc., 4700 Manufacturing Rd., 44135, pg. 1097 **PV**
Transportation Recoveries Inc., 6300 Wilson Mills Rd., 44143, pg. 1335 **PB**

Trelleborg Inc., 30700 Solon Industrial Pkwy., 44139, pg. 1423 **IT**
Tube Division, 1335 E. 171st St., 44110, pg. 1221 **PB**
Tube Form, Inc., 25840 Miles Rd., 44145, pg. 771 **PB**
Turbine Engine Components Textron, 23555 Euclid Ave., 44117, pg. 1589 **PB**
Turbo Industries, 6501 Barberton Ave., 44102, pg. 342 **PV**
Turner Construction Co., 100 Erieview Plaza, 44114, pg. 1645 **PB**
Tusar, Inc., 10800 Brookpark Rd., 44130, pg. 669 **PB**
Uddeholm Corporation, 7900 Hub Pkwy., 44125, pg. 1472 **IT**
UNGER COMPANY, 12401 Berea Rd., 44111-1090, pg. 1117 **PV**
United Financial Casualty Co., 6300 Wilson Mills Rd., 44143, pg. 1335 **PB**
United States Biomedical Corporation, 2611 Miles Rd., 44128, pg. 992 **IT**
The Universal Steel Co., 6600 Grant, 44105, pg. 256 **PV**
VWS, Inc., 11760 Berea Rd., 44111, pg. 440 **IT**
Victoria Financial Corporation, 5915 Landerbrook Dr., 44124, pg. 1660 **PV**
Victoria Fire & Casualty, 5915 Landerbrook Dr., 44124, pg. 1660 **PV**
Village Transport Corp., 6300 Wilson Mills Rd., 44143, pg. 1335 **PB**
Volvo Construction Equipment, 22221 St. Clair Ave., 44117, pg. 1477 **IT**
VOSS INDUSTRIES, INC., 2168 W. 25th St., 44113, pg. 1143 **PV**
WENZ-FM, 1041 Huron Rd., 44115, pg. 385 **PB**
WERE, 1041 Huron Rd., 44115, pg. 385 **PB**
WEWS-TV, 3001 Euclid, 44115, pg. 1448 **PB**
WKYC-TV, 1403 East 6th St., 44114, pg. 702 **PB**
WNCX, 1041 Huron Rd., 44115, pg. 385 **PB**
WATT, ROOP & CO., 1100 Superior Ave., 13th Fl., 44114, pg. 1154 **PV**
Webber Gage Div., 24500 Detroit Rd., 44145, pg. 1511 **PV**
Western International Media Corporation, Court House Sq., Ste. 350, 310 W. Lakeside Ave., 44113-1021, pg. 1167 **PV**
White Consolidated Industries, Inc., 11770 Berea Rd., 44111-1601, pg. 439 **IT**
Wilhold Inc., One American Rd., 44144, pg. 78 **PB**
Willamette Industries Inc., 4500 Emery Industrial Pkwy., 44128, pg. 1768 **PV**
Willis Corroon Corp. of Northern Ohio, Bond Court Bldg., Ste. 1700, 1300 E. Ninth St., 44114, pg. 1506 **IT**
Wilson Mills Land Company, 6300 Wilson Mills Rd., 44143, pg. 1335 **PB**
WYSE ADVERTISING, 25 Prospect West, 44115, pg. 1193 **PV**
Wyse Advertising/Cleveland, 25 Prospect West, 44115, pg. 1194 **PV**
Wyse Direct, 25 Prospect West, 44115, pg. 1194 **PV**
Xenia L.D. Corp., 10800 Brookpark Rd., 44130, pg. 670 **PB**
Zellerbach Division, 26401 Richmond Rd., 44146, pg. 1075 **PB**

Cleves

Graseby GMW, 145 South Miami, 45002, pg. 1268 **IT**

Clyde

Clyde Savings Bank Company, 137 W. Buckeye St., 43410, pg. 632 **PB**
Whirlpool Corp., Clyde Div., 119 Birdseye St., 43410, pg. 1765 **PB**

Columbus

ABB Industrial Systems, Inc., 650 Ackerman Rd., 43202, pg. 4 **IT**
AEP Generating Co., One Riverside Plaza, 43215, pg. 72 **PB**
AEP Resources Service Company, One Riverside Plaza, 43215, pg. 72 **PB**
Abitec, 525 W. 1st Ave., 43201, pg. 92 **IT**
ACORN PRODUCTS, INC., 500 Dublin Ave., 43216-1930, pg. 17 **PV**
Advanced Distribution System, Inc., 4181 Arlingate Plaza, 43228, pg. 911 **PB**
Akzo Nobel Coatings Inc., 1313 Windsor, 43211, pg. 48 **IT**
Allen Milk Co., P.O. Box 453, 43216, pg. 977 **PB**
Alliance Data Systems, 4590 E. Broad St., 43213, pg. 995 **PB**
Allied Eastern Co., 1611 Integrity Dr., 43209, pg. 1204 **PV**
ALLIED MINERAL PRODUCTS, INC., 2700 Scioto Pkwy., 43221, pg. 39 **PV**
Allied Security Inc., 1550 Old Henderson Rd., Ste. N160, 43220, pg. 40 **PV**
Allright Columbus Parking, Inc., 145 N. High St., 43215, pg. 42 **PV**
AMERICAN ELECTRIC POWER COMPANY, INC., One Riverside Plaza, 43215-2373, pg. 71 **PB**
American Electric Power Service Corp., One Riverside Plaza, 43215, pg. 72 **PB**
American Glassmith, Inc., 195 Phillipi Rd., 43228, pg. 67 **PV**
American Hardware Mutual Insurance Co., 471 E. Broad St., 43215, pg. 764 **PV**
American Health Packaging, 2550 John Glenn Ave., 43217, pg. 96 **PV**
American Merchants Casualty Co., 471 E. Broad St., 43215, pg. 764 **PV**
AmeriSource-Columbus Div., 1200 E. Fifth Ave., 43219, pg. 97 **PB**

Assurex Development Corporation, 6480 Busch Blvd., Ste. 320, 43229, pg. 366 **PB**
Automobile Club Insurance Company, 3590 Twin Creeks Dr., 43204, pg. 51 **PV**
Banc One Capital Corporation, 90 N. High St., 43215, pg. 175 **PB**
BANC ONE CORPORATION, 100 E. Broad St., 43271, pg. 172 **PB**
Banc One Credit Corporation, 100 E. Broad St., 43271, pg. 175 **PB**
Banc One Leasing Corporation, 100 E. Broad St., 43215, pg. 175 **PB**
Banc One Life Insurance Co., 100 E. Broad St., 43215, pg. 175 **PB**
Banc One Ohio Corporation, 100 E. Broad St., 43271, pg. 173 **PB**
Banc One Realty Columbus Corp., 100 E. Broad St., 43271, pg. 175 **PB**
Banc One Securities Corporation, 100 E. Broad St., 43215, pg. 175 **PB**
Banc One Services Corporation, 100 E. Broad St., 43215, pg. 175 **PB**
BANCINSURANCE CORP., 20 E. Broad St., 4th Fl., 43215, pg. 175 **PB**
The Bank of Tokyo-Mitsubishi, Ltd. (Columbus Corporate Banking), Huntington Ctr., Ste. 2492, 41 S. High St., 43215, pg. 157 **IT**
Bank One, Ohio Trust Company, N.A., 100 E. Broad St., 43271, pg. 175 **PB**
BATTELLE MEMORIAL INSTITUTE, 505 King Ave., 43201-2693, pg. 123 **PV**
Bekaert Corporation, 2320 International St., 43228, pg. 184 **IT**
Big Bear Stores Company, 770 W. Goodale Blvd., 43212, pg. 1270 **PB**
Borden Foods Corporation, 180 E. Broad St., 43215-3799, pg. 157 **PV**
BORDEN, INC., 180 E. Broad St., 25th Fl., 43215, pg. 157 **PV**
Borden International, Inc., 180 E. Broad St., 43215, pg. 158 **PV**
Borden Italian Foods, 180 E. Broad St., 43215, pg. 158 **PV**
Brooks Beverage Management, Inc., 1900 E. Dublin - Granville Rd., 43229, pg. 142 **PV**
Brown Steel Div., P.O. Box 16505, 43216, pg. 651 **PV**
Buckeye Steel Castings Company, 2211 Parsons Ave., 43085, pg. 1780 **PB**
Buckeye Union Insurance Co., 1111 E. Broad St., 43216, pg. 1010 **PB**
Building Material Industry Division, 650 Ackerman Rd., 43220, pg. 4 **IT**
BURGESS & NIPLE, LIMITED, 5085 Reed Rd., 43220, pg. 182 **PV**
Burns & Wilcox - Columbus Office, 6230 Busch Blvd. Ste. 403, 43229, pg. 609 **PV**
Business First of Columbus, Inc., 471 E. Broad St., Ste. 1500, 43215, pg. 19 **PV**
CGAS, Inc., 4770 Indianola Ave., 43214, pg. 585 **PB**
CNS-Community News Service Weekly Newspapers, 90A Northwoods Blvd., 43234, pg. 335 **PV**
CTL Steel Co., 375 E. Fifth Ave., 43201, pg. 243 **PV**
California Cash Management Company, One Nationwide Plaza, 43216, pg. 788 **PV**
Cigna Healthcare of Ohio, Inc., 445 Hutchinson Ave., Ste. 900, 43235, pg. 360 **PB**
Circle International, 3275 Alum Creek Ave., 43207, pg. 371 **PB**
CLARK GRAVE VAULT CO., 375 E. Fifth Ave., 43201, pg. 243 **PV**
Clinton Gas Marketing, 4770 Indianola Ave., 43214, pg. 585 **PB**
The Clinton Oil Company, 4770 Indianola Ave., 43214, pg. 585 **PB**
Colomet, Inc., 215 N. Front St., 43215, pg. 72 **PB**
Columbia Gas Distribution Companies, 200 Civic Center Dr., 43215, pg. 402 **PB**
Columbia Gas of Kentucky, Inc., 200 Civic Ctr. Dr., 43215, pg. 403 **PB**
Columbia Gas of Maryland, Inc., 200 Civic Ctr. Dr., 43215, pg. 403 **PB**
Columbia Gas of Ohio, Inc., 200 Civic Ctr. Dr., 43215, pg. 403 **PB**
Columbia Gas of Pennsylvania, Inc., 200 Civic Ctr. Dr., 43215, pg. 403 **PB**
COLUMBUS PIPE & EQUIPMENT COMPANY, 773 E. Markison Ave., 43207, pg. 257 **PV**
COLUMBUS SHOW CASE COMPANY, 850 W. Fifth Ave., 43212, pg. 257 **PV**
Columbus Southern Power Company, 215 N. Front St., 43215, pg. 72 **PB**
COMBI Block, Inc., 4800 Roberts Rd., 43228, pg. 1020 **IT**
Combibloc Inc., 4800 Roberts Rd., 43228, pg. 1156 **IT**
Compuserve Interactive Services, Inc., 5000 Arlington Center Blvd., 43220, pg. 66 **PV**
Conesville Coal Preparation Co., 215 N. Front St., 43215, pg. 72 **PB**
CONSOLIDATED STORES CORP., P.O. Box 28512, 300 Phillipi Rd., 43228-0512, pg. 437 **PB**
CRANE PLASTICS COMPANY, 2141 Fairwood Ave., 43207, pg. 286 **PV**
Dayton Rogers of Ohio, 2309 McGaw Rd. West, 43207, pg. 318 **PV**
Desco Advertising & Marketing, 150 E. Campus View Blvd., Ste. 250, 43235, pg. 327 **PV**
DESCO CORPORATION, 150 E. Campus View Blvd., Ste. 250, 43235, pg. 326 **PV**
DeVRY Institute of Technology, 1350 Alum Creek Dr., 43209, pg. 504 **PB**
THE DISPATCH PRINTING COMPANY, 34 S. Third St., 43216-1289, pg. 334 **PV**

PB - *U.S. Public Companies Volume*
PV - *U.S. Private Companies Volume*
IT - *International Public & Private Companies Volume*

1382

Geographic Index-U.S.

DYWIDAG Systems International, USA, Inc., 1474 Grandview Ave., 43212, pg. 424 **IT**

ERD Environmental, Inc., 2480 Creekway Dr., 43207, pg. 546 **PB**

Eagle Mountain Energy, Inc., 7626 E. Main St., 43213, pg. 585 **PB**

Eddie Bauer Mail Order Division, 2711 Intl. St., 43228-4604, pg. 1499 **PB**

ELECTRIC POWER EQUIPMENT CO., 60 E. Spring St., 43215, pg. 368 **PV**

Elmer's Products, Inc., 180 E. Broad St., 43215-3799, pg. 158 **PV**

Encore Computer, 6460 Busch Blvd., Ste. 123, 43229, pg. 580 **PB**

Environmental & Commercial Insurance, 2400 Corporate Exchange Dr., #270, 43231, pg. 684 **PV**

EVANS ADHESIVE CORP., 925 Old Henderson Rd., 43220, pg. 384 **PV**

BOB EVANS FARMS, INC., 3776 S. High St., 43207-0863, pg. 596 **PB**

EXECUTIVE JET AVIATION, INC., 625 N. Hamilton Rd., 43219-1825, pg. 388 **PV**

Express, One Limited Pkwy., 43230, pg. 995 **PB**

The Fifth Third Bank of Columbus, 180 E. Road St., 43215, pg. 621 **PB**

Formaldehyde, 1975 Watkins Rd., 43207, pg. 737 **PB**

G B Stores, 3241 Westerville Rd., 43224, pg. 972 **PV**

GSI Engineering, Inc., 2211 Parsons Ave., 43085, pg. 1780 **PB**

General Employment Enterprises, Inc., 88 E. Broad St., Ste. 1450, 43215, pg. 714 **PB**

GERBIG, SNELL/WEISHEIMER & ASSOC., INC., 8000 Ravine's Edge Ct., 43235, pg. 449 **PV**

BF Goodrich Flight Systems, Inc., 2001 Polaris Pkwy., 43240-2001, pg. 751 **PB**

HC HOLDINGS, 1285 Alum Creek Dr., 43209-2797, pg. 489 **PV**

HMS-Direct Columbus, 10 W. Broad St., 15th Fl., 43215, pg. 492 **PV**

HMS PARTNERS, One Columbus, Ten W. Broad St., 43215, pg. 491 **PV**

HMS Partners-Columbus, Ten W. Broad St., 14th Fl., 43215, pg. 492 **PV**

Hagglunds Drives Inc., 2275 International Street, 43228, pg. 670 **IT**

HARROP INDUSTRIES, INC., 3470 E. Fifth Ave., 43219, pg. 506 **PV**

High State/Investors Guaranty, 2500 Farmers Dr., 43085, pg. 110 **PV**

HIGHLIGHTS FOR CHILDREN, INC., 2300 W. Fifth Ave., 43215, pg. 528 **PV**

HOMEWOOD CORPORATION, 750 Northlawn Dr., 43214, pg. 537 **PV**

Hughes-Peters, Inc., 894 Freeway Dr., N., 43229, pg. 547 **PV**

HUNTINGTON BANCSHARES INC., Huntington Ctr., 41 S. High St., 43287, pg. 849 **PB**

Huntington Clothiers, Inc., 1285 Alum Creek Dr., 43209-2797, pg. 490 **PV**

The Huntington Investment Company, Huntington Ctr., 43287, pg. 850 **PB**

Huntington Investment Management Co., 41 High St., 43260, pg. 850 **PB**

The Huntington Mortgage Company, Huntington Ctr., 43287, pg. 850 **PB**

Huntington National Bank, Huntington Ctr., 43287, pg. 850 **PB**

The Huntington National Life Insurance Company, P.O. Box 1558, 43216, pg. 850 **PB**

The Huntington Service Company, 2361 Morse Rd., 43229, pg. 850 **PB**

The Huntington Trust Co., N.A., 41 S. High St., 43260, pg. 850 **PB**

HY-TEK MATERIAL HANDLING, INC., 2222 Port Rd., 43217-1177, pg. 550 **PB**

IRD Mechanalysis, Inc. (U.S.A.), 6150 Huntley Rd., 43229, pg. 789 **PB**

Inn Maid Products, 1105 Schrock Rd., 43229, pg. 977 **PB**

Insurance Intermediaries, Inc., 6460 Busch Blvd., 43229, pg. 789 **PV**

Intergraph Corporation, 65 E. State St., Ste. 1000, 43215, pg. 890 **PB**

Intimate Brands, Inc., Three Limited Pkwy., 43230, pg. 995 **PB**

Investors Fidelity Life Assurance Corp., 2211 Lake Climb Dr., Ste. 100, 43216, pg. 438 **PV**

Kubota Tractor Corp., 438 McCormick St., 43213, pg. 762 **IT**

Lancaster Colony Commercial Products, Inc., P.O. Box 630, 43216, pg. 977 **PV**

LANCASTER COLONY CORPORATION, 37 West Broad St., Ste. 500, 43215, pg. 976 **PV**

LEXFORD RESIDENTIAL TRUST, 41 S. High St., Ste. 2410, 43215, pg. 991 **PB**

Liebert Corporation, 1050 Dearborn Dr., 43229, pg. 573 **PB**

Limited Distribution Services, Two Limited Pkwy., 43230, pg. 995 **PB**

THE LIMITED, INC., Three Limited Pkwy., 43230, pg. 995 **PB**

Limited Real Estate, Three Limited Pkwy., 43230, pg. 995 **PB**

Limited Store Planning, Three Limited Pkwy., 43230, pg. 995 **PB**

Limited Stores, Three Limited Pkwy., 43216, pg. 996 **PB**

Limited, Too, 3885 Morse Rd., 43219, pg. 996 **PB**

LORD, SULLIVAN & YODER INC. MARKETING COMMUNICATIONS, P.O. Box 800, 250 Old Wilson Bridge Rd., 43085-0800, pg. 676 **PV**

Lydall Westex, 6767 Huntley Rd., 43229, pg. 1021 **PB**

MC2 Cyberspace, 707 Park Meadow Rd., 43081, pg. 955 **PV**

T. Marzetti Company, 1105 Schrock Rd., Ste. 600, 43229, pg. 977 **PV**

MAX & ERMA'S RESTAURANTS, 4849 Evanswood Dr., 43229, pg. 1060 **PV**

Menasha Corp., Murfin Division, 539 Industrial Mile Rd., 43228-2412, pg. 731 **PB**

Metal Forge, 291 Marconi Blvd., 43207, pg. 727 **PB**

MICO Insurance Company, 471 E. Broad St., 43215, pg. 764 **PV**

MIDLAND LIFE INSURANCE CO., 250 E. Broad, 43215, pg. 744 **PV**

Montgomery & Collins, Inc. of New Jersey, 100 Old Wilson Bridge Rd., Ste. 100, 43085-2297, pg. 366 **PV**

Montgomery & Collins, Inc. of Ohio, 100 Old Wilson Bridge Rd., Ste. 100, 43085-2297, pg. 366 **PB**

MORGAN LUMBER SALES CO., 800 Jasonway, 43214, pg. 761 **PV**

Motorists Life Insurance Company, 471 E. Broad St., 43215, pg. 764 **PV**

MOTORISTS MUTUAL INSURANCE CO., 471 E. Broad, 43215, pg. 764 **PV**

NBBJ, 1555 Lake Shore Dr., 43204, pg. 771 **PV**

NBD Bank (Ohio), 175 S. Third St., 43215, pg. 628 **PB**

NDS, 1700 17th Ave., 43219, pg. 918 **IT**

NATIONAL ELECTRIC COIL, 800 King Ave., 43212, pg. 782 **PV**

Nationwide Communications, Inc., One Nationwide Plaza, 43216, pg. 789 **PV**

Nationwide General Insurance Company, One Nationwide Plaza, 43216, pg. 789 **PV**

Nationwide HMO, Inc., One Nationwide Plaza, 43216, pg. 789 **PV**

NATIONWIDE INSURANCE ENTERPRISE, One Nationwide Plaza, 43215, pg. 788 **PV**

Nationwide Life Insurance Co., One Nationwide Plaza, 43216, pg. 789 **PV**

Nationwide Property & Casualty Insurance Company, One Nationwide Plaza, 43216, pg. 789 **PV**

Nestle Dairy Systems, Licensing Division, P.O. Box 1819, 43216, pg. 918 **IT**

Nestle Dairy Systems-Packaging/Machinery Division, P.O. Box 1819, 43216, pg. 918 **IT**

Nestle Ice Cream Co., P.O. Box 1869, 43216, pg. 918 **IT**

Nexus Healthcare, Inc., 4161 Arling Gate Plaza, 43228, pg. 304 **PB**

NIBCO Inc., 4531 Industrial Center Dr., 43207, pg. 798 **PV**

94th Aero Squadron of Columbus, Inc., Port Columbus Intl. Airport, 5030 Sawyer Rd., 43219, pg. 1023 **PV**

Noise Dairy Systems, LP, P.O. Box 1819, 43216, pg. 249 **PV**

NORSE DAIRY SYSTEMS, P.O. Box 1869, 43216, pg. 802 **PV**

NuArc Co., 909 Oakland Park, 43224, pg. 809 **PV**

OASIS CORP., 265 N. Hamilton Rd., 43213, pg. 810 **PV**

Ohio Auto Auction, 3905 Jackson Pike, 43123, pg. 283 **PV**

Ohio Indemnity Company, 20 E. Broad St., 4th Fl., 43215, pg. 175 **PV**

Ohio State Life Insurance Co., 2500 Farmers Dr., 43235, pg. 110 **PV**

OHIO TRANSMISSION CORPORATION, 666 Parsons Ave., 43206, pg. 813 **PV**

Olen Corporation, 4755 S. High St., 43207, pg. 631 **PV**

P/M Structural Parts Div., 2100 Advance Ave., 43207, pg. 619 **PV**

PSB Co., 555 W. Goodale St., 43215, pg. 1172 **PV**

Partech Communications Group, Inc., 3021 Bethel Rd., Ste. 208, 43220, pg. 1641 **PB**

Planes Moving & Storage Company Of Columbus, 2000 Dividend Dr., 43228, pg. 869 **PV**

PLASKOLITE INC., 1770 Joyce Ave., 43219, pg. 870 **PV**

PLASTIC SUPPLIERS, INC., 2887 Johnstown Rd., 43219, pg. 871 **PV**

Plastic Suppliers, Inc, 2400 Marilyn Lane, 43219, pg. 871 **PV**

Powertech, 1138 Chambers Rd., 43212-1798, pg. 736 **PV**

Public Employees Benefit Services Corp., One Nationwide Plaza, 43216, pg. 789 **PV**

Pulp & Paper Division, 650 Ackerman Rd., 43202, pg. 4 **IT**

Q3 STAMPED METAL, 777 Manor Park, 43228, pg. 897 **PV**

The Quality Bakery Co., Inc., P.O. Box 29147, 43229, pg. 977 **PB**

Republic Franklin Insurance Co., 2600 Corporate Exchange Dr., 43229, pg. 1130 **PV**

Reputation Management, One Columbus, Ten W. Broad St., 43215, pg. 492 **PV**

RESOURCE MARKETING, INC., 515 N. Park St., 43215, pg. 924 **PV**

Ross Products, 625 Cleveland Ave., 43215, pg. 13 **PB**

Roundy's-Columbus Division, Van Arlingale, 43228, pg. 948 **PV**

Roxane Laboratories, Inc., 1809 Wilson Rd., 43216, pg. 199 **IT**

SBC ADVERTISING, 707 Park Meadow Rd., 43081, pg. 955 **PV**

SBC Specialized Marketing, 707 Park Meadow Rd., 43081, pg. 955 **PV**

SMS-Columbus, 455 Hutchinson Ave., Ste. 900, 43235, pg. 1463 **PB**

SAFELITE AUTOGLASS, 1105 Schrock Rd., 43229, pg. 960 **PV**

I.H. Schlezinger, Inc., 1041 Joyce Ave., 43203, pg. 123 **PV**

SCHOTTENSTEIN STORES CORPORATION, 1800 Moler Rd., 43207, pg. 1172 **PV**

Scientific Advances Inc., 601 W. 5th Ave., 43201, pg. 123 **PV**

SecurityLink from Ameritech, 2461 McGaw Rd., 43207, pg. 98 **PB**

Service General, 6230 Busch Blvd., Ste. 403, 43229, pg. 609 **PV**

SHONAC CORPORATION, 1675 Watkins Rd., 43207, pg. 996 **PV**

Simco, Inc., 215 N. Front St., 43215, pg. 72 **PB**

Specialty Restaurants Corp., 2379 W. Fifth St., 43204, pg. 1023 **PV**

Specialty Restaurants Corporation, 679 W. Spring St., 43215, pg. 1023 **PV**

State Auto Life Insurance Company, 518 E. Broad, 43216, pg. 622 **PB**

State Auto P & C, 518 E. Broad St., 43216, pg. 1036 **PV**

STATE AUTOMOBILE MUTUAL INSURANCE CO., 518 E. Broad, 43215, pg. 1036 **PV**

Ed Stormont Sales, P.O. Box 273, 2570 East Cleft Dr., 43216, pg. 736 **IT**

Structure, Two Limited Pkwy., 43230, pg. 996 **PV**

SUPERIOR DIE TOOL AND MACHINE COMPANY, 2301 Fairwood Ave., 43207, pg. 1054 **PV**

The Sygma Network, Inc.-Columbus Central Division, P.O. Box 28523, 4265 Diplomacy Dr., 43228, pg. 1550 **PB**

SYMIX SYSTEMS, INC., 2800 Corporate Exchange Dr., 43231, pg. 1546 **PV**

Thermal Industries Inc., 7030 Huntley Rd., Ste. A, 43229-1053, pg. 491 **PV**

TROPIC COMMUNICATIONS INC., 3021 Bethel Rd., Ste. 208, 43220, pg. 1641 **PB**

Turner Construction Co., 65 E. State St., 43215, pg. 1645 **PB**

URS Greiner, Inc., 50 W. Broad St., 28th Fl., 43215, pg. 1658 **PB**

UnionTools, Inc., 500 Dublin Ave., 43215, pg. 17 **PV**

United HealthCare of Ohio, Inc., 3650 Olentangy River Rd., 43214-3459, pg. 1678 **PB**

Valley Fair & L.F. Widmann, 3241 Westerville Rd., 43224, pg. 972 **PV**

Value City Department Stores, Inc., 3241 Westerville Rd., 43224, pg. 972 **PV**

Value City Furniture, 1800 Moler Rd., 43207, pg. 972 **PV**

Victoria's Secret Catalog, 3925 Morris Crossing, 43219, pg. 995 **PV**

Viking Engraving Corp. Inc., 1432 N. Grant Ave., 43201, pg. 158 **PV**

WBNS Television & Radio, 770 Twin Rivers Dr., 43215, pg. 335 **PV**

Walker National, Inc., P.O. Box 18155, 43218, pg. 1147 **PV**

Warner Cable Communications, Inc., 1266 Dubin Rd., 43215, pg. 1611 **PB**

WASSERSTROM COMPANY, 477 S. Front St., 43215, pg. 1152 **PV**

Weldon, Inc., 2000 S. High, 43207, pg. 449 **IT**

Westpac Banking Corporation (Columbus Representative Office), Ste. 2870, The Huntington Ctr., 41 S. High St., 43215-6104, pg. 1496 **IT**

White Castle Distributing, Inc., 555 W. Goodale St., 43216, pg. 1172 **PV**

White Castle International Company, 555 W. Goodale St., 43215, pg. 1172 **PV**

WHITE CASTLE SYSTEM, INC., 555 W. Goodale, 43215, pg. 1171 **PV**

THE W.W. WILLIAMS COMPANY, 835 W. Goodale Blvd., 43212, pg. 1178 **PV**

World Book Financial Services, 100 E. Campus View Blvd., Ste. 370, 43235, pg. 218 **PB**

World Book, Inc., 100 E. Campus View Blvd., Ste. 370, 43235, pg. 218 **PB**

Worthington Custom Plastics, 1055 Dearborn Dr., 43085, pg. 1780 **PB**

Worthington Cylinder Corporation, 1085 Dearborn Dr., 43085, pg. 1780 **PB**

WORTHINGTON INDUSTRIES, INC., 1205 Dearborn Dr., 43085, pg. 1780 **PB**

Worthington Steel Co., 1127 Dearborn Dr., 43085, pg. 1780 **PB**

YENKIN-MAJESTIC PAINT CORPORATION, 1920 Leonard Ave., 43219, pg. 1195 **PV**

Zellerbach Division, 808 Rhoads Ave., 43205, pg. 1075 **PB**

Continental

Continental Telephone Co., P.O. Box 367, 88 E. Rice St., 45831, pg. 1571 **PB**

Socar of Ohio, Inc., P.O. Box 219, W. Rice St., 45831, pg. 1392 **PB**

Copley

PVS Chemicals, Inc., 3149 Copley Rd., 44321, pg. 828 **PV**

Cortland

Alphabet Design Center, 80 Erie St., 44410, pg. 1044 **PV**

Control Transformer Corp., 3701 Warren-Meadville Rd., 44410, pg. 113 **IT**

Coshocton

Armco Inc.-Coshocton Operations, P.O. Box 548, 43812, pg. 1164 **PB**

Clow Water Systems Corp., P.O. Box 479, 2266 S. Sixth St., 43812, pg. 725 **PV**

Cox Communications-Coshocton, 640 Walnut St., 43812, pg. 454 **PB**

Ennis Business Forms of Ohio, Inc., 24359 County Rd. #202, 43812, pg. 583 **PB**

Jll/Sales Promotion Associates, Inc., 545 Walnut St., 43812, pg. 598 **PV**

PB - U.S. Public Companies Volume
PV - U.S. Private Companies Volume
IT - International Public & Private Companies Volume

1383

Geographic Index-U.S.

School Annual Publishing Co., 545 Walnut St., 43812, pg. 598 — PV
Steel Ceilings Inc., 500 N. Third St., 43812, pg. 29 — PV

Cuyahoga Falls

Alside, 3773 State Rd., 44223, pg. 91 — PV
DAIRY MART CONVENIENCE STORES, INC., 210 Broadway E., 44222, pg. 476 — PB
The Fifth Third Bank, 2335 Second St., 44221, pg. 622 — PB
General Ionics, 3380 Cavalier Trail, 44224, pg. 912 — PB
GO JO INDUSTRIES, 3783 State Rd., 44223, pg. 458 — PV
Pneumatic Scale Corporation, 10 Ascot Pkwy., 44223, pg. 118 — PV
Schrader Bellows Division, 257 Huddleston Ave., 44221, pg. 1261 — PB
Spirol International Corp., P.O. Box 360, 321 Remington Rd., 44222, pg. 1026 — PV

Dayton

ABS General Contractors, Inc., P.O. Box 14585, 2589 Needmore Rd., 45414, pg. 996 — PV
Allright Dayton Parking, Inc., 100 N. Jefferson, 45402, pg. 42 — PV
Alro Group, Dayton, 821 Springfield St., 45403, pg. 46 — PV
AMCAST INDUSTRIAL CORPORATION, 7887 Washington Village Dr., 45401, pg. 63 — PB
American Aggregates Corp., 6450 Sand Lake Rd., 45414-2659, pg. 245 — IT
Ameritcon, Inc., P.O. Box 14585, 2589 Needmore Rd., 45414, pg. 996 — PV
Ampex Data Systems Corporation, 4130 Linden Ave., 45432, pg. 104 — PV
Apex Operation, 762 W. Stewart St., 45408, pg. 444 — PB
Appleton Papers-West Carrollton Mill, 1030 W. Alex Bell Rd., 45449, pg. 568 — IT
Astro, Inc., 4403 Dayton-Xenia Rd., 45432, pg. 1112 — PV
Automotive Aftermarket, North America, One Prestige Pl., P.O. Box 1004, 45401-1004, pg. 1045 — PB
Bee-Gee Shoe Corp., 3155 El-Bee Rd., 45439, pg. 367 — PV
L.M. Berry and Company, 3170 Kettering Blvd., 45401, pg. 208 — PB
BERRY NETWORK, INC., 3100 Kettering Blvd., 45439, pg. 137 — PV
CSD Dayton Office, 5100 Springfield Pike, Ste. 140, 45431-1231, pg. 1689 — PV
CAP Gemini America (Dayton Branch), 6450 Poe Ave. #416, 45414, pg. 263 — IT
CASSANO'S INC., 1700 E. Stroop Rd., 45429, pg. 218 — PV
Chemineer, Inc., 5870 Poe Ave., 45414, pg. 1393 — PB
CITFED BANCORP, INC., One Citizens Federal Ctr., 45402, pg. 376 — PB
CitFed Mortgage Corporation of America, One Citizens Federal Ctr., 45402, pg. 376 — PB
Citizens Federal Bank, F.S.B., One Citizens Federal Ctr., 45402, pg. 376 — PB
Cole-Layer-Trumble Company (CLT), 3199 Klepinger, 45406, pg. 317 — PV
Conaire Div., P.O. Box 943, 45401, pg. 1398 — IT
Construction & Mining Inc., P.O. Box 725, pg. 310 — PV
CRABAR BUSINESS SYSTEMS, 1129 Miamisburg Centreville Rd., 45449, pg. 283 — PV
D.P.&L. Community Urban Redevelopment Corp., Courthouse Plaza, 45402, pg. 473 — PV
DPL INC., P.O. Box 1247, 45401, pg. 473 — PB
Danis Clarkco Landfill Company, P.O. Box 725, 45401, pg. 310 — PV
THE DANIS COMPANIES, Two Riverplace, Ste. 200, 45405, pg. 310 — PV
Danis Environmental Management Co., P.O. Box 725, 45401, pg. 310 — PV
Danis Heavy Construction Co., Two River Pl., Ste. 200, 45405, pg. 310 — PV
Day International Printing Products Co., 333 W. First St., 45401, pg. 56 — PV
Dayflex Plastics, One Prestige Pl, P.O. Box 1004, 45401-1004, pg. 1045 — PB
Dayton Newspapers, Inc., 45 S. Ludlow St., 45402, pg. 281 — PV
Dayton Operations, 3100 Research Blvd., 45420, pg. 644 — IT
Dayton Power & Light Co., Courthouse Plaza S.W., P.O. Box 1247, 45401, pg. 473 — PB
Dayton Progress Corporation, 500 Progress Rd., 45449, pg. 617 — PB
Dayton Thermal Products Div., 1600 Webster St., 45401-1205, pg. 353 — PB
Delphi Chassis Systems, P.O. Box 1042, 2000 Forrer Blvd., 45401-1042, pg. 719 — PB
Deuer Manufacturing, Inc., 2985 Springboro W., 45439, pg. 1455 — PB
Digitron, 500 Webster St., 45404-1525, pg. 333 — PV
Digitron Kettering, 2801 Wilmington Pike, 45419-2154, pg. 333 — PV
EDD-Dayton, 444 Windsor Park Dr., 45459, pg. 204 — PB
EDD-Dayton Government, 446 Windsor Pk. Dr., 45459, pg. 205 — PV
The El-Bee Chargit Corp., 3155 Elbee Rd., 45439, pg. 367 — PV
THE ELDER-BEERMAN STORES CORP., 3155 El-Bee Rd., 45439, pg. 367 — PB
Farmers Insurance Group, 1377 E. Stroop Rd. Ste. 304, 45429-4900, pg. 111 — IT
FLOWSERVE CORPORATION, Miami Valley Research Park, 3100 Research Blvd., 45420, pg. 658 — PB
Forest Kraft Company, Courthouse Plaza N.E., 45463, pg. 1076 — PB
Giddings & Lewis Sheffield Measurement Systems, 721 Springfield St., 45403, pg. 1389 — IT

Globe Motors Division, 2275 Stanley Ave., 45404, pg. 787 — IT
GOSIGER INC., 108 McDonough St., 45402, pg. 466 — PV
Heidelberg Finishing Systems, 4900 Webster St., 45414, pg. 604 — IT
Hewitt Soap Co., 333 Linden Ave., 45403, pg. 597 — PV
Hewlett-Packard Company, 7887 Washington Village Dr., Ste. 100, 45459, pg. 815 — PB
IAMS COMPANY, 7250 Poe Ave., 45414, pg. 556 — PV
Industrial Distribution and OEM, North America, One Prestige Pl., P.O. Box 1004, 45401-1004, pg. 1045 — PB
Krug International Technology/Scientific Services, Inc., 3821 Colonel Glenn Hwy., 45431, pg. 968 — PB
KURZ-KASCH, INC., 2271 Arbor Blvd., 45401, pg. 637 — PV
LCC Holding Company, Courthouse Plaza N.E., 45463, pg. 1076 — PB
Landise Systems, 3199 Klepinger Rd., 45406, pg. 317 — PV
Lau Div., 2027 Home Ave., P.O. Box 1388, 45401, pg. 1398 — IT
M & M Restaurant Supply, 3581 Dayton Park Dr., 45414, pg. 619 — PV
M-B Pulp Company, Courthouse Plaza N.E., 45463, pg. 1076 — PB
MacGregor Park, Inc., Courthouse Plaza 45402, pg. 473 — PB
Mark IV Industrial, 1 Prestige Pl., 45401, pg. 1045 — PB
Mead Coated Board Intl., Inc., Courthouse Plaza N.E., 45433, pg. 1076 — PB
THE MEAD CORPORATION, Courthouse Plaza N.E., 45433, pg. 1074 — PB
Mead European Holdings, Inc., Courthouse Plaza, N.E., 45463, pg. 1076 — PB
Mead Foreign Holdings, Inc., Courthouse Plaza N.E., 45463, pg. 1076 — PB
Mead International Holdings, Inc., Courthouse Plaza N.E., 45463, pg. 1076 — PB
Mead Panelboard, Inc., Courthouse Plaza N.E., 45463, pg. 1076 — PB
Mead Pulp Sales, Inc., Courthouse Plaza N.E., 45463, pg. 1074 — PB
Mead School & Office Products, Courthouse Plaza N.E., 45463, pg. 1074 — PB
Mead Timber Co., Courthouse Plaza N.E., 45463, pg. 1076 — PB
Miami Mill, 125-129 Mill St., 45449, pg. 434 — IT
Miami Valley Broadcasting Corporation, 1414 Wilmington Ave., 45420, pg. 282 — PV
Miami Valley CTC, Inc., Courthouse Plaza, 45402, pg. 474 — PB
Miami Valley Development Co., Courthouse Plaza, 45402, pg. 474 — PB
Miami Valley Leasing, Inc., Courthouse Plaza, 45402, pg. 474 — PB
Miami Valley Lighting, Inc., Courthouse Plaza, 45402, pg. 474 — PB
Miami Valley Resources, Inc., Courthouse Plaza, 45402, pg. 474 — PB
Monrovia Nursery Co.-Oregon, 12600 S.E. Alderman, 97114, pg. 757 — PV
MOTO PHOTO, INC., 4444 Lake Center Dr., 45426, pg. 1136 — PV
NCR CORPORATION, 1700 S. Patterson Blvd., 45479, pg. 1146 — PB
Perma-Fix of Dayton, Inc., 300 S. W. End Ave., 45427, pg. 1279 — PB
Permacrete Products Corporation, 6450 Sand Lake Rd., 45414-2659, pg. 245 — IT
Plastic Trim, Inc., 3909 Research Blvd., 45430, pg. 919 — PB
PRICE BROTHERS CO., 367 W. Second St., 45402, pg. 883 — PV
PRIMUS INC., 3110 Kettering Blvd., 45439, pg. 884 — PV
PROJECTS UNLIMITED, INC., 3680 Wyse Rd., 45414, pg. 890 — PV
Pulp Asia Limited, Courthouse Plaza N.E., 45463, pg. 1076 — PB
Quality Chemicals, Inc., 1515 Nicholas Rd., 45418, pg. 345 — PB
REX STORES CORP., 2875 Needmore Rd., 45414, pg. 1384 — PB
Reyna Capital Corp., P.O. Box 1005, 45401, pg. 1385 — PB
THE REYNOLDS AND REYNOLDS COMPANY, 115 S. Ludlow St., 45402, pg. 1384 — PB
ROBBINS & MYERS, INC., 1400 Kettering Tower, 45423-1400 pg. 1393 — PB
SRA – Dayton, 101 Woodman Drive, Suite 18, 45431, pg. 958 — PV
SRL Operations, 2800 Indian Ripple Rd., 45440-3696, pg. 1136 — PV
Salem Mall, Inc., 1420 Salem Mall, 5200 Salem Ave., 45426, pg. 1408 — PB
Shook Building Group, P.O. Box 138806, 4977 Northcutt Pl., 45414, pg. 996 — PV
Shook Heavy And Environmental Group, P.O. Box 138806, 4977 Northcutt Pl., 45414, pg. 996 — PV
Shook, Incorporated, P.O. Box 138806, 4977 Northcutt Pl., 45414, pg. 996 — PV
SHOOK NATIONAL CORPORATION, 4977 Northcutt Pl., 45414, pg. 996 — PV
SHOPSMITH, INC., 6530 Poe Ave., 45414, pg. 1467 — PB
Spectra-Physics Laserplane Inc., 5475 Kellenburger Rd., 45424, pg. 1594 — PB
StacoEnergy Products Co., 301 Gaddis Blvd., 45403, pg. 260 — PV
THE STANDARD REGISTER COMPANY, 600 Albany St., 45408-1405, pg. 1505 — PB
Stanfast Inc., 2621 Dryden Rd., Ste. 106, 45439, pg. 1505 — PB
Sugar Creek Packing Co., 1241 N. Gettysburg Ave., 45427, pg. 1049 — PV
Superpetz, 36 W. Third St., 17801, pg. 1752 — PB

Tech Development Inc., 6800 Poe Ave., 45414, pg. 1242 — IT
Tomkins Corporation, 4801 Springfield St., 45431, pg. 1397 — IT
Tomkins Industries Inc., 4801 Springfield St., 45431, pg. 1397 — IT
UES, INC., 4401 Dayton-Xenia Rd., 45432, pg. 1112 — PV
VAN DYNE-CROTTY, INC., 903 Brandt St., 45401, pg. 1132 — PV
Varity Dayton Walther, 2800 E. River Rd., 45439, pg. 820 — IT
WDTN-TV, P.O. Box 741, 4595 S. Dixie Ave., 45439, pg. 516 — PV
WHIO, Inc., 1414 Wilmington Ave., 45420, pg. 282 — PV
Wilmer Service Line, P.O. Box 2237, 45401-2237, pg. 1385 — PB
S.J. Wolfe Division, 32 N. Main St., Ste. 647, 45402, pg. 1068 — PB
WOOLPERT, 409 E. Monument Ave., 45402-1261, pg. 1188 — PV
Zellerbach Division, 2551 Lance Dr., 45409, pg. 1075 — PB
Zephyer Properties, Inc., Courthouse Plaza N.E., 45463, pg. 1076 — PB

Defiance

Cox Communications-Defiance, 310 Jefferson St., 43512, pg. 454 — PV
Defiance Precision Products, Inc., 1125 Precision Way, 43512, pg. 493 — PV
DIEHL INC., 24 N. Clinton St., 43512, pg. 332 — PV
Diehl Specialties International, 24 N. Clinton St., 43512-1899, pg. 332 — PV
Motor Master Products, 815 Greenler Rd., 43512, pg. 1204 — PV
RURBAN FINANCIAL CORP., 401 Clinton St., 43512, pg. 1412 — PB
Rurban Life Insurance Company, 401 Clinton St., 43512, pg. 1413 — PB
Rurbanc Data Services, Inc., 401 Clinton St., 43512, pg. 1413 — PB
The State Bank and Trust Company, 401 Clinton St., 43512, pg. 1413 — PB
ZELLER CORP., 1307 Baltimore St., 43512-1903, pg. 1204 — PV
Zeller World Trade Corporation, P.O. Box 278, 43512, pg. 1204 — PV

Delaware

The Flxible Corp., 970 Pittsburgh Dr., 43015, pg. 444 — PV
Greif Bros. Corporation, 621 Pennsylvania Ave., 43015, pg. 763 — PB
GREIF BROTHERS CORPORATION, 425 Winter Rd., 43015, pg. 763 — PB
The Nippert Company, 801 Pittsburgh Dr., 43015, pg. 1016 — PV
Ranco Automotive Div., 555 London, 43015, pg. 1243 — IT

Delphos

THE COMMERCIAL BANK, 230 E. Second St., 45833, pg. 410 — PB
The Commerical Bank-Main Street, 246 N. Main St., 45833, pg. 410 — PB
I & K DISTRIBUTORS, INC., 1600 Gressel Dr., 45833, pg. 552 — PV

Delta

North Star BHP Steel LLC, 6767 Country Rd 9, 43515, pg. 226 — IT

Dennison

Resource America, Inc., Rte. 800, Stillwater Ave., 44621, pg. 1382 — PB

Dover

Amko Service Company, 44622, pg. 1320 — PB
Dover Chemical Corp., P.O. Box 40, 3676 Davis Rd. NW, 44622, pg. 553 — PV
GREER STEEL CO., 624 Blvd., 44622, pg. 479 — PV
INCA Presswood Pallets, Ltd., P.O. Box 248, 44622, pg. 678 — IT
MARLITE, 202 Harger St., 44622, pg. 705 — PV
Perma Glas-Mesh, Inc., 2201 Progress St., 44622-0039, pg. 1171 — IT
Perma Glass-Mesh Inc., 2201 Progress St., 44622-0039, pg. 1177 — IT
Simon-Duplex Inc., 120 Deeds Dr., 44622, pg. 1252 — IT

Dresden

THE LONGABERGER COMPANY, 95 Chestnut St., 43821, pg. 675 — PV

Dublin

ACCEL INTERNATIONAL CORPORATION, 475 Metro Pl. N., 43017, pg. 14 — PV
Acceleration Insurance Agency, Inc., 475 Metro Pl. N., 43017, pg. 14 — PV
Acceleration Insurance Agency of Indiana, Inc., 475 Metro Pl. N., 43017, pg. 14 — PV
Acceleration Life Insurance Agency, Inc., 475 Metro Pl. N., 43017, pg. 14 — PB

Acceleration National Insurance Company, 475 Metro Pl. N., 43017, pg. 14 **PB**
APPLIED INNOVATION INC., 5800 Innovation Dr., 43016, pg. 123 **PB**
Ashland Chemical, 5200 Paul G. Blazer Memorial Pkwy., 43017, pg. 139 **PB**
Cardinal Distribution, 5555 Glendon Ct., 43016, pg. 304 **PB**
CARDINAL HEALTH INC., 5555 Glendon Ct., 43016, pg. 304 **PB**
Comdisco Healthcare, Inc., 495 Metroplace S., Ste. 110, 43017, pg. 408 **PB**
Delavest, Inc., 4288 W. Dublin-Granville Rd., 43017, pg. 1754 **PB**
DOMINION HOMES, 5501 Frantz Rd., 43017, pg. 516 **PB**
Enron Acess, 655 Metro Place, S., 43017, pg. 584 **PB**
Ethix Midlands, 525 Metro Place N., 43017, pg. 795 **PV**
FAHLGREN, 655 Metro Place S., Ste. 700, 43017, pg. 391 **PV**
Fahlgren, P.O. Box 7159, 655 Metro Place S., Ste. 700, 43017, pg. 391 **PV**
Frigidaire Home Products, 6000 Perimeter Dr., 43017, pg. 439 **IT**
Gates/Arrow Commercial Systems Div., 284 Cramer Creek, 43017, pg. 133 **PB**
Gibson Appliances, 6000 Perimeter Dr., 43017, pg. 439 **IT**
Great Oaks Insurance Company, 4995 Bradenton Ave., Ste. 240, 43017-3521, pg. 786 **PB**
Ikon Office Solutions-Columbus, Cramer Creek Corporate Park, 350 Cramer Creek Ct., 43017, pg. 863 **PB**
Information Dimensions, 5080 Tuttle Crossing Blvd., 43016-2007, pg. 465 **PV**
INSILCO CORPORATION, 425 Metro Pl., N., Ste. 555, 43017, pg. 881 **PB**
Interchange Software Division, P.O. Box 7160, 4600 Lakehurst Ct., 43017-0760, pg. 1516 **PB**
Kelvinator Appliances, 6000 Perimeter Dr., 43017, pg. 440 **IT**
LCI INTERNATIONAL, INC., 4650 Lakehurst Ct., 43016, pg. 969 **PB**
Lancaster Colony Automotive Group, 299 Cramer Creek Court, 43017, pg. 977 **PB**
Progressive Rent-A-Car, Inc., 4288 W. Dublin-Granville Rd., 43017, pg. 1754 **PB**
Restaurant Finance Corporation, 4288 W. Dublin-Granville Rd., 43017, pg. 1754 **PB**
STANLEY STEEMER INTERNATIONAL, INC., 5500 Stanley Steemer Pkwy., 43016, pg. 1033 **PV**
STERLING COMMERCE, INC., 4600 Lakehurst Ct., 43016, pg. 1515 **PB**
WLP Leasing Co., 4288 W. Dublin-Granville Rd., 43017, pg. 1754 **PB**
Wendco Northwest Limited, 4288 W. Dublin-Granville Rd., 43017, pg. 1754 **PB**
Wendcreek Venture, 4288 W. Dublin-Granville Rd., 43017, pg. 1754 **PB**
Wendy Restaurant, Inc., 4288 W. Dublin-Granville Rd., 43017, pg. 1754 **PB**
Wendy's Capital Corporation, 4288 W. Dublin-Granville Rd., 43017, pg. 1754 **PB**
WENDY'S INTERNATIONAL INC., 4288 W. Dublin Granville Rd., 43017, pg. 1754 **PB**
Wendy's of N.E. Florida, Inc., 4288 W. Dublin-Granville Rd., 43017, pg. 1754 **PB**
Wendy's Old Fashioned Hamburgers of New York, 4288 W. Dublin-Granville Rd., 43017, pg. 1754 **PB**
Wenko Company, Ltd. (Korea), U.S. Office: 4288 W. Dublin-Granville Rd., 43017, pg. 1754 **PB**
Wentexas, 4288 W. Dublin-Granville Rd., 43017, pg. 1754 **PB**
Willis Corroon Administrative Services Corporation, 655 Metro Pl. S., 43017, pg. 1505 **IT**
Willis Corroon Corp. of Northern Ohio, 655 Metro Pl. S., Ste. 600, 43017, pg. 1506 **IT**

East Liverpool

East Liverpool Landfill, Inc., Y & O Rd., 43920, pg. 94 **PB**
THE HALL CHINA COMPANY, One Anna Ave., 43920, pg. 494 **PV**

East Sparta

D & H Tool and Die, 10505 Sandyville Rd. S.E., 44626, pg. 1124 **PV**
UNITED STATES CERAMIC TILE CO., 10233 Sandyville Rd., SE, 44626, pg. 1124 **PV**

Eastlake

ENPAC, 34335 Volkes Drive, 44095, pg. 592 **PB**
Gould Electronics Inc., 35129 Curtis Blvd., 44095, pg. 1591 **PB**
Gould Electronics Inc., Foil Division, 35129 Curtis Blvd., 44095, pg. 1592 **PB**

Edgerton

Edgerton Forge, Inc., 257 E. Morrison St., R.R. 2, Box 12, 43517, pg. 102 **PV**

Edon

Edon Machine Div., Box 8, 507 W. Indianna St., 43518, pg. 1475 **PB**

Elida

The Commercial Bank-Elida, 105 S. Greenlawn Ave., 45807, pg. 410 **PB**

Elyria

AlliedSignal Truck Brake Systems Company, 901 Cleveland St., 44036-2016, pg. 738 **IT**
Alltel Ohio, Inc., 363 Third St., P.O. Box 4033, 44035, pg. 56 **PB**
Crane Lear Romec Corp., 241 Abbe Rd. S., 44035-6239, pg. 457 **PB**
Electro Alloys, Abbey Rd & Taylor St., 44035, pg. 839 **PV**
ELYRIA FOUNDRY COMPANY, 120 Filbert St., 44036, pg. 373 **PV**
Elyria Savings & Trust National Bank, 105 Court St., 44035, pg. 646 **PB**
G.I. PLASTEK, Olive & Taylor Sts., 44035, pg. 435 **PV**
Hydraulic Valve Div., 520 Ternes Ave., 44036-2026, pg. 1261 **PB**
ITC Flavor & Seasoning Div., 110 Liberty Ct., 44035, pg. 459 **PB**
INVACARE CORPORATION, One Invacare Way, 44036, pg. 911 **PB**
Lortec Power Systems, Inc., 145 Keep Ct., 44035-2214, pg. 126 **IT**
Manoir Electroalloys Corporation, Taylor St. & Abbe Rd., 44035, pg. 570 **IT**
Ridge Tool Co., 400 Clark St., 44036, pg. 574 **PB**
The Timms Spring Company, 811 Taylor St., 44035, pg. 880 **PV**
Trio Products Inc., 250 Warden Ave., 44035, pg. 915 **PB**

Euclid

Motor Group, 24700 Euclid Ave., 44117-1794, pg. 1398 **PB**
Seika Electric Co., 775 Walnut Dr., 44132, pg. 1218 **IT**
STAMCO INDUSTRIES INC., 26650 Lakeland Blvd., 44132-2644, pg. 1029 **PV**

Fairborn

Miami Valley Publishing Company, Inc., 678 Fairfield - Yellow Springs Rd., 45324, pg. 539 **IT**
Northrop Grumman Corporation - Central Region, 2850 Presidential Dr., Ste. 100, 45324-6265, pg. 1199 **PB**

Fairfield

CFC Investment Corp., 6200 S. Gilmore Rd., 45014, pg. 368 **PB**
Cincinnati Casualty Co., 6200 S. Gilmore Rd., 45014, pg. 368 **PB**
CINCINNATI FINANCIAL CORP., 6200 S. Gilmore Rd., 45014, pg. 368 **PB**
Cincinnati Indemnity Company, 6200 S. Gilmore Rd., 45014, pg. 368 **PB**
Cincinnati Insurance Co., 6200 S. Gilmore Rd., 45014, pg. 368 **PB**
Cincinnati Life Insurance Co., 6200 S. Gilmore Rd., 45014, pg. 368 **PB**
First Finance Mortgage Company, 4783 Dixie Hwy., 45014, pg. 633 **PB**
Intermec Media Products, 9290 Le Saint Dr., 45014-5454, pg. 1699 **PB**
THE KRUSE COMPANY, 4275 Thunderbird Ln., 45014, pg. 636 **PV**
MERCANTILE STORES COMPANY, INC., 9450 Seward Rd., 45014, pg. 1089 **PB**
PEASE INDUSTRIES, INC., 7100 Dixie Hwy., 45014, pg. 845 **PB**
PERFORMANCE AUTOMOTIVE NETWORK, 5816 Dixie Hwy., 45014, pg. 853 **PV**
SKYLINE CHILI, INC., 4180 Thunderbird Ln., 45014, pg. 1475 **PV**
Jeff Wyler Olds, Cadillac, 5251 Dixie Hwy., 45014, pg. 1193 **PV**

Fairlawn

BIOPRODUCTS, INC., 320 Springside Dr., Ste. 300, 44333, pg. 145 **PV**
Gen Corp Inc., 175 Ghent Rd., 44333-3300, pg. 1411 **IT**
GENCORP INC., 175 Ghent Rd., 44333-3300, pg. 705 **PB**

Fayetteville

Fayetteville Tubular Products, Inc., P.O. Box 369, Railroad & Gamber Sts., 43521, pg. 481 **PB**

Findlay

Analytical Services Corporation, 16406 US Rte. 224 E., 45840, pg. 1207 **PB**
CENTREX CORPORATION, 750 Western Ave., 45840, pg. 225 **PV**
COOPER TIRE & RUBBER COMPANY, 701 Lima Ave., 45840, pg. 445 **PB**
The Cooper Tire Company, 701 Lima Ave., 45840, pg. 445 **PB**
Environmental Treatment & Technologies Corp., 16406 U.S. Rte. 224 E., 45839-0551, pg. 1208 **PB**
THE HERCULES TIRE & RUBBER COMPANY, 1300 Morrical Blvd., 45840, pg. 523 **PV**
Kuss Corporation, 1331 Broad Ave., 45840, pg. 468 **PB**

LaRiche Chevrolet-Cadillac, 215 E. Main Cross, 45840, pg. 651 **PV**
LaRiche Toyota-Subaru, 920 Plaza, 45840, pg. 651 **PV**
Marathon Ashland Petroleum LLC, 539 S. Main St., 45840, pg. 139 **PB**
Marathon Ashland Petroleum LLC Retain Marketing, 539 S. Main St., 45840, pg. 1662 **PB**
Marathon Ashland Pile Line LLC, 539 S. Main St., 45840, pg. 1662 **PB**
Marathon International Petroleum Supply Company, 539 S. Main St., 45840, pg. 1662 **PB**
OHM CORPORATION, 16406 U.S. Rte. 224 E., 45840, pg. 1207 **PB**
OHM Environmental Resources Management Corp., 16406 U.S. Rte. 224 E., 45839, pg. 1208 **PB**
OHM International, Inc., 16406 U.S. Rte. 224 E., 45839-0551, pg. 1208 **PB**
OHM Remediation Services Corp., P.O. Box 551, 16406 U.S. Rte. 224 E., 45839, pg. 1208 **PB**
Pan Ocean Energy Company, 539 S. Main St., 45840, pg. 1662 **PB**
The Peoples Banking Company, 301 S. Main St., 45840, pg. 1413 **PB**
Sundor Brands Inc., 4500 Fostoria Rd., 45839, pg. 1331 **PB**
Trinity Difco, 1501 N. Main St., 45840, pg. 1639 **PB**
Whirlpool Corp., Findlay Div., 4901 No. Main St., 45840, pg. 1765 **PB**

Forest

United Aircraft Products, P.O. Box 37, 200 Railroad St., 45843-0037, pg. 1262 **PB**

Fort Loramie

Marwil Products Company, 62 Elm St., 45845, pg. 137 **PB**

Fostoria

AlliedSignal Filters & Spark Plugs, 1600 N. Union St., 44830, pg. 51 **PB**
Atlas Crankshaft Corporation, Rte. 23 S., 44830, pg. 468 **PB**
Atlas, P.O. Box 846, 44830, pg. 468 **PB**
FOSTORIA INDUSTRIES, INC., 1200 N. Main St., 44830, pg. 421 **PV**
GRAY PRINTING CO., 401 E. North St., 44830, pg. 472 **PV**
National Electrical Carbon Corporation, P.O. Box J, 200 N. Town St., 44830, pg. 891 **IT**
ROPPE CORP., 1602 N. Union St., 44830, pg. 944 **PV**
SENECA WIRE & MANUFACTURING CO., 319 S. Vine St., 44830-1843, pg. 984 **PV**

Franklin

Digitron, Inc., 300 Conover Dr., 45005-1996, pg. 332 **PV**
Hepworth Refractories Inc., P.O. Box 666, 45005-0666, pg. 615 **IT**

Fredericktown

KOKOSING CONSTRUCTION COMPANY, INC., 17531 Waterford Rd., 43019, pg. 631 **PV**
Kokosing Materials, Inc., P.O. Box 334, 43109, pg. 631 **PV**

Fremont

CRESCENT MANUFACTURING COMPANY, 1310 Majestic Dr., 43420, pg. 289 **PV**
EPCO, Inc., 225 Cedar St., 43420, pg. 773 **IT**
THE FREMONT CO., 802 N. Front St., 43420, pg. 426 **PV**
Fremont News-Messenger, 1700 Cedar St., 43420, pg. 700 **PB**
Great Lakes Sugar Company, 1101 N. Front St., 43420, pg. 873 **PB**
LUDLOW COMPOSITES CORPORATION, 2100 Commerce Dr., 43420, pg. 680 **PV**

Gahanna

Unisource, 555 Office Center Pl., 43230, pg. 1671 **PB**

Galion

McClain Easy Pack, P.O. Box 607, 44833, pg. 1065 **PB**
Rosewood Manor, 935 Rosewood Dr., 44833, pg. 838 **PB**
Village Care Center, 925 Wagner Ave., 44833, pg. 838 **PB**

Gallipolis

Gallipolis Daily Tribune, 625 Third Ave., 45631, pg. 699 **PB**
Ohio Valley Publishing Co., 825 Third Ave., 45631, pg. 701 **PB**

Garfield Heights

Klockner-Moeller Corp., 5350 Transportation Blvd., #3, 44125, pg. 736 **IT**

Garrettsville

Warren Tool Group, P.O. Box 286, 10610 Freedom St., 44231, pg. 1181 **PV**

Geographic Index-U.S.

Germantown

DUPPS COMPANY, 548 N. Cherry St., 45327, pg. 348 PV

Gibsonburg

CHEMI-TROL CHEMICAL CO., 2776 C.R. 69, 43431, pg. 345 PB

Girard

EASCO INC., 706 S. State St., 44420, pg. 548 PB

Glenford

Glass Rock Plant, 2446 Glass Rock Rd., St. Rt. 204, 43739, pg. 1213 PB

Gomer

The Commercial Bank-Gomer Banking Center, 4310 Lincoln Hwy., 45809, pg. 410 PB

Greenfield

Computer Stock Forms, Inc., 324 S. Washington St., 45123, pg. 947 PV
Waddell Display Cases Div. of Ghent Mfg. Co., 512 S. Washington St., 45123, pg. 450 PV

Greenville

HUGHES SUPPLY CORP., 501 Gray Ave., 45331, pg. 547 PV

Grove City

Tigerpoly Manufacturing, Inc., 6231 Enterprise Pkwy., 43123, pg. 1390 IT
Tosoh SMD, Inc., 3600 Gantz Rd., 43123-1895, pg. 1407 IT

Groveport

Isomedix Operations Inc., 4405 Marketing Pl., 43125, pg. 1515 PB
RICART FORD INC., 4255 S. Hamilton Rd., 43125, pg. 927 PV
SUN TV & APPLIANCES, INC., 6600 Port Rd., 43125-9104, pg. 1532 PB
UNITED MCGILL CORP., One Mission Park, 43125, pg. 1122 PV

Hamilton

American Fire & Casualty Co., 136 N. Third St., 45025, pg. 1214 PB
CHEMCENTRAL/Cincinnati, 12 Standen Dr., 45015, pg. 232 PV
CONNECTOR MANUFACTURING COMPANY, 3501 Symmes Rd., 45015, pg. 264 PV
FIRST FINANCIAL BANCORP, 300 High St., 45011, pg. 632 PB
First National Bank of Southwestern Ohio, 300 High St., 45011, pg. 633 PB
Hamilton Division, 851 Walnut St., 45012, pg. 1517 PB
Hamilton Machining Center, 2175 Schlicter Dr., 45012, pg. 1517 PB
Hamilton Mill, Champion International Corporation, 601 North B St., 45013, pg. 334 PB
Hoesch Suspensions Inc., 8685 Berk Blvd., 45015, pg. 508 IT
Home Federal Bank, Third & Court Sts., 45011, pg. 633 PB
LESHNER MILLS. INC., 1010 Eaton Ave., 45013, pg. 660 PV
MOSLER INC., 8509 Berk Blvd., 45012, pg. 763 PV
Ocasco Budget, Inc., 136 N. Third St., 45025, pg. 1214 PB
OHIO CASUALTY CORPORATION, 136 N. Third St., 45025, pg. 1214 PB
Ohio Casualty Insurance Co., 136 N. Third St., 45025, pg. 1214 PB
The Ohio Casualty Insurance Group, 136 N. Third St., 45025, pg. 1214 PB
Ohio Security Insurance Co., 136 N. Third St., 45025, pg. 1214 PB
WESTERN STATES MACHINE COMPANY, 1798 Fairgrove Ave., 45011, pg. 1168 PV
Wright-Bernet, Inc., 3001 Symmes Rd., 45015, pg. 566 PB
Zeneca Specialty Inks, 4602 Mulhauser Rd., 45011, pg. 1525 IT

Hannibal

Ormet Primary Aluminum Corp., P.O. Box 176, State Rt. 7, 43931, pg. 820 PV

Harrison

Campbell Hausfeld Division of Scott Fetzer, 100 Production Dr., 45030, pg. 217 PB
CINCINNATI INCORPORATED, 7420 Kilby Rd., 45030, pg. 240 PV
HUBERT COMPANY, 9555 Dry Fork Rd., 45030, pg. 545 PV
Melben Products Inc., Production Dr., 45030, pg. 218 PB

Hartville

Lomak Operating Company, 1160 Sunnyside, 44632, pg. 1012 PB
Lomak Production Company, 1160 Sunnyside, 44632, pg. 1012 PB

Hayesville

Custom Hoists, Inc., 771 CR 30A W., 44838-0098, pg. 1506 PB

Hebron

Barzon Corporation, P.O. Box 796, Newark Industrial Pk., 43C25, pg. 763 PB
Bundy Corporation, Hebron Plant, 3600 Hebron Rd., 43025-1137, pg. 1340 IT
Dayton Precision Co., 171 O'Neill Dr. S.E., 43025, pg. 623 PV

Hicksville

Dotco, 600 Defiance Ave., 43526, pg. 444 PB
Hydraulic Valve Div., 373 Meuse Argonne, 43526, pg. 411 PB

Highland Heights

Namco Controls Corporation, 5335 Avion Park Dr., 44143, pg. 482 PB
Things Remembered, Inc., 5340 Avion Park Dr., 44143, pg. 397 PB
Tranzonic Industrial Textiles Division, 670 Alpha Drive, 44143, pg. 1632 PB

Hilliard

B. Elliott Inc., 4282 Reynolds Dr., 43026, pg. 449 IT
Gates, McDonald & Co., 3455 Mill Run Dr., 43026, pg. 789 PV
ITW Nirco, Inc., 4199 Weaver Court S., 43026, pg. 867 PB
Medex Inc., 3637 Lacon Rd., 43026, pg. 689 PB
MICRO ELECTRONICS, INC., 4119 Leap Rd., 43026, pg. 742 PV
RED ROOF INNS, INC., 4355 Davidson Rd., 43026-2491, pg. 369 PB
Vanner, Inc., 4282 Reynolds Dr., 43026, pg. 449 IT

Hillsboro

The Fifth Third Bank of Southern Ohio, 100 S. High St., 45133-0910, pg. 622 PB
ROTARY FORMS PRESS, INC., 835 S. High St., 45133, pg. 947 PV

Holland

Alpha Tube, 1302 Kittle Rd., 43528, pg. 17 PB
CCS, 1140 Corporate Dr., 43528, pg. 147 PV
Drivetrain Service Div., 6936 Airport Hwy., 43528, pg. 479 PB
GENERAL ALUM & CHEMICAL, 1630 Timberwolf Dr., 43529, pg. 443 PB
Millar Elevator Industries, Inc., 1530 Timberwolf Dr., 43528, pg. 1205 IT
Peterson Spring-Maumee Plant, 1625 Commerce Rd., 43523, pg. 857 PB
Reed National Company, 7301 International Dr., 43528-9412, pg. 1099 PB

Holmesville

Felsted Division, County Hwy. 245, 44633, pg. 689 PB

Howard

Millwood Plant, 26900 Coshocton Rd., 43028, pg. 1213 PB

Hubbard

TRUCK WORLD INC., 1610 Thomas Rd., 44425, pg. 1107 PV

Huber Heights

LITTLEFIELD, ADAMS & COMPANY, 6262 Executive Blvd., 45424, pg. 1001 PB
Sports Imprints/Fun Wear, 6262 Executive Blvd., 45424, pg. 1002 PB

Hudson

ALLTEL Communications Corporation, 100 Executive Pkwy., 44236, pg. 55 PB
ALLTEL Publishing Corporation, 100 Executive Pkwy., 44236, pg. 56 PB
ALLTEL Service Corporation, 100 Executive Pkwy., 44236, pg. 56 PB
FABRI-CENTERS OF AMERICA, INC., 5555 Darrow Rd., 44236, pg. 609 PB
THE FLOOD COMPANY, 1212 Barlow Rd., 44236, pg. 414 PV
Superior Thermal, Inc., 201 Sales Ave., 45030, pg. 360 PV
Hudson Elms Nursing Home, 563 E. Streetsboro Rd., 44236, pg. 838 PB
Kobelco Stewart Bolling Inc., 1600 Terex Rd., 44236, pg. 740 IT
Kobelco Stewart Bolling, Inc., 1600 Terex Rd., 44236, pg. 740 IT
The Little Tikes Company, 2180 Barlow Rd., 44236, pg. 1411 PB
Morse Controls, 21 Clinton St., 44236, pg. 857 PB
Ohio Div., 75 Milford Dr., Ste. 221, 44236, pg. 1683 PB

Independence

AGA Gas, Inc., 6055 Rockside Woods Blvd., 44131, pg. 13 IT
Burns & Wilcox Ltd., 6133 Rockside Rd., Ste. 201, 44131, pg. 610 PV
Cigna Insurance Company of Ohio, 5005 Rockside Rd., Ste. 815, 44131, pg. 366 PB
The Cleveland Electric Illuminating Company, 6200 Oak Tree Blvd., 44131, pg. 645 PB
Cognos Corp.-Cleveland Sales Office, 4807 Rockside Rd., Ste. 400, 44131, pg. 306 IT
FAIRMONT SNACK GROUP, INC., 6133 Rockside Rd., Ste. 208, 44131, pg. 392 PV
GREAT LAKES CONSTRUCTION CO., 6600 E. Schaaf Rd., 44131, pg. 474 PV
Great Lakes Region, Four Summit Park Dr., Ste. 200, 44131, pg. 1024 PB
Intergraph Corporation, 6111 Oak Tree Blvd., 44131, pg. 890 PB
INTERNATIONAL TOTAL SERVICES, Crown Centre, 5005 Rockside Rd., 44131, pg. 908 PB
Lockheed Martin Defense Systems, 6201 Ranchview Dr., 44131-6512, pg. 1008 PB
Merck Medco Managed Care, 4700 Rockside Rd., #200, 44131, pg. 1091 PB
Precision Tube Formers, 7717 Commerce Park Oval, 44131, pg. 771 PB
RESTAURANT DEVELOPERS CORP., 5755 Granger Rd., Ste. 200, 44131, pg. 925 PV
SMS-Cleveland, Three Summit Park Dr., 44131, pg. 1463 PB
SIFCO Selective Plating, 5708 Schaaf Rd., 44131, pg. 1471 PB

Jackson

Jackson Corp., 275 S. Bennett Ave., 45640, pg. 977 PB

Jackson Center

Airstream, Inc., 419 W. Pike St., 45334, pg. 1602 PB
THOR INDUSTRIES, INC., 419 W. Pike St., 45334, pg. 1602 PB

Johnstown

Broughton Foods Company, 257 W. Coshoton St., 43031, pg. 260 PB

Kent

CARTER-JONES COMPANIES, INC., 605 Tallmadge Rd., 44240, pg. 217 PV
Carter-Jones Lumber Co., 605 Tallmadge Rd., 44240, pg. 217 PV
THE DAVEY TREE EXPERT COMPANY, 1500 N. Mantua St., 44240, pg. 314 PV
GOUGLER INDUSTRIES, INC., 705 Lake St., 44240, pg. 466 PV
Kent Plant, 1510 St. Clair Ave., 44240, pg. 1044 PV
Krupp Plastics & Rubber Machinery Inc. (Rubber Division), 1010 W. Main St., 44240, pg. 510 IT
Lamb Electric Div., 627 Lake St., 44240, pg. 100 PB
Land O'Lakes Inc., 2001 Mogadore Rd., 44240-7274, pg. 646 PV
SCHNELLER, INC., 6019 Powder Mill Rd., 44240, pg. 971 PV
Synflex Division, 642 Middlebury Rd., 44240, pg. 689 PB

Kettering

Donohue Pulp & Paper Sales Corp., Ste. 344, 580 Lincoln Park Blvd., 45429, pg. 1075 IT

Kidron

KIDRON INC., P.O. Box 17, 44636, pg. 619 PV
Kidron, Inc., 13442 Emerson Rd., 44636, pg. 1097 PV

Kinsman

TARGET STAMPED PRODUCTS CORP., 8091 State Rte. 5, 44428, pg. 1069 PV

Lakewood

ZAREMBA GROUP, INC., 14600 Detroit Ave., Ste. 1500, 44107, pg. 1204 PV

Lancaster

Diamond Power Specialty Co., 2600 E. Main St., 43130, pg. 1068 PB
Lancaster Glass Corporation, 240 W. Main St., 43130, pg. 977 PB

PB - U.S. Public Companies Volume
PV - U.S. Private Companies Volume
IT - International Public & Private Companies Volume

State Electric Supply Company, P.O. Box 576, 319 Forest Rose Ave., 43130-0576, pg. 1036   **PV**

Lebanon

GHENT MANUFACTURING, INC., 2999 Henkle Dr., 45036, pg. 450   **PV**
Lucas Sumitomo Brakes Inc., P.O. Box 149, 1650 Kingsview Dr., 45036, pg. 819   **IT**

Lexington

Neer Manufacturing Company Inc., 265 S. Mill St., 44904, pg. 727   **PB**

Liberty Center

Structural Foam Plastics, P.O. Box 455, Township Rd., 43532, pg. 1048   **PV**

Lima

Arbor Health Care Company, 1100 Shawnee Rd., 45805, pg. 468   **IT**
The Commercial Bank-Allentown Rd. Branch, 2600 Allentown Rd., 45805, pg. 410   **PB**
The Commercial Bank-Cole St. Branch, 2285 Cole St., 45801, pg. 410   **PB**
Correctional Behavioral Solutions of Ohio, Inc., Allen Correctional Institute, 2338 North West St., 45801, pg. 1035   **PB**
International Brake Industries, Inc., 1840 McCullough St., 45801, pg. 1055   **PB**
Lima Communications Corp., P.O. Box 1689, 45802, pg. 147   **PV**
Marathon Electric, Lima, 200 E. Chapman Rd., 45802, pg. 1371   **PB**
Nickles Bakery of Ohio Inc., 1950 Sugar St., 45801, pg. 799   **PV**
Owners Insurance Co., 2325 N. Cole St., 45801, pg. 100   **PV**
RUDOLPH FOODS COMPANY, 6575 Bellefontaine Rd., 45804, pg. 950   **PV**
Southern Instruments, Inc., P.O. Box 5365, 45802, pg. 921   **PB**

Logan

Paramount Natural Gas Company, 63 Gallagher Ave., 43138, pg. 1280   **PB**
Paramount Transmission Corp., P.O. Box 391, 43138, pg. 1281   **PB**

London

London Industries, Inc., 350 E. High Street, 43140, pg. 1780   **PB**

Lorain

Hughes-Peters, Inc., 1875 N. Ridge Rd., E., Ste. L, 44055, pg. 547   **PV**
The Lorain Journal Company-The Morning Journal, 1657 Broadway, 44052, pg. 935   **PB**
Lorain Products, 1122 F St., 44052, pg. 921   **PV**
USS Kobe Steel, 1807 E. 28th St., 44055, pg. 741   **IT**

Louisville

Hewlett Packard Product Division, 512 W. Gorgas St., 44641-1332, pg. 816   **PB**
Transtec Environmental Inc., 3766 Tulane Ave. N.E., 44641, pg. 71   **PB**

Loveland

Amano Cincinnati - Cincinnati Branch Office, 130 Commerce Drive, 45140-7726, pg. 70   **IT**
Amano Cincinnati Inc., 130 Commerce Blvd., 45140, pg. 71   **IT**
BALDWIN PIANO & ORGAN COMPANY, 422 Wards Corner Rd., 45140-8390, pg. 169   **PB**
CINCINNATI UNITED CONTRACTORS, 9501 Union Cemetery Rd., 45140, pg. 240   **PV**
Chelsea Moore Company, Ste. 200, 396 Wards Corner Rd., 45140, pg. 1164   **PV**
Totes Incorporated, 10078 E. Kemper Rd., 45140, pg. 111   **PV**
The Wurlitzer Company, 422 Wards Corner Rd., 45140, pg. 169   **PB**

Macedonia

CENTURY PRODUCTS CO., 9600 Valley View Rd., 44056-9989, pg. 226   **PB**
Norandex Vinyl Products Co., 8450 S. Bedford Rd., 44056, pg. 1237   **PB**

Madison

Chesapeake Packaging Co./Madison, 3200 County Line Rd., 44057, pg. 347   **PB**
Hubbell Industrial Controls, Inc., 50 Edwards St., 44057, pg. 844   **PB**
Perfection Corporation, 222 Lake St., 44057-3189, pg. 1149   **IT**

Maineville

Matrix Technologies, Inc., 8603 S. Cove Dr., 45039, pg. 714   **PV**
U.S. Turbine Corporation, 7685 S. State Rte. 48, 45039, pg. 1127   **IT**

Malta

Malta Div.-Tomkins Industries, Inc., P.O. Box 397, 43758, pg. 1398   **IT**
The Residential Products Group, P.O. Box 397, 43758, pg. 1398   **IT**

Mansfield

Armco Inc.-Mansfield Operations, 913 Bowman St., 44901, pg. 131   **PB**
Barnes Pumps, Inc., 1485 Lexington Ave., 44907, pg. 457   **PB**
Beckley Cardy Group, 100 Paragon Pkwy., 44903-8101, pg. 190   **PB**
THE GORMAN-RUPP COMPANY, 305 Bowman St., 44903, pg. 754   **PB**
The Gorman-Rupp International Co., P.O. Box 1217, 305 Bowman St., 44901, pg. 754   **IT**
IPT Division, P.O. Box 2818, 883 Longview Ave. W., 44906, pg. 754   **PB**
Park Avenue Villa, 2124 Park Ave. W., 44906, pg. 838   **PB**
Therm-O-Disc Inc., 1320 S. Main St., 44907, pg. 573   **PB**
Warren Rupp, Inc., 800 N. Main St., 44901, pg. 862   **PB**

Mantua

Synflex Division, Main & Orchard Sts., 44255, pg. 689   **PB**

Maple Heights

FINAST, 17000 Rockside Rd., 44137, pg. 750   **IT**
Sherwood Foods, 16625 Granite Rd., 44137, pg. 994   **PV**

Marietta

THE AIROLITE COMPANY, 114 Westview Ave., 45750, pg. 29   **PV**
BROUGHTON FOODS COMPANY, 210 N. Seventh St., 45750, pg. 259   **IT**
Elkem Marietta, P.O. Box 299, 45750, pg. 447   **IT**
Elkem Metals Company, River View Road, P.O. Box72, 45750-0072, pg. 447   **IT**
Flexmag Industries, 107 Industry Rd., 45750, pg. 1420   **PB**
Forma Scientific Inc., Millcreek Road, 45750, pg. 1595   **PB**
The Times Co., 700 Channel Ln., 45750, pg. 700   **PB**

Marion

Na-Churs Plant Food Company, 421 Leader St., 43302, pg. 1096   **PV**
Ohio-American Water Co., 365 E. Center St., 43301-0506, pg. 95   **PV**
Todco, 1332 Fairground Rd. E., 43302, pg. 823   **PV**
Turco Products Division, P.O. Box 195, 43301-0195, pg. 446   **IT**
WYANDOT INC., 135 Wyandot Ave., 43302, pg. 1193   **PV**

Martins Ferry

Nickles Bakery, Inc., 1000 Broadway, 43935, pg. 799   **PV**

Marysville

BMY-Wheeled Vehicles, 13311 Industrial Pkwy., 43040, pg. 793   **PB**
DENISON HYDRAULICS, INC., 14249 Industrial Pkwy., 43040, pg. 324   **PV**
Hyponex Corporation, 14111 Scottslawn Rd., 43041, pg. 1447   **PB**
THE SCOTTS COMPANY, 14111 Scottslawn Rd., 43041, pg. 1446   **PB**

Mason

A-Mold Corp., 4600 Mason-Montgomery Rd., 45040, pg. 1427   **IT**
BERENFIELD CONTAINERS, INC., 1229 Castle Dr., 45040, pg. 135   **PV**
Berenfield Containers (MASON), Inc., 1229 Castle Dr., 45040, pg. 135   **PV**
Cincinnati Sales, 9540 Mason Montgomery, Ste. A, 45040, pg. 611   **PV**
CINTAS CORPORATION, 6800 Cintas Blvd., 45050, pg. 370   **PB**
Cognos Corp.-Cincinnati Sales Office, 4770 Duke Drive, Ste. 201, 45040-9010, pg. 306   **IT**
Creative Media Products, 7400 Industrial Row Dr., 45040, pg. 1055   **PV**
The FACS Group, 4705 Duke Dr., 45040, pg. 618   **PV**
Intergraph Corporation, 4900 Parkway Dr., Ste. 140, 45040-9300, pg. 890   **PB**
Makino Inc., 7680 Innovation Way, 45040, pg. 831   **IT**
Makino USA Inc., 7680 Innovation Way, 45040, pg. 831   **IT**
Mitsubishi Electric Mfg., 4773 Bethany Rd., 45040-9660, pg. 872   **IT**
PETS-N-SUCH INC., 1065 Reading Rd., 45040, pg. 859   **PV**

RELIANCE MEDICAL PRODUCTS, INC., 3535 Kings Mills Rd., 45040, pg. 1055   **PV**
STEELOX SYSTEMS INC., 5412 Courseview Dr., Ste. 300, 45040-8181, pg. 1038   **PV**
SUPERIOR LABEL SYSTEMS, INC., 7500 Industrial Road Dr., 45040, pg. 1055   **PV**
Superior Machine Systems, 7400 Industrial Row Dr., 45040, pg. 1055   **PV**
ASHLEY F. WARD, INC., 7490 Easy St., 45040, pg. 1149   **PV**

Massillon

CAMPBELL OIL CO., 611 S. Erie, 44648, pg. 204   **PV**
Central States Can Co., 700 16th St. SE, 44646, pg. 463   **PB**
Central States Can Co.-Composite Operations, 2101 Ninth St. S.W., 44646, pg. 463   **PB**
Countrymark Feed Plant, 8485 Navarre Rd. S.W., 44646-8814, pg. 279   **PB**
Engineered Fasteners Div., 240 Sixth St., N.W., 44646, pg. 557   **PB**
First National Bank in Massillon, One First National Plaza, 44648, pg. 646   **PB**
Fleming Foods of Ohio, Inc., P.O. Box 207, 46648, pg. 653   **PB**
Greif Board Corporation, 9420 Warmington Rd., 44648, pg. 763   **PB**
REPUBLIC ENGINEERED STEELS, INC., 410 Oberlin Rd., SW, 44648-0579, pg. 1378   **PB**
Superior's Brand Meats, 1888 Southway, S.E., 44646, pg. 427   **PV**

Masury

Berenfield Containers Ltd., 7838 Iron St., 44438, pg. 135   **PV**

Maumee

Aeroquip Corporation, 3000 Strayer, 43537, pg. 24   **PB**
AEROQUIP-VICKERS, INC., 3000 Strayer, 43537-0050, pg. 24   **PB**
Aerospace-Marine-Defense Group, 3000 Strayer Rd., 43537, pg. 24   **PB**
Aftermarket Production Div., 1480 Ford St., 43537, pg. 479   **PB**
THE ANDERSONS INCORPORATED, 480 W. Dussel Dr., 43537, pg. 111   **PB**
The Andersons Investment Services Corp., 480 Dussel Dr., 43537, pg. 111   **PB**
Automotive Distribution Sales Div., 1480 Ford St., 43537, pg. 479   **PB**
Charter Behavioral Health System of Toledo, Inc., 1725 Timberline Rd., 43537, pg. 1034   **PB**
Custer Pharmacy, 1020 Ford St., 43537, pg. 1453   **PB**
Dana World Trade Div., 1609 Henthorne Dr., 43537, pg. 479   **PB**
Dentsply Ransom & Randolph, 520 Illinois Ave., 43537, pg. 499   **PB**
DeVilbiss Automotive Refinishing Products, 1724 Indian Wood Circle, Ste. G, 43537-4051, pg. 865   **PB**
DeVilbiss Ransburg Industrial Coating Equipment, 1724 Indian Wood Circle, Ste. F, 43537-4050, pg. 865   **PB**
Fluid Product Sales Div., 1745 Indian Wood Cir., Ste. 160, 43537, pg. 479   **PB**
Food Town Supermarkets Division, 1020 Ford St., 43537, pg. 1453   **PB**
Gruber's Food Town, 1020 Ford St., 43537, pg. 1453   **PB**
Hickory Farms Catalogues of America, Inc., 1505 Holland Rd., 43537, pg. 525   **PV**
HICKORY FARMS, INC., 1505 Holland Rd., 43537, pg. 525   **PV**
ITW Finishing Systems & Products-North America, 1724 Indian Wood Circle, Ste. A, 43537-4005, pg. 866   **PB**
Industrial Americas Group, 1695 Indian Wood Cir., 43537, pg. 24   **PB**
MATRIX TECHNOLOGIES INC., 1760 Indianwood Cir., 43537-4006, pg. 714   **PV**
Northern Distributing Co., 1020 Ford St., 43537, pg. 1453   **PB**
Ransom & Randolph Division, 120 W. Wayne St., 43537, pg. 499   **PB**
SEAWAY FOOD TOWN, INC., 1020 Ford St., 43537, pg. 1452   **PB**
Seaway Properties, Inc., 1020 Ford St., 43537, pg. 1453   **PB**
THERMA-TRU CORP., 1687 Woodlands Dr., 43537, pg. 1079   **PV**
Tracy & Avery Food Town, 1020 Ford St., 43537, pg. 1453   **PB**
Vickers, Incorporated, 3000 Strayer, 43537-0632, pg. 24   **PB**
Vickers Industrial, 3000 Strayer Rd., 43537, pg. 24   **PB**

Mc Comb

CONSOLIDATED BISCUIT CO., 312 Radar Rd., 45858, pg. 265   **PV**

Mechanicsburg

Champaign Landmark, 140 S. Main St., 43044, pg. 227   **PV**

Medina

CORRPRO COMPANIES, INC., 1090 Enterprise Dr., 44256, pg. 451   **PB**

PB - *U.S. Public Companies Volume*
PV - *U.S. Private Companies Volume*
IT - *International Public & Private Companies Volume*

Geographic Index-U.S.

DISCOUNT DRUG MART INC., 211 Commerce Dr., 44256, pg. 334   PV

Imediate Pharmaceutical Services Inc., 211 Commerce Dr., 44256, pg. 334   PV

NASCO INDUSTRIES INC., 955 W. Smith Rd., 44256, pg. 774   PV

The Old Phoenix National Bank of Medina, P.O. Box 725, 44258, pg. 646   PB

Overseas Capital Corporation, 955 W. Smith Rd., 44256, pg. 774   PV

PAR INDUSTRIES, INC., 305 Lake Rd., 44258, pg. 838   PV

PLASTI-KOTE COMPANY INC., 1000 Lake Rd., 44256, pg. 870   PV

RPM, INC., 2628 Pearl Rd., 44258, pg. 1356   PV

Republic Powdered Metals, Inc., P.O. Box 724, 2628 Pearl Rd., 44256, pg. 1357   PB

A.I. ROOT COMPANY, 623 W. Liberty St., 44256, pg. 944   PV

Sealy Mattress Company, 1070 Lake Rd., 44258, pg. 979   PV

TRU-FIT PRODUCTS CORP., 460 Lake Rd., 44256, pg. 1107   PV

Wellman Engineering Resins, 538 West Liberty St., Unit C, Ste.7, 44256, pg. 1752   PB

Mentor

Aviation Product Support Inc., 7600 Tyler Blvd., 44060-4853, pg. 1569   PB

Caterpillar Industrial Inc., 5970 Heisley Rd., 44060, pg. 315   PB

Cyberex, Inc., 7171 Industrial Park Blvd., 44060, pg. 481   PV

Gas Turbine Fuel Systems Div., 9200 Tyler Blvd., 44060, pg. 1262   PB

ISK Biotech, 5966 Heisley Rd., 44060, pg. 689   IT

MILL-ROSE COMPANY, 7995 Tyler Blvd., 44060, pg. 746   PV

Ohio Sealants Inc., 7405 Production Dr., 44060, pg. 802   IT

Polychem Corporation, 6277 Heisley Rd., 44060, pg. 169   PV

SENTINEL CONSUMER PRODUCTS, INC., 7750 Tyler Blvd., 44060, pg. 984   PV

STERIS CORPORATION, 5960 Heisley Rd., 44060, pg. 1515   PB

Tamms Industries, 7405 Production Dr., 44060, pg. 803   IT

Metamora

Hydraulic Filter Div., 16810 Fulton County Rd. No. 2, 43540-9714, pg. 1260   PB

Miamisburg

Dayco Products Inc., One Prestige Place, 45342, pg. 1045   PB

Dayco Rubber Industrial Sales Division, One Prestige Pl., 45342, pg. 1045   PB

Dayco Rubber Products Co., One Prestige Pl., 45342, pg. 1045   PB

Dayflex Worldwide, One Prestige Pl., 45342, pg. 1045   PB

Dayton Superior Corporation, 721 Richard St., 45342, pg. 931   PV

Daytronic Corporation, 2589 Corporate Pl., 45342, pg. 126   IT

DIGITRON TOOL CO., INC., 8641 Washington Church Rd., 45342, pg. 332   PV

EG & G Mound Applied Technologies, P.O. Box 3000, One Mound Rd., 45342, pg. 543   PV

Hewlett-Packard Company, 9080 Springboro Pike, 45342, pg. 815   PB

HUFFY CORPORATION, 225 Byers Rd., 45342, pg. 846   PB

Huffy Service First, Inc., 8521 Gander Creek Dr., 45342, pg. 846   PB

ISOTEC, Inc., 3858 Benner Rd., 45342, pg. 938   IT

Janesville Products, 1010 N. Fourth St., 45342, pg. 924   PB

LEXIS-NEXIS, 9443 Springboro Pike, 45342, pg. 1096   IT

MIM Industries, Inc., 4301 Lyons Rd., 45342, pg. 229   IT

Monarch Marking Systems, 170 Monarch Ln., 45342, pg. 1266   PB

National City Mortgage Co., 3232 Newmark Dr., 45342-1820, pg. 1154   PB

Sabre Systems & Service Inc., 9111 Springboro Pike, 45342, pg. 890   IT

Super Food Services, Inc., 3233 Newmark Dr., 45342, pg. 1152   PV

Zellerbach Division, 3131 Newmark Dr., 45342, pg. 1074   PB

Middleburg

DataCard-Cleveland, 6902 Pearl Rd., Ste 304, 44130, pg. 312   PV

Emery Ocean Services, 6940A Engle Rd., 44130, pg. 281   PB

TIE Systems-Cleveland, 17535 Rosbough Dr., #108, 44130, pg. 1085   PV

URS Greiner, Inc., Plaza South-Three, 7271 Engle Rd., #300, 44130-8405, pg. 1658   PB

Union-Transport Corporation-Cleveland Office, 6909 Engle Rd., Ste. 9 & 10, 44130, pg. 1119   PV

Middlefield

Duncan Toys Company, 15981 ValPlast Rd., 44062, pg. 409   PV

Flambeau Products Corp., 15981 Val Plast Rd., 44062, pg. 409   PV

Kraftmaid Cabinetry, Inc., 16502 Industrial Pkwy., 44062, pg. 1053   PB

Kraftmaid Trucking, Inc., 16502 Industrial Pkwy., 44062, pg. 1053   PB

Universal Polymer & Rubber Co., P.O. Box 767, 15730 S. Madison Rd., 44062, pg. 56   PV

Middletown

AK STEEL CORPORATION, P.O. Box 600, 703 Curtis St., 45043, pg. 7   PB

Aeronca, Inc., 1712 Germantown Rd., 45042, pg. 829   PB

AKERS PACKAGING SERVICE INC., 2820 Lefferson Rd., 45044, pg. 29   PB

Bay West Paper Corp. Towel & Tissue Div., 700 Columbia Ave., 45044, pg. 1747   PB

CONTECH CONSTRUCTION PRODUCTS INC., 1001 Grove St., 45044, pg. 267   PV

THE CRYSTAL TISSUE CO., 3120 S. Verity Pkwy., 45042, pg. 294   PV

Folding Carton (Middletown), 407 Charles St., 45042, pg. 1270   IT

McGraw/Kokosing, Inc., P.O. Box 370, 45042, pg. 631   PV

The Sorg Paper Co., 901 Manchester Ave., 45042, pg. 1747   PB

Square D Middletown Plant, 1500 S. University Blvd., 45044, pg. 1208   IT

Sulzer Papertec Inc., P.O. Box 509, 45042, pg. 1305   IT

Thermo Black Clawson, Inc., 605 Clark St., 45042, pg. 1593   PB

Xerox Research, 5086 Moisman Rd., 45042-1672, pg. 1784   PB

Milan

Monroe Clevite, 33 Lockwood Rd., 44846, pg. 1577   PB

Milford

Bigg's Hyper Shoppes, Inc., 25 Whitney Dr., Ste. 122, 45150, pg. 1541   PB

THE BREWER COMPANY, 1354 U.S. Hwy 50, 45150, pg. 167   PV

Buckhorn Inc., 55 W. Techne Center Dr., 45150, pg. 1143   PB

Buckhorn Material Handling Group Inc., 55 W. Techne Center Dr., 45150, pg. 1143   PB

MIKE CASTRUCCI CHEVROLET, 1099 Lila Ave., 45150, pg. 219   PV

Cyprus Amax Coal Sales Corporation, 400 TechneCenter Dr., Ste. 320, 45150, pg. 471   PV

Fluid Conservation Systems Inc., 2001 Ford Cir., Ste. F., 45150, pg. 590   IT

INTRENET, INC., 400 Techne Ctr. Dr., Ste. 200, 45150, pg. 910   PB

Kvaerner Energy USA, 50 W. Techne Center Dr., Ste. K, 45150, pg. 770   IT

Packaging Business, One Better Way Rd., 45150, pg. 671   PB

SDRC Engineering Services Division, Inc., 2000 Eastman Dr., 45150, pg. 1525   PB

STRUCTURAL DYNAMICS RESEARCH CORP., 2000 Eastman Dr., 45150, pg. 1525   PB

Millbury

Guardian Transportation Corp., 24310 W. State Rt. 51, 43447, pg. 485   PV

Millersburg

Artwood Products, 7100 County Rd. 407, 44654, pg. 983   PV

SEMAC INDUSTRIES INC., 7100 County Rd. 407, 44654, pg. 983   PV

Minster

THE MINSTER MACHINE COMPANY, 240 W. Fifth St., 45865, pg. 751   PV

Mogadore

LumenX Company, 3400 Gilchrist Rd., 44260, pg. 56   PB

Monroe

BAKER CONCRETE CONSTRUCTION, INC., 900 N. Garver Rd., 45050, pg. 111   PV

Moreland Hills

DEVELOPERS DIVERSIFIED REALTY CORPORATION, 34555 Chagrin Blvd., 44022, pg. 502   PB

Mount Gilead

HPM CORPORATION, 820 Marion Rd., 43338, pg. 492   PV

Mount Hope

WAYNE DALTON CORPORATION, One Door Dr., 44660, pg. 1155   PV

Mount Sterling

Integrated Material Handling Company, 28 N. Clark St., 43143, pg. 1397   IT

Showa Aluminum Corp. of America, 10500 O'Day-Harrison Rd., 43143, pg. 1236   IT

Mount Vernon

ARIEL CORPORATION, 35 Blackjack Rd., 43050, pg. 81   PV

Jannock Steel Fabricating, Inc., 8800 Blackjack Rd., 43050, pg. 699   IT

Napoleon

Napco Plastics Co., 600 Filmore St., 43545, pg. 440   IT

Navarre

ALFRED NICKLES BAKERY, INC., 26 N. Main St., 44662, pg. 799   PV

Nelsonville

ROCKY SHOES & BOOTS, INC., 39 Canal St., 45764, pg. 1402   PB

New Albany

RAX RESTAURANTS, C/O Carpediem Management Co., 180 W. Gravellie Rd., Ste. A1, 43054, pg. 911   PV

New Boston

State Electric Supply Company, P.O. Box 3127, 3200 Rhodes Ave., 45662, pg. 1036   PV

New Bremen

CROWN EQUIPMENT CORPORATION, 40 S. Washington St., 45869, pg. 292   PV

Stamco Div., 125 S. Herman St., 45869, pg. 1124   PB

New Carlisle

Wenco Inc., P.O. Box 149, 45344-0149, pg. 1754   PB

New Lexington

Ludowici Celadon, SE Rte. One, 4757 Tile Plant Road, 43764, pg. 1171   IT

Ludowici Roof Tile, Inc., 4757 Tile Plant Rd., S.E., 43764, pg. 1171   IT

New Philadelphia

Joy/Green Fan Division, 338 S. Broadway, 44663, pg. 789   PB

Morgantown Machine Anderson Mavor, 464 Robinson Drive, 44663, pg. 281   IT

The Times Reporter, 629 Wabash Ave., N.W., 44663, pg. 935   PB

New Springfield

Mahoning Landfill, Inc., 3510 Garfield Rd., 44443, pg. 94   PB

Newark

THE ADVOCATE, 22 N. First St., 43055, pg. 23   PV

ALLTEL Ohio, Inc., 66 N. Fourth St., 43055, pg. 56   PB

Banc One-Newark, 15 N. Third St., 43055, pg. 173   PB

Corrugated Packaging, S. 21st & Hancock Sts., P.O. Box 870, 43055, pg. 737   PB

Cox Communications-Newark, 111 N. 11th St., 43055, pg. 455   PB

ENGLEFIELD, INC., 447 James Pkwy., 43055, pg. 377   PV

Larsan Manufacturing Co., Newark Indus. Park, Bldg. 12, 43055, pg. 575   PB

NGO Development Corporation, P.O. Box 517, 1500 Granville Rd., 43055-0517, pg. 1157   PB

NATIONAL GAS & OIL COMPANY, 1500 Granville Rd., 43055, pg. 1156   PB

National Gas & Oil Corp., P.O. Box 4970, 1500 Granville Rd., 43055-4970, pg. 1157   PB

Producers Gas Sales, Inc., P.O. Box 4970, 1560 Granville Rd., 43055-4970, pg. 1157   PB

Newbury

THE GREAT LAKES CHEESE CO., 9988 Kinsman Rd., 44065, pg. 473   PV

Niles

L.B. Foster Company-Niles Plant, 1195 Slat Springs Rd., 44446, pg. 676   PB

RMI Titanium Company, 1000 Warren Ave., 44446, pg. 1662 **PB**

North Bend

Consolidated Grain & Barge Co., P.O. Box 8, 300 Three Rivers Pkwy., 45052, pg. 694 **IT**

North Olmsted

Moen Incorporated, 25300 Al Moen Dr., 44070, pg. 675 **PB**

North Ridgeville

RELTEC Services, 38683 Taylor Woods Industrial Pkwy., 44039, pg. 921 **PV**
The Tobin Corporation, 35544 Lorain Rd., 44039, pg. 102 **PV**

Norton

Armin Plastics, Northeast Division, P.O. Box 1093, 44203-9493, pg. 1647 **PB**

Norwalk

Applied Curing Technology, Inc., P.O. Box 259, 41 E. Water St., 44857, pg. 1189 **PB**
Circon ACMI, 93 N. Pleasant, 44853, pg. 373 **PB**
Firelands Tool Rental, 39 Woodlawn Ave., 44857, pg. 586 **PV**
Industrial Powder Coatings, Inc., 202 Republic St., 44857, pg. 894 **PB**
Janesville Products, 156 S. Norwalk Rd., 44857, pg. 924 **PB**
NORWALK FURNITURE CORPORATION, 100 Furniture Pkwy., 44857, pg. 807 **PV**

Norwood

C.W. ZUMBIEL COMPANY, 2339 Harris Ave., 45212, pg. 1207 **PV**

Oak Hill

Cedar Heights Clay, P.O. Box 294, 45656, pg. 924 **PV**

Oberlin

Alden Press, 235 Artino St., 44074, pg. 1778 **PB**
Ciba Corning Diagnostics Corporation, 132 Artino St., 44074, pg. 973 **IT**

Old Washington

Broughton Foods Company, I-70 & S.R. 285, 43768, pg. 260 **PB**

Orrville

Enviromental Products Inc., 169 S. Main St., 44667-0900, pg. 1177 **PV**
Federal Packaging Corporation, 425 Collins Blvd., 44667, pg. 303 **PB**
J.M. SMUCKER COMPANY, One Strawberry Ln., 44667-0280, pg. 1480 **PB**
Steiner Turf Equipment Inc., 930 Penn Ave., 44667, pg. 1088 **IT**
THE WILL-BURT COMPANY, 169 S. Main, 44667-0900, pg. 1177 **PV**

Orwell

Orwell Plant, 7530 Staley Rd., 44076, pg. 1044 **PV**
Village Square Nursing Center, 7787 Stanley Rd., 44076, pg. 838 **PB**

Ottawa

The First National Bank of Ottawa, 405 E. Main St., 45875, pg. 1413 **PB**

Oxford

Square D Oxford Plant, 5735 College Corner Rd., 45056, pg. 1208 **IT**

Painesville

Coe Manufacturing Co, P.O. Box 520, 44077, pg. 249 **PV**
THE COE MANUFACTURING COMPANY, 609 Bank St., 44077, pg. 249 **PV**
CONVENIENT FOOD MART, INC., 467 N. State St., 44077, pg. 271 **PV**
Fasson Films, 250 Chester St., Bldg. 1, 44077, pg. 153 **PB**
Fasson Industrial (U.S.) Div., 250 Chester St., 44077, pg. 153 **PB**
Fasson Roll Div., 7670 Auburn Rd., 44077, pg. 153 **PB**
Federal Hose Manufacturing Corp., 25 Florence Ave., 44077, pg. 412 **PV**
Fluid Regulators Co., 313 Gillett St., 44077, pg. 594 **PB**
Materials Group North America, 7590 Auburn Rd., 44077, pg. 153 **PB**
Quantum, USI Division, P.O. Box 1054, 44077-1054, pg. 1350 **PB**

Ricera Inc., 7528 Auburn Rd., 44077, pg. 689 **IT**
SAS Rubber Company, 474 Newell St., 44077, pg. 1521 **IT**
Uniroyal Chemical Co., Inc., P.O. Box 460, 44077, pg. 460 **PB**
United States Wallboard Machinery, P.O. Box 520, 44077, pg. 249 **PV**

Pataskala

Mako Construction Co., 13338 E. Broad St., Rte. 16 P.O. Box A64, 43062, pg. 522 **PV**

Paulding

Atlas Alchem Plastics, Inc., 11708 Rd. 144, 45879, pg. 1496 **PB**

Payne

Taylor Products, Inc., P.O. Box 77, 45880, pg. 1071 **PV**

Pemberville

The Citizens Savings Bank Company, 132 E. Front St., 43450, pg. 1412 **PB**

Peninsula

EPI/Cleveland, 1600 W. Mill St., 44264, pg. 376 **PV**

Pepper Pike

Olympic Continental Resources, LLC, 30050 Chagrin Blvd., Ste. 220, 44124, pg. 1221 **PB**
THE TRANZONIC COMPANIES, 30195 Chagrin Blvd., 44124, pg. 1632 **PB**
Tranzonic Personal Care Division, 30195 Chagrin Bvld., 44124, pg. 1632 **PB**

Perry

Newport News Industrial Corp. of Ohio, P.O. Box 25, 44081, pg. 1180 **PB**
Zeneca Ag Products, 3647 Shepard Rd., 44081, pg. 1525 **IT**

Perrysburg

ABBEY ETNA MACHINE COMPANY, P.O. Box 408, 11140 Avenue Rd., 43552, pg. 9 **PV**
Alro Group, Perrysburg, 361 D St., 43551, pg. 46 **PV**
Brambles Equipment Services Inc., 28363 Glenwood Rd., 43551, pg. 211 **PB**
Rentway Truck Leasing, 12681 Eckel Junction Rd., 43551, pg. 1424 **IT**
Toledo Precision Machining Div., 8000 Chrysler Dr., 43551, pg. 353 **PB**

Pickerington

R.G. BARRY CORPORATION, 13405 Yarmouth Dr. N.W., 43147, pg. 192 **PB**

Piketon

Indiana Kentucky Electric Corporation, P.O. Box 468, 45661, pg. 813 **PV**
OHIO VALLEY ELECTRIC CORPORATION, P.O. Box 468, 45661, pg. 813 **PV**

Pioneer

Letts Industries, Pioneer Div., One Industrial Dr., 43554, pg. 661 **PV**
Universal Industrial Products Co., One Coreway Dr., 43554-0628, pg. 1677 **PV**

Piqua

Copperweld Miami Division, P.O. Box 912, 9054 N. County Rd., 25-A, 45356, pg. 662 **IT**
Copperweld Miami Industries, 9054 North County Rd., 45356, pg. 662 **IT**
Crane Pumps & Systems Inc., 420 Third St., 45356, pg. 457 **PB**
Evenflo Company, Inc., 1801 Commerce Dr., 45356, pg. 629 **PV**
The Fifth Third Bank of Western Ohio, National Association, 123 Market St., 45356-1117, pg. 622 **PB**
THE ORR FELT COMPANY, 750 S. Main St., 45356, pg. 820 **PV**
Sellers Cleaning Systems, 420 Third St., 45356, pg. 457 **PB**
Tri-Mark Inc., 8585 Industrial Park Dr., 45356, pg. 866 **PB**

Plain City

Ranco Inc., 8115 U.S. Rte. 42N, 43064, pg. 1243 **IT**
Ranco North America, 8115 U.S. Route 42 North, 43064, pg. 1243 **IT**
SELECT SIRES, INC., 11740 U.S. Rt. 42 N., 43064, pg. 982 **PV**

Plymouth

Autolift Industrial Lift Trucks, 607 Bell St., 44865, pg. 873 **PV**
PLYMOUTH INDUSTRIES, INC., 607 Bell St., 44865, pg. 873 **PV**

Pomeroy

The Daily Sentinel, 111 Court St., 45769, pg. 699 **PB**
L.B. Foster Company-Pomeroy Plant, 736 E. Main St., 45769, pg. 676 **PB**

Port Clinton

Scandura Ohio Inc., Bldg. 320-Erie Industrial Pk., 43452, pg. 113 **IT**

Portsmouth

Mid State Products Co., P.O. Box 1388, 45662, pg. 821 **PV**
OSCO INDUSTRIES INC., 11th & Chillicothe St., 45662, pg. 820 **PV**

Powell

Aeroflex Lintek Corp., 60 Grace Dr., 43065, pg. 24 **PB**
DRUG EMPORIUM, INC., 155 Hidden Ravines Dr., 43065, pg. 530 **PB**
Houston Venture, 155 Hidden Ravines Dr., 43065, pg. 530 **PB**

Ravenna

Norton Performance Plastics Co., 335 N. Diamond St., 44266-2153, pg. 1176 **IT**
Ravenna Arsenal, Inc., 8451 State Rte. 5, 44266, pg. 1219 **PB**

Reynoldsburg

Abercrombie & Fitch, Four Limited Pkwy., East, 43068, pg. 995 **PB**
Bath & Body Works, Seven Limited Pkwy. E., 43068, pg. 995 **PB**
Cacique, Five Limited Pkwy., 43068, pg. 995 **PB**
Green Tree Acceptance of Ohio, Inc., 6430 E. Main St., 43068, pg. 762 **PB**
Lane Bryant, Five Limited Pkwy. E., 43068, pg. 995 **PB**
Lippert Abrasives Inc., 6915 Americana Pkwy., 43068, pg. 518 **IT**
Victoria's Secret Stores, Four Limited Pkwy., 43068, pg. 995 **PB**

Richfield

Crestar Foods Inc., 3940 Congress Pkwy., 44286, pg. 805 **PB**
THE B.F. GOODRICH COMPANY, 4020 Kinross Lakes Pkwy., 44286-9368, pg. 751 **PB**

Rockford

The Fremont Co., P.O. Box 326, 150 Hickory St., 45882, pg. 427 **PV**

Rocky River

LESCO, INC., 20005 Lake Rd., 44116, pg. 989 **PB**
WORLD SHIPPING, INC., 1340 Depot St., Ste. 200, 44116, pg. 1190 **PV**

Roseville

Robinson-Ransbottom Pottery Company, County Rd. 32, Box # 7, 45309, pg. 169 **PV**

Rossford

Hunger Hydraulics, Limited, 63 Dixie Highway, P.O. Box 37, 43460, pg. 639 **IT**

Sabina

Bundy Corporation, Sabina Plant, 277 Kenyon Dr., 45169, pg. 1341 **IT**
Palm Harbor Homes, Rte. 22 E., 45169, pg. 1255 **PB**

Saint Paris

Federal Packaging Corporation, 310 State Rte. 235, 43072, pg. 303 **PB**

Salem

BLISS-SALEM, INC., 530 S. Ellsworth Ave., 44460-3000, pg. 149 **PV**
Crane Deming Pumps, 1453 Allen Rd., 44460, pg. 457 **PB**
ELECTRIC FURNACE CO., 435 W. Wilson St., 44460-0150, pg. 367 **PV**
HUNT VALVE, 1913 E. State St., 44460-2491, pg. 549 **PV**
Turner Machine Company, 435 W. Wilson St., 44460, pg. 368 **PV**

Sandusky

CEDAR FAIR, L.P., One Causeway Dr., 44870, pg. 319 — PB
Cedar Point, P.O. Box 5006, One Causeway Dr., 44871-5006, pg. 319 — PB
The Cedar Point Bridge Co., CN 5006, 44870, pg. 319 — PB
The Cedar Point Transportation Co., CN 5006, 44870, pg. 319 — PB
DISTRICT PETROLEUM PRODUCTS, INC., 1832 Milan Rd., 44870, pg. 336 — PV
Dixon Ticonderoga Company, 1706 Hayes Ave., 44870, pg. 515 — PB
Erie County Cablevision, P.O. Box 5800, 44870, pg. 147 — PB
The G&C Foundry Company, 2806 W. Monroe St., 44870, pg. 142 — PB
Ohio Edison Co. Western Div., 237 W. Washington Row, 44870, pg. 645 — PB
Periodical Publishers' Service Bureau, Inc., One N. Superior St., 44870, pg. 517 — PV
J.H. ROUTH PACKING CO., 4413 W. Bogart Rd., 44870, pg. 948 — PV
SANDUSKY INTERNATIONAL INC., 615 W. Market St., 44870, pg. 964 — PV
Sandusky Plastics, Inc., 400 Broadway, 44870, pg. 586 — PB
Stein Inc., 1622 First St., CN 5001, 44870, pg. 13 — IT
Tsubaki, Inc. - Engineering Chain Div., P.O. Box 5651, 1010 Edgewater Dr., 44870-1601, pg. 1425 — IT

Seville

Meadowview Care Center, 76 High St., 44273, pg. 838 — PB

Shaker Heights

OFFICEMAX, 3605 Warrensville Ctr. Rd., 44122-5203, pg. 1212 — PB

Sharon Center

THE RUHLIN COMPANY, 6931 Ridge Rd., 44274, pg. 951 — PV
A. Schulman, Inc., 1475 Wolf Creek Trail, 44274, pg. 1441 — PB

Shelby

Copperweld Shelby Division, 132 West Main St., 44875-1471, pg. 662 — IT
Crestwood Care Center, 225 W. Main St., 44875, pg. 838 — PB
Heritage Care Center, 100 Rogers Ln., 44875, pg. 838 — PB
The Shelby Insurance Companies, 175 Mansfield Ave., 44875, pg. 1718 — PB
Uforma Shelby Business Forms, 40 High School Ave., 44875, pg. 740 — PV

Shreve

Diamonite Plant, 453 W. McConkey St., 44676, pg. 618 — PB

Sidney

Alcoa Building Products, Inc., 2615 Campbell Rd., 45365, pg. 61 — PB
Baum USA, 1660 Campbell Rd., 45365, pg. 1293 — IT
Busch U.S., 615 N. Oak Ave., 45365, pg. 1124 — PB
ComPair LeRoi, P.O. Box 927, 211 E. Russell Rd., 45365, pg. 1242 — PB
Copeland Corporation, 1675 W. Campbell Rd., 45365-0669, pg. 573 — PB
THE MONARCH MACHINE TOOL COMPANY, 615 N. Oak St., 45365, pg. 1123 — PB
Norcold, 600 S. Kuther Rd., 45365, pg. 352 — PB
Ross Aluminum Foundries, 815 N. Oak Ave., 45365, pg. 355 — PV
The Stolle Corporation, 1501 W. Michigan Ave., 45365, pg. 61 — PB
WAGNERWARE CORPORATION, 440 Fair Rd., 45365, pg. 1146 — PV

Smithville

ELASTIC MATERIALS, INC., 200 Wellar Dr., 44677, pg. 367 — PV

Solon

Agency Auto Sales, Inc., 30000 Aurora Rd., 44139, pg. 1153 — PB
Agency Chrysler-Plymouth, Inc., 30000 Aurora Rd., 44139, pg. 1153 — PB
Agency Ford, Inc., 30000 Aurora Rd., 44139, pg. 1153 — PB
Allen Telecom Inc., 30500 Bruce Industrial Pkwy., 44139, pg. 45 — PB
American Consumer Products, 31100 Solon Rd., 44139, pg. 1142 — PB
Arrow/Schweber Electronics, 6573 E. Cochran Rd., 44139, pg. 133 — PB
Baldwin International, Inc., 30403 Bruce Industrial Pkwy., 44139, pg. 1150 — IT
BARDONS & OLIVER, INC., 5800 Harper Rd., 44139-1833, pg. 116 — PV
Brockway Standard Ohio, Inc., 30301 Carter St., 44139, pg. 164 — PB

Clestra Hauserman, Inc., 29525 Fountain Pkwy., 44139-4351, pg. 569 — IT
Cole Consumer Products, 31100 Solon Rd., 44139, pg. 1142 — PV
EDD-Cleveland, 31200 Solon Rd., Unit 11, 44139, pg. 204 — PV
ERICO INTERNATIONAL, 34600 Solon Rd., 44139, pg. 381 — PV
FIL (U.S.) Inc., 30403 Bruce Industrial Pkwy., 44139, pg. 1151 — IT
Food Division, 30003 Bainbridge Rd., 44139, pg. 916 — IT
Harshaw Filtrol, 6801 Cochran Rd., 44139-3907, pg. 46 — IT
J & J Snack Foods Corp., 5351 Naiman Pkwy., 44139, pg. 916 — PB
Lindberg Heat Treating Co., 6111 Cochran Rd., 44139, pg. 999 — PB
Matrix Essentials, Inc., 30601 Carter St., 44139, pg. 254 — PB
L.J. Minor Corporation, 30003 Bainbridge Rd., 44139, pg. 917 — IT
Murphy-Phoenix Co., 31900 Solon Rd., 44139, pg. 397 — PV
NATIONAL AUTO CREDIT INC., 30000 Aurora Rd., 44139, pg. 1152 — PV
Nestle Frozen, Refrigerated, and Ice Cream Companies, 30003 Bainbridge Rd., 44139, pg. 918 — IT
Replacement Rent-A-Car, 30000 Aurora Rd., 44139, pg. 1153 — PB
The Sacks Group, 5135 Naiman Pkwy., 44139, pg. 1107 — IT
Sherwin-Williams Diversified Brands, Inc., 31500 Solon Rd., 44139, pg. 1466 — PB
SIGNATURE BRANDS USA, INC., 7005 Cochran Rd., 44139, pg. 1472 — PB
SWAGELOK COMPANY, 29500 Solon Rd., 44139, pg. 1057 — PV
Total Management Systems, 71 Franklin's Row, 44139, pg. 566 — PB
Wessel Hardware, 31100 Solon Rd., 44139, pg. 1142 — PV
Woodward-Clyde, 30775 Bainbridge Rd., Ste. 200, 44139, pg. 1656 — PB

Springboro

Flowserve Corporation, Engineered Plastic Products Div., 705 Pleasant Valley Dr., 45066-1158, pg. 658 — PB

Springdale

Avon Manufacturing Lab., 175 Progress Pl., 45246, pg. 156 — PB
Avon Sales & Distribution Branch, 175 Progress Pl., 45246, pg. 156 — PB

Springfield

AKZO Coatings Inc., 1550 Progress Rd., 45505-4456, pg. 46 — IT
WILLIAM BAYLEY/FOLGER ADAM SECURITY, INC., 1200 Warder St., 45503, pg. 125 — PV
F.H. BONN COMPANY, 4300 Gateway Blvd., 45502, pg. 156 — PV
HUGO BOSCA CO., INC., 1905 W. Jefferson, 45506, pg. 160 — PV
FULMER SUPERMARKETS, INC., 1804 N. Limestone St., 45503, pg. 431 — PV
International Steel Wool Corporation, P.O. Box 1767, 45501, pg. 156 — PV
Ohio Eby Brown, 1982 Commerce St., 45501, pg. 359 — PB
Ohio Edison Co.-Springfield Div., 111 E. High St., 45501, pg. 645 — PB
Olan Mills Inc. of Ohio, 329 Mt. Vernon Ave., 45503, pg. 749 — PV
Parker Sweeper Company, 91 Bechtle Ave., 44504, pg. 587 — IT
Speedway SuperAmerica LLC, P.O. Box 1500, 45501, pg. 1662 — PB
Springfield Newspapers, Inc., 202 N. Limestone St., 45503, pg. 281 — PV
United Technologies Elliott, P.O. Box 239, 45501-0239, pg. 1690 — PB

Steubenville

ACI Standard, P.O. Box 56, 43952, pg. 891 — IT
WTOV, Inc., Box 9999, Altamont Hill, 43952, pg. 390 — PV

Stow

City Machine & Wheel Co., 1676 Commerce Dr., 44224, pg. 299 — PV
F.R. Gross Company, 1397 Commerce Dr., 44224, pg. 103 — PB
The C.P. Hall Company, 4460 Hudson Dr., 44224, pg. 495 — PV
MACtac Morgan Adhesive Company, 4560 Darrow Rd., 44224, pg. 210 — PB
Matco Tools, 4403 Allen Rd., 44224, pg. 482 — PB
Norton Chemical Process Products Corporation, 3855 Fishcreek Rd., 44224, pg. 1173 — IT
Wilkinson Company, Inc., 1530 Commerce St., 44224, pg. 368 — PV

Strasburg

Special Packaging, Inc., 216 12th St. N.E., 44680, pg. 304 — PB

Streetsboro

Alumitech, Inc., 10380 Rte. 43, 44241, pg. 1523 — IT

Strongsville

CRL Asset Management Corp., 17800 Royalton Rd., 44136, pg. 326 — PB
CENTIN Corporation, 15400 Pearl Rd., Ste. 240, 44136, pg. 913 — PB
CENTRAL RESERVE LIFE CORPORATION, 17800 Royalton Rd., 44136-5197, pg. 326 — PB
Central Reserve Life of North America Insurance Co., 17800 Royalton Rd., 44136, pg. 326 — PB
CHEMCENTRAL/Cleveland, 21600 Drake Rd., 44136, pg. 232 — PV
Eberhard Manufacturing, 21944 Drake Rd., 44136, pg. 548 — PB
Hewlett-Packard Company, 15885 Sprague Rd., 44136, pg. 815 — PB
MILK MARKETING INC., 8257 Dow Cir., 44136, pg. 745 — PV
NATIONAL ENGINEERING & CONTRACTING CO., 12608 Alameda Dr., 44136, pg. 782 — PV
SEQUENTIA INC., 15900 Foltz Industrial Pkwy., 44136, pg. 985 — PV
Transbulk, Inc., 12608 Alameda Dr., 44136, pg. 782 — PV
Tri State Steel Construction, 12608 Alameda Dr., 44136, pg. 782 — PV
Unibus, Inc., 15242 Foltz Industrial Pkwy., 44136, pg. 1319 — PB
Van Dorn Demag Corporation, 11792 Alameda Dr., 44136, pg. 837 — IT
Western Reserve Administrative Services, Inc., 17800 Royalton Rd., 44136, pg. 326 — PB

Stryker

Strydel, Inc., 201 Ellis St., 43557, pg. 1214 — PB

Sunbury

Nestle Beverage Company, P.O. Box 5000, 185 S. Columbus St., 43074-5000, pg. 918 — IT

Swanton

R & R Plastics, P.O. Box 177, 43558, pg. 431 — PV
Toledo Learning Center, Toledo Express Airport, 11600 W. Airport Service Rd., 43558, pg. 219 — PB

Tallmadge

Alro Specialty Metals, Tallmadge, 184 South Ave., 44278, pg. 46 — PV
Chemionics Corporation, 070 Munroe Falls Rd., 44278, pg. 234 — PV
Summit Plastic Co., 1169 Brittain Rd., 44278, pg. 974 — IT

Tiffin

Horizon Technology Group - Tiffin Division, 1988 County Rd. # 593, 44883, pg. 539 — PV
NATIONAL MACHINERY, 161 Greenfield St., 44883, pg. 785 — PV
Pettibone Tiffin Parts, 235 Miami St., 44883, pg. 860 — PV
Stacy Equipment Co., 325 Hall St., 44883, pg. 1158 — PV
Tiffin Enterprises, Inc., 458 Second Ave., 44883, pg. 98 — PB
WEBSTER INDUSTRIES INC., 325 Hall St., 44883, pg. 1157 — PV
Webster Mfg. Co., 325 Hall St., 44883, pg. 1158 — PV

Tipp City

DAP Inc., 855 N. 3rd St., 45371, pg. 1486 — IT
A.O. Smith Electrical Products Company, 531 N. Fourth St., 45371, pg. 1477 — PB

Toledo

Abros, Inc., 860 Curtis St., P.O. Box 940, 43697, pg. 86 — PV
Abtco, Inc., 2900 Hill Ave., 43607, pg. 20 — IT
Acklin Stamping Div., 1925 Nebraska Ave., 43607, pg. 1565 — PB
Allright Toledo, Inc., 332 N. Michigan Ave., 43624, pg. 43 — PV
AmeriSource-Toledo Div., 3145 Nebraska Ave., 43607, pg. 97 — PB
ART IRON, INC., 860 Curtis St., 43609, pg. 86 — PV
Auburndale Company, Inc., 4310 Lagrange St., 43612, pg. 1645 — PB
Bendix Toledo Stamping, P.O. Box 692, 43697-0692, pg. 51 — PB
Beta Tube, 7400 Airport Hwy., 43615, pg. 17 — PB
BLADE COMMUNICATIONS, INC., 541 N. Superior St., 43660, pg. 174 — PV
Bleim Steel Company, 1500 Coining Dr., 43612, pg. 845 — IT
BROWN MOTORS, 5625 W. Central Ave., 43615, pg. 174 — PV
Browning-Ferris Industries of Ohio & Michigan, Inc., P.O. Box 5069, Pt. Place Station, 43611, pg. 264 — PB
Buckeye Cablevision, 5566 Southwyck Blvd., 43614, pg. 147 — PV

PB - *U.S. Public Companies Volume*
PV - *U.S. Private Companies Volume*
IT - *International Public & Private Companies Volume*

1390

Geographic Index-U.S.

Buckeye Specialties Division, 2145 Tedrow St., 43614, pg. 1453 **PB**
CAPITAL TIRE, INC., 1001 Cherry St., 43608, pg. 206 **PV**
CHEMCENTRAL/Toledo, 4051 South Ave., 43615, pg. 232 **PV**
Dana Commercial Credit Corp. (Ohio), 1801 Richards Rd., 43607, pg. 479 **PB**
DANA CORPORATION, 4500 Dorr St., 43615, pg. 479 **PB**
Dart Trucking Company, Inc., 322 Matzinger Rd., 43612, pg. 94 **PB**
DeVilbiss Ransburg Industrial Liquid Systems (OH), 320 Phillips Ave., 43612, pg. 866 **PB**
Diamond Financial Holdings, Inc., 4500 Dorr St., 43615, pg. 480 **PB**
Doehler-Jarvis, Inc., 5400 N. Detroit Ave., 43612, pg. 796 **PB**
Excel Components, 64 Fearing Blvd., 43607, pg. 598 **PB**
Exothermics-Eclipse, Inc., 5040 Enterprise Blvd., 43612, pg. 360 **PB**
Fahlgren, One Seagate, Ste. 901, 43604-2396, pg. 391 **PV**
The Fifth Third Bank of Northwestern Ohio, National Association, 606 Madison Ave., 43604-1102, pg. 622 **PB**
Fiske Brothers Refining, Toledo Div., 1500 Oakdale, 43605, pg. 409 **PV**
Franklin Park Mall, Inc., 700 Franklin Park Mall, 43623, pg. 1408 **PB**
GIANT INDUSTRIES, 900 N. Westwood Ave., 43607, pg. 451 **PV**
Great Lakes Window, Inc., P.O. Box 1896, 43603-1896, pg. 1193 **PB**
H.S. Processing, 2401 Front St., 43605, pg. 519 **PV**
HEALTH CARE & RETIREMENT CORPORATION, One SeaGate, 43604-2616, pg. 801 **PB**
HEIDTMAN STEEL PRODUCTS, INC., 2401 Front St., 43605, pg. 519 **PV**
Hewlett-Packard Company, 5th Fl., One Maritime Plaza, 720 Water St., 43604, pg. 815 **PB**
KELLERMEYER CO., 1025 Brown Ave., 43607, pg. 612 **PV**
The Lathrop Company, 460 W. Dussel Dr., 43537, pg. 1645 **PB**
Libbey Owens Ford Co., 811 Madison Ave., 43624, pg. 1056 **IT**
Lion, 2040 S. Reynolds, 43614, pg. 1090 **PB**
MERIDIAN NATIONAL CORPORATION, 805 Chicago St., 43611, pg. 1095 **PB**
A. Mindel & Son, Inc., 4200 Creekside Ave., 43612, pg. 987 **PV**
THE NATIONAL SUPER SERVICE CO., 3115 Frenchmens Rd., 43607-2958, pg. 787 **PV**
Nekoosa Packaging Company, P.O. Box 697, 1660 Indianwood Circle, 43694-0697, pg. 736 **PB**
Nekoosa Packaging Corp., One Seagate, 43666, pg. 736 **PB**
Neste Resins Corporation, 6175 American Rd., P.O. Caller No. 64010, 43612, pg. 913 **IT**
New Mather Metals Inc., 5270 N. Detroit Ave., 43612, pg. 902 **IT**
Ottawa River Steel Co., 805 Chicago St., 43611, pg. 1095 **PV**
Owens-Brockway Glass Containers, One SeaGate, 43666, pg. 1238 **PB**
Owens-Brockway Plastic Containers, One SeaGate, 43666, pg. 1238 **PB**
Owens-Brockway Prescription Products, One SeaGate, 43666, pg. 1238 **PB**
OWENS CORNING, One Owens Corning Pkwy., 43659, pg. 1236 **PB**
Owens-Illinois Closure Inc., One SeaGate, 43666, pg. 1238 **PB**
OWENS-ILLINOIS, INC., One SeaGate, 43666, pg. 1238 **PB**
Perstorp Polyols Inc., 600 Matzinger Rd., 43612-2695, pg. 1038 **IT**
Port Lawrence Title & Trust Co., 616 Madison Ave., 43604, pg. 626 **PB**
J. Richard Industries, L.P., 3934 Concord St., 43612, pg. 249 **PV**
Riker Products, Inc., 4901 Stickney Ave., 43612, pg. 300 **PV**
Rowe Industries, P.O. Box 6877, 6225 Benore Rd., 43612, pg. 308 **PB**
Schuller Intl. Inc., P.O. Box 517, 43697-0517, pg. 927 **PV**
Service Products Buildings, Inc., 460 W. Dussel Dr., 43537, pg. 1645 **PB**
The Toledo Edison Company, 300 Madison Ave., 43652-0001, pg. 645 **PB**
Toledo Milk Processing, Inc., 1149 Grand Ave., 43606, pg. 1453 **PB**
Toledo Shiprepair Company, 2245 Front St., 43605, pg. 1041 **PB**
Toledo Stamping & Manufacturing Co., P.O. Box 596, 43607, pg. 707 **PB**
TUFFY ASSOCIATES CORP., 1414 Baronial Plaza Dr., 43615, pg. 1109 **PV**
Unitog Rental Facility, One Southland Ave., 43624, pg. 1693 **PB**
WTOL-TV, 730 N. Summit St., 43604, pg. 992 **PB**

Toronto

Hancock Manufacturing, Fifth & Cleveland Sts., 43964, pg. 299 **PV**

Trenton

Miller Brewing Company, 2525 Wayne Madison Rd., 45067, pg. 1289 **PB**

Troy

Brown-Bridge, 518 E. Water St., 45373, pg. 1022 **PB**
Hobart Brothers Co., 600 W. Main, 45373, pg. 866 **PB**
Hobart Corporation, 701 S. Ridge Ave., 45374, pg. 1322 **PB**
Ivex Packaging Corporation-Troy, 421 S. Union St., 45373, pg. 915 **PB**
Miller Automation, Inc. (OH), 1314 South Barnhart Rd., 45373, pg. 867 **PB**
Premark Food Equipment Group, World Headquarters Ave., 45374, pg. 1322 **PB**
Tri Dayton, 1275 Archer Dr., 45373, pg. 428 **PV**
Troy Operations, 2001 Corporate Dr., 45373, pg. 1475 **PB**
Worldwide Leasing, Hobart Square, 45373, pg. 866 **PB**

Twinsburg

ADVANCED LIGHTING TECHNOLOGIES, INC., 2307 E. Aurora Rd., Ste. 1, 44087, pg. 20 **PB**
Automated Label Systems, Inc., 8400 Darrow Rd., 44087, pg. 865 **PB**
THE GIBSON-HOMANS COMPANY, 1755 Enterprise Pkwy., 44087, pg. 451 **PB**
IER Division, 8589 Darrow Rd., 44087, pg. 689 **PB**
Earle M. Jorgensen Company/Cincinnati, 2060 Enterprise Pkwy., 44087, pg. 600 **PV**
KOOL SEAL, INC., 1499 Enterprise Pkwy., 44087, pg. 632 **PV**
North Coast Division, 8036 Bavaria Rd., 44087, pg. 518 **IT**

Uhrichsville

IMCO Recycling of Ohio Inc., 7335 Newport Rd., 44683, pg. 871 **PB**

Upper Sandusky

Bond Plastic Div., State Rd. 182 E., 43351, pg. 1000 **PB**
Hydraulics Inc., State Rte. 182 E., P.O. Box 337, 43351, pg. 560 **PB**

Urbana

CHAMPAIGN LANDMARK, INC., 304 Bloomfield Ave., 43078, pg. 227 **PV**
Q3 Industries, 605 Miami St., 43078, pg. 897 **PV**

Valley City

MTD PRODUCTS, INC., 5965 Grafton Rd., 44280, pg. 688 **PV**

Valley View

Gould Instrument Systems, Inc., 8333 Rockside Rd., 44125, pg. 1592 **PV**
KENDALE INDUSTRIES, INC., 7600 Hub Parkway, 44125, pg. 614 **PV**
KLECO CORP., 6161 Halle Dr., 44125, pg. 625 **PV**
Market Direct, 7640 Hub Pkwy., 44125, pg. 1177 **IT**
Triangle Machine Product Co., 6055 Hillcrest Dr., 44125, pg. 426 **PV**
TYLER ELEVATOR PRODUCTS, INC., 6161 Halle Dr., 44125, pg. 1112 **PV**

Van Wert

All America Insurance Company, 800 So. Washington, 45891, pg. 224 **PV**
Cafco, 800 So. Washington, 45891, pg. 224 **PV**
CENTRAL MUTUAL INSURANCE CO., 800 S. Washington, 45891, pg. 223 **PV**
KENNEDY MANUFACTURING COMPANY, 520 E. Sycamore St., 45891, pg. 614 **PV**
Norwest Bank Ohio, N.A., 114 E. Main St., 45891, pg. 1202 **PB**
Spring Lake Merchandise, Inc., 1200 N. Washington, 45891, pg. 948 **PV**
Teleflex Automotive, 1265 Industrial Ave., 45891, pg. 1569 **PB**

Vandalia

Circle Freight International USA, 3620 Lightner Rd., 45377-0310, pg. 371 **PB**
Circle International, 3620 Lightner Rd., 45377-0310, pg. 371 **PB**
Emery Worldwide Airlines, One Emery Plaza, Dayton International Airport, 45377, pg. 281 **PB**
McCauley Propeller Systems, P.O. Box 5053, 3535 McCauley Dr., 45377, pg. 1589 **PB**
Metromedia Steakhouses, Inc., Terminal Dr., 45377, pg. 736 **PV**
PSA Airlines, Inc., 3400 Terminal Dr., 45377, pg. 1680 **PB**
PAXAR Graphics, 815 S. Brown School Rd., 45377, pg. 1266 **PB**

Wadsworth

Admiral/CDT, P.O. Box 1003, 931 Seville Rd., 44281, pg. 287 **PB**
Admiral Heintz, Inc., 689 Weber Dr., 44281, pg. 1143 **PB**
Frank B. Black Research Center, 8711 Wadsworth Rd., P.O. Box 1001, 44281, pg. 844 **PB**

ROHRER CORPORATION, 717 Seville Rd., 44281, pg. 940 **PV**
Zeneca Specialty Inks, 471 E. Bergey St., 44281, pg. 1525 **IT**

Walbridge

Pre Finish Metals (EG) Inc., 30610 E. Broadway, 43465, pg. 226 **PB**
RUDOLPH/LIBBE, INC., 6494 Latcha Rd., 43465, pg. 950 **PV**
Walbridge Coatings, Inc., 30610 E. Broadway, 43465, pg. 879 **PB**

Walton Hills

Buckeye Biscuit Company, 7515 Northfield Rd., 44146, pg. 1069 **IT**

Wapakoneta

Amcast Automotive-Wapakoneta Plant, 13663 Short Rd., 45895, pg. 63 **PB**
Koneta Rubber Co. Div., P.O. Box 150, 45895, pg. 976 **PB**

Warren

Ajax Magnethermic Corp., 1745 Overland Ave. N.E., 44482, pg. 113 **IT**
Ajax Services Inc., P.O. Box 991, 44482, pg. 113 **IT**
Alcan Aluminum Corporation, 280 N. Park Ave., 44481, pg. 50 **IT**
Alphabet Division, 8700 E. Market St., 44484, pg. 1044 **PV**
American Waste Management Services, Inc., One American Way, 44484-5555, pg. 94 **PB**
AMERICAN WASTE SERVICES, INC., One American Way, 44484-5555, pg. 94 **PB**
American Welding & Manufacturing Co., Dietz Rd., 44483, pg. 425 **PV**
CSC, Ltd., 4000 Mahoning Ave., 44483, pg. 924 **PV**
Envirco Transportation Management, Inc., One American Way, 44484-5555, pg. 94 **PB**
Erieview Cartage, Inc., 1260 N. Park Ave., 44483, pg. 50 **IT**
Horizon Village Nursing & Rehabilitation, 2473 North Rd. N.E., 44483, pg. 838 **PB**
Imperial Skilled Care Center, 4121 Tod Ave., 44485, pg. 838 **PB**
Ohio Star Forge Co., 4000 Mahoning Ave., 44483, pg. 364 **IT**
Ridgecrest Care Center, 1926 Ridge Ave., 44484, pg. 838 **PB**
STONERIDGE, INC., 9400 E. Market St., 44484, pg. 1044 **PV**
SUPERIOR PRINTING CO., 3869 Niles Rd., 44484-3599, pg. 1055 **PV**
Thomas Steel Strip Corp., Delaware Ave. NW, 44485, pg. 756 **IT**
Titan Wheel Corporation Of Ohio, 250 Dietz Rd., 44483, pg. 1619 **PB**
Warren Plant, 101 Tidewater Rd., 44483, pg. 1214 **PB**
Washington Square Nursing Center, 202 Washington St. N.W., 44483, pg. 838 **PB**

Warrensville Heights

Baxter Tube Company, 25221 Miles Rd., 44122, pg. 1632 **PB**

Washington Court House

Auburn Manor, 375 Glenn Ave., 43160, pg. 838 **PB**
Bundy Corporation, Washington Court House Plant, 495 Old Chillicothe Rd., 43160-9053, pg. 1341 **IT**
CorTec Industries, 2351 Kenskill Ave., 43160, pg. 456 **PB**
Crestar Foods Inc., 1104 Clinton Ave., 43160, pg. 805 **PV**
Sugar Creek Packing Co., 2101 Kenskill Ave., 43160, pg. 1049 **PV**
SUGAR CREEK PACKING CO., 2101 1/2 Kenskill Ave., 43160, pg. 1049 **PV**
Vigoro Industries, Inc., 717 Robinson Rd., 43160, pg. 856 **PB**

Wauseon

Britt Industries, Inc., 525 Enterprise Dr., 43567, pg. 637 **PV**
FULTON INDUSTRIES INC., 135 E. Linfoot St., 43567, pg. 431 **PV**
Koncor Industries Div., 14614-H, 43567, pg. 1617 **PB**
Kurdziel Iron of Wauseon, Inc., 820 W. Leggett, 43567, pg. 637 **PV**
McCord Payen Inc., Sycamore & Potter, 43567, pg. 1334 **IT**
Small Parts, Inc.-Napco Division, 530 N. Linfoot St., 43567, pg. 1006 **PV**

Waynesburg

American Landfill, Inc., 7916 Chapel St., S.E., 44688, pg. 94 **PB**

Wellington

JENNINGS & CHURELLA CONSTRUCTION COMPANY, 311 Maple St., 44090, pg. 586 **PV**

PB - U.S. Public Companies Volume
PV - U.S. Private Companies Volume
IT - International Public & Private Companies Volume

Wellston

McNally Pittsburg Mfg. Corp., P.O. Box 228, 45692, pg. 1326   IT
Totino's/Wellston, 2403 S. Pennsylvania Ave., 45692-9569, pg. 411   IT

West Chester

ESCORT, INC., 5440 West Chester Rd., 45069-2950, pg. 383   PB
SCHUMACHER-DUGAN CONSTRUCTION, 6355 Centre Park Dr., 45069, pg. 973   PV

West Unity

Schlegel West Unity Inc., 214 Defiance St., 43570-9500, pg. 128   IT

Westerville

Capitol Manufacturing Co., P.O. Box 6103, 675 Brooksedge Blvd., 43086, pg. 793   PB
Dispatch Consumer Services, 7801 N. Central, P.O. Box 206, 43081, pg. 335   PV
Eaton IDT, 173 Heatherdown Dr., 43081, pg. 558   PB
Exel Logistics North America, 501 W. Schrock Rd., 43081, pg. 901   IT
Glencoe/Mc-Graw Hill, 936 Eastwind Dr., 43081-3374, pg. 1070   PB
Hewlett-Packard Company, 675 Brooksedge Blvd., 43081, pg. 815   PB
Ohio Utilities Company, 5481 Buenos Aires Blvd., 43081, pg. 380   PB
The Product Design Center, Inc., 921-126 Eastwind Dr., 43081, pg. 370   IT
SBC Public Relations, 707 Park Meadow Rd., 43081, pg. 955   PV

Westfield Center

WESTFIELD COMPANIES, One Park Cir., 44251, pg. 1169   PV

Westlake

DSM RIM Nylon, Inc., 1991 Crocker Rd., 44145, pg. 355   IT
The Scott Fetzer Company, 28800 Clemens Rd., 44145, pg. 217   PB
Grinnell Fire Protection Systems, 835 Sharon Dr., 44145, pg. 1386   IT
Grinnell Fire Protection Systems, 835 Sharon Dr., 44145, pg. 1647   PB
THE RICHARD E. JACOBS GROUP, 25425 Center Ridge Road, 44145, pg. 580   PV
Koyo Corporation of USA, Sales Division, 29570 Clemens Rd., 44145, pg. 760   IT
LAKE ERIE ELECTRIC, INC., 25730 First St., 44145, pg. 643   PV
NORDSON CORPORATION, 28601 Clemens Rd., 44145, pg. 1188   PB
Radiometer America Inc., 810 Sharon Dr., 44145-1598, pg. 1083   PB
Sachs Boge of America, 909 Crocker Rd., 44145, pg. 835   IT
United Consumer Financial Services Co., 865 Bassett Rd., 44145, pg. 218   PB
Western Enterprises Div., 875 Bassett Rd., 44145, pg. 218   PB

Wickliffe

Bailey Controls Company, 29801 Euclid Ave., 44092, pg. 449   IT
The Hall Chemical Company, 28960 Lakeland Blvd., 44092, pg. 461   PV
THE LUBRIZOL CORPORATION, 29400 Lakeland Blvd., 44092, pg. 1016   PB
PMC INDUSTRIES INC., 29100 Lakeland Blvd., 44092, pg. 827   PV

Willard

Mapa Pioneer Corporation, 512 E. Tiffin St., 44890, pg. 1409   IT

Williamsburg

DUALITE INC., One Dualite Ln., 45176, pg. 344   PV
Dualite Sales & Service, Inc., One Dualite Ln., 45176, pg. 344   PV

Willoughby

BUD INDUSTRIES, INC., 4605 E. 355th, 44094, pg. 178   PV
LAKE BUSINESS PRODUCTS, INC., 38322 Apollo Pkwy., 44094, pg. 643   PV
MCDONALD EQUIPMENT CO., 37200 Vine St., 44094-6346, pg. 721   PV
METAL SEAL & PRODUCTS, INC., 4323 Hamann Pkwy., 44094, pg. 734   PV
The News-Herald (Lake County), 7085 Mentor Ave., 44094, pg. 935   PB

Wilmington

ABX Air, Inc., 145 Hunter Dr., 45177, pg. 33   PB
GATOR FREIGHTWAYS, INC., 600 Gilliam Rd., 45177, pg. 441   PV
Hydro-electric Lift Trucks, Inc., 370 Davids Dr., 45177, pg. 243   PV
Hydro-electric Lift Trucks Inc., 370 Davids Dr., 45177, pg. 61   PB
Kurz-kasch, Inc., 185 Park Dr., 45177, pg. 637   PV
R & L Carriers, P.O. Box 271, 45177, pg. 441   PV
Units Sets, Inc., 115 Skimming Dr., 45177, pg. 947   PV

Winesburg

Case Farms of Ohio, P.O. Box 185, 44690, pg. 218   PV

Woodville

Redland Ohio Inc., P.O. Box 128, 43469-0128, pg. 1091   IT

Wooster

Akron Brass Company, 1450 Spruce St., 44691, pg. 1068   IT
Bell & Howell Publication Systems Company, 1909 Old Mansfield Rd., 44691, pg. 201   PB
Buckeye Container, P.O. Box 16, 44691, pg. 177   PV
BUCKEYE CORRUGATED INC., 2200 Benden Dr., 44691, pg. 177   PV
The Crown Divisions, 1654 Old Mansfield Rd., 44691, pg. 631   PB
The Gerstenslager Company, 1425 E. Bowman St., 44691, pg. 780   PB
Hawkins Markets, 2312 Akron Rd., 44691, pg. 1540   PB
Maintenance, Inc., 1051 W. Liberty St., 44691, pg. 1068   IT
Peoples Federal Savings Bank, 121 N. Market St., 44691, pg. 647   PB
Rubbermaid Home Products Div., 1147 Akron Rd., 44691, pg. 1411   PB
RUBBERMAID INCORPORATED, 1147 Akron Rd., 44691-6000, pg. 1411   PB
Stahl Div., 3201 W. Lincoln Way, 44691, pg. 218   PB
Wayne Steel, Inc., 1070 W. Liberty St. Extn., 44691, pg. 1101   PB
THE WOOSTER BRUSH COMPANY, 604 Madison Ave., 44691, pg. 1188   PV

Worthington

Chase Manhattan Mortgage Corporation, 200 Old Wilson Bridge Rd., 43085, pg. 338   PB
Dayco Swan Corporation, P.O. Box 509, 43085, pg. 1045   PB
G.E. Superabrasives, 6325 Huntley Rd., 43085, pg. 711   PB
Grumman Ohio Corp., 250 E. Wilson Bridge Road, Ste. 250, 43085, pg. 1198   PB
LIQUI-BOX CORPORATION, 6950 Worthington-Galena Rd., 43085, pg. 1000   PB
Mettler-Toledo Inc., 350 W. Wilson Bridge Rd., 43085, pg. 4   PV
PENCO-Ohio, P.O. Box 6007, 400 W. Wilson Bridge Rd., 43085, pg. 1508   IT
SRA McGraw Hill, 250 Old Wilson Bridge Rd., 43085, pg. 1070   PB
Specialty Foods Investment Inl., 900 Proprietors Rd., 43085, pg. 1780   PB
TIE Systems Ohio, 402 East Wilson Bridge Rd., Ste. A, 43085, pg. 1085   PV
WORTHINGTON FOODS INC., 900 Proprietors Rd., 43085, pg. 1790   PB

Xenia

New Systech Corporation, 245 North Valley Rd., 45385, pg. 783   IT
SuperValu, Inc.-Ohio Valley Div., 1003 Bellbrook Ave., 45385, pg. 1540   PB

Yellow Springs

VERNAY LABORATORIES, INC., 120 E. S. College St., 45387, pg. 1137   PV
YSI INCORPORATED, 1725 Brannum Ln., 45387, pg. 1195   PV

Youngstown

AMERICAN ARCHITECTURAL PRODUCTS, INC., 755 Boardman Canfield Rd., 44512, pg. 67   PB
American Church, 8401 Southern Blvd., 44512, pg. 60   PV
AMERICAN PAPER GROUP, INC., 8401 Southern Blvd., 44512, pg. 60   PV
American Paper Products, 8401 Southern Blvd., 44512, pg. 60   PV
Bliss Manufacturing Company, P.O. Box 4266, 44515, pg. 771   PB
Boardman Community Care Center, 5665 South Ave., 44512, pg. 838   PB
Browning-Ferris Industries of Ohio, Inc., 530 Glenwood Ave., 44502, pg. 264   PB
THE CAFARO CO., 2445 Belmont Ave., 44504, pg. 198   PV
Colonial Manor, 196 Colonial Dr., 44505, pg. 838   PB
COMMERCIAL INTERTECH CORP., 1775 Logan Ave., 44505, pg. 411   PB
Connecting Point Computer Services, 4845 Market St., 44708, pg. 471   PV
Danielli of America, 3805 Henricks Rd., 44515-0180, pg. 378   IT
THE EDWARD J. DEBARTOLO CORPORATION, 7620 Market St., 44513-9128, pg. 319   PV
HYNES INDUSTRIES INC., 3760 Oakwood Ave., 44515, pg. 552   PV
LTV Steel Tubular Products, 1315 Albert St., 44505, pg. 972   PB
The Metropolitan Savings Bank of Ohio, One Federal Plaza W., 44501, pg. 608   PB
National Uniform Service, 350 North Ave., 44502, pg. 690   PB
Northeast Ohio Correctional Facility, 2240 Hubbard Rd., 44505, pg. 451   PB
Ohio Alloy Steels Corporation, P.O. Box 1286, 219 S. Phelps St., 44501-1286, pg. 1617   PB
PHAR-MOR, INC., 20 Federal Plaza W., 445011, pg. 1284   PB
PHOTOGENIC MACHINE COMPANY, INC., 525 McClurg Rd., 44512, pg. 864   PV
Republic Hose Manufacturing Co., 1354 Albert St., Dept. 12, 44505, pg. 1423   IT
YSD INDUSTRIES, 3710 Henricks Rd., 44515, pg. 1194   PV

Zanesville

Armco Inc.-Zanesville Operations, 1724 Lindon Ave., 43701, pg. 131   PB
Benco Pet Foods, Inc., 22 S. First St., 43701, pg. 1360   PB
National PharmPak Services, Inc., 3540 E. Pike, 43701, pg. 304   PB
The New Bakery Company of Ohio, Inc., P.O. Box 2764, 750 Airport Rd., 43701, pg. 1754   PB
United Technologies Fabrications, P.O. Box 2158, 43702-2158, pg. 1690   PB

OKLAHOMA

Ada

Evergreen Mills Inc., 221 N. Rennie, 74820, pg. 1134   PV
PRE-PAID LEGAL SERVICES, INC., 321 E. Main St., 74821-0145, pg. 1320   PB

Altus

United Supermarkets, P.O. Box 557, 73521, pg. 494   PV

Alva

Wheeler Bros. Grain Co., 420 Santa Fe, 73717, pg. 1171   PV

Anadarko

Hollytex Carpet Mills, Inc., 505 N.E. Seventh St., 73005, pg. 535   PV

Ardmore

The Ardmore Daily Ardmoreite, 117 W. Broadway, 73402-1328, pg. 995   PV
Energy Development Corporation, 110 W. Broadway, 73402, pg. 1186   PB
NOBLE AFFILIATES, INC., 110 W. Broadway, 73401, pg. 1186   PB
Noble Trading, Inc., 110 W. Broadway, 73402, pg. 1186   PB
Samedan Oil Corporation, 110 W. Broadway, 73402, pg. 1186   PB
Total Petroleum, Inc., 142 Bypass, 73401, pg. 1663   PB

Bartlesville

ADAMS INVESTMENT COMPANY, 4100 S.E. Adams Rd., Ste. E103, 74006, pg. 16   PV
Applied Automation Inc., Pawhuska Rd., 74004, pg. 835   IT
Phillips Communications, Inc., Fourth & Keeler Ave., 74004, pg. 1291   PB
Phillips Gas Company, 1250 Adams Bldg., 74004, pg. 1291   PB
PHILLIPS PETROLEUM COMPANY, Fourth & Keeler Ave., 74004, pg. 1290   PB
Phillips Petroleum International Corporation, c/o Phillips Petroleum Company, 1156 B Adams Bldg., 74004, pg. 1291   PB
Phillips Pipe Line Company, 1250 Adams Bldg., 74004, pg. 1291   PB
Public Service Company of Oklahoma-Northern Div., 400 S. Johnstone, 74003, pg. 324   PB
REDA, Fourth & Dewey, 74003, pg. 298   PB

Bethany

Bethany Learning Center, P.O. Box 1640 Wiley Post Airpt, 7310 N.W. 50th St., 73008, pg. 218   PB

Bixby

AMERICAN FOUNDRY GROUP, INC., 14602 S. Grant, 74008, pg. 54   PV

PB - *U.S. Public Companies Volume*
PV - *U.S. Private Companies Volume*
IT - *International Public & Private Companies Volume*

1392

Geographic Index-U.S.

Broken Arrow

Continental Federal Saving & Loan, 701 W. New Orleans,
pg. 174 **PB**
EG & G Instruments-Process Measurements/Chandler,
2001 N. Indianwood Ave., 74012, pg. 543 **PB**
Mylon C. Jacobs Supply Co., 2701 N. Hemlock Ct., 74012,
pg. 963 **PV**
PACCAR Winch Division, 800 E. Dallas Ave., 74012,
pg. 1246 **PB**
Simulation Systems Division, 2700 N. Hemlock Cir., 74012,
pg. 218 **PB**

Burns Flat

ALLTEL Oklahoma, Inc., Clinton Sherman Airpark, P.O. Box
750, Bldg. 825, 73624, pg. 56 **PB**

Catoosa

AlliedSignal Environmental Catalysts, 1301 Main Pkwy.,
74015, pg. 51 **PB**
Eagle Electronics, P.O. Box 669, 74015, pg. 1016 **PB**
Erlanger Tubular Corporation, 5610 Bird Creek Ave., 74015,
pg. 1147 **PB**

Checotah

Dentures and Dental Services, 200 N. Broadway, 74426,
pg. 990 **PV**
SHARPE DRY GOODS CO., INC., 200 N. Broadway,
74426, pg. 990 **PV**

Chickasha

Delta Faucet of Oklahoma, Inc., P.O. Box 905, 73023,
pg. 1053 **PB**
Gabriel Shock Absorber Plant, P.O. Box 988, Methvin
Industrial, 73018, pg. 137 **PB**

Choctaw

Oklahoma Communication Systems, Inc., P.O. Box 220,
2495 Main St., 73020, pg. 1571 **PB**

Claremore

Centrilift, 200 W. Stuart Roosa Dr., 74017, pg. 167 **PB**
International Tubular Products, Inc., 401 E. 30th St. N.,
74017, pg. 14 **PV**
North American Galvanizing, 5100 S.W. Alliance Dr., 74017,
pg. 961 **PB**
Nupar, P.O. Box 225-B, Rte. 7, 74017, pg. 169 **PB**

Clinton

Acme Brick Co., 600 S. 28, P.O. Box 1025, 73601,
pg. 936 **PB**
ELK SUPPLY COMPANY, 103 Gary Blvd., 73601,
pg. 371 **PV**

Del City

Woodward-Clyde, 3000 Tower Dr., Ste. 456, 73115,
pg. 1656 **PB**

Dewey

Central States Multiplex, 2800 Industrial Pkwy., 74029,
pg. 16 **PV**

Duke

Hollis & Eastern Railroad Co., P.O. Drawer C, 73532,
pg. 1378 **PB**

Duncan

COOK MANUFACTURING CORPORATION, 3920 S. 13th
St., 73533, pg. 272 **PV**
Oklahoma National Bank of Duncan, 729 Main St., 73534,
pg. 630 **PB**
UNIVERSAL FIDELITY LIFE INSURANCE COMPANY,
2211 N. Hwy. 81, 73533, pg. 1127 **PV**

Durant

Durant Electronics, Inc., 2200 Arkansas Ave., 74701,
pg. 1047 **PV**

Edmond

Acme Brick Co., P.O. Box 14506, 500 E. Memorial Rd.,
73113, pg. 936 **PB**
Bryant Nursing Center, 1100 E. Ninth St., 73034,
pg. 839 **PB**
Continental Federal Saving & Loan, 18 S.E. 15th St.,
73103, pg. 174 **PB**
First National Bank of Edmond, 24 E. First St., 73083,
pg. 174 **PB**
First Oklahoma Bank & Trust Company of Edmond, 300 S.
Bryant, 73034, pg. 174 **PB**
Horizon Specialty Hospital, 1100 E. Ninth St., 73034,
pg. 839 **PB**

Lyntone Belts, P.O. Box 5110, 401 SW 33rd St., 73083,
pg. 442 **PV**
T.H. ROGERS LUMBER CO., 1717 State St., 73013,
pg. 940 **PV**
SofTechnics Inc., 200 E. Tenth St., Ste. A, 73034,
pg. 1012 **PV**

Enid

ATWOOD DISTRIBUTING, INC., 2717 N. Van Buren,
73701, pg. 98 **PV**
GROENDYKE TRANSPORTS, INC., 2510 Rock Island
Blvd., 73701, pg. 483 **PV**
Steco, 2215 S. Van Buren, 73702, pg. 153 **PV**
Uni-Steel Inc., 101 E. Illinois Ave., 73701, pg. 1101 **PB**

Frederick

Schlegel Oklahoma, Inc., Airport Industrial Park, 73542,
pg. 128 **IT**

Hinton

Great Plains Correctional Facility, P.O. Box 1018, 73047,
pg. 450 **PB**

Holdenville

Davis Correctional Facility, Rte. 4, Box 40, 74848,
pg. 450 **PB**

Hugo

CHOCTAW ELECTRIC CO-OP, P.O. Box 758, Hwy. 93 N.,
74743, pg. 238 **PV**

Jenks

First National Bank of Jenks, 700 W. Main, 74037,
pg. 174 **PB**
Kimberly-Clark, P.O. Box 3000, 74037-3000, pg. 959 **PB**

Kingfisher

KINGFISHER CO-OP ELEVATOR ASSOCIATION, One
Co-Op Way, 73750, pg. 621 **PV**

Lawton

Hewlett-Packard Company, 2210 W. Gore, Ste. 5, 73501,
pg. 815 **PB**
Public Service Company of Oklahoma-Western Div., 629
SW C Ave., 73501, pg. 324 **PB**

Lindsay

RURAL ELECTRIC CO-OP, N. Hwy. 76, 73052,
pg. 952 **PV**

Marietta

President Baking-Marietta, P.O. Box 249, 600 N. Hwy. 77,
73448, pg. 1069 **IT**

Marlow

EBI/AOA Division, 1801 W. Nabor Rd., 73055, pg. 231 **PB**

Maysville

Texaco USA, P.O. Box 846, 73057-0846, pg. 1583 **PB**

McAlester

Edison Plastics Co., P.O. Box 1810, One Edison Dr., 74502,
pg. 1179 **PV**
McAlester News-Capital & Democrat, Box 987, 500 S.
Second, 74502, pg. 1078 **PB**
McAlester Publishing Co., Box 987, 500 S. Second, 74502,
pg. 1078 **PB**
N.B.M. CORP., 2nd & Carl Albert Pkwy., 74502,
pg. 771 **PV**
Public Service Company of Oklahoma-Eastern Div., 109 E.
Carl Albert Pkwy., 74501, pg. 324 **PB**

Miami

BLITZ USA, INC., 404 26th Ave. N.W., 74354, pg. 149 **PV**

Midwest City

Midwest National Bank of Midwest City, 301 N. Midwest
Blvd., 73140, pg. 174 **PB**

Mill Creek

Autumn Rose Quarry, Inc., P.O. Box 88, 74856,
pg. 1396 **PB**

Moore

East Moore Nursing Center, 320 N. Eastern, 73160,
pg. 839 **PB**

Muskogee

American Alloy Plant No. II, 612 S. 45th St., 74403,
pg. 55 **PV**
American Bindry-South, 4803 Chandler Rd., 74403,
pg. 52 **PV**
ANDERSON WHOLESALE COMPANY, 2211 W. Shawnee,
74401, pg. 73 **PV**
Bush Brothers & Company Plant, 1900 North St., 74402,
pg. 189 **PV**
GRIFFIN MANUFACTURING CO., 111 S. Cherokee,
74403, pg. 481 **PV**
Oklahoma Press Publishing Co., 214-216 Wall St., 74401,
pg. 701 **PB**
W-P Milling Co., Inc., 1119 S. Cherokee St., 74402,
pg. 46 **PV**

Noble

UNITED DESIGN CORPORATION P.O. Box 1200, 73068,
pg. 1121 **PV**

Norman

Security National Bank & Trust Co. of Norman, 200 E. Main
St., 73069, pg. 630 **PB**
Sysco Food Services of Oklahoma, Inc., 2020 Industrial
Blvd., 73079, pg. 1552 **PB**

Okarche

Temtrol, Inc., 15 E. Oklahoma Ave., 73762, pg. 1193 **PB**

Oklahoma City

AAR Oklahoma, 6611 S. Meridian, 73159, pg. 1 **PB**
ACKERMAN MCQUEEN, INC., 1100 The Tower, 1601
N.W. Expressway, 73118, pg. 12 **PV**
ALL AMERICAN BOTTLING CORP., 15 N. Robinson, Ste.
1201, 73102, pg. 34 **PV**
All-American Bottling Financial Corp., 15 N. Robinson, Ste.
1201, 73102, pg. 34 **PV**
American Bearing Division, Inc., Six S. Pennsylvania Ave.,
73101, pg. 970 **PB**
AMERICAN FIDELITY CORP., 2000 Classon Blvd., 73106,
pg. 54 **PV**
American General Life Insurance Company of Oklahoma,
209 S.W. 89th St.,Stes. A,B & C, 73139, pg. 76 **PB**
Anadarko Petroleum Corp., One Leadership Sq., 211 N.
Robinson, Ste. 1400, 73102, pg. 107 **PB**
Anco Transportation Service, Inc., 5500 W. Reno, 73102,
pg. 1029 **PV**
C.R. Anthony Company, 701 N. Broadway, 73102,
pg. 1029 **PV**
Aramark Magazine & Book Division, Inc., P.O. Box 25489,
7000 N. Robinson, 73125, pg. 79 **PV**
BancTec Technologies, 3701 S. Thomas Rd., 73179,
pg. 177 **PB**
BLOOM ELECTRIC SERVICES, INC., 9525 W. Reno,
73127, pg. 150 **PV**
Boeing Bao, 5600 Liberty Parwat Ste. 700, 73170-9807,
pg. 240 **PB**
BRAUM ICE CREAM STORES INC., 3000 N.E. 63rd St.,
73121, pg. 166 **PV**
CMI CORPORATION, Interstate 40 & Morgan Rd., 73101,
pg. 278 **PB**
CMI Energy Conversion Systems, Inc., P.O. Box 1985,
73101, pg. 279 **PB**
CMI OIL Corporation, Interstate 40 & Morgan Rd., 73101,
pg. 279 **PB**
CMI Weighing Equipment Division, Interstate 40 & Morgan
Rd., 73128, pg. 279 **PB**
COBE Renal Care, Inc., P.O. 44500, 3631 SW 54th St.,
73119, pg. 667 **IT**
Cain's Coffee Co., 13131 N. Broadway Extension, 73114,
pg. 305 **PB**
Carlisle Food Service Products, 12 N.E. 36th St., 73105,
pg. 1045 **PB**
Cato Oil & Grease Co., P.O. Box 26868, 73126,
pg. 1045 **IT**
Ceco Door Products, 5201 S.W. 36th St., 73179,
pg. 1676 **PB**
CHEMCENTRAL/Oklahoma City, 7301 S.W. 29th, 73179,
pg. 232 **PB**
The Chesapeake Life Insurance Co., P.O. Box 548801, I44
Service Rd., 73154, pg. 1679 **PB**
Cigna Healthcare of Oklahoma, Inc., 5100 N. Brookline, 9th
Fl., 73112, pg. 360 **PB**
CLEMENTS FOODS CO., 6601 N. Harvey, 73116,
pg. 245 **PV**
Clements Vinegar Company, 1734 N.W. Sixth St., 73106,
pg. 245 **PV**
Climatemaster Inc., 7300 SW 44th St., 73179, pg. 970 **PB**
Corken, Inc., P.O. Box 12338, 3805 N.W. 36th St., 73157,
pg. 862 **PB**
Cox Communications-Oklahoma City, 2312 N.W. Tenth St.,
73107, pg. 455 **PB**
The Daily & Sunday Oklahoman, 9000 N. Broadway, 73114,
pg. 213 **PV**
Dayton Tire Company, 2500 S. Council Rd., 73124,
pg. 214 **IT**
Dayton Tire Company-Oklahoma City, 2500 S. Council Rd.,
73124, pg. 214 **IT**
DEVON ENERGY CORPORATION, 20 N. Broadway, Ste.
1500, 73102-8260, pg. 503 **PB**
Dewberry Design Group, 119 N. Robinson, Ste. 700, 73104,
pg. 329 **PV**

PB - *U.S. Public Companies Volume*
PV - *U.S. Private Companies Volume*
IT - *International Public & Private Companies Volume*

1393

Geographic Index-U.S.

Digital Communications of America, Inc., 300 N. Meridian, Ste. 115, 73107, pg. 872   PV
DUNCAN EQUIPMENT COMPANY, 3709 W. Reno, 73107, pg. 346   PV
Eagle Valve Co., Inc., 1500 S.E. 89th St., 73149, pg. 1746   PB
EATERIES, INC., 3240 W. Britton Rd., Ste. 202, 73120, pg. 555   PB
Ebsco Graphics, 1223 Linwood, 73106, pg. 359   PV
El Dorado Chemical, 16 S. Pennsylvania Ave., 73101, pg. 970   PB
Enogex Inc., 515 Central Pk. Dr., Ste. 600, 73105, pg. 1207   PB
Fiesta Restaurants, Inc., 3240 W. Britton Rd., Ste. 202, 73120, pg. 555   PB
FLEMING COMPANIES, INC., 6301 Waterford Blvd., 73126-0647, pg. 652   PB
Fleming Finance Corp., P.O. Box 26647, 6301 Waterford Blvd., 73126, pg. 653   PB
Foodbrands America, Inc., 1601 N.W. Expressway, Ste. 1700 W, 73118-1495, pg. 852   PB
Forest Siding Supply, Inc., 50 N. May, 73107, pg. 1080   PV
Globe Life And Accident Insurance Co., 204 N. Robinson, 73102, pg. 1622   PB
Globe Life And Accident Insurance Co. of Oklahoma, Inc., 1400 Quail Springs Pkwy. Plaza, 73184, pg. 1622   PB
Gold Medal Beverage Corp., 15 N. Robinson, Ste. 1201, 73102, pg. 34   PV
Governair Corporation, 4841 N. Sewall, 73118, pg. 1193   PB
Great Western Industrial Machinery Co.-Gwim, 800 W. Sheridan, 73101, pg. 970   PB
Grocery Supply of Oklahoma City, 1740 W. Main St., 73106, pg. 436   PV
Hadson Corporation, 101 Park Ave., Ste. 1400, 73102, pg. 119   PB
Hercules Energy Corp., 16 S. Pennsylvania Ave., 73107, pg. 970   PB
Hewlett-Packard Company, 3525 N.W. 56th St., Ste. C-100, 73112, pg. 815   PB
Hilb, Rogal and Hamilton Company of Oklahoma, 125 Park Ave., 73102, pg. 827   PB
HOMELAND HOLDING CORP., 2601 N.W. Expwy., Orl Ctr. East, 73112, pg. 832   PB
Homeland Stores, Inc., 2601 N.W. Expwy., Orl Center E., 73112, pg. 832   PB
Hydro Conduit Corp., P.O. Box 19380, 6200 S.W. 44th St., 73179, pg. 245   IT
Ikon Office Solutions, 280 Quadrum Dr., 73108, pg. 863   PB
Inter-Global Insurance Agency, 1400 Quail Springs Pkwy. Plaza, 73184, pg. 1622   PB
International Environmental Corp., 5000 S.W. Seventh, 73128, pg. 970   PB
International Environmental Export Corp., 5000 S.W. Seventh, 73128, pg. 970   PB
Jani King of Oklahoma, Inc., 3030 N.W. Expresway, 73112, pg. 582   PV
Tom Johnson Investment Management, Inc., Two Leadership Sq., 211 N. Robinson, Ste. 450, 73102, pg. 1673   PB
KEBC-AM, 101 N.E. 28th St., 73105, pg. 384   PB
KF Industries, 1500 S.E. 89th St., 73149, pg. 1746   PB
KFOR-TV, 444 E. Britton Rd., 73114, pg. 1174   PB
KJYO-FM, 50 Penn Pl., Ste. 1000, 73101, pg. 384   PB
KNRX-FM, 50 Penn Pl., Ste. 1000, 73118, pg. 384   PB
KTOK-AM, 50 Penn Pl., Ste. 1000, 73101, pg. 384   PB
KTST-FM, 101 N.E. 28th St., 73105, pg. 384   PB
KXXY-FM, 101 N.E. 28th St., 73105, pg. 384   PB
Ben E. Keith Co. of Oklahoma, 316 S. Blackwelder, 73108, pg. 611   PV
Kerr-McGee Chemical Corp., 123 Robert S. Kerr, 73102, pg. 952   PB
Kerr-McGee Coal Corp., 123 Robert S. Kerr, 73102, pg. 952   PB
KERR-MCGEE CORPORATION, Kerr-McGee Ctr., 123 Robert S. Kerr, 73102, pg. 952   PB
Kerr-McGee Petroleum Exploration & Production Division, P.O. Box 25861, 73125, pg. 952   PB
KIMRAY, INC., 52 N.W. 42nd St., 73118, pg. 620   PV
L & S Bearing Co., Six S. Pennsylvania Ave., 73107, pg. 970   PB
LSB Chemical Corp., 16 S. Pennsylvania Ave., 73107, pg. 971   PB
LSB INDUSTRIES, INC., 16 S. Pennsylvania Ave., 73107, pg. 970   PB
Laboratory Supply Company, 723 N. Ann Arbor, 73127, pg. 642   PV
The Lamson & Sessions Co., 6500 S. Interpace, 73115, pg. 976   PB
Land of AHHS, 50 Penn Pl., Ste. 1000, 73118, pg. 384   PB
Lexco Petroleum, 100 Broadway, 73102, pg. 174   PB
Liberty Bancorp, Inc., 100 N. Broadway, 73102, pg. 174   PB
Liberty Bank & Trust of Oklahoma City, 9350 S. Western, 73143, pg. 174   PB
Liberty Bank & Trust Company of Oklahoma City, P.O. Box 25848, Liberty Tower, 73125, pg. 174   PB
Liberty Mortgage Co., P.O. Box 25848, Liberty Tower, 73125, pg. 174   PB
Liberty Property Management Co., P.O. Box 25848, Liberty Tower, 73125, pg. 174   PB
Liberty Real Estate Co., P.O. Box 25848, Liberty Tower, 73125, pg. 175   PB
Little Giant Pump Company, 3810 N. Tulsa St., 73112, pg. 1566   PB
Louis Dreyfus Natural Gas Corp., 14000 Quail Springs Pkwy., Ste. 600, 73134-2600, pg. 342   PB
Lund Acquisition Corp., 7949 S. I-35, 73149, pg. 1020   PV
MACKLANBURG-DUNCAN CO., 4041 N. Santa Fe, 73118, pg. 692   PV

Mid-America Credit Life Assurance Co., P.O. Box 25848, Liberty Tower, 73125, pg. 175   PB
Mid-America Insurance Agency, Inc., P.O. Box 25848, Liberty Tower, 73125, pg. 175   PB
Mid-America Leasing Corp., P.O. Box 25848, Liberty Tower, 73125, pg. 175   PB
Mid-Continent Life Insurance Company, 1400 Classen Dr., 73106, pg. 655   PB
Moroch & Associates, Inc., 301 NW 63rd #590, 73116, pg. 762   PV
OGE ENERGY CORP., 101 N. Robinson, 73102-0321, pg. 1207   PB
OKLAHOMA PUBLISHING COMPANY, 9000 N. Broadway, 73114, pg. 813   PV
Frank Paxton Lumber Company, 1815 S. Agnew, Box 82215, 73148, pg. 585   PB
PENCO-Oklahoma, 818 N.W. 63rd St., Ste. 103, 731167604, pg. 1508   IT
Pepperoni Grill, 3240 W. Britton Rd., 73120, pg. 555   PB
The Phoenix Resource Companies, Inc., 6525 N. Meridian, Ste. 102, 73116-1491, pg. 119   PB
PREMIER PARKS INC., 11501 N.E. Expressway St., 73131, pg. 1323   PB
Production Operators, Inc. (Oklahoma City Office), 4141 N.W. Expwy., 73116, pg. 298   PB
Pyramid Electric Supply Co., Inc., 2034 NW Seventh St., 73106, pg. 1108   IT
Quail Creek Nursing & Retirement Center, 13500 Brandon Pl., 73142, pg. 839   PB
Quivera Mining Company, 6305 Waterford Blvd., Ste. 325, 731 8-1115, pg. 1118   PB
Rehabilitation Institute of Oklahoma, 707 N.W. Sixth St., 73102, pg. 1714   PB
Reynolds and Reynolds-Business Forms Division, 3909 N.W 36th, 73157, pg. 1385   PB
Rio Algom Mining Corp., 6305 Waterford Blvd., Ste. 325, 731 8-1115, pg. 1118   IT
ROCOR TRANSPORTATION COMPANIES INC., 4350 Will Rogers Pky. Ste. 300 S., 73108, pg. 938   PV
Seagate Control Data, P.O. Box 12313, 73157-2313, pg. 450   PB
SONIC CORPORATION, 101 Park Ave., Ste. 1400, 73102, pg. 1485   PB
Sonic Industries, Inc., 101 Park Ave., 73102, pg. 1485   PB
Sonic Restaurants, Inc., 101 Park Ave., 73102, pg. 1485   PB
Southwest Oilfield Construction Company, 5400 N.W. Grand Blvd., Ste. 450, 73112-5652, pg. 1329   PB
Southwest Title & Trust Company, 133 N.W. Eighth St., 73101, pg. 626   PB
Star Building Systems, 8600 S. I-35, 73149, pg. 1394   PB
Summit Export Corp., 518 N. Indiana, 73101, pg. 971   PB
Summit Machine Tool Mfg. Corp., 518 N. Indiana, P.O. Box 1402, 73101, pg. 971   PB
Technifom Corp., P.O. Box 1537, Six S. Pennslyvania Ave., 73101, pg. 971   PB
Times Journal Publishing, One N.W. Sixth, 73102, pg. 1415   PB
Tribonetics Co., Six S. Pennslyvania Ave., 73101, pg. 971   PB
UNC Lear Siegler, P.O. Box 11566, 3100 N. Interstate Hwy. 35, 73136-0566, pg. 710   PB
Union Transport Corporation-Oklahoma City Office, 1401 Cornell Pkwy., 73108, pg. 1120   PV
UNITED ENGINES, INC., 5555 W. Reno, 73127, pg. 1122   PV
WKY-AM, 50 Penn Pl., Ste. 1000, 73118, pg. 385   PB
Weatherford Enterra U.S., L.P., 6525 N. Meridan, Ste. 201, 73116, pg. 1749   PB
Willis Corroon Administrative Services Corporation, 3555 N.W. 58th St., Ste. 610, 73112, pg. 1505   IT
Zellerbach Division, 294 Quadrum Dr., 73108, pg. 1076   PB

Okmulgee

Kelco Div., P.O. Box 998, 74447, pg. 1125   PB

Perry

CHARLES MACHINE WORKS, INC., 1959 W. Fir Ave., 73077, pg. 230   PV

Ponca City

Continental Carbon Company, P.O. Box 551, 74602, pg. 286   IT
LINDSAY MANUFACTURING INC., Bldg. 3, Darr Industrial Park, 74601, pg. 668   PV

Poteau

ALLTEL Oklahoma, Inc., Poteau Industrial Park, 101 Kerr Ave., P.O. Box 460, 74953, pg. 56   PB

Pryor

Armin Plastics, One Armin Rd., 74361, pg. 1647   PB
Atochem, Sixth & Hunt, 74361, pg. 445   IT
Elkem-American Carbide Company (Pryor), P.O. Box 518, Carbide Rd., 74361-0518, pg. 33   IT
Grede-Pryor, Inc., P.O. Box 549, Hwy. 412 B, 74362-0549, pg. 476   PV
Interplastic Corporation, Hunt St. Mid-America Industrial Park, 74361, pg. 572   PB
MITCHELL COACH MANUFACTURING, 4 1/2 Mile S. Hwy. 69, 74361, pg. 753   PV
ORCHIDS PAPER PRODUCTS CO., Rte. 3, Box 69-B, 74361, pg. 819   PV

Primary Pulp & Paper Plant, Rte. 69-A, P.O. Box 578, 74362, pg. 736   PB
Pryor Foundry, Inc., P.O. Box 549, 74361, pg. 312   PB

Sand Springs

Flobend, 8635 W. 21st St., 74063, pg. 1639   PB
Total Distributors Supply Corporation, 900 E. Pecan, 74063-0517, pg. 1150   IT

Sapulpa

IMCO Investment Company, P.O. Box 1070, 74067, pg. 871   PB
Park Newspapers of Sapulpa, Inc., 16 S. Park St., 74067, pg. 1079   PB

Seminole

Georg Fischer Disa Goff Inc., P.O. Box 1607, One Pleasant Grove Rd., 74868, pg. 488   IT
GOFF Division Georg Fischer, P.O. Box 1607, One Pleasant Grove Rd., 74868, pg. 490   IT
Hayes Axle, Inc., 400 Harvey Rd., 74868, pg. 299   PV

Shawnee

Shawnee News-Star, P.O. Box 1688, 215 N. Bell, 74801-1688, pg. 995   PV

Stilwell

Stilwell Foods, Inc., Five E. Walnut, 74960, pg. 658   PB

Stonewall

Mid-America Telephone, Inc., P.O. Box 7, 74871, pg. 1571   PB

Tahlequah

Mid-Western Nursery Division, Hwy. 10 N., 74464, pg. 60   PV

Tonkawa

HMT Tonkawa Tank Company, Inc., 509 East B Ave., 74653, pg. 914   PB

Tulsa

Ackerman McQueen, Inc., 320 S. Boston Ave., Ste. 1200, 74103, pg. 13   PV
Acme Brick Co., P.O. Box 582590, 4103 Dawson Rd., 74115, pg. 936   PB
American Camper, 6501 E. Apache St., 74115, pg. 265   PV
American Econo-Therm, 8282 South Memorial, 74133, pg. 858   PB
AMERICAN NURSERY PRODUCTS, LLC, 7010 Soyale Ste 101, 74102, pg. 70   PV
Amoco Research Center, P.O. Box 591-N12, 74102, pg. 103   PB
ANCHOR GASOLINE CORPORATION, 114 E. 5th Street, 74103, pg. 70   PV
APCO ARGENTINA INC., P.O. Box 2400 MD47-17, One Wiliams Ctr., 74102-2400, pg. 119   PB
Ark-Mart, P.O. Box 582898, 74158, pg. 494   PV
Arkansas Valley Distributing, 9111 E. Pine, 74115, pg. 494   PV
Armin Plastics, Tyco Labs, 10001 E. 54th St., 74146-5720, pg. 1647   PB
Arrow/Schweber Electronics, 12111 E. 51st St., 74146, pg. 134   PB
BOK FINANCIAL CORP., Bank of Oklahoma Tower, 74192, pg. 163   PB
BS & B Safety Systems, P.O. Box 470590, 74147-0590, pg. 572   PV
Badger Meter, PMI, 7420 E. 46th Pl., 74145, pg. 165   PB
Badger Pipe Line Co., Cities Service Bldg., Box 300, 74102, pg. 1584   PB
Bank of Oklahoma, N.A., Bank of Oklahoma Tower, One Williams Ctr., 74192, pg. 163   PB
Berendsen Fluid Power, Inc., 1700 Mid-Continent Tower, 401 S. Boston, 17th Fl., 74103-4005, pg. 1284   IT
Bergen Brunswig Medical Corporation, 1140 S. Joplin, 74158, pg. 214   PB
BLUE CROSS AND BLUE SHIELD OF OKLAHOMA, 1215 S. Boulder Ave., 74119, pg. 151   PV
BlueLincs HMO, 1215 S. Boulder Ave., 74119, pg. 152   PV
BOVAIRD SUPPLY CO., 823 S. Detroit, 74120, pg. 162   PV
Braden Company, 5199 No. Mingo Rd., 74117, pg. 924   PV
Braden Manufacturing Co., 5199 N. Mingo Rd., 74117, pg. 924   PB
Brunswick Outdoor Recreation Group, 6101 E. Apache St., 74115, pg. 265   PB
CCI CORPORATION, 1901 N. Sheridan, 74115, pg. 193   PV
CIS Technologies, Inc., One Warren Place, 6100 S. Yale, Ste. 1900, 74136-1903, pg. 1155   PB
Callidus Technologies, Inc., 7130 S. Lewis, Ste. 635, 74136-5488, pg. 344   PB
Cam Cars, 5330 E. 31st St., 74135, pg. 354   PB
Canal Refining Company, 114 E. 5th St., 74103, pg. 71   PV
A.M. Castle & Co., 10838 E. Marshall #140, 74101, pg. 313   PB
Center Line, 1007 E. Admiral Blvd., 74120, pg. 457   PB

PB - U.S. Public Companies Volume
PV - U.S. Private Companies Volume
IT - International Public & Private Companies Volume

1394

Geographic Index-U.S.

CHEMCENTRAL/Tulsa, 4500 N. Peoria Ave., 74106, pg. 232 · PV
Citgo Caribbean Corporation, Warren Pl., 6100 S. Yale Blvd., 74136, pg. 1045 · IT
Citgo Petroleum Corporation, P.O. Box 3758, One Warren Pl., 74102, pg. 1045 · IT
Citgo Pipeline Company, 6100 S. Yale, 74136, pg. 1045 · IT
Clear Channel Metroplex, 5801 E. 41st St., Ste. 715, 74135, pg. 383 · PB
Clear Channel Television, Inc., 5416 S. Yale, Ste. 500, 74135, pg. 383 · PB
COBURN OPTICAL INDUSTRIES INC., 4606 S. Garnett Rd., Ste. 200, 74146, pg. 248 · PB
Continental Federal Saving & Loan, 6985 S. Lewis, pg. 174 · PB
Continental Federal Saving & Loan, 6660 S. Sheridan, pg. 174 · PB
Continental Federal Saving & Loan, 8015 E. 71st., pg. 174 · PB
Continental Industries Inc., 4102 S. 74th E. Ave., 74101, pg. 780 · PV
Cove Petroleum, 114 E. 5th St., 74103, pg. 71 · PV
CRANE CARRIER COMPANY, 1925 N. Sheridan, 74115, pg. 286 · PV
John Crane Lemco, 3311 Charles Page Blvd., 74127-8233, pg. 1339 · IT
The Crosby Group Inc., 2801 Dawson Rd., 74110, pg. 473 · IT
Curtis Equipment Co., Inc., 6577 E. 40th St., 74145, pg. 494 · PV
Dentsply Tulsa, 5001 E. 68th St., 74136, pg. 499 · PB
Dollar Rent A Car, 5330 E. 31st St., 74135, pg. 354 · PB
Dover Resources Inc., 4606 E. 67th St., Ste. 100, 74136, pg. 521 · PB
EDUCATIONAL DEVELOPMENT CORPORATION, 10302 E. 55th Pl., Ste. B, 74146-6515, pg. 564 · PB
Empire Foundry, 2729 Charles Page Blvd., 74127, pg. 457 · PV
Energy Companies Of ONEOK, P.O. Box 871, 100 W. Fifth St., 74102-0871, pg. 1226 · PB
Explorer Pipeline Co., 6846 So. Canton, 74136, pg. 1584 · PV
Fabricated Products Plant, 7311 E. 41st St., 74145, pg. 1062 · PB
Fadler, Inc., 6511 E. 44th St., 74145, pg. 494 · PV
First American Abstract & Title Co., 625 S. Detroit, 74120, pg. 625 · PB
Fo-Mac Division, 2621 N. Iroquois, 74106, pg. 689 · PB
Fluor Daniel Williams Brothers, 4500 S. 129th E. Ave., Ste. 200, 74134, pg. 660 · PB
Foodland, Inc., 9111 E. Pine, 74115, pg. 494 · PV
Foodtown, Inc., 9111 E. Pine, 74115, pg. 494 · PV
Gear Products Inc., 1111 N. 161st E. Ave., 74116, pg. 238 · PB
Geraghty & Miller Environmental Equipment, 10002-B E. 43rd St., 74146, pg. 607 · IT
Git N Go Inc., 8315 E. 73rd St., 74133, pg. 494 · PV
Global Pipeline Surveys, 2929 W. 21st St., 74107, pg. 1180 · PV
Green Tree Acceptance, Inc., 4500 S. Garnett Rd., Ste. 400, 74146, pg. 762 · PB
Gunnebo Johnson Corporation, 1240 N. Harvard, 74115, pg. 578 · IT
HM INTERNATIONAL, 5810 E. Skelly Dr., Ste. 1000, 74135, pg. 491 · PV
HALE-HALSELL COMPANY, 9111 E. Pine, 74115, pg. 494 · PV
Harley Gauge & Instrument Co., 4445 South 91st, 74147, pg. 880 · PB
Harley Industries, Inc., 4445 S. 91st E. Ave., 74145, pg. 880 · PB
Hart Industrial Supply Co., 4236 S. 74th E. Ave., 74145, pg. 970 · PB
Hathaway Motion Control Division, 10827 E. Marshall, 74116, pg. 799 · PB
Hathaway Motors & Instruments Division, 10816 E. Newton St., 74116, pg. 799 · PB
HELMERICH & PAYNE, INC., 1579 E. 21st St., 74114, pg. 808 · PB
Helmerich & Payne International Drilling Co., 1579 E. 21st St., 74114, pg. 808 · PB
Helmerich & Payne Properties, Inc., 1579 E. 21st St., 74114, pg. 808 · PB
Helmerich & Payne Rasco Inc., 1579 E. 21st St., 74114, pg. 808 · PB
Hewlett-Packard Company, 6655 S. Lewis, Ste. 105, 74136, pg. 815 · PB
Hilti Inc., 5400 S. 122nd E. Ave., 74146, pg. 620 · IT
Hilti Latin America, 5400 S. 122nd Ave., 74146, pg. 620 · IT
Hydro Conduit Corp., 3200 N. 129th E. Ave., 74158, pg. 245 · IT
INTERNATIONAL CHEMICAL COMPANY, 1887 E. 71st St., 74136, pg. 568 · PV
JL Media, Inc., 401 S. Boston, 74103, pg. 577 · PV
Earle M. Jorgensen Company/Tulsa, 7311 E. Pine St., 74115, pg. 600 · PV
Earle M. Jorgensen Honing Center/Tulsa, 2522 N. Columbia Pl., 74110, pg. 600 · PV
KAKC-AM, 5801 E. 41st St., Ste. 900, 74135, pg. 384 · PB
KJRH, 3701 S. Peoria, 74105, pg. 1448 · PB
KMOD-FM, 5801 E. 41st St., Ste. 900, 74135, pg. 384 · PB
KOAS-FM, 5801 E. 41st St., #900, 74135, pg. 384 · PB
KOKI-TV, Fox Plaza, 5416 S. Yale, 74135, pg. 384 · PB
KOTV Inc., 302 S. Frankfurt, 74120, pg. 209 · PB
KQLL-AM/FM, 5801 E. 41st St., #900, 74135, pg. 384 · PB
KINARK CORPORATION, 225 E. 73rd St., 74136, pg. 960 · PB

Klockner-Moeller Corp., 12626 E. 60th St., Ste. 101, 74146, pg. 736 · IT
KTUL, LLC, P.O. Box 8, 74101, pg. 854 · PV
LDDS WorldCom, P.O. Box 21348, 74121, pg. 1779 · PB
LEI Extras, Inc., 12000 East Skelly Dr., 74128-2486, pg. 1016 · PB
LaBarge, 11618 E. 51st St., 74146-5911, pg. 973 · PB
Larkin, Meeder & Schweidel-Tulsa, 2421 E. Skelly Dr., Ste. 104, 74105, pg. 651 · PV
Liberty Bank & Trust Company of Tulsa, 15 E. Fifth St., 74103, pg. 174 · PV
Lindberg Heat Treating Co., 4208 South 74th East Ave., 74145, pg. 999 · PB
Lowrance Avionics, 12000 E. Skelly Dr., 74128-2486, pg. 1016 · PB
LOWRANCE ELECTRONICS, INC., 12000 E. Skelly Dr., 74128-2486, pg. 1015 · PB
MPSI SYSTEMS INC., 8282 S. Memorial Dr., 74133, pg. 1027 · PB
Madison, Inc., 8500 New Sapulpa Rd., 74131, pg. 428 · PV
Maintenance Services Group, 7633 E. 63rd Pl., 4th Fl., 74133, pg. 773 · PV
Manhattan Construction Company, 111 W. Fifth St., 1000, 74103-4235, pg. 943 · PV
Mapco Coal Inc., 1717 S. Boulder Ave., 74119, pg. 1042 · PB
MAPCO INC., 1800 S. Baltimore Ave., 74119, pg. 1042 · PB
Mapco Natural Gas Liquids Inc., 1800 S. Baltimore Ave., 74119, pg. 1042 · PB
Mapco Petroleum Inc., 1800 S. Baltimore Ave., 74119, pg. 1042 · PB
Martin Reels, A Division of Zebco, 6101 E. Apache, 74101, pg. 265 · PB
MATRIX SERVICE COMPANY, 10701 E. Ute St., 74116, pg. 1057 · PB
McKissick Products Co., 2857 Dawson Rd., 74110, pg. 473 · IT
Member Service Life Insurance Co., 1215 S. Boulder Ave., 74114, pg. 152 · PV
Metals, Inc., 1010 W. 37th Pl., 74107, pg. 847 · PB
Mid-Continent Casualty Company, 1646 S. Boulder, 74119, pg. 75 · PV
Midwest Division, 8127 E. 21st St., 74129, pg. 38 · PB
Mintech, Inc.-Tulsa, 4608 S. Garnett, Ste. 100, 74146, pg. 1279 · PB
Moroch & Associates, Inc., 7941 E 57th St., Ste. 9, 74145, pg. 762 · PV
NMP Corp., P.O. Box 35493, 74153-0493, pg. 1763 · PB
NAMACO LLC, 7633 E. 63rd Pl., 4th Floor, 74133, pg. 773 · PB
Niject, 2320 One Williams Ctr., 74172, pg. 877 · PB
Niject Services Company, pg. 1320 · PB
Norris, P.O. Box 1496, 74101, pg. 521 · PB
Nuclear Upgrade, 1200 N. Peoria, 74106, pg. 55 · PV
Nutter Engineering, 643 W. 41st St., 74105, pg. 793 · PV
ONG Sayre Storage Co., P.O. Box 871, 100 W. Fifth St., 74102, pg. 1226 · PB
ONG Transmission Company, P.O. Box 871, 100 W. Fifth St., 74102-0871, pg. 1226 · PB
O-Z/Gedney, Nelson Firestop Products, 4041 S. Sheridan Rd., 74145, pg. 726 · PB
Oil Dynamics Inc., P.O. Box 470446, 7655 E. 46th St., 74147-0446, pg. 679 · PB
Oklahoma Natural Gas Company, 5848 E. 15th St., 74112, pg. 1226 · PB
ONEOK Gas Marketing, 100 W. Fifth St., 74103, pg. 1226 · PB
ONEOK INC., 100 W. Fifth St., P.O. Box 871, 74102-0871, pg. 1226 · PB
ONEOK Leasing Co., P.O. Box 871, 100 W. Fifth St., 74102-0871, pg. 1226 · PB
ONEOK Parking Co., PO Box 871, 100 W. Fifth St., 74102-0871, pg. 1226 · PB
ONEOK Products Co., PO Box 871, 100 W. Fifth St., 74102-0871, pg. 1226 · PB
ONEOK Resources Co., P.O. Box 871, 100 W. Fifth St., 74102-0871, pg. 1226 · PB
ONEOK Technology Co., 100 W. Fifth St., 74103, pg. 1226 · PB
The Original Chili Bowl, Inc., 9016 E. 46th St., 74145, pg. 1182 · PV
PacifiCare of Oklahoma, 7134 S. Yale Ave., Ste. 700, 74136, pg. 1251 · PV
PARKER DRILLING COMPANY, Eight E. Third St., 74103-3637, pg. 1259 · PB
Parker Drilling Company International Limited, 8 East Third St., 74103, pg. 1259 · PB
Patterson-Kelley Company, 4111 S. Darlington, 74135, pg. 793 · PB
Frank Paxton Lumber Company, 5420 S. 99th E. Ave., 74146, pg. 585 · PV
Pentastar Transportation Corp., 5330 E. 31st St., 74135, pg. 354 · PB
Perma-Fix Treatment Services, Inc., 2700 S. 25th West Ave., 74107, pg. 1180 · PV
Pigging Products, 10727 E. 55th Pl., 74145, pg. 1180 · PV
Public Service Company of Oklahoma, 212 E. Sixth St., 74119, pg. 324 · PB
Public Service Company of Oklahoma-Mantulsa Div., 212 E. Sixth St., 74119, pg. 324 · PB
Purolator Products Co., 6120 S. Yale Ave., 74136, pg. 1045 · PB
QUIKTRIP CORPORATION, 901 N. Mingo Rd., 74116, pg. 901 · PV
Reclamation Systems, Inc., 4608 Garnett, Ste. 100, 74146, pg. 1280 · PV
ROONEY BROTHERS COMPANY, 111 W. Fifth St., Ste. 1000, 74103-4235, pg. 943 · PV
Safety Railway Service-Tulsa, 2530 S. Yukon, 74107, pg. 412 · PV

Scamp Auto, 5330 E. 31st St., 74135, pg. 354 · PB
SNAPPY CAR RENTAL, INC., 411 S. Darlington, Ste. 500, 74135-6375, pg. 1010 · PV
SOONER PIPE & SUPPLY CORP., 1000 MidContinent Tower, 401 S. Boston, 74103, pg. 1014 · PV
Space Center, Inc., 1579 E. 21st St., 74114, pg. 808 · PB
Stainless Tubular Products, Inc., 1010 W. 37th Pl., 74107, pg. 847 · PB
Sterling Electronics, 5119 S. 110th East Ave., 74146, pg. 1051 · PB
TDW Building Corporation, 8506 E. 61st St., 74133, pg. 1180 · PV
TDW Services, Inc., 6801 S. 65th West Ave., 74101, pg. 1180 · PV
TDW Trading, Inc., 8506 E. 61st St., 74133, pg. 1180 · PV
Tartan, Inc., Unit 7087, 7001 E. 38th St., 74145, pg. 354 · PB
The Tearoom in Utica Square, Inc., 1579 E. 21st St., 74114, pg. 808 · PB
Terex Trucks, 5400 S. 49th West Ave., 74107, pg. 1581 · PB
TERRA NITROGEN COMPANY, L.P., 5100 E. Skelly Dr., Ste. 800, 74135, pg. 1581 · PB
Texaco Refining & Marketing, Inc., P.O. Box 1650, 1437 S. Boulder, 74102, pg. 1583 · PB
Thomson Training & Simulation, 7041 E. 15th St., P.O. Box 1677, 74101, pg. 1384 · IT
Thrifty Rent-a-Car System, Inc., 5330 E. 31st, 74135, pg. 354 · PB
Thrifty World Headquarters, 5330 E. 31st St., 74135, pg. 354 · PB
Transok, Inc., 110 W. 7th St., 74101, pg. 1136 · IT
Tulsa Manufacturing Plant, 6801 South 65th West Ave., 74131-2444, pg. 1180 · PB
Union-Transport Corporation-Tulsa Office, 3168 S. 108 E. Ave., Ste. 380, 74146, pg. 1120 · PB
UNIT CORPORATION, Kensington Tower, Ste. 1000, 7130 S. Lewis, 74136, pg. 1672 · PB
Unit Drilling Company, 7130 S. Lewis Ave., Ste. 1000, 74136, pg. 1672 · PB
Unit Petroleum Company, 7130 S. Lewis Ave., Ste. 1000, 74136, pg. 1672 · PB
Utica Square Shopping Center, Inc., 1579 E. 21st St., 74114, pg. 808 · PB
Valmont, P.O. Box 2620, 74101-2620, pg. 1707 · PB
Valu-Fare Foods, Inc., 9111 E. Pine, 74115, pg. 494 · PV
Valu-Foods, Inc., P.O. Box 582807, 74158-2807, pg. 494 · PV
WESTWOOD CORPORATION, 5314 S. Yale, Ste. 1100, 74135-6251, pg. 1763 · PV
THE WILLIAMS COMPANIES, INC., P.O. Box 2400, One Williams Ctr., 74172, pg. 1769 · PB
Williams Field Services, One Williams Ctr., 45th. Fl., 74172, pg. 1769 · PB
Williams Natural Gas Company, One Williams Center, 74172, pg. 1769 · PB
Williams Pipe Line Co., One Williams Center, 74172, pg. 1769 · PB
Williamson International Corp., 8506 E. 61st St., 74133, pg. 1180 · PV
T.D. WILLIAMSON, INC., P.O. Box 2299, 74101, pg. 1179 · PV
WORLD PUBLISHING COMPANY, 315 S. Boulder, 74103, pg. 1190 · PB
WORLDWIDE SPORTS & RECREATION, INC., 7130 S. Lewis Ave., Ste. 850, 74136, pg. 1191 · PV
XETA CORPORATION, 4500 S. Garnett Rd., Ste. 1000, 74146, pg. 1783 · PB
Yuba Heat Transfer Division, 2121 N. East Ave., P.O. Box 3158, 74116, pg. 264 · PV
Zebco, 6101 E. Apache St., 74115, pg. 265 · PB
Zellerbach Division, 4901 W. 66th St., 74131-2601, pg. 1075 · PB
John Zink Co., 11920 E. Apache, 74116, pg. 628 · PV

Vinita

Labinal Aero Plant, 820 N. Wilson St., 74301-1610, pg. 786 · IT
Labinal Components & Systems Inc., 820 N. Wilson St., 74301-1610, pg. 786 · IT

Walters

COTTON ELECTRIC CO-OP, 226 N. Broadway, 73572, pg. 278 · PV

Watonga

AT&L Railroad, P.O. Box 29, 73772, pg. 1171 · PV
WHEELER BROTHERS GRAIN CO., 501 W. Russworm, 73772, pg. 1171 · PV

Waurika

Red River Sand & Gravel Company, Rt. 1 Box 108, 73573, pg. 1585 · PB

Westville

Baldor Electric Company, P.O. Box 305, Industrial Park Rd., 74965, pg. 169 · PB

Woodward

Deepwater Chemicals, Inc., 1210 Airpark Rd., 73801, pg. 1395 · IT
Woodward Cable TV, Inc., 1117 11th St., 73801, pg. 1611 · PB

Geographic Index-U.S.

OREGON

Albany

Albany Democrat-Herald, 600 Lyon St. S.W., 97321, pg. 983 **PB**
Discovery Plastics, Inc., 3700 Western Way N.E., 97321-7447, pg. 904 **PV**
Formaldehyde, P.O. Box 1068, 2190 Old Salem Rd., 97321, pg. 737 **PB**
National Frozen Foods Corporation - Albany, 745 S.W. 30th Ave., 97321, pg. 783 **PB**
Northwest Industries, Inc., 125 E. 34th Ave. S.W., 97321, pg. 1640 **PV**
OREGON FREEZE DRY, INC., 525 25th Ave., S.W., 97321, pg. 819 **PV**
Oregon Metallurgical Corporation, 530 34th Ave. S.W., 97321-0177, pg. 43 **PB**
Stone Forest Industries, P.O. Box 338, 2703 S. Pacific Blvd., 97321, pg. 1521 **PB**
Valley Group, Inc., P.O. Box 1119, 2450 14th Ave. S.E., 97321, pg. 1257 **IT**
Wah Chang, 1600 N.E. Old Salem Rd., 97321-0136, pg. 44 **PB**

Ashland

The Daily Tidings, 1661 Siskiyou Blvd., 97520, pg. 983 **PB**

Aurora

Elixir Industries, P.O. Box 9, 19527 Grim Rd., 97002, pg. 371 **PV**

Beaverton

All American Technologies of Portland, Inc., 1815 N.W. 169th Pl., Ste. 6025, 97006, pg. 42 **PB**
American International Forest Products, Inc., 5560 S.W. 107th Ave., 97005, pg. 669 **PB**
Arrow/Schweber Electronics, 9275 S.W. Nimbus Ave., 97005, pg. 134 **PB**
Bergen Brunswig Drug Company, 6505 S.W. 110th Ct., 97008, pg. 214 **PB**
Cache Scientific, Inc., P.O. Box 4013, 47076, pg. 1567 **PB**
Carat ICG (Portland, OR), 3800 S.W. Cedar Hills Blvd., Ste. 225, 97005, pg. 207 **PV**
EDD-Portland, 8705 S.W. Nimbus Ave., Ste. 100, 97008, pg. 205 **PB**
Eaton Corp. Div., 13725 S.W. Millikan Way, 97005, pg. 556 **PB**
First Consumers National Bank, 9300 SW Gemini, 97005, pg. 1499 **PB**
IMS Division, 9525 S.W. Gemini Dr., 97005, pg. 290 **PB**
Intergraph Corporation, 8625 S.W. Cascade Blvd., Ste. 250, 97008, pg. 890 **PB**
Jaco Electronics Inc., 4900 S.W. Griffith Dr., Ste. 129, 97005, pg. 920 **PB**
LEUPOLD & STEVENS, INC., 14400 N.W. Greenbrier Pkwy., 97006, pg. 662 **PV**
Milgray/Oregon, Inc., 8705 S.W. Nimbus Ave., 97008, pg. 207 **PB**
Nike Apparel, 3900 S.W. Murray Blvd., 97005, pg. 1184 **PB**
Nike Footwear, 3900 S.W. Murray Blvd., 97005, pg. 1184 **PB**
NIKE, INC., One Bowerman Dr., 97005-6453, pg. 1184 **PB**
Nike Latin American Headquarters, One Bowerman Dr., 97005, pg. 1184 **PB**
ORCAD INC., 9300 S.W. Nimbus Ave., 97008, pg. 1230 **PB**
Photon Kinetics, Inc., 9405 S.W. Gemini Dr., 97008-7160, pg. 1376 **PB**
PLAID PANTRIES, INC., 10025 S.W. Allen Blvd., 97005, pg. 868 **PV**
PROTOCOL SYSTEMS, INC., 8500 S.W. Creekside Pl., 97008-7107, pg. 1336 **PB**
SEQUENT COMPUTER SYSTEMS, INC., 15450 S.W. Koll Pkwy., 97006, pg. 1459 **PB**
Symantec Corporation - Beaverton Site, 15220 N.W. Greenbriar Pkwy., Ste. 200, 95014-2132, pg. 1545 **PB**
Tektronix Federal Systems, Inc., P.O. Box 500, D/S 50-FSI, 97077-0001, pg. 1567 **PB**
Teppan Restaurants, 9205 S.W. Cascade Ave., 97005, pg. 212 **PB**
TIMBERLINE SOFTWARE CORPORATION, 9600 S.W. Nimbus, 97008-7163, pg. 1609 **PB**
Tyco Toys, Inc., 8585 S.W. Hall St., 97005, pg. 1058 **PB**
Westco Products/Northwest, 6555 S.W. 111th St., 97005, pg. 244 **PB**
Western Intl. Forest Prods., Inc., 8285 S.W. Nimbus Ave. # 131, 97005, pg. 669 **PV**
Whittaker Communications, Inc., 15275 S.W. Koll Pkwy., 97006, pg. 1767 **PB**

Bend

Awbrey Glen Golf Club, Inc., 2500 Aubrey Glen Dr., 97701, pg. 172 **PV**
BROOKS RESOURCES CORPORATION, 296 S.W. Columbia St., 97701, pg. 172 **PV**
Brooks Resources Sales Corp., 296 SW. Columbia St., Ste. A, 97702, pg. 172 **PV**
Mount Bachelor Village Corp., 19717 Mt. Bachelor Dr., 97705, pg. 172 **PV**
Northland Furniture Co., LLC, 681 S.E. Glenwood, 97709, pg. 77 **PV**

Boardman

Boeing Agri-Industrial Co., P.O. Box 139, 98108, pg. 242 **PB**

Boring

VANPORT MANUFACTURING, INC., 28590 S.E. Wally Rd., 97009, pg. 1134 **PV**

Brookings

C & K MARKET, INC., 615 Fifth St., 97415, pg. 191 **PV**

Canby

Gypsum Firedoor Core Plant, 505 N.E. Third St., 97013, pg. 737 **PB**

Central Point

Central Point Lumber Co., 594 S. Front St., 97502-2723, pg. 1729 **PB**

Clackamas

AmeriSource-Portland Div., 10151 S.E. Jennifer St., 97015, pg. 97 **PB**
Enway Inc., 10320 S.E. Highway 212, 97015, pg. 1262 **IT**
GEM TOP MFG., INC., 8811 S.E. Herbert Ct., 97015, pg. 443 **PV**
WARN INDUSTRIES, INC., 12900 SE Capps Rd., 97015, pg. 1150 **PV**

Coburg

Mill-Log Equipment Co., Inc., 94401, pg. 1646 **PB**
MONACO COACH CORPORATION, 9130 Coburg Industrial Way, 97408, pg. 1123 **PB**
Monaco Coach Corporation, 91320 Industrial Pkwy., 97408, pg. 1123 **PB**

Condon

Condon TV Systems, Inc., 119 W. Gilliam, 97823, pg. 1571 **PB**
Home Telephone Co., 119 W. Gilliam, 97823, pg. 1571 **PB**

Coos Bay

The World, 350 Commercial Ave., 97420, pg. 1343 **PB**

Coquille

Douglas Fir Stud & Plywood Mill, P.O. Box 610, Hwy. 42 S., 97423, pg. 737 **PB**

Cornelius

Hazelnut Growers of Oregon, 401 N. 26th Ave., 97113, pg. 1051 **PV**

Corvallis

Corvallis Gazette-Times, 600 S.W. Jefferson St., 97330, pg. 983 **PB**
Evanite Fiber Corp., Crystal Lake Pike, 97339, pg. 535 **PV**

Cottage Grove

Cottage Grove Sentinel, P.O. Box 35, 116 N. Sixth St., 97424, pg. 983 **PB**
Poly-Craft Systems, 195 Palmer Ave., 97424-0518, pg. 229 **PB**

Culver

Bramco, Inc., Seventh & C Sts., P.O. Box 167, 97734, pg. 478 **PV**

Dillard

RLC INDUSTRIES CO., Old Hwy. 99 S., 97432, pg. 905 **PV**
Roseburg Forest Products Co., Old Hwy. 99 S., 97432, pg. 905 **PV**
Roseburg Resources Co., Old Hwy. 99 S., 97470, pg. 905 **PV**
Scott Timber Co., Old Hwy. 99 S., 97432, pg. 905 **PV**

Durkee

Ash Grove Cement-Western Region Cement Plant, P.O. Box 5, 97905, pg. 88 **PV**

Eugene

Atlas Cylinder, 29289 Airport Rd., 97402-0079, pg. 1261 **PB**
Dynamix, Inc., 1600 Mill Race Dr., 97403, pg. 321 **PB**
ElJay Division, 86470 Franklin Blvd., 97405, pg. 1365 **PB**
Fir Plywood Plant, 1651 So. F. St., 97477, pg. 737 **PB**
GUARD PUBLISHING COMPANY, 3500 Chad Dr., 97408, pg. 485 **PV**
Hardwood Plywood Plant, 1900 Irving Rd., P.O. Box 1618, 97440, pg. 737 **PB**
Hewlett-Packard Company, 1600 Valley River Dr., Ste. 160, 97401, pg. 815 **PB**
MURPHY COMPANY, P.O. Box 2810, 97402, pg. 768 **PV**
Murphy International, P.O. Box 2810, 97402, pg. 768 **PV**
Murphy Plywood, P.O. Box 2810, 97402, pg. 768 **PV**
Murphy Properties, Inc., P.O. Box 2810, 97402, pg. 768 **PV**
Murphy Timber, P.O. Box 2810, 97402, pg. 768 **PV**
Neste Resins Corporation, 1600 Valley River Dr., Ste. 390, 97401, pg. 913 **IT**
Softwood Veneer, 1900 Irving Rd., 97402, pg. 738 **PB**
Spectra-Physics Scanning Systems Inc., 959 Terry St., 97402-9120, pg. 1594 **IT**
Stewart Smith West, Inc., 1200 Executive Pkwy., 97401, pg. 1509 **IT**
Ventek Inc., 4217 W. 5th, 97402, pg. 20 **PB**
Willamette Industries, Inc., 85647 Hwy. 99 S., 97405-9542, pg. 1769 **PB**
William's Bakery, P.O. Box 1375, 97440, pg. 1124 **PV**
Willis Corroon Corp. of Eugene, 1577 Pearl St., 97401-4010, pg. 1505 **IT**

Forest Grove

Gray & Company, P.O. Box 218, 97201, pg. 876 **PV**
Matsushita Electronic Materials, Inc., 4114 Heather St., 97116, pg. 848 **IT**
MERIX CORPORATION, P.O. Box 3000, 1521 Poplar Ln., 97116, pg. 1096 **PB**
PORTLAND FOOD PRODUCTS COMPANY, 2331 23rd Ave., 97116, pg. 876 **PV**

Gladstone

THOMASON AUTO GROUP, 19405 S.E. McLoughlin, 97027, pg. 1083 **PV**

Glide

Glide Lumber Products Co., 1577 Glide Loop Rd., 97443-9711, pg. 1729 **PB**

Grants Pass

Guidance & Control Systems, 1001 Redwood Hwy. Spur, 97526-2387, pg. 1002 **PB**
MetOne, Inc., 481 California Ave., 97526, pg. 1250 **PB**

Gresham

Fujitsu Microelectronics - Mfg., 21015 S.E. Stark St., 97030-2099, pg. 527 **IT**
Gresham Outlook, P.O. Box 747, 97030, pg. 983 **PB**

Hermiston

Hermiston Foods, Inc., 2250 Hwy. 395 S., 97838, pg. 802 **PV**
Marlette Homes, Inc., 400 Elm St., 97838, pg. 1442 **PB**

Hillsboro

Epson Portland Inc., 3950 NW Aloclek Place, 97124, pg. 1219 **IT**
Fujitsu Computer Products of America - Mfg., 7300 N.E. Evergreen Pkwy., 97124, pg. 526 **IT**
LATTICE SEMICONDUCTOR CORPORATION, 5555 N.E. Moore Ct., 97124, pg. 979 **PB**
THRUSTMASTER, INC., 7175 N.W. Evergreen Pkwy., #400, 97124, pg. 1607 **PB**

Hood River

Hanel Lumber Co., Inc., 4865 Hwy. 35, 97031, pg. 538 **PV**
Western Power Products, Inc., 900 Portway Ave., 97031, pg. 444 **PB**

Junction City

Country Coach, Inc., 135 E. First St., 97448, pg. 1159 **PB**

Klamath Falls

JELD-WEN, INC., 3250 Lakeport Blvd., 97601, pg. 585 **PV**
U.S. TIMBERLANDS COMPANY, L.P., P.O. Box 10, 6400 Hwy. 66, 97601, pg. 1688 **PB**

Lake Oswego

THE APOGEE COMPANIES, INC., 15455 Hallmark Dr., Ste. 100, 97035, pg. 77 **PV**
Diachem Pacific Northwest Inc., 5285 SW Meadows Rd., 97035, pg. 1086 **IT**
Intervest-Mortgage Investment Company, 5285 S.W. Meadows Rd., Ste. 320, 97035-3227, pg. 1516 **PB**
Norpac Services, Inc., P.O. Box 2249, 97035, pg. 802 **PV**
PacifiCare of Oregon, Five Centerpointe Dr., Ste. 600, 97035, pg. 1251 **PB**
Piper Jaffray Inc., 5285 S.W. Meadows Rd., Ste. 495, 97035-3229, pg. 1302 **PB**
Southern Pacific Funding Corporation, One Centerpointe Dr., Ste. 500, 97035, pg. 872 **PB**
Systems Northwest, Bldg. One, 4000 S.W. Kruse Way Pl., Ste. 300, 97035, pg. 1114 **IT**

PB - U.S. Public Companies Volume
PV - U.S. Private Companies Volume
IT - International Public & Private Companies Volume

Zenith Media Services, Inc., 5285 SW Meadows, Ste. 232, 97035, pg. 1204 **PV**

Lebanon

Lebanon Express, P.O. Box 459, 97355, pg. 983 **PB**

McMinnville

Atlas-Alchem Plastics-Oregon, 4150 Riverside Dr., 97128, pg. 1496 **PB**
Cascade Steel Rolling Mills, Inc., 3200 No. Hwy. 99 W., 97128, pg. 1440 **PB**
EVERGREEN INTERNATIONAL AVIATION, INC., 3850 Three Mile Ln., 97128-9496, pg. 386 **PV**
Farmers Insurance Group, 1571 N. Hwy. 99W, 97128-2726, pg. 111 **IT**
Hazelwood Farms Bakeries, Inc., P.O. Box 916, 2803 Orchard Ave., 97128, pg. 1541 **PB**

Medford

ADVANCED MACHINE VISION CORP., 2067 Commerce Dr., 97504, pg. 20 **PB**
Bear Creek Corporation, 2518 S. Pacific Hwy., 97501, pg. 1518 **IT**
Bear Creek Gardens, Inc., 2518 S. Pacific Hwy., 97501, pg. 1518 **IT**
Bear Creek Stores, Inc., 2518 S. Pacific Hwy., 97501, pg. 1518 **IT**
Harry and David, P.O. Box 712, 97501, pg. 1518 **IT**
Jackson & Perkins, 2518 S. Pacific Hwy., 97501, pg. 1518 **IT**
Medite Corporation, 2685 N. Pacific Hwy., 97501, pg. 999 **PV**
SRC Vision, P.O. Box 1666, 97501, pg. 20 **PV**
SHERMS THUNDERBIRD MARKET, 753 S. Grape, 97501, pg. 993 **PV**

Mill City

HOOD LUMBER CO., P.O. Box 377, 97360, pg. 538 **PV**

Milwaukie

Cascade Pacific Engineering, Inc., 12300 S.E. Mallard Way, Ste. 205, 97222, pg. 1379 **PV**
Clarke Electronics, 17402 S.E. Plymouth Ct., 97267, pg. 1720 **PB**
DARK HORSE COMICS, INC., 10956 S.E. Main St., 97222, pg. 311 **PV**
Komfort Corporation, 3701 S.E. Naef Rd., 97268, pg. 1602 **PB**
Lamplighter Homes, Inc., 13625 S.E. McLaughlin, 97222, pg. 333 **PB**
Orchids Etc., 5456 S.E. International Way, 97222, pg. 1518 **IT**
Stanley Hydraulic Tools Div., 3810 S.E. Naef Rd., 97267, pg. 1509 **PB**

Newberg

A-DEC, INC., 2601 Crestview Dr., 97132, pg. 2 **PV**

Newport

CENTRAL LINCOLN PEOPLE'S UTILITY DISTRICT, P.O. Box 1126, 97365, pg. 223 **PV**
Newport-News Times, P.O. Box 965, 97365, pg. 984 **PB**

North Powder

North Powder Lumber Co., 105 Second St., 97867, pg. 1730 **PB**

Nyssa

Amalgamated Sugar Co., P.O. Box 1766, 97913, pg. 48 **PV**
American Fine Foods, Inc. (Nyssa Plant), 100 E. Locust St., 97913, pg. 349 **PB**

Ontario

RED APPLE, INC., 555 S.W. Fourth Ave., 97914, pg. 915 **PV**

Oregon City

Cladwood Div. (Central Office), 427 Main St., 97045, pg. 1270 **IT**
Smurfit Newsprint Corporation, 427 Main St., 97045, pg. 1271 **IT**

Philomath

Pacific Softwoods Co., 950 Clemens Mill Rd., 97370, pg. 1730 **PB**
Philomath Forest Products Co., 1701 Chapel Rd., 97370-9557, pg. 1730 **PB**

Portland

Ackerley Communications of the Northwest-Portland, 715 N.E. Everett, 97232, pg. 15 **PB**
Adidas International, 541 N.E. 20th St., Ste. 207, 97232, pg. 24 **IT**

Alaskan Copper Companies, P.O. Box 5067, 2440 S.E. Raymond, 97208, pg. 31 **PV**
Alcatel, 15540 North Lombard, 97217, pg. 52 **IT**
American Steel LLC, 4033 N.W. Yeon Ave., 97210, pg. 1375 **PV**
Ameritech, 3500 N.E. 82nd Ave., 97220-5118, pg. 97 **PB**
Ash Grove Cement Company Sales Office, 6720 S.W. Macadam Ave., 97219, pg. 87 **PV**
Ash Grove Cement-Western Region Lime Plant, 13939 N. Rivergate Blvd., 97203, pg. 88 **PV**
Associated Administrators, Inc., 2929 N.W. 31st St., 97210, pg. 918 **PV**
Atlas Copco Wagner Inc., P.O. Box 20307, 97220-0307, pg. 96 **IT**
Bank of America Oregon, P.O. Box 6400, 97228, pg. 180 **PB**
The Bank of Nova Scotia, 888 S.W. 5th Ave., Ste. 750, 97004, pg. 156 **IT**
Bank of Tokyo-Mitsubishi, Ltd., 1211 S.W. 5th Ave., 97204, pg. 157 **IT**
BENSON INDUSTRIES, INC., 1650 N.W. Front #250, 97209, pg. 133 **PV**
Biamp Systems Corp., 14130 N.W. Science Park Dr., 97229, pg. 911 **PV**
Blount, Inc. Oregon Cutting Systems Division, 4909 SE International Way, 97269-2127, pg. 238 **PB**
Boeing of Portland, P.O. Box 20487, 97220, pg. 240 **PB**
Brim Health Care, 305 N.E. 102nd Ave., 97220, pg. 168 **PV**
Brim Healthcare, 305 N.E. 102nd Ave., 97220, pg. 168 **PV**
BRIM, INC., 305 N.E. 102nd Ave., 97220, pg. 168 **PV**
Browning-Ferris Industries of Oregon, Inc., 9363 N. Columbia Blvd., 97203, pg. 264 **PB**
Buckeye Pacific Corp., Inc., 5410 S.W. Macadam Ave., 97201, pg. 669 **PB**
BURNS BROS. INC., 516 S.E. Morrison St., 97214, pg. 187 **PV**
The Business Journal of Portland, Inc., Ten N.W. 10th St., Ste. 200, 97209, pg. 19 **PV**
BYERS INDUSTRIES, INC., 6800 N.E. 59th Pl., 97218, pg. 191 **PV**
Byers Transport Willamette, 6800 N.E. 59th Pl., 97218, pg. 191 **PV**
CF2GS, 614 S.W. 11th Ave., 97205, pg. 194 **PV**
CH2M Hill Industrial Design Corp., Parkside Plaza, 2020 S.W. Fourth, 3rd Fl., 97201, pg. 195 **PV**
CKS Partners/Portland, 320 S.W. Oak St., 97201, pg. 195 **PV**
CTC Consulting, 4380 S.W. Macadam Ave., Ste. 450, 97201, pg. 1688 **PV**
The Campbell Group, Inc., One S.W. Columbia., Ste. 1720, 97258, pg. 1672 **PB**
Canron Fabrication Corporation - Western Division, P.O. Box 30149, 4600 N.E. 138th Ave., 97230, pg. 695 **IT**
CAP Gemini America (Portland Branch), 6915 S.W. Macadam Ave., Ste. 100, 97219, pg. 264 **IT**
Cartall Div., 4720 S.E. 17th Ave., 97202, pg. 846 **PV**
Cascade Empire Corporation, 4900 S.W. Meadows, St. 400, 97035, pg. 669 **PV**
Cavenham Forest Industries Inc., 1500 S.W. First Ave., 97201, pg. 593 **IT**
Centralia Mining Company, 700 NE Multnomah, Ste. 1600, 97232, pg. 1251 **PB**
CHEMCENTRAL/Portland, 10821 N. Lombard St., 97203, pg. 232 **PV**
CHRISTENSON ELECTRIC, INC., 111 S.W. Columbia, Ste. 480, 97201, pg. 238 **PV**
Circle A.W. Products, Co., 13885 S.W. 72nd Ave., 97223, pg. 1471 **PB**
Circle Freight International USA, 12555 N.E. Marx St., 97230, pg. 371 **PB**
Coast RV, Inc., 7914 S.E. 82nd St., 97266, pg. 388 **PB**
Columbia Grain, Inc., 111 S.W. Columbia St., Ste. 1200, 97201-5844, pg. 845 **IT**
Columbia Willamette Development Co., 121 S.W. Salmon St., 97204, pg. 585 **PV**
Columbia Willamette Leasing, Inc., 121 S.W. Salmon St., 97204, pg. 585 **PV**
Community Psychiatric Centers of Oregon, Inc., 10300 S.W. Eastridge, 97225, pg. 1712 **PV**
Congress Financial (Northwest), 101 S.W. Main, 97204, pg. 447 **PV**
Consolidated Metco, Inc., 13940 N. Rivergate Blvd., 97203, pg. 1710 **PB**
CONTINENTAL PAPER RECYCLING LLC, 6950 S.W. Hampton, #200, 97224, pg. 269 **PV**
COPELAND LUMBER YARD, INC., 901 N.E. Glisan St., 97232, pg. 274 **PV**
Creative Process, Inc., 5497 SE International Way, 97222, pg. 1122 **PV**
Custom Casting, 2141 N.W. 25th Ave., 97210, pg. 383 **PV**
DSU Leasing, Inc., 4810 N. Basin Ave., 97217, pg. 306 **PV**
D.S.U.-PETERBILT & GMC, INC., 4810 N. Basin Ave., 97217, pg. 306 **PV**
DavisElen Advertising, Inc., 101 S.W. Main St., Ste. 300, 97204, pg. 316 **PV**
Design Systems Inc., 133 S.W. 2nd Ave. Ste. 304, 97204-3526, pg. 13 **PV**
Drake Construction Company, 437 Columbia Blvd., 97217, pg. 347 **PV**
DYWIDAG Systems International, USA, Inc., 7225 S.W. 86th St., 97223, pg. 424 **IT**
EB5 CORPORATION, 2232 E. Burnside St., 97214, pg. 353 **PV**
Earthmoving Equipment Div., 2141 N.W. 25th Ave., 97210, pg. 383 **PV**
ELECTRO SCIENTIFIC INDUSTRIES, INC., 13900 N.W. Science Park Dr., 97229-5497, pg. 568 **PB**
EMCON Northwest, Inc., 7504 Southwest Bridgeport Rd., 97224, pg. 571 **PB**

Energy National, Inc., Ste. 900, 500 N.E. Multnomah, 97232, pg. 1252 **PB**
Energy West Mining Company, 700 NE Multnomah, Ste. 1600, 97232, pg. 1251 **PB**
Ennis Business Forms of Oregon, Inc., 2811 N.E. Riverside Way, 97211, pg. 583 **PB**
ESCO CORPORATION, 2141 N.W. 25th Ave., 97296, pg. 382 **PV**
Esco International, 2141 N.W. 25th Ave., 97210, pg. 383 **PV**
Farmers Insurance Group, 13333 S.W. 68th Pkwy., 97223-8304, pg. 111 **IT**
First American Title Insurance Co. of Oregon, 1700 S.W. Fourth Ave., Ste. 102, 97201, pg. 626 **PB**
First Interstate Bank of Oregon, N.A., 1300 S.W. Fifth Ave., 97201, pg. 1753 **PB**
FIRSTCORP, 7145 S.W. Varnes, 97223, pg. 408 **PV**
Fiskars-Gerber, 14200 S.W. 72nd Ave., 97223, pg. 492 **IT**
Fleming Foods West, P.O. Box 22107, 97222, pg. 653 **PB**
FLIR SYSTEMS, INC., 16505 S.W. 72nd Ave., 97224, pg. 654 **PB**
FONE AMERICA, INC., 12323 S.W. 66th Ave., 97723, pg. 661 **PB**
Forest City Trading Group, Inc., 10250 S.W. Greenburg Rd., 97223, pg. 669 **PB**
Fort James Western Transportation, 3710 N.W. Front Ave., 97210, pg. 672 **PB**
Foss Maritime Co., 9030 N.W. St. Helen's Rd., 97231, pg. 1092 **PV**
Franz Bakery, P.O. Box 14769, 97214, pg. 1124 **PV**
Freightliner Corp., 4747 N. Channel Ave., 97217, pg. 368 **IT**
GWC Properties, Inc., 808 S.W. 15th Ave., 97205, pg. 719 **PV**
Glenrock Coal Company, 700 NE Multnomah, Ste. 1600, 97232, pg. 1251 **PB**
Globe Furniture Rentals, 16290 S.W. 72nd St., #2, 97224, pg. 458 **PV**
Granplex, Inc., Portland Branch, One S.W. Columbia St., Ste. 430, 97258-2021, pg. 927 **IT**
Gregg Foods of Portland, Inc., 4000 N.E. Marx Dr., 97220, pg. 158 **PV**
HAMPTON RESOURCES INC., 9400 S.W. Barnes Rd., 97225, pg. 498 **PV**
HANNA-SHERMAN INTERNATIONAL, INC., 2000 Hanna Dr., S.E., 97222, pg. 499 **PV**
Hercules Inc.-Portland, 3366 N.W. Yeon, 97210-1526, pg. 810 **PB**
Hewlett-Packard Company, 15115 S.W. Sequoia Pkwy., 97224, pg. 815 **PB**
Hillhaven West, Park Royal Convalescent Center, 2430 N.W. 97210, pg. 1714 **PB**
Hoffman Construction Company of Oregon, 1300 S.W. Sixth Ave., 97201, pg. 532 **PV**
HOFFMAN CORPORATION, 1300 S.W. Sixth Ave., 97201, pg. 532 **PV**
Hoffman Mechanical Corporation, 1300 S.W. Sixth Ave., 97201, pg. 532 **PV**
Hoffman Structures, Inc., 1300 S.W. Sixth Ave., 97201, pg. 532 **PV**
Hyster Overseas Capital Corporation, 2701 NW Vaughn St., Ste. 900, 97210, pg. 1149 **PB**
Ikon Office Solutions-Oregon, 12100 S.W. Garden Place, 97223, pg. 864 **PB**
Industra Inc., 15055 S.W. Sequoia Pkwy., Ste. 100, 97224, pg. 74 **PV**
INX Incorporated/Midland Color Company, 2663 N.W. St. Helen's Rd., 97210, pg. 1311 **IT**
K.F. Jacobson Co., 4315 S.E. McLoughlin Blvd., 97202, pg. 836 **PV**
Jantzen, 411 N.E. 19th St., 97232, pg. 1702 **PB**
JOHNSON ACOUSTICAL & SUPPLY CO., 2001 N.W. 19th Ave., 97209, pg. 590 **PV**
Earle M. Jorgensen Company/Portland, 6650 N. Ensign St., 97217, pg. 600 **PV**
KFXX/KGON, Inc., 4614 S.W. Kelly Ave., 97201, pg. 378 **PV**
KOIN-TV, 140 S.W. Columbia St., 97201, pg. 983 **PB**
KPTV Television, Inc., 735 S.W. 20th Pl., 97205, pg. 352 **PV**
Kaiser Permanente, Northwest Division, 2701 N.W. Vaughn, Ste. 300, 97210-5398, pg. 605 **PV**
KARAKAS, VANSICKLE, OUELLETTE ADVERTISING & PUBLIC RELATIONS, 200 S.W. Market St., Ste. 1400, 97201, pg. 607 **PV**
Kentrox Industries, Inc., 14375 N.W. Science Park Dr., 97229, pg. 4 **PB**
Key Bank of Oregon, 1211 S.W. Fifth Ave., Ste. 300, 97204, pg. 954 **PB**
KINDERCARE LEARNING CENTERS, INC., 825 N.E. Halladay, Ste 1400, 97232, pg. 961 **PB**
Kintetsu World Express Inc., 12430 N.E. Marx St., 97230, pg. 735 **IT**
Kysor Panel Systems, 7320 N.E. 55th Ave., 97218, pg. 1445 **PB**
Laclede Chain Manufacturing Plant, P.O. Box 10636, 97210, pg. 974 **PB**
Land O'Lakes Inc., 15840 N. Simmons Rd., 97203-6425, pg. 646 **PV**
LANDA, INC., 13705 N.E. Airport Way, 97230, pg. 646 **PV**
Liberty Northwest Insurance Corp., 825 N.E. Multnomah St., 97232, pg. 666 **PV**
THE CHAS. H. LILLY CO., 14546 N. Lombard St., 97203, pg. 667 **PV**
Lips Propeller Inc., Swan Island Shipyard, Bldg. 64, P.O. Box 17161, 97217, pg. 812 **IT**
LOUISIANA PACIFIC CORPORATION, 111 S.W. Fifth Ave., 97204, pg. 1015 **PB**
M & T PARTNERS, 15350 Southwest Sequoia Pkwy., #300, 97224, pg. 684 **PV**

PB - U.S. Public Companies Volume
PV - U.S. Private Companies Volume
IT - International Public & Private Companies Volume

MRI Corporation, 3200 N.W. Yeon Ave., 97210, pg. 1440 **PB**
HERBERT MALARKEY ROOFING COMPANY, 3131 N. Columbia Blvd., 97217, pg. 698 **PV**
MCCALL OIL & CHEMICAL CORP., 808 S.W. 15th Ave., 97205, pg. 719 **PV**
McCall Oil Real Estate Corporation, 808 S.W. 15th Ave., 97205, pg. 719 **PV**
McCall Properties, Inc., 808 S.W. 15th Ave., 97205, pg. 719 **PV**
Meier & Frank, 621 S.W. Fifth Ave., 97204, pg. 1064 **PB**
Merchants Information Solutions, Inc., 6623 N.E. 78th Ct., Ste. B9, 97218, pg. 1106 **PB**
FRED MEYER INCORPORATED, 3800 S.E. 22nd Ave., 97202, pg. 1103 **PB**
Fred Meyer Stores, 3800 S.E. 22nd Ave., 97202, pg. 1103 **PB**
Miller Brands, Inc., 5825 N.E. Skyport Way, 97218, pg. 1289 **PB**
Ming Surveyors, Inc., 1300 S.W. Sixth Ave., 97201, pg. 532 **PV**
Mitsui & Co. (U.S.A.), Inc., 200 S.W. Market St., 97201, pg. 879 **IT**
Mt. Hood Life Insurance, Inc., 309 SW Sixth Ave., 97204, pg. 1681 **PB**
NCS Abacus, 921 Southwest Washington St., Ste. 410, 97205-2822, pg. 1155 **PB**
NNG Energy Systems, Inc., 230 N.W. Second Ave., 97209, pg. 1200 **PB**
NNG Financial Corporation, 220 N.W. Second Ave., 97209, pg. 1200 **PB**
NACCO Materials Handling Group, Inc., 2701 N.W. Vaughn, Ste. 300, 97210, pg. 1149 **PB**
NESS HOLDING CO., 6645 N. Ensign, 97217, pg. 791 **PV**
Nickel Ads, 7818 S.E. Stark St., 97215, pg. 984 **PB**
North Pacific Insurance Company, 1675 S.W. Marlow Ave., 97225, pg. 543 **IT**
NORTH PACIFIC LUMBER COMPANY, P.O. Box 3915, 815 N.E. Davis St., 97232, pg. 805 **PV**
NORTHWEST NATURAL GAS COMPANY, 220 N.W. Second Ave., 97209, pg. 1200 **PB**
Northwest Pacific Indemnity Co., 1500 S.W. First Ave., Ste. 1000, 97201, pg. 355 **PB**
Norwest Division, 17401 N.E. Halsey St., 97230-6099, pg. 518 **PB**
Omark Properties, Inc., 4909 S.E. International Way, 97222, pg. 239 **PB**
OMNI PRODUCTS, INC., 975 S.E. Sandy Blvd., 97214, pg. 816 **PV**
OMNI Products, Inc., 2330 N.E. Columbia Blvd., 97208, pg. 816 **PV**
121 S.W. Salmon St. Corp., 121 S.W. Salmon St., 97204, pg. 585 **PB**
Oregon Automobile Insurance Company, 1675 S.W. Marlow Ave., 97225, pg. 543 **PV**
Oregon Natural Gas Development Corp., 220 N.W. Second Ave., 97209, pg. 1200 **PB**
OREGON STEEL MILLS, INC., 1000 Broadway Bldg., 1000 S.W. Broadway, Ste. 2200, 97205, pg. 1230 **PB**
PCC Exports, Inc., 4650 S.W. Macadam Ave., Ste. 440, 97201-4254, pg. 1320 **PV**
Paccom Leasing Corporation, Ste. 775, 825 N.E. Multnomah, 97232, pg. 1252 **PB**
Pacific Generation Company, 500 N.E. Multnomah St., Ste. 900, 97232, pg. 1252 **PB**
PACIFIC METAL COMPANY, 3400 SW Bond Ave., 97201, pg. 832 **PV**
Pacific Minerals, Inc., 700 NE Multnomah, Ste. 1600, 97232, pg. 1252 **PB**
Pacific One Bank, 401 S.W. 5th Ave., 97204, pg. 635 **PB**
Pacific Power & Light Company, 700 N.E. Multnomah, Ste. 1600, 97232, pg. 1251 **PB**
Pacific Square Corporation, 220 N.W. Second Ave., 97209, pg. 1200 **PB**
PACIFICORP, 700 N.E. Multnomah #1600, 97232-4116, pg. 1251 **PB**
PacifiCorp Aviation (Holdings), Inc., 825 N.E. Multnomah, Ste. 775, 97232, pg. 1252 **PB**
PacifiCorp Credit, Inc., Ste. 775, 825 N.E. Multnomah, 97232, pg. 1252 **PB**
PacifiCorp Financial Services, Inc., Ste. 775, 825 N.E. Multnomah, 97232, pg. 1252 **PB**
PacifiCorp Group Holdings Company, Ste. 1600, 700 N.E. Multnomah, 97232-4116, pg. 1251 **PB**
PacifiCorp Trans, Inc. Ste. 125, 729 N.E. Oregon St., 97232, pg. 1252 **PB**
Pacwest Center, 1211 S.W. Fifth Ave., 97204, pg. 873 **IT**
R.B. PAMPLIN CORP., 900 S.W. Fifth Ave., Ste. 1800, 97204, pg. 835 **PV**
Paper Products Marketing, 806 S.W. Broadway, Ste. 300, 97205, pg. 72 **IT**
PECO MFG. CO., INC., 4707 S.E. 17th Ave., 97202, pg. 846 **PV**
PENDLETON WOOLEN MILLS, INC., 220 N.W. Broadway, 97209, pg. 848 **PV**
Piper Jaffray Inc., One Main Pl., 101 S.W. Main St., Ste. 1040, 97204-3279, pg. 1302 **PB**
Piper Jaffray Inc., One Main Pl., 101 S.W. Main St., Ste. 820, 97204-3216, pg. 1303 **PB**
Piper Jaffray Inc., One Main Pl., 101 S.W. Main St., Ste. 1940, 97204-3279, pg. 1303 **PB**
Piper Jaffray Inc., 200 Market, 200 S.W. Market St., Ste. 1800, 97201-5745, pg. 1303 **PB**
POPE & TALBOT, INC., 1500 S.W. First Ave., 97201, pg. 1316 **PB**
Pope & Talbot Inc., P.O. Box 5171, 97207, pg. 1317 **PB**
Port Center Restaurant Corp., 4575 N. Channell Ave., 97217, pg. 1023 **PV**
PORT OF PORTLAND, 700 N.E. Multnomah, 97232, pg. 876 **PV**

Portland Auto Auction, 3000 N. Hayden Island Dr., 97217, pg. 283 **PV**
Portland General Electric Co., 121 S.W. Salmon St., 97204, pg. 584 **PB**
Portland General Holdings, Inc., 121 S.W. Salmon St., 97204, pg. 585 **PB**
Portland Terminal, 5880 N.W. St. Helens Rd., 97210, pg. 692 **PB**
Portland Terminal Railroad Co., Union Station, Rm. 209, 800 N.W. 6th, 97209, pg. 1668 **PB**
Portland Traction Co., 1640 S.E. Water Ave., 97214, pg. 1668 **PB**
ARTHUR A. POZZI CO., INC., 5550 S.W. MacAdam Ave., Ste. 230, 97201, pg. 878 **PV**
Precision Asbestos Abatement Company, 8025 N.E. Killingsworth, 97218, pg. 532 **PV**
PRECISION CASTPARTS CORP., 4650 S.W. Macadam Ave., Ste. 440, 97201-4254, pg. 1320 **PB**
Precision Construction Company, 8025 N.E. Killingsworth, 97218, pg. 532 **PV**
Precision Interconnect, 16640 SW 72nd Ave., 97224, pg. 8 **PB**
Premier Edible Oils Corp., P.O. Box 83599, 97283, pg. 872 **IT**
Proler Environmental Services, Inc., 3200 N.W. Yeon Ave., 97210, pg. 1440 **PB**
Proler International Corp., 3200 N.W. Yeon Ave., 97210, pg. 1440 **PB**
Proler Recycling, Inc., 3200 N.W. Yeon Ave., 97210, pg. 1440 **PB**
Proleride Transport Systems, Inc., 3200 N.W. Yeon Ave., 97210, pg. 1440 **PB**
Proprietory Products Group, 2141 N.W. 25th Avenue, 97210, pg. 383 **PV**
Qualivest Capital Management, Inc., 111 S.W. Fifth Ave., Ste. 1500, 97204, pg. 1681 **PB**
QualMed Plans for Health-Oregon, 4800 Macadam Ave., Ste. 400, 97201, pg. 678 **PV**
RP alpha/Portland, Pacific Business Park, Bldg. 1, 4900 N.E. 122nd Ave., 97230, pg. 950 **PV**
REGENCE BLUECROSS BLUESHIELD OF OREGON, 100 S.W. Market St., 97201, pg. 917 **PV**
Regence Life & Health Insurance Co., P.O. Box 1271, 97207, pg. 918 **PV**
RENTFAK CORPORATION, One Airport Ctr., 7700 N.E. Ambassador Pl., 97220, pg. 1377 **PV**
Rexam Graphics, P.O. Box 3849, 12238 N. Portland Rd., 972 7, pg. 1107 **IT**
Rhone-Poulenc Basic Chemicals Co., 4429 Suttle Rd., 972 7, pg. 1110 **IT**
Riedel-Smith Environmental Services, Foot of N. Portsmouth, 97028, pg. 1478 **PV**
Riedel Waste Disposal Systems, 4611 N. Channel Ave., 972 7, pg. 1478 **PV**
Rollins Hudig Hall of Oregon, Inc., 1211 S.W. 5th Ave., 972 4, pg. 117 **IT**
Ross Island Sand & Gravel Co., Inc., 4315 S.E. McLoughlin Blvd., 97202, pg. 836 **PV**
RUNDEL PRODUCTS, INC., 13233 N.E. Jarrett St., 97230, pg. 951 **PV**
SLC Technologies, 10831 S.W. Cascade Blvd., 97223, pg. 138 **PV**
Ann Sacks Tile & Stone, Inc., 8120 N.E. 33rd Dr., 97211, pg. 630 **PV**
SCHNITZER STEEL INDUSTRIES, INC., 3200 N.W. Yeon Ave., 97210, pg. 1439 **PB**
Sealy Mattress Company - Portland, 13635 N. Lombard, 97203, pg. 979 **PV**
Security Pacific Bank Oregon, 1001 S.W. Fifth Ave., 97204, pg. 182 **PB**
Security Pacific Oregon Bancorp, 1001 S.W. Fifth Ave., 97204, pg. 182 **PB**
Smith Technologies Corp., 4611 N. Channel Ave., 97217, pg. 1478 **PV**
STANDARD INSURANCE CO., 1100 S. W. Sixth, 97204, pg. 1031 **PV**
Stone Mill Foods, P.O. Box 10144, 2140 N.W. Quimby, 97210, pg. 802 **PV**
Subaru Northwest Region, 8040 N.E. 33rd Dr., 97211, pg. 523 **IT**
Subaru of America Western, Inc., 8040 N.E. 33rd Dr., 97211, pg. 523 **IT**
Sulzer Bingham Pumps Inc., 2800 N.W. Front Ave., 97210, pg. 1305 **IT**
Sunne Controls Div., 4720 S.E. 17th Ave., 97202, pg. 846 **PV**
TIE Systems-Portland, 9220 S.W. Barbur Blvd., #107, 97219, pg. 1085 **PV**
TMP Worldwide, Inc., 600 N.W. 14th Ave., Ste. 100, 97209, pg. 1064 **PV**
TMP Worldwide/Recruitment Division, 600 N.W. 14th Ave., Ste. 10, 97209, pg. 1065 **PV**
TRM COPY CENTERS CORPORATION, 5208 N.E. 122nd. Ave., 97230-1074, pg. 1558 **PV**
Takenaka (U.S.A.) Corporation, Portland Office, 0718 S.W. Bancroft, 97201, pg. 1351 **IT**
TEMP-CONTROL MECHANICAL CORP., 4800 N. Channel, 97217, pg. 1075 **PV**
TreeSource, Inc., 10260 S.W. Greenburg Rd., Ste. 900, 97223-5519, pg. 1729 **PB**
Tucker Rocky Distributing, 2424 N.E. Riverside Way, 97211, pg. 639 **PV**
Tule Hub Services Co., 121 S.W. Salmon St., 97204, pg. 585 **PB**
United Employers Ins., 6566 SE Lake Rd., 97222, pg. 1122 **PB**
UNITED GROCERS INC., 6433 S.E. Lake Rd., 97222-2198, pg. 1122 **PV**
UNITED STATES BAKERY, 315 N.E. Tenth Ave., 97232, pg. 1124 **PV**

U.S. Bancorp Brokerage, 111 SW 5th St., 97204, pg. 1681 **PB**
U.S. Bancorp Insurance Agency, Inc., 309 S.W. Sixth Ave., 97204, pg. 1681 **PB**
U.S. Bancorp Leasing & Financial, 111 S.W. 5th Ave., 97204, pg. 1681 **PB**
U.S. Bank Insurance Agency, 309 SW 6th Ave., 97204, pg. 1681 **PB**
United States National Bank of Oregon, 111 S.W. 5th Ave., 97204, pg. 1681 **PB**
Vantageparts, 2222 N.W. Raleigh St., Ste. A, 97209, pg. 281 **PB**
WTD INDUSTRIES, INC., 10260 S.W. Greenburg Rd., Ste. 900, 97223-5519, pg. 1729 **PB**
Weiss Scientific Glass Blowing Co., Inc., 14380 NW Science Park Dr., 97229, pg. 1408 **IT**
Western International Media Corporation, 4380 S.W. Macadam, Ste. 170, 97201, pg. 1167 **PV**
Western Pulp & Paper Div., 900 S.W. Fifth Ave., 97204, pg. 736 **PB**
Western Timber Co., 10260 S.W. Greenburg Rd., Ste. 900, 97223-5519, pg. 1729 **PB**
Western Wood Prods. Mfg. Div., 900 S.W. Fifth Ave., 97204, pg. 736 **PB**
WIEDEN & KENNEDY, INC., 320 S.W. Washington, 97204, pg. 1175 **PV**
WILLAMETTE INDUSTRIES, INC., 1300 S.W. Fifth Ave., Ste. 3800, 97201, pg. 1768 **PB**
Willamina Lumber Co. Inc., 9400 S.W. Barnes Rd., 97225, pg. 498 **PV**
WILLIAMS CONTROLS, INC., 14100 S.W. 72nd Ave., 97224, pg. 1769 **PB**
Willis Corroon Corp. of Portland, 1800 S.W. Fourth Ave., 97201, pg. 1507 **IT**
WOODWARD & DICKERSON, 50 S.W. 2nd Ave., 5th Fl., 97204, pg. 1188 **PV**
Woodward-Clyde, 111 S.W. Columbia St., Ste. 990, 97201, pg. 1656 **PB**
World Trade Center Northwest Corporation, 121 S.W. Salmon St., 97204, pg. 585 **PB**
Worldwide Paper Factors Inc., 806 S.W. Broadway, Ste. 300, 97205, pg. 72 **IT**
Zellerbach Division, 9111 Northeast Columbia Blvd., 97220, pg. 1075 **PB**

Prineville

OCHOCO LUMBER COMPANY, 416 Combs Flat Rd., 97754, pg. 811 **PV**
LES SCHWAB TIRE CENTERS, 646 Madras Hwy., 97754, pg. 974 **PV**

Redmond

Columbia Medical, Inc., P.O. Box 1530, 97756, pg. 1700 **PB**
Schlosser Casting Company, 345 N.E. Hemlock, 97756, pg. 970 **PV**

Riddle

Glenbrook Nickel Company, P.O. Box 85, 5093 Riddle By-Pass Road, 97469, pg. 307 **IT**

Roseburg

Applied Sciences Division, 17271 N. Umpqua Highway, 97470, pg. 198 **PV**

Salem

AGRIPAC INC., 325 Patterson N.W., 97304, pg. 26 **PV**
CAPITOL CHEVROLET CADILLAC GEO SUBARU INC., 2711 Mission St. S.E., 97302, pg. 206 **PV**
Carriage Hill Foods, 1735 S. Lincoln Ave., 44460, pg. 427 **PV**
Country Mutual Northwest Regional Office, 2150 Country Dr. S., 97302-2209, pg. 279 **PV**
First Security Bank of Oregon, 580 State St., N.E., 97301, pg. 637 **PB**
HMO Oregon, 201 High St., S.E., 97309, pg. 918 **PV**
Health Maintenance Oregon, 201 High St. S.E., 97309, pg. 918 **PV**
IFF Concentrates, Inc., 2340 Hyacinth N.E., 97303, pg. 899 **PB**
Jannock Steel Fabricating, Inc., 4570 Ridge Dr., N.E., 97303, pg. 699 **IT**
Microflect Company, Inc., 3575 25th St., S.E., 97302, pg. 1707 **PV**
Mitsubishi Silicon America, 1351 Tandem Ave., N.E., 97303, pg. 875 **IT**
MORROW WEST BEACH, 2600 Pringle Rd. S.E., 97302, pg. 1134 **PB**
Salem Manufacturing Facility, 1351 Tandem Ave., N.E., P.O. Box 7748, 97303, pg. 875 **IT**
Statesman-Journal Co., 280 Church St. N.E., 97309, pg. 701 **PB**
Waremart Inc., 3601 State St., 97301, pg. 1150 **PV**
Wilsey Foods, Inc., 3371 Portland Rd. N.E., 97303, pg. 879 **IT**

Springfield

The Kingsford Products Co., 3315 Marcola St., 97477, pg. 387 **PB**
McKenzie Towables By Monaco, 5280 High Banks Rd., 97448, pg. 1123 **PB**
Neste Resins Corporation, 475 North 28th St., P.O. Box 270, 97477, pg. 913 **IT**

PB - U.S. Public Companies Volume
PV - U.S. Private Companies Volume
IT - International Public & Private Companies Volume

1398

Geographic Index-U.S.

Shorewood Packaging Corporation of Oregon, 500 International Way, 97477-1080, pg. 1468 **PB**
Springfield News, P.O. Box 139, 97477, pg. 984 **PB**
TIMBER PRODUCTS COMPANY, LP, 305 S. Fourth St., 97477, pg. 1086 **PV**

Stayton

NORPAC FOODS, INC., 930 W. Washington St., 97383-0458, pg. 802 **PV**

Sutherlin

Softwood Veneer, Hastings Ave., P.O. Box 1146, 97479, pg. 738 **PB**

Tangent

Barenbrug Research USA, P.O. Box 239, 32080 Old Highway 34, 97389, pg. 166 **IT**
Barenbrug USA, 33477 Hwy. 99E, 97389, pg. 166 **IT**

Tigard

Bergen Brunswig Medical Corp., 14160 S.W. 72nd Ave., 97224, pg. 214 **PB**
Central Sprinkler Company, 7500 S.W. Tech Center Drive, 97223, pg. 327 **PB**
Pro Shop (Portland, OR), 7100 S.W. Sandberg, 97223, pg. 861 **PB**
SCR, INC., 7320 S.W. Hunziker Rd., Ste. 207, 97223, pg. 955 **PV**
Shimizu America Corporation-Portland Office, 7100 S.W. Hampton Dr., Ste. 231, 97223, pg. 1233 **IT**
Tillamook Food Sales, 12520 S.W. 68th St., Ste. B, 97223, pg. 1086 **PV**
WERSHOW-ASH-LEWIS, 7340 S.W. Hunziker Rd., Ste. 220, 97223, pg. 1162 **PV**

Tillamook

Oregon Coast Foods, 4175 Hwy. 101 N., 97141, pg. 1086 **PV**
TILLAMOOK COUNTY CREAMERY ASSN., 4175 Hwy. 101 N., 97141, pg. 1086 **PB**
Trask River Lumber Co., 5900 Moffett Rd., 97141-9621, pg. 1730 **PB**

Toledo

Grocery Bags & Sacks, One Butler Branch Rd., P.O. Box 580, 97391, pg. 737 **PB**
Primary Pulp & Paper Plant, One Butler Branch Rd., P.O. Box 580, 97391, pg. 736 **PB**

Troutdale

CASCADE CORPORATION, 2201 N.E. 201st, 97060, pg. 310 **PV**
Hawkeye Construction, Inc., 1500 N.E. Graham Rd., 97060, pg. 1029 **PB**
Reynolds Metals Company-Troutdale, 5100 NE Sun Dial Rd., 97060, pg. 1386 **PB**

Tualatin

Association Sand & Gravel, P.O. Box 363, 19585 S.W. 118th Ave., 97062, pg. 246 **IT**
Autodesk Portland, S. Center Bldg. J, 7644 S.W. Mohawk, 97062, pg. 149 **PB**
Colonial Pacific Leasing Corp., 7659 Mohawk St., 97602, pg. 1303 **PB**
Hydro Conduit Corp., P.O. Box 363, 19585 SW 118th Ave., 97062, pg. 246 **IT**
JAE Oregon, Inc., 11555 S.W. Leveton Dr., 97062, pg. 701 **IT**
Oregon Culvert Co., Inc., 10780 SW Tualatin-Sherwood Rd., 97062, pg. 1305 **PB**
Portland Chain Mfg. Co., 12475 S.W. Herman Rd., 97062, pg. 1158 **PV**
Puget Plastics Corporation, 11555 S.W. Myslony Rd., 97062, pg. 80 **PB**
Seaboard Life (USA), P.O. Box 339, 7630 S.W. Mohawk, 97062, pg. 464 **IT**
Successful Money Management Seminars, Inc., 12100 Tualatin Rd., 97062, pg. 1376 **PB**

Weston

SMITH FROZEN FOODS, INC., P.O. Box 68, Depot St., 97886, pg. 1008 **PV**

White City

Down River Forest Products, Inc., 1790 Ave. G, 97503, pg. 763 **PB**
MILLENNIUM TECHNOLOGY SERVICES, INC., 1050 Antelope Rd., 97503, pg. 746 **PV**

Wilsonville

G.I. JOE'S INC., 9805 Boeckman Rd., 97070, pg. 435 **PV**
Graphic Arts Supply Division, 26100 S.W. 95th Ave., Ste. 200, 97070, pg. 205 **PB**
Hewlett-Packard Company, 9255 S.W. Pioneer Ct., 97070, pg. 815 **PB**

HOLLYWOOD ENTERTAINMENT CORP., 25600 S.W. Parkway Ctr. Dr., 97070, pg. 535 **PV**
In Focus Services, Inc., 27700B S.W. Pkwy. Ave., 97070, pg. 873 **PB**
IN FOCUS SYSTEMS, INC., 27700B S.W. Pkwy. Ave., 97070-9215, pg. 873 **PB**
Intelledex Vision Products, 27350 SW 95th Ave., Suite 3038, 97070-7709, pg. 568 **PB**
Kao Infosystems Company, 9025 Southwest Hillman, 97070, pg. 717 **IT**
MENTOR GRAPHICS CORPORATION, 8005 S.W. Boeckman Rd., 97070-7777, pg. 1086 **PB**
Motif, Inc., 27700A S.W. Parkway Ave., 97070, pg. 873 **PB**
Perstorp Analytical Inc. Division Alpkem, 9445 S.W. Ridder Rd., Ste. 310, 97070, pg. 1039 **IT**
Sight & Sound, 9750 S.W. Hillman Ct., 97070, pg. 780 **PB**
Sysco Food Services of Portland, Inc., 26250 W. Parkway Ctr. Dr., 97070, pg. 1552 **PB**
T.G.U.S. Corp., 9450 SW Commerce Cir., Ste. 110, 97070, pg. 1348 **IT**
Tektronix Asia, Limited, P.O. Box 1000, 26600 S.W. Parkway, 97070, pg. 1567 **PB**
Tektronix Development Company, P.O. Box 1000, D/S 63-LAW, 97070-1000, pg. 1567 **PB**
Tektronix Europe, Inc., P.O. Box 1000, 26600 S.W. Pkwy., 97070, pg. 1567 **PB**
Tektronix Funding Corporation, P.O. Box 1000, D/S 63-LAW, 97070-1000, pg. 1567 **PB**
TEKTRONIX, INC., 26600 S.W. Pkwy. Ave., 97070, pg. 1567 **PB**
Tektronix International, Inc., P.O. Box 1000, 26600 S.W. Parkway, 97070, pg. 1567 **PB**
Tektronix Properties, Inc., P.O. Box 1000, D/S 63-LAW, 97070-1000, pg. 1567 **PB**

Woodburn

Smucker Woodburn Plant, 1440 Silverton Rd., 97071, pg. 1480 **PB**

PENNSYLVANIA

Adamstown

BOLLMAN HAT CO., 110 E. Main St., 19501-0517, pg. 155 **PV**

Akron

Cadmus Journal Services-Tapsco, 309 Colonial Dr., 17501, pg. 291 **PB**

Allentown

APCI (U.K.), Inc., 7201 Hamilton Blvd., 18195-1501, pg. 30 **PB**
APD Cryogenics Inc., 1833 Vultee St., 18103, pg. 894 **PB**
AIR PRODUCTS AND CHEMICALS, INC., 7201 Hamilton Blvd., 18195-1501, pg. 30 **PB**
Air Products Europe, Inc., 7201 Hamilton Blvd., 18195, pg. 30 **PB**
Air Products Hydrogen Co., Inc., 7201 Hamilton Blvd., 18195, pg. 30 **PB**
Air Products International Corp., 7201 Hamilton Blvd., 18195-1501, pg. 31 **PB**
Air Products of Puerto Rico, Inc., 7201 Hamilton Blvd., 18195-1501, pg. 31 **PB**
Air Products Ref-fuel Holding Corp., 7201 Hamilton Blvd., 18195-1501, pg. 31 **PB**
Air Products Ref-fuel of Connecticut (S.E.), Inc., 7201 Hamilton Blvd., 18195-1501, pg. 31 **PB**
Air Products Ref-fuel of Hempstead, Inc., 7201 Hamilton Blvd., 18195, pg. 31 **PB**
Alpo Pet Foods, Inc., Rte. 309 & Pope Rd., 18104, pg. 917 **IT**
BDW Corp., Two N. Ninth St., 18101, pg. 1244 **PB**
BioChem ImmunoSystems, Inc., 100 Cascade Dr., 18103, pg. 196 **IT**
BONNEY FORGE CORPORATION, Cedar & Meadow Sts., 18102, pg. 156 **PB**
BUCKEYE PARTNERS, L.P., 3900 Hamilton Blvd., 18103, pg. 266 **PB**
Buckeye Pipe Line Company, L.P., 3900 Hamilton Blvd., 18103, pg. 266 **PB**
Buckeye Tank Terminals L.P., 3900 Hamilton Blvd., 18103, pg. 266 **PB**
CBR Investment Corporation of America, 7660 Imperial Way, 18195-1016, pg. 605 **IT**
CEP Group, Inc., Two N. Ninth St., 18101, pg. 1244 **PB**
Chrysler First Business Credit Corporation, Commerce Plaza III, Ste. 150, 5050 Tilghman St., 18104, pg. 354 **PB**
Dorney Park & Wildwater Kingdom, 3830 Dorney Park Rd., 18104, pg. 319 **PB**
EBELING & REUSS COMPANY, 6500 Chapmans Rd., 18106, pg. 358 **PV**
Everglades Pipe Line Company, L.P., 3900 Hamilton Blvd., 18103, pg. 266 **PB**
First National Bank of Saxton, 911 Church St., 16678, pg. 1222 **PB**
Fuller Company (Allentown), South 10th and Mill Streets, 18103, pg. 475 **IT**
GSF Energy Inc., 7201 Hamilton Blvd., 18195, pg. 31 **PB**
Greene Manor Coal Co., Two N. Ninth St., 18101, pg. 1244 **PB**
Hawthorne ABE, 600 Hayden Cir., Hangar 7, 18103, pg. 512 **PV**
Heidelberg Cement Inc., 7660 Imperial Way, 18195-1016, pg. 605 **IT**

Interstate Energy Co., Two N. Ninth St., 18101, pg. 1244 **PB**
JP Foodservice, Inc.-Allentown, 1135 N. Plymouth St., 18103, pg. 918 **PB**
JAMISON PLASTIC CORPORATION, 5001 Crackersport Rd., 18104, pg. 581 **PV**
Lady Jane Collieries, Inc., Two N. Ninth St., 18101, pg. 1244 **PB**
Laurel Pipe Line Company, L.P., 3900 Hamilton Blvd., 18103, pg. 267 **PB**
Lehigh Portland Cement Company, 7660 Imperial Way, 18195-1016, pg. 605 **IT**
Mack Leasing System, 2100 Mack Blvd., 18105, pg. 1102 **IT**
Mack Trucks, Inc., 2100 Mack Blvd., 18105, pg. 1102 **IT**
Middletown Oxygen Co., Inc., 7201 Hamilton Blvd., 18195, pg. 31 **PB**
The Morning Call, 101 N. 6th St., 18101, pg. 1616 **PB**
NationsCredit, 1105 Hamilton, 18101, pg. 1165 **PB**
PP&L RESOURCES, Two N. 9th St., 18101-1179, pg. 1244 **PB**
Pacific Anchor Chemical Corporation, 7201 Hamilton Blvd., 18195, pg. 31 **PB**
Pennsylvania Coal Resources Corp., Two N. Ninth St., 18101, pg. 1244 **PB**
Pennsylvania Power & Light Company-Lehigh Div., Rts. 22 & 309, 827 Hausman Rd., 18106-0500, pg. 1244 **PB**
Power Markets Development Company, Two N. Ninth St., 18101, pg. 1244 **PB**
PRECISION ROLL GRINDERS, INC., 6356 Chapmans Rd., 18106, pg. 880 **PV**
Realty Co. of Pennsylvania, Two N. Ninth St., 18101, pg. 1244 **PB**
Sky Bros. Inc., 1135 N. Plymouth St., 18103, pg. 918 **PB**
Stockton CoGen (I), Inc., 7201 Hamilton Blvd., 18195, pg. 31 **PB**
Trexlertown Properties, Inc., 7201 Hamilton Blvd., 18195, pg. 31 **PB**

Allison Park

GLENSHAW GLASS CO. INC., 3140 William Flinn Hwy., 15101, pg. 457 **PV**

Altoona

BOYER CANDY COMPANY INC., 821 17th St., 16602, pg. 162 **PV**
Federated Fry Metals, Inc., 6th Ave. & 41st St., 16602, pg. 328 **IT**
THE HITE COMPANY, Beale Ave & 31st St., 16603-1754, pg. 531 **PV**
ITEMS INTERNATIONAL/AIRWALK, INC., 1540 E. Pleasant Valley Blvd., 16602, pg. 576 **PV**
JP Foodservice, Inc.-Altoona, Burns Ave. & Canan Station, 16601, pg. 918 **PB**
Keystone Financial Service Group, Inc., P.O. Box 1783, 16603, pg. 956 **PB**
Mid-State Bank, 1130 12th Ave., 16603, pg. 956 **PB**
SHEETZ, INC., 5700 Sixth Ave., 16602, pg. 991 **PV**
Sky Bros. Inc., Burns Ave. & Canan Station, 16601, pg. 918 **PB**
Small Tube Products Co., Inc., Spring Meadows, 16603, pg. 1775 **PB**
Thermal Industries Inc., 810 S. 12th St., 16602-6246, pg. 491 **PV**
WARD TRUCKING CORP., Second Ave. & Seventh St., Greenwood, 16602, pg. 1149 **PV**

Alum Bank

Exact Level, Pleasantville Indus. Pk., 15521, pg. 1511 **PB**

Ambler

BRADFORD-WHITE CORPORATION, 321 Norristown Rd., Ste. 250, 19002-2755, pg. 164 **PV**
Henkel Chemical Specialties Div., 300 Brookside Ave., 19002, pg. 610 **IT**
Henkel Organic Products Div., 300 Brookside Ave., 19002, pg. 610 **IT**
Johnson Press, 160 N. Main St., 19002-5712, pg. 592 **PV**

Ambridge

Interstate Steel Supply Co. of Pittsburgh, 81 Century Dr., 15003, pg. 1100 **PB**

Archbald

Lockheed Martin Tactical Defense Systems, John F. Kennedy Dr., 18403-1598, pg. 1009 **PB**

Ardmore

CRS Financial Services, Inc., 50 Rittenhouse Pl., 19003, pg. 1374 **PB**
GRANT MARKETING COMMUNICATIONS, Cricket Terrace Ctr., 19003, pg. 470 **PV**
HAJOCA CORP., 127 Coulter Ave., 19003, pg. 494 **PV**
DANIEL J. KEATING CO., 326 Lancaster Ave., 19003, pg. 610 **PV**
KINGSWOOD ADVERTISING, INC., Cricket Terrace Ctr., 19003, pg. 622 **PV**
Kingswood Interactive, Cricket Terrace Ctr., 19003, pg. 622 **PV**

PB - U.S. Public Companies Volume
PV - U.S. Private Companies Volume
IT - International Public & Private Companies Volume

Geographic Index-U.S.

1399

Ashland

Laubeck Corporation, Laubenstein Division, 418 S. Hoffman Blvd., 17921, pg. 653 **PV**

Aston

Engineering Systems Co., 2550 Market St., 19014-3426, pg. 313 **PV**
PHONETICS, INC., 901 Tryens Rd., 19014, pg. 863 **PV**
PYROMET, INC., Five Commerce Dr., 19014, pg. 897 **PV**

Atglen

Quebecor Printing Atglen Inc., P.O. Box 465, Rte. 372, Lower Valley Rd., 19310, pg. 1076 **IT**

Athens

Ingersoll Rand - Power Tool Div., 101 N. Main St., 18810-1707, pg. 877 **PB**

Auburn

GenCorp Decorative Product Manufacturing Div., P.O. Box 429, Old Hickory La., 17922, pg. 706 **PB**

Avondale

Edlon Products, Inc., 117 State Rd., 19311-0667, pg. 1393 **PB**

Bala Cynwyd

AAMCO TRANSMISSIONS, INC., One Presidential Blvd., 19004, pg. 9 **PV**
Belmont Industries, Inc., 225 City Line Ave., 19004, pg. 903 **PV**
CAP Gemini America (Philadelphia Branch), 150 Monument Rd., Ste. 100, 19004, pg. 264 **IT**
CONNELLY CONTAINERS, INC., Righters Ferry Rd., 19004, pg. 264 **PV**
L.F. DRISCOLL CO., Nine Presidential Blvd., 19004, pg. 343 **PV**
ENTERTAINMENT COMMUNICATIONS, 401 City Ave., Ste. 409, 19004, pg. 378 **PV**
KEATING BUILDING CORP., One Bala Ave., 19004, pg. 610 **PV**
KEYSTONE FOODS CORPORATION, 401 City Ave., Ste. 800, 19004, pg. 619 **PV**
OCE, Three Bala Plaza E., Ste. 217, 19004, pg. 994 **PB**
PRIMAVERA SYSTEMS, INC., Two Bala Plaza, 19004, pg. 884 **PV**
SANI-MIST, INC., 45 E. City Line Ave., Ste. 375, 19004, pg. 965 **PV**
Sequent Computer Systems, Inc., 401 City Ave., Ste. 900, 19004, pg. 1459 **PB**
Shadow Broadcast Services, 555 City Ave., Ste. 1000, 19004, pg. 1763 **PV**
WWF PAPER CORPORATION, Two Bala Plaza, 19004, pg. 1145 **PV**
Waverley Mineral Corporation, 555 City Line, 19004, pg. 803 **IT**

Barnesville

Frontier Communications-Lakewood, Inc, P.O. Box 189, RR #1, Box 212A, 18214, pg. 683 **PB**

Bath

Keystone Cement Co., 7311 Airport, 18014-0058, pg. 741 **PB**

Beaver

Michael Baker, Jr., Inc., 4301 Dutch Ridge Rd., 15009, pg. 168 **PB**

Beaver Falls

Koppel Steel Corp., P.O. Box 750, Sixth Ave. & Mount, 15010, pg. 1147 **PB**
MOLTRUP STEEL PRODUCTS COMPANY, 14th St. & Second Ave., 15010, pg. 756 **PV**
Reeves Bank, 1217 Seventh Ave., 15010, pg. 607 **PB**

Beaver Springs

The JPM Company, 254 Snyder Ave., 17812, pg. 919 **PB**
Mattern Hatchery, Rte. 1, Box 240, 17812, pg. 374 **PV**

Bedford

L.B. Foster Company-Bedford Plant, Bedford Industrial Park, 15522, pg. 676 **PB**
JLG Industries, Inc., Industrial Park, Weber Ln., 15522, pg. 918 **PB**

Belle Vernon

THE GUTTMAN GROUP, 200 Speers St., 15012, pg. 488 **PV**
Guttman Oil, Inc., 200 Speers St., 15012, pg. 489 **PV**
Mon River Towing Inc., 200 Speers St., 15012, pg. 489 **PV**

Belleville

Fairmont Products, P.O. Box 977, 15 Kishacoquillas St., 17004, pg. 490 **PB**

Bensalem

ABB STAL Refrigeration, 3580 Progress Dr., 19020, pg. 4 **IT**
AIRLINE HYDRAULICS CORPORATION, I-95 & Street Rd., 19020, pg. 29 **PV**
American Travellers Corporation, 3220 Tillman Dr., 19020, pg. 433 **PB**
Brandt, Inc., 1750 Woodhaven Dr., 19020, pg. 387 **IT**
CMS Gilbreth Packaging Systems, 3300 State Rd., 19020, pg. 558 **PV**
CHARMING SHOPPES, INC., 450 Winks Ln., 19020-6759, pg. 335 **PB**
Edgcomb Metals, 555 State Rd., 19020, pg. 572 **IT**
FPA CORPORATION, One Greenwood Sq., 3333 Street Rd., Ste. 101, 19020, pg. 608 **PB**
Fashion Bug, 450 Winks Ln., 19020, pg. 336 **PB**
Fashion Bug Plus, 450 Winks Ln., 19020, pg. 336 **PB**
Fire Protection Industries, Inc., 1765 Woodhaven Rd., 19020, pg. 321 **IT**
GILES & RANSOME, INC., 2975 Galloway Rd., 19020, pg. 453 **PV**
Iveco Trucks Of North America Inc., 3433 Progress Dr., 19020, pg. 484 **IT**
Olde English Equine Insurance Agency, Inc., P.O. Box 5017, 19020, pg. 908 **PB**
Orleans Corporation, 3333 Street Rd., 19020, pg. 608 **PB**
Ransome Engine, 2975 Galloway Rd., 19020, pg. 453 **PV**
Ransome Lift, 2975 Galloway Rd., 19020, pg. 453 **PV**
Schutte & Koerting Division, 2233 State Rd., 19020, pg. 604 **PV**
STRATEGIC DISTRIBUTION INC., 3220 Tillman Dr., Ste. 200, 19020, pg. 1523 **PB**
Transilwrap Co. of Philadelphia, 320 Camer Dr., 19020, pg. 1097 **PV**
United General Life Insurance, 3220 Tillman Dr., 19020, pg. 433 **PB**

Berlin

Snyder Berlin, 1313 Stadium Dr., 15530, pg. 887 **PV**

Berwick

Berwick Industries, Inc., P.O. Box 428, Bombay Ln. & Ninth St., 18603, pg. 284 **PB**
DELUXE HOMES OF PA., INC., 499 W. Third St., 18603, pg. 323 **PV**
Raisio, Inc., P.O. Box 347, 18603, pg. 1086 **IT**
Strick Corp., 9th & Oak STS, 18603, pg. 1787 **PB**

Berwyn

AMP Inc. Lytel/Netcom Division, 1000 Westlakes Dr. Ste. 150, 19312-2409, pg. 8 **PB**
BARCLAY WHITE INCORPORATED, 22 Cassatt Ave., 19312, pg. 115 **PV**
CHAPMAN MANAGEMENT GROUP, 1235 W. Lakes Dr., Ste. 260, 19312, pg. 229 **PV**
DEVON DIRECT MARKETING & ADVERTISING, INC., 200 Berwyn Pk., 19312, pg. 329 **PV**
International Rehabilitation Associates, Inc., 1205 Westlakes Dr., Ste. 300, 19312, pg. 362 **PB**
Intracorp Peer Review Organization, Inc., 1205 Westlakes Dr., 19312, pg. 362 **PB**
PQ CORPORATION, 1200 W. Swedesford Rd., 19312-1077, pg. 827 **PV**
Pepper, Hamilton & Scheetz, 1235 Westlakes Dr., Ste. 400, 19312-2401, pg. 851 **PV**
Provident Mutual Life & Annuity Company of America, 1050 West Lake Dr., 19312, pg. 892 **PV**
PROVIDENT MUTUAL LIFE INSURANCE CO., 1050 West Lake Dr., 19312, pg. 891 **PV**
SMS-Philadelphia, 100 Berwyn Pk., 19312, pg. 1463 **PV**
Tokai Financial Services, Inc., 1055 Westlakes Dr., 19312, pg. 1391 **PV**
Total Renal Care, 1180 W. Swedesford Rd., 19312, pg. 1625 **PB**
UNISOURCE WORLDWIDE, INC., 1100 Cassatt Rd., 19312, pg. 1670 **PB**

Bethlehem

ALCOM PRINTING GROUP, INC., 2285 Ave. A, 18017, pg. 33 **PV**
BIEC International Inc., Park Plaza, 3400 Bath Pike, 18017, pg. 226 **IT**
BETHLEHEM STEEL CORPORATION, 1170 8th Ave., 18016-7699, pg. 226 **PB**
Bethlehem Steel-Structural Products Division, 701 E. Third St., 18016, pg. 226 **PB**
Centec Roll Corporation, RR 5 Box 5217, Applebutter Rd., 18015-9538, pg. 839 **PV**
First Valley Corporation, One Bethlehem Plaza, 18018, pg. 1528 **PB**
First Valley Leasing, Inc., One Bethlehem Plaza, 18018, pg. 1528 **PB**
First Valley Life Insurance Company, One Bethlehem Plaza, 18018, pg. 1528 **PB**
Fuller Company, Lehigh Valley Indus. Pk., 2040 Ave. C, 18017-2188, pg. 475 **IT**
Fuller-Kovako Corporation, 3225 Schoenersville Rd., 18016-0805, pg. 475 **IT**

Birdsboro

BEACON CONTAINER CORPORATION, 700 W. First St., 19508, pg. 125 **PV**
F.M. BROWN SONS, INC., P.O. Box 67, Furnace St., 19508, pg. 174 **PV**
Teltron Technologies, Inc., Two Riga Ln., 19508, pg. 1720 **PB**

HDW Electronics, 5897 Colony Dr., 18017, pg. 1070 **IT**
M.A. Hanna Engineered Materials, 177 Micron Rd., 18017, pg. 781 **PB**
Harris Rebar Atlantic, Inc., 1700 Riverside Drive, 18015, pg. 598 **IT**
HYGRADE METAL MOULDING MFG. CORP., 1990 Highland Ave., 18020, pg. 552 **PV**
I-R Equipment Sales, 1495 Valley Center Pkwy., 18017, pg. 876 **PB**
JUST BORN, INC., 1300 Stefko Blvd., 18017, pg. 602 **PV**
Pennsylvania Cellular Telephone Corp., 1655 Valley Center Pkwy., 18017, pg. 1708 **PB**
PIERCING PAGODA, INC., 3910 Adler Pl., 18017, pg. 1296 **PB**
SKF Specialty Products, Lehigh Valley Corp. Center, 1530 Valley Center Pkwy., 18017, pg. 1157 **IT**
SERVICE TIRE TRUCK CENTERS, INC., 2255 Ave. A, 18017, pg. 987 **PV**
Summit Bank, One Bethlehem Plaza, 18018, pg. 1528 **PB**
Technology Systems Corporation, 3400 Bath Pike, Ste. 200, 18017, pg. 1425 **PB**
Willis Corroon Corp. of Penn., 1495 Valley Ctr. Pkwy., 18017, pg. 1506 **IT**

Blandon

Allentown Cement Co. Inc., P.O. Box 619, 19510-0199, pg. 1201 **IT**
Campbell's Fresh, Inc., P.O. Box 169, 19510, pg. 299 **PB**
CAN CORPORATION OF AMERICA, P.O. Box 170, Excelsior Industrial Park, 19510, pg. 204 **PV**
Scancem Industries, Inc., P.O. Box 199, 19510-0199, pg. 1201 **IT**

Bloomsburg

Champion Valley Farms, 6670 Low St., 17815, pg. 806 **PB**
Haleyville Drapery, 7040 New Barwick Hwy., 17815, pg. 491 **PB**
THE MAGEE CARPET COMPANY, 480 W. Fifth St., 17815, pg. 694 **PV**
Unitog Rental Facility, 899 Market St., 17815, pg. 1693 **PB**

Blossburg

WARD MANUFACTURING, INC., 115 Gulick St., 16912, pg. 1149 **PV**

Blue Bell

AVO INTERNATIONAL, 510 Township Line Rd., 19422, pg. 9 **PV**
Alternative Computer Company, 490 Norristown Rd., #50, 19422, pg. 711 **PV**
C&D CHARTER POWER SYSTEMS, 1400 Union Meeting Rd., 19422, pg. 271 **PB**
C & D TECHNOLOGIES, INC., 1400 Union Meeting Rd., 19422, pg. 272 **PB**
Cognos Corp-Philadelphia Sales Office, 1 Sentry Pkwy., Ste. 6000, 19422, pg. 306 **IT**
Corporate Health Administrators, Inc., 980 Jolly Rd, P.O. Box 1109, 19422, pg. 26 **PB**
CRAFTEX MILLS OF PENNSYLVANIA, 450 Sentry Pkwy., 19422-0795, pg. 284 **PV**
Earth Sciences Consultants, Inc. (Ohio Valley Opers.), 490 Norristown Rd., Ste. 250, 19422, pg. 94 **PB**
H & M Mexico, Inc., 985 Jolly Rd., 19422, pg. 522 **PV**
Henkels & McCoy Equipment Co., Inc., Jolly Rd., 19422, pg. 522 **PV**
HENKELS & MCCOY, INC., 985 Jolly Rd., 19422, pg. 522 **PV**
Martin Marietta Stategic Systems, 1787 Sentry Pkwy. W., 19422, pg. 1007 **PB**
PCM Construction, Inc., 985 Jolly Rd., 19422, pg. 522 **PV**
PENNSYLVANIA MANUFACTURERS CORP., The PMA Bldg., 380 Sentry Pkwy., 19422-2328, pg. 1272 **PB**
Selas Fluid Processing Corp., Five Sentry Pkwy. E., Ste. 204, 19422, pg. 811 **PB**
Spectra-Physics USA, Inc., 595 Skippack Pike, Ste. 300, 19422, pg. 1289 **IT**
Symix Systems Inc., 1767 Sentryx Pkwy. W., Ste. 311, 19422, pg. 1547 **IT**
UNISYS CORPORATION, Township Line & Union Meeting Rd., 19424, pg. 1671 **PB**
United States Health Care Systems of Pennsylvania, Inc., 980 Jolly Rd., P.O. Box 1109, 19422, pg. 26 **PB**
U.S. Health Insurance Company, 980 Jolly Rd., P.O. Box 1109, 19422, pg. 26 **PB**
U.S. Healthcare Dental Plan, Inc. (Delaware), 980 Jolly Rd., P.O. Box 1109, 19422, pg. 26 **PB**
U.S. Healthcare Dental Plan, Inc. (New Jersey), 980 Jolly Rd., 19422, pg. 26 **PB**
U.S. Healthcare Dental Plan, Inc. (Pennsylvania), 980 Jolly Rd., P.O. Box 1109, 19422, pg. 26 **PB**
U.S. Healthcare, Inc., 980 Jolly Rd., 19422, pg. 26 **PB**
U.S. Healthcare, Inc. (Delaware), 980 Jolly Rd., P.O. Box 1109, 19422, pg. 26 **PB**
U.S. Healthcare, Inc. (Maryland), 980 Jolly Rd., P.O. Box 1109, 19422, pg. 26 **PB**

PB - *U.S. Public Companies Volume*
PV - *U.S. Private Companies Volume*
IT - *International Public & Private Companies Volume*

U.S. Healthcare Properties, Inc., 980 Jolly Rd., P.O. Box 1109, 19422, pg. 27   **PB**
U.S. Mental Health Systems, Inc., 980 Jolly Rd., 19422, pg. 27   **PB**
United States Physicians Care Systems, Inc., 980 Jolly Rd., P.O. Box 1109, 19422, pg. 27   **PB**
U.S. Quality Algorithms, Inc., 980 Jolly Rd., P.O. Box 1109, 19422, pg. 27   **PB**
Volt Directory Services, One Sentry Pkwy., 19422, pg. 1724   **PB**
Woodward-Clyde, 1400 Union Meeting Rd., Ste. 202, 19422, pg. 1656   **PB**
Yarway Corporation, 480 Norristown Rd., 19422, pg. 1650   **PB**

Blue Ridge Summit

ISP Minerals Inc., Rt. 116, 17214, pg. 858   **PB**

Boalsburg

Nuson Inc., P.O. Box 540, 1020 E. Boal Ave., 16827, pg. 755   **IT**

Boyertown

Electronic Materials & Refractory Metals Div., 300 Holly Rd., 19512, pg. 289   **PB**
Headlamp Facility, Second & Jefferson Sts., 19512, pg. 442   **PB**
NATIONAL PENN BANCSHARES, INC., Philadelphia & Reading Ave., 19512-0547, pg. 1158   **PB**
National Penn Bank, P.O. Box 547, 19512-0547, pg. 1159   **PB**
National Penn Investment Company, P.O. Box 547, 19512, pg. 1159   **PB**
National Penn Life Insurance Company, P.O. Box 547, 19512, pg. 1159   **PB**

Brackenridge

Allegheny Ludlum-Brackenridge, 100 River Rd., 15014, pg. 43   **PB**

Bradford

Bradford Electronic Inc., 550 High St., 16701-0930, pg. 1722   **PB**
W.R. Case & Sons Cutlery Company, Owens Way, 16701, pg. 1207   **PV**
Trico Industries, Inc., 57 Holley Ave., 16701, pg. 1247   **PB**
ZIPPO MANUFACTURING COMPANY, 33 Barbour St., 16701, pg. 1207   **PV**

Breezewood

Frontier Communications of Breezewood, Inc., P.O. Box 303, S. Breezewood Rd., 15533, pg. 683   **PB**

Bridgeville

Consolidated Graphic Communications, 1901 Mayview Rd., 15017, pg. 333   **PB**
Interform Corporation, 1901 Mayview Rd., 15017, pg. 333   **PB**
Ionics, Incorporated, P.O. Box 99, 15017, pg. 912   **PB**
Krupp Wilputte Corp., 1370 Washington Pike, 15017, pg. 512   **IT**
ROKOP CORPORATION, 400 Old Pond Rd., 15017, pg. 941   **PV**

Bristol

Falcon Associates, 416 Green Ln., 19007, pg. 29   **PB**
Ferag Inc., P.O. Box 137, 190 Rittenhouse Cir., 19007-0137, pg. 1484   **IT**
JONES APPAREL GROUP, INC., 250 Rittenhouse Cir., 19007, pg. 933   **PB**
Land Instruments International, Inc., 2525 Pearl Buck Rd., 19007, pg. 798   **IT**
Material Handling Equipment Co., 2501 Durham Rd., 19007, pg. 754   **PV**
MODERN GROUP LTD., 2501 Durham Rd., 19007, pg. 754   **PV**
Modern Handling Equipment Co., 2501 Durham Rd., 19007, pg. 755   **PV**
Moreco Inc., 2501 Durham Rd., 19007, pg. 755   **PV**
Robern, Inc., 7 Wood Ave., 19007, pg. 630   **PV**
Scanforms, Inc., Keystone Park, 181 Rittenhouse Cir., 19007, pg. 228   **PB**
Stokes-Merrill, Two Pearl Buck Court, 19007, pg. 1379   **IT**
Taylor & Francis Philadelphia, 1900 Frost Rd., Ste. 101, 19007, pg. 1358   **IT**
TRIMFIT, INC., 1900 Frost Rd., #111, 19007, pg. 1103   **PV**
Unitog Rental Facility, 420 Howell St., 19007, pg. 1693   **PB**
West Mill Clothes, Tuxedo Accessories Div., Keystone Industrial Park, 257 Rittenhouse Circle, 19007, pg. 1163   **PV**
Y.K.K. (U.S.A.) Inc., 171 Rittenhouse Circle, 19007, pg. 1515   **IT**

Brookville

Brookville Telephone Company, 186 Main St., 15825, pg. 56   **PB**

Broomall

M.A. BRUDER & SONS, INCORPORATED, 600 Reed Rd., 19008, pg. 175   **PV**
Germantown (USA) Co., 505 Parkway Dr., 19008, pg. 555   **IT**
Keeler Instruments Inc., 456 Parkway, 19008, pg. 590   **IT**
PENNSYLVANIA CRUSHER CORP., 600 Abbott Dr., 19008-0100, pg. 850   **PV**
RADIO DIRECT RESPONSE, 630 Parkway, 19008, pg. 906   **PV**

Bryn Mawr

INDEPENDENT PUBLICATIONS, INC., 945 Haverford Rd., 19010-3814, pg. 559   **PV**
Newbold's Asset Management Inc., 950 Haverford Rd., 19010-3845, pg. 1673   **PB**
PSC Services Group, Inc., 762 Lancaster Ave., 19010, pg. 1287   **PB**
PHILADELPHIA SUBURBAN CORPORATION, 762 Lancaster Ave., 19010-3489, pg. 1287   **PB**
Philadelphia Suburban Water Company, 762 Lancaster Ave., 19010, pg. 1287   **PB**
Utility & Municipal Services, Inc., 762 Lancaster Ave., 19010, pg. 1287   **PB**

Burnham

FREEDOM FORGE CORPORATION, 500 N. Walnut St., 17009, pg. 425   **PV**
Standard Steel, 500 N. Walnut St., 17009, pg. 425   **PV**

Bushkill

Resorts USA Inc., P.O. Box 447, Rte. 209, 18324, pg. 1087   **IT**

Butler

AGR INTERNATIONAL, INC., 615 Whitestown Rd., 16001, pg. 5   **PV**
Advocate Services, Inc., P.O. Box 1021, 19 Grant Ave., 16001, pg. 1108   **PV**
Armco Inc.-Butler Opers., 101 Three Degree Rd., 16001, pg. 131   **PB**
Ervin Amasteel Div., 681 E. Butler Rd., 16001, pg. 382   **PV**
Heckett MultiServ, P.O. Box 1071, 612 N. Main St., 16003, pg. 793   **PB**
Magnetics, P.O. Box 391, 16003, pg. 1020   **PV**
T.W. PHILLIPS GAS AND OIL CO., 205 N. Main St., 16001, pg. 862   **PB**
SPANG & COMPANY, 100 Brugh Ave., 16003, pg. 1020   **PV**

Callery

BYRNES & KIEFER COMPANY, 131 Kline Ave., 16024, pg. 191   **PV**
Charlie's Specialties Inc., 131 Kline Ave, 16042, pg. 191   **PV**
Herr-Voss Corp., P.O. Box AB, 130 Main St., 16024, pg. 961   **PV**

Camp Hill

Appleton Papers-Harrisburg, 2850 Appleton, 17011, pg. 567   **IT**
Arnold Transportation Services, 4410 Industrial Park Rd., 17011, pg. 132   **PB**
Clarity Vision, 100 Senate Ave., 17011, pg. 529   **PV**
Consumers Car Care Corporation, 1200 Camp Hill By-Pass, 17011, pg. 438   **PB**
CONSUMERS FINANCIAL CORPORATION, 1200 Camp Hill By-Pass, 17011, pg. 437   **PB**
Consumers Life Insurance Company, 1200 Camp Hill By-Pass, 17001-0026, pg. 438   **PB**
Consumers Reinsurance Company, 1200 Camp Hill By-Pass, 17011, pg. 438   **PB**
Eagle Managed Care, P.O. Box 546, 17001, pg. 1391   **PB**
GANNETT FLEMING AFFILIATES, INC., 207 Senate Ave., 17011, pg. 439   **PV**
Grandview Surgery Center, 205 Grandview Ave., 17011, pg. 803   **PB**
HARSCO CORPORATION, 350 Poplar Church Rd., 17001-8888, pg. 792   **PB**
HEMPT BROTHERS, INC., 205 Creek Rd., 17011, pg. 521   **PV**
Insurer Physician Services Organization, 1800 Center St., 17089, pg. 529   **PV**
Keystone Railway Equipment Company, P.O. Box 456, 3420 Simpson Ferry Rd., 17011, pg. 1711   **PV**
PNC Bank, P.O. Box 8874, 4242 Carlisle Pike, 17011, pg. 1243   **PB**
RITE AID CORPORATION, 30 Hunter Ln., 17011, pg. 1390   **PB**
L.B. SMITH, INC., 2001 State Rd., 17001-0134, pg. 1009   **PV**
Taylor-Wharton Gas Equipment, 1011 Mumma Rd., 17001, pg. 793   **PB**
True Temper Hardware Company, 465 Railroad Ave., 17011, pg. 846   **PB**
United Concordia Companies Inc., 100 Senate Ave., 17011, pg. 529   **PV**

Canonsburg

American Specialty Foods, R.D. #1 Box 216B, 15317, pg. 1107   **PV**
Cegelec AEG Automation Systems Corp., 701 Technology Dr., 15317-9587, pg. 52   **IT**
CENTIMARK CORPORATION, South Pointe, 12 Grandview Cir., 15317, pg. 222   **PV**
Colonial Iron Works, 135 Meadow Ln., 15317, pg. 376   **PV**
Greenery Rehabilitation & Skilled Nursing Center, 2200 Hill Church-Houston Rd., 15317, pg. 839   **PB**
Mobil Chemical Co., 162 Fawn Valley Dr., 15317-2706, pg. 1118   **PB**

Canton

Frontier Communications of Canton, Inc., P.O. Box 216, Four N. Center St., 17724, pg. 683   **PB**

Carbondale

Glass Products, Inc., Clindo Dr., 18407, pg. 84   **IT**
LAUBECK CORPORATION/CROSS, 166 Dundaff St., 18407, pg. 652   **PV**
PIONEER AMERICAN HOLDING COMPANY, 41 N. Main St., 18407, pg. 1298   **PB**

Carlisle

Carlisle SynTec Inc., 1285 Ritner Hwy., 17013, pg. 305   **PB**
DAILY EXPRESS, INC., 1072 Harrisburg Pike, 17013, pg. 307   **PV**
Edwards Super Food Stores, 1149 Harrisburg Pike, 17013, pg. 749   **PB**
Financial Trust Corp., 1415 Ritner Hwy., 17013, pg. 956   **PB**
FROG SWITCH & MANUFACTURING COMPANY, 600 East High St., 17013, pg. 429   **PV**
GS Electric, 1700 Ritner Hwy., 17013, pg. 726   **PB**
Giant Food Stores Inc., 1149 Harrisburg Pike, 17013, pg. 750   **IT**
Land O' Lakes, 405 Park Dr., 17013, pg. 646   **PV**
Masland, 50 Spring Rd., 17013, pg. 981   **PB**
PIEZO CRYSTAL CO., 100 K St., 17013, pg. 865   **PV**
Reeves-Hoffman Div., 400 W. North St., 17013-2248, pg. 286   **PB**
Stoner Associates Inc., P.O. Box 86, 1170 Harrisburg Pike, 17013-0086, pg. 1226   **IT**

Carnegie

Adience Inc., 27 Nobletown Rd., 15106, pg. 58   **PB**
Browning-Ferris Industries of Pennsylvania, Inc., P.O. Box 448, 15106, pg. 264   **PB**
Jani King of Pittsburgh, Inc., 100 W. Mall Plaza, 15106, pg. 582   **PV**
Kraton Fabricators, 530 Bell Ave., 15106, pg. 376   **PV**
MALLET & CO., Arch Street Extension, 15106, pg. 698   **PV**
National Mine Service Company, Distribution Div., Carnegie Office Park, Bldg. 6, 800 N. Bell Ave., Ste. 110, 15106, pg. 281   **IT**
Salem Erectors, Arch St. Ext., 15106, pg. 961   **PV**
Salem Furnace Co., Arch St. Ext., P.O. Box 2222, 15106, pg. 961   **PV**
Salem International Services Inc., Arch St. Extension, 15106, pg. 961   **PV**
Union Electric Steel Corp., P.O. Box 465, 15106, pg. 103   **PB**
Viviano Macaroni Co., 15106, pg. 158   **PV**

Catasauqua

Fuller Company (Catasauqua), Front & Willow Sts., 18032, pg. 475   **IT**
ROCK HILL MATERIALS COMPANY, 339 School St., 18032-1832, pg. 938   **PV**

Centre Hall

Hanover Foods, P.O. Box 193, 16828, pg. 499   **PV**

Chalfont

ANSUTECH, Inc., 500 Horizon Dr., Ste. 505, 18914, pg. 938   **IT**
Comark Communications, Inc., 500 Horizon Dr., Ste. 503, 18914, pg. 1383   **IT**
Material Handling Systems Div., 400 Highpoint Dr., 18914, pg. 605   **PB**

Chambersburg

MARTIN'S FAMOUS PASTRY SHOPPES, 1000 Potato Row Ln., 17201, pg. 710   **PV**
OLIVER OIL COMPANY, INC., 875 S. Main St., 17201, pg. 815   **PV**
Pennsylvania Cellular Telephone Corp., 791 Wayne Ave., 17201, pg. 1708   **PB**
Public Opinion, 77 N. Third St., 17201, pg. 700   **PB**
Quest Diagnostic-Chambersburg, 144 S. Eighth St., 17201, pg. 1351   **PB**
T B Wood's Incorporated, 440 N. Fifth Ave., 17201, pg. 1562   **PB**
TB WOOD'S CORPORATION, 440 N. Fifth Ave., 17201, pg. 1562   **PB**
Value Stationery, Inc., P.O. Box 507, 17201, pg. 89   **PB**

Geographic Index-U.S.

Chester

BALDT, INC., 801 W. 6th St., 19013, pg. 112 **PV**
DEE PAPER COMPANY, Front & Broomall, 19016-0320, pg. 320 **PV**
KeyStone Center, 2001 Providence Rd., 19013, pg. 1697 **PB**
PSG, 3300 W. Fourth St., 19013, pg. 1774 **PB**

Chester Springs

Chester Springs Distribution Point, 55 Pottstown Pike, Ste. 500, 19425, pg. 247 **PV**

Cheswick

A.M. Castle & Co., 491 Nixon Rd., 15024, pg. 313 **PB**
Strick Corp., Russelton Rd., 15024, pg. 1787 **PB**

Chicora

Allegheny Heat Treating, 1024 Kittanning Pike, 16025-2030, pg. 412 **PB**

Clairton

TYK Refractories Co., 301 Brickyard Rd., 15025, pg. 1345 **IT**

Clarendon

Berenfield Containers (CLARENDON), Inc., 31 Railroad St., 16313, pg. 135 **PV**

Clarks Mills

L & N Metallurgiacal Products Co., P.O. Box 111, 16114, pg. 616 **IT**

Clarks Summit

Beloit Manhattan Inc., Ivy Park, P.O. Box 155, 18411, pg. 789 **PB**

Claysburg

Atlantic Homes Div., P.O. Box 343, Off Rte. 220, 16625, pg. 332 **PB**

Clearfield

Crescent Brick-Clearfield Division, P.O. Box 1110, 16830, pg. 924 **PV**
KURTZ BROS., INC., P.O. Box 392, 400 Reed St., 16830, pg. 637 **PV**

Cleona

HAUCK MFG. CO., 100 N. Harris St., 17042, pg. 510 **PV**

Clifton Heights

CAPP, INC., 201 Marple Ave., 19018-0127, pg. 207 **PV**
Servo Components, Broadway and Marple Aves., 19018-2495, pg. 1003 **PV**

Coatesville

Brandywine Valley Railroad Company, 50 First Ave., 19320, pg. 1020 **PV**
Hoppe's A Brunswick Company, Airport Industrial Mall, 19320, pg. 266 **PB**
LI Service Company, 50 S. First Ave., 19320, pg. 1020 **PV**
LUKENS INC., 50 S. First Ave., 19320-0911, pg. 1019 **PB**
Lukens Steel Company, ARC Bldg., Modena Rd., 19320, pg. 1020 **PB**
PENGUIN INDUSTRIES, INC., 116 Quarry Rd., 19320, pg. 849 **PV**
Somat Corporation, 855 Fox Chase, 19320, pg. 1322 **PB**

Collegeville

COLLEGEVILLE FLAG & MFG. COMPANY, 24 W. 4th. Ave., 19426, pg. 252 **PV**
Collegeville/Imagineering L.P., 70 E. 3rd Ave., 19426, pg. 252 **PV**
Dermik Laboratories, Inc., 500 Arcola Rd., 19426, pg. 1110 **IT**
Rahns Specialty Metals, Inc., P.O. Box 990, 19426-0990, pg. 572 **IT**
Rhone-Poulenc Rorer - U.S., 500 Arcola Rd., 19426-0107, pg. 1110 **IT**
Rorer-Inter-American Corp., 500 Arcola Rd., 19426, pg. 1111 **IT**
SUPERIOR TUBE COMPANY, 3900 Germantown Pike, 19426-3112, pg. 1056 **PV**
USV (P.R) Development Corporation, 500 Arcola Rd., P.O. Box 1200, 19426-0107, pg. 1111 **IT**

Colmar

Capital Controls Company Inc., 3000 Advance Ln., 18915, pg. 1226 **IT**
Fichtel & Sachs Industries, Inc., 92 Country Line Rd., 18915, pg. 835 **IT**

New Yorker Boiler Co., Inc., Rte. 309, P.O. Box 184, 18915, pg. 270 **PB**
R&B, INC., 3400 E. Walnut St., 18915-1800, pg. 1354 **PB**
Severn Trent (Del) Inc., 2980 Advance Ln., 18915, pg. 1226 **IT**
Thomeast Inc., P.O. Box 488, Rte. 309 & Advance Ln., 18915, pg. 1384 **IT**

Columbia

COLONIAL METALS CO., 217 Linden St., 17512, pg. 253 **PV**
NCS Document Operations, 3975 Continental Dr., 17512-9779, pg. 1155 **PV**
United States Lock & Hardware Co., 166 Bridge St., 17512, pg. 1196 **PV**

Concordville

Creed Co., P.O. Box 700, 19331, pg. 1145 **PB**
Danco Products, P.O. Box 700, 19331, pg. 1145 **PB**
THE FIBRE-METAL PRODUCTS COMPANY, Baltimore Pike & S. Brenton Lake Rd., 19331, pg. 402 **PV**
Futty & Company, P.O. Box 700, 19331, pg. 1145 **PB**
IA CONSTRUCTION CORP., Rte. 202, P.O. Box 8, 19331, pg. 552 **PV**
Plumbmaster Inc., P.O. Box 700, 19331, pg. 1145 **PB**
SOUTHCO. INC., 210 Brinton Lake Rd., 19331, pg. 1014 **PV**
Southco International, 210 Brinton Lake Rd., 19331, pg. 1015 **PV**
WATKINS SYSTEM INC., Rte. 202, 19331, pg. 1153 **PV**

Conestoga

Safe Harbor Water Power Corp., RD 2, P.O. Box 97, 17516, pg. 172 **PB**
TURKEY HILL DAIRY, INC., 2601 River Rd., 17516, pg. 1109 **PV**

Connellsville

Anchor Hocking, 1840 Baldridge Ave., 15425-5202, pg. 1177 **PB**

Conshohocken

ASBURY AUTOMOTIVE GROUP, One Tower Bridge, Ste. 1440, 19428, pg. 87 **PV**
Badix Systems Inc., Lee Parie, 19428, pg. 1527 **PV**
FINNAREN & HALEY, INC., 901 Washington St., 19428, pg. 405 **PV**
FISHMAN & TOBIN, INC., Bldg. E-3, 625 Ridge Pike, 19428, pg. 408 **PV**
FLORIG EQUIPMENT COMPANY, INC., 906 Ridge Pike, 19428, pg. 415 **PV**
Franklin-Burlington Plastics, Elm & Harry St., 19428, pg. 496 **PB**
Hale Products Inc., 700 Spring Mill Ave., 19428, pg. 862 **PB**
Jani King of Philadelphia, Inc., Bldg. E, Ste. 203, 625 Ridge Pike, 19428, pg. 582 **PV**
LTCB-MAS Investment Management, Inc., One Tower Bridge, Ste. 1000, 19428, pg. 816 **IT**
Miller, Anderson & Sherrerd, 1 Tower Bridge, 19428, pg. 1132 **PB**
QUAKER CHEMICAL CORPORATION, Elm & Lee Sts., 19428-0809, pg. 1346 **PB**
RESCO PRODUCTS, INC., 1302 Conshohocken Rd., 19428, pg. 924 **PV**
RUMSEY ELECTRIC COMPANY, 15 Colwell Ln., 19428, pg. 651 **PV**
Spring Mill Corp., 901 Washington St., 19428, pg. 406 **PV**
U.S. BIOSCIENCE, INC., 1 Tower Bridge, Ste. 400, 19428, pg. 1681 **PB**
Universal Steel of Pennsylvania, 1100 East Hector St., 19428-2374, pg. 256 **PV**
Upper Merion & Plymouth Railroad, Box 404, 19428, pg. 1020 **PB**
Weathe- Barrier Inc., 901 Washington St., 19428, pg. 406 **PV**

Coraopolis

Baker Environmental, Inc., Airport Office Park, Bldg. 3, 420 Rouser Rd., 15108, pg. 168 **PB**
CHEMCENTRAL/Pittsburgh, 3000 Casteel Dr., 15108, pg. 232 **PV**
DQE INC., 500 Cherrington Pkwy., 15108-3193, pg. 474 **PB**
FORT PITT ACQUISITIONS, INC., 400 Chess St., 15108, pg. 419 **PV**
Framesi USA, Inc./Roffler Industries, Inc./Casa di Colore, Inc., 400 Chess St., 15108, pg. 419 **PV**
Italimpianti of America, Incorporated, Airport Office Park, Rouser Road, Bldg. 4, 15108, pg. 655 **IT**
Mannesmann Demag Wean Company, 345 Rouser Rd., 15108, pg. 837 **IT**
RPS Inc., 1000 RPS Dr., 15108, pg. 604 **PB**

Cornwells Heights

Philips Consumer Electronics, 3599 Meadow Ln., 19020, pg. 1055 **IT**

Corry

Associated Spring, 226 S. Center St., 16407, pg. 190 **PB**

Associated Spring-Raymond, 380 Sciota St., 16407, pg. 190 **PB**
CorryHiebert Corporation, 844 E. Columbus Ave., 16407, pg. 772 **PB**
ERIE PLASTICS, One Plastics Rd., 16407, pg. 381 **PV**
MCINNES STEEL COMPANY, 441 E. Main St., 16407, pg. 722 **PV**
Raymond Merchandise, 380 Sciota St., 16407, pg. 190 **PB**

Cressona

Alumax Extrusions, Inc., P.O. Box 187, 53 Pottsville St., 17929-0187, pg. 60 **PB**

Croydon

Aydin Electro-Fab Div., 960 River Rd., 19020, pg. 158 **PB**
PHILADELPHIA RESERVE SUPPLY COMPANY, 400 Mack Dr., 19021, pg. 861 **PV**

Curwensville

HOWES LEATHER CORPORATION, 101 Meadow St., 16833, pg. 543 **PV**

Dallas

Commonwealth Telephone Co., P.O. Box 800, Rte. 309, 18612, pg. 415 **PB**
COMMONWEALTH TELEPHONE ENTERPRISES, INC., 100 CTE Dr., 18612, pg. 415 **PB**
Offset Paperback Mfrs. (BPMC), Rt. 309, 18612, pg. 191 **IT**

Danboro

PENN ENGINEERING & MANUFACTURING CORP., Old Easton Rd., 18916, pg. 1269 **PB**

Danville

Kennedy Van Saun Corp., Two Beaver St., 17821, pg. 1326 **IT**
Montour Bank, 1519 Bloom Rd., 17821, pg. 1222 **PB**
Valve Division, 601 E. Market St., 17821-2135, pg. 1559 **PB**

Darlington

Pittsburgh Tube Darlington Div., 305 Cannelton Rd., 16115, pg. 868 **PV**

Delano

The Ohio Mattress Company Licensing & Components Group, Majic Industrial Park, 18220, pg. 979 **PV**

Delaware Water Gap

Heico Chemicals, Inc., Rte. 611 N., Box 160, 18327, pg. 297 **PB**
INSTRUMENT SPECIALTIES COMPANY, Shielding Way, 18327-0136, pg. 565 **PV**
Shawnee Press, Inc., One Waring Dr., 18327-1099, pg. 768 **PV**

Delmont

Menasha Corp., POLY Hi Solidur, 200 Industrial Dr., 15626-1015, pg. 731 **PV**

Denver

Covance Research Products, Inc., P.O. Box 7200, 17517, pg. 454 **PB**
KALAS MANUFACTURING, INC., 25 Main St., 17517, pg. 606 **PV**
Quinlan Pretzel Co., Inc., 3rd & Washington Sts., 17517, pg. 158 **PV**
SUNLINE COACH CO., INC., 245 S. Muddy Creek Rd., 17517, pg. 1053 **PV**

Devault

DEVAULT FOODS, One Devault Ln., 19432, pg. 329 **PV**

Devon

G.E. Capital Modular Space, 426 W. Lancaster Ave., 19333, pg. 712 **PB**

Dillsburg

Capitol Engineering, P.O. Box 445, 124 W. Church St., 17019-0445, pg. 329 **PV**

Douglassville

AMERICAN CRANE & EQUIPMENT CORP., 531 Old Swede Rd., 19518, pg. 52 **PV**
Kiwi Brands, 447 Old Swede Rd., 19518-1239, pg. 1433 **PB**
STV Architects, 205 W. Welsh Dr., 19518, pg. 1421 **PB**
STV Construction Services, 205 W. Welsh Dr., 19518, pg. 1421 **PB**

PB - *U.S. Public Companies Volume*
PV - *U.S. Private Companies Volume*
IT - *International Public & Private Companies Volume*

Geographic Index-U.S.

STV Environmental, 205 W. Welsh Dr., 19518, pg. 1421 **PB**
STV GROUP, INC., 205 W. Welsh Dr., 19518, pg. 1421 **PB**

Downingtown

Paragon Inc., 275 W. Uwehlen Ave., 19335, pg. 1771 **PB**
Reynolds Metals Company-Downingtown, 520 Maple Ave., 19335, pg. 1385 **PB**
SOFTMART, INC., 450 Acorn Ln., 19335, pg. 1012 **PV**

Doylestown

Anthony and Sylvan Pools Corporation, Route 611, 18901, pg. 593 **PB**
DVI, INC., 500 Hyde Park, 18901, pg. 476 **PB**
International Exploration, Inc., 212 N. Main St., 18901, pg. 546 **PB**
TRIBORO ELECTRIC CO., 260 N. Broad St., 18901, pg. 1102 **PV**

Dresher

SELAS CORPORATION OF AMERICA, 2034 Limekiln Pike, 19025, pg. 1454 **PB**

Drums

EASTERN ENVIRONMENTAL SERVICES, INC., Rte. 309 N., 18222, pg. 549 **PB**

Du Bois

McDowell Mfg. Co. Inc., P.O. Box 665, 15801, pg. 300 **PV**
Pennway Express, Inc., Shaffer Rd. & Rt. 255, 15801, pg. 1271 **PB**

Dunmore

GERTRUDE HAWK CHOCOLATES, INC., Nine Keystone Pk., 18512-1538, pg. 449 **PV**

Duryea

Schott Glass Technologies, Inc., 400 York Ave., 18642, pg. 1523 **IT**

East Butler

Castle Rubber Co., W. Tenth St., 16029, pg. 1258 **PB**
Home & Garden Show Place, One Servistar Way, 16003, pg. 1108 **PV**
Taylor Rental, One Servistar Way, 16029, pg. 1108 **PV**
TruServ Lumberyards/Home Centers, One Servistar Way, 16003, pg. 1108 **PV**

East Earl

CONESTOGA WOOD SPECIALTIES CORP., 245 Reading Rd., 17519, pg. 262 **PV**

East Greenville

Brown Printing East, P.O. Box 5, 18041, pg. 190 **IT**
Knoll Intl., Inc., 1235 Water St., 18041, pg. 627 **PV**

East Stroudsburg

Carbon Products Operation Inc., 100 Stokes Ave., 18301, pg. 891 **IT**
Hayward Laboratories, 18301, pg. 175 **PV**
Imperial Cosmetics, 855 Crowe Rd., 18301, pg. 239 **IT**
Mack Printing Group (East Stroudsburg Div.), 34 N. Crystal St., 18301, pg. 692 **PV**
Pocono Fabricators, 100 Burson St., 18301, pg. 793 **PB**

East Texas

Day-Timers, Inc., 1 Willow Lane, P.O. Box 67, 18046, pg. 674 **PB**

Easton

Berenfield Containers (NORTHEAST), Inc., Seven McFadden Rd., 18042, pg. 135 **PV**
THE BETHLEHEM CORPORATION, 25th & Lennox Sts., 18045, pg. 225 **PB**
Bethlehem Intl. Sales Corp., P.O. Box 348, 18044, pg. 226 **PV**
Binney & Smith Inc., 1100 Church Lane, 18042, pg. 496 **PV**
Crayola Products Div., 1100 Church Ln., 18044, pg. 496 **PV**
Hallmark Art Products & International Div., PO Box 431, 1100 Church Ln., 18044, pg. 496 **PV**
Hallmark Educational Products Div., 1100 Church Lane, 18044, pg. 496 **PV**
Harvel Plastics, Inc., P.O. Box 757, 18042, pg. 502 **PB**
International Women's Apparel Group, P.O. Box 469, 18044, pg. 796 **PB**
Laneco Inc., 3747 Hecktown Rd., 18043-3234, pg. 1541 **PB**
MACK PRINTING COMPANY, 1991 Northampton St., 18042, pg. 691 **PV**
SI/Baker, Inc., 600 Kuebler Rd., 18040, pg. 1418 **PB**

SI HANDLING SYSTEMS, INC., 600 Kuebler Rd., 18040, pg. 1418 **PB**
VICTAULIC COMPANY OF AMERICA, 4901 Kesslersville Rd., 18040, pg. 1138 **PV**
Victaulic Fire Safety Company LLC, P.O.Box 31, 18044-0031, pg. 1138 **PV**
Victaulic International, 4901 Kesslerville Rd., 18042, pg. 1138 **PV**
Victaulic Tool Company, P.O. Box 31, 1326 Tatamy Rd., 18042, pg. 1138 **PV**

Ebensburg

L. ROBERT KIMBALL & ASSOCIATES, 615 W. Highland Ave., 15931, pg. 619 **PV**
Pennsylvania Mines Corp., P.O. Box 367, 15931, pg. 1244 **PB**
Rushton Mining Co., P.O. Box 367, 15931, pg. 1244 **PB**

Eddystone

Fresh World, 630 Baldwin Twr., 19022, pg. 454 **IT**
WEFA, Inc., 800 Baldwin Tower, 19022, pg. 1325 **PB**

Edwardsville

Jewelcor Travel Services, Inc., Gateway Shopping Center, 18704, pg. 587 **PV**

Eighty Four

84 LUMBER COMPANY, Rte. 519, 15330, pg. 366 **PV**

Elizabeth

Twin Rivers Towing Co., Box 387, 15037, pg. 531 **PB**

Elizabethtown

Fleetwood Homes of Pennsylvania, Inc.-Elizabethtown, P.O. Box 530, Industrial Rd., 17022, pg. 651 **PB**

Ellwood City

Ellwood City Forge, Commercial Ave., 16117, pg. 373 **PV**
ELLWOOD GROUP, INC., Commercial Ave., 16117, pg. 373 **PV**
Emess Lighting Inc., One Early St., 16117, pg. 453 **IT**
The International Metals Reclamation Company, Inc., U.S. Steel Industrial Pk., Rte. 488, 16117, pg. 672 **IT**

Emlenton

Grafo Colloids Division, 105 Eighth St., 16373, pg. 518 **IT**

Emmaus

RODALE PRESS, INC., 33 E. Minor St., 18098, pg. 939 **PV**
Simon-Atlantico Inc., Colebrook Ave., 18049, pg. 1252 **IT**

Emporium

American Centered Technologies, P.O. Box 149, 15834, pg. 612 **PB**
MALLERY LUMBER CORP., HC3, Box #1, 15834, pg. 698 **PV**

Enola

AMALGAMATED AUTOMOTIVE INDUSTRIES, INC., 125 N. Enola Dr., Ste. 208, 17025, pg. 48 **PV**

Ephrata

L.B. Foster Company-Ephrata Plant, 440 Wenger Dr., 17522, pg. 676 **PB**
HAMILTON EQUIPMENT, INC., 567 S. Reading Rd., 17522, pg. 497 **PV**
Mack Printing Group (Ephrata Div.), 300 W. Chestnut, 17522, pg. 692 **PV**
Simon Ladder Towers Inc., 64 Cocalico Creek Rd., 17522, pg. 1252 **IT**

Erie

Autoclave Engineers, 2930 W. 22nd. St., 16506, pg. 1010 **PV**
Bay City Forge Operations, 1802 Cranberry St., 16514, pg. 1794 **PB**
CDA Distributors, 900 State St., 16501, pg. 903 **PB**
Cast Metals Operations, 1301 Raspberry St., 16514, pg. 1794 **PB**
EFCO INC., 1253 W. 12th St., 16512, pg. 353 **PV**
Erie Bronze & Aluminum Co., 6300 W. Ridge Rd., 16505, pg. 722 **PV**
Erie Coca-Cola Bottling Company, 2209 West 50th St., 16506, pg. 393 **PB**
ERIE FAMILY LIFE INSURANCE COMPANY, 100 Erie Insurance Pl., 16530, pg. 590 **PB**
Erie Indemnity Company, 100 Erie Insurance Place, 16530, pg. 591 **PB**
Erie Insurance Exchange, 100 Erie Insurance Place, 16530, pg. 591 **PB**
Erie Insurance Group, 100 Erie Insurance Pl., 16530, pg. 591 **PB**
Erie Press Systems, 1253 W. 12th, 16512, pg. 353 **PV**

ERIEZ MAGNETICS, 220 Ashbury Rd., 16506, pg. 381 **PV**
FMC-Smith Meter Co., 1602 Wagner Ave., 16514, pg. 605 **PV**
Flagship City Insurance Company, 100 Erie Insurance Pl., 16530, pg. 591 **PB**
Kold Draft, 1525 E. Lake Rd., 16511-1031, pg. 1117 **PV**
Lord Corp., Industrial Adhesives & Coatings Div., 2000 W. Grandview Blvd., 16509, pg. 676 **PV**
Marketing & Project Development, One Zurn Pl., 16514-2000, pg. 1794 **PB**
Master Mold, 3230 W. 22nd St., 16586, pg. 870 **PV**
McInnes Rolled Rings, 1533 E. 12th St., 16511, pg. 722 **PV**
Mellon Bank, N.A.-Northern Region, 1128 State St., 16501, pg. 1085 **PB**
MORRIS COUPLING CO., 2240 W. 15th St., 16505, pg. 762 **PV**
National Fuel Gas Supply Corp., 1100 State St., 16512, pg. 1156 **PB**
PNC Bank, 717 State St., 16566, pg. 1243 **PB**
PNC Bank, P.O. Box 8480, 901 State St., 16553, pg. 1243 **PB**
PNC Bank Mortgage Center, Sumner E. Nichols Bldg., 155 W. Eighth St., Ste. 316, 16501, pg. 1243 **PB**
Penn Erie Div., 2315 W. 23rd. St., 16506, pg. 870 **PV**
Pioneer Tool & Mold, Inc., 3001 W. 15th St., 16586, pg. 870 **PV**
PLASTEK GROUP, 2425 W. 23rd. St., 16506, pg. 870 **PV**
Plastek Industries, Inc., 2425 W. 23rd St., 165086, pg. 870 **PV**
Presque Isle Insurance Div., 3910 Caughey Rd., Ste 200, 18506, pg. 215 **PB**
RENT-WAY, INC., 3230 W. Lake Rd., 16505, pg. 1377 **PB**
SNAP-TITE, INC., 2930 W. 22nd St., 16506, pg. 1010 **PV**
Spectrum Control, Connecting Devices Div., 6000 W. Ridge Rd., 16506, pg. 1497 **PB**
SPECTRUM CONTROL, INC., 6000 W. Ridge Rd., 16506, pg. 1497 **PB**
Spectrum Molding, 2425 W. 23rd St., 16586, pg. 870 **PV**
Triangle Tool Co., 3230 W. 22nd St., 16586, pg. 870 **PV**
UNIFLOW MANUFACTURING CO., 1525 E. Lake Rd., 16511, pg. 1117 **PV**
Zurn Drainage and Control Systems Ltd., One Zurn Pl., 16514, pg. 1795 **PB**
ZURN INDUSTRIES, INC., One Zurn Pl., 16514-2000, pg. 1794 **PB**
Zurn Plumbing Products Group, One Zurn Pl., 16514, pg. 1794 **PB**

Etters

BERG Electronics Group, Inc., 825 Old Trail Rd., 17319, pg. 213 **PB**

Evans City

Butler Auto Auction, 21095 Rte. 19 N., 16033, pg. 282 **PV**

Exeter

PRIDE HEALTH CARE, INC., 182 Susquehanna Ave., 18643, pg. 883 **PV**

Export

AWS Remediation, Inc., One Triangle Dr., 15632, pg. 94 **PB**
Advanced Metallurgy, Inc., Murray Corp. Park, 1003 Corporate Dr., 15632, pg. 1564 **PB**
ALLTEL Answering Service, Inc., P.O. Box E, Old William Penn Hwy., 15632, pg. 55 **PB**
Alltel Pennsylvania, Inc., 4792 Old William Penn Hwy., P.O. Box E, 15632, pg. 56 **PB**
Antech Ltd., One Triangle Dr., 15632, pg. 94 **PB**
Earth Sciences Consultants, Inc., One Triangle Dr., 15632, pg. 94 **PB**
Fulmer Company, Inc., Westmoreland Industrial Park 3, 3004 Venture Ct., 15632, pg. 891 **IT**
Oliver Rubber Co., White Valley Industrial Park, #2 Burland Rd., 15632, pg. 1504 **PV**

Exton

ALstrip East, One Tabas Ln., 19341, pg. 43 **PB**
Bell Atlantic TeleProducts Corp., 456 Creamery Way, 19341, pg. 203 **PB**
BENTLEY SYSTEMS, INC., 690 Pennsylvania Ave., 19341, pg. 134 **PB**
CHEMICAL LEAMAN CORPORATION, 102 Pickering Way, 19341, pg. 233 **PV**
Chemical Leaman Tank Lines, Inc., 102 Pickering Way, 19341-0200, pg. 233 **PV**
Chemical Properties, Inc., 102 Pickering Way, 19341, pg. 233 **PV**
Comprehensive Benefits Service Co., Inc., 740 E. Lancaster Pike, Ste. 200, 19341-2856, pg. 635 **PV**
ERM-EnviroClean, 855 Springdale Dr., 19341, pg. 379 **PB**
ENVIRONMENTAL RESOURCES MANAGEMENT, 855 Springdale Dr., 19341, pg. 378 **PV**
EnviroPower, 102 Pickering Way, 19341, pg. 233 **PV**
Exton Square, Inc., 100 Exton Sq., P.O. Box 325, 19341, pg. 1407 **PB**
INTELLIGENT ELECTRONICS, INC., 411 Eagleview Blvd., 19341, pg. 887 **PB**
International Envelope Company, 2 Tabas Ln., 19341-2753, pg. 70 **PB**
Axel Johnson Ore & Metals, Inc., 215 Welsh Pool Rd., 19341, pg. 710 **IT**

NTH Consultants, Ltd., 860 Springdale Dr., 19341,
pg. 772 **PV**
NETZSCH INCORPORATED, 119 Pickering Way, 19341-
1393, pg. 792 **PV**
Power Purchasing, Inc., 102 Pickering Way, 19341-0200,
pg. 233 **PB**
Quala Systems, Inc., 102 Pickering Way, 19341-0200,
pg. 233 **PV**
The Suburban Advertiser, 315 E. Lancaster Pike, 19341,
pg. 935 **PB**
Tank Service Co., 102 Pickering Way., 19341, pg. 233 **PB**
Therakos, Inc., 437 Creamery Way, 19341, pg. 929 **PB**
WOLFINGTON BODY COMPANY, P.O. Box 218, 19341,
pg. 1186 **PV**
XL Connect, 411 Eagleview Blvd., 19341, pg. 888 **PB**

Eynon

CASKET SHELLS, INC., 432 First St., 18403, pg. 218 **PV**

Fairfield

Quebecor Printing Fairfield Inc., P.O. Box 717, 100 N. Miller
St., 17320, pg. 1076 **IT**

Fairless Hills

A.M. Castle & Co., 299 Canal Rd., 19030, pg. 313 **PB**
General Felt, Fairless Hills, 259 Canal Rd., 19030,
pg. 1094 **PV**
Laclede - Fairless Branch, Fairless Works, 19030,
pg. 974 **PB**
Strick Lease, Inc., 225 Lincoln Hwy., 19030, pg. 1787 **PB**

Fairview

PHB DIE CASTING, 7900 W. Ridge Rd., 16415,
pg. 826 **PV**
PHB Machining Division, 1850 W. Ridge Rd., 16415,
pg. 826 **PV**
PHB Plastic & Rubber Molding Division, 8152 W. Ridge
Rd., 16415, pg. 826 **PV**
Spectrum Control, Filter Products Group, 8061 Avonia Rd.,
16415, pg. 1497 **PB**

Fallsington

Tri-Lite Plastics, Inc., Seven Headley Pl., 19054,
pg. 233 **IT**

Felton

Key Plastics, Inc., P.O. Box 160, 17322-0160, pg. 618 **PV**

Fleetwood

C. ROHER INC., 18 W. Poplar St., 19522, pg. 940 **PV**

Folcroft

Dayton Superior Corp., 3 Horne Dr., 19032, pg. 932 **PB**
Union-Transport Corporation-Philadelphia Office, 1600
Delmar Dr., 19032, pg. 1120 **PV**

Ford City

Eljer Industries, 1301 Eljer Way, 16226, pg. 1795 **PB**

Fort Littleton

JLG Industries, Inc., Route 522, 17223, pg. 918 **PB**

Fort Washington

Advanta Mortgage Corp. USA, 500 Office Center Dr., Ste.
400, 19034, pg. 22 **PB**
Aydin Controls Div., 414 Commerce Dr., 19034,
pg. 158 **PB**
Berdel, Inc., 455 Pennsylvania Ave., 19034, pg. 1272 **PB**
Berfia, Inc., 455 Pennsylvania Ave., 19034, pg. 1272 **PB**
Burren, Inc., 455 Pennsylvania Ave., 19034, pg. 1272 **PB**
Connectware, Inc. LLC, Valley Green Corp. Center, 7111
Valley Green Rd., 19034, pg. 8 **PB**
COTTMAN TRANSMISSION SYSTEMS, INC., 240 New
York Dr., 19034, pg. 278 **PV**
The GMR Group, 1300 Virginia Dr., Ste. 210, 19034,
pg. 1224 **PB**
Honeywell, Inc., 1100 Virginia Dr., 19034-3260, pg. 834 **PB**
Larmes, Inc., 455 Pennsylvania Ave., 19034, pg. 1272 **PB**
McNeil Consumer Products Company, 7050 Camp Hill Rd.,
19034-2292, pg. 928 **PB**
PENNSYLVANIA REAL ESTATE INVESTMENT TRUST,
455 Pennsylvania Ave., Ste. 135, 19034, pg. 1272 **PB**
Pilling Weck, 420 Delaware Dr., 19034, pg. 1569 **PB**
Polyphase Instruments Co., 175 Commerce Dr., 19034,
pg. 1315 **PB**
PRIME BANCORP, INC., 7111 Valley Green Rd., 19034,
pg. 1326 **PB**
RA, Inc., 455 Pennsylvania Ave., 19034, pg. 1272 **PB**
SAFEGUARD BUSINESS SYSTEMS, INC., 455 Maryland
Dr., 19034, pg. 960 **PB**
Safeguard Financial Corp., 455 Maryland Dr., 19034,
pg. 960 **PV**
Sumitomo Machinery Corporation of America, 501 Office
Center Dr., Ste. 260, 19034, pg. 1314 **IT**

Forty Fort

40 FORT EYE ASSOCIATES, One Arlington Rd., 18704,
pg. 420 **PV**
Harte-Hanks Direct Marketing/Pennsylvania, 900 Rutter
Ave., 18704-4906, pg. 794 **PB**
VIVIAN MILLWORKS, 61 Elizabeth St., 18704,
pg. 1143 **PV**

Fountainville

BRT Corporation, 5525 Swamp Rd., 18923, pg. 1246 **PB**

Franklin

Corrugated Products Division, P.O. Box 395, State Rte. 8 &
62, 16343, pg. 763 **PB**
Mining Machinery Group, 120 Liberty St., 16323,
pg. 789 **PB**

Franklin Center

The Franklin Mint, U.S. Rte. One, 19091, pg. 941 **PV**

Frazer

AMERICAN SWEETNERS, INC., 11 Lee Blvd., 19355,
pg. 63 **PV**
Bell Atlantic Customer Services International, Inc., 50 E.
Swedesford Rd., 19355, pg. 202 **PB**
Bell Atlantic Software and Systems Solutions, 50 E.
Swedesford Rd., 19355, pg. 203 **PB**
ESSEX GRAIN PRODUCTS, INC., Nine Lee Blvd., 19355,
pg. 383 **PV**
National Liberty Corporation, Liberty Park, 20 Moores Rd.,
19355, pg. 26 **IT**
Norwood Industries, Inc., 57 Morehall Rd., 19355,
pg. 987 **PV**
Westcode Inc., 90 Great Valley Pkwy., 19355, pg. 127 **IT**

Fredericksburg

FARMER'S PRIDE, INC., W. Main St., 17026, pg. 395 **PV**

Freeland

Garland Commercial Industries, Inc., 185 E. South St.,
18224, pg. 188 **IT**

Freeport

Independent Tool & Die, Silverville Rd., 16229, pg. 810 **PV**
Oberg Carbide Punch & Die, Oberg Dr., 16229,
pg. 810 **PV**
OBERG INDUSTRIES CORP., P.O. Box 368, Silverville Rd.,
16229-0315, pg. 810 **PV**
Oberg Mfg. Co., Silverville Rd., 16229, pg. 810 **PV**

Gettysburg

Dal Keystone, 211 N. Fourth St., 17325-1604, pg. 308 **PV**
Herff Jones Yearbooks, 525 Boyds School Rd., 17325-
8015, pg. 524 **PV**

Gibsonia

United Sciences Inc., 5310 N. Pioneer Rd., 15044,
pg. 208 **IT**

Gilbertsville

Eclipse Combustion, Inc., 112 Martin Ave., 19525,
pg. 360 **PV**

Girard

Morlite, 321 Mechanic St., 16417, pg. 821 **IT**
PHB Tool & Die, 711 Beaver St., 16417, pg. 826 **PV**

Glassport

Olympic Mill Services, 12 Monongahela Ave., 15045,
pg. 1108 **PV**
TUBE CITY INC., 12 Monongahela Ave., 15045,
pg. 1108 **PV**

Glen Rock

AMP Inc. Lytel Division, P.O. Box 382, RT 2 Hwy. 616 N.,
17327-9585, pg. 8 **PB**
Adhesive Research, Inc., P.O. Box 100, 17327,
pg. 1091 **PV**
Stewart Connector Systems, Inc., R.D.2, P.O. Box 2020,
17327, pg. 881 **PB**

Glenolden

American Tech Manufacturing Corporation, P.O. Box 93,
322 Oak Lane, 19036-0093, pg. 590 **IT**
Vickers Tedeco Div., 24 E. Glenolden Ave., 19036-2107,
pg. 25 **PB**

Glenshaw

Glenshaw Glass Co. Inc., 1101 William Flinn Hwy., 15116,
pg. 457 **PV**

Goodville

Rutt Custom Cabinetry, P.O. Box 129, 17528, pg. 507 **PV**

Greencastle

Citizens National Bank of Southern Pennsylvania, 35 N.
Carlisle St., 17225, pg. 1542 **PB**
Jerr-Dan Corporation, 1080 Hykes Rd., 17225, pg. 537 **PB**

Greensburg

Allegheny Pittsburgh Coal Co., Cabin Hill, 15601,
pg. 42 **PB**
Greengate Mall, Inc., 1300 Greengate Mall, Lincoln Hwy.,
15601, pg. 1407 **PB**
Old Republic Insurance Co., P.O. Box 789, 15601,
pg. 1218 **PB**
OVERLY MANUFACTURING CO., 574 W. Otterman St.,
15601, pg. 823 **PV**
Quest Diagnostic-Greensburg, Central Medical Arts Bldg.,
Old Rte. 30, 15601, pg. 1351 **PB**
Southwest National Bank of Pennsylvania, P.O. Box 760,
15601, pg. 1493 **PB**
SOUTHWEST NATIONAL CORPORATION, P.O. Box 760,
15601, pg. 1493 **PB**
SULCUS COMPUTER CORP., Sulcus Ctr., 41 N. Main St.,
15601, pg. 1527 **PB**
Sulcus Investment Corp., 41 N. Main St., 15601,
pg. 1527 **PB**
Sulcus Law Management Services, Inc., 41 N. Main St.,
Ste. 201, 15601, pg. 1527 **PB**
Sunrise Leasing Corporation, 231 S. Main St., Ste. 304,
15601, pg. 1535 **PB**
TRIBUNE REVIEW PUBLISHING CO., 622 Cabin Hill Dr.,
15601, pg. 1102 **PV**
West Penn Power Co., 800 Cabin Hill Dr., 15601,
pg. 42 **PB**

Greenville

Damascus Bishop Tube Co., 795 Reynolds Industrial Park
Rd., 16125, pg. 842 **IT**
Greenville Tube Co., 316 Hadley Rd., 16125, pg. 336 **PB**
KNOLL, INC., 1235 Water St., 18041, pg. 627 **PV**
Neward Paperboard Products Mercer Div., P.O. Box 29,
Arlington Dr., 16125, pg. 796 **PV**

Grove City

CaliTek Corporation, 900 Liberty St., 16127, pg. 967 **PV**
Ivex Packaging Corporation-Grove City, P.O. Box 1128, 660
Barkeyville Rd., 16127, pg. 915 **PB**
SATEC SYSTEMS INC., 900 Liberty St., 16127,
pg. 967 **PV**

Gulph Mills

Henkel Corporation Fine Chemicals Div., 2200 Renaissance
Blvd., Ste. 200, 19406, pg. 610 **IT**

Hamburg

Hood & Company, P.O. Box 485, 19526, pg. 572 **IT**
Pennsylvania Steel Foundry & Machine Company, Third &
Arch Sts., 19526-0128, pg. 142 **PB**
Quest Diagnostic-Hamburg, c/o Laurel Living Ctr., RD3,
Box 3835, 19526, pg. 1351 **PB**
Wenco Inc., P.O. Box 455, 19526-0455, pg. 1754 **PB**

Hanover

ESAB Consumables, P.O. Box 517, 801 Wilson Ave.,
17331, pg. 281 **IT**
The Esab Group, Inc., P.O. Box 517, 801 Wilson Ave.,
17331, pg. 281 **IT**
ESAB Welding & Cutting Products, 801 Wilson Ave., 17331,
pg. 281 **IT**
Hanover Direct Pennsylvania, Inc., 340 Poplar St., 17331,
pg. 782 **PB**
HANOVER FOODS CORPORATION, P.O. Box 334, 17331,
pg. 499 **PV**
Hanover Shoe Co., 240 Kindig Ln., 17331, pg. 297 **IT**
Hanover Wire Cloth, 500 E. Middle St., 17331, pg. 193 **PV**
Miller Chemical & Fertilizer Corp., Radio Rd., 17331,
pg. 33 **PV**
THE SHERIDAN GROUP, 450 Fame Ave., 17331,
pg. 993 **PV**
The Sheridan Press, Inc., Fame Ave., 17331, pg. 993 **PV**
SNYDER'S OF HANOVER, INC., 555 Centennial Ave.,
17331, pg. 1011 **PV**
UTZ QUALITY FOODS, INC., P.O. Box 338, 17331,
pg. 1130 **PV**

Harleysville

HARLEYSVILLE GROUP, 355 Maple Ave., 19438-2297,
pg. 786 **PB**
Harleysville Life Insurance Co., 355 Maple Ave., 19438-
2297, pg. 787 **PB**
Harleysville Mutual Insurance, 355 Maple Ave., 19438-2297,
pg. 787 **PB**

PB - *U.S. Public Companies Volume*
PV - *U.S. Private Companies Volume*
IT - *International Public & Private Companies Volume*

1404

Harleysville Services Inc, 355 Maple Ave., 19438, pg. 787 **PB**
Huron Insurance Co., 335 Maple Ave., 19438-2297, pg. 787 **PB**
Mainland Insurance Co., 355 Maple Ave., 19438, pg. 787 **PB**
MET-PRO CORPORATION, 160 Cassell Rd., 19438, pg. 1100 **PB**
Mid-America Insurance Co., 355 Maple Ave., 19438-2297, pg. 787 **PB**
Pennland Insurance Co., 355 Maple Ave., 19438-2297, pg. 787 **PB**
The Pittman Company, 343 Godshall Dr., 19438, pg. 1270 **PB**
Strobic Air Corp., 160 Cassell Rd., 19438, pg. 1100 **PB**

Harmony

Deaktor/Sysco Food Services Co., One Whitney Dr., 16037, pg. 1551 **PB**

Harrisburg

AMP Automotive/Consumer Div., P.O. Box 3608, 17105, pg. 7 **PB**
AMP Capital Goods, P.O. Box 3608, 17105, pg. 7 **PB**
AMP Distributor Marketing Div., P.O. Box 3608, 17105, pg. 7 **PB**
AMP INCORPORATED, 470 Friendship Rd., 17111, pg. 7 **PB**
AMP Industrial Div., P.O. Box 3608, 17105, pg. 7 **PB**
CLEVELAND BROTHERS EQUIPMENT CO., INC., 5300 Paxton St., 17111, pg. 245 **PV**
D&H DISTRIBUTING COMPANY, 2525 N. Seventh St., 17110, pg. 300 **PV**
Dauphin Deposit Bank and Trust Company, 213 Market St., 17101, pg. 64 **IT**
Dayton Parts, Inc., P.O. Box 5795, 3500 Industrial Rd., 17110, pg. 919 **PB**
ESL, Inc., P.O. Box 2361, 17105, pg. 850 **PV**
Eastern Industries, 635 Lucknow Rd., 17110, pg. 1028 **PV**
Ganflec Corporation, P.O. Box 67100, 17106-7100, pg. 439 **PV**
Gannett Fleming, Inc., P.O. Box 67100, 17106-7100, pg. 439 **PV**
Gannett Fleming Investment Corporation, P.O. Box 67100, 17106-7100, pg. 439 **PV**
Gannett Fleming Valuation and Rate Consultants, Inc., P.O. Box 67100, 17106-7100, pg. 439 **PV**
Harrisburg Stamp Co., 2741 Paxton St., 17111, pg. 59 **PV**
Harrisburg Television, Inc, 3235 Hoffman St., 17110, pg. 854 **PV**
HealthAmerica of Central Pennsylvania, 2601 Market Pl., 17110-9339, pg. 454 **PB**
HERSHEY CREAMERY COMPANY, 301 S. Cameron, 17101, pg. 524 **PB**
Hewlett-Packard Company, Heatherwood Industrial Pk., 50 Dorchester Rd., 17112-0080, pg. 815 **PB**
Inservco Insurance Services, Inc., P.O. Box 2361, 17105, pg. 850 **PV**
KEYSTONE FINANCIAL INC., One Keystone Plaza, Front & Market St., 17105-3660, pg. 956 **PB**
Thomas J. Lipton Company, 523 S. 17th St., 17105, pg. 1435 **IT**
Mellon Bank, N.A.-Commonwealth Region, Ten S. Market Sq., 17101, pg. 1085 **PB**
MONY Brokerage, Inc., P.O. Box 8009, 17105-8009, pg. 769 **PV**
NORCAM Construction Company, P.O. Box 1577, 1511 N. Cameron, 17105, pg. 934 **PV**
Northeast Marketing Div., 4309 N. Front St., 17110, pg. 296 **PV**
Sysco Food Services Company, Union Square Industrial Park, 3905 Corey Rd., 17109, pg. 1551 **PB**
PENCO-Pennsylvania, 1800 Linglestown Rd., Ste. 208, 17110, pg. 1508 **IT**
PENN NATIONAL INSURANCE, P.O. Box 2361, 17105, pg. 850 **PV**
Pennsylvania Cellular Telephone Corp., Gateway Corporate Center, 6360 Flank Dr., Ste. 800, 17112, pg. 1708 **PB**
Pennsylvania Power & Light Company-Harrisburg Div., 1801 Brookwood St., 17105, pg. 1244 **PB**
Pepper, Hamilton & Scheetz, 200 One Keystone Plaza, 17108-1181, pg. 851 **PV**
Precision Solar Controls, 635 Lucknow Rd., 17110, pg. 1028 **PV**
Protection Services, 635 Lucknow Rd., 17110, pg. 1028 **PV**
Quest Diagnostic-Harrisburg, 2151 Linglestown Rd., 17110, pg. 1351 **PB**
Raisio Inc., 4755 Linglestown Rd., Ste. 401, 17112, pg. 1086 **IT**
Richfood Pennsylvania, 3900 Industrial Rd., 17110-2945, pg. 1389 **PB**
RITTER BROS., INC., 1511 N. Cameron St., 17103, pg. 933 **PV**
SCHAEDLER BROTHERS, INC., 1030 S. 13th St., 17104, pg. 969 **PV**
Service Supply Corporation, 7205 Paxton St., 17111, pg. 1040 **PV**
Square D Co., 3500 Industrial Rd., 17110, pg. 1208 **IT**
STABLER COMPANIES, INC., 635 Lucknow Rd., 17110, pg. 1028 **PB**
Stabler Construction Company, 635 Lucknow Rd., 17110, pg. 1028 **PV**
STEPHENSON EQUIPMENT, INC., 7201 Paxton St., 17111, pg. 1040 **PV**
Stroehmann Bakeries, 3996 Paxton St., 17111, pg. 1495 **IT**

The Sygma Network of Pennsylvania, 4000 Industrial Rd., 17110, pg. 1551 **PB**
Synertech, P.O. Box 69300, 17106, pg. 529 **PV**
TV HOST INC., 3935 Jonestown Rd., 17109, pg. 1066 **PV**
WHP-TV, 3300 N. 6th St., 17110, pg. 385 **PB**
Willis Corroon Administrative Services Corporation, 1800 Linglestown Rd., Ste. 208, 17110, pg. 1505 **IT**
Work Area Protection, 635 Lucknow Rd., 17110, pg. 1028 **PV**

Harrison City

Daedal Division, P.O. Box 500, 1400 Sandy Hill Rd., 15636-0500, pg. 1259 **PB**

Hatboro

Air-Shields Inc., 330 Jacksonville Rd., 19040, pg. 1468 **IT**
Broadband Networks Group, 2200 Byberry Rd., 19040, pg. 716 **PB**
Elastomeric Technologies, Inc., 2940 Turnpike Dr., 19040, pg. 1598 **PB**
HULL CORPORATION, 3535 Davisville Rd., 19040, pg. 547 **PV**
Lydall Manning-Hatboro Operation, 2800 Turnpike Dr., 19040, pg. 1021 **PV**
Seatronics Company, 25 Sunset Ln., 19040, pg. 1593 **PB**

Hatfield

Brooks Instrument, 407 W. Vine St., 19440, pg. 574 **PB**
Furnival/State Machinery Co., 2240 Bethlehem Pike, 19440, pg. 744 **IT**
Green Bay Supply Co., Inc., 2331 Topaz Dr., 19440, pg. 307 **PB**
Hatfield Auto Auction, P.O. Box 309, Rte. 309, 19440, pg. 1649 **PV**
HATFIELD QUALITY MEATS, 2700 Funks Rd., 19440, pg. 510 **PV**
Republic Environmental Systems, Inc., 21 Church Rd., 19440, pg. 1050 **PB**
Republic Environmental Systems (Pennsylvania), Inc., 2337 N. Penn Rd., 19440, pg. 1050 **IT**
ROSENBERGERS DAIRIES, INC., 847 Forty Foot Rd., 19440, pg. 945 **PV**
Simco, 2257 N. Penn Rd., 19440, pg. 865 **PB**
Trotter Soft Pretzels, Inc., 8th & Squirrel Lane, 19440, pg. 916 **PB**

Hazleton

ABB Operations & Maintenance, RR # 1, Box 381-A, 18201, pg. 4 **IT**
BARLETTA MATERIALS & CONSTRUCTION, P.O. Box 10, 18201, pg. 116 **PV**
Bucilla Corporation, One Oak Ridge Rd., 18201-9764, pg. 352 **PV**
Composite Products, Inc., R.D. 1, Box 409-D1, 417 NE Bldg., 18201, pg. 1053 **PB**
Down River Forest Products, Inc., Valmont Industrial Pk., 450 Jaycee Dr., 18201, pg. 763 **PB**
Forbo Industries Inc., Humboldt Indus. Park, 18201, pg. 497 **IT**
Hazleton Pumps Inc., 225 N. Cedar St., 18201-0488, pg. 967 **IT**
Hershey Chocolate U.S.A., Humboldt Industrial Park, Box 340, 18201, pg. 812 **PB**
Ivex Packaging Corporation-Polymerization and Extrusion Division, P.O. Box 658, 600 Dietrich Ave., 18201, pg. 915 **PB**
Pocono Knits, Inc., 100 E. Diamond, 18201, pg. 1201 **PV**
Quebecor Printing Hazleton Inc., Humboldt Industrial Pkwy Rt 924 S., 18201, pg. 1076 **IT**
Quebecor Printing Hazleton Inc., Humboldt Industrial Pkwy., Rte. 924 S., 18201, pg. 1076 **IT**
Stationery House, VIP Division, 64 N. Conahan Dr., 18201, pg. 89 **PB**
Structural Reinforcement Products, Inc., 409-A Forest Rd., 18201, pg. 1206 **IT**
JACK YOUNG ASSOCIATES, 100 E. Diamond Ave., 18201-0522, pg. 1201 **PV**

Hermitage

Advanced Monobloc Corporation, One Llodio Dr., 16146, pg. 238 **IT**
Ellwood Crankshaft & Machine Company, 2727 Freeland Rd., 16148, pg. 373 **PV**
F.N.B. Building Corporation, 3320 E. State St., 16148, pg. 607 **PV**
F.N.B. CORPORATION, One F.N.B. Blvd., 16148, pg. 607 **PB**
First National Bank of Pennsylvania, 3320 E. State St., 16148, pg. 607 **PB**
GEORGE & THOMAS CONE CO., 3435 Lamor Rd., 16148, pg. 448 **PV**
Mortgage Service Corporation, 3320 E. State St., 16148, pg. 607 **PB**
Regency Finance Company, 3320 E. State St., 16148, pg. 607 **PB**

Herndon

Mahanoy & Mahantongo Telephone Company, P.O. Box 336, R.D. #1, 17830, pg. 1571 **PV**

Hershey

American Commonwealth Management Services Company, Inc., P.O. Box 460, Corner Sanbeach & Boathouse Rds., 17033, pg. 95 **PB**
Hershey Chocolate U.S.A., 14 E. Chocolate Ave., 17033, pg. 812 **PB**
HERSHEY FOODS CORPORATION, 100 Crystal A Dr., 17033-0810, pg. 811 **PB**
Hershey International, 100 Crystal A Dr., 17033, pg. 812 **PB**
Hershey Pasta and Grocery Group, 100 Crystal A Dr., 17033, pg. 812 **PB**
PNC Bank, P.O. Box 809, Nine W. Chocolate Ave., 17033, pg. 1243 **PB**
Pennsylvania-American Water Co., 800 W. Hersheypark Dr., 17033, pg. 95 **PB**
H.B. Reese Candy Co., 925 Reese Ave., 17033, pg. 812 **PB**

Hidden Valley

Hidden Valley Resort, One Craighead Dr., 15502, pg. 617 **PV**

Hollidaysburg

Hollidaysburg Trust Company, 224 Allegheny St., 16648, pg. 1222 **PB**
JAMES INDUSTRIES INC., Beaver St. Extension, 16648, pg. 580 **PV**

Hollsopple

FirstMiss Steel, Inc., P.O. Box 509, 15935-0509, pg. 344 **PB**

Homer City

Packaging and Material Handling Equipment Div., 57 Cooper Ave., 15748, pg. 606 **PB**

Homestead

American Shear Knive Co., 501 W. 7th Ave., 15120, pg. 89 **PV**
ASKO, INC, 501 W. 7th Ave., 15120, pg. 89 **PV**

Honesdale

Park Newspapers of Honesdale, Inc., 220 Eighth St., 18431, pg. 1078 **PB**
Wayne Independent, 220 Eighth St., 18431, pg. 1078 **PB**

Horsham

Advanta Insurance Companies, Commonwealth Corp. Ctr., 200 Tournament Dr., 19044, pg. 22 **PB**
American Bank Note Co., 680 Blair Mill Rd., 19044, pg. 68 **PB**
American Bank Note Company, 680 Blair Mill Rd., 19044-2222, pg. 68 **PB**
American Meter Company, 300 Welsh Rd., Bldg. 1, 19044-2234, pg. 1149 **IT**
AYDIN CORPORATION, 700 Dresher Rd., 19044, pg. 158 **PB**
Aydin Displays (East), 700 Dresher Rd., 19044, pg. 158 **PB**
Aydin Telecom Division, 700 Dresher Rd., 19044, pg. 158 **PB**
BetzDearborn Metals Process Group, 200A Precision Dr., 19044, pg. 226 **PB**
BetzDearborn Water Management Group, 200 Witmer Rd., 19044, pg. 226 **PB**
ContiMortgage Corporation, 500 Enterprise Rd., Ste. 150, 19044, pg. 439 **PB**
Conversion Systems, Inc., 200 Welsh Rd., 19044, pg. 587 **PB**
Decision Data, 400 Horsham Rd., Ste. D, 19044-2175, pg. 645 **IT**
Dynamic Graphics Inc., 945 Horsham Rd., 19044, pg. 191 **IT**
Encore Computer Corp., Horsham Business Center, Bldg. 3, Ste. 100, 300 Welsh Rd., 19044, pg. 580 **PB**
ENVIROSOURCE, INC., 1155 Business Center, 19044, pg. 587 **PB**
EnviroSource-International Mill Service, 1155 Business Center Dr., 19044-3454, pg. 587 **PB**
Fairfield Group, 200 Gibralter Rd., 19044, pg. 985 **PB**
GMAC Mortgage Corporation, 100 Witmer Rd., 19044-0963, pg. 720 **PB**
General Employment Enterprises, Inc., 110 Gibralter Rd., Ste. 105, 19044, pg. 714 **PV**
GENERAL INSTRUMENT CORPORATION, 101 Tournament Dr., 19044, pg. 716 **PB**
Honeywell Leeds & Northrup International, 795 Horsham Rd., 19044, pg. 834 **PB**
Independence Capital Management, Inc., 600 Dresher Rd., 19044, pg. 849 **PB**
Kasser/Laird Distilling Co., 419 Sargon Way, Unit 8, 19044, pg. 643 **PV**
Keystone Bank, 601 Dresher Rd., 19044, pg. 956 **PB**
Lockheed Martin Training & Technical Services, Lakeside Plaza One, 100 Lakeside Plaza, 19044, pg. 1009 **PB**
MENLEY & JAMES LABORATORIES, INC., Commonwealth Corporate Ctr., 100 Tournament Dr., 19044, pg. 1086 **PB**

Geographic Index-U.S.

Nutri/System Inc., 410 Horsham Rd., 19044, pg. 859 **PV**
Reed Technology and Information Services-Government Services, 275 Gibraltar Rd., 19044, pg. 1096 **IT**
Reed Technology and Information Services Inc., One Progress Dr., 19044, pg. 1096 **IT**
Stroehmann Bakeries, L.C., P.O. Box 848, 255 Business Ctr. Dr., 19044, pg. 1495 **IT**
TSI Argus Research Laboratories & Center for Photobiology, 905 Sheehy Dr., 19044, pg. 733 **PB**

Hummelstown

AYCOCK, INC., 8261 Derry St., 17036, pg. 103 **PV**

Huntingdon

ELCO Corporation, Huntington Industrial Park, 16652, pg. 775 **IT**
Penn Central National Bank, 431 Penn St., 16652, pg. 1222 **PB**

Huntingdon Valley

American Bank Note Company, 1448 County Line Road, 19006, pg. 68 **PB**
Bostik Inc., 1740 Cty Line Rd., 19006-1702, pg. 1409 **IT**
HEALTHCARE SERVICES GROUP, INC., 2643 Huntingdon Pike, 19006, pg. 803 **PB**
TOLL BROTHERS, INC., 3103 Philmont Ave., 19006, pg. 1620 **PB**

Indiana

Eastern American Energy Corp., 2281 Airport Prof. Bldg., 15701, pg. 357 **PV**
Eighty Four Coal Co., 655 Church St., 15701, pg. 1395 **PB**
Helvetia Coal Co., 655 Church St., 15701, pg. 1395 **PB**
Kent Coal Mining, 655 Church St., 15701, pg. 1395 **PB**
Keystone Coal Mining Corp., 655 Church St., 15701, pg. 1395 **PB**
National Mine Service, Inc., 795 Old Rte. 119 N., 15701, pg. 280 **IT**
ROCHESTER & PITTSBURGH COAL COMPANY, 655 Church St., 15701, pg. 1395 **PB**
Season-All Industries, Inc., 1480 Wayne Ave., 15701, pg. 267 **IT**
United Eastern Coal Sales Corp., 655 Church St., 15701, pg. 1395 **PB**
Westco Coal Co., 655 Church St., 15701, pg. 1395 **PB**

Indianola

Medrad, Inc., One Medrad Dr., 15051, pg. 1204 **IT**

Industry

Great Lakes Terminal & Transport of Pennsylvania, P.O. Box 281, 15052, pg. 435 **PV**

Irvine

NATIONAL FORGE COMPANY, One Front St., 16329, pg. 783 **PV**

Irwin

T-R Printing & Publishing, P.O. Box 280, 15642, pg. 1102 **PV**

Ivyland

Hartell Div., 70 Industrial Dr., 18974, pg. 1534 **PB**
Milton Roy Company, 201 Ivyland Rd., 18974-0800, pg. 1534 **PB**

Jeannette

ELLIOTT COMPANY, 901 N. Fourth St., 15644, pg. 373 **PV**
Lightcraft, P.O. Box 259, 15644, pg. 749 **PV**
New Elliott Corporation, N. Fourth St., 15644, pg. 432 **IT**

Jenkintown

SPS TECHNOLOGIES, INC., 101 Greenwood Ave., Ste. 470, 19046, pg. 1419 **PB**
Unbrako Div., 301 Highland Ave., 19046, pg. 1420 **PB**

Johnsonburg

Willamette Industries, Inc., 100 Center St., 15845, pg. 1768 **PB**

Johnstown

BT FINANCIAL CORPORATION, BT Financial Plaza, 551 Main St., 15901, pg. 163 **PB**
Bedford Associates, Inc., BT Financial Plaza, 551 Main St., 15901, pg. 164 **PB**
CROWN AMERICAN REALTY TRUST, P.O. Box 879, 15907, pg. 461 **PB**
DRS Laurel Technologies, 423 Walters Ave., 15904, pg. 475 **PB**
Dairy Dell, Inc., 400 Franklin St., 15901, pg. 1271 **PV**
GKI Electronic Enclosure Division-Johnstown, 110 Sunray Dr., 15905, pg. 717 **PB**
GPU Energy, 1001 Broad St., 15907-2437, pg. 695 **PB**

GPU Generation Corporation, 1001 Broad St., 15906-2498, pg. 695 **PB**
JOHNSTOWN CORPORATION, 545 Central Ave., 15902, pg. 595 **PV**
Johnstown Wire Technologies, Inc., 124 Laurel Ave., 15906, pg. 344 **PV**
Laurel Bank, 532-534 Main St., 15901, pg. 164 **PB**
Laurel Community Development Corporation, 551 Main St., 15901, pg. 164 **PB**
Laurel Trust Company, BT Financial Plaza, 551 Main St., 15901, pg. 164 **PB**
Penn Machine Company, 106 Station St., 15905, pg. 281 **IT**
SCM Metal Products Inc., 101 Bridge St., 15902-2904, pg. 594 **IT**
Sunrise Properties, 319 Washington St., 15901, pg. 1271 **PB**

Jonestown

Supreme MidAtlantic Corporation, 411 Jonestown Rd., 17038, pg. 1542 **PB**

Karns City

Penreco, 138 Petrolia St., 16041, pg. 1273 **PB**

Kennett Square

Bostonian Wholesale Division, 520 S. Broad St., 19348, pg. 297 **IT**
C & J Clark America, Inc., 520 S. Broad St., 19348, pg. 297 **IT**
C & J Clark Direct Marketing Division, 520 S. Broad St., 19348, pg. 297 **IT**
C & J Clark Retail, Inc., 520 S. Broad St., 19348, pg. 297 **IT**
Calico Corners, 203 Gale Ln., 19348, pg. 386 **PV**
Clark Shoe Co., 520 S. Broad St., 19348, pg. 297 **IT**
Detaclad Division, 220 Gale Ln., Ste. 5, 19348, pg. 539 **PB**
EVERFAST INC., 203 Gale Ln., 19348, pg. 386 **PV**
GENESIS HEALTH VENTURES, INC., 148 W. State St., 19348, pg. 728 **PB**
Printed Circuitry Div., Layfette & Mulberry Sts., 19348, pg. 772 **PB**
Seneca Foods-Kennett Division, Cypress & West St., 19348, pg. 1457 **PB**

Kimberton

MONSEY-BAKOR, Coldestream Rd., 19442, pg. 757 **PV**

King of Prussia

AMERICAN FOODSERVICE CORP., 400 Drew Ct., 19406, pg. 54 **PV**
Buten, Division of Duron, 711 First Ave., 19406, pg. 349 **PV**
Centeon, L.L.C., 1020 First Ave., 19406-1310, pg. 628 **IT**
Central Sprinkler Company, 201 King Manor Rd., 19406, pg. 327 **PB**
Cochrane, Inc., 800 Third Ave., 19406, pg. 456 **PB**
ENV Services, Inc., 1016 W. Eighth Ave., 19406, pg. 517 **PB**
EGGLAND'S BEST, INC., 842 First Ave., 19406, pg. 366 **PV**
ELECTRO-SCIENCE LABORATORIES, INC., 416 E. Church Rd., 19406, pg. 369 **PB**
Envirosafe Services, Inc., 900 E. 8th Ave., Ste. 200, 19406, pg. 587 **PB**
Ethical Nutriment, Inc., 842 First Ave., 19406, pg. 366 **PV**
FOSTER MANAGEMENT CO., 1018 Ninth Ave., 19406, pg. 421 **PV**
GAI Construction Services, Inc., 1150 First Ave., Ste. 405, 19406, pg. 434 **PV**
GAI Consultants, Inc., 1150 First Ave., Ste. 405, 19406, pg. 434 **PV**
INTERDIGITAL COMMUNICATIONS CORP., 781 3rd Ave., 19406, pg. 889 **PB**
InterDigital Patents Corporation, 2200 Renaissance Blvd., Ste. 100, 19406, pg. 889 **PB**
Intergraph Corporation, 1018 W. 9th St., Ste. 300, 19406-1238, pg. 890 **IT**
The King of Prussia Courier, 707 W. Dekalb Pike., 19406, pg. 935 **PV**
Lindenmeyr Munroe, 3300 Horizon Dr., 19406, pg. 224 **PV**
The M&T Company, Valley Forge Park Office Bldg., 1018 W. Ninth Ave., Ste. 313, 19406, pg. 277 **PV**
MAACO ENTERPRISES INC., 381 Brooks Rd., 19406, pg. 888 **PV**
NASON AND CULLEN GROUP INCORPORATED, 500 N. Gulph Rd., Ste. 150, 19406-0988, pg. 775 **PV**
Nason and Cullen Inc., 500 N. Gulph Rd., Ste. 100, 19406, pg. 775 **PV**
NOVACARE INC., 1016 W. Ninth Ave., 19406, pg. 1203 **PB**
OWOSSO CORPORATION, The Triad Building, 2200 Renaissance Blvd., 19406, pg. 1238 **PB**
PREMIER DENTAL PRODUCTS COMPANY, 3600 Horizon Dr., 19406, pg. 881 **PV**
Premier Refractories International Inc., 901 E. Eighth Ave., 19406, pg. 58 **PB**
RBS/PNCF Inc., 455 S. Gulph Rd., 19406, pg. 1244 **PB**
RYKA INCORPORATED, 555 S. Henderson Rd., Ste. B, 19406, pg. 1414 **PV**
SKF USA Inc., 1100 First Ave., 19406-0907, pg. 1157 **IT**
SMC Environmental Services Group Inc., 501 Allendale Rd., 19406, pg. 1717 **PB**

Senior Engineering Co.-Eastern Region, 154 Hansen Acess Rd., 19406, pg. 1222 **IT**
Senior Engineering Services Co. (Head Office), 154 Hansen Access Rd., 19406, pg. 1222 **IT**
Silverman's Dental Supplies Inc., 420 Feheley Dr., 19406, pg. 710 **IT**
SmithKline Beecham Clinical Laboratories, Inc., 620 Freedom Bus. Ctr., Ste. 400, 19406, pg. 1264 **IT**
Starboard Data Services, Inc., 771 Fifth Avenue, 19406, pg. 86 **PV**
UGI CORPORATION, 460 N. Gulph Rd., 19406, pg. 1653 **PB**
UGI Enterprises, 460 N. Gulph Rd., 19406, pg. 1653 **PB**
URS Greiner, Inc., 671 Moore Rd., 19406, pg. 1653 **PB**
Universal Health Realty Income Trust, 367 S. Gulph Rd., 19406, pg. 1697 **PB**
UNIVERSAL HEALTH SERVICES, INC., 367 S. Gulph Rd., 19406, pg. 1697 **PB**
Wells Fargo Alarm Services, Inc., 780 Fifth Ave., 19406, pg. 246 **PB**
ZUCKERMAN-HONICKMAN INC., 191 S. Gulph Rd., 19406, pg. 1207 **PV**
Zyan, Inc., 1012 W. 9th Ave., Ste. 100, 19406, pg. 421 **PV**

Kingston

ANESCO, 517 Pierce St., 18704-0053, pg. 74 **PV**
Royer Industries, Inc., 158 Pringle St., 18704, pg. 1066 **IT**
Royer/Mogensen, Inc., 158 Pringle St., 18704, pg. 1066 **IT**
Strober Building Supply Centers, Inc., 695 Wyoming Ave., 18704, pg. 403 **PV**

Kittanning

ALLTEL Pennsylvania, Inc., 201 N. Jefferson St., 16201, pg. 56 **PB**
5 Rubber Corporation, 1655 Orr Ave., 16201, pg. 1504 **PB**

Kulpsville

Clemens Country Kitchen (CCK), Bldg. 2, 1555 Bustard Rd., 19443, pg. 245 **PV**
CLEMENS MARKETS INC., Bldg. 1, 1555 Bustard Rd., 19443, pg. 245 **PV**
Nice Specialty Bearings, Detwiler Rd., 19443-0307, pg. 1157 **IT**

Lafayette Hill

NATIONAL LABEL COMPANY, 2025 Joshua Rd., 19444, pg. 785 **PV**

Lake City

COPES-VULCAN INC., Martin & Rice Aves., 16423, pg. 274 **PV**
Van Air Systems, Inc., 350 Mechanic St., 16423, pg. 354 **PV**

Lakeville

Cove Haven, Inc., Rte. 590, 18483, pg. 1512 **PB**

Lancaster

A.S.M. Industries, 41 Industrial Cir., 17601, pg. 985 **PV**
Agricultural Warehousing, 500 Running Pump Rd., 17607, pg. 552 **PV**
All Size Corrugated, P.O. Box 4544, 17604, pg. 177 **PV**
Alumax Aluminum Corp., Mill Products, 1480 Manheim Pike, 17604, pg. 59 **PB**
AMERIFOODS INC., 2060 Old Philadelphia Pk., 17602, pg. 65 **PV**
Anderson Bakery Co., Inc., 2060 Old Philadelphia Pike, 17602, pg. 65 **PV**
ARMSTRONG WORLD INDUSTRIES, INC., 313 W. Liberty St., 17604, pg. 131 **PB**
Automatic Timing & Controls, 1827 Freedom Rd., 17601, pg. 327 **PV**
BURNHAM, 1241 Harrisburg Ave., 17603, pg. 270 **PB**
Cadmus Journal Services, Inc., 3575 Hempland Rd., 17604, pg. 291 **PB**
Cadmus-Lancaster Manufacturing, 3575 Hempland Rd., 17604, pg. 291 **PB**
Childcraft Education Corp., 2920 Old Tree Dr., 17603, pg. 513 **PB**
Clark Filter, 3649 Hempland Rd., 17601, pg. 381 **PB**
J.L. Clark Lancaster Div., 303 N. Plum St., 17604, pg. 381 **PB**
CLOISTER PURE SPRING WATER CO., INC., P.O. Box 3229, 17603-3229, pg. 247 **PV**
Coast RV, Inc., 175 Greenfield Rd., 17601, pg. 388 **PB**
Commonwealth Insurance Managers, 2929 Lititz Pike, Box 3010, 17604, pg. 1216 **PB**
CoreStates Bank, 1097 Commercial Ave., 17601, pg. 446 **PB**
Crowley Frozen Desserts, Inc., P.O. Box 7007, 1801 Hempstead Rd., 17604, pg. 752 **IT**
Danaher Tool Group, P.O. Box 3767, 805 Estelle Dr., 17601-3767, pg. 480 **PB**
DODGE REGUPOL, INC., 715 Fountain Ave., 17601, pg. 337 **PV**
Elgood-Mayo Corp., 1817 Colonial Village La., 17601, pg. 439 **PV**
Flexsteel Division, Pitney Rd., 17604, pg. 654 **PB**
FULTON FINANCIAL CORP., One Penn Sq., 17602, pg. 687 **PB**

PB - U.S. Public Companies Volume
PV - U.S. Private Companies Volume
IT - International Public & Private Companies Volume

1406

Goschen Hoppen - Home Mutual Insurance Co., 2929 Lititz Pike, Box 3010, 17604, pg. 1216 **PB**

Hamilton Arms Nursing & Rehabilitation Center, 336 S. West End Ave., 17603, pg. 729 **PB**

Hamilton Precision Metals, P.O. Box 3014, 1780 Rohrerstown Rd., 17604-3014, pg. 944 **PB**

Hanover Foods Corp., Plum & Liberty Sts., 17604, pg. 499 **PV**

HealthGuard of Lancaster, 280 Granite Run Dr., 17601, pg. 529 **PV**

Heil Trailer International, 3249 Hempland Rd., 17604, pg. 520 **PB**

HERLEY INDUSTRIES, INC., 10 Industry Dr., 17603, pg. 811 **PB**

Herley Vega Industry, 10 Industry Dr., 17603, pg. 811 **PB**

Herrmidifier Co., Inc., 1812 Colonial Village Ln., 17605, pg. 1639 **PB**

HIGH INDUSTRIES, INC., 1853 William Penn Way, 17605, pg. 528 **PV**

THE HOLIDAY INN LANCASTER HOST HOTEL & CONFERENCE CENTER, 2300 Lincoln Hwy. E., 17602, pg. 534 **PV**

Hopper Soliday & Co., Inc., 1825 Oregon Pike, 17601, pg. 65 **IT**

HYDRO/KIRBY AGRI SERVICE, INC., 500 Running Pump Rd., 17607, pg. 552 **PV**

IDENTICARD SYSTEMS, INC., 40 Citation Ln., 17601, pg. 557 **PV**

Installation Products Div., 313 Liberty St., 17604, pg. 132 **PB**

IREX CORPORATION, 120 N. Lime St., 17602, pg. 913 **PB**

Kemps Foods, Inc., 1801 Hempstead Rd., 17604, pg. 752 **IT**

KERR GROUP, INC., 500 New Holland Ave., 17602, pg. 952 **PB**

KUNZLER & COMPANY, INC., 652 Manor St., 17604, pg. 636 **PV**

Lancaster Leaf Tobacco Co. of Pennsylvania, P.O. Box 897, 17603, pg. 1695 **PB**

LANCASTER MALLEABLE CASTINGS COMPANY, 1170 Lititz Ave., 17601, pg. 645 **PV**

Lancaster Plant-Kellogg U.S.A., 205 O State Rd., 17604, pg. 947 **PB**

Lindenmeyr Munroe, 3041 Industry Dr., 17603-4025, pg. 224 **PV**

MXL Industries, Inc., 1764 Rohrerstown Rd., 17601, pg. 694 **PB**

Neffsville Mutual Fire Insurance Co., 2929 Lititz Pike, Box 3010, 17604, pg. 1216 **PB**

Nissin Foods (U.S.A.) Co., Inc., Masako Pl., 2901 Hempland Rd., 17601, pg. 949 **IT**

OLD GUARD INSURANCE GROUP, 2929 Lititz Pike, Box 3010, 17604, pg. 1216 **PB**

Old Guard Mutual Fire Insurance Co., 2929 Lititz Pike, Box 3010, 17604, pg. 1216 **PB**

Old Guard Mutual Insurance Co., 2929 Lititz Pike, Box 3010, 17604, pg. 1216 **PB**

OMNI Products, Inc., 223 Wohlsen Way, 17601, pg. 816 **PV**

Pennsylvania Cellular Telephone Corp., 260 Granite Run Dr., 17601, pg. 1708 **PB**

Pennsylvania Power & Light Company-Lancaster Div., 1701 Manheim Pike, 17604, pg. 1244 **PB**

SFP Corporation, 500 New Holland Ave., 17602, pg. 952 **PB**

Sensenich Propeller Manufacturing Co., Inc., 519 E. Airport Rd., 17601-5100, pg. 861 **PV**

ServiceMaster Manufacturing Services, Greenfield Industrial Park, 1828 William Penn Way, 17601, pg. 1462 **PB**

2929 Service Corporation, 2929 Lititz Pike, Box 3010, 17604, pg. 1216 **PB**

WGAL-TV, 1300 Columbia Ave., 17604-7127, pg. 1344 **PB**

WestCon, 1827 Freedom Rd., 17604, pg. 327 **PV**

Y & S Candies, 400 Running Pump Rd., 17603, pg. 812 **PB**

Landisville

A.H. HOFFMAN, INC., 77 Cooper Ave., 17538, pg. 532 **PV**

Hoffman Seeds, Inc., 144 Main St., 17538, pg. 532 **PV**

Langhorne

Cabot Medical Corporation, 2021 Cabot Blvd. W., 19047, pg. 373 **PB**

Crestview, 262 Tollgate Rd., 19047, pg. 729 **PB**

DiMark, Inc., 2050 Cabot Blvd. W., 19047, pg. 793 **PB**

EXACT EQUIPMENT CORPORATION, 850 Town Center Dr., 19047, pg. 387 **PV**

Earle M. Jorgensen Company/Philadelphia, 58 Cabot Blvd., 19047, pg. 600 **PV**

Lenox Brands, 900 Wheeler Way, 19047, pg. 261 **PB**

Lenox Collections, 900 Wheeler Way, 19047, pg. 261 **PB**

National Video, Inc., One Summit Sq., Ste. 200, 19041, pg. 1755 **PB**

Sesame Place, 100 Sesame Rd., 19047, pg. 114 **PB**

Systems Bio Industries, 2021 Cabot Blvd. W., 19047, pg. 445 **IT**

WEST COAST ENTERTAINMENT INC., Rt. 413, Double Woods Rd., One Summit Square, Ste. 200, 19047, pg. 1755 **PB**

Lansdale

Central Sprinkler Company, Third St. & Cannon Ave., 19446, pg. 327 **PB**

CENTRAL SPRINKLER CORPORATION, 451 N. Cannon Ave., 19446, pg. 327 **PB**

Gasboy International, Inc., Eighth St. & North Valley Forge Rd., 19446, pg. 1620 **PB**

R.A. INDUSTRIES, INC., Welsh Rd., 19446, pg. 902 **PV**

The Reporter Equitable Publishing Co., 307 Derstine Ave., 19446, pg. 701 **PB**

SprinkCAD, 1215 Walnut St., 19446, pg. 327 **PB**

Tracor Aerospace Electronics Systems, Inc., 305 Richardson Rd., 19446-1485, pg. 1627 **PB**

Large

DICK CORPORATION, 900 Rte. 51, 15025, pg. 331 **PV**

Ebara Solar, Inc., 811 Rte. 51 S., 15025, pg. 432 **IT**

Latrobe

JLK Direct Distribution Inc., State Rte. 981 S., 15650, pg. 951 **PB**

KENNAMETAL INC., Rte. 981 S., 15650, pg. 950 **PB**

Kennametal Metalworking Systems Div., Rte. 981 S., 15650, pg. 950 **PB**

Latrobe Brewing Co., 119 Jefferson St., 15650, pg. 680 **IT**

Latrobe Special Products Div., 2626 S. Ligonier, 15650, pg. 1617 **PB**

Latrobe Steel Company, 2626 S. Ligonier, 15650, pg. 1617 **PB**

Mining and Construction Division, P.O. Box 231, 15650, pg. 950 **PB**

Pakco Industrial Ceramics, Inc., 55 Hillview Ave., 15650, pg. 1174 **IT**

Quest Diagnostic-Latrobe, 1100 Ligonier St., 15650, pg. 1351 **PB**

VR/Wesson Hydro Carbide, P.O. Box 363, 15650, pg. 612 **PB**

Laureldale

Empire Steel Castings, Inc., 1501 Frush Valley Rd., 19605, pg. 142 **PB**

Lawrence

BLACK BOX CORPORATION OF PA, 1000 Park Dr., 15055, pg. 235 **PB**

Black Box Corporation of Pennsylvania, 1000 Park Dr., 15055, pg. 235 **PB**

Lebanon

ARNOLD INDUSTRIES, INC., 625 S. Fifth Ave., 17042, pg. 132 **PB**

Hauck Manufacturing Company Inc., P.O. Box 90, 100 N. Harris St., 17042, pg. 1149 **IT**

Hedlund-Martin Inc., 25 Keystone Dr., 17042, pg. 704 **PB**

Keystone Heritage Group, Inc., P.O. Box 1285, 555 Willow St., 17042, pg. 687 **PB**

LEBANON SEABOARD CORPORATION, 1600 E. Cumberland St., 17042, pg. 656 **PV**

Lebanon Valley Farmers Bank, 555 Willow St., 17042, pg. 688 **PB**

New Penn Motor Express, Inc., 625 S. Fifth Ave., 17042, pg. 132 **PB**

San Giorgio Macaroni, 249 Guilford St., 17042, pg. 812 **PB**

WEABER, INC, RR #4 Box 1255, 17042, pg. 1155 **PV**

Leechburg

Allegheny Ludlum-Bagdad, P.O. Box 565, 15656, pg. 43 **PB**

Allegheny Ludlum-Leechburg, P.O. Box 565, 15656, pg. 43 **PB**

Leetsdale

MULACH STEEL CORPORATION, 100 Leetsdale Industrial Dr., 15056, pg. 766 **PV**

Lehighton

BLUE RIDGE PRESSURE CASTINGS, INC., P.O. Box 208, 18235, pg. 153 **PV**

Lemoyne

Dialysis Corporation of Harrisburg, 27 Miller St., Ste. 120, 17043, pg. 1080 **PB**

Leola

Elixir Industries, 304 East Main, P.O. Box 312, 17540, pg. **PV**

ROSS TECHNOLOGY CORP., 104 N. Maple Ave., 17540, pg. 946 **PV**

Lester

Circle Freight International USA, 1019 4th Ave., 19029, pg. 370 **PB**

Olympic Steel - Philadelphia Division, Ten Industrial Hwy., 19113, pg. 1221 **PB**

Levittown

Lower Bucks Cablevision, Inc., 2320 Trenton Rd., 19056, pg. 1611 **PB**

Lewis Run

MCCOURT LABEL CO., 20 Egbert Ln., 16738, pg. 720 **PV**

Lewisburg

THE JPM COMPANY, Rte. 15 N., 17837, pg. 919 **PB**

Pennsylvania House Casegoods, 137 N. Tenth St., 17837-1388, pg. 975 **PB**

Lewistown

Krautkramer-Branson, Inc., 50 Industrial Park Rd., 17044, pg. 574 **PB**

Marlette Homes, Inc., 30 Industrial Pk., 17044, pg. 1442 **PB**

Quest Diagnostic-Lewistown, 21 S. Brown St., 17044, pg. 1351 **PB**

The Russell National Bank, P.O. Box 70, 17044, pg. 1222 **PB**

Library

Consolidation Coal Research & Development, 4000 Brownsville Rd., 15129, pg. 531 **PB**

United Technologies Services, P.O. Box 64, 15129-0064, pg. 1690 **PB**

Lima

PILOT AIR FREIGHT CORP., 314 N. Middletown Rd., 19037, pg. 865 **PV**

Limerick

Cetrk USA, 640 N. Lewis Rd., 19468, pg. 1569 **PB**

Sermatech International, 155 S. Limerick Rd., 19468, pg. 1569 **PB**

Sermatech Middle Atlantic, 155 S. Limerick Rd., 19468, pg. 1570 **PB**

Teleflex Marine, 640 N. Lewis Rd., 19468, pg. 1569 **PB**

Linesville

MFG Tray Co., E. Erie St., 16424, pg. 756 **PV**

Linwood

Foamex International Inc., 1000 Columbia Ave., 19061, pg. 1094 **PV**

Foamex, L.P., 1000 Columbia Ave., 19061, pg. 1094 **PV**

General Felt Industries, Inc., 1000 Columbia Ave., 19061, pg. 1094 **PV**

Lionville

The Bentley-Harris Manufacturing Co., 241 Welsh Pool Rd., 19353, pg. 1334 **IT**

Axel Johnson Metals, Inc., 215 Welsh Pool Rd., 19353, pg. 709 **IT**

THE WEST COMPANY, INCORPORATED, 101 Gordon Dr., 19341, pg. 1755 **PB**

Lititz

Farmers First Bank, 24 N. Cedar St., 17543, pg. 1542 **PB**

Phillips & Jacobs/North, 123 W. Airport Rd., 17543, pg. 1329 **PB**

Susque-Bancshares Leasing Co., Inc., 26 N. Cedar St., 17543, pg. 1542 **PB**

Susque-Bancshares Life Insurance Company, 26 N. Cedar St., 17543, pg. 1542 **PB**

SUSQUEHANNA BANCSHARES, INC., 26 N. Cedar St., 17543, pg. 1542 **PB**

Susquehanna Bancshares South, Inc., 26 N. Cedar St., 17543, pg. 1543 **PB**

Wilbur Chocolate Co., Inc., 20 No. Broad St., 17543, pg. 210 **PV**

Woodstream Corporation, 69 N. Locust St., 17543, pg. 566 **PB**

Littlestown

Craftlite, 100 Craftway, 17340, pg. 730 **PB**

Loganton

Sugar Valley Telephone Co., P.O. Box 37, South St., 17747, pg. 1572 **PB**

Lower Burrell

Braeburn Alloy Steel, River Rd., 15068, pg. 193 **PV**

Lucernemines

Morgantown Machine Anderson Mavor, U.S. 119 S. Lucerne Rd., 15754, pg. 281 **IT**

Lyon Station

EAST PENN MFG. CO., Deka Rd., 19536, pg. 357 **PV**

Geographic Index-U.S.

Geographic Index-U.S.

Macungie

ALLEN ORGAN COMPANY, 150 Locust St., 18062, pg. 45 **PB**

Malvern

Acme Markets, 75 Valley Stream Pkwy., 19355-0710, pg. 93 **PB**
AMERISOURCE HEALTH CORP., 300 Chester Field Pkwy., 19355, pg. 96 **PB**
CANA Inc., 490 Lapp Rd., 19355, pg. 55 **IT**
Centocor Diagnostics Div., 200 Great Valley Pkwy., 19355, pg. 323 **PB**
CENTOCOR, INC., 200 Great Valley Pkwy., 19355-1307, pg. 323 **PB**
Centocor Partners III, L.P., 244 Great Valley Parkway, 19355, pg. 323 **PB**
Centocor Pharmaceutical Division, 200 Great Valley Pkwy., 19355, pg. 323 **PB**
ENSONIQ, 155 Great Valley Pkwy., 19355, pg. 377 **PV**
Family Pharmacy General Office, 300 Chesterfield Pkwy., 19355, pg. 97 **PB**
IKON OFFICE SOLUTIONS, INC., 70 Valley Stream Pkwy., 19355, pg. 862 **PB**
Joy Environmental Technologies, Inc., One Country View Rd., 19755, pg. 789 **PB**
Nilfisk of America Inc., 300 Technology Dr., 19355, pg. 932 **IT**
Osram Sylvania Inc., 101 Lindenwood Dr., Ste. 450, 19355, pg. 1245 **IT**
SMS International Division, 51 Valley Stream Pkwy., 19355, pg. 1463 **PB**
SMS Physician Services Division, 51 Valley Stream Pkwy., 19355, pg. 1463 **PB**
SMS Properties Corp., 51 Valley Stream Pkwy., 19355, pg. 1463 **PB**
SMS Services Corp., 51 Valley Stream Pkwy., 19355, pg. 1463 **PB**
Sanchez Computer Associates, Great Valley Corporate Ctr., 40 Valley Stream Pkwy., 19355, pg. 1425 **PV**
Sanofi Research Division, 9 Great Valley Parkway, 19355, pg. 445 **PB**
SHARED MEDICAL SYSTEMS CORPORATION, 51 Valley Stream Pkwy., 19355, pg. 1463 **PB**
Smiths Industries Aerospace & Defense Systems Inc.-Malvern, 255 Great Valley Pkwy., 19355, pg. 1268 **IT**
SYSTEMS & COMPUTER TECHNOLOGY CORPORATION, Four Country View Rd., 19355, pg. 1552 **PB**
VISHAY INTERTECHNOLOGY, INC., 63 Lincoln Hwy., 19355-2120, pg. 1721 **PB**
Vishay Resistive Systems, 63 Lincoln Hwy., 19355-2120, pg. 1722 **PB**
WAVE, P.O. Box 3050, 19355, pg. 1780 **PB**
The Worthington Steel Company-Pennsylavnia, P.O. Box 3050, 19355, pg. 1780 **PB**

Manheim

FENNER DRIVES, 311 W. Stiegel St., 17545-1010, pg. 400 **PV**
Fuller Company (Manheim), 236 South Cherry Street, 17545-1020, pg. 475 **IT**
HARRINGTON HOISTS, INC., 401 W. End Ave., 17545, pg. 504 **PV**
LIFT-ALL CO., INC., 102 S. Heintzelman St., 17545, pg. 667 **PV**
UNIVERSAL COMPOSITES-U.S.C., 123 E. Stiegel St., 17545, pg. 1126 **PV**

Marcus Hook

Marcus Hook, PA Refinery, P.O. Box 426, 2nd & Green Streets, 19061, pg. 1530 **PB**

Marion

Martin's Snack Division, 6647 Molly Pitcher Hwy. South, 17235, pg. 710 **PV**

Mars

JAMES AUSTIN CO., 115 Downriver Rd., 16046, pg. 99 **PV**
ROESSING BRONZE CO., Myoma Rd., 16046, pg. 939 **PV**

Marshalls Creek

Pocono Palace, Inc., Rte. 209, 18335, pg. 1512 **PB**

Martinsburg

Cove Shoe Company, 107 Highland St., 16662, pg. 217 **PB**

McConnellsburg

JLG INDUSTRIES, INC., One JLG Dr., 17233-9533, pg. 918 **PB**
Waring Products Div., First St. & Lincoln Hwy. W., 17233, pg. 286 **PB**

McMurray

Information Transmission Systems Corp., 102 Rahway Rd., 15317-3349, pg. 4 **PB**
Voltec, 3075 Washington Rd., 15317, pg. 968 **PV**

Meadow Lands

Tamrock Group U.S., P.O. Box 540, 455 Race Track Rd., 15347, pg. 1353 **IT**

Meadville

CHANNELLOCK, INC., 1306 S. Main St., 16335, pg. 229 **PV**
DAD'S PRODUCTS CO., INC., Mill St., 16335, pg. 306 **PV**
MEADVILLE FORGING CO., P.O. Box 459, 16335, pg. 726 **PV**
SECO WARWICK CORPORATION, 180 Mercer St., 16335, pg. 980 **PV**

Mechanicsburg

Continental Medical Systems, Inc., P.O. Box 715, 600 Wilson Ln., 17055, pg. 839 **PB**
Eastman Kodak Adw Inc., 336 Heinz St., 17055-3212, pg. 555 **PB**
Morgan Distribution, P.O. Box 2003, 17055, pg. 1132 **PB**
PNC Bank, South Central, Main & Market Sts., 17055, pg. 1243 **PB**
Pasco U.S.A., Inc., 4913 Gettysburg Rd., 17055, pg. 1024 **IT**
SelectRehab, 600 Wilson Ln., 17055, pg. 839 **PB**
Thermal Industries Inc., Wesley Plaza, 17055-3174, pg. 491 **PV**

Media

Barnett International/PAREXEL, Rosetree Corp. Ctr., 1400 N. Providence Rd., Ste. 200, 19063, pg. 1258 **PB**
Business Information Technology, Rosetree Corporate Ctr., 1400 N. Providence Rd., Ste. 5000, 19063, pg. 356 **PB**
IRD Mechanalysis, Inc., 1400 Providence Rd., Ste. 3035, 19063, pg. 789 **PB**
Imagine Educational Products, Inc., 1400 N. Providence Rd., Ste. 3055, 19063, pg. 1186 **PB**
NOBEL EDUCATION DYNAMICS, INC., Rose Tree Corp. Center II, 1400 N. Providence Rd., Ste. 3055, 19063, pg. 1185 **PB**
Rocking Horse Development Corporation, 1400 N. Providence Rd., Ste. 3055, 19063, pg. 1186 **PB**
WAWA, INC., 260 Baltimore Pike, 19063, pg. 1155 **PV**

Melrose Park

GMAC Mortgage Corporation of Pennsylvania, 1333 W. Chetenham Ave., 19126, pg. 720 **PB**

Mercer

Adesa Pittsburgh Auto Auction, Rte. 62, 16137, pg. 116 **PB**

Middleburg

Thor America, 37 Old 522 St., 17842, pg. 1602 **PB**

Middletown

Allegheny Airlines, Inc., Bldg. 601, Harrisburg Intl. Airport, 17057, pg. 1680 **PB**
Bindley Western, Middletown Division, 1001 Air Park Dr., 17057, pg. 228 **PB**
Environmental Restoration Systems, Inc., 3240 Schoolhouse Rd., 17057, pg. 976 **PV**
Mack Remanufacturing Center, 2800 Commerce Dr., 17057-3204, pg. 1102 **IT**
Olivetti Supplies, Inc., Harrisburg Intl. Airport, 137 Fourth St., 17057, pg. 1002 **IT**
PETROLEUM PRODUCTS CORP., 900 Eisenhower Blvd., 17057, pg. 859 **PV**
RE Wright Environmental, Inc., 3240 Schoolhouse Rd., 17057, pg. 976 **PV**
Wright Laboratory Services, Inc., 34 Dogwood Ln., 17057, pg. 976 **PV**

Mifflintown

EMPIRE KOSHER POULTRY, INC., River Rd., 17059, pg. 374 **PV**

Milford

Altec Lansing Technologies, Inc., Rte. 6 & 209, 18337, pg. 479 **PV**
Pike County Light & Power Co., 219 1/2 Broad St., 18337, pg. 1229 **PB**

Millersburg

Brubaker Tool Corp., 200 Front St., 17061, pg. 368 **PV**

Milton

Schult Homes Corporation, 30 Industrial Pk. Rd., 17847, pg. 1442 **PB**

Mohnton

Gai-Tronics Corporation, 400 E. Wyomissing Ave., 19540, pg. 1430 **PB**

Monaca

Anchor Hocking, 400 Ninth St., 15061-1864, pg. 1177 **PB**
Nova Chemicals, Inc., 400 Frankfurt Road, 15061, pg. 971 **IT**
Pittsburgh Tube Monaca Div., 1817 Pennsylvania Ave., 15061, pg. 868 **PV**
Zinc Corporation of America, 300 Frankfort Rd., 15061, pg. 540 **PV**

Monroeville

American Cablevision of Monroeville, Inc., 200 James Place, 15146, pg. 1610 **PB**
AMERICAN HOME IMPROVEMENT, 9001 Rico Rd., Bldg. 9, 15146, pg. 56 **PB**
GAI Construction Monitoring Services, Inc., 570 Beatty Rd., 15146, pg. 434 **PV**
GAI CONSULTANTS, INC., 570 Beatty Rd., 15146, pg. 433 **PV**
GCH Acquisition Corp., Corporate One, Building II, 4075 Monroeville Blvd., Ste. 400, 15146, pg. 1347 **IT**
INTERNATIONAL TECHNOLOGY CORPORATION, 2790 Mosside Blvd., 15146, pg. 907 **PB**
Nuclear and Advanced Technology Division, 4350 Northern Pike, 15146, pg. 273 **PB**
#1 COCHRAN, INC., 4200 William Penn Hwy., 15146, pg. 809 **PV**
Olander & Brophy, Inc., 2300 Eldo Rd., 15145, pg. 847 **PB**
Ragnar Benson, Inc., 4055 Monroeville Blvd., Ste. 210, 15146, pg. 99 **PV**
Thermal Transfer Corp., 1100 Rico Rd., 15146, pg. 29 **PB**
TRANSTAR HOLDINGS, L.P., P.O. Box 68, 135 Jamison Lane, 15146, pg. 1097 **PV**
US Steel Technical Center, 4000 Tech Ctr. Drive, 15146-3057, pg. 1662 **PB**
Westinghouse Energy Center, 4350 Northern Pike, 15146, pg. 273 **PB**
Woodhaven Care Center, 2400 McGinley Rd., 15146, pg. 733 **PV**

Montgomeryville

Aydin Raytor Div., Mongomeryville Industrial Ctr., Commerce Dr., 18936, pg. 158 **PB**
Books Management, Inc., 979 Bethlehem Pike, 18936, pg. 491 **PB**
EG & G Optoelectronics Montgomeryville, 221 Commerce Drive, 18936, pg. 543 **PB**
ITW Philadelphia Resins, 130 Commerce Dr., 18936, pg. 867 **PB**
Microsemi RF Products, Inc., 140 Commerce Dr., 18936, pg. 1107 **PB**
SURGICAL LASER TECHNOLOGIES, INC., 147 Keystone Dr., 18936, pg. 1542 **PV**
TosoHaas Company, 156 Keystone Dr., 18936, pg. 1408 **IT**
Zink & Triest, 111 Commerce Dr., 18936, pg. 1090 **PV**

Montoursville

Beacon Container of PA, 326 Maple St., 17754, pg. 125 **PV**
Schnadig Corp., 17754, pg. 971 **PV**

Montrose

STOREROOM SOLUTIONS INC., 71 Grow Ave., 18801, pg. 1045 **PV**

Moon Township

CENTRIA, 1005 Beaver Grade Rd., 15108-2944, pg. 225 **PV**
PITTSBURGH TUBE CO., Cherrington Corp. Ctr., 600 Club House Dr., Ste. 200, 15108-3195, pg. 867 **PV**

Morgantown

Kayeness, Inc., 115 Thousand Oaks Blvd., Ste. 102, 19543, pg. 138 **PV**
McNeilus Companies, Hemlock Rd., 19543, pg. 725 **PV**
MORGAN TRAILER MANUFACTURING CO., One Morgan Way, 19543, pg. 761 **PV**

Morrisville

CHEMCENTRAL/Philadelphia, Four Steel Rd. E., 19067, pg. 232 **PV**
Pre Finish Metals Inc.-Morrisville, 1295 Newford Mill Rd., 19067, pg. 1057 **PB**

Mount Bethel

Wildon Industries, Inc., Rte. 512, P.O. Box 176, 18343, pg. 129 **IT**

Mount Holly Springs

Ahlstrom Filtration, Inc.-Mt. Holly Springs Mill, 122 W. Butler St., 17065-0238, pg. 35 **IT**

PB - U.S. Public Companies Volume
PV - U.S. Private Companies Volume
IT - International Public & Private Companies Volume

1408

McCoy Electronics Co., 100 Watts St., P.O. Box B, 17065, pg. 1209 **PB**

Mount Jewett

PTC Thermistor Div., Drawer 1, 16704, pg. 208 **IT**

Mount Joy

FIRST MOUNT JOY CORPORATION, 15 Mount Joy St., 17552, pg. 407 **PV**
NEW STANDARD CORPORATION, 125 Pinkerton Rd., 17552, pg. 794 **PV**
Rollman Supply Company, Nine Joy St., 17552, pg. 407 **PV**
The Sico Company, 15 Mt. Joy St., 17552, pg. 407 **PV**
Spangles' Flour Mills of Mt. Joy, 17552, pg. 1176 **PV**

Mount Pleasant

Sony Display Systems, P.O. Box Sony, 15666, pg. 1284 **IT**

Mount Pocono

Paradise Stream, Inc., 18344, pg. 1512 **PB**

Mount Wolf

Corrugated Packaging, 25 Walnut St., 17347, pg. 737 **PB**
NEW YORK WIRE CO., 152 N. Main St., 17347, pg. 795 **PV**

Mountain Top

Communication Microwave Corp., P.O. Box 69, 18707, pg. 1384 **IT**
CORNELL IRON WORKS, INC., Crestwood Industrial Park, 18707, pg. 276 **PV**
Cornell Storefront Systems, Inc., Crestwood Industrial Park, 18707, pg. 276 **PV**
Dowty Aerospace Turbine Engine Components Group, P.O. Box 68, Crestwood Industrial Park, 18707-0068, pg. 1337 **IT**
Huls America Inc., Crestwood Industrial Park, Oakhill Rd., 18707, pg. 1455 **IT**
King Fifth Wheel Co., Crestwood Industrial Pk., P.O. Box 68, 18707, pg. 1337 **IT**

Murrysville

BECKWITH MACHINERY COMPANY, 4565 William Penn Hwy., 15668, pg. 129 **PV**
Ellson Equipment Co., Inc., 3820 Old Wm. Penn Hwy., 15668, pg. 360 **PV**
Respironics, Inc., 1001 Murray Ridge Dr., 15668-8550, pg. 1383 **PB**

Myerstown

Quaker Alloy, Inc., 200 E. Richland Ave., 17067, pg. 142 **PB**

Narberth

Jacob Sigel Triad, Sabine & Essex Aves., 19072, pg. 921 **PB**

Nazareth

Essroc Materials Inc., 3251 Bath Pike, 18019, pg. 292 **IT**
Hi-Pure Chemicals, Inc., P.O. Box 351, 731 Englert St., 18064, pg. 1219 **PB**
The Lamson & Sessions Co., 635 E. Lawn Rd., 18064, pg. 976 **PB**
Transilwrap Company, Inc., 615 Daniels Rd., 18064, pg. 1097 **PV**

Nesquehoning

Westchester Plastics, Green Acres Industrial Pk., 18240, pg. 100 **PB**

New Bethlehem

Citizens Utilities Company of Pennsylvania, 214-216 Lafayette St., 16242, pg. 380 **PB**
H.B. DeViney Co., 300 Keck Ave., 16242, pg. 1480 **PB**

New Brighton

TUSCARORA INCORPORATED, 800 Fifth Ave., 15066, pg. 1646 **PB**

New Britain

BATEMAN BROTHERS LUMBER CO., INC., 89 Sand Rd., 18901, pg. 122 **PV**

New Castle

Feed Screws Div., 1399 Countyline Rd., 16101, pg. 104 **PB**
FIRST WESTERN BANCORP, INC., 101 E. Washington St., 16101, pg. 642 **PB**

First Western Bank, National Association, 101 E. Washington St., 16101, pg. 642 **PB**
First Western Trust Services Co., 101 E. Washington St., 16101, pg. 642 **PB**
New Castle Industries, Inc., 1399 Countyline Rd., 16101, pg. 104 **PB**
New Castle Refractory Co., 915 Industrial St., 16102, pg. 515 **PB**
Pennsylvania Power Co., One E. Washington St., 16103-0891, pg. 645 **PB**
Shaw-Perkins Inc., 205 W. Washington St., P.O. Box 1486, 16103, pg. 913 **PV**
Tanner Plating Div., 925 Industrial St., 16102, pg. 104 **PB**
Universal-Rundle Corp., 217 N. Mill St., 16101, pg. 1193 **PB**

New Holland

Automatic Timing & Controls, Inc., 114 Earland Dr., 17757, pg. 327 **PV**
BC-USA, 400 S. Custer Ave., 17557, pg. 201 **IT**
Bongrain Cheese USA, 400 S. Custer Ave., 17557, pg. 201 **IT**
Certified Food Service of PA, Inc., 112 Short St., 17557, pg. 1529 **PB**
East Smithfield Farms, Inc., 150 W. Jackson St., 17557, pg. 201 **IT**
Ford New Holland, 500 Diller Ave., 17557-0903, pg. 483 **IT**
Ford New Holland Credit, Inc., 208 E. Main St., 17557, pg. 483 **IT**
Frontier Communications of Pennsylvania, Inc., P.O. Box 1902, 37-43 Diller Ave., 17757, pg. 684 **PB**
Major Smith Inc., 158 W. Jackson St., 17557, pg. 201 **IT**

New Hope

TEL-SAVE HOLDINGS, INC., 6805 Rte. 202, 18938, pg. 1568 **PB**

New Kensington

Robicon, 500 Hunt Valley Dr., 15068, pg. 528 **PV**

New Kingstown

VALK MANUFACTURING COMPANY, 66 E. Main St., 17072-0428, pg. 1131 **PV**

New Oxford

Aero Oil Corp., 230 Lincolnway E., 17350, pg. 741 **PB**

New Stanton

SuperValu, Inc.-Pittsburgh Div., P.O. Box 1000, 400 Paintersville St., 15672, pg. 1540 **PB**

Newtown

Aydin Vector Div., P.O. Box 328, 47 Friends Ln., 18940, pg. 158 **PB**
DUNMORE CORPORATION, 207 Penns Trail, 18940, pg. 346 **PV**
Eurotherm Recorders Inc., One Pheasant Run, 18940, pg. 466 **IT**
EXAR Corp.-Southeast, 293 Centinel Ave., 18940, pg. 598 **PB**
France Compressor Products Division, 104 Pheasant Run, 18940, pg. 402 **PV**
Plastomer Products Div., 23 Friends Lane, 18940, pg. 402 **PB**

Newtown Square

ARCO Chemical Co., 3801 West Chester Pike, 19073, pg. 144 **PB**
Mobil Chemical Co., 3801 W. Chester Pike, 19073-2320, pg. 1118 **PB**
Poe & Brown of Pennsylvania, 3603 Winding Way, 19073, pg. 1312 **PB**
Vester Corporation, 3400 Westchester Pike, Ste 201, 19073, pg. 86 **PV**

Norristown

Burns & Roe Environmental Services, 2570 Blvd. of the Generals, 19403, pg. 187 **PV**
Collegeville Advertising, Bldg. 200, Washington Sq., 2750 Blvd. of the Generals, 19403, pg. 1422 **PB**
Colonial Penn Insurance Co., 2650 Audobon Rd., 19403, pg. 712 **PB**
H.S. Crocker Co., Inc., Valley Forge Corp. Ctr., 19403, pg. 290 **PV**
FCA Transaction Services, Inc., Valley Forge Business Center, 601 General Washington Ave., Ste. 600, 19403, pg. 471 **IT**
GENUARDI FAMILY MARKETS INC., 805 E. Germantown Pike, 19401, pg. 447 **PV**
Handy & Harman Tube Co., Inc., Twnshp. Line & Whitehall Rd., 19401, pg. 780 **PB**
Laramie Tire Distributors Inc., 700 Markley St., 19404, pg. 1312 **PB**
NATIONAL FIBERSTOCK CORPORATION, 2051 Potshop Ln., 19403, pg. 782 **PV**
NovaCare Employee Services, Inc., Valley Forge Corp. Ctr., 2621 Van Buren Ave., 19403, pg. 1203 **PB**

SETON COMPANY, 1000 Madison Ave., 19403, pg. 987 **PV**
STREAMLIGHT INC., 1030 W. Germantown Pike, 19403, pg. 1047 **PV**
The Times Herald, 410 Markley St., 18404, pg. 935 **PV**
TSENG LABS, Courthouse Plaza, 18 W. Aries St., 19401, pg. 1643 **PB**

North East

BETTER BAKED FOODS, INC., 56 Smedley St., 16428, pg. 141 **PV**
RIDG-U-RAK, INC., 120 South Lake St., 16428, pg. 930 **PV**

North Huntingdon

Chambers USA Waste, Inc., 310 Leger Rd., 15642-1148, pg. 1686 **PB**

North Versailles

FlexRx, 1810 Lincoln Hwy., 15137, pg. 1091 **PB**

North Wales

BIF, Sumneytown Pike, 19454, pg. 726 **PB**

Northumberland

FURMAN FOODS, INC., P.O. Box 500, 17857, pg. 431 **PV**
Mohawk Flush Doors, Inc., P.O. Box 112, U.S. Rte. 11, 17857, pg. 1067 **IT**

Oakmont

BECO ENGINEERING COMPANY, P.O. Box 443, 800 Third St., 15139, pg. 129 **PV**
EDGEWATER STEEL COMPANY, 300 College Ave., 15139-2199, pg. 364 **PV**

Oaks

DETTRA FLAG COMPANY, 120 Montgomery Ave., 19456, pg. 328 **PV**
Fleming Foods of Pennsylvania, Inc., Egypt & Greentree Rd., 19456, pg. 653 **PB**
PENCO PRODUCTS, P.O. Box 378, Brower Ave., 19456, pg. 848 **PV**
SEI Financial Services Company, Freedom Valley Dr., 19456, pg. 1417 **PB**
SEI INVESTMENTS, One Freedom Valley Dr., 19456, pg. 1417 **PB**

Oil City

NSO Co., Rouseville Rd., 16301, pg. 1110 **IT**

Old Forge

PANEL PRINTS, INC., 1001 Moosic Rd., 18518, pg. 836 **PV**

Olyphant

WILLIAM BROJACK LUMBER COMPANY, RD # 1, P.O. Box 482, 18447, pg. 171 **PV**
WEA Manufacturing, 210 N. Valley Ave., 18447, pg. 1612 **PB**

Orwigsburg

Dixon Wearever Inc., Rte. 61, 17961, pg. 515 **PB**

Ottsville

MODERN CONCRETE SEPTIC TANK COMPANY, Durham Rd., 18942, pg. 754 **PV**
Wehrung Family Home Center, Route 611, 18942, pg. 754 **PV**

Oxford

Tasty Baking-Oxford, 700 Lincoln St., 19363, pg. 1561 **PB**

Palmerton

Horsehead Resource Development Company, Inc., 401 Delaware Ave., 18071, pg. 540 **PV**
Palmer Water Co., 6 94th St., 18071, pg. 540 **PV**

Paoli

AMETEK, INC., Station Sq., 19301, pg. 99 **PB**
Orga Card Systems Inc., 19 East Central Ave., 19301, pg. 1070 **IT**

Paradise

DENLINGER, INC., 3246 Lincoln Hwy. E, 17562, pg. 324 **PV**

Geographic Index-U.S.

PB - *U.S. Public Companies Volume*
PV - *U.S. Private Companies Volume*
IT - *International Public & Private Companies Volume*

1409

Peach Glen

KNOUSE FOODS INC., 800 Peach Glen/Idaville Rd., 17375-0001, pg. 627   **PV**

Perkasie

PERKASIE INDUSTRIES CORPORATION, 50 E. Spruce St., 18944, pg. 854   **PV**

Petrolia

PSG, Hwy. 268, 16050, pg. 1774   **PB**

Philadelphia

AIC Holdings, Inc., Two Liberty Plaza, 1601 Chestnut St., 19192, pg. 362   **PB**
AIG Life Insurance Company, 2005 Market, 19103, pg. 84   **PB**
AT&T Communications, 1500 Market St., 15th Fl., 19102, pg. 10   **PB**
ACTION MANUFACTURING CO., 100 E. Erie, 19134, pg. 15   **PV**
ADELPHIA LAMP & SHADE INC., 5000 Paschall Ave., 19143, pg. 17   **PV**
Adwin Equipment Co., 2301 Market St., 19103, pg. 1268   **PB**
Adwin Realty Co., 2301 Market St., 19103, pg. 1268   **PB**
Agusta Aerospace Corporation, 3050 Red Lion Rd., 19114, pg. 32   **IT**
ALDAN INDUSTRIES, 2701 E. Tioga St., 19134-6184, pg. 33   **PV**
ALL-LUMINUM PRODUCTS, INC., 10981 Decatur Rd., 19154-3297, pg. 34   **PV**
Allied Advertising Agency, Public Relations, 2218 Race St., 19103, pg. 38   **PV**
Allied Insurance Company, Two Liberty Plaza, 1601 Chestnut St., 19192, pg. 362   **PB**
ALLIED MERCANTILE COMPANY, 1720 Chestnut St., 19103, pg. 39   **PV**
Allied Security Inc., 7900 Bustleton Ave., 19152, pg. 41   **PV**
ALMO CORP., 9815 Roosevelt Blvd., 19114, pg. 44   **PV**
ALPHA SHIRT CO., INC., 401 E. Hunting Park Ave., 19124, pg. 45   **PV**
AMERICAN PACKAGING CORPORATION, 2900 Grant Ave., 19114, pg. 60   **PV**
American Risk Associates, Ltd., 1818 Market St., 19103, pg. 317   **PV**
ANGELO BROTHERS CO., 12401 McNulty Rd., 19154, pg. 74   **PV**
Anthropologie, 1809 Walnut St., 19103, pg. 1700   **PB**
Anzon, 2545 Aramingo Ave., 19125, pg. 328   **IT**
ARAMARK CORP., Aramark Tower, 1101 Market St., 19107, pg. 78   **PV**
Aramark Corporation, Aramark Tower, 1101 Market St., 19107, pg. 79   **PV**
Aramark Services of Texas, Inc., 1101 Market St., 19107, pg. 79   **PV**
Aramark Sports & Entertainment Services Inc., 1101 Market St., 19107, pg. 79   **PV**
Ascom Automation Inc., 444 N. Third St., 19123, pg. 86   **IT**
ATLANTIC METALS CORPORATION, Orthodox St. at Delaware River, 19137, pg. 95   **PV**
Atlas Co. of Boston, Inc., 2121 E. Huntington St., 19125, pg. 581   **PV**
AtoHaas North America Inc., 100 Independence Mall W., 19106, pg. 1403   **PB**
Automotive Service Equipment Div., 1735 Market St., 19103, pg. 605   **PB**
BACPE, Inc., 1717 Arch St., 19103, pg. 202   **PB**
BAP-Durham, Inc., 1717 Arch St., 34th Fl., 19103, pg. 202   **PB**
BAP-1810 Arch Land Parcel, Inc., 1717 Arch St., 34th Fl., 19103, pg. 202   **PB**
BAP-1760 Market, Inc., 1717 Arch St., 34th Fl., 19103, pg. 202   **PB**
BAP-1310 North Court House, 1717 Arch St., 34th Fl., 19103, pg. 202   **PB**
BAP-Tustin, Inc., 1717 Arch St., 34th Fl., 19103, pg. 202   **PB**
BHC Securities, Inc., One Commerce Sq., 2005 Market St., 19103-3212, pg. 647   **PB**
BHCM Inc., One Commerce Sq., 2005 Market St. 19103-3212, pg. 647   **PB**
BSA Advertising, Inc., 11 Penn Center, Ste. 625, 19103-2996, pg. 108   **PB**
BACHMANN INDUSTRIES, INC., 1400 E. Erie Ave., 19124, pg. 109   **PV**
Bank Hapoalim (Philadelphia), 1515 Market St., 19102, pg. 149   **IT**
Bankers Standard Insurance Company, Two Liberty Pl., 1601 Chestnut St., 19192, pg. 365   **PB**
Baum Printing House, Inc., 9985 Gantry Rd., 19115, pg. 1735
Bell Atlantic Administrative Services, Inc., 1717 Arch St., 19103, pg. 202   **PB**
Bell Atlantic Capital Advisors, Inc., 1717 Arch St., 19103, pg. 202   **PB**
Bell Atlantic Enterprises Corporation, 1717 Arch St., 19103, pg. 202   **PB**
Bell Atlantic Foundation, 1717 Arch St., 19103, pg. 202   **PB**
Bell Atlantic Information Systems, Inc., 1717 Arch St., 19103, pg. 202   **PB**
Bell Atlantic Investment Development Corporation, 1717 Arch St., 19103, pg. 202   **PB**

Bell Atlantic Land Development, Inc., 1717 Arch St., 19103, pg. 202   **PB**
Bell Atlantic MM Holdings, Inc., 1717 Arch St., 19103, pg. 202   **PB**
Bell Atlantic-PA, 1717 Arch St., 18th Fl., 19103, pg. 203   **PB**
Bell Atlantic Personal Communications, Inc., 1717 Arch St., 19103, pg. 203   **PB**
Bell Atlantic Properties, Inc., 1717 Arch St., 19103, pg. 203   **PB**
Bell Atlantic Properties II, Inc., 1717 Arch St., 19103, pg. 203   **PB**
Bell Atlantic Property Holdings, Inc., 1717 Arch St., 34th Fl., 19103, pg. 203   **PB**
Bell Atlantic Ventures XXI, Inc., 1717 Arch St., 19103, pg. 203   **PB**
Bell Atlantic Ventures II, Inc., 1717 Arch St., 19103, pg. 203   **PB**
John Benjamins North America Inc, 821 Bethlehem Pike, 19118, pg. 187   **IT**
Bermudez-Binswanger, 2 Logan Sq., 19103, pg. 144   **PV**
BERWIND CORPORATION, 3000 W. Tower, Centre Sq., 1500 Market St., 19102, pg. 138   **PB**
Berwind Financial Group, 3000 W. Tower, Centre Sq., 1500 Market St., 19102, pg. 139   **PV**
Berwind Property Group, Inc., 1500 Market St., 19102, pg. 138   **PV**
BFG Railway Investors LP, 3000 W. Tower, Center Square, 1500 Market St., 19102, pg. 139   **PV**
Bienfang Paper Div., One Commerce Sq., 2005 Market St., 19103, pg. 849   **PB**
BINSWANGER, 2 Logan Square, 19103, pg. 144   **PV**
Binswanger Management Corp., 2 Logan Sq., 19103, pg. 144   **PV**
Binswanger Realty Group, 2 Logan Sq., 19103, pg. 144   **PV**
BROOKS PROVISIONS INC., 3445 S. Front St., 19148, pg. 172   **PV**
Earle Palmer Brown Public Relations, One Liberty Pl., 1650 Market St., 19103, pg. 174   **PV**
BURGOYNE, INC., 2030 E. Byberry Rd., 19116, pg. 182   **PV**
Burholme Woods Joint Venture, 6425 Rising Sun Ave., 19111, pg. 1326   **PB**
BUTCHER & CO., INC., 1528 Walnut St., Ste. 2100, 19102, pg. 189   **PV**
Butcher Energy, 1528 Walnut St.Ste 2100, 19102, pg. 189   **PV**
BUTLER FOODS, INC., 2300 E. Butler, 19137, pg. 190   **PV**
CDI CORP., 1717 Arch St., 35th Fl., 19103-2768, pg. 276   **PB**
CDI Corporation, 1717 Arch St., 35th Fl., 19103-2768, pg. 277   **PB**
CG Projects, Inc., P.O. Box 41400, 2001 Market St., 19101-1400, pg. 432   **PB**
CMAC INVESTMENT CORPORATION, 1601 Market St., 12th Fl., 19103, pg. 278   **PB**
CR Quality Services, Inc., 2001 Market St., 19101, pg. 432   **PB**
CRC Properties, Inc., 2001 Market St., 19101, pg. 432   **PB**
CRR Industries, Inc., P.O. Box 41400, 2001 Market St., 19101-1400, pg. 432   **PB**
CRR Investments, Inc., P.O. Box 41400, 2001 Market St., 19101-1400, pg. 432   **PB**
CSS INDUSTRIES, INC., 1845 Walnut St., Ste. 800, 19103, pg. 283   **PB**
The Camden Fire Insurance Assn., 436 Walnut St., 19105, pg. 543   **IT**
Capital Cities/ABC Owned Television Stations, 4100 City Line Ave., 19131, pg. 512   **PB**
The Care Pavilion of Walnut Park Plaza, 6212 Walnut St., 19139, pg. 729   **PB**
CAREERS USA INC., 1825 JFK Blvd., 19103, pg. 209   **PV**
Case Paper Co., Inc., 499 E. Tioga, 19134, pg. 218   **PV**
CEDAF FARMS COMPANY, INC., 2609 E. York St., 19125, pg. 221   **PV**
Century Indemnity Company, Two Liberty Plaza, 1601 Chestnut St., 19192, pg. 365   **PB**
Century Reinsurance Company, Two Liberty Plaza, 1601 Chestnut St., 19192, pg. 365   **PB**
Charter Fairmount Behavioral Health System, Inc., 561 Fairmorne Ave., 19128, pg. 1034   **PB**
Cheltenham Nursing & Rehabilitation Center, 600 W. Cheltenham Ave., 19126, pg. 729   **PB**
Cheltenham-York Road Nursing & Rehabilitation Center, 7101 Old York Rd., 19126, pg. 729   **PB**
Chemical Products Group, 1735 Market St., 19103, pg. 605   **PB**
Chesterton Binswanger Capital Advisors, 2 Logan Sq., 19103, pg. 144   **PV**
Chestnut Hill National Bank, 9 W. Evergreen Ave., 19118, pg. 1159   **PB**
THE CHILDREN'S HOSPITAL OF PHILADELPHIA, 34th St. & Civic Ctr. Blvd., 19104-4399, pg. 236   **PB**
Cigna Bond Services, Inc., Two Liberty Pl., 1601 Chestnut St., 19192, pg. 362   **PB**
Cigna Conference Facilities, Inc., One Liberty Pl., 1650 Market St., 19192, pg. 358   **PB**
CIGNA CORP., One Liberty Pl., 1650 Market St., 19192-1550, pg. 356   **PB**
Cigna Direct Marketing Company, Two Liberty Plaza, 1601 Chestnut St., 19192, pg. 362   **PB**
Cigna Employers Insurance Company, Two Liberty Pl., 1601 Chestnut St., 19192, pg. 366   **PB**
Cigna Excess & Surplus Insurance Services, Inc. (PA), 1601 Chestnut St., 19192, pg. 363   **PB**
Cigna Fire Underwriters Insurance Company, Two Liberty Plaza, 1601 Chestnut St., 19192, pg. 365   **PB**
Cigna Foundation, One Liberty Pl., 1650 Market St., 19192, pg. 357   **PB**

Cigna Healthcare Benefits, Inc., 1601 Chestnut St., 19192, pg. 359   **PB**
Cigna Insurance Company, Two Liberty Plaza, 1601 Chestnut St., 19192, pg. 365   **PB**
Cigna Loss Control Services, Inc., Two Liberty Pl., 1601 Chestnut St., 19192, pg. 364   **PB**
Cigna Managed Care Benefits Company, 1601 Chestnut St., 19192, pg. 360   **PB**
Cigna Property & Casualty Insurance Company, Two Liberty Plaza, 1601 Chestnut St., 19192, pg. 364   **PB**
Cigna Reinsurance Company, Two Liberty Pl., 1601 Chestnut St., 19192, pg. 365   **PB**
Cigna Road & Travel Club, Inc., Two Liberty Plaza, 1601 Chestnut St., 19192, pg. 362   **PB**
Cigna Run-Off Services, Inc., Two Liberty Pl., 1601 Chestnut St., 19192, pg. 365   **PB**
Cigna Worldwide, Incorporated, Two Liberty Plaza, 1601 Chestnut St., 19192, pg. 363   **PB**
Cobbs Creek Nursing Center, 6900 Cobbs Creek Pkwy., 19142, pg. 729   **PB**
COLONIAL BEEF CO., 3333 S. Third St., 19148, pg. 253   **PV**
Colonial Penn Life Insurance Company, 399 Market St., 19181, pg. 433   **PB**
Comcast Cable Communications, Inc., 1500 Market St., 19107, pg. 407   **PB**
COMCAST CORPORATION, 1500 Market St., 19102, pg. 406   **PB**
CoMed Communications, Inc., 210 W. Washington Sq., 19106, pg. 1083   **PV**
Commonwealth Land Title Insurance Company, Eight Penn Ctr. Plaza, 19103, pg. 1374   **PB**
Commonwealth Relocation Services, Inc., Eight Penn Ctr. Plaza, 19103, pg. 1374   **PB**
Connecticut General Fire & Casualty Insurance Company, Two Liberty Plaza, 1601 Chestnut St., 19192, pg. 365   **PB**
Connelly Paper Mill, 4368 Main St., 19127, pg. 264   **PV**
CONRAIL, INC., Two Commerce Sq., Ste. 19-A, 19103, pg. 431   **PB**
Cooke & Bieler, Inc., 1700 Market St., Ste. 3222, 19103, pg. 1673   **PB**
CoreStates Bank, N.A., Broad & Chestnut Sts., 19101, pg. 446   **PB**
CoreStates Capital Corp., Broad & Chestnut Sts., 19101, pg. 446   **PB**
CoreStates Capital Markets Group, Broad & Chestnut Sts., 19107, pg. 446   **PB**
CORESTATES FINANCIAL CORP., PNB Bldg., Broad & Chestnut Sts., 19107-3494, pg. 446   **PB**
CoreStates Holding, Inc., Philadelphia Natl. Bank Bldg., Broad & Chestnut Sts., 19101-7558, pg. 447   **PB**
Corestates Securities Corp., Philadelphia Natl. Bank Bldg., Broad & Chestnut Sts., 19101-7558, pg. 447   **PB**
Cravens, Dargan & Company, Pacific Coast, Two Liberty Pl., 1601 Chestnut St., 19192, pg. 365   **PB**
Cravens, Dargan & Company, Pacific Coast of New York, Inc., Two Liberty Pl., 1601 Chestnut St., 19192, pg. 366   **PB**
Crown Cork & Seal, Americas Division, One Crown Way, 19154-4599, pg. 463   **PB**
CROWN CORK & SEAL COMPANY, INC., One Crown Way, 19154-4599, pg. 462   **PB**
Crown Cork & Seal Company, Inc.-Subsidiaries Division, One Crown Way, 19154-4599, pg. 463   **PB**
D&Z Microelectronics, 1818 Market St., 19103, pg. 317   **PV**
D&Z Utility Services, 1818 Market St., 19103, pg. 317   **PV**
D&Z Construction Services, 1818 Market St., 19103-3672, pg. 317   **PV**
Day & Zimmerman Infrastructure, 1818 Market St., 19103, pg. 317   **PV**
DAY & ZIMMERMANN, INC., 1818 Market St., 19103, pg. 316   **PV**
Day & Zimmermann International, Inc., 1818 Market St., 19103, pg. 317   **PV**
Day & Zimmermann LLC, 1818 Market St., 19103, pg. 317   **PV**
DEB SHOPS, INC., 9401 Blue Grass Rd., 19114, pg. 474   **PB**
Delaware Management Holdings, Inc., 1 Commerce Sq., 2005 Market St., 19103-7042, pg. 997   **PB**
DELAWARE RIBBON MANUFACTURERS, INC., P.O. Box 15271, 2531 N. Trenton Ave., 19125, pg. 322   **PV**
Delaware Valley Wool Scouring Co., 3419 Richmond St., 19117, pg. 1121   **PV**
Dilks Stamp Co., 1613 Sansom St., 19103, pg. 58   **PV**
DIMELING, SCHREIBER & PARK, 1629 Locust St., 19103, pg. 333   **PV**
DOLPHIN & BRADBURY, INC., 1617 JFK Blvd., Ste. 1140, 19103-1811, pg. 338   **PV**
Durand Inc., 112 008 Roosevelt Blvd., 19154, pg. 638   **PV**
ESIS International, Inc., Two Liberty Plaza, 1601 Chestnut St., 19192, pg. 366   **PB**
Eastern Pennsylvania Development Co., 2301 Market St., 19103, pg. 1268   **PB**
Eastern Pennsylvania Exploration Co., 2301 Market St., 19103, pg. 1268   **PB**
Elf Atochem North America, Agrichemicals Div., 2000 Market St., 19103-7885, pg. 446   **IT**
Elf Atochem North America, Basic Chemicals Div., 2000 Market St., 19103, pg. 446   **IT**
Elf Atochem North America, Fluorochemical Div., 2000 Market St., 19103-3222, pg. 446   **IT**
Elf Atochem North America, 2000 Market St., 19103-3222, pg. 445   **IT**
Esis, Inc., Two Liberty Pl., 1601 Chestnut St., 19192, pg. 366   **PB**
EWING COLE CHERRY BROTT, 100 N. 6th St., 19106, pg. 387   **PV**
FMC Corp. Pharmaceutical & Bioscience Products Div., 2000 Market St., 19103, pg. 605   **PB**

Geographic Index-U.S.

FMC Corp., Agricultural Products Group, 1735 Market St., 19103, pg. 605 **PB**
FMC Food Ingredients Div., 1735 Market St., 19103, pg. 605 **PB**
FMC Alkali Chemicals Div., 1735 Market St., 19103, pg. 605 **PB**
FMC Peroxygen Chemicals Div., 1735 Market St., 19103, pg. 605 **PB**
FMC Phosphorus Chemicals Div., 1735 Market St., 19103, pg. 605 **PB**
Fairview Care Center of Bethlehem Pike, 184 Bethlehem Pike, 19118, pg. 729 **PB**
Fairview Care Center of Papermill Rd., 850 Papermill Rd., 19118, pg. 729 **PB**
Fanta Furniture, 10981 Decatur Rd., 19154-3297, pg. 35 **PV**
FARM JOURNAL INC., Centre Sq. W., 1500 Market St., 28th Fl., 19102, pg. 394 **PV**
5601 Medical Plaza, 56th & Chestnut Sts., 19139, pg. 729 **PB**
Frank H. Fleer Corp., 10th & Somerville, 19123, pg. 1052 **PB**
Four Seasons Hotel, One Logan Sq., 19103, pg. 502 **IT**
Frankford Abstract Co., 6500 Castor Ave., 19149, pg. 956 **PB**
THE FRANKLIN INSTITUTE, 222 N. 20th St., 19103, pg. 424 **PV**
Franklin Real Estate Co., 225 S. 15th St., 19102, pg. 72 **PB**
H. FREEMAN & SON, INC., 3601 Island Rd., 19153, pg. 426 **PV**
Gemini Bakery Equipment Co., 9990 Gantry Rd., 19115, pg. 511 **IT**
General Accident Insurance, 436 Walnut St., 19106-3786, pg. 543 **IT**
General Employment Enterprises, Inc., 1617 JFK Blvd., Ste. 930, 19103, pg. 714 **PV**
General Felt Industries, Inc., 2121 E. Wheatsheaf Ln., 19137, pg. 1094 **PV**
Genesis ElderCare, 5601 Chestnut St., 19139, pg. 728 **PB**
Girard Point Refinery, 3144 W. Passyunk, 19145, pg. 1530 **PV**
GOLDENBERG CANDY COMPANY, 7701 State Rd., 19136, pg. 461 **PV**
G.B. Goldman Paper Co., 2201 E. Allegheny Ave., 19134, pg. 233 **PV**
Goldman, Sachs & Co., Mellon Bank Ctr., 1735 Market St., 26th Fl., 19103, pg. 462 **PV**
ALBERT M. GREENFIELD & COMPANY, 1880 JFK Blvd., 11th Fl., 19103, pg. 477 **PV**
Hanley & Belfus, Inc., 210 S. 13th St., 19107, pg. 1479 **PV**
HARRIS, BAIO & McCULLOUGH INC., 520 S. Front St., 19147, pg. 504 **PV**
Hatboro Manor Professional Condominiums, 6425 Rising Sun Ave., 19111, pg. 1326 **PV**
HAWTHORNE ADV., INC., 399 Market St., 19181, pg. 512 **PV**
Helios Capital Corporation, Ten Penn Ctr., 17th Fl., 1801 Market St., 19103, pg. 1530 **PV**
Heraeus Electro-Nite Co., 9901 Blue Grass Rd., 19114, pg. 616 **IT**
Holmes Protection of Philadelphia, Inc., 701 Callowhill St., 19123, pg. 1649 **PV**
Hornor, Townsend & Kent, 1601 Market St., 19103, pg. 849 **PV**
HUNT CORPORATION, One Commerce Sq., 2005 Market St., 19103, pg. 848 **PB**
Hunt International Div., One Commerce Sq., 2005 Market St., 19103, pg. 849 **PB**
INA Corporation, Two Liberty Pl., 1601 Chestnut St., 19192, pg. 362 **PB**
INA Special Risk Facilities, Inc., Two Liberty Pl., 1601 Chestnut St., 19192, pg. 366 **PB**
INA Tax Benefits Reporting, Inc., 1601 Chestnut St., 19192, pg. 362 **PB**
INAC Corp., Two Liberty Plaza, 1601 Chestnut St., 19192, pg. 366 **PB**
Image ReproGraphics, 1818 Market St., 19103, pg. 317 **PV**
Inapro, Inc., Two Liberty Pl., 1601 Chestnut St., 19192, pg. 366 **PB**
Indemnity Insurance Company of North America, Two Liberty Plaza, 1601 Chestnut St., 19192, pg. 366 **PB**
Independence Square Properties, Independence Sq., 19172, pg. 849 **PV**
Institute For Scientific Information, 3501 Market St., 19104, pg. 1600 **PV**
Insurance Company of North America, Two Liberty Plaza, 1601 Chestnut St., 19192, pg. 366 **PB**
Intercounty Newspaper, U 220 Ridge Ave., 19128, pg. 935 **PV**
Interstate Steel Supply Company, 1800 E. Byberry Rd., 19116, pg. 1100 **PV**
JWG Associates, Inc., 306 Cherry St., 19106, pg. 579 **PV**
CHARLES JACQUIN ET CIE, INC., 2633 Trenton Ave., 19125, pg. 580 **PV**
Janney Montgomery Scott Inc., 1601 Market St., 19103, pg. 849 **PV**
Jetro Cash & Carry, 3535 S. 10th Ave., 19148, pg. 587 **PV**
JETRONIC INDUSTRIES, INC., 4200 Mitchell St., 19128, pg. 926 **PB**
JORDON COMMERCIAL REFRIGERATOR CO., 2200 Kennedy, 19137, pg. 599 **PV**
KYW TV, Independence Mall E., 19106, pg. 275 **PB**
KINGSBURY, INC., 10385 Drummond Rd., 19154, pg. 622 **PV**
A.C. KISSLING, INC., 161 E. Allen St., 19125, pg. 624 **PV**
The LL Holding Company, Inc., 1717 Arch St., 34th Fl., 19103, pg. 203 **PB**
LP Associates, Two Liberty Pl., 1601 Chestnut St., 19192, pg. 365 **PB**

LPA Associates, Two Liberty Pl., 1601 Chestnut St., 19192, pg. 365 **PB**
LPB Associates, Two Liberty Pl., 1601 Chestnut St., 19192, pg. 365 **PB**
LPC Associates, Two Liberty Pl., 1601 Chestnut St., 19192, pg. 365 **PB**
LPD Associates, Two Liberty Pl., 1601 Chestnut St., 19192, pg. 365 **PB**
LPY Associates, Two Liberty Pl., 1601 Chestnut St., 19192, pg. 365 **PB**
LPZ Associates, Two Liberty Pl., 1601 Chestnut St., 19192, pg. 365 **PB**
LA FRANCE CORPORATION, 8425 Executive Ave., 19153, pg. 640 **PV**
Latimer & Buck, Inc., 121 S. Broad St., 13th Fl., 19107, pg. 985 **PB**
LAVELLE COMPANY, 275 Geiger Rd., 19115, pg. 653 **PV**
AL PAUL LEFTON CO., INC., 100 Independence Mall W., 19106-2399, pg. 658 **PV**
Levy United News, 850 E. Luzerne St., 19124, pg. 664 **PV**
Lewis & Norwood, General Agents, Inc., Two Liberty Pl., 1601 Chestnut St., 19192, pg. 366 **PB**
Life Insurance Company of North America, Two Liberty Plaza, 1601 Chestnut St., 19192, pg. 362 **PB**
Life Sciences International, 1818 Market St., 19103, pg. 317 **PV**
J.B. Lippincott Company, 227 E. Washington Sq., 19105, pg. 1513 **IT**
Lipschutz Brothers Inc, 1310-12 N. 4th St., 19122, pg. 103 **IT**
Arthur D. Little, Inc., Floor 3, 1760 Market St., 19103, pg. 670 **PV**
Marketdyne International, Inc., Two Liberty Plaza, 1601 Chestnut St., 19192, pg. 366 **PB**
MARQUETTE COPPERSMITHING CO., INC., P.O. Box 4584, 19131-6584, pg. 706 **PV**
Martin/F. Weber Company, 2727 Southampton, 19154, pg. 710 **PV**
Martin Marietta Management & Data Systems, P.O. Box 8048, 19101, pg. 1007 **PB**
Mayo Center, 650 Edison Ave., 19116, pg. 729 **PB**
The McCloskey Corporation, 7600 State Rd., 19136, pg. 1074 **PV**
Mellon PSFS, Mellon Bank Ctr., 1735 Market St., 19102-2386, pg. 1085 **PB**
DAVID MICHAEL & CO. INC., 10801 Decatur Rd., 19154, pg. 740 **PV**
Midlantic Bank, N.A., Centre Square, 1500 Market St., 19102, pg. 1242 **PB**
Montgomery & Collins, Inc. of Pennsylvania, Bourse Bldg., 21 S. Fifth St., Ste. 870, 19106-3409, pg. 366 **PB**
Moran Towing of Pennsylvania, 2799 S. Delaware Ave., 19148, pg. 761 **PV**
NAO, INC., 1284 E. Sedgley Ave., 19134, pg. 771 **PV**
NPS Energy Services, Inc., 1818 Market St., 19103, pg. 317 **PV**
NYT Video News International, 150 S. Independence Mall W., Ste. 1140, 19106, pg. 1174 **PB**
NYT Video News International, Public Ledger Bldg., 150 S. Independence Mall W. #1140, 19106, pg. 1176 **PB**
NAMICO, INC., 4601 Flat Rock Rd., 19127, pg. 774 **PV**
NATIONAL MEDIA CORPORATION, 11 Penn Ctr., 1835 Market St., Ste. 1100, 19103, pg. 1158 **PB**
National Publishing Co., 24th & Locus St., 19101, pg. 453 **PV**
W.H. Newbold, 1500 Walnut St., 19102, pg. 476 **IT**
94th Aero Squadron of Philadelphia, Inc., No. Philadelphia Airport, 2750 Red Lion Rd., 19154, pg. 1023 **PV**
NORTH AMERICAN PUBLISHING COMPANY, 401 N. Broad St., 19108, pg. 803 **PV**
Northeast Marketing-Philadelphia Business Center, Two Logan Sq., 18th & Arch Sts., Ste. 1650, 16th Fl., 19103, pg. 649 **PV**
NuArc Co., 9810 Ashton Rd., 19114, pg. 809 **PV**
Oxford Health Plans (PA), Inc., Independence Sq. W., Curtis, 601 Walnut St., Ste. 900, 19106, pg. 1239 **PB**
PMA Reinsurance Corporation, Mellon Bank Ctr., 1735 Market St., 19103-7590, pg. 1272 **PB**
PNC Bank, 100 S. Broad St., 19101, pg. 1243 **PB**
PNC Corp., Broad & Chestnut Sts., 19101, pg. 1243 **PB**
PNC Discount Brokerage, 1 PNC Plaza, 19102, pg. 1242 **PB**
Pacific Employers Insurance Company, Two Liberty Plaza, 1601 Chestnut St., 19192, pg. 365 **PB**
PACIFICO AUTO GROUP, 6701 Essington Ave., 19153, pg. 832 **PV**
PACOR, INC., 1900 N. Sixth St., 19122, pg. 833 **PV**
PARISI INC./ROYAL STORE FIXTURE, 3031 Red Lion Rd., 19114, pg. 839 **PV**
PEARL-PRESSMAN-LIBERTY COMMUNICATIONS GROUP, 912 N. 5th St., 19123, pg. 845 **PV**
PECO ENERGY COMPANY, 2301 Market St., 19101, pg. 1268 **PB**
PECO Energy Power Co., 2301 Market St., 19103, pg. 1268 **PB**
PEIRCE-PHELPS, INC., 2000 N. 59th St., 19131, pg. 847 **PV**
Penn Central Communications Corp., 2001 Market St., 19101, pg. 432 **PV**
Penn CMO Corporation, Independence Sq., 19172, pg. 850 **PV**
THE PENN COMPANIES, 10909 Dutton Rd., 19154, pg. 849 **PV**
Penn Insurance & Annuity Co., Independence Sq., 19172, pg. 850 **PV**
THE PENN MUTUAL LIFE INSURANCE COMPANY, 19172, pg. 849 **PV**
PENNOCK, 3027 Stokley St., 19129, pg. 850 **PV**
The Penns Landing Marina Corporation, 1717 Arch St., 34th Fl., 19103, pg. 203 **PB**

Pennsylvania General Insurance Company, 436 Walnut St., 19105, pg. 543 **IT**
Pennsylvania Parking, Inc., 1201 Walnut St., 2nd Fl., 19107, pg. 43 **PV**
THE PEP BOYS-MANNY, MOE & JACK, 3111 W. Allegheny Ave., 19132, pg. 1276 **PB**
PEPPER, HAMILTON & SCHEETZ, 3000 Two Logan Square, 18th & Arch Sts., 19103-2799, pg. 851 **PV**
Perfecseal Company, 9800 Bustleton Ave., 19115, pg. 210 **PB**
PHILADELPHIA COCA-COLA BOTTLING CO., 725 E. Erie Ave., 19134, pg. 861 **PV**
Philadelphia Daily News, P.O. Box 8527, 400 N. Broad St., 19101, pg. 964 **PB**
The Philadelphia Inquirer, 400 N. Broad, 19130, pg. 964 **PB**
Philadelphia International Investment Corp., Broad & Chestnut Sts., 19101, pg. 447 **PB**
Philadelphia Newspapers, Inc., 400 N. Broad St., 19130, pg. 964 **PB**
Philadelphia Terminal, 3300 N. Delaware Ave., 19134, pg. 692 **PB**
THE PHILLIES-A LIMITED PARTNERSHIP, Veterans Stadium, 3501 S. Broad St., 19148, pg. 861 **PV**
PINCUS BROS., INC., Independence Mall East, 19106, pg. 875 **PV**
Piping Design Div., P.O. Box 4584, 19131, pg. 706 **PV**
A. POMERANTZ & COMPANY, 701 Market St., Ste. 7000, 19106, pg. 875 **PV**
Potomac Insurance Co. of Illinois, 436 Walnut St., 19105, pg. 543 **IT**
POWELL ELECTRONICS INC., S. Island Rd. & Enterprise Ave., 19153, pg. 877 **PV**
Premium Recovery Services International, Inc., Two Liberty Pl., 1601 Chestnut St., 19192, pg. 366 **PB**
Prime Abstract, Inc., 6425 Rising Sun Ave., 19111, pg. 1326 **PB**
Prime Bank, 6425 Rising Sun Ave., 19111, pg. 1326 **PB**
Prime Financial, Inc., 6425 Rising Sun Ave., 19111, pg. 1326 **PB**
Process & Industrial Division, 1818 Market St., 19103, pg. 317 **PV**
Protection Technology, 1818 Market St., 14th Fl., 19103, pg. 317 **PV**
Quaker City Stamp Co., 4234 Macalester Ave., 19124, pg. 59 **PV**
Raytheon Engineers & Constructors International, 30 S. 17th St., 19103, pg. 1366 **PB**
Reading Entertainment Inc., One Penn Sq. W., 30 S. 15th St., Ste. 1300, 19102-4813, pg. 456 **PB**
Reclamizer, 10501 Decatur Rd., 19154, pg. 1039 **PV**
Recovery Services International, Inc., Two Liberty Plaza, 1601 Chestnut St., 19192, pg. 366 **PB**
Reliance Insurance Company, Four Penn Ctr. Plaza, 19103, pg. 1374 **PB**
Reliance Reinsurance Corp., Two Penn Ctr. Plaza, 19102, pg. 1374 **PB**
Reliance Standard Life Insurance Company, 2501 Parkway, 19130-2499, pg. 496 **PB**
Reliance Surety Corp., Four Penn Ctr. Plaza, 19103, pg. 1374 **PB**
RESOURCE AMERICA, INC., 1521 Locust St., 19102, pg. 1382 **PB**
REUBEN ORGANIZATION, 200 S. Broad St., 3rd Fl., 19102, pg. 925 **PV**
S.D. RICHMAN SONS, INC., 2435 E. Wheatsheaf Ln., 19137, pg. 929 **PV**
RIGHT MANAGEMENT CONSULTANTS, INC., 1818 Market St., 33rd Fl., 19103-3614, pg. 1390 **PB**
Rittenhouse Care Center, 1526 Lombard St., 19146, pg. 729 **PB**
ROHM AND HAAS COMPANY, 100 Independence Mall W., 19106-2399, pg. 1403 **PB**
Rohm and Haas Philadelphia Inc., 100 Independence Mall W., 19106-2399, pg. 1403 **PB**
ROOSEVELT PAPER CO., 7601 State Rd., 19136-3496, pg. 943 **PV**
Rowland Service Corporation, 6425 Rising Sun Ave., 19111, pg. 1326 **PV**
SPD TECHNOLOGIES, 13500 Roosevelt Blvd., 19116, pg. 957 **PV**
Sadtler Research Laboratories, 3316 Spring Garden St., 19104, pg. 230 **PV**
The St. Lawrence & Adirondack Railway Co., 2001 Market St., 19104, pg. 432 **PB**
W.B. Saunders Company, The Curtis Ctr., Independence Sq. W., 19106, pg. 784 **PB**
Saxony Distillers Et Cie, Inc., 2633 Trenton Ave., 19125, pg. 580 **PV**
Senior Publications Holdings, Inc., 1500 Market St., Centre Square, E. Tower, 12th Fl., 19102, pg. 539 **IT**
The 1792 Company, Two Liberty Pl., 1601 Chestnut St., 19192, pg. 365 **PV**
SMITH-EDWARDS-DUNLAP COMPANY, 2867 E. Allegheny Ave., 19134, pg. 1007 **PV**
SmithKline Beecham Corporation, One Franklin Plaza, 19101-7929, pg. 1264 **IT**
SmithKline Beecham Pharmaceuticals, One Franklin Plaza, 19101, pg. 1265 **IT**
Soabar Products Group, 7722 Dungan Rd., 19111, pg. 153 **PB**
Soabar Systems Division, 7722 Dungan Rd., 19111, pg. 153 **PB**
SORBEE INTERNATIONAL LTD., 9990 Global Rd., 19115, pg. 1014 **PV**
SOUTHEASTERN PENNSYLVANIA TRANSPORTATION AUTHORITY, 1234 Market St., 19107-2385, pg. 1015 **PV**
SOUTHWARK METAL MANUFACTURING COMPANY, 1600 Washington Ave., 19146, pg. 1018 **PV**

Geographic Index-U.S.

STERLING PAPER CO., 2155 E. Castor Ave., 19134, pg. 1041 **PV**
Stewart Smith East, Inc., 400 Market St., Ste. 1103, 19106-2511, pg. 1508 **PB**
Stokes Vacuum Inc., 5500 Tabor Rd., 19120, pg. 426 **IT**
SUN COMPANY, INC., Ten Penn Ctr., 1801 Market St., 19103-1699, pg. 1530 **PB**
Sun Company, Inc. (R&M), Ten Penn Ctr., 1801 Market St., 19103-1699, pg. 1530 **PB**
Sun Refining & Marketing Co. Lubes Div., 1801 Market St., 19103-1699, pg. 1530 **PB**
Sun Refining & Marketing Co. Operations Div., Ten Penn Center, 1801 Market St., 19103-1699, pg. 1530 **PB**
Susquehanna Electric Co., 2301 Market St., 19103, pg. 1268 **PB**
Susquehanna Power Co., 2301 Market St., 19103, pg. 1268 **PB**
Sysco Food Services of Philadelphia, Inc., 666 Packer Ave., 19148, pg. 1552 **PB**
TBC Financial Services, 2801 Hunting Park Ave., 19129, pg. 1561 **PB**
TCV, Inc., P.O. Box 41400, 2001 Market St., 19101-1400, pg. 432 **PB**
TMP Worldwide, Inc., Benjamin Franklin Bus. Ctr., 9th & Chestnut St., Ste. T-110, 19107, pg. 1064 **PV**
TASTY BAKING COMPANY, 2801 Hunting Park Ave., 19129, pg. 1561 **PB**
Thermal Industries Inc., 3665 Richmond St., 17055-3174, pg. 491 **PB**
TED THOMAS ASSOCIATES INC. ADVERTISING, 210 W. Washington Sq., 19106, pg. 1083 **PV**
Thyssen Specialty Steels, Inc., 10430 Drummond Rd., 19154, pg. 1388 **IT**
Tierney & Partners, 200 S. Broad St., 19102, pg. 1641 **PV**
Tops 'N Bottoms of New York, Inc., 9401 Blue Grass Rd., 19114, pg. 491 **PB**
Towers Perrin Reinsurance, The Melon Bank Center, 1500 Market St., 19102, pg. 1093 **PV**
Trilog, Inc., One Logan Sq., Ste. 1600, 19103, pg. 362 **PB**
Triumph Releasing Corporation - Mid-Atlantic Territory, 1617 John F. Kennedy Blvd., Ste. 800, 19103-1808, pg. 1282 **IT**
Turner Construction Co., 10 Penn Center, Ste. 700, 19103, pg. 1645 **PB**
USF Insurance Company, 1760 Market St., 19103, pg. 328 **PB**
Unisource, 7575 Brewster Ave., 19153, pg. 1671 **PB**
United States Name Plate, 8425 Executive Ave., 19153, pg. 640 **PV**
US Reprographics, Inc., 261 S. 22nd St., 19103, pg. 1176 **PB**
URBAN OUTFITTERS, INC., 1809 Walnut St., 19103, pg. 1700 **PV**
VOX MEDICA CORPORATION, 210 W. Washington Sq., 19106, pg. 1143 **PV**
WCAU-TV, City Line & Monument Aves., 19131, pg. 712 **PB**
WPHL-TV, Inc., 5001 Wynnefield Ave., 19131, pg. 1636 **PB**
WPVI-TV, 4100 City Line Ave., 19131, pg. 512 **PB**
Water-Side, Inc., 1800 John F. Kennedy Blvd., 19103, pg. 203 **PB**
THE WEIGHTMAN GROUP, 2129 Chestnut St., 19103, pg. 1159 **PV**
WESTERN SKY INDUSTRIES, INC., 1500 Market St., 12th Fl., East Tower, 19102, pg. 1168 **PV**
FRANK W. WINNE & SON, INC., 44 N. Front St., 19106, pg. 1183 **PV**
WOLF, BLOCK, SCHORR & SOLIS-COHEN, Packard Bldg., 12th Fl., 15th & Chestnut Sts., 19102, pg. 1185 **PV**
Wyeth-Ayerst Laboratories, Inc., P.O. Box 8299, 19101-1245, pg. 80 **PB**
Xerox Research, 1700 Market St., 19103-3913, pg. 1784 **PB**
H.L. Yoh Group LLC, 1818 Market St., 20th Flr., 19103, pg. 317 **PV**
Yoh Staffing Services, 1818 Market St., 19103, pg. 317 **PV**

Philipsburg

Shain/Shopbilt, 509 Hemlock St., 16866, pg. 156 **PV**

Phoenixville

AMERICAN INKS & COATINGS CORP., 330 Pawlings Rd., 19460, pg. 56 **PV**
Phoenixville Newspapers, Inc., 225 Bridge St., 19460, pg. 935 **PB**

Pipersville

AMP Inc. Lytel Division, 61 Chubb Way, 18947, pg. 8 **PB**
ERD Environmental, Inc., 6025 Easton Rd., 18949, pg. 546 **PB**

Pittsburgh

ABN AMRO Bank, N.V. (Pittsburgh), One PPG Place, Ste. 2950, 15222-5400, pg. 10 **IT**
Adtrans Pittsburgh, 1501 Lebanon Church Rd., 15236-1491, pg. 369 **IT**
Affiliated Building Services, Inc., Four Northshore Ctr., 15212, pg. 322 **IT**
Ahlstrom Process Equipment Inc., 300 Mt. Lebanon Blvd., Rm. 207C, 15234, pg. 34 **IT**
Air-Scent International, Ridc Industrial Pk., 290-298 Alpha Dr., 15238, pg. 1056 **PV**

Alcoa Steamship Co., Inc., 1501 Alcoa Bldg., 24th Fl., 15219, pg. 61 **PB**
Allegheny Development Corp., One Oxford Ctr., 301 Grant St., 15279, pg. 474 **PB**
Allegheny Rail Products, 415 Holiday Dr., 15220, pg. 676 **PB**
ALLEGHENY TELEDYNE INCORPORATED, 1000 Six PPG Pl., 15222-5479, pg. 43 **PB**
Alliance Ventures, Inc., Fifth Ave. Pl., 120 Fifth Ave., 15222-3099, pg. 529 **PV**
ALLIED SECURITY, INC., 2840 Library Rd., 15234, pg. 40 **PV**
Altegra Credit Company, 150 Allegheny Center Mall, 15212, pg. 1154 **PB**
ALUMINUM COMPANY OF AMERICA, The Alcoa Bldg., 425 Sixth Ave., 15219-1850, pg. 60 **PB**
American Bank Note Company, 1101 Commonwealth Bldg., 316 Fourth Ave., 15222, pg. 68 **PB**
AMPCO-PITTSBURGH CORPORATION, 600 Grant St., Ste 4600, 15219-2700, pg. 103 **PB**
Apollo Gas Co., 800 Regis Ave., 15236, pg. 1661 **PB**
Aristech Chemical Corporation, 600 Grant St., 15219-2704, pg. 872 **IT**
ARMCO INC., One Oxford Center, 301 Grant St., 15219-1415, pg. 131 **PB**
BHP Trading Inc., 2593 Wexford Bayne Rd., Ste. 106, 15235, pg. 226 **IT**
BTR-Measurement & Flow Control Division, 400 N. Lexington Ave., 15208, pg. 125 **IT**
BABCOCK LUMBER COMPANY, 2220 Palmer St., 15218, pg. 108 **PV**
BACHARACH INC., 625 Alpha Dr., 15238, pg. 109 **PV**
Baker Mellon Stuart Construction, Inc., One N. Shore Ctr., 15212, pg. 168 **PB**
MICHAEL BAKER CORPORATION, P.O. Box 12259, 15231, pg. 168 **PB**
Bayer Corporation, One Mellon Ctd., 500 Grant St., 15219-2507, pg. 172 **PB**
Bayer Corporation, Bldg. # 4, 100 Bayer Rd., 15205-9741, pg. 172 **IT**
Bayer Corporation/Fibers, Organics & Rubber Division, 100 Bayer Rd., 15205-9741, pg. 172 **IT**
BEARING SERVICE COMPANY, 500 Dargan St., 15224, pg. 127 **PV**
Beck/Arnley Worldparts Corp., 6905 Susquehana St., 15208, pg. 561 **PB**
Binks Manufacturing Company, 3601 Library Rd., pg. 229 **PB**
BRIDGES & COMPANY, INC., 1300 Brighton Rd., 15233, pg. 168 **PV**
Bronze Div., 1315 W. Liberty Ave., 15226, pg. 1059 **PB**
CBS CORPORATION, 11 Stanwix St., 15222-1384, pg. 273 **PB**
CCF Mellon Partners, One Mellon Bank Ctr., Ste. 4150, 15258-0001, pg. 342 **IT**
CNG Energy Services Corporation, P.O. Box 15746, One Park Ridge Ctr., 5th Fl., 15244-0746, pg. 435 **PB**
CNG Power Services Corporation, P.O. Box 15746, One Park Ridge Center, 15244-0746, pg. 435 **PB**
CABLE DESIGN TECHNOLOGIES CORPORATION, Foster Plaza 7, 661 Anderson Dr., 15220, pg. 287 **PB**
CALGON CARBON CORPORATION, 400 Calgon Carbon Dr., 15205, pg. 292 **PB**
Calgon Carbon Corp., Neville Island, P.O. Box 717, 15230, pg. 293 **PB**
Calgon Corporation, 5700 Campbells Run Rd., 15205, pg. 455 **IT**
Callery Chemical Co., P.O. Box 429, 15230, pg. 1114 **PB**
Capintec Instruments Inc., 540 Alpha Dr., 15238, pg. 205 **PV**
THE CARBIDE/GRAPHITE GROUP, INC., One Gateway Ctr., 19th Fl., 15222, pg. 304 **PB**
Carnegie Natural Gas Co., 800 Regis Ave., 15236, pg. 1661 **PB**
Celegec Automation Projects Inc., D.L. Clark Bldg., 503 Martindale St., 5th Fl., 15212, pg. 53 **IT**
Challenger Electrical Equipment Corp., 5 Parkway Center, 15220, pg. 558 **PB**
CHATWINS GROUP, INC., 300 Weyman Plaza, Ste. 340, 15236, pg. 231 **PV**
CHICAGO HOLDINGS, INC., 1000 RIDC Plaza, 15238, pg. 234 **PV**
Columbia Energy Services Corporation, Bldg. 200, Ste. 201, 2581 Washington Rd., 15241, pg. 402 **PB**
THE CONAIR GROUP, INC., One Conair Dr., 15202, pg. 261 **PB**
Consol, 1800 Washington Rd., 15241, pg. 531 **PB**
Consol, 1800 Washington Rd., 15241, pg. 1081 **IT**
CONSOLIDATED NATURAL GAS COMPANY, CNG Tower, 625 Liberty Ave., 15222-3199, pg. 435 **PB**
Consolidated Natural Gas Service Co., Inc., CNG Tower, 625 Liberty Ave., 15222-3199, pg. 435 **PB**
Contraves Inc., 615 Epsilon Dr., 15238, pg. 998 **IT**
Copperweld International Co., Four Gateway Center, Ste. 2200, 15222, pg. 662 **PB**
Copperweld Tubing, Four Gateway Ctr., Liberty Ave., 15200, 15222, pg. 662 **PB**
Cornerstone Natural Gas, Inc.-Pittsburgh, 2551 Washington Rd., Ste. 810, 15241, pg. 567 **PB**
Corrugated Packaging, One 28th St., 15222, pg. 736 **PB**
CREATIVE PRODUCTIONS, 7500 Thomas Blvd., 15208, pg. 258 **PV**
CROWN COAL & COKE CO. INC., 200 Nine Pkwy. Ctr., 15220, pg. 292 **PV**
DQE Energy Services, One N. Shore Center, 12 Federal St., 15210, pg. 474 **PB**
Davy Dravo Division, One Oliver Plaza, 15222, pg. 774 **IT**
Davy International, 1 Oliver Plaza, 15222, pg. 773 **IT**
Davy Pittsburgh, One Oliver Plaza, 15222, pg. 774 **IT**
Delta International Machinery Corp., 246 Alpha Dr., 15238, pg. 1273 **PB**

DRAVO CORPORATION, 3600 One Oliver Plaza, 15222-2682, pg. 527 **PB**
Dravo Leasing Co., One Oliver Plaza, 15222, pg. 527 **PB**
Dravo Lime Company, 3600 One Oliver Plaza, 15222, pg. 527 **PB**
Dreyfus Investment Services Corp., Union Trust Bldg., Rm. 179, 15259, pg. 1085 **PB**
Duquesne Enterprises, One Oxford Centre, 301 Grant St., 15279, pg. 474 **PB**
Duquesne Light Company, One Oxford Ctr., 301 Grant St., 15279, pg. 474 **PB**
EG & G Environmental, Inc., Foster Plaza, Ste. 400, 681 Andersen St., 15220, pg. 543 **PB**
EPI Wall Systems, 1844 Ardmore Blvd., 15221, pg. 376 **PV**
ERI Realty, Inc., 420 Boulevard of the Allies, 15219, pg. 589 **PB**
ERI Services, 420 Blvd. of the Allies, 15219-1393, pg. 589 **PB**
ET Storage Company, 3500 Park Ln., 15275, pg. 590 **PB**
EAT N PARK RESTAURANTS, 100 Park Manor Dr., 15205-1099, pg. 358 **IT**
Eickhoff Corporation, 200 Park W. Dr., 15230, pg. 542 **IT**
Elkem-American Carbide Company (Pittsburgh), Park West Office Center, P.O. Box 37, 15230, pg. 33 **PB**
Elkem Materials Inc., P.O. Box 266, 15230-0266, pg. 447 **IT**
Elkem Metals Company, P.O. Box 266, 15230, pg. 447 **IT**
Engineered Construction-Pittsburgh, 3400 Grand Ave., 15225, pg. 1304 **PB**
ENGINEERED PRODUCTS, INC., 1844 Ardmore Blvd., 15221, pg. 376 **PV**
Equitable Gas Co., Allegheny Center Mall, Ste. 2000, 15212, pg. 589 **PB**
Equitable Gas-Energy Co., 420 Blvd. of Allies, 15219, pg. 589 **PB**
Equitable Pipeline Company, 420 Boulevard of the Allies, 15219, pg. 590 **PB**
Equitable Resources Energy Company, 420 Blvd. of the Allies, 3rd. Fl., 15219, pg. 589 **PB**
EQUITABLE RESOURCES, INC., 420 Blvd. of the Allies, 15219-1393, pg. 589 **PB**
Equitable Resources Marketing Company, 420 Blvd. of the Allies, Mezzanine Level, 15219, pg. 590 **PB**
Equitable Storage Company, 420 Boulevard of the Allies, 15220, pg. 590 **PB**
Equitech Division, 420 Blvd. of the Allies, 15219, pg. 590 **PB**
Equitrans, Inc., 3500 Park Ln., 15275, pg. 590 **PB**
Falconbridge U.S. Inc., Twin Towers, 4955 Steubenville Pike, Ste. 245, 15205-9604, pg. 434 **IT**
Fisher Scientific Company, 2000 Park Ln., 15275-1126, pg. 337 **PV**
Fluid Polymers, 128 First St., 15238, pg. 337 **PB**
L.B. FOSTER COMPANY, 415 Holiday Dr., 15220-2793, pg. 675 **PB**
GP Instrument Services, 2045 Rt. 286, 15239, pg. 694 **PB**
THE GAGE COMPANY, 3000 Liberty Ave., 15201, pg. 437 **PB**
General Nutrition Centers, 921 Penn Ave., 15222, pg. 725 **PB**
General Nutrition Franchising, Inc., 921 Penn Ave., 15222, pg. 725 **PB**
GENERAL NUTRITION, INC., 921 Penn Ave., 15222, pg. 725 **PB**
General Nutrition Services, Inc., 921 Penn Ave., 15222, pg. 725 **PB**
GIANT EAGLE, INC., 101 Kappa Dr., 15238, pg. 450 **PV**
Giant Eagle Market Co., 101 Kappa Dr., 15238, pg. 450 **PV**
Golf Digest Information Systems, Inc., 135 Delta Dr., 15238, pg. 1174 **PB**
Grant Steel Corp., Third & Oliver, 15110, pg. 256 **PV**
Green Tree Acceptance, Inc., 300 Weyman Plaza, 15236, pg. 762 **PB**
HAMBURG BROTHERS, 40 24th St., 15222, pg. 497 **PV**
Harbison-Walker Refractories, 600 Grant St., 15221, pg. 748 **PB**
Health Education Center Inc., Fifth Ave. Pl., 120 Fifth Ave., 15222-3099, pg. 529 **PV**
HealthAmerica Pennsylvania, Inc., Five Gateway Ctr., 60 Blvd. of the Allies, 15222, pg. 454 **PB**
H.J. HEINZ COMPANY, 600 Grant St., 15219, pg. 805 **PB**
Heinz U.S.A. Div., 1062 Progress, 15212, pg. 805 **PB**
Hewlett-Packard Company, 111 Zeta Dr., 15238, pg. 815 **PB**
HIGHMARK INC., Fifth Ave. Pl., 120 Fifth Ave., 15222-3099, pg. 528 **PV**
Hilb, Rogal and Hamilton Company of Pittsburgh, Inc., Warner Centre, 333 Forbes Ave., 15222, pg. 827 **PB**
THE HILLMAN COMPANY, 1900 Grant Bldg., 15219-2381, pg. 530 **PV**
Hoechstetter Printing Company, Inc., 218 N. Braddock Ave., 15208, pg. 1735 **PB**
Hoogovens Technical Services USA, Inc., 200 Fleet St., Ste. 6000, 15220, pg. 755 **IT**
The Huntington Acceptance Company, Greentree Commons, 381 Mansfield Ave., Ste. 200, 15220, pg. 850 **PB**
Ikon Office Solutions-Pittsburgh, 601 Holiday Dr, Foster Plaza 3, 15220, pg. 864 **PB**
Interactive Instructional Systems Inc., Two Gateway Ctr., 15222, pg. 1089 **IT**
Intergraph Corporation, Campbell's Run Bus. Ctr., 500 Business Ctr. Dr., 15205-4325, pg. 890 **IT**
Iron Age Corporation, Robinson Plaza Three, Ste. 400, 15205-1024, pg. 401 **PV**
Iron Age Holdings Corporation, Robinson Plaza Three, Ste. 400, 15205-1024, pg. 401 **PV**
J & J Snack Foods Corp., 333 N. Braddock St., 15208, pg. 916 **PB**

PB - *U.S. Public Companies Volume*
PV - *U.S. Private Companies Volume*
IT - *International Public & Private Companies Volume*

Geographic Index-U.S.

J & L Specialty Products Corp., One PPG Place, 15222, pg. 572 **IT**
Jannock Vinyl Group, Foster Plaza Seven, 661 Andersen Dr., 15220-2746, pg. 699 **IT**
KDKA-Radio & KDKA-TV, One Gateway Center, 15222, pg. 275 **PB**
Kaufmann's, 400 Fifth Ave., 15219, pg. 1063 **PB**
Ketchum Advertising/Pittsburgh, Six PPG Place, 13th Fl., 15222-5488, pg. 616 **PV**
KETCHUM COMMUNICATIONS INC., Six PPG Pl., 15222-5488, pg. 616 **PV**
KETCHUM, INC., Three Gateway Center., Ste. 1726, 15222, pg. 617 **PV**
KEYSTONE BREWERS, INC., 3340 Liberty Ave., 15201, pg. 618 **PV**
Keystone Health Plan West, Inc., Fifth Ave. Pl., 120 Fifth Ave., 15222-3099, pg. 529 **PV**
Kop-Coat, 1850 Koppers Bldg., 426 Seventh Ave., 15219, pg. 1357 **PV**
Kvaerner Davy, One Oliver Plaza, 15222-2682, pg. 774 **IT**
Ladbroke Racing Corporation, Foster Plaza 9, 750 Holiday Dr., 15220, pg. 788 **IT**
Lake Region Medical, Inc., 620 Alpha Dr., 15238, pg. 643 **PV**
Laurel Capital Advisors, One Mellon Bank Ctr., 15258, pg. 1085 **PB**
Le Nickel Inc., Park West Office Center, Bldg. 1, Ste. 430, 15275, pg. 661 **IT**
LePage's, Inc., 120 Delta Dr., 15238, pg. 598 **PV**
Limbach Constructors, Inc., Four Northshore Ctr., 15212, pg. 322 **IT**
Limbach Holdings, Inc., Four Northshore Ctr., 15212, pg. 321 **IT**
The Linc Corp., Four Northshore Ctr., 15212, pg. 322 **IT**
LOI, 2000 Oxford Dr., Bethel Park, 15241, pg. 1149 **IT**
MAN GHH Corp., 5700 Corporate Drive, Ste. 800, 15237, pg. 824 **IT**
MCS, Inc., 400 Penn Center Blvd., Bldg. 4, 10th Fl., 15235, pg. 1099 **PB**
MPS CORPORATION, 150 Park Dr., 15056, pg. 687 **PV**
MARC, Four Station Sq., Ste. 500, 15219, pg. 701 **PV**
MARC Direct, Four Station Sq., 15219, pg. 701 **PV**
MARC Promotion, Four Station Sq., 15219, pg. 701 **PV**
MARC Public Relations, Four Station Sq., 15219, pg. 701 **PV**
Market Place Print, Inc., 4800 USX Tower, 600 Grant St., 15219, pg. 701 **PV**
MATTHEWS INTERNATIONAL CORP., Two North Shore Ctr., 15212, pg. 1059 **PB**
Matthews Intl. Corp.-Graphic Systems Div., 1910 Cochran Rd., 15220, pg. 1060 **PB**
Matthews International Marking Systems Div., 6515 Penn Ave., 15206, pg. 1059 **PB**
Matthews International Memorial Division, 1315 W. Liberty Ave., 15226, pg. 1059 **PB**
Matthews Intl. Trading Corp., Two North Shore Ctr., 15221, pg. 1060 **PB**
MCKEAN OLDSMOBILE COMPANY, 5001 Liberty Ave., 15224, pg. 722 **PV**
C.S. McKee & Company, Inc., One Gateway Center, 8th Fl., 15222, pg. 1673 **PV**
McNally Wellman, 4800 Grand Ave., 15225-1522, pg. 1326 **PV**
MELLON BANK CORPORATION, One Mellon Bank Ctr., 15258, pg. 1084 **PB**
Mellon Bank, N.A., One Mellon Bank Ctr., 15258-0001, pg. 1085 **PB**
Mellon Bond Associates Corp., Mellon Bank Ctr., 15258, pg. 1085 **PB**
Mellon Equity Associates Corp., Mellon Bank Ctr., 15258, pg. 1085 **PB**
J.W. Messner, Inc., 4955 Steubenville Pike, Ste. 219, 15205-9604, pg. 734 **PV**
MINE SAFETY APPLIANCES CO., RIDC Industrial Park, 121 Gamma Dr., 15238, pg. 1114 **PB**
Mine Safety Appliances Co., P.O. Box 426, 15230, pg. 1114 **PB**
Minerals and Mining Group, 600 Grant St., 50th Fl., 15219, pg. 748 **PB**
Mock Seed Company, 929 Beaver Ave., 15233, pg. 981 **PV**
Montauk, One Oxford Ctr., 15279, pg. 474 **PB**
Morgan Technical Services, Inc, Two North Shore Plaza, 15219, pg. 761 **PV**
MUNROE, INC., 1820 N. Franklin St., 15233, pg. 767 **PV**
MYLAN LABORATORIES, INC., 1030 Century Bldg., 130 Seventh St., 15222, pg. 1143 **PB**
NVR Settlement Services, 300 Bilmar Dr., Ste. 250, 15205, pg. 1148 **PB**
NationsBank Leasing Corporation, Three Gateway Ctr., Ste. 300, 15222, pg. 1163 **PB**
Nora Transmission Co., 420 Blvd. of the Allies, 15219, pg. 590 **PB**
Olympia International, 600 Grant St., Ste. 3246, 15219, pg. 1221 **PV**
PG Publishing Co., 34 Boulevard of the Allies, 15222, pg. 147 **PV**
PNC BANK CORP., One PNC Plaza, 249 Fifth Ave., 15222-2707, pg. 1242 **PB**
PNC Bank, N.A., Fifth Ave. & Wood St., 15222, pg. 1243 **PB**
PNC Capital Corp., Fifth Ave. & Wood St., 15222, pg. 1243 **PB**
PNC Commercial Corporation, Fifth Ave. & Wood St., 15222, pg. 1243 **PB**
PNC ESOP Funding Corporation, Fifth Ave. & Wood St., 15222, pg. 1243 **PB**
PNC Funding Corp., Fifth Ave. & Wood St., 15222, pg. 1243 **PB**

PNC International Bank, One PNC Plaza, 15265, pg. 1243 **PB**
PNC International Finance, N.V., Fifth Ave. & Wood St., 15222, pg. 1243 **PB**
PNC Leasing Corp., One PNC Plaza, 15265, pg. 1243 **PB**
PNC Life Insurance Company, Pittsburgh National Bldg., Fifth Ave. & Wood St., 15222, pg. 1243 **PB**
PNC Realty Holding Corporation, Fifth Ave. & Wood St., 15222, pg. 1244 **PB**
PNC Securities Corp., One PNC Plaza, 15265, pg. 1243 **PB**
PNC Securities Corp., Fifth Avenue & Wood St., 15222, pg. 1244 **PB**
PNC Venture Corporation, Fifth Ave. & Wood St., 15222, pg. 1244 **PB**
PPG INDUSTRIES, INC., One PPG Pl., 15272, pg. 1245 **PB**
PANNIER CORPORATION, 207 Sandusky St., 15212, pg. 837 **PV**
The Peoples Natural Gas Co., 625 Liberty Ave., 15222-3197, pg. 435 **PB**
PINACO, 300 Sixth Ave., 15222, pg. 1244 **PB**
PITT-DES MOINES, INC., 3400 Grand Ave., 15225, pg. 1304 **PB**
PITTSBURGH ASSOCIATES, 600 Stadium Cir., 15212, pg. 867 **PV**
Pittsburgh Brewing Company, 3340 Liberty Ave., 15201, pg. 619 **PV**
Pittsburgh, Chartiers & Youghiogheny Railway Co., Ste. 780, Commerce Court, Four Station Sq., 15219, pg. 432 **PB**
Pittsburgh Corning Corporation, 800 Presque Isle, 15239, pg. 449 **PV**
Pittsburgh Gear Company, Neville Island, 15255, pg. 417 **PV**
Pittsburgh Pirates, 600 Stadium Circle, 15212, pg. 867 **PV**
Pittsburgh Stadium Concessions, Inc., 100 Stadium Cir., 15212, pg. 79 **PV**
Polaroid Corp.- Camera Division, 201 Penn Center Blvd., 15235-5435, pg. 1313 **PB**
Portec Inc., Railway Maintenance Products Div., P.O. Box 38250, 900 Freeport Rd., 15238-8250, pg. 1318 **PB**
Power Piping Company, Four Allegheny Ctr., 15212, pg. 1029 **PB**
Property Ventures, Ltd., One Oxford Ctr., 301 Grant St., 15279, pg. 474 **PB**
Resorcoh Inc., 701 Rodi Rd., Ste. 102, 15235, pg. 798 **PV**
RESPIRONICS, INC., 1501 Ardmore Blvd., 15221-4401, pg. 1383 **PB**
Rimoldi of America Inc., 400 N. Lexington Ave., 15208, pg. 1118 **IT**
Royston Laboratories, 128 First St., 15238, pg. 337 **PV**
SMS-Pittsburgh, Foster Plaza #9, 750 Holiday Dr., 15220, pg. 1463 **PB**
THE ST. GEORGE GROUP, INC., CNG Tower, 625 Liberty Ave., Ste. 1600, 15222, pg. 960 **PV**
Salem Corporation, P.O Box 2222, 15230, pg. 961 **PV**
SALEM GROUP, INC., P.O. Box 2222, 15230, pg. 961 **PV**
SAUER INDUSTRIES, INC., P.O. Box 40320, 32 51st St, 15201, pg. 967 **PV**
SCHNEIDER'S DAIRY, INC., 726 Frank St., 15227, pg. 971 **PV**
Sears Logistics Services, 27 51st St., 15201-2707, pg. 1452 **PB**
Senstar Capital Corporation, 301 Grant St., 15219, pg. 984 **PV**
Sequent Computer Systems, Inc., Two Gateway Ctr., Ste. 620, 15222, pg. 1459 **PB**
Shandon Lipshaw Inc., 171 Industry Dr., 15275, pg. 1595 **PB**
SmithKline Beecham Consumer Healthcare, 100 Beecham Dr., 15205, pg. 625 **IT**
SmithKline Beecham Consumer Healthcare, U.S., 100 Beecham Dr., 15205, pg. 1264 **IT**
SNAVELY FOREST PRODUCTS, INC., 600 Delwar Rd., 15236, pg. 1010 **PV**
SPEC HOLDINGS INC., 55 Alpha Dr. W., 15238, pg. 1022 **PV**
Stadtlander Drug Company, Inc., 600 Penn Center Blvd., 15235-5810, pg. 338 **IT**
Stadtlander HMI, 2030 Ardmore Blvd., 15221, pg. 338 **IT**
Standard Property Corporation, Fifth Ave. Pl., 120 Fifth Ave., 15222-3099, pg. 529 **PV**
Stern Advertising, Inc., Seven Parkway Center, 15220, pg. 1041 **PV**
Sumitomo Corporation of America, 2750 U.S. Steel Bldg., 600 Grant St., 15219, pg. 1312 **IT**
SURCO PRODUCTS, INC., RIDC Industrial Pk., 292 Alpha Dr., 15238, pg. 1056 **PV**
Suriname Aluminum Company, 425 6th Ave., 15219, pg. 61 **PB**
Tamarkin Co., Inc., 101 Kappa Dr., 15238, pg. 451 **PV**
Tamrock Service, Penn Ctr. W. 4, Ste. 1200, 15276, pg. 1353 **IT**
Technology Group, 600 Grant St., 50th Fl., 15219, pg. 748 **PB**
Thermal Industries, Inc., 301 Brushton Ave., 15221, pg. 490 **PV**
Thermal Industries Inc., 301 Brushton Ave., 15221-2168, pg. 491 **PV**
TIPPINS INCORPORATED, 435 Butler St., 15223, pg. 1088 **PV**
Trafalgar House Construction Inc., 1 Oliver Plaza, 15222, pg. 774 **IT**
Trans-General Life & Casualty Group, Inc., Fifth Ave. Pl., 120 Fifth Ave., 15222-3099, pg. 529 **PV**
Trans-General Life Insurance Company, Fifth Ave. Pl., 120 Fifth Ave., 15222-3099, pg. 529 **PV**
Trumbull Investments, Inc., P.O. Box 98100, 15227, pg. 1107 **PV**

Turner Construction Co., 850 Porter Bldg., 601 Grant St., 15219, pg. 1645 **PB**
URS Greiner, Inc. Mid-Atlantic, Bldg. One, Ste. 202, Penn Center W., 15276, pg. 1659 **PB**
USX CORPORATION, 600 Grant St., 15219-4776, pg. 1661 **PB**
USX Credit, 600 Grant St., 15219-4776, pg. 1661 **PB**
USX Engineers & Consultants, Inc., 600 Grant St., 15219-4776, pg. 1662 **PB**
USX Realty Development, 600 Grant St., 15219-4776, pg. 1661 **PB**
Union Switch & Signal Inc., 1000 Technology Dr., 15219, pg. 77 **IT**
U.S. Steel International, Inc., 600 Grant St., 15219, pg. 1662 **PB**
US Steel Mining Co., Inc., 600 Grant St., 15219-4776, pg. 1662 **PB**
Unitel Video, Inc. - Mobile Production Headquarters, 4100 Steubenville Pike, pg. 1692 **PB**
Unsmoke International, Ridc Industrial, 292 Alpha Dr., 15238, pg. 1056 **PV**
Vinylium Corp., 301 Brushton Ave., 15221, pg. 491 **PV**
Voest-Alpine Industries, Inc.-USX Project Office, Kossman Bldg., 100 Forbes Ave., Ste. 1110, 15222, pg. 1470 **IT**
Voest-Alpine Services and Technologies Corp.-Material Handling Equipment, 2209 Babcock Blvd., 15237, pg. 1471 **IT**
WCI International Company, Three Pkwy. Ctr., 15220, pg. 440 **IT**
WPXI Inc., 11 Television Hill, 15214, pg. 282 **PV**
WTAE-AM, 400 Ardmore Blvd., 15221, pg. 1418 **PB**
WTAE Division, 400 Ardmore Blvd., 15221, pg. 516 **PV**
WTAE-TV, 400 Ardmore Blvd., 15221, pg. 516 **PV**
WVTY-FM, 400 Ardmore Blvd., 15221, pg. 1418 **PB**
Weight Watchers Gourmet Food Company, 1062 Progress St., 15212, pg. 806 **PB**
WESCO Distribution, Inc., Commerce Ct., Ste. 700, Four Station Sq., 15219, pg. 244 **PB**
Western International Media Corporation, 1910 Cochran Rd., Ste. 260, 15220, pg. 1167 **PV**
Western Pennsylvania Caring Foundation, Inc., Fifth Ave. Pl., 120 Fifth Ave., 15222-3099, pg. 529 **PV**
Westinghouse Communication & Information Systems, 11 Stanwix St., 15222, pg. 273 **PB**
Westinghouse Communications, Inc. (WesComm), 902 Brinton Rd., 15221, pg. 273 **PB**
Westinghouse Industries & Technologies Group, Westinghouse Bldg., 15222, pg. 273 **PB**
Westinghouse Power Systems Group, Westinghouse Bldg., 15222, pg. 273 **PB**
Wiegand Industrial-Chromalox, 701 Alpha Dr., 15238, pg. 573 **PB**
Williams & Company, Inc., 901 Pennsylvania Ave., 15233, pg. 1055 **PV**
Williams House of Metals, Inc., 901 Pennsylvania Ave., 15233, pg. 1055 **PV**
Willis Corroon Corp. of Pittsburgh, One N. Shore Ctr., 15212, pg. 1507 **IT**
Zellerbach Division, 2200 Liberty Ave., Ste. 107, 15222, pg. 1075 **PV**

Pittston

S L C GRAPHICS, LP, 50 Rock St., Hughestown Borough, 18640, pg. 955 **PV**

Plumsteadville

Scott Environmental Technology, Rte. 611 N., 18949, pg. 546 **PB**
SCOTT SPECIALTY GASES, 6141 Easton Rd., 18949, pg. 977 **PV**

Plymouth Meeting

Aston Brooke Development Laboratory, 620 W. Germantown Pike, Ste. 200, 19462, pg. 1309 **PV**
Conrail Direct, One Plymouth Meeting, Ste. 610, 19462, pg. 432 **PB**
Corson Lime Company, 500 Stenton Ave., 19462, pg. 1685 **PB**
Elkay Plastics Co., Inc., Stock Service Center, 4110 Butler Pike, Unit B-105, 19402, pg. 372 **PV**
Ikea North America, Inc., Plymouth Commons, 496 W. Germantown Pike, 19462, pg. 660 **IT**
KLEINERT'S, INC., Meetinghouse Business Ctr., 120 W. Germantown Pike, Ste. 100, 19462-1420, pg. 625 **PV**
Merchants Despatch Transp. Co., One Plymouth Meeting, 19462, pg. 432 **PB**
Plymouth Meeting Mall, Inc., 1150 Plymouth Meeting Mall, 19462, pg. 1407 **PB**
SMITH ENVIRONMENTAL TECHNOLOGIES CORP., One Plymouth Meeting, 19462, pg. 1477 **PV**
Smith Environmental Technologies Corp., One Plymouth Meeting, 19462, pg. 1478 **PV**
STRATTON MANAGEMENT COMPANY, Plymouth Meeting Exec. Campus, 610 W. Germantown Pike, Ste. 300, 19462, pg. 1046 **PV**
TELEFLEX INCORPORATED, 630 W. Germantown Pike, Ste. 450, 19462, pg. 1569 **PB**
Trans Leasing International, Inc.-Northeast Region, 610 W. Germantown Pike, Ste. 170, 19462, pg. 1628 **PB**

Pottstown

J. FEGELY INC., 1810 W. High St., 19464, pg. 399 **PV**
Fishing Tackle Div., P.O. Box 357, 19464, pg. 486 **PV**
GUDEBROD, INC., 274 Shoemaker Road, 19464, pg. 486 **PV**

PB - U.S. Public Companies Volume
PV - U.S. Private Companies Volume
IT - International Public & Private Companies Volume

Geographic Index-U.S.

Industrial Sewing Thread Div., P.O. Box 357, 19464, pg. 486 **PV**
Mrs. Smith's Bakery of Pennsylvania, South & Charlotte Streets, 19464, pg. 658 **PV**
Neapco, Inc., Queen & Bailey Sts., 19464, pg. 1113 **PV**
Nichifu America, Inc., 398 Circle of Progress, 19464, pg. 927 **IT**
Mayer Pollack Steel Corporation, P.O. Box 759, 19464, pg. 874 **PV**
THE POLLOCK CORP., Industrial Hwy. & Keim Rd., 19464, pg. 874 **PV**
Rixie Paper Products, P.O. Box 478, H & Quinter St., 19464, pg. 1486 **PB**
Surgical Div., P.O. Box 357, 19464, pg. 486 **PV**
U.S. AXLE, INC., 275 Shoemaker Rd., 19464-6434, pg. 1124 **PV**

Pottsville

Howard Products, 14th & Laurel Sts., 17901, pg. 1124 **PV**
Pennsylvania National Bank, One S. Centre St., 19526, pg. 956 **PB**
READING ANTHRACITE CO., 200 Mahantongo St., 17901, pg. 913 **PV**
United Metal Receptacle Corp., 14th & Laurel Sts., 17901, pg. 1124 **PV**
UNITED RECEPTICAL, INC., 14th & Laurel Sts., 17901, pg. 1123 **PV**

Quakertown

Durable Specialties Division, 45 N. 4th St., 18951, pg. 620 **PB**
Fasson Roll Materials Div., P.O. Box 756, 18951, pg. 153 **PB**
E.W. KNAUSS & SON, INC., 625 E. Broad St., 18951, pg. 626 **PV**
Magikitch'n, Inc., 180 Penn-Am Dr., 18951, pg. 1065 **PB**

Radnor

AIRGAS, INC., 259 Radnor Chester Rd., Ste. 100, 19087-8675, pg. 33 **PB**
BNP Cooper NEFF, Three Radnor Corp. Ctr., 19087, pg. 163 **IT**
Bestinfo, 100 Matsonford Rd., 19087, pg. 890 **PB**
Capital Analysts, Incorporated, 250 King of Prussia Rd., 19087, pg. 1164 **PV**
CASTLE ENERGY CORPORATION, 1 Radnor Corp. Ctr., Ste. 250, 100 Matsonford Rd., 19087, pg. 313 **PB**
Chilton Research Services, 201 King of Prussia Rd., 19089, pg. 1096 **IT**
1838 BOND-DEBENTURE TRADING FUND, Five Radnor Corporate Ctr., Ste. 320, 19087-4571, pg. 566 **PB**
FIDELITY MUTUAL LIFE INSURANCE CO., 250 King of Prussia Rd., 19087, pg. 403 **PV**
FREEDOM CHEMICAL COMPANY, 100 Matsonford Rd., Ste. 170, 19087, pg. 425 **PV**
PENN VIRGINIA CORPORATION, One Radnor Corporate Ctr., 100 Matsonford Rd., Ste. 200, 19087, pg. 1271 **PB**
SUPERIOR GROUP, INC., Three Radnor Corp. Ctr., Ste. 400, 19087, pg. 1055 **PV**
TV Guide Magazine, 100 Matsonford Rd., 19088, pg. 925 **IT**
Willis Corroon Administrative Services Corporation, Building One, Ste. 400, 100 Matsonford Rd., 19087-4582, pg. 1505 **IT**
Willis Corroon Corp. of Penn., One Radnor Corporate Center, 100 Matsonford Rd., Ste. 400, 19087-4582, pg. 1507 **IT**
Willis Corroon International/Americas, Building One, Ste. 400, 100 Matsonford Rd., 19087-4582, pg. 1507 **IT**
Willis Faber North America, Inc.-Pennsylvania, Bldg. One, Ste. 400, 100 Matsonford Rd., 19087-9050, pg. 1504 **IT**
Wyeth-Ayerst International, Inc., 150 Radnor Chester Rd., 19057, pg. 80 **PB**
Wyeth-Ayerst Laboratories-Domestic, 145 King of Prussia Rd., 19087, pg. 80 **PB**
Wyeth-Ayerst Laboratories-Research & Development, 145 King of Prussia Rd., 19087, pg. 80 **PB**

Reading

AEL Leasing Co., Inc., P.O. Box 13428, 19612-3428, pg. 9 **IT**
American Commercial Credit Corp., P.O. Box 13428, 19612-3428, pg. 9 **IT**
American Refractories Co., 1250 Clarion St., 19601, pg. 903 **PV**
ARROW INTERNATIONAL, INC., 2400 Bernville Rd., 19605, pg. 135 **PB**
BACHMAN COMPANY, 50 N. Fourth St., 19601, pg. 109 **PB**
Baldwin Hardware Corporation, 841 E. Wyomissing Blvd., 19612, pg. 1053 **PB**
Baldwin Hardware Service Corporation, 841 E. Wyomissing Blvd., 19611, pg. 1053 **PB**
Bank of Pennsylvania, P.O. Box 15210, 50 N. Fifth St., 19601, pg. 64 **IT**
BERKS PRODUCTS CORPORATION, 726 Spring St., 19603, pg. 136 **PV**
BOSCOV'S DEPARTMENT STORE, INC., 4500 Perkiomen Ave., 19606, pg. 160 **PV**
The Business Outlet, Inc., 200 Penn Ave., 19611, pg. 9 **PV**
CARPENTER TECHNOLOGY CORPORATION, 101 W. Bern St., 19601, pg. 307 **PB**
DSM Engineering Plastic Products, 2120 Fairmont Ave., 19605, pg. 354 **IT**

DIETRICH'S MILK PRODUCTS, INC., 100 McKinley Ave., 19605-2117, pg. 332 **PV**
Dimensions Inc., 641 McKnight St., 19601, pg. 300 **IT**
ELBECO INCORPORATED, 4203 Pottsville Pike, 19605, pg. 367 **PV**
EXIDE CORPORATION, P.O. Box 14205, 645 Penn St., 19612, pg. 600 **PB**
GAICO, 2675 Morgantown Rd., 19607, pg. 841 **PV**
Horrigan American Inc., Horrigan American Bldg., Flying Hills Corp. Ctr., #6 Commerce Dr., 19607, pg. 9 **IT**
Integrated Press Systems, One Birchmont Dr., 19606, pg. 881 **PV**
Interstate Container Corporation, Grace & Meade Sts., 19611, pg. 573 **PV**
J & J Snack Foods Corp., Five Spring Valley Rd., 19605, pg. 916 **PV**
Lucent Technologies, 2525 N. 12th St., 19604, pg. 1017 **PB**
Luden's Inc., P.O. Box 15087, 200 N. Eighth St., 19612-5087, pg. 812 **PV**
Metropolitan Edison Co., 2800 Pottsville Pike, 19640-0001, pg. 695 **PB**
Morton Chemical Powder Coatings, Flying Hills Corp. Ctr., 5 Commerce Dr., 19607, pg. 1135 **PV**
NARROW FABRIC INDUSTRIES, INC., Seventh & Reading Aves., 19611, pg. 774 **PV**
R.M. PALMER COMPANY, 77 Second Ave., 19611, pg. 835 **PV**
Parish Div., P.O. Box 13445, 19612-3445, pg. 479 **PV**
Pennsylvania Cellular Telephone Corp., 125 Morgantown Rd., 19611, pg. 1708 **PB**
Pennsylvania Electric Company, 2800 Pottsville Pike, 19640-0001, pg. 695 **PB**
Penske Logistics, Rte. 10, 19603, pg. 851 **PV**
Penske Truck Leasing Company LP, Rte. 10, 19603, pg. 850 **PV**
PREMIER MILL CORP., One Birchmont Dr., 19606, pg. 881 **PV**
Premier Mill Corp., Exeter Industrial Park, One Birchmont Dr., 19606, pg. 881 **PV**
Quest Diagnostic-Reading, 4418 Pottsville Pike, 19605, pg. 1351 **PB**
READING BODY WORKS, INC., Hancock Blvd. & Gerry St., 19611, pg. 913 **PV**
READING EAGLE COMPANY, 345 Penn St., 19603, pg. 913 **PV**
Reading Tube Corp., Rte. 61, 19605, pg. 202 **PV**
Regional Aircraft Services, RR9 Box 9400, Reading Regional Airport, 19605, pg. 1099 **PV**
SOCO Chemical, Inc., Pottsville Pike & Huller Ln., 19612-3788, pg. 1458 **IT**
SALIENT 3 COMMUNICATIONS, INC., Rte. 10 & Pheasant Rd., 19607, pg. 1429 **PB**
Sovereign Bank F.S.B., P.O. Box 12646, 19612, pg. 1494 **PB**
Sovereign Investment Corp., P.O. Box 12646, 19612, pg. 1494 **PB**
SURG CAL SPECIALTIES, 340 Morgantown Rd., 19611, pg. 1056 **PV**
Textile Chemical Co., Inc., Pottsville Pike & Huller Ln., 19612-3788, pg. 1458 **IT**
UGI Utilities, Inc., P.O. Box 13009, 225 Morgantown Rd., 19612-3009, pg. 1653 **PB**
WGM Safety Corporation, 205 Washington St., 19603, pg. 462 **IT**
WRAW-AM, 1265 Perkoimen Ave., 19602, pg. 385 **PB**
WRFY FM, 1265 Perkoiment Ave., 19602, pg. 385 **PB**
Windsor Service, Inc., 2415 Kutztown Rd., 19605, pg. 494 **PV**
Yuasa-Exide, Inc., 2366 Bernville Rd., 19605, pg. 1522 **IT**

Red Lion

REDCO CORPORATION, E. Broadway & Redco Ave., 17356, pg. 915 **PV**
SPECIALTY INDUSTRIES, INC., 120 N. Charles St., 17356, pg. 1022 **PV**
YORKTOWNE, INC., 100 Redco Ave., 17356, pg. 1196 **PV**

Reedsville

ATL Echo Ultrasound, Box 118, 17084-9772, pg. 12 **PB**
C-COR Electronics, Inc., 60 Flexnet Dr., 17084, pg. 272 **PB**

Rheems

JOHN COPES FOOD PRODUCTS, INC., 156 W. Harrisburg Ave., 17570, pg. 274 **PV**

Richland

CARLOS R. LEFFLER INC., 225 E. Main St., 17087, pg. 358 **PV**

Ridgway

Mascotech Sintered Components, Inc., Steis Dr., Boot Jack Hill, 15853, pg. 1055 **PB**
Motion Control Industries, Inc., Gillis Ave., 15853, pg. 305 **PV**

Ridley Park

Boeing Helicopters, Stewart Ave. & Industrial Hwy., 19078, pg. 241 **PB**

Roaring Spring

Appleton Papers-Spring Mill, 100 Paper Mill Rd., 16673, pg. 568 **IT**

Robesonia

ASSOCIATED WHOLESALERS INC., P.O. Box 67, Rte. 422, 19551, pg. 93 **PV**

Royersford

AMERICAN MACHINE & TOOL COMPANY, INC., P.O. Box 70, 19468, pg. 58 **PV**
Citizens Utilities Home Water Company, 135 N. Fourth St., 19468, pg. 380 **PB**
NES, Inc., 826 N. Lewis Rd., 19468, pg. 546 **PB**

Saint Davids

Elkins-Sinn, Inc.-Lederle, 555 E. Lancaster Ave., 19087, pg. 79 **PB**
1st Main Line Bank, 528 E. Lancaster Ave., 19087, pg. 1159 **PB**

Saint Marys

Carbone of America, Graphite Materials Div., 215 Stackpole St., 15857-1488, pg. 1028 **IT**
KEYSTONE POWDERED METAL COMPANY, 1935 State St., 15857-0313, pg. 619 **PV**
Keystone Thermometrics Corporation, 967 Windfall Rd., 15857, pg. 208 **IT**
Pure Carbon Company, 441 Hall Ave., 15857, pg. 891 **IT**

Saint Peters

Pennsylvania Granite Corp., P.O. Box 510, 19470, pg. 1396 **PB**

Saltsburg

Breeze Industrial, 100 Aero-Seal Dr., 15681-9594, pg. 1632 **PV**
Federal Laboratories, P.O. Box 305, One Tunnelton Rd., 15681-0305, pg. 1030 **PV**

Sandy Lake

Spang Power Control, P.O. Box 457, Lake St., 16145, pg. 1020 **PV**

Saxonburg

eV Products, 375 Saxonburg Blvd., 16056, pg. 1647 **PB**
Quantum, 438 Saxonburg Blvd., 16056-9407, pg. 1350 **PB**
SYLVAN INC., 333 Main St., 16056-0249, pg. 1545 **PB**
II-VI INCORPORATED, 375 Saxonburg Blvd., 16056, pg. 1647 **PB**

Sayre

PAXAR Apparel Identification Systems, One Wilcox St., 18840, pg. 1266 **PB**
RYNONE MANUFACTURING CORPORATION, N. Thomas Ave., 18840, pg. 953 **PV**
Susquehanna Division, P.O. Box 160, 206 S. Keystone Ave., 18840, pg. 439 **PB**
Waverly Gas/Valley Cities Gas, 523 S. Keystone Ave., 18840-0340, pg. 1148 **PB**

Schuylkill Haven

ALPHA MILLS CORP., 122 Margaretta St., 17972, pg. 45 **PV**
Tamaqua Cable Products Corp., One Tamaqua Blvd., 17972, pg. 417 **IT**

Scotrun

Brookdale Resorts, Inc., P.O. Box 400, 18355, pg. 1512 **PB**

Scottdale

Duraloy Technologies, P.O. Box 81, Bridge St., 15683, pg. 839 **PV**

Scranton

Anemostat Products, 888 N. Keyser Ave., 18504-9723, pg. 286 **PB**
Chesapeake Packaging Co./Scranton, 301 Green Ridge St., 18501, pg. 518 **PB**
Haddon Craftsmen, Inc., 1001 Wyoming Ave., 18509, pg. 523 **PV**
Herff Jones, Fine Papers, 1509 Maple St., 18505, pg. 523 **PV**
ICS Learning Systems, Inc., 925 Oak St., 18515, pg. 783 **PB**
International Correspondence Schools, Inc., 925 Oak St., 18515, pg. 783 **PB**
J & J Snack Foods Corp., P.O. Box 3777, 18505, pg. 916 **PB**

PB - *U.S. Public Companies Volume*
PV - *U.S. Private Companies Volume*
IT - *International Public & Private Companies Volume*

Geographic Index-U.S.

MACtac Scranton Facility, P.O. Box 1106, 18501, pg. 210 **PB**
McKinney Products Company, 820 Davis St., 18505, pg. 18 **IT**
NBD Incorporated, 925 Oak St., 18515, pg. 783 **PB**
NYT Video Productions, 16 Montage Mountain Rd., 18507, pg. 1174 **PB**
National Book Company Inc., Keystone Industrial Park, 18512, pg. 807 **PV**
National Learning Systems, Inc., 925 Oak St., 18515, pg. 783 **PB**
PNC Bank, P.O. Box 231, 201 Penn Ave., 18501, pg. 1243 **PB**
The Paper Magic Group, Inc., The Scranton Ctr., 401 Adams Ave., 18510-2025, pg. 284 **PB**
PENN SECURITY BANK AND TRUST CO., 150 N. Washington Ave., 18503-1848, pg. 1270 **PB**
Pennsylvania Cellular Telephone Corp., Siniaw Plaza, Route 6, 18508, pg. 1708 **PB**
Sandvik Steel Co., P.O. Box 1220, 18501, pg. 1185 **IT**
Simplex Construction Co. Inc., Simplex Dr., 18504, pg. 1001 **PV**
SIMPLEX INDUSTRIES, INC., Keyser Valley Indus. Park, 1 Simplex Dr., 18504, pg. 1001 **PV**
WNEP-TV, 16 Montage Mountain Rd., 18507, pg. 1174 **PB**

Selinsgrove

K & L Feeds, R.D. 1, 17870, pg. 374 **PV**
SUN BANCORP, INC., 2-16 S. Market St., 17870, pg. 1529 **PB**
Sun Bank d/b/a Snyder County Trust Company, 2-16 S. Market St., 17870, pg. 1529 **PB**
Sun Bank d/b/a Wastontown National bank, 2-16 S. Market St., 17870, pg. 1529 **PB**

Sewickley

MERITCARE, INC., 400 Broad St., Ste. 203, 15143, pg. 733 **PV**

Shady Grove

Grove WorldWide, 1565 Buchanan Trail East, 17256, pg. 593 **IT**

Shamokin

Roaring Creek Division, Lock Box AA, 204 E. Sunbury St., 17872-0909, pg. 439 **PB**

Sharon

Medal Distributing Co., 330 Vine St., 16146, pg. 1748 **PB**
Mercer Company, 200 Stewart Ave., 16146, pg. 256 **PV**
JOHN REYER COMPANY, City Center, 16146, pg. 926 **PV**
Sawhill Tubular Div., P.O. Box 11, 16146, pg. 131 **PB**
SHARON TUBE COMPANY, 134 Mill St., 16146, pg. 990 **PV**
Shenango Valley Water Co., P.O. Box 572, 665 S. Dock St., 16146, pg. 439 **PB**

Sharon Hill

Kintetsu World Express Inc., 301 Henderson Dr., 19079, pg. 735 **IT**

Sharpsville

Dean Dairy Products Co., P.O. Box 69, 16150, pg. 490 **PB**

Sheffield

Long Oil Coolers, Inc., 108 Horton St., 16347, pg. 815 **IT**

Shinglehouse

Frontier Communications-Oswayo River, Inc., P.O. Box 159, 24 Academy St., 16748, pg. 684 **PB**

Shippenville

Astro Homes, Box 189, 16254, pg. 318 **PB**

Simpson

Gentex Optics, Inc., 324 Main St., 18407, pg. 462 **IT**

Sinking Spring

HI Products Inc., 3145 Skillington Rd., 19608, pg. 533 **PV**
HOFMANN INDUSTRIES, INC., 3145 Shillington Rd., 19608, pg. 533 **PV**
KB Alloys, Inc., 2917 Windmill Rd., 19608, pg. 249 **PV**
Reading Paperboard Corporation, 3110 Papermill Rd., Rt. #5, 19603, pg. 304 **PB**

Skippack

HAINES KIBBLEHOUSE, P.O. Box 196, 2052 Lucan Rd., 19474, pg. 494 **PV**
Palmer International, Inc., 2036 Lucon Rd., 19474, pg. 835 **PV**

Somerset

Fleetwood Folding Trailers, Inc., P.O. Box 111, R D 2, 15501, pg. 651 **PB**
Gilmour Manufacturing Co., Drumall Industrial Pk., 15501, pg. 575 **PB**
Somerset Welding & Steel, Inc., P.O. Box 735, 15501, pg. 930 **PV**
Sunrise Medical Respiratory Products Division, 1200 E. Main St., 15501, pg. 1536 **PV**

Souderton

MOYER PACKING COMPANY, 249 Allentown Rd., 18964, pg. 765 **PV**
Shelly Bros., Inc., P.O. Box 115, 18964, pg. 163 **PV**

Southampton

ENVIRONMENTAL TECTONICS CORPORATION (ETC), County Line Industrial Park, 125 James Way, 18966-3877, pg. 587 **PB**
Grinnell Fire Protection Systems, 1100 Industrial Hwy., 18966-4009, pg. 1386 **IT**
Grinnell Fire Protection Systems, 1100 Industrial Hwy., 18966-4009, pg. 1648 **PB**
Land O'Lakes, Inc., 1225 Industrial Hwy., 18966, pg. 646 **PV**
M & C SPECIALTIES COMPANY, 90 James Way, 18966, pg. 684 **PV**
NEFA Corporation, 723 Street Rd., 18966, pg. 1326 **PB**
QC, Inc., 1205 Industrial Hwy., 18966, pg. 646 **PV**
VIR, Inc., 105 James Way, 18966, pg. 45 **PB**

Spartansburg

Spartywood Products, Inc., Fairview Rd., 16434, pg. 983 **PV**

Spring Grove

P.H. GLATFELTER COMPANY, 228 S. Main St., 17362, pg. 746 **PB**
The Glatfelter Pulp Wood Co., 228 S. Main St., 17362, pg. 746 **PB**
Nearby Eggs, Inc., RD #2, 17362, pg. 1529 **PB**
Spring Grove National Bank, Ten S. Main St., 17362, pg. 1542 **PB**
The Spring Grove Water Co., 228 S. Main St., 17362, pg. 746 **PB**

Spring House

ADVANTA CORP., P.O. Box 844, Welsh & McKean Rds., 19477, pg. 22 **PB**
MOORE PRODUCTS CO., Sumneytown Pike, 19477-0900, pg. 1128 **PB**
Silverstream Center, 905 Penllyn Pike, 19477, pg. 729 **PB**
Springhouse Corporation, 1111 Bethlehem Pike, 19477, pg. 1100 **IT**
The Villa, 905 Penllyn Pike, 19477, pg. 729 **PB**

Spring Mills

Vespa Laboratories, Inc., R.D. NBR 1, 16875, pg. 288 **IT**

Springfield

Newport News Reactor Services, Inc., 1260 E. Woodland Ave., 19064, pg. 1180 **PB**

State College

C-COR ELECTRONICS, INC., 60 Decibel Rd., 16801, pg. 272 **PB**
Centre Daily Times, Inc., 3400 E. College Ave., 16801, pg. 964 **PB**
HRB Systems, 300 N. Science Park Rd., 16804-0060, pg. 1365 **PB**
GLENN O. HAWBAKER, INC., 325 W. Aaron Dr., 16803, pg. 511 **PV**
Kinko's Service Corp., 321 Rear E. Beaver Ave., 16801, pg. 622 **PV**
Locus, Inc., P.O. Box 740, 16804, pg. 942 **PB**
Maxtech, Inc., 2120 Old Gatesburg Rd., 16803, pg. 1718 **PV**
Mellon Bank, N.A.-Central Region, 122 W. College Ave., 16801, pg. 1085 **PB**
Nittany Printing & Publishing Co., Box 89, 3400 E. College Ave., 16801, pg. 964 **PB**
Omega Bank, N.A., P.O. Box 298, 16804, pg. 1222 **PB**
OMEGA FINANCIAL CORPORATION, 366 Walker Dr., 16804, pg. 1222 **PB**
Pennsylvania Cellular Telephone Corp., 2601 College Ave., 16801, pg. 1708 **PB**
Peoples National Bank of Central Pennsylvania, P.O. Box 298, 16804, pg. 1222 **PB**
Ruetgers-Nease Corporation, 201 Struble Rd., 16801, pg. 1148 **IT**
State Gas & Oil Company Division, 477 E. Beaver Ave., 16801, pg. 1664 **PB**
UNI-MARTS, INC., 477 E. Beaver Ave., 16801-5690, pg. 1664 **PB**

Steelton

Bethlehem Steel-PA Steel Technologies Inc., Front & Swatara Sts., 17113, pg. 226 **PB**

Stowe

Doehler-Jarvis, Pottstown Inc., 400 Old Reading Pike, 19464, pg. 796 **PB**
Flagg Brass, 1020 W. High St., 19464, pg. 63 **PB**

Stoystown

RIGGS INDUSTRIES, INC., Rte. 30 W., 15563, pg. 930 **PV**
Somerset Steel, Rte 30 W., 15563, pg. 930 **PV**

Stroudsburg

Absorbent Manufacturing & Technology, Inc., 1 Foundry ST., 18360, pg. 546 **PV**
Pennsylvania Cellular Telephone Corp., 1250 N. Ninth St., Ste. 4, 18360, pg. 1708 **PB**

Sunbury

Anthracite Industries, Inc., P.O. Box 112, Anthracite Rd., 17801, pg. 87 **PV**
Sunbury Textiles, P.O. Box 768, Miller St., 17801, pg. 432 **PV**
Weis Food Service, 1000 S. 2nd St., 17801, pg. 1752 **PB**
WEIS MARKETS, INC., 1000 S. Second St., 17801, pg. 1751 **PB**

Swiftwater

Connaught Laboratories, Inc., Rte. 611, P.O. Box 187, 18370, pg. 1109 **IT**

Tamaqua

Lehigh Asphalt, Paving & Construction, Rte. 209, 18252, pg. 116 **PV**
J.E. Morgan Knitting Mills Inc., Rte. 54, R.D. 2, Box 390, 18252, pg. 386 **IT**

Taylor

CONTEMPRI HOMES, INC., P.O. Box 96, Stauffer Industrial Park, 18517, pg. 439 **PB**

Telford

ACCU-SORT SYSTEMS, INC., 511 School House Rd., 18969, pg. 11 **PV**
FARM & HOME OIL COMPANY, 3115 State Rd., 18969, pg. 394 **PV**

Temple

SuperValu, Inc.-Reading Div., West Tuckerton Rd., 19560, pg. 1540 **PB**

Terre Hill

TERRE HILL CONCRETE PRODUCTS, INC., Rte. 897 S., 17581, pg. 1077 **PV**

Thomasville

Medusa Minerals Co, P.O. Box 23, Beisecker Rd., 17364, pg. 1084 **PB**

Throop

Sandvik Saws & Tools Co., 19 Keystone Indus. Park, 18512, pg. 1185 **IT**

Tipton

C-COR Electronics, Inc., P.O. Box 109, 7 Park Ave., 16684, pg. 272 **PB**

Titusville

FRONTIER FOUNDRY, INC., 221 S. Perry St., 16354, pg. 430 **PV**
Queen Cutlery Co., 507 Chestnut St., 16354, pg. 1462 **PB**

Trevose

Allied Bond & Collection Agency, Inc., One Allied Dr., Neshaminy Interplex, 19053, pg. 1667 **PB**
BETZDEARBORN INC., 4636 Somerton Rd., 19053-6783, pg. 226 **PB**
BRENNTAG Interchem, Inc., Three Neshaminy Interplex, Ste., 103, 19053, pg. 1458 **IT**
CRAFTMATIC INDUSTRIES, INC., 2500 Interplex Dr., 19053, pg. 284 **PV**
Craftmatic Organization, Inc., 2500 Interplex Dr., 19053, pg. 284 **PV**
FAULKNER CADILLAC INC., Rte. One & Old Lincoln Hwy., 19053, pg. 397 **PV**
Gensym Corporation, Philadelphia Area Office, Six Neshaminy Interplex, Ste. 215, 19053, pg. 731 **PB**

Geographic Index-U.S.

KORMAN SERVICES, L.P., Two Neshaminy Interplex, 19053, pg. 632 **PV**
TECHNITROL, INC., 1210 Northbrook Dr., Ste. 385, 19053, pg. 1564 **PB**

Tullytown

ATLANTIC CONCRETE PRODUCTS, INC., 8900 Old Rte. 13, 19007-0098, pg. 95 **PV**
Ikselah Corporation, P.O. Box 132, 19007, pg. 1339 **PB**

Tyrone

C.C.K., Inc., P.O. Box 276, 16686, pg. 637 **PV**
Quality Chemicals, Inc., P.O. Box 216, 16686-0216, pg. 344 **PB**

Union City

MFG Union City Operations, 55 Fourth Ave., 16438, pg. 756 **PV**
Molded Fiber Glass Co., 55 Fourth Ave., 16438, pg. 756 **PV**
Snap-Tite Hose, Inc., 217 Titusville Rd., 16438, pg. 1010 **PV**
Snap-Tite, Inc., 201 Titusville Rd., 16438, pg. 1010 **PV**
Union City Chair Co., 18 Market St., 16438, pg. 170 **PV**

Uniontown

O.C. CLUSS LUMBER CO., P.O. Box 696, 15401, pg. 248 **PV**

Upper Darby

Meenan Oil/Young Supply Co., 8301 Lansdowne Ave., 19082, pg. 729 **PV**
United Technologies Tel MIS, 8049 W. Chester Pike, 19082-1317, pg. 1690 **PB**

Valley Forge

AMP Inc. Flexible Film Sensors, P.O. Box 799, 19482-0799, pg. 7 **PB**
ALCO INDUSTRIES, INC., P.O. Box 937, 19482, pg. 32 **PV**
AmeriGas, Inc., P.O. Box 858, 19482, pg. 1653 **PB**
AmeriGas Partners, L.P., P.O. Box 965, 19482, pg. 1653 **PB**
AmeriGas Propane, P.O. Box 965, 19482, pg. 1653 **PB**
Atochem Services Inc., P.O. Box 799, 19482-0799, pg. 445 **IT**
Bell Atlantic Directory Graphics, Inc., Valley Forge Corp. Center, 2500 Monroe Blvd., 19484-3050, pg. 203 **PB**
CertainTeed Corporation, P.O. Box 860, 750 E. Swedesford Rd., 19482, pg. 1170 **IT**
CertainTeed Corporation Foundation, 750 E. Swedesford Rd., 19482, pg. 1171 **PB**
CertainTeed Foreign Sales Corp., P.O. Box 860, 19482, pg. 1171 **IT**
CertainTeed International, Inc., P.O. Box 860, 750 E. Swedesford Rd., 19482, pg. 1171 **IT**
CertainTeed Ventures, Inc., 750 E. Swedesford Rd., 19482, pg. 1171 **IT**
CertainTeed Weaving Corp., P. O. Box 860, 19482, pg. 1171 **IT**
Ecophon CertainTeed, Inc., 750 E. Swedesford Rd., 19482, pg. 1171 **IT**
Hewlett-Packard Company, 2750 Monroe Blvd., 19482, pg. 815 **PB**
Hollow Spheres Business, P.O. Box 840, 19482, pg. 827 **PV**
HOUGHTON INTERNATIONAL INC., Madison & Van Buren, 19482, pg. 541 **PV**
ICI Aerospace, 2550 Eisenhower Rd., 19482, pg. 663 **IT**
Inorganic Colloids Business, P.O. Box 840, 19482, pg. 827 **PV**
Lake Keowee Country Club, Inc., P. O. Box 860, 19482, pg. 1171 **IT**
ROBERT E. LAMB, INC., 939 Jefferson Ave., P.O. Box 821, 19482, pg. 644 **PV**
Manatee Holding Company, P.O. Box 860, 750 E. Swedesford Rd., 19482, pg. 1176 **PV**
Martin Marietta Regional Manufacturing Operation, 680 American Ave., 19406, pg. 1007 **PB**
National Integrity Life Insurance Co., Liberty Park, 19493, pg. 27 **IT**
Potters Industries, Inc., Corporate Hdqtrs., P.O. Box 840, 19482-0840, pg. 827 **PV**
Providian Life & Health Insurance Co., Liberty Park, 19493, pg. 27 **IT**
Saint-Gobain Corporation, P.O. Box 860, 750 E. Swedesford Rd., 19482, pg. 1177 **IT**
Saint-Gobain Delaware Corporation, P.O. Box 860, 750 E. Swedesford Rd., 19482, pg. 1177 **IT**
Transicoil, Inc., P.O. Box 9011, 19485, pg. 538 **IT**
THE VANGUARD GROUP, INC., Vanguard Financial Ctr., 19482, pg. 1133 **PV**
Vanguard Real Estate Fund II, P.O. Box 2600, 19482, pg. 1134 **PV**
Veterans Life Insurance Co., Liberty Park, 19493, pg. 26 **IT**
Wolverine Vinyl Siding, 750 E. Swedesford Rd., 19482, pg. 1171 **IT**

Vandergrift

Allegheny Ludlum-Vandergrift, 130 Lincoln Ave., 15690, pg. 43 **PB**

Verona

American Beverage Corporation, One Daily Way, 15147, pg. 752 **IT**

Warfordsburg

H.B. MELLOTT ESTATE, INC., Rte. 1 Box 25, 17267, pg. 730 **PV**

Warminster

Alfa Laval Separation Inc., 955 Mearns Rd., 18974, pg. 1378 **IT**
Alfa-Laval Sharples, 955 Mearns Rd., 18974, pg. 1378 **IT**
Bailey Fischer & Porter Company, 125 E. County Line Rd., 18974-4995, pg. 449 **IT**
W. ATLEE BURPEE CO., 300 Park Ave., 18974, pg. 187 **PV**
CRC Industries, Inc., 885 Louis Dr., 18974, pg. 138 **PV**
Hull/Finmac, Inc., 14 Bonair Dr., 18974, pg. 547 **PV**
Midland Seaboard Printing Ink, Inc., 841 Nina Way, 18974, pg. 1311 **IT**
BENJAMIN OBDYKE, INC., John Fitch Industrial Pk., 65 Steamboat Dr., 18974, pg. 810 **PV**
Pressure Products Industries, 900 Louis Dr., 18974, pg. 1055 **PV**

Warren

BLAIR CORPORATION, 220 Hickory St., 16366-0001, pg. 236 **PB**
DELUXE STORAGE SYSTEMS, INC., 151 Struthers St., 16365, pg. 323 **PV**
Struthers Wells Corp., 1003 Pennsylvania Ave. W., 16365, pg. 1048 **PV**
Unitec Refining Company, 15 Bradley St., 16365, pg. 915 **PV**
Unitec Refining Inc., 15 Bradley St., 16365, pg. 915 **PV**

Warrendale

AMERICAN EAGLES OUTFITTERS INC., 150 Thornhill Dr., 15095-0788, pg. 53 **PV**
FORE SYSTEMS, INC., 1000 FORE Dr., 15086-7502, pg. 667 **PB**
Joy Mining Machinery, Thornhill Industrial Park, 177 Thorn Hill Rd., 15086, pg. 790 **PB**
Joy Mining Machinery, 177 Thorn Hill Rd., 15068, pg. 789 **PB**
Metallurgical Products Co., P.O. Box 777, 15095, pg. 727 **PV**

Warrington

ChemPump, 175 Titus Ave., 18976, pg. 456 **PB**
JOMAR, INC., 863 Easton Rd., 18976, pg. 595 **PV**
Porsche Motorsports North America, Inc., 18976, pg. 1063 **IT**

Washington

Advanced Coil Industries, 175 Plumpton Ave., 15301, pg. 74 **PV**
Allegheny Ludlum-Washington Plant, 500 Green St., 15301, pg. 43 **PB**
CAMALLOY, INCORPORATED, 1960 N. Main St., 15301, pg. 202 **PV**
Cerdec Corporation, W. Wylie Ave., 15301, pg. 292 **PB**
Consolidation Coal Co.-Eastern Region, 450 Race Track Rd., 15301, pg. 531 **PB**
Cox Communications-Washington, 140 Park Ave., 15301, pg. 455 **PB**
Dynamet Inc., 195 Museum Rd., 15301, pg. 307 **PB**
Senior Conflow Inc., 270 Meadowlands Blvd., 15301, pg. 1222 **IT**
Superior Valve Company, 2200 N. Main St., 15301, pg. 53 **PB**
West Penn Wire/CDT, P.O. Box 762, 2833 W. Chestnut St., 15301, pg. 287 **PB**
X-Mark/CDT, 2001 N. Main St., 15301, pg. 287 **PB**

Waterford

TROYER POTATO PRODUCTS, INC., Rte. 97 South, 16441, pg. 1106 **PV**

Watsontown

Hoeganaes Corp., P.O. Box 37, 17777, pg. 893 **PB**

Wayne

American Software, Inc., Northeast, 1265 Drummers Ln., Ste. 201, 19087, pg. 91 **PB**
Architecture, 99 Old Eagle School Rd., Ste. 1010, 19087, pg. 1446 **IT**
Arnold Advertising, 530 E. Swedesford Rd., Ste. 101, 19087, pg. 84 **PV**
Astra Merck Inc., 725 Cheterbrook Blvd., 19087, pg. 93 **IT**
Comcast Cellular Communications, Inc., 480 E. Swedesford Rd., 19087, pg. 407 **PB**
Day & Zimmerman Information Solutions, 151 S. Warner Rd., Ste. 322, 19087, pg. 317 **PV**
Desjarcins Laurentian Life Assurance, 640 Lee Road, Ste. 303, 19087, pg. 396 **IT**

EnerTech Capital Partners, 435 Devon Park Dr., Ste. 410, 19087, pg. 1424 **PB**
FCA Holdings, Inc., 998 Old Eagle School Rd., Ste. 1205, 19087, pg. 471 **IT**
Financial Collection Agencies of Pennsylvania Inc, The Woods, Ste. 1205, 998 Old Eagle School Rd., 19087, pg. 471 **IT**
Graphic Packaging Corporation, 955 Chesterbrook Blvd., 19087, pg. 3 **PB**
Horan Goldman Companies Inc., 485 Devon Park Dr., Ste. 115, 19087-0288, pg. 705 **IT**
Hospital Group of America, 1265 Drummers Ln., Ste. 107, 19087, pg. 442 **PB**
Integrated Systems Consulting Group, 575 E. Swedesford Rd., 19087, pg. 1425 **PB**
Internet Capital Group, 800 The Safeguard Bldg., 435 Devon Park Dr., 19087, pg. 1425 **PB**
Johnson Matthey Inc., 460 E. Swedesord Rd., 19087, pg. 713 **IT**
LUMBERMENS MERCHANDISING CORPORATION, 137 W. Wayne Ave., 19087, pg. 680 **PV**
THE McCLURE GROUP, 1325 Morris Dr., Chesterbrook, 19087, pg. 719 **PV**
Pilgrim Baxter & Associates, 1255 Drummer Ln., Ste. 300, 19087, pg. 1673 **PB**
Recon Consultants, Inc., 998 Old Eagle School Road, Ste. 1205, 19087, pg. 471 **IT**
SCP Private Equity Partners, 800 The Safeguard Bldg., 435 Devon Park Dr., 19087, pg. 1424 **PB**
SEI Benefit Services Corporation, 680 E. Swedesford Rd., 19087, pg. 1417 **PB**
SEI Financial Management Corporation, 680 E. Swedesford Rd., 19087, pg. 1417 **PB**
Safeguard International Group, 800 The Safeguard Bldg., 435 Devon Park Dr., 19087, pg. 1424 **PB**
SAFEGUARD SCIENTIFICS, INC., 800 The Safeguard Bldg., 435 Devon Park Dr., 19087-1945, pg. 1424 **PB**
Smiths Industries Aerospace & Defense Systems Inc.-Finance Dept., 435 Devon Park Dr., Ste. 101, 19087, pg. 1268 **IT**
Structured Financial Capital Inc., 998 Old Eagle School Rd., 19087, pg. 471 **IT**
Suburban Publications, Inc., P.O. Box 409, 134 N. Wayne Ave., 19087, pg. 935 **PB**
SUNGARD DATA SYSTEMS INC., 1285 Drummers Ln., 19087-1586, pg. 1534 **PB**
SunGard Planning Solutions Inc., 1285 Drummers Ln., 19087, pg. 1535 **PB**
Sungard Recovery Services Group, 1285 Drummers Ln., 19087, pg. 1535 **PB**
SunGard Technology Systems Group, 1285 Drummers Lane, 19087-1586, pg. 1535 **PB**
TL Ventures, 800 The Safeguard Bldg., 435 Devon Dr., 19087, pg. 1424 **PB**
TRIUMPH GROUP, INC., Four Glenhardie Corp. Ctr., 1255 Drummers Ln., Ste. 200, 19087-1565, pg. 1640 **PB**
Western Interactive Media, Three Glen Hardie Corp. Ctr., 1265 Drummers Ln., Ste. 106, 19087, pg. 1166 **PV**

Waynesboro

Beck Manufacturing, Inc., East 9th St., 17268, pg. 146 **PV**
BITREK CORPORATION, 330 E. Ninth St., 17268, pg. 145 **PV**
Elite Personalized Creations, 725 Clayton Ave., 17268, pg. 89 **PB**
Frick Company, 100 C.V. Ave., 17268, pg. 1788 **PB**
Landis, 20 E. Sixth St., 17268-2050, pg. 1699 **PB**
Regency Engravers, Inc., 725 Clayton Ave., 17268, pg. 89 **PB**
Regency Thermographers, 725 Clayton Ave., 17268, pg. 89 **PB**

Waynesburg

Cyprus Emerald Resources Corporation, P.O. Box 871, 15370, pg. 471 **PB**

West Chester

API Harowe, 110 Westtown Rd., 19380, pg. 90 **PB**
Allister Manufacturing Co., 304 Willowbrook Lane, 19382, pg. 1376 **PB**
ALOETTE COSMETICS, INC., 1301 Wright's Ln. E., 19380, pg. 57 **PV**
AMKOR ELECTRONICS, INC., 1345 Enterprise Dr., 19380, pg. 66 **PV**
Ampex Data Systems Corporation, 1012 Rock Creek Rd., 19380, pg. 104 **PB**
Brandywine Hall Care Center, 800 W. Miner St., 19382, pg. 728 **PB**
The Daily Local News, 250 N. Bradford Ave., 19382, pg. 934 **PB**
Delchester Oil Co. Inc., 841 Lincoln Ave., 19380-0596, pg. 518 **PV**
Gagliardi Brothers Inc., 700 N. Five Point Rd., 19380, pg. 805 **PB**
LASKO METAL PRODUCTS, INC., 820 Lincoln Ave., 19380, pg. 652 **PV**
LENAPE FORGE, INC., 1280 Lenape Rd., 19382, pg. 659 **PV**
Mars-Philadelphia, 217 Willowbrook Lane, 19382, pg. 707 **PV**
METABO CORPORATION, 1231 Wilson Dr., 19380, pg. 734 **PV**
QVC, Inc., 1365 Enterprise Dr., 19380, pg. 407 **PB**
QVC, INC., 1200 Wilson Dr., 19380, pg. 897 **PV**
QVC, Inc., 1365 Enterprise Dr., 19380, pg. 1555 **PB**
RedGo Properties, Inc., 401 Willowbrook Ln., 19382, pg. 1376 **PB**

PB - *U.S. Public Companies Volume*
PV - *U.S. Private Companies Volume*
IT - *International Public & Private Companies Volume*

1416

Geographic Index-U.S.

RELM WIRELESS CORP., 342 Willowbrook Ln., 19382, pg. 1376 **PB**
Universal Promotions, Inc., 217 Willowbrook Lane, 19382, pg. 707 **PV**
VTG USA Inc., 1234 West Chester Pike, 19380, pg. 1070 **IT**
VWR SCIENTIFIC PRODUCTS, 1310 Goshen Pky., 19380, pg. 1703 **PB**
Weston International, Inc., One Weston Way, 19380, pg. 1761 **PB**
ROY F. WESTON, INC., One Weston Way, 19380-1499, pg. 1761 **PB**

West Conshohocken

Modern Hilift Equipment Co., 1165 Matsonford Rd., 19428, pg. 755 **PB**
R.M. SHOEMAKER CO., One Tower Bridge, 100 Front St., 19428, pg. 996 **PV**

West Elizabeth

Hercules Inc.-Jefferson, P.O. Box 567, 15088-2520, pg. 810 **PB**

West Middlesex

T. BRUCE SALES, INC., Carbough St., 16159, pg. 175 **PV**

West Mifflin

Keywell Co., 890 Noble Dr., 15122, pg. 619 **PV**
Transport USA, Inc., 1200 Lebanon Rd., 15122, pg. 389 **PB**
TRUMBULL CORPORATION/P.J. DICK, INC., 1020 Lebanon Rd., 15122-0100, pg. 1107 **PV**

West Pittsburg

REACTIVE METALS & ALLOYS CORPORATION (REMACOR), P.O. Box 366, Rt. 168, 16160, pg. 913 **PV**
Shaw-Perkins, Inc., P.O. Box 366, Rte. 168, 16160, pg. 913 **PV**

West Point

Berwind Pharmaceutical Services, Inc., Moyer Blvd., 19486, pg. 139 **PV**
Colorcon, Moyer Blvd., 19486, pg. 139 **PV**
Merck Human Health Division (U.S. Human Health), Sumneytown Pike, 19486, pg. 1091 **PB**
Rotelle, Inc., 301 Morris Rd., 19486, pg. 1389 **PB**

Westchester

Groundwater Technology Government Services, Inc., 1220 Ward Ave., Ste. 200, 19380, pg. 660 **PB**

Westfield

Electri-Cord Manufacturing Co., 312 E. Main St., 16950, pg. 990 **PB**

Wexford

Class One Research, 602 Wiltshire Ct., 15090-7468, pg. 383 **PB**
LANDAU BUILDING CO., 9855 Rinaman Rd., 15090, pg. 646 **PV**
TRU-WELD GRATING, INC., 2000 Corporate Dr., 15090, pg. 1107 **PV**

White Haven

EMCEE BROADCAST PRODUCTS, INC., Susquehanna St. Ext., 18661, pg. 570 **PB**

White Mills

Chroma Video, Inc., Park St. & Riverside Dr., 18473, pg. 1720 **PB**

Whitehall

Lehigh Securities Corporation, 1457 MacArthur Rd., 18052, pg. 1528 **PB**

Wilkes-Barre

Action Lift, 1500 Hwy. 315, 18711, pg. 728 **PV**
Bridon American Corp., Hanover Industrial Park, 18703, pg. 215 **IT**
Bright Star Industries, Inc., 380 Stewart Rd., 18706, pg. 1341 **PB**
Citadel Broadcasting Co., East Mountain Corporate Ctr., 600 Baltimore Dr., 18702, pg. 241 **PV**
Louis Cohen and Sons, Inc., Fellows Ave., 18702, pg. 728 **PV**
Franklin First Savings Bank, 44 W. Market St., 18773, pg. 632 **PB**
JEWELCOR COMPANIES, 100 N. Wilkes-Barre Blvd., 4th. Fl., 18702, pg. 587 **PV**
THE LION BREWERY, INC., 700 N. Pennsylvania Ave., 18705, pg. 1000 **PB**
MEDICO INDUSTRIES, INC., 1500 Hwy. 315, 18711, pg. 728 **PV**

Mellon Bank, N.A.-Northeastern Region, Eight W. Market St., 18711, pg. 1085 **PB**
MUSKIN LEISURE PRODUCTS, INC., 401 E. Thomas St., 18705-3897, pg. 768 **PV**
PG Energy, Inc., One PEI Ctr., 18711, pg. 1271 **PB**
PG Energy Services, One PEI Ctr., 18711, pg. 1272 **PB**
Pennsylvania Cellular Telephone Corp., 277 Mundy St., 18702, pg. 1708 **PB**
PENNSYLVANIA ENTERPRISES INC., One PEI Ctr., 18711, pg. 1271 **PB**
Pennsylvania Power & Light Company-Northeast Div., 1190 E. Mountain Dr., 18702-7907, pg. 1244 **PB**
Rykoff-Sexton, Inc., 613 Baltimore Dr., 18702, pg. 918 **PB**
THETA Land Corporation, One PEI Ctr., 18711, pg. 1272 **PB**
The Times Leader, 15 N. Main St., 18711, pg. 964 **PB**
The Times Leader, 15 N. Main St., P.O. Box 730, 18711, pg. 963 **PB**
Tru-Form, 1141 Hgwy. 315, 18702-6928, pg. 1338 **IT**
U.S. Food Service, 1603 Baltimore Dr., 18702, pg. 918 **PB**
Valley Manufacturing Corporation, P.O. Box 626, 120 Hazle St., 18703-0626, pg. 1338 **IT**

Williamsburg

Charter Cove Forge Behavioral Health System, Inc., New Beginnings Rd., 16693, pg. 1034 **PB**

Williamsport

BRODART COMPANY, 500 Arch St., 17705, pg. 170 **PV**
Brodart Sales Co., 500 Arch St., 17705, pg. 170 **PV**
Cox Communications-Williamsport, 330 Basin St., 17701, pg. 455 **PB**
Grovenberg, Four Quality St., 17701, pg. 1077 **PB**
The HON Co., Williamsport Plant, 1201 W. Third St., 17701, pg. 772 **PB**
Keystone Brokerage, Inc., 110 W. Fourth St., 17701, pg. 956 **PB**
Lunaire Environmental, Four Quality St., 17701, pg. 1077 **PB**
LUNDY CONSTRUCTION CO., INC., Arch St. & Reach Rd., 17701, pg. 681 **PV**
Northern Central Bank, 102 W. Fouth St., 17701, pg. 956 **PB**
OHD Thermacore Div., OHD Corp., 3200 Reach Rd., 17701, pg. 822 **PV**
Pennpower Inc., 25 W. 3rd St., Ste. 803, 17701, pg. 1353 **IT**
Pennsylvania Cellular Telephone Corp., 2495 E. Third St., 17701, pg. 1708 **PB**
Quest Diagnostic-Williamsport, 410 Locust St., 17701, pg. 1352 **PB**
Schneider Farms Dairy, 1860 E. Third St., 17703, pg. 971 **PV**
Tampella Power Corp., P.O. Box 3308, 2600 Reach Rd., 17701-0308, pg. 1354 **IT**
TENNEY ENVIRONMENTAL, P.O. Box 3246, Four Quality St., 17701, pg. 1076 **PV**
Textron Lycoming, 652 Oliver St., 17701, pg. 1589 **PV**
TRIMTEX CO. INC., 400 Park Ave., 17701, pg. 1103 **PV**
Williamsport National Bank, 329 Pine St., 17701, pg. 1543 **PB**

Willow Grove

Allegro MicroSystems Inc., 3900 Welsh Rd., 19090, pg. 1188 **IT**
ASPLUNDH TREE EXPERT CO., 708 Blair Mill Rd., 19090, pg. 89 **PV**
KULICKE & SOFFA INDUSTRIES, INC., 2101 Blair Mill Rd., 19090, pg. 968 **PB**
NEWAGE INDUSTRIES INC., 2300 Maryland Rd., 19090-1799, pg. 796 **PV**
QUAD SYSTEMS CORPORATION, 2405 Maryland Rd., 19090, pg. 898 **PB**
TINIUS OLSEN TESTING MACHINE CO., INC., Easton Rd., 19090, pg. 1088 **PV**

Wilmerding

WABCO-Freight Car, P.O. Box 67, 15148, pg. 1761 **PB**
WABCO-Locomotive, P.O. Box 68, 15148, pg. 1761 **PB**
WESTINGHOUSE AIR BRAKE COMPANY, 1001 Air Brake Ave., 15148, pg. 1760 **PB**

Wind Gap

Blue Mountain Consolidated Water Company, 20 E. Center St., 18091, pg. 379 **PB**

Windber

Reitz Coal Company, 509 15th St., 15963, pg. 139 **PV**
Wilmore Coal Company, 509 15th St., 15963, pg. 138 **PV**

Windsor

BMY Co., P.O. Box 444, RR 1, 17366-9777, pg. 793 **PB**

Womelsdorf

Double H Boot Co., 30 N. Third St., 19567, pg. 217 **PB**

Woodland

Walker Lumber & Supply, Inc., P.O. Box 60, 16881, pg. 502 **PV**

Woolrich

WOOLRICH, INC., One Mill St., 17779, pg. 1188 **PV**
Woolrich Store Div., Park Ave., 17779, pg. 1188 **PV**

Worcester

PALMER INTERNATIONAL, INC., 2955 Skippack Pike, 19490, pg. 834 **PV**

Wormleysburg

Pennsylvania Cellular Telephone Corp., 902 N. Front St., 17043, pg. 1708 **PB**

Wymissing

Citizens Utilities Water Company of Pennsylvania, Four Wellington Blvd., 19610, pg. 380 **PB**

Wyncote

Hillcrest Center, 1245 Church Rd., 19095, pg. 729 **PB**

Wyomissing

Cott Corporation - North East US Region, 1090 Spring Street, 19610, pg. 337 **IT**
Glen-Gery Corporation, P.O. Box 7001, 1166 Spring St., 19610-6001, pg. 658 **IT**
Investors Trust Company, 2201 Ridgewood Rd., 19610-1190, pg. 1159 **PB**
PENN NATIONAL GAMING, INC., 825 Berkshire Blvd., Ste. 203, 19610, pg. 1270 **PB**
SOVEREIGN BANCORP, INC., 1130 Berkshire Blvd., 19610, pg. 1494 **PB**
Systems Assembly Div., 1105 Berkshire Blvd., Ste. 310, 19610, pg. 479 **PB**
VF CORPORATION, 1047 N. Park Rd., 19610, pg. 1702 **PB**
VF International, 1047 North Park Rd., 19610, pg. 1702 **PB**

York

Acco Chain & Lifting Products, P.O. Box 792, 76 Acco Dr., 17405, pg. 473 **IT**
Air Products Group, 631 S. Richland Dr., 17403, pg. 1789 **PB**
Amerifoods Snacks, 1120 Zinns Quarry Rd., 17404, pg. 65 **PV**
Applied Systems, 631 So. Richland Ave., 17403, pg. 1788 **PV**
B-H Computers, 445 W. Philadelphia St., 17405, pg. 830 **PV**
B-H Laboratories, Inc., 978 Loucks Mill Rd., 17402, pg. 830 **PV**
BMY Co., P.O. Box 1512, 17405-1512, pg. 793 **PB**
J.E. BAKER CO., 232 E. Market St., 17403, pg. 112 **PV**
BLOCKHOUSE CO., INC., 3285 Farmtrail Rd., 17402, pg. 150 **PV**
Bon Ton Foods, Inc., 1120 Zinns Quarry Rd., 17404, pg. 65 **PV**
THE BON TON STORES, INC., 2801 E. Market St., 17402, pg. 244 **PB**
Buchart Horn Inc., 445 W. Philadelphia St., 17405, pg. 245 **PV**
C P CONVERTERS, INC., 15 Grumbacher Rd., 17402, pg. 192 **PV**
Combat Systems Division, Wolf's Church Rd., 17405, pg. 213 **PV**
Danskin, 305 State St., 17405, pg. 483 **PB**
Dentsply Ash, P.O. Box 872, 570 W. College Ave., 17405, pg. 499 **PB**
Dentsply Cavitron, P.O. Box 872, 570 W. College Ave., 17405, pg. 499 **PB**
Dentsply International, P.O. Box 872, 570 W. College Ave., 17405, pg. 499 **PB**
DENTSPLY INTERNATIONAL INC., 570 W. College Ave., 17405, pg. 498 **PB**
Dentsply Latin American Export, P.O. Box 872, 570 W. College Ave., 17405, pg. 499 **PB**
Dentsply Trubyte, P.O. Box 872, 570 W. College Ave., 17405, pg. 499 **PB**
DONLEE TECHNOLOGIES INC., 693 N. Hills Rd., 17402-2211, pg. 339 **PV**
Emons Finance Corp., 96 S. George St., 17401, pg. 578 **PB**
Emons Industries, Inc., 96 S. George St., 17401, pg. 578 **PB**
Emons Logistics Services Inc., 96 George St., 17401, pg. 578 **PB**
Emons Railroad Group, Inc., 96 S. George St., 17401, pg. 578 **PB**
EMONS TRANSPORTATION GROUP, INC., 96 S. George St., 17401, pg. 578 **PB**
Fincor Electronics, 3750 E. Market St., 17402, pg. 857 **PB**
First Maryland Intl. Banking Corp., 96 S. George St., Ste. 510, 17401, pg. 64 **IT**
Gunnebo Corporation, P.O. Box 1589, 180 S. Hartman St., 17405, pg. 578 **IT**
Hercon Environmental Corporation, P.O. Box 786, 17405, pg. 802 **PB**
Herculite Products, Inc., P.O. Box 786, 17405, pg. 802 **PV**
KBA-Motter Corp., 3900 E. Market St., 17402, pg. 742 **IT**
KBA-Motter Corp., 3900 E. Market St., 17402, pg. 1341 **PB**

Geographic Index-U.S.

Maryland & Pennsylvania Railroad, 96 S. George St., 17401, pg. 579 **PB**
McCrory Stores Div., 2955 E. Market St., 17402, pg. 721 **PV**
Meiji Seika Kaisha, Ltd. - York Office, 1725 Seventh Ave., 17403, pg. 855 **IT**
Newark Paperboard Products Mercer Div., 2510 N. George St., 17402, pg. 796 **PV**
PACE RESOURCES, INC., 40 S. Richland Ave., 17404, pg. 829 **PV**
Pennsylvania Cellular Telephone Corp., Prospect Commerce Center, 1803 Mount Rose Ave., 17403, pg. 1708 **PB**
THE PFALTZGRAFF CO., 140 E. Market St., 17401, pg. 860 **PV**
The Pfaltzgraff Co., 140 E. Market St., 17401, pg. 860 **PV**
Print-O-Stat, Inc., 1011 W. Market St., 17405, pg. 830 **PV**
St. Lawrence & Atlantic Railroad, 96 S. George St., 17401, pg. 578 **PB**
SHIPLEY COMPANIES, 550 E. King St., 17405, pg. 994 **PV**
D.F. Stauffer Biscuit Co., Belmont & Sixth Ave., 17403, pg. 855 **IT**
Svedala Industries Inc., 240 Arch St., 17403, pg. 1325 **IT**
TIGHE INDUSTRIES, INC., 333 E. 7th Ave., 17404, pg. 1086 **PV**
TOPFLIGHT CORP., 160 E. Ninth Ave., 17404, pg. 1091 **PV**
Unitary Products Group, 631 S. Richland Ave., 17403-3445, pg. 1788 **PV**
Voith Hydro, Inc., E. Berlin Rd., 17404, pg. 1473 **IT**
WPMT Channel 43, 2005 South Queen St., 17403-4806, pg. 1636 **PV**
WSBA AM/FM, Box 910, 17402, pg. 860 **PV**
WELDON MACHINE TOOL, INC., 1800 W. King St., 17404, pg. 1161 **PV**
The York Bank and Trust Company, 107 W. Market St., 17401, pg. 65 **IT**
YORK BARBELL CO., INC., 3300 Board Rd., 17402, pg. 1196 **PV**
YORK BUILDING PRODUCTS CO., INC., 1020 N. Hartley St., 17405, pg. 1196 **PV**
YORK INTERNATIONAL CORPORATION, P.O. Box 1592, 631 S. Richland Ave., 17403, pg. 1788 **PV**
York Paint, P.O. Box 3056, 3990 E. Market St., 17402-0056, pg. 444 **PB**
YORK WALLCOVERINGS INC., 750 Linden Ave., 17405, pg. 1196 **PV**
Yorkrail Inc., 96 S. George St., 17401, pg. 579 **PV**
Yorktowne Paperboard Corp., 1001 Loucks Mill Rd., 17402, pg. 796 **PV**

Youngwood

Cherry Creek Golf, P.O. Box K, 15697, pg. 749 **PV**
JHJ Realty, P.O. Box K, 15697, pg. 749 **PV**
MILLSTEIN INDUSTRIES, P.O. Box K, 15697, pg. 749 **PB**
Powerex Inc., Hillis St., 15697, pg. 873 **IT**

PUERTO RICO

Aguada

Telecom Solutions Puerto Rico, Inc., Industrial Park, Bldg. Seven, P.O. Box 1046, 00602-1046, pg. 1547 **PB**

Aguadilla

CARIBE EXPRESS, Bldg. 1102, Parallel Rd., Ramey, 00604, pg. 211 **PV**
Caribe Freight, Edificio Caribe Freight, Aeropuerto International de las Americas, 00603, pg. 211 **PV**
Disposable Safety Wear Inc., R.D. #107, KMO, 3 Borinquen, 00603, pg. 548 **PB**
Hewlett-Packard Puerto Rico, P.O. Box 4048, Hwy. 110 N., 00605, pg. 816 **PB**
Mo-Ka Shoe Corp., Borinquen Rd., 00603, pg. 1752 **PB**
Puerto Rico Safety Corporation, R.D. #107, KMO, 3 Borinquen, 00603, pg. 548 **PB**
Puerto Rico Safety Equipment Corporation, R.D. #107, KMO, 3 Borinquen, 00603, pg. 548 **PB**
Sensormatic Electronics de Puerto Rico, BO Montana, Poblado, KM 5.8 State Rd. 110, 00690-0627, pg. 1457 **PB**
Wolverine Boot Co., Rd. 111, Km. 2.3 Insular Rd., 00603, pg. 1775 **PB**

Aguas Buenas

Cutler-Hammer Puerto Rico, Road 174, Km 22, 00607, pg. 556 **PB**

Arecibo

Pharmacia & Upjohn Manufacturing Co., Hwy. 2, KM 60.0, 00612, pg. 1048 **IT**
Superior Industries Intl., P.O. Box 1954, 00613, pg. 1539 **PB**

Barceloneta

Abbott Hospitals Inc., RD 2 KM 58 3, 00617, pg. 13 **PB**
Bristol Myers Barceloneta Inc., Rd. 2, Km. 56.4, 00617, pg. 254 **PB**

Bayamon

Kenwood Service Corporation-Puerto Rico Branch, BMS-328, P.O. Box 607061, 00960-7061, pg. 730 **IT**
A.J. Oster Caribe, Inc., Bldg. 18, Central Industrial Corujo, Hato Tejas, 00619, pg. 1219 **PB**
Puerto Rico Container Co., Road No. 2, Corujo Industrial Park, 00961, pg. 1666 **PB**
Pulte Puerto Rican Operations, P.O. Box 1998, 00619, pg. 1345 **PB**
Thomas & Betts Caribe, Inc., P.O. Box 2421, 00619, pg. 1598 **PB**
W & S Distributors, Inc., P.O. Box 1650, 00960, pg. 132 **IT**
Wang Computadoras, Inc., Avenida Santa Juanita CC-20, 00956, pg. 1737 **IT**

Caguas

The Clorox Co. of Puerto Rico, Rd. 798, Km. 0.9, Bo. Rio Canas, 00625, pg. 387 **PB**
Ferrero Inc., Road 1, Km 29.4, 00625, pg. 480 **IT**
Garrido y Compania, 105 Betances St., 00726, pg. 1527 **PB**
Johnson & Johnson Hemisferica, P.O. Box 4986, 00726-4986, pg. 928 **PB**
Johnson & Johnson Medical Caribbean, Call Box 4987, 00726-4987, pg. 928 **PB**
St. Jude Puerto Rico, Inc., Caguas W. Indus. Park, Lot 20, B S., 00625, pg. 1428 **PB**

Canovanas

Chiron, Canovanas Industrial Pk., Rd. 118, Lot 17, 00729, pg. 350 **PB**
Milgray Electronics/P.R., Inc., P.O. Box 1603, Calle No. 1 (Carr. # 188), 00629, pg. 206 **PB**

Caparra Heights

Arrow/Schweber Electronics, 00922, pg. 134 **PB**
Hewlett-Packard Company, Texaco Plaza, Ste. 100, Street 1 Lot 2, 00920-1705, pg. 813 **PB**
Honeywell S.A., 26 Ortegon St., 00968, pg. 835 **PB**
Velco, PO Box 11917, 00922, pg. 176 **PB**

Carolina

Acme/Chaston Puerto Rico, Charlyn Indus. Park, P.O. Box 4580, 00628, pg. 694 **PB**
Atlantic Pump & Equipment Co. of Puerto Rico, Bldg. #6, Industr. Villate, Rd. 190, Ste. 51, 00984, pg. 846 **PB**
Circle Freight International USA, P.O. Box 4837, 00984-4837, pg. 370 **PB**
Crown Cork de Puerto Rico, Inc., K12H6 65th Infantry Ave., 00986, pg. 463 **PB**
El San Juan Hotel & Casino, 6063 Isla Verde Ave., 00979, pg. 1265 **PB**
Gerber Products Company of Puerto Rico, Inc., P.O. Box 1769, 00628, pg. 973 **IT**
IPR Pharmaceuticals, Inc., P.O. Box No. 1967, 00984, pg. 1524 **IT**
Kodak Caribbean Limited, Campo Rico & 246 St., Country Club, 00987, pg. 551 **PB**
Eli Lilly and Company, Inc., Carr 3 Km 12.6, 00630, pg. 993 **PB**
Eli Lilly Industries, Inc., Call Box 1198, Pueblo Station, 00986-1190, pg. 993 **PB**
Newell Puerto Rico, Ltd., P.O. Box 3379, 00984-3379, pg. 1177 **PB**
Orion Research Puerto Rico, Inc., Industrial Ville Park, Carrigo KM 1.5, Edificio #3, 00630, pg. 1592 **PB**
Pueblo International, Inc.-P.R. Div., Loiza Expwy. Corner of Campo Rico Ave., 00630, pg. 894 **PV**
Red Star de Puerto Rico, S.A., Apartado 3428, 00984, pg. 1696 **PB**
3M Puerto Rico, Inc., Puerto Rico Industrial Park, P.O. Box 100, 00986-0100, pg. 1605 **PB**
WHG Resorts & Casinos, 6063 E. Isla Verde Ave., 00979, pg. 1265 **PB**
Williams Hospitality Group Inc., 6063 E. Isla Verde Ave., 00959, pg. 1265 **PB**

Catano

Bacardi-Martini Caribbean Corporation, 165 St., Km. 2.6, 00962, pg. 132 **IT**
Island Express, Royal Ind. Park, Bldg. D-1, BO. Palmas, 00650, pg. 211 **PV**
Mallinckrodt Caribe, Inc., Bariio Palmas Bldg., Expresso de Diego, 00632, pg. 1039 **PB**
National Can Puerto Rico Inc., Las Palmas Industrial Division, Carretera 869, km 1.1, 00962, pg. 1029 **IT**
Nestle Puerto Rico, Inc., Road 869, Km. 3.4 Bo. Palmas, 00632, pg. 917 **IT**

Cayey

B & C Bottlers Corp., P.O. Box 1187, 00633, pg. 131 **IT**
Olay Co., Inc., Box OL, CUC Station, 00633, pg. 1330 **PB**

Ceiba

Corox Controls Inc., KM 0.9, P.O. Box 444, Road 978, 00735, pg. 1243 **IT**

Cidra

KNOGO Caribe, Inc., Road No. 172, Km. 9.5, 00639, pg. 1458 **PB**
Millipore Cidra, Inc., P.O. Box 11977, 00739, pg. 1113 **PB**
Millipore/Puerto Rico, KM 7.7, State Rd. 172, 00639, pg. 1112 **PB**
Rexam Medical Packaging, 50 Calle Baldorioly, 00739, pg. 1107 **IT**
Tech Group Puerto Rico, State Rd. #1, KM 48.7, BO Bretiz, 00625, pg. 1071 **PV**

Condado

Stephen Gould of Puerto Rico, Inc., 884 Ashford Ave., Ste. 1-A, 00907, pg. 468 **PV**

Dorado

Emulex Caribe Inc., State Rd. 693, Km. 7.5, Borado Indus. Subdivision, Lot #5, 00646, pg. 579 **PB**

Fajardo

El Conquistador Resort & Country Club, 1000 El Conquistador Ave., 00738, pg. 1265 **PB**
Pall Biomedical Puerto Rico, Carr. #194 Pall Blvd. 98, 00738, pg. 1254 **PB**
Pall Puerto Rico, Inc., P.O. Box 729, 00738, pg. 1254 **PB**

Guayama

Ayerst-Wyeth Pharmaceuticals, Inc., P.O. Box 208, 00785, pg. 79 **PB**
Guayama Correctional Center, P.O. Box 2520, 00784, pg. 450 **PB**
Latas De Aluminio Reynolds, Inc., P.O. Box 2937, 00785, pg. 1386 **PB**
Ohmeda Caribe, Inc., Rd. No. 3, KM. 142.5, 00784, pg. 121 **IT**

Guaynabo

Electro-Biology, Inc., #1 Electro-Biology Blvd., Los Frailes Industrial Pk., 00657-1359, pg. 231 **PB**
Guerlain Puerto Rico Inc., Glamour Corp. Carretera 24, Km 2.6 Parque Industrial Amelia, 00965, pg. 780 **IT**
Metropolitana de Prestamos, Inc., Villa Caparra, State Rd. # 2, Km. 6.8, 00966, pg. 176 **PB**
Microsoft Caribbean Inc., pg. 1108 **PB**
Motorola de Puerto Rico, Inc., Metro Office Park, Marginal Ave. Kennedy, pg. 1138 **PB**
NRG Distribution Corporation, Caparra Hills Indus. Pk., Calle Tabonuco #2, Officina 100, 00968-3098, pg. 1115 **IT**
PUERTO RICAN CEMENT CO., INC., P.O. Box 364487, 00936-4487, pg. 1341 **PB**
R.J. Reynolds Tobacco Company P.R., Rd. 165 Buchanan to Catano, 00657, pg. 1355 **PB**
Turner Caribe, Inc., B-5 Camino Alejandrino, Villa Clementina, 00657, pg. 1646 **PB**
Union-Transport Corporation-San Juan Office, Zona Libre Comercial, Edisicio #3, Pueblo Viejo, 00920, pg. 1120 **PV**
Whitehall Laboratories, Caparra Hills, Marginal Ave., 00968, pg. 81 **PB**
Young & Rubicam Puerto Rico, Inc., Pueblo Viejo, Nine Munet Ct., 00968, pg. 1198 **PV**

Gurabo

Insituform de Puerto Rico, Inc., P.O. Box 3068, P.R. 189 KM 5.9, 00778, pg. 882 **PB**
Praxair Puerto Rico, Inc., 00658, pg. 1320 **PB**

Hato Rey

Alberto-Culver (P.R.), Inc., Bankers Finance Tower, 654 Munoz Rivera Ave., 00918, pg. 38 **PB**
Banco Central Corp. (Puerto Rico), 221 Ponce de Leon Ave., 00917, pg. 139 **IT**
Banco Santander Puerto Rico, Ponce de Leon 207, 00919, pg. 143 **IT**
BanPonce Corporation, 209 Munoz Rivera Ave., 00918, pg. 176 **PB**
Leo Burnett Inc., Hato Rey Tower, 268 Munoz Rivera Ave., Ste. 2200, 00918, pg. 185 **PV**
Caribbean American Life Assurance Company, 273 Ponce De Leon Ave., 00913, pg. 67 **PB**
Cigna Insurance Company of Puerto Rico, Plaza Scotiabank, Ponce de Leon Ave., 00917, pg. 364 **PB**
Economy International Service Inc., P.O. Box 1247, 00920, pg. 6 **PV**
Empresas ICA Sociedad Controladora (Puerto Rico), 270 Munoz Rivera Ave., Ste. 658, 00918, pg. 454 **IT**
Engraph Puerto Rico, Duarte 27, 00917, pg. 1486 **PB**
Financial Collection Agencies, IBM Tower, 654 Munoz Rivera Ave., Ste. 1813, 00918, pg. 471 **IT**
First Brands Puerto Rico, 268 Ponce De Leon Ave., Ste. 1103, 00918, pg. 627 **PB**
Hewlett-Packard Puerto Rico, Esu. Calle Ochoa, 101 Munoz Rivera Ave., 00918, pg. 815 **PB**
Memorex Telex P.R., Inc., Mercantil Plaza Bldg Ste. 1601, Ponce de Leon Ave., 00919, pg. 857 **IT**
Merck Sharp & Dohme Quimica de Puerto Rico, Inc., Scotia Bank Bldg., 273 Ponce de Leon Dr., Ste. 1201, 00918, pg. 1091 **PB**

PB - *U.S. Public Companies Volume*
PV - *U.S. Private Companies Volume*
IT - *International Public & Private Companies Volume*

Moore Business Forms de Puerto Rico, S.A., 120 E. Roosevelt St., 00919, pg. 889 **IT**

Oki Semiconductores (Puerto Rico) Inc., Fiddler, Gonzalez & Rodriguez, Chase Manhattan Bank Bldg., 00936, pg. 1000 **IT**

Pan American Corporation, Avda. Chardon/C. Gonzalez, pg. 333 **IT**

Pan American Finance Corporation, Avda. Chardon/C. Gonzalez, pg. 333 **IT**

Pan American Insurance Company, Avda. Chardon/C. Gonzalez, pg. 333 **IT**

Popular Consumer Services, Inc., 209 Munoz Rivera Bldg., 00901, pg. 176 **PB**

Popular Securities, Inc., 1020 Popular Ctr., 00918, pg. 176 **PB**

Preferred Risk Insurance Company, Avda. Chardon/C. Gonzalez, pg. 333 **IT**

Puerto Rican American Insurance Company, Avda. Chardon/C. Gonzalez, pg. 333 **IT**

Puerto Rican Insurance Agency Inc., Avda. Chardon/C. Gonzalez, pg. 333 **IT**

Rorer (Caribbean) Corp., 43-44 A Buonomo St., 00936, pg. 1111 **IT**

SMS-San Juan, 654 Luis Munoz Riviera Ave., 00918, pg. 1463 **PB**

Santander Overseas Bank (Puerto Rico), Ponce de Leon 207, 00919, pg. 143 **IT**

Scotiabank de Puerto Rico, Plaza Scotiabank, 273 Ponce de Leon Ave., 00917, pg. 156 **IT**

SmithKline Beecham Consumer Products, P.O. Box 1149, 52 Angel Duonomo St., 00919, pg. 1264 **IT**

Humacao

Alcon (Puerto Rico) Inc., P.O. Box 3000, Carr. 925 Km. 1.0, Bo. Junquito, 00661, pg. 916 **IT**

Danbury Pharmacal Puerto Rico Inc., Humacao Industrial Park, State Road Three, Km 76.9, 00792, pg. 969 **PV**

Dentco, Inc., Road No. 3 K.M. 76.9, 00661, pg. 237 **PB**

Denver Chemical (PR) Inc., Rd. 3 Km. 76 Hm. 9, 00661, pg. 310 **PB**

Medtronic Med Rel, Inc., Road 909, Km. 0.4, Bo. Mariana, 00792, pg. 1083 **PB**

Microsoft Puerto Rico, Inc., Humacao Industrial Park, Road Three, KM 77.0 vice 77.8, 00661, pg. 1108 **IT**

Peerless Tube Co. of Puerto Rico, Inc., 00661, pg. 1269 **PB**

Reedco, Inc., Road No. 3 Km. 76.9, 00661, pg. 237 **PB**

Sandoz Pharmaceuticals Corp., P.O. Box 16629, 00791, pg. 974 **IT**

Squibb Manufacturing Inc., Road 3, Km. 75.5, 00661, pg. 254 **PB**

Suttle Caribe, Inc., HC 01 Box 16620, P.R. Rd. No. 3 Km 82.3, 00791-9731, pg. 415 **PB**

Syntex Puerto Rico, Inc., pg. 1122 **IT**

Isabela

Isabela Shoe Corp., P.O. Box 357, Rd. 2 Km., 111.2 Bo Mora, 00662, pg. 217 **PB**

Kent Meters, Inc., P.O. Box 225, Carr 112-Km 2.3, 00662, pg. 4 **IT**

The Outdoor Footwear Company, P.O. Box 869, Rd. 112, K2H3 Moraward, 00662, pg. 1609 **PB**

Isla Verde

Sensormatic del Caribe, 69 Atlantic View, 00913, pg. 1457 **PB**

Juana Diaz

BancTec (Puerto Rico), Inc., Luis Lorrens Torres Indus. Pk., Kilometer Marker No. 66.9, Rd. 149, 00795, pg. 177 **PB**

Juncos

Amgen Manufacturing, Inc., Kilometer 24.6, State Rd. 31, 00777-4060, pg. 101 **PB**

Lehigh Press-Puerto Rico, 00777, pg. 659 **PV**

Las Piedras

Ceramco Manufacturing Co., 183 State Rd., 00671-9738, pg. 499 **PB**

Chesebrough-Pond's Mfg. Co., P.O. Box 66, 00671, pg. 1435 **IT**

Sonoco Containers of Puerto Rico, Inc., P.O. Box 411, 00671, pg. 1486 **PB**

Sonoco of Puerto Rico, Inc., KM 19.9 Las Piedras to San Lorenzo Rd., 00671, pg. 1486 **PB**

Luquillo

AMI Gibson, Inc., P.O. Box G, 00673, pg. 1564 **PB**

Chemetronics Caribe Inc., Rte. 992 Mata de Platano, 00673, pg. 1500 **IT**

Interstate Uniform Manufacturing of Puerto Rico, Inc., Rd. 922 KMO.2, Box F, 00673, pg. 1665 **PB**

Manati

Caribe Biochemicals, Inc., P.O. Box 735, 00701, pg. 531 **PB**

Roche Products Inc., pg. 1121 **IT**

Rorer Puerto Rico Inc., 604 Rd. Bo. San Jose, 00701, pg. 1111 **IT**

Schering-Plough Pharmaceuticals, P.O. Box 486, Carretera Estal No. 686, Kilometroos, 00674, pg. 1438 **PB**

Mayaguez

Aramark Uniform Services of Puerto Rico, Guanajibo Industrial Park, 00708, pg. 79 **PV**

Bristol-Myers Squibb Company of Puerto Rico Inc., Road 114, Foreign Trade Zone 7, 00709, pg. 254 **PB**

Bumble Bee International Inc., El Malecon Rd., P.O. Box 3268, 00709, pg. 526 **PV**

Central States Can Co. of Puerto Rico, Inc., P.O. Box 3268, Marina Station, 00681, pg. 463 **PB**

Star-Kist Caribe, Inc., P.O. Box 3051, Rd. 64, 00680-6031, pg. 806 **PB**

Storage Technology-Puerto Rico, Guanajibo Industrial Zone, Rd.114, Kilometer 1.5, 00708, pg. 1523 **PB**

WESTERNBANK OF PUERTO RICO, 19 W. McKinley St., 00681, pg. 1760 **PB**

Old San Juan

D'Jesco, Inc., P.O. Box S-1653, 00903, pg. 6 **PV**

Fleishman-Hillard Caribbean, Antiguo Edificio El Mundo, 254 San Jose, 2nd Fl., 00901, pg. 411 **IT**

Orocovis

Kaufel International Inc., P.O. Box 2109, 00720, pg. 725 **IT**

Ponce

Boehringer Mannheim Pharm, Box 7085 Punto Oro Industrial, 00732-7085, pg. 331 **IT**

Checkpoint Systems, Inc. Puerto Rico, Sabanetas Industrial Park, 00732, pg. 343 **PB**

Echlin-Ponce, Inc., Industrial Park, 00731, pg. 560 **PB**

Fibras Ceramicas, Inc., Bo. El Tuque, KM, 25.7, 00731, pg. 893 **IT**

Molex Caribe, Ponce Harbor Indus. Pk., 1305 Santiago de los Caballero Ave., 00731, pg. 1122 **PB**

Ponce Regional Institutions, Banrio Canas, Las Cucharas, Puerto Rico State Rd. #2, 00731, pg. 451 **PB**

Ponce Salt Industries Corp., P.O. Box 1749, 00731, pg. 1135 **PB**

PONCEBANK, F.S.B., Villa and Concordia Sts., 00731, pg. 1316 **PB**

Popular Finance, Inc., El Senorial Condo., Ste. 613, 10 Salud St., 00731, pg. 176 **PB**

Storage Technology-Puerto Rico, P. O. Box 7334, Hwy. 127, Lot #13, El Tugue Industl. Pk., 00731, pg. 1523 **PB**

Puerto Real

Stanric, Inc., P.O. Box 128, 00740, pg. 1503 **PB**

Quebradillas

Glamourette Fashion Mills, P.O. Box 1557, 00742, pg. 779 **PB**

Ramey

Caribbean Air Service Dominicana, Parallel Rd., Bldg. #1102, 00604, pg. 211 **PV**

Rio Grande

Security Plastics Caribe, Inc., Box 910, State Rd. 3, KM 23.3, Calle A Urbanizacion Industrial, 00743, pg. 981 **PV**

Rio Piedras

Browning-Ferris Industries of Puerto Rico, Inc., P.O. Box 29499, 65th Infantry Station, 00929, pg. 264 **PB**

Forest Laboratories Caribe, Inc., 123 De Diego Ave., 00922, pg. 670 **PB**

ISP (Puerto Rico) Inc., Ste. 206B, Iturregui Plaza, 65th Infanteria Ave., 00924, pg. 858 **PV**

Olivetti de Puerto Rico Inc., Calle Ganges 114, Urb. El Paraiso, 00926, pg. 1002 **IT**

Sealy Mattress Company of Puerto Rico, El Commandante Indus. Ctr., #1 San Maracos, 00924, pg. 979 **PB**

Sein Mendez Laboratories, Inc., 126 De Diego Ave., 00922, pg. 670 **PB**

Sabana Grande

Loctite Puerto Rico, Inc., P.O. Box 669, 00747, pg. 611 **IT**

San Juan

AGA Puerto Rico Corp., P.O. Box 363868, 00936-3868, pg. 13 **IT**

ADI Puerto Rico, Mario Julia Industrial Park, #15-A Street, pg. 1307 **PB**

Aladdin Synergetics, Inc., P.O. Box 194111, 00910, pg. 31 **PV**

Analytical Technologies, Inc., P.O. Box 70175, 00936, pg. 131 **IT**

Avon Products, Inc., Puerto Rico Branch G.P.O. Box 3774, 00936, pg. 156 **PB**

Bacardi Corporation, P.O. Box 363549, 00936-3549, pg. 131 **IT**

BANCO POPULAR DE PUERTO RICO, Banco Popular Ctr., Hato Rey, 209 Munoz Rivera Ave., 00918, pg. 175 **PB**

Bausch & Lomb Puerto Rico, Inc., P.O. Box 3869, 00936, pg. 194 **PB**

Butterworth of Puerto Rico Inc., Edificio Pello, Paseo de Covadonga 52, 00906, pg. 1095 **IT**

Caribbean Cement Carriers Corporation, G.P.O. Box 364487, 00936-4487, pg. 1342 **PB**

Carrier Puerto Rico, P.O. Box 9357, 00908, pg. 1691 **PB**

Clairol Caribe, P.O. Box 4707, 00936, pg. 254 **PB**

Condado Plaza Hotel & Casino, 999 Ashford Ave., 00907, pg. 1265 **PB**

CUNA Mutual Group-Puerto Rico, P.O. Box 2219, 00936-2219, pg. 296 **PV**

DE LA CRUZ & ASSOCIATES, P.O. Box 11885, 00922-1885, pg. 318 **PV**

Desarrollos Multiples Insulares, Inc., G.P.O. Box 4487, 00936, pg. 1342 **PB**

Det Norske Veritas, P.O. Box S-2467, 400 Gomercio St., 00902, pg. 396 **IT**

Dow Jones Telerate Puerto Rico, Inc., 416 Ponce de Leon, Ste. 1105, 00918, pg. 525 **PB**

Esis International (Puerto Rico), Inc., Plaza Scotiabank, 273 Ponce De Leon Ave., 00917, pg. 366 **IT**

Executive Airlines, P.O. Box 38082, Airport Station, 00937-0082, pg. 9 **PB**

Florida Lime Corp., G.P.O. Box 4487, 00936, pg. 1342 **PB**

John H. Harland Co. of Puerto Rico, P.O. Box 3427, 00936, pg. 786 **PB**

John Crane Caribe, P.O. Box 29779, 00929-0779, pg. 1339 **IT**

Key Communications, Inc., P.O. Box 11885, 00922-1885, pg. 318 **PV**

Kimberly-Clark Puerto Rico, Inc., Industrial Park, P.O. Box 191859, 00919, pg. 959 **PB**

Lexis Law Publishing, Paseo Covandonga 52, 00906, pg. 1096 **IT**

MDI Puerto Rico, Inc., Scotiabank Bldg., Old San Juan, P.O. Box S-2152, 00903, pg. 1137 **PB**

Molinas de Puerto Rico, GPO Box G-1960, 00936, pg. 426 **PB**

Molinas de Puerto Rico, G.P.O. Box G 1960, 00936, pg. 427 **PB**

The Pipelines of Puerto Rico, Inc., GPO Box 2768, 450 Ponce de Leon Ave., 00905, pg. 1584 **PB**

Popular Home Mortgage, Inc., 268 Ponce de Leon Ave., 00918, pg. 176 **PB**

Popular Leasing and Rental, Inc., Tres Monjitas Indus. Devel., M-1046 Federico Costa St., 00903, pg. 176 **PB**

Popular Leasing & Rental, Inc., G.P.O. Box 50045, 00903, pg. 176 **PB**

PUERTO RICO TOURISM COMPANY, Paseo La Princesa, pg. 894 **PV**

Schindler Corporation of Puerto Rico, pg. 1205 **IT**

Security National Life Insurance Co., Avda. Munoz Rivera 396, pg. 334 **IT**

The Shell Company (Puerto Rico) Ltd., Puerto de Tierra, 450 Ponce de Leon Ave., 00901, pg. 1141 **IT**

Shell (Puerto Rico), G.P.O. Box 2768, 00936, pg. 1136 **IT**

Texaco Puerto Rico, Inc., Box S-4429, 00905, pg. 1583 **PB**

Toyota de Puerto Rico Corp., 1064 Munoz Rivera Ave., Rio Piedras, 00919-5467, pg. 1412 **PB**

Universal Insurance Co., Metro Office Pk., Marginal Rd.-Kennedy Ave., 00936, pg. 962 **PB**

San Lorenzo

E-Z-EM Caribe, Inc., Ramal 916, Barrio Cerro Gordo, 00754, pg. 540 **PB**

Santa Isabel

Sundstrand Electrical Systems Div., P.O. Box 19, Playa Industrial Park, 00757, pg. 1534 **PB**

Santurce

Automax Finance, P.O. Box 9146, 00908-0146, pg. 644 **PB**

Best Foods Caribbean, Inc., Centro Europa Bldg., 1492 Ponce DeLeon Ave., 00907, pg. 224 **PB**

Caribe Grolier, Inc., Stop 23, 601 Del Parque St., 4th Fl., 00909, pg. 794 **IT**

Charter Behavioral Health of Puerto Rico, Inc., Caso Bldg., Ste. 1504, 1225 Ponce de Leon Ave., 00907, pg. 1033 **PV**

Charter Medical of Puerto Rico, Inc., Caso Bldg., Ste. 1504, 1225 Ponce de Leon Ave., 00907, pg. 1035 **PV**

Comet Rice of Puerto Rico, Inc., Corbian Plaza, GM3, 1607 Ponce de Leon, 00907, pg. 591 **PB**

First Federal Finance Corporation, P.O. Box 9146, 00908-0146, pg. 644 **PB**

FIRSTBANK PUERTO RICO, 1519 Ponce de Leon Ave.-Stop 23, 00908-0146, pg. 644 **PB**

Hallmark Puerto Rico, Inc., Calle Del Parque 607 A, 00909, pg. 496 **PV**

Kodak Rahola, Inc., Ave. Ponce de Leon 1006, PDA 15, 00908, pg. 551 **PB**

Lucent Technologies Puerto Rico Inc., 950 ponce de Leon Ave., 00907, pg. 1018 **PB**

Novo Nordisk A/S, Santurce Medical Mall 302/303, 1801 Ponce de Leon Ave., 00909, pg. 987 **IT**

Polaroid Caribbean Corp., Centro de Seguros Bldg., Ponce de Leon 701, Miramar, 00907, pg. 1313 **PB**

Wometco de Puerto Rico Inc., Calle del Parque, #601, Quiento piso, parada 23, 00909, pg. 1186 **PV**

Geographic Index-U.S.

Toa Alta

TII Industries, Inc., P.O. Box 433, 00953, pg. 1556 **PB**

Toa Baja

First Leasing & Rental Corporation, P.O. Box 2489, 00951-2662, pg. 644 **PB**
Mitsubishi Motor Sales of Caribbean Inc., Carretera No. 2, Km 20.1, Barrio Candelaria, pg. 876 **IT**

Trujillo Alto

El Conquistador Development Corp., Carretera 175-K-10-2, 00936, pg. 988 **PB**

Vega Alta

The West Company of Puerto Rico, Inc., Industrial Park, State Hwy. #2, KM 30.7, 00762, pg. 1755 **PB**

Vega Baja

Motorola Electronica de Puerto Rico, Inc., Rd. 686 KM. 170 Cabo Carbie Ind. Park, 00764, pg. 1138 **PB**

Villalba

Medtronic Puerto Rico, Inc., Calle Box 6001, Road 149, Km. 56.3, 00766-6001, pg. 1083 **PB**

Yabucoa

Caribbean Outerwear Corp., RD 3 Km 96.9, 00767, pg. 1032 **PV**
Yabucoa, PR Refinery, P.O. Box 186, 00767, pg. 1530 **PB**

RHODE ISLAND

Bristol

Advanced Polymers Corp., 386 Metacom Ave., 02809, pg. 689 **PB**
Bristol & Warren Gas Company, 25 Gooding Ave., 02809, pg. 1706 **PB**
Furon Co., 386 Metacom Ave., 02809, pg. 689 **PB**

Centredale

Contaminant Recovery Systems, 140 Waterman Ave., 02911, pg. 592 **PB**

Coventry

The Coventry Courier, 800 Washington St., 02816, pg. 934 **PB**
GameScape, Inc., 2006 Nooseneck Hill Rd., 02816, pg. 767 **PB**

Cranston

AMF Lang's Bowlarama Inc., 225 Niantic Ave., 02907-3121, pg. 7 **PV**
Bercen Inc., 1381 Cranston St., 02920, pg. 287 **PV**
Chapman Equipment Company, 970 Wellington Ave., 02910, pg. 334 **PV**
Cox Communications-Rhode Island, 111 Comstock Pkwy., 02920, pg. 455 **PB**
CRANSTON PRINT WORKS COMPANY, 1381 Cranston St., 02920, pg. 286 **PV**
Davol Inc., 100 Sockanossett Crossroad, 02920, pg. 189 **PB**
ESL Inc., 36 Western Industrial Dr., 02921-3403, pg. 1558 **PB**
C.I. HAYES, INC., 800 Wellington Ave., 02910, pg. 513 **PV**
JAN-CO., INC., 35 Sockanosset Cross Rd., 02920, pg. 581 **PV**
North Safety Products, Safety Equipment Division, 2000 Plainfield Pike, 02921, pg. 1243 **IT**
TACO INCORPORATED, 1160 Cranston St., 02920, pg. 1066 **PV**
TECHNIC INCORPORATED, One Spectacle St, 02910-9650, pg. 1071 **PV**
Todd Enterprises, 530 Wellington Ave., 02910, pg. 231 **PV**

Cumberland

CCL Custom Manufacturing, Martin St., 02864-5361, pg. 238 **IT**
MOSSBERG INDUSTRIES, INC., 160 Bearhill Rd., 02864, pg. 763 **PV**
R.J. Development & Exploration Co., P. O. Box 7900, 1595 Mendon Rd., 02864, pg. 1706 **PB**
J.T. Slocomb Co., One Front St., 02864, pg. 1006 **PV**
Valley Gas Co., P. O. Box 7900, 1595 Mendon Rd., 02864, pg. 1706 **PB**
Valley Propane, Inc., P. O. Box 7900, 1595 Mendon Rd., 02864, pg. 1706 **PB**
VALLEY RESOURCES, INC., P.O. Box 7900, 1595 Mendon Rd., 02864-0700, pg. 1706 **PB**
Vamco, P. O. Box 7900, 1595 Mendon Rd., 02864, pg. 1706 **PB**

East Greenwich

Cherry Semiconductor Corp., 2000 S. County Trail, 02818, pg. 346 **PB**
The East Greenwich Pendulum, 580 Main St., 02818, pg. 934 **PB**
Graphic Instruments, 1900 S. County Trail, 02818, pg. 481 **PB**
Pendulum, 580 Main St., 02818, pg. 935 **PB**
Stanley Fastening Systems, Briggs Dr., 02818, pg. 1509 **PB**

East Providence

A&Z HAYWARD, INC., 655 Waterman Ave., 02914, pg. 3 **PV**
B.A. BALLOU & CO. INC., 800 Waterman Ave., 02914, pg. 112 **PV**
Dairy Mart East, Inc., South Broadway, 02914, pg. 476 **PB**
Handy & Harman Precious Metals Products Division, 231 Ferris Ave., 02914, pg. 780 **PB**
Trifari Jewelers, 3400 Pawtucket Ave., 02915, pg. 757 **PV**
WPRI-TV, 25 Catamore Blvd., 02914, pg. 385 **PB**

Esmond

NEW ENGLAND STONE INDUSTRIES, INC., 15 Branch Pike, 02917-1223, pg. 793 **PV**

Fiskeville

Arkwright, Inc, 538 Main St., 02823, pg. 994 **IT**

Greenville

HART ENGINEERING CORPORATION, 29 Lark Industrial Pkwy., 02828, pg. 507 **PV**

Johnston

Affiliated FM Insurance Co., Allendale Park, 02919, pg. 37 **PV**
ALLENDALE MUTUAL INSURANCE CO., 1301 Atwood Ave., 02919, pg. 37 **PV**
Appalachian Insurance Co., Allendale Park, 02919, pg. 37 **PV**
New Providence Corp., Allendale Park, 02919, pg. 37 **PV**

Kenyon

Kenyon Industries, Inc., 36 Sherman Ave., 02836, pg. 778 **PB**

Lincoln

ATX International, Inc., One Albion Rd., 02865, pg. 461 **PB**
ATX Marketing Co., One Albion Rd., 02865, pg. 461 **PB**
AMICA MUTUAL INSURANCE CO., 100 Amigo Way, 02865, pg. 66 **PV**
Blackstone Valley Electric Co., Washington Hwy., 02865, pg. 549 **PB**
A.T. CROSS CO., One Albion Rd., 02865-3700, pg. 460 **PB**
A.T. Cross Export Co., One Albion Rd., 02865, pg. 461 **PB**
NCS Recognition Products Group, 6 Blackstone Pl., Unit 600, 02865-1112, pg. 1155 **PB**
Technical Materials, Inc., Five Wellington Rd., 02865, pg. 256 **PB**
Windmoeller & Hoelscher Corp., 23 New England Way, 02865, pg. 1511 **IT**

Middletown

Newport Electric Corporation, 12 Turner Rd., 02840, pg. 550 **PB**
Newport Learning Center, 344 Aquidneck Avenue, 02842, pg. 219 **PB**
Trimble Navigation Ltd., Northeast Sales/Technical Support, 438 E. Main Rd., Irongate #1, 02840, pg. 1638 **PB**

Newport

Sailing Business, 5 John Clark Rd., 02840, pg. 1174 **PB**
Sailing World, Five John Clarke Rd., 02840, pg. 1174 **PB**

North Kingstown

Brown & Sharpe Intl. Capital Corp., 200 Frenchtown Rd., 02852, pg. 260 **PB**
BROWN & SHARPE MANUFACTURING COMPANY, Precision Park, 200 Frenchtown Rd., 02852-1700, pg. 260 **PB**
The Standard Times, 13 W. Main St., 02852, pg. 935 **PB**
Toray Plastics (America), Inc., 50 Belver Ave., 02852, pg. 1400 **IT**

Pawtucket

American Insulated Wire Corp., 36 Freeman St., 02862, pg. 663 **PV**
COLFAX, INC., 38 Colfax St., 02860, pg. 252 **PV**
COOLEY, INC., 50 Esten Ave., 02860, pg. 273 **PV**
Copperweld Metallon Div., 690 Narragansett Park Dr., 02861, pg. 662 **IT**

DARLENE JEWELRY MANUFACTURING COMPANY, 483 Main St., 02860, pg. 311 **PV**
Elmwood Sensors, Inc., 500 Narragansett Park Dr., 02861, pg. 125 **IT**
Hasbro Foreign Sales Corp., 1027 Newport Ave., 02861, pg. 797 **PB**
HASBRO, INC., 1027 Newport Ave., 02862-1059, pg. 797 **PB**
Hasbro Toy Division, 1027 Newport Ave., 02861, pg. 797 **PB**
KEY CONTAINER CORPORATION, 21 Campbell St., 02862, pg. 617 **PV**
Monet Jewelers, Two Lonsdale Ave., 02860, pg. 757 **PV**
New England Newspapers, Inc.-The Times, 23 Exchange St., 02862, pg. 935 **PB**
PAWTUCKET FASTENERS INC., 327 Pine St., 02860, pg. 844 **PV**
Playskool, Inc., 1027 Newport Ave., 02861, pg. 797 **PB**
TEKNOR APEX COMPANY, 505 Central Ave., 02861, pg. 1073 **PV**
Teknor Color Company, 505 Central Ave., 02861, pg. 1073 **PV**
Tonka Corporation, 1027 Newport Ave., 02862, pg. 797 **PB**
Vitrus, Inc., 881 Main St., 02860, pg. 1566 **PB**
Wellman Engineering Resins, 100 Armistice Blvd., 02860, pg. 1752 **PB**

Portsmouth

Raytheon Electronics Systems, 1847 W. Main Rd., 02871, pg. 1364 **PB**

Providence

AFC CABLE SYSTEMS, INC., 50 Kennedy Plaza, Ste. 1250, 02903, pg. 6 **PB**
Admiral Packaging Inc., Ten Admiral St., 02940, pg. 1119 **PV**
Alcatel Transcom, P.O. Box 5714, 02903-0714, pg. 55 **IT**
AMERICAN MATHEMATICAL SOCIETY, INC., 201 Charles St., 02904-2213, pg. 59 **PV**
American Silicon Products, Inc., 15 Clarkson St., 02908, pg. 328 **PB**
Arconium Specialty Alloys, 50 Simms Ave., 02909, pg. 328 **IT**
Barber-Colman Indev, 1 Richmond Sq., 02906, pg. 1242 **IT**
BONANZA BUS LINES, INC., One Bonanza Way, 02904, pg. 156 **PV**
Citizens Financial Group, Inc., One Citizens Plaza, 02903, pg. 1132 **PV**
Citizens Financial Services Corporation, One Citizens Plaza, 02903, pg. 1132 **IT**
Clifford Metal, 200 Cortiss St., 02904, pg. 651 **PV**
COKEN COMPANY, INC., 150 Colfax St., 02905, pg. 250 **PV**
Cookson America Inc., One Cookson Pl., 02903, pg. 328 **IT**
Coto Wabash, 55 Dupont Dr., 02907, pg. 351 **PV**
Curtman Division, 623 Atwells Ave., 02909-2413, pg. 1116 **PV**
DIMEO CONSTRUCTION COMPANY, 75 Chapman St., 02905, pg. 333 **PV**
Drake Petroleum Company, Inc., P.O. Box 2616, Elmwood Station, 02907, pg. 1151 **PV**
EXCELL MANUFACTURING COMPANY, 200 Chestnut St., 02903, pg. 387 **PV**
Federal Products Co., 1144 Eddy St., 02905, pg. 594 **PB**
Fleet Capital Leasing, 50 Kennedy Plaza, 02903, pg. 650 **PB**
Fleet Credit Corporation, 50 Kennedy Plaza, 02903, pg. 650 **PB**
Fleet Equity Partners, 111 Westminster St., 02903, pg. 650 **PB**
Fleet Investment Services, 50 Kennedy Plaza, 02903, pg. 650 **PB**
Fleet National Bank, 111 Westminster St., 02903, pg. 649 **PB**
Fleet Precious Metals, Inc., 111 Westminster St., 02903, pg. 650 **PB**
Fleet Real Estate, Inc., 111 Westminster St., 02903, pg. 650 **PB**
Fleet Services Corp., P.O. Box 366, 02901, pg. 650 **PB**
GILBANE BUILDING COMPANY, Seven Jackson Walkway, 02903, pg. 452 **PV**
Gilbane Properties, Inc., Seven Jackson Walkway, 02940, pg. 453 **PV**
Harcros Chemicals Inc., 275 Allens Ave., 02905, pg. 598 **IT**
Herff Jones, Jewelry, 226 Public St., 02940, pg. 523 **PV**
The Hospital Trust Leasing Corporation, One Hospital Trust Plaza, 02903, pg. 184 **PB**
Inso Providence Corp., 1 Richmond Sq., 02906, pg. 882 **PB**
K&M Associates, 425 Dexter St., 02907, pg. 69 **PB**
LIN Central Broadcasting Corporation (WOTV), Four Richmond Sq., Ste. 200, 02906, pg. 11 **PB**
Mortgage Guarantee & Title Co., 450 Veterans Memorial Pkwy., 02914-5342, pg. 626 **PB**
NARRAGANSETT CAPITAL INC., 50 Kennedy Plaza, 02903, pg. 774 **PV**
Narragansett Electric Co., 280 Melrose St., 02901, pg. 1171 **PB**
Narragansett Energy Resources Company, 280 Melrose St., 02901, pg. 1171 **PB**
New England Trust Company, 144 Westminster St., 02903, pg. 637 **PB**
Newport America Corporation, 100 Weybosset St., 02903, pg. 1337 **PB**

PB - *U.S. Public Companies Volume*
PV - *U.S. Private Companies Volume*
IT - *International Public & Private Companies Volume*

1420

Geographic Index-U.S.

NORTEK, INC., 50 Kennedy Plaza, 02903-2360, pg. 1192 — PB
Oster Alloys, 50 Sims Ave., 02909, pg. 329 — IT
Patience Realty Corporation, 100 Weybosset St., 02903, pg. 1337 — PB
PROVIDENCE ENERGY CORPORATION, 100 Weybosset St., 02903, pg. 1337 — PB
Providence Energy Services, 100 Weybosset St., 02903, pg. 1337 — PB
Providence Gas Co., 100 Weybosset St., 02903, pg. 1337 — PB
Providence Journal Broadcasting Corp., 75 Fountain St., 02902, pg. 209 — PB
Providence Journal-Bulletin, 75 Fountain St., 02902, pg. 209 — PB
Quebecor Printing Federated Inc., 369 Prairie Ave., 02905, pg. 1078 — PB
Quebecor Printing Providence Inc., 99 W. River St., 02940-2617, pg. 1077 — IT
RIHT Financial Corporation, One Hospital Trust Plaza, 02903, pg. 184 — PB
RIHT Life Insurance Company, One Hospital Trust Plaza, 02903, pg. 184 — PB
Resource Monitors, Inc., 100 Weybosset St., 02903, pg. 1337 — PB
Rhode Island Hospital Trust National Bank, One Hospital Trust Plaza, 02903, pg. 184 — PB
Sheffield Insurance Co., 86 Weybossett St., 02903, pg. 1622 — PB
The Stone Building Company, 780 Allens Ave., 02905, pg. 334 — PV
Textron Financial Corporation, 40 Westminster St., P.O. Box 6687, 02940-6687, pg. 1590 — PB
TEXTRON, INC., 40 Westminster St., 02903-2525, pg. 1588 — PB
UNCAS MANUFACTURING COMPANY, 623 Atwells Ave., 02909-2413, pg. 1116 — PV
UNION INDUSTRIES, INC., 10 Admiral St., 02908, pg. 1119 — PV
Union Paper Co., Ten Admiral St., 02908, pg. 1119 — PV
WWBB, 75 Oxford St., 02905-9329, pg. 385 — PB
WWRX, 75 Oxford St., 02905-9329, pg. 385 — PB
WARREN EQUITIES INC., One Warren Way, 02905, pg. 1151 — PV

Rumford

ADP Marshall Contractors Inc., 75 Newman Ave., 02916, pg. 660 — PB
AlliedSignal, Automotive Aftermarket, 105 Pawtucket Ave., 02916-2422, pg. 51 — PV

Slatersville

Philips Components-Discrete Products Division, One Providence Pike, P.O. Box 278, 02876-0278, pg. 1054 — IT

Slocum

Carbon Technology Inc., S. County Trail, 02877, pg. 891 — IT

Smithfield

B.T. Equipment Co., Inc., 115 Lydia Ann Rd., 02917, pg. 453 — PV
Bacou U.S.A., Inc., 10 Thurber Blvd., 02917, pg. 132 — IT
Elan Pharma Inc., Two Thurber Blvd., 02917, pg. 436 — IT
Rendva, 20 Thurber Blvd., 02917, pg. 549 — PB
Uvex Safety, Inc., 10 Thurber Blvd., 02917, pg. 132 — IT

Wakefield

Narragansett Times, 171 Main St., 02880, pg. 935 — PB
Southern Rhode Island Newspapers, 187 Main St., 02879, pg. 935 — PB

Warren

American Tourister, Inc., 91 Main St., 02885, pg. 1430 — PB

Warwick

Burgmann Seals America, Inc., Seven Hall St., 02818, pg. 233 — IT
EG & G Sealol Eagle, 15 Pioneer Ave., 02888, pg. 544 — PV
EG & G Sealol Engineered Products Division, 15 Pioneer Ave., 02888, pg. 542 — PV
The Jean Coutu (PJC) USA Inc., 50 Service Rd., 02888, pg. 840 — IT
KENNEY MANUFACTURING COMPANY, 1000 Jefferson Blvd., 02886, pg. 615 — PV
Metropolitan Property & Casualty Insurance Co. (Met P&C), P.O. Box 350, 700 Quaker Ln., 02886, pg. 737 — PV
National Diecasting Machinery, 33 Plan Way, Bldg. 7, 02886, pg. 906 — PV
Ostby & Barton Co., 487 Jefferson Blvd., 02886, pg. 386 — PV
A.J. Oster Company, Summit East, 300 Centerville Rd., 02886, pg. 1219 — PV
PLAN INTERNATIONAL USA, INC., 155 Plan Way, 02886, pg. 869 — PV
United HealthCare Plans of New England, Inc., 475 Kilvert St., Metro Ctr., 02886, pg. 1678 — PB
Vemaline Products, 487 Jefferson Blvd., 02886, pg. 386 — PV
VICTORIA CREATIONS, INC., 30 Jefferson Park Rd., 02888, pg. 1139 — PV

West Greenwich

GTECH CORPORATION, 55 Technology Way, 02817, pg. 767 — PB

West Kingston

AMERICAN POWER CONVERSION CORPORATION, 132 Fairgrounds Rd., 02892, pg. 89 — PB

West Warwick

Amtrol Inc., 1400 Division Rd., 02893, pg. 300 — PV
PAUL ARPIN VANLINES, INC., 99 James P. Murphy Hwy., 02893, pg. 85 — PV
ASTRO-MED, INC., 600 E. Greenwich Ave., 02893, pg. 141 — PB
Battenfeld of America, 31 James P. Murphy Industrial Hwy., 02893, pg. 825 — IT
John Brown, Inc., 1600 Division Rd., 02893, pg. 774 — IT
Cox Communications-Providence/Weymouth, 9 J.P. Murphy Hwy., 02893-2381, pg. 455 — PV
Dryvit Systems, Inc., One Energy Way, 02893, pg. 1357 — PB
Trafalgar House Holdings Inc., 1600 Division Rd., 02893, pg. 774 — IT
VICTOR CORPORATION, 618 Main St., 02893, pg. 1138 — PV

Westerly

BESS EATON DONUT FLOUR CO., INC., 79 Tom Harvey Rd., 02891, pg. 139 — PV
Guild Music Division, 60 Industrial Dr., 02891, pg. 400 — PV
MOORE COMPANY, 36 Beach St., 02891, pg. 759 — PV
South County Gas Company, P.O. Box 554, 02891, pg. 1337 — PB
WASHINGTON TRUST BANCORP, INC., 23 Broad St., 02891, pg. 1744 — PB
The Washington Trust Company, 23 Broad St., 02891, pg. 1744 — PB

Woonsocket

ACS INDUSTRIES, INC., 160 Hamlet Ave., 02895, pg. 3 — PV
ACS Industries, Inc., Fiber Operation, 148 Hamlet Ave., 02895, pg. 4 — PV
CVS CORP., One CVS Dr., 02895, pg. 287 — PB
The Evening Call Publishing Co.-The Call, P.O. Box A, 75 Main St., 02895-0992, pg. 934 — PB
GMS CORPORATION, 168 Campeau St., 02895, pg. 435 — PV
Hanora Spinning, Inc., 159 Singleton St., 02895, pg. 637 — PB
K2 Bike, 115 Front St., 02895, pg. 940 — PB
TECH INDUSTRIES, INC., 85 Fairmount St., 02895, pg. 1071 — PV

Wyoming

The Chariho Times, 1171 Main St., 02898, pg. 934 — PB
VIBCO INC., 75 Stilson Rd., 02898, pg. 1138 — PV

SOUTH CAROLINA

Abbeville

Flexible Technologies Inc., P.O. Box 888, Carwellyn Rd., 29620, pg. 1267 — IT
Pirelli Cable, Power Cable Div., P.O. Box 250, 29620, pg. 1059 — IT

Aiken

AIKEN ELECTRIC COOPERATIVE INC., P.O. Box 417, 29802, pg. 28 — PV
Aiken Electric Satellite, P.O. Box 417, 29802, pg. 28 — PV
Carlisle Tire & Wheel Company, 23 Windham Blvd., 29805, pg. 305 — PB
Du Pont Srp, Bldg. 707 5 C, 29808, pg. 531 — PV
The Ohio Brass Co., 2200 Richland E., 29801, pg. 844 — PB
Westinghouse Savannah River Co., Savannah River Site, P.O. Box 616, Road 1, 29802, pg. 273 — PB

Anderson

Associated Fuel Pump Systems Corp., 110 Scotts Bridge Rd., 29622, pg. 205 — IT
Automotive Electronic Control Systems, Inc., Hwy. 81 at I-85, 29622, pg. 205 — IT
Fairway Ford of Anderson, 39 Clemson Blvd., 29622, pg. 392 — PV
Glen Raven Mills, Inc.-Custom Fabrics Division-Equinox Plant, 200 Jackson St., 29622-1658, pg. 456 — PV
Glen Raven Mills, Inc.-Custom Fabrics Division-Equinox Finishing Plant, 107 Service Rd., 29622, pg. 456 — PV
Hampshire Designers Inc., P.O. Box 2667, 215 Commerce Blvd., 29622, pg. 778 — PV
HAMPSHIRE GROUP, LTD., 215 Commerce Blvd., 29621, pg. 778 — PB
Independent Publishing Company, 1000 Williamston Rd., 29621, pg. 794 — PB
Mikron Corp. Anderson, 103 Clemson Research Blvd., 29625, pg. 866 — IT

Andrews

Atochem, P.O. Box 288, 29510-0288, pg. 445 — IT
PHOENIX MEDICAL TECHNOLOGY, INC., Rte. 521 W., 29510, pg. 1292 — PB

Arcadia

MAYFAIR MILLS, INC., 1885 Hayne St., 29320, pg. 718 — PV

Barnwell

Carolina Metals, Inc., Hwy. 80, 29812, pg. 1511 — PV

Beaufort

Alcoa South Carolina, Inc., 211 Charles St., 29902, pg. 61 — PB
Buford Gazette, P.O. Box 399, 1556 Salem Rd., 29901, pg. 1065 — PV
Minster Machine Company-Beaufort Operation, Industrial Park, Parker Dr., 29903, pg. 751 — PV
Orleans Food Co., 29902, pg. 158 — PV
Pirelli Jerome Inc., P.O. Box 4428, Beaufort County Industrial Park, 29903, pg. 1059 — IT

Beech Island

Kimberly-Clark Home Healthcare, P.O. Box 112, 29842-0112, pg. 959 — PB

Bennettsville

Marley Electric Heating Company, 470 Beauty Spot Rd. E., 29512-2700, pg. 1676 — PB

Bishopville

American Natl. Can Co., P.O. Box 564, 29010, pg. 1029 — IT
Reeves Brothers, Inc. (Bishopville Div.), P.O. Box 472, Rte. 2, Dixon Dr., 29010, pg. 507 — PV

Blenheim

Davis Wood Products, Inc.-South Carolina Div., 3067 Screwpin Rd., 29516, pg. 316 — PV

Bluffton

Sun City Hilton Head, Eight Buckingham, Plantation Dr., 29910, pg. 495 — PB

Blythewood

Knurr USA East, 120 Northpoint Ct., 29016, pg. 739 — IT
POLICY MANAGEMENT SYSTEMS CORPORATION, One PMSC Ctr., 29016, pg. 1314 — PB
Policy Management Systems Information and Administration Services, Inc., One PMS Center, 29016, pg. 1314 — PB

Camden

Builders Transport, Inc., P.O. Box 7005, 29020-7005, pg. 267 — PB
BUILDERS TRANSPORT, INCORPORATED, 2029 W. DeKalb St., 29020-7005, pg. 267 — PB
Builders Transport of Texas, Inc., P.O. Box 7005, 29020-7005, pg. 267 — PB
CCG Corp., P.O. Box 7005, 29020-7005, pg. 267 — PB
Whiting Metals, Inc., Hwy. I-20, P.O. Box 190, 29020, pg. 1548 — PB

Carlisle

Cone Finishing Company, 3863 Carlisle/Chester Hwy., 29031, pg. 430 — PB
Webb Forging, P.O. Box 400, 29031, pg. 1156 — PV

Catawba

Bowater Coated Paper & Pulp Div., 5300 Cureton Ferry Rd., 29704, pg. 248 — PB

Cayce

CMC-Cayce, 603 Godley St., 29033, pg. 412 — PB
MPX Systems, Inc., 440 Knox Abbot Dr., 29033, pg. 1436 — PB
SMI Miscellaneous, 2804 Taylors Rd., 29033, pg. 412 — PB
SMI Steel South Carolina, 310 New State Rd., 29033, pg. 412 — PB

Chapin

FRED B. JOHNSTON COMPANY, INC., 300 E. Boundry Rd., 29036, pg. 595 — PV
Weisz Graphics, 300 E. Boundry Rd., 29036, pg. 595 — PV

Ryobi America Corp., 5201 Pearman Dairy Rd., 29625-8950, pg. 1151 — IT
Ryobi Electric Tool Mfg., 1424 Pearman Dairy Rd., 29625, pg. 1151 — IT
Ryobi Motor Products, 5201 Tearman Dairy Rd., 29625, pg. 1151 — IT

PB - *U.S. Public Companies Volume*
PV - *U.S. Private Companies Volume*
IT - *International Public & Private Companies Volume*

1421

Geographic Index-U.S.

Charleston

Albright & Wilson Americas Inc., 2151 King St. Extension, 29405, pg. 49 **IT**
Atlantic National Corporation, 6543 Fain St., 29411, pg. 512 **PV**
WILLIAM M. BIRD & CO., INC., 1142 Morrison Dr., 29403, pg. 145 **PV**
CNB INTERNATIONAL, INC., 171 Church St., Ste. 140, 29401, pg. 196 **PB**
CNB International, L.L.C., 171 Church St., Ste. 140, 29401, pg. 196 **PB**
CAMERON & BARKLEY COMPANY, 2864 Azalea Dr., 29405, pg. 203 **PV**
W.C. Caye & Co., 145 Williman St., 29403, pg. 220 **PV**
Charleston Containers Shops Inc., 1601 Oceanic St., 29405, pg. 1214 **IT**
Charleston Financial Services, Inc., P.O. Box 118068, 29423-8068, pg. 634 **PB**
Charleston Supply, 1791 King St. Extension, 29405, pg. 91 **PV**
Charleston Tool Services, 2301 Leeds Ave., 29405, pg. 468 **PB**
Charter Behavioral Health System of Charleston, Inc., 2777 Speissegger Dr., 29405-8299, pg. 1033 **PB**
Circle International, 4725E Arco Ln., 29418, pg. 371 **PB**
Diesel ReCon Charleston, 2301 Leeds Ave., 29405, pg. 468 **PB**
Dillard, A ResourceNet International Company, 7370 A Spartan Blvd., 29418, pg. 902 **PV**
Dowty O Rings North America - Charleston, 4275 Arcon Ln., 29418, pg. 1338 **IT**
Engineering Test Services, 2301 Leeds Ave., 29405, pg. 468 **PB**
Evans Rule Co., Inc., 6555 Fain St., 29418, pg. 1511 **PB**
EVENING POST PUBLISHING CO., 134 Columbus St., 29403-4800, pg. 385 **PV**
First Federal Savings & Loan Association of Charleston, 34 Broad St., 29401, pg. 634 **PB**
FIRST FINANCIAL HOLDINGS, INC., 34 Broad St., 29401, pg. 634 **PB**
Goer Manufacturing Co., 4500 Mariott Dr., N., 29418, pg. 904 **PV**
Hawthorne Airport Services, Inc., 6543 Fain St., 29411, pg. 512 **PV**
Hawthorne Aviation, 6543 Fain St., 29411, pg. 512 **PV**
HAWTHORNE CORP., 6543 Fain St., 29406, pg. 512 **PV**
Hawthorne Properties, Inc., 6543 Fain St., 29411, pg. 512 **PV**
Hawthorne Services, Inc., 6543 Fain St., 29411, pg. 512 **PV**
Healthsource South Carolina, Inc., 146 Fairchild St., 29492, pg. 360 **PB**
The Intertech Group Inc., 4838 Jenkins Ave., 29406, pg. 113 **IT**
KINETCO, 2301 Leeds Ave., 29405, pg. 468 **PB**
Line Equipment Sales Co., Inc., 551 Meeting St., 29403, pg. 1130 **PV**
Arthur D. Little Program Systems Management Company, Ste. 201, 5300 International Boulevard, 29418-6936, pg. 670 **PV**
MICHAEL BUSINESS MACHINES CORPORATION, 3134 Industry Dr., 29418, pg. 740 **PV**
Nordic Synthesis, Inc., Two Gillon St., Ste. A, 29401, pg. 297 **PB**
North Safety Products, 4090 Azalea Dr., 29405, pg. 1243 **IT**
North Safety Products, Hand Protection Division, 4090 Azalea Dr., P.O. Box 70729, 29505, pg. 1243 **IT**
PEARLSTINE DISTRIBUTORS INC., 4550 Gaynor Ave., 29406, pg. 845 **PV**
Gene Reed Chevrolet, 8199 Rivers Ave., N., 29406, pg. 1095 **PV**
RUSCON CORP., 149 E. Bay St., 29401, pg. 952 **PV**
SASIB Beverage & Food N.A., Inc., P.O. Box 118008, 300 Eagle Rd., 600 SE Creek, 29423, pg. 1194 **IT**
Scott & Stringfellow, Inc., 288 Meeting St., Second Fl., 29401, pg. 1446 **PV**
Sea Containers North American Operations & Accounting Group, 1601 Oceanic St., 29405, pg. 1214 **IT**
SouthTrust Bank of Charleston, 145 King St., 29401, pg. 1492 **PB**
Tencarva Machinery Company, 2460 Remount Rd., Suite 107, 29418, pg. 1076 **PV**
Unisun Insurance Co., One S. Park Cir., 29407, pg. 1231 **PB**
UTILITIES CONSTRUCTION CO., INC. OF SOUTH CAROLINA, 1890 Milford St., 29405, pg. 1130 **PV**
WCSC-TV, P.O. Box 186, 29420, pg. 926 **PB**
Westvaco Corporation-Chemical Div., 3950 Faber Place Dr., 29405, pg. 1762 **PB**

Cheraw

Cheraw Plant, 815 State Rd., 29520, pg. 444 **PB**
CHERAW YARN MILLS, INC., U.S. Hwy. 1 S., 29520, pg. 233 **PV**

Chesnee

Reeves Brothers, Inc. (Chesnee Div.), P.O. Box 128, 604 S. Alabama St., 29323, pg. 507 **PV**
Watts Regtrol, 815 Pickens St., 29323-1625, pg. 1746 **PB**

Chester

Carolina Tank Corp., 527 Mahlon Dr., 29706, pg. 968 **PB**
The News and Reporter, P.O. Box 250, 104 York St., 29706, pg. 648 **PV**

Schlegel Carolina Div., P.O. Box 190, 29706, pg. 128 **IT**
Sequa Chemicals, Inc., One Sequa Dr., 29706, pg. 1459 **PB**

Clemson

Jacobs Chuck Manufacturing, PO Box 592, One Jacobs Rd. 29631, pg. 481 **PB**

Clinton

Anderson Hardwood Floors, Old Laurens Rd., 29325, pg. 1032 **PV**
E.L. Mansure Div., P.O. Box 502, 29325, pg. 1094 **PV**
STANDARD PLYWOODS, INC., Old Laurens Rd., 29325, pg. 1032 **PV**

Clover

S.E. HUFFMAN CORP., 1050 Huffman Way, 29710, pg. 546 **PV**
Springfield Manufacturing LLC, 901 Ultra Dr., 29710, pg. 546 **PV**

Columbia

AEA of Columbia, 1825 Laurel St., 29282, pg. 1377 **PB**
Agency Specialty Inc., 1420 Lady St., 29201, pg. 1454 **PB**
AMBAC INTERNATIONAL CORP., I-77 at Killian Rd., 29203, pg. 48 **PV**
ANCHOR CONTINENTAL INCORPORATED, 2000 S. Beltline Blvd., 29205, pg. 70 **PV**
Ben Arnold Co., Inc., 700 Gervais St., 29201, pg. 83 **PV**
ASSOCIATED INDUSTRIAL SUPPLY, INC., 1207 Lincoln St., Suite 200, 29201, pg. 91 **PV**
BEARING DISTRIBUTORS, INC., 930 S. Stadium Rd., 29202, pg. 127 **PV**
BenefitAmerica, 1200 Colonial Life Blvd., 29210, pg. 1699 **PB**
BURRISS CORP., 508 Evelyn Dr., 29210, pg. 188 **PV**
CMI INDUSTRIES, INC., 1301 Gervais, Ste. 700, 29201, pg. 95 **PV**
Carolina Eastman Co., P.O. Box 1782, 29202-1782, pg. 350 **PV**
Carolina First Mortgage Company, 1420 Lady St., 29201, pg. 306 **PB**
Carolina Reprographics, pg. 1736 **PV**
Catawba Insurance Co., 1501 Lady St., 29201, pg. 454 **PB**
THE CLIMATIC CORP., 2270 LeGrand Rd., 29223, pg. 246 **PV**
Colonial Companies, Inc., 1200 Colonial Life Blvd., 29210, pg. 699 **PB**
Colonial Life & Accident Insurance Co., 1200 Colonial Life Blvd., 29210, pg. 1699 **PB**
Columbia Farms Distribution, P.O. Box 168, 29202, pg. 255 **PV**
COLUMBIA LUMBER & MANUFACTURING CO., P.O. Box 23269, 29224, pg. 255 **PV**
Columbia Supply, P.O. Box 729, 823 Gervais St., 29201, pg. 91 **PV**
Columbia Training Center, 7901 Farrow Rd., 29203, pg. 450 **PB**
Colwood Co., Inc., P.O. Box 23289, 29224, pg. 255 **PV**
CONGAREE CONSTRUCTION CO., INC., 1634 Pineview Rd., 29209, pg. 263 **PV**
Consolidated American Insurance Co., 1501 Lady St., 29201, pg. 1454 **PB**
Consolidated Cargo Carriers, 650 Rosewood Dr., 29201, pg. 266 **PV**
CONSOLIDATED SYSTEMS, INC., 650 Rosewood Dr., 29201, pg. 266 **PV**
DEFENDER SERVICES, INC., 9031 Garrners Ferry Rd., 29202, pg. 320 **PV**
Dillard, A ResourceNet International Company, 721 Vine St., 29202, pg. 902 **PV**
Fitton & Pittman, Inc., 1504 Elmon St., 29230, pg. 1056 **PV**
Fleet Mortgage Group, Inc., 1333 Main St., 29211, pg. 650 **PV**
Forest Lake Travel Service, Inc., Forest Lake Office Ctr., Four Monckton Blvd., 29206, pg. 1454 **PV**
Green Tree Acceptance, Inc., One Windsor Cove, 29223, pg. 752 **PV**
HARDAWAY CONCRETE CO., INC., 2001 Taylor St., 29204, pg. 501 **PV**
Harley Valve & Instrument Co., P.O. Box 11267, 29211, pg. 880 **PV**
Helicoflex Co., P.O. Box 9889, 2770 The Boulevard, 29290, pg. 1028 **IT**
Hewlett-Packard Company, Brookside Pk., Ste. 122, One Harbison Way, 29210, pg. 815 **PB**
Hewlett-Packard Company, 250 Berryhill Rd., Ste. 111, 29210, pg. 815 **PB**
V.B. HOOK & CO., INC., P.O. Box 13503, 29201, pg. 518 **PV**
JIM HUDSON, PONTIAC, OLDSMOBILE GMC, 7201 Sumter Hwy., 29209, pg. 545 **PV**
Investors National Life Insurance Co., 1420 Lady St., 29201, pg. 1454 **PB**
M.B. KAHN CONSTRUCTION CO., INC., 101 Flintlake Rd., 29223, pg. 604 **PV**
KLINE IRON & STEEL CO., INC., 1225 Huger St., 29201, pg. 626 **PV**
LAIDLAW ENVIRONMENTAL SERVICES, INC., 1301 Gervais St., Ste. 300, 29201, pg. 975 **PB**
MASHBURN CONSTRUCTION COMPANY, 1410 Laurel St., 29201, pg. 711 **PV**
MCCRORY CONSTRUCTION CO., INC., 1280 Assembly St., 29201, pg. 720 **PV**

NBSC Corporation, 1457 Main Street, 29202, pg. 1549 **PB**
NationsBank South Carolina Corporation, 1801 Main St., 29201, pg. 1163 **PB**
NationsBank South Carolina, N.A., 1301 Gervais St., 29202, pg. 1163 **PB**
Plasti-Line Columbia, Inc., 1829 Shop Rd., 29201, pg. 1309 **PB**
Policy Management Systems International, Ltd., P.O. Box 10, 29202, pg. 1314 **PB**
Premium Service Corp., 1508 Washington St., 29201, pg. 1454 **PB**
Primesouth, Inc., P.O. Box 212129, 29221, pg. 1436 **PB**
PULLIAM MOTOR COMPANY, 2800 Two Notch Rd., 29204, pg. 894 **PV**
RPR & ASSOCIATES, INC., P.O. Box 11348, 29211, pg. 905 **PV**
Republic Automotive Parts Sales, Inc., 1825 Laurel St., 29201, pg. 1378 **PV**
REPUBLIC CONTRACTING CORP., 869 Pepper St., 29209, pg. 923 **PV**
Richtex Corporation, Brickyard Rd. at Frost Ave., 29230, pg. 699 **PV**
SCT Utilities Systems, Inc., Carolina Research Park, Nine Science Ct., 29203-9344, pg. 1552 **PB**
SMI-Owen Steel Company, 824 Green St., 29201, pg. 413 **PB**
SMI-Owen Supply Company, 831 Blossom St., 29201, pg. 412 **PB**
SMI Rebar South Carolina, 2105 S. Beltline, 29201, pg. 412 **PB**
SMI Specialties, 801 Blossom St., 29201, pg. 413 **PB**
SCANA, 440 Knox Abbott Dr., 29033, pg. 1436 **PB**
SCANA CORPORATION, Palmetto Ctr., 1426 Main St., 29201-2845, pg. 1436 **PB**
SCANA Energy Marketing Inc., 7909 Parklane Dr., 29223, pg. 1436 **PB**
SCANA Resources, Inc., 1426 Main St., 29218, pg. 1436 **PB**
Seibels, Bruce & Co., 1501 Lady St., 29201, pg. 1454 **PB**
THE SEIBELS BRUCE GROUP, INC., 1501 Lady St., 29202, pg. 1453 **PB**
ServiceCare, Inc., P.O. Box 7815, 29202, pg. 1436 **PB**
Shakespeare Fishing Tackle, 3801 Westmore Dr., 29223, pg. 940 **PB**
Shakespeare Monofilament, P.O. Box 4060, 29204, pg. 940 **PB**
WILBUR SMITH ASSOCIATES, 1301 Geruis St., Ste. 1500, 29201, pg. 1009 **PV**
South Carolina Electric & Gas Co. (SCE&G), 1426 Main St., 29201, pg. 1436 **PB**
South Carolina Fuel Co., Inc., 1426 Main St., 29218, pg. 1436 **PB**
South Carolina Generating Co., Inc., 1426 Main St., 29218, pg. 1436 **PB**
South Carolina Insurance Company, 1501 Lady St., 29201, pg. 1453 **PB**
South Carolina National Corporation, 1426 Main St., 29226, pg. 1730 **PB**
South Carolina Pipeline Corporation, I-20 Alpine Rd., 29206, pg. 1436 **PB**
Southeastern Coated Products, 650 Rosewood Dr., 29201, pg. 266 **PV**
Square D Company, 8821 Garners Ferry Rd., 29209, pg. 1208 **IT**
The State Printing Company, Inc., 1210 Key Rd., 29201, pg. 1736 **PV**
The State-Record Company, 1401 Shop Rd., 29201, pg. 964 **PV**
Sunbird Boat Co., Inc., 1501 Shop Rd., 29201, pg. 478 **PV**
Tencarva Machinery Co., 1405 Old Dairy Road, 29201, pg. 1076 **PV**
TERMINIX SERVICE, INC., 3618 Fernandino Rd., 29210, pg. 1077 **PV**
THOMAS & HOWARD CO., P.O. Box 23659, 29224-3659, pg. 1081 **PV**
Thomas & Howard Co., P.O. Box 23659, 29224-3659, pg. 1082 **PV**
United Companies Lending Corp. (South Carolina), P.O. Drawer 61047, 4700 Forest Dr., 29260, pg. 1675 **PB**
WARQ, 1900 Pineview Rd., 29209, pg. 384 **PB**
WIS-TV, P.O. Box 367, 1111 Bull St., 29202, pg. 992 **PB**
WWDM, 1900 Pineview Rd., 29209, pg. 385 **PB**
Wachovia Bank of South Carolina, 1401 Main St., 29226, pg. 1730 **PB**
Wachovia Bank of South Carolina, N.A., 1401 Main St., 29202, pg. 1730 **PB**
J.B. White, One Riverland Mall, 29204, pg. 1090 **PB**
Willis Corroon Corp. of South Carolina, 1441 Main St., 29201, pg. 1507 **IT**
Willis Corroon Corp. of South Carolina, 1276 Assembly St., 29201, pg. 1507 **IT**

Conway

AVX Conway Plant, 2875 Hwy. 501, 29526, pg. 775 **IT**
Aberdeen Mfg. Corp. Conway Plant, 16th Ave., 29526, pg. 1094 **PV**
Columbia Supply, Conway, P.O. Box 349, 1509 Third Ave., 29526, pg. 91 **PV**
EMBERS CHARCOAL COMPANY, INC., P.O. Box 870, 29528, pg. 373 **PV**
First Southeast Insurance Agency, P.O. Box 1740, 29526, pg. 634 **PB**
Glendinning Marine Products, Inc., 4753 Highway 90, 29526, pg. 1705 **PV**
Peoples Federal Savings & Loan Association, 1601 11th Ave., 29526-4136, pg. 634 **PB**
Southern Hardwood Sawmill, City 5, 1906 Country Club Dr., 29526, pg. 508 **PB**
Terex Cranes, Hwy. 501 E., 29526, pg. 1581 **PB**

PB - *U.S. Public Companies Volume*
PV - *U.S. Private Companies Volume*
IT - *International Public & Private Companies Volume*

1422

Geographic Index-U.S.

UNIBLEND SPINNERS, INC., 4701 Adrian Hwy., 29526, pg. 1117 **PV**

Darlington

Clanton's Auto Auction, Highway 34 W., 29532, pg. 282 **PV**
DARLINGTON VENEER COMPANY, 225 Fourth St., 29532, pg. 311 **PV**
Diamond Hill Plywood Company, 600 E. Broad St., 29532, pg. 311 **PV**
Nucor Cold Finish-South Carolina, P.O. Box 525, 29532, pg. 1205 **PB**
Nucor Steel-South Carolina, N. Hwy. 52, 29532, pg. 1205 **PB**

Dillon

Dorsey Trailers, Inc., P.O. Box 1688, 1063 Bass Lake Pl., 29536-1688, pg. 520 **PB**

Duncan

Alcoa Fujikura Ltd., 150 Ridgeview Cir., 29334, pg. 525 **IT**
Grace Packaging, I-85 and Hwy 290, 29334, pg. 755 **PB**
Hayssen, 225 Spartan Green Blvd., 29334, pg. 118 **PV**
One Price Clothing of Puerto Rico, Inc., Commerce Park, Hwy. 290, 29334, pg. 1225 **PV**
ONE PRICE CLOTHING STORES, INC., Commerce Park, Hwy. 290, 1875 E. Main St., 29334, pg. 1225 **PB**

Easley

Ahlstrom Process Equipment Inc. Pump Factory, P.O. Box 2069, 29641-2069, pg. 34 **IT**
Ahlstrom Process Equipment Inc., P.O. Box 2069, 29641, pg. 34 **IT**
Danfoss Fluid Power, 1201 Pelzer Hwy., 29640, pg. 377 **IT**
HOLLINGSWORTH SACO LOWELL CORPORATION, INC., 183 Rolling Hills Circle, 29640, pg. 535 **PV**
Imperial Die Casting, Griffin Mill & Brazil Rds., 29640, pg. 903 **PV**
MPC Easley, P.O. Box 1569, Liberty Highway, 29641, pg. 851 **IT**

Edgefield

MARTIN COLOR-FI, 306 Main St., 29824, pg. 1052 **PV**
Tranter Inc.-Edgefield Div., P.O. Box 570, 29824, pg. 522 **PB**

Edisto Island

Fairfield Ocean Ridge, One King Cotton Rd., 29438, pg. 610 **PB**

Fairfax

King Seely Thermos Company, P.O. Box 890, Hwy. 321 S., 29827-0890, pg. 558 **PB**

Florence

ESAB Equipment/Automation, P.O. Box 100545, Ebenezer Rd., 29501-0545, pg. 281 **IT**
Florence Industrial Supply, P.O. Box 5717, 1403 Success Way, 29502, pg. 91 **PV**
La-Z-Boy East, 901 No. Douglas, 29501, pg. 973 **PB**
Nytron Inductors, 2295 Hossmeyer Rd., 29501-0556, pg. 1722 **PV**
POWERS CONSTRUCTION CO., INC., 3091 S. Cashua Dr., 29501, pg. 878 **PV**
Socar, Inc., National Cemetery Rd., 29501, pg. 1392 **PB**
SOUTHEASTERN STEEL COMPANY, Koppers Rd., 29501, pg. 1015 **PV**
SUPERIOR MACHINE COMPANY OF SOUTH CAROLINA, INC., P.O. Box 5419, 29502, pg. 1055 **PV**
Trayco of S.C., Inc., 1307 National Cemetary Rd., 29502, pg. 352 **PV**
Vulcraft Div., 1501 W. Darlington St., 29502, pg. 1206 **PB**
Wellman Man-Made Fibers Div., P.O. Box 100542, 29501, pg. 1752 **PB**
Wellman Polymer Products Div., P.O. Box 100542, 29501, pg. 1753 **PV**
YOUNG PECAN COMPANY (A PARTNERSHIP), 1200 Pecan St., 29501, pg. 1201 **PV**

Fort Lawn

MORRISON TEXTILE MACHINERY CO., 6044 Lancaster Hwy., 29714, pg. 762 **PV**

Fort Mill

Baldor Electric Company, 2499 Deerfield Dr., 29715, pg. 169 **PB**
City Club of Charlotte, 4225 Pleasant Rd., 29715, pg. 610 **PB**
OWSLEY & SONS, INC., Gold Hill Rd. at I-77 S., 29716-1449, pg. 824 **PV**
N. Schlumberger (USA) Inc., 1299 Schlumberger Dr., 29715, pg. 1206 **IT**
SPRINGS INDUSTRIES, INC., 205 N. White St., 29716, pg. 1499 **PB**

Fountain Inn

Flowers Baking Co. of Fountain Inn, Inc., 1405 South Main St., 29644, pg. 657 **PB**
Vermont American Corporation-Fountain Inn Div., 800 Woodside Ave., 29644, pg. 575 **PB**
Wilson Sporting Goods Co., 206 Georgia St., 29644, pg. 73 **IT**

Gaffney

Autocam South Carolina, Inc., 348 Huntington Dr., 29341, pg. 148 **PB**
Nestle Frozen/Refrigerated Food Co., P.O. Box 1419, Highway 29 South, Route 7, 29340, pg. 918 **IT**
PEELERS RUG COMPANY, INC., 1224 Champion Ferry Rd., 29341, pg. 846 **PV**

Goose Creek

Haarman & Reimer Aroma Chemicals, 1636 Bushy Park Rd., 29445, pg. 173 **IT**
QUOIZEL INC., Six Corporate Pkwy., 29445, pg. 901 **PV**

Graniteville

Graniteville Company, 133 Marshall St., 29829, pg. 103 **PV**
Woodhead Specialty Fabrics, 131 Marshall St., 29829, pg. 103 **PV**

Great Falls

REPUBLIC FASTENER PRODUCTS CORP., 1827 Waterview Dr., 29055, pg. 923 **PV**

Greenville

Albany Mount Vernon Dryers, P.O. Box 5837, 29606, pg. 36 **PB**
American Sahm Corporation, 180 Commerce Dr./Pelham Rd., 29615, pg. 1169 **IT**
AMICO-Greenville Distr. Center, P.O. Box 26534, 29616, pg. 30 **PV**
BB&T of South Carolina, P.O. Box 408, 29602, pg. 160 **PB**
Bausch & Lomb Personal Products Division-SC, 8507 Pelham Rd., 29615, pg. 194 **PB**
BI-LO Inc., 208 Industrial Blvd., 29607, pg. 749 **PB**
Blue Ridge Finance Co., Inc., 355 Woodruff Rd., Ste. 210, 29606, pg. 306 **PV**
BOWATER INCORPORATED, 55 E. Camperdown Way, 29602, pg. 247 **PB**
BUILDER MARTS OF AMERICA, INC., One Independence Pointe, 29615, pg. 179 **PV**
CF Investment Company, 200 E. Camperdown Way, 29601, pg. 306 **PB**
Carolina First Bank, 102 S. Main St., 29601, pg. 306 **PB**
CAROLINA FIRST CORPORATION, 102 S. Main St., 29601, pg. 306 **PB**
Carolina Steel-Greenville Plant, P.O. Box 128, 29602, pg. 214 **PV**
Coats & Clark Inc., P.O. Box 24998, 29616, pg. 300 **IT**
Cosmos Broadcasting Corp., 2000 Wade Hampton Blvd., 29615, pg. 992 **PB**
DAVIS ELECTRICAL CONSTRUCTORS, INC., 429 N. Main St., 29601, pg. 315 **PV**
Day & Zimmermann Services, 33 Villa Rd., Ste. 200, 29615, pg. 317 **PV**
Day International Textile Products, P.O. Box 2065, 29602-2065, pg. 56 **PV**
Day & Zimmerman Construction Inc., 33 Villa Rd., Ste. 400, 29615, pg. 317 **PV**
DELTA WOODSIDE INDUSTRIES, INC., 233 N. Main St., Ste. 200, 29601, pg. 497 **PB**
Dillard, A ResourceNet International Company, 2930 Whitehorse Rd., 29602, pg. 902 **PB**
Dodge Mechanical Group, P.O. Box 499, 29602-0499, pg. 1398 **PB**
Eclipse Combustion, Inc., P.O. Box 14034, 146 Pilot Rd., 29609, pg. 360 **PV**
Equipment Resources, Inc., P.O. Box 47, 29602, pg. 180 **PV**
FAIRWAY FORD, INC., 2323 Laurens Rd., 29607, pg. 392 **PV**
First Union National Bank of South Carolina, P.O. Box 1329, One Insignia Pl., 29601, pg. 640 **PB**
Gates/Arrow Commercial Systems Div., 39 Pecham Ridge Dr., 29615, pg. 133 **PB**
General Nutrition Products, Inc., 1050 Woodruff Rd., 29607, pg. 725 **PV**
Grace Logistics Services, Patewood Plaza, Ste. 270, 30 Patewood Dr., 29615, pg. 755 **PB**
The Greenville News, 305 S. Main St., 29602, pg. 699 **PB**
Heritage Lincoln-Mercury, 2424 Laurens Rd., 29607, pg. 392 **PV**
Hewlett-Packard Company, 545 N. Pleasanburg Dr., Ste. 100, 29607, pg. 815 **PB**
Hewlett-Packard Company, 101 W. 14th St., Bldg. 2, Ste. 10, 27835, pg. 815 **PB**
HomeAdd Financial Corporation, 850 S. Pleasanburg Dr., 27834, pg. 1358 **PB**
Imaging Technologies Services, 353 W. McBee Ave., 29602, pg. 1735 **PB**
Industra Inc., 545 N. Pleasanturg Dr., Ste. 300, 29607, pg. 74 **IT**
INSIGNIA FINANCIAL GROUP, INC., One Insignia Plaza, 29602, pg. 881 **PB**

Insignia Residential Group, Insignia Financial Plaza, 29602, pg. 881 **PB**
Intergraph Corporation, Brookfield Plaza, 201 Brookfield Pkwy., Ste. 120, 29607, pg. 890 **PB**
JPS Automotive L.P., 29 Stevens St., 29605, pg. 1095 **PV**
JPS Converter & Industrial Corp., 33 Stevens St., 29605, pg. 578 **PV**
JPS TEXTILE GROUP, INC., 555 N. Pleasantburg Dr., Ste. 202, 29607, pg. 578 **PV**
Jacobs Sirrine Engineers, Inc., B1041 East Butler Rd., 29608-5456, pg. 921 **PB**
KAEPA INC., 1500 Poinsette Hwy., Entrance C, 29609, pg. 604 **PV**
LIBERTY CORPORATION, Wade Hampton Blvd., 29615, pg. 991 **PB**
Liberty Investment Group, Inc., 2000 Wade Hampton Blvd., 29615, pg. 992 **PB**
Liberty Life Insurance Company, 2000 Wade Hampton Blvd., 29615, pg. 992 **PB**
Lockheed Aeromod Center, Inc., 1044 Terminal Road, 29605, pg. 1007 **PB**
MARSHALL & WILLIAMS CO., 301 Airport Rd., 29606, pg. 708 **PV**
MCLAUGHLIN MANUFACTURING COMPANY, 2006 Perimeter Rd., 29605, pg. 724 **PV**
McLaughlin Manufacturing Co. of S.C., P.O. Box 8954, Sta. A, 2006 Perimeter Rd., 29604, pg. 724 **PV**
Michelin Americas Small Tires (MAST), P.O. Box 19001, 29602-9001, pg. 322 **IT**
Michelin North America, One Parkway S., 29615, pg. 322 **IT**
Mount Vernon Dryer Fabrics, P.O. Box 5837, 29606, pg. 835 **PV**
Mount Vernon Mills, Inc., One Insignia Financial Plaza, Ste. 700, 29601, pg. 835 **PV**
Mount Vernon Mills, Inc., Riegel Textile Div., P.O. Box 3478, 29602, pg. 835 **PV**
Multimedia Newspaper Company, 305 S. Main St., 29602, pg. 699 **PB**
Multimedia Publishing of South Carolina, Inc., 305 S. Main St., 29601, pg. 699 **PB**
National Electrical Carbon Corporation, 251 Forrester Dr., 29607, pg. 891 **IT**
Olympic Steel - Southern Division, Five Century Dr., Ste. 220, 29607, pg. 1221 **PB**
ORDERS DISTRIBUTING CO., 501 Congaree Rd., 29607, pg. 819 **PV**
PYA/Monarch, Inc., 80 International Dr., Ste. 200, 29615, pg. 1433 **PB**
C.H. Patrick & Co., Inc., P.O. Box 2526, 29602, pg. 751 **PV**
Piedmont Olsen Hensley, Inc., P.O. Box 1717, 29602, pg. 607 **IT**
Pierce National Life Insurance Co., 2000 Wade Hampton Blvd., 29602, pg. 992 **PB**
Poe Supply, 215 Pelham Davis Cir., 29615, pg. 91 **PV**
POTTER-SHACKELFORD CONSTRUCTION CO., 80 Villa Rd., 29615, pg. 877 **PV**
RSI HOLDINGS INC., 28 E. Court St., 29601, pg. 1358 **PB**
Rust Environment and Infrastructure, 15 Brendan Way, 29615, pg. 1366 **PB**
Rust Environment & Infrastructure, Inc., 15 Brendan Way, 29615, pg. 1745 **PB**
SOS International, 100 Fluor Daniel Dr., 29607, pg. 660 **PB**
SHEALY ELECTRICAL WHOLESALERS, 27 River St., 29601, pg. 991 **PV**
SPAN-AMERICA MEDICAL SYSTEMS INC., 70 Commerce Dr., 29615, pg. 1495 **PB**
Suitt Construction Company, Inc., 1400 Cleveland St., 29607, pg. 106 **PV**
UMBRO INTERNATIONAL, INC., 1500 Poinsett Hwy., 29609, pg. 1116 **PV**
U.S. Finishing, 3335 Old Buncombe Rd., 29602, pg. 54 **PV**
WYFF-TV, 505 Rutherford St., 29609, pg. 1344 **PB**
Wangner Systems Corporation, 525 Old Piedmont Hwy., 29605-4691, pg. 1418 **IT**
Willis Corroon Corp. of South Carolina, One Insignia Fin. Plaza, Ste. 900, 29601, pg. 1507 **IT**
WORLD ACCEPTANCE CORPORATION, 108 Frederick St., 29607, pg. 1778 **PB**

Greenwood

Columbia Supply, Greenwood, 2428 Hwy. 72-221, 29649, pg. 91 **PV**
Environmental Resorts Inc., Greenwood Bldg., 29646, pg. 479 **PV**
Fuji Photo Film, Inc., 211 Pucketts Ferry Rd., 29649, pg. 524 **IT**
Greenwood Development Co., Greenwood Bldg., 29646, pg. 479 **PV**
GREENWOOD MILLS, INC., 104 Maxwell Ave., 29646, pg. 479 **PV**
Greenwood Plant, 104 Stoneridge Ct., 29649, pg. 1044 **PV**
Greenwood Warehouse Co., Greenwood Bldg., 29646, pg. 479 **PV**
GEORGE W. PARK SEED CO., INC., Hwy. 254 N. Cokesbury Rd., 29647, pg. 839 **PV**
Titan Wheel, 111 Industrial Park Rd., 29649-0198, pg. 1618 **PB**

Greer

Hoechst Polyester Film Products Division, One Hood Rd, 29652, pg. 626 **IT**
Holiday RV Superstores, Inc., 198 Bob Ledford Dr., 29651, pg. 829 **PB**
RYAN'S FAMILY STEAK HOUSES, INC., 405 Lancaster Ave., 29650, pg. 1413 **PB**

Geographic Index-U.S.

Stevcoknit Fabrics Company, P.O. Box 1500, 29652, pg. 498 **PB**
Tencarva Machinery Co., Pelham Industrial Pk., 29651, pg. 1076 **PV**
Unimark Plastics Company, 1303 Batesville Rd., 29650-9379, pg. 57 **PV**
Union-Transport Corporation-Greenville/Spartanburg Office, Ste. 7C, Craftsman Ct., 29650, pg. 1119 **PV**

Hampton

Chambers Medical Technologies, Inc., 100 Nix St., 29924, pg. 1686 **PB**

Harleyville

Giant Cement Company, P.O. Box 218, 29448, pg. 741 **PB**
Giant Resource Recovery Company (Grr!), P.O. Box 218, Hwy. 453, 29448, pg. 741 **PB**

Hartsville

Sonoco Adhesives Division, P.O. Box 160, 29550, pg. 1486 **PB**
Sonoco Consumer Packaging Group, P.O. Box 160, 29550, pg. 1486 **PB**
Sonoco Forest Products Division, P.O. Box 160, 29550, pg. 1486 **PB**
Sonoco Industrial Products Division, P.O. Box 160, 29550, pg. 1486 **PB**
Sonoco International Division, P.O. Box 160, 29550, pg. 1486 **PB**
SONOCO PRODUCTS COMPANY, N. Second St., 29550-3305, pg. 1485 **PB**
Sonoco Special Products Group, P.O. Box 160, 29550, pg. 1486 **PB**
Talley Metals Technology, Inc., Box 2498, 29550, pg. 308 **PB**

Hickory Grove

Hickson Corporation, P.O. Box 248, 29717, pg. 619 **IT**

Hilton Head Island

Atlantic Savings Bank FSB, 200 Merchant, 29926, pg. 1730 **PB**
ETHIKA CORPORATION, 107 The Executive Center, 29928, pg. 595 **PB**
Hilton Head Island Packet, P.O. Box 5727, 1 Pope Ave., 29928, pg. 1065 **PB**

Hollywood

METAL TRADES, INC., 4194 Hwy. 165, 29449, pg. 734 **PV**

Honea Path

Torrington Co.-Precision Components, P.O. Box 565, 29654-0565, pg. 877 **PB**

Inman

INMAN MILLS, 300 Park Rd., 29349, pg. 564 **PV**

Irmo

MICHAEL J. MUNGO COMPANY, INC., 441 Western Lane, 29063, pg. 767 **PV**

Jefferson

Caro Knit (Jefferson Plant), P.O. Box 366, So. Main St., 29718-0366, pg. 514 **PB**

Johnsonville

Wellman Engineering Resins Div., P.O. Drawer 188, Hwys. 41/51 N., 29555-0188, pg. 1752 **PB**
Wellman Man-Made Fibers Div., P.O. Box 188, Hwys. 41/51 N., 29555-0188, pg. 1752 **PB**
Wellman Recycling Div., P.O. Box 188, Hwy. 41/51 N., 29555, pg. 1753 **PB**
Wellman Wool Div., P.O. Drawer 188, Hwys. 41/51 N., 29555-0188, pg. 1753 **PB**

Johnston

Mount Vernon Mills, Inc., Riegel Consumer Products Div., P.O. Box E, 29832, pg. 835 **PV**

Kingstree

FARMERS TELEPHONE CO-OP, 1101 E. Main St., 29556, pg. 395 **PV**
Firestone Building Products Company-Kingstree Plant, Rte. 4, Box 350-B, 29556, pg. 214 **IT**

La France

Mount Vernon Mills, Inc., LaFrance Industries, P.O. Box 500, 29656, pg. 835 **PV**

Lake City

The Coleman Company, P.O. Box 1119, Hwy. 341, 29560, pg. 691 **PV**

Lancaster

Chesterfield Division, P.O. Box 111, Highway 9, 29721, pg. 1500 **PB**
Joslyn Clark Controls, Inc., P.O. Box 945, Rt. 4, Rock Hill Hwy., 29720, pg. 481 **PB**
The Lancaster News, 701 N. White St., 29720, pg. 648 **PV**
Nucor Wire, P.O. Box 2079, 1553 Cashey Rd., 29720, pg. 1205 **PB**
Rail Products Division, 1888 Riverside Rd., 29720, pg. 65 **PV**
Rexam Performance Products, P.O. Box 800, 29721, pg. 1106 **IT**
Thomas & Betts Lehigh Lancaster, P.O. BOX P.O. Box, 29721-1209, pg. 1597 **PB**

Landrum

BOMMER INDUSTRIES, INC., 19810 Ashville Hwy., 29356, pg. 156 **PV**
Simkins Carolina Folding Box Div., 1205 S. Shamrock Ave., 29356, pg. 1000 **PV**

Langley

Air Products, P.O. Box 1330, 29834, pg. 30 **PB**

Laurens

Ceramtec North America, One Technology Pl., 29360-0089, pg. 860 **IT**
Palmetto Spinning Corp., 1100 Church St., 29360, pg. 1052 **PB**
Wal-Mart Distribution Center, P.O. Box 2000, 29360-2000, pg. 1733 **PB**

Leesville

COLUMBIA FARMS INC., P.O. Box 577, 29070, pg. 255 **PV**

Lexington

ALLTEL South Carolina, Inc., 106 N. Church St., P.O. Box 1046, 29071, pg. 56 **PB**
Barenbrug Southeast, P.O. Box 1817, 239 Cedatcrest Rd., 29017, pg. 167 **IT**
CMC-Lexington, 2308 Two Notch Rd., 29072, pg. 412 **PB**
Cooper Power Tools Division, 670 Industrial Dr., 29072, pg. 444 **PB**
GLASSMASTER COMPANY, 126 Glassmaster Rd., 29072, pg. 745 **PV**
Golden State Foods-South Carolina Division, 2588 Old Two Notch Rd., 29072, pg. 461 **PV**
Lexington Plant, 670 Industrial Ave., 29072, pg. 444 **PB**
Pirelli Cable, Fiber Optic Div., 7000 Industrial Dr., 29072, pg. 1059 **IT**
SOUTHEASTERN FREIGHT LINES, INC., 420 Davega Rd., 29073, pg. 1015 **PV**

Liberty

Champion Aviation Products, 1230 Old Norris Rd., 29657, pg. 443 **PB**
Ohio Gear/Richmond Gear - Liberty Div., 1208 Old Norris Rd., 29657, pg. 1370 **PB**

Lugoff

COGSD LL TOOL PRODUCTS, INC., 1001 Guion Dr., 29078, pg. 250 **PV**
Wateree Textile Corp., 412 Grove St., 29078, pg. 845 **IT**

Lyman

Lyman, P.O. Box 517, 29365, pg. 1222 **IT**
Senior Engineering, P.O. Box 517, 29365, pg. 1222 **IT**

Manning

SPROTT OIL CO., INC., P.O. Box 1392, 29102, pg. 1027 **PV**
The Starflo Corporation, Rte. 5, Box 472, 29102, pg. 877 **PV**

Marion

AVM Inc., P.O. Box 729, 29571, pg. 137 **PB**
Blumenthal Mills, Hwy. 76 W., 29571, pg. 153 **PV**
Heritage Sportswear, 505 Manning St., 29571, pg. 1472 **PB**
Raytex Finishing Co., P.O. Box 884, 576 Bypass, 29571, pg. 430 **PB**

Mauldin

National Cabinet Lock, Inc., 200 Old Mill Rd., 29662, pg. 270 **PV**

McBee

MAR-MAC MANUFACTURING COMPANY, INC., Highway One, N., 29101, pg. 701 **PV**
A.O. Smith Water Products Company, Hwy. 1 N., 29101, pg. 1477 **PB**

McClellanville

McClellanville Telephone Co., Inc., Drawer 888, 1130 Hwy. 45, 29458, pg. 1571 **PB**

McCormick

Mount Vernon Mills, Inc., Consumer Products Div. (McCormick), Augusta Hwy., 29835, pg. 835 **PV**

Moncks Corner

Industrial Acoustics Company S.C. Inc., P.O. Box 579, 29461, pg. 875 **PB**

Mount Holly

Alumax of South Carolina Mt. Holly, P.O. Box 1000, U.S. Hwy. 52, 29445, pg. 60 **PB**
J.W. Aluminum Company, 435 Old Mt. Holly Rd., 29445, pg. 1736 **PB**

Mount Pleasant

Charleston Television, Inc., 210 W. Coleman Blvd., 29464, pg. 1078 **PB**
WCIV, LLC, 88 Allbritton Blvd., 29464, pg. 854 **PV**
John Wieland Homes of South Carolina, Inc., 496 LaMesa Dr., 29464, pg. 1175 **PV**

Myrtle Beach

AVX Corporation, P.O. Box 867, 17th Ave. S., 29577, pg. 775 **IT**
AVX Leaded Products Div., P.O. Box 867, 17th Ave. S., 29577, pg. 775 **IT**
The Anchor Bank, 2002 Oak St., 29577-3145, pg. 111 **PB**
ANCHOR FINANCIAL CORPORATION, 2002 Oak St., 29577-3145, pg. 111 **PB**
Atlantic Reprographics, pg. 1736 **PB**
Cox Communications-Myrtle Beach, 1901 Oak St., 29577, pg. 455 **PB**
General Commercial Packaging, Inc., P.O. Box 808, 29578, pg. 1049 **PV**
SANDS INVESTMENTS, INC., 201 74th Ave. N., 29572, pg. 964 **PV**
The Sun News, 914 Frontage Rd. E., 29577, pg. 964 **PB**
Sun Publishing Company, Inc., Frontage Road East, 29577, pg. 964 **PB**
Vanguard Cellular Systems of South Carolina, Inc., 918 Frontage Rd E., 29577, pg. 1708 **PB**
WACCAMAW CORPORATION, 3200 Pottery Dr., 29577, pg. 1145 **PV**

Newberry

Precision Fiberglass, 101 Park Ave., 29108, pg. 692 **PV**
Shakespeare Composites & Electronics, Box 733, Rt. #3, 29108, pg. 940 **PB**
Thomas & Howard Co., P.O. Box 38, 29108, pg. 1082 **PV**

North Augusta

CMC-North Augusta, 1119 Atomic Rd., 29841, pg. 412 **PB**

North Myrtle Beach

Fairfield Myrtle Beach, Inc., 3405 S. Ocean Blvd., 29582, pg. 611 **PB**

Orangeburg

COX WOOD PRESERVING CO., Cannon Bridge Rd., 29116, pg. 283 **PV**
Frigidaire Home Products, P.O. Box 1687, S. Carolina Hwy. & Old Cameron Rd., 29116, pg. 440 **IT**
Jacobs Applied Technology, Inc., 1525 Charleston Hwy., 29115-1327, pg. 921 **PB**
Koyo Corporation of USA, Hwy. 601 North, 29115, pg. 760 **IT**
Koyo Corporation of USA, Manufacturing Division, Hwy. 601 North, 29115, pg. 760 **IT**
Orangeburg Industrial Supply, 1885 Joe S. Jeffords Hwy., SE, 29116, pg. 91 **PV**
Orangeburg Trucking, Inc., P.O. Drawer 1186, 29115, pg. 1521 **PB**
Radar Systems, P.O. Box 1163, 29116, pg. 1364 **PV**
The Starflo Corporation, Hwy 301 N., Crosscreek Rd., 29115, pg. 877 **PV**

Pacolet

Spartan Minerals Corp., 520 Calico Dr., 29372, pg. 605 **PB**

Pageland

Conbraco Industries-Apollo Division, P.O. Box 125, 29728-0125, pg. 261 **PV**

PB - *U.S. Public Companies Volume*
PV - *U.S. Private Companies Volume*
IT - *International Public & Private Companies Volume*

1424

Pickens

BLUE RIDGE ELECTRIC COOPERATIVE INC., Box 277, 734 W. Main St., 29671, pg. 153 — **PV**
THE KENT MANUFACTURING CO., Hwy. 183, 29671, pg. 615 — **PV**
Ryobi Motor Products, P.O. Box 35, 29671, pg. 1151 — **IT**

Rock Hill

ATOTECH U.S.A. INC., 1750 Overview Dr., 29732, pg. 97 — **PV**
CKC, 600 Huey Rd., 29730, pg. 89 — **PV**
Chicago Pneumatic Tool Company, 1800 Overview Dr., 29730, pg. 96 — **IT**
International Carolina Glass Corp., 780 Cel-River Rd., 29730, pg. 895 — **PV**
Meco Metal Finishing USA Inc., 445 Bryant Blvd., 29732, pg. 1064 — **IT**
Meco USA Inc., 445 Bryant Blvd., 29732, pg. 1064 — **IT**
OSTROW TEXTILE CO., INC., 923 Standard & High Sts., 29731, pg. 821 — **PV**
PAXAR Apparel Identification Systems, 1595 Cedar Line Dr., 29730, pg. 1266 — **PV**
Plej's Linen Supermarket, 923 Standard & High St., 29731, pg. 821 — **PV**
Rock Hill Herald, 132 W. Main St., 29730, pg. 1066 — **PB**
SMITH ENTERPRISES, 1953 Langston St., 29730, pg. 1007 — **PV**
Star Paper Tube, Inc., 1379 McDow Dr., 29732, pg. 304 — **PB**
United States Aluminum-Carolina, 720 Cel-River Road, 29730, pg. 895 — **PB**

Roebuck

THE FELTERS COMPANY, P.O. Drawer 228, 29376, pg. 400 — **PV**

Russellville

Formaldehyde, P.O. Box 147, 29476, pg. 737 — **PB**

Saint Stephen

Albany International/Press Fabrics Division, P.O. Box 608, 29479, pg. 36 — **PB**

Seneca

Bostik Inc., P.O. Box 1619, Wells Hwy. # 1619, 29678-1346, pg. 1409 — **IT**
Duke Power Oconee Nuclear Station, P.O. Box 1439, Hwy. 130, 29679-1439, pg. 534 — **PB**
Dynacast, Walhalla Hwy., 29678, pg. 300 — **IT**
Square D Seneca Plant, 1990 Sandifer Blvd., 29678, pg. 1208 — **IT**

Simpsonville

BKI, 2812 Grandview Dr., 29681, pg. 1506 — **PB**
FTZ Industries, Inc., 515 Palmetto Dr., 29681, pg. 558 — **PV**
Fiberweb North America Inc., 840 S.E. Main St., 29681, pg. 113 — **IT**
KEMET CORPORATION, 2835 Kemet Way, 29681, pg. 949 — **PB**
Kemet Electronics Corporation, 2835 Kemet Way, 29681, pg. 949 — **PB**

Spartanburg

Adidas America, 5675 N. Blackstock Rd., 29303, pg. 24 — **IT**
Adidas Central Distribution, 100 International Dr., 29301, pg. 24 — **IT**
ADVANTICA RESTAURANT GROUP, INC., 203 E. Main St., 29319-0001, pg. 22 — **PV**
AMERICAN FAST PRINT, LIMITED, I-85 & Bryant Rd., 29303, pg. 53 — **PV**
ASSOCIATED PETROLEUM CARRIERS, 1746 Union Rd., 29302, pg. 92 — **PV**
Beverage-Air Co., P.O. Box 5932, 29304, pg. 1496 — **PB**
Blackman Uhler Chemical Co., Croft Industrial Park, 2155 W. Croft Circle, 29302, pg. 1548 — **PB**
COMMUNITY CASH STORES, 3001 N. Blackstock Rd., 29301, pg. 259 — **PV**
Denny's, Inc., 203 E. Main St., 29319, pg. 23 — **PB**
DIVERSCO, INC., Rd. 57, 29302, pg. 336 — **PV**
DRAPER TEXMACO, INC., 951 S. Pine St., 29302-331-1, pg. 342 — **PV**
Flowers Baking Co. of South Carolina, Hearon Cir., 7001 Asheville Hwy., 29303, pg. 657 — **PB**
Gateway Additive Company, 201 Henry Pl., 29304, pg. 1016 — **PB**
General Wholesale Company, 360 Daniel Morgan Ave., 29301, pg. 446 — **PV**
Hoechst Celanese Corp. Spunbond Products, P.O. Box 5887, 29304, pg. 626 — **IT**
Imaging Technologies, 657 No. Church St., 29303, pg. 1735 — **PB**
Industrial Coated Fabrics Group, U.S. Hwy. 29 S., 29304, pg. 507 — **PV**
Isomedix Operations Inc., 2072 Southport Rd., Hwy. 295, 29301, pg. 1515 — **PB**
JBL Div., 3025 W. Croft Circle Dr., 29302-0201, pg. 1262 — **PB**
Kohler Co. (SC), P.O. Box 1987, 29304, pg. 630 — **PV**

KUSTERS CORPORATION, I-85 at 101 Zima Park Dr., 29304, pg. 637 — **PV**
Lockwood Greene Engineers, Inc., 1500 International Dr., 29304, pg. 633 — **IT**
Mahlo America Inc., P.O. Box 2825, 29304, pg. 830 — **IT**
MILLIKEN & COMPANY, Mailstop M-285, P.O. Box 1926, 29304, pg. 748 — **PV**
Milliken Fine Goods Div., P.O. Box 1926, 29304, pg. 748 — **PV**
Milliken Finished Apparel Div., P.O. Box 1926, 29304, pg. 748 — **PV**
Milliken Industrial Div., P.O. Box 1926, 29304, pg. 749 — **PV**
Milliken Interior Furnishings Div., P.O. Box 1926, 29304, pg. 749 — **PV**
PIEDMONT MECHANICAL, INC., 116 John Dodd Rd., 29303, pg. 865 — **PV**
PINNACLE COATING & CONVERTING, INC., 212 National Ave., 29303, pg. 866 — **PV**
Progress Lighting, P.O. Box 5704, 29304, pg. 1684 — **PV**
Prym-Dritz Corporation, 950 Brisack Rd., 29304, pg. 1499 — **IT**
Quincy Family Steak House, 203 E. Main St., 29301, pg. 23 — **PB**
Reeves Brothers, Inc., Highway 29 S., 29301, pg. 507 — **PV**
Reeves-Industrial Coated Fabrics Plant, Highway 29 South, 29301, pg. 507 — **PV**
Reeves International, Highway 29 S., 29301, pg. 507 — **PV**
Rexam Custom, P.O. Box 8429, 5670 N. Blackstock Rd., 29305-8429, pg. 1106 — **IT**
J.M. SMITH CORP., 450 Wofford St., 29301, pg. 1008 — **PV**
Smith Premium Services, 450 Wofford St., 29301, pg. 1008 — **PV**
Smith Wholesale Drug Div., 450 Wofford St., 29301, pg. 1008 — **PV**
Southern Fineblanking, P.O. Box 2748, 801 No. Main St.-Cowpens, 29304, pg. 737 — **IT**
SPARTAN MILLS, 805 Spartan Blvd., 29301, pg. 1020 — **PV**
Spartanburg Herald-Journal, 189 W. Main St., 29301, pg. 1175 — **PB**
Spartanburg Steel Products, P.O. Box 6428, 1290 New Cut Rd., 29304, pg. 300 — **PV**
Sulzer Ruti Inc., P.O. Box 5332, 29304, pg. 1307 — **IT**
SYNALLOY CORPORATION, P.O. Box 5627, 29304, pg. 1547 — **PB**
Thomas & Howard Co., P.O. Box 6250, 29304, pg. 1082 — **PV**
Transidyne General Corporation, 400 Herald Journal Park, 29303, pg. 1761 — **PB**
WABCO-Passenger Transit, P.O. Box 11, 29304, pg. 1761 — **PV**
Zima Corporation, I-85 at Zima Park, 29301, pg. 637 — **PV**

Summerville

Baker Material Handling Corp., 2450 W. 5th North St., 29484, pg. 810 — **IT**
CAPITAL IMAGING, 2745 W. 5th North St., 29483, pg. 206 — **PV**
GIANT CEMENT HOLDING INC., 320-D Midland Pkwy., 29485, pg. 741 — **PB**
HORIZON DISTRIBUTION INC., 1101 N. Main St., 29483, pg. 539 — **PV**
Syn Strand Inc., P.O. Box 2007, 215 Deming Way, 29484, pg. 1202 — **IT**
Westvaco Development Corp., P.O. Box 1990, 29484, pg. 1762 — **PB**
Williams Technologies, Inc., 211 Farmington Road, 29484-1548, pg. 1179 — **PV**

Sumter

Bosch Braking Systems-North America, Sumter Plant, Sumter Industrial Park, 29151, pg. 205 — **IT**
Crescent/Xcelite, Sumter Indus. Park, 29154, pg. 444 — **PV**
The National Bank of South Carolina, One Broad St., 29150, pg. 1549 — **PB**
Suburban Propane Group, Inc., 319 N. Main St., 29150, pg. 1436 — **PB**
Sumbank Life Insurance Co., 13 E. Canal St., 29150, pg. 1549 — **PB**
U.S. Broach & Machine Company, Bypass 378 Frontage Rd., P.O. Box 1649, 29150, pg. 102 — **IT**

Taylors

APAC/Ballenger Paving Company, Inc., 900 W. Lee Rd., 29687, pg. 139 — **PV**
Carotell Paper Board Corporation, Alexander Dr., 29687, pg. 303 — **PB**
South Carolina Steel, 113 E. Warehouse Ct., 29687, pg. 412 — **PB**
Staflex/Harotex, P.O. Box 1106, 29687, pg. 504 — **PV**

Timmonsville

Carolina Cut Sheets, Palmetto Industrial Pk., Hwy. 76, 29161, pg. 333 — **PB**

Travelers Rest

SWISS-M-TEX, L.P., 50 S. End Circle, 29690, pg. 1059 — **PV**
T & S BRASS & BRONZE WORKS, INC., Two Saddleback Cove, 29690, pg. 1061 — **PV**

Trenton

Menardi-Criswell, One Maxwell Drive, 29847, pg. 636 — **IT**
Salem Carpet Mills, Hwy. 19, 29847, pg. 1464 — **PB**

Union

CONSO PRODUCTS COMPANY, 513 N. Duncan Byp., 29379, pg. 434 — **PB**
Duraco Products Inc. of South Carolina, P.O. Box 867, Hwy. 9 Adamsburg, 29379, pg. 348 — **PV**
Paragon Plastics, Inc., Rice Ave. Extension, 29379, pg. 304 — **PB**

Walterboro

CCX Fiberglass Products, P.O. Box 1148, Industrial Area Rd., 29488, pg. 193 — **PV**

Ware Shoals

Mount Vernon Mills, Smith & Waters, Inc., Nation Rd., 29692, pg. 835 — **PV**

Wellford

Sybron Chemicals Inc., Highway 29A, 29385, pg. 1544 — **PB**

West Columbia

Capital Auto Auction Inc., I-26 at Exit 119, Frontage Rd., 29171, pg. 1648 — **PB**
Capital City Manufacturing Company, P.O. Box 1130, 29171, pg. 542 — **PV**
Charter Rivers Behavioral Health System, Inc., 2900 Sunset Blvd., 29169, pg. 1035 — **PB**
Digitron, 601 Center St., 29169-7219, pg. 333 — **PV**
Fairmont Tamper, P.O. Box 20, 2401 Edmund Rd., 29171-0020, pg. 793 — **PB**
LOXCREEN COMPANY, 1630 Old Dunbar Rd., 29169, pg. 679 — **PV**
SMI Joist South Carolina, 850 Taylor St., 29033, pg. 412 — **PB**
Southern Plastics Co., 2121 Old Dunbar Rd., 29172, pg. 233 — **IT**
Southern Post South Carolina, 1540 Pine Ridge Dr., 29172, pg. 413 — **PB**

Westminster

Eaton Corporation, U.S. Engine Valve Corporation, P.O. Box 277, Intersections 123 & 111, 29693, pg. 557 — **PB**
U.S. Engine Valve Corporation, P.O. Box 277, 29693, pg. 558 — **PB**

Williamston

THE JOURNAL, P.O. Box 369, 106 W. Main, 29697, pg. 601 — **PV**
Mount Vernon Mills, Inc., Williamston, P.O. Box 339, 29697, pg. 835 — **PV**

Williston

Dixie-Narco, Inc., Dixie-Narco Blvd., 29853, pg. 1065 — **PB**
Williston Manufacturing Co., Kelly St., 29853, pg. 542 — **PV**
Williston Telephone Co., Box 100, 15 West St., 29853, pg. 1572 — **PB**

Winnsboro

FAIRFIELD ELECTRIC COOPERATIVE, 3129 US Hwy. 321 N., 29180, pg. 391 — **PV**
The HON Co., Winnsboro Plant, N. Highway 321, 29180, pg. 772 — **PV**
The JPM Company of South Carolina, Inc., Route 321, 29180, pg. 919 — **PB**
Winnsboro Assembly Division, U.S. Rt. 321 & S.C. Rt. 269, 29180, pg. 1103 — **IT**

Woodruff

Mount Vernon Mills, Inc., Woodruff, P.O. Box 459, 29388, pg. 835 — **PV**

York

Ovako Ajax, Inc., P.O. Box 860, 500 Wallace Way, 29745, pg. 1157 — **IT**

SOUTH DAKOTA

Aberdeen

Aberdeen News Company, Box 4430, 124 S. Second, 57402, pg. 963 — **PB**
Hub City, Inc., 2914 Industrial Ave., 57402-1089, pg. 1371 — **PV**
THE RIVET GROUP L.L.C., 1910 Eighth Ave., N.E., 57401, pg. 934 — **PV**
Sheldahl, Inc. (Aberdeen), 715 North County 19, 57401, pg. 1465 — **PB**
Super 8 Motels, Inc., 1910 Eighth Ave., N.E., 57402-4090, pg. 322 — **PB**

Alcester

ALKOTA CLEANING SYSTEMS, INC., 110 Iowa St., 57001, pg. 34 — **PV**

Geographic Index-U.S.

Big Stone City

Big Stone Cheese Factory, P.O. Box 8, 57216,
pg. 1040 **PV**

Brandon

Allied Oil & Supply, Inc, 26043 478th Ave., I 90-Exit 402,
57005, pg. 39 **PV**

Britton

Britton Operation, E. Hwy. Ten, 57430, pg. 1465 **PB**

Brookings

DAKTRONICS, INC., 331 32nd Ave., 57006, pg. 478 **PB**
LARSON MANUFACTURING COMPANY, 2333 Eastbrook
Dr., 57006, pg. 652 **PV**
Piper Jaffray Inc., 518 Main Ave., 57006-0787,
pg. 1300 **PB**
Star Circuits, 405 Railroad St., 57006, pg. 478 **PB**

Canton

Bidwell Div., P.O. Box 97, 57013, pg. 279 **PB**

Colman

Sioux Valley Rural Television, P.O. Box 20, 57017,
pg. 1004 **PV**
**SIOUX VALLEY SOUTHWESTERN ELECTRIC
ASSOCIATION,** Junction Hwy. 34 & 77, 57017,
pg. 1004 **PV**
T & R ELECTRIC SUPPLY COMPANY, INC., P.O. Box
180, Hwy. 34 W., 57017, pg. 1061 **PV**

Deadwood

Gilt Edge Mine, Two Gilt Edge Rd., 57732, pg. 477 **PB**

Elk Point

CMI Load King Trailer Division, P.O. Box 427, 57025,
pg. 279 **PB**

Huron

Grant, Inc., 33 Third St. S.E., 57350, pg. 1201 **PB**
Lewis Drug Huron, 1950 Dakota Ave. S., 57350,
pg. 665 **PV**
Nekota Resources Inc., 33 Third St., 57350, pg. 1201 **PB**
Northwestern Energy Corp., 33 Third St., 57350,
pg. 1201 **PB**
Northwestern Networks, Inc., 33 Third St. S.E., 57350-1318,
pg. 1201 **PB**
NORTHWESTERN PUBLIC SERVICE, 33 Third St. S.E.,
57350-1318, pg. 1200 **PB**
Northwestern Systems, Inc., 33 Third St. S.E., 57350-1318,
pg. 1201 **PB**
Prostrollo Motor Sales, Inc., 500 4th St., N.E., 57350,
pg. 891 **PV**

Lead

Golden Reward Mine, Fantail Creek Rd., #141, 57754,
pg. 243 **IT**
Golden Reward Mine, Fantail Creek Rd., #141, 57754,
pg. 477 **PB**
Homestake Mine, P.O. Box 875, 630 E. Summit, 57754-
0875, pg. 833 **PB**
Wharf Mine, HC 37, Box 811, 57754-9710, pg. 243 **IT**
Wharf Resources Ltd., HC 37, 57754-9710, pg. 243 **IT**

Madison

EAST RIVER ELECTRIC COOPERATIVE, 121 S.E. First
St., 57042, pg. 357 **PV**
NEW APPLE LINES, INC., 212 S.W. Second St., 57042,
pg. 792 **PV**
PROSTROLLO MOTOR COMPANY, 1001 S. Washington
St., 57042, pg. 891 **PV**
ROSCO MANUFACTURING CO., 1001 S.W. First St.,
57042, pg. 944 **PV**

Milbank

Milbank Insurance Co., E. Hwy. 12, 57253, pg. 1131 **IT**

Mitchell

Piper Jaffray Inc., 102 W. Fifth Ave., 57301-1955,
pg. 1302 **PB**
RANDALL STORES, INC., 101 W. 23rd Ave., 57301,
pg. 909 **PV**
Toner Product Division, P.O. Box 70, 901 North Foster St.,
57301-0070, pg. 1405 **IT**

North Sioux City

GATEWAY 2000, 610 Gateway Dr., 57049-2000,
pg. 703 **PB**

Philip

Dakota Case Inc., 180 E. Hwy. 57567, pg. 636 **PV**
KROFAM INC., 180 E. Hwy. 14, 57567, pg. 636 **PV**
Scotchman Industries, Inc., 180 E. Hwy. 14, 57567,
pg. 636 **PV**

Pierre

Piper Jaffray Inc., 221 W. Capitol Ave., Ste. 101, 57501-
2408, pg. 1302 **PB**

Rapid City

BLACK HILLS CORPORATION, 625 Ninth St., 57709,
pg. 235 **PB**
Black Hills Power & Light Company, 625 Ninth St., 57709,
pg. 235 **PB**
BRINK ELECTRIC CONSTRUCTION COMPANY, 2950 N.
Plaza Dr., 57702, pg. 169 **PV**
Federal Beef Processors South, P.O. Box 2130, 1330 West
Chicago, 57709, pg. 435 **PV**
Gillette Dairy of the Black Hills, Inc., P.O. Box 2553, 1699
Sedivy Ln., 57705-2553, pg. 1152 **PB**
Hills Materials Co., P.O. Box 2320, 57709, pg. 806 **PV**
Hubbard Feeds, 426 Omaha St., 57701, pg. 1116 **IT**
Magnum Diamond, One Concourse, 57701, pg. 350 **PB**
MIDWEST TIRE & MUFFLER, INC., 4700 N. I-90 Service
Rd., 57701, pg. 745 **PV**
NORTHWESTERN ENGINEERING CO., P.O. Box 2320,
57709, pg. 806 **PV**
Piper Jaffray Inc., 726 St. Joseph St., 57701-2785,
pg. 1302 **PB**
Rapid City Journal, 507 Main St., 57701, pg. 984 **PB**
SODAK GAMING, INC., 5301 S. Hwy. 16, 57701,
pg. 1482 **PB**
Universal Transport, 3600 Universal Dr. 57702, 57709,
pg. 1424 **IT**
Western Production Company, 625 9th St., P.O. Box 1400,
57709, pg. 236 **PB**
Wyodak Resources Development Corp., 625 Ninth St.,
57709, pg. 236 **PB**

Salem

Feterl Mfg. Co., 411 Center Ave. W., P.O. Box 398, 57058,
pg. 1676 **PB**

Sioux Falls

Aerostar International, P.O. Box 5057, 57117-5057,
pg. 1361 **PB**
Building Products Inc. of S.D., 1500 Industrial, 57104,
pg. 180 **PV**
CCL Label, P.O. Box 5037, 1209 W. Bailey, 57117-5037,
pg. 238 **IT**
Charter Sioux Falls Behavioral Health System, Inc., 2812 S.
Louise Ave., 57106, pg. 1035 **PB**
Citibank (South Dakota), 701 E. 60th St. N., 57104,
pg. 377 **PB**
Dial Bank, 3201 N. Fourth Ave., 57104-0700, pg. 1202 **PB**
L.G. EVERIST INC., 300 S. Phillips Ave., Ste. 200, 57117-
5829, pg. 386 **PV**
Flow Control Division, P.O. Box 5707, 57117, pg. 1361 **PB**
Golden Sun Feeds, Inc., 101 S. Marion Rd., 50112,
pg. 895 **PV**
Green Tree Acceptance, Inc., P.O. Box 1465, 57101,
pg. 762 **PB**
Hutchinson Technology Inc., Sioux Falls, 3401 Fourth Ave.
N., 57104, pg. 851 **PB**
KSFY-TV, 300 No. Dakota Ave., 57102, pg. 912 **PV**
Land O'Lakes Inc., 1501 W. 10th St., 57104-3307,
pg. 646 **PV**
Lewis Drug Distribution Center, 3701 S. Western Ave.,
57105, pg. 665 **PV**
Lewis Drug Eastgate, 1301 E. 10th St., 57103, pg. 665 **PV**
LEWIS DRUG, INC., 2701 S. Minnesota Ave., Ste 1,
57105, pg. 665 **PV**
Lewis Drug Southeast, 4409 E. 26th St., 57103,
pg. 665 **PV**
Lewis Drug Southgate, 500 W. 41st St., 57105,
pg. 665 **PV**
Lewis Drug Westgate, 2700 W. 12th St., 57104,
pg. 665 **PV**
Lewis Drugs Southwest, 5500 W. 41st St., 57106,
pg. 665 **PV**
Midland National Life Insurance Co., One Midland Plaza,
57193, pg. 963 **PV**
MIDWEST COAST TRANSPORT L.P., 1600 E. Benson
Rd., 57104, pg. 744 **PV**
NSP-Sioux Falls Region, 500 W. Russell St., 57014,
pg. 1195 **PB**
Northwestern Growth Corp., 125 S. Dakota Ave., Ste. 1100,
57104, pg. 1201 **PB**
Norwest Agricultural Credit, Inc., 101 N. Phillips Ave.,
57117-6035, pg. 1201 **PB**
Norwest Bank South Dakota, N.A., P.O. Box 1028, 57117,
pg. 1203 **PB**
Piper Jaffray Inc., 201 S. Phillips Ave., 57102-0717,
pg. 1302 **PB**
RAVEN INDUSTRIES, INC., 205 E. Sixth St., 57104-5931,
pg. 1361 **PB**
SCHOENEMAN BROTHERS COMPANY, 305 E. Eighth St.,
57103-7022, pg. 972 **PV**
SENCORE, INC., 3200 Sencore Dr., 57107, pg. 983 **PV**
Sioux Falls Argus Leader, 200 S. Minnesota Ave., 57102,
pg. 701 **PB**

SIOUX FALLS CONSTRUCTION COMPANY, 800 S.
Seventh Ave., 57104, pg. 1003 **PV**
Starmark, Inc., 600 E. 48th St. N., 57104, pg. 1054 **PB**
Tel-Drug, Inc., 3101 S. Carolyn Ave., 57106, pg. 362 **PB**
Thompson Bros., Inc., 3605 Teem Dr., 57101, pg. 66 **PV**
Western Surety Company, 202 S. Phillips Ave., 57102,
pg. 303 **PB**

Spearfish

Paramount Technical Products, Inc., 2600 Paramount Dr.,
P.O. Box 1042, 57783, pg. 1357 **PB**

Sturgis

Dakota Farms Cheese, Inc., 2350 W. Main St., 57785,
pg. 646 **PV**

Watertown

BUILDING PRODUCTS INC., 405 First Ave., N.E., 57201,
pg. 180 **PV**
Faultless Nutting, 505 W. Airport Dr., 57201, pg. 473 **IT**
Simon-Telelect Inc., P.O. Box 1150, 600 Oakwood Rd.,
57201, pg. 1252 **IT**
Twin City Die Castings Co., 122 Cessna St. N.W., 57201,
pg. 1111 **PV**

Webster

DAKOTAH, INC., One N. Park Ln., 57274, pg. 477 **PB**

Winner

Grossenburg Concrete, HC 59 Box 1, 57580-7801,
pg. 483 **PV**
GROSSENBURG IMPLEMENTS, INCORPORATED, HC 59
Box 1, 57580-7801, pg. 483 **PV**

Yankton

Dale Electronics, Yankton Division, P.O. Box 180, East
Hwy. 50, 57078-0180, pg. 1722 **PB**
Gehl Power Products, Inc., 900 Ferdig Ave., 57078,
pg. 704 **PB**
Hastings Filters, 1901 Hastings Dr., 57078, pg. 382 **PB**
M-Tron Industries, Inc., 100 Douglas Ave., 57078,
pg. 1022 **PB**
Portec, Inc.-Construction Equipment Div., 700 W. 21st St.,
57078, pg. 1318 **PB**
The Yankton Printing Company, P.O. Box 56, 319 Walnut,
57078-0056, pg. 995 **PV**

TENNESSEE

Adamsville

Adamsville Telephone Co., P.O. Box 405, 38310,
pg. 329 **PB**
Aqua Glass Corp., P.O. Box 412, Industrial Park, 38310,
pg. 1053 **PB**
Tombigbee Transport Corporation, Industrial Park, 38310,
pg. 1053 **PB**

Alcoa

PDS Agency, Inc., 115 N. Calderwood St., 37701,
pg. 1334 **PB**
PROFFITT'S, INC., 115 N. Calderwood St., 37701,
pg. 1333 **PB**
Proffitt's Investment Inc., 115 N. Calderwood St., 37701,
pg. 1334 **PB**
Proffitt's of Tri-Cities, Inc., 115 N. Calderwood, 37701,
pg. 1334 **PB**
Tapoco, Inc., P.O. Box 9128, 37701, pg. 61 **PB**

Antioch

Bergen Brunswig Drug Company, 12980 Old Hickory Rd.,
37013, pg. 214 **PB**
Rohm Electronics, Eastern Sales Div., 3034 Owen Dr.,
Jackson Business Park, 37013, pg. 1125 **IT**

Arlington

Dow Corning Wright, 5677 Airline Rd., 38002-9501,
pg. 523 **PV**
WRIGHT MEDICAL TECHNOLOGY, 5677 Airline Rd.,
38002, pg. 1192 **PV**

Ashland City

Apcom Inc., Hwy. 49 South, 37015, pg. 1037 **PV**
STATE INDUSTRIES INC., 500 Bypass Rd., 37015,
pg. 1036 **PV**
Timco, Inc., 13 Bluegrass Dr., 37015, pg. 234 **PV**

Athens

Frigidaire Company Range Products, 202 Hicks, 37303,
pg. 439 **IT**
Heil Trailer International, P.O. Box 160, 37303, pg. 520 **PB**
Mayfield Dairy Farms Inc., P.O. Box 310, 806 E. Madison
Ave., 37303, pg. 490 **PB**
Textron Automotive Trim Operations, 2110 Charles C.
Redfern Dr., 37303, pg. 1590 **PB**

Bartlett

Smith & Nephew ENT, 2925 Appling Rd., 38135, pg. 1263   **IT**

Baxter

Leisure Life, Inc., P.O. Box 60, 215 Fourth Ave. N., 38544, pg. 34   **PB**

Bells

UNITED FOODS, INC., Ten Pictsweet Dr., 38006-0119, pg. 1677   **PB**

Blountville

Tri-City Bank and Trust Company, 3416 Hwy. 126, 37617-0277, pg. 642   **PB**

Brentwood

Alcoa Fujikura Ltd., 105 Westpark Dr., 37027, pg. 60   **PB**
Alcoa Fujikura Ltd., 105 Westpark Dr., 37027, pg. 525   **IT**
American Color Graphics, 100 Winners Circle, 37027, pg. 1132   **PB**
American Rehability Services, Inc., 111 Westwood Pl., Ste. 210, 37027, pg. 1257   **PB**
RAY BELL CONSTRUCTION CO. INC., 255 Wilson Pike Circle, 37027, pg. 131   **PV**
Berol Corporation, 105 West Park Dr., 370267, pg. 1178   **PB**
Boston Weatherhead Div., P.O. Box 1708, 37024-1708, pg. 479   **PB**
Brentwood Label Group, One Maryland Farms, 37027, pg. 1529   **IT**
Ceco Door Products, 750 Old Hickory Blvd., Ste. 150, 37027, pg. 1676   **PB**
COLUMBIA CORPORATION, Kingsport Bldg., 215 Centerview Dr., Ste. 255, 37027, pg. 255   **PV**
Comdata Corporation, 5301 Maryland Way, 37027, pg. 331   **PB**
Comdisco Healthcare and Scientific Group, Two Brentwood Commons, 750 Old Hickory Blvd., Ste. 150, 37027, pg. 408   **PB**
Community Health Systems, Inc., 155 Franklin Rd., Ste. 400, 37027-4660, pg. 419   **PV**
Crain Communications, Nashville, 104 E. Park Dr., Ste. 315, 37027-7504, pg. 285   **PV**
Crestar Food Products, Inc., 750 Old Hickory Blvd., Ste. 250, 37027, pg. 805   **PB**
Empire Berol U.S.A., 105 Westpark Dr., 37027, pg. 1178   **PB**
Fox Ridge Homes, 5115 Maryland Way, Ste. 300, pg. 1148   **PB**
Gabriel Ride Control Products Division HQ, 100 Westwood Pl., Ste. 300, 37027, pg. 137   **PB**
Gol-Pak Corp., 214 Overlook Ct., Ste. 105, 37027, pg. 278   **PB**
Healthsource Tennessee, Inc., 5409 Maryland Way, Ste. 200, 37027, pg. 360   **PB**
Hickory Specialties, Inc., 783 Old Hickory Blvd., 37027, pg. 596   **PB**
January & Associates, Inc., 5560 Franklin Pike Cir., 37027, pg. 287   **PV**
MANCHESTER TANK & EQUIPMENT COMPANY, 1749 Mallory Ln., Ste. 400, 37027, pg. 699   **PV**
Murray Export Sales B. V., P.O. Box 268, 37027, pg. 1397   **IT**
The Murray Ohio Mfg. Co., 219 Franklin Rd., 37027, pg. 1397   **IT**
Noranda Aluminium, 1 Brentwood Commons, Ste. 175, 750 Old Hickory Blvd., 37027, pg. 434   **IT**
Provident Music Group, One Maryland Farms, Ste. 200, 37027, pg. 1529   **PB**
QUORUM HEALTH GROUP, INC., 103 Continental Pl., 37027, pg. 1353   **PB**
Quorum Health Resources, Inc., 105 Continental Pl., 37027, pg. 1354   **PB**
REPUBLIC AUTOMOTIVE PARTS, INC., 500 Wilson Pike Cir., Ste. 115, 37024-2088, pg. 1377   **PB**
SMS-Nashville, Three Maryland Farms Blvd., 37027, pg. 1463   **PB**
Sanford Beroc Corp., 105 W. Park Dr., 37027, pg. 1178   **PB**
SERVICE MERCHANDISE COMPANY, INC., 7100 Service Merchandise Dr., 37027, pg. 1461   **PB**
The Shannon Group, 5214 Maryland Way, Ste. 300, 37027, pg. 1041   **PB**
STATE VOLUNTEER MUTUAL INSURANCE CO., 101 W. Park Dr., 37027, pg. 1037   **PV**
UCG Energy Corporation, 7106 Crossroads Blvd., Ste. 228, 37027, pg. 146   **PB**
United Cities Gas Company, 5300 Maryland Way, 37027, pg. 146   **PB**
United Clays, Inc., 7003 Chadwick Dr., Ste. 100, 37027, pg. 1487   **IT**
Vivra Health Advantage, Inc., 5310 Maryland Way #300, 37027, pg. 1724   **PB**
WINDY HILL PET FOOD CO., Highwood Plaza 11, 103 Powell Ct., Ste 200, 37027, pg. 1182   **PV**

Bristol

Affiliated Laboratories, 501-550 Fifth Ave., 37620, pg. 1264   **IT**
Aquamine, LLC, 247-A Vancetank Rd., 37620, pg. 1138   **PV**

Bristol Metals, L.P., P.O. Box 1589, 390 Bristol Metals Rd., 37620, pg. 1548   **PB**
Bristol Motor Speedway, P.O. Box 3966, 37625, pg. 1498   **PB**
Hewlett-Packard Company, 1816 Volunteer Pkwy., Ste. P, 37620, pg. 815   **IT**
SmithKline Beecham Laboratories, 501 Fifth St., 37620, pg. 1264   **IT**

Brownsville

First State Bank, Six N. Washington, 38012, pg. 1669   **PB**
Kleer-Vu, Kleer Vu Dr., 38012, pg. 962   **PV**
LASCO Fluid Distribution Products, 540 Lasco St., 38012, pg. 1398   **IT**

Bruceton

Tennessee Telephone Company, P.O. Box 155, 204 E. Broad St., 38317, pg. 1572   **PB**

Calhoun

Bowater Newsprint Division, 5020 Hwy. 11 S., 37309, pg. 248   **PB**

Caryville

A & S Building Systems, Inc., Hwy. 25 N., 37714, pg. 1146   **PB**

Centerville

NationsBank/Hickman County, 116 Church St., 37033, pg. 1163   **PB**

Chattanooga

ABB C-E Power Products Manufacturing, 911 W. Main St., 37402, pg. 3   **IT**
Accu-Cast, 1911 Crutchfield St., 37406, pg. 456   **PB**
Ahlstrom Filtration, Inc.-Chattanooga Mill, 105 W. 45th St., 37409, pg. 35   **PB**
Ahlstrom Filtration, Inc., Krystal Bldg., One Union Sq., Ste. 810, 37409, pg. 35   **PB**
Alco Chemical, 909 Mueller Dr., 37406, pg. 1435   **IT**
Allright Tenn. Inc., 737 Market St., Ste. 309, 37402, pg. 43   **PV**
American Institutional Foods, P.O. Box 367, 37401, pg. 6   **PV**
AMERICAN MANUFACTURING COMPANY, 3600 N. Hawthorne St., 37406, pg. 58   **PV**
AmeriSource-Chattanooga Div., 200 N. Holly St., 34704, pg. 97   **PB**
AmSouth Bank, 601 Market Ct., 37402, pg. 105   **PB**
ARCADE INC., 1815 E. Main St., 37404, pg. 79   **PV**
Astec Financial Services, Inc., 4101 Jerome Ave., 37407, pg. 141   **PB**
Astec, Inc., 4101 Jerome Ave., 37407, pg. 141   **PB**
ASTEC INDUSTRIES, INC., 4101 Jerome Ave., 37407, pg. 141   **PB**
Athens Paper Co., Inc., 2005 Amnicola Hwy., 37422, pg. 94   **PV**
Bergen Brunswig Medical Corporation, 2710 Amnicola Hwy., 37401, pg. 97   **PB**
Big River Grille & Brewery Works, 100 E. 10th St., Ste. 600, 37402, pg. 1396   **PV**
Brach & Brock Confections Inc., 4120 Jersey Pike, 37422, pg. 163   **PV**
Brooks, Montague & Associates, Inc., 603 James Bldg., 735 Broad St., 37402, pg. 1155   **PV**
Burner Systems International, Inc., 2806 E. 50th St., 37407, pg. 351   **PV**
BUSTER BROWN APPAREL, INC., 2001 Wheeler Ave., 37406, pg. 189   **PB**
CBL & ASSOCIATES PROPERTIES, INC., One Park Pl., 6148 Lee Hwy., 37421, pg. 273   **PB**
Cannon Equipment, 950 Riverside Dr., 37401, pg. 646   **IT**
Casting Materials Division, 3101 Alton Park Blvd., 37410-1014, pg. 525   **PB**
CAVALIER CORPORATION, 1105 E. Tenth St., 37403, pg. 220   **PB**
Chattanooga Cable T.V. Company, 2030 E. Polymer Dr., 37421, pg. 1447   **PV**
CHATTANOOGA CHOO-CHOO HOLIDAY INN, 1400 Market St., 37402, pg. 231   **PV**
Chattanooga Paperboard Corporation, 2100 Rossville Ave., 37408, pg. 303   **PB**
CHATTEM, INC., 1715 W. 38th St., 37409, pg. 341   **PB**
Chattem, Inc., Consumer Products Division, 1715 W. 38th St., 37409, pg. 341   **PB**
Commercial Metals Co., 400 E. 20th St., 37408, pg. 413   **PB**
Dillard, A ResourceNet International Company, 501 Cumberland St., 37404, pg. 902   **PV**
THE DIXIE GROUP, INC., 1100 S. Watkins St., 37404, pg. 514   **PB**
Dixie Industries, Inc., 3510 N. Orchard Knob Ave., 37406-7600, pg. 406   **PB**
DOUBLE-COLA CO.-USA, 3350 Broad St., 37408-3090, pg. 341   **PV**
Eclipse Combustion, Inc., P.O. Box 4808, 401 N. Market St., 37405, pg. 360   **PV**
Fillauer, Inc., 2710 Amnicola Hwy., 37406, pg. 214   **PB**
First American National Bank, 725 Broad St., 37402, pg. 624   **PB**
First Tennessee Bank - Chattanooga, 701 Market St., 37402-4886, pg. 639   **PB**

FROST COMPANY, 6830 Lee Highway, 37421, pg. 430   **PV**
Gibraltar Steel Corporation of Tennessee, 401 River Terminal Rd., 37406, pg. 742   **PB**
Heatec, Inc., 5200 Wilson Rd., 37410, pg. 141   **PB**
Heil Environmental Industries, Eastgate Ctr., 37414, pg. 520   **PB**
Hydro Conduit Corp, P.O. Box 23056, 3950 Cromwell Road, 37422, pg. 245   **IT**
ISS Southern Management Company, 951 Eastgate Loop, Ste. 1000, 37411, pg. 656   **IT**
KRYSTAL COMPANY, Krystal Bldg., One Union Sq., 37402, pg. 636   **PV**
Landmark Web Printing, Riverside Indusl Pk, Ste. J, 1548 Riverside Dr., 37406, pg. 648   **PV**
Mills & Lupton Supply Co., P.O. Box 1639, 749 E. 12th St., 37401, pg. 847   **PB**
OLAN MILLS, INC., 4325 Amnicola Hwy., 37406, pg. 749   **PV**
NA Industries, Inc., P.O. Box 5407, 2651 Riverport Rd., 37406, pg. 939   **IT**
National Posters, Inc., 1001 Latta St., 37406, pg. 786   **PV**
NATIONAL PRINT GROUP, INC., 2464 Amnicola Hwy., 37406, pg. 785   **PV**
NationsBank/Chattanooga, 633 Chestnut St., 37450, pg. 1163   **PB**
NORTH AMERICAN ROYALTIES, INC., 200 E. Eighth St., 37402, pg. 803   **PB**
Plant Engineering Consultants, 6135 Airways Blvd., 37421, pg. 1562   **PV**
PROVIDENT COMPANIES, INC., One Fountain Sq., 37402, pg. 1337   **PB**
Provident Life and Casualty Insurance Co., One Fountain Sq., 37402, pg. 1338   **PB**
Provident Life Capital Co., One Fountain Sq., 37402, pg. 1338   **PB**
Provident National Assurance Co., One Fountain Sq., 37402, pg. 1338   **PB**
Roadtec, Inc., 800 Manufacturers Rd., 37405, pg. 141   **PB**
SCT YARNS, INC., 1800 S. Watkins St., 37404, pg. 956   **PV**
Sandoz Consumer Pharmaceutical, P.O. Box 6339, 715 Market St., 37402-4806, pg. 974   **IT**
Seaboard Farms of Chattanooga, 414 W. 16th St., 37408-1001, pg. 1449   **PB**
SHERMAN & REILLY, INC., 400 W. 33rd St., 37410, pg. 993   **PV**
SIGNAL APPAREL COMPANY, INC., 200 Manufacturers Rd., 37405, pg. 1472   **PB**
Signal Knitwear, 200 Manufacturers Rd., 37405, pg. 1472   **PB**
Silverdale Facilities, 7609 Standifur Gap Rd., 37402, pg. 451   **PB**
Sisken Steel, 1901 River Front Pkwy., 37401, pg. 1375   **PB**
Spectra National, 1401 Godson Ave., 37406, pg. 786   **PV**
SunTrust Bank, Chattanooga, N.A., 736 Market St., 37402, pg. 1538   **PB**
Tencarva Machinery Co., Warehouse Two, Bay 10, 4295 Cromwell Rd., Suite 409, 37421-2172, pg. 1075   **PV**
Tennessee-American Water Co., 1101 Broad St., P.O. Box 6338, 37401, pg. 95   **PB**
TOP FLIGHT, INC., 1300 Central Ave., 37408-1515, pg. 1091   **PV**
UPB of Chattanooga, 835 Georgia Ave., 37402, pg. 1669   **PB**
WDEF AM/FM, 3300 Broad St., 37408, pg. 1078   **PB**
WDEF-TV, 3300 Broad St., 37408, pg. 1078   **PB**
Willis Corroon Corp. of Chattanooga, One Republic Centre, Ste. 1100, 633 Chestnut St., 37450, pg. 1505   **IT**
World Pacific Ullenberg Corp., 701 Cherokee Blvd., Ste. E, 37405, pg. 861   **PB**

Church Hill

Quebecor Printing Hawkins, P.O. Box 1967, Hwy. 11W S., 37642, pg. 1076   **IT**

Clarksville

Bosch Braking Systems-North America, Clarksville Plant, 780 Arcata Blvd., 37040, pg. 204   **IT**
Community Newspapers, 200 Commerce St., 37040, pg. 701   **PB**
Leaf-Chronicle Co., 200 Commerce St., 37040, pg. 699   **PB**
Precision Printing & Packaging, 801 Alfred Thun Rd., 37040-9373, pg. 115   **PB**
Quebecor Printing Clarksville, 451 Arcata Blvd., 37040, pg. 1076   **IT**
TileCera, Inc., 300 Arcata Blvd., 37040, pg. 1239   **IT**
Vulcan Corporation, P.O. Box 709, 1151 College St., 37041, pg. 1725   **PB**

Cleveland

American Uniform Co., 2180 N. Parker St. N.E., 37311, pg. 1039   **PV**
Cleveland Bank & Trust Company, 775 Raider Dr., pg. 639   **PB**
Cleveland Chair Company, 370 Ninth St. S.E., 37364, pg. 579   **PV**
Duracell USA TN Packaging, Tasso Rd., 37312, pg. 743   **PB**
HARDWICK CLOTHES INC., 3800 Old Tasso Rd., 37312, pg. 502   **PV**
Harrington & King, South, Inc., 3939 Michigan Ave., 37311, pg. 504   **PV**
Harrington & King South, Inc., 3939 Michigan Ave., 37311, pg. 504   **PV**
JACKSON FURNITURE INDUSTRIES, 1910 King Edward Ave., 37364, pg. 579   **PV**

Johnston Coca-Cola Bottling Group, Inc., Highway 64 Bypass, 37311, pg. 393   **PB**
Manufacturers Chemical LP, P.O. Box 2788, 4325 Old Tasso Rd., 37320-2788, pg. 1548   **PB**
Manufacturers Soap & Chemical Co., P.O. Box 2788, 37320-2788, pg. 1548   **PB**
Maytag Cleveland Cooking Products, P.O. Box 2790, 37320, pg. 1064   **PB**
Maytag Customer Service, 240 Edwards St. S.E., 37311, pg. 1064   **PB**
Newly Weds Foods, Inc., 187 Industrial Ln., S., 37311, pg. 797   **PV**
President Baking-Bishop Div., P.O. Box 3720, 37320, pg. 1069   **IT**
SCM Specialty Chemicals Inc., P.O. Box 2606, 37320-2606, pg. 594   **IT**
Schering-Plough Healthcare Products, P.O. Box 2850, 37320-2850, pg. 1438   **PB**
United Knitting, Inc., 310 Industrial Dr., 37311, pg. 538   **PB**
Zeneca Specialty Inks, 3730 Old Tasso Rd. NE, 37312, pg. 1525   **IT**

Clifton

South Central Correctional Center, Carroll Dr., 38425, pg. 451   **PB**

Clinton

Benton Plastics, Inc., 190 J.D. Yarnell Industrial Park Rd., 37716, pg. 537   **PB**
DH Compounding Co., P.O. Box 70, 37716, pg. 781   **PB**
Titan Tire Corporation of TN, 520 J.D. Yarnell, Industrial Pkwy., 37716, pg. 1618   **PB**

Collegedale

MCKEE FOODS CORPORATION, 10000 McKee Rd., 37315, pg. 723   **PV**
Sovex Natural Foods, P.O. Box 2178, 37315, pg. 723   **PV**

Collierville

THE ALPHA CORPORATION OF TENNESSEE, 175 Commerce Rd., 2nd Fl., 38017, pg. 44   **PV**
Alpha/Owens Corning LLC, P.O. Box 610, 38027-0610, pg. 45   **PV**
Chroma-Tek, 920 Hwy. 57 E., 38017, pg. 45   **PV**
Glasteel Industrial Laminates, 175 Commerce Rd., 38017, pg. 45   **PV**
Glasteel Tennessee, Inc., P.O. Box 521, 38017, pg. 45   **PV**
Therapy Management Associates, LLC, 165 N. Main St., Ste. 101, 38017, pg. 1642   **PB**

Columbia

American Bank Note Company, 711 Armstrong Ln., 38401, pg. 68   **PB**
Coca-Cola Bottling Works of Columbia, 1516 Nashville Hwy., 38401, pg. 392   **PB**
Columbia Specialties, Inc., Industrial Park- Rte. 4, 38401, pg. 615   **PB**
FIRST FARMERS & MERCHANTS NATIONAL BANK, 816 S. Garden St., 38401, pg. 407   **PV**
JRN, INC., 201 W. Seventh St., 38401, pg. 578   **PV**
Spontex, Inc., Santa Fe Pike, 38401, pg. 1409   **IT**
Wabash Fibre Box Co.-Columbia, 971 Greenlick Ct., 38401, pg. 1170   **PV**

Como

Como Grain Co., Hwy. 54, 38223, pg. 1145   **PV**

Cookeville

Dacco, Inc., P.O. Box 2789, 5 Dacco Dr., 38502, pg. 598   **PV**
Dixie Royal Homes, Inc., 38501, pg. 392   **PV**
First Tennessee Bank - Cookeville, 345 S. Jefferson Ave., 38501, pg. 639   **PB**
Fleetguard, Inc., Rte. 8, 38501, pg. 468   **PB**
Flowserve Corporation, Valve Div., 1978 Foreman Dr., 38501, pg. 658   **PB**
Harris Metals, 2315 Hilham Rd.-Highway 136, 38501, pg. 999   **PV**
Norwalk Furniture Corporation of Tennessee, P.O. Box 2370, Burgess Falls Rd., 38502-2370, pg. 808   **PV**
TRW Vehicle Safety Systems Inc., 1400 Old Salem Rd., 38502-3027, pg. 1559   **IT**
TUTCO, 500 Gould Dr., 38501, pg. 1268   **IT**
UPB of the Cumberlands, Ten W. Broad St., 38501, pg. 1669   **PB**
Volunteer Tool & Die, 1010 Volunteer Dr., 38501, pg. 1037   **PV**

Cordova

Blazer Financial Services, 8001 Centerview Pkwy., 38018, pg. 1741   **PB**
ICI Acrylics Inc., 7275 Goodlets Farm Pkwy., 38018, pg. 663   **IT**
Jimmy Dean Foods, 8000 Centerview Pkwy., Ste. 400, 38018, pg. 1433   **PB**
Sara Lee Meats, 8000 Centerview Pkwy., Ste. 300, 38018, pg. 1434   **PB**
SmithKline Beecham Pharmaceuticals, 65 Germantown Ct. Ste. 217, 38018-4245, pg. 1264   **IT**

Tabuchi Electric Company of America, 65 Germantown Rd., Ste. 107, 38018, pg. 1346   **PB**
UNION PLANTERS CORPORATION, 7130 Goodlett Farm Pkwy., 38018, pg. 1668   **PB**

Cornersville

Tennessee Telephone Company, P.O. Box 7, 37407, pg. 1572   **PB**

Counce

Tennessee River Pulp & Paper Co., P.O. Box 33, 38326, pg. 1579   **PB**

Covington

TURNER HOLDING LLC, 653 Turner Ln., 38019, pg. 1109   **PV**

Crossville

Crossville Ceramics Company, P.O. Box 1168, 38557, pg. 297   **PV**
Elixir Industries, Cumberland County Indus. Park, P.O. Box 628, 38557, pg. 371   **PV**
First National Bank of Crossville, 812 N. Main St., 38555, pg. 1669   **PB**
Turner, Day & Woolworth Handle Corp., 205 N. Webb Ave., 38555, pg. 669   **PV**

Dandridge

Bush Brothers & Company Plant, 3885 Hwy. 411, 37725, pg. 189   **PV**
First Tennessee Bank - Dandridge, Hwy. 2570, 37725, pg. 639   **PB**

Dayton

La-Z-Boy Tennessee, Walnut Grove Rd., 37321, pg. 973   **PB**
POLYLOOM CORP. OF AMERICA, 1131 Broadway, 37321, pg. 875   **PV**

Dickson

Premdor Entry Systems, One Premdor Dr., 37055, pg. 1067   **IT**
Quebecor Printing Dickson Inc., P.O. Box 686, 1665 Old Columbia Rd., 37055, pg. 1076   **IT**
Quebecor Printing Dickson Inc., P.O. Box 686, Colesburg Rd., 37055, pg. 1078   **IT**
Teksid Aluminum Foundry, R.R. 7, Box 319, 37055, pg. 483   **IT**
TENNSCO CORPORATION, 201 Tennsco Dr., 37055, pg. 1077   **PV**

Dresden

American West Trading Co., 100 Hilcrest, 38225, pg. 1073   **PB**
Ringier America, Dresden Division, 273 Evergreen, 38225, pg. 1778   **PB**

Dunlap

Dunlap Division, P.O. Box 1329, 37327, pg. 1565   **PB**

Dyer

Dyer Grain Co., Hwy. 45, 38330, pg. 1145   **PV**

Dyersburg

Bekaert Corporation, P.O. Box 1407, One Bekaert Rd., Industrial Park, 38024, pg. 184   **IT**
Centex Forcum-Lannom, Inc., 350 Jere Ford Hwy., 38024, pg. 224   **PB**
Dyer-Lauderdale Farmers Co-op, P.O. Box 550, 38024, pg. 1076   **PV**
DYERSBURG CORPORATION, 1315 Phillips St., 38024, pg. 538   **PB**
Dyersburg Fabric, 1315 E. Phillips St., 38024, pg. 538   **PB**
Electric Research and Manufacturing Cooperative, Inc. (ERMCO), 2225 Industrial Rd., 38024, pg. 82   **PB**
Firestone Industrial Products Company-Dyersburg, 1901 Sylvan Rd., 38024, pg. 214   **IT**
First Tennessee Bank - Dyersburg, 205 N. Main, 38024, pg. 639   **PB**
M.A. Hanna Rubber Compounding, 150 So. Connell Ave., 38024, pg. 781   **PB**
HECKETHORN MFG. COMPANY, INC., 2005 Forrest St., 38024, pg. 519   **PV**

Elizabethton

Elizabeth on Twins Baseball Club, Holly Ln., 37643, pg. 751   **PV**
General Shale Products Corp., P.O. Box 608, 37644, pg. 843   **IT**
J.W. Window Components, Inc., 386 Hwy. 91, 37643, pg. 1736   **IT**

Erin

ITW Southern Gage Co., P.O. Box 509, Midway Dr., 37061, pg. 867   **PB**
Southern Gage Inc., 49 Midway Dr., 37061, pg. 45   **PV**
UPB of North Central Tennessee, 100 Main St., 37061, pg. 1669   **PB**

Erwin

NN BALL & ROLLER, INC., 800 Tennessee Rd., 37650, pg. 1146   **PB**

Fairview

France Div., 726 Fairview Blvd., 37062, pg. 217   **PB**

Fayetteville

Copperweld Bimetallics Products Co., P.O. Box 70, 254 Cotton Mill Rd., 37334, pg. 662   **IT**
Copperweld Fayetteville Division, P.O. Box 70, 254 Cotton Mill Rd., 37334, pg. 662   **IT**
HAROLD MOORE & ASSOCIATES, INC., 1798 Wilson Pkwy., 37334, pg. 759   **PV**

Franklin

CPS Corporation, 1715 Columbia Hwy., 37065, pg. 422   **PV**
First Tennessee Bank - Franklin, 236 Public Sq., 37064, pg. 639   **PB**
Georgia/Durango Boot Company, 1810 Columbia Hwy., 37064, pg. 1684   **PB**
INTERNATIONAL COMFORT PRODUCTS, 501 Corporate Drive, Suite 200, 37064, pg. 898   **PB**
TOM JAMES COMPANY, 263 Seaboard Ln., 37067, pg. 580   **PV**
JAMISON BEDDING, INC., 238 Bedford Way, 37064, pg. 581   **PV**
MCKINNON BRIDGE CO., 205 Eddy Ln., 37064, pg. 723   **PV**
Southern Services Inc., W. Harpeth Rd., 37064, pg. 1286   **IT**
Sumiden Wire Products Corp., 710 Marshall Stuart Dr., 37055, pg. 1313   **IT**
United Cities Gas Co., IL/TN/MO Div., 377 Riverside Dr., Ste. 300, 37064, pg. 146   **PB**
John Wieland Homes of Tenessee, Inc., 128 Holiday Court, Ste. 110, 37064, pg. 1175   **PV**

Gainesboro

Nielsen, 122267 N. Grundy Quarles Hwy., 38562, pg. 460   **IT**

Gallatin

AlliedSignal-Jidosha Kiki Corporation, 801 Industrial Dr., 37066, pg. 51   **PB**
Bosch Braking Systems-North America, Gallatin Plant, 375 Belvedere Dr., 37066, pg. 204   **IT**
Byron's, Inc., 349 W. Main St., 37066, pg. 928   **PV**
First Tennessee Bank - Gallatin, 668 Nashville Pike, 37066, pg. 639   **PB**
Fleetwood Homes of Tennessee, Inc./Westmoreland Plant/ Pleasant Grove, P.O. Box 1139, Airport Rd., 37066, pg. 651   **PB**
GF OFFICE FURNITURE LTD., 525 Steam Plant Rd., 37066, pg. 434   **PV**
Hoeganaes Corp., P.O. Box 1276, 37066, pg. 893   **PB**
Linatex Corporation of America, P.O. Box 889, 1550 Airport Rd., 37066, pg. 599   **IT**

Germantown

Borden Foods, Inc., 2195 Germantown Rd. South, Ste. 100, 38138, pg. 158   **PV**
EZON PRODUCTS, INC., 1900 Exeter Rd., 38138, pg. 388   **PV**
Intergraph Corporation, 2593 Cedarville Dr., 38138-6009, pg. 890   **PB**
SCHILLING COMPANIES, INC., 7516 Enterprise, Ste. 2, 38138, pg. 970   **PV**
Schilling Motors, Inc., 7516 Enterprise, Ste. 2, 38138, pg. 970   **PV**
Timber Products Co., 3059 Forest Hill Rd., 38138, pg. 1086   **PV**

Goodlettsville

Anchor Wire Corporation of Tennessee, 425 Church St., 37072, pg. 1590   **PB**
Bank of Goodlettsville, 112 Long Hollow Pike, 37072, pg. 1669   **PB**
Liberty Financial Services, 907 Two Mile Pkwy., Ste. D-7, 37072, pg. 173   **PV**
Malone & Hyde, Inc.-Goodlettsville, 500 S. Cartwright St., 37072, pg. 653   **PB**

Greenback

Pyron Metal Powders, Inc., 6621 Hwy. 441 S., 37742-2158, pg. 1524   **IT**

PB - *U.S. Public Companies Volume*
PV - *U.S. Private Companies Volume*
IT - *International Public & Private Companies Volume*

Greenbrier

Atwood Mobile Products, P.O. Box R, 6320 Kelly Willis Rd., 37073, pg. 598 **PB**

Greeneville

Bundy Corporation, Greenville Plant, 455 T. Elmer Cox Dr., 37743, pg. 1340 **IT**

Chardon Electrical Components, Inc., P.O. Box 638, 37744, pg. 229 **PV**

John Deere Power Products, Inc., Rte 3, Box 45, 37743, pg. 492 **PB**

Doehler-Jarvis, Greenville Inc., Rufe Taylor Rd., 37743, pg. 796 **PB**

First Tennessee Bank - Greeneville, 206 N. Main St., 37743, pg. 639 **PB**

Greeneville Metal Manufacturing, Inc., 711 Campbell Dr., 37743, pg. 1180 **PB**

Hurd Locks, 603 Bohannon Ave., P.O. Box 1450, 37744, pg. 102 **PV**

MECO CORPORATION, 1500 Industrial Rd., 37745, pg. 726 **PV**

Naturalle Springs, Inc., 1616 Industrial Rd., pg. 106 **PV**

Zinc Products Company, 2500 Old Stage Rd., 37743-8950, pg. 57 **PB**

Halls

URS Greiner, Inc., P.O. Box 66, 38040-0066, pg. 1658 **PB**

Harriman

Bayou Steel Corporation (Tennessee), 2404 S. Roane St., 37748, pg. 197 **PB**

Harriman Record, P.O. Box 261, 510 Devonia St., 37748, pg. 648 **PV**

UPB of the Tennessee Valley, 200 Roane St., 37746, pg. 1669 **PB**

Hartsville

GENERAL SPRING, INC., 245 Warehouse Ln., 37074-0176, pg. 445 **PV**

Hendersonville

Globe Business Furniture, Inc., 90 Volunteer Dr., 37075, pg. 512 **PV**

Green Tree Acceptance, Inc., 181 E. Main, 37075, pg. 762 **PB**

ITW Dynatec, 31 Volunteer Dr., 37075, pg. 867 **PB**

SHOLODGE, INC., 130 Maple Dr., N., 37075, pg. 1467 **PB**

Henry

Atlantic Homes Div., P.O. Box 100, 38231, pg. 332 **PB**

Mark I Molded Plastics of Tennessee, Inc., Cardinal Ave., 38231, pg. 599 **PB**

Hillsboro

General Shale Products Corp.-Cumberland Mountain Sand Div., P.O. Box 99, 37342, pg. 844 **IT**

Hixson

CHATTANOOGA GROUP, INC., 4717 Adams Rd., 37343, pg. 231 **PV**

Hohenwald

First Citizens Bank of Hohenwald, P.O. Box 2207, 10 East Main St., 38462, pg. 1669 **PB**

Humboldt

Union Planters Bank of West Tennessee, 1214 Main St., 38343, pg. 1669 **PB**

Wilson Sporting Goods Co., 2330 Ultra Dr., 38343, pg. 73 **IT**

Jackson

ADM Milling Co., P.O. Box 609, 38302, pg. 128 **PB**

Coca-Cola Bottling Co. of Jackson, Inc., 2650 N. Parkway E., 38301, pg. 391 **PB**

Enco-Jackson, 3836 Highway 45 N., 38305, pg. 375 **PV**

First American National Bank, Main St. at Highland Ave., 38301, pg. 624 **PB**

First Tennessee Bank - Jackson, 110 W. Baltimore, 38301, pg. 639 **PB**

ITW Finishing Systems & Products, 99 Whalley, 38301, pg. 866 **PB**

Jackson Sun, Inc., 245 W. Lafayette, 38301, pg. 701 **PB**

Maytag/Jackson Dishwashing Products, 2500 Dr. F.E. Wright Rd., 38302-0700, pg. 1064 **PB**

Porter-Cable Corporation, P.O. Box 2468, 38302-2468, pg. 1274 **PB**

Tri-State Mack Inc., 2560 Hollywood Dr., 38305, pg. 1101 **PV**

UPB of Jackson, 118 Liberty, 38301, pg. 1669 **PB**

Volunteer Bank, 301 E. Main St., 38301, pg. 176 **PB**

Johnson City

Alemite Div., Rte. 9, P.O. Box 104AA, Roweland Dr., 37601, pg. 127 **IT**

American Water Heat Group, 500 Princeton Rd., 37601, pg. 1287 **PB**

AmeriSource-Johnson City Div., 410 Princeton Rd., 37601, pg. 97 **PB**

Denise Lingerie, 717 Rowland Dr., 37601, pg. 542 **PV**

Dentsply Tulsa, 3111 Hanover Rd., 37604, pg. 499 **PB**

Enco-Johnson City Division, 2704 S. Roan St., 37601, pg. 375 **PV**

First Tennessee Bank - Johnson City, 1919 N. Roan St., 37601, pg. 639 **PB**

Fleming Foods of Tennessee, Inc., 3000 Buffalo St., 37601, pg. 653 **PB**

FREE SERVICE TIRE COMPANY, INC., 126 Buffalo St., 37601, pg. 425 **PV**

General Shale Products Corp., 3211 N. Roan St., 37602, pg. 843 **IT**

Gordon's Inc., 815 Love St., 37601, pg. 688 **PV**

HAMPTON PRINT WORKS, INC., 2212 Buffalo Rd., 37604, pg. 498 **PV**

LAND-O-SUN DAIRIES, INC., 2900 Bristol Hwy., 37601, pg. 646 **PV**

Marley Plastics Holdings (USA) Inc., 3211 N. Roam St., P.O. Box 3547 CRS, 37602, pg. 843 **IT**

Marley Roof Tiles Holdings (U.S.A.) Inc., 3211 N. Roan St., 37602, pg. 844 **IT**

Marley (U.S.A.) Holding Corporation, 3211 N. Roan St., 37602, pg. 843 **IT**

NationsBank/Tri-Cities, P.O. Box 1818, 37606, pg. 1163 **PB**

SunTrust Bank, Northeast Tennessee, 207 Mockingbird Lane, 37605, pg. 1538 **PB**

Superior Industries-Johnson City, 655 Woodlyn Rd., 37605, pg. 1539 **PB**

Tencarva Machinery Co., 2831 E. Oakland Ave., 37602, pg. 1076 **PV**

United Cities Gas Co., VA/ETN Div., P.O. Box 60, 108 W. 10th Ave., 37601, pg. 146 **PB**

WJHL-TV, 338 E. Main St., 37601, pg. 1078 **PB**

Kenton

Kenton Grain Co., 405 Maple Heights, 38233, pg. 1145 **PV**

Wade Gin Co., 105 E. Taylor St., 38233, pg. 1146 **PV**

Wade Land Co., 405 Maple Heights, 38233, pg. 1146 **PV**

TOM WADE CO., 201 E. Church, 38233, pg. 1145 **PV**

Kingsport

AFG Industries, Inc., P.O. Box 929, 37662, pg. 84 **IT**

CDI Engineering Group, Inc., 1905 American Way, 37660, pg. 277 **PB**

Donihe Graphics, 766 Brookside Dr., 37660, pg. 333 **PB**

EASTMAN CHEMICAL COMPANY, P.O. Box 431, 37662, pg. 550 **PB**

Equitable Resources Exploration Division, Two Executive Park Pl., 1989 E. Stone Dr., 37660, pg. 589 **PB**

First American National Bank, 415 Broad St., 37662, pg. 624 **PB**

First Tennessee Bank - Kingsport/Bristol, 235 E. Center St., 37660, pg. 639 **PB**

General Shale Products Corp., P.O. Box 448, 37662, pg. 843 **PB**

Heritage National Healthplan of Tennessee, Inc., 2578 E. Stone Dr., Ste. A, 37660, pg. 492 **PB**

Penn Virginia Oil & Gas Company, 999 Executive Park Blvd., Ste. 300, 37660, pg. 1271 **PB**

Quebecor Printing Kingsport Inc., P.O. Box 711, Press & Roller Sts., 37662, pg. 1076 **IT**

Quebecor Printing Sherwood, P.O. Box 3948, 2400 Sherwood Rd., 37664, pg. 1076 **IT**

Tri-State Concrete Products Co., Inc., Hwy. 11 W., 37665, pg. 843 **IT**

Kingston

Professional Loss Control, P.O. Box 585, 37763, pg. 795 **PB**

Profit Management Corp., I-40 at Gallaher Rd., 37763, pg. 393 **PV**

Roane County News, P.O. Box 610, 204 Franklin St., 37763, pg. 648 **PV**

Kingston Springs

Mid Packaging Group, Inc., 167 Luyben Hills Rd., 37082, pg. 304 **PB**

Knoxville

ABB Environmental Systems (ABBES), 1400 Centerpoint Blvd., 37932-1966, pg. 4 **IT**

Alcoa Recycling Co., 1100 Riverview Tower, 900 S. Gay St., 37902, pg. 61 **PB**

Allen & Hoshall, 9950 Kingston Pk., 37922, pg. 36 **PV**

American Limestone Co., 2209 Blount Ave., 37901, pg. 138 **PB**

Appalachian Realty Co., P.O. Box 238, 37901, pg. 493 **PV**

Athens Distributing Co., Inc., 4420 A Middlebrook Pike, 37921, pg. 94 **PV**

AZTEX ENTERPRISES, 5222 Middlebrook Pike, 37921, pg. 104 **PV**

Bendix Atlantic Inflater Co., 1601 Mid Park Rd., 37921-5919, pg. 51 **PB**

BIKE ATHLETIC CO., 2801 Red Dog Dr., 37914, pg. 143 **PV**

Blue Ridge Printing, 1485 Amhurst Rd., 37909, pg. 333 **PV**

Browning-Ferris Industries of Tennessee, Inc., P.O. Box 272, 37901, pg. 264 **PB**

BUSH BROTHERS & COMPANY, P.O. Box 52330, 37950, pg. 189 **PV**

CMH Homes, Inc., P.O. Box 15169, 37901, pg. 383 **PB**

CMH Manufacturing, Inc., P.O. Box 15169, 37901, pg. 383 **PB**

CMH Parks, Inc., P.O. Box 15169, 37901, pg. 383 **PB**

CSI Services, 835 Innovation Dr., 37932, pg. 573 **PB**

CLAYTON HOMES, INC., 623 Market St., 37902, pg. 382 **PB**

Computational Systems Inc., 835 Innovation Dr., 37932, pg. 572 **PV**

ConAgra Feed Ingredient, P.O. Box 671, 37901, pg. 426 **PB**

Concord Telephone Exchange, P.O. Box 22610, 37933-0610, pg. 1571 **PV**

Dillard, A ResourceNet International Company, 5900 Middlebrook N.W., 37950, pg. 902 **PV**

East Tennessee Natural Gas Co., P.O. Box 10245, 1575 Downtown W. Blvd., 37919, pg. 567 **PB**

Enco-Knoxville, 4615 Coster Rd., 37912, pg. 375 **PV**

Ennis Business Forms Tenn Inc., 4214 Greenway Rd., 37918-2109, pg. 583 **PB**

Ever-Tite Coupling Products, 5320 S. National Dr., 37914, pg. 762 **PV**

Fairfield Purchasing & Design, Inc., W. 40 Trade Ctr., 207 Center Park Dr., 37922, pg. 611 **PB**

Fidelity National Title Insurance Company of Tennessee, 408 Cedar Bluff Rd., Ste. 140, 37923, pg. 621 **PB**

First American National Bank, P.O. Box 511, 505 S. Gay St., 37901, pg. 624 **PB**

First Tennessee Bank - Knoxville, 800 Gay St., 37901, pg. 639 **PB**

First Vantage-Tennessee, P.O. Box 200, 620 Market St., 37901-0200, pg. 641 **PB**

General Shale Products Corp., 1740 Riverside Dr., 37915, pg. 843 **IT**

GOODY'S FAMILY CLOTHING, INC., 400 Goody's Ln., 37922, pg. 753 **PB**

Stephen Gould of Tennessee, Inc., Southern Sta. Bldg., Ste. 104, 182A Market Place Blvd., 37922, pg. 468 **PV**

Growth Management Corp., 4300 Rutledge Pike, 37914, pg. 392 **PV**

THE H.T. HACKNEY CO., 502 S. Gay St., 37901, pg. 493 **PV**

Hackney Petroleum, Inc., P.O. Box 238, 37901, pg. 493 **PV**

Heritage National Healthplan of Tennessee, Inc., Executive Tower I, 408 N. Cedar Bluff, Ste. 400, 37909, pg. 492 **PV**

Hewlett-Packard Company, One Energy Ctr., Ste. 200, 725 Pellissippi Pkwy., 37932, pg. 815 **PV**

Home & Garden Television, 9701 Madison Ave., 37932, pg. 1447 **PB**

House-Hasson Hardware Co., 3125 Water Plant Rd., 37914, pg. 335 **PV**

IT Corp., 312 Directors Dr., 37923, pg. 908 **PB**

Innco Management Corp., 8167 Kingston Pike, 37919, pg. 392 **PV**

J & S Leasing Inc., 1810 Ailor Ave., 37921, pg. 1155 **PB**

KELSO OIL COMPANY, 641 Atlantic Ave., 37912, pg. 1155 **PV**

Kenesaw Leasing Inc., 900 S. Gay St., 37902, pg. 1155 **PB**

Kern's Bakeries, Incorporated, 2110 Chapman Hwy., 37920, pg. 547 **PB**

Knox Allright, Inc., 517 W. Clinch Ave., 37901, pg. 43 **PB**

Knox Porcelain Corp., 2706 Mynders Ave., 37921, pg. 308 **PV**

Knoxville News-Sentinel Company, 208 W. Church Ave., 37950-9038, pg. 1448 **PB**

KNOXVILLE UTILITIES BOARD, 626 Gay St., S.W., 37902, pg. 627 **PV**

LAY'S FINE FOODS, 400 E. Jackson Ave., 37905, pg. 655 **PV**

Midsouth Machine & Service Company, 3001 Alcoa Hwy., 37920, pg. 1726 **PB**

NBC Bank, FSB (Knoxville), 9040 Executive Park Dr., 37916, pg. 1155 **PB**

Philips Consumer Electronics, One Philips Dr., 37914-1810, pg. 1054 **IT**

PILOT CORPORATION, 5508 Lonas Rd., 37909, pg. 865 **PV**

Pilot Receivables Corporation, 7401 Kingston Pike, 37919, pg. 865 **PV**

PLASTI-LINE, INC., P.O. Box 59043, 37950-9043, pg. 1308 **PB**

Precision Disc Corp., 5055 S. National Dr., 37914, pg. 803 **PV**

Pride Oil Co., Inc., 5414 Clinton Hwy., 37912, pg. 613 **PV**

REGAL CINEMAS INC., 7132 Commercial Park Dr., 37918, pg. 1371 **PB**

Reily Foods & Co., 3434 Mynatt Ave., NW, 37919, pg. 919 **PV**

Rentenbach Constructors Incorporated, 2400 Sutherland Ave., 37919, pg. 923 **PV**

RENTENBACH ENGINEERING COMPANY, 2400 Sutherland Ave., 37919, pg. 923 **PV**

Robertshaw Tennessee, 2318 Kingston Pike, 37901-0400, pg. 1243 **IT**

Screen Art, 1801 Mid Park Dr., 37921, pg. 1486 **PB**

Scripps Howard Cable T.V. Company, 614 N. Central Ave., 37917, pg. 1448 **PB**

Sea Ray, 2600 Sea Ray Blvd., 37914, pg. 266 **PB**

Silver Furniture Co., Inc., 2742 Hancock St., 37917, pg. 352 **PB**

Geographic Index-U.S.

Geographic Index-U.S.

STAR SALES CO., INC., 1803 N. Central, 37917, pg. 1035   PV
SunTrust Bank, East Tennessee, N.A., 700 East Hills Ave., 37915, pg. 1538   PB
Tank Service, Inc., P.O. Box 3386, 37917, pg. 521   PB
Tencarva Machinery Co., 3508 Overlook Circle, 37919, pg. 1075   PV
Tennessee Telephone Company, 7407 Andersonville Pike, 37938, pg. 1572   PB
Tennessee Tubebending Inc., 5320 S. National Dr., 37914, pg. 762   PV
TENNESSEE VALLEY AUTHORITY, 400 W. Summit Hill Dr., 37902-1499, pg. 1580   PB
WM. S. TRIMBLE COMPANY, INC., 2200 Atchley St., 37920, pg. 1103   PV
UPB of East Tennessee, 900 Gay St., 37902, pg. 1669   PB
Valmet Inc.- Enerdy Division, 2200 Sutherland Ave., Ste. B-201, 37919, pg. 1448   IT
Vanderbilt Mortgage & Finance, Inc., P.O. Box 15169, 37901, pg. 383   PB
Volunteer Fabricators, Inc., P.O. Box 238, 37901, pg. 493   PV
Vulcan Materials Company-Midsouth Div., 3001 Alcoa Hwy., 37920, pg. 1726   PB
WBIR, Inc., 1513 Hutchinson Ave., 37917, pg. 702   PB
WMYU-FM, 8419 Kingston Pike, 37919, pg. 923   PB
Whittle Communications L.P., 333 Main Ave., 37902, pg. 1614   PB
Willis Corroon Corp. of Knoxville, 6322 Deane Hill Dr., 37939-2820, pg. 1506   IT
Zellerbach Division, 2821 N. Central St., 37917, pg. 1075   PB
Zellweger Uster, Inc., 456 Troy Cir., 37919, pg. 618   IT

La Vergne

Ammco Tools, Inc., 1601 J.P. Hennessy Dr., 37086, pg. 480   PB
Bergen Brunswig Medical Corporation, 1135 Heil Quaker Blvd., Ste. 200, 37086, pg. 214   PB
Bridgestone/Firestone Tire Manufacturing Operations-Lavergne, I-24 & Waldron Rd., 37086, pg. 213   IT
CORD Logistics, 1135 Heil Quaker Blvd., Ste. 100, 37086, pg. 304   PB
Hennessy/Coats Division, 1601 J.P. Hennessy Dr., 37086, pg. 481   PB
Hennessy Industries, Inc., 1601 J.P. Hennessy Dr., 37086, pg. 481   PB
Ingram Library Services, Inc., 1125 Heil Quaker Blvd., 37086, pg. 563   PV
Ingram Merchandising Service Inc., 1125 Heil Quaker Blvd., 37086, pg. 563   PV
Ingram Periodicals Inc., 1117 Heil Quaker Blvd., 37086-7000, pg. 563   PV
Kex Products, Inc., P.O. Box 600, 1435 Heil Quaker Blvd., 37086, pg. 138   PV
Perfect Equipment Corp., 1435 Heil Quaker Blvd., Box 600, 37086, pg. 138   PV
Publisher Resources Inc., 1125 Heil Quaker Blvd., 37086, pg. 563   PV
Tennessee Book Company, 1109 Heil Quaker Blvd., 37086-9962, pg. 563   PV
TENNESSEE FARMERS CO-OP, 200 Waldron Rd., 37086, pg. 1076   PV
Tennessee Telephone Company, P.O. Box 100, 37086-0100, pg. 1572   PB

Lafayette

Lafayette Manufacturing, 915 Red Boiling Springs Rd., 37083, pg. 957   PB

Lawrenceburg

Excel of Tennessee, 2200 Helton Dr., 38464, pg. 598   PB
The Murray Ohio Mfg. Co., Hannon Dr., 38464, pg. 1397   IT
Tridon Inc., 101 Motivation Dr., 38464-7371, pg. 11   PB

Lebanon

Commercial Steering Division, P.O. Box 250, 37088-0250, pg. 1558   PB
CRACKER BARREL OLD COUNTRY STORE, INC., Hartmann Dr., 37088-0787, pg. 455   PB
First Tennessee Bank - Lebanon, 249 W. Main St., 37087, pg. 639   PB
Hartmann Luggage & Leather Goods Group, 1301 Hartmann Dr., 37087, pg. 261   PB
Kenneth O. Lester, Inc., 216 Hartman Dr., 37087, pg. 1278   PB
SHENANDOAH MILLS, INC., P.O. Box 369, 143 S. Cumberland St., 37087, pg. 992   PV
Tennessee Woolen Mills, 218 N. Maple St., 37087, pg. 1296   PB
Toshiba America Consumer Products Manufacturing Div., 1420 Toshiba Dr., 37087, pg. 1405   IT
Wynn's-Precision, Inc., 104 Hartmann Dr., 37087, pg. 1783   PB

Lewisburg

Cosmolab Div., 37091, pg. 629   PV
International Comfort Products Corp., P.O. Box 128, 37091, pg. 898   PB
NationsBank/Marshall Co., 101 West Commerce St., 37091, pg. 1163   PB
Peoples & Union Bank, Public Sq., 37091, pg. 639   PB

WALKER DIE CASTING, INC., 1125 Higgs Rd., 37091, pg. 1147   PV

Lexington

CM Chain Division, State Road 22A, 38351, pg. 405   PB
Central State Bank, 28 Church St., 35351, pg. 1669   PB
Delavan Commercial Products Division, 20 Delavan Dr., 38351, pg. 401   PB

Loudon

Maremont Exhaust System Division, 2400 Industrial Pk. Blvd., 37774, pg. 137   PB
Maremont Exhaust Systems Product Division, 2400 Maremount Parkway, 37774, pg. 137   PB
Metal Resources, Inc., Blair Bend Industrial Park, 388 Williamson Dr., 37774, pg. 871   PB
A.E. Staley Manufacturing Co., 198 Blair Bin Dr., 37774, pg. 1357   IT

Louisville

Gilbert/Commonwealth International, Inc., Rt. 4, 1302 Topside Rd., 37777, pg. 841   PV

Lynchburg

Jack Daniels Distillery, P.O. Box 199, Hwy. 55, 37352, pg. 261   PB

Madison

Hillhaven Convalescent Center Madison, 431 Larkin Springs Rd., 37115, pg. 1713   PB
Peterbilt Motors Co., 430 Myatt Dr., 37115, pg. 1247   PB
Pirelli Armstrong Southeast Division, 710 Myatt Dr., P.O. Box 359, 37116, pg. 1058   IT

Manchester

Temco Fireplace Products, Inc. (Manchester), 1324 McArthur St., 37355, pg. 1576   PB
Volunteer Engineering, Inc., 1021 Volunteer Pkwy., 37355, pg. 315   PV

Maryville

First Tennessee Bank - Maryville, 101 W. Broadway, 37801, pg. 639   PB
MasterCraft Boat Company, 869 Binfield Rd., 37801-7642, pg. 689   PV
Schlegel Tennessee, Inc., 1713 Henry G. Ln. St., Blount County Ind. Pk., 37801, pg. 128   IT

Mason

West Tennessee Detention Facility, 555 Finde Naifeh Dr., 38049, pg. 451   PB

McKenzie

Windy Hill Pet Food Co., Old Hwy. 22, 38201, pg. 1182   PV

McMinnville

General Shale Products Corp.-McMinnville Concrete Div., P.O. Box 699, 37110, pg. 844   IT
Powermatic, 619 Morrison St., 37110, pg. 502   PB

Memphis

A.P.S., 601 So. Dudley St., 38104, pg. 10   PB
Added Dimensions, 3742 Lamar Ave., 38118, pg. 318   PB
Aero Electronics Incorporated, 3900 Willow Lake Blvd., 38118, pg. 731   PB
Agrolinz Inc., 7777 Walnut Grove Rd., 38120, pg. 356   IT
ALLEN & HOSHALL, INC., 2430 Poplar Ave., 38112, pg. 36   PV
ALLEN & OHARA, INC., 3385 Airways Blvd., 38116, pg. 36   PV
Allright System Parking, Inc., 8 South Third St, Concourse Level, 38103, pg. 43   PV
American Home Shield Corporation, 860 Blue Ridge Lake Blvd., 38120, pg. 1461   PB
ANDERSON-TULLY CO., 1242 N. 2nd St., 38107, pg. 73   PV
The Answer, 3742 Lamar Ave., 38118, pg. 318   PB
Apollo Express, Inc., 965 Ridge Lake Blvd., Ste. 103, 38120, pg. 1046   PB
Art Graphic Converters, Inc., 710 S. Fourth St., 38126, pg. 1193   PB
Aster Insurance Ltd., 1023 Cherry Rd., 38117, pg. 790   PB
Athens Paper Co., Inc., 4155 Newgetwell, 38118, pg. 94   PV
AUTOZONE, INC., 123 S. Front St., 38103, pg. 150   PB
B&M Printing Co., Inc., 2500 Lamar Ave., 38114, pg. 713   PV
Bagpak Div., 6400 Poplar Ave., 38107, pg. 901   PB
W.M. BARR & CO., INC., 2105 Channel Ave., 38113, pg. 117   PV
BELZ ENTERPRISES, 100 Peabody Place, Ste. 1400, 38103, pg. 132   PV
Bemis Paper Bag Division, P.O. Box 9417, 38109, pg. 210   PB

Binswanger Glass Company, 965 Ridge Lake Blvd., 38117, pg. 129   IT
BLUFF CITY DISTRIBUTING CO., INC., 3339 Fontaine Rd., 38116, pg. 153   PB
Boatmen's National Mortgage Inc., 4041 Knight Arnold Rd., 38118, pg. 1165   PB
Boyd Gaming Corporation, 2600 Nonconnah, Ste. 152, 38132, pg. 249   PB
Brother Industries (USA) Inc., P.O. Box 341347, 2950 Brother Blvd., 38133, pg. 229   IT
Browning-Ferris Industries of Kentucky, Inc., 2605 Nonconnah Blvd., Ste. 105, 38132, pg. 263   PB
Browning-Ferris Industries of South Atlantic, Inc., 2605 Nonconnah Blvd., Ste. 105, 38132, pg. 264   PB
BRYCE LLC CORPORATION, 4505 Old Lamar, 38118, pg. 177   PV
Buckeye Cellulose Corp., 2899 Jackson Ave., 38108, pg. 1331   PB
Buckleigh, Inc., 755 Crossover Ln., 38117, pg. 1335   PB
Buckman Laboratories Inc., 1256 N. McLean Blvd., 38108, pg. 180   PV
BUILDING PLASTICS, INC., 3263 Sharpe Ave., 38111, pg. 180   PV
BULAB HOLDINGS, INC., 1256 N. McLean Blvd., 38108, pg. 180   PV
Bulldog Co., 4533 Old Lamar Ave., 38118, pg. 1176   PB
CCL Custom Manufacturing, 1725 S. Third St., 38109, pg. 238   IT
JOHN J. CAMPBELL CO., INC., 6012 Resources Dr., 38134, pg. 204   PV
D. CANALE FOOD SERVICES, INC., Seven W. Georgia Ave., 38103, pg. 204   PV
Capricorn Transportation, Inc., 965 Ridge Lake Blvd., Ste. 103, 38120, pg. 1046   PB
Carat ICG, 5830 Mount Moriah, Ste. 6, 38115, pg. 207   PV
CATHERINES STORES CORPORATION, 3742 Lamar Ave., 38118, pg. 317   PB
Charter Lakeside Behavioral Health System, Inc., 2911 Brunswick Rd., 38134, pg. 1034   PB
Check Consultants Incorporated, 8275 Tournament Dr., Ste. 300, 38138, pg. 639   PB
CHOCTAW, INC., 1975 Nonconnah Blvd., 38132, pg. 238   PV
Circle International, Interstate Industrial Park, 2931 Lakeview Rd., 38116, pg. 371   PB
Cleo Inc., 4025 Viscount, P.O. Box 18520, 38118, pg. 284   PB
The Coca-Cola Bottling Co. of Memphis, Tennessee, 499 S. Hollywood St., 38111, pg. 393   PB
Commerce Capital Management, Inc., One Commerce Sq., 38150, pg. 1155   PB
Commerce Finance Company, One Commerce Sq., 38150, pg. 1155   PB
Commerce General Corporation, One Commerce Sq., 38150, pg. 1155   PB
Commerce Investment Corporation, One Commerce Sq., 38150, pg. 1155   PB
The Commercial Appeal, 495 Union Ave., 38103, pg. 1447   PB
CONCORD EFS, INC., 2525 Horizon Lake Dr., Ste. 120, 38133, pg. 429   PB
Concord National Bank, Inc., 2525 Horizon Lake Dr., Ste. 120, 38133, pg. 429   PB
CONLEY FROG/SWITCH & FORGE CO., 387 E. Bodley, 38109, pg. 263   PV
Continental Aviation Underwriters, Inc., 5100 Poplar Ave., 38137, pg. 1374   PB
CONWOOD COMPANY L.P., 813 Ridge Lake Blvd., 38120, pg. 272   PV
Cornwall & Stevens Co., Inc., 850 Ridge Lake Blvd., Ste. 103, 38120, pg. 688   PV
THE COURT COMPANY, 5605 Murray Rd. #103, 38119-3868, pg. 279   PV
CUMMINS MID-SOUTH, INC., 666 Riverside Dr., 38103, pg. 295   PV
Danek Medical Inc., 3092 Directors Row, 38131, pg. 1482   PB
Danek Sales Corporation, 3092 Directors Row, 38131, pg. 1482   PB
BUD DAVIS CADILLAC, INC., 5433 Poplar Ave., 38119, pg. 314   PV
DeLeuw, Cather & Company, 5885 Ridgeway Center, 38112, pg. 841   PV
DELTA FOREMOST CHEMICAL CORP., 3915 Air Park St., 38118, pg. 322   PV
Delta Life & Annuity Co., 530 Oak Court, Ste. 200, 38117, pg. 59   PV
Delta Life Corporation, 530 Oak Court, Ste. 200, 38117, pg. 59   PV
Diesel ReCon, 5765 Summer Trees Dr., 38134, pg. 468   PB
Diesel ReCon, 2680 Pershing St., 38112, pg. 468   PB
DOBBS BROTHERS MANAGEMENT, 5170 Sanderlin Ave., 38117, pg. 337   PV
Dobbs International Services, Inc., 5100 Poplar Ave., 38137, pg. 1718   PB
Dorfile Company, P.O. Box 18937, 4533 Old Lamar Ave., 38118, pg. 1177   PB
Doubletree Corporation, 755 Crossover Ln., 38117, pg. 1335   PB
Dover Elevator International, Inc., P.O. Box 2177, 38101, pg. 521   PB
DUNAVANT ENTERPRISES, INC., 3797 New Getwell Rd., 38118, pg. 346   PV
EJP Corporation, 755 Crossover Ln., 38117, pg. 1335   PB
EPAM Corporation, 755 Crossover Ln., 38117, pg. 1335   PB
ESI-Air, Inc., 1023 Cherry Rd., 38120, pg. 790   PB
ESI Mortgage Development Corporation, 755 Crossover Ln., 38117, pg. 1335   PB

PB - U.S. Public Companies Volume
PV - U.S. Private Companies Volume
IT - International Public & Private Companies Volume

ECONOCOM-USA INC., 965 Ridge Lake Blvd., Ste. 207, 38120, pg. 361 **PV**
Embassy Development Corporation, 755 Crossover Ln., 38117, pg. 1335 **PB**
Embassy Equity Development Corporation, 755 Crossover Ln., 38117, pg. 1335 **PB**
Embassy Pacific Equity Corporation, 755 Crossover Ln., 38117, pg. 1335 **PB**
Embassy Suites Club No. 1, Inc., 755 Crossover Ln., 38117, pg. 1335 **PB**
Embassy Suites Club No. 2, Inc., 755 Crossover Ln., 38117, pg. 1335 **PB**
Embassy Suites (Puerto Rico), Inc., 755 Crossover Ln., 38117, pg. 1335 **PB**
Embassy Syracuse Development Corporation, 755 Crossover Ln., 38117, pg. 1335 **PB**
Enco-Memphis, 5394 Lamar Ave., 38118, pg. 375 **PV**
FDX CORPORATION, 2005 Corporate Ave., 38118, pg. 603 **PB**
FT Mortgage, 4990 Poplar, 3rd fl., 38117, pg. 639 **PB**
FEDERAL COMPRESS & WAREHOUSE COMPANY, INC., 165 Madison Ave., Ste. 1400, 38103, pg. 398 **PV**
Federal Express Aviation Services Inc., P.O. Box 727, 38194, pg. 604 **PB**
Federal Express International, Inc., P.O. Box 727, 38194, pg. 604 **PB**
Federal Express Leasing Corp., P.O. Box 727, 38194, pg. 604 **PB**
Federal Express Logistics, Inc., P.O. Box 727, 38194, pg. 604 **PB**
Federal Express Redevelopment Corp., P.O. Box 727, 38194, pg. 604 **PB**
Fedex Customs Brokerage Corp., P.O. Box 727, 38194, pg. 604 **PB**
Fedex International Transmission Corp., P.O. Box 727, 38194, pg. 604 **PB**
First American National Bank, P.O. Box 183, 44 N. Second St., 38103, pg. 624 **PB**
First Commercial Bank, N.A. of Memphis, 6263 Poplar, 38119, pg. 630 **PB**
First Tennessee Bank - Memphis, 165 Madison Ave., 38103, pg. 639 **PB**
First Tennessee Bank National Association, 165 Madison Ave., 38103, pg. 639 **PB**
First Tennessee Brokerage, Inc., 4655 Poplar Ave., 38117, pg. 639 **PB**
First Tennessee Capital Assets Corporation, 843 Crossover Ln., Ste. 240, 38117, pg. 639 **PB**
FIRST TENNESSEE NATIONAL CORPORATION, 165 Madison Ave., 38103, pg. 638 **PB**
FISCHER COMPANIES, 3347 Pearson Rd., 38118, pg. 408 **PV**
FRED'S INC., 4300 New Getwell Road, 38118, pg. 680 **PB**
Furman Wholesale Lumber Branch, 4341 Old Lamar, 38118, pg. 431 **PV**
GKN North America Services Inc., P.O. Box 240909, 38124-0909, pg. 535 **IT**
General Employment Enterprises, Inc., 5100 Poplar Ave., Ste. 270, 38137, pg. 715 **PB**
Goldman, Sachs & Co., 6075 Poplar Ave., Ste. 720, 38119, pg. 462 **PV**
Great Dane Trailers Tennessee, Inc., 1095 Harbor Ave., 38113, pg. 1030 **PV**
GUARDSMARK, INC., 22 S. Second St., 38103, pg. 486 **PV**
HMI Electric, 3980 Pilot, 38118, pg. 518 **PV**
HMS/Memphis, 7500 Capital Dr., 38138, pg. 492 **PV**
The C.P. Hall Company, P.O. Box 13303, 38113, pg. 495 **PV**
Hammermill Papers, 6400 Poplar Ave., 38197-7000, pg. 902 **PB**
Hampton Inns, Inc., 6799 Great Oaks Rd., Ste. 100, 38138, pg. 1335 **PB**
Hardin's-Sysco Food Services, Inc., 4359 B.F. Goodrich Blvd., 38118-7306, pg. 1551 **PB**
Harland Bartholomew & Associates Inc., 2701 Union Ave. Extended, 38112, pg. 841 **PV**
Harrah's Alberta Investment Corporation, 1023 Cherry Rd., 38117, pg. 790 **PB**
HARRAH'S ENTERTAINMENT, INC., 1023 Cherry Rd., 38117-5423, pg. 790 **PB**
Harrah's Illinois Corporation, 1023 Cherry Rd., pg. 790 **PB**
Harrah's Operating Company, Inc., 1023 Cherry Rd., 38117, pg. 790 **PB**
Harrah's PTY. Limited, 1023 Cherry Rd., 38117, pg. 790 **PB**
HEAVY MACHINES, INC., 3926 E. Raines Rd., 38118, pg. 518 **PV**
Helena Chemical Company, Clark Tower, 6075 Poplar Ave., Ste. 500, 38119, pg. 845 **IT**
Hewlett-Packard Company, 889 Ridge Lake Blvd., Ste. 100, 38119, pg. 815 **PB**
Highland Capital Management Corporation, 165 Madison Ave., 38103-3723, pg. 639 **PB**
Hillhaven Convalescent Center Memphis, 6025 Primacy Pkwy., 38138, pg. 1713 **PB**
Hohenberg Bros. Company, P.O. Box 193, 38101, pg. 210 **PV**
Hospital Staffing Services of Tennessee, Inc., 5705 Stage Rd., Ste. 201, 38134, pg. 840 **PB**
A.C. Humko, 6410 Poplar Ave., 38119, pg. 92 **IT**
HUNTER FAN COMPANY, 2500 Frisco Ave., 38114, pg. 549 **PV**
CHUCK HUTTON CHEVROLET COMPANY, 2471 Mt. Moriah, 38115, pg. 550 **PV**
Hyde Insurance Agency, Inc., 3030 Poplar Ave., 38111, pg. 653 **PB**
INX International, 3085 Fleetbrook, 38116, pg. 1311 **IT**
ISK BioSciences, 6075 Poplar Ave. Ste. 306, 38119, pg. 689 **IT**

ISP Filters Inc., 4436 Malone Rd., 38118, pg. 858 **PB**
IDEAL CHEMICAL & SUPPLY COMPANY, 4025 Air Park St., 38118, pg. 557 **PV**
Idealease of Memphis, 3340 Pearson Rd., pg. 743 **PV**
Ike's, 4727 Burbank Rd., 38118, pg. 653 **PB**
INMAN CONSTRUCTION CORPORATION, 5100 Poplar Ave., Ste. 1210, 38137, pg. 564 **PV**
Instrument Associates, Inc., 2455 Harber Ave., 38113-0217, pg. 1430 **PB**
Jani King of Memphis, Inc., 2725 S. Mendenhall Rd., Ste. 27, 38115, pg. 582 **PV**
Jefferson-Pilot Data Services, Inc., 785 Crossover Ln., Ste. 141, 38117, pg. 925 **PB**
The Jordan Co., 4661 Burbank Rd., 38118, pg. 1163 **PB**
Earle M. Jorgensen Company/Memphis, 1340 Channel Ave., 38113, pg. 600 **PV**
Jupiter Transportation, Inc., 965 Ridge Lake Blvd., 38120, pg. 1046 **PB**
KEMMONS WILSON, INC., 1629 Winchester Rd., 38116, pg. 613 **PV**
King Cotton Foods, 1837 Harbor Ave., 38113, pg. 1433 **PB**
KNOWLEDGE TREE INC., 1217 Getwell, 38122, pg. 627 **PV**
Kraft Food Ingredients Corp., 8000 Horizon Center, 38133, pg. 1288 **PB**
Laclede - Memphis Branch, P.O. Box 13207, 1175 Harbor Ave., 38113, pg. 974 **PV**
LANGSTON COMPANIES, 1760 S. Third St., 38109, pg. 650 **PV**
Levcon, Inc., 400 W. Trigg, 38106, pg. 700 **PV**
LINKOUS CONSTRUCTION COMPANY, INC., 324, 6750 Poplar, Ste. 517, 38138, pg. 669 **PV**
Mark Lipman Div., 22 S. Second St., 38103, pg. 486 **PV**
Lithograph Printing Company, Inc., 4222 Pilot Dr., 38118, pg. 713 **PV**
M & H Financial Corp., 1991 Corporate Ave., 38132, pg. 653 **PB**
M&H Retail Food Group, 1991 Corporate Ave., 38132, pg. 653 **PB**
MCDR, INC., 5100 Wheelis St., Ste. 200, 38117, pg. 686 **PV**
M.S. CARRIERS, INC., 3171 Directors Row, 38131, pg. 1027 **PB**
Mail Well Services Inc., 3001 Lakeview Rd., 38116, pg. 1328 **PB**
Malone & Hyde, Inc.-Drug Distributors, 4681 Burbank Rd., 38118, pg. 653 **PB**
Manitowoc Debanking Technology, 3926 E. Raines Rd., 38118, pg. 518 **PV**
MANUFACTURERS CONSOLIDATION SERVICE, INC., 618 OakLeaf Office Ln., 38117, pg. 700 **PB**
MARK VII, INC., 965 Ridge Lake Blvd., Ste. 103, 38120, pg. 1046 **PB**
Marshall Steel, Inc., 1555 Harbor Rd., 38113, pg. 1513 **PB**
MASTER GRAPHIC, INC., 2500 Lamar Ave., 38114, pg. 713 **PV**
MAYER MYERS PAPER COMPANY, 1769 Latham St., 38101, pg. 718 **PV**
Megamarkets, Inc., 1451 Union Ave., 38104, pg. 653 **PB**
Memphis Beverage Production Company, Inc., 499 S. Hollywood St., 38111, pg. 393 **PV**
MEMPHIS GROUP, INC., 3900 Willow Lake Blvd., 38118, pg. 730 **PV**
MEMPHIS LIGHT, GAS & WATER, 220 S. Main St., 38103, pg. 731 **PV**
Memphis Plant-Kellogg U.S.A., 2168 Frisco, 38114, pg. 947 **PB**
Memphis Publishing Co., 495 Union Ave., 38103, pg. 1448 **PB**
Memphis Title Company, 200 Jefferson Ave., Ste. 200, 38103, pg. 626 **PB**
Mercury Printing Company, Inc., 2929 Convair Rd., 38132, pg. 1736 **PB**
MID AMERICA INTERNATIONAL TRUCKS, INC., 1750 E. Brooks Rd., 38116, pg. 743 **PB**
Mid-South Comprehensive Home Health, 5705 Stage Rd., Ste. 201, 38134, pg. 841 **PB**
MID-SOUTH MILLING COMPANY, INC., 710 Oakleaf Office Ln., 38117-487, pg. 744 **PV**
Monroe Properties, Inc., One Commerce Sq., 38150, pg. 1155 **PB**
Morgan Asset Management, Inc., 50 Front St., 38103, pg. 1131 **PB**
Morgan Keegan & Company, Inc., Morgan Keegan Tower, 50 Front St., 38103, pg. 1131 **PB**
Morgan Keegan Funding Corp., 50 Front Street, 38103, pg. 1131 **PB**
MORGAN KEEGAN, INC., Morgan Keegan Tower, 50 N. Front St., 38103, pg. 1131 **PB**
Morgan Keegan Insurance Agency of Louisiana, Inc., 50 Front St., 38103, pg. 1131 **PB**
Morgan Keegan Managed Futures, Inc., 50 Front St., 38103, pg. 1131 **PB**
Morgan Keegan Mortgage Company, Inc., 50 Front St., 38103, pg. 1131 **PB**
MUELLER INDUSTRIES, INC., Atrium Z, 6799 Great Oaks Rd., Ste. 200, 38138, pg. 1141 **PB**
Multiform, Inc., 710 S. Fourth St., 38126, pg. 1193 **PV**
National Bank of Commerce, One Commerce Sq., 38150, pg. 1155 **PB**
National Bedding Co., 736 S. Dudley, 38104, pg. 780 **PV**
NATIONAL COMMERCE BANCORPORATION, One Commerce Sq., 38150, pg. 1154 **PB**
National Commerce Bank Services, Inc., One Commerce Sq., 38150, pg. 1155 **PB**
NATIONAL SAFETY ASSOCIATES, 4260 E. Raines Rd., 38118, pg. 786 **PV**
NationsBank/Memphis, P.O. Box 1503, 38101, pg. 1163 **PB**

NationsBank of Tennessee, 200 Madison Ave., 38103, pg. 1165 **PB**
Neptune Trucking, Inc., 965 Ridge Lake Blvd., Ste. 103, 38120, pg. 1046 **PB**
The New York Times Broadcasting Service, Inc., 803 Channel 3 Dr., 38103, pg. 1173 **PB**
The New York Times Company Broadcasting Group, 803 Channel 3 Dr., 38103, pg. 1173 **PB**
nexAir, 363 Walnut, 38101, pg. 797 **PV**
NEXAIR, LLC, 1385 Corporate Ave., 38132, pg. 797 **PV**
94th Aero Squadron of Memphis, Inc., 2561 Democrat Rd., 38118, pg. 1023 **PV**
Nisco Steel Services, Inc., 3779 Knight Road, 38118, pg. 947 **IT**
Nissan Forklift Corporation, North America, 2900 Datsun Drive, 38186, pg. 945 **IT**
Nissin Foods (U.S.A.) Plant, 4789 Cromwell, 38118, pg. 950 **IT**
Norfen Life Insurance Company, 165 Madison Ave., 38103, pg. 639 **PB**
ORGILL, INC., 2100 Latham St., 38109, pg. 819 **PV**
Orion Express, Inc., 965 Ridge Lake Blvd., Ste. 103, 38120, pg. 1046 **PB**
OZARK MOTOR LINES, 3934 Homewood Rd., 38118, pg. 825 **PV**
PCS Nitrogen, 3175 Lenox Park Blvd., Ste. 400, 38115-4256, pg. 1064 **IT**
PS...Plus Sizes, Plus Savings, 3742 Lamar Ave., 38118, pg. 318 **PB**
Pacific Hotels, Inc., 755 Crossover Ln., 38117, pg. 1335 **PB**
Pemko Manufacturing, 5535 Distribution Dr., 38141, pg. 848 **PB**
Peoplemark, Inc., 22 S. Second St., 38103, pg. 486 **PV**
PERFORMA ENTERTAINMENT REAL ESTATE, INC., 203 Beale St., Ste. 300, 38103, pg. 853 **PV**
Perkins Family Restaurants, 6075 Poplar Ave. Ste. 800, 38119-4709, pg. 925 **PV**
Perma-Fix of Memphis, 901 E. Bodley, 38106, pg. 1280 **PB**
Piggly Wiggly Co., 1991 Corporate Ave., 38132, pg. 653 **PB**
PLANT MAINTENANCE SERVICE CORPORATION, 3000 Fite Rd., 38127, pg. 869 **PV**
Plough U.S.A., 3030 Jackson Ave., 38151, pg. 1438 **PB**
POWER & TELEPHONE SUPPLY COMPANY, 2673 Yale Ave., 38112-3335, pg. 877 **PV**
PROCESS SYSTEMS INC., 1790 Kirby Pkwy., Ste. 300, 38138, pg. 888 **PV**
Process Systems, Inc. Construction Co., 1790 Kirby Pkwy. Ste. 300, 38138, pg. 888 **PV**
PROMUS HOTEL CORPORATION, 755 Crossover Ln., 38117, pg. 1335 **PB**
Quality Incentive & Travel, 1991 Corporate Ave., 38132, pg. 653 **PB**
Quality Stamp, 4690 Hungerford Rd., 38118, pg. 653 **PB**
Quebecor Printing Memphis Inc., 828 E. Holmes Rd., 38116, pg. 1076 **IT**
Recognition Division, 8300 Winchester Rd., 38181, pg. 934 **PB**
Response Oncology, Inc., 1775 Moriah Woods Blvd., 38117, pg. 1449 **PB**
Retail Services, 1451 Union Ave., 38104, pg. 653 **PB**
Retailer Development, 1991 Corporate Ave., 38132, pg. 653 **PB**
Scholl U.S.A., 3030 Jackson Ave., 38151, pg. 1438 **PB**
Screen Graphics, Inc., 285 Union Ave., 38103, pg. 713 **PV**
SEABROOK WALLCOVERINGS, INC., 1325 Farmville Rd., 38122, pg. 978 **PV**
Sealy Mattress Company of Memphis, 4120 Air Trans Rd., 38181, pg. 979 **PV**
Sedgwick, Inc., 1000 Ridgeway Loop Rd., 38120, pg. 1218 **IT**
Sedgwick Noble Lowndes, 1000 Ridgeway Loop Rd., 38120, pg. 1218 **IT**
SEESSEL HOLDINGS, INC., 1745 Union Ave., 38104, pg. 981 **PV**
ServiceMaster Consumer Services Company, 860 Ridge Lake Blvd., 38120, pg. 1461 **PB**
ServiceMaster Diversified Health Services, Inc., 5050 Poplar Ave., Ste. 1800, 38157, pg. 1462 **PB**
ServiceMaster Residential/Commercial Services Co., 860 Ridge Lake Blvd., 38120, pg. 1461 **PB**
Shelby County Training Center, 3420 Old Getwell Rd., 38103, pg. 451 **PB**
SHELBY GROUP INTERNATIONAL, INC., 5321 E. Shelby Dr., 38118, pg. 991 **PV**
Smith & Nephew North America, 1450 Brooks Rd., 38116, pg. 1263 **IT**
Smith & Nephew Orthopedics, 1450 Brooks Rd., 38116, pg. 1263 **IT**
Smucker Memphis Plant, 4740 Burbank Rd., 38118, pg. 1480 **PB**
SOFAMOR DANEK GROUP, INC., 1800 Pyramid Pl., 38132, pg. 1482 **PB**
Southern Interiors, 2541 Farrisview Blvd., 38118, pg. 491 **PV**
SOUTHERN LEATHER CO., INC., 274 Monroe Ave., 38103, pg. 1016 **PV**
Southern Uniforms Div., 3459 Summer, 38133, pg. 1539 **PB**
SOUTHLAND FORD STERLING TRUCK, 673 E. Brooks Rd., 38116, pg. 1018 **PV**
SPARTAN AUTOMATIC RETAILERS, 3761 Lamar Ave., 38118, pg. 1020 **PV**
Springhill Papers Div., 6400 Poplar Ave., 38197, pg. 900 **PB**
Square D Co., Central Distribution Ctr., 4575 Pleasant Hill Rd., 38118, pg. 1208 **IT**

PB - *U.S. Public Companies Volume*
PV - *U.S. Private Companies Volume*
IT - *International Public & Private Companies Volume*

Geographic Index-U.S.

TENNESSEE **DIRECTORY OF CORPORATE AFFILIATIONS**

Station and Cable Services Div., 785 Crossover Ln., Ste. 141, 38117, pg. 925 **PB**
Sterilization Services of Tennessee, 2396 Florida St., 38109, pg. 46 **PV**
Super D Drug Stores, 4895 Outland Center Dr., Ste. 101, 38118, pg. 642 **PV**
TBC CORPORATION, 4770 Hickory Hill Rd., 38141, pg. 1553 **PB**
TMP Worldwide, Inc., 889 Ridge Lake Blvd., Ste. 210, 38120, pg. 1064 **PV**
TVESCO, INC., 296 Adams Ave., 38101, pg. 1066 **PV**
Tall Trees, 3335 Old Getwell Rd., 38118, pg. 451 **PB**
Taurus Trucking, Inc., 965 Ridge Lake Blvd., Ste. 103, 38120, pg. 1046 **PB**
Tencarva Machinery Co., 3725 Getwell Cove, 38118, pg. 1075 **PV**
Tennessee Refinery, P.O. Box 2930, 38103-2930, pg. 1042 **PB**
The Terminix International Company, 860 Ridge Lake Blvd., 38120, pg. 1461 **PB**
THOMAS & BETTS CORPORATION, 8155 T & B Blvd., 38125, pg. 1597 **PB**
Thomas & Betts Electronics Division, 1555 Lynnfield Rd., 38119, pg. 1597 **PB**
Thomas & Betts Reznor Division, 1555 Lynnfield Rd., 38119, pg. 1598 **PB**
The Thompson's Company, 825 Crossover Ln., Ste. 240, 38117, pg. 1466 **PB**
Three States Supply Co., Inc., 666-E. H. Crump Blvd., 38216, pg. 1113 **PV**
TRI-STATE ARMATURE & ELECTRIC WORKS, 330 E. Calhoun Ave., 38126, pg. 1100 **PV**
TRI-STATE MACK INC, 494 E.H. Crump Blvd., 38126, pg. 1101 **PV**
Tri-State Leasing, 494 E.H. Crump Blvd., 38126, pg. 1101 **PV**
True Temper Sports Division, 8275 Tournament Dr., Ste. 200, 38125, pg. 233 **PB**
TruGreen-ChemLawn, 860 Ridge Lake Blvd., 38120, pg. 1461 **PB**
Turner Holding LLC, 2040 Maidson Ave., 38174, pg. 1109 **PV**
URS Greiner, Inc., 5885 Ridgeway Center Pkwy., #218, 38120, pg. 1658 **PB**
US1 Alliance Corp., One Commerce Sq., 38150, pg. 1155 **PB**
Union Planters Bank, 6200 Poplar Ave., 38103, pg. 1669 **PB**
Union-Transport Corporation-Memphis Office, 3035 Directors Rd., Ste. 2172, 38131, pg. 1119 **PV**
United Cement Co., 2050 Hunter Ave., 38108, pg. 628 **IT**
United Paint Co., 404 E. Mallory St., 38109, pg. 1466 **PB**
U.S. Container Div., 6400 Poplar Ave., 38197, pg. 903 **PB**
Universal Fasteners, 4821 Cromwell Ave., 38118, pg. 1515 **IT**
Universal Financial Services, 3385 Airways Blvd., Ste. 229, 38116, pg. 1127 **PV**
UNIVERSAL LIFE INSURANCE COMPANY, 480 Linden Ave., 38126, pg. 1127 **PV**
VP Buildings, 6000 Poplar Ave., Ste. 400, 38119, pg. 972 **PB**
Varco-Pruden Buildings, 6000 Poplar Ave., Ste. 400, 38119, pg. 1677 **PB**
Varsity Intropa, 2525 Horizon Lake Dr., 38133, pg. 1389 **PB**
Varsity Spirit Corporation, 2525 Horizon Lake Dr., 38133, pg. 1389 **PB**
Varsity Spirit Fashions, 2525 Horizon Lake Dr., 38133, pg. 1389 **PB**
Varsity USA, 2525 Horizon Lake Dr., 38133, pg. 1389 **PB**
WDIA-AM, 112 Union Ave., 38103, pg. 384 **PB**
WEGR, 203 Beale St., 38103, pg. 384 **PB**
WPTY-TV, 2701 Union, Ste. 100, 38112, pg. 385 **PB**
WREC, 203 Beale St., 38103, pg. 385 **PB**
WREG-TV, 803 Channel 3 Dr., 38103, pg. 1174 **PB**
WRXQ, 203 Beale St., 38103, pg. 385 **PB**
WANG'S INTERNATIONAL, INC., 4250 E. Shelby Dr., 38118, pg. 1149 **PV**
WEST UNION CORPORATION, 35 Union Ave., Ste. 300, 38103, pg. 1163 **PV**
Western International Media Corporation, 6000 Poplar Ave., Ste. 215, 38120, pg. 1167 **PV**
WURZBURG, INC., 710 S. Fourth St., 38126, pg. 1192 **PV**
Zellerbach Division, 4821 Cromwell Ave., 38118, pg. 1075 **PB**
Zeneca Pharmaceuticals, 1755 Kirby Pkwy., Ste. 250, 38120, pg. 1525 **IT**

Milan

Acco Controls, 5200 Industrial Dr., 38358, pg. 472 **IT**
Ceco Door Products, 9159 Telecom Dr., 38358-3432, pg. 1676 **PB**
Douglas & Lomason Company, 3000 Kefauver Dr., 38358, pg. 830 **IT**
Sandvik Windsor Corp., P.O. Box 470, 38358, pg. 1185 **IT**

Morrison

Bridgestone/Firestone Tire Manufacturing Operations-Warren County, 725 Bridgestone Dr., 37357, pg. 213 **IT**
Calsonic Yorozu Corporation, 2000 Mountain View Dr., 37357, pg. 944 **IT**

Morristown

Bank of East Tennessee, 201 W. Morris Blvd., 37816, pg. 1669 **PB**
The Berkline Corporation, One Berkline Dr., 37813, pg. 432 **PV**
First Tennessee Bank - Morristown, 1112 W. First North St., 37814, pg. 639 **PB**
Flowers Baking Co. of Morristown, 1725 W. First N. St., 37816, pg. 657 **PB**
Hale Brothers, Inc., 530 E. Main, 37816, pg. 1278 **PB**
Pioneer Plastics Corporation, 325 DeSoto Ave., 37814, pg. 867 **PV**
PRECISION PARTS CORP., 5727 Superior Dr., 37814, pg. 879 **PV**
SHELBY WILLIAMS INDUSTRIES, INC., 150 Shelby Williams Dr., 37813, pg. 1464 **PB**
Shelby Williams Textiles, P.O. Box 1028, 37816, pg. 1465 **PB**
Southern Electric Supply Co., Inc., 3415 W. Andrew Johnson Hwy., 37814, pg. 1108 **IT**

Mount Juliet

Tennessee Telephone Company, P.O. Box 1000, 37122, pg. 1572 **PB**

Mount Pleasant

D&A Technology, 201 Canaan Rd., 38474, pg. 85 **IT**
ITW Shippers Paper, 1203 N. Main St., 38474, pg. 867 **PB**
Rhone-Poulenc Agrochemical Div., Arrow Mines Rd., Box 352, 38474, pg. 1111 **IT**

Mountain City

FPC, Inc., P.O. Box 506, Rt. 3, Johnson County Industrial Park, 37683, pg. 551 **PB**

Murfreesboro

First Tennessee Bank - Murfreesboro, 305 W. Northfield Blvd., 37130, pg. 639 **PB**
General Slicing/Red Goat Disposers, 1152 Park Ave., 37129, pg. 1506 **PB**
Lewis Bros. Bakeries (TN), 847 Scott Dr., 37129, pg. 665 **PV**
Perfect Equipment Corp., 855 Scott St., Box 942, 37130, pg. 138 **PV**
Procon Products, 910 Ridgely Rd., 37130, pg. 1506 **PB**
United Service Equipment Company, 1152 Park Ave., 37129, pg. 1507 **PB**

Nashville

ADI, 6615 Robertson Ave., 37209, pg. 1076 **PV**
ADT Automotive, Inc., 435 Metroplex Dr., 37211, pg. 1648 **PB**
ADT Truck & Equipment Auctions, Inc., 435 Metroplex Dr., 37211, pg. 1648 **PB**
AGC Life Insurance Co., American General Center, 37250, pg. 76 **PB**
ATC, Inc., 3050 Sidco Dr., 37204, pg. 1427 **IT**
Abingdon Press, 201 Eighth Ave. S., 37203, pg. 1123 **PV**
AFFILIATED PUBLISHERS, INC., 1009 16th Ave. S., 37212, pg. 26 **PV**
ALADDIN INDUSTRIES, INCORPORATED, 703 Murfreesboro Rd., 37210, pg. 30 **PV**
Aladdin Synergetics, Inc., 555 Marriott Dr., Ste. 400, 37214, pg. 31 **PV**
J. ALEXANDERS CORPORATION, 3401 W. End Ave., Ste. 260, 37203, pg. 40 **PB**
Allen & Hoshall, 402 Bana Dr., Bldg. 100, Ste. 208, 37217, pg. 36 **PV**
ALLEY-CASSETTY COAL CO., #2 Oldham St., 37213, pg. 37 **PV**
Allied Clinical Laboratories, Inc., 2515 Park Plaza, 37203, pg. 973 **PB**
Allied Security Inc., 1161 Murfreesboro Rd., #415, 37217, pg. 41 **PV**
Allright Nashville Parking, Inc., McKendree Parking Ctr., 140 Sixth Ave. N., 37203, pg. 42 **PV**
American General Life & Accident Insurance Co., American General Center-Nashville, 37250-2205, pg. 76 **PB**
American General Property Insurance Company, American General Ctr., 37250, pg. 76 **PB**
AMERICAN HEALTHCORP INC., One Burton Hills Blvd., 37215, pg. 78 **PB**
Ameristar Capital Markets, Inc., Fourth & Union, 37237, pg. 624 **PB**
Amusement Business, 14 Music Circle East, 37203, pg. 1446 **IT**
ATHENS PAPER CO. INC., 1898 Elmtree Dr., 37210, pg. 94 **PV**
B & G WHOLESALERS, INC., 337 28th Ave., N., 37209, pg. 105 **PV**
Beck/Arnley Worldparts Corp., 1020 Space Park South, P.O. Box 110910, 37222, pg. 561 **PB**
Berwind Industries, Inc., One Lakeview Pl., Ste. 305, 37214, pg. 138 **PV**
Bindley Western, Tennessee Wholesale Division, 200 Cumberland Bend, 37228, pg. 229 **PB**
BLEVINS INC., 421 Hart Ln., 37216, pg. 149 **PV**
JOHN BOUCHARD & SONS COMPANY, 1024 Harrison St., 37203, pg. 161 **PV**
J.C. BRADFORD & CO., 330 Commerce St., 37201, pg. 163 **PV**
BRAID ELECTRIC COMPANY, 299 Cowan St., 37213, pg. 165 **PV**
Brentwood Benson Publishing Group, 365 Great Circle Rd., 37228, pg. 1529 **IT**
Bridgestone/Firestone, Inc., One Bridgestone Pk., 37214, pg. 213 **IT**
Bridgestone/Firestone, Inc., 50 Century Blvd., 37214, pg. 213 **IT**
Bridgestone/Firestone Off Road Tire Company, 565 Marriott Dr., Ste. 600, 37214, pg. 213 **IT**
Bridgestone/Firestone Tire Manufacturing Operations, 565 Marriott Dr., Ste. 500, 37214, pg. 213 **IT**
Bridgestone/Firestone Tire Sales Company, One Bridgestone Park, 37214, pg. 213 **IT**
THE BUNTIN GROUP, 1001 Hawkins St., 37203, pg. 181 **PV**
Buntin Out of Home Media, 1001 Hawkins St., 37203, pg. 181 **PV**
CCA International, Inc., 102 Woodmont Blvd., 37205, pg. 451 **PB**
CUC Travel Services Inc., 49 Music Square W., 37203, pg. 320 **PB**
Captain D's Restaurant, 1727 Elm Hill Pike, 37210, pg. 1467 **PB**
Castner Knott Co., 618 Church St., 37219, pg. 1090 **PB**
Caterpillar Financial Receivables Inc., 3322 West End Ave., 37203-0903, pg. 315 **PB**
Caterpillar Financial Services Corporation, 3322 W. End Ave., Ste. 610, 37203, pg. 315 **PB**
Caterpillar Insurance Services Corporation, 3322 W. End Ave., Ste. 610, 37203, pg. 316 **PB**
Centex-Rodgers Construction Company, 2620 Elm Hill Pike, Ste. 400, 37214, pg. 322 **PB**
CENTRAL PARKING CORP., 2401 21st St., Ste. 200, 37212, pg. 326 **PB**
Chemrock Corporation, 1101 Kermit Dr., Ste. 420, 37217, pg. 903 **PV**
Chemrock Corporation, 2601 Osage St., 37208, pg. 903 **PV**
Cigna Healthcare of Tennessee, Inc., 1801 West End Ave., Ste. 800, 37202, pg. 360 **PB**
Circle International, 2603 Elm Hill Pike, Ste. 1, 37214, pg. 371 **PB**
Citicorp Insurance Services, Inc., 601 Mainstream Dr., 37228, pg. 377 **PB**
Cleaning Specialty Company, 814 Cherokee Ave., 37207, pg. 566 **PB**
COLUMBIA/HCA HEALTHCARE CORPORATION, P.O. Box 550, 37203, pg. 403 **PB**
ComAlloy International Company, 481 Allied Dr., 37211-3333, pg. 1441 **PB**
CORRECTIONS CORPORATION OF AMERICA, 10 Burton Hills Blvd., 37215, pg. 450 **PB**
Country Delite, 1401 Church St., 37203, pg. 1526 **PB**
COVENTRY CORPORATION, 53 Century Blvd., Ste. 250, 37214, pg. 454 **PB**
CREST CADILLAC COMPANY, 2121 Metro Ctr. Blvd., 37228, pg. 289 **PV**
Crest Cadillac, Inc., 2121 Metrocenter Blvd., 37228, pg. 712 **PV**
CUMMINGS INC., 200 12th Ave. S., 37203, pg. 295 **PV**
Davidson County Juvenile Detention Center, 100 Woodland St., 37213, pg. 450 **PB**
Digi International, 618 Grassmere Park Dr., #3, 37211, pg. 507 **PB**
DOBSON & JOHNSON, INC., 3841 Green Hills Village Dr., 37215, pg. 337 **PV**
Dockers Footwear, 1415 Murfreesboro Rd., Ste. 430, 37217, pg. 728 **PB**
DOLLAR GENERAL CORPORATION, 104 Woodmont Blvd., Ste. 500, 37205, pg. 515 **PB**
East-West Design Group, 1001 Hawkins St., 37203, pg. 181 **PV**
ENCO MATERIALS, INC., 110 N. 1st. St., 37213, pg. 375 **PV**
ENVOY CORPORATION, Two Lakeview Dr., 15 Century Blvd., Ste. 600, 37214, pg. 587 **PB**
FFV Aerotech Inc., Ten Airways Blvd., 37217, pg. 276 **IT**
FISI Madison Financial Corporation, 49 Music Sq. W., 37203, pg. 320 **PB**
Fairfield Nashville, 2415 McGavock Pike, 37214, pg. 611 **PB**
Fifth Quarter, 1727 Elm Hill Pike, 37210, pg. 1467 **PB**
FIRST AMERICAN CORPORATION, 300 Union St., 37237-0811, pg. 624 **PB**
First American National Bank, P.O. Box 1351, First American Ctr., 326 Union St., 37237, pg. 624 **PB**
First American Trust Company, N.A., First American Ctr., 360 Union St., 37237, pg. 624 **PB**
First Amtenn Life Insurance Company, First American Ctr., 37237, pg. 624 **PB**
First Tennessee Bank - Nashville, 511 Union St., 37219, pg. 639 **PB**
First Union National Bank of Tennessee, 150 Fourth Ave. N., 37219, pg. 640 **PB**
Flagship Airlines, Two International Plaza, Ste. 900, 37210, pg. 9 **PB**
Fleetguard Inc., 402 BNA Dr., Ste. 500, 37217, pg. 468 **PB**
Gaylord Broadcasting Co., 2806 Opryland Dr., 37214, pg. 704 **PB**
GAYLORD ENTERTAINMENT CO., One Gaylord Dr., 37214, pg. 704 **PB**
Gaylord Entertainment/Opryland USA, One Gaylord Dr., 37214, pg. 704 **PB**
The General Shoe Warehouse, Genesco Park, 37202, pg. 728 **PB**
GENESCO INC., 1415 Murfreesboro Rd., 37217-2829, pg. 728 **PB**
GIBSON MUSICAL INSTRUMENTS, INC., 1818 Elm Hill Pike, 37210, pg. 451 **PV**
HCA International Co., One Park Plaza, 37203, pg. 405 **PB**
HCA Psychiatric Co., One Park Plaza, 37203, pg. 405 **PB**
W.L. HAILEY & COMPANY, INC., 2971 Kraft Dr., 37204, pg. 494 **PV**
HARDAWAY CONSTRUCTION CORP. OF TENNESSEE, INC., 615 Main St., 37206, pg. 501 **PV**

Geographic Index-U.S.

PB - *U.S. Public Companies Volume*
PV - *U.S. Private Companies Volume*
IT - *International Public & Private Companies Volume*

HealthWise of America, 102 Woodmont Blvd., Ste. 110, 37205, pg. 1678 PB
Hewlett-Packard Company, 44 Vantage Way, Ste. 160, 37228, pg. 815 PB
Horace Small Apparel Company, 350 28th Ave. N., 37209, pg. 635 IT
HORNER RAUSCH OPTICAL COMPANY EAST, INC., 968 Main, 37206, pg. 540 PV
HOSPITAL AFFILIATES DEVELOPMENT CORPORATION, 3310 W. End Ave., Ste. 460, 37203, pg. 540 PV
Hospital Development Co., One Park Plaza, 37203, pg. 405 PB
Hydra-Sports Corporation, 100 Oceanside Drive, 37204, pg. 478 PV
Ikon Office Solutions-Nashville, 2994 Sideo Dr., 37204, pg. 863 PB
Ingram Barge Company, One Belle Meade Place, 4400 Harding Rd., 37205, pg. 563 PV
Ingram Coal Company, One Belle Meade Place, 4400 Harding Rd., 37205, pg. 563 PV
INGRAM INDUSTRIES INC., One Belle Meade Pl., 4400 Harding Rd., 37205-2290, pg. 562 PV
Ingram Production Company, One Belle Meade Place, 4400 Harding Rd., 37205, pg. 563 PV
Innovative South, 1201 Antioch Pike, 37211, pg. 565 PV
Intergraph Corporation, 5211 Linbar Dr., Ste. 510, 37211-3137, pg. 890 PB
International Diverse Foods, 189 Spence Lane, 37210, pg. 663 PV
JACKSON MSC, 801 Airpark Center Dr., 37217, pg. 579 PV
Jani King of Nashville, Inc., 301 Pluspark Blvd., 37212, pg. 582 PV
Jarman Shoe Co., Genesco Park, 37202, pg. 728 PB
Johnston & Murphy Co., 1415 Murfreesboro Rd., 37217, pg. 728 PB
Johnston & Murphy Retail/Wholesale Stores, Genesco Park, 37202, pg. 728 PB
Laboratory Supply Company, 336 Wilhagan Rd., 37217, pg. 642 PV
Laredo Boot Co., Genesco Park, 37202, pg. 728 PB
Lee, Robinson & Steine, Inc., First American Ctr., 37237, pg. 624 PB
Lee's Famous Recipe Restaurant, 3343 Perimeter Hill Dr., Ste. 200, 37211, pg. 906 PV
Lewis Bros. Bakeries, 702 Murfreesboro Rd., 37210, pg. 665 PV
M & H Dairy, 1401 Church St., 37203, pg. 653 PB
MAGNETEK, INC., 26 Century Blvd., Ste. 600, 37214, pg. 1037 PB
MagneTek Lighting Products Group, 26 Century Blvd., 37214, pg. 1037 PB
The Marble Company, 3102 Ambrose, 37207, pg. 149 PV
Marta Technologies, Inc., 311 Plus Park Blvd., 37217, pg. 46 PB
MedTrac, Inc., 26 Century Blvd., 37214, pg. 1504 IT
Mercury Air Center, 635 Hanger Ln., 37217, pg. 1093 PB
Metro Davidson Co. DF, 5115 Harding Pl., 37211, pg. 450 PB
Mitre Sports (U.S.), 2214 Metro Center Blvd., Ste. 200, 37217, pg. 1036 IT
Mitsui & Co. (U.S.A.), Inc., 25 Century Blvd., 37214, pg. 879 IT
Music City News, 1302 Division St., 37203, pg. 701 PB
Nashville Auto Auction Inc., 1450 Lebanon Rd., 37210, pg. 1649 PB
Nashville Bank of Commerce, 1700 Elm Hill Pike, 37210, pg. 1155 PB
Nashville Crawdaddy, Inc., 14 Oldham St., 37213, pg. 1023 PV
NASHVILLE MACHINE CO. INC., 530 Woodycrest Ave., 37210-4394, pg. 774 PV
NASHVILLE STEEL CORP., 7211 Centennial Blvd., 37209, pg. 775 PV
NASHVILLE WIRE PRODUCT CO., 199 Polk Ave., 37210, pg. 775 PV
National Specialty Services, Inc., 556 Metroplex Dr., 37211, pg. 304 PB
NationsBank of Tennessee, NationsBank Plaza, 37239, pg. 1163 PB
NationsBank Realty Services Corp., One Commerce Pl., 37219, pg. 1164 PB
Nationsbank/Tennessee, One Commerce Pl., 37219, pg. 1163 PB
Nautica Footwear, 1415 Murfreesboro Rd., 37217, pg. 728 PB
THOMAS NELSON INC., Nelson Pl. at Elm Hill Pike, 37214, pg. 1167 PB
94th Aero Squadron of Nashville, Inc., 1362-A Murfreesboro Rd., 37217, pg. 1023 PV
Nortel, 200 Athens Way, 37228, pg. 970 IT
Northern Telecom, Northern Telecom Plaza, #200 Athens Way, 37228-1397, pg. 969 IT
Northern Telecom Finance Corporation, Northern Telecom Plaza, 220 Athens Way, 37228-1399, pg. 969 IT
Northern Telecom - National Repair & Distribution Center, 640 Massman Dr., 37210, pg. 970 IT
O'CHARLEY'S INC., 3038 Sidco Dr., 37204, pg. 1211 PB
One Stop Supply, Inc., 1133 Polk Ave., 37210, pg. 847 PB
Robert Orr-Sysco Food Services Co., One Hermitage Plaza, 37209, pg. 1551 PB
OUIMET CORP., 2967 Sidco Dr., 37204, pg. 821 PV
PENCO-Tennessee, Willis Corroon Plaza, 26 Century Blvd., 37124, pg. 1508 IT
Palmer Plaza, Limited, P.O. Box 1115, 1801 West End Ave., 37203, pg. 361 PB
Pargo's Restaurants, 1727 Elm Hill Pike, 37210, pg. 1467 PB
THE PARMAN CORPORATION, 1740 Ed Temple Blvd., 37208, pg. 840 PV
Parman Lubricants, 7101 Cockeral Bend Blvd., 37209, pg. 840 PV
Parmart Stores, 1740 Ed Temple Blvd., 37208, pg. 840 PV
Parthenon Insurance Co., 3401 West End, 37203, pg. 405 PB
Patten-Beers Constructors, 1901 21st Ave. South, 37212, pg. 1261 IT
Pearl Drum Center, 408 Harding Indus. Dr., 37211, pg. 452 PV
Permanent General Companies, 633 Thompson Lane, 37204, pg. 563 PV
Philip Metals/Steiner-Liff, 710 1st St., 37213, pg. 1050 IT
PHYCOR, INC., 30 Burton Hills Blvd., Ste. 400, 37215, pg. 1293 PB
PolyGram Records, Inc., 66 Music Square W., 37203, pg. 1052 IT
Pony U.S.A., 2214 Metro Ctr. Blvd., Ste. 200, 37228, pg. 1036 IT
Provident Music Distribution, 468 McNally Dr., 37211, pg. 1529 IT
PURITY DAIRIES INC., 360 Mufreesboro Rd., 37210, pg. 895 PV
Quebecor Printing Nashville, 2501 Powell Ave., 37204, pg. 1076 IT
R & R Uniforms, 350 28th Ave. N., 37209, pg. 635 IT
C.B. RAGLAND COMPANY, P.O. Box 40587, 37204, pg. 907 PV
Rail Systems, Inc., Airpark Center V, 505 Airpark Center Dr., 37217, pg. 961 PB
Red Kap Industries, 545 Marriott Dr., 37214, pg. 1702 PB
Reference Pathology Laboratory, Inc., P.O. Box 90908, 210 25th Ave. N., Ste. 1217, 37203, pg. 973 PB
Regions Bank/Middle Tennessee, P.O. Box 305171, 37230-5171, pg. 1372 PB
Reunion Records, 2908 Poston Ave., 37203, pg. 1529 IT
ROGERS GROUP INC., 421 Great Circle Rd., 37228, pg. 939 PV
STS Services Inc., 555 Marriott Dr., Ste. 805, 37217, pg. 277 PB
SHONEY'S, INC., 1727 Elm Hill Pike, 37210, pg. 1467 PB
Shoney's Restaurant Div., 1727 Elm Hill Pike, 37210, pg. 1467 PB
SmithKline Beecham Clinical Laboratories, 2545 Park Plaza, 37203, pg. 1265 IT
Sony Music, Nashville, 34 Music Sq. E., 37203-4323, pg. 1284 IT
Southern Hospitality Corporation, P.O. Box 48, 37202, pg. 488 PB
SouthTrust Bank of Middle Tennessee, 1801 West End Ave., 37201, pg. 1492 PB
SOUTHWESTERN/GREAT AMERICAN INC., 2451 Atrium Way, 37214, pg. 1018 PV
STANDARD CANDY CO., INC., 715 Massman Dr., 37210-3787, pg. 1030 PV
STAR TRANSPORTATION, INC., P.O. Box 100925, 1116 Polk Ave., 37224, pg. 1035 PV
Stewart Smith Group, Inc., Willis Corroon Plaza, 26 Century Blvd., 37214, pg. 1508 IT
Stewart Smith Southeast, Inc., Willis Corroon Plaza, 26 Century Blvd., 37214, pg. 1508 IT
SunTrust Bank, Nashville, N.A., Third National Bank Building, 201 4th Ave. N., 37219, pg. 1538 PB
SunTrust Banks of Tennessee, Inc., 201 4th Ave. N., 37219, pg. 1538 PB
Surgical Care Affiliates, Inc., 102 Woodmont Blvd., Ste. 610, 3705-2212, pg. 803 PB
TAYLOR IMPRESSION, INC., 1705 Charlotte Ave., 37203, pg. 1070 PV
Temco Fireplace Products, Inc., 301 S. Perimeter Park Dr., Ste. 227, 37211, pg. 1576 PB
Tencarva Machinery Co., 839 Fesslers Pkwy., 37210, pg. 1075 PV
Tennessean Newspapers, Inc., 1100 Broadway, 37203, pg. 701 PB
TENNESSEE DRESSED BEEF COMPANY, 50 Van Buren St., 37208, pg. 1076 PV
Tennessee Insurance Co., 633 Thompson Ln., 37204, pg. 563 PV
Tennessee Valley Life Insurance Co., One Commerce Pl., 37219, pg. 1163 PB
Thermal Industries Inc., 1106 Elm Hill Pike, Ste. 120, 37210-3519, pg. 491 PV
I.C. THOMASSON ASSOCIATES, INC., 2120 Eighth Ave., So., 37204, pg. 1083 PV
TOP BILLING INC., 1222 16th Ave., S., Ste. 24, 37212, pg. 1091 PV
TRACTOR SUPPLY CO., 320 Plus Park Blvd., 37217, pg. 1627 PB
Trans Financial Bank, 814 Church St., pg. 1628 PB
Trans Financial Bank of Tennessee, F.S.B., 814 Church St., 37202, pg. 1628 PB
Trans Financial Bank Tennessee, N.A., 814 Church St., pg. 1628 PB
Transcorp, 102 Woodmont Blvd., 37205, pg. 451 PB
Transplatinum Service Corp., 5042 Linbar Dr., 37210, pg. 1155 PB
Tridon Inc., P.O. Box 1600, 37202-1600, pg. 11 PB
Turner Construction Company, 555 Marriott Dr., Ste. 210, 37210, pg. 1645 PB
UPB of Middle Tennessee, 401 Union St., 37219, pg. 1669 PB
Underwriters Management Associates, Inc., Willis Corroon Plaza, 26 Century Blvd., 37124, pg. 1508 IT
United Companies Mortgage of Tennessee, Inc., P.O. Box 140395, 2401 Lebanon Rd., 37214, pg. 1675 PB
THE UNITED METHODIST PUBLISHING HOUSE, 201 Eighth Ave. S., 37203, pg. 1122 PV
Unitog Rental Facility, 1700 State, 37203, pg. 1693 PB
THE UPPER ROOM, 1908 Grand Ave., 37212, pg. 1129 PV
Volunteer Leather Co., Genesco Pk. 140, 37202, pg. 728 PB
WTVF, 474 James Robertson Pkwy., 37219, pg. 647 PV
WERTHAN PACKAGING, INC., 1400 8th Ave. N., 37208, pg. 1162 PV
Willis Corroon, 26 Century Blvd., 37214, pg. 1504 IT
Willis Corroon Administrative Services Corporation, Willis Corroon Plaza, 26 Century Blvd., 37124, pg. 1505 IT
Willis Corroon Administrative Services, Inc., 26 Century Blvd., 37214, pg. 1504 IT
Willis Corroon Advanced Risk Management Services, Willis Corroon Plaza, 26 Century Blvd., 37214, pg. 1505 IT
Willis Corroon Americas, 26 Century Blvd., 37214, pg. 1505 IT
Willis Corroon Construction Division, Willis Corroon Plaza, 26 Century Blvd., 37124, pg. 1504 IT
Willis Corroon Corp., Willis Corroon Plaza, 26 Century Blvd., 37214, pg. 1504 IT
Willis Corroon International/Americas, Willis Corroon Plaza, 26 Century Blvd., 37214, pg. 1508 IT
Willis Corroon Property & Casualty Programs Div., 26 Century Blvd., 37214, pg. 1508 IT
Willis Faber North America, Inc.-Tennessee, Willis Corroon Plaza, 26 Century Blvd., 37124, pg. 1504 IT
Zellerbach Division, Ten Center, 566 Mainstream Dr., 37228, pg. 1075 PB

New Tazewell

Century Telephone of Claiborne, Inc., P.O. Box 100, 507 Main St., 37825-0100, pg. 330 PB
Claiborne Telephone Co., P.O. Box 100, 37825, pg. 330 PB
England/Corsair, 402 Old Knoxville Hwy., 37825, pg. 972 PB

Newport

Falcon-Newport, 810 W. Hwy. 25/70, 37821, pg. 611 PB

Oak Ridge

Boeing Aerospace & Electronics, Oak Ridge, 767 Boeing Rd., 37830, pg. 240 PB
EG & G Instruments, 801 S. Illinois Ave., 37831-0895, pg. 543 PB
EG & G Instruments Applied Research, 801 S. Illinois Ave., 37831-2011, pg. 543 PB
EG & G Ortec, 100 Midland Rd., 37831, pg. 543 PB
Lockwood Greene Technologies, P.O. Box 3562, 1201 Oak Ridge Tpke., Ste. 101, 37831-3562, pg. 633 IT
Martin Marietta Energy Group, P.O. Box 2009, 37831-8001, pg. 1007 PB
Martin Marietta Uranium Enrichment Operations, 702 South Illinois, Ste. B-201, 37830, pg. 1007 PB
NationsBank/Eastern, 795 Main St., 37831, pg. 1163 PB
The Oak Ridger, 785 Oak Ridge Turnpike, 37830-3446, pg. 995 PV
Oxford Instruments-Nuclear Measurements Group, 601 Oak Ridge Tpke., 37830-7079, pg. 1018 IT
Pathway Bellows, Inc., 115 Franklin Rd., 37831-3027, pg. 521 PB

Old Hickory

Genesee A & B, Inc., P.O. Box 429, 1409 Robinson Rd., 37138-0429, pg. 446 PV
Reemay Inc., Industrial Rd., 70 Old Hickory Blvd., 37138, pg. 113 IT
Stratos Boat Company, Ltd., 931 Industrial Rd., 37138, pg. 478 PV

Oneida

Hartco Flooring Company, 300 S. Main St., 37841, pg. 1322 PB

Ooltewah

THE ARNOLD PALMER GOLF COMPANY, 6201 Mountain View Rd., 37363, pg. 132 PB
MILLER INDUSTRIES, INC., P.O. Box 120, 37363, pg. 1112 PB

Paris

KESTERSON FOOD COMPANY, INC., 200 Hwy. 69 N., 38242, pg. 616 PV
Plumley Companies, 100 Plumley Dr., 38242, pg. 480 PB
Union Planters Bank of Northwest Tennessee, 914 E. Wood St., 38242, pg. 1669 PB

Parsons

Tennessee Telephone Company, P.O. Box 610, 302 E. Main St., 38363, pg. 1572 PB

Pigeon Forge

Airport '82 Associates Ltd., P.O. Box 10, 3124 Tammy King Rd., 37863, pg. 392 PV
FAMILY INNS OF AMERICA, INC., 3124 Tammy King Rd., 37863-0010, pg. 392 PV
Lucky Inns of America, Inc., P.O. Box 10, 37863, pg. 393 PV
Regional Development Corp., P.O. Box 10, 37863, pg. 393 PV

PB - *U.S. Public Companies Volume*
PV - *U.S. Private Companies Volume*
IT - *International Public & Private Companies Volume*

Kenneth M. Seaton Enterprises, P.O. Box 10, 37863, pg. 393 **PV**
Tri-Management Corp., P.O. Box 10, 37863, pg. 393 **PV**

Pikeville

Excel Systems, 132 Ferro Rd., 37367, pg. 598 **PB**

Piney Flats

Modern Forge/Tennessee, Tri County Industrial Pk., 37686, pg. 754 **PV**
THE PATY COMPANY, 220 Piney Flats Rd., 37686, pg. 844 **PV**

Portland

Albany International Appleton Wire Div., P.O. Box 508, 37148, pg. 36 **PB**
Albany International/Industrial Eng Process Fabrics Division, P.O. Box 508, 214 Kirby Rd., 37148, pg. 36 **PB**
Associated Building Systems, 124 Kirby Dr., 37148, pg. 699 **IT**
The Crown Group-Portland Plant, 133 Davis St., 37148, pg. 293 **PV**
Kirby Building Systems, Inc., 124 Kirby Dr., 37148, pg. 699 **IT**

Powell

ALLTEL Tennessee, Inc., 2104 Emory Rd., P.O. Box 620, 37849, pg. 380 **PB**

Pulaski

Pulaski Rubber Co., P.O. Drawer I, 38478, pg. 902 **PV**
SunTrust Bank, South Central Tennessee, N.A., 225 W. Madison, 38478, pg. 1538 **PB**

Ripley

Ripley Graphics, 1236 American Way, 38063, pg. 78 **PB**

Rockwood

Akzo Nobel Fortafil Fibers Inc., P.O. Box 357, 121 Cardiff Valley Rd., 37854, pg. 48 **IT**
Rockwood Times, P.O. Box 297, N. Kingston Ave., 37854, pg. 648 **PV**

Rogersville

Dennison Transoceanic Corporation, 530 W. Main St., 37857, pg. 153 **PB**

Rossville

Kellogg Convenience Food Plant, 80 Morrison Rd., 38066, pg. 947 **PB**

Rutherford

Kellwood Sportswear, 302 N. Trenton St., 38369, pg. 948 **PB**

Selmer

HENCO, INC., P.O. Box 547, Selmer Industrial Park, 38375, pg. 521 **PV**

Sequatchie

Sequatchie Handle Works, Inc., P.O. Box 140, 37374, pg. 669 **PV**

Sevierville

E-Z BOWZ, INC., 117 S. Boulevard, 37862, pg. 352 **PV**
Sevierville Facility, Wagner Lighting Division, Ray L. Reagan Industrial Park, 1130 Wagner Dr., 37862, pg. 442 **PB**

Shelbyville

American Natl. Can Co., P.O. Box 757, 37160, pg. 1029 **IT**
Calsonic Mfg. Corp., One Calsonic Way, 37160, pg. 944 **IT**

Smithville

General Shale Products Corp.-Smithville Concrete Div., Hays St., 37166, pg. 844 **IT**

Smyrna

All-Care Professional Services, Inc., 988 Mayfield Dr., 37167, pg. 841 **PB**
Nissan Motor Mfg. Corp., U.S.A., 983 Nissan Dr., 37167, pg. 945 **IT**
Perrigo of Tennessee, One Swan Dr., 37167, pg. 1280 **PB**
Square D Company, 330 Weakley Rd., 37167, pg. 1208 **IT**

Somerville

First State Bank of Fayette Co., 16880 Hwy. 64, 38055, pg. 1669 **PB**

South Pittsburg

Galaxy Carpet Mills, Inc., P.O. Box 348, 37380, pg. 1121 **PB**
Salem Carpet Mills, P.O. Box 703, 37380, pg. 1464 **PB**

Sparta

General Shale Products Corp.-Sparta Concrete Div., 101 S. Wilson St., 38583, pg. 844 **IT**
Thomas Lighting-Sparta Opers., Rte. 70 S., 38583, pg. 1599 **IT**
Wilson Sporting Goods Co., 4600 Roberts Matthew Hwy., 38583, pg. 73 **IT**

Springfield

All American Homes of Tennessee, Inc., P.O. Box 890, 102 Evergreen Dr., 37172, pg. 388 **PB**
ALstrip South, 197 Evergreen Dr., 37172, pg. 43 **PB**
Frigidaire Home Products-Range Products, 1100 Industrial Dr., 37172, pg. 440 **IT**
HOLLINGSWORTH OIL CO. INC., 1503 Memorial Blvd., 37172, pg. 535 **PV**
Perstorp Components Inc.-Springfield, 2409 Industrial Dr., 37172, pg. 1040 **IT**
Unarco Material, 701 16th Ave. E., 37172, pg. 922 **PV**
Wilson Sporting Goods Co., 601 Central Ave., 37172, pg. 73 **IT**

Strawberry Plains

CBP Resources, 9300 Johnson Rd., 37871, pg. 192 **PV**

Sweetwater

Tennessee Packaging, Longmeadow Rd., 37874, pg. 177 **PV**
Vestal Manufacturing, 176 Industrial Park Rd., 37874, pg. 1737 **PB**

Tellico Plains

Tellico Telephone Company, Inc., P.O. Box 9, 37385, pg. 1572 **PB**

Toone

Kilgore Operations, Kilgore Dr., 38381, pg. 47 **PB**

Trenton

Trenton Division, P.O. Box 128, 38382, pg. 1566 **PB**
Trenton Mills, Factory St., 38382, pg. 538 **PB**

Tullahoma

Sverdrup Technology, Inc., 600 William Northern Blvd., P.O. Box 884, 37388, pg. 1057 **PV**
System Service Division, 1308 S. Washington St., 37388, pg. 466 **PB**
Tennessee Dickel Distilling Co., Cascade Spring Branch Rd., Coffee Country, 37388, pg. 412 **IT**
Wilson Sporting Goods Co., 303 Wilson Ave., 37388, pg. 73 **IT**

Union City

NationsBank/Union City, P.O. Box 370, 38261, pg. 1163 **PB**

Vonore

NATIONAL SEATING CO., 200 National Dr., 37885, pg. 786 **PV**

Wartburg

Morgan County News, P.O. Box 346, 224 Maiden St., 37887, pg. 648 **PV**

Waverly

Global Power Company, 4801 W. Trace Creek Rd., 37185, pg. 74 **IT**
Houston Products, 4801 W. Trace Creek Rd., 37185, pg. 74 **IT**

Waynesboro

Tennessee Telephone Company, P.O. Box 433, South Main St., 38485, pg. 1572 **PB**

White House

SCT B Inc., P.O. Box 737, 100 SCT Dr., 37188, pg. 1176 **IT**

Whiteville

Hardeman Co. Correctional Facility, P.O. Box 549, 2520 Union Springs Rd., 38075, pg. 450 **PB**

Winchester

Regions Bank/Winchester, P.O. Box 500, 37398, pg. 1373 **PB**

Woodbury

Bank of Commerce, 200 Public Sq., 37190, pg. 1669 **PB**
General Shale Products Corp.-Woodbury Concrete Div., McMinnville Hwy., 37910, pg. 844 **IT**

TEXAS

Abilene

Abilene Reporter News, N. First & Cypress, 79601, pg. 793 **PB**
Block Plant, P.O. Box 6633, 2065 Oak, 79604, pg. 936 **PB**
FIRST FINANCIAL BANKSHARES, INC., 400 Pine St., 79601-5128, pg. 633 **PB**
First National Bank of Abilene, 400 Pine St., 79601-5128, pg. 633 **PB**
First State Bank N.A., Abilene, 547 Chestnut St., 79602, pg. 874 **PB**
General Dynamics, Abilene Facility, 300 Wall St., 79603-6435, pg. 709 **PB**
Gooch Packing Co., Inc., P.O. Box 2738, 79604, pg. 909 **PV**
Hewlett-Packard Company, 3303 N. Third, Ste. G, 79603, pg. 815 **PB**
INDEPENDENT BANKSHARES, INC., 547 Chestnut St., 79602, pg. 874 **PB**
West Texas Utilities Co., 301 Cypress, 79604, pg. 324 **PB**
West Texas Wholesale Supply Co., 4th & Plum, 79604, pg. 335 **PV**

Addison

TGI Friday's, Inc., 14665 Midway Rd., 75244, pg. 212 **PV**
Telpar, Inc., 4181 Centurion Way, 75244, pg. 890 **IT**
UNC ARTEX, 15502 Weight Brothers Dr., 75001, pg. 710 **PB**
Wine World Estates, 4004 Belt Line Rd., Ste. 100, 75244, pg. 917 **IT**

Alamo

Crest Fruit Co., 100 N. Tower Rd., 78516, pg. 1506 **PB**
Speedling Incorporated Alamo Transplants Division, P.O. Box 730, 78516, pg. 1024 **PV**

Allen

Matra Communication USA Inc, 601 Intecom Dr., 75002, pg. 795 **IT**
QUEST MEDICAL, INC., One Allentown Pkwy., 75002-4211, pg. 1352 **PB**

Alvin

Pipe Repairs, Inc., 1019 S. Hood, 77511, pg. 1562 **PB**
Premier Polymers, Inc., Box 353, 4000 E. Hwy. 6, Rte. 6, 77511, pg. 370 **IT**
TEAM, INC., 1019 S. Hood St., 77511, pg. 1562 **PB**
Team Industrial Services, Inc., 1019 S. Hood, 77511, pg. 1562 **PB**
TECO Manufacturing, Inc., 1019 S. Hood, 77511, pg. 1562 **PB**

Amarillo

Affiliated Finance Inc., 1401 W. Farmers Ave., 79118, pg. 25 **PV**
AFFILIATED FOODS, INC., 1401 W. Farmers Ave., 79118, pg. 25 **PV**
Affiliated Funding Inc., 300 N. Taylor, 79105, pg. 25 **PV**
Amarillo Hardware Company, 622 Grant St., 79101, pg. 335 **PV**
Block Plant, P.O. Box 31058, 2801 E. Third, 79104, pg. 936 **PV**
CACTUS FEEDERS, INC., 2209 W. Seventh St., 79116-3050, pg. 198 **PV**
Diamond Shamrock Credit Card Center, 112 W. Eighth, 79105, pg. 1663 **PV**
Flo-Line Filters, Inc., 1501 S. Johnson, 79105, pg. 855 **PV**
Friona Agriculture Credit Corp., P.O. Box 15568, 79105, pg. 429 **PV**
FRIONA INDUSTRIES, L.P., 900 Amarillo Natl. Bank Bldg., 410 S. Taylor St., Ste. 900, 79101, pg. 429 **PV**
GILVIN-TERRILL INC., P.O. Box 9027, 79105, pg. 455 **PV**
Hewlett-Packard Company, 3613 S. Georgia, Ste. 104, 79109, pg. 815 **PB**
Hilb, Rogal & Hamilton Company of Amarillo, 1800 Washington, Ste. 400, 79105, pg. 827 **PB**
IBP-Amarillo, P.O. Box 30500, 79187, pg. 852 **PB**
NitroMite Fertilizer, 4211 1-40 W., Ste. 200, 79106, pg. 1663 **PB**
Quixx Corporation, P.O. Box 12033, Tyler at Sixth, 79101, pg. 1170 **PB**
Randall County Feed Yard, Rte. 4, Box 99, 79119, pg. 429 **PV**

U.S. LOCATED COMPANIES TEXAS

Southwestern Public Service Company, SPS Tower, Tyler at Sixth, 79101, pg. 1170 **PB**
TCA Cable of Amarillo, Inc., 6654 Canyon Dr., 79109, pg. 1553 **PB**
TECH SPRAY, INC., 1011 N.W. First St., 79107, pg. 1071 **PV**
United Filters, Inc., 1501 S. Johnson, 79101, pg. 855 **PV**
Utility Engineering Corporation, 5601 I-40 W., 79101, pg. 1170 **PB**

Angleton

BENCHMARK ELECTRONICS INC., 3000 Technology Dr., 77515, pg. 210 **PB**
Intermedics Inc., 4000 Technology Dr., 77515, pg. 1307 **IT**
Sulzermedica USA Inc., 4000 Technology Dr., 77515, pg. 1307 **IT**

Arlington

Accessory Design Group, Ltd., 690 E. Lamar Blvd., Ste. 300, 76011, pg. 1560 **PB**
Altai Development Laboratory, 624 Six Flags Dr., Ste. 150, 76011, pg. 1309 **PB**
AMERICAN EXCELSIOR COMPANY, 850 Ave. H E., 76011, pg. 53 **PV**
The Arlington Citizen-Journal, 1111 W. Abram, 76004, pg. 512 **PB**
Atlas-Alchem Plastics-Texas, 840 N. Great Southwest Pkwy., 76011, pg. 1496 **PB**
BERRYMAN PRODUCTS, INC., 3800 E. Randol Mill Rd., 76011, pg. 138 **PV**
Bowman Distribution, 1111 Great N. Southwest Pkwy., 76011, pg. 190 **PB**
Burns & Wilcox - Arlington Office, 2261 Brookhollow Plaza Dr., Ste.209, 76006, pg. 609 **PV**
CPC of Texas, Inc., 1011 N. Cooper St., 76011, pg. 1712 **PB**
DAIRY FARMERS OF AMERICA, INC., 1600 E. Lamar Blvd., 76011, pg. 307 **PV**
Dallas-Ft. Worth Suburban Newspapers, Inc., 1000 Ave. H, E., 76011, pg. 209 **PB**
Dayton Rogers of Texas, 1107 Commercial Blvd. N., 76017, pg. 318 **PV**
ElectroCom Automation L.P., 2910 Ave. F, 76011-5276, pg. 1244 **IT**
FIRST CASH, INC., 690 E. Lamar Blvd., Ste. 400, 76011, pg. 627 **PB**
GATX Logistics, Inc.-Texas (Public), 2023 Exchange Dr., 76011, pg. 692 **PB**
General Magnaplate Texas, 801 Ave. G. East, 76011, pg. 717 **PB**
Green Tree Acceptance of Texas, Inc., 1600 E. Pioneer Pkwy., Ste. 300, 76010, pg. 763 **PB**
Heritage Oaks, 1112 Gibbins Rd., 76011, pg. 839 **PB**
D.R. HORTON, INC., 1901 Ascension Blvd., Ste. 100, 76006, pg. 840 **PB**
ITW Electronic Component Packaging, 3400 Ave. E., 76011-5235, pg. 866 **PB**
INNOSERV TECHNOLOGIES, INC., 320 Westway Pl., 76018-1099, pg. 879 **PB**
InnoServ Technologies, Inc., 4330 Beltway, Ste. 200, 76018, pg. 880 **PB**
Interturbine Dallas Casings, 2800 Avenue East, 76011, pg. 1690 **PB**
Johnson & Johnson Medical, Inc., P.O. Box 90130, 2500 Arbrook Blvd., 76004-3130, pg. 928 **PB**
Johnson Storage & Moving, Cleburne, 625 107th St., 76111, pg. 594 **PV**
Kinro, Inc., 4381 Green Oaks Blvd. W., 76016, pg. 529 **PB**
Lockheed Support Systems, Inc., 1600 E. Pioneer Pkwy., Ste. 440, 76010, pg. 1009 **PB**
MBS HOLDING, INC., 3403 E. Abram St., 76010, pg. 685 **PV**
MARTIN SPROCKET & GEAR, INC., 3100 Sprocket Dr., 76015, pg. 709 **PV**
Mayfield Building Supply Co., 3403 E. Abram, 76010, pg. 686 **PV**
Meritex Plastics Industries, Inc., 3301 E. Randol Mill Rd., 76011, pg. 867 **PB**
MORITZ CADILLAC-BMW INC., 2001 N. Collins, 76011, pg. 761 **PV**
Nationwide Acceptance, 912 113th St., 76011, pg. 917 **PV**
SALADMASTER, 912 113th St., 76011, pg. 961 **PV**
Saladmaster, Inc., 912 113th St., 76011, pg. 917 **PV**
Shoals Supply, Inc., 4381 Green Oaks Blvd. W., 76016, pg. 529 **PB**
Six Flags Hurricane Harbor, 1800 E. Lamar Blvd., 76006, pg. 1611 **PB**
Six Flags Over Texas, 2201 Rd. to Six Flags, 76010, pg. 1612 **PB**
Southwest Region, 3015 Ave. E East, 76011, pg. 617 **PB**
TBAC - Prince Gardner, Inc., 690 E. Lamar Blvd., Ste. 330, 76011, pg. 1560 **PB**
TANDY BRANDS ACCESSORIES, INC., 690 E. Lamar Blvd., Ste. 200, 76011, pg. 1560 **PB**
Tandy Signs, 1908 S. Peyco Dr., 76017, pg. 1560 **PB**
Texas Division, 1001 Oakmead Dr., 76011, pg. 518 **IT**
Tucker Housewares, P.O. Box 5467, 721 111th St., 76011, pg. 1118 **PB**
VANDERGRIFF CHEVROLET GEO, 1200 W. I-20, 76017, pg. 1133 **PV**
WBAP-KSCS Radio, Inc., 2221 E. Lamar, Ste. 400, 76006, pg. 512 **PB**
WEBB BUILDERS HARDWARE, 3016 Avenue E East, 76011, pg. 1156 **PV**
Floyd West & Company, 1250 E. Copeland Rd., Ste. 900, 76011, pg. 609 **PV**
Wet-N-Wild, A Six Flags Water Park, 1800 East Lamr Blvd., 76006, pg. 1612 **PB**

Arp

Baker / Altech, Highway 64, 75750, pg. 602 **PV**

Athens

Athens Brick Co., Flat Creek Rd., 75751, pg. 1585 **PB**
Structural Bearings Div., FM 2495 at Progress Way, 75751, pg. 689 **PB**

Atlanta

Anthony Forest Div., S. Louis St., 75551, pg. 76 **PV**

Austin

ADCS, Inc., 6805 Capital of Texas Hwy., 78731, pg. 12 **PB**
AMP Recycling, 1704 Howard Ln., 78664, pg. 413 **PB**
APV Glacier Industries, 3409 Executive Center Dr., 78731, pg. 1240 **IT**
AU Management Corp., 1230 Highland Mall, 78752, pg. 1409 **PB**
ADAMS EXTRACT CO., INC., 11206 IH-35 S., 78747, pg. 16 **PV**
Advanced Microcontroller Division, 6501 William Cannon Dr. W., 78735, pg. 1137 **PB**
Alabama Renal Stone Institute, Inc., 1301 Capitol of Texas Hwy., 78746, pg. 1327 **PB**
Allright Parking of Austin, Inc., 720 Brazos T., Ste. S-14, 78701, pg. 43 **PV**
American City Business Journals, Inc., 1301 S. Capitol Texas Hwy., Ste. B-224, 78746, pg. 19 **PV**
American Innovations, Ltd., 12112 Technology Blvd., 78729, pg. 491 **PV**
AMERICAN TELEVISION TIME, INC., 207 Barsana Ave., 78737, pg. 63 **PV**
Analysis & Applied Research Div., 6500 Tracor Ln., 78725-2070, pg. 1627 **PB**
ARRHYTHMIA RESEARCH TECHNOLOGY, INC., 5910 Courtyard Dr., Ste. 300, 78731, pg. 133 **PB**
AST Research, Inc., Seven Village Cir., 76262, pg. 1182 **IT**
AUSTIN JET LTD., 1721 Wilshire Blvd., 78722, pg. 100 **PV**
Austron Inc., Exit 248 N. Interstate Hwy. 35, 78761, pg. 488 **PB**
Automatic Signal/Eagle Signal, 8004 Cameron Rd., 78754, pg. 1245 **IT**
L.G. Balfour Co., Inc., 7211 Circle S. Rd., 78745, pg. 258 **PV**
Barton Creek Capital, Inc., 504 Alocka St., 78701, pg. 1554 **PB**
BERNARD JOHNSON YOUNG INC., 2600 Lake Austin Blvd., #12101, 78703, pg. 136 **PV**
Burnup & Sims of TX, 2716 E. Fifth, 78767, pg. 1056 **PB**
CCI/TRIAD CORPORATION, 6207 Bee Cave Rd., 78746, pg. 193 **PV**
C.P. Rehab Corp. of Delaware, 1301 Capitol of Texas Hwy., 78746, pg. 1327 **PB**
CSC Financial Services Group, 9500 Arboretum Blvd., 78759-6399, pg. 422 **PB**
CSIC Microcontroller Division, 6501 William Cannon Dr. W., 78735, pg. 1137 **PB**
CALCASIEU LUMBER COMPANY, 4501 Burleson Rd., 78744, pg. 200 **PV**
Carbomedics, Inc., 1300 E. Anderson Ln., 78752, pg. 1307 **IT**
Centex Materials, Inc., P.O. Box 2252, 78768, pg. 322 **PB**
Charter Behavioral Health System of Austin, Inc., 8402 Cross Park Dr., 78754, pg. 1033 **PB**
Circle International, 1514 Ed Bluestein Rd., Ste. 206, 78721, pg. 372 **PB**
Clear Channel Radio, Inc., 811 Barton Springs Rd., Ste. 967, 78704, pg. 383 **PB**
Columbia Scientific Industries Corporation, 11950 Jollyville Rd., 78720, pg. 1500 **IT**
Columbia Universal Life Insurance Company, 11044 Research Blvd., Bldg. A, Fifth Fl., 78759, pg. 79 **PB**
COMMEMORATIVE BRANDS, INC., 7211 Circle S Rd., 78745, pg. 258 **PV**
Commercial Metals-Austin Inc., 710 Industrial Blvd., 78745, pg. 413 **PB**
Consolidated Wholesale Lumber Co., 4501 Burleson Rd., 78744, pg. 200 **PV**
Continental Homes of Austin, L.P., 4515 Seton Ctr. Pkwy., 78759, pg. 441 **PB**
Countermeasures & Combat Systems Division, 6500 Tracor Ln., 78725-2070, pg. 1627 **PB**
Cryco Quartz, Inc., 8107 Altoga Dr., 78724, pg. 1408 **IT**
Cryco Twenty Two, Inc., 8107 Altoga Dr., 78724, pg. 1408 **IT**
Crystal Semiconductor Corporation, 4210 S. Industrial St., 78760, pg. 375 **PB**
Customer Service & Brand Strategy, 5601 William Cannon Blvd., 78735, pg. 1137 **PB**
Cutter Aviation, 811 W. Howard Ln., 78753-9744, pg. 299 **PV**
DAC International, Inc., 6702 McNeil Drive, 78729, pg. 187 **PB**
Dairyland County Mutual Insurance Co., 305 E. Huntland, 78752, pg. 985 **PV**
Defense Systems Div., 6500 Tracor Ln., 78725-2070, pg. 1627 **PB**
Dell Marketing Corporation, 2214 W. Braker Lane, 78758, pg. 495 **PB**
Digital Signal Processing Division, 6501 William Cannon Dr. W., 78735, pg. 1137 **PB**
Dresser Industries Wayne Division, 3814 Jarrett Way, 78728, pg. 528 **PB**
DURHAM TRANSPORTATION, INC., 9011 Mountain Ridge Rd., Ste., 200, 78759-7222, pg. 348 **PV**
EMC Test System, L.P., 2205 Kramer Ln., 78758, pg. 546 **PB**
Eagle Signal Controls, 8004 Cameron Rd., 78753, pg. 481 **PB**
Electra Communications, 5000 Plaza on the Lake, Ste. 100, 78746, pg. 556 **PV**
Electrical Products Division, 3M Austin Ctr, Bldg. A130-4N-1, 1801 River Place Blvd., 78726-9000, pg. 1605 **PB**
Electronic Products Division, 3M Austin Ctr, Bldg A130-3N-27, 6801 River Place Blvd., 78726-9000, pg. 1605 **PB**
Epsilon Industrial, 2215 Grand Ave. Pkwy., 78728, pg. 1593 **PB**
Espey Huston Associates, Inc., 206 S. Wild Basin Rd., Ste. 300, 78746-3343, pg. 826 **PV**
Farm Credit Bank of Texas, La Costa Office Park, 6210 Hwy. 290 E., 78723, pg. 398 **PV**
Fast Static RAM Division, 3501 Ed Bluestein Blvd., 78721, pg. 1137 **PB**
Featherlite Building Products Operation, 2824 Real Street, 78741, pg. 936 **PB**
FINANCIAL INDUSTRIES CORP., The Austin Centre, 701 Brazos, 12th Fl., 78701, pg. 622 **PB**
First American Flood Data Services, 11902 Burnett Rd., 78758, pg. 625 **PB**
Fogarty Klein & Partners Yellow Pages, Inc., 1150 Lakeway Dr., Ste. 150, 78734, pg. 416 **PV**
Four Seasons Hotel, 98 San Jacinto Blvd., 78701, pg. 502 **IT**
GSD&M, 828 W. 6th St., 78703, pg. 436 **PV**
General Employment Enterprises, Inc., Bldg. 2, Ste. 205, 1250 Capital of Texas Hwy., 78746, pg. 715 **PB**
Genus, Inc., 2209 Woodward St., 78744, pg. 732 **PB**
Hart Distribution Services, 3106 Longhorn Blvd., 78759, pg. 507 **PV**
Hart Forms & Services, 11500 Metric Blvd., Ste. 300, 78758, pg. 507 **PV**
HART GRAPHICS INC., 8000 Shoal Creek Blvd., 78757, pg. 507 **PV**
HEALTHCARE AMERICA, INC., 1407 W. Stassney Ln., 78745, pg. 515 **PV**
Hewlett-Packard Company, 1826-P Kramer Ln., 78758, pg. 815 **PB**
Holt, Rinehart and Winston School Division, 1627 Woodland Ave., 78741, pg. 783 **PB**
IPC Technologies, Inc., 10300 Metric Blvd., 78758, pg. 651 **IT**
IXC COMMUNICATIONS, INC., 1122 Capital of Texas Hwy S., 78746, pg. 556 **PV**
Intergraph Corporation, Ecehelon Iii, 9420 Research Blvd., Ste. 330, 78759, pg. 890 **PB**
Intermedics Orthopedics, Inc., 990 Spectrum, 78717, pg. 1307 **IT**
InternContinental Life Corp., The Austin Centre, 701 Brazos, Ste. 1400, 78701, pg. 622 **PB**
Jaco Electronics, Inc., 2120-M Braker Ln., 78758, pg. 921 **PB**
KEYI-FM, 811 Barton Springs, Ste. 967, 78704, pg. 384 **PB**
KFON-AM, 811 Barton Springs, Ste. 967, 78704, pg. 384 **PB**
KHFI-FM, 811 Barton Springs, Ste. 967, 78704, pg. 384 **PB**
KPEZ-FM, 811 Barton Springs, Ste. 967, 78704, pg. 384 **PB**
KTBC, 119 E. Tenth St., 78701, pg. 926 **IT**
KVUE-TV, Inc., 3201 Steck Ave., 78758, pg. 702 **PB**
KXAN, 908 W. Martin Luther King Blvd., 78701, pg. 11 **PB**
Koslow's, 10000 U.S. Hwy. 183, 79759, pg. 597 **PB**
LaVaca Realty Co., 504 Lavaca, Ste. 800, 78701, pg. 1491 **PB**
Lithotripters, Inc., 1301 Capital of Texas Hwy., Ste. C300, 78746, pg. 1327 **PB**
Lockheed Austin Division, P.O. Box 17100, 78760, pg. 1008 **PB**
Lone Star Produce Acquisition Corp., 8110 Springdale Rd., 78724, pg. 682 **PB**
MOS Digital-Analog Integrated Circuits Division, 3501 Ed Bluestein Blvd., 78721, pg. 1137 **PB**
MEDIATEX COMMUNICATIONS CORPORATION, P.O. Box 1569, 78767-1569, pg. 727 **PV**
Medtronic Carbon Implants, Inc., 8605 Cross Park Dr., 78754, pg. 1083 **PB**
Mercado Gas Services, 504 Lavaca, Ste. 800, 78701, pg. 1491 **PB**
Milgray/Austin, 11824 Jollyville Rd., 78759, pg. 206 **PB**
Motorola MCTG, 6501 William Cannon Dr. W., 78735, pg. 1138 **PB**
Motorola MMTG, 3501 Ed Bluestein Blvd., 78721, pg. 1137 **PB**
Mutual Signal Corporation of Michigan, 5000 Plaza on the Lake, Ste. 100, 78746, pg. 556 **PV**
NCS Information Services, 2201 Donley Dr., Ste. 100, 78758-8758, pg. 1155 **PB**
NWL 806 Main, Inc., 850 E. Anderson Ln., 78752, pg. 1161 **PB**
NWL Financial, Inc., 850 E. Anderson Ln., 78752, pg. 1161 **PB**
NWL Investments, Inc., 850 E. Anderson Ln., 78752, pg. 1161 **PB**
NWL Properties, Inc., 850 E. Anderson Ln., 78752, pg. 1161 **PB**
NWL Services, Inc., 850 E. Anderson Ln., 78752, pg. 1161 **PB**
NALLE PLASTICS INC., 220 E. St. Elmo, 78745, pg. 773 **PV**
NATIONAL INSTRUMENTS CORP., 6504 Bridge Point Pkwy., 78730, pg. 1157 **PB**

PB - *U.S. Public Companies Volume*
PV - *U.S. Private Companies Volume*
IT - *International Public & Private Companies Volume*

Geographic Index-U.S.

Geographic Index-U.S.

NATIONAL WESTERN LIFE INSURANCE COMPANY, 850 E. Anderson Ln., 78752-1602, pg. 1161   **PB**
NationsBank of Texas, P.O. Box 4218, 919 Congress Ave., 78701, pg. 1164   **PB**
NYLIFE Administration Corp., 800 San Jacinto Center, 98 San Jacinto Blvd., Ste. 800, 78701, pg. 795   **PV**
Norteno Pipeline Co., 504 Lavaca, Ste. 800, 78701, pg. 1491   **PB**
Ohio Litho Inc., 1301 Capitol of Texas Hwy., 78746, pg. 1327   **PB**
Origin Systems, Inc., 12940 Research Blvd., 78750, pg. 569   **PB**
PCI, 12416 Hymeadow Dr., 78750, pg. 826   **PV**
Palladin Financial, Inc., 504 Alocka St., 78701, pg. 1554   **PB**
Parker Kinetic Designs, 8303 Mopac, Ste. 240C, 78759, pg. 1259   **PB**
PERVASIVE SOFTWARE INC., 8834 Capital of Texas Hwy., 78759, pg. 1280   **PB**
Powered by Motorola, 6501 William Cannon Dr. W., 78735, pg. 1137   **PB**
Premium Polymers Inc., 9721 Hwy. 290 E., 412   **PV**
Prime Cardiac Rehabilitation Services, Inc., 1301 Capitol of Texas Hwy., 78746, pg. 1327   **PB**
Prime Diagnostic Corp. of Florida, 1301 Capitol of Texas Hwy., 78746, pg. 1327   **PB**
Prime Diagnostic Services, Inc., 1301 Capitol of Texas Hwy., 78746, pg. 1327   **PB**
Prime Kidney Stone Treatment, 1301 Capitol of Texas Hwy., 78746, pg. 1327   **PB**
Prime Lithotripsy Services, Inc., 1301 Capitol of Texas Hwy., 78746, pg. 1327   **PB**
Prime Lithotripter Operations, Inc., 1301 Capitol of Texas Hwy., 78746, pg. 1327   **PB**
Prime Management, Inc., 1301 Capital of Texas Hwy., Ste. C300, 78746, pg. 1327   **PB**
Prime Medical Operating, Inc., 1301 Capitol of Texas Hwy., 78746, pg. 1327   **PB**
PRIME MEDICAL SERVICES, INC., 1301 Capital of Texas Hwy., Ste. C300, 78746, pg. 1327   **PB**
R.R. Litho, Inc., 1301 Capitol of Texas Hwy., 78746, pg. 1327   **PB**
Radian International LLC, 8501 Mo-Pac Blvd., 78720-1088, pg. 522   **PV**
Rehab Leasing Corp., 1301 Capitol of Texas Hwy., 78746, pg. 1327   **PB**
RISC Microprocessor Division, 6501 William Cannon Dr. W., 78735, pg. 1137   **PB**
Ross Technology, Inc., 5316 Hwy. W. 290, 78735, pg. 526   **IT**
SAS Institute, Inc., 11920 Wilson Parke Ave., 78726, pg. 966   **PV**
SCHLOTZSKY'S, INC., 203 Colorado St., 78701, pg. 1439   **PV**
7-UP/RC of Austin, 3411 Hidalgo St., 78702, pg. 470   **PV**
Shepler's Austin, 4123 Todd Ln., 78760, pg. 413   **PV**
Sheshunoff Information Services, Inc., One Texas Center, 505 Barton Springs Rd., Ste. 1100, 78704, pg. 1601   **PB**
SICOLAMARTIN INC., 9442 Capital of Texas Hwy. N., Arboretum Plaza Two, Ste. 400, 78759, pg. 998   **PV**
Solectron Texas, P.O. Box 149188, 12455 Research Blvd., 78714-9188, pg. 1483   **PB**
SOUTHERN UNION COMPANY, 504 Lavaca, Ste. 800, 78701, pg. 1491   **PB**
Southern Union Gas Co., 504 Lavaca St., 78701, pg. 1491   **PB**
Steck-Vaughn Company, 8701 N. MoPac Expwy., Ste. 200, 78759-8364, pg. 784   **PB**
Steck-Vaughn Distribution Company, 4515 Seton Ctr. Pkwy., Ste. 300, 78759, pg. 784   **PB**
Steck-Vaughn Publishing Corporation, 4515 Seton Ctr. Pkwy., Ste. 300, 78759, pg. 784   **PB**
Sterling Electronics, 11500 Metric Blvd., Ste. 495, 78758, pg. 1051   **PB**
Sun Medical Technologies, Inc., 1301 Capital of Texas Hwy., Ste. C300, 78746, pg. 1327   **PB**
Superior Dairies, Inc., 600 E. First St., 78701, pg. 158   **PV**
TCC INDUSTRIES, 504 Alocka St., Ste. 1004, 78701, pg. 1554   **PB**
TNL Flight Services, Inc., 2105 Donley Dr., 78758, pg. 1638   **PB**
TR Navigation Corporation, 210 Donley Dr., 78758, pg. 1638   **PB**
Tandem Computers MCC, 14231 Tandem Blvd., 78728, pg. 417   **PB**
Temple-Inland Financial Services, Inc, P.O. Box 40, 78701, pg. 1575   **PB**
Temple-Inland Mortgage Corporation, 901 S. Mopac Expressway, 78746, pg. 1575   **PB**
Texas Copy Systems, Inc., 3019 Alvin DeVane, Bldg. 4, Ste. 400, 78741-7418, pg. 864   **PB**
TEXAS ELECTRIC COOPERATIVES, INC., 8140 Burnet Rd., 78757, pg. 1078   **PV**
Texas Instruments Information Technology Group, 12501 Research Blvd., 78759, pg. 1586   **PB**
Texas Litho, Inc., 1301 Capitol of Texas Hwy., 78746, pg. 1327   **PB**
Texas Monthly, Inc., P.O. Box 1569, 78767, pg. 727   **PV**
Tracor Aerospace, Inc., 6500 Tracor Ln., 78725-2070, pg. 1627   **PB**
TRACOR, INC., 6500 Tracor Ln., 78725-2000, pg. 1627   **PB**
Transactive Corporation, 1627 Woodland Ave., 78741, pg. 767   **PB**
Travis County Title Company, 4515 Seton Ctr. Pkwy., Ste. 110, 78759, pg. 441   **PB**
Tremetrics, Inc., 2215 Grand Ave. Pkwy., 78728-3812, pg. 1595   **PB**
Trimble Navigation Ltd., Texas, 2105 Donley Dr., 78758, pg. 1638   **PB**

Trivoli Systems Inc., 9442 Capital of Texas Hwy. N., 78759, pg. 896   **PB**
United HealthCare of Texas, Inc., 1250 Capital of Texas Hwy., Bldg. One, Ste. 400, 78746, pg. 1678   **PB**
VTEL CORPORATION, 108 Wild Basin Rd., 78746, pg. 1703   **PB**
Vaughan & Sons, Inc. Multi-Family Sales, 7500 Hwy. 71 W., Ste. 204, 78735, pg. 1135   **PV**
VINDICATOR TECHNOLOGIES, 98301 US Hwy 290 W., Bldg. 2, 78736, pg. 1141   **PV**
Visible Changes of Austin, 6001 Airport, 78752, pg. 1141   **PV**
WHOLE FOODS MARKET, INC., 601 N. Lamar Blvd. # 300, 78703, pg. 1767   **PB**
Woodward-Clyde, First State Bank Bldg., 300 Highland Mall Blvd., Ste. 300, 78752, pg. 1656   **PB**
Xetel Corporation, 2525 Brockton Dr., 78758, pg. 1125   **IT**

Avalon

CSC Disposal and Landfill, Inc., 76623, pg. 1379   **PB**

Bartlett

Bartlett State Jail, P.O. Box 650, 76511-0650, pg. 450   **PB**

Bastrop

Design Security Inc., Rte. 6, Box 835, 78602, pg. 328   **PV**

Batson

Batson Mill LP, P.O. Box 444, 77519, pg. 1179   **PB**

Baytown

Alloys International, 1901 Ellis School Rd., 77521, pg. 865   **PB**
Exxon Chemical Polymers, Eng., P.O. Box 2953, 77522-2953, pg. 601   **PB**
Koppel Steel-Baytown, P.O. Box 770, 77522, pg. 1147   **PB**
Natural Gas Odorizing, 3601 Decker Dr., 77520, pg. 1210   **PB**

Beaumont

Allright Beaumont Company, 338 Crockett St., 77701, pg. 42   **PV**
American Valve & Hydrant Co., P.O. Box 3608, 77704, pg. 52   **PV**
Beaumont Enterprise, 380 Main St., 77701, pg. 517   **PV**
Entergy Gulf States, Inc., 350 Pine St., 77701, pg. 586   **PB**
Harley Valve & Instrument, 4780 23rd St., 77705, pg. 880   **PB**
HELENA LABORATORIES CORPORATION, 1530 Lindbergh, 77707, pg. 519   **PV**
Hewlett-Packard Company, P.O. box 7511, 3560 Delaware, Ste. 104, 77706, pg. 815   **PB**
Physician Sales & Services Inc., 2155 IH 10 E., 77701, pg. 1294   **PB**
Shepler's Beaumont, 7055 S. Major Dr., 77705, pg. 413   **PB**
Southern Iron & Metal Co., 5250 College St., 77707, pg. 413   **PB**
Southern States Steel Company, 9675 Walden Rd., 77707, pg. 412   **PV**
Sysco Food Services of Beaumont, Inc., 6000 Tram Rd., 77713, pg. 1551   **PB**
Taylor Home Health Inc., 2865 Laurel, 77702, pg. 885   **PB**
TEXAS METAL WORKS, INC., 937 Pine St., 77701, pg. 1078   **PV**

Bedford

RELTEC Systems, 2100 Reliance Pkwy., 76021, pg. 921   **PV**
Square D Co., 3301 Airport Freeway # 212, 76021, pg. 1208   **IT**

Bellaire

Crown Central Pipe Line Co., 4747 Bellaire Blvd., 77401, pg 462   **PB**
Crown-Rancho Pipe Line Corp., 4747 Bellaire Blvd., 77401, pg. 462   **PB**
Graphic Arts Supply Division, 1303 N. 1st St., 77401, pg. 205   **PB**
HydroGEN Supply, Inc., pg. 1320   **PB**
Phillips Alaska Natural Gas Corporation, 6330 W. Loop S., 77401, pg. 1291   **PB**
Phillips Gas Supply Corporation, 6330 W. Loop S., 77401, pg. 1291   **PB**
Voest-Alpine International Corp., 6575 W. Loop S., Ste. 730, 77401, pg. 1470   **PB**
Voest-Alpine Steel Corp.-Tubulars, 6575 West Loop S., Ste. 730, 77401, pg. 1471   **IT**

Belton

Tarco of Texas, Inc., 2403 E. 6th St., 76513, pg. 1069   **PV**

Big Spring

Fina Oil & Chemical Co. (Big Spring), P.O. Box 1311, 79721, pg. 1044   **IT**

Big Wells

RCLJ Construction, Inc., Fm Rd. 468, 78830, pg. 1379   **PB**

Boerne

C&L COMMUNICATIONS, INC., Rte. 10 W., 78006, pg. 191   **PV**

Bonham

Seven Oaks Care Center, 901 Seven Oaks Rd., 75418, pg. 839   **PB**

Borger

Engineered Carbons Inc., 1111 Penn Ave., 79007, pg. 65   **PV**

Bovina

SHERLEY GRAIN COMPANY, 503 Gardner Ave., 79009, pg. 993   **PV**

Brady

Brady Plant, P.O. Box 429, 76825-0429, pg. 1213   **PB**

Breckenridge

Breck Operating Corp., 300 N. Breckenridge Ave., 76424, pg. 1037   **PV**
Crest Ridge Homes, Inc., 1000 Industrial Blvd., 76424, pg. 333   **PB**
STATES, INC., 300 N. Breckenridge Ave., 76424, pg. 1037   **PV**

Bremond

TNP ONE, P.O. Box 37, Hwy 6, Robertson County, 76629, pg. 1557   **PB**

Brenham

BLUE BELL CREAMERIES, L.P., 1101 S. Horton Loop, # 577, 77833, pg. 150   **PV**
Ohio-Sealy Mattress Manufacturing Co.-Houston, Hwy. Loop 290, P.O. Box 593, 77833, pg. 979   **PV**
Valmont/ALS, 255 Valmont Dr., 77833, pg. 1707   **PB**

Bridgeport

Acme Brick Co., 102 Main St., P.O. Box 368, 76026, pg. 936   **PB**
Bridgeport Correction Facility, 222 Lake Rd., 76426, pg. 450   **PB**
TXI Aggregate Transportation Company, Bridgeport Stone Plant 515, 76026, pg. 1585   **PB**

Brownfield

Brownfield Correction Facility, 2002 Lamesa Hwy., 79316, pg. 450   **PB**
GOODPASTURE, INC., 214 S. Sixth St., 79316, pg. 464   **PV**

Brownsville

AMFELS Inc., P.O. Box 3107, Hwy. 48, 78521, pg. 731   **IT**
CTS Brownsville/Electromechanical, Business Unit, 1100 Roosevelt St., 78521, pg. 285   **PB**
Duro Paper Bag Mfg. Co., P.O. Box 4380, 78523, pg. 349   **PV**
MERCANTILE BANK, 835 E. Levee, P.O. Box 2219, 78522, pg. 731   **PV**
Spanish Meadow Nursing Center, 1040 FM 802, 78521, pg. 839   **PB**
Trico Technologies Corporation, 1995 Billy Mitchell Blvd., 78521, pg. 1397   **IT**
United Technologies Motor Systems, 904 Billy Mitchell Blvd., 78521-5602, pg. 1690   **PB**
Valley Grande Manor, 901 Wild Rose Ln., 78520, pg. 839   **PB**

Brownwood

Kohler Co. (TX), P.O. Box 1709, 76801, pg. 630   **PV**

Bryan

Fields Financial Services, Inc., 1716 Briarcrest Dr., Ste. 800, pg. 942   **PB**

Buda

Capitol City Steel Co., 900 N. IH 35, 78610, pg. 413   **PB**
Texas-Lehigh Cement Co., P.O. Box 610, 78610, pg. 323   **PB**

Burleson

THOMAS CONVEYOR COMPANY, 555 N. Burleson Blvd., 76028, pg. 1082   **PV**

PB - *U.S. Public Companies Volume*
PV - *U.S. Private Companies Volume*
IT - *International Public & Private Companies Volume*

1436

Burnet

Southwestern Graphite Co., P.O. Box 883, 78611, pg. 515 **PB**

Caldwell

Sherman Wire of Caldwell, Inc., P.O. Box 879, 77836, pg. 955 **PB**

Campbell

Republic/Maloy Landfill & Sanitation, Route 1 Box 343, 75422, pg. 1379 **PB**

Canton

Heritage Manor Canton, 901 W. College St., 75013, pg. 839 **PB**

Canutillo

Commercial Metals Company, P.O. Box 508, 79835, pg. 413 **PB**

Carrollton

ALTO Papers Company, 2425 Camp Dr., Ste. 150, 75006, pg. 164 **PV**
Amano Cincinnati - Dallas Branch Office, 1321 Valwood Parkway, Ste. 400, 75006-6889, pg. 70 **IT**
Antec Group, 1620 Crosby Rd., 75006, pg. 117 **PB**
Arrow Industries, Inc., 2625 Belt Line Rd., 75006-5498, pg. 426 **PB**
Arrow/Schweber Electronics, 3220 Comandor Dr., 75006, pg. 134 **PB**
BMW of North America, Inc.-Southwestern Region, 1730 Briercroft Ct., 75006, pg. 177 **IT**
BRAC Credit Corp., 3414 Midcourt Rd., Bldg. 2, 75006, pg. 178 **PV**
BEAUTICONTROL COSMETICS, INC., 2121 Midway Rd., 75006, pg. 198 **PB**
Bergen Brunswig Drug Company, 1841 Monetary Ln., 75006, pg. 214 **PB**
Bergen Brunswig Medical Corporation, 2150 Hutton, 75006, pg. 214 **PB**
Bimar Bakeries, 1925 E. Beltline Rd., Ste. 530, 75006, pg. 575 **IT**
Broder Bros. Co. of Dallas, 2425 Camp Ave., #100, 75806, pg. 171 **PB**
Capstone Electronics Div., 3220 Comandor Dr., 75006, pg. 134 **PB**
Casa Bonita, Inc., 3033 Kellway, Ste. 122, 75006, pg. 278 **PB**
Comdata Transceiver, 1421 Champion Dr., Ste. 101, 75006, pg. 331 **PB**
COMPUTER LANGUAGE RESEARCH, INC., 2395 Midway Rd., 75006, pg. 421 **PB**
Dallas Aerospace, Inc., pg. 187 **PB**
DeCorp, 1401 Valwood Parkway, 75006, pg. 948 **PB**
EA Engineering, Science & Technology, Inc., 1420 Valwood Pky., Ste. 170, 75006, pg. 541 **PB**
Earthgrains Co., 1820 N. Josey Ln., 75006, pg. 547 **PB**
Eclipse Combustion, Inc., 1614 S. Broadway, Ste. 208, 75006, pg. 360 **PV**
Electronic Form Systems, 1555 Valwood Pkwy., 75006, pg. 1385 **PB**
Electronic Tax Systems, Inc., 2395 Midway Rd., 75006, pg. 421 **PB**
Elkay Plastics Co., Inc., Stock Service Center, 1580 North I-35, 75006, pg. 372 **PV**
Enterprise Service Solutions, P.O. Box 1100, 75006-5495, pg. 729 **PB**
Fast-Tax, 2395 Midway Rd., 75006, pg. 421 **PB**
Forney Corporation, 3405 Wiley Post Rd., 75006, pg. 1500 **IT**
GATX Logistics (DWC), Inc., 1701 Vantage Dr., 75006, pg. 691 **PB**
Golden Eagle Systems, 1201 W. Crosby, 75006, pg. 1431 **PB**
Greenlee Lighting Inc., 1300 Hutton St., 75006, pg. 971 **PB**
Halliburton Energy Services, 2601 Beltline Rd., 75006, pg. 776 **PB**
Harris Adacom Network Services, 1100 Venture Ct., 75006-5412, pg. 729 **PB**
Hathaway Process Instrumentation, 1840 Hutton Dr., Ste. 200, 75006, pg. 799 **PB**
Heritage Gardens, 2135 N. Denton Dr., 75006, pg. 839 **PB**
Hilton Reservations Worldwide, 2050 Chennault Dr., 75006-5096, pg. 829 **PB**
I Can't Believe It's Yogurt, 3361 Boyington Dr., Ste. 200, 75006, pg. 1520 **IT**
ILD Communications, Inc., 2155 Chenault, Ste. 410, 75006, pg. 887 **PB**
INTELLICALL, INC., 2155 Chenault, Ste. 410, 75006-5023, pg. 887 **PB**
Jani King of Dallas, 3440 Sojourn St., Ste. 270, 75006, pg. 582 **PV**
LEATHER CENTER, INC., 2724 Realty Rd., 75006, pg. 656 **PV**
Lehigh Press-Carrollton, 1228 Crowley Rd., 75506, pg. 659 **PB**
Leviton, 1615 Diplomat Dr., 75006-6848, pg. 663 **PV**
Long Automotive, Inc.-Dallas Aftermarket Div., 2301 McDaniel Dr., 75006, pg. 815 **IT**
Lotto Sport U.S.A., 1900 Surveyor Blvd., 75006, pg. 819 **IT**

McKesson Corporation, 1220 Senlac Dr., 75006, pg. 1073 **PB**
Nelson Westerberg Atlas, 3214 Commander Dr., 75006, pg. 1164 **PB**
NIBCO, 2055 Luna Rd., Ste. 156, 75006, pg. 798 **PV**
OPTEK TECHNOLOGY, INC., 1215 W. Crosby Rd., 75006, pg. 1227 **PB**
Para Systems Inc., 1455 Le May Dr., 75007, pg. 260 **PV**
PREMIER METAL PRODUCTS CO., 1525 N. Interstate 35 E., 75006, pg. 881 **PB**
PRIME SOURCE INC., 1800 John Connally Dr., 75006, pg. 884 **PV**
Primedia Workplace Learning, 1303 Marsh Ln., 75006-5430, pg. 1328 **PV**
Prok International USA Inc., Ste. A17, Crosby Business Park, 1225 E. Crosby, 75006, pg. 1353 **IT**
Rent Roll, Inc, 2395 Midway Rd., 75006, pg. 421 **IT**
SGS-Thomson Microelectronics, Inc., Mail Station 735, 1310 Electronics Dr., 75006-5039, pg. 1153 **IT**
Sumitomo Machinery Corporation of America, 1420 Halsey Way # 130, 75007, pg. 1314 **IT**
Syseca Inc., 1840 Hutton Dr., #190, 75006, pg. 1384 **IT**
TIE Systems Gulfcoast, 2430 Lacy Ln., Ste 116, 75007, pg. 1085 **PV**
Tidel Engineering, Inc., 2310 McDaniel Dr., 75006, pg. 1608 **PB**
Venture Engineering, 2019 McKenzie Dr., Ste. 109, 75006, pg. 757 **PB**
WESTERN EXTRUSIONS, 1735 Sandy Lake Rd., 75006, pg. 1165 **PV**
WorldCom/IDB Systems, 3236 Skylane Dr., 75006, pg. 1779 **PB**
Y.K.K. (U.S.A.) Inc., 1624 W. Crosby, Ste. 144, 75006, pg. 1515 **IT**

Castroville

Hydro Conduit Corp., San Antonia Hwy. 90, 5415 Mechler Lane, 78009, pg. 246 **IT**

Cedar Park

Antec Group, 505 Cypress Creek, 78613, pg. 116 **PB**
M/D Totco Instrumentation, 1200 Cypress Creek Rd., 78613, pg. 1709 **PB**

Celina

WILLARD GRAIN & FEED, INC., 104 Ash St., 75009, pg. 1177 **PV**

Center

Center Fixture Operations, P.O. Box 1775, 1010 Logansport, 75935, pg. 496 **PV**

Channelview

Western Towing Company, 18350 Market St., 77530, pg. 961 **PB**
3ummit Performance Dist. Inc., P.O. Box 9964, 15473 Interstate 10E, 77530, pg. 1233 **PB**

Cleburne

First National Bank in Cleburne, 403 N. Main, 76031, pg. 633 **PB**
Keene Distributors, 105 Healthway Dr., 76031, pg. 752 **IT**
Kimberly-Clark Durafab, Inc., 1102 E. Kilpatrick, 76031, pg. 959 **PB**
Marti Electronics, 421 Marti Drive, 76033, pg. 531 **PV**
Rangaire Inc., 501 S. Wilhite, 76031, pg. 1193 **PB**
Supreme Corporation of Texas, 500 W. Commerce, 76033, pg. 1542 **PB**
Texas Lime Co., P.O. Box 851, 76033, pg. 1685 **PB**

Cleveland

Cleveland Pre-Release Center, 901 E. Fifth St., 77327, pg. 450 **PB**

College Station

Alcatel Network System, Inc., P.O. Box 7170, 77844-7170, pg. 55 **IT**
Hewlett-Packard Company, 301 Arguello, Ste. 102, 77840, pg. 815 **PB**
O.I. CORPORATION, 151 Graham Rd., 77842-9010, pg. 1208 **PB**
Shepler's College Station, 580-A Graham Rd., 77845, pg. 413 **PB**

Commerce

AWC Manufacturing Facility, 804 Fourth St., 75428, pg. 1193 **PB**
Montgomery Elevator Controls Division, U.S. Hwy. 11, 75428, pg. 746 **IT**

Conroe

Crane Defense Systems, Rte. 20, Box 1126, Hwy. 105, FM3083, 77301, pg. 456 **PV**
Eckerd Drug Co., 2061 Interstate 45 S., 77302, pg. 917 **PB**
Quaker Chemical Environmental Products Division, 10001 Hwy. 105 W., Ste 110, 77303, pg. 1346 **PB**
Shepler's Conroe, 2309 N. Frazier, 77303, pg. 413 **PB**

Synergistics Industries (TX) Inc., 9733 Meador Rd., 77303-2335, pg. 734 **PB**

Converse

Block Plant, P.O. Box 67, 400 Gibbs Sprawl Rd., 78109, pg. 936 **PB**

Coppell

DUPEY MANAGEMENT CORP., 500 Airline Dr., 75019, pg. 348 **PV**
Four Seasons Air Conditioning Div., 100 S. Royal Ln., 75019, pg. 1503 **PB**
MINYARD FOOD STORES, INC., 777 Freeport Pkwy., 75019, pg. 752 **PV**
Minyard Properties, Inc., 777 Freeport Pkwy., 75019, pg. 752 **PV**
TST/IMPRESO, INC., 652 Southwestern Blvd., 75019, pg. 1066 **PV**

Corpus Christi

Allright Corpus Christi, Inc., One Shoreline Plaza, #733, 78403, pg. 42 **PV**
American Chrome & Chemicals, Inc., P.O. Box 9912, Buddy Lawrence Dr., 78408, pg. 598 **IT**
Bay Area Medical Center, 7101 S. Padre Island Dr., 78411, pg. 404 **PB**
Bayview Hospital, 6629 Woolridge Rd., 78414, pg. 404 **PB**
BERRY CONTRACTING, 1414 Corn Products Rd., 78409, pg. 137 **PV**
Block Products Plant, P.O. Box 4732, 3822 Agnes, 78469, pg. 936 **PB**
Briner Paint Manufacturing Co., Inc., 3713 Agnes St., 78405-3097, pg. 1358 **PB**
Central Power and Light Company, 539 N. Carancahua St., 78401-2802, pg. 324 **PB**
Charter Behavioral Health System of Corpus Christi, Inc., 3126 Rodd Field Rd., 78414, pg. 1034 **PB**
Columbia-Bay Area, 5656 S. Staples, Ste. 108, 78411, pg. 404 **PB**
Commercial Metals Company, 4614 Agnes St., 78405, pg. 413 **PB**
Corpus Christi Caller-Times, 820 N. Lower Broadway, 78401, pg. 793 **PB**
Encycle/Texas, Inc., 5500 Upriver Rd., 78403, pg. 138 **PB**
Enterra Compressions Co., P.O. Box 9258, 78469, pg. 1749 **PB**
Harbor View Care Center, 1314 Third St., 78401, pg. 839 **PB**
Hewlett-Packard Company, 4646 Corona Dr., Ste. 120, 78411, pg. 815 **PB**
Hilb, Rogal and Hamilton Company of Corpus Christi, 5733 S. Padre Island Dr., 78412, pg. 827 **PB**
HITOX CORPORATION OF AMERICA, 418 Peoples St., Ste. 500, 78401, pg. 829 **PB**
Horizon Specialty Hospital - Corpus Christi, 1310 Third St., 78404, pg. 839 **PB**
Horton Automatics Div., 4242 Baldwin Blvd., 78405, pg. 823 **PB**
International Resistive Company Inc., 422 S. Staples St., 78411, pg. 1344 **IT**
SAM KANE BEEF PROCESSORS, INC., 9001 Leapard St., 78409, pg. 607 **PV**
Medicenter, Corpus Christi, 1314 Third St., 78404, pg. 1714 **PB**
Mercury Air Center, 355 Pinson Rd., 78469-9155, pg. 1093 **PB**
Principal Health Care of Texas, Inc., 555 N. Caranahua, Ste. 500, 78478, pg. 886 **PB**
RHG Corpus Christi, 3206 Reid Dr., #12A, 78404, pg. 1151 **IT**
Republic New York Investment Corp., First City Bank Tower, Box 118, 78477, pg. 1380 **PB**
Reynolds Metals Company-Oil & Gas, 615 Leopard, Ste.630, 78476-2201, pg. 1386 **PB**
Safety Steel Service, Inc., 6802 Safety Steel Dr., 78412, pg. 412 **PB**
Semtech Corpus Christi, 121 International Blvd., 78406, pg. 1456 **IT**
7-UP of Corpus Christi, 3127 Cabaniss Pkwy., 78415, pg. 470 **PB**
Shepler's Corpus Christi, 2786 45th St., 78405, pg. 413 **PB**
Texas Sunbelt Cement, P.O. Box 9294, 78408, pg. 323 **PB**
Trademark Press, Inc., 2346 Horne Rd., 78415, pg. 794 **PB**
WHATABURGER, INC., 4600 Parkdale Dr., 78411, pg. 1170 **PV**

Corrigan

Corigan Plant, Wood Products Div., P.O. Box 100-S, 75939, pg. 334 **PB**

Corsicana

COLLIN STREET BAKERY, 401 W. Seventh Ave., 75110, pg. 252 **PV**
Midway Home Entertainment Inc., 1800 S. Business Hwy. 45, 75110, pg. 1727 **PB**

Crosby

A-Z Terminal Corporation, 1919 Crosby Dayton Rd., 77532, pg. 1014 **PV**

Geographic Index-U.S.

Crowley

AZTEC MANUFACTURING CO., 400 Tarrant, 76036, pg. 159 **PB**

Cypress

Baker/MO Services, Inc., 18119 Telge Rd., 77429, pg. 168 **PB**
INTERNATIONAL CENTER FOR ENTREPRENEURIAL DEVELOPMENT, INC., One Kwik-Kopy Ln., 77410, pg. 568 **PV**

Dallas

ADT Security Systems Southwest, 1375 River Bend Dr., 75247, pg. 1649 **PB**
AEP-SPAN, 5100 E. Grand Ave., 75223, pg. 1676 **PB**
AM Can, P.O. Box 655888, 75265-5888, pg. 685 **PB**
AST Bearings, 2448 Walnut Ridge St., 75229, pg. 157 **PB**
AST Research, Inc, Ste. 600, LB22, 5005 LBJ Fwy., 75244, pg. 1182 **IT**
AT&T Datatek Inc., 3801 Realty Rd., 75244-2214, pg. 10 **IT**
ATC COMMUNICATIONS GROUP, INC., 5950 Berkshire Ln., Ste. 1650, 75225, pg. 11 **PB**
AVO International, 4651 S. Westmoreland, 75237, pg. 1335 **IT**
AVO Multi-Amp Institute, 4555 S. Westmoreland, 75237, pg. 1335 **IT**
AVO Multi-Amp Services Corp., 4651 S. Westmoreland, 75237, pg. 1335 **IT**
AVW Audiovisual, Inc., 2241 Irving Blvd., 75207, pg. 426 **PV**
Adolphus Hotel, 1321 Commerce St., 75202, pg. 800 **PV**
ADVENTURE TOURS USA, INC., 10726 Piano Rd., 75238, pg. 22 **PV**
AFFILIATED COMPUTER SERVICES, INC., 2828 N. Haskell, 75204, pg. 27 **PB**
Air Pro, 4921 Olson Dr., 75227, pg. 685 **PB**
AirTouch Paging, 12221 Merit Drive, 75251, pg. 34 **PB**
ALFORD REFRIGERATED WAREHOUSE, INC., 318 Cadiz St., 75207, pg. 33 **PV**
Allianz Life Insurance Co., P.O. Box 50, 75221, pg. 58 **IT**
Allied Premium Finance, 2727 Turtle Creek Blvd., 75219, pg. 346 **IT**
Allied Security Inc., 1140 Empire Central, #120, 75247, pg. 40 **PB**
Allright Parking System, 1700 Commerce Pl., Ste. 732, 75201, pg. 43 **PV**
ALLTEL Distribution, Inc., 10730 Composite Dr., 75220-1277, pg. 55 **PB**
Aloe-Vera of America, 9600 Dilworth, 75243, pg. 418 **PV**
American Bank Note Company, 5307 E. Mockingbird Ln., Ste. 705, 75206-5109, pg. 68 **PB**
American City Business Journals, Inc., 4131 N. Central Expwy., Ste. 310, 75204, pg. 19 **PV**
American Consumer Services Inc., 2909 N. Buckner Blvd., 75228, pg. 1623 **PB**
AMERICAN EAGLE GROUP, INC., 12801 N. Central Expwy., Ste. 800, 75243, pg. 71 **PB**
American Eagle Lines, P.O. Box 223752, 75222, pg. 685 **PB**
American Iron & Metal Co., 2215 S. Good-Latimer, 75226, pg. 413 **PB**
American Life & Accident Insurance Company, 2909 N. Buckner, 75221, pg. 1622 **PB**
AMERICAN PAD AND PAPER COMPANY, 17304 Preston Rd., Ste. 700, 75252-5613, pg. 88 **PB**
American Petrofina Holding Co., Fina Plaza, 8350 North Central Expwy., 75206, pg. 1044 **IT**
Americana Foods, Inc., 3333 Dan Morton Dr., 75236, pg. 1554 **PB**
AmeriServe Food Distribution, Inc., 14841 Dallas Pkwy., 75240-2100, pg. 533 **PV**
AMRESCO, Inc., 700 N. Pearl St., 75201-7424, pg. 287 **PV**
AMTECH CORPORATION, 19111 Dallas Pkwy., Ste. 300, 75287-3106, pg. 105 **PB**
Amtech Logistics Corporation, 17304 Preston Rd., Ste. 305, 75252, pg. 432 **PB**
Amtech Systems Corporation, 19111 Dallas Pkwy., Ste. 300, 75287-3106, pg. 105 **PB**
Antares Alliance Group, 17304 Preston Rd., Ste. 1200, 75252, pg. 528 **IT**
Anthem Health Plans of Texas, 5055 Keller Springs Rd., 75248, pg. 76 **PV**
ASSOCIATED AIRCRAFT SUPPLY COMPANY, 6020 Cedar Springs Rd., 75235, pg. 89 **PV**
ASSOCIATED MATERIALS INCORPORATED, 2200 Ross Ave., Ste. 4100 E., 75201, pg. 91 **PV**
Associated Spring, 3443 Morse Dr., 75221, pg. 190 **PB**
Associates Commercial Corporation, 300 E. Carpenter Fwy., P.O. Box 650363, 75265-0363, pg. 663 **PB**
Associates Financial Life Insurance Company, P.O. Box 660028, 75266-0028, pg. 663 **PB**
Associates Financial Services Corporation, 250 Carpenter Fwy., 75266-0237, pg. 663 **PB**
Associates First Capital Corporation, P.O. Box 660237, 250 Carpenter Freeway, 75266-0237, pg. 663 **PB**
Associates Insurance Company, P.O. Box 660028, 75266-0028, pg. 663 **PB**
Associates Insurance Group, Inc., P.O. Box 660028, 75266-0028, pg. 663 **PB**
Associates International Management Company, P.O. Box 660237, 75266, pg. 663 **PB**
Associates National Mortgage Corporation, P.O. Box 226586, 76265, pg. 663 **PB**

Associates Real Estate Financial Services Company, Inc., P.C. Box 660237, 75266, pg. 663 **PB**
Associates Relocation Management Company, Inc., P.O. Box 650042, 75265-0042, pg. 663 **PB**
Athletic Training Equipment Company, Inc., 1901 Diplomat Dr., 75234, pg. 1499 **PB**
ATMOS ENERGY CORPORATION, Three Lincoln Centre, 5430 LBJ Frwy., Ste. 160, 75240, pg. 145 **PB**
ATRIUM COMPANIES, INC., 1341 W. Mockingbird, Ste. 1200 W., 75247, pg. 98 **PV**
Austin Bridge & Rd., Inc., 11143 Goodnight Lane, 75229, pg. 99 **PV**
Austin Commercial, Inc., 3535 Travis St., 75204, pg. 99 **PV**
AUSTIN INDUSTRIES, INC., 3535 Travis Ste. 300, 75204, pg. 99 **PV**
Autodesk, 15303 Dallas Pkwy., Ste. 1410 LB42, 75248, pg. 149 **IT**
AVATEX CORPORATION, 5910 N. Central Expwy., Ste. 1780, 75206, pg. 151 **PB**
AVIALL, INC., 2075 Diplomat Dr., 75234-8989, pg. 154 **PB**
Aviall, Inc., 2075 Diplomat, 75234, pg. 154 **PB**
Award Foods, Inc., 4202 Dan Morton Dr., 75236, pg. 752 **PV**
BRC HOLDINGS, 1111 W. Mockingbird Ln., Ste.1400, 75247, pg. 163 **PB**
BSA Advertising, Inc., 4835 LBJ Freeway, Ste. 230, 75244, pg. 108 **PV**
Baby Doe's, Inc., 3305 Harry Hines Blvd., 75201, pg. 1023 **PV**
Baker Support Services, Inc., 4801 Spring Valley Rd., Ste. 125, 75244, pg. 168 **PB**
BancTec Financial Systems, 4435 Spring Valley Rd., pg. 177 **PB**
BANCTEC, INC., 4851 LBJ Frwy., 75240, pg. 176 **PB**
BancTec Service Corp., 4435 Spring Valley Rd., 75244, pg. 177 **PB**
Bank of America Texas, P.O. Box 619005, 75261-9005, pg. 180 **PB**
Bank One, Texas Corp., 1717 Main St., 75201, pg. 173 **PB**
W.O. Bankston Enterprises Inc., 4755 McEwen Rd., 75244, pg. 1379 **PV**
W.O. Bankston Lincoln Mercury, 4747 LBJ Fwy., 75240, pg. 1379 **PV**
W.O. Bankston Nissan Inc., 13130 Preston Rd., 75240, pg. 1379 **PV**
Banque Paribas-Dallas, 2121 San Jacinto St., Ste. 930, 75201, pg. 319 **IT**
Barrow, Hanley, Mewhinney & Strauss, Inc., One McKinney Plaza, 3232 McKinney Ave., 15th Fl., 75201, pg. 1672 **PB**
Basic Resources, Inc., 1601 Bryan St., 75201, pg. 1587 **PB**
Bear, Stearns & Co. Inc., Dallas, 300 Crescent Ct., Ste. 200, 75201, pg. 198 **PB**
BeautiControl International, Inc., P.O. Box 815189, 75381-5189, pg. 198 **PB**
Belden Associates, 3102 Oaklawn Ave., Ste. 500, 75219, pg. 1447 **IT**
Bellaire Corporation, 14785 Preston Rd., Ste. 1100, 75240, pg. 1149 **PB**
A.H. BELO CORPORATION, 400 S. Record St., 16th Fl., 75202, pg. 209 **PB**
Bennigan's, 12404 Park Central Dr., 75251, pg. 736 **PV**
BERRY-BROWN ADVERTISING, INC., 3100 McKinnon, Ste. 1100, 75201-1046, pg. 137 **PV**
Bestolite Corp., 1111 W. Mockingbird Ln., 75247, pg. 900 **PV**
Bindley Western, Dallas Division, 4217 Mint Way, 75237, pg. 228 **PB**
Bird Life Designs, 4450 Alpha Rd., pg. 1591 **PB**
Block Plant, 3815 Singleton Blvd., P.O. Box 560725, 75247, pg. 936 **PB**
Blockbuster Entertainment Group, P.O. Box 509010, 75250, pg. 775 **PV**
Bonanza Restaurants, 12404 Park Central Dr., 75251-1899, pg. 736 **PV**
Bonnet Resources Corp., 1717 Main St., 75265, pg. 175 **PB**
Booth/Crystal Tips, 2007 Royal Ln., 75229, pg. 1445 **PB**
Bowne of Dallas, Inc., 1931 N. Industrial Blvd., Ste. 111, 75207, pg. 249 **PB**
W. Braun Co., 10480 Shady Trail, Ste. 102, 75220, pg. 166 **PB**
Bridgford Frozen-Rite Foods, 1601 Good-Latimer Expwy., 75226, pg. 252 **PB**
BRIERLEY & PARTNERS, 1201 Main St., Ste. 2500, 75202, pg. 168 **PV**
Briggs Weaver Vinson, 5000 Harry Hines Blvd., 75235, pg. 963 **PB**
BRINKER INTERNATIONAL, INC., 6820 LBJ Frwy., 75240, pg. 253 **PB**
BRISTOL HOTELS & RESORTS, 14275 Midway Rd., 75244, pg. 253 **PB**
Brookhollow Corp., 7610 Stemmons Fwy., 75247, pg. 1585 **PB**
Brookhollow of Virginia, Inc., 7610 Stemmons Freeway, 75247, pg. 1585 **PB**
Brown & Root Development, Inc., 1300 W. Mockingbird Ln., 75247-4976, pg. 775 **PB**
Brown Brothers Harriman Trust Co. of Texas, 1150 Trammell Crow Ctr., 2001 Ross Ave., 75201, pg. 173 **PV**
Bruce Hardwood Floors, 16803 Dallas Pkwy., 75248, pg. 1534 **PB**
Business Travel Management, Inc., 8777 Stemmons Fwy., 75247, pg. 711 **PV**
BusLease, Inc., 1250 Slocum St., 75207, pg. 326 **IT**
CCC Conveyors, Inc., P.O. Box 59448, 2466 Glenda Ln., 75229-4511, pg. 351 **PV**

CMC Steel Holding Co., 7800 Stemmons Freeway, 75247, pg. 412 **PB**
CSC Logic, Inc., 9330 LBJ Freeway, Ste. 500, 75243, pg. 422 **PB**
CSW Communications, Inc., P.O. Box 660164, 1616 Woodall Rodgers Fwy., 75266-0164, pg. 324 **PB**
CSW Credit, Inc., 1616 Woodall Rodgers Frwy., 75266-0164, pg. 324 **PB**
CSW Energy, Inc., 1616 Woodall Rodgers Frwy., 75266-0164, pg. 324 **PB**
CSW Financial Inc., 1616 Woodall Rodgers Frwy., 75266-0164, pg. 324 **PB**
CSW Leasing, Inc., 1616 Woodall Rodgers Frwy., 75202, pg. 324 **PB**
CTX Mortgage Co., Inc., 3333 Lee Pkwy., 75219, pg. 323 **PB**
Cable & Wireless Communications Inc.-Texas, 8111 LBJ freeway, Ste. 670, 75251, pg. 247 **IT**
Cadbury Beverages Seven Up, 8144 Walnut Hill Lane, 75231, pg. 248 **IT**
CAMELOT COMMUNICATIONS, INC., 8140 Walnut Hill, Ste. 700, 75231, pg. 203 **PV**
CAMERON ASHLEY BUILDING PRODUCTS, INC, 11651 Plano Rd., 75243, pg. 298 **PB**
Campbell Sales, 16775 Addison Rd., Ste. 350, 75248, pg. 299 **PB**
CAP Gemini America (Dallas Branch), Two Galleria Towers, 13455 Noel Rd., 75240, pg. 263 **IT**
CAPITAL SENIOR LIVING, INC., 14160 Dallas Pkwy., Ste. 300, 75240, pg. 302 **PB**
CAPSTEAD MORTGAGE CORPORATION, 2711 N. Haskell Ave., Ste. 900, 75204, pg. 303 **PB**
The Care Group of Texas, Inc., 4334 Lemmon Ave., 75219, pg. 305 **PB**
Care Line, Inc., 4334 Lemmon Ave., 75234, pg. 305 **PB**
Catellus Management Corporation, 5429 LBJ Fwy., Ste. 600, 75240, pg. 315 **PB**
Celanese Inc., 1601 W. LBJ Freeway, 75234, pg. 624 **IT**
Centennial Homes Inc., 5720 LBJ Freeway, Hines Blvd., Parkplace 3, 75240, pg. 1764 **PB**
Centex Construction Company, 2728 N. Harwood, 75201-1516, pg. 322 **PB**
Centex Construction Group, Inc., 2728 N. Harwood, 75201-1516, pg. 322 **PB**
Centex Construction Products, Inc., 3710 Rawlins, Ste. 1600, 75219, pg. 322 **PB**
CENTEX CORPORATION, 2728 N. Harwood, 75201-1516, pg. 322 **PB**
Centex Real Estate Corp./Centex Homes, 3333 Lee Pkwy., 75219, pg. 323 **PB**
CENTRAL AND SOUTH WEST CORPORATION, 1616 Woodall Rodgers Fwy., 75202-0164, pg. 324 **PB**
Central and South West Services, Inc., 1616 Woodall Rodgers Fwy., 75266-0164, pg. 324 **PB**
Cerner Corporation -South Central Region, 8235 Douglas, Ste. 1000, 75225-6010, pg. 331 **PB**
Chaco Energy Co., 1601 Bryan St., 75201-3411, pg. 1587 **PB**
Chancellor Radio Broadcasting Co., 12655 N. Central Expwy., Ste. 405, 75243, pg. 335 **PB**
CHARLES CURTAIN COMPANY, INC., 1352 Crampton St., 75207, pg. 229 **PV**
Charter Builders, Inc., 10105 W. Technology Blvd., 75220, pg. 896 **IT**
The Charter Group, Inc., 1200 N. Central Exprwy., Ste.1300, 75222-3687, pg. 1257 **IT**
Charter Group, Inc., P.O. Box 223687, 12001 N. Central Expressway, Ste. 1300, 75222-3687, pg. 1257 **IT**
CHEMCENTRAL/Dallas, 2500 Vinson St., 75212, pg. 232 **PV**
CHIEF AUTO PARTS, One Lincoln Center, 5400 LBJ Fwy., Ste. 200, 75240, pg. 236 **PV**
Chromium Corp., Wellington Centre, 14643 Dallas Pkwy., Ste. 900, 75240, pg. 568 **PB**
Chubb Lloyds Insurance Co. of TX, Maxus Energy Tower, 717 N. Harwood, 75201, pg. 355 **PB**
Cigna Health Network, Inc., P.O. Box 540144, 75354, pg. 359 **PV**
CINEMARK USA, INC., 7502 Greenville Ave., Ste. 800, 75231, pg. 240 **PV**
Circle International, 1245 Royal Lane N., DFW Airport, 75261, pg. 372 **PB**
Claudius Peters Inc., 4141 Blue Lake Cir., 75244, pg. 131 **IT**
Club Corp Realty, 3030 LBJ Fwy., Ste. 700, 75234, pg. 247 **PV**
CLUB CORPORATION INTERNATIONAL, 3030 LBJ Fwy., Ste. 700, 75234, pg. 247 **PV**
Club Corporation of America, 3030 LBJ Fwy., Ste. 500, 75234, pg. 247 **PV**
Club Resorts Holding, Inc., 3030 LBJ Fwy., Ste. 700, 75234, pg. 247 **PV**
Coda Energy, Inc., 5735 Pineland Dr., Ste. 300, 75231, pg. 584 **PB**
COHO ENERGY, INC., 14785 Preston Rd., Ste. 860, 75240, pg. 396 **PB**
Columbia/H.C.A., Two Galleria Tower, 13455 Noel Rd., 20th Fl., 75248, pg. 404 **PB**
Columbia Medical Center Dallas Southwest, 2929 S. Hampton Rd., 75224, pg. 404 **PB**
Columbia Tri-Star Television Distribution - Dallas, 8117 Preston Rd., Ste. 510, 75225, pg. 1282 **IT**
Comerica Bank Texas, 1909 Woodall Rodgers Fwy., 75201, pg. 409 **PB**
CoMet Steel, Inc., 4846 Singleton Blvd., 75212, pg. 412 **PB**
Commercial Aircraft Division, 9314 W. Jefferson Blvd., 75211, pg. 1198 **PB**
Commercial Guaranty Insurance Company, P.O. Box 660028, 75266-0028, pg. 663 **PB**

PB - *U.S. Public Companies Volume*
PV - *U.S. Private Companies Volume*
IT - *International Public & Private Companies Volume*

1438

Geographic Index-U.S.

COMMERCIAL METALS COMPANY, 7800 Stemmons Fwy., 75247, pg. 411 PB
Commercial Metals Co.-Dallas Trading Div., 7800 Stemmons Fwy., 75247, pg. 413 PB
Communications Technology Corporation, 4000 McEwen Dr., 75234, pg. 480 PB
COMPONENTS CORPORATION OF AMERICA, 717 N. Harwood #2555, 75201, pg. 259 PV
Composite Structures International, Inc., 4115 Keller Springs Rd., Ste. 224, 75244, pg. 1357 PB
CompuCom Systems, Inc., 7171 Forest Ln., 75230, pg. 1424 PB
COMPUSA, 14951 N. Dallas Pkwy., 75240, pg. 420 PB
Comverse Network Systems, 16775 Addison Rd., Ste. 201, 75248, pg. 425 PB
Condo, Hotel & Resort Management, 3710 Rawlins Ave., Ste. 1500, 75219-4236, pg. 778 PB
Connolly Tool & Machine Co., 2605 Brenner Dr., 75220, pg. 583 PB
Consolidated X-Ray Service Corporation, 10931 Indian Trail; P.O. Box 20195, 75220, pg. 337 IT
Constitution Life Insurance Co., 500 N. Akard, 75201, pg. 1018 PV
Consumer Support Services, Inc., 2909 N. Bruckner Bvld., 75228, pg. 1623 PB
Continental Electronics Corporation, 4212 S. Buckner Blvd., 75227-0879, pg. 1563 PB
CONTINENTAL MORTGAGE AND EQUITY TRUST, 10670 N. Central Expwy., Ste. 300, 75231, pg. 441 PB
CONTRAN CORPORATION, Three Lincoln Ctr., 5430 LBJ Fwy., Ste. 1700, 75240, pg. 270 PV
Conwell Corp., P.O. Box 655888, 75265-5888, pg. 685 PB
Cornerstone Health Management, 5080 Spectrum Dr., Ste. 920 West, 75248, pg. 1257 PB
Cornerstone Natural Gas, Inc., 8080 N. Central Expwy., Ste. 1200, 75206, pg. 567 PB
Cornerstone Pipeline Co., 8080 N. Central Expwy., 75206, pg. 567 PB
Corrosion Technologies Intl., 2121 San Jacino St., Ste. 2880, 75201, pg. 748 PB
Costain Process Inc., 10931 Indian Trail; P.O. Box 20195, 75220, pg. 337 IT
COUNTY SEAT STORES, INC., 17950 Preston Rd., Ste. 1000, 75252, pg. 279 PV
CRACKEN, HARKEY, STREET & CO., LLC, 5956 Sherry Ln., Ste. 1401, 75225, pg. 283 PV
Crain Communications, Dallas, 8950 N. Central Expwy., Ste. 114, 75231-6415, pg. 285 PV
Culco, Inc., 14303 Inwood Rd., 75240, pg. 909 PV
Cullum Development Co., 14303 Inwood Rd., 75244, pg. 909 PV
Cullum Distribution Center, Inc., 14303 Inwood Rd., 75240, pg. 909 PV
Custom Laminates, Inc., 2700 S. Westmoreland Ave., 75233, pg. 1530 PB
Cybertek Corporation, 7800 Stemmons Fwy., Ste. 800, 75247-1560, pg. 1314 PB
Daewoo International America Corp. - Dallas, 5005 LBJ Freeway, Ste. 740, 75244, pg. 357 IT
Dal-Tile Corp., 7834 Hawn Fwy., 75217, pg. 308 PV
DAL-TILE INTERNATIONAL, 7834 Hawn Fwy., 75217, pg. 308 PV
Dalfort Aerospace, 7701 Lemmon Ave., 75209, pg. 1253 IT
Dallas Auto Auction Inc., 5333 West Kiest Blvd., 75236-1055, pg. 1648 PB
Dallas Flower Market, Inc., 2636 Farrington St., 75207, pg. 326 PV
Dallas Global Travel, 2817 Forest Ln., 75234, pg. 478 PB
DALLAS GOLD & SILVER EXCHANGE, INC., 2817 Forest Ln., 75234, pg. 478 PB
The Dallas Morning News, Inc., Communications Center, 508 Young St., 75202, pg. 209 PB
Dallas Moving System Inc., 2537 Willowbrook St., 75220, pg. 1171 PV
DALLAS SEMICONDUCTOR CORPORATION, 4401 S. Beltwood Pkwy., 75244-3292, pg. 478 PB
DAVE & BUSTER'S, 2751 Electronic Ln., 75220, pg. 488 PB
Davenport Data Processors Inc., 12850 Spurling Rd., Second Fl., 75230, pg. 181 PB
Dayton Superior Corp., 4835 Reading St., 75247, pg. 932 PV
Decibel Products, Inc., 8635 N. Stemmons Fwy., 75247-3701, pg. 46 PB
Dext Company of TX, 3915 Hallifax St., 75247, pg. 1444 PB
Diamond Energy Operating Co., 5735 Pineland Dr., Ste. 300, 75231, pg. 584 PB
DocuCorp International, 5910 N. Central Expy., Ste. 800, 75206, pg. 1425 PB
Donruss Trading Card Co., 1845 Woodall Rodgers Fwy., 75201, pg. 866 PV
Dr. Pepper Co., 8144 Walnut Hill Ln., 75231, pg. 248 IT
Dr Pepper/Seven Up No. America, 8144 Walnut Hill Ln., 75265-4372, pg. 248 IT
Dr Pepper/Seven-Up Fountain Foodservice, 8144 Walnut Hill Ln., 75231-4372, pg. 248 IT
DRESSER INDUSTRIES, INC., 2001 Ross Ave., 75201, pg. 528 PB
Dresser Oil Tools, 4949 Joseph Hardin Dr., 75236, pg. 528 PB
Dugan Valva Contess-Dallas, 4514 Cole Ave., Ste. 1400, 75205, pg. 345 PV
DUGGAN INDUSTRIES, INC., 3901 S. Lamar St., 75215, pg. 345 PV
E-Systems Medical Technology Systems, P.O. Box 660023, 75266-0023, pg. 1365 PB
EDD-Dallas, 14110 Dallas Pkwy., Ste. 170, 75240, pg. 204 PB
EDS, International, Commercial and Communications Groups, 7171 Forest Lane, 75230, pg. 570 PB
EG & G Services Information Technologies, 1950 N. Stemmons Frwy., Ste. 3060, 75207-3199, pg. 544 PB
ESY Export Co., Inc., P.O. Box 660248, 75266, pg. 1365 PB
Eagle General Agency, 2727 Turtle Creek Blvd., 75219, pg. 346 IT
EAGLE LINCOLN MERCURY INC., 6200 Lemmon Ave., 75209, pg. 355 PV
Edelman Worldwide, Inc., 3131 Turtle Creek Blvd., #504, 75219, pg. 362 PV
El Chico Restaurants, Inc., 12200 Stemmons Fwy., Ste. 100, 75234, pg. 283 PV
ELCOR CORPORATION, Wellington Centre, Ste. 1000, 14643 Dallas Pkwy., 75240-8871, pg. 567 PB
Eljer Manufacturing/HVAC Group, Evergreen Center, Ste. 205, 17120 N. Dallas Pkwy., 75248, pg. 1794 PB
Eljer Plumbingware, 17120 Dallas Pkwy., 75248, pg. 1794 PB
Elk Corporation of Dallas, Wellington Centre, 14643 Dallas Pkwy., Ste. 1000, 75240, pg. 568 PB
Encore Computer, 8111 LBJ Freeway, Ste. 300, 75251, pg. 580 PB
Endevco Producing Co., 8080 No. Central Expwy., 75206, pg. 567 PB
ENSCO INTERNATIONAL INCORPORATED (ENSCO), 1445 Ross Ave., Ste. 2700, 75202-2792, pg. 585 PB
ENSERCH Corporation, ENSERCH Center, 300 S. St. Paul St., 75201-5598, pg. 1587 PB
Enserch Gas Co., 300 S. St. Paul, 75201, pg. 1587 PB
Environmental Service Insurance Co., 1111 W. Mockingbird, 75247, pg. 900 PV
EvansGroup, 3100 Monticello Ave., 6th Fl., 75205, pg. 385 PV
EXCEL COMMUNICATIONS, INC., 8750 N. Central Expwy., Ste. 2000, 75231, pg. 598 PB
Excelis, Inc., 1750 Viceroy Dr., 75235, pg. 625 PB
FFE Transportation Services, Inc., P.O. Box 655888, 75265-5888, pg. 685 PB
Family Service Life Insurance Co., P.O. Box 29018, 75221, pg. 1622 PB
Federal Parts, 9249 King James Rd., 75247, pg. 1503 PB
FEDERAL RESERVE BANK OF DALLAS, 2200 N. Pearl St., 75201, pg. 399 PV
FERGUSON INTERNATIONAL, INC., 1900 W. Northwest Hwy., 75220, pg. 401 PV
FERGUSON MANUFACTURING & EQUIPMENT COMPANY, INC., 4900 Harry Hines Blvd., 75235, pg. 401 PV
Fina, Inc., Fina Plaza, 8350 N. Central Expwy., 75206, pg. 1044 IT
Fina Oil & Chemical Co. (Dallas), 8350 N. Central Expwy., 75206, pg. 1044 IT
Financial Security Assurance Inc., The Crescent, 100 Crescent Court, 75201, pg. 623 PB
Fireman's Fund Insurance Co. of Texas, P.O. Box 2519, 1999 Bryan St., 75201, pg. 59 IT
FIRST SOUTHWEST COMPANY, 1700 Pacific Ave., Ste. 500, 75201-4652, pg. 407 PV
First USA Capital Markets, Inc., 1601 Elm St., 75201, pg. 174 PB
First USA, Inc., 1601 Elm St., 75201, pg. 174 PB
FIRST WORTHING COMPANY, 8144 Walnut Hill Ln., Ste. 550, 75231, pg. 408 PV
Albert Fisher North America, The Colonnade Bldg., 15303 Dallas Pkwy., Ste. 1250, 75248, pg. 491 IT
FITZ & FLOYD, 13111 N. Central Expwy., Ste. 100, 75243, pg. 409 PV
Fleishman-Hillard, Inc., Texas Commerce Tower, 2200 Ross Ave., Ste. 4600 E., 75201, pg. 411 PV
Fleming Foods of Texas, Inc., 15110 Dallas Pkwy., Ste. 500, 75248, pg. 653 PB
The Focus Agency, Inc., 200 Crescent Ct., Ste. 700, 75201, pg. 1224 PB
Fogarty Klein & Partners, One McKinney Plaza, 3232 McKinney Ave., Ste. 610, 75204, pg. 416 PV
FOXWORTH-GALBRAITH LUMBER CO., 17111 Waterview Pkwy., 75252, pg. 423 PV
FREEMAN DECORATING CO., 1421 W. Mockingbird Ln., 75247-4105, pg. 426 PV
Freeman Exhibit Co., 8301 Ambassador Rd., 75247, pg. 426 PV
FRESH AMERICA CORP., Lincoln Center One, 5400 LBJ Freeway, Ste. 1025, 75240, pg. 681 PB
Friction Inc., 5108 Cockrell Hill Rd., 75211, pg. 560 PB
FRIENDLY CHEVROLET CO. INC., 5601 Lemmon Ave., 75209, pg. 428 PV
FROZEN FOOD EXPRESS INDUSTRIES, INC., 1145 Empire Central Pl., 75247-4309, pg. 685 PB
Fruehauf Finance Company, P.O. Box 660237, 75266, pg. 663 PB
Furman Lumber Company Inc., 9708 Skillman, Ste. 102, 75243, pg. 431 PV
Furman Wholesale Lumber Branch, 11050 Plano Rd., 75238, pg. 431 PV
GCI Dallas, Inc/GCI Texas, Inc, 7901 Carpenter Freeway, 75247, pg. 470 PV
GH Hensley Industries, Inc., 2108 Joe Field Rd., 75229, pg. 439 PV
GLI Holding Company, 15110 N. Dallas Pkwy., 75248, pg. 765 PB
GLI Venture Company, 15110 N. Dallas Pkwy., 75248, pg. 765 PB
GAS EQUIPMENT COMPANY, INC., 11616 Harry Hines, 75229, pg. 440 PV
General Employment Enterprises, 3010 LBJ Fwy., Ste. 1200, 75234, pg. 714 PB
General Employment Enterprises, Inc., 1950 Stemmons Fwy., Ste. 5001, 75207, pg. 715 PB
General Felt Industries, Inc., 10726 Doric St., 75220, pg. 1095 PV
General Magnetic, 5252 Investment Dr., 75211, pg. 1369 PB
General Merchandise Distributors, Inc., 3400 Dan Morton Dr., 75211, pg. 653 PB
Gifford-Hill-American, Inc., P.O. Box 569470, 75356, pg. 99 PB
Gifford-Hill Cement Company of South Carolina, 2515 McKinney Ave., 75201, pg. 593 IT
Gifford-Hill Company, 2515 McKinney, 75201, pg. 593 IT
GLAZER'S WHOLESALE DRUG CO. INC., 14860 Landmark Blvd., 75240, pg. 455 PV
GLEASON/CALISE/ASSOCIATES, INC., 16775 Addison Rd., Ste. 500, 75248, pg. 455 PV
Glitsch International, 4900 Singleton Blvd., 75266, pg. 628 PV
GLOBAL INDUSTRIAL TECHNOLOGIES, 2121 San Jacino St., Ste. 2500, 75201, pg. 747 PB
Global Special Risks, Inc. of Texas, Lock Box 120, 3131 McKinney Ave., Ste. 400, 75204, pg. 1503 IT
Goldman, Sachs & Co., 100 Crescent Ct., Ste. 1000, 75201, pg. 462 PV
GORGES/QUIK-TO-FIX FOODS, 9441 LBJ Fwy., Ste. 214, 75243, pg. 465 PV
Gould Paper Corporation, 3131 Turtle Creek Blvd., Ste. 307, 75219, pg. 467 PV
Stephen Gould of Texas, Inc., 15820 Midway Rd., 75244, pg. 468 PV
GREYHOUND LINES, INC., 15110 N. Dallas Pkwy., Ste. 101, 75248, pg. 765 PB
Grocery Supply of Dallas, 1135 S. Lamar St., 75215, pg. 436 PV
Guaranty F.S.B., 8333 Douglas Ave., 75225, pg. 1575 PB
HCBECK, 1700 Pacific Ave., Ste. 3800, 75201, pg. 490 PV
HDR Architecture, 12700 Hillcrest Rd. Ste. 125, 75230-2048, pg. 206 IT
HI Property, Inc., 4550 Spring Valley Rd., 75234, pg. 537 PV
HSC Securities Corporation, 3710 Rawlins Ave., Ste. 1500, 75219, pg. 778 PB
HAAS, WHEAT & PARTNERS, 300 Crescent Court, Ste. 1700, 75201, pg. 492 PV
Hackney Inc., 2525 Stemmons Freeway, 75207-2401, pg. 1639 PB
Hadeler Law Media Management, 5430 LBJ Frwy., Ste. 1100, 75240, pg. 493 PV
HADELER SULLIVAN EWING, Three Lincoln Centre, 5430 LBJ Frwy., Ste. 1100, 75240, pg. 493 PV
Hadeler White Public Relations, 5430 LBJ Frwy., Ste. 1100, 75240, pg. 493 PV
HAGGAR CORPORATION, 6113 Lemmon Ave., 75209, pg. 774 PB
HALL FINANCIAL GROUP, INC., 750 N. Saint Paul St., Ste. 200, 75201-3241, pg. 495 PV
Hall-Mark Computer Products, 11333 Pagemill Rd., 75243, pg. 155 PB
HALLIBURTON COMPANY, 3600 Lincoln Plaza, 500 N. Akard St., 75201-3391, pg. 775 PB
Halliburton Energy Services, Inc., 3600 Lincoln Plaza, 500 N. Akard St., 75201-2600, pg. 776 PB
Hallwood Commercial Real Estate, Inc., 3710 Rawlins Ave., Ste. 1500, 75219, pg. 778 PB
THE HALLWOOD GROUP INCORPORATED, 3710 Rawlins Ave., Ste. 1500, 75219-4236, pg. 777 PB
Hallwood Hotels Inc., 3710 Rawlins, Ste 1500, 75219, pg. 778 PB
Hallwood Realty Corporation, 3710 Rawlins Ave., Ste. 1500, 75219-4236, pg. 778 PB
Hallwood Realty Investors Inc., 3710 Rawlins Ave., Ste. 1500, 75219-5588, pg. 778 PB
Hallwood Realty Partners, L.P., 3710 Rawlins, Ste. 1500, 75219, pg. 778 PB
Health Economics Corporation, 1300 W. Mockingbird Ln., 75247, pg. 588 PB
Heritage Forest Lane, 9009 Forest Ln., 75243, pg. 839 PB
Heritage Press, Inc., 8939 Premier Row, 75247, pg. 1735 PB
Hewlett-Packard Company, 7920 Elmbrook, Ste. 120, 75247, pg. 815 PB
HICKS, MUSE, TATE & FURST INC., 200 Crescent Ct., Ste. 1600, 75201, pg. 526 PV
Hilb, Rogal and Hamilton Company of Dallas, 5520 LBJ Freeway, 6th Fl., 75240, pg. 827 PB
HINDERLITER HEAT TREATING, INC., 10543 Doric Street, 75220, pg. 530 PV
HOAK CAPITAL, 13355 Noel Rd., Ste. 1050, 75240, pg. 531 PV
Hogan Systems, Inc., 5525 L.B.J. Fwy., 75240, pg. 422 PB
HOLLY CORPORATION, 100 Crescent Ct., Ste. 1600, 75201-6927, pg. 830 PB
Holly Petroleum, Inc., 100 Crescent Ct., Ste. 1600, 75201, pg. 830 PB
Holman Boiler Works, Inc., 1956 Singleton Blvd., 75212, pg. 274 PV
HOME INTERIORS & GIFTS, INC., 4550 Spring Valley Rd., 75244, pg. 536 PV
Horizon Specialty Hospital - Dallas, 7850 Brookhollow Rd., 75235, pg. 839 PB
Housewares Holding Company, 14785 Preston Rd., Ste. 1100, 75240, pg. 1149 PB
Howmedica Leibinger Inc., 14540 Beltwood Pkwy., 75244, pg. 1282 PB
Huber, Hunt & Nichols, Inc., 4099 McEwen Dr., Ste. 400, 75244, pg. 548 PV
Hugoton Capital Limited Partnership (HCLP), 2001 Ross Ave., Ste. 2600, 75201, pg. 1300 PB
HUITT-ZOLLARS, INC., 3131 McKinney Ave., Ste. 600, 75204, pg. 547 PV

Geographic Index-U.S.

PB - U.S. Public Companies Volume
PV - U.S. Private Companies Volume
IT - International Public & Private Companies Volume

CAROLINE HUNT TRUST ESTATE, 100 Crescent Court, Ste. 500, 75201, pg. 548 — PV

Hunt Oil Central Exploration Division, Fountain Place, 1445 Ross at Field, 75202-2785, pg. 548 — PV

HUNT OIL COMPANY, Fountain Place, 1445 Ross at Field, 75202-2785, pg. 548 — PV

Hutchinson Wil-Rich Manufacturing Co., 4645 N. Central Expwy., 75205, pg. 1063 — IT

HYDROSCIENCE, INC., 2659 Nova Dr., 75229, pg. 552 — PV

Hydrotex Inc., P.O. Box 560707, 1165 Empire Central Place, 75356-0707, pg. 892 — IT

ICI Explosives USA Inc., 15301 Dallas Pkwy., Suite 1200, 75248, pg. 663 — IT

IDX Systems Corporation-Dallas, 4901 LBJ Fwy., Ste. 400, 75244-6125, pg. 854 — PB

IKOS Systems, Inc., 9330 LBJ Freeway, Ste. 900, 75243, pg. 864 — PB

IXL Cabinets, 16803 Dallas Pkwy., 75248, pg. 1634 — PV

Iberia Air Lines of Spain, 8111 LBJ Fwy., Ste. 945, 75251, pg. 575 — IT

Ikon Office Solutions-Dallas, 14875 Landmark Blvd., 75240, pg. 863 — PB

The Ingersoll Group, 2501 Cedar Springs Rd., Ste. 400, 75201, pg. 651 — PV

InteCom, 5057 Keller Springs Rd., 75248, pg. 794 — PB

Integra Resort Management, Inc., 3710 Rawlins Ave., Ste. 1500, 75219-4236, pg. 778 — PV

Integral Corp., P.O. Box 151369, 75315, pg. 1019 — PV

Intergraph Corporation, 8111 LBJ Frwy., Ste. 1400, 75251, pg. 890 — PB

INTERNATIONAL WINE ACCESSORIES, INC., 11020 Audelia Rd., Ste. B-113, 75243, pg. 572 — PV

INTERPHASE CORPORATION, 13800 Senlac, 75234-8823, pg. 908 — PB

INTERVOICE, INC., 17811 Waterview Pkwy., 75252, pg. 910 — PB

Italia Advertising, Two Lincoln Ctr., 5420 LBJ Fwy., Ste. 1250, 75240, pg. 576 — PV

ITOCHU Cotton, Inc., 4311 Oak Lawn Dr., Ste. 350, 75219, pg. 694 — IT

JC Penney Business Services, 5001 Spring Valley Rd., 75244-3910, pg. 917 — PB

JC Penney Properties, Inc., P.O. Box 659000, 75265-9000, pg. 917 — PB

JC Penney Purchasing Corp., P.O. Box 10001, 75301, pg. 917 — PB

JLH Advertising, Inc., P.O. Box 815189, 75381-5189, pg. 198 — PV

JWG Associates, Inc., 4600 Greenville Ave., 75206, pg. 579 — PV

Jackhammer, 8750 N. Central Expwy., Ste. 1400, 75231-6437, pg. 929 — PB

Jamieson Film Company, Inc., 10425 Olympic Dr., 75220, pg. 551 — PV

Jani King Franchising, Inc., 16885 Dallas Pkwy., 75248, pg. 581 — PV

Jani King, Inc., 16885 Dallas Pkwy., 75248, pg. 581 — PV

JANI KING INTERNATIONAL, INC., 16885 Dallas Pkwy, 75248, pg. 581 — PB

Jani King Leasing Corp., 4950 Keller Springs Rd., Ste. 190, 75248, pg. 582 — PV

Jefferies & Company, Inc., 13355 Noel Rd., Ste. 1400, 75240, pg. 925 — PB

JERELL, INC., 1431 Regal Row, 75247, pg. 586 — PV

Jesse R. Dawson State Jail, Dallas County State Jail, 106 Commerce St., 75207, pg. 450 — PB

Johnson Ladders, 700 S. Ewing, 75203, pg. 477 — PV

S.C. Johnson & Son Inc., 15301 Dallas Pkwy. Ste. 760, LB 77, 75248-4672, pg. 592 — PV

JONES BLAIR COMPANY, 2728 Empire Central, 75235, pg. 596 — PV

Earle M. Jorgensen Company/Dallas, 2030 W. Commerce St., 75208, pg. 600 — PB

KDAF, 8001 Carpenter Freeway, 75247, pg. 926 — IT

KDAF (WB), 8001 John Carpenter Fwy., 75247, pg. 1636 — PB

KDFW, 400 N. Griffin, 75202, pg. 926 — IT

KHKS-FM, 8235 Douglas, Ste. 300, 75225, pg. 335 — PV

Kaiser Permanente, Southwest Division, 12720 Hillcrest Rd., Ste. 600, 75230, pg. 605 — PV

Keystone Automotive Industries, Inc.-Dallas, 4949 Sharp St., Ste. 101, 75247, pg. 955 — PB

KEYSTONE CONSOLIDATED INDUSTRIES, INC., 5430 LBJ Fwy., Ste. 1740, 75240, pg. 955 — PB

KIMBERLY-CLARK CORPORATION, P.O. Box 619100, 75261-9100, pg. 958 — PB

Kinepak, Incorporated, 15301 Dallas Pkwy., Ste. 1200, 75248, pg. 664 — IT

The Knape Group, 2501 Cedar Springs, Ste. 560, 75201, pg. 651 — PV

KNOX OIL OF TEXAS INC., 5001 L.B.J. Fwy., Ste. 1020, 75244, pg. 627 — PV

Korn/Ferry International, 3232 Lincoln Plaza, 500 North Akard St., 75201, pg. 633 — PB

Korn/Ferry International - High Technology Research Center, 17440 Dallas Pkwy. # 127, 75287, pg. 633 — PB

Koslow's, 9100 N. Central Expwy., 75231, pg. 597 — PB

The L & B Group, North Park Central, 8750 N. Central Expwy., Ste. 800, 75231-6431, pg. 1673 — PB

LG&E Natural, Inc., 2777 Stemmouse Fwy., Ste. 700, 75207, pg. 970 — PB

LGM Omega, Inc., 4521 Brass Way, 76236, pg. 1222 — PB

LARKIN MEEDER & SCHWEIDEL, 2501 Cedar Springs Rd., 4th Fl., 75201, pg. 651 — PV

LASTING PRODUCTS, INC., 2115 W. Valley View Rd., 75234, pg. 652 — PV

Latitude, 7007 Twin Hills, Ste. 300, 75231, pg. 929 — PV

Leader National Insurance Company, 4100 Harry Hines Blvd., 75219, pg. 75 — PB

LEVENSON & HILL, INC., Plaza of the Americas, 600 N. Pearl St., Ste. 910, 75201, pg. 662 — PV

Lilly Industries, Inc., 2518 Chalk Hill Rd., 75212, pg. 994 — PB

LINCOLN PROPERTY COMPANY, 500 N. Akard, Ste. 3300, 75201, pg. 668 — PV

Louis London Dallas, 2515 McKinney Ave., Ste. 1585, 75201, pg. 674 — PV

Lone Star Energy Co., 301 S. Harwood, 75201, pg. 1587 — PB

Lone Star Gas Co., 301 S. Harwood St., 75201, pg. 1587 — PB

Lone Star Pipeline Company, 300 S. St. Paul, 75201-5598, pg. 1587 — PB

Lone Star Steel Company, P.O. Box 803546, 5501 LBJ Freeway, Ste. 1200, 75380-3546, pg. 1012 — PB

LONE STAR TECHNOLOGIES, INC., 5501 LBJ Fwy., 1200, 75240, pg. 1012 — PB

Long Mile Rubber Company, 5550 LBJ Freeway, Ste. 200, 75240, pg. 1504 — PB

Long-Term Credit Bank of Japan, Limited, 2200 Ross Ave., Ste. 4700 W., 75201, pg. 816 — IT

Lucent Netcare Messaging Services, 17080 Dallas Pkwy., 75248-1986, pg. 1018 — IT

M & S Systems, Inc., 2861 Congressman Ln., 75220, pg. 1193 — PV

MBNA Hallmark Information Systems, Hallmark Ctr., 16001 N. Dallas Pkwy., 75248, pg. 1023 — PB

MC II Corp., 1745 Hinton St., 75235, pg. 1763 — PV

MEPC AMERICAN PROPERTIES, 15303 Dallas Pkwy., Ste. 400, 75248, pg. 686 — PV

Machinery Sales & Supply Co., 11237 Stemmons Frwy., 75229, pg. 971 — PB

Magnaview Inc., 1240 Profit Dr., 75247, pg. 1720 — PV

MAGUIRE OIL CO., 1201 Elm St., Ste. 4000, 75270, pg. 596 — PV

MALIBU ENTERTAINMENT WORLDWIDE, 717 N. Harwood, Ste. 615, 75201, pg. 1039 — PB

MARCUS CABLE COMPANY, L.P., 2911 Turtle Creek Blvd., Ste. 1300, 75219, pg. 702 — PB

MarketSource Corporation, 7502 Greenville Ave., Ste. 500, 75231, pg. 705 — PB

MARLOW INDUSTRIES, 10451 Vista Park Rd., 75238, pg. 705 — PV

Marquette National Life Insurance Co., 717 N. Harwood, 75201, pg. 1018 — PB

MARY KAY CORPORATION, 4300 W. Grove Dr., 75248, pg. 710 — PV

Mary Kay Cosmetics, Inc., 13835 Senlac Dr., 75234, pg. 711 — PV

Mary Kay, Inc., 16251 N. Dallas Pkwy., 75248-2696, pg. 711 — PV

Massey Cadillac, Inc., 11501 E. Northwest Hwy., 75218, pg. 713 — PV

Materials Research Corp., 12160 Abrams Road, Ste. 217, 74243, pg. 1283 — IT

Curtis Mathes Corporation, 10911 Petal St., 75238, pg. 1057 — PB

CURTIS MATHES HOLDING CORP., 10911 Petal St., 75238, pg. 1057 — PB

Maxum Health Corp., 11617 Central Expwy., Ste. 132, 75243, pg. 881 — PB

Maxus Energy Corporation, 717 N. Harwood St., 75201-6594, pg. 1515 — IT

MAYNARD OIL CO., 8080 N. Central Expwy., Ste. 660, 75206, pg. 1064 — PB

Mechanics Tool Div., 12827 Valley Branch Ln., 75234, pg. 1509 — PV

Media Recovery Inc.-Dallas, TX, 7929 Brookriver Dr., Ste. 200, 75247, pg. 1064 — PV

Mercury Air Center, 4400 Glenn Curtiss Dr., 75248, pg. 1093 — PV

Mesa Capital Corporation, 2001 Ross Ave., Ste. 2600, 75201, pg. 1300 — PB

Mesa Holding Limited Partnership (MHLP), 2001 Ross Ave., Ste. 2600, 75201, pg. 1300 — PB

Mesa Midcontinent Limited Partnership (MMLP), 2001 Ross Ave., Ste. 2600, 75201, pg. 1300 — PB

Mesa Operating Limited Partnership (MOLP), 2001 Ross Ave., Ste. 2600, 75201, pg. 1300 — PB

Milgray/Dallas, Inc., 16610 N. Dallas Pkwy., 75248, pg. 206 — PV

Miller Freeman Inc., 13760 Noel Rd., # 500, 75240, pg. 1443 — IT

Mitsubishi Silicon America-Southwest Regional Sales Office, 17304 N. Preston Rd., Ste. 800, 75252-5645, pg. 875 — IT

Mobil Pipe Line Company, P.O. Box 900, 75221-10900, pg. 1118 — PB

MonkeyHaus Design, Three Lincoln Ctr., 5430 LBJ Frwy., Ste. 100, 75240, pg. 493 — PV

Montgomery & Collins, Inc. of Texas, 3030 LBJ Freeway, Ste. 130, 75244-7773, pg. 366 — PB

The Morning Star Group, 5956 Sherry Ln., Ste. 1500, 75225, pg. 1527 — PB

MOROCH & ASSOC., INC., 3625 N. Hall, Suite 1200, 75219, pg. 762 — PV

Motel 6 Operating L.P., 14651 Dallas Pkwy., Ste. 500, 75240, pg. 21 — IT

Motorola USA, 4950 Bent Tree Plaza, 75248, pg. 1138 — IT

NMI Corporation, 14110 N. Dallas Pkwy., Ste. 300, 75240, pg. 900 — PV

NATIONAL BANNER COMPANY, INC., 11938 Harry Hines Blvd., 75229, pg. 780 — PV

NATIONAL ENERGY GROUP, INC., 4925 Greenville Ave., Ste. 1400, 75206, pg. 1156 — PB

National Hand Tools, 12827 Valley Branch Lane, 75237, pg. 1509 — PV

National Precision Products, 2840 Reward Ln., 75220, pg. 145 — PV

NationsBank Mortgage Corporation, 1707 Pacific Ave., Sixth Fl., Tower II, 75201, pg. 1165 — PB

NationsBank of Texas, N.A., 901 Main St., 75202, pg. 1163 — PB

NationsBank of Texas National Bank Properties Inc., P.O. Box 83000, 75283, pg. 1163 — PB

NationsBank of Texas National Bank Services Corporation, 1401 Elm St., 75283, pg. 1163 — PB

NationsBank of Texas National International Co., Pacific & Ervay Sts., 75201, pg. 1163 — PB

NationsBank of Texas National Leasing Corp., P.O. Box 146, 75221, pg. 1163 — PB

NationsBank of Texas National Life Insurance Co., P.O. Box 83000, 75283, pg. 1163 — PB

NationsBank of Texas National Money Orders Inc, P.O. Box 2048, 75221, pg. 1163 — PB

NationsBank of Texas National Ventures Group Inc., P.O. Box 225961, Pacific & Ervay Sts., 75265, pg. 1163 — PB

NationsBank Texas Corporation, 901 Main St., 75202, pg. 1163 — PB

Navajo Crude Oil Purchasing, 100 Crescent Court St., 75201, pg. 830 — PB

Navajo Holdings, Inc., 100 Crescent Court, Ste. 1600, 75201-1880, pg. 830 — PB

Navajo Western Asphalt Company, 100 Crescent Court, Ste. 1600, 75201-1880, pg. 830 — PB

Neiman Marcus Co., One Marcus Sq., 1618 Main St., 75201, pg. 785 — PB

The Neogard Corporation, 2732 Empire Central, 75235, pg. 596 — PV

New America Financial, Inc., 3131 Turtle Creek Blvd., Ste. 1300, 75219, pg. 644 — PB

New Line Cinema-Dallas, 6060 North Central, 75206, pg. 1614 — PB

Niagara Portfolio Management Corporation, 15660 N. Dallas Pkwy., Ste. 600, 75248, pg. 955 — PB

Nobel Insurance Agency, 8001 LBJ Fwy., 75234, pg. 951 — IT

Nobel Insurance Group, 8001 LBJ Fwy., Ste. 300, 75251, pg. 951 — IT

Nobel Lloyds Insurance Company, 8001 LBJ Fwy., 75251, pg. 951 — IT

The North American Coal Corporation, 14785 Preston Rd., Ste. 1100, 75240-7891, pg. 1149 — PB

North American Coal Royalty Company, 14785 Preston Rd., Ste. 1100, 75240-7891, pg. 1149 — PB

Northern Trust Bank of Texas, N.A., 2020 Ross Avenue, 75201, pg. 1197 — PB

Northern Trust Bank of Texas, N.A., 5540 Preston Rd., 75205, pg. 1197 — PB

NU-KOTE INTERNATIONAL, 17950 Preston Rd., Ste. 690, 75252, pg. 1205 — PB

Occidental Chemical Corporation, Mktg. Support-NR, 5005 LBJ Frwy., 75244, pg. 1210 — PB

Oliver Rubber Co., 6840 Forest Park Rd., 75235, pg. 1505 — PB

Olympic Pipe Line Co., P.O. Box 900, 75221, pg. 1584 — PB

Omega Environmental Services, 5565 Redbird Ctr. Dr., Ste. 130, 75237, pg. 1222 — PV

Omniflight Helicopters, Inc., 4650 Airport Parkway, 75248, pg. 817 — PV

OMNIFLIGHT, INC., 4650 Airport Parkway, 75248, pg. 816 — PV

Openconnect Systems, Inc., 1120 Empire Central Pl., 75247, pg. 361 — PB

Optigraphics Inc., 1845 Woodall Rodgers Fwy., 75201, pg. 866 — PV

ORYX ENERGY, 13155 Noel Rd., 75240-5067, pg. 1232 — PB

Outdoor Services, 2711 N. Haskell Ave. # 2150, 75204, pg. 1166 — PV

OVERHEAD DOOR CORPORATION, 6750 LBJ Fwy., Ste. 1200, 75240, pg. 822 — PV

Overhead Door Corp. of Texas, 2170 French Settlement Rd., 75212, pg. 823 — PV

PC SERVICE SOURCE, INC., 2350 Valley View Ln., 75234, pg. 1240 — PB

PMC CAPITAL INC., 17290 Preston Rd., Ste. 300, 75252, pg. 1242 — PB

PS Trading, Inc., 17742 Preston Rd., 75252, pg. 1245 — PB

PacifiCare of Texas, 1420 W. Mockingbird Ln., Ste. 800, 75247, pg. 1251 — PV

Pages Drugs, 14303 Inwood Rd., 75234, pg. 909 — PV

PALM HARBOR HOMES, INC., 15303 Dallas Pkwy., Ste. 800-LB 35, 75248, pg. 1254 — PB

PARK PLACE MOTORCARS, LTD., 4023 Oak Lawn, 75219, pg. 840 — PV

PATRIOT AMERICAN HOSPITALITY, INC., 1950 Stemmons Fwy., Ste. 6001, 75207, pg. 1265 — PB

Payson Services, Inc., 2688 Freewood Dr., 75220, pg. 844 — PV

Pearle Inc., 2534 Royal La., 75229, pg. 396 — PV

Pearle Vision Express, 2534 Royal La., 75229, pg. 397 — PB

Pearle Vision, Inc., 2534 Royal Lane, 75229, pg. 397 — PB

PEERLESS MFG. CO., 2819 Walnut Hill Ln., 75354, pg. 1268 — PB

Pepsi-Cola South, 4100 Alpha Rd., Ste. 300, 75244, pg. 1277 — PB

PEROT SYSTEMS CORPORATION, 12377 Merit Dr., Ste. 1100, 75251, pg. 854 — PV

PETRO-HUNT CORPORATION, 3900 Thanksgiving Tower, 75201, pg. 858 — PV

Petrofina Delaware, Incorporated, Fina Plaza, 8350 N. Central Expwy., 75206, pg. 1044 — IT

Philips Information Systems, 15301 Dallas Pkwy., Ste. 300, 75248-4690, pg. 1055 — IT

Phillips Driscopipe, Inc., 12200 Ford Rd., 75234, pg. 1291 — PB

PILLOWTEX CORPORATION, 4111 Mint Way, 75237, pg. 1296 — PB

PINNACLE BRANDS, INC., 1845 Woodall Rodgers Fwy., Ste. 1300, 75201, pg. 866 **PV**

Pinnacle Trading Card Co., 1845 Woodall Rodgers Fwy., 75201, pg. 866 **PV**

Pizza Hut, Inc., 14841 N. Dallas Pkwy., 75240, pg. 1636 **PB**

PIZZA INN, INC., 5050 Quorum Dr., Ste. 500, 75240, pg. 1307 **PB**

Plastic Suppliers Inc., 4526 Bronze Way, 75236, pg. 871 **PB**

Plastics Manufacturing Company, 2700 S. Westmoreland Ave., 75233, pg. 1530 **PV**

POLYPHASE CORPORATION, 16885 Dallas Pkwy., 75248, pg. 1315 **PB**

Ponderosa Steakhouse, 12404 Park Central Dr., 75251, pg. 736 **PB**

Posadas USA Inc., 5950 Berkshire Ln., 75225-5846, pg. 576 **IT**

POST Buckley Schuh & Jernigan, 599 Summerside Dr., Ste.202, 75252, pg. 826 **PV**

The PowerBase Marketing Group, 2501 Cedar Springs Rd., Ste. 400, 75201, pg. 651 **PV**

Pratt Casino Corporation, 13455 Noel Rd., 75240, pg. 761 **PB**

Principal Financial Securities, 1445 Ross Ave., Ste. 2300, 75202, pg. 885 **PV**

Prior Gaskets Inc., 4874 Olson Dr., 75227, pg. 300 **PV**

Pro-Cut Products, Inc., 10901 Alder Circle, 75355, pg. 1171 **IT**

PRO-LINE CORPORATION, 2121 Panoramic Circle, 75212, pg. 887 **PV**

Publicis/Bloom, 3500 Maple Ave., Ste. 450, 75219, pg. 469 **PV**

Publicis Public Relations, 3500 Maple Ave., 75219, pg. 470 **IT**

PUBLISHERS EQUIPMENT CORPORATION, 16660 Dallas Pkwy., Ste. 1100, 75248, pg. 1341 **PB**

Quebecor Printing Dallas Inc., 4800 Spring Valley Rd., 75209, pg. 1076 **PB**

Quemetco, Inc., 1111 W. Mockingbird Ln., 75247, pg. 900 **PV**

Quemetco Metals Limited, Inc., 1111 W. Mockingbird Ln., 75247, pg. 900 **PV**

Quemetco Realty, Inc., 1111 W. Mockingbird Ln., 75247, pg. 900 **PV**

QUEXCO INCORPORATED, 2777 Stemmons Frwy., 75207, pg. 900 **PV**

RLI Claims/P&C, Graystone Center, Ste. 1020, 3010 LBJ Fwy., 75234, pg. 1356 **PB**

RSR Corporation, 1111 W. Mockingbird Ln., 75247, pg. 900 **PV**

RADICA USA LIMITED, 13628-A Beta Rd., 75244, pg. 906 **PB**

Radio Metroplex Inc., 3500 Maple Ave., Ste. 1600, 75219-3906, pg. 860 **PV**

Reddy Ice, 3535 Travis, Ste. 170, 75204, pg. 1527 **PB**

Reed Travel Publishing-Dallas, Two Forest Plaza, Ste. 730, 12201 Merit Dr., 75251, pg. 1097 **IT**

REGENCY LINCOLN MERCURY, INC., 11810 E. Northwest Hwy., 75218, pg. 918 **PV**

Regions Bank/Paulding County, P.O. Box 108, 30163-3801, pg. 1372 **PB**

Republic Beverage Co., 2535 Manana St., 75220, pg. 150 **PB**

Republic Diversified Services, Inc., 2727 Turtle Creek Blvd., 75219, pg. 346 **IT**

Republic Financial Services, Inc., 2727 Turtle Creek Blvd., 75219, pg. 346 **PV**

Republic Fire & Casualty Insurance Company, 2727 Turtle Creek Blvd., pg. 346 **PV**

Republic Group No. Two, 2727 Turtle Creek Blvd., 75219, pg. 346 **PV**

Republic Gypsum Company-Dallas Office, P.O. Box 750, 75221-0750, pg. 1378 **PB**

Republic Insurance Company, 2727 Turtle Creek Blvd., 75219, pg. 346 **PV**

Republic Lloyds, 2727 Turtle Creek Blvd., 75219, pg. 346 **PV**

Republic Underwriters Insurance Co., 2727 Turtle Creek Blvd., 75219, pg. 346 **PV**

Republic-Vanguard Life Insurance Co., 2727 Turtle Creek Blvd., 75219, pg. 346 **IT**

Republic-Vanguard Reinsurance Co., 2727 Turtle Creek Blvd., 75219, pg. 346 **IT**

Revere Smelting & Refining Corp., 1111 W. Mockingbird Ln., 75247, pg. 901 **PV**

Rexene Corporation, 5005 LBJ Fwy., Ste. 500, 75244, pg. 549 **PB**

Richards, Brock, Miller, Mitchell & Assoc. Inc., 7007 Twin Hills, Ste. 200, 75231, pg. 929 **PV**

Richards/Gravelle, 8750 N. Central Expwy., Ste. 1200, 75231-6437, pg. 929 **PV**

Richards/Gravelle Public Relations, 8750 N. Central Expwy., Ste. 1200, 75231-6437, pg. 929 **PV**

THE RICHARDS GROUP, INC., 8750 N. Central Expwy., Ste. 1200, 75231-6437, pg. 929 **PV**

Riteway Trucking, 1111 W. Mockingbird Ln., 75247, pg. 900 **PV**

River Ranch - Southwest, 4721 Simonton Road, 75244, pg. 491 **PV**

RIVER RANCH SOUTHWEST, INC., 4721 Simonton Rd., 75244, pg. 934 **PV**

Robinson Nugent-Dallas, Inc., 2640 Tarna Dr., 75229, pg. 1395 **PB**

Robinson Nugent, Inc., 2640 Tarna Dr., 75229, pg. 1394 **PB**

Rochester Gauges Inc. Of Texas, 11616 Harry Hines Blvd., 75229, pg. 440 **PV**

Romacorp, Inc., 9304 Forest Ln., Ste. 200, 75243-8953, pg. 1147 **PB**

Rosewood Corporation, 100 Crescent Ct., Ste. 1700, 75201, pg. 548 **PV**

ROSEWOOD PROPERTY COMPANY, 500 Crescent Ct., Ste. 300, 75201, pg. 946 **PV**

Ruppman Marketing Technologies, Inc., 9019 Clayco Dr., 75243, pg. 952 **PV**

S.Two Systems Corporation, 15301 Dallas Pkwy., Ste. 600, 75248, pg. 1524 **PB**

SA-SO COMPANY, 1341 W. Mockingbird Ln., Ste. 1200E, 75247, pg. 955 **PB**

SCR Division, 2819 Walnut Hill Ln., 75229, pg. 1268 **PB**

SEI Corporation, 8585 N. Stemmons Fwy., Ste. 1100, 75247-3805, pg. 1417 **PB**

SEI HOLDING CORP., 750 N. St. Paul St., Ste. 530, 75201, pg. 956 **PV**

Salem Carpet Mills, P.O. Box 333, 2861 Merrell Rd., 75229, pg. 1464 **PB**

SAMMONS ENTERPRISES, INC., 300 Cresent Ct. Ave., Ste. 700, 75201, pg. 963 **PV**

Sandoz Agro Corporation, 12005 Ford Rd., Ste. 800, 75234, pg. 974 **PV**

Santa Fe International Corporation, Two Lincoln Ctr., 5420 LBJ Frwy., Ste. 1100, 75240, pg. 765 **IT**

Santa Fe Minerals Inc., Two Galleria Tower, Ste. 1100, 13455 Noel Rd., 75240-6620, pg. 765 **IT**

Selkirk HVAC, 17120 Dallas Pkwy., 75248-1144, pg. 1795 **PB**

Selkirk Metalbestos, 17120 Dallas Pkwy., Ste. 205, 75248, pg. 1794 **PB**

Seltec Selective Technology Inc., DFW Airport, 1100 N. 27th Ave., Ste. 200, 75261-0870, pg. 1528 **IT**

Sequent Computer Systems, Inc., 15303 Dallas Pkwy., Ste. 1350, 75248, pg. 1459 **PB**

Serco Company, 4030 LaReunion, #150, 75212, pg. 1676 **PB**

7-Eleven Stores, P.O. Box 711, 2711 N. Haskell Ave., 75204, pg. 693 **IT**

SEWELL VILLAGE CADILLAC CO., 7310 Lemmon Ave., 75209, pg. 988 **PV**

Sharp Electronics Corporation, P.O. Box 619035, 1025 Royal Lane, 75261-9035, pg. 1229 **IT**

Shawflex Inc., Office 20, 18333 Preston Rd., Ste. 460, 75252, pg. 1231 **IT**

Singapore Airlines Ltd., 8500 Stemmons Fwy., Ste. 1060, 75247, pg. 1374 **IT**

SmithKline Beecham Clinical Laboratories, 8000 Sovereign Row, 75247, pg. 1265 **IT**

Snavely Forest Products, Inc., P.O. Box 59907, 75229, pg. 1010 **PV**

SNELLING PERSONNEL SERVICES, 12801 N. Central Expwy., Ste. 700, 75243, pg. 1010 **PV**

SOURCE SERVICES CORPORATION, 5580 LBJ Fwy., Ste. 300, 75240, pg. 1488 **PV**

Southern County Mutual Insurance Company, 2727 Turtle Creek Blvd., 75219, pg. 346 **IT**

SOUTHERN FOODS GROUP, 3114 S. Haskell, 75227, pg. 1016 **PV**

Southern Insurance Co., 2727 Turtle Creek Blvd., 75219, pg. 346 **IT**

Southern Underwriters Insurance Company, 2727 Turtle Creek Blvd., 75219, pg. 346 **IT**

The Southland Corporation, 2711 N. Haskell Ave., 75204-2906, pg. 693 **PB**

SOUTHWEST AIRLINES CO., 2702 Love Field Dr., 75235, pg. 1493 **PB**

Southwest Jet Fuel Co., P.O. Box 36646, 75235, pg. 1493 **PB**

Southwest Marketing Div., 4455 LBJ Freeway, Ste. 1008, 75244, pg. 296 **PV**

Southwest Region, 13155 Noel Rd., 13th Fl., 75240, pg. 1024 **PV**

Southwestern Bell Telecom, 1440 Empire Central, 75249, pg. 1416 **PV**

Southwestern Electric Service Co., 1601 Bryan St., Ste. 10-020, 75201, pg. 1588 **PB**

Southwestern Financial Corp., 8100 Carpenter Frwy., 75247, pg. 1585 **PB**

Southwestern Financial Services Corp., 500 N. Akard, 75201, pg. 1018 **PV**

Southwestern Life Insurance Company, 500 N. Akard, 75201, pg. 1018 **PV**

Spinnaker Industries, Inc., 600 N. Pearl St., 75201, pg. 1022 **PB**

SPORT SUPPLY GROUP, INC., 1901 Diplomat Dr., 75234, pg. 1499 **PB**

Sprint Business, 5420 LBJ Freeway, 75240, pg. 1501 **PB**

Sprint's Long Distance Div., 5420 LBJ Freeway, 75240, pg. 1501 **PB**

Square D Co., 1111 Regal Row, 75247, pg. 1208 **PB**

Standard-Pacific-Texas, 1321 Greenway, Suite 250, 75038, pg. 1504 **PB**

Stanfast, Inc., 4132A Billy Mitchell, 75244, pg. 1505 **PB**

State Fair Foods, 4639 Irving Blvd., Ste. 304, 75247, pg. 1434 **PB**

State Farm County Mutual Insurance Co. of Texas, 17301 Preston Rd., 75379, pg. 1036 **PV**

State Farm Lloyds, 17301 Preston Rd., 75379, pg. 1036 **PV**

Statex Petroleum, Inc., 1801 Royal Lane, Ste. 110, 75229, pg. 1245 **PB**

Steak and Ale Restaurants, 12404 Park Central Dr., 75251, pg. 736 **PV**

STEAKLEY CHEVROLET GEO SUBARU INC., 6411 E. Northwest Hwy., 75231, pg. 1037 **PV**

STERLING SOFTWARE, INC., 300 Crescent Ste. 1200, 75201-7832, pg. 1516 **PB**

Stewart Smith Southwest, Inc, 1201 Elm St., Ste. 1960, 75270, pg. 1508 **IT**

SUIZA FOODS CORPORATION, 3811 Turtle Creek Blvd., Ste. 1300, 75219, pg. 1526 **PB**

Sullivan Transfer Co., 3817 Irving Blvd., 75247, pg. 426 **PV**

Summers Group, 6700 LBJ Fwy., Ste. 3200, 75240, pg. 1108 **IT**

SUN COAST INDUSTRIES, INC, 2700 S. Westmorland Ave., 75233, pg. 1529 **PB**

Sunbelt National Mortgage Corporation, 2974 LBJ Freeway, 75234, pg. 639 **PB**

SUNRISE ENERGY SERVICES, INC., 4925 Greenville Ave., 75206, pg. 1053 **PV**

Support Terminal Services, Inc., 17304 Preston Rd., 75252, pg. 942 **PV**

Symbol, 1805 Royal Ln., Ste. 103, 75229, pg. 1546 **PB**

Sysco Food Services of Dallas, 14330 Gillis Rd., 75244-3717, pg. 1551 **PB**

TCI Cablevision of Dallas, Inc., 400 N. St. Paul, 75201, pg. 1555 **PB**

TD INDUSTRIES INC., 13850 Diplomat Dr., 75234, pg. 1063 **PV**

TIC Investment Corp., 4645 N. Central Expwy., 75205, pg. 1064 **PV**

TIC UNITED CORPORATION, 4645 N. Central Expressway, 75205, pg. 1063 **PV**

TLPartnership, 200 Crescent Ct., Ste. 900, 75201, pg. 1224 **PV**

TMP Worldwide, Inc., 12225 Greenville Ave. Ste. 750, 75243, pg. 1064 **PV**

TMP Worldwide/Recruitment Division, 12225 Greenville Ave., Ste. 750, 75243, pg. 1065 **PV**

TU Electric, 1601 Bryan St., 75201-3411, pg. 1588 **PB**

TU Services, 1601 Bryan St., 75201, pg. 1588 **PB**

TXI Aviation, Inc., 8350 Denton Dr., 75235, pg. 1585 **PB**

TXI Structural Products, Inc., 1910 Chalkhill Rd., 75212, pg. 1585 **PB**

TXI Transportation Company, 7610 Stemmons Freeway, 75207, pg. 1585 **PB**

Taivan Corp., P.O. Box 6, 2777 Stemmons Frwy., Ste. 600, 75207, pg. 1347 **IT**

TARRAGON REALTY INVESTORS, 3100 Monticello Ave., Ste. 200, 75205, pg. 1561 **PB**

Taurus Energy Co., 5735 Pineland Dr., Ste. 202, 75231, pg. 584 **PB**

Taurus Energy Corp., 9400 N. Central Expwy., Ste. 510, 75231, pg. 584 **PB**

Taylor Publishing Co., 1550 W. Mockingbird Ln., 75235, pg. 881 **PB**

Taymetric (U.S.A) Inc., 2526 Manana Drive, Ste. 100, 75220, pg. 1359 **IT**

TEMTEX INDUSTRIES INC., One Lincoln Ctr., 5400 LBJ Fwy., Ste. 1375, 75240, pg. 1575 **PB**

Tenet HealthSystem HealthCorp, 14001 Dallas Pkwy., Ste. 105, 75240, pg. 1577 **PB**

Tenet HealthSystem Hospitals, Inc., 14001 Dallas Pkwy., Ste. 105, 75240, pg. 1577 **PB**

Tenet HealthSystem Medical, Inc., 14001 Dallas Pkwy., Ste. 105, 75240, pg. 1577 **PB**

TEXAS INDUSTRIES, INC., 1341 W. Mockingbird Ln., #700W., 75247-6913, pg. 1585 **PB**

Texas Instruments Consumer Products Div., 7800 Banner Dr., 75251, pg. 1586 **PB**

TEXAS INSTRUMENTS INCORPORATED, 13500 N. Central Expwy., 75243, pg. 1585 **PB**

Texas Instruments Semiconductor Group, P.O. Box 655012, 13500 No. Central Expwy, 75243, pg. 1586 **PB**

Texas Pacific Indemnity Co., Maxus Energy Tower, 717 N. Harwood, Ste. 300, 75201, pg. 355 **PB**

Texas Resin, 2728 Empire Central, 75235, pg. 596 **PV**

Texas Utilities Communications Inc., 1601 Bryan St., 75201-3411, pg. 1588 **PB**

TEXAS UTILITIES COMPANY, Energy Plaza, 1601 Bryan St., 75201-3411, pg. 1586 **PB**

Texas Utilities Fuel Co., 1601 Bryan St., 75201-3411, pg. 1588 **PB**

Texas Utilities Mining Co., 1601 Bryan St., 75201-3411, pg. 1588 **PB**

Texas Utilities Properties Inc., 1601 Bryan St., 75201-3411, pg. 1588 **PB**

Thai Airways Intl. Ltd.-Dallas, 8700 N. Stemmons Fwy., Ste. 408, 75247, pg. 1381 **IT**

TimeMed Labeling Systems, Inc., 2808 McGowan St., 75203, pg. 1087 **PV**

Todays Temporary, Inc., 18111 Preston Rd., Ste. 700, 75252-5409, pg. 1517 **PV**

Tom Thumb Food & Pharmacy, 14303 Inwood Rd., 75244, pg. 909 **PV**

TRAMMELL CROW COMPANY, 3400 Trammell Crow Ctr., 2001 Ross Ave., 75201, pg. 1628 **PV**

Trammell Crow Interests, 3200 Trammell Crow Center, 2001 Ross Ave., 75201, pg. 1628 **PB**

Transamerica Real Estate Information Companies, Two Lincoln Ctr., 5420 LBJ Freeway, Ste. 1400, 75240, pg. 1630 **PV**

TRANSCONTINENTAL REALTY INVESTORS, INC., 10670 N. Central Expressway, Ste. 300, 75231, pg. 1630 **PB**

Transilwrap Company, Inc., 1118 Quaker St., 75207, pg. 1097 **PV**

Transport Insurance Co., 4100 Harry Hines Blvd., 75219, pg. 75 **PV**

TRIANGLE FOOD SERVICES CO., 16970 Dallas Pkwy., Ste. 701, 75248, pg. 1102 **PV**

TRIANGLE PACIFIC CORPORATION, 16803 Dallas Pkwy., 75248, pg. 1634 **PB**

Tricon Restaurants International, 14841 Dallas Pkwy., 75240, pg. 1637 **PB**

Trinity Construction Products, 2525 Stemmons Fwy., 75207-2401, pg. 1639 **PB**

TRINITY INDUSTRIES INC., 2525 Stemmons Fwy., 75207-2401, pg. 1638 **PB**

Trinity Leasing, 2525 Stemmons Freeway, 75207, pg. 1639 **PB**

Trinity Metal Components, P.O. Box 568887, 75356-8887, pg. 1639 **PB**

PB - *U.S. Public Companies Volume*
PV - *U.S. Private Companies Volume*
IT - *International Public & Private Companies Volume*

1441

Geographic Index-U.S.

Trinity Railcar Leasing, 2525 Stemmons Freeway, 75207, pg. 1639 **PB**
Trinity Transportation, Inc., 2525 Stemmons Freeway, 75207, pg. 1639 **PB**
Trinity Universal Insurance Co., P.O. Box 65028, 75265-5028, pg. 1694 **PB**
Triple D Supply Corp., 5501 LBJ Freeway, Ste. 810, 75240, pg. 1070 **PB**
TriStar Pictures Southern Division, Northcreek Place I, 9461 LBJ Frwy., Ste. 128-C, 75243, pg. 1283 **IT**
TRITON ENERGY LIMITED, 6688 N. Central Expwy., Ste. 1400, 75206, pg. 1640 **PB**
Triumph Releasing Corporation - Southwestern Territory, 12770 Merit Dr., Ste. 702, 75251-1503, pg. 1282 **IT**
TUESDAY MORNING CORPORATION, 14621 Inwood Rd., 75244, pg. 1644 **PB**
Turner Construction Company, 5429 LBJ Fwy., Ste. 550, 75248, pg. 1646 **PB**
TYLER CORPORATION, 2121 San Jacinto St., Ste. 3200, 75201, pg. 1651 **PB**
Uddeholm Corporation, 7901 Sovereign Row, 75247, pg. 1472 **IT**
Union Banker Insurance Co., 500 N. Akard, 75201, pg. 1018 **PV**
UNION PACIFIC CORPORATION, 1717 Main St., Ste. 5900, 75201, pg. 1667 **PB**
United Advertising Publications, Inc., Ste. 450, 15400 Knoll Trail, 75248, pg. 1443 **IT**
United American Insurance Co., 2909 N. Buckner Blvd., 75228, pg. 1623 **PB**
UNITED INSURANCE COMPANIES, INC., 4001 McEwen, Ste. 200, 75244, pg. 1679 **PB**
United States Auto Club, Motoring Division, Inc., P.O. Box 660460, 75266-0460, pg. 663 **PB**
U.S. Brass, 17120 Dallas Pkwy., 75248-1144, pg. 1794 **PB**
USLIFE Insurance Services Corporation, 1355 River Bend Dr., Ste. 300, 75247, pg. 77 **PB**
USLIFE Real Estate Services Corp., 1355 River Bend Dr., Ste. 100, 75247, pg. 77 **PB**
USLIFE Systems Corporation, 1380 River Bend Dr., 75247, pg. 77 **PB**
UNITED STATES LIME & MINERALS, 12221 Merit Dr., Ste. 500, 75251, pg. 1684 **PB**
U.S. TRAILS, 2711 LBJ Fwy., Ste. 200, 75234, pg. 1688 **PB**
U.S. Yellow Pages, 2711 N. Haskell Ave., Ste. 2150, 75204, pg. 1168 **PV**
Unitog Rental Facility, 2151 W. Commerce, 75212, pg. 1693 **PB**
Universal Belo Productions, 400 S. Record St., 75202, pg. 210 **PB**
UNIVESCO INC., 6210 Campbell Rd., Ste. 140, 75248, pg. 1128 **PB**
Utell International-Dallas, 500 N. Akard, Ste. 1910, 75201, pg. 1098 **IT**
Utica Lloyds of Texas, 11910 Greenville Ave., 75243, pg. 1130 **PV**
Utica National Insurance Co. of Texas, 11910 Greenville Avenue, 75243, pg. 1130 **PV**
Valhi, Inc., Three Lincoln Ctr., 5430 LBJ Fwy., Ste. 1700, 75240, pg. 270 **PV**
VANTAGE COMPANIES, 2911 Turtle Creek Blvd., Ste. 450, 75219, pg. 1134 **PV**
VAREL MANUFACTURING CO., 9230 Denton Dr., 75235, pg. 1134 **PV**
VARI-LITE INTERNATIONAL, 201 Regal Row, 75247, pg. 1709 **PB**
VingCard Systems Inc., 9333 Forest La., 75243, pg. 18 **IT**
Vinson Supply Company, 3010 LBJ Freeway, Ste. 800, 75234, pg. 963 **PB**
Voest-Alpine International Corp.-Tumco Project Office, 1511 Bryan St., Ste. 1515, 75266-0268, pg. 1471 **IT**
W & B Refrigeration Service Co., 660 Ft. Worth Ave., 75202, pg. 685 **PB**
WFAA-TV, Communications Center, Young & Houston Sts., 75202, pg. 209 **PB**
Wall Street Deli, Inc., 4356 Spring Valley Rd., 75244, pg. 1734 **PB**
Watson Electric, 320 S. Walton, 75226, pg. 1151 **PV**
West Hudson, Inc. (Healthcare Consulting Services), Two Lincoln Ctr., Ste. 1355, 75240, pg. 45 **PB**
West Morris Properties, Inc., 1111 W. Mockingbird, 75247, pg. 901 **PB**
Western International Media Corporation, 2711 N. Haskell Ave., Ste. 2150, 75204, pg. 1167 **PV**
WHITEHALL CORPORATION, 2659 Nova Dr., 75229, pg. 1765 **PB**
WHOLESALE ELECTRONIC SUPPLY, 2809 Ross Ave., 75201, pg. 1174 **PV**
Wickersham Hunt Schwantner, 3131 McKinney Ave., Ste. 850, 75204, pg. 84 **PV**
Williamhouse of Texas, 1234 Roundtable Dr., P.O. Box 470108, 75247, pg. 89 **PB**
Willis Corroon Administrative Services Corporation, Lincoln Center II, 5420 LBJ Freeway, Ste. 1400, 75240-2652, pg. 1505 **IT**
Willis Corroon Corp. of Texas, Two Lincoln Ctr., 5420 LBJ Frwy., Ste. 1400, 75240-2652, pg. 1507 **IT**
Willis Corroon Financial Services Corp., Two Lincoln Center, 5420 LBJ Freeway, 75240, pg. 1507 **IT**
THE WISER OIL COMPANY, 8115 Preston Rd., Ste. 400, 75225, pg. 1773 **PB**
HOWARD B. WOLF, INC., 3809 Parry Ave., 75226, pg. 1774 **PB**
Wolverine Pipe Line Co., P.O. Box 900, 75221, pg. 1584 **PB**
Word, Incorporated, 1501 LBJ Freeway, Ste. 650, 75234, pg. 704 **PB**
World Tableware, Inc., 6500 Greenville Ave., Ste. 400, 75206, pg. 1056 **IT**

Wyatt Cafeterias Inc., 16970 Dallas Pkwy., Ste. 701, 75248, pg. 1102 **PV**
A.P. WYOTT, 729 3rd. Ave., 75226, pg. 1193 **PV**
RODNEY D. YOUNG INSURANCE, P.O. Box 224467, 75222, pg. 1202 **PV**
Zeneca Specialty Inks, Box 560765, 5117 Norwood Rd., 75356, pg. 1525 **IT**
Zenith Finance & Construction Co., P.O. Box 1046, 75221, pg. 413 **PB**

Dallas-Fort Worth Airport

AMR Investment Services, Inc., P.O. Box 619616, 4333 Amon Carter Blvd., 75261-9616, pg. 9 **PB**
AMR Services Corporation, P.O. Box 619616, 4333 Amon Carter Blvd., 75261, pg. 9 **PB**
Circle International, c/o Sekin Transport, 1245 Royal Lane N., 75261, pg. 371 **PB**
Circle International, 1245 Royal Ln. N., 75261, pg. 372 **PB**
GTE Information Services Incorporated, 2200 W. Airfield Dr. 75261, pg. 696 **PB**
Simmons American Eagle Airlines, P.O. Box 612527, 75261, pg. 10 **PB**

Darrouzett

Equity Country Inc., P.O. Box 325, pg. 396 **PV**

Decatur

Poco Graphite, Incorporated, 1601 So. State St., 76234, pg. 1698 **PB**

Deer Park

Disposal Systems, Inc., 2525 Battleground Rd., 77536, pg. 694 **PB**
Flexitallic LP, 6915 Highway 225, 77536, pg. 413 **PB**
GNI Chemical Corporation, 2525 Battleground Rd., 77536, pg. 694 **PB**
THE GNI GROUP, INC., 2525 Battleground Rd., 77536, pg. 693 **PB**
Houston Marine Containers Inc., 1718 W. 13th St., 77536, pg. 1214 **IT**
Interox America, 1230 Battleground Rd., 77536, pg. 1278 **IT**
Resource Transportation Services, Inc., 2525 Battleground Rd., 77536, pg. 694 **PB**
Riedel-Smith Environmental Services, 1110 Howard Dr., 77536, pg. 1478 **PB**
San Jacinto Manor, 206 W. Ave. P, 77536, pg. 839 **PB**
Sea Containers U.S. Gulf Inc., 1718 W. 13th St., 77536, pg. 1214 **IT**

Del Rio

Douglas & Lomason Company, #8 Johnson Blvd., 78840, pg. 330 **IT**

Denison

Reedrill Inc., 3501 S. SM Hwy. 1417, 75020, pg. 1325 **IT**

Denton

Acme Brick Co., P.O. Box 806, 220 E. Daniels, 76202, pg. 936 **PB**
Peterbilt Motors Co., 1700 Woodbrook St., 76205-7864, pg. 1247 **PB**
Peterbilt Motors Co., 3200 Airport Road, 76205, pg. 1247 **PB**
Sally Beauty Company, Inc., 3900 Morse St., 76205-6333, pg. 38 **PB**

Desoto

GATX Logistics, Inc.-Texas, 2050 Kestrel Ave., 75115, pg. 692 **PB**

Diboll

Temple-Inland Forest Products Corporation, 303 S. Temple, 75941, pg. 1575 **PB**
Temple-Inland Forest Products Corp.-Building Products Group, 303 S. Temple, 75941, pg. 1575 **PB**
Temple-Inland Forest Products Corp.-Forests Division, 303 S. Temple, 75941, pg. 1575 **PB**
TEMPLE-INLAND INC., 303 S. Temple, 75941-0814, pg. 1574 **PB**

Double Oak

Daher Golden Eagle - Dallas, 325 Lake Trail Ct., 75067, pg. 749 **PB**

Dumas

Swift Independent Packing Co., P.O. Box 524, Schroeder Industrial Park, 79029, pg. 427 **PB**

Earth

Spring Lake Feed Yard, P.O. Box 718, 78031, pg. 429 **PV**

Eastland

Eastland National Bank, 201 East Main St., 76448, pg. 633 **PB**

Eden

Eden Detention Center, P.O. Box 605, 76837-605, pg. 450 **PB**

Edinburg

IEC Edinburg, Texas, 1920 Industrial Park Dr., 78539, pg. 855 **PB**

Edmonson

EDMONSON WHEAT GROWERS, INC., Hwy. 194, 79032, pg. 364 **PV**

El Campo

El Campo Aluminum Co., 702 Gladys St., Rte. 3, 77437, pg. 1386 **PB**

El Paso

Acme Boot Co., Inc., 40 Walter Jones Blvd., 79906, pg. 394 **PV**
Allright Parking El Paso, Inc., 601 Magoffin Ave., 79901, pg. 43 **PV**
Block Products Plant, P.O. Box 9977, 525 Americas Ave., 79990, pg. 936 **PB**
Boeing North America, Autonetics Electronics Sys Div., 9556 Railroad, 79924-6318, pg. 241 **IT**
Clarostat Centers & Controls Group, 12055 Rojas Dr., Ste K, 79936, pg. 127 **IT**
Columbia Back Institute, 1700 N. Oregon, Ste. G-50, 79902, pg. 404 **PB**
Columbia Behavioral Center, 1155 Idaho, 79902, pg. 404 **PB**
Columbia Diagnostic Center, 1900 N. Oregon, Ste. 600, 79902, pg. 404 **PB**
Columbia LifeCare Center, 1810 Murchison, 79902, pg. 404 **PB**
Columbia Medical Center-East, 10301 Gatewa W., 79925, pg. 404 **PB**
Columbia Medical Center-West, 1801 N. Oregon, 79902, pg. 404 **PB**
Columbia Reg. Oncology, 101 Rim Rd., 79902, pg. 404 **PB**
Copamex Paper, 444 Executive Center Blvd., 79902-2392, pg. 330 **IT**
COWTOWN BOOT COMPANY, 11401 Gateway W., 79936, pg. 281 **PV**
Cutter Beechcraft, 6825 Comvair, 79225, pg. 299 **PV**
Dale Electronics, El Paso Div., P.O. Box 26728, 79926-6728, pg. 1722 **PB**
Dale Electronics Resistor Network, 1462 Lionel Dr., 79936, pg. 1722 **PB**
Diesel ReCon, 20 Zane Gray, 79906, pg. 468 **PB**
El Paso Baking Co., Inc., 301 N. Dallas, 79901, pg. 657 **PB**
EL PASO ELECTRIC COMPANY, Kayser Ctr., 100 N. Stanton, 79901, pg. 567 **PB**
El Paso Herald-Post, Mills & Kansas Sts., 79999, pg. 1441 **PB**
El Paso Times, Inc., 401 Mills Ave., 77901, pg. 700 **PB**
FTX, Inc., P.O. Box 9519, 79985, pg. 613 **PB**
Farah Clothing, Inc., P.O. Box 9519, 79985, pg. 613 **PB**
FARAH INCORPORATED, 4171 N. Mesa, 79902-1433, pg. 612 **PB**
Farah International, Inc., P.O. Box 9519, 79985, pg. 613 **PB**
Farah Mfg. Co. of New Mexico, P.O. Box 9519, 79985, pg. 613 **PB**
Farah Manufacturing Services, Inc., P.O.Box 9519, 79985, pg. 613 **PB**
Farah Sales Corp., P.O. Box 9519, 79985, pg. 613 **PB**
Farah U.S.A., Inc., P.O. Box 1433, 79985, pg. 613 **PB**
Favesa S.A. de C.V., (Mexico), 15 Leigh Fisher, Ste. 400, 79906, pg. 982 **PB**
Grocery Supply of El Paso, 9300 Ste. E Billy the Kid, 79907, pg. 436 **PV**
Handgards Inc., 901 Hawkins Blvd., 79915-1202, pg. 499 **PV**
Healthcare Diagnostics Centers, 1800 Lee Travino, Ste. C-1, 79936, pg. 405 **PB**
Helen of Troy, Consumer Products Div., 6827 Market Ave., 79915, pg. 807 **PB**
HELEN OF TROY CORPORATION, 6827 Market Ave., 79915, pg. 807 **PB**
Helen of Troy, Professional Salon Div., 6827 Market Ave., 79915, pg. 807 **PB**
Hewlett-Packard Company, 5700 Cromo Dr., 79912, pg. 815 **PB**
Hillhaven Convalescent Center El Paso, 2301 N. Oregon St., 79902, pg. 1713 **PB**
Horizon Specialty Hospital - El Paso, 2311 N. Oregon, 79902, pg. 839 **PB**
HUNT BUILDING CORPORATION, 4401 N. Mesa, Ste. 201, 79902, pg. 468 **PV**
Hydro Conduit Corp., 5515 McNutt Rd., 79932, pg. 245 **IT**
Interfab, 309 West Overland, 79901, pg. 786 **PV**
Isomedix Operations Inc., 1435 Isomedix Pl., 79936, pg. 1515 **PB**
J & J Register Div., 12504 Weaver Road, 79927, pg. 1515 **IT**
KHEY-AM/FM, 2419 N. Piedras, 79930, pg. 384 **PB**

PB - *U.S. Public Companies Volume*
PV - *U.S. Private Companies Volume*
IT - *International Public & Private Companies Volume*

1442

Geographic Index-U.S.

KPRR-FM, 2419 N. Piedras, 79930, pg. 384 **PB**
Kintetsu World Express Inc., Butterfield Trail Indus. Park, 15-D Zane Grey Blvd., 79906, pg. 735 **IT**
Tony Lama Co., Inc., 1137 Tony Lama St., 79915, pg. 937 **PB**
Leviton, 7800 Trade Ctr. Ave., 79912-8407, pg. 663 **PB**
Manufacturers Folding Carton, Inc., 10237 Allway, 79925, pg. 1521 **PB**
Mizuno Mexico USA, Inc., c/o 42 Butterfield Circle, 79906, pg. 885 **IT**
Mountain View Place, 1600 Murchison Rd., 79902, pg. 839 **PB**
NATIONAL RESTAURANT SUPPLY COMPANY, 320 W. San Antonio, 79901, pg. 786 **PV**
Norwest Bank El Paso, N.A., 221 Kansas St., 79901, pg. 1201 **PB**
OMC El Paso, Bldg. A, Ste. C, 11130 Rogs Dr., 79935, pg. 478 **PV**
PEC El Paso, 1325 Pendale Rd., 79936, pg. 871 **PV**
PSI International, 4717 Hondo Pass, Ste. B, 79904, pg. 1522 **IT**
PASOTEX CORPORATION, 310 N. Mesa, Ste. 614, 79901, pg. 842 **PV**
Peyton Meats, 9730 Railroad Dr., Ste. 200, 79924, pg. 75 **PB**
Phelps Dodge Refining Corp., 6999 N. Loop, 79998, pg. 1287 **PB**
Physical Therapy Center, 1527 Brown Bldg. C, 79902, pg. 405 **PB**
Price's Creameries, P.O. Box 3008, Station A, 600 N. Piedras St., 79923, pg. 491 **PB**
Productos Electronicos Laguna, P.O. Box 20039, 79998-0039, pg. 1383 **IT**
Radco Sportswear, Inc., P.O. Box 9519, 79985, pg. 613 **PB**
Security Capital Pacific Trust, 7777 Market Center Ave., 79912, pg. 981 **PV**
Stewart Warner Instruments Corporation, 1320 Goodyear Dr, Unit A, 79936, pg. 1043 **PV**
Sun City Redi-Mix Inc., 425 N. Americas Ave., 79907-7008, pg. 573 **IT**
Sunwest Bank of El Paso, P.O. Box 9697, 79987, pg. 1165 **PB**
Texas Apparel, 600 Sunland Park Dr., Bldg. 5, Ste. 500, 79912, pg. 1429 **PB**
Transportation Electronics Division, 11801 Miriam Dr., Ste. B-1, 79936, pg. 1045 **PV**
TRI-STATE WHOLESALE ASSOCIATED GROCERS, INC., 1000 Hawkins, 79915, pg. 1101 **PV**
United Technologies Furukawa Corporation (UTF), 6070 Gateway East, Ste. 316, 79905, pg. 530 **IT**
Value Clothing Company, Inc., 8889 Gateway West, 79925, pg. 613 **PB**
Value Slacks, Inc., 8889 Gateway West, 79925, pg. 613 **PB**
Young Pecan Company West, Inc., 2211 E. Missouri, Ste. E 239 D, 79903, pg. 1201 **PB**

Eldorado

AmerCable, 350 Bailey Rd., 71730-6600, pg. 91 **PV**

Ennis

Elk Corporation of Texas, P.O. Box 500, 75119, pg. 568 **PB**
ENNIS BUSINESS FORMS, INC., 107 N. Sherman St., 75119, pg. 583 **PB**
OMNI Products, Inc., 3901 S. Hwy. I-45, 75119, pg. 816 **PV**
Tropar Mfg. Co., Inc., 2313 N. Preston St., 75119, pg. 1105 **PV**

Euless

BEI Defense Systems Company, 11312 S. Pipeline Rd., 76040, pg. 160 **PB**
Menasco Aerosystems Division, Hgwy. 157 & Pipeline Rd., 76040-7012, pg. 402 **PB**
Warrantech Automotive, Inc., 1441 Westpark Fwy., 76040, pg. 1740 **PB**
Warrantech Consumer Product Services, Inc., 150 Westpark Way, 769040, pg. 1740 **PB**
Warrantech Direct, Inc., 1441 Westpark Fwy., 76040, pg. 1740 **PB**

Evadale

Temple-Inland Forest Products Corp.-Bleached Paperboard Group, Hwy. 105, 77615, pg. 1575 **PB**

Farmers Branch

BRW Paper Co., Inc., 14035 Distribution Way, 75234, pg. 467 **PV**
Binks Manufacturing Company, 14340 Proton Rd., 75244-3594, pg. 229 **PB**
Kubota Tractor Corp., 1378 Benchmark Drive, 75234, pg. 762 **IT**
Thermalloy, Inc., 2021 W. Valley View, 75234, pg. 208 **IT**

Fate

Mayfield Swain Rockwall, 812 W. Holiday Dr., 75132-0159, pg. 686 **PV**

Flatonia

SMITH FARMS, INC., 403 S. Colorado, 78941, pg. 1008 **PV**

Fort Worth

A & A International, Inc., 1200 One Tandy Ctr., 76102, pg. 1560 **PB**
AMR CORPORATION, 4333 Amon Carter Blvd., 76155, pg. 9 **PB**
AMR Eagle, Inc., 4333 Amon Carter Blvd., 76155, pg. 9 **PB**
AST Fort Worth Final Assembly, Western Center Facility, 2400 Western Ctr. Blvd., 76131, pg. 1182 **IT**
Acme Brick Co., 2821 W. Seventh St., 76107, pg. 936 **PB**
Aerospace Technology, One Ridgemar Centre, 6500 W. Fwy., Ste. 600, 76116, pg. 351 **PV**
Alcon Eye Care, Inc., 6201 South Freeway, 76134, pg. 916 **IT**
Alcon Laboratories, Inc., 6201 S. Freeway, 76134, pg. 916 **IT**
Alcon Pharma, Inc., 6201 South Freeway, 76134, pg. 916 **IT**
Alcon Surgical, 6201 S. Freeway, 76134, pg. 916 **IT**
Alcon Systems, Inc., 6201 South Freeway, 76134, pg. 916 **IT**
Alliance Flight Training Academy, 2250 Alliance Blvd., 76177, pg. 218 **PV**
Allied Electronics Inc., 7410 Pebble Dr., 76118, pg. 155 **PB**
Allright Parking Corporation, 210 W. Sixth St., Ste. 1101, 76102, pg. 43 **PV**
American Airlines Cargo, 4225 Amon Carter Blvd., 76155, pg. 9 **PB**
American Airlines, Inc., 4333 Amon Carter Blvd., 76155, pg. 9 **PB**
American Cometra, Inc., 500 Throckmorton St., Ste. 2500, 76102, pg. 562 **IT**
American Health and Life Insurance Co., 777 Main St., P.O. Box 2548, 76113, pg. 1633 **PB**
American Modular Technologies, L.L.C., 3421 N. Sylvania Ave., 76111, pg. 69 **PV**
AMERICREDIT CORP., 200 Bailey Ave., 76107-1221, pg. 96 **PB**
AmeriServe of Fort Worth, 1201 John Burgess Dr., 76140, pg. 533 **PV**
AMERITRUCK DISTRIBUTION CORPORATION, 301 Commerce St., Ste. 1101, 76102-5384, pg. 65 **PV**
Anvil Products, Box 4434, 76106, pg. 1651 **PB**
BFX HOSPITALITY GROUP, INC., 226 Bailey Ave., Ste. 101, 76107, pg. 160 **PB**
Bailey Hats, 3201 N.E. Loop 820, Ste. 275, 76137-2434, pg. 155 **PB**
Banknote & Securities Division, 5500 Airport Fwy., 76117, pg. 1517 **PB**
BASS ENTERPRISES PRODUCTION COMPANY, 201 Main St., Ste. 31100, 76102, pg. 122 **PV**
Bernal Division, 5700 E. Belknap St., 76117, pg. 1517 **PB**
Blancett, 100 E. Felix St, 76116-3548, pg. 906 **PV**
THE BOMBAY COMPANY, INC., 550 Bailey Ave., Ste. 700, 76107, pg. 244 **PB**
The Bombay Company, 550 Bailey, Ste. 400, 76107, pg. 244 **PB**
Brazos Point, Inc., 6032 Jacksboro Hwy., 76135, pg. 322 **PB**
Bunge Foods, P.O. Box 163289, 76161, pg. 753 **IT**
BURLINGTON NORTHERN SANTA FE CORPORATION, 2650 Lou Menk Dr., 76131-2830, pg. 268 **PB**
CA Pawn, Inc. of Ohio, Cash America Intl. Bldg., 1600 W. Seventh St., 76102-2599, pg. 312 **PB**
Cargo Furniture & Accents, 1400 Everman Pkwy., 76140, pg. 1561 **PV**
Cash America, Inc. of Kentucky, Cash America Intl. Bldg., 1600 W. Seventh St., 76102-2599, pg. 312 **PB**
Cash America, Inc. of Louisiana, Cash America Intl. Bldg., 1600 W. Seventh St., 76102-2599, pg. 312 **PB**
Cash America, Inc. of North Carolina, Cash America Intl. Bldg., 1600 W. Seventh St., 76102-2599, pg. 312 **PB**
Cash America, Inc. of Oklahoma, Cash America Intl. Bldg., 1600 W. Seventh St., 76102-2599, pg. 312 **PB**
Cash America, Inc. of South Carolina, Cash America Intl. Bldg., 1600 W. Seventh St., 76102-2599, pg. 312 **PB**
Cash America, Inc. of Tennessee, Cash America Intl. Bldg., 1600 W. Seventh St., 76102-2599, pg. 312 **PB**
CASH AMERICA INTERNATIONAL, INC., Cash America Intl. Bldg., 1600 W. Seventh St., 76102-2599, pg. 312 **PB**
CENTRAL ADVERTISING AGENCY, 100 Throckmorton, Ste. 300, 76102, pg. 222 **PV**
Central U.S., 1200 Country Club Ln., Ste. 102, 76112, pg. 1540 **PB**
Ceramic Cooling Tower Co., 1100 Northway Dr., 76131, pg. 68 **PV**
Champion Int'l. Corp., 1901 Windsor Pl., 76110, pg. 334 **PB**
Coast RV, Inc., 7133 Burns St., 76118, pg. 388 **PB**
Color Tile, Inc., 515 Houston St., 76102, pg. 686 **IT**
Cometra Oil & Gas, Inc., 500 Throckmorton St., Ste. 2500, 76102, pg. 562 **IT**
Commercial Metals Company, 601 N. Throckmorton, 76106, pg. 413 **PB**
Computalog Drilling Services Inc., 7450 Winscott Rd., 76126, pg. 325 **PV**
Computalog Holdings Inc., 7450 Winscott Rd., 76126, pg. 325 **PV**
Computalog U.S.A., Inc., 7450 Winscott Rd., 76126, pg. 325 **IT**

Computer City, 300 W. Third St., Ste. 2000, 76102, pg. 1560 **PB**
Con-Way Southern Express, Inc., 14500 Trinity Blvd., Ste. 118, 76155, pg. 281 **PB**
Con-Way Truckload Services, 2322 Gravel Dr., 76118, pg. 281 **PB**
Continental Life Insurance Company, 714 Main St., 76102, pg. 433 **PB**
Coventry Health & Life Insurance, 200 Bailey Ave., 76107, pg. 454 **PB**
CROUCH SUPPLY COMPANY, INC., 902 S. Jennings Ave., 76104, pg. 291 **PV**
Cummins Natural Gas Engines, Inc., 8713 Airport Freeway, Ste. 316, 76180, pg. 468 **PB**
Dallas Airline Learning Center, P.O. Box 612786, 2201 W. Airfield Dr., 75261, pg. 218 **PB**
DEEN WHOLESALE MEAT COMPANY, INC., 813 E. Northside Dr., 76102, pg. 320 **PV**
Development Association, Inc., 1400 Everman Pkwy., 76140, pg. 1561 **PB**
Dickies Operational Wear, 509 W. Vickery Blvd., 76101, pg. 1179 **PV**
Direct Fuels, L.P., 2801 Glenda Ave., 76117, pg. 604 **PV**
The Dryden Press, a Division of Holt, Rinehart and Winston College Division, 301 Commerce St., Ste. 3700, 76102, pg. 783 **PB**
THE DUNLAP COMPANY, 200 Greenleaf, 76107, pg. 346 **PV**
Entwistle, 5801 Curzon, 76107, pg. 378 **PV**
ESCO ELEVATOR CORP., 4720 Esco Dr., 76140, pg. 383 **PV**
FFP Financial Services, L.P., 2801 Glenda Ave., 76117, pg. 604 **PV**
FFP MARKETING COMPANY, INC., 2801 Glenda Ave., 76117-4391, pg. 604 **PB**
Facility Works Inc., 4100 International Plaza, Tower II, 76109, pg. 1557 **PV**
Farmers Insurance Group, 4101 Airport Fwy., 76117-6202, pg. 111 **IT**
Florida Cash America, Inc., Cash America Intl. Bldg., 1600 W. Seventh St., 76102-2599, pg. 312 **PB**
Fort Worth Auto Auction, 2245 Jacksboro Hwy., 76114, pg. 283 **PV**
Fort Worth Learning Center, 9601 Trinity Blvd., 76053, pg. 218 **PB**
FORT WORTH LUMBER COMPANY, 9101 South Freeway, 76140, pg. 419 **PV**
Foster Mortgage Corporation, 6000 Western Pl., 76107, pg. 839 **PB**
Frank Paxton Lumber Company, 2900 Bryan Ave., Box 1225, 76101, pg. 585 **PV**
Freeman Products, 2310 Franklin Dr., 76106, pg. 1105 **PV**
GATX Logistics, Inc.-Texas, 13700 S. Eagle Pkwy., 76178, pg. 692 **PB**
GSB Investment Management, Inc., 301 Commerce St., 1501, 76102, pg. 1673 **PB**
Galderma Laboratories, 3000 Altamesa Blvd., 76163, pg. 918 **IT**
Georgia Cash America, Inc., Cash America Intl. Bldg., 1600 W. Seventh St., 76102-2599, pg. 312 **PB**
Graphic Arts Division, P.O. Box 1293, 76101, pg. 419 **PV**
Green Oaks Park Hotel, 6901 W. Freeway, 76116, pg. 1517 **PB**
Healthsource North Texas, Inc., 1612 Summit Ave., Ste. 302, 76102, pg. 360 **PB**
Hehr Power Systems, 4616 Fairlane Ave., 76119, pg. 519 **PV**
Heritage Estates, 201 Sycamore School Rd., 76134, pg. 839 **PB**
Heritage Western Hills, 8001 Western Hills Blvd., 76018, pg. 839 **PB**
Holt, Rinehart and Winston College Division, City Ctr. Tower II, Ste. 3700, 301 Commerce St., 76102-4137, pg. 783 **PB**
Houston General Insurance Co., P.O. Box 2932, 4055 International Plaza, 76113-2932, pg. 1392 **IT**
HOWELL INSTRUMENTS INC., 3479 W. Vickery Blvd., 76107, pg. 543 **PV**
Institutional Services, Inc., 777 Main St., Ste. 2500, 76102, pg. 1482 **PB**
International Benefit Service Corporation, 2200 Continental Plaza, 76102, pg. 362 **PB**
INTERTAN INC., 201 Main St., Ste. 1805, 76102, pg. 910 **PB**
JRC CANIDA, INC., 4000 Sandshell Dr., 76137, pg. 578 **PV**
Justin Boot Company, 610 W. Daggett, 76104, pg. 937 **PV**
JUSTIN INDUSTRIES, INC., 2821 W. Seventh St., 76101, pg. 936 **PB**
KXAS-TV, 3900 Barnett St., 76103, pg. 11 **PB**
BEN E. KEITH COMPANY, 601 E. Seventh St., 76102, pg. 611 **PV**
Ben E. Keith Co., P.O. Box 2628, 76113, pg. 611 **PV**
KEVCO, INC., University Ctr. I, 1300 S. University Dr., Ste. 200, 76107, pg. 952 **PB**
Kimberly-Clark Tecnol, 7201 Industrial Park Blvd., 76180, pg. 959 **PB**
Kysor Panel Systems, P.O. Box 13248, 76117, pg. 1445 **PV**
Lisa Motor Lines, Inc., P.O. Box 4529, 76164, pg. 685 **PB**
Lockheed Fort Worth Company, Lockheed Blvd., 76101-0748, pg. 1007 **PB**
LOMAK PETROLEUM INC., 500 Throckmorton St., Ste. 2104, 76102, pg. 1012 **PB**
LUBRICATION ENGINEERS, INC., 3851 Airport Frwy., 76111, pg. 679 **PV**
LUSKEYS WESTERN STORES, INC., 101 N. Houston, 76102-2080, pg. 681 **PV**
Mesa Environmental, 3125 W. Bolt St., 76110-5813, pg. 1300 **PB**

Geographic Index-U.S.

Middleton Transportation Co., 1801 Mony St., 76146, pg. 685 **PB**
Miller Brewing Company, 7001 S. Freeway, 76134-4098, pg. 1289 **PB**
Motorola Messaging Systems Product Group, 5401 N. Beach St., 76137, pg. 1137 **PB**
MRS. BAIRD'S BAKERIES, INC., 7301 S. Frwy., 76134, pg. 765 **PV**
NTS, 6100 Western Pl., 76107, pg. 631 **PB**
NATIONAL FINANCIAL INSURANCE COMPANY, 777 Main St., Ste. 900, 76102, pg. 782 **PV**
Nokia Mobile Phones Manufacturing (USA) Ltd., 5650 Alliance Gateway, 76178, pg. 952 **IT**
ODG, 611 East Northside Dr., 76106, pg. 1774 **PV**
Ohio-Sealy Mattress Manufacturing Co.-Fort Worth, 6550 Wuliger Way, 76180, pg. 979 **PV**
Ozarka/Oasis Water Co., 4302 Buckingham Rd., 76155, pg. 919 **IT**
PMB Enterprises West, Inc., 3500 Noble Ave., 76111, pg. 1255 **PB**
Paktronics Controls, Inc., 7415 Whitehall St., 76118, pg. 716 **PV**
Palm Harbor Homes, 6901 Bowman Roberts Road, 76179, pg. 1255 **PB**
Pamex of Texas, Inc., P.O. Box 7407, 76111, pg. 1255 **PB**
PANCHO'S MEXICAN BUFFET, INC., 3500 Noble Ave., 76111, pg. 1255 **PB**
PANGBURN CANDY COMPANY, 2000 White Settlement Rd., 76107, pg. 836 **PV**
PharmChem Laboratories, Inc.-Texas Division, 7606 Pebble Dr., 76118, pg. 1285 **PB**
PIER 1 IMPORTS, INC., 301 Commerce St., Ste. 600, 76102, pg. 1295 **PB**
PIONEER OIL COMPANY INC., 3420 E. Vickery, 76105, pg. 866 **PV**
Practitioners Publishing Co., 3221 Collinsworth, 76107, pg. 1601 **PB**
RadioShack, 100 Throckmorton Ste. 300, 76102, pg. 1560 **PB**
Reynolds Metals Company-Fort Worth, 6600 Roy Rogers Blvd., 76140, pg. 1385 **PB**
Richmond Screw Anchor Company, 7214 Burns St., Richland Hills, 76118, pg. 932 **PV**
Ryon's Saddle & Ranch Supply, 2601 N. Main, 76106, pg. 681 **PV**
SOCO California Properties, Inc., 777 Main St., Ste. 2500, 76102, pg. 1482 **PB**
SOCO Holdings Inc., 777 Main St., Ste. 2500, 76102, pg. 1482 **PB**
SOCO Thomasville, Inc., 777 Main St., Ste. 2500, 76102, pg. 1482 **PB**
SOCO Wattenberg Corporation, 777 Main St., Ste. 2500, 76102, pg. 1482 **PB**
Sabre Decision Technologies, 4255 Amon Carter Blvd., 76155, pg. 10 **PB**
The SABRE Group Holdings, 4255 Amon Carter Blvd., 76155, pg. 10 **PB**
SABRE Travel Information Network, 4255 Amon Carter Blvd., 76155, pg. 10 **PB**
SAMSILL CORPORATION, 4301 Mansfield Hwy., 76119, pg. 963 **PV**
Satellite Technology Group, 4700 Amon Carter Blvd., 76155, pg. 1433 **IT**
Sav-On, Inc., 2720 Cullen, 76107, pg. 1561 **PB**
SNYDER OIL CORPORATION, 777 Main St., Ste. 2500, 76102, pg. 1481 **PV**
SOUTHWESTERN PETROLEUM CORPORATION, 534 N. Main St., 76106, pg. 1019 **PV**
Star-Telegram Newspaper, Inc., 400 W. Seventh St., 76102, pg. 964 **PB**
Sterling Electronics, 2200 William D. Tater Ave., 76051, pg. 1052 **PB**
Stevens Corp., 5500 Airport Frwy., 76117, pg. 1517 **PB**
STEVENS INTERNATIONAL, INC., 5500 Airport Frwy., 76117, pg. 1517 **PB**
Stratoflex Aerospace/Military Connectors Div., 220 Roberts Cut-Off Rd., 76114-0398, pg. 1260 **PB**
Sunbelt Nursery Group Inc., 6500 W. Fwy., Ste. 600, 76116, pg. 715 **PB**
TNP ENTERPRISES, INC., 4100 International Plaza, Tower II, 76109, pg. 1557 **PB**
TNP Operating Company, 4100 International Plaza, Tower II, 76109, pg. 1557 **PB**
Tandy Cabinets, 701 N. Hampton, 76102, pg. 1560 **PB**
Tandy Cable Products, 1924 8th. Ave., 76110, pg. 1560 **PB**
TANDY CORPORATION, 100 Throckmorton, Ste. 1800, 76102, pg. 1560 **PB**
Tandy Leather Co., 1400 Everman Pkwy., 76140, pg. 1561 **PB**
Tandy Packaging, 801 N.E. 38th St., 76106, pg. 1560 **PB**
Tandy Transportation, 2560 E. Long Ave., 76137, pg. 1560 **PB**
Tandy Wire & Cable, 3500 McCart, 76110, pg. 1560 **PB**
Tandy Wire Fabrication, 1924 8th Ave., 76110, pg. 1560 **PB**
TANDYCRAFTS, INC., 1400 Everman Pkwy., 76140, pg. 1561 **PB**
Tarmac Texas, 1200 Summit Ave., Ste. 740, 76102, pg. 1356 **IT**
Tejas Western Outlet, 101 N. Houston, 76102-2080, pg. 681 **PV**
Texas Generating Company, Tower II, 4100 International Plaza, 76109, pg. 1557 **PB**
Texas Motor Speedway, P.O. Box 500, 76101-2500, pg. 1498 **PB**
Texas-New Mexico Power Co., 4100 International Plaza, Tower II, 76113, pg. 1557 **PB**
TEXAS PACIFIC GROUP, 201 Main St., 76102, pg. 1078 **PV**
TEXAS REFINERY CORP., One Refinery Place, 840 N. Main St., 76106, pg. 1078 **PV**

Thomasville Energy Corporation, 777 Main St., Ste. 2500, 76102, pg. 1482 **PB**
Toll Road Restaurant Corp., 1900 Ben St., 76103, pg. 1023 **PV**
Town & Country Homes, 4501 Mark IV Pkwy., 76161, pg. 319 **PB**
Transport Holdings Inc., 714 Main St., 76102, pg. 433 **PB**
Transport Life Insurance Co., 714 Main St., 76102, pg. 433 **PB**
URS Greiner, Inc., 4100 Amon Carter Blvd., Ste. 108, 76155, pg. 1658 **PV**
Uniden America Corporation, 4700 Amon Carter Blvd., 76155, pg. 1433 **IT**
Union Pacific Resources Company (UPRC), Burnett Plaza, 801 Cherry St., 76102, pg. 1668 **PB**
Universal Blueprint Paper Co., 327 Bryan Ave., 76104, pg. 1176 **PV**
Voyager American Insurance Company, Ltd., 110 West Seventh St., 76102, pg. 68 **PB**
Voyager Indemnity Insurance Company, 110 West Seventh St., 76102, pg. 68 **PB**
Voyager Life Insurance Company, 110 West Seventh St., 76102, pg. 68 **PB**
Voyager Property and Casualty Insurance Company, 110 West Seventh St., 76102, pg. 68 **PB**
Voyager Service Warranties, Inc., 110 West Seventh St., 76102, pg. 68 **PB**
WILLIAMSON-DICKIE MFG. CO., 319 Lipscomb, 76104, pg. 1179 **PV**
Willis Corroon, City Ctr. II, 301 Commerce St., Ste. 3050, 76102, pg. 1504 **IT**
Wilsey Foods, Inc., 1100 DeFiel Rd., 76131, pg. 879 **IT**
Winn-Dixie Texas, Inc., 5500 S. Freeway, 76115, pg. 1772 **PB**
Wolfe Nursery, 500 Terminal Rd., 76106, pg. 715 **PB**

Freeport

American Rice, Inc.-Freeport, 505 Port Rd., 77541, pg. 591 **PB**
Davco Equipment, Inc., 1744 W. Fourth St., Ste. 208, 77541, pg. 658 **PB**
GULF STATES, INC., 6711 E. Hwy. 332, 77541, pg. 487 **PB**
Rhone-Poulenc Basic Chemicals Co., P.O. Box 917, 77541, pg. 1110 **IT**
Rhone-Poulenc Fine Inorganic Chemical Div., 6213 Hwy. 332 E., 77541, pg. 1110 **IT**
Sentry Polymers, Inc., P.O. Box 2076, 5500 E. Hwy. 332, 77541, pg. 1357 **PB**
Testronics, 6711 E. Hwy. 332, 77541, pg. 487 **PV**

Friendswood

BJ Software Systems, 1560 W. Bay Area Blvd., Ste. 220, 77546, pg. 1593 **PB**

Friona

Friona Feed Yard, P.O. Box 369, 79035, pg. 429 **PV**
Hi-Pro Animal Health, P.O. Box 519, 79035, pg. 429 **PV**
Hi-Pro Feed, P.O. Box 519, 79035, pg. 429 **PV**

Frisco

Bankston Ford of Frisco, Ltd. Co., Preston Rd. & Hwy. 121, 75034, pg. 1379 **PB**

Galena Park

CONTAINER CARE INTERNATIONAL, 500 Mayo Shell Rd., 77547, pg. 266 **PV**
Galena Park Terminal, 906 Clinton Dr., 77547, pg. 692 **PB**
Texmark Chemicals Inc., 900 Clinton Sr., 77547, pg. 233 **PV**

Galveston

American Fire & Indemnity Co., One American Indemnity Plaza, 77550, pg. 83 **PB**
American Indemnity Company, One American Indemnity Plaza, 77550, pg. 83 **PB**
AMERICAN INDEMNITY FINANCIAL CORP., 2115 Winnie St., 77550, pg. 83 **PB**
American National Growth Fund, Inc., One Moody Plaza, 77550, pg. 87 **PB**
American National Income Fund, Inc., One Moody Plaza, 77550, pg. 87 **PB**
AMERICAN NATIONAL INSURANCE COMPANY, One Moody Plaza, 77550, pg. 87 **PB**
American National Investment Accounts, One Moody Plaza, 77550, pg. 87 **PB**
American National Life Insurance Co. of Texas, One Moody Plaza, 77550, pg. 87 **PB**
American National Triflex Fund, Inc., One Moody Plaza, 77550, pg. 87 **PB**
Anrem Co., One Moody Plaza, 77550, pg. 88 **PB**
Commercial Metals Company, P.O. Box 3100, 77552, pg. 413 **PB**
Commercial Metals Company, 71st & Post Office St., 77550, pg. 413 **PB**
Farmers Copper & Industrial Supply, 202 37th St., 77550, pg. 422 **PV**
Farmers Marine Copper Works, 1908 Strand Ave. B, 77550, pg. 422 **PV**
FOUR WINDS INVESTMENT CORP., 1908 Strand Ave. B, 77550, pg. 422 **PV**
SM&R Capital Funds Inc., One Moody Plaza, 77550, pg. 88 **PB**

Securities Management & Research, One Moody Plaza, 77550, pg. 88 **PB**
Standard Life & Accident Insurance Co., One Moody Plaza, 77550, pg. 88 **PB**
Sunrise Leasing Corporation, 2301 Strand, Ste. 237, 77550, pg. 1535 **PB**
Texas General Indemnity Co., One American Indemnity Plaza, 77550, pg. 83 **PB**
United States National Bank, P.O. Box 179, 2201 Market St., 77553, pg. 467 **PB**

Garland

Ampco Saftey Tools, Dallas Div., 204 Barnes Dr., 75042, pg. 67 **PV**
Bergman Manufacturing, 1200 N. Glenbrook, 75040, pg. 313 **PV**
Corrugated Packaging, P.O. Box 461696, 2510 W. Miller Rd., 75046, pg. 737 **PB**
CUPLEX, INC., 1500 E. Hwy. 66, 75040, pg. 297 **PV**
Eckerd Drug Co., 4409 Action St., 75042, pg. 917 **PB**
Garland Operations, 2975 Miller Park N., 75042-7799, pg. 126 **IT**
HATCO, INC., 601 Marion Dr., 75042, pg. 510 **PV**
INNER CERAMIC USA, 2333 S. Jupiter, 75041, pg. 564 **PB**
Intelligence, Information & Aircraft Integration Systems, 501 South Jupiter St., 75042, pg. 1364 **PB**
Interceramic Manufacturing Inc., 2333 S. Jupiter Rd., 75041, pg. 680 **IT**
Intercontinental Mfg. Co., P.O. Box 461148, 1200 N. Glenbrook Dr., 75046, pg. 313 **PV**
International Power Machines Corporation, 2975 Miller Park North, 75042-7799, pg. 126 **IT**
Lortec Power Systems Natl. Sls. Office, 2975 Miller Park N., 75042-7799, pg. 126 **IT**
METRO LABEL CORP., 3366 Miller Pk. S., 75042, pg. 1495 **PV**
Old Merchandise Company, 402 W. I-30, 75043, pg. 1495 **PB**
Otis Merla Systems, 300 Kirby St., 75046, pg. 776 **PB**
Power Product Group, 2975 Miller Park North, 75042, pg. 126 **IT**
PRESTIGE FORD, 3401 S. Garland Ave., 75041, pg. 882 **PV**
Prior Remanufacturers, Inc., 315 International Rd., 75046, pg. 300 **PV**
Ridg's Finer Foods, 2340 Forest Lane, 75040, pg. 1288 **PB**
Royale Paint & Body, 2766 W. Kingsley, 75041, pg. 918 **PV**
Scientific Communications, Inc., 2908 National Dr., 75041, pg. 112 **PB**
SOFTECHNICS INC., 310 E. Interstate Hwy. 30, Ste. M-105, 75043, pg. 1012 **PV**
SOFTWARE SPECTRUM, INC., 2140 Merritt Dr., 75041, pg. 1483 **PB**
Spaghetti Warehouse Construction, 402 W. I-30, 75043, pg. 1495 **PB**
SPAGHETTI WAREHOUSE, INC., 402 W. I30, 75043, pg. 1495 **PB**
TELSCO INDUSTRIES, 3301 W. Kingsley Rd., 75041, pg. 1074 **PV**
Weather-Matic Div., 3301 W. Kingsley Rd., 75041, pg. 1074 **PV**

Garrison

Acme Brick Co., P.O. Box 428, Hwy. 95, 75946, pg. 936 **PB**

Georgetown

Georgetown Jet Center, Inc., 217 Corsair Dr., 78628, pg. 187 **PB**
Manitex, Inc., P.O. Box 1609, 3000 S. Austin Avenue, 78627-1609, pg. 1041 **PB**
Sun City Georgetown, 5535 Williams Dr., 78628, pg. 495 **PB**
Tessco Group, Inc., 300 Industrial Ave., 78626, pg. 394 **PB**
Triple S Plastics, Texas Central, 107 ACM Way, 78626, pg. 1640 **PB**

Gonzales

Southern Clay Products Inc., 1212 Church St., 78629, pg. 802 **IT**
Southwestern Explosives, P.O. Box 1558, 78629, pg. 100 **PV**

Gorman

Texas Central Railroad, 620 McCall St., 76454, pg. 145 **PV**

Graham

Detectors, Inc., 804 Loving Rd., 76450, pg. 727 **PV**
MEDIA RECOVERY, INC., FNB, Second & Elm, St. 407, 76450, pg. 726 **PV**
Media Recovery Inc.-Texas, 804 Loving Rd., 76046, pg. 727 **PV**
Media Recovery Intl., FNB, Second & Elm, Ste. 407, 76450, pg. 727 **PV**

Grand Prairie

API Katema Inc., 2300 W. Marshall Dr., 75051, pg. 90 **PB**

PB - *U.S. Public Companies Volume*
PV - *U.S. Private Companies Volume*
IT - *International Public & Private Companies Volume*

1444

Geographic Index-U.S.

Accessory Services-Texas, 1038 Santerre Dr., 75050, pg. 710 **PB**
Aetrium-FSA, 734 W. North Carrier Pkwy., 75050, pg. 27 **PB**
Air Liquide Northern Div., 801 W/N Carrier Pkwy., 75050-1003, pg. 37 **IT**
American Eurocopter Corp., 2701 Forum Dr., 75052-7099, pg. 29 **IT**
AmeriSource-Dallas Div., 1229 Ave. R, 75050, pg. 97 **PB**
Baker Hughes Mining Tools, Inc., 1600 S. Great Southwest Pkwy., 75053, pg. 166 **PB**
BOLLINGER INDUSTRIES INC., 602 Fountain Pkwy., 75050-1407, pg. 243 **PB**
Burns Drilling Company, 2505 N. Hwy. 360, Ste. 800, 75050, pg. 785 **PB**
C.E. Services, 2895 113th St., 75050, pg. 527 **IT**
A.M. Castle & Co., 2602 Pinewood Dr., 75051, pg. 313 **PB**
DYWIDAG Systems International, USA, Inc., 1169 Ruggles Dr., 75050, pg. 424 **IT**
Electrovert, 1111 W. No Carrier Pkwy., Ste. 200, 75050, pg. 328 **IT**
Genesee Precision Fabricating, 1470 Ave. T, 75050, pg. 446 **PV**
Genesee Stamping, 1470 Ave. T, 75050, pg. 446 **PV**
H.A.C. Corp., 537 Camden Dr., 75050, pg. 527 **PB**
Harken Bahrain Oil Company, 2505 N. Hwy. 360, Ste. 800, 75050, pg. 785 **PB**
Harken Exploration Company, 2505 N. Hwy., Ste. 800, 75050, pg. 785 **PB**
Harken Resource Management Company, 2505 N. Hwy. 360, Ste. 800, 75050, pg. 785 **PB**
Harte Hanks Shopper Dallas Fort Worth, 1302 Avenue T., 75050, pg. 794 **PB**
Insituform Texark, Inc., 3001 Roy Orr Blvd., 75050, pg. 882 **PB**
Interturbine Dallas Airfoil, 1170-111th St., 75050, pg. 1690 **PB**
Kennedy & Mitchell, Inc., 2505 N. Hwy. 360, Ste. 800, 75050, pg. 785 **PB**
Labinal Aero & Defense Systems, Inc.-Technofan Inc., 2709 Forum Dr., 75051, pg. 786 **IT**
Microturbo, Inc., 2709 Forum Dr., 75052, pg. 787 **IT**
NuArc Southwestern Div., 2610 W. Marshall, Ste. 6, 75051, pg. 809 **PV**
PASSAT LAUNDRY SYSTEMS, 2425 109th St., 75050, pg. 842 **PV**
Pratt & Whitney, 1170-111th St., 75050, pg. 1690 **PB**
Reed Plastics (TX), 1309 Ave. H East, 75050, pg. 974 **IT**
Texstars Inc., P.O. Box 534036, 802 Ave. J E., 75050, pg. 114 **IT**
Trencor, Inc., 3545 E. Main St., 75050, pg. 141 **PB**
Turbomeca Engine Corporation, 2709 Forum Dr., 75051, pg. 787 **IT**
U.S. Brick, Inc., Bldg. D., 840 Greenview Dr., 75050, pg. 699 **IT**
WESTGATE FABRICS, INC., 1000 Fountain Parkway, 75050, pg. 1169 **PV**
Zimmerman & Partners Advertising, Inc., 2821 S.E. Eighth St. #110, 75051, pg. 1206 **PV**

Grandview

Great Southwest Telephone Corp., P.O. Drawer 429, 76050, pg. 56 **PB**

Grapevine

Adaptec - Central Region, 1701 W. Northwest Hwy., Ste. 290, 76051, pg. 19 **PB**
BABBAGE'S ETC. LLC, 2250 Willim D. Tate Ave., 76051, pg. 108 **PV**
Charter Grapevine Behavioral Health System, Inc., 2300 William D. Tate Ave., 76051, pg. 1034 **PB**
Circle Freight International USA, 1085 E. Northwest Hwy., 76051, pg. 371 **PB**
Circle International, 1085 E. Northwest Hwy., 76051, pg. 371 **PB**
Continental Homes of Dallas, L.P., 621 W. College St., 76051, pg. 441 **PV**
Jannock Steel Fabricating, Inc., 404 E. Dallas Rd., 76051, pg. 699 **IT**
MSC Southwest Regional Office, 1000 Main St., Ste. 190, 76051, pg. 1031 **PB**
Major Aerospace Accounts, 1000 Main St., 76051, pg. 1031 **PB**
Metroplex Behavioral Healthcare Services, Inc., 1000 S. Main St., Ste. 100, 76051, pg. 1036 **PB**
Union-Transport Corporation-Dallas Office, 755 Port America Pl., Ste. 300, 76051, pg. 1119 **PV**

Greenville

Crown Door Corp., 6308 Industrial Dr., 75401, pg. 1067 **IT**
Glen Oaks Hospital, 301 E. Division, 75401, pg. 1697 **PB**
Powell ESCO Company, P.O. Box 1039, 75403, pg. 1319 **PB**
Raytheon E-Systems, P.O. Box 6056, 75403-6056, pg. 1365 **PB**
Serv-Air, Inc., P.O. Box 6669, 75403-6669, pg. 1366 **PB**
Trico Industries, Inc., 6325 Trico Lane, 75401, pg. 1247 **PB**
WING INDUSTRIES, INC., 6202 Industrial Dr., 75402, pg. 1183 **PV**
Wing Industries South Central, 6202 Industrial Dr., 75401, pg. 1183 **PV**

Groves

Sabine Transportation Company, P.O. Box 1528, 7200 Hwy. 87 E., 77619, pg. 962 **PB**

Hallsville

The Sabine Mining Co., (Operations Office), P.O. Box 659, 75650, pg. 1149 **PB**

Harlingen

Continental/Murray, 1305 E. Oklahoma, 78550, pg. 268 **PV**
General Dynamics Harlingen, 2800 Airport Dr., 78550, pg. 709 **PB**
HYGEIA DAIRY CO., INC., 720 S. F St., 78550, pg. 552 **PV**
7-UP/RC of Harlingen, 915 Ed Carey Dr., 78550, pg. 470 **PV**
Sun Valley Health Care Center, 2204 Pease St., 78550, pg. 839 **PV**

Helotes

Statewide Transport, Inc., P.O. Box 992, 78023, pg. 1726 **PB**

Hempstead

VF Factory Outlet Stores, 805 Factory Outlet Dr., 77445-5604, pg. 1702 **PB**

Henderson

Anderson Hickey, Inc., 1610 Industrial Dr., 75653, pg. 512 **PV**

Hereford

ARROWHEAD MILLS, INC., 110 S. Lawton, 79045, pg. 86 **PV**
Hereford State Bank, 212 East 3rd St., 79045, pg. 633 **PB**

Hillsboro

TOWNE SQUARE FURNITURE, INC., 402 Hawkins, 76645, pg. 1093 **PV**

Houston

ABB Randall Corporation, 10255 Richmond, 77042, pg. 5 **IT**
ABN AMRO Bank, N.V. (Houston), Three Riverway, Ste. 1600, 77056, pg. 10 **IT**
ABS Integrated Services, 16855 Northchase Dr., 77060-6008, pg. 51 **PV**
ABS Marine Services, Inc., 16855 Northchase Dr., 77060, pg. 51 **PV**
ABS Quality Evaluations, Inc., 16855 Northchase Dr., 77060, pg. 51 **PV**
ACR GROUP, 3200 Wilcrest, Ste. 440, 77042-6019, pg. 3 **PB**
ACS Mistermesh, 211 Industry Rd., 77053, pg. 4 **PB**
Ada Crude Oil Company, 6910 Fannin, 77030, pg. 19 **PB**
AM Management Corp., 555 Almeda Mall, 77075, pg. 1409 **PB**
AMRI Inc., P.O. Box 41068, 77241-1068, pg. 721 **IT**
ANR Credit Corporation, Nine Greenway Plaza, 77046, pg. 389 **PB**
ANR Development Corporation, Nine Greenway Plaza, 77046-0995, pg. 389 **PB**
ANR Production Co., Coastal Tower, Nine Greenway Plaza, 77046, pg. 389 **PB**
ANR Venture Management Co., Coastal Tower, Nine Greenway Plaza, 77046-0995, pg. 389 **PB**
APC Operating Partnership, L.P., 2000 Post Oak Blvd., Ste. 100, 77056-4400, pg. 119 **PB**
APS HOLDING CORPORATION, World Houston Plaza, 15710 John F. Kennedy Blvd., Ste. 700, 77032-2347, pg. 10 **PB**
A.P.S., Inc., 15710 JFK Blvd., Ste. 700, 77032, pg. 10 **PB**
ATS Omega, Inc., 3355 W. 11th St., 77008, pg. 1222 **PB**
ADAMS RESOURCES & ENERGY, INC., 5 Post Oak Park, Ste. 77027, pg. 18 **PB**
Adams Resources Exploration Corp., 6910 Fannin, 77030, pg. 19 **PB**
Aero Service Corp., 3600 Briarpark, 77042-4299, pg. 1003 **PB**
AeroMexico, 13405 N.W. Freeway, Ste. 140, 77040, pg. 31 **IT**
Aggregate Haulers Inc., 5511 Renwick, 77081, pg. 1058 **PB**
AGRA Monenco, Inc., 11757 Katy Fwy., Ste. 820, 77079, pg. 31 **IT**
Aim Equity Funds, Inc., Eleven Greenway Pl., 77046, pg. 685 **IT**
Aim Family of Funds, 11 Greenway Plaza, Ste. 1919, 77046, pg. 685 **IT**
Air France (Southwestern Region), Ste. 3220, One Allen Center, 500 Dallas St., 77002, pg. 561 **IT**
Air Liquide America Corporation, 2700 Post Oak Blvd., Ste. 1800, 77056, pg. 37 **IT**
Air Liquide Southern Div., 3535 W. 12th St., 77008, pg. 37 **IT**
Aker Oil & Gas Technology, Inc., Kirkwood Atrium, 11757 Katy Freeway, Ste. 700, 77079, pg. 42 **IT**

Aker Omega Inc. (AE), 11757 Katy Freeway, Ste. 1300, 77079, pg. 42 **IT**
Alfa Laval Saunders Inc., 16516 Air Center Blvd., 77032, pg. 1378 **IT**
All-American Systems, P.O. Box 40338, 77240, pg. 1146 **PB**
Allied Indus., Inc., P.O. Box 61248, 77208, pg. 775 **PB**
Allied Security Inc., 9100 S. West Fwy., #123, 77074, pg. 40 **PV**
ALLRIGHT CORPORATION, 1111 Fannin, Ste. 1300, 77002, pg. 42 **PV**
Allright Parking of Texas, Inc., 815 Walker St., Ste. 1047, 77002, pg. 43 **PV**
Almeda Mall, Inc., 555 Almeda Mall, 77075, pg. 1409 **PV**
Alpha Olefins North America Inc., 9800 Centre Pkwy., Ste. 870, 77036, pg. 1196 **IT**
Amerac Energy Corp., 1201 Louisiana Ave., Ste. 3350, 77002-5609, pg. 1490 **PB**
Amerada Hess Corp., One Allen Ctr., 500 Dallas St., 77002, pg. 65 **PB**
Ameri-Forge Corporation, 13770 Industrial Rd., 77015, pg. 748 **PB**
American City Business Journals, Inc., One W. Loop S., Ste. 650, 77027, pg. 19 **PV**
American Eco Corporation, 11011 Jones Rd., 77070, pg. 74 **IT**
AMERICAN GENERAL CORPORATION, 2929 Allen Pkwy., 77019-2155, pg. 76 **PB**
American General Life Insurance Company, 2727 Allen Pkwy., 77019, pg. 76 **PB**
American Oil & Gas Corporation, 333 Clay St., Ste. 2000, 77002-9817, pg. 937 **PB**
AMERICAN ONCOLOGY RESOURCES, INC., 16825 Northchase Dr., 77060, pg. 88 **PB**
American Rice Inc., 16825 Northchase Dr., Ste. 1600, 77060, pg. 591 **PB**
American Thermoplastics Corporation, 1235 Kress St., 77020, pg. 30 **PB**
American Trading & Production Corporation, Oil & Gas Div., 77010, pg. 64 **PV**
Ameron Fiberglass Pipe Group, 13405 Northwest Fwy., Ste. 117, 77040, pg. 99 **PB**
AMICO-Houston Distr. Center, 415 A North Wayside Dr., 77020, pg. 30 **PV**
Amoco Gas Company, 550 Westlake Park Blvd., 77079, pg. 1136 **IT**
Anadarko Algeria Corporation, P.O. Box 3915, 77253-3915, pg. 107 **PB**
Anadarko Marketing Company, P.O. Box 1330, 77251-1330, pg. 107 **PB**
Anadarko Oil & Gas Company, 16855 Northchase Dr., 77251, pg. 107 **PB**
Anadarko Petroleum Corp., Ste. 200, 16801 Greenspoint Park Dr., 77060, pg. 107 **PB**
ANADARKO PETROLEUM CORPORATION, 17001 Northchase Dr., 77060, pg. 107 **PB**
Anadarko Trading Company, P.O. Box 1330, 77251-1330, pg. 107 **PB**
Anedco, Inc., 10429 Koenig Rd., 77034-4028, pg. 1016 **IT**
APACHE CORPORATION, One Post Oak Central, 2000 Post Oak Blvd., Ste. 100, 77056-4400, pg. 119 **PB**
Apache International Finance, N.V., 2000 Post Oak Blvd., Ste. 100, 77056-4400, pg. 119 **PB**
Apache International, Inc., 2000 Post Oak Blvd., Ste. 100, 77056-4400, pg. 119 **PB**
APPLETREE MARKETS, 7676 Hillmont, Ste. 300, 77040, pg. 78 **PV**
Applied Drilling Technology Inc., 10777 Westheimer, Ste. 700, 77042, pg. 748 **PB**
ARDCO/Traverse Lift, 322 Riley Rd., 77047, pg. 859 **PV**
Arrow/Schweber Electronics, Ste. 100, 10899 Kinghurst St., 77099, pg. 134 **PB**
Arrowlift Systems, 4803 Cripple Creek, 77017-5935, pg. 769 **PV**
Arthur D. Little, Inc., First City Tower Bldng., 1001 Fannin St., Ste. 2050, 77002-6778, pg. 670 **PV**
Associated Technologies, Inc., c/o American Ecology Corp., 5333 Westheimer, Ste. 1000, 77058-5407, pg. 71 **IT**
Atlantic Machine Tools Inc., 11629 No. Houston-Rosslyn, 77086, pg. 585 **IT**
Atwood Deep Seas, Ltd., P.O. Box 4558, 77210, pg. 358 **PB**
Atwood Falcon I, Ltd., P.O. Box 4558, 77210, pg. 358 **PB**
Atwood Oceanics Drilling Co., 15835 Park Ten Place Dr., 77084, pg. 146 **PB**
ATWOOD OCEANICS, INC., 15835 Park Ten Place Dr., 77084, pg. 146 **PB**
Austin Industrial, Inc., 8031 Airport Blvd., 77061, pg. 99 **PV**
Auto-trol Technology Corp.-Houston, 2550 N. Loop W., Ste. 750, 77092, pg. 148 **PV**
Automatic Power, Inc., 213 Hutcheson St., 77223, pg. 1289 **IT**
BFI Acquisition, 757 N. Eldridge, 77079, pg. 263 **PB**
BFI Aviation Services, Inc., 8402 Nelms, Ste. 4, 77079, pg. 263 **PB**
BFI Energy Systems, Inc., P.O. Box 3151, 77253, pg. 263 **PB**
BFI Energy Systems of Bergen County, Inc., P.O. Box 3151, 77253, pg. 263 **PB**
BFI Energy Systems of Plymouth, Inc., P.O. Box 3151, 77253, pg. 263 **PB**
BFI Energy Systems of Texas, Inc., P.O. Box 3151, 77253, pg. 263 **PB**
BFI Waste Systems, 757 N. Eldridge, 77079, pg. 263 **PB**
BHP Petroleum (Americas) Inc., 1360 Post Oak Blvd., Ste. 500, 77056-3020, pg. 225 **IT**
BHP Trading Inc., 1360 Post Oak Blvd, Ste. 200, 77056-3020, pg. 226 **IT**

Geographic Index-U.S.

Geographic Index-U.S.

BJ Coil Tech, 5005 Mitchendale, Ste. 250, 77092, pg. 161 **PB**
BJ SERVICES COMPANY, 5500 N.W. Central Dr., 77210-4442, pg. 161 **PB**
BJ-Titan Services Company (Partnership), P.O. Box 4442, 5500 Northwest Central Dr., 77092, pg. 166 **PB**
BMC SOFTWARE, INC., 2101 CityWest Blvd., 77042-2827, pg. 162 **PB**
BS & B Process Systems, Inc., 2727 Allen Pkwy., Ste. 910, 77019-2100, pg. 572 **PV**
BSA Advertising, Inc., 1700 West Loop S., Ste. 1130, 77027, pg. 108 **PV**
Baby Doe's, Inc., 8505 Cypress St., 77012, pg. 1023 **PV**
Baker-CAC, Inc., 17015 A Aldine-Westfield Rd., 70073, pg. 166 **PB**
Baker Hughes Drilling Technologies, P.O. Box 4740, 3900 Essex Ln., Ste. 800, 77027, pg. 166 **PB**
BAKER HUGHES INCORPORATED, 3900 Essex Ln., Ste. 1200, 77027-5177, pg. 165 **PB**
Baker Hughes INTEQ, 1999 Rankin Rd., 77073, pg. 166 **PB**
Baker Hughes Process Systems Company, 6650 Roxburg, Ste. 180, 77041, pg. 166 **PB**
Baker Hughes Production Tools, Inc., 3900 Essex Ln., Ste. 1200, 77027, pg. 166 **PB**
Baker Oil Tools, 6023 Navigation Blvd., 77011, pg. 167 **PB**
Baker Oil Tools, 9100 Emmott Rd., 77040-0129, pg. 167 **PB**
Baker Petrolite Corporation, 3900 Essex Ln., Ste. 300, 77027, pg. 166 **PB**
Banco Nacional de Mexico, First Interstate Plaza, 1000 Louisiana St., Ste. 6920, 77002, pg. 574 **IT**
Bank of Montreal - Houston, 700 Louisiana St., Ste. 4400, 77002, pg. 154 **IT**
The Bank of Nova Scotia, 1100 Louisiana, Ste. 3000, 77002, pg. 156 **IT**
The Bank of Tokyo-Mitsubishi, Ltd. (Houston Agency), 1100 Louisiana St., Ste. 2800, 77002-5216, pg. 157 **IT**
Banque Paribas-Houston, 1200 Smith St., 77002, pg. 319 **PB**
Barkers Landing #3 Joint Venture, 1600 Barker's Point Ln., 77079, pg. 365 **PB**
Baroid Drilling Fluids Division, 3000 N. Sam Houston Pkwy. E., 77032, pg. 528 **PB**
Basis Petroleum, Inc., One Allen Ctr., 500 Dallas Ave., Ste. 3200, 77002-4709, pg. 1704 **PB**
BATTLE MOUNTAIN GOLD COMPANY, 333 Clay St., Ste. 4200, 77002, pg. 193 **PB**
Bayou City Barge Lines, 6910 Fannin, 77030, pg. 19 **PB**
Bechtel Petroleum & Chemical, 3000 Post Oak Blvd., 77056, pg. 128 **PV**
Becon Construction Company, Inc., 3000 Post Oak Blvd., 77056, pg. 128 **PV**
Big Ball Sports, 5708 Sheppard Dr., 77091, pg. 1472 **PB**
Big Sandy Gas Company, 15375 Memorial Dr., 77079, pg. 289 **PB**
Bindley Western, Houston Division, 3562 E. T.C. Jester, 77018, pg. 228 **PB**
Bindley Western, Southwestern Division, 3562 T.C. Jester E., 77018, pg. 229 **PB**
BLACK ROGERS SULLIVAN GOODNIGHT, INC., 5851 San Felipe, Ste. 100, 77057, pg. 147 **PV**
Blackhawk Holding Company, 1300 Main St., Ste. 1520, 77027, pg. 1623 **PB**
Blimpie International, Inc., 2620 Fountainview, Ste. 327, 77057, pg. 236 **PB**
Bohler, 1625 W. Sam Houston Pkwy. N., 77043, pg. 1471 **IT**
Bowen Tools, 2400 Crockett, 77007, pg. 858 **PB**
Bowman Distribution, 404 Garden Oaks Blvd., 77018, pg. 190 **PB**
BRANCE KRACHY COMPANY, INC., 4411 Navigation Blvd., 77011-1035, pg. 165 **PV**
Daniel Breen and Co., 700 Louisiana St., Ste. 2650, 77002, pg. 313 **IT**
Brooklyn Interstate, 2121 Sage Rd., Ste. 380, 77056-4301, pg. 259 **PB**
Brown & Root Civil, 4100 Clinton Dr., 77020-6299, pg. 775 **PB**
Brown & Root Environmental, 10200 Bellaire Blvd., 77072-5299, pg. 775 **PB**
Brown & Root Inc., 4100 Clinton Dr., 77001-6299, pg. 775 **PB**
Brown & Root Industrial Services, 4100 Clinton Dr., 77020-6299, pg. 775 **PB**
Brown & Root International, Inc., P.O. Box 3, 77001, pg. 775 **PB**
Brown & Root Petroleum and Chemicals, 4100 Clinton Dr., 77020-6299, pg. 775 **PB**
Brown & Root Power & Mfg., 4100 Clinton Dr., 77020-6209, pg. 775 **PB**
Brown & Root Services Corporation, 4100 Clinton Dr., 77020-6299, pg. 775 **PB**
Brown & Root U.S.A. Inc., P.O. Box 3, 77001, pg. 775 **PB**
John Brown E & C Corporate Offices (U.S.), 7909 Parkwood Circle Dr., 77272, pg. 774 **IT**
R.J. Brown America, Inc., 1111 Wilcrest Green, Ste. 250, 77042, pg. 766 **IT**
Browning-Ferris, Inc., P.O. Box 3151, 77253, pg. 263 **PB**
Browning-Ferris Industries Chemical Services, Inc., P.O. Box 3151, 77253, pg. 263 **PB**
BROWNING-FERRIS INDUSTRIES, INC., 757 N. Eldridge, 77079, pg. 262 **PB**
Browning-Ferris Industries of Central Jersey, Inc., P.O. Box 3151, 77253, pg. 263 **PB**
Browning-Ferris Industries of Hawaii, Inc., P.O. Box 3151, 77253, pg. 263 **PB**
Browning-Ferris Industries of Washington, Inc., P.O. Box 3151, 77253, pg. 264 **PB**
Browning-Ferris Industries of Wyoming, Inc., P.O. Box 3151, 77253, pg. 264 **PB**

Browning-Ferris Services, Inc., P.O. Box 3151, 77001, pg. 264 **PB**
Burgmann Seals America, Inc., 9009 Pine Hill, Ste. 212, 77041, pg. 233 **IT**
BURLINGTON RESOURCES INC., 5051 Westheimer, Ste. 1400, 77056, pg. 269 **PB**
Buttes Drilling-C Company, 2801 Post Oak Blvd., Ste. 400, 77056, pg. 1383 **PB**
C & L Processors Partnership, P.O. Box 2197, 77258, pg. 531 **PB**
CB Commercial Real Estate Group Central Division, 2500 W. Loop S., Ste. 100, 77027, pg. 272 **PB**
CGG American Services Inc., 2500 Wilcrest St., Suite 200, 77042, pg. 241 **IT**
CIG Exploration, Inc., Coastal Tower, Nine Greenway Plaza, 77046-0995, pg. 390 **PB**
CRSS Capital, Inc., 1177 W. Loop S., 77027, pg. 1415 **IT**
CRSS Inc., 1177 W. Loop S., Ste. 800, 77027, pg. 1415 **IT**
CRSS International, Inc., 4848 Loop S., 77227, pg. 922 **PB**
CSC Credit Services, Inc., 652 North Belt E., Ste. 400, 77060, pg. 423 **PB**
CSR Central, 16701 Greenspoint Park Dr., Ste. 350, 77060, pg. 245 **PB**
CABOT OIL & GAS CORPORATION, 15375 Memorial Dr., 77079, pg. 289 **PB**
Cabot Oil & Gas Marketing Corporation, 15375 Memorial Dr., 77079, pg. 289 **PB**
Cabot Petroleum North Sea Limited, 15375 Memorial Dr., 77079, pg. 289 **PB**
CABVAL, 14811 St. Mary's Ln., Ste. 150, 77079, pg. 301 **PB**
Caldyne, Inc., Tenneco Bldg., P.O. Box 2511, 77001, pg. 1579 **PB**
Caleb Brett USA Inc., 8866 Gulf Freeway, Ste. 500, 77087, pg. 571 **IT**
CAMCO Drilling Group, 6501 Navigation, 77011, pg. 298 **PB**
CAMCO INTERNATIONAL INC., 7030 Ardmore St., 77054, pg. 297 **PB**
Camco International Inc., 7030 Ardmore, 77054, pg. 298 **PB**
Camco Products & Services Company, 7030 Ardmore, 77054, pg. 298 **PB**
CAMDEN PROPERTY TRUST, 3200 Southwest Fwy., Ste. 1500, 77027, pg. 298 **PB**
CAMERON, 13013 Northwest Fwy., 77040, pg. 298 **PB**
CAP Gemini America (Houston Branch), 1700 West Loop South, Ste. 1200, 77027, pg. 264 **PB**
Capitol County Mutual Fire Insurance Co., P.O. Box 73416, 19627 I-45 North, 77273, pg. 1374 **PB**
The Care Group of Texas, Inc., 2525 W. Bellfort, 77054, pg. 305 **PB**
CareerStaff Unlimited, Inc., 3040 Post Oak Blvd., 77056, pg. 1531 **PB**
Carter-Holt Harvey Roofing USA, Inc., 773 Bradfield, 77060, pg. 905 **PB**
A.M. Castle & Co., 6501 Bingle Rd., 77092, pg. 313 **PB**
Catalyst Resources, Inc, 7600 W. Tidwell, Ste. 500, 77040, pg. 1039 **PB**
Cathodic Protection Services Company, 8420 West Glen, 77036, pg. 297 **PV**
Cathodic Protection Services Company, 8420 West Glen, 77036, pg. 1213 **PB**
Cemex, S.A. de C.V. - Houston, One Riverway, Ste. 2200, 77056, pg. 278 **IT**
Centra 2000, Inc., 1350 NASA Rd. One, Ste. 202, 77058, pg. 148 **PB**
CENTRAL UNITED LIFE INSURANCE CO., 2727 Allen Pkwy., 6th Fl., 77019-2115, pg. 225 **PV**
Centrilift, 1010 Rankin Rd., 77073, pg. 167 **PB**
Challenger Minerals Inc., 10777 Westheimer, Ste. 700, 77042, pg. 748 **PB**
CHAMPION HEALTHCARE CORPORATION, 515 W. Green Rd., Ste. 800, 77067, pg. 333 **PB**
Champion Recycling Corporation, 2350 N. Belt E., Ste. 600, 77032, pg. 334 **PB**
Champion's Residential Treatment Center, 14320 Walters Rd., 77014, pg. 404 **PB**
Channel Industries Gas Co., P.O. Box 2511, 77001, pg. 1579 **PB**
Charlotte Laboratory, 9800 Kincey Ave., Ste. 100, 77058, pg. 829 **PB**
CHEMCENTRAL/Houston, 8425 Market St., 77029-2419, pg. 232 **PB**
CHEMICAL EXCHANGE INDUSTRIES, 3131 W. Alabama, Ste. 211, 77098, pg. 232 **PV**
Chemisolv, 5200 Cedar Crest Blvd., 77087, pg. 1460 **PB**
Chevron TCI Inc., 5959 Corporate Dr., 77036-2305, pg. 348 **PB**
Chevron USA Production Co., P.O. Box 1635, 77251-1635, pg. 348 **PB**
Children's Nursing Services, Ltd., 2525 W. Bellfort, 77054, pg. 305 **PB**
China Airlines Ltd., 11 Greenway Plaza, Ste. 2714, 77046, pg. 285 **IT**
Christian Mutual Life Insurance Co., 2727 Allen Pkwy, 6th Fl., 77019-2115, pg. 225 **PV**
Circle Freight International, 15851 Vickery Dr., 77032, pg. 370 **PB**
Circle International, 15851 Vickery Dr., 77032, pg. 371 **PB**
Citrus Corp., 1400 Smith St., 77002, pg. 585 **PB**
CLIFFS DRILLING COMPANY, 1200 Smith St., Ste. 300, 77002, pg. 386 **PB**
Co-Counsel, Inc., Three Riverway, 77056, pg. 1221 **PB**
Coastal Border Gas Sales, Inc., Nine E. Greenway Plaza, 77045, pg. 390 **PB**
THE COASTAL CORPORATION, Coastal Tower, Nine Greenway Plaza, 77046-0995, pg. 389 **PB**
Coastal Javelina, Inc., Nine E. Greenway Plaza, 77046, pg. 390 **PB**

Coastal Natural Gas Company, Nine E. Greenway Plaza, 77046, pg. 390 **PB**
Coastal Oil & Gas Corp., Coastal Tower, Nine Greenway Plaza, 77046-0995, pg. 390 **PB**
Coastal Oil Chelsea, Inc., Nine Greenway Plaza, 77046, pg. 390 **PB**
Coastal Power Production Company, Coastal Tower, Nine Greenway Plaza, 77046-0995, pg. 390 **PB**
Coastal States Gas Transmission Company, Nine E. Greenway Plaza, 77046, pg. 390 **PB**
Coastal States Management Corp., Coastal Tower, Nine Greenway Plaza, 77046-0995, pg. 390 **PB**
Coastal States Trading, Inc., Coastal Tower, Nine Greenway Plaza, 77046-0995, pg. 390 **PB**
Coastal Travel Mart, Inc., Nine Greenway Plaza, 77046, pg. 390 **PB**
CoastalDril, Inc., Nine E. Greenway Plaza, 77046, pg. 390 **PB**
Coflexip & Services Inc., 7660 Woodway, Ste. 390, 77063, pg. 304 **IT**
CogniSeis Development, Inc., 2401 Portsmouth, 77098-3903, pg. 1563 **PB**
Comet American Marketing, 16825 Northchase Dr., Ste. 1600, 77060, pg. 591 **PB**
Comet Enterprises, Inc., P.O. Box 3151, 77253, pg. 264 **PB**
Commercial Metals Co., 2015 Quitman, 77026, pg. 413 **PB**
CommLink, 9920 Cypresswood Dr., 77070, pg. 809 **PB**
COMPAQ COMPUTER CORPORATION, 20555 State Hwy. 249, 77070-2698, pg. 417 **PB**
Compass Bancshares, Inc., 24 Greenway Plaza, 77046, pg. 419 **PB**
Compass Bank Houston, 24 Greenway Plaza, 77046, pg. 419 **PB**
Composite Thread Protectors, Inc., 17720 Hwy. 90 E., 77049, pg. 963 **PV**
Computer Systems and Applications Inc., Two Chasewood Park, 20405 State Hwy. 249, Ste. 600, 77070, pg. 1226 **IT**
Concrete Products Group, 1200 Smith St., Suite 2400, 77002, pg. 1489 **PB**
Condea Vista Company, 900 Threadneedle, 77079, pg. 325 **PB**
Conoco, 600 N. Dairy Ashford, 77097, pg. 531 **PB**
Conoco Inc., 600 N. Dairy Ashford, 77079, pg. 531 **PB**
CONSOLIDATED GRAPHICS, INC., 5858 W. Heimer, Ste. 200, 77057, pg. 265 **PB**
Continental Airline Holdings, Inc., 2929 Allen Pkwy., 77019, pg. 1202 **IT**
CONTINENTAL AIRLINES, 2929 Allen Pkwy., 20th Fl., 77019, pg. 439 **PB**
Continental Carbon Company, 333 Cyprus Run, Ste. 100, 77094, pg. 286 **IT**
Continental Coffee, P.O. Box 9389, 77261, pg. 1348 **PB**
Continental Express, 15333 JFK Blvd., Gateway Two, Ste. 600, 77032, pg. 439 **PB**
Cook Inland, 11851 Ormandy St., 77035, pg. 521 **PB**
Cooper Industries Foundation, 600 Travis, Ste. 5800, 77002, pg. 444 **PB**
COOPER INDUSTRIES, INC., 600 Travis St., Ste. 5800, 77002, pg. 442 **PB**
CORAL OIL & GAS INC., 600 Travis, Ste. 6110, 77002, pg. 275 **PV**
Corporate Express Delivery Systems, 11 Greenway Plaza, Ste. 250, 77046, pg. 449 **PB**
Corporate Express Delivery Systems Southwest, Inc., 8211 Laporte Frwy., 77012, pg. 449 **PB**
Cosbel Petroleum Corp., Coastal Tower, Nine Greenway Plaza, 77046-0995, pg. 390 **PB**
Coscol Marine Corp., Coastal Tower, Nine Greenway Plaza, 77046-0995, pg. 390 **PB**
Coscol Petroleum Corp., Coastal Tower, Nine Greenway Plaza, 77046-0995, pg. 390 **PB**
Counce Finance Corporation, Tenneco Bldg., P.O. Box 2511, 77001, pg. 1578 **PB**
Cranberry Pipeline Corporation, 15375 Memorial Dr., 77079, pg. 289 **PB**
CREEKSIDE INDUSTRIAL, 4600 Post Oak Pl., 77027, pg. 288 **PV**
THE CRISPIN COMPANY, 2929 Allen Pkwy. Ste. 2222, 77019, pg. 290 **PV**
Criterion Catalyst Company L.P., 16825 Northchase Dr., Ste. 1000, 77060, pg. 1136 **IT**
Cron Chemical, Inc., 6015 Murphy Ave., 77031, pg. 1071 **PB**
MICHAEL CURRAN & ASSOCIATES, 7700 San Felipe, Ste. 340, 77063, pg. 297 **PV**
Cypress Acquisition, Inc., P.O. Box 1637, 77251-1637, pg. 1517 **PB**
DCA of Texas, Inc., 5855 Sovereign, Ste. No. 127, 77036, pg. 988 **PB**
DDD Energy, 50 Briar Hollow Ln. W., Seventh Fl., 77027, pg. 1454 **PB**
DI International, Inc., 450 Gears Rd., #625, 77067, pg. 765 **IT**
DMD Dresser Measurement Operation, 10201 Westheimer, Bldg. 9, 77042, pg. 528 **PB**
DSI Staff Connxions Southwest, 2 North Point Dr., Ste. 110, 77060, pg. 508 **PB**
DSI Transports, Inc., 15600 J.F.K. Blvd., 77032, pg. 1285 **IT**
DSM Hydrocarbons Americas, Inc., Four Greens Point, 16945 Northchase Dr., Ste. 120, 77060, pg. 355 **IT**
Dai-ichi Kangyo Bank, Ltd.-Houston, Interfirst Plaza, Ste. 4940, 1100 Louisiana, 77002, pg. 359 **IT**
Daniel Automation Company, 9753 Pine Lake Dr., 77055, pg. 483 **PB**
Daniel Flow Products, Inc., 9720 Katy Rd., 77224, pg. 483 **PB**
DANIEL INDUSTRIES, INC., 9753 Pine Lake Dr., 77055, pg. 482 **PB**

PB - *U.S. Public Companies Volume*
PV - *U.S. Private Companies Volume*
IT - *International Public & Private Companies Volume*

1446

Daniel Valve Company, 19191 Hempstead Hwy., 77041, pg. 483 **PB**
Dan-Loc Bolt & Gasket, Inc., 725 N. Drennan, 77003, pg. 413 **PV**
Datatel, Inc., 50 Briar Hollow Ln. W., Seventh Fl., 77027, pg. 1454 **PV**
Dayton Superior Corp., 6417 Toledo, 77008, pg. 932 **PV**
Delnor Corp., P.O. Box 2289, 5599 San Felipe, Ste. 600, 77252, pg. 1070 **IT**
Delta Steel Inc., 5599 San Felipe, Ste. 600, 77056, pg. 1070 **PB**
Destec Energy, Inc., 2500 City West Blvd., Ste. 150, 77042, pg. 1146 **PB**
DETOX, Inc., c/o American Ecology Corp., 5333 Westheimer, Ste. 1000, 77056-5407, pg. 71 **PB**
Deutag Marketing & Technical Services Inc., 16945 Worthcase Dr., 77060, pg. 1069 **IT**
DiaLogos, Inc., 5851 San Felipe, Ste. 100, 77057, pg. 147 **PV**
Diamond Offshore Drilling, Inc., 15415 Katy Frwy., 77094-1810, pg. 1011 **PB**
DigiCourse, Inc., 3120 Rogerdale Rd., Ste. 150, 77042, pg. 643 **PV**
Dixie Bulk Transport, Inc., 1775 St. James Pl., Ste. 300, 77056, pg. 962 **PB**
Dixie Canal Group, P.O. Box 1537, 1775 St. James Pl., Ste. 300, 77251-1537, pg. 961 **PB**
Dixie Canal Group, 2102 Broadway, 77012, pg. 961 **PB**
Dixie Carriers, Inc., 1775 St. James Pl., Ste. 300, 77251-1537, pg. 962 **PB**
Dixie Fuels Limited, P.O. Box 1537, 1775 St. James Pl., Ste. 300, 77251-1537, pg. 962 **PB**
Dixie Fuels II Limited, P.O. Box 1537, 1775 St. James Pl., Ste. 300, 77251-1537, pg. 962 **PB**
Dixie Linehaul Group, P.O. Box 1537, 1775 St. James Pl., Ste. 300, 77251-1537, pg. 961 **PB**
Dixie Marine, Inc., 1775 St. James Pl., Ste. 300, 77056, pg. 962 **PB**
Dixie River Tow Group, P.O. Box 1537, 1775 St. James Pl., Ste. 300, 77251-1537, pg. 961 **PB**
DOMAIN ENERGY CORPORATION, 16801 Greenspoint Park Dr., Ste. 200, 77060, pg. 515 **PB**
Domain Energy Finance Corporation, 16801 Greenspoint Park Dr., Ste. 200, 77060, pg. 516 **PB**
Domain Energy International Corporation, 16801 Greenspoint Park Dr., Ste. 200, 77060, pg. 516 **PB**
Domain Energy Production Corporation, 16801 Greenspoint Park Dr., 77060, pg. 516 **PB**
Domain Energy Ventures Corporation, 16801 Greenspoint Park Dr., Ste. 200, 77060, pg. 516 **PB**
Domco Inc. Floor Products (Texas), 1705 N. Oliver St., 77007-3821, pg. 415 **IT**
Doty Laboratories, Inc., 8866 Gulf Freeway, Ste. 500, 77017, pg. 671 **IT**
Downhole Seismic Services, 3600 Briarpark, 77042-4299, pg. 1003 **PB**
Dresser-Rand Sales, 1200 W. Sam Houston Pkwy. N., 77043, pg. 529 **PB**
Drillers Inc., 2427 Kelly Ln., 77066, pg. 765 **PB**
Dry Hole Oil & Gas Corporation, 1300 Main St., Ste. 1520, 77027, pg. 1623 **PB**
Duke Energy International, L.L.C., 5400 Westheimer Ct., 77056, pg. 534 **PB**
Dungey & Associates, 11601 Katy Frwy., Ste. 109, 77079, pg. 644 **PB**
DuPont Merck Pharm Co., 15355 Vantage Pkwy. W., Ste. 252, 77032-1965, pg. 1091 **PB**
E-Z Serve Convenience Stores, Inc., P.O. Box 922021, 77292-2021, pg. 540 **PB**
E-Z SERVE CORP., 2550 N. Loop W., Ste. 600, 77092, pg. 540 **PB**
EDD-Houston, 10700 Richmond, Ste. 263, 77042, pg. 205 **PB**
EEX CORPORATION, 2500 City W. Blvd., Ste. 1400, 77046, pg. 542 **PB**
EJL Advertising/Houston, 2121 Sage Rd., Ste. 200, 77056, pg. 673 **PB**
EMS Southwest Region Office, One Riverway #1700, 77056, pg. 565 **PB**
ENGY, Inc., 5 Post Oak Park, Ste. 1760, 77027, pg. 547 **PB**
ESI, Inc., P.O. Box 3151, 77253, pg. 264 **PB**
EVI, INC., Five Post Oak Pk., Ste. 1760, 77027-3415, pg. 547 **PB**
EVI International, Inc., Five Post Oak Park, Ste. 1760, 77027-3415, pg. 547 **PB**
Eagle Frieght Services, 3202 Igloo, 77032, pg. 547 **PB**
Eagle Mexico, International Airport, Lodestar, 77032, pg. 547 **PB**
Eagle Oceanics, Inc., 15835 Park Ten Place Dr., 77084, pg. 146 **PV**
Eagle Transportation Services, 3838 N. Sam Houston Pkwy. E. #150, 77032, pg. 547 **PB**
EAGLE USA AIRFREIGHT, Intercontinental Airport, 3214 Lodestar, 77032, pg. 547 **PB**
Eagle USA Airfreight, Intercontinental Airport, 3214 Lodestar, 77032, pg. 547 **PB**
Eagle USA Charter Services, 3838 N. Sam Houston Pkwy. E. #150, 77032, pg. 547 **PB**
Eagle USA Information Services, Intercontinental Airport, 3214 Lodestar, 77032, pg. 547 **PB**
Eagle USA International, 3838 Sam Houston Pkwy. E., #420, 77032, pg. 547 **PB**
Eagle USA Logistics Services, 3838 N. Sam Houston Pkwy. E. #150, 77032, pg. 547 **PB**
Eagle USA Tradshow Services, International Airport, 3214 Lodestar, 77032, pg. 547 **PB**
Eastern Oil Well Services, 2900 Wilcrest Dr., 77042, pg. 1329 **PB**
Eastex Energy Inc., First Interstate Bank Plaza, 1000 Louisiana, Ste., 1100, 77002, pg. 567 **PB**

Eastex Gas Production Co., First Interstate Bank Plaza, 1000 Lousiana, Ste. 1100, 77002, pg. 567 **PB**
Eastex Gas Transmission Co., First Interstate Bank Plaza, 1000 Louisiana, Ste. 1100, 77002, pg. 567 **PB**
Eastex Hydrocarbons, Inc., First Interstate Bank Plaza, 1000 Louisiana, Ste. 1100, 77002, pg. 567 **PB**
Edelman Worldwide, Inc., One Greenway Plaza, #700, 77046, pg. 362 **PV**
El Paso Energy, P.O. Box 2511, 77252, pg. 567 **PB**
EL PASO NATURAL GAS CO., 1001 Louisiana, 77002, pg. 567 **PB**
Elf Exploration Inc., 1000 Louisiana, Ste. 3800, 77002, pg. 445 **IT**
Elf Trading, Inc., 5847 San Felipe, Ste. #2100, 77057, pg. 445 **IT**
Ellwood Texas Forge, Inc., 12500 Amelia, 77001, pg. 373 **PV**
Empresas ICA Sociedad Controladora (Houston), 1424 W. Sam, Houston Pkwy., Ste. 280, 77043, pg. 454 **IT**
Enercop Gas Marketing, 5555 San Felipe, Ste. 1200, 77056, pg. 938 **PB**
Energy Valve Division, 1020 Rankin Rd., 77073, pg. 528 **PB**
Energy Ventures Mid East, Inc., 5 Post Oak Park, Ste. 1760, 77027-3415, pg. 547 **PB**
ENGINEERS & FABRICATORS CO., 3501 W. 11th St., 77008, pg. 377 **PV**
Enraf Inc., 500 Century Plaza Dr., Ste. 120, 77073, pg. 389 **IT**
Enron Americas, Inc., P.O. Box 1188, 77251, pg. 584 **PB**
Enron Capital & Trade Resources, P.O. Box 1188, 77251-1188, pg. 584 **PB**
ENRON CORP., 1400 Smith St., 77002-7369, pg. 584 **PB**
Enron Liquid Services Corp., P.O. Box 1188, 77251, pg. 584 **PB**
Enron Liquids Services Corp., P.O. Box 1188, 77251, pg. 584 **PB**
Enron Oil & Gas Co., P.O. Box 1188, 77251, pg. 584 **PB**
Enron Oil Trading & Transportation Co., P.O. Box 1188, 77251, pg. 584 **PB**
Enron Operations Corp., P.O. Box 1188, 77251, pg. 584 **PB**
ENTERPRISE PRODUCTS COMPANY, 2727 N. Loop W., Ste. 700, 77008, pg. 377 **PB**
Enterra Petroleum Equipment Group, Inc., 1360 Post Oak Blvd., Ste. 1000, 77040, pg. 1749 **PB**
Entex, P.O. Box 2628, 1600 Smith St., 77252-2628, pg. 843 **PB**
ENVIRON Corporation, 1980 Post Oak Blvd., Ste. 2120, 77056, pg. 1285 **PB**
EQUITY FUND ADVISORS INC., Ste. 500, 550 Post Oak Blvd., 77027, pg. 380 **PV**
Ercon Development Co., 8800 Jamael, Ste. 190, 77040, pg. 769 **PV**
Esso Eastern Inc., 820 Gessner, 77024, pg. 601 **PB**
Excavator Enterprises, Inc., Tenneco Bldg., P.O. Box 2511, 77001, pg. 1578 **PB**
Exsol, Inc., 50 Briar Hollow Ln. W., Seventh Fl., 77027, pg. 1454 **PB**
Exxon Chemical Asset Management Partnership, 13501 Katy Freeway, pg. 601 **PB**
Exxon Chemical Company, Westlake Plaza, 13501 Katy Fwy., 77079-1398, pg. 601 **PB**
Exxon Coal and Minerals Company, 2401 S. Gessner, 77063-2005, pg. 601 **PB**
Exxon Company, U.S.A., 800 Bell St., 77252, pg. 601 **PB**
Exxon Computing Services Company, 800 Bell, 77002, pg. 601 **PB**
Exxon Exploration Company, 233 Benmar, 77060, pg. 601 **PB**
Exxon Pipeline Company, 800 Bell Street, 77002-7426, pg. 601 **PB**
Exxon Upstream Technical Computing Company, P.O. Box 4449, 77210-4449, pg. 601 **PB**
Exxon Yemen Inc., 820 Gessner, 77024, pg. 601 **PB**
FMC Energy & Transportation Equipment Group, 1777 Gears Rd., 77067, pg. 605 **PB**
Fairfield Industries, Inc., 10627 Kinghurst, 77099, pg. 391 **PV**
Falcon Drilling Company Inc., 1900 West Loop S., Ste. 1800, 77027, pg. 1354 **PB**
Farmers Insurance Group, 17422 N.W. Fwy., 77040-1002, pg. 111 **IT**
Ferrellgas Houston, 16800 Greenspoint Park Dr., 77060, pg. 618 **PB**
Fidelity Gas Systems, Inc., c/o Petrocorp, 16800 Greenspoint Park Dr., Ste. 300, 77060, pg. 358 **PV**
FIESTA MART INC., 5235 Katy Frwy., 77007, pg. 403 **PV**
Financial Collection Agencies (1990) Inc., One Westheimer Pl., Ste. 306, 2620 Fountainview, 77057-7861, pg. 471 **IT**
FINGER FURNITURE COMPANY, INC., 4001 Gulf Fwy., 77003, pg. 405 **PV**
First American Title Insurance Co. of Texas, Inc., 11490 Westheimer, Ste. 600, 77077, pg. 626 **PB**
First Interstate Bank of Texas N.A., 808 Travis, 77002, pg. 1753 **PB**
Fish International Co., 1990 S. Post Oak Rd., Suite 200, 77056-3846, pg. 604 **PV**
Fish International Engineers, 1990 S. Post Oak Rd., Suite 200, 77056-3846, pg. 604 **PV**
Fish Service Corporation, 1990 S. Post Oak Rd., Suite 200, 77056-3846, pg. 604 **PV**
Fisk Electric Company, 111 T. C. Jester Blvd., 77007, pg. 16 **PV**
Fleishman-Hillard, Inc., 2800 Post Oak Rd. Blvd., Ste. 6060, 77056, pg. 411 **PV**
Flexibox Inc., 2407 Albright, 77017, pg. 426 **IT**
THE FLEXITALLIC GROUP, INC., 450 Gears Rd., Ste. 790, 77067, pg. 413 **PV**

Florida Gas Transmission Co., P.O. Box 1188, 77251, pg. 585 **PB**
Fluid Control Division, 1777 Gears Rd., 77067, pg. 605 **PB**
FOGARTY KLEIN & PARTNERS, 7155 Old Katy Rd., Ste. 100, 77024, pg. 415 **PV**
Fogarty Klein & Partners, 7155 Old Katy Rd., Ste. 200, 77024, pg. 416 **PV**
Fogarty Klein & Partners Direct, 7155 Old Katy Rd., Ste. 200, 77024, pg. 416 **PV**
Fogarty Klein & Partners Public Relations, 7155 Old Katy Rd., Ste. 200, 77024, pg. 416 **PV**
Foley's, 1110 Main St., 77002, pg. 1063 **PV**
Foratex Inc., 11211 Katy Frwy., 77079, pg. 496 **IT**
Forest Oil New Ventures, 1331 Lamar St., Ste. 676, 77010, pg. 670 **PB**
Forged Products, 6505 N. Houston Rosslyn Rd., 77091, pg. 299 **PV**
Forwest Inc., 11211 Katy Frwy., 77079, pg. 496 **IT**
L.B. Foster Company-Langfield Yard, 6500 Langfield Rd., 77092, pg. 676 **PB**
Four Seasons Hotel, 1300 Lamar St., 77010, pg. 502 **IT**
Franklin Brine Treatment Corporation, 15375 Memorial Dr., 77079, pg. 289 **PB**
FRIEDMAN INDUSTRIES, INC., 4001 Homestead Rd., 77028, pg. 682 **PB**
Friendswood Development Company, 17001 Northchase Rd., 77060-3105, pg. 988 **PB**
FUGRO GROUP COMPANIES, 6100 Hillcroft, 77081, pg. 430 **PB**
Fuji Bank, Houston, One Houston Center, Ste. 4100, 1221 McKinney St., 77010, pg. 519 **IT**
Furness North America Inc., 11811 E. Freeway, Ste. 660, 77029, pg. 530 **IT**
Futronix Systems, 12614 Hempstead Hwy., 77092-4527, pg. 951 **PB**
GCO Minerals Co., P.O. Box 4258, 77210, pg. 902 **PV**
GPM Gas Corporation, 1300 Post Oak Blvd., Ste. 800, 77056, pg. 1291 **PB**
GPM Gas Gathering L.L.C., 1300 Post Oak Blvd., Ste. 800, 77056, pg. 362 **PB**
GSE Living Technology, Inc., 19103 Gundle Rd., 77073, pg. 770 **PB**
R.J. GALLAGHER CO., 7901 El Rio, 77054, pg. 438 **PV**
GALLERY FURNITURE, 6006 N. Freeway, 77076, pg. 438 **PV**
GALVESTON-HOUSTON COMPANY, 4900 Woodway, Ste. 1200, 77056, pg. 438 **PB**
GAMMA BIOLOGICALS INC., 3700 Mangum Rd., 77092-5408, pg. 698 **PB**
Gellatly Hankey Marine Services, 8866 Gulf Freeway, 77017, pg. 672 **PV**
General Employment Enterprises, Inc., 2603 Augusta, Ste. 850, 77057, pg. 714 **PV**
GENERAL HOMES CORPORATION, 6671 Southwest Fwy., Ste. 600, 77074, pg. 444 **PV**
Georex Inc., 3602 W. Chase Dr., 77042, pg. 241 **IT**
GERLAND CORP., 3131 Pawnee, 77002, pg. 449 **PV**
Gibson-Homas, 1919 Cross Timbers Rd., pg. 451 **PV**
Global Businesses, 1111 Bagby, 77002-2543, pg. 1583 **PB**
Global Marine Drilling Co., 777 N. Eldridge Rd., 77079, pg. 748 **PB**
GLOBAL MARINE INC., 777 N. Eldridge Rd., 77079, pg. 748 **PB**
Global Special Risks, Inc. of Houston, 5847 San Felipe, Ste. 3100, 77057, pg. 1503 **IT**
OTTO GOEDECKE, INC., 1900 W. Loop S., Ste. 940, 77027-3206, pg. 458 **PV**
Gold Lance, Inc., 1920 N. Memorial Way, 77007, pg. 1625 **PV**
Goldman, Sachs & Co., 1000 Louisiana St., Ste. 550, 77002, pg. 462 **PV**
GOODMAN MANUFACTURING, 1501 Seamist St., 77008, pg. 464 **PV**
Gotaverken Arendal Inc., 12200 Northwest Fwy., Ste. 330, 77092, pg. 278 **IT**
Gowan, Inc., 5550 Airline Dr., 77022, pg. 372 **PV**
GRANT GEOPHYSICAL INC., 16850 Park Row, 77084, pg. 470 **PB**
Grant Prideco, Inc., 363 N. Sam Houston Pkwy. E., Ste. 1660, 77060-2409, pg. 547 **PB**
Great Lakes Carbon Corp., 4 Greenspoint Plaza, 16945 Northchase Dr., Ste. 2200, 77060, pg. 540 **PB**
Great Western Metals Inc., 14121 Gulf Freeway, 77034, pg. 422 **PV**
Greenspoint Marriott Restaurant Corporation, 255 North Belt E., 77060, pg. 361 **PV**
GREY WOLF, INC., 10370 Richmond Ave., Ste. 600, 77042, pg. 765 **PB**
GROCERS SUPPLY CO. INC., 3131 E. Holcombe Blvd., 77021, pg. 483 **PV**
Grocers Supply Convenience Stores, 3131 E. Holcombe Blvd., 77021, pg. 483 **PV**
Grocers Supply International, 411 Brisbane, 77061, pg. 483 **PV**
Grocers Supply Produce, 3000 Hicks St., 77021, pg. 483 **PV**
GROUP MAINTENANCE AMERICA CORP., 1800 W. Loop S., Ste. 1375, 77027, pg. 766 **PV**
GROUP 1 AUTOMOTIVE, INC., 950 Echo Ln., Ste. 350, 77024, pg. 767 **PV**
Max Gruenhut International Inc. USA, 15851 Vickery Dr., 77032, pg. 372 **PB**
Gulf Coast District, 2427 Kelly Ln., 77066, pg. 75 **PB**
Gulf Energy Development Corp., 1301 McKinney St., Ste. 700, 77010, pg. 1136 **IT**
Gulf Energy Gathering & Processing Corp., 1301 McKinney St., Ste. 700, 77010, pg. 1136 **IT**
Gulf Energy Marketing Co., 1301 McKinney St., Ste. 700, 77010, pg. 1136 **IT**
Gulf Energy Pipeline Co., 1301 McKinney St., Ste. 700, 77010, pg. 1136 **IT**

Geographic Index-U.S.

GULF STATES TOYOTA, INC., 7701 Wilshire Pl., 77040, pg. 488 PV
Gulfmark Energy Inc., 6910 Fannin, 77030, pg. 19 PB
GULFMARK OFFSHORE INC., Five Post Oak Pk., Ste. 1170, 77027, pg. 769 PB
Gulfstar Energy, Inc., 16801 Greenspoint Park Dr., Ste. 200, 77060, pg. 516 PB
Gumout Division, Pennzoil Pl., 77252, pg. 1273 PB
GUNDLE/SLT ENVIRONMENTAL, INC., 19103 Gundle Rd., 77073, pg. 769 PB
HMO Texas, L.C., 820 Gessner, Ste. 1000, 77024, pg. 1470 PB
HMT Inc., 4422 F.M. 1960 W., Ste. 350, 77068, pg. 914 PB
HMT Inspection & Engineering Services, 900 S. Loop W., 77054, pg. 914 PB
HWC Distribution Corp., 10201 N. Loop E., 77029, pg. 55 PB
Hale Oil Field Products Co., 10105 West Gulf Bank Rd., 77040, pg. 1746 PB
Matthew Hall & Co., 111 T.C. Jester, Ste. 150, 77007, pg. 16 IT
Halliburton Energy Services, Halliburton Ctr., 5151 San Felipe, 77056-3610, pg. 776 PB
Halliburton Environmental Technologies, Inc., P.O. Box 3, Bldg. 3, 77001, pg. 776 PB
Haltermann Ltd., 16717 Jacintoport Blvd., 77015, pg. 590 IT
Hamilton Financial Services Corp., 340 N. Sam Houston Pkwy. E., Ste. 100, 77060, pg. 644 PB
Hanwa American Corp., 98000 Richmond, Ste. 515, 77042, pg. 595 IT
Harbor Financial Mortgage Corp., 340 N. Sam Houston Pkwy. E., Ste. 100, 77060, pg. 644 PB
Harbor Financial Property Management Inc., 340 N. Sam Houston Pkwy. E., Ste. 100, 77060, pg. 644 PB
HARCOR ENERGY, INC., Five Post Oak Park, 4400 Post Oak Pkwy., Ste. 2220, 77027, pg. 782 PB
HEATH CONSULTANTS INCORPORATED, 9030 Monroe Rd., 70061, pg. 518 PV
Herberts-O'Brien Inc., 9800 Genard Rd., 77041, pg. 626 IT
Hewlett-Packard Company, 10535 Harwin Dr., 77036, pg. 815 PB
Hi/LO Automotive, Inc., 2575 W. Bellfort, 77054, pg. 1230 PB
HIGHLANDS INSURANCE CO., 10370 Richmond Ave., 77042-4123, pg. 826 PB
Hilb, Rogal and Hamilton Company of Houston, 14825 St. Mary's Lane, Ste. 100, 77079, pg. 827 PB
HOT SHOT DELIVERY INC., 701 Shepherd Dr., 77270, pg. 541 PV
Household Products, 5822 Armour Dr., 77020, pg. 387 PB
Houston Cellular Telephone Co., 1195 W. Loop North, Ste. 190, 77055, pg. 11 PB
Houston Chronicle, 801 Texas Ave., 77002, pg. 517 PV
Houston Division, 12012 Wickehecter, Ste. 150, 77079, pg. 1683 PV
Houston Engineers, P.O. Box 567, 1616 E. Freeway, 77020, pg. 1181 PV
The Houston Exploration Company, 1331 Lamar, 77010, pg. 259 PB
Houston Industries Energy, Inc., P.O. Box 61446, 77208-1446, pg. 843 PB
HOUSTON INDUSTRIES INCORPORATED, P.O. Box 4567, 77210, pg. 842 PB
Houston Laboratory, 900 Gemini Ave., 77058, pg. 829 PV
Houston Learning Center, 7525 Fauna St., 77061, pg. 218 PB
Houston Lighting & Power Company, P.O. Box 1700, 77251, pg. 843 PB
Houston Oil & Minerals Exploration Co., 1100 Louisiana St., 77001, pg. 1578 PB
Houston Pipe Line Co., P.O. Box 1188, 77251, pg. 584 PB
Houston Processing Center, 15850 Export Plaza Dr., 77032, pg. 450 PB
Houston Steel Service Company of Texas, 5321 Westpark Dr., 77056, pg. 412 PB
Houston Warwick Inc., 5701 Main St., Ste. 1100, 77005, pg. 1134 IT
HOWELL CORPORATION, 1500 Howell Bldg., 1111 Fannin St., 77002-6923, pg. 843 PB
Howell Gas Management Co., 1500 Howell Corp. Bldg., 1111 Fannin, 77002, pg. 844 PB
Howell Petroleum Corp., 1500 Howell Corp. Bldg., 1111 Fannin, 77002, pg. 844 PB
J.M. Huber, Oil & Gas Div., 1900 West Loop S., Flrs. 16 & 17, 77027, pg. 545 PV
Hudson Engineering & Project Management Services, P.O. Box 218218, 77218, pg. 1068 PB
Hudson Engineering Corp., 801 Eldridge St., 77079, pg. 1068 PB
Hughes Christensen, P.O. Box 2522539, 77252, pg. 166 PB
Joe D. Hughes, Inc., P.O. Box 96469, 77013, pg. 776 PB
Humphreys Mineral Industries, Inc., 2801 Post Oak Blvd., Ste. 400, 77056, pg. 1383 PB
Hunt Oil Gulf Coast Exploration Division, Brookhollow Central Three, 2950 North Loop W., Ste. 900, 77092, pg. 548 PV
Hycalog, 9777 W. Gulf Bank Rd., Ste. 15, 77040, pg. 298 PB
HYDRIL COMPANY, 3300 N. Sam Houston Pkwy., E., 77032-3411, pg. 551 PV
Hydril Technology Center, P.O. Box 60458-77205, 77272, pg. 551 PV
Hydro Conduit Corp., P.O. Box 553509, 11403 N. Houston Rosslyn Rd., 77255, pg. 245 IT
Hydro Conduit Corp., P.O. Box 60297, 16701 Greenspoint Park Dr., Ste. 350, 77060, pg. 245 IT

Hydrocarbon & Chemical Processing Division, 6001 Savoy Dr., Ste. 400, 77036, pg. 4 IT
Hydrocarbon Development Corp., 1301 McKinney St., Ste. 700, 77010, pg. 1136 IT
ICIS LOR-USA, 3730 Kirby Dr., Ste. 1030, 77098, pg. 1094 IT
ICO, INC., 11490 Westheimer, Ste. 1000, 77077, pg. 853 PB
IDM CONTROLS, 9510 Houston Rosslyn Rd., 77088, pg. 554 PV
IDM Equipment Company, 11616 Galayda Rd., 77086, pg. 555 PV
IRD Mechanalysis, Inc., 2525 W. Bellfort, 77054-5024, pg. 789 PB
IRI INTERNATIONAL CORPORATION, 10000 Louisiana, Ste. 5900, 77002, pg. 858 PB
ITOCHU Industrial Machinery, Inc., 7950 Blankenship Dr., 77055, pg. 695 IT
ITOCHU International Petroleum Co., Ltd., 5847 San Felipe Plaza, Ste. 1100, 77057, pg. 695 IT
ITOCHU Pipe & Tube, Inc., 1001 Fannin St., Ste. 2450, 77002, pg. 695 IT
Ideal Concrete, Off 9600 Clinton Dr., 77020, pg. 628 IT
Igloo Products Corporation, 1001 W. Sam Houston Pkwy., N., 77043, pg. 265 PB
Ikon Office Solutions-Houston, 280 Post Oak, Ste. 3200, 77056, pg. 863 PB
Indoco Inc., P.O. Box 3151, 77253, pg. 264 PB
The Industrial Bank of Japan, Limited (Houston), Three Allen Ctr., Ste 4850, 333 Clay St., N.E., 77002, pg. 674 IT
Industrial Services, Ste. 100, 16340 Park Ten. Pl., 77084, pg. 396 PB
Industrial Water Treatment Co., 3535 W. 12th, 77008, pg. 37 PB
INNOVATIVE VALVE TECHNOLOGY, INC., Two Northpoint Dr., 77073, pg. 880 PB
Intake Water Co., Tennecco Bldg., P.O. Box 2511, 77001, pg. 1579 PB
Integrated Technologies, 10205 Westheimer Road, 77042-4299, pg. 1004 PB
Interamerican Foods Corporation, C.P. 77002-45-01, 1200 Smith St., Ste. 3060, 77002, pg. 1346 PB
Intergraph Corporation, 675 Bering Dr., Ste. 200, 77057, pg. 890 PB
Intergraph Corporation, 17629 El Camino Real, Ste. 160, 77058, pg. 890 PB
The International Commercial Bank of China, 811 Rusk, Ste. 1355, 77002, pg. 683 IT
International Disposal Corporation of Indiana, P.O. Box 3151, 77253, pg. 264 PB
International Disposal Corporation of Kansas, P.O. Box 3151, 77253, pg. 264 PB
International Paint Powder Coatings Div., 6001 Antoine, P.O. Box 924224, 77292, pg. 339 IT
International Paint Southwest Div., 6001 Antoine, P.O. Box 10762, 77292, pg. 339 IT
INTERNATIONAL SYSTEMS & CONTROLS CORP., 2727 Allen Pkwy., 77019, pg. 572 PV
International Tool & Supply Company, Inc., 4669 S.W. Fwy., Ste. 400, 77027, pg. 684 IT
Interox America, P.O. Box 27328, 77227, pg. 1278 IT
Interpak Terminals, Inc., 8790 Wallisville Rd., 77029, pg. 724 PV
Intertel, Inc., 6955 Port West Dr., Ste. 190, 77024, pg. 203 PB
Intsel Southwest, P.O. Box 41041, 11310 W. Little York, 77041, pg. 1029 PB
ITEQ, INC., 2727 Allen Pkwy., Ste. 760, 77019, pg. 914 PB
JGC Corporation, Ste. 800, 10370 Richmond Ave., 77042, pg. 697 IT
JGC (U.S.A.), Inc., 10370 Richmond Ave., Ste. 800, 77042, pg. 697 IT
Jacobs Constructors, Inc., 4848 Loop Central Dr., 77081-2211, pg. 921 PB
Jacobs Engineering Group Inc., 4848 Loop Central Dr., 77081-2211, pg. 921 PB
Japan Energy USA, Inc., 1980 Post Oak Blvd., Ste. 7030, 77056, pg. 702 IT
Jefferies & Company, Inc., 909 Fannin St., Ste. 3100, 77010, pg. 925 PV
Jiffy Lube International, Inc., P.O. Box 2967, 77002-2967, pg. 1272 PB
Jiffy Lube International of Maryland, Inc., P.O. Box 2967, 77252-2967, pg. 1272 PB
Joffko Cameroon Corporation, 6815-A Lindbergh St., 77087, pg. 589 PV
JOFFKO INTERNATIONAL, 8038 El Rio, 77054, pg. 589 PV
JOHNSON SUPPLY & EQUIPMENT CORP., 10151 Stella Link, 77025, pg. 594 PB
Earle M Jorgensen Company/Houston, 5311 Clinton Dr., 77020, pg. 600 PB
Joy Environmental Technologies, Inc., 10700 North Freeway, 77037, pg. 789 PV
K-Bin Inc., Wesleyan Tower, 24 Greenway Plaza, Suite 811, 77046, pg. 1234 IT
KBXX-FM, 24 Greenway Plaza, Ste. 1508, 77046, pg. 384 PB
KCS Energy Marketing, Inc., 5555 San Felipe, Ste. 1200, 77056, pg. 939 PB
KCS Energy Services, Inc., 5555 San Felipe, Ste. 1200, 77056, pg. 939 PB
KCS Michigan Resources, Inc., 5555 San Felipe, Ste. 1200, 77056, pg. 939 PB
KCS Pipeline Systems, Inc., 5555 San Felipe, Ste. 1200, 77056, pg. 939 PB
KCS Resources, Inc., 5555 San Felipe, Ste. 1200, 77056, pg. 939 PB
KHOU-TV Inc., 1945 Allen Pkwy., 77019, pg. 209 PB

KHTV-TV, 7700 Westpark, 77063, pg. 1636 PB
KHYS-FM, 24 Greenway Plaza, Ste. 1508, 77046, pg. 384 PB
KIKK AM/FM, 24 Greenway Plaza, 77046, pg. 274 PB
KILT AM/FM Radio, 4810 San Felipe Rd., 77056, pg. 274 PB
KJOJ-AM/FM, 2400 Greenway Plaza, Ste. 1508, 77046, pg. 384 PB
KKBQ-AM/FM, 11 Greenway Plaza, Ste. 2022, 77046, pg. 335 PB
KMJQ-FM, 24 Greenway Plaza, Ste. 1508, 77046, pg. 384 PB
KPRC-AM, 11767 Katy Fwy., Ste. 1170, 77079, pg. 384 PB
KPRC-TV, 181 S.W. Freeway, 77074, pg. 1743 PB
KRIV, 3935 W. Westheimer Rd., 77027, pg. 926 IT
KSEV-AM, 11767 Katy Fwy., Ste. 1170, 77079, pg. 384 PB
KTI FISH, 1990 Post Oak Blvd., Ste. 200, 77056-3846, pg. 604 PV
KTRK Television, Inc., 3310 Bissonnet, 77005, pg. 512 PB
Kaiser Aluminum Corporation, 5847 San Felipe, Ste. 2600, 77257-2887, pg. 1062 PB
Kaw Pipeline Co., P.O. Box 42130, 77042, pg. 1584 PB
Kawasaki Steel America, Texas Commerce Tower, 600 Travis St., Ste. 6375, 77002, pg. 726 IT
The M.W. Kellogg Company, 601 Jefferson Ave., 77002, pg. 528 PB
Kennell & Company Insurance Managers, Inc., 2450 Fondren, Ste. 200, 77063, pg. 1257 PB
Kent Datacomm Corp., 7433 Harwin Dr., 77036, pg. 951 PB
KENT ELECTRONICS CORP., 7433 Harwin Dr., 77036-2015, pg. 951 PB
Keppel Marine Agencies Inc., Texas Commerce Bank Bldg., 5177 Richmond Ave., Ste. 1065, 77056, pg. 731 IT
Kern River Corporation, 1010 Milam St., 77002, pg. 1578 PB
Kern River Gas Supply Corporation, 1010 Milam St., 77002, pg. 1579 PB
Kern River Service Corporation, 1010 Milam St., 77002, pg. 1578 PB
KETTLE RESTAURANTS, 2855 Mangum St., 77092, pg. 617 PV
Keystone International Holdings Corp., P.O. Box 40010, 77240, pg. 1650 PB
Keystone Valves and Controls, Inc., P.O. Box 40010, 9700 W. Gulf Bank Dr., 77040, pg. 1650 PB
Keystone Valvtron, Inc., 7230 Empire Central Dr., 77040, pg. 1650 PB
KIRBY CORPORATION, 1775 St. James Pl., Ste. 200, 77056, pg. 961 PB
Kobelco America Inc., 10515 Harwin Dr., Ste. 139A, 77036, pg. 740 IT
Koch Otto H. York Co., Inc., 6611 Killough Rd., 77086, pg. 628 PV
Korn/Ferry International, 1100 Louisiana, Ste. 2850, 77002, pg. 633 PV
Kronos, Inc., 16825 Northchase Dr., Ste. 1200, 77060, pg. 270 PV
KRUG INTERNATIONAL CORP., 1290 Hercules Dr., Ste. 120, 77058, pg. 967 PB
Krug Life Sciences Inc., 1290 Hercules Dr., Ste. 120, 77058, pg. 968 PB
Kvaerner Earl and Wright, Inc., 11111 Wilcrest Green, Ste. 250, 77042, pg. 771 IT
Kvaerner National Inc., 1255 N. Post Oak Rd., 77055-7213, pg. 770 IT
LTB, 12 Greenway Plaza, Ste. 528, 77046, pg. 668 PB
LTB Ward Constructors, Inc., 3000 Richmond Ave., Ste. 200, 77098, pg. 347 PV
Lachmar, 5400 Westheimer Ct., 77056, pg. 535 PB
LAFEHR CHAN TECHNOLOGIES, 1155 Dairy Ashford Rd., Ste. 500, 77079, pg. 642 PV
Lamons Metal Gasket Co., 3600 Canal St., 77011, pg. 1054 PV
Landmark Graphics Corporation, 15150 Memorial Dr., 77079-4304, pg. 776 PB
LANDRY'S SEAFOOD RESTAURANTS INC., 1400 Post Oak Blvd., Ste. 1010, 77056, pg. 977 PB
Larcom Insurance Company, Ltd., 5847 San Felipe, Ste. 3300, 77057, pg. 1325 PB
LASMO America Inc., 12 Greenway Plaza, 8th Floor, 77046-1291, pg. 804 IT
Laughlin Environmental, Inc., 5402 Lewndale St., 77023, pg. 1379 PV
LINBECK CONSTRUCTION CORP., 3810 W. Alabama, 77027, pg. 667 PV
Lindberg Heat Treating Co., 8316 E. Freeway, P.O. Box 24147, 77029, pg. 999 PB
Liqui-Box Corp., 7112 Cavalcade, 77028, pg. 1001 PB
Living Centers of America, 15415 Katex Fwy., Ste. 800, 77094, pg. 1257 PB
Living Earth Technology Co., 5625 Crawford Rd., 77041, pg. 1379 PV
Lockheed Engineering & Sciences Co., Inc., 2625 Bay Area Blvd., 77058, pg. 1009 PB
Lockheed Environmental Systems & Technologies Company, Citicorp Center, 1200 Smith St., Ste. 900, 77002-3400, pg. 1009 PB
Lockheed Martin Space Information Systems, Marina Plaza, Ste. 500, 82450 Shore Blvd., 77058, pg. 1009 PB
Lockwood Andrews & Newnam, Inc., 1500 City West Blvd., 77042, pg. 309 PV
LONG REACH HOLDINGS INC., 12300 Amelia Dr., 77045, pg. 675 PB
Long Reach Manufacturing, 12300 Amelia Dr., 77045, pg. 675 PV
Loomis-Fargo & Co., 2500 City West Blvd., Ste. 900, 77042, pg. 245 PB

PB - U.S. Public Companies Volume
PV - U.S. Private Companies Volume
IT - International Public & Private Companies Volume

1448

Geographic Index-U.S.

Louisiana Intrastate Gas Corporation, 200 Westlake Park Blvd., 77079, pg. 590 PB
Lyondell-Citgo Refining Company, Ltd., 12000 Lawndale, 77017, pg. 1022 PB
Lyondell Licensing, Inc., One Houston Center, 1221 McKinney St., 77253-3646, pg. 1022 PB
LYONDELL PETROCHEMICAL COMPANY, One Houston Ctr., 1221 McKinney St., Ste. 1600, 77010, pg. 1022 PB
M & C Brokerage Services, Inc., 24 Greenway Plaza, Ste. 1201, 77046, pg. 366 PB
M-I L.L.C., 1201 Louisiana, 9th Fl., 77002, pg. 776 PB
MAC EQUIPMENT INC., 13813 Fm 529, 77041, pg. 685 PV
MCF Controls Inc., 1110 N. Post Oak Bvld., Ste. 345, 77055, pg. 647 IT
MG Natural Gas Corporation, 1000 Louisiana, Ste. 6600, 77002, pg. 862 IT
MG Refining & Marketing, Inc., 1000 Louisianna, Ste. 6600, 77002, pg. 862 IT
MHIA Houston Technical Service Branch, 10795 Hammerly, Ste. 350 B, 77043, pg. 874 IT
MMI PRODUCTS, INC., 515 W. Greens Rd., Ste. 710, 77067, pg. 687 PV
MMLJ, INC., P.O. Box 70527, 77270-0527, pg. 687 PV
MW Petroleum Corp., 2000 Post Oak Blvd., Ste. 100, 77056-4400, pg. 119 PB
MWJR. Petroleum Corp., 2000 Post Oak Blvd., Ste. 100, 77056-4400, pg. 119 PB
Machinery Acceptance Corporation, P.O. Box 1637, 77251-1637, pg. 1517 PB
Machinery Sales & Supply Co., 8510 S. Loop E., 77017, pg. 971 PB
Mannesmann Oilfield Tubulars Corporation, 1990 Post Oak Blvd., Ste. 1700, 77056, pg. 835 IT
Mannesmann Pipe & Steel Corp., 1990 Post Oak Blvd., 18th Fl., 77056, pg. 838 IT
Marathon Oil Company, P.O. Box 3128, 77253, pg. 1661 PB
Mark Products, 10502 Fallstone Rd., 77099, pg. 1231 IT
Marlin Drilling Co., Inc., Park Tower South, 1333 West Loop South, Ste. 780, 77027, pg. 1579 PB
Masoneilan North American Operations, P.O. Box 60078, 77205-0078, pg. 528 PB
Masterbilt Fixtures, Inc., 3131 E. Holcombe Blvd., 77021, pg. 483 PV
MAXXAM INC., 5847 San Felipe, Ste. 2600, 77257-2887, pg. 1062 PB
MAXXAM Property Company, P.O. Box 572887, 5847 San Felipe, Ste. 2600, 77257-2887, pg. 1062 PB
STERLING MCCALL TOYOTA GROUP, 9400 Southwest Fwy., 77074, pg. 719 PV
The McClure Group/American Teledirect, 222 Pennbright, Ste. 304, 77090, pg. 720 PV
McCullough, An Atlas Wireline Services Operation, P.O. Box 1407, 10205 Westheimer Rd., 77251-1407, pg. 1004 PB
Media Recovery Inc.-Houston, TX, 5301 Hollister St., 77040, pg. 727 PV
MediaU.S.A., 5851 San Felipe, Ste. 225, 77057, pg. 147 PV
Men's Wearhouse, 5803 Glenmont Dr., 77081, pg. 1086 PB
Meridian Oil Holding Inc., 2919 Allen Pkwy., 10th Fl., 77019, pg. 269 PB
THE MERIDIAN RESOURCE CORPORATION, 15995 N. Barkers Landing, Ste. 300, 77079, pg. 1095 PB
Metallic Building Company, P.O. Box 40338, 77240, pg. 1146 PB
METALS USA, INC., Three Riverway, Ste. 600, 77056, pg. 1100 PB
MIDCOAST ENERGY RESOURCES, INC., 1100 Louisiana, Ste. 2950, 77002, pg. 1109 PB
MidCon Gas Products Corp., 3200 S.W. Freeway, 77027-7523, pg. 1210 PB
MidCon Gas Services Corp., 3200 S.W. Freeway, 77027-7523, pg. 1210 PB
MidCon Texas Pipeline Operator, Inc., 3200 S.W. Fwy., 77027-7523, pg. 1210 PB
Midwest Steel Building Company, P.O. Box 40338, 77240, pg. 1146 PB
Midwestern Gas Marketing Company, 1010 Milam St., pg. 1579 PB
Midwestern Gas Transmission Co., Tenneco Bldg., P.O. Box 2511, 77001, pg. 567 PB
Milgray/Houston, Inc., 12000 Richmond Ave., 77082, pg. 206 PB
The Minute Maid Company, 2000 St. James Pl., 77056, pg. 392 PB
Mitrans Corporation, Ste. 587, 6776 Southwest Frwy., 77074, pg. 874 IT
Mitsubishi Caterpillar Forklift America Inc. (MCFA), 2011 W. Sam Houston Pkwy. N., 77043, pg. 316 PB
Mitsubishi Caterpillar Forklift America Inc. (MCFA), 2011 W. Sam Houston Pkwy. N., 77043, pg. 874 IT
Mitsui & Co. (U.S.A.), 1000 Louisiana St., 77002, pg. 879 IT
Mobil Petrochemicals Div., Intercontinental Center, 15600 J.F.K. Blvd., Ste. 906, 77032-2343, pg. 1118 PB
MOGAS INDUSTRIES, INC., P.O. Box 11529, 77293-1529, pg. 755 PV
Mont Belvieu Land Company, 1010 Milam St., pg. 1578 PB
Monterey's Acquisition Corp., 3838 N. Sam Houston Pkwy. E., Ste. 520, 77032, pg. 758 PV
MONTEREY'S ACQUISITION CORPORATION, 3838 N. Sam Houston Pkwy. E., Ste. 520, 77032, pg. 758 PV
Morgan-Hayes Div., 1620 Austin, 77002, pg. 1764 PB
J.P. Morgan Investment Management Inc., One Houston Ctr., 1221 McKinney St., 77010-2009, pg. 1129 PB
J.P. Morgan Securities Inc., One Houston Ctr., 1221 McKinney St., Ste. 3131 & 3150, 77010-2009, pg. 1129 PB
Moroch & Associates, Inc., 5177 Richmond #5005, 77056, pg. 762 PV
Motorola USA, 6100 Corporate Dr., #230, 77036-3425, pg. 1138 PB
Mustang Industrial Equipment Co., 7607 Wallisville Rd., 77020, pg. 769 PV
Mustang Power Systems, 12800 N. W. Fwy., 77040, pg. 769 PV
MUSTANG TRACTOR & EQUIP. CO., 12800 N.W. Fwy., 77040, pg. 768 PV
N & N Inc., 5701 Main St., Ste. 1100, 77005-1895, pg. 1134 IT
NCI BUILDING SYSTEMS, INC., 7301 Fairview, 77041, pg. 1145 PB
NCT U.S.A. Inc., 5 Post Oak Park, Ste. 1250, 77027, pg. 913 IT
NGC CORPORATION, 1000 Louisiana, Ste. 5800, 77002-5050, pg. 1146 PB
NI Tubulars, Inc., Three Riverway, Ste. 800, 77056, pg. 947 IT
NL Industries, Inc., Two Greenspoint Plaza, 16825 Northchase Dr., Ste. 1200, 77060, pg. 270 PV
NS Pipe Technology, c/o Nippon Steel U.S.A., Inc., 110 Louisiana St., Suite 4400, 77002, pg. 940 IT
NW Management Corp., P. O. Box 10650, 555 Northwest Mall, 77292, pg. 1409 PB
Nabors Drilling International Limited, 515 W. Greens Rd., Ste. 1200, 77067, pg. 1148 PB
Nabors Drilling USA, Inc., 515 W. Greens Rd., Ste. 1200, 77067, pg. 1149 PB
NABORS INDUSTRIES, INC., 515 W. Greens Rd., Ste. 1200, 77067-4525, pg. 1148 PB
NAGASCO, Inc., 2000 Post Oak Blvd., Ste. 100, 77056-4400, pg. 119 PB
National-Oilwell/Dreco Holdings, Inc., 10000 Richmond Ave., Ste. 400, 77042, pg. 1158 PB
Naitonal-Oilwell/Dreco Inc., 10000 Richmond Ave,. Ste. 400, 77042, pg. 1158 PB
NATIONAL-OILWELL INC., P.O. Box 4638, 77210-4638, pg. 1158 PB
National Service Center, 14275 Northwest Frwy., 77040, pg. 1573 PB
National Tower Trunking Systems, Inc., 6020 W. 34th St., 77092, pg. 1138 PB
National Triple R, Inc., c/o American Ecology Corp., 5333 Westheimer, Ste. 1000, 77056-5407, pg. 71 PB
Neste Chemicals Holding Inc., 4400 Post Oak Pkwy., Five Post Oak Rd., Ste. 1230, 77027, pg. 913 IT
Neste Chemicals Holding Inc., 440 Post Oak Pkwy., Five Post Oak Park, Ste. 1230, 77027, pg. 913 IT
Neste Corporate Holding Inc., 4400 Post Oak Pkwy., Five Post Oak Park, Ste. 1230, 77020, pg. 913 IT
Neste Crude Oil, Inc., Five Post Oak Park, Ste. 1220, 77027, pg. 914 IT
Neste Oil Services, Inc., Five Post Oak Park, Ste. 1220, 77027, pg. 914 IT
Neste Petroleum, Inc., 4400 Post Oak Pkwy., Five Post Oak Park, Ste. 1220, 77027, pg. 914 IT
Neste Petroleum (Products), Inc., 440 Post Oak Pkwy., Five Post Oak Park, Ste. 1220, 77027, pg. 914 IT
New Tenn Company, 1010 Milam St., 77002, pg. 1578 PB
Nichimen America, Inc., Houston Branch, Three Riverway, Ste. 1260, 77056, pg. 928 IT
Nippon Oil Exploration U.S.A. Limited, 5847 San Felipe, Ste. 2800, 77057, pg. 937 IT
Nippon Steel U.S.A., Inc., InterFirst Plaza, 1100 Louisiana St., Ste. 4400, 77002-5268, pg. 940 IT
NOBLE DRILLING CORPORATION, 10370 Richmond Ave., Ste. 400, 77042, pg. 1186 PB
Noble Drilling International, Inc., 10370 Richmond Ave., Ste. 400, 77042, pg. 1186 PB
Noble Drilling Services Inc., 10370 Richmond Ave., Ste. 400, 77042, pg. 1186 PB
Noble Drilling (U.S.) Inc., 10370 Richmond Ave., Ste. 400, 77042, pg. 1186 PB
Noble Gas Marketing, Inc., 350 Glenborough, Ste. 180, 77067, pg. 1186 PB
Noble-National Joint Venture, 10370 Richmond Ave., Ste. 400, 77042, pg. 1186 PB
Noble Offshore Corporation, 10370 Richmond Ave., Ste. 400, 77042, pg. 1186 PB
J.S. Nolen & Associates, 16225 Park 10 Pl., Ste. 560, 77084, pg. 1004 PB
NorAm Energy Corp., 1600 Smith St., 77002-2628, pg. 843 PB
Norriseal Controls, P.O. Box 40525, 77240, pg. 521 PB
Northern Trust Bank of Texas, N.A., 700 Rusk St., 77002, pg. 1197 PB
Northern Trust Bank of Texas, N.A., 2701 Kirby Dr., 77098, pg. 1197 PB
Northwest Mall, Inc., P.O. Box 10650, 555 Northwest Mall, 77292, pg. 1409 PB
Nowsco Inc., 9821 Katy Fwy., Ste. 750, 77024, pg. 990 IT
Nowsco Pipeline Services Inc., P.O. Box 8898, 77249, pg. 990 IT
Nowsco Well Service Inc., 9821 Katy Fwy., Ste. 750, 77024, pg. 990 IT
Nowsco Well Service Ltd.-United States, 9821 Katy Fwy., Ste. 750, 77024, pg. 990 IT
NUEVO ENERGY COMPANY, 1331 Lamar, Ste. 1650, 77010, pg. 1206 PB
Nurses Inc., 9703 Richmond Ave., 77042, pg. 1285 IT
OCEANEERING INTERNATIONAL, INC., 11911 FM 529, 77041, pg. 1211 PB
Oceaneering Intervention Engineering, 11911 FM 529, 77041, pg. 1211 PB
Oceaneering Production Systems, 11911 FM 529, 77041, pg. 1211 PB
Oceaneering Space Systems, 16665 Space Center Blvd., 77058-2268, pg. 1211 PB
Olicom Americas - Latin America, 9950 Cypresswood Dr., Ste. 222, 77070, pg. 1001 IT
Olicom Americas - South, 9950 Cypresswood Dr., Ste. 222, 77070, pg. 1001 IT
Omsco Industries, 6418 Esperson St., 77011, pg. 1231 IT
OPICOIL Houston, Inc., 3040 Post Oak Blvd., Ste. 800, 77056, pg. 286 IT
OSHMAN'S SPORTING GOODS, INC., 2302 Maxwell Ln., 77023, pg. 1233 PB
Outdoor Systems, Inc. of Texas, 1600 Studemont, 77007, pg. 1235 PB
Owen Health Care, Inc., 9800 Centre Pkwy., Ste. 1100, 77036, pg. 304 PB
Oyo Corporation U.S.A., 9777 W. Gulf Bank Rd., Ste. 5, 77040, pg. 1019 IT
OYO Geosciences Corporation, 9777 W. Gulf Bank Rd., Ste. 5, 77040, pg. 1019 IT
PB - KBB Inc., 11757 Katy Freeway, Ste. 600, 77079, pg. 1069 IT
PCC Energy Inc., c/o Petrocorp, 16800 Grennspoint Park Dr., Ste. 300, 77060, pg. 358 PB
PCC Flow Technologies, Inc., 16801 Greenspoint Park Dr., Ste. 350, 77060-2312, pg. 1320 PB
PDI (Production.Design.Interactive), 5851 San Felipe, Ste. 220, 77057, pg. 147 PV
PDVSA Services, Inc., 11490 Westheimer, Ste. 1000, 77077, pg. 1045 IT
PG&E Energy Trading, 1100 Louisiana St., Ste. 1000, 77002, pg. 1241 PB
Pabco Metals Corporation, 11811 North Fwy., Ste. 265, 77060, pg. 449 PV
The Pace Consultants, Inc., 4848 Loop Central Dr., 77081-2211, pg. 921 PB
Pakhoed USA Inc., 2000 West Loop S., Ste. 2200, 77027, pg. 1147 IT
Palais Royal, 10201 Main St., 77025, pg. 1029 PV
Paloma Production Co. Inc., 12320 S. Main St., 77235, pg. 845 PV
Pan Canadian Energy Services, 1200 Smith, 77027, pg. 259 IT
Parsons Construction Services, Inc., 8412 Mosley Rd., 77075, pg. 842 PV
Parsons Process Group Inc., 9920 Gulf Freeway, 77034, pg. 842 PV
Pearce Equipment Leasing, 12320 S. Main St., 77235, pg. 845 PV
PEARCE INDUSTRIES INC., 12320 S. Main St., 77035, pg. 845 PV
Pearce International Inc., 12320 S. Main St., 77235, pg. 845 PV
Pearson Longman Inc., 7030 Ardmore St., 77054, pg. 1026 IT
PEMEX, 3600 S. Gessner, 77063, pg. 1046 IT
PENNZOIL COMPANY, 700 Milam, 77002, pg. 1272 PB
Pennzoil Exploration & Production Co., Pennzoil Place, 77252, pg. 1272 PB
Pennzoil Products Co., 700 Milam St., 77002-2967, pg. 1272 PB
Pennzoil Sulphur Co., Pennzoil Pl., P.O. Box 2967, 77252, pg. 1273 PB
People's Choice-TV of Houston, Inc., 7272 Pinemont Dr., 77040, pg. 1274 PB
Pepper-Lawson Construction, Inc., 16420 Park Ten Place Drive, Suite 520, 77084, pg. 851 PV
Petreco Baker Hughes Company, 5455 Old Spanish Trail, 77023, pg. 166 PB
Petrobras America Inc., 10777 Westheimer, Ste. 625, 77042, pg. 1042 IT
Petrocarbon Developments Inc., 1730 Nasa Rd. 1, 77058, pg. 337 IT
Petrocorp, 300 N. Atrium, 16800 Greenspoint Pk. Dr., 77060, pg. 358 PB
Petrocorp Incorporated, 16800 Greenspoint Park Dr., 77060, pg. 358 PB
Petrocorp Management, Inc., c/o Petrocorp Inc., 16800 Greenspoint Park Dr., Ste. 300, 77060, pg. 358 PB
Petrocorp Private Drilling Ltd. 1984-1, c/o Petrocorp Inc., 16800 Greenspoint Park Dr., Ste. 300, 77060, pg. 358 PB
Petrocorp Private Drilling Ltd. 1985-1, c/o Petrocorp Inc., 16800 Greenspoint Park Dr., Ste. 300, 77060, pg. 358 PB
Petrocorp Private Drilling Limited Partnership 1983-1, c/o Petrocorp Inc., 16800 Greenspoint Park Dr., Ste. 300, 77060, pg. 358 PB
Petrocorp Reserve Acquisition Fund, Ltd. 1, c/o Petrocorp Inc., 16800 Greenspoint Park Dr., Ste. 300, 77060, pg. 358 PB
Petroleum Supply Company, 5847 San Felipe, Ste. 3300, 77057, pg. 1325 PB
Philadelphia American Life Insurance Company, 3121 Buffalo Speedway, 77098, pg. 853 PB
Philip Industrial Services Group, 5151 San Felipe, Ste. 1600, 77056-3609, pg. 1050 IT
Pioneer Concrete of America, 800 Gessner, Ste.1100, 77024, pg. 1058 IT
Pioneer Concrete Of Texas, Inc., 800 Gessner, Ste. 1100, 77024, pg. 1058 IT
PIPECO SERVICES, 8223 Willow Pl. S., Ste. 190, 77070, pg. 867 PV
Pipetronix Inc., 2207 Oil Center Ct., 77073, pg. 1070 IT
Piping Resources, 8011 Blankenship, 77055, pg. 162 PV
Plains Marketing & Transportation, 1600 Smith St., Ste. 1300, 77002, pg. 1308 PB
PLAINS RESOURCES INC., 1600 Smith, Ste.1500, 77002, pg. 1307 PB

PB - *U.S. Public Companies Volume*
PV - *U.S. Private Companies Volume*
IT - *International Public & Private Companies Volume*

Geographic Index-U.S.

Poe & Brown of Texas, 10700 N.W. Fwy., Ste. 100, 77092, pg. 1312 **PB**
POGO PRODUCING COMPANY, Five Greenway Plaza, Ste. 2700, 77046-0504, pg. 1312 **PB**
Pogo Producing Company, International Division, P.O. Box 2504, 77252-2504, pg. 1313 **PB**
Pogo Producing Company, Onshore Division, P.O. Box 2504, 77252-2504, pg. 1313 **PB**
Polyflex Business Unit, 4263 Dacoma, 77092-8607, pg. 1260 **PB**
Pool Company (Texas), Inc., 10375 Richmond Ave., 77042, pg. 1316 **PB**
POOL ENERGY SERVICES CO., 10375 Richmond Ave., 77042, pg. 1316 **PB**
PORT OF HOUSTON AUTHORITY, 111 East Loop N., 77029, pg. 876 **PV**
Post Acute Division, 15415 Katy Fwy., Ste. 800, 77094, pg. 1256 **PB**
Powell Electrical Mfg. Co., 8550 Mosley Dr., 77075-1180, pg. 1319 **PB**
POWELL INDUSTRIES, INC., 8550 Mosley Dr., 77075-1180, pg. 1319 **PB**
Precision Clean Piping, Inc., 9814 Whithorn Dr., pg. 722 **PB**
PRIDE INTERNATIONAL, INC., 5847 San Felipe, Ste. 3300, 77057, pg. 1324 **PB**
Pride International, Ltd., 5847 San Felipe, Ste. 3300, 77057, pg. 1325 **PB**
PRIME BANCSHARES INC., 12200 Northwest Fwy., 77092, pg. 1326 **PB**
Prime Operating Company, 2900 Wilcrest Dr., 77042, pg. 1329 **PB**
Pro Shop (Houston, TX), 1102 Fellows Rd., 77047, pg. 861 **PV**
Production Management Corporation, 1980 Post Oak Blvd., 77056, pg. 889 **PV**
Production Operators Inc., 11302 Tanner Rd., 77041, pg. 298 **PB**
Production Operators, Inc., 11302 Tanner Rd., 77041, pg. 298 **PB**
Propak Systems Inc., 16420 Park 10 Pl., Ste. 130, 77084, pg. 1071 **IT**
Protosoft Development Laboratory, 17629 El Camino Real MS 400, 77058-3051, pg. 1309 **PB**
Pulte Houston Division, 17171 Park Row Blvd., Ste. 190, 77084, pg. 1344 **PB**
QUANEX CORPORATION, 1900 W. Loop S., #1500, 77027, pg. 1349 **PB**
Quintana Environmental Services, Inc., 601 Jefferson, Ste. 3800, 77002, pg. 901 **PV**
QUINTANA PETROLEUM CORP., 601 Jefferson St., Ste. 3800, 77002, pg. 901 **PV**
Quintana Petroleum Services, 601 Jefferson, 77002, pg. 901 **PV**
R&B FALCON CORPORATION, 1900 West Loop S., Ste. 1800, 77027, pg. 1354 **PB**
RBC Realty Inc., 9753 Pine Lake Dr., 77055, pg. 483 **PB**
RDC Marine, Inc., 5450 Transco Tower, 77056-6196, pg. 1410 **PB**
Racal NCS Inc., 3624 Westchase, 77042, pg. 1083 **IT**
Radio Holland Group Head Office-Houston, 8943 Gulf Freeway, 77017, pg. 1152 **IT**
Ragland Manufacturing Company Inc., 2000 Silber Rd., 77055, pg. 895 **PB**
RANDALLS FOOD MARKETS, INC., 3663 Briar Park Dr., 77042, pg. 909 **PV**
Randalls Warehouse Corporation, 10700 Telge Rd., 77095, pg. 909 **PV**
Ranger Oil Company, 910 Travis St., Ste. 2160, 77002, pg. 1086 **IT**
Ransome/Tempil, 3511 W. 12th, 77008, pg. 37 **IT**
RAWSON-KOENIG, INC., 2301 Central Pkwy., 77092, pg. 1362 **PB**
Raytheon Environmental Services Company, 1250 W. Sam Houston Pkwy., 77042, pg. 1366 **PB**
Reading & Bates Corporation, 901 Threadneedle, Ste. 200, 77079-2902, pg. 1354 **PB**
Reading & Bates Development Co., 901 Threadneedle, Ste. 200, 77079, pg. 1354 **PB**
Reading & Bates Drilling Co., 901 Threadneedle, 77079, pg. 1354 **PB**
Reed Tool Company, 6501 Navigation, 77011, pg. 298 **PB**
RELIABILITY INCORPORATED, 16400 Park Row, 77084, pg. 1373 **PB**
Republic Beverage Company, 9835 Genard Rd., 77041, pg. 149 **PV**
Residential Service, Inc., P.O. Box 3151, 77253, pg. 264 **PB**
Reunion Energy Company, 2801 Post Oak Blvd., Ste. 400, 77056, pg. 1383 **PB**
Reunion Operating Company, 2801 Post Oak Blvd., Ste. 400, 77056, pg. 1383 **PB**
Rex Supply Company, 3715 Harrisburg Blvd., 77003, pg. 889 **PV**
Reynolds Metals Company-Houston, 10000 N. Loop E., 77029, pg. 1385 **PB**
Rheox, 16825 Northchase Dr., Ste. 1200, 77060, pg. 270 **PV**
RICE FOOD MARKETS INC., 5333 Gulfton, 77081, pg. 927 **PV**
RICE, SANGALIS, TOOLE & WILSON, 5847 San Felipe, Ste. 4350, 77057, pg. 928 **PV**
Ridgway's, Inc., 5711 Hillcroft Ave., 77036, pg. 1176 **PV**
Rig-A-Lite Co., 8500 Hanson Rd., 77075, pg. 159 **PB**
River Oaks Trust Company, 2001 Kirby, 77019, pg. 419 **PB**
RIVES CARLBERG, 2800 Post Oak Blvd., Ste. 3400, 77056-6106, pg. 934 **PV**
RIVIANA FOODS INC., 2777 Allen Pkwy., 77019-2141, pg. 1392 **PB**

Riviana International Inc., 2777 Allen Pkwy., 77019, pg. 1392 **PB**
Rockland Pipeline Company, 1000 Louisiana, Ste. 2310, 77002, pg. 562 **IT**
Rockwater Co., 333 Sam Houston Pkwy. E., Ste. 395, 77050, pg. 776 **PB**
Ross Hill Controls, 1530 Sam Houston Pkwy. N., 77043, pg. 553 **IT**
ROWAN COMPANIES, INC., 5450 Transco Tower, 2800 Post Oak Blvd., 77056-6196, pg. 1409 **PB**
RUSKA INSTRUMENT CORPORATION, 3601 Dunvale, 77063, pg. 952 **PV**
S & S (Dihall) Cogeneration, Inc., P.O. Box 1637, 77251-1637, pg. 1517 **PB**
S&S Domestic International Sales Corp., P.O. Box 1637, 77251-1637, pg. 1517 **PB**
S&S Energy Products, 2707 N. Loop W., 77008, pg. 711 **PB**
SAIC Comsystems, 17049 El Camino Real 202, 77058-2611, pg. 976 **IT**
SC Polymers Inc., 2000 Post Oak Blvd., Ste. 2450, 77056, pg. 1255 **IT**
SEI Corporation, 3040 Post Oak Blvd., Ste. 445, 77056, pg. 1417 **IT**
SGB Construction Services, Inc., 14942 Talcott, 77015, pg. 396 **IT**
SGI Integrated Graphic Systems, 14902 Sommermeyer, St. 120 77041, pg. 971 **PB**
SMC McEver Inc., 6200 Savoy Dr., Ste. 800, 77036, pg. 1717 **PB**
ST Environmental Services Corp. (II), Park 10, 16337 Park Row, 77084, pg. 1226 **PB**
STB Corporate Development, Inc., STB Corp. Devel., Inc., Ste. 3120, Nine Greenway Plaza, 77046, pg. 1317 **IT**
Sakura Bank - Houston Agency, 1100 Louisiana, Ste. 2900, 77002, pg. 1179 **IT**
Samuel Specialty Metals Inc., 5022 Ashley Ct., 77041, pg. 964 **PV**
Sandvik Rock Tools, Inc., 8760 Clay Rd., 77080, pg. 1185 **IT**
Sanifill, Inc., 2777 Allen Pkwy., Ste. 700, 77008, pg. 1686 **PB**
SANTA FE ENERGY RESOURCES, INC., 1616 S. Voss Rd., Ste. 1000, 77057, pg. 1431 **PB**
Santa Fe Offshore Construction Co., 12941 I-45 No., Ste. 833 77060, pg. 765 **PB**
Saunders Valve, Inc., 16516 Air Center Blvd., 77032, pg. 1379 **IT**
Saw Construction Corporation, One Allen Ctr., 500 Dallas St., Ste. 2800, 77002, pg. 1519 **PB**
SCANA Petroleum Resources, Inc., 1200 Smith St., Ste. 500, 77002-4308, pg. 1436 **PB**
Schlumberger Oilfield Services, 1325 S. Dairy Ashford, 77077, pg. 1439 **PB**
Schlumberger Technology Corporation, 811 Dallas Ave., 77002, pg. 1439 **PB**
Schott's Bakery, Inc., 3000 Washington Ave., 77007, pg. 658 **PV**
A. Schulman, Inc., 363 N. Sam Houston Pkwy. E., Ste. 480, 77060, pg. 1441 **PB**
Sea River Maritime, Inc., 800 Bell Street, 77002-7426, pg. 601 **PV**
Sea-3, Inc., Houston, 1111 Bagby St., Ste. 2640, 77002, pg. 1096 **PV**
Seaco Texas Properties Inc., P.O. Box 590125, 77259, pg. 1213 **IT**
SEACOR SMIT INC., 11200 Westheimer, Ste. 850, 77042, pg. 449 **PB**
SEAGULL ENERGY CORPORATION, 1001 Fannin, Ste. 1700, 77002-6714, pg. 1450 **PB**
Seagull Energy E & P, Inc., 1001 Fannin, Ste. 1700, 77002, pg. 450 **PB**
Seitel Data Corp., 50 Briar Hollow Ln. W., Seventh Fl., 77027, pg. 1454 **PB**
Seitel Gas & Energy Corp., 50 Briar Hollow Ln. W., Seventh Fl., 77027, pg. 1454 **PB**
Seitel Geophysical, Inc. dba Eagle Geophysical, Inc., 50 Briar Hollow Ln. W., Seventh Fl., 77027, pg. 1454 **PB**
SEITEL, INC., 50 Briar Hollow Ln. W. 7th Fl., 77027, pg. 1454 **PB**
Seitel International, Inc., 50 Briar Hollow Ln. W., Seventh Fl., 77027, pg. 1454 **PB**
Seitel Offshore Corp., 50 Briar Hollow Ln. W., Seventh Fl., 77027, pg. 1454 **PB**
Seneca Resources Corp., 1201 Louisiana, Ste. 400, 77002, pg. 156 **PB**
Sequent Computer Systems, Inc., Greenway Exec. Business Ctr., 11 Greenway Plaza, Ste. 1404, 77046, pg. 459 **IT**
SERV-TECH, INC., 5200 Cedar Crest Blvd., 77087, pg. 450 **PB**
SERVICE CORPORATION INTERNATIONAL, 1929 Allen Pkwy., 77019, pg. 1460 **PB**
Setpoint Inc., 14701 St. Mary's Ln., 77079, pg. 53 **IT**
Sheldon Mill, Champion International Corporation, P.O. Box 23011, 77228-3011, pg. 334 **PB**
Shell Chemical Co., One Shell Plaza, 77002, pg. 1136 **IT**
Shell Development Co., One Shell Plaza, 77252, pg. 1136 **IT**
Shell Oil Company, One Shell Plaza, 900 Louisiana, 77002, pg. 1136 **IT**
Shell Pipe Line Corp., Two Shell Plaza, 77252, pg. 1136 **IT**
Shepler's Houston South, 9103 Almeda Rd., 77054, pg. 413 **PB**
Shepler's Houston West, 2001 Brittmoore Rd., 77043, pg. 413 **PB**
Shintech Inc., Wesleyan Tower, 24 Greenway Plaza, Ste. 811, 77046, pg. 1234 **IT**
Silver Springs Nursing & Rehabilitation Center, 12350 Wood Bayou Dr., 77013, pg. 839 **PB**

Singapore Airlines Ltd., 3701 Kirby Dr., Ste. 1290, 77098, pg. 1374 **IT**
Six Flags Astroworld/Six Flags Waterworld/Six Flags Houston, 9001 Kirby Dr., 77054, pg. 1611 **PB**
Skadden, Arps, Slate, Meagher & Flom LLP, 1600 Smith St., Ste. 4460, 77002, pg. 1004 **PV**
Smith Environmental Technologies Corp., 16010 Barkers Pt. Lane, Ste. 600, 77079, pg. 1477 **PB**
Howard Smith Screen Co., P.O. Box 666, 77012, pg. 776 **PB**
SMITH INTERNATIONAL, INC., 16740 Hardy St., 77032, pg. 1478 **PB**
Smith Tool Company, Inc., 16740 Hardy St., 77032, pg. 1478 **PB**
SmithKline Beecham Labs, 8933 Interchange Dr., 77054-2507, pg. 1265 **IT**
SOCO International, Inc., 2010 N. Main, 77009, pg. 1482 **PB**
Software Interfaces Development Laboratory, 1400 Broadfield, Ste. 600, 77084, pg. 1309 **IT**
Solvay America Inc., 3333 Richmond Ave., 77098-3009, pg. 1278 **IT**
Solvay Interox America, 3333 Richmond Ave., 77098-3009, pg. 1277 **IT**
Solvay Polymers Inc., 3333 Richmond Ave., 77098-3007, pg. 1278 **IT**
Sonat Exploration Company, Four Greenway Plaza, 77046, pg. 1485 **PB**
Sonat Exploration GOM Inc., 1201 Louisiana, Ste. 3200, 77002, pg. 1485 **PB**
South Padre Land Co., 2727 Allen Pkwy., 77019, pg. 77 **PB**
Southdown Cement Group, 1200 Smith St., Suite 2400, 77002, pg. 1489 **PB**
SOUTHDOWN, INC., 1200 Smith St., Ste. 2400, 77002-4486, pg. 1488 **PB**
SOUTHERN MINERAL CORPORATION, 500 Dallas St., Ste. 2800, 77002-4708, pg. 1490 **PB**
Southern Post Company, 14340 Torrey Chase Blvd., # 360, 77014, pg. 412 **PB**
Southwest Chemical/Services, 2625 Bay Area Blvd.-Ste. 520, 77058, pg. 781 **PB**
Southwestern Bell Printing Company, 2627 N. Loop W., Ste.120, 77008, pg. 1415 **PB**
Southwestern Energy Production Co., 5151 San Felipe, Ste. 700, 77056-3608, pg. 1494 **PB**
Spar Operations and Engineering Corporation, 16915 El Camino Real, Ste. 260, 77058, pg. 1288 **PB**
Sperry-Sun Drilling Services Division, 3000 Sam Houston Pkwy. E., 77032, pg. 528 **PB**
Sphere Supply, Inc., 16643 Jacintoport Blvd., P.O. Box 96555, 77213, pg. 765 **PB**
Sprecher & Schuh N. America, 15503 W. Hardy, 77060, pg. 1397 **PB**
Spring Engineers of Houston Ltd., 9740 Tanner Rd., 77041, pg. 956 **PV**
Sprint Paranet, 1776 Yorktown, Ste. 300, 77056, pg. 1501 **PB**
STAGE STORES, INC., 10201 Main St., 77025, pg. 1028 **PV**
Stand-Cote Industrial Coatings Div., P.O. Box 87, 77001, pg. 1032 **PB**
Standard-Pacific-Texas, Inc., 15995 N. Barker's Landing, Suite 295, 77079, pg. 1504 **PB**
STANDCO INDUSTRIES, INC., 2701 Clinton Drive, 77020, pg. 1032 **PV**
Standco Oilfield Products Div., 2701 Clinton Dr., 77020, pg. 1032 **PV**
Star Furniture Company, 16666 Barker Springs Rd., 77084, pg. 221 **PB**
Steel Systems Inc., P.O. Box 40338, 77240, pg. 1146 **PB**
STERLING CHEMICALS HOLDINGS, INC., 1200 Smith St., Ste. 1900, 77002-4312, pg. 1515 **PB**
Sterling Chemicals, Inc., 1200 Smith St., Ste. 1900, 77002-4312, pg. 1515 **PB**
Sterling Electronics Corporation, 4201 Southwest Fwy., 77027, pg. 1051 **PB**
Sterling Rubber & Gasket, P.O. Box 87, 77001, pg. 1032 **PV**
Sterling Steel Company, 2001 Brittmoore Rd., 77043, pg. 412 **PB**
Stewart & Stevenson de las Americas, Inc., P.O. Box 1637, 77251-1637, pg. 1517 **PB**
Stewart & Stevenson Holdings, Inc., P.O. Box 1637, 77251-1637, pg. 1517 **PB**
Stewart & Stevenson International, Inc., P.O. Box 1637, 77251-1637, pg. 1517 **PB**
Stewart & Stevenson Overseas, Inc., P.O. Box 1637, 77251-1637, pg. 1517 **PB**
Stewart & Stevenson Realty Corporation, P.O. Box 1637, 77251-1637, pg. 1518 **PB**
STEWART & STEVENSON SERVICES, INC., 2707 N. Loop W., 77008, pg. 1515 **PB**
Stewart & Stevenson Transportation, Inc., P.O. Box 1637, 77251-1637, pg. 1518 **PB**
Stewart & Stevenson (U.K.) Limited, P.O. Box 1637, 77251-1637, pg. 1518 **PB**
Stewart & Stevenson Vehicle Services, Inc., P.O. Box 1637, 77251-1637, pg. 1518 **PB**
C. Jim Stewart & Stevenson, Inc., P.O. Box 1637, 77251-1637, pg. 1517 **PB**
STEWART INFORMATION SERVICES CORPORATION, 1980 Post Oak Blvd., 77056, pg. 1518 **PB**
Stone & Webster Oil Company, Inc., One Allen Ctr., 500 Dallas St., Ste. 2800, 77002, pg. 1519 **PB**
The Sumitomo Bank, Ltd.-Houston Agency, NationsBank Center, 700 Louisiana St., Ste. 1750, 77002, pg. 1309 **IT**
Sumitomo Corporation of America, 1000 Louisiana, Ste. 6800, 77002, pg. 1312 **IT**

PB - *U.S. Public Companies Volume*
PV - *U.S. Private Companies Volume*
IT - *International Public & Private Companies Volume*

1450

Geographic Index-U.S.

Sumitomo Metal U.S.A. Corp., 333 Clay St., Ste. 3650, 77002, pg. 1316 IT
SunAmerica Corporate Finance, 1800 W. Loop S., Ste. 1110, 77027-3211, pg. 1533 PB
Sunbelt Supply Co., 8363 Market St., 77029, pg. 847 PB
Sundowner Offshore Services, Inc., 2707 N. Loop W., Ste. 510, 77008, pg. 1149 PB
SWIFT ENERGY COMPANY, 16825 Northchase Dr., Ste. 400, 77060-6098, pg. 1543 PB
Swiftdrill, Inc., 15835 Park Ten Place Dr., 77084, pg. 146 PB
Symtronix Corporation, 10500 Westoffice Dr., Ste. 215, 77042-5326, pg. 1563 PB
Syntron, Inc., 17200 Park Row, 77084-4925, pg. 1563 PB
SYSCO CORPORATION, 1390 Enclave Pkwy., 77077-2099, pg. 1550 PB
Sysco Food Services of Houston, Inc., 535 Portwall, 77029-5316, pg. 1551 PB
T&L Omega, Inc., 5712 Yale, 77076, pg. 1222 PB
TCI International Sales Corp., Tenneco Bldg., P.O. Box 2511, 77001, pg. 1578 PB
TPC Corporation, 200 WestLake Park Blvd., Ste. 1000, 77079, pg. 1252 PB
TRI Realty, Inc., P.O. Box 2511, 1100 Milam Bldg., 77001, pg. 312 PB
TRMI Holdings Inc., 1111 Bagby St., 77002, pg. 1583 PB
Takumei Kumiai Holdings, Inc., P.O. Box 1637, 77251-1637, pg. 1518 PB
TAUBER OIL COMPANY, 55 Waugh Dr., Ste. 700, 77007, pg. 1069 PV
Taywood Energy Services Inc., One Allen Centre, 77024, pg. 1359 IT
TECH-SYM CORPORATION, 10500 Westoffice Dr., Ste. 200, 77042-5391, pg. 1563 PB
Tejas Gas Corporation, 1301 McKinney, Suite 700, 77010-9600, pg. 1136 IT
Tejas Gas Systems, Inc., 1301 McKinney St., Ste. 700, 77010, pg. 1136 IT
Tejas-Gulf Corp., 1301 McKinney, Ste. 700, 77010, pg. 1136 IT
Tejas Hydrocarbons Co., 1301 McKinney St., Ste. 700, 77010, pg. 1136 IT
TeleCheck Services, Inc., 5251 Westheimer, 77056, pg. 631 PB
Telxon-Products Division, 6333 Rothway St., 77040, pg. 1573 PB
10 Minute Oil Change, Pennzoil Place, 77252, pg. 1272 PB
Tenneco Alaska, Inc., Tenneco Bldg., P.O. Box 2511, 77001, pg. 1578 PB
Tenneco Asset Management Co., P.O. Box 2511, 77001, pg. 1578 PB
Tenneco Asset Planning Co., P.O. Box 2511, 77001, pg. 1578 PB
Tenneco China Trade Inc., 1010 Milam St., pg. 1578 PB
Tenneco Coal Co., 1100 Milam Bldg., P.O. Box 2511, 77001, pg. 1579 PB
Tenneco Coal Conversion Co., 1100 Milam Bldg., P.O. Box 2511, 77001, pg. 1579 PB
Tenneco Coal Gasification Co., 1100 Milam Bldg., P.O. Box 2511, 77001, pg. 1579 PB
Tenneco Communications Corportion, 1100 Milam St., 77002, pg. 1578 PB
Tenneco Corporation, Tenneco Bldg., P.O. Box 2511, 77001, pg. 1578 PB
Tenneco Credit Corp., P.O. Box 2511, 77001, pg. 1578 PB
Tenneco Domestic International Sales Corp., Tenneco Bldg., P.O. Box 2511, 77001, pg. 1578 PB
Tenneco Financial Services, Inc., P.O. Box 2511, Two Shell Plaza, Ste. 2000, 77001, pg. 1578 PB
Tenneco Foreign Sales Corporation, 1010 Milam St., pg. 1578 PB
Tenneco Gas Marketing Company, P.O. Box 2511, 77001, pg. 1579 PB
Tenneco Gas Pipeline Group, Tenneco Bldg., P.O. Box 2511, 77001, pg. 1578 PB
Tenneco Gas Processing Company, 1010 Milam St., pg. 1579 PB
Tenneco Gas Supply Corp., 1010 Milam St., pg. 1579 PB
Tenneco Insurance Ventures, P.O. Box 2511, Two Shell Plaza, Ste. 2000, 77001, pg. 1578 PB
Tenneco International Inc., Tenneco Bldg., P.O. Box 2511, 77001, pg. 1578 PB
Tenneco International N.V., Tenneco Bldg., P.O. Box 2511, 77001, pg. 1578 PB
Tenneco Management Company, 1010 Milam St., 77002, pg. 1578 PB
Tenneco Minerals Co. of Australia Inc., P.O. Box 2511, 77001, pg. 1579 PB
Tenneco Minerals Co.-Nevada, 1010 Milam St., pg. 1579 PB
Tenneco Norge, Inc., Tenneco Bldg., P.O. Box 2511, 77001, pg. 1578 PB
Tenneco Ocean Metals Development Corp., Tenneco Bldg., P.O. Box 2511, 77001, pg. 1578 PB
Tenneco Phosphate, Inc., Tenneco Bldg., P.O. Box 2511, 77001, pg. 1578 PB
Tenneco Realty, Inc., P.O. Box 2511, 77252, pg. 1578 PB
Tenneco SNG, Inc., Tenneco Bldg., P.O. Box 2511, 77001, pg. 1579 PB
Tenneco Sudan, Inc., Tenneco Bldg., P.O. Box 2511, 77001, pg. 1578 PB
Tenneco Synfuels Co., Tenneco Bldg., P.O. Box 2511, 77001, pg. 1578 PB
Tenneco Uranium, Inc., Tenneco Bldg., P.O. Box 2511, 77001, pg. 1579 PB
Tenneco Ventures,Inc., P.O. Box 2511, 77001, pg. 1578 PB
Tennessee Argentina, S.A., Tenneco Bldg., P.O. Box 2511, 77001, pg. 1578 PB
Tennessee Gas Marketing Company, 1010 Milam St., pg. 1579 PB
Tennessee Gas Transmission Co., Tenneco Bldg., P.O. Box 2511, 77001, pg. 567 PB
Tennessee/New England Pipeline Company, pg. 1579 PB
Tennessee Trailblazer Gas Co., Tenneco Bldg., P.O. Box 2511, 77001, pg. 567 PB
TEPPCO Partners L.P., 2929 Allen Pkwy., 77019, pg. 534 PB
Tesoro Marine Services, 9426 Telephone Rd., 77075, pg. 1582 PB
Tetra Tech NUS, Inc., 4100 Clinton Dr., 77020-6299, pg. 1582 PB
Texas Auto Auction Services, Inc., 14450 W. Rd., 77041, pg. 283 PV
Texas Bank N.A., 2010 N. Main St., 77009, pg. 626 PB
Texas Bank N.A., 2929 Allen Pkwy., 77019, pg. 626 PB
Texas Cold Finished Steel, Inc., 1300 Baker, 77002, pg. 412 PB
Texas Commerce Bank, 712 Main St., 77002, pg. 339 PB
Texas Commerce Bank, N.A., 712 Main St., 77252, pg. 339 PB
Texas Eastern Products Pipeline Company, L.P., 1919 Allen Pkwy., 77252-2521, pg. 535 PB
Texas Eastern Transmission Corp., 5400 Westheimer Ct., 77252, pg. 535 PB
Texas First Securities Corp., 1360 Post Oak Blvd., 77055, pg. 1244 PB
Texas Hobby Auto Auction, 800 Brisbane Rd., 77061, pg. 283 PV
Texas Instruments Consulting, 3355 W. Alabama St. Ste. 1100, 77098-1718, pg. 1586 PB
Texas Instruments Facilities, Semiconductor, P.O. Box 1443, 77251-1443, pg. 1586 PB
Texas Iron Works Inc., 12320 S. Main St., 77235, pg. 845 PV
Texas Metal Fabricating, 7000 Old Kathy Rd., 77024, pg. 1639 PB
TEXAS MICRO, INC., 5959 Corporate Dr., Ste. 1600, 77036, pg. 1586 PB
Texas Microsystems Inc., 5959 Corporate Dr., Ste. 1600, 77036, pg. 1586 PB
Texas-New Mexico Pipe Line Co., P.O. Box 52332, 77052, pg. 1584 PB
TEXAS PETRO CHEMICALS, 8600 Park Place, 77017, pg. 1078 PV
Texas Tank Ship Agency, Inc., Coastal Tower, Nine Greenway Plaza, 77046-0995, pg. 390 PB
Thermon Heat Tracing Services, Inc. I, 2810 Mowery Rd., 77045, pg. 1080 PV
CHARLIE THOMAS DEALERSHIPS, 12215 Gulf Fwy., 77034, pg. 1082 PV
TIDEL TECHNOLOGIES, INC., 5847 San Felipe, Ste. 900, 77057, pg. 1608 PB
Tidewater Compression Service, Inc., P.O. Box 40009, 77240, pg. 1608 PB
Tokheim Investment Corp., 1080 W. San Houston Pkwy. North Ste. 113, 77043, pg. 1620 PB
Torch Energy Advisors, Incorporated, 1221 Lamar, Ste. 1600, 77010-3039, pg. 1623 PB
Torch Energy Corp., 1221 Lamar, Ste. 1600, 77027, pg. 1623 PB
Torch Operating Co., 1300 Main St., Suite 1520, 77027, pg. 1623 PB
Toromont Process Systems Inc., Northwoods Industrial Park, 12227-D FM529, 77041, pg. 1401 IT
Toronto-Dominion (Texas), Inc., 909 Fannin St., Suite 1700, 77010, pg. 1401 IT
Toshiba International Corp. Industrial Div., 13131 W. Little York Rd., 77041, pg. 1405 IT
TradeStar Investments, Inc., 5599 San Felipe, Ste. 1400, 77056, pg. 647 PB
TRAILER WHEEL & FRAME COMPANY, 8222 North Fwy., 77037, pg. 1095 PV
Trans-American Steamship Agency, 5005 Mitchelldale St., 77092-7235, pg. 1418 IT
Trans-Ohio Pipeline Co., P.O. Box 2521, 77252, pg. 535 PB
TRANSAMERICAN NATURAL GAS CORPORATION, 1300 E. North Belt, Ste. 310, 77032-2949, pg. 1096 PV
TransCanada Energy USA Inc., 4 Greenspoint Plaza, 16945 Northcase Drive, 77060, pg. 1417 IT
Transcontinental Gas Pipe Line Corp., 2800 Post Oak Blvd., 77056, pg. 1769 PB
TRANSOCEAN OFFSHORE, INC., Four Greenway Plaza, 77046, pg. 1631 PB
Transwestern Pipeline Co., P.O. Box 1188, 77251, pg. 585 PB
Trendmaker Homes Inc., 333 Cypress Run, Ste. 300, 77094, pg. 1764 PB
TRIBBLE & STEPHENS CO., 8580 Katy Hwy., Ste. 320, 77024-1800, pg. 1102 PV
Triton Engineering Services Company, 1201 Dairy Ashford, Ste. 100, 77079, pg. 1186 PB
Trunkline Gas Co., 5400 Westheimer Ct., 77056, pg. 534 PB
Trunkline LNG Co., 5400 Westheimer Ct., 77056, pg. 535 PB
TUBOSCOPE INCORPORATED, 2835 Holmes Rd., 77051, pg. 1643 PB
TUBULAR SERVICES, INC., 1010 McCarty Dr., 77029, pg. 1108 PV
Turner Construction Co., 2900 Weslayan Rd., P.O. Box 27927, 77027, pg. 1645 PB
UCISCO Inc., pg. 1320 PB
U.N. Alloy Steel Div., 9021 Spikewood, 77078, pg. 1001 IT
U.N.A. Corp., 9021 Spikewood, 77078, pg. 1001 IT
Uncle Ben's, Inc., 5721 Harvey Wilson Dr., 77020, pg. 707 PV
Unichem, 14505 Torrey Chase, Ste. 201, pg. 161 PB
Union Bank of Switzerland, 1100 Louisiana Plaza, Ste. 4500, 77002, pg. 1440 IT
UNION TEXAS PETROLEUM HOLDINGS, 1330 Post Oak Blvd., 77252, pg. 1669 PB
Union-Transport Corporation-Houston Office, 14130 Chrisman St., 77039, pg. 1119 PV
Unisource, 4414 Hollister St., 77040, pg. 1671 PB
US Ecology, Inc., c/o American Ecology Corp., 5333 Westheimer, Ste. 1000, 77056-5407, pg. 71 PB
U.S. HOME CORPORATION, 1800 W. Loop S., 77252, pg. 1682 PB
USA WASTE SERVICES, INC., 1001 Fannin St., Ste. 4000, 77002, pg. 1686 PB
U.S. Pipeline, Inc., 363 N. Sam Houston Pkwy. E., Ste. 300, 77060, pg. 31 IT
UNITED WASTE SYSTEMS, INC., First City Tower, 1001 Fannin, Ste. 4000, 77002, pg. 1691 PB
Universal Surety of America, 950 Echo Ln., Ste. 250, 77024, pg. 303 PB
Unoc Equipment & Supply L.L.C., 5555 San Felipe, 77056, pg. 316 PB
Uson Corporation, 5215 Hollister, 77040, pg. 1405 PB
VALLEN CORPORATION, 13333 Northwest Fwy., 77040-6086, pg. 1705 PB
Vallen Safety Supply Company, P.O. Box 3587, 77253, pg. 1705 PB
Valley Gas Transmission, Inc., 1301 McKinney St., Ste. 700, 77010, pg. 1136 IT
Van Leer Flexibles, Inc., 9505 Bamboo Rd., 77041, pg. 1146 IT
Van Leeuwen Pipe & Tube Corp., 15333 Hempstead Road, 77040, pg. 1449 IT
VANGUARD ENERGY CORP., 1111 North Loop W., Ste. 1100, 77008, pg. 1133 PV
Varco Best Products, 12950 W. Little York Rd., 77041, pg. 1709 PB
Varco BJ Drilling Systems, 12950 W. Little York Rd., 77041, pg. 1709 PB
The Variable Annuity Life Insurance Co., 2929 Allen Pkwy., 77019, pg. 76 PB
VenGas Marketing Company, P.O. Box 4263, 77210, pg. 1519 PB
VenGas Pipeline Company, P.O. Box 4263, 77210, pg. 1519 PB
Venture Distribution Company, P.O. Box 4263, 77210, pg. 1519 PB
Venture Pipeline Company, P.O. Box 4263, 77210, pg. 1519 PB
Venture Processing Company, P.O. Box 4263, 77210, pg. 1519 PB
Venture Resources, Inc., P.O. Box 4263, 77210, pg. 1519 PB
VERITAS DGC INC., 3701 Kirby Dr., Ste., 112, 77098, pg. 1136 PV
Veritas DGC Inc, 3701 Kirby Dr., 77098, pg. 1136 PV
Veritas DGC INC, 3701 Kirby Dr., 77098, pg. 1137 PV
Virginia Indonesia Company, One Houston Center, 1221 McKinney Street, 77010, pg. 804 IT
VISIBLE CHANGES, 1303 Campbell Rd., 77055, pg. 1141 PV
Vista Life Insurance Company of Texas, 400 E.N. Belt Dr., 77060, pg. 664 PB
Voest-Alpine Trading U.S.A. Corp., 363 N. Belt, Ste. 1580, 77060, pg. 1471 IT
WFI INTERNATIONAL, INC., 4407 Haygood, 77022, pg. 1144 PV
WPI Waste Carriers, Inc., c/o American Ecology Corp., 5333 Westheimer, Ste. 1000, 77058-5407, pg. 71 PB
Wainoco Oil & Gas Company, 100000 Memorial Dr., Ste. 600, 77024-3411, pg. 1732 PB
WAINOCO OIL CORPORATION, 10000 Memorial Dr., Ste. 600, 77024-3411, pg. 1732 PB
Wainoco Resources, Inc., 10000 memorial Dr., 77024-3411, pg. 1732 PB
Wall Street Deli, Inc., 5730 Teague Rd., 77041, pg. 1734 PB
Wallpapers-To-Go, 16825 N. Chase, #900, 77060-4586, pg. 1175 PV
THE WALWORTH COMPANY USA, 8383 Commerce Pk. Dr., Ste. 608, 77036-7425, pg. 1149 PV
Warren Electric Company, 2929 McKinney, 77003, pg. 1151 PV
WARREN ELECTRIC GROUP, 2929 McKinney, 77003, pg. 1151 PV
Warren Electric Telecommunications-Utilities Company, 1005 Ennis, 77003, pg. 1151 PV
Warren Petroleum Company, 1000 Louisiana, Ste. 5800, 77002, pg. 1146 PB
Watts Automatic Control Valves, Inc., 8550 Hansen Rd., 77075, pg. 1747 PB
Watts Regulator/Watts ACV, 8550 Hansen, 77075-1006, pg. 1746 PB
Waukesha-Pearce Industries, 12320 S. Main St., 77235, pg. 845 PV
Weatherford, 11909 Spencer Rd. (FM 529), 77041-3011, pg. 1749 PB
Weatherford, 11909 Spencer Rd., (FM 529), 77041-3011, pg. 1749 PB
WEATHERFORD ENTERRA INCORPORATED, 1360 Post Oak Blvd., Ste. 1000, 77056, pg. 1749 PB
Weatherford U.S., Inc., 515 Post Oak Blvd., 77027, pg. 1749 PB
Weatherford U.S., Inc., 1360 Post Oak Blvd., Ste. 1000, 77056, pg. 1749 PB
WEBB, MURRAY & ASSOCIATES, 2525 Bay Area Blvd., 77058, pg. 1157 PV
WEDGE ENERGY GROUP INC., 1415 Louisiana St., 30th Fl., 77002, pg. 1158 PV
DAVID WEEKLEY HOMES, 1300 Post Oak Blvd., Ste. 1000, 77056, pg. 1158 PV

PB - *U.S. Public Companies Volume*
PV - *U.S. Private Companies Volume*
IT - *International Public & Private Companies Volume*

Geographic Index-U.S.

WEINERS STORES, INC., 6005 Westview, 77055, pg. 1160 **PV**
WEINGARTEN REALTY INVESTORS, 2600 Citadel Plaza Dr., Ste. 300, 77008, pg. 1751 **PB**
Wellhead Equipment Division, 1777 W. Gears Rd., 77067, pg. 605 **PB**
Wellnite Services, pg. 1320 **PB**
The Westcap Corporation, 1301 Fannin St., 23rd Fl., 77002, pg. 1161 **PB**
WESTERN ATLAS INC., 10205 Westheimer Rd., 77042, pg. 1757 **PB**
Western Atlas International, Inc., 10205 Westheimer, 77042, pg. 1757 **PB**
Western Atlas Logging Services, 10205 Westheimer Rd., 77042-4299, pg. 1757 **PB**
Western Atlas Software, 10205 Westheimer, 77042, pg. 1004 **PB**
Western E & P Services, 10205 Westheimer Rd., 77042-4299, pg. 1757 **PB**
Western Geophysical, 10001 Richmond Ave., 77042-4299, pg. 1757 **PB**
Western Indemnity Insurance Company, 820 Gessnor, Ste. 1200, 77024-4259, pg. 685 **PB**
Western International Media Corporation, 11200 Westheimer, Ste. 520, 77042, pg. 1167 **PV**
Western National Corporation, 5555 San Felipe, Ste. 900, 77056, pg. 76 **PB**
Western National Life Insurance Co., 5555 San Felipe, 77056, pg. 76 **PB**
Western Star Underwriters, Inc., 8275 El Rio St., Ste. 100, 77054, pg. 667 **PB**
Wetmore & Company, 1645 W. Sam Houston Pkwy., N., 77043, pg. 1736 **PB**
White Star Steel, 2200 Harbor Blvd., 77020, pg. 775 **PV**
Wholesome Dairy, 2025 Herman Dr., 77004, pg. 158 **PV**
WICKS 'N STICKS, LTD, 16825 N. Chase, #900, 77060, pg. 1175 **PV**
Williams Brothers Construction, 3800 Milam S.W. Fwy., 77006-5159, pg. 198 **PB**
Williams Telecommunications Systems, Inc., 2800 Post Oak Blvd., Level 25, 77056, pg. 1769 **PB**
Willis Corroon Aerospace-Southwest Region, P.O. Box 27408, One Riverway, Ste. 900, 77056, pg. 1505 **IT**
Willis Corroon Corp. of Texas, One Riverway, Ste. 900, 77056, pg. 1507 **IT**
Willis Corroon Marine & Energy, One Riverway, Ste. 900, 77056, pg. 1508 **IT**
WILSON INDUSTRIES INC., 1301 Conti St., 77002, pg. 1181 **PV**
WINDSOR QUALITY FOOD CO., LTD., 3355 W. Alabama, Ste. 730, 77098, pg. 112 **PV**
Winter Haven, 6534 Stuebner-Airline Rd., 77091, pg. 839 **PB**
Wolf's Head Oil Company, P.O. Box 2967, 77002-2967, pg. 1273 **PB**
WOOD GROUP PRESSURE CONTROL, 1441 Park Ten Blvd., 77084, pg. 1775 **PB**
Woodlands Millwork I, Ltd., 5401 Lacondale St., 77023, pg. 1067 **PB**
Woodward-Clyde, One Northwind Plaza, 7600 W. Tidwell, Ste. 400, 77040, pg. 1656 **PB**
World Fuel Services, Inc., 15333 JFK Blvd., Ste. 528, 77032, pg. 906 **PB**
Wyatt Field Service Co., P.O. Box 3052, 77253, pg. 801 **PV**
Wyle Electronics-Houston, 2901 S. Wilcrest, Ste. 120, 77042, pg. 1457 **IT**
Wyman-Gordon Forgings Inc, 10825 Telge Rd., 77095-5038, pg. 1782 **PB**
Wyman-Gordon Forgings, Inc., 10825 Telge Rd., 77095, pg. 1782 **PB**
Xerox Research, 5151 San Felipe St., 77056-3607, pg. 1784 **PB**
YRJ Corporation, 5711 Hillcroft, 77036, pg. 1176 **PV**
Yokohama Tire Corp., 9455 W. Winghoot, 77041, pg. 1521 **IT**
Bernard Johnson Young Inc., 3000 Wilcrest, 2nd Fl., 77042, pg. 136 **PV**
ZAPATA CORPORATION, 1717 St. James Pl. # 550, 77056, pg. 1789 **PB**
Zenith Media Services, Inc., Three River Way, Ste. 1100, 77056, pg. 1204 **PV**
Zeolyst International, 16825 Northchase Dr., 77060-6029, pg. 827 **PV**

Howe

OLD AMERICA STORES, 811 N. Collins Fwy. 75 N., 75459, pg. 1215 **PB**

Humble

Daher Golden Eagle, 120 Standifer Drive, 77338, pg. 749 **PB**
GOLDEN EAGLE GROUP, INC., 120 Standifer Dr., 77338, pg. 749 **PB**
Hydril Rubber Opers., 18000 E. Tex Frwy., 77396, pg. 551 **PV**
Zimmermann & Jansen Inc., 620 N. Houston Ave., 77347, pg. 1528 **IT**

Hurst

Bell, 600 E. Hurst Blvd., 76053-8030, pg. 115 **IT**
Bell Helicopter Textron, 600 E. Hurst Blvd., 76053, pg. 1588 **IT**
Boyles Galvanizing Co., 305 N.E. Loop 820, 76053, pg. 960 **PB**
Hewlett-Packard Company, 1550 Norwood Dr., Ste. 303, 76054, pg. 815 **PB**

Ingleside

Aker Gulf Marine, FM 1089, P.O. Box C, 78362, pg. 42 **IT**
Peterson Builders, Inc.-Ingleside Div., FM-1069, 78362, pg. 857 **PV**

Irving

ALIC, Incorporated, 600 E. Las Colinas Blvd., Ste. 640, 75015, pg. 364 **PB**
AMP Inc. Lytel Division, 1231 Greenway Dr. Ste. 450, 75038-2528, pg. 8 **PB**
Abloy Security Inc., 6015 Commerce Dr., Ste. 450, 75063, pg. 18 **PB**
Ackerman McQueen, Inc., 600 Commerce Tower, 545 E. John Carpenter Frwy., 75062, pg. 13 **PB**
Advanced Telemarketing Corp., 8001 Bent Branch Dr., 75063-6024, pg. 11 **PB**
Allen & Hoshall, 4545 Fuller Dr., Ste. 326, 75038, pg. 36 **PV**
Amatron, 2727 Chemsearch Blvd., 75062, pg. 1145 **PB**
American Allsafe Co., 2727 Chemsearch Blvd., 75062, pg. 1145 **PB**
America's Beverage Co., 1331 E. Airport Frwy., 75062, pg. 967 **PB**
Ancon Insurance Company, Inc., 225 E. John W. Carpenter Frwy., 75062-2298, pg. 601 **PB**
Atrium Companies, Inc., 2100 Union Bower Rd., 75061-6957, pg. 98 **PB**
Bankers Standard Fire & Marine Company, 600 E. Las Colinas Blvd., 75039, pg. 365 **PB**
Bankston Nissan in Irving, Inc., 1500 East Airport Fwy., 75062, pg. 1379 **PB**
Boeing Aerospace & Electronics, Irving, 3131 Story Rd., W., 75038, pg. 240 **PB**
Boeing Electronics, Inc., P.O. Box 2707, 75061, pg. 240 **PB**
Brink's Home Security, Inc., 18880 Esters Blvd., 75063, pg. 1305 **PB**
CMI Lloyds, 1200 Walnut Hill Ln., 75062, pg. 348 **PB**
Caltex Petroleum Corporation, 125 E. John Carpenter Fwy., 75062-2794, pg. 348 **PB**
Caltex Services Corp., 125 E. John Carpenter Fwy., 75062-2238, pg. 348 **PB**
Caraloe, Inc., P.O. Box 168128, 75038, pg. 309 **PB**
CARRINGTON LABORATORIES, INC., 2001 Walnut Hill Ln., 75038, pg. 309 **PB**
Central Sprinkler Company, 1780 Hurd Drive, 75038, pg. 327 **PB**
Certified Labs, 2727 Chemsearch Blvd., 75062, pg. 1145 **PB**
CHANCELLOR MEDIA CORPORATION, 433 E. Las Colinas Blvd., Ste. 1130, 75039, pg. 335 **PB**
Cigna Dental Health of Texas, Inc., 600 E. Las Colinas Blvd., Ste. 1000, 75039, pg. 358 **PB**
Cigna Healthcare of Texas, Inc., 600 E. Las Colinas Blvd., Ste. 1100, 75039, pg. 360 **PB**
Cigna Insurance Company of Texas, 600 E. Las Colinas Blvd., 75039, pg. 365 **PB**
Cigna Lloyds Insurance Company, 600 E. Las Colinas Blvd., 75039, pg. 365 **PB**
Claricom, 8101 Ridgepoint Dr., 75063, pg. 111 **PV**
Coast to Coast Corporation, 600 E. Las Colinas, Ste. 650, 75039, pg. 306 **PB**
Cognos Corp.-Dallas Sales Office, 222 W. Las Colinas Blvd., Ste. 1450, 75039-5429, pg. 306 **IT**
COLORTYME, INC., 1231 Greenway Dr., Ste. 900, 75038, pg. 255 **PV**
Communications Software Division, 5215 N. O'Connor Blvd., Ste. 1500, 75039, pg. 1516 **PB**
Cott Corporation - South Central Region, 1425 Greenway Drive, Suite 380, 75038, pg. 337 **IT**
Current Technology, Inc., 3001 N. Story, 75038, pg. 480 **PB**
DALLAS PETERBILT, INC., 515 N. Loop 12, 75061, pg. 309 **PB**
DALLAS STARS, 211 Cowboys Pkwy., 75063, pg. 309 **PV**
DARLING INTERNATIONAL, INC, 251 O'Connor Ridge Blvd., Ste. 300, 75038, pg. 484 **PB**
DeVRY Institute of Technology, 4801 Regent Blvd., 75063, pg. 504 **PB**
Dobbins Jewlers Inc., 901 W. Walnut Hill Ln., 75038, pg. 1789 **PB**
Dyna Systems, 2727 Chemsearch Blvd., 75062, pg. 1145 **PB**
Exxon Asset Management Company, 225 E. John W. Carpenter Freeway, 75062-2298, pg. 601 **PB**
EXXON CORPORATION, 5959 Las Calinas Blvd., 75039-2298, pg. 601 **PB**
F.P.A., INC., 1000 E. Airport Frwy., 75062, pg. 389 **PV**
First American Real Estate Tax Service, Inc., 1400 Corporate Dr., pg. 625 **PB**
First American Tax Valuation, 5615 Highpoint Dr., 75038, pg. 625 **PB**
First Gibralter Bank, 1925 W. John Carpenter Fwy., 75063, pg. 181 **PB**
Flow-Quip Texas, Inc., Union Bower Business Park, 400 Union Bower Ct., Ste. 416, 75061, pg. 162 **PB**
FootAction USA, 7880 Bent Branch Dr., Ste. 100, 75063, pg. 661 **PB**
Fritz Air Freight, 125 E. John Carpenter Fwy. 900, 75062, pg. 683 **PB**
GTE California Incorporated, 600 Hidden Ridge, 75038, pg. 697 **PB**
GTE Hawaiian Telephone Company Incorporated, 600 Hidden Ridge, 75038, pg. 697 **PB**
GTE North Incorporated, HQE04B12, 600 Hidden Ridge, 75038, pg. 696 **PB**
GTE Northwest Incorporated, 600 Hidden Ridge, 75038, pg. 697 **PB**
GTE South Incorporated, HQE04B12, 600 Hidden Ridge, 75038, pg. 697 **PB**
GTE Southwest Incorporated, 600 Hidden Ridge, 75038, pg. 697 **PB**
GTE Supply, 5615 High Point Dr., 75038, pg. 697 **PB**
J. Gordon Gaines of Texas, Inc., 511 E. John W. Carpenter Frwy., Ste 310, 75062, pg. 1623 **PB**
Global Moving & Storage, Inc., 3151 E. Carpenter Frwy., 75062, pg. 458 **PV**
Gulf Insurance Company, 4800 Fuller Dr., 75038, pg. 1633 **PB**
HD VEST FINANCIAL SERVICES, 6333 N. State Hwy. 161, 4th Fl., 75038, pg. 770 **PB**
HARKEN ENERGY CORPORATION, 5605 N. MacArthur Blvd., Ste. 400, 75038, pg. 785 **PB**
Harmon Publishing, 415 E. Airport Fwy., 75062, pg. 1443 **IT**
Hewlett-Packard Company, 3301 W. Royal Ln., 75063, pg. 815 **PB**
Hitachi Semiconductor (America), Inc., 1505 Walnut Hill Lane, 75016, pg. 622 **IT**
IMCO Management Partnership L.P., Central Tower, Williams Sq., 5215 N. O'Connor Blvd., Ste. 940, 75039, pg. 871 **PB**
INA County Mutual Insurance Company, 600 E. Las Colinas Blvd., Ste. 650, 75039, pg. 366 **PB**
IMCO RECYCLING INC., Central Tower at Williams Sq., 5215 N. O'Connor Blvd., Ste. 940, 75039, pg. 870 **PB**
IRVING CONVENTION & VISITORS BUREAU, 3333 N. MacArthur, Ste. 200, 75062, pg. 575 **PB**
JHC Holding Corp., 901 W. Walnut Hill Ln., 75038, pg. 1789 **PB**
Jewel Recovery, LP, 901 W. Walnut Hill Ln., 75038, pg. 1789 **PB**
Jeweler's Financial Service, Inc., 901 W. Walnut Hill Ln., 75038, pg. 1789 **PB**
Kernite, 2727 Chemsearch Blvd., 75062, pg. 1145 **PB**
Kintetsu Intermodal Inc., 8732 W. Royal Ln., 75063, pg. 735 **IT**
Kintetsu World Express Inc., 8732 W. Royal Ln., 75063, pg. 735 **IT**
Kumagai International USA Corporation, 122 W. Capenter Fwy., 75039, pg. 764 **IT**
Las Colinas Inn & Conference Center, 3501 N. MacArthur Blvd., Ste. 416, 75062, pg. 502 **IT**
Lone Star Container Sales Corp., 700 N. Wildwood Dr., 75017, pg. 674 **PV**
LONE STAR CORRUGATED CONTAINER CORPORATION, 700 N. Wildwood Dr., 75017, pg. 674 **PV**
LubraSystems, 2727 Chemsearch Blvd., 75062, pg. 1022 **PB**
THE M/A/R/C GROUP, 7850 N. Belt Line Rd., 75063, pg. 1022 **PB**
M/A/R/C Marketing and Research Counselors, Inc., 7850 N. Belt Line Rd., 75060, pg. 1023 **PB**
Mantek, 2727 Chemsearch Blvd., 75062, pg. 1145 **PB**
DAVID MCDAVID AUTO DEALERSHIP, 3600 W. Airport Fwy., 75062, pg. 721 **PV**
Memorex Telex Corp., 545 E. John Carpenter Fwy., 75062, pg. 857 **IT**
MICHAELS STORES, INC., 8000 Bent Branch Dr., 75063, pg. 1104 **PB**
Mitsui & Co. (U.S.A.), Inc., 600 E. Las Colinas Blvd., Ste. 1212, 75039, pg. 879 **IT**
Mitsumi Electronics Corp., 6210 N. Beltline Rd., Ste.170, 75063, pg. 884 **IT**
Mohawk Laboratories Div., 2727 Chemsearch Blvd., 75062, pg. 1145 **PB**
NCH CORPORATION, 2727 Chemsearch Blvd., 75062, pg. 1145 **PB**
NCS Regional Resource Center, 8304 Esters Blvd., Ste. 860, 75063-2234, pg. 1155 **PB**
National Chemsearch, 2727 Chemsearch Blvd., 75062, pg. 1145 **PB**
National Group Marketing Corp., 5005 Royal Lane, 75063, pg. 433 **PB**
NewsEdge Corp., 320 Decker Dr., Ste. 100, 75062, pg. 1180 **PB**
Nippon Oil (U.S.A.) Limited - Dallas Office, Caltex House, Ste. 1020A, 125 E. John Carpenter Fwy., 75062, pg. 937 **IT**
Nokia Inc., 2300 Valley View Ln., Ste. 100, 75062, pg. 952 **IT**
Nokia Investor Relations/USA, 2300 Valley View Ln., Ste. 100, 75062, pg. 952 **IT**
North Central Texas Independant Practice Association, P.A., 600 E. Colinas Blvd., Ste. 1100, 75039, pg. 360 **PB**
Omni Hotels, 420 Decker Dr., 75062, pg. 1065 **PV**
PharMerica-Regional Office, 9901 E. Valley Ranch Pkwy., 75063, pg. 1286 **PB**
PIONEER NATURAL RESOURCES CO., 1400 Williams Sq. W., 5205 N. O'Connor Blvd., 75039, pg. 1299 **PB**
Production Oil Tools, 1425 Greenway Dr., 75038, pg. 547 **PB**
Pulte Dallas Division, 1431 Greenway Dr. Ste. 700, 75038, pg. 1344 **PB**
QUAKER STATE CORPORATION, 225 E. John Carpenter Fwy., 75062, pg. 1348 **PB**
RP alpha/Dallas, Crestwood Ctr., Ste. 2275, 1200 Walnut Hill Ln., 75038, pg. 950 **PV**
SHOWBIZ PIZZA TIME, INC., 4441 W. Airport Fwy., 75062, pg. 1468 **PB**
Siplast Inc., Xerox Centre, 222 W. Colinas Blvd., 75039, pg. 659 **IT**
A.O. Smith Water Products Company, 5605 N. MacArthur Blvd., Ste. 360, 75038, pg. 1477 **PB**

PB - *U.S. Public Companies Volume*
PV - *U.S. Private Companies Volume*
IT - *International Public & Private Companies Volume*

Geographic Index-U.S.

Southwestern Regional Office, P.O. Box 152010, 1200 Walnut Hill Lane, 75015, pg. 224 **PV**

TBWA Chiat/Day Dallas, 251 O'connor Ridge, Ste. 100, 75038, pg. 1062 **PV**

TRT HOLDINGS INC., 420 Decker Dr., 75062, pg. 1065 **PV**

Tampella Power Corp., Williams Sq., Ste. 200, 5215 N. O'Connor, 75039, pg. 1354 **IT**

Targetbase Marketing, 7850 N. Beltline Rd., 75060, pg. 1023 **PB**

Targetbase Marketing International, 7850 N. Betline Rd., 75060, pg. 1023 **PB**

Temerlin McClain, 201 E. Carpenter Fwy., 75062, pg. 1642 **PB**

Tri-Gas Inc., 4545 Fuller Dr., Ste. 200, 75038, pg. 939 **IT**

Tucker-Rocky Distributing, 1775 Hurd Dr., 75038, pg. 639 **PV**

Union Standard Insurance Company, 122 W. Carpenter Fwy., 75039-2180, pg. 216 **PB**

WCM Co., 2727 Chemsearch Blvd., 75062, pg. 1145 **PB**

Western Interactive Media, 4425 W. Airport Fwy., Ste. 230, 75062, pg. 1166 **PV**

Westinghouse Residential Security Systems, 4221 W. John Carpenter Fwy., 75063, pg. 273 **PB**

X-Ergon, 2727 Chemsearch Blvd., 75062, pg. 1145 **PB**

ZHCL Corp., 901 W. Walnut Hill Ln., 75038, pg. 1789 **PB**

Zale Acquisition Corp., 901 W. Walnut Hill Ln., 75038, pg. 1789 **PB**

Zale Corp., 901 W. Walnut Hill Ln., 75038, pg. 1789 **PB**

ZALE CORPORATION, 901 W. Walnut Hill Ln., 75038-1003, pg. 1789 **PB**

Zale Delaware, Inc., 901 W. Walnut Hill Ln., 75038, pg. 1789 **PB**

Zale Holding Co., 901 W. Walnut Hill Ln., 75038, pg. 1789 **PB**

Zale Life Insurance Co., 901 W. Walnut Hill Ln., 75038, pg. 1789 **PB**

Zale Puerto Rico Inc., 901 W. Walnut Hill Ln., 75038, pg. 1789 **PB**

Jasper

Jasper News-Boy, P.O. Box 1419, 302 N. Wheeler, 75951, pg. 517 **PV**

Jewett

Northwestern Resources Company, P.O. Box 915, 75846-0915, pg. 1127 **PB**

Junction

The Paks Corp., P.O. Box 325, 76849, pg. 899 **PB**

Katy

ACADEMY CORPORATION, 1800 N. Mason Rd., 77449, pg. 11 **PV**

Houston Division, 23623 Colonial Park Way, Ste. 200, 77493, pg. 38 **PB**

Pepper-Lawson, 4555 Katy Hocley Cut-off Rd., 77449, pg. 851 **PV**

Kaufman

Aberdeen Mfg. Corp. Kaufman Plant, P.O. Box 70, 74142, pg. 1094 **PV**

Keller

Mayfield Swain/Keller, 201 Golden Triangle, 76244, pg. 686 **PV**

Kerrville

Alpine Terrace, 746 Alpine Dr., 78028, pg. 1256 **PB**

Edgewater Care Center, 1213 Water St., 78028, pg. 1256 **PB**

The Hills, 2300 Chalet Trail, 78028, pg. 1257 **PB**

Hilltop Village, Hilltop Circle, 78028, pg. 1257 **PB**

LDB CORPORATION, 444 Sidney Baker S., 78028, pg. 639 **PV**

LDB Food Services, Inc., 444 Sidney Baker S., 78028, pg. 639 **PV**

Leslie Place, 600 Leslie Dr., 78028, pg. 1257 **PB**

MOONEY AIRCRAFT CORPORATION, Louis Schreiner Field, 78028, pg. 759 **PV**

Mr. Gatti's, Inc., 444 Sidney Baker S., 78028, pg. 639 **PV**

Kilgore

Kilgore First National Bank, 910 N. Kilgore St., 75662, pg. 630 **PB**

MARTIN GAS CORPORATION, 101 E. Sabine, 75662, pg. 709 **PV**

Pak-Sher Co., 2500 N. Longview, 75662, pg. 1062 **PV**

Skeeter Products, Inc., One Skeeter Rd., 75662, pg. 689 **PV**

Vertex Antenna Division, P.O. Box 1277, 2600 N. Longview St., 75663, pg. 1718 **PB**

VERTEX COMMUNICATIONS CORPORATION, 2600 N. Longview St., 75663, pg. 1717 **PB**

Kingsville

C&C Bakery Inc., 2600 E. Corral Avenue, 78363, pg. 575 **IT**

Kingwood

Baker CAC, 22001 Northpark Dr., 77339-3804, pg. 1593 **PB**

CH & A Corporation, CH&A Centre, 2218 Northpark Dr., 77339, pg. 1153 **IT**

Century Contractors West Inc., Four Kingwood Pl., Ste. 200, 77339, pg. 950 **PB**

EnviroTech Controls, Inc., 22001 N. Park Dr., 77339, pg. 1594 **PB**

Houston Atlas, 22001 Northpark Dr., 77339-3804, pg. 1593 **PB**

Westronics, Inc., 22001 North Park Dr., Ste. 100, 77339-3804, pg. 1593 **PB**

La Grange

7-Up of LaGrange, TX, 189 S. Brown, 78945, pg. 470 **PV**

La Porte

Hickham Industries Inc., 11518 Old La Porte Rd., 77571, pg. 1305 **IT**

Lake Dallas

Century Telephone of Lake Dallas, Inc., 450 Main St., 75065, pg. 329 **PB**

Lancaster

Brass-Craft Holding Co., 300 G. Pecan, 75146, pg. 1053 **PB**

Brass-Craft Western Company, 300 G. Pecan, 75146, pg. 1053 **PB**

Lane City

Solvay, 1230 Battleground Rd., 77453, pg. 1278 **IT**

Laredo

Barry of Laredo, 4519 E. Corridor, 78043, pg. 192 **PB**

Carrier Corp. Latin Amer Opers, 1211 San Dario Ave. Ste. 579, 78040-4505, pg. 1689 **PB**

Daher Golden Eagle - Laredo, 4460 Trade Ctr., 78041, pg. 749 **PB**

INTERNATIONAL BANCSHARES CORP, 1200 San Bernardo Ave., 78040, pg. 568 **PV**

ABB Kent Taylor Inc., 610 Maher Ave., 78041, pg. 4 **IT**

The Laredo Coca-Cola Bottling Company, Inc., 1402 Industrial Blvd., 78041, pg. 393 **PB**

Laredo Morning Times, 111 Esperanza Dr., 78041, pg. 517 **PV**

Laredo Processing Center, Rte. Four, 78041, pg. 450 **PB**

Montoi Mattel Toys, 5819 Riverside Dr. Ste. 400, 78041-2584, pg. 1058 **PB**

UETA, Inc., P.O. Box 2689, 78041, pg. 103 **IT**

League City

AMERICAN HOMESTAR CORPORATION, 2450 S. Shore Blvd., 77573, pg. 83 **PB**

Garden State Life Insurance Company, Marina Plaza, 2450 South Shore Blvd., Ste. 401, 77573-2964, pg. 88 **PB**

South Shore Harbour Development, 3027 FM 2094, Ste. 200, 77573, pg. 88 **PB**

Leander

SOUTHWEST RECREATIONAL INDUSTRIES INC., 701 Leander Dr., 78646, pg. 1018 **PV**

Lewisville

American Nut Co., P.O. Box 247, 75067, pg. 245 **PV**

Clements Nut Co., P.O. Box 247, 614 E. Main St., 75067, pg. 245 **PV**

Grandy's, Inc., 997 Grandy's Ln., 75067-2599, pg. 61 **PV**

Raytheon TI Systems, P.O. Box 405, 2501 S. Hwy. 121, 75067, pg. 1365 **PB**

Swain Building Materials, 902 N. Mill St., 75057, pg. 686 **PV**

TNP Enterprises, Inc.-North Central Region, 2139 N. Stemmons, 75067, pg. 1557 **PB**

ULTRAK INC., 1301 Waters Ridge Dr., 75057, pg. 1663 **PB**

Liberty

Liberty County Jail/Juvenile Center, P.O. Box 10069, 77575-1006, pg. 450 **PB**

Liberty Hill

Meridell Achievement Center, P.O. Box 87, 78642, pg. 1697 **PB**

Littlefield

Littlefield Feed Yard, Box 727, 79339, pg. 429 **PV**

Livingston

Lake Livingston Telephone Company, 1231 Stevens Ln., 77351, pg. 1571 **PB**

Lone Star

Friedman Industries, Inc., Farm Rd. 250, P.O. Box 437, 75668, pg. 682 **PB**

Longview

Capacity of Texas, Inc., 401 Capacity Drive, Loop 281 S.E., 75604, pg. 400 **PB**

Delta Distributors, Inc., 610 Fisher Rd., 75604-5299, pg. 1458 **IT**

Friedman Industries, 1121 Judson Rd., 75601, pg. 682 **PB**

Heritage Manor Longview, 112 Ruthlynn Dr., 75601, pg. 839 **PB**

Le Tourneau, Inc., 2400 S. McArthur St., 75603, pg. 1410 **PB**

Lebus Manufacturing Co., 900 Fisher Rd., 75604-4709, pg. 473 **IT**

Longview National Bank, 213 N. Fredonia St., 75601, pg. 630 **PB**

Mustang Pipeline Company, P.O. Box 7444, 75607-7444, pg. 551 **PB**

Norris Cylinder Company, 5035 FM 1845, 75607, pg. 1054 **PB**

Precipitair Pollution Control, 3000 Marshal Rd., 75601, pg. 320 **PB**

Stemco Truck Products Division, 300 E. Industrial Blvd., 75606, pg. 402 **PB**

Surplus Warehouse-Longview, 4013 Estes Pkwy., 75603, pg. 120 **PV**

Texas Eastman Co., P.O. Box 7444, 75607, pg. 550 **PB**

Vertex Control Systems, P.O. Box 150590, 75615, pg. 1718 **PB**

Vertex Integrated Satellite Antenna Technology Division, 1915 Harrison Rd., 75604, pg. 1718 **PB**

Lubbock

Bell Dairy Products, Inc., 201 University, P.O. Box 2588, 79408, pg. 490 **PB**

Charter Plains Behavioral Health System, Inc., 801 N. Quaker Ave., 79408, pg. 1035 **PB**

Cox Communications-Lubbock, 6710 Hartford Ave., 79413, pg. 455 **PB**

Elmer's Weights, 1020 S.E. Loop 289, 79404, pg. 243 **PB**

Energas Company, P.O. Box 1121, 79408, pg. 145 **PB**

FURR'S/BISHOPS, INC., 6901 Quaker Ave., P.O. Box 6747, 79413-6747, pg. 689 **PV**

HIGGINBOTHAM-BARTLETT CO., 8302 Indiana Ave., 79423, pg. 527 **PV**

Horizon Specialty Hospital - Lubbock, 1409 Ninth St., 79401, pg. 839 **PB**

Norwest Bank Texas, N.A., 1500 Broadway, 79401, pg. 1203 **PB**

PLAINS CO-OP OIL MILL, 2901 Ave. A, 79404, pg. 868 **PV**

PLAINS COTTON CO-OP ASSOCIATION, 3301 E. 50th St., 79404, pg. 868 **PV**

Snook & Aderton, Inc., 1702 Ave. F, 79401, pg. 360 **PV**

Texas Instruments Lmos, Consumer Products, P.O. Box 10508, 79408-3508, pg. 1586 **PB**

Texas, New Mexico & Oklahoma Coaches, Inc., P.O. Box 1800, 79408-1800, pg. 766 **PB**

UNITED SUPERMARKETS INC., 7830 Orlando, 79423, pg. 1126 **PV**

Lufkin

BROOKSHIRE BROS., LTD., 1201 Ellen Trout Dr., 75904, pg. 172 **PV**

CONTRACTORS SUPPLIES, INC., 303 Webber, 75901, pg. 270 **PV**

Formaldehyde, 1429 E. Lufkin Ave., P.O. Box 938, 75902, pg. 737 **PB**

LUFKIN INDUSTRIES, INC., 601 S. Raguet, 75901, pg. 1019 **PB**

Lufkin Industries, Inc., Boundary Division, 601 Raquet, 75901, pg. 1019 **PB**

Lufkin Mill, Champion International Corporation, P.O. Box 149, 75901, pg. 334 **PB**

Lufkin National Bank, 203 S. First St., 75901, pg. 630 **PB**

Parkwood Place, 300 N. Bynum, 75904, pg. 839 **PB**

PERRY BROTHERS, INC., 107 W. Lufkin Ave., 75904, pg. 854 **PV**

Magnolia

Oceaneering Multiflex, 38553 FM 1774 S., 77355, pg. 1211 **PB**

Malakoff

Malakoff Industries, P.O. Box 487, 75148, pg. 1386 **PB**

Mansfield

Ropak Southwest Inc., 1501 E. Dallas St., 76063, pg. 812 **IT**

Geographic Index-U.S.

Marble Falls

Texas Granite Corp., Hwy. 1431 W., 78654, pg. 251   PV

Marshall

Polymer Chemicals Group, Hwy. 59, 75671, pg. 1774   PB

Mc Kinney

Montgomery Elevator Division, 2101 Couch Dr., 75069,
pg. 746   IT
Texas Bank N.A., 321 N. Central Expwy., 75070,
pg. 626   PB

Mc Queeney

Acme Brick Co., P.O. Box 158, F. M. 725, 78123,
pg. 936   PB

McAllen

Charter Palms Behavioral Health System, Inc., 1421 E.
Jackson Ave., 78502, pg. 1035   PB
Hewlett-Packard Company, 801 Nolana Ave., Ste. 205,
78504, pg. 815   PB
Hilb, Rogal & Hamilton Company of McAllen, 121 W.
Pecan-Drawer 3785, 78502, pg. 827   PB
Invamex, S.A. de C.V., 4324 W. Military Hwy., 78530,
pg. 911   PB
JONES & JONES, INC., 1821 S. 18th St., 78503,
pg. 596   PV
Jones Financial Services, 1821 S. 18th St., 78503,
pg. 596   PV
Kimball Electronics Group, 3600 Formosa Ave., Ste. 2,
78503, pg. 957   PB
Lambda Electronics, 3801 W. Military Hwy., 78501,
pg. 1241   IT
McAllen Medical Center, 301 W. Expwy. 83, 78503,
pg. 1697   PB
McAllen Pipe & Supply Div., 100 N. First St., 78502,
pg. 1682   PB
The Monitor, P.O. Drawer 760, 78504, pg. 425   PV
Packaged Products Division, 200 N. First St., 78501,
pg. 1191   PV
PEC Rio Grande Valley, 3700 Ursula Ave., 78503,
pg. 871   PV
Security Plastics West, Inc., 3900 W. Military Hwy., 78503,
pg. 981   PV
Shimizu America Corporation-McAllen Office, One Park Pl.,
100 Savannah Ave., Ste. 370, 78503, pg. 1233   IT
Valley Coca-Cola Bottling Company, Inc., 2400 Exprwy. 83
W., 78501, pg. 393   PV
Valley Onions, P.O. Box 2345, 78502, pg. 344   PV
Zenith Electronics Corp. of TX, 6601 S. 33rd St., 78503,
pg. 1790   PB
Zentrans, Inc., 6601 S. 33rd St., 78503, pg. 1790   PB

Mesquite

THE FIGARO COMPANY, INC., 3601 Executive Blvd.,
75149-2711, pg. 404   PV
FRITZ INDUSTRIES INC., 500 Sam Houston Rd., 75149,
pg. 429   PV
Heritage Place, 825 W. Kearney, 75149, pg. 839   PB
Lucent Technologies, 3000 Skyline Dr., 75149-1802,
pg. 1017   PB

Midland

Block Plant, P.O. Box 991, 3505 W. Industrial, 79702,
pg. 936   PB
TOM BROWN, INC., 508 W. Wall, Ste. 500, 79701,
pg. 262   PB
Clint Hurt Drilling, Drawer 10627, 1501 Taylor, 79701,
pg. 953   PB
Compressor Systems, Inc., Drawer A, 79701, pg. 1027   IT
Cox Communications-Midland, 2530 S. Midkiff, 79704,
pg. 455   PV
DAWSON GEOPHYSICAL COMPANY, 208 S. Marienfeld
St., 79701, pg. 489   PB
EDDINS-WALCHER COMPANY, 2406 West Wall Ave.,
79701, pg. 362   PV
Midland Production District Office, 1204 Wilco Bldg., 415
W. Wall St., 79702, pg. 548   PV
Midland Reporter-Telegram, 201 E. Illinois St., 79701,
pg. 517   PV
OEL, Ltd., 415 W. Wall, Ste. 2000, 79701, pg. 568   PB
Plains Petroleum Operating Company, 415 West Wall St.,
Ste. 1000, 79701, pg. 191   PV
Production Operators, Inc. (Midland-Odessa Office), Six
Desta Dr., Ste. 3335, 79705, pg. 298   PV
Texas Instruments Security, P.O. Box 60448, 79711-0448,
pg. 1586   PB
Yale E Key, Inc., Drawer 10627, 1501 Taylor, 79701,
pg. 953   PB

Midlothian

Chaparral Steel Co., Rte. 1, Box 1100, 76065,
pg. 1585   PB
North Texas Cement Company, P.O. Box 520, 900 Gifco
Rd., Hwy. 67, 76015, pg. 88   PV
TXI Cement Company, 245 Ward Rd., 76065, pg. 1585   PB

Millsap

Acme Brick Co., Route 1, Box AB 1, 76066, pg. 936   PB

Mineral Wells

Antenna Products Corp., 101 S.E. 25th Ave., 76067,
pg. 289   PB
BUTLER VENTAMATIC CORP., P.O. Box 728, 76068,
pg. 190   PV
Cantex Inc., P.O. Box 340, 76068, pg. 1312   IT
Mineral Wells Correction Facility, 759 Heintzelman Rd.,
76067-9211, pg. 450   PB
PERRY EQUIPMENT CORPORATION, Wolters Industrial
Park, P.O. Box 640, 76068, pg. 855   PV

Mount Pleasant

Dekoron Wire & Cable Division, 1300 Industrial Blvd.,
75455, pg. 689   PB
Pilgrim's Pride West Division, P.O. Box 371, Monticello Rd.,
75456, pg. 1296   PB

Nacogdoches

NACOMA PRODUCTS, INC., 7516 U.S. 59 N., 75961,
pg. 773   PV
Stone Fort National Bank, Nacogdoches, 300 E. Main,
75961, pg. 630   PV
Surplus Warehouse-Nacogdoches, 2596 South St., 75961,
pg. 120   PV

Nash

Munitions Technology Division, 527 S. Kings Hwy., 75569,
pg. 317   PV

Navasota

Schult Homes Corporation, 2215 Industrial Dr., 77868,
pg. 1442   PB

Nederland

Moran Towing of Texas, Inc., 2300 Hwy. 365, Ste. 570,
77627, pg. 761   PV

New Braunfels

APG Lime Corp., Rte. 6, Box 662, 78132, pg. 761   PB
The Coleman Company, 766 Hwy. 306, 78130, pg. 691   PV
DETEX CORPORATION, 302 Detex Dr., 78130,
pg. 327   PV
Flexonics Expansion Joints, 2400 Longhorn Industrial Dr.,
78130, pg. 1222   IT
Steel Form Div., 1155 Church Hill Dr., 78130, pg. 932   PV
Wal Mart Distribution Center, 3900 Ih 35 N., 78132-5038,
pg. 1733   PB

Nocona

ALLTEL Texas, Inc., 117 E. Oak St., P.O. Box 120, 76255,
pg. 56   PB
Nocona Boot Co., East Hwy. 82, P.O. Box 599, 76255,
pg. 937   PB

North Richland Hills

BATES CONTAINER, INC., 6433 Davis Blvd., 76180,
pg. 122   PV

Odessa

CHEMCENTRAL/Odessa, 105 Pronto Ave., 79762,
pg. 232   PV
Commercial Metals Company, 3501 W. Second St., 79763,
pg. 413   PB
Dynagen Inc., P.O. Box 2032, 2000 E. Pool Rd., 79760,
pg. 327   IT
Odessa Exploration, Inc., 6010 Hwy. 191, Ste. 210, 79762,
pg. 953   PB
Parker Technology, Inc., Route 1, Box 210, 79765,
pg. 1259   PB
SIVALLS, INC., 2200 E. 2nd St., 79761, pg. 1004   PV
Textron Compressor Components, P.O. BOX 1209, 79760-
1209, pg. 1590   PB
Turner Bit Services, 2431 W. 42nd, 79764, pg. 1134   PV
Weatherford, 2912 E. I-20, 79766, pg. 1749   PB

Orange

Beaird Industries, Inc. of Orange, 91 Front St., 77630,
pg. 1639   PB
Firestone Synthetic Rubber & Latex Company-Orange,
1006 Farm Rd., 77630, pg. 214   IT
A. Schulman, Inc.-Dispersion Plant, 3007 Burnett, 77630,
pg. 1441   IT
Texas Polymer Services, Inc., 6522 Interstate Hwy. 10 W.,
77632, pg. 1441   PB

Orange Grove

ORANGE GROVE CO-OPERATIVE, Hwy. 359 Soyars,
78372, pg. 818   PV

Overton

B.M. Moore Pre-Release Center, 8500 North FM 3053,
75684, pg. 450   PB

Palestine

First National Bank, Palestine, 100 Ave. A, 75802,
pg. 630   PB
Wal Mart Distribution Center, 201 Old Elkhart Rd., 75801-
5931, pg. 1733   PB

Pampa

W-B SUPPLY CO., P.O. Drawer 2479, 111 N. Naida,
79065, pg. 1144   PV

Paris

Campbell Soup (Texas) Inc., P.O. Box 9016, 75460,
pg. 299   PB
Oliver Rubber Co., Loop 28, 75460, pg. 1504   PB
Southwestern Foundries, P.O. Box 897, 75460,
pg. 457   PB
Surplus Warehouse-Paris, 1236 N. Main, 75460,
pg. 120   PV

Pasadena

Akzo Chemicals Inc., 13000 Baypark Rd., 77507,
pg. 47   IT
Bayou Cogeneration, 11777 Bayarea Blvd., 77507,
pg. 37   IT
Graver Tank & Mfg. Co., Inc., 10101 Bay Area Blvd.,
77507, pg. 914   PB
The Lamson & Sessions Co., 4395 Pasadena Frwy., 77508,
pg. 976   PB
Pasadena Terminal, 530 N. Witter, 77506, pg. 692   PB
Simpson Pasadena Paper Co., P.O. Box 872, 77501,
pg. 1003   PV
WPI Transportation, Inc., 131 N. Richey, 77506, pg. 71   PB
Zeneca Inc. (Bayport), 5757 Underwood Rd., 77507,
pg. 1525   IT

Pearland

ASSOCIATED EQUIPMENT CO., INC., 1603 N. Main,
77581, pg. 90   PV
Eclipse Combustion, Inc., 2508 Westminster, 77581,
pg. 360   PV
Wedge Dia-Log, P.O. Box 14103, 120 Dixie Farm Rd.,
77581, pg. 1158   PV

Perryton

PERRYTON EQUITY, 202 S. Amherst, 79070, pg. 855   PV

Pharr

Shepler's Rio Grande Steel, Hwy. 281 & E. Owasa, 78577,
pg. 413   PB

Pittsburg

PILGRIM'S PRIDE CORPORATION, 110 S. Texas, 75686,
pg. 1296   PB

Plainview

ADM Milling Co., P.O. Box 1000, 1208 Columbia, 79072,
pg. 128   PB
GEBO DISTRIBUTING CO., INC., 3109 Olton Rd., 79073,
pg. 442   PV
Plainview Daily Herald, 820 Broadway, 79072, pg. 517   PV
Wal Mart Distribution Center, 3101 N. Quincy, 79072-1951,
pg. 1733   PB
ZIPP INDUSTRIES, P.O. Box 1450, 79079-1450,
pg. 1207   PV

Plano

Amanda Fielding, 6501 Legacy Dr., 75024-3698,
pg. 917   PB
Applications Management Group, 6620 Chase Oaks Blvd.,
75023, pg. 1516   PB
ARCO Intl. Oil & Gas Co., 2300 W. Plano Pkwy., 75075,
pg. 144   PB
Boeing Aerospace & Electronics, Inc., 7801 S. Stemons
Freeway, 75065, pg. 240   PB
Charter Behavioral Health System of Dallas, Inc., 6800
Preston Rd., 75024, pg. 1034   PB
Compass Bank, 1420 Independence, 75075, pg. 419   PB
Corrugated Packaging, 1800 E. Plano Pkwy., 75074,
pg. 737   PB
DSC COMMUNICATIONS CORPORATION, 1000 Coit Rd.,
75075, pg. 475   PB
Daisytek Incorporated, 500 N. Central, 75074, pg. 477   PB
DAISYTEK INTERNATIONAL CORPORATION, 500 N.
Central Expwy., 75074, pg. 477   PB
EDS, Financial and Insurance Group, 5400 Legacy Dr.,
75024, pg. 570   PB
ELECTRONIC DATA SYSTEMS CORPORATION, 5400
Legacy Dr., 75024, pg. 569   PB
Frito-Lay Company, 7701 Legacy Dr., 75024-4099,
pg. 1277   PB

PB - *U.S. Public Companies Volume*
PV - *U.S. Private Companies Volume*
IT - *International Public & Private Companies Volume*

Gustafson, Inc., 1400 Preston Rd., Ste. 40, 75903, pg. 460   **PB**
Harte-Hanks Community Newspapers, Inc., c/o Plano Star Courier, P.O. Box 860248, 75086, pg. 793   **PB**
Heritage Manor Plano, 1621 Coit Rd., 75075, pg. 839   **PB**
Heritage Park, 3208 Thunderbird Ln., 75075, pg. 839   **PB**
JC PENNEY COMPANY, INC., 6501 Legacy Dr., 75024-3698, pg. 916   **PB**
JC Penney Europe, Inc., 6501 Legacy Dr., 75024, pg. 917   **PB**
JC Penney Financial Services, Inc., 2700 W. Plano Pkwy., 75075, pg. 917   **PB**
J.C. Penney Life Insurance Company, 2700 W. Plano Pkwy., 75075, pg. 917   **PB**
JC Penney Reinsurance Company, 2700 W. Plano Pkwy., 75075, pg. 917   **PB**
JCP Realty, Inc., 6501 Legacy Dr., 10001, pg. 917   **PB**
Latin America Operation, 6620 Chase Oaks Blvd., 75023, pg. 1516   **PB**
Luminator, 1200 E. Plano Pkwy., 75074, pg. 1045   **PB**
Metrologic South Central Region, 3401 Custer Rd., Ste. 115, 75023, pg. 1102   **PB**
Micropolis Corporation, 4975 Preston Park Blvd., Ste. 320, 75093, pg. 742   **PV**
Mixit, 6501 Legacy Dr., 75024, pg. 917   **PB**
Muratech America, Inc., 6400 International Pkwy., Ste. 1500, 75093, pg. 897   **IT**
PAGING NETWORK, INC., 4965 Preston Park Blvd., Ste. 600, 75093, pg. 1252   **PB**
Portfolio Interiors by J.C. Penney, 6501 Legacy Dr., 75075, pg. 917   **PB**
Priority Fulfillment Services, Inc., 500 N. Central Expwy., 75074, pg. 477   **PB**
SASIB Bakery North America Inc., 808 Stewart Ave., 75074, pg. 1194   **IT**
Senlsys, 1600 W. Plano Pkwy., 75075, pg. 127   **IT**
Smartfoods, Inc., 7701 Legacy Dr., 75024-4099, pg. 1277   **PB**
SMITH SYSTEM MANUFACTURING COMPANY, P.O. Box 860415, 75086, pg. 1009   **PV**
Sterling Software Application Development Division, 6620 Chase Oaks Blvd., 75023, pg. 1516   **PB**
Systems Management Group, 6620 Chase Oaks Blvd., 75023, pg. 1516   **PB**
Tandem Telecommunications Systems, Inc., 1255 W. 15th St., 75075, pg. 417   **PB**
United States Brass Corporation, P.O. Box 37, 901 Tenth St., 75074, pg. 1795   **PB**
Zeneca Pharmaceuticals, 500 N. Central Expressway, Ste. 231, 75074-6744, pg. 1525   **IT**

Port Aransas

Mustang Telephone Co., P.O. Box 98, 78373, pg. 329   **PB**

Port Arthur

Afram Carriers, Inc., 7200 Hwy. 87 E., 77642, pg. 962   **PB**
Clark Oil & Refining Corp.-Port Arthur Refinery, 1801 S. Gulfway Dr., 77640, pg. 243   **PV**
Fina Oil & Chemical Co. (Port Arthur), P.O. Box 849, 77640, pg. 1044   **IT**
Kirby Tankships, Inc., 7200 Hwy. 87 E., 77642, pg. 962   **PB**
Sabine Transportation Company, 7200 Hwy. 87 E., 77642, pg. 962   **PB**
Standard Alloys & Manufacturing, KCS & 4th St., 77640, pg. 153   **PV**
Texaco USA, P.O. Box 1608, 77641-1608, pg. 1583   **PB**
The Turner Group, 6201 Procter St. Ext., 77642, pg. 74   **IT**
U.S. Intec, Inc., 1212 Brai Dr., 77643, pg. 433   **PV**

Port Neches

AMERIPOL SYNPOL CORP., 1215 Main St., 77651, pg. 65   **PV**
Block Plant, 1600 Main, 77651, pg. 936   **PB**

Poynor

Fairway District Production Office, P.O. Box 138, 75782, pg. 548   **PV**

Rhome

J&L Tank, P.O. Box 247, 76078, pg. 521   **PB**

Richardson

Alcatel Network Systems, Inc. (TX), 1225 N. Alma Rd., 75081, pg. 55   **IT**
Alcatel Telecom, 1225 N. Alma Rd., 75081, pg. 55   **IT**
All American Semiconductor of Texas, Inc., 1819 Firman Dr., Ste. 127, 75081, pg. 41   **IT**
Anritsu America, Inc.-Central Region, 800 E. Campbell Rd., 75081, pg. 77   **IT**
Aromat South Central Sales Office, 850 E. Arapaho Rd., Ste. 210, 75081, pg. 848   **IT**
BRSG/Maples Public Relations, 801 E. Campbell Rd., Ste. 330, 75081, pg. 147   **PV**
BLUE CROSS & BLUE SHIELD OF TEXAS, INC., 901 S. Central Expwy., 75080, pg. 152   **PV**
Collins International Service Company, 3200 W. Renner Rd., 75082-2402, pg. 1397   **PB**
Compass Bank Dallas, 1600 Promenade Tower, 75080, pg. 419   **PB**
COMSAT RSI, 900 Alpha Dr., 75081, pg. 424   **PB**
Convex Technology Center - Hewlett-Packard, 3000 Waterview Pkwy., 75080, pg. 815   **PB**

Cyrix Corporation, 2703 N. Central Expwy., 75080-2010, pg. 1160   **PB**
Data Communications & Networks, 2435 N. Central Expwy., 75080, pg. 969   **IT**
Electrospace Systems, Inc., 1301 E. Collins Blvd., 75081, pg. 1365   **IT**
Ericsson Business Communications, Inc., 500 Industrial Dr., Ste. 300, 75081, pg. 1364   **IT**
Ericsson Components, Inc., 1010 E. Arapaho Rd., 75081, pg. 1364   **IT**
Ericsson, Inc., 1010 E. Arapaho Rd., 75081, pg. 1364   **IT**
Ericsson Network Systems, Inc., 730 International Pkwy., 75081, pg. 1364   **IT**
Ericsson North America, Inc., 1010 E. Arapaho Rd., 75081, pg. 1364   **IT**
Ericsson Radio Systems, 740 E. Campbell Rd., 75081, pg. 1365   **IT**
FOSSIL INC., 2280 N. Greenville Ave., 75085, pg. 420   **PV**
Fujitsu Network Transmission Systems Inc., 2801 Telecom Pkwy., 75082, pg. 526   **IT**
Furmanite Worldwide, Inc., 2435 N. Central Expwy., Ste. 700, 75080, pg. 942   **PV**
Gerber Garment Technology, Inc., 1200 N. Bowser Rd., 75083, pg. 740   **PV**
Group Life & Health Insurance Company, 901 S. Central Expwy., 75080, pg. 152   **PV**
Hanover Lloyd's Insurance Company, 801 E. Campbell Rd., 75081, pg. 54   **PB**
Hanover Texas Insurance Management Company, Inc., 801 E. Campbell Rd., 75081, pg. 54   **PB**
Heritage Village, 1111 Rockingham Dr., 75080, pg. 839   **PB**
Hewlett-Packard Company, 930 E. Campbell Rd., 75081, pg. 815   **PB**
Intermec Southwest, 850 N. Greenville Rd., Suite 150, 75081, pg. 1004   **PB**
Jaco Electronics, Inc., 1209 N. Glenville Dr., 75081, pg. 921   **PB**
Jerdon Products, Inc., 1810 N. Glenville Dr., 75081, pg. 1771   **PB**
Kaneb Pipe Line Partners, L.P., 2435 N. Central Expwy., 7th Fl., 75080, pg. 942   **PV**
KANEB SERVICES, INC., 2435 N. Central Expwy., 7th Fl., 75080, pg. 942   **PV**
LEBLANC COMMUNICATIONS, INC., 1755 N. Collins Blvd., Ste. 325, 75080, pg. 656   **PV**
Lennox Global Ltd., 2100 Lake Park Blvd., 75080, pg. 659   **PV**
Lennox Industries Inc., 2100 Lake Park Blvd., 75080, pg. 659   **PV**
LENNOX INTERNATIONAL INC., 2100 Lake Park Blvd., 75080, pg. 659   **PV**
Levtech, Inc., 250 E. Arapaho Rd., 75081, pg. 1011   **IT**
Marshall Erdman & Assoc., Inc., 880 Dorothy Dr., Ste. 800, 75081, pg. 380   **PV**
Motorola Nortel, 2435 N. Central Expwy., 75080, pg. 1138   **PB**
Network Support Products, 1850 N. Greenville Ave., 75081-1854, pg. 792   **PB**
NetworkMCI Services, 2400 N. Glenville Dr., 75082, pg. 1024   **PB**
ODS NETWORKS, INC., 1101 E. Arapaho Rd., 75081, pg. 1206   **PB**
Olicom Inc., Headquarters Americas, 1680 N. Prospect Dr., 75081, pg. 1001   **IT**
Orthofix Inc., 250 E. Arapaho Rd., 75081, pg. 1011   **IT**
Owens Country Sausage, Inc., 1403 E. Lookout Dr., 75081, pg. 596   **PB**
Phillips Coal Company, 2929 N. Central Expwy., 75080, pg. 1291   **PB**
RELIABLE CHEVROLET, 800 N. Central Expwy., 75080, pg. 920   **PV**
SMS-Dallas, 800 E. Campbell Rd., Ste. 295, 75081, pg. 1463   **PB**
STB SYSTEMS, INC., 1651 N. Glenville, Ste. 210, 75081, pg. 1421   **PB**
SAFECO Lloyds Insurance Co., P.O. Box 586, 75080, pg. 1423   **PB**
Sanmina Corporation-Richardson Plant, 1250 American Pkwy., 75081, pg. 1431   **PB**
Semtech Central Region, 1701 Greenville Ave., Ste. 106, 75081, pg. 1456   **PB**
Titus Products Div., 990 Security Row, 75081, pg. 1398   **IT**
Transport Systems Group, 2240 Campbell Creek Blvd., 75082, pg. 4   **PB**
USDATA Corporation, 2435 N. Central Expwy., 75080-2722, pg. 1425   **PB**
Wyle Electronics-Dallas, 1810 N. Greenville Ave., 75081, pg. 1457   **IT**

Roanoke

Hydro Conduit Corp., P.O. Box 1230, 3/4 m. NE from I SH 114 & I 35W, 76262, pg. 245   **IT**
Nokia Telecommunications Inc., Seven Village Circle, Ste. 100, 76262, pg. 953   **IT**

Robstown

Texas Ecologists, Inc., Petronilla Rd., 78380, pg. 71   **PB**

Rosharon

Davenport Mammoet Heavy Transport Inc., 20525 FM 521 Rd., 77583, pg. 1144   **PV**

Round Rock

AMP Packaging Systems, Inc., 700 E. Jeffrey Way, 78664, pg. 8   **PB**

Block Plant, P.O. Box 425, 508 McNeil Rd., 78681, pg. 936   **PB**
Carroll Touch, Inc., 811 Paloma Dr., 78664, pg. 8   **PB**
Cyclean, Inc., 1000 S. I-H35, 78681, pg. 316   **PB**
DELL COMPUTER CORPORATION, One Dell Way, 78682-2222, pg. 495   **PB**
Shepler's Round Rock, 3203 S. IH 35, 78664, pg. 413   **PB**
Sysco Food Services of Austin, Inc., 101 Chisholm Trail, 78681-5098, pg. 1551   **PB**
TN Technologies, 2555 North IH-35, 78664-2015, pg. 1593   **PB**
Tellabs Texas Inc., 601 Jeffrey Way, 78664-2424, pg. 1573   **PB**
Westinghouse Motor Company, 5100 IH-35 at Westinghouse Rd., 78681, pg. 275   **PB**

San Angelo

Barry Distribution of San Angelo, 3301 Barry Ave., 76904, pg. 192   **PB**
Barry of San Angelo, 2880 Loop 306, 76904, pg. 192   **PB**
HIRSCHFELD, INC., 112 W. 29th St., 76903, pg. 530   **PV**
Hirschfeld Steel Company, Inc., 112 W. 29th St., 76903, pg. 531   **PV**
River Crest Hospital, 1636 Hunter's Glen, 76901, pg. 1697   **PB**
San Angelo National Bank, 301 W. Beauregard, 76903, pg. 633   **PB**
San Angelo Standard, Inc., 34 W. Harris, 76903, pg. 794   **PB**
Wendland Manufacturing Corporation, P.O. Box 808, 76902, pg. 176   **PV**

San Antonio

ADT Security Systems Texas, 140 Heimer, 78232-5028, pg. 1649   **PB**
AT Supply, Inc., 4703 Shavano DR., Ste. 104, 78249, pg. 1573   **PB**
ADTEC DETENTION SYSTEMS, 7816 Jones Maltberger Rd., 78216, pg. 18   **PV**
Alamo Forest Products, Inc., 10800 Sentinel Dr., 78217-0258, pg. 1135   **PV**
ALAMO INDUSTRIAL GROUP, P.O. Box 231, 78291-0231, pg. 31   **PV**
Alamo Iron Works, P.O. Box 231, 78291, pg. 31   **PV**
Alamo Lumber Company, 10800 Sentinel Dr., 78217-0258, pg. 1135   **PV**
All-American Co., 6846 Alamo Downs Pkwy., 78238, pg. 1389   **PB**
Allied Security Inc., 8546 Broadway, Ste. 212, 78217, pg. 40   **PV**
Allright San Antonio Parking, Inc., 405 N. St. Marys, Ste. 920, 78295, pg. 43   **PV**
American Detention Services, Inc., 8799 Crownhill Blvd., 78209, pg. 18   **PV**
ANCIRA ENTERPRISES INC., 6111 Bandera, 78238, pg. 71   **PV**
Aquila Gas Pipeline Corporation, 100 NE Loop 410, Ste. 1000, 78216, pg. 1701   **PB**
AST Research, Inc., 9311 San Pedro Ave., Ste. 700, 78216, pg. 1181   **PV**
Bausch & Lomb Eyewear Division-TX, 5335 Castroville Rd., 78227, pg. 194   **PV**
BENSON AUTOMOTIVE WORLD, 100 Sandall, Ste. 210, 78216, pg. 133   **PV**
Bergen Brunswig Drug Company, 1949 Hormel Dr., 78219, pg. 214   **PB**
Besser/APPCO, 442 N. N.W. White Rd., 78219, pg. 139   **PV**
BLOCK DISTRIBUTING COMPANY, 827 Coliseum Rd., 78219, pg. 149   **PV**
Bromley, Aguilar & Associates, 321 Alamo Plaza, 78205, pg. 692   **PV**
Builders Square, Inc., 9725 Datapoint Dr., 78229, pg. 477   **PB**
Business Journal Publications, 8200 IH-10 W., Ste. 300, 78230, pg. 19   **PV**
H.E. BUTT GROCERY CO., 646 S. Main Ave., 78204, pg. 190   **PV**
CCMCS, Inc., 14607 San Pedro, Ste. 200, 78232, pg. 383   **PB**
Carmun International, 702 San Fernando St., 78207, pg. 646   **IT**
Charter Health Management of Texas, Inc., 6800 Park Ten Blvd., Ste. 275-W, 78213, pg. 1034   **PB**
Charter Real Behavioral Health System, Inc., 8550 Huebner Rd., 78240, pg. 1035   **PB**
CHEMCENTRAL/San Antonio, 1107 E. Southcross Blvd., 78214, pg. 232   **PB**
Chromalloy Gas Turbine Corp., 4430 Director Dr., 78219, pg. 1458   **PB**
Clarke American Corp., 10931 Laureate Dr., 78249, pg. 267   **IT**
CLEAR CHANNEL COMMUNICATIONS, INC., 200 Concord Plaza, Ste. 600, 78216, pg. 383   **PB**
Coast RV, Inc., 4706 Macro Dr., 78218, pg. 388   **PV**
COCA-COLA BOTTLING CO. OF THE SOUTHWEST, One Coca-Cola Pl., 78219, pg. 248   **PV**
BARTLETT COCKE, INC., 8706 Lockway, 78217, pg. 249   **PV**
Continental Homes of San Antonio, L.P., 14206 N. Brook, 78232, pg. 441   **PB**
Cott Corporation - South Central Region, 4238 Director Drive, 78219, pg. 337   **IT**
CULLEN/FROST BANKERS, INC., 100 W. Houston St., 78296, pg. 467   **PB**
Daltex General Agency, 100 W. Houston St., 78205, pg. 467   **PB**

Geographic Index-U.S.

Dalworth Concrete Products, Inc., 1900 Rilling Rd., 78214, pg. 417 **PV**

Datapoint Corporation, 8410 Datapoint Dr., 78229-8500, pg. 384 **IT**

Datapoint Development Center, Inc., 8400 Datapoint Dr., 78229-8500, pg. 384 **IT**

Datapoint-DISC, Inc., 8400 Datapoint Dr., 78229-8500, pg. 384 **IT**

The Dee Howard, P.O. Box 469001, 78246, pg. 653 **PV**

EG & G Automotive Research, 5404 Bandera Rd., 78238-1993, pg. 544 **PB**

EA Engineering, Science & Technology, Inc., 7330 San Pedro. Ste. 536, 78216, pg. 541 **PV**

ELDORADO CHEMICAL COMPANY, 14350 Lookout Rd., 78233, pg. 367 **PV**

FAIRCHILD AEROSPACE CORPORATION, 10823 N.E. Entrance, 78216, pg. 391 **PV**

Fairchild Dornier USA, 10823 N.E. Entrance, 78216, pg. 391 **PV**

Fogarty Klein & Partners, Commerce Bldg., 314 E. Commerce St., Ste. 800, 78205, pg. 416 **PV**

Frost Brokerage Services, Inc., 100 W. Houston St., 78205, pg. 467 **PV**

Frost National Bank, P.O. Box 1600, 100 W. Houston, 78296, pg. 467 **PB**

Gesco International, P.O. Box 690188, 78269, pg. 189 **PB**

GRANT-LYDICK BEVERAGE CO., 4518 Seguin Rd., 78220, pg. 470 **PV**

Green Tree Acceptance of Texas, Inc., 823 Vantage Dr., Ste. 1050, 78230, pg. 762 **PV**

Grocery Supply Company-San Antonio, 2330 Roosevelt, 78210, pg. 436 **PV**

CURTIS C. GUNN, INC., 227 Broadway, 78205, pg. 488 **PV**

Gunn Pontiac GMC, Inc., 12526 I35 N., 78209, pg. 488 **PV**

HARTE-HANKS COMMUNICATIONS, INC., Harte-Hanks Tower, 200 Concord Plaza Dr., Ste. 800, 78216, pg. 793 **PB**

Harte-Hanks Television, Inc. (KENS-TV), 5400 Fredricksburg Rd., 78229, pg. 794 **PB**

HASSLOCHER ENTERPRISES, INC., 8520 Crownhill Blvd., 78209, pg. 510 **PV**

Hewlett-Packard Company, 14100 San Pedro Ave., Ste. 100, 78233, pg. 815 **PB**

Horizon Specialty Hospital - San Antonio, 7310 Oak Manor Dr., 78229, pg. 839 **PV**

THE DEE HOWARD COMPANY, 9610 John Saunders Intl. Airport, 78216, pg. 542 **PV**

Humana Health Plan of Texas, Inc., 8431 Fredricksburg, 78224, pg. 848 **PV**

International Cancer Screening Labs, 3370 Nacogdoches, Ste. 100, 78217, pg. 436 **PV**

Interplastic Distribution Group, 10940 Laureate Dr., Ste.8250, 78249, pg. 572 **PV**

Jani King of San Antonio, Inc., 40 Northeast Loop 410, Ste. 527, 78216, pg. 582 **PV**

JUDSON-ATKINSON CANDIES, INC., 831 S. Flores, 78204, pg. 602 **PV**

Jugos del Valle Distribution, 40 N.E. Loop 410, 78216-5828, pg. 716 **IT**

KAJA-FM, 6222 N.W. 1-10, 78201, pg. 384 **PB**

KMOL Television, Inc., 1103 Navarro, 78205, pg. 352 **PB**

KQXT Radio, 6222 N.W. I-10, 78201, pg. 384 **PB**

KSAT-TV, 1408 N. Saint Mary, 78215, pg. 1743 **PV**

KSJL-FM, 6222 N.W. I-10, 78201, pg. 384 **PB**

KTKR-AM, 6222 N.W. I-10, 78201, pg. 384 **PB**

Kaufman and Broad of Texas, Ltd., 4800 Fredricksburg Rd., 78229, pg. 945 **PB**

KINETIC CONCEPTS, INC., 8023 Vantage Dr., 78230-4726, pg. 620 **PB**

Krug Life Sciences Inc., 1313 S.E. Military Dr., Ste. 110, 78214, pg. 968 **PV**

LQ-Cigna I, 10010 San Pedro Ave., 78279, pg. 361 **PB**

LQ-Cigna II, P.O. Box 790064, 10010 San Pedro Ave., pg. 361 **PB**

LA QUINTA INNS, INC., 112 E. Pecan, 78205, pg. 972 **PB**

LABATT FOOD SERVICE, 4500 Industry Pk., 78218, pg. 641 **PV**

LEONARD & HARRAL PACKING CO., 647 Steves Ave., 78210, pg. 660 **PV**

LOTS OFF CORPORATION, 8750 Tesoro Dr., 78217-0555, pg. 1014 **PV**

LUBY'S CAFETERIAS, INC., 2211 N.E. Loop 410, 78217, pg. 1017 **PB**

MG PRODUCTS, 8154 Bracken Creek, 78266, pg. 1026 **PB**

Main Plaza Corporation, 100 W. Houston St., 78205, pg. 467 **PB**

MCCOMBS AUTOMOTIVE, 9000 Tesoro Dr., Ste. 122, 78217, pg. 720 **PV**

Media Recovery Inc.-San Antonio, TX, 12000 Crown Point Dr., Ste. 120, 78216, pg. 727 **PV**

Medical Center Nursing Facility, 7302 Oak Manor Dr., 78229, pg. 839 **PB**

MILLER CURTAIN CO., INC., 1734 Centennial, 78211, pg. 746 **PV**

Mining Group, 7550 IH 10, Ste.1400, 78229, pg. 1134 **PB**

Moroch & Associates, Inc., 4047 Broadway, 78209, pg. 762 **PV**

NS Management Corp., 2000 N. Star Mall, 78216, pg. 1409 **PB**

NORTH PARK LINCOLN MERCURY INC., 9207 San Pedro, 78216, pg. 805 **PV**

North Star Mall, Inc., 2000 N. Star Mall, 78216, pg. 1409 **PB**

Omega Environmental Services, 4412 Bluemel, 78240, pg. 1222 **PV**

Pearl Container Co., 245 Newell, 78215, pg. 954 **PV**

PENCO-Texas, 342 W. Woodlawn Ave., Ste. 100, 78212-3314, pg. 1508 **IT**

PIONEER FLOUR MILLS, 129 E. Guenther, 78204, pg. 866 **PV**

PLAY BY PLAY TOYS & NOVELTIES, INC., 4400 Tejasco, 78218, pg. 1309 **PB**

Procermex Inc., 8004 West Ave., 78213-1870, pg. 115 **PB**

The Psychological Corp., 555 Academic Ct., 78204-2498, pg. 784 **PB**

Quality Service Tank Lines, Inc., 13550 Toepperwein Rd., 78233-4036, pg. 1424 **IT**

Redland Credit Corporation, 17910 I-H 10 West, 78257, pg. 1091 **IT**

Redland Finance Inc., 17910 I-H 10 West, 78257, pg. 1091 **IT**

Redland Funding Corporation, 17910 I-H 10 W., 78257, pg. 1091 **IT**

Redland Stone Products Co., 17910 I-H10 West, 78257, pg. 1091 **IT**

A.I. Root Co., 529 S. Flores St., 78204, pg. 944 **PV**

Rouse Central Park Shopping Center, Inc., 246 Central Park Mall, 78316, pg. 1409 **PB**

SBC COMMUNICATIONS INC., 175 E. Houston, 78205, pg. 1415 **PB**

SRA - San Antonio, 1777 N.E. Loop 410, Suite 510, 78217, pg. 958 **PB**

SAGE ENERGY COMPANY, 10101 Reunion Pl., Ste. 800, 78216-4158, pg. 1426 **PV**

San Antonio Auto Auction, 1500 Ackerman Rd., 78219, pg. 283 **PB**

San Antonio Div., 14800 San Pedro, Ste. 200, 78232, pg. 1683 **PB**

San Antonio Division, 121 Interpark Blvd., Ste. 300, 78216, pg. 38 **PB**

San Antonio Express News, Ave. E. & Third St., 78205, pg. 517 **PV**

San Antonio Learning Center, 9027 Airport Blvd., P.O. Box 16540, 78216, pg. 219 **PB**

Sea World of Texas, 10500 Sea World Dr., 78251, pg. 114 **PB**

Shepler's San Antonio, 4911 Whirlwind Dr., 78217, pg. 413 **PB**

SIGNTECH USA, LTD., 4669 Hwy. 90, 78237, pg. 999 **PV**

Silver Creek Manor Nursing Center, 9014 Timber Path, 78250, pg. 1257 **PB**

Six Flags Fiesta Texas, 1700 Interstate Highway 10 W., 78257, pg. 1611 **PB**

Stanley Smith Security, Inc., 3355 Cherry Ridge, Ste. 200, 78230, pg. 1286 **IT**

SmithKline Beecham Clinical Laboratories, 601 N. Frio, 78207, pg. 1265 **IT**

Sony Microelectronics, One Sony Pl., 78245, pg. 1284 **IT**

Southern Steel Company, P.O. Box 2021, 78297, pg. 361 **PV**

Southwestern Bell Media Ventures, 175 E. Houston Room 6B05, 78205, pg. 1415 **PB**

Southwestern Bell Messaging Services, 4801 N.W. Loop 410. Ste. 850, 78229, pg. 1416 **PB**

STAR FOOD PROCESSING, INC., 3444 E. Commerce St., 78220-1323, pg. 1034 **PV**

STEVES & SONS, INC., P.O. Drawer S, 78211, pg. 1042 **PV**

STRAFCO, INC., 1964 S. Alamo, 78204-1918, pg. 046 **PV**

Subaru Southwest Region, 12615 San Pedro Ave., P.O. Box 32906, 78216, pg. 523 **IT**

SUPERIOR AUCTIONEERS & MARKETING, INC., P.O. Box 792427, 78279-2427, pg. 1054 **PV**

Surlean Meat Co., 1545 S. San Marcos St., 78207, pg. 660 **PV**

Sysco Food Services-San Antonio, Inc., 5711 FM 78, 78244-1005, pg. 1552 **PB**

TACO CABANA, 8918 Tesoro Dr., 78217, pg. 1559 **PB**

Tampo Industries Inc., P.O. Box 7248, 1146 West Laurel St., 78285, pg. 1420 **IT**

TESORO PETROLEUM CORPORATION, 8700 Tesoro Dr., 78217-6218, pg. 1581 **PB**

Texas Homestead Mortgage Co., 4800 Fredricksburg Rd., 78229, pg. 945 **PB**

Texas Transportation Co., 312 Pearl Pkwy., 78215, pg. 954 **PV**

TRISTAR CORP., 12500 San Pedro. Ste. 500, 78216, pg. 1640 **PB**

USAA Buying Service, USSA Bldg., 9800 Fredricksburg Rd., 78288, pg. 1114 **PV**

USAA Federal Savings Bank, USAA Bldg., 9800 Fredricksburg Rd., 78288, pg. 1114 **PV**

USAA Investment Management Co., USAA Bldg., 9800 Fredricksburg Rd., 78288, pg. 1114 **PV**

USAA Life Insurance Co., USAA Bldg., 9800 Fredricksburg Rd., 78288, pg. 1115 **PV**

USAA (UNITED SERVICES AUTOMOBILE ASSOCIATION), 9800 Fredricksburg Rd., 78288, pg. 1114 **PV**

USLD Communications Corp., 9311 San Pedro, Ste. 300, 78216, pg. 969 **PB**

ULTRAMAR DIAMOND SHAMROCK CORPORATION, 6000 N. Loop, 1604 W., 78269-6000, pg. 1663 **PB**

U.S. Brick-San Antonio, 11131 Nacogdoches Rd., 78217, pg. 699 **IT**

VALERO ENERGY CORPORATION, 7990 W. Hwy. 10, 78230-4715, pg. 1704 **PB**

Valero Marketing & Supply Company, 7990 W. Hwy. 10, 78230-4515, pg. 1704 **PB**

Valero Refining Company, 7990 W. Hwy. 10, 78230-4715, pg. 1704 **PB**

VAUGHAN & SONS, INC., 10800 Sentinel Dr., 78217-0258, pg. 1134 **PV**

Visible Changes of Texas, 7400 San Pedro, 78216, pg. 1141 **PV**

Vulcan Materials Company-Southwest Div., 800 Isom Rd., Ste. 330, 78216, pg. 1726 **PB**

WOAI-AM, 6222 N.W. 1-H10, 78201, pg. 385 **PB**

Whitmire Micro-Gen Research Laboratories Incorporated, 10700 Sentinel Dr., 78217, pg. 592 **PV**

Wise & Associates/S&W Technical Services, 8122 Datapoint Dr. #930, 78229, pg. 1161 **PB**

Woodward-Clyde, 12702 Toepperwein, Ste. 201, 78233, pg. 1657 **PB**

YANTIS CORPORATION, 5425C NFM 1604E, 78247, pg. 1195 **PV**

York Intl./Reco, 5680 E. Houston St., 78220, pg. 1789 **PB**

H.B. ZACHRY, 527 Logwood, 78221, pg. 1203 **PV**

H.B. Zachry Company, 527 Logwood, 78221, pg. 1203 **PV**

San Marcos

Cellex Manufacturing, Inc., 208 Therman Dr., 78666, pg. 1080 **PV**

MCCOY'S BUILDING SUPPLY CENTERS, 1200 IH-35 North, 78666, pg. 720 **PV**

Rohr, Incorporated-HTA Aerostructures, Inc., 2005 Technology Way, 78666, pg. 751 **PB**

Southern Post Company-Texas, 440 Wonder World Dr., 78666, pg. 412 **PB**

THERMON MANUFACTURING COMPANY, 100 Thermon Dr., 78666, pg. 1080 **PV**

Trico Industries, Inc., 2503 Hunter Rd., 78666. pg. 1247 **PB**

Wide-Lite, 500 Wonderworld Dr., 78667, pg. 730 **PB**

Scroggins

Texaco Worldwide Exploration & Production, P.O. Box 6, 75480-0006, pg. 1583 **PB**

Seagoville

Surplus Warehouse-Seagoville, 104 Simonds Rd., 75159, pg. 120 **PV**

Sealy

Acme Brick Co., P.O. Box 397, 562 Peters-San Felipe Rd., 77474, pg. 936 **PB**

Sebastian

SEBASTIAN COTTON & GRAIN CORP., 6th & David Ramirez, 78594, pg. 980 **PV**

Seguin

ALAMO GROUP, INC., 1502 E. Walnut, 78155, pg. 34 **PB**

CMC Steel Fabricators, Inc., Steel Mill Rd., 78155, pg. 412 **PB**

Hexcel KnYtex, 2301 Hwy. 46 N., 78155, pg. 824 **PB**

Horowitz Salvage, 1558 N. Austin St., 78155, pg. 412 **PB**

SMI Rail, P.O. Box 911, 78156-0911, pg. 413 **PB**

Structural Metals, Inc., Steel Mill Rd., 78155, pg. 412 **PB**

Sherman

Heritage Country Manor, 505 N. FM1417, 75090, pg. 839 **PB**

Sherman Wire, Hwy. 56 W. & Gibbons Rd., 75090, pg. 955 **PB**

Texas Instruments Gpl, P.O. Box 84, 75091-0084, pg. 1586 **PB**

Shiner

BASSICK BY KASPAR, Hwy. 95 N., 77984, pg. 122 **PV**

KASPAR WIRE WORKS, INC., Hwy. 95 N., 77984, pg. 608 **PV**

Slaton

G & H Castings Corporation, 1470 Industrial Dr., 79364, pg. 861 **PB**

Turbine Division, P.O. Box 708, 79364, pg. 861 **PB**

Snyder

Patterson Drilling Co., 4510 Lamesa Hwy., 79549, pg. 1265 **PB**

PATTERSON ENERGY, INC., 4510 Lomesa Hwy., P.O. Box 1416, 79550, pg. 1265 **PB**

South Houston

Gulf State Specialties, Inc., P.O. Box 508, 77587, pg. 487 **PV**

GULF STATES ASPHALT COMPANY, INC., 300 Christy Pl., 77587, pg. 487 **PV**

Southlake

Texas National Bank, 3205 E. Hwy. 114, 76092, pg. 633 **PB**

Spring

Canusa - CPS, 2408 Timberloch Pl., 77380, pg. 1231 **IT**

Gensym Corporation, South Central Regional Office, 10077 Grogan's Mill Rd., Ste. 100, 77380, pg. 731 **PB**

MITCHELL ENERGY & DEVELOPMENT CORP., 2001 Timberloch Pl., 77380, pg. 1117 **PB**

NAO, P.O. Box 7889, 77387, pg. 771 **PV**

PB - U.S. Public Companies Volume
PV - U.S. Private Companies Volume
IT - International Public & Private Companies Volume

1456

Geographic Index-U.S.

Schlegel Lining Technology, Inc. P.O. Box 7730, 77380, pg. 128   **IT**

Shaw Pipeline Services, Inc., 2408 Timberloch Pl, Bldg. C-8, 77380-1038, pg. 1231   **IT**

Trimble Navigation Ltd., Houston Sales/Technical Support, 1440 Lakefront, Ste. 110, 77380, pg. 1638   **PB**

Stafford

Anderson, Greenwood & Co., 3950 Greenbriar, 77477, pg. 1650   **PB**

Enraf-Nonius Tank Inventory Systems Inc., 12503 Exchange Dr., Ste. 536, 77477, pg. 389   **IT**

Flanders Air Seal Filters Housings Inc., 1112 Staffordshire, 77477, pg. 648   **PB**

Furman Wholesale Lumber Branch, 13246 Murphy Rd., 77477, pg. 431   **PV**

GROVE VALVE & REGULATOR COMPANY, 11100 W. Airport Blvd., 77477, pg. 484   **PV**

INPUT/OUTPUT, INC., 1104 W. Airport Blvd., 77477, pg. 880   **PB**

Klockner-Moeller, 4141 Greenbriar Dr., 77477, pg. 736   **IT**

Klockner-Moeller, Greenbriar S.W. Industrial Pk., 4141 Greenbriar Dr., 77477, pg. 736   **IT**

LeFebure, South, 12603 Executive Dr., Ste. 810, 77477-3603, pg. 387   **IT**

Makita U.S.A. Inc.-Houston, 12701 Directors Dr., 77477-3701, pg. 831   **IT**

Monarch Homes Inc., 11104 W. Airport Blvd., Ste. 240, 77477, pg. 1510   **PV**

TABS Direct (Operating Div.), 1002 Texas Pkwy., 77477, pg. 482   **PV**

Stephenville

Stephenville Bank & Trust Co., 2201 W. South Loop, 76401, pg. 633   **PB**

Stratford

Smoot Grain Co., Inc., 202 S. Poplar St., 79034, pg. 128   **PB**

Sugar Land

Argon Medical, 104 Industrial Blvd., 77478, pg. 1063   **PB**

Bailey Network Management, P.O. Box 5012, 12808 W. Airport Blvd., 77487-5012, pg. 449   **IT**

Baylor Company, 500 Industrial Rd., 77478, pg. 1134   **IT**

Begemann Inc, 500 Industrial Rd., 77478-2898, pg. 1134   **IT**

Bergen Brunswig Drug Company, 1227 W. Airport Blvd., 77478, pg. 214   **PB**

Case Management, 104 Industrial Blvd., 77478, pg. 1063   **PB**

Continental Holdings Inc., 12910 Jess Pirtle Blvd., 77478-2850, pg. 1011   **PB**

Dow Hickam Pharmaceuticals Inc., 10410 Corporate Dr., 77478, pg. 1143   **PB**

ECO Resources, Inc., 12550 Emily Ct., 77478, pg. 1494   **PB**

Fluor Daniel Houston, P.O. Box 5014, One Fluor Dr., 77487-3899, pg. 660   **PB**

Fort Bend Utilities Co., 198 Kempner, 77487, pg. 872   **PB**

HSC Export Corporation, P.O. Box 9, 77487, pg. 872   **PB**

Henley Healthcare, 104 Industrial Blvd., 77478, pg. 1063   **PB**

The Heronhill Corporation, 623 Lakeshore, 77478, pg. 1359   **IT**

Holly Sugar Corporation, P.O. Box 9, 77487-0009, pg. 872   **PB**

IMPERIAL HOLLY CORPORATION, 8016 Hwy 90-A, 77478, pg. 872   **PB**

Imperial Sweetner Distributors, Inc., 198 Kempner, 77487, pg. 872   **PB**

K-Tec Electronics, 1111 Gillingham Ln., 77478, pg. 951   **PB**

Kvaerner FSSL Inc., 525 Julie Rivers Dr., 77478-2835, pg. 770   **IT**

MARINE DRILLING COMPANIES, INC., One Sugar Creek Ctr. Blvd., Ste. 600, 77478-3556, pg. 1044   **PB**

Mazda Motor of America, Inc. Gulf Region, 13100 Southwest Fwy., 77478, pg. 849   **IT**

Nalco/Exxon Energy Chemicals, L.P., P.O. Box 87, 77487, pg. 1150   **PB**

Sermatech Southwest, 12505 Reed Rd. #100, 77478-2876, pg. 1570   **PB**

Spirit Energy 76, One Sugar Creek Pl., 14141 S.W. Frwy., 77478, pg. 1698   **PB**

Sulphur Springs

Fidelity Express Money Order Company Division, 130 Hillcrest Dr., 75482, pg. 436   **PV**

GSC ENTERPRISES, INC., 130 Hillcrest Dr., 75482, pg. 436   **PV**

Grocery Supply Company Division, 130 Hillcrest Dr., 75482, pg. 436   **PV**

The HON Co., Sulphur Springs Plant, 906 Hillcrest Dr., 75482, pg. 772   **PB**

NORTHEAST TEXAS FARMERS CO-OP, 428 N. Jackson, 75482, pg. 805   **PV**

Sunray

Continental Carbon Company, St. Rte. 1, Box 15, 79084, pg. 286   **IT**

McKee Complex, HCR Rte. 1, Box 36, 79086-9705, pg. 1663   **PB**

Sweetwater

First National Bank of Sweetwater, 201 Elm St., 79556, pg. 633   **PB**

Taylor

Decorel Incorporated, One Intercraft Plaza, 76574, pg. 1177   **PB**

Holson Burnes Group, One International Plaza, 76574, pg. 1177   **PB**

Intercraft Company, One Intercraft Plaza, 76574, pg. 1177   **PB**

Temple

ADMC Inc, 1302 Industrial Blvd., 76503, pg. 86   **PV**

ARTCO-BELL CORPORATION, 1302 Industrial Blvd., 76503, pg. 86   **PV**

McLane Company, Inc., 4747 McLane Pkwy., 76504, pg. 1733   **PB**

McLane Food Service, 3015 Center St., 76501, pg. 1733   **PB**

Merit Distribution Services, Inc., 3407 S. 31st St., 76502, pg. 1733   **PB**

Surplus Warehouse-Temple, 1401 S. First St., 76504, pg. 120   **PV**

Texas Instruments Printers, P.O. Box 6102, 76503, pg. 1586   **PB**

Ralph Wilson Plastics Co., 600 General Bruce Dr., P.O. Box 3507, 76501, pg. 1322   **PB**

Wilsonart International, Inc., 2400 Wilson Pl., 76503, pg. 1322   **PB**

Texarkana

TRUMAN ARNOLD COMPANIES, 701 S. Robison Rd., 75504, pg. 84   **PV**

Coca-Cola Bottling Co. of Texarkana, 1930 New Boston Rd. & Reading Ave., 75501-3506, pg. 393   **PB**

Colgate-Palmolive IPD, 303 Falvey Ave., 75501-6620, pg. 1733   **PB**

E-Z MART STORES, INC., 602 W. Falvey, 75504, pg. 353   **PV**

Firstbank, P.O. Box 5608, 75501, pg. 641   **PB**

Hibernia National Bank of Texas, 2318 Richmond, 75503, pg. 825   **PB**

State First National Bank, Texas, 2000 Richmond Rd., 75503, pg. 630   **PB**

Texas City

BETHURUM RESEARCH & DEVELOPMENT, INC., 502 Sixth St., N., 77590, pg. 141   **PV**

Bushwhacker Associates, Inc., 502 Sixth St. N., 77590, pg. 141   **PV**

ISP Technologies Inc., State Hwy. 146 & Industrial Rd., 77590, pg. 859   **PB**

TNP Enterprises, Inc.-Gulf Coast Region, P.O. Box 2190, 702 36th St. N., 77592-2190, pg. 1557   **PB**

Three Rivers

Three Rivers Refinery, P.O. Box 490, 301 Leroy St., 78701, pg. 1663   **PB**

Tomball

Flow Control Equipment, 10906 FM 2920, 77375, pg. 1393   **PB**

HMT Sentry Systems, Inc., 23834 Tomball Pkwy., 77375, pg. 914   **PB**

Tulia

Swisher County Cattle Co., P.O. Box 129, 79088, pg. 429   **PV**

Tyler

BROOKSHIRE GROCERY, 1600 W.S.W. Loop. 323, 75701, pg. 172   **PV**

CELEBRITY INCORPORATED, 4520 Old Troop Rd., 75707, pg. 319   **PB**

Flowers Baking Co. of Tyler, Inc., 1200 W. Erwin St., 75702, pg. 657   **PB**

La Gloria Oil & Gas Co., 425 McMurrey Dr., 75702, pg. 462   **PV**

McMurrey Pipe Line Company, 425 McMurrey Dr., 75702, pg. 462   **PV**

Surplus Warehouse-Tyler, Rte. 12, Box 12808, NE Loop 323, 75708, pg. 120   **PV**

TCA CABLE TV, INC., 3015 S.S.E. Loop 323, 75701, pg. 1553   **PB**

TCA Management Company, 3015 S.E. Loop 323, 75713-0489, pg. 1553   **PB**

Telecable Associates, Inc., P.O. Box 130489, 75713, pg. 1553   **PB**

Teleservice Corporation of America, P.O. Box 130489, 75713, pg. 1553   **PB**

Texas Community Antennas, Inc., P.O. Box 130489, 75713, pg. 1553   **PB**

Texas Telecable, Inc., P.O. Box 130489, 75713, pg. 1553   **PB**

The Trane Company, Unitary Products Group, 6200 Troup Hwy., 75707, pg. 92   **PB**

Tyler Bank & Trust, 100 E. Ferguson, 75702, pg. 630   **PB**

Uvalde

Dean Foods Vegetable Co., P.O. Box 367, 2369 Hacineda Rd., 78802, pg. 490   **PB**

Venus

Venus Pre-Release Center, 1100 Hwy. 1807, 76084, pg. 451   **PB**

Vernon

Rhone-Poulenc, 201 Harrison St., 76384-3327, pg. 1109   **IT**

WRIGHT BRAND FOODS, INC., 1306 Main St., 76384, pg. 1192   **PV**

Victoria

Commercial Metals Company, 398 Coletoville Rd. E., 77905, pg. 413   **PB**

Hilb, Rogal and Hamilton Company of Victoria, 2403 N. Laurent, 77901, pg. 827   **PB**

Safety Railway Service, P.O. Box 1819, Aloe Field @ Hwy. 59, 77902, pg. 412   **PB**

Saw Drilling, Inc., P.O. Box 4630, 77903, pg. 1519   **PB**

Seadrift Coke, L.P., Hwy. 185 South, 77983, pg. 304   **PB**

7-UP of Victoria, 3704 Billy Dr., 77901, pg. 470   **PV**

Victoria Regional Medical Center, 101 Medical Dr., 77904, pg. 1697   **PB**

Vidor

STANLEY STORES, INC., P.O. Box 998, 77670, pg. 1033   **PV**

Waco

Aigner Products Division, 1001 Jewel Dr., 76702, pg. 152   **PB**

Aire Serve Heating & Air Conditioning, Inc., 1010 N. University Parks Dr., 76707, pg. 538   **PB**

Alamo Steel Company, 321 Old Dallas Rd, 76705, pg. 412   **PB**

American-Amicable Life Insurance Company of Texas, 425 Austin Ave., 76701, pg. 1271   **PB**

American Income Life Insurance Company, 1200 Wooded Acres, 76710, pg. 1622   **PB**

BRAZOS ELECTRIC POWER COOPERATIVE, INC., 2404 La Salle, 76706, pg. 166   **PV**

Brazos Fuel Company, Inc., P.O. Box 2585, 76702, pg. 166   **PV**

CENTRAL FREIGHT LINES, INC., 5601 W. Waco Dr., 76702-2638, pg. 223   **PV**

DEALERS ELECTRICAL SUPPLY CO., 2320 Columbus, 76701, pg. 318   **PV**

Down River Forest Products, Inc., 7201 Imperial Dr., 76712, pg. 763   **PB**

THE DWYER GROUP, INC., 1010 N. University Parks Dr., 76707, pg. 537   **PB**

Easy Gardener Inc., 3022 Franklin Ave., 76710, pg. 1682   **PB**

Fabrication Plant/Custom Products, 2825 Gholson Rd., 76704-1110, pg. 1177   **PB**

FIRSTCITY FINANCIAL CORPORATION, 6400 Imperial Dr., 76712, pg. 644   **PB**

Fleetwood Homes of Texas, Inc., 1101 Foundation Dr., 76710, pg. 651   **PB**

Fleetwood Homes of Texas, Inc.-Waco/Gholson Rd., 2801 Gholson Rd., 76703, pg. 651   **PB**

General Business Services, Inc., 1010 N. University Parks Rd., 76707, pg. 538   **PB**

Huck International Industrial Fastener Division, P.O. Box 8117, 8001 Imperial Dr., 76710, pg. 1597   **PB**

Ikon Office Solutions, 2121 W Waco Dr., 76707, pg. 863   **PB**

K-D Manitou, Inc., 3120 Gholson Rd., P.O. Box 4547, 76705, pg. 834   **IT**

Olan Mills Inc. of Texas, 701 W. Loop 340, 76702, pg. 749   **PV**

Mr. Appliance Corp., 1010 N. University Parks Dr., 76707, pg. 538   **PB**

Mr. Electric Corporation, 1010 N. Universtiy Parks Dr., 76707, pg. 538   **PB**

Mr. Rooter Corporation, 100 N. University Parks Dr., 76707, pg. 538   **PB**

National Public Service Ins. Co., 425 Austin Ave., 76701, pg. 77   **PB**

PMSI Ltd., 204 Woodhew, 76712, pg. 1314   **PB**

Pioneer American Insurance Company, 425 Austin Ave., 76701, pg. 1271   **PB**

PLANTATION FOODS INC., 2510 E. Lake Shore Dr., 76705, pg. 869   **PV**

Policy Management Systems Life, Inc., 204 Woodhew Dr., 76712, pg. 1314   **PB**

Rainbow International Carpet Dyeing & Cleaning Co., 1010 N. University Parks Dr., 76707, pg. 538   **PB**

Raytheon E-Systems, P.O. Box 154580, 7500 Maehr Rd., 76715-4580, pg. 1365   **PB**

SBS ENTERPRISES INC., 6301 Imperial Dr., 76710, pg. 955   **PV**

ALLEN SAMUELS CHEVROLET GEO, 1625 N. Valley Mills Dr., 76710, pg. 964   **PV**

Shepler's Waco, 321 Old Dallas Rd., 76705, pg. 413   **PB**

Spenco Medical Corporation, P.O. Box 2501, 76702-2501, pg. 955   **PV**

Texas Life Insurance Company, Texas Ctr., 900 Washington Ave., 76701, pg. 738   **PV**

Geographic Index-U.S.

Trust Life Insurance Company, 5400 Bosque Blvd., 76710, pg. 1622 **PB**
E.K. Williams, 1010 N. University Parks Rd., 76707, pg. 538 **PB**
WOLF MANUFACTURING COMPANY, 1801 W. Waco Dr., 76707, pg. 1186 **PV**

Waller

Bettis Corporation, P.O. Box 508, 77484, pg. 482 **PB**

Waskom

Aztec Manufacturing (Waskom), Hwy. 80 E., 75692, pg. 159 **PB**

Waxahachie

AEP Industries, Inc., P.O. Box 306, 6250 N. Hwy. 35 E., 75165, pg. 5 **PB**
International Extrusion Corporation-Texas, 200 Singleton Dr., 75165, pg. 895 **PB**
United States Aluminum Corp.-Texas, 200 Singleton Dr., 75165, pg. 895 **PB**

Weatherford

Weatherford National Bank, 101 N. Main, 76086, pg. 633 **PB**

Webster

Alimak Elevator Company, P.O. Box 57117, 16920 Texas Ave., Ste. C13, 77598, pg. 34 **PV**

Wichita Falls

ABB Control Inc., 1206 Hatton Rd., 76302, pg. 4 **IT**
BURK ROYALTY CO., 726 Scott St., 10th Fl., 76301-2623, pg. 182 **PV**
CAVALIER HOMES, INC., 719 Scott Ave., Ste. 600, 76301, pg. 318 **PB**
Cerbay Company, Arrowhead Industrial Pk., 211 Randy Dr., 76307, pg. 1171 **IT**
ELX Group, 5000 Central Fwy., 7306, pg. 439 **IT**
Fleetwood Homes of Texas, P.O. Box 3545, 2400 Burkburnett Rd., 76304, pg. 651 **PB**
Kibo Compressor Corp., 726 Scott St., 10th Fl., 76301, pg. 183 **PV**
Vetrotex CertainTeed Corporation, 4515 Allendale Rd., 76310, pg. 1171 **IT**
Wichita Falls Times & Record News, 1301 Lamar, 76307, pg. 794 **PB**

Willis

Capro, Inc., 300 So. Cochran, 77378, pg. 1569 **PB**

Winters

WINTERS WELDING WORKS, INC., 1400 S. Main, 79567, pg. 1183 **PV**

Wolfe City

Ennis-Texas Tag, P.O. Bin D, 75496, pg. 583 **PB**

Woodlands

BetzDearborn Hydrocarbon Process Group, 9669 Grogans Mill Rd., 77380, pg. 226 **PB**
DMD, 1007 Grogans Mill Rd., Ste. 460, 77380, pg. 528 **PB**
Dresser Valve & Controls Div., 10077 Grogans Mill Rd., Ste. 500, 77380, pg. 528 **PB**
Engineered Construction Division, 10200 Grogans Mill Road, Ste. 300, 77380, pg. 1304 **PB**
INTERBIO INC., 2204 Timberloch Pl., Ste 260, 77380, pg. 566 **PV**
Liquid Energy Corporation, 2001 Timberloch Pl., 77380, pg. 1117 **PB**
MND Energy Corporation, 2001 Timberloch Pl., 77380, pg. 1117 **PB**
Microbe Masters, 2204 Timberloch Pl., Ste 260, 77380, pg. 567 **PV**
PDM International Ltd., 10200 Grogan's Mill Rd., Ste. 300, 77380, pg. 1304 **PB**
PDM Latin America Ltd., 10200 Grogan's Mill Rd., 77380, pg. 1304 **PB**
Quantum Corporation, 25277 Grograns Mill Rd., #125, 77380, pg. 1350 **PB**
Southwestern Gas Pipeline, Inc., 2001 Timberloch Pl., 77380, pg. 1117 **PB**
TETRA TECHNOLOGIES, 25025 I-45 N., 77380, pg. 1582 **PB**
The Wing Group, 1610 Woodstead Ct., Ste. 220, 77380, pg. 1760 **PB**

Wortham

Mexia Fabricators, Inc., 1005 N. Ave. A, 76693, pg. 424 **PB**

Wylie

Carlisle Coating & Waterproofing, 903 W. Kirby St., 75098, pg. 305 **PB**

Sanden International (U.S.A.), Inc., 601 S. Sanden Blvd., 75098-4999, pg. 1184 **IT**

UTAH

Bingham Canyon

Kennecott Utah Copper Corporation, 8362 W. 10200 S., 84006-1197, pg. 1119 **IT**

Bountiful

Amcor, Inc., P.O. Box 868, 84011-0868, pg. 242 **IT**
Pro Image, 563 W. 500 South, Ste. 330, 84010, pg. 1377 **PB**
Telos Field Engineering, 530 W. 1500 S., 84010, pg. 1573 **PB**
Telos Systems Solutions, 530 W. 1500 S., 84010, pg. 1573 **PB**

Brigham City

Defense & Launch Vehicles Division, P.O. Box 689, 84302-0689, pg. 1597 **PB**
FLYING J. INC., 50 W. 990 S., 84302, pg. 415 **PV**
Nucor Cold Finish-Utah, P.O. Box 637, 84302, pg. 1205 **PB**
Nucor Grinding Balls, P.O. Box 637, 84302, pg. 1205 **PB**
Southern Post Company-Utah, 920 W. 600 N., 84302, pg. 412 **PB**
Thiokol Propulsion Group, P.O. Box 707, 84302-0707, pg. 1597 **PB**
Thiokol Science and Engineering, P.O. Box 707, 84302-0707, pg. 1597 **PB**
Thiokol Space Operations, P.O. Box 707, 84302-0707, pg. 1597 **PB**

Cedar City

American Azide Corporation, 10622 W. 6400 W., 84720, pg. 88 **PB**
The Coleman Company, 597 N. 1500 West, 84720, pg. 691 **PV**
DCI of Utah Inc., 1024 Production Rd., 84720, pg. 301 **PV**
Halotron, Inc., 10622 W. 6400 W., 84720, pg. 88 **PV**
Western Electrochemical Company, 10622 W. 6400 N., 84720, pg. 88 **PB**

Clearfield

Asbury Fluxmaster, P.O. Box 160067, Building D-10, Freeport Ctr., 84016, pg. 87 **PV**
LIFETIME PRODUCTS INC., Freeport Ctr. Bldg. D-11, 84016, pg. 667 **PV**
National-Oilwell/Dreco, P.O. Box 160410, 84016, pg. 1158 **PB**
Poli-Twine Western Inc., P.O. Box 1255, Bldg. A-16-A, Freeport Center, 84016, pg. 1362 **IT**
Sentinel Consumer Products, Inc., P. O. Box 1417, Freeport Ctr., 84016, pg. 984 **PB**

Draper

BALLARD MEDICAL PRODUCTS, 12050 Lone Peak Pkwy., 84020, pg. 171 **PB**

Helper

Morgantown Machine, P.O. Box 176H, 84526, pg. 281 **IT**

Hyrum

E.A. Miller Company, 410 N. 200 W., 84319, pg. 428 **PB**

Kaysville

Clover Club Foods, Inc., 95 E. 200 N., 84037, pg. 469 **PV**
El Molino Foods, Inc., 100 W. North St., 84037, pg. 158 **PV**
Granny Goose Foods, 95 E. 200 N., 84037, pg. 469 **PV**

Layton

J.C. Bangerter & Sons, Ltd., P.O. Box 703, 695 N. Angel St., 84041, pg. 66 **PV**

Leamington

Ash Grove Cement-Western Region Cement Plant, A6 West, 84648, pg. 88 **PV**

Lehi

Western States Energy, P.O. Box 195, 84043, pg. 664 **IT**

Logan

Bourns Integrated Technologies Division, 1400 N. 1000 W., 84321-1900, pg. 161 **PV**
Herff Jones Yearbooks, P.O. Box 3288, 84321, pg. 524 **PV**
HyClone Laboratories Inc., 1725 S. HyClone Rd., 84321, pg. 1037 **IT**
ICON HEALTH & FITNESS, INC., 1500 S. 1000 W., 84321, pg. 556 **PV**

LEGRAND JOHNSON CONSTRUCTION CO., 1000 S. Main, 84321, pg. 591 **PV**

Magna

Alliant Techsystems-Magna, P.O. Box 98, 84044-0098, pg. 47 **PB**
Hercules Inc.-Magna, P.O. Box 98, 84044-0098, pg. 810 **PB**
Kennecott Holdings Corporation, 8315 W. 3595 S., 84044, pg. 1119 **IT**

Midvale

Baxter Research Medical, Inc., 6864 S. 300 W., 84047-1001, pg. 196 **PB**
Benchmark, Inc., 6864 South 300 W., 84047, pg. 196 **PB**
CheckRite International, 7050 Union Park Ctr., 84047, pg. 484 **PB**
EDD-Salt Lake City, 6912 S. 185 W., #B, 84047, pg. 205 **PB**
IDS Deposit Corp., 6985 Union Park Ctr., Ste. 235, 84047, pg. 73 **PB**
Instore Satellite Network/Business TV, 7050 Union Park Ctr., 84047, pg. 484 **PB**
Kaufman and Broad Utah Division, 6975 Union Park Ctr., Ste. 120, 84047, pg. 945 **PV**
NORBEST, INC., 6875 S. 900 E., 84047, pg. 801 **PV**
Research Industries Corp., 1847 W. 2300 South, 84047, pg. 196 **PB**
Utah Auto Auction, 1650 W. 500 S., 84087, pg. 283 **PV**
UTAH MEDICAL PRODUCTS, INC., 7043 S. 300 W., 84047, pg. 1700 **PB**
Woodward-Clyde, 6925 Union Pk. Ctr., Ste. 110, 84047, pg. 1656 **PB**

Moab

PCS Potash - Moab, P.O. Box 1208, 84532, pg. 1064 **IT**
Southern Paving Co., 5101 E. Old Airport Rd., 84532, pg. 591 **PV**

Murray

Bergen Brunswig Medical Corporation, 4080 S. 500 W., Ste. E, 84157, pg. 214 **PB**
Browning-Ferris Industries of Utah, Inc., 155 A. W. Central Ave., 84107, pg. 264 **PB**
First USA Financial Services, Inc., 6056 Fashion Sq. Dr., Ste. 201, 84107, pg. 174 **PB**
Milgray/Utah, Inc., 310 E. 4500 S., 84107, pg. 207 **PB**
LARRY H. MILLER GROUP, 5650 S. State St., 84107, pg. 747 **PV**
Skaggs Telecommunications Services, Inc., 935 W. Bullion St., 84123, pg. 93 **PB**

North Salt Lake

Aero Tech Manufacturing Inc., 395 W. 1100 North, 84054, pg. 1400 **IT**
HUGHES CONSTRUCTION, INC., 900 N. Redwood Rd., 84054, pg. 546 **PV**
PRODUCERS LIVESTOCK, 230 W. Center St., 84054, pg. 888 **PV**

Ogden

THE AMALGAMATED SUGAR COMPANY LLC, 2427 Lincoln Ave., 84401, pg. 48 **PV**
AMERICAN NUTRITION, INC., 2890 Reeves, 84402, pg. 60 **PV**
ANDERSON LUMBER COMPANY, 4700 S. Harrison Blvd., 84403, pg. 72 **PV**
B & K STEEL & SUPPLY, INC., 2393 S. 1900 W., 84401, pg. 105 **PV**
BANK OF UTAH, 2605 Washington Blvd., 84401, pg. 114 **PV**
Best Western Ogden Park Hotel, 247 24th St., 84401, pg. 1537 **PB**
Bourns Sensors & Controls Division, 2533 N. 1500 W., 84404-2647, pg. 161 **PV**
Bowman & Kemp Rebar, 2397 S. 1900 W., 84401, pg. 105 **PV**
Bowman & Kemp Steel & Supply Company, 2393 S. 1900 W., 84401, pg. 105 **PV**
Control Systems Division-Commercial, 1425 W. 2675 N., 84404-2696, pg. 1262 **PB**
Fraser Valley Forest Inc., P.O. Box 12276, 2525 North Hwy. 89, 84412-2276, pg. 1067 **IT**
GSL Solar Consultants & Advisors, Inc., P.O. Box 1190, 84401, pg. 505 **PV**
Medical Meadow Gold Dairies, Inc., 1104 E. Country Hills Dr., 84403, pg. 1016 **PV**
The Ogden Union Railway and Depot Co., 198 W. 28th St., 84401, pg. 1668 **PB**
STANDARD EXAMINER, 455 23rd St., 84401, pg. 1031 **PV**
THIOKOL CORPORATION, 2475 Washington Blvd., 84401-2398, pg. 1596 **PB**
Thiokol Public Relations, 2475 Washington Blvd., 84401-2398, pg. 1597 **PB**
Young Electric Signs Ogden Division, P.O. Box 1880, 2767 Industrial Dr., 84402-1880, pg. 1201 **PV**

Orem

Corel Corporation, 567 E. Timpanogos Pkwy., 84057-2399, pg. 331 **IT**
MITY-LITE, INC., 1301 W. 400 N., 84057, pg. 1118 **PB**

PB - *U.S. Public Companies Volume*
PV - *U.S. Private Companies Volume*
IT - *International Public & Private Companies Volume*

1458

NOVELL, INC., 1555 N. Technology Way, 84097, pg. 1203 — PB

Park City

Olympia Park Hotel, P.O. Box 4439, 1895 Sidewinder Dr., 84604, pg. 1537 — PB

Price

Cyprus Plateau Mining Corporation, P.O. Drawer PMC, 84501, pg. 471 — PB
National Mine Service Company, Price Div., P.O. Drawer 798, 84501, pg. 281 — IT

Provo

Alpnet, 750 North 200 W., Ste. 307, 84103, pg. 58 — PB
Charter-Provo School, Inc., P.O. Box 1441, 4501 N. University Ave., 84604, pg. 1035 — PB
The Daily Herald, P.O. Box 717, 84603, pg. 1343 — PB
Folio Products Group, 5072 North 300 West, 84604, pg. 1227 — PB
NATURE'S SUNSHINE PRODUCTS, INC., P.O. Box 19005, 75 E 1700 S, 84605, pg. 1166 — PB
NU SKIN INTERNATIONAL, 75 W. Center St., 84606, pg. 808 — PV
Piper Jaffray Inc., Knight Block Bldg., One East Center St., Ste. 100, 84606-3152, pg. 1301 — PB
Sii Mega Diamond, 275 W. 2230 N., 94601, pg. 1478 — PB

Roy

IOMEGA CORPORATION, 1821 W. Iomega Way, 84067, pg. 912 — PB

Saint George

National Parks Transportation, Inc., 444 S. River Rd., 84770, pg. 1476 — PB
ROCKY MOUNTAIN COMPANY, 825 Industrial Rd., 84770, pg. 938 — PV
Scenic Airlines, Inc., 444 S. River Rd., 84770, pg. 1476 — PB
SkyWest Airlines, Inc., 444 S. River Rd., 84770, pg. 1476 — PB
SKYWEST INC., 444 S. River Rd., 84790, pg. 1476 — PB

Salt Lake City

AFS Insurance Services, Inc., 1812 S. Empire Rd., 84130, pg. 90 — PV
AT&T Universal Card Service, 5201 Amelia Earhart Dr., 84116-2857, pg. 11 — PB
Air Seal West, 1911 S. 3850 W. St., 84104, pg. 648 — PB
All American Semiconductor of Salt Lake, Inc., 4455 South 700 E., #303, 84107, pg. 41 — PB
Allen Communication, 5 Triad Ctr., Fifth F., 84180, pg. 1616 — PB
ALPNET INC., 4460 S. Highland Dr., Ste. 100, 84124, pg. 58 — PB
American Investment Bank, NA, 200 E. South Temple, 84111-1241, pg. 990 — PB
American Procurement & Logistics Company, 155 N. 400 West, 84103, pg. 93 — PB
AMERICAN STORES COMPANY, 709 E. South Temple, 84102-1205, pg. 92 — PB
American Stores Properties, Inc., 348 E. South Temple, 84111, pg. 93 — PB
Anderson Electrical Sales, 6 E. Cordella Ave., 84115, pg. 736 — IT
ARNOLD MACHINERY COMPANY, 2975 W. 21st S., 84119, pg. 84 — PV
Arrow/Schweber Electronics, 1946 W. Parkway Blvd., 84119, pg. 134 — PB
Artel Utah Scientific, Inc., 4750 Wiley Post Way, 84116, pg. 86 — PV
ASSOCIATED FOOD STORES INC., 1850 W. 2100 South, 84130, pg. 644 — PV
Atwood Mobile Products, 1874 S. Pioneer Rd., 84104, pg. 598 — PB
Bard Access Systems, 5425 W. Amelia Earnhart Dr., 84116, pg. 189 — PB
Beneficial Life Insurance, 36 S. State St., Ste. 1310, 84111, pg. 327 — PV
Bergen Brunswig Drug Company, 1765 Fremont Dr., 84104, pg. 214 — PB
Blackhawk Coal Co., Ste. 400 Deseret Bldg., 84111, pg. 72 — PB
Bonneville International Corp., Broadcast House, #5, Triad Ctr., 84180, pg. 327 — PB
BONNEVILLE PACIFIC CORPORATION, 50 W. 300 S. St., Ste. 300, 84101, pg. 244 — PB
Boon Edam Inc., 4050 So. 500 W. Complex 27, 84123, pg. 202 — IT
Bud Bailey Construction Inc., 244 W. 300 N., 84147, pg. 1059 — PV
Burns & Wilcox - Salt Lake City Office, 420 East South Temple, Ste. 330, 84111, pg. 610 — PV
A.M. Castle & Co., 660 S. 500 W., 84104, pg. 313 — PB
Celsius Energy Company, 79 S. State, 84147, pg. 1352 — PB
Central Sprinkler Company, 2915 South West Temple, 84115, pg. 327 — PB
Ceramatec, 24255 S. 900 West, 84119, pg. 448 — IT
Chase Manhattan of Utah, 370 E. S. Temple St., Ste. 150, 84111, pg. 338 — PB
Christensen Products, 4446 W. 1730 S., 84104, pg. 981 — PB
Cigna Healthcare of Utah, Inc., 5295 S. 320 W. No. 280, 84107, pg. 360 — PB

Coast RV, Inc., 3800 W. 2100 S., 84120, pg. 388 — PB
Coastal States Energy Co., 175 E. 400 S., Ste. 800, 84111, pg. 390 — PB
Community Psychiatric Centers of Utah, Inc., 1400 E. 4500 S. Holiday, 84124, pg. 1712 — PB
CompHealth, Inc., 4021 S. 700 East, 84107, pg. 839 — PB
Control Equipment Co., 353 W. 2880 S., 84115, pg. 360 — PV
COOKIE TREE INC., 4122 S. 500 W., 84123, pg. 273 — PV
Cream O'Weber Dairy Inc., P.O. Box 26248, 84126-0248, pg. 490 — PB
CUMMINS INTERMOUNTAIN DIESEL, 1030 South, 300 West, 84101, pg. 295 — PB
DWF of Salt Lake, Inc., 1765 S. 300 W., 84115, pg. 326 — PB
DAW TECHNOLOGIES, INC., 2700 South 900 W., 84119, pg. 489 — PB
Deseret Book Co., 40 E. S. Temple, 84111, pg. 327 — PV
DESERET MANAGEMENT CORPORATION, 60 East S. Temple, Ste. 575, 84111, pg. 327 — PV
Deseret News, 157 Regent St., 84111, pg. 327 — PV
Desktop Graphics, 600 Komas Dr., 84108, pg. 596 — PB
Devoe & Raynolds, 2179 S. 300 W., #1, 84115, pg. 663 — IT
EDO Acoustic Products, 2645 S. 300 W., 84115, pg. 542 — PB
EDO Ceramics, 2645 S. 300 W., 84115-2968, pg. 542 — PB
EDO Fiber Science, 506 N. Billy Mitchell Rd., 84116-2896, pg. 542 — PB
EDO Industrial Products Division, 2645 S. 300 W., 84115-2968, pg. 542 — PB
EDO Western Corporation, 2645 South 300 West, 84115, pg. 542 — PB
Education & Entertainment, 600 Komas Dr., 84108, pg. 596 — PB
Eimco Process Equipment Co., P.O. Box 300, 669 W. 200 S., 84110, pg. 166 — PB
EIS, Inc., 1347 S. 300 West, 84115, pg. 368 — PV
Entrada Industries, Inc., 79 S. State St., P.O. Box 11070, 84147, pg. 1352 — PB
EnviroTech PumpSystems, 440 W. 800 S., 84110, pg. 1489 — IT
EQUITY OIL COMPANY, Ten W. Third S. St., Ste. 806, 84110-0959, pg. 590 — PV
EURO RSCG DAHLIN SMITH WHITE, LLC, Four Triad Ctr., Ste. 400, 84180, pg. 384 — PV
EVANS & SUTHERLAND COMPUTER CORPORATION, 600 Komas Dr., 84108, pg. 595 — PB
EVANSGROUP, 110 Social Hall Ave., 84111, pg. 385 — PB
EvansGroup (Public Relations), 110 Social Hall Ave., 84111, pg. 385 — PB
Firetrol Protection Systems, Inc., 142 W. 2260 South, 84115-2510, pg. 1795 — PB
First American Title Co. of Utah, 330 E. Fourth S., 84111, pg. 625 — PB
FIRST HEALTH Strategies, pg. 635 — PB
First Interstate Bank of Utah, N.A., 180 S. Main St., 84101, pg. 1753 — PB
First Security Bank of Utah, N.A., 79 S. Main St., 10th Fl., 84111, pg. 637 — PB
First Security Business Investment Corp., 79 S. Main St., 10th fl., 84111, pg. 637 — PB
FIRST SECURITY CORPORATION, 79 S. Main St., 84111-0006, pg. 637 — PB
First Security Information Technology, Inc., 260 N. Charles Lindbergh Dr., 84116, pg. 637 — PB
First Security Insurance, Inc., 405 S. Main St., 8th Fl., 84110, pg. 638 — PB
First Security Investment Management, Inc., 61 S. Main St., 5th Fl., 84111, pg. 638 — PB
First Security Investor Services, Inc., 61 S. Main St., 1st Fl., 84111, pg. 638 — PB
First Security Leasing Co., 381 E. Broadway, 84111, pg. 638 — PB
First Security Life Ins. Co. of Arizona, 405 S. Main St., 8th Fl., 84110, pg. 638 — PB
First Security Processing Services, Inc., 381 East Broadway, 84111, pg. 638 — PB
First Security Service Company, 15 E. 100 S., 4th fl., 84111, pg. 638 — PB
Fleet Call of Utah, Inc., 141 E. First S., 84111, pg. 1180 — PB
Fleming Foods West, P.O. Box 26828, 84126, pg. 653 — PB
FRANKLIN COVEY, 2200 W. Pkwy. Blvd., 84119, pg. 679 — PB
General Implement Distributors, 2955 W. 21st S., 84119, pg. 84 — PV
Gibbons & Reed Company, 1000 N. Warm Springs Rd., 84116, pg. 759 — PV
GRANITE FURNITURE CO., 1050 E. 2100 S., 84106, pg. 469 — PB
Guidance & Control Systems, 2211 W. N. Temple, 84116, pg. 1002 — PV
HARMON CITY, INC., 3540 S. 4000 W., Ste. 500, 84120, pg. 503 — PV
Health 'n' Home Corporation, 136 E. South Temple, 84111, pg. 93 — PV
Hercules Incorporated Graphite Fibers, Gate 15, Bldg. 9370, 4700 W. 5400 S., 84118-0748, pg. 810 — PV
Hewlett-Packard Company, 3530 W. 2100 South St., 84130, pg. 815 — PV
Hillhaven Convalescent Center Salt Lake City, 41 S. Ninth E., 84102, pg. 1713 — PB
Hughes Christensen Co., 1937 So. 300 W., Ste. 150, 84115, pg. 166 — PV
Humana Health Plan of Utah, Inc., 10 Exchange Pl., 84111, pg. 848 — PB
HUNTSMAN CORPORATION, 500 Huntsman Way, 84108, pg. 549 — PV
Huntsman Corporation, 500 Huntsman Way, 84108, pg. 549 — PV

Insituform Rockies, Inc., P.O. Box 236, 408 E. Bridlewood Dr., 84107, pg. 882 — PB
INTERMOUNTAIN FARMERS ASSOCIATION, 1147 W. 2100 S., 84119, pg. 568 — PV
INTERMOUNTAIN HEALTH CARE INC., 36 S. State St., Ste. 2200, 84111, pg. 568 — PV
Interstate Land Corp., P.O. Box 45433, 180 East First South, 84111, pg. 1352 — PB
Johnson Matthey Refining, Inc., 4603 W. 2100 S., 84120, pg. 713 — IT
KSL Radio, Broadcast House, #5 Triad Ctr., 84180, pg. 327 — PV
KSL-TV, Broadcast House, #5 Triad Ctr., 84180, pg. 327 — PV
KTVX Television, Inc., 1760 Fremont Dr., 84104, pg. 352 — PB
Kennecott Energy and Coal Company, P.O. Box 11248, 84147, pg. 1119 — IT
Kern River Gas Transmission, 295 Chipeta Way, 84108, pg. 1769 — PV
Key Bank of Utah, P.O. Box 30815, 50 S. Main Street, 84130-0815, pg. 954 — PB
Kinross Gold Corporation, Suite 820, 185 South State Street, 84111, pg. 734 — IT
LAMB ENGINEERING & CONSTRUCTION CO., 125 Walton Ave., 84115, pg. 644 — PV
Lamb Leasing & Lamb Brothers General, 125 Walton Ave., 84115, pg. 644 — PV
Leucadia Financial Corporation, 529 E. South Temple, 84102-1089, pg. 990 — PB
Little America Hotels, 500 S. Main St.mple, 84101, pg. 1003 — PV
MRS. FIELDS' ORIGINAL COOKIES, INC., 462 W. Bearcat Dr., 84115, pg. 688 — PV
MACROTECH PLYSEAL, INC., 1754 W. 500 S., 84104, pg. 693 — PV
Market Development Inc., 1850 W. 2100 S., 84130, pg. 90 — PV
Market Information Corporation (BMI), 3 Triad Ctr., Ste. 100, 84180, pg. 484 — PV
MARTIN DOOR MFG., INC., 2828 S. 900 W., 84119, pg. 708 — PV
MAVERIK COUNTRY STORES, INC., 880 W. Center St., 84054, pg. 715 — PV
Megahertz Holding Inc., 605 N. 5600 W., 84116, pg. 1115 — PV
Mining Services International, 5284 S. Commerce Dr., Ste. C-244, 84107-7930, pg. 1115 — PB
MONROC, INC., 1730 N. Beck St., 84116, pg. 1124 — PB
Montek Div., 2268 S. 3270 W., 84119, pg. 1366 — PB
Mountain Fuel Supply Company, 180 E. First S., 84111, pg. 1352 — PV
National Procurement & Logistics Company, 709 E. South Temple, 84102, pg. 93 — PB
Northwest Pipeline Corp., 295 Chipeta Way, 84108, pg. 1769 — PV
OEC MEDICAL SYSTEMS, INC., 384 Wright Brothers Dr., 84116, pg. 1207 — PB
Osco Drug, 155 N. 400 W. Ste. 300, 84103, pg. 93 — PB
PST VANS, INC., 1901 W. 2100 St. S., 84119, pg. 1246 — PB
Pacificare of Utah, 35 W. Broadway, 84101, pg. 1251 — PB
Pax Company, 580 W. 1300 St. S., 84115, pg. 1207 — PV
Piper Jaffray Inc., 215 S. State St., Ste. 100, 84111-2331, pg. 1302 — PB
Preferred/Kahler Associates, 150 West 500 S., 84101, pg. 1357 — PB
Pretzel Time Inc., 462 W. Bearcat Dr., 84115, pg. 688 — PV
Psomas Associates, 339 E. 3900 South St., Ste. 201A, 84107, pg. 893 — PV
Quaker State Q-Lube, Inc., 1385 W. 2200 S., 84119, pg. 352 — PB
QUESTAR CORPORATION, 180 E. 100 South St., 84145-0433, pg. 1352 — PB
Questar Development Corporation, 180 East First South, 84111, pg. 1352 — PB
Questar InfoComm, 180 E. First S., 84147, pg. 1352 — PB
Questar Pipeline Company, 79 S. State St., 84147, pg. 1352 — PB
R&R Advertising, 837 E. South Temple, 84102, pg. 902 — PV
Rx America, 369 Billy Mitchell Way, 84116, pg. 93 — PV
RADIX CORPORATION, 4855 Wiley Post Way, 84116, pg. 906 — PV
RHODES INTERNATIONAL, INC., 1949 S. 4250 W., 84104, pg. 927 — PV
Roberts & Schaefer Company-Salt Lake City, 5225 Wiley Post Way, Ste. 300, 84116, pg. 371 — PB
SMS-Salt Lake City, 175 S.W. Temple, 84101, pg. 1463 — PB
Salt Lake City Airline Learning Center, 201 N. 2200 W., 84116, pg. 219 — PB
Salt Lake City Buzz, 80 W. 1300 S., 84115, pg. 751 — PV
Sav-on, 709 E. South Temple, 84102, pg. 93 — PB
SINCLAIR OIL CORP., 550 E. South Temple, 84130, pg. 1003 — PV
Smith's Food & Drug Centers, Inc., 1550 S. Redwood Rd., 84104, pg. 1103 — PB
STANDARD INDUSTRIES, INC., 3500 S. West Temple, 84115, pg. 1031 — PV
Star Buffet, Inc., 440 Lawndale Dr., 84115-2917, pg. 278 — PV
STEINER CORPORATION, 505 E. S. Temple St., 84102, pg. 1039 — PV
Steiner Foreign Linen Division, 505 E. S. Temple St., 84102, pg. 1039 — PV
Steiner U.S. Linen Div., 505 E. S. Temple St., 84102, pg. 1039 — PV
Sterling Electronics, 1615 W. 2200 S., 84119, pg. 1051 — PB
Summit Family Restaurants, Inc., 440 Lawndale, 84115, pg. 278 — PB

PB - U.S. Public Companies Volume
PV - U.S. Private Companies Volume
IT - International Public & Private Companies Volume

Geographic Index-U.S.

Symskaya Exploration, Inc., P.O. Box 959, 10 W. Third S., Ste. 806, 84110-0959, pg. 590 **PB**
Sysco Intermountain Food Services, Inc., 1659 S. Industrial Rd., 84104, pg. 1552 **PB**
TIE Systems Utah, 2371 S. Presidents Dr., Ste B, 84120, pg. 1085 **PV**
TMP Worldwide/Recruitment Division, 311 S. State St., Ste. 250, 84111, pg. 1065 **PV**
Terrace Villa Convalescent Center, 4600 S. Highland Dr., 84117, pg. 1715 **PB**
Textile Care Services, Inc., 5120 W. Amelia Earhart Dr., 84116, pg. 1537 **PB**
Union Pacific Motor Freight, 1800 Beck St., 84116-1219, pg. 1668 **PB**
Union-Transport Corporation-Salt Lake City Office, 1959 S. 4130 W., Unit D, 84104, pg. 1120 **PV**
Unique Mining Systems, Inc., 175 E. 400 S., Ste. 800, 84111, pg. 390 **PB**
United HealthCare of Utah, 7910 S. 3500 E., Ste. 100, 84121-0409, pg. 1678 **PB**
U.S. Bank of Utah, 107 S. Main, 84111, pg. 1681 **PB**
Universal Resources Corporation, 79 S. State, 84111, pg. 1352 **PB**
University Inn Associates, 480 Wakara Way, 84108, pg. 1537 **PB**
Utah Power & Light, One Utah Ctr., Ste. 2200, 201 S. Main, 84140, pg. 1251 **PB**
Varian X-Ray Tube Products, 1678 S. Pioneer Rd., 84104-4298, pg. 1710 **PB**
Vickers Truck Equipment, 2255 S. 2940 W., 84119, pg. 84 **PV**
Wasatch Villa Convalescent Nursing Home, 2200 E. 33rd St., 84109, pg. 1715 **PB**
Westco Products/Intermountain, 805 W. 2500 South, 84119, pg. 244 **IT**
Western International Media Corporation, Five Triad Ctr., Ste. 450, 84180, pg. 1167 **PV**
Wexpro Company, 79 S. State St., 84147, pg. 1352 **PB**
R.C. Willey Home Furnishings, 2301 S. 300 W., 84115, pg. 221 **PB**
Willis Corroon Corp. of Utah, 4001 S. 700 E., Ste. 420, 84107, pg. 1507 **IT**
WILSON PRODUCTS CO., 1811 W. 1700 S., 84104, pg. 1181 **PB**
YOUNG ELECTRIC SIGN COMPANY, 2401 Foothill Dr., 84109, pg. 1201 **PV**
Young Electric Signs Salt Lake City, P.O. Box 25728, 1148 S. 300 W., 84125-0728, pg. 1201 **PV**
Zellerbach Division, 225 S. 300 E., 84115, pg. 1075 **PB**
ZIONS BANCORPORATION, One S. Main, Ste. 1380, 84111, pg. 1792 **PB**
ZIONS CO-OPERATIVE MERCANTILE INSTITUTION, 2200 South 900 W., 84137, pg. 1793 **PB**
Zions Credit Corporation, 37 West 100 South, 84101, pg. 1793 **PB**
Zions Data Service Co., 2200 S. 3270 W., 84119, pg. 1793 **PB**
Zions First National Bank, One S. Main, Ste. 200, 84111, pg. 1793 **PB**
Zions Insurance Agency, Inc., J. C. Penney Bldg., 310 S. Main, Ste. 308, 84101, pg. 1793 **PB**
Zions Investment Securities, Inc., 1345 Kennecott Bldg., 84133, pg. 1793 **PB**
Zions Life Insurance Co., J. C. Penney Bldg., 310 S. Main, 84101, pg. 1793 **PB**
Zions Mortgage Company, 4460 Highland Dr., 84124, pg. 1793 **PB**
Zion's Securities Corp., 102 E.S. Social Hall Ave., 84111, pg. 327 **PV**

Sandy

Becton Dickinson Infusion Therapy, Inc., 9450 S. State St., 84707, pg. 199 **PB**
Beehive Machinery Co., P.O. Box 5002, 9100 S. 500 W., 84091-5002, pg. 1160 **PV**
DOD Electronics Corporation, 8760 S. Sandy Pkwy., 84070, pg. 787 **PB**
Human Affairs International Inc., 10150 S. Centennial Pkwy., 84070, pg. 1036 **PB**
Isomedix Operations Inc., 9120 S. 150 E., 84070, pg. 1515 **PB**
MINING SERVICES INTERNATIONAL, INC., 8805 S. Sandy Pkwy., 84070, pg. 1115 **PV**
PENCO-Utah, 8160 S. Highland Dr., Ste. 203, 84093, pg. 1508 **IT**
Prime Option Services, 10200 S. 280 West, 84070, pg. 1132 **PB**
RECOMP, INC., 9710 S. 700 E., Ste. 101A, 84070, pg. 914 **PV**

South Jordan

MERIT MEDICAL SYSTEMS, INC., 1600 W. Merit Pkwy., 84095, pg. 1096 **PB**

Spanish Fork

Banta Information Services Group, 2600 N. Main St., 84660-9596, pg. 188 **PB**
Longview Fibre Co. Western Container Division, 2220 N. Main, 84660, pg. 1014 **PB**
PDM Steel Service Center-Spanish Fork, 1100 North 300 West, 84660, pg. 1305 **PB**

Springville

Nestle Frozen/Refrigerated Food Co., P.O. Box 3000, 815 W. Ray Klauck Way, 84663, pg. 918 **IT**

Valmont Industries, Inc., 1535 Mountain Springs Pkwy., 84663, pg. 1707 **PB**
Valtek International, 1350 N. Mountain Springs Pkwy., 84663-0903, pg. 658 **PB**

Tooele

Akzo Salt of Utah, 1428 James Palmer Rd., 84074, pg. 48 **IT**
EG & G Defense Materials Division, 11600 Stark Rd., 84074, pg. 543 **PB**
Mercur Mine, P.O. Box 838, Mercur Canyon Rd., 84074-0838, pg. 169 **PB**

Tremonton

La-Z-Boy Utah, 350 W. Tenth N., 84337, pg. 973 **PB**

Vernal

Weatherford US Inc., 1150 E. 1500 S., 84078, pg. 1749 **PB**

Vineyard

GENEVA STEEL, 10 S. Geneva Rd., 84058, pg. 729 **PB**

West Jordan

Amtech, 8050 S. 1300 West, 84088, pg. 594 **PB**
Interstate Brick Company, 9780 S. 5200 West, 84088, pg. 830 **PV**
R-Cubed Composites Inc., 3392 W. 8600 South, 84088-9706, pg. 1037 **IT**

Woods Cross

CHEMCENTRAL/Salt Lake City, 2465 S. 1100 W., 84087, pg. 232 **PB**
Pipe Fabricating & Supply Company, 2398 S. 1100 W St., 84087, pg. 867 **PV**

VERMONT

Arlington

MACK MOLDING COMPANY INC., Warm Brook Rd., 05250, pg. 691 **PV**

Barre

Granite Savings Bank & Trust Company, 36 N. Main St., 05641, pg. 187 **PB**

Barton

Community National Bank, P.O. Box K, Church St., 05822, pg. 416 **PB**

Bellows Falls

WHITNEY BLAKE COMPANY OF VERMONT, INC., Industrial Dr., 05101, pg. 148 **PV**

Bennington

BENNINGTON IRON WORKS, INC., Harmon Rd., 05201, pg. 133 **PV**
BIJUR LUBRICATING CORPORATION, 50 Kocher Dr., 05201, pg. 143 **PV**
Courtaulds Structural Composites Inc., P.O. Box 618, 6, Shields Dr., 05201, pg. 338 **IT**
Green Mountain Steel Erectors Inc., P.O. Box 798, Harmon Rd., 05201, pg. 133 **PV**
Intergraph Corporation, 145 Convent Ave., 05201, pg. 890 **PB**
Kindergard, 160 Benmont Ave., 05201, pg. 1030 **PB**
MACE SECURITY INTERNATIONAL, INC., 160 Benmont Ave., 05201, pg. 1030 **PB**
NASTECH Corp., One Shields Dr., Rte. 2, 05201, pg. 903 **IT**

Berlin

CAPITAL CITY PRESS, INC., Airport Rd., 05602, pg. 205 **PV**

Bethel

BETHEL MILLS, INC., One N. Main St., 05032, pg. 141 **PV**
Bethel Mills Kitchen & Bath, P.O. Box 61, 05032, pg. 141 **PV**

Bradford

BRADFORD OIL COMPANY, INC., Jcts. Rtes. 5 & 25, 05033, pg. 164 **PV**

Brandon

Vermont Tubbs, Inc., P.O. Box 369, One Tubbs Ave., 05733, pg. 215 **PV**

Brattleboro

Banknorth Mortgage Company, 425 Western Ave., 05301, pg. 187 **PB**
C & S WHOLESALE GROCERY INC., P.O. Box 821, Old Ferry Rd., 05301, pg. 192 **PV**
ERD Environmental, Inc., 205 Main St., 05302, pg. 546 **PB**
FIBERMARK INC., P.O. Box 498, 161 Wellington Rd., 05302, pg. 620 **PB**
First Vermont Bank & Trust Company, 215 Main St., 05301, pg. 187 **PB**
HOLSTEIN ASSOCIATION USA, INC., One Holstein Pl., 05302-0808, pg. 536 **PV**
Holstein-Friesian Services, Inc., One Holstein Pl., 05301, pg. 536 **PV**
Office Products Division, P.O. Box 498, 161 Wellington Rd., 05302, pg. 620 **PB**
Quebecor Printing Book Press Inc., Putney Rd., 05301, pg. 1078 **IT**
TRI-S Environmental Consulting, 205 Main St., 05301, pg. 546 **PB**
VERMONT FINANCIAL SERVICES CORP., 100 Main St., 05301, pg. 1716 **PB**
Vermont National Bank, 100 Main St., 05301, pg. 1716 **PB**
Vermont Yankee Nuclear Power Corp., Ferry Rd., P.O. Box 169, 05301, pg. 328 **PB**

Burlington

Alcoa International Finance Company, Five Burlington Sq., 4th Fl., 05401, pg. 60 **PB**
Alcoa International Holdings Corp., Five Burlington St., 05401, pg. 60 **PB**
Alcoa Properties, Inc., Five Burlington Sq., 4th Fl., 05402-1491, pg. 61 **PB**
Alcoa Securities Corporation, Five Burlington Sq., 05401, pg. 61 **PB**
BANKNORTH GROUP INC., P.O. Box 5420, 300 Financial Plaza, 05401, pg. 186 **PB**
Birchwood Terrace Healthcare, 43 Starr Farm Rd., 05401, pg. 1712 **PB**
Blodgett Combi, 50 Lakeside Ave., P.O. Box 4489, 05401, pg. 1064 **PB**
G.S. Blodgett Corporation, 50 Lakeside Ave., 05401, pg. 1064 **PB**
Blodgett International, 50 Lakeside Ave., 05402, pg. 1064 **PB**
The Blodgett Oven Co., Inc., 50 Lakeside Ave., 05401, pg. 1064 **PB**
Burlington Free Press, 191 College St., 05401, pg. 700 **PB**
Capital National Insurance Company, c/o Downs, Rachlin & Martin, 7 Burlington Square, Ste. 600, 05401, pg. 1207 **PB**
Chittenden Bank, Two Burlington Sq., 05402, pg. 351 **PB**
CHITTENDEN CORPORATION, Two Burlington Sq., 05402, pg. 350 **PB**
Dwight Asset Management Company, P.O. Box 1590, 125 College St., 05402-1590, pg. 1673 **PB**
EDLUND COMPANY, INC., 159 Industrial Pkwy., 05401, pg. 364 **PV**
Frontier Communications of New England, 29 Church St., 05402, pg. 684 **PB**
General Dynamics Armament Systems, Lakeside Ave., 05401, pg. 709 **PB**
Green Mountain Propane Gas Co., 346 Shelburne St., 05401-4938, pg. 761 **PB**
The Howard Bank, N.A., 111 Main St., 05401, pg. 187 **PB**
IDX SYSTEMS CORPORATION, 1400 Shelburne Rd., P.O. Box 1070, 05402-1070, pg. 854 **PB**
Key Bank of Vermont, 149 Bank St., 05402, pg. 954 **PB**
MCKENZIES OF VERMONT, INC., 160 Flynn Ave., 05401, pg. 723 **PV**
North Group Realty, 300 Financial Plaza, 05401, pg. 187 **PB**
Skandia International Risk Management (Vermont), Inc., P.O. Box 64649, 346 Shelburne Rd., 05406-4649, pg. 1257 **IT**
The Stratevest Group, N.A., 111 Main St., 05401, pg. 187 **PB**
Three Rivers Insurance Company, Five Burlington Sq., 05401, pg. 61 **PB**
Tiara Insurance Company, Seven Burlington Sq., 05401, pg. 462 **PB**
Vermont Transit Co., Inc., 135 St. Paul St., 05401, pg. 766 **PB**
Willis Corroon Management (Vermont) Ltd., 76 Paul St., Ste. 501, 05401, pg. 1505 **IT**

Cabot

Cabot Creamery Co-Operative Inc., 130 Main St., 05647, pg. 26 **PV**

Colchester

Bombardier Capital Group, 1600 Mountain Dr., 05446, pg. 200 **IT**
Bombardier Capital Inc., 1600 Mountain Dr., 05446, pg. 200 **IT**
Champlain Cable Corp., 12 Hercules Dr., 05446, pg. 637 **IT**
Jordan's Foods-Colchester Division, Hercules Dr., P.O. Box 70, 05446, pg. 599 **PV**
Polhemus Inc., P.O. Box 560, One Hercules Dr., 05446, pg. 605 **PV**

PB - *U.S. Public Companies Volume*
PV - *U.S. Private Companies Volume*
IT - *International Public & Private Companies Volume*

1460

Geographic Index-U.S.

Derby

COMMUNITY BANCORP, P.O. Box 259, Derby St., 05829, pg. 416   **PB**

Community National Bank, P.O. Box 259, 05829, pg. 416   **PB**

Derby Line

Community National Bank, P.O. Box 455, Main St., 05830, pg. 416   **PB**

Essex

Huber & Suhner Inc., P.O. Box 400, One Allen Martin Dr., 05451, pg. 637   **IT**

Essex Junction

Essex Plant, Belden Wire & Cable, P.O. Box 148, 05453, pg. 201   **PB**

KOMBI, LTD., Six Thompson Dr., 05451-8767, pg. 631   **PV**

Graniteville

ROCK OF AGES CORPORATION, 772 Graniteville Rd., 05654, pg. 1396   **PB**

Hinesburg

Stella Foods, Inc., Main St., 05461, pg. 1040   **PV**

Island Pond

Community National Bank, P.O. Box 441, Main St., 05846, pg. 416   **PB**

Killington

Killington Limited, Box 2450, RR 1, 05751, pg. 61   **PV**

Ludlow

Ludlow Telephone Co., 111 Main St., 05149, pg. 1571   **PB**

Manchester

THE ORVIS COMPANY, INC., U.S. Rte. Historic 7A, 05254, pg. 820   **PV**

Montpelier

Administrative Services, Inc., National Life Dr., 05604, pg. 785   **PV**

Equity Services, Inc., One National Life Dr., 05604, pg. 785   **PV**

Miami Valley Insurance Co., Crosstown Rd., 05602, pg. 474   **PB**

NATIONAL LIFE INSURANCE COMPANY, National Life Dr., 05604, pg. 785   **PV**

National Life Investment Management Co., Inc., National Life Dr., 05604, pg. 785   **PV**

Redstone Properties, Inc., National Life Drive, 05604, pg. 785   **PV**

Sentinel Administrative Service Corporation, National Life Dr., 05604, pg. 785   **PV**

Sentinel Advisors, Inc., National Life Dr., 05604, pg. 785   **PV**

Mount Snow

Mount Snow Resort, Mount Snow, 05356, pg. 61   **PV**

Newfane

Zone VI Studios, Inc., 05345-0219, pg. 202   **PV**

Newport

Citizens Utilities Company, P.O. Box 604, 05855, pg. 380   **PB**

Community National Bank, P.O. Box 266, Main St., 05855, pg. 416   **PB**

The Newport Daily Express, Hill St., 05855, pg. 1343   **PB**

Northern Vermont Railroad, P.O. Box 39, 05855, pg. 575   **PV**

North Bennington

Advanced Polymers Division, Water St., 05257, pg. 689   **PB**

Chem Fab Corporation, 13 Water St., 05257, pg. 344   **PB**

North Springfield

Fellows Corporation, Precision Dr., 05150, pg. 461   **PV**

Vermont USA Machine Tool Group, Precision Dr., 05150, pg. 461   **PV**

Northfield

Northfield Telephone Co., Box 30, Seven Park Sq., 05663, pg. 1571   **PB**

Perkinsville

Perkinsville Telephone Co., Inc., P.O. Box 157, Upper Falls Rd., 05151, pg. 1571   **PB**

Proctor

Omya, Inc., 61 Main St., 05765, pg. 1061   **IT**

Pluess-Staufer Industries, Inc., 61 Main St., 05765, pg. 1061   **IT**

Randolph

Waterbury Companies, Inc., S. Pleasant St. Ext., 05060, pg. 308   **PB**

Richmond

HARRINGTON'S OF VERMONT, INC., 618 Main St., 05477, pg. 504   **PV**

Rutland

C.V. Realty, Inc., 77 Grove St., 05701, pg. 328   **PB**

CARRIS FINANCIAL GROUP, 439 West St., 05701, pg. 215   **PV**

Carris Reels, Inc., 439 West St., 05701, pg. 215   **PV**

CASELLA WASTE SYSTEMS, INC., 25 Greens Hill Ln., 05701, pg. 312   **PB**

Catamount Energy Corporation, 71 Allen St., 05701, pg. 328   **PB**

Catamount Investment Corporation, 77 Grove St., 05701, pg. 328   **PB**

CENTRAL VERMONT PUBLIC SERVICE CORPORATION, 77 Grove St., 05701, pg. 327   **PB**

Connecticut Valley Electric Co., 77 Grove St., 05701, pg. 328   **PB**

Smart Energy Services, Inc., 77 Grove St., 05701, pg. 328   **PB**

Vermont Electric Power Co., Inc., P.O. Box 548, Pinnacle Ridge Rd., 05702, pg. 328   **PB**

Saint Albans

Barry Callebaut, 400 Industrial Park Dr., 05478, pg. 252   **IT**

Bertek, Inc., 110 Lake St., 05478, pg. 1143   **PB**

Central Vermont Railway, Inc., Two Federal St., 05478, pg. 258   **IT**

A.N. DERINGER, INC., 64-66 N. Main St., 05478, pg. 326   **PV**

The Fonda Group, Inc., 21 Lowernewton St., 05478, pg. 421   **PV**

Franklin-Lamoille Bank, Eight N. Main St., 05478, pg. 187   **PB**

Saint Johnsbury

Community National Bank, RR2 Box 36A, Corner of I-91 Access Rd., 05819, pg. 416   **PB**

Northern Petroleum, P.O. Box 540, 05819, pg. 164   **PV**

Shelburne

THE SHELBURNE CORPORATION, Rte. 7 S., 05482, pg. 991   **PV**

Shelburne Husky Div., P.O. Box 158, 05482, pg. 991   **PV**

THE VERMONT TEDDY BEAR COMPANY, INC., 2236 Shelburne Rd., 05482, pg. 1716   **PB**

South Burlington

BEN & JERRY'S HOMEMADE INC., 30 Community Dr., 05403, pg. 210   **PB**

GMP Real Estate Corp., 25 Green Mountain Dr., P.O. Box 850, 05402, pg. 761   **PB**

GREEN MOUNTAIN POWER CORPORATION, 25 Green Mountain Dr., 05402-0850, pg. 761   **PB**

LANE PRESS, INC., 1000 Hinesburg Rd., 05403, pg. 650   **PV**

Lease-Elec, Inc., P.O. Box 850, 25 Green Mountain Dr., 05402, pg. 761   **PB**

Mountain Energy, Inc., 25 Green Mountain Dr., 05403, pg. 761   **PB**

PIZZAGALLI CONSTRUCTION CO., 50 Joy Dr., 05403, pg. 868   **PV**

Titania Insurance Company of America, Lakewood Commons, Ste. 200, 123 Shellburn Rd., 05403, pg. 1731   **PB**

Vermont Energy Resources, Inc., 25 Green Mountain Dr., P.O. Box 850, 05402, pg. 761   **PB**

Vermont Gas Systems, Inc., 85 Swift St., 05403, pg. 542   **IT**

Springfield

Browning-Ferris Industries of Vermont, Inc., P.O. Box 121, 05156, pg. 264   **PB**

Bryant Grinder Corp., 257 Clinton St., 05156, pg. 461   **PV**

Disposal Specialists, Inc., P.O. Box 121, 05156, pg. 264   **PB**

J & L Metrology Company, Inc., N. Precision Dr., 05150, pg. 461   **PV**

Miltope Corporation Vermont Facility, 76 Pearl St., 05156, pg. 1114   **PB**

Stockbridge

Advanced Animations, Inc., Rte. 107, 05772, pg. 1703   **PB**

Stowe

TRAPP FAMILY LODGE, INC., 42 Trapp Hill Rd., 05672, pg. 1098   **PV**

Stratton Mountain

Stratton Corporation, Stratton Mountain, RRI Box 145, 05155-9406, pg. 685   **IT**

Swanton

Canstar Apparel Inc., 50 Jonergin Dr., 05488, pg. 1184   **PB**

I.F.C. USA Corp., Rd. 78 Swanton Industrial Park, 05488, pg. 696   **IT**

Sunhill Food Of Vermont, Inc., 14 Jonergin Dr., 05488, pg. 1464   **IT**

Vermont Fasteners Manufacturing, Rd. 78 Swanton Industrial Park, 05488, pg. 696   **IT**

Troy

Community National Bank, P.O. Box 127, Rte. 101, 05868, pg. 416   **PB**

Vergennes

Simmonds Precision Engine Systems, 100 Parton Rd., 05491, pg. 752   **PB**

Warren

Sugarbush, RR1 Box 350, 05674, pg. 62   **PV**

Waterbury

GREEN MOUNTAIN COFFEE ROASTERS, INC., 33 Coffee Lane, 05676, pg. 761   **PB**

West Burke

Burke Lumber Co., P.O. Box 210, Rte. 5, 05871-0210, pg. 1729   **PB**

West Rutland

Killington Wood Products, Inc., P.O. Box 696, 05702, pg. 215   **PV**

Westminster Station

BURTCO, INC., P.O. Box 40, Rt. 123, 05159, pg. 188   **PV**

Burtco Metal Systems, Conn River Bridge Rd., 05159, pg. 188   **PV**

White River Junction

CDF Northeast, Nine Harnson Ave., 05001, pg. 298   **PB**

LOGIC ASSOCIATES, INC., 221 Christian St., 05001, pg. 673   **PV**

Williston

Champion/Jogbra, Inc., 13 Avenue D Sport Pl., 05495, pg. 1433   **PB**

KBA-Planeta North America Inc., Three Hurricane Ln., 05495-0900, pg. 742   **IT**

Rossignol Ski Co., Industrial Rd., 05495, pg. 1127   **IT**

Thermo Consulting Engineers, 2A Williston Park, 05495, pg. 1594   **PB**

Wilmington

Haystack Ski Resort at Mount Snow, Coldbrook Rd., 05363, pg. 61   **PV**

Windsor

CONE-BLANCHARD MACHINE COMPANY, Seven Everett Ln., 05089, pg. 262   **PV**

Winooski

BIO-TEK INSTRUMENTS, INC., Highland Industrial Pk., 05404, pg. 144   **PV**

County Data Corp., 136 W. Canal St., 05404, pg. 70   **PB**

TWINCRAFT, INC., Two Tigan St., 05404, pg. 1111   **PV**

Woodstock

Woodstock National Bank, 21 Elm St., 05091, pg. 187   **PB**

VIRGIN ISLANDS (U.S)

Charlotte Amalie

AMI Industries F.S.C., Inc., P.O. Box 309420, 00803, pg. 401   **PB**

Geographic Index-U.S.

Air Products World Trade, Inc. c/o Chase Trade, Inc., P.O. Box 309420, 55-11 Curacao Gade, 00803-9420, pg. 31 PB
Bell Atlantic Foreign Sales Corporation, CitiBank Bldg., Veteran's Dr., Ste. 208, 00801, pg. 202 PB
Essef Manufacturing FSC, Inc., Ste. A & AN, Upper Level Drake's Passage, 00802, pg. 592 PB
G.D. International, Ltd., Citibank Bldg., Ste. 208, Veterns Dr., 00801, pg. 1219 PB
LITTLE SWITZERLAND, INC., 161-B Crown Bay Cruise Dock, 00802, pg. 1001 PB
Salem Foreign Sales Corp., 5144 Dronningens Gade, Ste. 300, 00802, pg. 961 PV
West International Sales Corporation, Chase Trade, Inc., 55-11 Curacoo Gade, 00803, pg. 1755 PB

Christiansted

TDW Foreign Sales Corp., 1A Gallows Bay, 00820, pg. 1180 PV

Frederiksted

Mt. Eagle Corporation, P.O. Box 33, 00840, pg. 261 PB

Saint Croix

Hercules Overseas Corporation, pg. 810 PB
Hess Oil Virgin Islands Corp., P.O. Box 127, Kingshill Post Office, 00851, pg. 65 PB
M21 Industries, Inc., P.O. Box 1547, Frederiksted, 00801, pg. 502 PB
Millipore Intertech (V.I.), Inc., The Chase Manhattan Bank, N.A., No. 4 Orange Grove, 00820, pg. 1113 PB
Presto Export Ltd., c/o ChasePro, P.O. Box 309420, 00803, pg. 1159 PB

Saint Thomas

ABN-AMRO Trust Company (Virgin Islands), Guardian Bldg., 2nd Fl., Havensight, Charlotte Amalie, 00801, pg. 11 IT
API-FS Corporation, 5 Norre Gade, 00801-8080, pg. 90 PV
Abbey Etna Foreign Sales Corporation, 00801, pg. 9 PV
Analogic Foreign Sales Corp., 00801, pg. 109 PB
Bared Jewelers, Sparky's, 30 Main St., 00802, pg. 103 IT
Camtronics Foreign Sales Corp., 00801, pg. 109 PB
Caterpillar Export Limited, P.O. Box 10332, Charlotte Amalie, 00801, pg. 315 PB
Devcon Crown Bay Corp., Crown Bay Marina, Ste. 528, 00802, pg. 502 PV
Ebasco V.I. Inc., c/o De Vos & Co., 5 Norre Gade, Charlotte Amalie, 00801, pg. 1587 PB
Keithley Foreign Sales Corp., 5 Norre Gade, Charlotte Amalie, 00801, pg. 947 PB
Mead Export, Inc., Citibank Bldg., Veterans Dr., Ste. 208, 00801, pg. 1076 PB
Motorola Foreign Sales Corporation, Chase Financial Center, 11A & 11B Curacao Gade, 00804, pg. 1138 PB
Olin Export Trading Corporation, 24 Dronningens Gade, 00801, pg. 1219 PB
The Raymond Export Corporation, 49A-50A Kongens Gardens, 00801, pg. 123 IT
Timberland International Sales Corporation, Chase Financial Center, 11A & 11B Curacao Gade, 00804, pg. 1609 PB
V.I. Cement & Building Products, Inc., P.O. Box 7368, 00801, pg. 502 PB
The Virgin Islands Daily News, 4-5 Wimmelshaft Gade, P.O. Box 7638, 00801, pg. 702 PB
Vulcan International, Ltd., The Guardian Bldg., 2nd Fl., Havensight, pg. 1726 PB

VIRGINIA

Abingdon

The Dosco Corp., P.O. Box 324, Rt. 10, 24210-9306, pg. 124 IT
First Virginia Bank-Mountain Empire, P.O. Box 1038, 498 Cummings St., 24202-1038, pg. 642 PB
Hapco/American Div., Hillman Hwy., 24210, pg. 351 PV
K-VA-T, P.O. Box 1158, 201 Trigg St., 24212, pg. 603 PB

Alexandria

Alexandria Sales, 1800 Duke St., 22314, pg. 611 PB
ALLIED PLYWOOD CORP., 6189 Grovesdale Ct., 22310, pg. 40 PV
ASTRE CORPORATE GROUP, P.O. Box 25766, 22313, pg. 93 PV
The Atrium Development Co., 777 Duke St., 22314, pg. 1613 PB
Betac Corporation, 2001 N. Beauregard St., 22311, pg. 140 PB
BETAC INTERNATIONAL CORPORATION, 2001 N. Beauregard St., 22311, pg. 140 PV
BOAT AMERICA CORP., 880 S. Pickett St., 22304, pg. 153 PV
BOWL AMERICA, INCORPORATED, 6446 Edsall Rd., 22312, pg. 248 PB
Cadmus Magazines, 1800 Diagonal Rd., Ste. 420, 22314, pg. 291 PB
Celsius Inc., 1800 Diagonal Rd., Ste. 230, 22314, pg. 278 PB
CelsiusTech Inc., 1800 Diagonal Rd., Ste. 230, 22314, pg. 278 IT
Circle International, 205 South Whiting St., Ste. 315, 22304, pg. 372 PB

Crown America Life Insurance Company, 201 N. Union St., Ste. 140, 22314, pg. 468 IT
CUISINE SOLUTIONS, INC., 85 S. Bragg St., Ste. 600, 22312, pg. 466 PB
FFV Finance Inc., 1800 Diagonal Rd., Ste 280, 22314, pg. 278 IT
Falkland Partners, 201 N. Union St., Ste. 300, 22314, pg. 361 PB
Federal Integrated Systems Corp., 1600 N. Beauregard St., 22311, pg. 570 PB
GP Taurio, Inc., 1901 N. Beauregard St., 22311, pg. 694 PB
HADRON, INC., 4900 Seminary Rd., Ste. 800, 22311, pg. 773 PB
HALIFAX CORPORATION, P.O. Box 11904, 5250 Cherokee Ave., 22312, pg. 775 PB
Halifax Engineering, Inc., 5250 Cherokee Ave., 22312, pg. 775 PB
Halifax Technical Services, 5250 Cherokee Ave., 22312, pg. 775 PB
Harris Data Services Corporation, 1201 E. Abingdon Dr., Ste. 300, 22314, pg. 791 PB
Harris Washington Operations, Harris Parkway Bldg., 1201 E. Abingdon Dr., Ste. 300, 22314, pg. 792 PB
Jane's Information Group, 1340 Braddock Pl., Ste. 300, 22314-1651, pg. 1601 IT
Mazo Lerch Company, Inc., 4720 Eisenhower Ave., 22304, pg. 918 PB
The Mercury Group, 201 N. Union St., Ste. 520, 22314, pg. 13 PV
METROCALL, INC., 6677 Richmond Hwy., 22306, pg. 1102 PB
MICRODYNE CORPORATION, 3601 Eisenhower Ave., Ste. 300, 22304, pg. 1105 PB
National Journal Daily Briefings, 3129 Mt. Vernon Ave., 22305, pg. 785 PV
Networking Products, 3601 Eisenhower Ave., 22304, pg. 1105 PB
Robinson Terminal Warehouse Corp., Two Duke St., 22314, pg. 1743 PB
Sammler Kabinett, Inc., 777 Duke St., 22314, pg. 1613 PB
Scott & Stringfellow, Inc., 320 King St., Ste. 301, 22314, pg. 1446 PV
Sharp Electronics Corporation, 5825 Barclay Drive, Ste. 3, 22315, pg. 1229 IT
STEPHENSON, INC., 5731 General Washington Dr., 22312, pg. 1040 PV
Sycom Services Inc., 4900 Seminary Rd., Ste. 800, 22311, pg. 773 PB
Thomson Corporation of America, 99 Canal Center Plaza, 22314, pg. 1383 IT
Time-Life Books (Europe), Inc., 777 Duke St., 22314, pg. 1613 PB
Time-Life Customer Service, 777 Duke St., 22314, pg. 1613 PB
Time-Life, Inc., 2000 Duke St., 22314, pg. 1613 PB
Veda Design Group, 1800 N. Beauregard St., 22311, pg. 1136 PV
Veda Incorporated, 2001 N. Beauregard St., Ste. 1200, 22311, pg. 1136 PV
Veda International, Inc., 2001 N. Beauregard St., Ste. 1200, 22311, pg. 1136 PV
VERIDIAN, 2001 N. Beauregard St., Ste. 1200, 22311, pg. 1136 PV
Virginia-American Water Co., P.O. Box 25405, 2223 Duke St., 22313, pg. 96 PB
Wall Street Deli, Inc., 5568 General Washington Dr., Ste. A207, 22312, pg. 1734 PB
Washington Operations, 1201 E. Abingdon Dr., Ste. 500, 22314, pg. 791 PB
Weichert Insurance Agent, Inc., 1700 Diagonal Rd., 22314, pg. 1159 PV
Weichert Realty Career Development, 1700 Diagonal Rd., 22314, pg. 1159 PV
Weichert Realty, Inc., Station Center, 1700 Diagonal Rd., 22314, pg. 1159 PV

Altavista

The Lane Company, Inc., E. Franklin Ave., 24517, pg. 688 PB

Amelia Court House

Amelia Telephone Co., P.O. Box 76, Amelia Ave., 23002, pg. 1571 PB

Amherst

Buffalo Air Handling, Zane Snead Dr., RR3Box 423, 24531-9803, pg. 103 PB
Virginia Fibre Corp., P.O. Box 339, 24521, pg. 764 PB

Annandale

Acacia Federal Mortgage Corp., 7023 Little River Tpke., 22003, pg. 11 PB
JWK INTERNATIONAL CORP., 7617 Little River Tpke., 22003, pg. 579 PV
TMP Worldwide/Recruitment Division, 7535 Little River Tpke., 22003, pg. 1065 PV

Arlington

AES Americas, 1001 N. 19th St., 22209, pg. 5 PB
AES CORPORATION, 1001 N. 19th St., 22209, pg. 5 PB
AES Enterprise, 1001 N. 19th St., 22209, pg. 5 PB
AM General Corporation, 2345 Crystal Dr., Ste. 808, 22202, pg. 922 PV

Advanced Marine Enterprises, Inc., 1725 Jefferson Davis Hwy., Ste. 1300, 22202, pg. 1182 PB
AES Aurora, 1001 N. 19th St., 22209, pg. 5 PB
Allied Security Inc., 200 N. Glebe Rd., #909, 22203, pg. 40 PV
ANSER (ANALYTIC SERVICES INC.), 1215 Jeff Davis Hwy., Ste. 800, 22202-3251, pg. 75 PV
ARGOSystems, Inc., 2301 Jefferson Davis Hwy., Ste. 1519, 22202, pg. 240 PB
Arthur D. Little, Inc., Colonial Place One, 2111 Wilson Blvd., Ste. 1000, 22201-3001, pg. 670 PV
BAII/NZ, Inc., 1300 N. 17th St., 15th Fl., 22209, pg. 202 PB
Bell Atlantic Argentina, Inc., 1300 N. 17th St., Ste. 1510, 22209, pg. 202 PB
Bell Atlantic Asia, Inc., 1300 N. 17th St., Ste. 1510, 22209, pg. 202 PB
Bell Atlantic International, Inc., 1300 N. 17th St., Ste. 1510, 22209, pg. 202 PB
Bell Atlantic Network Services, Inc., 1310 N. Court House Rd., 22201, pg. 202 PB
Bell Atlantic Puerto Rico, Inc., 1300 N. 17th St., Ste. 1510, 22209, pg. 203 PB
Bell Atlantic Systems Integration Corp., 1550 Wilson Blvd., 5th Fl., 22209, pg. 203 PB
CACI INTERNATIONAL INC, 1100 N. Glebe Rd., 22201, pg. 272 PB
Claritas, Inc., 1525 Wilson Boulevard, 22209-2411, pg. 1447 IT
Communications Technology Group, 2100 Washington Blvd., 22204-5710, pg. 1199 PB
DRS Technologies, Inc., 1215 S. Jefferson Davis Hwy., Ste. 1004, 22202, pg. 474 PB
Digi International Federal Systems, 2231 Crystal Dr., Ste. 500, 22202, pg. 507 PB
EDO Washington Office, 2001 Jefferson Davis Hwy., 22202, pg. 542 PB
ENVIRON International, 4350 N. Fairfax Dr., 22203, pg. 1285 PB
The Ericsson Corporation, President's Office, 2101 Wilson Blvd., Ste. 402, 22201, pg. 1364 IT
Ericsson Network Systems, Inc., 2101 Wilson Blvd., Ste. 402, 22201, pg. 1365 IT
Federal Home Loan Mortgage Corporation (Freddie Mac)-Northeast Region, 2231 Crystal Dr., Ste. 900, 22202, pg. 615 PB
GANNETT COMPANY, INC., 1100 Wilson Blvd., 22234, pg. 698 PB
Gannett New Media, 1000 Wilson Blvd., 22229, pg. 699 PB
Gannett News Service, Inc., 1000 Wilson Blvd., 22229, pg. 700 PB
Gannett Satellite Information Network, Inc., 1000 Wilson Blvd., 22229, pg. 700 PB
Gannett Supply Corp., 1100 Wilson Blvd., 22234, pg. 699 PB
Hecht's, 685 N. Glebe Rd., 22203-2199, pg. 1063 PB
THE IDI GROUP COMPANIES, 901 N. Stuart St., Ste. 1110, 22203, pg. 554 PV
ISA Information Systems Services, 2800 Shirlington Rd., 22206, pg. 566 PV
INTEGRATED SYSTEMS ANALYSTS, INC., 2800 Shirlington Rd., Ste. 1100, 22206, pg. 566 PV
Intergraph Corporation, Crystal Park 4, 2345 Crystal Dr., Ste. 415, 22202, pg. 890 PB
Israel Aircraft Industries International Inc., 1700 N. Moore St., Ste. 1210, 22209, pg. 690 IT
Italian Aerospace Industries, 1235 Jefferson Davis Hwy., Ste. 500, 22202, pg. 654 IT
Jacobs Engineering Group Inc., 1300 N. 17th St., Ste. 601, 22209, pg. 921 PB
KASTLE SYSTEMS LLC, 1501 Wilson Blvd., 22209, pg. 608 PV
Kodak Commercial & Information Systems Marketing, 1155 Wilson Blvd., 22209, pg. 551 PB
Logicon Operating Systems Division, 2100 Washington Blvd., 22204, pg. 1199 PB
M.A.I., 1901 N. Moore St., Ste. 804, 22209, pg. 795 IT
MCI Mass Markets, 1200 S. Hayes St., 22202, pg. 1024 PB
M.C.N. SAT US, 1901 N. Moore St., Ste. 804, 22209, pg. 792 IT
Martin Marietta Fleet Combat System Services, 2011 Crystal Dr., Ste. 905, 22202, pg. 1007 PB
Matra Aerospace Inc., 1735 Jefferson Davis Hwy., Suite 807, 22202, pg. 795 IT
THE MILLS CORPORATION, 1300 Wilson Blvd., Ste. 400, 22209, pg. 1113 PB
Moffet, Larson, & Johnson, 1110 N. Glebe Rd., 22201, pg. 1743 PB
NCS Information Technology & Federal Systems, 4301 Wilson Blvd., Ste. 200, 22203-4196, pg. 1155 PB
NATIONAL ELECTRICAL MANUFACTURERS ASSOCIATION, 1300 N. 17th St., Ste. 1847, 22209-3801, pg. 782 PV
Northrop Grumman Corporation - Washington, D.C., 1000 Wilson Blvd., Ste. 2300, 22209-2278, pg. 1199 PB
Northrop Grumman International, Inc., 1000 Wilson Blvd., Ste. 2300, 22209-2278, pg. 1198 PB
OCE, 2300 Clarendon Blvd., 22201-3367, pg. 994 IT
Pitney Bowes Management Services, 1777 N. Kent St., 22209-2110, pg. 1304 PB
Polaroid Corp.- Camera Division, 2111 Wilson Blvd., 22201-3001, pg. 1313 PB
Raytheon Systems Company, 1100 Wilson Blvd., 22209, pg. 1364 PB
ReliaStar Employer Financial Services Company, 4601 Fairfax Dr., 22203, pg. 1376 PB
Reltech Development Laboratory, 4601 N. Fairfax Dr., Ste. 1050, 22203-1547, pg. 1309 PB

PB - *U.S. Public Companies Volume*
PV - *U.S. Private Companies Volume*
IT - *International Public & Private Companies Volume*

1462

Geographic Index-U.S.

ROSENTHAL AUTOMOTIVE ORGANIZATION, 1100 S. Glebe Rd., 22204, pg. 946 **PV**
SHL Systemhouse - Latin America Operations, 1010 N. Glebe Rd., Ste. 200, 22201-5700, pg. 1154 **IT**
SPC International Corp., 1000 Wilson Blvd., 22209, pg. 1061 **PV**
SRA INTERNATIONAL INC., 2000 15th St. N., 22201, pg. 957 **PV**
Smiths Industries Aerospace & Defense Systems Inc.-Washington D.C., 1225 Jefferson Davis Hwy., Ste. 1100, 22202, pg. 1268 **PB**
Spar Aviation Services, 2231 Crystal Dr., Ste. 500, 22202-3736, pg. 1288 **IT**
SYSTEM PLANNING CORP., 1000 Wilson Blvd., 22209, pg. 1061 **PV**
Thiokol Government Relations, 1735 Jefferson Davis Hwy., Ste. 1001, 22202-3461, pg. 1597 **PB**
Thomson-CSF, Inc., 2231 Crystal Dr., Ste. 814, 22202, pg. 1384 **IT**
TriData Inc., 1000 Wilson Blvd., 22209, pg. 1061 **PV**
Turner Construction Co., 4601 N. Fairfax Dr., 22203, pg. 1645 **PB**
United Defense L.P., 1525 Wilson's Blvd., 22209-2411, pg. 213 **PV**
United Services Life Insurance Co., 4601 Fairfax Dr., 22203, pg. 1376 **PB**
US Airways Fuel Corporation, 2345 Crystal Dr., 22227, pg. 1680 **PB**
US AIRWAYS GROUP, INC., 2345 Crystal Dr., 22227, pg. 1680 **PB**
US Airways, Inc., 2345 Crystal Dr., 22227, pg. 1680 **PB**
US Airways Leasing & Services, Inc., 2345 Crystal Dr., 22227, pg. 1680 **PB**
USA Today, 1000 Wilson Blvd., 22229, pg. 700 **PV**
Washington Business Journal, Inc., 2000 14th St. N., Ste. 500, 22201, pg. 20 **PV**
Wyle Laboratories-Eastern Operations, 2001 Jefferson Davis Hwy., 22202, pg. 1193 **PV**

Ashburn

Coherent Communications Systems Corp., 45085 University Dr., 20147-2745, pg. 1424 **PB**
enterWorks.com, inc., 19886 Ashburn Rd., 20147, pg. 1573 **PV**
TELOS CORPORATION, 19886 Ashburn Rd., 20147, pg. 1573 **PB**
Telos International Corp., 19886 Ashburn Rd., 20147, pg. 1573 **PB**
Telos Systems Integration, 19886 Ashburn Rd., 20147, pg. 1573 **PB**
United Litho, Inc., 21800 Beaumede Cir., 20147, pg. 993 **PV**

Ashland

Albright & Wilson, Inc., 10487 Lakeridge Pkwy., 23005, pg. 49 **IT**
Bear Island Paper Co., P.O. Box 2119, 23005, pg. 166 **PV**
Bear Island Paper Co., P.O. Box 2119, 23005, pg. 525 **PB**
Bear Island Timberlands Company, L.P., P.O. Box 2119, 23005, pg. 1743 **PB**
Bondioli & Pavesi Inc., 104 Sycamore Dr., 23005, pg. 201 **IT**
Hanover Manufacturing Corporation, 411 Leadbetter Pl., 23055, pg. 1386 **PB**
HOHNER/HSS INC., Lakeridge Pk., 10223 Sycamore Dr., 23005, pg. 533 **PV**
Lydall Transport, Ltd., 10970 Richardson Rd., 23005-3228, pg. 1021 **PB**
Mobil Mining & Minerals Company, 96 Lakeridge Ave., 23005-6683, pg. 1118 **PB**
WORSHAM SPRINKLER COMPANY, 10991 S. Richardson Rd., 23005, pg. 1191 **PV**

Baileys Crossroads

MOZEL DEVELOPMENT CORP., 6031 Leesburg Pike, 22041, pg. 765 **PV**

Bassett

Bassett Chair Co., Two Main St., 24055, pg. 193 **PB**
Bassett Furniture Co., Two Main St., 24055, pg. 193 **PB**
BASSETT FURNITURE INDUSTRIES, INCORPORATED, 3525 Fairystone Pkwy., 24055, pg. 193 **PB**
J.D. Bassett Mfg. Co., Two Main St., 24055, pg. 193 **PB**
Bassett Superior Lines, Two Main St., 24055, pg. 193 **PB**
Bassett Table Co., Two Main St., 24055, pg. 193 **PB**
National Mount Airy, Two Main St., 24055, pg. 193 **PB**
Weiman, P.O. Box 670, 24055, pg. 193 **PB**

Bedford

Bedford Bulletin, P.O. Box 331, 402 E. Main St., 24523-0331, pg. 648 **PV**
Bunker Hill Foods Inc., Hwy. # 122 S., 24523, pg. 219 **PV**
Piedmont Metal Products, Inc., P.O. Box 546, 24523, pg. 1770 **PB**

Berryville

Berryville Graphics Inc., P.O. Box 272, Springsbury Rd., 22611, pg. 191 **IT**
Bertelsmann Printing & Manufacturing Corp., P.O. Box 272, Springsbury Rd., 22611, pg. 191 **IT**

Blacksburg

Electro-Tec Corp., 1501 N. Main St., 24060, pg. 946 **PB**
Kollmorgen Virtual Motion Group, 1700 Kraft Dr., Ste. 1350, 24060, pg. 965 **PB**
Litton Poly-Scientific, 1213 N. Main St., 24060, pg. 1003 **PB**
Poly-Scientific Div., 1213 N. Main St., 24060-3127, pg. 1003 **PB**
Scott & Stringfellow, Inc., 2807 S. Main St., Ste. 240, 24060, pg. 1446 **PB**

Blue Ridge

General Shale Products Corp., P.O. Box 306, 24064, pg. 844 **IT**

Bluefield

Freightliner Enterprise Corp., 600 Mountain Lane, 24605, pg. 368 **IT**

Bracey

Ahlstrom Process Equipment Inc., P.O. Box 322, 23919, pg. 34 **IT**

Bristol

American Longwall Rebuild Inc., P.O. Box 1749, 24203, pg. 789 **PB**
Bristol Compressors, Inc., 649 Industrial Park Dr., 24210, pg. 1788 **PB**
Bristol Concrete Prods. Corp., 111 E. Mary St., 24201, pg. 843 **IT**
Bristol Lingerie, 203 Bob Morrison Blvd., 24201, pg. 542 **PV**
Carolina Steel-Fab Shop, 14781 Industrial Pk. Rd., 24202, pg. 214 **PV**
Dillard, A ResourceNet International Company, Eight Coronet Dr., 24203, pg. 902 **PB**
First American Federal Savings Bank, 110 Piedmont Ave., 24201, pg. 624 **PB**
Moore's Quality Snack Foods, Inc., P.O. Box 1909, 24203, pg. 158 **PV**
THE UNITED COMPANY, 1005 Glenway Ave., 24201, pg. 1121 **PV**

Buchanan

Groendyk, Inc., 1735 Main St., 24066, pg. 56 **PV**

Buena Vista

Bontex International (F.S.C.), P. O. Box 751, 24416, pg. 734 **PB**

Burke

THE VAN METRES COMPANIES, 5252 Lyngate Ct., 22015, pg. 1132 **PV**

Cedar Bluff

Triangle Mining Equipment Co. Inc., P.O. Box 270, Claypool Hall, 24609, pg. 473 **PB**

Chantilly

AMERICAN SYSTEMS CORPORATION, 14200 Park Meadow Dr., 20151, pg. 63 **PV**
BCI Incorporated, 5160 Parkstone Dr., Ste. 190, 22221-3813, pg. 116 **PB**
British Aerospace Holdings Inc., 15000 Conference Center Dr., Ste. 200, 20151, pg. 218 **IT**
Casa Aircraft USA Incorporated, Avion Business Park, 3810 Concorde Pkwy., Ste. 1000, 22021, pg. 1224 **IT**
Comstor, 14116 Newbrook Dr., 22201, pg. 711 **PB**
Data National, 3800 Concorde Pkwy., 20151, pg. 1724 **PB**
De La Rue Faraday, 4250 Pleasant Valley Rd., 22021, pg. 387 **IT**
Thomas De La Rue Inc., 4260 Pleasant Valley Rd., 22021-1213, pg. 387 **IT**
Dynex Technologies, 14340 Sullyfield Cir., 20151, pg. 1591 **PB**
THE FAIRCHILD CORPORATION, 300 W. Service Rd., 22021, pg. 610 **PB**
GENERAL KINETICS INCORPORATED, 14130 Sully Field Cir., Ste. C, 20151, pg. 716 **PB**
GENICOM CORPORATION, 14800 Conference Ctr. Dr., Ste. 400, 20151, pg. 729 **PB**
Gensym Corporation, Mid-Atlantic Area Office, 5180 Parkstone Dr., Ste. 110, 22021, pg. 731 **PB**
Media General Cable of Fairfax County Inc., 14650 Lee Rd., P.O. Box 468, 22021, pg. 1078 **PB**
Mitek Systems, Inc., 4506 Daly Dr., Ste. 500, 20151, pg. 1118 **PB**
Secure Communications Division, 14130-C Sullyfield Circle, 22021, pg. 717 **PB**
Share Technologies - Fairchild, P.O. Box 10804, 300 W. Service Rd., 22021, pg. 1568 **PB**
Teleo Communications Group, 4219 Lafayette Center Dr., 20151, pg. 598 **PB**
VSI Corporation, P.O. Box 10803, 300 W. Service Rd., 22021, pg. 610 **PB**

Charlottesville

American Phone Centers, Inc., P.O. Box 7871, 361 Greenbriar Dr., 22906, pg. 407 **PB**
American Telecommunications Corporation, 1180 Seminole Trail, 22901, pg. 407 **PB**
Avionics Specialities, Inc., P.O. Box 6400, 22906-6400, pg. 25 **PB**
Badger Fire Protection Inc., Rte. 29 N., 22906, pg. 1500 **IT**
BETTER LIVING INC., Rte. 29 North, 22906, pg. 141 **PV**
Charter Behavioral Health System of Charlottesville, Inc., 2101 Arlington Blvd., 22903-1593, pg. 1033 **PB**
Charter MOB of Charlottesville, Inc., 1023 Millmont Ave., 22901, pg. 1035 **PB**
COMDIAL CORPORATION, 1180 Seminole Trail, 22906, pg. 407 **PB**
Comdial Enterprise Systems, Inc., 1180 Seminole Trail, 22901, pg. 407 **PB**
Comdial Telecommunications International, Inc., 1180 Seminole Trail, 22901, pg. 407 **PB**
Frank IX & Sons, Inc., P.O. Box 276, Ware St., 22902, pg. 423 **PV**
GE Fanuc Automation Corporation, P.O. Box 8106, 22906, pg. 477 **IT**
GE Fanuc Automation Corporation, P.O. Box 8106, 22906, pg. 711 **PB**
GE Fanuc Automation North America, Inc., P.O. Box 8106, 22906, pg. 477 **IT**
Lexis Law Publishing, 701 E. Water St., 22902, pg. 1096 **IT**
Litton Marine Systems, 1070 Seminole Trail, 22901, pg. 1003 **PB**
Micropolis Corporation, 310 Barracks Hill, 22901, pg. 742 **PV**
Money Market Directories, 320 E. Main St., 22901, pg. 1071 **PB**
Saunders Oil Co., Inc., 205 7th St., S.W., 22901, pg. 968 **PV**
Scott & Stringfellow, Inc., 103 E. Water St., Ste. 201, 22902, pg. 1446 **PB**
Wachovia Bank, 200 E. Main St., 22901, pg. 1730 **PB**
Westmoreland Energy, Inc., 300 Preston Ave., 22901, pg. 1761 **PB**

Chatham

Ennis Eastern Div., P.O. Box 490, 24531, pg. 583 **PB**

Chesapeake

CBP Resources-Norfolk Division, P.O. Box 1126, 23320, pg. 192 **PV**
DRS Technical Services, 737 Volvo Pkwy., Ste. 150, 23320, pg. 474 **PB**
EDO Combat Systems, 1801 E. Sara Dr., 23320-2014, pg. 542 **PB**
EXECUTIVE PRODUCTIVITY SYSTEMS, INC., P.O. Box 15539, 23328, pg. 388 **PV**
Fleet Support Center, 825 Greenbrier Cir., Ste. 101, 23320, pg. 110 **PB**
Hewlett-Packard Company, 840 Greenbrier Cir., Ste. 101, 23320, pg. 815 **PB**
Household Credit Services, 1421 Kristina Way, 23320-8917, pg. 842 **PB**
Lafarge Calcium Aluminate, Foot of Ohio St., 23324, pg. 791 **IT**
Lifetouch National School Studios Inc., 2210 Paramont Ave., 23320, pg. 667 **PV**
Lips Propellers, Inc., 3617 Koppens Way, 23323, pg. 812 **IT**
Marine Systems, Inc.-East Coast, 2032 Atlantic Ave., 23324-3004, pg. 961 **PB**
MONEY POINT DIAMOND CO., 4300 Buell St., 23324, pg. 757 **PV**
Sadler Materials Corp., 4606 Bainbridge Blvd., 23320, pg. 656 **PB**
Scott & Stringfellow, Inc., 3115 Western Branch Blvd., Ste. 115, 23321, pg. 1445 **PB**
Sumitomo Machinery Corporation of America, 4200 Holland Blvd., 23323, pg. 1314 **IT**
Tencarva Machinery Co., 933 Corporate Ln., 23320, pg. 1076 **PV**
Virginia Operations, 401 Volvo Pkwy., 23320, pg. 871 **IT**
Volvo Penta of the Americas, Inc., 1300 Volvo Penta Dr., 23320, pg. 1477 **IT**

Chester

Van Leeuwen Pipe & Tube Corp., 13341 Kingston Avenue, 23836, pg. 1450 **IT**

Chilhowie

American Mine Tool Co., 1027 Kendall Rd., 24319, pg. 950 **PB**
Natalie Knitting Mills, Hwy. 11-E. Rouse Industrial Park, 24319, pg. 779 **PB**

Christiansburg

Hubbell Lighting Inc., 2000 Electric Way, 24073, pg. 844 **PB**
Pulaski Furniture-Christiansburg, P.O. Box 479, 405 W. Cambria St., 24073, pg. 1343 **PB**

PB - *U.S. Public Companies Volume*
PV - *U.S. Private Companies Volume*
IT - *International Public & Private Companies Volume*

Geographic Index-U.S.

Geographic Index-U.S.

Clifton Forge

First National Bank of Clifton Forge, 511 Main St., 24422,
pg. 1039   **PB**

Clover

Clover Yarns, P.O. Box B-8, 24534, pg. 247   **PV**

Coeburn

DAVIS MINING & MANUFACTURING, Miners Professional
Bldg., 24230, pg. 315   **PV**

Colonial Heights

Heritage Merchandising Co., Inc., 2701 Boulevard, 23834,
pg. 1272   **PB**
Hill Phoenix, 1925 Ruffin Mill Rd., 23834, pg. 521   **PB**

Courtland

Hancock Peanut Company, Hwy. 58 W. Business, 23837,
pg. 763   **PV**

Crozet

ACME DESIGN TECHNOLOGY, CO., 1000 Allview Dr.,
22932, pg. 13   **PV**
Acme Visible Records, 1000 Allview Dr., 22932, pg. 13   **PV**

Crozier

National Card Control, Inc., 1700 Cardwell Rd., 23039,
pg. 321   **PB**

Culpeper

Fairfax Building Systems, 651 Maddox Dr., 22701,
pg. 391   **PV**
Scott & Stringfellow, Inc., 130 E. Davis St., 22701,
pg. 1446   **PB**

Damascus

CM Hoist Division, P.O. Box 41, Rte. 1, 24236-9601,
pg. 405   **PB**

Danville

Dan River Cotton Co., Inc., 2291 Memorial Dr., 24541,
pg. 479   **PB**
Dan River Danville Mfg. Div., P.O. Box 261, 24543,
pg. 479   **PB**
DAN RIVER INC., 2291 Memorial Dr., 24541, pg. 478   **PB**
Dan River Inc.-Home Furnishings & Related Prods., Div. I,
P.O. Box 261, 24543, pg. 479   **PB**
Dan River Inc.-Riverside Div., P.O. Box 261, 24543,
pg. 479   **PB**
DIMON, INCORPORATED, 512 Bridge St., 24541,
pg. 509   **PB**
Florimex Worldwide, Inc., 512 Bridge St., 24541,
pg. 510   **PB**
Hickson DanCHem Corporation, 1975 Richmond Blvd.,
24540, pg. 619   **IT**
Lockley Manufacturing Division, Halifax Rd., 24543,
pg. 378   **PV**
C.M. Offray & Son, 255 Stinson Dr., 24540, pg. 812   **PV**
Scott & Stringfellow, Inc., 201 Patton St., 24541,
pg. 1446   **PB**
Servitex, Inc., 270 Piney Forest Rd., 24541, pg. 782   **PV**
Shorewood Packaging Corporation of Virginia-Danville
Operations, 145 Cane Creek Blvd., 24540-5609,
pg. 1468   **PB**
Southern Processors, Inc., P.O. Box 1707, 24543,
pg. 1695   **PB**
Virginia Tobacco Co., Inc., P.O. Box 1081, 24543,
pg. 1695   **PB**
Virsa, Inc., P.O. Box 906, 24543, pg. 1695   **PB**

Dayton

Shady Brook Farms, P.O. Box 158, 22821, pg. 937   **PV**

Dillwyn

KYANITE MINING CORPORATION, P.O. Box 486, 23936,
pg. 638   **PV**

Dublin

BBA Friction Inc., 3994 Pepperell Way, 24084-3837,
pg. 113   **IT**
Pulaski Furniture-Dublin, P.O. Box 1169, 24084,
pg. 1343   **PB**

Duffield

Penn Virginia Coal Company, U.S. Hwy. 58, 421 W., 24244,
pg. 1271   **PB**

Dulles

AMERICA ONLINE INCORPORATED, 22000 AOL Way,
20166-9323, pg. 66   **PB**

ORBITAL SCIENCES CORPORATION, 21700 Atlantic
Blvd., 20166, pg. 1229   **PB**

Eastville

The Eastville Bank, P.O. Box 7, 16485 Lankford Highway,
23347, pg. 1089   **PB**

Edinburg

Automatic Service Co. of Virginia, N. Virginia Branch, P.O.
Box 218, 22824, pg. 8   **PV**
Rocco Farm Foods, Inc., 19992 Senedo Rd., 22824,
pg 937   **PV**

Fairfax

AMERICAN MANAGEMENT SYSTEMS, INC., 4050 Legato
Rd., 22033, pg. 86   **PB**
BTG, INC., 3877 Fairfax Ridge Rd., 22030-7448,
pg. 164   **PB**
BROWN AUTOMOTIVE GROUP, 10287 Lee Hwy., 22030,
pg. 173   **PV**
Burns & Roe Industrial Services Company, 2812 Old Lee
Hwy., Ste. 120, 22116, pg. 187   **PB**
CDM Federal Programs Corporation, 13135 Lee Jackson
Memorial Hwy. Ste. 200, 22033, pg. 204   **PV**
CORT BUSINESS SERVICES CORPORATION, 4401 Fair
Lakes Ct., 22033, pg. 451   **PB**
DeLeuw Cather & Co., 10521 Rosehaven St., 22030-2837,
pg. 841   **PV**
DEWEERRY & DAVIS, 8401 Arlington Blvd., 22031,
pg. 329   **PV**
EG & G Dynatrend, 3702 Pender Dr., 22030, pg. 544   **PB**
Edison Mission Energy, 12500 Fair Lakes Cir., Ste. 200,
22033-3804, pg. 564   **PB**
FGI Research, Washington, 11350 Random Hills Rd., Ste.
800, 22030, pg. 389   **PV**
GUEST SERVICES, INC., 3055 Prosperity Ave., 22031,
pg. 486   **PV**
ICF Incorporated, 9300 Lee Hwy., 22031, pg. 853   **PB**
ICF Information Technology, Inc., 9300 Lee Hwy., 22031,
pg. 853   **PB**
ICF KAISER INTERNATIONAL INC., 9300 Lee Hwy.,
22031-1207, pg. 852   **PB**
ISM Soccer Inc., 4300 Fair Lakes Ct., Ste. 300A, 22033,
pg. 393   **IT**
Information & Engineering Technology, 12700 Fair Lakes
Cir. 22033, pg. 351   **PV**
International Marketing & Refining Division, 3225 Gallows
Rd. 22037-001, pg. 1118   **PB**
IsoQuest, Inc., 3900 Jermantown Rd., Ste. 400, 22030-
4900, pg. 958   **PV**
Logicon Geodynamics Eastern Division, 11781 Lee Jackson
Memorial Hwy. Ste. 400, 22033, pg. 1199   **PB**
THE LONG & FOSTER COMPANIES, INC., 11351 Random
Hills Rd., 22030, pg. 674   **PV**
The Long & Foster Real Estate, Inc., 11351 Random Hills
Rd., 22030, pg. 674   **PV**
Mobil Land Development Corporation, 3225 Gallows Rd.,
#FLR4D, 22037-0001, pg. 1118   **PB**
MOBIL OIL CORPORATION, 3225 Gallows Rd., 22037-
000 , pg. 1118   **PB**
Mobil South, Marketing & Refining Division, 3225 Gallows
Rd., 22037-001, pg. 1118   **PB**
OMEGA WORLD TRAVEL, INC., 3102 Omega Office Park,
22031-2400, pg. 816   **PV**
Pulte Virginia Division, 10600 Arrowhead Dr., Ste. 225,
22030, pg. 1345   **PB**
Richmond American Homes of Virginia, Inc., 3701 Pender
Dr., Ste. 200, 22030, pg. 1025   **PB**
Risk Science International Inc., 11166 Main St., Ste. 110,
22030, pg. 117   **PB**
SRA - Fairfax, 4350 Fair Lakes Ct., 22033, pg. 958   **PV**
TRW Systems Integration Group, One Federal Systems
Park Dr., 22033-4411, pg. 1558   **PB**
Tolk, Inc., 8401 Arlington Blvd., 22031, pg. 329   **PB**
U.S. Marketing and Refining Division, 3225 Gallows Rd.,
22037-0001, pg. 1118   **PB**
UUNET Technologies, Inc., 3060 Williams Dr., 22031,
pg. 1779   **PB**

Falls Church

Bell Atlantic, 2980 Fairview 7th Flr., 22042-4525,
pg. 202   **PB**
CAPITAL ONE FINANCIAL CORPORATION, 2980
Fairview Park Dr., Ste. 1300, 22042, pg. 302   **PB**
CREATIVE HAIRDRESSERS, 2815 Hartland Rd., 22043,
pg. 287   **PV**
FCW Publishing Corp., 3110 Fairview Park Dr., Ste. 1040,
22042, pg. 569   **PV**
Falls Church Div., 7700 Arlington Blvd., 22046,
pg. 1365   **PB**
FINNAIR, 122 E. Broad St., 22046, pg. 486   **IT**
FINNAIR, 122 East Broad St., 22046, pg. 486   **IT**
First Virginia Bank, 6400 Arlington Blvd., 22042-2336,
pg. 641   **PB**
FIRST VIRGINIA BANKS, INC., One First Virginia Plaza,
6400 Arlington Blvd., 22042-2336, pg. 641   **PB**
First Virginia Insurance Services, Inc., 6402 Arlington Blvd.,
22042-2398, pg. 642   **PB**
First Virginia Life Insurance Company, 6400 Arlington Blvd.,
22042, pg. 642   **PB**
First Virginia Mortgage Company, 6402 Arlington Blvd.,
Ste.1300, 22042, pg. 642   **PB**
GENERAL DYNAMICS CORPORATION, 3190 Fairview
Park Dr., 22042-4523, pg. 708   **PB**
The Hair Cuttery, 2815 Hartland Rd., 22043, pg. 287   **PV**

Hewlett-Packard Company, 3141 Fairview Park Dr., Stes.
240 & 300, 22042, pg. 815   **PB**
Integrated Business Services, 3160 Fairview Park Dr.,
22042, pg. 423   **PB**
Logicon Syscon Corporation, 8110 Gatehouse Rd., 22042-
1212, pg. 1199   **PB**
Optimum Public Relations (U.S.) Inc., 7700 Leesburg Pike,
Ste. 270, 22043, pg. 336   **IT**
SRA - Falls Church, One Skyline Pl., Ste. 1300, 5205
Leesburg Pike, 22041, pg. 958   **PV**
Systems Engineering Div., Virginia Technology Center, 3160
Fairview Park Dr., 22042, pg. 423   **PB**
WILLIAMS INDUSTRIES, INC., 2849 Meadow View Rd.,
22042, pg. 1769   **PB**
Williams Steel Erection Co., Inc., 2849 Meadow View Road,
22042, pg. 1770   **PB**

Farmville

Carbone of America, Commutation Components Div. Hwy.
115 & 460 West, 23901, pg. 1028   **IT**
Dunnington-Beach Tobacco Co., P.O. Box 468, 23901,
pg. 1694   **PB**

Ferrum

Bank of Ferrum, 315 N. Main St., 24088, pg. 1038   **PB**

Forest

First Community Bank, P.O. Box 195, Rte. 221 Forest Sq.
Shopping Ctr., 24551, pg. 1039   **PB**
Grayson Electronics Corporation, 306 Enterprise Dr.,
24551, pg. 46   **PB**

Fredericksburg

BookCrafters U.S.A. Inc., Lee Hill Industrial Park, P. O. Box
892, 22401, pg. 70   **PB**
THE FREE LANCE-STAR PUBLISHING CO., 616 Amelia
St., 22401-3887, pg. 424   **PV**
Friction Park, 1000 Falls Run Industrial Park, 22401,
pg. 560   **PB**
Media General Cable of Fredericksburg, Inc., 1310 Belman
Rd., 22401, pg. 1078   **PB**
The National Bank of Fredericksburg, 2403 Fall Hill Ave.,
22404, pg. 1089   **PB**
Radio Stations WFLS FM & WYSK-AM-FM, 616 Amelia St.,
22401-3886, pg. 425   **PV**
SMI Rebar Virginia, 9434 Crossroads Pkwy., 22408,
pg. 412   **PB**

Front Royal

PEN-TAB INDUSTRIES, INC., 167 Kelley Dr., 22630,
pg. 848   **PV**

Gainesville

Atlantic Research Corporation, 5945 Wellington Rd., 20155-
1633, pg. 1458   **PB**

Galax

The Gazette, Box 68, 108 W.Stuart Dr., 24333,
pg. 648   **PV**

Glasgow

General Shale Products Corp., Rte. One, Box 1, 24555,
pg. 844   **IT**

Glen Allen

Bergen Brunswig Drug Company, 9900 Jeb Stuart Pkwy.,
23060, pg. 214   **PB**
Caliber One Indemnity Company, 4551 Cox Rd., 23060,
pg. 1272   **PB**
Car Max, 4212 Park Place Ct., 23060, pg. 374   **PB**
Cigna Healthcare of Virginia, Inc., 4050 Innslake Dr., 23060,
pg. 360   **PB**
Compute PX, Innsbrook Corporate Center, 4200 Park Place
Ct., 23060-3328, pg. 1008   **PV**
Essex Insurance Co., 4551 Cox Rd., 23060, pg. 1046   **PB**
FIRST HEALTH Services, 4300 Cox Rd, 23060,
pg. 635   **PB**
Hamilton Beach/Proctor-Silex, Inc., 4421 Waterfront Dr.,
23060, pg. 1149   **PB**
Hewlett-Packard Company, 4401 Waterfront Dr., Ste. 150,
23060, pg. 815   **PB**
HILB, ROGAL AND HAMILTON COMPANY, 4235 Innslake
Dr., 23060, pg. 826   **PB**
Intergraph Corporation, Innbrook Corporate Ctr., 4405 Cox
Rd., 23060, pg. 890   **PB**
Markel American Insurance Co., 4551 Cox Road, 23060,
pg. 1046   **PB**
MARKEL CORPORATION, 4551 Cox Rd., 23060,
pg. 1046   **PB**
Markel Insurance Co., 4551 Cox Road, 23060,
pg. 1046   **PB**
Markel Service, Inc., 4551 Cox Rd., 23060, pg. 1046   **PB**
OWENS & MINOR INC., 4800 Cox Rd., 23060,
pg. 1236   **PB**
THE PITTSTON COMPANY, 1000 Virginia Ctr. Pkwy.,
23058, pg. 1305   **PB**
RESOURCE MORTGAGE CAPITAL, INC., 10900 Nuckols
Rd., Ste. 300, 23060, pg. 1382   **PB**

PB - *U.S. Public Companies Volume*
PV - *U.S. Private Companies Volume*
IT - *International Public & Private Companies Volume*

RICHFOOD HOLDINGS, INC., 4860 Cox Rd., Ste. 200, 23060, pg. 1388 **PB**
Richmond International Forest Products, Inc., Innsbrook Corporate Ctr., 4228 Parkplace Ct., 23060, pg. 669 **PB**
S & K FAMOUS BRANDS, INC., 11100 W. Broad St., 23060, pg. 1414 **PB**

Gordonsville

Klockner Barrier Films, P.O. Box 300, Klockner Rd., 22942, pg. 737 **IT**
Klockner Capital Corp., P.O. Box 750, 22942, pg. 737 **IT**
Klockner-Hooper Packaging Machinery, P.O. Box 500, Kloeckner Rd., 22942, pg. 737 **IT**
Klockner Pentaplast of America, Inc., 3585 Klockner Rd., 22942, pg. 737 **IT**
Liberty Fabrics-Gordonsville Division, P.O. Box 308 22942, 22942, pg. 340 **IT**

Great Falls

MSC Washington, D.C. Office, 10738 Wynkoop Dr., 22066, pg. 1031 **PB**

Grottoes

Reynolds Metals Company-Grottoes, P.O. Box 128, RCN Caverns Rd., 24441, pg. 1385 **PB**

Hampton

Atlantic Homes Corp., Two Eaton St., Ste. 1100, 23669, pg. 473 **PV**
Great Atlantic Hospitality Co. Inc., Two Eaton St., Ste. 1100, 23669, pg. 473 **PV**
Great Atlantic Management Co. Inc., Two Eaton St., Ste. 1100, 23669, pg. 473 **PV**
THE GREAT ATLANTIC MANAGEMENT COMPANY, Two Eaton St., Ste. 1100, 23669, pg. 473 **PV**
Lucas Control Systems Products, 1000 Lucas Way, 23666-1573, pg. 820 **IT**
Northrop Grumman Corporation - Eastern Region, 1919 Commerce Dr., Ste. 455, 23666-4269, pg. 1199 **PB**
Pressure Systems, Inc., 34 Research Dr., 23666, pg. 1130 **IT**
Wyle Laboratories-Eastern Operations, 3200 Magruder Blvd., 23666, pg. 1193 **PV**

Harrisonburg

AMP Inc. Lytel Division, 1175 N. Main St., 22801-4630, pg. 8 **PB**
Banta Book Group-Harrisonburg, 3330 Willow Spring Rd., 22801, pg. 188 **IT**
Cassco Ice & Cold Storage, Inc., 217 S. Liberty St., 22801, pg. 1727 **PB**
Chesapeake Western Railway, 141 West Bruce St., 22801, pg. 1191 **PB**
COMSONICS, INC., 1350 Port Republic Rd., 22801, pg. 260 **PB**
Harrisonburg Auto Auction, Exit 62 & Interstate 81, 3560 Early Rd., 22801, pg. 282 **PV**
May Supply Company, Inc., 1775 Erickson Ave., 22801, pg. 1727 **PB**
Rocco Building Supplies Inc., P.O. Box 669, 22801, pg. 937 **PV**
Rocco Farms, 1620 S. Main St., 22801, pg. 937 **PV**
Rocco Feeds, Inc., P.O. Box 549, 22801, pg. 937 **PV**
ROCCO INC., One Kratzer Rd., 22802, pg. 937 **PV**
Rocco Realty Inc., 1 Kratzer Ave., 22821, pg. 937 **PV**
Scott & Stringfellow, Inc., 560 Neff Ave., Ste. 400, 22801, pg. 1445 **PB**
SHENANDOAH MFG. CO. INC., P.O. Box 839, 22801, pg. 992 **PV**
Sysco Food Services of Virginia, Inc., P.O. Box 20020, Rt. 11 S., 22801-7520, pg. 1552 **PB**
Victor Tube Corp., 810 N. Main St., 22801, pg. 239 **IT**
Wetsel Seed Company, P.O. Box 791, 22801, pg. 1017 **PV**

Hartwood

DC Division, P.O. Box 38, State Rte. 748, 22471, pg. 1161 **PB**

Herndon

AIB Software Development Laboratory, 1145 Herndon Pkwy., Ste. 200, 22070, pg. 1309 **PB**
Adtechs Corporation, 2411 Dulles Corner Park, Ste. 520, 22071, pg. 697 **IT**
Airbus Industrie of North America, Inc., 198 Van Buren St., Ste. 300, 20170, pg. 39 **IT**
BHP Minerals, 200 Fairbrook Dr., Ste. 204, 22070-5200, pg. 224 **IT**
Cerner Corporation -Mid-Atlantic Region, 2201 Cooperation Way, Ste. 301, 22071-3024, pg. 331 **PB**
ComSkill Learning Centers, Inc., 13515 Dulles Technology Dr., 22071, pg. 859 **PB**
Continental Dynamics, Inc., 620 Herndon Pkwy., Ste. 220, 22070, pg. 110 **PB**
Data Systems and Services Division, 2411 Dulles Corner Park, 22071, pg. 1198 **PB**
EIS INTERNATIONAL INC., 555 Herndon Pkwy., 20170, pg. 544 **PB**
Food Technology Corporation, 13505 Dulles Technology Dr., 22071, pg. 717 **PB**
ITC LEARNING CORP., 13515 Dulles Technology Dr., 20171, pg. 859 **PB**

InteliData, 13873 Park Center Rd., Ste. 230, 22071, pg. 1780 **PB**
LICOM, 607 Herndon Pkwy., 22070, pg. 1702 **PB**
Mitel, Inc., 205 Van Buren St., Ste. 400, 20170-5336, pg. 870 **IT**
NATIONAL RURAL UTILITIES COOPERATIVE FINANCE CORPORATION, Woodland Park, 2201 Cooperative Way, 20171-3025, pg. 786 **PV**
NETRIX, CORP., 13595 Dulles Technology Dr., 22171, pg. 791 **PB**
Network Solutions, Inc., 505 Huntmar Park Dr., 22070, pg. 976 **PV**
Newbridge Networks Inc., 593 Herndon Pkwy., 22070-5241, pg. 924 **IT**
Noell Inc., 2411 Dulles, 20171, pg. 1070 **IT**
Parsons Brinckerhoff Construction Services, Inc., 465 Spring Park Place, 22070, pg. 841 **PV**
Pulse Communications, Inc., 2900 Towerview Rd., 22071, pg. 1463 **PB**
SMS-Washington, D.C., 2411 Dulles Corner Pk., 22071, pg. 1463 **PB**
Tarmac America, Inc., 13873 Park Center Rd., 22071, pg. 1355 **IT**
Trimble Navigation Ltd., Washington, D.C., Monroe Bus. Ctr. 1, 610 Herndon Pkwy., B-3 Ste. 600, 22070, pg. 1638 **PB**
World Airways, Inc., 13873 Park Center Rd., Ste. 490, 22071, pg. 1780 **PB**
World Flight Crew Services, 13873 Park Center Rd., Ste. 490, 22071, pg. 1780 **PB**
WORLDCORP, INC., 13873 Park Ctr. Rd., Ste. 490, 20171, pg. 1779 **PB**
WorldServ, 2214 Rock Hill Rd., 22070, pg. 767 **PB**

Hillsville

Bank of Carroll, P.O. Box 699, 24343, pg. 1038 **PB**
PAXAR Woven Labels, P.O. Box 127, 24343, pg. 1266 **PB**

Hopewell

Aqualon-Hopewell, 1111 Hercules Rd., 23860-5245, pg. 810 **PB**

Hot Springs

The Homestead L.C., U.S. Rte. 220, 24445, pg. 247 **PV**

Independence

Nautilus International, 709 Powerhouse Rd., 24348, pg. 498 **PB**

Jarratt

Nearby Eggs, Inc., Old Halifax Rd., 23867, pg. 1529 **PB**
Softboard Plant, Allens Road, P.O. Box 367, 23867, pg. 738 **PB**

Lebanon

Pittston Minerals Group, Inc., 448 N.E. Main St., 24266, pg. 1305 **PB**
Teleflex Automotive, Russell County Indus. Park, Rt. 71, 24266, pg. 1569 **PB**

Leesburg

CAE Electronics Inc.-New York, 750 Miller Drive S.E., 20175, pg. 237 **IT**
Charter Springwood Behavioral Health System, Inc., Box 50, Rte. 4, 22075, pg. 1035 **PB**
Cowles History Group, Inc., 741 Miller Dr., S.E., Ste. D2, 22075, pg. 281 **PV**
PRECISION TUNE AUTOCARE INC., 748 Miller Dr. S.E., Ste. G-1, 22075, pg. 1321 **PV**
Xerox International Center for Training & Management Development, P.O. Box 2000, 22075, pg. 1785 **PB**

Lexington

Scott & Stringfellow, Inc., 158 S. Main St., 24450, pg. 1446 **PB**

Lorton

Omega Environmental Services, 8433 Backlick Rd., Ste. 201, 22079, pg. 1222 **PB**

Lynchburg

Aerofin Corp., 4621 Murray Pl., 24506, pg. 103 **PB**
Allright Parking Virginia, Inc., P.O. Box 742, Tenth & Commerce Key Bldg., 24505, pg. 43 **PV**
AmeriSource-Lynchburg Div., 9221 Timberlake Rd., 24502, pg. 97 **PB**
Automatic Service Co. of Virginia, Lynchburg Branch, P.O. Box 10278, 3224 Odd Fellow Rd., 24506, pg. 8 **PV**
Babock & Wilcox Fuel Co. (B & WF CO), P.O. Box 10935, 3315 Old Forest Rd., 24506-0935, pg. 305 **IT**
CRADDOCK-TERRY INC., 601 12th St., 24504, pg. 284 **PV**
Dillard, A ResourceNet International Company, 2001 Enterprise Dr., 24501, pg. 902 **PB**
Ericsson GE Mobile Communications Distribution, Mountain View Rd., Room 1652, 24502, pg. 1364 **IT**
Ericsson GE Mobile Communications Inc., Mountain View Rd., 24502, pg. 1365 **IT**

First Colony Life Insurance Co., 700 Main St., P.O. Box 1280, 24505, pg. 711 **PB**
C. B. FLEET CO., INC., 4615 Murray Place, 24502, pg. 410 **PV**
Flowers Baking Co. of Lynchburg, Inc., 1905 Hollins Mill Rd., 24503, pg. 657 **PB**
Framatome Cogema Fuels, P.O. Box 10935, 3315 Old Forest Rd., 24506-0935, pg. 503 **IT**
Home Showcase Products, 1000 Robins Rd., 24506, pg. 1101 **PV**
ITW Paktron, 1205 McConville Rd., 24502, pg. 866 **PB**
Lynchburg Graphics Service Center, 1011 Creekside Dr., 24502, pg. 518 **PB**
Massey's, 601 12th St., 24504, pg. 284 **PV**
Mrs. Giles Country Kitchens, Inc., 125 Oakley Ave., 24501, pg. 596 **PV**
PROGRESS PRINTING COMPANY, 3523 Waterlick Rd., 24502, pg. 890 **PV**
Scott & Stringfellow, Inc., 810 Main St., 24504, pg. 1446 **PB**
Irma Shorell, Inc., 1000 Robins Rd., 24506, pg. 1101 **PV**
Simplimatic Engineering Co., P.O. Box 11709, Wards Ferry Rd., 24506, pg. 463 **PB**
Starmark of Virginia, Inc., One Millrace Rd., 24502, pg. 1054 **PB**
TRI TECH LABORATORIES, INC., 1000 Robins Road, 24506, pg. 1101 **PV**
Universal Shoe Mfg. Co., P.O. Box 10088, 24506, pg. 284 **PV**
WSET Incorporatd, 2320 Laughorn Rd., 24501, pg. 854 **PV**
Wynn's-Precision Fluid Sealing Div., P.O. Box 11708, 24506, pg. 1783 **PB**

Madison Heights

DACAM Corp., P.O. Box 310, Hwy. 766, Kings Rd., 24572, pg. 814 **PV**
Lynchburg Service Center, Elon Industrial Park, 24572, pg. 214 **PV**
OLD DOMINION BOX CO., INC., 300 Elon Rd., 24572, pg. 814 **PV**

Manassas

Dominion Semiconductor, L.L.C., 9600 Godwin Dr., 22110, pg. 1405 **IT**
Lockheed Martin Advanced Projects, 9500 Godwin Dr., Bldg. 400, Third Fl., 22110, pg. 1008 **PB**
Scott & Stringfellow, Inc., 9113 Church St., 20110, pg. 1446 **PB**
Williams Bridge Co., 8587 J.D. Reading Dr., 22150, pg. 1770 **PB**
Williams Equipment Corporation, 8587 J. D. Reading Dr., 22110, pg. 1770 **PB**

Marion

General Shale Products Corp., Rte. 4, Box 127, 24354, pg. 843 **IT**
Marley Mouldings Inc., P.O. Box 610, 24354, pg. 843 **IT**

Martinsville

American Furniture Company, Incorporated, 128 E. Church St., 24112, pg. 974 **PB**
Bassett-Walker, Inc., P.O. Box 5423, Walker Rd., 24115, pg. 1702 **PB**
W.M. Bassett Furniture Co., Rives Rd., 24112, pg. 193 **PB**
Courtaulds Performance Films Inc., PO Box 5068, 24115, pg. 339 **IT**
Dominion Stores, Inc., 101 Commonwealth Blvd., 24112, pg. 1644 **PV**
HOOKER FURNITURE CORPORATION, 440 E. Commonwealth Blvd., 24112, pg. 538 **PV**
MAINSTREET BANKGROUP INCORPORATED, 200 E. Church St., 24115, pg. 1038 **PB**
MainStreet Trust Company, N.A., One Ellsworth St., 24112, pg. 1039 **PB**
NATIONWIDE HOMES, INC., 1100 Rives Rd., 24115, pg. 788 **PV**
Piedmont Trust Bank, One Ellsworth St., 24112, pg. 1039 **PB**
Pulaski Furniture-Martinsville, P.O. Box 3431, 24115, pg. 1343 **PB**
Scott & Stringfellow, Inc., Druid Hills Centre, 1077 Spruce St., 24112, pg. 1446 **PB**
TULTEX CORPORATION, 380 Beaver Creek Dr., 24112, pg. 1644 **PB**

Mc Lean

America, 8808 L, Tysons Corner Center, 22102, pg. 130 **PB**
Analysis & Technology, Inc., 7926 Jones Branch Dr., Ste. 600, 22102, pg. 109 **PB**
Applied Science Associates, Inc., Ste. 600, 7926 Jones Branch Dr., 22102, pg. 109 **PB**
Arnold Advertising, 8300 Greensboro Dr., Ste. 1200, 22102, pg. 84 **PV**
Auto-trol Technology Corp.-Virginia, 2010 Corporate Ridge, Ste. 700, 22102, pg. 148 **PV**
Autodesk, Inc., 1420 Spring Hill Rd., Ste. 600, 22102, pg. 149 **PB**
BDM International, Inc., 1501 BDM Way, 22102, pg. 1558 **PB**
BPA International - McLean, 8201 Greensboro Dr., #1055, 22102, pg. 107 **PV**

Data General Services, 7927 Jones Branch Dr. Ste. 200, 22102-3305, pg. 485 — PB
Dynalectric Company, 1420 Spring Hill Rd., Ste. 500, 22102, pg. 571 — PB
FEDERAL HOME LOAN MORTGAGE CORPORATION, 8200 Jones Branch Dr., 22102, pg. 615 — PB
Federal Systems Group, 1650 Tysons Blvd., Ste 800, 22102, pg. 1516 — PB
Federal Systems Integration Corporation, 7900 Westpark Dr., 22102, pg. 316 — IT
First American Metro Corp., 1751 Pinnacle Dr., 22102, pg. 640 — PB
G.E. Spacenet Corporation, 1750 Old Meadow Rd., 22102, pg. 711 — PB
HFS Inc., 7900 Westpark Dr., 22102, pg. 316 — IT
Hicks & Associates Inc., 1710 Goodridge Dr., Ste. 1300, 22101, pg. 976 — PV
ITT Defense & Electronics, Inc., 1650 Tysons Blvd., 22102, pg. 859 — PB
Integrated Systems Operations, 7900 Westpark Dr., 22102, pg. 1784 — PB
KCI Communications, Inc, 1750 Old Meadow Rd., Ste. 300, 22102, pg. 784 — PV
Market Facts, Inc., 1650 Tysons Blvd., 22102, pg. 1047 — PB
MARS, INCORPORATED, 6885 Elm St., 22101, pg. 707 — PV
Mid-Atlantic Region, 8200 Greensboro Dr., 22102, pg. 1024 — PB
MILLER & SMITH, INC., 1568 Spring Hill Rd., 22102, pg. 746 — PV
NVR Financial Services, Inc., 7601 Lewinsville Rd., Ste. 302, 22102, pg. 1148 — PB
NVR, INC., 7601 Lewinsville Rd. Ste. 300, 22102, pg. 1148 — PB
NVR Mortgage, 7601 Lewinsville Rd., Ste. 302, 22102, pg. 1148 — PB
NATIONAL INFORMATION CORPORATION, 1750 Old Meadow Rd., 22102, pg. 784 — PV
National Institute of Business Management, Inc., 1750 Old Meadow Rd. Ste. 301, 22102, pg. 785 — PV
NEXTEL COMMUNICATIONS, 1505 Farm Credit Dr., 22102, pg. 1180 — PB
PRC, Inc., 1500 PRC Dr., 22102, pg. 1003 — PB
PLANNING SYSTEMS INC., 7923 Jones Branch Dr., 22102-3304, pg. 869 — PB
Primark Storage Leasing Corporation, 8251 Greenboro Dr., 22102, pg. 1325 — PB
Prism-Dae, Inc., 7926 Jones Branch Dr., Ste. 600, 22102, pg. 110 — PB
Professional Assistance, Inc., 8251 Greensboro Dr., Rm. 630, 22102, pg. 203 — PB
Quality Systems Inc., 8201 Greensboro Dr., Ste. 1200, 22102, pg. 1627 — PB
Rosendorf/Evans, Tyson's Corner Ctr., 22101, pg. 597 — PB
ROWE FURNITURE CORP., 1650 Tysons Blvd., Ste. 710, 22102, pg. 1410 — PB
SAIC, 1710 Goodridge Dr., 22102, pg. 976 — PB
Sequent Computer Systems, Inc., 1430 Springhill Rd., Ste. 400, 22102, pg. 1459 — PB
STACKIG ADVERTISING AND PUBLIC RELATIONS, 7680 Old Springhouse Rd., 22102, pg. 1028 — PV
Sun Microsystems Federal Inc., 7900 W. Park Dr., Ste. A110, 22102, pg. 1531 — PB
Wang Fed Inc., 7900 Westpark Dr., 22102, pg. 1737 — PB
Xerox Custom Systems Division, 7900 Westpark Dr., 22102, pg. 1784 — PB

Mechanicsville

AMF REECE INCORPORATED, 8080 AMF Dr., 23111, pg. 7 — PV
American Environmental Products, Inc., 210 Conner Rd., 23111, pg. 1741 — PB
Hanover Bank, 7021 Mechanicsville Tpke., 23111, pg. 1039 — PB
Richfood, Inc., 8258 Richfood Rd., 23116, pg. 1389 — PB
West Park Tobacco Inc., Clock Tower Bldg., 7443 Lee Davis Rd., Ste. 305, 23111, pg. 1101 — IT

Merrifield

The Riggs National Bank of Virginia, 8315 Lee Hwy., 22116, pg. 1390 — PB

Middleburg

JACK KENT COOKE, INC., Kent Farms, P.O. Box 2110, 20117, pg. 273 — PV

Midlothian

ABB Gas Turbine Business, 5309 Commonwealth Ctr. Pkwy., 23112, pg. 4 — IT
ABB Power Generation Inc., 5309 Commonwealth Ctr., 23112, pg. 3 — IT

Milford

Gypsum Joint Systems Plant, P.O. Box 129, 22514, pg. 737 — PB

Montvale

Shredded Products Corp., P.O. Box 159, Rte. 460 E., 24122, pg. 1392 — PB

Mount Crawford

RIDDLEBERGER BROS., INC., P.O. Box 27, 22841, pg. 930 — PV

Mount Jackson

Mount Jackson Press, Inc., 1868 Judd's Dr., 22842, pg. 855 — PV

New Market

Howell Metal Company, State Rte. 728, 574 Depot Rd., 22844, pg. 413 — PB

Newington

Marshall Erdman & Assoc., Inc., 8550 Cinder Bed Rd., # 1300, 22122, pg. 380 — PV
S.T. RESEARCH, 8419 Terminal Rd., 22122, pg. 958 — PV

Newport

ICELAND SEAFOOD CORPORATION, 190 Enterprise Dr., 23603, pg. 556 — PV

Newport News

Allright Parking Virginia, Inc., 2501 Washington Ave., Ste. 300 23607, pg. 43 — PV
BHA Group, 11840 Canon Blvd., 23606, pg. 161 — PB
BASIC CONSTRUCTION COMPANY, 538 Oyster Point Rd., 23602, pg. 121 — PV
THE BIONETICS CORPORATION, 11833 Canon Blvd., Ste. 100, 23606, pg. 145 — PV
Blessings Corporation, 200 Enterprise Dr., 23603, pg. 1179 — PV
COBE Renal Care, Inc., Copeland Industrial Pk., 5000 Chestnut Ave., 23605, pg. 667 — IT
C.S. Polymer, Inc., 11900 Canon Blvd., 23606, pg. 261 — IT
Canon Virginia, Inc., 12000 Canon Blvd., 23606-4299, pg. 261 — IT
The Daily Press, Incorporated, 7505 Warwick Blvd., 23607, pg. 635 — PB
Edison Plastics Co., 240 Enterprise Dr., 23603, pg. 179 — PV
Edison Plastics Co., Oakland Technical Center, 230 Enterprise Dr., 23603, pg. 1179 — PV
Ferguson Enterprises, Inc., 618 Bland Ave., 23609, pg. 512 — IT
Flight International Aviation, Inc., Newport News, Williamsburg Intl. Airport, 23602, pg. 654 — PB
THE FLIGHT INTERNATIONAL GROUP, INC., Newport News/Williamsburg Intl. Airport, 23602, pg. 654 — PB
Flight International, Inc., Newport News, Williamsburg Intl. Airport, 23602, pg. 654 — PB
HL Farm Corp., P.O. Box Drawer 0, 4100 Chestnut Ave., 23605, pg. 808 — IT
Liebherr-America Inc., 4100 Chestnut Ave., 23605, pg. 808 — IT
MUNCK AUTOMATION TECHNOLOGY, 161 Enterprise Dr., 23603, pg. 767 — PV
Newpor News Industrial Corp., 230-41st St., 23607, pg. 1180 — PB
Newpor News Offshore Systems Corp., 230-41st St., 23607, pg. 1180 — PB
NEWPORT NEWS SHIPBUILDING, INC., 4101 Washington Ave., 23607, pg. 1179 — PB
Noland Air Conditioning/Refrigeration Div., 2700 Warwick Blvd. 23607, pg. 1187 — PB
NOLAND COMPANY, 80 29th St., 23607, pg. 1187 — PB
Noland Electrical Div., 2700 Warwick Blvd., 23607, pg. 1187 — PB
Noland Industrial Div., 2700 Warwick Blvd., 23607, pg. 1187 — PB
Noland Properties, Inc., Central Fidelity Natl. Bank, 2700 Washington Ave., Ste. 400, 23607, pg. 1188 — PB
NVIEW CORPORATION, 860 Omni Blvd., 23606, pg. 1206 — PB
Plymkraft, Inc., P.O. Box 1577, Warwick Station, 23601, pg. 256 — PV
Shorewood Packaging Corporation of Virginia-Williamsburg Operations, 815 Chapman Way, 23602-1310, pg. 1468 — PB

Norfolk

Airforce Pipeline Inc., Three Commercial Pl., 23510, pg. 1191 — PB
The Alabama Great Southern Railroad Co., Three Commercial Pl., 23510, pg. 1191 — PB
ARGOSystems, Inc., 2550 Ellsmere Ave., Ste. B, 23513, pg. 240 — PB
Arrowood-Southern Company, Three Commerical Pl., 23510, pg. 1190 — PB
Arrowood Southern Executive Park Inc., Three Commercial Pl., 23510, pg. 1190 — PB
The Atlanta & Charlotte Air Line Railway Co., Three Commercial Pl., 23510, pg. 1191 — PB
Atlantic & East Carolina Railway Company, Three Commercial Pl., 23510, pg. 1191 — PB
Atlantic Investment Company, Three Commercial Pl., 23510, pg. 1190 — PB
Be-Lo Markets Inc., 1157 Production Rd., 23502, pg. 203 — PV
CAMELLIA FOOD STORES, INC., 1157 Production Rd., 23502, pg. 203 — PV

Camp Lejeune Railroad Company, Three Commercial Pl., 23510, pg. 1191 — PB
Careerweb, 150 W. Brambleton Ave., 23510, pg. 647 — PV
Cash Flow, Inc., Royster Building, Fifth Fl., Two Commercial Pl., 23510, pg. 1163 — PB
Central of Georgia Railroad Company, Three Commercial Pl., 23510, pg. 1191 — PB
Charlotte-Southern Corporation, Three Commercial Pl., 23510, pg. 1190 — PB
The Cincinnati, New Orleans & Texas Pacific Railway Co., Three Commercial Pl., 23510, pg. 1191 — PB
Citico Realty Co., Three Commercial Pl., 23510, pg. 1191 — PB
DWF of Norfolk, 5315 Henneman Dr., 23513, pg. 326 — PV
Diesel Marine Norshipco, P.O. Box 2100, 23501, pg. 802 — PV
Dillard, A ResourceNet International Company, 3666 Progress Rd., 23502, pg. 902 — PV
Eastern Shore Markets, Inc., 1157 Production Rd., 23502, pg. 203 — PV
Elberton Southern Railway Co., Three Commercial Pl., 23510, pg. 1191 — PB
Farm Fresh, Inc., 7530 Tidewater Dr., 23505, pg. 1388 — PB
Flagship, 150 Brambleton Ave., 23510, pg. 649 — PV
Flowers Baking Co. of Norfolk, P.O. Box 2860, 23501-2860, pg. 657 — PB
The Georgia Midland Railway Co., Three Commercial Pl., 23510, pg. 1191 — PB
Georgia Southern & Florida Railway Co., Three Commercial Pl., 23510, pg. 1191 — PB
Harley Valve & Instrument, 1447 W. 27th St., 23508, pg. 880 — PB
Harris Technical Services Corp., 5365 Robin Hood Rd., Ste. A-3, 23513, pg. 792 — PB
High Point, Randleman, Asheboro and Southern Railroad Co., Three Commercial Pl., 23510, pg. 1191 — PB
Hillhaven Rehabilitation Convalescent, 1005 Hampton Blvd., 23507, pg. 1713 — PB
Hub Furniture Store, 800 Tidewater Dr., 23504, pg. 921 — PV
Infinet Operations, 740 Duke St., 23510, pg. 649 — PV
Intergraph Corporation, Dominion Tower, Ste. 2215, 999 Waterside Dr., 23510, pg. 890 — PB
Interstate Railroad Co., Three Commercial Pl., 23510, pg. 1191 — PB
Lake Erie Dock Co., Three Commercial Pl., 23510, pg. 1191 — PB
Lambert's Point Barge Company, Inc., Three Commercial Pl., 23510, pg. 1190 — PB
Lambert's Point Docks, Inc., Three Commercial Pl., 23510, pg. 1190 — PB
Lamberts Point Stevedore & Terminals Co., P.O. Box 28, Foot of Orapaks St., Ste. 201, 23501, pg. 472 — PV
LANDMARK COMMUNICATIONS, INC., 150 W. Brambleton Ave., 23510, pg. 647 — PV
Landmark Specialty Publications, Inc., 150 W. Brambleton Ave., 23510, pg. 649 — PV
Memphis & Charleston Railway Co., Three Commercial Pl., 23510, pg. 1191 — PB
MILLER OIL CO., INC., 1000 E. City Hall Ave., 23504, pg. 747 — PV
Mobile & Birmingham Railroad Co., Three Commercial Pl., 23510, pg. 1191 — PB
Moran Towing of Virginia, Life Saving Building, 109 E. Main St., 23510, pg. 761 — PV
NS Fiber Optics, Inc., Three Commercial Pl., 23510, pg. 1190 — PB
NS Transportation Brokerage Corporation, Three Commercial Pl., 23510, pg. 1190 — PB
NYT Shared Services Center, Inc., Ste. 7000, World Trade Ctr., 23510, pg. 1176 — PV
NationsBank Insurance Agency, Inc., P.O. Box 600, 23501, pg. 1163 — PB
NationsBank Life Insurance Co., P.O. Box 600, 23501, pg. 1164 — PB
The Nickel Plate Improvement Co., Inc., Three Commercial Pl., 23510, pg. 1191 — PB
Norfolk and Portsmouth Belt Line R.R. Co., 147 Granby St., 23510, pg. 1191 — PB
Norfolk and Western Railway Company, Three Commercial Pl., 23510, pg. 1191 — PB
NORFOLK SHIPBUILDING & DRYDOCK CORPORATION, 750 W. Berkley Ave., 23523, pg. 802 — PV
NORFOLK SOUTHERN CORPORATION, Three Commercial Pl., 23510-9219, pg. 1190 — PB
Norfolk Southern Industrial Development Corp., Three Commercial Pl., 23510, pg. 1190 — PB
Norfolk Southern Properties, Inc., Three Commercial Pl., 23510-2191, pg. 1190 — PB
Norfolk Southern Railway Company, Three Commercial Pl., 23510-2191, pg. 1191 — PB
Norshipco Industrial Enterprises, P.O. Box 2100, 23501, pg. 802 — PV
The North Carolina Midland Railroad Co., Three Commercial Pl., 23510, pg. 1191 — PB
Owens & Minor, Inc, 4502 Progress Rd., 23502, pg. 1236 — PB
Pocahontas Development Corporation, Three Commercial Pl., 23510, pg. 1192 — PB
Pocahontas Land Corporation, Three Commercial Pl., 23510, pg. 1192 — PB
Saunders Oil Co., Inc., 817 Pollard St., 23504, pg. 968 — PV
Scott & Stringfellow, Inc., 2400 Dominion Center, 999 Waterside Dr., 23510, pg. 1446 — PB
Shenandoah-Virginia Corporation, Three Commercial Pl., 23510, pg. 1191 — PB
SMITHFIELD FOODS, INC., 999 Waterside Dr., Ste. 900, 23510, pg. 1479 — PB
The South Western Rail Road Co., Three Commercial Pl., 23510, pg. 1191 — PB

PB - *U.S. Public Companies Volume*
PV - *U.S. Private Companies Volume*
IT - *International Public & Private Companies Volume*

Southern Rail Terminals, Inc., Three Commercial Pl., 23510, pg. 1191 **PB**
Southern Rail Terminals of North Carolina, Inc., Three Commercial Pl., 23510, pg. 1191 **PB**
Southern Railway-Carolina Div., Three Commercial Pl., 23510, pg. 1191 **PB**
Southern Region Coal Transport, Inc., Three Commercial Pl., 23510, pg. 1191 **PB**
Southern Region Industrial Realty, Inc., Three Commercial Pl., 23510, pg. 1190 **PB**
Southern Region Materials Supply, Inc., Three Commercial Pl., 23510, pg. 1191 **PB**
Southern Region Motor Transport, Inc., Three Commercial Pl., 23510, pg. 1191 **PB**
Spirit Cruises, Inc., 501 Front St., 23510, pg. 1274 **IT**
State University Railroad Co., Three Commercial Pl., 23510, pg. 1191 **PB**
Tarmac Virginia, Inc., 1151 Azelea Garden Rd., 23502, pg. 1356 **IT**
Tennessee, Alabama & Georgia Railway Co., Three Commercial Pl., 23510, pg. 1191 **PB**
Tennessee Railway Co., Three Commercial Pl., 23510, pg. 1191 **PB**
The Toledo Belt Railway Co., Three Commercial Pl., 23510, pg. 1191 **PB**
Trader Publishing Company, 100 W. Plume St., 23510, pg. 649 **PV**
Triple Crown Services, Inc., Three Commercial Pl., 23510, pg. 1192 **PB**
Virginia & Southwestern Railway Co., Three Commercial Pl., 23510, pg. 1191 **PB**
Virginia Holding Corporation, Three Commercial Pl., 23510, pg. 1190 **PB**
Virginia Natural Gas, Inc., 5100 E. Virginia Beach Blvd., 23502-3488, pg. 436 **PB**
The Virginian-Pilot, 150 W. Brambleton Ave., 23510, pg. 649 **PV**
WJCD-FM, 1003 Norfolk Sq., 23502, pg. 385 **PB**
WMYK-FM, 1003 Norfolk Sq., 23502, pg. 385 **PB**
WOWI-FM, 1003 Norfolk Sq., 23502, pg. 385 **PB**
WSVY-FM, 1003 Norfolk Sq., 23502, pg. 385 **PB**
WTKR-TV, 720 Boush St., 23510, pg. 1174 **PB**
WVEC-TV, Inc., 613 Woodis Ave., 23510, pg. 209 **PB**
Watters & Martin Inc., 3800 Village Ave., 23502, pg. 335 **PV**
Yadkin Railroad Co., Three Commercial Pl., 23510, pg. 1191 **PB**

Onley

Farmers & Merchants Bank-Eastern Shore, P.O. Box 623, 25275 Lankford Hwy., 23418, pg. 1089 **PB**

Orange

Kollman Div., 14100 Old Gordonsville Rd., 22960, pg. 575 **PB**
VIRGINIA METAL INDUSTRIES, INC., 12314 Old Gordonsville Rd., 22960, pg. 1141 **PV**

Petersburg

Brenco, Inc., Petersburg Industrial Park, 23804, pg. 1710 **PB**
FSA Rebuilding of Virginia, Inc., Petersburg Industrial Pk., 23804, pg. 1711 **PB**
Maclin-Zimmer McGill Tobacco Company, Inc., P.O. Box 550, 23804, pg. 1695 **PB**
ROPER BROS. LUMBER CO., INC., 130 Pocahontas St., 23803, pg. 944 **PV**
SEWARD INC., 434 High St., 23803, pg. 988 **PV**
VIRGINIA FIRST FINANCIAL CORP., Franklin & Adams Streets, 23803, pg. 1721 **PB**
Virginia First Savings Bank, F.S.B., Franklin & Adams Streets, 23803, pg. 1721 **PB**
Carl Zeiss Optical, Inc., 1015 Commerce St., 23803, pg. 1523 **IT**

Portsmouth

THE SMITHFIELD COMPANIES, INC., The Smithfield Bldg., 311 County St., Ste. 203, 23704, pg. 1479 **PB**
WAVY-Television, Inc., 801 Wavy St., 23704, pg. 11 **PB**

Pulaski

Accentrics Division, One Pulaski Sq., 24301, pg. 1342 **PB**
Carftique, Inc., One Pulaski Sq., 24301, pg. 1342 **PB**
JEFFERSON MILLS, INC., Valley & Commerce Sts., 24301, pg. 584 **PV**
PULASKI FURNITURE CORPORATION, One Pulaski Sq., 24301, pg. 1342 **PB**
Ridgeway Clock Company, One Pulaski Square, 24301, pg. 1343 **PB**
XALOY, INC., 102 Xaloy Way, 24301, pg. 1194 **PV**

Radford

Kollmorgen SMG, 201 Rock Rd., 24141, pg. 965 **PB**

Reston

Alcatel ITS Inc., 12030 Sunrise Valley Dr., 22091-3409, pg. 55 **IT**
Avitas Inc., 1835 Alexander Bell Dr., 22091, pg. 396 **IT**
BEST SOFTWARE, INC., 11413 Isaac Newton Sq., 20190, pg. 223 **PB**
CNG International Corp., Two Fountain Sq., Ste. 600, 11921 Freedom Dr., 20190-5608, pg. 435 **PB**

COLUMBIA ENERGY GROUP, 12355 Sunrise Valley Dr., Ste. 300, 20191-3420, pg. 402 **PB**
Comsearch Applied Technology, Inc., 2002 Edmund Hally Dr., 22091, pg. 46 **PB**
Comsearch, Inc., 2002 Edmund Halley Dr., 22091, pg. 46 **PB**
Comverse Network Systems, 11911 Freedom Dr., Ste. 530, 20190, pg. 425 **PB**
Data Architecture & Engineering, 2100 Reston Pkwy., 20191, pg. 1024 **PB**
Dataproducts Corp., 12200 Sunrise Valley Dr., 22091-3447, pg. 620 **IT**
DYNCORP, 2000 Edmund Halley Dr., 20191, pg. 351 **PV**
Earth Station Div., 2002 Edmund Halley Dr., 22091, pg. 46 **PB**
Enterprise Management, 2000 Edmond Halley Dr., 22091, pg. 351 **PV**
Eurotherm Circuits Inc., 1808 Michael Faraday Ct., 22090, pg. 466 **PB**
Eurotherm Controls Inc., 11485 Sunset Hills Rd., 22090-5286, pg. 466 **PB**
Eurotherm Drives Inc., 1808 Michael Faraday Ct., 22090, pg. 466 **PB**
GDC Federal Systems, Inc., 11260 Roger Bacon Dr., 22090, pg. 708 **PB**
Global One, 12490 Sunrise Valley Dr., 22096, pg. 1501 **PB**
Intergraph Corporation, Regional Training Ctr., 12347-B Sunrise Valley Dr., 22091, pg. 890 **PB**
Intergraph Corporation, 2051 Mercator Dr., 22091, pg. 890 **PB**
Lafarge Corporation, P.O. Box 4600, 20195-1415, pg. 788 **IT**
Litton Computer Services-Eastern Regional Data Center, 1831 Michael Faraday Dr., 22090-5298, pg. 1002 **PB**
MARYLAND & VIRGINIA MILK PRODUCERS COOPERATIVE ASSOCIATION, INC., 1985 Isaac Newton Sq., 20190, pg. 1289 **PB**
Molson Breweries U.S.A. Inc., 11911 Freedom Dr., Ste. 1100, 22090, pg. 1289 **IT**
PHP HEALTHCARE CORPORATION, 11440 Commerce Park Dr., Ste.300, 20191-1544, pg. 1241 **PB**
Pracon, 1800 Robert Fulton Dr., 22091, pg. 1100 **IT**
Product Distribution & Directory Publishing, 12490 Sunrise Valley Dr., 22096, pg. 1501 **PB**
Rolls-Royce Inc., 11911 Freedom Dr., 22090-5602, pg. 1127 **IT**
Sky Courier, 1851 Alexander Bell Dr., 22091, pg. 33 **IT**
SOFTWARE AG AMERICAS, INC., 11190 Sunrise Valley Dr., 20191, pg. 1482 **PB**
TBWA Chiat/Day Washington, D.C., 11921 Freedom Dr., Ste. 970, 22090, pg. 1062 **PV**
Terrestrial Microwave Services Div., 2002 Edmund Halley Dr., 22091, pg. 46 **PB**
Tracor Enterprise Solutions, Inc., 11400 Commerce Park Dr., 20191, pg. 1627 **PB**
VM Software Division, 1800 Alexander Bell Dr., 22091, pg. 1516 **PB**

Rich Creek

Dollinger Corporation, 101 Spruce St., 24147, pg. 1676 **PB**

Richmond

ABB Steam Power Generation Company, 1200 Willis Rd., 23237, pg. 4 **IT**
ABB Turbine Manufacturing & Service, 1200 Willis Rd., 23237, pg. 4 **IT**
AJD, 3301 Castlewood Rd., 23234, pg. 510 **PV**
AMF Azalea Bowl, 1741 Dumbarton Rd., 23227-3323, pg. 7 **PV**
AMF BAKERY SYSTEMS, 2115 W. Laburnum Ave., 23227, pg. 7 **PV**
AMF Bowling Centers Inc., 7275 Glen Forest Dr., 23226-3755, pg. 6 **PV**
AMF BOWLING WORLDWIDE, 8100 AMF Dr., 23211, pg. 1634 **PV**
APPX Software Inc., 1100 Boulder Pkwy., 23225, pg. 1277 **PB**
ALBEMARLE CORPORATION, 330 S. Fourth St., P.O. Box 1335, 23218, pg. 37 **PB**
Alfa Laval Thermal Inc., 5400 International Trade Dr., 23231, pg. 1378 **IT**
Allegheny Pepsi-Cola Bottling Company, 3008 Mechanicsville Pike, 23223, pg. 1277 **PB**
Allright Parking Virginia, Inc., 100 Virginia St., 23219, pg. 43 **PV**
Ambulatory Services, Inc., 4301 Meadowdale Blvd., 23234, pg. 403 **PV**
Amer Air Filters, 8410 Sanford Dr., 23228-2811, pg. 3 **PV**
American Church, 3801 Caroline Ave., 23222, pg. 60 **PV**
American Inks & Coatings Corp., Ink Division, 111 Agency Ave., 23225, pg. 56 **PV**
The Arnold Agency, Riverfront Plaza West Tower, 901 E. Byrd St., 14th Fl., 23219, pg. 84 **PV**
Automotive Rebuilders, 1500 Chamberlayne Ave., 23230, pg. 929 **PV**
Beacon Press, Inc., 4731 Eubank St., 23231, pg. 1077 **PV**
Bell Atlantic-VA, 600 E. Main St., 23219, pg. 203 **PB**
Best Products Co., Inc., 1400 Best Plaza, 23227, pg. 990 **PV**
Bleu Water Company, 1706 Roseneath Rd., 23230, pg. 223 **PV**
Bunzl Extrusion, 3951 Westerre Pkwy., Ste. 300, 23233, pg. 232 **IT**
CSX CORPORATION, One James Ctr., 901 E. Cary St., 23219-4031, pg. 284 **PB**
Cadmus-Byrd Manufacturing, 2901 Byrdhill Rd., 23228, pg. 290 **PB**

CADMUS COMMUNICATIONS CORPORATION, 6620 W. Broad St., Ste. 240, 23230, pg. 290 **PB**
Cadmus/GE Print Services, 6620 W. Broad St., Ste. 230, 23230, pg. 291 **PB**
Cadmus Journal Services, 2901 Byrdhill Rd., 23261, pg. 291 **PB**
Cadmus Journal Services, Inc., 2901 Byrdhill Rd., 23228-5867, pg. 291 **PB**
Cadmus Magazines, 2901 Byrdhill Rd., 23228, pg. 291 **PB**
Cadmus Promotional Printing, P.O. Box 26549, 2015 W. Laburnum Ave., 23261, pg. 291 **PB**
Cadmus Promotional Printing, 2901 Byrdhill Rd., 23228, pg. 291 **PB**
CAP Gemini America (Richmond Branch), 808 Moorefield Park Dr., 23236, pg. 264 **IT**
Capital Resources of Virginia, Inc., 15 Dove Ct., pg. 657 **PV**
Capitoline Investment Services, Inc., 919 E. Main St., 23219, pg. 458 **PV**
THE CARDWELL MACHINE COMPANY, 2831 Cardwell Rd., 23234, pg. 209 **PV**
CARPENTER CO., 5016 Monument Ave., 23230, pg. 214 **PV**
Carter Ryley Thomas-EPB, One East Cary St., 23219, pg. 174 **PV**
CENTRAL COCA-COLA BOTTLING COMPANY, INC., Corporate Headquarters, 1706 Roseneath Rd., 23230, pg. 222 **PV**
Chambers USA Waste, Inc., 2114 Bellemead Rd., 23224, pg. 1686 **IT**
Chappell Agency Inc., 6415 Rigsby Rd., 23226, pg. 736 **IT**
Charter Behavioral Health System of Central Virginia, Inc., 1500 Westbrook Ave., 23227, pg. 1033 **PB**
Charter Westbrook Behaviorl Health System, Inc., 1500 Westbrook Ave., 23227, pg. 1035 **PB**
CHESAPEAKE CORPORATION, 1021 E. Cary St., 23219, pg. 346 **PB**
Chesapeake Packaging Co., 2104 W. Laburnum Ave., Ste. 209, 23221, pg. 346 **PB**
Chesapeake Packaging Co./Richmond, 5600 Lewis Rd., 23150, pg. 347 **PB**
CHRISTIAN CHILDREN'S FUND, INC., 2821 Emerywood Pkwy., 23294, pg. 238 **PV**
Circuit City Central Div., 12201 Gayton Rd., 23233, pg. 374 **PB**
Circuit City Northeast Division, 9950 Mayland Dr., 23233, pg. 374 **PB**
CIRCUIT CITY STORES, INC., 9950 Mayland Dr., 23233, pg. 374 **PB**
Colony Insurance Company, 9201 Forest Hill Ave., Ste. 200, 23235, pg. 430 **PV**
Colony Management Services, 9201 Forest Hill Ave., Ste. 200, 23235, pg. 430 **PV**
Columbia Propane Corp., 800 Moorefield Pk. Dr., 23236, pg. 403 **PB**
Commonwealth Gas Services, Inc., 800 Moorefield Pk. Dr., 23236, pg. 403 **PB**
Commonwealth Propane, Inc., 800 Moorefield Pk. Dr., 23236, pg. 403 **PB**
Crestar Bank, 919 E. Main St., 23219, pg. 458 **PB**
CRESTAR FINANCIAL CORPORATION, Crestar Center, 919 E. Main St., 23261-6665, pg. 458 **PB**
Crestar Insurance Agency Incorporated, 919 E. Main St., 23219, pg. 458 **PB**
Crestar Mortgage Corporation, 901 Semmes Ave., 23224, pg. 458 **PB**
Crestar Securities Corporation, 919 E. Main St., 23219, pg. 458 **PB**
Datura Development Laboratory, 8155 Staples Mill Rd., 23228, pg. 1309 **PB**
Dillard, A ResourceNet International Company, 2100 Jefferson Davis Hwy., 23234, pg. 902 **PB**
Domestic Uniform Rental, 1321 No. 17th St., 23219, pg. 338 **PV**
Dominion Capital, Inc., P.O. Box 26532, 23261, pg. 516 **PB**
Dominion Energy, Inc., P.O. Box 26532, 23261, pg. 516 **PB**
Dominion Energy Services Company, P.O. Box 26532, 23261, pg. 516 **PB**
Dominion Financing, Inc., P.O. Box 26532, 23261, pg. 516 **PB**
Dominion Lands, Inc., P.O. Box 26532, 23261, pg. 516 **PB**
DOMINION RESOURCES, INC., Riverfront Plaza, W. Tower, 901 E. Byrd St., 23219, pg. 516 **PB**
Duplex Envelope Co., 3801 Carolina Ave., 23222, pg. 903 **PB**
Electrical Equipment Company, 1807 Blvd. W., 23230, pg. 368 **PB**
ESKIMO PIE CORPORATION, 901 Moorefield Park Dr., 23236, pg. 592 **PB**
ESTES EXPRESS LINES, INC., 1100 Commerce Rd., 23224, pg. 384 **PV**
ETHYL CORPORATION, 330 S. Fourth St., 23218-2189, pg. 595 **PB**
Fidus Instrument Corp., 7400 White Pine Rd., 23237, pg. 233 **IT**
Filter Products Division, 110 Tredegar St., 23219, pg. 620 **PB**
Filtrona Richmond Company, 8401 Jefferson Davis Hwy., 23237, pg. 232 **PB**
Financial Collection Agencies (1990) Inc., 1500 Forest Ave., Ste. 224, 23229, pg. 471 **IT**
First Virginia Bank-Colonial, 700 E. Main St., 23219-2653, pg. 641 **PB**
Formex, Inc. - Permanent Steel Forms, P.O. Box 24129, 23224, Formex Rd., 23224, pg. 1222 **PB**
FORT JAMES CORPORATION, 120 Tredegar St., 23219, pg. 670 **PB**

PB - *U.S. Public Companies Volume*
PV - *U.S. Private Companies Volume*
IT - *International Public & Private Companies Volume*

1467

Geographic Index-U.S.

Front Royal Insurance Company, 9201 Forest Hill Ave., Ste. 200, 23235, pg. 430 **PV**
G.D. Packaging Machinery Inc., 501 Southlake Blvd., 23236, pg. 531 **IT**
GES Environmental, Inc., 8040 Kimway Dr., 23228, pg. 1222 **PB**
Galen of Virginia, Inc., 4114 E. Parham Rd., 23228, pg. 404 **PB**
G.E. Financial Assurance, 6604 W. Broad St., 23230, pg. 712 **PB**
General Medical Corp., 8741 Landmark Rd., 23228, pg. 1073 **PB**
GENERAL SERVICES CORPORATION, 2922 Hathaway Rd., 23225, pg. 445 **PV**
Gifford-Hill Concrete Products Inc., 2900 Terminal Ave., 23234, pg. 593 **IT**
HCA-Cluster, 9100 Arboretum Pkwy., Ste. 140, 23226, pg. 403 **PB**
Halifax Technology Services Company, 2215 Tomlynn St., 23230, pg. 775 **PB**
HEILIG-MEYERS COMPANY, 2235 Staples Mill Rd., 23230, pg. 804 **PB**
Heilig Meyers Furniture Co., 2235 Staples Mill Rd., 23230, pg. 804 **PB**
Home Beneficial Corporation, 3901 W. Broad St., 23230, pg. 76 **PB**
Home Beneficial Life Insurance Co., 3901 W. Broad St., 23230, pg. 77 **PB**
Ikon Office Solutions-Richmond, 2211 Dickens Rd., 20230, pg. 864 **PB**
Interbake Foods Inc., 2220 Edward Holland Dr., 23230-2519, pg. 1495 **IT**
James Transportation, P.O. Box 2218, 23217, pg. 672 **PB**
Jefferson-Pilot Communications Co. of Virginia, 5710 Midlothian Tpke., 23201, pg. 926 **PB**
KSB Inc., 4415 Sarellen Road, 23231, pg. 721 **IT**
Kjellstrom & Lee, Inc., Vistas at Brookfield, 5516 Flamouth St., Ste. 200, 23230, pg. 453 **PV**
Latco, Inc., 1501 N. Hamilton St., 23230, pg. 1695 **PB**
LAWYERS TITLE INSURANCE CORPORATION, 6630 W. Broad St., 23230, pg. 981 **PB**
The Life Insurance Co. of Virginia, 6610 W. Broad St., 23230, pg. 712 **PB**
Lindenmeyr Munroe, 5654 Eastport Blvd., 23231, pg. 224 **PV**
MACTAVISH MACHINE MANUFACTURING COMPANY, 9001 Hermitage Rd., 23228, pg. 693 **PV**
Manufacturers Life Mortgage Securities Corporation, 901 E. Cary Street, Ste. 1610, 23219, pg. 840 **IT**
The Martin Agency, One Shockoe Plaza, 23219-4132, pg. 678 **PV**
The Martin Agency, One Shockoe Plaza, 23219-4132, pg. 909 **PB**
A.T. Massey Coal Company, Inc., Four N. Fourth St., 23219, pg. 660 **PB**
Media General Financial Services, Inc., 333 E. Grace St., 23219-0001, pg. 1078 **PB**
MEDIA GENERAL, INC., 333 E. Grace St., 23219-6100, pg. 1077 **PB**
MEGA Advertising, Inc., 333 E. Grace St., 23219, pg. 1078 **PB**
Mentor Investment Group, 901 E. Byrd St., 23219, pg. 640 **PB**
Modern Merchandising, Inc., P.O. Box 26303, 23260, pg. 990 **PV**
NationsBank Capital Management Corporation, 1111 E. Main St., 23261, pg. 1163 **PB**
NationsBank Equity Mortgage Corporation, 3600 W. Broad St., Ste. 452, 23230, pg. 1163 **PB**
NationsBank Futures Corporation, Sovran Center Pavillion, 12th & Main Sts., 23219, pg. 1163 **PB**
NationsBank Investment Corporation, 12th and Main Sts., 23219, pg. 1163 **PB**
NationsBank Virginia, 1111 E. Main St., 23219-3500, pg. 1163 **PB**
M.F. Neal & Co.,Inc., 4400 Williamsburg Rd., 23219, pg. 689 **PV**
Omega Environmental Inc., 8040 Kimway Rd., 23228, pg. 1222 **PB**
Overnite Transportation Co., 1000 Semmes Ave., 23218-1212, pg. 1668 **PB**
PM Terminals, Inc., P.O. Box 34370, 23234, pg. 859 **PV**
PPD Pharmaco (Analytical Laboratory), 2240 Dabney Rd., 23230, pg. 1285 **PB**
PENCO-Virginia, 7400 Beaufont Springs Dr., Ste. 300, 23225, pg. 1508 **IT**
Pepsi-Cola Bottling Company of Richmond, Inc., 300 Mechanicsvile Pike, 23223, pg. 1277 **PB**
PERFORMANCE FOOD GROUP COMPANY, 6800 Paragon Pl., Ste. 500, 23230, pg. 1278 **PB**
Phipps & Bird, 8741 Landmark Rd., 23228, pg. 1073 **PB**
Pocahontas Foods, USA, 7420 Ranco Rd., 23228, pg. 1278 **PB**
Potomac Digital, Inc./Scott Data, 2720 Enterprise Pkwy., 23229, pg. 711 **PB**
Power Equipment Co., 1307 W. Main St., 23220, pg. 360 **PV**
Properties Division, 6603 W. Broad St., 23261, pg. 1386 **PB**
Quebecor Printing Richmond Inc., 7400 Impala Dr., 23228, pg. 1078 **IT**
Rail Bearing Service Corp., 2510 Professional Rd., 23235, pg. 1617 **PB**
Raschig Corp., 5000 Osborne Tpke., 23231, pg. 827 **PV**
Rehrig International, 901 N. Lombardy St., 23220, pg. 287 **PV**
Reynolds Aluminum Recycling Co., 6601 W. Broad St., 23261, pg. 1386 **PB**
REYNOLDS METALS COMPANY, 6601 W. Broad St., 23230, pg. 1385 **PB**
Reynolds Metals Company-Bellwood, 1900 Remat Rd., 23237, pg. 1385 **PB**
Richfood Dairy, 1505 Robin Hood Rd., 23220, pg. 1389 **PB**
Richmond Foundry and Manufacturing Co., 8500 Sanford Dr., 23238, pg. 601 **PV**
Richmond Leasing, 4515 W. Broad St., 23230, pg. 929 **PV**
RICHMOND MOTOR COMPANY, 4600 W. Broad St., 23230, pg. 929 **PV**
Richmond Newspapers, Inc., 333 E. Grace St., 23219, pg. 1079 **PB**
Richmond Paperboard Corporation, 111 Hull St., 23234, pg. 304 **PB**
Rincon Securities, Inc., P.O. Box 26532, 23219, pg. 516 **PB**
Robertshaw Controls Company, 1701 Byrd Ave., 23230, pg. 1243 **IT**
San-J Intl. Inc., 2880 Sprouse Dr., 23231, pg. 1183 **IT**
SASIB Corporation of America, 7527 Whitepine Rd., 23237-2216, pg. 1194 **IT**
SAUNDERS OIL COMPANY, INC., 1200 W. Marshall St., 23220, pg. 968 **PV**
Scott & Stringfellow Capital Management, Inc., Mutual Bldg., 909 E. Main St., 23219, pg. 1445 **PB**
SCOTT & STRINGFELLOW FINANCIAL, INC., Mutual Bldg., 909 E. Main St., 23219, pg. 1445 **PB**
Scott & Stringfellow, Inc., P.O. Box 1575, 23218-1575, pg. 1445 **PB**
Scott & Stringfellow, Inc., 909 E. Main St., 23219, pg. 1445 **PB**
Scott & Stringfellow, Inc., 808 Moorefield Park Dr., Ste. 110, 23236, pg. 1446 **PB**
Shorewood Packaging Corporation of Virginia, 6767 Forest Hill Ave., Ste. 234, 23225-1851, pg. 1468 **PB**
Southern Health Services, Inc., 9881 Maryland Ave., 23233, pg. 454 **PB**
SOUTHERN STATES COOPERATIVE, INC., 6606 W. Broad St., 23230, pg. 1017 **PV**
Southwestern Tobacco Co., Inc., 1501 N. Hamilton St., 23230, pg. 1695 **PB**
Sterilization Services of Virginia, 5674 Eastport Blvd., 23231, pg. 46 **PV**
Sterling Electronics, 711 Moorefield Dr., 23231, pg. 1051 **PB**
Style Weekly, 1118 W. Main St., 23220, pg. 649 **PV**
Tarmac-LoneStar, Inc., 3011 Dock St., 23223, pg. 1355 **IT**
Tencarva Machinery Co., 2231 E. Belt Blvd., 23224, pg. 1076 **PV**
Thermal Industries Inc., 3309 W. Leigh St., 23230-4411, pg. 491 **PV**
THIS END UP FURNITURE, 23 S. 13th. St., 23219, pg. 1081 **PV**
Thompson, Siegel & Walmsley, Inc., P.O. Box 6883, 5000 Monument Ave., 23230, pg. 1674 **PB**
Tredegar Film Products, 1100 Boulders Pkwy., 23225, pg. 1634 **PB**
TREDEGAR INDUSTRIES INC., 1100 Boulders Pkwy., 23225, pg. 1633 **PB**
TRIGON BLUE CROSS & BLUE SHIELD, 2015 Staples Mill Rd., 23230, pg. 1637 **PB**
Tuff Stuff Publications, Inc., P.O. Box 1637, 1934 E. Parnham Rd., 23060, pg. 291 **PB**
Turner Construction Company, 7204 Glen Forest Dr., Ste. 300, 23226, pg. 1646 **PB**
URS Greiner, Inc., 5540 Falmouth St., Ste. 203, 44130-8405, pg. 1658 **PB**
UKROP'S SUPER MARKETS, 600 Southlake Blvd., 23236, pg. 1115 **PV**
United Companies Lending Corp. (Virginia), 2112 W. Laburnum, Ste. 100, 23260, pg. 1675 **PB**
UNITED DOMINION REALTY TRUST, INC., Ten S. Sixth St., 23219, pg. 1677 **PB**
UNIVERSAL CORPORATION, 1501 N. Hamilton St., 23230, pg. 1694 **PB**
Universal Leaf Export Company, Inc., 1501 Hamilton St., 23230, pg. 1695 **PB**
Universal Leaf Tobacco Company, Inc., 1501 N. Hamilton St., 23230, pg. 1694 **PB**
Universal Wilton Inc., 1501 N. Hamilton St., 23230, pg. 1695 **PB**
Virginia Electric and Power Company, One James River Plaza, 23219, pg. 516 **PB**
VIRGINIA TOURISM CORP., 901 E. Byrd St., W-19, 23219-0798, pg. 1141 **PV**
WFS Clearing Services, 901 E. Byrd St., 23219, pg. 640 **PB**
WRNL-FM, 200 N. 22nd St., 23212, pg. 385 **PB**
WRVA-AM, 200 N. 22nd St., 23223, pg. 385 **PB**
WRVQ-FM, 3245 Basie Rd., 23228, pg. 385 **PB**
WRXL-FM, 3245 Basie Rd., 23228, pg. 385 **PB**
WTVR-AM/FM, 3314 Cutshaw Ave., 23230, pg. 385 **PB**
WWBT-TV, P.O. Box 12, 23201, pg. 926 **PB**
WWF Paper Corporation - Mid Atlantic, 4245 Carolina Ave., 23261, pg. 1145 **PV**
Wachovia Bank, 1021 E. Cary St., 23219, pg. 1730 **PB**
Wachovia Mortgage, 219 E. Broad St., 23219, pg. 1731 **PB**
R.P. Watson Co., 1501 N. Hamilton St., 23230, pg. 1695 **PB**
Westvaco Corporation-Consumer Packaging Div., 320 Hull St., 23224, pg. 1762 **PB**
Wheat First Butcher Singer, Inc., 901 E. Byrd St., 23219, pg. 640 **PB**
Whitby, Inc., 1211 Sherwood Ave., 23261, pg. 1427 **IT**
Williams Constructors, 938 E. 4th St., 23208, pg. 1178 **PV**
Williams Crane & Rigging, Inc., 938 E. 4th St., 23208, pg. 1178 **PV**
WILLIAMS INTERNATIONAL INDUSTRIES, INC., 938 E. 4th St., 23218, pg. 1178 **PV**
W.H. Winstead Company, 1501 N. Hamilton St., 23230, pg. 1695 **PB**
Zellerbach Division, 2100 Tomlynn St., 23230, pg. 1075 **PB**
Zeneca Specialty Inks, 3411 Shaw Ln., 23224, pg. 1525 **IT**

Ridgeway

Ridgeway Clock Company, P.O. Box 407, 24148, pg. 1343 **PB**
Triwood, Inc., S.R. 782, Box 589A, 24148, pg. 193 **PB**

Ripplemead

APG Lime Corp., Rte. 635, 24150-9728, pg. 761 **PB**

Roanoke

ANR Venture Eagle Point Company, 310 First St., 24011, pg. 389 **PB**
ANR Venture Fulton Company, 310 First St., 24011, pg. 389 **PB**
A.P.G. Lime Corp., 3959 Electric Rd., Ste. 100, 24018-4512, pg. 761 **PB**
Allright Roanoke Parking, Inc., 33 W. Salem Ave., 24011, pg. 43 **PV**
Appalachian Power Company, 40 Franklin Rd., 24011, pg. 72 **PB**
Asbury Equipment, 4501 Brentwood Ct., 24018, pg. 87 **PV**
BellSouth Communication Systems, Inc., 1936 Blue Hills Dr., NE, 24012, pg. 209 **PB**
BellSouth Products, Inc., 1936 Blue Hills Dr., 24012, pg. 209 **PB**
Chesapeake Packaging Co./Roanoke, 802 Kyle Ave., 24012, pg. 347 **PB**
Coastal Development Company, 310 First St., 24011, pg. 390 **PB**
Coastal Power Revere Company, 310 First St., 24011, pg. 390 **PB**
Coastal Remediation Company, 310 First St. SW, 24011, pg. 390 **PB**
Coca-Cola Bottling Co. of Roanoke, 235 Shenandoah Ave., N.W., 24033, pg. 392 **PB**
Cox Communications-Roanoke, 5400 Fallowater Ln. S.W., 24014, pg. 455 **PB**
Dominion Bankshare Corporation, P.O. Box 13327, 24033, pg. 640 **PB**
ENCAP Systems, Inc., 1202 Franklin Road, 24016, pg. 513 **PV**
First Citizens Bank of Virginia Corporation, 3601 Thiglane Rd., Ste. 6, 24019, pg. 629 **PB**
First Union National Bank of Virginia, 213 S. Jefferson St., 24040, pg. 640 **PB**
First Virginia Bank-Southwest, 601 S. Jefferson St., 24011-2414, pg. 642 **PB**
Government Forms & Systems, Inc., 1825 Blue Hill Cir., 24012, pg. 782 **PV**
HSMM Facilities, Inc., 1202 Franklin Rd., S.W., 24016, pg. 513 **PV**
Hanover Direct Virginia, Inc., One Avery Rd., 24012, pg. 782 **PV**
HAYES, SEAY, MATTERN & MATTERN, INC., 1315 Franklin Rd. S.W., 24016, pg. 513 **PV**
Hewlett-Packard Company, 2800 Electric Rd., Ste. 100, 24018, pg. 815 **PB**
Highland Propane Company, 519 Kimball Ave., N.E., 24016, pg. 1393 **PB**
ITT Gallium Arsenide Technology Center, 7670 Enon Drive, 20419, pg. 859 **PB**
ITT Night Vision, 7635 Plantaion Road, 20416, pg. 860 **PB**
Kingsport Power Co., 40 Franklin Rd., P.O. Box 2021, 24022, pg. 72 **PB**
Nelson-Roanoke Corp., 901 11th St. N.E., 24012, pg. 335 **PV**
Old Dominion Life Insurance Co., 2301 Brambleton Ave., S.W., 24015, pg. 992 **PV**
The Orvis Company, 1711 Blue Hills Dr., 24012, pg. 820 **PV**
PM Foods Inc., 3000 Ogden Rd., 24014, pg. 859 **PV**
PM Properties Inc., 3000 Ogden Rd., 24014, pg. 859 **PV**
PM Transport, Inc., 4939 Starkey Rd., 24018, pg. 859 **PV**
PETROLEUM MARKETERS, INC., 3000 Ogden Rd., 24014, pg. 859 **PV**
Putnam Graphic Innovations, Inc., 1825 Blue Hill Cir., 24012, pg. 782 **PV**
RBX Corporation, 5221 ValleyPark Dr., 24019-3074, pg. 56 **PV**
ROANOKE ELECTRIC STEEL CORPORATION, P.O. Box 13948, 24038-3948, pg. 1392 **PB**
ROANOKE GAS COMPANY, 519 Kimball Ave., N.E., 24016, pg. 1392 **PB**
The Roanoke Times, 201 Campbell Ave., 24011, pg. 649 **PV**
Rubatex Corporation, 5221 Valley Park Dr., 24019-3079, pg. 56 **PV**
SPC Company of Virginia, Inc., 2807 Mary Linda Ave., N.E., 24012-5655, pg. 1468 **PB**
Scott & Stringfellow, Inc., 601 S. Jefferson St., Ste. 160, 24011, pg. 1446 **PB**
SHENANDOAH LIFE INSURANCE COMPANY, 2301 Brambleton Ave., S.W., 24015, pg. 992 **PV**
Southern Utah Fuel Co., Crestor Bank Bldg., 310 First St., 24011, pg. 390 **PB**
Stop In Food Stores, 3000 Ogden Rd., 24014, pg. 859 **PV**
Tencarva Machinery Co., 3646 Aerial Way Dr., Suite 1, 24018, pg. 1076 **PV**
Transkrit Corporation, 1825 Blue Hill Cir., 24012, pg. 782 **PV**
WSLS-TV, 401 Third St. S.W., 24011, pg. 1078 **PB**

PB - *U.S. Public Companies Volume*
PV - *U.S. Private Companies Volume*
IT - *International Public & Private Companies Volume*

Rocky Mount

Fleetwood Homes of Virginia, Inc., Hwy. 40 W. RFD, 24151, pg. 651 **PB**
MW Manufacturers Inc., 433 N. Main St., 24151, pg. 593 **IT**
NEWBOLD CORPORATION, 450 Weaver St., 24151, pg. 796 **PV**

Rosslyn

AST Research, Inc, Ste. 800, 1560 Wilson Blvd., 22209, pg. 1182 **IT**
INTERSTATE RESOURCES, INC., 1800 N. Kent St., Ste. 1200, 22209-2145, pg. 573 **PV**

Saint Paul

FOURNIER FURNITURE, One Fournier Pl., 24283, pg. 422 **PV**

Salem

Carbone of America, Chemical Equipment Div., 540 Branch Dr., Box 1189, 24153, pg. 1028 **IT**
Carter Machinery Company, Inc., 1330 Lynchburg Tpke., 24153, pg. 315 **PB**
Dillard, A ResourceNet International Company, 1885 Apperson Rd., 24153, pg. 902 **PB**
John W. Hancock Jr., Inc., Diuguids Ln., Dept. TR, 24153, pg. 1392 **PB**
LAYMAN CANDY COMPANY, INC., 1637 E. Main St., 24153, pg. 655 **PV**
Medeco Security Locks, Inc., 3625 Allegheny Dr., 24153-0330, pg. 828 **PB**
RESCO Steel Products Corp., 438 Kessler Mill Rd., 24153, pg. 1544 **PB**
Sybron Chemicals Inc., 111 Kessler Mill Rd., 24153, pg. 1544 **PB**
Valleydale Foods, Inc., 1013 Iowa St., 24153, pg. 1479 **PB**

Saltville

First Community Bank of Saltville, Box B, 205 E. Main St., 24370, pg. 1039 **PB**
Titan Wheel Corporation of Virginia, 227 Allison Gap Rd., 24370, pg. 1619 **PB**

Sandston

Cadmus, 5301 Lewis Rd., 23150, pg. 290 **PB**
Cadmus Creative, 5301 Lewis Rd., 23150, pg. 290 **PB**
Cadmus Financial Communications, 5301 Lewis Rd., 23150, pg. 291 **PB**
Cadmus Promotional Printing, 5301 Lewis Rd., 23150, pg. 291 **PB**
Cadmus-Richmond Manufacturing, 5301 Lewis Rd., 23150, pg. 291 **PB**
STERNHEIMER BROTHERS INC., 5501 Ferncroft Rd., 23150, pg. 1042 **PV**

Smithfield

Gwaltney of Smithfield, Ltd., 601 N. Church St., 23430, pg. 1479 **PB**
Smithfield Division, P.O. Box 487, 23431, pg. 1479 **PB**
The Smithfield Packing Co., Inc., Hwy. No. 10, 501 N. Church St., 23430, pg. 1479 **PB**

Somerset

General Shale Products Corp., P.O. Box 523, 22972, pg. 844 **IT**

South Hill

PEEBLES, INC., One Peebles St., 23970, pg. 846 **PV**

Springfield

AR Division of Telenex, 7401 Boston Blvd., 22153, pg. 727 **PB**
Allied Plywood Corp., 6732 Industrial Rd., 22151, pg. 40 **PV**
Allnewsco, Inc., 7600D Boston Blvd., 22153, pg. 854 **PV**
Army Times Publishing Co., 6883 Commercial Dr., 22159, pg. 699 **PB**
Cardinal Concrete Co., P.O. Box 725, 22150, pg. 656 **PB**
EROL'S INTERNET, 7921 Woodruff Ct., 22151, pg. 382 **PV**
FAIRFAX LUMBER & MILLWORK COMPANY INC., 7622 Backlick Rd., 22150, pg. 391 **PV**
Gannett Offset, 6883 Commercial Dr., 22159, pg. 699 **PB**
Gannett Offset-Springfield Plant, 6883 Commercial Dr., 22159, pg. 700 **PB**
Gannett Telemarketing Inc., 6883 Commercial Dr., 22159, pg. 699 **PB**
Hydro Conduit Corp., 6800 Loisdale Rd., 22150, pg. 246 **IT**
INTERSTATE VAN LINES, INC., 5801 Rolling Rd., 22152, pg. 573 **PV**
LogEtronics Corporation, 7001 Loisdale Rd., 22150, pg. 6 **PB**
REICO, INC., 6790 Commercial Dr., 22151, pg. 919 **PV**
S&G Concrete Co., P.O. Box 606, 22150, pg. 656 **PB**
VERSAR INC., 6850 Versar Ctr., 22151, pg. 1717 **PB**

Versar Risk Management, Inc., 6850 Versar Ctr., 22151, pg. 1717 **PB**
Virginia Concrete Co., Inc., 6860 Commerical Dr., 22150, pg. 656 **PB**
WASHINGTON GAS LIGHT CO., 6801 Industrial Rd., 22151, pg. 1740 **PB**

Stanley

Crown Door Corp., P.O. Box 98, 22851, pg. 1067 **IT**

Stanleytown

STANLEY FURNITURE CO. INC., 1641 Fairystone Park Hwy., 24168, pg. 1508 **PB**

Staunton

The Daily News Leader, 11 N. Central, 24401, pg. 699 **PB**
McQuay Int'l, P.O. Box 2510, 24402-2510, pg. 3 **PV**
Scott & Stringfellow, Inc., 119 S. Augusta St., 24401, pg. 1446 **PB**
Staunton Leader Publishing Co., P.O. Box 59, 24401, pg. 701 **PB**

Sterling

ATR Support, 20 Export Dr., 20164, pg. 653 **IT**
Analytical Surveys, Inc. - Northeast Division, Two Pidgeon Hill Dr. Ste. 340, 22170, pg. 110 **PB**
Asia-Pacific Space & Communication Limited, 22070 Broderick Dr., 20166, pg. 218 **IT**
BMW of North America, Inc.-Mid-Atlantic Region, 21545 Ridgetop Cir., 20166, pg. 177 **IT**
Billcom Exposition & Conference, 45365 Vintage Park Plaza, Ste. 200, 20166, pg. 1446 **IT**
Circle Freight International USA, Dulles International Airport, 22660 Executive Dr., Ste. 110, 20166, pg. 370 **PB**
COMSAT RSI, Inc., 1501 Moran Rd., 20166, pg. 424 **PB**
Costco Wholesale, Inc.-Eastern Division, 46000 Manekin Plaza, 22166, pg. 452 **PB**
Diamond Paper Corporation, 21955 Cascades Pkwy., 20166, pg. 467 **PV**
Dowty Aerospace Aviation Services, P.O. Box 5000, Staverton West, Sully Rd., 20167, pg. 1337 **IT**
GeoTrans, Inc., 46050 Manekin Plaza, Ste. 100, 21066, pg. 1582 **PB**
Laux Communications, Inc., 1501 Moran Rd., 20166, pg. 424 **PB**
Messier-Dowty Customer Support Center- Americas, P.O. Box 49, 20167, pg. 1340 **IT**
Messier Services Inc., 45635 Willow Pond Plaza, 20164, pg. 1165 **IT**
NATIONAL ELECTRONICS WARRANTY CORPORATION, 44873 Falcon Pl., Ste. 174, 20166, pg. 782 **PV**
Saab Aircraft of America Inc., 21300 Ridgetop Circle, 20166, pg. 687 **IT**
Satellite Networks Division, 1501 Moran Rd., 22170, pg. 424 **PB**
Union-Transport Corporation-Washington, DC Office, 22660 Executive Dr., Ste. 122, 20166, pg. 1120 **PV**
World Trade Transport of Virginia, 22 Export Drive, 20164, pg. 749 **PB**

Strasburg

CHEMSTONE CORP., P.O. Box 71, 22657, pg. 233 **PV**
Judd's, Inc., 294 Front Royal Rd., 22657, pg. 855 **PV**
Lear Corporation, E. Queen St., 22657, pg. 982 **PB**

Stuart

CMI Industries, Inc., P.O. Box 519, 24171, pg. 195 **PV**
First Bank of Stuart, P.O. Box 352, Blue Ridge & Main Sts., 24171, pg. 1039 **PB**

Stuarts Draft

Hershey Chocolate U.S.A.-Stuarts Draft Plant, Box 1028, 24477, pg. 812 **IT**

Suffolk

Allied Colloids Inc., 2301 Wilroy Rd., 23434, pg. 62 **IT**
BIRDSONG CORPORATION, 612 Madison Ave., 23434, pg. 145 **PV**
Golden State Foods-Suffolk, 1391 Progress Rd., 23434, pg. 461 **PV**
Nestle Beverage Company, 1370 Progress Rd., 23434, pg. 918 **IT**

Tappahannock

SouthTech, Inc., P.O. Box 126, 22560, pg. 261 **IT**

Tazewell

Clinch River Corp., P.O. Box 60, Rte. Six, 24651, pg. 370 **PV**

Timberville

Rocco Quality Foods, Co-op Drive, 22853, pg. 937 **PV**
WLR FOODS, INC., 800 Co-op Dr., 22853, pg. 1727 **PB**

Toano

Williamsburg Foods, Inc., 8012 Hankins Industrial Park, 23168, pg. 1479 **PB**

Verona

American Safety Razor Company, Razor Blade Lane, 24482-0500, pg. 597 **PV**

Vienna

ALLIED RESEARCH CORPORATION, 8000 Towers Crescent Dr., Ste. 750, 22182, pg. 48 **PB**
Allied Research Corporation Limited, 8000 Towers Crescent Dr., Ste. 750, 22182, pg. 49 **PB**
Andreas Galleries, Inc., 8545 Leesburg Pike, 22182, pg. 650 **PV**
BSA Advertising, Inc., 8130 Boone Blvd., 22182, pg. 108 **PV**
Box Hill Federal Systems, 8150 Leesburg Pike, Ste. 600, 22182, pg. 249 **PB**
CAP Gemini America (Management Consulting Branch), 8381 Old Courthouse Rd., Ste. 300, 22180, pg. 264 **IT**
Cable & Wireless Communications Inc., 8219 Leesburg Pike, 22182, pg. 247 **IT**
Cable & Wireless Management Services, 1919 Gallows Rd., 22182, pg. 247 **IT**
Cable & Wireless of North America, Inc., 1919 Gallows Rd., 22182, pg. 247 **IT**
CAP Gemini America (Washington D.C. Branch), 8391 Old Courthouse Rd., Ste. 350, 22180, pg. 264 **IT**
Cognos Corp.-Washington, D.C. Sales Office, 1593 Springhill Rd., Ste. 510, 22182-9675, pg. 306 **IT**
COMMTEK COMMUNICATIONS, CORP., 8330 Boone Blvd., Ste. 600, 22182, pg. 258 **PV**
Coscan Land, Inc., 8521 Leesburg Pike, Ste. 200, 22180, pg. 228 **IT**
Covance Laboratories, 9200 Leesburg Tpke., 22180, pg. 454 **PB**
Decisions & Design, Inc., 8150 Leesburgh Pike, Ste. 500, 22182, pg. 406 **PB**
Engineering Research Associates, 1595 Springhill Rd., 22182-2235, pg. 1365 **PB**
EXCALIBUR TECHNOLOGIES CORPORATION, 1921 Gallows Rd., Ste. 200, 22182, pg. 598 **PB**
FELD PRODUCTIONS, 8607 Westwood Center Dr., 22182, pg. 399 **PV**
GRC INTERNATIONAL, INC., 1900 Gallows Rd., 22182, pg. 695 **PB**
H.B.L., Inc., 8545 Leesburg Pike, 22182, pg. 650 **PV**
Interealty Corporation, 1951 Kidwell Dr., 22182, pg. 797 **PV**
International Business Services, Inc., 8150 Leesburgh Pike, Ste. 500, 22182, pg. 406 **PB**
International Relocation Insurance Services Inc., 1921 Gallows Road, Ste. 750, 22182-3900, pg. 1503 **PB**
Jani King of Washington D.C., Inc., 8245 Boone Blvd, Ste. 708, 22182, pg. 568 **PV**
KEMRON ENVIRONMENTAL SERVICES, INC., 8150 Leesburg Pk., 22182, pg. 614 **PV**
JIM KOONS MANAGEMENT, 2000 Chainbridge Rd., 22182, pg. 632 **PV**
LANDMARK SYSTEMS CORPORATION, 8000 Towers Crescent Dr., 22182-2700, pg. 649 **PV**
LANTZSCH-ANDREAS ENTERPRISES, INC., 8545 Leesburg Pike, 22182-2283, pg. 650 **PV**
MCImetro, 8521 Leesburg Pike, 22182, pg. 1024 **PB**
MFS International, Inc., 8100 Boone Blvd., Ste. 500, 22182, pg. 1779 **PB**
MHM SERVICES INC., 8000 Tower Crescent Dr., Ste. 810, 22182, pg. 1027 **PB**
Micro Card Technologies Inc., 8000 Towers Crescent Dr., 22182, pg. 316 **IT**
N.E.T. Federal, 8300 Boone Blvd., Ste. 600, 22182-2626, pg. 1169 **PB**
NEWS HOLDINGS CORP., 1951 Kidwell Dr., 22182, pg. 797 **PV**
Optima Direct, Inc., 8100 Boone Blvd., 22182-2642, pg. 1224 **PB**
Ringling Bros., Barnum & Bailey Combined Shows, Inc., 8607 Westwood Center Dr., 22182, pg. 400 **PV**
SSE TELECOM, INC., 8230 Leesburg Pike, Ste. 710, 22182, pg. 1421 **PB**
Scott & Stringfellow, Inc., 8133 Leesburg Pike, Ste. 570, 22182, pg. 1446 **PB**
Vie de France Bakery Yamazaki, Inc., 2070 Chain Bridge Rd., Ste. 500, 22182, pg. 1519 **IT**
Willis Corroon Corp. of Virginia, 1921 Gallows Rd., Ste. 750, 22182, pg. 1507 **IT**

Virginia Beach

American Systems Engineering Corporation, 2829 Guardian Ln., Ste. 200, 23452, pg. 976 **PV**
Cavalier Hotel Corp., 42nd St. & Atlantic Ave., 23451, pg. 638 **PV**
Cooper Bearings, 5795 Thurston Ave., 23455, pg. 946 **PB**
Cox Cable Hampton Roads, Inc., 5200 Cleveland St., 23462, pg. 455 **PB**
International Family Entertainment, Inc., 2877 Guardian Ln., 23452, pg. 927 **IT**
Medicenter, Virginia Beach, 1148 First Colonial Rd., 23454, pg. 1714 **PV**
METRO INFORMATION SERVICES, Reflection 2, Ste. 300, 200 Golden Oak Ct., 23452, pg. 1102 **PB**
Mohawk Marketing, P.O. Box 62229, 23462, pg. 869 **IT**
RHG Norfolk/RH Defense Systems Inc., 2703 Avenger Dr., 23452, pg. 1151 **IT**

Geographic Index-U.S.

L.M. SANDLER & SONS, 448 Viking Dr., Ste. 220, 23452, pg. 964   PV
Schiess-America Corp., 529 Central Dr., Ste. 101, 23454, pg. 860   IT
Scott & Stringfellow, Inc., 1080 Laskin Rd., Ste. 102, 23451, pg. 1445   PB
Servitex, Inc., 5616 Shell Rd., 23455, pg. 782   PV
Stihl Inc., P.O. Box 2015, 536 Viking Dr., 23452, pg. 1301   IT
Stihl Parts, Inc., 520 Viking Dr., 23452, pg. 1301   IT
Susquehanna Radio Corp., 168 Business Park Dr., Ste. 201, 23462, pg. 860   PV
The Vacation Store, 5501 Greenwich Rd., Ste. 200, 23462, pg. 649   PV

Warrenton

Scott & Stringfellow, Inc., 550 Broadview Ave., Ste. 101, 20186-2036, pg. 1446   PB

Waynesboro

BAUGHER CHEVROLET-BUICK INC., 2551 W. Main, 22980, pg. 123   PV
Genicom Corporation, One Genicom Dr., 22980-1999, pg. 729   PB
Park Newspapers of Waynesboro, Inc., 544 W. Main St., 22980, pg. 1079   PB
Poly-Bond Inc., 1020 Shenandoah Village Drive, 22980, pg. 415   IT

West Point

Chesapeake Forest Products Co., 19th & Main Sts., 23181, pg. 346   PB
Chesapeake Paper Products Co., 19th & Main Sts., 23181, pg. 347   PB
Delmarva Properties, Inc., P.O. Box 1700, 23181, pg. 347   PB
Stonehouse, Inc., P.O. Box 1700, 23181, pg. 347   PB

Williamsburg

Busch Gardens Williamsburg, One Busch Gardens Dr., 23187, pg. 114   PB
COLONIAL WILLIAMSBURG FOUNDATION, Henry St. & Prince George St., 23187, pg. 254   PV
EA Engineering, Science & Technology, Inc., Busch Corporate Ctr., 460 McLaws Cir., Ste. 115, 23185, pg. 541   IT
Fairfield Williamsburg, 133 Waller Mill Rd., 23187, pg. 611   IT
First Virginia Bank-Commonwealth, 171 Monticello Ave., 23185-2812, pg. 641   PB
Lucent Technologies, P.O. Box 1357, 23187-1357, pg. 1017   PB
MORGAN PRODUCTS LTD., 469 McLaws Cir., 23185-5645, pg. 1132   PB
Munck Softech, 5428 Old Towne Rd., 23188, pg. 767   PV
Scott & Stringfellow, Inc., 1138 Professional Dr., 23185, pg. 1445   PB
Water Country USA, 176 Water Country Pkwy., 23185, pg. 114   PB

Winchester

Abex Friction Products, 2410 Papermill Rd., 22601, pg. 443   PB
AMERICAN WOODMARK CORPORATION, 3102 Shawnee Dr., 22601-4208, pg. 96   PB
Argo Instruments Inc., 1013 Fort Collier Rd., 22601, pg. 839   IT
Hershey Pasta Group Winchester, Inc., 300 Park Center Dr., 22603, pg. 812   PB
JOUAN, INC., 170 Marcel Dr., 22602, pg. 601   PV
Melnor Inc., P.O. Box 2840, 22604-2040, pg. 1234   IT
NATIONAL FRUIT PRODUCT COMPANY, 550 Fairmont Ave., 22601-3931, pg. 783   PV
O'SULLIVAN CORPORATION, 1944 Valley Ave., 22601-6306, pg. 1234   PB
PAC Manufacturing & Distributing Co., 131 Kentmere Ct., 22603, pg. 1321   PV
PERRY ENGINEERING COMPANY, INC., 1945 Millwood Pike, 22602, pg. 854   PV
Precision Scientific Inc., 110-B Industrial Dr., 22602, pg. 601   PV
Scott & Stringfellow, Inc., One S. Cameron St., 22601, pg. 1446   PB
Sensycon Corporation, 210A Fort Collier Rd., 22603, pg. 835   IT
Shenandoah Gas Co., Rte. 81 at Exit 79, 22601, pg. 1741   PB
Swiss Prestige, Inc., P.O. Box 1608, 188 Brook Rd., 22603, pg. 697   IT
VDO Instruments, Inc., 188 Brooke Rd., 22603, pg. 839   IT
VDO Yazaki Corporation, 188 Brooke Rd., 22603, pg. 839   IT

Woodbridge

Amano Pioneer Credit Corp., 4328 Ridgewood Ctr. Dr., 22194, pg. 71   IT
FICON Corporation, 14011 Telegraph Rd., 22192, pg. 84   PB
Green Tree Acceptance, Inc., P.O. Box 4488, 22194, pg. 762   PB
Universal Dynamics, Inc., P.O. Drawer X, 13600 Dabney Rd., 22194-0396, pg. 484   IT

Virginia First Mortgage, 1308 Devil's Reach Rd., 22184, pg. 1721   PB

Wytheville

The Polymer Corporation, Bluefield Hwy., 24382, pg. 355   IT

WASHINGTON

Aberdeen

Piper Jaffray Inc., 110 W. Market St., Ste. 6206, 98520-6206, pg. 1300   PB

Addy

Northwest Alloys, Inc., 1560A Marble Valley Rd., 99101, pg. 31   PB

Airway Heights

E Z LCADER CORPORATE, P.O. Box 879, 99001, pg. 352   PV

Anacortes

Tecnal Corporation, 708 N. Texas Rd., 98221, pg. 457   IT

Arlington

U.S. Marine Division, 17817 59th Ave. N.E., 98223, pg. 266   PB
Washington Culvert Co., 6523 188 N.E., 98223, pg. 305   PB

Asotin

Asotin Telephone Co., 126-2nd St., P.O. Box 399, 99402, pg. 1571   PB

Auburn

Auburn General Hospital, 20 Second St. N.E., 98002, pg. 1696   PB
Boeing Fabrication Division, 1002 15th S.W., 98002, pg. 240   PB
Bowman Distribution, Bldg. B, Ste. 100, 2302 W. Valley Hwy. N., 98001, pg. 190   PB
Dynacraft, 650 Milwaukee Ave. N., 98001, pg. 1246   PB
Insulate LLC, 5001 D St., N.W., 98001, pg. 1171   IT
MILES SAND & GRAVEL COMPANY, 1201 A M St., S.E., 98002, pg. 745   PV
Puget Sound Auto Auction, Inc., 621 37th N.W., 98002, pg. 1649   PB
Tim's Cascade Style Potato Chips, P.O. Box 2302, 98001, pg. 887   PV
Utility Vault Co., Inc., 2808 A St. S.E., P.O. Box 588, 98071, pg. 242   PB
VALLEY PONTIAC BUICK GMC, INC., 3104 Auburn Way N., 98002, pg. 1132   PV

Bainbridge Island

Ingalls Moranville Advertising/Seattle, 4447 Blakely Ave., N.E., 98110, pg. 316   PV
Port Townsend Paper Corporation, 750 Ericksen Ave., N.E., 98110, pg. 586   IT

Bellevue

AST Research, Inc, Ste. 900, Plaza Center Bldg., 10900 N.E. 8th St., 98004, pg. 1182   IT
Ace Novelty Fun Service Division, 13434 N.W. 16th, 98005, pg. 1309   PB
AirTouch Cellular - Western Region, 3350 161 Ave., S.E., 98008, pg. 34   PB
Allied Security Inc., 13400 Northrup Way, Ste. 23, 98005, pg. 4   PV
Arrow/Schweber Electronics, 1432 N.E. 21st. St., 98007, pg. 134   PB
ASYMETRIX LEARNING SYSTEMS, INC., 110 110th Ave., NE, 93004, pg. 93   PV
ATTACHMATE, 3617 131st Ave. S.E., 98006, pg. 98   PB
BHP Trading Inc., Ste. 120, 1300 114th Ave. S.E., 98004, pg. 226   IT
Boeing Computer Services, 2810 160th Ave. S.E., 98008, pg. 240   PB
Boeing Computer Support Services, Inc., 2800 160 Ave., S.E., 98008, pg. 240   PB
Boeing Information & Support Services, 2810 160th Avenue S.E., 98008, pg. 241   PB
Bright Star Technology,Inc., Suite 200, 3380 146th Pl. S.E., 98007, pg. 321   PB
Burns & Wilcox - Seattle Office, 15015 Main St. Ste. 210, 98007, pg. 610   PV
BURNSTEAD CONSTRUCTION COMPANY, 1215 120th Ave., N.E., Ste. 201, 98005, pg. 187   PV
Cascade Design Automation Corp., 3650 131st Ave. S.E., Ste. 650, 98006, pg. 1000   IT
Cerner Corporation -Northwest Region, 3245 146th Pl. S.E., Ste. 100, 98007, pg. 331   PB
DMR Group, Inc., 3245 146 Place S.E., Ste. 230, 98007, pg. 523   PB
Daewoo International America Corp. - Seattle, Plaza Center, Ste. 1105, 10900 N.E. 8th St., 98004, pg. 357   IT

Danzas Corporation, 3650 131st Ave. S.E., Ste. 700, 98006, pg. 382   IT
Design Systems Inc., P.O. Box 3984, 98009, pg. 606   IT
The William Dierickx Company, 3075 112th N.E., Ste. 100, 98004, pg. 863   PB
Dowty Aerospace Marketing, Quadrant Plaza Bldg., 11100 N.E. 8th St., Ste. 610, 98004, pg. 1337   IT
EA Engineering, Science & Technology, Inc., 155 108th Ave. N.E., Ste. 400, 98004, pg. 541   IT
Esca Corporation, 11120 N.E. 33rd Pl., 98004, pg. 53   IT
ESTERLINE TECHNOLOGIES CORPORATION, 10800 N.E. Eighth St., Ste. 600, 98004, pg. 594   PB
Fibres International, Inc., P.O. Box 1691, 98009, pg. 269   PV
Frigoscandia North America Inc., P.O. Box 3984, 98009, pg. 606   PB
Hanson Engineers, 1621 114th Ave. S.E., Ste. 200, 98004, pg. 500   PV
Harding Lawson Associates, Infrastructure, Inc., 13810 S.E. Eastgate Way, 98005-4440, pg. 785   PB
Harza Northwest, Inc., 520 Corporate Center, Ste. 200, 2353 130th Ave., N.E., 98005, pg. 509   PV
Hewlett-Packard Company, 15815 S.E. 37th St., 98006, pg. 815   PB
InterConnections, Inc., 14711 N.E. 29 Pl., 98007, pg. 579   PB
Intergraph Corporation, 11130 N.E. 33rd Pl., 98004, pg. 890   PB
MSC Seattle Technical Office, 14205 S.E. 36th St., 98006, pg. 1031   PB
MetLife Capital Holdings, Inc., 10900 N.E. Fourth St., Ste. 500, 98004-5853, pg. 737   PV
Microsoft Press, 3075 112th Ave., N.E., 98004, pg. 1107   PB
NEXTLINK COMMUNICATIONS INC., 155 108th Ave. N.E., 8th Fl., 98004, pg. 1181   PB
Nichimen America, Inc., Seattle Branch, 12310 N.E. Eighth St., 98005, pg. 928   IT
NORTH COAST ELECTRIC COMPANY, 110 110th Ave., N.E., Ste. 616, 98004, pg. 804   PV
PACCAR Financial Corp., Business Center Bldg., 777 106th Ave. N.E., 98004, pg. 1247   PB
PACCAR INC., 777 106th Ave., N.E., 98004, pg. 1246   PB
PACCAR Leasing Corporation, Paccar Bldg., 777-106th Ave. N.E., 98004, pg. 1247   PB
PACCAR Sales North America, Inc., 777 106th Ave. NE, 98004, pg. 1247   PB
PENFORD CORP., 777 108th Ave. N.E., Ste. 2390, 98004-1688, pg. 1269   PB
Piper Jaffray Inc., 500-108th Ave. N.E., Ste. 1600, 98004-5500, pg. 1301   PB
PIZZA HAVEN INC., Ste. 101, 14645 Bel-Red. Rd., 98007-3929, pg. 868   PV
PTI Environmental, 15375 S.E. 30th Pl., Ste. 250, 98007, pg. 609   PB
Puget Sound Energy Co., 411 108th Ave. N.E., 98004-5515, pg. 1342   PB
PUGET SOUND ENERGY, INC., 411 108th Ave., N.E., 98004-5515, pg. 1342   PB
Puget Western, Inc., 19515 N. Creek Pkwy., Ste. 310, 98009, pg. 1342   PB
The Quadrant Corporation, 11100 N.E. 8th St., Ste. 500, 98004, pg. 1764   PB
QUALITY FOOD CENTERS, INC., 10116 N.E. Eighth St., 98004, pg. 1349   PB
QualMed Plans for Health-Washington, 520 Corp. Ctr., Bldg. C, 2331 130th Ave., # 200, 98005, pg. 678   PV
Quebecor Interactive Electronic Publishing Group, 11811 N.E. First, 98005, pg. 1076   IT
SDL Construction, 3150 Richards Rd. S.E., 98005, pg. 719   PV
SMS-Seattle, 3055 112th Ave. N.E., Ste. 200, 98004, pg. 1463   PB
STI Optronics, 2755 Northup Way, 98004, pg. 1289   IT
Security Pacific Leasing Corporation, 800 Koll Ctr., 500 108th Ave., N.E., 98004-5560, pg. 182   PB
Sierra On-Line, Inc., 3380 146th Place SE., Ste. 300, 98007, pg. 321   PB
The Sumitomo Trust & Banking Co., Ltd., 500 108th Ave. N.E. Ste. 2500, 98004, pg. 1317   IT
TCI West, 2233 112th Ave. N.E., 98004, pg. 1555   PB
Tellus, Inc., One Bellevue Ctr., Ste. 500, 411 108th Ave., N.E., 98004-5515, pg. 1342   PB
TOPLINE IMPORTS, INC., 3650 131st Ave. SE, Ste. 150, 98006, pg. 1091   PV
URS Greiner, Inc., Park Heights Bldg., 1800 112th Ave., NE, # 100W-15, 98004, pg. 1659   PB
Unigard Indemnity Co., 15805 N.E. 24th St., 98008, pg. 345   IT
Unigard Insurance Co., 15805 N.E. 24th St., 98008, pg. 345   IT

Bellingham

ALLSOP, INC., 4201 Guide Meridian, 98226, pg. 44   PV
The Bellingham Herald, 1155 State St., 98225, pg. 700   PB
Canfor U.S.A., Bellingham Division, 4395 Curtis Rd., 98225, pg. 260   IT
First American Title Co. of Bellingham, Ste. B, 215 Commercial St., 98226, pg. 625   PB
HAGGEN, INC., 2211 Rimland Dr., 98226, pg. 493   PV
KVOS Television Corp., 1151 Ellis St., 98227, pg. 16   PB
Lignin Products, P.O. Box 1236, 98227, pg. 737   PB
Lummi Fisheries Supply, 851 Coho Way, 98225, pg. 429   PB
MORSE HARDWARE COMPANY, 1025 N. State St., 98225, pg. 763   PV
Piper Jaffray Inc., 104 Unity St., 98225-4418, pg. 1302   PB
Primary Pulp & Paper Plant, 300 Laurel St., P.O. Box 1236, 98225, pg. 736   PB

Softride, Inc., 4208 Guide Meridian, # 2, 98225, pg. 44 **PV**

Trans Ocean Products, Inc., 350 West Orchard Dr., 98225, pg. 845 **IT**

Bothell

ABB Phoenix Controls, 22310 20th Ave., S.E., 98021, pg. 4 **IT**

ATL ULTRASOUND, INC., 22100 Bothell Everett Hwy., 98021, pg. 11 **PB**

Alpine Industries, Inc., 19720 Bothell Everett Hwy., 98012, pg. 194 **PV**

Autodesk, Inc., Bothell Technical Center, 1725 220th St. S.E., Ste. C101, 98021, pg. 149 **PB**

CELLPRO, INCORPORATED, 22215 26th Ave., S.E., 98021, pg. 320 **PB**

EDD-Bellevue, 19119 North Creek Pkwy., Ste. 102, 98011, pg. 204 **PB**

EMCON Northwest, Inc., 18912 N. Creek Pkwy., Ste. 210, 98011, pg. 571 **PB**

Hydro Energy Development Corp., 19515 N. Creek Pkwy., Ste. 310, 98011, pg. 1342 **PB**

Leviton Telecom, 2222 222nd St. S.E., 98021-4416, pg. 663 **PB**

Market Entry Omega, 19805 North Creek Pkwy., 98041-3005, pg. 1222 **PB**

Matsushita Avionics Systems, 22333 29th Dr. S.E., 98021, pg. 847 **IT**

Metanetics Corp., 22310 20th Ave., S.E., Ste. 100, 98021-8446, pg. 1573 **PB**

Microsoft Corporation Mfg. & Distr. Ctr., 21919 20th Ave. S.E., 98021, pg. 1108 **PB**

Motorola Mobile Data Division, 19807 N. Creek Pkwy., 98011-8214, pg. 1138 **PB**

OMEGA ENVIRONMENTAL INC., 19805 Northcreek Pkwy., 98011, pg. 1221 **PB**

Panlabs International Operations, 11804 N. Creek Pkwy. S., 98011-8805, pg. 827 **IT**

Precor, Inc., 20001 N. Creek Pkwy., 98011, pg. 1322 **PB**

Puget Energy Inc., 19515 N. Creek Pkwy., Ste. 310, 98011, pg. 1342 **PB**

Quinton Instrument Company, 3303 Montevilla Pkwy., 98021-8906, pg. 80 **PB**

THURMAN INDUSTRIES, INC., 2122 20th Ave., SE, Ste. 4157, 98021, pg. 1084 **PV**

TRAVELING SOFTWARE INC., 18702 N. Creek Pkwy., 98011, pg. 1098 **PV**

Wright Group Publishing, Inc., 19201 120th Ave. N.E., 98011, pg. 1636 **PB**

Bremerton

Bremerton Sun, 545 Fifth St., 98310, pg. 1447 **PB**

SRA Pacific Northwest Operations, 120 Washington Ave., Suite 204, 98337, pg. 958 **PV**

Burlington

National Frozen Foods Corporation - Burlington, 200 Washington Ave., 98233, pg. 783 **PV**

Camas

Ahlstrom Recovery Inc.-Western Region, 1725 N.W. Lacamas Dr., 98607, pg. 34 **IT**

Heraeus Shin-Etsu America Inc., 4600 N.W. Pacific Rim Blvd., 98607, pg. 616 **IT**

Sharp Flat Display Manufacturing Company, 5700 Northwest Pacific Rim Blvd., 98607, pg. 1229 **IT**

Sharp Laboratories of America, Inc., 5700 Northwest PacificRim Blvd., 98607, pg. 1229 **IT**

Sharp Microelectronics Technology, Inc., 5700 Northwest Pacific Rim Blvd., 98607, pg. 1229 **IT**

Centralia

Hardel Builders Center, 402 E. Suma Ave., 98931, pg. 501 **PV**

Chehalis

Lamplighter Homes, Inc., P.O. Box 333, 98532, pg. 333 **PB**

Moduline Industries, Inc., P.O. Box 1106, 124 Habien Rd., 98532, pg. 333 **PB**

National Frozen Foods Corporation - Chehalis, 188 Sturdevant Rd., 98532, pg. 783 **PV**

Chelan

Piper Jaffray Inc., 312 E. Trow Ave., Ste. 202, 98816, pg. 1302 **PB**

TROUT-BLUE CHELIAU, INC., Eight Howser Rd., 98816, pg. 1105 **PV**

Colville

VAAGEN BROTHERS LUMBER, INC., 565 W. 5th, 99114, pg. 1131 **PV**

East Wenatchee

Dole Northwest, 201 S. Union St., 98802, pg. 515 **PB**

Ellensburg

SCHAAKE CORPORATION, P.O. Box 128, 98926, pg. 969 **PV**

Ephrata

PUBLIC UTILITY DISTRICT NO. 2 OF GRANT COUNTY, P.O. Box 878, 98823, pg. 893 **PV**

Everett

Achilles USA, Inc., 1407 80th St., S.W., 98203, pg. 22 **IT**

AGRA Foundations Inc., 10108 32nd Ave. W., 98204, pg. 31 **IT**

Associated Sand & Gravel Co., Inc., 6300 Glenwood Ave., 98203, pg. 245 **IT**

Daily Herald Co., P.O. Box 930, 1213 California Ave., 98206, pg. 1743 **PB**

FLUKE CORPORATION, 6920 Seaway Blvd., 98203, pg. 659 **PB**

Fluke International Corporation, 6920 Seaway Blvd., 98203, pg. 659 **PB**

Intermec Technologies Corporation, 6001 36th Ave. W., 98203-9280, pg. 1699 **PB**

Kimberly-Clark, Everett, P.O. Box B, 98206, pg. 958 **PB**

LEE GROCERY COMPANY, 1930 Merrillck Pway, Ste. A, 98203, pg. 657 **PV**

Millstone Coffee, Inc., 729 100th St., S.E., 98208, pg. 1331 **PB**

Piper Jaffray Inc., 2825 Colby Ave., Ste. 300, 98201-3529, pg. 1301 **PB**

777 Program, 3303 W. Casino Rd., 98204, pg. 240 **PB**

Solectron Washington, Inc., 8600 Soper Hill Rd., Ste. A, 98205-1256, pg. 1483 **PB**

Tramco Inc., 11323 30th Ave. W., 98204, pg. 752 **PB**

UNC Aerostructures-Washington, Building C-19, Paine Field, 98204, pg. 710 **PB**

Federal Way

Green Tree Acceptance, Inc., 33330 8th Ave. S, Ste. 210, 98003, pg. 762 **PB**

McLean, 1911 S.W. Campus Dr. # 128, 98023-6473, pg. 1791 **PV**

Northwest Marketing Div., P.O. Box 4989, 98063-4989, pg. 296 **PV**

The Park at Dashpoint, 31736 50th Ln. S.W., 98023, pg. 163 **PB**

Westwood Shipping Lines, 33663 Weyerhaeuser Way South, 98003, pg. 1764 **PB**

WEYERHAEUSER COMPANY, 33663 Weyerhaeuser Way S., 98003, pg. 1764 **PB**

Weyerhaeuser Financial Services, Inc., 33650 Sixth Ave. S., 98003, pg. 1764 **PB**

Weyerhaeuser Forest Products Company, 33663 Weyerhaeuser Way S., 98003, pg. 1764 **PB**

Ferndale

THE AMERICAN GROUP, 2090 Thornton St., 98248, pg. 56 **PV**

Intalco Aluminum Corp., P.O. Box 937, 4050 Mountain View Rd., 98248, pg. 60 **PB**

Fife

L & L Plant Soil Division, 2507 Frank Albert Rd., Ste. 130, 98424, pg. 638 **PV**

Print Northwest Company, L.P., 4918 20th St. E., 98424, pg. 1076 **IT**

Quebecor Integrated Media, 4101 D Industry Dr. E., 98424, pg. 1076 **IT**

Grandview

Smucker Grandview Plant, P.O. Box 608, 98930, pg. 1480 **PB**

Greenbank

Citadel Broadcasting Company, 1256 E. Dines Point Rd., 98253, pg. 241 **PV**

Hoquiam

ENTERPRISES INTERNATIONAL INC., Blaine & Firman, 98550, pg. 377 **PV**

Lamb Grays Harbor Co, P.O. Box 359, 98550, pg. 378 **PV**

Ovalstrapping, Inc., 206 Firman St., 98550, pg. 378 **PV**

Issaquah

BMC West, 5210 E. Lake Sammamish Pkwy. S.E., 98027-7012, pg. 433 **PV**

Costco, Inc.-Northwest Region, 999 Lake Dr., 98027, pg. 452 **PB**

COSTCO WHOLESALE, 999 Lake Drive, 98027, pg. 451 **PB**

Daewoo America Development, Inc., 4135 Providence Point Dr., S.E., 98027, pg. 358 **IT**

Danaher Controls, 310 3rd N.E., 98027-3300, pg. 480 **PB**

LAKESIDE INDUSTRIES, 6505 226th Pl., S.E., 98027, pg. 644 **PV**

North American Energy Services Co., Inc., 999Lake Dr., Ste. 310, 98027, pg. 1127 **PB**

ZETEC, INC., 1370 N.W. Mall, 98027, pg. 1205 **PV**

Kelso

Columbia Analytical Services, Inc., 1317 S. 13th St., 98626, pg. 571 **PB**

Kennewick

Dyna-Pak Div., 900 E. Chemical Dr., 99336, pg. 832 **PV**

Lamb-Weston, Inc., 8701 W. Gage Blvd., 99336, pg. 427 **PB**

Piper Jaffray Inc., 8203 W. Quinault Ave., Ste. 100, 99336, pg. 1303 **PB**

Scitec Corporation, 415 N. Quay, 99336, pg. 74 **PV**

Staveley/NDT Technologies Inc., 421 North Quay, 99336, pg. 1299 **IT**

Kent

Air Conditioning Co., Inc., 6952 South 220th St., 98032, pg. 28 **PV**

American Natl. Can Co., 1220 N. Second Ave., 98032, pg. 1029 **IT**

Atlas Copco Robbins, P.O. Box 97027, 98064-9727, pg. 96 **IT**

BPI Inc., Bldg. K, 20608 - 87th Ave. S., 98031, pg. 772 **PB**

Bergen Brunswig Drug Company, 19220 64th Ave. S., 98032, pg. 214 **PB**

Boeing Defense & Space Group, 20403 68th Ave. S., 98032, pg. 240 **PB**

Brower Company, 7043 S. 190th St., 98032, pg. 124 **PV**

Cedartone Specialties, P.O. Box 10, 98035-0010, pg. 1071 **IT**

Central Sprinkler Company, 19307 70th Ave. South, 98032, pg. 327 **PB**

Chandler Attwood Limited, 21412 84 Ave. S., 98032, pg. 772 **PB**

CHEMCENTRAL/Seattle, 7601 S.190th St., 98032, pg. 232 **PV**

Circle Freight International USA, 23119 66th Ave. S., 98032, pg. 370 **PB**

Crane Creek Cedar, P.O. Box 10, 98035-0010, pg. 1071 **IT**

Derby Cycle Corporation, 22710 72nd Ave. S., 98032, pg. 394 **IT**

DIADORA AMERICA, INC., 6419 S. 228th St., 98032, pg. 330 **PV**

Dreyer's Northwest Division, 6846 S. 224th St., 98032, pg. 529 **PB**

Electronic Systems Division, 20403 68th Ave. S., 98032, pg. 241 **PB**

FLOW INTERNATIONAL CORPORATION, 23500 64th Ave. S., 98032, pg. 656 **PB**

FlowMole Export Sales Corporation, 22404 66th Ave. South, 98032-4801, pg. 1701 **PB**

Fraser Valley Forest Inc., 6409 S. 149th St., 98032, pg. 1067 **IT**

Graphic Arts Supply Division, 6823 S. 220th St., 98032, pg. 205 **PB**

Haskel Controls, Ste. H-103, 19115 W. Valley Hwy., 98032-2110, pg. 798 **PB**

Hathaway Systems Northwest, 7661 S. 180th St., 98032, pg. 799 **PB**

Heart Interface Corporation, 21440 68th Ave. S., 98032-2416, pg. 1705 **PB**

Howard Manufacturing, 21255 76th Ave. S., 98032, pg. 477 **PV**

Hunter Douglas Fabrication Company, 7015 South 212, 98032, pg. 639 **IT**

Hytek Finishes Co., 8127 S. 216th St., 98032, pg. 594 **PB**

Earle M. Jorgensen Company/Seattle, 22011 76th Ave. S., 98032, pg. 600 **PV**

Lunstead, A Haworth Co., 8655 S. 208th St., 98031, pg. 512 **PV**

Lynden Transport, Inc., 6250 S. 228th Rd., 98032, pg. 684 **PV**

M.A. Hanna Resin Distribution, 22239 76th Ave. S., 98136, pg. 781 **PB**

MAGNOLIA HI-FI, INC., 6305 S. 231st St., 98032, pg. 696 **PV**

Merlino's Macaroni, Inc., 8247 S. 194th, 98032, pg. 158 **PV**

Miller Brands, Inc., 6030 S. 196th St., 98032, pg. 1289 **PB**

Northwest Dietetic Supply, Inc., 7036 South 190th St., West Valley Dist. Center, 98031, pg. 752 **IT**

PACIFIC FOODS, INC., 21612 88th Ave. S., 98031, pg. 831 **PV**

Propulsion Systems Division, 7600 212th Ave. S.W., 98032, pg. 240 **PB**

Quest Int'l., 21414 68th Ave. S., 98032-2439, pg. 1435 **IT**

RECREATIONAL EQUIPMENT, INC., 6750 S. 228th, 98032, pg. 914 **PV**

Reynolds Metals Company-Seattle, 7416 S. 228, 98032, pg. 1386 **PB**

Ropak Northwest Inc., Bldg. F, 20024 87th Ave. S., 98031, pg. 812 **PB**

SMITH BROTHERS FARMS, INC., 27441 68th Ave., S., 98032, pg. 914 **PV**

South Seattle Auto Auction, 19443 77th Ave. S., 98064-5189, pg. 283 **PV**

Sysco Food Services of Seattle, Inc., 22820 54th Ave. S., 98032, pg. 1552 **PB**

United Graphics, Inc., 21409 72nd Ave. S., 98032, pg. 188 **PB**

UTILX CORPORATION, 22404 66th Ave. So., 98032-4801, pg. 1701 **PB**

Wajax Pacific Fire Equipment Inc., 19308 68th Ave. S., Box 88540, 98032-2139, pg. 1485 **IT**

Willis Corroon Administrative Services Corporation, Building A, Ste. 108, 19011 W. Valley Hwy., 98032, pg. 1505 **IT**

Geographic Index-U.S.

Y.K.K. (U.S.A.) Inc., 7113 S. 216th St., 98032,
pg. 1515   IT

Kirkland

AT&T Wireless Services, 5000 Carillon Point, 98033,
pg. 11   PB
AGRA Earth & Environmental, Inc., 11335 NE 122 Way,
Ste. 100, 98034, pg. 31   IT
Hoffman Construction Company of Washington, Ste. 265,
135 Lake St. S., 98033, pg. 532   PV
InVireChem, 1500 Seventh Ave., S., 98033, pg. 829   PV
Kenworth Truck Company, 10630 N.E. 38th Pl., 98033-
1000, pg. 1246   PB
LAMONTS APPAREL, INC., 12413 Willows Rd. N.E.,
98034, pg. 975   PB
LIN Cellular Group, c/o LIN Broadcasting Corp., 5295
Carillon Corporation, 98033, pg. 11   PB
NOBLE HOUSE HOTELS AND RESORTS, 25 Central
Way, Ste. 400, 98033, pg. 800   PV
PSR, 13467 64th Pl., N.E., 98034, pg. 828   PB
PACCAR International, 10604 N.E. 38th Pl., 98033,
pg. 1246   PB
PACE INTERNATIONAL L.P., 500 Seventh Ave., S.,
98033, pg. 829   PV
ROYAL OAK MINES INC., 5501 Lakeview Dr., 98033,
pg. 1410   PB
Sound Elevator, P.O. Box 2699, 98033, pg. 521   PB
Van Waters & Rogers, 6100 Carillon Point, 98033,
pg. 1147   IT
Van Waters & Rogers Inc., 6100 Carillon Point, 98033,
pg. 1147   IT
WALL DATA INCORPORATED, 11332 N.E. 122nd Way,
98034-6931, pg. 1734   PB

Lacey

CAPITAL DEVELOPMENT CO., 691 Sleater-Kinney Rd.
S.E., Ste. 100, 98503, pg. 205   PV
Cubic Applications, Inc., 4550 3rd Ave S.E., 98503,
pg. 466   PB
Lamplighter Homes, Inc., P.O. Box 3000, 99 B S. Sound
Center, 98503, pg. 333   PB
Lamplighter Homes, Inc., 6325 Martin Way, 98506,
pg. 333   PB
Moduline International, Inc., P.O. Box 3000, 99 B S. Sound
Ctr., 98509, pg. 333   PB

Lake Stevens

Eclipse Combustion, Inc., 10708 Lakeview Dr., 98258,
pg. 360   PV

Liberty Lake

EGGHEAD, INC., 22705 E. Mission, 99019-8553,
pg. 566   PB
Olsy North America Inc., 22425 E. Appleway Ave., 99019-
9534, pg. 1002   IT

Longview

Longfibre Ltd., P.O. Box 639, pg. 1014   PB
LONGVIEW FIBRE COMPANY, End of Fibre Way, 98632,
pg. 1013   PB
North Pacific Paper Corporation (NORPAC), Box 2069,
98632, pg. 938   IT
Reynolds Metals Company-Longview, 4012 Industrial Rd.,
98632, pg. 1385   PB
Solvay Interox America, 3500 Industrial Way, 98632,
pg. 1278   IT

Lynden

LTI, Inc., P.O. Box 433, 98264, pg. 683   PV

Lynnwood

BFC Frontier, 101, 19217-36 Avenue West, 98036,
pg. 118   IT
CARVER CORPORATION, 20121 48th Ave. W., 98046,
pg. 310   PB
Cineplex Odeon Corporation -Seattle, 18421 Alderwood
Mall Blvd., 98036, pg. 293   IT
Connelly Skis, Inc., 20621 50th St., 98036, pg. 1388   IT
HARRIS FORD, INC., 20006 64th Ave., W., 98036,
pg. 506   PV
ID Solutions, 6825 216th St. S.W., 98036, pg. 566   PV
INTELLIGENT CONTROLS INC., 6825 216th St. S.W.,
98036, pg. 566   PV
Little Nickel Want Ads, 3619 148th St., 98037, pg. 983   PB
Materiel Division, 20818 44th Ave. W., 98046, pg. 240   PB
Simrad Inc., 19210 33rd Ave., W., 98036, pg. 1252   IT
Trade Products, 2807 Lincoln Way, 98046, pg. 1526   PB
Trimble Navigation Ltd., Northwest Sales/Technical
Support, 3400 188th St., Ste. 335, 98037-4708,
pg. 1638   PB

Marysville

WELCO LUMBER COMPANY, P.O. Box 125, 98270,
pg. 1161   PV

McCleary

Simpson Door Company, 400 Simpson Ave., 98557,
pg. 1003   PV

Mercer Island

Farmers New World Life Insurance Co., 3003 77th Ave.
S.E., 98040, pg. 110   IT
GERRY SPORTSWEAR COMPANY, 2955 80th Ave., S.E.,
98040, pg. 449   PV
Mambosock, 2955 80th Ave., S.E., 98040, pg. 449   PV
Market Facts, Inc., 7900 S.E. 28th St., Ste. 200, 98040,
pg. 1047   PB
Square D Co., 7525 S.E. 24th St. #320, 98040,
pg. 1208   IT
Transamerica Glass, Inc., 9675 SE 36th St., 98040,
pg. 1336   IT

Mill Creek

NYK Bulkship-Seattle, 2230 160th Place S.E., 98012,
pg. 941   IT

Morton

Morton Forest Products Co., 247 Priest Rd., 98356-9404,
pg. 1730   IT
Tubafor Mill Inc., P.O. Box U, Hwy. 7, 98356, pg. 1071   IT

Moses Lake

AlliedSignal Avionics Communications Systems, 7966
Andrews St. N.E., 98837-3210, pg. 51   PB
National Frozen Foods Corporation - Moses Lake, P.O. Box
54, 98837, pg. 783   PV

Mount Vernon

Dynacare-Washington, 1310 E. Division St., 98273,
pg. 425   IT
First Insurance Agency, Inc., 406 Second Street, 98273,
pg. 1740   PB
PACCAR Technical Center, 1261 Hwy. 237, 98273,
pg. 1246   PB

Mountlake Terrace

Commercial Design Architects/HEPY, 6608 216th St., Ste.
100, 98043, pg. 503   PV
DATAMARINE INTERNATIONAL, INC., 7030 220th S.W.,
98043, pg. 486   PB
LLOYD CONTROLS, INC., 21414 66th Ave., W., 98043,
pg. 672   PV
SEA, Inc., 7030 220th St., S.W., 98043, pg. 487   PB

Mukilteo

TONE COMMANDER SYSTEMS, 11609 49th Pl. W.,
98275-4255, pg. 1090   PV

Ocean Shores

Piper Jaffray Inc., 837 Point Brown Ave. N.W., 98569,
pg. 1303   PB

Olympia

Albany Mount Vernon Dryer Fabric, P.O. Box 1798, 98507,
pg. 36   PB
Corrugated Packaging, 1203 Fones Rd., P.O. Box 547,
98507, pg. 736   PB
First American Title Co. of Thurston County, 510 Plum St.,
S.E., Ste. 200, 98501, pg. 625   PB
Hardel Builders Center, 415 Olympia Ave. N.E., 98501,
pg. 501   PV
HARDEL MUTUAL PLYWOOD CORPORATION, 1515 W.
Bay Dr., 98502, pg. 501   PV
Louis Kemp Seafood Co., 3400 25th Ave.SW, 98512,
pg. 1652   PB
The Olympian, 1268 E. Fourth St., 98507, pg. 701   PB
Sunset Life Insurance Co. of America, 3200 Capitol Blvd.,
98501, pg. 943   PB

Pasco

AGRINORTHWEST, INC., 2810 W. Clearwater Ave., 99336,
pg. 26   PV
IBP-Pasco, P.O. Box 4239, 99302, pg. 852   PB
Tri-City Auto Auction, Inc., 3333 Railroad Ave., 99302,
pg. 1649   PB
Tri-City Herald, P.O. Box 2608, 99302, pg. 1066   PB
Valmont Northwest, 1619 E. Hillsboro Rd., 99301,
pg. 1707   PB

Poulsbo

Piper Jaffray Inc., 19735 10th Ave. N.E., Ste. N203, 98370-
7549, pg. 1303   PB
POPE RESOURCES, 19245 10th Ave. N.E., 98370,
pg. 1317   PB

Prosser

Milne Food Products, Inc., 804 Bennett Ave., 99350,
pg. 811   PV
Milne Fruit Products, 804 Bennett Ave., 99350-1267,
pg. 811   PV

Puyallup

Lamplighter Homes, Inc., 15535 Meridian E., 98373,
pg. 333   PB
Lamplighter Homes, Inc., 15513 Meridian Ave. S., 98373,
pg. 333   PB
Pierce County Herald, 822 E. Main St., 98371,
pg. 1066   PB

Raymond

Pacific Hardwoods-South Bend Co., 819 Ocean St., 98577-
2905, pg. 1730   PB
Pronova Biopolymer Inc., 1725 Ocean Ave., 98577,
pg. 961   IT

Redmond

AG Industries, Inc., 15335 N.E. 95th St., 98052, pg. 40   IT
ANI America, Inc., 2889 152nd Ave. N.E., Ste. D, 98052,
pg. 101   IT
All American Agency Facilities, 8060 165th Ave., N.E.,
98052, pg. 216   PB
AlliedSignal Commercial Avionics Systems, P.O. Box 97001,
15001 N.E. 36th St., 98073-9701, pg. 50   PB
Apex Computer Co., 4500 150th Ave., NE, 98052,
pg. 332   PB
APPLIED MICROSYSTEMS CORPORATION, 5020 148th
Ave., N.E., 98052, pg. 123   PB
Bard Diagnostic Sciences, 12277 134th Ct., N.E., Ste. 100,
98052, pg. 189   PB
The Cadman Companies, P.O. Box 538, 98073,
pg. 605   IT
Cascadia Technology Corporation, 2877 152nd Ave. N.E.,
98052, pg. 1203   PB
Color Control, Inc., 3820 150th Ave. NE, 98052,
pg. 194   PV
DATA I/O CORPORATION, 10525 Willows Road N.E.,
98052, pg. 486   PB
Eddie Bauer, Inc., 15010 N.E. 36th St., 98052,
pg. 1499   PB
Helly-Hansen (US), Inc., 17275 N.E. 67th Ct., 98052,
pg. 1010   IT
Interpoint, 10301 Willows Rd., 98073, pg. 457   PB
LANOGA CORPORATION, P.O. Box 97040, 17946 NE
65th St., 98073, pg. 650   PV
MICROSOFT CORPORATION, One Microsoft Way, 98052-
6399, pg. 1107   PB
National Energy Production Corporation, 18578 NE 67th
Court, 98073, pg. 1795   PB
Nintendo of America, 4820 150th Ave., N.E., 98052,
pg. 932   IT
Nippon Suisan U.S.A., 15400 N.E. 90th St., 98073,
pg. 940   IT
O'Brien International, Inc., 14615 N.E. 91st, 98052-3459,
pg. 689   PV
Pacific Electro-Dynamics, Inc., 11465 Willow Rd. N.E.,
98052, pg. 1219   PB
PHYSIO-CONTROL CORPORATION, 11811 Willows Rd.,
98052-1013, pg. 1294   PB
Plateau Electric Construction Inc., 14960 N.E. 31st Cir.,
98052, pg. 65   PB
RENA-WARE DISTRIBUTORS INC., 8383 158th Ave.,
N.E., 98052, pg. 922   PV
The Rho Company, 4002 148th Ave., N.E., 98052,
pg. 409   PB
SAFECO Life and Health Insurance Companies, 15411 N.E.
51st St., 98052, pg. 1423   PB
SPACELABS MEDICAL, INC., 15220 N.E. 40th St., 98073,
pg. 1494   PB
Trigon Packaging Corporation, 6812 185th Ave. NE, 98052,
pg. 1451   PB
UniSea Foods, Inc., 15110 N.E. 90th St., 98052-3524,
pg. 940   IT
Virtual Vision, Inc., 7659 178th Pl., N.E., 98052-4953,
pg. 1573   PB
Wyle Electronics-Seattle, 15385 N.E. 90th St., 98052,
pg. 1458   IT
ZURN/NEPCO, 18578 N.E. 67th Ct., 98073, pg. 1795   PB

Renton

ACME POULTRY COMPANY, INC., 600 S.W. Seventh St.,
98055, pg. 13   PV
E.J. BARTELLS CO., 700 Powell Ave., S.W., 98055,
pg. 118   PB
E.J. Bartells Material Management Co., 700 Powell Ave.,
S.W., 98057, pg. 118   PB
Beef Distributors, Inc., 600 Powell Ave., 98055, pg. 611   PV
Bergen Brunswig Medical Corporation, 300 S.W. 27th St.,
98055, pg. 214   PB
Boeing Commercial Airplane Group, N. 8th & Park Ave. N.,
98055, pg. 240   PB
Cello Bag Company, Inc., 1217 S.W. 7th St., 98055,
pg. 72   IT
Engineering Division, N. Eighth & Park Ave., 98055,
pg. 240   PB
Farman Brothers Pickle Company, 14410 S.E. Petrovitsky,
Ste 201, 98058, pg. 887   PV
KEENERS, INC., 600 Powell Ave., S.W., 98055,
pg. 611   PV
Kenworth Truck Co., Howser Way N., 98055, pg. 1246   PB
Longacres Park, Inc., 1621 SW 16 St., 98055, pg. 242   PB
PACCAR Automotive Inc., 1400 N. 4th St., 98055,
pg. 1247   PB
PACCAR Parts, 750 Houser Way, N., 98055, pg. 1246   PB
Renton Waterfront Restaurant Corp., 1011 W. Perimeter
Rd., 98055, pg. 1023   PV

PB - U.S. Public Companies Volume
PV - U.S. Private Companies Volume
IT - International Public & Private Companies Volume

1472

Geographic Index-U.S.

737/757 Programs, N. Eighth & Park Ave. N., 98055, pg. 240 — **PB**

TIE Systems Northwest, 500 Naches Ave. S.W., Ste 101, 98055, pg. 1085 — **PV**

TSR, Inc., P.O. Box 707, 98057-0707, pg. 1185 — **PB**

Unisource (West Region), 1000 Dardale Ave. S.W., 98055, pg. 1671 — **PB**

WIZARDS OF THE COAST, 1801 Lind Ave. S.W., 98055, pg. 1185 — **PV**

Republic

Kettle River Gold Mine, Echo Bay Minerals, P.O. Box 1019, 921 Fish Hatchery Rd., 99166, pg. 562 — **PB**

Richland

BCS Richland Inc., 825 Jadwin Ave., 99352, pg. 241 — **PB**

Geosafe Corporation, 2950 George Washington Way, 99352, pg. 123 — **PV**

Hewlett-Packard Company, 1845 Terminal Dr., Ste. 150, 99352, pg. 815 — **PB**

ICF Kaiser Hanford Company, P.O. Box 888, 99352, pg. 853 — **PB**

Penford Food Ingredients Company, 216 1st St., 99352, pg. 1269 — **PB**

Ridgefield

Brudi, Inc., 26709 N.W. 19th Ave., 98642-9348, pg. 675 — **PV**

Seatac

Kintetsu World Express Inc., Seatac Industrial Park Bldg. 4, 18900 Des Moines Memorial Dr., 98148, pg. 735 — **IT**

Seattle

ABN AMRO Bank, N.V. (Seattle), One Union Sq., Ste. 2323, 98101, pg. 10 — **IT**

J.R. ABBOTT CONSTRUCTION, INC., 3512 Airport Way, 98134, pg. 9 — **PV**

ACE TANK & EQUIPMENT CO., 1143 Elliott Ave. West, 98119, pg. 12 — **PV**

Ackerley Communications of the Northwest-Seattle, 3601 Sixth Ave. S., 98134, pg. 15 — **IT**

THE ACKERLEY GROUP, 1301 Fifth Ave., Ste. 4000, 98101, pg. 15 — **PB**

ACTIVE VOICE CORPORATION, 2901 3rd Ave., Ste. 500, 98121, pg. 17 — **PB**

Adobe Systems Incorporated, 411 First Ave. S., 98104-2871, pg. 20 — **PV**

AIRBORNE FREIGHT CORPORATION, 3101 Western Ave., 98121, pg. 32 — **PB**

AIRSENSORS, INC., 708 Industry Dr., 98188, pg. 33 — **PV**

ALASKA AIR GROUP, INC., 19300 Pacific Hwy. S., 98188, pg. 35 — **PB**

Alaska Airlines, Inc., 19300 Pacific Hwy. S., 98188, pg. 35 — **PB**

Alaska Boat Co., P.O. Box 5030 University Station, 98105, pg. 1150 — **PV**

Alaska Marine Lines, Inc., 5615 W. Marginal Way, S.W., 98106, pg. 683 — **PV**

ALASKAN COPPER COMPANIES, 3223 6th Ave., S., 98134, pg. 31 — **PV**

ALLIANCE MANAGEMENT, INC., 2200 6th Ave., Ste. 770, 98121, pg. 38 — **PV**

AlliedSignal Avionics Communications Systems, P.O. Box 75381, 98125-0381, pg. 51 — **PB**

AMAZON.COM, INC., 1516 Second Ave., 4th Fl., 98101, pg. 62 — **PB**

AMERICAN PASSAGE MEDIA CORPORATION, 401 Second Ave. W., 98119, pg. 60 — **PV**

American Red Ball International, Inc., 9750 Thrid Ave. N.E., Ste. 200, 98115, pg. 97 — **PV**

Arctic Alaska Fisheries Corporation, 1900 W. Nickerson St., 98119, pg. 1652 — **PB**

Arctic Alaska Seafoods, Inc., Pier 91, Bldg. 392, C-119, 98119, pg. 1652 — **PB**

Ash Grove Cement-Seattle Western Region Cement Plant, 3801 E. Marginal Way So., 98134, pg. 88 — **PV**

ASSOCIATED GROCERS, INC., 3301 S. Norfolk St., 98118, pg. 90 — **PV**

Augat, Inc., Communications Division, 2414 SW Andover, 98106, pg. 1598 — **PV**

BE & C Engineers Inc., 14675 Interurban Ave. S., 98168, pg. 241 — **PV**

Bank and Office Interiors, 5601 6th Ave. S., 98108, pg. 107 — **PV**

The Bank of Tokyo-Mitsubishi, Ltd. (Seattle Branch) 1201 Third Ave., Ste. 1100, 98101, pg. 157 — **IT**

THE BARTELL DRUG COMPANY, 4727 Denver Ave. S., 98134, pg. 118 — **PV**

BAUGH CONSTRUCTION COMPANY, 900 Poplar Pl., S., 98144, pg. 123 — **PV**

ROBERT E. BAYLEY CONSTRUCTION, 205 Columbia St., 98104, pg. 125 — **PV**

F.B. Beattie & Company, Inc., Westlake Center, 1601 Fifth Ave., Ste. 1500, 98101, pg. 1423 — **PB**

R.W. BECK, INC., 1001 Fourth Ave., Ste 2500, 98154, pg. 128 — **PV**

Belshaw Brothers, Inc., 1750 22nd Ave. S., 98144-4590, pg. 188 — **IT**

BERGSTROM CAPITAL CORPORATION, 505 Madison, Ste. 220, 98104, pg. 215 — **PB**

Bering Marine Corporation, P.O. Box 3757, 98124, pg. 683 — **PV**

Binks Manufacturing Company, 1749 First Ave. S., 98134-1441, pg. 229 — **PB**

Bird-Johnson Company-Seattle Operations, 4451 14th Ave. NW, 98107-4696, pg. 709 — **IT**

Boeing Advanced Systems, P.O. Box 3707, 98124, pg. 240 — **PB**

THE BOEING COMPANY, 7755 E. Marginal Way S., 98108, pg. 239 — **PB**

Boeing Electronics, Inc., 7755 E. Marginal Way S., 98108, pg. 240 — **PB**

Boeing Military Airplanes Division, 9725 E. Marginal Way S., 98108, pg. 241 — **PB**

The Bon Marche, Inc., 1601 Third Ave., 98181, pg. 617 — **PB**

Bowhead Equipment Company, P.O. Box 3757, 98124, pg. 683 — **PV**

BrandSolutions, 190 Queen Anne Ave. N., 98109, pg. 385 — **PV**

Broadcast Programming, 2211 Fifth Ave., 98121, pg. 531 — **PV**

CF2GS, 1008 Western Ave., Ste. 201, 98104, pg. 194 — **PV**

CGC Energy, Inc., 222 Fairview Ave. N., 98109, pg. 311 — **PV**

CGC Properties Inc., 222 Fairview Ave. N., 98109, pg. 311 — **PV**

CGC Resources, Inc., 222 Fairview Ave. N., 98109-5312, pg. 311 — **PV**

CAP Gemini America (Seattle Branch), 16400 S. Center Pkwy., Ste. 200, 98188, pg. 264 — **IT**

CAPITAL INDUSTRIES, INC., 5801 Third Ave., S., 98108, pg. 206 — **PV**

Carrier Building System & Services, 655 S. Orcas St., 98108-2648, pg. 1689 — **PB**

Cascade Land Leasing Co., 222 Fairview Ave. N., 98109, pg. 311 — **PV**

CASCADE NATURAL GAS CORPORATION, 222 Fairview Ave. N., 98109, pg. 311 — **PB**

Cigna Healthcare of Washington, Inc., 2940 Columbia Ctr., 701 Fifth Ave., 98101, pg. 360 — **PB**

Columbia Services, Inc., 1201 Third Ave., 98101, pg. 311 — **PV**

Commodore Financial Corp., 2300 W. Commodore Way, 98199, pg. 703 — **PV**

Composite Research & Management Company, 1201 Third Ave., 98101, pg. 1742 — **PB**

Container Care International, One South Idaho, 98134, pg. 267 — **PV**

Cruising Equipment Company, 6315 Seaview Ave. NW, 98107-2664, pg. 1705 — **PB**

Customer Services Division, 2925 S. 112th, 98168, pg. 240 — **PB**

D International Inc., Queen Anne Square, Ste. 507, 220 W. Mercer St., 98119, pg. 364 — **IT**

D.W. Close Company, 3317 Third Ave. S., 98124, pg. 1029 — **PV**

DWF of Seattle, 330 Terry Ave. N., 98109, pg. 326 — **PV**

Dairy Export Co., Inc., 635 Elliott Ave., 98119, pg. 311 — **PV**

DARIGOLD, INC., 635 Elliott Ave., W., 98119, pg. 311 — **PV**

Dayton Superior Corporation, 500 S. Lander St., 98134, pg. 932 — **PV**

Sam Dick Industries, Inc., 1140 N.W. 46th St., 98107, pg. 360 — **PV**

DOLAN NORTHWEST LLC, 222 Second Ave. Extension S., 98104, pg. 338 — **PV**

Douglas Management Company, P.O. Box 3757, 98124, pg. 683 — **PV**

EDERER INC., 2925 First Ave. S., 98134, pg. 363 — **PV**

Ederer Services, Inc., 2925 First Ave. S., 98134, pg. 364 — **PV**

Electronic Transaction Corporation, 11000 Lake City Way, 98125, pg. 498 — **PV**

Elkay Plastics Co., Inc., Stock Service Center, 500 S. Brandon, 98108, pg. 372 — **PV**

Emerald Warehouse & Distribution Services, 21 S. Nevada St., 98134, pg. 1038 — **PV**

Empire Life Insurance Company, 1203 Third Ave., 6th Fl., 98101, pg. 1742 — **PV**

EvansGroup, 190 Queen Anne N., 98109-4924, pg. 385 — **PV**

EvansGroup Technology, 190 Queen Anne Ave. North, 98109-4924, pg. 385 — **PV**

Expeditors International Ocean, Inc., 19119 - 16th Ave. So., 98188, pg. 600 — **PV**

EXPEDITORS INTERNATIONAL OF WASHINGTON, INC., 19119 16th Ave. S., 98104, pg. 600 — **PB**

First Columbia Escrow, Inc., 1201 Third Ave., 98101, pg. 1742 — **PB**

First Interstate Bank of Washington, N.A., 999 Third Ave., 98104, pg. 1753 — **PB**

First National Insurance Co. of America, SAFECO Plaza, 98185, pg. 1423 — **PB**

Fisher Broadcasting Inc., 100 Fourth Ave. N., 98109, pg. 648 — **PB**

FISHER COMPANIES INC., 600 University St., Ste. 1525, 98101-3185, pg. 647 — **PB**

Fisher Mills, Inc., 3235 16th Ave., S.W., 98134, pg. 648 — **PB**

Fisher Properties Inc., 600 University St., Ste. 1525, 98101, pg. 648 — **PB**

FISHERIES SUPPLY COMPANY, 1900 N. Northlake Way # 10, 98103, pg. 408 — **PV**

Food Services of America, 4025 Dell Ridge Way, S.W., Ste. 400, 98106, pg. 987 — **PV**

Foss Maritime Co., 660 W. Ewing St., 98119, pg. 1092 — **PV**

Four Seasons Olympic Hotel, 411 University St., 98101, pg. 502 — **IT**

Franz Seattle, 2901 Sixth Ave. S., 98134, pg. 1124 — **PV**

Full House Sports & Entertainment, 190 Queen Anne Ave., N., 98109, pg. 16 — **PB**

FUTUREWORKS, 190 Queen Anne Ave., N., Ste. 320, 98109, pg. 385 — **PV**

GATX Terminals Corp., 2720 13th Ave., S.W., 98134, pg. 692 — **PB**

GB Distribution LLC, 4711 Denver S., 98134, pg. 118 — **PV**

G.E. Capital Assurance, Two Union Sq., 601 Union St., Ste. 5600, 98101, pg. 712 — **PB**

GNA Corp., 56002 Union Sq., 98101, pg. 712 — **PB**

Gai's Northwest Bakeries, 2006 S. Weller St., 98144, pg. 1124 — **PV**

General Insurance Co. of America, Safeco Plaza, 98185, pg. 1423 — **PB**

General Travel Services, Inc., 1201 Third Ave., 18th Fl., 98101, pg. 1742 — **PB**

THE GENERRA COMPANY, 316 Occidental Ave. S., Ste. 410, 98104, pg. 446 — **PV**

Genetic Systems Corporation, 3005 First Ave., 98121, pg. 445 — **IT**

Golden Alaska Seafoods, Inc., 400 Market Pl. One, 2001 Western Ave., 98121, pg. 928 — **IT**

Graphic Jackets, 4797 First Ave., S., 98134, pg. 827 — **PV**

Gray Line of Alaska, 300 Elliott Ave., West, 98119, pg. 306 — **PB**

Gray Line of Seattle, 720 South Forest, 98134, pg. 306 — **PB**

Griffin Envelope, Inc., 4301 E. Marginal Way S., 98134-1198, pg. 1038 — **PV**

HALLIDIE MACHINERY COMPANY, INC., 2200 Sixth Ave. S., 98134, pg. 495 — **PV**

Hanwa American Corp., Seattle Branch, 900 Fourth Ave., Bank of California Center, Ste. 1640, 98164, pg. 595 — **IT**

James Hardie Gypsum Washington, 5931 E. Marginal Way S., 98134, pg. 597 — **IT**

HART CROWSER, INC., 1910 Fairview Ave. E., 98102, pg. 507 — **PV**

HERRING NEWMAN, 414 Olive Way, Ste. 300, 98101, pg. 524 — **PV**

Holiday House, Inc., 1201 Third Ave., 18th Fl., 98101, pg. 1742 — **PB**

Holland America Line Westours, 300 Elliott Ave. W., 98119, pg. 306 — **PB**

Horizon Air Industries, 19521 Pacific Hwy. S., 98188, pg. 35 — **PB**

Hosho America Inc., 1111 Third Ave., Ste. 1860, 98101, pg. 733 — **IT**

IDX Systems Corporation-Seattle, 1001 Forth Ave. Plaza, Ste 1500, 98154-1144, pg. 854 — **PB**

ICICLE SEAFOODS, INC., 4019 21st Ave. W., 98199, pg. 556 — **PV**

IMMUNEX CORPORATION, 51 University St., 98101, pg. 871 — **PB**

Immunex Manufacturing Corporation, 51 University St., 98101, pg. 871 — **PB**

Immunex Research and Development Corporation, 51 University St., 98101, pg. 871 — **PB**

Industra Inc., 16300 Christensen Rd., Ste. 300, 98188, pg. 74 — **IT**

Ingersoll Rand Tool & Hoist, P.O. Box 24046, 98124-0046, pg. 877 — **PB**

INTERPACIFIC INVESTORS SERVICES, 2623 Second Ave., 98121-1294, pg. 572 — **PV**

INX Incorporated/Midland Color Company, 4029 First Ave., S., 98134, pg. 1311 — **IT**

J.W. Messner, Inc., 609 Tower Bldg., 1809 7th Ave., 98101, pg. 734 — **PV**

JAY JACOBS, INC., 1530 Fifth Ave., 98101-1677, pg. 922 — **PB**

KBSG/KNDD-AM/FM, 1730 Minor St., Ste. 2000, 98101, pg. 378 — **PV**

KEBE, 190 Queen Anne Ave. N., 98109, pg. 792 — **PV**

KJR-AM, 190 Queen Anne Ave. N., 98109, pg. 792 — **PV**

KJR-FM, 190 Queen Anne Ave. N., 98109, pg. 792 — **PV**

Kawaguchi Travel Services, Inc., 1201 Third Ave., 18th Fl., 98101, pg. 1742 — **PB**

Thomas Kemper Lager, 1201 1st Ave. S., 98134, pg. 1345 — **PB**

Thomas Kemper Soda Company, 1201 1st Ave. S., 98134, pg. 1345 — **PB**

Kenworth Truck Co., 8801 E. Marginal Way S., 98108, pg. 1246 — **PB**

Key Trust Company of the Northwest, AT&T Gateway Tower, 700 Fifth Ave., 98111, pg. 954 — **PB**

Knik Construction Co., Inc., P.O. Box 3757, 98124, pg. 683 — **PV**

Koito Manufacturing Co.-Seattle Office, Ste. 5900, Gateway Tower, 700, 5th Ave., 98104-5059, pg. 743 — **IT**

Korn/Ferry International, One Union Sq., 600 University St., #311, 98101-1114, pg. 633 — **PV**

Korry Electronics Co., 901 Dexter Ave. N., 98109, pg. 594 — **PV**

Kvaerner Eureka Inc., 4200 23rd Ave. W., 3rd Fl., 98199, pg. 770 — **IT**

Kvaerner Fish Process, Seattle, 4200 23rd Avenue West, 98199, pg. 770 — **IT**

Kyokuyo America Corp., 2201 6th Ave. Ste. 1300, 98121, pg. 777 — **IT**

Land O'Lakes Inc., 200 W. Mercer St., Ste. 205, 98119-3958, pg. 646 — **PV**

Lilly Industries, Inc., 13535 Monster Rd., 98178, pg. 995 — **PB**

LINDAL CEDAR HOMES, INC., 4300 S. 104th Pl., 98178, pg. 998 — **PB**

Arthur D. Little, Inc., 1313 Plaza 600 Bldg., 98101, pg. 670 — **PV**

Lloyd Electric Apparatus Co., 7126 W. Marginal Way, S.W., 98106, pg. 672 — **PV**

Longview Fibre Co. Western Div., 5901 E. Marginal Way S., 98134, pg. 1014 — **PB**

Lucent Technologies, 2601 4th Ave., 98121, pg. 1017 — **PB**

Lynden Air Freight, Inc., One Union Sq., 600 Univ. St., 10th Fl., 98101, pg. 683 — **PV**

PB - *U.S. Public Companies Volume*
PV - *U.S. Private Companies Volume*
IT - *International Public & Private Companies Volume*

Geographic Index-U.S.

1473

Lynden Financial Services, Inc., P.O. Box 3757, 98124, pg. 684 — PV

Lynden Forwarding, Inc., One Union Sq., 600 Univ. St., 10th Fl., 98101, pg. 684 — PV

LYNDEN INCORPORATED, 18000 Pacific Hwy. S., Ste. 800, 98188, pg. 683 — PV

Lynden Logistics, Inc., P.O. Box 3757, 98124, pg. 684 — PV

MB Paper, 1505 Peoples National Bank Bldg. 1415 5t, 98171, pg. 829 — IT

MSR, 3800 First Ave. S, 98134, pg. 914 — PV

Magnet Properties, 2200 6th Ave., Ste. 770, 98121, pg. 38 — PV

Marco Seattle, Inc., 2300 W. Commodore Way, 98199, pg. 703 — PV

MARINE CONSTRUCTION & DESIGN CO., 2300 W. Commodore Way, 98199, pg. 703 — PV

Marine Systems, Inc.-West Coast, 950 N.W. Leary Way, 98107, pg. 961 — PB

Merchants Information Solutions, Inc., 415 S. Brandon St., 98108, pg. 1106 — PB

Merrill/Seattle, 1000 Second Ave., Ste. 1650, 98104, pg. 1097 — PB

Microsoft University, 6846 42nd Ave. N.E., 98115-7536, pg. 1108 — PB

Mill Maple Properties, Inc., 1201 Third Ave., 98101, pg. 1742 — PB

Mill Plain Four, Inc., 1201 Third Ave., 98101, pg. 1742 — PB

Mill Plain Three, Inc., 1201 Third Ave., 98101, pg. 1742 — PB

Mill Plain Two, Inc., 1201 Third Ave., 98101, pg. 1742 — PB

Mitsui & Co. (U.S.A.), 1001 Fourth Ave., 98154, pg. 879 — IT

Mitsui Foods Export, 1001 Fourth Ave., Ste. 4000, 98154, pg. 879 — IT

Momentum, 355 Treck Dr., 98188, pg. 1329 — PB

Murphey Favre Housing Managers, Inc., 1201 Third Ave., 15th Fl., 98101, pg. 1742 — PB

Murphey Favre, Inc., 1201 Third Ave., 98101, pg. 1742 — PB

Murphey Favre Properties, Inc., 1191 2nd Ave., 98101, pg. 1742 — PB

Mutual Travel, Inc., 1201 Third Ave., 18th Fl., 98101, pg. 1742 — PB

Muzak Limited Partnership, 2901 Third Ave., Ste. 400, 98121, pg. 222 — PV

NATIONAL FROZEN FOODS CORP., 2371 Eastlake Ave. E., 98102, pg. 783 — PV

ALLEN NELSON & CO., 1906 California Ave., S.W., 98116, pg. 790 — PV

NEORX CORPORATION, 410 W. Harrison St., 98119, pg. 791 — PB

NEW CENTURY MEDIA, 190 Queen Anne Ave., N., 98109, pg. 792 — PV

New Oji Paper Co., Ltd., 2610 First Interstate Ctr., 999 Third Ave., 98104-4050, pg. 998 — IT

Nichirei Foods, 2033 6th Ave., Ste. 900, 98121, pg. 928 — IT

Nippon Paper Industries Company Limited Seattle Office, Two Union Square, 601 Union St., Suite 5535, 98101, pg. 938 — IT

NORDSTROM, INC., 1501 Fifth Ave., 98101-1603, pg. 1190 — PB

North American Acceptance Corporation, 1201 Third Ave., 98101, pg. 1742 — PB

Northern Life Insurance Company, 1110 Third Ave., 98101, pg. 1375 — PB

Northwest Parking Services Inc., 721 First Ave., 98104, pg. 43 — PV

Nozaki America, Inc., Seattle Branch, Bank of California Bldg., 900 Fourth Ave., Ste. 3031, 98164, pg. 990 — IT

OCEAN BEAUTY SEAFOODS, 1100 W. Ewing St., 98119, pg. 810 — PV

THE ODOM CORPORATION, 26 S. Hanford, 98134, pg. 811 — PV

Oncomembrane, Inc., 1201 Third Ave., Ste. 5300, 98101, pg. 1013 — IT

Onoda Northwest, Inc., 5975 E. Marginal Way S., 98134, pg. 284 — IT

Outdoor Services, 720 Olive Way, Ste. 1500, 98101, pg. 1166 — PV

PNMR Securities, SAFECO Plaza, 98185, pg. 1423 — PB

PPG INC., 4797 First Ave., S., 98134, pg. 827 — PV

PACIFIC LUMBER & SHIPPING CO., 1301 Rainier Bank Tower, Ste. 3131, 98101, pg. 832 — PV

PACIFIC NORTHERN INC., North Tower, Ste. 200, 100 W. Harrison, 98119, pg. 832 — PB

Pacific Trail, Inc., 1700 Westlake Avenue N., Ste. 200, 98109, pg. 673 — PV

PacifiCare of Washington, 600 University St., Ste. 700, 98101, pg. 1251 — PB

Peter Pan Seafoods, Inc., 2200 Sixth Ave., 10th Fl., 98121, pg. 928 — IT

Piper Jaffray Inc., IBM Bldg., 1200 Fifth Ave., Ste. 1700, 98101-3161, pg. 1302 — PB

Pirelli Jacobson, Inc., 28th Ave. N.W., 98107, pg. 1059 — IT

PLUM CREEK TIMBER CO., L.P., 999 Third Ave., Ste. 2300, 98104, pg. 1311 — PB

Port Chatham Packing Company, Pier 89, 1240 16th Ave. W., 98119, pg. 556 — PV

Preservative Paint Company, 5400-5410 Airport Way S., 98108, pg. 613 — PV

Preston Properties of Arizona, Inc., 1201 Third Ave., 98101, pg. 1742 — PB

Preston Properties of California, Inc., 1201 Third Ave., 98101, pg. 1742 — PB

Preston Properties Texas, Inc., 1201 Third Ave., 98101, pg. 1742 — PB

Preston Property Management Company, 1201 Third Ave., 98101, pg. 1742 — PB

Preston Ridge Financial Services Corporation, 1201 Third Ave., 98101, pg. 1742 — PB

Qualex Inc., 1904 3rd Ave., Ste. 425, 98109, pg. 551 — PB

RHG Seattle, P.O. Box 58084, 3251 S. 176th, Ste. 112, 98138, pg. 1151 — IT

Re-Union Division, 1848 Westlake Ave. N., 98109, pg. 980 — PV

Red Ball Corporation, 9750 Third Ave. N.E., Ste. 200, 98115, pg. 97 — PV

ReliaStar Financial Marketing Corp., One Union Sq., 600 University St., Ste. 1720, 98101, pg. 1376 — PB

RESTAURANTS UNLIMITED, 1818 N. Northlake Way, 98103, pg. 925 — PV

ROMAC INDUSTRIES, INC., 1064 Fourth Ave. S., 98134, pg. 942 — PV

S & W Construction Services Inc, 400 N. 34th St., Ste. 100, 98103, pg. 989 — PV

SS Service Corporation, 1201 Third Ave., 98101, pg. 1742 — PB

SAFECO Select Markets Division, 1601 Fifth Ave., Ste. 1500, 98101, pg. 1423 — PB

Safecare Company, Gateway Tower, 700 Fifth Ave., Ste. 2600, 98104-5026, pg. 1423 — PB

SAFECO Asset Management Company, SAFECO Plaza, 98185, pg. 1423 — PB

SAFECO CORPORATION, SAFECO Plaza, 98185, pg. 1423 — PB

SAFECO Credit Company, Inc., SAFECO Plaza, 98185, pg. 1423 — PB

SAFECO Insurance Co. of America, SAFECO Plaza, 98185, pg. 1423 — PB

SAFECO Mutual Funds, SAFECO Plaza, 98185, pg. 1423 — PB

SAFECO National Insurance Co., SAFECO Plaza, 98185, pg. 1423 — PB

SAFECO Properties, Inc., Gateway Tower, 700 Fifth Ave., Ste. 2600, 98104-5026, pg. 1423 — PB

SAFECO Property & Casualty Insurance Companies, SAFECO Plaza, 98185, pg. 1423 — PB

SAFECO Securities, Inc., SAFECO Plaza, 98185, pg. 1423 — PB

SAFECO Services Co., SAFECO Plaza, 98185, pg. 1423 — PB

SAFECO Surplus Lines Insurance Co., SAFECO Plaza, 98135, pg. 1423 — PB

SAFECO Trust Company, 1409 Fifth Ave., Second Fl., 98101, pg. 1423 — PB

Seafirst Corporation, 701 5th Ave., 98104, pg. 181 — PB

Seafirst Insurance Corporation, P.O. Box 3977, 98124, pg. 181 — PB

Seattle Airline Learning Center, 1505 S. 192nd St., 98148, pg. 219 — IT

The Seattle Business Journal, Inc., 720 Third Ave., Ste. 800, 98104-1811, pg. 20 — IT

SEATTLE CITY LIGHT, 700 Fifth Ave., Ste. 3100, 98104-5037, pg. 1086 — PB

SEATTLE PACIFIC INDUSTRIES, INC., 1848 Westlake Ave. N., 98109, pg. 980 — PV

SEATTLE PACKAGING CORPORATION, 3701 S. Norfolk St., 98118, pg. 980 — PV

Seattle Post-Intelligencer, 101 Elliott Ave. W., 98119-4220, pg. 517 — PV

SEATTLE TIMES COMPANY, 1120 John St., 98109, pg. 980 — PV

Seattle WA Steel Division, 2424 SW Andover, 98106-1100, pg. 232 — PV

Security Pacific Investments, Inc., P.O. Box 3598, 98124-3598, pg. 182 — PB

SELLEN CONSTRUCTION COMPANY, 228 Ninth Ave., N., 98109, pg. 982 — PV

Sequent Computer Systems, Inc., Pacific First Centre, 1420 Fifth Ave., Ste. 2900, 98101, pg. 1459 — PB

SERVICES GROUP OF AMERICA, 4025 Dell Ridge Way S.W., Ste. 500, 98106, pg. 987 — PV

SHANNON & WILSON, INC., 400 N. 34th St., Ste. 100, 98103-8600, pg. 989 — PV

Shannon & Wilson Intl., 400 N. 34th St., 98103, pg. 989 — PV

Signature Travel, Inc., 1201 Third Ave., 18th Fl., 98101, pg. 1742 — PB

SIMPSON INVESTMENT CO., 1201 Third Ave., Ste. 4900, 98101-3045, pg. 1003 — PB

Simpson Paper Co., 1301 Fifth Ave., Ste. 1900, 98101-2943, pg. 1003 — PV

Sirach Capital Management, Inc., 3323 One Union Sq., 600 University St., 98101, pg. 1674 — PB

SKYWAY LUGGAGE CO., 30 Wall St., 98121, pg. 1005 — PV

A.O. Smith Water Products Company, P.O. Box 3675, 98124, pg. 1097 — PB

SmithKline Beecham Clinical Laboratories, 1737 Airport Way S., Ste. 200, 98134, pg. 1265 — IT

STARBUCKS COFFEE COMPANY, 2401 Utah Ave. S., 98134, pg. 1510 — PB

STEVEDORING SERVICES OF AMERICA, 1131 S.W. Klickitat Way, 98134, pg. 1042 — PV

Stusser Electric Company, 660 S. Andover St., 98108, pg. 265 — PV

The Sumitomo Bank, Ltd.-Seattle Representative Office, 1201 Third Ave., Ste. 5320, 98101, pg. 1309 — IT

Sumitomo Corporation of America, Two Union Sq., 601 Union St., Ste. 4500, 98101, pg. 1312 — IT

Superior Blends, 5118 14th NW, 98107, pg. 1652 — PB

Superior Reprographics, 1927 5th Ave. S., 98101, pg. 413 — PV

TCI Cablevision of Washington, Pioneer Bldg., 600 First Ave., Ste. 500, 98104, pg. 1555 — PB

TMP Worldwide, Inc., 10700 Meridian Ave. N., Ste. 201, 98133, pg. 1064 — PV

Talegen Corporation, 1011 Western Ave., Ste. 1000, 98104, pg. 1734 — PB

Targeted Genetics Corp., 51 University St., 98101, pg. 87 — PB

Tesoro Refining, Marketing & Supply Co., 999 Third Ave., # 4000, 98104, pg. 1582 — PB

Thaw & Walrus, Inc., 8300 Military Rd. So, 98108, pg. 914 — PV

TIME OIL COMPANY, 2737 W. Commodore Way, 98199, pg. 1086 — PV

TODD PACIFIC SHIPYARDS CORP., 1801 16th Ave. S.W., 98134, pg. 1619 — PB

Togiak Fisheries Inc., 1914 N. 34th, 98103, pg. 845 — IT

TOTEM RESOURCES CORPORATION, 1100 Olive Way, Ste. 1100, 98101, pg. 1092 — PV

Trident Seafood Corporation, 5303 Shilshole Ave., N.W., 98107, pg. 429 — PB

Tucci Benucch, W. Lake Ctr., 400 Pine St., Ste. 352, 98101, pg. 661 — PV

Turner Construction Co., 601 Union St., Ste. 400, 98101, pg. 1645 — PB

Union-Transport Corporation-Seattle Office, 1200 S. 192nd St., Ste. 301, 98148, pg. 1120 — PV

Unionbay Division, 1848 Westlake Ave. N., 98109, pg. 980 — PV

U.S. Bank of Washington N.A., 1414 4th Ave., 98101, pg. 1681 — PB

VanFed Appraisal Company, 1201 Third Ave., 98101, pg. 1742 — PB

VanFed Investment Services, Inc., 1201 Third Ave., 98101, pg. 1742 — PB

VanFed Mortgage Company, 1201 Third Ave., 98101, pg. 1742 — PB

VITAMILK DAIRY, INC., 427 N.E. 72nd St., 98115, pg. 1142 — PV

Volt Services Group, 1501 Fourth Ave., 98101, pg. 1724 — PB

WM Financial, Inc., 1201 Third Ave., 98101, pg. 1742 — PB

WM Life Insurance Company, 1203 Third Ave., 6th Fl., 98101, pg. 1742 — PB

WM Trust Company, 1201 Third Ave., 98101, pg. 1742 — PB

WRQ, INC., 1500 Dexter Ave. N., 98109, pg. 1145 — PV

WARDS COVE PACKING COMPANY, 88 E. Hamlin St., 98109, pg. 1149 — PV

WASHINGTON FEDERAL SAVINGS, 425 Pike St., 98101, pg. 1740 — PB

Washington Mutual Federal Savings Bank, 1201 Third Ave., 98101, pg. 1742 — PB

WASHINGTON MUTUAL INC., 1201 Third Ave., 98101, pg. 1741 — PB

Washington Mutual Life Insurance Services, Inc., 1201 Third Ave., 98101, pg. 1742 — PB

Washington Services, Inc., 425 Pike St., 98101, pg. 1740 — PB

Westco Products/Seattle, 9883 40th Ave. S., 98118, pg. 244 — IT

Western Alaska Fisheries Inc., 1111 Third Ave., 98101, pg. 845 — IT

Western International Media Corporation, 720 Olive Way, Ste. 1500, 98101, pg. 1167 — PV

Westin Hotels & Resorts, The Westin Bldg., 2001 Sixth Ave., 98121, pg. 1512 — PB

Westmark Hotels, Alaska, 300 Elliott Ave., West, 98119, pg. 306 — PV

Westward Seafoods, Inc., 1111 3rd Ave. Bldg., Ste. 2250, 98101, pg. 845 — IT

Whitney International, 2201 6th Ave., Ste. 1300, 98121, pg. 777 — IT

Willawa Fishing Co., 2300 W. Commodore Way, 98199, pg. 703 — PV

Willis Corroon Corp. of Seattle, 4200 Columbia Ctr., 701 Fifth Ave., 98104, pg. 1507 — IT

Willis Corroon, Inc., 4200 Columbia Center, 701 Fifth Ave., 98104, pg. 1507 — IT

WindowVisions, Inc., 4300 S. 104th Pl., P.O. Box 24426, 98124, pg. 999 — PV

Winmar Company, Gateway Tower, 700 5th Ave. N.E., Ste. 2600, 98104-5026, pg. 1423 — PB

The Winn Art Group, Ltd., 6015 Sixth Ave. S., 98108, pg. 503 — PV

Woodward-Clyde, 440 Bank of California Ctr., 1501 Fourth Ave., Ste. 1500, 98101, pg. 1657 — PB

The Yokohama Rubber Co., Ltd., 17680 W. Valley Hwy., Tukwila, 98188, pg. 1521 — IT

Zellerbach Division, Gateway Corporate Center, 13035 Gateway Dr., Ste.119, 98108, pg. 1075 — PB

ZymoGenetics, Inc., 1201 Eastlake Ave. E., 98102, pg. 987 — IT

Sedro Woolley

Sedro-Woolley Lumber Co., 109 Jameson St., 98284-1572, pg. 1730 — PB

Selah

TREE TOP, INC., 220 E. Second Ave., 98942, pg. 1098 — PV

Shelton

Simpson Timber Co., 215 N. Third St., 98584, pg. 1003 — PV

Silverdale

Technical Services Division, 10300 Silverdale Way, N.W., 98383-1072, pg. 1627 — PB

Snohomish

Harvest State Feed, Inc., 311 Maple St., 98290, pg. 508 — PV

Geographic Index-U.S.

Spokane

Action Mortgage Company, 510 W. Riverside, 99201, pg. 1516 **PB**
AgAmerica, FCB, W. 601 First Ave., 99204, pg. 398 **PV**
ALLIED SECURITY, INTERNATIONAL, W. 425 Second Ave., 99204, pg. 41 **PV**
Bergen Brunswig Medical Corporation, E. 715 Sprague St., 99202, pg. 214 **PB**
Boeing Spokane, P.O. Box AMF 757, 99219, pg. 241 **PV**
THE CALKINS MANUFACTURING COMPANY, 3108 East Ferry Ave., 99202, pg. 201 **PV**
CHEMCENTRAL/Spokane, 6308 E. Sharp, 99212, pg. 232 **PV**
Columbia Lighting, Inc., 3808 Sullivan Rd., 99216, pg. 1684 **PV**
COLUMBIA PAINT & COATINGS, P.O. Box 4569, 99202, pg. 256 **PV**
Cominco American Incorporated, 15918 E. Euclid Avenue, 99216-1815, pg. 308 **IT**
Compass Group, Inc., W. 510 Riverside St., Ste. 309, 99201, pg. 1681 **PB**
Cox Communications-Spokane, 1717 E. Buckeye, 99207, pg. 455 **PB**
E Z Loader Boat Trailers, Inc., N. 717 Hamilton, 99202, pg. 353 **PV**
First American Title Co. of Spokane, E. 40 Trent, 99202, pg. 625 **PB**
Harbor Financial Services, 111 N. Wall, 99201, pg. 1516 **PB**
Hewlett-Packard Company, N. 1225 Argonne Rd., 99212, pg. 815 **PB**
Inland Empire Division, P.O. Box 13000, N. 609 Argonne Rd., 99213, pg. 38 **PB**
ITRON INC., 2818 N. Sullivan Rd., 99216, pg. 914 **PB**
Jannock Steel Fabricating, Inc., E. 6207 Desmet Ave., 99212, pg. 699 **IT**
Jensen Distribution Services, W. 314-324 Riverside Ave., 99201, pg. 335 **PV**
KEY TRONIC CORPORATION, 4424 N. Sullivan Rd., 99216, pg. 953 **PB**
Lamplighter Homes, Inc., 13721 E. Sprague, 99216, pg. 333 **PB**
METROPOLITAN MORTGAGE & SECURITIES CO., INC., 911 W. Sprague Ave., 88204, pg. 738 **PV**
Metwest Mortgage Services, Inc., 929 W. Sprague Ave., 99204, pg. 738 **PV**
Murphey Favre Securities Services, Inc., 601 Riverside Ave., 9th Fl., 99201, pg. 17 **PV**
Neste Resins Corporation, Bldg. N. 3, Spokane Industrial Park, 99216, pg. 913 **IT**
Nickel Nik, North 1409 Maple St., 99201, pg. 984 **PV**
OXARC INC., E. 4003 Broadway Ave., 99220, pg. 825 **PV**
PEGASUS GOLD CORPORATION, 601 W. First Ave., Ste. 1500, 99204, pg. 1269 **PB**
Peirone Produce Company, 524 Trent, 99202, pg. 1114 **PV**
Pentzer Corporation, P.O. Box 3727, E. 1411 Mission Ave., 99220, pg. 1744 **PB**
Piper Jaffray Inc., Seafirst Financial Ctr., 601 W. Riverside Ave., Ste. 1200, 99201-0929, pg. 1302 **PB**
Plum Creek Manufacturing, N. 3808 Sullivan Rd., Bldg. 27, 99216, pg. 1311 **PB**
POTLATCH CORPORATION, 601 W. Riverside Ave., Ste. 1100, 99201, pg. 1318 **PB**
QualMed Plans for Health-Spokane, W. 201 N. River Dr., Ste. 300, 99201, pg. 678 **PB**
ROSAUERS SUPERMARKETS, INC., W. 1815 Garland, 99205, pg. 944 **PV**
Snyder Bakery, P.O. Box 305, 99210, pg. 1124 **PV**
L.H. Sowles Company, Inc., E. 11808 Mansfield #3, 99206, pg. 1019 **PV**
STERLING FINANCIAL CORPORATION, 111 North Wall St., 99201-0696, pg. 1516 **PB**
SuperValu, Inc.-Spokane Div., 11016 E. Montgomery Ave., 99206, pg. 1541 **PB**
URM Development Corp., North 7511 Freya, 99220, pg. 1114 **PV**
URM Insurance Agency, North 7511 Freya, 99220, pg. 1114 **PV**
URM STORES, INC., N. 7511 Freya, 99207, pg. 1114 **PV**
WAGSTAFF INC., 3910 N. Flora Rd., 99216, pg. 1146 **PV**
THE WASHINGTON WATER POWER COMPANY, E. 1411 Mission Ave., 99202, pg. 1744 **PB**
Western United Life Assurance Company, 929 W. Sprague Ave., 99204, pg. 738 **PV**
Zellerbach Division, North Valley Business Park, 11303 E. Montgomery, Ste. 3, 99206, pg. 1075 **PB**

Stanwood

TWIN CITY FOODS, INC., P.O. Box 699, 98292, pg. 1111 **PV**

Sumner

NuArc Northwestern Div., P.O. Box 7348, 98390, pg. 809 **PV**

Tacoma

ACH, Inc., S. 19th & Union St., 98405, pg. 403 **PB**
Almond Roca International, 1940 E. 11th St., P.O. Box 1596, 98401, pg. 173 **PV**
Atlas Foundry & Machine Co., 3021 S. Wikeson St., 98409, pg. 1063 **PV**
BROADCAST SUPPLY WORLDWIDE, INC., 7012 27th St., W., 98466, pg. 170 **PV**
BROWN & HALEY, 1940 E. 11th St., 98421, pg. 173 **PV**

BUFFELEN WOODWORKING COMPANY, 1901 Taylor Way, 98421, pg. 179 **PV**
Cablecraft Inc., 4401 S. Orchard St., 98411, pg. 1110 **PV**
Commencement Bay Mill Company, 801 Portland Ave., 98421, pg. 1003 **PV**
CONCRETE TECHNOLOGY CORP., 1123 Port of Tacoma Rd., 98421, pg. 262 **PV**
DWF of Tacoma, 5211 S. Washington, 98406, pg. 326 **PV**
Graphic Arts Supply Division, 2108 Tacoma Ave. S., 98402, pg. 205 **PV**
Harley Valve & Instrument, 2007 E. Stewart St., 98421, pg. 880 **PB**
Harris Rebar Seattle, Inc., Bldg. 9326, 401 Alexander Ave., 98421, pg. 598 **IT**
INTERSTATE DISTRIBUTOR COMPANY, 11707 21st Ave. S., 98444, pg. 573 **PV**
Key Bank of Washington, 1119 Pacific Ave., 98401, pg. 954 **PB**
MANKE LUMBER COMPANY, INC., 1717 Marine View Dr., 98422, pg. 699 **PV**
Nalleys Fine Foods, 3303 S. 35th St., 98409, pg. 887 **PV**
The News Tribune, 1950 S. State St., 98405, pg. 1066 **PV**
Pace Industries Puget Division, Inc., 2101 Mildred St. W., 98466, pg. 986 **PB**
Parker Paint Manufacturing Co. Inc., 3003 S. Tacoma Way, 98409, pg. 1501 **PV**
Perstorp Xytec, Inc., P.O. Box 99057, 9350 47th Ave. S.W., 98499, pg. 1037 **IT**
PICKERING INC., 1616 E St. Paul Ave., 98421, pg. 864 **PV**
Pick's Cove Marina, 1940 East D St., 98421, pg. 865 **PV**
Piper Jaffray Inc., P.O. Box 1258, 98401-1258, pg. 1301 **PB**
PREMIER INDUSTRIES, INC., 1019 Pacific Ave., Ste. 1501, 98402, pg. 881 **PV**
Regency Thermographics of Washington, Inc., 3801 S. Union Ave., 98409, pg. 89 **PB**
Republic Automotive Parts Sales, Inc., 2404 Center St., 98409, pg. 1378 **PB**
ROMAN MEAL COMPANY, 2101 S. Tacoma Way, 98409, pg. 942 **PV**
FRANK RUSSELL COMPANY, 909 A St., 98402, pg. 952 **PV**
Frank Russell Securities, Inc., 909 A St., 98402, pg. 952 **PV**
Frank Russell Trust Co., 909 A St., 98402, pg. 952 **PV**
JOSEPH SIMON & SONS, INC., 2202 E. River St., 98421-1595, pg. 1001 **PV**
Simpson Tacoma Kraft Co., P.O. Box 2133, 98421, pg. 1003 **PV**
Spanaway Lumber Co., 19111 38th Ave. East, 98446-1189, pg. 1003 **PB**
SuperValu, Inc.-Tacoma Div., 1525 E. D St., 98421, pg. 1541 **PB**
SUPERVALU International, 495 E. 19th St., 98421, pg. 1541 **PB**
T&W FINANCIAL CORPORATION, 6416 Pacific Hwy. E., 98424, pg. 1552 **PB**
Toray Composites (America), Inc., 19002 50th Ave. E., 98446, pg. 1400 **IT**
U.S. Oil & Refining Co., 3001 Marshall Ave., 98421, pg. 1086 **PV**
WDK, Inc., 300 Middle Waterway, 98421, pg. 999 **PB**
Weyerhaeuser Co. Fiber Div., 98477, pg. 1764 **PB**

Tukwila

CONTINENTAL MILLS, INC., 18125 Andover Pk. W., 98188, pg. 269 **PV**
Nordstrom Distribution, Inc., 1201 Andover Park E., 98188-3961, pg. 1190 **PB**
PENCO-Washington, 6300 Southcenter Blvd., Ste. 210, 98188, pg. 1508 **IT**
Shasta Beverage Inc., 1227 Andover Park E., 98188-3906, pg. 1153 **PB**

Tumwater

Pabst Brewing Co./Tumwater, Schmidt Pl. & Custer Way, 98502, pg. 954 **PV**
Tumwater Lumber Co., 8277 Center St., S.W., 98501-7227, pg. 1730 **PB**

Vancouver

Ahlstrom Process Equipment Inc., 1111 Main St., Ste. 710, 98661, pg. 34 **IT**
CADET MANUFACTURING COMPANY, 2500 W. Fourth Plain Blvd., 98660, pg. 198 **PV**
Cascade Autovon Co., 805 Broadway, 98660, pg. 1252 **PB**
Cascadia Transport, 12004 N.E. 95th St., Ste. 860, 98682, pg. 683 **PV**
DRYPER'S CORP., 801 S.E. Assembly Ave., 98661, pg. 344 **PV**
Elixir Industries, Bldg. #3, 2000 East Columbia Way, 98661, pg. 371 **PV**
First American Title Co. of Clark County, 108 E. Mill Plain Blvd., 98660, pg. 625 **PB**
Gem State Utilities Corporation, 805 Broadway, 98660, pg. 1252 **PB**
General Steel Corporation, 3000 S.E. Hiddenway, Ste. 40-A, 98881, pg. 1305 **PV**
GOULD PACKAGING, INC., 1200 W. Eighth St., 98660, pg. 466 **PV**
Great Western Malting Co., P.O. Box 1529, Foot of West 11th St., 98668-1529, pg. 428 **PB**
Heritage Hillhaven Nursing Home, 3605 Y St., 98663, pg. 1713 **PB**
Hillhaven Convalescent Center Vancouver, 400 E. 33rd St., 98663, pg. 1713 **PB**

Hydro Agri-Vancouver, 9013 N.E. Hwy. 99, Ste. W, 98665, pg. 961 **IT**
Inter Island Telephone Co., Inc., 805 Broadway, 98660, pg. 1252 **PB**
International Communications Holdings, Inc., 805 Broadway, 98660, pg. 1252 **PB**
Kamyr, Inc., 1111 Main St., Ste. 710, 98660, pg. 34 **IT**
Kyocera Industrial Ceramics Corp., 5713 E. Fourth Plains Blvd., 98661, pg. 776 **IT**
Lamplighter Homes, Inc., 13002 N.E. Hwy. 99, 98686, pg. 333 **PB**
Micropump Corporation, 1402 N.E. 136th Ave., 98684, pg. 862 **PB**
Northwestern Telephone Systems, Inc., 805 Broadway, 98660, pg. 1252 **PB**
PAC PAPER INC., 6416 N.W. Whitney Rd., 98665, pg. 828 **PV**
Pacific Telecom Cable, Inc., 805 Broadway, 98660, pg. 247 **IT**
Pacific Telecom Cellular, Inc., 805 Broadway, 98668, pg. 1252 **PB**
Pacific Telecom, Inc., 805 Broadway, 98668, pg. 330 **PB**
RHG Portland, P.O. Box 16126, 7601-H N.E. Hazel Dell Ave., 98665, pg. 1151 **IT**
SEH America Inc., 4111 N.E. 112th Ave., 98662-6776, pg. 1234 **IT**
Silgan Containers, 2601 N.W. Lower River Rd., 98660, pg. 1473 **PB**
Telephone Utilities of Alaska, Inc., 805 Broadway, 98660, pg. 1252 **PB**
Telephone Utilities of Eastern Oregon, Inc., 805 Broadway, 98660, pg. 1252 **PB**
Telephone Utilities of Oregon, Inc., 805 Broadway, 98660, pg. 1252 **PB**
Telephone Utilities of Washington, Inc., 805 Broadway, 98660, pg. 1252 **PB**
Vancouver Terminal, P.O. Box 1207, Foot of West 16th, 98660, pg. 692 **PB**
WESTOWER CORPORATION, 7001 N.E. 40th Ave., 98661, pg. 1762 **PB**

Vashon

K2 Corporation, P.O. Box 509, 19215 Vashon Hwy., 98070, pg. 940 **PB**

Walla Walla

Piper Jaffray Inc., 26 E. Main St., Ste. Four, 99362-1801, pg. 1303 **PB**
Stokely USA, Inc., 1164 Dell Avenue, 99362, pg. 1519 **PB**
WALLA WALLA GRAIN GROWERS, INC., P.O. Box 310, 99362, pg. 1148 **PV**
Walla Walla Union Bulletin, First & Poplar Sts., 99362, pg. 980 **PV**

Washougal

Fiberweb Washougal Inc., 3720 Grant St., 98671, pg. 113 **IT**

Wenatchee

Piper Jaffray Inc., 517 N. Mission St., 98801-2048, pg. 1302 **PB**
WASHINGTON STATE APPLE COMMISSION, 2900 Euclid, 98801, pg. 1152 **PV**
Zellerbach Division, 527 Pierre Ave. N., 98801, pg. 1076 **PB**

Winlock

Shakertown 1992, Inc., 1200 Kerron St., 98596, pg. 296 **IT**

Woodinville

Ace Novelty Company, Inc., 15000 Woodinville-Redmond Rd., Ste. 600, 98072, pg. 1309 **PV**
Baldor Electric Company, 1500 Woodinville-Redmond Rd., B-800, 98072-9042, pg. 169 **PB**
MACKIE DESIGNS, INC., 16220 Wood Red Rd. N.E., 98072, pg. 1030 **PB**
Spectrum Glass Co., 24305 Woodinville-Snohomish Hwy., 98072, pg. 296 **IT**
Stimson Lane Ltd., 14111 N.E. 45th, 98072, pg. 1661 **PB**

Woodland

Down River Forest Products, Inc., 1497 Down River Dr., 98674, pg. 763 **PB**

Yakima

A & B Plastics, Inc., 50 W. Arlington St., 98902, pg. 232 **IT**
Dowty Aerospace Yakima, P.O. Box 9907, 98909, pg. 1337 **IT**
Lamplighter Homes, Inc., 1522 So. First St., 98901, pg. 333 **PB**
Longview Fibre Co. Western Container Div., 2001 Longfibre Ave., 98909, pg. 1014 **PB**
Milky Way, Inc., 1602-A Rudkin Rd., 98901, pg. 683 **PV**
NOEL CANNING CORPORATION, 1001 S. First St., 98901, pg. 800 **PV**
SNOKIST GROWERS, 18 W. Mead, 98902, pg. 1011 **PV**
Snyder Bakery, 16 N. Third Ave., 98902, pg. 1124 **PV**

PB - U.S. Public Companies Volume
PV - U.S. Private Companies Volume
IT - International Public & Private Companies Volume

Geographic Index-U.S.

STADELMAN FRUIT L.L.C., 314 S. 2nd Ave., 98902, pg. 1028 **PV**
Zellerbach Division, 21 W. Washington Ave., 98902, pg. 1075 **PB**

WEST VIRGINIA

Alloy

Elkem Alloy, P.O. Box 613, 25002-0813, pg. 447 **IT**

Ashford

Mining Services International, HC 64, Box 807, 25009, pg. 1115 **PB**

Beckley

Bank of Raleigh, One Park Ave., 25802, pg. 836 **PB**
HORIZON BANCORP, INC., One Park Ave., 25802-2803, pg. 836 **PB**
Mining Controls, Inc., P.O. Box 1141, 25801, pg. 370 **PV**

Belle

Du Pont Belle Plant, 901 W. DuPont Ave., 25015-1555, pg. 531 **PB**

Beverly

Colonial Millwork, Inc., P.O. Box 436, 25653, pg. 706 **PV**

Bluefield

Bluefield Gas Company, 4699 E. Cumberland Rd., 24701, pg. 1393 **PB**
Eimco Coal Machinery Inc., 210 Bland St., 24701, pg. 1352 **IT**
Flowers Baking Co. of West Virginia, U.S. Rte. 52 N., 24701, pg. 657 **PB**
RISH EQUIPMENT COMPANY, Airport Rd. Near U.S. 52, 24701, pg. 932 **PV**
Scott & Stringfellow, Inc., 105 Law & Commerce Bldg., 24701, pg. 1446 **PB**
Tabor Machine Co., P.O. Box 3037, Bluewell Station, 24701, pg. 371 **PV**
Tele Scripps Cable, 1901 Leatherwood Ln., 24701, pg. 1448 **PB**

Bridgeport

Fourco Glass Co., P.O. Box 890, 26330, pg. 84 **IT**
PDC Securities, Inc., P.O. Box 26, 26330, pg. 1280 **PB**
PETROLEUM DEVELOPMENT CORPORATION, 103 E. Main St., 26330, pg. 1280 **PB**
Riley Natural Gas, 103 E. Main St., pg. 1281 **PB**

Buckhannon

HAWG Hauling & Disposal, Inc., Rte. 1, Box 84A, 26201, pg. 403 **PB**
Union Drilling Division, Drawer 40, 26201, pg. 590 **PB**

Chapmanville

Logan Manufacturing, 110 Phico, pg. 1032 **PV**

Charles Town

Charles Town Races, Flowing Springs Rd., 25414, pg. 1270 **PB**

Charleston

Alamco, Inc., 900 Pennsylvania Ave., 25302, pg. 403 **PB**
Bell Atlantic-WV, 1500 MacCorkle Ave. S.E., 25314, pg. 203 **PB**
Bluefield Valley Water Works Co., P.O. Box 1906, 25327, pg. 96 **PB**
Broughton Foods Company, 1931 W. Washington St., 25312, pg. 260 **PB**
Cannelton Inc., 101 Washington St. E., 25301, pg. 471 **PB**
Cannelton Industries, Inc., 101 Washington St. E., 25301, pg. 471 **PB**
Carlton, Inc., 209 Washington St. W., 25362, pg. 694 **PV**
Charleston Division, 1565 Hansford St., 25311, pg. 333 **PB**
Coca-Cola Bottling Co. of West Virginia, Inc., 300 Kanawha Blvd. E. #306, 25301, pg. 392 **PB**
Columbia Gas Transmission Corp., 1700 MacCorkle Ave., S.E., 25314, pg. 403 **PB**
Columbia Gulf Transmission Co., 1700 MacCorkle Ave., 25314, pg. 403 **PB**
Columbia Natural Resources, Inc., 900 Pennsylvania Ave., 25302, pg. 403 **PB**
EASTERN AMERICAN ENERGY CORPORATION, 501 E. 56th St., S.E., 25304-2393, pg. 357 **PV**
Eastern Associated Coal Corp., 800 Laidley Tower, 25324, pg. 594 **IT**
GAI Consultants, Inc., 315 70th St.S.E., 25304, pg. 434 **PV**
Hewlett-Packard Company, 501-56th St., 25304, pg. 815 **PB**
INDUSTRIAL RUBBER PRODUCTS COMPANY, 815 Court St., 25301, pg. 561 **PV**
Kentucky Berwind Land Company, 1050 One Valley Sq., 25301, pg. 138 **PV**

McJunkin - Appalachain, 835 Hillcrest Dr., 25311, pg. 722 **PV**
MCJUNKIN CORPORATION, 835 Hillcrest Dr., 25311, pg. 722 **PV**
Medical Assurance of West Virginia, 110 Association Dr., 25311, pg. 1080 **PB**
Mountain States Airgas, 1 Oregon St., 25312, pg. 33 **PB**
Mountaineer Gas Services, Inc., 414 Summers St., 25301, pg. 357 **PV**
Peabody Coal Co., 800 Laidley Tower, 25324, pg. 594 **IT**
PERSINGERS, INC., 520 Elizabeth St., 25311, pg. 855 **PV**
Stone & Thomas Merchandising Offices, Lee & Dickinson Sts., 25326, pg. 1044 **PV**
Valley Air, P.O. Box 6516, 3000 Edens Fork Rd., 25362, pg. 672 **PV**
Valley Bell Dairy Co., 508 Roane, 25302, pg. 158 **PV**
West Virginia-American Water Co., P.O. Box 1906, 500 Summers St., 25327, pg. 96 **PB**
West Virginia Cellular Telephone Corp., 701 Lee St., 25301, pg. 1708 **PB**

Clarksburg

Broughton Foods Company, Rte. 2, 26301, pg. 260 **PB**
CNG Transmission Corporation, 445 W. Main St., 26301, pg. 435 **PB**
Champion Industries, Inc., 700 N. South R., 26301, pg. 333 **PB**
Hope Gas, Inc., P.O. Box 2868, Bank One Ctr., 26302-2868, pg. 435 **PB**
State Electric Supply Company, P.O. Box 986, Old Rte. 50 E., 26301, pg. 1036 **PV**

Dunbar

Allied Security Inc., 1222 Leone Lane, 25064, pg. 40 **PV**
Gilbert & Bennett, P.O. Box 158, 25064, pg. 453 **PV**

Fairlea

West Virginia Power, 280 Seneca Trail, 24902, pg. 1701 **PB**

Fairmont

B & J Operations Company, Inc., 103 Adams St., 26554, pg. 850 **PB**
Browning-Ferris Industries of West Virginia, Inc., 97 10th St., 26554, pg. 264 **PB**
O.C. Cluss Lumber Co., 215 Mill St., 26554, pg. 248 **PV**
HELMICK CORPORATION, 10th St. & Minor Ave., 26554, pg. 520 **PV**
Industrial Contracting of Fairmont, Inc., P.O. Box 2648, 26554, pg. 961 **PV**
Industrial Resources, Inc., P.O. Box 2648, 26554, pg. 961 **PV**
McHal Corporation, 2011 Pleasant Valley Rd., P.O. Box 1587, 26554, pg. 961 **PV**
Monongahela Power Co., 1310 Fairmont Ave., 26554, pg. 42 **PB**
Mountaineer Resources, Inc., P.O. Box 2648, 26554, pg. 961 **PV**
Salem Electric Company, P.O. Box 1587, 2011 Pleasant Valley Rd., 26554, pg. 961 **PV**
Tampella Power Corp., 2030 Pleasant Valley Rd., 26555, pg. 1354 **IT**
West Virginia Electric Corp., 2011 Pleasant Valley Rd., P.O. Box 1587, 26554, pg. 962 **PV**

Glen Morgan

ICI Explosives, P.O. Box 175, 25847, pg. 664 **IT**

Grafton

Corrugated Packaging, P.O. Box 49, 26354, pg. 737 **PB**

Halltown

Republic Paperboard Company-Halltown Mill, P.O. Box 10, 25423-0010, pg. 1378 **PB**

Harrisville

Troy Mills, Inc., 625 N. Pennsylvania Ave., 26362, pg. 1106 **PV**

Hazelton

Coastal Lumber Company, P.O. Box 237, 26535, pg. 248 **PV**

Hedgesville

LCS Services, Inc., Allensville Rd., 25427, pg. 1686 **PB**

Hinton

National Bank of Summers, P.O. Box 220, 25951, pg. 836 **PB**

Hundred

Bank of Hundred, P.O. Box 248, 26575, pg. 850 **PB**

Huntington

Arch Coal, Inc., 2205 Fifth Street Rd., 25701, pg. 139 **PB**
CHAMPION INDUSTRIES, 2450-90 First Ave., 25703, pg. 333 **PB**
Chiron Vision, Rte. 2, Industrial Ln., 25702, pg. 350 **PB**
Corrugated Products Division, P.O. Box 3068, 409 Buffington St., 25702, pg. 763 **PB**
ERD Environmental, Inc., 801 Madison Ave., Rm. 200, 25773, pg. 546 **PB**
J.H. FLETCHER & CO., 402 High St., 24705, pg. 412 **PV**
The Herald-Dispatch, 946 Fifth Ave., 25701, pg. 701 **PB**
Huntington Division, 2450-90 First Ave., 25703, pg. 333 **PB**
Inco Alloys International, Inc., 3200 Riverside Dr., 25705-1771, pg. 672 **IT**
LOGAN CORPORATION, 555 7th Ave., 25701, pg. 672 **PV**
STATE ELECTRIC SUPPLY CO., 2010 2nd Ave., 25703, pg. 1036 **PV**
Stationers, Inc., 1945 Fifth Ave., 25703, pg. 333 **PB**
STEEL OF WEST VIRGINIA, INC., 17th & 2nd Sts., 25703, pg. 1513 **PB**
WSAZ-TV, 645 Fifth Ave., 25721, pg. 984 **PB**
West Virginia Cellular Telephone Corp., 4341 Route 60 E., Bldg. #2, 25705, pg. 1708 **PB**
West Virginia Pump & Supply Company, 1551 Jackson Ave., 25704, pg. 861 **PB**

Jane Lew

Pittsburgh Tube Jane Lew Div., P.O. Box 875, Industrial Park Rd., 26378, pg. 868 **PV**

Kenova

Dart Trucking Company, Inc., 1807A Rte. 7, 25530, pg. 94 **PB**

Keyser

Alliant Techsystems-Rocket Center, P.O. Box 210, 26726-0210, pg. 47 **PB**
Upland Resources, Inc., P.O. Box 429, 26726, pg. 1762 **PB**

Lester

A.L. Lee Corp., Rte. 54 S., P.O. Box 99, 25865, pg. 961 **PV**

Lewisburg

ABB Process Analytics, P.O. Box 831, 843 N. Jefferson St., 24901, pg. 5 **IT**
Greenbrier Valley National Bank, P.O. Box 387, 24901-0387, pg. 836 **PB**

Mabscott

WRM, INCOPORATED, 144 Whitestick St., 25871, pg. 1144 **PV**

Marlinton

First Citizens Bank & Trust Company-West Virginia, 201 Eigth St., 24954, pg. 629 **PB**
First National Bank in Marlinton, 300 Eighth St., 24954, pg. 836 **PB**

Martinsburg

Quebecor Printing Martinsburg, P.O. Box 11, 1989 Arcata Blvd., 25401, pg. 1076 **IT**

Masontown

Mountain State Telephone Co., Depot St., 26542, pg. 380 **PB**

Millville

Millville Quarry Inc., P.O. Box 166, Blair Rd., 25432, pg. 166 **IT**

Milton

SuperValu, Inc.-Milton Div., P.O. Box 386, James River Tpke., 25541, pg. 1540 **PB**

Morgantown

EG & G Technical Services of West Virginia, Morgantown Energy Tech. Ctr., 3610 Collins Ferry Rd., 26507-0880, pg. 543 **PB**
Euro-Suites, 501 Chestnut Ridge Rd., 26505, pg. 1537 **PB**
Greer Limestone Co., Greer Bldg., 26505, pg. 479 **PV**
Huntington National Bank, P.O. Box 853, 26507-0853, pg. 850 **PB**
Lakeview Resort & Conference Center, One Lakeview Dr., 26505, pg. 1537 **PB**
Morgantown Machine & Hydraulics, Inc., Rte. 5, Box 250, 26505, pg. 280 **IT**
Mylan Pharmaceuticals Inc., 781 Chestnut Ridge Rd., 26505, pg. 1143 **PB**

PB - U.S. Public Companies Volume
PV - U.S. Private Companies Volume
IT - International Public & Private Companies Volume

National Mine Service Company, 696 Fairmont Rd., 26505, pg. 281 · IT

Moundsville

Consolidated Coal Co., P.O. Box 537, 26041, pg. 531 · PB

New Haven

Central Operating Co., P. O. Box 389, 25265, pg. 72 · PB

Newell

THE HOMER LAUGHLIN CHINA COMPANY, Harrison St., 26050-1299, pg. 653
MARSH BELLOFRAM CORP., State Rte. Two, Box 305, 26050, pg. 707
Newell Bridge & Railway Company, Sixth Harrison St., 26050-0593, pg. 653 · PV
The Newell Company, Harrison St., 26050-1249, pg. 653 · PV

Nitro

CONCORP, INC., P.O. Box 425, 25143, pg. 262 · PV
Union Boiler Co., P.O. Box 425, 25143, pg. 262 · PV

Parkersburg

Ames Company, 3801 Camden Ave., 26102, pg. 1683 · PB
Fahlgren, Rosemar Rd. & Seminary Dr., 26102, pg. 391
G.E. Specialty Chemicals, U.N.B. Square, 5th & Avery Sts., 26102, pg. 711
Orange County Cellular Telephone Corp., 3417 Murdoch Ave., 26101, pg. 1708 · PB
Parkersburg Division, 405 Ann St., 26101, pg. 333 · PB
UNITED BANKSHARES, INC., 514 Market St., 26101, pg. 1674 · PB

Parsons

The Kingsford Products Co., Hwy. 219, P.O. Box 464, 26287, pg. 387 · PB

Poca

Tampella Power Corp., 178 Spruce La., 25159, pg. 1354 · IT

Point Pleasant

Point Pleasant Register Co., 200 Main St., 25550, pg. 701 · PB

Powellton

Cyprus Kanawha Corporation, P.O. Box 30, 25161, pg. 471 · PB

Princeton

Norris Screen & Mfg., Inc., 403 S. Wickham Ave., 24740, pg. 370 · PV

Ravenswood

Peake Energy, Inc., P.O. Box 8, State Rte. 2 & Pleasantview Rd., 26164, pg. 1078 · PV
Ravenswood Aluminum Corp., P.O. Box 98, Rte. Two S., 93940, pg. 328 · PB

Snowshoe

Snowshoe Resort, Inc., P.O. Box 10, 26209, pg. 685 · IT

South Charleston

LOGAN & KANAWHA COAL CO., 96 MacCorkle, 25303, pg. 672 · PV
Panhandle Pipe & Supply Co., Inc., 4821 McClung St., 25309, pg. 847 · PB
South Charleston Sewage Treatment Co., P.O. Box 8515, Browne St., 25303, pg. 1667 · PB
South Charleston Stamping & Manufacturing, 3100 Mac Corkle, SW, 25303, pg. 1030 · PV

Spelter

Meadowbrook Co., P.O. Box 184, Main St., 26438, pg. 331 · PV

Summersville

Bright of America, Inc., 300 Greenbrier Rd., 26651, pg. 223 · PB

Switzer

National Mine Service Company, Logan Div., P.O. Box 250, 25647, pg. 281 · IT

Vienna

MARMAC CORPORATION, P.O. Box 6129, 26105, pg. 705 · PV
Schuller Intl. Inc., P.O. Box 5130, 26105-5130, pg. 927 · PB

Washington

L.B. Foster Company-Parkersburg Plant, Rte. 892, Dupont Rd., 26181, pg. 676 · PB

Weirton

Alpo Pet Foods, Inc., 1000 Hamilton Rd., 26062, pg. 917 · IT
WEIRTON STEEL CORPORATION, 400 Three Springs Dr., 26062-4989, pg. 1751 · PB

Wheeling

Best Western Wheeling Inn. 949 Main St., 26003, pg. 162 · PV
BOURY ENTERPRISES, 1315 Main St., 26003, pg. 162 · PV
Centre Foundry & Machine Co., 74 Warnwood Ave., 26003, pg. 351 · PV
OGDEN NEWSPAPERS, INC., 1500 Main St., 26003, pg. 812 · PV
ORMET CORPORATION, 1233 Main St., 26003, pg. 820 · PV
PAR ENTERPRISES, INC., 1535 Market St., 26003, pg. 838 · PV
Riverside Restaurant, c/o Best Western, 949 Main St., 26003, pg. 162 · PV
STONE & THOMAS, 1030 Main St., 26003, pg. 1044 · PV
T.J.'s Sports Garden Restaurant, 808 National Rd., 26003, pg. 162 · PV
VALLEY NATIONAL GASSES INC., 67 43rd St., 26003, pg. 1132 · PV
Wheeling Corrugating Co., 1134-1140 Market St., 26003, pg. 1727 · PB
Wheeling-Pittsburgh Steel Corporation, 1134 Market St., 26003, pg. 1727 · PB
Wheeling Power Company, 51 16th St., P.O. Box 751, 26003, pg. 73 · PB

White Sulphur Springs

First Citizens Bank & Trust Company-White Sulphur Springs, P.O. Box 40, 24986, pg. 629 · PB
The Greenbrier, 300 West Main St., 24986, pg. 284 · PB

Williamstown

Walker Systems, Inc., 1000 Innovation Dr., 26187, pg. 1184 · PV

WISCONSIN

Abbotsford

ABBYLAND FOODS, INC., 502 E. Linden St., 54405, pg. 10 · PV
Liberia Mfg. Co., 101 W. Linden St., 54405, pg. 491 · PB

Adams

Castle Rock Container Co., Grove St., 53910, pg. 436 · PB

Adell

Ecological Chemical Products Co., W-5280 S. County Trunk A, 53001, pg. 531 · PB

Algoma

WISCONSIN LABEL CORPORATION, 1102 Jefferson St., 54201, pg. 1184 · PV

Alma

Tenney Telephone Co., P.O. Box 26, 120 S. Main St., 54610, pg. 1572 · PB

Antigo

SHELDONS' INC., 626 Center St., 54409-2496, pg. 992 · PV

Appleton

AAL Capital Management Corp., 4321 N. Ballard Rd., 54919, pg. 28 · PV
Ahlstrom Process Equipment Inc., 4351 W. College Ave., Ste. 402, 54914, pg. 34 · IT
AID ASSOCIATION FOR LUTHERANS, 4321 N. Ballard Rd., 54919-0001, pg. 27 · PV
Appleton Papers Inc., 825 E. Wisconsin Ave., 54912, pg. 567 · IT
I. Bahcall Steel & Pipe Inc., P.O. Box 1054, 975 N. Mead St., 54911-1054, pg. 1150 · IT
Central National-Gottesman Inc., 911 N. Lyndale Dr., 54914, pg. 224 · PV
CREATIVE GROUP INC., 619 N. Lynndale Dr., 54914, pg. 287 · PV

Duralam, Inc., P.O. Box 862, 54912, pg. 966 · PV
Engineered Fabrics/T.S.I., 600 E. Atlantic St., 54913, pg. 36 · PB
Fox River Paper Company, 100 W. Lawrence, 54913, pg. 422 · PV
FOX VALLEY CORPORATION, 100 W. Lawrence St., 54911, pg. 422 · PV
Green Tree Acceptance, Inc., 1500 N. Casa Lome Dr., 54915, pg. 762 · PB
INTEGRITY MUTUAL INSURANCE COMPANY, 2121 E. Capitol Dr., 54911, pg. 566 · PV
JanSport, P.O. Box 1817, 54913, pg. 1702 · PB
M & I Bank Fox Valley, 221 W. College Ave., 54912, pg. 1050 · PB
Miller Electric Manufacturing Co., 1635 West Spencer St., 54912, pg. 867 · PB
Miller Thermal, Inc., 555 Communications Dr., 54912, pg. 867 · PB
The Paper Factory of Wisconsin, Inc., 600 E. Hancock St., 54911, pg. 742 · PB
Pierce Manufacturing, Inc., 2600 American Dr., 54915, pg. 1233 · PB
Piper Jaffray Inc., Giltedge Bldg., 4321 W. College Ave., Ste. 102, 54914-3983, pg. 1301 · PB
RAYOVAC Corporation, 2600 North Ballard, 54912, pg. 912 · PV
Sulpaco West, 600 E. Hancock St., 54912, pg. 1050 · PV
Svedala Industries Inc., 2600 N. Roemer Rd., 54915, pg. 1325 · IT
Unisource, 1800 W. Rogers Ave., 54912, pg. 1671 · PB
Valleycast, Inc., P.O. Box 1714, 54913-1714, pg. 1017 · IT
Valmet Inc.- Appleton Division, P.O. Box 2339, 54913, pg. 1448 · IT
Voith Inc., P.O. Box 2337, 2200 N. Roemer Rd., 54913, pg. 1473 · IT
Voith Sulzer Paper Technology, North America, Inc., 2200 N. Roemer Rd., 54913, pg. 1308 · IT
Williamhouse Sales Corporation, 3800 Wisconsin Ave., 54915-5739, pg. 89 · PB

Arcadia

Gold'n Plump Poultry, Inc., 502 W. Main, 54612, pg. 577 · PV

Ashland

M & I Bank, 100 Main St. E., 54806, pg. 1050 · PB

Augusta

Bush Brothers & Company Plant, 600 S. Highway St., 54727, pg. 189 · PV

Baldwin

CTS Corp., Connector Products, 1560 Tenth Ave., 54002, pg. 285 · PB

Baraboo

Baraboo-Sysco Food Services, Inc., 910 South Blvd., 53913-2793, pg. 1550 · PB
FLAMBEAU CORPORATION, 801 Lynn Ave., 53913, pg. 409 · PV
Flambeau Corporation, 801 Lynn Ave., 53913, pg. 409 · PV
Flambeau Plastics Co., 801 Lynn Ave., 53913, pg. 409 · PV
FOREMOST FARMS USA COOPERATIVE, E10889A Penny Ln., 53913, pg. 418 · PV
Foremost Ingredient Group, E. 10889A Penny Lne., 53913, pg. 418 · PV

Barron

JEROME FOODS INC., 34 N. Seventh St., 54812, pg. 586 · PV

Bear Creek

Flanagan Bros. Trucking Co., 400 Clark St., 54922, pg. 887 · PV
Great Lakes Kraut Co., 400 Clark St., 54922, pg. 887 · PV

Beaver Dam

Power Gear, 950 Green Valley Rd., 53916, pg. 124 · PB

Belgium

Lakeside Packing Co., 705 Main St., 53004-9512, pg. 644 · PV

Belleville

Federal Industries, Inc., 215 Federal Ave., 53508, pg. 1506 · PB

Beloit

ABC SUPPLY COMPANY, INC., One ABC Pkwy., 53511, pg. 3 · PV
Beloit Corporation, One Saint Lawrence Ave., 53511, pg. 789 · PB
Durst Div., P.O. Box 298, 53511, pg. 1370 · PB
Enzyme Bio-Systems, Ltd., 2600 Kennedy Dr., 53511, pg. 448 · PB

Geographic Index-U.S.

Fairbanks Morse Engine Division, 701 Lawton Ave., 53511, pg. 401 **PB**
Frito-Lay Inc., 2810 Kennedy Dr., 53511, pg. 1277 **PB**
Kerry Ingredients, 352 E. Grand Ave., 53511, pg. 732 **IT**
M & I Bank of Beloit, 500 E. Grand Ave., 53511, pg. 1050 **PB**
NATIONAL BEDDING CO., 1500 Lee Ln., 53511, pg. 780 **PV**
Papermaking Machinery & Systems, One St. Lawrence Ave., 53511-3311, pg. 789 **PB**
REGAL-BELOIT CORPORATION, 200 State St., 53511, pg. 1370 **PB**

Berlin

Berlin Glove Co., P.O. Box 230, 150 W. Franklin St., 54923, pg. 136 **PV**
BERLIN GLOVE COMPANY LTD., 150 W. Franklin, 54923-0230, pg. 136 **PV**
Mid-Western, 150 W. Franklin, 54923, pg. 136 **PV**
Senior Engineering Co.-Berlin, P.O. Box 89, 242 S. Pearl St., 54923-0089, pg. 1222 **IT**

Big Bend

Orley Meyer, 22400 Edgewood Ave., 53103, pg. 1041 **PB**

Black Earth

Black Earth Telephone Co., Inc., 1125 Mills, 53515, pg. 1571 **PB**

Bonduel

Bonduel Telephone Co., 229 E. Green Bay St., 54107, pg. 1571 **PB**

Brillion

Brillion Iron Works, Inc., 200 Park Ave., 54110, pg. 933 **PB**
Dean Foods Vegetable Company, 235 E. Ryan, 54110, pg. 490 **PB**

Bristol

Billiards Div. of Brunswick, 87th St. & 196th Ave., 53104, pg. 265 **PB**

Brokaw

Wausau Papers - Printing & Writing Div., Second St., 54417-0305, pg. 1747 **PB**

Brookfield

Arrow/Schweber Electronics, 200 N. Patrick Blvd., 53045, pg. 134 **PB**
BADER RUTTER & ASSOC., INC., Bishop's Woods Centre, 13555 Bishop's Court, 53005, pg. 110 **PV**
Binks Manufacturing Company, 12705 Robin Ln., 53005-3125, pg. 229 **PB**
Fiserv CIR, Inc., 255 Fiserv Dr., pg. 647 **PB**
FISERV, INC., 255 Fiserv Dr., 53045, pg. 647 **PB**
Harnischfeger Corp., 13400 Bishop's Lane, 53005, pg. 740 **IT**
Hewlett-Packard Company, 275 N. Corporate Dr., 53005, pg. 815 **PB**
HYDRITE CHEMICAL COMPANY, 300 N. Patrick Blvd., 53045, pg. 551 **PV**
Jani King of Milwaukee, Inc., 17400 W. North Ave., Ste. 106, 53045, pg. 582 **PV**
M & I Northern Bank, 3155 N. 124th St., 53005, pg. 1050 **PB**
Milwaukee Electric Tool Corp., 13135 W. Lisbon Rd., 53005, pg. 96 **IT**
Motorola Galvin Center, 325 N. Corporate Dr. Ste. 220, 53045-5828, pg. 1138 **PV**
National Account Systems, Inc., 180 N. Executive Dr., 53005, pg. 1267 **PB**
Newport News Technical Services, Inc. (Wisconsin), Maplewood Exec. Center, 250 N. Sunnyslope Rd., 53005, pg. 1180 **PB**
Norlight Telecommunications Inc., 275 N. Corporate Dr., 53045, pg. 601 **PV**
PAYCO AMERICAN CORPORATION, 180 N. Executive Dr., 53005, pg. 1267 **PB**
Payco-General American Credits, Inc., 180 N. Executive Dr., 53005, pg. 1267 **PB**
Professional Recoveries, Inc., 180 N. Executive Dr., 53005, pg. 1267 **PB**
Stolper-Fabralloy Co. LLC, 115 N. Janecek Rd., 53045-6155, pg. 1640 **PB**
University Accounting Service, Inc., 180 N. Executive Dr., 53005, pg. 1267 **PB**
Wisconsin Wire & Steel, 4320 N. 126th St., 53005, pg. 1061 **PB**

Brown Deer

Charter Northbrooke Behavioral Health System, Inc., 46000 W. Schroeder Dr., 53223, pg. 1035 **PB**
KRIER FOODS, INC., 4555 W. Schroeder Dr., Ste. 190, 53223, pg. 636 **PV**
M & I Data Services, Inc., 4900 W. Brown Deer Rd., 53223, pg. 1050 **PB**
WAGO Corporation, 9085 N. Deerbrook Trail, 53223, pg. 209 **IT**

Burlington

Burlington, Brighton & Wheatland Telephone Co., P.O. Box 250, 7610 McHenry St., 53105, pg. 1571 **PB**
LAVELLE INDUSTRIES INC., 665 McHenry St., 53105, pg. 653 **PV**
M & I Bank of Burlington, 200 S. Pine St., 53105, pg. 1050 **PB**
Nestle Chocolate & Confections Company, 637 S. Pine St., 53105, pg. 917 **IT**

Butler

APITECH, 1300 W. Silver Spring Dr., 53001, pg. 124 **PB**
APPLIED POWER INC., 13000 W. Silver Spring Dr., 53007-0325, pg. 124 **PV**
Enerpac U.S., 13000 W. Silver Spring Dr., 53007, pg. 124 **PB**
INLAND DETROIT DIESEL ALLISON CO., 13015 W. Custer Ave., 53007-0916, pg. 564 **PV**
Power-Packer U.S., 1300 W. Silver Spring Dr., 53001, pg. 124 **PB**

Caledonia

Metro Milwaukee Auto Auction, 561 S. Hwy. 41, 53108, pg. 282 **PV**

Cambria

Dean Foods Vegetable Company, P.O. Box 237, 53923, pg. 490 **PB**

Cashton

Motorola Radius, P.O. Box 203, 54619-0203, pg. 1138 **PB**

Cecil

Frontier Communications-Lakeshore, Inc., 111 E. Freeborn St., 54111, pg. 683 **PB**

Cedar Grove

Dean Foods Vegetable Company, 307 S. Commerce, 53013, pg. 490 **PB**

Cedarburg

Amcast Automotive-Cedarburg Plant, N39 W5789 Hamilton Rd., 53012, pg. 63 **PB**
M & I Mortgage Corp., W. 57 N14280 Doerr Way, 53012-3103, pg. 1051 **PB**
Marigold Foods, Inc., W. 55 N. 155 McKinley Blvd., 53012, pg. 752 **IT**
Wabash Pioneer Container Division, N143 W6049 Pioneer Rd., 53012-0045, pg. 1170 **PV**

Chilton

M-B COMPANIES INC. OF WISCONSIN, 1200 So. Park St., 53014, pg. 684 **PV**

Chippewa Falls

Duncan Creek Inc., 1251 First Ave., 54729, pg. 712 **PV**
Hubbard Scientific, 1120 Halbleib Rd., 54729, pg. 71 **PB**
Jacob Leinenkugel Brewing Co., P.O. Box 368, One Jefferson Ave., 54729-0368, pg. 1289 **PB**
B.A. Mason, 1313 First Ave., 54729, pg. 712 **PV**
MASON SHOE MFG. CO., 1251 First Ave., 54729, pg. 712 **PV**
SPECTRUM INDUSTRIES, INC., 1600 Johnson St., 54729, pg. 1024 **PV**
Wissota Trader Ltd., 1313 First Ave., 54729, pg. 712 **PV**

Clear Lake

Land O'Lakes Dairy Foods, 600 1st Ave. W., 54005, pg. 646 **PV**

Clintonville

FWD/SEAGRAVE FIRE APPARATUS, INC., 105 E. 12th St., 54929, pg. 390 **PV**
Frontier Communications of Wisconsin, Inc., 26 W. 12th St., 54929, pg. 584 **PB**

Columbus

Rhodes International, Hwy. 16 W., P.O. Box 410, 53925, pg. 927 **PV**

Combined Locks

Appleton Papers-Locks Mills, 531 Prospect, 54113, pg. 567 **IT**

Cross Plains

ZANDER'S CREAMERY INC., 1300 Main St., 53528, pg. 1203 **PV**

Cudahy

CRANE MANUFACTURING, 6000 S. Buckhorn Ave., 53110, pg. 286 **PV**
Patrick Cudahy Inc., 3500 E. Barnard, 53110, pg. 1479 **PB**
Kintetsu World Express Inc., 6212 Ace Industrial Dr., 53110, pg. 734 **IT**
Lucas-Milhaupt, Inc., 5656 S. Pennsylvania Ave., 53110, pg. 780 **PB**
Milwaukee Cylinder Division, 5877 S. Pennsylvania Ave., 53110, pg. 124 **PB**
Northern Engineering Corp., P.O. Box 410, 6000 Buckhorn Ave., 53110, pg. 286 **PV**
Union-Transport Corporation-Milwaukee Office, 2100 B E. College Ave., 53110, pg. 1120 **PV**
VILTER MANUFACTURING CORPORATION, 5555 S. Packard Ave., 53110, pg. 1140 **PV**

Curtiss

Abbyland Pork Rack, 539 N. Meridan St., 54422, pg. 10 **PV**

Dale

A & N Leasing, Box 170, 54931, pg. 986 **PV**
SERVICE MOTOR COMPANY, W. 9614 Hwy. 10, 54931, pg. 986 **PV**

Dane

Menasha Corp., Traex Division, 101 Traex Plaza., 53529, pg. 731 **PV**

Darien

Dean Foods Vegetable Company, P.O. Box 398, 53114, pg. 490 **PB**

Darlington

Colman Motor Products, Inc., 1 Colman Lane, 53530, pg. 1242 **IT**

De Forest

ABS GLOBAL INC., P.O. Box 459, 6908 River Rd., 53532, pg. 3 **PV**

De Pere

Associated Mortgage, Inc., 301 N. Broadway, 54115, pg. 140 **PB**
MEGTEC, P.O. Box 5030, 54115, pg. 1459 **PB**
Nicolet Division, 200 Main Ave., 54115, pg. 903 **PB**
Nicolet Paper Company, 200 Main Ave., 54115, pg. 903 **PB**
Richco Structures, Red Maple Rd., pg. 929 **PV**
SASIB Packaging North America Inc.-Wrapper Division, 1416 Fortune Ave., 54115, pg. 1194 **IT**
Shade/Allied, Inc., 700 Heritage Rd., 54115, pg. 89 **PB**
SIERRA COATING TECHNOLOGIES, 1820 Enterprise Dr., 54115, pg. 998 **PV**

Deerfield

LSJ Sportswear Inc., P.O. Box 528, 54 Golf Car Rd., 53531, pg. 732 **PV**
Wisconsin Fineblanking, P.O. Box 468, One Grand Ave., 53531, pg. 737 **IT**

Delavan

Ajay Leisure Products, Inc., 1501 E. Wisconsin St., 53115, pg. 34 **PB**
AJAY SPORTS INC., 1501 E. Wisconsin St., 53115, pg. 34 **PB**
Andes Candies Inc., 1400 E. Wisconsin St., 53115, pg. 163 **PV**
M & I Bank of Delavan, 104 N. Fifth St., 53115, pg. 1050 **PB**
Sta-Rite Foreign Sales Corporation, 175 Wright St., 53115, pg. 1767 **PB**
Sta-Rite Industries, Inc., 293 S. Wright St., 53115, pg. 1767 **PB**
Sta-Rite Water Systems, 293 S. Wright St., 53115, pg. 1767 **PB**
Water Systems Group, 293 S. Wright St., 53115, pg. 1767 **PB**
Waukesha Cherry-Burrell, 611 Sugar Creek Rd., 53115, pg. 1677 **PB**

Dodgeville

LANDS' END, INC., Lands' End Ln., 53595, pg. 977 **PB**

Eagle River

M & I Bank of Eagle River, First & Wall Sts., 54521-1089, pg. 1050 **PB**

East Troy

Buell Motorcycle Company, 2286 Church St., Unit C, 53120, pg. 786 **PB**

PB - *U.S. Public Companies Volume*
PV - *U.S. Private Companies Volume*
IT - *International Public & Private Companies Volume*

1478

Geographic Index-U.S.

Moxness Products East Troy Division, 2030 Young St., 53120, pg. 124 **PB**

Eau Claire

Hutchinson Technology, Inc., Eau Claire, 2435 Alpine Rd., 54703, pg. 851 **PB**
M & I Community State Bank, 301 Water St., 54703, pg. 1050 **PB**
MENARDS, INC., 4777 Menard Dr., 54703, pg. 731 **PV**
National Defense Corp., 3925 N. Hastings Way, 54703, pg. 1159 **PB**
NATIONAL PRESTO INDUSTRIES, INC., 3925 N. Hastings Way, 54703-3703, pg. 1159 **PB**
Northwest Fabrics & Crafts, 2520 Mall Dr., 54701, pg. 779 **PV**
PDM Bridge, PDM Bridge Headquarters, 2800 Melby St., 54703, pg. 1305 **PB**
Piper Jaffray Inc., 3408 Oakwood Mall Dr., 54701-7672, pg. 1301 **PB**
River City Refuse Removal, Inc., 1102 Menomonie St., 54701, pg. 264 **PB**
WRR Environmental Services Co., Inc., 5200 State Rd. 93, 54701-9808, pg. 1792 **PB**

Elkhorn

Frank Holton Co., 320 N. Church St., 53121, pg. 657 **PV**
Intertractor America Corporation, 960 Proctor Dr., 53121, pg. 1511 **IT**
Leblanc Case Co., 320 1/2 N. Church St., 53121, pg. 657 **PV**

Elm Grove

A. Bradley Presence Sensing, P.O. Box 804, 53122-0804, pg. 1397 **PB**

Fennimore

RAYOVAC Corporation, P.O. Box 128, 100 Rayovac Ct., 53809, pg. 912 **PV**

Fond Du Lac

J.F. AHERN CO., 855 Morris St., 54935, pg. 27 **PV**
Automation Control, 660 S. Military Rd., 54936-1658, pg. 1389 **IT**
Giddings & Lewis Automation Technology, 142 Doty St., 54935, pg. 1389 **IT**
Giddings & Lewis, Inc., 142 Doty St., 54935, pg. 1389 **IT**
Mercury Marine, 6250 W. Pioneer Rd., 54935, pg. 265 **PB**
Service Motor Co., N 5560, Hwy. 151, 54937, pg. 986 **PV**
STEENBERG HOMES, INC., 300 Rolling Meadows Dr., 54937-1257, pg. 1039 **PV**
Waterford Foods Inc., 325 Tompkins St., 54935, pg. 102 **IT**
Wells Mfg. Corp., 26 S. Brooke St., 54935-4007, pg. 1113 **PV**

Fort Atkinson

J-STAR INDUSTRIES, INC., 801 Janesville Ave., 53538, pg. 576 **PV**
JONES DAIRY FARM, Jones Ave., 53538, pg. 596 **PV**
Moore's Food Service Products, 801 Rockwell St., 53538, pg. 805 **PB**
Nasco, 901 Janesville Ave., 53538, pg. 446 **PV**
Nasco International, Inc., 901 Janesville Ave., 53538-0901, pg. 446 **PV**
Redi-Serve Foods, 1200 Industrial Dr., 53538, pg. 817 **PV**

Franksville

Thomas A. Edison Technical Center, 11131 Adams Rd., 53126, pg. 443 **PB**

Germantown

THE F. DOHMEN COMPANY, W 194 N 11381 McCormick Dr., 53022, pg. 338 **PV**
INDEPENDENT METALS, N115 W18945 Edison Dr., 53022-0247, pg. 559 **PV**
Milwaukee Seasonings, Inc., N114 W18937 Clinton Dr., P.O. Box 339, 53022, pg. 224 **PB**
Recreational Products Div., N. 117 W. 18456 Fulton Dr., 53022, pg. 205 **PB**
SCM, W. 168 N. 11318 Western Ave., 53022-3242, pg. 594 **IT**
Smith & Nephew Rehabilitation Inc., N105W13400 Donges Bay Rd., 53022, pg. 1263 **IT**
DAVID WHITE, L.L.C., W. 209 N. 11845 Insurance Pl., 53022, pg. 1765 **PB**
DAVID WHITE, L.L.C., W. 209 N. 11845 Insurance Pl., 53022, pg. 1765 **PV**

Grafton

Engine and Gear Service Division, 900 North St., 53024, pg. 1565 **PB**
Tecumseh Products Co. Engine & Transmission Group, 900 North St., 53024, pg. 1566 **PB**

Grantsburg

MCNALLY INDUSTRIES, INC., 216 S. Pine St., 54840, pg. 724 **PV**

Green Bay

American Foods Group, 544 Acme St., 54302, pg. 54 **PV**
AMERICAN FOODS GROUP, INC., 544 Acme St., 54302, pg. 54 **PV**
American Medical Security Holdings, Inc., 3100 AMS Blvd., 54313, pg. 1692 **PB**
ASSOCIATED BANC-CORP, 112 N. Adams St., 54307, pg. 140 **PB**
Associated Bank Green Bay, 200 N. Adams, P.O. Box 19006, 54307-9006, pg. 141 **PB**
Associated Commercial Mortgage, Inc., 2001 S. Webster Ave., 54305-1073, pg. 140 **PB**
Associated Investment Services, Inc., 230 Cherry St., 54301, pg. 140 **PB**
BAY INDUSTRIES INC., 2929 Walker Dr., 54311, pg. 124 **PV**
Bay Insulation, 1330 Elizabeth St., 54302, pg. 124 **PV**
Dakota Pork Industries, 544 Acme St., 54302, pg. 54 **PV**
Dean Foods Vegetable Company, 520 N. Broadway, 54303, pg. 490 **PV**
Dean Pickle & Specialty Products Co., 857-897 School Pl., 54307, pg. 490 **PV**
Employers Health Insurance Company, 1100 Employers Blvd., 54344, pg. 847 **PB**
Erving Paper Products, Inc., 2954 Gross St., 54307-3006, pg. 382 **PV**
FIRST NORTHERN CAPITAL CORP., 201 N. Monroe Ave., 54301, pg. 636 **PB**
GenCorp Specialty Product Div., 1701 Cornell Rd., 54313, pg. 706 **PB**
Good Humor/Breyers Ice Cream, 909 Packerland Dr., 54303, pg. 1435 **IT**
Green Bay Dressed Beef Company, 544 Acme St., 54302, pg. 54 **PV**
GREEN BAY PACKAGING INC., 1700 N. Webster Ct., 54302, pg. 476 **PV**
Green Bay Press-Gazette, P.O. Box 19430, 54307, pg. 700 **PB**
Hewlett-Packard Company, 1400 Lombardi Ave., Ste. 105, 54304, pg. 815 **PB**
IMPERIAL, INC., 789 Packer Dr., 54304, pg. 558 **PV**
Intertape Polymer Group, 2612 S. Broadway, 54304, pg. 685 **IT**
Iowa Pork Industries, Inc., 544 Acme St., 54302, pg. 54 **PV**
Label Products & Design Division, 1836 Sal St., 54308, pg. 602 **PV**
M & I Bank Northeast, 310 W. Walnut St., 54306, pg. 1050 **PB**
Moore Response Graphics, P.O. Box 19050, 54307-9050, pg. 890 **IT**
Norwest Bank Wisconsin Green Bay N.A., 908 S. Fisk St., P.O. Box 19600, 54307-9600, pg. 1203 **PB**
PACKERLAND PACKING CO., 2580 University Ave., P.O. Box 23000, 54305, pg. 833 **PV**
Piper Jaffray Inc., 2301 Riverside Dr., 54301-1996, pg. 1301 **PB**
Schneider Communications, 3061 S. Ridge Rd., 54306, pg. 684 **PB**
SCHNEIDER NATIONAL, INC., 3101 S. Packerland Dr., 54304, pg. 971 **PV**
SCHREIBER FOODS, INC., 425 Pine St., 54301-5179, pg. 972 **PV**
SHOPKO STORES, INC., P.O. Box 19060, 54307-9060, pg. 1467 **PB**
STELLA FOODS, INC., 1088 Springhurst Dr., 54304, pg. 1040 **PV**
SuperValu, Inc.-Great Lakes Div.-Green Bay, 451 Joannes Ave., 54304, pg. 1540 **PB**
WFRV-TV, 1181 E. Mason, 54301, pg. 275 **PB**
WLUK-TV, 787 Lombardi Ave., 54304, pg. 1685 **PB**
WPS Energy Services, Inc., 677 Baeten Rd., 54304, pg. 1728 **PB**
WPS Leasing, Inc., 700 N. Adams St., 54301, pg. 1728 **PB**
WPS Power Development, Inc., 677 Baeten Rd., 54304, pg. 1728 **PB**
WPS RESOURCES CORP., 700 N. Adams St., 54301, pg. 1728 **PB**
Wisconsin Protective Coatings Corp., 614 Elizabeth St., 54302, pg. 1358 **PB**
Wisconsin Public Service Corporation, 700 N. Adams St., 54301, pg. 1728 **PB**

Greenfield

EVERBRITE, INC., 4949 S. 110th St., 53228, pg. 386 **PV**

Hales Corners

The Equitable Bank, 5225 S. 108th St., 53130, pg. 380 **PV**

Hartford

Aubrey Manufacturing Company, P.O. Box 140, 53027, pg. 1193 **PB**
Broan Mfg. Co., Inc., 926 W. State St., 53027, pg. 1193 **PB**
Hartford Care Center, 1202 E. Sumner St., 53027, pg. 840 **PB**

Hartland

Camtronics Ltd., 900 Walnut Ridge Dr., 53029, pg. 109 **PB**
DORNER MANUFACTURING CORP., 580 Industrial Dr., 53029, pg. 340 **PV**
M & I Lake Country Bank, 112 E. Capitol Dr., 53029, pg. 1050 **PB**

Pharmacia & Upjohn, 31812 W. Hwy. K, 53029, pg. 1048 **IT**

Haven

Richco Structures, Hwy. FF, 53083, pg. 929 **PV**

Hawkins

Century Telephone Co. of Northern Wisconsin, 425 Ellingson Ave., 54530, pg. 330 **PB**

Hilbert

Sargento Foods Inc., P.O. Box 289, 460 Eighth St., 54129, pg. 966 **PV**
THIEL CHEESE CO., N. 7630 County Rd. BB, 54129, pg. 1081 **PV**

Horicon

John Deere Horicon Works, 400 N. Vine St., 53032-1291, pg. 492 **PB**
Steel Service Systems Inc., 301 Industrial Dr., 53032, pg. 1101 **PB**

Hortonville

Fox Valley Steel & Wire Co., P.O. Box 130, 111 N. Douglas St., 54944, pg. 956 **PB**

Hudson

Duro Paper Bag Mfg. Co., P.O. Box 247, 54016, pg. 349 **PB**
ERICKSON OIL PRODUCTS, INC., 1231 Industrial St., 54016, pg. 381 **PV**
ERICKSON'S DIVERSIFIED CORP., 700 First St., 54016, pg. 381 **PV**
Freedom Valu Centers, Inc., 1231 Industrial St., 54016, pg. 381 **PV**

Hustisford

Wagner Casters and Wheels, 331 Riverview Dr., 53034, pg. 1146 **PV**

Iola

KRAUSE PUBLICATIONS, INC., 700 E. State St., 54990, pg. 635 **PV**
Scandinavia Telephone Co., Box 317, 155 Main St., 54945, pg. 1571 **PB**

Ixonia

NRV, Inc., P.O. Box 347, N8155 American St., 53036, pg. 47 **PV**

Jackson

Sysco Food Services of Eastern Wisconsin, One Sysco Dr., 53037, pg. 1551 **PB**
WISCONSIN PHARMACAL CO., INC., One Repel Rd., 53037, pg. 1185 **PV**

Janesville

Accudyne Corporation, 340 N. Franklin St., P.O. Box 1429, 53545, pg. 47 **PB**
Akzo Chemicals Inc., 114 E. Conde St., 53546, pg. 47 **IT**
Allied International-American Eagle Trading Corp., P.O. Box 997, 3533 Bell St., 53547, pg. 694 **IT**
Gilman, 305 W. Delavan Dr., 53547-1367, pg. 1389 **IT**
Lab Safety Supply Inc., 401 S. Wright Rd., 53546-8729, pg. 758 **PB**
M & I Bank of Janesville, 100 N. Main St., 53547-5000, pg. 1050 **PB**
Oleochemicals & Derivatives Group, 2001 Afton Rd., 53545, pg. 1774 **PB**
SWING-N-SLIDE CORP., 1212 Barberry Dr., 53545, pg. 1543 **PB**
Wisconsin & Southern Railroad Company, 203 S. Pearl St., 53545-4521, pg. 1184 **PV**

Johnson Creek

Ransomes Inc., P.O. Box 469, One Bobcat Ln., 53038, pg. 1088 **IT**

Kaukauna

Thermo Electron Wisconsin, Inc., 820 Hyland Ave., 54130, pg. 1593 **PB**

Kenosha

Alfa Laval Inc., P.O. Box 840, 9201 Wilmot Rd., 53141-0840, pg. 1378 **IT**
Alfa Laval Pumps Inc., 9201 Wilmot Rd., 53141, pg. 1378 **IT**
DAIRYLAND GREYHOUND PARK, INC., 5522 104th Ave., 53144, pg. 307 **PV**
Dairyland Marketing Services, Inc., 5522 104th Ave., 53144, pg. 307 **PV**

PB - *U.S. Public Companies Volume*
PV - *U.S. Private Companies Volume*
IT - *International Public & Private Companies Volume*

Eaton Corporation, Electric Drives Division, 3122 14th Ave., 53141, pg. 556   PB
G&H Products Corp., 7600 57th Ave., 53141, pg. 1378   IT
JOCKEY INTERNATIONAL, INC., 2300 60th St., 53140, pg. 588   PV
LAWTER INTERNATIONAL, INC., One Terra Way, 8601 95th St., 53142-7716, pg. 980   PB
G. LEBLANC CORPORATION, P.O. Box 1415, 7001 Leblanc Blvd., 53141-1415, pg. 656   PV
MGI Pumps, Inc., 9201 Wilmot Rd., 53141-1426, pg. 1378   IT
Macwhyte Co., 2906 14th Ave., 53141, pg. 68   PV
Martin Band Instrument Co., 9009 Sheridan Rd, 53143, pg. 657   PV
Ocean Spray Cranberries-Kenosha Plant, 7800 S. 60th Ave., 53142-4009, pg. 811   PB
Outokumpu Copper Kenosha, Inc., 1420 63rd St., 53143, pg. 1017   IT
Snap-on Diagnostics, 2801 80th St., 53141-1410, pg. 1480   PB
Snap-on Financial Services, 2801 80th St., 53141-1410, pg. 1481   PB
Snap-on Industrial, 2801 80th St., 53141-1410, pg. 1481   PB
Snap-on Tools, 2801 80th St., 53141-1410, pg. 1481   PB
SNAP-ON TOOLS CORPORATION, 2801 80th St., 53141-1410, pg. 1480   PB
Snap-on Tools International, Ltd., 2801 80th St., 53141, pg. 1481   PB
Tri-Clover Inc., 9201 Wilmot Rd., 53141, pg. 1379   IT
Vista International Packaging Inc., 1126 88th Place, 53140, pg. 840   PB

Kewaskum

REGAL WARE, INC., 1675 Reigle Dr., 53040, pg. 917   PV

Kewaunee

Kewaunee Engineering Corp., 520 N. Main St., 52416, pg. 703   PV
Vollrath-Kewaunee Plant, 23 Kilbourn St., 54216-0336, pg. 1143   PV

Kiel

Land O'Lakes, Inc., 1125 Eighth St., 53042-4804, pg. 646   PV

Kimberly

InterLake Papers, Inc., 433 N. Main St., 54136, pg. 436   PB

Kohler

JOHNSONVILLE FOODS, INC., 950 Woodlake Rd., 53044, pg. 595   PV
KOHLER COMPANY, 444 Highland Dr., 53044, pg. 630   PV

La Crosse

AlliedSignal Laminate Systems, P.O. Box 1448, 230 N. Front St., 54602-1448, pg. 51   PB
American Down & Textile Company, 455 Park Pl., 54601, pg. 782   PB
Century Area Long Lines Inc., 206 Fifth Ave., 54601, pg. 330   PB
Century Telephone, Region III, 1905 Ward Ave., 54601, pg. 329   PB
Company Store Holdings, Inc., 455 Park Plaza, 54601, pg. 782   PB
CONSOLIDATED MIDWEST, INC., 3600 Hwy. 157, 54603, pg. 265   PV
Culligan, 729 La Crosse St., 54601-3349, pg. 467   PV
DAIRYLAND POWER COOPERATIVE, 3200 East Ave. S., 54601-0817, pg. 307   PV
Everbrite LaCrosse, 3145 Airport Rd., 54601, pg. 386   PV
FIRST FEDERAL CAPITAL CORP., 605 State St., 54601, pg. 632   PB
First Federal Savings Bank La Crosse-Madison, 605 State St., 54601, pg. 632   PB
Great Lakes Cheese of La Crosse Wisconsin, Inc., 2220 Enterprise, 54601, pg. 474   PV
INLAND PRINTING CO., 2009 W. Ave. S., 54601, pg. 564   PV
KWIK TRIP INC., 1626 Oak St., 54603, pg. 637   PV
La Crosse Tribune, 401 N. Third St., 54601, pg. 983   PB
M & I Bank of LaCrosse, 3500 U.S. Hwy. 16, 54601, pg. 1050   PB
Metz Baking Company (WI), 334 Fifth Ave. S., 54601, pg. 1022   PV
Midwest Bottle Gas Company, 3600 Hwy. 157, 54602, pg. 266   PV
Norwest Bank La Crosse, N.A., P.O. Box 1688, 54601-3200, pg. 1202   PV
Piper Jaffray Inc., First Bank Pl., 201 Main St., Ste. 500, 54601-3283, pg. 1302   PB
W.A. ROOSEVELT CO., 2727 Commerce St., 54601, pg. 943   PV
Scandia Down Shops Limited, 455 Park Plaza, 54601, pg. 782   PV
The Trane Company North American Commercial Group, 3600 Pammel Creek Rd., 54601-7599, pg. 92   PB

Lake Geneva

Citizens National Bank of Lake Geneva, P.O. Box 432, 401 Broad St., 53147, pg. 643   PB
O.G. Hoyer Inc., 201 Broad St., 53147, pg. 1378   IT
Albert Trostel Packings Ltd., 901 Maxwell St., 53147, pg. 1105   PV
Willis Corroon Administrative Services Corporation, 846 Main St., Ste. 202, 53147, pg. 1505   IT

Lake Mills

APV Gaulin, 100 CP Ave., 53551, pg. 1241   IT
Engineering & Manufacturing Div., 100 S. CP Ave., 53551, pg. 1240   IT
Hamlin, Inc., 612 E. Lake St., 53551, pg. 251   PB

Lena

Frigo Cheese Corp., P.O. Box 19024, 54307-9024, pg. 1040   PV

Little Chute

BEL/KAUKAUNA USA, 1500 E. North Ave., 54140, pg. 130   PV

Lodi

DEC Alkar Div., 105 Spring St., 53555, pg. 301   PV

Madison

American Energy Management, P.O. Box 1231, 53701, pg. 1033   PB
American Family Brokerage, Inc., 6000 American Pkwy., 53783, pg. 53   PV
American Family Financial Services, Inc., 6000 American Pkwy., 53783, pg. 53   PV
American Family Insurance Company, 6000 American Pky., 53783-0001, pg. 53   PV
American Family Life Insurance Co., 6000 American Pkwy., 53783-0001, pg. 53   PV
AMERICAN FAMILY MUTUAL INSURANCE CO., 6000 American Pkwy., 53783-0001, pg. 53   PV
American Family Mutual Insurance Co., 6000 American Pkwy., 53783, pg. 53   PV
American Standard Insurance Company of Ohio, 6000 American Pky., 53783-0001, pg. 53   PV
American Standard Insurance Company of Wisconsin, 6000 American Pkwy., 53783, pg. 53   PV
AMERICAN TV & APPLIANCE OF MADISON, INC., 2404 W. Beltline Hwy., 53713, pg. 64   PV
Association of Credit Union League Executives, P.O. Box 431, 53701-0431, pg. 288   PV
AUTO GLASS SPECIALISTS, 1200 John Q. Hammonds Dr., 53717, pg. 100   PV
Belmont Telephone Company, 2801 International Lane, 53740, pg. 1022   PB
Berg Co., 1911 S. Stoughton Rd., 53716, pg. 301   PB
Bou-Matic, 1919 S. Stoughton Rd., 53716, pg. 301   PV
Browning-Ferris Industries of Wisconsin, Inc., 3083 Highway MM, 53711, pg. 264   PB
CMG Mortgage Insurance Company, 5910 Mineral Point Rd., 53705, pg. 296   PV
Capitol Facilities Corp., 4610 University Ave., Ste. 1400, 53705, pg. 302   PV
CAPITOL INDEMNITY CORPORATION, 4610 University Ave., Ste. 1400, 53705-0900, pg. 302   PV
Capitol Indemnity Corporation, 4610 University Ave., 53705, pg. 302   PV
Capitol Specialty Insurance Corporation, 4610 University Ave., 53705, pg. 302   PV
Central Wisconsin Development Corporation, P.O. Box 1231, 53701, pg. 1033   PB
Chicago Consolidated, 1849 Wright St., 53704, pg. 533   PB
Colonial Manor Nursing & Convalescent Hospital, 110 Belmont Rd., 53714, pg. 1712   PV
Country Kitchen International, Inc., P.O. Box 44434, 53744, pg. 624   PV
Covance Laboratories, 3301 Kinsman Blvd., 53704, pg. 454   PB
Credit Union Benefits Services, Inc., 5710 Mineral Point Road, 53705, pg. 288   PV
Credit Union Foundation, P.O. Box 431, 53701-0431, pg. 288   PV
CREDIT UNION NATIONAL ASSOCIATION, 5710 Mineral Point Rd., 53701-0431, pg. 288   PV
Cuba City Telephone Exchange Co., 2801 International Lane, 53740, pg. 1022   PB
CUMIS Insurance Society, Inc., P.O. Box 391, 53701-0391, pg. 296   PV
CUNA Mortgage Corporation, P.O. Box 1332, 53701-1332, pg. 296   PV
CUNA Mutual Insurance Agency, Inc., P.O. Box 391, 53701-0391, pg. 296   PV
CUNA MUTUAL INSURANCE SOCIETY, 5910 Mineral Point Rd., 53705, pg. 296   PV
CUNA Mutual Investment Corporation, P.O. Box 391, 53701-0391, pg. 296   PV
CUNA Service Group, Inc., 5710 Mineral Point Rd., 53705, pg. 288   PV
DEC INTERNATIONAL, INC., 1919 S. Stoughton Rd., 53716, pg. 301   PV
Deere Credit Services, Inc., 8402 Excelsior Drive, 53717, pg. 492   PB
DEMCO INC., 4810 Forest Run Rd., 53704, pg. 323   PV

ENSERV, Inc., P.O. Box 192, 222 W. Washington Ave., 53703, pg. 1728   PB
MARSHALL ERDMAN AND ASSOCIATES, INC., 5117 University Ave., 53705, pg. 380   PV
Famous Footwear, 7010 Mineral Point Rd., 53713-1701, pg. 262   PB
Farm Plan Corporation, 8402 Excelsior Dr., 53717, pg. 492   PB
Filene Research Institute, 5910 Mineral Point Rd., 53705, pg. 288   PV
J.H. FINDORFF & SON, INC., 601 W. Wilson St., 53703, pg. 405   PV
First Wisconsin Asset Management, Inc., One S. Pinckney St., 53703, pg. 643   PB
Fiskars Inc., 636 Science Dr., 53711, pg. 492   IT
Fiskars Inc.-Special Markets, 636 Science Dr., 53711, pg. 492   IT
Flambeau Micro Co., 3696 Burke Rd., 53704, pg. 409   PV
Great Lakes Energy Corp., P.O. Box 1231, 53701, pg. 1033   PB
Heartland Development Corporation, 222 W. Washington Ave., 53703, pg. 1728   PB
Heartland Energy Group, Inc., 222 W. Washington Ave., 53703, pg. 1728   PB
Heartland Energy Services, Inc., 222 W. Washington Ave., 53703, pg. 1728   PB
Heartland Properties, Inc., 222 W. Washington Ave., 53701-2115, pg. 1728   PB
Heurikon Corporation, 8310 Excelsior Dr., 53717, pg. 422   PB
Integrated Communications Services, Inc., 333 W. Mifflin St., Ste. Two, 53703, pg. 1570   PB
KITCHEN INVESTMENT GROUP, 6410 Enterprise Lane, 53719, pg. 624   PV
M & I Madison Bank, One W. Main St., 53703, pg. 1050   PB
MADISON DAIRY PRODUCE COMPANY, 1002 E. Washington Ave., 53703, pg. 694   PV
MADISON GAS AND ELECTRIC COMPANY, 133 S. Blair St., 53701, pg. 1032   PB
Madison Newspapers, Inc., 1901 Fish Hatchery, 53713, pg. 984   PB
MAGAEL, Inc., P.O. Box 1231, 53701, pg. 1033   PB
MAUTZ PAINT CO., 939 E. Washington Ave., 53703, pg. 704   PV
Metz Baking Company - Gardner Div., 3401 E. Washington Ave., 53704, pg. 1022   PV
Midvale Plaza, P.O. Box 8685, 53708-8685, pg. 784   PV
NGL Financial Services Inc., Two E. Gillman St., 53703-1194, pg. 784   PV
NGL Holdings Inc., Two E. Gilman St., 53703-1494, pg. 784   PV
NGL Investment Services Inc., Two E. Gilman St., 53703-1491, pg. 784   PV
NATIONAL GUARDIAN LIFE INSURANCE COMPANY, Two E. Gilman St., 53703-1494, pg. 784   PV
Nicolet Analytical, 5225 Verona Rd., 53711, pg. 1593   PB
Nicolet Test & Measurement Division, 5225 Verona Rd., 53711, pg. 1593   PB
Northern Capital Management, Inc., 8018 Excelsior Dr., Ste. 300, 53717, pg. 1673   PB
L.L. OLDS SEED COMPANY, 2901 Packers Ave., 53704, pg. 814   PV
Oscar Mayer Foods Corp., P.O. Box 7188, 53707, pg. 1288   PB
PERSOFT, INC., P.O. Box 44953, 465 Science Dr., 53744-4953, pg. 856   PV
Piper Jaffray Inc., 406 Science Dr., Ste. 110, 53711-1069, pg. 1301   PB
RMT, Inc., 744 Heartland Trail, 53717, pg. 1728   PB
RAYOVAC CORPORATION, 601 Rayovac Dr., 53711-2497, pg. 912   PV
RAYOVAC Corporation, 2317 Winnebago St., 53704, pg. 912   PV
REAC, Inc., P.O. Box 192, 222 W. Washington Ave., 53703, pg. 1728   PB
RESEARCH PRODUCTS CORPORATION, 1015 E. Washington Ave., 53703, pg. 924   PV
Sani-Matic Systems, 1915 S. Stoughton Rd., 53708, pg. 301   PV
SCHOEP'S ICE CREAM, INC., 514 Division St., 53704, pg. 972   PV
Sterling Plastics Co., 2514 Fish Hatchery Rd., 53713-2407, pg. 1178   PV
SUB-ZERO FREEZER CO., INC., 4717 Hammersley Rd., 53711, pg. 1048   PV
TDS Computing Services, Inc., 301 S. Westfield Rd., 53705, pg. 1572   PV
TDS Telecommunications Corporation, P.O. Box 5158, 301 S. Westfield Rd., 53705, pg. 1570   PB
Tektronix NewStar, Inc., 6400 Enterprise Ln., 53719, pg. 1567   PB
UNIVERSITY BOOK STORE, 711 State St., 53703, pg. 1127   PV
WPL HOLDINGS, INC., 222 W. Washington Ave., 53703, pg. 1727   PB
Warman International Ltd., 2701 S. Stoughton Rd., 53716-3315, pg. 967   IT
Wisconsin Power & Light Company, 222 W. Washington Ave., 53703, pg. 1728   PB
Wisconsin River Power Co., 222 W. Washington Ave., 53703, pg. 1728   PB
Wisconsin State Journal, 1901 Fish Hatchery Rd., 53708, pg. 984   PB
World Council of Credit Unions, 5810 Mineral Point Rd., 53705, pg. 288   PV

Manitowoc

HERESITE PROTECTIVE COATINGS INC., P.O. Box 250, 822 S. 14th St., 54221-0250, pg. 523   PV

PB - *U.S. Public Companies Volume*
PV - *U.S. Private Companies Volume*
IT - *International Public & Private Companies Volume*

1480

INVINCIBLE OFFICE FURNITURE, 842 S. 26th St., 54220, pg. 575　**PV**
LAKESIDE FOODS, INC., PO Box 1327, 508 Jay St., 54221-1327, pg. 643　**PV**
THE MANITOWOC COMPANY, INC., 500 S. 16th St., 54220, pg. 1040　**PB**
Manitowoc Engineering Co., 2401 S. 30th St., 54220, pg. 1041　**PB**
Manitowoc Ice, Inc., 2110 S. 26th St., 54221, pg. 1041　**PB**
Mirro Company, 1512 Washington St., 54221, pg. 1177　**PB**
NORTHERN LABS, INC., 4701 Custer St., 54220, pg. 805　**PV**

Marathon

MARATHON CHEESE CORP., 304 East St., 54448, pg. 701　**PV**

Marinette

Ansul Fire Protection, One Stanton St., 54143, pg. 1650　**PB**
Ansul Incorporated, One Stanton St., 54143, pg. 1648　**PB**
MARINETTE MARINE CORPORATION, 1600 Ely St., 54143-0198, pg. 703　**PB**
SpecialtyChem Products Corporation, Two Stanton St., 54143, pg. 173　**IT**

Marshfield

Figi's, Inc., 3200 S. Maple Ave., 54449, pg. 623　**PB**
Graham Manufacturing Co., 1920 E. 26th St., 54449, pg. 18　**IT**
Hub City Foods, 1700 S. Alemie, 54449, pg. 653　**PB**
M & I Central Bank & Trust, 101 W. Fourth St., 54449, pg. 1050　**PB**
MARSHFIELD CLINIC, 1000 N. Oak Ave., 54449, pg. 708　**PV**
Wick Bldg. Systems Inc. Manufactured Homes Div., 2301 E. 4th St., 54449, pg. 1174　**PV**

Mauston

DUMORE CORPORATION, 1030 Veteran St., 53948, pg. 346　**PV**

Mayville

M & I Bank of Mayville, 209 Horicon St., 53050, pg. 1050　**PB**
MAYVILLE ENGINEERING CO., INC., 715 South St., 53050, pg. 718　**PV**
Mayville Metal Products Division, First & Highland, P.O. Box 28, 53050, pg. 264　**PV**

Mazomanie

Roundy's General Merchandise Division, 400 Walter Rd., 53560, pg. 948　**PV**
Wick Building Division, P.O. Box 38, 405 Walter Rd., 53560, pg. 1174　**PV**
WICK BUILDING SYSTEMS, 404 Walter Rd., 53560, pg. 1174　**PV**
Wicks Homes Division, P.O. Box 188, 400 Walter Rd., 53560, pg. 1174　**PV**

Medford

Hurd Millwork Company, Inc., 575 S. Whelen Ave., 54451, pg. 1113　**PV**

Menasha

Akrosil, 206 Garfield Ave., 54952, pg. 903　**PB**
Akrosil Division, P.O. Box 8001, 206 Garfield St., 54952, pg. 901　**PB**
Albany International Appleton Wire Div., 435 Sixth St., 54952, pg. 36　**PB**
Banta Book Group, P.O. Box 60, Curtis Reed Plaza, 54952-0060, pg. 188　**PB**
BANTA CORPORATION, 225 Main St., 54952, pg. 187　**PB**
Banta Digital Group, 1457 Earl St., 54952-0390, pg. 188　**PB**
Banta Packaging & Fulfillment, 675 Brighton Beach Rd., 54952-0060, pg. 188　**PB**
Central Products Company, Inc., 748 Fourth St., 54952, pg. 1022　**PB**
Gilbert Paper, 430 Ahnaip St., 54952, pg. 1074　**PB**
NGL American Life, 1483 Kenwood Ctr., 54952, pg. 784　**PV**
Wisconsin Tissue Mills, Inc., P.O. Box 489, 54952, pg. 347　**PB**

Menomonee Falls

APV Refinery Products Corp., N90 W14555 Commerce Dr., 53051, pg. 1241　**IT**
Ahern Fire Protection, N56W16743 Ridgewood Dr., Ste. 800, 53051, pg. 27　**PV**
Alro Specialty Metals, Menomonee Falls, N49 W13545 Campbell Dr., 53051, pg. 46　**PV**
ARANDELL CORPORATION, N82 W. 13118 Leon Rd., 53051, pg. 79　**PV**
Arandell-Schmidt, N82 W. 13118 Leon Rd., 53051, pg. 79　**PV**
Associated Financial Center, Ltd., N88 W16554 Main St., 53051, pg. 140　**PB**

Associated Leasing, Inc., N88 W16554 Main St., 53052-0010, pg. 140　**PB**
Associated Realty, Inc., P.O. Box 10, N88 W16554 Main St., 53052-0010, pg. 140　**PB**
Auro Tech, Inc., N. 92 W. 14224 Anthony Ave., 53052, pg. 899　**PB**
BRADLEY CORPORATION, W. 142 N. 9101 Fountain Blvd., 53051, pg. 164　**PB**
COUSINS SUBMARINES, N83 W13400 Leon Rd., 53051, pg. 280　**PV**
Cousins Subs Systems, Inc., N83 W13400 Lean Rd., 53051, pg. 280　**PV**
KOHL'S CORPORATION, N. 56 W. 17000 Ridgewood Dr., 53051-7027, pg. 636　**PV**
KUHLMAN, INC., N57 WI 3666 Reichert Ave., 53051, pg. 636　**PV**
M & I Bank of Menomonee Falls, N82 W15415 Appleton Ave., 53051, pg. 1050　**PB**
Pryon Corporation, N. 93 W. 14575 Whittaker Way, 53051, pg. 1336　**PB**
Traub-Hermle Corporation, W. 134 N. 5235 Campbell Dr., 53051, pg. 1419　**IT**

Menomonie

First American Bank Wisconsin, P.O. Box 107, 54751, pg. 167　**PV**
Wal Mart Distribution Center, 6100 3M Dr., 54751-4930, pg. 1733　**PB**

Mequon

APS Resources, 6219 W. Eastwood Ct., 53095, pg. 613　**PV**
Control & Information Group, 6400 W. Enterprise Dr., 53092, pg. 1397　**PV**
Hayes Brake, 5800 W. Donges Bay Rd., 53092, pg. 299　**PV**
M.W. KASCH COMPANY, 5401 W. Donges Bay Rd., 53092, pg. 608　**PV**
Mark Net World, 1355 Towne Square Rd., 53092, pg. 108　**PV**
Rockwell Automation Drive Systems, 6400 W. Enterprise Dr., 53092, pg. 1397　**PB**
Schwarz Pharma Inc., 6140 W. Executive Dr., 53092, pg. 1211　**IT**
SUPER SKY PRODUCTS, INC., 10301 N. Enterprise Dr., 53092, pg. 1054　**PV**
Telsmith, Inc., 10910 N. Industrial Dr., 53092, pg. 141　**PB**

Merrill

CHURCH MUTUAL INSURANCE CO., 3000 Schuster Lane, 54452, pg. 239　**PV**
M & I Citizens American Bank, 900 E. Main St., 54452, pg. 1050　**PB**
WEINBRENNER SHOE COMPANY, INC., 108 So. Polk St., 54452, pg. 1160　**PV**

Middleton

Gen Trac, 2228 Evergreen Rd., 53562, pg. 934　**PV**
Madison National Life Insurance Co., Inc., 6120 University Ave., 53562, pg. 446　**PV**
The Neumayer Company, 2309 Evergreen Road, 53562, pg. 1016　**IT**
Noran Instruments, Inc., 2551 West Beltline Hwy., 53562, pg. 1593　**PB**
PLEASANT COMPANY, 8400 Fairway Place, 53562-0998, pg. 872　**PV**
Springs Window Fashions Division, 7549 Graber Rd., 53562, pg. 1500　**PB**
Woodward-Clyde, 8383 Greenway Blvd., 53562, pg. 1656　**PB**

Milton

BURDICK, INC., 15 Plumb St., 53563, pg. 181　**PV**

Milwaukee

ABC DeCo, Inc., 532 E. Capitol Dr., 53212, pg. 2　**PV**
AMB DEVELOPMENT GROUP LLC, 219 N. Milwaukee St., 53202, pg. 6　**PV**
AR ACCESSORIES GROUP, INC., 4300 W. Brown Deer Rd., 53223, pg. 7　**PV**
Stacy Adams Shoe Co., 234 E. Reservoir Ave., 53212, pg. 1763　**PV**
Advanced Detection Systems, 4740 W. Electric Ave., 53219, pg. 1136　**PV**
AgriStor Credit Corp., P.O. Box 2000, 53122, pg. 1477　**PB**
Aldrich Chemical Co., 940 W. St. Paul Ave., 53233, pg. 1471　**PB**
Allen-Bradley Global Sales & Support Group, 1201 S. Second St., 53204, pg. 1397　**PB**
Allen-Bradley Packaged Control Products, 788 N. Jefferson St., 53202-3718, pg. 1397　**PB**
Allied Tool Products Inc., 8355 W. Bradley Rd., 53223, pg. 617　**PV**
Allright Parking of Milwaukee, Inc., 744 N. Fourth St., Ste. 225, 53203, pg. 43　**PV**
Alpha Property & Casualty Insurance Co., 803 W. Michigan, 53233, pg. 1694　**PB**
American Appraisal Asia, Inc., 411 E. Wisconsin Ave., Ste. 2100, 53202, pg. 50　**PV**
AMERICAN APPRAISAL ASSOCIATES, INC., 411 E. Wisconsin Ave., Ste. 1900, 53202, pg. 49　**PV**
American Appraisal Capital Services, Inc., 411 E. Wisconsin Ave., 53202, pg. 50　**PV**

American Appraisal China, Inc., 411 E. Wisconsin Ave., Ste. 2100, 53202, pg. 50　**PV**
The American Appraisal Co., 411 E. Wisconsin Ave., 53202, pg. 50　**PV**
Ameritech, 722 N. Broadway, 53202, pg. 97　**PB**
Amity, 4300 W. Brown Deer Rd., 53223, pg. 7　**PB**
AMPCO METAL INCORPORATED, 1745 S. 38th St., 53215, pg. 67　**PV**
Applied Biochemist Inc., 6120 W. Douglas Ave., 53218, pg. 802　**IT**
Appraisal Services, Inc., 250 E. Wisconsin Ave., 53202, pg. 141　**PB**
Aqua-Chem Inc., P.O. Box 421, 53201, pg. 824　**IT**
Arnold Advertising, 316 N. Milwaukee St., Ste. 100, 53202, pg. 84　**PV**
Asahi Breweries U.S.A., Inc., 1110 N. Old World Third St., Ste. 300, 53203, pg. 83　**IT**
Associated Spring, 434 W. Edgerton Ave., 53207, pg. 190　**PB**
Associated Trust Company, Inc., 515 W. Wells, 53201-0522, pg. 140　**PB**
ASTRONAUTICS CORPORATION OF AMERICA, P.O. Box 523, 4115 N. Teutonia Ave., 53201-0523, pg. 93　**PV**
Autodesk, 1110 N. Old World Third, Ste. 359, 53203, pg. 149　**PB**
Autotrol Corporation, 5730 N. Glen Park Rd., 53209, pg. 1234　**PB**
B&G Realty, Inc., 250 E. Wisconsin Ave., 53202, pg. 1044　**PB**
BVK/MCDONALD, 250 W. Coventry Ct., 53217, pg. 108　**PV**
BADGER METER, INC., 4545 W. Brown Deer Rd., 53223-0099, pg. 164　**PB**
Badger Meter Industrial Div., 4545 W. Brown Deer Rd., 53223, pg. 165　**PB**
Badger Meter Utility Div., 4545 W. Brown Deer Rd., 53223, pg. 165　**PB**
Badger Service Co., 231 W. Michigan St., 53201, pg. 1773　**PB**
BADGER TRUCK CENTER, INC., 2326 W. St. Paul Ave., 53233, pg. 110　**PV**
Ball Products, Inc., 2300 S. 51st St., 53219, pg. 1215　**PB**
Banc One Building Management Corporation, 111 E. Wisconsin Ave., 53202, pg. 173　**PB**
Banc One Leasing Co., 111 E. Wisconsin Ave., 53201, pg. 173　**PB**
Banc One Services Corporation, 1000 N. Market St., 53201, pg. 174　**PB**
Bank One, International Services Corporation, 111 E. Wisconsin Ave., 53202, pg. 173　**PB**
Bank One Venture Corporation, 111 E. Wisconsin Ave., 53202, pg. 174　**PB**
Bank One, Wisconsin, 111 E. Wisconsin Ave., 53202, pg. 174　**PB**
Bank One Wisconsin Bankcard Corporation, 1000 N. Market St., 53201, pg. 174　**PB**
Bank One Wisconsin Investment Services Corporation, 111 E. Wisconsin Ave., 53202, pg. 174　**PB**
BANKMANAGERS CORP., 7540 W. Capitol Dr., 53216, pg. 114　**PV**
Banta Merchandising Products, 5111 S. Ninth St., 53221-0926, pg. 188　**PB**
Belarus Machinery, Inc., 7075 W. Parkland Ct., 53223, pg. 101　**IT**
Bell Atlantic Services, 2514 S. 102nd St. Ste. 180, 53227-2142, pg. 203　**PB**
Boston Store, 331 W. Wisconsin Ave., 53203, pg. 309　**PB**
Bradley Washroom Accessories Div., 7020 Parkland Ct., 53223, pg. 164　**PV**
Brady International Co., P.O. Box571, 53201-0571, pg. 250　**PB**
Brady Precision Tape Co., P.O. Box 571, 53201-0571, pg. 250　**PB**
Brady Service Co., 727 W. Glendale Ave., 53201, pg. 250　**PB**
Brady USA, Inc., P.O. Box 571, 53201-0571, pg. 250　**PB**
W.H. BRADY CO., P.O. Box 571, 53201-0571, pg. 250　**PB**
Brewery Ingredients Group, 4215 N. Port Washington Ave., 53212, pg. 349　**IT**
Briggs & Stratton Corp., 1706 S. 68th St., 53214-4949, pg. 252　**PB**
Bruner Water Treatment Systems, 700 W. Virginia St., Ste. 700, 53204, pg. 467　**PV**
Budgetel Inns, Inc., 250 E. Wisconsin Ave., 53202, pg. 1044　**PB**
CMI Group, Inc., 424 N. Fourth St., 53203, pg. 1462　**PB**
CT&I Corp. of Wisconsin, 6030 N. 60th St., 53218, pg. 235　**PV**
CAP Gemini America (Milwaukee Branch), 10150 W. National Ave., Ste. 200, 53227, pg. 264　**IT**
CARSON PIRIE SCOTT & CO., 331 W. Wisconsin Ave., 53203, pg. 309　**PB**
Castaways of Wisconsin, Inc., 550 N. Harbor Dr., 53202, pg. 1023　**PV**
Central Steel & Wire Company, 4343 S. Sixth St., 53221, pg. 327　**PB**
Charter Milwaukee Behavioral Health System, Inc., 11101 W. Lincoln Ave., 53227, pg. 1035　**PB**
CHRISTIANA COMPANIES, INC., 777 E. Wisconsin Ave., Ste. 3380, 53202, pg. 352　**PB**
Circle Freight International USA, 241 W. Edgerton Ave., 53207, pg. 370　**PB**
Circle Freight International USA, 241 W. Edgerton, 53207, pg. 371　**PB**
COMMERCE GROUP CORP., 6001 N. 91st St., 53225-1795, pg. 410　**PB**
Commerce/Sanseb Joint Venture, 6001 North 91st St., 53225-1795, pg. 410　**PB**
Corrugated Packaging, 5600 W. Good Hope Rd., 53223, pg. 737　**PB**

PB - U.S. Public Companies Volume
PV - U.S. Private Companies Volume
IT - International Public & Private Companies Volume

1481

Geographic Index-U.S.

CRAMER-KRASSELT, 733 N. Van Buren, 53202, pg. 285 — PV
Cramer-Krasselt, 733 N. Van Buren, 53202, pg. 286 — PV
Cramer-Krasselt Public Relations, 733 N. Van Buren St., 53202, pg. 286 — PV
Crestwood Bakery, 1710 S. 108th St., 53214, pg. 653 — PV
Cutler-Hammer Eaton Corporation, 4201 N. 27th St., 53216, pg. 556 — PB
DWF of Milwaukee, Inc., 425 W. Walnut, 53212, pg. 326 — PV
Dairy Ingredients Group, 4215 N. Point Washington Ave., 53212, pg. 349 — IT
Data Retrieval Corp. of America, 11801 W. Silverspring Dr., 53225, pg. 1602 — PB
Delco Electronics Corporation, P.O. Box 471, 53201, pg. 720 — PB
DELTA RESINS & REFRACTORIES, INC., 6263 N. Teutonia Ave., 53209, pg. 323 — PV
Diabetes Shoppe, 2122 N. Prospect Ave. #200, 53202, pg. 97 — PB
Dings Dynamics Co., 4740 W. Electric Ave., 53219, pg. 1136 — PV
Kelley Dock Systems, 6720 N. Teuronia, 53209, pg. 612 — PV
Douglas Dynamics, Inc., 7777 N. 73rd. St., 53223, pg. 131 — PB
Downey, Inc., 2203 W. Michigan St., 53233, pg. 602 — PV
Duni Inc., 5300 N. Sherman Blvd., 53209, pg. 421 — IT
EMS Central Regional Office (Corporate), 12000 W. Park Pl., 53224, pg. 565 — PB
Eaton Corporation, Specific Industry Control Division, 4265 North 30th St., 53216, pg. 557 — PB
EFFECTIVE MANAGEMENT SYSTEMS, 12000 W. Park Pl., 53224-3026, pg. 565 — PB
Elan Insurance Services, Inc., 777 E. Wisconsin Ave., 53202, pg. 643 — PB
Elan Investment Services, Inc., 777 E. Wisconsin Ave., 53202, pg. 643 — PB
Elan Life Insurance Company, First Wisconsin Ctr., 777 E. Wisconsin Ave., 53202, pg. 643 — PB
Elan Title Services, Inc., First Wisconsin Ctr., 777 E. Wisconsin Ave., 53202, pg. 643 — PB
Erie Manufacturing Co., 4000 S. 13th St., 53221, pg. 1241 — IT
F.W.S.F. Corporation, First Wisconsin Ctr., 777 E. Wisconsin Ave., 53201, pg. 643 — PB
The Falk Corporation, 3001 W. Canal St., 53208-4200, pg. 1534 — PB
Far-Mor Biochem, P.O. Box 18999, 6120 W. Douglas Ave., 53218, pg. 802 — IT
Financial Collection Agencies (1990) Inc., 5678 W. Brown Deer Rd., Ste. 102P, 53223-6027, pg. 471 — IT
First Amer. Finance Corp., 250 E. Wisconsin Ave., 53202, pg. 1044 — PB
First Bank N.A., 201 W. Wisconsin Ave., 53259, pg. 1680 — PB
First Community Investment Corp., First Wisconsin Ctr., 777 E. Wisconsin Ave., 53202, pg. 643 — PB
FIRSTAR CORPORATION, 777 E. Wisconsin Ave., 53202, pg. 642 — PB
Firstar Corporation Arizona, First Wisconsin Ctr., 777 E. Wisconsin Ave., 53202, pg. 643 — PB
Firstar Corporation Illinois, First Wisconsin Ctr., 777 E. Wisconsin Ave., 53202, pg. 643 — PB
Firstar Corporation of Minnesota, First Wisconsin Ctr., 777 E. Wisconsin Ave., 53202, pg. 643 — PB
Firstar Development Corporation, First Wisconsin Ctr., 777 E. Wisconsin Ave., 53202, pg. 643 — PB
Firstar Export Credit Limited, First Wisconsin Ctr., 777 E. Wisconsin Ave., 53202, pg. 643 — PB
Firstar Information Services Corporation, 777 E. Wisconsin Ave., 53202, pg. 643 — PB
Firstar Leasing Corporation, First Wisconsin Center, 777 E. Wisconsin Ave., 53202, pg. 643 — PB
Firstar Mortgage Corporation, 777 E. Wisconsin Ave., 53202, pg. 643 — PB
Firstar Real Estate Services, Inc., 777 E. Wisconsin Ave., 53202, pg. 643 — PB
Fleck Controls, 20580 Enterprise Ave., 53008, pg. 1273 — PB
Fortis Life, P.O. Box 3050, 501 W. Michigan, 53201-3050, pg. 499 — IT
Fortis Long Term Care, 501 W. Michigan Ave., 53201, pg. 499 — IT
Fortis Sales, 501 W. Michigan, 53201, pg. 499 — IT
FOSTER PONTIAC, INC., 3636 S. 27th St., 53221, pg. 421 — PV
GB Electrical, Inc., 6101 N. Baker Rd., 53209, pg. 124 — PB
G.E. Medical Systems, P.O. Box 414, 53201, pg. 710 — PB
GFG Corporation, 7611 N. 73rd St., 53223, pg. 395 — IT
Grace Cocoa/Ambrosia Chocolate, 12500 W. Carmen Ave., 53225-6199, pg. 128 — PB
Graham, 8800 W. Bradley Rd., 53224, pg. 377 — IT
Graham Transmissions Inc/Graham Gear Systems, Inc, 8800 W. Bradley Rd., 53224, pg. 377 — IT
Great Lakes Biochemical Co., Inc., 6120 W. Douglas Ave., P.O. Box 18999, 53218, pg. 802 — IT
GREDE FOUNDRIES, INC., 9898 W. Bluemound Rd., 53226, pg. 476 — PV
Grede Transport, Inc., 9898 W. Bluemound Rd., 53226, pg. 476 — PV
Grinnell Supply Sales Division, 1819 W. Saint Paul Ave., 53233-2633, pg. 1648 — PB
Grover Piston Ring Division, 2759 S. 28th St., 53215, pg. 689 — PB
Halper Bros., 233 E. Chicago St., 53201, pg. 920 — PV
Chr. Hansen, Inc., 9015 W. Maple St., 53214-4298, pg. 288 — IT
HARLEY-DAVIDSON, INC., 3700 W. Juneau Ave., 53208, pg. 786 — PB

Harley-Davidson Motor Company, P.O. Box 653, 3700 W. Juneau Ave., 53201, pg. 786 — PB
HELWIG CARBON PRODUCTS, INC., 8900 W. Tower Ave., 53224, pg. 521 — PB
Hercules Inc.-Milwaukee, 5228 N. Hopkins, 53209, pg. 810 — PB
Homespan Realty Co., Inc., 6001 N. 91st St., 53225-1795, pg. 410 — PB
Humana Wisconsin Health Organization Insurance Corporation, 111 W. Pleasant St., 53212, pg. 848 — PB
Hydro-Stack Products, 2300 S. 51st St., 53219, pg. 1215 — PB
Hydura Products, 2300 S. 51st St., 53219, pg. 1215 — PB
INX International, 5501 W. Mill Rd., 53218, pg. 1311 — IT
Industrial Control Group, 1201 S. 2nd St., 53204, pg. 1397 — PB
INSTRUMENTARIUM IMAGING, INC., 300 W. Edgerton Ave., 53207, pg. 565 — PV
Jaeger Baking Co., 918 W. Somers St., 53205, pg. 1022 — PV
JASON INCORPORATED, 411 E. Wisconsin Ave., Ste. 2500, 53202, pg. 923 — PB
JOHNSON CONTROLS, INC., 5757 N. Green Bay Ave., 53209, pg. 932 — PB
Johnson Controls, Inc., Battery Group, 5757 N. Green Bay Ave., 53201, pg. 932 — PB
Johnson Controls, Inc., Controls Group, 507 E. Michigan St., 53202, pg. 932 — PB
Johnson Controls International, Inc., 507 E. Michigan St., 53201, pg. 932 — PB
Johnson Controls-Milwaukee, 1701 W. Civic Dr., 53209, pg. 932 — PB
Journal Broadcast Group, Inc., 720 E. Capitol Dr., 53212, pg. 601 — PV
JOURNAL COMMUNICATIONS INC., 333 W. State St., 53201, pg. 601 — PV
K & G OF WISCONSIN, INC., 2207 W. Wisconsin Ave., 53201, pg. 602 — PV
KM Development Corp., 710 N. Plankinton St., 53203, pg. 1206 — PV
Kabelschlepp America Inc., 7100 W. Marcia Rd., 53223-3363, pg. 721 — IT
KELLEY COMPANY, INC., 6720 N. Teuronia, 53209, pg. 612 — PV
Koss Classics Ltd., 4129 North Port Washington Ave., 53212, pg. 966 — PB
KOSS CORPORATION, 4129 N. Port Washington Ave., 53212, pg. 966 — PB
Kramer International, Inc., 114 E. Pittsburgh Ave., 53204, pg. 142 — PB
Landmark Construction Corp., 710 N. Plankinton Ave., 53203, pg. 1206 — PV
LAUGHLIN/CONSTABLE, INC., 207 E. Michigan St., 53202, pg. 653 — PV
LiphaTech, Inc., 3101 W. Custer Ave., 53209, pg. 812 — IT
Louis London Advertising & Sales Promotion, 1110 N. Market St., Ste. 300, 53202, pg. 674 — PV
Longview Fibre Co. Central Container Div., 3832 N. Third St., 53212, pg. 1014 — PB
LOUIS ALLIS COMPANY, 427 E. Stewart, 53201, pg. 677 — PV
M & I Brokerage Services, Inc., 770 N. Water St., 53202, pg. 1050 — PB
M & I Capital Markets Group, Inc., 770 N. Water St., 53202, pg. 1051 — PB
M & I First National Leasing Corp., 250 E. Wisconsin Ave., Ste. 1400, 53202, pg. 1051 — PB
M & I Investment Management Corp., 1000 N. Water St., 53202, pg. 1051 — PB
M & I Marshall & Ilsley Bank, 770 N. Water St., 53202, pg. 1050 — PB
M & I Ventures Corporation, 770 N. Water St., 53202, pg. 1051 — PB
MGIC INVESTMENT CORPORATION, MGIC Plaza, 250 E. Kilbourn Ave., 53202, pg. 1026 — PB
MSC/EMAS Development, 4300 W. Brown Deer Rd., 53223, pg. 1031 — PB
MSC Engineering/Electromagnetics Applications Department, 9076 N. Deerbrook Trail, 53223-2434, pg. 1031 — PB
MSC Midwest Regional Office, 4300 W. Brown Deer Rd., 53223, pg. 1031 — PB
MSC Milwaukee Office, 4300 W. Brown Deer Rd., 53223, pg. 1031 — PB
Mainline Industrial Distributors, Inc., 8475 N. 87th St., 53224, pg. 123 — PB
MANPOWER INC., 5301 N. Ironwood Rd., 53217, pg. 1042 — PB
Marc Plaza Corp., 250 E. Wisconsin Ave., 53202, pg. 1044 — PB
THE MARCUS CORPORATION, 250 E. Wisconsin Ave., 53202, pg. 1044 — PB
Marcus Hotel Corp., 250 E. Wisconsin Ave., 53202, pg. 1044 — PB
Marcus Restaurants Inc., 250 E. Wisconsin Ave., 53202, pg. 1044 — PB
Marcus Theatres Corp., 250 E. Wisconsin Ave., 53202, pg. 1044 — PB
MARQUETTE MEDICAL SYSTEMS, INC., 8200 W. Tower Ave., 53223, pg. 1047 — PB
MARSHALL & ILSLEY CORPORATION, 770 N. Water St., 53202, pg. 1049 — PB
Marshall & Ilsley Trust Company, 1000 N. Water St., 53202, pg. 1051 — PB
Master Lock Company, 2600 No. 32nd St., 53210, pg. 675 — PB
MAYNARD STEEL CASTING COMPANY, 2856 S. 27th St., 53234, pg. 718 — PV
Medical Advances Inc., 10437 Innovation Dr., 53226, pg. 894 — PB

MERIDIAN INDUSTRIES, INC., 100 E. Wisconsin, Ste. 2750, 53202, pg. 732 — PV
Metal Treating, Inc., 1575 W. Pierce St., 53204, pg. 1592 — PB
Midland Color Company, 11217 W. Becher St., 53227, pg. 1311 — IT
Miller Brewing Company, P.O. Box 482, 53201-0482, pg. 1289 — PB
H.C. MILLER COMPANY, 8111 N. 87th St., 53224, pg. 747 — PV
MILWAUKEE BUCKS, INC., 1001 N. Fourth St., 53203, pg. 749 — PB
Milwaukee Container Div., 8500 W. Tower Ave., 53224, pg. 1289 — PB
Milwaukee Grey Iron, 1501 S. 83rd, 53214, pg. 579 — PV
Milwaukee Guardian Insurance Inc., 803 W. Michigan, 53233, pg. 1694 — PB
Milwaukee Insurance Group, 803 W. Michigan St., 53201-0621, pg. 1694 — PB
Milwaukee Journal Sentinel, 333 W. State St., 53203, pg. 601 — PV
Milwaukee Lock Company, 2600 N. 32nd St., 53210, pg. 675 — PB
Milwaukee Safeguard Insurance Co., 803 W. Michigan, 53233, pg. 1694 — PB
Morgan Matroc Inc.-Midwest Sales Division, 8989 N. Port Washington Rd., Ste. 203, 53217, pg. 893 — IT
Mortgage Guaranty Insurance Corporation, MGIC Plaza, 250 E. Kilbourn Ave., 53202, pg. 1026 — PB
National Health Services, Inc., 10909 W. Greenfield Ave., 53214, pg. 433 — PB
Marshall W. Nelson & Assoc., 2110 W. Silver Spring Dr., 53209, pg. 360 — PV
Network EPO, Inc., 111 W. Pleasant St., 52312, pg. 848 — PB
Nordco, Inc., 182 W. Oklahoma Ave., 53207, pg. 1209 — PB
North Star Print Group Inc., 5100 W. Brown Deer Rd., 53223, pg. 601 — PV
Northern Computers, Inc., 5007 S. Howell Ave., 53207, pg. 64 — PB
NORTHWESTERN MUTUAL LIFE INSURANCE CO., 720 E. Wisconsin Ave., 53202, pg. 807 — PB
Norwest Bank of Wisconsin, 100 E. Wisconsin Ave., 53202, pg. 1202 — PB
Nunn-Bush Shoe Co., 234 E. Reservoir Ave., 53212, pg. 1763 — PB
OMC Milwaukee, 6101 N. 64th St., 53218-1562, pg. 478 — PV
THE OILGEAR COMPANY, 2300 S. 51st St., 53219, pg. 1215 — PV
The Old Line Life Insurance Co. of America, 707 N. 11th St., 53201, pg. 77 — PB
THE OLDENBURG GROUP COMPANIES, 8600 W. Bradley, 53224, pg. 814 — PV
Pabst Brewing Co./Milwaukee, 622 Vienna St., 53212, pg. 954 — PV
Petrodyne Products, 2300 S. 51st St., 53219, pg. 1215 — PV
Pfister Corporation, 250 E. Wisconsin Ave., 53202, pg. 1044 — PB
Pharmacia & Upjohn Biotech Inc., 2202, North Bartlett Ave., 53202, pg. 1047 — PB
Piccadilly Advertising Agency, Inc., 6001 N. 91st St., 53225, pg. 410 — PB
Piper Jaffray Inc., 411 E. Wisconsin Ave., Ste. 1700, 53202-4409, pg. 1302 — PB
PRESSED STEEL TANK CO., INC., 1445 S. 66th St., 53214, pg. 882 — PV
PrimeCare Health Plan, Inc., 1233 N. Mayfair Rd., 53226, pg. 1678 — PB
RE Services, Inc., First Wisconsin Ctr., 777 E. Wisconsin Ave., 53202, pg. 643 — PB
Red Star Bio Products, 433 E. Michigan St., 53202, pg. 1695 — PB
Red Star Yeast & Products Div., 433 E. Michigan St., 53202, pg. 1695 — PB
RELIABLE KNITTING WORKS, 233 E. Chicago St., 53202, pg. 920 — PV
Rexnord Corporation, 4701 W. Greenfield Ave., 53214, pg. 127 — IT
REXWORKS INC., 445 W. Oklahoma Ave., 53207, pg. 926 — PV
Reynolds Metals Company-Milwaukee, 8500 W. Tyler Ave., 53224-2894, pg. 1385 — PB
Richter-Schroeder Company, Inc., 1110 N. Old World Third St., Ste. 320, 53203, pg. 1051 — PB
RITE-HITE CORPORATION, 8900 N. Arbon Dr., 53223, pg. 933 — PV
Rite-Hite Division, P.O. Box 23043, 53229, pg. 933 — PV
Rite-Hite Door Division, P.O. Box 53229, 53229, pg. 933 — PV
Rite-Hite Frommelt Division, P.O. Box 23043, 53229, pg. 933 — PV
Rockwell Automation, 1201 S. Second St., 53204, pg. 1397 — PB
Rolfs, 4300 W. Brown Deer Rd., 53223, pg. 7 — PB
ROMAN ELECTRIC COMPANY, INC., 640 S. 70th St., 53214, pg. 942 — PV
Roundy's, Milwaukee Division, 11300 W. Burleigh St., 53201, pg. 948 — PV
Rouse-Milwaukee Garage Maintenance, Inc., The Grand Ave., Ste. 5, 275 W. Wisconsin Ave., 53203, pg. 1409 — PB
Rouse-Milwaukee, Inc., The Grand Avenue, Ste. 5, 275 W. Wisconsin Ave., 53203, pg. 1409 — PB
SAFECO Administrative Services, Inc., 9275 N. 49th St., Ste. 300, 53223, pg. 1423 — PB
Salem Products, 2300 S. 51st St., 53219, pg. 1215 — PB
San Luis Estates, Inc., 6001 N. 91st St., 53225-1795, pg. 410 — PB
San Sebastian Gold Mines, Inc., 6001 N. 91st St., 53225, pg. 410 — PB

PB - U.S. Public Companies Volume
PV - U.S. Private Companies Volume
IT - International Public & Private Companies Volume

1482

Geographic Index-U.S.

Sax Arts & Crafts, 100 A East Pleasant St., 53212, pg. 1687 **PB**
Senior Engineering Co.-Milwaukee, P.O. Box 27906, 2514 S. 102nd St., Ste. 110, 53227, pg. 1222 **IT**
Siemens Power Corp., 1040 S. 70th St., 53214, pg. 1246 **IT**
Sight and Sound, 1135 S. 70th St., 53214, pg. 749 **PB**
Signature Flight Support, 923 E. Layton Ave., Mitchell Field, 53207, pg. 114 **IT**
Simon Aerials Inc., 10600 W. Brown Deer Rd., 53224, pg. 1252 **PB**
Siva Truck Leasing Inc., 2301 W. St. Paul Ave., 53233, pg. 110 **PV**
A.O. SMITH CORPORATION, One Park Plaza, 11270 W. Park Pl., 53224, pg. 1476 **PB**
EVERETT SMITH GROUP, LTD., 800 N. Marshall St., 53202, pg. 1007 **PV**
SMITH INVESTMENT COMPANY, P.O. Box 23976, 53223-0976, pg. 1008 **PV**
Southeastern Wisconsin Products Co., Inc., 500 W. Edgerton Ave., 53207, pg. 299 **PB**
Spincraft Wisconsin, 2455 Commerce Dr., 53151, pg. 1506 **PB**
Square D Automation Products, 4041 N. Richards St., 53212, pg. 1208 **IT**
Square D Company, 4080 N. First St., 53212, pg. 1208 **IT**
Square D Co.-Transformer Bus. Div., 4080 N. First St., 53212, pg. 1208 **IT**
Standing Rock Campground, 6001 N. 91st St., 53225-1795, pg. 410 **PB**
Star Language Center - LLC, 8111 N. 87th St., 53224, pg. 747 **PV**
STERLING, INC., 5200 W. Clinton Ave., 53223, pg. 1041 **PV**
STRATTEC SECURITIES CORPORATION, 333 W. Good Hope Rd., 53209, pg. 1523 **PB**
SYBRON INTERNATIONAL CORPORATION, 411 E. Wisconsin Ave., 24th Fl., 53202, pg. 1544 **PB**
Syndesis Development Corp., 231 W. Michigan St., 53201, pg. 1773 **PB**
Systems & Services Div., 507 E. Michigan St., 53201, pg. 932 **PB**
Systems Group, 1201 S. 2nd St., 53204, pg. 1398 **PB**
TCF Bank Wisconsin, 500 W. Brown Deer Rd., 53217, pg. 1554 **PB**
TLC, 11430 W. Burleigh, 53222, pg. 352 **PB**
TMP Worldwide, Inc., 611 E. Wisconsin Ave., 53202, pg. 1064 **PV**
Time Insurance, 501 W. Michigan, 53201, pg. 499 **IT**
Towler Products, 2300 S. 51st St., 53219, pg. 1215 **PB**
Towne Realty, Inc., 710 N. Plankinton Ave., 53203, pg. 1206 **PV**
Tricor Direct, Inc., P.O. Box 571, 53201-0571, pg. 250 **PB**
ALBERT TROSTEL & SONS CO., 10201 W. Lincoln, Ste. 405, 53227, pg. 1105 **PV**
Tulip Corp., Milwaukee Div., 714 E. Keefe Ave., 53215, pg. 1109 **PB**
Tyton Corporation, P.O. Box 23055, 7930 N. Faulkner Rd., 53224, pg. 208 **IT**
United Health, Inc., 105 W. Michigan St., 53203, pg. 468 **IT**
United Insurance Corporation of America, 310 W. Wisconsin Ave., 53203, pg. 1694 **PB**
UNITED WISCONSIN SERVICES, INC., 401 W. Michigan St., 53203, pg. 1692 **PB**
Universal Developers, Inc., 6001 N. 91st St., 53225-1795, pg. 410 **PB**
UNIVERSAL FOODS CORPORATION, 433 E. Michigan St., 53202, pg. 1695 **PB**
FRED USINGER, INC., 1030 N. Old World Third St., 53203, pg. 1119 **PV**
VENTUREDYNE, LTD., 10201 W. Lincoln Ave., Ste. 400, 53227, pg. 1136 **PV**
Vilter Export Corp., 2217 S. First St., 53207, pg. 1141 **PV**
WISN-AM, 759 N. 19th St., 53233, pg. 1418 **PB**
WISN Division, 759 N. 19th St., 53233, pg. 516 **PV**
WISN-TV, 759 N. 19th St., 53233, pg. 516 **PB**
WKKV-FM, 2400 S. 102nd St., Ste. 230, 53227, pg. 385 **PB**
WLTQ-FM, 759 N. 19th St., 53233, pg. 1418 **PB**
E.R. WAGNER MANUFACTURING, 4611 N. 32nd St., 53209, pg. 1146 **PV**
Wayne Chemical Corporation, 546 So. Water St., 53204, pg. 599 **IT**
WESTERN INDUSTRIES, INC., 1215 N. 62nd St., 53213, pg. 1165 **PV**
WESTERN STATES ENVELOPE CO., P.O. Box 2048, 53201-2048, pg. 1168 **PV**
WEYCO GROUP, INC., 234 E. Reservoir Ave., 53212-1188, pg. 1763 **PB**
WICOR, INC., 626 E. Wisconsin Ave., 53202, pg. 1767 **PB**
Williams Steel & Supply Co., 999 W. Armour Ave., 53221, pg. 1101 **PV**
Willis Corroon Corp. of Wisconsin, One Plaza E., 330 E. Kilbourn Ave., Ste. 1400, 53202-3195, pg. 1507 **IT**
Willis Corroon Financial Services Corp., 330 E. Kilbourn Ave., Ste. 1400, 53202-3195, pg. 1507 **IT**
WISCONSIN & SOUTHERN RAILROAD CO., 5300 N. 33rd St., 53209, pg. 1184 **PV**
Wisconsin Electric Power Company, 231 W. Michigan St., 53201, pg. 1773 **PB**
WISCONSIN ENERGY CORPORATION, 231 W. Michigan St., 53201, pg. 1773 **PB**
Wisconsin Gas Company, 626 E. Wisconsin Ave., 53202, pg. 1767 **PB**
WISCONSIN MACHINE AND TOOL CORPORATION, 225 S. Curtis St., 53214, pg. 1185 **PV**
Wisconsin Michigan Investment Corp., 231 W. Michigan, 53201, pg. 1773 **PB**
Wispark Corporation, 231 W. Michigan St., 53201, pg. 1773 **PB**

Wisvest Corporation, 231 W. Michigan St., 53201, pg. 1773 **PB**
Witech Corporation, 231 W. Michigan St., 53201, pg. 1773 **PB**
Worldmark Inc., P.O. Box 571, 53201-0571, pg. 250 **PB**
WROUGHT WASHER MFG., INC., 2100 S. Bay St., 53207, pg. 1192 **PB**
Zellerbach Division, 3200 S. Third St., 53207, pg. 1075 **PB**
ZILBER, LTD., 710 N. Plankinton Ave., 53203, pg. 1206 **PV**

Mondovi

Frontier Communications of Mondovi, Inc., 217 S. Eau Claire St., 54755, pg. 684 **PB**
MARTEN TRANSPORT, LTD., 129 Marten St., 54755, pg. 1052 **PB**

Monroe

Beatrice Cheese, 105 Third St., 53566, pg. 426 **PB**
JOSEPH HUBER BREWING CO., INC., 1208 14th Ave., 53566, pg. 545 **PV**
THE SWISS COLONY, INC, 1112 Seventh Ave., 53566, pg. 1059 **PV**

Mosinee

Mosinee Paper International, Inc., 1244 Kronenwetter Dr., 54455, pg. 1747 **PB**
SNE Enterprises, Inc., 888 South View Dr., 54455, pg. 1193 **PB**
WAUSAU-MOSINEE PAPER CORPORATION, 1244 Kronenwetter Dr., 54455-9099, pg. 1747 **PB**
Wausau-Mosinee Papers Export Corporation, 1244 Kronenwetter Dr., 54455, pg. 1748 **PB**
Wausau-Mosinee Papers International, Inc., 1244 Kronenwetter Dr., 54455, pg. 1748 **PB**

Mount Horeb

PEC Wisconsin, 1204 E. Lincoln St., 53572, pg. 871 **PV**

Mukwonago

Seaquist Closures, 711 Fox St., 53149, pg. 125 **PV**

Nashotah

CONTROLLED SYSTEMS OF WISCONSIN, INC., N. 44 W32882 Watertown Plank Rd., 53058, pg. 271 **PV**
DICKTEN & MASCH MANUFACTURING CO., N44 W. 33341 Watertown Plank Rd., 53058, pg. 331 **PV**

Necedah

BEST POWER, N. 9246 Hwy. 80, 54646, pg. 140 **PV**

Neenah

ABT Building Products Corporation, One Neenah Ctr., Ste. 600, 54956, pg. 20 **IT**
American Natl. Can Co., P.O. Box 702, 54956, pg. 1029 **IT**
Associated Bank, National Association, P.O. Box 408, 100 W. Wisconsin Ave., 54956, pg. 140 **PB**
Atlas Tag & Label Inc., P.O. Box 638, 54957, pg. 145 **PB**
Banta Healthcare Products, 570 Enterprise Dr., Box 804, 54957-0806, pg. 188 **PB**
Bergstrom Paper Div., Bergstrom Rd., 54956, pg. 746 **PB**
Household Products Sector, 401 N. Lake St., 54956, pg. 958 **PB**
International Consumer & Service Sector, 401 N. Lake St., 54956, pg. 958 **PB**
JEWELERS MUTUAL INSURANCE COMPANY, 24 Jewelers Park Dr., 54957-0468, pg. 587 **PV**
K-C Advertising, Inc., N. Lake St., 54956, pg. 959 **PB**
K-C Aviation Inc., N. Lake St., 54956, pg. 959 **PB**
KRC (Hewitt) Inc., P.O. Box 688, 375 Byrd Ave., 54957-0688, pg. 1202 **IT**
J.J. KELLER & ASSOCIATES, INC., 3003 W. Breezewood Ln., 54957-0368, pg. 612 **PV**
Kimberly-Clark Computer Services, Inc., 401 N. Lake St., 54956, pg. 959 **PB**
Kimberly-Clark International Services Corp., N. Lake St., 54956-0349, pg. 959 **PB**
Kimfibers Ltd., 401 N. Lake St., 54956, pg. 959 **PB**
MENASHA CORPORATION, 1645 Bergstrom Rd., 54956, pg. 731 **PV**
Menasha Corp., Printed Systems Div., 1271 Dillingham Rd., 54957, pg. 731 **PV**
Menasha Development Corporation, P.O. Box 367, 54957-0367, pg. 731 **PV**
Menasha Foreign Sales Corporation, P.O. Box 367, 54957-0367, pg. 731 **PV**
Menasha Transport Inc., 1649 Bergstrom Rd., 54957, pg. 731 **PV**
NEENAH FOUNDRY COMPANY, 2121 Brooks Ave., 54956, pg. 790 **PV**
Neenah Paper, P.O. Box 211, 135 N. Commercial St., 54956, pg. 958 **PB**
Outlook Graphics, 1180 American Dr., 54957-0748, pg. 1235 **PB**
OUTLOOK GROUP CORPORATION, 1180 American Dr., 54956, pg. 1235 **PB**
Outlook Label Systems, Inc., P.O. Box 755, 2411 Industrial Dr., 59457, pg. 1235 **PB**

Zeneca Specialty Inks, 830 Ehlers Rd., 54956, pg. 1525 **IT**

Neillsville

Badger Telecam, Inc., 420 Hewett St., 54456, pg. 1571 **PB**

New Berlin

A&A MANUFACTURING CO., 2300 S. Calhoun Rd., 53151, pg. 1 **PV**
ABB Flexible Automation, 2487 S. Commerce Dr., 53151, pg. 4 **IT**
Bank One, Mortgage Company, 15525 W. National Ave., 53151, pg. 174 **PB**
Bradner Smith & Co. of Wisconsin, 2255 S. 162nd St., 53151-2203, pg. 165 **PV**
CHEMCENTRAL/Milwaukee, 2400 S. 170th St., 53151, pg. 232 **PV**
Crawler Systems, 17028 West Victor Rd., 53151, pg. 511 **IT**
Dataforms, Inc., 16600 Glendale Dr., 53151, pg. 1385 **PB**
Dewco Milwaukee Sales, 5660 S. Westridge Dr., 53151, pg. 1178 **PB**
Drives & Metals Systems Division, 16250 W. Glendale Dr., 53131-2840, pg. 4 **IT**
Eskimo Flavors, 2400 S. Calhoun Rd., 53151, pg. 592 **PB**
Franklin Tool & Mfg. Co., 16680 W. Cleveland Ave., 53151, pg. 1192 **PV**
HK SYSTEMS, INC., 2855 S. James Dr., 53151, pg. 491 **PV**
Industrial Automation Division, 2487 S. Commerce Dr., 53131, pg. 4 **IT**
INDUSTRIAL TOWEL & UNIFORM, 2700 S. 160th St., 53151, pg. 561 **PV**
Lindberg Heat Treating Co., 16167 W. Rogers Dr., 53151, pg. 999 **PB**
Petron Corporation, 16700 Glendale Dr., 53151, pg. 1158 **PV**
Ringier America, New Berlin Division, 16555 W. Rogers Dr., 53151, pg. 1778 **PB**
Sax Arts & Crafts, Inc., 2405 S. Calhoun Rd., 53151, pg. 1687 **PB**
Sumitomo Electric Carbide Manufacturing, Inc., P.O. Box 511110, 5635 S. Westridge Dr., 53151-1110, pg. 1313 **IT**
TEKRA CORPORATION, 16700 W. Lincoln Ave., 53151, pg. 1073 **PV**
Zerand Division, 15800 W. Overland Dr., 53151, pg. 1517 **PB**

New Franken

Service Motor Co., Hwy. 54 & 57, 54229, pg. 986 **PV**

New Glarus

BCS Wireless, P.O. Box 730, 98 Hwy. 69 N., 53574, pg. 609 **PB**

New Holstein

Lauson Engine Div., 1604 Michigan Ave., 53061, pg. 1566 **PB**

New London

Hillshire Farm Company, Rte. No. 4, 54961, pg. 1433 **PB**

New Richmond

Frontier Communications-St. Croix, Inc., P.O. Box 318, 154 E. Sceind St., 54017, pg. 684 **PB**
SIG Holding USA Inc., 869 S. Knowles Ave., 54017-1797, pg. 1156 **IT**
ST. CROIX PRESS, INC., 1185 S. Knowles Hwy. 65, 54017, pg. 960 **PV**

Niagara

Niagara of Wisconsin, 1101 Mill St., 54151-1496, pg. 436 **PB**
Niagara of Wisconsin Paper Corp., 1101 Mill St., 54151, pg. 436 **PB**

Oak Creek

Eder Industries, Inc., 2250 W. Southbranch Blvd., 53154, pg. 124 **PB**
Midwest Express Airlines, Inc., 6744 S. Howell Ave., 53207, pg. 1111 **PB**
MIDWEST EXPRESS HOLDINGS, INC., 6744 S. Howell Ave., 53154, pg. 1111 **PB**
Ph. Orth Co., 7350 S. Tenth St., 53154-0067, pg. 244 **IT**
Outlook Packaging, Inc., 2025 W. South Branch Blvd., 53154-4948, pg. 1236 **PB**
Prime Manufacturing Company, 7730 S. 6th St., 53154, pg. 1711 **PB**

Oconomowoc

FIBERESIN INDUSTRIES INC., P.O. Box 88, 37031 E. Wisconsin Ave., 53066, pg. 402 **PV**
Menasha Corp., Orbis Division, 1055 Corporate Center Dr., 53066, pg. 731 **PV**
Oconomowoc Canning Company, 1055 Corporate Center Dr., 53066, pg. 1519 **PB**

Geographic Index-U.S.

Outlook Foods, Inc., 132 S. Concord Rd., 53066, pg. 1235 **PB**
QUEST TECHNOLOGIES, INC., 510 S. Worthington, 53066, pg. 900 **PV**
ROCKY ROCOCO CORPORATION, 105 E. Wisconsin Ave., Suite 204, 53066-207, pg. 938 **PV**
STOKELY USA, INC., 1230 Corporate Ctr. Dr., 53066, pg. 1518 **PB**

Oconto Falls

Plas-Techs, Inc., 750 Ralph Lemorande Dr., 54154, pg. 165 **PB**

Oshkosh

Basic American Metal Products, 3331 N. Shore Dr., 54901, pg. 404 **PV**
Corrugated Packaging, 413 E. Murdock St., P.O. Box 199, 54902, pg. 736 **PB**
Integrated Material Handling Company, 3255 Medalist Dr., 54901, pg. 1397 **IT**
Lapham Hickey Steel (WI), 2585 W. 20th Ave., 54903, pg. 651 **PV**
MILES KIMBALL COMPANY, 41 W. 8th Ave., 54901, pg. 745 **PV**
Milprint Inc., P.O. Box 2968, 2200 Badger Ave., 54903-2968, pg. 210 **PB**
Morgan Manufacturing, 523 Oregon St., 54901, pg. 1132 **PB**
OSHKOSH B'GOSH, INC., 112 Otter Ave., 54901, pg. 1232 **PB**
OSHKOSH TRUCK CORPORATION, 2307 Oregon St., 54901, pg. 1233 **PB**
Rexam Extrusions, 3555 Moser St., 54901, pg. 1106 **IT**
Square D Co., 3300 Medalist Dr., 54901, pg. 1208 **PB**
TOP BRANDS, INC., 520 W. 15th Ave., 54901, pg. 1091 **PV**
WISCONSIN AUTOMATED MACHINERY CORP., 123 Jackson St., 54901, pg. 1184 **PV**

Palmyra

Clearwater Mill, Inc., R.R. #1, P.O. Box 427, 53156, pg. 653 **PB**

Park Falls

Flambeau Mill, 200 N. First Ave., 54552, pg. 434 **IT**

Peshtigo

BADGER PAPER MILLS, INC., 200 W. Front St., 54157, pg. 165 **PB**

Pewaukee

CENTURY FENCE COMPANY, N. 11 W. 24711 Silvernail Rd., 53072, pg. 226 **PV**
Ikon Office Solutions-Milwaukee, 23050 Paul Rd., 53072, pg. 863 **PB**
QUAD/GRAPHICS, INC., Duplainville Rd., 53072-4195, pg. 897 **PV**
ROUNDY'S, INC., 23000 Roundy Dr., 53072, pg. 948 **PV**
Stark Candy Company, Candy Lane & Hickory, 53072, pg. 1113 **PV**

Phillips

PHILLIPS PLASTICS CORPORATION, Seven Long Lake Dr., 54555, pg. 862 **PV**

Platteville

Old Wisconsin Cheese Co., Inc., 1085 E. Mineral St., 53818, pg. 178 **PV**

Pleasant Prairie

CHICAGO LOCK COMPANY, 10100 88th Ave., 53158, pg. 235 **PB**
Nitro Steel Div., 9855 80th Ave., 53158, pg. 1349 **PB**
SuperValu, Inc.-Great Lakes Div.-Pleasant Prairie, 7400 95th St., 53158-0330, pg. 1540 **PV**
Tetra-Pak Processing Systems, 8400 Lakeview Pkwy., Ste. 500, 53158, pg. 1379 **IT**

Plover

Banta Global Turnkey, 1200 Disk Dr., 54467-0220, pg. 188 **PB**
Plover BLFC Branch, 5680 Plover Rd., 54467, pg. 943 **PV**

Plymouth

Great Lakes of Wisconsin, 2602 County Rd. PP, 53073, pg. 474 **PV**
ITW Screen Process Specialist, Ltd., 1700 Sunset Dr., 53073, pg. 867 **PB**
PLYMOUTH CREAMERIES, INC., 322 Schuartz St., 53073, pg. 872 **PV**
SARGENTO FOODS INC., One Persnickety Pl., 53073, pg. 966 **PV**
Sargento Foods Inc. - Consumer Products Div., One Persnickety Pl., 53073, pg. 966 **PV**
Sargento Foods Inc.- Food Service Div., One Persnickety Pl., 53073, pg. 966 **PV**

Toro Worldwide Parts Distribution Center, 3424 County Rd., PF, 53073, pg. 1624 **PB**

Port Edwards

Georgia-Pacific Nekoosa Operations, 100 Wisconsin River Dr., 54469-1492, pg. 736 **PB**
Georgia-Pacific Port Edwards Operations, 100 Wisconsin River Dr., 54469-1492, pg. 736 **PB**

Port Washington

ALLEN-EDMONDS SHOE CORP., 201 E. Seven Hills Rd., 53074, pg. 36 **PV**
Cook Composites & Polymers, P.O. Box 966, 217 Freeman Dr., 53074, pg. 1409 **IT**
Modern Equipment Co., Inc., 336 S. Spring St., 53074, pg. 33 **PV**
OmniQuip International, Inc., 222 E. Main St., 53074, pg. 500 **PV**
SIMPLICITY MANUFACTURING, INC., 500 N. Spring St., 53074, pg. 1002 **PV**
Woodore, 3820 Hwy. KW, 53074, pg. 37 **PV**

Portage

Appleton Papers-Portage Plant, 2500 W. Wisconsin, 53901, pg. 567 **IT**
Mox-Med, Inc., 2316 W. Wisconsin St., 53901, pg. 124 **PV**
PENDA CORPORATION, 2344 W. Wisconsin St., 53901, pg. 848 **PV**
RAYOVAC Corporation, 2851 Portage Rd., 53901, pg. 912 **PV**
Spartech Plastics, 1325 Adams St., 53901, pg. 1496 **PB**
TRIENDA CORPORATION, N7660 Industrial Rd., 53901, pg. 1103 **PV**

Prairie Du Sac

MUELLER SPORTS MEDICINE, INC., One Quench Dr., 53578, pg. 766 **PV**

Racine

API-Gettys Corporation, 2701 No. Green Bay Rd., 53404, pg. 90 **PB**
Agricultural Equipment Div., J.I. Case, 700 State St., 53404, pg. 311 **PB**
Robert Bosch Fluid Power Corporation, 7505 Durand Ave., 53406, pg. 204 **IT**
CASE CORPORATION, 700 State St., 53404, pg. 311 **PB**
The Case Corporation, 700 State St., 53404, pg. 311 **PB**
Case Engine Holding Company, Inc., 700 State St., 53404, pg. 311 **PB**
J.I. Case Credit Corp., 700 State St., 53404, pg. 312 **PB**
J.I. Case International Sales, 700 State St., 53404, pg. 312 **PB**
J.I. Case Leasing Corporation, 700 State St., pg. 312 **PB**
J.I. Case Threshing Machine Company, 700 State St., pg. 312 **PB**
Case Ventures Corporation, 700 State St., pg. 312 **PB**
COLOR ARTS, INC., 1840 Oakdale Ave., 53406, pg. 254 **PV**
Construction Equipment Div., 700 State St., 53404, pg. 311 **PB**
Danfoss Fluid Power, 8635 Washington Ave., 53406-3773, pg. 377 **IT**
Danfoss Fluid Power, a division of Danfoss, Inc., 8635 Washington Ave., 53406, pg. 377 **IT**
Dremel, 4915 21st St., 53406, pg. 574 **PB**
General Magnaplate Wisconsin, 2924 Rapids Dr., 53404, pg. 717 **PV**
Grand Detour Plow Company, 700 State St., pg. 1578 **PB**
Harris Metals, 4210 Douglas Ave., P.O. Box 248, 53401, pg. 999 **PB**
Hedland, 2200 South St., 53404, pg. 906 **PV**
In-Sink-Erator, 4700 21st St., 53406, pg. 573 **PB**
Jacobsen Textron, 1721 Packard Ave., 53403-2564, pg. 589 **PB**
S.C. JOHNSON & SON, INC., 1525 Howe St., 53403-5011, pg. 592 **PV**
Johnson Venture Capital, Inc., 1525 Howe St., 53403, pg. 592 **PV**
The Journal Times, 212 Fourth St., 53403, pg. 983 **PB**
Lovdahl Manufacturing, 5200 Douglas Ave., 53402, pg. 637 **PV**
M & I Bank of Racine, 441 Main St., P.O. Box 757, 53403, pg. 1050 **PB**
MASTER APPLIANCE CORP., 2420 18th St., 53403, pg. 713 **PV**
MODINE MANUFACTURING COMPANY, 1500 DeKoven Ave., 53403-2552, pg. 1121 **PB**
Moxness Products, Inc., 1914 Indiana St., 53405, pg. 124 **PB**
PENCO Wisconsin, 8330 Corporate Dr., Ste. One, 53406, pg. 1508 **IT**
Printing Developments, Inc., 2010 Indiana St., 53405, pg. 717 **PB**
Pugh Marina, 200 Dodge St., 53402, pg. 894 **PV**
PUGH OIL COMPANY, 200 Dodge St., 53402, pg. 894 **PV**
RACINE FEDERATED, INC., 2200 South St., 53404, pg. 906 **PV**
RAINFAIR, INC., 3600 S. Memorial Dr., 53403, pg. 906 **PV**
Rydelle Laboratories, 1525 Howe St., 53403, pg. 592 **PV**
Service Parts Supply Div., 700 State St., 53404, pg. 311 **PB**
Surgitek, 3037 Mt. Pleasant St., 53404, pg. 253 **PB**

TWIN DISC, INCORPORATED, 1328 Racine St., 53403, pg. 1646 **PB**
Walker Europe, Inc., 1201 Michigan Blvd., 53402, pg. 1578 **PB**
Webster Company, Inc., 1900 Clark St., 53403, pg. 377 **IT**
White Flash Oil Co., 200 Dodge St., 53402, pg. 894 **PV**
The Wyco Tool Co., 2200 South St., 53404, pg. 906 **PV**
YOUNG RADIATOR COMPANY, 2825 Four Mile Rd., 53404, pg. 1201 **PV**

Randolph

Busse Brothers Inc., 124 N. Columbus St., 53956, pg. 866 **PV**

Random Lake

TIMES PRINTING COMPANY, INC., 100 Industrial Dr., 53075, pg. 1087 **PV**

Reedsburg

Columbia ParCar Corp., 350 N. Dewey Ave., 53959, pg. 409 **PV**
Gerber Products Division-Baby Care, P.O. Box 120, 728 Booster Blvd., 53959, pg. 973 **IT**
Seats Incorporated, 1515 Industrial St., 53959, pg. 410 **PV**

Rhinelander

The Daily News, P.O. Box 778, 54501, pg. 1343 **PB**
M & I Merchants Bank, Seven N. Brown St., 54501, pg. 1050 **PB**
Wausau-Mosinee Papers Specialty Papers Group, 515 W. Davenport St., 54501, pg. 1747 **PB**

Rice Lake

AMSCO, 311 W. Coleman St., 54868, pg. 1350 **PV**
RICE LAKE WEIGHING SYSTEMS, 230 W. Coleman St., 54868, pg. 927 **PV**
Roosevelt Rice Lake Branch, 310 W. Coleman, 54868, pg. 943 **PV**

Ripon

CONDON OIL COMPANY, INC., 126 E. Jackson St., 54971, pg. 262 **PV**
JMS Specialty Foods, Inc., 126 Jefferson St., 54971, pg. 1480 **PB**
LYKE CORPORATION, 656 Douglas St., 54971, pg. 682 **PV**
M & I Central State Bank, 333 Blackburn St., 54971, pg. 1050 **PB**
Raytheon Appliances, P.O. Box 990, 54971-0990, pg. 1366 **PB**
RIPON FOODS, INC., 420 E. Oshkosh, 54971, pg. 931 **PV**
Wellman Extrusions, Inc., P.O. Box 130, Vermont St., 54971, pg. 1753 **PB**

Rothschild

Sterling Building Systems, Inc., 10805 Bus. Hwy. 51, 54474, pg. 1154 **PV**
WAUSAU HOMES, INC., 10805 Bus. Hwy. 51, 54474, pg. 1154 **PV**

Saint Croix Falls

NV-Mannor, 1105 E. Pine St., 54024, pg. 800 **PV**
NOBLES MFG. INC., 1105 E. Pine St., 54024, pg. 800 **PV**

Saint Francis

EZ Paintr Corp., 4051 S. Iowa Ave., 53235, pg. 1177 **PB**
HARNISCHFEGER INDUSTRIES, INC., 3600 S. Lake Dr., 53235-3716, pg. 788 **PB**

Saint Nazianz

Badger Farm Systems, Inc., 511 E. Main St., 54232, pg. 748 **PV**
Miller Finance Corp., 511 E. Main St., 54232, pg. 748 **PV**
MILLER-ST. NAZIANZ, INC., 511 E. Main St., 54232-0127, pg. 748 **PV**

Sauk City

Fiskars Inc.-Wallace Div., 780 Carolina St., 53583, pg. 492 **IT**

Schofield

Hoffer's Glass Fab, 5103 Janice Ave., 54476, pg. 239 **PV**
Hoffer's Inc., 4601 Camp Phillips Rd., 54476, pg. 239 **PV**

Seymour

PROVIMI VEAL CORPORATION, W. 2103 Country Rd., 54165, pg. 892 **PV**
Service Motor Co., 831 N. Main, pg. 986 **PV**

PB - *U.S. Public Companies Volume*
PV - *U.S. Private Companies Volume*
IT - *International Public & Private Companies Volume*

Shawano

M & I Bank of Shawano, N.A., 101 N. Main St., 54166, pg. 1050   **PB**

Sheboygan

Corrugated Packaging, 1927 Erie Ave., P.O. Box 729, 53082, pg. 736   **PB**
ECLIPSE MANUFACTURING COMPANY, 1828 Oakland Ave., 53081, pg. 361   **PV**
ENZOPAC, INC., 4350 S. Taylor Dr., 53081, pg. 379   **PV**
Kohler Co. Generator Div., Country Trunk LS, 53083, pg. 630   **PV**
M & I Bank S.S.B., 1441 N. Taylor Dr., 53082, pg. 1050   **PB**
NEMSCHOFF CHAIRS, INC., 2218 Julson Ct., 53081, pg. 791   **PV**
Old Wisconsin Sausage, 2107 S. 17th St., 53081, pg. 178   **PV**
POLAR WARE COMPANY, 2806 N. 15th St., 53083, pg. 873   **PV**
SCHREIER MALTING CO., 704 S. 15th St., 53081, pg. 972   **PV**
SCHULTZ SAV-O STORES, INC., 2215 Union Ave., 53082-0419, pg. 1442   **PB**
TORKE COFFEE ROASTING COMPANY, 3455 Paine Ave., 53081, pg. 1092   **PV**
Verifine Dairy Products Corp., 1616 Erie St., 53082, pg. 491   **PB**
VINYL PLASTICS INCORPORATED, 3123 S. 9th St., 54664, pg. 1141   **PV**
THE VOLLRATH COMPANY, L.L.C., 1236 N. 18th St., 53081, pg. 1143   **PV**
WIGWAM MILLS, INC., 3402 Crocker Ave., 53081, pg. 1175   **PV**

Sheboygan Falls

CURT G. JOA, INC., P.O. Box 903, 100 Crocker Ave., 53085-0903, pg. 588   **PV**
Johnsonville Sausage, Inc., County Trunk J, 53085, pg. 595   **PV**
RICHARDSON INDUSTRIES, INC., 904 Monroe St., 53085, pg. 929   **PV**
Richardson Lumber Co., 904 Monroe St., 53085, pg. 929   **PV**
Richardson's Furniture Emporium, 202 Pine St., 53085, pg. 929   **PV**

Sherwood

Stockbridge & Sherwood Telephone Co., Inc., Box 159, N 287 Military Rd., 54169, pg. 1572   **PB**

Shiocton

Bush Brothers & Company Plant, P.O. Box 27, 54170, pg. 189   **PV**

Shullsburg

MCCOY GROUP INC., Hwy. 11, 53586, pg. 720   **PV**

Slinger

Titan Wheel Corporation of WI, P.O. Box 376, 465 W. Washington St., 53086, pg. 1619   **PB**

Solon Springs

Mosinee Industrial Forest Division, P.O. Box 238, 54873, pg. 1747   **PB**

South Milwaukee

BUCYRUS INTERNATIONAL, 1100 Milwaukee Ave., 53172, pg. 177   **PV**
Minserco, Inc., 1100 Milwaukee Ave., 53172, pg. 177   **PV**

Sparta

Monroe County Telephone Co., 311 S. Court, 54656, pg. 330   **PB**

Spring Green

M & I Bank Southwest, 209 E. Jefferson St., 53588, pg. 1050   **PB**

Stanley

Stanley Drying Company, P.O. Box 120, 54768, pg. 301   **PV**

Stevens Point

THE COPPS CORP., 2828 Wayne St., 54481, pg. 275   **PV**
Crestline Distribution Facility, 2116 Wood St., 54481, pg. 1193   **PV**
Dairyland Insurance Co., 1800 N. Point Dr., 54481, pg. 985   **PV**
First Financial Bank, FSB, 1305 Main St., 54481, pg. 140   **PB**
First Financial Corporation, 1305 Main St., 54481, pg. 140   **PB**

Joern's Sunrise Medical, 5001 Joerns Dr., 54481, pg. 1536   **PB**
M & I Mid-State Bank, 1245 Main St., 54481, pg. 1050   **PB**
Middlesex Insurance Co., 1800 N. Point Dr., 54481, pg. 985   **PV**
NOEL OLSON GROUP, 1145 Clark St., 54481, pg. 800   **PV**
SENTRY INSURANCE, A MUTUAL COMPANY, 1800 N. Point Dr., 54481, pg. 984   **PV**
Sentry Insurance, A Mutual Company, 1800 N. Point Dr., 54481, pg. 985   **PV**
Service Motor Co., 6693 Hwy. 66, pg. 986   **PV**
Stevens Point Brewery, 2617 Water St., 54481, pg. 300   **PV**
WORZALLA PUBLISHING CO., INC., 3535 Jefferson St., 54481, pg. 1191   **PV**

Stoughton

Zalk Joseph Fabrications, Inc., 400 Industrial Cir., 53589, pg. 860   **PV**

Sturgeon Bay

Bay Shipbuilding Co., 605 N. Third Ave., 54235, pg. 1041   **PB**
Emerson Motor Company, 821 Neenah Ave., 54235, pg. 573   **PV**
MTI Leasing, Ltd., 49 E. Yew St., 54235, pg. 703   **PV**
MARINE TRAVELIFT, INC., 49 E. Yew St., 54235, pg. 703   **PV**
PETERSON BUILDERS, INC., 41 North Third Ave., 54235, pg. 857   **PV**
Shuttlelift, Inc., 49 E. Yew St., 54235, pg. 703   **PV**

Sturtevant

ANDIS COMPANY, 1800 Renaissance Blvd., 53177, pg. 73   **PV**
JOHNSON WORLDWIDE ASSOCIATES, INC., 1326 Willow Rd., 53177, pg. 932   **PB**
PUTZMEISTER, INC., 1733 90th St., 53177, pg. 896   **PV**

Sun Prairie

General Casualty Company of Wisconsin, One General Dr., 53596, pg. 345   **IT**

Superior

Barko Hydraulics, Banks Ave. & Bayfront, 54880, pg. 859   **PV**
Duluth, Winnipeg & Pacific Railway Co., Rt. 2, Box 3008, 54880, pg. 258   **IT**
Lakehead Pipe Line Co., Inc., 119 N. 25 St. E., 54880, pg. 652   **IT**
M & I Bank, 1425 Tower Ave., 54880, pg. 1050   **PB**
Superior Water, Light & Power Company, 1230 Tower Ave., 54880, pg. 1116   **PB**

Sussex

Huffy Sports Company, N53 W24700 S. Corp. Cir., 53089, pg. 846   **PB**

Tomah

BURNSTAD BROTHERS, INC., 701 E. Clifton, 54660, pg. 187   **PV**

Two Rivers

Aristo Manufacturing Co., 1704 Monroe St., 54241, pg. 735   **PV**
THE METAL WARE CORP., 1700 Monroe St., 54241, pg. 734   **PV**
Outdoor Technologies Wisconsin, 1429 Wentker Ct., 54241, pg. 822   **PV**
Paragon Electric Co., Inc., 606 Parkway Blvd., 54241, pg. 1243   **IT**

Union Grove

Alling-Lander, 1524 15th Ave., 53182, pg. 1370   **PB**
Danfoss Fluid Power - Mini Steering Units Div., 1101 S. Sylvannia Ave., 53182, pg. 377   **IT**
Grove Gear Div., 1524 15th Ave., 53182, pg. 1370   **PB**

Verona

American Systems Technologies, 421 S. Nine Mound Rd., 53593, pg. 2   **PB**
Mt. Vernon Telephone Co., P.O. Box 95, 113 No. Main St., 53593, pg. 1571   **PB**

Vesper

Central State Telephone Co., P.O. Box 125, 106 N. Virginia St., 54489, pg. 1571   **PB**

Viroqua

Frontier Communications of Viroqua, Inc., P.O. Box 91, 114 E. Court St., 54665, pg. 684   **PB**

Walworth

Iseli Company, 402 North Main St., 53184, pg. 481   **PB**
Kikkoman Foods, Inc., P.O. Box 69, 53184, pg. 733   **IT**
MINIATURE PRECISION COMPONENTS, Walworth Industrial Park, 53184, pg. 750   **PV**

Waterloo

PERRY GRAPHIC COMMUNICATIONS, INC., 575 W. Madison St., 53594, pg. 855   **PV**
Trek Bicycle Corporation, 801 W. Madison St., 53594, pg. 1099   **PV**
TREK CORPORATION, 801 W. Madison St., 53594, pg. 1099   **PV**
Waterloo Malting Co., Inc., P.O. Box 67, 53594, pg. 1289   **PB**

Watertown

Blue M Electric Co., 304 Hart St., 53094, pg. 726   **PB**
Cutler-Hammer Products, 901 S. 12th St., 53094, pg. 556   **PB**
Lindberg, A General Signal Company, 304 Hart St., 55094, pg. 727   **PB**
M & I Bank South Central, 205 N. Second St., 53094, pg. 1050   **PB**

Waukesha

ALLOY PRODUCTS CORP., 1045 Perkins Ave., 53187-0529, pg. 42   **PV**
Beatrice Cheese Co., 770 N. Springdale Rd., 53186, pg. 426   **PB**
Blackhawk Collision Repair Inc., 2120 Pewaukee Rd., 53188, pg. 805   **PV**
COOLIDGE GLASS CO., INC., W226 N758 Eastmound Dr., 53186-1656, pg. 273   **PV**
Cooper Power Systems, 2300 Badger Dr., 53188-5951, pg. 443   **PB**
CRITICARE SYSTEMS, INC., 20925 Crossroads Cir., 53186, pg. 459   **PB**
Dover Diversified, 2607 N. Grandview Blvd., 53188, pg. 521   **PV**
EDD-Milwaukee, W. 226, N. 900 Eastmound Dr., 53186, pg. 205   **PB**
ELECTRONIC TELE-COMMUNICATIONS, INC., 1915 MacArthur Rd., 53188, pg. 570   **PB**
Envirex, 1901 S. Prairie Ave., 53186, pg. 61   **PB**
Fleming Company, 1200 W. Sunset Dr., 53186-6597, pg. 653   **PB**
H&K Holdings, Inc., 880 Bahcall Ct., 53187, pg. 737   **IT**
H&K Machines, Inc., 880 Bahcall Ct., 53187, pg. 737   **IT**
HWC Export Sales Corporation, 2120 Pewaukee Rd., 53188, pg. 805   **PV**
HEIN-WERNER CORPORATION, 2120 Pewaukee Rd., 53188, pg. 805   **PB**
Hein-Werner of Canada, Ltd., P.O. Box 1606, 53187-1606, pg. 805   **PB**
HOLOUBEK INC., W238 N1800 Rockwood Dr., 53188, pg. 536   **PV**
Intelligraphics International, 741 N. Grand Ave., 53186, pg. 110   **PB**
Intercare Technologies, Inc., 20875 Crossroads Circle, Ste. 300, 53186, pg. 459   **PB**
Intergraph Corporation, 20725 Watertown Rd., Ste. K, 53186, pg. 891   **PB**
J & L Fiber Services, Inc., 809 Philip Dr., 53186, pg. 789   **PB**
KALMBACH PUBLISHING CO., 21027 Crossroads Circle, 53187, pg. 606   **PV**
Lappin Electric Company, W. 229 N. 1420th Westwood Dr, Unit A., 53188, pg. 265   **PV**
McHugh Software International, 2071 Swensen Dr., Ste. 400, 53186, pg. 866   **PV**
ORTHO-KINETICS, INC., W220 N507 Springdale Rd., 53186, pg. 820   **PV**
PLASTIC ENGINEERED COMPONENTS INC., N14 W23833 Stone Ridge Dr., Ste. 310, 53188, pg. 870   **PV**
Quality Casting Company, 1908 Mac Arthur Rd., 53186, pg. 741   **PV**
Safway Steel Products Inc., N14 W23833 Stone Ridge Dr. Ste. 400, 53188, pg. 1389   **IT**
Sanofi Bio Industries, 620 Progress Ave., 53186, pg. 445   **IT**
Sentry Drugs, Inc., 1200 W. Sunset Dr., 53186, pg. 653   **PB**
Sentry Markets, Inc., 1200 W. Sunset Dr., 53186, pg. 653   **PB**
Store Equipment, Inc., 1200 W. Sunset Dr., 53186, pg. 653   **PB**
Svedala Industries Inc., 20965 Crossroads Cir., 53186, pg. 1326   **IT**
THP United Enterprises, N14 W23833 Stone Ridge Dr., Ste. 400, 53188, pg. 1389   **IT**
Waukesha Bearings Corp., PO Box 798, 53187, pg. 521   **PV**
Waukesha Engine Division, 1000 W. St. Paul Ave., 53188-4999, pg. 528   **PV**
WAUKESHA FOUNDRY INC., 1300 Lincoln Ave., 53186, pg. 1154   **PV**
Wisconsin Insurance Management, Inc., 300 Wisconsin Ave., 53186, pg. 141   **PB**

Waunakee

Scientific Protein Laboratories, Inc., 700 E. Main St., 53597, pg. 80   **PB**

PB - *U.S. Public Companies Volume*
PV - *U.S. Private Companies Volume*
IT - *International Public & Private Companies Volume*

Geographic Index-U.S.

Suttle Press, Inc., P.O. Box 370, 1000 Uniek Dr., 53597, pg. 1570 **PB**

Waunakee Telephone Co., Inc., 103 Bacon St., 53597, pg. 1572 **PB**

Waupaca

ADD, Inc., P.O. Box 267, 54981, pg. 601 **PV**
AmeriTruck Refrigerated Transport, Inc., 455 Industrial Dr., 54981, pg. 66 **PV**
Moore-O-Matic, Inc., 419 Oak St., 54981, pg. 1193 **PB**
Waupaca Foundry Inc., Tower Rd., 54981, pg. 1389 **IT**

Waupun

ALTO DAIRY COOPERATIVE, P.O. Box 550, N. 3545 County EE, 53963-0550, pg. 47 **PV**
NATIONAL RIVET & MANUFACTURING COMPANY, 21 E. Jefferson St., 53963, pg. 786 **PV**

Wausau

Associated Bank North, 303 S. First Ave., 54401, pg. 140 **PB**
Case CE Div.-Wausau, P.O. Box 1087, 54401, pg. 311 **PB**
Employers Insurance of Wausau, 2000 Westwood Dr., 54401, pg. 788 **PV**
Employers Life Ins. Co. of Wausau, 2000 Westwood Dr., 54401, pg. 789 **PV**
Fiskars Hand Tool Division, 7811 W. Stewart Ave., 54401, pg. 492 **IT**
Fiskars Inc., P.O. Box 8027, 7811 W. Stewart Ave., 54401, pg. 492 **IT**
Fiskars Inc., 7811 W. Stewart Ave., 54401, pg. 492 **IT**
THE HAMMERBLOW CORP., 1000 First St., 54403, pg. 498 **PV**
M & I First American Bank, 500 Third St., 54402-8008, pg. 1050 **PB**
Marathon Electric Manufacturing Corp., 100 E. Randolph, 54401, pg. 1371 **PB**
PDM Bridge, 3526 W. Sherman St., 54401, pg. 1305 **PB**
Piper Jaffray Inc., First American Ctr., 500 Third St., Ste. 305, 54401-4857, pg. 1302 **PB**
Wausau Daily Herald, 800 Scott St., 54401, pg. 700 **PB**
Wausau Metals Corp., 1415 West St., 54401, pg. 120 **PB**
Wausau Metals, Nanik Division, 7200 Stewart Ave., 54402, pg. 1500 **PB**
Wausau Service Corp., 2000 Westwood Dr., 54401, pg. 789 **PV**
Wausau Underwriters Insurance Co., 2000 Westwood Dr., 54401, pg. 789 **PV**
Wipfli, Ullrich, Bertelson, 500 3rd St., Ste. 303, 54402-8010, pg. 566 **PB**

Wauwatosa

Ato-Findley, Inc., 11320 Watertown Plank Rd., 53226-3434, pg. 445 **IT**
BRIGGS & STRATTON CORPORATION, 12301 W. Wirth St., 53222, pg. 252 **PB**
Briggs & Stratton International Sales, 12301 W. Wirth St., 53222, pg. 252 **PB**
Briggs & Stratton Corp., 3300 N. 124th St., 53222-3106, pg. 252 **PB**
A.M. Castle & Co., 3000 N. 114th St., 53226, pg. 313 **PB**
EQUITABLE SAVINGS & LOAN ASSOCIATION, 2290 N. Mayfair Rd., 53226, pg. 380 **PV**
Federated Bank, S.S.B., 2600 N. Mayfair Rd., 53226, pg. 643 **PB**
Fireman's Fund Insurance Co. of Wisconsin, 3333 N. Mayfair, 53222, pg. 59 **IT**
Earle M. Jorgensen Company/Milwaukee, 11610 W. North Ave., 53226, pg. 600 **PV**
Kohl's Food Stores, 11100 W. Burleigh Ave., 53222-3212, pg. 1375 **IT**
Nordic Systems, Ltd., 11400 W. Bluemound, Ste. 300, 53226, pg. 410 **PV**

West Bend

RUSS DARROW GROUP, 4524 Dollar Dr., 53095, pg. 311 **PV**
ENGER-KRESS COMPANY, 151 Wisconsin St., 53095, pg. 376 **PV**
First Church Financing Corporation, 215 N. Main St., 53095, pg. 1792 **PB**
GEHL COMPANY, P.O. Box 179, 53095-0179, pg. 704 **PB**
M & I First National Bank, 321 N. Main St., 53095, pg. 1050 **PB**
SERIGRAPH, INC., 3801 E. Decorah Rd, 53095, pg. 985 **PV**
Weasler Engineering Inc., Hwy. 45 N., 53095, pg. 249 **PV**
The West Bend Co., 400 Washington, 53095, pg. 1322 **PB**
Ziegler Asset Management, Inc., 215 N. Main St., 53095-3348, pg. 1792 **PB**
B.C. Ziegler & Co., 215 N. Main St., 53095-3348, pg. 1792 **PB**
Ziegler Collateralized Securities, 215 N. Main St., 53095, pg. 1792 **PB**
THE ZIEGLER COMPANIES, INC., P.O. Box 118, 215 N. Main St., 53095-3348, pg. 1791 **PB**
Ziegler Financing Corp., 215 N. Main St., 53095, pg. 1792 **PB**
Ziegler Leasing Corp., 215 N. Main St., 53095-3348, pg. 1792 **PB**

Weyauwega

Benson Corp., 512 N. Mill St., 54983, pg. 443 **PV**

Whitewater

Polymer Technologies, 420 N. Universal Blvd., 53190, pg. 692 **PV**
WEILER & COMPANY, INC., 116 E. Main St., 53190, pg. 1160 **PV**

Winneconne

Ingersoll Equipment Co., Inc., P.O. Box 5001, 54986, pg. 1129 **IT**

Wisconsin Rapids

ADVANTAGE LEARNING SYSTEMS, INC., 2911 Peach St., 54494, pg. 22 **PB**
Biron Div., 621 Biron Dr., 54494, pg. 436 **PB**
CONSOLIDATED PAPERS, INC., P.O. Box 8050, 54495-8050, pg. 436 **PB**
Consolidated Water Power Co., 231 First Ave. N., 54494, pg. 436 **PB**
Converting Div., 231 First Ave. N., 54494, pg. 436 **PB**
Firstar Wisconsin Rapids, 311 W. Grand Ave., 54494, pg. 643 **PB**
Hotel Mead Corp., 451 E. Grand Ave., 54494, pg. 436 **PB**
Mead Realty Corp., 214 W. Grand Ave., 54494, pg. 436 **PB**
NORTHLAND CRANBERRIES, INC., 800 First Ave. S., 54495-8020, pg. 1197 **PB**
WildHawk, Inc., 800 First Ave. S., 54495, pg. 1197 **PB**

WYOMING

Buffalo

Johnson County Title Company, Inc., 71 N. Main St., 82834, pg. 626 **PB**

Casper

B & B HOMES CORPORATION, 3283 N. Nine Mile Rd., 82604, pg. 105 **PV**
Belle Fourche Pipeline Co., 895 W. River Cross Rd., 82602, pg. 1107 **PV**
Black Hills Trucking Co., 895 W. River Cross Rd., 82602, pg. 1107 **PV**
Casper Wyoming Production District Office, 800 Werner Ct., Ste. 150, 82601, pg. 548 **PV**
CRUM ELECTRIC SUPPLY CO., INC., 1165 English Ave., 82601, pg. 293 **PV**
Eighty Eight Oil Co., 895 W. River Cross Rd., 82602, pg. 1107 **PV**
First Interstate Bank of Wyoming N.A., 104 S. Wolcott St., 82601, pg. 1753 **PB**
Mini Mart, Inc., 907 N. Poplar, Ste. 260, 82602, pg. 967 **PB**
Northern Gas Company, P.O. Box 2800, 82602-2800, pg. 937 **PB**
Norwest Bank Wyoming, N.A., P.O. Box 2799, 82601, pg. 1202 **PB**
Piper Jaffray Inc., 120 S. Durbin St., 82601-2512, pg. 1302 **PB**
RISSLER & MCMURRY COMPANY, 3245 N. Salt Creek Hwy., 82601, pg. 933 **PV**
Toolpusher Supply Co., 895 W. River Cross Rd., 82601, pg. 1107 **PV**
TRUE COMPANIES, 895 W. River Cross Rd., 82601, pg. 1107 **PV**
True Drilling Co., 895 W. River Cross Rd., 82602, pg. 1107 **PV**
True Geothermal Energy Co., 895 W. River Cross Rd., 82601, pg. 1107 **PV**
True Oil Co., 895 W. River Cross Rd., 82602, pg. 1107 **PV**
True Ranches, 895 W. River Cross Rd., 82602, pg. 1107 **PV**
True Wyoming Beef, 895 W. River Cross Rd., 82601, pg. 1107 **PV**
Westowns Disposal Systems, Inc., 2583 Bryan Evansville Rd., 82602, pg. 265 **PB**
Woodward-Clyde, 110 W. Second St., Ste. 285, 82601, pg. 1656 **PB**
Wyoming Concrete Products Co., 725 Bryan Stock Trail, 82609, pg. 208 **PV**
WYOMING MACHINERY COMPANY, 5300 W. Old Yellowstone, 82604, pg. 1193 **PV**

Cheyenne

American Wyott Corporation, 1938 Wyott Dr., 82007, pg. 1193 **PV**
Cheyenne Light, Fuel & Power Co., 108 W. 18th St., 82001, pg. 1170 **PB**
CHEYENNE OUTFITTERS, INC., P.O. Box 12013, 82003, pg. 234 **PV**
Dynacare-Wyoming, 800 E. 20th St., Ste. 206, 82001, pg. 425 **IT**
First American Title Guaranty Agency of Cheyenne, 1810 Pioneer Dr., 82001, pg. 625 **PB**
FLEISCHLI OIL COMPANY, INC., 2350 W. Lincoln Way, 82001, pg. 410 **PV**
Frontier Refining, Inc., 2700 E. 5th St., 82001, pg. 1732 **PB**
Johnson Storage & Moving, Cheyenne, 204 N. American Rd., 82001, pg. 594 **PV**
Key Trust Company of the West, 1800 Carey Ave., 82001, pg. 954 **PB**

Mountain Towers Healthcare, 3129 Aracia Dr., 82001, pg. 1714 **PB**
Options and Choices, Inc., 2232 Dell Range Blvd., Ste. 305, 82009, pg. 1699 **PB**
TACO JOHN'S INTERNATIONAL, INC., 808 W. 20th St., 82001, pg. 1066 **PV**
UNICOVER CORPORATION, 1934 Wyott Dr., 82007, pg. 1117 **PV**

Cody

Shoshone Title Insurance & Abstract Company, 1002 13th St., 82414, pg. 626 **PB**
WYO L.P. Gas, 125 W. Yellowstone Ave., 82414, pg. 581 **PB**

Douglas

Converse Land Title Company, 313 Center St., 82633, pg. 625 **PB**

Evansville

Little America Refining, Inc., P.O. Box 510, 82636, pg. 1003 **PV**

Gillette

ICI Explosives, P.O. Box 2560, 82716, pg. 664 **IT**
LARRYS, INC., 2020 Schoonover Rd., 82718, pg. 652 **PV**
MGTC, Inc., P.O. Box 1749, 82717-1749, pg. 1758 **PB**
Piper Jaffray Inc., 222 S. Gillette Ave., Ste. 600, 82716-3745, pg. 1303 **PB**
Powder River Coal Company, Caller Box #3034, 1013 Boxelder, 82717-3034, pg. 594 **IT**

Green River

FMC Wyoming Corp., 20 Miles W. on West Vaco Rd., 82935, pg. 605 **PB**
Rhone-Poulenc Basic Chemicals Co., P.O. Box 513, 82935, pg. 1110 **IT**
Wyoming Land Title Company, 189 N. First W., 82935, pg. 626 **PB**

Greybull

BIG HORN CO-OP MARKETING ASSOCIATION, 346 S. 6th, 82426, pg. 143 **PV**

Hanna

Cyprus Shoshone Coal Corporation, P.O. Box 830, 82327, pg. 471 **PB**

Jackson

DATA BROADCASTING CORPORATION, 3490 Clubhouse Dr. I-2, 83001, pg. 484 **PB**
MEDTECH INC., 3510 N. Lake Creek Dr., 83001, pg. 728 **PV**
Teton Land Title Company, 140 S. Cache, 83001, pg. 626 **PB**

Kemmerer

FMC Wyoming Corp., P.O. Box 750, 83101, pg. 605 **PB**

Lander

Fremont County Title Company, 130 Eugene St., 82520, pg. 626 **PB**

Laramie

BANNER ASSOCIATES INC., 620 Plaza Ct., 82070, pg. 114 **PV**
Mountain Cement Company, P.O. Box 339, 82070, pg. 323 **PB**
TRC Mariah Associates, Inc., 605 Skyline Dr., 82070, pg. 1558 **PB**

Pinedale

First American Title Guaranty Agency of Sublette County, 17 S. Fremont Ave., 82941, pg. 625 **PB**

Point of Rocks

Mining Services International, Exit 130, I-80 E., Hwy. 377, 84107-7930, pg. 1115 **PB**

Powell

Big Horn Redi-Mix, 245 Park Ave., pg. 1124 **PB**

Rawlins

First American Title Guaranty Agency of Carbon County, 820 W. Spruce, Box 1647, 82301, pg. 625 **PB**
Park Manor Nursing & Convalescent Home, 542-16th St., 82301, pg. 1714 **PB**

PB - U.S. Public Companies Volume
PV - U.S. Private Companies Volume
IT - International Public & Private Companies Volume

Geographic Index-U.S.

Riverton

Fremont Mannor Nursing & Convalescent Home, 1002
    Forest Dr., P.O. Box 833, 82501, pg. 1712   **PB**
GILPATRICK CONSTRUCTION COMPANY, INC, 714 W.
    Monroe, 82501, pg. 454   **PV**

Rock Springs

First Security Bank of Wyoming, 1400 Dewar Dr., 82901,
    pg. 637   **PB**
Kimberly Manor Nursing and Convalescent Home, 1325
    Sage St., 82901, pg. 1714   **PB**
Morgantown Machine Anderson Mavor, 38 Purple Sage
    Rd., 82901, pg. 280   **IT**

Sheridan

Piper Jaffray Inc., 21 E. Works St., 82801-3642,
    pg. 1302   **PB**

Sundance

First American Title Guaranty Agency of Crook County, 307
    Main St., 82729, pg. 625   **PB**

Teton Village

JACKSON HOLE SKI RESORT, 7658 N. Teewinot, Chairlift
    Rd., 83025, pg. 579   **PV**

Thermopolis

First American Title Guaranty Agency of Hot Springs
    County, 534 Big Horn Dr., 82443, pg. 625   **PB**

Torrington

Goshen County Abstract & Title, 2019 Main St., 82240,
    pg. 626   **PB**

Worland

PENCO-Wyoming, P.O. Box 579, 121 S. Ninth St., 82401,
    pg. 1508   **IT**

MASTER GEOGRAPHIC INDEX TO NON-U.S. LOCATED COMPANIES

ALBANIA

Tirana

CIBA-GEIGY Services Limited-Scientific Office, Rruga L. Gurakuqi, pg. 980 **IT**
Deminex Albania Petroleum GmbH, Bogdan St. 38, pg. 1461 **IT**
Groupe ADA, Adriatika DFS Albania, 1 Place Skenderbeg, pg. 817 **PB**
The World Bank, Deshmoret e 4 Shkurtit, pg. 1189 **PV**

ALGERIA

Algiers

BHP Petroleum (Algerie) Inc., 5 Du Chemin Maclay, pg. 225 **IT**
Daewoo Corp. - Algiers, pg. 358 **IT**
Det Norske Veritas, Rue No. 12 Lot 36, Les Vergers Birkhadem, pg. 397 **IT**
Digital Equipment Algeria, Hotel El Aurassi, Niveau C/ Bureau 13, pg. 507 **PB**
ESAB Bureau de Liaison, 90, rue Hassiba Ben Bouali, pg. 282 **IT**
Fin.Co-Algeria, 29 Blvd. Zirout Youcef, pg. 654 **IT**
Krupp Maschinentechnik GmbH, Bureau de Liaison, 33, Rue No. 1, pg. 510 **IT**
Mitsui & Co., Ltd., 17, rue Gadouche Abdelkader, El-Biar, pg. 881 **IT**
Neste Algerie S.A.R.L., Villa Machee Allah, 5 bis Chemin Maclay, pg. 914 **IT**
Pechiney AIM-Rep. Office in Algeria, 38-44, rue Didouche Mourad, pg. 1031 **IT**
Pfizer Pharm Algerie (PPA), Mo. 15, rue 4, pg. 1283 **PB**
Rhone-Poulenc S.A., Blvd. Colonel Bougara, 27, pg. 1113 **IT**
SNC-Lavalin, 2, rue Ribolet, pg. 1162 **IT**
Sandvik S.A. Bureau de Liasion, pg. 1187 **IT**
Shell d'Exploration, pg. 1137 **IT**
Societa Ital. per Condotte D'Acqua-Algeria, Blvd. des Martyres 15, pg. 655 **IT**
Societe Algerienne d'Hotellerie, De Loisirs et d'Immobilier, Pins Maritimes, pg. 358 **IT**

Cheraga

Hewlett-Packard Trading S.A., Bureau de Liaison Alger, 71, Lot. Benachour, pg. 822 **PB**
Tamrock Bureau de Liaison Alger, 12, route de Ain-Benian, pg. 1353 **IT**

Constantine

Italstrade-Algeria, Hamma Bouziane, pg. 655 **IT**

Hydra

Bureau BASF Algerie, 13, Rue Arezki Abri, pg. 107 **IT**
CIBA-GEIGY Services S.A., Bureau de Liason, 4, rue Mohamed Hadj Ahmed, pg. 980 **IT**
Novo Nordisk A/S, Bureau de Liaison, 5, Rue Abri Arezki, pg. 987 **IT**
Ram Representative Office-Algeria, Chemin Gadouche, AEK, Lotissement Altitude, Nr. 7, pg. 741 **IT**
Repsol Exploracion Algerie, S.A., 40 Rue Parmentier, pg. 1105 **IT**
Telefonaktiebolaget LM Ericsson Bureaux Techniques d'Algerie, Val d'Hydra lot Nr 50, pg. 1370 **IT**

Tlemcen

SITEL-Societe Industrielle Algerienne de Telecommunications, Zone Industrielle, Route de Chetouane, pg. 1370 **IT**

ANGOLA

Cabinda

Algoa Oil de Cabinda, Ltd., C.P. 405, pg. 5 **IT**

Luanda

Banco Mundial, Edificio BPC, Rua Alfredo Troni, pg. 1189 **PV**
Banque Paribas-Angola, Rua Dr. Alfredo Troni-Predio do B.P.A., pg. 319 **IT**
Blackwood Hodge (Angola) Ltda., Vale do Soroca, pg. 231 **IT**
Braspetro Angola, Rua Pedro Felix Machado, 51-2 Andar, pg. 1042 **IT**
CIBA-GEIGY Trading and Marketing Services Co. Ltd., Rua Conselheiro, pg. 980 **IT**
Daewoo Corp. - Luanda, pg. 358 **IT**
Det Norske Veritas, c/o Agenang, Rua Gomes de Sousa, pg. 397 **IT**
Equator Trade Services Limited, Rua Alfredo Troni, Edificio BPC, Andar Direit, pg. 580 **IT**
Fina Petroleos de Angola, S.A.R.L., av. Rainha Ginga, 128, pg. 1044 **IT**
Mitsui & Co., Ltd., Av. 4 de Fevereiro No. 37 3 Andar, Porta, pg. 881 **IT**
Nova Cimangola S.A.R.L., Av. 4 de Fevereiro, 42, pg. 1201 **IT**
Shell Company of West Africa Ltd., Avenida 4 de Fevreiro No. 42, pg. 1137 **IT**
Sodexho Angola S.A., pg. 1275 **IT**
Statoil Angola, BP Exploration, Rua Alfredo Trony, 15-A-16, pg. 1298 **IT**
Texaco Petroleos de Angola S.A.R.L., Caixa Postal 5897, pg. 1584 **PB**

ARGENTINA

Buenos Aires

AGA Argentina SACIFIMR, Piedras 383-2 piso, pg. 13 **IT**
A.I. Ocean S.A., Bernardo de Irigoyen, 308, pg. 14 **IT**
AMP S.A. Argentina, 4 de Febrero, pg. 9 **PB**
Acer Argentina, pg. 22 **IT**
Aceros Boehler S.A., Presidente Sarmiento 1297 esq., Lafuente, 1870 Avellaneda, pg. 1471 **IT**
Aceros Fortuna S.A., Donado 1149, pg. 515 **IT**
Aconcagua Seguros de Retiro, S.A., Lavalle 348, pg. 333 **IT**
Aerolineas Argentinas, C/Bouchard, 547, pg. 575 **IT**
Agfa-Gevaert Argentina S.A., pg. 174 **IT**
Aguas Argentinas, Reconquiste 823, pg. 824 **IT**
Alcon Laboratories Argentina S.A., pg. 918 **IT**
Alfa-Laval S.A., Casilla de Correo 62, pg. 1379 **IT**
All Computers S.A., Cerrito 1138, Piso 9, pg. 816 **PB**
Allianz RAS Argentina, S.A. de Seguros Generales, San Martin 550, pg. 60 **IT**
Amoco Argentina Oil Co., Maipu 942, pg. 102 **PB**
Amway Argentina, Inc., Maipu 939-P.B., pg. 69 **PV**
Ansaldo Argentina S.A., Av. Del Libertador 498, pg. 654 **IT**
Arcoplus Argentina, General JOse Maria Paz 451, Florida, pg. 576 **IT**
Cia. Argentina de Telefonos, S.A., Belgrano 894, pg. 1365 **IT**
Ascensores Schindler S.A., pg. 1205 **IT**
Asea Brown Boveri S.A., pg. 8 **IT**
Autolatina Argentina S.A., Avda. Henry Ford y Panamericana, pg. 1475 **IT**
BASF Argentina S.A., Av. Corrientes 327, pg. 105 **IT**
BHF-Bank Representative Office, Reconquista 144, piso 12, pg. 120 **IT**
BHP Petroleum (Argentina) Inc., Avenida Eduardo Madero 1020, pg. 225 **IT**

BNL - Fondiaria Inversiones Argentinas S.A., Juncal 1319, pg. 136 **IT**
BYK Liprandi S.A.C.e.l., pg. 66 **IT**
Babcock Argentina S.A., Cangallo, 925 60 Piso, pg. 473 **IT**
Bagley S.A., Moreno 877, Piso 12, pg. 379 **IT**
Banca Nazionale del Lavoro S.A., (Head Office), Florida 40, pg. 137 **IT**
BANCO DE LA NACION ARGENTINA, Bartolome Mitre 326, pg. 140 **IT**
BANCO DE LA PROVINCIA DE BUENOS AIRES, Avenida San Martin 108, 22nd Floor, pg. 140 **IT**
Banco do Brasil S.A.-Argentina, Calle Sarmiento 487, pg. 141 **IT**
Banco Interfinanzas S.A., Sarmiento 332, 8th Fl., pg. 347 **IT**
Banco Mundial, Piso 12, Avenida Leandro N. Alem 628-30, pg. 1189 **PV**
Banco Popular Argentino, Florida, 201 (esquina Cangallo), pg. 140 **IT**
BANCO QUILMES, Tte. Gral. J.D. Peron 564, pg. 142 **IT**
Banco Santander, Rivadavia 611 - piso 11,, pg. 144 **IT**
Banco Santander Argentina, Avda. Leandro N. Aleu 356, pg. 143 **IT**
Banco Santander-Argentina, Calle Esmeralda 55, Piso 10, pg. 143 **IT**
Bank of America NT&SA, 537-25 de Mayo, 1st Fl., pg. 182 **PB**
Bank Hapoalim (Buenos Aires), Sarmiento 944, Piso 13, pg. 149 **IT**
Bank of Boston, Banco de Boston, Florida 99, pg. 184 **PB**
The Bank of New York, 25 de Mayo 195, 9th Fl., pg. 179 **PB**
The Bank of New York, S.A., 25 de Mayo 199, 9th Floor, pg. 179 **PB**
Bankers Trust New York Corporation, BT Rio de la Plata, S.A.C.F. San Martin No. 128/142, pg. 186 **PB**
Banque Europeenne pour l'Amerique Latine (BEAL) S.A., Calle Teniente, General Juan Domingo Peron, 338, pg. 1493 **IT**
Bayer Quimicas Unidas S.A., pg. 175 **IT**
Benckiser Cosmetics Argentina S.A., pg. 185 **IT**
Berkley International, S.A., Av. Santa Fe 8462 Piso, pg. 216 **IT**
Berlitz Schools of Languages of Argentina S.A., Avenida Santa Fe 1605, pg. 222 **PB**
Bodegas Chandon S.A., Florida 378, pg. 782 **IT**
Bonifica-Argentina, Calle Sarmiento 1967 4 Piso, pg. 655 **IT**
Robert Bosch Argentina SA, Avda. Cordoba 5160/64, pg. 205 **IT**
Boston Compania Argentina de Seguros S.A., Suipacha 268, pg. 364 **PB**
Boston Compania Argentina de Seguros S.A., Suipacha 268-Pisos 3 y 4, pg. 1700 **PB**
Boston Inversora De Valores S.A., Sarmiento 539, 10th Floor, Of.2, pg. 185 **PB**
The Boston Investment Group S.A., Sarmiento 539, 10th Floor, Of.1, pg. 185 **PB**
Boston Overseas Financial Corporation S.A., Sarmiento 539, 8th Floor, pg. 185 **PB**
Bridgestone/Firestone de la Argentina S.A.I.C., Anartida Argentina 2715, pg. 222 **IT**
Bull Argentina SACI, Carlos Pellegrini 1363, pg. 315 **IT**
Leo Burnett Co. Inc., Carlos Pellegrini 1363, 12th Fl., pg. 185 **PV**
CINBA SA, Don Bosco 3672 2 Piso, pg. 409 **IT**
CNL Bull, Piso 10 Capital Federal, pg. 318 **IT**
CTI Compania de Telefonos del Interior S.A., Avenida Pte. Rogue Saenz, Para 832, Piso 4, pg. 697 **PB**
CTI Norte Compania de Telefonos del Interior S.A., Avenida Pte. Rogue Saenz, Para 832, Piso 4, pg. 697 **PB**
CW Comunicaciones S/A, Av Belgrano 406-Piso 9, pg. 569 **PV**
Caja Reaseguradora de Argentina, S.A., pg. 335 **IT**
Camea S.A., Casilla de Correo, 1900, pg. 51 **IT**
Carrefour Argentine S.A., avenue del liberador 95, pg. 272 **IT**

PB - U.S. Public Companies Volume
PV - U.S. Private Companies Volume
IT - International Public & Private Companies Volume

1489

The Chase Manhattan Bank, N.A., 25 de Mayo 130/140, pg. 340 **PB**

Chase Manhattan Trading S.A., 25 de Mayo 158, pg. 340 **PB**

Checkpoint Systems S.A., Avda Del Libertador 3799, pg. 343 **PB**

Christensen Roder Argentina S.A., pg. 1174 **IT**

CIBA-GEIGY Argentina S.A.I.C. y F., Ramallo 1851, pg. 976 **IT**

CIBA-GEIGY Argentina S.A.I.C. y F., Zarate Plant, pg. 976 **IT**

Circle Freight International Argentina S.A., 25 De Mayo 596, 17th Fl., pg. 372 **PB**

Clorox Argentina S.A., Castro Barros 2050, 1770 Aldo Bonzi, pg. 387 **PB**

Coasin, S.A., Verrey Del Pino 4071, pg. 817 **PB**

Columbia Pictures of Argentina, Inc., Ayacucho 520, pg. 1282 **IT**

Compania Aseguradora Argentina S.A., Avenida P.te R. Saenz Pena 555, pg. 61 **IT**

Compania De Radiocomunicaciones Moviles S.A., Tucuman 744, Piso 8, pg. 208 **PB**

Compania Ericsson S.A.C.I., Belgrano 964, pg. 1365 **IT**

Copetro, S.A., Av. Leandro N. Alem, pg. 540 **PV**

Coppermol S.A., Ricardo Rojas 401, Piso 4, pg. 303 **IT**

Corafin S.A.C.I.F.A., Calle Suipacha 268, pg. 363 **PB**

Cosmeticos Avon, S.A.C.I., Casilla de Correo 1447, pg. 156 **IT**

Crown Cork de Argentina, S. A., Castilla De Dorreo, 072, One Aprida 4755, pg. 464 **PB**

Cyanamid de Argentina S.A.I.C., Charcas 5051, pg. 80 **PB**

Daewoo Corp. - Buenos Aires, San Jose 4th Fl., Rm. 401-2, pg. 358 **PB**

Dai-Ichi Kangyo Bank, Ltd.-Buenos Aires, Av. Davila 270 Piso 2, pg. 361 **IT**

Danzas Argentina S.A., Reconquista 458-7, pg. 382 **IT**

Dart Argentina S.A., Av del Libertador #498, Piso 314, pg. 1322 **PB**

Deitec S.A., Tucuman 540, Piso 12, pg. 1180 **PB**

DeKalb Argentina, S.A., Maipu 1252 5th Fl., pg. 493 **PB**

Deminex Argentina SA, Esmeralda 719, pg. 1461 **IT**

Det Norske Veritas, Suipacha 1067, 1st Floor, pg. 396 **IT**

Deutsche Babcock Argentina S.A., Avenida Belgrano 427, 6 Piso, pg. 398 **IT**

Deutsche Bank AG (Buenos Aires), pg. 404 **IT**

Dignitas S.A., Calle Pellegrini 1135, pg. 364 **PB**

Domain Argentina S.A., pg. 516 **PB**

Ducilo S.A., Casilla de Correo 1888, Correo Central, pg. 533 **PB**

Dumez-GTM, Galeria Jardin, pg. 823 **IT**

Dun & Bradstreet SA, Av. Leandro N. Alem 928 Piso 1, pg. 536 **PB**

Duperial S.A.I.C., Paseo Colon 285, 1330 Capital Federal, pg. 664 **PB**

Dyckerhoff & Widmann AG Sucursal Buenos Aires, Maipu 464, piso 5, pg. 424 **IT**

EAMI Hornos Industriales, S.A., Formosa 279 6-20, pg. 361 **PV**

ECI Telecom (Argentina), Cerrito 1070, pg. 643 **IT**

EMI-Odeon SAIC, Av. San Martin 3590, (1602) Florida, pg. 427 **IT**

Eaton I.C.S.A Axle & Foundry Divisions, Avenida Cordova 679, 3rd Fl., pg. 558 **PB**

Echlin Argentina S.A., pg. 561 **PB**

Editorial Medica Panamericana S.A., Marcelo de Alvear 2145, pg. 1748 **IT**

Elaboradora Argentina de Cereales, S.A., Virrey Del Pino 2458, pg. 1348 **IT**

Electricite de France, Palacio Urquiza, Avenida de Mayo 749 - Piso 2, pg. 437 **IT**

Electroclor S.A., Paseocolon 285, 1330 Capital Federal, pg. 664 **IT**

S.A. Electrolux, Anchorena 665171 C. P. 1170, pg. 444 **IT**

Empresas ICA Sociedad Controladora (Argentina). Av. Presidente Roque Saenz, Pena No. 832, piso 4, pg. 454 **IT**

Erven Lucas Bols S.A., Casilla de Correo No. 1, Correo Central, pg. 751 **IT**

Esso Sociedad Anonima Petroleum Argentina, Carlos Maria Della, pg. 602 **PB**

Ethika AFJP, Sarmiento 663 Piso 4, (1316), pg. 886 **PV**

EURO RSCG, Callao 1033 6o, pg. 602 **IT**

FMC Argentina, S.A. C.I., Y.F., Ave. E, Madero 1020-16O, pg. 606 **PB**

Fama S.A., Ave. Comodoro Pedro Zanni 250, pg. 654 **IT**

Ferro Enamel Argentina, S.A., Casilla de Correo 2553, Correo Central, pg. 619 **PB**

Fiat Concord S.A., Cerrito 1290, pg. 483 **IT**

Fiat Concord SAIC, Cerrito 1290, pg. 484 **IT**

Fidelio Technologies Sucursal Argentina, pg. 1106 **PB**

Filtros Mann S.A., Casilla de Correo 57, pg. 484 **IT**

Fortinox S.A., Donado 1149, pg. 515 **IT**

Fuchs Argentina S.A., Belgrano 2551, pg. 517 **IT**

H.B. Fuller Argentina S.A.I.C, Paraque Industrial Pilar, Ruta 8 Km 60 Calle 3, pg. 687 **PB**

GO International de Argentina S.A., Sarmiento 663 3 Piso, pg. 776 **PB**

Gaseba S.A., Suipacha 1111, Piso 5, pg. 541 **IT**

Gerber Argentina, Aligen SA, AV Corrientes 222, pg. 973 **IT**

Gillette Argentina S.A., Casilla de Correo No. 694, Avenida del Libertador 8526, pg. 744 **PB**

Givaudan-Roure S.A., pg. 1120 **IT**

Gowland/ADD, San Martin 323 Piso 13, 1004, pg. 1200 **PV**

Gowland Publicidad S.A., Florida 868, 1st & 2nd Fls., pg. 1642 **PV**

Grace Argentina S.A., Primera Junta 550, 1878 Quilmes, pg. 755 **PB**

Graffiti/DMB&B, Uruguay 1112, pg. 304 **PV**

Groupe SEB Argentina, Avenida Pueyrredon 2446, pg. 568 **IT**

HSBC Roberts S.A., 25 de Mayo 258, pg. 583 **IT**

Halliburton Argentina S.A., Viamonte 1133, pg. 777 **IT**

Heller-Sud Servicios Financieros S.A., Maipu 311 Piso 1, pg. 521 **IT**

Henkel Argentina S.A., Casilla di Correo 3496, pg. 611 **IT**

Herbalife International Argentina, S.A., Gral. Belgrano 2272, 1611 Don Torcuato, Partido de Tigre, pg. 809 **PB**

Hewlett-Packard Argentina, S.A., Montaneses 2140/50/60, pg. 818 **IT**

Hoesch Argentina S.A.I.y.C., Sucursal 37, pg. 508 **IT**

Honeywell S.A.I.C., Belgrano 1156, pg. 835 **IT**

Honoris Compania de Seguros de Vida S.A., Cerrito 740, pg. 364 **PV**

Huber S.A.I.C., Peru 545, pg. 1157 **IT**

Hughes Tool Company S.A.C.I.F.I., Maipu 942-5 Piso, pg. 167 **IT**

IBM Argentina, S.A., Pie de las Catalinas 275, pg. 896 **PB**

IDC Argentina, CW Communications S/A, pg. 570 **PV**

IGT Argentina S.A., Sarmiento 944, 9 Piso/20, pg. 900 **PB**

ING Bank Buenos Aires, Ingeniero Butty 220, Piso 21, pg. 649 **IT**

ING Bank Buenos Aires, Bartolome Mitre 760, 6th Floor, pg. 649 **IT**

ING Baring Argentina S.A., L.N. Alem 628, Floor 15, pg. 649 **IT**

ING Baring Securities Argentina, L.N. Alem 628, Floor 14, pg. 649 **IT**

ING Baring Sociedad de Bolsa (Argentina), Ingeniero BUtty 220, Piso 21, pg. 649 **IT**

ING Insurance Seguros de Vida, Edificio Catalinas Plaza, Ingeniero Butty 220, Piso 21, pg. 650 **IT**

Iberoasistencia Argentina S.A., Avda. Cordova, pg. 334 **IT**

Iguazu Compania de Seguros, San Martin 442, pg. 1531 **IT**

InCem S.A., 25 De Mayo 596, pg. 512 **IT**

Independencia Compania Argentina de Seguros S.A., Corrients 821, pg. 216 **PB**

Intalcable Argentina, Calle San Martin 320, pg. 655 **IT**

Interraco S.R.L., Florida 537-Local 288, pg. 822 **IT**

International Flavors & Fragrances S.A.C.I., Parque Industrial Oks, pg. 899 **IT**

Iochpe-Maxion Argentina S.A., Calle Reconquista 656, 8 piso, pg. 688 **IT**

Ishihara Argentina S.A., Reconquista 656, Piso 9, pg. 689 **IT**

Isotex, Bouchard y Enz, pg. 1176 **IT**

Italimpianti-Argentina, Florida, 1-7 Piso, pg. 655 **IT**

Itsemap Austral, S.A., Avda. Figueroa, pg. 333 **IT**

John Crane Argentina, Pasaje Carabelas 241-PISO 7, pg. 1339 **IT**

Johnson & Johnson de Argentina, S.A., Casilla de Correo 79 pg. 930 **PB**

S.C. Johnson & Son de Argentina S.A.I.C., Av. Marquez 2249, pg. 593 **PV**

KSB Compania Sudamericana de Bombas S.A., pg. 721 **IT**

Karl-Lutz Ammann, Representante del Commerzbank AG, Avda. Corrientes 456, pg. 312 **IT**

Kasdorf S.A., pg. 991 **IT**

Kellocg Company Argentina S.A.C.I.F., General Roca 4735, 1602 Florida, pg. 947 **PB**

Kleinwort Benson Argentina SA, Esmeralda 130, 7 Piso, pg. 420 **IT**

Kluber Lubrication Argentina S.A., pg. 506 **IT**

Kodak Argentina S.A.I.C., Prilidiano Pueyrredon 2989, 1607 Villa Adelina, Pcia., pg. 552 **PB**

Kolynos SAIC, Tnte. Gral. J.D. Peron 925, 1 Piso, pg. 81 **PB**

KONE Ascensores S.A., Ciudad de la Paz 123, pg. 747 **IT**

Korn/Ferry International, Avenida Quintana 585, 6th Fl., pg. 633 **IT**

La Franco Penn Life Compania De Segures De Vida S.A., Avenida Corrientas 330, pg. 1271 **PV**

LA NACION S.A., Bouchard 557, pg. 785 **IT**

Landis & Staefa (Argentina) S.A.I.y.C., Pietrqs 338-3 Piso 13, pg. 800 **IT**

Ediciones Larousse Argentina SA, Valentin Gómez 3530, pg. 240 **IT**

Le Carbone-Lorriane S.A.I.C., Erezcano 3051, pg. 1030 **IT**

Lever y Asociados SACIF, Traga 1163, pg. 1438 **IT**

Arthur D. Little de Argentina S.A., Av. Leandro N. Alem 1110; Piso 2, pg. 670 **PV**

Loctite Argentina, Montaneses 24-34, pg. 611 **IT**

L'Oreal Prodesca S.A., 381 Avenue Presidente, N45, pg. 819 **IT**

Lucas Indiel Argentina S.A., Av. San Martin 4205, 1752, Lomas Del Mirador, pg. 820 **IT**

Lucent Technologies Argentina S.A., Esmeralda 55, Capital Federal, pg. 1018 **PB**

Mannesmann Rexroth SAIC, pg. 839 **IT**

MAPFRE Aconcagua Cia. de Seguros, S.A., Lavalle 348, pg. 333 **IT**

MAPFRE Argentina, Lavalle 348, pg. 333 **IT**

MAPFRE Soft Argentina S.A., Cordoba, 1450, pg. 335 **IT**

Marcam Argentina S.A., Juramento 2059, 1st Fl., pg. 1043 **PB**

MARCO DEL PONT S.A., 2368 Warnes Ave., pg. 842 **IT**

Mary Kay Cosmetics, S.A., Corrientes 345, pg. 711 **PV**

Massalin Particulares S.A., Av. Leandro M. Alem 466, pg. 1101 **IT**

Mathieu Argentina, Avenida Dorrego 2622, P5 C, pg. 346 **IT**

McCair Argentina SA, Ruta 226, pg. 850 **IT**

Medtronic Latin America, Inc., Juramento 2550, 4th Floor, pg. 1084 **PB**

Merceces-Benz Argentina S.A., Casilla Correo 3890, pg. 368 **IT**

Metropolitan Life Seguros de Vida, S.A., Avenida Madero 942, pg. 738 **PV**

MICROS Systems Latino America, Cerrito 268, pg. 1107 **PB**

MICROS Systems Latino America y Caribe, pg. 1107 **PB**

Miluz SAICIF, Zufriategui 4501, pg. 43 **IT**

Mitsui Argentina S.A., 25 de Mayo 555, Piso 17, pg. 882 **IT**

Monofort, San Martin 379, Piso 3, pg. 1177 **IT**

Morgan Guaranty Trust Company, Av. Corrientes 411, pg. 1130 **PB**

J.P. Morgan Argentina Sociedad de Bolsa S.A., Av. Corrientes 411, pg. 1130 **PB**

Motorola de Comercializacion y Servicios S.A., pg. 1139 **PB**

NIFE Argentina S.A., Jose Leon Suarez 2244, pg. 54 **IT**

NYK-Buenos Aires, Av. Corrientes 327, 4 piso (1043), pg. 941 **IT**

Nacional Financiera, 25 De Mayo NR. 555 4th Floor, pg. 904 **IT**

Nahuelsat S.A., pg. 367 **IT**

Nalco Argentina S.A., 1001 Capital Federal, Av. Leandro N. Alem 712-100, pg. 1150 **PB**

Nedlloyd (Argentina) S.A., pg. 1145 **IT**

Nestle Argentina S.A., pg. 920 **IT**

S.A. Nestle de Productos Alimenticios, pg. 921 **IT**

Neumaticos Goodyear SA, Manuel Ocampo 1170, pg. 753 **PB**

Nicoll Eterplast, Peribebuy 1492, pg. 430 **IT**

A.C. Nielsen (Argentina) S.A., Rivadavia 620-3 er. Piso, pg. 1183 **PB**

NOBLEX ARGENTINA S.A.C. E I., Palestina 980, pg. 951 **IT**

Northrup King Semillas S.A., pg. 983 **IT**

Novell Argentina, Av. Leandro N. Alem 1110 9, pg. 1204 **PB**

Novo Nordisk, Avenida Del Libertador 222, pg. 987 **IT**

Nowsco Well Service Ltd.-Argentina, Avenida Leandro N., pg. 990 **IT**

NUEVO FEDERAL S.A., Av. Crovara 48, pg. 990 **IT**

O.P.E.S.S.A., Av. Roque Saenz Pena 777, pg. 1515 **IT**

OTRASA, Sarmiento 778, Piso 4, pg. 1515 **IT**

Ocye S.A., Cordoba 1856 piso 9, pg. 823 **IT**

Olivetti Argentina S.A.C. e I., Calle Suipacha 1109, pg. 1003 **IT**

Oracle Argentina S.A., Leandro Alem Avda. 1002, pg. 1228 **IT**

Orbea Argentina Sociedad Anonima, Paseo Colon 285, 1330 Capital Federal, pg. 665 **IT**

Organon Argentina S.A., 25 Sucursal, pg. 45 **IT**

Osram Argentina S.A.C.I., Ramos Mejia 2456, pg. 1244 **IT**

Owens-Corning Canos S.A., Monsenor Magliano 3049/55, pg. 1237 **PB**

Panalpina Transportes Mundiales S.A., pg. 1023 **IT**

PENAFLOR S.A., Juan B. Justo 1015, pg. 1032 **IT**

Pepsi-Cola Argentina, S.A.C.I., Maipu 938, pg. 1277 **PB**

Peroxides Argentinos SA, 3421 Dr. Romula S. Nalon, pg. 47 **IT**

Petrobras Argentina, Calle Reconquista, 1166, pg. 1042 **IT**

Pfizer S.A.C.I., Virrey Loreto 2477, pg. 1282 **PB**

Phonogram S.A.I.C., Calle Moreno 2038, pg. 1052 **IT**

Pioneer Argentina, S.A., 25 De Mayo 460-4th Floor, pg. 1299 **PB**

Pirelli Argentina de Mandatos S.A., Maipu 757, P60, pg. 1059 **IT**

Pirelli Cables SAIC, Avenida Argentina 6784, pg. 1059 **IT**

Plus Ultra, Compania Argentina de Seguros S.A., Avenida Pte R. Saenz Pena 555, pg. 62 **IT**

PolyGram Disco S.A., Hipolito Yrigoyen 1622, pg. 1053 **IT**

Pond's Argentina S.A.I.C., Av Marquez Y Martin Fierro, pg. 1436 **IT**

Praxair Argentina S.A., pg. 1320 **PB**

Princor Compania de Seguros de Retiro S.A., Sarmiento 663 Piso 4, (1316), pg. 886 **PV**

Prinlife Compania de Seguros de Vida S.A., Sarmiento 663 Piso 4, (1316), pg. 886 **PV**

Providencia Compania Argentina de seguros S.A., Calle Reconquista 572, pg. 92 **IT**

Providencia Compania de Seguro de Retiro S.A., Calle Reconquista 572, pg. 92 **IT**

Quaker Chemical S.A., Suipacha 472, pg. 1347 **PB**

RNBNY-Buenos Aires Office, Bartolome Mitre 343, pg. 1381 **PB**

RNBNY Representative Office-Argentina, 890 Calle Florida, pg. 1381 **PB**

Refinerias de Maiz S.A.I.C.F., Tucuman 117, pg. 448 **IT**

Reinter BC, San Martin 140- Piso 100- 1004, pg. 1502 **IT**

Renault Argentina, Oro 1744, pg. 1103 **IT**

Repsol Exploration Argentina, S.A., Avda. Libertador, 602, pg. 1105 **IT**

Rhone-Poulenc Argentina S.A., Avenida de Mayo 676, pg. 1112 **IT**

Rockwell Argentina S.A., Avenida Cordoba 4970, pg. 1399 **PB**

Rodamientos FAG, pg. 469 **IT**

Rorer Argentina S.A., Division Farmaceutica Primera, Junta, pg. 1111 **IT**

SHL Systenhouse Argentina S.A., Esmeralda 130, Piso 9, pg. 1154 **IT**

SKF Argentina S.A., Peru 545, pg. 1158 **IT**

STET-Argentina, Maipu 1300 Piso 21, pg. 656 **IT**

Salvat Editores Argentina, SA, Adolfo Albina, 1609 friso 80F. 7, pg. 796 **IT**

SANCOR COOPERATIVAS UNIDAS LIMITADAS, Tacuari 202, 12th Fl., pg. 1183 **IT**

Sandoz Argentina S.A.I.C., pg. 984 **IT**

Sandvik Bahco Argentina S.A.C.e.I., Casilla de Correo 5594, pg. 1187 **IT**

Savaglio TBWA & Associados S.A., 11 de Septiembre 839, pg. 1063 **PV**

PB - *U.S. Public Companies Volume*
PV - *U.S. Private Companies Volume*
IT - *International Public & Private Companies Volume*

1490

Geographic Index-Non U.S.

R.P. Scherer Argentina S.A.I.C., Av. Marquez 691, (Camino de Cintura), pg. 1438 **PB**
Schering Argentina S.A.I.C., pg. 1204 **IT**
Search Organization de Seguridad, S.A., Tronador 543, pg. 1731 **PB**
Semillas Meriel, pg. 1299 **PB**
Servicios Ticket SA, Sarmiento 944, 3 etage, pg. 21 **IT**
Servired YPF S.A., Av. Roque Saenz Pena 777, pg. 1515 **IT**
Seven-Up Concessiones S.A., pg. 1278 **PB**
Shell Argentina de Petroleo, Avenida Presidente Roque Saenz, pg. 1141 **IT**
Siemens S.A., Av. Pte. Julio A. Roca 516, pg. 1248 **IT**
Singapore Tourist Promotion Board - Buenos Aires, Ayacucho 1474-3 y 4 Pisos, pg. 1254 **IT**
Sintyal Otsuka Pharmaceutical S.A., Salguero Plaza 5th Floor, Jeronimo Salguero 2686, pg. 1014 **IT**
Smith International de Argentina, S.A., Cerrito 200-Piso 6, pg. 1478 **PB**
SmithKline & French Inter-American Corp., Sucursal Argentina, pg. 1265 **IT**
SmithKline Beecham Division Veterinaria, Bolivar 391-2nd Floor, pg. 1266 **IT**
Sodexho Argentina S.A., Talcahuano 778 - 3, pg. 1275 **IT**
Stafford-Miller Argentina S.A., Juhin 508, pg. 237 **PB**
Standard Wool Argentina S.A., pg. 1502 **PB**
Stolt-Nielsen S.A., pg. 1302 **IT**
Sud America Seguros-Argentine, Roque Saenz Pena 530, pg. 321 **IT**
Suiza de Reaseguros S.A., Bouchard 547, Piso 19, pg. 1333 **IT**
Sullair Argentina S.A., Goncalves Dias 1145, pg. 1534 **PB**
Sulzer Argentina S.A., pg. 1306 **IT**
The Sumitomo Bank, Ltd.-Buenos Aires Representative Office, Reconquista 336, 8 Piso 1335, pg. 1309 **IT**
Sun Chemical Inks S.A., Calle 95 No. 1127 - Ex Monteagodo, pg. 371 **IT**
Sun Chemical S.A., 565 Rodriguez Pena, pg. 371 **IT**
Supermercados Mayoristas Makra S.A., Ricardo Gutierrez 3647, pg. 1156 **IT**
Surassur, S.A., Lavalle 445, pg. 333 **IT**
Swiss Bank Corporation, 25 de Mayo 55, Piso 15, pg. 1330 **IT**
SylvaPen Distribuidora S.A.C.I.Y.F., Ruta Panamericana Km. 38, pg. 745 **PB**
Tamrock Argentina S.A., Corrales 1727/29, pg. 1353 **IT**
Taylor Instrumentos, S.A., Calle 37 (Ex Julio a Roca) 2522, 1650 Vi, pg. 6 **IT**
Thomson-CSF S.A., Lavalle 534-4 Piso, pg. 1385 **IT**
3M Argentina S.A.C.I.F.I.A., Los Arboles 842, 1686 Hurlingham, pg. 1606 **PB**
Tibsa, Maipu 1300 Piso no 10, pg. 1415 **IT**
Timken Argentina S.R.L., Av. Almafuerte 737, pg. 1617 **PB**
Topps Argentina S.A., Alicia Moreau De Justo 1148, 4th Floor, 1107, pg. 1622 **PB**
Total Research Argentina, Parana 1097 - Piso 12, pg. 1625 **PB**
Toyota Argentina S.A., Montesquieu 425, pg. 1413 **IT**
Transistemas S.A., Tucuman 744, Piso 6, pg. 924 **IT**
Triton Argentina, Inc., pg. 1640 **PB**
UBS Representative Office, Avenida Santa Fe 846, pg. 1441 **IT**
UTE, Cordoba 1856 piso 6, pg. 824 **IT**
Union Carbide Argentina S.A.I.C.S., Ave. Leandro N. Alem, pg. 1667 **IT**
Utell International-Argentina, Esmeralda 719, pg. 1098 **IT**
Valvulas Worcester de Argentina S.A., Peru 1345, pg. 551 **IT**
Van Leer Argentina S.A., pg. 1146 **IT**
Van Leer Envases-Envasa Plas S.A., pg. 1147 **IT**
VARTA Baterias SAICyF, Avda. Ricardo Balbin, pg. 1452 **IT**
Vidrieria Argentina SA, Corrientes 1386, pg. 1057 **IT**
Voest-Alpine Argentina S.A., Defensa 363-69, pg. 1472 **IT**
Volkswagen Argentina S.A., pg. 1475 **IT**
Wandel & Goltermann & Co., Argentina, Montaneses 2599, pg. 1486 **IT**
Wang Export Services, Inc., Bartolome Mitre 777 6-C, pg. 1738 **PB**
Waverly Hispanica S.A., Scalabrini Ortez 2394.3B, pg. 1748 **PB**
The West Company Argentina S.A., Avda Ader 2811, pg. 1755 **PB**
West Merchant Bank Limited, Av. Conientes 415, Piso 7, pg. 1494 **IT**
Whitehall Laboratorios S.A., Pte. Peron 949, 9 piso, pg. 82 **PB**
John Wyeth Laboratorios S.A., Casillo de Correo 2498, pg. 82 **PB**
Xerox Argentina I.C.S.A., Jaramilo 1595, Casilla de Correos 1664, pg. 1785 **PB**
Y.P.F. Gas S.A., Ave. Roque Saenz Pena 777, pg. 1515 **IT**
Y.P.F., S.A., Ave. Roque Saenz Pena 777, Piso 4, pg. 1515 **IT**
Young & Rubicam de Buenos Aires, Paseo Colon 275, Piso 13, pg. 1200 **PV**
Zeneca SAIC, Av. Leandro N. Alem 1134, 12th Floor, pg. 1527 **IT**
Zurich Compania de Seguros, San Martin 442, pg. 1531 **IT**
Zurich Iguazu Compania de Seguros de Retiro S.A., San Martin 442, pg. 1532 **IT**

Cordoba

Bertrand Faure Argentina SA, Av. Velez Sarsfield 2930, pg. 193 **IT**
Corporacion Cementera Argentina S.A. (CORCEMAR), Chacabuco 187, Piso 1, pg. 629 **IT**

JUAN MINETTI S.A., Malaqueno Casa de Correo 16, pg. 869 **IT**
PAB SA, Av. Circunvalacion s/n, Esq. av. Las Rosas B Alejandro Carbo, pg. 193 **IT**

Corrientes

Plantaciones Mesopotamicas, Catamarca, 1046, pg. 333 **IT**

Francisco Astelarra

Principal International Argentina, S.A., Capital Fed., Sarmiento 663, pg. 886 **PV**

Haedo

AGCO ARGENTINA S.A., Valentin Gomez 577, pg. 30 **IT**
Astra S.A. Productos Farmaceuticos y Quimicos, Agerich 536, pg. 94 **IT**

Lavalle

Colgate-Palmolive S.A.I.C., Avenida Antartida Argentina 2269, pg. 399 **PB**
Georg Fischer, Inc., pg. 488 **IT**

Lopez

Volvo Sudamericana SACI, Av. Libertador 1296, pg. 1478 **IT**

Mar del Plata

Alpesca, S.A., Posadas 458, pg. 909 **IT**

Mendoza

CR International Corporation, Talchuano 699, Villa Nueva, pg. 302 **PB**
ICSA (Ingenieria y Computacion, S.A.), Necochea 183, pg. 1032 **IT**
Pool International Argentina S.A., Rodriguez Pena 680, pg. 1316 **PB**
Sunshine Argentina, Inc., Julio A. Roca 326, pg. 1536 **PB**

Merlo

Pirelli Neumsticos, Cervantes 1901, pg. 1059 **IT**

Munro

Bayer Argentina S.A., Ricardo Gutierrez 3652, pg. 175 **IT**

Neuquen

Argentina Division (Drillers International S.A.), Cornelio Saavedra 169, pg. 75 **PB**
Drillers International S.A., Cornelio Saavedra 169, pg. 765 **PB**

Olivos

Productos Roche S.A. Quimica e Industrial, pg. 1121 **IT**

Quilmes

Chr. Hansen Argentina S.A.I.C., Casilla de Correo 20, pg. 289 **IT**
Industrias Electricas de Quilmes, 12 de Octubre 2130, pg. 1368 **IT**

Rosario

La Union Gremial Compania Argentina de Seguros S.A., pg. 216 **PB**

San Fernando

FATE S.A., Av. Blanco Encalada 3003, pg. 478 **IT**
Lametal del Norte S.A., pg. 1146 **IT**

San Isidro

Bertrand Faure Argentina SA, Roque Saenz Pena 308 - Piso 4 y 5, pg. 193 **IT**
Compania MSA de Argentina, S.A., Dardo Rocha 1444, pg. 1114 **PB**

San Juan

Battle Mountain Gold (Argentina), Angel de Rojas 575 (Sur), pg. 193 **PB**
Duperial 9 de Julio S.A.I.C., Ruta 20 y Eusebio Zapata -, Las Chacritas, pg. 664 **IT**
Orbea 9 de Julio S.A.I.C., Ruta 20 y Eusebio Zapata, Las Chacritas Departamento, pg. 665 **IT**
Strauss 9 de Julio S.A.I.C., Ruta 20 y Eusebio Zapata, Las Chacritas Departamento, pg. 665 **IT**
Van Leer Argentina S.A., pg. 1146 **IT**

San Martin

AGA S.A., Calle 54 No. 2075, pg. 13 **IT**
Freudenberg S.A. Telas sin Tejer, pg. 505 **IT**
Nobleza-Piccardo SAICF, Ave. 85, No. 645, pg. 111 **IT**
Parker Hannifin Argentina SAIC, Avda. Pte. Arturo U Illia 2064, pg. 1263 **PB**

San Miguel

CIBA-GEIGY Argentina S.A.I.C. y F., Pharma Production Plant, pg. 976 **IT**

San Miguel de Tucuman

Scania Argentina S.A., Casilla Correo No. 3 Central, pg. 687 **IT**

Tortuguitas

Glasurit de Argentina S.A., Avda. de los Constituyentes 1758, pg. 105 **IT**

Ushuaia

Sanelco S.A., Av. Perito Moreno 1651, pg. 1192 **IT**

Victoria

Bundy Argentina SA, Juncal 3561-C.P. 1644, pg. 1342 **IT**

ARUBA

Oranjestad

Ballast Nedam Aruba N.V., L.G. Smith Boulevard, pg. 134 **IT**
Ballast Nedam Dredging Caribbean/Latin America, Van Dragtstraat 6, pg. 134 **IT**
DKB Finance (Aruba) A.E.C., Frankrijkstraat No. 1, pg. 361 **IT**
MTBC Finance (Aruba) A.E.C., Frankrijkstraat 1, pg. 877 **IT**

AUSTRALIA

Abbotsford

Robert Bryce & Co., Ltd., 64 Trenerry Crescent, pg. 682 **IT**
Dentsply (Australia) Pty. Ltd., 204-206 Gipps St., pg. 499 **PB**
Hewlett-Packard Australia Ltd., 126-142 Trenerry Crescent, pg. 818 **PB**
Melbourne Brewery, Southampton Crescent, pg. 501 **IT**
Tidewater Port Jackson Marine Pty. Limited, 663 Victoria Street, Ste. 6, pg. 211 **IT**

Acacia Ridge

Brisbane Market Mill, 341 Bradman Street, pg. 227 **IT**

Adelaide

AIS Media Adelaide, 29 Sydenham Rd., pg. 394 **IT**
Adelaide Brewery, 34-36 Rosberg Rd., pg. 501 **IT**
Australian Guarantee Corporation Limited - South Australia, Ten Pulteney St., pg. 1496 **IT**
Australian Submarine Corporation, pg. 277 **IT**
AxTrade (Australia) Pty Ltd., 10th Level, Citi Center, 11 Hindmarsh Square, pg. 710 **IT**
Bundy Asia Pacific, 492 Churchill Road, pg. 1341 **IT**
Bundy Tubing Co. (Australia) Pty. Ltd., G.P.O. Box 2051, pg. 1341 **IT**
CelsiusTech Australia Pty Ltd, Endeavour House, Module 6, 4th Avenue, Technology Park, pg. 278 **IT**
Commonwealth Bank of Australia-South Australia, 96 King William St., GPO Box 1551, pg. 313 **IT**
DMR Group Australia Pty. Ltd., MLC Centre, Level 5, 100 Pirie St., pg. 528 **IT**
DAIRY VALE CO-OP. LTD., 154 Caulfield Ave., pg. 372 **IT**
Elders Limited, 27 Currie St., pg. 500 **IT**
Elders - South Australia, 27 Currie St., pg. 501 **IT**
G.W. Falland & Co., Pyap St., pg. 372 **IT**
Freesia, 158 Railway Terr., pg. 372 **IT**
Harris Scarfe Ltd., 81 Rundle Mall, pg. 597 **IT**
International Public Relations, Pty. Ltd., 19 Rundle St., pg. 1227 **IT**
Kockums Pacific Pty Ltd., 1st Fl., 251 Hutt St., pg. 277 **IT**
Makita (Australia) Pty. Ltd.-Adelaide, 45 Birralee Road, pg. 831 **IT**
F R Mayfield, 43-69 Sturt St., pg. 16 **IT**
Michell NBD Limited, 70 Hindmarsh Square, 4th Fl., pg. 628 **PB**
NYK Line-Adelaide, 83 Lipson Street, pg. 941 **IT**
National Mutual South Australia, 80 King William St., pg. 908 **IT**
Pacific Marine Batteries Pty. Ltd., pg. 1452 **IT**
Phillips Henderson Ward Limited, 1/F, Pearl Assurance House, 32 Grenfell Street, pg. 583 **IT**
Robertson Leo Burnett Pty. Ltd., 99 Frome St., pg. 186 **PV**
SOUTHCORP HOLDINGS LTD., State Bank Center, Level 23, 91 King William St., pg. 1287 **IT**

PB - *U.S. Public Companies Volume*
PV - *U.S. Private Companies Volume*
IT - *International Public & Private Companies Volume*

1491

Geographic Index-Non U.S.

TMP Worldwide Pty Ltd., 211 Flinders Street, pg. 1342   **IT**
Tektronix Australia Pty. Limited-Adelaide, pg. 1567   **PB**
Tretolite Pty. Limited, 31 Flemington St., pg. 166   **PB**
Weatherford Australia Pty. Ltd., 7 Wyn Street, pg. 1750   **PB**
Westpac - South Australia, 2-8 King William St., pg. 1496   **IT**
Willis Corroon Richard Oliver Pty. Ltd., Level 1, 190 Flinders Street, pg. 1509   **IT**

Albany

Albany Glass, Cockburn Rd., pg. 129   **IT**

Albert Park

Mildara Blass Wines, 170 Bridport St., pg. 501   **IT**

Albury

Cooper Tools Pty. Ltd., 519 Nurigong St., pg. 445   **PB**
Twin Disc (Pacific) Pty. Ltd., 110 Baronia St., pg. 1647   **PB**
Van Leer Australia Pty. Ltd., pg. 1146   **IT**
Willis Corroon Richard Oliver Pty. Ltd., 539 Kiewa Street, pg. 1509   **IT**

Alexandria

AEI Australia Pty. Ltd., 23 O'Riordan St., pg. 30   **PB**
Consumer Foods Group, 5/476 Gardeners Road, pg. 555   **IT**
Daisytek Australia Pty. Ltd., 1727 Power Ave., Unit 11, pg. 477   **PB**
GF Food Services, 5/476 Gardeners Road, pg. 555   **IT**
GF International Limited, 5/476 Gardeners Rd., pg. 555   **IT**
Honeywell Leeds & Northrup Australia Pty. Ltd., 147 McEvoy, pg. 834   **PB**
Kenner Parker (Australia) Ltd., 102-108 Bourke Rd., pg. 797   **PB**
KONE Elevators (Australia) Pty. Ltd., 205 Euston Road, pg. 748   **IT**
Morganite Australia Pty. Limited, 65 Bourke Rd., pg. 895   **IT**
Morganite Carbon Division, 65 Bourke Rd., pg. 895   **IT**
Morganite Ceramic Fibres Pty. Limited, 65 Bourke Rd., pg. 894   **IT**
PGF International Pty. Limited, 11-21 Mandible Street, pg. 604   **IT**
PolyGram Records Pty. Ltd., 122 McEvoy St., pg. 1053   **IT**
Schering Pty. Ltd., 27-31 Doody St., pg. 1204   **IT**
Sealed Air Australia, 3 Burrows Road, pg. 1451   **PB**
Suntory (Aust.) Pty. Ltd., 22-26 Mandible St., pg. 1322   **IT**
Turbomeca Australasia Pty Limited, Unit 11, 17-21 Bowden Street, pg. 787   **IT**

Altona

Auseon, Karoit Creek Road, pg. 734   **PB**
BHP Fastener Products, Westgate Drive, pg. 226   **IT**
Van Leer Australia Pty. Ltd., pg. 1146   **IT**
Yokohama Tyre Australia Pty., Ltd., 91 Dohertys Road, pg. 1521   **IT**

Ararat

Packard CTA Pty. Ltd., 18 Gordon St., pg. 723   **PB**

Archerfield

Hastings Deering (Australia) Limited, 99, Kerry Rd., pg. 1250   **IT**

Arncliffe

Rorer Australia Pty. Ltd., 172 Princes Hwy., pg. 1111   **IT**

Artarmon

Acacia Technologies Australia/New Zealand, 407 Pacific Highway, pg. 420   **PB**
Aisin (Australia) Pty. Ltd., 71 Dickson Ave., pg. 39   **PB**
Allergan Australia (Pty.) Ltd., Five George Pl., pg. 46   **PB**
Chiron Vision Australia, pg. 350   **PB**
Datamarine International Australia Pty. Ltd., 6-8 George Pl., pg. 487   **PB**
Datapoint Corp. Pty. Ltd., 66-76 Dickinson Ave., pg. 384   **IT**
Denver Equipment Pty., Ltd., 1st. Fl., 40 Dickson Ave., pg. 1326   **IT**
FoxVideo (South Pacific) Pty., Ltd., 407 Pacific Hgwy., 4th Level, pg. 926   **IT**
Howmedica Investments Pty. Ltd., 20 Carlotta St., pg. 1282   **PB**
Lordco (Australia) Pty. Ltd., P.O. Box 565, pg. 6   **PB**
Mosby - Williams & Wilkins Pty. Ltd., 39 Herbert St., Unit 19, pg. 1748   **PB**
Parker Pen (Australia) Pty. Ltd., 73 Reserve Rd., pg. 745   **PB**
Pficonprod Pty. Ltd., 20 Carlotta Ave., pg. 1282   **PB**
Royal Copenhagen & Georg Jensen Pty. Ltd., 46 Whiting St., pg. 1135   **IT**
S.D. Investments Pty. Ltd., 20 Carlotta St., pg. 1282   **PB**
Sun Microsystems Australia Pty. Ltd.-Sydney, Unit 2, 49-53 Hotham Parade, pg. 1532   **PB**
TDK (Australia) Pty. Ltd., 22 Lams Rd., pg. 1336   **IT**
Wallace & Tiernan Pacific Pty. Ltd., 89-93 Reserve Road, pg. 61   **PB**
Warman Group, 1 Marden Street, pg. 967   **IT**

Warman International Ltd., 1 Marden Street, pg. 967   **IT**

Auburn

Corning Australia Pty. Limited, 305 Parramatta Rd., pg. 448   **PB**
Raychem (Australia) Pty. Limited, Unit 1b, 107 Carnavon St., pg. 1362   **PB**
Siegling Australia Pty. Ltd., pg. 498   **IT**
Southern Cubic Pty. Ltd., Unit A, 41-49 St. Hilliers Rd., pg. 466   **PB**
Steelmark-Eagle & Globe, Manchester Rd. West, pg. 100   **IT**
TAB Products Pty. Ltd., 32 Hampstead Road, pg. 1559   **PB**
Trelleborg Pty. Ltd., 265 Parramatta Road, pg. 1423   **IT**

Austinmer

The Ramtite Co. (Australia) Pty. Ltd., 70 Lawrence Hargrave Dr., pg. 6   **IT**

Balcatta

PETERS & BROWNES FOODS LTD., 22 Geddes Street, pg. 1040   **IT**

Ballarat

Australian Timken Proprietary Ltd., 21-53 Learmonth Rd., pg. 448   **PB**
Bendix Mintex Pty., Ltd., P.O. Box 631, Elizabeth St., pg. 54   **PB**
McCain Foods (Australia) Pty, Ltd., pg. 850   **IT**

Balmain

Baldwin Graphic Equipment Pty., 6/323A Darling St., pg. 170   **PB**
MacGREGOR (AUS) Pty. Ltd., 59 Lilyfield Rd., pg. 670   **IT**

Balwyn

Tektronix Australia Pty. Limited-Balwyn, pg. 1567   **PB**

Banksmeadow

Australian Perlite, 20-22 McPherson St., pg. 803   **IT**

Bankstown

John Crane Australia Pty, Ltd., 166 Eldridge Rd., pg. 1339   **IT**
Frigoscandia Food Process Systems Pty Ltd, pg. 607   **PB**
Hawker de Havilland Ltd., P.O. Box 30, pg. 128   **IT**
Eli Lilly Australia Pty. Limited, 112 Wharf Rd., pg. 993   **PB**
Otis Elevator Co. Pty. Ltd., 122 Canterbury Rd., pg. 1691   **PB**
Outboard Marine Corporation Australia Pty. Ltd., 34 Canterbury Road, P.O. Box 92, pg. 478   **PV**
Polarcup (Australia) Ltd., 406 Marion Street, pg. 638   **IT**
Shakespeare (Australia) Pty. Ltd., Canterbury Rd., Ste. 6/38-42, pg. 940   **PB**

Barton

Westpac - Australian Capital Territory, Westpac Chambers, 53 Blackall St., pg. 1496   **IT**

Bassendean

Donhad Armco Pty. Ltd., 18-22 Jackson St., pg. 391   **IT**

Baulkham Hills

Amersham Australia Pty. Ltd., pg. 992   **IT**
Check Point Software Technologies (Australia) Ltd., 4 Gabrielle Avenue, pg. 342   **PB**
Cyanamid Australia, Pty., Ltd., 5 Gibbon Rd., pg. 80   **PB**
Gambro Pty Ltd., pg. 668   **IT**
Wyeth Australia Pty. Ltd., 5 Gibbon Rd., pg. 82   **PB**

Bayswater

Dunlop Skega, pg. 1323   **IT**
Instron Pty. Ltd., 15 Stud Road, pg. 883   **PB**
Kitchen Products Div., 841 Mountain Hwy., pg. 1287   **IT**
M.E. Mack Valves Pty. Limited, 30 Burgess Rd., pg. 1222   **IT**
PACCAR Australia Pty. Ltd., 64 Canterbury Rd., pg. 1247   **PB**
PACCAR Financial Pty, Ltd., 64 Canterbury Rd., pg. 1247   **PB**
Quality Heat Treatment, 18 Turbo Dr., pg. 530   **PB**
Thermon Australia, Private Bag 32, P.O. Box Bayswater 3153, pg. 1081   **PV**

Bell Bay

Comalco Aluminium (Bell Bay) Limited, pg. 307   **IT**
Tasmania Electro Metallurgical Company Pty Ltd (TEMCO), Temco Road, pg. 224   **IT**

Belmont

North Exploration (Western Region), 154 Abernathy Road, pg. 967   **IT**

Belrose

Bull HN Information Systems Australia Pty Ltd., 2 Minna Close, pg. 317   **IT**
Bull HN Information Systems Wholesale Pty. Ltd., 2 Minna Close, pg. 317   **IT**

Bendigo

Swan Hill Milk Distributors Pty. Ltd., 93 Bannister St., pg. 1074   **IT**

Bennetts Green

ANI Strata Products, 25 Pacific Highway, pg. 100   **IT**

Bentley

Delta West Pty. Ltd., 15 Brodie Hall Drive, pg. 1049   **IT**
Intergraph Corp. Pty. Ltd., Technology Park, Unit Two, Four Brodie Hall Dr., pg. 891   **PB**

Beresfield

Australian Poultry Ltd., Hawthorne Street, pg. 555   **IT**

Berkeley Vale

SICO South Pacific, Lot 36 Craftsman Ave., pg. 998   **PV**

Berrimah

BHP Petroleum Pty. Ltd., Lot 4233 Pruen Road, pg. 225   **IT**

Beverly

Hannaford Seedmaster Services Australia (Pty) Ltd., 52 East Avenue, pg. 460   **PB**

Blackburn

Allen-Bradley Pty. Limited, 37 Chapman Street, pg. 1399   **PB**
COBE Laboratories Pty Ltd.-Melbourne, 17, King Street, pg. 667   **IT**
Hewlett-Packard Australia Ltd., 31-41 Joseph St., pg. 818   **PB**

Blacktown

ABB Asea Brown Boveri Pty. Ltd., P.O. Box 747, pg. 2   **IT**
Boral Concrete Products Pty. Ltd., 57-69 Tattersall Rd., pg. 203   **IT**
Dexion (Australia) Pty. Ltd., Tattersall Rd., pg. 893   **PB**
Harvest Products Pty. Ltd., 34 Tattersall Rd., pg. 682   **IT**
Sharp Corporation of Australia Pty. Ltd., No. 1 Huntingwood Dr., pg. 1229   **IT**

Blackwater

Blackwater Mine, pg. 223   **IT**

Bondi Junction

Nokia Mobile Phones Australia Pty. Ltd., Level 15, Tower 2, pg. 952   **IT**
Nucletron PTY Limited, Suite 3, 2nd Floor, 79-85 Oxford Street, pg. 389   **IT**
Quarterdeck Office Systems Australia Pty. Ltd., Plaza 11, 500 Oxford St., pg. 1351   **PB**
Travel Industries Automated Systems Pty Limited (TIAS), GPO Box 387, pg. 38   **IT**
VMark Asia-Pacific Pty. Ltd., Ste. 1704, Bondi Junction Plaza, pg. 129   **PB**

Boronia

Angus Fire Armour (Australia) Pty Ltd., 4/1001 Mountain Highway, pg. 1500   **IT**
Glaxo Wellcome Australia Ltd., 1061 Mountain Hwy., pg. 553   **IT**
Honeywell-Measurex Pty. Ltd., 175 Boronia Rd., Stes. 3 & 4, 1st Flr., pg. 834   **PB**
Pacific Fire Hose Pty Ltd., 1001 Mountain Highway, pg. 1500   **IT**

Botany

Australian Chemical Holdings Ltd., 49-61 Stephen Rd., pg. 810   **PB**
Bayer Australia Ltd., 47-67 Wilson St., pg. 175   **IT**
Colour Services, 19-21 Wilson St., pg. 803   **IT**
A.C. Hatrick Chemicals Pty. Limited, 49 Stephen St., pg. 811   **PB**
IPC Corporation (Australia) Pty Ltd., Unit 4, 12 Lord Street, pg. 651   **IT**
Kennametal Australia Pty. Ltd., 73 Banksia St., pg. 951   **PB**
Nalco Australia, Anderson Street, pg. 1150   **IT**
Solvay Interox Chemicals Pty. Ltd., pg. 1280   **IT**

Box Hill

Albright & Wilson Specialties P/L, 313 Middleborough Rd., pg. 50   **IT**

PB - *U.S. Public Companies Volume*
PV - *U.S. Private Companies Volume*
IT - *International Public & Private Companies Volume*

1492

Jardine Matheson Victoria Ltd., 532 Station St.,
   pg. 705   IT
Marcam Australia Pty., Ltd., Second Fl., 532 Station St.,
   pg. 1043   PB
Taylor Instrument Pty. Ltd., 275 Middleborough Road,
   pg. 6   IT

Boyne

Boyne Smelters Limited, Handley Dr., pg. 307   IT

Braeside

Armstrong-Nylex Pty. Ltd., 3 Mills Rd., pg. 132   PB
Battenfeld Australia Pty. Ltd., 114-116 Boundary Road,
   pg. 825   IT
R.P. Scherer Holdings Pty. Ltd., 217-221 Governor Road,
   pg. 1438   PB

Braybrook

Valmet-Boustead Pty. Ltd., 14-28 South Rd., pg. 1449   IT

Brisbane

ACI Resources Ltd., 137 Montague Rd., pg. 128   IT
AIS Media Brisbane, Level 3, 454 Upper Edward,
   pg. 15   IT
ANZ Queensland, 324 Queen St., pg. 98   IT
Abbot Point Bulkcoal Pty. Ltd, 410 Ann Street, pg. 827   IT
Apple Computer Ltd., 279 Grey St., pg. 121   PB
ARCO Coal Australia, Inc., 10 Eagle St., pg. 144   PB
Australian Guarantee Corporation Limited - Queensland,
   AGC House, Tank St. & North Quay, pg. 1496   IT
BHP Coal, Riverside Centre, 123 Eagle Street, pg. 223   IT
Bankers Trust Australia Limited, Level 8, Riverside Centre,
   pg. 186   IT
Bill Acceptance Corporation Limited - Queensland, 37th Fl.,
   10 Eagle St., pg. 1496   IT
Blair Athol Coal, 10 Eagle St., pg. 128   IT
Bowen Coke Pty. Ltd., 410 Ann St., pg. 827   IT
Bucyrus (Australia) Proprietary Ltd., 9th Floor G.W.A.
   House, 10 Market Street, pg. 177   PV
Bundaberg Sugar Company, pg. 1357
Burns, Philp Pacific Division, 5 Cribb St., pg. 237   IT
Burson-Marsteller, 12th Fl., Bank of NZ Bldg., 410 Queen
   St., pg. 1198   PV
Carpentaria Gold Pty. Ltd., 410 Ann St., pg. 827   IT
Colinta Holdings Pty. Ltd., 410 Ann St., pg. 827   IT
Collinsville Coal Co. Pty. Ltd., 410 Ann St., pg. 827   IT
COMALCO LIMITED, 12 Creek Street, pg. 307   IT
Comalco Minerals & Alumina, Comalco Place, 12 Creek St.,
   pg. 307   IT
Commonwealth Bank of Australia-Queensland, 240 Queen
   St., pg. 313   IT
Computer Maintenance of Australia Pty. Ltd., 25 Donkin St.,
   pg. 317   IT
Curragh Coal, 15-23 Adelaide St., pg. 128   IT
DMR Group Australia Pty. Ltd., Level 8, 307 Queen St.,
   pg. 528   PB
Daiwa House (Australia) Pty. Ltd., Ste. 4, Level 3, Cavill
   Pk., 46 Cavill Ave., pg. 374   IT
Elders - Queensland, 10 Felix St., pg. 501   IT
Energy Power Systems PNG Pty. Limited, 180 Kerry Rd.,
   pg. 316   PB
Gearhart Australia Limited, 25th Fl., MLC Ctr., CNR.,
   pg. 776   PB
Hewlett-Packard Australia Ltd., 10 Payne Rd., pg. 818   PB
ICI Valchem, Newson Street, pg. 1525   IT
Industrial Galvanizers Corporation Pty. Ltd., 6th Fl. Barclay
   Mowlem Bldg., 973 Fairfield Rd., pg. 391   IT
Intergraph Corp. Pty. Ltd., 7th Fl., 126 Margaret St.,
   pg. 891   PB
International Public Relations, Pty Ltd., Netpac Terraces, 39
   Leopard St., pg. 1227   IT
Kinney Shoes (Australia), Ltd., 140 Melbourne St.,
   pg. 1778   PB
LGT Asset Management Ltd., pg. 810   IT
M.I.M. Exploration Pty. Ltd., 410 Ann Street, pg. 827   IT
M.I.M. HOLDINGS LTD., M.I.M. Plaza, 410 Ann St.,
   pg. 827   IT
Magellan Petroleum Australia Ltd., 145 Eagle Street, 10th
   Fl., pg. 1037   PB
Makita (Australia) Pty. Ltd.-Brisbane, 78 Pritchard Road,
   pg. 831   IT
Mitsui & Co. (Australia), 18th Fl., Colonial Mutual Bldg.,
   pg. 880   IT
Mount Isa International Pty. Ltd., 410 Ann St., pg. 827   IT
Mount Isa Mines (Coal Finance) Limited, 410 Ann St.,
   pg. 827   IT
NYK Line-Brisbane, 9th Floor, 444 Queen Street,
   pg. 941   IT
National Mutual Queensland, 144 Edward St., pg. 908   IT
Nevitts Limited, Level 12, Comalco Place, 12 Creek Street,
   pg. 583   IT
Newlands Coal Pty. Ltd., 410 Ann St., pg. 827   IT
Oaky Creek Coal Pty. Ltd., 410 Ann Street, pg. 827   IT
Palmer Tube, 146 Ingram Rd., pg. 101   IT
Port Curtis Moulders Pty. Ltd., CNR Montague Rd. & Hope
   57, pg. 1074   IT
Q.U.F. INDUSTRIES LTD., Cnr. Montague Rd. & Hope St.,
   pg. 1074   IT
Q.U.F. Milk Marketing, Montague Rd. & Hope St.,
   pg. 1074   IT
Queensland Alumina Limited, G.P.O. Box 374, 4001,
   pg. 52   IT
Queensland Alumina Limited, G.P.O. Box 374, 4001,
   pg. 1063   PB
SSB Advertising Brisbane, 90 Petrie Terrace, pg. 394   IT

Sanwa Australia Finance Limited, Level 20, Waterfront
   Place, One Eagle Street, pg. 1190   IT
Tektronix Australia Pty. Limited-Brisbane, pg. 1567   PB
Tenneco Oil & Minerals of Australia, Inc., 91 Robertson
   Street, Fortitude Valley, pg. 1580   IT
Total Energy Systems Limited, 3rd Floor Invicta House, 172
   Edward Street, pg. 1115   IT
Universal Transport Operations Pty. Ltd., 14 Edmondstone
   St., pg. 827   IT
Van Leer Australia Pty. Ltd., pg. 1146   IT
Veritas DGC INC, 5456 Brookes St., Bowen Hills,
   pg. 1137   PV
Westpac - Queensland, 260 Queen St., pg. 1496   IT
Willis Corroon Richard Oliver Pty. Ltd., 12 Creek Street,
   2nd Floor, pg. 1509   IT

Broadmeadows

Ericsson Australia Pty. Ltd., 61 Riggall Street, pg. 1366   IT
Ericsson Treasury Australia Pty. Ltd., 61 Riggall Street,
   pg. 1368   IT
Kubota Tractor (Australia) Pty. Ltd., 9-23, King William St.,
   pg. 763   IT
LM Ericsson Pty. Ltd., 61, Riggall St., pg. 1369   IT
Teleric Pty. Ltd., 61, Riggall St., pg. 1371   IT

Brooklyn

Brambles Bulk Haulage, McDonald Road, pg. 211   IT
Jotun Powder Coatings Pty. Ltd., 9, Cawley Rd.,
   pg. 715   IT

Brookvale

Artistcare Pty. Ltd., Locked Bag 3000, pg. 460   IT
Bevaloid Australia (Pty) Ltd., 84 Old Pitwater Rd.,
   pg. 1113   IT
Citizen Watches Australia Pty Ltd., 122 Old Pittwater Rd.,
   pg. 294   IT
Eaton Pty. Ltd. Controls Division, 32 Roger St.,
   pg. 559   PB
Fuji Photo Film Co., Ltd., Sydney Office, c/o Hanimex Pty.
   Ltd., 108 Old Pittwater Rd., pg. 525   IT
Geodimeter of Australia Pty. Ltd., 275 Harbord Rd.,
   pg. 1290   IT
Gestetner Australasia Limited, 108 Old Pittwater Road,
   pg. 1115   IT
Hanimex Pty. Limited, 108 Old Pittwater Road,
   pg. 1115   IT
Letraset Australia Pty. Ltd., Unit 5, 4 Skyline Place,
   pg. 461   IT
Lowrance Australia, 42/9 Powells Rd., pg. 1016   PB
Luxo Asia-Pacific Pty. Ltd., Unit 4, 98 Old Pittwater Road,
   pg. 821   IT
Luxo Australia Pty. Ltd., Unit 4, 98 Old Pittwater Rd.,
   pg. 821   IT
Prentice Hall of Australia Pty., Ltd., 7 Grosvenor Place,
   pg. 758   PV
Simplex Intl. Time Equip. Pty. Ltd., 32 Cross Street P.O.
   Box 561, pg. 1002   PV
Weir Engineering Pty. Ltd., pg. 1489   IT
The West Company Australia Pty. Ltd., 12/98 Old Pittwater
   Rd., pg. 1755   IT
Zellweger Pty. Ltd., pg. 618   IT

Bruce

Hewlett-Packard Australia Ltd., Thynne St., Fern Hill Park,
   pg. 818   PB

Brunswick

Bertolli Australia Pty Ltd., 108-112 Dawson St., pg. 655   IT

Bulimba

Getinge Australia Pty Ltd., 154 Lytton Road, pg. 551   IT

Bundall

Mineral Deposits Pty. Ltd., Level 5, Evandale Place, 142
   Bundall Road, pg. 224   IT

Bundoora

Mytton's Limited, 10 Mirra Ct., pg. 216   IT

Burnie

Lactos Pty. Ltd., Old Surrey Rd., pg. 201   IT
North Forests Burnie, pg. 967   IT
North Pine Products, Massy Greene Dr., pg. 967   IT
Tioxide Australia Proprietary Limited, pg. 665   IT

Burswood

Commonwealth Financial Services, 3rd Floor, 16-24 Elsie
   Street, pg. 313   IT
Outokumpu Mining Australia Pty. Ltd., 1st Floor Burswood
   Court, 141 Burswood Road, pg. 1016   IT

Cabramatta

Capral Aluminium-Foil, 11 Longfield Street, pg. 266   IT

Cairns

Cairns Brewery, 113 Spence St., pg. 501   IT

Camberwell

Amcor Fibre Packaging, 971-973 Burke Road, pg. 72   IT
Amcor Printing Papers Group, 685 Burke Road, pg. 72   IT
D & B Software Australia Pty. Ltd., Camberwell Office Park,
   19 Prospect Hill Rd., pg. 532   IT
Rohm & Haas Australia Pty. Ltd., 969 Burke Rd.,
   pg. 1404   PB

Camden Park

Herbalife Australasia Pty. Ltd., 123-125 Mooringe Ave.,
   pg. 809   PB

Camellia

Burns, Philp & Co., 15 Grand Ave., pg. 236   IT
James Hardie Building Products, 1 Grand Avenue,
   pg. 597   IT
Movements International Movers (NSW) Pty. Ltd., 3 Grand
   Ave., pg. 211   IT

Campbellfield

Andrew Australia, 153 Barry Rd., pg. 113   PB
Ford Motor Co. of Australia Ltd., 1735 Sidney Rd.,
   pg. 666   PB
Ford Sales Company of Australia Limited, 1735 Sidney Rd.,
   pg. 666   PB
Scania Australia Pty. Ltd., Private Mail Bag 11, pg. 687   IT

Campbelltown

Pirelli Cables Australia Limited, 135 Airds Rd., P.O. Box
   491, pg. 1059   IT

Camperdown

Bally Australia Pty. Ltd., 42/44 Gibbons St., pg. 997   IT
Carl Zeiss Pty. Ltd. Canberra Company, pg. 1523   IT

Campsie

Sunbeam Victa Holdings Ltd., Wade Street, pg. 539   IT

Canada Bay

WATTYL, 48 Walker St., pg. 1488   IT

Canberra

ANZ Australian Capital Territory, 25 Petrie Plaza,
   pg. 98   IT
AOFR Pty Limited, pg. 4   PB
AST Research, Suite 9, Level 11, Advance Bank Center,
   pg. 1182   IT
Alusuisse of Australia Ltd, pg. 68   IT
AST Research, Level 11 Advance Bank Centre,
   pg. 1182   IT
Australian Guarantee Corporation Limited - A.C.T., Law
   Society Bldg., 11 London Circuit, pg. 1496   IT
Commonwealth Bank of Australia-Australian Capital
   Territory, 2nd Fl., Bank House, London Circuit & Ainslie
   Ave., pg. 312   IT
International Public Relations, Pty Ltd., 35 Kennedy St.,
   pg. 1227   IT
Makita (Australia) Pty. Ltd.-Canberra, Unit 18, 157-161
   Gladstone Street, pg. 831   IT
Martin Marietta International, Inc., Perpetual Trustees Bldg.,
   3rd Fl. Unit 3, 10 Rudd St., pg. 1010   PB
Sequent Computer Systems (Australia), Level 6, Advance
   Bank Center, 60 Marcus Clarke St., pg. 1459   PB
Swiss Aluminium Australia Ltd., pg. 69   IT
Tektronix Australia Pty. Limited-Canberra, pg. 1567   PB

Canning Vale

Hagglunds Drives Pty Ltd, pg. 670   IT
Smith International Australia (Pty) Ltd., Unit 2, 30 Canvale
   Road, pg. 1478   PB
Van Leeuwen Pipe and Tube Western Australia Pty. Ltd.,
   31-35 Vulcan Rd., pg. 1450   IT

Cannington

Port Waratah Coal Services Pty. Ltd., Off Parker St.,
   pg. 949   IT

Capel

Westralian Sands Limited, Jenkin Road, pg. 689   IT

Caringbah

Dunphy Holding Pty. Ltd., Unit 5, 32 Endeavour Rd.,
   pg. 1232   IT
Florasynth Australasia Pty. Ltd., 30 Endeavor Rd.,
   pg. 173   IT
Kent Instruments Pty. Ltd., 70-78 Box Rd., P.O. Box 333,
   pg. 2   IT
Loctite (Australia) Pty. Ltd., 3 Endeavor Rd., pg. 611   IT

PB - *U.S. Public Companies Volume*
PV - *U.S. Private Companies Volume*
IT - *International Public & Private Companies Volume*

Parke-Davis Pty. Ltd., 32 Cawarra Road, pg. 1739   **PB**

Carlington

MD Holmen Australia & New Zealand Pty. Ltd., 7 Lloyds Ave., Ste. No. 6, pg. 886   **IT**
Svedala Australia (Carrington), pg. 1324   **IT**

Carlton Hill

Blackwell Scientific Publications (Australia) Pty. Ltd., 107 Barry St., pg. 197   **IT**

Carrum Downs

Aloette Cosmetics (Australasia) Pty. Ltd., 8 Aster Ave., pg. 57   **PB**

Castle Hill

Amway of Australia Pty. Ltd., 46 Carrington Rd., P.O. Box 202, pg. 70   **PV**
Australian AMP Pty. Limited, 13 Hudson Ave., pg. 9   **PB**
CIBA Vision Australia Pty Limited, Unit 1, 42 Carrington Rd., pg. 981   **IT**
CIBA Vision Care Australia, Unit 1, 42 Carrington Rd., pg. 981   **IT**
Harcros Timber Australia Pty. Ltd., 18 Victoria Ave., pg. 599   **IT**
Axel Johnson Steel Australia Pty Ltd., Corner of Gladstone Rd. & Victoria Ave., pg. 712   **IT**
Matchbox Collectibles Pty. Ltd., Unit 2, 13 Hoyle Ave., pg. 1059   **PB**
Mindscape International, Pty. Limited, 5/6 Gladstone Road, pg. 1027   **IT**
Parker Hannifin (Australia) (Pty.) Ltd., 9 Carrington Rd., pg. 1263   **PB**
Sunrise Medical Pty. Ltd., Unit 7, 15 Carrington Rd., pg. 1536   **PB**

Caversham

BRISTILE CLAY TILES, LTD., Harper St., pg. 216   **IT**

Chapel Hill

Sun Microsystems Australia Pty. Ltd.-Brisbane, 87 Moordale St., pg. 1532   **PB**

Charlestown

Van Leeuwen Pipe and Tube Eastern Australia Pty. Ltd., Unit 17/22, Smart Street, pg. 1450   **IT**

Charters Towers

Battle Mountain (Australia) Inc., Pajingo Mine, Claremont Rd., pg. 193   **PB**

Chatswood

Aetna International (Australia) Pty. Ltd., Interchange South Tower, 67 Albert Ave., pg. 27   **PB**
BOC Gases Australia Ltd., 799 Pacific Highway, pg. 121   **IT**
D & B Software Australia Pty Ltd., 19 Havilah St., Grnd. Fl., pg. 532   **IT**
Drill and Blast (Australia) Pty Limited, Level 6, 799 Pacific Hwy., pg. 664   **IT**
Epson Australia Pty. Ltd. (E.A.L.), 1/70 Gibbes Street, pg. 1219   **IT**
Fujitsu Australia Ltd., 475 Victoria Ave., pg. 528   **IT**
Genicom Pty. Ltd., 175 Gibbes Street, Unit 12, pg. 729   **PB**
Grinnell Asia Pacific Pty Limited, Level 11, 815 Pacific Hwy., pg. 1651   **PB**
IE Management Consultant Pty. Ltd., Level 5, South Tower, 1-5 Railway St., pg. 162   **PV**
Kvaerner R J Brown Pty Ltd, Level 5, 67 Albert Ave., pg. 767   **IT**
Linde (Australia) Pty. Ltd., pg. 811   **IT**
MBT (Australia) Pty. Ltd., 79 Victoria Ave., pg. 1465   **IT**
Mardev-Australia, Level 12, North Tower, Chatswood Plaza, 1-5 Railway Street, pg. 1094   **IT**
McKechnie Pacific, Ste. 1802, Level 18, Tower A, Zenith Centre, 821 Pacific Hwy., pg. 852   **IT**
NextLevel Systems (Australia), 815 Pacific Hwy., Level 10, Ste. 3, pg. 716   **PB**
Nortel Australia Pty. Limited, 475-495 Victoria Avenue, pg. 970   **IT**
Powell's Pest Control Pty. Ltd., 554 Pacific Hwy., pg. 1286   **IT**
Reed Business Information Pty. Limited, Tower 2, 475 Victoria Ave., pg. 1094   **IT**
Reed Travel Publishing-Australia, 8th Floor, North Tower, Chatswood Plaza, pg. 1097   **IT**
Reed Travel Publishing-Australia/South Pacific, Suite 801, North Tower, Chatswood Plaza, pg. 1097   **IT**
Rentokil (Pty.) Ltd., 554 Pacific Hwy., pg. 1286   **IT**
Sun Microsystems of Australia Pty. Ltd., 1st Level, Aetna Centre, 475-495 Victoria Ave., pg. 1532   **PB**
Tyco Grinnell Australia Pty Ltd, Level 11, 815 Pacific Hwy., pg. 1651   **PB**
Tyco International Pty Ltd., Level 11, 815 Pacific Hwy., pg. 1651   **PB**
UPM-Kymmene Paper Pty Ltd., Suite 307, 282 Victoria Avenue, pg. 1430   **IT**
Utell International-Australia, Suite 801, North Tower, Chatswood Plaza, 1-5 Railway Street, pg. 1098   **IT**

Volvo Australia Pty. Ltd., pg. 1477   **IT**
Wormald Australia Pty Limited, Level 11, 815 Pacific Hwy., pg. 1651   **PB**

Cheltenham

OCE-Australia Finance Pty. Ltd., pg. 994   **IT**
OCE-Australia Limited, 89 Tulip St., pg. 994   **IT**
P&S Australia Pty Ltd., pg. 1202   **IT**

Chippendale

Reed Exhibition Companies-Australia, 97 Chippen Street, pg. 1097   **IT**
Thomson Australian Holdings Pty. Ltd., 47 Chippen St., pg. 1601   **PB**

Chipping Norton

Daikin Australia Pty. Ltd., 77-83 Alfred Rd., pg. 365   **IT**

Chiswick

BHP Reinforcing Products, Blackwall Point Road, pg. 226   **IT**

Chullora

Franklins Holdings Ltd., 62 Hume Highway, pg. 703   **IT**
Franklins Limited, 62 Hume Hwy., pg. 703   **IT**
Grace Express, 41 Roberts Road, pg. 211   **IT**

City Beach

Barrick Gold, 32 Templetenia Crescent, pg. 169   **IT**

Clayton

ACI Liquitainers, 314 Ferntree Gully Rd., pg. 128   **IT**
Robert Bosch (Australia) Pty Ltd., CNR. Ctr. & McNaughton Rds., pg. 205   **IT**
Chiron Mimotopes, 11 Duerdin St., pg. 350   **PB**
Energy Power Systems Australia Pty. Limited, 17-55 Nantilla Rd., pg. 316   **PB**
Hallmark Asia/Pacific Region, 611 Blackburn Road, pg. 496   **PV**
Hallmark Cards Australia Ltd., 611 Blackburn Rd., pg. 496   **PV**
Kiwi Brands Pty. Ltd., 610 Heatherton Rd., pg. 1434   **PB**
McCormick Foods Australia Pty. Ltd., Private Bag 31, 71 Fairbank Rd., pg. 1067   **PB**
Nissan Motor Manufacturing Co. (Australia) Ltd., Center Rd., pg. 945   **IT**
Philmac Pty Limited, 36 Bendix Dr., pg. 555   **IT**
Refrigeration Div., 1092 Center Rd., pg. 1287   **IT**
Regency, 1503 Centre Road, pg. 851   **IT**
S & B Altim, pg. 129   **IT**
Shimadzu Australia Manufacturing Pty. Ltd., 5 Buckland St., pg. 1232   **IT**

Clovelly Park

Mitsubishi Motors Australia Ltd., 1284 South Rd., pg. 876   **IT**

Coburg

Kodak (Australasia) Pty. Ltd., 173 Elizabeth St., pg. 552   **PB**
Pacific Film Laboratories, 173-179 Elizabeth St., pg. 552   **PB**

Coldstream

Domaine Chandon Australia Pty Ltd, Green Point, Maroondah Hwy., pg. 782   **IT**

Collie

Worsley Alumina Pty. Ltd., Gastaldo Rd., pg. 1387   **PB**

Concord West

Westinghouse Brake & Signal Co. Ltd., pg. 128   **IT**

Condell Park

Fairfax Community Newspapers Pty. Limited, 47 Allingham Street, pg. 477   **IT**
Sanden International Oceania (Australia) Pty. Ltd., 54 Allingham Street, pg. 1184   **IT**

Coopers Plains

Yokohama Tyre Australia Pty., Ltd., 622 Boundary Road, pg. 1522   **IT**

Cottlesloe

Gray Tool Company, c/o Donald H. Dobson & Co., Pty. Ltd., pg. 5   **IT**

Cremorne

EMI Music Australia, pg. 427   **IT**
THORN EMI Australia Limited, pg. 427   **IT**

Crows Nest

CHEP Australia, 70-76 Alexander, pg. 211   **IT**
IDC Australia, 88 Christie St., St. Leonards, pg. 570   **PV**
IRD Mechanalysis (Australia) Pty. Limited, 337 Pacific Hwy., pg. 790   **PB**
ITC Australasia PTY Ltd., Level 1, 272 Pacific Highway, pg. 859   **PB**
Intel Australia Pty. Ltd., pg. 887   **PB**
Interleaf Australia, Pty. Ltd., pg. 893   **PB**
MSI Australia Pty. Ltd., Ste. 9, No. 9 Myrle Street, pg. 1546   **PB**
Melitta Catering Pty. Ltd., pg. 857   **IT**
Melitta House of Coffee Pty. Ltd., pg. 857   **IT**
Sola Basic Australia Ltd., 109 Alexander, pg. 727   **PB**

Croydon

Black & Decker (Australasia) Pty. Limited, pg. 234   **IT**
Emhart Australia Pty. Ltd., 286-288 Maroondah Hwy., pg. 234   **PB**
Spectra-Physics Pty. Ltd., 25 Research Drive, pg. 1290   **IT**

Dampier

BHP Petroleum Pty. Ltd., Lot 313 Supply Base, King Bay Road, pg. 225   **IT**

Dandenong

ACI Fibreglass, Frankston Rd., pg. 128   **IT**
Beecham (Australia) Pty. Ltd., Private Mail Bag 34, 300 Frankston Rd., pg. 1265   **IT**
Fairfax Community Newspapers Pty. Ltd., 142 Frankston Street, pg. 477   **IT**
H.B. Fuller Co. Australia Pty., Ltd., 16-20 Redgum Dr., pg. 687   **PB**
Gambro Pty Ltd., 27 Healey Rd., pg. 668   **IT**
H.J. Heinz Company Australia Ltd., 43-65 Princes Hwy., P.O. Box 57, pg. 807   **PB**
Ingersoll-Rand (Australia) Proprietary Ltd., Private Mail Bag 42, pg. 878   **PB**
Linatex Australia Pty. Ltd., 44-80 Sinclair Rd., pg. 599   **PB**
Marine Power Australia, Pty. Ltd., 132-140 Frankston Road, pg. 266   **PB**
Nichiyu Australia Pty., P.O. Box 461, pg. 97   **IT**
Nissan Castings Australia Pty. Ltd., 260-284 Frankston Road, pg. 945   **IT**
Nissan Motor Co. (Australia) Pty. Ltd., 260-284 Frankston Road, pg. 945   **IT**
PQ Australia Pty., Ltd., Lot 2, Ruhr Ct., pg. 827   **PV**
Panduit Aust. Pty. Ltd., 30-36 Kitchen Rd., pg. 836   **PV**
SAB WABCO Pty. Ltd., P.O. Box 685, pg. 271   **IT**
Van Leeuwen Pipe and Tube Eastern Australia Pty. Ltd., Lot 5, Dana Court, pg. 1450   **IT**

Darra

Mack Trucks Australia Pty. Ltd., P.O. Box 364, pg. 1103   **IT**
Westinghouse Industry Services-Queensland, 56 Archerfield Rd., pg. 275   **PB**

Darwin

ANZ Northern Territory, 43 The Mall, pg. 98   **IT**
Australian Guarantee Corporation Limited - Northern Territory, Mitchell Plaza, 28 Mitchell St., pg. 1496   **IT**
DMR Group Australia Pty. Ltd., 24 Cavenagh St., pg. 528   **IT**
Darwin Glass, Bishop St., pg. 129   **IT**
MGM Grand Australia Pty, Ltd., Gilruth Ave., Mindil Beach, pg. 1027   **IT**
Makita (Australia) Pty. Ltd.-Darwin, 34 Bishop Street, pg. 832   **IT**
Westpac - Northern Territory, 2nd. Fl., Pasapley Bldg., 19 Smith St. Mall, pg. 1496   **IT**
Woodward-Clyde, Esanda Bldg.-Ground Fl., 70 Cavenagh St., pg. 1657   **PB**

Deakin

DMR Group Australia Pty. Ltd., 2 Napier Close, Suite 5, pg. 528   **IT**

Deer Park

Metropolitan Women's Correctional Facility, Riding Boundry Road, pg. 451   **PB**

Deewhy

Avon Products Pty. Ltd., P.O. Box 180, pg. 156   **PB**
Colby Engineering Pty. Ltd., pg. 838   **IT**
Givaudan-Roure Pty. Ltd., 96 South Creek Rd., pg. 1120   **IT**
International Flavors & Fragrances (Australia) Pty. Ltd., 156 S. Creek Rd., pg. 899   **PB**
JEOL (Australasia) Pty. Ltd., 17 Villiers Place, pg. 697   **IT**
MAN GHH Australia Pty. Ltd., 99a South Creek Rd., pg. 824   **IT**
Nicholas Products Pty. Ltd., pg. 1121   **IT**

PB - *U.S. Public Companies Volume*
PV - *U.S. Private Companies Volume*
IT - *International Public & Private Companies Volume*

1494

Roche Products (Pty.) Ltd., 4-10 Inman Rd., pg. 1122   IT
Valpak Pty. Ltd., Unit 37, Dee Why Industrial Estate, pg. 949   IT

Devon Park

Orlando Wyndham, 33 Exeter Terrace, pg. 567   IT

Dingley

Fischer Imaging Australia Pty., Ltd., Five Fir St., 3172, pg. 647   PB
Nationwide Bearings Pty. Ltd., 399-401 Lower Dandenong Rd., pg. 1157   IT
Scholl International (ANZ) Pty. Ltd., 354-356 Boundary Rd., pg. 1209   IT
Scholl International (NZ) Ltd., 354-356 255a Boundary Rd., pg. 1210   IT

Double Bay

ORIX Australia Corporation Limited, Level 1, 4-10 Bay St., pg. 1009   IT

Dulwich

Hewlett-Packard Australia Ltd., 191 Fullerton Rd., pg. 818   PB
Young & Rubicam Adelaide Pty. Ltd., 182-184 Fullarton Rd., First Fl., pg. 1198 PV

Dysart

Norwich Park Mine, pg. 223   IT
Saraji Mine, pg. 223   IT

East Brisbane

Telxon Australia Pty., Ltd., Suite 1A/96 Lytton Road, pg. 1574   PB

Eastwood

Goodman Fielder Milling & Baking Group, Level 4, 33-43 Rowe Street, pg. 555   IT
Goodman Fielder Mills Ltd., Level 4, 33-43 Rowe St., pg. 555   IT
Quality Bakers Australia Ltd., Level 4, 33-43 Rowe St., pg. 555   IT

Edgecliff

Australasian HMT Pty. Ltd., pg. 914   PB
Carlson Marketing Group (Aust.) Pty. Limited, pg. 212   PV

Edwardstown

Bridgestone Australia Ltd., 1028-1042 South Rd., pg. 214   IT
Portal Aird Publications Pty. Ltd., U3, 5 Lindfield Avenue, pg. 503   PB

Elizabeth

Fasson Pty. Ltd., Hewittson Rd., pg. 154   PB

Emerald

Crinum Mine, Locked Bag No. 1, pg. 224   IT
Gregory Mine, LockedBag No. 1, pg. 223   IT

Emu Plains

BHP House Framing, Lot 1 Russell Street, pg. 226   IT

Enfield

Tate Access Floors, 50 Cosgrove Rd., pg. 905   PB

Epping

Acuson Pty. Ltd., 51 Rawson St., pg. 18   PB
Australian Guarantee Corporation Limited - New South Wales, 12 Langston Pl., pg. 1496 IT
Chesebrough-Pond's International Ltd., 44 Oxford, pg. 1436   IT
CRANE GROUP LIMITED, Level 3, 242 Beecroft Rd., pg. 340   IT
Driver-Harris Australia, Childs Road, pg. 723   IT
Ecolab Pty. Ltd., 242 Beecroft Rd., pg. 562   PB
Telxon Australia Pty. Limited, 4 Cambridge Street, pg. 1573   PB
Van Leer Australia Pty. Ltd., pg. 1146   IT
WD-40 Company (Australia), Century Plaza, Ste. 23, Level 2, 41 Rawson St., pg. 1726 PB

Ermington

ESAB Australia Pty. Ltd., 129-137 Beaconsfield St., pg. 282   IT
Reckitt & Colman Products Pty. Ltd., 33 Hope Street, pg. 1090   IT

Everard Park

Jardine Matheson Distributors Ltd., 16 Anzac Hwy, pg. 705   IT

Fairfield

Le Carbone-Lorraine Australia Pty. Ltd., 75 Sparks Avenue, pg. 1030   IT
Linde Gas Pty. Ltd., pg. 811   IT
NS Komatsu Pty., Ltd., Lisbon & Mandarin Streets, pg. 745   IT

Fawkner

W.R. Grace Australia Ltd., 1126 Sydney Road, pg. 755   PB

Five Dock

BHP Wire Products, Blackwell Point Road, pg. 226   IT
Sydney Wire Mill, Blackwall Point Road, pg. 226   IT

Footscray

Smorgon Consolidated Industries, 433 Somerville Rd., pg. 1269   IT
Smorgon Cyclone Rural, 433 Somerville Rd., pg. 1269   IT
West Footscray Engineering Works Pty. Ltd., 54 Cross St., pg. 392   IT

Forestville

Abu Garcia Pty. Ltd., pg. 822   PV

Fortitude Valley

AST Research, Level 2, K-Tower, Onr Wickham Terrace & Ballow St., pg. 1182   IT
Brisbane Brewery, 18 Malt St., pg. 501   IT
TMP Worldwide Pty Ltd., 88 Brunswick St., pg. 1342   IT

Fremantle

Matilda Bay Brewing Co. Ltd., 130 Stirling Highway, pg. 501   IT
NYK Line-Fremantle, Port Cinema Bldg., 70 Adelaide Street, pg. 941   IT
Perth Brewery, 130 Stirling Highway, pg. 501   IT
Standard Wool (Australia) Pty. Ltd., P.O. Box 618, pg. 1502   PB
United Transport (WA) Pty. Ltd., Kautsford St., pg. 211   IT

Frenchs Forest

ADC Telecommunications Australia Pty. Ltd., Level 1, Bldg. F, Forest Corporate Park, pg. 4   PB
Alcon Laboratories (Australia) Pty. Ltd., Allambie Grove Business Park, 25 Frenchs Forest Rd., pg. 918 IT
Ascomation Pty. Ltd., Unit 12, Allambie Grove, P.O. Box 631, pg. 576   PB
COBE Laboratories Pty Ltd.-Sydney, 3/17 Rodborough Road, pg. 667   IT
Cabletron Systems, Inc.-Australia, Unit 8, Allambie Grove Business Estate, pg. 288   PB
Carter-Wallace (Australia) Pty. Limited, 6 Aquatic Dr., pg. 310   PB
Dell Computer Pty. Ltd., Unit 3, Aquatic Dr., pg. 496   PB
Fujitsu ICL Australia Pty. Limited, 14 Rodborough Rd., pg. 529   PB
Lexmark Australia, Locked Bag 519, pg. 991   PB
Nitto Denko (Australia) Pty. Ltd., Unit D, 15 Rodborough Rd., pg. 950   IT
Outokumpu Mintec Australia Pty. Ltd., 5 Skyline Place, pg. 1017   IT
Supaflo Technologies Pty., Ltd., 5 Skyline Place, pg. 1017   IT
Wang Australia Pty. Ltd., Austlink Corporate Park, 2 Minna Close, pg. 1737   PB
Zimmer Australia Pty. Limited, 1/1 Skyline Place, pg. 256   PB

Fyshwick

Sharp Corporation of Australia Pty. Ltd., Unit 3, Centre Ct., 1 Pirie St., pg. 1229 IT

Gardenvale

Svedala Australia (Gardenvale), pg. 1324   IT

Geelong

Olin Australia Limited, Hays Road, Point Henry, pg. 1220   PB
Senior Tift-Queensland, 97 Granite Rd., pg. 1223   IT
Volclay Standard Pty. Ltd., Chowie St., pg. 64   PB

Girraween

Van Leeuwen Pipe and Tube Eastern Australia Pty. Ltd., 214-222 Toongabbie Road, pg. 1450 IT

Gladesville

BHP Building and Construction Products, 476 Victoria Road, pg. 226   IT
Germantown International, 230 Victoria Road, pg. 555   IT
James Hardie Plumbing & Pipelines, 450 Victoria Road, pg. 597   IT
Ingredients Group, Level 4, 230 Victoria Road, pg. 555   IT
Leiner-Davis International Limited, Level 2, 230 Victoria Road, pg. 555   IT
Poultry Group, Level 2, 230 Victoria Road, pg. 555   IT
Starch Australia, Level 4, 230 Victoria Rd., pg. 555   IT

Gladstone

Barney Point Coal Terminal, pg. 223   IT
QAL Gladstone Plant, Parsons Point, pg. 1062   PB

Glebe

Zomba Production Music (Australia) Pty Limited, pg. 1529   IT

Glen Iris

AST Research, 1601 Malvern Road, pg. 1182   IT
Quest Leisure Products (Aust) Pty. Ltd., 601 Malvern Road, pg. 707   IT

Glen Waverley

Ansell International, 530 Springvale Rd., pg. 1021   IT
Electrolux Pty. Ltd., P.O. Box 57, pg. 440   IT
Mercedes-Benz (Australia) Pty. Ltd., Dunlop Rd. 12-20, pg. 368   IT
NEC Australia Pty. Ltd., 635 Ferntree Gully Rd., pg. 901   IT

Glenorchy

North Western Shipping and Towage Company Pty. Ltd., Prince of Wales Bay, 4 Hornby Road, pg. 211   IT

Gordon

Royal Doulton Australia Pty. Limited, 17-23 Merriwa Street, pg. 1135   IT
Textron Pacific Limited, 910 Pacific Highway, 3rd Flr., pg. 1590   PB

Gosford

Albany International Pty., Ltd., P.O. Box 417, pg. 37   PB
Ashton/Scholastic Pty. Ltd., P.O. Box 579, pg. 1440   PB

Granville

Borden Australia (Pty) Ltd., 46 Wellington Road, pg. 159   PV
Capral Aluminium-Extrusion, Shirley Street, pg. 266   IT
CAPRAL ALUMINIUM LIMITED, Unwin Street, pg. 266   IT
Capral Aluminium-Sheets, Shirley Street, pg. 266   IT
Capral Aluminium-Trading, Unwin Street, pg. 266   IT
Carbon Mechanical Products Pty Limited, Nine Harbord St., pg. 891   IT
Voest-Alpine (Australia) Pty. Ltd., Two Darcy St., pg. 1472   IT

Greenacres

Chr. Hansen Pty. Ltd., P.O. Box 193, pg. 289   IT
MQF Pty. Ltd., 52 Wentworth St., pg. 936   IT

Greenfields

Van Leeuwen Pipe and Tube Eastern Australia Pty. Ltd., Lot 129 Salisbury Highway, pg. 1450   IT

Greenwich

Fuller-F.L. Smidth (Pacific) Pty. Ltd., Level 4, 156 Pacific Highway, pg. 475   IT

Griffith

TMP Worldwide Pty Ltd., 131 Canberra Ave., pg. 1342   IT

Groote Eylandt

Groote Eylandt Mining Company, Alyangula, pg. 224   IT

Guildford

Bohler Steels Pty. Ltd., 129-135 McCredie Rd., pg. 1471   IT

Hackney

Woodward-Clyde International, 25 North Terrace, pg. 1658   PB

PB - U.S. Public Companies Volume
PV - U.S. Private Companies Volume
IT - International Public & Private Companies Volume

Geographic Index-Non U.S.

1495

Hallam

Major Furnace and Engineering Pty., Ltd., 33 Wedgewood
   Road, pg. 1455   PB

Hastings

Sheet & Coil Products Victoria, Western Port Works,
   pg. 227   IT

Hawthorn

BHP Minerals International Exploration Inc., 801 Glenferrie
   Road, pg. 224   IT
BMC Software (Australia) Pty. Ltd., The Atrium, 290
   Burwood Rd., pg. 162   PB
Kamyr Pty Ltd., 1 Oxley Rd., pg. 771   IT
Kvaerner Boving (ANZ) Pty Ltd, One Oxley Rd.,
   pg. 772   IT
Kvaerner Pulping Pty Ltd., 1, Oxley Rd, pg. 768   IT
Pacific Brands, 25 Camberwell Road, pg. 1021   IT
Pacific Distribution, 818 Glenferrie Rd., pg. 1021   IT
Paper Agencies (Aust.) Pty. Ltd., 554 Burwood Rd.,
   pg. 458   IT
Silenus Laboratories Pty Limited, Five Guest St., 3122,
   pg. 665   IT
Spalding Australia Pty. Ltd., Spalding House, 116 Church
   St., 3122, pg. 630   PV
Telxon Australia Pty., Ltd., 2 Domville Avenue,
   pg. 1573   PB

Herdsman

Allen-Bradley Pty. Limited, First Floor Building C, 345
   Harborne Street, pg. 1399   PB

Hilton

Sharp Corporation of Australia Pty. Ltd., 136-140 Burbridge
   Road, pg. 1229   IT

Hindmarsh

Dunlite Power Generation Pty. Ltd., 11 Manton St.,
   pg. 469   PB

Hobart

Australian Guarantee Corporation Limited - Tasmania, 161
   Collins St., pg. 1496   IT
Australian Newsprint Mills, 21 Kirksway Place, pg. 495   IT
Cooperative Motors Ltd., 267 Argyle St., pg. 597   IT
G.P. Fitzgerald & Co. Ltd., 91 Collins St., pg. 597   IT
Hobart Brewery, Port Tower Bldg., Evans St., pg. 501   IT
International Public Relations, Pty Ltd., Sydney Lodge, 57
   Brisbane Street, Sandy Bay, pg. 1227   IT
Makita (Australia) Pty. Ltd.-Hobart, 3/65, Albert Road,
   pg. 832   IT
National Mutual Tasmania, 119 Macquarie St., pg. 908   IT
North Forest Products, 7-9 Franklin Wharf, pg. 967   IT
Shadforths Limited, Level 3, 111 Macquarie Street,
   pg. 583   IT
TMP Worldwide Pty Ltd, 183 Macquarie Street,
   pg. 1342   IT
Westpac - Tasmania, 28 Elizabeth St., pg. 1496   IT
Willis Corroon Richard Oliver Pty Ltd., 6th Floor, 152
   Macquarie Street, pg. 1509   IT

Homebush

FSE Pty. Ltd., Unit 4, 149 Arthur St., pg. 1111   IT
Kenwood Electronics Australia Pty. Ltd., 8 Figtree Dr.,
   pg. 730   IT
Sanyo Australia Pty. Ltd., 7 Figtree Dr., pg. 1192   IT

Hornsby

Check Technology Pty Limited, 5/8 Leighton Pl.,
   pg. 342   PB
Eurotherm Pty Ltd., Unit 3, 6-18 Bridge Rd., pg. 466   IT
Knorr-Brake Ausrtialia Pty. Limited, 2/45-47 Salisbury Rd.,
   pg. 738   IT
Kolmar (Aust.) Pty Ltd., 45 King Road, pg. 239   IT
Sulzer Australia Pty. Limited, pg. 1306   IT

Hunters Hill

qad.australia pty ltd, Level 1, 71-75 Gladesville Rd.,
   pg. 1345   PB

Huntingdale

Email Limited-Building Products Group, Edward St.,
   pg. 450   IT
Morlynn Ceramics Pty Limited, 1353 North Rd.,
   pg. 893   IT

Huntingwood

Guiness Finance Australia Limited, 4 Distillers Place,
   pg. 412   IT

Ingleburn

BetzDearborn Australia Pty Limited, 69-77 Williamson Rd.,
   pg. 227   PB

Ipswich

Borallon, P.O. Box 782, pg. 451   PB

Jabiru

ERA Ranger Mine, Lot Bag 1, pg. 967   IT

Jolimont

Battle Mountain Gold (Australia), 76 Jersey St.,
   pg. 193   PB
Dentsply Australia, 50-54 Jersey Street, pg. 499   PB

Kalgoorlie

Svedala Australia (Kalgoorlie), pg. 1324   IT

Kallaroo

North Whitfords Estates Pty. Ltd., 11, Henderson Dr.,
   pg. 1359   IT

Kanowna

Kanowna Belle Gold Mines, Yarri Road, pg. 967   IT

Karrabin

ANI Engineering, Walloon Rd., pg. 100   IT
ANI Mineral Processing, Karrabin-Walloon Road,
   pg. 100   IT

Karridale

Beenup Mine, pg. 224   IT

Kemps Creek

CIBA-GEIGY Australia Ltd., Western Rd., pg. 976   IT

Kenmore

Gambrc Pty. Ltd., pg. 668   IT

Keon Park

Davies Shephard Pty. Ltd., Dunstans Court, pg. 2   IT

Kewdale

Grace (WA) Pty. Limited, 16 Valentine, pg. 211   IT
Sharp Corporation of Australia Pty. Ltd., 53-61 Kewdale
   Rd., pg. 1229   IT
Teledyne Australia, 1 Princess Street, Suite 501,
   pg. 44   PB
Western Geophysical (Australia), 447-449 Belmont Ave.,
   pg. 1005   PB
Yokohama Tyre Australia Pty., Ltd., 521 Abernethy Road,
   pg. 1522   IT

Kilsyth

Brilliant Lighting (Australia), Cantonbury Ln., pg. 453   IT
Eaton Pty. Ltd.-Truck Components Operations, 33-35
   Garden St., pg. 559   PB
Fleetguard Australia, 31 Garden St., pg. 469   PB
Henkel Australia Pty. Ltd., Canterbury Rd., pg. 611   IT

Kings Park

Rexroth Hydraulics Pty. Ltd., pg. 839   IT

Kingsgrove

Verosol Australia Pty.Ltd., 2 Garema Circuit, pg. 198   IT
Woodward Governor Company (Australia), P.O. Box 319/
   Unit 1-1 Wirega Ave., pg. 1776   PB

Kingston

Analysis & Technology Australia Pty Limited, 1st Floor,
   Andrew Arcade, 42 Giles Street, pg. 110   PB

Kirrawee

AEP Industries Australia Pty. Ltd., 162 Garnet Rd.,
   pg. 5   PB
Roehlen Industries Pty. Ltd. (Sidney Division), Unit 16, 429
   The Eoulevarde, pg. 1507   PB

Knoxfield

Mary Kay Cosmetics Pty. Ltd., 551 Burwood Hwy.,
   pg. 771   PV
Prok Group Limited, 2/45 Rushdale St., pg. 1353   IT
Screen Products Australian Pty Ltd, 77 Parkhurst Dr.,
   pg. 412   PV

Kurnell

Abbott Australia/Asia Pty. Ltd., Captain Cook Dr.,
   pg. 13   PB

Kurri Kurri

Capral Aluminium-Smelter, Hart Road, pg. 266   IT

Kyabram

Henry Jones Foods Pty., Ltd., Church Street, pg. 1480   PB

Labrador

Gold Coast Milk Pty. Ltd., Cnr. Gold Coast Hwy. & Pine,
   pg. 1074   IT
The Great Australian Pie Company Pty. Ltd., Brisbane Rd.
   & Wright's Pl., pg. 1074   IT

Lane Cove

AST Research ANZ Pty. Ltd., 706 Mowbray Rd., Unit S.,
   pg. 1182   IT
Brambles Record Management, 702 Mowbray Road,
   pg. 211   IT
Brambles Securities Services Limited, 702 Mowbry Road,
   pg. 211   IT
British Pharmaceuticals Pty. Ltd., 31-33 Sirius Rd.,
   pg. 44   IT
Diasonics Pty. Ltd., 1 Woodstock Pl., pg. 644   IT
Doubleday Australia Pty. Ltd., 91 Mars Rd., pg. 192   IT
W.A. FLICK & CO. PTY. LIMITED, Level 3, 18-20 Orion
   Rd., pg. 495   IT
Grolier Australia PTY Limited, 14 Mars Road, pg. 795   IT
Helene Curtis Australia Pty. Ltd., 2 Lincoln Street,
   pg. 1434   IT
International Correspondence Schools (Australasia) Limited,
   398 Pacific Hwy., pg. 784   IT
Janssen-Cilag Pty. Ltd., 706 Mowbray Rd., Locked Bag 30,
   pg. 929   PB
Ladysan, 18-20 Orion Road, pg. 496   IT
Merisel Australia, 4 Sirius Rd., pg. 1096   PB
Millipore Pty. Ltd., Private Bag 18 87-89, Mars Rd.,
   pg. 1113   PB
SAS Institute Australia Pty. Ltd., Private Bag No. 52,
   pg. 966   PV
Toshiba International Corporation Pty., Ltd., Unit 1, 9 Orion
   Rd., pg. 1406   IT
Tuta Laboratories (Australia) Pty., Ltd., 318-332 Burns Bay
   Road, pg. 1014   IT

Launceston

North Forest Products Tamar, pg. 967   IT

Laverton

Avesta Sheffield Pty. Ltd., pg. 222   IT
BHP Petroleum Pty Ltd., 171 Fitzgerald Road, pg. 225   IT
Granny Smith Joint Venture, pg. 1060   IT
S.C.I. Steel Mill Pty. Ltd., 105 Dohertys Rd., pg. 1269   IT
Westinghouse Electric Australasia Ltd.-Victoria Div., 14
   Somerleigh, pg. 275   PB

Leederville

TMP Worldwide Pty Ltd., 125 Cambridge Street,
   pg. 1342   IT

Lidcombe

Allen-Bradley Pty. Limited, 56 Parramatta Road,
   pg. 1399   PB
Australian Abrasives Pty. Ltd., 25 Nyrang St., pg. 1174   IT
Bell-IRH Industries Pty. Ltd., 1-5 Carter St., pg. 391   IT
Capral Aluminium-Aluminium Centers, 9 Carter Street,
   pg. 266   IT
Duck River Company, 25, Nyrang Street, pg. 1174   IT
Grace Removals, Carter Street, pg. 211   IT
Norton Pty. Ltd., 25 Nyrang Street, pg. 1175   IT
Svedala Australia, pg. 1324   IT
Vaughan Transport (Australia) Pty. Ltd., Hill Rd.,
   pg. 211   IT
Whitehall Laboratories Pty. Limited, 12 Victoria, pg. 82   PB

Lilydale

Rockwell Australia Limited, Corner Maroondah Hwy. &
   Sheep Rd., pg. 1399   PB

Lindfield

Wall Data Australia Pty. Ltd., Ste. 18, 12 Tryon Rd.,
   pg. 1734   PB

Liverpool

Amoco Chemicals Pty. Ltd., 28-34 Orange Grove Road,
   pg. 102   PB
Cottee's Foods, 42 Orange Grove Rd., pg. 248   IT

Lonsdale

Rainsfords Metal Products Pty. Limited, Sherriffs Rd.,
   pg. 217   IT

Mackay

BHP Australia Coal Ltd., Mackay Laboratory, pg. 227   IT
Thomas Borthwick & Sons (Australia) Pty. Ltd., pg. 936   IT

PB - *U.S. Public Companies Volume*
PV - *U.S. Private Companies Volume*
IT - *International Public & Private Companies Volume*

Hay Point Export Terminal, Mail Service 283, pg. 223   IT
Prok Group Ltd., pg. 1353   IT

Macleod

Bontex Australia, 20 Munro Street, pg. 734   PB

Maidstone

Croner-Tyco Toys Pty. Ltd., 10-22 Hampstead Rd.,
   pg. 1059   PB

Malaga

Australia Power Pty Ltd, 220 Montgomery Way,
   pg. 894   IT
Maxpro Systems, Unit 1, 25 Irvine Drive, pg. 1663   PB
Weatherford Australia Pty. Ltd., 17 Truganina Road,
   pg. 1750   PB

Malvern

Brambles Equipment & Forklifts, 259 Wattletree Road,
   pg. 211   IT
Intergraph Public Safety Pty., Ltd., 311 Glenferrie Road,
   3144, pg. 892   PB
qad.australia pty ltd., 1155 Malvern Rd., pg. 1345   PB

Mansfield

Sharp Corporation of Australia Pty. Ltd., 10 Dividend St.,
   pg. 1229   IT

Marayong

Van Leer Australia Pty. Ltd., pg. 1146   IT

Margaret River

Cape Mentelle Vineyards Limited, pg. 782   IT

Maribyrnong

Vickers Systems Pty., Ltd., 169 Rosamond Rd., pg. 25   PB

Mascot

A.I. Ocean (Australia) Pty. Ltd., 292 Coward St., pg. 14   IT
Airlink, 203 Coward St., pg. 1075   IT
Boeing International Corp., Sydney Airport Ctr., Level 3, 15
   Bourke Rd., pg. 242   PB
Meadow Lea Foods Ltd., 514 Gardeners Rd., pg. 555   IT
Nippon Express (Australia) Pty., Ltd., Unit 1 Mascot
   Airfreight, Terminal 154, pg. 934   IT
QANTAS AIRWAYS LTD., Qantas Centre, 203 Coward St.,
   pg. 1074   IT
Qantas Flight Catering, Jetbase Dr., pg. 1075   IT
Qantas Information Technology, 203 Coward St.,
   pg. 1075   IT
TNT Australia Pty. Limited, 52-60 Kent Road, pg. 1343   IT

Matraville

Kintetsu World Express (Australia) Pty. Ltd., Unit 5, 153
   Beauchamp Rd., pg. 735   IT
Pioneer Plasterboard Pty Ltd., 31 Military Road,
   pg. 791   IT
Rohm & Haas (Australia) Pty. Ltd., 60 Perry, pg. 1404   PB

Mayfield

Australian Manganese Company Pty Ltd., Off Industrial
   Drive, pg. 224   IT
BHP Refractories Pty Ltd., Gavey Street, pg. 227   IT
BHP Refractories Ltd. Research & Development, Gavey
   Street, pg. 227   IT
BHP Steel Sankey, Ingall Street, pg. 227   IT
Building & Industrial Products Research, Bull Street,
   pg. 227   IT
Newcastle Wire Mill, Bull St. Extended, pg. 226   IT
Rod & Bar Products Division, Selwyn Street, pg. 227   IT

Meadowbank

GEC-Marconi Systems Pty. Ltd., Faraday Park, Railway Rd.,
   pg. 546   IT
Laundry & Floor Care Div., 41-45 Belmore St.,
   pg. 1287   IT
Prok Group Limited, 125 Bowden St., pg. 1353   IT

Melbourne

AAV Australia, 180 Banks Street, pg. 477   IT
ACI Australia Limited, Level 28, 200 Queen St.,
   pg. 128   IT
ACI Computer Services, 31 Wolger Rd., pg. 128   IT
ACI Engineering, Level 28, 200 Queen St., pg. 128   IT
ACI Homes, Level 28, 200 Queens St., pg. 128   IT
ACI International Ltd., 32nd Level, 200 Queen St.,
   pg. 128   IT
ACI Milling Pty. Ltd., 200 Queen St., pg. 128   IT
ACI Operations Pty. Ltd., Level 28, 200 Queen St.,
   pg. 128   IT
ACI Plastics Closures, 4 Kingsway, pg. 128   IT
AIS Media South, Level 3, 570 St. Kilda Road, pg. 15   IT
ANZ McCaughan Securities Limited, 9th Floor, 360 Collins
   Street, pg. 98   IT

AST Research, 9th Floor, 390 St. Kilda Rd., pg. 1182   IT
Acmetrack, Level 28, 200 Queen St., pg. 129   IT
Acmil Industries Pty. Ltd., Level 28, 200 Queen St.,
   pg. 129   IT
Adriatic Life Ltd., 88, Albert Road, pg. 61   IT
Ahlstrom ANZ Pty Ltd., 14/209 Toorak Rd., pg. 34   IT
Albright & Wilson (Australia) Limited, 610 St. Kilda Road,
   pg. 49   IT
Alcoa of Australia Limited, 530 Collins St., 7th Fl.,
   pg. 62   PB
Alfa-Laval Hamilton Pty Ltd., P.O. Box 75, pg. 1379   IT
AlliedSignal Aerospace Service Corporation, Ste. D0608,
   Bldg. D, World Trade Center, pg. 52   IT
AlliedSignal (Australia) Sales Ltd. Fibers & Chemicals, 71
   Queens Rd.,2nd Fl., pg. 52   PB
AMCOR LIMITED, Southgate, pg. 71   IT
Ansett Transport Industries Ltd., Box 362F, pg. 925   IT
Armstrong York Pty., Ltd., pg. 265   IT
Austen & Butta, Shell Corner, 155 William St.,
   pg. 1137   IT
Australasian Online Systems Pty. Ltd., 470 St. Kilda D.,
   Level 2, pg. 417   PB
AUSTRALIA & NEW ZEALAND BANKING GROUP
   LIMITED, 100 Queen St., pg. 98   IT
Australia and New Zealand Banking Group Limited,
   International Banking Division, 20th Floor, 100 Queen
   Street, pg. 98   IT
Australian Glass Manufacturers Co., Level 28, 200 Queen
   St., pg. 128   IT
Australian Guarantee Corporation Limited - Victoria, 277
   Wiliam St., pg. 1496   IT
Australian Road Credit Limited, 33 Albert Rd., pg. 665   PB
BASF Australia Ltd., 500 Princes Highway, pg. 105   IT
BHF-Bank Liason Office, Level 7, Challenge Tower, 459
   Collins Street, pg. 120   IT
BHP Information Technology, 600 Bourke Street,
   pg. 225   IT
BHP Insurance, 600 Bourke Street, pg. 225   IT
BHP Manganese, 600 Bourke Street, pg. 224   IT
BHP Minerals, 600 Bourke Street, pg. 223   IT
BHP Petroleum, 120 Collins Street, pg. 224   IT
BHP Petroleum Pty Ltd., BHP Petroleum Plaza, 120 Collins
   St., pg. 225   IT
BHP Service Companies, 600 Bourke Street, pg. 225   IT
BHP Steel, BHP Tower-Bourke Place, 600 Bourke St.,
   pg. 225   IT
BHP Titanium Minerals, 600 Bourke Street, pg. 224   IT
BHP Transport, 600 Bourke Street, pg. 225   IT
BIAM Australia Pty Ltd., Level 11, 580 St. Kida St.,
   pg. 153   IT
BP Australia Ltd., 1 Albert Rd., pg. 220   IT
BRW Media, Level 2, 469 LaTrobe Street, pg. 477   IT
BTR Nylex Limited, 15th Fl., 390 St. Kilda Rd., 3004,
   pg. 128   IT
Bank Hapoalim (Melbourne), Bourke Place, Level 20, 600
   Bourke Street, pg. 149   IT
Bank in Liechtenstein (Frankfurt) GmbH Australia, Level 24,
   333 Collins Street, pg. 809   IT
The Bank of New York, Level 4, 90 William Street,
   pg. 179   PB
Bankers Trust Australia Limited, Level 27, 367 Collins St.,
   pg. 185   PB
Becton Dickinson Pty Ltd., 80 Rushdale St., pg. 200   IT
Bekaert (Australia) Pty. Ltd., pg. 540   IT
Bill Acceptance Corporation Limited - Victoria, 10th Flr.,
   227 William St., pg. 1496   IT
Bloch & Behrens Pty. Ltd., pg. 431   IT
Boral Australian Gypsum Ltd., 676 Lorimer St., pg. 203   IT
Brambles Seacargo, 4th Fl., 766 Elizabeth Street,
   pg. 211   IT
Brambles Shipping, 391 Plummer St., pg. 211   IT
Brambles Transport (Freight Forwarding) Division, 4th Fl.,
   Elizabeth St., pg. 211   IT
Britax Childcare Products Pty., 1521 Sydney Rd.,
   Campbellfield, pg. 216   IT
THE BROKEN HILL PROPRIETARY COMPANY LIMITED,
   BHP Tower, Bourke Place, 600 Bourke St., pg. 223   IT
Leo Burnett/Connaghan & May (VIC.) Pty. Ltd., 464 St.
   Kilda Rd., 5th Fl., pg. 185   PV
CQCA Mine, pg. 223   IT
CRA Limited, 55 Collins St., 33rd Fl., pg. 1119   IT
Cadbury Schweppes Australia Ltd, Cadbury Schweppes
   House, 636 St. Kilda Rd., pg. 248   IT
Campbell's Soups (Aust.) Pty. Ltd., 499 St. Kilda Rd.,
   Fawkner Center, pg. 299   PB
Caterpillar of Australia Ltd., 1 Sharps Rd., Tullmarine,
   pg. 316   PB
Chamberlain John Deere Pty. Ltd., 237 Rex Campbellfield,
   pg. 492   PB
Clarion Australia Pty., Ltd., Unit 17, 50 Keys Rd.,
   pg. 296   IT
Comalco Research & Technology, Level 38, 55 Collins St.,
   pg. 307   IT
Comalco Smelting, 441 St. Kilda Rd., pg. 307   IT
Commercial Hydraulics Pty. Ltd., 265 Ingles St.,
   pg. 411   IT
Commonwealth Bank of Australia-Victoria & Tasmania, 385
   Bourke St., pg. 313   IT
COMPUTER POWER GROUP LIMITED, 439 St. Kilda Rd.,
   pg. 325   IT
Continuum Australia Limited, 310 King Street, pg. 423   PB
Cookson Matthey (Australia), 26-28 Garden Blvd.,
   pg. 714   IT
County NatWest Australia Investment, Level 20, 333 Collins
   Street, pg. 911   IT
County NatWest Securities Australia Limited, Level 52, The
   Rialto, pg. 911   IT
D & D Tolhurst Ltd., 31 Queen St., pg. 257   IT
DMR Group Australia Pty. Ltd., Level 8, 1 Southbank Blvd.,
   pg. 528   IT

Dai-Ichi Kangyo Bank, Ltd.-Melbourne, 19th Floor, 359
   Collins St., pg. 361   IT
Daiwa Securities Australia Limited-Head Office, Level 48,
   Nauru House, 80 Collins St., pg. 375   IT
Danzas Pty. Ltd., 4 Tarmac Dr., pg. 382   IT
Data General Australia Pty. Ltd., 100 Dorcas S.,
   pg. 485   PB
Davy John Brown PTY Limited, 600 St. Kilda Rd,
   pg. 775   IT
Delhi Petroleum Pty. Ltd., 360 Elizabeth Street,
   pg. 601   PB
Delta Group Australia Pty. Ltd., 568 St. Kilda Rd.,
   pg. 391   IT
Deutsche Bank Australia Ltd., 1 Collins Street, pg. 405   IT
W.A. Deutsher Pty. Ltd., P.O. Box 154, 600 South Rd.,
   pg. 867   PB
W.A. Deutsher Pty. Ltd., 8-12 Jack Rd., pg. 867   PB
Deville Dumping & Containerisation Pty. Ltd., pg. 431   IT
Dresdner Bank AG, 367 Collins St., pg. 419   IT
Dun & Bradstreet (Australia) Pty. Ltd., 479 St. Kilda Rd.,
   pg. 536   PB
The East Asiatic Co. (Australia) Limited, pg. 431   IT
Eclipse Combustion & Industrial Equipment, 14 Aristoc
   Road, pg. 361   PV
Daniel J. Edelman Pty. Ltd., Level 1, 58 Market Street,
   pg. 363   PV
Edison Mission Energy Holdings Pty. Ltd., Southgate
   Complex, Level 20, HWT Tower, pg. 564   PB
Elder's Finance Group, Level 5, 351 Collins St.,
   pg. 501   IT
Elders - Victoria, 160 Queen St., pg. 501   IT
Electrolux Utility Services Pty. Ltd., Cnr. Alexandra Ave. &
   Chapel St. South Y, pg. 440   IT
Esanda Finance Corporation Limited, 85 Spring St.,
   pg. 98   IT
Esso Australia Resources Ltd., 360 Elizabeth St.,
   pg. 602   PB
Ferro Corporation (Australia) Pty. Ltd., 105-115 Cochranes
   Road, pg. 619   PB
Fiduciary Trust Company International, 101 Collins St.,
   pg. 621   PB
Fluor Daniel Australia Limited, Fluor House, 616 St. Kilda
   Rd., pg. 660   PB
Ford Credit Australia Limited, 24 Albert Rd., 7th Fl.,
   pg. 665   PB
Ford Credit Australia Wholesale Limited, 33 Albert Rd.,
   pg. 665   PB
Fragrance Services Pty. Ltd., pg. 1436   IT
Frionor Australia Pty. Ltd., 541 King Street, pg. 516   IT
Friskies Pet Care Pty. Ltd., pg. 920   IT
General Motors-Holden's Automotive Limited, Box 1714
   G.P.O., pg. 723   PB
Greenfields Woolscour Pty. Ltd., pg. 431   IT
Guerlain (Asia Pacific) Ltd., 407, City Rd., pg. 780   IT
HSBC Asset Management Australia Limited, 7/F, 99
   William Street, pg. 582   IT
HSBC Investment Funds Australia Limited, 99 William
   Street, pg. 582   IT
Harris & Dixon (Insurance Brokers) Pty. Ltd., 582, St. Kilda,
   pg. 90   IT
Wm. Haughton & Co. Ltd., 29 Palmerston Cres.,
   pg. 501   IT
Hercules Chemicals Investments Pty. Ltd., pg. 811   PB
Hoechst Australia Ltd., 606 St. Kilda Rd., pg. 626   IT
Hogan Systems Australia, 30 King St., pg. 422   PB
Holden's Engine Products Overseas Corporation, Locked
   Bag No. 1, pg. 723   PB
John Holland Constructions Pty Ltd., 492 St. Kilda Rd.,
   pg. 630   IT
John Holland Engineering Pty Ltd., 492 St. Kilda Rd.,
   pg. 630   IT
JOHN HOLLAND GROUP PTY. LTD., 492 St. Kilda Road,
   pg. 630   IT
Hugo Boss Holdings Pty. Ltd., pg. 638   IT
IBJ Australia Bank Limited, 16th Fl., 333 Collins St.,
   pg. 676   IT
ICI Australia Engineering Proprietary Ltd, 486 Albert St.,
   pg. 664   IT
ICI Australia Hospital Products Pty Ltd, ICI House, 1
   Nicholson St., pg. 664   IT
ICI Australia Ltd., pg. 1525   IT
ICI Instruments Pty Ltd, 1 Nicholson St., pg. 665   IT
Intergraph Corp. Pty. Ltd., 35 Cotham Rd., pg. 891   PB
International Division, 600 Bourke Street, pg. 226   IT
International Public Relations, Pty. Ltd., 33 Walsh Street,
   pg. 1227   IT
Isuzu-General Motors Australia Ltd., 858 Lorimer St.,
   pg. 693   IT
Isuzu-General Motors Australia Ltd., 858 Lorimer St.,
   pg. 725   PB
Jacobs Suchard (Australia) Pty. Ltd., pg. 1288   PB
Jetset Travel and Technology Holdings Pty. Ltd.,
   pg. 38   IT
KSB Ajax Pumps Pty. Ltd., pg. 721   IT
Keppel Prince Engineering Engineering Pty Ltd., Level 7, 3
   Bowen Crescent, pg. 731   IT
Kluber Lubrication Australia Pty. Ltd., pg. 507   IT
Kobe Steel, Ltd. (Melbourne), 30F, ANZ Tower, 55 Collins
   St., pg. 741   IT
Korn/Ferry International, Level 42, 80 Collins St.,
   pg. 633   PV
Kraft Holdings Limited, Salmon St. Port, pg. 1290   PB
LGT Asset Management Pty. Ltd., pg. 810   IT
Laura Ashley (Australia) Pty Ltd., 112-12 Buckhurst Street,
   pg. 804   IT
Lintas:Hakuhodo Australia Pty. Ltd., Level 12, 468 St. Kilda
   Rd., pg. 589   IT
Litton Precision Products (Australia), pg. 1004   PB
Logica Pty. Ltd., 30 Collins St., pg. 815   IT
Longman Cheshire Pty. Ltd., Longman Cheshire House,
   Kings Garden, pg. 1025   IT

PB - *U.S. Public Companies Volume*
PV - *U.S. Private Companies Volume*
IT - *International Public & Private Companies Volume*

Lurgi (Australia) Pty. Ltd., 230 Albert Rd., pg. 861 IT
MAN Automotive (Australia) Pty. Ltd., P.O. Box 167, pg. 825 IT
The Macmillan Co. of Australia Pty. Ltd., 107 Moray Street, pg. 1480 IT
Makita (Australia) Pty. Ltd.-Melbourne, 89 Rushdale Street, pg. 832 IT
Marcam Australia Pty., Ltd., Level 3, No. 9 Daane St., pg. 1043 PB
Marquette Electronics (Australia) Pty Ltd, pg. 1047 PB
Mattel Pty. Ltd., 461 Plumner St., pg. 1059 PB
MELBOURNE PORT CORPORATION, Level 48, Rialto South Tower, pg. 856 IT
Mettler-Toledo Ltd., 525 Graham St., pg. 4 PV
Mitsui & Co. (Australia) Ltd., 30th Fl., B.H.P. House, 140 William St., pg. 880 IT
Mobil Oil Australia Ltd., 2 City Rd., pg. 1119 IT
Morgan Guaranty Trust Company, 333 Collins St., 25th Fl., pg. 1130 PB
J.P. Morgan Australia Limited, 333 Collins St., 25th Fl., pg. 1130 PB
J.P. Morgan Australia Securities Limited, 333 Collins St., 25th Fl., pg. 1130 PB
J.P. Morgan Investment Management Australia Ltd., 333 Collins St., 25th Fl., pg. 1131 PB
Morgan Stanley Melbourne, Level 53, 101 Collins St., pg. 1133 PB
NYK Line-Melbourne, Level 18, Quantas House, 114 William Street, pg. 941 IT
National Australia Asset Management, Floor 6, 333 Collins Street, pg. 906 IT
NATIONAL AUSTRALIA BANK LIMITED, Floor 24, 500 Bourke St., pg. 906 PB
National Australia Financial Management Ltd., 342 Flinders St., pg. 906 IT
National Australia Trustees Ltd., 271 Collins St., pg. 906 IT
National Bank of Greece Melbourne Branch, pg. 907 IT
NATIONAL CONSOLIDATED, Level 14, 350 Collins St., pg. 908 IT
National Mutual Funds Management (Global) Ltd., Level 35, Rialto South Tower, 525 Collins St., pg. 908 IT
National Mutual Funds Management Ltd., Level 34, Rialto South Tower, 525 Collins Street, pg. 908 IT
NATIONAL MUTUAL HOLDINGS LIMITED, 447 Collins St., pg. 908 IT
The National Mutual Life Association of Australia Limited, 447 Collins St., pg. 909 IT
National Mutual Victoria, 8 Nicholson St., pg. 908 IT
Thomas Nelson Australia, 480 Latrobe, pg. 1601 PB
Nichimen Australia Ltd.-Melbourne, 14th Floor, 575 Bourke St., pg. 928 IT
Nippondenso (Australia) Pty. Ltd., 155 Bertie St., pg. 1414 IT
Nissan Finance Corporation Ltd., Nissan House, 210 Albert Road, pg. 945 IT
Nokia Telecommunications Pty. Ltd., 677 The Boulevard, pg. 954 IT
Nordson Australia Pty. Limited, 4-5 Harnett Close, pg. 1189 PB
Normalair-Garrett Mfg. Australia, 45 King St., pg. 53 PB
NORTH LIMITED, 476 St. Kilda Rd., pg. 967 IT
North West Shelf Development, pg. 1137 IT
Olefines Pty Ltd, 1 Nicholson St., pg. 1137 IT
Optical Waveguides Australia Pty,. Limited, Summit Road, Noble Park, pg. 449 PB
Oxford University Press, Australia, pg. 1019 IT
PAK Pacific Corp. Pty. Ltd., Dougharty Road, pg. 129 IT
PACIFIC DUNLOP LIMITED, Level 41, 101 Collins St., pg. 1021 PB
Pall Australia, 106 Talinga Rd., 3192, pg. 1254 PB
PepsiCo. Australia Pty. Ltd., pg. 1277 PB
Petroleum Refineries (Australia) Pty., Ltd., 2 City Rd., pg. 1120 PB
Philip Morris (Australia) Limited, One Little Collins Street, pg. 1290 PB
Pilkington Australasia Limited, Level 5/570 St. Kilda Rd., pg. 1057 IT
Pilkington (Australia) Operations Limited, Level 5, 570 St. Kilda Rd., pg. 1057 IT
Pizza Hut Properties Pty. Ltd., pg. 1637 PB
Polychrome (Australia) Pty. Ltd., 5/58 Queens Road, pg. 370 IT
Potter Warburg Asset Management Ltd., Level 16, Number 1 Collins St., pg. 1331 IT
Potter Warburg Pty. Ltd., Level 9, 530 Collins St., pg. 1331 IT
PRATT INDUSTRIES, Level 2, Dominion Bldg., 533 Little Lonsdale St., pg. 1066 IT
Puma Australia Pty. Ltd., 111 Keys Rd., pg. 1072 IT
R&H Australia Pty. Ltd., 287 Grant St., pg. 681 IT
Reed Books Australia, 22 Salmon Street, pg. 1094 IT
Rhone-Poulenc Australia Holdings Pty. Ltd., 100 York St., pg. 1112 IT
Rigby Heinemann, 22 Salmon Street, pg. 1095 IT
SSB Advertising Melbourne, 253 Park St., pg. 394 IT
The Sakura Bank - Melbourne Representative Office, Level 46, Melbourne Central, 360 Elizabeth Street, pg. 1180 IT
Sedgwick Limited, Sedgwick House, 555 Lonsdale Street, pg. 1218 IT
Sedgwick Noble Lowndes Limited, Sedgwick House, 555 Lonsdale Street, pg. 1218 IT
Sequent Computer Systems (Australia), 580 St. Kilda Rd., pg. 1459 PB
Shell Australia Ltd., Shell Corner, 155 William St., pg. 1137 IT
Shell Chemical (Australia), 155 William St., pg. 1137 IT
Shell Development (Australia) Pty. Ltd., 155 William St., pg. 1137 IT

Shell Refining (Australia) Pty. Ltd., 155 William St., pg. 1137 IT
Silenus Instruments Pty Ltd, One Nicholson St., pg. 665 IT
Smiths Industries Australia Pty Limited-Product Support Division, 209 Cecil St., pg. 1268 IT
Smorgon Fencing, 528 Ballarat Rd., pg. 1269 IT
Snow Brand Trading Australia, Pty., 4th Fl., 50 Queen St., pg. 1272 IT
Sonoco Pacific Pty., Ltd., Box 61, Heidelberg W., pg. 1449 PB
South Pacific Tyre, Somerton Hume Hwy., pg. 753 PB
SouthCorp Holdings Ltd.-Melbourne, 469 La Trobe St., pg. 1287 IT
Spring Properties Pty. Ltd., pg. 1024 IT
Stabilus Pty. Ltd., South Oakleigh, pg. 835 IT
Stolt-Nielsen Pty. Ltd., pg. 1302 IT
Stratus Computer PTY, Ltd., Level 10/5 Queen Rd., pg. 1524 IT
Sumikin Bussan International (Australia) Pty. Ltd., Level 21, 90 Collins St., Mezzanine Fl., pg. 1308 IT
Sumitomo Chemical Company, Ltd.-Melbourne Office, 47th Fl., Nauru House, 80 Collins St., pg. 1311 IT
Sumitomo Rubber Industries-Melbourne, Cnr. Bertie & Woodruff Streets, pg. 1317 IT
Sun Microsystems Australia Pty. Ltd.-Melbourne, 11-15 Waverly Rd., pg. 1532 PB
Sun Microsystems Australia Pty. Ltd.-Melbourne Demo, Level 46, Rialto 525 Collins St., pg. 1532 PB
Sungold Dairies Proprietary Ltd, pg. 1290 PB
Superannuation, 600 Bourke Street, pg. 225 IT
Swiss Re Australia Ltd., 31 Queen Street, pg. 1333 IT
Symbol Australia Pty. Ltd., 432 Saint Kilda Rd., 10th Fl., pg. 1546 PB
David Syme & Co. Limited, 250 Spencer St., pg. 477 IT
T & K Glass Co., Level 28, 200 Queen St., pg. 129 IT
TMP Worldwide Pty Ltd., 46-50 Chetwynd Street, pg. 1342 IT
Tandem Nonstop Pty. Ltd., 470 St. Kilda Rd., pg. 418 PB
TATTERSALLS, 787 Dandenong Rd., pg. 1357 IT
Taylor Woodrow (Victoria) Pty. Ltd., Level 28, 525 Collins St., pg. 1360 IT
Teac Australia Pty. Ltd., 106 Bay Street, pg. 1360 IT
Templeton Investment Management (Australia), Ltd., 10 Queens Rd., 1st Fl., pg. 680 IT
Texas Utilities Australia, Level 8 MLC Tower, pg. 1588 PB
D.W. Thorpe-Australia, 18 Salmon Street, pg. 1095 IT
Toronto Dominion Australia Ltd., State Bank Centre, Level 36, pg. 1401 IT
Toyota Finance Australia Ltd., Level 11, 55 Lavender Street, pg. 1414 IT
Toyota Motor Corporation, Australia Ltd. (TMCA), 155 Bertie Street, pg. 1414 IT
Toyota Motor Corporation, Australia Office, 155 Bertie St., pg. 1413 IT
Transworld (Australia) Pty. Ltd., 35 Collins Street, 24th Floor, pg. 191 IT
Trigon Viskase Pty. Ltd., 6 Plane Tree Avenue, pg. 451 IT
Unimet Pty Ltd., 7/539 Highett Rd., pg. 303 PB
Uniroyal Chemical Pty. Ltd., Three Bowen Crescent, pg. 260 PB
United Transport Services Pty. Ltd., L1, 19 Flemington Road, pg. 211 IT
Utell International-Australia, pg. 1098 IT
VDO Instruments Australia Pty. Ltd., Heidelberg West, pg. 839 IT
Valmet (ANZ) Pty. Ltd., P.O. Box 185, pg. 1448 IT
Varian Australia Pty. Ltd., 679 Springvale Rd., Mulgrove, pg. 1710 PB
Wandel & Goltermann Pty. Ltd., pg. 1486 IT
Western Staff Services Pty. Ltd., 100 Albert Rd., 6th Fl., pg. 1760 IT
Westpac - Victoria, 360 Collins St., pg. 1496 IT
Whiteley Chemicals (Victoria) Pty. Ltd., P.O. Box 12741, pg. 440 PV
Whybin.TBWA, 171 LaTrobe St., pg. 1063 IT
Willis Corroon Richard Oliver Pty. Ltd., 71 Queens Road, pg. 1509 IT
Woodside Petroleum Ltd., Level 40, 385 Bourke St., pg. 1137 IT

Melville

Hughes Tool Company of Australia Limited, P.O. Box 130, pg. 167 PB

Mentone

BTR Nylex Limited, Nepean Hwy., pg. 129 IT
CR Industries Pty. Ltd., 4 Shearson Crescent, pg. 1157 IT
EOC Normalien Australia Pty. Ltd., 2/65 Voltri Street, pg. 75 IT

Metraville

Bell Sports Australia, 3/153 Beauchamp Road, pg. 207 PB

Milperra

Goyen Controls Division, 268-292 Milperra Rd., pg. 1287 IT
Hyster Australia Pty. Ltd., #1 Bullecourt Ave., pg. 1149 PB
ITW Finishing Systems & Products Pty. Ltd., 23 Ashford Ave., pg. 868 PB

Milsons Point

Cerner Corporation Pty Ltd., Level 10, 52 Alfred Street, pg. 331 PB
S.C. Johnson & Son Pty. Ltd., P.O. Box 277, pg. 593 PV
Kimberly-Clark Australia Pty. Ltd., 20 Alfred Street, pg. 959 PB
Kraft Foods Limited, 68 Alfred South Street, pg. 1290 PB
Paper Agencies (Aust.) Pty. Ltd., Suite 5, Harbourlights, 102 Alfred Street, pg. 458 IT
Peabody Resources Limited, Level 17, 2 Dind Street, pg. 594 IT
Southcorp-Wine Group, Imun Reserve, pg. 1287 IT
Unisys Australia Limited, 30 Alfred St., pg. 1671 PB

Milton

Leo Burnett/Connaghan & May (QLD.) Pty. Ltd., 33 Park Rd., pg. 185 PV
Condreco Pty. Ltd., 4th Floor, Tandem House, 303 Coronation Drive, pg. 135 IT
Fidelio Australia (Pty) Ltd., 4 Park Road, pg. 1106 PB
Hewlett-Packard Australia Ltd., 50 McDougall St., pg. 818 PB
Jacaranda Wiley Ltd., 33 Park Road, pg. 1768 PB
Queensland Cement Ltd., 50 McDougall Street, pg. 629 IT
Woodward-Clyde, 49 Park Rd., pg. 1657 PB

Mitcham

Tucker Industries Pty. Ltd., P.O. Box 70, pg. 235 PB

Mitchell Park

Boart Longyear Pty. Ltd., 919-929 Marion Rd., pg. 76 IT

Mona Vale

Binks-Bullows (Aust.) Pty. Ltd., 5-7 By The Sea Road, pg. 229 PB

Moorebank

Boral Bricks Pty. Ltd., Nuwarra Rd., pg. 203 IT

Mooroolbark

Henkes-Harmon Industries, Pty. Ltd., 14 Summit Ct., pg. 788 PB

Morabbin

Autologic Information International Ltd. (Australia), 433-435 South Rd., pg. 1724 PB

Moranbah

Goonyella Mine, pg. 223 IT
Peak Downs Mine, pg. 223 IT
Riverside Mine, pg. 224 IT

Mordialloc

Fortress Security Pty Limited, P.O. Box 575, pg. 590 IT
Ilco Unican Australia (Pty.) Ltd., 5 Hinkler Rd., pg. 1432 IT
Kidde-Graviner Australia Pty. Limited, P.O. Box 721, pg. 1500 IT
Roehlen Industries Pty. Ltd. Mold-Tech Div., Factory 1/46 Dehavilland Rd., pg. 1507 IT
Roehlen Industries Pty. Ltd. Procon Pump Div., Factory 1/46 Dehavilland Rd., pg. 1507 PB
Terumo (Australia) Pty. Ltd., 24-32 Industrial Dr., pg. 1376 IT

Morley

Prok Group Ltd., pg. 1353 IT

Mortdale

Ademco-Sontrix (Australia) Pty. Ltd., 41 Barry Ave., pg. 1307 PB

Moss Vale

Joy Manufacturing Company (Pty) Ltd., Sydney Plant, Vale Rd., pg. 789 PB

Mount Druitt

InterTAN Australia Ltd., 91 Kurrajong, pg. 910 PB

Mount Isa

Mount Isa Mines Ltd., pg. 827 IT

Mount Macedon

Warner-Jenkinson Australia, 26 The Governors Drive, pg. 1696 PB

PB - *U.S. Public Companies Volume*
PV - *U.S. Private Companies Volume*
IT - *International Public & Private Companies Volume*

Mount Ommaney

NAPS Australia, P.O. Box 531, pg. 913   IT
Sigmaform Australia, Units 4 & 5, 49 Jijaws St., Sumner Pk., pg. 1363   PB

Mount Pleasant

Taylor Woodrow (Australia) Pty. Limited, 907 Canning Highway, pg. 1359   IT
Taylor Woodrow Corser Pty. Limited, P.O. Box 197, 907 Mt. Pleasant, pg. 1359   IT
Taylor Woodrow Homes Builders Pty. Ltd., P.O. Box 197, 907 Mt. Pleasant, pg. 1359   IT

Mount Waverley

Carlton Special Beverages, 405 Ferntree Gully Rd., pg. 501   IT
Email Limited-Metals Group, 88 Ricketts Rd., pg. 450   IT
Foster Wheeler Australia Pty. Ltd., 63 Wadham Parade, pg. 677   PB
Onga Pty. Ltd., 357 Ferntree Gully Rd., pg. 1767   PB

Mulgrave

Action Controls Pty. Ltd., 11/12-14 Miles St., pg. 15   PV
Aeroquip Division, Vickers Systems Pty. Ltd., 65-67 Glenvale Crescent, pg. 25   PB
BMW Australia Ltd., 783 Sprinvale Rd., pg. 178   IT
D.I.C. Australia Pty. Ltd., 21 McDonalds Lane, pg. 371   IT
Edwards Dunlop & Co. Pty. Ltd., 227 Wellington Rd., pg. 72   IT
EMTEC Magnetics Australia Pty. Limited, 700 Springvale Road (4th Floor), pg. 743   IT
Interbath-Australia, Pty. Ltd., Unit 35, Lot 4 Bunney Rd., pg. 566   PV
MacGregor Golf Australia pty. Ltd., 742 Springvale Road, pg. 73   IT
MCPHERSON'S LIMITED, 64 Geddes Street, pg. 852   IT
Melbourne Laboratories, 245 Wellington Road, pg. 227   IT
Miles Laboratories Australia Pty. Ltd., 500 Wellington Rd., pg. 175   IT
Moog Australia Pty. Ltd., Unit 1, 12-14 Miles St., pg. 1127   PB
Prok Group Ltd., 16 Miles Street, pg. 1353   IT
Wilson Sporting Goods Australia Pty. Ltd., 742 Springvale Rd., pg. 73   IT

Murarrie

Incitec Ltd, Paringa Rd., pg. 665   IT

Myaree

Senior Tift-Western Australia, 100 Norma Rd., pg. 1223   IT
Westinghouse Electric Australasia Ltd.-W.A. Division, 8 Playle St., pg. 275   PB

Neutral Bay

Kentucky Fried Chicken (Adelaide) Pty. Ltd., 40 Yeo St., pg. 1637   PB

Newcastle

Dentsply Australia, 125 Tudor Street, pg. 499   PB
Makita (Australia) Pty. Ltd.-Newcastle, 7 Gamma Close, pg. 832   IT
NYK Line-Newcastle, 4th Floor, 57 Hunter Street, pg. 941   IT
Newcastle Newspapers Pty. Limited, 28-30 Bolton Street, pg. 477   IT
Sandvik Hard Materials Pty. Ltd., pg. 1187   IT
Trans-Lux Pty. Ltd., 73 Broadmeade, pg. 1629   PB

Newstead

Dentsply Australia, 21 Ross St., pg. 499   PB

Noble Park

Remington Australia, 19 Overseas Dr., pg. 921   PV

North Adelaide

Telxon Australia Pty., Ltd., 145 Tynte Street, pg. 1573   PB

North Rocks

Alberto-Culver Co. (Australia) Pty. Ltd., 14 Loyalty Rd., pg. 38   PB
Novo Nordisk Bioindustrial Pty Ltd., 22 Loyalty Road, pg. 989   PB
Novo Nordisk Pharmaceuticals Pty. Ltd., 22 Loyalty Road, pg. 988   IT
Viking Office Products Pty. Ltd., 15-17 Loyalty Road, pg. 1721   PB

North Ryde

Biomet Australia Pty Ltd., 11 Lyon Pk. Rd., pg. 231   PB
Lucent Technologies Australia Pty. Ltd., 6-10 Talavera Rd., pg. 1018   PB

North Shore

Bekaert-BHP Steel Cord Pty. Ltd., 49-59 Seabeach Parade, P.O. Box 190, pg. 184   IT
Geelong Rod Mill, The Esplanade, pg. 227   IT
Geelong Wire Mill, Walchs Road, pg. 226   IT

Northbridge

Medtronic Australasia Pty. Ltd., 50 Strathallen Avenue, pg. 1083   PB

Northmead

J.I. Case (Australia) Pty., Ltd., Windsor Road, pg. 1579   PB
J.I. Case Credit Corporation of Australia Pty. Limited, Windsor Road, pg. 1579   PB
Fanner-PLP, 150 Briens Rd., pg. 1321   PB

Norwood

AIS Media, 29 Sydenham Road, pg. 15   IT
Dentsply Australia, 116 Fullaton Road, pg. 499   PB
Sun Microsystems Australia Pty. Ltd.-Adelaide, 78 Fullarton Rd., pg. 1532   PB

Notting Hill

FMC (Australia) Limited, 50-54 Howleys Rd., pg. 606   PB

Nottingham

Mallinckrodt Australia Pty. Ltd., Nine Ferntree Pl., pg. 1040   PB

Nowra

Keystone Pacific Pty. Ltd., P.O. Box 517, 114 Albatross Rd., pg. 1650   PB

Nunawading

Unbrako Pty. Ltd., Norcal Road, pg. 1420   PB

Oakden

Northfield Laboratories Pty Ltd., pg. 992   IT

Oakey

Oakey Abattoir Pty. Ltd., pg. 936   IT

Oakleigh

Cherry Australia Pty. Ltd., 14/104 Ferntree Gully Road, pg. 346   PB
Georg Fischer Pty Ltd., Suite 3, 41 Stamford Road, pg. 488   IT
SKF Australia Pty. Ltd., 17-21 Stamford Road, pg. 1158   IT

O'Connor

Atwood Oceanics Australia Pty Ltd., 35 Peel Rd., pg. 146   PB

Orange

Canon Office Machines (Australia) Pty. Ltd., 264 Peisley Street, pg. 263   IT

Osborne Park

Hewlett-Packard Australia Ltd., Herdsman Business Park, 66 Hasler Rd., pg. 818   PB

Padstow

Acheson A.N.Z. Pty. Ltd., 63 Davies Road, pg. 12   PV
First Brands Australia, 36 Gow Street, pg. 627   PB
The Lincoln Electric Co. Australia Pty. Ltd., 35 Bryant Street, pg. 996   PB
Pegler Hattersley Australia Pty. Ltd., 18 Gibson Avenue, pg. 550   IT
Selleys Chemical Co Pty Limited, One Gow St., pg. 665   IT
Stafford-Miller Ltd., 5-9 Enterprise Ave., pg. 237   PB

Pagewood

Kellogg (Aust.) Proprietary Ltd., 41-57 Wentworth Avenue, pg. 947   PB

Pannawonica

Pannawonica Mine, pg. 967   IT

Para Hills

Liebherr-Australia Pty. Ltd., 1 Kesters Road, pg. 808   IT

Parkes

North Exploration (Eastern Region), Cnr. Clarke & Alluvial Streets, pg. 967   IT
Northparkes Mines, pg. 967   IT

Parkside

Hewlett-Packard Australia Ltd., 153 Greenhill Rd., pg. 818   PB

Parramatta

Ademco Australia Pty. Ltd., Unit 5 Riverside Centre, 24-28 River Road West, pg. 1307   PB
Bently Nevada, Australia, Unit 13, pg. 134   PV
Blackwood Hodge (Australia) Pty. Ltd., Suite 202, 30 Cowper Street, pg. 231   IT
Bose Australia, 1 Sorrell Street, pg. 161   PV
Pharmacia & Upjohn Pty. Limited, P.O. Box 138, pg. 1049   IT
RailTek Australia Pty. Ltd., Level 1, 85 George Street, pg. 528   IT
SM-Cyclo of Australia Pty. Ltd., Suite 5, 5-9 Hunter Street, pg. 1315   IT
TMP Worldwide Pty Ltd., 12 Palmer St., pg. 1342   IT
Taylor Woodrow Property Holdings Pty. Ltd., Level 1, 96 Phillip Street, pg. 1360   IT

Pascoe

Ridge Tool (Australia) Pty., Ltd., pg. 577   PB

Payneham

Allen-Bradley Pty. Limited, Wellington Centre, 2 Portrush Road, pg. 1399   PB

Pendle Hill

CIBA-GEIGY Australia Ltd., 140 Bungaree Rd., pg. 976   IT

Pennant Hills

Chloride Power Electronics Pty. Limited, pg. 287   IT
CUNA Mutual Group-Australia, 380 Pennant Hills Road, pg. 296   PV
Imation Australia New Zealand Pty. Ltd., 423 Pennant Hills Rd., 8th Fl., pg. 870   PB

Perth

Australian Guarantee Corporation Limited - Western Australia, AGC House, 165 Adelaide Ter., pg. 1496   IT
BHP Iron Ore, 200 St. George's Terrace, pg. 224   IT
BHP Minerals International Exploration Inc., Level 3, Hyatt Centre, 3 Plain Street, pg. 224   IT
BHP Petroleum Pty. Ltd., Level 12, 221 St. George's Terrace, pg. 225   IT
Bankers Trust Australia Limited, CML Bldg., Level 5, 55 St., George's Terrace, pg. 186   PB
Barrick Gold, Level 2, 87 Colin St., pg. 169   IT
Brambles Manford, 8th Fl., Hammersley House, 191 St. George's Terrace, pg. 211   IT
Commonwealth Bank of Australia-Western Australia, 150 St. George's Terrace, GPO Box A32, pg. 313   IT
DMR Group Australia Pty. Ltd., 12 St. George Terrace, Level 6, pg. 528   IT
Dampier Salt Ltd., 1177 A. St., pg. 947   IT
Homestake Gold of Australia Limited, Cloisters Sq., pg. 833   PB
IBJ Australia Bank Limited, 37 St. George's Terrace. pg. 676   IT
International Public Relations, Pty Ltd., 22 Charles St., South Perth, pg. 1227   IT
JGC Engineers Australia Pty. Ltd., Royal Insurance Bldg.. 5th Fl., 105 street George's Terrace Private, pg. 697   IT
Kobe Alumina Associates (Australia) Pty. Ltd., 7th Floor, International House, 26 Street, Geoeges Terrace, pg. 741   IT
Makita (Australia) Pty. Ltd.-Perth, 31 Furnace Road, pg. 832   IT
Metro Brick Company Pty. Limited, 212 Adelaide Terr., pg. 216   IT
Mitsui & Co. (Australia), 22nd Flr., City Centre, 44 St. George's Te, pg. 880   IT
National Mutual Western Australia, 111 St. Georges Ter., pg. 908   IT
Nichimen Australia Ltd.-Perth, 2nd Fl., Allied House, 201 Adelaide Terr., pg. 928   IT
North Mining, Level 2, 12-14 St. Georges Terrace, pg. 967   IT
Peak Hill Mine, Level 2, 12-14 St. Georges Terrace, pg. 967   IT
Perth Linen Service, 141 West Prd. Mount Lawley, pg. 211   IT
Reynolds Yilgarn Gold Operations Limited, 8th Fl., Griffin Center, 28 The Esplanade, pg. 1387   PB
Robe River Iron Associates, Level 9, 12-14 St. Georges Terrace, pg. 967   IT
Sime Darby Australia Limited, 22 Bishop St., pg. 1251   IT

PB - *U.S. Public Companies Volume*
PV - *U.S. Private Companies Volume*
IT - *International Public & Private Companies Volume*

Singapore Tourist Promotion Board - Perth, 8th Floor, St. Goerges Court, 16 St. Georges Terrace, pg. 1254   IT
Supaflo Technologies Pty., Ltd., Ground Floor, 7 Kintail Road, pg. 1017   IT
Taywood Farms Pty. Ltd., 907 Canning Highway, pg. 1360   IT
Teamwork Constructions Pty. Limited, 909, Canning Highway, pg. 1360   IT
Tourism Malaysia - Perth Office, 56, William St., pg. 833   IT
Town & Country Bank Ltd., Chancery House, 37 St. George's Terrace, pg. 98   IT
Valtek Australia/Perth, 10 Thorogood St., pg. 659   PB
Van Leer Australia Pty. Ltd., pg. 1146   IT
Westpac - Western Australia, 109 St. George Terrace, pg. 1496   IT
Willis Corroon Richard Oliver Pty. Ltd., Quayside on Mill, Level 8, pg. 1509   IT
Woodside Offshore Petroleum Pty. Ltd., 1 Adelaide Terrace, pg. 1137   IT
Woodward-Clyde, 5th Floor, Eastpoint Plaza, 233 Adelaide Terrace, pg. 1657   PB

Port Kembla

Port Kembla Laboratories, Old Port Road, pg. 227   IT
Port Kembla Steelworks, Five Islands Road, pg. 227   IT
Sheet & Coil Products Division, Old Port Road, pg. 227   IT
Sheet & Coil Products New South Wales, Springhill Works, Springhill Road, pg. 227   IT
Slab & Plate Products Division, Five Islands Road, pg. 227   IT

Port MacQuarie

JLG Industries (Australia) Pty. Limited, 11 Bolwarra Rd., pg. 918   PB

Port Waratah

Newcastle Steelworks, Selwyn Street, pg. 227   IT
Rod & Bar Products Division, Selwyn Street, pg. 227   IT

Prahran

Australian Char Holding Pty., Ltd., 3rd Fl. Pran-Central, 32F, pg. 947   IT

Preston

Ericsson Defense Systems Pty. Ltd., pg. 1366   IT
Hugo Boss Australia Pty. Ltd., pg. 638   IT
Rockwell Light Vehicle Systems (Australia) Pty. Limited, 62 Albert St., pg. 1401   PB
Spicers Paper Limited, 44 Raglan St., pg. 72   IT
Square D Company Australia Pty. Limited, 2 Albert St., pg. 1209   IT
Van Leer Australia Pty. Ltd., pg. 1146   IT
Wrapping Specialists Pty. Ltd., 5 Powerdrill Road, pg. 160   PV

Prospect

Senior Tift-Prospect, 204 Prospect Rd., pg. 1223   IT

Punchbowl

Dennison Marking Systems, Pty. Ltd., 95 Bonds Rd., pg. 153   PB

Pymble

HLA Envirosciences Pty. Ltd., 55-65 Grandview St., pg. 785   PB
Otsuka Pharmaceutical Australia Pty. Ltd., Suite 103, 4-10 Bridge Street, pg. 1014   IT
Pharmaco PTY LTD, Pymble Corporate Center, 20 Bridge St., pg. 1285   PB
Pirelli Tyres Australia Pty. Ltd., 20 Bridge St., Bldg. 2, 1st Fl., pg. 1059   IT
Southcorp Appliance Group, 9-11 Bridge St., pg. 1287   IT
3M Australia Pty. Ltd., 950 Pacific Hwy., pg. 1606   PB

Pyrmont

AUSTRALIAN NATIONAL INDUSTRIES LIMITED, Level 5, Merlin Centre, 235 Pyrmont St., pg. 100   IT
CCA Systems, Pty. Ltd., 100 Harris St., pg. 418   PB
Shiseido (Australia) Pty. Limited, 100 Harris St., pg. 1235   IT
Symix Systems, Inc.-Australia, 100 Harris St., Second Fl., pg. 1547   PB

Queanbeyan

Brambles Textile Rental & Laundry Services, 53 Erin St., pg. 211   IT

Randburg

Munters Pty Ltd., 21 Lyn Rd., pg. 669   IT

Redfern

TNT LIMITED, TNT Plaza, Tower 1, Lawson Square, pg. 1342   IT

TNT Logistics, 9th Floor, TNT Plaza, Tower 1, Lawson Square, pg. 1343   IT

Regents Park

Bio-Rad Laboratories Pty. Limited, Unit 1, Block Y-1, 391 Park Rd., pg. 230   PB
Dussek Campbell Pty Ltd., 13/21 Clapham Road, pg. 236   IT
Elsag Bailey Pty Limited, pg. 449   IT
Liebert Corporation Australia Pty. Ltd., pg. 577   PB

Reservoir

Axel Johnson Corp. (Australia) AB, 1, Malua St., pg. 710   IT

Revesby

Cutting Edges Pty. Ltd., 25A Violet St., pg. 391   IT
MacDermid Australia Branch, 299 Canterbury Rd., pg. 1030   PB

Rhodes

Cutler Hammer Australia Pty. Ltd., 27 Leeds St., pg. 558   PB
Digital Equipment Corporation (Australia) Pty. Limited, 410 Concord Road, pg. 507   PB
Tonka Corp. Pty. Ltd., 810 Leeds St., pg. 798   PB

Richmond

Hamiltons of Melbourne Pty. Ltd., pg. 1063   IT
Hamiltons Pty. Ltd., pg. 1063   IT
Heidelberg Graphic Equipment Ltd.-Heidelberg Australia, 658 Church Street, pg. 605   IT
Moore Business Systems Australia Ltd., The Boulevard, pg. 389   IT
Moore Intelligent Imaging Systems Pty. Ltd., The Boulevard, pg. 389   IT
Porsche Cars Australia (Distribution) Pty. Ltd., pg. 1063   IT
Porsche Cars Australia (Finance) Pty. Ltd., pg. 1063   IT
Porsche Cars Australia Pty. Ltd., pg. 1063   IT
Rosella Lipton Pty. Ltd., 1490 Ferntree Gully Rd., pg. 1438   IT
Rothenberger Australia Pty. Ltd., 26 Terrace Rd., pg. 1129   IT
Siemens Ltd., 544 Church St., pg. 1247   IT
The Uncle Toby's Company Ltd., 580 Church St., pg. 555   IT
Woodward-Clyde, Riverwalk Complex, Level 3, 649 Bridge Rd., pg. 1657   PB
Y&R Mattingly, 21-31 Goodwood Street, pg. 325   PV
Young & Rubicam Mattingly, 21-31 Goodwood St., pg. 198   PV

Ridgley

North Forest Eucalypt Research Center, pg. 967   IT

Ringwood

Mentor Medical Systems, Australia, Unit 5/156-160 New St., pg. 1086   PB

Riverwood

Daihatsu Australia Pty. Ltd., 96 Belmore Rd., pg. 365   IT

Rockdale

Senior TIFT Australia Pty Limited, 2-6 Lindsay St., pg. 1223   IT

Rocklea

Grow Force Australia Limited, 1808 Ipswich Rd., pg. 664   IT
Prok Group Limited, 1463 Ipswich Rd., pg. 1353   IT

Rooty Hill

Sydney Steel Mill, 22 Kellogg Road, pg. 227   IT

Rosebery

Carbon Brush Mfg. Co., Pty Limited, 19 Roseberry Ave., pg. 894   IT
Haden Engineering Pty, 54 Rosebery Ave., pg. 586   IT
IGT-(Australia), Pty. Limited, 1 Rosebery Avenue, pg. 900   PB
Interurarium Australia Pty. Ltd., G.P.O. Box 4896, pg. 305   IT
Saarberg Coal Australia Pty. Limited, J. Rosebery Ave., pg. 1167   IT
Trimex Fty., 5 Crewe Pl., pg. 296   IT

Roseville

McGraw-Hill Book Co. Australia Pty. Ltd., 4 Barcoo St., pg. 1072   PB

Rowville

Milk Products Holdings (Australia) Pty Ltd, 830 Wellington Rd., pg. 923   IT
Optical Networks Pty. Ltd., 24 Laser Dr., pg. 1313   IT
Pegler Hattersley Australia Pty. Ltd., 3 Corporate Avenue, pg. 550   IT
Stegbar Bifold Doors, 949 Stud Rd., pg. 128   IT
Stegbar Windowalls Pty. Ltd., 949 Stud Rd., pg. 128   IT
Velcro Australia Pty. Ltd., 15 View Tech Place, pg. 1462   IT
Wander (Australia) Pty. Ltd., pg. 986   IT

Royal Exchange

Cleanaway, pg. 211   IT

Rydalmere

Bristol-Myers Company Pty. Limited, 320 Victoria Rd., pg. 255   PB
Bristol-Myers Marketing Services Pty. Ltd., 320 Victoria Rd., pg. 255   PB
Fanuc Oceania Pty. Limited, 21 Muriel Ave., pg. 478   IT
Hunter Douglas Holdings Ltd., 338-346 Victoria Rd., pg. 640   IT
Hunter Douglas Ltd.-Sydney, 338-346 Victoria Rd., pg. 640   IT
Kawasaki Motors Pty. Ltd., Unit Q, 10-16 South Street, pg. 726   IT
McKechnie Consumer Products Australasia, Units 4/8/9-40 Brodie St., pg. 851   IT
Milton Bradley Australia Pty. Ltd., Brodie St., pg. 798   PB
Shimadzu Oceania Pty. Ltd., Rydalmere Business Park, Unit T, 10-16 South St., pg. 1232   IT

Saint Kilda

Notifier Australia, Ste. 4, 400 St. Kilda Rd., pg. 1307   PB
United Australian Automotive Industries Ltd., 1st Fl., 245 Kilda Rd., pg. 725   PB

Saint Leonards

CSC Australia, 460 Pacific Highway, pg. 423   PB
Cognos Pty., Ltd., 110 Pacific Highway, Third Floor, pg. 306   IT
IDG Communications P/L, 88 Christie St., pg. 570   PV
Leighton Holdings Limited, 472 Pacific Highway, pg. 624   IT
Olin Australia Limited, 601 Pacific Hwy., Level 2, Ste. 1, pg. 1523   PB
Storage Technology Corporation, 174 Pacific Hwy., pg. 1523   IT
Tyco Investments (Australia) Limited, 601 Pacific Highway, 5th Flr., pg. 1651   PB
George Weston Foods Group, 100 Christie St., pg. 92   IT
Woodward-Clyde, Level 6-486-494 Pacific Hwy., pg. 1658   PB

Saint Marys

Crane Australia Pty. Ltd., 146-154 Dunheved Circuit, pg. 457   PB
Schenectady Australia Pty. Ltd., pg. 970   PV

Saint Peters

Dinol Australia Pty. Ltd., 64 Mary St., pg. 981   IT

Sale

International Sea Drilling Ltd., 332 Raglan St., pg. 1316   PB
Oceaneering Australia Pty. Ltd., 141 Patten St., pg. 211   IT
Oceaneering Australia Pty. Ltd., 141 Patten St., pg. 1211   PB
South Seas Drilling Co., 60 Cunninghame St., pg. 766   IT

Salisbury

Heating & Cooling Div., 26 Nylex Ave., pg. 1287   IT
Van Leeuwen Pipe and Tube Eastern Australia Pty. ltd., 268 Evans Rd., pg. 1450   IT

Schofields

PGH Bricks Pty. Ltd., pg. 128   IT
PGH Eureka Ceramics, pg. 128   IT

Scoresby

Australian Diagnostics Corporation Pty. Ltd., Two Keith Campbell Court, pg. 975   IT
Diesel ReCon Australia, Two Caribbean Dr., pg. 469   PB
Gillette (Australia) Pty., Limited, Five Caribbean Dr., pg. 744   PB
Landis & Staefa (Australia) Pty. Ltd., 15 Nyadale Dr., pg. 800   IT
Landis & Staefa (Australia) Pty. Ltd., 411 Ferntree Gully Rd., pg. 800   IT
Mentholatum Pty. Ltd., 12 Janine St., pg. 1126   IT
Motorola Australia Pty., Ltd., 6 Caribbean Drive, pg. 1139   PB

PB - *U.S. Public Companies Volume*
PV - *U.S. Private Companies Volume*
IT - *International Public & Private Companies Volume*

1500

Geographic Index-Non U.S.

Motorola Electronics Australia Pty., Ltd., 6 Caribbean Drive, pg. 1139 **PB**
NSK-RHP Australia Pty. Ltd., 11 Dalmore Dr., pg. 904 **IT**
RAECO, 75 Rushdale Street, pg. 462 **IT**
Sharp Corporation of Australia Pty. Ltd., 15 Koornang Rd., pg. 1229 **IT**
Valtek/Australia, 14 Dalmore Dr., pg. 659 **PB**

Seaford

Inductoheat Pty. Ltd., 62 Bardia Ave., pg. 560 **PV**

Seven Hills

Australian Radio Network, 2 Leabons Lane, pg. 386 **PB**
Cerebos Australia Limited, 92-96 Station Road, pg. 1322 **IT**
Howard Australia Pty. Ltd., 167 Prospect Highway, pg. 1387 **IT**
ITS Australia Pty., Ltd., 1A, 167 Prospect Highway, pg. 900 **PB**
Micro Warehouse (Australia) Pty Ltd., 2/11 Artisan Road, pg. 1104 **PB**
Nordson Australia Pty., Ltd., Unit 4, 6 Boden Rd., pg. 1189 **IT**
Quaker Chemical (Australasia) Pty. Ltd., 8 Abbott Road, pg. 1346 **PB**
Snap-on Tools (Australia) Pty. Ltd., Unit 6/110 Station Road, pg. 1481 **PB**
Suntester (Australia) Pty. Ltd., 13 Prince William Dr., pg. 1481 **PB**
Uniroyal Chemical Pty. Ltd., Unit 2, 13 Stanton Rd., pg. 460 **PB**
Van Leer Australia Pty. Ltd., pg. 1146 **IT**

Shortland

Newcastle Laboratories, Off Vale Street, pg. 227 **IT**

Silverwater

Abel Lemon & Bleakley, 26 Fariola St., pg. 803 **IT**
Australian Water Heater Division, 13 Rachael Close, pg. 1287 **IT**
Bleakley Fine Chemicals, 24 Fariola St., pg. 803 **IT**
Bridgestone Earthmover Tyres Pty. Ltd., 10 Rachael Close, pg. 214 **IT**
CAE Electronics (Australia) Pty. Ltd., 120 Silverwater Rd., pg. 238 **IT**
Cadillac Plastic, 3143 Vore St., pg. 781 **PB**
ITT Flygt Limited, Unit 31, Slough Estate, Holker St., pg. 860 **PB**
Lubrizol International, Inc., 28 River St., pg. 1016 **PB**
Olivetti Australia Pty. Ltd., 110 Silverwater Rd., pg. 1003 **IT**
Stone & Webster Engineering Pty. Limited, 1 Rachael Cl., pg. 1520 **PB**
Svedala Australia (Silverwater), pg. 1324 **IT**
Yokohama Tyre Australia Pty., Ltd., 44 Egerton Street, pg. 1521 **IT**
Yokohama Tyre Australian Pty., Ltd., 123-129 Silverwater Rd., pg. 1522 **IT**

Smithfield

Kanthal Australia Pty. Limited, pg. 724 **IT**
Mack Valves-NSW, 66 Victoria St., pg. 1223 **IT**
Mannesmann Demag Pty. Ltd., pg. 837 **IT**
Rocol/Molybond Laboratories Division, 106 Woodpark Rd., pg. 895 **IT**
Senior Australia Limited, 66 Victoria St., pg. 1222 **IT**
Valvoline (Australia) Pty. Ltd., Wetherill Park 2164, Private Bag # 2, pg. 140 **PB**

Somersby

Cosmetic Products Pty., Ltd., One Wella Way, pg. 1490 **IT**

Somerton

South Pacific Tyres, Hume Highway, pg. 1021 **IT**

Southbank

Carlton & United Breweries Ltd., 77 Southbank Boulevard, pg. 500 **IT**
Foster's Brewing Group, 77 Southbank Boulevard, pg. 501 **IT**
FOSTER'S BREWING GROUP LIMITED, 77 Southbank Boulevard, pg. 500 **IT**
Powercor Australia Limited, Level 3, 77 Southbank Blvd., pg. 1252 **PB**
WESTERN MINING CORPORATION HOLDINGS LIMITED, IBM Tower, Level 16, 60 City Road, pg. 1494

Southport

Electronic Arts Pty. Ltd., 4/46 Smith Street, pg. 569 **PB**
K-Tel (Australia) Pty. Limited, pg. 938 **PB**

Spotswood

ACI Closures, 61 Simcock Ave., pg. 128 **IT**
Queensland Glass Manufacturers Co., Booker St., pg. 128 **IT**

Spring Hill

Region Australia Tamcorp Australia Pty. Limited, Unit 3, 35 Astor Terrace, pg. 1353 **IT**
Tamrock Pty. Ltd., Unit 3, 35 Astor Terr., pg. 1353 **IT**

Springvale

Ancra Australia Pty. Ltd., 11 Bando Rd., pg. 71 **PV**
Baker Perkins Proprietary Limited, 10 Blissington St., pg. 1240 **IT**
Briggs & Stratton Australia Pty. Limited, Private Bag 48, pg. 252 **PB**
Trico Pty. Ltd., 820-850 Princes Hwy., pg. 1397 **IT**
Vermont American Australia, Ltd., 7 Longford Ct., pg. 578 **PB**

Stanmore

Lightnin Mixers Pty. Ltd., pg. 727 **PB**
World's Finest Chocolate Australia Pty. Ltd., 8 Bridge Rd., pg. 1191 **PV**

Stepney

Gerber Australia, Ltd., Simes Australia, 5 George St., pg. 973 **IT**

Subiaco

Sun Microsystems Australia Pty. Ltd.-Perth, 130 Hay St., pg. 1532 **PB**

Summer Hill

Papua-New Guinea Division, 2 Smith St., pg. 556 **IT**

Sunbury

DeZurik of Australia Pty., Ltd., Vineyards Road, pg. 727 **PB**

Sunshine

Fuchs Australia Pty., R & D Center, 49 McIntyre Rd., pg. 518 **IT**
GUD HOLDINGS LIMITED, 245 Sunshine Road, pg. 539 **IT**
Rockwell Standard of Australia Ltd., 70 Berkshire Rd., pg. 1402 **PB**
Senior Tift-Victoria, 5 Third Ave., pg. 1223 **IT**
SMORGON A.R.C., 518 Ballarat Road, pg. 1269 **IT**

Surrey Hills

AIS MEDIA, Level 1, 31 Buckingham St., pg. 15 **IT**
Advertising Investment Services Pty. Ltd., Level 1, 31 Buckingham St., pg. 394 **IT**
F.J. Benjamin Fashions (Aust) Pty. Ltd., 3rd Floor, 72 Cooper St., pg. 187 **IT**
Sheridan Australia Ltd., 10-14 Waterloo St., pg. 197 **PV**

Sutherland

BHP Civil Products, 127-141 Bath Road, pg. 226 **IT**

Sydney

AAV Business Communications, Level 3, 83-85 Chandos Street, pg. 477 **IT**
ABN-AMRO Australia Limited, ABN House, Level 14, 10 Spring St., pg. 11 **IT**
ACI Industries Pty. Ltd., Level 39, 100 Miller St., pg. 128 **IT**
ACS International Pty Limited, Level 1, 13-15 Castlereagh Street, pg. 242 **IT**
A.G.C. (Advances) Limited, AGC House, 130 Phillip St., pg. 1496 **IT**
A.G.C. (Finance) Limited, AGC House, 130 Phillip St., pg. 1496 **IT**
A.G.C. (General Finance) Limited, AGC House, 130 Phillip St., pg. 1496 **IT**
A.G.C. (Industrial) Limited, AGC House, 130 Phillip St., pg. 1496 **IT**
AMRAD Pharmacia & Upjohn Biotech, Unit A, 25-27 Paul street, pg. 1047 **IT**
AMS Management Systems Australia, MCL Centre Level 67, Martin Pl., pg. 86 **PB**
ANZ Funds Management, 68 Pitt Street, pg. 98 **IT**
ANZ Life Assurance Company Limited, 68 Pitt Street, pg. 98 **IT**
ANZ Managed Investments Limited, 68 Pitt St., pg. 98 **IT**
Acer Computer Australia Pty. Ltd., Tower A, Level 3, 112-118 Talavera Rd., pg. 22 **IT**
Addison-Wesley Publishers Pty. Ltd., Unit 1A, 6 Byfield St., pg. 1027 **IT**
Adecco Australia Pty Ltd., Level 22, 207 Kent St., pg. 24 **IT**
Alarmcom Security Pty. Ltd., Suite 5, 1059-1063 Victoria Road, pg. 1246 **IT**
Alcan South Pacific Ltd., Queen Victoria Bldg., P.O. Box Q282, 2000, pg. 51 **IT**
Alcatel STC Australia, pg. 56 **IT**
Alexander & Alexander Australia Holdings Ltd., 2 Market St., 19th Fl., pg. 117 **PB**
Alfa-Laval Pty Ltd., P.O. Box 282, Lidcombe, pg. 1379 **IT**

Alusuisse-Lonza Australasia Pacific Pty Ltd., pg. 68 **IT**
Amdahl Australia Pty. Ltd., 1 Pacific Highway, 9th Floor, pg. 527 **IT**
Amdahl Pacific Services Pty. Ltd., 1 Pacific Highway, pg. 527 **IT**
Amgen Australia Pty Ltd., Level 3, 65 Epping Rd., pg. 101 **PB**
Amoco Australia Petroleum Company, Phillips Bldg., 12th Flr., 15 Blue St., pg. 102 **PB**
Amro Australia Ltd., Level 28, MLC Centre, Martin Plaza, pg. 9 **IT**
Apple Computer Australia Pty. Ltd., 37 Waterloo Road, pg. 121 **PB**
Armstrong World Industries Pty. Ltd., 117 Wicks Rd., pg. 132 **PB**
Arnotts Limited, 170 Kent, pg. 299 **PB**
Asahi Bank Sydney Branch, 5th Fl., 25 Bligh St., pg. 82 **IT**
Asahi Finance (Australia) Ltd., 5th Fl., 25 Bligh St., pg. 83 **IT**
Asahi Investment Australia Ltd., Level 20, Gateway, 1 Macquarie Pl., pg. 85 **IT**
Asahi Property Australia Pty. Ltd., Level 20, Gateway, 1 Macquarie Pl., pg. 85 **IT**
Ascom Timeplex Australia Pty. Ltd., Level 21, York Street, pg. 87 **IT**
Astra Pharmaceuticals Pty. Ltd., pg. 94 **IT**
Australian Aluminium (Australuco) Limited, 31 Market St., 2000, pg. 51 **IT**
Australian Financial Review, Level 19, 201 Sussex St., pg. 477 **IT**
Australian Guarantee Corporation Limited, AGC House, 130 Phillip St., pg. 1496 **IT**
AUSTRALIAN MUTUAL PROVIDENT, Alfred Street, pg. 100 **IT**
AUSTRALIAN OIL & GAS CORPORATION LIMITED, Level 10, 74 Castlereagh Street, pg. 101 **IT**
Australian Thread Pty. Ltd., P.O. Box 69, Station Rd., pg. 299 **IT**
Australian Window Furnishings (NSW) Pty. Ltd., 1-15 Bennett Street, pg. 639 **IT**
Auto-trol Technology Australia, Ste. 1603, Northpoint, 100 Miller St., pg. 148 **PB**
Avnet VSI Electronics (Australia) Pty. Ltd., Unit C, Lyon Park Rd., pg. 155 **PB**
BBL Australia Limited, 56 Pitt Street, 25th Fl., pg. 148 **IT**
BGS Systems Pty. Ltd., Parkway House, 34 Burton Street, pg. 161 **PB**
BHP Engineering, Oracle Plaza, 181 Miller Street, pg. 225 **IT**
BHP Lifting & Industrial Products, 37-49 Pitt Street, pg. 226 **IT**
BHP Petroleum Pty. Ltd., Level 15, 1 Castlereagh Street, pg. 225 **IT**
BLE Capital Limited, 15th Flr., Endeavour House, 50 Pitt St., pg. 1496 **IT**
BT Australasia Pty Limited, BT Tower, Level 12, 1 Market Street, pg. 223 **IT**
Babcock Australia Holdings Ltd., 14th Fl., Babcock House, 140 Pacific Hwy, pg. 474 **IT**
Bain & Company Limited, Level 18, Grosvenor Pl., 225 George St., pg. 406 **IT**
Banca Nazionale del Lavoro, Royal Exchange Bldg.-Level 17, 56, Pitt Street, pg. 137 **IT**
Banco Santander, 210 Georges Street, 15th Floor, pg. 144 **IT**
BancTec (Australia) Pty. Limited, Level 2, 245 Pacific Highway, pg. 177 **PB**
Bank of America NT&SA, Level 18, Bank of America Centre, 135 King St., pg. 182 **PB**
Bank of Montreal - Australia, 33 York St., pg. 155 **IT**
The Bank of New York, Level 5, 179 Elizabeth St., pg. 179 **PB**
The Bank of Tokyo-Mitsubishi (Australia) Ltd., 1 Macquarie Pl., pg. 158 **IT**
Bankers Trust Australia Limited, Level 38, Australia Square, pg. 185 **PB**
Baring Asset Management (Australia) Ltd., Suite 5303, MLC Centre, 1929 Martin Place, pg. 648 **IT**
Baring Brothers Burrows & Co. Ltd., Level 9, 7 Macquarie Place, pg. 648 **IT**
Batey Kazoo, 3 Hickson Rd., pg. 117 **IT**
A.W. Baulderstone Holdings Pty. Ltd., Level 31, 101 Miller Street, pg. 196 **IT**
Bausch & Lomb Australia Pty. Ltd., 47 Epping Rd., pg. 195 **PB**
Beiersdorf (Australia) Ltd., pg. 183 **IT**
Bell Atlantic Australia Pty Limited, Level II, Lloyds Bank House, 35 Pitt St., pg. 204 **PB**
Benckiser Australia Pty. Ltd., pg. 185 **IT**
Bilfinger + Berger Australia Pty. Ltd., Level 31, 101 Miller Street, pg. 196 **IT**
Bill Acceptance Corporation Limited, 124 Phillip St., pg. 1496 **IT**
Blue Circle Southern Cement Limited, 1 McLaren St., pg. 203 **IT**
Boral Gas Limited, Level 39 AMP Centre, 50 Bridge St., pg. 203 **IT**
BORAL LIMITED, Level 39, AMP Centre, pg. 203 **IT**
Borland International (AUST) Pty Ltd., Level 6, 140 Sussex Street, pg. 246 **PB**
Bowater Industries Australia Ltd., Level 15, 275 Alfred Street, pg. 1107 **IT**
Bowthorpe Australia Pty. Ltd., pg. 208 **IT**
Brambles Container Services, 5th Fl., Underwood House, 37 Pitt St., pg. 211 **IT**
Brambles Holdings Limited, L11, 2 Elizabeth Plaza, pg. 211 **IT**
BRAMBLES INDUSTRIES LIMITED, Level 40 The Gateway, # 1 Mcquarie Place, pg. 210 **IT**

PB - *U.S. Public Companies Volume*
PV - *U.S. Private Companies Volume*
IT - *International Public & Private Companies Volume*

Brambles International Freight Pty. Limited, 5th Fl., Roden Cutler House, 24-28 Campbell Street, pg. 211   IT

Brambles Marine Services Pty. Ltd., 5th Fl., Underwood House, 37 Pitt St., pg. 211   IT

F. Braun & Co. Pty. Ltd., 11-17 Khartoum Rd., pg. 1489   IT

Brierley Investments Ltd., Level 41, Gateway, 1 Macquarie Place, pg. 215   IT

Brother Industries (Australia) Pty. Ltd., 7 Khartoum Rd., pg. 229   IT

Building & Industrial Products Division, 37-49 Pitt Street, pg. 225   IT

Burgmann Seals Australia Pty. Ltd., 48, Garema Circuit, pg. 234   IT

Leo Burnett/Connaghan & May Pty. Ltd., Leo Burnett House, Levels 3 & 4, pg. 185   PV

Burns & Roe Worley, One Chandos St., pg. 187   PV

BURNS, PHILP & COMPANY LIMITED, 7 Bridge St., pg. 236   IT

Butterworths Australia, 271-273 Lane Cove Road, pg. 1095   IT

CBFC Limited, 5 Hunter St., pg. 313   IT

CCH Australia Limited, 36-52 Talavera, pg. 1513   IT

CIBC Australia Holdings Limited, pg. 257   IT

CIBC Australia Limited, G.P.O. Box 3709, pg. 257   IT

CICA Superannuation Nominees, Pty., Ltd., 51 Berry St., pg. 118   PB

CIG Medishield Co., 11 Khartoum Rd., pg. 816   IT

CMC (Australia) Pty. Limited, Level 5, 4-8 Woodville Street, pg. 413   IT

CSA (Australasia) Pty Limited, Level 1, 13-15 Castlereagh Street, pg. 243   IT

CSR LIMITED, Level 24, 1 O'Connell Street, pg. 245   IT

Canon Australia Pty. Ltd., 1 Thomas Holt Dr., pg. 262   IT

Canon Finance Australia Pty. Ltd., 1 Thomas Holt Drive, pg. 262   IT

Canon Information Systems research Australia Pty. Ltd., One Thomas Holt Dr., pg. 262   IT

Carter Holt Harvey Plastic Products (Australia) Pty. Limited, pg. 905   IT

Castrol Australia Pty Ltd., ACD House, 13th Floor, 189 Kent Street, pg. 235   IT

Cathay Finance International (Holdings) Limited, 6th Floor, 275-281 George St., pg. 684   IT

Central Japan Railway Company-Sydney Office, Ste. 5203, The M.L.C. Centre, 19-29 Martin Pl., pg. 219   IT

Checkpoint Systems Australia Pty Ltd., 78 C Charles St., pg. 343   PB

Chichibu Onoda Cement Corporation-Australia, 225 Miller Street, pg. 284   IT

Cigna Insurance Australia Limited, CIGNA Bldg., 28-34 O'Connell St., pg. 364   PB

Cigna International Investment Advisors Australia Limited, 12th Fl., 28-34 O'Connell St., pg. 357   PB

Cigna Life Insurance Australia Limited, Cigna Bldg., 28-34 O'Connell St., 2000, pg. 364   PB

Cigna Superannuation Nominees Pty Limited, Cigna Bldg., 28-34 O'Connell St., pg. 364   PB

Clarify Inc.-Australia/Asia, Level 20, 99, Walker Street, pg. 382   PB

Club Mediterranee Australia Pty. Ltd., 500 George St., pg. 298   IT

Coca-Cola South Pacific, Ltd., 71 Circular Quay E., pg. 392   IT

Cogema Australia Pty. Ltd., Erskine House, Ste. 1, Level 10, pg. 305   IT

Colgate-Palmolive Pty. Ltd., C.P.O. Box 3964, 345 George St., 2000, pg. 399   PB

Columbia Pictures Television Pty. Ltd., 165 Walker St., pg. 1282   IT

Combined Ins. Co. of America, 51 Berry St., pg. 118   PB

Combined Insurance Co. of Australia, Ltd., 51 Berry St., pg. 118   PB

Combined Life Insurance Co. of Australia, Ltd., 51 Berry St., pg. 118   PB

Comdisco Australia Pty. Ltd., Level 18, 111 Pacific Highway, pg. 408   PB

Commerzbank AG-Australia, MLC Centre, Ste. 5301, 19-29 Martin Place, pg. 311   IT

COMMONWEALTH BANK GROUP, Level 3, 48 Martin Place, pg. 312   IT

Commonwealth Bank of Australia-Business Banking, Level 16, pg. 312   IT

Commonwealth Bank of Australia-Institutional Banking, Level 3, 48 Mrtin Place, pg. 312   IT

Commonwealth Bank of Australia-New South Wales, 2nd Fl., Pitt St. & Martin Pl., pg. 312   IT

Commonwealth Bank of Australia-Personal Banking, Level 15, 175 Pitt Street, pg. 313   IT

Commonwealth Bank of Australia-Technology, Operations & Property, Level 3, 48 Martin Place, pg. 313   IT

Commonwealth Development Bank, Level 21, 175 Pitt. St., pg. 313   IT

Compumod Pty. Ltd., 9th Fl., 309 Pitt St., pg. 1031   PB

Consolidated Wool Services Pty. Ltd., 5th Fl., Underwood House, 37 Pitt St., pg. 211   IT

Continuum Australia Limited, 201 Miller St., pg. 423   PB

Coty Australia Pty. Ltd., pg. 186   IT

County NatWest Australia Limited, Level 14, Grosvenor Place, 225 George Street, pg. 911   IT

County NatWest Corporate Finance Australia Limited, Level 16, Grosvenor Place, 225 George Street, pg. 911   IT

Crouse-Hinds (Australia) Pty. Ltd., 391 Park Road, Block X, pg. 445   PB

Crusader Insurance Company of Australia Limited, Cigna Bldg., 28-34 O'Connell St., pg. 364   PB

D.F.S. Australia Pty. Ltd., 145 George St., pg. 500   IT

DMR Group Australia Pty. Ltd., 155 George St., Level 7, pg. 528   IT

Daewoo Australia Pty. Limited, Ste. 405, Victoria Cross Bldg., 60 Miller St., pg. 357   IT

Dai-Ichi Kangyo Australia Limited, Level 57, MLC Centre 19-29, State Bank Centre, pg. 361   IT

Dai-Ichi Kangyo Bank, Ltd.-Sydney, Level 57, MLC Centre 19-29, Martin Pl., pg. 361   IT

Dai-ichi Life International (Australia) Limited, 36th Fl., AMP Centre, 50 Bridge St., pg. 362   IT

Dai Nippon Printing Co. (Australia) Pty. Ltd., Ste. 904, Level 9, KPMG Centre, pg. 363   IT

Daihatsu Diesel Mfg. Co., Ltd., Ste. 104, 1st Floor, 44 Miller St., pg. 364   IT

Daiwa Bank-Sydney, Level 14, Natl. Australia Bank, House, 255 George St., pg. 374   IT

Daiwa Finance Australia Limited, Level 14, Natl. Australia Bank, House, 255 George St., pg. 373   IT

Daiwa Securities Australia Limited-Sydney Branch, Level 17, pg. 376   IT

Data General Corp., pg. 486   PB

Datastream International (Sydney), Level 14, he Landmark, 34 George St., pg. 1326   IT

De La Rue Systems Imports Pty Limited, Level 21, 68 Pitt Street, pg. 387   IT

DELTA GOLD N.L., Level 16, 99 Walker Street, pg. 389   IT

Dentsply Australia, 72-80 Copper Street, pg. 499   PB

Dentsu Oceania Pty. Ltd., 4th Floor, 70 Riley Street, pg. 394   IT

Det Norske Veritas, Level 19, Northpoint, 100 Miller Street, pg. 398   IT

Deutsche Bank Australia Ltd. (Sydney), Level 20, Grosvenor Pl., pg. 405   IT

Deve Hydraulic Lifts Pty. Ltd., pg. 1205   IT

Deville (NSW) Pty. Ltd., pg. 431   IT

Dow Chemical (Australia) Ltd., pg. 523   PB

Dow Jones Markets (Australia) Pty Limited, 309 Kent St., Level 11, pg. 525   IT

Dresdner Australia Ltd., Level 20, No. 2 Market Street, pg. 419   IT

Dresdner International Financial Markets (Australia) Ltd., Level 20, No. 2 Market St., pg. 419   IT

Du Pont (Australia) Ltd., Northside Gardens, 168 Walker, pg. 532   PB

Duesbury's, 140 Sussex St., Level 8, pg. 211   IT

EASAMS (Australia) Ltd., Two Giffnock Av., pg. 543   IT

EEI-Australia, pg. 126   IT

Ebasco Australia Pty. Limited, Level 32, AMP Centre, 50 Bridge Street, pg. 1587   PB

Ecusta Australia Pty. Limited, 2-10 Amax Ave., pg. 746   PB

Daniel J. Edelman Pty. Ltd., Level 24, AGL Bldg., 111 Pacific Hwy., pg. 363   PV

Elders - New South Wales, 4 O'Connell St., pg. 501   IT

Elvy Pty. Ltd., 205 Clarence St., pg. 1052   IT

Email Limited-Industrial Products Group, Suite 3001, Level 3, Bayside Towers, 376 Bay St., pg. 450   IT

The Emmac, Inc., 14 F, The Royal Exchange Bldg., 56 Pitt St., pg. 364   IT

Energy Resources of Australia Ltd., 1 Macquarie Place, pg. 567   IT

EURO RSCG Partnership, Level 12, pg. 602   IT

Exxon Coal Australia Ltd., 60 Miller Street, pg. 602   PB

FAG Australia Pty. Ltd., pg. 469   IT

JOHN FAIRFAX HOLDINGS LIMITED, Level 19, 201 Sussex St., pg. 477   IT

John Fairfax Publications Pty. Ltd., Level 20, Darling Park, pg. 477   IT

Financial Security Assurance Inc., Hambros House, 167 Macquarie Street, pg. 623   PB

First Chicago Australia Ltd., 33 Pitt, pg. 628   IT

First Chicago Securities Ltd., 33 Pitt, pg. 628   PB

First State Computing Pty Ltd, Level 7, Underwood House, 37-43 Pitt Street, pg. 222   IT

Fletcher Challenge Australia Limited, Level 11, AMP Centre, 50 Bridge St., pg. 495   IT

Forbo Australia Pty. Ltd., pg. 497   IT

FORTUNE COMMUNICATION HOLDINGS LTD., Level 11, Westfield Towers, 100 William St., pg. 500   IT

Fuji International Finance (Australia) Limited, AIDC Tower-Maritime Centre, Level 28, 201 Kent St., pg. 521   IT

Furukawa Electric Co., Ltd. Australia, 333-339 George St., 7th Fl., pg. 530   IT

GATX Financial Services (Australia) PTY. Limited, Level 29, Chifley Tower, 2 Chifley Square, pg. 691   PB

GEC Australia Ltd., Two Giffnock Ave., pg. 546   IT

Gas Drive Systems, Unit C 28-32 Egerton St., pg. 1401   IT

Gelman Sciences Pty. Ltd., 27 Sirius Rd., Lane Cove, pg. 1253   PB

Georg Jensen Silver (NSW) Pty. Ltd, G 15/16 Gallery Leve, Centrepoint, pg. 1134   IT

Gilbarco Australia Ltd., 12-38 Talavera Rd., pg. 545   IT

Goldman Sachs Australia L.L.C., Level 48, Governor Phillip Tower, pg. 462   PV

GOODMAN FIELDER LIMITED, Level 42, 225 George St., pg. 555   IT

Grolier Limited New Zealand, 14 Mars Road, pg. 795   IT

HSBC James Capel Australia Limited, Level 11, 1 O'Connell Street, pg. 582   IT

Hachette Consolidated Australia, 54/58 Park Street, pg. 795   IT

Hachette Filipacchi Australia, 22 Wunulla Road - Point Piper, pg. 795   IT

Hakuhodo Australia Pty. Ltd., Office Suite Level 4, Tandem House, 76 Berry St., pg. 588   IT

Hapag-Lloyd (Australia) Pte. Ltd., pg. 596   IT

James Hardie Building Services, Level 6, 65 York Street, pg. 597   IT

JAMES HARDIE INDUSTRIES LTD., James Hardie House, Level 9, 65 York Street, pg. 596   IT

Harris Lenier Australia, 77 Berry St., pg. 791   PB

Harrisons & Crosfield (Australia) Ltd., 90 Arthur St., pg. 569   IT

Hayes Microcomputer Products Ltd., Level 10, pg. 801   PB

Health-Mor Acceptance Pty Ltd., pg. 771   PB

Heinemann Electric Pty. Ltd., 15 Mellor, pg. 557   PB

Heller Financial Services Limited, 234 Sussex Street, 6th Floor, pg. 521   IT

Hermes Precisa Australia Pty Ltd., pg. 579   IT

Hewlett-Packard Australia Ltd., 17-23 Talavera Rd., pg. 818   PB

Hochtief Limited, Level 20, National Mutual Ctr., 44 Market St., pg. 624   IT

Honeywell Australia Limited, 5, Thomas Holt Dr., pg. 834   PB

HongkongBank of Australia Limited, pg. 583   IT

Howden Group Australia Pty Limited, 97-103 Pacific Hwy., pg. 636   IT

Humphreys & Glasgow Pacific Pty. Limited c/o Fesler Russell & Co., Level 9, Shell House, 140 Phillip St., pg. 1587   PB

Norman J. Hurll & Co., 190 Bourke Road, pg. 361   PV

Husqvarna Pty. Ltd., Unit 1, Eden Park, 31 Waterloo Road, pg. 440   IT

IBJ Australia Bank Limited, Level 21, State Bank Center, 52 Martin Place, pg. 676   IT

IBJ Australia Corporation Limited, 29th Fl., Qantas Intl. Ctr., Corner George & Jamison Sts., pg. 676   IT

IBJ Australia Nominees Limited, 29th Fl., Qantas Intl. Ctr., Corner George & Jamison Sts., pg. 676   IT

IBM Australia Limited, Coonara Ave. West, pg. 896   PB

IBM Australia Rentals Pty. Ltd., Coonara Ave. West, pg. 896   PB

IBM Australia Services Pty. Ltd., Coonara Ave. West, pg. 896   PB

IHI Engineering Australia Pty. Ltd., 15th Floor, 213-219 Miller Street, pg. 689   IT

ING Mercantile Mutual Bank, 347 Kent Street, pg. 650   IT

Igetalloy-Kirby (Pty.), Ltd., pg. 1313   IT

Indosuez Australia Ltd., Level 30, 201 Kent, pg. 315   IT

The Industrial Bank of Japan, Limited (Sydney), 4th Fl. Qantas Intl. Ctr., Corner George & Jamison Sts., pg. 675   IT

INDUSTRIAL EQUITY LIMITED, Colonial Center 52, 52 Martin Place, pg. 676   IT

Intergraph Corp. Pty. Ltd., Macquarie Centre, 61c Talavera Road, pg. 891   PB

International Business Analysis Proprietary Limited, 9th Floor, 56 Berry St., pg. 1496   IT

International Public Relations, Pty Limited, 55 Falcon St., pg. 1227   IT

Itoham Foods (Australia) Pty. Ltd., Level 60, The M.L.C. Center, 19-29 Martin Pl., pg. 695   IT

Japan Energy (Australia) Pty. Ltd., Level 66, MLC Center 19-29, Martin Place, pg. 702   IT

Jardine Fleming Australia Limited, Level 14 Jardine Fleming House, 19 Pitt St., pg. 494   IT

Jardine Fleming Ord Minnett Pty Limited, Level 26, Grosvenor Place, 225 George Street, pg. 494   IT

Jardine Matheson (Australia) Ltd., Level 8, 66 Clarence St., pg. 705   IT

Johnson & Johnson International, 154 Pacific Hwy., pg. 930   IT

Johnson & Johnson Medical Pty. Ltd., 1-5 Khartoum Road, pg. 931   IT

D.R. Johnston Group Pty. Ltd., pg. 429   PB

DAVID JONES LIMITED, 86-108 Castlereagh Street, pg. 714   IT

Joy Corporation, pg. 256   IT

J.P. Morgan Australia Securities Limited, 1 O'Connell St., GPO Box 5248, pg. 1130   IT

Kawasho International (Australia) Pty., Ltd., Level 17, City Centre, 55 Market St., pg. 727   IT

Kelly Services Ltd., Level 21, 68 Pitt Street, pg. 949   PB

Kendall Australia Pty. Ltd., 22 Giffnock Ave., pg. 1647   PB

KEPCO Resources Australia, Level 38, The Chifley Tower, 2 Chifley Square, pg. 758   IT

Kidston Gold Mines Limited, G.P.O. Box 4315, Gold Fields House, 1 Alfred St., pg. 1060   IT

Kobe Steel Australia Pty. Ltd., Level 32, Gateway, 1 Macquarie Pl., pg. 741   IT

Konica Australia Pty., 22 Gittnock Ave., pg. 749   IT

Korn/Ferry International, One Alfred St., pg. 633   PV

LGT Asset Management Pty. Ltd., Level 6, 12-14 O'Connell Street, pg. 810   IT

LGT Unit Managers (Australia) Ltd., Level 6, 12-14 O'Connell Street, pg. 809   IT

LIEF International Pty. Ltd., LIEF 2nd Fl., 221 Miller St., pg. 1255   IT

LL&E Australia (Offshore) Pty. Limited, Level 21, 201 Miller Street, pg. 269   PB

LTCB Australia Limited, Level 34, Tower Building, Australia Square, pg. 816   IT

Lancaster Group Pty. Ltd., pg. 186   IT

Legal & General Assurance Holdings (Australia) Limited, Level 4, York Street, pg. 805   IT

Legion Telecall PTY Ltd., Suite 201, Level 2, 153 Walker Street, pg. 796   IT

LEND LEASE CORPORATION LIMITED, Level 46, Tower Building, Australia Square, pg. 806   IT

Lever & Kitchen Pty. Ltd., 71 York St., pg. 1437   IT

Linde Materials Handling Pty. Ltd., pg. 588   IT

Lintas:Hakuhodo Australia Pty. Ltd., The Denison, 8th Floor, 65 Berry Street, pg. 588   IT

Arthur D. Little International, Inc., Level 38, Gov. Phillip Tower, 1 Farrer Place, pg. 671   PV

Litton Precision Products (Australia), 414 Gardeners Rd., pg. 1004   PB

Lloyds Bank NZA Limited, Lloyds Bank House, pg. 813   IT

Lloyds International Ltd., Lloyds Bank House, 35 Pitt St., pg. 813   IT

Loewe Australia Pty Ltd, 63 Castlereagh St., pg. 782   IT

Louis Vuitton Australia Pty Ltd, 63 Castlereagh St., pg. 782   IT

Lummus Overseas Corp., 213-219 Miller St., pg. 6   IT

Luxottica Australia pty ltd., pg. 822 — IT
MLC Limited, 105-153 Miller Street, pg. 806 — IT
MMI Insurance Group, 2 Market Street, pg. 60 — IT
MSA (Australia) Pty. Ltd., 137 Gilba Road, pg. 1114 — PB
MacDonald Dettwiler Pty. Ltd., Level 7, 146 Arthur St., pg. 1230 — IT
Makita (Australia) Pty. Ltd., 92 Wetherill St., pg. 831 — IT
Makita (Australia) Pty. Ltd.-Sydney, 92 Wetherill Street, pg. 832 — IT
Mannesmann Trading Pty. Ltd., pg. 838 — IT
Marubeni Australia Ltd., 255 George St., pg. 845 — IT
Mase Westpac Australia Limited, Level 6, AMP Centre, 50 Bridge St., pg. 1496 — IT
The McArthur Shipping & Agency Company Pty. Ltd., 5th Fl., Underwood House, 37 Pitt St., pg. 211 — IT
Mead Packaging Proprietary Ltd., Level 30, Northpoint, pg. 1077 — PB
Medical Division, pg. 1406 — IT
The Meiji Life Insurance Company Sydney Office, 25th Level, 60 Margaret St., pg. 854 — IT
The Meijiseimei Property Australia Ltd., 25th Level, 60 Margaret Street, pg. 854 — IT
Memorex Telex Pty. Ltd., 3 Thomas Holt Drive, pg. 858 — IT
Mentor Graphics (Australia) Pty. Ltd., Ste. 404, Level 4, pg. 1087 — PB
Mercantile Mutual Holdings Limited, 347 Kent Street, pg. 650 — IT
Metal Manufactures Limited, Level 33, Gateway, One Macquarie Pl., pg. 120 — IT
Micropolis Limited, Level 21, 201 Miller Street, pg. 743 — PV
Microsoft Pty. Ltd., pg. 1108 — IT
Minemet Australia Pty. Ltd., 11th Level 185 Macquarie St., pg. 661 — IT
Mitsubishi Trust Australia Limited, Level 27, 2 Chifley Square, pg. 877 — IT
Mitsui & Co. (Australia) Ltd., 33rd Level, State Bank Center, 52 Martin Place, pg. 880 — IT
Mitsui Trust Finance (Australia) Ltd., Level 8, National Australia, Bank House, 255 George Street, pg. 883 — IT
Moody's Investors Service Pty. Ltd., Level 10, 55 Hunter Street, pg. 537 — PB
Morgan Grenfell Australia Ltd., 18th Fl., Royal Exchange Bldg, 56 Pitt St., pg. 406 — IT
Morgan Guaranty Trust Company, 1 O'Connell St., GPO Box 5248, pg. 1130 — PB
J.P. Morgan Australia Limited (Sydney), 1 O'Connell St., pg. 1130 — IT
Morgan Stanley Sydney, Level 33, The Chifley Tower, 2 Chifley Sq., pg. 1133 — IT
NCNB Australia Holdings Ltd., Level 55 MLC Centre, pg. 1166 — PB
NLI International Australia Limited, Level 34, The Chifley Tower, 2 Chifley Square, pg. 936 — IT
NUS International Pty. Ltd., 122-130 Arthur St., pg. 787 — PV
NYK Line (Australia) Pty. Ltd., Level 5, KPMG Bldg., 45 Clarence Street, pg. 941 — IT
Nabalco Pty. Ltd., 99 Walker, pg. 69 — IT
National Australia Bank/GATX, Level 27, Nab House, 255 George St., pg. 691 — IT
National Bank of Greece Sydney Branch, pg. 907 — IT
National Mutual New South Wales, 44 Market St., pg. 908 — IT
NatWest Capital Markets Australia Limited, Level 16, Grosvenor Place, 225 George Street, pg. 911 — IT
NatWest Markets Australia Limited, Level 16, Grosvenor Place, 225 George Street, pg. 911 — IT
Nedlloyd Australia Pty. Limited, pg. 1145 — IT
Neosid Australia Pty. Limited, 23/25 Percival Street, Lilyfield, pg. 1344 — IT
Nestle Australia Ltd., 60 Bathurst St., pg. 920 — IT
Nestle Confectionery Ltd., pg. 921 — IT
THE NEWS CORPORATION LIMITED, 2 Holt St., pg. 925 — IT
News Limited Of Australia, Two Holt St., pg. 925 — IT
Nichimen Australia Limited, Level 3, 60-70 Elizabeth St., pg. 928 — IT
A.C. Nielsen Pty., Ltd., 85 Epping Rd., pg. 1184 — PB
The Nikko Securities (Australia) Ltd., level 22, State Bank Centre, 52 Martin Place, pg. 931 — IT
Nippon Credit Australia Limited, Level 22, Gateway, 1 Macquarie Pl., pg. 933 — IT
Nippon Credit Bank Ltd.-Sydney, Level 22, Gateway, 1 Macquarie Pl., pg. 933 — IT
Nippon Meat Packers Australia Pty. Ltd., 15th Floor, 124 Walker St., pg. 936 — IT
Nippon Oil (Australia) Pty. Limited, Level 40, Governor, Phillip Tower, 1 Farrer Place, pg. 937 — IT
Nippon Steel Australia Pty., Limited, Level 24, No.1 York St., pg. 940 — IT
Nissho Iwai Australia Ltd., Level 17, 1 Macquarie Place, pg. 948 — IT
Nokia Mobile Phones R & D Center, Level 10, 100 William Street, pg. 952 — IT
Nokia Telecommunications Pty. Ltd., Level 8, 32 Walker Street, pg. 954 — IT
Nomura Australia Limited, Level 23, State Bank Centre, 52 Martin Place, pg. 956 — IT
North West Water Australia Pty. Ltd., Level 41, AMP Center, 50 Bridge Street, pg. 1444 — IT
Novell Australia, Level 18, 201 Miller St., pg. 1204 — PB
Obayashi Corporation-Sydney, Level 16, State Bank Centre, 52 Martin Place, pg. 996 — IT
Oil Drilling & Exploration Limited, 74 Castlereagh Street, pg. 101 — IT
OMRON Electronics Pty. Ltd., 71 Epping Road, pg. 1006 — IT
Optus Communications, OPTUS Centre, 101 Miller St., pg. 209 — PB
Oracle Systems Australia Pty. Ltd., No. 1 Pacific Hwy., pg. 1228 — PB

Oral-B Laboratories Pty. Limited, Fifth Fl., 221-223 Miller St., pg. 745 — IT
Ord Minnett Group Limited, Level 26, Grosvenor Pl., 225 George St., pg. 1496 — IT
OZEMAIL LIMITED, MDIS House, 39 Herbert Street, pg. 1019 — IT
P&O Australia Ltd., 160 Sussex St., pg. 1035 — IT
Panalpina World Transport (Pty) Limited, pg. 1023 — IT
Paramount Pictures (Australia) Pty. Ltd., 100 Miller St., Ste. 3501, pg. 777 — PV
Paribas Group (Australia) Limited, Level 11, 3 Spring St., pg. 321 — IT
Partnership Pacific Limited, 28th Level, StateW Bank Bldg., 52 Martin Pl., pg. 1496 — IT
Pechiney Corporation-Australian Branch, Level 9, 151 Macquarie Street, pg. 1031 — IT
Pfizer Pty. Ltd., 38 Wharf Rd., pg. 1282 — PB
Pharmacia & Upjohn (Australia) Pty. Ltd., 4 Byfield St., pg. 1050 — IT
The Pillsbury Company, 68 Pitt Street Ste. 2303, pg. 411 — IT
PIONEER INTERNATIONAL LTD., Level 46, Governor Phillip Tower, pg. 1058 — IT
Placer Pacific Limited, Level 16 Gold Fields House, 1 Alfred Street, pg. 1060 — IT
Pohang Steel Australia Pty, Ltd.(POSA), Suite C, Level 49, Governor Philip Tower, pg. 1062 — IT
Polaroid Australia Pty. Ltd., 31 Waterloo Rd., pg. 1314 — PB
Policy Management Systems Australia Pty Ltd., 3 Byfield St., pg. 1315 — IT
PolyGram Direct Marketing Australasia, 4th Fl., Westfield Towers, 100 William S., pg. 1053 — IT
Potter Warburg Asset Management, Level 60, MLC Ctr., Martin Pl., pg. 1331 — IT
Potter Warburg Ltd., 1 Farrer Pl., Level 25, pg. 1331 — IT
Prudential Corporation Australia Ltd., Carlton Centre, 55 Elizabeth Street, pg. 1073 — IT
Qantas Holidays, 141 Walker St., pg. 1075 — IT
Quadrant Industrial Ltd., 220 George St., pg. 528 — IT
Quantum Corporation Australia Branch, Norwich House-Level 4, 6-10 O'Connell Street, pg. 1350 — PB
Raleigh Nutritional Products Ltd., pg. 922 — IT
The Reader's Digest Association Pty. Limited, Reader's Digest Bldg., 26-32 Waterloo St., pg. 1368 — PB
Reader's Digest (Australia) Pty. Ltd., Reader's Digest Bldg., 26-32 Waterloo St., pg. 1368 — PB
Reckitt & Colman Pharmaceuticals, pg. 1090 — IT
Redland Australia Ltd., 7th Floor, 20 Loftus St., pg. 1092 — IT
Renison Goldfields Consolidated Limited, Gold Fields House, 1 Alfred St., pg. 595 — IT
Republic Mase Australia Ltd., Level 6, Amp Center, 50 Bridge St., pg. 1380 — PB
Reuters Australia Pty. Ltd., 2 Barrack St., pg. 1105 — IT
Revue Australia Pty. Ltd., Universal House, Pelican & Poplar Sts., pg. 1216 — IT
Ricon Pty Ltd, Unit 1, 32 Lilian Fowler Place, pg. 740 — IT
Rockwell Australia Limited, Level 6, 3 Thomas Holt Dr., pg. 1399 — IT
Rothmans Holdings Ltd., Level 42, Northpoint, 100 Miller St., pg. 1130 — IT
SAI Pty Ltd., Level 3, Imperial Arcade Office Tower, pg. 976 — PV
SBC Australia Limited, 225 George St., Level 6, pg. 1330 — IT
SSB Advertising Sydney, Level 4, 70 Riley Street, pg. 394 — IT
The Sakura Bank - Sydney Representative Office, 10th Fl., AMP Centre, 50 Bridge St., pg. 1180 — IT
Sakura Finance Australia Limited, 10th Fl., AMP Centre, 50 Bridge St., pg. 1180 — IT
Sanderson Computers Pty. Ltd., 132 Arthur St., 8th Fl., pg. 1185 — IT
Sandoz Australia Pty. Ltd., 54 Waterloo Road, pg. 984 — IT
Sandvik Australia Pty. Ltd., P.O. Box 23, pg. 1187 — IT
Sanpaolo-Sydney Representative Office, Level 10, Hambros House, 167 Macquario Street, pg. 692 — IT
Sanwa Australia Limited, AMP Centre, Level 30, 50 Bridge Street, pg. 1190 — IT
Sara Lee Holdings, Level 11, 1 York Street, pg. 1435 — PB
Sara Lee Personal Products Australia, Level 12, 1 Pacific Highway, pg. 1435 — PB
Schindler Lifts Australia Pty. Ltd., pg. 1205 — IT
ScotiaMocatta, Level 10, 345 George St., pg. 156 — IT
Sea Containers Australia Ltd., Ste. 2301. 1 Market Place, pg. 1214 — IT
Security Pacific Limited, National Australia Bank House, 255 George Street, pg. 183 — PB
SEIKO Australia Pty. Ltd., 89 Epping Rd., pg. 1218 — IT
Senior Flexonics Australia, pg. 1223 — IT
Sensormatic Australia Pty Limited, pg. 1457 — PB
Sequent Computer Systems (Australia) Pty. Ltd., 160 Pacific Highway, pg. 1459 — PB
Shimizu Corporation of Australia Pty. Ltd., Level 22, Westpac Plaza 60, pg. 1234 — IT
Shimizu International Finance (Australia) Ltd.-Sydney Office, Level 22, Westpac Plaza 60, pg. 1234 — IT
Simon-Carves Australia, 33 Paul Street, pg. 1252 — IT
Simon Engineering (Australia) Pty. Ltd., 33 Paul Street, pg. 1252 — IT
Singapore Tourist Promotion Board - Sydney, Level 11, Awa Building, 47, York Street, pg. 1254 — IT
Sinochem Australia Office, Unit 6, Lindsay St., pg. 1255 — IT
Skadden, Arps, Slate, Meagher & Flom, Level 26-Colonial, 52 Martin Pl., pg. 1005 — PV
Sonoco Pacific, Ltd., 14th Fl., 213 Miller St., pg. 1487 — PB
Ssangyong Australia Pty., Ltd., Level 5, Denision Bldg., 65 Berry St., pg. 1291 — IT

Ssangyong Resources Pty., Ltd., Level 5, Denison Bldg., 65 Berry Street, pg. 1293 — IT
Stamford Hotels & Resorts Pty Limited, Level 9, Stamford House, 20 Loftus Street, pg. 586 — IT
Standard Chartered Australia Limited, 11th Fl., 345 George St., pg. 1296 — IT
Standard Chartered Bank Australia Limited, 345 George St., pg. 1294 — IT
Starch Australasia, 170 Epping Rd., pg. 224 — PB
State Street Australia Ltd., 141 Walker St., pg. 1513 — PB
Steelcase Australia Pty. Ltd., Unit One, 37-69 Union St., pg. 1038 — PV
Stolt-Nielsen Pty. Ltd., pg. 1302 — IT
Stratus Computer PTY, Ltd., Level 14, 99 Walker St., pg. 1524 — PB
Streets Ice Cream Pty. Ltd., pg. 1438 — IT
Sulcus (Australia), 267 Pacific Hwy., pg. 1527 — PB
The Sumitomo Bank, Ltd.-Sydney Representative Office, The Chifley Tower, 2 Chifley Square, pg. 1310 — IT
Sumitomo International Finance Australia Limited, Level 40, The Chifley Tower, 2 Chifley Square, pg. 1310 — IT
Sumitomo Life Realty (Australia) Limited, Level 10 City Centre, 55 Market Street, pg. 1315 — IT
Sumitomo Metal Australia Pty. Ltd., Level 16, AMP Center, 50 Bridge St., pg. 1316 — IT
Sumitomo Metal Mining Oceania Pty. Ltd., Level 21, Governor Philip Tower, pg. 1316 — IT
The Sumitomo Trust & Banking Co., Ltd., Level 38, The Chifley Tower, Two Chiffley Sq., pg. 1318 — IT
Sumitomo Trust Finance (Australia) Limited, Level 38, The Chifley Tower, Two Chifley Sq., pg. 1318 — IT
The Sun-Herald, 201 Sussex St., pg. 477 — IT
Suzuki Australia Pty. Ltd., 7 Grand Ave., Camellia, pg. 1323 — IT
Swift and Company Ltd., 7 Bridge Street, pg. 682 — IT
Sydney Brewery, 26 Broadway, pg. 501 — IT
The Sydney Morning Herald, 201 Sussex St., pg. 477 — IT
Symantec Pty Ltd., 408 Victoria Rd., pg. 1546 — PB
Syntex Australia Limited, pg. 1122 — IT
TMP WORLDWIDE PTY LIMITED, 7-13 Parraween St., pg. 1342 — IT
Takashimaya Australia Pty., Ltd., MMI Centre, Kent St. Forecourt, Level 8, Two Market St., pg. 1350 — IT
Takashimaya Retailing Australia Pty., Ltd., 177 Sussex St., pg. 1350 — IT
Tektronix Australia Pty. Limited, 80 Waterloo Road, North Ryde, pg. 1567 — PB
THORN Australia Pty Ltd., AMP Centre, Level 35, 50 Bridge Street, pg. 1386 — IT
Thrifty System International, Pty. Ltd., 85 William Kings Cross, pg. 354 — PB
Tiffany & Co. (New York) Pty Limited, Level 26, AMP Centre, 50 Bridge St., pg. 1609 — IT
Tokai Australia Finance Corporation Limited, 19th Level, State Bank Center, 52 Martin Place, pg. 1391 — IT
The Tokio Marine Management (Australia) Pty. Ltd., pg. 1393 — IT
Tomago Aluminum Company Pty. Ltd., 3rd floor-Erskine House, 39-41 York Street, pg. 1032 — IT
Toppan Printing Co. (Australia) Pty. Ltd., Level 13, 179 Elizabeth Street, pg. 1399 — IT
Toshiba (Australia) Pty., Ltd., pg. 1406 — IT
Total Holdings (Australia) Pty. Ltd., Level 8, CML Bldg., 14 Martin Place, pg. 1409 — IT
Tourism Malaysia - Sydney Office, 65 York St., pg. 833 — IT
Toyo Trust Australia Limited, Level 19, AMP Centre, 50 Bridge Street, pg. 1411 — IT
Travelstrength Limited, 38-44 York St., pg. 313 — IT
UBS Australia Ltd., Level 4, 7 Macquairie Place, pg. 1440 — IT
Unilever Australia Ltd., pg. 1439 — IT
United Tankers Services Pty. Limited, 25 Wilson, pg. 211 — IT
Universal Studios Australia Pty. Ltd., Universal House, Pelican & Poplar Sts., pg. 1216 — IT
Universal Studios Music Australia, Universal House, Pelican & Poplar Sts., pg. 1216 — IT
VAW Australia Pty. Ltd., Level 7, Lavda House, 36 Carringdon St., pg. 1466 — IT
Viacom Intl. Pty. Ltd., 16th St., St. Martin's Tower, 31 Market St., pg. 779 — PV
Voest-Alpine (Australia) Pty. Ltd., 1602 Northpoint, pg. 1472 — IT
Wardley James Capel Corporate Finance Ltd., Level 10, 1 O'Connell Street, pg. 584 — IT
Wella (Australia) Cosmetic Suppliers Pty. Ltd., 29 Waterloo Rd., pg. 1490 — IT
Wellcome Australia Ltd., 53 Philips Cbrita, pg. 553 — IT
West Merchant Bank Limited, Level 29, 60 Margaret Street, pg. 1493 — IT
WestLB Australia and New Zealand, Level 29, 60 Margaret Street, pg. 1493 — IT
WESTPAC BANKING CORPORATION, 60 Martin Pl., pg. 1495 — IT
Westpac Financial Services Group Limited, 50 Pitt St., pg. 1496 — IT
Westpac Insurance Services (Brokers) Limited, 9th Fl., Wynard House, 301 George St., pg. 1496 — IT
Westpac Life Limited, 40 Pitt St., pg. 1496 — IT
Westpac - New South Wales, 60 Margaret St., pg. 1496 — IT
Westvaco Pacific Pty. Ltd., 1st Fl., 2SM Bldg., 182-186 Blues Point Rd., pg. 1763 — PB
Whitbread Restaurants (Australia) Ltd., pg. 1499 — IT
White & Lewis, 33 Berry Street, 4th Floor, pg. 1502 — IT
Willis Corroon Richard Oliver Pty. Ltd., 8th Floor, 2 Market Street, pg. 1509 — IT
Willis Faber & Dumas Limited, 1 Castlereagh St., pg. 1510 — IT
W.D. & H.O. Wills (Australia) Ltd., 71-79 Macquarie St., pg. 112 — IT

Wolters Kluwer Australia, Cnr. Talavera & Khartoum Roads, pg. 1513 IT
Wool Filters Intl., pg. 686 PB
The Wrigley Co. Pty. Ltd., Michigan Ave., pg. 1781 PB
Yamaichi Australia Ltd., Nine Castlereagh St., Level 27, pg. 1517 IT
York Toyota City, 101 William Street, pg. 1413 IT
Young & Rubicam Australia/New Zealand, 17th Floor, 65 Berry St., pg. 1198 PV
Zurich Australian Insurance Limited, 5 Blue Street, pg. 1531 IT
Zurich Australian Life Insurance Limited, 5 Blue Street, pg. 1531 IT
Zurich Investment Management Ltd., 5 Blue Street, pg. 1532 IT

Taree

Britax-Brylite Pty. Ltd., Hargreaves Dr., pg. 216 IT
Bryant Manufacturing Pty Limited, Hargreanes Dr., pg. 217 IT
Brylite Pty Limited, Hargreanes Dr., pg. 217 IT
Hiaba Pty Limited, Hargreanes Dr., pg. 217 IT

Taren Point

Oilgear/Towler Australia Pty. Ltd., 1a/45 Bay Rd., pg. 1215 PB
Toyota Motor Sales Australia Ltd., 2-28 Alexander Ave., pg. 1414 IT

Tea Gardens

Hawks Nest Mine, Mungo Brush Road, pg. 224 IT

Terrey Hills

Australian Geographic, 321 Mona Vale Road, pg. 477 IT
Radiometer Pacific Pty. Ltd., 45 Booralie Rd., pg. 1084 IT

Texas

Oakey Holdings Pty. Ltd., pg. 936 IT

Thomastown

CIBA-GEIGY Australia Ltd., 235 Settlement Rd., pg. 976 IT
Freudenberg Pty. Ltd., pg. 506 IT
PENTEX Australia Pty. Ltd., 227 Settlement Rd., pg. 983 IT
Puritan-Bennett Australia Pty. Ltd., 22 Wilgah St., pg. 1040 PB
Wajax (Australasia) Pty. Ltd., 2 Charnfield Ct., pg. 1485 IT
Webb-Conveyor Company of Australia Pty. Ltd., 20-22 MacQuarie Drive, pg. 1157 PV

Thornleigh

McDonald's System of Australia Ltd., 21-29 Central Ave., pg. 1069 PB

Tingalpa

Wadkin Australia, 39 Proprietary St., pg. 232 IT

Toorak

HARRIS SCARFE HOLDINGS LIMITED, 1st Fl., 521 Toorak Rd., pg. 597 IT
Onga Pty. Ltd., 689 Malvern Rd., pg. 1767 PB

Tooronga

COLES MYER LTD., 800 Toorak Rd., pg. 306 IT

Toowoomba

Pacific Seeds Pty Ltd., Corner Alderley St. & Anzac Ave., pg. 1525 IT
Pioneer Hi-Bred Australia Pty. Ltd., 371 Taylor Street, Locked Mail, pg. 1299 PB

Tottenham

Optix Australia Limited, 207 Sunshine Rd., pg. 1313 IT
Pacific Dunlop Cables Group, 207 Sunshine Rd., pg. 1021 IT

Townsville

Copper Refineries Pty. Ltd., Hunter St., Stuart, pg. 827 IT
Van Leer Australia Pty. Ltd., pg. 1146 IT
Yokohama Tyre Australia Pty., Ltd., 76 Leyland Street, pg. 1522 IT

Triabunna

North Forest Products Triabunna, pg. 967 IT

Tullamarine

Caterpillar Financial Australia Ltd., One Caterpillar Dr., pg. 315 PB
Circle International, Four Garden Dr., pg. 373 PB

Dural Leeds Pty. Ltd., Cnr. Sharps Rd. & Assembly Dr., pg. 639 IT
Honda Australia Pty., Ltd., Lot 95 Sharps Rd., pg. 635 IT
Omicron Proprietary Ltd., Lot 54-55 Keilor Dr., 3043, pg. 756 PB
Rockwell Australia Limited, Corner Sharps Rd. & Allied Dr., pg. 1399 IT
SASIE Beverage Australia, Unit 4, Lot 1, Trade Park Drive, pg. 1194 IT
Union-Transport (Aust) Pty Ltd, 2B International Trade Pk., pg. 1120 PV

Turner

Sun Microsystems Australia Pty. Ltd.-Canberra, 3rd Fl., 95 Northbourne Ave., pg. 1532 PB

Turramurra

Velsicol Australia Limited, Ten William St., pg. 1135 PV

Ultimo

DMB&B/Weekes Morris Osborn, 349 Bulwara Rd., pg. 304 PV

Unanderra

Heat Containment Industries Pty. Limited, Glastonbury Ave., pg. 394 IT
Stainless Products, Marley Place, pg. 227 IT

Varley

Outokumpu Mining Australia Pty. Ltd., Forrestania Nickel Mines, pg. 1016 IT

Vienna

SMH Osterreich Vertriebs GmbH, Kuefsteingasse 15, pg. 1161 IT

Villawood

Berendsen Fluid Power Pty. Ltd., 82 Biloela Street, pg. 285 IT
Epirez Construction Products Pty Limited, Two Seville St., pg. 492 IT
Procter & Gamble Australia, 24 Biloela St., pg. 1332 PB
Van Leer Australia Pty. Ltd., pg. 1146 IT
Westinghouse Electric Australasia Ltd., 49 Miowera Rd., pg. 275 PB

Wagga Wagga

Colborn-Dawes Australia (Pty.) Limited, pg. 1121 IT
Moore Paragon Australia Limited, pg. 889 IT

Waitara

Toro Australia Pty. Ltd., 9 Romsey, pg. 1624 PB

Wantirna

Esselte Meto Pty. Ltd., 80 Lewis Road, pg. 461 IT

Waratah

ANI Bradken, Maud St., pg. 100 IT
ANI Wear Resistant Products, Maud Street, pg. 100 IT
Commonwealth Steel Co. Ltd., Maud St., pg. 101 IT

Warriewood

Augat Pty Ltd., Unit 3/1 Vuko Pl., pg. 1598 PB
Huber & Suhner (Australia) Pty. Ltd., Unit 1, No. 1 Vuko Pl., pg. 637 IT

Warrnambool

Warrnambool Standard, 170-176 Koroit Street, pg. 477 IT

Waterloo

AlliedSignal Aerospace Limited, Unit B, 10-20 McEvory St., pg. 52 PB
Australian Power Products Pty Ltd, Seven Danks St., pg. 893 IT
Crown Corning Ltd., 866-882 Bourke St., pg. 128 IT
EMAIL LIMITED, Joynton Ave., pg. 450 IT
Farah Australia Pty. Limited, 715-721 Elizabeth St., pg. 613 PB
Kraft Foods Ltd., Yeast Extract Plant, O'Dea Avenue, pg. 1290 PB
Moore Products Co. (Australia) Pty. Ltd., Federation Business Centre, Unit 27, 198 Young St., pg. 1128 PB
Nira Australia Pty. Ltd., 10-20 McEvoy St., pg. 1369 IT

Welshpool

Delta Fasteners Pty. Ltd., 290-296 Welshpool Rd., pg. 391 IT
Elders - Western Australia, 72-82 Welshpool Rd., pg. 501 IT
Krupp Engineering (Australia) (Pty.) Ltd., 96 Ewing St., pg. 511 IT

Svedala Australia (Welshpool), pg. 1324 IT

Wentworthville

Boral Resources Ltd., Greystanes Rd., pg. 203 IT
Siebe Controls Australia, 115-121 Ballendella Rd., pg. 1244 IT

Westbury

Tasmanian Alkaloids Pty. Ltd., Birralee Rd., pg. 932 PB

Westgate

Aladdin Industries Pty. Ltd., P.O. Box 22, pg. 31 PV

Wetherill Park

Albright & Wilson (Australia) Ltd., 22 Davis Rd., pg. 49 IT
Aust-AMEC Pty., 70 Hassal St., pg. 16 IT
Austral Bronze Crane Copper Limited, pg. 340 IT
Australian Coleman, Inc., 5 Hallstrom Pl., pg. 691 PV
Davco Services, 67-69 Elizabeth St., pg. 803 IT
Esselte Australia Pty. Ltd., Locked Bag 47, pg. 461 IT
Flender (Australia) Pty. Ltd., 9, Nello Place, pg. 400 IT
Hosokawa Micron Australia Pty. Ltd., 1 Tooher Road, pg. 636 IT
Kohler Australia, Unit 7, 171-75 Newton Road, pg. 631 PV
McKechnie Metals, Lot 412 Victoria St., pg. 852 IT
Newly Weds Foods Asia/Pacific, 32 Davis Rd., pg. 797 PV
O.H. O'Brien Division, 192 Newtons Rd., pg. 895 IT
PENTEX Australia Pty. Ltd., 92 Hassall St., pg. 983 IT
Allen Taylor & Co. Limited, 360 Victoria St., pg. 203 IT
Thermos Pty. Ltd., Unit 2, 136 Newton Road, pg. 939 IT

Whyalla

Long Products Division, Port Augusta Road, pg. 227 IT
Whyalla Steelworks, pg. 227 IT

Wickham

Cape Lambert Operations, pg. 967 IT

Willoughby

Ilco Unican Australia (Pty.) Ltd., pg. 1432 IT
MTV Australia, TCN Channel 9, 24 Artarmon Road, pg. 779 PV
NIFE Australia Pty. Ltd., 6 McCabe Place, Chatswood 2067, pg. 54 IT
New Oji Paper Co., Ltd., 46 Frenchs Road, pg. 998 IT

Windsor

SMH Australia Ltd., 47 Wellington Street, pg. 1161 IT

Winnellie

Darwin Bakery Pty. Ltd., Winnellie Rd. &, pg. 1074 IT
Darwin Brewery, 14 Winnellie Rd., pg. 501 IT
Weatherford Australia Pty. Ltd., c/o P.O. Box 36971, pg. 1750 PB
Yokohama Tyre Australia Pty., Ltd., 426 Stuart Hwy. pg. 1522 IT

Wollongong

Breckett Pty. Limited, 156 Keira Street, pg. 211 IT
Collieries Division, Level 4, 90 Crown Street, pg. 226 IT
Illawarra Newspaper Holdings Pty. Limited, 282 Keira St., pg. 477 IT
Port Kembla Coal Terminal Ltd., Port Kembla Road, pg. 226 IT
Shaw Pipe Protection Pty. Ltd., Lot 22, West Dapto Road, pg. 1231 IT
Slab & Plate Products Division, 20 Crown, P.O. Box 1854, pg. 227 IT

Woodville

Sheridan Australia Ltd., Actil Ave., pg. 197 PV
Steiger Australia, Ltd., pg. 1580 PB

Wynard

Pickands Mather & Co. International, P.O. Box 353, pg. 386 PB

Wyong

Allied Colloids (Australia) Pty. Ltd., pg. 62 IT
Donaldson Australasia (Pty.) Ltd., P.O. Box 153, pg. 517 PB
Dulmison Pty. Limited, Dulmison Ave., pg. 893 IT
Fosroc Expandite (Australia) Pty. Ltd., 33 Lucca Road, North, pg. 236 IT
Weiser Lock Pty. Ltd., Lot 18, Lucca Rd., pg. 1055 PB

Yagoona

Bensons International Systems Pty. Ltd., 97 Rookwood Road, pg. 460 IT
Hawker Pacific Pty. Ltd., P.O. Box 172, pg. 128 IT

PB - *U.S. Public Companies Volume*
PV - *U.S. Private Companies Volume*
IT - *International Public & Private Companies Volume*

Geographic Index-Non U.S.

Yarram

Albright & Wilson (Australia) Ltd., Whitehall St., pg. 49 — IT
Christie's Australia Pty. Ltd., 1 Darling St., 290 — IT

Yennora

Comalco Foundry Products, Nelson Rd., pg. 307 — IT
Woolworths Limited, Cnr. Dursley & Fairfields Rds., pg. 676 — IT

AUSTRIA

Altenmarkt

Atomic Austria GmbH, Lackengasse 301, pg. 73 — IT

Amstetten

General Biscuits Osterreich (GBO), Industriestrasse 2, pg. 381 — IT

Aspach-Rientenau

Heil-und Mineralquellen GmbH, pg. 920 — IT

Asten

Dyckerhoff Austria Ausbauprodukte Ges.mbH, pg. 423 — IT

Bad Aussee

Rigips Austria GmbH, Unterkainisch 24, pg. 123 — IT

Baden

Wandel & Goltermann Ges.m.b.H, Postfach 13, pg. 1486 — IT

Bergheim

Herlitz Ges.m.b.H., Metzgerstr. 81A, pg. 616 — IT

Berndorf

FAG Austria Waelzlager AG, Ferd.-Poezl-Str. 2, pg. 469 — IT

Bernhardgasse

Morgan Austria GmbH, A-2340, pg. 891 — IT

Bischofshofen

Liebherr-Austria-Holding GmbH, Dr. Hans Liebherr Str. 4, pg. 808 — IT
Liebherr-Werk Bischofshofen GmbH, Dr. Hans Liebherr Str. 4, pg. 808 — IT

Bludenz

BIERBRAUEREI FOHRENBURG, Fohrenburgstr. 5, Postfach 192, pg. 194 — IT
Suchard Schokolade Ges.m.b.H, pg. 1289 — PB
Vorarlberger Zementwerke Loruns Nachfolger GmbH, Brunnenfelderstr. 59, pg. 791 — IT

Bohlerwerk

BOHLER Ybbstalwerke Ges.m.b.H., pg. 1470 — IT

Braunau

Hertwich Engineering GmbH, pg. 837 — IT

Bregenz

CIBA-GEIGY Gesellschaft mbH, Zweigstelle, Bregenz Hard, pg. 977 — IT
Volta Bregenz GmbH, Inder Braike 12, pg. 441 — IT

Breitenbrunn

Master Foods Austria GmbH, Eisenstaederstr. 80, pg. 707 — PV

Bruck

VOEST-ALPINE Austria Draht Ges.m.b.H., Bahnhofstrasse 2, pg. 1470 — IT

Brunn

Eomag AG - Erste Osterreichische Machinglasindustrie Brunn am Gebirge, Feldstr. 12, pg. 1056 — IT

Brunn am Gebirge

Avesta Sheffield GesmbH, pg. 221 — IT
Raychem Ges.m.b.H., Rennweg 85 Austria, pg. 1362 — PB
Scania Osterreich Ges.m.b.H., Postfach 50, pg. 687 — IT

Dornbirn

DORNBIRNER SPARKASSE, Bahnhof Str. #2, pg. 417 — IT
Kodak Fotoservice Gesellschaft m.b.H., Arlbergstrasse 7, pg. 553 — PB

Ebensee

Solvay Osterreich AG, Bahnhofstrasse 40, pg. 1280 — IT

Eferding

HALI-BUROMOBEL VERTRIEBS GESMBH, Karl-Schachinger Strasse 1, pg. 589 — IT

Eisenstadt

Landis & Staefa Leit- und Fernwirktechnik Ges.m.b.H, Neusiedlerstrasse 86, pg. 801 — IT

Elsbethen

DSI DYWIDAG -Systems International Ges. m.b.H., pg. 424 — IT

Enzersdorf

Bekaert Ges.m.b.H., Sudstadtzentrum 4/1 C2, pg. 184 — IT
Maschinenfabrik KBA Modling AG, Gabrielesstrasse 2-4, pg. 742 — IT

Eugendorf

BASF Lacke & Farben Vertriebsgesellschaft mbH, Gewerbegebiet Kalham, Gewerbestr. 25, pg. 106 — IT

Felixdorf

Charnaux Ges.m.b.H., pg. 618 — IT
Schiesser International Ges.m.b.H., pg. 618 — IT

Fieberbrunn

ZYMA-GEBRO Arzneimittel GmbH, pg. 986 — IT

Frankenmarkt

Oberdorfer Siebtechnik GmbH, Hohenwarth 1, pg. 1202 — IT

Fuerstenfeld

Verdichter Oe. G.m.b.H., Jahnstrasse 30, pg. 443 — IT

Glashutten

Collegium Glashutten Zentrum fur Kommunikation GmbH, pg. 312 — IT

Gleinstatten

Ziegelwerke Gleinstatten GmbH & Co. KG, pg. 1092 — IT

Gmunden

Elefanten-Schuh-Ges.m.b.H., pg. 505 — IT

Goetzis

Hewlett-Packard Vorarlberg, Wiedengasse 25, pg. 822 — PB

Gratkorn

K & P Leykam Austria, Brucker Strsse 21, pg. 757 — IT

Graz

AxPro Axel Johnson GesmbH, Exerzierplatzstrasse 85, pg. 710 — IT
Ed. AST & Co. Baugesellschaft mbH, Burgring 16, pg. 633 — IT
Hewlett-Packard Ges.m.b.H., Verkaufsbuero Graz, Grottenhofstrasse 94, pg. 820 — PB
ISS Servisystem GesmbH, Peter Rosegger Strasse 28, pg. 657 — IT
Jauch & Huebener, Lichtenfelsgasse 15, pg. 118 — PB
Maschinenfabrik Andritz AG, pg. 14 — IT
Otto-Versand GmbH, pg. 1015 — IT
Panalpina GmbH, pg. 1023 — IT
VOEST-ALPINE Stahlhandel AG, Waagner-Biro-Strasse 47, pg. 1470 — IT
Zollfreizonen-Betriebe GmbH, pg. 1023 — IT

Grosspetersdorf

Packard Electric Burgenland Ges.m.b.H., pg. 723 — PB
Packard Electric Europa Ges.m.b.H., Industriestrasse 1, pg. 723 — PB

Gunskirchen

Bombardier-Rotax GmbH Motorenfabrik, Welser Strasse 32, pg. 200 — IT

Hallein

Margaret Astor Cosmetics Ges.m.b.H., pg. 185 — IT
Benckiser Austria Ges.m.b.H., pg. 185 — IT
Halvic Kunststoffwerke GmbH, Solvay-Halvic Streabe, 6, pg. 1278 — IT
3 Pagen Handelsgesellschaft mbH, pg. 1015 — IT

Hard

Vorwerk Ges.m.b.H., pg. 1481 — IT

Herzogenburg

Georg Fischer Automobilguss Ges.m.b.H., Wiener Strasse 41-43, pg. 488 — IT
Georg Fischer Rohrleitungssystems GmbH, Sandgasse 16, pg. 490 — IT

Hirschegg

EAB Electronic Apparatebau GmbH, Durenbodenstrasse 7, pg. 1129 — IT

Hochfilzen

Tiroler Magnesit, A.G., pg. 904 — PV

Hohenems

Enka (Schweiz) GmbH, Abwicklung CH, pg. 46 — IT
Jauch & Huebener, Schlossplatz 13, pg. 118 — PB

Innsbruck

Bank fur Tirol und Vorarlberg AG, pg. 347 — IT
Hochtief Aktiengesellschaft Vorm. Gebr. Helfmann Ges.m.b.H., Rossaugasse 3, pg. 624 — IT
Jauch & Huebener, Michael-Gaismayr Strasse 11, pg. 118 — PB
Panalpina GmbH, pg. 1023 — IT

Inzing

Sodexho MM Catering GmbH, Dr. Gustav Markt. Weg 18, pg. 1275 — IT

Judenburg

STYRIA Federn Ges.m.b.H., Gussstahlwerkstrasse 20, pg. 1470 — IT
VOEST-ALPINE STAHL Judenburg Ges.m.b.H., Gussstahlwerkstrasse 21, pg. 1470 — IT

Kapfenberg

BOHLER Ges.m.b.H., Mariazallerstrasse 25, pg. 1470 — IT
Bohlerit Ges.m.b.H., pg. 1470 — IT

Kindberg

Voest-Alpine Stahlrohr Kindberg Ges.m.b.H., Alpinestrasse 17, pg. 1470 — IT

Kitzbuhel

Primagaz GmbH, St. Johanner Strasse 11, pg. 1155 — IT

Klagenfurt

Adidas Austria AG, pg. 24 — IT
Bank fur Karnten und Steiermark AG, pg. 347 — IT
Mazda Austria GmbH, Ernst-Diez-Strasze 3, pg. 849 — IT
Panalpina GmbH, pg. 1023 — IT
VOEST-ALPINE Stahlhandel AG, Sudring 252, pg. 1470 — IT

Klosterneuburg

Dell Computer GES.m.b.H, Inkustrasse 1-7, Haus H/7, pg. 496 — PB
Kali-Chemie Pharma Gesellschaft mbH, Donaustrasse 106, pg. 1279 — IT
Kali-Chemie Pharma GmbH, Donaustrasse 106, pg. 1279 — IT

Koflach

Koflach Sport GmbH, Alte Hauptstrasse 5-7, pg. 73 — IT

Korneuburg

Hoogovens Aluminium Verkauf GmbH, Laaerstrasse 7-9/2/1, pg. 755 — IT

Kottingbrunn

Battenfeld Automatisierungstechnik Ges.m.b.H., Wiener Neustadter Strasse 81, pg. 825 — IT
Battenfeld Kunststoffmaschinen Ges. m.b.H., Wiener Neustadter Strasse 81, pg. 825 — IT
Battenfeld Kunststoffmaschinen Ges. m. b. H., Wiener Neustaedter Strasse 81, pg. 826 — IT

PB - *U.S. Public Companies Volume*
PV - *U.S. Private Companies Volume*
IT - *International Public & Private Companies Volume*

Geographic Index-Non U.S.

Krems

Krems-Chemi GmbH, Hafenstrasse 77, pg. 175   IT
VOEST-ALPINE Krems Finaltechnik GmbH, Schmidhuettenstrasse 5, pg. 1470   IT
VOEST-ALPINE Krems Ges.m.b.H., Schmidhuettenstrasse 5, pg. 1470   IT

Krieglach

BWK Krieglach Bauwerkstoffe Ges. m. b. H., P.O. Box 8, pg. 1465   IT

Kufstein

Freudenberg Simrit Kufstein Ges.m.b.H., pg. 507   IT
Freudenberg Simrit Kufstein Ges.m.b.H. & Co. KG, pg. 506   IT
Simmerwerk Gesellschaft m.b.H., pg. 507   IT
Simmerwerke W. Simmer GmbH & Co. KG, pg. 506   IT

Kundl

Biochemie Gesellschaft m.b.H., Dr. Hans Bachman Str. 17, pg. 975   IT
Biozym Gesellschaft m.b.h., Dr. Hans Bachman Str. 17, pg. 986   IT
Sanabo Gesellschaft m.b.H., Dr. Hans Bachman Str. 17, pg. 984   IT

Lackenbach

Quarzsandwerk Gesellschaft mbH, pg. 1092   IT

Langendorf

MBT Austria Gesellschaft m.b.h., pg. 1465   IT

Lauterach

Gebruder Sulzer-Escher Wyss-Kaltetechnik GmbH, pg. 1306   IT
Sulzer Escher Wyss Kaltetchnik G.m.b.H., pg. 1306   IT

Leoben

VOEST-ALPINE Schienen GmbH, Kerpelystrasse 199, pg. 1470   IT
VOEST-ALPINE STAHL Donawitz Ges.m.b.H., Kerpelstrasse 199, pg. 1470   IT

Leobersdorf

Leobersdorfer Maschinenfabuk AG, Sudbahnstrasse 28, pg. 399   IT
Neumayer GmbH, Gunselsdorferstrasse 2, pg. 1017   IT
Julius Overhoff Ruckkuhltechnik Ges. m.b.H., Sudbahnstr. 28, pg. 400   IT

Lienz

Agrolinz Melamin GmbH, St. Peter Str. 25, pg. 356   IT
Astra Ges. m.b.H., Sudtirolerstrasse 6, pg. 93   IT
Bank fur Oberosterreich und Salzburg, pg. 347   IT
Chemserv Industrie Service Ges.m.b.H., St. Peter-Strasse 25, pg. 356   IT
DSM Chemie Linz GmbH, St.-Peter-Strasse 25, pg. 356   IT
Epipharm GmbH, Bannerstrasse 10, pg. 288   IT
Gartenhilfe Ges.m.b.H., St. Peter-Strasse 25, pg. 356   IT
Husqvarna Gesellschaft GmbH, Industriezeile 36, pg. 441   IT
Interkosmetik Ges.m.b.H., pg. 1490   IT
Krauss-Maffei Austria GmbH, pg. 836   IT
Liebherr-Werk Lienz GmbH, Dr. Hans Liebherr Strasse 1, pg. 808   IT
Linde Fodertechnik GmbH, pg. 810   IT
Network Systems Austria GmbH, Mozartstrasse 4, pg. 1522   PB
Panalpina GmbH, pg. 1023   IT
Rockwell Automation GesmbH, Backermuhlweg 1, pg. 1399   PB
VOEST-ALPINE Intertrading GmbH, Strasserau 6, pg. 1470   IT
VOEST-ALPINE Rohstoffhandel Ges.m.b.H., Strasserau 6, pg. 1470   IT
VOEST-ALPINE STAHL AG, Turmstrasse 41, pg. 1470   IT
VOEST-ALPINE STAHL Linz Ges.m.b.H., Turmstrasse 45, pg. 1470   IT
VOEST-ALPINE Stahlhandel AG, Lastenstr. 38, pg. 1470   IT

Linz

Jauch & Huebener, Mozartstrasse 11, pg. 118   PB
Tandem Computers Ges.m.b.H., Prinz-Eugen Str. 35-37, pg. 418   PB

Marchtrenk

VOAC Hydraulics GmbH, Muhlstrabe 2, pg. 1264   PB

Modling

Knorr-Bremse Ges.m.b.H., Steinfeldgergasse 12, pg. 738   IT
Dr. Techn. Josef Zelisko GMBH, Steinfeldergasse 12, pg. 738   IT
Zeneca Resins, Grutschgasse 2, pg. 1527   IT

Mollersdorf

Fichtel & Sachs Austria GmbH, pg. 835   IT

Murzzuschlag

Getinge GmbH, Bleckmanngasse 10, pg. 551   IT

Nenzing

Hydro Aluminium Nenzing GmbH, Austrasse 16, pg. 962   IT
Liebherr-Werk Nenzing GmbH, pg. 808   IT

Nettingsdorf

Nettingsdorfer Beteiligungs AG, pg. 1271   IT

Oberweis

Scapa-Kern Walzenservice GmbH, pg. 1203   IT

Parndorf

Pioneer Overseas, GES.mbH., Pioneerstrasse Industriegelaude, pg. 1299   PB
Pioneer Saaten AG, Pioneerstr., pg. 1299   PB

Pasching

G.L. Rexroth GmbH, pg. 838   IT
Traub-Heckert Austria GmbH, Industriepark 24, pg. 1419   IT

Perchtoldsdorf

Hartmann & Braun Austria, pg. 835   IT
Krupp Widia Vertriebsges. mbH, Salitergasse 7, pg. 510   IT
3M Oesterreich Ges mbH, Brunner Feldstrasse 63, P.O. Box 611, pg. 1607   PB

Pochlarn

Bramac Dachsysteme International GmbH, Fichenstrasse 10, pg. 1092   IT

Pottendorf

Forbo Wiener Teppichfabrik GmbH, pg. 498   IT

Puch

Milupa Gmbh, pg. 991   IT

Pucking

Adecco GmbH, Pinguinweg 5, pg. 24   IT

Radenthein

Oesterreichisch Heraklith, A.G., pg. 904   PV
Radex Austria, A.G., pg. 904   PV

Saint Gallen

Familia Lebensversicherungs-Gesellschaft, Teufenerstrasse, 25, pg. 91   IT

Saint Jakob

Magnifin Magnesiaprodukte GmbH, pg. 69   IT

Saint Margrethen

Cold Storage Warehouse AG St. Margrethen, pg. 866   IT

Saint Michael

Panalpina GmbH, pg. 1023   IT

Saint Polten

Gourmet Menu-Service GmbH & Co KG, Zdarskystr. 3, pg. 842   IT
J.M. Voith AG, Passauer Strasse 40, pg. 1473   IT

Saint Stefan

F.W. Schwing GmbH, P.O. Box 49, pg. 1211   IT

Salzburg

Akzo Coatings Ges. m.b.H., Elixhausen, P.O. Box 248, pg. 43   IT

ALLSPANN, Allgemeine Spannbetongesellschaft m.b.H., Christophorusstr. 12, pg. 424   IT
Austria Puma Dassler Ges.m.b.H., Munchner Bundesstrasse 119, pg. 1072   IT
BMW Austria Gesellschaft m.b.H., Siegfr. Marcus Strasse 24, pg. 178   IT
Bran & Luebbe G.m.b.H., Friedenstrasse 11, pg. 1379   IT
CIBA Corning Diagnostics GmbH, Traunstrasse 46, pg. 975   IT
Curver (Osterreich) GmbH, Mayrwies-Esch 392, pg. 353   IT
Danone Austria, Salzachweg 1, pg. 379   IT
Duni GmbH, Moosstrasse 41, pg. 421   IT
Eisenmetall Gesellschaft mbH, Habach 91, pg. 514   IT
Erste Salzburger Gipswerks-Gesellschaft Christian Moldan KG, Kellau 75, pg. 606   IT
Ford Bank Aktiengesellschaft (Austria), Fuerbergstrasse 51, pg. 665   PB
Ford Motor Co. (Austria) KG, Fuerbergstr. 51, pg. 666   PB
Fuchs Reiner Schmiermittel Ges. M.B.H., pg. 519   IT
GGK Salzburg, Aignerstr. 30, pg. 1335   IT
Gervais Danone Austria, Salzachweg 1, pg. 380   IT
Jauch & Huebener, Hubert-Sattler-Gasse 8, pg. 118   PB
Kluber Lubrication Austria Ges.m.b.H., pg. 506   IT
Kodak Fotoservice Gesellschaft m.b.H., Kieselhaus, Rainerstrasse 23, pg. 553   PB
Lancaster Group Ges.m.b.h., pg. 186   IT
Mannesmann Demag Fordertechnik GmbH, Gniglerstr. 57, pg. 837   IT
Melitta-Gesellschaft MbH & Co KG, pg. 857   IT
Mercedes-Benz Osterreich Vertriebsgesellschaft mbH, pg. 369   IT
AB Mikroelektronik GmbH, Josef-Brandstaetter-Str. 2, pg. 1344   IT
Mirabell Salzburger Confiserie-Und Bisquit-Ges.m.b.H, Hauptstrasse 14-16, pg. 1289   PB
Molto Ges.m.b.H., Hellbrunnerstrasse 7, pg. 1501   IT
Nedlloyd Road Cargo GmbH, pg. 1145   IT
Polita Gebaudereinigung Ges.m.b.H, pg. 1481   IT
Raab Karcher Austria GmbH, pg. 1458   IT
Reed Exhibition Companies-Austria, Bessarabierstarsse 83, pg. 1097   IT
Rothenberg Holding Ges.m.b.H., WalterstraBe 1, pg. 1129   IT
Rothenberger Werkzeug-und Maschinenhandelsgesellschaft m.b.H., WalterstraBe 1, pg. 1129   IT
SAIA-Burgess Ges.mbH, Schallmooser Hauptstrasse 38, pg. 1501   IT
Saltzburger Kredit-und Wechsel-Bank AG, Makartplatz 3, pg. 176   IT
Sensormatic Ges.m.b.H., Handelszentrum 7, pg. 1457   PB
Suzuki Austria Automobil Handels G.m.b.H., pg. 1323   IT
TakeFive Software, GmbH, pg. 886   PB
VB Heller Bank A.G., Alpenstrasse 54, pg. 521   IT
Valvoline Oil Co. GmbH, Braumuhlweg, 148, pg. 140   PB
VOEST-ALPINE Rohstoffhandel Ges.m.b.H., Paris-Lodron-Strasse 3 a, pg. 1470   IT
VOEST-ALPINE Stahlhandel AG, Munchner-Bundesstrasse 105, pg. 1470   IT
Walter Werkzeuge Salzburg Ges m.b.H. & Co., WalterstraBe 1, pg. 1129   IT
Wrigley Austria Ges.m.b.H., Joseph Waach Str. 11, pg. 1781   PB

Schruns

Hotel Lowen Schruns GmbH, Silvretta Strasse 8, pg. 808   IT

Schwanenstadt

Crown Cork Company (Austria), GmbH, Postfach 90, pg. 464   PB

Schwechat

Nordson GmbH (Austria), Concorde Business Park C 2/13, pg. 1189   PB
Tektronix GesmbH, pg. 1567   IT

Spielberg

Flender Austria Antriebstechnik AG, G. Bauknecht-Strasse 1, pg. 400   IT

Stadl Paura

Lambacher Hitiag Leinen AG, pg. 347   IT
Linde Gas GmbH & Co. KG, pg. 811   IT

Steyr

BMW Motoren Ges.m.b.H., Hinterbergerstrasse 2, pg. 178   IT
Faltec Tore Ges.m.b.H., Wolfernstrasse 17D, pg. 269   IT
Forbo Industrieprodukte Ges.m.b.H., pg. 497   IT
SKF Osterreich AG, Postfach 205, pg. 1159   IT
Steyr Nutzfahrzeuge AG, Schoenauerstrasse 5, pg. 825   IT
Steyr Walzlager Ges.m.b.H., pg. 1160   IT

Stockerau

Exel Osterreich, John Gutenberggasse 41, pg. 914   IT
Tel Mineralwolle AG, Prager Strasse 77, pg. 1176   IT
Vogel Pumpenfabrik, pg. 861   PB

PB - *U.S. Public Companies Volume*
PV - *U.S. Private Companies Volume*
IT - *International Public & Private Companies Volume*

Telfs

Interalpen-Hotel Tyrol GmbH, pg. 808   IT
Liebherr-Werk Telfs GmbH, Hans Liebherr Strasse 35, pg. 808   IT

Ternitz

Amada Austria GmbH, Wassergasse 1, pg. 70   IT
Schoeller-Beckmann Nooter Apparatetechnik GMBH, Hauptstrasse 2, pg. 801   PV

Traisen

Georg Fischer Fittings GmbH, Mariazeller Strasse 75, pg. 489   IT
Fittings Traisen Gmbh, Mariazeller Strasse 75, pg. 490   IT
VOEST-ALPINE STAHL Traisen Ges.m.b.H., Mariazallerstrasse 75, pg. 1470   IT

Traiskirchen

Semperit Reifen AG, Wienersdorfer Strasse 20-24, pg. 328   IT

Traun

Patex Chemie GmbH, pg. 811   PB

Treibach

Treibacher Chemische Werke AG, pg. 347   IT

Unterach

EBEWE Arzneimittel Ges.m.b.H., Mondseestr. 11, pg. 108   IT

Vienna

ABS Pumpen Ges.m.b.H., IZ-NO-Sud Strasse 2, M27, pg. 270   IT
AC Rochester Products Austria Ges.m.b.H, Gross Enzerdorfer Strasse 59, pg. 723   PB
AGA Ges.m.b.H., pg. 13   IT
AKG Acoustics, Lembockgasse 21-25, pg. 787   PB
AMP Osterreich G.m.b.H., Pilzgasse 31, pg. 9   PB
AWT International Trade & Finance AG, pg. 347   IT
Accor GmbH, Palmgasse 3, pg. 21   IT
Acer Computer HandelsgmbH, pg. 22   IT
Adria Bank AG, pg. 347   IT
Adria-Wien Pipeline, pg. 1138   IT
A. Ahlstrom Ges.m.b.H., Plenergasse 1/7, pg. 34   IT
Air Sea Charter Transport GmbH, pg. 1022   IT
Ajinomoto Osteuropa Handels-G.m.b.H., Kramergasse 1/5/8, pg. 40   IT
Alarmcom GmbH, Lainzerstrasse 54, pg. 1246   IT
Albright & Wilson GmbH (Austria), Walfischgasse, pg. 49   IT
Alcatel Austria A.G., Scheudgasse 41, pg. 55   IT
AG Alfa-Laval, Postfach 99, pg. 1379   IT
Alfa-Laval Stalltechnik G.m.b.H., Postfach 99, pg. 1379   IT
Algemene Bank Nederland (Osterreich) AG, Schottenring 35, pg. 12   IT
Allgemeine Immobilien Verwaltungs GmbH, Bauernmarkt 12, pg. 89   IT
Allgemeiner Kugellagervertrieb Polzl GmbH, pg. 469   IT
Alusuisse Austria GmbH, pg. 68   IT
Amdahl Computer Systeme Gesellschaft m.b.H., Alserbachstr 16, pg. 527   IT
Amway Gesellschaft M.B.H., Lohnergasse 2, pg. 70   PV
Analog Devices HDLSGESMBH, Heissgasse 51, pg. 108   PB
Anglo-Elementar Versicherungs-AG, Karntner Ring 12, pg. 60   IT
Apple Computer Ges.mbH, Rotenturmstrasse 103 top 12, pg. 121   IT
Ascom Austria Ges.mbH, Hohenbergstrasse 22, pg. 86   IT
Asea Brown Boveri AG, Wienerbergstrasse 11B, pg. 2   IT
Asea Brown Boveri Aktiengesellschaft mbH, Pernerstorfergasse 94, pg. 8   IT
Austria OBI-Systemzentrale, Hutteldorfer Str. 299, pg. 993   PV
Austria III, Daringergasse 6, pg. 1062   PV
AUSTRIAN AIRLINES, Fontanna Str. 1, pg. 101   IT
AUSTRIAN POSTAL & TELEGRAPH ADMINISTRATION, pg. 101   IT
AUSTRO-BAVARIA Investment AG, pg. 180   IT
AVABANK AG, pg. 712   PB
BASF Oesterreich (Austria) Ges.m.b.H., Hietzinger Hauptstrasse 119, pg. 106   IT
BM Beteiligungs Management GmbH, pg. 347   IT
BMC Software GmbH, Hebbelplatz 5, pg. 162   PB
Bally Gesellschaft mbH, Sterngasse 13, pg. 997   IT
Banco do Brasil S.A.-Austria, Tegetthoffstrasse 4, pg. 142   IT
Bang & Olufsen Ges. m.b.H., pg. 146   IT
Bausch & Lomb G.m.b.H., Handelskai 52, pg. 195   PB
Bayer Austria G.m.b.H., Am Heumarkt 10, pg. 175   IT
Bayerische Landesbank Girozentrale, Mahlerstr. 10-12, pg. 177   IT
Beiersdorf Ges. mbH, pg. 183   IT
BEKO, Modecenterstr. 22/A1, pg. 1031   PB
Bensdrop Ges. m.b.H., pg. 1436   IT
Berlitz Sprachschulen GmbH, Graben 13, pg. 222   PB
Bestobell Mobrey GESmbH, Donaustadstrasse, Donauzen Trum, pg. 854   IT

BetzDearborn Ges.m.b.H, Storchengasse 1, pg. 227   PB
Bio-Rad Laboratories, Ges.m.b.H., Auhofstrasse 78D, pg. 230   PB
Black & Decker Werkzeuge Vertriebasgesellschaft m.b.H., Erlaaerstrasse 165, pg. 234   PB
Bohler Uddeholm AG, pg. 1471   IT
BolsWessanen Beteiligung GmbH Osterreich, pg. 752   IT
Bombardier-Wien Schienenfahrzeuge AG, Donaufelder Strasse 73-79, pg. 200   IT
Bondioli & Pavesi GS.M.B.H, Siebenhirterstrasse 13A, pg. 201   IT
Robert Bosch AG, Geiereckstrasse 6, pg. 205   IT
L. Bosendorfer Klavierfabrik GmbH, Graf-Starhemberggasse 14, pg. 958   PB
Brewo Grundstucksverwaltungs GmbH, Wiedner Haupstrasse 5b, pg. 89   IT
Bristol-Myers Ges.m.b.H., Postfach 486, pg. 255   PB
Brother International G.m.b.H., Pfarrgasse 58, pg. 229   IT
Bruder Kunz Ges.m.b.H., pg. 856   IT
Bull AG, Linke Wienzeile 192, pg. 317   IT
Leo Burnett & Wirz, Gottfried-Keller-Gasse 2, pg. 184   PV
Burohaus Vermietungs und Verwaltungs GmbH & Co. KG, pg. 347   IT
CA Bau-Finanzierungsberatung GmbH, pg. 347   IT
CA-Consult International Investitionsprojektbberstungesellschaft m.b.h., pg. 347   IT
CA-EA Investment GmbH, pg. 347   IT
CA Fund Advisory Fonds Beratungs GmbH, pg. 347   IT
CA-Generali Versicherung AG, Gonzaagasse 16, pg. 89   IT
CA Global Futures Terminkontrakte AG, pg. 347   IT
CA Global Property Internationale Immobilien AG, pg. 347   IT
CA-GVG-Holding GmbH, pg. 347   IT
CA Immobilien Invest AG, pg. 347   IT
CA-Informations-Technologie Beratungs, pg. 347   IT
CA-Leasing GmbH, pg. 347   IT
CA Management-Systems-Consult GmbH, pg. 347   IT
CA-3 Banken Beteiligungsfonds AG, pg. 347   IT
CA-3 Banken Venture Fonds AG, pg. 347   IT
CA-Versicherungsdienst GmbH, pg. 347   IT
CA-Versicherungsholding GmbH, pg. 347   IT
CAIB-Austria Oeva GmbH, Volksgartenstrasse 3, pg. 212   IT
CAP Gemini Austria, Kaiserstrasse 65, pg. 264   IT
COFINEC (Compagnie Financiere pour l'Europe Centrale), Gusshausstrasse 2/2, pg. 240   IT
Canon East Europe Vertriebsgesellschaft mbH, Ober Laaer Strasse 233, pg. 262   IT
Canon GmbH, Zetschegasse 11, pg. 262   IT
Carbone-Lorraine GmbH, Reindorfgasse 5/11, pg. 1030   IT
Centro Internationale Handelsbank AG (Centrobank), Tegetthoffstrasse 1, pg. 420   IT
Chase Manhattan Bank (Austria), A.G., Parkring 12A, pg. 340   PB
Chemag Chemikalien-Handels Ges m.b.H., Hietzinger Hauptstrasse 119, pg. 107   IT
Chemia GmbH, Am Heumarkt 10, pg. 175   IT
CIBA-GEIGY Gesellschaft mbH, Breitenfurterstrasse 251, pg. 977   IT
CIBA Vision Austria, Modecenterstrasse 14, pg. 981   IT
Cincinnati Milacron Austria Aktiengesellschaft, P.O. Box 111, pg. 368   IT
Cincinnati Milacron Handelsgesellschaft mbH, pg. 368   PB
Cincinnati Milacron Holding Gesellschaft mbH, pg. 368   PB
Citibank (Austria) A.G., Lothringerstr. 7, pg. 378   PB
Coats Harlander G.m.b.H., Autokaderstrasse 31, pg. 300   IT
Colgate-Palmolive GmbH, Argentinierstrasse 22, pg. 398   PB
Comdisco Handelsgesellschaft m.b.H. Austria, Mahlerstrasse 7/22, pg. 408   PB
Commenda Baustoff A.G., Gonzagegasse 16, pg. 1501   IT
Commenda Baustoffgesellschaft mbH, Postfach 118, pg. 1278   IT
Compaq Computer GmbH, Wetteldorferstrasse 65, pg. 418   PB
COMPAREX Informationssysteme Ges.m.b.H., Hietzinger Hauptstrasse 119, pg. 108   IT
Componenta International GmbH, Nordwestbahnstrasse 83, pg. 1421   IT
Conquest Europe, Reisnerstrasse 29, pg. 1483   IT
John Crane Ltd., Eastern Europe Branch Office, Auhofstrasse 84/3/4/40, pg. 1339   IT
CREDITANSTALT-BANKVEREIN, Schottengasse 6-8, pg. 346   IT
Creditanstalt Investment Bank AG, pg. 347   IT
D.R.S. Restaurant Scheck-Sodexho GmbH, Hockegasse 19, pg. 1274   IT
DYWIDAG Spezialtiefbau Ges.m.b.h., pg. 424   IT
Daewoo Corp. - Vienna, pg. 358   IT
Daihatsu Autohandelsges M.B.H., Zetschegasse 13, pg. 365   IT
Danzas AG, pg. 382   IT
Data General Gesellschaft mbH, Ungargasse 37, pg. 486   PB
Dataproducts Handelsgesellschaft M.b.H., Hintere Zollamtstrasse 9/32, pg. 621   IT
DEMMER, MERLICEK & BERGMANN WERBEGESELLSCHAFT MBH, Lehargasse 9-11, pg. 392   IT
Det Norske Veritas, Wiener Strasse 89, pg. 397   IT
Deutsche Bank AG (Vienna), pg. 405   IT
Deutscher Container-Dienst Ges. mbH, pg. 596   IT
Die Hager, Seilerstaette 13, pg. 678   PV
Digital Equipment Corporation GmbH, Ziedlergasse 21, pg. 507   PB
Diners Club Austria AG, pg. 347   IT
Donau Chemie AG, Am Heumarkt 10, pg. 1112   IT

Dow Chemical Austria Gesellschaft mbH, Wohllebengasse 6, pg. 523   PB
Dow Jones Markets Ges.m.b.H., Praterstrasse 31, pg. 525   PB
Dun & Bradstreet Schimmelpfeng GmbH, Opernring 3-5, pg. 537   PB
Durkopp Adler Austria GmbH, Modecenterstrasse 14, pg. 469   IT
Dyckerhoff & Widmann Gesellschaft m.b.H., Stubenring 18, pg. 424   IT
EA - Generali AG, Landskrongasse 1-3, pg. 89   IT
EA-Generali AG, Landskrongasse 1-3, pg. 91   IT
EA Generali Risk Consult GmbH, Landskrongasse 1-3, pg. 89   IT
EA Generali Vermogensberatungs GmbH, Landskrongasse 1-3, pg. 89   IT
EMI Austria GesmbH, Webgasse 43, pg. 427   IT
ESAB Ges.m.b.H, Dirmhirngasse 110, pg. 282   IT
Eichler KG, Pernerstorfergasse 5, pg. 550   IT
Einlagensicherung der Banken und Bankiers GmbH, pg. 347   IT
Electricite de France, Karnterring 5-7, Top 505, pg. 438   IT
Electrolux Bedenpflegegerate Vertriebsgesellschaft GmbH, Postfach 51, pg. 440   IT
Elscint Central & Eastern Europe, Nobilegrasse 23-25, pg. 450   IT
Elster Gastechnic Produktions -und Vertriebsgesellschaft m.b.H, Heiligenstaederstrasse 45, pg. 1149   IT
Emhart Ges.m.b.H. (Austria), Missindorfstrasse 19-23, pg. 233   PB
EMTEC Magnetics ECE GmbH, Hietzinger Hauptstrasse 119, pg. 743   IT
Enka Osterreich Handelsgesellschaft mbH, 11 Reichstratsstrasse, pg. 46   IT
Enso Trading Handelsgesellschaft mbH, Gottfried Kellergsse 2/10, pg. 457   IT
Enso Trading Handelsgesellschaft mbH, pg. 457   IT
Ericsson Schrack AG, Pottendorfer Strasse 25-27, pg. 1367   IT
Erstallges Betriebskuche Landskrongasse GmbH, Landskrongasse 1-3, pg. 89   IT
Erste Allgemeine Versicherungs AG, Landskrongasse 1-3, pg. 89   IT
ERSTE BANK DER OESTERREICHISCHEN SPARKASSEN AG, Schuberring 5, pg. 459   IT
Esselte Meta Ges mbH, Jochen Rindt-Str. 13, pg. 461   IT
Esselte Vertriebsges. mbH, Kinskygasse 40-44, pg. 461   IT
EURO RSCG, Argentinierstr. 26, pg. 602   IT
EUROCONSULT Energie und Umwelt Beratungs GmbH, pg. 347   IT
Europaische Reiseversicherung AG, Johannegasse 20, pg. 89   IT
Europay Austria Zahlungsverkehrssysteme GmbH, pg. 347   IT
Eurotherm GmbH, Geiereckstrasse 18/1, pg. 466   IT
Factor-Bank, pg. 347   IT
Fasson Gesellschaft mbH, Theresiengasse 58, pg. 154   PB
Fina GmbH, Seidlgasse 22/5, pg. 1043   IT
Forbo Contel Handelsgesellschaft mbH, pg. 497   IT
Francesco Parisi Ges.m.b.H., Sonnwendgasse, 21, 4 Strasse, pg. 504   IT
Francesco Parisi G.m.b.H., Raum F 210, Flughafen Schwechat, pg. 504   IT
Frank & Schulte in Austria Ges. mbH, Paulanergasse 10, pg. 1459   IT
Freudenberg Vertriebs-KG in Austria, pg. 506   IT
GGK Occidental, Hietzinger Hauptstrasse 45, pg. 1335   IT
GGK Occidental Holding AG, Hietzinger Hauptstrasse 45, pg. 1335   IT
GGK Wien, Linzerstrasse 375, pg. 1336   IT
GGK Wien Werbeagentur GmbH, Linzer Str. 375, pg. 1336   IT
GKN Service-Austria GmbH, Slammastrasse 32, pg. 536   IT
Gambro Vertriebsgesellschaft m.b.H., Warneckestrasse 7, pg. 668   IT
Gebhardt Ventilatoren, GmbH, Handelskai 300, pg. 1054   PB
Gebruder Gross Ges.m.b.H., pg. 856   IT
Gebruder Sulzer Gesellschqaft mbH, Anlagen- und Gebaudetechnik, pg. 1306   IT
General Motors Austria Ges.m.b.H., Gross Enzerdorfer Strasse 59, pg. 721   PB
Generali Allgemeine Lebensversicherung AG, Landskrongasse 1-3, pg. 89   IT
Generali Ruckversicherung AG, Landskrongasse 1-3, pg. 89   IT
Geodimeter Handels Gesmbh, Vivenotgasse 48, pg. 1290   IT
Gesfo Gemeinnutzige Bau- und Siedlungs GmbH, pg. 347   IT
Gestetner Buromaschinen-Verkaufsgesellschaft m.b.H., Siemensstrasse 160, pg. 1115   IT
Glaxo Wellcome Pharma GmbH, Julius-Meinl-Gasse, pg. 553   IT
Grothusen Ges.m.b.H., Albert-Schweitzer-Gasse 5, pg. 739   IT
Grun + Bilfinger, Schonbrunner Strasse 213-215, pg. 196   IT
Grundstucke- und Gebaudeverwaltungs GmbH, pg. 347   IT
Gruner + Jahr Verlags-GmbH, Parkring 12, pg. 191   IT
Guerlain GmbH, Esslinggasse 9/3, pg. 780   IT
HALI-Buromobel Vertriebs GesmbH, Sranzosengraben 10, pg. 589   IT
Handelsbeteiligungs GmbH, pg. 347   IT
Chr. Hansen GmbH Niederlassung fur Osterreich, Sudbahnhof, 7 Strasse, pg. 289   IT

PB - *U.S. Public Companies Volume*
PV - *U.S. Private Companies Volume*
IT - *International Public & Private Companies Volume*

1507

Geographic Index-Non U.S.

Hapag-Lloyd Austria Ges. mbH, pg. 596   IT
Hapag-Lloyd Belgium N.V., pg. 596   IT
Henkel Austria Group, Erdbergstrasse 29, pg. 611   IT
Henkel Cosmetics Ges.mbH, pg. 612   IT
Hewlett-Packard Ges.m.b.H., Lieblgasse 1, pg. 820   PB
High-Tech Nachrichtentechnische Anlagen GmbH, pg. 1139   PB
Hoesch Bausysteme GmbH, Tenscherstr. 3, pg. 508   IT
Hoesch Rothe Erde Gesellschaft, Tenscherstr. 3, pg. 509   IT
Hoesch Stahlhandel GmbH, Operngasse 18, pg. 515   IT
Hoffmann-La Roche Wien GmbH, Jacquingasse 16-18, pg. 1121   IT
Honda Austria G.m.b.H., Richard Strauss Strasse 10, pg. 635   IT
Honeywell Austria GmbH, Handelskai 388, pg. 834   PB
Honeywell Bull AG, Linke Wienzeile 236, pg. 318   IT
Hospal Medizintechnische Produkte Ges.m.b.H., Nussdorferstrasse 38, pg. 668   IT
Howmedica G.m.b.H., Bacherplatz 10, pg. 1284   IT
Hubner-Gray Ges. m.b.H., Mushgasse 64, pg. 6   IT
Huls Austria Ges. mbH, Gonzagagasse 4, pg. 1455   IT
Hutter & Schrantz AG, pg. 347   IT
IBJ-CA Consult Handels-und Investitionsberatungsgesellschaft m.b.H., Landhausgasse 4/7, pg. 347   IT
IBM Oesterreich, Internationale Bueromaschinen Gesellschaft mbH, Obere Donaustrasse 95, pg. 897   PB
IBM Produktvertrieb Gesellschaft mbH, pg. 897   PB
ICI Oesterreich GmbH, Schwartzenbergplatz 7, pg. 665   IT
ICL International Computers GmbH, Meidlinger Hauptstrasse 51-53, pg. 529   IT
IDC Austria, Zieglergasse 6, pg. 570   PV
IDG Communications Verlagsges.mbH, Zieglergasse 6, pg. 570   PV
ING Bank Vienna, Neuer Market 2, pg. 649   IT
ING Finanzberatungs- und Leasing, Neuer Markt 2, pg. 650   IT
IPU - International, Hardtmuthgasse 53, pg. 550   IT
ISS Central Europe GesmbH, Brunner Strasse 85, pg. 656   IT
ISS Securisystem GesmbH, Brunner Strasse 85, pg. 1458   IT
ISS Servisystem GesmbH, Brunner Strasse 85, pg. 657   IT
ITT Flygt GmbH, Heinrich von Buol-Gasse 10, pg. 860   PB
Ideal-Standard, Pasettistrasse 32-35, pg. 92   IT
Imperial Hotels Austria AG, pg. 347   IT
Industrie-Immobilien-Verwaltung GmbH, pg. 347   IT
Industrie- und Forst Verwaltung AG, pg. 347   IT
Intergraph Gmb (Austria), Modecenterstrasse 14, pg. 892   IT
Internationale Bank fur Aussenhandel, A.G., Neuer Markt 1, pg. 447   PB
Interunfall Leasing, pg. 61   IT
Interunfall Versicherung AG, Tegetthoffstrasse 7, pg. 89   IT
INTROPA Beteiligungs GmbH, pg. 347   IT
Investkredit Holding, pg. 347   IT
Italimpianti Intl.-Austria, Weykingergasse 35, pg. 655   IT
Jacobs Kaffee Ges.m.b.H., Jacobsgasse 3, pg. 1288   PB
Janssen/Cilag G.m.b.H., Pfarrgasse 75, pg. 929   IT
Janssen/Cilag Pharmaceutica GmbH, Zweigniederlassung der Johnson, & Johnson, pg. 929   PB
Jauch & Huebener, Blechturmgasse 11, pg. 118   PB
Johnson Matthey & Co. GmbH., Steckhovengasse 12, pg. 714   IT
Julius Meinl Stores, P.O. Box 114, pg. 856   IT
KB Beteiligungs- und Verwatungs GmbH, pg. 347   IT
KME Austria Vertriebsgesellschaft m.b.H., Slama str. 48, pg. 719   IT
KSB Osterreich Ges.mbH, pg. 721   IT
Kenwood Manufacturing GmbH, Elektrogerate, Erzherzog Karl Strasse 57, pg. 730   IT
Kodak Gessellschaft m.b.H., Albert Schweitzer-Gasse 4, pg. 553   PB
Komplett-Burovermietungs GmbH, pg. 347   IT
KONE Sowitsch AG, Forchheimergasse 34, pg. 748   IT
Konica Gesellschaft mbH, Hofbauergasse 3, pg. 749   IT
Korn/Ferry International, Dr. Karl-Lueger-Ring 8, pg. 634   PV
'Kostlin' Nahrungsmittel Ein- und Ausfuhrandel Ges.m.b.H., pg. 856   IT
Krupp Hoesch Stahlvertriebs GmbH, Tenscherstr. 3, pg. 516   IT
Kuehne & Nagel GmbH, Warneckstr. 10, pg. 763   IT
Landis & Staefa (Osterreich) AG, Breitenfurterstrasse 148, pg. 801   IT
Laura Ashley GesmbH, pg. 804   IT
Lederwerke Gerhardus Beteiligungsgesellschaft mbH, pg. 507   IT
Lieferbeton AG, Handelskai 132, pg. 1081   IT
Eli Lilly & Elanco Ges.m.b.H., Huetteldorfstrasse 65, pg. 993   PB
Eli Lilly Ges.m.b.H., Huetteldorfstrasse 65, pg. 993   PB
Linde Kaltetechnik Ges.m.b.H., pg. 810   IT
Lista Betriebs- und Lagereinrichtungen Ges.m.b.H., pg. 812   IT
Lista Buroeinrichtungen Ges.m.b.H., pg. 812   IT
Arthur D. Little International GmbH, Palais Todesco, pg. 670   PV
Loctite Europa Gesellschaft mbH, Akaziengasse 34, pg. 611   IT
Loewa Warenhandel Ges.mbh, Oberlaaer Strasse 300-306, pg. 1375   IT
Louis Vuitton Osterreich Ges.m.b.H., Kohlmarkt 16, pg. 783   IT
Lubrizol Gesellschaft m.b.H., Nibelungengasse 13, pg. 1016   IT
Lucent Technologies Austria Ges.m.b.H., Brigittenauer Lande 50-54, pg. 1018   PB
Luwa Ges.m.b.H., pg. 617   IT

M.A.I.L. Finanzberatung GmbH, pg. 347   IT
Maclean Hunter GmbH, Loquaiplatz 12, pg. 1123   IT
Main-Donau (Rhein-Main-Donau) Speditions GmbH, pg. 1022   IT
Makita Werkzeug Gesellschaft m.b.H., Kolpingstrasse 13, pg. 832   IT
Management Data Datenverabeitungs- und Unternehmensberatung GmbH, pg. 347   IT
Mang/DMB&B, Vienna, Jacquingasse 16-18, pg. 305   PV
Mannesmann Handel GmbH, pg. 838   IT
Mannesmann Tally GmbH, pg. 840   IT
MARESI MARKENARTIKELVERTRIEB AKTIENGESELLSCHAFT, Werdertorgasse 5-7, Postfach 214, pg. 842   IT
Mautner Markhof International GmbH, pg. 753   IT
Mead Coated Board Europe Kartonvertriebs-A.G., Alserbachstrasse 14-16, pg. 1076   PB
Media EMAP Verlag GmbH, Loquaiplatz 12, pg. 451   IT
Medtronic GmbH, Handelskai 388/Top 852, pg. 1083   IT
Meinl Bank AG, Bauernmarkt 2, pg. 856   IT
JULIUS MEINL AG, pg. 856   IT
Julius Meinl Gourmet Ges.m.b.H., pg. 856   IT
Julius Meinl Grosshandels-Ges.m.b.H., Zeillergasse 3-5, pg. 856   IT
Julius Meinl Immobilien Verwaltungs-Vermietungs-vnol Leasing Ges.m.b.H., pg. 856   IT
Julius Meinl Nahrungsmittel Produktions Ges.m.b.H., pg. 856   IT
Memorex Telex Computer Products GesmbH, Wehlistrasse 27 A, pg. 857   IT
Merisel Austria, Traviatagasse 35, pg. 1096   PB
Mettler-Toledo Gesellschaft mbH, Favoritner Gewerbering 17, pg. 4   PV
Microsoft Gesellschaft m.b.H., pg. 1108   PB
Millipore Ges.m.b.H., Heitzinger Hauptstrasse 145, pg. 1113   PB
Mitsui & Co., Ltd., Opernringhof, Opernring I, Stiege E. Zim, pg. 881   IT
Mobil Oil Austria A.G., Schwarzenbergplatz 3, pg. 1119   IT
Monsanto GmbH, Hilton Center Am Stadtpark, pg. 1125   PB
Moore Ges.m.b.H., Paragonstrasse 2, pg. 889   IT
Motorola Center Computersysteme GesmbH, pg. 1139   PB
Motorola Ges.m.b.H., Gartengasse 21, pg. 1139   PB
Moulinex GmbH, Heilgenstaedter Laende 11, pg. 896   IT
MOVIECAM-VOEST-ALPINE kinematographische Gerate Ges.m.b.H., pg. 1470   IT
Munters Trocknungs Service Ges mbH, Dietrichgasse 18, pg. 669   IT
NETG Applied Learning GmbH, Rainergassel, pg. 784   IT
NIFE Ges.m.b.H., Liesing, Eduard Kittenberger-Gasse 56, pg. 53   IT
Nederman Ges.m.b.H., Dirmhirngasse 110, pg. 283   IT
Neste Chemicals Handelsgesellschaft mbH, Linke Wienzeile 236, pg. 914   IT
A.C. Nielsen Co., GmbH, Moeringgasse 20, pg. 1183   IT
NIKE GmbH, Donau Business Centre, pg. 1184   PB
Nordsee Ges. m.b.H., pg. 1438   IT
Novartis-Pharma GmbH, Brunnerstrasse 59, pg. 984   IT
Novell Austria, Theresianumgasse 7, pg. 1204   PB
Novo Nordisk A/S, Landstrasser Hauptstrasse 26, pg. 987   IT
Novo Nordisk A/S, Argentinierstrasse 21, pg. 989   IT
Novo Nordisk Pharma Gesellschaft mbH, Universitatsstrasse 11, pg. 988   IT
Nutricia Nahrungsmittel GmbH, pg. 992   IT
OAF & STEYR Nutzfahrzeuge OHG, Brunner Strasse 44, pg. 825   IT
OAG Gruppe A.G., pg. 1511   IT
OCE Osterreich Ges.m.b.H., Carlbergergasse 38, pg. 995   IT
OKB Vermogensverwaltungs- und Beteiligungsgesellschaft m.b.h., pg. 181   IT
OMV AG, Otto-Wagner-Platz 5, pg. 995   IT
OTOB Clearing Bank AG, pg. 347   IT
Oesterreichische Automobilfabrik, OEAF- Graef & Stift AG, Brunner Strasse 44-50, pg. 825   IT
OFA-Akkumulatoren Ges.m.b.H., Siebenhirtenstrasse 12, pg. 1452   IT
Olicom Austria, Mariahilfer Strasse 103/2/1/42a, pg. 1001   IT
Olivetti Austria G.m.b.H., Breitenfurter Strasse 317-319, pg. 1003   IT
OMRON Electronics Ges.m.b.H., Altmannsdorfer Strasse 142, pg. 1006   IT
Oracle Datenbanksysteme GesmbH, Schoepfleuthnergasse 25, pg. 1228   PB
ORAG Osterreichische Realitaten AG, pg. 347   IT
Organchemie Ges.m.b.H., Hietzinger Hauptstrasse 119, pg. 347   IT
Osterreichische Fernmeldetechnische Entwicklungs- und Forderungs- Ges.mbH, Arsenal, pg. 101   IT
Osterreichische Hotel- und Fremdenverkehrs GmbH, pg. 347   IT
OSTERFEICHISCHE INDUSTRIEHOLDING AG, Kantgasse 1, pg. 1012   IT
Osterreichische Investitionskredit AG, pg. 347   IT
Osterreichische Investment GmbH, pg. 347   IT
Osterreichische Kontrollbank AG, pg. 347   IT
Osterreichische Nestle GmbH, Emil Kralik G 6, pg. 922   IT
OSTERREICHISCHE POSTSPARKASSE AG, Georg Coch-Platz 2, pg. 1012   IT
Osterreichische Rohrbau GmbH, pg. 837   IT
Osterreichische Unilever Ges.m.b.H., Schenkenstr. 8-10, pg. 1438   IT
OSTERREICHISCHEN BUNDESBAHNEN GMBH, Elisabethstrasse 9, pg. 1012   IT
Pall Austria Filter GmbH, pg. 1254   PB
PAM Gas B.V., Zelinkagasse 2/4b, pg. 1155   IT
PAMPAM Warenhandel Ges.m.b.H., Sandleitengasse 41, pg. 856   IT

Panalpina Aktiengesellschaft Wien, pg. 1022   IT
Panalpina Lagerhaus-Immobilien GmbH, pg. 1023   IT
Panduit Corp., Zweigniederlassung, pg. 836   PV
Parker Hannifin N.M.F. GmbH, Handelskai 52, pg. 1261   PB
Pechiney Handelsgesellschaft mbH, Gumpendorferstrasse 65/11, pg. 1031   IT
Perlmooser Zementwerke AG, Operngasse 11, pg. 791   IT
Perstorp & Heinrich Puzelik Ges.m.b.H.-Div. Chemetic, Stachegasse 19, pg. 1037   IT
Perstorp & Heinrich Puzelik Ges.m.b.H-Div. Plastic, Stachegasse 19, pg. 1037   IT
Petrolite Handelsgesellschaft m.b.H., Bruner Strasse 105, pg. 166   IT
Pfizer Corporation Austria G.m.b.H., Mondscheingasse 16, pg. 1283   IT
Pfizer Med-Inform Beratungs G.m.b.H., Mondscheingasse 16, pg. 1283   PB
Pharmacia & Upjohn Biotech, Oberlaaer Strasse 251, pg. 1047   IT
Pharmacia & Upjohn Ges.m.b.H., Oberlaaer Strasse 251, pg. 1050   IT
Pharmacia & Upjohn LKB Instrument GmbH, Wurzbachgasse 18, pg. 1048   IT
Pirelli Gesellschaft M.B.H., Scherestrasse 16, pg. 1059   IT
Pitney Bowes Ges.b.H., Hosnedlgasse 35 Postfach 19, pg. 1304   PB
Pohang Iron & Steel Co., Ltd., Mariahilfer Strasse 136, pg. 1062   IT
Polaroid Austria A.G., Eitnergrasse 5A, pg. 1314   PB
PolyGram Record Services Ges. mbH, Kreilplatzl, pg. 1053   IT
Post Telecom Austria Beteiligungs Gmbh, Postgasse 8-10, pg. 101   IT
Pro Fleisch Be- und Verarbeitungs Ges.m.b.H., pg. 856   IT
Procter & Gamble Austria GmbH, Mariahilferstr. 77-79, pg. 1332   PB
RIL VIII Raifeisen Immobilien Leasing GmbH & Co., pg. 181   IT
Radex-Heraklith Industriebeteiligungs, A.G., Opernring 1, pg. 904   PV
Radio-Austria AG, Wiedner Haupstrabe 73, pg. 101   IT
RAIFFEISEN ZENTRALBANK OSTERREICH, Am Stadtpark 9, pg. 1084   IT
Refractories Consulting & Engineering GmbH, c/o Opernring 1 A-1010, pg. 904   PV
Reichhold Chemie GmbH, Breitenleer Strasse 97-99, pg. 370   IT
Renner Ges.m.b.H., pg. 856   IT
Rohol-Aufsuchungs, pg. 1158   IT
Rowenta-Vertriebsgesellschaft mbH, Deutschstrasse 5, pg. 569   IT
Ruf Datensysteme GmbH, pg. 618   IT
ST Liegendchaftsverwertungs AG, pg. 347   IT
Sachs Riedl GmbH, pg. 835   IT
St. Marx Branch, Marktareal, pg. 1084   IT
Sandoz Forschungsinstitut Gesellschaft m.b.H., Brunnerstrasse 59-65/Ob.:6, pg. 984   IT
Sandoz Forschungsinstitut Handelsgesellschaft m.b.H., pg. 984   IT
Sandvik in Austria Ges.m.b.H., Scheydgasse 44, pg. 1186   IT
Sandvik Process Systems Ges.m.b.H., P.O. Box 7, pg. 1187   IT
Sanpaolo Bank (Austria) A.G., Tuerkenstrasse 9-A, pg. 692   IT
Satel Fernseh- und Filmproduktions GmbH, pg. 347   IT
SCHENKER & Co. AG, pg. 1460   IT
Schering Wien Ges.m.b.H., Scheringgasse 2, pg. 1204   IT
Schindler Aufzuge und Fahrtreppen AG, pg. 1205   IT
Schmalback-Lubeca Austria Ges.m.b.H., pg. 1207   IT
Scholl Oesterreisch GmbH, Hutteldorferstrasse 46, pg. 1210   IT
Scholl s.r.o., c/o Scholl Oesterreich GmbH, Hutteldorferstrasse 46, pg. 1210   IT
Scholler Beteiligungs GmbH, pg. 181   IT
Scholler Dienstleistungs GmbH, pg. 181   IT
Scholler Holding AG, pg. 181   IT
Scholler Leasing Gesellschaft mbH, pg. 181   IT
Scholler Leasing Gesellschaft mbH & Co. KG, pg. 181   IT
Scholler Munzhandel GmbH, pg. 181   IT
Schollerbank AG, pg. 181   IT
Schweizerischer Bankverein, Naglergasse 25, pg. 1330   IT
Semperit AG Holding, pg. 347   IT
Senna Nohrungsmittel GmbH, Stockhammerngasse 19, pg. 842   IT
Sequent Computer Systems (Austria), Loisl-Spiel Zach, pg. 1459   PB
Sharp Electronics GmbH, Handelskai 342, pg. 1230   IT
Shell Austria AG, Renweg 12, pg. 1138   IT
Shimizu C.A. Ges.m.b.H., Gonzagagasse 15/2/4, pg. 1314   IT
Siegling-Austria Ges.m.b.H., pg. 498   IT
Siemens AG Oesterreich, Siemensstrasse 88-92, pg. 1247   IT
Siemens Nixdorf Informationssysteme Ges.m.b.H., Obere Donaustrasse 23-27, pg. 1245   IT
Skandia Leben AG, Postfach 10, pg. 1258   IT
SmithKline & French Intl., GmbH, Renning 17, pg. 1265   IT
Sony Ges.m.b.H., 23 Jochen Rindt-Str. 15, pg. 1284   IT
Sorbus Ges.mbH, Millergasse 16, pg. 204   PB
Stahl Chemical Industries bv GmbH, Bleibtreustrasse 2/1, pg. 1526   IT
Steyr Bus Gesmbh, Zweite Haidequerstrasse 3, pg. 1477   IT
Steyr-Daimler-Puch AG, pg. 347   IT
Steyr-Daimler-Puch Fahrzeugtechnik GmbH, pg. 347   IT
Strobelgasse 2, Strobelgasse 2, pg. 1377   IT
Substantia Gesellschaft m.b.H., Ketzergasse 118, pg. 1739   PB

PB - U.S. Public Companies Volume
PV - U.S. Private Companies Volume
IT - International Public & Private Companies Volume

Sukab Intertrade GesmbH, Taborstrasse 13, pg. 712   IT
Sulzer Infra Anlagen- und Gebaudetechnik Gesellschaft m.b.H, pg. 1306   IT
The Sumitomo Bank, Ltd.-Vienna Representative Office, 3rd Fl., Room No. 338, Borsegebaude, Borsegasse 11, pg. 1310   IT
Sumitomo Metal Industries, Ltd. (Vienna Liaison Office), Land Strasser Hauptstrasse, pg. 1316   IT
Sun Chemical AG, Perfektastrasse 82, pg. 371   IT
Sun Electric Austria G.m.b.H., Hochstrasse 18-20 A2380 Perchtoldsdorf, pg. 1481   PB
Svedala Austria, pg. 1324   IT
Swift Austria GmbH, Percostrasse, pg. 370   IT
Symbol Technologies GmbH, Prinz-Eugenstrasse 70, pg. 1546   PB
Technische Gase GmbH, Postach 139, pg. 14   IT
Tefal Handelsgesellschaft mbH, Deutschstrasse 5, pg. 568   IT
TEMPO-Vertriebsges fur hygienische Artikel m.b.H, Rudolfinergasse 12, pg. 1333   IT
Thomainfor, Franzosengraben 12, pg. 1385   IT
Thomson-CSF Austria GesmbH, Franzosengraben 12, pg. 1385   IT
Touristik Assekuranz Service GmbH, Storchengasse 1, pg. 89   IT
Trans Austria Gasleitung GmbH, pg. 429   IT
Tyco Toys (Osterreich) Ges.m.b.H., Gunoldstrabe, pg. 1059   IT
UPM-Kymmene Papier GmbH, Mariannengasse 14/2/3, pg. 1430   IT
Uniferm GmbH, Brede 4, pg. 1143   IT
Unifrost Nahrungsmittel Ges. m.b.H., Schenkenstrake 8-10, pg. 1439   IT
Union Carbide Austria GmbH, c/o Price Waterhouse, Prins-Eugen-Strasse 72, pg. 1667   PB
Universale-Bau AG, pg. 347   IT
Urban & Schwarzenberg GmbH, Frankgasse 4, pg. 1748   PB
VDO Austria GmbH, pg. 839   IT
VSH Beteiligungsgesellschaft m.b.H., pg. 181   IT
Valmet Ges.m.b.H., Franzosengraben 12, pg. 1448   IT
VARTA Batterie Ges.m.b.H., Postfach 35, Siebenhirtenstrasse 12, pg. 1452   IT
Vereinigte Kaffee-Grossrostereien 'Arabia-Mikado' Kaffeevertriebsges.m.b.H., pg. 347   IT
Vereinigte Papierindustrie-und Allgemeine Warenhandels AG, pg. 347   IT
Verlag Das Beste GmbH, Singerstrasse 2, pg. 1368   PB
Verlag Kremayr und Scheriau, Niederhofstr. 37, pg. 192   IT
Vermogensverwaltungsgesellschaft mbH, pg. 181   IT
Vienna Representative Office, Turkenstrasse 25, pg. 520   IT
VIMPEX Handelsgesellschaft mbH, pg. 458   IT
VOEST-ALPINE Rohstoffhandel Ges.m.b.H., Schottenfeldgasse 79, pg. 1470   IT
VOEST-ALPINE Stahlhandel AG, Lembockgasse 51, pg. 1470   IT
Voith-Elin Electronik GmbH, pg. 1473   IT
Volta Elektrowaren-Vertriebsgesellschaft GmbH, Postfach 51, pg. 441   IT
WABCO Westinghouse G.m.b.H., Hochstadtplatz 4, Postfach 49, pg. 92   PB
WAGO Kontakttechnik Ges mbH, Laxenburger Strasse 244, pg. 209   IT
Wander Gesellschaft m.b.H., pg. 986   IT
Werner & Pfleiderer AG Bakery Equipment, Tenscherstr. 3, pg. 511   IT
Werner & Pfleiderer Maschinentechnik Ges. mbH, Tenschnerstr. 3, pg. 511   IT
Wiener Allianz Lebensversicherungs-AG, Hiezinger Kai 101-105, pg. 62   IT
Wiener Allianz Versicherungs-AG, Heitzinger Kai 101-105, pg. 62   IT
Wienerberger Baustoffindustrie AG, pg. 347   IT
Wiener-Kuhlhaus Frigoscandia Ges.m.b.H., Franzogengraben, pg. 607   PB
Wirtschaftswoche Zeitschriften-Verlagsgesellschaft m.b.H. & Co. KG, Seidengasse 11, pg. 1479   IT
Yashica Handelsgesellschaft mbH, pg. 776   IT
Yokohama Austria GmbH, Kolbegasse 66, pg. 1521   IT
Young & Rubicam GmbH, Marc Aurel-Strasse 4, pg. 1199   PV
Zeidler GmbH, Schonbrunner Allee 28, pg. 97   IT
Zeneca Osterreich GmbH, Postfach 153, pg. 1527   IT
Zurich Kosmos Versicherungen AG, Schwarzenbergplatz 15, pg. 1532   IT

Viktring

Adidas Sportschuhfabriken Gmbh, Adi-Dassler-Gasse 2, pg. 25   IT

Voesendorf

Honeywell-Measurex International GmbH, Eisgrubengasse 2, pg. 833   PB
MSI Data Austria, 18 Ortsstrasse, pg. 1546   PB

Waldegg

Granges Metallhandels-ges. GmbH, Hauptstrasse 51, pg. 440   IT

Wartberg

Schiedel Kaminwerke GmbH, Auern 99, pg. 1092   IT

Weikendorf

Luxottica Vertriebsgesellshaft mbH, Birkengasse 4, pg. 822   IT

Wels

A. Ahlstrom Ges.m.b.H., Kienzlstrasse 13, pg. 34   IT
H.B. Fuller Austria GesmbH, Kaplanstrasse 30, pg. 687   PB
C.H. Knorr Nahrungsmittelfabrik, Ges. mb H., Knorrstrasse 8, Postfach 168. pg. 225   PB
Liebherr-Verkehrstechnik GmbH, Handelskai 134, pg. 808   IT
Martin Merkel Vertriebsgesellschaft mbH, Rablstraasse 25, pg. 860   IT

Wiener Neustadt

L. Bosendorfer Klavierfabrik GmbH, Gymelsdorfergasse 42, pg. 958   PB
Castrol Austria GmbH, 17-Noe-Sued Strasse 6, pg. 235   IT
Crawford Tor Ges.m.b.H., IZ No-Sud Strasse 7, Objekt 58/ B 4, pg. 269   IT
Flender Ges. m.b.h., IZ NO Sud, Strasse 4, Objekt 14, pg. 400   IT
Kvaerner Pulping Ges. mbh, Triester Strasse 14, pg. 768   IT
Parker Ermeto GmbH, Badener Str. 12, pg. 1261   PB
STILL Ges.m.b.H., pg. 811   IT
Toshiba Medical Systems Gesellschaft GmbH, Industriezentrum No-Sud Ricoweg 40, pg. 1407   IT
Uddeholm Tooling GesmbH, Industriezentrum NO-Sud, Str. 1, pg. 1472   IT

Wimpassing

Scapa-Kern GmbH, Triester Bundestrassa 26, pg. 1203   IT

Zistersdorf

Durr Anlagenbau Ges.m.b.H., Dur-Weg 2, pg. 422   IT

AZERBAIJAN

Baku

Caspian Shipyard Company Limited, 5th Fl.,Hajiyew Lane, pg. 731   IT
Energy Logistics Azerbaijan Ltd., pg. 749   PB
FELS Baku Ltd., 5th Fl., Hajiyew Lane, pg. 731   IT
Ram Representative Office-Azerbaijan, B. Safarogly Str. 539 KV, pg. 741   IT
Statoil Baku, BP Exploration, Ulitsa Krepostaya 42, pg. 1298   IT

BAHAMAS

Eleuthera

Windmere Island Club, pg. 1213   IT

Freeport

Bahamas Oil Refining Co. (BORCO), pg. 1046   IT
Guerlain Western Hemisphere Co. Ltd., Bonded Warehouse B, Queens Hwy., pg. 780   IT
Pegasus Engineering Ltd., W. Sunrise Hwy., pg. 922   PB
Uniroyal Chemical Company Limited, West Sunrise Highway, pg. 460   PB

Great Inagua

Inagua General Store, Ltd., Matthewtown, pg. 1135   PB
Morton Bahamas Ltd., Matthewtown, pg. 1135   PB

Nassau

Banco Santander Trust & Banking Corporation (Bahamas) Ltd., P.O. Box N-1682, Bahamas Financial Center, 3rd Fl., pg. 143   IT
Bank of Boston Trust Co. (Bahamas) Limited, Charlotte House, P.O. Box N3930, pg. 185   IT
The Bank of Nova Scotia International Limited, Scotiabank Building, Rawson Square, pg. 156   IT
The Bank of Nova Scotia Trust Company (Bahamas) Limited, Scotiabank Building, Rawson Square, pg. 156   IT
BankAmerica Trust & Banking Corp. (Bahamas) Ltd., BankAmerica House, E. Bay St., pg. 183   PB
Bankers Trust New York Corporation, Claughton House, pg. 186   PB
Bastogi International Ltd., St. Andrews Court, Frederic St. Steps, pg. 170   IT
Casu Transport Limited, pg. 431   IT
Cedrala Transport Limited, pg. 431   IT
Chase Manhattan Trust Cayman Ltd., P.O. Box N3708, pg. 340   IT
The Chase Manhattan Trust Corporation Limited, Shirley/ Charlotte Streets, pg. 341   PB
Cititrust (Bahamas) Ltd., pg. 379   IT
Colina Insurance Company Limited, 12 Village Road, pg. 363   PB
Coutts & Co (Bahamas) Limited, West Bay Street, pg. 911   IT
Coutts & Co Trust Holdings Limited, pg. 911   IT
Dai-ichi Life Bahama Limited, pg. 362   IT
Dan Merchanr Limited, pg. 431   IT
Dow Jones (Bahamas) Limited, c/o Higgs & Caroll, Madeira & Montrose Ave., pg. 525   PB
Dunkin' Donuts (Bahamas) Ltd., P.O. Box N-8340, pg. 63   IT
Equator Advisory Services Limited, Suite 102, Saffrey Square, Bank Lane and Bay Street, pg. 580   IT
Equator Bank Limited, Suite 102, Saffrey Square, Bank Lane & Bay Street, pg. 580   IT
Esso Standard Oil S.A. Limited, Windsor Field Rd., pg. 602   IT
Ferrier Lullin Bank & Trust (Bahamas) Limited, Swiss Bank House, East Bay Street, pg. 468   IT
Finance Corporation of Bahamas Limited, Bahamas Financial Centre, Charlotte Street, pg. 1131   IT
First RepublicBank Dallas, N.A., 50 Shirley St., pg. 1165   IT
Handelsfinanz-CCF Bank (International), P.O. Box 10441, pg. 343   IT
Hang Seng Bank (Bahamas) Limited, 2/F, Euro Canadian Centre, pg. 583   IT
Harris Trust & Savings Bank, P.O. Box N 7768, pg. 154   IT
Hercules International Trade Corp., Ltd. (HINTCO), pg. 811   PB
HongKong Bank (Bahamas) Limited, Claughton House, Corner Shirley and Charlotte Streets, pg. 583   IT
IBM Bahamas Limited, pg. 896   PB
ITB Corporation, pg. 1346   IT
The Industrial Bank of Japan Trust Company (Nassau Branch), NatWest Building, West Bay Street, pg. 675   IT
Kyoei Fire & Marine Investment (Bahama) Ltd., P.O. Box N-7788, West Bay St., pg. 777   IT
Lloyds Bank (Americas) Ltd., Bolam House, pg. 813   IT
Lloyds Bank International Ltd., Bolam House, pg. 813   IT
Morgan Guaranty Trust Company, Bahamas Financial Centre, Charlotte & Shirley Sts., pg. 1130   PB
Morgan Trust Company of The Bahamas Limited, Bahamas Financial Centre, Charlotte & Shirley Sts., pg. 1131   IT
Nassau/Bahamas Transatlantic bulk Carriers Inc., pg. 514   IT
Natcan Holdings International Limited, Charlotte House, Charlotte Street, pg. 907   IT
National Bank of Canada (International) Limited, Charlotte House, Charlotte Street, P.O. Box N3015, pg. 907   IT
NatWest International Trust Corporation (Bahamas) Limited, West Bay St., pg. 911   IT
NatWest International Trust Holdings Limited, pg. 911   PB
New World Development Corp. Ltd., pg. 447   PB
Paribas Suisse (Bahamas) Ltd., Woodstar East Bay St., pg. 321   IT
Polydex Pharmaceuticals Limited, Sandringham House, 83 Shirley Street, pg. 1063   IT
Rentokil Bahamas Ltd., Box N395, pg. 1286   IT
Republic National Bank of New York (Intl.) Ltd., pg. 1381   IT
The Royal Bank of Scotland (Nassau) Limited, 50 Shirley St., pg. 1133   IT
Santander Investment Bank, Bahamas Financial Center 3rd Fl., pg. 143   IT
Scotia Realty Bahamas Limited, Scotiabank Building, Rawson Square, pg. 156   IT
Shell Bahamas Ltd., Thompson Boulevard, pg. 1141   IT
The Sumitomo Trust & Banking Co., Ltd., pg. 1317   IT
Swiss Bank Corporation (Overseas) Ltd., Claughton House, Corner Shirley & Charlotte Sts., pg. 1332   IT
TGH Holdings, Ltd., Box N-7759, pg. 680   PB
Taiyo Life Investment (Bahamas), Ltd., Nat West Bldg., West Bay St., pg. 1349   IT
Texaco Bahamas Ltd., P.O. Box N4807, pg. 1584   IT
Tokio Marine International Fund (Bahama) Company Limited, West Bay St., pg. 1393   IT
Trident Enterprise Ltd., Bitco Building, pg. 298   IT
Wardley International Limited, Suite 102, Saffrey Square, Bank Lane and Bay Street, pg. 582   IT
Wireless Network Ventures Ltd., pg. 1140   IT

BAHRAIN

Manama

ANZ Grindlays Bank plc Offshore Banking Unit, 1st Floor, Manama Centre, pg. 99   IT
The Arab-Eastern Insurance Company Limited E.C., United Gulf Bank Bldg., 4th Fl., Diplomatic Area, pg. 1392   IT
Arabia Cigna Insurance Company Limited E.C., Manama Center, Ste. 404, 114 Government Rd., pg. 363   PB
BMMI Engineering Services, pg. 1128   PB
Bahrain Representative Office, pg. 1485   IT
Bankers Trust New York Corporation, First Fl., West Wing, Manama Centre, pg. 186   PB
Banque Paribas, Offshore Branch, Bahrein Tower-Ground Floor, pg. 319   IT
Banque Paribas-Bahrain, Full Commercial Branch, Bahrein Tower-Ground Floor, pg. 319   IT
Baring Asset Management (Bahrain) Ltd., Bahrain Commercial Complex, Suite 801, pg. 648   IT
Biokat International (Bahrain) EC, pg. 836   IT
COMSIP AL A'Ali W.L.L., pg. 53   IT
The Chase Manhattan Bank, N.A., pg. 339   PB

Geographic Index-Non U.S.

Commerzbank AG Representative Office-Bahrain, UGB Tower, 4th Floor, Diplomatic Area, pg. 311   **IT**
Dai-Ichi Kangyo Bank, Ltd.-Bahrain, 6th Floor, Part 3, Manama Centre, pg. 361   **IT**
Daiwa Middle East E.C., 7th Fl., The Tower, Bahrain Commercial Complex, pg. 375   **IT**
Delmon Ready Mixed Concrete & Products Co. W.L.L. (Bahrain), pg. 1092   **IT**
Det Norske Veritas, Manama Centre, Entrance No. 4, 5th Fl., pg. 398   **IT**
Deutsche Bank AG (Bahrain), P.O. Box 20619, Manama Ctr., Entrance 1, pg. 404   **IT**
Diamond Stationery Est., pg. 108   **IT**
Dresdner Bank AG, Yateem Centre, pg. 419   **IT**
Robert Fleming Holdings Limited, P.O. Box 2467, pg. 494   **IT**
Gajria Electronics, pg. 108   **IT**
Grindlays Bahrain Bank B.S.C. (c), Manama Centre, pg. 100   **IT**
Gulf Assist E.C., Manama Centre Building, Suite 587, pg. 334   **IT**
Gulf Petrochemical Industries Co., P.O. Box 5090, pg. 766   **IT**
Inchcape Middle East, Bldg. No. 57, AL Salmaniya Rd., Block 327, pg. 672   **IT**
The Industrial Bank of Japan, Limited (Bahrain), Manama Ctr., Entrance 4,4th Fl, pg. 675   **IT**
Intermarkets Bahrain, Al Fateh Bldg., Al Khalifa Rd., pg. 680   **IT**
The International Commercial Bank of China, Aboleatih Building, Block No. 319, Al-Hoora Area, pg. 683   **IT**
INVESTCORP INTERNATIONAL, pg. 686   **IT**
Jalal-Costain W.L.L., P.O. Box 5985, pg. 337   **IT**
Kobelco Middle East (E.C.), P.O. Box 2309, 1st Fl., Zayani House, pg. 741   **IT**
Lucent Technologies Middle East W.L.L., 1 Hedaga, 6th Fl., Government Avenue, pg. 1019   **IT**
Milk Products Holdings (Middle East) EC, Rm. 301, 3rd Fl., Entrance 3, Manama Ctr., pg. 923   **IT**
Mitsui & Co. (Middle East) E.C., Manama Center, Room No. 101, Part 2, pg. 882   **IT**
Mitsui & Co., Ltd., Manama Center, Rm. No. 101, Part 2, pg. 882   **IT**
National Bank of Pakistan-Manama, 9 Manama Centre, pg. 908   **IT**
Nikko Investment Banking (Middle East) E.C., 3rd Loor, Unitag House, Government Road, pg. 931   **IT**
Nippon Credit Bank Ltd.-Bahrain, Sheraton Tower, Gate 3, Isa Al-khabeer Ave., pg. 933   **IT**
Nissho Iwai Middle East E.C., Building No. 315, Block 317, Room No. 604-606, Diplomat Tower, pg. 948   **IT**
Nomura Investment Banking (Middle East) E.C., 10th & 11th Floor, BMB Centre, Diplomatic Area, pg. 957   **IT**
PENCO Process Engineering Co. W.L.L., Office No. 1, Bldg. 3636, Road 1862, pg. 550   **IT**
The Sakura Bank - Representative Office for the Middle East, 3rd Fl, Part II, Manama Center, Government Road, pg. 1180   **IT**
Standard Chartered Bank (Bahrain), Government Road, pg. 1295   **IT**
The Sumitomo Bank, Ltd.-Bahrain Representative Office, No. 406 & 407, Entrance 3, 4th, Fl., Manama Center, pg. 1309   **IT**
Sumitomo Finance (Middle East) E.C., No. 405 (Entrance 3, 4th fl.), Manama Centre, pg. 1310   **IT**
Telefon AB LM Ericsson Bahrain, Office no. 42, 4th floor, Building no. 44, Road no. 1701, pg. 1370   **IT**
Thomas De La Rue Ltd., House 17, Yateem Gardens, Building 2614, Road 2766, pg. 386   **IT**
Toyota Motor Corporation, Bahrain Representative Office, P.O. Box 3099, pg. 1413   **IT**
UBS Representative Office Ltd., Unitag House, 4th Fl., Government Avenue, pg. 1441   **IT**
Wael Pharmacy, P.O. Box 648, pg. 823   **PB**
Westpac Banking Corporation-Bahrain, Office 24, 4th. Flr., Kanoo Comml. Center, pg. 1497   **IT**
Willis Faber EC, Willis Faber WLL, pg. 1510   **IT**
Yamaichi International (Middle East) E.C., U.G.B. Building, Bldg. 440, Flat 21, Road 1705, Block 317, pg. 1518   **IT**
Yusuf Bin Ahmed Kanoo, pg. 110   **IT**
Zayani Computer Systems, 46 Tariq Bdg., Government Ave., pg. 824   **PB**
Zurich Insurance Services (Middle East) E.C., Suite 302, Entrance 2, Manama Centre, pg. 1532   **IT**

Sitra

Circle Freight International (Bahrain) Ltd., Bldg. 903, Road 115, Block 601, pg. 372   **PB**

BANGLADESH

Chittagong

CIBA-GEIGY (Bangladesh) Limited-Pesticides Plant, 10/11, Sholoshahar Light, pg. 976   **IT**
Lever Brothers Bangladesh Ltd., pg. 1437   **IT**
Mitsui & Co., Ltd., Chamber House, 4th Fl. Agrabad, Commerci, pg. 881   **IT**

Dhaka

ANZ Grindlays Bank plc Bangladesh, No. 2 Dilkusha C.A., pg. 98   **IT**
BASF Bangladesh Limited, H.R. Bhaban, 4th Fl., 26/1, Kakrail Rd., pg. 105   **IT**
BOC Bangladesh Ltd., pg. 121   **IT**
Bangladesh Tobacco Co. Ltd., pg. 111   **IT**

Bitopi Advertising Ltd., 822/3 Shewapara, (Bejum Rokeyo Sharani), pg. 184   **PV**
Blackwood Hodge (Bangladesh) Ltd., 56 Dilkusha Commercial Area, 2nd Fl., pg. 231   **IT**
Burroughs Wellcome & Co (Bangladesh) Ltd, pg. 553   **IT**
CIBA-GEIGY (Bangladesh) Ltd., House 50, Road 2A, Dhanmondi Resid. Area, pg. 976   **IT**
Det Norske Veritas, Wasa Bhaban, 1st Fl., 27/34, karwan bazar C/A, pg. 398   **IT**
Fisons (Bangladesh) Limited, pg. 1111   **IT**
Gestetner Bangladesh Ltd., 69-70 Motijheel Comml. Area, pg. 1115   **IT**
Habib Bank Ltd., 53 Motijheel, Commercial Area, pg. 584   **IT**
IBCS-Primax Software Ltd., House 4, Road 7, pg. 1228   **PB**
ICI Bangladesh Limited, Chamber Building, pg. 664   **IT**
Mitsui & Co., Ltd., BCIV Bhavan, 30-31 Dilkusha C.A., pg. 881   **IT**
National Bank of Pakistan-Dhaka, 79, Motijheel Commercial Area, pg. 908   **IT**
Nestle Bangladesh Ltd., pg. 921   **IT**
Network Marketing Limited, 35 Topkhana Rd., pg. 822   **PB**
Rhone-Poulenc Bangladesh Ltd., 29 Topkhana Rd., Ranma, pg. 1112   **IT**
SmithKline & French (Bangladesh) Ltd., 5 Dhanmondi Residential Area, pg. 1265   **IT**
Standard Chartered Bank (Bangladesh), 18-20 Motijheel Commercial Area, pg. 1295   **IT**
Telemach Limited, 25, Kakrail Road, pg. 550   **IT**
The World Bank, 3A Paribagh, pg. 1189   **PV**

Motijheel

The General Electric Company of Bangladesh Ltd., Magnet House, 72 Dilkusha Commercial Area, pg. 546   **IT**

Tongi

CIBA-GEIGY (Bangladesh) Limited-Pharmaceuticals Plant, Squibb Road, pg. 976   **IT**

BARBADOS

Barbados

Sandy Bay Hotel Limited, c/o Sandy Lane Hotel, pg. 684   **IT**

Bridgetown

American International Management Co. (Barbados) Ltd., ALICO Bldg., Cheapside, pg. 85   **PB**
Aroaima Bauxite Company Ltd., Nile House, West Indies, pg. 1386   **PB**
Atlantic International Reinsurance Company Ltd., ICB Building, Upper Roebuck Street, pg. 1333   **IT**
Bank of Commerce Trust Company Barbados Limited, pg. 257   **IT**
The Bank of Nova Scotia Trust Company (Caribbean) Limited, Broad Street, pg. 157   **IT**
The Barbados Light & Power Co. Ltd., C.P.O. Box 142, pg. 990   **PB**
British-American Tobacco Co. (Barbados) Ltd., pg. 111   **IT**
CCG Capital Limited, The Ernst & Young Bldg., Bush Hill, Bay St., pg. 326   **IT**
CCG Equipment Limited, The Ernst & Young Bldg., Bush Hill, Bay St., pg. 326   **IT**
CIEL Caribbean International Equipment Ltd., The Ernst & Young Bldg., Bush Hill, Bay St., pg. 326   **IT**
CLCL Caribbean Interantional Capital Ltd., The Ernst & Young Bldg., Bush Hill, Bay St., pg. 326   **IT**
Caribbean Antilles Molasses Co. Ltd., pg. 1357   **IT**
Chase Export Corporation, Collymore Rock, pg. 337   **PB**
Cirrus Logic International Ltd., Harbour Indus. Park, Bldg. 6, pg. 375   **PB**
Cognos Barbados Ltd., Alleyne House, White Park Rd., pg. 306   **PB**
Colgate-Palmolive, pg. 398   **IT**
European Finance Reinsurance Company Ltd., Chancery House, High Street, pg. 1333   **IT**
European International Reinsurance Company Ltd., Chancery House, High Street, pg. 1333   **IT**
HTI Export Ltd., pg. 851   **PB**
Henkel Chemicals (Barbados) Ltd., pg. 614   **IT**
Huron Capital Limited, The Ernst & Young Bldg., Bush Hill, Bay St., pg. 326   **IT**
International Distillers Caribbean, pg. 410   **IT**
MDI Caribe Limited, Bay Street, pg. 1139   **PB**
Manitowoc International Sales Corp., Bay St., pg. 1041   **PB**
Manulife Data Services Inc., The Ernst & Young Bldg., Bush Hill, Bay St., pg. 841   **IT**
Mobil Oil Barbados, Ltd., Garrison St. Michael, West Indies, pg. 1119   **IT**
Natcan Insurance Company Limited, Alleyne House, White Park Foad, pg. 907   **PB**
Science Applications International, Barbados, pg. 976   **PV**
Shaw International Limited, Bush Hill, Bay Street, pg. 1231   **PB**
Texaco Interamerican Exploration Co., pg. 1584   **PB**

Christchurch

Barclays Bank PLC, Caribbean, pg. 166   **IT**
Falconbridge International Ltd., Suite 201, Stevmar House, pg. 434   **IT**
Lucent Technologies Foreign Sales Corporation, c/c Chase Trade, Inc., Stevmar House, Ste. 2 Rockley, pg. 1019   **PB**

Saint Michael

Amgen Sales Corporation, c/o Corporate Services Ltd., Collymore Rock, pg. 101   **PB**
BNS International (Barbados) Limited, 3rd Floor, International Trading Centre, pg. 156   **IT**
Barbados Dairy Industries Ltd., pg. 923   **IT**
Camarin Limited, P.O. Box 1304, Collymore Rock, pg. 829   **PB**
Computers & Controls Barbados Ltd., Ste. 5, 1st Fl., W.I., pg. 817   **PB**
R.R. Donnelley Barbados, Bldg. 4, Wiley Industrial Park, WI, pg. 519   **PB**
Electrolux Ltd., Fontabelle, St. Michael, pg. 441   **IT**
Ensopack Ltd., pg. 458   **IT**
Reliance National (Barbados) Insurance, Ltd., P.O. Box 634C, W.I., pg. 1374   **PB**
Royal Bank of Canada Financial Corporation, Royal Bank House, The Garrison, P.O. Box 48B, pg. 1132   **IT**
Scotia Insurance (Barbdos) Limited, 3rd Floor, International Trading Centre, Warrens, pg. 156   **IT**
Soje/Lonsdale Advertising Inc, 11th Ave., pg. 1422   **PB**
UTILX International Product Sales Inc., The Financial Services Ctr., Bishop's Ct. Hill, pg. 1701   **IT**
Yogen Fruz (Barbados) Inc., Price Waterhouse Centre, Collymore Rock, pg. 1520   **IT**

Saint Thomas

Clearly Canadian International, Golden Anchorage House, 1st Fl, pg. 297   **IT**

Wildey

Moore Paragon (Caribbean) Limited, No. 7 Wildey Industrial Park, pg. 889   **IT**

BELARUS

Minsk

Robert Bosch t.a.a., Warwascheni 17, pg. 206   **IT**
CIBA-GEIGY Services Ltd., ul Krasnozwezdnaya, 8 kom 27, pg. 979   **IT**
Commerzbank AG Representative Office-Minsk, Tschitscherim Strasse 21, pg. 312   **IT**
Sandvik-Bisov, pg. 1186   **IT**
Vertretung der BASF in Belarus, Pr. Masherova 5, pg. 109   **IT**
The World Bank, 6A Partizansky Avenue, 5th Floor, pg. 1190   **PV**
Zeneca Minsk, Ul. Kazinta, 62, pg. 1527   **IT**

BELGIUM

Aalst

Amylum N.V., 10, Burchstraat, pg. 1357   **IT**
CAD Service NV, pg. 1357   **IT**
Campina N.V./S.A., Groeneweg 5b, pg. 254   **IT**
Dart Industries Belgium NV, 35, Pierre Corneliskaai, pg. 1357   **PB**
FMC Europe NV, Denderstraat 56, pg. 606   **PB**

Aalter

I.M.W.V. C.V., pg. 437   **IT**

Aarschot

Battenfeld Belgium N.V., Nieuwlandlaan 1A, pg. 825   **IT**
N.V. Duracell Batteries, S.A., 7 Nijverheidslaan, pg. 743   **PB**
S.A. DuraCell Benelux N.V., 7 Nijverheidslaan, pg. 743   **PB**
Swish Benelux NV/SA, pg. 925   **IT**

Aartselaar

CW Lease Belgium, Ingberthoeveweg 6, pg. 648   **IT**
ING Lease Belgium, Ingberthoeveweg 6,lok C, pg. 650   **IT**
Munters NV, Ingberthoeveweg 3E, pg. 669   **IT**
Rothenberger Benelux bvba, Antwerpsesteenweg 59, pg. 1129   **IT**
S.A. Tenneco Belgium (Poclain-Monroe-Petro-Tex) N.V., Boomsesteenweg 20, pg. 1580   **PB**

Alken

Gomala Imtech NV, Hendrikstraat 118, pg. 681   **IT**

Alleur

Notifier (Benelux) S.A., Avenue de l'Expansion, 16D, pg. 1307   **IT**
Nouvelles Editions Marabout, 30, avenue de l'Energie, pg. 796   **IT**

Anderlecht

Siegener Benelux SA/NV, Boulevard Paepsem 22, pg. 508   **IT**

PB - *U.S. Public Companies Volume*
PV - *U.S. Private Companies Volume*
IT - *International Public & Private Companies Volume*

1510

Geographic Index-Non U.S.

Ans

N.V. Lawn Comfort S.A., Parc Industrielle, 12 rue Wallonie, pg. 355   IT

Antwerp

ABN International Diamond Division, Pelikaanstraat 70-76, pg. 11   IT
ASLK-CGER, Lange Klarenstrasse 19, pg. 17   IT
Acer Belgium N.V., pg. 22   IT
Agfa-Gevaert N.V., Septestraat 27, pg. 174   IT
Allianz Nederland N.V. in Fa. Stanislas H. Haine S.A., Amerikalei 106, pg. 60   IT
Allianz Versicherungs-AG, Amerikalei 106, pg. 61   IT
ALMANIJ N.V., Schoenmarkt 33, pg. 65   IT
Amoco Fina N.V., Scheldelaan 6, pg. 102   PB
Analog Devices International Inc., Justitiestraat 18, pg. 108   PB
Antwerp Local Head Office, 20 Lange Gasthuisstraat, pg. 147   IT
Antwerpe Diamantbank, Pelikaanstraat 54, pg. 546   IT
Antwerpese Diamantbank N.V., 54 Pelikaanstraat, pg. 147   IT
BASF Antwerpen N.V., Haven 725, Scheldelaan 600, pg. 105   IT
BBL Flemish Region, 12 Lange Gasthuisstraat, pg. 147   IT
Bank of America NT&SA, Uitbreidingstraat 180, Box 6, pg. 182   PB
Banque Indosuez, Grote Markt 9, pg. 314   IT
Banque IPPA, Brusselsestraat 45, pg. 562   IT
Bayer Antwerpen N.V., Kanaaldok B1, pg. 174   IT
Bijhuis Antwerpen, Uitbreidingstraat 46, pg. 312   IT
BolsWessanen Coordination Center, pg. 752   IT
Boreas S.A. IARD, Lombardenvest 34, pg. 61   IT
CCMP N.V., Katwilgweg 15, pg. 678   IT
C.N.P. S.A., Eikenstraat 9, pg. 1415   IT
CPC-Monda N.V./S.A., St. Pietersvliet 7 bus 4, pg. 224   PB
Castrol NV, 107, Helmstreet, pg. 236   IT
Cat Pumps International N.V., Harmoniestr. 29, pg. 336   PV
Cinevideo Enterprises NV, pg. 720   IT
DCD (Belgium) N.V., pg. 596   IT
Damco Maritime (Belgium) N.V., pg. 1144   IT
De Vaderlandsche Insurance, Desguinlei 92, pg. 648   IT
De Vaderlandsche Spaarbank N.V., Desguinlei 92, pg. 648   IT
Det Norske Veritas, Amsterdamstraat 18, pg. 397   IT
Deutsche Bank AG (Antwerp), Postbus 228, Arenbergstraat 23, pg. 403   IT
Eij Imtech NV, Bisschoppenhof Straat 145, pg. 681   IT
Eij Imtech N.V., Bisschoppenhoflaan 145-149, pg. 682   IT
Eclipse Combustion bv, G. Blondeau & Zn. B.V.B.A., pg. 361   PV
S.A. Enso N.V. Enso West, Wilmarstraat, pg. 437   IT
Eurotherm BV (Belgian Branch), Herentalsebaan 71-75, pg. 466   IT
Fidelis NV, Schoenmarkt 33, pg. 65   IT
Fidelitas NV, Van Eycklei 14, pg. 65   IT
Fina Antwerp Olefins N.V., Scheldelaan 10, pg. 1043   IT
Fina Chemicals Antwerpen N.V., Scheldelaan 2-4, pg. 1043   IT
Fina Raffinaderij Antwerpen N.V., Scheldelaan 16, pg. 1044   IT
Ford Credit N.V., Boite Postal 37, Kanaaldok 200-204, pg. 666   PB
Ford Motor Company (Belgium) N.V., Boite Postal 37, pg. 666   PB
Gamatex N.V., Scheldelaan Kanaaldok B2, pg. 692   PB
General Motors Continental, Noorderlaan 75 Postbus 9, pg. 722   PB
Gerlach & Co. N.V., pg. 1144   IT
Getinge-D.S.E. NV, Napoleankaai 51, pg. 551   IT
Hydro Finance Consultancy NV, Lange Nieuwatraat 21-23, pg. 65   IT
IGAO, Uitbreidingstraat 584, pg. 437   IT
ITT Promedia N.V., Antwerp Tower, pg. 1447   IT
Imea C.V., pg. 437   IT
Indufor (1975) n.v., pg. 431   IT
Interensco N.V., 1 Stoopstraat, pg. 682   IT
Jacky S.A., pg. 920   IT
N.V. Jacky, S.A., Antwerp Tower, de Keyserlei 5, pg. 1437   IT
Axel Johnson & Co. N.V. Marin Division, Oudaan 22-24 Box 1, pg. 711   IT
KATOEN NATIE NV, Van Aerdtstraat33, pg. 724   IT
Kredietbank NV, Schoenmarkt 35, pg. 65   IT
Krefima NV, Mechelsesteenweg 180-184, pg. 65   IT
Lazare Kaplan Belgium N.V., pg. 981   PB
Livingston International Freight Belgium, Verbindingsdok O.K. 17, pg. 373   PB
Luber-Finer, Europe, N.V./S.A., Waterwilgweg, 4, pg. 1113   PV
MacGREGOR (BEL) N.V., Luithagen Haven 2e, pg. 670   IT
MacWarehouse, Frankrijklei 152, pg. 1104   PB
Maison Mathieu, 572   IT
MAISON MATHIEU, S.A., Van Putlei 14, pg. 846   IT
Mitsui & Co., Ltd., 20th Fl., Antwerp Tower, De Keyserlei 5, pg. 881   IT
Muller Liner Agencies N.V., Antwerp, 9, Ankerrui, pg. 682   IT
Muller-Thomsen Antwerpen, Styfselrui 44, pg. 682   IT
NYK Bulkship-Brussels, c/o Van Ommeran Antwerpen NV, 42 St. Paulusstraat, pg. 941   IT
NYK Line Benelux-Antwerp, Batavia Bldg., Amsterdamstraat 18, pg. 942   IT
Nedlloyd Lines Belgium N.V., pg. 1145   IT
Nedlloyd Road Cargo N.V., pg. 1145   IT

Neste Shipping Benelux, N.V., Britselei 3, Bus 1, pg. 915   IT
Nynas Petroleum N.V., 4e Havendok-Kaaien 279-285, pg. 915   IT
Omniver NV, Schoenmarkt 33, pg. 65   IT
Panalpina World Transport N.V., pg. 1023   IT
N.V. Perexma, pg. 1447   IT
Perstorp Flooring NV, Vlaamse Kaai 90, pg. 1039   IT
N.V. Prometal, Ijzerlaan 11, pg. 550   IT
Rabobank Belgie, Antwerp Branch, Frankrijklei 156-158, pg. 1082   IT
Red Band Services N.V., Britselei 15, bus 5, pg. 245   IT
Rickmers-Linie Belgium N.V., pg. 596   IT
SNC-Lavalin, Sint Pietersvliet, pg. 1162   IT
N.V. Sandoz Nutrition S.A., pg. 985   IT
SARCA N.V., pg. 811   IT
Saval N.V., 7, Griffinstraat, pg. 681   IT
Spectra-Physics Belgium BVBA, North Trade Bldg., pg. 1290   IT
Stinnes Belgium N.V., pg. 1460   IT
W. Swanstrom & Co. S.p.r.l., Italielei 217, bus 8, pg. 966   IT
Swift Kleefstoffen BvbA, Industrie Park Den Hoek, Volveld 21, pg. 370   IT
Taylor Instrument N.V., Maarschalk Gerardstraat 8, pg. 6   IT
Telekempo C.V., pg. 437   IT
Thyssen Haniel Logistics, Bourdeaux 8, pg. 1388   IT
Tijdschriften Uitgevers Maatschappij, Jan Blockxstraat 7, pg. 1447   IT
Trans Polymer International N.V., pg. 1145   IT
Union Carbide Benelux NV, 147, Noorderlaan, pg. 1667   PB
Union N.V., Antwerp Tower, de Keyserei 5, pg. 1439   IT
VGL Rail Cargo N.V., pg. 1145   IT
VRG Belgie NV, pg. 757   IT
Windmoller & Holscher N.V., Meir 44A, pg. 1511   IT
Wisapaper Benelux B.V., America House, Amerikalei 122/2A, pg. 1430   IT

Arlon

Interlux S.C., pg. 437   IT

Asse

N.V. Dell Computer S.A., Doornveld 1, B 15, pg. 496   PB
Polypenco NV, Industriezone, Hof te Bollebeeklaan 12, pg. 354   IT

Aubange

S.A. Espace Mobile International E.M.I., Zoning Industrial, pg. 301   IT

Awans

KONE Belgium S.A., Rue de Bruxelles 174, pg. 747   IT

Union-Transport N.V. S.A., Brucargo Bldg. 734, pg. 1120   PV

Balen

S.A. OmniChem N.V. Balen Plant, Dynamietlaan, pg. 41   IT

Baudour

AEP/Borden S.A., Route De Wallonie, pg. 5   PB
Pirelli S.A.C.I.C., Parc Industriel, pg. 1059   IT

Beersel

Century Oils N.V., pg. 517   IT
N.V. Dieetcentrum-Wander S.A., pg. 981   IT
Fardem NV, Industriezone A, Toekomstlaan 18, pg. 353   IT
Janssen Pharmaceutica N.V., 30 Turnhoutseweg, pg. 930   PB
Ortho Clinical Diagnostic N.V., Antwerpseweg 19-21, pg. 931   PB

Beloeil

Battaille S.A., Rue O. Battaille 172, pg. 728   IT
Engrais Battaille S.A., pg. 728   IT
Haumont Mestsoffen N.V., pg. 728   IT
S.A. Sabfran, Brunelle & Cie, pg. 728   IT

Ben-Ahin

Lafarge Refractaires Monolithiques Benelux, Chaussee d'Andennes 138, pg. 791   IT

Berchem

Bobst Benelux N.V., pg. 198   IT
Tioxide Europe NV/SA, Uitbreidingsstraat 66, pg. 666   IT
Trace Belgium, Coreman Sstraat 34, pg. 1095   PV
N.V. Van Melle S.A., Koninklijke Laan 76, pg. 1451   IT

Beringen

Beringen, Schoebroekstraat 20, pg. 1341   IT
Borealis N.V., Industrieweg, P.O. Box 13, pg. 914   IT
Hercules Belgium N.V., Postbus 1, Industrieweg Z/N, pg. 810   PB
Neste P.A.O. N.V., Industrieweg, P.O. Box 4, pg. 915   IT

Beveren

Berendsen PMC N.V./S.A., Keetberglaan 6, pg. 1285   IT
RQB Montagebedrif N.V., Keetberglaan 5, pg. 400   IT
Tevelo N.V., pg. 437   IT

Blehories

S.A. Legrain, rue de Pont de Moulde 33 A, pg. 301   IT

Boortmeerbeek

DYWIDAG-Systems International N.V., Industrieweg 25, pg. 424   IT

Bornem

BMW Belgium S.A./N.V., Lodderstr. 16, pg. 178   IT
BMW Coordination Center N.V., pg. 178   IT
S.A. Capsugel N.V., Rijksweg 11, pg. 1739   PB
N.V.A. Schulman Plastics, S.A., Pedro Colomalaan 25, pg. 1441   PB
N.V. Nutricia Belgie, pg. 992   IT
N.V.A. Schulman Plastics, S.A., Pedro Colomalaan 25, pg. 1441   PB
Sigma-Aldrich N.V., K. Cardijnplein, pg. 1472   PB

Braine-l'Alleud

Aisin Europe S.A., Parc Industriel de la Vallee du Hain 21, pg. 39   IT
Bubbe S.A., 11, avenue de l'Artisanat, pg. 295   IT
Eldon S.A., Avenue de L'Industrie 13, pg. 436   IT
Forbo Decor S.A., pg. 497   IT
Nairn Floors Benelux S.A., pg. 498   IT
O.C.A. S.A., Chaussee de Tubize 489, pg. 1415   IT
Seditel S.C., pg. 437   IT
UCB-Bioproducts SA, pg. 1427   IT
UCB SA Pharma Sector, pg. 1427   IT

Braine-le-Chateau

Ferguson Machine Co. S.A., Pare Industriel 33, pg. 457   PB

Brasschaat

Begemann Belgium N.V., Bredabaan 906, pg. 1134   IT
Begimmo N.V., Bredabaan 906, pg. 1134   IT
SKBM N.V., Bredabaan 906, pg. 1134   IT

Bruges

N.V. Beleggings-en Kredietkantoor Van Poperinge, Diksmuidse Heerweg 47, pg. 90   IT
De Clerck N.V., pg. 1207   IT
Genencor International N.V., Komvest 43, pg. 349   IT
Gist-Brocades Benelux N.V., St. Peterskaai 75, pg. 1142   IT
SNT Calberson, pg. 1164   IT
Tevewest N.V., pg. 437   IT

Brussels

ADC Europe NV, Belgicastraat 2, 1930 Zaventem, pg. 4   PB
ADT Europe, Saifi Tower, Ave. Louise 326, pg. 1649   PB
AGA nv/sa, Waversesteenweg 1519, pg. 13   IT
AGG - SA Alusuisse Guy Geisler NV, pg. 68   IT
AMP Belgium, pg. 8   PB
A.M.P. Transports, Chaussee de Mons 576, pg. 795   IT
AMS Management Systems Europe, SA, NV, Em. Jacqmainlaan 157-4th Fl., pg. 87   PB
ARI Group Europe, Bedryfspork Keiberg Excelsion Laan 9, pg. 1650   PB
ASB Interim, St. Lazaruslaan 10, pg. 1463   IT
AXA Belgium, Avenue de la Toison d'Or, pg. 19   IT
Aaciphar nv, 13 Marnixlaan, pg. 44   IT
Abay Engineering, Rue de Geneve, n4-Bte n 24, pg. 1361   IT
Accor TRB, Avenue Louise 326, pg. 21   IT
Accordination, Avenue Louise 326, pg. 21   IT
Adaptec Europe, S.A., Avenue Tedesco 5, pg. 21   PB
Aer Lingus, Avenue Louise 91/93, pg. 28   IT
Aeronet Europe, 19 Rue Capouillet, pg. 1573   PB
Agence Belge Bulow Bennet & Cie, Avenue de Tervueren 297, pg. 966   IT
Agence et Messageries de la Presse, 1, rue de la Petite-Ile, pg. 795   IT
Aidi Center S.P.R.L., Rue Osseghem 53, pg. 463   IT
Air Products S.A., Chaussee de Wavre, 1789, pg. 32   PB
Air Sea Broker Belgium N.V., pg. 1022   IT
Albright & Wilson B.V., Square Vergote 1, Box 1, pg. 49   IT
Alfa-Laval Flow Equipment, Ave. Louise 65, Bte. 9, pg. 1379   IT
S.A. Alfa-Laval N.V., 333, Rue du Progres, pg. 1379   IT
Alfigen S.A., pg. 1015   IT

Geographic Index-Non U.S.

Algemene Bank Nederland (Belgie) N.V., Regentlaan 53, pg. 12 IT
Allianz AG (EU Representative Office), Avenue des Arts 44, pg. 59 IT
AlliedSignal Chemicals, Saifi Tower, Avenue Louise, pg. 52 PB
AlliedSignal Europe S.A., Avenue Louise 480-Bte 4, pg. 52 PB
Allinsure, Rue du Damier, pg. 532 IT
Almaver NV, Verenigingstraat 44a, pg. 65 IT
Alpha Contact, 3 Montagne du Parc, pg. 546 IT
Alpha Credit, Rue Ravenstein 60, bte 15, pg. 546 IT
Alpha Life SA, Montagne du Parc 3, pg. 546 IT
Amcor Flexibles Europe, Avenue Hermann-Debroux 46, pg. 72 IT
Amgen N.V., Avenue Marcel Thirylaan 200, pg. 101 PB
Aniserco S.A., Rue Osseghem 53, pg. 463 IT
Ansul S.A., 63 rue de Stalle, pg. 1651 PB
Apple Computer SA, 105A, rue Colonel Bourg, pg. 121 PB
Aquinter S.A., Place du Trone 1, pg. 1415 IT
Aramark Belgium, S.A., Ave. Louise 326, pg. 79 PV
Arjo Wiggins Interservices S.A., Blvd. Leopold II 184, pg. 568 IT
Artic N.V. S.A., G. Huysmanspin 1 Lot, pg. 1064 PV
Asahi Chemical Industry - Brussels Office, Ave. Louise 326, pg. 84 IT
Asahi Property Belgium S.A./N.V., AG Bldg., Bd, Emile Jacqmain 53, pg. 85 IT
Ascom Hasler SA, 60, rue de la Fusee, pg. 87 IT
Ascom Timeplex SA, 10, rue de Geneve, pg. 87 IT
The Associated Press (Belgium) S.A., Boulevard Charlemagne, pg. 92 PV
Assurances de la Poste, Chaussee d'Anvers 167, pg. 562 IT
N.V. Astra Pharmaceuticals S.A., 16, rue des Trois Arbes, pg. 94 IT
Auto 5, Rue du Damier 26, pg. 533 IT
Auxfina, Avenue Van Nieuwenhuyse 6, pg. 562 IT
Auxinvest S.A., Place du Trone 1, pg. 1415 IT
Award Services SA, Chee. de Wavre 1789, pg. 532 IT
BASF Aktiengesellschaft EG-Verbindungsbuero, 50, Boulevard du Regent, pg. 105 IT
BASF Belgium S.A./N.V., Avenue Hamoir 14, Hamoirlaan 14, pg. 105 IT
BASF Polyurethane, Avenue Hamoir 14, Hamoirlaan 14, pg. 107 IT
BB Europe-Banco do Brasil N.V., Rue du Trone 14-16, pg. 141 IT
BBL Capital Management Corporation, 24 Ave. Marnix, pg. 147 IT
BBL Central Region, 60 Cours Saint Michel, pg. 147 IT
BBL Insurance, 60 Cours St. Michel, pg. 147 IT
BBL Insurance Brokerage, 60, Cours St. Michel, pg. 147 IT
BBL Life, 60 Cours St. Michel, pg. 147 IT
BDDP Belgique, 40, rue Souveraine, pg. 117 IT
BLD Europe S.A., Avenue Brugman 60, pg. 394 IT
BMG Ariola Belgium NV, Square Francois Riga 30/68, pg. 192 IT
Banca Monte Paschi Belgio, 24, rue Joseph II, pg. 147 IT
Banca Nazionale del Lavoro, Avenue Louise, 66 Bte. 6, pg. 137 IT
Banco di Napoli-Brussels, 66 Blvd. de l'Imperatrice, pg. 140 IT
Banco Hispano Americano-Benelux, S.A./NV, Rue de la Loi, 227, pg. 140 IT
Banco Santander, Chaussee de Forest, 26, pg. 144 IT
BANK BRUSSELS LAMBERT, Avenue Marmix 24, pg. 146 IT
Bank Card Company, Bd. E. Jacqmain, 159, pg. 147 IT
The Bank of New York, Avenue des Arts 35 Kunstlaan, pg. 179 PB
The Bank of Tokyo-Mitsubishi, Ltd. (Brussels Branch), Avenue des Arts 39, Bte. 1, pg. 158 IT
Bank of Yokohama (Europe) S.A., 287 Avenue Louise, pg. 159 IT
Bankers Trust New York Corporation, Rue des Colonies, 54 BTEI, pg. 186 PB
Banksys, 1442, chaussee de Haecht, pg. 147 IT
Banque Belgolaise, Cantersteen 1, pg. 546 IT
Banque de La Poste, Rue de la Chancellerie 1, pg. 547 IT
Banque Europeenne pour l'Amerique Latine (BEAL) S.A., Rue de l'Associataion 59, pg. 1493 IT
Banque Indosuez Belgique, Place Sainte Gudule 14, pg. 314 IT
Banque IPPA, Boulevard du Souverain 23, pg. 562 IT
Banque Nagelmackers SA, Place de Louvain 12, pg. 447 PB
BANQUE NATIONALE DE BELGIQUE, Boulevard de Berlaimont 14, pg. 162 IT
Banque Paribas Belgique, Boite 2, WTC, Tour de Paris et des Pays-Bas, pg. 319 IT
Barclays Bank PLC, Avenue Louise 65, pg. 166 IT
Bascule-Rest, Chee. de Waterloo 605, pg. 532 IT
Bayer Belgium S.A.-N.V., Louizalaan 143, pg. 175 IT
Bayer Owens/Corning Glasswool S.A., 178, Chaussee De La Hulpe, pg. 175 IT
Bazimo, Rue du Damier, 26, pg. 533 IT
S.A. Beiersdorf NV, Boulevard Industriel 30, pg. 183 IT
Bel RTL, 1, avenue Ariane, pg. 561 IT
Belfin S.A., Rue Royale 54, pg. 1415 IT
Belfox, 2, rue Henri Maus, pg. 147 IT
Belgamanche S.A., Place du Trone 1, pg. 1415 IT
Belgatom S.A., Avenue Ariane 7, pg. 1415 IT
S.A. Belge Le Carbone, 124, boulevard du Jubile, pg. 1030 IT
Belgian Pipe Control S.A., Rue Guimard 4, pg. 1415 IT
Belgian Shell, S.A., 47 Cantersteen, pg. 1138 IT
Belgica Insurance Holding S.A., 149, Avenue Louise, pg. 90 IT
Belgium Union des Assureurs, Belgique, 16, Place Rouppe, pg. 784 IT
Belgonucleaire S.A., Avenue Ariane 4, pg. 1415 IT
Belgoest S.A., 5, avenue du Col-Vert, pg. 1274 IT
Bell Atlantic Europe S.A., Twin House, 107 Rue Neerveld, pg. 204 PB
Bellsouth Europe, Ave. Louise 65, Bte. 3, pg. 208 PB
Benelux Division, pg. 423 PB
Bepac SC (Ropac Products), Rue de la Jonction 7, pg. 1339 IT
S.A. Bergiers N.V., Rue Bollinckxstraat, 28, pg. 281 IT
Berlitz Schools of Languages of Benelux S.A., 306-310 Avenue Louise, pg. 222 PB
Bernheim-Comofi, Rue du Trone 98, pg. 562 IT
BIC Benelux S.A., Ch. de Haecht 55, pg. 1273 IT
Bigg's SA, Av. des Olympiades, 20, pg. 533 IT
Bios-Coutelier SA, pg. 1427 IT
Black & Decker (Belgium) N.V., Weihoeki 1, pg. 234 PB
Bohler S.A., N.V. 77, Caussee de Ninove, pg. 1471 IT
Bombardier Eurorail, Avenue Louise, 65, pg. 200 IT
Bonifica-Belgium, Av. de Tervuren 32, B.te 29, pg. 655 IT
Robert Bosch Produktie NV, Rue Henri Genesse, 1, pg. 206 IT
N.V. Robert Bosch SA, Rue Henri Genesse, pg. 206 IT
Brambles Europe S.A., Avenue Herrmann-Debroux 44-46, pg. 212 IT
Brambles Industries Ltd., 18 Square de Meeus, pg. 212 IT
Brico Belgium SA, Rue du Damier, 26, pg. 533 IT
Bridgestone/Firestone Europe, S.A., Woluwe Office Park, pg. 214 IT
Bristol-Myers Belgium S.A, N.V., Chaussee De La Hulpe, Terhulpsestw. 185, pg. 255 PB
S.A. Brother International (Belgium) N.V., Industrialaan 32, pg. 229 IT
Bull Eurocenter, 41 ave. de Tervueren, pg. 318 IT
S.A. Bull N.V., 41 Ave. de Tervueren, pg. 318 IT
Leo Burnett Brussels, Chaussee de Wavre 1789, pg. 185 PV
CB Direct, Kolonel Bourgstraat 133, pg. 464 IT
CC Banque Belgique, Rue du Fosse aux Loups 32, pg. 144 IT
CCF Bussels, 46 Avenue des Arts, pg. 342 IT
C.E.A.I S.A., rue de l'Industrie, 52, pg. 1043 IT
CIWLT Mere & Succursales, 51-53 bd Clovis, pg. 21 IT
COMSIP Automation Benelux, S.A., 311, avenue de la Couronne, pg. 53 IT
CPC Europe Consumer Foods Division, 300 Avenue de Tervuren, pg. 224 PB
Cabot Plastics International, Avenue des Pleiades 11, pg. 289 PB
Cariplo (Bruxelles), Avenue Louise 250, pg. 275 IT
CARITAS Centrale d'Articles de Marques S.A., Rue de la Grenouillette 2 G-1, pg. 1101 IT
Carpenter Technology (Europe) S.A., Blvd. Auguste Reyers 207-209, pg. 308 PB
Caterpillar Commercial N.V., Chaussee de la Hulpe, pg. 316 PB
S.A. Cebelor, Rue Prince Baudouin 108, pg. 710 IT
Celsius Industries Corporation European Affairs Office, 33 Boulevard de la Cambre, pg. 278 IT
Cemstobel, Vaartstraat 59, pg. 1463 IT
Centre de Coordination Hachette Distribution Services, 1, rue de la Petite-Ile, pg. 795 IT
Centre International de Paiements Europ Assistance S.C., 75, Rue Bosquet, pg. 90 IT
N.V. Cerberus SA, Paepsem Business Park, pg. 1246 IT
N.V. Certanium Services S.A., Ave. Hipposcrateslaan No. 2, pg. 1068 IT
The Chase Manhattan Bank, N.A., Avenues des Arts 52, pg. 339 PB
Chaussem, 1, rue de la Petite-Ile, pg. 795 IT
S.A. Chaussures Bally Schoenen N.V., 8 Rue de Suisse, pg. 997 IT
Chefaro nv, 13 Marnixlaan, pg. 44 IT
Chemviron Carbon, Boulevard de Woluwe 60, pg. 293 PB
Chep Europ S.A., 18, Square de Meeus, pg. 212 IT
Cheque Restaurant, Rue du Doyenne, 56, pg. 1274 IT
Christiaensen International, Rue du Damier 26, pg. 533 IT
Chubb Insurance Company of Europe, 35 Square de Meeus, pg. 355 PB
Chuo Trust & Banking Company (Europe) S.A., Rue de la Loi 15, pg. 291 IT
Cigna Insurance Company of Europe, S.A.-N.V., Rue Belliard 9-11, pg. 364 PB
Cigna Life Insurance Company of Europe S.A.-N.V., Rue Belliard 9-11, pg. 364 PB
Cigna Reinsurance Company S.A.-N.V., Boulevard du Regent 37-40, pg. 365 PB
S.A. Cimenteries CBR, Chaussee de La Hulpe 185, pg. 605 IT
CINTA Compagnie Independante des Tabacs S.A., Avenue Georges Rodenbach 29, pg. 1101 IT
Citensy S.A., Rue Montoyer 63, pg. 1415 IT
Clairol Division, Ch. La Hulpe, Terhulpsestw. 185, pg. 255 PB
Clestra Hauserman Belgium, Athens Gallery 175, Bvld. Emile Jacqmainlaan 162, pg. 570 IT
Club Mediterranee S.A. Belge, 58 rue Ravenstein, pg. 298 IT
Club SA, Rue du Damier, 26, pg. 533 IT
Cobepa S.A., World Trade Center, pg. 321 IT
Cocetrel S.A., Place du Trone 1, pg. 1415 IT
COCKERILL SAMBRE, Chaussee de La Hulpe 187, pg. 301 IT
S.A. Cockerill Sambre Finances et Services C.S.F.S., 187 ch de le Hulpe, pg. 301 IT
Codic S.A., Clausee De La Hulpe 130, pg. 414 IT
Coditel Brabant S.A., Rue des Deux Eglises 26, pg. 1415 IT
Colgate-Palmolive Belgium, Ba de la Woluwe 58, pg. 398 PB
Comdisco Belgium S.P.R.I., pg. 408 PB
Commerzbank AG, Boulevard Louis Schmidt 87, pg. 311 IT
Compagnie Coppee de Developpement Industriel-CDI, 251, av. Louise, pg. 790 IT
Compagnie d'enterprises CFE, 164, chaussee de la Hulpe, pg. 823 IT
Compagnie Immobiliere de Belgique S.A., Avenue Jean Dubrucq 175 bte 1, pg. 1415 IT
Compagnie Internationale D'assurances et Reassurances (CIAR), 45, Rue de Treves, pg. 335 IT
COMPAREX Information Systems S.A./N.V., Boulevard General Wahis 16a, pg. 108 IT
S.A. Comptoir Finlandais N.V., Ave. des Gaulois 7, pg. 457 IT
ConAgra-Europe, Inc., Av. Tervueren 168, pg. 429 PB
Conception et Coordination Leopold S.A., Avenue Louise 500, pg. 1415 IT
Conquest Europe S.A., Gulledelle 98, pg. 1484 IT
Contassur Assistance-Conseil S.A., Place du Trone 1, pg. 1415 IT
Contassur S.A., pg. 437 IT
Coordination Center Volkswagen S.A., pg. 1475 IT
Corvita Europe S.A., Av. J Wybran 40 A 1070, pg. 1282 PB
Cote d'Or S.A., 40, rue Bara, pg. 1288 PB
S.A. John Crane Belgium N.V., 46 rue Grisa, pg. 1339 IT
CREDIT COMMUNAL DE BELGIQUE SA, Blvd. Pacheco 44, pg. 343 IT
Credit Lyonnais Belgium, 17, avenue Marnix, pg. 344 IT
Crock'in SA, Rue du Damier 26, pg. 533 IT
Crompton & Knowles Tertre SA., Ave. de la Reine 141, pg. 460 PB
N.V. Crown-Baele S. A., Industriepark, pg. 464 PB
Crush International, 1 rue de Philippe Le Bon, pg. 248 IT
D & B Software Belgium, Tour Leopold, pg. 532 IT
DB (Belgium) Finance S.A./N.V., 100, Blvd. du Souverain, pg. 403 IT
DMR Group (Belgium) S.A.-N.V., Rue de la Fusee 62, pg. 528 IT
DRI Europe, Inc., Rue Camille Lemonnier 1, pg. 1072 PB
DSM Belgium N.V., Boulevard du Souverain 100 Vorstlaan, pg. 355 IT
DSM Resins Belgium N.V., Nieuwbrugstraat 73, pg. 355 IT
Dai-Ichi Kangyo Bank, Ltd.-Brussels, Blue Tower, 13B, Avenue Louise 326, pg. 361 IT
Damixa S.A., Van Volxemlaan 328, pg. 1054 PB
Danone, Ave. De Broqueville, 12, pg. 379 IT
Darci Pharma SA, pg. 1427 IT
Data General S.A., 191 Boulevard Du Soverain Bte. 11, pg. 486 PB
Datapoint Belgium S.A., Rue de la Fusee 100 Bte. 13, pg. 384 IT
Delhaize the Lion Coordination Center S.A., Rue Osseghem 53, pg. 463 IT
Delimmo S.A., Rue Osseghem 53, pg. 463 IT
Delshop S.A., Rue Osseghem 53, pg. 463 IT
Dentsu Europe-Brussels, 475 Avenue Louise Bre 6, pg. 393 IT
Detrick Belge, rue du Magistrat, 2, pg. 789 IT
Deutsche Bank AG (Brussels), 100, Blvd. du Souverain, pg. 403 IT
Dexter Europe, Av. H. Debroux 15A, pg. 505 PB
Dicalite Europe Nord, S.A., Av. Louise 430-Bte. 2, pg. 903 PV
Dicalite Trading, S.A., Av. Louise, 430-BTE 2, pg. 903 PV
A.B. Dick S.A., Chaussee de Louvain 451, pg. 791 PV
Digital Equipment N.V./S.A., Luchtschipstraat 1, Rue de L'Aeromep, #1, pg. 508 PB
Diligentia Business Press nv, pg. 1445 IT
S.A. Dirame, Au Poplimont Laan 49, pg. 710 IT
Disport International, Rue du Damier 26, pg. 533 IT
Distrilease B.S.E.T., Rue du Damier 26, pg. 533 IT
Distripipe S.A., Rue Guimard 4, pg. 1416 IT
Distrirest, Rue du Damier 26, pg. 533 IT
Dour, Rue d'Argent 8, pg. 533 IT
Dow Jones Markets Belgium SA, 273 Avenue de Tervuren, pg. 525 PB
Dow Jones Publishing Company (Europe) Inc., Hilton Tower, Boulevard de Waterloo 39/7A, pg. 525 PB
Du Pont de Nemours (Belgium) S.A., Raketstraat, Rue de la Fusee 100, pg. 532 PB
Dun & Bradstreet Eurinform SA-NV, Avenue des Pleiades 73, Plejadenlaan 73, pg. 536 PB
Duphar & Cie S.N.C., Boulevard Emile Bockstael 122, pg. 1277 IT
S.A. Durco Europe N.V., 6 rue de Geneve, pg. 659 PB
EGT, Rue de la Grenouillette 2B, pg. 795 IT
EIB Brussels Branch, rue de la Loi 227, pg. 465 IT
EMC-Belgique, Rue de Trone 130, pg. 459 IT
EMI Belgium SA, Kolonel Bourgstraat 128, pg. 427 IT
EMI Music Publishing (Belgium) SA, 140B Ave. Eugene Plasky-B.13, pg. 427 IT
S.A. ESAB N.V., Avenue Jules Bordetlaan 15, pg. 282 IT
Ebam, Rue d'Argent 8, pg. 533 IT
Edelman Europe, Avenue de Tervuren BA, pg. 363 PV
Editeco S.A., Rue de Birmingham 131, pg. 1415 IT
Editions Francophones Belges sa (EFB), pg. 1447 IT
Eldon International S.A., 128, Avenue Moliere, pg. 436 IT
ELECTRABEL S.A., 8, Blvd. du Regent, pg. 436 IT
Electrafina, 24, Avenue Marnix, pg. 562 IT
Electric Protection Services (EPS), Saifi Tower, Ave. Louise 326, pg. 1650 PB
Electricite de France, 47/48 boulevard de Regent, pg. 438 IT
Electrolux-Martin S.A., Rue Nestor Martin 315, pg. 441 IT
Elkem Benelux S.A., Boulevard Charlemagne 27A, pg. 447 IT

PB - U.S. Public Companies Volume
PV - U.S. Private Companies Volume
IT - International Public & Private Companies Volume

Elsevier Training NV, Leuvensesteenweg 325, pg. 1100   IT
ELVIA Assurances S.A., Avenue des Arts 23, pg. 60   IT
EMTEC Magnetics Benelux N.V., Avenue Hamoirlaan 79, pg. 743   IT
S.A. Enso N.V., Ave. des Gaulois 7, pg. 457   IT
Equator, 82, avenue Brugmann, pg. 602   IT
Equinox Communications, Rue Lietart 16-18, pg. 1152   PV
Ericsson Business Communications NV/SA, 40 rue de la Fusee, pg. 1366   IT
Ericsson European Support Centre, 40 rue de la Fusee, pg. 1366   IT
Esplanade Leopold S.A., Avenue Louise 500, pg. 1416   IT
Esso Inc., Boulevard du Souverain 280, pg. 602   PB
ETABLISSEMENTS DELHAIZE FRERES ET CIE "LE LION" S.A., 53 rue Osseghem, pg. 462   IT
Etmofina S.A., rue de l'Industrie 52, pg. 1043   IT
Eufradis SPRL, Av. des Olympiades, 20, pg. 533   IT
Eurest Belgium SA, 51-53, bd Clovis, pg. 21   IT
Euro Reinsurance Brokers S.A., 149, Avenue Louise, pg. 91   IT
Eurocermex N.V., Rue Colonel Bourg107, pg. 115   PB
Euroclear Operations Centre, Boulevard Emile Jacqmain 151, pg. 1130   PB
Euroguard SA, Rue Mercelis, 31, pg. 533   IT
Eurolease, Rue des Colonies 62, pg. 547   IT
Europ Assistance Services S.A., 75, Rue Bosquet, pg. 91   IT
Europaea-Assurance Protection Jurdique S.A., 149, Avenue Louise, pg. 91   IT
Europay Belgium S.C., Rue E. Jacqmain 159, pg. 147   IT
European Owens-Corning Fiberglas SA, 178 Chaussee de La Hulpe, Box 7, pg. 1237   PB
Evelec S.A., pg. 437   IT
FAG Belgium S.A. N.V., pg. 469   IT
FCB Brussels, Avenue Louise 65, pg. 389   PV
FMC Europe, S.A./N.V., Ave. Louise 523, pg. 606   PB
FMC Food Machinery Europe, S.A., Ave. Louise, 523, pg. 606   PB
Falconbridge Europe S.A., 150, Chaussee de la Hulpe, Bte 15, pg. 434   IT
Falconbridge International S.A., 150, Chaussee de la Hulpe, Bte 18, pg. 434   IT
Fallek Chemical S.A., Ave. Franklyn Roosevelt 81, pg. 553   PV
Famibank S.A., pg. 379   PB
Family Buffets, Rue du Damier 26, pg. 533   IT
Ferrosan Healthcrafts NV/SA, Chaussee de Haecht 1801, pg. 989   IT
Fidabel NV, Regentlaan 54, pg. 65   IT
Fimagroup SA, Rue du Damier, 26, pg. 533   IT
Fimaser, Rue Neuve 77, pg. 533   IT
Fimeuse S.A., Place du Trone 1, pg. 1415   IT
Fina Europe S.A., rue du Commerce 93, pg. 1043   IT
Fina Exploration Norway, S.A. (FEN SA), rue-de l'Industrie, 52, pg. 1043   IT
Fina Exploration Norway, SCA (FENSCA), rue de l'Industrie, 52, pg. 1043   IT
Fina Insurance S.A., rue de l'Industrie 52, pg. 1043   IT
Fina Life S.A., rue de l'Industrie 52, pg. 1043   IT
Fina Marine S.A., rue de l'Industrie, 52, pg. 1043   IT
Finacta, 24, Avenue Marnix, pg. 561   IT
Finmeccanica-Belgium, Bd. du Regent 40, pg. 654   IT
Finop, Rue d'Argent 8, pg. 533   IT
Finpipe G.I.E., Rue Guimard 4, pg. 1416   IT
S.A. Firet, N.V., Dandermondesti 51, pg. 686   PB
Georg Fischer NV-SA, Vaartdijk 109-11 Digue du Camal, pg. 489   IT
Fleetguard International Corporation, 3 Avenue Val Duchesse, pg. 469   IT
Fleishman-Hillard Brussels, rue de L'Industrie, 11-bte 18, pg. 411   PV
Florixelles, 44, rue de Namur, pg. 782   IT
Forbo Krommenie S.A., Cartond e Wiartln 74, pg. 497   IT
Fortis, Boulevard Emile Jacqmain 53, pg. 500   IT
Fortis International N.V., Boulevard Emile Jacqmain 53, pg. 499   IT
Forum Leopold S.A., Avenue Louise 500, pg. 1416   IT
Fotolabo Club S.A., Rue des Pavots 50, pg. 501   IT
Fournex N.V., Avenue Louise 287, pg. 1265   IT
Francia-Lotus S.A., Avenue Victoria 22, pg. 672   PB
Fruitasol BV, 7 Avenue Edmond Candries, pg. 491   IT
G-Securities, Montagne due Parc 3, pg. 547   IT
GB LEX, Avenue du Nieuwenhuyse 6, pg. 562   IT
GB Unic SA, Rue Nueve, 111, pg. 533   IT
GFI TB La Mondiale Bull, 15 rue Vergote, pg. 318   IT
GGK Brussels, 100 Avenue Moliere, pg. 1335   IT
GIB Coordination Center, Rue de Damier, 26, pg. 533   IT
GIB GROUP, 20, Ave. des Olympiades, pg. 532   IT
GIEE Brico International, Rue de la Technologie 11-15, pg. 533   IT
N.V. GLS Logistical Service SA, pg. 836   IT
GPC Market Access Europe, 50 Rue d'Arlon, pg. 1225   PB
Gandalf Systems Belgium, Heizel Esplaned, pg. 541   IT
Garbarski EURO RSCG, rue du Doyenne 58, pg. 603   IT
Gecotec, Rue du Damier, 26, pg. 533   IT
Gecotec SA, Rue du Damier, 26, pg. 533   IT
Gelder Advertising, 28B Ave. E. Van Becelaere, pg. 1152   PV
Gemey Div., Rue da Peuplear 12, pg. 819   IT
General Dynamics International Corporation, 191 Boulevard du Souverain, Box 7, pg. 709   PB
Generale de Banque - Generale Bank, Montagne du Parc 3, pg. 546   PB
GENERALE DE BANQUE S.A., 3 Montagne du Parc, pg. 546   IT
Generali Belgium Holding S.A., 149, Avenue Louise, pg. 91   IT
Generali Belgium Invest S.A., 149, Avenue Louise, pg. 91   IT

Generali Belgium S.A., 149, Avenue Louise, pg. 91   IT
S.A. Geoter, Av. Jean Mernuoz, pg. 301   IT
Glaverbel S.A., Chee De La Hulpe 166, pg. 85   IT
Glaxo Wellcome Belgium S.A., Boulevard du Trioniphe 172, pg. 553   IT
Gralex S.A., 94 Gulledelle, pg. 605   IT
Gregg Interim, St Lazaruslaan 10, pg. 1463   IT
Gregg KnowHow, Albertline 2 - bus 3, pg. 1463   IT
Grey Europe/Brussels, Blvd. de la Woluwe 56, pg. 765   PB
Grinnell Europe s.a./n.v., 63 rue de Stalle, pg. 1651   PB
Group Fabricom S.A., Rue Gatti de Gamond 254, pg. 1415   IT
GROUPE BRUXELLES LAMBERT S.A., 24, Avenue Marnix, pg. 561   IT
S.C. Groupement Immobilier GROUPIMO, rue de la Sepence 3, pg. 301   IT
Habib Bank, 35, Square De Meeus, pg. 584   IT
S.A. Hartog N.V., Humaniteitslaan 292, pg. 1437   IT
Hasbro-MB S.A., Digue Du Canal, pg. 797   PB
Haseldonckx SA, BD, Leopold II, 184 Boite 9, pg. 567   IT
Hasselbach Belgium S.A. NV, 61 Rue de la Technologie, pg. 1468   IT
H.J. Heinz Branch Belgium, 178 Chausse De La Hulpe, pg. 806   PB
H.J. Heinz Central Europe S.A., Chaussee De La Hulpe 178, pg. 806   PB
Heita Belgique S.A., pg. 920   IT
Henkel Belgium S.A., 68 Avenue Du Port, pg. 612   IT
Henkel Benelux Gruppe, 16, Avenue du Port/Havenlaan 16, pg. 612   IT
Henkel Coordination Center N.V., S.A., 68 Avenue Du Port, pg. 612   IT
Henrijean & Cie. S.A., 2 Boulevard du Soverain, pg. 1049   PB
S.A. Hercules Europe N.V., pg. 811   IT
Hewlett-Packard Belgium S.A./N.V., Blvd. de La Woluwe, 100, pg. 818   IT
H.J. Heinz Northern Europe, Chaussee de La Hulpe 178, pg. 806   PB
Holmen Belgium NV/SA, Rue des Mimosas 22, pg. 885   IT
Honeywell Bull S.A., 28, Avenue Marnix, pg. 318   IT
Honeywell Europe S.A., Ave. du Bourget 3, pg. 834   IT
Hydro Agri Belgium S.A., Rue Neerveld 107, pg. 962   IT
Hydro Agri Europe Licensing & Engineering B.V., RueNeerveld 107, pg. 962   IT
Hydro Chemicals Belgium, Rue Neerveld 107, pg. 963   IT
Hydro Magnesium Marketing, rue Neerveld 107, pg. 963   IT
Hydro S.A., rue Neerveld 107, pg. 963   IT
IC Imtech NV, Industrie boulevard 28, pg. 681   IT
ING Bank Brussels, De Lignestraat 1, pg. 649   IT
ING Vastgoed SA, Kunstlaan 46,ert Chasseur, pg. 650   IT
ISK (Europe) SA., ITT Tower, 480, Avenue Louise, pg. 689   IT
ISS Airport Services S.A.-N.V., Rue des Megissieres 30-36, pg. 657   IT
ISS Food Hygiene S.A.-N.V., Rue des Megissiers 30-36, pg. 657   IT
ISS Healthcare S.A.-N.V., Rue des Megissiers 30-36, pg. 657   IT
ISS Servisystem S.A.-N.V., Rue des Megissiers 30-36, pg. 657   IT
ITW Belgium S.A./N.V., rue Bollinckx 205, pg. 868   PB
Iglo-Ola N.V., Montoyerstr. 51, pg. 1437   IT
Immobiliere de Beaufays, Rue du Damier, 26, pg. 533   IT
S.A. Immobiliere de la Chaussee Romaine, pg. 1205   IT
Immobiliere Tractebel S.A., Place du Trone 1, pg. 1415   IT
Immolease NV, Albertinaplien 2 bus 5, pg. 65   IT
Imodis, Rue de Damier 26, pg. 533   IT
Importation de Products Alimentaires s.a., Pagodenlaan 1020, Ave. des Pagodes 2921, pg. 655   IT
Imtech-Maintenance nv, Industrie boulevard 26, pg. 681   IT
Inchcape Belgium NV/SA, Rue Colonel Bourg 115, pg. 672   IT
Ingersoll-Rand Benelux S.A., Rue de Genevestraat 10, B.9, pg. 878   PB
Inno SA, Rue Nueve, 11, pg. 533   IT
Institut de Reescompte et de Garantie, 78, rue du Commerce, pg. 147   IT
Inter-Beton S.A., 94, Gulledelle, pg. 605   IT
Interbrands NV, pg. 752   IT
Intercosmetic S.A., 9, Gossetlan, pg. 1490   IT
Intergraph (Benelux) B.V., Riverside Business Park, pg. 891   PB
International Business Machines of Belgium S.A, VIctoria Regina Plantsoen 1, pg. 898   PB
International Equipment News Europe NV, Groenstraat 216, pg. 1099   IT
International Factors, Ave de la Couronne 358, pg. 147   IT
International Paper (Europe) S.A., 1150 Woluwe-Saint-Pierre, pg. 905   PB
Investco NV, Regentlaan 54 bus 2, pg. 65   IT
Iritecna-Begium, 40 Bd. du Regent, pg. 655   IT
Isover SA, World Trade Center No1, pg. 1176   IT
Jamont N.V., 92 rue de Treves, pg. 672   IT
John Hancock Intl. Services S.A., Avenue des Arts 44, BTE. 4, pg. 590   PV
S.A. Johnson Matthey NV., 6 Ave de Bale, pg. 714   IT
Knoll Belgium S.A./N.V., Avenue Hamoir 14, Hamoirlaan 14, pg. 108   IT
Koito Manufacturing Co.-Brussels Office, Avenue Louise 326 Boite 14, pg. 743   IT
KONE Corporate Office, Avenue E. van Nieuwenhuyse 6, pg. 747   IT
KONE International S.A., Avenue E.Van Nieuwenhuyse 6, pg. 748   IT
Konezo, Div. of Akzo Belgie n.v., Akzo Bldg., 13, Marnixlaan, pg. 44   IT

Konica Business Machines Belgium S.A./N.V., Rue du Jardinier 100, pg. 749   IT
Korn/Ferry International, 523, Avenue Louise, pg. 633   PV
KREDIETBANK N.V., Arenbergstraat 7, pg. 760   IT
Kronos Europe, Inc., Rue de L Hopital 31, pg. 271   PV
Kronos Worldwide Services SA/NV, Rue de l'Hopital 31, Lot 36, pg. 271   PV
Laboratoires Corvita S.A.R.L., c/o Corvita Europe S.A., Av. J Wybran 40 A 1070, pg. 1282   PB
Laboratory Div., Rue da Peuplear 12, pg. 819   IT
Landis & Staefa s.a./n.v., Av. des Anciens, pg. 801   IT
Lanier Worldwide, Inc.-European Division, Boulevard du Souverain, 100, pg. 791   PB
Larousse-Belgique, 25-27 rue Godefroid Kurth, pg. 240   IT
Laura Ashley NV, Rue de Namur 81/83, pg. 804   IT
Le Cheque Repas, Rue Marche-aux-Herbes, 105, pg. 1274   IT
Lee Europe N.V., Dreve De Bonne Odeur 20, pg. 1702   PB
SA Letraset Belgium NV, 33 Rue Gustave Schildknecht B5, pg. 461   IT
Lever N.V., Rue Montoyesstr. 51, pg. 1438   IT
Libamedi S.A., 11 Rue De La Bienvenue, pg. 81   PB
Eli Lilly Benelux, S.A., 52, Rue De L'etuve, pg. 993   IT
Arthur D. Little International, Inc., Blvd. de la Woluwe, 2, pg. 671   PV
Lloyds Bank (Belgium) S.A., 2 Avenue de Tervuren, pg. 813   IT
Locabel S.A., 71, ave. de Cortenbergh (Bte 5), pg. 147   IT
Lockheed Corporation (International) S.A., Chaussee de la Hulpe 130, pg. 1009   IT
Logica SA/NV, Rue Colonel Bourgstrasse 105, pg. 815   IT
Long Manufacturing, Ave. de la Tanche 2, pg. 815   IT
L'Oreal Belgilux SA, Rue da Peuplear 12, pg. 819   IT
L'Oreal Parfumerie, Van der Boogaurden 91, pg. 819   IT
L'Oreal Technique Professional Div., Rue da Peuplear 12, pg. 819   IT
Louis Vuitton Belgique, Ave. Louis 25, pg. 782   IT
Lowe Troost, Avenue Herrmmann Debroux 17, pg. 678   PV
Lucent Technologies Network Systems Belgium S.A./N.V., Rue des Deux 84, pg. 1018   PB
Lunch Garden, Rue d'Argent 8, pg. 533   IT
M.M.H. SA, Rue d'Argent, 8, pg. 22   IT
MSG SA Divisie Plantin, pg. 757   IT
MSI Data International, European Hdqtrs., Rue D'Arlon 15, pg. 1546   PB
Mabe, Rue d'Argent 8, pg. 533   IT
Maginvest, Rue de Damier 26, pg. 533   IT
Makhteshim-Agan International, Avenue Louise 283, pg. 831   IT
S.A. Mannesmann Import-Export Supply NV, pg. 838   IT
Marketing and Merchandising Holding, Rue d'Argent 8, pg. 533   IT
S.A. Marks and Spencer Belgium N.V., Blvd. E. Jacqmain 6, pg. 843   PB
Marquette Benelux n.v./s.a., pg. 1047   IT
Martin Marietta International, Inc., 375 Ave. Louise, pg. 1010   PB
Master Foods NV, 100 Boulevard Du Souverain, pg. 707   PV
Matra Datavision Ben, pg. 796   IT
Mazda Motor Parts Center (Europe) N.V., 1475 Chaussee De Haecht, pg. 849   IT
Mead Johnson Benelux S.A., Chausse De La Hulpe 185-187, pg. 256   PB
Media International Data s.a., 17, allees du Languedoc, pg. 1124   IT
Mediafina S.A., Place du Trone 1, pg. 1415   IT
Mercedes-Benz Belgium S.A./N.V, Ave. du Peage, 68 Tollaan, pg. 368   IT
Methods and Services Group S.A., 97, Avenue de Tervuren, pg. 319   IT
Methods & Services Group S.A., 97 ave. de Tervueren, pg. 318   IT
Microsoft N.V., pg. 1108   IT
Milliporre S.A.-N.V., Rue de la Fusse 60, Raketstraat, pg. 1113   PB
Mitsubishi Trust & Banking Corporation (Europe) S.A., 4th Floor, Le Regent, 40 Boulevard du Regent, pg. 877   IT
N.V. Mitsui & Co. Europe (Benelux) S.A., 14th Flr., A.G. Bldg., Box 15, pg. 880   IT
Mitsui Trust Bank (Europe) S.A., Avenue Louise, 287-Bte. 5, pg. 883   IT
Mobrey SA-NV, Rue Vandenboogaerdestraat 27, pg. 854   IT
Molnlycke S.A. Health Care, Ave. de Beaulieu 25, pg. 1326   IT
Monsanto Europe S.A., 270-272 Avenue de Tervuren, pg. 1125   IT
Morgan Guaranty Trust Company, Avenue des Arts 35, pg. 1130   PB
Morgan Guaranty Trust Company, 35, Ave. des Arts, pg. 1130   PB
J.P. Morgan Benelux S.A., 35, Avenue des Arts, pg. 1130   PB
S.A. Morgan, Rue Fernand Severin 54/58, pg. 891   IT
Morinaga Nutritional Foods Europe S.A., Place Saint-Lambert 14, pg. 895   IT
N.V. Morton Thiokol S.A., Avenue Louise 149, Box 8, pg. 1136   PB
Mutuelle Solvay S.C.S., Rue Keyenveld 58, pg. 1277   IT
N.V. Owens-Corning S.A., Chaussee de La Hulpe 178 Bte. 7, pg. 1237   PB
NRG Belgium S.A., Riverside Business Park, Nashuatec House, Boite 19, pg. 1116   IT
National Bank of Greece Brussels Branch, pg. 907   IT
National Utility Service, S.A., Avenue Louise 221, BTE 3, pg. 788   PV
Neste Chemicals Belgium N.V., Neste Coordination Center NV, Bazellaan 1, pg. 914   IT
Nestle Belgilux S.A., Rue de Birmingham, pg. 921   IT

PB - *U.S. Public Companies Volume*
PV - *U.S. Private Companies Volume*
IT - *International Public & Private Companies Volume*

Network Systems Belgium, Avenue Louise 66-Box 14, pg. 1523 **PB**
New Motorest SA, Rue du Damier, 26, pg. 533 **IT**
New Vanden Boore S.A., Chausee de Mons 700-706, pg. 441 **IT**
NextLevel Systems (Belgium), Avenue De L'Horizon, 32, pg. 716 **PB**
Nicolet Instrument Benelux, Av. P. Hymans 105, pg. 1594 **PB**
A.C. Nielsen Co. (Belgium) S.A., 56 Ave. de Arts, pg. 1183 **PB**
N.V. Nira Communication Systems, Minervastraat 8, pg. 1369 **IT**
N.V. Nissho Iwai (Benelux) S.A., 4 Rue de la Science, pg. 948 **IT**
Nobema S.A., Place du Trone 1, pg. 1415 **IT**
Nopri, Rue d'Argent 8, pg. 533 **IT**
Nopri SA, Rue d'Argent, 8, pg. 533 **IT**
NORIT Belgium N.V., Avenue deDeavlieu 25, pg. 958 **IT**
S.A. Novo Nordisk Pharma NV, Riverside Business Park, Boulevard International 55, pg. 988 **IT**
Numetrix S.A., Avenue Eugene de Molder IV, pg. 990 **IT**
Nynex Network Systems Company, Avenue Louise 106, pg. 204 **PB**
OCE-Belgium N.V./S.A., Avenue J. Bordet 32, pg. 994 **IT**
OCE-Interservices N.V./S.A., pg. 994 **IT**
N.V. Olin Europe S.A., Excelsiorlaan 59, pg. 1220 **PB**
S.A. Olivetti Belgium N.V., Place Madouplein 1, pg. 1003 **IT**
154 Testa, Boulevard Saint Michel 61, pg. 1377 **IT**
Oracle Belgium NV, Excelsiorlaan 28, B-1930, pg. 1228 **PB**
Orbotech S.A., Europe, rue de la Fusee 62, pg. 1007 **IT**
Overpelt-Plascobel, Inc., Rue du Marias 31, pg. 1442 **IT**
PCM Belgium, 32 rue Duysburgh, B. 21, pg. 356 **IT**
Pan European Publishing Co., Groenstraat 216, pg. 1099 **IT**
Panduit Belgium, Baron de Vironlaan 2, pg. 836 **PV**
Parfums Christian Dior SAB, Avenue Brugmann 71, pg. 783 **IT**
Parker Hannifin SA NV, Marcel Thirty Ct., 200D Avenue Marcel Thirylaan, pg. 1263 **PB**
Pechiney Belgium S.A., 24, rue de la Loi, pg. 1031 **IT**
Petresa International N.V., Hilton Tower, 25th Fl., Boulevard Waterloo, 39, pg. 323 **IT**
Petrofina International Group S.A., rue de L'Industrie 52, pg. 1044 **IT**
PETROFINA S.A., 52, rue de l'Industrie, pg. 1043 **IT**
Petrus S.A., 111, chaussee de Ruisbroek, pg. 1574 **PB**
Pfizer S.A., Rue Leon Theodor 102, pg. 1283 **PB**
Pharmacia & Upjohn Biotech Europe, Rue de la Fusee, pg. 1047 **IT**
Pharmacia & Upjohn Eurocentre, Rue de la Fusee 62 b2, pg. 1050 **IT**
Pharmacia & Upjohn S.A.N.V., Rue de la Fusee, pg. 1050 **IT**
Pharmaco International Holdings, Inc., Rue de la Fusee 66, pg. 1285 **PB**
Philips Industrie SA, 2, Place de Brouckere, pg. 1055 **IT**
NV Pijpleiding Antwerpen-Limburg-Luik, pg. 356 **IT**
Pirelli Bedding Benelux S.A., Galerie de la Porte Louise, 203, pg. 1059 **IT**
Pirelli Industrial Hoses S.A., Bat. D, Avenue du Port 104, pg. 1059 **IT**
Pirelli Tyres Benelux S.A., Avenue Louise 225, pg. 1059 **IT**
Pizza Hut, Av. Charles-Quint 420 B8, pg. 1499 **IT**
Polaroid (Belgium) NV, 113 rue Colonel Bourg, pg. 1314 **PB**
PolyGram Records S.A., 215, Rue Victor Hugo, pg. 1053 **IT**
POSCO Brussels Office, Blue Tower, Ave. Louise 326-BTE 33, pg. 1062 **PB**
Powercontracting S.A., Place du Trone 1, pg. 1415 **IT**
Powerfin S.A., Place du Trone 1, pg. 1415 **IT**
Press-Shop Alg., 150, boulevard Emile-Bockstael, pg. 796 **IT**
Primagaz Belgium N.V., Lambert Crickxstraat 19, pg. 1155 **IT**
Procter & Gamble Health & Beauty Care Belgium, Rue Philippe-Le-Bon 1, pg. 1332 **PB**
Procter & Gamble Laundry Cleaning & Paper Products Benelux, Rue Philippe-Le-Bon 1, pg. 1332 **PB**
Prometal S.A., Avenue de la Basilique, 106, pg. 550 **IT**
Promotion Leopold S.A., Avenue Louise 500, pg. 1416 **IT**
Pullman Belgium SA, 51-53, bd Clovis, pg. 21 **IT**
Quartier Leopold Realty S.A., 17, rue d'Idalie, pg. 1574 **PB**
Quattro DMB&B, Brussels, Avenue Rogier 18-20, pg. 305 **PV**
Quick International, Rue du Damier, 26, pg. 533 **IT**
Quick International Development, Rue du Damier, 26, pg. 533 **IT**
Quick Restaurants SA, Rue du Daimer, 26, pg. 533 **IT**
Quinton Hazell PLC, Brussels, pg. 561 **PB**
RTL TVi, 1, avenue Ariane, pg. 562 **IT**
RVS Verzekeringen NV, Henri Matisselaan 16, pg. 651 **IT**
Rabobank Belgie, Brussels Office, Louizalaan 327, pg. 1082 **IT**
Radio Contact, 33, avenue Telemaque, pg. 561 **IT**
N.V. Reader's Digest S.A., 29, Quai du Hainaut, pg. 1368 **PB**
Reader's Digest World Services, S.A., 29, Quai du Hainaut - Henegouwenkaai 29, pg. 1368 **PB**
N.V. Rentokil SA, Rogierlaan 385, pg. 1286 **IT**
Repsol S.A., Repsol Quimica, Avenue Louise, 327 (10o), pg. 1105 **IT**
Restaura S.A., 5, avenue du Col-Vert, pg. 1275 **IT**
Rhone-Poulenc Belgique S.A., Blvd. Sylvain Dupuislaan, 243, pg. 1112 **IT**
Rob, Bd de la Woluwe 28, pg. 533 **IT**
S.A. Roche Nicholas N.V., pg. 1121 **IT**

N.V. Roche S.A., 75 rue Dante, pg. 1122 **IT**
Rockwell Automation European Headquarters S.A./N.V., Avenue Herrmann Debroux, 46, pg. 1399 **PB**
S.A. Rorer N.V., Place du Champ de Mars, pg. 1112 **IT**
Royale Belge RE, Boulevard du Souverain 25, pg. 562 **IT**
Royale Belge S.A., Boulevard du Souverain 25, pg. 562 **IT**
Rubson Benelux S.A., Avenue du Port 73, pg. 614 **IT**
SAIT-RADIOHOLLAND GROUP S.A., Chaussee de Ruisbroek, 66, pg. 1151 **IT**
SAS International Hotels A/S, Boulevard du Regent 45, pg 1202 **IT**
SDRC Belgium N.V./S.A., Boulevard Lambermont Laan, 140, pg. 1525 **PB**
SKF Belgium S.A., Ave. de Bale 3, pg. 1158 **IT**
SKF Intertrade S.A., Rue du Bourdon 100, pg. 1158 **IT**
SMH Belgium SA, Dupuis Center, Boulevard Sylain Dupuis, 243, pg. 1161 **IT**
S.A. SNC-Lavalin Europe N.V., Avenue Louise 251, bte. 16, pg 1163 **IT**
S.N.T.M. S.A., Rue Guimard 4, pg. 1416 **IT**
S.P.T.E. S.A., Avenue Ariane 7, pg. 1415 **IT**
STB, 15 rue Vergote, pg. 318 **IT**
STET Belgium, 40 Bd. du Regent, pg. 656 **IT**
Saboma, Rue de Damier, 26, pg. 533 **IT**
Safe insurance, Rue du Damier 26, pg. 533 **IT**
St. Jude Medical Europe, Inc., Ave. Arianelaan 5, pg. 1428 **PB**
The Sakura Bank - Brussels Branch, Galilee Building, Avenue Galilee 5, pg. 1179 **IT**
Sandcz Management Services, pg. 985 **IT**
Sandcz S.A., 226, Chausee de Haecht, pg. 985 **IT**
Sandvik Benelux, Chaussee de Louvain 1188, pg. 1186 **IT**
Sanpaolo-Brussels Branch, 350 Ave. Louise, pg. 692 **IT**
Saprona S.A., Avenue Edouard Lacomble 21, pg. 212 **PV**
Sarimno, Rue d'Argent 8, pg. 533 **IT**
Sarme-Nopri Group, Rue d'Argent 8, pg. 533 **IT**
Sarme Shop, Rue d'Argent 8, pg. 533 **IT**
Sarmag, Rue d'Argent 8, pg. 533 **IT**
Saunier Duval Belgique S.A., rue de Birmingham 53, pg. 615 **IT**
Schauman B.V., 8, avenue des Gaulois, pg. 1429 **IT**
S.A. Schindler N.V., pg. 1205 **IT**
Scholl Belgium SA, 45 Rue Neuve, pg. 1209 **IT**
Selective Beauty International Div., Rue Vanden Bougaerde 91, pg. 819 **IT**
Shandwick S.A. Infopublic N.V., Blvd. Lambermont 436, pg. 1228 **IT**
Shef S.A., pg. 437 **IT**
Shimizu Benelux S.A., Avenue Marcel Thiry 204, pg. 1233 **IT**
Shizucka Bank (Europe) S.A., 283 Avenue Louise, Bte. 13, pg. 1236 **IT**
Sibeka, Rue Royal 52, pg. 1442 **IT**
Sibelgaz, Hotel Communal Saint-Josse-ten-Noode, pg. 437 **IT**
Siemens Nixdorf Information Systems S.A./NV, Chaussee de Cahrleroi M0-M6, pg. 1245 **IT**
Slamub, Rue du Daimer, 26, pg. 533 **IT**
SmithKline Beecham Pharma S.A., Avenue Louise 287, pg. 1266 **IT**
SmithKline Beecham Pharmaceuticals, European Division, c/o Fournex N.V., pg. 1264 **IT**
SmithKline Beecham S.A., Avenue Louise 287, pg. 1266 **IT**
Sobelair S.A., Av E. Mounier 2, pg. 1168 **IT**
Societe Espace Leopold S.A., Avenue Louise 500, pg. 1416 **IT**
Socoficex, 100 Boulevard Louis Schmidt, pg. 1333 **PB**
Sodal Corporation, Rue de Damier, 26, pg. 533 **IT**
Sodexo Belgique S.A., 5, avenue du Col-Vert, pg. 1275 **IT**
Sodif, Rue du Damier 26, pg. 533 **IT**
Sogem Gulledelle 92, pg. 1442 **IT**
Sogerfin, 24, avenue Marnix, pg. 147 **IT**
Soges-Fiducem S.A., 24, Ave. Marnix, pg. 147 **IT**
Soigest, Rue du Damier, 26, pg. 533 **IT**
Solvay Interox S.A., Rue du Prince Albert 33, pg. 1277 **IT**
SOLVAY S.A., Rue du Prince Albert 33, pg. 1277 **IT**
Solvic & Cie S.N.C., Rue du Prince Albert 44, pg. 1277 **IT**
Sonocc Europe, Ltd., Boulevard Du Souverain 100, pg. 487 **PB**
Sovedi Benelux-Belgium, 1385 Chaussee de Haecht, pg. -10 **IT**
Sparbaleg, Mettewielaan 272 b4, pg. 28 **IT**
SPADEL SA, 103 Rue Colonel Bourg, pg. 1287 **PB**
Spur Belgium, Manchesterstraat 25, pg. 851 **IT**
Squibb-Contavec SA, Av. Louise 130a, pg. 256 **PB**
Stampen S.A., pg. 312 **IT**
Standard & Poor's International S.A., Residence Charles Woeste, 306 Ave. Charles Woeste, pg. 1072 **PB**
Stigam, Rue d'Argent 8, pg. 533 **IT**
Stora Finance Brussels S.A., 480 Avenue Louise, pg. 1303 **IT**
Stream International, Avenue Adolphe Lacomble Laan 52, pg. 518 **PB**
S.A. Sulzer Belgium N.V., pg. 1306 **IT**
Sulzer Belgium S.A., pg. 1306 **IT**
The Sumitomo Bank, Ltd.-Brussels Branch, Avenue des Arts, 58, pg. 1309 **IT**
Sumitomo Rubber Industries-Brussels, 5-6 Square de Meeus, pg. 1317 **IT**
Sundstrand International Corp. S.A., Genevestraat 10, pg. 1534 **IT**
Swiss Life (Belgium), Rue de la Loi 82, pg. 1332 **IT**
Symbol Technologies International, Inc., Waterloo Office Park Bldg. B, Dreve Richelle 161, pg. 1546 **PB**
Synatom S.A., pg. 437 **IT**
Synerfi S.A., Boulevard du Souverain 288, pg. 547 **IT**
Syntex S.A., pg. 1122 **IT**

TBWA Belgium, 8 avenue Van Nieuwenhuyse, pg. 1063 **PV**
Tandem Computers SA/NV, Lozenberg 22, pg. 418 **PB**
Telfin S.A., Place du Trone 1, pg. 1415 **IT**
N.V. Telxon Belgium S.A., 150 Chausee de la Hulpe, pg. 1574 **PB**
Telxon Corporation, Belgium Branch, Chausse de La Hulpe 150 Bte 1, pg. 1574 **PB**
Temco Europe S.A., 17 rue d'Idalie, pg. 1574 **PB**
Temco Service Industries S.A., Headquarters, 17, rue'dIdalie, pg. 1574 **PB**
S.A. Texaco Petroleum N.V., Ave Louise 149, pg. 1584 **PB**
Texaco Services (Europe) Ltd., Ave. Louise 149, pg. 1584 **PB**
N.V. Texas Instruments Belgium SA, Mercure Centre, Rue de la Fusee 100, pg. 1586 **PB**
Thibaut - Colson - De Nef (TCD), Place de l'Alma 2, pg. 547 **IT**
Thomson-CSF, Avenue Louise 363, Boite 10, pg. 1385 **IT**
Thomson-CSF Passive Components Benelux, Avenue Louise, 363, Boite 10, pg. 1385 **IT**
3M Belgium N.V./S.A., 106 Boulevard, Hermeslaan 7, pg. 1606 **IT**
Thule International S.A., 128, Avenue Moliere, pg. 436 **IT**
Tierce Ladbroke SA, Chausee de Waterloo 715, pg. 788 **IT**
N.V. Tijdschriften Verening Vlaanderen, pg. 1447 **IT**
Tokio Marine & Fire Insurance Company (U.K.) Limited, c/o A.G. 1824-Compagnie Belge, D'Assurance Generales S.A., pg. 1392 **IT**
Toyo Trust & Banking (Europe) S.A., 287 Ave. Louise, pg. 1411 **IT**
Toyota Motor Corporation, Europe Office, 191-197, Boulevard du Souverain, BTE 2, pg. 1413 **IT**
N.V. Toyota Motor Europe Marketing & Engineering S.A., Avenue du Bourget 60, pg. 1414 **IT**
TRACTEBEL, 1 place du Trone, pg. 1414 **IT**
Tractebel Development S.A., Avenue Ariane 7, pg. 1415 **IT**
Tractebel Engineering International S.A., Avenue Ariane 7, pg. 1415 **IT**
Tractebel Industrie S.A., Avenue Ariane 7, pg. 1415 **IT**
Transcor S.A., 181, Chaussee de la Hulpe, pg. 562 **IT**
Transga, Boulevard du Souverain 25, pg. 562 **IT**
Trasys S.A., Avenue Ariane 7, pg. 1415 **IT**
Triosol, S.A., Boulevard E. Bockstael 122, pg. 1279 **IT**
UAB, Avenue Marcel Thiry 208, pg. 562 **IT**
UCB Pharma SA, pg. 1427 **IT**
UCB, S.A., Avenue Louise, pg. 1427 **IT**
UMCZ, Gulledelle 92, pg. 1442 **IT**
UPM-Kymmene (Belgium) S.A./N.V., Chaussee de la Hulpe, 181, pg. 1430 **IT**
Uniccomptoir, Rue du Damier, 26, pg. 533 **IT**
Union Minere Services & Finance, Gulledelle 92, pg. 1442 **IT**
UNION MINIERE, Rue du Marais 31, pg. 1441 **IT**
Union Special-Belgium, Rue de la Caserne, 90, pg. 716 **IT**
Unisys Belgium, Avenue du Bourget 20, pg. 1672 **IT**
VF Jeanswear-Europe, Dreve de Bonne Odeur, pg. 1702 **PV**
VNU World Directories, N.V., Ave. Louise, 480, pg. 1447 **IT**
Vadis S.P.R.L., Rue Osseghem 53, pg. 463 **IT**
Van Hemelrijck, Rue du Damier, 26, pg. 533 **IT**
Variety Music Corp. S.A., 30 Avenue de Roodebeek, pg. 1453 **IT**
Vattenfall European Affairs, Avenue de Tervuren 12, Bte 3, pg. 1472 **IT**
N.V. Vectur S.A., 1243 Chaussee de Haecht, pg. 1129 **PV**
Vedim SA, pg 1427 **IT**
Vendo (Benelux) S.A., Industrial Research Park NOH, Font St. Landry, pg. 1184 **IT**
Veratec S.A., Blvd. de la Woluwe 100, pg. 906 **PB**
Vermeulen-Raemdonck, Rue du Commerce, Handelsstraat, 10, pg. 147 **IT**
Vision Centers, Rue du Daimer, 26, pg. 533 **IT**
Voest-Alpine Industrie S.A., Passage International 6, pg. 1472 **IT**
S.A. Volkswagen Bruxelles N.V., Blvd de la ze Armee Britannique 201, pg. 1475 **IT**
Volkswagen Bruxelles S.A., pg. 1475 **IT**
Volkswagen Trading S.A., pg. 1475 **IT**
Volvo Cars Europe Marketing NV, Zelliksesteenweg 12, pg. 1477 **IT**
Volvo Construction Equipment, Chaussee de La Hulpe 130, pg. 1477 **IT**
Von Ernst Belgium Management S.A., pg. 181 **IT**
WABCO Automotive, Products Group, Boulevard du Souverain, 348, pg. 92 **PB**
WABCO Westinghouse, Ave. Van Volxem 164-166, pg. 92 **PB**
Wagons-Lits Tourisme SA, 51-53, bd Clovis, pg. 22 **IT**
N.V. Wander S.A., pg. 986 **IT**
N.V. Wellcome S.A., Industriezone III Aalst, pg. 553 **IT**
Werner & Pfleiderer P.V.B.A., St.-Lambertusstraat 141, pg. 511 **IT**
Westdeutsche Landesbank-Brussels Branch, Rue du Gouvernment Provisoire 19, pg. 1493 **IT**
Westinghouse Energy Systems International, Inc., 73 Rue de Stalle, pg. 275 **IT**
Westvaco Europe, S.A., Avenue de Tervueren 296D, pg. 1762 **PB**
Weyerhaeuser, S.A., 2/4 rue de Praetere, Bte 3, pg. 1764 **PB**
Wyeth S.A., 150 Chaussee de la Hulpe, pg. 82 **PB**
Yamanouchi Pharma B.V.-Brussels, Riverside Business Park, Internationalelaan 55, pg. 1519 **IT**
Young & Rubicam Belgium S.A., Dieweg 3B, pg. 1199 **PV**
Zeneca Colours, Ave. De Tervueren 13 B, pg. 1526 **IT**
Zeneca Plant Science, rue du Mail 95, pg. 1527 **IT**

PB - *U.S. Public Companies Volume*
PV - *U.S. Private Companies Volume*
IT - *International Public & Private Companies Volume*

Zenith Data Systems N.V., 41 ave. de Tervueren, pg. 318
Zimmer International, S.A., Klein Eilandstraat 5, pg. 257 **PB**
Zurich Compagnie d'Assurances, 76, Rue de la Loi, pg. 1530 **IT**
Zurich Compagnie d'assurances sur la vie, 76, Rue de la Loi, pg. 1529 **IT**
Zurich International (Belgique) S.A., 76, Rue de la Loi, pg. 1532 **IT**
Zyma Benelux S.A., rue de Wand 209-213, pg. 986 **IT**

Bueda

Begemann Rusland B.V., Speelhuislaan 173, pg. 1134 **IT**

Charleroi

Acec Automatisme, Avenue Emile Rousseau, pg. 54 **IT**
ACEC-OSI, Avenue Emile Rousseau, pg. 1415 **IT**
ASEA Jumet S.A., pg. 7 **IT**
S.A. Compagnie des Produits Siderurgiques COPROSID, pg. 301 **IT**
Fibelpar S.A., Boulevard Tirou 11, pg. 1416 **IT**
S.A. Proprete, Assainissement, Gestion de l"Environnement P.A.G.E., Av. Jean Memoz, pg. 301 **IT**
Pum Inox, Av. Jean Mernuoz, pg. 301 **IT**
S.A. Societe Caroloregienne de Laminage CARLAM, rue de l'usimenier, pg. 301 **IT**
S.A. Vulcain Environment, pg. 302 **IT**
S.A. Vulcain Industrie, pg. 302 **IT**
S.A. Ymos Belgium, pg. 302 **IT**

Clermont

Cegram S.A., Route de Liege, pg. 1030 **IT**

Couillet

S.A. Bureau International de Recherches pour la Destruction des Immondices B.I.R.D.I., pg. 301 **IT**

Deerlijk

N.V. Boucquillon S.A., Nijverheidslaan 38, pg. 1458 **IT**

Deinze

Radar N.V., pg. 1121 **IT**

Dendermonde

Intergem, Stadhuis, pg. 437 **IT**

Destelbergen

Zeneca nv, Schaessestrasse 15, pg. 1527 **IT**

Deurne

Crown Cork Company (Belgium) N.V., Belcrownlaan 2, pg. 464 **PB**
Crown Cork Coordination Center N.V., Belcrownlaan 2, pg. 464 **PB**
Delta Air Transport N.V., Antwerp Airport Box 4, pg. 1168 **IT**
ENVIRAS, Clara Snellingstraat 27, pg. 608 **IT**
Forbo Tapijt N.V., pg. 498 **IT**
GEDAS NV, Clara Snellingstraat 27, pg. 608 **IT**
Luxottica Belgium N.V., August Van de Wielelei 63/65, pg. 822 **IT**
Sun Electric Belgium N.V., Callifortlei 214, pg. 1481 **PB**

Diegem

ABS Belgium nv/sa, Vuurberg 25, pg. 270 **IT**
Accors Hotels Belgium, Olmenstraat Z/N, pg. 21 **IT**
Canon Benelux N.V./S.A., Bessenveldstraat 7, pg. 262 **IT**
Componenta Benelux/Branch Office Belgium, Vuuberg 49, pg. 1421 **IT**
Fidisco NV, Kosteraat 209, pg. 65 **IT**
ICL (Belgium) S.A., Bessenvledstraat 9, pg. 529 **IT**
Nokia Mobile Phones (Benelux) S.A., Airport Business Center, pg. 952 **IT**
Nokia Telecommunications Belgium, Airport Business Center, Vuurberg 80, pg. 953 **IT**
Scania Belgium sa-nv, President J. F. Kennedylaan 4, pg. 687 **IT**
Statoil Petrochemicals, John F. Kennedy Laan #3, pg. 1298 **IT**
Stratus Computer S.A., Bessenveldstraat, 25, pg. 1524 **PB**
Takenaka Belgium S.A., Airport Business Park, Berkenlaan 1, pg. 1351 **IT**
Teledyne Belgium S.A., Airport Business Center, pg. 44 **PB**
VB Autobatteijen B.V., Woluwelaan 34, pg. 1452 **IT**
VARTA Industriebatterie N.V. S.A., Woluwelaan 34, pg. 1452 **IT**
Wang Benelux S.A/N.V., Bessenveldstr. 21, pg. 1737 **PB**
Wang Europe S.A./N.V., Bessenveldstraat 21, pg. 1738 **PB**
Wolters Kluwer Belgium, Kouterveldstraat 14, pg. 1513 **IT**

Dilsen

Bandag Europe NV, Industrieterrein, pg. 178 **PB**

N.V. Immobilien en Grindexploitatlemaatschappij, Maasdijk z/n, pg. 135 **IT**

Doel

Aqualon Belgium N.V., Geslechtsstraat 2, pg. 810 **PB**

Dottignies

Kluber Lubrication Benelux S.A., pg. 506 **IT**

Drogenbos

Delhome S.A., Blvd. de l'Humanite 219, pg. 463 **IT**
Glaenzer-Seurre NV/SA, Avenue Mr. Paul Gilson Laan 441, pg. 536 **IT**
Lincoln Smitweld Belgium NV, Ave. Paul Gilson Laan 470, pg. 997 **PB**

Duffel

Cascade Duffel NV, Adolf Stocletlaan 23, pg. 274 **IT**
Dufalco NV, A. Stocletlaan 87, pg. 755 **IT**
Hoogovens Aluminium Building Systems NV, A. Stocletlaan 87, pg. 755 **IT**
Hoogovens Aluminium International NV, A. Stocletlaan 87, pg. 755 **IT**
Hoogovens Aluminium NV, 87 Adolf Stockletlaan, pg. 755 **IT**
Hoogovens Aluminium NV Profiel Centrum, A. Stocletlaan 87, pg. 755 **IT**
Hoogovens Aluminium Service Center NV, A. Stocletlaan 87, pg. 755 **IT**
Scott Continental N.V., Adolf Stockletlann 3, pg. 960 **PB**

Edegem

Supertransport, Drie Eikenstraat, 362, pg. 533 **IT**

Eeklo

Eeklo Mill, Korte Moeie 53, pg. 673 **PB**
Imewo, Stadhuis, pg. 437 **IT**

Eke

Bio-Rad Sanz, Begonia Straat 5, pg. 230 **IT**

Ensival

Houget Duesberg Bosson, 37, rue du Tissage, pg. 1206 **IT**

Erembodegem

Gates Europe, Dr. Carlierl 30, pg. 1396 **IT**
HyClone Europe, Industriezone 111, pg. 1037 **IT**
Moore Lithorex Direct Marketing Services N.V. S.A., 3 de Industriezone 9320, pg. 890 **IT**

Erpe

Pioneer Electronics Manufacturing NV, Industriepark, Joseph Cardijnstraat 31, pg. 1058 **IT**

Ertvelde

Fina Oleochemicals N.V., Assenedstraat 2, pg. 1043 **IT**

Essen

N.V. Van Leer Muno S.A., pg. 1147 **IT**

Etalle

Societe Generale de Grandes Sources Belges S.A., pg. 922 **IT**

Eupen

Cremar SA, pg. 838 **IT**
Freudenberg Haushaltsprodukte SCS, pg. 507 **IT**
Interest, Hotel de Ville, pg. 437 **IT**
S.A. Laserflash, Industriestrasse, 34, pg. 301 **IT**
Nomadis S.A., pg. 507 **IT**
TD Produktions- u. Handelsgesellschaft S.A., pg. 507 **IT**

Everberg

BIM S.A., Kwikstraat 4, pg. 1531 **PB**
Zeneca Agro, Everslaam 45, pg. 1526 **IT**

Feluy

Fina Chemicals Feluy S.A., Zoning Industriel, pg. 1043 **IT**
Fina Research S.A., Zone Industrielle C, pg. 1043 **IT**

Flemalle

Segal, Societe Cooperative, pg. 754 **IT**

Fleurus

Guerlain Benelux S.A., Zoning Industriel, pg. 780 **IT**

Rowenta Belgium S.A., Avenue de l'Esperance, pg. 569 **IT**
Tefal Belgium, Avenue de l'Esperance, pg. 568 **IT**

Forest

Interenergie S.C., pg. 437 **IT**

Fosses-la-Ville

Inatel S.C., pg. 437 **IT**

Frameries

Esco, Europe S.A., Rue des Frous-Chaux, pg. 383 **PV**
Lightnin Belgium, S.A., pg. 727 **PB**

Geel

Amoco Chemical Belgium N.V., Amocolaan, pg. 103 **PB**
B.A.T Benelux S.A., Heidebloemstraat 91, pg. 111 **IT**
Colorprofil N.V., 8, Lammerdries, Industrieterrein Geel-West, pg. 79 **IT**
Decosteel N.V., 10, Lammerdries, Industrieterrein Geel-West, Zone 4, pg. 79 **IT**
E.S.P. Europese Staalprefabricatle N.V., 8, Twee Molenstraat, Industrieterrein Geel-West, Zone 4, pg. 79 **IT**
Moduwall N.V., 6, Twee Molenstraat, pg. 80 **IT**
Stafford-Miller Continental, N.V. S.A., Nijverheidsstraat 9, pg. 237 **PB**
Velasques Sigarenfabrieken N.V., Heidebloemstraat 91, pg. 111 **IT**

Gembloux

Furon S.A./N.V., Chanssee de Tirlemont 100, pg. 689 **PB**
Whitehall Benelux S.A., Chaussee De Tirlemont 80, pg. 82 **PB**

Genk

ALZ N.V., Genk-Zuid, Zone 6A, pg. 79 **IT**
Amano Electronics Europe, N.V., Westerring 2, pg. 71 **IT**
DSM Specialty Compounds nv, pg. 355 **IT**
N.V. Elefant, pg. 506 **IT**
Elefant n.v.i.L., pg. 507 **IT**
Ford Werke AG - Genk Branch, Henry Fordiaan 8, pg. 666 **PB**
Iega, Gemeentehuis, pg. 437 **IT**
Nitto Europe N.V., Eikelaarstraat 22, pg. 951 **IT**
Rieter Automotive Belgium N.V., pg. 1117 **IT**
Sikel N.V., 3 Kanaaloever, pg. 79 **IT**
Tailor Steel N.V., 2, Kanaaloever, pg. 79 **IT**

Gent

Air Products N.V., pg. 31 **IT**
Almetal Holding N.V., 9, Scheepzatestraat, pg. 79 **IT**
Amersham Belgium NV/SA, Ottergemsesteenweg 644Z, pg. 992 **IT**
Banque Indosuez, Ajuinlei 1, pg. 314 **IT**
Biscuiterie Boone S.A., pg. 411 **IT**
DSM Moreels NV, Koopvaardijlaan 180-182, pg. 355 **IT**
GALTEC N.V., 51, John Kennedylaan, pg. 79 **IT**
Honda Europe N.V., Langerbruggestraat 104, pg. 635 **IT**
Kronos SA/NV, Langerbruggekaai 10, pg. 271 **PV**
Moore Belgium NV, Industrieweg 78-80, pg. 889 **IT**
PAXAR Benelux BvBA, Maaltecenter Blo G, Derbystraat 349, pg. 1266 **PB**
Perstorp Analytical, Dernystraat 49, pg. 1039 **IT**
Perstorp Components, Eddastraat 40, pg. 1040 **IT**
Prayon de Pauw N.V., pg. 268 **IT**
Rogers N.V., Afrikalaan 188, pg. 1403 **PB**
Schleicher & Schuell N.V. S.A., Meersstraat 138D, pg. 1206 **IT**
Sidmar N.V., John Kennedylaan 51, pg. 79 **IT**
N.V. Silicaatsteen, Staatstuinwijk 36, pg. 1199 **IT**
Stora Langerbrugge N.V., Wondelgemkaai 200, pg. 1304 **IT**
UCB SA Chemical, pg. 1427 **IT**
Volvo Europa Car NV, P.O. Box 273, pg. 1476 **IT**
Volvo Europa Truck NV, Smallaheerweg 31, pg. 1476 **IT**
Vynckier NV, Nieuwevaart, 51, pg. 546 **IT**
Vyncolit N.V., Nieuwevaart 51, pg. 1037 **IT**

Genval

SmithKline Beecham Pharma S.A., Rue du Tilleul, 13, pg. 1266 **IT**

Ghislenghien

Sun Chemical ECP S.A./N.V., 6, Chemin de Malplaquet, pg. 371 **IT**

Ghlin

Aluminium Europe S.A., En Abregle: "Aleurope S.A.", 1, route de Wallonie, pg. 1386 **PB**
Cartomills, S.A., Route de Douvrain 19, pg. 20 **IT**

Gilly

Hayward S.A., 245 Rue du Rond Point, pg. 514 **PV**

PB - *U.S. Public Companies Volume*
PV - *U.S. Private Companies Volume*
IT - *International Public & Private Companies Volume*

Geographic Index-Non U.S.

1515

Gosselies

Caterpillar Belgium S.A., 1, Avenue Des Etats-Unis, pg. 317 PB

Grace-Hollogne

Babcock Services (Belgium), pg. 474 IT

Grembergen

Norton S.A./N.V., Mechelsestraat 153, pg. 1175 IT
TrefilARBED Grembergen S.A., Zeelse Baan 83, pg. 80 IT

Grimbergen

Beamix-Bel S.A., Oostvaartdijk 10, pg. 606 IT
Caterpillar Logistics Services Belgium N.V., Humbeeksesteenweg 98, pg. 316 PB
Danzas N.V., Eppegemsesteenweg 31, pg. 382 IT
Norton Abrasives, Oude, pg. 1174 IT
Schiesser International Belgie N.V., pg. 618 IT

Groot-Bijgaarden

N.V. CIBA-GEIGY Agro S.A., Noordkustlaan 18, pg. 976 IT
S.A. CIBA-GEIGY NV, Noordkustlaan 18, pg. 978 IT
N.V. Johnson Wax Belgium S.A., Noordkustlaan 16 (B), pg. 593 PV
Johnson Wax Consumer Products, Noordkustlaan 16, pg. 593 PV
Johnson Wax Industrial Products (INNOCHEM), Noordkustlaan 16, pg. 593 PV
Lowara Belgium S.A., pg. 861 PB
OMRON Electronics N.V./S.A., Stationsstraat 24, pg. 1006 IT
Sensormatic (Belgium) S.A., Pastoor Cooremansstraat 3, pg. 1457 PB
Sharp Electronics (Europe) GmbH, Belgian Branch, T Hofveld4, pg. 1230 IT
N.V. Svedala S.A., pg. 1325 IT
Unifix (Belgium) S.A., Stationstraat 39, pg. 232 IT

Halle

Bordex (Belgium) N.V., pg. 159 PV
N.V. Huls Belgien S.A., Meiboomstraat 26, pg. 1455 IT

Hamme

Master Builders N.V., pg. 1465 IT

Hamont

Teckino Manufacturing b.v.b.a., Heikant 21, pg. 1395 PB

Harelbeke

Alarmcom N.V., Kortrijksesteenweg 321, pg. 1246 IT
VSK Group, Venetiglaan 39, Industrial Park, pg. 49 PB

Hasselt

BIK Interimkantoor, Leopoldplein 48, pg. 1574 PB
Pligas, Stadhuis, pg. 437 IT
N.V. Readymix Belgium S.A., 1-3 Kolonel Dusartplein, pg. 1081 IT
NV Charles Sternotte, Zeilstraat 2, pg. 754 IT
VCST Computer Services N.V., Universiteitslaan 9, pg. 1134 IT

Heist-op-den-Berg

Kemira Color N.V., Industriepark 16, pg. 729 IT
Vink N.V., Industriepark 7, pg. 1211 IT

Helchteren

S.A. Coal Waste Engineering, pg. 301 IT

Hemiksem

Bekaert-Tinsley, Heuvelstraat 184-186, pg. 183 IT
Technip Benelux, Nieuwe Dreef, 2620 Hemiksem, pg. 1361 IT

Herent

Cadsand Medica N.V., Timmerick 2, pg. 1284 PB
N.V. Verzekeringskantoor Paul Lamin, Mechelseteenweg, 455, pg. 92 IT

Herentals

BetzDearborn N.V., Toekomstlaan 54, pg. 227 PB
CPAC Europe N.V., Industriepark Klein Gent, pg. 282 PB
DYWIBEL N.V., Bertemsebaan 1, pg. 424 IT
Erie Controls Europe-NV, Industriepark, pg. 1241 IT
Fike Europe N.V., Toekomstlaan 52, pg. 404 PV
General Biscuits Belgie N.V., De Beukelaer-Pareinlaan 1, pg. 380 IT
N.V. Griffith Laboratories S.A., Toekomstlaan, Wolfstee Industriepark, pg. 481 PV

Knorr-Bremse Benelux B.V.B.A., Herenthoutseweg 190, pg. 738 IT
Structural Europe, Industriepark Wolfstee, pg. 593 PB
Wicona Benelux N.V., Diamantstraat, Industriezone Klein Gent, pg. 964 IT

Herk-de-Stad

Advanced Materials and Technologies N.V., Daelemveld 1113, pg. 1427 IT

Herstal

Browning SA, Parc Industrieldes Hauts-Sarts, pg. 617 IT
FN Herstal S.A., 33 Rue Voie de Liege, pg. 617 IT
HERSTAL S.A., 33 Rue Voie de Liege, pg. 617 IT
S.A. I.B.T., pg. 301 IT
Kennametal Hertel Belgium, S.A., Parc Industrial Des Hauts Sarts, pg. 951 PB
Pneu Uniroyal Englebert S.A., Parc Industriel des Hauts Sarts, pg. 327 IT
S.A. Folytuil, Parc Industriel des Hours Sorts, pg. 301 IT
S.A. Forges De Zeebrugge, 63, rue en Bois, pg. 1385 IT

Heusden

Perstorp Stamp, Heidestraat 69, pg. 1038 IT

Heverlee

AlliedSignal Europe N.V., Haasrode Research Park, pg. 52 PB
Conwed Plastics/N.V. S.A., Ambachtenlaan 17, Bus 2, pg. 990 PB
Nellcor Puritan Bennett Belgium N.V./S.A., Interleuvenlaan 62-8, pg. 1040 PB
Perlav-Euroclean, 88, Tweekleinwegenstraat, pg. 1574 PB
SAS Institute NV/SA, Interleuvenlaan 10, pg. 967 PV

Hollogne-sur-Geer

Agusta Aerospace Services A.A.S., S.A.-Belgio, Rue Dierain de Liege, pg. 32 IT

Hooglede

Sadef N.V., Bruggesteenweg 60, pg. 1472 IT

Houdeng-Goegnies

Ideal-Standard, Chaussee Paul Houtart, 88, pg. 92 PB

Houthalen

Heraeus Electro-Nite International N.V., Centrum-Zuid 1105, pg. 616 IT
Radiart Color NV, Europark 1046, pg. 1357 PB
Technum N.V., pg. 1415 IT

Huizingen

Century Oils Industries N.V., Industriezone, Heideveld 54, pg. 517 IT
Valvoline Belgium N.V., Industriezone Heideveld 54, pg. 140 PB

Huy

Bequet Paul, Chaussee d'Andenne, pg. 789 IT

Ivoz-Ramet

Phenix Aluminium S.A., pg. 755 IT
Segal SA, Chassee de Ramioul 50, pg. 756 IT
Segal s.c.r.l., 50, Chaussee de Ramioul, pg. 79 IT

Izegem

VANDEMOORTELE N.V., Prinse Albert Laan 12, pg. 1451 IT

Jumet

Settas S.A., pg. 673 IT

Kallo

N.V. KymTrans S.A., Land van Waaslann, Vrasenedok 1212, pg. 1430 IT
Lawter Intl. N.V., Haven 1520, pg. 981 PB
Lumipa_er N.V., Haven 1139, Land van Waaslaan 3, pg. _58 IT
MoDo Paper Benelux BV, Haven 1219, Hazopweg 6, pg. 887 IT
MoDo Papier Belgium, Hazopweg 6, pg. 886 IT
Statoil Antwerp NSP, St. Jansweg 2, pg. 1298 IT

Kalmthout

Copijn Belgie Boomchirurgen BVBA, De Lindenreef 57, pg. 608 IT

Kessel-Lo

Raychem N.V., 692, Diestsesteenweg, pg. 1362 PB

Kontich

AST Benelux, N.V., Prins Boudewijnlaan, 17 Bus 3, pg. 1182 IT
Anixter Antwerp, Satenrozen 7, pg. 116 PB
Epacar NV, pg. 757 IT
H.B. Fuller Belgium N.V./S.A., Duffelsesteenweg 79, pg. 687 PB
Knurr NV Belgie, Heivel dekens 9/A1, pg. 739 IT
Loctite Belgium N.V., Mechel Sesteenweg 313, pg. 611 IT
Seals N.V./S.A., Heiveldekens 22, pg. 689 PB
VAW Belgique S.A., pg. 1466 IT

Kortenberg

Alfa-Laval Agri N.V., Leuvensesteenweg 456, pg. 1379 IT
Scaldia-Buhrmann NV, pg. 757 IT

Kortrijk

Banque Indosuez, O.L. Vrouwestraat,41, pg. 314 IT
Barenbrug (Belgium) Maes NV/SA, Torkonjestraat 23, pg. 167 IT
Bekaert Coordinatiecentrum, President Kennedypark 27A, pg. 183 IT
N.V. BEKAERT S.A., President Kennedy Park 18, pg. 183 IT
Bekaert-Stanwick N.V., President Kennedypark 27D, pg. 183 IT
De Hallen-Kortrjk S.V., Doorniksesteenweg 216, pg. 1415 IT
De Kortrijkse Verzekering, Lange steenstaat, 20, pg. 19 IT
Kredietwaarborg NV, Minister Vanden Peereboomlaan 72, pg. 65 IT

La Louviere

I.E.H. S.C., pg. 437 IT
IGH, Hotel de Ville, pg. 437 IT

Lanaken

KNP Belgie NV, pg. 757 IT
KNP Press Paper NV, pg. 757 IT

Le Mesnil

Skega SA, 45 Rue Maurice Berteaux, pg. 1324 IT
Svedala Skega, pg. 1324 IT

Lebbeke

BARRY CALLEBAUT N.V., Aalstesesgraat 122, pg. 252 IT

Leiden

Anitec Image International B.V., Nieuwenjuizenweg 10, 2314 XR Leiden, pg. 904 PB

Lessines

Amphabel S.A., pg. 1523 IT

Leuven

S.A. Ajinomoto Coordination Center N.V., Industrial Research Park, pg. 40 IT
N.V. Bilfinger + Berger Belgium S.A., Interleuvenlaan 64, pg. 196 IT
CSI European Headquarters, Interleuvenlaan 64, Research Park Interleuven, pg. 573 PB
Donaldson Coordination Center, N.V., Interleuvenlaan, 1, pg. 517 PB
Donaldson Europe N.V., Interleuvenlaan, 1, pg. 517 PB
Gambro N.V./S.A., 11, Groenveldstraat, pg. 668 IT
INTERBREW S.A., Vaartstraat 94, pg. 679 IT
Loctite Luminescent Europe, Interleuvenlear 62-#8, pg. 611 IT
S.A. OmniChem N.V., Industrial Reseaech Park, pg. 41 IT
S.A. OmniChem N.V., Louvain-la-Neuve Plant, Industrial Research Park, pg. 41 IT
Ridge Tool, N.V., Research Park, pg. 577 PB
Terumo Europe N.V., Interleuvenlaan 40, pg. 1376 IT

Liege

Armstrong International, S.A., Parc Industrial Des Hauts-Sarts, pg. 83 PV
Banque Indosuez, Place Emile DuPont, 8, pg. 314 IT
Briko Depot SA, Place Marechal Foch 1, pg. 533 IT
CONSTRUCTIONS GENERALES ELECTRIQUES ER GAZIERES COGEGAZ S.A., 48 Rue de Fouruear, pg. 1149 IT
Distrisud, 35, boulevard de Froidmont, pg. 795 IT
Elkro S.P.R.L., pg. 1149 IT
Etablissement Charles Monseur S.A., Quai du Condroz 5, pg. 710 IT
S.A. Eurinbel, pg. 301 IT
Euroclean Wallonie S.A., 30, Quai de Coronmeuse, pg. 1574 PB
Frippiat S.A., Rue de Fragnee 57, pg. 463 IT
S.A. Heurbel, 16 Quoi Churchill, pg. 301 IT
Intermosane, Hotel de Ville, pg. 437 IT

PB - *U.S. Public Companies Volume*
PV - *U.S. Private Companies Volume*
IT - *International Public & Private Companies Volume*

Jacobs Belgique S.A., Ave. Georges Truffaut 45-46, pg. 1288 **PB**
Koffie Hag NV, Ave. Georges Truffaut 45-46, pg. 1289 **PB**
LOI Fours Industriels S.A., Rue, De Sragnee 165, pg. 1149 **IT**
S.A. P.A.G.E. Municipal, Sue des Petites Vignes 47, pg. 301 **IT**
Polytuil S.A., pg. 903 **PB**
Royale Belge Finance, Boulevard d'Avroy 37, pg. 562 **IT**
SNC-Lavalin, Bd. frere Orban, 25, pg. 1162 **IT**
S.A. Societe d'Operations Maritimes et Fluviales S.O.M.E.F., rue de Isle Sosimon 87, pg. 302 **IT**

Lier

Interteve, N.V., pg. 437 **IT**
MSA Belgium NV, Sterrenstraat 58/1, pg. 1114 **PB**
Monti NV, Antwerpsesteenweg 386, pg. 462 **IT**
Van Leer Belgium BV, pg. 1146 **IT**

Linkebeek

C.P.T.E. S.A., pg. 437 **IT**
Laborelec S.C., pg. 437 **IT**

Lint

Continental Can Europe Service Center N.V., pg. 1207 **IT**
Continental Can European Industries N.V., pg. 1207 **IT**
Sobemi N.V., pg. 1207 **IT**

Lokeren

Cobelplast N.V., pg. 1207 **IT**
Cobelplast Trading N.V., pg. 1207 **IT**
Teveoost N.V., pg. 437 **IT**

Lot

N.V. Mettler-Toledo S.A., Frans Walravensstraat 84, pg. 4 **PV**

Louveigne

Pfizer Animal Health S.A., Rue Laid Burnait 1, pg. 1283 **PB**

Lubbeek

Intergas C.V.B.A., pg. 437 **IT**

Maasmechelen

Esso N.V./S.A., Hermeslaan 2, pg. 602 **PB**
Graco N.V., Industreiterrein-Oude Bunders, Slakweidestraat 31, pg. 757 **PB**
Sumitomo Chemical Belgium S.A./N.V., Rittwegerlaan 52A, pg. 1311 **IT**

Malle

Iveka, Gemeentehuis, pg. 437 **IT**
Redland Koramic Bricks N.V., St. Jobbaan 58, pg. 1093 **IT**

Manage

Sigma Coatings S.A., Parc Industriel, pg. 1044 **IT**

Marche-En-Famenne

Telelux S.A., pg. 437 **IT**

Marchienne-ou-Pont

Dohmen S.A., Rue du Port 1, pg. 514 **IT**

Marchin

S.A. Toleries Delloye-Matthieu, pg. 302 **IT**

Mechelen

Autodesk B.V., Battelsesteenweg 455a, pg. 149 **PB**
S.A. CIBA Vision Benelux NV, Omega Business Park, Industrieterrein Mechelen Noord II, pg. 981 **IT**
Cummins Diesel N.V., Industriepark Noord 2, Blarenberglaan 4, pg. 468 **PB**
Dionex N.V., Wayenborgstraat 14, pg. 510 **PB**
Framatome Connectors Belgium N.V., Antoon Spinoystraat 8, pg. 503 **IT**
Iverlek, Stadhuis, pg. 437 **IT**
Krupp Hoesch Staal N.V., Motstraat 54, pg. 515 **IT**
Runoto Belgium, Businesspark E19, pg. 651 **IT**
N.V. Schering S.A./Belgien, pg. 1204 **IT**
Shimano Center Interbike N.V., Zandvoortstraat 6, pg. 1233 **IT**
Stelrad NV, 274 Oude Antwerpsebaan, pg. 268 **IT**

Meise

Gamma Holding Belgie N.V., pg. 540 **IT**

Melle

S.A. Oxyflash, pg. 301 **IT**

Melsbroek

Federal Express Europe & Co., Airport Building 119, pg. 604 **PB**

Melsele

Pioneer Electronic (Europe) NV, Haven 1087, pg. 1058 **IT**

Merelbeke

N.V. Life Technologies SA, Hundelgemsesteenweg 284, pg. 505 **PB**

Merksem

N & C Boost N.V., pg. 1392 **PB**

Mettet

Hepworth Minerals and Chemicals S.A., Route Hardichamps, pg. 615 **IT**

Milmort

Techspace Aero, Route de Liers, 121 Parc Industriel des Hauts Sarts, pg. 1166 **IT**

Mol

KTI Belgium N.V., Nijverheidsstraat 10, pg. 836 **IT**

Molenbeek

Interga S.C., pg. 437 **IT**

Mons

Akzo Chemie, Parc Industriel de Ghlin Baudour, pg. 46 **IT**
Organon Belgie nv, Parc Industriel de Ghlin Baudour, pg. 45 **IT**
Research-Cottrell (Belgium) S.A., pg. 29 **PB**

Monstreaux

Arjo Wiggins Belgium S.A., Rue Des Heures Claires 46, pg. 568 **IT**

Mont-Saint Guibert

S.A. Centre d'Enfouissement Technique de Mont-Saint-Guibert C.E.Te.M., rue des Sobliers, pg. 301 **IT**
Andre de Vriendt SA, pg. 757 **IT**
S.A. d'Exploitation de Sablieres a Mont-Saint-Guibert, rue des Soblienes, pg. 301 **IT**
S.A. Entreprise de Travaux et de Constructions ENTRACON, rue des Soblienes SB, pg. 301 **IT**
Papeteries de Mont Saint Guibert SA, pg. 757 **IT**

Mortsel

Dormer Tools N.V./S.A., pg. 1186 **IT**
ING Bank Antwerp, Eggestraat 30, pg. 649 **IT**

Mouscron

Simogel, Hotel de Ville, pg. 437 **IT**

Namur

British Industrial Sand SA, Avenue Reine Astrid 8, pg. 615 **IT**
Hach Europe, S.A./N.V., Ch. de Namur 1, pg. 773 **PB**
Ideg S.C., pg. 437 **IT**

Niel

Hoek Loos nv, pg. 811 **IT**

Nivelles

N.V. Allied Colloids Belgium S.A., pg. 62 **IT**
Blount Europe, S.A., Rue Buisson aux Loups, 8, pg. 238 **PB**
S.A. Dexion Redirack, Ch. de Namur 55, pg. 893 **PB**
Montepolimeri Belgio S.A., Rue de l'Industrie, 8, pg. 429 **IT**
Nivelles, 25 Rue De L'Industrie, pg. 1342 **IT**
Sedilec S.C., pg. 437 **IT**
Sweco Europe S.A., Chemin de La Vieille Cours, 10, pg. 578 **PB**
Twin Disc Intl., S.A., Ch. de Namur 54, pg. 1647 **PB**
T.D. Williamson S.A., 6 rue du Travail, pg. 1180 **PV**

Nossegem

Subaru Parts Europe NV/SA, Hermesstraat GC, pg. 523 **IT**

Obourg

S.A. Obourg, Rue des Fabriques 2, pg. 629 **IT**

Oevel

B.F. Goodrich Chemical (Belgie) N.V., Nijverheidstraat 30, pg. 752 **PB**

Olen

Praxair N.V., pg. 1320 **PB**

Oostende

CNO N.V., Oudenburgsesteenweg 102, pg. 107 **IT**
Daikin Europe N.V., Zandvoordestraat 300, pg. 365 **IT**
I.B.D., 28 Zandvoordestraat, pg. 795 **IT**
Milton Roy (Belgium) N.V., E. Vlietinckstraat 20, pg. 1534 **PB**
Monibel NV, Ankerstraat 2, pg. 491 **IT**
Mutoh Belgium N.V., Archimedesstraat 13, pg. 897 **IT**
Rokenj La Couronne NV, Zandvoordestraat 446, pg. 491 **IT**
Teveo N.V., pg. 437 **IT**

Orcq

Saint Brice S.A., pg. 1015 **IT**

Ostmalle

N.V. Southwestern Petroleum Europe S.A., Industrial Zone, pg. 1019 **PV**

Ottignies

Abbott S.A., 2, Rue du Bosquet, pg. 14 **PB**
UM Engineering, 4 Rue Du Bosquet, pg. 1442 **IT**

Oudenaarde

Bekaert Composites, S.A., Composites Dept., Industriepark De Bruwaan 2, pg. 183 **IT**
Dimeq NV, Westerring 21, pg. 389 **IT**
OIP N.V., Westerring 21, pg. 389 **IT**
Plavina & Cie S.N.C., Industriepark De Bruwaan, pg. 1277 **IT**

Ougree

S.C. Corporations Efficiency Growth Through Information Systems CEGIS, rue de la Gare, pg. 301 **IT**
S.C. Recherche et Developpement du Groupe Cockerill Sambre R.D.C.S., Domaine du Sant Treman, pg. 301 **IT**

Overijse

Chemviron Specialty Chemicals, Brusselsesteenweg 359, pg. 1091 **PB**
Phillips Petroleum Chemicals S.A., Steenweg op Brussel 355, pg. 1291 **PB**

Paal

N.V. Galenco, pg. 991 **IT**
N.V. Soprodal, pg. 992 **IT**

Pepinster

Cabot Plastics Belgium S.A., Rue Prevochamps 78, pg. 289 **PB**

Petit-Rechain

S.A. Durco Europe N.V., Parc Industriel, pg. 659 **PB**
Shur-Lok International, Pare Industriel, pg. 997 **PV**
Visol, S.A., Zoning Industrierl 4822, pg. 371 **IT**

Petit-Roeulz-Lez-Nivelles

MECAR S.A., 10 Rue Grinfaux, pg. 49 **PB**

Poperinge

BVBA Verzekeringskantoor Soenen, Casselstraat, 20, pg. 90 **IT**
N.V. Soenen Beleggings-en Kredietkantoor, Casselstraat, 20, pg. 92 **IT**

Puurs

Alcon-Couvreur N.V., pg. 918 **IT**
Grace Silica N.V., Nijverheidstraat 5, pg. 756 **PB**
Pharmacia & Upjohn Coordination Center N.V., Rijksweg 12, pg. 1049 **IT**
N.V. Pharmacia & Upjohn S.A., Rijksweg 12, pg. 1049 **IT**

Raeren

S.A. Hydro Aluminium Raeren N.V., Waldstrasse 55, pg. 963 **IT**

Ranst

n.v. Norske Skog Belgium s.a., Vaarstraat 128, pg. 966 **IT**

PB - *U.S. Public Companies Volume*
PV - *U.S. Private Companies Volume*
IT - *International Public & Private Companies Volume*

Rijkevorsel

Mondi Foods Belgium NV, Grammel 91, pg. 491   IT

Rixensart

SmithKline Beecham Biologicals S.A., Rue de l'Institut 89, pg. 1265   IT

Roeselare

Gaselwest, Stadhuis, pg. 437   IT
HACO N.V., 120 Oekenesestraat, pg. 585   IT

Ronse

Anc.Ets.Cyr.Cambier N.V., pg. 540   IT
S.A. Crawford Door N.V., Zoning Klein Frankrijk, 21, pg. 269   IT
Ideal Tape-Belgium, Industrie Zone, pg. 69   PB

Rotselaar

Havico N.V., pg. 1061   IT

Saint Genesius-Rode

Home Furnishing Lederland, 39, Chaussee de Waterloo, pg. 1463   IT

Saint Ghislain

Hepworth Refractories (Belgium) S.A., rue de la Rivierette, pg. 615   IT

Saint Pieters-Leeuw

ELCO NV-SA, E. Ghijsstr., pg. 775   IT
Keithley Instruments B.V., Bergensesteenweg 709, pg. 947   PB
Sealed Air N.V., Bergensesteenweg 709, pg. 1451   PB

Saint Truiden

C.V.T.-R & D Company N.V., Rekkestraat 2, pg. 1134   IT
Car Finance Belgium N.V., Rellestrat 2, pg. 1134   IT
Drive Medium R & D Company N.V., Rellestraat 2, pg. 1134   IT
H.M.Z. Belgium N.V., Industriezone V, Rellestraat 3, pg. 1134   IT
Ridge Tool Europe, S.A., Industriepark I, pg. 577   PB
Surface Treatment Company N.V., Nijverheidslaan 16, pg. 1134   IT
VCBV Coordinatiecentrum N.V., pg. 1134   IT
VCST Industrial Products N.V., Rellestraat 2, pg. 1134   IT
VCST N.V., Rellestraat 2, pg. 1134   IT
VCST Special Products N.V., Rellestraat 2, pg. 1134   IT
VCST Variabele Transmissie N.V., Groenstraat 60, pg. 1134   IT

Saint-Gilles

Siemens S.A., 116, Chaussee de Charleroi, pg. 1248   IT

Saint-Lambert-Woluwe

Interelec S.C., pg. 437   IT
NRG Services SA, Sint Lambertusplein 14, pg. 1116   IT

Saint-Martens-Latem

S.A. Meggitt Petroleum Systems NV, Kortrijksrsteenweg 126, pg. 854   IT

Saint-Michiels

BN Division, Vaardijkstraat 5, pg. 200   IT
Bombardier Eurorail, Vaartdijkstraat 7, pg. 200   IT

Saint-Niklaas

Ascona (Belgie) P.V.B.A., Europack 31, pg. 857   IT
Esselte NV Produktion, Industriepark-Noord 30, pg. 461   IT
Fuji Hunt Photographic Chemicals, N.V., Europark-Noord 21-22, pg. 524   IT
Fuji Medical Systems Benelux N.V., Europark-Noord 21A, pg. 524   IT
Guilford Texla N.V., Europark-Oost 20, pg. 769   IT
OCG Microelectronic Materials N.V., 17-18 Europark-Noord, pg. 1220   PB
N.V. Olin Hunt Specialty Products, 17-18 Europark-Noord, pg. 1220   PB
N.V. Olin Hunt Trading, 17-18 Europark Noord, pg. 1220   PB
Starke Diekstra NV, Residentie Boudelo, Hofstraat 40-48, pg. 608   IT
Tyco Toys (Belgium) N.V., Hooghamerstratt, 38, pg. 1059   PB
Tyco Toys (Benelux) N.V., pg. 1059   PB
N.V. Weiser Europe, S.A., Oude Molenstraat 106/2, pg. 1055   PB

Saint-Stevens-Woluwe

Air Products N.V./S.A., Leuvensesteenweg 48C, pg. 32   PB
Amdahl Belgium S.A., Wolwe Garden, Woluwedal 26, B4, pg. 527   IT
Cominco Resources Europe N.V., Leuvensesteenweg 325, pg. 308   IT
Ethyl Europe S.A., Woluwe Garden Officer, pg. 595   IT
Hollingsworth & Vose Europe NV, Woluwedal 12, Box 138, pg. 535   PV
N.V. Milupa S.A., pg. 992   IT
Premier Industrial Belgium S.A., Ave. Hipposcratelaan No. 2, pg. 1068   IT

Sambreville

Glaceries de Saint-Roch, Rue des Glaces Nationales 169, pg. 1172   IT
Sekurit Saint-Gobain Benelux, Rue des Glaces, pg. 1173   IT

Schelle

Medelec Northern Europe, Molenberglei 32, pg. 1467   IT

Schoten

Amalga N.V., Bredabaan 1263-1277, pg. 1210   IT
Indugas N.V., pg. 1320   PB
Liebig Benelux NV, Liebiglaan, 11, pg. 380   IT

Seilles

Pechiney Food Packaging Benelux, Parc Industrial, pg. 1031   IT

Seneffe

Hydalu s.a., Parc Industriel Zone C, pg. 962   IT
P.C. Wiaux, Z.I. Seneffe-Manage, Zone C, pg. 1442   IT
Stauffer Chemical Belgium, pg. 1526   IT

Seraing

S.A. Ameco, pg. 301   IT
S.A. Cockerill Forges and Ringmill C.F.R., Boite Postal 65, pg. 301   IT
S.A. Cockerill Mechanical Industries C.M.I., av. Greener, pg. 301   IT
S.C. Fours a Chaux de Ben-Ahin, pg. 301   IT

Soignies

MACtac Europe S.A., Boulevard Kennedy, pg. 210   PB

Sombreffe

Air Products/Spec Gas Facility, Zoning Industrial de Keumiee, pg. 32   PB

Stabroek

Bilfinger + Berger Bauaktiengesellschaft, Vossenpad 6, pg. 196   IT

Stavelot

L'Ardenne Prevoyante, Avenue des Demineurs 5, pg. 562   IT

Stembert

Bontex S.A., Rue Slar, pg. 734   PB

Strombeek-Bever

Medtronic Belgium, Boechoutlaan 55, pg. 1083   PB
Procter & Gamble Benelux S.A., Temselaan 55, pg. 1332   PB

Temse

N.V. Aro S.A., Eurolaan 3, pg. 877   PB
Edi, Kapelanielaan 8, pg. 1463   IT

Ternat

Akzo Coatings Belgium, Div. of Akzo Belgie nv, 38, Donkerstraat, pg. 43   IT
Bose N.V., Essenestraat 15, pg. 161   PV
Esselte Meto NV, Assesteenweg 117 A, pg. 461   IT
J.P. Janssen N.V., pg. 1144   IT
G.L. Rexroth SA, pg. 838   IT
Sarragan Benelux S.A., pg. 25   IT
Sauer-Sundstrand Benelux N.V., Industriezone Ternat, Industrielaan 13, pg. 1198   IT
Van Gend & Loos N.V., pg. 1145   IT

Terte

Kemira S.A./N.V., P.O. Box 6, Rue de la Carbo, pg. 728   IT
S.A. Societe Caroloregienne de Cokefaction CARCOKE, rue de Chevres, pg. 301   IT

Tervuren

S.A. Lancaster Group N.V., pg. 186   IT

Tessenderlo

Dow Chemical Belgium NV/SA, 14, Industriepark, pg. 523   PB
Eurogenetics N.V., Transportstraat 4, pg. 1408   IT
Limburgse Vinyl Maatschappij NV, H. Hartlaan, pg. 355   IT
Pittsburgh Corning Europe, N.V., Albertkade 1, pg. 449   PB
RBB NV, Aubruggestraat Industriepark-Paal-Noord, pg. 1092   IT
Tessenderlo Chemie, Stationstraat, pg. 459   IT
Tosoh Belgium N.V., Transportstraat 4, pg. 1408   IT
Union Electric Steel N.V., Industrie Park, pg. 104   PB

Tielrode

ABI Imtech NV, 224, Ruisstraat, pg. 681   IT

Tielt

Axxis NV, Industriepark Zuid, Wakkensesteenweg 47, pg. 354   IT
Erta NV, Industriepark Noord, Robert Tavernierlaan 2, pg. 354   IT
RPM Belgium N.V., Industriepark Nord H., Dunanstraat 11B, pg. 1357   PB

Tienen

S.A. Citrique Belge N.V., 249 Pastorijstraat, pg. 1121   IT
SES Europe N.V./S.A., Industriepark 15, pg. 1525   IT

Tongeren

Mann & Hummel Hydromation N.V., Luikersleenweg 220, pg. 484   IT
SKF European Distribution Centre, pg. 1158   IT

Tournai

Igeho, Hotel de Ville, pg. 437   IT
Reinshagen Tournai S.A., Rue de la Terre a Briques, pg. 723   PB

Tubize

Thomson-CSF, 28, rue des Freres Taymans, pg. 1385   IT

Turnhout

Anco N.V., Guldensporenlei 88, pg. 244   IT
Belgo-Factors, N.V., Steenweg op Tielen 51, pg. 547   IT
N.V. Fasson Indus. Div., Tieblokkenlaan 1, pg. 154   PB
Inamed B.V.B.A., Prinsenstraat 5, pg. 874   PB
McCain Foods Belgium N.V. (Belgium), 12, Everdongenlaan, pg. 850   IT
McCain Sunnyland Belgium, 12, Everdongenlaan, pg. 850   IT
Organon Teknika nv, Veedijk 58, pg. 45   IT
N.V. Red Band S.A., Everdongenlaan 25, pg. 245   IT

Uccle

JP Moreels S.A., 139, avenue de Fre, Residence La Source, pg. 782   IT

Verviers

Groupe Vervietois D'Assureurs S.A., Chaussee de Theux, 76, pg. 91   IT
Verviers Local Head Office, 27 Place Verte, pg. 147   IT

Veurne

Raiso Belgium N.V., Albert I-laan 78, pg. 1086   IT

Vilvoorde

Air Products N.V., Houtemse Steenweg 20, pg. 31   PB
N.V. Antriebstechnik Bauknecht N.V., Cyriel Buyssestraat 130, pg. 400   IT
S.A. Margaret Astor N.V., pg. 186   IT
Avesta Sheffield N.V., Luchthavenlaan, 25-27, pg. 222   IT
BASF Coatings & Inks Belgium N.V./S.A., Gustave Levisstraat 35, pg. 105   IT
S.A. Benckiser N.V., pg. 185   IT
Biffa Waste Services SA, Mechelsesteenweg 642, pg. 1226   IT
N.V. Biscuits Delacre S.A., Leavensesteenweg 260-262, pg. 300   PB
Blackwood Hodge (Belgie) N.V., Luchthavenlaan 23A, pg. 231   IT
Checkpoint Systems Belgium NV, Eurovil Business Center, Benalt Hanssensiaan 7, Bus. 1, pg. 343   PB
NV Flender Belge S.A., Cyriel Buyssestraat 130, pg. 400   IT
Gresser N.V., Luchthavenlaan 23A, pg. 231   IT
N.V. Kodak S.A., Steenstraat 20, pg. 554   PB
Komatsu Europe International N.V., Mechelsesteenweg, 586, pg. 744   IT
S.A. Levis, 167-199 Leuvensesteenweg, pg. 43   IT
S.A. Makita N.V., Mechelsesteenweg 323, pg. 832   IT

N.V. Maxon International S.A., Luchthavenlaan 16, pg. 717 **PV**
Societe Europeenne des Carburants S.A., Mechelseteenweg 520, pg. 533 **PB**
Uddeholm Tooling N.V., Luchthavenlaan 25-27, pg. 1472 **IT**
Van Leeuwen Buizen Belgium N.V., Schaarbeeklei 189, pg. 1450 **IT**

Vorst

S.B.T.N.V., pg. 1438 **IT**

Waarloos

Alken-Maes, Waarloosveld 10, pg. 381 **IT**

Walferdange

Prometal Luxembourg S.A., Rue de l'Eglise, pg. 550 **IT**

Wandre

Bundy Belgium SA, 55 Au Werihet, pg. 1341 **IT**

Waregem

Bekaert Textiles N.V., 22 Deerlijkseweg, pg. 540 **IT**
CAE Trislot N.V., Roterijstraat 134, pg. 238 **IT**

Waterloo

Binks International, S.A., Chaussee de Bruxelles 684, pg. 229 **PB**
Lucent Technologies Belgium S.A./N.V., Waterloo Office Park, Dreve Richelle 161, Bldg. M, pg. 1018 **PB**
Smith Corona S.A., pg. 1007 **PV**

Wavre

BBL Walloon Region, 10 Boulevard de l'Europe, Bte 10, pg. 147 **IT**
Braas Benelux S.A., 85 Rue Provinciale, pg. 1092 **IT**
Fun Stores, Place Cardinal Mercier 7, pg. 533 **IT**
Johnson-Saunders S.A., Avenue Vesale 10, pg. 712 **IT**
N.V. KSB Belgium S.A., pg. 721 **IT**
Kemira Agro Services S.A., Avenue Einstein 11, pg. 728 **IT**
Kemira International Services S.A., Avenue Einstein, pg. 729 **IT**
Kemira Pigments S.A., Avenue Einstein 11, pg. 729 **IT**
Pannevis Zaadteelt en Zaadhandel N.V., St. Katelijne, pg. 983 **IT**
Sun Chemical Servives S.A., 1 Rue Larmoyer, pg. 371 **IT**

Welkenraedt

Hexcel, S.A., Rue des 3 Bourdons 50, Parc Industriel, pg. 824 **PB**

Wemmel

S.A. Bang & Olufsen Belgium N.V., Koningin Astrid Laan 53, pg. 146 **IT**

Wervik

De Witte-Lietaer Industries N.V., pg. 540 **IT**
Van Rullen Freres SPRL, Menensesteenweg 274, pg. 1499 **IT**

Westerlo

Hertecant N.V., Lossing 22, pg. 222 **IT**

Wetteren

Bekintex N.V., Industriepark Kwatrecht, Neerhonderd 16, pg. 1283 **IT**
S.A. OmniChem N.V., Wetteren Plant, Cooppallaan 91, pg. 41 **IT**
Victaulic-Europe, Industrie Park, Kwatrecht Neerhonderd 37, pg. 1138 **PV**

Wevelgem

Bedruijencentrum Regio Kortrijk N.V., Vlamingstraat 4, pg. 1415 **IT**

Wijnegem

STILL N.V., pg. 811 **IT**
Toshiba Medical Systems NV/SA, Bijkhoevelaan 32C, pg. 1407 **IT**

Willebroek

S.A. New Denaeyer Thermal Industries N.D.T.I., pg. 301 **IT**

Wilrijk

Airtec Division, pg. 96 **IT**
Atlas Copco ACT, pg. 96 **IT**
Atlas Copco Airpower N.V., Boomsesteenweg 957, pg. 96 **IT**

Atlas Copco Compressor International, pg. 96 **IT**
Bailey-Fischer & Porter N.V., Elektronikalaan 12-14, pg. 449 **IT**
Biomet Europe Ltd., Fotografielaan 5, pg. 232 **PB**
Duni Belgium NV, Laarstraat 16, pg. 421 **IT**
KME Belgium b.v.b.a., St. Barostraat 78-80, pg. 719 **IT**
Mediplant N.V./S.A., Fotografielaan 5, pg. 232 **PB**
Victoria-Vesta N.V., Garden Square, Laarstraat 16, pg. 651 **IT**

Winksele

EOC Normalien Belgium n.v./s.a., Brusselsesteenweg 134, pg. 75 **IT**

Wondelgem

Zaden Labor C.V., pg. 986 **IT**

Yvoir

Societe d'Exploitation des Carrieres d'Yvoir SA, Rue de Redeau 36, pg. 135 **IT**

Zaventem

Amway Belgium Co., Ikaroslaan 4, pg. 69 **PV**
Angus Belgium SA, Excelsior Laan 33, pg. 1500 **IT**
Aritech Europe & Central Life Safety Europe, Excelsiorlaan 9, pg. 139 **PV**
BMC Software Belgium N.V.-S.A., Belgicastraat 2, pg. 162 **PB**
S.A. Balzers N.V., Minerrastraat 14, pg. 998 **IT**
Belgian Fuelling and Services Company, Mainard Center, Brussels National Airport, pg. 1168 **IT**
Bull Scion Services, Planet II Leuvensesteenweg, pg. 318 **IT**
CDR International NU/SA, Chaussee de Louvain, 510, pg. 413 **PV**
COBE International Ltd, 30, Mercuriustraat, pg. 667 **IT**
CW Rent Belgium N.V., Leuvensesteenweg 528, pg. 648 **IT**
S.A. Carnation N.V., Vierwinden 5, pg. 919 **IT**
S.A. CIBA Corning Diagnostics NV, Excelsiorlaan 49, pg. 975 **IT**
CiMatrix NV/SA, Horizoncentrum Gebouw 3 B14, Leuvensesteenweg 510, pg. 1395 **PB**
Circle Ziegler S.A. Airfreight, Brucargo, Bldg. 726-730, pg. 373 **PB**
Clairol Distribution Center, Brixtonin 9, pg. 255 **PB**
Compaq Computer N.V./S.A., Weiveldaan 2, pg. 418 **PB**
DSM Engineering Plastic Products, Weiveldlaan 41, bus 6, pg. 354 **IT**
Daihatsu Motor Co., Ltd., Hermesstraat 8C, pg. 365 **IT**
De Lage Landen Leasing N.V., Excelsiorlaan 87, pg. 1082 **IT**
Elscint NV/SA, Excelsiorlaan 35, Box 2, pg. 450 **IT**
Friskies Service Merchandising, pg. 920 **IT**
B.F. Goodrich Chemical Europe, Excelsiorlaan 40-42, pg. 752 **IT**
Hologic Europe N.V., Horizon Park, Leuvensesteenweg 510, pg. 831 **IT**
Hospal-COBE Renal N.V., 30, Mercuriusstraat, pg. 668 **IT**
ITT Flygt N.V./S.A., Vierwinden 5B, pg. 860 **PB**
Iggesund Benelux N.V., Ikaroslaan 2, pg. 886 **IT**
Info'Products Belgie NV, pg. 757 **IT**
Jurid N.V. (S.A.), pg. 53 **PB**
Kenwood Electronics Benelux N.V., Mechelsesteenweg 418, pg. 730 **IT**
Krups N.V., Brixtonlaan, 5, pg. 896 **IT**
Marcam Belgium N.V., Imperiastraat #8, pg. 1043 **PB**
Memorex Telex, Lozenberg 21, pg. 857 **IT**
S.A. Motorola, N.V., Excelsiorlaan 89, pg. 1140 **PB**
SA Netstal Belgium NV, pg. 836 **IT**
Nippon Express (Belgium) N.V./S.A., Brucargo Bldg. 723, pg. 934 **IT**
Nordson Belgium N.V., Industrieterrein Zaventem-Zuid, pg. 1189 **PB**
Novell Belgium, Excelsiorlaan 13, pg. 1204 **IT**
Pfizer European Service Center N.V., Hoge Wei 10, pg. 1283 **PB**
Pfizer Hospital Products (Belgium) N.V., Hoge Wei 8, pg. 1284 **PB**
Premark Food Equipment Group Belgium, N.V., Laan/Ave. Brixton 2A, pg. 1323 **PB**
Purina Protein Europe S.A., 13, Exelsion Laan, pg. 1360 **IT**
RAM Mobile Data Belgium S.C.S., Excelsiorlaan 48-50, pg. 208 **IT**
Ross Systems Europe N.V., Excelsiorin 36-38, pg. 1406 **PB**
SAB WABCO Benelux, Walenweg 73, pg. 271 **IT**
SAB WABCO N.V., Coordination Center, Imperiastraat 6, pg. 271 **IT**
SCA Packaging, Excelsiorlaan 79/81, pg. 1326 **IT**
SMS Belgium, Keiberg Estate, Excelsiorlaan, 4042, pg. 1463 **IT**
SABENA, Sabena House, Brussels National Airport, pg. 1168 **IT**
Sabena Interservice Center Limited, Bldg. 40, Brussels National Airport, pg. 1168 **IT**
Signode Belgium, E 40 Business Park, Sterrebeekstraat 179-D1 & D2, pg. 869 **PB**
Snack Ventures Europe, Imperiastraat 6, pg. 718 **PB**
Sobelease N.V., Leuvensesteenweg 373, pg. 1082 **IT**
N.V. Subaru Benelux S.A., 1, Weiveldaan, pg. 879 **IT**
Sysabel S.A., Chaussee de Louvain 573, pg. 1385 **IT**
Tanabe Europe N.V., Excelsiorlaan 83, pg. 1354 **IT**
Tanabe Seiyaku Co., Ltd.-European R & D Center, Excelsiorlaan 83, pg. 1354 **IT**

Tektronix N.V./S.A., Bedrijspark Keiberg, pg. 1568 **PB**
Thomainfor, Leuvensesteenweg 573, pg. 1385 **IT**
Warner-Lambert Belgium N.V., Excelsiorlaan 75-77, pg. 1739 **PB**

Zedelgem

Flandria Garden N.V., Torhoutsesteenweg 222, pg. 1072 **IT**
Superia N.V., Torhoutsesteenweg 222, pg. 1072 **IT**

Zeebrugge

S.A. Centrale Electrique de Zeebrugge, pg. 301 **IT**
Statoil Belgium, Achterhaven Zuid, Zone 5, pg. 1298 **IT**

Zelem

Martin Mathys, NV, pg. 1358 **PB**

Zellik

Delsey NV, Sphere Business Park, pg. 192 **IT**
Wambacq & Peeters NV, Relegemsestraat 9, pg. 463 **IT**
Wintrucks S.A., Isidoor Crockaertstraat 25, pg. 463 **IT**

Zonhoven

Muva Greetings S.A., Oudestratt 13B, pg. 78 **PB**

Zulte

Innovative Sputtering Technology IST, Karreweg 18, pg. 183 **IT**

Zwevegem

N.V. Acotech S.A., Bekaerstraat 2, pg. 183 **IT**
Bekaert Benelux N.V., Bekaerstraaat 2, pg. 183 **IT**
Bekaert Engineering, Meulebekestraat 139, pg. 183 **IT**
Bekaert International Trade, Bekaertstraat 2, pg. 183 **IT**
N.V. Bekaert S.A., Fibre Dept., Bekaerstraat 2, pg. 183 **IT**
N.V. Bekaert S.A., Dramix, Verzetslaan 3, pg. 184 **IT**
Delaware Computing Zwevegem, Blokkestraar 29A, pg. 183 **IT**

Zwijnaarde

Delaware Industrial Services N.V., Tochnologie Park 1, pg. 183 **IT**
Vlaamse Investeringsvennootschap (VIV), Bollebergen 2A bus 23, pg. 547 **IT**

Zwijndrecht

Borealis Antwerpen N.V., Nieuwe Weg 1, bus 3, pg. 914 **IT**

BELIZE

Belize

Belize Food Products Ltd., pg. 918 **IT**
Belize Telecommunications Limited, Esquivel Telecom Centre, St. Thomas Street, pg. 223 **IT**
Shell Belize, pg. 1141 **IT**
Sinochem Belize Ltd., 5604 Lizaraga Ave., pg. 1255 **IT**
Wackenhut Belize, Ltd., pg. 1731 **PB**

BENIN

Cotonou

Cimbenin S.A., pg. 1201 **IT**
Sodexho Benin, pg. 1275 **IT**
The World Bank, Zone Residentielle de la Radio, pg. 1189 **PV**

BERMUDA

Hamilton

Alcan (Bermuda) Ltd., P.O. Box HM 1386, pg. 50 **IT**
Alcan Finances (Bermuda) Ltd., pg. 51 **IT**
Alcan Trading (Bermuda) Limited, P.O. Box HM 1386, pg. 51 **IT**
American International Underwriters Overseas Ltd., P.O. Box 152, pg. 85 **PB**
Anderson Hill Insurance Limited, pg. 1277 **PB**
Applied Computer Technology, Kenwood Bldg., 17 Reid St., pg. 816 **PB**
Argent Insurance Co. Limited, Cumberland House, P.O. Box 2280, pg. 714 **IT**
Asia Financial Holdings, Ltd., Clarendon House, Church St., pg. 1391 **IT**
Associated Company Management of Ebasco Limited, Airlie House, pg. 1587 **PB**

Associates Diversified Investments Ltd., 1 Parliament St., pg. 665 **PB**
Atlantic Chemical Corporation Limited, Melborne House, pg. 1111 **IT**
B & L Insurance, Ltd., Windsor Pl., 18 Queen St., pg. 169 **PB**
THE BANK OF BERMUDA LIMITED, Six Front St., pg. 150 **IT**
The Bank of Bermuda Limited-Church Street Branch, 64 Church Street, pg. 151 **IT**
The Bank of Bermuda Limited-Par-La-Ville Branch, 30 Par-la-Ville Road, pg. 151 **IT**
Bausch & Lomb Bermuda, Limited, pg. 195 **PB**
Befico Limited, pg. 975 **IT**
Bermead Insurance Company Ltd., pg. 1076 **PB**
Brittany Holdings Ltd., Continental Building, Church Street, pg. 1044 **IT**
Burmah Oil Tankers Ltd., pg. 235 **IT**
Burmah Transport Holdings Ltd., pg. 235 **IT**
Caterpillar Insurance Co., Ltd., c/o Appleby Spurlin & Kempe, pg. 316 **PB**
Centre Investment Services Ltd., Crawford House, 23 Church Street, pg. 1531 **IT**
Centre Reinsurance (Bermuda) Ltd., Cumberland House, One Victoria St., pg. 1531 **IT**
Chemical Insurance Company Limited, Washington Mall, Phase 1, Church Street, pg. 975 **IT**
Chevron Overseas Petroleum Limited, 11 Church Street, pg. 348 **PB**
CIBA-GEIGY Finance & Investment Limited, Washington Mall, Phase 1, Church Street, pg. 976 **IT**
Cigna Fund Managers Limited, Victoria Hall, Victoria St., pg. 357 **PB**
Cigna International Asset Fund Ltd., Clarendon House, Church St. W., pg. 357 **PB**
Cigna International Brokers, Ltd., Victoria Hall, Victoria Street, pg. 364 **PB**
Cigna International Insurance Managers, Ltd., Victoria Hall, Victoria St., pg. 364 **PB**
Cigna International Reinsurance Company Ltd., Victoria Hall, Victoria St., pg. 364 **PB**
Cigna International Strategic Funds, L.P., c/o Cigna Intrn'l Ins. Mgrs., Victoria St., pg. 364 **PB**
Clayton Reinsurance, Ltd., Clarendon House, P.O. Box 1022, pg. 1374 **PB**
Coastal (Bermuda) Petroleum Limited, Sofia House, 48 Church St., pg. 390 **PB**
Coastal Stock Co., Ltd., Sofia House, 48 Church St., pg. 390 **PB**
Commercial Risk Partners Ltd., Continental Building, 25 Church Street, pg. 1152 **IT**
CORANGE LIMITED, P.O. Box HM 2026, pg. 330 **IT**
Coutts & Co (Bermuda) Limited, Crawford House, 23 Church Street, pg. 911 **IT**
Curtis Bay Insurance Co. Ltd., pg. 810 **PB**
Dairy Farm International Holdings Limited, Jardine House, 33-35 Reid St., pg. 703 **IT**
Dairy Farm Management Limited, Jardine House, 33-3 Reid St., pg. 703 **IT**
de Bes' Insurance Ltd., Belevedere Bldg., pg. 1764 **PB**
ELCO Insurance Company Ltd., pg. 993 **PB**
Eastern Insurance Company Ltd., P.O. Box 20111, pg. 1579 **PB**
Eastman Christensen Ltd., P.O. Box 1022, pg. 167 **PB**
Elan International Finance Ltd., 41 Cedar Ave., pg. 436 **IT**
Energy Services International Limited, Clarendon House, Church St. Station, pg. 316 **PB**
EXEL INSURANCE CO. LTD., Cumberland House, One Victoria St., pg. 467 **IT**
Exeter Reassurance Company, Ltd., Victoria Hall, pg. 738 **PV**
FMC Insurance Company Limited, pg. 606 **PB**
Fencourt Reinsurance Co. Ltd., Craig Appin House, Wesley St., HM 11, pg. 795 **PB**
Financial Reassurance Company, Ltd., pg. 665 **PB**
Forte (Bermuda) Limited, Reid House, Church Street, pg. 556 **IT**
Foster Wheeler Trading Co., Ltd., North Rock Enterprises Ltd., Clarendon House, pg. 677 **PB**
Four Stars Insurance Company, Cumberland House, 8th Floor, One Victoria St., pg. 1653 **PB**
GTE Reinsurance Company Limited, Jardine House, Reid St., pg. 697 **PB**
General Holdings Limited, pg. 447 **PB**
Golden Isles Assurance Co., Ltd., pg. 1036 **PB**
Grove Insurance Company Ltd., pg. 256 **PB**
HBA Insurance Ltd., 16 Church St., pg. 342 **PB**
HSBC Gibbs Harnett and Richardson Limited, 75 Front Street, pg. 582 **IT**
Harrington International Insurance Ltd., 69 Pitts Bay Road, pg. 1333 **IT**
High Ridge Co. Ltd., pg. 727 **PB**
Holborn Oil Trading Ltd., Sofia House, 48 Church St., pg. 390 **PB**
Hongkong Land Holdings Limited, Jardine House, 33-35 Reid St., pg. 704 **IT**
Hudson Reinsurance Company Limited, Skandia Intl. House, 16 Church St., pg. 1257 **IT**
Hudson Underwriting Ltd., Skandia Intl. House, 16 Church St., pg. 1257 **IT**
Insuratex, Ltd., pg. 268 **PB**
INTERNATIONAL CAPITAL EQUIPMENT LIMITED, Parkside Bldg., 3 Park Road, pg. 683 **IT**
International Risk Management Group Ltd., 69 Pitts Bay Road, pg. 1333 **IT**
J&H Marsh & McLennan Management Services (Bermuda) Ltd., 2nd Fl., Craig Appin House, Wesley St., pg. 1049 **PB**
JARDINE MATHESON HOLDINGS LIMITED, Jardine House, 33-35 Reid Street, pg. 703 **IT**
Jardine Strategic Holdings Ltd., Jardine House, 33-35 Reid St., pg. 703 **IT**
John Hancock Insurance Company of Bermuda Ltd., Clarendon House, Church St., pg. 590 **PV**
Axel Johnson Insurance Company Ltd., Sedgwick House, 031 Reid St., pg. 711 **IT**
K-Swiss International Ltd., Clarendon House, pg. 937 **PB**
KIC, Ltd., Global House, P.O. Box HM 2280, pg. 594 **IT**
LGT Asset Management Ltd., pg. 810 **IT**
LL&E Algeria, Ltd., 41 Cedar Ave., pg. 269 **PB**
LL&E Tunisia, Ltd., 41 Cedar Avenue, pg. 269 **PB**
LL&E Yemen, Ltd., 41 Cedar Ave., pg. 269 **PB**
Lucent Technologies (Bermuda) Ltd., Conyers, Dill & Pearlman, P.O. Box HM 666, Clarendon House, pg. 1019 **PB**
Mandarin Oriental International Limited, Jardine House, 33-35 Reid St., pg. 704 **IT**
ManuLife (International) Limited, 73 Front Rd., pg. 841 **IT**
ManuLife (International) P & C Ltd., 73 Front Rd., pg. 841 **IT**
The Marine Container Insurance Co. Ltd., 41, Cedar Ave., pg. 1213 **IT**
Navillus Insurance Ltd., pg. 159 **PV**
New York Life Insurance Worldwide Ltd., Seven Church St. West, pg. 795 **PV**
Newbury Insurance Co., pg. 738 **PV**
NOBEL INSURANCE LIMITED, pg. 951 **IT**
Norton Insurance Limited, 30 Cedar Avenue, pg. 1175 **IT**
Nutmeg Insurance Limited, c/o Conyers, Dill & Pearman, Clarendon House, Church Street, pg. 1219 **PB**
Old Fort Insurance Co., Ltd. (Bermuda), 12 Wesley St., pg. 998 **PB**
Omega II Insurance, Limited, Craig Appin House, pg. 1478 **PB**
Pan Arabian Insurance Company Limited, Clareden House, Church Street, pg. 364 **PB**
Paramount Television International Services Ltd., P.O. Box 704, #1 Parliament St., pg. 777 **PV**
Passenger Railroad Insurance Ltd., Craig Appin House, 8 Wesley St, pg. 69 **PV**
Pepsi-Cola (Bermuda) Limited, pg. 1277 **PB**
Pepsi-Cola International Limited, pg. 1277 **PB**
Piper Indemnity Ltd., Boyle Building, Church St., pg. 1210 **PB**
Plaskon Electronic Materials, Ltd., pg. 1404 **PB**
Plymouth Insurance Company Ltd., P.O. Box 824, pg. 1036 **PB**
Priestly Insurance Co. Ltd., P.O. HM 2250, Cumberland House, Level 6, pg. 122 **IT**
Regent International Insurance Company, Ltd., P.O. Box HM 1581, pg. 1374 **PB**
Ridgeway Insurance Co. Ltd., Dorchester House, pg. 960 **PB**
Riyad Insurance Company Ltd., Thirty Cedar Ave., pg. 363 **PB**
Rohm & Haas Holdings Ltd., pg. 1404 **PB**
Rollins Burdick Hunter Co. (Bermuda) Ltd., Cumberland House, 1 Victoria St., pg. 119 **PB**
SEA CONTAINERS LTD., 41 Cedar Avenue, pg. 1213 **IT**
Securitas Capital Partners I, L.P., 41 Cedar Avenue, pg. 1333 **IT**
Shell Bermuda, pg. 1141 **IT**
Sigma Insurance Company (Bermuda) Ltd., Cumberland House, One Victoria Street, pg. 1140 **PB**
Specialty Underwriters Reinsurance Facility, Victoria Hall, pg. 741 **PV**
Stockton Holdings Limited, Stockton House, 55Par-la-Ville Road, pg. 1010 **IT**
SwissRe Finance (Bermuda) Ltd., 41 Cedar Avenue, pg. 1333 **IT**
SwissRe Investments (Bermuda) Ltd., 41 Cedar Avenue, pg. 1333 **IT**
Syntex Pharmaceuticals International Limited, pg. 1122 **IT**
Tate & Lyle Commodites Ltd., pg. 1357 **IT**
Tate & Lyle Reinsurance Ltd., pg. 1357 **IT**
Teddington Company Limited, pg. 449 **PB**
Temple Insurance Company Limited, c/o Conyers, Dill & Pearman, pg. 360 **PB**
Terra Nova (Bermuda) Holdings Ltd., Clarendon House, Church Street West, pg. 365 **PB**
Trans European Natural Gas Pipeline Finance Company Limited, pg. 1149 **IT**
Transcon Insurance Ltd., American Intl. Bldg., P.O. Box 1737, pg. 667 **PB**
Tyco International Ltd., Cedar House, 41 Cedar Ave., pg. 1648 **PB**
Victoria Hall Company Limited, c/o Conyers, Dill & Pearman, Clarendon House, Church Street, pg. 363 **PB**
WTC Insurance Corp, Ltd., pg. 898 **PB**
Watlington Waterworks Limited, P.O. Box 630, pg. 912 **PB**
Willis Corroon Limited-Bermuda, F B Perry Building, Church Street, pg. 1509 **IT**
Willis Corroon Management Limited-Bermuda, F B Perry Building, Church Street, pg. 1509 **IT**
Woodlines Shipping Limited, 3 Park Rd., pg. 683 **IT**
X.L. Insurance Company, Ltd., One Victoria St., pg. 467 **IT**
Zurich International (Bermuda) Ltd., Crawford House, 50 Cedar Avenue, pg. 1532 **IT**

Pembroke

American International Co. Ltd., American Intl. Bldg., Richmond Rd., pg. 85 **PB**
BACARDI LIMITED, 65 Pitts Bay Rd., pg. 131 **IT**
PARTNERRE LTD., 106 Pitts Bay Road, pg. 1024 **IT**

Saint Georges

The Bank of Bermuda Limited-Airport Branch, Civil Air Terminal, Two Kindley Field Road, pg. 151 **IT**
The Bank of Bermuda Limited-St. Georges Branch, Four King's Square, pg. 151 **IT**
Esso Trading Company of Abu Dhabi, 25 Ferry Road, pg. 602 **PB**
Exxon Insurance Holdings, Inc., 25 Ferry Road, pg. 602 **PB**
Mediterranean Standard Oil Co., 25 Ferry Road, pg. 602 **PB**

Somerset

The Bank of Bermuda Limited-Somerset Branch, 31 Mangrove Bay Road, pg. 151 **IT**

BOLIVIA

Cochabamba

Spea-Bolivia, Calle Obispo Anaya 0213, pg. 655 **IT**

La Paz

ALCAMP, s.r.l., Edificio Mariscal Ballivlian, pg. 360 **PV**
Banco do Brasil S.A.-Bolivia, Avenida Camacho 1448, pg. 141 **IT**
Banco Mundial, Edificio BISA, Piso 9, pg. 1189 **PV**
Battle Mountain Gold (Bolivia), Calle Cordero N. 130, Casilla 7341, pg. 193 **PB**
CIBA-GEIGY Boliviana Ltda., Plaza Espana, Esq. Mendez, Acros, s/n mezzanine, pg. 976 **IT**
Hansa Ltda., Calle Yanacocha, Esquina Mercado, pg. 108 **IT**
IBM de Bolivia, S.A, pg. 897 **PB**
Minera Cominco Bolivia Ltda., Casilla 10580, pg. 308 **IT**
Siser Ltda., Gabriel Gozalvez 221, pg. 823 **PB**

Santa Cruz

AGA S.A., pg. 13 **IT**
BHP Petroleum (Bolivia) Inc., Casilla 3568, pg. 225 **IT**
CIBA-GEIGY Services A.G., Casilla de Correo 1968, pg. 979 **IT**
Tesoro Bolivia Petroleum Company, Av. San Martin Esq., Calle 5 Deste, Paseo Commercial, pg. 1582 **PB**

BOSNIA AND HERZEGOVINA

Sarajevo

Hermes, Kralja Tomislava 1, pg. 818 **PB**
TAS Tvornica Automobila Sarajevo, P.O. Box 1, pg. 1475 **IT**

BOTSWANA

Francistown

Sedgwick Insurance Brokers (Pty) Limited, Haskins Bldg., Blue Jacket Square, pg. 1297 **IT**

Gaborone

Barclays Bank of Botswana Limited, pg. 165 **IT**
Blackwood Hodge (Botswana) (Pty.) Ltd., Broadhurst Plot, pg. 231 **IT**
Cominco Resources (Botswana) (Pty.) Ltd., pg. 307 **IT**
Ericom Services Pty. Ltd., Axess House, Thlwane Road, Broadhurst Industrial, pg. 1366 **IT**
First National Bank Holdings (Botswana) LTD., First National Bank of, Botswanan House, Plot 884, pg. 487 **IT**
Heinemann Educational Botswana, P.O. Box 10103, pg. 1094 **IT**
H.J. Heinz (Botswana) (Proprietary) Ltd., Private Bag BR33, pg. 806 **PB**
Kgalagadi Soap Industries(Pty) Ltd., Private Bag BR33, pg. 806 **PB**
Longman Botswana (Pty) Ltd., Plot 784, Independence Ave., pg. 1025 **IT**
Macmillan Botswana Publishing Co., pg. 1479 **IT**
Martex Investments (Pty) Ltd, pg. 167 **IT**
Owens Corning Pipe Botswana (Proprietary) Ltd., Plot 43180, Phakalane Industrial Site, pg. 1238 **PB**
Refined Oil Products (Pty.) Ltd., Private Bag BR33, pg. 806 **PB**
Shell Coal Botswana, pg. 1136 **IT**
Shell Oil Botswana, pg. 1136 **IT**
Stanbic Bank Botswana Limited, Travaglini House, Old Lobatse Road, pg. 1293 **IT**
Standard Chartered Bank Botswana Limited, Box 496, 5th Fl., Standard House, pg. 1294 **IT**

BRAZIL

Amazonas

Lucent Technologies Network Systems do Brasil S.A., Rug Acara 200, Predio J/1, pg. 1019 **PB**

PB - *U.S. Public Companies Volume*
PV - *U.S. Private Companies Volume*
IT - *International Public & Private Companies Volume*

1520

Geographic Index-Non U.S.

Americana

Polyenka SA, Via Anhanguera, KM 129, pg. 46 — IT

Aracaju

Crown Cork do Brasil S.A., pg. 464 — PB

Aratu

Van Leer Embalagens Industriais do Brasil Ltda., pg. 1146 — IT

Araucaria

Novo Nordisk Bioindustrial do Brasil Ltda., R Prof Francisco Ribeiro, 683, pg. 989 — IT
Presidente Getulio Vargas Refinery, Rodovia do Xisto, BR 476, Km 16, pg. 1042 — IT
Van Leer Embalagens Industriais do Brasil Ltda., pg. 1146 — IT

Barra Manse

Companhia Metallurgica Barbara, Via Dr. Sergio Braga, 452, pg. 1176 — IT

Barueri

SADIA GROUP, Alameda Tocantins 525, pg. 1168 — IT

Bauru

American Bank Note Company, Al. Jurua N 474, pg. 68 — PB
Ascoval Industria e Commercio Ltda., Rodovia Presidente Castelo Branco, pg. 576 — IT
Ebara Industrias Mecanicas e Comercio Ltda., Rue Joaquim Marques de Figueiredo 2-31, pg. 432 — IT
Edisa Informatica S.A., Alameda Rio Negro, 750, pg. 817 — PB
Edisa Informatica S.A., Av. Aruana, 125-Tambore, pg. 817 — PB
Kluber Lubrication Lubrificantes Especiais Ltda., pg. 506 — IT
Lapa Alimentos S/A, Al. Tocantins, 525, pg. 1168 — IT
Mettler-Toledo Ind. E. Com. Ltda., Rua San Paulo, 291, pg. 4 — PV
Moore Formularios Limitada, Central Administrativo, Avenida Cavasi, 118, pg. 889 — IT
Pirelli S.A. Companhia Industrial Brasileira, Filial Cabos, Rua Amazonas 4-65, pg. 1059 — IT
Sadia Agroavicola S/A Industria E Comercio, Al Tocantins, 525, pg. 1168 — IT
Van Den Cientifica Ltda., Pca. das Violetas, pg. 823 — PB

Bela Vista

NSK do Brasil Industria e Comercio de Rolamentos Ltda., Rua Treze de Maio 1633, 14 Andar-Paraiso, pg. 904 — IT
T and S Servicos Industrias S/C Ltda., Av. Paulista, 807-21 Andar, pg. 1406 — IT

Belem

Brasilit da Amazonia, Rodovia Arthur Bernardes, pg. 1171 — IT
Mitsui Brasileira Imp. e Exp. Ltda., Rodovia BR-316 KM-3, pg. 882 — IT

Belo Horizonte

Bekaert Engineering do Brasil Ltda., Rua Paraiba, 330, pg. 184 — IT
Brooks-Sellos Da Seguranca Do Brazil Ltda, Rua Bolivar, 128, Barrri; Uniao, pg. 172 — PV
Bucyrus (Brasil) Ltda., Avenida Professor Magalhaes Penido, 439, pg. 177 — PV
Companhia Siderurgica Belgo-Mineira, Avenida Carandal 1115, Edificio Louis Ensch, 17-26 Andares, pg. 79 — IT
Edisa Informatica S.A. (Belo Horizonte), Av. Do Contorno, 6321, 11th andar, pg. 817 — PB
Fuji Electric do Brasil Industria e Comercio Ltda., Rua Guajajaras, pg. 522 — IT
Fuji Electric Nordeste S.A., Rua Guajajaras, pg. 522 — IT
Kilborn Do Brasil Ltda., Av. Brasil, 1666 - 14 Andar, pg. 1162 — IT
Mannesmann Administradora Ltda., pg. 839 — IT
Mannesmann FI-EL Florestal Ltda., pg. 839 — IT
Mannesmann SA, pg. 839 — IT
Minas da Serra Beral S.A., Av. do Contorno 5489, pg. 948 — IT
Mitsui Brasileira Imp. e Exp. Ltda., Avenida Afonso Pena 732 S/701-704, pg. 882 — IT
Samarco Mineracao SA, Rua Paraiba 1122, pg. 224 — IT
Svedala-FACO Belo Horizonte, pg. 1324 — IT
Usinas Siderurgicas de Minas Gerais S.A., Rua Timbiras 2349, pg. 949 — IT

Benevides

Amafrutas S.A., Rodovia BR 316, Km. 20, pg. 974 — IT

Betim

Gabriel Passos Refinery, Rodovia Fernai Dias, pg. 1042 — IT
Ritz-C.Industria E Comercio SA, pg. 577 — PB

Blumenau

Bermo Ltda., Rua Engo. Paul Werner 120, pg. 550 — IT
Tabacos Brasileiros, Ltda., pg. 1695 — PB

Boituva

Ellan Eletromecanica Ltda., Rua Antonio, pg. 739 — IT

Botucatu

Industria Aeronautica Neiva S.A., Rua Nossa Senhora de Fatima 360, pg. 452 — IT

Brasilia

BB Administradora de Cartoes de Credito S.A., SBS-Q.4-BL.A-Ed. Sede I, pg. 141 — IT
BB Corretora de Seguros e Administradora de Bens S.A., SCN-Quadra 1-BL.A-u-77, Ed. Number One, pg. 141 — IT
BB Financeira S.A. Credito Financiamento e Investimento, Setor Bancario Sul, Q.Y-BL.A-Ed. Sede I, pg. 141 — IT
BB Leasing-Arrendamento Mercantil, Setor Bancario Sul, pg. 141 — IT
BB-Tur-Viagens e Turismo, SETS 702/902-Lote B-Ed. General, pg. 141 — IT
BANCO DO BRASIL, Setor Bancario Sul, Edificio Sede III, pg. 141 — IT
Banco Mundial, Setor Comercial Sul, Quadra 1, Bloco H, pg. 1189 — PV
Edisa Informatica S.A. (Brasilia), SCS-Quadra 4, Edificio Brasal II-10o andar, pg. 817 — PB
Mitsui Brasileira Imp. e Exp. Ltda., SC5 Bloco-G Edificio Baracat, Salas 1601, pg. 882 — IT
Salles/DMB&B Publicidade S.A., SCS-Quadra 06-Bloco A #157, Ed. Bandeirantes-Salas 607/608, pg. 305 — PV
TELEBRAS S.A., SAS Quadra 6, pg. 1362 — IT

Brumadinho

Mannesmann Mineracao Ltda., pg. 839 — IT

Butanta

Kanaflex do Brasil Industria de Plasticos Ltda., Avenida Caxingui, pg. 948 — IT

Caieiras

Inmont Industria Quimica Ltda., Av. David Kasitzky, 580, pg. 108 — IT

Camacari

BASF S.A., Rua Benzeno, 765, Polo Petroquimico de Camacari, pg. 107 — IT
CPC-Companhia Petroquimica Camaccari Ltda., Rua Hidogenio, pg. 947 — IT
CIBA-GEIGY Quimica S.A., Rua Gama, 520, Area Industrial Norte, pg. 979 — IT
Ciquine-Companhia Petroquimica, Av. Joao Ursulo Ribeiro Coutinho, pg. 947 — IT
COBAFI, Companhia Bahiana de Fibras SA, Rua Eteno S/N, Polo Petroquimico, pg. 46 — IT
Polialden-Petroquimica S.A., Rua Hidrogeni, pg. 949 — IT

Campinas

Asgrow do Brasil Sementes Ltda., Caixa Postal 1564, pg. 1049 — IT
Bandag Do Brasil Ltda., Av. Mercedes Benz, pg. 178 — PB
Robert Bosch Ltda., Caixa Postal 1195, pg. 205 — IT
Burgmann do Brasil, Av. Sta. Izabel, No. 1721, pg. 233 — IT
Cia. Campineira de Alimentos, Rodovia Campinas Barao Geraldo, pg. 380 — IT
CERVEJARIAS KAISER BRASIL LTDA., Rua Barao de Jaguara, pg. 279 — IT
Deutsche Bank AG (Campinas), Rua Sacramento, 126-17o Andar, pg. 404 — IT
Edisa Informatica S.A. (Campinas), Rodovia D. Petro 1, pg. 817 — PB
Stumpp & Schuele do Brasil Industria e Comercio Limitada, Caixa Postal 1288, pg. 190 — PB
Woodward Governor (Reguladores) Ltda., Rua Joaquim Noerberto, 284, pg. 1777 — PB

Canoas

Iochpe-Maxion S.A., Av. Guilherme Schell, 10.160, pg. 688 — IT
Alberto Pasqualini Refinery, Av. Getulio Vargas 11001, pg. 1042 — IT
Stabilimento, Av. Guitherme Schell, pg. 654 — IT

Carapicuiba

Ridgid Ferramentas E Maguinas, Ltda., Caixa Postal 72, Shopping Center Iguatemi, pg. 577 — PB

Cascavel

Mitsui Brasileira Imp. e Exp. Ltda., Rodovia BR 277, KM 599, pg. 882 — IT

Caxias do Sul

Robertshaw do Brasil S.A., Caixa Postal 308, 95.100, pg. 1244 — IT

Celupa

Companhia Industrial Celulose e Papel Guaiba, Guaiba Rio Grande do Sul, pg. 857 — IT

Concordia

Sadia Concordia S.A. Industria e Comercio, Senador Atilio Fontana, 86, 89700-000, pg. 1168 — IT

Contagem

ABC Bull S.A. Telematic, Rua Haeckel Ben Hur, Salvador 800, pg. 318 — IT
Belgo-Mineira Bekaert Trefilarias Ltda., Avienda General David Sarnoff 909, pg. 184 — IT
ESAB S.A. Industria e Comercio, Rua Dezenove, 117, Cidade Industrial, pg. 282 — IT
Flender Brasil Ltda., pg. 400 — IT
Tecmise Componentes Automotivos S.A., Av. Joao Cesar de Oliveira, 4.205, pg. 688 — IT

Convica

Yamaha Motor do Brasil Ltda., Rod. Pres. Dutra, Km. 218.3, pg. 1516 — IT

Cotia

Mannesmann Demag Movicarga Ltda., pg. 837 — IT

Cravinhos

Zeneca Sementes Do Brasil, Via Anhanguera KM 296, pg. 1527 — IT

Cruzeiro

Maxion Componentes Estruturas Ltda, Rua Dr. Othon Barcellos, 83, pg. 688 — IT
Maxion Fund e Equipmentes Ferroviams Ltda, Rua Dr. Othon Barcellos, 83, pg. 688 — IT

Cubatao

Presidente Bernardes Refinery, Praca Marechal Stenio Caio A. Lima 1, pg. 1042 — IT

Cuiaba

Brasilit do Oeste, Rodovia des Imigrantes km 4.2, pg. 1171 — IT

Curitiba

ABS Industria de Bombas Centrifuges Ltda, Rua BT 3- Nr 701, pg. 270 — IT
Ahlstrom Equipamentos Ltda., Rua Presidente Faria, 248-10, pg. 34 — IT
Blount Industrial de Correntes Ltda., Rua Emilio Romani, No. 1630-Area Sul, pg. 239 — PB
Edisa Informatica S.A. (Curitiba), Rua Marechal Deodoro, 717-8o andar, pg. 817 — PB
Furukawa Industrial S.A. Produtos Eletricos (FISA), Rua Hasdrubal Bellegard, 820, Cidade Industrial Cx, pg. 531 — IT
Kamyr do Brasil Tecnica de Celulose Ltda., Caixa Postal 14.046, pg. 771 — IT
Kvaerner Brasfab Ltda, Rua Francisco Sobania, 1300 - CIC, pg. 767 — IT
Kvaerner Pulping Ltda., Rua Francicso Sobania, 1300-CIC, pg. 768 — IT
TI Brazil Industria E Comerico Ltda., Rua Rodolpho Hatschbach, 1431, pg. 1342 — IT
Van Leer Embalagens Moldadas Ltda, pg. 1146 — IT
Volvo do Brasil Veiculos Ltda., Caixa Postal 7981, pg. 1477 — IT

Diadema

Acos Villares Plant - Diadema, Av. Fagundes de Oliveira, 510, pg. 23 — IT
Donaldson do Brasil, Ltda., Av. Antonio Piranga, 2985, pg. 517 — PB
Industrias Metalurgicas Liebau S.A., Avenida Sete De Setembro 1370, pg. 473 — IT
Kanthal Brazil Ltda., pg. 724 — IT
MSA do Brasil, Ltda., Av. Roberto Gordon, 138, pg. 1115 — PB
Mojonnier do Brasil Industria e Commercio de Equipamentos, Rua Gema 230, S Judas Tadeu, pg. 1194 — IT
Rapistan Demag Industria e Comercio Ltda., pg. 838 — IT
Reifenhauser Ind. de Maquinas Ltda., Ave. Reifenhauser 240, pg. 1101 — IT
Rexroth Automacao Ltda, pg. 839 — IT

Robrasa-Rolamentos Especias Rothe Erde Ltda., Rua Lidia
Blank, No. 48, pg. 509 **IT**
Windmoller & Holscher do Brasil Ltda., Av. Casa Grande
1543, pg. 1511 **IT**

Duque de Caxias

Duque de Caxias Refinery, Rodivia Washington Luiz, Km
113,7, pg. 1042 **IT**

Embu

Vitrosul Industria e Comercio de Vidros Ltda., pg. 1523 **IT**

Feira de Santana

Industria de Sucos Bols Ltda., pg. 752 **IT**

Florianopolis

Edisa Informatica S.A. (Florianopolis), Rua Geronimo
Coelho, pg. 817 **PB**

Fortaleza

Asphalt Plant, Av. Leite Barbosa s/n, pg. 1042 **IT**
Ceras Johnson Ltda., pg. 593 **PV**

Gerais

Cofap-Arvin Sistemas De Exaustao LTDA., Rodovia Fernao
Dias, KM 843, pg. 137 **PB**
FMB S.A. - Productos Metallurgicos, BR 381 KM 11,
pg. 483 **IT**

Goiania

Inco Brasil Participacoes Ltda., pg. 673 **IT**

Guaiba

Cia. de Papel e Papelao Pedras Brancas, Vila Passo
Fundo, pg. 677 **IT**

Guaratingueta

Liebherr Brasil Ltda., Rodovia presidente Dutra, Km. 59,
Engenheiro Neiva, pg. 808 **IT**

Guarulhos

ABB SACE Limitada, Caixa Postal 196 and 197, pg. 7 **IT**
ABB SACE Limitada, Avenida Monteiro Lobato 3285,
pg. 8 **IT**
AlliedSignal Automotive, Ave. Julia Gaiolli 212/250,
pg. 52 **PB**
Cummins Brasil S.A., Rua Jati, 266, pg. 468 **PB**
Getoflex Metzler Industria e Comercio Ltda., Avenida
Rotary 281, pg. 130 **IT**
Industria Maquinas e Equipamentos Electricos Limitada,
Caixa Postal 196 & 197, pg. 3 **IT**
Norton Minerios Ltda., Rua-Joao- Zacharias, 119,
pg. 1175 **IT**
SKF do Brasil Ltda., Rodovia Presidente Dutra,
pg. 1158 **IT**
VDO do Brasil Medidores Ltda., pg. 839 **IT**
Warner-Lambert Industria E Comercio Ltda, pg. 1739 **PB**

Igarape Acu

Agroindustrial Biotropical Ltda., pg. 288 **IT**

Igarass

Norton do Nordeste S.A. Industria e Comercio, Rodovia, Br-
101 KM 249, pg. 1175 **IT**

Indaial

Albany International Feltros E Telas Industrias Ltda., Rua
Colorado, 350, pg. 37 **PB**
Filtros Mann Ltda., Alameda Filtros Mann 555, CEP 13344-
710, pg. 484 **IT**

Ipiranga

Christensen Roder Productos Diamantados Ltda., P.O. Box
30.600, pg. 1174 **IT**
Linhas Corrente Ltda., Rua Do Manifesto-750, pg. 301 **IT**

Itabuna

Companhia Produtora de Alimentos S.A., pg. 920 **IT**

Itajai

River Wood Produtos Florestais LTDA., Rau Reinaldo
Schmithausen, 2.927, pg. 927 **PB**

Itapeva

Extremultus Industria de Correias Ltda., pg. 497 **IT**
Itapeva, Rua Itarare, 12, pg. 677 **IT**

Itapissuma

Alconor S.A., Rodovia PE-35 Km. 3, pg. 62 **PB**

Itatiba

Bobst Brasil Ltda., pg. 198 **IT**

Itu

Jacuzzi do Brasil, Caixa Postal 285 Rodivia SP-79-Km. 53,
5, pg. 1684 **PB**
Starrett Industrial e Comercio Ltda., Avenida Laroy S.,
pg. 1511 **PB**

Jaboatao

AGANOR S.A., BR. 101 Sul Km 17/18, pg. 13 **IT**
BASF S.A., Av. Dr. Julio Maranhao, 3219, pg. 107 **IT**

Jacarei

Pneumatic Division; Industria e Comercio Ltda., Lucas
Nogueira Garcez, 2181, pg. 1264 **PB**

Jandira

H. Fuchs do Brazil S.A., Via Joao de Goes, KM1,214,
pg. 517 **IT**

Jardim Sao Judas

Christensen Roder Productos e Servicos de Petroleo Ltda.,
Rua Solimoes, 428, pg. 1174 **IT**

Joinville

Consul S.A., Rua Dona Francisca, pg. 1765 **PB**
Empresa Brasileira de Compressores S.A. (Embraco), Caixa
Postal D-27, pg. 1765 **PB**

Jundiai

Ideal-Standard Wabco Ind. E Com. Ltda, Rua Honorato
Spiandorim 189, pg. 92 **PB**
Van Melle Brasil Ltda., Caixa Postal 288, pg. 1451 **IT**

Limeira

Ajinomoto Interamericana Industria e Comercio, Ltda.,
Limeira Plant, Rodovia Anhanguera Km 131, pg. 40 **IT**
Pittler Maquinas Ltda., pg. 1128 **IT**

Louveira

Ahlstrom Papeis Ltda., Rua Armando Steck 770,
pg. 35 **IT**

Macau

Nam Kwong Petroleum & Chemicals Co., Ltd., 12th Fl.,
Nam Kwong Bldg., Av. Do Dr. Rodrigo Rodrigues,
pg. 1255 **IT**

Mairipora

Osato- Ajinomoto Alimentos S.A., Av. Tancredo de Almeida
Neves 875, pg. 41 **IT**
Schwing Equipamentos Industriais Ltda., Rod. Fernao Dias,
Km 56, pg. 1211 **IT**

Manaus

Construtora Shimizu do Brasil Ltda.-Manaus Office, Av.
Efigenio Sales, 976-V8, pg. 1233 **IT**
Ericsson Amazonia S.A., Av. Buriti 3000, pg. 1366 **IT**
Fios e Cabos Plasticos do Brasil S.A., Av. Buriti 3000,
pg. 1368 **IT**
Gillette da Amazonia S/A, Avenida Solimoes 800, Distrito
Industrial Castelo Branco, pg. 744 **PB**
Manaus Refinery, Estrada da Refinaria s/n, pg. 1042 **IT**
OMRON Components Eletro Eletronicos da Amazonia
Ltda., Av. Constantino Nery, 2800 Chapada,
pg. 1005 **IT**
Outboard Marine Motors de Amazonia Ltd., Rua Santa Cruz
Machado, 170, pg. 479 **PV**
Semp Toshiba Amazonas S.A., Rua Ica No. K500, Districo
Industrial de Suframa, pg. 1406 **IT**
Sharp do Brasil S.A. Industria de Equipamentos
Electronicos, Rua Acara #203, Distrio Industrial da
Suframa, pg. 1229 **IT**
Showpla Brasil Ltd., Rua S/No Esquina Eixo Norte Sul,
pg. 1237 **IT**
Verbatim do Amazonas Industrial Ltd., Av. Acai 287-A,
pg. 552 **PB**

Mataripe

Landulpho Alves Refinery, Rodovia BA 849 - Km 4,
pg. 1042 **IT**

Maua

Capuava Refinery, Av. Alberto S. Sampaio 1740,
pg. 1042 **IT**

Cofade-Sociedade Fabricadora de Elastomeros Ltda., Rua
Gen. Castilho de Lima, 150, pg. 107 **IT**

Novo Hamburgo

Stahl Brasil SA, Rua Bento Gonclaves 3144, pg. 1526 **IT**

Osasco

Battenfeld-Pugliese Equipamentos Ltda., Avenida Henry
Ford, 643, pg. 825 **IT**
CIMAF-Companhia Industrial e Mercantil de Artefatos de
Ferro, Av. Marechal Rondon 915, pg. 184 **IT**
Osram do Brasil Companhia de Lampadas Eletricas S.A.,
Av. do Gutonomistas 4229, pg. 1244 **IT**

Palmeira

Van Leer Embalagens Moldadas Ltda., pg. 1146 **IT**

Paraiba do Sul

Dentsply Brazil, Av. Marechal Castelo Branco, 200,
pg. 499 **PB**
Cia. Nordestina de Papel (CONPEL), BR 101, Km 06,
Municipio do Conde, pg. 677 **IT**

Parana

Novo Nordisk Bioindustrial do Brasil Ltda., Rua Prof.
Francisco Ribeiro, 683, pg. 988 **IT**

Paulinia

Paulinia Refinery, Rodovia SP 332, Km 132, pg. 1042 **IT**
Rhodiaco Industries Quimicas Ltda., pg. 103 **PB**

Paulista

Malharia Industrial do Nordeste S.A., Rodovia PE-18-km.2,
pg. 1279 **IT**

Perdizes

Sealed Air Brasil Ltda., Rua Eng. Francisco Azevedo, 243,
pg. 1451 **PB**

Petropolis

Dentsply Brazil, Rua Alice Herve, 86 Bingen, pg. 499 **PB**

Pindamonhangaba

Acos Villares Plant - Pindamonhangaba, Rodovia Luiz
Dumont Villares s/n Km 2, pg. 23 **IT**
TI Brazil Industria E Comerico Ltda., Av. Buriti 1087 Bairro
do Feital, 12400-000, pg. 1342 **IT**

Pocos de Caldas

Alcoa Aluminio S.A., Km. 10-Pocos de Caldas/Andradas
Highway, pg. 61 **PB**

Porto Alegre

Banco Santander, Rua Uruguay 155, pg. 144 **IT**
Cornealent Waicon de Brasil Industria e Comercio Ltda.,
Rua Dona Alzira 139, Passo da Mangue, pg. 195 **PB**
DHB-Componentes Automotivos, S.A., pg. 724 **PB**
Deutsche Bank AG (Porto Alegre), Rua dos Andradas,
1001-17o Andar, pg. 404 **IT**
Edisa Informatica S.A. (Porto Alegre), Rua dos Andradas,
1001, 10o andar, pg. 817 **PB**
ILSA-Fruticultura E Reflorestamento Ltda., Rua
Mostardeiro, 333 - 2o andar, pg. 688 **IT**
ING Servicos, Av. Carlos Gomes 111-cj 902, pg. 649 **IT**
Kodak Brasileira C.I.L., Av. Carlos Gomes 111, Conjunto
201, pg. 552 **IT**
SLC S.A. Industria e Comercio, Rua Bernardo Pires 128,
pg. 493 **IT**
Vanguarda Componentes Automotivos, S.A., Rua Pinto
Bandeira 368, pg. 722 **PB**
ZIVI S.A. CUTELARIA, Rua Visconde de Pelotas, 360,
pg. 1529 **IT**

Recife

Cia. Agro Industrial Igarassu, Rua Madre de Deus, 27,
pg. 677 **IT**
Banco Mundial, Edificio SUDENE, Cidade Universitaria,
pg. 1189 **PV**
Edisa Informatica S.A. (Recife), Av. Eng Abdias de
Carvalho, 111, pg. 817 **PB**
Kodak Brasileira C.I.L., Rua Paissandu 567-5 Andar Sala
601/602, pg. 552 **PB**
Nordesclor S.A., Rue Madre de Deus, 27, pg. 1219 **PB**
Usina Sao Jose S.A., Rua Madre de Deus, 27, pg. 678 **IT**
Cia. Usina Tiuma, Rua Madre de Deus, 27, pg. 678 **IT**

Resende

Industrias Quimicas Resende S.A., pg. 983 **IT**
Wander S.A., pg. 986 **IT**

PB - *U.S. Public Companies Volume*
PV - *U.S. Private Companies Volume*
IT - *International Public & Private Companies Volume*

1522

Rio de Janeiro

AGA S.A., Rua da Passagem, 123-6 andar, pg. 13 IT
ANZ Grindlays Bank plc Brazil, Av Nilo Pecanha, 50 Grupo 810, pg. 98 IT
ATA Combustao Tecnica S.A., Rua Divino Espirito, Santa 1100, Carangola, Petropolis, pg. 874 IT
Adecco do Brasil Ltda., Rua da Assemblea, 11/4 andar, pg. 24 IT
Albacora Field Development, Rua General Canabarro 500, pg. 1041 IT
Alcoa Mineracao S.A., 2/5 Maria Coelhode Agular Avenue, pg. 62 PB
Allianz-Bradesco (Rio de Janeiro Office), Praca Pio X. 79-10 andar, pg. 59 IT
Allied Domecq Brasil Industria e Comercio Ltda., Rua Lauro Muller, 116/Gr. 4104, Torre Rio Sul, pg. 63 IT
American Bank Note Company, Rua Peter Lund, N 146, pg. 68 PB
American Banknote Company Grafica e Servicos Ltda., Rua Peter Lund N 146, pg. 68 PB
Anritsu Electronica S.A., Av. Passos, 91 Sobrelojas 203-205, pg. 77 IT
APOLO PRODUTOS DE ACO S.A., Estrada Rio do Pao, pg. 78 IT
ARACRUZ CELULOSE S.A., Rua Lauro Muller, 116, 22nd Fl., pg. 78 IT
Atlas Sul Americana de Fomento Comercial Limitada, Avenida Rio Branco, 128, pg. 90 IT
Australia & New Zealand Banking Group Limited Brazil, Av Nilo Pecanha, 50 Grupo 810, pg. 99 IT
Autologic Information International, Rua Fonseca Teles, 18, pg. 1724 PB
Automatic Power RJ, Rua Eduardo Xavier 60, pg. 1289 IT
Aymore Group, Rua do Ouvidor 107, pg. 12 IT
BBBI Banco de Investimento, R. Senador Dantas, pg. 141 IT
BL Industria Otica, Ltda., Rua Leopolda 351, pg. 195 PB
Ballast Nedam Dredging, c/o Sotep S.A., Rua da Candelaria, 79-11, pg. 134 IT
Banco Boavista Interatlantico SA, Praca Pio X, 118, pg. 142 IT
Banco CCF Brazil, Rua Rodrigo Silva, 26-15 e 16 Andar, pg. 342 IT
Banco Chase Manhattan S.A., Praia de Botaofogo 228, 14th Floor, pg. 339 PB
Banco de Montreal S.A., Travessa Do Ouvidor, No. 4-16 Andar, pg. 155 IT
Banco Inter-Atlantico S.A., Av. Rio Branco 110, 33 andar, pg. 341 IT
Banco J.P. Morgan S.A., Avenida Almirante Barroso, pg. 1130 PB
Bank Hapoalim (Rio de Janeiro), Edificio Torre Rio Sul, Conjunto 2304, Botafogo, pg. 149 IT
Bank of Tokyo-Mitsubishi, Ltd. (Rio de Janeiro Representative Office), Praia de Botafogon 228, pg. 158 IT
Bankers Trust New York Corporation, Avenida Rio Branco, 114, 16th Fl., pg. 186 PB
Banque Paribas-Bresil, Rua da Assembleia, pg. 319 IT
Barracuda Field Development, Rua General Canabarro 500, pg. 1041 IT
Basic Engineering (SUPEN), Cidade Universitaria, Qd. 7, Ilha do Fundao, pg. 1042 IT
Bavaria Servicos de Representacao Comercial Ltda., pg. 180 IT
Bayerische Vereinsbank AG, Rua da Assembleia 10, pg. 180 IT
Belcosa Distribuidora de Cosmeticos Ltda., Estrada Marechal Miguel, Salazar Mendes de Morais, 747, pg. 1489 IT
Bob's Industria e Comercia Ltda., pg. 919 IT
Brascan Brazil, Rua Lauro Miller, 116-29 andar, pg. 435 IT
Carboindustrial, Av. Augusto Severo, 8-7 andar, pg. 447 IT
Ceras Johnson Ltda., Estrada dos Bandeirantes 3091, pg. 593 PV
Chase Manhattan Administracao E Servicios, S.A., Praia de Botafogo 374, pg. 339 PB
Chase Manhattan, S.A. Credito Financiamento Investimento, Praia de Botafogo 374, pg. 340 PB
Chase Manhattan, S.A. Distribuidora de Titulos E Valores Mobiliarios, Praia de Botafogo 374, pg. 340 PB
CIBA-GEIGY Quimica S.A., Estrada do Colegio, 170, pg. 979 IT
Cigna Brasil Empreendimentos Ltda., Av. Paulo de Frontin No. 628, pg. 363 PB
Cigna Seguradora S.A., Av. Paulo de Frontin, pg. 363 PB
Cimento Maua S.A., Av. Almirante Barroso, pg. 789 IT
Clube de Sucessos, Rua das Marrecas 39-3O, pg. 1052 IT
Cobra-Computadores e Sistemas Brasileiros, Estrada dos Bandeirantes, pg. 142 IT
Coca-Cola Industrias Ltda., Praia de Botafogo 374, pg. 392 PB
Commerzbank Rio de Janeiro Servicos Ltda. Representative Office, Av. Rio Branco 123, pg. 312 IT
Companhia Brasiliera Carbureto de Calcio, Praia do Flamengo, 200 17, pg. 1278 IT
Companhia Hotels Palace, Av. N.S. de Copacabana 327, pg. 1214 IT
Companhia Nacional de Cimento Portland (C.N.C.P.), Ave. Alm. Barroso 52-15, pg. 789 IT
Compania Nacional de Mineracao, Edificio Internacional Rio, Praio do Flamenco, pg. 1345 IT
Compania NHK Cimebra-Comercial Industrial e Mecanica Brasileira, Rovovia President Dutra Kmis, pg. 947 IT
Computerworld de Brazil, Barra da Tijuca, pg. 569 PV
Construtora Shimizu do Brasil Ltda.-Rio de Janeiro Office, Av. Rio Branco, 156, pg. 1233 IT
Credit Agricole (CNCA) Representative Office-Rio de Janeiro, Centro Empresarial Rio, Praia de Botafogo, n 228, pg. 341 IT
Cyanamid Quimica do Brasil Ltda., Caixa Postal 1039, pg. 81 PB
D & B Software do Brasil Ltda., Rua de Assembleia 100/25 Centro, pg. 532 IT
DG Bank - Brazil, Av. Alm. Barroso, 63/2709, pg. 352 IT
DPZ, Rua Visconde de Piraja, 351, pg. 352 IT
DEIND, Rua General Canabarri 500, pg. 1041 IT
Det Norske Veritas, Rua Sete de Setembro 55, 15/17 Fl., pg. 396 IT
DICOP, Av. Republica do Chile 65, pg. 1043 IT
Digital Equipment do Brasil Ltda., Avenida Presidente Wilson, 231-26th floor Andar, pg. 508 PB
DIPLAC, Rua General Canabarro 500, pg. 1041 IT
DITEP, Av. Republica do Chile 65, pg. 1042 IT
DITEQ, Av. Republica do Chile 65, pg. 1042 IT
E&P Research, Cidade Universitaria, Qd. 7, Ilha do Fundao, pg. 1042 IT
Edisa Informatica S.A. (Rio de Janeiro), Praia de Botafogo, pg. 817 PB
Editora Campus Ltda., Rua Sete de Setembro 11-16 Andar, pg. 1100 IT
Elevadores Otis S/A, Ave. President Wilson 231, pg. 1691 PB
Elevadores Schindler do Brasil S.A., pg. 1205 IT
Embratel-Empresa Brasiliera de Telecomunicagoes S.A., Ave. Pres. Vargas 1012, pg. 1362 IT
ENAVAL, Rua General Canabarro 500, pg. 1041 IT
Engineering Services (SEGEN), Rua General Canabarro 500, pg. 1041 IT
Esso Brasileira de Petroleo Limitada, Avenida Presidente Wilson 118, pg. 602 PB
Executive Superintendency for Exploration & Production (SUEX), Av. Republica do Chile 65, pg. 1041 IT
Exploration Coordination & Control (GECEX), Av. Republica do Chile 65, pg. 1041 IT
Fabrica Carioca de Catalisadores, 14 Av. Senador Dantas, 4th Fl., pg. 47 IT
Fiat do Brazil SA, Rua Santa Luzia 651, 24 Andar, pg. 484 IT
Florasynth Fragancias y Aromas Ltda., Rua Frei Fabiano N. 36, pg. 173 IT
FRONAPE, Rua Carlos Seidl 188, pg. 1043 IT
GO International Services Electro-Digital de Brazil, Ltda., Av. Nilo Pecanha, 50-Gr-509, pg. 776 PB
GEINP, Rua General Canabarro 500, pg. 1041 IT
Generali do Brasil Companhia Nacional de Seguros, Avenida Rio Branco, 128, pg. 91 IT
Geodesy (GEODES), Av. Republica do Chile 65, pg. 1041 IT
Geophysical Acquisition Technology (GETAG), Av. Republica do Chile 65, pg. 1041 IT
Geophysical Processing (GEPROG), Av. Republica do Chile 65, pg. 1041 IT
Geosource Industria e Commercio Ltda., Rua de Bloria 344-12 Andar Caixa, pg. 777 PB
Gestetner do Brasil, S.A. Sistemas Reprographicos, Rua Assuncao 119, pg. 1115 IT
GETRAN, Av. Republica do Chile 65, pg. 1041 IT
Gilletie do Brasil & Cia, Avenida Suburbana 561, pg. 744 PB
Goinbras Industria e Comercia do Brasil, Ltda., Av. Nilo Pecanha, 50-Gr.-509, pg. 777 PB
Gotaverken Energy do Brasil, Rua Lauro Muller, 116-conj. , 2601-2 Torre Rio Sul, pg. 771 IT
Gulf Offshore do Brasil, c/o BrasTech, Rua da Gloria, 290-20 andar, pg. 769 PB
Hispano-Suiza do Brasil Equipamentos Limitada, 311 Av. Rio Branco, n 311, 9 Andar, pg. 1165 IT
I.F.F. Essencias e Fragrancias Ltda., Avenida Brasil, pg. 899 PB
IMI Cornelius Brasil, Rua Santa Mariana, 21, pg. 646 IT
ING Servicos, Avenida Almirante Barroso, pg. 649 IT
Industria e Comercio Vitronac Ltda., pg. 1523 IT
The Industrial Bank of Japan, Limited (Rio de Janeiro), Avenida Rio Banca 143, 18 Andar, pg. 675 IT
Industrial Department (DEPIN), Av. Republica do Chile 65, 21st Floor, pg. 1042 IT
Industrial Research (SUPESQ), Cidade Universitaria, Qd. 7, Ilha do Fundao, pg. 1042 IT
Information Technology (GETINF), Av. Republica do Chile 65, pg. 1041 IT
Intercarbon do Brasil Ltda., Av. Rio Branco, 52/52 A-15 andar, pg. 1461 IT
Interpretation of Strategic Areas (GEIEST), Av. Republica do Chile 65, pg. 1041 IT
JPM Corretora de Cambio, Titulos e Valores Mobiliarios S.A. (Rio de Janeiro), Av. Almirante Barroso, 52, pg. 1130 PB
Key Perfuracoes Maritimas Limitada, Rua Mexico Nr. 31-D, pg. 765 IT
Walter Kidde S.A. Industria e Comercio, Rua Senador Dantas 76, 2000-Centro, pg. 594 IT
Knoll S.A. Produtos Quimicos e Farmaceuticos, Estrada dos Bandeirantes, 2400., pg. 109 IT
Kodak Brasileira C.I.L., Campo de Sao Cristovao # 268, pg. 552 PB
Kvaerner do Brasil Ltda, Ave. Nilo Pecanha 50, Grupo 1410, pg. 767 IT
Kvaerner Ships Equipment Ltda., Av. Nilo Pecanha 50, Groupo 517, pg. 768 IT
Editoria Larousse do Brasil, Ave. Almte Barrosa, 63s, pg. 240 IT
Latas De Aluminio, S/A-LATASA, 231-24th fl, Av. Presidente Wilson, pg. 1387 PB
Louis Vuitton Distribuicao Ltda, Rue Garcia d'Avila, 117, pg. 782 IT
Lubrizol do Brasil Aditivos LTDA, Estrada de Belford, pg. 1016 PB
Lucent Technologies Brasil Ltda., Torre do Rio Sul, Rio Lauro Muller 116, pg. 1018 PB
MacGREGOR (BRA) Ltda, rua Visconde de Inhauma 134, pg. 670 IT
Marlim Field Development, Rua General Canabarro 500, pg. 1041 IT
Material Supply (SESUP), Cidade Universitaria, Qd. 7, Ilha do Fundao, pg. 1042 IT
Leopoldo A. Miguez de Mello R&D Center, Cidade Universitaria, Qd. 7, pg. 1042 IT
Minasgas S.A. Distribuidora de Gas Combustivel, Avda Graca Aranha, pg. 1155 IT
Mineracao Marex Ltda., Praia de Botafogo, 440-15 Andar, pg. 224 IT
Mineracao Marex Ltda., 15th Floor, Praia de Botafogo 440/15, pg. 227 IT
Mineracao Rio do Norte S.A., P.O. Box 16230, pg. 52 IT
Mineracao Serras Do Sul Ltda., pg. 673 IT
Mitsubishi Chemical do Brasil Ltda., Pria de Botafogo, 228-Ala A, s/1702, pg. 871 IT
Mitsui Brasileira Imp. e Exp. Ltda., Praia do Flamengo 200, 14 And. Flamengo, pg. 882 IT
Montana Participacoes Limitada, Rua da Assembleia 10-Grupo 3301, pg. 1127 PB
Morgan Guaranty Trust Company, Av. Almirante Barroso, 52, pg. 1130 PB
J.P. Morgan Investimentos e Financas Ltda. (Rio de Janeiro), Av. Almirante Barroso, 52, pg. 1131 PB
Morganite Isolantes Termicos Limitada, Rua Darcy Pereora, 83, Distrito Industrial de, pg. 895 IT
Munters Tecnar (Tecnologia Ambiental), Rua Jaci 3, Penha, pg. 669 IT
NHK Cimebra Industria de Molas Ltda., Rodovia Presidente Dutra, KM 178, Nova Iguacu Estado, pg. 902 IT
NationsBank (Brazil) Branch, Av. Nilo Pecanha, 50-Conj. 2005, pg. 1166 PB
Network World Brazil, Rua Luiz Carlos Prestes, pg. 570 PV
Nippon Steel-Empreendimentos Siderurgicos Limitada, Praia de Botafogo, 228 Sla 602, pg. 940 IT
NUCLEST, Av. Republica do Chile 65, pg. 1042 IT
Omnia Minerios Ltda., 6 Carmo Ave., Rm. 1006, pg. 1387 PB
Petrobras Internacional S.A. (Braspetro), Rua General Canabarro, 500-10 o andar, pg. 1042 IT
PETROBRAS - PETROLEO BRASILEIRO S.A., Av. Republica do Chile, 65, Centro, pg. 1041 IT
Petrobras Quimica S.A. - Petroquisa, Av. Republica do Chile, pg. 1042 IT
Petroleum Systems Stratigraphy (GESIP), Av. Republica do Chile 65, pg. 1041 IT
PolyGram Do Brazil, Avenida Rio Branco 311 4O andar, P.O. Bo, pg. 1053 IT
Portocel-Terminal Especializado de Barra do Riacho, Rua Lauro Muller, 116, pg. 78 IT
POSTRADE Rio Office, Rua Lauro Muller, 116/1603, pg. 1062 IT
Purac Sinteses, Praca Pio X 15, pg. 245 IT
Quaker Brasil, Ltda., R Sao Jorge 99/195 Sao Goncalo, pg. 1348 PB
RNBNY Representative Office-Rio de Janeiro, Rua Sete di Setembro 99, pg. 1381 PB
Reader's Digest Brasil Ltda., c/o Escritorio De Advocacia, Jose Thomaz Nabuco, pg. 1368 PB
Reserves and Reservoirs Coordination and Control (GECOR), Av. Republica do Chile 65, pg. 1041 IT
Reservoir Technology and Simulation (GETEC), Av. Republica do Chile 65, pg. 1042 IT
Richardson-Vicks do Brasil Quimica e Farmaceutica Ltda., Ave. Almirante Barroso 63, Grupo 2415, pg. 1333 PB
Rigs and Special Well Services Coordination (GESEP), Av. Republica do Chile 65, pg. 1042 IT
Rioquima S.A., Avenida Beira Mar 200, 6/7 Andares, pg. 984 IT
Salles/DMB&B Publicidade S.A., Praia do Flamengo 200-18, pg. 305 PV
Santa Fe Offshore Construction Co., Rua Mexico 131-D-1002, pg. 766 IT
Santos Basin Development, Rua General Canabarro 500, pg. 1041 IT
Sao Marcos Empreendimentos e Participacoes S.A., Avenida Rio Branco, 128, pg. 92 IT
Shell Brasil SA, Praia de Botafogo 370, pg. 1141 IT
Shell Brasil SA (Petroleo), Praia de Botafogo 370, pg. 1141 IT
Sinochem Brasil Comercial Ltda., Av. Nilo Peganha 50, pg. 1255 IT
Smith International do Brasil Ltda., Rua Santa Luzia 651, Suite 2903, pg. 1478 PB
SmithKline Beecham Saude Animal, Avenida das Americas, 4790, pg. 1266 IT
Cia. Souza Cruz Industria e Comercio, Rua Candelaria, 66, pg. 112 IT
Souza Cruz, S.A., Rua Candelaria 66, pg. 112 IT
Stafford-Miller Farmaceutica, Ltda., Av. Erasamo Braga 299-8 Andar, pg. 237 PB
Standard Chartered Bank (Brazil), Rua da Ajuda 35, pg. 1295 IT
Stolt Comex Seaway Technologia Submarina S.A., pg. 1302 IT
Stolt-Nielsen Ltda., pg. 1302 IT
Sucos Refrigerantes Aguas Minerais Industria E Comercia, 256, Rua Ricardo Machado, pg. 919 IT
Suecobras Industria e Comercio Ltda., Rua Cachambi 713, pg. 271 IT
Sumare Processamento E Servicos S.A., Av. Paulo de Frontin, 628 Rio Comprido, 2nd Fl-Part, pg. 363 PB
Supergasbras Distribuidora de Gas S.A., Rua Sao Jose, pg. 1156 IT

PB - *U.S. Public Companies Volume*
PV - *U.S. Private Companies Volume*
IT - *International Public & Private Companies Volume*

Support Produtos Nutricionais Ltda., pg. 992   IT
Suramic Sucos Refrigerantes Aguas Minerais Industria e Comercio S.A., pg. 922   IT
Svedala-FACO Rio de Janeiro, pg. 1324   IT
Swedish Match do Brasil S/A, Rua Visconde De Piraja', pg. 1328   IT
Swiss Bank Corporation, Av. Rio Branco 99, pg. 1330   IT
TVX Participacoes Ltda., Edificio Internacional Rio, Praia Do Flamengo,154/5 Andar, pg. 1345   IT
Taloca Cafe S/C Ltda., Rua da Candelaria, pg. 1289   PB
Tate & Lyle do Brasil Servicos e Participacoes Ltda., pg. 1357   IT
Technical Information (SINTEP), Cidade Universitaria, Qd. 7, Ilha do Fundao, pg. 1042   IT
Technology Marketing (SECOMT), Cidade Universitaria, qd. 7, Ilha do Fundao, pg. 1042   IT
Tektronix Industria e Comercio Ltda.-Rio, pg. 1568   PB
Teledyne Brazil, Rua da Assembleia, 10 Sala 1124, pg. 44   PB
Temporal, A., Caixa Postal 3527, pg. 6   IT
Texaco Brasil S. A.-Produtos de Petroleo, R . Dom Gerardo 64, pg. 1584   PB
Thomson-CSF Eletronica Profissional Ltda, Avenida Presidente Wilson 231-Gr. 2504, pg. 1384   IT
Thomson-CSF Equipamentos do Brasil Ltda, Rua Cardoso de Morais, 433, pg. 1384   IT
Time Life International do Brazil Ltda., Rua Da Assemblia 10, pg. 1615   PB
Tintas Ypiranga Ltda., 14 Av. Senador Dantas, 4th Fl., pg. 47   IT
Toshiba International S.C. Ltda., Avenida Almirante Baroso 63, 20031, pg. 1406   IT
Transocean do Brasil Partipacoes S.A., Avenida Rio Branco, 128, pg. 92   IT
Trinova do Brazil S.A.-Divisao Aeroquip, Caixa Postal 2536, pg. 25   PB
Turbomeca do Brasil, Av. Alverada 2541, Setor A, Hangar 10, Bara de Tijuca, pg. 787   PB
UBS Representative Office, Praia de Botafogo 228-1.114, pg. 1441   IT
Unisys Eletronica Ltda., 31 Rua Teixeira de Freitas, pg. 1671   PB
Utell International-Brazil, Av. Nilo Pecanha 50, pg. 1098   IT
V&S Comunicacoes, Praia do Flamengo, 154/4 Andar, pg. 1200   PV
Van Den Cientifica Ltda., Rua Jose Bonifacio, pg. 823   IT
Van Leer Embalagens Industriais do Brazil Ltda., pg. 1146   PB
VARIG BRAZILIAN AIRLINES S.A., Av. Almirante Filho de Noronha, 365, pg. 1451   IT
Vitrofarma Industria e Comercio de Vidros S.A., pg. 1523   IT
Voest-Alpine do Brasil Equipamentos Industrials Ltda., Rua Sao Jose 70, pg. 1472   IT
Volvo Penta do Brasil-Industria Comercio de Motores Ltda., Caixa Postal 35004, pg. 1477   IT
Well Engineering and Technology (GETEP), Av. Republica do Chile 85, pg. 1042   IT
Westinghouse do Brasil S/A Electromar Division, Estrada Velha De Pavuna, 257, pg. 275   PB
S.A. White Martins, pg. 1320   IT
Wisconsin Consultar Engenharia, Ltd., Rua De Assembeia, pg. 50   PV
Xerox do Brasil S.A., Avenida Rodrigues Alves 261/275, pg. 1785   PB
York Willis Corroon SA, Avenida Almirante Barroso 22, pg. 1510   IT

Rio Claro

Uniroyal Quimica, S.A., Avenida Brasil,5333, pg. 460   PB

Salvador

Edisa Informatica S.A. (Salvador), Edif. Pituba Park Center, Av. Antonio Carlos Megalhaes, 1034, pg. 817   PB
Exportadora de Tabacos Trans-Continental Ltda., Ave Estados Unidos B 7th Fl., pg. 1502   IT
Hughes Tool do Brasil Equipamentos Industriais Ltda., Caixa Postal 1349, pg. 167   PB
Walter Kidde S.A. Industria e Comercio, Rodovia BR 324 Km 17, Simoes Filho, pg. 595   IT

Santa Cruz do Sul

Empreendimentos Agricola Pioneer Ltda., Rodovia BR-471, KM 49, pg. 1299   PB
Pioneer Agricultura Ltda., Distr. Industrial, BR-471, Km. 49, pg. 1299   PB
Pioneer Sementes Ltda., Distr. Industrial, pg. 1299   PB

Santo Amaro

Banco Chase Manhattan, S.A., Rua Zerbro Divino-1400, 2nd Floor, pg. 339   IT
Construtora Dumez-GTM Ltda, Ave. Alfredo Egydio de Souza, pg. 823   IT
Hyster Brasil Limitada, pg. 1149   PB
Moog Do Brasil, Rua Prof. Campos De Oliveira 338, pg. 1128   PB
Zeneca Brasil S.A., Caixa Postal 55094, Rua Verbo Divino, pg. 1526   IT

Santo Andre

B&D Electrodomesticos Ltda., Avenida Industrial 600, pg. 234   PB

Sensormatic Do Brazil Electronica Ltda., Rua Martin Alfonso de Souza, 202, pg. 1457   PB

Santos

Fujitsu Vitoria Computadores e Servicos, Ltda., Ave. Nossa, Senhora da Penha, 570 8-Andar, Praia do, pg. 528   IT
Paulista Containers Maritimos Ltda., Ave. Marginal da Via Anchieta, pg. 1214   IT
Stolthaven (Santos) Ltda., pg. 1302   IT

Sao Bernardo do Campo

BASF S.A., Estrada Samuel Aizemberg 1707, pg. 107   PB
Brastemp S.A., Ave. Albert Schweitzer 256, pg. 1765   PB
Consorcio Nacional Volkswagen Ltda., Via Anchieta s/n, Km 2385, pg. 665   PB
John Crane Brasil Industrial Ltda., pg. 1339   IT
Edisa Informatica S.A., Rua Bafin, 32-2o andar, pg. 817   PB
EMTEC da Amazonia S.A., Estr. Samuel Aizemberg, 1707, pg. 743   PB
Ericsson Sistemas de Energia Ltda., Av. Rbert Kennedy 74", Jardim Beatriz, pg. 1367   IT
Iochpe-Maxion S.A., Estrada dos Casa, 3.155, pg. 688   IT
Makita Do Brasil Ferramentas Eletricas LTDA., Rua Makita Brsil, No. 200 Bairro Dos Alvarengas, pg. 832   PB
Mercedes-Benz do Brasil S.A., Caixa Postal 202, pg. 368   IT
Perstcrp do Brasil Industria e Comercio Ltda.-Div. Chemitec, Avenida Piraporinha, 852, pg. 1037   IT
Perstcrp do Brasil Industria e Comercio Ltda-Decorative Laminate Div., Avinida Piraporinha, 852, pg. 1038   IT
Perstcrp do Brasil-Technical Laminate Division, Avienda Piraporinha,852, pg. 1040   IT
Scania do Brasil Ltda, Caixa Postal no 188, pg. 687   IT
Schlatter do Brasil, Av. Alvaro Guimaraes, 2487, pg. 1206   IT
Toshiba do Brasil S.A., Estrada dos Alvarengas 5500, Parqu Industrial dos Imigrantes, pg. 1406   IT
Toyota do Brasil S.A., Industria e Comercio, Avenida Piraporinha 1111, pg. 1414   IT
Transalme Sociedade de Representacoes Administracao e Orcanizacao Ltda., Km 23, 5 Estrada Marginal da Via Anchieta, pg. 1475   IT
Volkswagen do Brasil Ltda., pg. 1475   IT
Westirghouse do Brasil S/A Divisao Servicios Industriales, Rua Pindorama, 629-Vila Jordanopolis, pg. 275   PB

Sao Caetano do Sul

Acos Villares Sao Caetano Plant, Av. Dr. Ramos de Azevedo, 133, pg. 23   IT
Delco Remy Division, Avenida Goias 1805, pg. 721   PB
General Motors do Brasil Ltda., 1805 Banta Paula, Av. Goias, S. Caetano Do Sul, pg. 722   PB

Sao Goncalo

Lafarge Aluminoso Do Brazil, Usine de Guaxindiba, pg. 790   IT

Sao Jose dos Campos

EDE - Embraer Equipment Division, Rua Itabiana, 40, pg. 452   IT
EMBRAER-EMPRESA BRASILEIRA DE AERONAUTICA S.A., Av. Brig. Faria Lima 2170, pg. 452   IT
Ericson Packard Electric Componentes S.A., Rua Ambrosia Molina, 1090, pg. 724   PB
Kodak Brasileira C.I.L., Rodovia Presidente Dutra Km. 325, pg. 553   IT
KONE Elevadores Ltda., Av. Dr. Joao Batista de Souza, Soares, 4009, pg. 747   IT
Henrique Lage Refinery, Rodovia Presidente Dutra Km 147, pg. 1042   IT
Rockwell do Brasil Ltda., Rua Sebastiao Humel, Centro 395, pg. 1400   PB
TI Brazil Industria E Comercio Ltda., Rodovia Presidente Dutra, km 148, pg. 1342   IT

Sao Leopoldo

Rohm Brasileira Industria Quimica Ltda., pg. 1456   IT

Sao Luis

Alumar Consortium, BR 135, Km. 18, pg. 62   PB

Sao Mateus do Sul

Oil Shale Plant, Rodovia BR 476 - Km 143, pg. 1042   IT

Sao Miguel

Cia. Nicuel Tocantins, Av. Dr. Jose Artur Nova, 1309, pg. 677   IT
Cia. Nitroquimica Brasileira, Av. Dr. Jose Artur Nova, 185, pg. 677   IT

Sao Paulo

ABB Combustion Engineering Brasil, Av. Paulista 1471-160, pg. 5   PB
ABC Bull S/A Telematic, Av. Angelica 903, pg. 315   IT
AC Rochester Division (Sao Paulo), Av. Leopoldo Dedini No. * 363, pg. 721   PB

ADC Telecommunications do Brasil Ltda, Rua do Rocio 291 CJ52, pg. 4   PB
AGIP do Brasil S.A., Avenida Paulista, 2073 2 terraco, pg. 428   IT
AHP do Brasil, Rua Caetano Pinto No. 129-3 Andar-Bras, pg. 80   PB
AMP do Brasil, Rua. Ado Benatti 53, pg. 8   PB
Accor do Brasil, Avenue Paulista N 2313,9th Fl., pg. 21   IT
Acesita Sandvik Tubos Inox S.A., pg. 1187   IT
Acheson do Brasil Ind. e Com Ltda., Rua Howard A. Acheson Jr. 279, pg. 12   PV
Acos Phoenix-Boehler LTDA., Rua Freire da Silva 379, pg. 1471   IT
Acos Villares Mechanical Engineering Unit, pg. 23   IT
Acos Villares Plant - Mogi das Cruz, pg. 23   IT
ACOS VILLARES S.A., Av. Interlagos, 4455, pg. 23   IT
Acos Villares Steel Unit, pg. 23   IT
ADD Agency, Rua Gomes de Carvalho, 1356-5 Andar, pg. 1200   PV
Adidas do Brasil Ltda., pg. 24   IT
Agricur-Defensivos Agricolas Ltd., 7th Floor, CJ 71, Av. Brig Faria Lima 1698, pg. 830   IT
Air Products Gases Industriais Ltda., Praca Radialista Manoel de Nobrega, 65 C, pg. 31   PB
Aisin do Brasil Com. e. Ind. Ltda., Rua Abilio Soares, 367 1-Andar Sala C, pg. 39   IT
Ajinomoto Interamericana Industria e Comercio Ltda., Villa Mariana, Rua Joaquim Tavora 541, pg. 40   IT
Akzo Chemie Brasil, P.O. Box 12. 745, 1960 Estrada do Campo Limpo, pg. 46   IT
Akzo Coatings-Tintas Wanda, Raposo Tavares Km. 18, 5, pg. 43   IT
Alcan Aluminio do Brasil S.A., Av. Paulista 1106 14, pg. 50   IT
Alcan Empreendimentos Ltda., pg. 50   IT
Alcon Laboratorios do Brasil S.A., pg. 918   IT
Alfa-Laval Equipamentos Ltda., C.P. 2952, pg. 1379   IT
Allen-Bradley do Brasil Ltda., Rua Comendador Souza 194 - Agua Branca, pg. 1398   PB
Allergan-Lok Produtos, Farmaceuticos, Ltda., Avenida Diederichen, 1057, pg. 46   IT
Allianz-Bradesco Cia. Brasileira de Seguros, Av. Paulista, 1415-8 andar, pg. 59   IT
Allied Colloids do Brasil Ltda, pg. 62   IT
AlliedSignal Aerospace Service Corporation, Rua Tabapua, 41-cj-31, pg. 52   IT
AlliedSignal Automotive Ltda., Avenida Liberdade S/N, pg. 52   PB
AlliedSignal Automotive Ltda., Ave. Julia Gaiolli 212/250, pg. 52   PB
AlliedSignal Automotive Ltda-Campinas Plant, 13-100 Campinas, Rua Joao Felipe Xavier da Silva, 384, pg. 53   PB
AlliedSignal Chemicals do Brasil, Avenida Paulista 688, pg. 52   PB
Alpargatas Santista Textil S.A., pg. 1193   IT
Amapoly Industria e Comercio Ltda., Rua Urussui 300, C.P. 8001, pg. 1193   IT
America do Sul Leasing S.A. Arrendamento Mercantil, Avenida Paulista, 668-7 andar, pg. 521   IT
America Latina Companhia de Seguros, Rua 13 de Maio, pg. 1392   IT
American Bank Note Company, Rua Mazzini N 195 - Cambuci, pg. 68   PB
Amway Do Brasil LTDA., Av. Eng. Eusebio Stevaux 1257, pg. 69   PV
Anacomp do Brasil Ltda., Rua Arnaldo de Oliveira, 548, pg. 107   PB
Anderson, Clayton S.A., Av. Maria Coelho Aguiar, 215, pg. 1436   IT
Ansaldo do Brasil Equip Electromecanicos S.A., Av. Paulista 2073 - 5 Andar, pg. 654   PB
Aqualon do Braxil S.A., pg. 810   IT
A. Araujo S.A., Rua Maria Curupaiti 441, pg. 697   IT
Argos Companhia de Seguros, Rua Pedro Americo, 6803 Andar, pg. 355   PB
Arno-Skil Ferramentas Electricas Ltda., Ave. Arno 146, pg. 575   PB
Asahi Bank Sao Paulo Representative Office, Avenida Paulista 1938-18, pg. 83   IT
Ashland Partcipacoes Ltd., pg. 140   PB
Asland do Brasil Ltda., Rue Vergueiro 1883, pg. 790   IT
Astra Quimica e Farmaceutica Ltda., Rua Alexandre Dumas 2220, pg. 94   IT
Atlas Participacoes S/C Ltda., pg. 312   IT
Atochem SAIC, Caixa Postal 20945, pg. 446   IT
Autodesk Brazil, Rua Florida 1758-7 Andar, Brooklyn, pg. 149   PB
Autolatina, Comercio, Negocios e Participacoes Ltda., pg. 1474   IT
Autolatina Brasil S.A., Rua Prof. Manuelito de Ornella 303, pg. 665   PB
Autolatina Leasing S/A-Arrandamento Mercantil, pg. 665   PB
Automax Sistemas e Instrumentos de Control Ltda./Taylor, Av. do Cursino 1425/9 Dep. 04133, pg. 5   PB
Avesta Sheffield S.A., pg. 222   IT
Avon Cosmeticos, Ltda., Caixa Postal 12614, pg. 156   PB
Axios, Ltda., Rua Brasilio Luz, 535, pg. 1577   IT
BBX S/A, Rua Florida 1670, pg. 315   IT
BCN-Barclays Banco de Investimento S.A., Av. Paulista, 1842, 25th Fl., pg. 165   IT
BDF Nivea Ltda., pg. 183   IT
BFCE Brazil, Alameda Santos 705/CJTO 107, pg. 161   IT
BHF-Bank Representative Office, Avienda Brigadeiro Faria Lima, 1461, pg. 120   IT
BMG Ariola Music Ltda., Rua Dona Veridiana, 203, 5th Flr. CEP, pg. 192   IT

PB - U.S. Public Companies Volume
PV - U.S. Private Companies Volume
IT - International Public & Private Companies Volume

1524

Geographic Index-Non U.S.

BNCI Comercial Exportadora Ltda., Avenida Paulista 1842, 16 andar, pg. 339 — PB
BNL Consultoria e Servicios Ltda., Av. Paulista, 1294 - 4Andar, pg. 136
BNL Distribuidora de Titulos Val. Mob. S.A., Av. Paulista, 1294-3 e 4 Andar, pg. 136 — IT
BOC do Brasil Ltda., Rua Bernardo Wrona, pg. 121 — IT
BS CONTINENTAL S.A. UTILIDADES DOMESTICAS, Rua Sarapui, 164 Mooca, pg. 123
BYK Quimica e Farmaceutica Ltda., Rue do Estilo Barroco 712 3, pg. 66 — IT
Bailey do Brasil Instrumentos Industriais Ltda., pg. 449 — IT
Balzers Trechnovac Comercial Ltda., pg. 997 — IT
Banca BBA-Creditanstalt S.A., Avenida Paulista, 37, 19-20th Floors, pg. 347 — IT
Banco America do Sul S.A., Avenida Brigadeiro Luiz Antonio, 2020, pg. 521 — IT
Banco Banque Nationale de Paris Brasil S/A, Rua Joaquim Floriano 72, pg. 164 — IT
Banco BNL do Brasil S.A., Av. Paulista, 1294 4, pg. 137 — IT
BANCO BRADESCO S.A., Avenida Ipiranga, 282-10 andar, pg. 139
Banco CCF Brazil, Edificio l'Arche, Avienda Brigadeiro Faria Limza 3064, pg. 342 — IT
Banco Credibanco S.A., Avenida Paulista 1294, 20th Floor, pg. 179 — PB
Banco Crefisul de Investimento, S.A., pg. 378 — PB
Banco De Boston, Rua Libero Badaro, 487, pg. 184 — PB
Banco de Tokyo-Mitsubishi Brasil S/A, Avenida Paulista 1274, pg. 158 — IT
Banco Financial Portugues-Brazil, Rua Benjamim Constant 75, pg. 251 — IT
BANCO ITAU S.A., Rua Boa Vista, 176, pg. 142
Banco J.P. Morgan, S.A., Avenida Paulista, 1294, pg. 1130 — PB
Banco Nacional de Mexico, Nua Luigi Galvain 70, 1er piso Andar CJ1, pg. 574 — IT
Banco Norchem, S.A., Avenida Paulista 1842, pg. 339 — PB
Banco Santander, Av. Paulista 810 3-Andar, pg. 144 — IT
Banco Santander de Negocios, Avenida Paulista 37, pg. 144
Banco Sumitomo Brasileiro S.A., Avenida Paulista, N 949, pg. 1310 — IT
Bank Hapoalim (Sao Paulo), Rua Sergipe 475 CJ 501, pg. 150 — IT
Bank of America NT&SA, Rua Padre Joao Manoel 923, 14th Fl., pg. 182 — PB
The Bank of New York, Avenida Paulista 949, Conj 182, 18th Floor, pg. 179 — PB
Bankers Trust New York Corporation, Avenida Paulista 2439, 13 Andar, pg. 186 — PB
Banque Europeenne pour l'Amerique Latine (BEAL) S.A., Rua Bela Cintra, 952, pg. 1493 — IT
Bayer do Brazil S.A., Rue Domingos Jorge 1000, pg. 175 — IT
Berlimed-Productos Quimicos Farmaceulicos e Biologicos Ltda., Caixa Postal 21.457, pg. 1204 — IT
Berlitz Escola de Idiomas Ltda., Praca Charles Miller 16, pg. 221 — PB
Bermo Ltda., R. Dr. Jesuino Maciel 1583, pg. 550 — IT
Biogalenica Quimica e Farmaceutica Ltda., Av. Prof. Vincente Rao, 90, pg. 975 — IT
Bols Milani Ltd., Av. Brig. Faria Lima, 613-12th Fl., pg. 751 — IT
Bradesco Leasing S.A. Arrendamento Mercantil, Cidade de Deus, Vila Yara, Osasco, pg. 1009 — IT
Brasil Asistencia, Rua Sao Carlos Do Pinhal, 696 2., pg. 334 — IT
Brasil Beton, Rua Major Sertorio 128, pg. 790 — IT
Cia. Brasileira de Aluminio, Praca Ramos de Azevedo, 254, 3rd Fl., pg. 677 — IT
Brasilit S.A., Av. Pres. Juscelino,02-3 Andar, pg. 1171 — IT
Brasilpar Comercio e Participacoes S.A., Alameda Santos, 1357, 2e andar, pg. 321 — IT
Bridgestone/Firestone do Brasil Industria e Comercio Ltda., Av. Queiroz dos Santos, 1717, pg. 214 — IT
Brother International Corporation do Brazil, Alameda Nothmann, 354, pg. 229 — IT
Bucka, Spiero Comercio Industria e Importacao Ltda./ Walter Kidde S.A. Industria e Comercio, 2148 Ave. Santa Marina, pg. 594 — IT
Bull do Brasil Sistemas de Informaticao Ltda., Av. Angelica 903, pg. 315 — IT
Bull Engenharia de Sistemas Ltda., Rua 1670, pg. 315 — IT
Bundy Latin America, Rua Bandeira Paulista, 600 cj. 22/23, 04532-001, pg. 1342 — IT
Leo Burnett Publicidade, Ltda., Avendia das Nacoes Unidas, 12.995 - 14th/15th Floors, pg. 185 — PV
C-E Brasil Comercia e Industrial Ltda. Subsidiaria de Combustion Engineering, Avenida Paulista 1471, 16O, pg. 5 — IT
CBC Industrias Pesadas S.A., Rodovia D. Gabriel Paulino, Bueno Couto, Km. 68, Ermida, pg. 874 — IT
CCF Representacao e Assessoria S/C Ltda., Edificio l'Arche, Avenida Brigadeiro Faria Limza 3064, pg. 342 — IT
Canon do Brasil Industria e Comercio Limitada, Rua Domingos de Morais 1576, pg. 262 — IT
Carbono-Lorena S.A., Avenue Octalles Marcondes Ferreira, 460, pg. 1030 — IT
Carbosil Industrial Limitada, Av. Do Taboao 3265, pg. 894 — IT
Carillo, Pastore EURO RSCG, Av. Luis Carlos Berrini, pg. 603 — IT
Carrefour Commercio e Industria, Rua Paul Valery, 255, pg. 272 — IT
J.I. Case do Brasil & Cia (a Partnership), Avenida Jerome Case, 1951 Sorocaba, pg. 1579 — PB
Caterpillar Administracao e Participacoes Ltda., Av. Octalles Marcondes Ferreira, Ste. A, pg. 316 — PB

Caterpillar Brasil S.A., Caixa Postal 8239, pg. 316 — PB
Cebrace, 482, Avenida Santa Marina, pg. 1177 — IT
Cegelec Engenharia S.A., Alameda Jau 1754, pg. 53 — IT
Cerberus Ltda., Rua da Paz, 769, pg. 1246 — IT
CesviBrasil, S.A. Centro de Experimento e Seguranza Viana, Avda. Maria Coelho Aguiar, 215, pg. 333 — IT
Champion Papel e Celulose, S.A., Rua Libero Badaro 377, 8O Andar, pg. 334 — IT
M. Chandon do Brasil Ltda., Avenida Europa 863, pg. 782 — IT
Chemical Administracao e Consultoria Economico Financeira Ltda., Avenida Paulista 1842, pg. 341 — PB
Chilebras Metais Ltda., Avda. Sao Luiz 112, 5 Andar, pg. 303 — IT
Chr. Hansen Industria e Comercio Ltda., Caixa Postal 371, pg. 289 — IT
CIBA-GEIGY Quimica S.A., Av. Ibirama 518, Jardim Pirajussara, pg. 979 — IT
CIBA-GEIGY Quimica S.A., Av. Prof. Vicente Rao, 90, pg. 979 — IT
CIMINAS-Cimento Nacional de Minas S.A., Rua Verbo Divino 1488 - 6 andar, pg. 629 — IT
Citibank Brasil, Financiamento e Investimento, S.A., Ave. Ipiranga 855, pg. 378 — PB
Citicard S.A. Comercial Financiera y de Servicios, pg. 378 — PB
Coemea Ansaldo, Alameda Santos 2223, pg. 654 — IT
Coemsa, Avenida Paulista 2073, pg. 654 — IT
Colgate-Palmolive Ltda., Rua Rio Grande 752, pg. 398 — PB
Columbia Tri-Star Films of Brazil, Inc., Rua Santa Isabel 160, 7 Andar, pg. 1282 — IT
Combustherm, Av. Itatiba, pg. 361 — PV
Commercial Intertech do Brasil Ltda., Avenida Paulista, 460, pg. 411 — PB
Commerzbank Sao Paulo Servicos Ltda. Representative Office, Rua Pedroso Alvarenga 1208, pg. 312 — IT
Companhia Administradora Sao Lourenco, Avenida Juscelino Kubitscheck, pg. 1177 — IT
Companhia Adriatica de Seguros Gerais, Rua Dr. Cesario da Motta Junior 614, pg. 61 — IT
Companhia Brasileira de Estireno, Rua Paes Leme #524, 9' andar, pg. 1125 — IT
Companhia Goodyear do Brasil Produtos de Borracha, Avenida Paulista 854, pg. 753 — PB
Companhia Vidraria Santa Marina, Avenida Santa Marina, No. 482, pg. 1172 — IT
Companhia Vidraria Santa Marina, Avenida Santa Marina, pg. 1176 — IT
Concordia Companhia de Seguros, Av. Paulista 1471-1 Andar, pg. 777 — IT
Concrebras, S.A., Rua Major Sertorio, pg. 790 — IT
Conduphon Industria, Comercio, Representacao e Servicos Ltda., Rua Afonso Bras, 413 Conjuto A Vila, Nova Conceicao, pg. 530 — IT
Construtora Shimizu do Brasil Ltda.-Sao Paulo Office, Rua Treze de Maio, pg. 1233 — IT
Coparibe, Avenida Paulista, 1754, pg. 321 — IT
John Crane Brasil, Rua Arizona, 1366-8 andar, pg. 1340 — IT
DPZ-DUAILIBI, PETIT, ZARAGOZA, PROPAGANDA S.A., Av. Cidade Jardim, 280, pg. 352 — IT
Daewoo do Brazil Imp Exp. Ltd., Av. Paulista, pg. 358 — IT
Dai-Ichi Kangyo Bank, Ltd.-Sao Paulo, Avenida Paulista, 1274-11 andar, pg. 361 — IT
Daiwa Bank-Sao Paulo, 11th Fl., Edificio Kyoei, Paulista, Avenida Paulista 467/475, pg. 374 — IT
Daiwa do Brasil Textil Ltda., 1842-21 Andar, pg. 947 — IT
Dart do Brasil Industria e Comercio Ltda., 80, Sertaozinho St., pg. 1322 — PB
Data General Ltda., Rua Nebraska, pg. 486 — PB
Davy McKee Engenharia S/A, Rua Pires da Mota 838, pg. 775 — IT
Cia. de Seguros America do Sul Yasuda, Avenida Brigadeiro Luiz Antonio, pg. 521 — IT
Dennison do Brazil Commercial Ltda., Av. Eng., Alberto G. Zagotis 254, pg. 153 — PB
Detectar Desenvol Tecnicas y Admon. de Riesgos, Avda. Maria Coelho, pg. 334 — IT
Deutsche Bank AG (Sao Paulo), Rua Alexandre Dumas, 2200, pg. 404 — IT
DeVilbiss Ransburg Brazil, Rua Carmo do Rio Verde, 144, pg. 867 — IT
Donuts Comercio de Produtos Alimenticios, Ltda., pg. 64 — IT
Dorion S.A. Empreendimentos e Participacoes, pg. 175 — IT
Dormer Tools Ltda., pg. 1187 — IT
Du Pont do Brasil S.A., Caixa Postal 8112, pg. 532 — PB
Dun & Bradstreet Do Brasil Ltda, Av. Bernardina de Campos 98, pg. 536 — IT
Duracell do Brasil Industria & Comércio Ltda., Av. Eng. Eusebio Stevaux 2105, pg. 743 — PB
Durr do Brasil S.A., Rua Arnaldo Magnicaro, 500, pg. 422 — IT
Duta Ltda., pg. 422 — IT
Dynacast do Brazil Ltda., Alameda Rubia, pg. 301 — IT
Dynapac Equipamentos Industriais Ltd., Rod. Regis Bittencourt 3180, pg. 1420 — IT
Edisa Informatica S.A., Centro Empresarial, Av. Maria Coelho de Aguiar, 215, pg. 817 — PB
Elanco Quimica Limitada, pg. 993 — PB
Electrolux S.A., C.P. 3524, pg. 441 — IT
Electrolux-Servicos Soc. Commercial Ltda., P.O. Box 19.123, pg. 441 — IT
Elgin Brother Industrial Ltda., Caixa Postal 4575, pg. 230 — IT
Engranasa-Brazil, Rua J. Machado 250, pg. 617 — IT
EnviroTech Equipamentos Ltda., Rua Alonso Carbonell, pg. 1489 — IT
Equipamentos Cientificos Instron Ltd., Alameda Joaquim Eugenio, pg. 883 — PB

Ericsson do Brasil Comercio e Industria S.A., Rua Maria Prestes Maia 300, pg. 1366 — IT
Ericsson Telecomunicacoes S.A, Maria Prestes Maia, 300, pg. 1368 — IT
Esselte Meto Ind. e Com. Ltda., Rua General Bertoldo Klinger 150, pg. 461 — IT
Este Asiatico Comercio e Industria Ltda., pg. 431 — IT
Eterbas Tech Ltda., AV. Pres. Juscelino, pg. 1171 — IT
Eternit Bresil, Rua Doutor Fernandes, pg. 1171 — IT
Expasa Anstalt, Rua Urussui 300, C.P. 8001, pg. 1193 — IT
FMC do Brasil, S.A., Ave. Paulista, 1274-9th Fl., pg. 606 — PB
Fate do Brasil Ltda., Av. Thomas Edison 798, pg. 478 — IT
Ferro Enamel do Brasil I.C.L., Av. Senador Vergueiro no 2720, Rudge Ramos, pg. 619 — PB
Fiat Automisveis S.A., Av. Paulista 407, pg. 483 — IT
Finambra Impe. e Com. Equipamentos, Ltda., Praca Amadeu Amaral 47, pg. 1455 — IT
First RepublicBank Dallas, N.A. Representative Office, Ave Paulista 2439-2 Andar, pg. 1165 — PB
Fondo Educativo Interamericano, pg. 1027 — IT
Framatome do Brasil Conetores, Ltda., Estradado do Guarapiranga 2400, pg. 503 — IT
Freios Knorr Sistemas Ferroviarias Ltda., pg. 738 — IT
Fresinbra Indus. S.A., Caixa Postal 24.065, pg. 92 — PB
Freudenberg Componentes Ltda., pg. 505 — IT
Freudenberg Nao Tecidos Ltda., pg. 507 — IT
Freudenberg Nao-Tecidos Ltda. & Cia., pg. 505 — IT
Fuji Photo Film do Brasil Ltda., Avenida Vereador Jose Diniz, No. 3.400, pg. 524 — IT
Fujitsu do Brasil Comunica Cao Electronica Maqinas e Sevicos Limitada, Rua Manoel da Nobrega, 1280 2O Andar, C., pg. 528 — IT
Fundacao Iochpe, Av. das Nacoes Unidas, 17.891, pg. 688 — IT
Fundinox Ltda., pg. 1305 — IT
GGK Sao Paulo, R. Novo Horizonte, 78, pg. 1335 — IT
GKN Comercial Limitada, Rua Tabapua 479-9 And, pg. 536 — IT
Gates do Brasil Ind. e Com. Ltda., Rua Cesario Alvim 602/634, pg. 1396 — IT
Genconsultoria, Av. Paulista, 1754-14, pg. 547 — IT
General Electric do Brazil, S.A., Rua Antonio de Godoi 88-5, pg. 713 — IT
Generale Bank, Av. Paulista, 1754-14 Andar, pg. 547 — IT
Givaudan-Roure do Brasil Ltda., Av. Eng. Billings 2185, pg. 1120 — IT
Goldman, Sachs & Companhia, Av. Brig. Faria Lima, 2020-5 Andar-Cj. 54, pg. 462 — PV
Grace Especialidades Quimicos e Plasticas, Av. Mofarrej 619, Vila Leopoldina, pg. 755 — IT
Groupe SEB Do Brasil, Rua Serra da Borborema 105, pg. 568 — IT
Gumaco Industria E Comercio Ltda., Rua Maria Jose da Conceicao 166, pg. 705 — IT
Gunnebo do Brasil Ltda, Rua Vicosa do Ceara, 91, pg. 578 — IT
Gunsan Exportadora e Importadora Ltda., Av. Paulista, 2001, pg. 579 — IT
Hartmann & Braun do Brasil Controle e Instrumentacap Ltda., pg. 835 — IT
Harza-Hidrobrasileira Engenharia e Projetos Ltda, Rua Douter Bacelar, 91, Vila Clementino, pg. 509 — PV
Heinemann ELT-Brazil, Rua Carlos Comenale 281, pg. 1479 — IT
Henkel S/A. Industrias Quimicas, Av. das Nacoes Unidas, 10.989, Edificio Wilson Mendes Caldeira, pg. 613 — IT
Hercules do Brasil Produtos Quimicos Ltda., Av. Brigadeiro Raria Lima 1664, pg. 811 — IT
Hero Equipamentos Industrias Ltda., Rua Joao Ventura Batista, 622, pg. 967 — IT
Heublein do Brasil, Rua Arapore, 655, pg. 410 — IT
Hoesch Industria de Molas Ltda., Av. Abrahao Goncalves Braga, 4, pg. 508 — IT
Hoipart, Av. Pres. Juscelino, pg. 1171 — IT
Holset Brazil, Rua Jate, 266, pg. 469 — PB
Honda Motor do Brasil Ltda., Se Rue, Sena Madureira 1500, pg. 635 — IT
Honeywell Bull do Brasil S.A., Av. Angelica, 903-10A, pg. 318 — IT
Honeywell do Brasil & Cia., Rua Jose Alves Da Cunha, Lima, 172, pg. 834 — IT
Honeywell-Measurex do Brazil Controles de Processamento Ltda., Rua Coelho Neto, 329, pg. 833 — PB
Hoogovens Technical Service do Brasil Ltda., Avenida Paulista 1471, pg. 755 — IT
Houghton Brazil LTDA., Cx Postal 107 Capuava Mava, pg. 541 — PV
Hugo Boss do Brasil Ltda., pg. 638 — IT
Hugo Boss Holding (Brasil) Ltda., pg. 638 — IT
Huls do Brasil Ltda., Avenida Paulista 467/475 - 12 andar, pg. 1455 — IT
Hunter Douglas do Brazil Ltda., Av. Sao Gualter 931, pg. 640 — IT
Hutchison Mobile Data Limited, Av. Ibirapuera, 2033, 16th Floor, pg. 1139 — PB
Hydro Fertilizanted Ltda., rua Estela, pg. 963 — IT
ICC Comercio e Industria Ltds., Alameda Lorena 1304-14 Andar, pg. 554 — PV
ING Bank Sao Paulo, Rua Jorge Coelho, 16, pg. 649 — IT
ING Baring Corretora de Valores Mobiliaros, Rua Jorge Coelho, 1610 andar, pg. 649 — IT
ING Baring Securities do Brazil, Office 92, 9th Floor, pg. 649 — IT
ING Guilder, Rua Jorge Coelho, 16, pg. 650 — IT
ISS Servisystem Com. E. Ind. Ltda., Estrada da Ressaca No. 960, pg. 657 — IT
ISS Sulamericana Comercial Ltda., Estrada da Ressaca No. 960, pg. 657 — IT
ITW Mapri Industria e Comercio Ltda., Avenida Guarapiranga, 1389, pg. 868 — PB

PB - *U.S. Public Companies Volume*
PV - *U.S. Private Companies Volume*
IT - *International Public & Private Companies Volume*

1525

Geographic Index-Non U.S.

Ideal-Standard Brazil, Al. Jauaperi 299, pg. 92 PB
IGT-Do Brasil Promocoes E Servicos Ltda., Rua Porto Martins 546-3 Andar, pg. 900 PB
Indusquima S.A., Estr. Fernando Nobre 600, pg. 613 IT
Industria de Pneumaticos Firestone Ltda., Caixa Postal 8177, pg. 215 IT
Industria de Produtos Alimenticios Confianca S.A., pg. 920 IT
Industria e Comercio Metalurgica Atlas S.A., Av. Jose Gaspar de Oliveira, 21, pg. 677 IT
Industria Freios Knorr Ltda., pg. 738 IT
The Industrial Bank of Japan, Limited (Sao Paulo), Av. Paulista, 1842-21 Andar, pg. 675 IT
Industrias Brasileiras Artigos Refratarios S.A., Praca Ramos de Azevedo, 254, Ist Fl., pg. 677 IT
Industrias Farmaceuticas Fontoura Wyeth S.A., Rua Caetano Pinto 129, pg. 81 PB
Industrias Gessy Lever Ltda., Avda. Maria Coelhe Aguiar 215, Bloco C, 2nd Fl., pg. 1437 IT
S.A. INDUSTRIAS VOTORANTIM, Av. Rokui Betrone Jr., 999, pg. 677 IT
Intel Semicondutores do Brazil, Rue Florida, 1703-2, pg. 887 PB
Interelectrica Administracao e Participacoes Ltda., Rua Libero Badaro, 293, pg. 1452 IT
IOCHPE-MAXION S.A., Av. Eng. Luis Carlos Berrini, 1253, pg. 688 IT
Italimpianti Intl.-Brazil, Ave. dr. Cardoso de Mello 1855, pg. 655 IT
Itsemap do Brasil, Ltda., Rua Sao Carlos Pinhal 696, pg. 333 IT
JPM Corretora de Cambio, Titulos e Valores Mobiliarios S.A., Avenida Paulista, 1294, 8th Fl., pg. 1130 PB
Janssen Cilag Brazil, Avenida Nacoes Unidas, 12,955-29 Andar, pg. 929 PB
Jeumont-Schneider do Brasil, Av. Brigadeiro Faria Lima 2003-14 andar, pg. 706 IT
John Hancock Servicos Internacionais S/C., Ltda., Ave. Ipiranga 324 Building C Edifico Inv, pg. 590 PV
Axel Johnson do Brasil Ind. E. Com. Ltda., PO Box 1185, Av. Paulista, 2006 12th Fl., pg. 711 IT
K-C do Brasil Ltda., Caixa Postal 7238, pg. 959 PB
KSB Bombas Hidraulicas S.A., pg. 721 IT
Kawasaki do Brazil Industria E Comercio Ltda., Avenida Paulista 1294/1318-5, pg. 726 IT
Kellogg Brasil & CIA, Rua Augusto Ferreira de Morales, 602, pg. 947 PB
Kenwood ELectronics Brasil Ltda., Avenida Indianopolis 628, pg. 730 IT
Keystone do Brasil Ltda., Av. Antonio Bardella, Sorocabo, N. 3.000, pg. 1650 PB
Walter Kidde S.A. Industria e Comercio, 2148 Av. Santa Marina, pg. 594 IT
Komatsu do Brasil Ltda., Av. Paulista 1439-4 Andar CJ., pg. 744 IT
Korn/Ferry International, Condomino Transatlantico, Rue Verbo Divino, pg. 633 PV
Krupp Hoesch Stahlexport GmbH, c/o Polysius Tecnicos Ltda., Av. Brigadeiro Faria Lima, pg. 516 IT
Krupp Metalurgica Campo Limpo Ltda., Av. Alfried Krupp, 1050, pg. 508 IT
Kubota Brasil Ltda., Av. Fagundes De Oliveira 900, pg. 763 IT
Kyoei do Brasil Companhia de Seguros, Av. Paulista 475-16 andar, pg. 777 IT
Kyoei do Brasil Companhia de Seguros, pg. 777 IT
Kyoei do Brasil Empreendimentos Comerciais Ltda, pg. 777 IT
Kyoei do Brasil S/A-Empreendimentos Imobiliarios, pg. 777 IT
Kyoei Facom S/A-Centro de Computacao, pg. 777 IT
The Kyoei Mutual Fire & Marine Insurance Company, Av. Paulista, 1471-1 Andar, pg. 777 IT
Kyoei S/A-Centro de Check-ups Medicos, pg. 777 IT
Kyowa Hakko Do Brasil Ltda., Av. Paulista 949, 21-Andar, pg. 778 IT
Laboratorios Pfizer Ltd., Av. Pres. Tancredo de Almeida Neves, pg. 1284 PB
Laboratorios Wyeth-Whitehall Ltda., Caixa Postal No. 7156, pg. 81 PB
Laborterapica-Bristol Quimica e Farmaceutica Ltda., Rue Carlos Gomes 924, pg. 256 PB
Eli Lilly do Brasil Limitada, Avenica Morumbi 8264, pg. 993 PB
Lincoln Electric do Brasil, Ave. Torres de Oliveira, 329, pg. 997 PB
Littelfuse do Brasil, Rua Irapuru N 54-A, 02960070, pg. 1001 PB
Arthur D. Little Limitada, Avenida Brigadeiro Faria Lima, 1478, pg. 671 PV
Loctite Brasil Ltda., Av. Prof. Vernon Kriebel 91, pg. 611 IT
Lord Industrial Ltda., Via Anhanguera, Km. 63.5, pg. 676 PV
Lowe Loducca & Partners, Av. Naceos Unidas, pg. 678 PV
Lucent Technologies Multimedia Brasil S.A., Rua Dr. Gevalodo Compos, Mereira, 11th Fl., River Park Bldg., pg. 1019 PB
Luwa Climatecnica SA, pg. 617 IT
Luxottica Do Brasil Ltda., Av. Brig. Faria Lima 8880, pg. 822 IT
MTV Brasil, Avenida Prof. Alfonso Bovero #52, pg. 779 PV
Makro Atacadista S.A., Rua Carlos L. Carlucci, 519, pg. 1155 IT
Mannesmann Comercial SA, pg. 839 IT
Manville do Brasil, Rua Barao de Itapetinga 140 14 Andar, pg. 927 PB
MAPFRE do Brasil Consultoria e Servicios, Ltda., Rua Sao Carlos Pinhal 696, pg. 333 IT
Marcam Do Brasil, Alameda Ribeirao Preto 130, Con, 51-5 Andar Bela Vista, pg. 1043 PB
Matel Tecnologia de Teleinformatica S.A., Rua Maria Prestes Maia, 300, pg. 1369 IT
Mead Embalagens LTDA, Avenida Sao Gabriel, No. 333-16th Fl., pg. 1076 PB
The Meiji Life Insurance Company Sao Paulo Office, Rua 13 de Maio, pg. 854 IT
Meiji Seika do Brasil Ltda., Rua Tutoia 86, Paraiso, pg. 856 IT
Melitta do Brasil Industria e Comercio Ltda., Ave. Montero Lobato 1000, pg. 857 IT
Metallurg do Brazil Ltda., Rua Geraldo Flausino Gomes, 85-3 andar, pg. 735 PV
Michelin Industria e Comercio S/A, R. Monsenhor Andrade 114 Bras, pg. 322 IT
Microlite S.A. (Group), pg. 1452 IT
Microsoft Informatica Ltda., pg. 1108 PB
Midland Holding Participacao, Administracao e Representacoes Limitada, Avenida Brigadeiro Faria Lima 2020, pg. 580 IT
Millipore Industria e Commercio Ltda., Rua Prof. Campos de Oliveira, 430 Bairro: Jurubatuba-St. Amaro, pg. 1113 PB
Cia. Mineira de Metais, Praca Ramos de Azevedo, 254, pg. 677 IT
S.A. Mineracao de Amianto, Cana Brava, Caixa Postal 01,, pg. 1171 IT
Mitsubishi Brasileira de Industria Pesada Ltda. (MBI), Alameda dos Quinimuras, 187-3 andar, Planalto Paulista, pg. 874 IT
Mitsui Brasileira Imp. E Exp. Ltda., Avenida Bernardino de Campos, 98 Paraiso, pg. 882 IT
Mitsui do Brasil Trading S.A., Avenida Bernardino de Campos, 98 Paraiso, pg. 882 IT
Mobil Oil do Brasil (Industria e Commercio) Ltda., pg. 1119 PB
Molex Eletronica Ltda., Rua Capitao Francisco Teixeira, Nogueira #232 Bairro, pg. 1122 PB
Monroe Auto Pecas S.A., PCA Vereador Marcos Portiolli, pg. 1580 PB
Monsanto do Brasil Ltda. (Mobra S.A.), Rua Paes Leme no. 524 Edificio Passarelli, pg. 1125 PB
Moody's America Latina Ltda., World Trade Center, Av. das Nacoes Unidas, pg. 537 PB
Morgan Guaranty Trust Company, Avenida Paulista, 1294, pg. 1130 PB
J.P. Morgan Investimentos e Finances Ltda., Avenida Paulista, 1294, 8th Fl., pg. 1131 PB
Morganite do Brasil Industrial Limitada Refractories Division, Av. Jorge Alfredo, Camasmie 350, Parque, pg. 394 IT
Morganite do Brasil Industrial Limitada, Av. Jorge Alfreda, Camasmie 350, pg. 895 IT
Motorola do Brasil Ltda., Rua Paes Leme, 524, 5th Floor, pg. 1139 PB
Multibanco Internacional de Investimentos S.A. Sao Paulo Head Office, 24 de Maio 195, pg. 183 PB
Munters Brazil Indestria Comerico Ltda, Rua Formosa, 290, pg. 669 IT
NC Comercial Exportadora Ltda., Avenida Paulista 1842, pg. 339 PB
NHK Fastener do Brasil Industria e Comercio Ltda., AV. Francisco Monteiro 4140, Ribeivao Pires, pg. 902 IT
NIFE Brasil Sistemas Eletricos Ltda., Avenida Pires do Rio, 400 Itaquera, pg. 54 IT
NYK-Sao Paulo, c/o Lachman Agencias Maritimas S.A., pg. 941 IT
Nalco Brasil Ltda., Av. Das Nacoes Unidas, 17. 891, 11, pg. 150 PB
Nature's Sunshine Produtos Naturais Ltda., pg. 1167 PB
Nedlloyd do Brasil Navegacao Ltda., pg. 1145 IT
Nestle Industrial e Commercial Ltda., Av. das Nacoes Unidas, 12495, pg. 921 IT
A.C. Nielsen, Ltda., Av. Bernardino de Campos,98-14 Andar, pg. 1183 PB
Nippon Credit Bank Ltd.-Sao Paulo, Avenida Paulista 1274, pg. 933 IT
Nippon Express do Brasil Transportes Internacionals Ltda., Rua Fortaleza, 53, Bela Vista, pg. 934 IT
Nippon Meat Packers do Brasil Exp. E Imp. Ltda., Avenida Paulista, 807, Conj. 216/217, Bela Vista, pg. 936 IT
Nippon Steel Siderurgia Ltda., Av. Paulista, 949-22 Andar-Conjunto # 222, pg. 940 IT
Nissho Iwai do Brasil S.A., Av. Paulista, 1842-21 Andar CJS 215 A218, pg. 948 IT
Nissin-Ajinomoto Alimentos Ltda., Rua Soldado Ocimar Guimaraes da Silva, pg. 950 IT
Norchem Distribuidora de Titulos e Valores Mobiliarios S.A., Avenida Paulista 1842, pg. 339 PB
Nordson do Brasil Industria e Comercio Ltda., Alameda Araguaia, 451, pg. 1189 PB
Noroeste Chemical S.A. Arrendamento Mercantil Norchem, Avenida Paulista 1842, pg. 341 PB
Norsk Hydro Comercio e Industria Ltda., Al. Gabriel Monteiro da Silva, pg. 964 IT
Northern Telecom do Brasil Industria E Comercio Ltda., Av. das Nacoes Unidas, 17891, pg. 970 IT
Norton S.A. Industria e Comercio, Rua Joao, pg. 1175 IT
Nova Trading, Avenue Faria Lima 1885, 30th Fl., pg. 1389 IT
Novell Erazil, Alameda Ribeirao Preto, 130, pg. 1204 PB
Novo Nordisk A/S, Av Nacoes Unidas, 11.857-14, pg. 987 IT
Novo Nordisk Farmaceutica do Brasil Ltda., Av. Nacoes Unides, 11.857-14 andar, pg. 988 IT
OCE-Brasil Comercio e Industria Ltda., Avenica Caudido Portinari 1174, pg. 994 IT
Olin Brazil Ltda., Ave. Brig. Luiz Antonio 3779, pg. 1220 PB
Olivetti do Brasil S.A., Av. da Paulista 453, pg. 1003 IT
OMRON Business Sistemas Eletronicos Da America Latina Ltda., Ave. Paulista 949, 12-ander, pg. 1005 IT
OMRON Eletronika Do Brasil Ltda., 154 Vila Alexandria, pg. 1006 IT
Oracle do Brasil, Sistemas Limitadas, Rua Laplace,96-3rd Fl., pg. 1228 PB
Lab. Organon do Brazil Ltda., 375 Rua Joao Alfredo, pg. 45 IT
Oriento industria E commercio, Rua Correia Dis n 337-5,7,8 andar, pg. 790 IT
Otto Haensel Equipamentos Indstriais Ltda., Al Tocantins, 420 - Alphaville, pg. 737 IT
Owens-Corning Fiberglas A.S. Limitada, Av das Nacoes Unidas, N 17.891, 3rd Floor, Suite 301B, pg. 1237 PB
Oxigenio do Brasil S.A., Consolidee, pg. 37 IT
PLP Produtos Para Linhas Proformados Ltda., R. Santa Elvira 465, pg. 1321 PB
Pall Industrial do Brazil Ltda., Rua Jose Pedro da Silveira 61, pg. 1254 PB
Palupe-Comercio, Participacao e Servicos Ltda., R.da Consolacao, 247 Cj. 840, pg. 341 PB
Panalpina S.A., pg. 1023 IT
Papel de Imprensa, S.A., Av. Brig. Faria Lima, 1735 - No. 1 andar., pg. 495 IT
Paribas Do Brazil, av. Paulista, 37-cj. 72, pg. 321 IT
Parker Hannifin do Brazil Industria Comercio Ltda., Via Anhanguera, pg. 1263 PB
Parker Hannifin Industria e Comercio Ltda., Via Anhanguera, Km 25.5-Trevo Perus, pg. 1260 PB
Pechiney Brazil Ltda., Avenida Paulista 2202, 16 Andar Conj. 161, pg. 1031 IT
Peggy Sage Cosmeticos Ltda., 1065 Brooklim Paulista, pg. 1436 IT
Peroxidos do Brazil, Avenida Paulista 2001 - 14 andar, pg. 1279 IT
Petrocoque S.A., Caixa Postal 14, pg. 52 IT
Pharmacia & Upjohn Biotech do Brasil Ltda., Rua Wanderley 832/848, pg. 1047 IT
Phelps Dodge & Alcoa Fios e Cabos Electricos S.A., Centrol Empresarial de Sao, Paulo, Av. Maria Coelho Aguiar, pg. 1286 PB
Philips do Brasil-Walita Div., Prof. Campos de Oliveira, 605, pg. 1055 IT
Philips do Brazil Ltda., Av 9 de Julio 5229/57, pg. 1055 IT
Plantronics International do Brasil LTDA, Rua Joaquim Floriano, 636/131-Itaim, pg. 1308 PB
Plasticos Best SA, Avenida Paulista, 2202-3 Andar, pg. 1171 IT
Plasticos Plavinil S.A., Alameda Santos 2101-8 andar, pg. 1279 IT
Polaroid do Brazil Ltda., Rua Almirante Margues Leao, 408, pg. 1314 PB
Polo Industria e Comercio Ltda., pg. 811 PB
Polysius Projetos Ind. Ltda., Av. Brig. Faria Lima, pg. 512 IT
Pond's do Brasil Produtos de Beleza Ltda., R. Pensilvania, 1065 Brooklim, pg. 1436 IT
Power Transmission Industries do Brasil S.A., Caixa Postal 6064, pg. 1534 PB
Produtos Medico Hospitalares Elscint Ltda., Av. Corifu de Azevedo Marques 3596, pg. 450 IT
Produtos Roche Quimicos e Farmaceuticos S.A., Av. Englenheiro, pg. 1121 IT
Proquimo Prods. Quims Opot. Ltda., 5943 Av. Prof. Francisco Morato, pg. 45 IT
Protendidos DYWIDAG Ltda., Rua Marques de Itu, pg. 425 IT
Provifin Ltda, Avenida Europa 863, pg. 783 IT
PruServicos Participacoes, S.A., c/o Prudential Atlantic Companhia Brasileira de Seguros, Rua BoaVista, pg. 893 PV
Purina Alimentos Ltda., Av. Nacoes Unidas, 13.797, Conjunto Morumbi-Bloco 111-18 Andar, pg. 1360 PB
qad.brazil, Av. Dr. Chucra Zaidan, pg. 1345 PB
Quaker Chemical Industrial Comercio Ltda., Av. Bernardino De Campos, 98-9, pg. 1346 PB
Quaker Chemical Participacoes Ltda., Av. Bernardina De Campos, pg. 1347 PB
Raibobank do Brasil Ltda., Av. Brig. Faria Lima 2020, pg. 1082 IT
Raychem Produtos Irradiados Ltda, Rua Paes Leme, 524-7 andar, pg. 1363 PB
Reckitt & Colman Industrial Ltda., Rodovia Raposo Tavares 8015 (Km 18), pg. 1090 IT
Refinacoes de Milho, Brasil Ltda., Av. Eng. Luis Carlos Berrini, pg. 448 PB
Regional Office South Latin America, Rua Jorge Coelho, 16, pg. 651 IT
Renishaw Latino Americana Ltd., pg. 1103 IT
Rhodia Nordeste, Avenida Maria Coelho Aguiar 215, pg. 1109 IT
Rhodia S.A., Centro Empresarial, Av. Maria Goelho Aguiar 215, pg. 1112 IT
Rigesa, Ltda., Rua 13 DeMaio 755 Centro, Caxia Postal 161, pg. 1762 PB
Rimoldi da Amazonia Ind. e Com. Ltda., Maestro Gabriel Migliori 237, pg. 1118 IT
Robertshaw Pyrotec S.A., Estrada Dos Romeiros, 1.111 KM39.5, pg. 1244 IT
Rohm & Haas Brazil Ltda., Al Purus 105, Alphaville, pg. 1404 PB
Rohm Electronics Brasil Ltda., Av. Francisco Matarazzo, 404-7, pg. 1125 IT
Rolamentos FAG Ltda., Av. das Nacoes Unidas, pg. 469 IT
Rorer do Brasil Quimica E. Farmaceutica Ltda., Rue do Estilo Barrocco, pg. 1111 IT
SAB WABCO do Brasil SA, Rua Lauriano Fernandes Jr, 10, 05089-070 Vila Leopoldina, pg. 271 IT
SAMAB Cia. Industria e Comercio de Papel, pg. 458 IT

PB - *U.S. Public Companies Volume*
PV - *U.S. Private Companies Volume*
IT - *International Public & Private Companies Volume*

1526

Geographic Index-Non U.S.

SIG Industria e Comercio Ltda., Av. Jurua 606-Alphaville, pg. 1156 **IT**
SM-Cyclo Redutores Do Brasil Ltda., Av. Dr. Ulysses Guimars, pg. 1315 **IT**
SMH do Brazil, Av. Brigadeiro Faira Lima, pg. 1161 **IT**
SOFUNGE Ltda., Rua Bartolomeu Paes Nr., pg. 369 **IT**
Sachs Automotive Ltda., pg. 835 **IT**
Sack Instalacoes Siderurgicas Ltda., pg. 837 **IT**
Sadia Mato Grosso S/A, Al. Tocantins, 525, pg. 1168 **IT**
Sakata Seed do Brasil Ltda., Av. Paulista 1842-21, andar-conjs. 215A218, pg. 1178 **IT**
The Sakura Bank - Sao Paulo Representative Office, Avenida Paulista, 1274-12 Andar, pg. 1180 **IT**
Salles/DMB&B Publicidade S.A., Rua Borges Lagoa, 1328, pg. 305 **PV**
Salles/DMB&B Publicidade S.A., R. Borges Lagoa 1328, pg. 305 **PV**
Sandoz S.A., R. Henri Dunant 500, pg. 985 **IT**
Sandvik do Brasil S.A., Caixa Postal 21.261, pg. 1188 **IT**
Sandvik-Villares Wire Industria e Comerico Ltda., pg. 1188 **IT**
Sanpaolo-Sao Paulo Representative Office, Avenida Paulista 1842, pg. 692 **IT**
Santa Marina, 482, Avenida Santa Marina, pg. 1177 **IT**
Santa Veronica Empr Participationes S/C Ltda, Av. Pres. Juscelino, Kubitschek NR 1830, pg. 1171 **IT**
Sao Lourenco, Avenida Paulista 2202, pg. 1177 **IT**
SAO PAULO ALPARGATAS S.A., Rua Urussui 300 - Itaim Bibi, pg. 1193 **IT**
Saraiva S/A Livreiros Editores, Av. Marques de Sao, pg. 334 **IT**
SASIB S/A, Rod. Regis Bittencourt, pg. 1195 **IT**
Schenectady Brasil Limitada, Rue Campos Bicado 52, pg. 970 **PV**
Schering do Brasil Ltda., pg. 1204 **IT**
Schering Plough Brasil, Rua Cancioneiro De Evora 255, pg. 1439 **PB**
Seguradora Roma, S.A., Avda. Paulista 171-3 Andar, pg. 334 **IT**
Setal Instalacoes Industriais S.A., Av. Engenheiro Luiz Carlos Berrini, 801, pg. 6 **IT**
Sherwin-Williams do Brasil Industria e Comercio Limitada, Caixa Postal No. 546, pg. 1466 **PB**
Shimadzu do Brasil Representacao, Ltda., Avenida Paulista 726, pg. 1232 **IT**
Siderurgica Barra Mansa S.A., Av. Jose Cesar de Oliveira, 2l, 9th Fl., pg. 678 **IT**
Siemens S.A., Av. Mutinga, pg. 1248 **IT**
Sigla Equipamentos Eletricos Ltda., Av. Brigadeiro Faria Lima 2003, 14 andar, pg. 706 **IT**
Simpson Industries, Ltda. (Brazil), c/o Cummins Brazil Ltda., Holset VA Business, pg. 1475 **PB**
Singapore Tourist Promotion Board - Sao Paulo, World Trade Center - WTC, Av. das Nacoes Unidas, pg. 1254 **IT**
Skandinaviska Enskilda Banken - Sao Paulo, Centro Empresarial, Fario Lima, Ave. Brigadeira Faria Lima 2020, pg. 1259 **IT**
Sociedade Agricola Germinal Ltda., Av. Prof. Vicente Rao, 90, pg. 985 **IT**
Sodexho Brasil, Av. Joao Dias, 24, pg. 1275 **IT**
Sofegi Industria de Autopecas Ltda., Av. Piraporinha 251, 09891-000 San Bernardo do Campo, pg. 53 **PB**
Sogei do Brasil Publicidade Ltda., Alameda Campinas, pg. 1277 **IT**
Solvay do Brasil S/A, Alameda Santos 2101, pg. 1280 **IT**
Suessea Maquiuas S.A., Caixa Postal 03, pg. 1291 **IT**
Sulzer Brasil S.A., pg. 1305 **IT**
Sumitomo Chemical do Brasil Representacoes Limitada, Av. Paulista 949, pg. 1312 **IT**
Sun Electric do Brasil Comercio e. Industria Limitada, Commercio E. Industria Rua Costa Aguiar, pg. 1481 **PB**
Suntory Administracao e Desenvolvimento Ltda., Alameda Campinaz, No. 600, pg. 1322 **IT**
Swiss Bank Corporation, Rua Funchal, 573, pg. 1330 **IT**
Swiss Re Brasil Servicos e Participacoes Ltda, World Trade Center, Av. de Nacoes Unidas, pg. 1333 **IT**
TAM-Trasportes Aereos Regionais, Aeroporto de Congonhas, pg. 1464 **IT**
TDK do Brasil Ind. e Com. Ltda., pg. 1336 **IT**
TDK do Brasil Suzano Plant, Rua Dr. Libonati, S/No. Suzano, pg. 1337 **IT**
TNT Participacoes Ltda., Av. Morvan Dias Figueiredo, 6159, pg. 1343 **IT**
Takenaka do Brasil Construtora Ltda., Rua Deputado Joaquim Libanio, pg. 1351 **IT**
Tamrock Equipamentos Ltda., Rua Bacaetava, 264, pg. 1353 **IT**
Tech Data Brasil, Rua Sao Paulo, 137, pg. 1562 **PB**
Technip Cleplan, Avenida Paulista 2073, 24/25 Andares-Cojunto Nacional, pg. 1361 **PB**
Tecumseh do Brasil, Caiza Postal 54, pg. 1566 **PB**
Tektronix Industria e Comercio Ltda., Av. Das Nacoes Unidas, 13797-BL. III, pg. 1568 **PB**
Telxon Latin America, Rua Florida 1821-9 Brooklin Novo, pg. 1574 **PB**
Thomson-CSF Passive Components Brazil Ltda, Avenida Prof. Vicente Rao, 1620, pg. 1384 **IT**
3M Do Brasil Ltda., Rua. Verbogivino 1400, 7th Fl., pg. 1606 **IT**
Ticket Servicios Do Brasil, Alemado Santos 1293 2nd Fl., pg. 21 **IT**
Timken do Brasil S.A. Comercio e Industria Limitada, Rua Eng. Mesquita Sampaio 714, pg. 1618 **PB**
Topps Brasil Ltda., Rua Carmo do Rio Verde, 241 conj. 41, pg. 1622 **PB**
Trane do Brazil, Caixa Postal 362 Diaema, pg. 92 **PB**
TRANSBRASIL S.A. LINHAS AEREAS, Rua General Panteleao, Teles 40, Bairro Jardin Aeroporto, pg. 1416 **IT**

Traubomatic Ind. e Com. Ltda., rua Arnaldo Magniccaro, 364, pg. 1419 **IT**
Trinova Divisao Vickers System, Av. Julia Gaiolli No. 450, pg. 25 **PB**
Turner South America, Run Alexandre Dumas 2200 8 Andar, pg. 1646 **PB**
Tyton Hellermann do Brasil Industria e Comercio Ltda., Avenida Marginal Direita do Tiete, pg. 209 **IT**
UBS Representative Office, Edificio Grande Avenida, Av. Paulista 1754, 13 andar, pg. 1441 **IT**
UNIAO DE BANCOS BRASILEIROS S.A. (UNIBANCO), Avenida Eusebio Matoso 891, pg. 1431 **IT**
Union Carbide do Brasil S/A, Rue Dr. Eduardo de Souza Aranha, 153, pg. 1667 **PB**
Union-Transport Do Brasil Ltda, Rua Palacete das Aguias, 588/592, pg. 1120 **PV**
Uniroyal Quimica, S.A., Avenida Morumbi, 7 029, pg. 460 **IT**
Universal Studios Filmes do Brazil LTDA, Rua Said Aiach 305, Caixa Postal, pg. 1216 **IT**
Urba S.A. Industria e Comercio de Auto Pecas, Av. Sta. Marina 1357, pg. 561 **IT**
Utell International-Brazil, Rua de Consolacao, 2697-2 Andar, pg. 1098 **IT**
VDO Kienzle Comercio e Servicos Ltda., pg. 839 **IT**
Valvules Barbara S.A., Rua Frei Liberato de Gries, 548, pg. 1176 **IT**
Van Den Bergh/Anderson Clayton, Av. Maria Coelho Aguiar 215, Bl. C-8, pg. 1436 **IT**
Van Leer Embalagens Industriais do Brasil Ltda, Av. Des Nacoes Unidas 21102, pg. 1146 **IT**
Vera Cruz Consultoria Tecnica e Administracao de Fundos S/C LTDA., Avda. Maria Coelho Aguiar, 215, pg. 334 **IT**
Vera Cruz S.A. de Previdencia Privada, Avda. Maria Coelho, pg. 334 **IT**
Vera Cruz Seguradora, S.A., Avda. Maria Coelho, pg. 334 **IT**
VIACAO AEREA SAO PAULO S.A. (VASP), Aeroporto de Congonhas, pg. 1464 **IT**
Viacom Video-Audio Comunicacoes, Ltda., Alameda Jau', 1742-11 Andar, pg. 780 **PV**
Voith S.A. Maquinas e Equipamentos, Av. Paulista 2444, # 4 Andar, pg. 1473 **IT**
WAPSA Auto-Pecas Limitada, Rua Dr. Rubens Gomes Bueno, 478, pg. 206 **IT**
Wandel & Goltermann Instrumentacao Ltda. & Cia., Av. Eng. Luis Carlos Berrini, pg. 1486 **IT**
Weber Do Brasil Industria E Comercio Ltda., Avenida Interlagos 665, pg. 482 **IT**
Weldotron do Brasil, Rua Exavier Curada 60, pg. 1752 **PB**
The West Company Brasil Ltda., 3 Av NS Das Gracas 115, pg. 1755 **PB**
West Merchant Bank Limited, Av. Brig Faria Lima, 1541, Conj 18J, pg. 1494 **IT**
Westinghouse do Brasil S/A Marini e Daminelli Division, Av. Das Nacoes Unidas, 20828, pg. 275 **PB**
Whirlpool do Brazil S.A., Av. Brig Feria Lima, 2020, pg. 1765 **PB**
Yashica do Brasil-Exportacao e Industria Ltda., R Cruz e Souza 59, Aclimacao, pg. 776 **IT**
Yashica do Brasil-Industria e Comercio Ltda., R Cruz e Souza 59, Aclimacao, pg. 776 **IT**
Young & Rubicam Brazil, Av. Brigadeiro Faria Lima 2100, pg. 1200 **PV**
Zurich-Anglo Seguradora S.A., Rua Boa Vista, 314, 10 andar, pg. 1532 **IT**

Serra

Carboderivados S.A., R. Atalydes M. Souza s/n, CIVIT 1, pg. 447 **IT**
Hitachi Zosen Metalmecanica Ltda., BR 101 - KM8, pg. 947 **IT**

Sorocaba

Mannesmann Demag PIC Injetoras Industria e Comercio Ltda., pg. 837 **IT**
Metalac S.A. Industria e Comercio, Avenida Itavava, 4690, pg. 1420 **PB**
Poclain do Brasil S.A., Caxia Postal 650, pg. 1580 **PB**
R.P. Scherer do Brasil Encapsulacoes Ltda., Avenida Jerome Case, 1277, pg. 1438 **PB**
Svedala-Dynapac, pg. 1324 **IT**
Svedala-FACO, pg. 1324 **IT**
Svedala-FACO Sorocaba, pg. 1324 **IT**
Van Leer Embalagens Industriais do Brasil Ltda., pg. 1146 **IT**

Tabao da Serra

Svedala-FACO Taboao da Serra, pg. 1324 **IT**

Taubate

Mecanica Pesada S.A., pg. 824 **IT**

Toledo

Frigobras Companhia Brasileira de Frigorificos, Senador Atilio Fontana, 1191, 85900-000, pg. 1168 **IT**

Vacaria

Politubos S.A., Estrada Federal BR-116, pg. 1244 **IT**

Valinhos

Equipamentos Clark Ltda., Rue Clark 2061, pg. 559 **PB**

Varzea Grande

Sadia Oeste S.A. Industria e Comercio, al Julio Miller, 1650, 78115-902, pg. 1169 **IT**

Vespasiano

B.M.B. Belgo-Mineira Bekaert Artefatos de Arame Ltda., Rua das Nacoes, 2101, pg. 184 **IT**
Mannesmann Demag Ltda., pg. 837 **IT**

Vila Jaguara

LPC Industrias Alimenticias S.A., Avenida Candido Portinari, 1100, pg. 380 **IT**

Vila Olimpia

Toshiba Medical do Brasil Ltda., Ave. Pres. Juscelino Kubitschek, pg. 1407 **IT**

Vinhedo

Crown Cork do Brasil, S.A., Caixa Postal 84, pg. 464 **PB**
Fasson Produtos Adesivos Ltda., Rodovia Vinehedo-Viracopos, pg. 154 **PB**

Vitoria

Companhia Nipo-Brasileira de Pelotizacao-NIBRASCO, Ponta do Tubarao, pg. 903 **IT**
Construtora Shimizu do Brasil Ltda.-Vitoria Office, Av. Marcos de Azevedo, pg. 1233 **IT**
Edisa Informatica S.A. (Vitoria), Edificio Trade Center Cj 401, Av. Geronimo Moetiro, 1000, pg. 817 **PB**

BRUNEI DARUSSALAM

Bandar Seri Begawan

Accendo Technologies Sdn. Bhd., A-3, Kiarong Complex, Lebuhraya Sultan Haji, pg. 740 **IT**
Brunei Coldgas, pg. 1139 **IT**
Brunei LNG, pg. 1139 **IT**
Brunei Shell Marketing, pg. 1139 **IT**
GEC Brunei Sdn. Bhd., 1st Fl., Block A, No. 12, Lot, 20011, Bangunan Taman Alam, pg. 546 **IT**
International Computers (B) SDN.BHD, 146 Jalan Pemancha, 1st Floor, pg. 529 **IT**
The Islamic Bank of Brunei Berhad, Lot 159, Jalan Pemancha, pg. 362 **IT**
Kao Corporation (B) Sdn., Bdh., Lot 19997, Bangunan Taman Alam Gadong, pg. 718 **IT**
Komputer Wisman Sdn. Bhd., Ground Fl., Unit #1, Block A, Abdul Razak Complex, Jalan Gadong, pg. 822 **PB**
Mortgage & Finance Berhad, Shops 3-4, Goodwood Building, Mile 2 Jalan Gadong, pg. 583 **IT**
Standard Chartered Bank (Negara Brunei Darussalam), 51-55 Jalan Sultan, pg. 1295 **IT**
Standard Chartered Finance (Brunei) Berhad, Lot No. 1624, Ground Fl., Tang Ching Ying Bldg., pg. 1297 **IT**
Teamwork Sendirian Berhad, 501-503 Tech Guan Plaza Jalan Sultan, pg. 1360 **IT**
Veritas DGC INC, Room 408B, 4th Fl., Wisma Jaya, pg. 1137 **PV**
Willis Faber Insurance Brokers Sdn. Bhd., 607 6th Floor, Jalan Sultan Complex, pg. 1510 **IT**
Wiltshier Interiors (Brunei) Sdn. Bhd., P.O. Box 643, pg. 134 **IT**

Berakas

BHP Steel Building Products (B) Sdn Bhd, pg. 226 **IT**

Kuala Belait

Christensen Drilling Systems Sdnn. Bhd., Lot 4091 Jalan Kerma Negara, pg. 1174 **IT**
Det Norske Veritas/Russ Larkin & Associates, Jalan Lubok Jelutong, pg. 398 **IT**

Negara

Great Eastern Life Assurance Company-Brunei, Suite 1, 2nd Floor Badiah Complex, pg. 557 **IT**

Seria

Brunei Shell Petroleum Co Sdn Bhd, pg. 1139 **IT**

BULGARIA

Pleven

CIBA-GEIGY Services AG-TAO Pleven, San Stefano 22/A, pg. 979 **IT**

Sofia

AgroStar A.G., Sofiiski Geroi Str. bl 112 VH.B, pg. 974 **IT**

PB - *U.S. Public Companies Volume*
PV - *U.S. Private Companies Volume*
IT - *International Public & Private Companies Volume*

1527

Geographic Index-Non U.S.

Almagon, 8 Stefano St., pg. 710 IT
BASF EOOD, Iskarsko Chaussee 5, pg. 106 IT
BASF EOOD Knoll Pharma, Ewlogi Georgievstr. 62, pg. 106 IT
BNP-Dresdner Bank (Bulgaria) A.D., Narodno Sabrabie Squ. 11, pg. 418 IT
Robert Bosch FOOD, Nesabravka Str. Nr. 33A, pg. 205 IT
Leo Burnett Advertising, 63, Patriarch Evtimii Blvd., 2nd Floor, pg. 184 PV
Champions, 6A Jendov St., pg. 1199 PV
CIBA-GEIGY Services AG, Todor Atanasov str, bl 16, entr B, fl V, app 24, pg. 979 IT
CIBA-GEIGY Services AG-Technical Advisory Office, Sofiiski Geroi Str. bl 112, A, pg. 979 IT
CIBA-GEIGY Services SA-Technical Advisory Office, Sveta Gora Str. 17, et. 2, pg. 979 IT
Creditanstalt-Bulinvest Ltd., World Trade Center, Blvd. Dragan Tsankov 36, 3rd Fl., #303, pg. 348 IT
Daewoo Corp. - Sofia, pg. 358 IT
Danzas Bulgaria, Tzarigradsko Schosse Bul. No. 4, pg. 382 IT
Digital Equipment Bulgaria, Offices 201-202, interpred World Trade Center Sofia, pg. 507 PB
ESTESA, Bul Stambolijski N 24 Parterre, pg. 283 IT
Fanuc-Machinex Ltd., 24, Tzarigradsko Shausse, pg. 478 IT
Hartmann-Sun Chemical Ltd., Boulevard Zarigradsko Chaussee 47A, pg. 371 IT
Honeywell Eood, 14, Iskarsko Shosse, pg. 834 PB
IDG-Technika Communications Company, One H. Sminanski Blvd., pg. 570 PV
ING Bank Sofia, 7, Vassil Levski Street, pg. 649 IT
International Media Concepts/DMB&B, 1, Yury Venelin Street, pg. 304 PV
Interpartners Bulgaria, Vitosha Blvd. 86, pg. 1152 PV
Jotun Bulgaria Ltd., I Kukush, pg. 715 IT
Kanthal Bulgaria, pg. 723 IT
Mitsui & Co., Ltd. (Sofia), World Trade Center-Sofia, 16, Bulgaro-Savetska Droujba Blvd., pg. 882 IT
Novo Nordisk A/S, Baba Ilyitsa Str. bl. 80-A/12/apt. 45/46, pg. 987 IT
POAP-AD, 117a Tsarigradsko Shosse Blvd., pg. 371 IT
Raiffeisenbank (Bulgaria) A.D., Serdika str. 14, pg. 1085 IT
Ram Representative Office-Bulgaria, Tcherni Vruh Blvd., pg. 741 IT
SKF Sofia, Oboriste St., 43-A, pg. 1159 IT
Sandvik-Bulgaria, pg. 1186 IT
Tecnica, Tchervena Svesda, Block 20A; Ent 4, Apt. 69, pg. 823 PB
The World Bank, World Trade Ctr.-Sofia, 36 Dragan Tsankov Boulevard, pg. 1189 PV
Zeneca Bulgaria, 36 Dragan Tsankov Blvd., pg. 1526 IT

Stara Zagora

CIBA-GEIGY Services AG-TAO Stara Zagora, Otiez Paisi 87, pg. 979 IT

Varna

Keppel FELS Baltech Ltd., pg. 731 IT

BURKINA FASO

Ouagadougou

Banque Internationale du Burkina (BIB), Rue de la Chance, 01, pg. 548 IT
Banque Internationale pour le Commerce, L'Industrie et L'Agriculture du Burkina (BICIAB), Avenue Kwame N'Krumah, pg. 148 IT
The World Bank, Immeuble BICIA (3eme Etage), pg. 1189 PV

BURUNDI

Bujumbura

Banque Commerciale du Burundi Sarl, Chaussee Prince Louis Rwagasore, pg. 148 IT
Banque de Credit de Bujumbura, Avenue Patrice Lumumba, pg. 547 IT
Brasseries et Limonaderies du Burundi "Brarudi" S.A.R.L., Boulevard du 1er Novembre, pg. 608 IT
Fina BP Burundi S.A.R.L., Place de l'Independance 10, pg. 1044 IT
Panalpina S.A.R.L, pg. 1023 IT
The World Bank, Avenue du 18 Septembre, pg. 1189 PV

CAMEROON

Douala

Alucam-Soctral, BP 1090, pg. 1030 IT
Beriac, 1 Rue des Ecoles, pg. 1228 PB
Bull Cameroun, Immeuble C.N.P.S., Rue Ivy Douala, pg. 315 IT
CII-Honeywell Bull Cameroun SARL, Immeuble Viazzi et Aubriet, pg. 316 IT
COMSIP CAM, 5, rue Franqueville, pg. 53 IT
Camby, B.P. 215, pg. 207 IT
Cameroon Airlines, 3 Ave. Gen. de Goulle, pg. 561 IT
Centrachim Sarl, pg. 975 IT
CIBA-GEIGY Trading and Marketing Services Co. Ltd., Rue Prince Bell, pg. 980 IT
Cimenteries du Cameroun-CIMENCAM, pg. 790 IT
Det Norske Veritas, pg. 397 IT
Eastman Christensen (Cameroon) S.A.R.L., B.P. 3639, pg. 167 PB
Elf Serepca, 83, bd. Liberte, pg. 446 IT
FMC Cameroon SARL, S/C Caminfor, pg. 606 PB
Mitsui & Co. (Cameroun) Sarl, Avenue de General de Gaulle, pg. 880 IT
Nestle Cameroun S.A., pg. 921 IT
Pierre-Loti, pg. 21 IT
Plantations Pamol du Cameroon Ltd., pg. 1438 IT
R.T.I. Cameroon Distribution/Services, Bd de la libertes, Boite postale 3899, pg. 823 PB
Rhone-Poulenc Afrique Centrale, 2, boulevard de la Liberte, pg. 1112 IT
SITABAC Societe Industrielle des Tabacs du Cameroon, S.A. (Sitabac), pg. 1101 IT
Soc. Africaine des Produits Chemiques, Agricoles et Menagers SA (SAPCAM), Zone Industrielle Bonaberi, pg. 43 IT
Societe Camerounaise de Produits Alimetaires, Dietetiques et Autres (CAMAD), pg. 922 IT
Sodexho Cameroun, Rue Castelnau, pg. 1275 IT
Standard Chartered Bank Cameroon S.A., Boulevard de la Liberte, pg. 1294 IT

Yaounde

Bilfinger + Berger Bauaktiengesellschaft, c/o Groupement d'Entreprises, Bambui-Fundong, pg. 196 IT
CIBA-GEIGY Trading and Marketing Services Co Ltd, Deleg. techn. & scientif., pg. 980 IT
DYWIDAG CAMEROUN S.A.R.L., pg. 424 IT
Wackenhut Cameroon, pg. 1731 PB
The World Bank, Street 1.792, No. 186, pg. 1189 PV

CANADA

Abbotsford

DYWIDAG Systems International, USA, Inc., 2702 Ware St., Ste. 204, pg. 424 IT
On-Guard Mini-Storage Inc., 33966 Hazelwood Ave., pg. 253 IT
Snowcrest Packers Ltd., 1925 Riverside Rd., pg. 990 IT
Valley Rite-Mix Limited, 31601 Walmsley Rd., pg. 791 IT

Acton

Commercial Intertech Co. Ltd., 294 Quinn Street, Suite C, pg. 411 PB

Acton Vale

Peerless Carpet, 335 Roxton, pg. 1032 IT
PEERLESS CARPET CORPORATION, 335 Roxton Blvd., pg. 1032 IT

Agincourt

McCowan Mobile Mix, 1940 MCCowan Rd., pg. 629 IT
Renown Steel, 211 Nugget Ave., pg. 1262 IT

Airdrie

PROPAK SYSTEMS LTD., 505 E. Lake Blvd., pg. 1071 IT

Ajax

AEG Sorting Systems Inc., 167 Hunt St., pg. 1244 IT
Ajax Magnethermic Canada Ltd., 333 Station St., L1S 1S3, pg. 113 IT
C-Cor Electronics Canada, Inc., 377 MacKenzie Ave., Unit 5, pg. 272 PB
Du Pont Canada-Ajax, 408 Fairall St., pg. 532 PB
General Magnaplate Canada, 119 MacMaster Ave., pg. 717 PB
W.R. Grace & Co. of Canada Ltd., Grace Construction Products, 294 Clements Road West, pg. 755 PB
Kelley Atlantic, LTD, 457 Fairall St., pg. 613 PV
Mead Packaging (Canada) Ltd., 281 Fairall St., pg. 1076 PB
Messier-Dowty Inc., Toronto, 574 Monarch Avenue, L1S 2G8, pg. 1340 IT
Morton International, Ltd., 430 Finley Ave., pg. 1136 PB
Nokia Products Ltd., 575 Westney Road South, pg. 952 IT
Rogers Cable Systems, 700 Finley Ave., Unit No. 5, pg. 1123 IT
Volkswagen Canada, Inc., 777 Bayly St. W., pg. 1475 IT
Vorelco Ltd., 777 Bayly St. W., pg. 1475 IT

Allan

PCS Potash - Allan, pg. 1064 IT

Amherst

CKDH Radio-AM, 32 Church St., pg. 1124 IT
Premdor Inc.-Atlantic Division, Industrial Park, 23 Tupper Blvd., pg. 1067 IT

Amos

J.E. Therrien, Inc., 801 7th St., pg. 1075 IT

Anjou

Cascades Dismed Inc., 9950 Parkway Blvd., pg. 273 IT
E-Z-EM Canada Inc., 11100 Colbert St., pg. 540 PB
Equifax Canada, 7171 Jean Talon East, pg. 588 PB
Fibro Friction, 11060 Boulevard Pkwy., H1J 2H8, pg. 1503 PB
Les Papiers Graphiques Rolland, 10000 Ray-Lawson Blvd., pg. 274 IT
Telebec Ltee, 7151 Jean-Talon East, Ste. 310, pg. 116 IT

Annacis Island

Kamyr Construction, 1633 Cliveden Ave., pg. 35 IT

Armstrong

Kohler Ltd., RR3, C-1 Palisades, pg. 631 PV

Arnprior

Boeing Canada Technology Ltd., Arnprior Division, Baskin Dr. E., pg. 242 PB
Kao Infosystems Canada, Inc., 10 Didak Drive, pg. 717 IT
Kao Infosystems Canada Inc., P.O. Box 41, 10 Didak Drive, pg. 718 IT
Sandvik Steel Canada, 425 McCartney St., pg. 1188 IT
West End Systems Corporation, 39 Winner's Circle Drive, pg. 924 IT

Arthur

Coats Bell, 451 Smith St., pg. 299 IT

Aurora

Bunn-O-Matic Corp. of Canada Ltd., 280 Industrial Parkway S., pg. 181 PV
Engelhard Canada Limited, 100 Engelhard Dr., pg. 582 PB
Quebecor Printing Aurora, 275 Wellington St., East, pg. 1076 IT
Villeroy & Boch Tableware, Ltd., 38 Berczy St., pg. 1468 IT

Aylmer

Northern Telecom Canada Limited, Network Access Div., R.R. 2, Pink Road, pg. 969 IT

Ayr

Hayes-Dana Filter, Fitting & Gasket Div., Hwy. 401 & 97, R. R. 1, pg. 480 PB

Baie Comeau

Canadian Reynolds Metals Company, Ltd., Route Maritime, pg. 1386 PB
Manicouagan Power Co., Ste. 1405, Standard Life Bldg., 20, Marquette, pg. 1387 PB

Baie d'Urfe

Helene Curtis Ltd./Ltee., 19501 Clark Graham, pg. 1434 IT
Lawson Margo Packaging Corp., 19701 Ave. Clark Graham, pg. 69 IT
Pharmacia & Upjohn Biotech Inc., 500, Morgan Boulevard, pg. 1047 IT

Balmertown

Red Lake Mine, pg. 243 IT

Banff

Brewster Transport Co. Ltd., P.O. Box 1140, pg. 1719 PB

Barrie

Canplas Industries Ltd., 31 Patterson Rd., pg. 430 IT
Commerce Drug Canada Ltd., 25 Morrow Rd., pg. 494 PB
Cooper Industries (Canada) Inc., 164 Innisfil St., pg. 444 PB
Del Laboratories (Canada) Ltd., 25 Morrow Rd., pg. 494 PB
DeVilbiss Compressor Products, 50 Wood St., pg. 867 PB
DeVilbiss Ransburg Spray Equipment, 50 Wood St., pg. 868 PB
DeVilbiss Spray Booth Products, 50 Wood St., pg. 868 PB
GSW Thermoplastics Company, 26 Lorena St., pg. 538 IT
Hastings, Inc., 400 Huronia Rd., pg. 798 PB
InterTAN Canada Ltd., pg. 910 PB
Kolmar of Canada, 149 Victoria Street, pg. 239 IT
Mike's Mart, 85 Patterson Rd., pg. 1249 IT
The Municipal Savings & Loan Corporation, 70 Collier Street, pg. 907 IT
Theon Co. Ltd., 25 Morrow Rd., pg. 494 PB
West Bend of Canada Ltd., P.O. Box 6000, pg. 1323 PB

Bathurst

Brunswick Mining & Smelting Corp. Ltd., Mines Road, pg. 434 IT
Brunswick Mining Div., P.O. Box 3000, pg. 434 IT

PB - *U.S. Public Companies Volume*
PV - *U.S. Private Companies Volume*
IT - *International Public & Private Companies Volume*

Beamsville

Bass Block & Building Supplies, 4240 Bartlett Rd.,
pg. 629   IT
Clems Ready-Mix, pg. 629   IT
Enduro-Niagara Ltd., 4750 Christie Dr., pg. 935   PV
Hayes-Dana Service Parts Div., pg. 480   PB
Refrigeration & Air Conditioning Div., 4943 Union Street,
pg. 1264   PB

Beauceville

Imprimerie Quebecor L'Eclaireur, 205, 132e Rue,
pg. 1077   IT
Interglobe Printing Inc., 150, 181 Rue, pg. 538   IT

Beauport

Securespace Inc., 440 Ave. des Laurentides, pg. 253   IT

Becancour

Aluminerie de Becancour Inc. (A.B.I.), 5555 Pierre Thibault,
pg. 1030   IT
Norsk Hydro Canada, Inc., 7000, Boul. Raoul-Duchesne,
pg. 964   IT

Bedford

Air Nova, 1550 Bedford Hwy., 5th Fl., pg. 36   IT
CLEARWATER FINE FOODS INC., 757 Bedford Hwy.,
pg. 297   IT
Clearwater Lobster Limited, 757 Bedford Hwy., pg. 297   IT
NewCap Broadcasting, 1550 Bedford Highway, Suite 800,
pg. 924   IT

Beebe

Jomac Canada, 10 Bachelor St., pg. 595   PV
Rock of Ages Canada, Inc., pg. 1396   PB

Belleville

Belleville Center, 95 Hanna Ct., pg. 273   IT
Dussek Campbell Ltd., 30 Dussek St., P.O. Box 385,
pg. 236   IT
Mobil Chemical Canada, Ltd., 323 University Ave.,
pg. 1119   PB
Northern Telecom Canada Limited, Communications
Systems Div., 250 Sidney St., pg. 969   IT
Poli-Twine Canada (Belleville), pg. 1361   IT
Rexcan Circuits Inc., 161 Bridge Street, West, pg. 628   IT
Stewart Warner Corp. of Canada, Ltd., 349 MacDonald
Ave., pg. 127   IT
Svedala Industries Canada, 30 Franklin St., pg. 1324   IT
Wilson Sports Equipment Canada, Inc., 85 Davy Rd.,
pg. 73   IT

Beloeil

Galvano Division, 2620, rue Bernard-Pilon, pg. 696   IT

Bic

PURDEL, COOPERATIVE AGRO-ALIMENTAIRE, 155, St.
Jean Baptiste, pg. 1073   IT

Biggar

Prairie Malt Limited, pg. 1195   IT

Blacks Harbour

Connors Bros. Limited, Charlotte County, pg. 1495   IT

Blainville

Gaz Metropolitain, Inc.-Laurentians, 905 Michele Bohec,
pg. 541   IT

Blenheim

W.G. THOMPSON & SONS LTD., 122 George St.,
pg. 1381   IT

Boisbriand

Alloytec Mechanical, 599 Cure Boivin, pg. 256   IT
General Motors Canada Ste. Therese Div., 2500 Grand
Allee, pg. 722   PB
Lumec, Inc., 640 Cure Boivin Blvd., pg. 1599   PB

Boucherville

CIBA-GEIGY Canada Ltd., 550 Mortagne Blvd.,
pg. 976   IT
Delisle Foods Ltd., 100, rue de Lauzon, pg. 380   IT
Editions Francaises Inc., 1411 rue Ampere, pg. 240   IT
NGTC, 1350, rue Nobel, pg. 541   IT
Suzorite Mica Products Inc., 1475 Graham Bell Street,
pg. 1523   IT
Transcontinental Printing Inc. - Montreal, 1485, rue de
Coulomb, pg. 538   IT

Bowmanville

Dennison Manufacturing Canada, Inc., 200 Base Line Rd.,
pg. 153   PB

Bracebridge

Arbos Tree Service, pg. 119   PV
Rockwell International of Canada, 345 Ecclestone Drive,
pg. 1401   PB
Scandura Canada Inc., 700 Eccostone Dr., pg. 114   IT

Bradford

Asgrow Canada, Ltd., pg. 1049   IT
The Ontario Produce Co., 144 Dissette St., pg. 1012   IT

Bramalea

Besser Canada, Ltd., 387 Orenda Rd., pg. 139   PV
Brockhouse Canada Limited, 275 Orenda Rd., L6T 3T7,
pg. 426   IT
Bundy of Canada Ltd., 316 Orenda Rd., Brampton,
pg. 1341   IT
Jaguar Canada Inc., 8 Indell Lane, pg. 667   PB
Oakite Canada, Ltd., 115 East Dr., pg. 861   IT

Brampton

Air Products Canada, 2090 Steeles Ave. E., pg. 31   PB
Air Systems Ltd., 152 East Dr., pg. 1398   IT
American National Can Canada Inc., 180 Walker Dr.,
pg. 1029   IT
Anixter Toronto, 20 Wilkinson Rd., Units 13 & 14,
pg. 116   PB
Brampton Plant, 228 Queen St., pg. 672   PB
Buckhorn Canada Ltd., 8032 Torbram Rd., pg. 1143   PB
CFNY-FM Radio, 83 Kennedy Rd., South, pg. 1124   IT
CPI Corp., 46 Hedgedale Rd., pg. 283   PB
Chep Canada Inc., 76 Wentworth Court, pg. 212   IT
The Coe Mfg. Ltd., One Pleasant View Ave., pg. 249   PV
Componenta International Ltd., 1625 Steeles Avenue East,
Unit 3, pg. 1421   IT
ComputerLand Canada, 2000 Clark Blvd., pg. 1154   IT
Crosby Canada Ltd., 145 Heart Lake Rd., pg. 473   IT
DATA BUSINESS FORMS LIMITED, 2 Shaftsbury Ln.,
pg. 384   IT
Dynacare-Ontario, 115 Midair Ct., pg. 425   IT
Dynmark Plastics Inc., 159 Orenda Rd., pg. 1397   IT
Ferrum Inc., 14 Holtby Ave., pg. 414   IT
Gibbs Wire & Steel Company of Canada Ltd., 120 Walker
Dr., pg. 451   PV
Givaudan-Roure Inc., 98 Walker Dr., pg. 1120   IT
Goshen Rubber of Canada Ltd., 100 Stafford Dr.,
pg. 466   PV
Hosokawa Micron Ltd., 1940 Steeles Ave. E., pg. 636   IT
Huls Canada Inc., 235 Orenda Road, pg. 1455   IT
IMI Cornelius Canada, 31 Bram Steele Rd., pg. 646   IT
Johnson Matthey Limited, 130 Glidden Rd., pg. 714   IT
Kampgrounds of America (Canada) Ltd., 6-A Tilbury Court,
pg. 603   PV
Kmart (Canada) Ltd., 8925 Torbram Rd., pg. 963   PB
Lancaster Colony Canada, Inc., 1000 Clark Blvd.,
pg. 977   PB
LePage's Limited, 50 West Drive, pg. 613   IT
MD Foods Canada Inc., 20 Westwyn Court, pg. 826   IT
MLP Canada Limited, 123 Devon Rd., pg. 874   IT
MACtac North America, 100 Kennedy Rd. S., pg. 210   PB
Monserco Limited, 190 Wilkinson Road, pg. 993   IT
Moore Products Co. (Canada), Inc., P.O. Box 370,
pg. 1129   PB
Murray Canada, 155 Orenda Rd., pg. 1397   IT
Nacan Products Ltd., 60 West Drive, pg. 1436   IT
National Chemsearch of Canada Ltd., 245 Orenda Rd.,
pg. 1145   PB
Nippon Express Canada, Ltd., One Woodslea Rd.,
pg. 934   IT
Northern Telecom Canada Limited, 8200 Dixie Rd., Ste.
100, pg. 969   IT
NORTHERN TELECOM LIMITED, 8200 Dixie Rd., Ste.
100, pg. 968   IT
PROCHEM Mixing Equipment Ltd., 8032 Torban Rd.,
pg. 1393   PB
Peterbilt of Canada, 108 Summerlea Rd., pg. 1247   PB
Picker International Canada Inc., pg. 545   IT
Premdor Inc.-Mouldings Distribution, 10 Colony Ct.,
pg. 1067   IT
Reynolds and Reynolds (Canada) Ltd., 2100 Steeles Ave.
E., pg. 1385   PB
Rockwell International of Canada (Distribution Center),
Units 3 & 4, 80 Van Kirk Drive, pg. 1401   PB
Rockwell International of Canada (Regional Sales Center),
Units 3 & 4, 80 Van Kirk Dr., pg. 1401   PB
Rogers Cable TV-Brampton, 13 Hansen Rd. So.,
pg. 1122   IT
SHL Computer Innovations, 2000 Clark Boulevard,
pg. 1154   IT
Sealed Air of Canada Inc., 95 Glidden Road, pg. 1451   PB
Sonco Steel Tube Div., Ferrum Inc., 14 Holtby Ave.,
pg. 699   IT
Southwestern Petroleum Canada Ltd., 87 WestDrive, L6T
2J6, pg. 1019   PV
Spar Space Systems, 9445 Airport Road, pg. 1288   IT
Thermo Electric (Canada) Ltd., 12 Rutherford Rd. So.,
pg. 1080   PV
Transcontinental Digital Services, 66 Nugget Court,
pg. 538   IT

Transcontinental Printing Inc. - Brampton, 138 East Drive,
pg. 538   IT
Velcro Canada Inc., 114 East Dr., pg. 1462   IT
Via Post, 394 Orenda Road, pg. 538   IT
Washington Specialty Metals Canada, Inc., 150 Summerlea,
pg. 1020   IT
Wheel Care Retreading Inc., 1730 Steeles Ave. East, Ste.
2, pg. 274   IT

Brantford

Acheson Colloids (Canada) Ltd., P.O. Box 665, pg. 12   PV
Ascolectric Limited, 10 Airport Rd., pg. 575   PB
Brodart, 109 Roy Blvd., Braneida Ind. Pk., pg. 170   PV
Cascades Dominion Inc., 81 Elgin St., pg. 273   IT
Copeland Canada, Ltd., 145 Sherwood Dr., pg. 576   PB
Crown Mfg. Inc., 11 Spalding Drive, pg. 1237   PB
Dart Realty Co. Ltd., 109 Roy Blvd., Braneida Ind. Pk.,
pg. 170   PV
The Expositor, 53 Dalhousie St., pg. 631   IT
Financial Collection Agencies (International) Inc., Suite 310,
Ehton Market Square, One Market Street, pg. 470   IT
Gates Canada Inc., 300 Henry St., pg. 1396   IT
GUNTHER MELE LIMITED, 30 Craig Street, pg. 578   IT
S.C. Johnson & Son, Limited, One Webster St.,
pg. 593   PV
Keeprite Inc., 44 Elgin St., pg. 898   PB
Kester Solder Co. of Canada Ltd., 1 Prince Charles Rd.,
P.O. Box 474, pg. 1004   PB
Miura Boiler Co., Ltd. (Canada), 8 Copernicus Boulevard,
pg. 884   IT
Raymond Industrial Equipment Ltd., P.O. Box 1325,
pg. 123   IT
Rogers Cable TV-Brantford Div., 23 Harris Ave., P.O. Box
1074, pg. 1122   IT
SLACAN, 145 Roy Blvd., pg. 1262   IT
Sonoco Co., 33 Park Ave., E., pg. 1487   PB
Spalding & Evenflo Juvenile Furniture Company,
pg. 630   PV
Stelco Fasteners Ltd., Bldg. 5, 255 Henry St., pg. 1299   IT
WedTech Inc., 565 Greenwich St., pg. 854   PB
Zeneca Resins, 36 Easton Road, pg. 1527   IT

Breslau

Breslube Division of Safety-Kleen Canada Inc.,
pg. 1426   PB
Safety-Kleen Canada, Ltd., 300 Woolwich St. S.,
pg. 1426   PB

Brighton

Tokheim & Gasboy of Canada Limited, 40 Sharp Rd.,
pg. 1620   PB

Brockville

Avesta ABE Ltd., pg. 221   IT
Black & Decker Holdings (Canada) Inc., 100 Central Ave.,
pg. 234   PB
Brock Telecom Limited, 100 Strowger Boulevard,
pg. 969   IT
Enerstat Division- Erie Manufacturing Co. (Canada) Ltd.,
1600 California Ave., pg. 1241   IT
Gilbarco Canada Ltd., 1360 California Ave., pg. 545   IT
Permanent Lafarge, Hwy. #2 East, pg. 791   IT
Racal Filter Technologies, Inc., 1175 California Ave.,
pg. 1083   IT
Racal Protection Canada, 1175 California Ave.,
pg. 1083   IT
SPC Corporation, Limited, 1291 California Avenue,
pg. 1468   PB
Selkirk Canada Ltd., 130 No. Augusta Rd., pg. 1795   PB

Bromont

Imprimerie Quebecor Bromont, 99, rue de l'Aeroport,
pg. 1077   IT
Mitel Semiconductor, 18 Airport Blvd., pg. 870   IT

Bromptonville

Kruger Urban Forest Products, Inc., pg. 761   IT

Brooks

Barber Industries Ltd.-Service Center, 325B 8th St. East,
pg. 164   IT
Lakeside Farm Industries Ltd., Trans Canada Hwy.,
pg. 852   PB

Brossard

CASSIDY'S LTD., 2555 Matte Blvd., pg. 275   IT
Gaz Metropolitain, Inc.-Monteregie, 3657 rue Isabelle,
pg. 541   IT

Brownsburg

CXA Ltd., Maple Ave. S., pg. 664   IT

Buckingham

Albright & Wilson Amerique Limitee, 470 rue ERCO,
pg. 49   IT

PB - *U.S. Public Companies Volume*
PV - *U.S. Private Companies Volume*
IT - *International Public & Private Companies Volume*

Geographic Index-Non U.S.

1529

CANADA — DIRECTORY OF CORPORATE AFFILIATIONS

Burlington

ABB Process Analytics, 4410 Paletta Ct., pg. 5 IT
AGEMA Infrared Systems Ltd., 5230 S. Service Rd., pg. 1289 IT
Aisco Systems Inc., pg. 1017 IT
Amcast Industrial Ltd., 5276 John Lucas Dr., pg. 63 PB
Associated Spring, Ltd., 3100 Mainway, pg. 190 PB
BCL Magnetics, 5045 N. Service Rd., L7L 5H6, pg. 1075 PV
Beauticontrol Cosmetics Canada Ltd., 3375 N. Service Rd., pg. 199 PB
Bull Moose Tubes Ltd., 2170 Queensway Dr., pg. 265 IT
CCL Label, 3077 Mainway, pg. 238 IT
CCL Labeling Equipment, 3070 Mainway, pg. 238 IT
Canadian Building Systems Inc., 3455 North Service Road, pg. 698 IT
Canadian Equipment Finance Corporation, 1001 Chaplin Ave., Ste. 400, pg. 492 PB
Chrysler Credit Canada Ltd., 390 Brant St., Ste. 308, pg. 354 PB
COMMCORP Financial Services Inc., pg. 256 IT
Comstock Canada Ltd., 3455 Landmark Rd., pg. 572 PB
Contractors Machinery & Equipment, 1051 Heritage Rd., pg. 594 IT
Dairy Queen Canada, Inc., 5245 Harvester Rd., pg. 220 PB
John Deere Finance Limited, 1001 Champlaign Avenue, pg. 492 PB
Dinol Industrial Canada Inc., 1175 Appleby, Line Unit A2, pg. 982 IT
DOVER INDUSTRIES LIMITED, 4350 Harvester Rd., pg. 417 IT
Elliott Turbomachinery Canada, Inc., 955 Maple, pg. 373 PV
Elsag Bailey (Canada) Inc., 860 Harington Ct., pg. 449 IT
Fike Canada Inc., 4140 Morris Drive, pg. 404 PV
Fisher & Ludlow, 750 Appleby Line, pg. 598 IT
Gan Canada Insurance Company, 649 North Service Rd. W., pg. 564 IT
The Gan Company of Canada Ltd., 649 North Service Road West, pg. 564 IT
GAN General Insurance Company, 649 North Service Rd. W., pg. 564 IT
Genentech Canada Inc., 1100 Burloak Drive, 5th Floor, pg. 1120 IT
Gerrard-Ovalstrapping, 5330 South Service Road, L7L 5L1, pg. 378 PV
H.S.C. Canada Inc., 4205 Fairview St., pg. 505 PV
Hewlett-Packard (Canada) Ltd., 3325 North Service Rd., Unit 7, pg. 818 PB
H.H. Robertson, Inc., 1810 Ironstone Dr., pg. 1394 PB
Hoogovens Technical Services Technological & Operational Assistance Inc., 4210 S. Service Road, pg. 755 IT
Hoover Canada Inc., 4151 N. Service Rd., pg. 1065 PB
Howell Packaging, 3230 Mainway Ave., pg. 417 IT
I.D.Q. Canada, Inc., 5245 Harvester Rd., pg. 220 PB
Instron Canada, Inc., 969 Fraser Dr., pg. 883 PB
Johnson Worldwide Canada, Inc., 4180 Harvester Rd., pg. 933 PB
Keystone (Canada) Ltd., 1001 Century Dr., pg. 1650 PB
Koss Ltd., 2349 Fairview St., Unit 223, pg. 966 PB
Laidlaw Inc., 3221 North Service Rd., pg. 259 IT
Laidlaw Transit Limited, 3221 North Service Rd., pg. 259 IT
Laurel Steel, 5400 Harvester Road, pg. 598 IT
Liebherr-Canada Ltd., 1015 Sutton Dr., pg. 808 IT
Long Manufacturing Ltd.-Aftermarket Division, 5530 Harvester St., pg. 815 IT
Marcam Canada, 880 Laurentian Dr., pg. 1043 PB
Menasco Overhaul Division, 5415 N. Service Rd., pg. 402 PB
Mettler-Toledo Inc., 735 Toledo Court, pg. 4 PV
NEO Industries, 3370 South Service Road, pg. 1150 IT
Nalco Canada Inc., 1055 Truman St., pg. 1150 PB
Orange Julius Canada, Ltd., 5245 Harvester Rd., pg. 221 PB
Pacific Westeel, 3191 Mainway, pg. 698 IT
Quaker State Inc., 1101 Blair Rd., pg. 1348 PB
Quantum Inspection & Testing Ltd., 916 Gateway, pg. 273 PB
Republic Environmental Systems Ltd., 1455 Lakeshore Rd., Ste. 201N, pg. 1380 PB
Robinson Cone, 4350 Harvester Rd., pg. 417 IT
Shaklee Canada Inc., 952 Century Dr., pg. 1518 IT
Symix Cit, 3515 N. Service Rd., Third Fl., pg. 1547 PB
Tamrock Loaders Eimco Jarvis Clark Co. Ltd., 4445 Fairview Street, pg. 1353 IT
Thermal Ceramics, 1185 Walkers Line N., pg. 894 IT
Toledo Scale Canada Ltd., pg. 986 IT
Union Pump (Canada) Ltd., 4211 Mainway Dr., pg. 1119 PV
Watts Industries (Canada) Inc., 5435 N. Service Road, pg. 1747 PB

Burnaby

Accurate Door & Hardware Division, 5134 Stillcreek St., pg. 23 IT
Ames Taping Tools Co. of Canada Limited, 7779 Edmonds St., pg. 103 PV
Autodesk Canada Inc./Burnaby, 4170 Still Creek Dr., Ste. 200, pg. 149 PB
BC Telecom Inc., 3777 Kingsway, pg. 697 PB
Brian Controls Division, 4199 McConnell Drive, pg. 711 IT
Bulk Systems Management Ltd., 202, 4240 Manor Street, pg. 1424 IT
Canwel Distribution Ltd., 4603 Kingsway, Ste. 301, pg. 260 IT
Castleton Network Systems, Suite 1234, 4720 Kingsway, pg. 924 IT
Cineplex Odeon Corporation -Vancouver, 201-6200 McKay Avenue, pg. 293 IT
Commonwealth Construction Co., 4599 Tillicum St, pg. 143 PB
DIGITAL COURIER INTERNATIONAL INC., 8618 Commerce Court, pg. 413 IT
Du Pont Canada-Burnaby, Ste. 710, 4710 Kingsway, pg. 532 PB
Electronic Arts (Canada) Inc., 400-4400 Dominion Street, pg. 569 PB
Foundation Building West Inc., #101, 6400 Roberts Street, pg. 118 IT
Gibraltar Lock Co. Ltd., 6700 Beresford St., pg. 1054 PB
Glentel Inc., 8501 Commerce Court, pg. 1336 IT
Hamilton Hallmark (Canada) Ltd, 8610 Commerce Ct., pg. 155 PB
Intergraph Canada Ltd., Ste. 610, 4370 Dominion St., pg. 891 PB
LifeScan Canada Ltd., 2344170 Still Creek Dr., pg. 931 PB
THE LOEWEN GROUP, INC., 4126 Norland Ave., pg. 814 IT
Microsep International Corporation, 4599 Tillicum St., pg. 143 PB
Milgray/Western Canada, 4185 Still Creek Dr., pg. 207 PB
Nabob Foods Limited, 3131 Lake City Way, pg. 1289 PB
Nissin Foods (Canada) Inc., 217-1899 Willingdon Ave., pg. 950 IT
Office Depot Office Supply Warehouse, 4199 Lougheed Hwy, pg. 1212 PB
PMC Sierra, Inc., 105-8555 Baxter Place, pg. 1470 PB
Price/Costco, Inc.-Western Region, 3550 Brighton St., pg. 452 PB
Rogers Cable TV, 4710 Kingsway, 16th Fl., pg. 1122 IT
Scientific-Atlanta Canada, Inc., 7725 Lougheed Hwy., pg. 1443 PB
Siplast Canada Inc., 3650 Bonneville, Suite 110, pg. 659 IT
Southland Corp.-British Columbia Division, 3185 Willingdon Green, pg. 694 IT
Southland Corporation - Canada National Office, 3185 Willingdon Green, pg. 694 IT
Sulzer Bingham Pumps Inc., 4129 Lozells Ave., pg. 1305 IT
TCG INTERNATIONAL INC., 4710 Kingsway, Suite 2800, pg. 1336 IT
TSC Film Distribution, 4222 Manor Street, pg. 1343 IT
TSC SHANNOCK CORPORATION, 4222 Manor St., pg. 1343 IT
Tektronix Canada Inc.-Burnaby, 8666 Commerce Ct., pg. 1567 PB
Trax Music Vision Ltd., 4222 Manor Street, pg. 1343 IT
Weiser Inc., 6700 Beresford St., pg. 1055 PB
Weiser Lock Co. Ltd., 6700 Beresford St., pg. 1055 PB
Yokohama Tire Canada Inc., 4370 Dominion St., 3rd Fl., pg. 1521 IT

Calgary

ACTC Technologies, Ste. 350, 6715 8th St. N.E., pg. 317 IT
AEC Forest Products, 2400, 639 Fifth Ave. S.W., pg. 43 IT
AEC Oil & Gas, 2400, 639 Fifth Ave., SW, pg. 48 IT
AEC Pipelines, 2400, 639 Fifth Ave., SW, pg. 48 IT
AEC Power Ltd., 3900-421 Seventh Ave., S.W., pg. 49 IT
AM106/CJAY Radio, Broadcast House, Station E, pg. 1123 IT
AST Canada, Inc., Bow Valley Square 1V, Suite 1500, pg. 1182 IT
AGRA Earth & Environmental Limited, 221-18th St. SE, pg. 30 IT
AGRA INC., Royal Bank Tower, 335-8th Ave. S.W., Ste. 1900, pg. 30 IT
AGRA Inc., 335-8th Ave. S.W., Ste. 1900, pg. 30 IT
AGRIUM INC., 1033 Southpoint Rd., Ste. 426, pg. 31 IT
Air Products Canada Ltd., 7905 51st Street, S.E., pg. 31 PB
Aircraft of Canada Ltd., Ste. 320, pg. 1365 PB
ALBERTA ENERGY COMPANY, LTD., 3900 421-Seventh Ave., S.W., pg. 48 IT
Alberta Natural Gas Company Ltd., 3400, 237 Fourth Avenue S.W., pg. 1417 IT
Alberta Oil Sands Pipeline Ltd., 3900 421-Seventh Ave., S.W., pg. 48 IT
Alcan Price Extrusions Ltd., 7929-30th St. S.E., pg. 50 IT
Alenco, Inc., 3900 421-Seventh Ave., S.W., pg. 48 IT
Altana Exploration Company, 311 6th Ave. S.W.,13th Fl., pg. 1127 PB
Amoco Canada Petroleum Company Ltd., 240-4th Ave. S.W., pg. 103 PB
Amoco Canada Resources Ltd., 240-4th Ave. SW, pg. 103 PB
Andres Wines (Alberta) Ltd., 7530 Blackfoot Trail, S.E., pg. 76 IT
Anixter Calgary, 1155 40th Ave., N.E., pg. 115 PB
Apache Canada Ltd., 700 Ninth Ave., S.W., 10th Fl., pg. 119 PB
Atco Gas Services Ltd., 1400, 909-11 Ave. S.W., pg. 95 IT
ATCO GROUP CO., 909-11th Ave. S.W., Ste. 1500, pg. 95 IT
ATCO Structures Inc., 5115 Crowchild Trail S.W., pg. 95 IT
ATCO Travel, 1243 McKnight Blvd. N.E., pg. 95 IT
Auto-trol Technology (Canada) Ltd., 1144 29th Ave. N.E., Ste. 300, pg. 148 PB
Avnet Computer, #108 1144 29th Ave. NE, pg. 155 PB
BHP Petroleum (Canada) Inc., 400-4th Avenue, S.W., Ste. 2850, pg. 225 IT
Baker Oil Tools of Canada, Ltd., 700 736 8th Ave. S.W., pg. 167 PB
Bank of Montreal - Calgary, 350-Seventh Ave., S.W., pg. 153 IT
Bantrel Inc., 703-6th Avenue S.W., pg. 118 IT
BARBER INDUSTRIES INC., 605 Fifth Ave., S.W., Ste. 1220, pg. 164 IT
Barnwell of Canada Ltd., 639 5th Ave. S.W., pg. 191 PB
Bombardier Finance Inc., 6815A 40th Street S.E., pg. 200 IT
BOVAR Inc., 4 Manning Close NE, pg. 1424 IT
Brian Controls Division, 270, 2720 12th St. N.E., pg. 711 IT
Brookfield Homes-Western Region, 839 5th Ave. S.W., Ste. 400, pg. 228 IT
CFCN Communications Limited, Broadcast House, Station E, pg. 1123 IT
CFCN-TV (Calgary & Lethbridge), Broadcast House, Station E, pg. 1123 IT
CGG Geophysics Canada Ltd., Bank of Canada Bldg., Ste. 700, 404-6th Ave. S.W., pg. 241 IT
CGTX Calgary Office, 1225, 540 5th Ave. SW, pg. 693 PB
CU Power International Ltd., 800, 919-11th Ave. S.W., pg. 95 IT
CABRE EXPLORATION LTD., Suite 1400, 700 Ninth Ave., S.W., pg. 247 IT
CALGARY FLAMES HOCKEY CLUB, pg. 252 IT
Calgary Herald, 215-16th St. S.E., pg. 631 IT
The Calgary Sun, 2615-12th St. N.E., pg. 1320 IT
Canada Safeway Limited, 1020 64th Ave. N.E., pg. 1426 PB
CANADIAN AIRLINES CORPORATION, 700 Second St., S.W., pg. 255 IT
Canadian Airlines International Ltd., Ste. 2800, 700 Second St. S.W., pg. 256 IT
Canadian Cometra, Inc., pg. 562 IT
Canadian Forest Oil Ltd., 800 6th Ave., S.W., Suite 600, pg. 670 PB
Canadian Freightways Ltd., 4041A Sixth St. S.E., pg. 435 PB
Canadian Gas Gathering Systems II, Inc., 3000, 400-3 Avenue S.W., pg. 895 IT
Canadian Hunter Exploration Ltd., 2000, 605 - 5th Avenue S.W., pg. 433 IT
CANADIAN NATURAL RESOURCES LIMITED, 2000, 425-1st Street S.W., pg. 258 IT
Canadian Occidental Petroleum Ltd., 1500, 635-8th Ave. S.W., pg. 1210 PB
CANADIAN PACIFIC LIMITED, 1800 Bankers Hall East, pg. 258 IT
Canadian Pacific Railway, 401 9th Ave., S.W., pg. 258 IT
Canadian Roxy Petroleum Ltd., 421 Seventh Ave. S.W., pg. 1492 IT
Canadian Utilities Limited, 1500, 909-11th Ave. SW, pg. 95 IT
Canadian Western Natural Gas Company Limited, 909-11th Ave. S.W., pg. 95 IT
Cancarb Gas Services Limited, c/o TransCanada PipeLines Ltd., 111 Fifth Ave., S.W., pg. 1417 IT
Canrock Pipeline Company, Ltd., 1410 333-Fifth Ave., S.W., pg. 562 IT
Canuck Engineering Inc., 900 Monenco Place, pg. 31 IT
Capitol Pipe & Steel, 6120 40th St., S.E., pg. 256 IT
Chauvco Resources Ltd., 2900, 255 5 Avenue SW, pg. 1424 IT
Chevron Canada Resources Limited, Chevron Plaza, 500 Fifth Ave. S.W., pg. 348 PB
Chevron Standard Limited, 500 Fifth Ave., S.W., pg. 348 PB
CIBA-GEIGY Canada Ltd., Suite 850, Southland Tower, 10655 Southport Rd., S.W., pg. 976 IT
Cineplex Odeon Corporation -Calgary, 1705-16th Avenue N.W., pg. 293 IT
Coal Valley Project, 3900 421-Seventh Ave., S.W., pg. 49 IT
Coast RV, Inc., 7504 30th St., S.E., pg. 388 PB
Cognos Inc.-Calgary Sales Office, Bow Valley Square 4, Ste. 600, pg. 306 IT
COMPUTALOG LTD., 2000-530 Eighth Ave. S.W., pg. 325 IT
Confederation Leasing (Alberta) Limited, Ste. 1100, 311 6th Ave. S-W., pg. 325 IT
Consolidated Carma Corporation, 839 Fifth Ave., S.W., Ste. 800, pg. 229 IT
Core Laboratories-Canada Ltd., 1540 25th Ave., N.E., pg. 1004 PB
Cott Corporation - Pacific North West Region (Calgary), 4810 76 Avenue Southeast, pg. 337 IT
Crown Cork & Seal Canada, Inc., 4455 75th Ave. S.E., pg. 464 PB
Crows Nest Resources Limited, 525 3rd Ave., S.W., pg. 1138 IT
Cruise Canada, Inc., 2980-26th St., N.E., pg. 178 PV
DMR Group, Inc., 700 - 9th Ave. S.W., Suite 1190, pg. 527 IT
Daniel Canada, #114-4215-72 Ave. S.E., pg. 483 PB
Deminex (Canada) Ltd., 603 Seventh Ave. S.W., pg. 1461 IT
Devon Energy Canada Corporation, Bow Valley Sq. 4, Ste. 2400, 250 6th Ave. S.W., pg. 503 PB
Dowell Schlumberger Canada Inc., 801 6th Ave., S.W., pg. 1439 PB
Dresser Wheatley Division, 6875 9th St. N.E., pg. 529 PB
Du Pont Canada-Calgary, 10655 S. Port Rd. SW., Ste. 1000, pg. 532 PB
Du Pont Canada-Calgary Distribution, 4444-72nd Ave. SW, pg. 532 PB
DYWIDAG Systems International, USA, Inc., 3701-19th St. N.E., pg. 424 IT
Eclipse Combustion, #5, 3530-11A Street N.E., pg. 361 PV

PB - *U.S. Public Companies Volume*
PV - *U.S. Private Companies Volume*
IT - *International Public & Private Companies Volume*

Geographic Index-Non U.S.

Ellesmere Developments Ltd., 335-8th Ave. SW., pg. 31   IT
Enerflex Leasing, 7720 - 48 St. S.E., pg. 1400   IT
Enerflex Systems Ltd., 4949 76th Ave., S.E., pg. 1400   IT
ENERMARK INCOME FUND, Western Canada Place, 1900, 700 9th Avenue S.W., pg. 454   IT
Farm Electric Services Ltd., 110-12th Ave. S.W., pg. 1416   IT
Fedmet Tubulars, 1250-700 9th Ave. S.W., pg. 1150   IT
First Marathon Securities, Bankers Hall, 855 Second St., Ste. 4100, pg. 486   IT
Fletcher Challenge Petroleum Inc., 300 Fifth Ave. S.W., Ste. 2300, pg. 495   IT
Fluor Daniel Canada Inc., 10101 Southport Rd. S.W., pg. 660   PB
Fording Coal Ltd., Fording Place, 205-9th Ave., pg. 259   PB
GPC Communications (Calgary), 530 8th Ave. SW, Suite 1700, T2P 3S8, pg. 1225   PB
GPC Government Policy Consultants (Calgary), 530-8th Ave. S.W., Ste. 1700, pg. 1225   PB
Gas Tech Instrument Canada, Ltd., 1721 27 Avenue N.E., pg. 1593   PB
Genuine Parts Ltd., 5530-C 3rd St. S.E., pg. 732   PB
GREYHOUND LINES OF CANADA LTD., 877 Greyhound Way S.W., pg. 559   IT
GULF CANADA RESOURCES LTD., 401-9th Ave. S.W., pg. 577   IT
HCCO Energy Ltd., 1830 144 4th. S.W., pg. 782   PB
Halliburton Services, 550 6th Ave. S.W., pg. 777   PB
Harris Novatel, pg. 792   PB
Herbalife of Canada Ltd., 2916-5th Ave. N.E., Ste. 16, pg. 809   PB
Hewlett-Packard (Canada) Ltd., 150 Sixth Ave. S.W., pg. 818   PB
Highwood Resources, 324 8th Ave. S.W., Ste. 705, pg. 1411   PB
Hudson General Aviation Services Inc., 2000 Airport Road, pg. 846   PB
Hunt Oil Canadian Division Office, 1450-801 6th Ave., S.W., pg. 549   PV
Husky Oil Intl. Ltd., 707 8th Ave. S.W., pg. 640   IT
HUSKY OIL LTD., 707 8th Ave. S.W., pg. 640   IT
Husky Oil Mktg. Company, 707 8th Ave. S.W., pg. 640   IT
Husky Oil Operations Ltd., 707 8th Ave. S.W., pg. 640   IT
ICG Propane Inc., 150 6th Ave. S.W., pg. 1041   IT
IPL ENERGY INC., 2900 421 7th Avenue, S.W., pg. 651   IT
IRAD Development Ltd., 840-Seventh Ave., S.W., pg. 1444   PB
Ikon Office Solutions (Alberta), 1530-27 Ave. N.E., pg. 864   PB
In-Situ Research and Engineering Ltd., 840-Seventh Ave., S.W., pg. 1444   PB
Intera Information Technologies Corp., 1000, 645 7 Avenue SW, pg. 1424   IT
Intercomp Resoruce Development & Engineering (Canada) Ltd., 840-Seventh Ave., S.W., pg. 1444   PB
Intergraph Canada Ltd., 2912 Memorial Drive S.E., pg. 891   PB
Japan Airlines Company, Ltd., 1000, 340-12th Ave., S.W., pg. 700   IT
Kanelk Transmission Co. Ltd., 110-12th Ave., S.W., pg. 1416   IT
Kilborn SNC-Lavalin Inc., 700, 205-9th Avenue S.E., pg. 1162   IT
Kodak Canada Inc., 800 Fifth Ave. S.W., Ste. 1600, pg. 553   PB
Krupp Canada Inc., 405, 1177-11th Ave., S.W., pg. 511   IT
Kvaerner Process Systems Inc., 200, 1209-59th Ave. S.E., pg. 768   IT
LSI Logic Corporation of Canada, Inc., Petro-Canada Centre, Ste. 3410, pg. 971   PB
Lafarge Construction Materials, Deerfoot Trail & Southland Dr., S.E., pg. 791   PB
Lario Oil & Gas Company, 1711 Sun Oil Bldg., 500 4th Ave., S.W., pg. 651   PV
Laura Ashley Shops Ltd., Bankers Hall, Ste. 340, 315 Eighth Ave., S.W., pg. 804   IT
Lennox Industries (Canada) Ltd., 3916-70th Ave., S.E., P.O. Box 5460, pg. 660   PV
Lufkin Industries, 225 MacDougall Pl., 808 4th Ave. S.W., pg. 1019   PB
MacMillan Bloedel Inc., 34th Ave. & Ninth St. S.E., pg. 828   IT
Mammoet Canada Ltd., pg. 1144   IT
Mark Products, 1108 55th Avenue, S.E., pg. 1231   IT
MARK RESOURCES INC., 1300 800 5th Ave. SW, pg. 842   IT
Maxum Engineering Enterprises Ltd., 416 Monument Pl., pg. 31   IT
McKim Advertising Ltd., 237 8th Ave. S.E., Ste. 600, pg. 104   PV
MEDIA DUPLICATION INTERNATIONAL, 3807 9th Street, S.E., pg. 852   IT
Media Duplication International, 3807 9th Street, S.E., pg. 853   IT
Microcomp Management Ltd., 840-Seventh Ave., S.W., pg. 1444   IT
Milchem Canada Ltd., 600736 8th Ave. S.W., pg. 167   PB
Milne & Craighead Customs Brokers, Inc., 112 Fourth Avenue S.W., 19th Floor, pg. 435   PB
Mitsui & Co. (Canada), 1600-540 5th Ave., S.W., pg. 880   IT
Mobil Oil Canada, Ltd., pg. 1119   PB
Morrison Nuclear, Inc., 400 Third Ave., S.W., Ste. 2900, pg. 895   IT
MORRISON PETROLEUMS LTD., 400 Third Ave., S.W., Ste. 3000, pg. 895   IT
Murphy Oil Co., Ltd., 2100-555 4th Ave. S.W., pg. 1142   PB

NIC Resources, Inc., c/o Fenarty, Robertson, Fraser & Hatch, pg. 948   IT
Neste Canada Inc., Home Oil Tower, 324-8th Ave., S.W., Ste. 701, pg. 914   IT
Nomeco Exploration Canada, Inc., Ste. 775, Bank of Canada Bldg., pg. 280   PB
Norcen Energy Resources Limited, 715 Fifth Ave., S.W., pg. 434   IT
North Canadian Marketing, Suite 700, 112-4th Avenue S.W., pg. 434   IT
Northern Telecom Canada Limited, Business Products Div., 3705 - 35th St. N.E., pg. 969   IT
NORTHROCK RESOURCES LTD., 700 2nd St., S.W., Ste. 3500, pg. 970   IT
Nova Chemicals Ltd., 801 7th Ave. S.W., pg. 971   IT
NOVA CORPORATION, 801 7th Ave. S.W., pg. 971   IT
Nova Gas International Ltd., 801 Seventh Ave. S.W., pg. 971   IT
Nova Gas Transmission Ltd., 801 Seventh Ave. S.W., pg. 971   IT
Nowsco Well Service Ltd., 1300, 801 6th Ave. S.W., pg. 161   PB
NOWSCO WELL SERVICE LTD., #1300, 801 6th Avenue S.W., pg. 989   IT
NUBURN CAPITAL, 150 6th Ave. S.W., Ste. 1470, pg. 990   IT
NUMAC ENERGY INC., 321 6th Ave., pg. 990   IT
OCELOT ENERGY INC., 30th Floor, West Tower, Petro-Canada Center, pg. 996   IT
OYO Geospace Canada, Inc., Bay R, 1350 42nd Ave., pg. 1019   PB
PCL-Braun-Simons Ltd., 401 Ninth Ave. S.W., T2P 3C5, pg. 765   IT
Pamco Division, 8241 - 31 St. S.E., pg. 1400   IT
Pan-Alberta Gas Ltd., 500-707 Eighth Ave. S.W., pg. 971   IT
Pan-Alberta Resources Ltd., 3900 421-Seventh Ave., S.W., pg. 49   IT
PEMBINA PIPELINE CORPORATION, 707 8th Ave., SW, pg. 1032   IT
PETRO-CANADA, 150-6th Ave. S.W., pg. 1041   IT
Petwa Canada Ltd., 4120 23rd St., N.E., pg. 6   IT
Photon Systems Ltd., 520 Fifth Ave. S.W., pg. 1563   PB
POCO PETROLEUMS LTD., 3500, 250 - 6th Avenue S.W., pg. 1061   IT
Poli-Twine Canada (Calgary), 4216 54th Ave. S.E., pg. 1362   IT
Pounder Emulsions, Ltd., P.O. Box 6525, Station D, pg. 640   IT
Power and Compression Group, 8241 - 31 St. S.E., pg. 1400   IT
PRECISION DRILLING CORPORATION, Ste. 700, 112 4th Ave. S.W., pg. 1066   IT
Ranger Forest Products Ltd., 3900 421-Seventh Ave., S.W., pg. 49   IT
RANGER OIL LIMITED, Ste. 1600, 321 6th Ave., S.W., pg. 1086   IT
Rector Canada Ltd., 1600-717 Seventh Ave. S.W., pg. 6   IT
Rector-Gray, Ltd., 717 7th Ave., S.W., pg. 6   IT
RENAISSANCE ENERGY LTD., 425 First Street S.W., Ste. 3000, pg. 1102   IT
RIGEL ENERGY CORPORATION, 1900 255 5th Ave., S.W., pg. 1117   IT
Rigel Oil & Gas Ltd., 1900 255 5th Ave., S.W., pg. 1117   IT
Rigel Petroleum, Inc., 1900 255 5th Ave., S.W., pg. 1117   IT
Rigel Petroleum (NI) Limited, 1900 255 5th Ave., pg. 1117   IT
Rigel Petroleum UK Limited, 1900, 255 - 5th Avenue S.W., pg. 1117   IT
Roan Resources LTD, Cadillac Fairview Bldg., 1300 311 Sixth Ave. S.W., pg. 1127   PB
Rogers Cable TV-Alberta Limited, 3003 MacLeod Trail, pg. 1122   IT
Rogers CFAC-AM, 3320-17th Ave. S.W., pg. 1123   IT
Rogers Entertainment Inc., 5516A 3rd St. S.E., pg. 1123   IT
Ronalds Printing Calgary, 2626 N.E. 12th St., pg. 1077   IT
Rosemount Instruments Ltd., 808 55th Ave. N.E., pg. 577   PB
Royal LePage - Alberta Office, 144 4th Avenue, S.W., Ste. 900, pg. 1143   IT
SHL Systemhouse - Calgary, 240-4th Ave., S.W., 6th Fl., pg. 1154   IT
SNC-Lavalin, 909 5th Avenue S.W., pg. 1162   IT
Samedan Oil of Canada, Inc., 2905-500 Fourth Ave. S.W., pg. 1186   PV
SCEPTRE RESOURCES LIMITED, 400 Third Ave., S.W., Ste. 2000, pg. 1203   IT
Scott National, P.O. Box 2544, Stn. M, pg. 1012   IT
Sentinel Self-Storage Corporation, Ste. 1720, Sun Light Place, 10123-99th St., pg. 253   IT
Sequent Computer Systems (Canada) Ltd., 139 Woodmark Crescent S.W., pg. 1459   PB
Shaw Pipe Protection, 1900, 144 Fourth Ave., S.W., pg. 1231   IT
Shaw Pipeline Services Ltd., #6, 4452-64th Avenue, S.E., pg. 1231   IT
Shell Aerocentre, 1441 Aviation Park N.E., pg. 1138   IT
Shell Canada Ltd., pg. 1138   IT
Shell Canada Products Ltd., pg. 1138   IT
Southland Corp.-Prairies Division, 201-200 Rivercrest Dr. S.E., pg. 694   IT
Sun Microsystems of Canada-Western Canada, SunLife Plaza III, Suite 260, 112 Fourth Ave. S.W., pg. 1532   PB
Suncor Exploration & Production Group, 112 4th Ave. S.W., pg. 1320   IT
SUNCOR INC., 112-4th Ave. S.W., pg. 1320   IT
TIW Western, 7770 44th St., S.E., pg. 256   IT

TSC Shannock Corporation, 610-C 70th Ave. S.E., pg. 1343   IT
TALISMAN ENERGY INC., 2400 855-2nd St., S.W., pg. 1352   IT
Taro Industries Limited, 616 68 Avenue SE, pg. 1424   IT
Teamwork Developments Limited, 300 - 5th Ave. S.W., pg. 1360   IT
TELUS Advertising Services, 27F, 411-1 Street S.E., pg. 1374   IT
TELUS Mobility, 3030 -2 Avenue S.E., pg. 1374   IT
Telxon Canada Corporation, 119 14th Street N.W., Ste. 400, pg. 1574   PB
Thermon Heat Tracing Services, Inc., Bay 11, 1305-38 St. N.E., T2A 5P1, pg. 1081   PV
317070 Alberta Ltd., 400 Third Ave. S.W., Ste. 2000, pg. 1203   IT
Torchinsky Engineering Ltd, 206, 610-70 Ave. S.E., pg. 31   IT
Toromont Process Systems, 3615-34th St. N.E., pg. 1400   IT
Total Petroleum Canada Ltd., 1200 Standard Life Bldg., 639 Fifth Ave., S.W., Ste. 700, pg. 1409   IT
TRANSALTA CORPORATION, 110-12th Ave. S.W., pg. 1416   IT
TransAlta Energy Corporation, 110-12th Ave., S.W., pg. 1416   IT
TransAlta Enterprises Corporation, 110 12th Ave., S.W., pg. 1416   IT
TransAlta Fly Ash Ltd., 110-12th Ave., S.W., pg. 1416   IT
TransAlta Utilities, 110 12th Ave., S.W., pg. 1416   IT
TransCanada Energy Ltd, 3400, 237-Fourth Avenue S.W., pg. 1417   IT
TransCanada International Ltd., 3400, 237 Fourth Avenue S.W., pg. 1417   IT
TRANSCANADA PIPELINES LIMITED, TransCanada PipeLines Tower, 111 5th Ave. SW, pg. 1416   IT
Transcontinental Printing Inc. - Calgary, 5516 Fifth Street South East, pg. 538   IT
Tri-Line Expressways Ltd., 9559-40th St., S.E., pg. 1150   IT
Trimac Consulting Services, 700, 800 5 Avenue SW, pg. 1424   IT
TRIMAC CORPORATION, 2100, 800 Fifth Ave. S.W., pg. 1423   IT
Trimac Transportation System, 2100, 800 5th Ave. SW, pg. 1424   IT
Trimac Transportation-Western Division, 700, 800 5 Avenue SW, pg. 1424   IT
TriWaste Reduction Services Inc., 1700, 800 5 Avenue SW, pg. 1424   IT
Unigas, 150 Sixth Ave. S.W., Ste. 3520, pg. 1492   IT
Union Bank of Switzerland, 605-Fifth Ave. S.W., Ste. 805, pg. 1441   IT
Unocal Canada Limited, 150 6th Ave. S.W., pg. 1698   PB
Van Leeuwen Pipe & Tube (Canada) Inc., 4646 32nd Street S.E., pg. 1450   IT
Weatherford Canada Limited, 505 Third St., S.W., pg. 1750   PB
Westcoast Petroleum Ltd., 421 Seventh Ave. S.W., pg. 1492   IT
Western Cooperative Fertilizers Limited (WCFL), pg. 1195   IT
Western Gas Resources Canada, Inc., 2000 Bankers Hall, 855 Second Street S.W., pg. 1759   PB
Western Geophysical (Canada), 2612 37th Ave., N.E., pg. 1005   PB
Western Union Insurance Co., 333 5th Avenue,S.W., 16th Floor, pg. 651   PB
White Iron Film and Video Productions, 350, 708-11 Ave. S.W., pg. 1124   IT
Wilshire Oil of Canada, Ltd., 444 5th Ave. S.W., T2P 2T8, pg. 1770   PB
Wintershall Canada Ltd., 333 Fifth Ave. S.W., Ste. 700, pg. 110   IT
Wireless Networks Skyline - Northern Telecom Canada Limited, 5550 Skyline Way N.E., pg. 969   IT
Young & Rubicam Calgary, 1050, 1015-4th St., S.W., pg. 1200   PV
Zazula Process Equip. Ltd., 1526 10th Ave. S.W., pg. 6   IT

Cambridge

ATS AUTOMATION TOOLING SYSTEMS, INC., 250 Royal Oak Rd., pg. 18   IT
Allen-Bradley Canada Limited, 135 Dundas St., pg. 1398   PB
Appleton Electric Ltd., 750 Lawrence St., pg. 575   PB
BFC Industrial Nicholls-Radtke, 150 Sheldon Drive, pg. 118   IT
Babcock & Wilcox International, pg. 1068   PB
Bauer Sports, 445 Dobbie Dr., pg. 1184   PB
Bauer Sports, 63 Sheffield St., pg. 1184   PB
Butler Metal Products, 1574 Eagle St. N., pg. 113   IT
CIBA-GEIGY Canada Ltd., 1200 Franklin Blvd., pg. 976   IT
Dimplex North America, 1367 Industrial Road, pg. 554   IT
Dover Flour Mills, 140 King St. W., pg. 417   IT
Euroclean Canada Inc., 866 Langs Drive, pg. 441   IT
Fairway Group, 240 Holiday Inn Drive, pg. 631   IT
Florsheim, Inc., 1008 Queenston Rd., pg. 656   PB
Fuchs-Montgomery Company, Inc., 405 Dobbie Dr., pg. 518   IT
Getinge Sterilizing Equipment Inc., 180 Shearson Crescent, Unit 6, pg. 552   IT
Global Processing & Recycling Group, Shied-Tech Cambridge, pg. 748   PB
Gotaverken Energy Systems Ltd., 73 Water St. North, pg. 771   IT
Goulds Pumps Canada, Inc., 1700 Bishop St., pg. 861   PB
Hickman, Williams Canada, Inc., pg. 525   PV
Long Manufacturing Ltd., 401 Franklin Blvd., pg. 815   IT

PB - *U.S. Public Companies Volume*
PV - *U.S. Private Companies Volume*
IT - *International Public & Private Companies Volume*

Preformed Line Products Canada, 36 Raglan Pl., pg. 1321   **PB**
Rockwell International of Canada Ltd., 12 Raglin Place, pg. 1401   **PB**
Superior Graphite Ltd., 887 Langs Drive Unit #13, pg. 1055   **PV**
Toyota Motor Manufacturing Canada Inc., 1055 Fountain St., N., pg. 1414   **IT**
VicWest Steel Supply, 1670 Bishop St., pg. 698   **IT**
Westcan Chromalox, 1367 Industrial Rd., pg. 554   **IT**
Zehrmart Inc., 100 Holiday Inn Dr., pg. 1495   **IT**

Campbell River

Menzies Bay Division, pg. 828   **IT**
Stolt Sea Farm Inc., 1405 Spruce St., pg. 1302   **IT**

Campbellford

Cook Chocolate Canada Ltd., Second St., pg. 1191   **PV**
World's Finest Chocolate Canada Ltd., Second Street, pg. 1191   **PV**

Campbellton

CKNB-AM, 100 Water St., pg. 1124   **IT**

Campbellville

Leaver Mushrooms Co. Limited, 7399 Guelph Line, pg. 428   **PB**

Camrose

Camrose Pipe Company, 5302 39th St., pg. 1230   **PB**

Cap de la Madeleine

Cascades Lupel Inc., 700 Notre Dame, pg. 273   **IT**
Desencrage C.M.D. Inc., pg. 273   **IT**
Reynolds Aluminum of Canada, 290 St. Laurent Street, pg. 1387   **PB**

Carlyle

Talisman Energy Inc., Box 70, pg. 1352   **IT**

Carp

Pronexus, Inc., 123 Pinerdge Rd., R.R.3, pg. 17   **PB**

Centreville

Thomas Equipment Limited, pg. 850   **IT**

Chalk River

Atomic Energy of Canada Ltd., Chalk River Laboratories, pg. 97   **IT**

Chambly

Revomac, 2000 Boul. Industriel, pg. 696   **IT**

Chapleau

Chapleau Forest Products, pg. 828   **IT**

Chaplin

Saskatchewan Mineral Div., pg. 243   **IT**

Charlottetown

CFCY-AM/CHLQ-FM, 141 Kent St., pg. 1124   **IT**
The Guardian, 165 Prince Street, pg. 631   **IT**
Transatlantic Trust Corporation, 75 Rochford St., pg. 1197   **PB**

Chatham

CFCO Radio-AM, 21 Keil Dr., pg. 1123   **IT**
The Chatham Daily News, 45 Fourth Street, pg. 631   **IT**
DeKalb Canada Inc., 301 Richmond St., pg. 493   **PB**
Eaton Yale Ltd. Suspension Div., 566 Riverview Dr., pg. 559   **PB**
Pioneer Hi-Bred Limited, P.O. Box 730, #2 Highway W., pg. 1299   **PB**
Rockwell International Suspension Systems Company, 105 St. George St., pg. 1401   **PB**
Union Gas Limited, 50 Keil Dr. N., pg. 1492   **IT**

Chauvin

Talisman Energy Inc., pg. 1352   **IT**

Chelmsford

Falconbridge Explorations, 1977 McKenzie Rd., pg. 433   **IT**

Chemainus

Chemaius Sawmill Division, 9803 Croft St., pg. 828   **IT**

Chetwynd

Canadian Forest Products Ltd., Chetwynd Division, pg. 260   **IT**
Talisman Energy Inc., P.O. Box 1270, pg. 1352   **IT**

Chicoutimi

Elkem Chicoutimi, 2020 Chemin de la Reverse, pg. 448   **IT**
Gaz Metropolitain, Inc.-Saguenay/Lac St.-Jean, 1100 Bersimis Street, pg. 541   **IT**
Messaceries Saguenay, 2150-C, rue Fabien, pg. 539   **IT**
Port Saguenay/Baie des Ha! Ha!, Lafontaine St., pg. 255   **IT**

Chomedey

Farr Incorporated, 2785 Francis Hughes, pg. 614   **PB**
Favorite Products Co., 730 rue Salaberry, pg. 1215   **PB**

Churchill

Port of Churchill, P.O. Box 217, pg. 255   **IT**

Coaticook

Niedner Limited, 190 rue Cutting, pg. 1485   **IT**

Cobourg

Anamet Canada Inc., P.O. Box 550, pg. 70   **PV**
Cobourg Daily Star, 415 King Street West, pg. 631   **IT**
Cobourg Plant, 130 Willmott Street, pg. 201   **PB**

Collingwood

Canadian Mist Distillers Ltd., 202 MacDonald Rd., pg. 262   **PB**
Rogers Cable Systems, 4 Sandford Fleming Dr., pg. 1123   **IT**

Concord

Air Guard, 8001 Keele St., pg. 238   **IT**
Aloette Cosmetics of Canada, 89 Edilcan Dr., pg. 57   **PB**
Apple Auto Glass, Ltd., 360 Applewood Crescent, pg. 1336   **IT**
Arvin Automotive of Canada, Ltd., P.O. Box 270, pg. 137   **PB**
Beck Electric Manufacturing Company, 245 Drumlin Circle, pg. 955   **IT**
Boss Canada, Inc., 62 Bradwick Drive, pg. 1142   **PV**
Bowmar Distribution (Canada) Ltd., 267 North Revermede Road, pg. 190   **PB**
Cabano Kingsway Transport, 391 Creditstone Rd., pg. 1150   **IT**
Champion Parts (Canada) Ltd., 41 Courtland Ave., Unit #9, pg. 335   **PB**
Clarke Transport, Bowes Rd., pg. 924   **IT**
Con-Web Press Inc., 89 Connie Crescent, pg. 1076   **IT**
Cosma International Inc., 50 Casmir Ct., pg. 829   **IT**
Crown Cork & Seal Canada, Inc., 7900 Keele St., pg. 464   **PB**
Crown Cork of Canada Ltd., 7900 Keele St., pg. 464   **PB**
Decoma International Inc., 50 Casmir Ct., pg. 829   **IT**
Dufferin Aggregates, 3300 Hwy. 7, Ste. 400, pg. 628   **IT**
Dufferin-Custom Concrete Group, 3300 Highway 7, Ste. 400, pg. 628   **IT**
DYWIDAG Systems International, USA, Inc., 65 Bowes Rd., Unit #5, pg. 424   **PB**
Everest & Jennings/Graham-Field, Canada, 111 Snidercroft Rd., pg. 758   **PB**
The Glidden Company (Canada) Limited, c/o 8200 Keele St., pg. 664   **IT**
ICI Paints (Canada) Inc., 8200 Keele St., pg. 665   **IT**
ITW Plastiglide Ltd. of Canada/ ITW Fastex, 80 Sante Dr., pg. 869   **PB**
International Flavors & Fragrances (Canada) Ltd., 7330 Keele St., pg. 899   **PB**
INTERWOOD MARKETING GROUP, 2720 Steeles Ave. W., pg. 685   **IT**
K-G Packaging, 8001 Keele Street, pg. 238   **IT**
KIK Corporation Holdings Inc., pg. 222   **PV**
Lafarge Construction Materials, 7880 Keele St., 5th Floor, pg. 788   **IT**
Merisel Canada, 731 Millway Ave., pg. 1096   **PB**
North American Professional Products, 91 Caldari Rd., pg. 238   **IT**
Pipetronix Ltd., 50A Caldari Rd., pg. 1071   **IT**
Premdor Inc.-Door Distribution, 7171 Jane St., pg. 1067   **IT**
Premdor Mouldings Inc., 7725 Jane Street, pg. 1067   **IT**
Quebecor Printing Concord, 89 Connie Crescent, pg. 1077   **IT**
SCIEX, 714 Valley Dr., pg. 827   **IT**
Spalding Canada, 250 Courtland Ave., pg. 630   **PV**
Sunrise Medical Canada Inc., 237 Romina Dr., Unit 3, pg. 1536   **IT**
TECMAR TECHNOLOGIES INTERNATIONAL, INC., 7941 Jane St., Ste. 105, pg. 1361   **IT**
Tesma International Inc., 300 Edgeley Boulevard, pg. 830   **IT**
Toromont CAT, One Crothers Drive, pg. 1400   **IT**
TOROMONT INDUSTRIES LTD., One Crothers Drive, pg. 1400   **IT**

Contrecoeur

Stelco-McMaster Ltee, 2050 Route de Aceries, pg. 1299   **IT**

Copper Cliff

Inco Limited, Ontario Division, pg. 672   **IT**

Corner Brook

Corner Brook Pulp & Paper Limited, Mill Rd., pg. 761   **IT**
The Western Star, P.O. Box 460, pg. 632   **IT**

Cornwall

AlliedSignal Aerospace Canada, Electronic Systems, 2901 Marleau Ave., pg. 54   **PB**
Courtaulds (Canada) Inc., 1150 Montreal Rd., pg. 339   **IT**
Cyborg Systems of Canada, 2747 Marleau Ave., pg. 299   **PV**
Freudenberg Nonwovens Inc., 1020 Montreal Rd., pg. 506   **IT**
Lilly Industries, Inc., 1915 2nd Street W., pg. 995   **PB**
Roe Lee Canada Inc., 605 Boundary Road, pg. 1086   **IT**
Rogers Cable TV-Cornwall, 517 Pitt St., pg. 1122   **IT**
The Standard-Freeholder, 44 Pitt Street, pg. 631   **IT**
Techni-Therm Inc., 3330 Marleau Ave., pg. 416   **IT**
Transcontinental Printing Inc. - Cornwall, 1800 Vincent Massey Drive, pg. 538   **IT**

Corunna

Du Pont Canada-St. Clair River, Albert St., pg. 532   **PB**
Ethyl Canada, Inc., 220 St. Claire, pg. 595   **PB**

Coteau du Lac

Sorevco Inc., 25 Del'acier, pg. 414   **IT**

Cottam

Ciba Seeds(CIBA-GEIGY Canada Ltd.), Rural Rte. No. 3, pg. 976   **IT**

Cowansville

Albany International Canada, Inc., 300 Westmount St., pg. 37   **PB**

Cranbrook

Cominco Ltd., #1051 Industrial Road, No. 2, pg. 308   **IT**
CRESTBROOK FOREST INDUSTRIES LTD., 220 Cranbrook Street, pg. 348   **IT**

Dartmouth

Andres Wines (Atlantic) Ltd., 99 Wyse Rd., Ste. 350, pg. 76   **IT**
Anixter Halifax, 100 Wright Ave., pg. 115   **PB**
The Daily News, 11 Thornhill Drive, pg. 924   **IT**
Emco Supply Atlantic Division, 90 Wright Ave., P.O. Box 897, pg. 453   **PB**
Food Ingredients Limited, P.O. Box 2610, pg. 606   **IT**
Grow Group Canada Ltd., 55-A MacDonald Ave., pg. 663   **IT**
Helly-Hansen Canada Ltd., Landmark Place, 51 Raddal Avenue, pg. 1010   **IT**
Hermes Electronics, Inc., 40 Atlantic Street, pg. 1431   **IT**
Hewlett-Packard (Canada) Ltd., 201 Brownlow Ave., pg. 818   **PB**
Jacques Geosciences, Inc., 3 Spectacle Lake Dr., pg. 454   **PV**
Lawtons Drug Stores Limited, 236 Brownlow Ave., pg. 924   **IT**
MM Industra, Ltd., 61 Estates Road, pg. 74   **IT**
Major Foods Ltd., 131 Ilsley Ave., pg. 79   **PV**
Moirs Plant, Pleasant St., pg. 812   **PB**
NCC Specialty Publications, 900 Windmill Road, Unit 107, pg. 924   **IT**
NEWFOUNDLAND CAPITAL CORPORATION LIMITED, Suite 302, 800 Windmill Road, pg. 924   **IT**
Royal Insurance Atlantic Regional Centre, 120 Eileen Stubbs Ave., Ste. 301, pg. 1131   **IT**
TSC Shannock Corporation, 109 Ilsley Ave., pg. 1343   **IT**

Delhi

Bundy of Canada Ltd., 270 Argyle St., pg. 1341   **IT**
Delhi Industries Inc., 523 James St., pg. 1150   **IT**

Delta

AIM SAFETY COMPANY INC., 1600 Derwent Way, # 7, pg. 36   **PV**
Arnold Advertising, 6617 1A Avenue, pg. 84   **PV**
SM-Cyclo of Canada, Ltd., 740 Chester Road, pg. 1315   **IT**
Tilbury Cement Company, 7777 Ross Road, pg. 606   **IT**
Transcontinental Printing Inc. - Vancouver, 725 Hamstead Close, pg. 538   **IT**
Tristar Industries Ltd., Vantage Way, pg. 1473   **IT**

PB - *U.S. Public Companies Volume*
PV - *U.S. Private Companies Volume*
IT - *International Public & Private Companies Volume*

1532

Geographic Index-Non U.S.

WAJAX LIMITED, 8760 River Rd., pg. 1484 — IT
Westshore Terminals Ltd., One Roberts Bank, pg. 1491 — IT

Dollard des Ormeaux

Bentley Leathers Inc., 90A Brunswick Avenue, pg. 187 — IT
Brother International Corporation (Canada) Ltd., 1, rue Hotel de Ville, pg. 229 — IT

Don Mills

Addison-Wesley Publishers Ltd., 26 Prince Andrew Pl., pg. 1027 — IT
Advanced Monobloc Inc., 96 Scarsdale Road, pg. 238 — IT
Canadian Kawasaki Motors Inc., 25 Lesmill Rd., pg. 726 — IT
FTI FOODTECH INTERNATIONAL INC., 43 Railside Road, pg. 476 — IT
Financial Collection Agencies, Suite 406, 1090 Don Mills Road, pg. 470 — IT
Four Seasons Hotels & Resorts, 1165 Leslie St., M3C 2K8, pg. 502 — IT
FOUR SEASONS HOTELS INC., 1165 Leslie St., pg. 502 — IT
Grand & Toy Limited, 33 Green Belt Dr., pg. 243 — PB
Harlequin Enterprises Ltd., 225 Duncan Mill Rd., pg. 1402 — IT
Ingram & Bell Inc., 20 Bond Ave., pg. 826 — IT
IPEX, 50 Valleybrook Drive, pg. 695 — IT
Kenral Inc., 865 York Mills Rd., pg. 1049 — IT
Kraft Canada Inc., 95 Moatfield Dr., pg. 1288 — PB
Mappins Jewelers, 1440 Don Mills Rd., pg. 1036 — IT
NN Financial, 1 Concorde Gate, pg. 650 — IT
National Data Corporation of Canada Ltd., One Concore Gate, Ste. 700, pg. 1156 — PB
Oxford University Press Canada, 70 Winford Dr., pg. 1019 — IT
PEOPLES JEWELLERS CORPORATION, 1440 Don Mills Rd., pg. 1036 — IT
Pharmacia & Upjohn Company of Canada, 861 York Mills Rd., pg. 1049 — IT
Quebecor Printing MIL Inc., 180 Bond Ave., pg. 1077 — IT
Rogers Cable TV-Toronto Div., 855 York Mills, pg. 1122 — IT
ROYAL LEPAGE LIMITED, 39 Wynford Dr., pg. 1143 — IT
Royal LePage - Ottawa Office, 39 Wynford Dr., pg. 1143 — IT
Royal LePage Real Estate Services Ltd., 39 Wynford Drive, pg. 1143 — IT
Southam Inc., 1450 Don Mills Rd., pg. 631 — IT
TSC Shannock Corporation, 23-156 Duncan Mill Rd., pg. 1343 — IT
T.V. Times, 1450 Don Mills Road, pg. 632 — IT
Wackenhut of Canada Ltd., 26 Lesmill Rd., pg. 1731 — PB
Wrigley Canada Inc., 1123 Leslie St., pg. 1781 — PB

Dorval

APV Pavailler Canada, 619 rue Meloche, pg. 485 — IT
Aeroservices J.T. Inc., 975 Romeo Vachon Blvd. N., pg. 845 — PB
AST Canada, Inc., 1405 route Transcanadienne, pg. 1182 — IT
Atlas Copco Compressor Canada, 745 Montreal-Toronto Blvd., pg. 96 — IT
BPCO, 455 Fenelon Blvd., Ste. 110, pg. 453 — IT
Bombardier Aerospace, 400 Cote-Vertu Road, pg. 200 — IT
Bombardier Inc. Canadair, 400 Cote-Vertu Road, pg. 200 — IT
Catalina Lighting Canada, 250 Michel Jasmin, pg. 314 — PB
CIBA-GEIGY Canada Ltd., 215 Boul. Bouchard, pg. 976 — IT
CIBA-GEIGY Canada Ltd., 205 Boul. Bouchard, pg. 976 — IT
Coty Canada, 1255 Trans Canada Hwy., Ste. 200, pg. 186 — IT
Emergi-Lite Landmark Inc., 1811 Hymus Blvd., pg. 725 — IT
Farinon Canada Ltd., 657 Orly Ave., pg. 791 — PB
Gaz Metropolitain, Inc., 3150 Miller Street, pg. 541 — IT
Innotech Aviation Industries Ltd., 595 Stewart Graham Blvd., pg. 36 — IT
KAUFEL GROUP LTD., 1811 Hymus Blvd., pg. 724 — IT
Montreal Learning Center, 9555 Ryan Ave., pg. 219 — PB
Pan-Acc Transit Systems Inc., 1811 Hymus Blvd., pg. 725 — IT
Parkson Corporator, 9050 Ryan Ave., pg. 711 — IT
PREMIER CDN ENTERPRISES LTD., 1785 55th Ave., pg. 1067 — IT
Salomon Sports Ltd., 1904 St. Regis Blvd., pg. 1181 — IT
Sandoz Canada Ltd., 385 Bouchard Blvd., pg. 984 — IT
Securiplex Inc., 549 Meloche Street, pg. 1162 — IT
Selection Lighting Inc., 1811 Hymus Blvd., pg. 725 — IT
Sermatech Canada, 747 Riddle Ave., pg. 1570 — PB
Telxon Canada Corporation, Ltd., Carre Dorval, 455 Boul. Fenelon, Bureau 100, pg. 1574 — PB
Tenelux, 1811 Hymus Blvd., pg. 725 — IT
Twinpak Inc., 1255 Trans-Canada Highway, Suite 210, pg. 72 — IT
Zep Manufacturing, 660 Lepine St., pg. 1160 — PB

Downsview

ARC INTERNATIONAL CORPORATION, 4000 Chesswood Dr., pg. 17 — IT
Adidas (Canada) Ltd., 550 Oakdale Rd., pg. 24 — IT
Arc Sports, 4000 Chesswood Dr., pg. 17 — IT
Bank Hapoalim B.M., 3910 Bathurst Street, Suite 303, pg. 149 — IT
Bell Mobility Paging Inc., Ten Kodak Crescent, pg. 115 — IT

BIC Inc., 155 Oakdale Rd., pg. 1273 — IT
Bombardier Regional Aircraft Division, 123 Garratt Blvd., pg. 242 — PB
Canada Dry Division, 170 Athwell Dr., pg. 248 — IT
de Havilland Inc., 123 Garratt Boulevard, pg. 200 — IT
Diversified Stainless Steel of Canada, 98 Norfinch Dr., pg. 308 — PB
Essroc Canada, 949 Wilson Ave., pg. 292 — IT
Fischer & Porter (Canada) Ltd., 134 Norfinch Dr., pg. 449 — IT
Globe Spring & Cushion Co., Ltd., 4040 Chesswood Drive, pg. 987 — PB
Harrisons & Crosfield (Canada) Ltd., 777 Supertess Rd., pg. 599 — IT
Hugo Boss Canada Inc., 21 Codiac Crescent, pg. 638 — IT
Jones Apparel Group, Inc. Canada, 55 St. Regis Crescent North, pg. 933 — PB
Mirtone, 425 Alness St., pg. 727 — PB
Producto Diemakers Supplies Ltd., 620 Supertest Rd., pg. 889 — PV
Sumitomo Rubber Industries-Toronto, 470 Norfinch Drive, pg. 1317 — IT
Toronto Learning Center, 95 Garratt Blvd., pg. 219 — IT
TRIDEL ENTERPRISES INC., 4800 Dufferin Street, pg. 1423 — IT
Xomox Canada Ltd., 222 Norfinch Dr., M3N 1Y5, pg. 578 — PB

Drummondville

Americ Disc Inc., 2525, rue Canadien, pg. 539 — IT
Cascades Multi-Pro Inc., 495 Haggerty Street, pg. 273 — IT
Cascades P.S.H. Inc., 999 Rue Farrell, pg. 273 — IT
Cascades Sealed Air Inc., 2350 Boul Lemire, pg. 273 — IT
Celanese Cellulosics, 2575 St. Joseph, pg. 625 — IT
Emballages Cascades Drummondville Inc., 600 Rue Janelle, pg. 273 — IT
Plastichange International Inc., 500 Rue Lauzon, pg. 273 — IT
Swift Denim Inc., 575 des Ecoles, pg. 415 — IT
Transcontinental Printing Inc. - Drummondville, 1330, rue Michaud, pg. 538 — IT
Venmar Ventilation, Inc., 550 Boule Lemire, pg. 1194 — IT

Dryden

Golden Patricia Mine, P.O. Box 4000, pg. 169

Dubreuilville

Dubreuil Forest Products, Ltd., 21 rue des Pins, pg. 672 — PB

Duncan

DOMAN INDUSTRIES LIMITED, 435 Trunk Rd., 73rd Fl., pg. 414 — IT

Dunnville

Albright & Wilson Americas Limited, P.O. Box 130, pg. 49 — IT

East Angus

Cascades Cartech Inc., 248 Rue Wagner, pg. 273 — IT
Cascades East Angus Inc., 248 Rue Wagner, pg. 273 — IT

Edmonton

AST Canada, Inc., Sun Life Place-Execuplace, 10125-99th Street, Ste. 1840, pg. 1182 — IT
AGRA Foundations Limited, 7708 Wagner Rd., pg. 30 — IT
Alberta Envirofuels Inc., pg. 914 — IT
Alberta Oil Tool Div., 9530 60th Ave., T6E 0C1, pg. 522 — PB
Alberta Power Limited, 10035 105th St., pg. 95 — IT
Allarcom Pay Television Limited, 5324 Calgary Trail, Suite 200, pg. 1481 — IT
AltaSteel Ltd., 9401-E. 34th St., pg. 1299 — IT
Anixter Edmonton, 12759 149th St., pg. 115 — PB
Associated Valve, 4404 97th St., pg. 256 — IT
BFC Pipelines, pg. 118 — IT
Ballast Nedan Canada Ltd., 3200 Manulife Place, pg. 134 — IT
Banister Majestic, pg. 118 — IT
Barber Industries, Inc., 10358 65th Ave., pg. 164 — IT
Bettis Canada Limited, 4112 - 91A Street, pg. 483 — PB
Bowen Tools, Ltd., 4080 78 Ave., pg. 858 — PB
Brian Controls Division, 9833 45th Ave., pg. 711 — IT
Brown & Root Ltd., 3400 76th Ave., pg. 776 — PB
CES Thermal Services Limited-Alexander Fireproofing, 11503 - 160th St., pg. 74 — IT
CFRN-TV, 18520 Stony Plain Road, pg. 438 — IT
CKNG-FM/CHED-AM Radio, 5204 84 St., pg. 1124 — IT
Canadian Energy Services, 2204 - 84th Ave., pg. 74 — IT
CANADIAN WESTERN BANK, 10303 Jasper Ave., Ste. 2300, pg. 259 — IT
Centre Suite Hotel Ltd., Eaton Center Mall, pg. 325 — IT
Chieftain Development Co. Ltd., 1201 Toronto Dominion Tower, pg. 49 — IT
CHIEFTAIN INTERNATIONAL, INC., 1201 Toronto Dominion Tower, Edmonton Centre, pg. 284 — IT
Chieftain International (U.S.) Inc., 1201 Toronto Dominion Tower, pg. 284 — IT
Cognos Inc.-Edmonton Sales Office, Ste. 209, 8616-51st Ave., pg. 306 — IT
Comco Pipe and Supply Company, 5910-17 St., pg. 1150 — IT

Construction Services, 4404 97th St., pg. 256 — IT
DMR Group, Inc., 1500, 10020-101A Ave., pg. 527 — IT
Data Business Forms, 9815 42nd St., pg. 384 — IT
John Deere Finance Limited - Alberta, 1700-10123 99th Street, pg. 492 — PB
Domcor - Alberta, 15432-114th Avenue, pg. 415 — IT
Dynacare-Alberta, 14940-123 Avenue, pg. 425 — IT
Eastman Christensen Canada Ltd., 16230-112 Ave., pg. 167 — PB
Echo Bay Mines-Lupin Operations, 9818 International Airport, pg. 562 — PB
The Edmonton Journal, 10006 101 St., pg. 631 — IT
Edmonton Plant, 4610 76th Ave., pg. 672 — PB
The Edmonton Sun, 250, 4990-92nd Ave., pg. 1320 — IT
Emco Distribution Group Western Region, 14940 1- 121 A Ave., pg. 453 — IT
Financial Collection Agencies, Suite 600, Energy Square, 10109, pg. 470 — IT
Flowserve Duriron Canada Inc., 9044-18 Street, pg. 659 — PB
Frontec Corporation, 10035-105 Street, pg. 95 — IT
Frontec Logistics Corporation, 8th Fl., 10040-104 St., pg. 95 — IT
GPC Government Policy Consultants (Edmonton), 1100 Canada Trust Tower, 10104-103 Avenue, pg. 1225 — IT
General Business Forms, 102-9808 42nd Ave., pg. 384 — IT
Guardian Oilfield Services, 950 78th Avenue, pg. 1231 — IT
Hewlett-Packard (Canada) Ltd., 11120-178th St., pg. 818 — PB
Horne & Pitfield, 17220 Stony Plain Rd., pg. 1012 — IT
Hudson's Bay Company Acceptance Ltd., 501-10310 Jasper Ave., pg. 637 — IT
IPL International, IPL Tower, 10201 Jasper Ave., pg. 652 — IT
Ikon Office Solutions, 9897 34th Ave., pg. 864 — PB
Industra Service Corp. - Alberta, 2204 - 84th Avenue, pg. 74 — IT
Inland Cement Company, 12640 156th Street, pg. 606 — IT
Intergraph Canada Ltd., One Thornton Court, Ste. 1100, pg. 891 — PB
Interprovincial Pipe Line Inc., IPL Tower, 10201 Jasper Avenue, pg. 652 — IT
Interprovincial Pipe Line (NW) Ltd., IPL Tower, 10201 Jasper Ave., pg. 652 — IT
Kodak Canada Inc., 10180 101st St., Ste. 1680, pg. 553 — PB
Kvaerner National, Inc. Canadian Division, 9515-51 Ave. Edmonton, pg. 768 — IT
Labatt Breweries of Canada - Prairie Region, 4344-99 Street, pg. 679 — IT
Lafarge Construction Materials, 8635 Stadium Rd., pg. 791 — IT
Midwest Management (1987) Limited, 510 Ellis Drive, pg. 31 — IT
Midwest Pipeline Contractors Ltd., 490 Ellis Dr., pg. 31 — IT
Molson Alberta Brewery Ltd., 10449 121st St., pg. 887 — IT
National-Oilwell/Dreco, Suite 1340, Weber Ctr., 5555 Calgary Trail, pg. 1158 — PB
National-Oilwell/Dreco, 6415 75th St., pg. 1158 — PB
National-Oilwell/Dreco Holdings Ltd., 6415 75th St., pg. 1158 — PB
National-Oilwell Griffith Oil Tool & Trudril, 3660 - 93 St., pg. 1158 — PB
Northland Utilities (B.C.) Limited, 10035-105 St., pg. 95 — IT
Northland Utilities Enterprises Ltd., 10035 - 105 St., pg. 95 — IT
Northland Utilities (NWT) Limited, 10035 - 105 St., pg. 95 — IT
Northwestern Utilities Limited, 10035 - 105 St., pg. 95 — IT
Palmer Jarvis Advertising, 1000-10235 101 St., pg. 768 — IT
Panorama Apartments (Edmonton) Limited, Sun Life Plaza, Ste. 640, 10123-99th St., pg. 1319 — IT
Principal Plaza Leaseholds Ltd., 300, 8657 51st Ave., pg. 326 — IT
Quebecor Printing Edmonton, 18120 - 114th Ave., pg. 1077 — IT
Royal LePage, 10130 103 Street, Suite 2000, pg. 1143 — IT
SHL Systemhouse - Western Region, 10130-103 Street, Ste. 1420, pg. 1154 — IT
Sealy Canada, Ltd., 14550 112th Ave., pg. 979 — PV
Smith International Canada Ltd., 9205 51st Ave., pg. 1478 — PB
Solar Turbines Canada Ltd., 2510 84th Ave., pg. 317 — PB
Sun Microsystems of Canada-Edmonton, 413 Le Marchand Mansion, 11523-100th Ave., pg. 1532 — PB
Svedala Industries Canada Edmonton, 4320 81st Ave., pg. 1325 — IT
TSC Shannock Corporation, 14944 121 A. Ave., pg. 1343 — IT
TELUS CORPORATION, 10020-100 St. N.W., pg. 1374 — IT
TELUS Marketing Communications, Floor 24, 10020 100 Street, pg. 1374 — IT
Terochem Laboratories Limited a/k/a Raylo Chemicals, 8045 Argyll Rd., pg. 803 — IT
United Pipeline Systems, Inc, 7506 18th St., N.W., pg. 882 — PB
Valtek Controls, 9044 18th St., pg. 659 — PB
Van Leeuven Pipe & Tube (Canada) Inc., 211 E. Ocean Blvd. #300, pg. 1450 — IT
Varco BJ Drilling Systems, 10908 40A Ave., pg. 1709 — PB
WF Corroon-Alberta, 1200 Scotia Place, Tower 1, pg. 1502 — IT
Waterous Detroit Diesel-Allison Inc., 10025 51st Ave., pg. 1485 — IT
Weatherford Oil Tool Co. (1983) Ltd., 14435-116 Ave., pg. 1750 — PB
Westlund Industrial Supply Ltd., 3691-98 St., pg. 453 — IT
White Pass Systems Ltd., 16045 114th Ave., pg. 1150 — IT

PB - *U.S. Public Companies Volume*
PV - *U.S. Private Companies Volume*
IT - *International Public & Private Companies Volume*

1533

Geographic Index-Non U.S.

Willis Corroon Melling Ltd., 1200 Scotia Pl, 10060 Jasper Ave., pg. 1509   IT

Edson

Talisman Energy Inc., pg. 1352   IT

Elliot Lake

Rio Algom Limited, P.O. Box 1500, pg. 1118   IT

Elmira

Uniroyal Chemical Ltd., 25 Erb St., pg. 460   PB

Enfield

Litton Systems Canada Ltd. (Nova Scotia), 249 Aero Tech Dr., pg. 1005   PB

Esterhazy

PCS Potash - Esterhazy, pg. 1064   IT

Estevan

Estevan Brick Division, P.O. Box 40, pg. 698   IT

Etobicoke

ACC Long Distance, Ltd., 5343 Dundas St. W., Ste. 401, pg. 3   PB
Akzo Nobel Inc., 110 Woodbine Downs Blvd., Unit 4, pg. 428   IT
AlliedSignal Aerospace Canada, 255 Attwell Dr., pg. 53   PB
AlliedSignal Airline Services, Allied Signal Aerospace Canada, 255 Attwell Dr., pg. 53   PB
Amram's Distributing, Ltd., 315 Attwell Drive, pg. 223   IT
Aqualon Canada Inc., 5407 Eglinton Ave. West, Ste. 103, pg. 810   PB
Aromat Canada Inc., 109 Woodbine Downs Blvd., pg. 848   IT
ASTRO DAIRY PRODUCTS LTD., 25 Rakely Ct., pg. 95   IT
Atlas Alloys, 161 The West Mall, pg. 1118   IT
Baskin-Robbins Canada, 50 Ronson Dr., Ste. 131, pg. 63   IT
Bell Mobility Cellular Inc., 20 Carlson Ct., pg. 115   IT
Bernardin of Canada, Ltd., 120 The East Mall, pg. 56   PB
Best Foods Canada, Inc., 401 The West Mall, pg. 224   PB
Borden Foods Canada, 185 The West Mall, Ste. 1700, pg. 159   PV
CCL Custom Manufacturing, 2000 Kipling Avenue, pg. 239   IT
CCL Label, 35 McLachlan Dr., pg. 238   IT
Canada Life Casualty Insurance Company, 304 The East Mall, Ste. 400, pg. 254   IT
Candian Regional Airlines, 6th Fl., 191 The West Mall, pg. 256   IT
Cantel Paging, 5 Greensboro Dr., pg. 1123   IT
Canusa-EMI, 25 Bethridge Rd., pg. 1231   IT
Casco Inc., 401 The West Mall, pg. 448   IT
Celanese Canada Chemicals & Industrial Products Group, 195 The West Mall, Ste. 1000, pg. 625   IT
CHAPTERS INC., 90 Ronson Drive, pg. 280   IT
P.F. Collier & Son Ltd., 7 Daymall Ave., pg. 433   IT
Communications Technology (Canada) Ltd., 151 Carlingview Dr., pg. 480   PB
ConferTech Canada Inc., Leva Road, Ste. 213, pg. 683   PB
CONSUMERS PACKAGING INC., 777 Kipling Ave., pg. 326   IT
Corporate Foods Ltd., 10 Four Seasons Place, pg. 841   IT
DMC Telecom Canada Inc., 90 Claireport Cres., Ste. 8, pg. 508   PB
Dictaphone Canada Ltd.-Ltee., 630 The East Mall, pg. 1045   IT
The Walt Disney Company (Canada), 185 The West Mall, pg. 514   PB
Dominion Stores, 5559 Dundas Street West, pg. 1375   IT
Exide Electronics Canada, Inc., 380 Carling View Dr., pg. 126   IT
Federal Industries Metals Group, 180 Atwell Dr., Ste. 400, pg. 1150   IT
Financial Life Assurance Co. of Canada, 10 Four Seasons Place, 10 Fl., pg. 77   PB
Fraser Paper Limited, 185 West Mall, Ste. 1050, pg. 434   IT
General Mills Canada Inc., 1330 Martin Grove Rd., pg. 718   PB
Gilbey Canada Inc., 401 The West Mall, Ste. 700, pg. 409   IT
The Great Atlantic & Pacific Company of Canada Limited, 5559 Dundas Street West, pg. 1375   IT
Heidelberg Canada Graphic Equipment Ltd., 50 Worcester Rd., pg. 605   IT
Horizon International, 304 The East Mall, 7th Fl., pg. 1012   IT
Knape & Vogt Canada Inc., 340 Carlingview Dr., pg. 963   PB
Kohler Ltd., 110 Woodbine Downs Blvs, Unit 3, pg. 631   PV
LEP International Inc., 401 The West Mall, 6th Fl., pg. 571   PV
Lennox Industries (Canada) Ltd., 400 Norris Glen Rd., pg. 660   PV
Litton Systems Canada Ltd., 25 City View Dr., pg. 1005   PB
MDS Communicare, 100 International Blvd., pg. 827   IT

MDS Health Ventures Capital Corp., 100 International Blvd., pg. 827   IT
MDS INC., 100 International Blvd., pg. 826   IT
Manville Canada Inc., 295 The West Mall, pg. 927   PB
Metro Brewery, 50 Resources Road, pg. 679   IT
National Meats Inc., 550 kipling Ave., pg. 1207   IT
National Silicates Ltd., 429 Kipling Ave., pg. 827   PV
North Safety Products Siebe North Canada Ltd., 26 Dansk Court, pg. 1243   IT
THE OSHAWA GROUP LIMITED, 302 The East Mall, pg. 1012   IT
Parker & Amchem, 165 Rexdale Blvd., pg. 612   IT
Parmalat Canada Ltd., 405 The West Mall, 10th Fl., pg. 1023   IT
PenYork Properties, 4 Eva Road, Suite 427, pg. 249   IT
Philip Environmental/Delsan, 345 Horner Ave., pg. 1050   IT
Polaroid Canada Inc., 350 Carlingview Dr., pg. 1314   PB
Principal Marques Meat Co., 21 Medulla Ave., M8Z 5L7, pg. 841   IT
Quebecor Printing PE&E, 2250 Islington Ave., pg. 1077   IT
Rentway Inc., 1000, 185 The West Mall, pg. 1424   IT
Rogers Cable Systems, 80 Worcester Rd., pg. 1123   IT
Rouse Service (Canada) Limited, 25, The West Mall, pg. 1409   PB
Royal Insurance Ontario Regional Centre, Etobicoke Business Ctr., 405 The West Mall, pg. 1131   IT
Serca Food Services, Inc., 302 The East Mall, pg. 1012   IT
SHAW INDUSTRIES LTD., 25 Bethridge Road, pg. 1231   IT
Shawflex Inc., 25 Bethridge Rd., pg. 1231   IT
Sterling Pulp Chemicals, Ltd., 2 Gibbs Rd., pg. 1580   PB
Sunac America, 21 Four Seasons Place, 4th Fl., pg. 924   IT
Tarmac Canada Inc., 80 N. Queen St., pg. 1355   IT
Totes Canada Ltd., 77 Brown's Line, pg. 111   PV
Trans Canada Credit Corporation, 703 Evans Ave., Ste. 402, pg. 1202   PB
Versa Services Ltd., H11 Islenden, pg. 79   PV
WD-40 Products (Canada) Ltd., P.O. Box 220, pg. 1726   PB
Weston Bakeries Limited, 1425 The Queen's Way, pg. 1495   IT
John Wiley & Sons, Canada, Ltd., 22 Worcester Rd., pg. 1768   PB
The Yorkville Printing Group Limited, 8 Tidemore Avenue, pg. 538   IT

Falconbridge

Falconbridge Explorations, pg. 433   IT
Sudbury Division, pg. 433   IT

Farnham

Domco Inc., 1001 Yamaska Street East, pg. 415   IT
DOMCO INC., 1001 Yamaska Street East, pg. 415   IT
Les Publications CCH/FM Ltee, 33 rue Racine, pg. 1513   IT
Quebec Southern Railroad, pg. 575   PV

Fergus

GSW Pump Company, 599 Hill Street West, pg. 538   IT
GSW Water Heating Company, 599 Hill Street West, pg. 538   IT

Flin Flon

Cominco Ltd., pg. 308   IT

Florenceville

McCain Fertilizers Limited, pg. 850   IT
MCCAIN FOODS LIMITED, 107 Main Road, pg. 850   IT
McCain Produce Inc., pg. 850   IT
Valley Farms Limited, pg. 850   IT

Fort Erie

Erdle Perforating Co. Ltd., 41 Russell St., L2A 5M9, pg. 380   PV
Fleet Industries, P.O. Box 400, Gilmore Rd., L2A 5N3, pg. 829   IT
Irvin Aerospace Canada Ltd., 479 Central Ave., pg. 640   IT
ML Campbell & Fabulon, 224 Catherine St., pg. 1466   PB
Mentholatum Canada Ltd., 20 Lewis St., pg. 1126   IT

Fort McMurray

Air Products Canada Ltd., pg. 31   PB
Hewlett-Packard (Canada) Ltd., # 2, 8302 Fraser Ave., pg. 818   PB
Suncor Oil Sands Group, pg. 1320   IT

Fort Saint James

Canadian Forest Products Ltd., Fort St. James Division, pg. 260   IT

Fort Saint John

Canadian Forest Products Ltd., Fort St. John Diviison, R.R. #1, pg. 260   IT

Fort Saskatchewan

Northrup King Seeds Ltd., pg. 983   IT

Fredericton

Atomic Energy of Canada Ltd.-Atlantic Region, Suite 610, 570 Queen Street, pg. 97   IT
Atomic Energy of Canada Ltd.-Maritime Nuclear, 64 Alison Boulevard, pg. 97   IT
DMR Group, Inc., Carleton Place, Suite 830, King St., pg. 527   IT
NEW BRUNSWICK POWER CORPORATION, 515 King St., pg. 923   IT

Gatineau

Gatineau Office, 323 Rayol St., pg. 274   IT

Gentilly

Atomic Energy of Canada Ltd., 4160 Becancour Boulevard, pg. 97   IT

Georgetown

Curwood Packaging (Canada) Ltd., 114 Armstron Ave., pg. 210   PB
P.G. Bell Div., 60 Armstrong Avenue, pg. 698   IT

Gibbons

Du Pont Canada-Gibbons, 4608-50th Ave., pg. 532   PB

Glace Bay

Atomic Energy of Canada Ltd. pg. 97   IT
CAPE BRETON DEVELOPMENT CORPORATION, 95 Union St., pg. 265   IT

Gloucester

ABB Commercial Engineering Canada, 1410 Blair Pl., Ste. 600, pg. 5   IT
Atomic Energy of Canada Ltd., National Office, Suite 700, 1595 Telesat Court, pg. 97   IT
Brookfield Homes Development Corporation, 1811 St. Joseph Blvd., pg. 228   IT
TMI Communications Inc., 1601 Telesat Court, pg. 116   IT
Telesat Canada, 1601 Telesat Court, pg. 116   IT
Tellabs Ottawa, 1900 City Park Dr., Ste. 408, pg. 1573   PB

Granby

AGROPUR, 510 Principle St., pg. 31   IT
Amada Canada Ltd., 885 Ave. Georges Cros., pg. 70   IT
Bauer Apparel Inc., 1135 Boulevarde Industrial, pg. 1184   PB
Bell Sports Canada, 700 Bernard Street, pg. 207   PB
Bombardier Inc.-Industrial Division, 1001 J.A. Bombardier Street, pg. 200   IT

Grand Forks

Pope & Talbot Ltd., 570 68th Ave., pg. 1317   PB

Grande Prairie

Barber Industries Ltd.-Service Center, 9501-113th Ave., pg. 164   IT
Canadian Forest Products Ltd., Grande Prairie Operations, pg. 260   IT
Procter & Gamble Inc., pg. 1332   PB
Rogers CFGP-AM, 200 Windsor Ct., 9835-101st Ave., pg. 1123   IT
Talisman Energy Inc., 10940-92 Avenue, pg. 1352   IT

Grimsby

Fluid Connectors Group, Canada, South Durham Rd., pg. 1261   PB
John Deere Ltd., P.O. Box 1000, pg. 493   PB
Peller Wines of California, 697 S. Service Rd., pg. 76   PB
Reyco-Canada, Inc., pg. 926   PV

Guelph

Alcan Recycling, 240 Massey Road, pg. 50   IT
Armtec, 15 Campbell Road, pg. 698   IT
Blount Canada Ltd., 505 Edinburgh Rd. N., pg. 239   PB
Blount Holdings Ltd., 505 Edinburgh Rd. N., pg. 239   PB
John O. Butler Company (Canada), 515 Governors Rd., pg. 1320   IT
Court Galvanizing Limited, 138 Dawson Road, pg. 698   IT
Delta International Machinery, 644 Imperial Rd., pg. 1273   IT
Dowty Silcofab, 335 Woodlawn Road West, pg. 1338   IT
Frigoscandia Food Process Systems Inc., 367 Woodlawn West Rd., Ste. 805, pg. 607   PB
GSW INC., 150 Research La., Ste. 207, pg. 538   IT
Guelph Products, 500 Laird Rd., pg. 354   PB
INTERNATIONAL MUREX TECHNOLOGIES CORPORATION, 650 Woodlawn Rd. West, pg. 684   IT
Kenhar Products, P.O. Box 1508, N1H 6N9, pg. 311   PB
Langford Inc., 400 Michener Rd., pg. 81   PB
Little Tikes (Canada) Inc., 589 Massy Rd., pg. 1411   PB

PB - U.S. Public Companies Volume
PV - U.S. Private Companies Volume
IT - International Public & Private Companies Volume

1534

McNeil Consumer Products Company, 890 Woodlawn Rd. W., pg. 931 **PB**
National-Standard Co. Canada, 20 Campbell Rd., pg. 1161 **PB**
Polypenco Canada Ltd., 495 Laird Road, pg. 354 **IT**
Rogers Cable Systems, 18 Macdonell St., pg. 1123 **IT**
SIHI Pumps Ltd., 225 Speedvale Ave. W., pg. 1156 **IT**
Sandvik Process Systems Canada Ltd., 510 Governors Rd., pg. 1188 **IT**
Uniroyal Chemical Ltd., pg. 460 **PB**
Worthington Cylinder Canada, RR #7, Hwy. 24 S., pg. 1781 **PB**

Halifax

AST Canada Inc., 1496 Lower Water St., pg. 1182 **IT**
Bank of Montreal - Halifax, 5151 George St., pg. 153 **IT**
Bolands Limited, 19 Lakeside Park Dr., pg. 1012 **IT**
Brian Controls Division, Coywell Tower Ste. 812, pg. 711 **IT**
CHNS/CHFX Radio, 1313 Barrington St., pg. 842 **IT**
CSC, Halifax, Main Floor-TD Bldg., 1791 Barrington St., pg. 1482 **IT**
DMR Group, Inc., North American Life Building, 1770 Market St., Suite 502, pg. 527 **IT**
Dover Mills Limited, 730 Marginal Rd., pg. 417 **IT**
Eastern Elevator Limited, 110 Chain Lake Dr., Unit J, pg. 747 **IT**
Enercom Inc., pg. 971 **IT**
First Marathon Securities, Purdy's Wharf Tower II, 1969 Upper Water St., Ste. 204, pg. 486 **IT**
The Foundation Company - Halifax, 1387 Eastern Passage Hwy., Eastern Passage, pg. 118 **IT**
Green Line Investor Service, Central Guaranty Trust Tower, 1801 Hollis St., Ste. 230, pg. 1401 **IT**
Halifax Port Corporation, Ocean Terminals, P.O. Box 336, pg. 255 **IT**
Halterm Container Terminal, Pier C, Terminal Rd., pg. 924 **IT**
Ikon Office Solutions (Atlantic), 5445 Rainnie Dr., B3J 1P8, pg. 864 **PB**
Intergraph Canada Ltd., Ste. 500, Barrington Business Ctr., pg. 891 **PB**
Kodak Halifax, 1601 Lower Water St., Ste. 100, pg. 553 **PB**
MARITIME BROADCASTING SYSTEM LTD., 1313 Barrington St., pg. 842 **IT**
Maritime Life Assurance Co., 2701 Dutch Village Rd., pg. 590 **PV**
Maritime Telegraph & Telephone Company, Ltd., pg. 116 **IT**
Montrusco Associates, 1791 Barrington Street, Suite 1602, pg. 888 **IT**
NYK Line-Halifax, c/o Fairview Cave Container Terminal, pg. 942 **IT**
NOVA SCOTIA POWER INC., Scotia Sq. Complex, 1894 Barrington St., pg. 971 **IT**
Oland Breweries Limited, 3055 Aricola Street, pg. 679 **IT**
Palmer Refrigeration Ltd., 2631 King St., pg. 1766 **PB**
Prior Data Sciences Ltd., 5475 Spring Garden Road, Suite 601, pg. 1288 **IT**
SHL Systemhouse - Atlantic Region, 1660 Hollis St., Penthouse Ste., pg. 1154 **IT**
SEI Corporation, 1959 Upper Water St., Ste. 407, pg. 1417 **PB**
SNC-Lavalin, Park Lane Terraces, 5657 Spring Garden Road, Suite 200, pg. 1162 **IT**
Young & Rubicam Halifax, Brewery Business Centre, 1496 Lower Water St., pg. 1200 **PV**

Hamilton

Admiral Distribution Inc., 120 Nebo Road, Unit 4, pg. 539 **IT**
Ball Packaging Products Canada Inc., 391 Victoria Avenue N., pg. 171 **PB**
Baycoat, 244 Lanark St., pg. 414 **IT**
Baycoat Limited, 244 Lanark St., pg. 1299 **IT**
C&W Refractories, Ltd., 191 Victoria Ave. So., pg. 194 **PV**
CHCH-TV, 163 Jackson St., West, pg. 1124 **IT**
Canadian Puregas Equipment Ltd., 42 Niagara St., pg. 75 **PB**
John Crane Canada, Inc., 423 Green Rd., Stoney Creek, pg. 1339 **IT**
DOFASCO, INC., 1330 Burlington St. E., pg. 414 **IT**
Drummond McCall Inc., P.O. Box 3155, Station C, 410 Nash Rd. N., pg. 1150 **IT**
Elkem Sales & Marketing Service, 1685 Main St., W., Ste. 303, pg. 448 **IT**
Fortino's Supermarkets Ltd., 90 Glover Rd., pg. 1495 **IT**
Frost Wire Products, Ltd., 250 Lotteridge St., pg. 1299 **IT**
Gencab of Canada Ltd., 42 Niagara St., pg. 75 **PB**
Green Line Investor Service, 25 Main St. West, Ste. 1505, pg. 1401 **IT**
Hamilton Specialty Bar, 319 Sherman Ave. N., pg. 1262 **IT**
Hepworth Refractories (Canada) Limited, 350 Wentworth St. North, pg. 615 **IT**
H.H. Robertson, Inc., pg. 1394 **PB**
Hilton Works, P.O. Box 2030, pg. 1299 **IT**
Kelley Advertising Inc., 35 King St. E., Fifth Fl., pg. 765 **PB**
Langs Cold Storage Div., 590 Nash Rd. N., pg. 1012 **IT**
Lifesavers Plant, 100 Cumberland Ave., pg. 812 **PB**
Navistar International Corporation Canada, 120 King St. W., 9th Fl., pg. 1167 **PB**
Norton Canada Inc., pg. 1175 **IT**
Norton Capital Inc. (Canada), 3 Beach Road, pg. 1175 **IT**
PHILIP SERVICES CORP., 651 Burlington St. E., pg. 1050 **IT**

Porritts & Spencer Canada, Inc., LCD 1, 240 Lotteridge St., pg. 1203 **IT**
Procter & Gamble Inc., 1142 Burlington St. E., pg. 1332 **PB**
Redland Quarries Inc., 605 James Street North, pg. 1093 **IT**
Rheem Canada, Ltd., 128 Barton Street, W., pg. 1022 **IT**
H.H. Robertson Burford Plant, 61 Burford Rd., pg. 1394 **PB**
Rogers Cable Systems, 135 James St. South, Ste. 105, pg. 1123 **IT**
Rogers Cable TV-Hamilton, 695 Lawrence Rd., pg. 1122 **IT**
Royal Insurance Hamilton Regional Centre, Lloyd D. Jackson Sq., 110 King St. W., Ste. 500, pg. 1131 **IT**
RYCO-Alberici, Ltd., pg. 32 **PV**
The Spectator, Hamilton, 44 Frid St., pg. 631 **IT**
STELCO INC., 100 King St. W., pg. 1299 **IT**
Stelwire Ltd., 690 Strathearne Ave. N., pg. 1299 **IT**
Jervis B. Webb Company of Canada Ltd., 1647 Burlington St., E., pg. 1157 **PV**
Westinghouse Canada Inc., pg. 275 **PB**

Hartland

Day & Ross Inc., pg. 850 **IT**

Havelock

Havelock Lime Div., P.O. Box 59, pg. 243 **IT**

Hawkesbury

Amoco Fabrics & Fibers, Ltd., 1423 Cameron St., pg. 102 **PB**
KRC Rolls (Canada) Inc., pg. 1202 **IT**
Rogers Cable Systems, 1444 Aberdeen St., pg. 1123 **IT**

Hensall

General Coach, 73 Mill St., pg. 1602 **PB**

Hines Creek

Canadian Forest Products Ltd., Hines Creek Division, pg. 260 **IT**

Hornby

Dynapac Ltd., 7449 Trafalgar Road, pg. 1420 **IT**
Svedala Industries Canada Hornby, 7449 Trafalgar Rd., pg. 1325 **IT**

Hull

E.B. Eddy Forest Products Ltd., pg. 1495 **IT**
Intergraph Corporation, 200 Montcalm St. #100, J8Y 3B5, pg. 891 **PB**
Kimberly-Clark, Quebec, pg. 959 **PB**
Messageries de l'Outaouais, 220-A, rue Edmonton, pg. 539 **IT**

Huntsville

Canusa, Airport Road, pg. 1231 **IT**
Rogers Cable Systems, 20 West St., South, pg. 1123 **IT**

Hyde Park

Fleck Manufacturing Inc., Box 67, R.R. #1, pg. 955 **IT**

Iberville

ALIMENTS FLAMINGO, 700 Croisetiere Iberviule, pg. 57 **IT**
Thomas & Betts Ltd., 700 Thomas Ave., pg. 1598 **PB**

Ingersoll

CAMI Automotive, Inc., 300 Ingersoll St., pg. 722 **PB**
Infatool, Ingersoll Street, pg. 696 **IT**
Ingersoll Fasteners Division, 390 Thomas Street, pg. 696 **IT**
Ingersoll Machine and Tool Division, 347 King Street West, pg. 696 **IT**
Sivaco Ontario, 330 Thomas Street, pg. 696 **IT**

Innisfail

Manville Canada Inc. (Innisfail), pg. 927 **PB**

Islington

Carlson Marketing Group Ltd., 5353 Dundas Street West, M9B 6J3, pg. 212 **PV**
P. Lawson Travel, Ltd., 5353 Dundas St., W., Ste. 400, pg. 212 **PV**
Policy Management Systems Canada, Ltd., Valhalla Executive Ctr., Ste. 600, pg. 1315 **PB**

Jarvis

Capitol Equipment, 85 Talbot St., E., pg. 256 **IT**
Capitol Pipe Supports, 85 Talbot St., E., pg. 256 **IT**

Joliette

Imprimerie Quebecor Joliette, 585 St. Pierre St. S., pg. 1077 **IT**
Joliette Division, 260 Rue Saint Thomas, pg. 273 **IT**
Scapa Canada, Inc., pg. 1203 **IT**

Jonquiere

Cascades Jonquiere Inc., 4010 Chemim St-Andre, pg. 273 **IT**
The Roberval & Saguenay Railway Co., P.O. Box 1277, pg. 50 **IT**

Juskatla

Queen Charlotte Division, pg. 828 **IT**

Kamloops

Chemonics Industries (Canada) Ltd., 455 Dene Dr., pg. 591 **PB**
The Kamloops Daily News, 393 Seymour Street, pg. 631 **IT**
MOLY-COP Canada, pg. 1300 **IT**
Weyerhaeuser Canada Ltd., Mission Flats, pg. 1764 **PB**

Kanata

Atomic Energy of Canada Ltd.-Accelerators, 436b Hazeldean Road, pg. 97 **IT**
Compas Electronics, Inc., 100 Schnider Rd., pg. 36 **IT**
CrossKeys Systems Corporation, 362 Terry Fox Drive, pg. 924 **IT**
GMSI, Inc., 275 Michael Cowpland Dr., pg. 740 **PB**
Lumonics Inc., 105 Schneider Rd., pg. 1314 **IT**
MITEL CORPORATION, 350 Legget Drive, pg. 870 **IT**
NEWBRIDGE NETWORKS CORPORATION, 600 March Rd., pg. 923 **IT**
Newbridge Networks Corporation, P.O. Box 13600, pg. 924 **IT**
Nordion International Inc., 447 March Rd., pg. 827 **IT**
Pen-Stock, Inc., 260 Hearst Way, Ste. 313, pg. 155 **PB**
Prior Data Sciences Ltd., 240 Michael Cowpland Drive, pg. 1288 **IT**
Quantum Corporation, 135 Michael Cowpland, Ste. 301, pg. 1350 **PB**
Spar Applied Systems, 365 March Road, pg. 1288 **IT**
Televitesse Systems Incorporated, 603 March Road, pg. 924 **IT**
TimeStep Corporation, 600 March Road, pg. 924 **IT**

Kapuskasing

Spruce Falls Inc., One Government Rd., pg. 1375 **IT**

Kimberley

Air Products Canada Ltd., pg. 31 **PB**

Kingsey Falls

Boralex Inc., 404 Marie-Victorin St., pg. 273 **IT**
Cascades Conversion Inc., 404 Marie-Victorin St., pg. 273 **IT**
Cascades Energie Inc., 404 Marie-Victorin St., pg. 273 **IT**
Cascades Forma-Pak Inc., 404 Marie-Victorin St., pg. 273 **IT**
THE CASCADES GROUP, 404 Marie-Victorin St., pg. 273 **IT**
Cascades, Inc., 404 Marie-Victorin St., pg. 273 **IT**
Industries Cascades Inc., 467 Marie-Victorin St., pg. 273 **IT**
Kingsey Cogeneration Regd., 36 Lagaunesse St., pg. 273 **IT**
Papier Kingsey-Falls Div., 408 Ch. Marie Victorin RR1, pg. 273 **IT**
Plastiques Cascades Inc., 455 Rue Marie Victorin, pg. 273 **IT**
Recuperation Cascades Inc., 404 Marie-Victorin St., pg. 273 **IT**

Kingston

Alcan Rolled Products Company, 1 Lappan's Lane, pg. 50 **IT**
Canadian Erectors Pipe, 477 Rideau St., pg. 256 **IT**
Celanese Canada Textile Group, pg. 625 **IT**
Du Pont Canada-Kingston Research, pg. 532 **PB**
Du Pont Canada-Kingston Works, pg. 532 **PB**
Hewlett-Packard (Canada) Ltd., 496 Days Road, pg. 818 **IT**
Kingston Whig-Standard, 306 King Street East, pg. 631 **IT**
Knorr-Brake Ltd., 675 Development Dr., pg. 738 **IT**
C.E. MacPherson, 477 Rideau St., pg. 256 **IT**
Warner-Jenkinson Canada, River & Orchard Sts., pg. 1696 **PB**

Kingsville

Peterson Spring-Kingsville Plant, 208 Wigle Ave., pg. 857 **PV**

Kirkland

Gillette Canada Inc., 16700 Trans Canada, pg. 744 **PB**

PB - *U.S. Public Companies Volume*
PV - *U.S. Private Companies Volume*
IT - *International Public & Private Companies Volume*

Geographic Index-Non U.S.

1535

Hewlett-Packard (Canada) Ltd., 17500 Trans-Canada Hwy., pg. 818 **PB**
Ingersoll-Rand Canada, Inc., 3501 St. Charles Blvd., pg. 878 **PB**
Kirchimie Ltee., c/o Pfizer Canada Inc., 17300 Trans-Canada Hwy., pg. 1283 **PB**
Lambda Electronics, 16829b Hymus Blvd., pg. 1241 **IT**
Merck Frosst Canada Inc., 16711 Trans Canada Hwy., pg. 1092 **PB**
PQI Inc., 17300 Trans-Canada Hwy., pg. 1283 **PB**
Pfizer Canada, Inc., 17300 Trans Canada Hwy., pg. 1283 **PB**
Puritan-Bennett Canada (Kirkland), 3656 St. Charles Blvd., pg. 1040 **PB**
Svedala Industries Canada Quebec, pg. 1325 **IT**

Kirkland Lake

Barrick Gold, pg. 169 **IT**
Holt-McDermott Mine, P.O. Box 278, pg. 169 **IT**
Mines Assay Division, 953 Government Rd. W., pg. 23 **IT**
The Northern Daily News, 8 Duncan Avenue, pg. 631 **IT**

Kitchener

API of Canada Inc., 698 Wilson Ave., pg. 90 **PB**
Bank of Montreal - Kitchener, 7 Duke Street W., pg. 153 **IT**
Beatrice Corporation, 135 Ontonabee Dr., pg. 765 **PV**
Boehmers, 1060 Guelph St., pg. 629 **IT**
CHYM/CKGL Radio, 305 King St. West, pg. 1124 **IT**
CKCO-TV, 864 King St. W., pg. 438 **IT**
Canada Alloy Castings, Ltd., 529 Manitou Dr., pg. 142 **IT**
Dahlberg Sciences, Ltd., 500 Trillium Drive, Unit 15, pg. 194 **PB**
DARE FOODS LIMITED, 2481 Kingsway Dr., pg. 383 **IT**
Dukane Canada Ltd., 461 Manitou Dr., pg. 346 **IT**
ELECTROHOME LTD., 809 Wellington St. N., pg. 438 **IT**
Fowler Tools of Canada, pg. 422 **IT**
Hedstrom Canada, 130 Otonabee Dr., pg. 526 **PV**
KAUFMAN FOOTWEAR, 410 King Street, West, pg. 725 **IT**
Kitchener Center, Ste. 21-23, 20 Steckle Pl., pg. 273 **IT**
Knechtel Wholesale Grocers, pg. 1012 **IT**
Kvaerner Pulping Ltd., Executive Business Centre, Ste. 201, pg. 768 **IT**
MTD Products Limited, 97 Kent St., pg. 688 **PV**
F.E. Myers (Canada) Ltd./Ltee., 269 Trillium Dr., pg. 1274 **PB**
NBS Imprinter, 171 Webster Rd., pg. 898 **IT**
Perstorp Components, 51 Breithaupt St, pg. 1040 **IT**
Precision Resource Canadian Div., 50 Alpine Ct., pg. 880 **PV**
The Record, 225 Fairway Road, pg. 631 **IT**
Rogers Cable TV-Kitchener, 85 Grand Crest Place, pg. 1122 **IT**
SCHNEIDER CORP., 321 Cortland Ave. E., pg. 1207 **IT**
J.M. Schneider Inc., 321 Cortland Ave. East, pg. 1207 **IT**
Uniroyal Goodrich Canada Inc., pg. 322 **IT**
Waterloo Furniture Components Limited, 501 Manitou Dr., pg. 270 **PV**

L'Orignal

Ivaco Rolling Mills Limited Partnership, P.O. Box 322, pg. 696 **IT**

La Baie

MDF La Baie Inc., 5373, Chemin St. Anicet, pg. 1432 **IT**

La Guadeloupe

Shady Maple Farms Ltd., 786 8th St. E., pg. 806 **PB**

La Prairie

Fers et Metaux Recycles Ltee., 1975 Bvld. Ste. Elizabeth, pg. 1299 **IT**
Rose & Laflamme Co. Ltd., 300 rue St. Jacques, pg. 1195 **IT**
St. Lawrence Brick Division, 950 Godin St., pg. 698 **IT**

La Salle

ABB Drying, 8300 Saint Patrick, pg. 5 **IT**
Comfort Inc., 5600 Hochelega, pg. 698 **PB**
Contenants Greif Inc., 7000 Allard Street, pg. 764 **PB**
Foxboro Canada, Inc., 707 Dollard Ave., pg. 1243 **IT**
Gaz Metropolitain, Inc., 228b Cannes Brulees Street, pg. 541 **IT**
Guerlain Canada Ltd. Ltee., 9719 Clement, pg. 780 **IT**
Imprimerie Quebecor Graphique-Couleur, 2580, avenue Dollard, pg. 1077 **IT**
Imprimerie Quebecor Lasalle, 7743, rue Bourdeau, pg. 1077 **IT**
La Brasserie Labatt Limitee, 50 Labatt Avenue, pg. 783 **IT**
Les Mines Casa Berardi, 105-5th Avenue East, pg. 1345 **IT**
Peacock Inc., 8600 St. Patrick's Street, pg. 1489 **IT**
Prodair, Air Products Canada Ltd., 291 Rue Quinlan, pg. 32 **PB**
Ross-Ellis Printing Inc., 7399, rue Cordner, pg. 538 **IT**

Labrador City

Svedala Industries Canada Newfoundland, 10 1st Ave., Wabash Industrial Park, pg. 1325 **IT**

Lac des Iles

Uniboard Canada Inc.-LDI Division, 904 Rte. 309, pg. 1431 **IT**

Lac La Biche

Talisman Energy Inc., pg. 1352 **IT**

Lac-Beauport

Lac Beauport Office, 42, chemin de La Sapiniere, pg. 274 **IT**

Lachine

Accu-Sort Canada, 3231 Anatole-Carignan, pg. 11 **PV**
Anixter Montreal, 2075 52nd. Ave., pg. 115 **PB**
Antec Group, 2075 52nd Ave., pg. 117 **PB**
Berlex Canada, Inc., 2260 32nd Ave., pg. 1204 **PB**
Canadian Shade Tree Service, Ltd., 1540 Claire Crescent, pg. 314 **PV**
Canlyte Incorporated, 3015 Rue Louis Amos, pg. 730 **PB**
Clouston Foods Canada, 9960 cote de Liesse, pg. 492 **IT**
Cylinder Division, 2108 32nd Avenue, pg. 1262 **PB**
Emco Supply Eastern Region, 1820-46ieme Ave., pg. 453 **IT**
G.E. Canada Power Systems, 795 First Ave., pg. 713 **PB**
Joslyn Canada, 1560 55th Ave., pg. 482 **PB**
Lumacell Inc., 4460 Joseph Dubreuil, pg. 725 **IT**
Montreal Office, 2121 46th Ave., pg. 672 **PB**
N.B.S. Inc., 1101 46th Avenue, pg. 898 **IT**
NORDX/CDT, 150 Montreal-Toronto Blvd., pg. 287 **PB**
Portec Ltd., 2044-32nd Ave., pg. 1318 **PB**
Rexam Containers, 1795 32nd Ave., pg. 1107 **IT**
Roll-It, 1200 50th Ave., pg. 963 **PB**
Rolls-Royce Industries Canada Inc., 9500 Cote de Liesse, pg. 1127 **IT**
Stelfil Ltee., 303 St. Joseph Blvd., pg. 1299 **IT**
Valmet Canada Inc., 1, rue Provost, pg. 1448 **IT**
Valmet Canada Inc., Montreal Division, 1 rue Provost, pg. 1448 **IT**
VARTA Industrial Batteries Ltd., 5000 Rue Francois-Cusson, pg. 1452 **IT**
Wajax Manufacturing Limited, 1100 Norman St., pg. 1485 **IT**
Woolcan, 1880 32nd Ave., pg. 1188 **PV**
Zeneca Textile Colours, 2205 46th Ave., pg. 1527 **IT**

Lae Magantic

Premdor Inc.-Louvre Door, 4180 Villeneuve St., pg. 1067 **IT**

Lakeside

Clover Produce Limited, 1 Duck Pond Road, Lakeside Indus. Park, pg. 454 **IT**

Langley

Century Oils (Canada), Inc., 19829 99A Ave., pg. 518 **IT**
McGavin Foods Ltd., #220, 20353 64th Ave., pg. 841 **IT**
USNR, Ste. 200, 19670 92A Avenue, pg. 604 **IT**
Willis Corroon Melling Ltd., 5581 204th Street, pg. 1509 **IT**

Laval

BIOCHEM PHARMA INC., 275 Arramd Frappier, pg. 196 **IT**
BioChem Therapeutic Inc., 275 Armand-Frappier Blvd., pg. 196 **IT**
CARISTRAP INTERNATIONAL INC., 1760 Fortin Boulevard, pg. 271 **IT**
Costco, Inc.-Eastern Region, 300 Jacques Bureau, pg. 452 **PB**
Flowserve Duriron Canada Inc., 2345 Michelin, Ste. 200, pg. 659 **PB**
Grandma Food Products Limited, 2185 Francis Hughes Ave., pg. 460 **PB**
IAF BioVac Inc., 525 des Prairies Blvd., pg. 196 **IT**
Earle M. Jorgensen Company/Quebec, 1255 Ave. Laplace, pg. 600 **PV**
Kvaerner Hymac Inc., 1867 Berlier, pg. 770 **IT**
La Compagnie Foundation Limitee, 2540 Daniel Johnson, Ste. 1106, pg. 118 **IT**
Luxo Lamps Ltd., 1957 Rue de Chatelier, pg. 821 **IT**
Michelin North America (Canada) Inc., Les Tours Triomphe, 2540, Daniel-Johnson Blvd., pg. 822 **IT**
Parfums Christian Dior Canada, 1005, rue Berlier, pg. 783 **IT**
Perkins Papers, 2345 Autoroute, pg. 273 **IT**
SECURITY CHIMNEYS INTERNATIONAL LTD., 2125 Monterey St., pg. 1217 **IT**
TIW, 807 Marshall St., pg. 256 **IT**
UNIBOARD CANADA INC., 3080 Blvd. Le Carrefour, Ste. 400, pg. 1431 **IT**

Leamington

CHYR Radio-AM, 100 Talbot St., East, pg. 1124 **IT**

Leduc

Centra Gas Alberta Inc., Box 800, 5509 - 45th St., pg. 1492 **IT**

Lennoxville

CAE ScreenPlates Inc., 72 Queen St., pg. 237 **IT**

Lethbridge

Motion Industries (Canada), Inc., 236-36th St. North, pg. 732 **PB**

Levis

Assurance vie Desjardins-Laurentienne, 200, avenue des Commandeurs, pg. 396 **IT**
CONFEDERATION DES CAISSES DES JARDINS, 100 Ave. des Commandeurs, pg. 325 **IT**
DAVIE INDUSTRIES INC., 22 George D. Davie, pg. 385 **IT**
Mil Intermodal, 22 George D. Davie, pg. 385 **IT**

Lindsay

Bucyrus Blades of Canada Ltd., 199 St. David St., pg. 383 **PV**
Fleetwood Canada Ltd., 70 Mount Hope St., pg. 652 **PB**
Synergistics Industgries Limited - Packaging & Medical Products, 77 St. David Street, pg. 734 **PB**
Synergistics Industries Limited, 77 St. David Street, pg. 734 **PB**
Viskase Canada Inc., 150 Colborne St. E., pg. 586 **PB**

Lively

Tamrock EJC Canada Ltd., Walden Industrial Park, 100 Magill St., pg. 1353 **IT**

Liverpool

Bowater Mersey Paper Company, Ltd., P.O. Box 1150, pg. 248 **PB**

Lloydminster

Greif Containers, Inc., pg. 764 **PB**
Lloydminster Pool, Box 869, pg. 1195 **IT**

Logan Lake

Highland Valley Copper, P.O. Box 1500, pg. 308 **IT**
Highland Valley Copper, pg. 1118 **IT**

London

Agnew Group, 825 Bradley Ave., pg. 187 **IT**
Air Ontario, One Air Ontario Dr., London Airport, pg. 36 **IT**
AlliedSignal Turbocharging & Truck Brake Systems, 4474 Blakie Rd., Unit 135, pg. 53 **PB**
Amway of Canada, Ltd., 375 Exeter Rd., pg. 70 **PV**
Anixter London, 229 Consortium Court, pg. 115 **PB**
Bach-Simpson Ltd., 1255 Brydges St., pg. 944 **PB**
Beaver Foods Limited, 493 Dundas St., pg. 266 **IT**
THE BENTLEY AGNEW GROUP INC., 825 Bradley Avenue, pg. 187 **IT**
Bentley Group, 825 Bradley Ave., pg. 187 **IT**
Bowes Publishers Limited, 1147 Gainsboro Rd., pg. 1320 **IT**
CFPL-TV, One Communications Road, pg. 171 **IT**
The Canada Trust Company, Canada Trust Tower, 275 Dundas St., pg. 112 **IT**
Canada Trustco Mortgage Company, Canada Trust Tower, 275 Dundas St., pg. 112 **IT**
Carquest Canada Ltd., 246 Horton Street, N6B 1K9, pg. 445 **PV**
Cellex Manufacturing, Inc., 151 Meg Dr., pg. 1080 **PV**
Charterways Transportation Limited, 248 Pall Malh Street, Ste. 500, pg. 1213 **IT**
Delta Faucet of Canada, 420 Burbrook Pl., pg. 1053 **PB**
Emco Building Products, 620 Richmond St., pg. 453 **IT**
EMCO LIMITED, 620 Richmond St., 2nd Fl., pg. 452 **IT**
Essex Specialty Products, Inc., Canada, 980 Adelaide Street, So., pg. 524 **PB**
FARMATIC RESEARCH, INC., 45 Meg Dr., pg. 478 **IT**
Flowserve Duriron Canada Inc., 1215 Oxford Street West, pg. 659 **PB**
General Motors Canada Diesel Div., pg. 722 **PB**
Green Line Investor Service, 148 Fullarton St., Ste. 1506, pg. 1401 **IT**
HBO & Company Canada Ltd., 1195 Glenora Dr., pg. 770 **PB**
Hewlett-Packard (Canada) Ltd., 552 Newbold St., pg. 818 **PB**
Kaiser Aluminum & Chemical of Canada Limited, 3021 Gore Rd., pg. 1062 **IT**
Kellogg Canada Inc., 1097 Dundas St., East, pg. 947 **PB**
Lilly Industries, Inc., 65 Duke St., pg. 995 **PB**
London Brewery, 150 Simcoe Street, pg. 679 **IT**
London Center, 555 York St., pg. 273 **IT**
The London Free Press, 369 York Street, pg. 1320 **IT**
London Life Insurance Group, 255 Dufferin Ave., pg. 435 **IT**
Lorlea Architectural Systems Division, 300 Sovereigh Rd., pg. 698 **PV**
McCormick Canada, Ltd., 316 Rectory St., pg. 1067 **PB**

PB - *U.S. Public Companies Volume*
PV - *U.S. Private Companies Volume*
IT - *International Public & Private Companies Volume*

1536

Geographic Index-Non U.S.

Med+Care Health Services, G20-339 Wellington Rd. S., pg. 425 IT
Miracle Feeds Inc., 2100 Oxford St. E, pg. 432 PV
Perstorp Xytec, Inc., 231 Wychwood Park, pg. 1038 IT
Pope Technologies Ltd., pg. 469 IT
Rogers Cable Systems, 499 MacGregor Ave., pg. 1123 IT
Rogers Cable TV-London, P.O. Box 5800, pg. 1122 IT
Shoppers Drug Mart, Ltd., 1005 Wilton Grove Rd., pg. 112 IT
South Western Ontario Broadcasting Incorporated, 1 Communications Road, pg. 171 IT
Spartan Plastics Canada, 1015 Green Valley Rd., pg. 1020 PV
Sparton of Canada Ltd., 99 Ash St., pg. 1496 PB
Strike Rite Matches Ltd., pg. 127 PV
Summit Food Service Distributors, 580 Industrial Road, pg. 266 IT
Tecumseh Products of Canada Ltd., 185 Ashland Ave., pg. 1566 PB
3M Canada Inc., P.O. Box 5757, pg. 1606 PB
Wellington Insurance, Suite 500, 255 Queens Ave., pg. 651 IT
Wellington Insurance Company, 383 Richmond St., Ste. 700, pg. 435 IT

Long Harbour

Albright & Wilson Americas Limited, 1 Main Street, pg. 49 IT

Longueuil

ADC Telecom Canada Inc., 2147 de la Province, pg. 4 PB
THE JEAN COUTU GROUP (PJC) INC., 530, rue Beriault, pg. 340 IT
Deluxair Incorporated, 700 Place Trans-Canada, pg. 453 IT
DEMIX Beton/Agregats, 435 Trans-Canada Place, pg. 629 IT
DEMIX Construction, 435 Trans-Canada Place, pg. 629 IT
Hasbro Canada Inc., 2350 Rue De La Province, pg. 797 PB
Honeywell-Measurex, Inc., 1000 de Serigny St., pg. 833 PB
Ivex Packaging Corporation-Longueuil, 2355 Rue De La Province, pg. 915 PB
Natrel Inc., 101 Roland-Therrien Blvd., Ste. 600, pg. 32 IT
Pratt & Whitney Canada Inc., 1000 Marie-Victorin, pg. 1690 PB
RX Information Centre Ltd., 530, rue Beriault, pg. 340 IT
SNC-Lavalin, 2271 Fernand-Lafontaine Blvd., pg. 1162 IT
Services Securivol Inc., 530, rue Beriault, pg. 340 IT
SICO INC., 2505 rue de la Metropole, pg. 1239 IT

Lunenburg

Deep Sea Clam Company Limited, pg. 909 IT
NATIONAL SEA PRODUCTS LIMITED, P.O. Box 910, pg. 909 IT
Nautilus Industrial Relation Services Inc., pg. 909 IT
Scotia Trawler Equipment Limited, 280 Montague Street, pg. 909 IT

Magog

Imprimerie Quebecor Magog, 1500, rue Sherbrooke, pg. 1077 IT

Maitland

Du Pont Canada-Maitland, pg. 532 PB

Malartic

Barrick Gold, pg. 169 IT

Malton

Domtar Packaging Division, 6789 Airport Rd., pg. 416 IT
Playtex Apparel Canada, Ltd., 6363 Northam Dr., pg. 1433 PB
Wendy's Restaurants of Canada Inc., 6715 Airport Rd., Ste. 301, pg. 1754 IT

Marathon

Fort James-Marathon, Ltd., Mill Rd., pg. 672 PB
Woodlands License Management/Fibre Procurement, Bag JR, pg. 672 PB

Marieville

I.F.C. (Fasteners) Inc., 700, rue Ouellette, pg. 696 IT
Ifastgroupe and Company, Limited Partnership, 700, rue Ouellette, pg. 695 IT
Infasco Division, 700, rue Ouellette, pg. 696 IT
Sivaco Quebec, 800, rue Ouellette, pg. 696 IT

Markham

AMP of Canada Ltd., 20 Esna Park Dr., pg. 9 PB
Advanced Monobloc, 430 Steelcase Road East, pg. 238 IT
Allergan Inc., 625 Cochrane Dr., Ste. 1000, pg. 46 PB
Apple Canada Ltd., 7495 Birchmount Rd., pg. 121 PB
Ascom Canada Limited, 150 Steelcase Rd. W., pg. 86 IT
Atoma International, Inc., 36 Apple Creek Blvd., pg. 829 IT
Atomic Sports Canada, 250 Shields Court, Ste. 5, pg. 73 IT
Autodesk Canada Inc./Markham, 90 Allstate Pkwy., Ste. 201, pg. 149 PB
BancTec Canada Inc., 235 Hood Road, pg. 177 PB
Beaver Lumber Company Limited, 7303 Warden Ave., pg. 887 IT
Bently Nevada Canada ltd., 70 Gibson Dr., Unit 4, pg. 134 PV
Berendsen Fluid Power Ltd., 230 Denison Street, pg. 1285 IT
Borland Canada, 200 Konrad Crescent, pg. 246 PB
W. Braun Packaging, Canada Ltd., 400 Bentley St., Unit 8, pg. 166 PV
Brooks Instrument (Canada), pg. 576 PB
Bull HN Information Systems Ltd./Systems Informatiques Bull NH, 675 Cochrane Drive, pg. 317 IT
The Business Depot, Ltd., 30 Centurion Drive, pg. 1510 IT
Butterworths Canada, 75 Clegg Road, pg. 1095 IT
CCL Technologies, 430 Steelcase Road East, pg. 238 IT
Cabletel Communications Inc., 120 Gibson Dr., pg. 17 IT
Canadian Ad-Check Services Inc., 50 Acadia Ave., Ste. 210, pg. 1124 IT
Carsen Group Inc., 151 Telson Rd., pg. 301 PB
Chesebrough-Pond's (Canada) Inc., 150 Bullock Dr., pg. 1436 IT
Chesebrough-Pond's International Ltd., 150 Bullock Dr., pg. 1436 IT
Citizen Watch Co. of Canada, Ltd., 380 Bentley St., pg. 294 IT
Custom Concrete, 7655 Woodbine Ave., pg. 629 IT
Cyanamid Canada Inc., 88 McNabb St., pg. 80 IT
Daewoo Canada Ltd., 170 Alden Rd., pg. 357 IT
Elscint (Canada) Ltd., 60 Gough Rd., pg. 450 IT
Emerson Electric Canada Inc., P.O. Box 150, Hwy. 48, pg. 576 PB
Epson Manufacturing Ltd., 80 Telson Rd., pg. 1219 IT
Extendicare (Canada) Inc., 3000 Steeles Ave. East, 7th Fl., pg. 468 IT
EXTENDICARE INC., 3000 Steeles Ave. E., pg. 468 PB
FMC Finance Limited, 1650-2 Hood Rd., pg. 606 PB
FMC of Canada Limited, 30 Royal Crest Ct., Unit 11, pg. 606 PB
FMC of Canada Limited, 650-2 Hood Rd., pg. 606 PB
Fiskars Canada Inc., 1-201 Whitehall Drive, pg. 492 IT
Ford Electronics Manufacturing Corporation, 7455 Birchmount Rd., pg. 665 PB
GEAC COMPUTER CORPORATION LIMITED, 11 Allstate Pkwy., pg. 532 IT
GN Nettest, Datacom Division, 55 Renfrew Drive, pg. 537 IT
Hewlett-Packard (Canada) Ltd., 475 Hood Rd., Unit 2, pg. 818 PB
Humphrey Fluid Power Ltd., 570 Alden Road, Unit #10, pg. 548 PV
Hyundai Auto Canada Inc., 75 Frontenac Dr., pg. 641 IT
IBM Canada Limited, 3500 Steeles Ave. E., pg. 897 PB
IBM Canada Product Distribution Inc.-Distribution de Produits IBM Canada Incorporee, 3500 Steeles Ave. E., pg. 897 PB
IDenticam Systems Ltd., 145 Royalcrest Ct., pg. 557 PV
KnollPharma Inc., 100 Allstate Pkwy., Ste. 600, pg. 109 IT
Kubota Canada Ltd., 1495 Denison St., pg. 763 IT
LEGACY STORAGE SYSTEMS CORP., 43 Riviera Drive, pg. 805 IT
Letraset Canada Ltd., 170 Duffield Drive, pg. 461 IT
Lexmark Canada Inc., 160 Royal Crest Court, pg. 991 PB
MAGNA INTERNATIONAL INC., 36 Apple Creek Blvd., pg. 829 PB
Memorex Telex Canada Inc., 65 Allstate Pkwy., pg. 857 IT
Movado Group Inc., 80 Tiverton Ct., Ste. 602, pg. 1140 PB
Multilin, 215 Anderson Ave., pg. 713 PB
Nestle Foodservice Canada, 100 Alden Road, pg. 922 IT
A.C. Nielsen Co. of Canada, Ltd., 160 McNabb St., pg. 1183 PB
Nordson Canada Ltd., 1211 Denison St., pg. 1189 PB
Novell Canada, 3100 Steeles Ave. E., Ste. 500, pg. 1204 PB
O.E., Inc., 1490 Denison St., pg. 262 IT
Olivetti Canada Inc., 3190 Steeles Ave. E., pg. 1003 PB
Panduit Canada Ltd., 140 Amber St., pg. 836 PV
Pillsbury Canada Ltd., 675 Chochrane Dr., pg. 411 IT
Recoton Canada Inc., 65 Riviera Drive, Unit B, pg. 1369 PB
Remington Products (Canada) Inc., 475 Cochrane Dr., Unit #4, pg. 921 PV
Robin Hood Multifoods Inc., 60 Columbia Way, pg. 901 IT
S.C. Food Services (Canada) Inc., 500 Hood Road, pg. 1213 IT
Scan-Optics (Canada), Ltd., 7100 Woodbine Ave., Ste. 303, pg. 1436 PB
Scott's Food Services Inc., 500 Hood Rd., pg. 1213 IT
Scott's Management Services Inc., 500 Hood Road, pg. 1213 IT
SCOTT'S RESTAURANTS INC., 500 Hood Road, pg. 1213 IT
SEIKO Canada Inc., 115 Idema Rd., pg. 1218 IT
Semi-Tech Corp., 131 McNabb St., pg. 1220 IT
SEMI-TECH CORPORATION, 131 McNabb St., pg. 1220 IT
Skil Canada Ltd., Hwy. 48, pg. 577 PB
Smiths Industries Medical Systems Canada Limited, 301 Gough Rd., pg. 1269 IT
Smiths Industries North America Limited, 4 Denison St., pg. 1269 IT
Star Data Systems Inc., 7030 Woodbine Ave., Ste. 900, pg. 1077 IT

Steelcase Canada Ltd., One Steelcase Rd. W., pg. 1038 PV
Stirling Connectors, 211 Telson Rd., pg. 17 IT
Sun Microsystems of Canada, 100 Renfrew Dr., pg. 1532 PB
Tandem Computers Canada Limited, 11th Fl., 3100 Steeles Ave. East, pg. 417 IT
Telxon Canada Corporation, Inc., 80 Micro Court, Suite 100, pg. 1574 PB
Thomas Lighting-Canadian Division, 189 Bullock Dr., pg. 1599 PB
Tie Rack (Canada) Limited, 145 Renfrew, pg. 1389 IT
Toshiba of Canada, Ltd., 191 McNabb St., pg. 1407 IT
Toyota Credit Canada Inc., 80 Micro Ct., pg. 1413 IT
Tyton Hellermann Canada Incorporated, #28,3400 14th Ave., pg. 209 IT
Utell International-Canada, 75 Clegg Road, pg. 1098 IT
Vallen Safety Supply Company, Ltd., 25 Royal Crest Court, Unit #1, pg. 1705 PB
Wilson Sports Equipment Canada, Ltd., 145 Shleids Court, pg. 73 IT
YOGEN FRUZ WORLDWIDE INC., 8300 Woodbine Ave., pg. 1520 IT
Zenith Data Systems, 675 Cochrane Dr., pg. 317 IT

Medicine Hat

Cancarb Limited, 1702 Brier Park Crescent N.W., pg. 1417 IT
Medicine Hat News, 3257 Dunmore Rd., S.E., pg. 631 IT

Midland

Kindred Industries, P.O. Box 190, 1000 Kindred Rd., pg. 453 IT
NEBS Business Forms Limited, 330 Cranston Cres, pg. 1171 PB
Rogers Cable Systems, pg. 1123 IT

Millhaven

UTDC Systems, Taylor Kidd Blvd., pg. 200 IT

Milton

Agro Dynamics Canada Inc., 415 Industrial Ave., pg. 563 PB
Barrick Gold, 5437 Sleeles Avenue, pg. 169 IT
Cambridge-Lee Canada Ltd., 221 Nipissing Rd., pg. 202 PV
Canadian Meter Company, Inc., 3037 Derry Rd. West, pg. 1149 IT
Conchem, 180 Market Dr., pg. 790 IT
Derlan Aerospace Canada Limited, 180 Market Drive, pg. 395 PB
Distex Ind. Inc., 521 McGeachy Dr., pg. 560 PB
Komori Canada Ltd., 151 Steeles Ave. E., pg. 745 IT
Matthews Canada Ltd., 550 McGeeachie Dr., pg. 1060 PB
Rockwell International Suspension Systems Company, 150 Steeles Avenue, pg. 1401 PB
Toronto Auto Auction, 8277 Lawson Rd., pg. 283 PV
Volvo Truck North America Inc., 855 Steeles Ave. E., pg. 1477 IT

Minto

NB Coal Company Limited, Industrial Park, pg. 923 IT

Mirabel

Bell Helicopter Textron, 12800 Rue de L'Avenir, pg. 1590 PB
Kintetsu World Express Inc., 11850 Ave. Cargo A-H, Suite 227, pg. 735 IT
MATAC Cargo Ltd., Ste. 221, Air Freight Bldg. C, Montreal Intl. Airport, pg. 36 IT

Mission

THE CLARK GROUP, 33610 E. Broadway Ave., pg. 296 IT
Fraser Valley Forest Products Limited, 7116 Beatty Dr., pg. 1067 IT

Mississauga

ABS Pumps Corporation, 6315 Shawson Drive, Unit 13, pg. 270 IT
AGRA Plastics Inc., 7250 Danbro CRGS, pg. 30 IT
AST Canada, Inc., 375 Britannia Rd., Unit 1, pg. 1182 IT
AYP Canada, Inc., 1040 Jayson Ct., pg. 440 IT
Advance Automotive Industries, Inc., 6520 Viscount Rd., pg. 335 PB
Aladdin Canada, Inc., 750 Gana Ct., pg. 31 PV
Alcan Rolled Products Recycling, 2700 Matheson Blvd., 6th Floor, pg. 50 IT
Alcoa Inter-America Canada Ltd., 115A Matheson Blvd., Ste. 207, pg. 62 PB
Alcon Canada, Inc., 2145 Meadowpine Blvd., pg. 918 IT
Allders International (Canada) Limited, 400-2630 Skymark Ave., pg. 30 IT
AlliedSignal Canada Inc., Automotive Aftermarket, 7631 Bath Road, pg. 52 PB
AlliedSignal Chemicals Canada Inc., 50 Burnhamthorpe Rd. W., Ste. 904, pg. 52 PB
Amano Cincinnati - Toronto Branch Office, 270 Matheson Boulevard East, pg. 71 IT

PB - *U.S. Public Companies Volume*
PV - *U.S. Private Companies Volume*
IT - *International Public & Private Companies Volume*

1537

Geographic Index-Non U.S.

Amgen Canada Inc., 6733 Mississauga Rd., Ste. 303, pg. 101 **PB**
Angus Fire Limited, 1261 Shawson Dr., pg. 1500
Anixter Canada, 33 City Centre Dr., pg. 115 **PB**
Anixter Toronto, 5875 Chedworth Way, pg. 116 **PB**
Antec Group, 5875 Chedworth Way, pg. 117 **PB**
Aquaterra Corporation, Crystal Springs Div., 1200 Brittania Rd. E., pg. 381 **IT**
Arby's Canada, 6299 Airport Rd., Ste. 200, pg. 1635 **PB**
ARI Canada Limited, 1270 Central Parkway West, Suite 600, pg. 535 **PV**
Arrow Medical Products Ltd., 150 Brittania Rd. E., Unit 20, pg. 135 **PB**
Arthur-Jones Lithographing Limited, 1060 Tristar Dr., pg. 698 **IT**
Asbury Wilkinson Graphite & Foundry Supply Co., 1740 Argentia Rd., pg. 87 **PV**
Ashland Chemical Canada, Ltd., 2620 Royal Windsor Dr., pg. 139 **PB**
Astra Pharma Inc., 1004 Middlegate Rd., pg. 94 **IT**
Astro Polyfoam Ltd., 3939 Nashua Dr., pg. 756 **PB**
ATOMIC ENERGY OF CANADA LTD., 2251 Speakman Drive, pg. 97 **IT**
Atomic Energy of Canada Ltd., 2251 Speakman Drive, pg. 97 **IT**
Augat Electronics Inc., 285 Wratline Ave., pg. 1598 **PB**
Auto-trol, LTD., 5310 Explorer Dr., Ste. 110, pg. 148 **PB**
Avesta Sheffield Inc., 2140 Meadowpine Blvd., pg. 221 **IT**
Avnet Computer, 6705 Millcreek Dr., pg. 155 **PB**
BOC Canada Ltd., 5975 Falbourne Street, Unit 2, pg. 121 **IT**
Ball Superior Ltd., 1155 Birchview Dr., pg. 112 **PV**
BancTec (Canada), Inc., 405 Brittannia Rd., Unit 7, pg. 177 **PB**
Barringer Research Limited, 1730 Aimco Blvd., pg. 192 **PB**
Batten Converter Services, 1605 Argentia, pg. 698 **IT**
Battenfeld Canada Ltd., 940 A Westport Crescent, pg. 825 **IT**
Bauer Sports, 1330 Meyerside Dr., pg. 1184 **PB**
Bekaert Corporation, 1093 Meyerside Drive, pg. 184 **IT**
Bensons International Systems, 6494 Tomken Road, pg. 460 **IT**
BERG Electronics Canada, Inc., # 7 6695 Mill Creek Drive, pg. 213 **PB**
Bertrand Faure Components Ltd., 6141 Vipond Drive, pg. 193 **PB**
Best Universal Lock Ltd., 1155 Fewster Dr., pg. 223 **PB**
Betrand Faure Components Ltd. - Vipond Plant, 6141 Vipond Drive, pg. 193 **PB**
BetzDearborn Canada, Inc., 3451 Erindale Station Road, pg. 227 **PB**
BetzDearborn Inc., 3451 Erindale Station Rd., pg. 227 **PB**
Bio-Rad Laboratories (Canada) Ltd., 5149 Bradco Blvd., pg. 230 **PB**
Blistex Limited, 2395 Drew Rd., pg. 149 **PV**
Bloomfield Industries Canada Ltd., 5850 Keaton Crescent, pg. 1497 **PB**
Blue Streak-Hygrade Motor Products Ltd., 7680 Tranmere Dr., pg. 1503 **PB**
Robert Bosch Inc., 6811 Century Ave., pg. 205 **IT**
Braun Canada Ltd., 110 Matleson Blvd., pg. 744 **PB**
Brian Controls, 2360 Millrace Court, pg. 1489 **IT**
Brian Controls Division, 294 Watline Ave., pg. 711 **IT**
Bridgestone/Firestone Canada Inc., 4th Fl., 5770 Hurontario St., pg. 214 **PB**
Bridgestone/Firestone Canada, Inc., 5770 Hurontario St., Ste. 400, pg. 214 **PB**
Briggs & Stratton Canada Inc., 301 Ambassador Drive, pg. 252 **PB**
Brinkmann Instruments (Canada) Ltd., 6670 Campobello, pg. 169 **PV**
Bristol-Myers Equible Canada Inc., 2323 Argentia Rd., pg. 255 **PB**
Broan Limited, 1140 TriStar Dr., pg. 1194 **PB**
CCTF, 5266 Timberlea Blvd., pg. 453 **IT**
CGC Inc., 350 Burnhamthrope Rd. W., pg. 1660 **PB**
CGTX Inc., Plaza One, Ste. 206, 2000 Argentina Rd., pg. 604 **IT**
CGTX Toronto Office, 2000 Argentia Rd., pg. 693 **IT**
Cadbury Beverages Canada Inc., 2700 Matheson Blvd. East, pg. 248 **PB**
Calgon Carbon Canada, Inc., 6303 Airport Rd., Ste. 304, pg. 293 **PB**
Cam Am Casters, 2884 Slough St., pg. 1507 **PB**
Camco Canada, 1723 Lakeshore Road West, L5J 1J4, pg. 576 **IT**
Camco Inc., 2645 Skymark Ave., pg. 713 **PB**
N.C. Cameron & Sons, Ltd., pg. 1508 **PB**
Canada Malting Co. Limited, Plaza # 4, 2000 Argentia Rd., pg. 428 **PB**
Canada West Indies Molasses Co. Ltd., 33 City Centre Dr., Ste. 365, 1357 **IT**
Canadian Hardings Machine Tools Ltd., 415 Matheson Blvd. E., pg. 502 **PV**
Canadian Kenworth Co., Markbroough Pl., 6711 Mississauga Rd. N., 3rd Fl., pg. 1247 **PB**
Canadian Mini-Warehouse Properties, Ltd., 1550 Meyerside Dr., Unit 7, pg. 1341 **PB**
Canadian Satellite Communications Inc., 50 Burnhamthorpe Rd., W., pg. 1481 **IT**
Canon Canada Inc., 6390 Dixie Road, pg. 262 **IT**
Capitol Records-EMI of Canada Ltd., 3109 American Dr., pg. 427 **IT**
Card Technology Corp., 3198 Orlando Dr., pg. 898 **IT**
Carpenter Technology (Canada) Ltd., 7464 Tranmere Dr., Unit 2, pg. 308 **PB**
Carrier Canada Ltd., Meadowvale Atrium, 1900 Minnesota Ct., Suite 200, pg. 1691 **IT**
Carter Products, Canada, 6600 Kitimat Rd., pg. 310 **PB**
Cascade (Canada) Inc., 5570 Timberlea Blvd., pg. 311 **PB**

Caterpillar of Canada, 1550 Caterpillar Rd., pg. 316 **PB**
Chattem (Canada) Inc., 2220 Argentia Rd., pg. 342 **PB**
CIBA-GEIGY Canada Ltd., 6860 Century Ave., pg. 976 **IT**
CIBA Vision, 2150 Torquay Mews, pg. 981 **IT**
CIBA Vision Management Inc., 6515 Kitimat Rd., pg. 981 **IT**
CIBA Vision Sterile Manufacturing Inc., 6515 Kitimat Rd., pg. 981 **IT**
Cominco Ltd. Product Technology Center, 2280 Speakman Drive, pg. 308 **IT**
Connaught Novo Nordisk Inc., West Tower, 3rd Fl., 2700 Matheson Blvd. East, pg. 987 **IT**
Corvita Canada, Inc., 2395 Speakman Dr., pg. 1282 **PB**
Cott Corporation - North East Region (Ontario), 6525 Viscount Road, pg. 337 **IT**
Courtaulds Aerospace, 5676 Timberlea Blvd., pg. 339 **IT**
DHL International Express Ltd., Bldg. B, Ste. 400, 6205 Airport Rd., pg. 302 **PV**
Danka Business Systems Ltd., 5580 Explorer Drive, pg. 579 **IT**
Danzas (Canada) Ltd., 1600 Drew Road, pg. 382 **IT**
Data Genera (Canada) Ltd., Plaza 5, 2000 Argentia Rd., pg. 485 **PB**
Data I/O Canada Corporation, 6725 Airport Rd., Ste. 102, pg. 486 **PB**
DataCard Canada Inc., 5200 Orbitor Dr., pg. 312 **PV**
Design Electrical Manufacturing, 815 Gana Ct., pg. 955 **IT**
The Diebold Company of Canada Limited, 2100 Matheson Blvd. E., Ste. 102, pg. 506 **PB**
Distribupro, Inc., 5935 Airport Rd., pg. 420 **PB**
Docap (1985) Corporation, 6601 Goreway, Promenade Unit B, pg. 695 **IT**
Domcor - Ontario, 3545 Nashua Drive, pg. 415 **IT**
Dormer Tools, Inc., 6835 Century Ave., pg. 1188 **IT**
Dover Corp. (Canada) Ltd., 1551 Caterpillar Rd., pg. 522 **PB**
Dover Corporation (Canada) Ltd.-Turnbull Elevator Div., 1551 Caterpillar Rd., pg. 522 **PB**
Dresser Canada, Inc., 2135 Meadow Pine Blvd., pg. 529 **IT**
Du Pont Canada Inc., P.O. Box 2200, Streetsville, Postal Sta., pg. 532 **PB**
Dun & Bradstreet Canada Ltd., 5770 Hurontario St., pg. 536 **PB**
Duracell Canada Inc., 2333 N. Sheridan Way, pg. 743 **PB**
Dynamex Express, 3883 Nashua Dr., pg. 36 **IT**
EG & G Canada Limited Instruments Division, 6535 Millcreek Dr., Unit 58, pg. 544 **PB**
EIS Brake Manufacturing, Ltd., 6630 Tomken Road, L5T 1N1, pg. 1503 **PB**
ESAB Group Canada, Inc., 6010 Tomken Rd., pg. 282 **IT**
Eclipse Combustion, 1145 Westport Crescent, pg. 361 **PV**
Ecolab Canada, 5105 Tompkin Rd., pg. 562 **PV**
Electrolux Canada, 2470 Milltower Ct., pg. 370 **PV**
Emco Distribution, Plaza 3, 2000 Argentia Rd., pg. 453 **IT**
Epic Express, 7099 Torbram Rd., pg. 435 **PB**
Ericsson Communications, Inc., 6200 Kestral Rd., pg. 1366 **IT**
Ericsson GE Mobile Communications Canada, Inc., 6200 Kestral Rd., pg. 1366 **IT**
Ericsson GE Mobile Communications Canada, Inc., 5255 Satelite Drive, pg. 1371 **IT**
Ericsson GE Telecommunication Inc., 6200 Kestrel, pg. 1366 **IT**
Esselte Meto Canada, 5466 Timberlea Blvd., Unit 1, pg. 461 **IT**
Esselte Pendaflex Canada Inc., 6495 Tomken Rd., pg. 460 **IT**
Ethyl Canada, Inc., 350 Burnhamthorpe Rd. W., Ste. 600, pg. 595 **PB**
Evcon Supply Inc., 3115 Peppermill Court, pg. 1789 **IT**
Expressvu Inc., 1290 Central Parkway West, pg. 115 **IT**
F-P Electronics, 6030 Ambler Dr., pg. 1045 **PB**
Federal Industries Consumer Group, Inc., Ste. 520, 5925 Airport Rd., pg. 1150 **PB**
Fedmet International Inc., Airway Centre, 5925 Airport Rd., Ste. 520, pg. 1150 **PB**
Financia Collection Agencies (International) Inc., Unit # 4, 6715 Millcreek Drive, pg. 470 **PB**
Finstar Finance Inc., 6715 Millcreek Drive, Unit 4, pg. 471 **PB**
Fluke Electronics Canada Inc., 400 Brittania Rd. E., pg. 659 **PB**
Foundation Nuclear Managers, # 3, 2275 Speakman Dr., pg. 118 **IT**
Freightliner of Canada, Ltd., 3930 Nashua Drive, pg. 368 **IT**
Fuji Photo Film Canada, Inc., 275 Brittania Road East, pg. 524 **IT**
Fujitsu Canada, Inc., 2800 Matheson Blvd. E., pg. 527 **IT**
H.B. Fuller, Canada Inc., 880 Rangeview Rd., pg. 687 **PB**
G.E. Fanuc Automation Canada, 2300 Meadowvale Ave., pg. 713 **PB**
G.E. Plastic Canada, 2300 Meadowvale Blvd., pg. 713 **PB**
General Instrument of Canada Ltd., 1611 Courtney Park Dr. E., pg. 716 **PB**
Genicom Canada, Inc., 5170-A Timberlea Boulevard, L4W 2S5, pg. 729 **IT**
Gensym Canada Ltd., 6205 Airport Rd. Bldg. 8, Ste. 100, pg. 731 **IT**
Gerber Canada, 2415 Skymark Avenue, pg. 973 **IT**
Getinge/Castle Canada Limited, Unit Two, 2740 Matheson Blvd. E., pg. 551 **PB**
Glaxo Wellcome Inc., 7333 Mississauga Rd., North, pg. 553 **IT**
GLOBELLE CORPORATION, pg. 554 **IT**
Goldstar Canada Ltd., 7391 Pacific Circle, pg. 779 **IT**
Graco Canada Inc., 3400 American Dr., pg. 757 **PB**
Grinnell Canada Ltd., 135 Matheson Blvd., pg. 1651 **PB**
Guest International (Canada) Ltd., 55 Village Centre Place, Ste. 207, pg. 768 **PB**

Hamilton Hallmark (Canada) Ltd., 6705 Millcreek Drive, pg. 155 **PB**
Chr. Hansen Limited (Canada), 1146 Aerowood Dr., pg. 288 **IT**
HAWKER SIDDELEY CANADA INC., Ste. 700, 3 Robert Speck Pkwy., pg. 604 **IT**
Hazco Canada, Inc., 6541 Mississauga Rd., Unit B, pg. 1114 **PB**
Heinz Bakery Products, 3030 Orlando Dr., pg. 806 **PB**
Henkel Canada Ltd., 2290 Argentia Rd., pg. 612 **IT**
Hercules Canada Inc., Two Robert Speck Pkwy., pg. 810 **PB**
Hershey Canada Inc., 2350 Matheson Blvd. E., pg. 812 **PB**
Hoffmann-La Roche Ltd., 2455 Meadowpine Blvd., pg. 1121 **IT**
Hostess Frito-Lay Co., 700 Century Ave., Ste. 300, pg. 1277 **PB**
Hunt Canada, 5940 Ambler Dr., pg. 849 **PB**
Hunter Douglas Canada Inc., 2155 Drew Rd., Unit B, pg. 639 **IT**
Hussey Seating Co. (Canada) Ltd., 6185 Ordan Dr. # 14, pg. 550 **PV**
IPC Resistors Inc., 7615 Kimbel St., Unit 2, pg. 590 **PB**
IMAX CORPORATION, 2525 Speakman Drive, Sheridan Park, pg. 661 **PB**
Industrial Tires Incorporated, 3161 Wharton Way N., L4X 2B7, pg. 311 **IT**
Infasco Nut Division, 3990 Nashua Dr., pg. 696 **IT**
InfoWorks, 2655 N. Sheridan Way # 230, pg. 1225 **PB**
Inglis Limited, 1901 Minnesota Court, pg. 1765 **PB**
Interbath of Canada Ltd., 5556 Tomken Road, pg. 566 **PV**
Intercraft Industries of Canada, 3440 Wolfedale Rd., pg. 1178 **IT**
Intergraph Canada Ltd., 7070 Mississauga Road, Ste. 250, pg. 891 **PB**
Intermec Systems Corp., 7065 Tranmere Dr., Suite 3, pg. 1005 **PB**
International Power Machines Canada Ltd., 2798 Thamesgate Dr., pg. 126 **IT**
InterPost Systems Canada Inc., 6295 Northam Dr., Unit 14, pg. 720 **IT**
Jacuzzi Canada, 5880 Falbourne Street, pg. 1684 **PB**
Earle M. Jorgensen Company/Ontario, 1666 Shawson Drive East, pg. 600 **PV**
Juno Lighting Ltd., 1730 Sismet Rd., pg. 935 **PB**
KNOGO Canada, 7150 Torbram Rd., Unit 9, pg. 1458 **PB**
Kennametal, Ltd., 115B Matheson Blvd. W., Ste. 211, pg. 951 **PB**
Kenwood Electronics Canada Inc., 6070 Kestrel Rd., pg. 730 **IT**
KEPCO Toronto Office, 2275 Speakman, Unit 5, pg. 758 **IT**
Kimberly-Clark Inc., 90 Burnhamthorpe Road West, pg. 959 **PB**
Kintetsu World Express Inc., 6405 Northam Drive, pg. 735 **IT**
Kolmar Laboratories, 5090 Explorer Drive, pg. 239 **IT**
Konica Canada Inc., 1329 Meyerside Dr., pg. 749 **IT**
Krupp MaK Diesel Inc., 7555 Danbro Rd., pg. 509 **IT**
Krupp Plastics & Rubber Machinery (Canada), Inc., Uni 6, 2505 Dunwin Dr., pg. 510 **IT**
Kuehne & Nagel International Ltd., 5935 Airport Rd., Stes. 10 & 11, pg. 763 **IT**
Kyocera Canada, Inc., 6200 Dixie Rd., Unit 11, pg. 776 **IT**
Lawson Mardon Packaging Inc., 6733 Missisauga, Ste. 700, pg. 68 **IT**
Lawson Products Inc. (Ontario), 7315 Rapistan Court Rd., pg. 980 **PB**
Lincoln Canada Limited, 7017 Fir Tree Dr., pg. 1274 **PB**
Liuski International Toronto, Inc., 1830 Meyerside Ave., pg. 1005 **PB**
Lloydaire/Eljer Inc., 370 Universal Dr., pg. 1795 **PB**
Loctite Canada Inc., 270 Britannia Rd., E., pg. 611 **PB**
Long Manufacturing, Ltd., 6635 Ordan Dr., pg. 815 **IT**
Longlac Wood Industries Inc., 2000 Argentia Road, pg. 761 **IT**
Lowrance Canada, 919 Matheson Blvd., pg. 1016 **IT**
Luxottica Canada Inc., 947 Verbena Rd., pg. 822 **IT**
MTS Testing Systems Canada Ltd., Plaza 4, 2000 Argantia Rd., Suite 100, pg. 1029 **IT**
MacDermid Chemicals Inc., 4530 Fieldgate Dr., pg. 1030 **PB**
MacMillan Bathurst Inc., 2070 Hadwen Rd., pg. 20 **IT**
MAGELLAN AEROSPACE CORPORATION, 3160 Derry Road East, pg. 829 **PV**
Maritz Canada Inc., 1799 Argentia Rd., pg. 704 **PV**
Mark IV IVHS, 6030 Ambler Dr., pg. 1045 **PB**
Marks & Spencer Canada Inc., 3770 Nashua Dr., pg. 843 **PB**
Marks & Spencer Holdings Canada Inc., 3770 Nashua Dr., pg. 843 **PB**
Martin-Brower of Canada, Ltd., 30 Eglinton Avenue W., pg. 376 **PV**
Martin Sprocket & Gear, Inc., 896 Meyerside Dr., pg. 709 **PV**
Mary Kay Cosmetics Ltd., 5600 Ambler Dr., pg. 711 **PV**
Master Shield Building Products, 2441 Royal Windsor Dr., pg. 698 **IT**
Mattel Canada, Inc., 6155 Freemont Blvd., pg. 1059 **PB**
Medtronic of Canada, 6733 Kitimat Rd., pg. 1084 **PB**
Melburn Truck Lines, 2215 Royal Windsor Dr., pg. 1262 **IT**
Mentor Graphics (Canada) Limited, 2655 N. Sheriday Way, Ste. 230, pg. 1087 **PB**
Metallurg (Canada) Limited, 2700 Matheson Blvd. E., pg. 735 **PV**
Metroland Printing & Distributing, 3125 Wolfedale Rd., pg. 1402 **IT**
Micro Warehouse Canada Limited, 1551 Caterpillar Road, pg. 1104 **PB**

PB - *U.S. Public Companies Volume*
PV - *U.S. Private Companies Volume*
IT - *International Public & Private Companies Volume*

Microsoft Canada Co., 320 Matheson Blvd. W., pg. 1108 PB
Milgray/Toronto, Inc., 2783 Thames Gate Drive, pg. 207 PB
Millipore Ltd., 3688 Nashua Dr., pg. 1113 PB
Mississauga Center, 3190 Caravelle Dr., pg. 273 IT
Mississauga Center, 3300 Orlando Dr., pg. 273 IT
Mississauga Office, 6135 Kennedy Rd, pg. 274 IT
Mizuno Canada Limited, 5206 Timberlea Blvd., pg. 885 IT
Monsanto Canada, Inc., 2330 Argentia Rd., pg. 1125 PB
Moore Business Forms & Systems Ltd., 5500 Explorer Dr., pg. 889 IT
Morganite Canada Corporation, 6300 Northam Dr., pg. 895 IT
Mosler Canada, 280 Britannia Rd. E., pg. 92 PB
Multiple Pakfold Forms, 130 Matheson Blvd., Unit 5, pg. 384 IT
Munters Inc., 6180 Kitimat Rd., Unit 16, pg. 669 IT
NBS Card Services, 3206 Orlando Dr., pg. 898 IT
NBS TECHNOLOGIES, INC., 5935 Airport Rd., Ste. 600, pg. 898 IT
NBS Technologies Inc., 5935 Airport Rd., Ste. 600, pg. 898 IT
NMB Precision Inc., 370 Britannia Road, pg. 868 IT
NSK-RHP Canada Inc., 5585 McAdam Rd., pg. 904 IT
National Electrical Carbon Canada, 6300 Northam Dr., pg. 892 IT
National Fleet & Lease, 6500 Mississauga Rd., pg. 354 PB
Nederman Canada Ltd., 6010 Tomken Rd., pg. 283 IT
Neste Resins Canada, 5865 McLaughlin Rd., Unit 3, pg. 915 IT
Neste Resins Corporation, Unit 3, 5865 McLaughlin Rd., pg. 915 IT
Network Systems Corporation, 5710 Timberlea Blvd., Ste. 207, pg. 1523 PB
New Balance Canada Inc., 1495 Bonhill Rd., Unit 11, pg. 792 PV
New Hermes, Ltd., 1561 Courtneypark Dr. East, pg. 794 PV
Newport Instruments Canada Corp., 2650 Meadowvale Blvd., Ste. 3, pg. 1179 PB
Nikon Canada Inc., 1366 Aerowood Dr., pg. 931 IT
Nissan Canada Finance, Inc., 5290 Orbitor Dr., pg. 945 IT
Nissan Canada Inc., 5290 Orbitor Dr., pg. 945 IT
Northline Coupling Systems Ltd., 1815 Meyerside Dr., pg. 391 IT
Novo Nordisk Canada, Inc., 2700 Matheson Blvd. E., 3rd Floor, West Tower, pg. 988 IT
Nutone Canada Inc., 6300 Tomken Road, pg. 1499 IT
Olin Canada Inc., 3 Robert Speck Pkwy., pg. 1220 PB
Oracle Corporation Canada, 110 Matheson Blvd. W., Suite 100, pg. 1228 PB
Oral-B Laboratories Inc., 974 Lakeshore Rd. E., pg. 745 PB
Orenda Aerospace Corporation, 3160 Derry Road East, pg. 829 IT
Orenda (Canada), 3160 Derry Rd. E., pg. 604 IT
Oshawa Foods, 6355 Viscount Rd., pg. 1012 IT
Outokumpu Mintec Canada Ltd., 6495 Northam Dr., pg. 1017 IT
Owens-Corning Ontario Holdings Inc., 3,Robert Speck Parkway, Suite 800, pg. 1237 PB
PCL Courier Holdings Inc., 5310 Explorer Drive, pg. 36 IT
PHH Vehicle Management Services Canada, 350 Burnhamthorpe Rd. W., pg. 321 PB
PPG Canada Inc., 2301 Royal Windsor Dr., pg. 1245 PB
PACCAR Financial Services Ltd., Markborough Pl., 6711 Mississauga Rd. N., pg. 1247 PB
PACCAR of Canada Ltd., 6711 Mississauga Rd. N., pg. 1247 PB
Pakfold Business Forms, 7765 Tranmere Dr., pg. 384 IT
Pall (Canada) Ltd., 7205 Mill Creek Dr., pg. 1254 PB
Paperboard Industries Corporation, 7830 Tranmere Dr., pg. 273 IT
Peabody Engineering Canada Ltd., 3176 Ridgeway Dr., Ste 55, pg. 1066 IT
Pechiney World Trade (Canada) Inc., 3525 Meadowvale Blvd., pg. 1031 IT
Pentax Canada Inc., 3131 Universal Drive, pg. 85 IT
Perma-Flex (Canada) Inc., 6015 Kestrel Rd., pg. 1203 IT
Pharmacia & Upjohn Inc., 2280 Argentia Road, pg. 1050 IT
PharmaPlus Drugmarts Limited, 5935 Airport Rd., Ste. 500, pg. 1012 IT
Pioneer Standard Canada Inc., 3415 American Drive, pg. 1300 PB
Pitney Bowes of Canada Ltd.-Leasing Div., Promontory 1, Ste. 200, 2695 North Sheridan Way, pg. 1304 PB
Polychrome Corp. (Canada) Co., Ltd., 1745 Bonhill Road, Units 6 & 7, pg. 370 IT
Power Indusries Ltd., 7407 Bren Rd., pg. 878 PV
PREMDOR INC., 1600 Britannia Rd., E., pg. 1066 IT
Premdor Inc.-Flush Door Plant, 1600 Britannia Rd., pg. 1067 IT
Prior Data Sciences Ltd., 1550 Enterprise Road, Suite 120, pg. 1288 IT
Pro-Pastries Inc., 1774 Drew Road, pg. 806 PB
Procter & Gamble Inc., 3333 Unity Dr., pg. 1332 PB
Pyroil Canada Limited, 1330 Crestlawn Dr., pg. 955 IT
QMS Canada, 2600 Skymark Ave., Unit 5, pg. 1346 PB
RBC Insurance Holdings Inc., 55 City Centre Drive, Ste. 1100, pg. 1131 IT
Ralston Purina Canada Eveready Div., 2500 Royal Windsor Dr., pg. 1360 PB
Ralston Purina Canada Inc., 2500 Royal Windsor Dr., pg. 1360 PB
Rapistan Demag Ltd., 7300 Rapistan Ct., pg. 838 IT
Rauland-Borg (Canada) Inc., 4025 Sladeview Crescent, Unit 4, 5 & 6, pg. 911 PV
Rawlings Canada, 2285 Dunwin Dr., Unit 15, pg. 1362 PB
Raypak Canada, Ltd., 2805 Slough St., pg. 1022 IT
Ready Bake Foods Inc., 2095 Meadow Vale Blvd., pg. 1495 IT
Reichhold Limited, Four Robert Speck Pkwy., Ste. 700, pg. 370 IT
Rhone-Poulenc Canada, Ltd., Pllaza 3, Ste. 400, 2000 Argentia Rd., pg. 1112 IT
Richardson Electronics Canada Ltd., 6185 Tomken Rd., Units 3-5, pg. 1388 PB
Robertshaw Controls Canada Inc., 5785 Kennedy Road, pg. 550 IT
Robertshaw Controls (Canada) Inc., 5785 Kennedy Rd., pg. 1244 IT
Rogers Cable TV-Mississauga Div., 3573 Wolfdale Rd., pg. 1122 IT
Rolland Inc., Distribution Division, 3190 Caravelle Drive, pg. 273 IT
Ross Data Canada Ltd., Bldg. B, Ste. 100, 6205 Airport Road, pg. 1406 PB
Rothenberger Tools Canada Inc., 1675 Sismet Rd., Unit No. 8, pg. 1129 IT
Royal LePage, 5770 Hurontario Street, Suite 200, pg. 1143 IT
Rubbermaid Canada Inc. Consumer Products, 2562 Stanfield Rd., pg. 1411 PB
RUSSEL METALS INC., 1900 Minnesota Ct., Ste. 210, pg. 1149 IT
Safeguard Business Systems Limited, 420 Britannia Rd. E., Ste. 102, pg. 960 PV
Sandvik Canada Inc., 6835 Century Ave., pg. 1188 IT
Sanofi Canada, 6235 Tonken Rd., pg. 445 IT
Schneider Group, 6630 Campobello Rd., pg. 1208 IT
A. Schulman Canada Ltd., 5770 Hurontario St., Ste. 602, pg. 1441 PB
Schwank, 210 Brunel Rd., pg. 853 PV
Scott Paper Limited, 1900 Minnesota Court, Ste. 125, pg. 762 IT
Seal Group, 4120 Ridgeway Drive Unit #35, pg. 1262 PB
Sensormatic Canada, Inc., 3090 American Drive, pg. 1457 PB
Sequent Computer Systems (Canada) Ltd., 50 Burnhamthorpe Road, W. Ste. 508, pg. 1459 PB
ServiceMaster of Canada Ltd., 6540 Tomken Rd, pg. 1462 PB
Sharp Electronics of Canada Ltd., 335 Britannia Rd. East, pg. 1230 IT
Shimizu Canada Engineering Corporation, 4300 Village Centre Ct., pg. 1234 IT
Siegling Canada Ltd., 3220 Orlando Dr., pg. 498 IT
Sifto Canada, Inc., 5430 Timberlea Blvd., pg. 505 PV
Silicon Graphics Canada Inc., 2550 Matheson Blvd. East, pg. 1474 PB
Simplex Intl. Time Equip. Co. Ltd. (Canada), 6300 Viscount Rd., pg. 1002 PV
Slant-Fin, Ltd./Ltee, 6450 Northam Dr., pg. 1005 PV
Snap-on Tools of Canada, Ltd., 2325 Skymark Ave., pg. 1481 PB
Sonoco Containers, Inc., 90 Burnhamthorpe Rd. West, #1504, pg. 1487 PB
Spar Aviation Services, 7785 Tranmere Drive, pg. 1288 IT
Specialty Steels, 2525 Meadowvale Blvd., pg. 1032 IT
Spectra-Physics Canada, Inc., 1510 Drew Rd., Unit 16, pg. 1290 IT
Springs Canada, Ltd., 6345 Dixie Rd., Ste. 200, pg. 1500 PB
Square D Canada, 6675 Rexwood Rd., pg. 1209 IT
Star Expansion Shields Ltd., 6680 Excelsior Ct., pg. 1034 PV
L.S. Starrett Company of Canada, 1244 Kamato Rd., pg. 1511 PB
Stream International, 2185 Skymark Ave., pg. 518 PB
Subaru Canada Inc., 5770 Hurontario Street, Ste. 500, pg. 523 IT
Sun Chemical Ltd., 5925 Airport Road, Ste. 410, pg. 371 IT
Sunbeam Corporation (Canada) Limited, 5979 Falbourne St., pg. 1533 PB
Svedala Industries Canada Mississauga, 3136 Mavis Rd., pg. 1325 IT
Symbol Technologies Canada Inc., 2540 Matheson Blvd. E., pg. 1546 PB
Symix Systems Inc., 2700 Matheson Blvd. E., Ste. 210, pg. 1547 PB
Synergistics Chemicals, Inc., 5915 Airport Road, Ste. 425, pg. 734 PB
Synergistics Industries Limited, 5915 Airport Road, Suite 425, pg. 734 PB
TNT North America and Canada Inc., 5280 Maingate Drive, pg. 1343 IT
TSC Shannock Corporation, 5582 Ambler Drive, pg. 1343 IT
Tastemaker, Inc., 5285 Creekbank Rd., pg. 811 PB
Teac Canada Ltd., 5939 Wallace Street, pg. 1360 IT
Tech Data Canada, Inc., 1305 Meyerside Dr., pg. 1562 PB
Tellabs Communications CDA, 2433 Meadowvale Blvd., pg. 1573 PB
Terumo Medical-Toronto, 6390 Kestrel Rd., pg. 1376 IT
THORN EMI (Canada) Inc., 3109 American Drive, pg. 428 IT
Thrifty Canada, Ltd., 6050 Indian Line, pg. 354 PB
Time Electronics, 420 Britannia Rd., Ste. 108, pg. 155 PB
Trans-Lux Canada Ltd., 5446 Gorvan Dr., pg. 1629 PB
TransLogic Corp., 1200 Aerowood Dr., pg. 1387 IT
Transport International Pool of Canada Limited, 2300 Meadowvale Blvd., pg. 713 PB
Tube-Fab Ltd., 15 Ellen St., pg. 771 PB
Tyco Canada Ltd., 7420B Bramalea Rd., pg. 1059 PB
Uddeholm Limited, 6659 Ordan Dr., pg. 1472 IT
Union Air Transport Inc., L4V 1S1, pg. 1120 PV
United Media Canada, 6557C Mississauga Rd., pg. 1448 PB
United Parcel Service of Canada, 3195 Airway Dr., pg. 1123 PV
VWR Canlab, 2360 Argentia Rd., pg. 1704 PB
Valvoline Canada Ltd., 905 Winston Churchill Blvd., pg. 140 PB
Vermont American Canada, Inc., 1226 Cardiff Blvd., pg. 578 PB
Vibco Vibration Products, 2215 Dunwin Dr., pg. 1138 PV
Viewlogic Systems, Inc., 3 Robert Speck Pkwy., Ste. 900, pg. 1548 PB
Vivitar Canada Limited, 6535 Millcreek Dr., Unit 35, pg. 1116 IT
WBF Technologies, 4240 Sherwoodtowne Blvd., pg. 193 IT
Weber Marking Systems Canada ltd., 6180 Danville Rd., pg. 1157 PV
Wells Manufacturing Canada Ltd., 1080 Meyerside Dr., pg. 1113 PV
Westroc Industries Limited, 2424 Lakeshore Rd., W., pg. 123 IT
Westvaco Canada, Ltd., 5915 Airport Rd., Ste. 712, pg. 1762 PB
Wheel Tronic Inc., 1125 Aerowood Dr., pg. 1481 PB
Whitehall-Robins Inc., 5975 Whittle Rd., pg. 82 PB
Whitehall-Robins Laboratories Ltd., 5975 Whittle Rd., pg. 82 PB
Willson Stationers, 6625 Millcreek Dr., pg. 1150 IT
Windmere Consumer Products, Inc., 2160 Dunwin Dr., pg. 1771 PB
Wine Rack, 6660 Kennedy Road #20, pg. 1468 IT
Woodhead Canada Ltd., 1090 Brevik Pl., pg. 1776 PB
Work Wear Canada, 6299 Airport Rd., pg. 690 PB
Yale-Corbin Canada Limited, 3160 Orlando Dr., pg. 1499 IT
The Yorkville Printing Group Limited, 3175 Airway Dr., pg. 538 IT
Zeneca Pharma Inc., 2505 Meadowvale Blvd., pg. 1527 IT
Zimmer of Canada Limited, 2323 Argentia Rd., pg. 257 PB

Moncton

Brian Controls Division, 500 St. George St., pg. 711 IT
CKCW-AM/CFQM-FM, 1000 St. George Blvd., pg. 1124 IT
Cognos Inc.-Moncton Sales Office, 1133 Saint George Blvd., Ste. 400, pg. 306 IT
Datacor/ISM (Information Systems Management Atlantic Corp.), 644 Main St., pg. 230 IT
Financial Collection Agencies, Terminal Plaza Building, 5th Floor, 1222 Main Street, pg. 470 IT
Hewlett-Packard (Canada) Ltd., 535 Edinburgh Dr., pg. 818 PB

Mont Laurier

Uniboard Division Mont Laurier, 845, rue J.B. Reid, pg. 1431 IT

Mont Royal

Ericsson Research Canada, 8400 Decarie Blvd., pg. 1367 IT
Florasynth Canada, Inc., 5800 Andover Ave., pg. 173 IT

Mont-Tremblant

Mont Tremblant Resort, Inc., 3005 chemin Principal, pg. 685 IT

Montreal

ABN AMRO Bank Canada (Montreal), Ste. 860, 2000 Peel St., pg. 11 IT
AXA Assurances, 2020, rue Universite, pg. 19 IT
AXA Canada, 2020, rue Univeriste, pg. 19 IT
Abbott Laboratories Ltd.-Mfg., 5400 Cote de Liesse, pg. 14 PB
ABITIBI-CONSOLIDATED INC., 800 Rene-Levesque Blvd W., pg. 19 IT
Acces Capital, 1981, avenue McGill College, pg. 249 IT
Acces Capital Quebec, 1981, Avenue McGill College, pg. 249 IT
Aciers Francosteel Canada, 5890 Monkland, pg. 572 IT
Adriatic Insurance Company of Canada, 465 Rene Levesque Blvd. West, pg. 61 IT
AGRA Monenco Quebec, Inc., 2045 Stanley Street, 11th Floor, pg. 30 IT
Air Canada Vacations Inc., 1440 St. Catherine St. W., Ste. 800, pg. 36 IT
Akzo Salt Limited, 507 Place Barnes, pg. 43 IT
ALCAN ALUMINIUM LIMITED, 1188 Sherbrooke Street West, pg. 50 IT
Alcan International Limited, 1188 Sherbrooke Street W., pg. 50 IT
Alcan Smelters & Chemicals Ltd., 1188 Sherbrooke West, pg. 50 IT
O.B. Allan Jewellers, 1240 Phillips Sq., pg. 197 IT
ALLIANCE FOREST PRODUCTS INC., 1000 Dela Gauchetierre West, pg. 57 IT
AlliedSignal Aerospatiale Canada Inc., 200 Laurentien Blvd., pg. 53 PB
Alpha Forest Products Inc., 1250 Rene-Levesque Blvd., West, pg. 1104 IT
Alpnet, 2020 University St., Ste. 1520, pg. 58 PB
Armstrong World Industries Canada Ltd., 6911 Boulevard Decarie, pg. 132 PB
Atomic Energy of Canada Ltd., 1155 Metcalfe Street, pg. 97 IT

PB - *U.S. Public Companies Volume*
PV - *U.S. Private Companies Volume*
IT - *International Public & Private Companies Volume*

Audrey Resources, 800 Rene Levesque West, Ste. 850, pg. 253
AVENOR, INC., 1250 Rene-Levesque Blvd. W., 21st Fl., pg. 101　IT
BA Banknote Yvon Boulangar, 2325, rue Dandurand, pg. 1077　IT
BCE Capital Inc., 1000, rue de La Gauchetiere O., pg. 115　IT
BCE INC., 1000, rue de la Gauchetiere Ouest, pg. 114　IT
BCP GROUP LTD., Montreal World Trade Ctr., 393 St. Jacques West, 9th Fl., pg. 116　IT
BNY Financial Corporation-Canada, 500 Rene-Levesque Boulevard West, pg. 179　PB
BOS (Beauchesne Ostiguy & Simard), 3575 Boulevard St. Laurent, pg. 1062　PV
BTS, 4551 Rue De Bullion, pg. 205
Bank Hapoalim B.M., La Tour Xerox, 1, Place Alexis Nihon, pg. 149　IT
Bank of Ireland Asset Management (Canada), 1250 Rene Levesque Blvd. W., Ste. 2200, pg. 153　IT
Bank of Montreal - Montreal, 129, rue Saint-Jacques, pg. 153　IT
The Bank of Tokyo-Mitsubishi (Canada), Tour Banque Nationale, 600 de la Gauchetiere, pg. 158　IT
Banque Nationale de Paris (Canada), 1981 McGill College, pg. 164　IT
Baton Broadcast Sales, Suite 1803, 1010 Sherbrooke Street West, pg. 171　IT
Bauer Sports Inc., 5705 Ferrier St., Ste. 200, pg. 1184　PB
Bedarco Nooter, Inc., 5745 Place Turcot, pg. 801　PV
Belair Insurance Company, 5455 Saint Andre Street, pg. 648　IT
Bell Canada, McGill College Bureau 901, 1800 Avenue, pg. 115　IT
Bell Canada International, inc., 1000, rue de La Gauchetiere O., pg. 115　IT
Bell Local Services, 700, rue de La Gauchetiere O., pg. 115　IT
Bimcor Inc., 1000, rue de La Gauchetiere O., pg. 115　IT
BioChem ImmunoSystems Inc., 10900 Hamon Street, pg. 196　IT
HENRY BIRKS & SONS (1993) INC., 1240 Phillips Square, pg. 196　IT
Blackville Lumber Inc., 1250 Rene Levesque Blvd. West, Ste. 3800, pg. 1104　IT
BOMBARDIER INC., 800 Rene-Levesque Blvd. West, pg. 199　IT
Bombardier Motorized Consumer Products Group, 800 Rene Levesque Blvd. W., pg. 200　IT
Bombardier Real Estate Ltd., 2000 Mansfield St., Ste. 404, pg. 200　IT
Bombardier Recreational Products, 800 Rene-Levesque Blvd. West, pg. 200　IT
Boston Factors of Canada, Inc., 500 Rene Levesque, Ste. 1400, pg. 185　PB
Brian Controls Division, 2445 Duncan Rd., pg. 711　IT
Bristol-Myers Squibb Canada Inc., 2365 Cote de Liesse Rd., pg. 256　PB
CF Cable TV Inc., 405 Ogilvie Avenue, pg. 240　IT
CFCF INC., 405 Ogilvy Ave., pg. 240　IT
CFCF 12, 405 Ogilvy Avenue, pg. 241　IT
CGTX, Inc., 1600 Rene Leuesque Blvd. W., pg. 693　PB
Cadel Div., 1080, Montee de Liesse, pg. 1426　IT
Cadev, 413, rue Saint-Jacques, pg. 249　IT
Cadim, 383, rue Saint-Jacques, pg. 249　IT
CAISSE DE DEPOT ET PLACEMENT DU QUEBEC, 1981, Avenue McGill College, pg. 249　IT
Calvin Bullock, Ltd., 630 Rene-Levesque Blvd. West, Ste. 2690, pg. 1319　IT
Cambinex Exploration, 800 Rene Levesque West, Suite 850, pg. 253　IT
CAMBIOR INC., 800 Rene Levesque Blvd. W., Ste. 850, pg. 253　IT
Camro Inc., 5781 Notre Dame East, pg. 713　PB
Canadelle, Inc., 4405 Metropolitan Boulevard East, pg. 1434　PB
Canadian Adhesives Ltd., 420 Marien Avenue, pg. 1466　IT
Canadian Limited, 1080 Beaver Hall, pg. 1513　IT
Canadian Liquid Air Ltd.-Air Liquide Canada Ltee, IBM Marathon Bldg., 1250 Blvd. Rene Levesque W., pg. 37　IT
Canadian Liquidaire Properties Ltd., 1250 Blvd. Rene Levesque W., pg. 37　IT
Canadian Marconi Company, 2442 Trentonm Ave., pg. 545　IT
CANADIAN NATIONAL RAILWAY COMPANY, 935 de La Gauchetiere St. W., pg. 258　IT
Canadian Steel Foundries, Ltd., 5227 Norte Dame St., E., pg. 142　PB
Canagex Investments Limited, 800 Place Victoria, pg. 396　IT
Canatom Inc., 2020 University Street, Suite 2200, pg. 31　IT
Capital Communications CDPQ, 1981, avenue McGill College, pg. 249　IT
Capital d'Amerique CDPQ, 1981, avenue McGill College, pg. 249　IT
Capital International CDPQ, 1981, avenue McGill College, pg. 249　IT
Cascades Paperboard International Inc., Ste. 300, 772 Sherbrooke St. West, pg. 273　IT
Celanese Canada, Inc., 800 Rene-Levesque Blvd. West, pg. 625　IT
CertainTeed Manatee Insulation Ltd., 5 Place Ville Marie, Suite 1700, pg. 1176　IT
Champlain Productions Inc., 405 Ogilvy Avenue, pg. 241　IT
The Chase Manhattan Bank of Canada, 600 de la Gauchetiere St., W., pg. 340　PB

Cineplex Odeon Corporation -Montreal, 2388, rue Beaubien est., pg. 293　IT
Cipa Industries, Inc., 26 Amos Place Bonaventure, pg. 695　IT
Cognos Inc.-Montreal Sales Office, 500, Place d'Armes, Ste. 2820, pg. 306　IT
Comdisco Canada Ltd., 1801 McGill College, Ste. 1020, pg. 408　PB
Coming Event Fashions Ltd., 3901 Jarry St., East, pg. 1235　IT
Communications Maclean Hunter inc., 1955, ch Cote-de-Liesse, Ste. 113, pg. 1123　IT
Compo Em, 2055, rue Peel, pg. 538　IT
COOPERATIVE FEDEREE DE QUEBEC, 9001 de L'Acadie Blvd., Ste. 200, pg. 330　IT
COSCIENT GROUP INC., 300 Leo-Pariseau Street, Suite 2400, pg. 335　IT
Cosmair Canada Inc., 2115 Crescent, pg. 819　IT
Cossette Communication-Marketing (Montreal) Inc., 2100, Drummond, pg. 336　IT
Crane Canada Inc., 5850 Cote de Liesse Rd., 5th Fl., pg. 457　PB
Credit Lyonnais Canada, 2000 Rue Mansfield, pg. 344　IT
Crown Cork & Seal Canada, Inc., 10000 Meilleur, pg. 464　IT
CULINAR INC., 2 Complexe Desjardins, Ste. 2700, pg. 348　IT
DMB&E Montreal, 1001 Sherbrooke St. E., Ste. 600, H2L 1L3, pg. 304　PV
DMR Group, Inc., 1200 McGill College Ave., Ste. 2300, pg. 527　IT
D'Allairds, 333 Chabanel St. W., pg. 843　IT
Dayton Superior Canada Ltd., 8251 Metropolitan Blvd. E., pg. 932　PV
J.L. de Ball Canada Inc., 385 Louvin West, pg. 552　IT
J.L. de Ball Canada Inc., 433 Chabanel S.W., Ste. 1015, pg. 552　IT
J.L. de Ball-Girmes of America, Inc., 433 Chabanel, Rm. 1015, pg. 552　IT
DESJARDINS-LAURENTIAN FINANCIAL CORPORATION, 1 Complex Desjardin, CP 10500, pg. 396　IT
Distex Ind. Inc., 105 Rue Colbert, pg. 560　PB
Dominion Industrial Fabrics Company, 1950 Sherbrooke St., W., pg. 415　IT
DOMIN ON TEXTILE INC., 1950 Sherbrooke St., W., pg. 415　IT
Domtar Forest Products, 395 de Maisonnouve Blvd. W., pg. 416　IT
DOMTAR INC., 395 de Maisonneuve Blvd. W., pg. 416　IT
Doucet, Inc., 1240 Phillips Sq., pg. 197　IT
Du Pont Canada-Montreal, pg. 532　PB
Eclipse Combustion, 2095 Madison Avenue, pg. 361　IT
Edelman Houston Group, 2015 rue Peel, Bureau 500, pg. 363　PV
Edifice Dorchester-Commerce, Inc., 1155 Ouest, Blvd. Dorchester, pg. 256　IT
Editions d'enseignements-religieux F.P.R. Inc., 2715 ch. Cote Ste-Catherine, pg. 1077　IT
Editions Wilson & Lafleur, Martel Ltee, 40 Notre Dame St. E., pg. 1076　IT
Emballages Cascades P.A.T. Inc., 15300 Rue Sherbrooke E., pg. 273　IT
EnRoute Card Inc., 1000 Sherbrooke St. W., Suite 2200, pg. 36　IT
Ericsson Communications, Inc., 8400 Decarie Blvd., 3rd. Flr., pg. 1366　IT
Essilor Canada Ltee., 295 rue Deslauriers, pg. 462　IT
FEDERATION DES CAISSES POPULAIRES DESJARDINS, 1, complexe Desjardins, pg. 479　IT
Federation Insurance Company of Canada, 1000 De la Gauchetiere St. West, pg. 90　IT
Financial Collection Agencies, Ground Floor, 9697 Saint Laurent Boulevard, pg. 470　IT
First Marathon Securities, 1 Place Ville Marie, pg. 486　IT
Forbo Industries Inc., pg. 497　IT
Fuji Bank Canada (Montreal Branch), 500 Rene Levesque Blvd. W., Ste. 705, pg. 521　IT
GPC Communications (Montreal), 740, rue St. Maurice, pg. 1225　PB
G.T.C. TRANSCONTINENTAL GROUP LTD., 1, Place Ville Marie, pg. 538　IT
GAZ METROPOLITAIN & COMPANY, 1717 du Havre Street, pg. 541　IT
The Gazette, 250 St. Antoine St. West, pg. 631　IT
Gelman Sciences, Inc. (Canada), 2535 DeMiniac, pg. 1253　PB
General Trust Investment Funds Ltd., 1100 University, pg. 907　IT
General Trust of Canada, 1100 University, pg. 907　IT
GENFOOT INC., 554 Montee de Liesse, pg. 549　IT
Geyser Creation Inc., 2100, Drummond, pg. 336　IT
Giltex Hosiery, 3195 Chemin Bedford, pg. 1434　PB
Goldman Sachs Canada, Place de la Cathedrale, 600 Boul. de Maisonneuve Ouest, pg. 462　PV
Grapheme Inc., 2100 Drummond, pg. 336　IT
GROUPE MORROW INC., 1555 rue Peel, pg. 566　IT
Hachette Canada, 4001 A, boulevard Robert, pg. 795　IT
Hako Minuteman Ltd.(Canada), 84 E. Brunswick Blvd., pg. 587　IT
Hang Ten, 554 Montee de Liesse, pg. 549　IT
Hanna, 554 Montee de Liesse, pg. 549　IT
Hebdo Mag. Inc., 130 de Liege Est., pg. 321　PB
Heinemann Electric Canada Ltd., 343 Deslauriers, pg. 557　PB
Hilton Canada Inc., 9 Frontenac, Place Bonaventure, pg. 788　IT
Hitachi Data Systems Inc., 380 Cote Saint Antoine St., pg. 622　IT
Hoogovens Aluminium Quebec and Company Ltd., 2020 University Street, Suite 1334, pg. 755　IT

Frank W. Horner Inc. (Canada), 5485 Ferrier St., pg. 310　PB
Howmet-Cercast Inc., 3905 Industrial Blvd., pg. 213　PV
Hudon et Deaudelin Ltee, 11281 Albert Hudon, pg. 1012　IT
HYDRO-QUEBEC, 20th Fl., 75 Rene Levesque West, pg. 640　IT
Hydrogeo Canada Inc., 455 Rene-Levesque Blvd. West, pg. 1162　IT
Hydro-Quebec International, 400, boul. de Maisonneuve est, pg. 640　IT
Hypotheques CDPQ, 1981, avenue McGill College, pg. 249　IT
ING Canada, 405 de la Concorde Street, pg. 650　IT
Iberia Air Lines, 2020 University St., Ste. 1310, pg. 575　IT
Ideal Parking, Inc., Five Complexe, Place Desjardins, pg. 44　PV
Ilco Unican Inc. (Capitol Division), 5795 de Gaspe St., pg. 1432　IT
Ilco Unican Inc. (Dominion Lock Division), 7301 Decarie Blvd., pg. 1432　IT
Ilco Unican Inc. (Electronic Access Controls Division), 7301 Decarie Blvd., pg. 1432　IT
Imasco Limited, 600, de Maisonneuve Blvd. W., pg. 112　IT
Impact Recherche, 2100 Drummond, pg. 336　IT
Imperial Tobacco Limited, 3810 St. Antoine St. West, pg. 112　IT
Imprimerie Quebecor Barclay, 6600, rue St-Urbain, bureau 402, pg. 1077　IT
Imprimerie Quebecor Inc., 612 St. Jacques St., pg. 1077　IT
Imprimerie Quebecor Montreal, 8000, avenue Blaise-Pascal, pg. 1077　IT
Infradev International, 2190, rue Crescent, pg. 249　IT
Interim Services (Canada) Ltd., 1253 McGill College Ave., Ste. 250, pg. 892　PB
International Correspondence Schools Canadian Ltd., 7475 Sherbrooke St., pg. 784　PB
International Paints (Canada) Ltd., 6615 Park Ave., pg. 339　IT
Intra-Acoustics Company, Ltd., 1001 Domesinare Blvd. West, Ste. 950, pg. 875　PV
Iron-Ore Company of Canada, 1010 Sherbrooke West, Ste. 2500, pg. 967　IT
THE IVACO GROUP, 770, Sherbrooke St. West, 20th Floor, pg. 695　IT
Ivanhoe, 413, rue Saint Jacques, pg. 249　IT
JEOL Canada, Inc., 5757 Cavendish Boulevard, Suite 101, pg. 697　IT
JANIN, 8200, boulevard Decarie, pg. 823　IT
Japan Airlines Company, Ltd., Ste. 1702, Sun Life Bldg., 1155 Metcalfe St., pg. 701　IT
Jet Tours Canada, 2000 Rue Mansfield, Suite 1510, pg. 560　IT
Jeumont-Schneider Quebec inc., 406, Saint-Francois-Xavier, Ste. 101, pg. 706　IT
Johnson & Johnson Inc., 7101 Notre Dame St., pg. 930　PB
Axel Johnson, Inc., Montee de Liesse, pg. 711　IT
Kamik, 554 Montee de Liesse, pg. 549　IT
Klockner Stadler Hurter, Ltd., 1400 Rue Du Fort, pg. 1081　IT
Kodak Canada Inc., 14 Place du Commerce, Ile des Soeurs, pg. 553　PB
Kraft Limited-Kraft Limitee, 8600 Devonshire Rd., pg. 1290　PB
Kronos Canada Inc., 4 Place Ville Marie, Ste. 500, pg. 271　PV
KRUGER INC., 3285 Bedford Rd., pg. 761　IT
L.N.G. Plant, 11201 Henri-Bourassa Blvd. East, pg. 541　IT
Lafarge Canada Inc., 606 Cathcart, Ste. 800, pg. 789　IT
Lally, McFarland & Pantello Advertising Canada Ltd., 1425 Rene Levesque Blvd. W., Ste. 902, pg. 603　IT
Laurentian Bank of Canada, 1981 McGill College Ave., pg. 396　IT
The Laurentian Group Corporation, 1100 Rene-Levesque Blvd. W., pg. 396　IT
Laurentian Trust of Canada, 425 de Maisonneuve Blvd. W., pg. 396　IT
Laurentien Cable TV Inc., 405 Ogilvy Avenue, pg. 241　IT
Les Editions du Feu Vert, 5148, boulevard Saint-Laurent, pg. 539　IT
Les Editions Transcontinental Inc., 1100, boulevard Rene-Levesque Ouest, pg. 539　IT
Les Hebdos Transcontinental, 6455, rue Jean-Talon Est, pg. 539　IT
Les Messageries de Presse Internationale, 4001, boulevard Robert, pg. 796　IT
Les Publications MDN Inc., 612 St. Jacques Rd., pg. 1076　IT
Levesque, Beaubien and Company Inc., 1155 Metcalfe, 5th Floor, pg. 907　IT
Linatex Canada Inc., 5235 Henri Bourassa Blvd. W., pg. 599　IT
Litho Acme, 85, rue de Castelnau Ouest, pg. 538　IT
Lockheed Martin EDS-Canada, 6111 Royalmount Ave., pg. 1009　PB
Magazines Maclean Hunter Quebec, 1001, bd de Maisonneuve Ouest, pg. 1123　IT
MALETTE QUEBEC, INC., 625 Blvd. Rene Levesque West, Ste. 800, pg. 833　IT
Manac Solutions, Five Place Ville Marie, Ste. 1230, pg. 872　PV
Market Facts of Canada, Ltd., 1200 McGill College, pg. 1047　PB
George S. May Canada, Ltd., 615 Rene Levesque Blvd. W., Ste. 1100, pg. 717　PV
McLean Brothers, 1000 Wellington, pg. 698　PV
McQuay Int'l, 6969 Transcanadienne 142, pg. 3　PV

PB - *U.S. Public Companies Volume*
PV - *U.S. Private Companies Volume*
IT - *International Public & Private Companies Volume*

1540

Geographic Index-Non U.S.

Merrill Corporation-Montreal, 1000, rue Wellington, H3C 1V4, pg. 1097 **PB**
Mircor Inc., 612, rue St-Jacques, pg. 1075 **IT**
Mitsui & Co. (Canada), 5 Place Ville Marie, Ste. 3333, pg. 880 **IT**
Molson Brewery Quebec Limited, 1555 Notre Dame St., E., pg. 887 **IT**
Molson Sports and Entertainment, Montreal Forum, 1260 de La Gauchetiere Street West, pg. 887 **IT**
Montreal Fast Print, 9500 Blvd. St. Laurant, pg. 54 **PV**
Montreal Port Corporation, Port of Montreal Bldg., Cite du Havre, Wing No. 1, pg. 255 **IT**
Montreal Trustco, 1800 McGill College Ave., pg. 155 **IT**
Montreal Trustco-Corporate Services Div., 1800 McGill College Ave., pg. 155 **IT**
Montreal Trustco-Financial Operations & Control Div., 1800 McGill College Ave., pg. 155 **IT**
Montreal Trustco Investment Management Services, 1800 McGill College Ave., pg. 155 **IT**
Montreal Trustco-Personal Services Division, 1800 McGill College Ave., pg. 155 **IT**
MONTRUSCO ASSOCIATES, INC., 1501, Avenue McGill College, pg. 888 **PB**
Morgan Stanley Montreal, Tour McGill, 1501 McGill College Ave., Ste. 2310, pg. 1133 **PB**
NBC Clearing Services Incorporated, 1155 Metcalfe, pg. 942
NBC Export Development Corporation Inc., 600 de La Gauchetiere West, 5th Floor, pg. 907
NYK Line-Montreal, 800 Rene-Levesque West, Suite 2740, pg. 942 **IT**
Natcan Investment Management Inc., 1100 University, pg. 907
Natcan Trust Company, 600 de La GauchetiereWest, pg. 907 **IT**
NatExport, 600 de La Gauchetiere West, 5th Floor, pg. 907 **IT**
National Bank Financial Services Inc., 600 de La Gauchetiere West, 6th Floor, pg. 907 **IT**
National Bank Information Corporation Inc., 600 de La Gauchetiere West, pg. 907 **IT**
National Bank Life Insurance Company, 600 de La Gauchetiere West, 6th Floor, pg. 907 **IT**
NATIONAL BANK OF CANADA, 600 de la Gauchetiere St., W., pg. 907 **IT**
National Bank of Greece Canada Branch, pg. 907 **IT**
National Bank Securities Inc., 1100 University, pg. 907 **IT**
National Bearings Limited, 451 Lebeau Blvd., pg. 1485 **IT**
National Tobacco Co. of Canada, 3810 St. Antoine St., pg. 1661 **PB**
Newcastle Coated Paper Inc., 1250 Rene Levesque Blvd. West, Ste. 3800, pg. 1104 **IT**
Nikon Optical Canada Inc., 5075 Fullum St., Ste. 100, pg. 931 **IT**
Jay Norris Canada Inc., 10210 Boul. Pie IX, pg. 1150 **IT**
Northern Cable Holdings Ltd., 405 Ogilvy Avenue, pg. 241 **IT**
Nouveler, 1080, rue de la Gauchetiere ouest, pg. 640 **IT**
NOVERCO, Edifice Unitel, 740, rue Notre-Dame-Ouest, Bureau 1400, pg. 541 **IT**
NOVERGAZ, Edifice Unitel, 740, rue Notre-Dame-Ouest, Bureau 1400, pg. 541 **IT**
Oceanex, pg. 924 **IT**
177229 Canada Inc., 770 Sherbrooke Street West, pg. 696 **IT**
The Optimum Financial Corporation Ltd., 50, Place Cremazie, 12th Flr., pg. 435 **IT**
Optimum Inc., 2100, Drummond, pg. 336 **IT**
Panalpina World Transport (Eastern) Ltd., pg. 1023 **IT**
Patterson Dental Canada Inc., 1205 Henri Bourassa Blvd. W., pg. 1265 **PB**
Peoples, 5590 Royal Mount Ave., pg. 843 **IT**
Photosur Geomat International Inc., 5160 Decarie Blvd., Suite 300, pg. 1162 **IT**
Popcorn Communications, 2598-A, St-Zotique Est, pg. 293 **IT**
Prism Communications Ltee, 360 Notre Dame St. W., Ste. 500, pg. 209 **IT**
Provigo Distribution, 1611 Cremazie Boulevard East, pg. 1073 **IT**
PROVIGO INC., 1611 Cremazie East, pg. 1072 **IT**
Publications economiques, 1100, boulevard Rene-Levesque Ouest, pg. 539 **IT**
Publicis BCP Montreal Inc., Montreal World Trade Ctr., 413 St. Jacques W., 9th Fl., H2Y 1N9, pg. 116 **IT**
Publicis BCP Promotion Inc., Montreal World Trade Ctr., 413 Saint-Jacques St., 9th Fl., pg. 116 **IT**
Publicite McKim Ltee., 1155 Blvd. Rene Levesque W., 28th Flr., pg. 104 **PV**
QIT-Fer Et Titane, 770 Sherbrooke St. W., pg. 1119 **IT**
Quebec Cartier Mining Co., 1801 McGill College Ave., pg. 414 **IT**
Quebecor Communications, Inc., 612 Saint-Jacques Street, pg. 1076 **IT**
QUEBECOR INC., 612 Saint-Jacques Street, pg. 1075 **IT**
Quebecor Multimedia Inc., 612 Saint-Jacques Street, pg. 1076 **IT**
Quebecor Printing, Inc., 612 Saint-Jacques St., pg. 1076 **IT**
Quebecor Printing (USA) Holdings Inc., 612 St. James St. West, pg. 1078 **IT**
REITMANS (CANADA) LIMITED, 250 Sauve St., W., pg. 1102 **IT**
Reitmans Inc., 250 Sauve St. W., pg. 1102 **IT**
REPAP ENTERPRISES INC., 1155 Rene-Levesque Blvd. W., Ste. 2500, pg. 1104 **IT**
Repap International Inc., 1250 Rene-Levesque Blvd. West, Ste. 3800, pg. 1104 **IT**
Repap New Brunswick Inc., 1155 Rene-Levesque Blvd. West, pg. 1104 **IT**

Republic National Bank of New York (Canada), 1981 McGill College Ave., pg. 1381 **PB**
Reseau de Television Quatre Saisons Inc., 405 Ogilvy Avenue, pg. 241 **IT**
Rhone-Poulenc Rorer Canada Inc.-Ethical Division, 8580 Esplanade, pg. 1113 **IT**
Ross-Ellis Ltd., 300 Rue Ann, pg. 538 **IT**
Royal LePage - Quebec Office, 2001 University St., Ste. 1500, pg. 1143 **IT**
RoyNat, 1800 McGill College, pg. 155 **IT**
SEI Corporation, 1002 Sherbrooke St. W., Ste. 2520, pg. 1417 **PB**
SHL Systemhouse - Quebec Region, 740 Notre Dame W., Ste. 860, pg. 1154 **IT**
SITQ Immobilier, 380, rue Saint-Antoine Ouest, pg. 249 **IT**
SNC - Aker Offshore Inc. (AE), 2 Place Felix-Martin, pg. 42 **IT**
SNC-Lavalin, 1100 Rene-Levesque Blvd. West, pg. 1162 **IT**
SNC-LAVALIN GROUP INC., 455 Rene-Levesque Blvd. West, pg. 1161 **IT**
SNC-Lavalin Inc., 485 McGill Street, 11th Floor, pg. 1162 **IT**
Saint Jacques Vallee Young & Rubicam, Inc., 1600 Rene Levesque Blvd. W., pg. 1200 **PV**
St. Lawrence Cement Inc., 1945 Graham Blvd., pg. 628 **IT**
Sanyo Industries Canada Inc., 5660, Royalmount Ave., pg. 1192 **IT**
Seagram Canada, 1430 Peel St., pg. 1217 **IT**
THE SEAGRAM COMPANY LTD., 1430 Peel St., pg. 1214 **IT**
Shannock Quebec Audio and Video Inc., 8569 Dalton Road, pg. 1343 **IT**
SHIRMAX LEASING LTD., 3901 Jarry Street East, pg. 1235 **IT**
Shirmax Retail Ltd., 3901 Jarry St., East, pg. 1235 **IT**
SIDOCI, Ste. 200, 5345 l,Assomption Blvd., pg. 528 **IT**
Signode Fasteners, 6785 St. Jacques, pg. 869 **PB**
SOCANAV INC., 623 Rene Levesque Blvd. W., Ste. 600, pg. 1272 **IT**
Societe d'energie de la Baie James, 500, boul. Rene-Levesque ouest, pg. 640 **IT**
SOCIETE GENERALE DE FINANCEMENT DU QUEBEC, 600 de La Gauchetiere W., Ste. 1700, pg. 1274 **IT**
Soderma, 1501, rue McGill College, pg. 539 **IT**
Sodexho Canada Inc., 774, rue Saint-Paul Ouest, pg. 1275 **IT**
Sofinov, 1981, avenue McGill College, pg. 249 **IT**
SOFTIMAGE Inc., 3510 St.-Lauren Blvd., Ste. 500, pg. 1108 **PB**
Speizman Canada, Inc., 5205 boul. Metropolitain est., pg. 1498 **PB**
Stahl Canada Limited, 380 Deslauriers, pg. 1526 **IT**
Steinberg Inc., 1801 McGill College, Rm. 750, pg. 1272 **IT**
Sudler & Hennessey/Gall Inc., 5690, ave. Royalmount, pg. 1200 **PV**
Sudler & Hennessey: Gall Inc., 4700 Le La Savame, Office 200, pg. 1200 **PV**
Sun Life of Canada, 1155 Metcalfe Street, pg. 1319 **IT**
Sun Life of Canada Benefit Management Limited, Dominion Square, pg. 1319 **IT**
Swiss Bank Corporation (Canada), 800 Rene Levesque Blvd. West, Suite 1620, pg. 1332 **IT**
TQM Pipeline Partnership, 1 Place Ville-Marie, pg. 541 **IT**
Tele-Direct (Publications) Inc., 1600 blvd. Rene-Levesque O, pg. 116 **IT**
Teleglobe Canada Inc., 1000 de La Gauchetiere W., pg. 1373 **IT**
TELEGLOBE, INC., 1000 rue de La Gauchetiere W., pg. 1373 **IT**
Teleglobe, Inc., 1000 de la Gauchetiere W., pg. 1373 **IT**
Teleglobe World Mobility, 1000 de la Gauchetiere W., pg. 1373 **IT**
Telemedia Communications Inc., 1411 Peel St., Ste. 300, pg. 1373 **IT**
TELEMEDIA INC., 1411 Peel St., Ste. 300, pg. 1373 **IT**
TEMBEC INC., Rene Levesque Blvd. W., Ste. 2790, pg. 1374 **IT**
Tioxide Canada Inc., Ste. 100, 9999 Cavendish Blvd., pg. 665 **IT**
Touch Infopublicite Inc. (Infomercials), Montreal World Trade Ctr., 380 Saint Anfoine St., bureau 5300, pg. 116 **IT**
Traction Div., 4915, rue Cote Vertu, H4S 1E2, pg. 1426 **IT**
Tramo Holding Inc., pg. 1023 **IT**
Trans Quebec & Maritimes Pipeline, 1 Place Ville Marie, Ste. 2220, pg. 1417 **IT**
Transcontinental Publications Inc., 1100 boulevard Rene-Levesque Ouest, pg. 539 **IT**
Transfinition, 8800, boulevard Pie IX, pg. 538 **IT**
Trench Electric, Four Farnham, C.P. 253, pg. 113 **IT**
UAP, INC., 7025 Ontario Street East, pg. 1426 **IT**
UNICAN SECURITY SYSTEMS LTD., 7301 Decarie Blvd., pg. 1432 **IT**
Unimedia Inc., 600 Blvd. de Maisonneuve West, Ste. 3200, pg. 632 **IT**
Union Bank of Switzerland (Canada), 2000 McGill College Avenue, pg. 1441 **IT**
Union Special (Canada) Ltd., 5205 Metropolitan Blvd. East, Ste. 1, pg. 716 **IT**
Vachon Division, Two Complexe Desjardins, Ste. 2700, pg. 348 **IT**
Vale-Harmon Enterprises, Ltd., 2700 Brabant-Marineau Rue, pg. 788 **PB**
Velan Inc., 2125 Ward Ave., pg. 400 **IT**
Voyage Assistance International S.A., 59, Rue St. Jacques, pg. 90 **IT**

WF Corroon Canada Inc., 1130 Sherbrooke St. W., Ste. 1500, pg. 1502 **IT**
WWF-Canada, Inc., 11970 Blvd. Albert-Hudon, pg. 1145 **PV**
Wajax Industries Limited, 770 Sherbrooke St. W., Ste. 1750, pg. 1485 **IT**
Warburg Asset Management Canada Ltd., Ste. 603, 1080 Beaver Hall Hill, pg. 1331 **IT**
WESTBURNE INC., 6333 Decarie Blvd., Room 400, pg. 1491 **IT**
Willis Corroon Aerospace of Canada Ltd., 1130 Sherbrooke St. W., Ste. 1500, pg. 1509 **IT**
Willis Corroon Melling Inc., 1130 Sherbrooke St. W., Ste. 1500, pg. 1509 **IT**
Willis Corroon Melling Inc., 1130 Sherbrooke St. West, Suite 1500, pg. 1509 **IT**
Wilson & Lafleur, Limitee, 40 Notre-Dame St. E., pg. 1076 **IT**
Wirth Ltd., P.O. Box 780, Station A, pg. 1150 **IT**
Y & S Candies Plant, 4211 Rouen, pg. 812 **IT**
Yamaichi International (Canada) Limited/Limitee, 600 de Maisonneuve Blvd. W., pg. 1517 **IT**
York Research Canada, Inc., 1000 De La Gauchetiere St. W., pg. 1789 **PB**
York Windpower Corp., 1000 De La Gauchetiere St. W., pg. 1789 **PB**

Moose Jaw

The Clorox Company of Canada Ltd., 501 Hight St., pg. 387 **PB**
Moose Jaw Plant, Box 10, pg. 387 **PB**

Mount Forest

Acme Ruler Co. Ltd., 351 Foster St. North, pg. 17 **PB**
Long Manufacturing Ltd., 205 Industrial Dr., pg. 815 **IT**

Mount Pearl

Newfoundland Containers Ltd., 110 Clyde Avenue, pg. 273 **IT**
SNC-Lavalin, 1118 Topsail Road, pg. 1162 **IT**

Nackawick

St. Anne Chemical Co., Ltd., P.O. Box 1000, pg. 841 **PV**
St. Anne Industries Ltd., Main Rd., pg. 841 **PV**
St. Anne - Nackawic Pulp Co., Ltd., P.O. Box 1000, pg. 841 **PV**

Nanaimo

Hewlett-Packard (Canada) Ltd., 321 Wallace St., Ste. 5, pg. 818 **PB**
Vancouver Island Stevedoring Co. Ltd., 1826 Fremont Rd., pg. 828 **IT**

Nanoose Bay

South Island Woodlands, pg. 828 **IT**

Nanticoke

Air Products Canada Ltd., Regional Road 3, pg. 31 **PB**
Lake Erie Steel Company Ltd., General Delivery, pg. 1299 **IT**

Nepean

Air Products Canada Ltd., 17 Enterprise Ave., Unit C, pg. 31 **PB**
Air Products Canada Ltd., 185 Corkstown Road, MS 22, pg. 31 **PB**
Avnet Computer, 190 Colonnade Rd., pg. 155 **PB**
Bell-Northern Research Ltd., 3500 Carling Ave., pg. 116 **IT**
Brian Controls Division, 9 Antares Dr., pg. 711 **IT**
Fitel Photomatrix Inc., 18 Bentley Ave., pg. 530 **IT**
Gandalf Canada Ltd., 130 Colonnade Rd. S., pg. 540 **IT**
GANDALF TECHNOLOGIES INC., 130 Colonnade Rd. S., pg. 540 **IT**
Interoptics, 14 Capella Ct., pg. 1314 **IT**
KONE Wood Ltd., Bois KONE Ltee, 106 Colonnade Rd., Ste. 220, pg. 14 **IT**
Northern Telecom Canada Limited, Data Networks Div., 1431 Merivale Rd., pg. 969 **IT**
Spar Aerospace, Bldg. 65, 3701 Carling Ave., pg. 1288 **IT**

Neufchatel

Gaz Metropolitain, Inc.-Quebec, 2300 Jean-Perrin Street, pg. 541 **IT**

Neuville

Primes de Luxe Inc., 279 rue des Erables, pg. 1150 **IT**

New Glasgow

The Evening News, pg. 631 **IT**
Kimberly-Clark, Nova Scotia, P.O. Box 549-1D, pg. 959 **PB**

New Liskeard

Northern Telephone Limited, 25 Paget St., pg. 115 **IT**

PB - *U.S. Public Companies Volume*
PV - *U.S. Private Companies Volume*
IT - *International Public & Private Companies Volume*

New Westminster

Allmac Lumber Ltd., Ste. 305, 625 Agnes St., pg. 1071   IT
Callaway Chemical Limited, 1035 Derwent Way, pg. 1726   PB
Canadian Energy Services, 401 Salter St., pg. 74   IT
Canadian Forest Products Ltd., Panel & Fibre Division, 430 Canfor Ave., pg. 260   IT
Ideal Cement Company (B.C.) Ltd., 20 Capilano Way, pg. 628   IT
Industra Service Corporation, 401 Salter St., pg. 74   IT
Industra Thermal Service Corporation, 401 Salter St., pg. 74   IT
Labatt Breweries British Columbia, 210 Brunette Avenue, pg. 679   IT
Market Facts of Canada, Ltd., Royal City Centre, 610 Sixth St., Ste. 235, pg. 1047   PB
New Westminster Division, pg. 828   IT
E.R. Probyn Export Ltd., Suite 305, 625 Agnes Street, pg. 1071   IT
E.R. PROBYN LTD., Ste. 305, 625 Agnes St., pg. 1071   IT
Probyn Log, Ltd., Ste. 305, 625 Agnes St., pg. 1071   IT

Newcastle

Alcell Technologies Inc., pg. 1104   IT
CFAN-AM, 245 Pleasant St., pg. 1123   IT
Manheim's Oshawa Dealers Exchange, Hwy. 401 at Exit 425, pg. 283   PV
Miramichi Pulp & Paper Inc., 345 Curtis Rd., pg. 1104   IT

Newmarket

Asdor Ltd., 1255 Nicholson Road, pg. 61   PB
Dixon Ticonderoga Inc., 220 Pony Dr., Unit 4, pg. 515   PB
Engine Control Systems, Ltd., 165 Pony Dr., pg. 1016   PB
Flender Power Transmission Inc., 1151 Gorham St., Units 11-14, pg. 400   IT
Rogers Cable TV-Newmarket Div., 20 Gladman Ave., pg. 1122   IT

Niagara Falls

Bissell Ltd., Box 1003, 6934 Kinsmen Court, pg. 145   PV
Bright's & Martin's Foods, P.O. Box 90, pg. 411   PB
Day-Timers of Canada, Limited, 4875 Kent Ave., pg. 674   PB
Ekco Canada, Inc., 5781 Allen Ave., pg. 566   PB
Lubrizol Canada Ltd., P.O. Box 598, pg. 1016   PB
Norton Advanced Ceramics of Canada Inc., 8001 Daly Street, pg. 1174   IT
Oneida Canada Ltd., 8699 Stanley Ave., pg. 1226   PB
VINCOR INTERNATIONAL, 4887 Dorchester Rd., pg. 1468   IT
Zippo Manufacturing Company of Canada Limited, 6158 Allandale Ave., pg. 1207   PV

Niagara on the Lake

Foster Wheeler Ltd. (Canada), 509 Glendale Ave. E., pg. 677   PB
InniskilIin Wines, Inc., RR #1, Niagara Parkway, pg. 1468   IT

Nisku

Bently Nevada Canada Ltd., 1906 4th St., pg. 134   PV
Bucyrus-Erie Co. of Canada Ltd., 1310 8th Street, pg. 177   PV
Lufkin Machine Co. Ltd., 1107 8A Street, pg. 1019   PB
Marclin Westeel Division, 1609-8th Street, pg. 698   IT
Nabors Drilling Limited, pg. 1149   PB
National-Oilwell/Dreco Industrial, 506 -17 Ave., pg. 1158   IT
National-Oilwell/Dreco Rig Technology & Construction, 506 -17 Ave., pg. 1158   PB
O.J. Pipelines Corp., Box 169, 1409 Fourth St., pg. 996   PB
Weatherford Canada Ltd., 1306-5th Street, pg. 1750   PB

Nobel

Nobel Plant, Woods Rd., pg. 538   IT

North Bay

Boart Longyear Inc., P.O. Box 330, pg. 76   IT
CKNY/CHNB-TV, 245 Oak St. E., pg. 171   IT
Northmar Distributors, 495 Oak St. W., pg. 1249   IT
The Nugget, 259 Worthington St., W., pg. 631   IT
Rogers Cable Systems, 240 Fee St., pg. 1123   IT
Skega Canada Ltd., 28 Commerce Cres RR 3, pg. 1323   IT
Skega Ltd., 28 Commerce Cres RR 3, pg. 1324   IT
Svedala Skega, 28 Commerce Cres RR 3, pg. 1325   IT

North Vancouver

A&W FOOD SERVICES OF CANADA INC., 171 W. Esplanade, Ste. 300, pg. 1   IT
Honeywell-Measurex Devron, 500 Brooksbook Ave., pg. 833   PB
Olympic Industries, Inc., 221 W. Esplanade, Ste. 402, pg. 670   PB

North York

AXA Insurance, 5700 Yonge St., Ste. 1400, pg. 19   IT
Amdahl Canada Limited, 12 Concorde Pl., Ste. 100, pg. 527   IT
Benckiser Inc., 2005 Shepard Ave. East, pg. 185   IT
Bertrand Faure Components Ltd. - Norfinch Plant, 320 Norfinch Drive, pg. 193   IT
Blackwood Hodge (Canada) Ltd., Ten Suntract Rd., pg. 231   IT
Blackwood Hodge Equipment Ltd., Ten Suntract Rd., pg. 231   IT
Brookfield Homes-Eastern Region, 100 Sheppard Ave. E., Ste. 920, pg. 228   IT
CCH Canadian Ltd., 990 Sheppard Ave. East, Ste. 300, pg. 1513   IT
CANADIAN ERECTORS LTD., 100 Shepard Ave. E., Ste. 930, pg. 256   IT
Centra Gas Ontario Inc., 245 Yorkland Blvd., pg. 1492   IT
Clarendon Imports Inc., 1500 Don Mills Rd., pg. 1130   IT
Cognos Inc.-Toronto Sales Office, North American Life Center, Tower II, 12th Fl., 5700 Younge St., pg. 306   IT
Continental General Tire Inc., 490 Norfinch Drive, pg 327   IT
Custom Cheques of Canada, 360 Magnetic Dr., pg. 1077   IT
Davis & Henderson Limited, 2 Lansing Sq., Ste. 1101, pg. 384   IT
Dell Computer Corporation, 155 Gordon Baker Road, Suite 501, pg. 496   PB
Fuji Graphic Systems Canada Inc., 88 St. Regis Crescent South, pg. 524   IT
Fujitsu Systems Business of Canada, Inc., 5140 Yonge St., Ste. 2000, pg. 527   IT
Head Office Reference Laboratory, Ltd., 1140 Shephard Ave. West, Unit 1, pg. 1449   PB
H.J. Heinz Co. of Canada Ltd., 5700 Yonge St., 21st Fl., pg. 806   PB
Honeywell Limited, The Honeywell Centre, 155 Gordon Baker Rd., pg. 835   PB
House of Craven Ltd., 1500 Don Mills Rd., pg. 1130   IT
Household Financial Corporation Limited, 100 Sheppard Ave. East, pg. 842   PB
ICI Canada Inc., 90 Sheppard Ave. E., pg. 664   IT
IDC Canada, 501 Oakdale Road, pg. 570   PV
ING Trust Company of Canada, 111 Gordon Baker Road, pg. 650   IT
Janssen/Ortho Inc., 19 Greenbelt Dr., pg. 930   IT
Loblaw Companies Limited, 6220A Yonge St., pg. 1495   IT
MSA Canada, Inc., 148 Norfinch Drive, pg. 1114   PB
Marsulex Inc., 111 Gordon Baker Rd., Ste. 300, pg. 599   IT
McGraw-Hill Information Systems Co. of Canada Ltd., 270 Yorkland Boulevard, pg. 1072   IT
Motorola Canada Ltd./Motorola Canada Limitee, 3900 Victoria Park Ave., pg. 1139   IT
National Utility Service (Canada) Ltd., Cosmopolitan Centre, 111 Gordon Baker Rd., pg. 787   PV
Nestle Canada Inc., 25 Sheppard Ave., West, pg. 921   IT
NOMA INDUSTRIES LIMITED, 4100 Yonge St., Ste. 502, pg. 954   IT
Norsten Canada Inc., 251 Consumers Rd., 9th Fl., pg. 1192   PB
Norvista, 20 York Mills Road, Suite 402, pg. 486   IT
Owens-Corning Canada, 5140 Yonge Street, pg. 1237   PB
Premark Canada Inc., 190 Railside Rd., pg. 1323   PB
Procter & Gamble Inc., 4711 Yonge St., pg. 1331   PB
qad.inc., 5650 Yonge Street, pg. 1345   PB
Rockwell International of Canada Switching Systems, Suite 620, Yorkland Boulevard, M2J 5C1, pg. 1401   PB
Rothmans Benson & Hedges Inc., 1500 Don Mills Rd., pg. 1130   IT
Rothmans Inc., 1500 Don Mills Rd., pg. 1129   IT
Savin Canada Inc., 4100 Yonge Street, Ste. 600, pg. 1116   IT
SLATER INDUSTRIES INC., Yonge Corp. Centre, Ste. 410, 4100 Yonge St., pg. 1262   IT
Southam Magazine and Information Group, 1450 Don Mills Road, pg. 631   IT
Sunoco Group, 36 York Mills Road, pg. 1320   IT
TSN COMMUNICATIONS, 2225 Sheppard Ave. E., pg. 1343   IT
Unisys Canada Inc., 2001 Sheppard Ave., E., pg. 1671   PB
Volvo Canada Ltd., 175 Gordon Baker Rd., pg. 1477   IT
Volvo Canadian Holdings Ltd., 175 Gordon Baker Rd., pg. 1477   IT
Wyeth Ltd., pg. 82   IT
Xerox Canada Holdings Inc., 5650 Yonge St., pg. 1785   PB
Xerox Canada Ltd., 5650 Yonge St., pg. 1785   PB
Yamaha Motor Canada Ltd., 480 Gordon Baker Rd., pg. 1516   IT

Nuns Island

Data Business Forms, 1 place de Commerce, Ste. 400, pg. 384   IT
Formules d'Affaires Data, 1 place de Controller, Ste. 400, pg. 384   IT

Oakville

AGRA International Limited, 2010 Winston Park Drive, pg. 30   IT
Acuson Canada, Ltd., 644 Speers Rd., 3rd Floor, pg. 18   IT
AGRA Cambrian Inc., 100-2010 Winston Park Drive, pg. 30   IT
AGRA CI Power Limited, 2010 Winston Park Drive, Suite 100, pg. 30   IT
AGRA Inc., 2010 Winston Park Road, pg. 30   IT
AGRA Monenco, 2010 Winston Park Drive, Ste. 100, pg. 30   IT
AGRA Vadeko Inc., 2902 South Sheridan Way, Ste. 103, pg. 30   IT
Amersham Canada Limited, 1166 S. Service Rd. W., pg. 992   IT
Amicon Canada Ltd., 2333 Wyecroft Rd., pg. 1113   PB
Atlas Van Lines (Canada) Ltd., 485 N. Service Rd., pg. 97   PV
Atochem Canada Inc., 700 Third Line, pg. 446   IT
Autologic Information International, Inc., 2401 Royal Windsor Dr., pg. 1724   PB
Baker Cummins, Inc., 461 N. Service Rd. West, pg. 915   PB
Bay Mills Limited, 305 Church St., Ste. 200, pg. 1177   IT
Biomet Canada, Inc., 790 Redwood Sq., Unit One, pg. 231   PB
Brunswick International (Canada) Limited, 355 Iroquois Shore Rd., pg. 266   PB
C & J Clark Canada, Ltd., 2881 Brighton Road, pg. 297   IT
Canadian Road Credit Company, Limited, The Canadian Road, pg. 665   IT
CanAmera Foods, 2190 South Service Road West, pg. 1195   IT
Clarion Canada Inc., 2239 Winston Park Dr., pg. 296   IT
Dionex Canada Ltd., 586 Argus Rd., Ste. 4, pg. 510   PB
Dufferin Construction, 505 North Service Rd. East, pg. 628   IT
Fanchem, Ltd., 1141 S. Service Road, West, Unit A, pg. 828   PV
Ferro Industrial Products Ltd., 354 Davis Rd., pg. 619   PB
Fieldfresh Farms Inc., 886 Sinclair Rd., pg. 1012   IT
Ford Credit Canada Ltd., The Canadian Road, pg. 665   PB
Ford Motor Co. of Canada Ltd, pg. 666   PB
Jannock Steel Fabricating Company, 1296 South Service Rd. W., pg. 698   IT
Jenisys Engineered Products, 1296 S. Service Road W., pg. 698   IT
LONG MANUFACTURING, LTD., 656 Kerr St., pg. 815   IT
Lubrizol Canada Ltd., 277 Lakeshore, Rd. East, Suite 204, pg. 1016   PB
Mannesmann Demag Material Handling Ltd., 1155 N. Service Rd., West, pg. 840   IT
McCain Refrigerated Foods Inc., 550 Spears Road, pg. 850   IT
Menasco Aerospace Ltd., 1400 S. Service Rd. West, pg. 402   PB
Mirrlees Blackstone (Canada) Ltd., 355 Wyecroft Rd., L6K 2H2, pg. 125   IT
OMRON Dualtec Automotive Electronics, Inc., 2270 Bristol Circle, pg. 1005   IT
Otis Canada Inc., 710 Dorval Dr. Ste. 700, pg. 1691   PB
Raleigh Industries of Canada Ltd., 2124 London Lane, pg. 394   IT
Roberts Pharmaceutical of Canada, 400 Iroquois Shore Rd., pg. 1394   PB
Royal Life Insurance Company of Canada, Royal Life Bldg., 277 Lakeshore Rd. E., pg. 1130   IT
Rubbermaid Canada Inc. Commercial Products, 2130 S. Service Rd. W., pg. 1411   PB
SM-Cyclo of Canada, Ltd., 870 Equestrian Court, pg. 1315   IT
Searle Canada Inc., 400 Iroquois Shore Rd., pg. 1126   PB
SmithKline Beecham Canada, Inc., 2030 Bristoll Circle, pg. 1265   IT
SmithKline Beecham Pharmaceuticals Inc., 2030 Bristol Cir., pg. 1266   IT
Trimac Transportation-Eastern Division, 2284 Wyecroft Road, pg. 1424   IT
VicWest Steel Division North American Building Products, 1296 South Service Rd. W., pg. 698   IT
Wella Canada Inc., 2071 S. Service Rd. W., pg. 1489   IT

Oliver

General Coach, Ninth St. E., pg. 1602   PB

Orangeville

Douglas & Lomason Company, 81 Centennial Rd., pg. 830   IT
Greening Donald Co. Ltd., 16 Commerce Road, pg. 1389   IT
Nature's Sunshine Products of Canada, Ltd., 191 C-Line #11, pg. 1167   PB
Synergistics Industries Limited, 17 Tideman Drive, pg. 734   PB

Orillia

Coast RV, Inc., 381 W. St. S., pg. 388   PB
KFW Canada, Inc., Progress Industrial Pk., RR #1, pg. 1338   IT
Kubota Metal Corporation (Fahramet Division), 25 Commerce Rd., pg. 763   IT
Otaco Seating Co., Ltd., Harvie Settlement Rd., pg. 61   PV
Polytech Netting Industries, Forrest Home Indus. Park, P.O. Box 2312, pg. 1362   IT
Tritech, 301 Forest Ave., L3V 6R9, pg. 1424   IT
Uniplast Industries, Inc., 301 Forest Ave., pg. 1424   IT
Wynn's-Precision (Canada) Ltd., 255 Hughes Rd., pg. 1783   PB

PB - *U.S. Public Companies Volume*
PV - *U.S. Private Companies Volume*
IT - *International Public & Private Companies Volume*

Orleans

Tampella Power Corporation, 210 Centrum Blvd., Ste. 209, pg. 1354 IT

Oshawa

General Motors of Canada Ltd., 1908 Colonel Sam Drive, pg. 722 PB
Klockner-Pentaplast of Canada, Inc., Oshawa Executive Center, Ste. 604, pg. 737
Mentor Medical Systems, Canada, 1333 Boundary Rd., L1J 6Z7, pg. 1086 PB
North American Van Lines Canada Ltd., 850 Champlain Ave., pg. 1192 PB
Rogers Cable TV-Pine Ridge, 301 Marwood Dr., pg. 1122 IT
Snowden Rubber Industries, 846 Farewell Ave., pg. 1423 IT

Ottawa

AMS Management Systems Canada Inc., 180 Elgin St., Ste. 700, pg. 86 PB
AST Canada, Inc., 155 Queen Street, Ste. 900, pg. 1182 IT
AGRA Spectrocan Limited, 1145 Hunt Club Road, Ste. 600, pg. 30 IT
AlliedSignal Aerospace Canada Ocean Defense Systems, 50 O'Connor St., Ste. 1222, pg. 53 PB
Anixter Ottawa, 1335 Carling Ave., Suite 109, pg. 115 PB
Avenor Inc., 1145 Hunt Club Rd., Ste. 400, pg. 102 IT
B.A. Bank Note, 975 Gladstone Ave., K1N 8V4, pg. 1077 IT
Bakermet Inc., 2555 Sheffield Rd., pg. 695 IT
Bank of Montreal - Ottawa, Place Bell Canada, 160 Elgin St., pg. 153 IT
Bofors Canada Ltd, 130 Albert St., Ste. 416, pg. 278 IT
CJOH-TV, 1500 Merivale Rd., pg. 171 IT
CSC, Ottawa, 155 Queen St., 9th Fl., Suite 808, pg. 1482 IT
CANADA PORTS CORPORATION, 99 Metcalfe St., pg. 255 IT
Canadian Stebbins Engineering & Mfg. Co. Ltd., 2700 Lancaster Rd., pg. 1037 PV
Chargex Ltd./Chargex Ltee, 50 O'Connor St., Ste. 1015, pg. 257 IT
COGNOS INC., 3755 Riverside Dr., pg. 305 IT
Cognos Inc.-Ottawa Sales Office, 275 Slater Street, Ste. 700, pg. 306 IT
COREL CORPORATION, 1600 Carling Ave., pg. 331 IT
DMR Group, Inc., Constitution Sq., 360 Albert St., Suite 600, pg. 527 IT
Data Images, 1283 Algoma Rd., pg. 1004 PB
Eddy Paper Company Limited, pg. 1495 IT
FS Canada, Inc., 2460 Lancaster Rd., pg. 818 PV
Fenco MacLaren Inc., 170 Laurier Ouest Avenue, Suite 1100, pg. 1162 IT
Financial Collection Agencies, Suite 700, 170 Metcalfe Street, pg. 470 IT
GPC Government Policy Consultants (Federal), 350 Albert St., Ste. 1600, K1R 1A4, pg. 1225 PB
GPC International Holdings, 350 Albert St., Ste. 1600, pg. 1225 PB
Green Line Investor Service, Constitution Sq., 350 Albert St., Ste. 250, pg. 1401 PB
Hewlett-Packard (Canada) Ltd., 2670 Queensview Dr., pg. 818 PB
Howe AGRA Limited, 1160 Hunt Club Rd., #600, pg. 31 IT
JDS Fitel Inc., 570 Heston Drive, pg. 531 IT
Kamyr Canada Inc., Royal Bank Centre, 90 Sparks St., Ste. 1132, pg. 35 IT
Kodak Canada Inc., 55 Metcalfe St., Ste. 270, pg. 553 PB
Lansdowne Technologies Inc., 275 Slater St., Ste. 1001, pg. 259 IT
Litton Systems Canada Ltd., 220 Laurier Ave. W., Ste. 730, pg. 1005 PB
Lockheed Canada, 2421 Lancaster Rd., pg. 1009 PB
Loeb Inc., 1430 Blair Place, pg. 1073 IT
Martin Marietta Canada Ltd., 50 O'Connor St., Ste. 1450, pg. 1009 PB
Metropolitan Life Insurance Company Of Canada, 99 Bank Street, pg. 738 PV
Mil Systems Engineering, Ste. 200, 1150 Morrison Dr., pg. 385 IT
Modern Building Cleaning Inc., 1470 Triole St., pg. 79 PV
Montrusco Associates, 350 Sparks Street, Suite 211, pg. 888 IT
Ottawa Center, 2773 Lancaster Rd., pg. 273 IT
The Ottawa Citizen, 1101 Baxter Rd., pg. 631 IT
The Ottawa Sun, 380 Hunt Club Rd., pg. 1320 IT
Port Colbourne, 99 Metcalfe St., pg. 255 IT
Port of Belledune, 99 Metcalfe St., pg. 255 IT
Port of Prescott, 99 Metcalfe St., pg. 255 IT
Riverside Terrace (Ottawa) Limited, 225 Metcalf St., Ste. 308, pg. 1319 IT
Rogers Cable Systems, 475 Richmond Rd., pg. 1123 IT
Royal Insurance Ottawa Regional Centre, Constitution Sq., 360 Albert St., Ste. 500, pg. 1131 IT
Royal LePage - Ottawa Office, 220 Laurier Ave. W., Ste. 900, pg. 1143 IT
SAIC Canada, 56 Sparks St., Ste. 306, pg. 976 PV
SHL International, 50 O'Connor Street, Suite 501, pg. 1154 IT
SHL SYSTEMHOUSE, 50 O'Connor St., Ste. 501, pg. 1154 IT
SHL Systemhouse - Canada/Asia, 50 O'Connor St., Ste. 501, pg. 1154 IT

SHL Systemhouse - Ottawa Region, 50 O'Connor St., Ste. 501, pg. 1154 IT
SNC-Lavalin, 170 Laurier Oest Avenue, Suite 1100, pg. 1162 IT
Southam News Service, 151 Sparks Street, Ste. 200, pg. 631 IT
Sun Microsystems of Canada-Ottawa, 955 Green Valley Crest, Ste. 165, pg. 1532 PB
Tektronix Canada Inc.-Ottawa, pg. 1567 PB
Texas Instruments Canada, 301 Moodie Dr. Ste. 102, pg. 1586 PB
Victor Temporary Services, Ltd., 130 Albert St., Ste. 19C, pg. 892 IT
W1310/CKBY Radio, 112 Kent St., Ste. 1900, pg. 1124 IT
Willis Corroon Melling Inc., 75 Albert St., Ste. 205, pg. 1509 IT

Outremont

Flashmedia Advertising Inc., 932 Champagneur St., pg. 1076 IT

Owen Sound

Canadian Cement Ltd., 2125 16th Ave. E., pg. 1084 PB
Cylinder Division, P.O. Box 38, 1000 6th Street East, pg. 1262 PB
Rogers Cable Systems, 1040 20th St., East, pg. 1123 IT
Sun Times, 290 Ninth St. E., pg. 632 IT
The Sun Times, 290 9th St. E., pg. 631 IT
Transcontinental Printing Inc. - Owen Sound, 1749 20th Street East, pg. 538 IT

Paris

Mary Maxim, Ltd., pg. 716 PV

Pembroke

CHRO-TV, Forest Lea Rd., pg. 171 IT

Penetanguishene

Advanced Monobloc Inc., 163 Robert Street East, pg. 238 IT

Perth

Albany International Canada-Perth, pg. 37 PB
Brown Shoe Co. of Canada Ltd., 1857 Rogers Rd., pg. 262 PB

Peterborough

Baskin Robbins Production Facility, 375 Aylmer St., pg. 63 IT
EMAB Canada Div., P.O. Box 4250, pg. 441 IT
FISHER GAUGE LIMITED, 194 Sophia St., pg. 491 IT
Fishercast, 194 Sophia Street, pg. 491 IT
Fishertech, 194 Sophia Street, pg. 491 IT
G.E. Canada, Peterborough, 107 Park St. North, pg. 713 PB
JPE Canada Inc., 775 Technology Dr., K9J 6Z8, pg. 919 PB
Kendall Canada Ltd., 1100 Curity Ave., pg. 1647 PB
Messier-Dowty Electronics, 2000 Fisher Dr., pg. 1340 IT
Milltronics, 1954 Technology Dr., pg. 1150 IT
Outboard Marine Corp. of Canada Ltd., 910 Monaghan Rd., pg. 478 PV
Peterborough Port Hope Ready Mix, 3391 Parkhill Rd. E., pg. 629 IT
The Quaker Oats Co. of Canada Ltd., Quaker Park, pg. 1348 PB
Rogers Cable Systems, 685 The Queensway, pg. 1123 IT
Strano Syssco Foodservice Limited, 65 Elmdale Road, pg. 1552 PB

Pickering

Checkpoint Canada, 1815 Ironstone Manor-Unit 3, L1W 3W9, pg. 343 PB
Fisons Corporation Limited, 1851 Sandstone Manor, pg. 1111 PB
Hubbell Canada Inc., 870 Brock Rd. S., pg. 845 PB
Konica Business Machines Canada, Ltd., 1503 Sandy Beach Rd., pg. 749 IT
Mazda Canada, Inc., 821 Brock Road South, pg. 695 IT
Puritan-Bennett Canada Ltd., 1915 Clements Rd., Unit 7, pg. 1040 PB
Supreme/Mirro, 915 Sandy Beach Rd., pg. 1178 PB

Pinawa

Atomic Energy of Canada Ltd., Whiteshell Laboratories, pg. 97 IT

Plattsville

Carborundum Abrasives Inc./Carborundum Abrasifs Inc., 28 Albert St., pg. 1174 PV
CIBA-GEIGY Canada Ltd.-Honeywood Research Farm, pg. 976 IT

Pointe Noire

Wabush Mines, pg. 414 IT

Pointe-Claire

Albany Engineered Systems-Canada, 805 Bancroft, pg. 1593 PB
Auto-trol, LTD., 1 Holiday St., Ste. 500, pg. 148 PB
Autodesk Canada Inc./Montreal, East Tower, 5th Fl., 1 Holiday St., pg. 149 PB
Avon Canada, Inc., 5500 Trans Canada Hwy., pg. 156 PB
Bayer (Canada) Inc., 7600 Transcanada Hwy., pg. 175 IT
Bobst Canada, Inc., 274 Avenue Labrosse, pg. 198 IT
The Canadian Salt Co. Ltd., 755 St. John's Blvd., pg. 1135 PB
A.M. Castle & Co. (Canada), Inc., 835 Selkirk Avenue, pg. 313 PB
COTT CORPORATION, 333 Avro Ave., pg. 337 IT
Cott Corporatoin - North East Region (Quebec), 333 Avro Avenue, pg. 337 IT
Det Norske Veritas, 183 Place Frontenac, pg. 396 IT
Du Pont Canada-Pointe Claire, 6000 route, pg. 532 PB
GFI Inc., 180 Labrosse Ave., pg. 725 IT
ITT Flygt, 300 Labrosse Ave., pg. 860 PB
Kemira Paper Chemicals Canada, Inc., 1 Holiday St., E. Tower Level 5, pg. 728 IT
Lorentzen & Wettre Canada Inc., 125 Hymus Blvd., pg. 271 IT
Mallinckrodt Canada, Inc., 7500 Trans Canada Hwy., pg. 1040 PB
Manufacture Leviton du Canada, 165 Hymus Blvd., pg. 663 PV
Milgray/Montreal, 6600 Trans Canada Highway, pg. 207 IT
Plantronics Canada Limited, c/o Andrews & Associates, 225 Hymus Blvd., Ste. 10, pg. 1308 PB
Prior Data Sciences Ltd., Ste. 130, 6600 Transcanada Hwy., pg. 1288 IT
Quebecor Photolitho, 2400, route Trans-Canada, pg. 1077 IT
Siemens Canada Ltd., 7300 Trans Canada Hwy., pg. 1247 IT
Staveley Weighing Systems Canada, Inc., 217 Brunswick Blvd., pg. 1299 IT
Sulzer Canada Inc., pg. 1306 IT
Tektronix Canada Inc.-Pte. Claire, pg. 1567 PB

Polaris

Cominco Ltd.-Polaris Operations, Little Cornwallis Island, pg. 308 IT

Port Alberni

Estevan Division, 3406 - 3rd. Ave., pg. 828 IT
Forest Industries Flying Tankers Limited, R.R. #3 Lakeshore Dr., pg. 828 IT
Franklin River Division, pg. 828 IT
MacMillan Bloedel Limited - Alberni Pacific Div., 2500 1st Avenue, pg. 828 IT
MacMillan Bloedel Limited, Building Materials - Alberni Region, 4259 6th Avenue, pg. 828 IT
MacMillan Bloedel Specialties, 4000 Stamp Ave., pg. 828 IT
Somass Division, 3500 Harbour Rd., pg. 828 IT

Port Colborne

P.C. Drop Forgings Division, 837 Reuter Road, pg. 695 IT

Port Coquitlam

Candraft Detailing, Inc., 1424 Broadway St., Ste. 100, pg. 1305 PB
Coast Steel Fabricators Ltd., 1515 Kingsway Ave., pg. 31 IT
Esco Ltd., 1855 Kingsway, B3C 1C1, pg. 383 PV
Flowserve Duriron Canada Inc., 2540 Shaughnessy, Ste. 200, pg. 659 PB
Rogers Cable TV-Fraser, 1820 Kingsway Ave., pg. 1122 IT
Sysco/Konings Wholesale, 1346 Kingsway Ave., pg. 1552 PB
Web Press Graphics Ltd., 1589 Kebet Way, pg. 1077 IT

Port Hardy

BHP Minerals Canada Ltd., pg. 227 IT

Port Hawkesbury

Stora Forest Industries, pg. 1304 IT

Port Hope

Atomic Energy of Canada Ltd., Port Hope Field Office, Suite 104, 67 John Street, pg. 97 IT
CASHWAY BUILDING CENTRES LTD., 205 Peters St., pg. 274 IT
Port Hope Evening Guide, 64 John Street, pg. 631 IT
Textron Automative Trim Operations, 128 Peter St., pg. 1590 PB

Port McNeill

Port McNeill Div., pg. 828 IT

Port Moody

Andres Wines (B.C.) Ltd., 2120 Vintner St., pg. 76 IT

PB - *U.S. Public Companies Volume*
PV - *U.S. Private Companies Volume*
IT - *International Public & Private Companies Volume*

Geographic Index-Non U.S.

Port Robinson

Esquire Canada, Inc., 125 South Street North, pg. 1047   PV

Portage la Prairie

CIBA-GEIGY Canada Ltd.-Elm River Research Farm, pg. 976   IT
Outdoor Technologies - Canada, 815 Phillips St., pg. 822   PV

Powell River

Powell River Division, 6270 Yew St., pg. 828   IT

Preissac

Bousquet Complex, 2 Bousquet Road, pg. 169   IT

Prescott

Newell Window Furnishings Co., 606 Hyde St., pg. 1178   PB
Warnaco of Canada Limited, 707 St. Lawrence Ave., pg. 1738   PB

Prince Albert

CKBI/CIPA-TV, Prince Albert, 22-Tenth St. W., pg. 171   IT

Prince George

B.C. Chemicals Limited, pg. 260   IT
Canadian Forest Products Ltd., Clear Lake Division, Suite 5, 1257 4th Ave., pg. 260   IT
Canadian Forest Products Ltd., Isle Pierre Division, Bag Service, pg. 260   IT
Canadian Forest Products Ltd., Netherlands Division, pg. 260   IT
Canadian Forest Products Ltd., Prince George Pulp & Paper Mills Div., P.O. Box 6000, pg. 260   IT
Northwood Forest Industries, Ltd., P.O. Box 9000, pg. 1076   PB
Northwood Pulp & Timber Ltd., P.O. Box 9000, pg. 1076   PB
The Prince George Citizen, 150 Brunswick St., pg. 631   IT

Prince Rupert

Prince Rupert Port Corporation, 110 Third Ave., W., pg. 255   IT

Princeville

Altra Marine Products, Inc., 65 St. Henri St., pg. 479   PV

Quebec

Ascenseurs Drolet KONE Inc., 1730, Ave. Newton, pg. 747   IT
Beaudry Maple Products, Inc., pg. 159   PV
Bel-Air Fence Branch, 2400, rue Chappe, pg. 695   IT
Bertolli Canada Inc., 1680 Fleetwood Rd., pg. 655   IT
Bomem, Inc., pg. 835   IT
Bridgeston/Firestone Tire Manufacturing Operations-Joliette, 1200 Firestone Blvd., pg. 213   IT
CSA Recherche Ltee, 445, ave St-Jean Baptiste, Suite 100, pg. 243   IT
COSSETTE COMMUNICATION MARKETING, 437 Grande Allee E., pg. 335   IT
Cossette Communication-Marketing (Quebec) Inc., 437 Grande-Allee E., pg. 336   IT
J.B. Dionne Ltd., 151 Rioux, pg. 1074   IT
Donohue Inc., 801 Chemin Saint-Louis, pg. 1075   IT
Donohue Malbaie, Inc., 801 Chemin St. Louis, pg. 1174   PB
Donohue Matane, Inc., 801, chemin Saint-Louis, pg. 1075   IT
GPC Government Policy Consultants (Quebec), 1150, Claire Fontaine, G1R 5G4, pg. 1225   IT
Groupe Beton Quebec, 780 St. Joseph Blvd., pg. 629   IT
Hewlett-Packard (Canada) Ltd., 1165 Boul. Le Bourgneuf, Ste. 200, pg. 818   PB
Impact Recherche, 437 Grande-Allee E., pg. 336   IT
JFD Distribution, 15739, rue pierrefonds, pg. 539   IT
Le Concorde, 1225 Place Montcalm., pg. 1011   PB
Les Messageries Publi-Nord, 31, boulevard de la Seigneurie, pg. 539   IT
Les Messageries Publi-Tech, 710, rue Bouvier, pg. 539   IT
Phillips-Fitel Inc., 234 Rue Leonidas Rimouski, pg. 531   IT
Port of Quebec Corporation, 150 Dalhousie St., pg. 255   IT
Promotion Blitz Inc., 425 Grande-Allee E., pg. 336   IT
Quebec & Maritimes Div. St. Lawrence Cement, 780 St. Joseph Blvd., pg. 629   IT

Red Deer

Superior Emergency Vehicles, Ltd., 6430 Goldenwest Ave., pg. 617   PB

Regina

CKCK-TV, #1 Hwy. E., pg. 171   IT

CIBA-GEIGY Canada Ltd., 484 Henderson Dr., pg. 976   IT
Data Business Forms, 445 Mawwell Crescent, pg. 384   IT
DEGELMAN INDUSTRIES LTD., 272 Industrial Dr., pg. 388   IT
Financial Collection Agencies, Suite 200, 2332 11th Avenue, pg. 470   IT
Heartland Livestock Services, CDSL Tower, Suite #205, 1900 Albert Street, pg. 1195   IT
Hewlett-Packard (Canada) Ltd., 1848 McAra St., pg. 818   PB
Hylar Metal Products, pg. 388   IT
Kalium Chemicals, Ltd., 1200-1801 Hamilton St., pg. 856   IT
Koyl Commercial Real Estate Services Ltd., 1914 Hamilton Street, Suite 900, pg. 1143   IT
Molson Saskatchewan Brewery Ltd., 1300 Dewdney Ave., pg. 887   IT
Palmer Jarvis Advertising, 1401 Chateau Towers, 1920 Broad St., pg. 1022   IT
Printwest Communications, 1150 8th Avenue, pg. 1195   IT
SHL Systemhouse - Regina, 2500 Victoria Ave., Ste. 704, pg. 1154   IT
SGI Canada Insurance Services Ltd., 2260 11th Ave., pg. 1195   IT
SASKATCHEWAN GOVERNMENT INSURANCE, SGI, 2260-11th Avenue, pg. 1195   IT
SASKATCHEWAN WHEAT POOL, 2625 Victoria Avenue, pg. 1195   IT
SASKFOR MacMillan, 1055 Fleury Street, pg. 829   IT
SASKPOWER, 2025 Victoria Avenue, pg. 1195   IT
SaskPower Commercial, 2025 Victoria Avenue, pg. 1196   IT
Tampella Power Canada, Inc., 2022 Cornwall Street, Suite 105, pg. 1354   IT

Rexdale

Cadillac Plastic (Canada) Ltd., 91 Kelfield St., M9W 5A4, pg. 781   PB
Canron Inc., 100 Disco Road, pg. 695   PB
Carrier Ontario, 101 Claireville Dr., pg. 1691   PB
Circle Freight International (Canada) Ltd., 81 Kelfield St., Unit 10, pg. 372   PB
Cleveland Twist Drill Canada Limited, 23 Fasken Dr., pg. 950   PB
Craftwell Containers & Packaging Limited, 61 Baywood Road, pg. 761   IT
Danisco Ingredients Canada Inc., 10 Carlson Ct., Ste. 580, pg. 378   IT
Dayton Superior Canada Ltd., 396 Atwell Dr., pg. 932   PV
A.B. Dick Company of Canada, Ltd., 94 Brockport Dr., pg. 791   PV
Duro-Test Canada, 419 Attwell Dr., pg. 349   PB
Echlin Canada Inc., 500 Carlingview Dr., pg. 560   PB
Fabrication Operations East, 100 Disco Road, pg. 695   IT
Max Gruenhut International Canada Inc, 81 Kelfield Street, Unit 10, pg. 373   PB
Handy & Harman of Canada Ltd., 290 Carlingview Dr., pg. 780   PB
Kamro Lighting Products Ltd., 24 Vulcan St., pg. 725   PB
Kellogg Canada Inc., 6700 Finch Ave. W., pg. 947   PB
Kinetics, Inc., A Haworth Co., 110 Carrier Dr., pg. 512   PV
Lawter Intl. (Canada) Inc., 29 Iron St., pg. 981   PB
The Master's Workshop Corporation, 306 Rexdale Blvd., Units 1-9, pg. 1124   IT
Melitta Canada Inc., 75 Westmore Dr., pg. 857   IT
Mott's Canada Division, 170 Attwell Drive, pg. 248   IT
NVF Industries of Canada Ltd., 10 McLachlan Dr., pg. 772   PV
Periphonics Corporation, 151 Carlingview Drive, pg. 1279   PB
Schweppes Canada Division, 170 Attwell Drive, pg. 248   IT
Trimfit Company Limited, 375 Rexdale Blvd., pg. 1103   PV
Victaulic Company of Canada Limited, 65 Worcester Road, pg. 1138   PV
Xtek Canada, Ltd., 1344 Martingrove Rd., pg. 1194   PV
York Lithographing, 8 Tidemore Ave., pg. 1123   IT

Richardson

Regina Seed Processors Ltd., pg. 1195   IT

Richmond

A-R Technologies, #220-13155 Delf Place, pg. 829   IT
A-R Technologies, 13155 Delf Pl., Ste. 220, pg. 604   IT
AST Canada, Inc., 5600 Parkwood Way, Ste. 550, pg. 1182   IT
AGRA Foundations (Pacific) Limited, 206 11240 Bridgeport Road, pg. 30   IT
AGRA Marine Construction Limited, 16031 River Rd., pg. 30   IT
Air BC, 4740 Agar Dr., pg. 36   IT
Air Products Canada Ltd., 9751 Van Horne Way, pg. 31   PB
AlliedSignal Aerospace Canada, Aeromarine, 4440 Stark St., pg. 50   PB
Anixter Vancouver, Ste. 140, 13480 Crestwood Pl., pg. 116   PB
Antec Group, Unit 140-13480 Crestwood Pl., pg. 117   PB
Canadian Art Prints, 160-6551 Westminster Highway, pg. 503   IT
Comdisco Canada Ltd., 10691 Shellbridge Way, Ste. 130, pg. 408   PB
Daewoo Corp. - Vancouver, 3830 Jacombs Rd., Ste. 103, pg. 358   PB
Denny's of Canada, 125-10551 Shellbridge Way, pg. 23   PB

Domcor - British Columbia, 2471 Simpson Road, pg. 415   IT
Fields Stores, 3751 Viking Way, pg. 637   IT
Force 10 Marine Ltd., 23080 Hamilton Rd., pg. 1705   PB
GAULT DISTRIBUTORS INC., 3960 Jacombs Rd., Unit 150, pg. 541   IT
GRANDETEL TECHNOLOGIES INC., 13500 Maycrest Way, Suite 135, pg. 556   IT
Hewlett-Packard (Canada) Ltd., 10691 Shellbridge Way, pg. 818   PB
International Aviation Terminals Inc., pg. 1494   IT
Kirkland & Rose Ltd., 2480 Viking Way, pg. 244   IT
MCL Pile Driving, 206 11240 Bridgeport Road, pg. 30   IT
MDI, 11411 Number Five Rd., pg. 1139   PB
MacDonald Dettwiler & Associates Ltd., 13800 Commerce Pkwy., pg. 1229   PB
Merchants Information Solutions, Ltd., 135-3751 Shell Road, pg. 1106   PB
Prior Data Sciences Ltd., 10691 Shellbridge Way, pg. 1288   IT
Prism Systems Inc., 140 13551 Commerce Pkwy., pg. 969   IT
SLOCAN FOREST PRODUCTS LTD., 240-10451 Shellbridge Way, pg. 1263   IT
VTS Properties Ltd., P.O. Box 23960, pg. 1494   IT
Van Waters & Rogers Ltd., 9800 Van Horne Way, pg. 1147   IT

Richmond Hill

Abisko Mfg., Inc., 50 Mural St., Unit 8, pg. 412   PV
Allied Broadcast Equipment, Canada, 10 West Pearce St., Unit 6, pg. 791   PB
Anchor Hocking Canada Div., 9120 Leslie St., Ste. 205, pg. 1178   PB
Ascom Timeplex Canada Inc., 30 Fulton Way, pg. 87   IT
Ascom Timeplex Inc., 30 Fulton Way, pg. 87   IT
Black & Decker Canada Inc., 125 Mural St., pg. 234   PB
Bose Ltd., 8-35 E. Beaver Creek Rd., pg. 161   PV
CHT Steel Company Inc., 300 Newkirk Road, pg. 1299   IT
Cerberus Pyrotronics, 50 East Pearce Street, pg. 1246   IT
CIBA Corning Canada Inc., 28 Fulton Way, Unit 1, pg. 976   IT
Compaq Canada, Inc., 111 Granton Dr., Ste. 101, pg. 418   PB
Corning Canada Inc., 33 West Beaver Creek Rd., pg. 448   PB
Moulinex Canada Ltd., 10 Sims Crescent, pg. 896   PB
Quebecor Imaging (Alphatext), 10481 Yonge St., pg. 1077   IT
Quebecor Printing Richmond Hill, 10481 Yonge St., pg. 1077   IT
Quinton Electro Physiology, 200 W. Beaver Creek Rd., Unit 1, pg. 82   PB
Reynolds Extrusion Company, 500 Edward Ave., pg. 1387   PB
Royal Bank Action Direct Inc., 260 East Beaver Creek Road, Ste. 200, pg. 1131   IT
Sacor Inc., 80 W. Beaver Creek, Ste. 6, pg. 350   PB
Scholastic-Canada, Ltd., 123 Newkirk Rd., pg. 1440   PB
Sorbus Canada Limited, 91 Granton Drive, pg. 204   PB
Suzuki Canada Inc., 100 E. Beaver Creek Rd., pg. 1323   IT
TXbase Systems, Inc., 225 East Beaver Creek Road, Ste. 200, pg. 91   PB
Titleflex Canada, 128 Centre St. E., pg. 1341   IT

Rimouski

Quebec-Telephone, 6 Rue Jules-A-Brillant, pg. 697   PB

Riviere-du-Loup

Premier Tech Ltee, 454 Temiscouata, pg. 1068   IT

Rock Forest

Techno Caoutchouc Inc., pg. 274   IT

Rouyn-Noranda

Anixter Rouyn, 205 Industrial Blvd., pg. 116   PB
Barrick Gold, pg. 169   IT
Doyon Mine, P.O. Box 970, pg. 169   IT
Falconbridge Explorations, 8, rue Doyon, pg. 433   IT
Gaz Metropolitain, Inc.-Abitibi-Temiscamingue, 145 Quebec Blvd., pg. 541   IT
Tembec Forest Products Inc., 100 Dallaire Ave., pg. 1375   IT

Saanichton

AST Canada Inc., 2231 Cooperidge Dr., pg. 1182   IT

Sackville

Atlantic Wholesalers Ltd., Four Charlotte St., pg. 1495   IT

Saint Alphonse-de-Granby

Granford Manufacturing, Inc., 127 Rang Parent, pg. 753   PB

Saint Catharines

Bazaar & Novelty, 301 Louth St., pg. 1526   PB

PB - U.S. Public Companies Volume
PV - U.S. Private Companies Volume
IT - International Public & Private Companies Volume

CSE Marine Services Inc., 340 Lakeshore Rd. East, pg. 259 — IT
CANADIAN SHIPBUILDING & ENGINEERING LTD., 340 Lakeshore Rd. E., pg. 259 — IT
Canal Marine, 157 Cushman Rd., pg. 259 — IT
Colloids Canada Inc., 321 Welland Ave., pg. 1113 — IT
Dana Canada Inc., One Saint Paul St., pg. 480 — PB
General Motors Canada Components Div., 570 Glendale Ave., pg. 722 — PB
General Motors Canada Engine Div., 570 Glendale Ave., pg. 722 — PB
General Motors Canada Foundry Div., 570 Glendale Ave., pg. 722 — PB
Hamilton Marine & Engineering Ltd., 340 Lakeshore Rd. East, pg. 259 — IT
Niagara Structural Steel, 23 Smith St., pg. 256 — IT
Niagarasteel, 23 Smith St., pg. 256 — IT
Penberthy Div., 21 Keefer Rd., pg. 711 — IT
Port Weller Dry Docks, 340 Lakeshore Rd. East, pg. 259 — IT
The St. Catharines Standard, 17 Queen Street, pg. 631 — IT
TIW, 23 Smith St., pg. 256 — IT
TECSYN INTERNATIONAL, INC., 113-115 Cushman, pg. 1361 — IT

Saint Jean-sur-Richelieu

Clough Chemical Co., Ltd., pg. 199 — IT
Formica Canada, Inc., 25 Mercier St., pg. 129 — IT
Oerlikon Aerospace, Inc., 225, boul. du Seminaire sud, pg. 998 — IT

Saint John

AGRA Shawmont Limited, Bally Rou Place, 280 Torbay Road, pg. 30 — IT
Albright & Wilson Americas Limited, P.O. Box 2220, pg. 49 — IT
Anixter St. Johns, 10 Austin St., O'Leary Park, pg. 116 — PB
BRUNCOR, INC., One Brunswick Sq., pg. 230 — IT
CIOK-FM Radio, 400 Main St., pg. 1124 — IT
DMR Group, Inc., One Brunswick Sq., Suite 1602, pg. 528 — IT
Fredericton Business Park Ltd., One Brunswick Square, pg. 230 — IT
New North Media Inc., 1 Brunswick Square, Germain Street, pg. 230 — IT
Quebecor Printing Atlantic Saint John, pg. 1077 — IT
Saint John Port Corporation, 133 Prince William St., pg. 255 — IT
Stolt Sea Farm Inc., Bayside Drive, pg. 1302 — IT
Thornes, 331 Chelsey Dr., pg. 336 — PV

Saint Johns

Atlantic Explosives, 34 Pippy Pl., pg. 664 — IT
The Evening Telegram, pg. 631 — IT
Financial Collection Agencies, Suite 201, Bond Building, 53 Bond Street, pg. 470 — IT
FISHERY PRODUCTS INTERNATIONAL LTD., 70 O'Leary Avenue, pg. 492 — IT
Hewlett-Packard (Canada) Ltd., 1 Anderson Ave., pg. 818 — PB
Kvaerner Rosenberg Newfoundland Ltd., 100 New Gower St., Ste. 200, pg. 768 — IT
Labatt Breweries of Newfoundland, Leslie Street, pg. 679 — IT
Newfoundland Geosciences, Ltd., 607 Torbay Rd., pg. 431 — PV
NewTel Communications, Fort William Bldg., P.O. Box 2110, pg. 115 — IT
NewTel Enterprises Limited, Fort William Building, 10 Factory Lane, pg. 115 — IT
Noble Drilling (Canada) Ltd., Baine Johnston Centre, 4th Floor, pg. 1187 — PB
Nodeco (Hibernia Project), Box 61, Atlantic Place, pg. 823 — IT
Robinson-Blackmore Express, 36 Austin St., pg. 924 — IT
St. John's Port Corporation, 3 Water St., pg. 255 — IT
Vinland Industries Ltd., New Gower St., Ste. 200, pg. 770 — IT

Saint Leonard

Domcor - Quebec, 6150 des Grandes Prairies, pg. 415 — IT
FAUCHER INDUSTRIES INC., 6363, boul. Des Grande Prairies, pg. 479 — IT
Gaz Metropolitain, Inc., 9065 Champ-d'eau Street, pg. 541 — IT
Hospal-Gambro Limitee, 8220 Pascal Gagnon, pg. 668 — IT
Interglobe Montreal Inc., 4475, boulevard des Grandes-Prairies, pg. 538 — IT
Kearney-National Canada Ltd., 9240 Blvd. Langeoier, pg. 351 — PV
Les Produits Duvernay Ltee, 4711 Bd Couture, pg. 1177 — IT
Papier Malette, 101 Route du Moulin, pg. 833 — IT
Thermo Electron (Canada), 6875 Bombardier St., pg. 1596 — PB

Saint Remi-de-Napierville

Synergistics Industries Limited, 177 rue St. Andre, pg. 734 — PB
Synergistics Industries Limited, 177 rue. St. Andre, pg. 734 — PB

Saint Thomas

Brass-Craft Canada, Ltd., 35 Curran Road, pg. 1054 — PB
Canadian Timken Ltd., 1055 Talbot St., pg. 1617 — PB
Gorman-Rupp of Canada Ltd., 70 Burwell Rd., pg. 754 — PB
A. Schulman Canada Ltd., 400 S. Edgeware Rd., pg. 1442 — PB
Therm-O-Disc (Canada) Limited, 95 Edgeware Road, N5P 4C4, pg. 578 — PB

Saint-Augustin-De-Desmaures

Air Products Canada Ltd., pg. 31 — PB

Saint-Bruno

Coast RV, Inc., 1545 Maria-Victoria, pg. 388 — PB
Metropole Litho Inc., 1201-1203 Marie-Victorin Blvd., pg. 538 — IT
Transportation Equipment Group, 1101 Parent St., pg. 200 — IT
Transportation Equipment Group-North America, 1101 Parent St., pg. 200 — IT

Saint-Cesaire

D.D. Bean & Sons (Canada) Ltd., pg. 127 — PV

Saint-Constant

Charles River Canada, Inc., 188 La Salle St., pg. 195 — PB

Saint-Felicien

Laberge & Laberge Ltee., 1 Laberge, pg. 416 — IT

Saint-Georges

Panneaux Malette-OSB Inc., 775 122nd St., pg. 833 — IT

Saint-Germain

Bois J.L.P. Inc., Autoroute 20, Sortie 170, pg. 987 — PB

Saint-Hubert

MPM Media Rive-Sud, 3400, boulevard Losch, pg. 539 — IT

Saint-Hyacinthe

Griffin Canada Inc., 1375 Brouillette St., pg. 68 — PV
Le Groupe Commerce, 2450 Girouard Street West, pg. 650 — IT
Les Vins Andres du Quebec Ltee., 3755 Picard St., pg. 76 — IT
St. Jude Medical Ltd., 2550 Blvd. Vanier, pg. 1428 — PB
Transcontinental Printing Inc. - Saint-Hyacinthe, 2700, rue Casavant Ouest, pg. 538 — IT

Saint-Janvier

Messier-Dowty Inc., Montreal, 13000 du Parc, pg. 1340 — IT

Saint-Jean

Imprimerie Quebecor St-Jean, 142, rue St-Pierre, pg. 1077 — IT

Saint-Jerome

Bauer Sports, 1200 International Blvd., pg. 1184 — PB
Rolland Inc., 2 Rolland Ave., pg. 273 — IT
Rolland Inc., Two Rolland Ave., pg. 273 — IT
Rolland Inc., Fine Papers Division, 2 Rolland Avenue, pg. 274 — IT
St. Jerome Paper Mill, 455 Roland Ave., pg. 274 — IT

Saint-Laurent

ABB in Canada, 8585 Transcanada Hwy. S., pg. 7 — IT
ABC-Ademco Security Products, 601 McCaffrey, pg. 1306 — PB
Abbott Laboratories Ltd., 8401 TransCanada Hwy., pg. 13 — PB
AIR CANADA, Air Canada Center, pg. 36 — IT
Ayerst, McKenna & Harrison Inc., 1025 Blvd. Laurentien, pg. 80 — IT
BCE Mobile Communications Inc., 8501 TransCanada Highway, pg. 115 — IT
Bel-Air Fence Division, 400, rue Deslauriers, pg. 695 — IT
Bell Mobility Radio Inc., 8501 Transcanadian Hwy., Ste.200, pg. 115 — IT
W. Braun Packaging, Canada Ltd., 100 Alexis Nikon Blvd., #964, pg. 166 — PV
British Steel Canada Inc., Ste. 405-6505, Trans-Canada Hwy., pg. 222 — IT
CAE Electronics, Ltd., 8585 Cote de Liesse St., pg. 237 — IT
CCL Label, 5490 Boulevard Thimens, pg. 238 — IT
Crompton & Knowles of Canada, Ltd., 1850 Beaulec Ville, pg. 460 — PB
DataCard Canada Inc., 4915 Rue Dobrin, pg. 312 — PV
Delta Air Lines Marketing, Ste: 110, 3300 Cote Vertu, pg. 497 — PB
DYWIDAG Systems International, USA, Inc., 100 Alexis Nihon Blvd., Ste. 216, pg. 424 — IT
Encore Informatique Limitee, 100 Alexis Nihon Blvd., Ste. 270, pg. 580 — PB
Getinge/Castle Canada Limited, 3610 Poirier Blvd., pg. 551 — IT
Groupe Constructo, 1500, boulevard Jules-Poitras, pg. 539 — IT
Hamilton Hallmark, 7575 Trans Canada Hwy., Ste. 600, pg. 155 — PB
INTERTAPE POLYMER GROUP INC., 110 E. Montee de Liesse, pg. 684 — IT
Jac Jacobsen Enterprises, Inc., 6315 Cote de Liesse, pg. 821 — IT
Kamyr Enterprises Inc., 5055 Rue Levy, pg. 35 — IT
Lamson & Sessions Ltd., 414 Isabey, pg. 976 — IT
Les Editions Transcript Publishing, 1500, boulevard Jules-Poitras, pg. 539 — IT
MPM Media, 529, boulevard Lebeau, pg. 539 — IT
MITCHEL-LINCOLN PACKAGING, 3737 Thimens Blvd., pg. 870 — PB
NORDX/CDT, 105 Marcel-Laurin Boulevard, pg. 287 — IT
Northern Telecom Canada Limited, Outside Plant Div., 105 Laurentien Blvd., pg. 969 — IT
Northern Telecom Canada Limited, Telecom Distribution Division, 105 Laurentien Blvd., pg. 969 — IT
Panneaux Vicply Inc., 5605 Cypinot Street, pg. 1432 — IT
Pirelli Tire Inc., 9800 Trans Canadienne, pg. 1059 — IT
Pittway Corp. of Canada, 601 McCaffrey, pg. 1307 — PB
PolyGram Inc., 6000 Cote de Liesse, H4T 1E3, pg. 1053 — IT
Publi-Home Distributors Ltd., 523, boulevard Lebeau, pg. 539 — IT
Purolator, 6395 Cote de Liesse, pg. 36 — IT
Refrigeration Hussmann Ltee., 6160 Rte. TransCanadienne, pg. 1766 — PB
Reseau Publi-Maison, 525, boulevard Lebeau, pg. 539 — IT
Rockwell Internationale du Canada Avionics & Communications, Suite 100, 6500 TransCanada Highway, H4T 1X4, pg. 1400 — PB
Rogers Cantel Mobile Communications Inc., 6315 Cote de Liesse, pg. 1122 — IT
Royal LePage, 9900 Cavendish Boulevard, Suite 100, pg. 1143 — IT
SKW Canada Inc., 750 Laurentian Blvd., Ste. 300, pg. 1466 — IT
SKW Chemicals Canada Inc., 750 Laurentien Blvd., Ste. 300, pg. 1466 — IT
SM-Cyclo of Canada, Ltd., 226 Migneron Street, pg. 1315 — IT
Sharp Electronics of Canada, 9710 Rte. Transcanadienne, pg. 1230 — IT
Shimano Canada Ltd., 3393 Griffith St., pg. 1233 — IT
Shorewood Packaging Corporation of Canada, Limited, 6500 Autoroute Trans-Canadienne, pg. 1468 — PB
Sun Microsystems of Canada-Eastern Canada, 555 Dr. Frederik Philips Blvd., pg. 1532 — IT
Tellabs St. Laurent Transport Group, 3403 Griffith St., pg. 1573 — IT
Titanium Ltd/Ltdee, 5055 Rue Levy, pg. 35 — IT
Transcontinental Printing Inc., 395, boulevard Lebeau, pg. 538 — IT
Transmedia, 1500, boulevardJules-Poitras, pg. 538 — IT
VG Instruments Canada Inc., pg. 1595 — PB

Saint-Romvald

Imprimerie Quebecor St-Romuald, 470, 3e Avenue, Centre ind., pg. 1077 — IT

Sainte-Anne-de-Bellevue

Spar Satellite Systems, 21025 Trans Canada Hwy., pg. 1288 — IT

Sainte-Foy

Air Alliance, 6th Ave., pg. 36 — IT
Brian Controls Division, 3107 Sasseville, Ste. 41, pg. 711 — IT
Cognos Inc.-Quebec City Sales Office, 2600, boul. Laurier, Ste. 2730, pg. 306 — IT
DMR Group, Inc., Place Iberville Trois, 2960 Laurier Blvd., Suite 400, pg. 527 — IT
Detroit Diesel - Alison Canada, 2997 Rue Natt, pg. 1485 — IT
Domcor - Quebec, 2665, Dalton Street, pg. 415 — IT
Financial Collection Agencies, Bureau 220, 3060 Rue Maricourt, pg. 470 — IT
Guay, Blouin, & Associates, Inc., Place Iberville I, 1195 Rue de Lavigerie, Suite 180, pg. 1509 — IT
Kodak Canada Inc., 2954 Blvd. Laurier, Ste. 30, pg. 553 — PB
Les Papiers Graphiques Rolland, 2893 Kepler Ave., pg. 274 — IT
Litho Acme Quebec, 2057, rue Branly, pg. 538 — IT
Montrusco Associates, 2600 Boulevard Laurier, Suite 860, pg. 888 — IT

Sainte-Marie-Beauce

Bose Canada, Inc., Parc Industrial, pg. 161 — PV

Sainte-Therese-de-Blainville

Luxo Ltd./Sverige Inc., 30 Place Sicard, pg. 822 — IT

PB - *U.S. Public Companies Volume*
PV - *U.S. Private Companies Volume*
IT - *International Public & Private Companies Volume*

Geographic Index-Non U.S.

1545

Sarnia

Air Products Canada Ltd., 390 Indians, pg. 31 **PB**
Blue Water Broadcasting Limited, 1415 London Road, pg. 1123 **IT**
Brian Controls Division, 880 Philip St., pg. 711 **IT**
CKTY/CFGX, 1415 London Road, pg. 1123 **IT**
Cabot Canada Ltd., 350 Wilton St., pg. 289 **PB**
Dow Chemical Canada, Inc., 1086 Modeland Rd., pg. 523 **PB**
Kilborn SNC-Lavalin Inc., 201 North Front Street, Suite 401, pg. 1162 **IT**
Nova Chemicals (Canada) Ltd./Nova Chimie (Canada) Ltee., 201 N. Front Street, pg. 971 **IT**
The Observer (Sarnia), 140 Front Street North, pg. 631 **IT**
Rogers Cable Systems, 1421 Confederation St., pg. 1123 **IT**
Sunoco Sarnia Refinery, 1900 River Road, pg. 1320 **IT**

Saskatoon

Amok Ltd., 817-825 45th St. West, pg. 305 **IT**
Anixter Saskatoon, 302 50th Eaststreet, pg. 116 **PB**
Atomic Energy of Canada Ltd.-Western Region, 446A 2nd Avenue North, pg. 97 **IT**
BBS Saskatchewan Incorporated, 216 First Ave. N., pg. 171 **IT**
Bioriginal Food & Science Corp., #1-411 Downey Road, pg. 1195 **IT**
CFP Foods, Box 190, pg. 1195 **IT**
CFQC-TV, 216 First Ave. N., pg. 171 **IT**
CSC, Saskatoon, 2313 Hanselman Pl., pg. 1482 **IT**
Cogema Canada Ltee. (CCI), 817-825 45th St. West, pg. 305 **IT**
Hewlett-Packard (Canada) Ltd., 2175 Airport Dr., Ste. #1, pg. 818 **IT**
Infra Ready Products Ltd., 850C 56th Street East, pg. 1195 **IT**
Interprovincial Cooperative Limited (IPCO), pg. 1195 **IT**
Kilborn SNC-Lavalin Inc., 357 Third Avenue South, pg. 1162 **IT**
Nashua Photo Limited, 1725 Quebec Avenue, pg. 1152 **PB**
PCS Potash - Cory, pg. 1064 **IT**
PCS Potash - Patience Lake, pg. 1064 **IT**
POTASH CORPORATION OF SASKATCHEWAN INC., Suite 500, 122-1st Avenue South, pg. 1064 **IT**
Siecor Corporation, Holiday Park Industrial Centre, 1370 Fletcher Rd., pg. 449 **PB**
Weninger Industries Division, pg. 698 **IT**
Western Automotive Rebuilders, 1302 Quebec Ave., pg. 23 **IT**

Sault Sainte Marie

ALGOMA STEEL INC., 105 West Street, pg. 56 **IT**
CHBX/CJIC-TV, 119 E. St., pg. 171 **IT**
Rogers Cable Systems, 23 Manitou, pg. 1123 **IT**
The Sault Star Ltd., P.O. Box 460, 145 Old Garden River Rd., pg. 631 **IT**

Sayabec

Uniboard Division Sayabec, 152 Route Pouliot, pg. 1431 **IT**

Sayward

Eve River Division, pg. 828 **IT**
Kelsey Bay Div., pg. 828 **IT**

Scarborough

Alfa-Laval Ltd., 101 Milner Ave., pg. 1379 **IT**
The Amazing Video Network, 5590 Finch Avenue East, pg. 293 **IT**
American Locker Co. of Canada Ltd., 931 Progress Ave., Unit #5, pg. 86 **PB**
Ancra Canada, 235 Nugget Ave., pg. 71 **PV**
Atlantic Service Co., Ltd., 62 Howden Rd., pg. 165 **IT**
BFC Buildings, 3600 Midland Avenue, pg. 118 **IT**
BFC Civil, 3600 Midland Avenue, pg. 118 **IT**
BFC CONSTRUCTION CORPORATION, 3660 Midland Avenue, pg. 118 **IT**
BFC Utilities, 3660 Midland Avenue, pg. 118 **IT**
BATON BROADCASTING INCORPORATED, 9 Channel Nine Court, pg. 170 **IT**
BECKER MILK CO. LTD., 671 Warden Ave., pg. 182 **IT**
Bick's Pickles & Relishes, 333 Progress Ave., pg. 901 **PB**
Bowdens Media Monitoring Limited, 2206 Eglinton Ave. East, Ste. 190, pg. 1124 **IT**
Burgess Saia Co. Inc., 70 Ironside Cres, Unit 7, pg. 1500 **IT**
CFTO-TV, Nine Channel Nine Ct., pg. 171 **IT**
COBE Canada Ltd., 5736 Finch Avenue, pg. 667 **IT**
Canadian Locker Co., Ltd., 931 Progress Ave., Unit #5, pg. 86 **PB**
Canadian Thermos Products Ltd., 2040 Eglinton Ave. E., pg. 938 **IT**
Canefco Limited, 50 Milne Ave., pg. 368 **PV**
Casio Canada, Ltd., 2100 Ellesmere Rd., Ste. 240, pg. 274 **IT**
CINRAM LTD., 2255 Markham Rd., pg. 293 **IT**
Cinram Video Centre, 5590 Finch Avenue East, pg. 293 **IT**
Cliffside Utility Contractors, 3660 Midland Avenue, pg. 118 **IT**

Commercial Union Life Assurance Company of Canada, 300 Consilium Place, pg. 308 **IT**
The Consumers' Gas Company Ltd., 500 Consumers Rd., pg. 652 **IT**
The Continuum Company, Inc. (Canada), 2206 Eglinton Ave. East, Ste. 300, pg. 423 **PB**
Crane National Vendors Co., Ltd., 595 Middlefield Rd., Unit 20 pg. 456 **PB**
Dawn Distributors, 3400 Pharmacy Ave., Unit 12, pg. 1168 **PB**
Dextran Products Limited, 421 Comstock Road, pg. 1063 **IT**
Directory Distributing Associates, Inc., 1800 Ellesmere Ave., pg. 334 **PV**
Du Pont Canada-Scarborough, 75 Venture Dr., pg. 532 **PB**
Eaton Yale Ltd. Industrial Control Division, 45 Progress Ave., pg. 559 **PB**
Econolite Canada, Inc., 1650 Midland Ave., pg. 362 **PV**
First Brands (Canada) Corp., 100 Consilium Pl., pg. 627 **PB**
The Foundation Company, 3660 Midland Avenue, pg. 118 **IT**
Framatome Connectors, 1530 Birchmont Rd., pg. 503 **IT**
Fujitsu Systems Business of Canada - Customer Support, 60 Milner Ave., pg. 527 **IT**
Fuller-F.L. Smidth Canada Limited, 10 Thournmount Dr., pg. 475 **IT**
Graseby Goring Kerr Canada Inc., Unit 63, 705 Progress Ave., pg. 1268 **IT**
The Griffith Laboratories Ltd., 757 Pharmacy Ave., pg. 481 **PV**
Handleman Company of Canada Ltd., 10 Newgale Gate, pg. 780 **PB**
Home Depot Canada, 426 Ellesmere Rd., pg. 832 **PB**
Honda Canada Inc., 715 Milner Ave., pg. 635 **IT**
Howden Group Canada Limited, 1510 Birchmount Rd., pg. 636 **IT**
ITW Construction Products, 225 Nantucket Blvd., pg. 868 **IT**
JVC Canada Inc., 21 Finchdene Square, pg. 847 **IT**
The Jackson-Lewis Company, 3660 Midland Avenue, pg. 118 **IT**
Laura Secord, Inc., 1500 Birchmount Rd., pg. 920 **IT**
Leviton, 35 Dynamic Dr., pg. 663 **PV**
Eli Lilly Canada Inc., 3650 Danforth Avenue, pg. 993 **PB**
Marke Source Corporation, 815 Middlefield Rd., pg. 705 **PV**
Milwaukee Electric Tool (Canada) Ltd., 755 Progress Ave., pg. 18 **IT**
Molex Electronics Ltd., 85 Select Ave., pg. 1122 **PB**
NIFE Corporation, 125 Nantucket Blvd., pg. 54 **IT**
Nelson Canada, 1120 Birchmount, pg. 1601 **PB**
Newell Industries Canada, Inc., 1645 Warden Ave., Ste. 101, pg. 1178 **PB**
Noma Inc., 375 Kennedy Rd., pg. 955 **IT**
Noma Industrial Cords Company, 120 Mack Ave., pg. 955 **IT**
Noma Tooling Enterprises, 110 Mack Ave., pg. 955 **IT**
Omron Canada, Inc., 885 Milner Ave., pg. 1005 **IT**
Organon Canada Ltd., 200 Consilium Pl., Ste. 700, pg. 45 **IT**
PIC Realty Canada Inc., 200 Consilium Place, pg. 893 **PV**
Parker Pen Canada Limited, 380 Finchdene Square, pg. 745 **PB**
Philips Canada Ltd., 601 Milner Ave., pg. 1055 **IT**
Philips Electronics Ltd., 601 Milner Ave., pg. 1055 **IT**
POLYDEX PHARMACEUTICALS LIMITED, 421 Comstock Road, pg. 1062 **IT**
Prentice Hall Canada, Inc., 1870 Birchmount Road, pg. 778 **PV**
Proctor Silex Canada, Inc., Ten Milner Business Ct., Ste. 600, pg. 1150 **PB**
Prudential Fund Management Canada Ltd., 200 Consilium Pl., pg. 893 **PV**
Prudential of America General Insurance Co. (Canada), 200 Consilium Place, pg. 893 **PV**
Quality Music, 410 Passmore Ave., pg. 1075 **IT**
Quality Service Plan, Inc. Canada, 45 Ironside Cres, pg. 1368 **IT**
QUALITY SPECIAL PRODUCTS, 410 Passmore Ave., pg. 1075 **IT**
Quebecor Printing Haughton, 851 Middlefield Rd., pg. 1077 **IT**
Reed Exhibition Companies-Canada, 3761 Victoria Park Ave., Unit 1, pg. 1096 **IT**
Rexam Containers, 1200 Ellesmere Rd., pg. 1107 **IT**
Richard De Boo Publishers, Corp. Plaza, 2075 Kennedy Rd., pg. 1601 **PB**
Rotex Canada Inc., 1410 Birchmount Road, pg. 462 **IT**
Royal Doulton Canada Limited, 850 Progress Avenue, pg. 135 **IT**
C.J. Rush Inc., 189 Milner Ave., pg. 395 **IT**
SKF Canada Ltd., 40 Executive Court, pg. 1158 **IT**
Safer, Ltd., 3 Paulman Court, pg. 1390 **PB**
Saft Batteries Ltd., 125 Nantucket Blvd., pg. 55 **IT**
Scarborough Center, 345 Passmore Ave., pg. 273 **IT**
Schenectady Canada Ltd., 319 Comstock Rd., pg. 970 **PV**
Schindler Elevator Corporation, 40 Cowdray Ct., pg. 1205 **IT**
Scientific-Atlanta Canada, Inc., 120 Middlefield Rd., pg. 1443 **PB**
Scotia Mortgage Corporation, 2201 Eglinton Ave. E., pg. 156 **IT**
H.A. Sheldon, Inc., 2220 Midland Ave., Unit 68AA, pg. 1560 **PB**
Shorewood Packaging Corporation of Canada, Ltd., 2220 Midland Ave., pg. 1468 **PB**
Signode Canada, 115 Ridgetop Rd., pg. 869 **PB**
SILCOFP LIMITED, 10 Commander Blvd., pg. 1249 **IT**
A.G. SIMPSON CO. LIMITED, 675 Progress Ave., pg. 1252 **IT**

Smith Corona (Canada) Ltd., pg. 1007 **PV**
T-Fal Canada Inc., 257 Finchdene Square, Unit 1, pg. 568 **IT**
Tech-Met Canada Ltd., 80 Milner Ave., Unit 9, pg. 575 **PB**
Thomson Healthcare Communications, 1120 Birchmount Rd., pg. 1602 **PB**
Tootsie Roll of Canada, Ltd., c/o Osler-Hoskin & Harcourt, 260 Brimley Rd., pg. 1621 **PB**
Toronto Carton Corporation Limited, 44 Rolark Drive, pg. 1468 **PB**
Toyota Canada Inc., 1, Toyota Place, pg. 1414 **IT**
Transamerica Life Insurance Co.-Canada, 300 Consilium Place, pg. 1630 **PB**
Trench Electric, 71 Maybrook Dr., pg. 113 **IT**
Trench Electric, 390 Midwest Rd., pg. 113 **IT**
Tri-Clover Canada, 101 Milner Ave., pg. 1379 **IT**
W/A Music Corporation, Nine Channel Nine Ct., pg. 171 **IT**
Wallace & Tiernan Canada, Inc., 925 Warden Avenue, pg. 61 **PB**
Wandel & Goltermann Inc., 21 Rolark Dr., pg. 1486 **IT**
Wang Canada Limited, 150 Middlefield Rd., pg. 1737 **PB**
Wang Canada Ltd., 150 Middlefield Road, pg. 1737 **PB**
Warner-Lambert Canada, Inc., 2200 Eglinton Ave. East, pg. 1739 **IT**

Scoudouc

Cott Corporation - Atlantic Canada Region, 4 Eddison Ave., pg. 337 **IT**

Sept-Iles

Norsteel Limited, 234 Des Pionniers, pg. 256 **IT**
Port of Sept-Iles, 421 Arnaud St., pg. 255 **IT**
Svedala Industries Canada Quebec, pg. 1325 **IT**

Shaunavon

Talisman Energy Inc., Box 1177, pg. 1352 **IT**

Shawinigan

Bandag Canada, Ltd., 5230 Royal Boulevard, pg. 178 **PB**

Sherbrooke

American Biltrite (Canada) Ltd., 200 Bank St., J1H 4K3, pg. 69 **PB**
Distribution publicitaire Estrie, 4447, boulevard Industriel, pg. 539 **IT**
Gaz Metropolitain, Inc.-Eastern Townships, 240 Leger Street, pg. 541 **IT**
Metrolitho, 4001, boulevard Portland, pg. 538 **IT**

Sherwood Park

AGRA Land Surveys Ltd., 130 Sioux Road, pg. 30 **IT**

Simcoe

Simcoe Leaf Tobacco Company, Ltd., 401 Second Ave., W., pg. 1695 **PB**

Slave Lake

Barber Industries Ltd.-Service Center, #6, 216 Birch Rd. N.E., pg. 164 **IT**

Smiths Falls

Hershey Canada Inc.-Smith Falls Plant, Hershey Drive, pg. 812 **PB**
SPC Corporation, Limited, Six Hershey Drive, pg. 1468 **PB**

Snow Lake

New Britannia Mine, pg. 1345 **IT**

Sorel

Sorel Forge Inc., 100 McCarthy St., pg. 1262 **IT**

Sparwood

Mining Services International, Rural Route 1, Highway 3, pg. 1115 **PB**

Squamish

BHP Rail Products, 39601 Galbraith Rd., pg. 226 **IT**
Squamish Gas, 38152 Second Ave., pg. 114 **IT**

Stellarton

Amleco Leasing Limited, 115 King St., pg. 454 **IT**
Atlantic Shopping Centres Limited, 115 King St., pg. 454 **IT**
EMPIRE COMPANY LIMITED, 115 King St., pg. 453 **IT**
Empire Theaters Limited, 115 King St., pg. 454 **IT**
Kepec Resources Limited, 115 King St., pg. 454 **IT**
Sobey Inc., 115 King St., pg. 454 **IT**
Sobey Leased Properties Limited, 115 King St., pg. 454 **IT**

Stephenville

Hope Brook Mine, P.O. Box 294, pg. 1411 — PB

Stittsville

Xilinx, Inc., 34 Hampel Crescent, pg. 1786 — PB

Stoney Creek

Battlefield Equipment Rentals, 880 South Service Road, pg. 1400 — IT
Brabant Newspapers Ltd., 333 Arvin Ave., pg. 631 — IT
Canadian Ferro Hot Metal Specialties, Ltd., 345 Arvin Ave., pg. 1214 — PB
DSM Engineering Plastics, 233 Arvin Ave., pg. 46 — IT
GSW Heating Products Company, 455 Arvin Avenue, pg. 538 — IT
Hagglunds Drives Inc., 853 Arvin Avenue, pg. 670 — IT
Harris Rebar, 318 Arvin Avenue, pg. 598 — IT
IRD Mechanalysis Limited, 903 Barton St., Unit 6, pg. 790 — PB
Zeneca Corp., pg. 1526 — IT

Stouffville

Cable Tech Company Limited, 5769 Main St., pg. 955 — IT
Erie Manufacturing Co. (Canada) Ltd., RR #3, 15437 Hwy. 48, pg. 1241 — IT

Stratford

AlliedSignal Canada Inc., Automotive Aftermarket, 305 Romeo Street, South, pg. 52 — PB
AlliedSignal Canada Inc.-Filters & Spark Plugs Canada, 305 Romeo St. South, pg. 54 — IT
ATAPCO Canada, Ltd., pg. 64 — PV
Canadian Fabricated Products, 1172 Erie St., pg. 354 — PB
Dominion Controls Company, 617 Douro St., pg. 473 — IT
FAG Bearings Limited, 801 Ontario St., pg. 469 — IT
National Trust Company, 1 Ontario St., pg. 910 — IT
Samsonite of Canada, 753 Ontario St., pg. 1430 — PB
A.O. Smith-Enterprises Ltd., 768 Erie St., pg. 1477 — PB
Standard Products (Canada) Ltd., 1030 Erie St., pg. 1505 — PB
T B Wood's Canada Ltd., 750 Douro Street, pg. 1562 — PB

Strathroy

E.J. Brooks Industries, Ltd., 412 High St. E, pg. 172 — PV
Dover Corporation (Canada) Ltd.-Industrial Div., 111 McNab St., pg. 522 — PB
VARI-FORM, 233 Lothian Ave., pg. 1341 — IT

Streetsville

CTS of Canada, Ltd., 80 Thomas St., pg. 286 — PB
Canada Brick Div., P.O. Box 668, pg. 698 — IT
Jannock Brick Group-Head Office, P.O. Box 668, pg. 698 — IT

Sudbury

Anixter Sudbury, 1899 LaSalle Blvd., pg. 116 — PB
BBS Ontario Incorporated, 699 Frood Rd., pg. 171 — IT
CICI/CKNC-TV, 699 Frood Rd., pg. 171 — IT
Hewlett-Packard (Canada) Ltd., 1500 Paris St., pg. 818 — PB
Sudbury Center, 1350 Kelly Lake Rd., pg. 274 — IT
The Sudbury Star, 33 MacKenzie Street, pg. 631 — IT
Svedala Industries Canada Ontario, 955 Cambrien Heights Dr., pg. 1325 — IT

Surrey

Cott Corporation - Pacific North West Region (Surrey), 15050 - 54A Avenue, pg. 338 — IT
DYWIDAG-Systems International Canada Ltd., 19433 96 Avenue, pg. 424 — IT
Ewos Canada Ltd., 7721 - 132nd Street, pg. 349 — IT
Peace River Transmission Co., Ltd., 16705 Fraser Hwy., pg. 114 — IT
Prok International Canada Inc., Unit 101-18919, 96th Avenue, RR #4, pg. 1353 — IT
Revelstoke Home Centers, 19550 92nd Ave., pg. 1490 — IT
Rogers Cable TV-Surrey, 10445 138th St., pg. 1122 — IT
Royal LePage - British Columbia Office, 14888, 104th Avenue, Suite 206, pg. 1143 — IT
Titan Steel & Wire Co., 11041 Elevator Rd., V3V 2R8, pg. 741 — IT
Trus Joist MacMillan Limited, #5, 15355-102A Ave., pg. 1556 — PB
Trus Joist (Western) Ltd., #5, 15355 102 A Ave., pg. 1556 — PB
Willis Corroon Melling Co., 5746 176A Street, pg. 1509 — IT

Sussex

CJCW-AM, Maple Ave./Aiton Rd., pg. 1124 — IT
PCS Potash - New Brunswick, pg. 1064 — IT

Sydney

Cape Breton Post, 255 George Street, pg. 631 — IT
Micronav International Inc., 104 Marine Dr., pg. 546 — IT

Taylor

Canadian Forest Products Ltd., Taylor Division, pg. 260 — IT

Temiscaming

Sulphite Pulp, George Petty Rd., pg. 1375 — IT
Tembec Inc. Pulp Div., George Petty Rd., pg. 1375 — IT

Terrebonne

Filpac, Inc., 100, Rue Langlois, pg. 233 — IT

Texada Island

Ash Grove Cement-Western Region Quarry, pg. 87 — PV

Thamesville

R.J. Simpson Mfg. Co. (Canada) Ltd., Hwy. 21 No., P.O. Box 69, pg. 1475 — PB

The Pas

Tolko Manitoba, Inc., #10 Highway North, pg. 1395 — IT

Thetford Mines

Distex Ind. Inc., 2885 Smith Blvd., North, pg. 560 — PB

Thompson

Inco Limited, Manitoba Division, pg. 672 — IT

Thornhill

Beneficial Canada Inc., 8500 Leslie St., pg. 211 — PB
Canac Kitchens Ltd, 360 John St, pg. 630 — PV
Cole, Sherman & Associates Ltd., 75 Commerce Valley Dr., E., pg. 1657 — IT
Genicom ESSC, 100 Commerce Valley Drive E., L3T 7R1, pg. 729 — PB
NIKE Canada Ltd., 175 Commerce Valley Drive West, pg. 1184 — IT
Weetabix of Canada (Mfg.) Limited, 300 John St., Ste. 501, pg. 1488 — IT

Thorold

The Beaver Wood Fiber Company, Alanburg Rd., pg. 739 — PB
The Exolon-ESK Company of Canada Ltd., 181 Queen St., pg. 600 — PB
Georgia-Pacific Building Materials Sales, Ltd., Alanburg Rd., pg. 739 — IT
Optech Research & Engineering, Allanburg Road, pg. 1075 — IT

Thunder Bay

Anixter Thunder Bay, 1112 Russell St., Unit 5, pg. 116 — PB
Howe Monenco Inc., 95 North Cumberland Street, pg. 31 — IT
Pascol Engineering, P.O. Box 2690, pg. 259 — IT
Robin's Foods Inc., 725 Hewitson Street, pg. 1195 — IT
Rogers Cable Systems, 1635 Pacquette Rd., pg. 1123 — IT
Serca Food Service-Fitzsimmons Div., 840 North McKellar St., pg. 1012 — IT
Thunder Bay Terminals Ltd., P.O. Box 1800, Station F, pg. 1150 — IT
Valmet Canada Inc. - Enerdry, P.O. Box 3255, pg. 1448 — IT

Tilbury

Reliance Steel Fabricators Limited, 96 Lyon Ave. North, pg. 75 — IT
Rockwell International of Canada, 28 Mill Road, Highway No. 2, pg. 1401 — PB

Tillsonburg

Eberhard Hardware Manufacturing Ltd., 67 Goshen St., pg. 548 — PB
Fleck Manufacturing Inc., 80 Brock St. E., pg. 955 — IT
Freudenberg NOK, 65 Spruce St., pg. 505 — IT
Mastico Industries, Ltd., pg. 1117 — IT
NCC Publishing, 25 Townline Rd., pg. 924 — IT
Sachs Automotive Components, Inc., 95 Spruce St., pg. 835 — IT
Standard Commercial Tobacco Co. of Canada Ltd., Hwy. 3 W., pg. 1502 — PB

Timmins

CITO/CFCL-TV, 681 Pine St. N., pg. 171 — IT
The Daily Press, 187 Cedar Street South, pg. 631 — IT
Falconbridge Explorations, P.O. Box 1140, 571 Moneta Avenue, pg. 434 — IT
Malette Inc., P.O. Box 1100, pg. 1375 — IT
Outokumpu Mines Ltd., Timmins Office, Suite 30A, Algonquin Blvd. East, pg. 1016 — IT
Pamour Mine, pg. 1411 — PB

Toronto

ABN AMRO Bank Canada (Toronto), IBM Tower, Ste.3402, Toronto Dominion Centre, pg. 11 — IT
AIU Canada Ltd., 145 Wellington St., pg. 85 — PB
ACKLANDS LIMITED, 945 Wilson Avenue, pg. 23 — IT
Adason Properties Limited, 181 University Ave., Ste 2000, pg. 254 — IT
Aetna Canada Holdings Ltd., Aetna Tower, 79 Wellington St. West, pg. 27 — PB
Akzo Chemie Ltd., 100 University Ave., Ste. 906, pg. 47 — PB
Alberto-Culver Canada, Inc., 506 Kipling Ave., pg. 38 — PB
Alcan Canada Products, Ltd., P.O. Box 269, Toronto Dominion Ctr., pg. 50 — IT
Alias Wavefront, 210 King St., E., pg. 1474 — IT
ALLIANCE COMMUNICATIONS CORPORATION, 121 Broad St. E., Ste. 1500, pg. 57 — IT
Allianz Canada, 425 Bloor Street, Suite 500, pg. 59 — IT
Allied Advertising Public Relations Canada, Inc., 21 St. Clair Ave. E., Ste. 701, pg. 38 — PV
Aluma Systems Corp., 4810 Dufferin St., pg. 1423 — IT
AMBROSE CARR LINTON CARROLL INC., 939 Eglinton Ave. E., pg. 71 — IT
American Appraisal Canada, Inc., 310 Front St. W., Ste. 800, pg. 50 — PV
AMERICAN ECO CORPORATION, 154 University Ave., Ste. 200, pg. 73 — PV
Ammirati & Puris Ltd./Toronto, One First Canadian Pl., Ste. 5900, pg. 67 — PV
Arnold Advertising, 175 Bloor St. E., pg. 84 — PV
The Associated Press, Ltd., 36 King St., E., pg. 92 — PV
H.A. Astlett & Co. Ltd., 8 King St. E., Ste. 907, pg. 682 — IT
Atlas Asset Management Inc., Waterpark Place, 20 Bay Street, Ste. 1402, pg. 865 — IT
BASF Canada Inc. - Coatings & Colorants, 345 Carlingview Dr., pg. 105 — IT
BBDO Canada, 2 Bloor St. W., pg. 104 — PV
BBS Productions Inc., pg. 171 — IT
BLH Electronics, Canada Division, 41 Horner Avenue, Unit 5, pg. 1289 — IT
BMC Software Canada, 32 Park Rd., pg. 162 — PB
BMG Music Canada, 150 John St., 6th Fl., pg. 192 — IT
Banca Nazionale del Lavoro of Canada, 95 Wellington Street West, Suite 2100, pg. 137 — IT
Banco Central Canada, 330 Bay St., pg. 140 — IT
Banco Nacional de Mexico, One First Canadian Pl., Ste. 3430, pg. 574 — IT
Bank of America Canada, #4 King St. West, 18th Flr., pg. 182 — PB
Bank of Boston Canada, Ste. 500, P.O. Box 23, pg. 184 — PB
BANK OF MONTREAL, First Canadian Place, 21st Floor, pg. 153 — IT
Bank of Montreal Investor Services Limited, 302 Bay St., pg. 153 — IT
Bank of Montreal - Toronto, 302 Bay St., pg. 153 — IT
THE BANK OF NOVA SCOTIA, Scotia Plaza, pg. 155 — IT
The Bank of Nova Scotia Properties, Scotia Plaza, 44 King Street West, pg. 155 — IT
The Bank of Tokyo-Mitsubishi (Canada), Ste. 2100, Royal Bank Plaza, South Tower, pg. 158 — IT
Bankers Trust Bank of Canada, Royal Bank Plaza, North Tower, Ste. 1200, pg. 186 — PB
Banque ABN du Canada, IBM Tower, Ste. 3402, pg. 12 — IT
Banque Paribas Du Canada, Exchange Tower, 2 First Canadian Pl., Ste. 2520, pg. 319 — IT
Bantam Book Canada Inc., 105 Bond St., pg. 191 — IT
Barclays Bank of Canada, P.O. Box 377, Ste. 3500, pg. 165 — IT
Baring International Investment (Canada), 150 King Street West, Suite 2408, pg. 648 — IT
Barrick Gold, 21st Fl., N. Tower, pg. 169 — IT
BARRICK GOLD CORPORATION, Royal Bank Plaza, South Tower, Suite 2700, pg. 168 — IT
Barrick Gold Resources Corporation, Royal Bank Plaza, South Tower, 200 Bay Street, Suite 2700, pg. 169 — IT
Barrick Minerals (Canada) Inc., 24 Hazelton Ave., pg. 169 — IT
Bass, 345 Carlinview Drive, pg. 975 — IT
Baton Broadcast Sales, Suite 300, 2 Bloor Street West, pg. 171 — IT
Batten Graphics, 543 Richmond St. W., pg. 1437 — PB
Battle Mountain Canada Ltd., Royal Trust Tower, Ste. 2500, 77 King St. W., Dominion Ctr., pg. 193 — IT
The Bay, 401 Bay St., Ste. 501, pg. 637 — IT
Bayer Foreign Investments Ltd. (Bayforin), 77 Belfield Rd. Etobicoke, pg. 175 — IT
Bayerische Landesbank Girozentrale, BCE Place, Ste. 2210, 181 Bay St., pg. 177 — IT
Beacon Eye Centre Inc., 181 Bay St., Ste. 150, BCB Place, pg. 604 — IT
Bell Horizon Services, 483 Bay Street, pg. 115 — IT
Bensimon Byrne DMB&B Toronto, 2 Bloor St. W., Ste. 1400, pg. 303 — PV
Berlitz Language Centers of Canada Ltd., 130 Bloor St. W., Ste. 603, pg. 222 — IT
Bimcor Inc., 181 Bay Street, pg. 115 — IT
Binks Manufacturing Co. of Canada, Ltd., 14 Vansco Road, pg. 229 — PB
BlackRock Ventures Inc., 30 Soudan Avenue, Ste. 500, pg. 1089 — IT
Block Drug Co. (Canada) Ltd., 36 Northline Rd., pg. 237 — PB
The Boeing Company Canada Ltd., pg. 242 — PB
The Boiler Inspection & Insurance Co. of Canada, Eight King St E., pg. 795 — PB
Bondware, 191 New Toronto St., pg. 417 — IT
Bowne of Canada Inc., 60 Gervais Dr., pg. 249 — PB

BOZELL RETAIL, 121 Bloor St., East, 10th Floor, pg. 209 IT
Braemar Apparel Inc., 637 Lakeshore Blvd. West, pg. 425 IT
Brascade Resources Inc., BCE Place, 181 Bay St., Ste. 4400, pg. 433 IT
Bristol Babcock Canada, 234 Attwell Dr., Rexdale, pg. 473 IT
Brookfield Homes, BCE Pl., 181 Bay St., Ste. 4300, pg. 228 IT
Brookfield Homes Development Corporation, 3111 Dufferin St., pg. 228 IT
Brookfield Homes Ltd., BCE Place,., 181 Bay St., Ste. 4300, pg. 228 IT
BROOKFIELD PROPERTIES CORPORATION, BCE Pl., 181 Bay St., pg. 228 IT
Bulova Watch Company Limited, 105 Bartley Dr., pg. 1011 PB
Bunting Warburg Inc., BCE Pl., 161 Bay Street, Ste. 4100, pg. 1331 IT
Leo Burnett Company Ltd., North Tower, 175 Bloor St. E., pg. 185 PV
Bytex DataCom Ltd., 40 Holly St., pg. 1522 PB
CAE INC., Ste. 3060, Royal Bank Plaza, pg. 237 IT
CCL Custom Manufacturing, 994 Islington Avenue, pg. 239 IT
CIBC Mortgage Corporation, Commerce Court West, pg. 256 IT
CIBC Securities, Inc., Commerce Court West, pg. 256 IT
CIBC Ventures, Inc., Commerce Court West, pg. 256 IT
The CIBC Wood Gundy Corporation, Commerce Ct. West, 7th Fl., pg. 256 IT
CIBC Wood Gundy Inc., 161 Bay St., pg. 256 IT
CIGL HOLDINGS LTD., 200 King St. W., pg. 241 IT
CIMCO Refrigeration, 65 Villiers Street, pg. 1400 IT
CKYC-AM Radio, One Yonge St., 25th Fl., pg. 1124 IT
CLMS Realty Ltd., Ste. 800, 130 Adelaide St. W., pg. 254 IT
CMI-Toronto, 250 Bloor St. E., Ste. 1520, pg. 287 PV
CSA Managed Gold Mutual Funds, 145 King Street, W., Ste. 2700, pg. 243 IT
CSA MANAGEMENT INC., 145 King Street, W., Ste. 2700, pg. 243 IT
CT Financial Services, Inc., 161 Bay Street, pg. 112 IT
Cabot Place Ltd., 250 Bloor St. E, pg. 840 IT
Cadbury Chocolate Canada, Inc., 277 Gladstone Ave., pg. 248 IT
Cambridge Leaseholds Limited, Ste. 300, 95 Wellington St. W., pg. 253 IT
CAMBRIDGE SHOPPING CENTRES LIMITED, 95 Wellington St. W. Ste. 300, pg. 253 IT
Camdev Properties Inc., 40 King St. Ste. 2700, pg. 993 IT
Campbell Soup Company Ltd., 60 Birmingham St., pg. 299 PB
THE CANADA LIFE ASSURANCE COMPANY, 330 University Ave., pg. 254 IT
Canada Life Capital Corporation, 330 University Ave., pg. 254 IT
Canada Life Investment Management Limited, 130 Adelaide St. West, Ste. 804, pg. 255 IT
Canada Life Mortgage Services Ltd., 130 Adelaide St. W., Ste. 800, pg. 255 IT
Canada Life Securing Corporation, 330 University Ave., pg. 255 IT
Canadian Broadcast Sales, 48 St. Clair Ave. W., pg. 1482 IT
The Canadian Coleman Co., Ltd., 15 N. Queen St., pg. 691 PV
Canadian Coleman Supply Co., Inc., 15 N. Queen St., pg. 691 PV
CANADIAN IMPERIAL BANK OF COMMERCE, Commerce Court, pg. 256 IT
Canadian Pacific Hotels & Resorts Inc., One University Ave., pg. 258 IT
Canadian Press Clipping Services, 720 King St., West, Ste. 515, pg. 1124 IT
Canadian Publishing, Maclean Hunter Bldg., 777 Bay St., pg. 1123 IT
CANADIAN TIRE CORPORATION LIMITED, 2180 Yonge St., pg. 259 IT
Candev Financial Services Ltd., 93A King St. E., pg. 115 IT
Cantay Holdings Inc., 250 Bloor St. East, pg. 840 IT
CARA OPERATIONS LIMITED, 230 Bloor St. W., pg. 266 IT
Carbone of America (LCL) Ltd., 496 Evans Ave., pg. 1028 IT
Cardiovascular Innovations Canada, Inc., Ste. 2500, BCE Pl., 181 Bay St., pg. 1282 PB
Carlton Cards, Ltd., 1460 The Queensway, pg. 78 PB
Castrol Canada Inc., 3620 Lake Shore Blvd. W., pg. 235 IT
Caterpillar Financial Services Limited, pg. 315 PB
The Chase Manhattan Bank of Canada, 100 King St. W., Ste. 6900, pg. 340 IT
Checkpoint Communications, 421 Mount Pleasant Rd., pg. 1123 IT
Cho Hung Bank of Canada, 2 Sheppard Avenue East, Ste. 1100, pg. 288 IT
Chocolate Products Co. Ltd., P.O. Box 235, 335 Judson St., pg. 1495 IT
Chubb Insurance Co. of Canada, One Financial Pl., 1 Adelaide St. E., Ste. 1600, pg. 355 PB
Church & Dwight Co., Inc. Ltd., 75 The Donway West, pg. 356 PB
Cigna Insurance Company of Canada, 2 First Canadian Place, pg. 366 PB
Cigna Life Insurance Company of Canada, 250 Yonge Street, Suite 1400, pg. 362 PB
Cincinnati Milacron-Canada Ltd., 122 N. Queen St., pg. 368 PB

CINEPLEX ODEON CORPORATION, 1303 Yonge St., pg. 292 IT
The Citadel Assurance Companies, 1075 Bay Street, pg. 346 IT
Citibank Canada, Citibank Plaza, 123 Front St., W., Ste. 1900, pg. 378 PB
Clarify Inc.-Canada, 1 Young Street, Suite 1801, pg. 382 PB
Classco Benefit Services Limited, 330 University Ave., pg. 255 IT
CLUB MONACO INC., 430 King St. West, pg. 298 IT
Cluett, Peabody Canada Inc., 45 St. Clair Ave. W., pg. 194 PB
CO-STEEL INC., Scotia Plaza, Ste. 5010, P.O. Box 130, pg. 298 IT
Coats Patons, 1001 Roselawn Ave., pg. 300 IT
Colgate-Palmolive Canada Inc., 99 Vanderhoof Ave., pg. 398 PB
Collectibles Plant, 45 Samor Rd., pg. 672 PB
Columbia Health Care, Inc., 20 Elinton Ave., West, Suite 1007, M4R 1K8, pg. 1531 PB
Combined Insurance Company of America, 980 Yonge St., pg. 118 IT
Comdisco Canada Ltd., Royal Bank Plaza, N. Tower, 200 Bay St., Ste. 2200, pg. 408 IT
Cominco Ltd., 2200-120 Adelaide Street West, pg. 308 IT
Commerce & Industry Insurance Co. of Canada, 145 Wellington St., pg. 85 PB
Commercial Financial Corporation Limited, 95 King St. E., Ste. 500, pg. 115 IT
Commercial Union Assurance Company of Canada, Commercial Union Tower, 100 Wellington Street West, pg. 308 IT
Commercial Union of Canada Holdings Ltd, Toronto Dominion Centre, pg. 308 IT
Commerzbank AG-Canada Representative Office, Royal Bank Plaza, South Tower, Ste. 3190, pg. 311 IT
Compagnie d'Assurance du Quebec, 10 Wellington St. E., pg. 1131 IT
Computer Task Group of Canada Inc., Sun Life Center, 150 King St. W., pg. 423 IT
Confed Investment Counselling Limited, 250 Bloor St. East, pg. 325 IT
CONFEDERATION LIFE INSURANCE COMPANY, One Mount Pleasant Rd., pg. 325 IT
Confederation Trust Company, One Mount Pleasant Road, pg. 326 IT
Consolidated Fastfrate, 2525 St. Clair Ave., W., pg. 1150 IT
Continental PIR Communications, Inc., 160 Bloor Street, Ste. 500, pg. 1226 IT
The Continuum Company, Ltd., 1881 Young St., pg. 423 IT
Cooper & Beatty, 401 Wellington St. W., pg. 698 IT
Coscient-Astral Distribution, Royal Le Pge Bldg., Ste. 1020, 33 Yonge St., pg. 335 IT
Cossette Communication-Marketing (Toronto) Inc., 931 Yonge St., pg. 336 IT
Cott Corporation - Central Division, 207 Queen's Quay West, pg. 337 IT
Cott Corporation - North East Division, 207 Quenn's Quay West, pg. 337 IT
COUNSEL CORPORATION, Ste. 1300 The Exchange Tower, 130 King Street West, pg. 338 IT
Crawford & Company Insurance Adjusters Ltd., 185 The West Mall, Ste. 1200, pg. 458 PB
Credit Union of Central Canada, 300 The East Mall, pg. 1085 IT
CROSBIE & COMPANY INC., One First Canadian Pl., Ste. 980, pg. 348 IT
Crown Life Investment Management Company (CLIMCO), 120 Bloor St. E., pg. 468 IT
Cylinder Division, 530 Kipling Avenue, pg. 1262 PB
D & B Software, 10 Bay St., Ste. 400, pg. 532 IT
DMR Group, Inc., 252 Adelaide St. East, pg. 528 IT
Dai-Ichi Kangyo Bank (Canada), Suite 5025, Commerce Court West, pg. 362 IT
Dai-Ichi Kangyo Bank, Ltd.-Toronto, pg. 361 IT
Dai-ichi Life International (Canada), Inc., T-D Bank Tower, Ste. 2008, pg. 362 IT
Daisytek (Canada) Inc., 35 Valley Wood, pg. 477 PB
Daiwa Bank Canada, Sun Life Tower, pg. 373 IT
Daiwa Securities Canada Limited, Ste. 904, 105 Adelaide St. W., pg. 376 IT
Danbel Industries Inc., 222 Inslington Ave., pg. 955 IT
Davy International, Canada, Ste. 1100, 480 University Ave., pg. 775 IT
Dayton Progress of Canada, 1107 Barmac Dr., pg. 617 PB
Deluxe Toronto Limited, 380 Adelaide St., W., pg. 1087 IT
Dentsu-Cadence Canada, Inc., 438 University Avenue, 19th Floor, pg. 393 IT
DERLAN INDUSTRIES LIMITED, 145 King St. E., Ste. 500, pg. 395 IT
Destination Products International, Inc., 207 Queen's Quay West, Suite 885, pg. 338 IT
Deutsche Bank AG (Canada), 222 Bay St. Ste. 1200, pg. 404 IT
Dombur Investments Limited, 250 Bloor St. East, pg. 840 IT
Domgroup Ltd., 184 Front St. East, Ste. 400, pg. 631 IT
The Dominion Realty Company Limited, Commerce Court West, pg. 256 IT
Donohue Recycling Inc., 95 Commissioners Street,Suite 800, pg. 1075 IT
Doubleday Canada Ltd., 105 Bond St., pg. 192 IT
Dow Jones Canada, Inc., 155 University Ave., pg. 525 PB
Dow Jones Markets Canada, Inc., 60 Yonge Street, pg. 525 IT
Dresdner Bank Canada, 2 First Canadian Place, pg. 419 IT

DYLEX LIMITED, 637 Lake Shore Blvd., W., pg. 425 IT
DYNACARE, INC., 20 Eglinton Ave. W., Ste. 1600, pg. 425 IT
EPS/Entertainment Programming Services Ltd., 720 King St. West, Ste. 600, pg. 1282 IT
ESS-FOOD Canada, Inc., 48 Yonge St. W, Ste. 1001, pg. 429 IT
Ebasco Services of Canada Limited, Royal Bank Plaza, South Tower, pg. 1587 PB
EDPERBRASCAN CORPORATION, BCE Place, Ste. 4400, 181 Bay Street, pg. 433 IT
Everest Insurance Company of Canada, Scotia Plaza, 40 King Street West, pg. 597 IT
Export Finance Corporation of Canada Limited, Commerce Court West, pg. 257 IT
FAHNESTOCK VINER HOLDINGS INC., 20 Eglinton Ave. W., Suite 1110, pg. 476 IT
FAIRFAX FINANCIAL HOLDINGS LIMITED, 95 Wellington St., W., Ste. 800, pg. 476 IT
Falconbridge Limited, Ste. 1200, 95 Wellington St. West, pg. 433 IT
The Family Channel Inc., BCE Place, 181 Bay St., pg. 1482 PV
Famous Players Inc., 146 Bloor St. W., pg. 779 PV
Financial Collection Agencies, 4th Floor, 3200 Dufferin, pg. 470 IT
The Financial Post, 333 King St. East, pg. 1320 IT
FIRST MARATHON INC., 2 First Canadian Pl., Ste. 3200, pg. 486 IT
First Marathon Securities Limited, 2 First Canadian Place, pg. 486 IT
Firstcom Marketing Inc., 4100 Young St., Ste. 300, pg. 1200 PV
Fleming Canada Partners Inc., Ste. 1105, 100 Yonge St., pg. 493 IT
Fort James Canada, Inc., 137 Bentworth Ave., pg. 672 PB
Fortress Scientific Limited, 155 St. Regis Crescent South, pg. 826 IT
Forum Corporation of Canada, Ltd., 10 Bay St., #1512, pg. 420 PV
Four Seasons Hotel, 21 Avenue Rd., pg. 502 IT
Sally Fourmy & Associates, 30 Duncan St., pg. 113 PB
Fuji Bank Canada, Canada Trust Tower, Ste. 2800, BCE Pl., 161 Bay St., pg. 521 IT
GATX National Leasing, Ltd., Sun Life Tower, 150 King St., Ste. 2411, pg. 691 PB
GPC Communications (Ontario), 200 King St. W., Ste. 1702, M5H 3T4, pg. 1225 PB
GPC Government Policy Consultants (Ontario), 200 King St. W., Ste. 1702, M5H 3T4, pg. 1225 PB
Galileo Canada Distribution Systems Inc., 330 Front St. West, pg. 36 IT
GEE, JEFFERY & PARTNERS ADVERTISING INC., 154 Pearl Street, Suite 300, pg. 542 IT
The Gemini Group Limited Partnership, 330 Front St. West, pg. 36 IT
General Motors Acceptance Corporation of Canada Limited, Center Tower, 3300 Bloor St. W., Ste. 2800, pg. 720 PB
Geodimeter of Canada Ltd., 41 Horner Ave., Unit 5, pg. 1290 IT
Glengarry and Stormont Railway Company, 150 King St. West, pg. 1319 IT
Global Travel Computer Holdings Ltd., 365 Bloor St. E., pg. 36 IT
Gold Circle Insurance Co., 14th Floor, 200 King St. W., pg. 558 IT
Goldcorp Inc., 145 King St., W., Ste. 2700, pg. 243 IT
Goldman Sachs Canada, 150 King St., West, Ste. 1201, pg. 462 PV
Goody Canada Limited, 45 Samor Rd., pg. 1177 PB
Gould Electronics (Canada) Ltd., Shawmut Div., 88 Horner Ave., pg. 1592 PB
Grapheme Inc., 931, Yonge Street, pg. 336 IT
Great Lakes Power Inc., 181 Bay St., Ste. 4400, pg. 433 IT
Green Forest Lumber Corporation, 194 Merton St., pg. 828 IT
Green Line Investor Service, The Exchange Tower, 2 First Canadian Place, Ste. 3160, pg. 1401 IT
GREYVEST CAPITOL INC., 20 Adelaide St. E., Ste. 1300, pg. 559 IT
Greyvest Technology Inc., 20 Adelaide St. E., Ste. 1300, pg. 559 IT
Griffin Bacal Volny, 45 St. Clair Ave. W., 4th Fl., pg. 480 PV
Grolier Limited, 16 Overlea Blvd., pg. 794 IT
Grolier Limited Canada, 16 Overlea Boulevard, pg. 795 IT
Groupe Accor of Canada Inc., Two Berkeley St., Ste. 301, pg. 21 IT
Guthrie Canadian Investments Limited, 40 University Ave, Suite 1020, pg. 113 IT
HMI Acceptance Corp., pg. 771 PB
HMI Incorporated, pg. 771 PB
Haden Schweitzer Canada Inc., Toronto Dominion Bank Tower, 55 King St., 36th Fl., pg. 586 IT
The Halifax Insurance Company, 75 Eglinton Avenue East, pg. 648 IT
HARRISON, YOUNG, PESONEN & NEWELL INC., 1240 Bay St., Ste. 500, pg. 598 IT
Harrowston Capital Corporation, 181 Bay St., Ste. 3826, pg. 599 IT
HARROWSTON CORPORATION, 181 Bay Street, Ste. 3820, pg. 599 IT
Harrowston Developments Corporation, Ste. 3820, 181 Bay St., pg. 599 IT
Harry Rosen Inc., 11 Adelaide St. W., Suite 200, pg. 425 IT
Hilroy, 250 Bowie Ave., pg. 20 IT
Houghton Canada Inc., 100 Symes Rd., pg. 541 PV
Household Rental Systems, pg. 771 PB

PB - *U.S. Public Companies Volume*
PV - *U.S. Private Companies Volume*
IT - *International Public & Private Companies Volume*

HUDSON'S BAY COMPANY, 401 Bay St., Ste. 501, pg. 637   **IT**
Huls Canada Inc., 34 Industrial St., pg. 1455   **IT**
Humphreys & Glasgow (Canada) Limited c/o McTaggart, Stone, Winters & Herridge, 390 Bay St., Ste. 2600, pg. 1587   **PB**
IPCF Properties Inc., 22 St. Clair Ave. E., pg. 1495   **IT**
ITT Sheraton Hotels, 123 Queen St. W., pg. 1512   **PB**
ITT Sheraton Inns Canada, 123 Queen St. W., pg. 1512   **PB**
Iberia Air Lines of Spain, 102 Bloor St. W., Ste. 400, pg. 575   **IT**
Imbank Nominees Limited, Commerce Court West, pg. 257   **IT**
IMPACT/FCB, 245 Eglington Avenue East, Suite 200, pg. 389   **PV**
The Imperial Life Assurance Co., 95 St. Clair Ave., W., M4V 1N7, pg. 396   **IT**
Imperial Oil Limited, 111 St. Clair Ave. W., pg. 602   **IT**
INACAN Holdings Ltd., Scotia Plaza, Ste. 3800, 40 King St. W., pg. 366   **IT**
INCO LIMITED, 145 King St. W., Ste. 1500, pg. 672   **IT**
Inco Specialty Powder Products, pg. 672   **IT**
The Industrial Bank of Japan (Canada), Box 29, Ste. 1102, pg. 676   **IT**
The Industrial Bank of Japan, Limited (Canada), Box 29, Ste., 1102, 100 Yonge St., pg. 675   **IT**
Ingersoll-Rand Canada, Inc., 51 Worcester Road, pg. 878   **IT**
INMET MINING CORPORATION, Ste. 3400, Aetna Tower, 79 Wellington St. W., pg. 678   **IT**
Intercon Security Limited, 40 Sheppard Avenue West, pg. 699   **IT**
International Commercial Bank of Cathay, 150 York St., Ste. 910, pg. 684   **IT**
The International Commercial Bank of China, 270 Spadina Ave., pg. 684   **IT**
International Paper Canada, Inc., 6 Curity Avenue, pg. 905   **PB**
International Power Machines Canada Ltd., Ste. 2500, Commerce Court W., pg. 126   **IT**
Irwin Sports, Inc., 43 Hanna Ave., pg. 688   **IT**
IRWIN TOY LTD., 43 Hanna Ave., pg. 688   **IT**
Ivex Packaging Corporation-Canadian Region, 40 Butterick Rd., pg. 915   **PB**
J&H Marsh & McLennan Ltd., Canada Trust Tower, BCE Pl., pg. 1049   **PB**
Jannock Imaging Companies Limited, 553 Richmond St. W., pg. 698   **IT**
JANNOCK LIMITED, Scotia Plaza, Suite 5205, 40 King Street West, pg. 698   **IT**
Jugobanka (Toronto Rep.), 401 Bay St., pg. 716   **IT**
Juki Corporation, c/o/ B&W Sewing Machine Co., 75 Colville Rd., pg. 717   **IT**
Junors, 16 Goodrich Rd., pg. 1150   **IT**
KSB Pumps, Inc., 65 Queen St. West, Ste. 405, pg. 721   **IT**
Keane Canada, Inc., 439 University Ave., Ste. 500, pg. 946   **PB**
Kelley Advertising Inc., 1881 Yonge St., 5th Fl., pg. 765   **PB**
Kelly Services Canada, Ltd., One University Ave., Ste. 300, pg. 949   **PB**
Kenner Products (Canada) Limited, 43 Hanna Ave., pg. 798   **PB**
KEY Radio Limited, 1 Yonge St., Ste. 2416, pg. 1124   **IT**
Kilborn SNC-Lavalin Inc., 2200 Lakeshore Blvd. West, pg. 1162   **IT**
KINROSS GOLD CORPORATION, Scotia Plaza, 40 King St. W., 57th Fl., pg. 734   **IT**
Kodak Canada Inc., 3500 Eglington Ave. W., pg. 553   **PB**
Korn/Ferry International, Scotia Plaza, 40 King St. W., Ste. 3918, pg. 633   **PV**
Kuwait Airways, Canada, 77 Bloor St. W., pg. 764   **IT**
LGT Asset Management, Inc., Royal Trust Tower, TD Centre, Ste. 4001, pg. 810   **IT**
Labatt Breweries of Canada, Labatt House, 181 Bay Street, BCE Place, pg. 679   **IT**
Labatt Brewing Company Limited, Labatt House, BCE Pl., pg. 679   **IT**
LaFarge Concrete Products, 1224 Lawrence Ave., W., pg. 789   **IT**
Lafarge Materials, 1224 Lawrence Ave., W., pg. 789   **IT**
Lally, McFarland & Pantello, 175 Bloor St. E., #704, pg. 603   **IT**
Lancaster Canada Inc., 10 Bay St., Ste. 905, pg. 186   **IT**
Lancia-Bravo Foods, 58A Hook Ave., pg. 159   **PV**
Laurentian Financial Services, 310 Front Street W., pg. 396   **IT**
Lever Pond's Limited, 1 Sunlight Park Rd., pg. 1438   **IT**
Lexam Explorations Inc., 145 King Street, W., Ste. 2700, pg. 243   **IT**
The Lincoln Electric Co. of Canada Ltd., 179 Wicksteed Avenue, pg. 997   **PB**
Lipton, 160 Bloor St. East, pg. 1438   **IT**
Arthur D. Little of Canada Ltd., 67 Yonge St., Ste. 400, pg. 671   **PV**
Little Brown & Co. (Canada) Ltd., 148 Yorkville Ave., pg. 1615   **PB**
Logica Inc., 55 University Ave., Ste. 1710, pg. 814   **IT**
Louis Vuitton Canada Inc., 110 Bloor St. West, pg. 782   **IT**
Lurgi Canada Ltd., 100 Adelaide St. W., pg. 861   **IT**
Mac Cosmetics, 233 Carlton St., pg. 594   **PB**
Mack Canada Inc., 1350 The Queensway, pg. 1103   **IT**
MACKENZIE FINANCIAL CORPORATION, 150 Bloor Sreet West, pg. 828   **IT**
Maclean Hunter Broadcasting, 777 Bay St., pg. 1123   **IT**
Maclean Hunter Mailing Services, Unit 410, 500 Keele St., pg. 1124   **IT**
Maclean Hunter Publishing Ltd., 777 Bay St., pg. 1123   **IT**

The Magnetic North Corporation, 70 Richmond St., East, Ste. 100, pg. 1124   **IT**
The Magnetic South Corporation, 550 Queen St. East, Ste. 205, pg. 1124   **IT**
ManuCab Ltd., 250 Bloor St. E., pg. 840   **IT**
The Manufacturers Life Insurance Company of America, 200 Bloor St. East, pg. 840   **IT**
The Manufacturers Life Insurance Company of Michigan, 200 Bloor St. East, pg. 840   **IT**
Manufacturers Life Property Corporation, 250 Bloor St., E., pg. 840   **IT**
Manufacturers Life Services Canada Limited, 200 Bloor St. East, pg. 840   **IT**
Manulife Bank of Canada-Regional Lending Unit, 33 Yonge Street, Ste. 607, pg. 840   **IT**
ManuLife Computer Corp. Ltd., 200 Bloor St., E., pg. 840   **IT**
Manulife Financial, 250 Bloor Street East, pg. 840   **IT**
Manulife Financial Holdings Limited, 250 Bloor St., E., pg. 840   **IT**
ManuLife Financial Services Limited, 200 Bloor St., E., pg. 840   **IT**
MANULIFE FINANCIAL (THE MANUFACTURERS LIFE INSURANCE COMPANY), 200 Bloor St., East, M4W 1E5, pg. 840   **IT**
ManuLife Investment Holdings Limited, 200 Bloor St. East, pg. 840   **IT**
ManuLife Investment Management Corporation, 250 Bloor St., E., pg. 840   **IT**
MAPLE LEAF FOODS INC., 30 St. Clair Ave. W., pg. 841   **IT**
Marietta Canada, Inc., 35A Jutland Rd., pg. 703   **PV**
Market Facts of Canada, Ltd., 77 Bloor St., W., pg. 1047   **PB**
Marubeni Canada Ltd., Canada Trust Tower BCE Place, 161 Bay St., Ste. 2300, pg. 845   **IT**
Master Builders Technologies Ltd., 29 Kincourt St., pg. 1465   **IT**
MCCLELLAND & STEWART, 481 University Ave., Ste. 900, pg. 851   **IT**
McDonald's Restaurants of Canada Ltd., McDonald's Place, pg. 1069   **PB**
McLean McCarthy Limited, 222 Bay St. Ste. 1100, pg. 405   **IT**
MediaLinx Interactive Inc., 181 Bay Street, pg. 115   **IT**
The Meiji Life Insurance Company Toronto Office, 199 Bay St., Ste. 4121, pg. 854   **IT**
Mellon Bank Canada, Royal Bank Plaza, P.O. Box 153, pg. 1086   **PB**
Mellon Fund Administration Ltd, 44 Victoria St., pg. 1086   **PB**
Mercedes-Benz Canada Inc., 849 Eglinton Ave. E., pg. 368   **IT**
William M. Mercer Limited, BCE Place, 161 Bay St., pg. 840   **PB**
Merrill Corporation-Toronto, 401 Wellington St. W., 4th Fl., M5V 1E8, pg. 1097   **PB**
Merrill Lynch Canada Inc., Merrill Lynch Canada Tower, 200 King St. W., pg. 1098   **PB**
Metall Mining Corporation, Ste. 3400, Aetna Tower, 79 Wellington Street West, pg. 862   **IT**
Midland Walwyn Capital Inc., 181 Bay Street, pg. 865   **IT**
MIDLAND WALWYN INC., 181 Bay Street, Suite 400, pg. 865   **IT**
Midland Walwyn Insurance Services Limited, 181 Bay Street, Suite 400, pg. 865   **IT**
Herman Miller, Ltd., Ste. 400 11 Adelaid St. W., pg. 1112   **IT**
Mitsui & Co. (Canada) Ltd., Royal Bank Plaza, Ste. 3333, South Tower, pg. 880   **IT**
Modern Building Cleaning Inc., Islington & Evans Box 950, pg. 79   **PV**
Molson Breweries, 175 Bloor Street East, pg. 887   **IT**
THE MOLSON COMPANIES LIMITED, 40 King Street West, Suite 3600, pg. 887   **IT**
Montgomery KONE Elevator Co. Ltd., 80 Horner Avenue, pg. 748   **IT**
Montrusco Associates, The Exchange Tower, 130, King Street West, Suite 1580, pg. 888   **IT**
Moody's Canada Inc., BCE Place 181 Bay Street, Ste. 1610, pg. 537   **PB**
MOORE CORPORATION LIMITED, 1 First Canadian Place, pg. 888   **IT**
J.P. Morgan Canada, Royal Bank Plaza, South Tower, Ste. 2200, pg. 1130   **IT**
J.P. Morgan Securities Canada Inc., Royal Bank Plaza, South Tower, Ste. 2200, pg. 1131   **IT**
Morgan Stanley Canada Ltd., BCE Pl., 181 Bay St., Ste. 3700, P.O. Box 776, pg. 1133   **PB**
Morguard Investments Limited, Toronto, One University Avenue, Ste. 1500, pg. 738   **PV**
The Mortgage Insurance Company of Canada, 1 Dundas St. W., Ste. 1600, pg. 241   **IT**
Motion & Control Group, 530 Kipling Avenue, pg. 1261   **PB**
NBD Bank, Canada, North Tower, Royal Bank Plaza, Ste. 1601, pg. 628   **PB**
NLI International Canada Inc., Suite 4620, 1 First Canadian Place, pg. 936   **IT**
NLI Properties Canada Inc., Suite 4620, 1 First Canadian Place, pg. 936   **IT**
NYK Line (Canada) Inc., 1 Yonge Street, Suite 1101, pg. 942   **IT**
Nanisivik Mines Ltd., 12th Fl., 20 Toronto St., pg. 1138   **IT**
National Reinsurance Company of Canada, 55 University Ave., Suite 1200, pg. 443   **PV**
NATIONAL TRUSTCO INC., One Financial Pl., 3rd. Fl., One Adelaide St. E., pg. 909   **IT**
National Westminster Bank of Canada, Suite 3350,200 Bay Street, South Tower, Royal Bank Plaza, pg. 911   **IT**
Neosid (Canada) Limited, 10 Vansco Road, pg. 1344   **IT**

The Nesbitt Thomson Corporation Limited, Sun Life Tower, 150 King St. W., pg. 153   **IT**
Neste Shipping Canada Ltd., Waterpark Pl., 10 Bay St., Ste. 320, pg. 915   **IT**
Nestle Confectionery, 72 Sterling Rd., pg. 922   **IT**
NEWCOURT CREDIT GROUP INC., 181 Bay St., Ste. 3500, pg. 924   **IT**
NewsEdge Canada, Inc., 1 Eglinton Ave. E., Ste. 501, pg. 1180   **PB**
Nichimen Canada Inc., Ste. 2206, 20 Queen St. West, pg. 928   **IT**
Nissho Iwai Canada Ltd., 150 King St. West, Ste. 1506, pg. 948   **IT**
Nomura Canada Inc., Ste. 5830, 1 First Canadian Place, pg. 957   **IT**
Noranda Forest Inc., Toronto-Dominion Bank Tower, Ste. 4414, pg. 434   **IT**
Noranda Inc., BCE Place, Ste. 4100, 181 Bay St., pg. 433   **IT**
Noranda Minerals, One Adelaide St. E., Ste. 2700, pg. 434   **IT**
Northern Pigment, 36 Towns Road, pg. 1150   **PB**
The Northern Trust Company-Canadian Representative Office, B.C.E. Place, 161 Bay St., Ste. 4540, pg. 1197   **PB**
Notifier Canada, pg. 1306   **PB**
NUMETRIX LTD., 655 Bay St., Ste. 1200, pg. 990   **IT**
O&Y PROPERTIES CORPORATION, 40 King St. W., Ste. 2700, pg. 993   **IT**
Olicom Americas - Canada, 145 Wellington St., West, Suite 750, pg. 1001   **IT**
Olsten Staffing Services, 77 Bloor St. W., pg. 1221   **PB**
OLYMPIA & YORK DEVELOPMENTS LTD., 2 First Canadian Place, Bay Street, pg. 1004   **IT**
ONEX CORPORATION, 161 Bay Street., 40th Floor, pg. 1006   **IT**
ONTARIO HYDRO, 700 University Ave., pg. 1007   **IT**
Ontario Limited, 321 Bloor St. East, pg. 326   **IT**
The Ontario Produce Co., 165 The Queensway, pg. 1012   **IT**
Opinac Energy Corporation, Toronto Dominion Bank Tower, Toronto-Dominion Ctr., pg. 1181   **PB**
Optimum Inc., 931 Yonge Street, pg. 336   **IT**
Outdoor Services, 175 Bloor St. E., S. Tower 7th Fl., pg. 1168   **PV**
Outokumpu Mines Ltd., Ste. 4650, 1 First Canadian Place, pg. 1016   **IT**
PHH Toronto, 40 University Ave., Ste. 300, pg. 321   **PB**
Panalpina Inc., 25 Ontario St., pg. 1023   **IT**
Paramount Productions, Inc., 146 Bloor St. West, pg. 777   **PV**
Parfums Givenchy Canada Ltd., 165 Carlton St., pg. 783   **IT**
Paribas Bank of Canada, 77 King St., pg. 321   **IT**
Paribas Participation Ltd., TD Center, Royal Trust Tower, Ste. 4104, pg. 321   **IT**
Pepsi-Cola Canada, Ltd., 1255 Bay Rd., pg. 1277   **PB**
The Perrier Group of Canada Ltd., 180 Jardin Dr., pg. 922   **PB**
PETERSBURG LONG DISTANCE INC., 166 Pearl St., pg. 1040   **IT**
Pier 1 Imports Canada, 221 Yonge St., pg. 1295   **PB**
Pitney Bowes of Canada Ltd., 2200 Young St., Ste. 100, pg. 1304   **PB**
Playtex Apparel Canada, Ltd., Toronto, 370 King St. W., Ste. 250, pg. 1433   **PB**
Polysar Rubber Corporation, 200, 444 Yonge St., pg. 175   **IT**
Potash Company of Canada Ltd. (Potacan), Suite 1905, Box 48, 200 King Street West, pg. 109   **IT**
Premetalco Inc., Mo Belfield Road, pg. 1071   **IT**
Premier Fastener Ltd., 271 Attwell Dr., pg. 1068   **IT**
Principal Marques Inc., 21 Medulla Ave., pg. 599   **IT**
Progress Lighting Canada, 25 Ingram Dr., pg. 1684   **PB**
Promo Marketing Canada, Inc., 3300 Bloor Street West, 14th Floor, pg. 212   **PV**
Promotion Blitz Inc., 931 Yonge Street, pg. 336   **IT**
Publicis BCP Direct Inc., 1200 Bay St., Ste. 1200, pg. 116   **IT**
Publicis BCP Toronto Inc., 1200 Bay St., Ste. 1200, pg. 116   **IT**
Quarterdeck Office Systems Canada, Inc., 70 York St. #1220, pg. 1351   **PB**
RAI Corporation Canada, 1235 Bay Street, pg. 655   **PB**
RBC Dominion Securities Ltd., pg. 1131   **IT**
Ranco Controls Canada, Ltd., 221 Evans Ave., pg. 1243   **IT**
RAYROCK YELLOWKNIFE RESOURCES INC., 30 Soudan Ave., Ste. 500, pg. 1089   **IT**
Reckitt & Colman Canada Inc., 2 Wickman Rd., pg. 1090   **IT**
Redpath Industries Ltd., 95 Queens Key East, pg. 1357   **IT**
Reed Stenhouse Companies Ltd., Reed Stenouse Towers, pg. 1118   **PB**
Regal Greetings & Gifts, 939 Eglinton Ave., E., pg. 1150   **IT**
Reichhold Ltd., 1919 Wilson Ave., pg. 370   **IT**
Republic National Bank of New York (Canada), 3055 Bathurst St., pg. 1381   **PB**
Rio Algom Exploration, Inc., 120 Adelaide St. W. Ste. 2400, pg. 1118   **IT**
RIO ALGOM LIMITED, 120 Adelaide St. W., Ste. 2600, pg. 1118   **IT**
Roche Macaulay & Partners, 22 St. Clair Avenue East, pg. 678   **PV**
Rochester & Pittsburgh Coal Company (Canada) Ltd., 130 Adelaide St., W., pg. 1395   **IT**
Roden Stores Inc., 95 Ingram Dr., pg. 1007   **IT**
Rogers CFTR-AM, 25 Adelaide St. E., pg. 1123   **IT**
Rogers CHFI-FM, 25 Adelaide St. E., pg. 1123   **IT**

PB - *U.S. Public Companies Volume*
PV - *U.S. Private Companies Volume*
IT - *International Public & Private Companies Volume*

ROGERS COMMUNICATIONS, INC., Suite 6400, Scotia Plaza, pg. 1122 **IT**
Roins Holdings Limited, 10 Wellington St. E., pg. 1131 **IT**
Royal Bank Export Finance Co. Ltd. (REFCO), 6th Fl., 180 Wellington St., W., pg. 1131 **IT**
ROYAL BANK OF CANADA, Royal Bank Plaza, 200 Bay St., pg. 1131 **IT**
Royal Insurance Company of Canada, 10 Wellington St. E., pg. 1131 **IT**
Royal LePage Real Estate Services Ltd., 33 Yonge St., Ste. 900, pg. 1143 **IT**
Royal Mutual Funds Inc., Royal Trust Tower, P.O. Box 7500, Station A, pg. 1131 **IT**
Rust Craft Canada, Inc., 1460 The Queensway, pg. 78 **PB**
S & C Electric Canada Ltd., 90 Belfield Rd., pg. 954 **PV**
SAS Institute (Canada) Inc., BCE Place, 181 Bay St., pg. 967 **PV**
SBC Portfolio Management (Canada) Inc., 207 Queen's Quay West, Suite 780, pg. 1332 **IT**
SCOR Canada Reinsurance Company, BCE Place Canada Trust Tower, 161, Bay Street, Suite 5000, pg. 1152 **IT**
SEI Corporation, 70 York St., Ste. 1040, pg. 1417 **PB**
SHL Systemhouse - Central Canada Region, 55 York St., 7th Fl., pg. 1154 **IT**
SMH Swiss Watches & Microelectronics (Canada) Ltd., 555, Richmond Street, West, pg. 1161 **IT**
St. Anne Pulp Sales Co. Ltd., 250 Bloor Street E., Ste. 1420, pg. 841 **PV**
ST. CLAIR PAINT AND WALLPAPER CORPORATION, 10 Carson St., pg. 1170 **IT**
St. Clair Pipelines, Unicorp. Bldg., 21 St. Clair Ave. E., pg. 1492 **IT**
The Sakura Bank (Canada), Commerce Court West, Suite 3601, pg. 1180 **IT**
Sanpaolo-Toronto Representative Office, 1, First Canadian Place, Ste. 2640, pg. 692 **IT**
Sanwa Bank Canada, BCE Place, Canada Trust Tower, P.O. Box 525, pg. 1190 **IT**
Sanyo Canada Inc., 50 Beth Nealson Dr., pg. 1192 **IT**
Sanyo E.T. Canada Inc., 50 Beth Nealson Dr., pg. 1192 **IT**
Saturday Night Magazine Limited, 184 Front St. E., Ste. 400, pg. 631 **IT**
Schlumberger Canada Limited, 41st Floor, 1 First Canadian Place, pg. 1439 **PB**
Scotia Capital Markets, Scotia Plaza, 40 King Street, West, pg. 156 **IT**
Scotia Discount Brokerage Inc., 7th Floor, 1 Richmond Street West, pg. 155 **IT**
Scotia Life Insurance Company, 4th Floor, 100 Yonge Street, pg. 155 **IT**
Scotia Properties Quebec Inc., Scotia Plaza, 44 King Street West, pg. 156 **IT**
Scotia Realty Limited, Scotia Plaza, 44 King Street West, pg. 156 **IT**
ScotiaMcLeod Inc., P.O. Box 433, Commercial Union Tower, pg. 156 **IT**
Sears Canada, Inc., 222 Jarvis St., pg. 1452 **PB**
The Second Cup, 175 Bloor Street, East, pg. 266 **IT**
Sherway Center Limited, 330 University Ave., pg. 255 **IT**
Shiseido Cosmetics (America) Ltd., 468 Queens St. East #212, pg. 1235 **IT**
Shoppers Drug Mart, Ltd., 225 Yorkland Blvd., pg. 112 **IT**
Shopping Centre Group, Ste 300, 95 Wellington St. West, pg. 253 **IT**
Sierra Creative Communications Inc., 26 Soho Street, Suite 200, pg. 293 **IT**
Simon Marketing Consulting (Canada) Ltd., 931 Yonge St., 3rd Fl., M4W 2H2, pg. 1001 **PV**
Singapore Tourist Promotion Board - Toronto, The Standard Life Centre, 121 King Street West, Suite 1000, pg. 1254 **IT**
Skadden, Arps, Slate, Meagher & Flom LLP, Ste. 1820, North Tower, pg. 1005 **PV**
Skandia Canada Reinsurance Company, Ste. 1600, 55 University Ave., pg. 1258 **IT**
W.H. Smith Canada Ltd., 113 Merton Street, pg. 1150 **IT**
Smithbooks, 113 Merton St., pg. 1150 **IT**
SPAR AEROSPACE LIMITED, 121 King St. W., Ste. 1800, pg. 1287 **IT**
Spectrum Mutual Fund Services Inc., 55 University Ave, Mezzazine, pg. 1319 **IT**
Spectrum United Mutual Funds, Inc., 55 University Ave., Mezzazine, pg. 1319 **IT**
Speedy Muffler King, Inc., 365 Bloor St. E., pg. 1578 **PB**
Stackpole Limited, 550 Evans Ave., pg. 1028 **PV**
STARCAN CORPORATION, BCE Place, pg. 1297 **IT**
State Bank of India (Canada), Royal Bank Plaza, P.O. Box 81, Ste. 400, pg. 1297 **IT**
State Street Canada, Inc., 100 King St. West, Ste. 3500, pg. 1513 **PB**
Stolt Sea Farm Inc., 4100 Yonge St., Ste. 513, pg. 1302 **IT**
Stone & Webster Canada, Ltd., Yonge-Eglinton Centre, 2300 Yonge St., pg. 1520 **PB**
StorageTek Canada, Inc., 51 International Blvd. Rexdale, pg. 1523 **PB**
The Stormont Electric Light & Power Company Limited, 150 King St. West, pg. 1319 **IT**
Stratus Computer Corporation, 120 Adelaide St. W., pg. 1524 **PB**
Stringer Veroni Ketchum Advertising, 160 Bedford Rd., Ste. 307, pg. 617 **PV**
STROUD RESOURCES LTD., 330 Bay Street, Suite 304, pg. 1304 **IT**
Sudler & Hennessey/Gall Inc., 60 Bloor St. West, pg. 1200 **PV**
The Sumitomo Bank of Canada, Ernst & Young Tower, Ste.1400, pg. 1310 **IT**
Sumitomo Canada Ltd., Ste. 7010, P.O. Box 258, pg. 1312 **IT**
The Sumitomo Trust & Banking Co., Ltd., P.O. Box 439, 1 First Canadian Place, Ste. 6920, pg. 1318 **IT**
Summit-Canada, 1460 The Queensway, pg. 78 **PB**
SUN LIFE ASSURANCE COMPANY OF CANADA, Sun Life Centre, 150 King Street West, pg. 1318 **IT**
Sun Life Dealer Services Corp., 150 King St. West, Ste. 1010, pg. 1319 **IT**
Sun Life Distribution Services Inc., 150 King St. West, Ste. 1010, pg. 1319 **IT**
Sun Life Financial Holdings Inc., 150 King Street West, Ste. 1400, pg. 1319 **IT**
Sun Life of Canada, 225 King St. West, pg. 1319 **IT**
Sun Life of Canada Investment Management Limited, 438 University Ave., pg. 1319 **IT**
Sun Life Trust Company, 36 Toronto Street, pg. 1319 **IT**
SUN MEDIA CORPORATION, 333 King St., E., pg. 1320 **IT**
Swiss Bank Corporation (Canada), 207 Queen's Quay W., Ste. 780, pg. 1331 **IT**
Swiss Re Life Canada, 99 Yorkville Avenue, pg. 1333 **IT**
Swiss Reinsurance Company Canada, 99 Yorkville Avenue, pg. 1333 **IT**
Symantec/Delrina, 895 Don Mills Rd., 500-2 Park Ctr., pg. 1545 **PB**
System Sensor Canada, pg. 1307 **PB**
TBWA Chiat/Day Toronto, 10 Lower Spadina, pg. 1063 **PV**
TIW Stress Relieving, 944 Lakeshore Blvd., E., pg. 256 **IT**
TMP Worldwide Ltd., 184 Front St. East, Ste. 201, pg. 1065 **PV**
TNTI, 245 Eglinton Ave. E., Ste. 300, pg. 1642 **PB**
TVX GOLD INC., Ste. 4300, Canada Trust Tower, BCE Place, 161 Bay Street, pg. 1345 **IT**
Templeton Heritage Ltd., 4 King St., W., pg. 680 **PB**
Templeton Management Limited, 4 King St., W., pg. 680 **PB**
Textron Canada Ltd., 40 King St. W., pg. 1590 **PB**
Thai Airways Intl. Ltd.-Toronto, 20 Dundas St., Ste. 1133, pg. 1381 **IT**
Thomson Canada Limited, Toronto Dominion Bank Tower, Ste. 2706, pg. 1602 **PB**
Time Canada Ltd., 175 Bloor St. E 602 N., pg. 1615 **PB**
Tokai Bank Canada, Box 84, Ste. 2401, Sun Life Ctr., pg. 1391 **IT**
Torcad Limited, 275 Norseman St., pg. 1299 **IT**
Torfeaco Industries Ltd., 545 Trethewey Dr., pg. 1296 **PB**
Toronto Blue Jays Baseball Club, Inc., 1 Blue Jays Way, Ste. 3200, pg. 680 **IT**
THE TORONTO DOMINION BANK, Toronto-Dominion Ctr., pg. 1401 **IT**
Toronto Plant, 137 Bentworth Ave., pg. 672 **PB**
Toronto Star Newspapers Ltd., One Yonge Street, pg. 1402 **IT**
The Toronto Sun Publishing Corporation, 333 King St. East, pg. 1320 **IT**
TORSTAR CORPORATION, One Yonge Street, 6th Fl., pg. 1402 **IT**
Trane Co. of Canada, 401 Horner Ave., pg. 92 **PB**
Transatlantic Holdings Inc., 145 Wellington Street West, pg. 84 **PB**
Transatlantic Holdings, Inc.-Toronto, 145 Wellington Street West, pg. 85 **PB**
Transcontinental Sports Publications, 777 Bay Street, Suite 2700, pg. 539 **IT**
Triarch Corporation Ltd., 55 University Ave., Ste. 320, pg. 447 **PB**
Trilon Financial Corp., 181 Bay St., Ste. 4420, pg. 434 **IT**
Triumph Releasing Corporation - Canadian Territory, 1300 Yonge St., Ste. 606, pg. 1282 **IT**
Trivest Insurance Network Ltd., 33 Yonge St., Ste. 1100, pg. 435 **IT**
TRIZECHAHN CORPORATION, 181 Bay St., Suite 3900, pg. 1424 **IT**
The Trust Company of Bank of Montreal, 302 Bay St., pg. 153 **IT**
Trust Corporation of Canada, P.O. Box 7500, Station A, pg. 1131 **IT**
Tundra Books Inc., 481 University Ave., Ste. 802, pg. 851 **IT**
The UCS Group, 36 Toronto St., Ste. 1200, pg. 792 **IT**
UPM-Kymmene Canada, 60 Bloor St. West, pg. 1430 **IT**
UNICORP CANADA CORPORATION, Canada Trust Tower, BCE Place, Suite 2320, 161 Bay Street, pg. 1433 **IT**
Unilever Canada Limited, 160 Bloor St. East, pg. 1439 **IT**
Union Bank of Switzerland (Canada), 154 University Avenue, pg. 1441 **IT**
Union Energy Inc., Unicorp Bldg., 21 St. Clair Ave. E., pg. 1492 **IT**
United Parking Services, Inc., 214 King W., pg. 326 **PB**
Urban Group, Ste. 300, 95 Wellington St. West, pg. 253 **IT**
Urban Outfitters Canada, Inc., 235 Yonge St., pg. 1700 **PB**
Veedol (Canada) Ltd., 3660 Lake Shore Blvd. W., pg. 236 **IT**
Vernon Rentals & Leasing Inc., 1209 King Street West, pg. 559 **IT**
Viacom Canada Ltd., 45 Charles St. E., pg. 779 **PV**
Viacom Enterprises Canada Ltd., 45 Charles St. E., pg. 779 **PV**
VITRAN CORPORATION INC., 70 University Ave., Ste. 350, pg. 1469 **IT**
WF Corroon-Ontario, 20 Adelaide Street East, Ste. 300, pg. 1502 **IT**
WMC International Ltd., 181 Bat Street, BCE Place, Ste. 3000, pg. 1494 **IT**
WABCO Standard Inc., 1401 Dupont Street, pg. 92 **PB**
The Watt Design Group Inc., 300 Bayview Avenue, pg. 338 **IT**
Wellington Trust Company, 95 King St. E., pg. 115 **IT**
Western Assurance Company, 10 Wellington St. E., pg. 1131 **IT**
Western Broadcast Sales Ltd., 1600-55 Bloor St. W., pg. 1482 **IT**
Western International Media Corporation, 175 Bloor St. E., S. Tower, 7th Fl., pg. 1168 **PV**
WestLB Toronto Branch, Box 52, Ste. 1704, 95 Wellington St. W., pg. 1493 **IT**
Weston Foods, 22 St. Clair Ave. East, pg. 1495 **IT**
GEORGE WESTON LIMITED, 22 St. Clair Avenue East, pg. 1494 **IT**
Weston Resources, 22 St. Clair Ave. East, pg. 1495 **IT**
WHEATON RIVER MINERALS LTD., 330 Bay Street, pg. 1498 **IT**
Willis Corroon Melling Inc., 20 Adelaide Street East, Suite 300, pg. 1509 **IT**
Wiltshire Canada, Inc., 1 Yonge St., Ste. 1014, pg. 852 **IT**
Winners Apparel Ltd., 65 Densley Ave., pg. 1557 **PB**
Wolf Advertising Limited, 35 Prince Arthur Ave., pg. 1186 **PV**
Wolf-Campbell Public Relations, 35 Prince Arthur Ave., pg. 1186 **PV**
Young & Rubicam Ltd., 60 Bloor St. W., pg. 1200 **PV**
Carl Zeiss Canada Ltd., 45 Valleybrook Dr., pg. 1523 **IT**
Zellers Inc., 401 Bay Street, Suite 700, pg. 637 **IT**
ZEMEX CORPORATION, Canada Trust Tower, BCE Place, Ste. 3750, pg. 1523 **IT**
Zurich Indemnity Company of Canada, 400 Unversity Avenue, pg. 1531 **IT**
Zurich Insurance Company, 400 University Ave., pg. 1531 **IT**
Zurich Investment Management Ltd., 400 University Avenue, pg. 1532 **IT**

Trail

Cominco Ltd., Metal Production Division, pg. 308 **IT**
Cominco Ltd.-Research Div., pg. 308 **IT**
West Kootenay Power, 1290 Esplanade, pg. 1701 **PB**

Trenton

BICC Pyrotenax, 250 West St., pg. 120 **IT**
Domtech Holdings, Inc., 40 Davis St., pg. 990 **PB**

Trois Rivieres

Gaz Metropolitain, Inc.-Mauricie, 929 Pere-Daniel Street, pg. 541 **IT**
Les Messageries de la Mauricie, 645, rue du Pere Daniel, pg. 539 **IT**
Port of Trois Rivieres, 1545 de Fleuve St., pg. 255 **IT**
Scierie Parent Inc., 3300 Bellefeuille Street, pg. 761 **IT**

Truro

The Daily News, pg. 631 **IT**

Val d'Or

Acces Capital Abitibi-Temiscaminque, 640, 3 Avenue, pg. 249 **IT**
Explonor, Inc., 615 Avenue Centrale, pg. 664 **IT**
Gaz Metropolitain - Val d'Or, 1153 boul. des Foreurs, pg. 541 **IT**
Imprimerie Quebecor Lebonfon, 1051, rue de l'Eccho, pg. 1077 **IT**
Uniboard Division Unires, 970 de L'Echo, pg. 1431 **IT**
Uniboard Division Val d'Or, 2700, boul, Industriel, pg. 1431 **IT**

Valcourt

Bombardier Credit Ltd., 5571 Saint-Joseph St., pg. 200 **IT**

Valleyfield

Alcolac Ltd., 490 Dufferin St., pg. 1113 **IT**
Celfortec Inc., pg. 698 **IT**
Synergistics Industries Limited, 451 rue Jeanne Mance, pg. 734 **PB**

Vancouver

ABN AMRO Bank Canada (Vancouver), Vancouver Center, Ste. 2510, 650 W. Georgia St., pg. 11 **IT**
Alaskan Copper Companies, 225 North Road, pg. 31 **PV**
Alpac Construction & Surveys Limited, #900, 1333 West Broadway, pg. 114 **IT**
Asia Minerals Corp., 777 Hornby St., Ste. 1480, pg. 1411 **PB**
Atomic Energy of Canada Ltd.-Accelerators, Suite 900, 1281 West Georgia Street, pg. 97 **IT**
B C SUGAR REFINERY, LTD., 123 Roger Street, pg. 103 **IT**
BC GAS INC., 1111 W. Georgia Street, pg. 114 **IT**
BC Gas Utility, 1111 W. Georgia St., pg. 114 **IT**
B.C. HYDRO, 333 Dunsmuir St., 16th Fl., pg. 114 **IT**
BHP Steel Canada Inc., 740 Nicola Street, pg. 227 **IT**
Balfour Guthrie Forest Products Inc., 1285 West Pender St., Ste. 600, pg. 260 **IT**
Bank of Montreal - Vancouver, 595 Burrard St., pg. 153 **IT**
Barrick Gold, 698 Seymour St., Ste. 204, pg. 169 **IT**
Barrick Gold, Swik 204-698 Seymar St., pg. 169 **IT**
BenguetCorp Canada Ltd., c/o Richards Buell Sutton, 300-1111 Melville St., pg. 187 **IT**
British Columbia Packers Limited, P.O. Box 5000, pg. 1495 **IT**

PB - *U.S. Public Companies Volume*
PV - *U.S. Private Companies Volume*
IT - *International Public & Private Companies Volume*

Brookfield Homes Partners, 1075 W. Georgia St., Ste. 1300, pg. 228 **IT**
Bryant, Fulton & Shee, 1500 W. Georgia St., Ste. 1100, pg. 678 **PV**
CAE Machinery Ltd., 3550 Lougheed Hwy., pg. 237 **IT**
CESL Engineering Limited, 1636 W. 75th Ave., pg. 307 **IT**
Cambridge Western Leaseholds Limited, Ste. 301, North Office Tower, 650 West 41st, Avenue, pg. 253 **IT**
Canadian Forest Products Ltd., 2800-1055 Dunshuir St., pg. 260 **IT**
Canadian Forest Products Ltd., Eburne Saw Mills Division, 1700 W. 75th Ave., Ste. 301, pg. 260 **IT**
Canadian Limited, One Bentall Centre, 505 Burrard Street, pg. 1513 **IT**
Canadian Transport Company, 600-1285 W. Pender St., pg. 805 **PV**
Canadian Western Trust, 2236 Park Place, 666 Burnard Street, pg. 259 **IT**
Canadian White Pine Division, 3450 E. Kent, pg. 828 **IT**
Canall Resources Inc., 1901-1030 W. Georgia St., pg. 1255 **IT**
CANFOR CORPORATION, 2900-1055 Dunsmuir St., pg. 260 **IT**
Canusa Wood Products Ltd., 1281 West Georgia Street, pg. 864 **IT**
CellularVision Canada Ltd., 1960-505 Burrard Street, pg. 1482 **IT**
Centra Gas Inc., 1333 W. Georgia St., pg. 1492 **IT**
Chemetics International Company Ltd Vancouver Operations, 1818 Cornwall Ave., pg. 774 **IT**
Chevron Canada Limited, 1050 W. Pender St., pg. 348 **PB**
CLEARLY CANADIAN BEVERAGE CORP., 1900-999 West Hastings St., pg. 297 **IT**
Cognos Inc.-Vancouver Sales Office, 1166 Alberni St., Ste. 1505, pg. 306 **IT**
Columbia Brewing Company, 1220 Erikson Street, pg. 679 **IT**
COMINCO, LTD., Ste. 500, 200 Burrard Street, pg. 307 **IT**
Cominco Ltd., 500-200 Burrard Street, pg. 308 **IT**
Cominco Ltd., 7th Floor, 409 Granville Street, pg. 308 **IT**
Consolidated Footwear Co., Ltd., Suite 820, 1140 West Pender St., pg. 695 **IT**
CONSOLIDATED VISCOUNT RESOURCES LTD., The Marine Bldg., pg. 326 **IT**
Cossette Communication-Marketing (Vancouver) Inc., 220 Cambie St., Ste., Ste. 350, pg. 336 **IT**
Crestbrook Forest Industries Ltd - Vancouver, 1055 West Hastings Street, Ste. 1200, pg. 348 **IT**
Custom Cheques of Canada, 1375 McLean Dr., pg. 1077 **IT**
DMR Group, Inc., 601 West Cordova St., Suite 295, pg. 528 **IT**
Descente Canada Inc., 1445 Charles St., pg. 396 **IT**
Durum (Australia) Pty. Ltd., 1200-1090 West Pender Street, pg. 422 **IT**
DURUM ENERGY CORP., 1200-1090 West Pender St., pg. 422 **IT**
Durum Energy Corp., Sucursal Del Peru, 1200-1090 West Pender Street, pg. 422 **IT**
Empress Foods Ltd., 7280 Fraser St., pg. 1426 **PB**
FACS Records Centre Inc., pg. 1494 **IT**
Financial Collection Agencies, Suite 1400, 800 West Pender Street, pg. 470 **IT**
First Marathon Securities, 400 Burrard St., Ste. 2000, pg. 486 **IT**
Fisons Western Corporation, 1212 W. Broadway Ave., #500, pg. 1111 **IT**
Fleming Canada Partners Inc., Ste. 600, 999 W. Hasting St., pg. 493 **IT**
Fletcher Challenge Canada Limited, Toronto Dominion Tower, 700 W. Georgia St., pg. 495 **IT**
Fluor Daniel Wright Limited, 1075 W. Georgia St. Ste. 500, pg. 660 **PB**
Four Seasons Hotel, 791 W. Georgia St., pg. 502 **IT**
GPC Government Policy Consultants (Vancouver), Suite 550, V6E 4H1, pg. 1225 **PB**
General Paint Ltd., 950 Raymur Ave., pg. 1501 **IT**
Goldman Sachs Canada, 200 Burrard St., Ste. 1630, pg. 462 **PV**
GREAT PACIFIC ENTERPRISES INC., 1600-1055 W. Hastings St., pg. 557 **IT**
HSBC Capital Canada, Inc., Suite 1610, 885 West Georgia Street, pg. 583 **IT**
Hanwa Co., Ltd.-Vancouver Branch, Ste. 501, 777 W. Broadway, pg. 596 **IT**
The Hokkaido Takushoku Bank, Ltd. (Vancouver), Suite 3220, Park Place, 666 Burrard Street, pg. 627 **IT**
HOLLINGER INC., 1827 W. Fifth Avenue, pg. 630 **IT**
Homestake Canada Inc., 1100-1055 W., Georgia St., pg. 833 **PB**
HongKong Bank of Canada, Suite 400, 885 West Georgia Street, pg. 583 **IT**
Howe Sound Pulp & Paper Limited, 2900-1055 Dunsmuir St., pg. 260 **IT**
Hughes Leitz Optical Technologies, Ltd., 328 Ellen St., pg. 722 **PB**
Ikon Office Solutions (British Columbia), 1875 Boundary Rd., pg. 864 **PB**
Indo-Pacific Energy Ltd., 1200-1090 West Pender Street, pg. 422 **IT**
The Industrial Bank of Japan (Canada), Vancouver Ctr., Ste.2420, 650 W. Georgia St., pg. 676 **IT**
Inland Pacific Enterprises, Ste. 1600, 1095 W. Pender St., pg. 114 **IT**
The International Commercial Bank of China, 1095 W. Pender St., Ste. 1250, pg. 684 **IT**
INTRAWEST CORPORATION, 200 Burrard Street, Ste. 800, pg. 685 **IT**
Kawasho International Canada Ltd., 595 Burrard St., pg. 727 **IT**

Kelly Douglas & Company Limited, 3189 Grandview Hwy., pg. 1495 **IT**
KEPCO Vancouver Office, #1240-200 Cranville Street, pg. 758 **IT**
Kiena Gold Mines, Ltd., 1600, 1055 Dunsmuir St., pg. 1060 **IT**
Kilborn SNC-Lavalin Inc., Kilborn Building, 1380 Burrand Street, Suite 400, pg. 1162 **IT**
Kingcome Navigation Company Ltd., 55 Rogers St., pg. 828 **IT**
Kodak Canada Inc., 840 Howe St., Ste. 300, pg. 553 **PB**
Kvaerner Masa Marine Inc., 1441 Creekside Dr., Ste. 570, pg. 771 **IT**
Lafarge Concrete Ltd., 268 Kent Ave. S.E., pg. 789 **IT**
Lafarge Construction Materials Pacific/Western Region, 1770 West 7th Ave., Ste.401, pg. 789 **IT**
MacMillan Bloedel Building Materials Ltd., P.O. Box 340, Station A, pg. 828 **IT**
MacMillan Bloedel Building Materials - Western Region, pg. 828 **IT**
MACMILLAN BLOEDEL LIMITED, 925 W. Georgia St., pg. 828 **IT**
MacMillan Bloedel (Pacific) Limited, 925 W. Georgia St., pg. 828 **IT**
McKim Advertising Ltd., 1200-1066 W. Hastings St., pg. 104 **PV**
McLean, 400 375 Water St., pg. 1791 **PB**
METHANEX CORPORATION, 1800 Waterfront Centre, 200 Burrard Street, pg. 862 **IT**
Mitsui & Co. (Canada), Four Bentall Centre, 33rd Flr., 1055 Dunsmuir St., V7X 1E6, pg. 880 **IT**
Molson Brewery B.C. Ltd., 1550 Burrard St., pg. 887 **IT**
Montrusco Associates, 200 Granville Street, Suite 1333, pg. 888 **IT**
NKK Corporation Inc., P.O. Box 49168, Four Bentall Centre, Suite 3394, pg. 903 **IT**
NATIONAL REAL ESTATE SERVICES, INC., 1188 W. Georgia St., 19th Fl., pg. 909 **IT**
Newhawk Gold Mines LTD., 625 Howe St., Ste. 860, pg. 833 **PB**
Newmont Exploration of Canada, 808 West Hastings St., Suite 900, pg. 1179 **PB**
Nichimen Canada Inc. Vancouver Branch, Ste. 521, 999 Canada Pl., pg. 928 **IT**
Nippon Paper Industries Company Limited Vancouver Office, 1102 777 W. Broadway, pg. 938 **IT**
Nissho Iwai Coal Development (Canada) Ltd., St. 2624, 1055 Dunsmuir St., pg. 948 **IT**
North American Metals Corp., 700 W. Pender St., Ste. 1500, pg. 1498 **IT**
Oji Paper Co. Ltd., 2784-1055 Dunsmuir St., Bentall Postal Station, pg. 998 **IT**
Old Spaghetti Factory (Canada) Ltd., 53 Water St., pg. 1495 **PB**
Olivieri Foods, 1175 Union St., pg. 841 **PB**
Optimum Public Relations (Vancouver) Inc., #350, 220 Cambie Street, pg. 336 **IT**
Pacific Elevators Limited, 400-111 West Hastings Street, pg. 1195 **IT**
Pacific Forest Products Limited, 1000-1040 W. Georgia St., pg. 102 **IT**
Pacific Northern Gas Ltd., 1185 W. Georgia St., pg. 1492 **IT**
Pacific Press Ltd., 2250 Granville St., pg. 631 **IT**
PALMER JARVIS COMMUNICATIONS, 1600-777 Hornby St., pg. 1022 **IT**
Pentax Canada-Vancouver, pg. 85 **IT**
PETROSUL INTERNATIONAL LTD., Ste. 500, 1199 West Nasting Street, pg. 1046 **IT**
PLACER DOME INC., P.O. Box 49330, Bentall IV, pg. 1060 **IT**
Placer Dome North America, 600 - 1055 Dunsmuir Street, pg. 1060 **IT**
Pohang Steel Canada Ltd.(POSCAN), 1440-650 West Georgia St., pg. 1062 **IT**
Prince Rupert Grain Ltd., 900-1055 West Hastings St., pg. 1195 **IT**
The Province, 2250 Granville Street, pg. 631 **IT**
Qantas Airways Ltd., Ste. 1714, Four Bentall Centre, pg. 1075 **IT**
Quebecor Merrill Canada Inc., 950 Homer St., 2nd Fl., pg. 1077 **IT**
Quebecor Printing Vancouver, 1070 S.E. Marine Dr., pg. 1077 **IT**
Racal Canada Inc., 1495 Franklin Street, pg. 1083 **IT**
Raisio Chemicals Canada Inc., Suite 312-1285 West Broadway, pg. 1086 **IT**
Rogers CKWX-AM, 2440 Ash St., pg. 1123 **IT**
Rogers Sugar, 123 Rogers St., pg. 103 **IT**
Royal LePage - British Columbia Office, 777 Dunmuir St., pg. 1143 **IT**
S & M Developments Limited, Sun Life Plaza, Ste. 700, 1100 Melville St., pg. 1319 **IT**
SHL Systemhouse - Asia/Pacific, 1500 West Georgia St., Ste. 750, pg. 1154 **IT**
SEI Corporation, One Bentall Centre, 505 Burrard St., Ste. 420, pg. 1447 **PB**
SNC-Lavalin, 1075 West Georgia, 12th Floor, pg. 1162 **IT**
SANDWELL INC., Park Place, 666 Burrard St., pg. 1188 **IT**
Saratoga Processing Company Limited, 1333 W. Georgia St., pg. 1492 **IT**
Seaboard Life, 2165, West Broadway, pg. 464 **IT**
Security Pacific Bank Canada, 574, Four Bentall Ctr., pg. 183 **PB**
Sequent Computer Systems (Canada) Ltd., 1400-400 Burrard Street, pg. 1459 **PB**
SHATO HOLDINGS LTD., 4088 Candy St., Ste. 300, pg. 1060 **IT**
Sigma Mines (Quebec) Ltd., 1600, 1055 Dunsmuir St., pg. 1060 **IT**

SKEENA CELLULOSE INC., 666 Burrard St., Ste. 2300, pg. 1261 **IT**
Sterling Newspapers Ltd., 1827 W. Fifth Ave., pg. 632 **IT**
Sumitomo Canada Ltd.- Vancouver Office, Ste. 1900, 777 Dunsmuir St., pg. 1313 **IT**
Sumitomo Metal Mining Canada Ltd., 602-700 W. Georgia St., pg. 1316 **IT**
Sun Life Savings & Mortgage Corp., 310-885 Dunsmuir St., pg. 1319 **IT**
Sun Microsystems of Canada-Vancouver, 1285 W. Pender, St., Ste. 206, pg. 1532 **PB**
Svedala Industries Canada British Columbia, Suite 407, 1112 West Pender, pg. 1325 **IT**
Swiss Bank Corporation (Canada), Four Bentall Centre, 1055 Dunsmuir St., Ste. 2724, pg. 1332 **IT**
Taylor, Pearson & Carson Division, 3525 Cornatt Rd., pg. 23 **IT**
Teleflex (Canada) Ltd., 3831 N. 6 Rd., pg. 1570 **IT**
The Bank of Tokyo-Mitsubishi (Canada), 666 Burrard St., Ste. 2410, pg. 158 **IT**
The Sakura Bank (Canada), Vancouver Office, Three Bentall Centre, Ste. 3131, 595 Burrard St., pg. 1180 **IT**
Tourism Malaysia - Vancouver Office, 830 Burrard St., pg. 833 **IT**
Trans Mountain Enterprises of British Columbia Limited, #900, 1333 West Broadway, pg. 114 **IT**
Trans Mountain Holdings Ltd., #900, 1333 West Broadway, pg. 114 **IT**
Trans Mountain Housing Ltd., #900, 1333 West Broadway, pg. 114 **IT**
Trans Mountain Oil Pipe Line Corp., #900, 133 West Broadway, pg. 114 **IT**
Trans Mountain Petroleums Ltd., #900, 1333 West Broadway, pg. 114 **IT**
Trans Mountain Pipeline Company Ltd., 1333 W. Broadway, Ste. 900, pg. 114 **IT**
TRIMIN ENTERPRISES, INC., Ste. 638, 35 Water St., pg. 1424 **IT**
Valmet Canada Inc.-Western Canada Operations, Suite 1220, 1200 W. 73rd Avenue, pg. 1448 **IT**
Vancouver Port Corporation, 1900-200 Granville St., pg. 255 **IT**
The Vancouver Sun, 2250 Granville St., pg. 631 **IT**
Voest-Alpine Canada Corp., 1450 Creekside Dr., Ste. 300, pg. 1472 **IT**
WF Corroon-Vancouver, 555 West Hastings Street, 1100, pg. 1502 **IT**
WIC Entertainment Ltd., 1960-505 Burrard St., Suite 1960, pg. 1482 **IT**
WIC Radio Ltd., 505 Burrard St., Suite 1960, pg. 1482 **IT**
WIC Television Ltd., 505 Burrard Street, pg. 1482 **IT**
WIC WESTERN INTERNATIONAL COMMUNICATIONS LTD., 1960-505 Burrard St., pg. 1481 **IT**
Weldwood of Canada Limited, 1055 W. Hastings St., pg. 334 **PB**
WEST FRASER TIMBER CO. LTD., 1100 Melville St., Ste. 1000, pg. 1490 **IT**
West Hastings (GMO) Holdings Inc., 1066 West Hastings St., Ste. 1920, pg. 326 **IT**
WESTAR GROUP LTD., 1055 W. Hastings St., Suite 1600, V6E 2H2, pg. 1491 **IT**
Westcoast Cellufibre, 8890 Manitoba St., pg. 261 **IT**
WESTCOAST ENERGY INC., 1333 West Georgia Street, pg. 1492 **IT**
WESTERN CORPORATE ENTERPRISES INC., 200-1199 W. Hastings, pg. 1494 **IT**
Western International Media Corporation, 1155 Robson St., Ste. 401, pg. 1167 **PV**
Western Pool Terminals Limited, 400-111 West Hastings Street, pg. 1195 **IT**
Westim Resources Ltd., 1055 Dunsmuir St., Ste. 904, pg. 435 **IT**
Weyerhaeuser Canada Limited, 11th Fl., 1100 Melville, pg. 1764 **PB**
Whitbread Investments Ltd., 1700-1075 W. Georgia St., pg. 1499 **IT**
Williams & Mackie, 50 W. Second Ave., pg. 1150 **IT**
Willis Corroon Aerospace of Canada Ltd., 555 W. Hastings St., Ste. 1100, pg. 1509 **IT**
Willis Corroon Melling of Canada, 555 W. Hastings St., Ste. 1100, pg. 1509 **IT**
Young & Rubicam Ltd., 1100 Melville St., Suite 910, pg. 1200 **PV**

Vanier

Anixter Quebec City, 355 rue Marais, pg. 116 **PB**
Stihl Eastern Canada Ltd., 3200 Watt, pg. 1301 **IT**

Vaudreuil

EG & G Canada, Ltd. Optoelectronics, 22001 Dumberry Rd., pg. 544 **PB**
Noranpac, 400 Forbes St., pg. 273 **IT**

Vaughan

Paramount Canada's Wonderland, 9580 Jane St., pg. 776 **PV**

Verdun

Albright & Wilson Amerique Limitee, 2772 Marie - Victorin, pg. 49 **IT**
Intergraph Canada Ltd., 14 Place Du Commerce, Ste. 300, pg. 891 **PB**

PB - *U.S. Public Companies Volume*
PV - *U.S. Private Companies Volume*
IT - *International Public & Private Companies Volume*

Vernon

Lavington Planer Division, pg. 1395   IT
TOLKO INDUSTRIES LTD., P.O. Box 39, 3203 30th Ave., pg. 1395   IT

Victoria

Centra Gas British Columbia Inc., 1675 Douglas St., pg. 1492   IT
DMR Group, Inc., 32-560 Johnson St., pg. 528   IT
GPC Government Policy Consultants (Victoria), 1005 Broad St., Ste. 200, V8W 2A1, pg. 1225   PB
Green Line Investor Service, 1175 Douglas St., Ste. 700, pg. 1401   IT
Hewlett-Packard (Canada) Ltd., 121-3350 Douglas St., pg. 818   PB
Hewlett-Packard (Canada) Ltd., 771 Vernon Ave., Unit 410, pg. 818   PB
Palmer Jarvis Advertising, 1002 Wharf St., 3rd Fl., pg. 1022   IT
Ready-Lite Mfg. Ltd., 6828 Kirkpatrick Crescent, pg. 725   IT
Rogers Cable TV-Victoria, 861 Cloverdale Ave., pg. 1122   IT
Rogers CJVI-AM, 817 Fort St., pg. 1123   IT

Victoriaville

Noranpac, 400 Bolaventure Blvd., pg. 273   IT

Ville d'Anjou

BG Checo Construction, 7151 rue Jean-Talon Est., Ste. 1000, pg. 53   IT
Berkline, Inc., 8491 Ernest Cormier, pg. 432   PV
Cegelec Entreprises, Inc., 7151 rue Jean-Talon Est., Ste. 1000, pg. 53   IT
Francon-Lafarge, 7101 Les Galeries d'Anjou, pg. 791   IT
Les Editions CEC Inc., 8101, boul. Metropolitain E., pg. 794   IT
Premdor Inc.-Quebec Division, 8500 Rue Grenache, pg. 1067   IT
Transcontinental Printing Inc. - Transmag, 10807, rue Mirabeau, pg. 538   IT
West Penetone Inc., 10900 Secant St., pg. 1158   PV

Ville Marie

Temlam Inc., 48 Boivin St., pg. 1375   IT

Ville Saint Laurent

Bessey Juice Inc., 4216 Thimmens Boulevard, pg. 337   IT
CONSOLTEX GROUP INC., 8555 Auto Route Transcanadian, pg. 326   IT
Hudson General Aviation Services, Inc., 100 Alexis Nihon, Ste.400, pg. 846   PB
PAXAR Canada, 4939 Levy St., pg. 1266   PB
Pier 1 Imports Canada, 3015 Brabant-Marineau, pg. 1295   PB
Sensormatic Canada, Inc., 2755 Rue Paulus, pg. 1457   PB
Westburne Industrial Enterprises, Ltd., 505 Locke St., pg. 1492   IT
Westburne Supply, Inc., 505 Locke St., pg. 1492   IT

Ville Vanier

Charcuterie la Tour Eiffel Inc., 485 rue Lavoie, pg. 850   IT

Vimont

ALIMENTATION COUCHE TARD INC., 1600 Boul. Saint Martin E., Ste. 28, pg. 57   IT

Wallaceburg

Benn Iron Foundry, Ltd., Four Mason Street, pg. 271   IT
Eaton Yale Ltd. Suspension Div., 100 Mason St., pg. 559   PB
Emco Custom Products Group, 125 Mason Street, pg. 453   IT
Waltec Components, 125 Mason St., pg. 453   IT
Waltec Engineering, 75 Mason St., pg. 453   IT

Warburg

Talisman Energy Inc., pg. 1352   IT

Waterloo

Hayes Microcomputer Products (Canada) Ltd., 295 Philip St., pg. 801   PB
Heron Industries Limited, 440 Phillip St., pg. 1150   PB
La-Z-Boy Canada Ltd., 55 Columbia St. E., pg. 973   PB
Manulife Bank of Canada, 500 King St. North, pg. 840   IT
Northfield Metal Products Ltd., 195 Bathurst Drive, pg. 987   PB
Raytheon Canada Limited, 400 Phillip St., pg. 1366   PB
Weber Plastics Co. Ltd., 134 Dearborn Place, pg. 987   PB

Waterville

WATERVILLE TG INC., Ten Depot, B/S 4500, pg. 1487   IT

Watford

Androck Products/Newell Bulldog, 335 Wall St., pg. 1178   PB

Wawa

Algoma Ore Division, pg. 57   IT

Welland

Canadian Tire Acceptance Ltd., 555 Prince Charles Drive, pg. 259   IT
GenCorp Vehicle Sealing Div., John-Bernard Sts., pg. 706   PB
Premier Refractories (Canada) Ltd., Prince Charles Dr., pg. 58   PB
Stelpipe Ltd., 200 Dain Ave., pg. 1299   IT
Welland Forge Div., Centre St., pg. 474   IT
Welland Pipe Ltd., 615 Rusholme Rd., pg. 1299   IT
Whiting Equipment Canada, Inc., 350 Alexander St., pg. 1173   PV

West Hill

AEP Canada, Inc., 595 Coronation Dr., pg. 5   PB
AtoHaas Canada Inc., 2 Manse Rd., pg. 1403   PB
Rohm & Haas Canada Inc., 2 Manse Rd., pg. 1404   PB
Valspar, Inc., 645 Coronation Drive, pg. 1707   PB
Witco Canada, Inc., 565 Coronation Dr., pg. 1774   PB

Westmount

Alesa Alusuisse Engineering Canada Ltd., 245 Ave. Victoria, pg. 68   IT
CANCOM, 4269 St. Catherine St., W., Ste. 201, pg. 470   IT
FCA INTERNATIONAL LTD., 376 Victoria Ave., pg. 470   IT
Financial Collection Agencies (International) Inc., 376 Victoria Avenue, pg. 470   IT
The Reader's Digest Association (Canada) Ltd., 215 Redfern Ave., pg. 1368   IT
SAND TECHNOLOGY SYSTEMS, 4141 Sherbrook St. W., Ste. 410, pg. 1183   IT

Weston

Angelica International, Ltd., 35 Suntract Rd., pg. 113   PB
EZ Paintr Canada, 1155 Barmac Dr., pg. 1178   PB
Emco Supply Central Region, 65 Huxley Rd., pg. 453   IT
MacMillan Bloedel Inc., 50 Oak St., pg. 828   IT
Maple Leaf Meats, 150 Bartor Rd., pg. 841   IT
Mark IV Automotive Canada Inc., 46 Norelco Dr., pg. 1045   PB
National Grocers Co. Ltd., Six Monogram Pl., pg. 1495   IT
Northern Telecom Canada Limited, Telecom Services Div., 30 Norelco Dr., pg. 969   IT
Reynolds Metals Company-Weston, 40 Ironside Crescent, Ste. 789, pg. 1387   PB
Serca Food Service-Hickeson Div., 500 Fenmar Dr., pg. 1012   IT
Tektronix Canada Inc., 785 Arrow Rd., pg. 1567   PB
F.W. Woolworth Co. Ltd., Canada, 100 Mainshep Rd., pg. 1778   PB

Wetaskiwin

Tru-Weld LTD, pg. 1107   PV

Wheatley

Omstead Foods Limited, 1 Erie St. S., pg. 806   PB

Whistler

Blackcomb Skiing Enterprises Ltd., 4545 Blackcomb Way, pg. 685   IT
Whistler Mountain Holdings, Limited, 4545 Black Comb Way, pg. 685   IT

Whitby

Andrew Antenna Co. Ltd., 606 Beech St., pg. 113   PB
BMW Canada Inc., 920 Champlain Ct., pg. 178   IT
Croven Crystals Limited, 300 Beech St., pg. 354   PB
Du Pont Canada-Whitby, 201 S. Blair St., pg. 532   IT
EDS of Canada Ltd., 1615 Dundas St. E., pg. 570   PB
Isomedix Corporation (Canada), 184 Crown Ct., pg. 1515   PB
Makita Canada Inc., 1950 Forbes St., pg. 832   IT
Matheson Gas Products Canada, Inc., 530 Watson Street East, pg. 938   IT
McGraw-Hill Ryerson, Ltd., 300 Water St., pg. 1072   PB
Up-Right Scaffolds, 108 Industrial Dr., pg. 1128   PV

White Rock

Willis Corroon Melling Ltd., 15245 Russell Avenue, pg. 1509   IT

Whitehorse

Elvins Equipment Sales Limited, 9175 Alaska Hwy., pg. 1445   IT
Northwestel Inc., 301 Lambert St., pg. 115   IT

The White Pass & Yukon Corp. Limited, P.O. Box 4070, pg. 1150   IT
White Pass Transportation Limited, P.O. Box 4070, pg. 1150   IT
Yukon Alaska Transport Ltd., pg. 684   PV
The Yukon Electrical Co. Ltd., P.O. Box 4190, pg. 95   IT

Wiarton

Wiarton Echo Group, 573 Berford St., pg. 632   IT

Willowdale

ADT Security Systems Canada, 5734 Yonge St., pg. 1649   PB
ACCO Canada Inc., 501 McNicoll Ave., pg. 674   PB
Atria North-Phase II, 2235 Sheppard Ave. East, pg. 1162   IT
The Borden Company Limited (Canada), Ste. 300, 250 Consumers Rd., pg. 159   PV
CCL INDUSTRIES, INC., 105 Gordon Baker Road, Ste. 800, pg. 238   IT
CCL Label, 105 Gordon Baker Road, pg. 238   IT
A.B. Cairns Limited, 2025 Sheppard Ave East, pg. 1359   IT
Connaught Laboratories Limited, 1755 Steeles Ave. West, pg. 1109   IT
Dieffenbacher Toronto, 200 Consumer Rd., Ste. 200, pg. 413   IT
The Discovery Channel, 2225 Sheppard Ave. E., pg. 1343   IT
Epson Canada Limited, 550 McNicol Ave., pg. 1219   IT
The Fitness Institute, 2235 Sheppard Ave. East, pg. 806   IT
General DataComm, 2255 Sheppard Ave., East, Ste. 410, pg. 708   PB
GRAFTON FRASER INC., 1210 Sheppard Ave., E., Ste. 401, pg. 556   IT
The Great Eastern Insurance Company, 20 York Mills Rd., pg. 794   PB
Hallmark Cards Canada, 2 Hallcrown Pl., pg. 496   PV
HARRIS STEEL GROUP INC., 4120 Yonge St., Ste. 404, pg. 597   IT
The Hartford Fire Insurance Company, 20 York Mills Rd., pg. 794   PB
Hartford Insurance Group of Canada, 20 York Mills Rd., pg. 794   PB
The Hartford Life Insurance Company, 20 York Mills Rd., pg. 794   PB
London-Canada Insurance Company, 20 York Mills Rd., pg. 795   PB
Maclean Hunter Micropublishing, 4601 Yonge St., pg. 1124   IT
Monarch Construction Ltd., 2025 Sheppard Ave. East, pg. 1359   IT
Monarch Development Corporation, 2025 Sheppard Avenue East, pg. 1359   IT
The Monarch Group, 2025 Sheppard Ave. East, pg. 1359   IT
Octel Messaging Division, 4110 Yonge St., #506, pg. 1018   PB
Pacific Automotive Co-operation, Inc., Suite 1408, 2 Sheppard Avenue East, pg. 1413   IT
Quebecor Litho Plus, 390 Consumers Rd., pg. 1076   IT
Royal LePage, 2235 Sheppard Avenue East, Suite 1600, pg. 1143   IT
The Sports Network (TSN), 2225 Sheppard Ave. E., Ste. 100, pg. 1343   IT
Tab Products of Canada, Ltd., 130 Sparks Ave., pg. 1559   PB
Todays Temporary, Ltd., 505 Consumers Rd., Ste. 510, pg. 277   PB
Universal Studios Canada Ltd., 2450 Victoria Park Ave., pg. 1216   IT
Zurich Life Insurance Co. of Canada, 2225 Shepherd Ave. East, pg. 1532   IT

Windsor

ANCHOR LAMINA INC., 2590 Ouellette, pg. 75   IT
CHWI-TV, 75 Riverside Drive East, pg. 171   IT
Canadian Brine Ltd., 30 Prospect Ave., pg. 1135   PB
Chrysler Canada Ltd., 2450 Chrysler Centre, pg. 354   PB
DNN Galvanizing Corporation, 300 Sprucewood Ave., pg. 414   IT
Dieffenbacher North America, 1720 N. Talbot Rd., pg. 413   IT
Essex Manufacturing, 2950 Metcalfe St., pg. 665   PB
Ford Ensite International Inc. (Canadian), 2950 Metcalfe St., pg. 665   PB
General Motors Canada Transmission Div., 1550 Kildare Road, pg. 722   PB
Hiram Walker & Sons Limited, pg. 63   IT
Hull-Thomson Limited, 3315 Devon Dr., pg. 1150   IT
ITW Maple Roll Leaf, 2285 Ambassador Dr., pg. 868   PB
Kasle of Canada LTD, 715 Sprucewood Ave., pg. 608   PV
Lamb Technicon, 225 Eugenie St., pg. 1004   PB
Lican Medical Products Ltd., 5120 Halford Dr., pg. 374   IT
Peterson Spring-Windsor Plant, 2995 Dexiel Dr., pg. 857   PV
Ross Roy Communications Canada, Limited, 1737 Walker Rd., pg. 946   PV
Spirol Ind. Ltd., 3103 St. Etienne Blvd., pg. 1026   PV
The Windsor & Hantsport Railway Co. Ltd., 2 Water Street, pg. 575   PV
The Windsor Star, 167 Ferry St., pg. 632   IT

Wingham

CKNX-TV, 215 Carling Terrace, pg. 171   IT

PB - *U.S. Public Companies Volume*
PV - *U.S. Private Companies Volume*
IT - *International Public & Private Companies Volume*

Winkler

Ecusta Fibres Ltd., 346 Norquay Dr., pg. 746 **PB**

Winnipeg

AgPro Grain, 1504-201 Portage Avenue, pg. 1195 **IT**
Air Products Canada Ltd., 2230 Main Street, pg. 31 **PB**
Anixter Winnipeg, 199 Omands Creek Blvd., pg. 116 **PB**
Automotive Accessory Co., Ltd., 771 Main St., pg. 1113 **PV**
Bank of Montreal - Winnipeg, 333 Main St., pg. 153 **IT**
Bayco Industries, 2200 Logan Ave., pg. 395 **IT**
Boeing Canada Technology Ltd., Winnipeg Division, 99 Murray Park Rd., pg. 242 **PB**
Brian Controls Division, 43 Scurfield Blvd., pg. 711 **IT**
Bristol Aerospace Limited, 660 Berry Street, pg. 829 **IT**
Bristol Aerospace Ltd., 660 Berry St., pg. 1127 **IT**
BTR Aerspace Group, 1780 Wellington Ave., Ste. 200, pg. 127 **IT**
CAE Vanguard, Ltd.-Manitoba, 15 Bury Street, pg. 237 **IT**
CCL Label, 80 Paramount Road, pg. 238 **IT**
Canadian Media Distributors, 1465 St. James Street, pg. 539 **IT**
Canadian Pool Agencies Ltd., 1007-220 Portage Avenue, pg. 1195 **IT**
Cargill Ltd., The Cargill Bldg., 300-240 Graham Ave., pg. 210 **PV**
Carter Day Industries (Canada) Ltd., 1425 Whyte Ave., pg. 217 **PV**
Centra Gas Manitoba Inc., 444 St. Mary Ave., pg. 1492 **IT**
Chase Canada, 19 Otter St., pg. 337 **PB**
Codville Distributors, 1800 Inkster Blvd., pg. 1012 **IT**
Cognos Inc.-Winnipeg Sales Office, 5 Donald St., Ste. 200, pg. 306 **IT**
The Creamette Co. of Canada Ltd., 303 Stanley St., pg. 159 **PV**
Custom Cheques of Canada, 100 Irene St., pg. 1077 **IT**
Data Business Forms, 101 Irene St., pg. 384 **IT**
Domcor - Manitoba, 1310 Mountain Avenue, pg. 415 **IT**
ENSIS CORPORATION INC., 1120-200 Graham Ave., pg. 455 **IT**
Falconbridge Explorations, 21C Murray Park Road, pg. 433 **IT**
Federal Industries Industrial Group, Inc., 200 Graham Ave., Ste. 1120, pg. 1150 **IT**
Federal Industries Transport Group, 201 Portage Ave., Ste. 3100., pg. 1150 **IT**
Frank Fair Industries Ltd., 1149 St. Matthew Ave., pg. 326 **IT**
GWL Realty Advisors Co., 100 Osborne St. North, pg. 558 **IT**
GENDIS INC., 1370 Sony Pl., pg. 542 **IT**
Gold Circle Insurance Co., 100 Osborne St. North, pg. 558 **IT**
THE GREAT-WEST LIFE ASSURANCE COMPANY, 100 Osborne St. North, pg. 557 **IT**
Green Line Investor Service, 360 Main St., Ste. 520, pg. 1401 **IT**
Hach Sales & Service Canada Ltd., 1313 Border Stree, Suite 34, pg. 773 **PB**
Hayhurst Elias Dudek, Inc., Four Fort St., pg. 827 **PB**
Herff Jones of Canada, 1315 Inkster Blvd., pg. 524 **PV**
Hewlett-Packard (Canada) Ltd., 1825 Inkster Blvd., pg. 818 **PB**
Hilb, Rogal and Hamilton Company of Canada, Limited, Four Fort St., pg. 828 **PB**
Kelly Douglass Westfair Foods Ltd., 101 Weston St., pg. 1495 **IT**
Kilborn SNC-Lavalin Inc., 200-1600 Ness Avenue, pg. 1162 **IT**
Kodak Canada Inc., 360 Main St., Ste. 110, pg. 553 **PB**
Lafarge Construction Materials, 222 Provencher Blvd., pg. 791 **IT**
MANITOBA HYDRO, 820 Taylor Ave., pg. 834 **IT**
Maple Leaf Meats, 870 Lagimodiere, pg. 841 **IT**
McKim Communications Limited, McKim Courtyard, 3rd Fl., 100 Osborne St., pg. 104 **PV**
Motor Coach Industries Ltd., 1149 St. Matthews Ave., pg. 326 **IT**
Motorways (1980) Limited, 60 Eagle Dr., pg. 1150 **IT**
Palmer Jarvis Advertising, 400 St. Mary Ave., 5th Fl., pg. 1022 **IT**
Pool Insurance, 1007-220 Portage Avenue, pg. 1195 **IT**
POWELL EQUIPMENT LTD., 1455 Buffalo Pl., pg. 1066 **IT**
Powlift Trucks & Systems, 1525 Dublin Ave., pg. 1066 **IT**
RIDLEY CANADA LIMITED, 24th Fl., Richardson Bldg., One Lombard Place, pg. 1116 **IT**
SHL Systemhouse - Winnipeg, 363 Broadway, Ste. 350, pg. 1154 **IT**
Soo Line Mills Limited, Seven Higgins Ave., pg. 1495 **IT**
Standard Arrow Ltd., 33 Allen Dyne Rd., pg. 127 **IT**
Stevenson & Company Limited, 385 St. Mary Avenue, pg. 1143 **IT**
Sun Microsystems of Canada-Winnipeg, 485 Edward Ave., W., pg. 1532 **IT**
TSC Shannock Corporation, 1692 Dublin Ave., Unit #2, pg. 1343 **IT**
Teshmont Consultants Inc., 1190 Waverley Street, pg. 31 **IT**
Transcontinental Printing Inc. - Winnipeg, 55 Dunlop Avenue, pg. 538 **IT**
UNITED GRAIN GROWERS LTD., TD Centre, 201 Portage Avenue, pg. 1442 **IT**
Westeel Agricultural Products Division, P.O. Box 792, pg. 698 **IT**
Wholesale Heating Supplies, 669 Century St., pg. 453 **IT**

XCAN Grain Pool Ltd., 1200-201 Portage Avenue, pg. 1195 **IT**
Zeneca Seeds, Unit 6, 75 Scurfield Blvd., pg. 1527 **IT**

Winona

ANDRES WINES LTD., Kelson Avenue and South Service Road, pg. 75 **IT**
E.D. SMITH, 944 Hwy. # 8, pg. 1263 **IT**
Winona S.A.R.L., pg. 76 **IT**

Woodbridge

Automax Controls, Inc., 120 Vinyl Ct., pg. 658 **PB**
Bell & Howell Ltd., 360 Hanlan Road, pg. 201 **PB**
Caterpillar Commercial Services Ltd., 3700 Steeles Ave. W., pg. 316 **PB**
Dentsply Canada, 161 Vinyl Ct., pg. 499 **PB**
Flowserve Duriron Canada, 120 Vinyl Court, pg. 659 **PB**
Forbo Wallcoverings Ltd., 200 Vinyl Ct., pg. 498 **IT**
Imprimerie Quebecor Canada, 7 Director Ct., Ste. 202, pg. 1077 **IT**
Standco Canada, Ltd., 279 Trowers Rd., Unite 1, pg. 1420 **PB**
Transport Graphicor Inc., 8 Director Ct., Ste. 104, pg. 1075 **IT**
Triad Systems Canada Ltd., 5 Director Ct., Ste. 102, pg. 193 **PV**

Woodstock

AT&T Business Communication, Main Street, pg. 11 **PB**
Cambridge Industries - Woodstock, 969 Juliana Dr., pg. 202 **PV**
CONTRANS CORPORATION, pg. 328 **IT**
Firestone Fibers & Textiles Company-Woodstock Plant, 1200 Dundas St. E., pg. 214 **IT**
Firestone Textiles Company, 1200 Dundas St. E., pg. 214 **IT**
General Seating of Canada Limited, 1000 Ridgeway Rd., pg. 902 **IT**
Laidlaw Carriers Inc., P.O. Box 1210, 1179 Ridgeway Rd., pg. 328 **IT**
Ralston Purina Canada Agri-Division, 404 Main St., pg. 1360 **PB**
Standard Tube Canada Inc., 193 Givins St., pg. 699 **IT**
Thomas Built Buses of Canada, Ltd., pg. 1082 **PV**
VARI-FORM, 193-A Givins Street, pg. 1341 **IT**

Woss

Canadian Forest Products Ltd., Englewood Logging Division, pg. 260 **IT**

Wynyard

Lakeside Processors, pg. 1195 **IT**

Yarmouth

Pick O' Sea Fisheries, Ltd., pg. 297 **IT**

Yarrow

Fraser Valley Forest Products Limited-Flush Door Plant, 41916 Central Rd., pg. 1067 **IT**

Yellowknife

Air Products Canada Ltd., pg. 31 **PB**
Giant Mine, P.O. Box 3000, pg. 1411 **PB**
Hewlett-Packard (Canada) Ltd., #105 4920-54 Avenue, pg. 818 **PB**
Northwest Territorial Airways Ltd., Postal Service 9000, Yellowknife Intl. Airport, pg. 36 **IT**

Yorkton

CKOS/CICC TV, 95 E. Broadway, pg. 171 **IT**

CAPE VERDE

Ilha do Sal

Shell de Cabo Verde, Amilcar Cabral Intl. Airport, pg. 1137 **IT**

Sao Vincente

Det Norske Veritas, pg. 397 **IT**

CAYMAN ISLANDS

Georgetown

Asahi Bank Cayman Branch, P.O. Box 707, West Bay Rd., pg. 82 **IT**
Asahi Finance (Cayman) Ltd., pg. 83 **IT**
Banco di Napoli-Cayman Islands, 3rd Fl. W. Winding Bldg., pg. 140 **IT**
Banco do Brasil S.A.-Cayman Islands, Elizabethan Square, Phase III, Building, 4th Floor, Sheden Road, pg. 141 **IT**
Bank Hapoalim (Cayman) Ltd., pg. 149 **IT**
Bank of Bermuda (Cayman) Limited, P.O. Box 513 G.T., 3rd Fl., British American Tower, pg. 151 **IT**

The Bank of New York Trust Company (Cayman) Limited, Butterfield House, Fort Street, pg. 179 **PB**
BankAmerica Trust & Banking Corp. (Cayman) Ltd., Fort St., P.O. Box 1092, pg. 183 **PB**
Bankers Trust (Cayman) International, Ltd., P.O. Box 1967, pg. 186 **PB**
Bayerische Hypotheken-und Wechsel-Bank AG (Cayman Islands), Royal Bank Bldg., pg. 176 **IT**
Bel (Cayman) Limited, Maples & Calder, Attorneys at Law, pg. 146 **IT**
Bermuda Trust (Cayman) Ltd., P.O. Box 513 G.T., 3rd Fl., British American Tower, pg. 151 **IT**
Brasilian American Merchant Bank, Cardinal Ave., Scotia Bldg. 2 Fl., pg. 142 **IT**
Braspetro Oil Services Co. - Brasoil, West Wind Building, pg. 1042 **IT**
Brown Brothers Harriman Trust Co. (Cayman) Ltd., Butterfield House, Fort Street, pg. 173 **PV**
CIBC Bank and Trust Company (Cayman) Limited, P.O. Box 694, pg. 257 **IT**
CIBC Holdings (Cayman) Limited, pg. 257 **IT**
Canadian Imperial Fund Managers (Cayman) Limited, CIBC Bldg., Edward St., pg. 257 **IT**
Charter Medical (Cayman Islands) Ltd., Caledonian Bank & Trust Swiss Bank Bldg., pg. 1036 **PB**
Charter Medical International, Inc, Caledonian House, Caledonian Bank & Trust Swiss Bank Bldg., pg. 1036 **PB**
Chiyoda Investment Cayman Limited, Edward St., pg. 287 **IT**
Cigna Mezzanine Holdings, Inc., c/o MeesPierson (Cayman) Ltd., Cayside Galleries, pg. 357 **PB**
Cititrust (Cayman) Ltd., pg. 379 **PB**
Club Med, Inc., Cayman International Trust Bldg., pg. 341 **IT**
Crediop Overseas Bank Ltd., P.O. Box 707, West Bay Rd., pg. 341 **IT**
Dai-Ichi Kangyo Bank, Ltd-Cayman Island, pg. 360 **IT**
Dalton Holdings Ltd., pg. 256 **IT**
Ebasco Cayman Limited, c/o Maples and Calder P.O. Box 309, pg. 1587 **IT**
Ellesmere Britannia Ltd., P.O. Box 1698, West Bay Road, pg. 31 **IT**
Enserch Far East Ltd., P.O. Box 1043, pg. 1587 **PB**
Equipment Assurance Ltd., P.O. Box 694, pg. 177 **PV**
Equipment Leasing Limited, pg. 776 **PB**
Ferrier Lullin Cayman Bank & Trust, c/o Swiss Bank & Trust Corp., pg. 480 **IT**
Goldman Sachs (Cayman) Trust, Limited, P.O. Box 896, Harbour Centre, pg. 462 **PV**
IBJ Schroder Bank & Trust Company (Cayman Branch), West Wind Bldg., pg. 675 **IT**
J&H Marsh & McLennan Management Services (Cayman) Ltd., P.O. Box 2196, B.W.I., pg. 1049 **PB**
Kredietbank Grand Cayman Branch, P.O. Box 694, pg. 760 **IT**
MEGAL Finance Company Ltd., pg. 1149 **IT**
Midland Bank Trust Corporation (Cayman) Limited, Midland Bank Trust Building, Mary Street, pg. 583 **IT**
Morgan Grenfell (Cayman) Limited, P.O. Box 1984, Elizabethan Sq., pg. 406 **IT**
Morgan Trust Company of the Cayman Islands Ltd., c/o CIBC Bank & Trust Company (Cayman), pg. 1131 **PB**
NCNB National Bank, Grand Cayman Branch, P.O. Box 1040, pg. 1166 **IT**
NatWest International Trust Corporation (Cayman) Limited, West Bay Rd., pg. 911 **IT**
Nippon Credit Bank Ltd.-Grand Cayman, West Wind Building, pg. 933 **IT**
The Northern Trust Co., P.O. Box 501, pg. 1197 **PB**
RNBNY Branch Office-Cayman Islands, Albert Panton St., pg. 1381 **PB**
Republic National Bank of New York (Cayman) Limited, P.O. Box 500, pg. 1381 **PB**
Rollins Burdick Hunter (Cayman) Limited, pg. 119 **PB**
STB Finance Cayman Limited, pg. 1318 **IT**
The Sakura Bank - Cayman Branch, CIBC Building, Edward Street, pg. 1179 **IT**
Sherwin-Williams Cayman Islands Ltd., pg. 1466 **PB**
The Sumitomo Bank, Ltd.-Cayman Branch, pg. 1309 **IT**
The Sumitomo Trust & Banking Co., Ltd., c/o The Sumitomo Trust, International Business Opers. Dept., pg. 1317 **IT**
Swiss Bank & Trust Corporation Ltd., The Swiss Bank Bldg., Fort St., pg. 1332 **IT**
Taiyo Investment of Cayman Inc., Edward St., pg. 1349 **IT**
Takugin Finance (Cayman) Limited, P.O. Box 309, pg. 627 **IT**
Ucamar Shipping & Transportation Co., pg. 777 **PB**
United States Trust Co. of New York, pg. 1688 **PB**
Von Ernst Trust & Co. Ltd., pg. 181 **IT**
World Trade & Marketing Ltd., c/o Maples & Calder, P.O. Box 309, pg. 1621 **PB**

Grand Cayman

Ambroveneto International Bank Ltd., c/o Coutts House, West Bay Road, pg. 138 **IT**
BB Leasing Company Ltd., Caledonian House, pg. 141 **IT**
BNP Private Bank & Trust Cayman Limited, Piccadilly Ctre., pg. 164 **IT**
Bank of America NT&SA, Anchorage Centre, Fort St., pg. 182 **PB**
The Bank of Nova Scotia Trust Company (Cayman) Limited, Cardinal Avenue, pg. 156 **IT**
Caymadrid International Limited, pg. 252 **IT**
Coutts & Co (Cayman) Limited, West Bay Road, pg. 911 **IT**
Enichem Finance (Overseas) Ltd., Citco Bldg., pg. 429 **IT**
Fionia (C.I.Properties) Limited, pg. 431 **IT**

FTCI-Cayman Ltd., pg. 621 — PB
HSBC Trustee (Cayman) Limited, Midland Bank Trust Building, Mary Street, pg. 583 — IT
Helen of Troy (Cayman) Ltd., West Bay Road, pg. 807 — PB
The Kyoei-Seimei Investment Cayman Co., Ltd., pg. 777 — IT
LGT Bank in Liechtenstein (Cayman) Ltd., The Swiss Bank Building, pg. 810 — IT
Long-Term Credit Bank of Japan, Limited - Grand Cayman, c/o CIBC Bank & Trust Co. (Cayman) Ltd., pg. 816 — IT
Meonia Insurance Brokers Limited, pg. 431 — IT
The Mitsubishi Trust & Banking Corporation, c/o Morgan Grenfell (Cayman), Elizabethan Square, pg. 876 — IT
The Mitsui Trust and Banking Company - Cayman, c/o The Bank of Nova Scotia, Trust Company (Cayman) Limited, pg. 883 — IT
Northern Trust Cayman International, Ltd., pg. 1197 — PB
Sakura Capital Funding (Cayman) Limited, Maples and Calder, Cayman International Trust Buildings, pg. 1180 — IT
Sakura Finance (Cayman) Limited, Maples and Calder, Cayman International Trust Buildings, pg. 1180 — IT
Seagate Technology Singapore, Ltd., pg. 1450 — PB
Selandia Insurance Company Limited, pg. 431 — IT
TOHO Life Cayman Ltd., CIBC Bldg., Edward St., pg. 1390 — IT
Willis Corroon Management (Cayman) Ltd., pg. 1505 — IT

CENTRAL AFRICAN REPUBLIC

Bangui

Banque Mondiale, Rue des Missions, pg. 1189 — PV

CHAD

Moundou

Brasseries du Logone S.A., pg. 1436 — IT
Shell Tchad, pg. 1137 — IT
Shell Tchadienne, pg. 1137 — IT

N'djamena

The World Bank, Quartier Curvette St. Martin, N'Djamena Chad, pg. 1189 — PV

CHILE

Antofagasta

Antofagasta Mine, Avenida Angamos 721, pg. 228 — IT
Coloso Port Mine, c/-Casilla 690, pg. 228 — IT
Compania Minera Zaldivar, Balmaceda # 2536, Of. 403, pg. 1016 — IT
Escondida Mine, c/-Casilla 690, pg. 228 — IT
Minera Cominco Resources Chile Ltda., Antonio toro 945, pg. 308 — IT
Outokumpu Tecnica-Chile Ltda., Los Immigrates #720, Of. #3, pg. 1017 — IT
Svedala Chile, pg. 1324 — IT
United Sistema De Tuberias Ltda., Casilla 1390, pg. 882 — PB

Chuquicamata

Chuquicamata Division, Casilla 9-D, pg. 302 — IT

Concepcion

Volterra S.A., Ejercito 399, pg. 938 — IT

Copiapo

Outokumpu Tecnica-Chile Ltda., Plaza Comercio, Local #3, pg. 1017 — IT

Coronel

Ewos Chile S.A., Parque Industrial Escuadron, pg. 349 — IT
Pacific Protein, Avenida Pedro Aguirre Cerda S/N, pg. 350 — IT

Correo Central

Cia Ericsson de Chile S.A., Gertrudis Echenique, No 30-22 Piso, Torres Las Condes, pg. 1366 — IT

Iquique

Kodak Chilena S.A.F., Manzana 11 Sitios 204-24, pg. 553 — PB

La Serena

Barrick Gold, Barrios Industrial, Sitio 58, Alto Penuelas, pg. 169 — IT
Barrick Gold, Barrios Industrial, pg. 169 — IT
El India and Tambo Mines, Barrio Industrial, Sitio No. 58, Alto Penuelas, pg. 169 — IT

Las Condes

Minera Homestake Chile, S.A., Nueva Tajamar 481, pg. 833 — PB

Los Andes

Andina Division, Casilla 6-A, pg. 302 — IT

Maipu

AGA Chile S.A., Repr. Casilla 164, pg. 13 — IT

Puerto Varas

Lechera del Sur S.A., pg. 920 — IT

Punta Arenas

Standard Wool (Chile) S.A., KM13 5 Ruta 9 Norte, pg. 1502 — PB

Rancagua

El Teniente Division, Millan 1040, pg. 302 — IT
Talleres Rancagua Division, Avenida Estacion 01200, pg. 302 — IT

San Antonio

Dow Quimica Chilena S.A., Antonio Nunez de Fonseco 871, pg. 524 — PB

San Pedro

Papeles Bio Bio S.A., Pedro Aguirre Cerda No. 1054, Casilla 1097, pg. 495 — IT

Santiago

ACF Minera Ltda., Benjamin 2926 B, Las Condes, pg. 354 — IT
ADN/ADD, Benjamin 2935, Oficina 901, pg. 1200 — PV
AGA S.A., pg. 13 — IT
ANZ Banking Group Limited Chile, Miraflores 222, 22nd Floor, pg. 98 — IT
ASC, Ltda., Austria 2041, pg. 816 — PB
Acer Chile, pg. 22 — IT
Acma S.A., Senador Jaime Guzman 3609, pg. 184 — IT
Administracion y Mandatos La Transadina, Agustinos 1127, pg. 333 — IT
Administradora de Fondos de Pensiones Qualitas, New York 80, 11th Fl., pg. 1258 — IT
Aetna International Chile S.A., Coyancura 2270 Piso 10, pg. 27 — PB
Agencias Bancarias Copachile, San Sebastian 2839, Oficina 803, pg. 319 — IT
Aguas Purificadas Ltda., Argomedo 440, pg. 549 — IT
Alfa-Laval S.A.C.I., P.O. Box 1177, pg. 1379 — IT
Algas Marinas S.A., pg. 810 — PB
Allianz Bice Compania de Seguros de Vida S.A., Nueva York 9, pg. 59 — IT
Allianz Compania de Seguros S.A., Tenderini 82, Piso 3y8, pg. 59 — IT
Amway Chile, Coronel Periera 72, Piso 7, pg. 69 — PV
Ascensores Schindler (Chile) S.A., pg. 1205 — IT
Asea Brown Boveri S.A., Vicun a Mackenna 1602, Casilla 3555, pg. 3 — IT
Atlas Industries Chile S.A., Av. Tobalaba, No. 155, pg. 361 — PV
Autodesk Chile, Marchant Pereira 201 Piso 9, pg. 149 — PB
BASF Chile S.A., Av. Carrascal 3851, pg. 105 — IT
BDF de Chile S.A., pg. 182 — IT
Banco del Desarrollo, Alameda 949, 3 piso, pg. 341 — IT
Banco do Brasil S.A.-Chile, Avenida Apoquindo, 3001, pg. 141 — IT
Banco Santander-Chile, Estado 10, Oficina 601, pg. 143 — IT
Banco Santander Chile, S.A., Augustinas 920, pg. 144 — IT
Bank Hapoalim (Santiago), Av. Apoquindo 3721, pg. 149 — IT
Bank of America NT&SA, Agustinas 1465, pg. 182 — PB
Bank of Boston, Moneda 799, pg. 184 — PB
Bankers Trust New York Corporation, Ahumada 11, Piso 11, pg. 186 — PB
BanRenta Compania de Seguros de Vida S.A., BanRenta, Ave. Apoquindo 2942, pg. 186 — PV
Barrick Chile Ltda., Av. Pedro de Valdivia 100, pg. 169 — IT
Bayer de Chile S.A., Carlos Fernandez 260, pg. 175 — IT
BEAL - Santiago, Edificio Fundacion, Miraflores 178, Piso 14, Of. 1401, pg. 1494 — IT
Bellsouth Chile S.A., Av. El Bosque Sur 130 Piso 14, pg. 208 — IT
Bellsouth Comunicaciones S.A., Av. El Bosque Norte 0134, pg. 208 — IT
Berlitz Escuelas de Idiomas Ltda., Padre Mariano No. 305, pg. 222 — IT
Boart Longyear Ltda., Las Dalias 2900 (Macul), pg. 76 — IT
Boston Inversiones Servicios Y Administracion Ltda., Moneda 799, 5 Piso, pg. 185 — PB
Brandeis Chile Ltda., Avenida A. Vespucio Sur. 80, pg. 1030 — IT
Brother International de Chile, Ltda., La Pastora 169, pg. 229 — IT
Bucyrus Chile Ltda., Casilla 16846-Providencia, Avda 11 de Sepiembre 2055, pg. 177 — PV
Buenaventura S.A., pg. 1139 — PB

Bull Chile Informatica Ltda., Avenida Holland 1158, pg. 315 — IT
Leo Burnett Chile, Apoquindo 3000, Pisos 7 y 8, pg. 185 — PV
CMS Chile S.A., pg. 672 — IT
Caja Reaseguradora de Chile, S.A., Avda. Apoquindo, pg. 335 — IT
Canon Chile S.A., Avenida Providencia 1979 Entrepiso, pg. 262 — IT
Castrol Chile SA, pg. 235 — IT
Cemento Polpaico S.A., Amunategui 178, 5 piso, pg. 629 — IT
Centenario S.A., pg. 919 — IT
The Chase Manhattan Trust Corporation Limited, Augustinas 1235, pg. 341 — PB
Chilena Consolidada Seguros de Vida S.A., Pedro de Valdivia 195, pg. 1531 — IT
Chilena Consolidada Seguros Generales S.A., Pedro de Valdivia 195, pg. 1531 — IT
CIBA-GEIGY Ltda., Francisco Meneses 1980, pg. 978 — IT
Cigna Compania de Seguros (Chile) S.A., Calle Nueva York #80, 9th Fl., pg. 363 — IT
Cigna Compania de Seguros de Vida (Chile) S.A., Calle Nueva York #80, 9th Fl., pg. 364 — PB
Cigna Salud Isapre S.A., Almirante Lorenzo, pg. 364 — PB
Cimenta, Admon. de Fondos de Inversion, S.A., Agustinas 1141, piso 5, pg. 335 — IT
Circle Freight International Agencia Chilena, Callao 2970, Of. 203 Las Condes, pg. 372 — PB
Citibank, N.A. Santiago, Ahumada 40, pg. 378 — IT
Coats Cadena SA, Exposicion, pg. 300 — IT
Coca Cola de Chile, S.A., pg. 392 — PB
Cocesa Ingenieria Y Construccion S.A., Bilbao 523, Providencia, pg. 1313 — IT
CODELCO CHILE (CORPORACION NACIONAL DEL COBRE DE CHILE), Huerfanos 1270, pg. 302 — IT
Comercial Anglo Chilena, California 2231, Providencia, pg. 410 — IT
Compania de Seguros de Vida Euroamerica, S.A., Agustinos 1127, pg. 333 — IT
Compania de Seguros Generales Euroamerica S.A., Agustinos 1127, pg. 333 — IT
Compania de Seguros La Chilena Consolidada, Pedro de Valdivia 195, pg. 1531 — IT
Compania Ericsson de Chile S.A., Av. Libertador Bernardo, pg. 1365 — IT
Compania Minera Cerro Colorado Limitada, 11th Fl., Las Urbinas 53, pg. 1118 — IT
Compania Minera Disputada de Las Condes S.S., Pedro de Valdivia 291, pg. 601 — PB
Compania Minera Mantos de Oro, Piso 15, Av. 11 de Septiembre 2353, pg. 1060 — IT
Compania Minera Riochilex S.A., Jose Antonio Soffia 2747, pg. 1118 — IT
Compania Minera Zaldivar S.A., Av. El Bosque N. 130, Piso 6, pg. 1016 — IT
Compania Nacional de Mineria CNM Lda., Ave. 11 de Septiembre, 2353, pg. 1345 — IT
Compania Nacional de Rentas, Avda. Apoquindo 4499, pg. 335 — IT
Compania Telefonos Chile (C.T.C.), C/San Martin, 50, 5 Piso, Casilla 16-D, pg. 1373 — PB
Conasan, S.A., pg. 429 — IT
Constructora Dumez de Chile, Calle Las Urbinas, 46, pg. 823 — IT
Continental-Lensa S.A., David Arellano #1872, Independencia, pg. 1563 — PB
Copachile, 57-29 Santiago, pg. 321 — IT
Cosmeticos Avon, Ltda., Casilla 70.003, Correo 7, pg. 156 — PB
Crown Cork de Chile, S.A.I., Casilla 9342, pg. 464 — PB
Crown Cork de Chile S.A., Comino A. Melipiua,10700, pg. 464 — PB
Cyanamid Chile Ltda., Antonio Varas 671, pg. 80 — PB
DMB&B Chile S.A., Avda. Presidente Kennedy, 5118, 4th Fl., pg. 303 — PV
DSB-Dresdner Bank, Huerfanos 1219, pg. 419 — IT
Daewoo Chile S.A., Santa Rosa 356, pg. 358 — IT
Daewoo Motor Chile S.A., Av. Las Condes, pg. 358 — IT
Danzas Chile S.A., Rosal 331, Of. 21, pg. 382 — IT
Data General Chile C.A., Suecia 392 La Providencia, pg. 485 — PB
Davy McKee Chile Ltda., Av Apoquindo 3721, 19th Fl., pg. 775 — IT
DuraCell Chile Ltda., Av. Pedro de Valdivia North, pg. 743 — PB
Duratec, Avenida Jorge Alessandri, pg. 430 — IT
EMI Odeon Chilena SA, P.O. Box No. 186-D, pg. 427 — IT
Esis International Asesorias Limitada, Moneda 1123, pg. 363 — PB
Electrolux (Chile) Limitada, Casilla 16447; Correo No. 9, pg. 441 — IT
ENAEX S.A., Renato Sanchez 3859, pg. 1115 — PB
Envases Modernos (CHH) S.A., pg. 905 — PB
EURO RSCG Graffiti, Mar del Plata, 19-26, pg. 603 — IT
Ewos Chile S.A., Avda. Pedro de Valdivia 0193, pg. 349 — IT
The Export-Import Bank of Korea, Rm. 512, Forum Bldg., Providencia 2653, pg. 467 — IT
Fabrimetal S.A., San Gerardo, pg. 748 — IT
Falconbridge Chile S.A., Av. 11 de Septiembre 2353, pg. 434 — IT
Financiera Fusa, S.A., Moneda 840, pg. 335 — IT
Fluor Daniel Chile, S.A., Marchant Pereira 221, 7th Fl., Casilla 341-1, Correo 21, pg. 660 — PB
Fondo Educativo Interamericano, pg. 1027 — IT
Foster Wheeler Chile, S.A., Evanisto Lillo 112, pg. 677 — PB
Frederick & Valenzuela/TBWA, Silvina Hurado 1725, pg. 1062 — PV
H.B. Fuller Chile, S.A., Camino Lo Espejo 1350, pg. 687 — PB

PB - *U.S. Public Companies Volume*
PV - *U.S. Private Companies Volume*
IT - *International Public & Private Companies Volume*

1554

Garantias y Credito de Chile S.A., Bandera 84, pg. 335 IT
General Motors Chile S.A., Industria Automotriz, Camino Amelipeloya 9797, pg. 721 PB
Gerber Chile, S.A., Palacio Riesco, pg. 973 IT
Gestetner Chile S.A., San Pio X 2464, pg. 1115 IT
Gist-Brocades Chili S.A., Los Conquistadores 1700, Piso 12, pg. 1142 IT
Goodyear de Chile S.A.I.C., Camino a Melipilla Km. 16, pg. 753 PB
Grace Quimica Cia. Ltda., Lago Rinihue 02220, pg. 756 PB
Max Gruenhut Chile, Apoquindo 3076, P.8, pg. 373 PB
Hanel, S.A., Importadora Instrumental y, Laboratorio, pg. 818 PB
Heller Net-Sud, Augustinas 640, Piso 14, pg. 521 IT
Henkel Chile S.A., pg. 612 IT
Honeywell S.A., Eliodoro Yanez 2887, pg. 835 PB
Hormoquimica de Chile Ltda., 1582 Loreley, pg. 44 IT
IBM de Chile S.A.C, pg. 897 PB
ICI Chile SA, Avda. 11 de Septiembre 2237, Piso 6, pg. 665 IT
ING Bank Santiago de Chile, Avenida Nueva Tajamar 481, pg. 649 IT
ING Barings Chile Ltda., Av. Nueva Tajamar 481, pg. 650 IT
ING Compania de Inversiones y Servicios Ltda., Avenida Nueva Tajamar 481, pg. 650 IT
Inco Chile Ltda., pg. 673 IT
Indepro Ingenieria Ltda., pg. 1017 IT
Industrias de Maiz y Alimentos S.A., Av. el Bosque 0440, pg. 447 PB
Indutinta, S.A., Av. Vicuna MacKenna No. 4525, pg. 371 IT
Inmobiliaria Condominio Parque Zapallar S.A., Avda. Apoquindo 4499, piso 8, pg. 335 IT
International Flavors & Fragrances, Coyancura 2241 of.82, pg. 899 PB
Inversiones Chase Manhattan Limitada, Augustinas 1235, pg. 341 PB
Inversiones Ibericas S.A., Avda. Apoquindo, pg. 335 IT
Inversiones Ina Limitada, Calle Nueva York #80, 9th Fl., pg. 364 PB
Inversiones North (Chile) Ltda., San Sebastian 2839 Office 702, pg. 967 IT
Investment Management Co. Chile SA, 22/F, Miraflores 178, pg. 583 IT
Jacuzzi (Chile) S.A., Camino Melipilla 6843, pg. 1684 PB
John Crane Chile, LOTA 2267 OF.202, pg. 1340 IT
Johnson & Johnson de Chile S.A., Classificador 1333 Correo Central, pg. 930 PB
KSB Chile S.A., pg. 721 IT
Kamyr Chile S A C el, Casilla 53000, pg. 771 IT
Kilborn Inc. y Compania Limitada, Tajamar 183, Oficina 101, pg. 1162 IT
Kleinwort Benson Limited, Avenida Ricardo Lyon 2489, pg. 420 IT
Kodak Chilena S.A.F., Alonso Ovalle 1180, pg. 553 PB
Korn/Ferry International, Enrique Foster Sur 39, 12th Fl., pg. 634 PV
Kvaerner Chile S.A., Avda. 11 de Septiembre 1860, pg. 767 IT
Kvaerner Chile S.A., Casilla 16610, pg. 771 IT
Laboratorios Wyeth Inc., Casilla 263-V, Correo 21, pg. 81 PB
Ladeco S.A., Avda. Libertador B. O'Higgins, 107, pg. 575 IT
Le Carbone-Lorraine Industria y Comercio Ltd., Calle Santa Fe, pg. 1030 IT
Leasing Andino S.A., Edificio Eurocentro, Moneda 970, Piso 8, pg. 1009 IT
Lefersa Alimentos S.A., Pan Americana Norte 600, pg. 1143 IT
Lever Chile S.A., pg. 1437 IT
Loctite Corp. Chile Ltda., Av. Salvadore 443, pg. 611 IT
LOOK, Eleodoro Yanez 1804, pg. 553 PB
Louis Vuitton Chile Ltda, Enrique Foster 119, Las Condes, pg. 782 IT
Lubrizol de Chile, Ltda., Edificio Nueva de Lyon, Nuevea de Lyon 124, Office 201, 2nd fl., pg. 1016 PB
MSA de Chile Ltda., Avda. Salvador 1434, pg. 1114 PB
MAPFRE Chile Reaseguros, S.A., Avda. Apoquindo, pg. 334 IT
MAPFRE Chile Seguros, S.A., Avda. Apoquindo 4499, pg. 333 IT
Maquinas y Herramientas Black & Decker de Chile S.A., pg. 234 PB
Mary Kay Cosmetics Chile S.A., Los Conquistadores #2817, pg. 711 PV
Mathieu Chile, Seminario 109, piso 3, pg. 846 IT
Mattel Chile S.A. (Chile), AVDA Vicuna MacKenna 2301, Casilla 466-V, Correo 21, pg. 1059 PB
Mead Packaging Chile Limitada, pg. 1076 PB
Microsoft Chile S.A., pg. 1108 PB
Minera BHP de Chile Inc., Av. Apoquindo 4499, 12 Piso, pg. 224 IT
Minera Cominco Resources Chile Ltda., Callao 3332, pg. 308 IT
Minera Escondida Limitada, Avenida Apoquindo, 3200 Piaso-7, pg. 227 IT
Minera Outokumpu Chile S.A., San Sebastian 2839, Las Condes, Oficina 902, pg. 1016 IT
Minera Rayrock Inc. Chile, Isidora Goyenchea 2925, Oficina 202, Casilla 190, pg. 1089 IT
Mitsui Chilena Commercial Ltda., Calle Agustinas 1235, 7 Piso, pg. 882 IT
J.P. Morgan Chile Ltda., Gertrudis Echenique 30, Oficina 122, pg. 1130 PB
Motorola Chile S.A., Avenida Providencia, No. 2653, pg. 1139 PB
Mueblas Andes, Rura 68 No. 6910, pg. 553 PB
Nalco Productos Quimicos de Chile S.A., Bucarest 196, Piso 1 Providencia, pg. 1151 PB
Nanbei Ltd., Marchant Pereira 160, pg. 525 PB
Nestle Chile S.A., pg. 921 IT
Nippon Meat Packers, Inc. (Chile) Y Compania Limitada, Eliodoro Yanez, pg. 936 IT
Nissho Iwai (Chile) LTDA, Luis Thayer Ojeda 166, pg. 948 IT
Norton Chile S.A., pg. 1175 IT
Novell Chile, Avda. Pedro de Valdivia 176, pg. 1204 PB
Nueva Vision, Hernando de Aguirre 939, pg. 553 PB
Olivetti de Chile S.A., Santa Elena n. 1587, pg. 1003 IT
Oracle Chile, Marchant Pereira #10, Piso 17, pg. 1228 PB
Outokumpu Tecnica-Chile Ltda., Seminario # 90, 2 Piso, pg. 1017 IT
Pachon S.A. Minera, La Concepcion 177, Piso 4, pg. 253 IT
Panalpina Chile Transportes Mundiales Ltda., pg. 1023 IT
Parsons Overseas Co. Chile Limitada, Galvarino Gallardo 2125, pg. 842 PV
Pegasus Minera De Chile LTDA, La Gloria 36, pg. 1269 PB
Pepsi-Cola Chile Consultores Ltda., Pedrode Valdivia 0193 Casilla 13540 Corr, pg. 1277 PB
Petroleos Transandinos YPF S.A., Gertrudis Echenique 30, Piso 12, pg. 1515 IT
Pharmacia & Upjohn Compania Limitada, Eliodoro Yanez 1939, pg. 1049 IT
Placer Dome Latin America, Av. Gertrudis Echenique 30, 14th Floor, Torre Las Condes, pg. 1060 IT
Productos Alimenticios Savory S.A.I.C., pg. 922 IT
Productos de Acero S.A. Prodinsa, El Milagros 455, pg. 185 IT
Productos Farmoquimicos Roche Ltda., pg. 1121 IT
Productos Gillette Chile Limitada, Mons. Sotero Sanz 55 Piso 11, pg. 745 PB
Productos Quimicos CIBA-GEIGY Ltda., Francisco Meneses 1980, Casilla 9993, pg. 983 IT
Prolam/Young & Rubicam S.A., Triana 857, pg. 1200 PV
Publicaciones en Computacion Ltda., Avenida Pedro de Valdivia, pg. 570 PV
Quebrada Blanca, Avenida Los Leones 212, pg. 308 IT
Quimica Flesch, S.A., Av. Vicuna MacKenna No. 4815, pg. 371 IT
Quimica Harting S.A., pg. 614 IT
Quimica Sol S.A., Av. Vucuna MacKenna No. 4815, pg. 371 IT
RNBNY Branch Office-Santiago, Huerfanos, pg. 1381 PB
Raychem Industrial Y Comercial Limitada, Manuel Montt 1693, Providencia, pg. 1362 PB
Reader's Digest Chile, Limitada, Huelen 95, 3er Piso, Depto. 31, pg. 1368 PB
Refractorios Chilenos S.A. (RECSA), Carretera Panamericana Nortz 3076, pg. 748 PB
Representacion del Deutsche Bank AG (Santiago), pg. 405 IT
Rhodia-Merieux Chile, Ramon Subercaseaux 1528, Casilla 3456, pg. 1112 IT
Rimplex, S.A., Casilla 30, Coreo 29, pg. 823 PB
Rockwell Automation Dodge-Chile, Burgos 212, Dept. 32, pg. 1399 PB
Rockwell-Collins International, Inc., Aeropuerto los Cerrillos-, Hangar Bonir, pg. 1400 PB
Roerig S.A., Av. Tajamar 183, 2nd Fl., pg. 1284 PB
SKF Chilena S.A.I.C., Av. Vicuna MacKenna 655, pg. 1158 IT
SM-Cyclo Chile, Av. Ricardo Lyon 1601, pg. 1315 IT
SMM Group, Gertrudis Echenique 30, Torre Las Condes, Oficina No. 123, pg. 1316 IT
Sandoz Colorquimica Ltda., pg. 984 IT
Sandoz Farmaceutica Ltda., pg. 984 IT
Sandvik Chile S.A., P.O. Box 14510, pg. 1187 IT
Santander Merchant, S.A., Andres Bello 2777, Piso 16, pg. 144 IT
Schiesser Inversiones Chile Ltda., pg. 618 IT
Scientific-Atlanta Chile Y Compania Limitada, Avda. 11 de Septiembre 2155, pg. 1443 PB
Semillas Pioneer Chile Ltda., Coyancura 2241, Piso 3, pg. 1299 PB
Shell Chile SA Comercial e Industrial, Av. Providencia No. 1979, pg. 1142 IT
Singapore Tourist Promotion Board - Santiago, Edificio Banco Sudamericano, Andres de Fuenzalida 17 Of. 62, pg. 1254 IT
Sociedad Constructora y de Inversiones Martin Zamora Ltd., Avda. Apoquindo 4499, piso 8, pg. 335 IT
Sodexho Chile, Williams Rebolledo 1799, pg. 1275 IT
Sodexho Pass Chile-Cheque Restaurant, Avda. Santa Maria 0824, pg. 1275 IT
SONDA LTDA., pg. 508 PB
Sudamerica de Salud, Agustinos 1127, pg. 333 IT
Sulzer Sistemas e Instalaciones (Chile) S.A., pg. 1306 IT
Sur Asistencia, San Crecence 81, piso 7, pg. 334 IT
Svedala Chile, pg. 1324 IT
Swiss Bank Corporation, Miraflores 222, Piso 27, pg. 1330 IT
TVX Minera de Chile, Av. 11 de Septiembre, 2353, Piso 13, pg. 1345 IT
Tamrock EJC Chile S.A., Loteo Las Esteras Norte, pg. 1353 IT
Tasman Chile S.A., Av. Apoquindo 3076, Piso No. 6, pg. 495 IT
Telcel - Chile S.A., pg. 1140 PB
Telefonica Chile, S.A., Monsenor Sotero Saenz, pg. 1372 IT
Texaco Chile S.A.C., Comino A Melipilla 9330, pg. 1584 PB
Thomson-CSF (Chile) Ltda, Alonso Ovalle, 1626, pg. 1384 IT
3M Chile S.A., 1001 Santa Isabel, pg. 1606 PB
Tintas Graficas S.A., Williams Rebolledo No. 1717, pg. 109 IT
Union de Bancos Suizos, Edificio Torre del Bosque, Avenida El Bosque 177, pg. 1441 IT
Utell International-Chile, Anunategui no 277, pg. 1098 IT
Valmet Chile Ltda., Av. Nueva Tajamar 555, Oficina 1402, pg. 1448 IT
Van Leer Chile S.A., pg. 1146 IT
Voest-Alpine Chile Ltda., Moneda 1160-10, pg. 1472 IT
Vulco SA, Casilla 821, pg. 1489 IT
Wackenhut Chile, S.A., Ave., Ejercito 171, pg. 1731 PB
Wang Export Services, Inc., pg. 1738 PB
West Merchant Bank Limited, Avda. Libertador Bernardo O'Higgins 949, pg. 1494 IT

Talcahuano

Industrias Chilenas de Alambre Inchalam S.A., Casilla 7-D, pg. 185 IT

Valparaiso

Det Norske Veritas, Blanco 1215, Of. 805, Edificio Nautilus, pg. 397 IT

Vina del Mar

Quimica S.C. Johnson & Son Chilena S.A.C.I., Casilla 35-D, pg. 593 PV
Skega Chilena S.A., Casilla 277, pg. 1323 IT

CHINA

Beijing

AES China Generating, 3/F., Jinqiao Bldg., #1, Jianguomenwai Ave., pg. 5 PB
AST Research Inc., Beijing Representative Office, Unit 28-32 Level 7, China World Tower, pg. 1182 IT
Acer Market Services, Ltd., pg. 22 IT
Air Products China Inc., Beijing New Century Hotel, Office Tower, pg. 31 PB
Airbus Industrie Beijing, 3005 Jing Guang Centre, pg. 39 IT
Ajinomoto Co., Inc., Beijing Office, 0903 China World Tower, China World Trade Center No.1, pg. 40 IT
Allen-Bradley Enterprise Xiamen Ltd., Everbright Building No. 6, Room 1314, pg. 1398 PB
Allianz Beijing Representative Office, Office C 211 B, Beijing Lufthansa Center, pg. 59 IT
AlliedSignal China Inc., AlliedSignal Aerospace Services Corporation, Lido Commercial Centre A1-514, Jichang Road, Jiang Tai Road, pg. 52 PB
Amdahl (China) Limited, Room 1613, 16th Floor, Everbright Building, pg. 527 IT
Asahi Bank Beijing Representative Office, Ste. 2513, China World Tower, China World Trade Ctr., No 1, pg. 83 IT
Asahi Chemical Industry - Beijing, Room 930, China World Tower, China World Trade Center, pg. 84 IT
Autodesk China, Ste. 1892-1893, Pana Tower, No. 36 Haidian Rd., pg. 149 PB
BASF Beijing Representative Office, Room 214, 2nd Fl., Lido Commercial Bldg., pg. 105 IT
BHP Petroleum (China) Inc., 2nd Fl., Golden Bridge Mansion, West Entrance, A1 Jianguomenwai Avenue, pg. 225 IT
Bailey Beijing Controls Company Ltd., pg. 449 IT
Baldwin Printing Control Equipment (Beijing) Company, Ltd., Rm 115, Juyuan Office Bldg., No 33 Juer Alley, pg. 170 PB
Banca Nazionale del Lavoro, CITIC Building-10th floor, Office no. 2- 19, pg. 137 IT
Banco do Brasil S.A.-Beijing Representative Office, China World Trade Center, China World Tower, Room 1426, pg. 142 IT
Banco Santander, Unit 23-01, Landmark Building, 8 North Dongsanhuan Road, pg. 144 IT
Bank Brussels Lambert, Beijing, Beijing Lufthansa Centre, Office Unit C 317, pg. 148 IT
Bank of America NT&SA, Unit 22-23, Level 27 China, World Tower, China World Trade Centre, pg. 182 PB
BANK OF CHINA, 410 Fuchengmen Nei Dajie, pg. 152 IT
Bank of Montreal - China, Noble Tower, 22 Jianguomenwai Da Jie, pg. 155 IT
Bank of Yokohama Beijing, 2209 China World Tower, China World Trade Center, No.1, pg. 159 IT
Banque Paribas, Beijing Hotel, Batiment Central-Suite 3136, pg. 319 IT
Barclays Bank PLC, SCITE Tower, 12th Fl., 22 Jianguomenwai Dajie, Rm. 1211, pg. 165 IT
Barrick Power Gold Corporation of China Limited, Hong Kong Macau Centre, Dong Si Shi Tiao Li Jiao Qiao, pg. 169 IT
Bausch & Lomb China, Inc., No. 37, Xingfu St., Chong Wen District, pg. 195 PB
Bayerische Vereinsbank AG, Unit 10, 10 Liangma Tower, pg. 180 IT
Beijing AGIE Industrial Electronics Ltd., Mapo Shunyi County, pg. 488 IT
Beijing Airport Foods Service Co., Ltd., Beijing Capital Airport, pg. 1322 IT
Beijing AP Beifen Gases Industry Co. Ltd., Wen-Quan, Haidian District, pg. 32 PB
Beijing AP Beifen Gases Industry Company, Ltd., Wenquan Haidianqu District, pg. 32 PB
Beijing Automated Computer Systems Co. Ltd., Beijing, Rm. 1707-1708, Kun Tai Bldg., 10 Chao Wai Da Jie, pg. 242 IT

PB - *U.S. Public Companies Volume*
PV - *U.S. Private Companies Volume*
IT - *International Public & Private Companies Volume*

CHINA DIRECTORY OF CORPORATE AFFILIATIONS

Beijing Beiling Special Automobile Co., Ltd., 62 Kunminghu Nan-lu, pg. 692 IT
Beijing ChinaTuhsu Makro Property Co. Ltd., 3rd Bld. No. 28 An Wai Dong Hou Xiang, pg. 1155 IT
Beijing Chinefarge Cement Limited Liability Co., Huaibei Town, Huairou County, pg. 791 IT
Beijing CIBA-GEIGY Pharma Ltd., 5th Fl. Huayu Mansion, A3 Long Tan Road, pg. 975 IT
Beijing Crown Can Company Ltd., Xiao Tianzhue Village, pg. 465 PB
Beijing Dentsu Advertising Co., Ltd., 8th Floor, Bldg. F, Fuhun, Mansion, No. 8 North Avenue, pg. 393 IT
Beijing Descente Co., Ltd., 19 Changping Shisanling Shuiku, Yangshan Xi Road, pg. 396 IT
Beijing East Palace Apartment Co., Ltd., No.25, Zaoying Rd., pg. 374 IT
Beijing Eastern Rohm and Haas Company, Limited, pg. 1403 PB
Beijing - Fanuc Mechatronics Co., Ltd., Xibajianfang Beizhan, Dongzhimen Wai, pg. 478 IT
Beijing GOT Business Computer System Co. Ltd., Rm. 405, Wan Lian Bldg. # 19, North Sanhuan, Middle Road, pg. 1005 IT
Beijing Huade Lining Materials Industry Co. Ltd., 1, Fa Tou Dong Li, pg. 1322 IT
Beijing Huade Metal Packaging Container Co. Ltd., 4, Fa Tou Dong Li, pg. 1322 IT
Beijing Ji Tong-Bellsouth Communication & Information Engineering Co., Ltd., Beijing Ambassador Mansion, No. B21 Jiu Xian Qiao Rd., pg. 208 PB
Beijing JiAi Pharmaceuticals Limited Liability Company, National Institute of Pharmaceuticals, pg. 915 PB
Beijing Lufthansa Center Co., Ltd., 50 Liangmaqiao Rd., pg. 358 IT
Beijing Mitsukoshi Restaurant Ltd., Beijing Fortune Bldg. 1F, 5-Dong San Kwan Bei-lu, pg. 884 IT
Beijing Nokia Hang XingTelecoms Systems Co. Ltd., No. 11 Hepingli Dongjie, pg. 953 IT
Beijing Office, c/o Beijing Hotel Room # 1613, No. 33 East Chang An Street, pg. 871 IT
Beijing Office, Ste. 909, Beijing Fortune Bldg 5, Dong Sanhuan Bei-Lu, pg. 1519 IT
Beijing Praxair Inc., pg. 1320 PB
Beijing Representative Office, 26-02 CITIC Building, 19 Jianguo, Menwai Dajie, pg. 1517 IT
Beijing Shimadzu Medical Equipment Co., Ltd., No. 6 Langjiayuan Jianguomenwai Avenue, pg. 1232 IT
Beijing Toto Co., Ltd., Gao Xin Jianzhu Cailao Gongye, pg. 1410 IT
Beijing Wacoal Co., Ltd., Jia 34, Guang Qu Beili Chong, pg. 1484 IT
Beijing Wire Communications Plant, 14 Jiuxianqiao Road, pg. 739 IT
Beijing Zhong An Fire Security Electronics Company Ltd., 48 Cheng Fu Road, pg. 1246 IT
Beijing Zhuli Diantong Optoelectronics Technology Co., Ltd., pg. 1313 IT
Bellsouth China, Inc., Beijing Lufthansa Centre, Ste., C507, 50 Liangmaqiao Rd., pg. 208 PB
BERG Electronics Beijing Office, Room 405, 4/F Tower A, Beijing Keluh Building, pg. 213 PB
Bilfinger + Berger Bauaktiengesellschaft, Beijing Representaive Office, Office Building-Unit S. 1B, pg. 196 IT
Boeing China, Inc., Beijing Hotel, Rm. 1536, pg. 242 PB
Leo Burnett Advertising Co., Ltd.-Beijing, 12 Office Tower, Hong Kong Macau Center, pg. 184 PV
C-E International, Ste. 1325, Friendship Hotel, pg. 5 IT
CMC International (S.E. Asia) Pte. Ltd., 22/F Full Link Plaza, Suite 2207B, No. 18 Chaoyangmenwai Ave., pg. 413 PB
CPC Foods Co. Ltd. Beijing, pg. 224 PB
Cariplo (Beijing), 706 Cvik Tower, 22 Jianguomenwai Da Je, pg. 275 IT
Carrefour China, 1F/132, 136 Zhongfa Investment Bldg., pg. 272 IT
Chang Cheng-Takenaka Construction Co., Ltd., Beijing International Wanglian Bldg. 5F, pg. 1351 IT
The Chase Manhattan Bank, N.A., RMS 1629-31, pg. 340 PB
Chichibu Onoda Cement Corporation-Beijing, Beijing Hotel Dong-Lou, Room 1209, No. 33, pg. 284 IT
China Computerworld, Room 312 Haowei Bldg., No. 25 Beitaipingzhuang Rd., pg. 569 PV
China Computerworld/PC World China, Room 312 Haowei Building, pg. 569 PV
China Hewlett-Packard Company Ltd., Level 5, West Wing Office, China World Trade Center, No. 1, pg. 816 PB
China Infoworld, 20B FuXing Rd., pg. 569 PV
China International Petroleum & Chemicals United Co., Rm. 2508, Capital Mansion, No. 6 Xin Yuan South Rd., pg. 1254 IT
China Kang Fu International Leasing Co., Ltd., Bldg., No. 3, Xiyuan Hotel, Erligou, Hai-dian District, pg. 521 IT
CHINA NATIONAL CEREALS, OILS & FOODSTUFFS CORPORATION (COFCO), 6-11th Floors, Jing Xing Bldg., 2A Dong San Huan Bei Lu, pg. 285 IT
CHINA NATIONAL TECHNICAL IMPORT & EXPORT CORPORATION (CNTIC), Jiu Ling Building, No. 21, Xi San Huan Bei Lu, pg. 285 IT
China Orient Leasing Co., Ltd., 408-410, Donghi Office Bldg., No. 23, Xibahe Xili, pg. 1009 IT
China Prospering Building Design Joint Venture Corporation Ltd., 406, Hualongjie Nanheyan, pg. 1233 IT
China Schindler Elevator Co. Ltd., pg. 1205 IT
China United Petroleum Co., Room 135, Exhibition Centre, pg. 1254 IT
China Universal Leasing Co., Ltd., Rm. 7066, Mezzanine Fl., West Bldg., Beijing Hotel, pg. 1190 IT
China Yanshan United Foreign Trade Co. Ltd., Yan Fang Rd., pg. 1254 IT
Chugai Pharmaceutical Co. Ltd.-Beijing, China World Trade Center, 510 China World Tower, pg. 291 IT
CIBA-GEIGY (China) Limited, Room 3312 Jing Guang Centre, Hu Jia Lou, Chao, pg. 976 IT
CIBA-GEIGY (Hong Kong) Limited-Beijing Liaison Office, Room 3311, Jing Guang Centre, Hu Jia Lou, Chao Yang Qu, pg. 977 IT
Citic Golden Tiger Group Co., Ltd., The Business Bldg., Second Happiness Village, pg. 579 IT
Citizen Watch (China) Co., Ltd., Tian Zhu Lu 7 Hao, Tian Wei 2, Jie, Tian Zhu Kong Gang Gong Ye Qu, pg. 294 IT
Coherent Inc.-Beijing, Unit 517, 5th Floor, Tower 2, Bright China Chang An Building, pg. 395 PB
Cometals China, Inc., 22/F Full Link Plaza, Suite, 2206-2207A, No. 18 Chaoyangmenwai Ave., pg. 414 PB
Commerzbank AG-Beijing Representative Office, Representative Office, 8-4 CITIC Intl. Bldg., 8th Fl., pg. 311 IT
Commonwealth Bank-Beijing, 2910 China World Towers, pg. 313 IT
Comstream, A Spar Company, China World Trade World Ctr., No. 1 Jianguomenwai Ave., Ste. 2309, pg. 1288 IT
Credit Agricole (CNCA) Representative Office-Beijing, Ste. 1207-8, Scite Twr., pg. 341 IT
Cummins Corporation, China World Tower, Ste. 917, No. 1 Jian Gou Men Wai, pg. 468 PB
DMB&B Beijing, Rm. 601 N. Bldg., EAS Tower, No. 21 Xiao Yun Rd., Sanyuan, pg. 303 PV
DSM China, Citic Building 26E, 19 Jianguomenwai Dajie, pg. 355 IT
Dai-Ichi Kangyo Bank, Ltd.-Beijing, 1718 Beijing Fortune Bldg., 5 Dong Sanhuan Bei-Lu, pg. 361 IT
Daiko Pacific International Advertising Co., No. 8 Exhibition Hall, China International, Exhibition Centre, pg. 366 IT
Dainippon Ink & Chemicals, Inc., Room 902, Beijing Fortune Bldg, 5, Dong San Huan Bei Lu, pg. 372 IT
Daiwa Bank-Beijing, Room No. 1118, Beijing Fortune, Bldg., 5 Dong Sanhuan Beilu, pg. 373 IT
Dell Computer Corporation, Beijing Representative Office, Section A, 3/F Beijing Science, pg. 496 PB
Dentsu Beijing Office, 1518, Beijing Fortune Bldg., 5 Dong San Huan, pg. 393 IT
Dentsu Young & Rubicam Advertising Co., Ltd. (Beijing), Room 1115, 11th Floor, Office Tower 2, Henderson Centre, pg. 325 PV
Deutsche Bank AG (China), 2620-24 China World Tower, China World Trade Center, pg. 404 IT
Digital Equipment China Incorporated, 6/F., Office Tower, New Century Hotel, pg. 507 PB
Dresdner Bank AG, International Bldg., 6th Fl., Office #1, Jianguo Menwai Dajie, pg. 419 IT
Dumez-GTM Chine, Landmark Building 1610, 8 North Dongsanhuan Road, pg. 823 IT
ECI Telecom China, 14 Fl. Bldg. A.,Fu Hua Mansion, #8 Chao Yang Men Bei Avenue, pg. 643 IT
EG & G China Representative Office, Fuhua Plaza-12B-C, Tower A, 8 North Chao-Yang-Men Ave., pg. 544 PB
EMS China Limited, Room 1222 Beijing Hotel, pg. 566 PB
ESAB Representative Office, Unit 912 Landmark Tower, No 8 N. Dongsanhuan Rd., pg. 282 IT
Edelman Worldwide China, Hong Kong Macau Centre, 11th Fl., Office Tower, 100027, pg. 363 PV
Electricite de France, Beijing Chang AN Club 5-6, 10 Dong Chang An Street, pg. 437 IT
Elkem Representative Office - Beijing, Room 606, EAS Tower, No. 21, Xiao Yun Road, pg. 447 IT
Enso-Eurocan (H.K.) Ltd., Rm. 682, Tianlun Dynasty Hotel, pg. 457 IT
Exide Electronics International/IPM, pg. 126 IT
Finnigan MAT China, Inc., Rm. 3702, Friendship Hotel, pg. 1596 PB
Fischer Imaging China, BO7, Block H, No. 40, Liangmaqiao Road, pg. 647 PB
Fluor Daniel China, Inc., 2701 Landmark Building, 8 North Dongsanhuan Road, pg. 660 PB
Fuji Photo Film Co., Ltd., Beijing Representative Office, Beijing Fortune Bldg., No. 817, Dong Sanhuan Bei-lu, pg. 524 IT
Fujisawa Beijing, 621 Beijing Fortune Bldg., 5 dong Sanhuan Bei-lu Chao, pg. 525 IT
Furukawa Electric Co., Ltd. Beijing, 2305, China World Tower, No. 1, Jian Guo Men Wai Avenue, pg. 530 IT
GSI (Beijing) Hosiery Co., Ltd., Niushan District, Shunyi, pg. 579 IT
Gan S.A. China, Room 711, Level 7 Tower B, Beijing Cojco Plaza, pg. 565 IT
Generale Bank, Zijin Guest House, Bldg. 3, 1st Fl., 9 Chong Wenmen Xidajie, pg. 547 IT
Gestetner Office Equipment (China) Co. Ltd., 10 Bei Yi Tiao, pg. 1115 IT
Getinge AB Beijing, Zi Wei Hotel, Rm. 909, No. 40 Shi Jingshan Rd., pg. 551 IT
Goldman Sachs (China) L.L.C., Unit 1102-04 Landmark Bldg., 8 N. Dongsanhuan Rd., pg. 462 PV
Hakuhodo Inc., Rm. 507, Beijing Fortune Bldg., No. 5 Dong, pg. 588 IT
Hanwa Co., Ltd.-Beijing Branch, Rm. 808 Beijing Fortune Bldg., 5 Dong San Huan Bei-lu, pg. 595 IT
Henkel (China) Investment Co. Ltd., pg. 612 IT
Hitachi Zosen Beijing, Room 1201,Beijing Fortune Bldg, 5, Dong San Huan Bei Lu, pg. 623 IT
The Hokkaido Takushoku Bank, Ltd. (Beijing), Ste. 2601, Jing Guang Centre, Hujialou, Chaoyang District, pg. 627 IT
Honeywell China Inc., Zhong Wei Ke Yi Office Bldg., 2nd Fl. A34, Dong Huan Bei Ku, pg. 834 PB
Hoogovens Technical Services China, Suite 405, CATIC Plaza, 18 Beichen E. Road, pg. 755 IT
Huls AG Beijing Liason Office, Unit 1410, Scite Tower, 22 Jianguomanwai Dajie, pg. 1455 IT
I&S Corporation (Beijing Office), 8F Chang Fu Gong Office Bldg., Jian Guo Men Wai Dajie, pg. 642 IT
ING Bank Beijing, Room 1510, Landmark Bldg., No. 8, North Dongsanhuan Road, pg. 649 IT
ING Consultants, Room 1509, Landmark Bldg., No. 8, North Dongsanhuan Road, pg. 649 IT
ING Insurance International, Room 1508, Landmark Bldg., No. 8, N. Dongsanhuan Road, pg. 650 IT
IPC Information Technology (Beijing), Suite 202, Beijing Tong Heng Tower, pg. 651 IT
IPM Beijing Office, N. 50 Liangmagiao Rd., pg. 126 IT
IR International Holdings, Inc., Beijing Hui Yan Intl. Apt., Building C, #1205, pg. 907 PB
Imation Beijing Branch Office, Rm. 702, Tower A, Vantone New World Plaza, pg. 870 PB
The Industrial and Commercial Bank of China, 15 Cuiwei Road, pg. 1328 IT
The Industrial Bank of Japan, Limited (Beijing), 8th Fl., Chang-Fu-Gong Bldg., Jia 26, Jianguomenwai St., pg. 675 IT
Intalcable-China, c/o Jing Guang Centre, 35F, Hotel Llu Jailou, pg. 655 IT
Intergraph China, Inc., 4th Floor Polo Building, 6 GUanghuaxili, Jianguomenwai, pg. 891 PB
International Flavors & Fragrances, pg. 899 PB
International Union Leasing Co., Ltd., Rm. 1609, Beijing Fortune Bldg, 5 Dongsanhuan-Beilu, Chaoyang District, pg. 957 IT
Japan Energy Corporation-Beijing Office, No. 5 Bldg., Zijin Guest House, pg. 702 IT
Jardine Matheson (China) Ltd., 2718 China World Tower, China World Trade Centre, No. 1, pg. 705 IT
Axel Johnson (China) Ltd., Beijing Liaison Office, Room 611, Asia-Pacific Bldg., pg. 711 IT
Keithley Instruments China, Yuan Chen Xin Bldg., Rm. 705, No.12 Yumin Road, Dewai Median, pg. 947 PB
Kennametal (China) Limited, No. 192 Andingmenwai Street, pg. 951 PB
KEPCO Beijing Office, Level 6, 14-46, China World Tower, pg. 758 IT
Kerr-McGee China Petroleum Ltd., Fortune Center, pg. 952 PB
Knoll Beijing, Room 512, Tower A COFCO Plaza, pg. 108 IT
Kobe Steel, Ltd. (Beijing), Suite 2926, China World Tower, China World Trade Center, pg. 741 IT
Kodak (China) Limited, Unit 1-2, Level 4, West Wing Office, China World Trade Ctr., pg. 553 PB
Konica Beijing Office, Rm. No. 2339, Minzu Hotel,51 Fuxingmen, pg. 749 IT
Korn/Ferry International, Ste. 606, Landmark Bldg., 8 N. Dongsamhuan Rd., pg. 634 PV
Kubota Corp.-Beijing Office, Room 1551, New Century Office, Tower, No. 6 Southern Rd., pg. 762 IT
Kvaerner Hydro Power, Beijing Representative Office, Level 10, China World Tower, No. 1 Jiang Guo Men Wai Avenue, pg. 767 IT
Kyowa Hakko Kogyo Co., Ltd., 10004, Beijing Fortune Bldg., Room 420, No. 5, Dong San Huan Bei Lu, pg. 778 IT
Lucent Technologies (China) Co., Ltd., 7th & 9th Flrs., CVIK Pl. No. 22, Jian Guo Men, pg. 1018 PB
MTS Systems China Ltd., Xi Yuan Hotel, Suites 674, 675, 676, 691, pg. 1029 PB
Martin Marietta International, Inc., Level 29, Unit 1-2, China World Tower, pg. 1009 PB
Mathieu (China), pg. 846 IT
The Meiji Life Insurance Company Beijing Office, 2631, China World Tower, 1 Jian Guo Men Wai Avenue, pg. 854 IT
Merita Bank Ltd., Beijing Representative Office, 905 Landmark Twr., 8 N. Dongsanhuan Rd., pg. 859 IT
MetLife Beijing Representative Office, 1006 China World Tower, 1 Jian Guo Men Wai Ave., pg. 738 PV
Microsoft Corporation-Beijing, pg. 1108 PB
Mikron Beijing Office, San J1 Li Mansion, Room 501, No. 6 The East Quarter, pg. 867 IT
Millipore China, Ltd., Asia Pacific Bldg., Ste. 1101-1106 & 16, pg. 1113 PB
Mitsui & Co., Ltd., 1702 International Bldg., 19 Jianwai Street, pg. 881 IT
Mitsukoshi Ltd.-Beijing Office, Beijing Fortune Bldg. 10F, 5 Dong San Kwan Bei Lu, pg. 884 IT
J.P. Morgan & Co. Incorporated, 27/F, CITIC Bldg., No. 19, Jianguomenwai Dajie, pg. 1130 PB
Morgan Stanley Beijing, 21st Fl., Everbright Bldg., 6 Fu Xing Men Wai Ave., pg. 1133 PB
Motorola China Inc., China World Trade Tower, 1, Jian Guo Men Wai Ave., Rm. 1517, pg. 1139 PB
Munters Air Treatment Equipment Co. Ltd., Shajing Village West Sunyi, pg. 669 IT
Munters Beijing Ltd., Rm. 1008, Changwen Men Hotel, 2 W. Changwen Men St., pg. 669 IT
NKK Corporation Beijing Office, 1720, Beijing Fortune Bldg., pg. 903 IT
NYK-Beijing, Rm. 1810, Guo Mao Da Sha, 18th Floor, Jian Guo Men Wai Jei 1 Hao, pg. 941 IT
National Mutual Beijing, No. 408 Office Building, 8 Xinzhong Xi Jie Gongti Bei Lu, pg. 908 IT
New Brunswick Scientific Co., Inc., Taicheng Commercial Business, Complex No. 8, Da Hui Si Road, pg. 1170 PB
Nippon Credit Bank Ltd.-Beijing, Changfugong Office Building, A26 Jianguo-Menwai St., 7th Fl., pg. 933 IT
Nippon Life - Beijing Representative Office, Changfugong Office Building, 3rd Floor, Jia 26, Jianguomenwai Dajie, pg. 936 IT
Nippon Steel Corporation-Beijing Rep. Office, 8th fl.-Chang Fu Gong Center, Jiam Guo Men Wai Da Jie, pg. 940 IT

PB - *U.S. Public Companies Volume*
PV - *U.S. Private Companies Volume*
IT - *International Public & Private Companies Volume*

1556

Geographic Index-Non U.S.

Nissin Cofco Foods Co., Ltd., Room 2J, Guomen Building, No. 1, pg. 950   IT

Nokia Representative Office, International Club, Rm. #88, 21 Jianguomenwai Ave., pg. 953   IT

Nomura CITIC International Economic Consultants Co., Ltd., 1705, 17th Floor, Beijing, Fortune Bldg., 5 Dongsanhuan-Beilu, pg. 957   IT

Nortel Post & Telecommunications Technical Ins., No. 18 Shun San Tiao, pg. 970   IT

Novell China, Fl. 6, Annex Bldg., Sinochem Mansion, A2 Fuxngmanwai Ave., pg. 1204   PB

Novo Nordisk A/S, Shangdi Zone, Fourth Street 9, pg. 987   IT

Novo Nordisk A/S (Tianjin) Biotechnology Co. Ltd., Fourth Street No 9, Shangdi Zone, Haidian District, pg. 988   IT

OCE Office Equipment (Beijing) Co. Ltd., pg. 994   IT

Obayashi Corporation-Beijing, Beijing Fazhan BLD 1010, Dong Sanhuan Beilu 5, pg. 995   IT

OMRON (China) Co., Ltd., 7F, Chang Fu Gong Office Bldg., A-26, pg. 1005   IT

Oracle China Inc., Beijing Yanshan Hotel, Apt. Bldg. Ste. 1605-1608, pg. 1228   PB

Oxford Instruments, Room 508, Instrimpex Building, 6 Xizhimen Wai Street, pg. 1018   IT

Pall Filter (Beijing) Co., Ltd., No. 12 Dongdaqiao Rd., Chao Yang Men Wai, 100020, pg. 1254   IT

Parker Hanrifin Hong Kong Ltd., Suite 01B, 5th Floor, CITIC Building, pg. 1263   PB

Pechiney Asia Pacifique Services, Representative Office, Soite Tower, Rm. 1105, pg. 1031   IT

Perstorp Unidur Beijing Office, Room 111, Ever Bright Building, No. 6 FuXingMen Wai Avenue, pg. 1038   IT

Pharmacia & Upjohn Biotech (China) Ltd., Bejing Yanshan Hotel, Room 1202/1104, pg. 1047   IT

POSCO Beijing Office, 1707, China World Trade Center, No. 1 Jian Guo Men Wai Avenue, pg. 1062   IT

Principal International China, Unit B2003, Vantone New World Plaza, pg. 886   PV

Principal Mutual Life Insurance Co., B2003, Vantone New World Plaza, 2 Fu Chen Men Wai Avenue, 100037, pg. 886   PV

Quantum Hong Kong Ltd. PRC Branch, Beijing Rep. Office, Room 9-10, 13th Floor, Everbright Office Building, pg. 1350   PB

RNBNY Representative Office-Beijing, Unit 22-01, Landmark Bldg., 8 N. Dongsanhuan Rd., pg. 1381   PB

RZB Beijing, Beijing International Club, 1st Floor, Room 111, pg. 1084   IT

Reed Business Information-China, 28 Dong Hou Xiang, Andingmen Wai, pg. 1094   IT

Renishaw's Representative Office, Room 524, China Travel Service Tower, pg. 1103   IT

Rhone-Poulenc Chine, Bureau de Representation, Beijing Hong Kong Macao Center, pg. 1112   IT

Rockwell Automation (Hong Kong) Limited, Room 1307 Everbright Bldg., No. 6, Fu Xing Men Wai Avenue, pg. 1399   IT

Rockwell-Collins International, Room 1218, Everbright Building, No. 6, Fu Xing Men Wai Avenue, pg. 1400   IT

SAS Institute Ltd., Beijing Representative Office, Rm. 203, Tong Heng Tower, pg. 967   PV

SNC Lavalin - Beijing, China World Tower, Suite 2325, No. 1 Jian Guo Men Wai Ave., pg. 1162   IT

The Sakura Bank - Beijing Representative Office, 3rd Floor, Changfugong Office Bldg., pg. 1179   IT

Samsung China Headquarters, Room 909, China World Trade Center No. 1, pg. 1183   IT

Sandvik China Ltd., pg. 1187   IT

Sanpaolo-Beijing Representative Office, China World Trade Center, 2646 China World Tower, pg. 691   IT

Santa Fe Braun Intl. Ltd., Beijing Hotel, Rm. 4008, pg. 765   IT

SASIB Machinery (China) Company Limited, Room 411-413, Estoril House, pg. 1195   IT

Scientific-Atlanta, Inc., Suite 1406, Block B, Lucky Tower, 100027, pg. 1443   PB

Shandwick China, Room 211, Beijing BondTak Financial, pg. 1227   IT

Shimadzu Beijing Office, 2nd Fl., Chang Fu Gong Bldg., Jian Guo Men Wai Da Jie, pg. 1232   IT

Shougang NEC Electronics Co., Ltd., No. 45 Badachu Street, pg. 901   IT

Siemens Ltd.-Beijing, China, 7, Waugijing Zhoughuan Naulu, pg. 1247   IT

Sinochem Electronic Information Technology Co. Ltd., 12th Fl., Yulong Hotel, No. 40 Fucheng Rd., pg. 1254   IT

Sinochem Finance Co. Ltd., 6th Fl., Yulong Hotel, No. 40 Fucheng Rd., pg. 1254   IT

Sinochem International Advertising & Exhibition Co. Ltd., 6th Fl., Yulong Hotel, No. 40 Fucheng Rd., pg. 1254   IT

Sinochem International Chemicals Co. Ltd., 8th Fl., Yulong Hotel, No. 40 Fucheng Rd., pg. 1254   IT

Sinochem International Fertilizer Co. Ltd., 10th Fl., Yulong Hotel, No. 40 Fucheng Rd., pg. 1255   IT

Sinochem International Industry Co. Ltd., 4th Fl., Yulong Hotel, No. 40 Fucheng Rd., pg. 1255   IT

SINOCHEM INTERNATIONAL PETROLEUM CO. LTD., Tower A-2, Fuxingmen Wai Dajie, pg. 1254   IT

Sinochem International Rubber Co. Ltd., 4th Fl. & 9th Fl., Yulong Hotel, Hotel, No. 40 Fucheng Rd., pg. 1255   IT

Sinochem Intertrans Co. Ltd., 10th Fl., Yulong Hotel, No. 40 Fucheng Rd., pg. 1255   IT

Sinochem Li Yan Ping Garment Co., Room 549, Textile Industry, Ministry Bldg., No. 12 E. Chang An Ave., pg. 1255   IT

Sinochem Plastics Co. Ltd., 8th Fl., Yulong Hotel, No. 40 Fucheng Rd., pg. 1255   IT

Sinochem Research Institute of International Oil & Chemical Trade, 6th Fl., Yulong Hotel, No. 40 Fucheng Rd., pg. 1255   IT

Sinochem Trading Development Co. Ltd., 6th Fl., Yulong Hotel, No. 40 Fucheng Rd., pg. 1255   IT

Sinopec-Ebara Machinery Co., Ltd., No. 15 Beisanhuan Donglu, Box 142, Beijing Chemical Engineering, pg. 432   IT

Sinopec Honeywell (Tianjin) Ltd., 5th Golden Peacock Arts World, Zhuangjiao Bldg., Hepingli, pg. 835   PB

Skadden, Arps, Slate, Meagher & Flom LLP, East Wing Office, Level 4, China World Trade Ctr., pg. 1004   PV

Skandinaviska Enskilda Banken - Beijing, Landmark Tower, 8 North Dongsanhuan Road, pg. 1259   IT

Sony Corp.-Peoples Republic of China, 4088-91 Beijing Hotel, pg. 1283   IT

Steelcase Asia Inc.-China, 4H Estoril Ct., 100027, pg. 1038   PV

Stratus Computer, Inc., Tm. 960, New Century Officer Tower, pg. 1524   PB

The Sumitomo Bank, Ltd.-Beijing Representative Office, 2902, Jing Guang Centre, Hujialou Chaoyang District, pg. 1309   IT

Sumitomo Chemical Bejing, 1012, Beijing Fortune Bldg. 5, Dong San Huan Beilu, pg. 1311   IT

Sumitomo Electric Industries, Ltd., pg. 1314   IT

Sumitomo Metal Industries, Ltd. (Beijing Office), 701 Beijing Fortune Bldg., 5 Dong San Huan Bei Lu, pg. 1316   IT

The Sumitomo Trust & Banking Co., Ltd., 5th Fl., Chang Fu Gong Office Bldg., pg. 1318   IT

Sun Microsystems of California (Services) Ltd., Beijing Representative Office, 100046, pg. 1532   PB

Svedala China, pg. 1323   IT

Svenska Handelsbanken Beijing, CITIC Bldg. No. 15-05, 19 Jianguomenwai Daijie, pg. 1327   IT

Swiss Bank Corporation, 3624 China World Tower, No. 1, Jian Guo Men Wai Avenue, pg. 1330   IT

Swiss Reinsurance Company-Beijing Representative Office, Unit 1110 Landmark Building, 8 North Dongsanhuan Road, pg. 1333   IT

Takeda Chemical Industries, Ltd., Room 1204, Scite Tower, Jianguo men Wai Da Jie, pg. 1350   IT

Tamrock (China) Ltd., Room 4755, Media Centre, B11 Fuxinglu, pg. 1353   IT

Telefonaktiebolaget LM Ericsson China, Level 11, China World Tower, 1 Jianguomen Wai Dajie, pg. 1370   IT

Toppan Printing Co., Ltd., Beijing Representative Office, pg. 1399   IT

Toray Industries, Inc.-Beijing Office, Beijing Fortune Bldg., No. 802, 5, Dong San Huan Bei-Lu, pg. 1400   IT

Toshiba (China) Co., Ltd., Room No.2810, Level 28 China, World Tower, No. 1 Jian Guo Men Wai Ave., pg. 1406   IT

Toto Beijing Branch, 3317 CWTC Tower, No. 1 Jianguomenwai Avenue, pg. 1410   IT

Toto (Beijing) Co., Ltd., Beijing Xisanqi High-Tech Bldg, Xisanqi East Haidian District, pg. 1410   IT

Toto (China) Co. Ltd., 3317 CWTC, No. 1 Jianguomenwai Avenue, pg. 1410   IT

Toyota Motor Corporation, Beijing Representative Office, Room No. 3606, pg. 1413   IT

Triton China, Inc. LLC-Beijing, pg. 1640   PB

Union Bank of Switzerland, Beijing Representative, Suite 1610, China World Tower, 1, Jian Guo Men Wai Avenue, pg. 1441   IT

Union-Transport Ltd, No 10 Dong Zhi Men South Rd., Room 711, 100027, pg. 1120   PV

Utell International-China, Unit #06-02, The Gateway, No. 10 Ya Bao Road, pg. 1098   IT

VG Instruments-China Office, pg. 1595   PB

Valmet Corp.-Beijing Representative Office, Room 760, Hong Kong Macau Centre Office Bldg., pg. 1448   IT

Wandel & Goltermann Beijing Officer, Room 728, Wang Fu Jing Grand Hotel, pg. 1486   IT

WestLB Beijing, Beijing Lufthansa Centre, Suite C 613, pg. 1493   IT

Westpac Banking Corp. - China, Ste. 506, Tower of Science, & Technology Exchange Corporation, pg. 1497   IT

Willis Corroon Overseas Ltd., Room 919, Beijing Asia Jinjang Hotel, pg. 1509   IT

The World Bank, No. 2 Fu Cheng Lu, Diaoyutai State Guest House, pg. 1189   PV

Yulong Hotel, Beijing, No. 40 Fucheng Rd., pg. 1255   IT

Zeneca Sino-Pharma Development Consultancy Company Limited, Room 802, Jing Guang New World Hotel, pg. 1527   IT

ZEXEL Corporation Beijing Representative Office, Rm. 1005, Beijing Fortune Bldg, Dong San Huan Bei Lu, pg. 1528   IT

Zhong Da Enterprise Corp., Room 1003, 9th Building,No. 1, Flat Hui, Yuan, Chinese Overseas Apt., pg. 1348   IT

Zurich Insurance Company, Bejing Rep. Office, Rm. 612, CIVK Tower, pg. 1531   IT

Changchun

Owens-Corning Changchun Guan Dao Company Ltd., Changchun Economic & Tech, Development Zone, pg. 1237   PB

Changsha

Hunan Kansai Automotive Coatings Co., Ltd., No. 216 Deya Rd., pg. 723   IT

Hunan Resun-Albright & Wilson Industrial Co., Ltd., 1 Liuyanghe Lu, pg. 50   IT

Changshu

Sharp Office Equipments (Changsu) Co., Ltd., Huange Road, pg. 1230   IT

Wuxi Sharp Electronic Components Co., Ltd., Wuxi National High & New, Tech Industries Development Zone, pg. 1230   IT

Changzhou

Changzhou Hurai New Material Co., Ltd., No. 1, Changchen Road, pg. 371   IT

FAW-Volkswagen Automotive Company Co. Ltd., Dongfend St., 39-1, pg. 1475   IT

Chengdu

AST Research Inc.-Chengdu Representative, Room 318 Tian Ge Tower, 2nd Section, Ring Road No. 1, pg. 1182   IT

Beijing Automated Computer Systems Co. Ltd., Rm. 6, 1/F Nan Yi Building, 2 Consulate Avenue, pg. 242   IT

ChuanShi Christensen Diamond Bit Company, Ltd., 3, Erxiang Qiao West Jie, pg. 1174   IT

SWUMC (South West United Machinery Corporation), 89 Wuhouci St., pg. 1032   PB

Shimadzu Chengdu Office, Room No. 931, Tibet Hotel, 10 Ren Min Bei Lu, pg. 1232   IT

Chongqing

Chongquing Kansai Paint Co., Ltd., A9, Dangui Industrial District, Naping Economy & Tech. Development Zone, pg. 723   IT

Chongquing Si You Continuous Casting Machine Technical Engineering Co., Ltd., 1 Shuang Gang Road, pg. 874   IT

Nippon Paint (Chongqing) Chemicals Co., Ltd., Heshangshan Industrial Zone, pg. 937   IT

Qingling Motors Co., Ltd., 1 Xiexing Rd., pg. 693   IT

The Sumitomo Bank, Ltd.-Chongqing Representative Office, 3F Holiday Inn Yangtze Chongqing, pg. 1309   IT

Dalian

Banque Paribas-Dalian, Hotel Dalian - Suite 422, pg. 319   IT

Burgmann Dalian, No. 278 Cujin Road, pg. 234   IT

Canon Dalian Business Machines, Inc., Da Qing Road, pg. 262   IT

Chichibu Onoda Cement Corporation-Dalian, Dalian Minhang Dasha, Room 707, No. 143, pg. 284   IT

Daewoo (Dalian) Office, Dalan Intl. Hotel, Rm. 911-914, 9 Stalin Road, pg. 358   IT

Dai-Ichi Kangyo Bank, Ltd.-Dalian, Room 206, Dalian Hotel, 4 Zhongshan Square, pg. 361   IT

Dalian Civil Aviation Hotel Co., Ltd., 143 Zhongshan Rd., pg. 374   IT

Dalian Dali Steel Works Co., Ltd., Qi Jia Gou, Ge Zheng Pu, pg. 623   IT

Dalian Ericsson Communication Company Ltd., No. 9 Lian Shan Street, Sha He Kou District, pg. 1365   IT

Dalian Fuji Electric Motor Co., Ltd., No. 1 Nenjiang Rd., Dalian Economic & Tech. Devel. Zone, pg. 522   IT

Dalian Morgan Refractory Materials Limited, 142 Chun Liu St., pg. 894   IT

Dalian Nissan Guangming Gas Co., Ltd., 3, Nenjiang Road, Dalian Economic & Technical Development, pg. 939   IT

Fuji Electric Dalian Co., Ltd., Dalian Industrial Park 25-3-1, Dalian Economic & Tech. Devel. Zone, pg. 522   IT

The Industrial Bank of Japan, Limited (Dalian), 8th Floor, Dalain Civil Aviation Hotel, pg. 675   IT

KHI (Dalian) Computer Technology Co., Ltd., Training Center of the Dalian, Maritime College Ling Shui Qiao, pg. 726   IT

Liaoning Liao Bian Advanced Fashion Garments Co., Ltd., Tangia Village, pg. 579   IT

Mitsui & Co., Ltd., Room 201, Dalian Binguam, pg. 881   IT

North China International Leasing Co. Ltd., Rooms 602-613, Dalian Hotel, pg. 1297   IT

Obayashi Corporation-Dalian, 17th Floor,, AnGang Building, FengGuang St. No. 1, pg. 995   IT

OMRON (Dalian) Co., Ltd., Song Jiang Lu, 3 Hao, Dalian Econimic & Tech. Devel. Zone, pg. 1005   IT

Pfizer Pharmaceuticals Ltd., 22 Daqing Road, 116600, pg. 1282   PB

Rohm Electronics Dalian Co., LTD., No. 0519001 29-1/2, Dalian Economic & Technical, pg. 1125   IT

The Sakura Bank - Dalian Representative Office, 17th Floor, Senmao Building, 147 Zhongshan Road, pg. 1179   IT

Sinochem Dalian Training Centre, No. 3 Langhua St., pg. 1254   IT

Sinochem Liaoning Imp. & Exp. Co. Ltd., No. 3 Gangwan St., pg. 1255   IT

The Sumitomo Bank, Ltd.-Dalian Representative Office, Room #703, Dalian Civil, Aviation Htl., pg. 1309   IT

Toshiba Dalian Co. Ltd., Cui Zhu Quarter An Shan Road, pg. 1406   IT

Toto Dalian Co., Ltd., 29-9, Dalian Industrial Park, pg. 1410   IT

Dongguan

Dongguan Chao Ba Batteries Co. Ltd., No. 1-2 Tung Yi Road, Wan Yip Industries Area (138), pg. 537   IT

Dongguan Pulse Electronics Co. Ltd., #1, Industrial District, pg. 1564   PB

Dongguan Yinfea Battery Products Co. Ltd., No. 1-2 Tung Yi Road, Wan Yip Industries Area (138), pg. 537   IT

Nestle Dongguan Ltd., pg. 921   IT

Sun Kwong Metal Manufacturing Co. Ltd., pg. 707   PB

PB - U.S. Public Companies Volume
PV - U.S. Private Companies Volume
IT - International Public & Private Companies Volume

Geographic Index-Non U.S.

Donghuang

Molex China, Weixin Road, Xinwei Village, pg. 1123   PB

Erligou

The MacNeal-Schwendler Company, Ltd., Beijing Office, Room 5124, Xi-Yuan Hotel, pg. 1032   PB

Foshan

Foshan Crown Can Company Ltd., 16 Qing gong San Lu, pg. 465   PB
Foshan Easy-Opening End Company Ltd., 16 Qing gong San Lu, pg. 465   PB

Fujian

Allen-Bradley Enterprise Xiamen Ltd., 38 Yue Hua Road, pg. 1398   PB
Asahi Bank Fuzhou Representative Office, Fuzhou Lakeside Hotel Rm. 1436, No. 1 Hu Bin Rd., pg. 83   IT
CWI International China, Ltd., No. 6, Xing-Hua Rd., pg. 1749   PB
Fujian International Leasing Company Limited, Seg. C, 13th Fl., Intl. Bldg., Wu Si Rd., pg. 83   IT

Fushun

CNTIC Fushun Import & Export, No. 1, Dehui Road, Xinfu District, pg. 285   IT

Guangdong

Battenfeld Chen Extrusion Systems Ltd., Fengxiang Road, pg. 825   IT
Foshan Hua Nan Bundy Tubing Co Ltd., Qian Jin Road, 528041, pg. 1341   IT
Guangdong Nortel Telecommunications Switching Equipment Limited, Gui Zhou Rong Li Industrial Park, pg. 970   IT
Guangdong Otsuka Pharmaceutical Co., Ltd., New High-Tech District, pg. 1014   IT
Guangdong Sanyo Air Conditioners System Manufacturing Ltd., 11 Bi Tany West 2nd St., pg. 1192   IT
Guangdong Shunde Nissin Foods Co., Ltd., Beijiao Economic Industrial Zone, pg. 950   IT
Huaming Pharmaceuticals Co. Ltd. of Shantou, S.E.Z., 2nd Road Longhu, pg. 856   IT
Keystone Valve (China) Ltd., 189 Industrial Area, Heng Gang, pg. 1650   PB
Lilly Industries, Inc., Lot 3 Xintang District Adminstration, pg. 995   PB
The Mentholatum (Zhongsham) Pharmaceuticals Co., Ltd., The Second Industrial Estates, Sam Heung, pg. 1126   IT
Nippon Paint (Guang Dong) Co., Ltd., Shui kou long hu Industrial Zone, pg. 937   IT
Outokumpu Copper Tube (Zhongshan) Ltd., Huangpu Town, pg. 1017   IT
Owens-Corning (Guangzhou) Fiberglas Co. Ltd., Xia Yuan Lu, Donji Industrial Zone, pg. 1237   PB
Shanton Meiji Pharmaceuticals Co., Ltd., 2nd Road Lonbhu, Lohghu Industrial District, pg. 856   IT
Shunde Donnelly Zhen Hua Automotive Systems Co. Ltd., 9 Ronggang Rd., pg. 519   PB
Tandy Electronics (China) Ltd., Gu Tang Au Industrial District, pg. 1561   PB

Guangzhou

Allianz Guangzhou Representative Office, Room 738, Garden Tower, Garden Hotel, pg. 59   IT
Amway China, 8/F, Guangzhou Book Centre, No. 123 Tianhe Road, pg. 69   PV
BASF Guangzhou, Room 901-913, Garden Tower, pg. 106   IT
BHP Steel Building Products (Guangzhou) Ltd., Room 1312-1313 Main Block, Gitic Plaza, 339 Huanshi Dong Lu, pg. 226   IT
Banque Paribas-Guangzhou, China Hotel Office Tower, Block N-951, pg. 320   IT
Beijing Automated Computer Systems Co. Ltd., Guangzhou, Rm. 2001-2005, Flat 20, Blk 4, Dong Jun Plaza, pg. 242   IT
Leo Burnett (China) Advertising Co., Ltd.-Guangzhou, Gitic Plaza, Rm. 1003-1004, 339 Huanshi Dong Lu., pg. 184   PV
CNTIC South China Import & Export Co., 18/F Hua Le Building, 53 Hua Le Road, pg. 285   IT
CPC (Guangzhou) Foods Ltd., pg. 224   PB
China Century Cement Ltd., 12/F, Jinbao Tower, 110 Hengfu Road, pg. 605   PB
China United International Leasing Co., Ltd., Block D&E, 19th Floor, Hua Le Building, North Tower, pg. 1180   IT
Chugai Pharmaceutical Co., Ltd., Suite 1314, pg. 291   IT
CIBA-GEIGY (China) Limited-Guangzhou Branch Office, Room 1359 China Hotel Office Tower, pg. 976   IT
DMB&B Guangzhou, Rm. 1808 World Trade Center, Complex, South Tower, pg. 303   PV
Daewoo Corp. - Guanzghou, pg. 358   IT
Dai-Ichi Kangyo Bank, Ltd.-Guangzhou, Room 2560, Dong Fang Hotel, Liu Hua Lu 1 Hao, pg. 361   IT
Dainippon Ink & Chemicals (HK) Ltd., Room 1240, 12th Floor, Garden Tower, Huanshi Road East 368, pg. 372   IT
Daiwa Bank-Guangzhou, Room #1032, The Garden Tower, 368 Huanshi Dong Lu, pg. 373   IT
Dentsu Young & Rubicam Advertising Co., Ltd. (Guangzhou), 23/F CITIC Plaza Office Tower, 233 Tian He North Rd., pg. 325   PV
Edelman Worldwide China, Ste. 706, Garden Tower, 368 Huan Shi Dong Lu, pg. 363   PV
FCB/MegacoM, Room 1608 Block B, Tianxiu Building, pg. 389   PV
H.B. Fuller (China) Adhesives, Ltd., 10 Bihau St., Jin Xiu Nan Lu, Guangzhou Economic & Tech. Devel. Zone, pg. 687   PB
Generale Belgian Bank, Room 1204-1205 Garden Tower, Garden Hotel, pg. 547   IT
Green Cross Guangzhou Pharmaceutical Co., Ltd., 14 Baohua Central Street, Baohua Road, pg. 558   IT
Guangdong Ericsson Engineering Company Ltd., Garden Tower, Rooms 744, 717, 368 Huanshi Dong Lu, pg. 1368   IT
Guangzhou Chia Tai Makro (JiaJing) Co. Ltd., 19th Fl., Hua-Le Building, 53 Hua-Le Road, pg. 1155   IT
Guangzhou Henkel Chemical Products Co. Ltd., pg. 611   IT
Guangzhou Representative Office, Room 2502, South Tower, Guangzhou World Trade Center Complex, pg. 744   IT
Heinz-UFE Ltd., Yan Tang, Sha He, pg. 807   PB
ING Insurance International, Room 1019 Garden Tower, Garden Hotel, 368 Huanshi Dong Lu, pg. 650   IT
IPM Guangzhou Office, 109 Liu Hua Rd., pg. 126   IT
Industrial & Commercial International Leasing Co., Ltd., Room No. 2728, Dongfang Hotel, pg. 1391   IT
The Industrial Bank of Japan, Limited (Guangzhou), Rm. 1252, Garden Twr., 368 Huanshi Dong Lu, pg. 675   IT
International Flavors & Fragrances, Guangzhou Econ. & Tech. Devel., Lot No. S-1 Jin Bi Rd., pg. 899   PB
Jotun Ocean Paint Co. Ltd., pg. 715   IT
Lonza Guangzhou Fin Chemicals Ltd., pg. 69   IT
McCormick (Guangzhou) Food Company, Ltd., pg. 1067   PB
Mitsui & Co., Room 2770, pg. 880   IT
NYK-Guangzhou, Unit C, 19th Floor, Guangdong Intl. Bldg., Annex A, 339, pg. 942   IT
The Sakura Bank - Guangzhou Branch, 7th Fl., Main Building, Guangzhou International Hotel, pg. 1179   IT
Sanshui Redland Building Materials Co. Ltd., Room 844, Garden Tower, 368 Huanshi Donglu, pg. 1093   IT
Shimadzu Guangzhou Office, Room No. 607,China Hotel Tower, Liuhua Road, pg. 1232   IT
Sinochem Hotel, Guangzhou, No. 58 Zhanqian Rd., pg. 1254   IT
Stratus Computer, Inc., Rm. 1803, North Tower, Guangzhou World Trade Ctr., pg. 1524   PB
Sumiden Wire Products Guangzhou Co., Ltd., pg. 1313   IT
The Sumitomo Bank, Ltd.-Guangzhou Branch, 11th Fl., South Tower, Guangzhou World Trade Center Complex, 510060, pg. 1309   IT
Toto Guangzhou Branch, Room 1905, World Trade Center, North Building No. 371-375, pg. 1410   IT
Toyota Motor Corporation, Guangzhou Office, Room No. 2666, pg. 1413   IT
Wrigley Chewing Gum Company Ltd., East of Friendship Rd., pg. 1781   PB

Guilin

Guilin Henkel Detergents & Cleaning Products Co. Ltd., pg. 611   IT
Guilin-Nokia Telecom., No. 98, Liuhe Rd., pg. 954   IT

Haikou

CNTIC Hainan Industrial Co., 19/F Block A, International Trade Building, pg. 285   IT

Hainai

The Sumitomo Bank, Ltd.-Yangpu Branch, Yangpu Economic Development Zone, pg. 1309   IT

Hainan

Sinochem Hainan Co. Ltd., 7th Fl., Anhai Bldg., Longkun Rd., pg. 1254   IT

Hangzhou

Hangzhi Machinery & Electronics Co., Ltd., 6, Jiao Gong Rd., pg. 1405   IT

Harbin

Sinochem Heilongjiang Imp. & Exp. Co. Ltd., No. 17 Yiman St., pg. 1254   IT

Hebei

Langfang Nippon Paint Co. Ltd., Langfang Econ. & Tech. Development Zone, pg. 937   IT

Hohhot

CNTIC North China Import & Export Co., Room 1513-1515, Zhaojun Hotel, pg. 285   IT

Huiyang

CNTIC Huizhou Import & Export Co., Danshui, pg. 285   IT

Huizhou

GP Batteries (China) Ltd., Gu Tang Au Industrial District, pg. 537   IT
Huizhou Advance Battery Technology Co. Ltd., 3-6 H. Qisheng Ind. District, 1B Maidi Road, pg. 537   IT
Huizhou Power Pack Co. Ltd., Da Shu Ling Vil, Xiaojinkou, pg. 537   IT
Superior Metal Printing (Huiyang) Co. Ltd., Dong Jiang Industrial Zone, pg. 1322   IT
T.G. Battery Co. (China) Ltd., Gu Tang Au Industrial District, pg. 538   IT

Jiangmen

Wah Kong Pecision (Jiangmen) Ltd., pg. 295   IT

Jiangsu

Advantest (Suzhou) Co., Ltd., #06-15/16 A Block, 5 Xing Han Road, pg. 25   IT
Chang Jiang Float Glass Co., Ltd., Economic & Technology Developm, ent Zone, pg. 1348   IT
Komatsu Changlin Construction Machinery Corp., Heng Sheng Road, New High-Tech Indus. Devel. Zone, pg. 745   IT
Komatsu Changlin Foundry Corporation, Changzhou South-East Economic Develop., pg. 745   IT
Nalco Chemical (Suzhou) Co., Ltd., New Asia Fast Food Bldg. #208, pg. 1150   PB
Nanjing Owens Corning XPS Foam Co. Ltd., 6th floor, 82 Taiping North Road, pg. 1237   PB
Rockwell LVS Zhenjiang Co., Ltd. Light Vehicle Systems, 62 Paomashan, Zhong Shan West Road, pg. 1401   PB
Suzhou Hongda Enzyme Co. Ltd., West ShaXi Town, pg. 989   IT
Yangzhong Tektronix Electronic Instrument Co., Ltd., 10 Jin Xing Road, pg. 1568   PB

Jiangyin

China Bekaert Steel Cord Co., Ltd., No. 4 Binjiang Xincun, Binjiang Developing Zone, pg. 185   IT
Makita (China) Co., Ltd., Huangpujiang Road, Kunshan Economic & Technical Development, pg. 832   IT
Shimano (Kunshan) Bicycle Components Co., Ltd., Kunshan Economic &, Technical Development Zone, pg. 1233   IT

Jinan

Showa Plastics (Jinan) Co. Ltd., No. 520 South Jiwang Road, pg. 1237   IT

Kunshan

Kunshan Huade Metal Packaging Container Co. Ltd., 342, Beimen Rd., pg. 1322   IT

Lianyungang

China Jiangsu Suntory Foods Co., Ltd., Haizhou, pg. 1322   IT
China Liaohua United Foreign Trade Co. Ltd., Hong Wei District, pg. 1254   IT
TDK Dalian Corporation, No. 30 Industrial Estate, Dalian Economic & Technical Devel. Zone, pg. 1336   IT

Liaoyang

Liaoning-Liebherr Hydraulic Excavator Co. Ltd., Liuerpu Economic Development Zone, pg. 807   IT
Liaoning Liebherr Wheel Loader Co. Ltd., Liuerpu Economic Development Zone, pg. 807   IT

Nanchang

Jiangling-Isuzu Motors Co., Ltd., 199 Yingbin North Road, pg. 693   IT

Nanjing

Chichibu Onoda Cement Corporation-Nanjing, Gunandu Hotel, Room 706, No. 208, pg. 284   IT
Condea Nanjing Chemical Company, No. 68 Fang Shui Road Large, Chang Lu Town, Dachang District, pg. 325   IT
NYK-Nanjing, Apartment A, 11th Floor, Changjiang Trading Bldg., pg. 942   IT
Nanjing Ericsson Communication Company Ltd., D-01 Building, Zone of High, and New Technology Pukou, pg. 1369   IT
Nanjing Goulds Pumps Limited, 17 Xieng Zhou Rd., pg. 861   PB
Nanjing Sharo Electronics Co., Ltd, 4/F Hua Xin Building, No. 9 Guan Jia Qiao, pg. 1229   IT
Nanjing Technology I/E Corp., 7/F, No. 187, Zhu Jiang Road, pg. 285   IT
Nanjing Toto Co., Ltd., No. 2 West Dongarn Rd., Jiangning Economic & Technical Devel., pg. 1410   IT
Sinochem Jiangsu Imp. & Exp. Co., No. 50 Zhonghua Rd., pg. 1255   IT

PB - *U.S. Public Companies Volume*
PV - *U.S. Private Companies Volume*
IT - *International Public & Private Companies Volume*

Ningbo

NYK-Ningbo, Room No. 3310, Building No. 3, East Seaport Hotel, 52 Cai Hong Road, pg. 942 **IT**
Ningbo CNTIC United Import & Export Co., 10-12 Shuguang Road, pg. 285 **IT**
Sinochem Ningbo Imp. & Exp. Co. Ltd., 11th-12th Flrs., Hualian Bldg., No. 21 Jiang Xia St., pg. 1255 **IT**
Van Leer Ningbo, pg. 1147 **IT**

Qingdao

AT&T Qingdao Power Systems Company Ltd., Huite Industrial City, Hi-Tech Industrial Park, pg. 1018 **PB**
AT&T Qingdao Telecommunications Systems Ltd., Hui-Te Industrial City Hi-Tech Industrial Park, pg. 1018 **PB**
AT&T Qingdao Telecommunications Equipment Ltd., Hui-Te Industrial City Hi-Tech, Industrial Park, pg. 1018 **PB**
Asahi Bank Qingdao Representative Office, 5th Fl., Hua-He International, Leasing Bldg., pg. 83 **IT**
CIBA-GEIGY (China) Limited-Qingdao Office, Haitian Hotel, Phase 2, Room 960-964, 39, pg. 976 **IT**
Daewoo Corp., 15, Shaoguan Ru, pg. 358 **IT**
Ebara Qingdao Co. Ltd., Banghai Rd., pg. 432 **IT**
Mitsui & Co., Room 1100, pg. 880 **IT**
NYK-Qingdao, 17th Floor, Penavico Bldg., 21 Wuxia Road, lu, pg. 941 **IT**
Qingdao Ciba Agro Co., Ltd., No. 1 Hangzhouzhi Road, pg. 983 **IT**
Qingdao Daewoo Stone Co., Ltd., Zhudi Lancun Zhen Jimo, pg. 358 **IT**
Qingdao Float Glass Co., Ltd., Hongshiya Town, Jiaonan City, pg. 1348 **IT**
Qingdao Rolled Glass Co., Ltd., Hongshiya Town, pg. 1348 **IT**
Qingdao Ssangyong Apparel Co., Ltd., 5, Chengbei 3rd Road, pg. 1291 **IT**
Sinochem Nandaihe Training Centre, Nandaihe Holiday Village, pg. 1255 **IT**
Sinochem Shandong Imp. & Exp. Co. Ltd., No. 6 Hua Yang Rd., pg. 1255 **IT**

Qinhuangdao

Hua Yan Bundy Tubing Corporation, No.1 Qinhuangdao Economic & Technical, pg. 1341 **IT**

Rizhao

Yanri CWM Co., Ltd., Huanghai Rd. 1, pg. 697 **IT**

Shaanxi

Shanxi Japan Energy Lubricants Co., Ltd., pg. 702 **IT**
Shianfu Optical Fiber and Cables Co., Ltd., 20 Tao Yuan Road, Xian, pg. 531 **IT**

Shandong

Komatsu Shantui Construction Machinery Co., Ltd., Hong Xing East Road, pg. 744 **IT**
Shandong Nissin Foods Co., Ltd., Opposite Garden Farm, pg. 950 **IT**

Shanghai

AMP Shanghai Connector, Ltd., pg. 9 **PB**
ASDC (Applied Software Development Center), 851 Zhong San Rd., South No. 2, pg. 1031 **PB**
AST Research Inc., Shanghai Intl. Trade Centre, 2200 Yan An Road West, pg. 1182 **IT**
Advanced Semiconductor Manufacturing Corporation of Shanghai, 385 Hong Cao Road, pg. 970 **IT**
Advantest Shanghai Ltd., Room 1803-1806, New Caoheijng Tower, pg. 25 **IT**
Air Products China, Room 2201 Shartex Plaza, 88 Zunyi Nan Road, pg. 31 **PB**
Ajinomoto Co., Inc., Shanghi Office, 220 Yan An Rd. (W), pg. 40 **IT**
Allen-Bradley Enterprise Xiamen Ltd., Floor 27-B Jin Ming Bldg., 8 Xun Yi Road South, pg. 1398 **IT**
Allianz Shanghai Representative Office, Hotel Equatorial Shanghai, 707 Office Complex, pg. 59 **IT**
Amano International Trading (Shanghai) Co. Ltd., Room No. 901, Zhongdian Mansion, 1029 Laoshan Road W., pg. 71 **IT**
Asahi Bank Shanghai Branch, Room 1403, Shanghai International Trade Center, pg. 82 **IT**
Asahi Chemical Industry - Shanghai Office, Room 1811, Shanghai International Trade Center, pg. 84 **IT**
Australia & New Zealand Banking Group Limited China, 201A West Wing Office Complex, Equatorial Hotel, 65 Yanan Road West, pg. 99 **IT**
BASF Shanghai Rep. Office, 19 F., East Ocean Centre, Yanau Road East, pg. 107 **IT**
BFCE China, Rm. 2710, Union Bldg., 100 Yan An Rd. (East), pg. 161 **IT**
BHP Steel Building Products (Shanghai) Ltd., Lot 15, Kang Qiao Industrial Zone, pg. 226 **IT**
Baldwin Printing Control Equipment (Beijing) Co., Ltd., No. 38, Ln. 339, Wuzhong Rd., pg. 170 **PB**
Banca Nazionale del Lavoro, Ruijin Building, 10th floor, Office n 1004, 205 Maoming Road South, pg. 137 **IT**
Banco Santander, Hab 523, Hotel Yangtze New World, pg. 144 **IT**
The Bank of New York, Dynasty Business Ctr., Rm. 503, 457 Wulumuqui Road N., pg. 179 **PB**

The Bank of Tokyo-Mitsubishi, Ltd. (Shanghai Branch), Ruijing Bldg., Rm. 2107, 205 Maoming South Rd., pg. 158 **IT**
Bank of Yokohama Shanghai, Room No. 1411, Ruijin Bldg., 205 Mao Ming Nanlu, pg. 159 **IT**
Banque Paribas-Shanghai, Shanghai Jin Jiang Club, Room 58134, pg. 320 **IT**
Bayerische Landesbank Girozentrale, 1233 Si Ping Lu, pg. 177 **IT**
Beijing Automated Computer Systems Co. Ltd., Shanghai, 12/F, Suite A, 331 Tong Ren Road, pg. 242 **IT**
Beijing Dentsu Shanghai Branch (Dentsu Shanghai), 9 F, Sino-Australia Shanghai, Wan Zhong Building, pg. 393 **IT**
Bekaert Asia Shanghai Office, 2505 Shartex Plaza, 88 Zun Yi Nan Lu, pg. 184 **IT**
BellSouth Shanghai Centre, Ltd., Suites 431-435, Portman Shanghai Centre, pg. 208 **PB**
BERG Electronics Shanghai Office, Room 1118, Jin Du Mansion, 277 Wu Xing Road, pg. 213 **PB**
Burgmann Shanghai Ltd., No. 127-8 Wenijing Road, pg. 234 **IT**
Leo Burnett (Shanghai) Advertising Co., Ltd., 325 ChangLe Rd., pg. 185 **PV**
Butler (Shanghai), Inc., Timwell Industrial Park, pg. 271 **PB**
CNTIC Shanghai Import & Export Co., Suite 53238, Block 3, Jinjiang Club, pg. 285 **IT**
CPC (Shanghai) Foods Co., pg. 224 **PB**
Cambrex PRC, 6/F Shanghai Nan Wai Tan Bldg., 760 Zhong Shan Nan Rd., pg. 297 **PB**
Canon International (Shanghai) Co., Ltd., 5F (West) 2# Building, Pudong Waigaoqaio Free Trade Zone, pg. 263 **IT**
Casco Signal Ltd., 1150 Qui Jang Road, pg. 1195 **IT**
Caterpillar Shanghai Engine Company, Ltd., pg. 316 **IT**
China Hewlett-Packard Co., Ltd., Shanghai Center Office Bldg., Room 635-650, pg. 816 **IT**
China Jinshan Associated Trading Corporation, 4th Fl., Jinshan Hotel, pg. 1254 **IT**
Chugai Pharmaceutical Co., Ltd.-Shanghai, Suite 561, Shanghai Centre, 1376 Nanjing Xi Lu, pg. 291 **IT**
CIBA-GEIGY (China) Limited-Shanghai Branch, 3/F, Building 4, 471 Gui Ping Road, pg. 976 **IT**
Commerzbank AG-Shanghai, Central Place, 16, He Nan Road South, 7th Floor, pg. 311 **IT**
Commomnwealth Bank-Shanghai, 805 Union Building, pg. 313 **IT**
DG Bank - Shanghai, Room 510, Bund Center Bldg., 555 Zhongshan East Road (2), pg. 352 **IT**
DMB&B Shanghai, Rm. 201, West Block, Shanghai Universal Centre &, pg. 304 **PV**
Daewoo Corp. - Shanghai, pg. 358 **IT**
Daewoo Securities - Shanghai Representative Office, Suite 20-EF, Shanghai TV & Broadcasting Tower, #651, pg. 359 **IT**
Dai-Ichi Kangyo Bank, Ltd.-Shanghai, Room No. 1107, Ruijin Bldg., 205 Mao Ming Nan-Lu, pg. 361 **IT**
The Daiei, Inc., Shanghai International Trade, 2200 Yan-an-xi Road, pg. 364 **IT**
Daihatsu Diesel Mfg. Co., Ltd., Room No. 804-806, Electric Building 430, pg. 364 **IT**
Dainippon Ink & Chemicals, Inc., Room 404, Shanghai Union Bldg., 100 Yanan East Road, pg. 372 **IT**
Daiwa Bank-Shanghai, Room 1903, Shanghai, International Trade Centre, pg. 374 **IT**
Danzas China Ltd., Unit G, 8/fl., 1590 Yan An W. Road, pg. 382 **IT**
Dentsu Shanghai Office, Room 1113, 11F., Shanghai International, pg. 393 **IT**
Dentsu Young & Rubicam Advertising Co., Ltd. (Shanghai), 1802-1804 Rm., Shui On Plaza, 333 Huai Hai Middle Rd., pg. 325 **PV**
Diebold Financial Equipment Company, Ltd., 45 Caoxi Bei Road, pg. 506 **IT**
Dresdner Bank AG, Ruijin Bldg., 26th Fl., 205, Maoming Rd. South, pg. 419 **IT**
Dun & Bradstreet International Consultant (Shanghai) Ltd., 363 Chang Ping Road, pg. 536 **IT**
Durr GmbH Shanghai Office, Rm. 603, New Town Mansion, 55 Loushanguan Rd., pg. 422 **IT**
Edelman Worldwide China, 88 Ton Ren Lu, Rm. 4008, 200040, pg. 363 **PV**
Gambro Medical Products Co. Ltd. Shanghai, Minhang Economic & Tech. Devel. Zone, pg. 668 **IT**
Garden Hotel Shanghai Mitsukoshi, 58 Maoming Nan-lu, pg. 884 **IT**
Generale Bank, 601, 6th Fl. Office Bldg., Equatorial Hotel, pg. 547 **IT**
Goldman Sachs (China) L.L.C., Ste. 505, Shanghai Centre, 1376 Nanjing Xi Lu, pg. 592 **PV**
Grace China Ltd., Minhang Economic & Technological Zone, pg. 755 **PB**
Graco (HK) Limited, Shanghai Intl. Trade Ctr. Ltd., Toom 1807, 2200, Yan An West Road, pg. 757 **PB**
Hagglunds China Ltd., Room 313, Bund Center, 555 E. Zhongshan Road (2nd), pg. 670 **IT**
Hakuhodo Inc., Rm. 213, Hong Kong City, Mansion 117, Hong Kong Rd., pg. 588 **IT**
Hanwa Co., Ltd.-Shanghai Branch, Rm. 2205, Shartex Plaza No. 88, Zun-yi South Rd., pg. 595 **IT**
Henkel-Kemeng Cosmetics Ltd., pg. 613 **IT**
Hitachi Zosen Shanghai, Rm.304A, Golden Bridge Mansion, 2077 Yan An Road (W), pg. 623 **IT**
ING Bank Shanghai, 2nd Floor, Central Place, 16 Henan Road South, pg. 649 **IT**
ING Barings Securities International, Suite 538, East Tower, The Shanghai Centre, pg. 650 **IT**
ING Insurance International, 2nd Floor, Central Place, 16 Henan Road South, pg. 650 **IT**
IPM Shanghai Liasion Office, Room 8017, Shanghai Hotel, 505 Wulumuqi Road N., pg. 126 **IT**

Imation Shaghai Branch Office, 10/F Jiu Shi Fu Xin Mansion, 918 Huaihai Zhong Rd., pg. 870 **PB**
The Industrial Bank of Japan, Limited (Shanghai), Rm.1601, Shanghai Intl. Trade Center, pg. 675 **IT**
International Flavors & Fragrances, pg. 899 **PB**
Jardine Fleming Securities Ltd. Services, 11-B Jin ming Bldg., Block 11, 8 Zun Yi Rd., S., pg. 494 **IT**
Jiangsu Ciba Agrochemicals Co., Ltd., 403, Building 15, 46 Lingyuan Lu, pg. 983 **IT**
Jinco Nonferrous Metals Co., Ltd., pg. 673 **IT**
J.P. Morgan & Co. Incorporated, Shanghai Ctr., East Tower, Rm. 665, pg. 1130 **PB**
KSB Shanghai Pump Co. Ltd., pg. 721 **IT**
Kodak (China) Limited, Rm. 1212 Rui Jin Bldg., 205 Mao Ming South Rd., pg. 553 **PB**
Komatsu (Shanghai) Ltd., Rooms 249-254, International Trade Plaza, pg. 744 **IT**
Kredietbank Shanghai Branch, Unit 1-4, 15 F Marine Tower, 1 Pudong Avenue, Pudong, pg. 760 **IT**
Kyowa Hakko Kogyo Co., Ltd., 1376 Nanjing Rd., W., Room 702, pg. 778 **IT**
Landis & Staefa China Co. Ltd., Jin Jiang Hotel, Room No. 3521/2/3, pg. 800 **IT**
Lucent Technologies of Shanghai, Ltd., 704 Yi San Rd., pg. 1018 **IT**
Lucent Technologies (Shanghai) International Enterprises, Ltd., Rm. 204, Xin Yi Bldg., No. 2005 Yang Gao Rei Rd., pg. 1018 **IT**
MacGREGOR (CHN) Ltd., Rm. 601-602, Park Hotel, 170 Nanjing Rd. W., pg. 670 **IT**
Mary Kay Cosmetics China, 11th Floor, Juishi Renaissance Mansion, pg. 711 **PV**
MetLife Shanghai Representative Office, Ste. 809-810, Overseas Chinese Mansion, pg. 738 **PV**
Mettler Toledo Instruments (Shanghai) Ltd., 4th Floor Building A-4, 471 Gui Ping Road, pg. 4 **IT**
Minebea Co., Ltd. - Shanghai Office, Room 2311, Rui Jin Building, No. 205, Mao Min Road South, pg. 869 **IT**
Minebea Electronics & Hi-Tech Components (Shanghai) Ltd., Xi Cai, pg. 868 **IT**
Mitsui & Co., Room 1100, pg. 881 **IT**
Morgan Stanley Shanghai, Ste. 700B, 7/F, W. Wing, Shanghai Ctr., 1376 Nan Jing Xi Lu, pg. 1133 **PB**
NKK Corporation-Shanghai Office, Room 208, Shanghai International Trade Center, pg. 903 **IT**
NYK-Shanghai, 8th Floor, Central Place, No. 16, He Nan Road South, pg. 942 **IT**
Neste Shangai Office, Suite 19-E, Shanghai Broadcasting & Television Tower, pg. 915 **IT**
New Oji Paper Co., Ltd., Room No. 1225 Galaxy Hotel, 888 Zhong Shan Xi Road, pg. 998 **IT**
Nippon Life - Shanghai Representative Office, Room 1715, Shanghai International Trade Centre, pg. 936 **IT**
Nippon Paint (China) Co., Ltd., 22 Area, Wang Qiao Development Zone, pg. 937 **IT**
Nissho Iwai (Shanghai) Corporation, pg. 948 **IT**
Nitto Denko (Shaghai Pu Dong New Area) Co., Ltd., Wai Gao Qiao Free Trade Zone, D6C-9A, Building Block 1-3, pg. 950 **IT**
Nokia Shanghai Representative Office, No. 211, Jiang Su Road, pg. 953 **IT**
Nordson China Co., Ltd., 828 Xin Jin Qiao Road, pg. 1189 **PB**
Norton Performance Plastics (Shanghai), 198 Beidou Road, pg. 1175 **IT**
Novellus Systems Shanghai, 603-611, No. 300, Tian-Lin Rd., pg. 1205 **PB**
Nwe Brunswick Scientific Co., Inc., Ocean Petroleum Building, 583 Ling Ling Road, pg. 1170 **PB**
Obayashi Corporation-Shanghai, Shanghai International Trade Centre 1912, pg. 996 **IT**
OMRON (Shanghai) Co., Ltd., Jinhai Road, Block No. 77, Jin Qiao Export Processing District, pg. 1006 **IT**
OMRON Shanghai Computer Corporation, Meike Building, 14F, 1 Tianyaoqiao Road, pg. 1006 **IT**
Oracle China Inc., American Intl at Shanghai Ctr, Rm 560, pg. 1228 **PB**
Owens-Corning (Shanghai) Fiberglas Co., Ltd., 5 Shanghai Dazhong, Building Materials General Factory, pg. 1237 **PB**
Pacific Leasing Corporation, Room No. 1001, Lianyidasha, Yan'an Donglu 100, pg. 817 **IT**
Parker Hannifin Hong Kong Ltd., Rm. 703, Dynasty Bus. Center, No. 457 N. Wu Lu Mu Qi Road, pg. 1263 **PB**
Pharmacia & Upjohn Biotech (China) Ltd., Room 1112, Electric Power, 430 Xu Jia Hui Road, pg. 1047 **IT**
POSCO Shanghai Office, RM. 1301 Shanghai Intl. Trade, 2200 Yan An Road, W., pg. 1062 **IT**
POSEC Shanghai Office, Rm. 1301, Shanghai Intl. Trade, 2200 Yan AN Road, W., pg. 1062 **IT**
qad.china, 8-9/F Sandra Bldg., 196 Xin Jin Qiao Rd., pg. 1345 **PB**
Raychem Pacific Cable Accessories Limited, G/F, 481 Gui Ping Lu, Cao He Jing Hi-Tech Development Park, pg. 1363 **IT**
Rieter Jingwei Textile Machinery Ltd., pg. 1117 **IT**
Rockwell-Collins International, Inc., Suite 1310, New Town Mansion, 55 Loushanguan Road, pg. 1400 **PB**
STR Shanghai Office, Yi Tong Bldg., 470, 8F-L Zhong Shan Rd (N), P.C. 200071, pg. 1027 **PV**
SVC Shanghai Voith Paper Machinery Ltd., pg. 1473 **IT**
The Sakura Bank - Shanghai Branch, 5th Floor, Ruijin Building, 205 Maoming Nan Road, pg. 1179 **IT**
Sealed Air Packaging (Shanghai) Co. Ltd., No. 223 Fute North Road, pg. 1451 **PB**
Shanghai Agmet Electro-Science Laboratory, Ltd, 2nd Fl., Bldg. 12A1, # 223 N. Fort Fe Te Rd., pg. 369 **PB**
Shanghai Bao Tai Long Concrete Products Co., Ltd., No. 4 Building Huan Long Yuan, He Qing Industry Zone, Pudong, pg. 1293 **IT**

Geographic Index-Non U.S.

Shanghai Bi Ba Batteries Co. Ltd., Shanghai Pu Dong Area, Jing Qiao Export &, pg. 537 **IT**
Shanghai Chugai Pharmaceutical Co., Ltd., 1404-1406 Shanghai Medical Mansion, pg. 291 **IT**
Shanghai Ciba Gao-Qiao Chemical Company Ltd., Rm 405, Building No. 15, 48 Ling Yuan Lu, pg. 985 **IT**
Shanghai Ciba Gao-Qiao Chemical Company Ltd.-Pudong Site Office, 451 Dong Tang Lu, pg. 985 **IT**
Shanghai CIBA-GEIGY Animal Health Limited, Building No. 8, 46 Ling Yuan Road, pg. 985 **IT**
Shanghai Ciba Vision Contact Lenses Co., Ltd., 829 Jiang Ning Road, pg. 985 **IT**
Shanghai Corning Engineering Corporation, Room 506, #10 Mei Lin Nan Lu, pg. 449 **PB**
Shanghai Crown Packaging Company Ltd., Y-107 Yam Dang Rd., pg. 465 **PB**
Shanghai Donnelly Fu Hua Window Systems Company, Ltd., 700 Yaohua Rd., pg. 519 **PB**
Shanghai Ebara Engineering and Services Co., Ltd., No. 369 Dongwuwei Road, pg. 432 **IT**
Shanghai General Biscuits Foods Co. Ltd., 440 Cao Bao Rd., pg. 381 **IT**
Shanghai Henkel Chemicals Ltd., pg. 614 **IT**
Shanghai Henkel Oleochemicals Ltd., pg. 614 **IT**
Shanghai Henkel-Teroson Adhesives and Coatings Ltd., pg. 614 **IT**
Shanghai Huanghe DHA Pharmaceutical Co., Ltd., 250 Feng Yang Road, pg. 603 **IT**
Shanghai Huili Kansai Paint Co., Ltd., Tangdong Zhoupu, pg. 723 **IT**
SHANGHAI INDUSTRIAL CONSULTANTS, Suites 101-110, Jing An Guest House, pg. 1228 **IT**
Shanghai International Finance Company Limited, Office Bldg. 420, The Shanghai Centre, pg. 1190 **IT**
Shanghai International Realty Co., Ltd., Room 1506, Shanghai, International Trade Centre, pg. 374 **IT**
Shanghai JinJiang Battery Co. Ltd., Xinlu Station North, Shangchuan Road, pg. 537 **IT**
Shanghai Johnson & Johnson Ltd., International Business Center, 660 Xin Hua Road, pg. 932 **PB**
Shanghai JSD Electronics Co., Ltd., 16 Cang Wu Road, Cao He Jing Special Development Zone, pg. 954 **IT**
Shanghai Kenwood Electronics Co., Ltd., 60 Rongle E. Rd., Songjiang, pg. 731 **IT**
Shanghai Liebherr Machinery Equipment Co., Ltd., No. 1118 Kui Zhao Road, pg. 809 **IT**
Shanghai Long Feng Food Additives Co., Ltd., Sheshan Town, Songjiang, pg. 372 **IT**
Shanghai Lucent Technologies Transmission Equipment Co., Ltd., 1700 Yi Shan Rd., pg. 1018 **PB**
Shanghai Master Builders Co., Ltd., pg. 985 **IT**
Shanghai McCormick Seasoning & Foodstuffs Company, Limited, 550 Zhu Mei Road, pg. 1067 **PB**
Shanghai Miura Boiler Co., Ltd. (China), 90 Yao-Hua Road, Branch New Pu-Dong Districk, pg. 884 **IT**
Shanghai Mizuno Corporation Ltd., Shen Xiang Town, pg. 885 **IT**
Shanghai Morgan Carbon Company Limited, 4250 Long Wu Rd., pg. 892 **IT**
Shanghai Nissin Noodles Foods Co., Ltd., 200, 2/F, Kangping Road, pg. 950 **IT**
Shanghai Nortel Semiconductor Corporation, 4/F Tian Lin Building, 300 Tian Lin Road, pg. 970 **IT**
Shanghai Office, Jinjiang Hotel Room 212, Moaming S. Road, pg. 578 **IT**
Shanghai OMRON Automation System Co., Ltd., 500 Omron Road, Jin Qiao Export Processing District, pg. 1006 **IT**
Shanghai OMRON Control Components Co., Ltd., Jinhai Road, Block No. 77, Jin Qiao Export Processing District, pg. 1006 **IT**
Shanghai Pulong Concrete Products Co., Ltd., 1453 Chuanbei Highway Pudong, pg. 1293 **IT**
Shanghai Representative Office, Room 2403, Union Building, Yanan-Donglu 100, pg. 1517 **IT**
Shanghai Roche Pharmaceuticals Limited, pg. 1122 **IT**
Shanghai Shared Data Network Co., 11th Fl., Shanghai Trade Ctr., Office Block, pg. 651 **IT**
Shanghai Sharp Electronics Co., Inc, Block 24, Jinqiao Export Processing Zone, pg. 1229 **IT**
Shanghai Showa Plastics Co. Ltd., 888 Beiqing Road, pg. 1237 **IT**
Shanghai SMPIC Brother Industries, Ltd., 5 Wenzhi lu, pg. 230 **IT**
Shanghai SPS Biao Wu Fastener Co. Ltd., 181 Hu Yi Road, Nanxiang, pg. 1420 **PB**
Shanghai Tektronix Electronic Instrument Co. Ltd., 631 Jiangning Road, pg. 1567 **PB**
Shanghai-Volkswagen Automotive Company Ltd., Luo Pu Rd., pg. 1475 **IT**
Shanghai Yadie Fashion Co., Ltd., 664-9, Xietu-Lu, pg. 1484 **IT**
Shanghai Yin Tong Trust Co., Ltd., 4th Fl., Da-ru Hotel, pg. 1010 **IT**
Shimadzu Shanghai Office, Room 58147, Block 3, JIn Jiang Club, pg. 1232 **IT**
Singapore Tourist Promotion Board - Shanghai, #202A, Main Building, Hotel Equtorial Shanghai, pg. 1254 **IT**
Sinochem Shanghai Imp. & Exp. Co. Ltd., No. 27 Zhong Shan Dong Yi Rd., pg. 1255 **IT**
Sinochem Shanghai Pudong Trading Co. Ltd., Rooms 401 & 402, Baishu, Mansion, No. 1230, Zhong Shan Bei Yi Rd., pg. 1255 **IT**
Southcorp Holdings, Rm. L, 6th Fl., Wanzhong Commercial Bldg., pg. 1287 **IT**
Standard Chartered Bank, Merchant Bank Services, Level 7, Shanghai Centre, 1376 Nanjing Rd. West, pg. 1296 **IT**
Stratus Computer, Inc., Ste. 5C, Jing Ming Bldg., 8 Zun Yi Rd., S., pg. 1524 **PB**
Sulzer Shanghai Eng. and Mach. Works Ltd., pg. 1306 **IT**
The Sumitomo Bank, Ltd.-Shanghai Branch, Ste. 205, Shanghai International Trade Center, pg. 1309 **IT**
Swiss Bank Corporation, 812-812, 8th Fllor, Shanghai Intl. Trade Center, pg. 1330 **IT**
3M China Limited, 10/F, Newtown Mansion, 55 Lou Shan Guan Rd., pg. 1606 **PB**
Toppan Printing Co., (Shanghai) Ltd., Shanghai Intl. Shopping Ctr., Room 904, B Bldg., pg. 1399 **IT**
Toppan Printing Co., (Shanghai) Ltd., No. 5583 Hu Nan Road, pg. 1399 **IT**
Toshiba Technology Development (Shanghai) Co., Ltd., Suite 350, Shanghai Ctr. 1376, Nanjing West Road, pg. 1407 **IT**
Toto Shanghai Branch, Room 201B, Shanghai Intl. Trade Center Ltd., pg. 1410 **IT**
Union Bank of Switzerland, Union Building, Room 1904, 100 Yanan Road (E), pg. 1441 **IT**
United Leasing Company, Limited, Rm. 2007, 20th Fl., Shanghai, Union Bldg., 100 Yanan Rd. (East), pg. 1411 **IT**
Wander (Shanghai) Nutrition Ltd., pg. 986 **IT**
WestLB Shanghai, Rui Jin Building, Room 2301, 205, Maoming Nan Road, pg. 1493 **IT**

Shantou

Shantou Henkel Consumer Adhesives & Building Chemicals Co. Ltd., pg. 614 **IT**

Shaoxing

Shaoxing Redland Building Materials Co., Inc., Tingchechang, pg. 1093 **IT**

Shenyang

Hua Tong International Leasing Co., Ltd., 2nd Fl., Taishan Hotel No. 22 Taishan Road, pg. 1181 **IT**
ING Bank Shenyang, Room 328, Liaoning Hotel, No. 97, Zhongshan Street, pg. 649 **IT**
Liaoning Liebherr Diesel Engine Co. Ltd., Hunhepu, pg. 807 **IT**
Novo Nordisk Shenyang Biochemical Processin Co. Ltd., Hua Hai Road, No 4 Yu Fang Industrial Village, pg. 989 **IT**
Shenmei Daily Use Products Limited Company, No. 123 Hezuo St., pg. 745 **PB**
Shenyang ITT Flygt Jinbei Pump Co., Ltd., Honghu North Street No. 1, pg. 860 **PB**
Shenyang Kansai Paint Co., Ltd., No. 69, Kunsan West Road, pg. 723 **IT**
Shenyang NETS System Integration Co., Ltd., No. 3-11 Wenhua Road, pg. 1406 **IT**
Shenyang Nissan Gas Co., Ltd., No. 18, Taishad Road, pg. 959 **IT**
Shenyang Nortel Telecommunications Co., Ltd., 79 Nanshi Street, pg. 970 **IT**
Shenyang Office, Liaoning Binguan Rm. 301, pg. 579 **IT**
Shenyang Yamanouchi Pharmaceutical Co., Ltd., No. 54 Xinghua Nan Street, pg. 1519 **IT**
Shimadzu Sheyang Office, Room No. 351, Liao Bin Guan, No. 97, Zhongshan Road, pg. 1232 **IT**
The Sumitomo Bank, Ltd.-Shenyang Representative Office, Room No. 608, Gloria Plaza Hotel Shenyang, pg. 1310 **IT**

Shenzhen

Beijing Automated Computer Systems Co. Ltd., Shenzhen, Rm 1005-1007, Office Tower, Yue Hai Hotel, Shen Nan Zhong Road, pg. 242 **IT**
Beijing Sanyo Electronics (Shekou) Ltd., 4th Floor Block D2, Hua Jay Industrial Bldg., pg. 1191 **IT**
Brother Corporation (Asia) Ltd., Buji Nanling Factory, Golden Gardens Ind., pg. 229 **IT**
CNTIC Shenzhen Import & Export Co., 18/F Real Estate Building, South Ren Min Road, pg. 285 **IT**
Champion Stationary Manufacturing Company Ltd., pg. 707 **PB**
Changchun Sanyo Electronics (Shekou) Co., Ltd., Hua Jay Industrial Bldg., Flat A,B 4th Fl., Blk 3, pg. 1191 **IT**
China International Finance Company Limited (Shenzhen), 33rd Fl., International Bldg., 23 Jian She Rd., pg. 1310 **IT**
Chun Wang Industrial Gases, Limited, Song Hu Rd., She Kou Indus. Zone, pg. 32 **PB**
Fuji Electric Technology and Service (Shenzhen) Co., Ltd., No. 44 Dongjiao St., pg. 522 **IT**
The Hokkaido Takushoku Bank, Ltd. (Shenzhen), 16/F Shenzhen Intl. Fin. Bldg., 23 Jianshe Rd., pg. 627 **IT**
Huagiang Sanyo Electronics Co., Ltd., 34 Shennan Road, pg. 1192 **IT**
IDG Shenzhen, Information Center Bldg., Suite 388, pg. 570 **PV**
ING Bank Shenzen, 32nd Floor, Shenzen Development Centre, pg. 649 **IT**
Intergraph (Shenzhen) Company Ltd., 2809 Blk B, Tian An International Building, pg. 892 **PB**
Jardine Fleming Securities Ltd., Rm. 901 Development CTN, Fenmin Rd., S., pg. 494 **IT**
KONE Elevators (Shenzhen) Co. Ltd., Rm. 1608-C Shenzhen Tian An, Intl. Bldg., South Renmin Road, pg. 747 **IT**
Mitsui & Co., (Hong Kong) Ltd., Rms. 617/618, Friendship Commercial Mans, pg. 880 **IT**
Olympus (Shenzhen) Industrial Ltd., pg. 1005 **IT**
Sanyo Electric (Shekou) Ltd., Blk. 3, Hua Jay Industrial Bldg., pg. 1192 **IT**
Sanyo Semiconductor (Shekou) Ltd., Blk. 6, Hua Jay Industrial Bldg., pg. 1192 **IT**
Seagate Technology Co. Ltd., 3rd Floor, Kaifa Complex, Caitian Lu, Futian Industrial District, pg. 1450 **PB**
Shenzhen CIC-Amersham Isotope Co Limited, 6A Hseung Mei Lu, pg. 993 **IT**
Shenzhen Communication Cable, pg. 968 **PB**
Shenzhen-DIC Co., Ltd., Nanshan Road, pg. 372 **IT**
Shenzhen Jiadianbao Electrical Products Co., Ltd., Feng Huang Gang Village, Xia An Zhen, pg. 314 **PB**
Shenzhen Representative Office, 2611, Block B, Tian An International Bldg., pg. 943 **IT**
Shenzhen Sylva Electrochemical Ltd., No. 3B Dongjiao Street, pg. 537 **IT**
Showa Plastics (Shenzhen) Co. Ltd., Blk 28 Hexi Industrial District, pg. 1237 **IT**
Sinochem Shenzhen Industry Co. Ltd., 15th Fl., Jin Wei Bldg., 23 Jia Bin Rd., pg. 1255 **IT**
Songgang Electronics Wire Works, pg. 1313 **IT**
South China International Leasing Company Limited, International Financial Bldg., 31st Fl., 23 Jianshe Rd., pg. 627 **IT**
Standard Chartered Bank, Merchant Bank Services, 4th Fl., Hoi Yin Commercial, Bldg., Jia Bin Rd., pg. 1296 **IT**
Tong Guang-Nortel Limited Liability Company, Chiwan Road, pg. 970 **IT**
Toppan Printing Co., (Shenzhen) Ltd., No. 27 Industrial Zone, Chuang Ye Rd., Baoan District, pg. 1399 **IT**
Triton China, Inc. LLC-Shekou, pg. 1640 **PB**

Shijiazhuang

Sinochem Hebei Imp. & Exp. Co. Ltd., No. 8 Jichang Rd., pg. 1254 **IT**

Shuangcheng

Nestle Shuangcheng Ltd., pg. 921 **IT**

Sichuan

Chongqing Tektronix Electronic Instrument Co., Ltd., 1-1 Dian Ce Cun, Jian Xin Road North, pg. 1567 **PB**

Siping

Siping Henkel Detergents and Cleaning Products Co. Ltd., pg. 614 **IT**

Suzhou

Nippon Paint (Suzhou) Co., Ltd., Miduqiao, pg. 937 **IT**
Suzhou Esca Step Co. Ltd., pg. 1205 **IT**
Suzhou Littelfuse OVS Co. Ltd., 6, Xinghai Street, Suzhou Industrial Park, pg. 1001 **PB**
Suzhou Schindler Elevator Co., pg. 1205 **IT**
Suzhou Watts Valve Factory, 679 Renmin Road, pg. 1747 **PB**

Teda

Dentsply Dental (Tianjin) Co., Ltd., 1st Floor, Block C, Tai Feng Industrial & Trade Building, pg. 499 **PB**

Tianjin

AST Computer (China) Ltd., Block A & B, 2 & 3/F, No. 133, Dong Ting Rd., pg. 1182 **IT**
Bohai & MHI Platform Engineering Co., Ltd., pg. 874 **IT**
CNTIC Tianjin Import & Export Co., Rms. 203-205, Friendship Hotel, pg. 285 **IT**
China Otsuka Pharmaceutical Co., Ltd., Xin Hua Road 176, pg. 1014 **IT**
Cho Hung Bank, Tianjin Branch, Rm. 1901, Tianjin Intl. Bldg., pg. 288 **IT**
Danfoss (Tianjin) Ltd., Road 3, Tianjin Wuqing Development Area, pg. 377 **IT**
Gambro Jr. China Ltd., Block 4, Ming He Avenue, pg. 667 **IT**
John Crane Tianjin Ltd., 13 Miyun 1st Branch Road, pg. 1339 **IT**
Lucent Technologies of Tianjin Cable Co. Ltd., Yi Bai Rd., Hebei District, pg. 1018 **PB**
Mitsui & Co., Room 630, pg. 880 **IT**
Motorola China Electronics Ltd., Dongting Lu and Di Si Da Jie Tianjin, pg. 1139 **PB**
Novo Nordisk (China) Biotechnology Co. Ltd., 11/F, Tianjin International, Development Bldg., pg. 989 **IT**
Pfauter Gmt Service Center, 122 Dongting Rd., pg. 617 **IT**
Port of Tianjin Commercial Bonded Warehousing & Service Co. Ltd., pg. 1144 **IT**
Rohm Electronics (Tianjin) Co., Ltd., 55-7 X1 Qing Economic & Technical Devel., pg. 1125 **IT**
The Sakura Bank - Tianjin Branch, Room No. 1210, Tianjin International Building, pg. 1179 **IT**
Sinochem Tianjin Imp. & Exp. Co. Ltd., No. 58 Nanjing Rd., pg. 1255 **IT**
Technip Tianchen, 521 Jing Jin Road, pg. 1361 **IT**
Tianchi-Mitel Telecommunications Corporation, 1 Dongting 1st Avenue, pg. 870 **IT**
Tianjin Kollmorgen Industrial Drives Corp., Ltd., 81 Sima Rd., Hebei District, pg. 966 **PB**
Tianjin Beacon Kansai Paint & Chemicals Co., Ltd., Beicang Rd., pg. 723 **IT**
Tianjin Figaro Electronic Co., Ltd., Tianjin Economic, Technological Development Zone, pg. 1394 **IT**
Tianjin Henkel Detergents & Cleaning Products Co. Ltd., pg. 614 **IT**
Tianjin International Leasing Co., Ltd., Room IC, Astor Hotel, 33, Taier Zhuang Rd., pg. 1181 **IT**

PB - *U.S. Public Companies Volume*
PV - *U.S. Private Companies Volume*
IT - *International Public & Private Companies Volume*

1560
Geographic Index-Non U.S.

Tianjin Jinzhu Wiring Systems Co., Ltd., pg. 1314 IT
Tianjin Kansai Paint & Chemicals Co., Ltd., 42, No. 5 Avenue, Tianjin Econ. & Tech. Development Zone, pg. 723 IT
Tianjin Kerma Laboratories, Zhang Gui, Zhuang Beikong, pg. 239 IT
Tianjin Liming Cosmetics Joint Industrial Co., Tianjin Economic, & Technological Development Area, pg. 1490 IT
Tianjin Representative Office, Room 2202, Tianjin Intl. Bldg., 75, Nanjing's Road, pg. 520 IT
Tianjin-Shimadzu Hydraulic Equipment Co., Ltd., No. 7 Chang Jiang Road, Tianjin Hi-Tech Industry Park, pg. 1232 IT
Tianjin Takeda Pharmaceuticals Co., Ltd., Economic Development Area, Xiging District, pg. 1351 IT
Tianjin Tanabe Seiyaku Co., Ltd., 491 Huanghe Road, pg. 1354 IT
Tianjin Tanggu Watts Valve Co., Ltd., 5 Yong Tai Road, pg. 1747 PB
Tianjin Tianwei Seasoning Co., Ltd., No. 7 Bohai Rd., pg. 41 IT
Tianjin Wix Filter Corp., Shiyan Da Lou Hou, Xincun, Zhongshanman, pg. 480 PB

Tonglu

Fuchunjiang Fuji Electric Co., Ltd., Gongren Rd., pg. 522 IT

Tung Guan

Dongguan Sanxing Socks Co., Ltd., Yantian District, pg. 579 IT

Wuhan

AGRA Construction (Wuhan China) Limited, No. 420 Yingwu Avenue, pg. 31 IT
Beijing Automated Computer Systems Co. Ltd., Wuhan, Room 705-706, 80 Zhongnan Road, pg. 242 IT
Wuhan Bundy Fluid Systems Co. Ltd., 12 Industrial Land, Zhuan Yang Street, pg. 1341 IT

Wujiang

Suzhou Lanlian-Fuji Instruments Co., Ltd., Songlin Economic Economic & Tech., pg. 522 IT

Wuxi

Astra (Wuxi) Pharmaceutical, 3/F No. 2 Xi Nan Yi Road, pg. 94 IT
Leaf China, Zhong Qiao, pg. 638 IT
Sino-Sweed Pharmaceutical Corp Ltd., Mashan, pg. 94 IT
Wuxi-MSA Safety Equipment Co., Ltd., 305 Xicheng Road, pg. 1115 PB
Wuxi Okuda Garment Co. Ltd., Wuhe Bridge Lixin Road, pg. 579 IT
Wuxi Quaker Chemical Co. Ltd., 97 Wu Qiao Xi Road, pg. 1347 PB
Wuxi Sanwa Garment Materials Co., Ltd., Huangangxiang Quanfeng-Lu, 1, pg. 579 IT

Xiamen

Beijing Automated Computer Systems Co. Ltd, Xiamen, Rm. 405-4066, Zhen Ye Bldg., North Hubing Road, pg. 243 IT
CNTIC Strait I/E Corp., Suite 719, Bailu Hotel, Hu Yuan Road, pg. 285 IT
Dai-Ichi Kangyo Bank, Ltd.-Xiamen, #915, East Ocean Bldg. Hotel, # 1 Bldg., Zhongshan Road, pg. 361 IT
Linde-Xiamen Forklift Truck Corporation Ltd., pg. 810 IT
Sinochem Xia Men Co. Ltd., Flats B & D, 9th Fl. Huguang, Mansion, Hubin E. Rd., pg. 1255 IT
Xiamen International Bank (XIB), 52 Lujian Road, pg. 817 IT
Xiamen Jinwoong Enterprise Co., Ltd., 9th Fl., Ximdeco Building, Huli Industrial Zone, pg. 707 IT
Xiamen Tiger Medicals Co., Ltd., 2/F No. 17 Building, Yi Bin Road, pg. 604 IT

Xian

CNTIC North West Import & Export Co., 15th Floor, Huoju Building, Gaoxin Road, pg. 285 IT
IR International Holdings, Inc., 202 Zhuque St., pg. 907 PB
Valmet-Xian Paper Machinery Co. Ltd., No. 4th E. Pang Rd., pg. 1448 IT
Xian-Janssen Pharmaceutical Ltd., 34, Wanshou Rd. North, pg. 932 PB
Xi'An System Sensor Electronics, Ltd., No. 11 E. Xiao 2 Hai Rd., pg. 1307 PB

Xiangcheng

Lianhua Ajinomoto Co., Ltd., pg. 41 IT

Xinjiang

CNTIC Tianshan Import & Export Co., People's Hall, No. 45, North Youhao Road, pg. 285 IT
International Flavors & Fragrances, pg. 899 PB

Xuzhou

Caterpillar Xuzhou Ltd., 5 Sudi Rd. North, pg. 316 PB

Xuzhou Liebherr Concrete Machinery Co. Ltd., Jinshanqiao Economic &, Technological Development Zone, pg. 808 IT
Xuzhou Rockwell Axle Co., Ltd., 6 East Kuangshan Road, pg. 1402 PB

Yantai

Donnelly Yantai Electronics Corp. Ltd., Yantai Economic Technology, Development Zone, pg. 519 PB
Kendall Yantai Medical Products Co. Ltd., No. 1 Tianchi Road, Yantai Economic & Tech. Devel. Zone, pg. 1648 PB
Permea China, Ltd., Nanjiiao, pg. 32 IT
Yantai Ebara Air Conditioning Equipment Co., Ltd., Middle of Yongda Road, Fushan New 8, High TechnologyIndustrial, pg. 432 IT
Yantai Huada Chemicals Industry Co., Ltd., South Xingfu Road, pg. 372 IT

Yingkou

China Yingkou-Fuchs Oil Company Ltd., 1 Wenhua Li, Wenhua St., pg. 518 IT

Zhaoqing

Henkel Cosmetics Zhaoqing Ltd., pg. 612 IT

Zhengzhou

The Yellow River International Leasing Co., Ltd., Fl. 7, Agriculture Bldg., 6, Jingsam Rd., pg. 362 IT

Zhuhai

CNTIC Zhuhai Import & Export Co., Rm. 401, 402, Building 18, Lianhuashan, Jida, pg. 285 IT
Canon Zhuhai, Inc., No. 3, Industrial Bldg., Beijing Industrial District, pg. 262 IT
Sinochem Zhu Hai Co., Ltd., No. 2 Liyuan, Jiuzhou Rd., pg. 1255 IT
Torita Corporation Ltd., Torita Electronic City, Ming Zhu North Road, pg. 651 IT
Zhuhai Brother Industries Co., Ltd., 2nd Gang Road, pg. 230 IT
Zhuhai Golden Coast Winner Food Products Ltd., Food Indstrial City, Golden Coast, Sanzao Chun Garden, pg. 950 IT

Zibo

Shandong Zibo Kinhua-Chemferm Industrial Pharm. Ltd., 14, Dongyilu, pg. 1143 IT

COLOMBIA

Barranquilla

Aluminio Reynolds, Santo Domingo, S.A., Calle 79, No. 40-362, pg. 1386 PB
Det Norske Veritas, Carrera 59-C No. 79-180, pg. 397 IT

Bogata

OCENSA, Calle 78 No. 11-17, pg. 1417 IT
Proyectos Energeticos, Calle 100, No. 8A-55, pg. 1417 IT
VARTA S.A., pg. 1452 IT
Wandel & Goltermann Andina Ltda., A.P. 55052, pg. 1486 IT

Bogota

AGA-FANO S.A., Apartado Aereo 3624, pg. 13 IT
Acer Computer Colombia, pg. 22 IT
Alisa, S.A., pg. 159 PV
American Pipe and Construction International, Calle 193 No.3102, pg. 99 PB
Amoco Colombia Petroleum Company, Carrera 9, No. 74-08, pg. 102 PB
Amway Colombia, Calle 18 No.68D-04, pg. 69 PV
Ansaldo de Colombia S.A., Edificio Seguros Fenix, Carrera 7, - N. 32/33, pg. 654 IT
Ascensores Schindler de Colombia S.A., pg. 1205 IT
Asea Brown Boveri Ltda., pg. 8 IT
Asistencia Plus, S.A., Carrera 13, no. 98, 89, pg. 333 IT
Automotores Capital LTDA., Carerra 7, no. 74, 36, pg. 333 IT
BASF Quimica Colombiana S.A., Calle 100 Nro. 51-44, pg. 107 IT
BHF-Bank Representative Office, Centro Comercial Hds, Santa Barbara, Calle 114, No. 6A-92, pg. 120 IT
Banco Internacional de Colombia, S.A., Avenida Jimenez 8-89, pg. 378 IT
Banco Mundial, pg. 1189 PV
Banco Santander de Negocios, Carrera 7, n. 71, Torre A, pg. 144 IT
Bank of America NT&SA, Carrera 7a, No. 71-52, Torre B, 4th Fl., pg. 182 PB
Bankers Trust New York Corporation, Carrera Septima 7436, 4th Fl., pg. 186 PB
Bausch & Lomb de Columbia S.A., pg. 195 PB
BEAL - Bogota, Calle 93-A, 14-17, Of. 703, pg. 1493 IT
Black & Decker de Colombia S.A., Diagonal 17, No. 28-29, pg. 234 PB

Braspetro Columbia, Calle 70, No 7-30, Piso 3, pg. 1042 IT
Bristol Farmaceutica, S.A., Calle 12 No. 41-49, pg. 255 PB
Bundy Colombia S.A., pg. 1342 IT
Leo Burnett Columbiana, S.A., Carrera 13 No. 89-59, pg. 185 PV
CCF Bogota, Calle 93 - n 1262, Oficina 304, pg. 342 IT
Camecanica, S.A., Calle 22, no. 19, 31, pg. 333 IT
Carbone-Lorraine de Colombia S.A., Carrera 40 No 16-21, pg. 1030 PB
Carvajal, S.A., Calle 93 # 15-40, pg. 816 PB
Casa Cientifica, Calle 30A No 6-22, pg. 816 PB
Cementos Boyaca S.A., Carrera 7a, No. 32-33, Edificio Seguros Fenix, Piso 8, pg. 629 PB
Cerro Matoso, pg. 1141 PB
The Chase Manhattan Bank, N.A., Carrea 9A, #99-02, pg. 340 PB
Chevron Petroleum Company of Colombia, Apartado Areo 3631, pg. 348 IT
CIBA-GEIGY Colombiana S.A., Apartado Aereo 12323, Calle 11, No. 65-51, pg. 976 IT
Cigna Seguros de Colombia S.A., Calle 72, No. 10-51, pg. 363 PB
Citibank, N.A. Bogota, Cra 13, pg. 378 PB
Colcarga Transporte Internacional/Union-Transport, Calle 44A No. 93-12, pg. 1120 PV
Cia. Colombiana de Alimentos Lacetos, S.A., pg. 159 PV
Comestibles La Rosa S.A., pg. 920 IT
Communicacion Celular S.A. (COMCEL), Calle 90, No. 14/37, pg. 116 IT
Compania Celular de Colombia COCELCO, S.A., pg. 1373 PV
Compania Colombiana de Financiamentos, S.A., pg. 379 PB
Compania Colombiana de Grasas "Cogra-Lever" S.A., Calle 13, No. 45-46, pg. 1436 IT
Compania de Asistencia de los Andes, S.A., Carrera 11, No. 93, B-09, pg. 334 IT
Compania del Norte y Oriente para Inversiones, S.A., Carrera 7, No. 74, 36, pg. 333 IT
Compania Granadina de Seguros de Vida S.A., Carrera 10a, pg. 91 IT
Compania Granadina de Seguros S.A., Carrera 10a, pg. 91 IT
Compania Suiza de Reaseguros, Oficina de Asesoria Tecnica, Calle 72, No. 12-65,Pisa 9, pg. 1333 IT
Compumundo, Avenida 15 No. 107-80, pg. 817 PB
Computerworld-Columbia, Carrera 90, pg. 569 PV
Comteco S.A., pg. 1306 IT
Construcciones Capital LTDA., Carrera 7, no. 74, 36, pg. 333 IT
CUNA Mutual Group-Latin America, World Trade Center, Calle 100, No. 8A-55, pg. 297 PV
Cyanamid de Columbia SA, Carrera 62, #12-61, pg. 80 PB
Daewoo (Latin America) Ltd., pg. 358 IT
Danzas Ltda, Av. El Dorado No 97.03, Int. 1, pg. 382 IT
Du Pont de Colombia S.A., Apartado Aereo 15024, pg. 532 PB
Electrolux S.A., Calle 36 No. 6-13; Apartado Aereo 4416, pg. 441 PB
Empresas ICA Sociedad Controladora (Colombia), Carrera 9A No. 99-02, Ofna. 806 A, Barrio La Castellana, pg. 454 IT
Equilux S.A., Apartado Aereo 8669, pg. 441 IT
Equipelectro, World Trade Center de Bogota, Carrera 8-a, N - 99.51, pg. 321 IT
Ericsson de Colombia S.A., Carrera 13 No. 27-47, Piso 13, pg. 1366 IT
Florasynth Ltda., Carrerra 98, pg. 173 IT
Fondo Educativo Interamericano, pg. 1027 IT
Foster Wheeler Andina, S.A., Kilometre 20 Carretera Central del Norte, pg. 677 PB
Frutera Colombiana S.A., Calle 72, No. 13-23, pg. 447 PB
General Motors Colmotores, S.A., Avenida Boyaca 3681, S., pg. 722 IT
Gerber Colombia, Calle 21, N 69, pg. 973 IT
Gestetner Colombia S.A., Calle 69a 5-60, pg. 1115 IT
Givaudan-Roure S.A., Carrera 44, pg. 1120 IT
Grace Colombia S.A., Calle 18, pg. 755 PB
Grancol, Asesoramiento Y Servicios Ltda., Carrera 13, No. 26-45, pg. 364 PB
Grandes Marcas SA, Carrera 35 # 58-83, Interior 2, pg. 409 IT
Hanwa Co., Ltd.-Bogata Branch, Carrera 11 #86-32, Oficina 604 Apartado Aereo #093260, pg. 595 IT
Helmerich & Payne (Colombia) Drilling Co., Calle 79B, No. 7-46, pg. 808 PB
Hughes Tool Company S.A., Apartado Aero 29697, pg. 167 PB
IBM de Colombia, S.A., pg. 897 PB
IDC Columbia/Inviarco Ltda., Avenida Carrera 90, pg. 570 PV
ING Bank Bogota, Calle 73 No 7-06, pg. 649 PB
ING Baring Securities (Andean Pact), Carrera 7, No. 7152, pg. 649 PB
Industrias del Maiz S.A., pg. 447 PB
Instituto de Idiomas Colombia, S.A., Avenida 13, No. 88-20, pg. 222 IT
Instrumentacion, Ltda., Calle 115 No. 11A-10, pg. 822 IT
International Columbia Resources Corporation, Carrera 7 No. 36-45, pg. 602 IT
International Distillers Colombia, Diagonal 151 N0. 31-41, pg. 410 IT
Inversiones Araucaria, Carrera 11 No 93 B-109, pg. 335 IT
Inversiones Capital, S.A., Carrera 7, no. 74, 36, pg. 333 IT
Invertrans S.A. de Bogota, pg. 1022 IT
Inviarco Ltd., Carrera 5-D No 166-19, Apt. 401, pg. 570 PV

Geographic Index-Non U.S.

Janssen Farmaceutica S.A., Avenida El Dorado #98-51, pg. 929   PV
John Crane Colombia, Carrera 30 no.91-33, pg. 1340   IT
S.C. Johnson & Son Colombiana S.A., Apartado Aereo 29632, pg. 593   PV
Kellogg de Colombia S.A., Calle 17 No. 68A-75, pg. 947   PB
Kleinwort Benson Limited, Carrera 7, No. 32-33, Edificio Seguros Fenix No. 1601, pg. 420   IT
Knoll Colombiana S.A., Calle 100 No. 51-41, pg. 108   IT
Kodak Columbiana, Ltd., Avenida El Dorado 78A-93, pg. 553   PB
Korn/Ferry International, Carrera 7A No. 74-56, Piso 19, pg. 633   PV
La Federal Compania de Seguros, S.A., Apartado Aerlo No. 26931, pg. 355   IT
Laboratorios Wyeth Inc., Laboratorios Ayerst-Hormona, S.A., Apartado Aereo 862, pg. 81   IT
Ediciones Larousse Colombiana Ltda., Apartado Aereo 75548, pg. 240   IT
LASMO Oil (Colombia) Limited, pg. 804   IT
Arthur D. Little de Columbia, Ltda., Edificio Premium 98, Diagonal 97 No. 17-60, pg. 670   PV
Loctite de Colombia S.A., Calle 13, pg. 611   IT
Makro de Colombia S.A., Cra. 39 193-63 Autopista Norte, pg. 1155   PB
Marquinarias Ingersoll-Rand de Colombia S.A., Apartado Aereo 89655, pg. 877   PB
Materiales Industriales S.A., Apartado Aereo 80046, pg. 904   PV
Mathieu C.A., pg. 846   IT
Mathieu Colombia, Carrera 13 N, 90-20, pg. 846   IT
Medina Regal, Calle 14, No. 34-40, Apartado 20776, pg. 917   PV
Microbit Computadores, Calle 90 No. 10-26, pg. 822   PB
Microsoft Colombia Inc., pg. 1108   PB
Milchem Western Hemisphere Inc., Edificio Agricola de Seguros, Calle 67, No. 7-94, 9th Fl., pg. 167   PB
Mitsui de Colombia S.A., Cra 7, No. 24-89 Piso 15, Edificio Colpa, pg. 882   PB
Mobil Ami, S.A., Apartado Aereo 8401, pg. 1119   PB
Morgan Grenfell (Colombia), Calle 33, No. 6-94-Of. 504, pg. 405   IT
NationsBank (Colombia) Branch, Carrera 7 #32-33 Oficina 1301, pg. 1166   IT
Nature's Sunshine de Colombia, pg. 1166   IT
Nestle de Colombia, pg. 921   IT
A.C. Nielsen de Colombia, S.A., Calle 80, NR. 5-81, pg. 1183   PB
Nissho Iwai de Columbia S.A., pg. 948   IT
Northern Telecom de Colombia S.A., Carrera 14, No. 94-81, pg. 970   PB
Novell Colombia, World Trade Center, Calle 100 #8A-49, pg. 1204   PB
Occidental De Colombia, Inc., Edificio Colon Calle 77A, No. 11-32, pg. 1210   PV
Olivetti Colombiana S.A., Edificio Internacional, Carrera 13, n. 26-45, pg. 1003   IT
Oracle Colombia, Calle 100, No.8A-55, pg. 1228   PB
Panalpina S.A., pg. 1023   IT
Petroleum Drilling Services Columbia Pty., Ltd., Aparta do Qereo 91036, pg. 777   PB
Pfizer S.A., Autopista Sur #70-64, pg. 1282   PB
Productora Andina de Acidos y Derivados Ltda, Transversal 6, No. 14-60, Zona Industrial Cazuxa, pg. 1578   PB
Productos Roche S.A., pg. 1121   IT
Productos Stahl De Colombia SA, Carrera 67 # 71A-50 Sur, pg. 1525   IT
Promotora Capital LTDA., Carrera 7, no. 74, 36, pg. 333   PV
Promotora MAPFRE Caribe Carima, S.A., Carrera 7, n. 74-36, pg. 334   IT
Quimica Nalco de Colombia, S.A., Calle 77 No. 15-80 Of. 610, pg. 1151   IT
Quimica Schering Colombiana S. A., Apartado Aereo 3559, pg. 1204   IT
Reader's Digest Colombia S.A., c/o Cardenas & Cardenas, Abogados, pg. 1368   PB
Reaseguradora Hemisferica, S.A., Carrera 11, No. 93 B-109, pg. 335   IT
Repsol Exploracion Colombia S.A., Transversal, 21, pg. 1105   IT
Rhone-Poulenc Colombia Ltda., Sector Quimica, Avenida de las Americas 53A-19, pg. 1112   IT
A.H. Robins International, S.A., Carrera 27 Nos 8-46 to 8-70, pg. 82   PB
Rohm & Haas Colombia S.A., pg. 1404   IT
Rorer, S.A., Apartado Aero 28359, Carrera 15 #118-49, pg. 1114   IT
SAIC Colombia, Limitada, Calle 100 8A-49, Torre B, pg. 976   PV
SKF Colombia S.A., Carrera 7, No. 73-47, pg. 1158   IT
SNC-Lavalin, Calle 79A #8-63, Piso 4, pg. 1162   IT
STA (Sistemas de Tecnologia Avanzada, S.A.), pg. 508   PV
Saboresy Fragancias S.A., Diagonal 61 #89-A-45, pg. 900   PB
Sancho S.A., Torre Sancho, Calle 98 No. 903, Piso 2, pg. 1422   PB
Sandoz Colombiana S.A., pg. 984   IT
Sandvik Colombia S.A., Apartado 19927, pg. 1188   IT
Seguros Caribe, S.A., Carrera 7, No. 74,36, pg. 333   IT
Servicios Corporativos, S.A., Carrera 7, no. 74, 36, pg. 333   IT
Shell Colombia S.A., Carrera 7, 73-47, pg. 1142   IT
Siemens S.A., Carrera 65, No. 11-83, pg. 1248   IT
Skandia Holding de Colombia S.A., Avenida 19 No. 113-30, Apartado Aereo 100327, pg. 1258   IT
Skandia Seguros De Vida S.A., Avenida 19 No. 113-30, pg. 1258   IT

Skandia Sociedad Fiduciaria SA, Avenida 19 No. 113-30, Apartado Aereo 100327, pg. 1258   IT
Smith International South America, Inc., Calle 100 No. 8A-55, World Trade Center, pg. 1478   PB
Sodexho Colombia S.A., Calle 114 A No. 22 A 60, pg. 1275   IT
Sodexho Pass Colombia, Cra. 7a. No. 71-52, pg. 1275   IT
Solar Electronica, Calle 125 (Avenida 127), pg. 823   IT
Specia Colombia, Avenida de Las Americas 53A 19/45, pg. 1114   IT
Swiss Bank Corporation, Calle 80 No. 10-43, Piso 6, pg. 1330   IT
Taloca & Cia Ltda, Apartado Aereo 15835, pg. 1289   IT
3M Colombia S.A., Apartado Aereo 11091, Avenida El Dorado No. 78A-93, pg. 1606   PB
Tipiel Colombia, Calle 38 # 8 - 62 Piso 3, pg. 1361   IT
Toyota Motor Corporation, Bogota Representative Office, World Trade Center, Torre B, Oficina 617, Calle 100, pg. 1413   IT
TransGas de Occidente S.A., Edificio Teleport Bus. Park, Calle 114 No. 9-45, pg. 1417   IT
Triton Columbia, Inc., Carrera F. No. 32-33, pg. 1640   PB
UBS Representative Office, Edificio Seguros Tequendama, Carrera 7, No. 26-20, Piso 25, pg. 1441   IT
Unipharma S.A., Diagonal 45, No. 93-43, pg. 1048   IT
Utell International-Colombia, Carrera 12 No 90-20, pg. 1098   IT
Van Leer Envases de Colombia S.A., pg. 1147   IT
Vehidata, S.A., Calle 93 bis, no. 19, 31, pg. 334   IT
The West Company of Colombia, S.A., Carrera 98 No. 41A-23 Interior 15, pg. 1756   PB
Xerox de Colombia S.A., pg. 1785   PB
Young & Rubicam Bogota, Calle 93 A, No. 13-A07, pg. 1200   PV

Bucaramanga

CentrOriente, Carrera 29 No. 45-94 Piso 9, pg. 1417   IT

Cali

Arena de Colombia SA, pg. 25   IT
Beiersdorf S.A., pg. 183   IT
Carton de Columbia, S.A., Apartado Aereo 219, pg. 1271   IT
CIBA-GEIGY Colombiana S.A., Planta Arroyohondo, Autopista Cali-Yumbo, Km 5, pg. 976   IT
Colgate-Palmolive CIA, Apartado Aereo 2324, pg. 398   PB
Columbina Meiji S.A., Carrera 1 No. 24-56, pg. 856   PB
FACOMEC S.A., Calle 37, No. 1-18, pg. 1368   IT
Goodyear de Colombia S.A., Yumbo (Valle), pg. 753   PB
Henkel Colombiana S.A., pg. 612   IT
Home Products Inc., Autopista Cali-Yumbo Km 2, Urbanizacion Acopi, pg. 81   PB
Industrias del Maiz S.A., pg. 448   IT
Johnson & Johnson de Colombia S.A., Calle 15 # 31-146, pg. 930   PB
Maizena S.A., Avenida 3 Norte No. 71-80, Autopista Cali, pg. 447   IT
Productora de Papeles S.A. (PROPAL), Apartado Aereo 4412, pg. 906   PB
Productos Quaker, S.A., Carrera 5, 6A, pg. 1348   PB
Sonoco Colombiana S.A., Apartado Aereo No. 6958, pg. 1487   PB
Stepan Colombiana, Calle 28 No. 4, pg. 1514   PB
Young & Rubicam S.A., Avenida 5A Norte #20-83, pg. 1200   PV

Cartagena

CIBA-GEIGY Colombiana S.A., Planta de Cartagena, KM 6 Carretera Mamonal, pg. 976   IT
Productora Andina de Acidos y Derivados Ltda, Zona Industrial Mamomal Km 12, Apartado Aereo, pg. 1578   PB
Van Leer Envases de Costa Rica S.A., pg. 1147   IT

Envigado

Nordson Andina Limitada, Centro Multiple Las Vegas, Carrera 48, # 48-5-75, pg. 1189   PB

Itagul

Termaq, Autopista Sur No. 24-52, pg. 361   PV

Medellin

Colombiana Kimberly S.A., Apartado Aereo 51906, pg. 959   PB
Compania Latinoamerica de Software (LASC), Carrera 43A-No. 1A Sur-69, pg. 1043   PB
Crown Litometal, S.A., Apartado Aereo, pg. 465   PB
Empresa de Refractarios Colombianos S.A., Apartado Aereo 865, pg. 903   PV
Enka de Colombia S.A., Edificio Camacol, Carrera 63, N 49 A 31, pg. 46   PV
Griffith Colombia S.A., P.O. Box 8589, pg. 481   PV
Nopco Colombiana S.A., pg. 614   PB
Owens Corning Andercol Tuberias, Apartado Aero 2065, pg. 1237   PB
United Aceros Boehler S.A., Calle 29 No. 46-66, pg. 1472   IT
Y&R Medellin, Sur-91, Ste.1101-1102, Carrera 43A No. 9, pg. 1200   IT

Pereira

Colombiana Universal de Papeles S.A., Apartado Aereo, pg. 959   PB
Papeles Nacionales S.A., Apart. Aereo 483, pg. 762   IT
Suzuki Motor De Colombia S.A., Calle 22, No. 5-32, pg. 1323   IT

CONGO

Brazzaville

Banque Mondiale, Immeuble Arc (5eme etage), pg. 1189   PV
Bull Congo, 43 ave. Paul Doumer, pg. 315   IT
CII-Honeywell Bull Congo SARL, 43, Avenue Paul-Doumer, pg. 318   IT
Elf Congo, av. Foch/Lumumba, pg. 446   IT
Societe des Ciments du Congo S.A., P.O. Box 14510, Avenue du Port No. 300, pg. 1200   IT
Union Congolaise De Banques, Avenue Amilcar Cabral, pg. 548   IT

Kinshasa

Banque Commerciale Zairoise, Boulevard du 30 juin, pg. 547   IT
Barclays Bank Szarl, 191 Avenue d L'Equateur, pg. 166   IT
Brasseries, Limonaderies et Malteries du Zaire "Bralima" S.A.R.L., 912 Avenue du Flambeau, pg. 608   IT
C.I.E. Computer and Industrial Engineering, 25, Ave. de la Justice, pg. 817   IT
CIBA-GEIGY Services SA-Bureau Regional Kinshasa, 66, Avenue Lieutenant-Colonel, pg. 980   IT
Citibank (Zaire) S.A.R.L., Corner Ave. Lukasa et Ngongo Lutete, pg. 379   IT
Compagnie des Margarines, Savons et Cosmetiques au Zaire s.a.r.l., pg. 1436   IT
Fina Congo S.A.R.L., 652, av. Lt Colonel Lukasa, pg. 1044   IT
Fina Rep S.P.R.L., Av. Lieutenant Col. Lukasa, 652, pg. 1044   IT
SARL GB Zaire, Ave. de l'O.U.A., pg. 534   IT
GB Zaire SARL, Avenue de l'O.U.A., pg. 534   IT
Genie Mechanique Zairose, S.A.R.L, B.P. 11199, pg. 724   PB
Mitsui & Co., Ltd., Avenue des Aviateurs, pg. 881   IT
Plantations Lever au Zaire s.a.r.l., pg. 1438   IT
Sedec s.a.r.l., Av. Des Aviateurs 713, pg. 1438   IT
SEP Congo S.A.R.L., avenue des Petroles 1, Zone de la Gombe, pg. 1044   IT
Societe Financiere de Developpement, pg. 447   PB
Societe Zairo-Suisse de Produits Chimiques S.a.r.l., pg. 986   IT
Stanbic Bank Zaire s.z.a.r.l., Avenue de la Mongala, No. 12, pg. 1294   IT
Union de Banques Congolaises, Coin de l'Avenue de la Nation, et de l'Avenue des Aviateurs, pg. 149   IT
Zaire Mobil Oil, 3900 PC Ave. de la Republic du Tchad, pg. 1119   PB

Pointe Noire

Det Norske Veritas, pg. 397   IT
Panalpina Transports Mondiaux Congo S.A.R.L., pg. 1023   IT
Socorest, pg. 1275   IT
Weatherford Services S.A., pg. 1750   PB

COOK ISLANDS

Alofi

Westpac Banking Corp. - Niue, Main St., pg. 1497   IT

Avarua

Westpac Banking Corp. - Cook Islands, Main Rd., pg. 1497   IT

Rarotonga

Australia & New Zealand Banking Group Limited Cook Islands, Development Bank Building, pg. 99   IT
Bermuda Trust (Cook Islands) Limited, Bank of Bermuda House, Tutakimoa Road, pg. 151   IT
HSBC Trustee (Cook Islands) Limited, pg. 583   IT

COSTA RICA

Alajuela

Kre-Lon, S.A., Apartado 11-40002, pg. 1462   IT
Pharos de Costa Rica S.A., Saret Aeropuerto, Parque Industrial y Zona Franca, pg. 1290   IT
Productos Agroindustriales del Caribe S.A., pg. 447   PB
Suttle Costa Rica S.A., Parque Industrial, pg. 416   PB

Barrio Francisco Peralta

Leo Burnett-Costa Rica, De Pollos Kentucky, 100 Metros al Este Y 250 Metros Sur, pg. 185   PV

PB - U.S. Public Companies Volume
PV - U.S. Private Companies Volume
IT - International Public & Private Companies Volume

1562

Geographic Index-Non U.S.

Guadalupe

Motorola de Centroamerica, S.A., Apartado 442-2100, pg. 1139   PB

Heredia

Formularios Moore de Costa Rica S.A. de CV, 200 Metros Norte y, 200 Metros Weste, de Cameterio, pg. 889   IT
Industrias Merrimac Incorporada, S.A., Free Trade Zone Pk., Bldg. # 5, pg. 1098   PB
Pfizer S.A., Zona Franca Ultrapark, La Aurora, pg. 1282   PB
Pfizer Zona Franca S.A., Zona Franca Ultrapark, La Aurora, pg. 1282   PB

San Jose

Amway Costa Rica, La Uruca, Faco, pg. 69   PV
Asesores Publicitarios, S.A., Edificio Asesores, Apartado 6947-1000, pg. 1200   PV
ATH Costa Rica, Edif. D-Piso 1, San Pedro, 150 metros Oeste de la, pg. 176   PB
B&D de Costa Rica, S.A., 100 Mts. Surde Acuaductos y, Alcantarillados, Paseo Los Estudiantes, pg. 234   PB
BASF de Costa Rica, S.A., Edificio Irma, 2do Piso, Avenida Central, Calles 29-33, pg. 105   IT
Banco Santander, Edificio Centro Colon 9 Of. 5, Paseo Colon, calles 38 & 40, pg. 144   PB
Bonifica-Costa Rica, Officina Central Golfito, 76 Afortada, pg. 655   IT
Citicorp S.A., Calle 4 y, Avenida Central de la Artilleria, pg. 379   PB
Coca-Cola Interamerican Corporation, pg. 392   PB
Colgate-Palmolive (Central America), Inc., Calle 26-28, Avenida 3 Bis, pg. 398   PB
Crown Cork CentroAmericana S.A., P.O. Box 504-1000, pg. 464   PB
Cyanamid Inter-American Corporation, Apartado Postal 10229, pg. 81   PB
Distribuidora de Manufacturas Centro-Americanas, S.A., 250 Mts al Norte y 50 al Oeste, pg. 959   PB
Dole Latin America, Edificio Rodfon, Calles 5 y 7, Avenida 1, pg. 515   PV
Eaton Controles Industriales, S.A., Apartado Postal 10156, pg. 558   PB
Empresas Bristol de Costa Rica, S.A., 350 Mts. Oeste de Rancho Luna, pg. 256   PB
Ensabladora Centroamericana de Costa Rica S.A., Apartado 2884-1000, pg. 1413   IT
Envases Industriales de Costa Rica, S.A., Limon Apdo 151, pg. 739   IT
Ericsson de Costa Rica, Edificio Cristal, Piso 2, Local No. 1, Avenida I, Calles 1 y 3, pg. 1366   IT
Fotograbado Industrial Centro-Americano S.A., Apartado 6055, pg. 1349   IT
IBM de Costa Rica, S.A., pg. 897   PB
I.S. de Costa Rica, S.A., Calle 25, Avenida, pg. 822   PB
Industria Ceramica Costarricense, S.A., Apartado Postal 4120, pg. 92   IT
Industria Nacional de Cemento S.A., pg. 630   IT
S.A. Industrial Curacao Costa Rica, Ave Central Frente, Libreria Universal, San Jose, pg. 280   IT
S.C. Johnson de Centroamerica S.A., Apartado Postal #4971, pg. 593   PV
Kativo Chemical Industries, S.A., 225 Metros Al Oeste de Lacsa en la Uruca, pg. 687   PB
Keca de Centroamerica S.A., Apartado 3860-1000, pg. 458   PB
Laboratorios Griffith de Centro America S.A., Apd. 7-2820 (1000), pg. 481   PV
Lucent Technologies de Costa Rica S.A., Edificio Centro Colon, Piso Septimo, Paseo Colon, pg. 1018   PB
Microsoft de Centroamerica S.A., pg. 1108   PB
Monsanto de Costa Rica, S.A., P.O. Box 987-1007, Centro Colon, pg. 1125   PB
Nedlloyd Lineas Agencias S.A., pg. 1145   PB
Oracle de Costa Rica S.A., Edificio Delfos, Piso 2, pg. 1228   PB
Pozuelo, S.A., pg. 1392   PB
Productos de Concreto S.A., pg. 629   PB
Productos Gerber de Centroamerica, S.A., Contiguo Al Hotel Holland House, pg. 973   IT
Productos Nestle (Costa Rica) S.A., pg. 922   IT
Productos Roche S.A., pg. 1121   IT
Quimica Henkel Centroamericana de Costa Rica S.A., pg. 613   IT
Republic Tobacco Co. S.A., 800 Mts. Este Iglesia de Zapote, pg. 111   IT
Rio Minerales, Apartado 6753, pg. 1498   IT
Rohm & Haas Centro America S.A., pg. 1404   PB
Sandoz Latinoamerica S.A., pg. 985   IT
Scott Paper Co. de Costa Rica, S.A., Calle La Asuncion De Belen, pg. 960   PB
Square D Company Centroamerica, S.A., 1.5 KM Oeste de la Embajada Americana, pg. 1209   IT
3M Costa Rica, S.A., P.O. Box 10119, pg. 1606   PB
USRB S.A., pg. 707   IT
Union Publicitaria, DMB&B, Sabana Sur, do Universal, 100 m Sur, 50 ote, 75 Sur, pg. 305   PV
Universal Foods Products International Ltd., Calle 1, Avs. 1/3, pg. 1696   PB
Van Leer Envases de Costa Rica S.A., pg. 1147   PB
Wackenhut, S.A., pg. 1732   PB
Yrajos Hermanos Sucesores, S.A., Apartado 10-096, pg. 570   PV
Zeneca Costa Rica, S.A., PO Box 247-1150, 250 Mts. Norte de Rapifreno, pg. 1526   IT

Turrialba

Rawlings Costa Rica, pg. 1362   PB

COTE D'IVOIRE
Abidjan

Ste. Abidjanaise, Avenue Delafosse-Prolongee, Route AB02 01, pg. 21   IT
BASF Afrique de l'Ouest S.A.R.L., Bd. Achalme, No.3, pg. 105   IT
Banque Atlantique Cote D'Ivoire (BACI), Immeuble El Nasr, Avenue General de Gaulle, pg. 547   IT
Banque Internationale pour le Commerce et l'Industrie de la Cote d'Ivoire (BICICI), Av. Franchet d'Esperey, pg. 148   IT
Banque Paribas Cote d'Ivoire, 17, Avenue Terrasson de Fougeres, pg. 319   IT
Blackwood Hodge (Cote d'Ivoire) S.A.R.L., Boulevard du Port Dietaing 11, pg. 231   IT
Blohorn S.A., Zi De Vridi, pg. 1436   IT
Bull Cote d'Ivoire, Blvd. Roume, pg. 315   IT
CFCI S.A., 8 Rue De Tessieres, pg. 1436   IT
CII-Honeywell Bull Cote-d'Ivoire S.A., Nour-al-Hyat, pg. 316   IT
Chevron International Trading Company-West Africa, Immeuble, Le Jeceda (B41), Blvd. de la Republique, pg. 348   PB
CIBA-GEIGY Services SA, 01 Boite Postale 3996, pg. 980   IT
Colgate-Palmolive C.I.S.A., 08 BP 19, Boulevard Giscard D'Estang, pg. 398   PB
Compagnie Africaine de Preparations Alimentaires CAPRAL Nestle, pg. 920   IT
Compagnie Financiere de la Cote d'Ivoire, Rue Gourgas-Tour Bici-Ci, pg. 149   IT
Det Norske Veritas, Soc. Abidjanaise D'Expertics, Sabex 01, pg. 397   IT
Engineering Business Concept, 21, Route du Canal, pg. 817   PB
The Export-Import Bank of Korea, 04, B.P. 674, pg. 467   IT
Hydrochem C.I., Vridi 07, pg. 963   IT
Mitsui & Co., Ltd., 11, avenue Joseph Anoma, pg. 882   IT
NOVALIM-Nestle, pg. 922   IT
Rhone-Poulenc Sante C.I., Marcory Residential, 18 bis, bd de Lorraine, pg. 1114   IT
S.I.T.I. (Ste. Ivoirienne des Techniques de l'Informatique), Immeuble le General, Av. General de Gaulle, pg. 823   IT
SKF Abidjan S.A.R.L., 18 Abidjan 969, pg. 1158   IT
Setao, 15, rue du Chevalier de Clieu B.P. 925, pg. 207   IT
Shell Cote d'Ivoire, Rue des Petroliers, pg. 1137   PB
Shell Ivoirienne, pg. 1137   IT
Soc. Abidjanaise d'Expansion Chimique (SAEC) SA, P.O. Box 2578, pg. 43   IT
SOCHIM Cote-d'Ivoire SA, 01 Boite Postale 3715, pg. 985   IT
Societe Generale de Banques en Cote D'Ivoire, 5-7 Avenue Joseph Anoma, pg. 548   IT
Societe Ivoirienne de Cables (Sicable), B.P. 35, pg. 1060   IT
Societe Ivoirienne de Prefabriques et d'Accessoires Industriels S.A., 15 Bos Postale 449, pg. 949   IT
Societe Ivoirienne pour l'Application de Technologies, 81, Bd de Marseille, 02, pg. 1370   IT
Sodexho Cote D'Ivoire, pg. 1275   IT
Texaco Cote d'Ivorie, Zone Du Canal De Virdi, pg. 1584   PB
Toles Ivoire S.A. Societe de Galvanization de Toles en Cote Ivoire, Boite Postale 20902, pg. 949   IT
Uniwax S.A., pg. 1439   IT
The World Bank, Booker Washington & Jacques AKA Sts., pg. 1189   PV
Zurich Compagnie d'Assurances, 7, Blvd. Roume, pg. 1531   IT

CROATIA
Golubovec

Schiedel Proizvodnja Dimnjaka d.d., Golubovec 26, pg. 1092   IT

Rijeka

Det Norske Veritas, Riva 16, pg. 397   IT
MacGREGOR (HRV) d o o, Nikole Cara 6, pg. 671   IT

Samobor

Fuchs Maziva D.O.O., Josipa Jelacica 205, pg. 517   IT

Split

Bonifica-Croatia, Provoboraca 14, pg. 655   IT

Varazdin

KONTO d.o.o. Cakovecka 14, pg. 246   PB

Zagreb

BASF Aktiengesellschaft Predstavnistvo u Hrvatskoj, Vlaska 40, pg. 105   IT

Robert Bosch d.o.o., Culinecka cesta 44, pg. 205   IT
Bull D.O.O. - Croazia, Krsnjavoga, 15, pg. 318   IT
Fin.Co-Croatia, Mihanoviceva Ul. 1, pg. 654   IT
Henkel Croatia d.o.o., pg. 612   IT
Hermes, Gruska 6, pg. 818   PB
Huls Austria GmbH-Zagreb Office, Avenija Vukovar 271, pg. 1455   IT
LM Ericsson International (Croatia) AB, Meduliceva 1/1, pg. 1369   IT
Merkantile Inozemna, Svacicev trg 6, pg. 1369   A/S
Nikola Tesla, Krapinska 45, pg. 1369   IT
Novo Nordisk A/S, Poslouni Toranj Chromos, pg. 987   A/S
Raiffeisenbank Austria d.d., Mihanoviceva 36, pg. 1085   IT
SKF Services d.o.o., Svacicev trg 6, pg. 1159   IT
Swisscolor D.O.O., N. Kaciceva 12, pg. 986   IT
TEHNOKOM, Vocarska 15, pg. 550   IT
Vestretung des Knoll AG, Planinska bb, pg. 110   IT
Zeneca International Ltd., 54000 Osijek, pg. 1526   IT

CUBA
Havana

BASF Dominica S.A., Sucursal de Cuba, pg. 106   IT
Det Norske Veritas, EDIF.Focsa Apto. 4-H, Calle 17 Y M, pg. 397   IT
ING Bank Havana, 5ta. Avenida No. 6407, pg. 649   IT
Mitsui & Co., Ltd., Calle 12, No. 301, Miramar, pg. 881   IT
Netherlands Caribbean Bank Cuba, 5ta Avenida No. 6407, pg. 1159   IT
Pharmacia & Upjohn Biotech AB, Calle 3: A B, Entre 92 y 94, pg. 1047   IT
Productos CIBA SA, Calle A No. 460, pg. 983   IT
Sandoz Quimico Farmacetica Cubana S.A., pg. 985   IT
AB Sandvik International, pg. 1188   IT
Zeneca International Ltd., Cuba, Calle 4 no 715 entre 7ma y 6, pg. 1526   IT

CYPRUS
Limassol

Cyprus Cement Company Ltd., 172 St. Andrew Street, pg. 629   IT
Det Norske Veritas, Foloune House, Office No. E2, 5th Fl., pg. 397   IT
Flowtite Offshore Services Ltd., 284, Arch Makarios III Avenue, Fortuna Court, pg. 1237   PB
GE/Fuji Electric Co., Ltd., Nicolaou Pentadromos Centre, Office 908, pg. 522   IT
Moody's Interbank Credit Service Ltd., Arianthi Court, 50 Ayias Zonis Street, pg. 537   PB

Nicosia

B.A.T (Cyprus) Ltd., pg. 111   IT
Bull Middle East Pte. Ltd., 70 Makarios Ave., pg. 315   IT
Cooperative Central Bank Ltd.-Insurance Dept., Gregorios Afxentiou Street, pg. 60   IT
Cycom Computer Products Ltd., Marilena Bldg., 5th Fl., 12 Princess De Tyra St., pg. 1228   IT
Cyprus Popular Bank (Finance) Limited, 11-13 Archbishop Makarios III Avenue, pg. 581   IT
The Cyprus Popular Bank Ltd., Popular Bank Building, 39 Archbishop Makarios III Ave., pg. 581   IT
De La Ma/TBWA, 36 Grivas Dighenis Ave., pg. 1062   PV
Demonax Computer Services Limited, 11-13 Archbishop Makarios III Avenue, pg. 581   IT
Demstar Ltd., 30 Grivas Dhigenis Ave., pg. 817   PB
Dow Jones Markets Cyprus Limited, Apt. 201A, Kriticos Bldg., 38 AndreasArouzos St., pg. 525   PB
Eldon Cyprus, P.O. Box 7576, pg. 436   IT
Gnomi Advertising, 4th Fl., 2 Christodoulous Sozos St., pg. 304   PV
S.C. Johnson Company Limited, Etyk Bldg., Eight Preveza St., pg. 593   PV
Laiki Factors Limited, 11-13 Archbishop Makarios III Avenue, pg. 581   IT
Laiki Insurance Co. Limited, 11-13 Archbishop Makarios III Avenue, pg. 581   IT
Laiki Investments Limited, 9/F, Cronos Court, 66 Archbishop Makarios III Avenue, pg. 581   PB
Mobil Oil Cyprus, P.O. Box 1344, pg. 1119   PB
Monenco AGRA Techmaster Ltd., 21 Academias Avenue, pg. 31   IT
S.A. Petrides & Son Limited, 39, Ay. Nicolaos Str., Off G. Grivas Digenis Ave., pg. 1369   IT
Popular Bank Computers Limited, 11-13 Archbishop Makarios III Avenue, pg. 581   IT
Raychem Technologies Limited, Membr House, 21 Akademias Ave., pg. 1363   PB
Royal Skandia Life Assurance Ltd., Office 102, 23 Armenias Ave., pg. 1257   IT
Shell Cyprus Trading Company Ltd, 8 Prevezis St., pg. 1140   IT
Spima Ltd., P.O. Box 5038, pg. 97   IT
Swiss Bank Corporation, Afemia House, 2nd floor, No. 201, 70 Arch. Makarios III Avenue, pg. 1330   IT
Telerexa Ltd., Valentine House, 8 Stassandrou St., pg. 823   PB
P.M. Tseriotis Ltd., pg. 109   IT
Wackenhut Security Cyprus, 15, Vasili Michaelides St., pg. 1732   PB

Paphos

MoDo Paper Ltd., pg. 887   IT

PB - *U.S. Public Companies Volume*
PV - *U.S. Private Companies Volume*
IT - *International Public & Private Companies Volume*

Geographic Index-Non U.S.

Norske Skog (Cyprus) Ltd., 51, Griva Dighenis Ave.,
pg. 966   **IT**
Propak Systems (Cyprus) Limited, Gloria House, Office 104,
3 Kinyraf St., pg. 1071   **IT**

CZECH REPUBLIC

Beroun

Cement Bohemia Praha a.s., Kubatova 65, pg. 605   **IT**
Linde Frigera spol. s.r.o., pg. 810   **IT**

Bratislava

Commerzbank AG Representative Office-Bratislava,
Pribinova 25, pg. 311   **IT**
KSB Cerpadla a Armatury, pg. 721   **IT**
Robert Bosch spol. s.r.o., Kutlikova 17, pg. 206   **IT**

Brno

Beton Mix Brno a.s., Slamenikova 23, pg. 605   **IT**
Bilfinger + Berger stavebni s.r.o., Dvorakova, pg. 196   **IT**
Bobst Eastern Europe spol. s.r.o., pg. 198   **IT**
Brother International, S.R.O., Veveri 102, pg. 230   **IT**
Forbo s.r.o., pg. 498   **IT**
ING Bank Brno, Nam. Svobody 13/Jansja 1, pg. 649   **IT**
IVO-EKO s.r.o., Moravske Namesti 3, pg. 660   **IT**
Makita S.R.O., Prazakova 51/53, pg. 832   **IT**
Medata Czechoslovakia spol.sr.o., Slamova 34,
pg. 712   **IT**
Nordson CS, spol.s.r.o., Strama 43-61600, pg. 1189   **PB**
Rexroth SRO, pg. 839   **IT**
Sterkovny a piskovny Brno. a.s., Prikop 15-17, pg. 606   **IT**
Sun Chemical s.r.o., Uboz 8, pg. 371   **IT**
Svedala s.r.o., pg. 1323   **IT**

Ceska Lipa

Autobaterie spol.s.r.o., Dubicka 958, pg. 1452   **IT**
VARTA AKU spol. s.r.o., Dubicka 958, pg. 1452   **IT**

Ceske Budejovice

Robert Bosch spol. s.r.o., Knezskodvorska 26, pg. 206   **IT**

Chomutov

Sandvik Chomutov, pg. 1186   **IT**

Chynov

Avesta Sheffield sro, Zahostice 39, pg. 222   **IT**

Decin

Aluminum Decin spol. s.r.o., pg. 68   **IT**
Ferox A.S., pg. 32   **PB**

Hradec Kralove

Arrow Czech Republic, Int'l CR, as, Trazka 209,
pg. 135   **PB**
CIBA-GEIGY Services AG, Veverkova 1349, pg. 979   **IT**
Pechiney Strojobal, Slezska 839, pg. 1031   **IT**

Hranice

Krytina Hranice spol. s r.o., pg. 1092   **IT**

Jablonec

Knorr-Autobrzdy S.R.O., Vzdusna 25, pg. 738   **IT**

Jesenice u Prahy

Eurocon, Budejovicka 59, pg. 667   **IT**

Jilemnice

kaminSOS Obnova kaminu spol. s r.o., Doleni ulice 167,
pg. 1092   **IT**

Kasperske Hory

TVX Bohemia Dulni a.s., ul. Douha 95, pg. 1345   **IT**

Koprivnice

Tatrarex Precision Castings spol. s.r.o., Stefanikova 1163,
pg. 756   **IT**

Kourim

Lonza Biotec sro, pg. 69   **IT**

Liberec

BEKO spol. s.r.o., Ujezu 2, pg. 1031   **PB**
CIBA-GEIGY Services AG, pg. 979   **IT**
ING Bank Liberec, Masarykova 12, pg. 649   **IT**
Rockwell LVS - Liberec a.s., Ceske Mladeze 452,
pg. 1401   **PB**

Litomerice

Cizkovicka Cementarna A Vapenice, A.S., CS-411 12
Ciskovice, pg. 790   **IT**

Lysa

PREFA Lysa nad Labem a.s, pg. 425   **IT**

Mesto-Touskov

Deva a.s., pg. 991   **IT**

Mimon

Falcon Mimon, A.S., Hrezdovska 644, pg. 611   **PB**

Mlada Boleslav

Bundy s.r.o., Ptacka 20, pg. 1342   **IT**
SKODA, Automobilova a.s., Trida Vaclava Klementa,
pg. 1475   **IT**

Mokra

Cementarny a Vapenky Mokra, pg. 605   **IT**

Nehvizdy

Schiedel spol. s r.o., Horosanska 235, pg. 1092   **IT**

Okrisky

Mann Filtr Jipap s.r.o., Pribyslavice, pg. 484   **IT**

Olomouc

Jauch & Huebener spol. s.r.o., Polska 29, pg. 118   **PB**

Opocno

NMV Opocno a.s., pg. 992   **IT**
Nutricia Mlecna a.s., pg. 992   **IT**

Oslavany

Neumeyer CR, spol. sr.o, Padochovska 28, pg. 755   **IT**

Ostrava

American Power Conversion, Plzenska 4-6, pg. 89   **PB**
AutoCont A.S., Nemocnicni 12, pg. 739   **IT**
Cherry SRO, Moricovska 265, pg. 346   **PB**

Otrokovice

Barum Continental spol. s.r.o., pg. 327   **IT**

Pardubice

Cheming A.S., Pernerova 168, pg. 1415   **IT**

Plzen

Bayerische Landesbank Girozentrale, Perlova 7,
pg. 177   **IT**

Prachovice

Ceva Prachovice a.s., pg. 629   **IT**

Prague

AGA GAS spol.s r.o., Molakova 576, pg. 13   **IT**
AGIP Praha Ltd., Platnersca 4, pg. 428   **IT**
APP Systems, Kotorska 16/1599, pg. 1228   **PB**
Adecco CR Spol s.r.o., Narodni 33, pg. 24   **IT**
Adidas CSFR Spol.s.KO., pg. 24   **IT**
Adverta, Opletalova 19, pg. 1152   **PV**
Air Products S.R.O., pg. 32   **PB**
Alarmcom S.R.O., Na Dolinach 34, pg. 1246   **IT**
Allianz poistovna, a., Rimska 12, pg. 60   **IT**
American Appraisal, Ltd., Podolska 50, pg. 50   **PV**
Amway Czech Republic, Nad Kazanku 29, pg. 69   **PV**
Anglicka Business Center, Na Prikope 14, pg. 90   **IT**
Margaret Astor spol.s.r.o., pg. 185   **IT**
Atlas A.S., Delnicka 3, pg. 463   **IT**
Autodesk s.r.o., Jeseniova 1, pg. 150   **PB**
AxTrade Czechoslovakia, Na porici 6, pg. 710   **IT**
BASF spol. s.r.o., Korunovacni 6/103, pg. 107   **IT**
BNP-Dresdner Bank (CR) a.s., Vitezna 1, pg. 418   **IT**
BV Finance Praha s.r.o., pg. 180   **IT**
Bayerische Landesbank Girozentrale, U Prasne Brany 3,
pg. 177   **IT**
Beiersdorf spol. s.r.o., pg. 183   **IT**
Benckiser spol. s.r.o., pg. 186   **IT**
Berlitz Schools of Languages Czechoslovakia Spol.sr.o, Na
Porici 12, pg. 222   **PB**
Berner CZ, Na Piskach 61, pg. 189   **IT**
Borland SRO, Tynsky dvur 10, pg. 246   **PB**
Robert Bosch Vertriebsgesellschaft mbH, Pod visnovkou
25/1661, pg. 205   **IT**
Bramac spol. sr.o., Sokolovska 278, 6. posch.,
pg. 1092   **IT**

Bratri Bohlerove A.S., Pohnertova 1725, pg. 1472   **IT**
Bull SPOL S.R.O., Karlovo Ramesti 24, pg. 317   **IT**
Leo Burnett Advertising Spol.SR.O, Nad Vysinkou 15,
pg. 184   **PV**
CAC Leasing a.s., Prague, Josefska 6/34-Oettingensky
palac, pg. 348   **IT**
CPC Foods A.S., 1BC, Pobrenzi 3, pg. 225   **PB**
Canon CZ spol s.r.o., Mala Strana, pg. 262   **IT**
Cerberus S.R.O., Brezanska 2, pg. 1246   **IT**
Ceska Reklamni/TBWA, Vaclavske nam. 39, pg. 1062   **PV**
Chemie Linz Prag s.r.o., U pujcovny 2, pg. 356   **IT**
Chr. Hansen Czech Republic, s.r.o. K. Zizkovu 4,
pg. 289   **IT**
CIBA-GEIGY Services AG, Nam bratri Synku 10/477,
pg. 979   **IT**
Ciba-Geigy Services AG, Zyma Department, Na krivce 64,
pg. 979   **IT**
City Radio, Korunni 98, pg. 561   **IT**
Cokoladovny, Modranska 27, pg. 922   **IT**
Commenda C.R. s.r.o., Matechova 3, pg. 1501   **IT**
Commerzbank AG-Prague Branch, Jugoslavska 1,
pg. 311   **IT**
Credit Commercial de France, c/o Zivnostenska Banka, Na
Prikope 20, pg. 343   **IT**
Creditanstalt a.s., Siroka 5, ul. 5, pg. 348   **IT**
Czechia Superhobby Systemova centrala s.r.o., Krizikova
42, pg. 993   **IT**
DMB&B Prague, Liliova 4, 110 00 Praha 1, pg. 304   **PV**
Daewoo Corp. - Prague, Koonspool Bldg., Room No. 754,
pg. 358   **IT**
Danchem AG, Pod Visnovkou 25/1661, pg. 382   **IT**
Dell Computer SRO, Ossadni 12a 170 00, pg. 496   **PB**
Delnemo A.S., Delnicka 3, pg. 463   **IT**
Delvita A.S., Delnicka 3, pg. 463   **IT**
Deutsche Bank AG (Prague), Hotel Jalta, Vaclavske nam.
45, pg. 404   **IT**
Digital Equipment s.r.o., Na Pankraci 26, pg. 508   **PB**
Dun & Bradstreet spol s.r.o., Spalena 17, pg. 537   **PB**
Durkopp Adler CR s.r.o., Jugoslavska 29, pg. 469   **IT**
EOC Normalnien Praha S.r.o., Moskevska 63, pg. 75   **IT**
ESAB s.r.o., Ratajova 8/1113, pg. 282   **IT**
Electricite de France, Americka 17, pg. 437   **IT**
Elkem Representative Office - Czech Republic,
Jungmannova 11/23, pg. 447   **IT**
EURO RSCG, Praha, Vinohradska 60, pg. 602   **IT**
Europe 2 Prague, Nadrazni 56, pg. 795   **IT**
EuroTel Praha Lta, Olsanska 6, pg. 204   **PB**
EXPOCHEM s.r.o., Radlicka 2, pg. 458   **IT**
Ferrosan International A/S, Blanicka 28, pg. 989   **IT**
Fleming Investments Limited, Celetna 19, pg. 494   **IT**
Frionor C.R. a.s., Evropska 178, pg. 516   **IT**
Fuchs Oil Co. (CZ) Spol. s r.o., Tynska 21, pg. 518   **IT**
Gastra spol. s.r.o., K Zizkovu 4, pg. 638   **IT**
Generale Bank, Oettingen Palace, Josefska, 6-Mals Strana,
pg. 547   **IT**
Gerlach Spol Sro, pg. 1144   **IT**
Groupe SEB CR, Bubenska 55, pg. 568   **IT**
Heidelberger Zement - Cement Europe East, Central
Europe Branch, Evropska 178, pg. 606   **IT**
Heinemann ELT-Central Europe, Senovazne nam 24,
pg. 1479   **IT**
Henkel CR. s.r.o., pg. 612   **IT**
Herlitz Spol. S.r.o., Ve zlibku 1800, pg. 616   **IT**
Hewlett-Packard Ceskoslovensko spol.s.r.o., Novodvorska
82, pg. 819   **PB**
Honeywell Ssro, Budejovicka 1, pg. 835   **PB**
Huls CR, Kodanska 46, pg. 1455   **IT**
Hydro Czechoslovakia s.r.o., Dusni 10, pg. 963   **IT**
IDG Czechoslovakia, Seydlerova 2451/11, pg. 570   **PV**
IDV Czech Republic, International Business Centre, 6th
Floor, Pobrezni 3, pg. 410   **IT**
ING Bank Prague, IBC Building, Tower A, 9th Floor,
pg. 649   **IT**
IR International Holdings, Inc., Novodvorska 994,
pg. 907   **PB**
ISS Servisystem s.r.o., Jankovcova 2, pg. 657   **IT**
Immobiliengesellschaft Ost Haegle spol. s.r.o., pg. 310   **IT**
Intergraph CR, Podbabska 20, 160 46 Praha 6, 160-46,
pg. 891   **PB**
JWT/ARK Communications, Vysehrdaska 43, pg. 1484   **IT**
Jauch & Huebener, U. Pate baterie 8-10, pg. 118   **PB**
Juki (Europe) G.m.b.H-Prague Office, Antala Staska 78/
1357, pg. 717   **IT**
KSB Pumpy + Armatury spol. sr.o., pg. 721   **IT**
Kanthal Prague, pg. 723   **IT**
Knoll spol. s.r.o., Kounicka 70, pg. 109   **IT**
KONE Lifts a.s., Pod sancemi 196, pg. 747   **IT**
Korn/Ferry International, Valdstejnska 150/4, pg. 634   **PV**
Kredietbank Representative Office (Prague), Senovazne
Namesti 19, pg. 760   **IT**
Krupp Hoesch Stahlexport GmbH, Jiri Zazvorka,
Famfulikova 1139, pg. 515   **IT**
Landis & Staefa Praha s.r.o., Pocernicka 96, pg. 801   **IT**
Linde chladici technika spol. s.r.o., pg. 810   **IT**
Linde Technoplyn a.s., pg. 811   **IT**
Arthur D. Little International, Inc., Konviktska 24,
pg. 671   **PV**
Logica s.r.o., Vaclavske nam. 66/, pg. 815   **IT**
Lucent Technologies s.r.o., Navrstach 23/970,
pg. 1018   **PB**
Makro CR spol. s.r.o., Vodickova 20, pg. 1155   **IT**
Mannesmann Anlagenbau Bohemia Moravia SRO,
pg. 837   **IT**
Mary Kay Czech Republic S.R.O., Zitna 18, pg. 711   **PV**
Medata Czechoslovakia spol.s.r.o., U Krcske Vodarny 939/
1a, pg. 712   **IT**
Julius Meinl a.s., pg. 856   **IT**
Microsoft S.R.O., pg. 1108   **PB**
Mitsui & Co., Ltd., Belehradska 130, 12000, pg. 881   **IT**
Mona spol. sr.o., Zitna 18, pg. 1445   **IT**

PB - *U.S. Public Companies Volume*
PV - *U.S. Private Companies Volume*
IT - *International Public & Private Companies Volume*

1564

J.P. Morgan International Ltd., Mala Stupartska 7, pg. 1131   **PB**
Motorola S.R.O., Celakovskeho Sady No. 4, pg. 1140   **PB**
Moulinex, Karlovo Namesti 28, pg. 896   **IT**
Nationale-Nederlanden Zivotni Pojist'ovna, U Prasne Brany 1, pg. 651   **IT**
Neste Oy Chemicals, Trojska 13a, pg. 915   **IT**
Nestle Food S.r.o., pg. 921   **IT**
Nikon s.r.o., Stepanska 45/640, pg. 931   **IT**
Nokia Telecommunications, Nitranska 6, Vinondrany, pg. 953   **IT**
NORD/LB - Prague, U Prasne brany 3, pg. 958   **IT**
Novell Czech Republic, Olbrachtova 3, pg. 1204   **PB**
Novo Nordisk A/S, Blanicka 28, pg. 987   **IT**
OB Heller A.S., Kristanova 3, pg. 521   **IT**
OCE-Czech-Republic s.r.o., pg. 994   **IT**
Ocel Styria A.S., Pohnertova 1723, pg. 1472   **IT**
OMRON Electronics Spol SRO, Srobarova 6, pg. 1006   **IT**
PAL-VDO Instruments SRO, pg. 839   **IT**
Parker Hannifin Corporation, Novodvorska 1010/14, pg. 1263   **PB**
Pechiney CSFR-Rep. Office of Pechiney Handelsgesellschaft & Brandeis in Czechoslovakia, c/o O.A.C. Commerical Admin., Centre, pg. 1031
Perry Machinery Czech S.R.O., pg. 855   **PV**
Pfizer s.r.o., Lihovarska 14/1847, pg. 1284   **PB**
Prague Office, Vjame 8, pg. 1345   **IT**
Primaplyn s.r.o., Baarova 2, pg. 1155   **IT**
Prumyslovy Penzijni Fond, a.s., Na Strzi 63, pg. 651   **IT**
R.R.M. Prague, Celetna 17, pg. 796   **IT**
Raiffeisenbank a.s., Vodickova 38, pg. 1085   **PB**
Rakona, pg. 1333   **PB**
Reader's Digest Vyber, K Rot unde 89/4, pg. 1368   **IT**
Reemtsma International Praha spol. s.r.o., Bartolomejska 11, pg. 1101   **IT**
Rekord Nutricia s.r.o., pg. 992   **IT**
Roche s.r.o., pg. 1122   **IT**
Rockwell Automation s.r.o., Nad Vroskou horou 88/4, pg. 1400   **PB**
SKF Loziska A.S., U Mestanskeho Pivovaru 7, pg. 1159   **IT**
S.M.P., Na Florenci, 33, pg. 823   **IT**
Sandvik Czechoslovakia s.r.o., pg. 1186   **IT**
Scholl Spol sro, Na Jarove 4, pg. 1210   **IT**
Schrack-Ericsson spol. s.r.o. Czech Republic, Legerova 22-24, pg. 1369   **IT**
Sequent Computer Systems, s.r.o., K Zizkovu 4, pg. 1460   **PB**
Shimizu (CS) Spol. SR. O., Nad Svanhem 7, pg. 1234   **IT**
SkoFIN s.r.o., pg. 1475   **IT**
SkoLEASE, pg. 1475   **IT**
Sodexho Catering S.R.O., Zeleny Pruh 1294/52, pg. 1275   **IT**
Sodexho Pass-Gastrotur, El. Krasnohorske 9, pg. 1275   **IT**
STILL CR spol.s.r.o., pg. 811   **IT**
Sulzer Praha s.r.o., pg. 1306   **IT**
Telecomspol SRO, pg. 720   **IT**
3M Czech Republic, spol. sr.o., pg. 1606   **PB**
Toyota Motor Czech spol. sr.o, Svehlova 1900, pg. 1414   **IT**
UBS Representative Office, Parizska 3, pg. 1441   **IT**
Utell International-Czech Republic, C/O Brooks Travel, pg. 1098   **IT**
VDO Instruments SRO, pg. 839   **IT**
Vorwerk CS s.r.o., pg. 1481   **IT**
Vytahy Schindler A.S., pg. 1205   **IT**
Westdeutsche Landesbank Prague, Kralodvorska 11, pg. 1493   **IT**
Willis Corroon s.r.o., Podskalska 24, pg. 1509   **IT**
Wilson Sporting Goods CS spol sro, Nad Vrsovskou Horou 88-4, pg. 73   **IT**
WoodCommerz a.s., pg. 312   **IT**
Wrigley Czechoslovakia, Ltd., Wrigley Spol. sr.o, pg. 1781   **PB**
Wrigley, spol. s.r.o., Goncarenkova 12, pg. 1781   **PB**
Wuestenrot stavebni sporitelna a.s., Janackovo Nabr. 41, pg. 1514   **IT**
Young & Rubicam Prague, Na Kozacce 7, pg. 1199   **PV**
Zeneca (CZ) s.r.o., Cinska 4, pg. 1526   **IT**
Zurich Pojistovna, Organizacni slozka, pg. 1531   **IT**

Pratta

Gerber CS Ltd., Nuslova 2277, pg. 973   **IT**

Prerov

Gambro-Meopta S.R.O., Kabelikova 1, pg. 668   **IT**

Pribram

Georg Fischer Disa s.r.o., pg. 489   **IT**

Pribyslavice

JIP-PACK A.S., pg. 1146   **IT**

Slapanice

Krytina Slapanice a.s., Krbitovni 1643, pg. 1092   **IT**

Sumavska

AMP Czech s.r.o., CR-61254 Brno, pg. 8   **PB**

Svitavy

Westvaco Svitavy, SPOL. S.R.O., Tabak A.S., Zavod, pg. 1763   **PB**

Tabor

Lecotex, Mesicka 276, pg. 193   **IT**

Tremosnice

SAB WABCO CS, s.r.o., pg. 271   **IT**

Usti nad Labem

Corro-Coat (CZ) a.s., pg. 715   **IT**
Jotun Spolchemie a.s., Veleslavinova 3, pg. 715   **IT**
Van Leer Obaly a.s., pg. 1147   **IT**

Usti nad Orlici

Rieter Elltex a.s., pg. 1117   **IT**

Vamberk

ESAB Vamberk a.s., Smetanovo nabrezi 334, pg. 282   **IT**

Zlin

IPC Corporation spol.s.r.o, Tr 2 Kvetna 3070, pg. 651   **IT**

Znojmo

Obalex, A.S., pg. 440   **PB**

DENMARK

Aaby

Brenderup Trailers A/S, Fabriksvej 4, pg. 436   **IT**
Trailers International A/S, Fabriksvej 4, pg. 436   **IT**

Aalborg

DMT Dansk Mobiltelefon I/S, Skelagerveg 1, pg. 209   **PB**
Dan Tegl Tag A/S, Korsgarde 8, pg. 1092   **IT**
Electrolux Elmotor A/S, Svendborgvej 2, pg. 441   **IT**
Fibertex A/S, pg. 431   **IT**
Rothenberger-Exact A/S, Faborgvej 8, pg. 1129   **IT**
Svanehoj International A/S, pg. 1065   **IT**
Tagentreprise Nord A/S, pg. 659   **IT**

Abyhoj

Ciba-Geigy A/S, Egsagervej 16, pg. 976   **IT**

Albertslund

ASEA Skandia Havemanns El A/S, Vallensbaekvej 46, pg. 7   **IT**
Astra Danmark A/S, Roskildevej 22, pg. 93   **IT**
Cerberus A/S, Herstedostervej 29, pg. 1246   **IT**
Nordson Danmark A/S, Laehegnet 75, pg. 1189   **PB**
RT REKLAMEBUREAU A/S, Vallensbaek Torvevej 9, pg. 1081   **IT**
Rockwell Automation A/S, Herstedostervej 27-29, pg. 1399   **PB**
S & W Medico Teknik A/S, Herstedvang 8, pg. 1468   **IT**
TA Control A/S, Vaerkstedsgaarden 18, pg. 670   **IT**

Allerod

AST Research, pg. 1182   **IT**
AMETEK Denmark, Gydevang 32-34, pg. 100   **PB**
Munters Fugtteknik A/S, c/o Polygon A/S, Rypevang 5, pg. 669   **IT**
Nutricia A/S, pg. 992   **IT**
Pharmacia & Upjohn Biotech, Gydevang 21, pg. 1047   **IT**
Rosemount A/S, Hejvrevang 11, pg. 577   **PB**
Time/system Danmark a/s, Gydvang 25, pg. 73   **IT**
Time/System International, Gydevang 25, pg. 73   **IT**

Apenrade

Kraftwerk EV3 1/S, Flenborgvej 185, pg. 1457   **IT**

Ardew

Label-Aire A/S, Industrivej 9, pg. 641   **PV**

Arhus

FAG Danmark A/S, pg. 469   **IT**
O.G. Hoyer A/S, Soren Nymarksvej 13, pg. 1378   **IT**
A/S Kelvin Hughes, Marselis Boulevard 175, pg. 1268   **IT**
SCAN-AD GRUPPEN A/S, Skolegade 19B, pg. 1198   **IT**
Sun Chemical Hartmann A/S, Skejby Nordlandsvej 313, pg. 371   **IT**
Tagentreprise Midt A/S, pg. 659   **IT**
Travel Shop Arhus, Parkalle 9, pg. 1301   **IT**

Baarn

Allied Colloids Nederland B.V., pg. 62   **IT**

Bagsvaerd

NOVO NORDISK A/S, Novo Alle, pg. 987   **IT**
Novo Nordisk A/S, Krogshojvej 30, pg. 987   **IT**
Novo Nordisk A/S, Krogshojvej 55, pg. 989   **IT**
Novo Nordisk Engineering A/S, Krogshojvej 30, 7th Floor, pg. 987   **IT**
Novo Nordisk Farmaka Danmark A/S, Aslaksvej 3, pg. 987   **IT**

Ballerup

Alfa-Laval Nirex Engineering A/S, Metalbuen 20, pg. 1379   **IT**
BMC Software A/S, Lautrup Center, Borupvang 2B, pg. 162   **PB**
Robert Bosch A/S, Telegrafvej 1, pg. 205   **IT**
Dansk Uni-Cardan A/S, Baltorpbakken 10, pg. 535   **IT**
EAC Date ApS, pg. 430   **IT**
C.G. Jensen A/S, Baltorpvej 154, pg. 1261   **IT**
Erik Levison A/S, pg. 431   **IT**
Luxo Danmark A/S, Tempovej 27-29, pg. 821   **IT**
Nea-Lindberg A/S, Industriparken 39-43, pg. 475   **IT**
RM Industrial Group A/S, Industriparken 40, pg. 476   **IT**
Siemens A/S, Borupvang 3, pg. 1247   **IT**
Tefal Danmark A/S, Energivej, 42A, pg. 568   **IT**
Topdanmark, Borupvang 4, pg. 464   **IT**

Billund

Lego Overseas A/S, pg. 805   **IT**
LEGO SYSTEM A/S, Aastvej, pg. 805   **IT**

Birkerod

Acer Scandinavia A/S, pg. 22   **IT**
Amersham Denmark ApS, 2 Blokken II, pg. 993   **IT**
Beiersdorf (Denmark) A/S, Klinthoj Vaenoe 8-12, pg. 183   **IT**
Compaq Computer A/S, Bregnerodvej 133, pg. 418   **PB**
Datateam Danmark A/S, Datavej 58, pg. 710   **IT**
Elu Maskiner A/S, Bistrupvej, 172, pg. 234   **PB**
Georg Fischer A/S, Klintehoj Vaenge 17, pg. 489   **IT**
Hewlett-Packard A/S, Kongevejen 25, pg. 818   **PB**
Janssen-Cilag A/S, Postboks 149, pg. 929   **PB**
R. Ancker Jorgensen A/S, 18 Topstykket, pg. 153   **PB**
Mobil Oil Danmark A/S, Birkerod Kongevej 64, pg. 1119   **PB**
Moog Buhl Automation, 24 Topstykket, pg. 1128   **PB**
Polaroid a.s., Blokken 75, pg. 1314   **PB**
Ren-Vask A/S, Kongevejen 53-57, pg. 441   **IT**
Tandem Computers A/S, Kongegen 2-4, pg. 417   **PB**

Bjerringbro

HTH Kokkener A/S, Heimdalsvej 8, pg. 1302   **IT**

Brabrand

Danisco Ingredients, Edwin Rahrs Vej 38, pg. 378   **IT**

Brande

Dansk Orretfoder a.s., M. Erichsensvej 35, pg. 961   **IT**

Brondby

Agro-kemi a/s, Gammelager 1, pg. 174   **IT**
Ascom Nordic A/S, Park Alle 295, pg. 87   **PV**
Bose A/S, Industriazej 7, pg. 160   **PV**
Danish Pack, Banemarksvej 38, pg. 378   **IT**
GN Nettest Holding, Kirkebjerg Alle 86, pg. 536   **IT**
GN Nettest, Telecom Division, Kirkebjerg Alle 90, pg. 536   **IT**
A/S Helly-Hansen, Nyager 3, pg. 1010   **IT**
LM Ericsson A/S, Kirkebjerg Alle 86, pg. 1368   **IT**
LYCOM A/S, NKT Alle 75, pg. 1019   **PB**
MDI Scandinavia A/S, Midtager 20, pg. 1139   **PB**
Motorola A/S, Midtager 20, pg. 1139   **PB**
NILFISK A/S, Sognevei 25, pg. 932   **IT**
Outokumpu Danmark A/S, Vallensbaekvej 45, pg. 1015   **IT**
Outokumpu Danmark A/S, Vallensbaekvej 6, pg. 1017   **IT**
SKF Danmark A/S, Sdr. Ringvej 55, pg. 1158   **IT**
Scanpoint Technology A/S, Vibeholms Alle 22, pg. 466   **PB**
Siegling Danmark A/S, pg. 498   **IT**
Volvo Personvage Danmark A/S, Postbox 176, pg. 1478   **IT**

Bronshoj

Daekko Presenning Kompagni A/S, Kabbelevej 32-34, pg. 441   **IT**
RADIOMETER A/S, Akandevej 21, pg. 1083   **IT**
Radiometer Medical A/S, Akandevej 21, pg. 1083   **IT**

Charlottenlund

Axel Johnson A/S, Jaegersborg Alle 14, pg. 711   **IT**
Kjellbergs Successors A/S, Jagersborg Alle 14, pg. 712   **IT**

Copenhagen

ABB Industri A/S, Ved Vesterport 6, pg. 2   **IT**
ACTE Nordic Components A/S, Titangade 15, pg. 188   **IT**
AGA A/S, Vermlandsgade 55, pg. 13   **IT**

PB - *U.S. Public Companies Volume*
PV - *U.S. Private Companies Volume*
IT - *International Public & Private Companies Volume*

1565

Geographic Index-Non U.S.

Adecco Aps, Amagertorv 7, pg. 24   IT
Aer Lingus, Vesterbrogade 1C, pg. 28   IT
Aktieselikabet ESAB, Trekronergade 92, pg. 281   IT
Alicon Bormaeglerselkab A/S, Kobmagergade 9, pg. 12   IT
Ambrasoft International, Strodamvej 50, pg. 1002   IT
Amerada Hess A/S, Gronnegade 10, pg. 65   PB
Andrex Radiation Products A/S, Halfdansgade 8, pg. 867   PB
Ansaldo Volund A/S, Ameliegade 37, pg. 654   IT
The Associated Press A/S, 55 Road Rup Lad Ser, pg. 92   PV
BASF Danmark A/S, Ved Stadsgraven 15, pg. 105   IT
Banque Paribas-Denmark, Hammerensgade 4, pg. 319   IT
Bausch & Lomb Danmark A/S, Vesterbrogade 124 B4 Sal., pg. 195   PB
Berlitz International Danmark A/S, Vimmelskaftet 42A, pg. 222   PB
Betech A/S, Titangade 13, pg. 188   IT
Bloch & Behrens ApS, pg. 430   IT
Leo Burnett Denmark, Vesterbrogade 2B, pg. 185   PV
Carbone Danmark A/S, Teglvaerkegade 37, pg. 1030   IT
Castrol A/S, Esplanade 7, pg. 235   IT
CelsiusTech Systems AB, Prags Boulevard 80, pg. 278   IT
Chase Invest A/S, Vognmagergade 10, pg. 339   PB
The Chase Manhattan Bank, N.A., pg. 340   PB
Christiania Bank-Copenhagen Representative Office, Toldbodgade 10, pg. 289   IT
CIBA-GEIGY A/S, Lyngbyvej 172, pg. 976   IT
Citibank, N.A. Copenhagen, Industriens Hus, pg. 378   PB
Commerce, Oster Faelled Torv 6-8, pg. 470   IT
Commerzbank AG-Copenhagen Representative Office, Raadhuspladsen 4, pg. 311   IT
Compass Group-Scandanavian Division, 45 Nyropsgade, pg. 325   IT
The Continuum Company, Inc. (Denmark), Regus House, 3 Larsbjornsstrade, pg. 423   IT
DS Industries ApS, pg. 430   IT
DAGBLADET BOERSEN A/S, Moentergade 19, pg. 359   IT
DANISCO A/S, Langebrogade 1, pg. 378   IT
Danisco Distillers, Langebrogade 4, pg. 378   IT
Danisco Foods, Langebrogade 1, pg. 378   IT
Danisco Sugar, Langebrogade 1, pg. 378   IT
A/S Dansk Shell, Shell Huset, 2 Kampmannsgade, pg. 1138   IT
Dansk Signal Industri A/S, Stamholmen 175, pg. 1365   IT
Dansk Styropack, pg. 1138   IT
Danske Landmaend K/S, Kalvebod Brygge 20, pg. 826   IT
Data General ApS, Fabriksparken 38 Glostrup, pg. 485   PB
Denmark Plant, pg. 443   IT
Dial Forsikring A/S, Frederiksborggade 15, pg. 1257   IT
Dicalite Scandinavia, Rysensteensgade, 1, pg. 903   PV
Dow Jones Markets Danmark A/S, Vesterbrogade 1C, 4th Fl., pg. 525   PB
Dun & Bradstreet Danmark A/S, Egegaardsvej 39, pg. 536   PB
EAC Marketing Services Ltd. A/S, pg. 431   IT
EAC Shipping Ltd. A/S, pg. 431   IT
EAC Timber Ltd. A/S, pg. 431   IT
EMI-Medley, Vognmagerade 10, pg. 427   IT
ESAB A/S, Trekronorgade 92, pg. 282   IT
ESS-FOOD, Axelborg, Axeltorv 3, pg. 429   IT
The East Asiatic Company (Korea) Ltd. ApS, pg. 431   IT
THE EAST ASIATIC COMPANY LTD. A/S, Company House, 7 Midtermolen, pg. 430   IT
EMTEC Magnetics Nordic A/S, Ved Stadsgraven 15, pg. 743   IT
Enator A/S, Lille Strandstraede 20 C, pg. 278   IT
Engineering Company, Dalager 10, pg. 361   PV
Enso Danmark A/S, Vognmagergade 7, pg. 457   IT
Ericsson Computer Products, Sluseholmen 8, pg. 1366   IT
Ericsson Mobile Communications, Sluseholmen 8, pg. 1367   IT
Ericsson Standard Components, Sluseholmen 8, pg. 1367   IT
EURO RSCG, Copenhagen, Vangehusvej 19, pg. 602   IT
Fasson A/S, Marielundvej 46D, pg. 154   PB
A/S Findus, Masnedoegade 20, pg. 920   IT
Ford Credit A/S, 1, Sluselholmen, pg. 666   PB
Ford Motor Company A/S, 1, Sluselholmen, pg. 666   PB
Forlaget Det Beste A/S, Jagtvej 169B, pg. 1368   PB
Freudenberg Building Systems A.S., pg. 506   IT
GGK Copenhagen, Toldbodgade 49, pg. 1335   IT
GN Ejendomme, Kongens Nytorv 26, pg. 537   IT
GN GREAT NORDIC LTD., Kongens Nytorv 26, pg. 536   IT
GN Great Northern Telegraph Company, Kongens Nytorv 26, pg. 536   IT
GN Netcom A/S, Bispevej 4, pg. 537   IT
Georg Jensen Silver, Amagertorv 4, pg. 1134   IT
Georg Jensen Silversmithy Ltd., 45, Smallegade, pg. 1134   IT
Glaxo Danmark a/s, DK-605 Brondby, pg. 553   IT
Granges Metalock A/S, Vallenbacksvej 6, pg. 441   IT
Handelsbanken Copenhangen, Amaliegade 3-5, pg. 1327   IT
Harttung Fasteners A/S, Marielundvej 48A, pg. 233   PB
Herbalife Denmark ApS, pg. 809   PB
Holmegaards Glass, 15 Oestergade, pg. 1134   IT
Honeywell Bull A/S, Otto Monsteds Plads 9, pg. 318   IT
Horst & Sons Forlag A/S, Dr. Tvaergade 5, pg. 197   IT
Huls Nordic AB-Denmark Branch Office, Company House, Midtermolen 7, pg. 1455   IT
Hydro Aluminium Rolled Products, Parken, Oster Alle 48, pg. 963   IT
IBM Danmark-Produkt Distribution Selskab A/S, Danish Div., pg. 898   PB
ISS Catering A/S, Rentemestervej 62, pg. 656   IT
ISS Data A/S, Rentemestervej 60-62, pg. 656   IT
ISS Hospital Service A/S, Montmestervej 31, pg. 656   IT

ISS Rengoringsservice, Montmestervej 31, pg. 656   IT
ISS Scandinavia A/S, Rentemestervej 62, pg. 656   IT
ISS Specialservice, Montmestervej 31, pg. 656   IT
ISS Tele Response, Rentemestervej 162, pg. 656   IT
Illums Bolighus, Amagertorv 10, pg. 1134   IT
Intel Denmark, pg. 887   PB
Inter-Scan Airfreight A/S, 3C Fuglebaekvej, pg. 1120   PV
International Nutrition Co. ApS, pg. 431   IT
Axel Johnson Lab System A/S, Strandboulevarden 64, pg. 711   IT
K & E Trykfarver, Ved Stadsgraven 15, pg. 108   IT
KKKK A/S, Islands Brygge 22, pg. 1459   IT
KSB A/S, Rodovre, pg. 721   IT
Kelly Vikarer, Amagertorv 11, pg. 949   PB
Kemira Danmark A/S, Company House, Midtermolen 7, pg. 728   IT
Kenwood A/S, Brognenen 8, 2635 Ishoj, pg. 730   IT
KONE Elevator A/S, Lygten 37, pg. 747   IT
Kraft Foods A/S, Vasbygade 45, pg. 1290   PB
LM Ericsson Finans A/S, Sluseholmen 8, pg. 1368   IT
LM Ericsson International A/S Denmark, Sluseholmen 8, pg. 1369   IT
Arthur D. Little International, Inc., Bredgade 56, pg. 671   PV
Livsforsikrings-Aktieselskabet Utrecht, Radhuspladsen 4, pg. 499   IT
Louis Vuitton Danmark A/S, 3 Ny Ostergade, pg. 782   IT
MAN B & W Diesel A/S, Teglholmsgade 41, pg. 824   IT
Medi-Lab A/S, pg. 1121   IT
Mettle-Toledo A/S, Lyngbyvej 172, pg. 4   PV
Mostrups Forlag A/S, pg. 1602   PB
Motorola A/S, Artilerivej 126, pg. 1139   PB
Multi Finans A/S, Kobmagergade 57, 1sal, pg. 1257   IT
Munksgaard International Booksellers & Publishers Ltd., Norrebrogade 35, pg. 197   IT
NY*BO*E, Otta Mousteds Gade 7, pg. 993   IT
Nestle Danmark A/S, Masnedoegade 20, pg. 921   IT
Nevi Danmark A/S, Frederiksborggade 15, pg. 1257   IT
Nielsen Marketing Research A/S, Strandboulevarden 89, pg. 1184   PB
Nokia Mobile Phones, Fredrikskaj, pg. 952   IT
Norden Banking Group, Silkegade 8, pg. 1328   IT
Norsk Hydro Danmark a.s, Industriens Hus, Vesterbrogade 1 C, pg. 964   IT
Norsk Hydro Olie a.s, Vester Sogade 10, pg. 964   IT
Norsk Hydro Udforskning, Vester Sogade 10, pg. 964   IT
Nutricia Danmark A/S, pg. 992   IT
NYKREDIT, Otto Mosteds Plads 9, pg. 993   IT
Nykredit Bank A/S, Bredgade 40, pg. 993   IT
OCE-Danmark AS, Kornmarksvei 6, pg. 994   IT
Olivetti A/S, Lersoe Parkalle 107/111, pg. 1003   IT
Pharmacia & Upjohn AS, Overgaden neden vandet 7, pg. 1049   IT
Philips Danmark A/S, Prags Blvd. 80, pg. 1055   IT
Philips Lys A/S, Prags Blvd. 80, pg. 1055   IT
Plus Fack A/S Haustrup EKCO, pg. 69   IT
RNBNY Representative Office-Copenhagen, Nytorv 5, 1st Fl., pg. 1381   PB
Hans Reitzels Forlag A/S, Dronningens Tvaergade 5, pg. 197   IT
Repscl Quimica, Ehlersvej, 9, pg. 1105   IT
Royal Copenhagen Antiques, 6 Amagertorv, pg. 1134   IT
Royal Copenhagen Porcelain, Amagertorv 6, pg. 1134   IT
Royal Copenhagen Retail A/S, Amagertorv 6, pg. 1134   IT
SAS Institute A/S, Kobmagerade 9a, pg. 967   PV
SAS Service Partner A/S, Kristen Bernikows Gade 1, pg. 1202   IT
Sandcz A/S, Titangade 9 A, pg. 984   IT
Sandvik A/S, pg. 1186   IT
Sandvik Bahco Norden A/S, pg. 1186   IT
Scan-Ad Kobenhavn A/S, Dronningens Tvaergade 30, pg. 1198   IT
Scan Care A/S, Montemestervej 31, pg. 656   IT
Scan Gobain Glass A/S, Vibevej 20,2, pg. 1173   IT
Schiesser International A/S, pg. 618   IT
Thomas Schmidt Demag Materialehandtering A/S, pg. 838   IT
Scholl Danmark A/S, P.O. Box 1890, Yderlandsvej 15-17, pg. 1209   IT
Skancia Investment Management, Hojbro Plads 10, pg. 1258   IT
Skancinavisk Henkel A/S, pg. 614   IT
Skancinaviska Enskilda Banken, Copenhagen, Landmaerket 10, pg. 1259   IT
Skil Denmark A/S, Gl Koge Landevej 57, pg. 577   IT
F.L. Smidth & Co. A/S, Vigerslev Alle 77, pg. 475   IT
Statoi Danmark A/S, Sankt Annae Plads 13, pg. 1298   IT
Storage Technology Denmark, Stamholmen 149, pg. 1523   PB
TBWA Copenhagen, Kalkbraenderilobskaj 6, pg. 1063   PV
Telecom Scandinavia A/S, 2nd Floor, Norre Voldgade 27, pg. 796   IT
The Tokio Marine & Fire Insurance Company (U.K.) Limited, c/o Hansen & Klein Insurance, 7 Christian IX's Gade, pg. 1392   IT
Uni-Dan A/S, Melerbuen 6-12, pg. 1438   IT
Voest-Alpine Danmark ApS, Vesterbrogade 10, pg. 1472   IT
Western Service A/S, 54 Kobmagergade, pg. 1760   IT
Wibroe, Duckert & Partners, Landemaerket 29, pg. 678   PV
Willis Corroon A/S, Christian IX' Gade 7, 3rd Floor, pg. 1509   IT
World Tourist, Zved Vestertorv 4, pg. 22   IT
Young & Rubicam Copenhagen, Enhjorningens Bastion, Langebrogade 6V., pg. 1199   PV
Zeneca AS, Islands Brygge 41, pg. 1526   PV
Zurich Forsikring, Radhuspladsen 75, pg. 1531   IT
Zurich Livsforsikring, Radhuspladsen 75, pg. 1530   IT

Dragor

Avia Radio A/S, Hangar 141, pg. 2   PB
Nordisk Aviation Products a.s., Kobenhavns Lufthavn Syd, pg. 964   IT
Perstorp Form, Neelsvej 26, pg. 1038   IT

Eg

Micro Warehouse, Denmark APS, Gaseagervej # 12, pg. 1104   PB

Esbjerg

The Borden Co. A/S, Limfjordsvej 4, pg. 159   PV
Borden Ost A/S, pg. 159   PV
Cocio Chokolademaelk, Baunehojvej 13, pg. 159   PV
Esbjerg Glas A/S, Sp. Mollevej 97, pg. 1172   IT
Gray Tool Co. (Europe), Uglivigvej 2, pg. 5   IT
Kemira Miljo A/S, Made Industrivej 19, pg. 728   IT
Shell of Esbjerg, Esbjerg Airport, pg. 1138   IT
A/S Vestfrost, Spangsbjerg Mollevej 100, pg. 441   IT

Espergaerde

Polar Seals ApS; PTFE-Packing Mfg. Operation, Bjergvangen, pg. 1262   PB
Sandvik Hard Materials A/S, Hojvangen 21, pg. 1186   IT

Faborg

Dansk Traeemballage A/S, Banevej 3, pg. 476   IT

Farum

Munters A/S, Ryttermarken 4, pg. 669   IT
Carl Munters ApS, Farum Gydevej 89, pg. 669   IT
Oracle Danmark A/S, Ryttermarken 15-21, pg. 1228   PB

Fredericia

ER-Electric A/S, Vejlevej 123, pg. 3   IT
A/S Ernst Voss Fabrik, Slesvigga de 4, pg. 441   IT
Ewos Aqua A/S, Fabriksvej 1, pg. 349   IT
Hydrogas Danmark a.s, Rode Bank 120, pg. 963   IT
Kemira Danmark A/S, Kongensgade 107, pg. 728   IT
I.C. Moeller A/S, Treldevej 191, pg. 3   IT
Rahbekfisk AS, Vesthavnen, pg. 491   IT
Stelform A/S, Vejlbyvej 31, pg. 1088   IT
A/S Voss Komfur Service, Postbox 113, pg. 441   IT

Frederiksberg

DMB&B Reklamebureau A/S, Sankt Knuds Vej 41, pg. 304   PV
Esselte A/S, Norde Fasanvej 117-119, pg. 460   IT
Eurotherm Danmark A/S, Finsensvej 86, pg. 466   IT
Intergraph CAD/CAM (Denmark) A/S, Roskildevej 39, pg. 891   IT
International Marketing & Promotions, Sankt Knuds Vej 41, pg. 304   PV
Pechiney Denmark, Frydendalavej 23, pg. 1031   IT
ROYAL COPENHAGEN A/S, Smallegade 45, pg. 1134   IT

Frederikshavn

Stena Line A/S, Stena Terminalen, pg. 1300   IT
Stena Line Hoffmanns Hotel, Tordenskjoldsgade 3, pg. 1300   IT
Stena Line Hotel Frederikshavn, Tordenskjoldsgade 14, pg. 1300   IT

Gentofte

B&K Ultrasound A/S, Sandtoften #9, pg. 109   PB
Dansk Kenral A.p.S., Ericavej 149, pg. 1049   IT
Enka Danmark A/S, 50 Gentoftegade, pg. 46   IT
Steno Diabetes Center, Niels Steensensvej 2, pg. 987   IT

Gilleleje

NMB Minebea GmbH, Solvaenget 15, pg. 868   IT

Gjern

Cekan/CDT, pg. 287   PB

Glamsbjerg

G.W. Sprinkler A/S, Kastanievej 15, pg. 1500   IT

Glostrup

Albright & Wilson Denmark AS, Siestavej 7;1, pg. 49   IT
BERG Electronics DK, Naverland 2, pg. 213   PB
Boliden Bergsoe A/S, Hvissingev. 116, pg. 1423   IT
Brodrene Dahl A/S, 370 Park Alle, pg. 359   IT
Cinet Danmark A/S, Naverland 1C, pg. 710   IT
Cinet Periferi A/S, Naverland 1C, pg. 710   IT
Colgate-Palmolive A/S, Smedeland 9, pg. 398   PB
DDF Dental Depotet Flex A/S, Naverland 11, pg. 710   IT
DanTransport A/S, Kornmarksvej 12-20, pg. 476   IT
DanTransport Holding A/S, Kornmarksvej 12-20, pg. 476   IT

PB - *U.S. Public Companies Volume*
PV - *U.S. Private Companies Volume*
IT - *International Public & Private Companies Volume*

1566

Geographic Index-Non U.S.

Duracell Scandinavia ApS, Naverland 8, pg. 744 — **PB**
Granges Danmark A/S, Vallenbacksvej 6, pg. 441 — **IT**
Granzow A/S, Ejby industrivej 26, pg. 678 — **IT**
ITT Flygt A/S, Ejby Industrivej 60, pg. 860 — **PB**
Ludvigsen & Hermann A/S, Fabriksparken 37, pg. 278 — **IT**
Molex-G. Ostervig A/S, Paul Bergsoes Vej 16, pg. 1122 — **PB**
Monsanto A/S, Smedeland 6, pg. 1125 — **PB**
OMRON Electronics A/S, Odinsvej 15, pg. 1005 — **IT**
Raychem A/S, Formervangen 12-16, pg. 1362 — **PB**
3M A/S, Postboks 1393, Fabriksparken 15, pg. 1606 — **PB**
Uddeholm A/S, Fabriksparken 26, pg. 1472 — **IT**
Yamanouchi Pharma a/s, Naverland 3, pg. 1519 — **IT**

Grasten

Danfoss Drives A/S, pg. 377 — **IT**

Grena

BASF Health and Nutrition (BHN), Bredstrupvej 42, pg. 106 — **IT**
Danisco Paper, Korsgade 22, pg. 378 — **IT**
Lion Ferry A/S, Faergevej 1, pg. 1300 — **IT**
SAPA A/S, Rolshojvej 8, pg. 441 — **IT**
Stena Line Hotel Grena, Kystvej 32, pg. 1300 — **IT**

Greve

Nilfisk Danmark A/S, Agenavej 16-18, Postbox 120, pg. 932 — **IT**

Grindsted

Winther & Heide's EFTF. A/S, Adinsvej 12-14, pg. 359 — **IT**

Haderslev

Nitodan A/S, H.C. Orstedsvej 4, pg. 932 — **IT**
Scan-Ad Haderslev A/S, Naffet 2, pg. 1198 — **IT**
Tagentreprise Syd og Fyn A/S, pg. 659 — **IT**

Hasselager

Bridgestone Tire Co. A/S, Jegstrupvej 7, pg. 214 — **IT**
Danfoss Videk, Jegstrupvej 3, pg. 377 — **IT**
Danvalve A/S, Stormosevej 10, pg. 377 — **IT**

Havdrup

FPS Power Systems A/S, Kildebrogardsvej 11 C, pg. 492 —
Fiskars Power Systems A/S, Kildebrogardsvej 11 C, pg. 492 —
Scan Globe A/S, 23 Ulvevej, pg. 923 — **PV**

Havndal

All Plast A-S, Vesterbro 65, pg. 460 — **IT**

Hedehusene

Melitta A/S, Flongvej 12, pg. 857 — **IT**
Microsoft Danmark ApS, pg. 1108 — **PB**

Hedensted

Neste Thermisol A/S, Lundagervej 20, pg. 915 — **IT**

Hellerup

Det Norske Veritas, Tuborg Parkvej 8, 3rd Floor, pg. 396 — **IT**
UPM-Kymmene Papir A/S, Strandvejen 58, pg. 1430 — **IT**

Helsinge

Clestra Hauserman Scandinavia, Bymosevej 14, pg. 570 — **IT**

Helsingor

Ejendomsselskabet Tretorn A/S, Sundtoldvej 8 E, pg. 1257 — **IT**
MMC Danmark A.S., Provestenvej 50, pg. 876 — **IT**

Herlev

Aksel Skaarup & Co. A/S, Vasekaer 6-8, pg. 739 — **IT**
Analog Devices APS, Hoerkaer 20, pg. 108 — **PB**
Anco Herlev, Lyskaer 2, pg. 1429 — **IT**
Anco Trae A/S, Lyskaer 2, pg. 1429 — **IT**
BancTec Danmark A/S, Dynamouej 11, pg. 177 — **PB**
Danfoss System Automatik, Horkaer 12 B, pg. 377 — **IT**
DANSK INDUSTRI SYNDIKAT A/S, 17, Herlev Hovedgade, pg. 658 — **IT**
Esselte Meto A-S, Transformervej 14, pg. 461 — **IT**
Georg Fischer Disa A/S, 17 Herlev Hovedgade, pg. 489 — **IT**
Freudenberg Danmark A.S., pg. 506 — **IT**
Freudenberg Simrit A.S., pg. 506 — **IT**
W.R. Grace A/S, Generalorvej 8D, pg. 755 — **PB**
ICOPAL A/S, 38 Mileparken, pg. 658 — **IT**
A/S Industrihaerdiet, Herlov Hovedgade 15, pg. 476 — **IT**
Letraset AS, Marielundvej 30, pg. 461 — **IT**
MacGREGOR (DNK) A/S, Smedeholm 11, pg. 670 — **IT**

Nordisk Elektronics A/S, Transformervej 17, pg. 712 — **IT**
Nordisk Mikrosystem ApS, Transformervej 17, pg. 712 — **IT**
Ostjyllands Asfaltfabrik I/S, pg. 659 — **IT**
A/S Ruko, Marielundvej 20, pg. 18 — **IT**
Scania Danmark A/S, Generatorvej 12, pg. 687 — **IT**
Schindler Elevatorer A/S, pg. 1205 — **IT**
Sensormatic A/S (Denmark), Smedeholm 13A, pg. 1457 — **PB**
Sonderjyllands Asfaltfabrik I/S, pg. 659 — **IT**
Tagentreprise Ost A/S, pg. 659 — **IT**

Herning

Thygesen & Brother Symaskiner A/S, Hammershusvej 5, pg. 230 — **IT**

Hillerod

Mercedes-Benz Danmark AS, pg. 368 — **IT**
Novell Danmark, Helsingorsgade 52, pg. 1204 — **PB**

Hjorring

Internationale Gas Apparatur A/S, Antholtvej 1, pg. 1149 — **IT**
Intralox A/S, Egholmvej 3, pg. 643 — **PV**
Norse Crown Seafood A/S, Sct. Cathrine vej 31, pg. 1390 — **IT**
Rocol Danmark, Parallelvej 48, pg. 892 — **IT**

Hobro

Cardo Door Production A/S, Lupinvej 12, pg. 269 — **IT**
Faltec Porte A/S, Lupinvej 12, pg. 269 — **IT**

Holbaek

Proces-Styring ApS, Boerstenbindervej 4, pg. 1040 — **IT**

Holeby

Danisco Seed, Hojbygardvej 14, pg. 378 — **IT**

Holstebro

Dantek Holstebro A.p.S., pg. 506 — **IT**
Kluber Lubrication A.S., pg. 506 — **IT**
Kluber Lubrication Skandinavien A.S., pg. 506 — **IT**

Holte

Danapak A.m.b.a., Kongevejen 100, pg. 826 — **IT**
ISS Finans A/S, Kongevejen 195, pg. 656 — **IT**
ISS-INTERNATIONAL SERVICE SYSTEM A/S, Kongevejen 195, pg. 656 — **IT**
ISS University Hotel, Kongevejen 195, pg. 656 — **IT**

Horsens

Alcatel Kirk, Ane Staunings Vej 21, pg. 56 — **IT**
Danisco Flexible, HAttingvej 10, pg. 378 — **IT**
Makita Werkzeug GmbH-Denmark Office, Sandovej 11, pg. 832 — **IT**
Schubert Seals A/S, Fuglevangsvej si, pg. 1755 — **PB**

Horsholm

Akzo Chemie Danmark A/S, 26-28 Hovedgaden, pg. 47 — **IT**
Akzo Plastics Danmark A/S, 26-28 Hovedgaden, pg. 45 — **IT**
ALK A/S, Boge Alle 10-12, pg. 288 — **IT**
Chr. Hansen A/S, Boge Alle 10-12, pg. 288 — **IT**
Chr. Hansen Bio Systems A/S, Boge Alle 10-12, pg. 288 — **IT**
CHR. HANSEN HOLDING A/S, 10-12 Boege Alle, pg. 288 — **IT**
Dell Computer A.S. Denmark, Slotsmarken 11, pg. 496 — **PB**
Digital Equipment Corp. A.S., Aadalsvej 99, pg. 507 — **PB**
Diosynth Scandinavia, 26-28 Hovedgaden, pg. 44 — **IT**
Krupp Hoesch Stahl Aps, Hovedgaden 55 B, pg. 515 — **IT**
Milupa A/S, pg. 991 — **IT**
Neste Kemi Danmark A/S, Slotsmarken 12, pg. 915 — **IT**
Sonofon, Lyngsoe Alle 3, pg. 537 — **IT**
Statoil A/S Petrokemi, Hovedgaden 6, pg. 1298 — **IT**

Hvidovre

Diatom Verktoj A/S, Avedoreholmen 84, pg. 678 — **IT**
Electrolux Constructor, Hammerholmen 24-32, pg. 441 — **IT**
Frigoscandia A/S, Kanalholmen 25-29, pg. 606 — **PB**
Kgl. Brand A/S, Stamholmen 159, pg. 1257 — **IT**
Kali-Importen A/S, Biblioteksvej 51, pg. 108 — **IT**
Kanthal Norden AB, pg. 723 — **IT**
Nevi Finans A/S, Stamholmen 159, pg. 1257 — **IT**
Pfizer A/S, Vestre Gade 18, pg. 1283 — **PB**
G.L. Rexroth A/S, pg. 838 — **IT**
Roche A/S, pg. 1121 — **IT**
THORN Denmark, Gungevej 17, pg. 1386 — **IT**
THORN EMI Danmark A/S, Gungevej 17, pg. 428 — **IT**

Ikast

Bundy A/S, Romersvej 9, pg. 1341 — **IT**

Ishoj

Brother International Maskinaktieselskab A/S, Baldersbaekvej 18, pg. 229 — **IT**
A. Hansen's Amagerfroe A/S, Torslundevej 120, pg. 982 — **IT**
IWO A/S, Judusfrigrnen 7-9, pg. 441 — **IT**
Parker Hannifin Danmark A/S, Industrigrenen 11, pg. 1263 — **PB**
Ridgid Vaerktoj A/S, Postboks 55, Baldersbaekvej 24-26, pg. 577 — **PB**
SKA Storkokken, Industrigrenen 7-9, pg. 441 — **IT**
Vectur Aluminumstallningar, Baldersbaekrej 33, pg. 1128 — **PV**

Kabnhavn

Huls Danmark A/S, Capella/Hjornevej 4, pg. 1455 — **IT**

Kalundborg

Gyproc A/S, Hareskovvej 12, pg. 1200 — **IT**
Novo Nordisk A/S, Hallas Alle, pg. 987 — **IT**
Statoil A/S Kalundborg, pg. 1298 — **IT**

Karlslunde

DNP Denmark A/S, Skruegangen 2, pg. 363 — **IT**
Distributoren Interelko A/S, Silovej 18, pg. 710 — **IT**
Lowara Denmark, pg. 861 — **PB**

Karup

Danish Aerotech A/S, Flyvestation Karup, pg. 475 — **IT**

Kastrup

Circle Leman Air Freight, 149 Amager Landevej, pg. 373 — **PB**
Eli Lilly and Company Denmark APS, Tommerup Stationsvej 10, pg. 993 — **PB**
Nunc A/S, Kamstrupvej 90, pg. 130 — **IT**

Kibaek

Askov Mini-Kibaek Specialfabrik Aps, pg. 1205 — **IT**

Kirke Hyllinge

Danish Freeze-Drying ApS, pg. 430 — **IT**

Koge

FeF Chemicals A/S, Kobenhavnsvej 216, pg. 987 — **IT**
Lawter Intl. APS, Varkstedsvej 7-9, pg. 981 — **PB**
Pharmacia & Upjohn Koge Chemicals A/S, Kobenhavnsvej 140, pg. 1048 — **IT**
Primagaz Danmark A/S, Kosanvej, pg. 1155 — **IT**
Sun Chemical A/S, Gl. Lyngvej 2, pg. 371 — **IT**

Kokkedal

Berendsen PMC A/S, Kokkedal Industripark 12, pg. 1284 — **IT**
Kaalunds Produktion A/S, pg. 613 — **IT**
NIKE International Ltd.-Denmark, Kokkedal Industripark 101, pg. 1184 — **PB**

Kolding

Danfoss A/S Automatic Controls Div., Albuen 29, pg. 377 — **IT**
Dani-Tech A/S, Jernet 27, pg. 201 — **IT**
De danske Mejeriers Faellesindkeb amba, Bronzevej 1, pg. 826 — **IT**
Decra A/S, pg. 658 — **IT**
Indiana Tube Danmark A/S, pg. 780 — **PB**
Jotun-Danmark A/S, Jernet 6, pg. 714 — **IT**
Jotun Danmark A/S, pg. 715 — **IT**
LKM Group A/S, Postbox 74; DK-6000, pg. 1379 — **IT**
Merrild Kaffe, Laerkevej, pg. 1434 — **PB**
Reifenhauser Maskiner A/S, Toldbodgade 16, pg. 1101 — **IT**
Steel Paints A/S, Jernet 6, pg. 715 — **IT**
STILL Scandinavia A/S, pg. 811 — **IT**

Kolind

Perstrup Beton Industri A/S, pg. 1199 — **IT**

Korsor

CIBA Vision Danmark A/S, pg. 981 — **IT**
Kodak & H-Color A/S, Kodakvej 6, pg. 552 — **PB**
Scanglas A/S, Glasvej 2, pg. 1173 — **IT**

Kvistgaard

Saab Danmark A/S, Postbox 34, pg. 687 — **IT**

Lille Skensved

Copenhagen Pectin A/S, pg. 810 — **PB**

PB - *U.S. Public Companies Volume*
PV - *U.S. Private Companies Volume*
IT - *International Public & Private Companies Volume*

Logumkloster

Hydro Aluminium Automotive, Project Group Space Frame,
Industrivej 20, pg. 962 IT

Losning

Hydro Aluminium Hydro Trans, Hoymarksvej 5, pg. 962 IT

Lunderskov

GKN Wheels Nagbol A/S, Nagbol, pg. 535 IT

Lyngby

Borealis Holding A/S, Lyngby Hovedgade 96, pg. 914 IT
Caterpillar Commercial ApS, Firskovvej 4, pg. 317 PB
Electrolux A/S, Lundtoftevej 160, pg. 441 IT
Forbo A/S, Norgaarosvej 26, pg. 497 IT
Getinge Vaxjo A/S, Firskovvej 25b, pg. 552 IT
Greenlux A/S, Lundtofrevej 160, pg. 441 IT
Honeywell A/S, Lyngby Hovedgade 98, pg. 834 PB
Husqvarna A/S, Lundtoftegardsvej 99, pg. 441 IT
IBM Danmark A/S, Danish Div., Ngmoellezeg 91,
pg. 897 PB
IBM Danmark A/S, Nymollevsj 85, pg. 1043 PB
OLICOM A/S, Nybrovej 114, pg. 1001 IT
Olicom Nordic, Nybrovej 114, pg. 1001 IT
A/S Scan-Atlas Husholdningsapparater, Lundtdfteved,
pg. 441 IT
Skandinavisk Benckiser A/S, pg. 186 IT

Lynge

Effectona A/S, Noglegardsvej 10, pg. 1490 IT
Expandites Secomastic A/S, Smodevangen 5, pg. 236 IT

Lystrup

TERMA Elektronik AS, Hovmarken 4, pg. 1370 IT

Mariager

Dansk Salt I/S, 17 Hadsunvej, pg. 44 IT

Middelfart

Lydex A/S, Falstersvej 11/P.O. Box 99, pg. 1580 PB

Moldrup

B&C Danmark A/S, pg. 1091 IT
B&C Danmark Betontagstensvaerkene A/S, Postbox 40,
pg. 1092 IT

Naerum

Bruel & Kjaer Measurements A/S, Skodborgvek 307,
pg. 14 IT
Wellcome Danmark A/S, pg. 553 IT

Naestved

Danfoss System Hydraulik A/S, Aderupvej 41, pg. 377 IT
Icopal Tagentreprise SV Sjaeland A/S, pg. 658 IT
Neopac A/S, Grimstrupvej 185, pg. 864 IT

Nivaa

ISS Darenas International A/S, Teglbuen 10, pg. 656 IT

Noerresundby

Bates Emballage A/S, Stigsborgvej 36, pg. 476 IT
Kemira Danmark A/S, Limfjordsvej 27, pg. 728 IT
Shell of Aalborg, Aalborg Airport, pg. 1138 IT

Nordborg

DANFOSS A/S, pg. 376 IT
Danfoss A/S Automatic Controls Div., pg. 377 IT
Danfoss A/S Building Controls Div., pg. 377 IT
Danfoss A/S Burner Controls Div., pg. 377 IT
Danfoss A/S Household Compressors Div., pg. 377 IT
Danfoss A/S Instrumentation, pg. 377 IT
Danfoss A/S Mobile Hydraulics Div., pg. 377 IT

Nyborg

Nyborg Plast International A/S, Tasingevej 1, pg. 476 IT

Nykobing

Simonsen & Sons Limited, Mogelvangs Plads 7,
pg. 894 IT

Odense

Asea Brown Boveri Danmark A/S, Petersmidvej 1,
pg. 8 IT
Jacobs Suchard Kaffe A/S, Tagtaeckervej 8, pg. 1289 PB
KME Danmark ApS, Landbrugsvej 8, pg. 719 IT
Nordfoil Odense Flexible A.p.S., pg. 441 IT
SK Emballage A/S, Thorslundsvej 7, pg. 476 IT

Scan-Ad Odense A/S, Christiansgade 70, pg. 1198 IT
Stora Dalum A/S, Dalumvej 116, pg. 1303 IT
Thrige Agro A/S, Tolderlundsvej 3, pg. 1386 IT
Thrige Electric, Tolderlundsvej 3, pg. 1387 IT
Thrige-Titan A/S, Tolderlundsvej 3, pg. 1387 IT
THRIGE-TITAN GROUP, Tolderlundsvej 3, pg. 1386 IT
Wormald International (Scandinavia) A/S, Teglvaerksveg
47, pg. 1651 PB

Olgod

HTH Kokkener A/S, Industrivej 6, pg. 1302 IT

Pandrup

Dancall Telecom A/S, Klokkestobervej 4, pg. 206 IT

Pedersborg

Baxenden Scandinavia ApS, Fulbyvej 2, pg. 1774 PB

Randers

Avery Etikettering A/S, Tjaerbyvei 90, pg. 153 PB
Neopac A/S, pg. 864 IT
Nilfisk-Gerni A/S, Myntevej 2, pg. 932 IT
Vink AS, Kristrup Engvej 9, pg. 1210 IT

Rastatt

BWR GmbH, pg. 355 IT

Ringe

International ELCO, A.p.S., Algade 7, pg. 775 IT

Ringkobing

Lydig af Scandinavia A/S, Vesterland 6-8, pg. 787 PB

Ringsted

Delsey A/S, Norretov 14, 1, pg. 192 IT

Risskov

A/S Fibo, Voldbergvej 16, pg. 1200 IT
Hewlett-Packard A/S, Voldbjergvej 14-18, pg. 818 PB
Kodak & H-Color A/S, Lystrupvej 62, pg. 552 PB
A/S P. Wallmann & Co., Nordlandsvej 76-78, pg. 966 IT

Rodekro

Nordisk Bygge Kemi A/S, Hallandsvej 1, pg. 1466 IT

Roedovre

A/S Akerlund & Rausing, Hojnaaesvej 83, pg. 33 IT
Alfa-Laval Zeta A/S, Krondalvej 7, pg. 1379 IT
Duni A/S, Brandstrupvej 10, pg. 421 IT
Electrolux-Wascator A/S, Roskuldeva 527, pg. 441 IT
Radiometer International A/S, Valhojs Alle 176,
pg. 1083 IT
Schering A/S, Fjeldhammerveij 8, pg. 1204 IT
Struers A/S, Valhojs Alle 176, pg. 1083 IT

Roskilde

Bekaert A/S, Algade 26, pg. 184 IT
Life Technologies A/S, pg. 505 PB
Nordisk Case A/S, Industrivej 3-7, P.O. Box 159,
pg. 1580 PB
Sodra Timber AB, Sotoften 3, pg. 1276 IT
Svend Mullers Emballagefabrik ApS, pg. 1146 IT
Unicon Beton Holding A/S, Kogevej 172, pg. 475 IT

Seden

Mix-A-Mix A/S, pg. 1054 PB

Silkeborg

DAB-SILKEBORG A/S, P.O. Box 309, Kejlstrupvej 71,
pg. 350 IT
Danfoss A/S Comfort Div., Harupvaenget 11, pg. 377 IT
Fiskars Danmark A/S, Postbox 360, pg. 492 IT

Skanderborg

Tretorn A/S, Gronlandsvej 8, pg. 1072 IT

Skive

Nordisk Aluminium a.s., Ulvevej 2, pg. 964 IT
Nordsten, Gyrovej 1-5, pg. 1386 IT
VG Glas, Hjortevej 3, pg. 1173 IT

Skovlunde

CPC Foods A/S, Mileparken 9, pg. 225 PB
HyperVision A/S, Meterbuen 6-12, pg. 146 IT
Axel Johnson Teknik A/S, pg. 712 IT
SASIB Bakery Nordic A/S, Tonsbakken 10, pg. 1194 IT
Tektronix A/S, pg. 1567 PB
Wasabrod A/S, Mileparken 18, pg. 986 IT

Wisapak Multicoate A/S, Literbuen 17, pg. 1430 IT

Slagelse

Svedala Danmark, pg. 1323 IT

Smorum

ALNAB/Scana Armatur A/S, Kong Svenda Vej 65,
pg. 549 IT

Soeborg

Alfa-Laval Separation A/S, Maskinvej 5, pg. 1378 IT
Berendsen Components A/S, 8 Telefonvej, pg. 1284 IT
Berendsen Textil Service A/S, 1 Klausdalsbrovej,
pg. 1284 IT
Ferrosan A/S, Sydmarken 5, pg. 987 IT
Ferrosan Danmark A/S, Sydmarken 5, pg. 987 IT
Ferrosan International A/S, Sydmarken 5, pg. 987 IT
Fisons A/S, Rosenkaeret 22 B, pg. 1111 IT
International Rectifier Company (Great Britain) Limited,
pg. 907 PB
Landis & Staefa Danmark A/S, Tobaksvejen 21,
pg. 800 IT
Opel Danmark, Tobaksvejen 22, pg. 723 PB
Rhone-Poulenc Danmark A/S, Gladsaxevej 378,
pg. 1112 IT
SOPHUS BERENDSEN A/S, 1, Klausdalsbrovej,
pg. 1284 IT

Sollerod

Dansk Slurry Seal I/S, pg. 658 IT
Dansk Vejrenovering I/S, pg. 658 IT

Stenlose

VB Autobatteri A/S, Postbox 29, Knud Bro Alle 1,
pg. 1452 IT
VARTA Batteri A/S, Postbox 29, Knud Bro Alle 1,
pg. 1452 IT

Struer

BANG & OLUFSEN A/S, Peter Bangs Vej 15, pg. 145 IT
DIAX Telekomm A/S, Faelledvej 17, pg. 1365 IT
Foodane A/S, Kjelksmarkvej 2, pg. 1464 IT
VESTJYSKE SLAGTERIER, Havnevej 8, pg. 1464 IT

Svendborg

Nordisk Kelloggs A/S, Ostre Havnevej 25, pg. 948 PB
VASA I/S, pg. 659 IT

Tastrup

Crawford Door A/S, Taastrupggaardsvej 8, pg. 269 IT
Crown Cork Co. (Scandinavia) A/S, Hoerskaetten 13,
pg. 464 PB
Domus Forsikringsaktieselskabet A/S, Banestroget 21,
pg. 61 IT
Ericsson Radio Systems A/S, Tastrupgardsvej 10,
pg. 1367 IT
Forsikringsaktieselskabet (RAS) Allianz Nordeuropa,
Banestroget 21, pg. 60 IT
Henkel Barnangen A/S, pg. 612 IT
Hoogovens Aluminium Danmark A/S, Helgeshoj Allee 24,
pg. 755 IT
Kodak A/S, Dybendal Alle 10, pg. 552 PB
Krupp MaK Scandinavia A/S, Taastrupgardsvej 20-22,
pg. 510 IT
Metsa-Serla Tissue A/S, Maekaervej 5, pg. 864 IT
Millipore AS, Roskildevej 342, pg. 1113 PB
MoDo Danmark A/S, Selsmosevej 2, pg. 887 IT
Nokia Telecommunications A/S, Horskatten 3, pg. 953 IT
Nordeuropa Forsikringaktieselskabet A/S, Banestroget 21,
pg. 62 IT
Perstorp A/S Decorative Laminate, Kogevej 12,
pg. 1038 IT
Perstorp Chemitec A/S, Kogevej 164, pg. 1037 IT
Perstorp Gulv A/S, Kogevej 12, pg. 1039 IT
Unitruck A/S, Rugvaenget 22, pg. 97 IT

Thisted

Alkaline Batteries A/S, Tigervoj 1, pg. 537 IT

Tinglev

Danfoss A/S Tinglev Fabrikken, Mads Clausensvej 75,
pg. 377 IT

Tjaereborg

Tjaereborg Sten og Grus I/S, Ndr. Strandvej 33,
pg. 1092 IT

Tollose

Battenfeld Danmark A/S, Stengaardsvej 7, pg. 825 IT

Tommerup

Dampa A/S, Hojelykkevej 4, pg. 475 IT
Nyborg Vas kerimaskiner A/S, pg. 441 IT

PB - U.S. Public Companies Volume
PV - U.S. Private Companies Volume
IT - International Public & Private Companies Volume

1568

Geographic Index-Non U.S.

Tonder

Heat Transfer Tonder, Hydrovej 6, pg. 962   **IT**
Hydro Aluminium Tonder, Bygmestervej 7, pg. 963   **IT**

Tureby

Sonesson Indretning ApS, Turebyvej 1, pg. 23   **IT**

Vaerlose

ABS Pumper A/S, Kirke Vaerlosevej 14, pg. 270   **IT**
Gestetner A/S, Lejrvej 25, pg. 1115   **IT**
Netstal Skandinavien A/S, pg. 836   **IT**
Norske Skog Danmark A.S., Kr. Vaerlosevej 95,
   pg. 966   **IT**

Valby

Aalborg Portland Holding A/S, Vigerslev Alle 77,
   pg. 475   **IT**
FLS Automation A/S, Ramsingsvej 32, pg. 475   **IT**
FLS Cement Investments A/S, Vigerslev Alle 77,
   pg. 476   **IT**
FLS Data A/S, Ramsingsvej 7, pg. 476   **IT**
FLS Energy A/S, Vigerslev Alle 77, pg. 476   **IT**
FLS Finance A/S, Vigerslev Alle 77, pg. 476   **IT**
FLS INDUSTRIES A/S, Vigerslev Alle 77, pg. 474   **IT**
FLS Maskinteknik A/S, Gammel Koge Landevej 22,
   pg. 475   **IT**
FLS Miljo A/S, Ramsingsvej 30, pg. 475   **IT**
FLS Real Estate A/S, Vigerslev Alle 77, pg. 476   **IT**
IDC Scandinavia A/S, Carl Jacobsens Vej 25, pg. 571   **PV**
IDG Denmark A/S, Carl Jacobsens Vej 25, pg. 570   **PV**
F.L. Smidth-Fuller Engineering A/S, Vigerslev Alle 77,
   pg. 475   **IT**

Vallensbaek

Avesta Sheffield A/S, pg. 221   **IT**
Gambro Medicoteknik A/S, Jydekrogen 8, pg. 668   **IT**
Linatex A/S, Vejlegardsvej 38, pg. 678   **IT**
Nordisk Simplex A/S, Vejlegardsvej 34, pg. 1088   **IT**
Oki Systems (Danmark) A.S., Park Alle 382, pg. 1000   **IT**
Ostermann Petersen Bros. Ltd., Jydekrogen 40,
   pg. 1202   **IT**

Vamdrup

Glasuld A/S, Ostermarksvej 4, pg. 1176   **IT**

Varde

Optiroc A.S., Sonderskovvej 120, pg. 1200   **IT**

Vedbaek

Elkem Danmark a/s, Kohavevej 3, pg. 447   **IT**
Krups A/S, Staktoften 22, pg. 896   **IT**
Moulinex A/S, SCA, Staktoften 22, pg. 896   **IT**

Vejen

Alfa Solo Margarinefabrikken AS, Vestergade 2,
   pg. 1436   **IT**
KE-Burgmann A/S, Park Alle 34, pg. 234   **IT**

Vejle

Alfa-Laval Agri Scandinavia A/S, Rytterskolen Hojen,
   pg. 1379   **IT**
Landis & Staefa Maleteknik A/S, Islandsvej 1, pg. 801   **IT**
Soren Berggreen & Co. A/S, Bodkervej 3, pg. 864   **IT**

Viborg

Frionor Danmark A/S, Raunsbjergvej 69, pg. 516   **IT**
Viborg Asfaltfabrik I/S, pg. 659   **IT**
Vildsund Asfaltfabrik I/S, pg. 659   **IT**

Viby

AMP Danmark, Gunnar Clausens Vej 36, pg. 8   **PB**
Andelssmar A.m.b.a., Skanderborgvej 277, pg. 826   **IT**
Danfoss A/S Viby Fabrikken, Jens Juuls Vej 9, pg. 377   **IT**
Korn-og Foderstof Kompagniet (KFK) A/S, Grondalsvej 1,
   pg. 964   **IT**
MD FOODS, Skanderborgvej 277, pg. 826   **IT**
MD Foods Ingriedients amba, Skanderborgvej 277,
   pg. 826   **IT**
Mejeriernes Maelkedisponeringsselskab A.m.b.a,
   Skanderborgvej 277, pg. 826   **IT**
Mejeriernes Produktionsselskab A.m.b.a., Skanderborgvej
   277, pg. 826   **IT**

Videbaek

Danmark Protein A/S, Norre Vium, Sonderrupvej, 11,
   pg. 1279   **IT**

Virum

Burmeister & Wain Energi A/S, Teknikerbyen 23,
   pg. 398   **IT**
Cabelco ApS, Abildgaardsvej 45, pg. 1365   **IT**

Nordisk Factoring A/S, Teknikerkyen 21, pg. 521   **IT**

DJIBOUTI

Djibouti

BCI Mer Rouge, Place Lagarde, pg. 163   **IT**
Shell Djibouti, Jetee Duparachy, pg. 1137   **IT**
Sodeca, Aeroport de Djibouti, pg. 560   **IT**
Sodras (Societe Djiboutienne de restauration Aeronotique
   et de Servces), pg. 560   **IT**

DOMINICAN REPUBLIC

Bonao

Falconbridge Dominicana, C. por A., pg. 434   **IT**

LaRomana

Echlin Dominicana, S.A., pg. 561   **PB**

LaVega

Checkpoint Carriben, Apartado 30-C, pg. 343   **PB**

San Cristobal

H.B. Fuller Dominicana, S.A., Apartado No. 004, Piedra
   Blanca, pg. 687   **PB**

San Pedro de Marcoris

TII Dominicana Inc., Calle Lateral No. 2, Solar 6, Section
   3B, pg. 1556   **PB**

Santiago

Sanitarios Dominicanos, S.A., P.O. Box 910, pg. 92   **PB**

Santo Domingo

AGA-Quinsa S.A., pg. 13   **IT**
BASF Dominicana S.A., Edificio Scotiabank-5to Piso, Ave.
   John F. Kennedy/Lope de Vega, pg. 106   **IT**
B.F.C. Antilles-Guyane, pg. 314   **IT**
Banco Santander, Jose Amado Soler 57, pg. 144   **IT**
Leo Burnett Inc., Prolongacion Calle Arabia No. 17,
   pg. 185   **PV**
Caribe Freight, Las Americas A Ero Puerto, pg. 211   **PV**
The Chase Manhattan Bank, N.A., Apartado 1408, Avenida
   John F. Kennedy & Tiradentes, pg. 697   **PB**
Checkpoint Carriben, Zona Franca Industrial, Los
   Alcarrizos, pg. 343   **PB**
CIBA-GEIGY Caribe S.A., Calle H N 17, Esq. Diagonal,
   pg. 976   **IT**
Colgate-Palmolive, Inc., Avenida Maximo Gomez Esquina,
   pg. 398   **IT**
Compania Dominicana de Telefonos, C. por A., Abraham
   Lincoln 1101, P.O. Box 1377, pg. 697   **IT**
CUNA Mutual Group-Dominican Republic, 16 de Agosto
   No. 35, pg. 296   **PV**
Curacao Trading Company (Dominicana) C. Por A., Av.
   Leopoldo Navarro 28, pg. 280   **IT**
ELCO Dominicana, S.A., Calle el Vergel No. 8, Ensanche el
   Vergel, pg. 993   **PB**
Electrolux Lagares C. por A., Apartado 1851, pg. 441   **IT**
ESACOMP, Edificio Mercantil Del Caribe, Avenbida John F.
   Kennedy No. 11, pg. 817   **PB**
Etiquetas Internacionales, Inc., San Isidro St., Km. 17,
   pg. 132   **IT**
Ideal Dominicana, S.A., Avenida Independencia #506,
   pg. 628   **IT**
Knorr Alimentaria, pg. 224   **PB**
Kodak Dominicana, Av. Charles Sumner No. 17,
   pg. 553   **IT**
Minera Hispaniola, S.A., Edif. Plza Compostela, Ste.301,
   Avenida John F. Kennedy, Esquina Calle #7,
   pg. 302   **IT**
NRG Del Caribe SA, Pedro Henriquez Urena Street,
   Tiradentes Avenue, pg. 1116   **IT**
Productos Avon, S.A., Apartado Postal 21727, pg. 156   **PB**
Productos Del Tropico C. por A., pg. 160   **PV**
Productos Roche Dominicana, S.A., pg. 1121   **IT**
Publicitaria Cumbre, Jose Contreras No. 14, pg. 1422   **PB**
Quimica Dominicana, pg. 1141   **IT**
Refineria Dominicana de Petroleo, S.A., pg. 1141   **IT**
Sandoz Dominica, C. por A., pg. 984   **IT**
Shell Company (W.I.) Ltd, Edificio Alico 3rd Floor, Ave.
   Abraham Lincoln, pg. 1141   **IT**
Sociedad Dominicana de Conservas y Alimentos S.A.,
   pg. 916   **IT**
Staff/DMB&B, Edificio Concordia, Ste. 211, C/Jose A.
   Soler, Esq. A. Lincoln, pg. 305   **PV**
3M Dominicana S.A., Ave. Luperon, pg. 1606   **PV**
Wackenhut Dominicana, S.A., Paseo de los Locutores N36,
   pg. 1731   **PB**
Young & Rubicam Damaris, C. por A., Avenida de los
   Proceres, Corner Erik Leonard Ekman, pg. 1200   **PV**
Zeneca Dominicana SA, Fantino Falco, no. 7 Naco,
   pg. 1526   **IT**

ECUADOR

Cuenca

Ferro Ecuatoriana S.A., P.O. Box 01-01-1118, pg. 619   **PB**

Guayaquil

Balmanta S.A., Box 3842, pg. 172   **PB**
Bolivar, Compania de Seguros del Ecuador, Pinchincha Y
   Nueve, Pichincha 307 5th Flr., pg. 355   **PB**
Citibank, N.A. Guayaquil, Avenida 9 de Octubre y Chile,
   pg. 378   **PB**
Colgate-Palmolive Del Ecuador, S.A., Calle 10 Y Av. D.
   Comin, pg. 398   **PB**
Compania Ecuatoriana de Balsa S.A., Box 3842,
   pg. 172   **PB**
Creacional/DMB&B, Costanera 611 Y Las Morijas,
   pg. 303   **PV**
Det Norske Veritas, Los Ceibos Calle 7a, 122, pg. 396   **PB**
Ecuatoriana de Sal y Productos Quimicos C.A. (ECUASAL),
   Rocafuerte 742-746, pg. 1135   **PB**
Empacadora Ecuatoriana-Danesa (ECUADASA) S.A.,
   pg. 431   **IT**
H.B. Fuller Ecuador, S.A., Casilla Postal 09-01-7441,
   pg. 687   **PB**
Granjas Porcinas del Ecuador (Granporsa) S.A.,
   pg. 431   **IT**
Home Products Inc., CDLA. Urdesa Norte, Calle Ira. No.
   106-108, pg. 81   **PB**
Johnson & Johnson del Ecuador S.A., Circunvalacion Sur
   #309 Entre, pg. 930   **PB**
Johnsonwax del Ecuador S.A., P.O. Box 874, pg. 593   **PV**
La Cemento Nacional C.A., Via a la Costa Km 7 1/2,
   pg. 630   **IT**
La Nacional Compania de Seguros Generales S.A.,
   Panama 809 y V.M. Rendon, pg. 91   **IT**
La Nacional Compania Inmobiliaria, Panama 809 y V.M.
   Rendon, pg. 91   **IT**
Lubricantes y Tambores del Ecuador, C.A., Casilla No.
   6071, pg. 1584   **PB**
Maderas Secas C.A. (Maseca), Box 3842, pg. 172   **PB**
Mead Johnson Ecuador, S.A., Edificio Mecanos Ave.
   America 3er Piso, pg. 256   **PB**
Mitsui del Ecuador S.A., Edificio Seguros Condor, P. Ycasa
   302, 4, pg. 882   **IT**
Morfecor, C.A., Rocafuerre No. 742-746, pg. 1135   **PB**
Productos del Pacifico S.A., Box 3842, pg. 172   **PB**
Publicitas C.A., 1 ero de Mayo, 812 y Los Rios,
   pg. 1422   **PB**
Swiss Bank Corporation, Av. 9 de Octubre 2101 y,
   pg. 1330   **IT**
3M Ecuador C.A., KM 1.5 Via Duran Tambo, pg. 1606   **PB**

Guayas

Bristol-Myers Ecuatoriana, S.A., Ave. De Las Americas Edif.
   Mecanos Piso 3, pg. 255   **PB**
Laboratorios Bristol del Ecuador S.A., Ave. De Las
   Americas Edif Mecanos Piso 3, pg. 256   **PB**

Quito

AGA del Ecuador C.A., P.O. Box 17-01-2512, pg. 13   **IT**
Armenonic del Ecuador, S.A., Inaquito Torre de Marfil, Ave.
   Amazonas #3233, pg. 949   **IT**
BASF Ecuatoriana S.A., Valladolid 511 y Madrid,
   pg. 106   **IT**
Banco Mundial, Edifico Corp. Fin. Nacional, Calle Juan
   Leon Mera #130 y Ave. Patria, pg. 1189   **PV**
CCF Quito, P.O. Box 17 07 9022, Avenida 12 de Octubre,
   pg. 342   **IT**
C.Y.E.D.E. Cia, Ltda., Avenida Eloy Alfaro 1749 Belgica,
   pg. 816   **PB**
CIBA-GEIGY Ecuatoriana SA, pg. 976   **IT**
Condor Mine S.A., Ave 6 de Diciembre 2816, y James
   Orton, Edificio Josueth Gonzalez, pg. 1345   **IT**
Corporacion Microsoft del Ecuador, pg. 1108   **PB**
Digicom Cia. Ltda., Avenida de Los Shyris, pg. 817   **PB**
Ecuasistem, Av. Patria 640 y Amazonas, pg. 569   **PV**
Ecuatoriana de Lubricantes, pg. 1141   **IT**
Ecuatoriana de Petroquimicos Petrolite S.A., Edificio
   Albatros, Av. de los Shyris, pg. 166   **PB**
Ecuavia Oriente S.A., Casilla de Correo, 3418,
   pg. 1281   **PB**
C.A. Electrolux, Casilla 2235, pg. 441   **IT**
General Motors Del Ecuador S.A., pg. 722   **PB**
Helmerich & Payne del Ecuador, Inc., Avenida Republica
   1650 y Azuay, pg. 808   **PB**
IBM del Ecuador, C.A., pg. 897   **PB**
ING Bank Quito, Av. Amazinas 4545 y Pereira, pg. 649   **IT**
Ideal-Alambrec S.A., Casilla 19-124 M, pg. 185   **IT**
Indi Servicios C. Ltda., Av. Eloy Alfaro 939 Y Amazonas,
   pg. 363   **IT**
Inedeca S.A., pg. 920   **IT**
Intairdril Ltd., pg. 1316   **IT**
MAPFRE Ecuador, S.A., Av. Amazonas, 353, pg. 333   **IT**
Mathieu Ecuador, Av. Gaspar de Villaroel 1211,
   pg. 846   **IT**
Milchem Western Hemisphere Inc., Avenida de la
   Republica, 1954 y 10 deAgosto, Segundo Piso,
   pg. 167   **PB**
Mitsui del Ecuador S.A., Edificio Francisco de Orellana
   Avenida O, pg. 882   **IT**
Morgan Grenfell (Ecuador), Calle Ramiro Barba,
   pg. 405   **IT**
Nalco Ecuador S.A., Avenida Eloy Alfaro, pg. 1150   **PB**
Nestle Ecuador S.A., pg. 921   **IT**

Nissho Iwai del Ecuador S.A., Av. 12 de Octubre No. 1942 Y Cordero, pg. 948 **IT**
Nutrinsa, S.A., pg. 160 **PV**
Occidental Exploration and Production Company, Av. Rio Amazonas 3837 y Corea, 10 Piso, Oficino 1001, pg. 1210 **PB**
Omnibus BB Transportes, S.A., Kilometro 5 1/2 Panamericana Norte, pg. 723 **PB**
Panalquita, Panalpina Transportes Mundiales Ecuador S.A., pg. 1023 **IT**
S.B. Penick Del Ecuador, S.A., pg. 447 **PB**
Pfizer C.A., Baron de Carondelet No. 621, pg. 1282 **PB**
Quimica Borden Ecuatoriana, S.A., pg. 160 **PV**
Rivas & Herrera C./Young & Rubicam, Checoslavaquia, 620 y Suiza, pg. 1200 **PV**
Roche Ecuador S.A., pg. 1121 **IT**
Rorer De Ecuador, S.A., Nattermann Ecuatoriano C.A., Casilla 9243 (Almagro) Azeniza, pg. 1111 **IT**
Sandoz Latinoamericana (Ecuador) S.A., pg. 985 **IT**
Seguridad Movil del Ecuador, S.A., Valladolid N936y Cordero Casilla N4791, pg. 1731 **IT**
Sistemas de Informacion Decision C.A., Reina Victoria 562, pg. 823 **PB**
Square D Company Andina S.A., Ave. 10 De Agosto, pg. 1209 **PB**
Telefonos Ericsson C.A., Hernandez de Giron 452 y Av. America, pg. 1371 **IT**
Texaco Petroleum Co., pg. 1584 **PB**
Triton Ecuador Inc., LLC, pg. 1640 **PB**
Uniplex, Cristobal Gangotena, 326 y Coruna, pg. 1229 **PB**
Valencia y Asociados Publicidad, Av. Coruna 1311 y San Ignacio, pg. 186 **PV**
Wackenhut del Ecuador, S.A., Valladolid 936y Cordero Casilla 4791, pg. 1731 **PB**
Xerox del Ecuador, S.A., pg. 1785 **PB**

Sangolqui

Enkador S.A., Parroquina Selva Alegre, pg. 46 **IT**

EGYPT

Alexandria

Alexandria Automotive Company SAE, Ave. Victor Emmannuell III, pg. 665 **PB**
Det Norske Veritas, Ibrahim Abdel-Sayed & Patrice Lomomba, pg. 397 **IT**
R.P. Scherer Egypt, P.O. Box 49 Sidi Gaber, pg. 1438 **PB**
Suez Electronics S.A.E., Alexandria, 42, Saad Zaghloul Street, pg. 1152 **IT**

Cairo

Air Malta - Cairo, Nile Hilton Commercial Ctr., Executive Suite 34, 2 Tahir Square, pg. 38 **IT**
Arab Elevators Co., pg. 1205 **IT**
Arab International Insurance Company, 28 Talaat Harb Street, pg. 61 **IT**
BASF Aktiengesellschaft, 11, Aboul Feda Street, pg. 105 **IT**
Bankers Trust New York Corporation, 17 Kasr el Nil St., 3rd Fl., pg. 186 **PB**
Banque du Caire Barclays Intl. Bank SAE, 12 Midan El Sheikh Youssef, pg. 165 **IT**
Banque Indosuez, 9 Mariette Pacha Street, pg. 315 **IT**
Banque Paribas-Egypte, 6A rue Gankhi, (ci-devant rue El Salsoul), pg. 320 **IT**
Bull Egypte, World Trade Center, 11-13 Corniche El Nil, pg. 316 **IT**
Bureau Rhone-Poulenc, 2 rue Samanoud, pg. 1112 **IT**
CCF Cairo, BP 2687, 26 Mahmoud Bassiouni St., 4th Fl., pg. 343 **IT**
Cairo Foods Industries SAE, Nine Hussein Ahmed Rashad St., pg. 806 **PB**
CIBA-GEIGY Egypt SAE, 4, Yanbu St., Dokki, pg. 976 **IT**
CIBA-GEIGY Ltd.-Technical Assistance Office, 4, Yanbu Street, pg. 978 **IT**
CIBA-GEIGY Plastics (Egypt) S.A.E., 4, Yanbu Street, pg. 978 **IT**
CIBA-GEIGY-Scientific Office Pharmaceuticals, 14, Saray El Ezbekia, pg. 979 **IT**
Citibank, N.A. Cairo, 4 Ahmed Pasha St., pg. 378 **PB**
Commerzbank AG Representative Office-Cairo, Banque Misr Tower, 153 Mohamed Farid Street, pg. 311 **IT**
Corro-Coat Egypt Ltd., pg. 715 **IT**
Credit International d'Egypte, 46 El Batal Amhed Abdel Aziz St., pg. 343 **IT**
Daewoo Corp. - Cairo, pg. 358 **IT**
Darwish Consulting Engineers, 27, Nazih Khalifa St. (Ex Baroon), pg. 606 **IT**
Deminex Egypt, P.O. Box 1146, pg. 1461 **IT**
Deutsche Bank AG (Cairo), 23 Kasr el Nil Street, pg. 404 **IT**
Dresdner Bank AG, Nile Tower Bldg. 12th Fl., 21/23 Giza St., Giza, pg. 419 **IT**
ESAB Egypt, 1 Sherifein St., pg. 282 **IT**
Egybrit, 7 el Thawra St. El Korba, pg. 97 **IT**
Egypt Otsuka Pharmaceutical Co., S.A.E., 10th of Ramadan City, pg. 1014 **IT**
Egyptian Aluminium Products Company, 4, Wisa Wassef St., By Kobri El Gamaa, Giza, pg. 1386 **IT**
Egyptian British Bank S.A.E., Abu El Feda Building, 3 Abu El Feda Street, Zamalek, pg. 581 **IT**
Egyptian Fund Management Group, 3 Ahmed Nessim Street, pg. 343 **IT**
El-Mohandes Jotun Egypt, 20 Hosny El Ashmawy St., pg. 715 **IT**
Gearhart M.E. Holdings, Inc., pg. 776 **PB**

General Motors Egypt S.A.E., Abu El Fida Bldg., 3 Abu El Fide St., pg. 692 **IT**
General Motors Egypt S.A.E., Abu El Fida Bldg., 3 Abu El Fide St., pg. 724 **PB**
General Trading & Chemicals Co., 26, Sherif Street, pg. 108 **IT**
Gillette Internile S.A.E., 29, Abu El Feda St., pg. 745 **PB**
Gist-Brocades Egypt S.A.E., P.O. Box 2038, pg. 1142 **IT**
Gray Tool International Corporation, c/o Engineering & Consulting, 11 Gabelaya Street, pg. 6 **IT**
Gulf of Suez Petroleum Company, Palestine St., 4th Sector, pg. 102 **PB**
Honeywell Egypt Ltd., 33 Nabei Al Wakkad St., pg. 834 **IT**
Industrie de Froid S.A.E., Kaliub, pg. 920 **IT**
Intermarkets Egypt, 42 Abdel Monheim Riad St., pg. 680 **IT**
International Flavors & Fragrances, pg. 899 **IT**
Japan Airlines Company, Ltd., Nile Hotel, Tahrir Square, pg. 700 **IT**
John Crane Middle East - Western Region, 5 Moharam Shawki Street, pg. 1339 **IT**
Johnson & Johnson (Egypt) S.A.E., 24 Abdul Moneim Haffaz Street, pg. 930 **PV**
Johnson Wax, 44 El Tayaran St., pg. 593 **PV**
Knoll Scientific Office, 3 Amman Square, pg. 109 **IT**
Kodak (Egypt) S.A., 20 Adley St., pg. 553 **PB**
Lockheed Corporation (International) S.A., 105 Omar Ibn El Khattab St., Ninth Fl., Apt. 93, pg. 1009 **PB**
MFA Misr Freight Agencies S.a.r.l., 64, Gameat El Dowal Al Arabia Str., pg. 383 **IT**
MISR-America International Bank S.A.E., 5 Midan El Saraya Kobra, pg. 183 **IT**
MISR DYWIDAG, 24 Haroun St., pg. 425 **IT**
MISR Pioneer Seed Co. S.A.E., 9b Army Forces Bldg., In Front of Workers University, pg. 1299 **PB**
Marryat & Scott Egypt-S.A., 20 Abu Bakr El Sedik St Mohandessin, pg. 748 **IT**
Mass Publishing, 9 El Tahrir Str., pg. 1748 **PB**
Medequip, 1 Shafik Ghorbal St., pg. 822 **PB**
Mitsui & Co., Ltd., No. 6 Ebn Zanki St., Zamalek, pg. 881 **IT**
Mobil Oil Egypt (S.A.E.), 1097 Cornish el Nil, pg. 1119 **IT**
National Bank of Greece Cairo Branch, pg. 907 **IT**
National Bank of Pakistan-Cairo, 64 Gameat Al-Dawal, Al Arabia Street, pg. 908 **IT**
National Dehydration Company, pg. 1067 **PB**
Noaman Engineering Co., 10, Dessouk Str., Agouza, pg. 550 **IT**
Norsk Hydro Exploration Egypt a.s, House 10, Road 261, pg. 964 **IT**
Novo Nordisk A/S, World Trade Ctr., Office Tower, 8th Floor, 1191 Corniche El Nil, pg. 988 **IT**
Oracle Egypt, 59, Iran St., pg. 1228 **PB**
Orascom, 160, 26th July St., pg. 822 **PB**
Pechiney Moyen-Orient, 9, Dessouk Street, pg. 1031 **IT**
Pfizer Egypt S.A.E., 47 Ramses St., Postal Code 11511, pg. 1282 **PB**
Ram Representative Office-Egypt, 14 Alys Str., pg. 741 **IT**
Raychem Egypt Ltd., 8 Midan Haynet El Tadris, pg. 1362 **PB**
Santa Fe International (Egypt) Inc., P.O. Box 341, pg. 765 **IT**
Schindler Ltd., pg. 1205 **IT**
Shell Winning NV, 6 Hassan el Sheriey St., pg. 1140 **IT**
Shimadzu Mid-East Consulting Office, Abu El Feda Bldg, 14th Fl., 3 Abu Feda Street, Zamalek, pg. 1232 **IT**
Societa Ital. per Condotte D'Acqua-Egypt, Nile Hilton Hotel, pg. 655 **IT**
The Sumitomo Bank, Ltd.-Cairo Representative Office, 12th Fl., Nile Tower Bldg., 21-23 Giza St., pg. 1309 **IT**
Swisspharma S.A.E., El Sawah St., pg. 986 **IT**
Systems and Projects Engineering Co., 132, El Tahreer Street, Dokki, pg. 1370 **IT**
Telefonaktiebolaget LM Ericsson Egypt, 1, Wadi El Nil, Mohandeseen, pg. 1370 **IT**
The World Bank, World Trade Ctr., 15th Fl., 1191 Corniche El-Ni., pg. 1189 **PV**

Giza

AMA Leo Burnett, El Nahda Tower, 7th Fl., 21 Ahmed Orab St., pg. 184 **IT**
The Bank of New York, 9 Abdelmounim Riyad St., Dokki, pg. 179 **PB**
DMB&B Egypt Ltd., 126 El Nile St. Dokki, 3rd Fl., Apt. 8, pg. 303 **PV**
Egypor Trade, 42 El-Zhraa St., pg. 817 **PB**
Kubota Corp.-Cairo Office, Nile Tower Bldg., 12th Fl., 21-23 Guize St., pg. 762 **IT**
Misr International Bank S.A.E., 54 El Batal Ahmed Abdel Aziz St. El., pg. 1181 **IT**
Rovigyp Ltd., pg. 1122 **IT**

Heliopolis

General Dynamics Services Company, 105 Omar EBN El Khattab Street, pg. 709 **PB**
General Dynamics Services Company, 7 Aflaton St., pg. 709 **PB**
General Dynamics Services Company, 49 Beirut St., pg. 709 **PB**
Geosource Co. (Cayman) Ltd., 9, Dr. E1 Mahrouki Street, pg. 777 **PB**
Laing Projects BV, 16 Mohamed El Mandy Street, pg. 797 **IT**

Ismailia

Goldstar Egypt Electronics S.A.E., P.O. Box No. 14, pg. 779 **IT**

Maadi

Amoco Egypt Oil Company, 14, Road 252, pg. 102 **PB**
Repsol Exploration Egypt S.A., 58 Rd., 105, pg. 1105 **IT**

Sadat City

Van Leer Egypt L.L.C., pg. 1146 **IT**

EL SALVADOR

Nueva San Salvador

Kimberly-Clark de Centro America S.A., Apartado Postal No. 145, pg. 959 **PB**

San Salvador

BASF de El Salvador, S.A. de C.V., Paseo Gral. Escalon y 79. Av. Norte, pg. 105 **IT**
Banco de Santander, Suba Reforma, 183 - apdo. B, Apdos. Manuel Henry Calderon, pg. 144 **IT**
Black & Decker De El Salvador S.A. de C.V., Condominio Plaza Orleans, Local LB-1, Calle Arce, pg. 234 **PB**
Cigarreria Morazan SA de CV, Km. 5, Blvd. del Ejercito Nacional Soyapango, pg. 111 **IT**
Citibank, N.A. San Salvador, Torre Roble, pg. 378 **PB**
Compania Mercantil Intercontinental, S.A. de C.V., Edif. Plaza Cristal, 3er piso, 79a Av. Sur, pg. 107 **IT**
Cronos/DMB&B, 75 Avenida Norte 620, pg. 303 **PV**
Dada Dada & Cia S.A. de C.V., 21 Avenida Norte y, 3a Calle Poniente, Edificio Ericsson 1er, pg. 1365 **IT**
Distribuidora Shell de El Salvador SA, KM 11.5, Carrera al Puerto, pg. 1141 **IT**
Empresas ICA Sociedad Controladora (El Salvador), Tercera Calle Poniente No. 3977, pg. 454 **IT**
Eurolatina, Calle Circunvalacion, 296 Colonia San Benito, pg. 606 **IT**
Ipesa de El Salvador S.A., 29 Avenida Norte 1223, pg. 822 **PB**
Kativo El Salvador, S.A., 23 Ave. Sur, 12th-14th Calle Poniente, pg. 687 **PB**
Lemusimun, S.A. de C.V./Y&R, Blvd. Orden de Malta No. 5, Urbanizacion Santa Elena, pg. 1200 **PV**
Lucent Technologies El Salvador S.A. de C.V., Avenida Olympia 3742, pg. 1018 **PB**
McCormick de Centro America, S.A., C.A., pg. 1067 **PB**
Mineral San Sebastian S.A., Apdo. Postal 01-166, Av. Antiguo Cuscatlan 13, pg. 410 **IT**
Molinos El Salvador, S.A., Apartado Postal 327, pg. 411 **IT**
Moore Business Forms de Centro America, S.A. de C.V., Blvd. Del Ejercito, pg. 889 **IT**
Productos Nestle (El Salvador) S.A., pg. 922 **IT**
Publicidad Diaz, S.A. de C.V., 67 Avenida Norte, #120, pg. 186 **PV**
Quimica Henkel Centroamericana de El Salvador S.A., pg. 613 **IT**
Refineria Petrolera Acajutla, S.A., pg. 1141 **IT**
Rorer de Centro America S.A. de C.V., Edif. Industries Quimilas, 3er, Piso Blvd., Venezuela Col Roma, pg. 1111 **IT**
San Cristobal Mill & Plant, El Divisadero, pg. 410 **PB**
Shell Quimica de El Salvador, pg. 1141 **IT**
Sun Chemical de Centro America, S.A. de C.V., Boulevard Del Ejercito National Km 5 1/2, pg. 371 **IT**
TACA INTERNATIONAL AIRLINES, S. A., Alto Edifico Caribe 2nd Piso, Paseo General de Escalon, pg. 1346 **IT**
Telefonaktiebolaget LM Ericsson El Salvador, Piso 40, Edificio Ericsson, 21 Av. Norte y 3a Calle Poniente, pg. 1370 **IT**
Telefonaktiebolaget LM Ericsson Sucursal El Salvador, 21 Av. Norte 3a, Calle Poniente, Edificio Ericsson, pg. 1370 **IT**
3M Interamerica, Inc., Calle Chaparrastique No. 11, Urbanizacion Industrial Santa Elena, pg. 1606 **IT**
Wackenhut El Salvador, S.A., Calle Loma Linda No. 327, pg. 1731 **PB**

Santa Rosa de Lima

Commerce/Sanseb, Canton San Sebastian, pg. 410 **PB**
San Sebastian Gold Mines, Inc., Canton San Sebastian, pg. 410 **PB**

ESTONIA

Aseri

Aseri Tellis AS, Kordoni 1, pg. 1200 **IT**

Kohtla-Jarve

Perstorp Eesti AS, Ahtme mnt. 6, pg. 1038 **IT**

Maakond

AS Neopac-Elkson, Joelahtme vald, pg. 863 **IT**
Rae Betoon AS, Lagedi, Raevalt, pg. 1201 **IT**

PB - *U.S. Public Companies Volume*
PV - *U.S. Private Companies Volume*
IT - *International Public & Private Companies Volume*

Parnu

Fibo ExClay Eesti AS, Haademeeste, pg. 1200　IT
AS Rannila Profiil, Turba 5, pg. 1088　IT

Tabasalu

Balti Pakend Ltd., Rannamoisa Tee 2 D-E, pg. 33　IT

Tallinn

AS Lumiforest, Parnu mnt 20-2, pg. 457　IT
Ahlstrom Ltd., Ravala pst. 8, B 208, pg. 33　IT
Algol-Eesti AS, Vana-Narva mnt. 27, pg. 15　IT
Amer-Es AS, Kesk-Sojamae 3, pg. 72　IT
Balti Pakend, Ravala pst. 8, B 208, pg. 33　IT
Baltic Power (Estonia) Ltd., Ravala Pst 8-C-811,
　pg. 1453　IT
Bergemann-Ilmarine AG, Mustamae tee 5, pg. 398　IT
Berner Eesti AS, Narva maantee 7, IV krs/floor, h/room 40,
　pg. 189　IT
CIBA-GEIGY Services S.A., Ravola pst 6, pg. 980　IT
CIBA-GEIGY TAO, Narva mnt. 24, pg. 980　IT
Combitrans Eesti A.S., Manniku tee 102, pg. 1430　IT
AS Eesti AGA, Parnu mnt. 139F, pg. 14　IT
AS Eesti Varv, Liimi 5, pg. 729　IT
AS Estivo, Lai TN 27, pg. 660　IT
Estonian Transoil, Tobiase8, pg. 914　IT
Estravel, Suur-Karja 15, pg. 486　IT
Hansa Kindlustus, Narva Mnt. 24, pg. 1425　IT
AS Kandur, Mustamae Tee 4, pg. 748　IT
AS Kemi Vesi, Jarvecana tee 3, pg. 729　IT
Kontuur-Leo Burnett/Estonia, Parnu mnt. 142a,
　pg. 184　PV
Oy LM Ericsson Ab, Parnu mnt 137, pg. 1368　IT
Leaf Baltics, Adamsoni 2, pg. 638　IT
AS Leibur, Kadaka Tee 76 A, pg. 349　IT
Merita Bank Ltd.-Tallinn Branch, Harju 6, pg. 859　IT
Neste Oil Eesti, Tobiase 8, pg. 915　IT
Nokia Telecommunications, Ravala pst. 8 B 308,
　pg. 953　IT
Optiroc Esti AS, Narva Mnt 40, pg. 1200　IT
Pakenso Eesti AS, Laki 5, pg. 458　IT
Raisio Nordic Eesti AS, Roosikrantsi 10 A-4, pg. 1085　IT
Releplex AS, Mureli 3, pg. 1210　IT
Rudus Eesti AS, Peterburi mnt. 94, pg. 1201　IT
Statoil, Eesti Statoil A/S, Liivalaia 29-57, pg. 1298　IT
Svedala Estonia, pg. 1324　IT
Svenska Handelsbanken Tallinn, Suur-Karja 3, floor 2,
　pg. 1327　IT
SwissRe Advisers Tallinn, Lai Tanav 27, pg. 1333　IT
AS Traffic Service, Tobiase 8, pg. 915　IT
UPM-Kymmene Baltica, Ravala Avenue 8, B202,
　pg. 1430　IT
Vattenfall Estonia OU, Ahtri 12, pg. 1453　IT
Velsicol Eesti A.S., Parnu Mnt. 16, Tuba 9, pg. 1135　PV
The World Bank/Maailmapank, Kohtu 8, Rooms 68.73.74 &
　75, pg. 1190　PV
Zeneca Pharma, pg. 1527　IT

ETHIOPIA

Addis Ababa

BASF (Ethiopia) Limited P.L.C., House 538/38, Ware da 21,
　Kebele 04, pg. 106　IT
CIBA-GEIGY Trading and Marketing Services Co. Ltd.,
　pg. 980　IT
Mitsui & Co., Ltd., 5th Fl., Savings & Mortgage Bldg., Ras
　A, pg. 881　IT
Shell Ethiopia Ltd., Higher 19, Kebele 47, Hse 280 Debre
　Zeit Road, pg. 1137　IT
The World Bank, Africa Avenue Bole Road, pg. 1189　PV

FAROE ISLANDS

Hoyvik

Hans Hansen, Djupagilsvegur 34, pg. 966　IT

Torshavn

Det Norske Veritas, Vestara Bryggja, pg. 397　IT

FIJI

Ba

Nestle (Fiji) Ltd., pg. 921　IT

Lami

BJN (Fiji) Limited, Nukuwatu St., pg. 664　IT
ICI Fiji Limited, pg. 665　IT

Samabula

BHP Steel Building Products South Pacific Ltd., Lakeba
　Street, pg. 226　IT

Suva

Australia & New Zealand Banking Group Limited Fiji, ANZ
　House, pg. 99　IT

BOC Gases Fiji Ltd., pg. 121　IT
Carlton Brewery (Fiji) Limited, 122-164 Foster Rd., Walu
　Bay, pg. 501　IT
Colgate-Palmolive (Fiji) Ltd., C.P.O. Box 1195, 112 Rodwell
　Rd., pg. 998　PB
Det Norske Veritas, pg. 398　IT
Digital Equipment Corporation, pg. 507　PB
Hanimex (Fiji) Limited, c/o Munro, Leys & Co., Level 3,
　Pacific House, pg. 1115　IT
Westpac Banking Corp. - Fiji, Sixth Fl., Civic House, Town
　Hall Rd., pg. 1497　IT
Westpac Banking Corporation-Pacific Islands Div., Sixth Fl.,
　Civic House, Town Hall Rd., pg. 1497　IT

FINLAND

Aanekoski

Metsa-Sellu Oy, pg. 863　IT
Nokia Cellular Systems PMR Terminals, Aanekoskentie 70,
　pg. 953　IT

Aetsa

Finnish Chemicals Oy, pg. 1430　IT

Ahtari

Inha Works Ltd., Saarikylantie 21, pg. 492　IT

Anjalankoski

Akerlund & Rausing Oy, IK-Kotelo, pg. 32　IT
Enso Cartonboards Oy Ltd., pg. 456　IT
Enso-Yhteispalvelut Oy, pg. 457　IT
Inkeroinen Sawmill, pg. 456　IT

Degerby

Transmast Ltd., Kopparnas, pg. 660　IT

Espoo

Oy AGA Ab, Karapellontie 2, pg. 13　IT
OY ALGOL AB, Karapellontie 6, pg. 15　IT
AST Research Finland Oy, pg. 1182　IT
Algol Central Storage Depot, Karapellontie 6, pg. 15　IT
Ascom Energy Systems OY, P.O. Box 63, pg. 87　IT
BOC Ohmeda Oy, pg. 122　IT
Bailey-Fischer & Porter Oy, Lautamiehentie 1, pg. 449　IT
Bergtronics DY, Piispankailiontic 17, pg. 213　PB
Robert Bosch Oy, Tekniikantie 4A, pg. 205　IT
Braun Finland Oy, Nittykatu 8, pg. 744　PB
CPC Foods Oy, Ahventie 4A, pg. 225　PB
Carlor Finland Oy, Ruukinkuja 4, pg. 1030　IT
Oy Crawford Door AB, Luoteisrinne 4 D, pg. 269　IT
Digital Equipment Corporation Oy, 7 Niittymaentie,
　pg. 507　PB
Dun & Bradstreet Finland Oy., Sinimaentie 14 B,
　pg. 536　IT
Oy Esmi Ab, Olarinluoma 14, pg. 32　IT
Oy Emulsio AB, Mankimiehentie 10, pg. 370　IT
Enviropower Research & Development, R & D Department,
　Tekniilantie 12, pg. 1353　IT
Oy Erho AB, Karapellontie 6, pg. 15　IT
FAG Finland Oy, pg. 469　IT
FPS Power Systems Oy AB, P.O. Box 54, pg. 492　IT
OY Ferrosan AB, Vavarsvagen 8, pg. 989　IT
Fidenta Oy, Nihtisillante 3, pg. 859　IT
Fiskars Power Systems, pg. 127　IT
Gasum Oy, Keilranta 6, pg. 913　IT
Hewlett-Packard OY, Piispankalliontie 17, pg. 821　PB
Honeywell-Measurex Oy, Sinikalliontie 9, PL 91,
　pg. 833　PB
Honeywell OY, Ruukintie 8, pg. 835　PB
Huhtamaki Finance Oy, Lansituulentie 7, pg. 638　IT
HUHTAMAKI OY, Lansituulentie 7, pg. 638　IT
Icopal OY, Lant. Teollisuuskato 10, pg. 659　IT
Intergraph (Finland) Oy, Piispantilankuja 4, pg. 892　PB
K-instituuti OY, Siikajarventie 88-90, pg. 732　IT
Kemira Agro Oy, Research Center, Luoteisrinne 2,
　pg. 727　IT
Leaf Group B.V., Lansituulentie 7, pg. 638　IT
Oy Luxottica Finland AB, Sinikalliontie 12, pg. 822　IT
Oy Mecman, pg. 839　IT
Merita Life Assurance Ltd., Asemakuja 2, pg. 859　IT
Oy Metsa-Botnia AB, Revontulentine 6, pg. 863　IT
METSA-SERLA CORPORATION, Revontulentie 6,
　pg. 863　IT
Mikrokemia Oy, Keilaranta 6, P.O. Box 45, pg. 913　IT
Millipore Oy, Ruukinkuja 1, pg. 1113　PB
NAPS International, Keilaniemi, P.O. Box 3, pg. 913　IT
NCT Norden AB, Keilaniemi, P.O. Box 20, pg. 913　IT
Nellcor Puritan Bennett Finland Oy, Kappelitie 6B,
　pg. 1040　PB
Nemarc Shipping Company c/o Neste Shipping,
　pg. 772　IT
Oy Neoremedia AB, Karapellontie 6, pg. 15　IT
Neste Alfa Oy, Keilaniemi, P.O. Box 28, pg. 914　IT
Neste Aviation and Marine Sales, Meistentie 1, P.O. Box
　22, pg. 913　IT
Neste Kide Oy, Miestentie 1, pg. 913　IT
Neste Liikennepalvelu Oy, Miestentie 1, pg. 913　IT
NESTE OY, pg. 912　IT
Neste Oy, Chemicals, Keilaniemi, pg. 913　IT
Neste Oy, Gas LPG International, Keilaranta 6, P.O. Box
　21, pg. 913　IT

Neste Oy International Trading & Supply, Keilaniemi, P.O.
　Box 20, pg. 913　IT
Neste Oy, Shipping, Keilaniemi, P.O. Box 29, pg. 913　IT
Neste Yrityspalvelu Oy, Miestentie 1, P.O. Box 4,
　pg. 913　IT
Nobel Elektroniikka Oy Ab, Hyttimestarintie 6, pg. 1290　IT
Nokia Cellular Systems, Upseerinkatu 1, pg. 953　IT
Nokia Cellular Systems Mobile Switching, Hiomotie 8,
　pg. 953　IT
Nokia Cellular Systems Private Mobile Radio (PMR),
　Kilonkalio 7, pg. 953　IT
Nokia Mobile Phones, Metsanneidonkuja 6., pg. 951　IT
Nokia Network and Access Systems, Karanityntie 1,
　pg. 953　IT
Nokia Telecommunications, Keilalalidente 4, pg. 952　IT
Nokia Telecommunications Access Systems, Karaniityntie
　1, pg. 953　IT
Noptor Oy, Keilaniemi, P.O. Box 2, pg. 913　IT
Novell Finland, Sinimaentie 10 C, pg. 1204　PB
Novo Nordisk A/S, District Office Baltics, Pihatorma 1A,
　pg. 987　IT
Novo Nordisk Farma OY, Pihatorma 1A, pg. 988　IT
Olivetti (Suomi) OY, Luoteisrinne 4, pg. 1003　IT
OMRON Electronics O.Y., Metsanpojankuja 5,
　pg. 1006　IT
Opel Oy, Kutonjantie 8, pg. 723　PB
Oracle Finland Oy, Piispanportti 10, pg. 1228　PB
Outokumpu Base Metals Oy, Riihitontuntie 7 A,
　pg. 1016　IT
Outokumpu Castform Oy, pg. 1017　IT
Outokumpu China Oy, pg. 1015　IT
Outokumpu Copper Products Oy, Riihitontuntie 7 A,
　pg. 1016　IT
Outokumpu Engineering Contractors Oy, pg. 1017　IT
Outokumpu Engineering Services Oy, pg. 1017　IT
Outokumpu Harjavalta Metals Oy, pg. 1016　IT
Outokumpu Mining Oy, pg. 1016　IT
Outokumpu Mintec Oy, pg. 1017　IT
OUTOKUMPU OYJ, Riihitontuntie 7B, pg. 1015　IT
Outokumpu Rossisja Oy, pg. 1015　IT
Outokumpu Technology Oy, P.O. Box 86, pg. 1017　IT
Outokumpu Wenmec Oy, pg. 1017　IT
Pechiney Suomi-Rep. Office of Pechiney Denmark in
　Finland, Komeetankuja 1B, pg. 1031　IT
Perstorp Lattiat, Lintuvaarantie 23, pg. 1039　IT
Pfizer Oy, Tapiontori, pg. 1283　PB
Pharmacia & Upjohn Biotech, Sinikalliontie 3, pg. 1047　IT
Polarcup Group Headquarters, Lansituulentie 7,
　pg. 638　IT
Rintekno Oy, pg. 1361　IT
Roche Oy, pg. 1121　IT
SAB Nife OY, Kuutamokatu 2A, Box 19, pg. 54　IT
SAS Institute Oy, Sinikalliontie 10 PL 80, pg. 967　PV
Oy SKF AB, Backsankan 3, Olarsbacken, pg. 1158　IT
Sensormatic OY, Olarinlvoma 16, pg. 1458　PB
Sun Chemical Oy, Pieni Teollisuuskatu 2, pg. 371　IT
Sun Microsystems AB, Sinikalliontie 12, pg. 1531　PB
Oy Suomen Allied Colloids, pg. 62　IT
Oy Suomen Bofors Ab, pg. 278　IT
Oy Suomen Huls Ab, Sinimaentie 10 A, pg. 1456　IT
Suomen 3M Oy, PL 26, pg. 1606　PB
Suomen Vesimittarit Oy, Karapellontie 6, pg. 15　IT
TAPIOLA-YHTIOT, Revontulentie 7, pg. 1354　IT
Tellabs Oy, Ls Sinikallionan Tie 7, pg. 1573　PB
Oy VB Autonakut Ab, Kutojantje 1, pg. 1452　IT
Oy VARTA AB, Kutojantje 1, pg. 1452　IT
Viikinkikaapeli Oy, Brynstensvagen 10, pg. 1371　IT
Wellpharma Oy, pg. 553　IT

Fiskars

Ferraria Oy AB, pg. 492　IT
Fiskars Oy AB, pg. 492　IT

Grankulla

Hydro Aluminium Suomi Oy, Thurmansallen 8, pg. 963　IT

Haapavesi

Haapavesi Power Plant, pg. 660　IT

Halikko

ADI Data Furniture, Vanha Turuntie, pg. 460　IT

Hameenlinna

Acuson OY, pg. 18　PB
Hameenlinna Tube Works, pg. 1088　IT
Hameenlinna Works, Harvialantie 420, pg. 1088　IT
Herlitz Oy AB, Makelantie 7, pg. 616　IT
Melia Ltd., P.O. Box 509, pg. 1085　IT
Metform Division, pg. 1088　IT
Polarcup Finland, Polarpakintie, pg. 638　IT
Raisio Feed Ltd, Myllarinkatu 3, pg. 1085　IT
Strip Products, Harvialantie 420, pg. 1088　IT
Strip Products, pg. 1088　IT
Vanaja Power Plant, pg. 660　IT

Hamina

Neste Resins Oy, Oljysatamantie 16, P.O. Box 80,
　pg. 913　IT
Procurement Area South of Finland, pg. 455　IT
Summa Mills, pg. 457　IT
Zeofinn Oy, pg. 545　PV

PB - *U.S. Public Companies Volume*
PV - *U.S. Private Companies Volume*
IT - *International Public & Private Companies Volume*

1571

Geographic Index-Non U.S.

Hanko

Cebal Printal OY, Hopearanta, pg. 1030 IT

Harjavalta

Kemira Agro Oy, pg. 728 IT
Lansi-Suomen Voima Oy, pg. 1428 IT
Outokumpu Harjavalta Metals Oy, pg. 1016 IT

Hauho

Kesko - Training & Experimental Farm, Hahkialantie 30, pg. 732 IT

Heinola

Finnish Fibreboard Ltd., Viilukatu 11, pg. 1428 IT
Perstorp Form Oy, P.O. Box 1, pg. 1038 IT

Helsingfors

Artek oy ab, Hiekkakivintie 3, pg. 1072 IT
Det Norske Veritas, Skinnbyxvagen 3, pg. 397 IT
TopComp Elektronik Finland, Melkogatan 18, pg. 1371 IT

Helsinki

ABS Pumput OY, Hoylaamotie 16, pg. 270 IT
AMP Finland OY, Valimotie 1A, pg. 8 PB
Academic Bookstore, Keskuskatu 1, pg. 1301 IT
Afora Ltd., c/o Combustion Engineering, Process Automation Business, pg. 5 IT
A. AHLSTROM CORPORATION, Etelaesplanadi 14, pg. 32 IT
A. Ahlstrom Corporation, Sentnerikuja 2, pg. 32 IT
Ahlstrom Consumer Products Ltd., Sentnerikuja 2, pg. 32 IT
Ahlstrom Machinery, Sentnerikuja 2, pg. 33 IT
Ahlstrom Machinery, PL 5, pg. 34 IT
Ahlstrom Machinery Ecomachinery, Sentnerikuja 2, pg. 33 IT
Ahlstrom Machinery Recovery Boilers & Heat Engineering, Sentnerikuja 2, pg. 33 IT
Akerlund & Rausing Oy, pg. 32 IT
Alcatel SEP, Valimoite 13, pg. 56 IT
Alfa-Laval Agri-Scandinavia OY, Svetsargatan 7, pg. 1379 IT
Oy Alfa-Laval Zeta AB, PL 11, pg. 1379 IT
Amadeus Finland Oy, Dagmarinkatu 4, pg. 485 IT
AMER GROUP LTD., Makelankatu 91, pg. 72 IT
Amer Sport Oy, Makelankatu 91, pg. 72 IT
Amerpap Oy, pg. 863 IT
AREA Travel Agency Ltd., Paivarinnankatu 1, pg. 485 IT
ASEA Skandia Oy, pg. 7 IT
Oy Aurinkomatkat-Suntours Ltd., Dagmarinkatu 4, pg. 485 IT
Auto-Bon Oy, Vihdintien Autoalo, pg. 72 IT
Auto-Span OY, Hitsaajankatu 7 B, pg. 732 IT
Axmarine Oy, Lapinlahdenkaru 21c, pg. 712 IT
BASF Oy, Annankatu 42C, pg. 106 IT
B.A.T Finland, Vattuniemenkater 10, pg. 111 IT
Oy Ballograf BIC AB, pg. 1273 IT
Oy Bang & Olufsen ab, Kvortanegatan 1, pg. 146 IT
Banque Indosuez, Keskuskatu 7, pg. 314 IT
Oy Bausch & Lomb Finland A.B., Atomitie 5C, pg. 195 PB
Oy Berlitz AB, Kaivokatu 10 A 8. Krs., pg. 221 PB
BERNER LTD., Etelaranta 4B, pg. 189 IT
Oy Bristol-Myers (Finland) AB, pg. 255 PB
Canon Oy, Kornetintie 3, pg. 263 IT
Cerberus Finland Oy AB, Italahdenkalu 18C, pg. 1246 IT
CIBA-GEIGY OY, Pasilanraitio 5, pg. 978 IT
CIBA Vision Finland OY, Fredriksberginkatu 2, pg. 981 IT
Citibank Oy, Aleksanterinkatu 48, pg. 378 PB
Clavis Maris Finlandiae Oy, Munkholmsg. 1, pg. 771 IT
Oy Comdax Ab, Italahdenkatu 22 A, pg. 710 IT
CULTOR LTD., Kyllikinportti 2, pg. 349 IT
DMB&B Helsinki, Runeberginkatu 5A, pg. 303 PV
OY DAGMAR AB, Lonnrotinkatu 25, pg. 359 IT
Dell Computer Oy, Vattuniemenranta 2, pg. 496 PB
Dinol Oy, P.O. Box 140, Italahdenkatu 23 A, pg. 982 IT
Dow Jones Markets Finland OY, Etelaesplanadi 22A, 4th Fl., pg. 525 PB
Dow Suomi OY, Bulevard 1, Simonkatu 8 B, pg. 524 PB
Oy EMI Finland AB, Arinatie 6E, Box 28, pg. 427 IT
ESAB Oy, Rosavagen 18, pg. 282 IT
EleComp, Munkkiniemen puistotie 25 A, pg. 746 IT
Oy Electrolux Ab-ASAB, P.B. 15, pg. 441 IT
Oy Electrolux Ab-ELEKTRO HELIOS, Indusprig 1A, pg. 441 IT
Oy Electrolux Ab, P.B. 15, pg. 441 IT
Enator Ryhma Oy, Hiomotie 6 B, pg. 278 IT
Enka Suomi Oy, 2 Sahkottajankatu, P.O. Box 231, pg. 46 IT
ENSO OYJ, Kanavaranta 1, pg. 455 IT
Enso Publication Papers Oy Ltd., Box 309, pg. 457 IT
Oy Ericsson Radiopuhelin AB, Melkogatan 18, pg. 1367 IT
Espe oy, Vattuniemankatu 5, pg. 1138 IT
Esselte Meto, Ruosilantie 14, pg. 461 IT
Esselte Meto Finland, Ruosilantie 12, pg. 461 IT
Esselte Oy, Kutomotie 2, pg. 461 IT
Euroc Betong & Ballast AB, P.O. Box 49, pg. 1200 IT
ExClay Suomi Oy, pg. 1200 IT
FHP, Freudenberg Household Products Oy AB, pg. 506 IT
Fasson Tarra Oy, Linnanherrankuja 1, pg. 154 PB
Oy Fernofelt AB-Forming & Fabrics Dryer Plant, Ruosilantie 10, pg. 37 PB
Fina Chemicals, PL 21, pg. 1044 IT
Finland Travel Bureau Ltd., Kaivokatu 10A, pg. 485 IT
FINNAIR OY, Helsinki Airport, Tietotie 11 A, pg. 485 IT
Finnair Travel Services Oy, Dagmarinkatu 4, pg. 485 IT
Oy Finnmatkat-Finntours Ltd., Dagmarinkatu 4, pg. 485 IT
Finnsugar Bioproducts, Kyllikinportti 2, pg. 349 IT
Fiskars Consumer Oy Ab, Malmin Kauppatie 8 B, pg. 492 IT
FISKARS OY AB, Mannerheimintie 14, pg. 492 IT
Flavoring AB, Kyllikinportii 2, pg. 349 IT
Flende Oy, Korppaanmaentie 17 CL 6, pg. 400 IT
Oy Forbo AB, pg. 497 IT
Oy FORD Ab, 6146 Henry Fordgatan, pg. 665 PB
Foster Wheeler Energia Oy, Sentnerikuja 2, pg. 677 PB
Gas Systems, Finland Oy, Vahijarvi, pg. 361 PV
Oy Getinge AB, Mannerheimsvagan 79, pg. 551 IT
Gotaverken Oy, Erottajankatu 11, pg. 771 IT
W.R. Grace Oy, Teerisuonkuja 5, pg. 756 PB
Grako OY, Lauttasaarentie 1, pg. 78 PB
Oy Guerlain AB, Sornaister Rantatie 27B, pg. 780 IT
Hagglunds Drives Oy, Sienitie 9, pg. 670 IT
Handelsbanken Helsinki, Etalaranta 8, pg. 1327 IT
Oy Helsingen Huuttokauppakamari, Sornaisten rantatie 29, pg. 859 IT
Helsingen Pantti-Osakeyhtio, Iso Roobetinkatu 17-19 D 24, pg. 859 IT
Henkel Nopco Oy, pg. 614 IT
Oy Hercofinn Ab, PL 724, 00101, pg. 810 PB
Hobby Hall, Hameentie 157, pg. 1301 IT
Oy Honeywell Bull AB, Alexanderin Katu, pg. 318 IT
Huoneistokeskus Oy, Melkonkatu 16A, pg. 858 IT
Huoneistomarkkinointi Oy, Mannerheimintie 4, pg. 858 IT
Hydro Plast OY, Fabiansgatan 12 G 49, pg. 963 IT
Hydro Supra Chemicals Oy, Fabiansgatan 12 G 49, pg. 963 IT
ISS Suomi Oy, Laulukuja 6, pg. 656 IT
IVO Service Substations, Viikintie 3, pg. 660 IT
IVO Transmission Services Ltd., Urho Kekkosen katu 2, pg. 660 IT
Icopal Helsinki Oy, pg. 659 IT
Icopal Kouvola Oy, pg. 659 IT
Icopal Kuopio Oy, pg. 659 IT
Icopal Tampere Oy, pg. 659 IT
Icopal Turku Oy, pg. 659 IT
Imatra Steel Oy Ab, John Stenbergin ranta 2, pg. 863 IT
IMATRAN VOIMA OY, Malminkatu 16, pg. 660 IT
Industrial Bank of Finland Ltd., Aleksanterinkau 36 A, pg. 859 IT
Intel Finland OY, pg. 887 PB
Oy International Business Machines Ab, pg. 898 PB
International Marketing & Promotions Helsinki, Runeberginkatu 5A, pg. 304 PV
International Rectifier Company (Great Britain) Limited, Billskogavagen 19, pg. 907 PB
INTERRENT OY, Hitsaajankatu 7 C, pg. 684 IT
Axel Jonnson Oy, Italahdenkatu 22 b A, pg. 712 IT
Oy Jotun Scanpol AB, Melkogatan 28 e, pg. 715 IT
K-Cash & Carry Ltd., Kruunuvuorenkatu 5, pg. 732 IT
K-linkki Oy, Yla-Malmintori 6 A, pg. 732 IT
K-Tel International Finland O.Y., Hameentie 157A, pg. 938 PB
K-Yhtio Oy, Satamakatu 3, pg. 732 IT
Kamyr Oy, Erottajankatu 11, pg. 771 IT
Oy Karl Beus AB, Etelaranta 4A, pg. 189 IT
Kemira Agro Oy, Porkkalankatu 3, pg. 727 IT
Kemira Chemicals Oy, Porkkalankatu 3, pg. 728 IT
Kemira Engineering Oy, pg. 728 IT
KEMIRA OY, Porkkalankatu 3, pg. 727 IT
Kemira Pigments Oy, Porkkalankatu 3, pg. 729 IT
Kerana Oy, pg. 659 IT
Kesko Export Ltd., Kanavakatu 3 A, pg. 732 IT
KESKO LTD., Satamakatu 3, pg. 732 IT
Oy Kolmostelevisio Ab, Ilmalantori 2, pg. 828 IT
KONE CORPORATION, P.O. Box 8, Kartanontie 1, pg. 746 IT
KONE Elevators Export, P.O. Box 8, pg. 746 IT
KONE Elevators Finland, P.O. Box 51, pg. 746 IT
KONE Finance Corporation, Munkkiniemen puistotie 25, pg. 746 IT
Oy Konwell AB, Hankasuontie 11 A, pg. 550 IT
Korpivaara Oy, Itakeskuksen Autotalo Vibynkatu 3, pg. 72 IT
Kvaerner Masa-Yards Inc., Helsinki New Shipyard, Munkkisaarenkatu 1, pg. 771 IT
Kvaerner Pulping Oy, Erottajankatu 11, pg. 768 IT
Oy Liesmyynti-Spisforsaljning AB, pg. 441 IT
Lohja Rudus Oy AG, P.O. Box 49, pg. 1200 IT
Oy Lorentzen & Wettre Ab, P.O. Box 15, pg. 271 IT
Lowe Brindfors, Tehtaankatu 27-29a, pg. 678 PV
MK-Mainos Oy, Kruunuvuorenkatu 4, pg. 732 IT
MTV FINLAND, Ilmalantori 2, pg. 827 IT
MTV-palvelukiinteistot, Ilmalantori 2, pg. 828 IT
Oy Maritim AB, Batbyggarvagen 1, pg. 1011 IT
Masterfoods Oy, Kolmas Linji 22, pg. 707 PV
Materials Handling Division, Sahaajankatu 3, pg. 15 IT
Oy McCormick Ab, pg. 1067 PB
MEIJERIOSUUSKUNTA/MEJERIANDELSLAGET MILKA, Paivalaisente 2, pg. 854 IT
Oy Mercantile Ab Graphische Industrie, Viljatie 2, pg. 109 IT
Merita Bank Ltd., Aleksanterinkatu 30, pg. 858 IT
Merita Capital Ltd., Aleksanterinkatu 36 A, pg. 859 IT
Merita Customer Finance Ltd., Sornaistenkatu 1, pg. 859 IT
Merita Finance Ltd., Sornaistenkatu 1, pg. 859 IT
Merita Fund Management Ltd., Fabianinkatu 29 B, pg. 859 IT
MERITA LTD., Alexksanterinkatu 30, pg. 858 IT
Merita Real Estate Ltd., Asemapaallikonkatu 7, pg. 859 IT
Merita Securities Ltd., Fabianinkatu 29 B, pg. 859 IT
METRA CORPORATION, John Stenbergin ranta 2, pg. 862 IT
Micro Warehouse, Finland OY, Hiomotie 6B, pg. 1104 PB
Microsoft Oy, pg. 1108 PB
Mitsui & Co. Europe (Finland) OY, Toolonkatu 8-A, pg. 880 IT
Mobil Oil Oy A.B., Keskuskatu 7, pg. 1119 PB
Monsanto Oy, Mannerheimintie 15, pg. 1126 PB
Munters Oy, pg. 669 IT
Nestle-Findus Oy, pg. 921 IT
OY NOKIA AB/NOKIA GROUP, Etelaesplanadi 12, pg. 951 IT
Nokia Multimedia Network Terminals, Mannerheimintie 4, pg. 952 IT
Nordberg Group, Fabianinkatu 9A, pg. 1428 IT
Norden Banking Group, c/o Aktia Sparbank, Mannerheimintie 14, pg. 1328 IT
Norden Banking Group, Mikaelsgatan 4, pg. 1328 IT
Nordic-Hotel Oy, Hotel Inter-Continental Helsinki, pg. 485 IT
Nordson Finland Oy, Pihkatie 4, pg. 1189 PB
Oy Nortec Electronics Finland Ab, Italahdenkatu 22, pg. 712 IT
Optiroc Oy AB, Box 49, pg. 1200 IT
Oy Talentum Ab, Malminkatu 30, pg. 570 PV
Paasivaara Oy, pg. 1438 IT
Papyrus Oy, pg. 431 IT
PARTEK CORPORATION, Sornaisten Rantatie 23, pg. 1024 IT
Partita Ltd., Pohjoisesppladadi 27C, pg. 859 IT
Pitney Bowes Oy, Melkonkat 9, pg. 1304 PB
Oy Polarkesti AB, Iso Roobertinkatu 30, pg. 1274 IT
POSTIPANKKI LTD., Unioninkatu 20, pg. 1064 IT
Prospectus Ltd., Mikonkatu 1 B, pg. 859 IT
Puumerkki Oy, Takkatie 14, pg. 456 IT
Oy Qtronic AB, Italahdenkatu 22, pg. 712 IT
Rauma Ltd., Fabianinkatu 9A, pg. 1428 IT
RAUTARUUKKI OY, pg. 1088 IT
Rautaruukki Oy, Fredrikinkatu 51-53, pg. 1088 IT
Rhone-Poulenc Oy, Viljatie 4, B.P. 53, pg. 1113 IT
Oy Richardson-Vicks A.B., Mannerheimintie 15A, pg. 1332 PB
W. Rosenlew Ltd., Fabianinkatu 9B, pg. 1428 IT
Oy Saab-Auto Ab, P.O. Box 92, pg. 1449 IT
Sandoz Oy, pg. 985 IT
Oy Scan-Auto AB, P.O. Box 24, pg. 686 IT
Schindler Hissi Oy, pg. 1205 IT
Sedwick Johnson Oy, Bulevardi 34 A, pg. 712 IT
Sesto, Stockmannintie 1 H, pg. 1301 IT
Oy Shell Ab, Nejlikkaire 17, pg. 1138 IT
Siemens Osakeytioe, pg. 1247 IT
SILJA OY Ab, Bulevardi 1A, pg. 899 IT
Skandia Life Assurance Co. Ltd. - Helsinki, Fredrikinkatu 63 A8, 5 krs., pg. 1256 IT
Skandinaviska Enskilda Banken Helsinki, Unionsgatan 30, pg. 1259 IT
Skanska Oy, pg. 1261 IT
Statoil Finland OY, Svetsargatan 4, pg. 1298 IT
Steel Structure Division, Fredrikinkatu 51-53, pg. 1088 IT
OY STOCKMANN AB, Aleksanterinkatu 52 B, pg. 1301 IT
Stockmann Automotive Sales Div., Kutomotie 1A, pg. 1301 IT
Stockmann Department Store Div., Kutomotie I C, pg. 1301 IT
Storage Technology Finland, Sirikalliontie 10, pg. 1523 PB
Oy Suomen Henkel AB, pg. 614 IT
Suomen Nestle Oy, pg. 922 IT
Suomen Rehu Oy, Kyllikinportti 2, pg. 349 IT
Suomen Sandvik Oy, P.O. Box 52, pg. 1187 IT
Suomen Unipol Oy, Lapinrinne 1 B, pg. 15 IT
Tektronix Oy, Larin Kyostin Tie 4, pg. 1568 PB
Telivo Ltd., Malminkatu 16, pg. 661 IT
Thorn Finland Oy, Hitsaajankatu 1, pg. 1386 IT
Tietokesko Oy, Satamakatu 3, pg. 732 IT
Time/System Finland Oy, World Trade Center, Aleksanterinkatu 17, pg. 73 IT
Oy Tulenkestavaat Tiliet, A.B., Bolevardo 17C14, pg. 904 PV
UPM-KYMMENE CORPORATION, pg. 1427 IT
UPM-Kymmene Paper Division, Etelaesplanadi 2, pg. 1428 IT
UPM-Kymmene Timber, Fabianinkatu 9 B, pg. 1430 IT
Oy Uddeholm AB, Postboks 8, pg. 1472 IT
Unitas Congres Center Ltd., Ramsinniementie 14, pg. 859 IT
Utell International-Finland, Mannerhelmintle 102, pg. 1098 IT
VPV EURO RSCG, Fredrikinkatu 33A, pg. 603 IT
VTI Hamlin Oy, pg. 251 PB
VV-Auto Oy, Hitsaajankatu 7 B, pg. 732 IT
Vaasa Bakeries Ltd., Kyllikinportti 2, pg. 349 IT
Vaasamills Ltd., Kyllikinportti 2, pg. 349 IT
Oy Valitut Palat - Reader's Digest Ab, Sentnerikuja 5, pg. 1368 PB
Valmet Automation Inc., Panuntie 6, pg. 1449 IT
VALMET CORPORATION, Panuntie 6, pg. 1447 IT
Vattenfall Oy, Aleksanterinkatu 15 B, pg. 1453 IT
Oy Werner & Pfleiderer AB, Fredrikinkatu 48A, pg. 511 IT
Wettex OY AB, pg. 506 IT
Widni Oy, Valuraudantie 12, pg. 712 IT
Williams de Broe Pankkiiriliike Oy Finland, Pohjoisesplanadi 25A, pg. 148 IT
OY Willis Faber AB, Rikhard Nymansvag 9B, pg. 1510 IT
Young & Rubicam Finland, Munkkisaarenkatu 2, pg. 1199 PV
Young & Rubicam Finland Oy, Munkkisaarenkatu 2, pg. 1199 PV
Zeneca Oy, Mannerheimintic 160A, pg. 1527 IT

PB - *U.S. Public Companies Volume*
PV - *U.S. Private Companies Volume*
IT - *International Public & Private Companies Volume*

Hirvlax

Monas Feed Oy AB, Monasvagen 442, pg. 1085   IT

Hollola

BetzDearborn OY, Tarmontie 6, pg. 227   PB
KONE Wood Oy, pg. 14   IT
Roxon Companies Oy, Keskikankaantie 19, pg. 1353   IT
Roxon Komponentit Oy, Keskikankaantie 19, pg. 1353 IT
Roxon Oy, Keskikankaantie 19, pg. 1353   IT
Valmet Corporation Roll Handling, Muovitie 1, pg. 1448 IT

Hyvinkaa

Isover Ahlstrom OY, Kerkkolankatu 37-39, pg. 1176   IT
KONE Elevators, BU 2, P.O. Box 670, pg. 746   IT
Perel Oy, Torpankatu 28, pg. 740   IT

Imatra

Enso Forest Development Oy Ltd., Kuparintie 47, pg. 455 IT
Imatra Paperboards, pg. 456   IT
Imatra Power Plant, Valvomontie 2 A, pg. 660   IT
Insinooritoimisto N. Liukkonen Oy, Lappeentie 12, pg. 660 IT
Neste Oy, Natural Gas, Raikkolantie 170, pg. 913   IT
Plastilon Oy, Muovikuja 7, pg. 913   IT
Tainionkoski Paper Mill, pg. 457   IT

Inkoo

IVO Service Thermal Power, pg. 660   IT
Inkoo Power Plant, pg. 660   IT

Jamsankoski

Genencor International Europe Oy, Teollisuustie 15, pg. 349 IT
UPM-Kymmene - Jamsankoski, pg. 1428   IT

Jarvenpaa

Oy Fennofelt AB-Press Fabric Plant, Puurtajankatu 27, pg. 37 PB
Tako Carton Plant Ltd., pg. 863   IT
Valmet Corporation Calenders, Wartsilankatu 100, pg. 1448 IT
Valmet Corporation Coaters and Reels, Wartsilankatu 100, pg. 1448 IT
Valmet Corporation Production, Wartsilankatu 100, pg. 1448 IT
Valmet Corporation Winders, Wartsilankatu 100, pg. 1448 IT
Valmet Dura Oy, Wartsilankatu 100, pg. 1448   IT

Joensuu

Abloy Oy, Wahlforssinkatu 20, pg. 18   IT
Joensuu Mill, Sirkkalantie 17, pg. 1429   IT
Joensuu Power Plant, Iiksenvaarantie 2, pg. 660   IT
Ladenso Oy, pg. 456   IT
Mecakone Oy, Pamilonkatu 25, pg. 1353   IT

Jokioinen

OFA Oy Ab, pg. 578   IT

Jorvas

Oy LM Ericsson Ab, pg. 1368   IT

Joutseno

Finnish Chemicals Oy, pg. 1430   IT

Jyska

Enermet Ltd., pg. 660   IT

Jyvaskyla

Hewlett-Packard OY, Vainonkatu 9C, pg. 821   PB
Jyvaskyla Mills, Saynatsalo, pg. 1429   IT
Rauhalahti Power Plant, Kuokkalantie 4, pg. 660   IT
Valmet Corporation Foundry, P.O. Box 587, pg. 1448 IT
Valmet Corporation Paper Machines, P.O. Box 587, pg. 1448 IT
Valmet Corporation Service Development, P.O. Box 587, pg. 1449 IT

Kaarina

Beiersdorf Oy, pg. 183   IT
Case Traktori OY, P.O. Box 5, pg. 1579   PB
MacGREGOR Group, Hallimestarinkatu 6, pg. 670   IT

Kaipiainen

Raisio Chemicals Ltd., Siilotie 5, pg. 1085   IT
Raisio Feed Ltd., pg. 1085   IT
Raision Lateksi Oy, Tarkkelystie 4, pg. 1085   IT
Oy Raisional Ab, Siilotie 7, pg. 1085   IT

Kaipola

UPM-Kymmene - Kaipola, pg. 1428   IT

Kajaani

Sensodec Oy, pg. 1449   IT
UPM-Kymmene - Kajaani, pg. 1428   IT
Valmet Automation Kajaani Ltd., pg. 1449   IT

Kangas

Sealed Air Oy, Kaavakuja 3, pg. 1451   PB

Kankaanpaa

Kankaanpaa Works, Rautatienkatu 19, pg. 1088   IT

Kantvik

Finnsugar Ltd., pg. 349   IT
Porkkala Sugar Refinery, pg. 349   IT

Karhula

Ahlstrom Alcore Ltd, P.O. Box 100, pg. 32   IT
Ahlstrom Alcore Ltd., pg. 33   IT
Ahlstrom Glassfibre Ltd.-Karhula Plant, P.O. Box 18, pg. 32 IT
Ahlstrom Machinery Fiber Line, P.O. Box 18, pg. 33 IT
Ahlstrom Machinery Karhula Steel Foundry, P.O. Box 18, pg. 33 IT
Ahlstrom Machinery Pump Industry, P.O. Box 18, pg. 34 IT
Ahlstrom Machinery Pump Industry After Sales, P.O. Box 18, pg. 34 IT
Ahlstrom Machinery Pumps Inc., P.O. Box 18, pg. 33 IT
Valmet Corporation Printing Paper Machines, P.O. Box 600, pg. 1448 IT
Wisapak Oy Ab, Karhula Factory, pg. 1429   IT

Kauttua

Ahlstrom Kauttua Ltd., P.O. Box 55, pg. 35   IT
Akerlund & Rausing Oy, P.O. Box 100, pg. 32   IT
Jujo Thermal OY, pg. 938   IT
Lansi-Suomen Kaynnissapito Oy, pg. 660   IT

Kemi

Enso Fine Papers Oy, pg. 456   IT
Fortek Oy, pg. 456   IT
Outokumpu Chrome Oy, Kemi Mine, pg. 1018   IT
Veitsiluoto Publication Papers Oy, pg. 457   IT

Kemijarvi

Kemijarven Sellu Oy, pg. 456   IT
Salcomp Oy, Heralampi, pg. 951   IT

Kempele

LK Products Oy, Takatie 6, pg. 952   IT

Kerava

Ifi OY, Posliinitehtaankatu 1, pg. 501   IT
Teknolon Oy, Siokalliontie 6, pg. 1210   IT
Vink Finland OY, Silokalliontie 6, pg. 1210   IT

Kirkkonismmi

Gyproc Oy, pg. 1200   IT

Kittila

Kittila Wood Oy, Pitkakumpu 14 a, pg. 456   IT

Kiukainen

Mykora Oy, pg. 728   IT

Klaukkala

Plast-Teknik Curver OY, Kylvajantie 9, pg. 356   IT

Kokemaki

Raisio Group plc, P.O. Box 28, pg. 1085   IT

Kokkola

Kemira Agro Oy, pg. 728   IT
Kokkola Power Plant, Outokummuntic 12, pg. 660   IT
Outokumpu Zinc Oy, pg. 1016   IT

Kolho

Perstorp IKI Oy Decorative Laminate, pg. 1038   IT

Korso

Korpivaara Oy - Forklifts, Korpivaarantie 1, pg. 72 IT

Korpivaara Oy - Toyota Group, Korpivaarantie 1, pg. 72   IT

Kotka

Oy Finnterminals AB, pg. 1428   IT
Kotka Mills, pg. 457   IT
Laminating Papers Ltd., pg. 457   IT
Svedala Oy Kotka, pg. 1325   IT
Vaasanmylly Oy, Kotka Factory, Suursaarenkatu, pg. 349 IT
Xyrofin Oy, Sokeritehtaantie, pg. 350   IT

Kouvola

Tehdaspuu Oy, P.O. Box 139, pg. 1429   IT

Kulloo

Norlatex Oy, pg. 913   IT

Kuopio

Kuopio Mill, Itkonniemenkatu 29, pg. 1429   IT
Kuopion Matkatoimisto Oy, Kauppakatu 22, pg. 485   PB
Roibox Oy, pg. 834   PB
SO Oviteollisuus OY, Sammonkatu 4, pg. 1302   IT
Savo Procurement Area, pg. 455   IT
Savon Sellu Oy, pg. 863   IT

Kuusankoski

Finnish Chemicals Oy, pg. 1430   IT
Oy Finnish Peroxides Ab, pg. 1430   IT
Kymi Paper Mill, pg. 1428   IT
Kymi Paper Mills Ltd., pg. 1428   IT

Lahti

Bretec Oy, Taivalkatu 8, pg. 1352   IT
Corenso United Oy Ltd., P.O. Box 4, pg. 456   IT
Custom Accessories Scandinavia Oy, Vaaksakatu 3, pg. 298 PV
Detec International Oy, pg. 1352   IT
Formeca Oy, Mustapuronkatu 2, pg. 456   IT
Pakenso Oy, pg. 456   IT
Pilkington Lahden Lasitehdas Oy, pg. 1056   IT
Rammer Oy, Taivalkatu 8, pg. 1352   IT
Schauman Wood Oy, Niemenkatu 16,, pg. 1428   IT
Schauman Wood Oy, Niemenkatu 16, pg. 1430   IT

Laitila

Metpela Oy, Turuntie 41, pg. 729   IT

Lappeenranta

Combitrans Oy, Terminaalinkatu 15, pg. 1428   IT
Kaukas Oy, pg. 1428   IT
Kaukas Sawn Goods Industry, pg. 1428   IT
Kymmene Logistics Oy, Laserkuja 6, pg. 1428   IT
Processed Timber Products, pg. 1428   IT
Svedala Oy Lappeenranta, pg. 1325   IT

Lappohja

Lappohja Works, Satamatie 56, pg. 1088   IT

Lapua

Oy Kationi Ab, Simpsiontie 682, pg. 1085   IT
Lapuan Metalli Oy, Metallitie 3, pg. 1353   IT

Leppiniemi

IVO Service, North Finland, Pyhakoskentie 10, pg. 660 IT
Oulujoki Power Plants, Pyhakoskentie 10, pg. 660   IT

Lieksa

Akerlund & Rausing Oy, Kerantie 11, pg. 32   IT

Liljendal

Liljendals Bruk A.B., PL 524/A, pg. 869   PB

Luhtapohja

Pamilo Oy, pg. 661   IT

Luoma-Aho

Rannila Steel Oy, Vimpelintie 661, pg. 1088   IT

Mantta

Ahlstrom Machinery Mantta Pump Factory, pg. 33   IT
Serla Oy, pg. 863   IT

Mantyharju

Exel Oy, P.O. Box 29, pg. 913   IT

Masaby

Suomen Astra Oy, pg. 94   IT
Svedala Oy, pg. 1325   IT

Masala

Landis & Staefa Suomi Oy, Masalantie 330, pg. 801   IT

Massy

MET S.A., 19, Avenue Carnot, pg. 1369   IT

Mietoinen

Raisio Chemicals Ltd., Kaskistentie 9, pg. 1085   IT

Mikkeli

Ahlstrom Glassfibre Ltd.-Mikkeli Plant, Insinoorinkatu 2,
  pg. 32   IT
Mikkelin Matkatoimisto, Porrassalmenkatu 23, pg. 485   IT
Viljavuuspalvelu Oy, Graanintie, pg. 728   IT

Muurla

A. Jalander Oy, Muurlantie 101 B, pg. 727   IT

Naantali

Finnsugar Bioproducts, Naantali Factory, Satamatie 2,
  pg. 349   IT
Naantali Power Plant, Satamatie 16, pg. 660   IT
Neste Oy, Naantali Refinery, Naantali Refinery, pg. 914   IT

Nastola

Cultarom, Nastola Factory, Maitotie 4, pg. 349   IT
Edward Mendell Co., Maitotie 4, pg. 1269   PB

Nokia

Finbow Oy, Siuronvaltatie 158, pg. 1449   IT
Melia Ltd., Rounionkatu 55, pg. 1085   IT
Nokia Mill, pg. 673   PB
Nokian Paperi Oy, pg. 673   PB
Nokian Tyres, pg. 954   IT

Noormarkku

A. Ahlstrom Corporation, pg. 32   IT

Oulainen

Oulainen Works, pg. 1088   IT

Oulu

Enso Paperikemia Oy, pg. 456   IT
Forchem Oy, pg. 456   IT
Hewlett-Packard Finland Field OY, Valtatie 57, pg. 819   PB
Kemira Chemicals Oy, Tutkimuskeskus, pg. 728   IT
NE-Products Oy, Teknologiantie 18, pg. 952   IT
Nokia Cellular Systems Base Stations, Kaapelitie 4,
  pg. 953   IT
Nokia Mobile Phones R & D, Tutkijantie 4, pg. 952   IT
Oulun Kumitehdas Oy, Lumijoentie 2, pg. 1449   IT
Raisio Feed Ltd., P.O. Box 68, pg. 1085   IT
Rautaruukki Engineering, Kiilakiventie 1, pg. 1089   IT
Svedala Oy Oulu, pg. 1325   IT
Transtech, Kiilakiventie 1, pg. 1088   IT

Outokumpu

Outokumpu Mining Oy, Tehtaankatu 2, pg. 1016   IT
Outokumpu Oyj, Tietokumpu, pg. 1015   IT
Turula Works Inc., pg. 1017   IT

Paimio

Sahkolahteenmaki Oy, pg. 8   IT

Pankakoski

Pankakoski Boards Oy Ltd., pg. 456   IT

Pargas

Finnsementti Oy Ab, pg. 1198   IT
Pargas Plant, pg. 1198   IT

Perttila

Lohja Abetoni Oy AB, pg. 1199   IT

Pieksamaki

Svedala Oy Pieksamaki, pg. 1325   IT

Pietarsaari

Oy JA-RO AB, pg. 1018   IT
Oy Nautor AB, pg. 1428   IT
Wisaforest Oy Ab, Alholmintie 43, pg. 1429   IT

Wisapak Oy Ab, pg. 1429   IT
Wisapak Oy Ab, Pietarsaari Factory, pg. 1429   IT

Piikkio

Kvaerner Masa-Yards Inc., Piikkio Works, pg. 771   IT

Pori

Oy Algol Ab, Pori Sales Office, Teljankatu 8, pg. 15   IT
Oy Kalmar LMV, PI 165, pg. 1421   IT
Meri-Fori Power Plant, Tankoluoto, pg. 660   IT
Outokumpu Castform Oy, pg. 1017   IT
Outokumpu Harjavalta Metals Oy, Copper Refinery,
  pg. 1016   IT
Outokumpu Plating Oy, pg. 1016   IT
Outokumpu Poricopper Oy, P.O. Box 60, pg. 1016   IT
Outokumpu Research Oy, pg. 1015   IT
Outokumpu Superconductors Oy, pg. 1017   IT
Rauma Ecoplanning, pg. 1428   IT
Rauma Offshore Contracting Oy, pg. 1428   IT

Porvoo

Borealis Polymers Oy, PL 330, pg. 913   IT
Enso Timber Oy Ltd., pg. 456   IT
John Crane Finland, Engineered Sealing Systems, Kipinatie
  2 B, PL 88, pg. 1339   IT
Neste Oy, Chemicals, P.O. Box 20, pg. 913   IT
Neste Oy, Porvoo Refinery, Technology Centre, P.O. Box
  310, pg. 914   IT
Tolkkimen Sawmill, P.O. Box 39, pg. 456   IT

Puhos

Puhos-Board Oy, Lepikontie 23 A, pg. 1428   IT

Pulkkila

Pulkkila Works, Lehtolantie 36, pg. 1088   IT

Pyhasalmi

Outokumpu Mining Oy, Pyhasalmi Mine, pg. 1016   IT

Raahe

August Lindberg Oy, pg. 1088   IT
Oy JIT-Trans Ltd, pg. 1088   IT
Raahe Steel Works, pg. 1088   IT
Rautaruukki Information Systems, pg. 1089   IT
Rautaruukki Steel, P.O. Box 93, pg. 1088   IT
SKJ-yhtiot Oy, Niittykatu 5, pg. 1088   IT

Raisio

Avesta Sheffield Oy, Vanha Nuorikkalantie, pg. 222   IT
Melia Ltd., Raisionkaari 55, P.O. Box 101, pg. 1085   IT
Raisio Catering Oy, Raisionkaari 55, pg. 1085   IT
Raisio Chemicals Ltd., pg. 1085   IT
Raisio Engineering Ltd., Raisiokaari 60, pg. 1085   IT
Raisio Feed Ltd., Raisionkaari 55, pg. 1085   IT
RAISIO GROUP, Raisiokaari 55, pg. 1085   IT
Raisio Group plc, Raisionkaari 55, P.O. Box 101,
  pg. 1085   IT
Raisio Group plc, Raisionkaari 55, pg. 1085   IT
Raisio Group plc-Margarine, Raisionkaari 55, P.O. Box 101,
  pg. 1085   IT
Oy Raisional Ab, Raisionkaari 55, pg. 1085   IT
Valmet-Raisio Oy, Kerrolankatu 4, pg. 1448   IT

Rauma

Consilium Bulk Oy, Kaivopuistonitie 31, pg. 131   IT

Riihimaki

Sako Oy, Sakonkatu 2, pg. 954   IT
Valmet Corporation Roll Coatings, Kapalamaenkatu 11,
  pg. 1449   IT

Rovaniemi

Bombardier-Nordtrac Oy, Teollisuustle, pg. 200   IT

Ruotsinpyhtaa

A. Ahlstrom Corporation-Stromfors Works, pg. 32   IT

Sahaajankatu

Gambro AB Oy, FI-00811 Helsinki, pg. 667   IT

Salo

Ahlstrom Machinery Salo Works, pg. 34   IT
Nokia Display Products Inc., Salorankatu 5-7, pg. 951   IT
Nokia Display Products Oy, Salorankatem 5-7, pg. 951   IT
Nokia Industrial Electronics, Salorankatu 5-7, pg. 951   IT
Sucros Ltd., Sokerikatu 1, pg. 349   IT
Oy Suomen Plasmaschinen AB, Kaakelitehtaankatu 2,
  pg. 825   IT

Savonlinna

Ahlstrom Aquaflow Ltd., pg. 34   IT

Ahlstrom Machinery Chemical Recovery, pg. 33   IT
Ahlstrom Machinery Savonlinna Engineering Works, P.O.
  Box 34, pg. 34   IT
Saimaa Procurement Area, pg. 455   IT

Siilinjarvi

Kemira Chemicals Oy, pg. 728   IT

Sorsakoski

Finnbend Oy, pg. 222   IT
Finnpipe Oy, pg. 222   IT

Taivalkoski

Ulea Oy Taivalkoski Sawmill, pg. 456   IT

Tammerfors

Kvaerner Tamturbine Oy, Etu-Hankkionkatu 1, pg. 772   IT
Svedala Oy Plant, pg. 1325   IT
Svedala Oy Tammerfors, pg. 1325   IT

Tampere

Bronto Skylift Oy AB, Teerivuorenkatu 28, pg. 617   PB
Oy Electrolux Ab-HUSQVARNA, Box 676, pg. 441   IT
Oy Electrolux Ab-PARTNER, Box 676, pg. 441   IT
Oy Electrolux Ab-TAMMERMATIC, Box 206, pg. 441   IT
Enviropower, Osuusmyllynkatu 13, pg. 1353   IT
Freudenberg OY, pg. 506   IT
K-Luotto Oy, Tammelan puistokatu 21 A, pg. 732   IT
Kesoil Oy, Tammelanpuistokatu 21, P.O. Box 296,
  pg. 913   IT
Korpivaara Oy, Tammer-Auto, Hatanpaavaltatie 38,
  pg. 72   IT
Lielahti CTMP Mill, pg. 863   IT
Martin Merkel Finland Oy, Pispalan Valtatie 139,
  pg. 859   IT
Neopac Oy, pg. 863   IT
Nokia Cellular Systems Mobile Switching, Hatanpaanvaltatie
  34 A, pg. 953   IT
Nokia Mobile Phones Cellular Data, Sinitaival 5,
  pg. 952   IT
Pilkington Lamino Oy, pg. 1057   IT
Power Engineering Ltd., Lapintie 1, pg. 1353   IT
Region CIS, P.O. Box 100, pg. 1352   IT
Oy Skega Ab, pg. 1323   IT
Oy Steamservice Ab, Aleksanterinkatu 21, pg. 1353   IT
Tako Board Mill, Hallituskatu 1, pg. 863   IT
Tako Carton Plant Ltd., pg. 863   IT
Tampella Power Inc., Kelloportinkatu 1 D, pg. 1353   IT
Tampella Power Inc. Manufacturing Facility, Etu-
  Hankkionkatu 1, pg. 1353   IT
Tampere Sales Office & Storage Depot, Nuutisarankatu 15,
  pg. 15   IT
TAMROCK CORP., P.O. Box 256, pg. 1352   IT
Tamrock Drills, pg. 1352   IT
Tamrock Oy, Pihtisulunkatu 9, pg. 1352   IT
Tamrock Oy Northern Europe, Pispalanvaltatie 91,
  pg. 1352   IT
Tamrock Region CIS, c/o Tamrock Oy, Pihtisulunkatu 9,
  pg. 1353   IT
Oy Tamrotor Ab, pg. 1352   IT
Valmet Automation Inc.-Control Systems, P.O. Box 237,
  pg. 1449   IT
Valmet Automation Inc.- Field Instruments, P.O. Box 237,
  pg. 1449   IT
Valmet Corporation Board Machines, P.O. Box 267,
  pg. 1448   IT
Valmet Corporation Stock Preparation, P.O. Box 506,
  pg. 1448   IT

Tervakoski

Tervakoski Oy, pg. 456   IT

Tiukka

Oy Uni-Pak Ab, pg. 456   IT

Tohmajarvi

SKF Tohmac Transmission Oy, pg. 1159   IT

Toijala

Foodie Oy, Ilomaentie 25, pg. 1085   IT
Toijala Works, Hameentie 100, pg. 1088   IT

Tornio

Kandelinin Seuraajat Oy, Jaakarinkatu 4, pg. 1018   IT
Outokumpu Chrome Oy, pg. 1018   IT
Outokumpu Polarit Oy, pg. 1018   IT
Outokumpu Steel Oy, P.O. Box 82, pg. 1018   IT
Tornion Pakkauslava Oy, Roytta, pg. 456   IT

Turku

DCA-Instruments Oy, Telekatu 14, pg. 1088   IT
EG & G Wallac Oy, Mustionkatu 6, pg. 544   PB
Fidelio Nordic Oy, Pitkamaenkatu 4 B, pg. 1106   PB
Finnewos Aqua Oy, Rydonnotko 4, pg. 349   IT
Hissi-Ala Oy, Sampsankatu 6, pg. 746   IT
Huhtamaki Oy, Karsamaentie 35, pg. 638   IT

PB - *U.S. Public Companies Volume*
PV - *U.S. Private Companies Volume*
IT - *International Public & Private Companies Volume*

Keskometalli Oy, Rydonnotko 1, pg. 732 — IT
Kvaerner Masa-Yards Inc., Turku New Shipyard, Telakkakatu, pg. 771 — IT
Leaf Finland, Karsamaentie 35, pg. 638 — IT
Leiras Oy, Pansiontie 47, pg. 639 — IT
Oy Leverindus AB, pg. 1438 — IT
Nutricia Fennica Oy, pg. 992 — IT
Outokumpu Mintec Oy, Mustionkatu 2, pg. 1017 — IT
Perimistoimisto Contant Oy, Aurakatu 8, pg. 859 — IT
Tamrock Loaders Ara Oy, P.O. Box 434, pg. 1352 — IT
Turku Sales Office & Storage Depot, Lansilaituri 7, pg. 15 — IT
Turun Saippua Oy, pg. 1438 — IT
Valmet Corporation - Air Systems, pg. 1448 — IT
Viable Bioproducts Ltd., pg. 992 — IT
Oy Wrigley Scandinavia Ab, Ilpoisvagen 9, pg. 1781 — PB

Tuusula

AMER TOBACCO Ltd., Amerintie 1, pg. 72 — IT
Avesta Sheffield Oy, pg. 222 — IT
SH-Trade Oy, Teollisuustie 17, pg. 222 — IT

Uimaharju

Enocell Oy, pg. 455 — IT
Karelia Procurement Area, pg. 455 — IT

Urjala

Parker Hannifin Oy Finn Filter Division, pg. 1263 — PB

Uusikaupunki

Kemira Agro Oy, pg. 728 — IT

Vaasa

FFI Production Oy, Myllykatu 20, pg. 349 — IT
Kemira Chemicals Oy, pg. 728 — IT
Kemira Safety Oy, pg. 729 — IT
Vaasa Sales Office, Kauppapuistikko 15, pg. 15 — IT

Valkeakoski

Forchem Oy - Valkeakoski, pg. 456 — IT
Kemira Fibres Oy, P.O. Box 24, pg. 728 — IT
UPM Pack, Lempaalantie 20, pg. 1430 — IT
United Paper Mills Ltd., pg. 1429 — IT

Vammala

Isora Oy, P.O. Box 48, pg. 913 — IT
Outokumpu Mining Oy, Orivesi Mine, pg. 1016 — IT

Vantaa

Aarne Laaksonen Oy, Nittyvillankuja 3, pg. 568 — IT
Aluma Metalli, pg. 441 — IT
Ascom Fintel OY, Ralssitie 7c, pg. 87 — IT
Auto-Bon Oy, Makituvantie 3, pg. 72 — IT
Berendsen Components OY, 10 Virkatie, pg. 1284 — IT
Berendsen PMC Oy AB, 10 Virkatie, pg. 1285 — IT
Black & Decker Oy, Ayrikuja, 3, pg. 234 — PB
Oy Colly Company AB, Valimotie 8, pg. 678 — IT
Electric Rails Ltd., Rajatorpantie 8, pg. 660 — IT
Ermaco Oy, Nonkanummentie 2, pg. 230 — IT
Finnair Gateway Ravintolat Oy, Helsinki-Vantaa Airport, pg. 485 — IT
Finnaviation Oy, Teknikontie, pg. 485 — IT
Finncatering Oy, Valimokuja 2, pg. 485 — IT
Finnish Rich Coffee Ltd., Kuriiritie 5, pg. 732 — IT
HTH Keittiot Oy, Kielotie 7B, pg. 1302 — IT
Hellermann Finland, Kutoradantie 11, pg. 209 — IT
ICL Finland OY, pg. 529 — IT
Ih-Kunnossapito Oy, Rajatorpantie 8, pg. 660 — IT
Is-Plan Oy, Virtatie 9, pg. 660 — IT
IVO Generation Services Ltd., Rajatorpantie 8, pg. 660 — IT
IVO International Ltd., Rajatorpantie 8, pg. 660 — IT
IVO Service, Rajatorpantie 8, pg. 660 — IT
IVO Service Industry, Rajatorpantie 8, pg. 660 — IT
K-Maatalousyhtiot Oy, Kuriiritie 10-12, pg. 732 — IT
Kanthal Norden AB, pg. 723 — IT
Karair oy, Lentajantie 1 B, pg. 485 — IT
Kesko - Agricultural & Builders' Supplies Div., Kuriiritie 10-12, pg. 732 — IT
Kesko Central Warehouse One, Kuriiritie 5, pg. 732 — IT
Kesko Central Warehouse Two, Jokiniementie 31, pg. 732 — IT
Kesped Ltd., Jokiniementie 31, pg. 732 — PB
Kodak Oy, Ayritie, Veromiehen teollisuusalue, pg. 554 — PB
Koltek Oy, Kuussillantie 18, P.O. Box 118, pg. 1379 — IT
Koneportaat Oy, Koyhamaentie 17, pg. 746 — IT
Korpivaara Moottorialan Luotto Oy, Korpivaarantie 1, pg. 72 — IT
Korpivaara Oy, Kaivokselan Autotalo, Vanha Kaarelantie 31, pg. 72 — IT
LIC Care Oy, Hakkilankaari 1C, pg. 551 — IT
Oy Lining AB, Riihikuja 5, pg. 678 — IT
Neste Air, Helsinki Vantaa Lentoasema, pg. 913 — IT
Oy Novatool AB, Valimotie 8, pg. 678 — IT
Oy Paperi-Dahlberg Ab, Riihikuja 4, pg. 1428 — IT
Parker Hannifin Oy (Finland), Ylastontie 16, pg. 1263 — PB
Oy Pharmacia & Upjohn AB, Rajatorpantie 41 C, pg. 1049 — IT
Raychem Oy, Tiilitie 10, pg. 1362 — PB
Rexroth Oy, pg. 839 — IT
Seppala, Tikkurilantie 62, pg. 1301 — IT

Oy Sigma AB, Vetokuja 2, pg. 97 — IT
TA Control Oy, Kellokukantie 2, pg. 670 — IT
Tikkurila Oy, Kuninkaalantie 1, pg. 729 — IT
Toyota Estonia Ltd., Korpivaarantie 1, pg. 72 — IT
Viking Coffee Oy, Kuriiritie 5, pg. 643 — IT
Oy Volvo-Auto Ab, Edesvagen 1, pg. 1477 — IT
YTM Industrial Oy, Riihikuja 5, pg. 678 — IT

Varkaus

Ahlstrom Automation Oy, pg. 34 — IT
Ahlstrom Machinery Paivarinne Works, P.O. Box 137, pg. 33 — IT
Ahlstrom Machinery Recovery Boilers, P.O. Box 184, pg. 34 — IT
Ahlstrom Machinery Recovery Boilers & Heat Engineering, P.O. Box 137, pg. 33 — IT
CAE ScreenPlates-Finland, Kiertotic 27, pg. 238 — IT
Foster Wheeler Energia Oy, pg. 677 — PB
Varkauden Matkatoimisto Oy, Ahlstraminkatu 8, pg. 485 — IT

Vihanti

Raisio Group plc, pg. 1085 — IT

Vihtavuori

Kemira Metalkat Oy, pg. 728 — IT

Viiala

Viiala Mill, Tehtaantie, pg. 1429 — IT

Villmanstrand

Lappeenranti Plant, pg. 1198 — IT

Vimpeli

Rannila Steel Oy, Kalkkimaentie 1, pg. 1088 — IT

Virkkala

Udanmaan Sacha Oy, Marttatuvantie 1, pg. 661 — IT

Virrat

Killin Voima Oy, pg. 661 — IT

Voikkaa

Voikkaa Paper Mill, pg. 1428 — IT

Vuohijarvi

Kalso-Teollisuus Oy, Siikakoskentie 88, pg. 1428 — IT

FRANCE

Abondant

CXR SA, Rue de L'Ornette, pg. 1108 — PB

Agde

Agde Office, Rue de la Digue, pg. 784 — IT

Aigues-Vives

Societe Anonyme CIBA-GEIGY, Usine d'Aigues-Vives, pg. 985 — IT

Aix-en-Provence

Guigues S.A., 70, rue Pierre Duhem-Z.I. Les Milles, pg. 1361 — IT
Mistral Travaux, LeLigoures, Place Romee de Villeneuve B, pg. 206 — IT
Orangina France, B.P. 1000, pg. 566 — IT
Technip - Aix-en-Provence Branch, 70, rue Pierre Duheim, pg. 1360 — IT
Tektronix S.A.-AeP, pg. 1568 — PB

Ajaccio

Corse Composites Aeronautiques, Parc de L'Industriel'Ajaccio, pg. 1166 — IT

Albi

Calvel, pg. 1163 — IT

Alencon

SNTR Calberson, pg. 1164 — IT

Ales

Perstorp Analytical Anadis, 91, avenue des Pins d'Alep, pg. 1039 — IT
Svedala France, pg. 1324 — IT

Alfortville

Dela, 26 rue Marcel Bourdarias, pg. 570 — IT

Algolsheim

Fotolabo Club (France) S.A., Route de Volgelsheim, pg. 501 — IT

Alizay

Modo Paper Aipap, Z.I. du Clos Pre, pg. 887 — IT
Modo Paper Alicel, Z.I. du clos Pre, pg. 887 — IT
MoDo Paper Alizay, ZI du Clos Pre, pg. 887 — IT

Ambares

Cirma Enterprise, 12, av. du Chemin-de-la-Vie, pg. 53 — IT
Hydro Agri France Usine d'Ambares, Usine d'Ambares, Avenue des Industries, pg. 962 — IT

Ambes

Engrais d'Ambes, Engrais d'Ambes, Chemin De Pietru, pg. 961 — IT

Amboise

Allen France SA, 330 rue de Colombier, pg. 1268 — IT
Bundy SNC, Boulevard de l'Industrie, pg. 1342 — IT
Hydrochim, S.A., 2 Quai de Violettes, pg. 1219 — PB

Amiens

Calberson Picardie, pg. 1163 — IT
Cyclam SA, 75 rue Robert le Coq, pg. 1339 — IT
Eurolysine S.A., Plant, Z.I., rue de Vaux, pg. 41 — IT
La Ruche Picarde, 75, Rue Sully, pg. 98 — IT
SAB WABCO S.A., Zone Industrielle de Longpre, pg. 271 — IT
Sturge S.A., 66 Rue Sully, pg. 1113 — IT

Ancenis

Compagnie Francaise de Manutention, Bd Pierre et Marie Curie, pg. 834 — IT
MANITOU BF, Z.I. 430 Route de L'Aubiniere, pg. 834 — IT
Toyota Industrial Equipment Europe S.A.R.L., 250, Boulevard Robert-Schuman, pg. 1414 — IT

Ancerville

La Meusienne, pg. 571 — IT

Angers

Bull Electronics Angers, 331 ave. Patton, pg. 316 — IT
Dusolier, pg. 1163 — IT
Motorola Electronique Automobile, 8, Blvd. Charles Detriche, pg. 1139 — PB
Thyssen Ascenseurs Holding S.A., pg. 1387 — IT

Anglet

France Jardineries, Z.A. de Jorlis, Blvd. du Bab, pg. 276 — IT

Anizy-le-Chateau

Hydro Aluminium Pinon s.n.c., Rue de 7eme B.C.A., pg. 963 — IT

Annay

Slugro S.A., pg. 985 — IT

Annecy

ENTREMONT S.A., 25 Faubourg des Balmettes, B.P. 29, pg. 458 — IT
EURO RSCG Quartet, 16 rue des Mouettes, pg. 601 — IT
SALOMON S.A., METZ-TESSY, pg. 1181 — IT
Societe Industrielle de Combustible Nucleaire (SICN), 4, rue du Radar, pg. 305 — IT

Annemasse

Parker Hannifin RAK S.A., Ville-La-Grand, 17 rue des Buchillons, pg. 1261 — PB
SEFEA S.A., 15, rue de Valery, pg. 1161 — IT

Annoeullin

Claeys Semences, 9, rue de Touraihe, pg. 790 — IT

Annonay

Cereal Wander, pg. 975 — IT
Laboratoires Faure, 29 route de Californie, pg. 983 — IT

Antibes

Scubapro France S.A., Nova Antipolis, Les Terriers Nord, pg. 933 — PB

PB - *U.S. Public Companies Volume*
PV - *U.S. Private Companies Volume*
IT - *International Public & Private Companies Volume*

1575

Geographic Index-Non U.S.

Antony

Amway France, 14, Avenue Francois-Sommer, pg. 69   **PV**
Analog Devices S.A., Parc de Haute, Technologie D'Antony II, pg. 108   **PB**
Ascom SA, 5, rue Jacques Rueff, pg. 87   **IT**
Bekaert France, Parc de Haute Technologie, 23, rue Alexis de Tocqueville, pg. 184   **IT**
Bobst S.A., pg. 198   **IT**
Chugai-Rhone-Poulenc SNC, 20 Avenue Raymond Aron, pg. 291   **IT**
Claudius Peters S.A., Centre A'Affaires D'Antony, 2 Rue de La Renaissance, pg. 131   **PB**
The Kendall Co., 15 rue Marcelin Berthelot, pg. 1647   **PB**
Kidde Dexaero S.A., 4 Rue Henri Poincare, pg. 1500   **IT**
Komori France S.A., 19, Rue Georges Besse, Parc de Haute Technologie II, pg. 745   **IT**
Polychrome France S.A., 8 Avenue Francois Arago, pg. 370   **IT**
Presstech Controls SA, 4 Rue de Alexis de Tocqueville, pg. 790   **PB**
Sensormatic (France) S.A., Parc De Haute Technologie, 7 rue Alexis de Tocqueville, pg. 1457   **PB**
Symbol Technologies S.A., Centre d'Affaires d'Antony, 3 Rue de la Renaissance, pg. 1546   **PB**
RP Tanabe, 20 Avenue Raymond Aron, pg. 1354   **IT**
Teac France S.A., 17 Rue Alexis-de-Tocqueville, pg. 1360   **IT**
Thomson-CSF Services & Systemes Sol Spatiaux, 34, av. Leon Jouhaux, pg. 1383   **IT**

Arbois

Manoir Industries, 83 Avenue Pasteur, pg. 570   **IT**

Archamps

Phoenix Technologies Ltd., Batiment Hera, International Business Park, pg. 1292   **PB**

Arcueil

ISS France S.A., 50 Avenue Gabriel Peri, pg. 656   **IT**
Matra Telecommunications Paris-Loire, 10-12, avenue de la Convention, pg. 793   **IT**
Thomson-CSF, 1, avenue Aristide Briand, pg. 1382   **IT**

Argenteuil

Briggs & Stratton France S.A.R.L., 2 rue Gay Moquet, pg. 252   **PB**
CEPE, 44, avenue de la Glaciere, pg. 1381   **IT**
Ciap S.A., 5 Rue Guy Moquet, pg. 994   **IT**
DIC France S.A.R.L., 107/111 rue du Moulin Sarrazin, pg. 372   **IT**
Etablissement d'Argenteuil, 1, Avenue du Parc, pg. 383   **IT**
General Motors France Automobiles S.A., 1-9 Avenue du Marais, Angle Quai de Bezons, pg. 722   **PB**
Givaudan-Roure S.A., pg. 1120   **IT**
KME France S.A.R.L, 141/145 Rue Michel Carre, pg. 719   **IT**
Kubota Europe S.A., 19-25, rue Jules Vercruysse, Z.I., pg. 763   **IT**
Metco S.A., pg. 1307   **IT**
Pain Jacquet S.A., rue Michel Carre, pg. 1021   **IT**
Protec-Feu S.A., 16, rue Ambroise Croizat, pg. 1071   **IT**
Sevcon SA, 12 Rue Jean Poulmarch, pg. 1563   **PB**

Armentieres

Becquet S.A., pg. 1015   **IT**

Arpajon

Chr. Hansen France S.A., pg. 289   **IT**

Arras

Oldham France SA, pg. 125   **IT**
SNT Calberson Arras, pg. 1164   **IT**

Asnieres-la-Giraud

Combibloc S.a.r.l., 1, rue d'Anjou, pg. 1156   **IT**

Asnieres-sur-Seine

DMB&B Paris, 20 rue des Jardins, pg. 304   **PV**
FHP Vileda S.A., pg. 506   **IT**
FRB Connectron SA, 9-11 Rue H.G. Fontaine, pg. 1268   **IT**
GEC Composants S.A., 2 Rue Henri Bergson, pg. 546   **IT**
International Marketing & Promotions, 20, rue des Jardins, pg. 304   **PV**
Le Magnesium Industriel, Tour d'Asnieres, pg. 1028   **IT**
Microfusion, Tour d' Asnieres, 4 Avenue Laurent Cely, pg. 1028   **IT**
Reed Travel Group-France, 14 rue des Parisiens, pg. 1097   **IT**
SNC GEC Composants et Cie, 2 Rue Henri Bergson, pg. 546   **IT**
Societe Francaise des Ascenseurs KONE, Centre d'Affaires Objectif 2, 2, rue Louis Armand, pg. 748   **IT**
Softec, 42, rue Gallieri, pg. 793   **IT**

Toyota Motor Corporation, Paris Branch Office, c/o S.I.D.A.T. Toyota France, 3 Rue de Normandie, pg. 1413   **IT**

Assesse

Wilson-Fiberfil International SA, 2 Rue de l'Industrie, pg. 46   **IT**

Athis-Mons

Heudebert, 4-6, rue Edouard Vaillant, pg. 380   **IT**
Sanders, 17 Quai de l'Industrie, pg. 459   **IT**

Aubagne

Pons, Z.I. des Paluds, Avenue de la Floride, pg. 1382   **IT**
Socaco S.A., B.P. 548, Zone Industrielle, pg. 1060   **IT**

Aubergenville

Komatsu France S.A., 21 29, Rue du Clos Reine, pg. 744   **IT**
Les Jardins de Flins, CD 14, Flins-sur-Seine, pg. 781   **IT**
Rieter Automotive France S.A., pg. 1117   **IT**

Aubervilliers

Arus Group, 173-179, boulevard Felix Faure, pg. 79   **IT**
Forbo Tapis S.a.r.l., pg. 498   **IT**
Intertuft S.a.r.l., pg. 498   **IT**
Kiffer et Hamaide, 83-85 Ave. Victor Hugo, pg. 789   **IT**
Georges Lang Continu S.A., 45 Avenue Victor Hugo, pg. 889   **IT**
Longometal, pg. 571   **IT**
SARL MD Ile De France, pg. 302   **IT**
Matra Communication, 51, rue Victor-Hugo, pg. 793   **IT**
Prolifix, 111 Ave. Victor Hugo, pg. 789   **IT**
R.T.I. Realisations Telematiques Internationales), 155 Avenue Jean jaure, pg. 823   **PB**
SAR-Societe d'Applications Routieres, 44, rue Sadi Carnot, pg. 789   **IT**

Audincourt

ECIA-Equipments Et Composants Pour L'industrie Automobile, pg. 1021   **IT**

Audry

Usines Laprade, pg. 571   **IT**

Aulnay-sous-Bois

Brother France S.A., 8 et 10, Rue Nicolas Robert, pg. 229   **IT**
FMC Food Machinery France, S.A., pg. 606   **PB**

Aumale

SFAM Societe Francaise d'Ampoules Mecaniques SARL, pg. 1523   **IT**

Auneau

Polarcup France S.A., Route de Roinville, pg. 638   **IT**

Aurillac

Lacassagne, pg. 1164   **IT**

Autheuil

Van Leer Fibre & Plastique France S.A., pg. 1147   **IT**

Auxerre

Morvar Paris, pg. 1164   **IT**

Auxonne

Service Genetiques S.A.R.L., Chemin de L'Enseigure, pg. 299   **PB**
Thomson Television Components France, pg. 1384   **IT**

Avallon

SKF Slewing Bearings (RKS S.A) Route de Vassy, pg. 159   **IT**

Avignon

SNT Calberson Avignon, pg. 1164   **IT**

Avon

Corning Europe Inc., pg. 449   **PB**
Corning France, S.A., 44 Avenue De Valvins, pg. 449   **PB**

Avrille

Kollmorgan Artus, Chemin du Champ des Martyrs BP9, pg. 966   **PB**

Bagneux

Eurodif SA, 116, av. Aristide-Briand, pg. 305   **IT**
Keraglass, Rue Saint-Laurent, pg. 1172   **IT**
Melox, 116, avenue Aristide-Briand, pg. 305   **IT**
Selection du Reader's Digest S.A., 1 a 7 Avenue Louis Pasteur, pg. 1368   **PB**
Thomson-CSF Airsys, 7,9 rue des Mathurins, pg. 1382   **IT**
Thomson-CSF NCS France, 7/9, rue des Mathurins, pg. 1382   **IT**
Thomson Shorts Systemes S.A., 9, rue des Mathurins, pg. 1383   **IT**

Bagnolet

Cafe St-Louis, Rue J. Jaures 40, pg. 534   **IT**
Cascades Commercialisation S.A., Les Mercuriales, Tour Ponant, pg. 274   **IT**
Cascades S.A., Les Mercuriales, Tour Ponant, 40 Jean Jaures, pg. 274   **IT**
Cerrap, Rue J. Jaures 40, pg. 534   **IT**
DataCard France S.A., Tour Gallieni II 36, Ave. Gallieni, pg. 313   **PV**
Elscint France S.A., 19-21 rue Jean Lolive, pg. 450   **IT**
Estevenon, Rue J. Jaures 40, pg. 534   **IT**
France Quick, Rue J. Jaures 40, pg. 534   **IT**
Free Time, Rue J. Jaures 40, pg. 534   **IT**
General de Bazar, Rue J. Jaures 40, pg. 534   **IT**
La Rose D'Anjou, Rue J. Jaures 40, pg. 534   **IT**
Le Pactole, Rue J. Jaures 40, pg. 534   **IT**
L'Eclairage Technique S.A., 163 Ave. Gallieni, pg. 453   **IT**
London House, Rue J. Jaures 40, pg. 534   **IT**
Milupa S.A., pg. 992   **IT**
MOULINEX S.A., 11, Rue Jules-Ferry, pg. 896   **IT**
Munters Services SA, 6, Rue Sadi Carnot, pg. 669   **IT**
Negoce Pierre, Rue J. Jaures 40, pg. 534   **IT**
Nice Gare, Rue J. Jaures 40, pg. 534   **IT**
Restaurap, Rue J. Jaures 40, pg. 534   **IT**
S.P.R.B., Rue J. Jaures 40, pg. 534   **IT**
Takenaka Belgium S.A. - France Branch, 36, Avenue du General de Gaulle, pg. 1351   **IT**
Tir a Locques, Rue J. Jaures 40, pg. 534   **IT**

Bagnols-sur-Ceze

Marcoule Plant, pg. 305   **IT**

Baillargues

Baillargues Office, R.N. 113, pg. 784   **IT**

Bailleul

Nordlys SA, Avenue de l'Europe, Zone Industrielle de la Blanche Maison, pg. 415   **IT**

Bailly

Land Instruments Sarl, 7 Parc des Fontenelles, pg. 798   **IT**

Balaives

Vynex s.r.l., pg. 423   **IT**

Balan

Cestidur Industries SA, Zone Industrielle, Front de Bandiere, pg. 354   **IT**

Ballainvilliers

Gould Electronique SA, Test & Measurement, 57 Rue Saint Sauveur, pg. 1592   **PB**

Barbizon

Suspa France SARL, Rue des Plantes, pg. 1322   **IT**

Barlin

Societe de Transmissions Automatiques, Z. I. de Ruitz, B.P. 82, pg. 1102   **IT**

Bayonne

Duverger, pg. 1163   **IT**
Milchem France S.A.R.L., 6 Residence du Parc Avenue du B.A.B., pg. 167   **PB**

Beacouze

Skil France, S.A., Ave. De La Fontaine, pg. 577   **PB**

Beaucaire

Le Vitrage du Midi, ZI BP 68, pg. 1172   **IT**

Beauchamp

ITW de France SA, 305 Chaussee Jules Cesar, pg. 868   **PB**

Beaugency

Bertrand Faure Equipements SA, Route d'Orleans,
pg. 192 — IT

Beaumont-Hague

La Hague Plant, pg. 305 — IT

Beaune

Thomson-CSF Passive Components, 74, route de Savigny,
pg. 1382 — IT

Beaurepaire-d'Isere

Alisere S.A., pg. 68 — IT
COPAL SNC, pg. 68 — IT
Copal, Route de Marcollin, pg. 1028 — IT
Lawson Mardon Boxal France S.A., pg. 68 — IT

Beauvais

DSM Engrais France SA, Zone Industrielle No. 2, 6, Allee
Bernard Palissy, pg. 355 — IT
4P Emballages France, pg. 1146 — IT

Begles

S.A. des Papeteries de Begles, 91, quai du President
Wilson, pg. 789 — IT

Beinheim

R.P. Scherer S.A., 74, Rue Principale, pg. 1438 — PB

Belfort

Danzas, pg. 1163 — IT
GEC Alsthom-Intermagnetics S.A., 3 Ave. de Trois Chenes,
pg. 56 — IT
GEC Alsthom-Intermagnetics S.A., 3 Ave. de Trois Chenes,
pg. 894 — PB
Nipson Printing Systems, 28 rue Thierry Mieg, pg. 316 — IT
Societe d'Investissement et d'Industrialisation de Belfort
(SYBEL), 1 rue de Morimont, pg. 316 — IT
Societe Europeenne de Renovation et de Reparation
Informatique de Belfort (SERRIB), 6 ave. des Usines,
pg. 316 — IT

Bellegard

Societe des Adhesifs de Bellegarde-Ain S.A., 19 rue de
Savoie, pg. 1203 — IT
Sylea Harness Assembly Plant, pg. 785 — IT

Bellegarde-sur-Valserine

Anciens Establissements Goyot et Cie, Rue Brazza,
pg. 1507 — PB

Belleme

Key Plastics France SA, Zone Industrielle, Route du Mans,
pg. 618 — PV
Smith International France, S.A.R.L., pg. 1478 — PB

Bellerive-sur-Allier

Carpenter Technology (France) SARL, 77, Avenue Fernand
Auberger, pg. 308 — PB

Bellignat

Battenfeld France S.A., Agence d'Oyonnax, Zone
Industrielle Sud, pg. 825 — IT
Billion SA, pg. 836 — IT

Bennwhir Gare

Miroiterie du Rhin, Rue de l'Industrie, pg. 1172 — IT

Benouville

Les Jardins de Benouville, Route de Caen, Car Ferry,
pg. 781 — IT

Berck

Laboratoire Portex S.A., Zone Industrielle de la Vigogne,
pg. 1268 — IT

Bergues

Continental Can France S.A., pg. 1207 — IT
Continental Can G.I.E., pg. 1207 — IT
Continental PET France S.A., pg. 1207 — IT

Bernay

Bifurcated Engineering France S.A., 1, Rue de Menneval,
pg. 297 — IT
Societe Conditionnement et Industrie S.A., pg. 922 — IT
Zeneca Sopra, rue des Canadiens, pg. 1527 — IT

Besancon

Calparc Bat. D., 10, Rue Taco, pg. 816 — PB
Du Pont de Nemours (France) S.A., Besancon Plant,
pg. 532 — PB
G.T.F.C., Zone Industrielle de Thiese-B.P. 942, pg. 206 — IT
S.I.S., 32 rue Tenne Rouge, pg. 569 — IT
Sormel, Z.I. de Chateaufarine, B.P. 1565, pg. 793 — IT

Bethune

Beau Marais S.A. (France), 483 Rue de Beau Marais,
pg. 850 — IT
Firestone France S.A., B.P. 3, pg. 214 — IT
Schenectady Europe, S.A., pg. 970 — PV

Beziers

Beziers Office, 7, Rue Paul Langevin, Zone Industrielle,
pg. 784 — IT
LA MERIDIONALE DES BOIS ET MATERIAUX, 84 Ave.
22 du 22 Aoult 1944, pg. 784 — IT
Littorale Oenologie S.A., 27, Quai du Pont Neuf,
pg. 1143 — IT

Bezons

AGIE France Swiss EDM Sarl, 125-129 Rue Casimir-Perier,
pg. 488 — IT
Chemie Linz France S.A.R.L., 9, rue Marcel Paul,
pg. 356 — IT
DSM Resins France S.A., 119, Rue Salvador Allende,
pg. 355 — IT
Disco Hi-Tec France Sarl, 50, Rue de Pontoise,
pg. 413 — IT
Perstorp Analytical S.A., 1, Rue Jean Carrasso,
pg. 1040 — IT
Perstorp France, 1, rue Jean Carrasso, pg. 1040 — IT
Perstorp S.A.-Div. Bakelite, 1, Rue Jean-Carrasso,
pg. 1037 — IT
Perstorp S.A.-Div. Components France, 1, Rue Jean
Carrasso, pg. 1040 — IT
Perstorp S.A. Flooring Division, 1, Rue Jean Carrasso,
pg. 1039 — IT
Seltra, 9 rue Charles Francois Daubigny, pg. 807 — IT
Standard Products Industrial, 9, Rue Louis - Rameau,
pg. 1505 — PB

Biard

Etablissement de Poitiers, 24, avenue Marcel Dassault,
pg. 383 — IT

Biarritz

Etablissement de Biarritz, pg. 383 — IT

Biesles

Sodipan Biessard, 40-42 Quai des Roches, pg. 673 — PB
Wrigley S.A., pg. 1781 — PB

Bievres

Brossard, Parc Burospace 26, Route De La Paine De Gisy,
pg. 1435 — PB
Gandalf S.A., 16,Burospace, pg. 541 — IT
GrandMet Foods France, Parc Burospace No. 26,
pg. 408 — IT

Bihorel

Schauman S.A., 216 route de Neufchatel, pg. 1429 — IT

Billere.

Weatherford France, S.A., 94A Avenue, pg. 1750 — PB

Biot

Societe Anonyme Mediterraneene de Salaisons,
pg. 429 — PB

Bischwiller

SOCAMIC Ste. de Caoutchouc et de Produits Chimiques
S.a.r.l., Boite Postal No. 11, pg. 1167 — IT

Blagnac

AIRBUS INDUSTRIE, 1, Rond Point Maurice Bellonte,
pg. 39 — IT
AlliedSignal Aerospace Service Corporation, Centrada, Ave.
Didier Daurat, pg. 52 — IT
Avions de Transport Regional - ATR, 1, Allee Pierre Nadot,
pg. 654 — IT
Cryotechnologies S.A., 4, rue Marcel Doret, pg. 1381 — IT
B.F. Goodrich Aerospace, 64 Chemin Barrieu, pg. 752 — PB
Rockwell-Collins France, S.A., 6 avenue Didier Daurat,
pg. 1400 — PB
Sextant Avionique, Centre Avionique de Toulouse, 15, av.
Didier-Daurat, pg. 1382 — IT
Technofan, ZAC du Grand Noble, 10, place Marcel
Dassault, pg. 786 — IT

Blanc Mesnil

Canon France S.A., Z.I. du Coudray, pg. 262 — IT
GAZ et Thermique Controle S.A.R.L., Rue de la Victorie,
pg. 1149 — IT
Hasbro S.A., Centre D'Affairs Paris Nord, Immeuble
Ampere, pg. 797 — PB
Organisation de Vente des Produits Fasson S.a.r.l., Zone
Industrielle du Coudray Rue Isac N, pg. 154 — PB
Uddeholm S.A., B.P. 243, pg. 1472 — IT

Blanquefort

C.V.B.G. (Consortium Vinicole de Bordeaux et de la
Gironde), Dourthe Kressmann, pg. 751 — IT
Doc Francois, 4 Rue Pierre et Marie Curie, pg. 98 — IT
G.C.A., 4, Ave. du Port-du-Roy, pg. 206 — IT
Gravey S.A., Z.I. 40, rue Georges-Guynemer, pg. 784 — IT

Blere

Rimoldi France S.A., 1-3, Rue Des Freres Lumiere,
pg. 1118 — IT

Blois

B. I. P., 3, rue des Allies, pg. 791 — IT
Banque Regionale, 7 rue Gallois, pg. 563 — IT
Distriservice, 14, boulevard Rene Gentils, pg. 792 — IT
Laboratoire LaChartre S.A., 126 ave de Veedome,
pg. 1331 — PB
Lucas Diesel Systems, 9 Boulevard de l'Industrie,
pg. 820 — IT
Sograph, 14, boulevard Alexis Carrel, pg. 793 — IT
Swift Adhesifs S.A., Allee Robert Schuman, pg. 370 — IT

Bobigny

Meules Deplanque, 43, rue Saint-Andre, pg. 1173 — IT
Papeteries de Montevrain SA, 153 Rue de Stalingrad,
pg. 567 — IT
Tech Data France, 26, avenue Henri Barbusse,
pg. 1563 — PB
Valeo-Lighting, 34, rue Saint-Andre, pg. 240 — IT

Bohain-en-Vermandois

Bohain Jeumont Cables, 48, rue Paulin Pecqueux,
pg. 706 — IT

Bois-d'Arcy

BMW France S.A., pg. 178 — IT
Fimacom - Financiere Matra Communication, Rue Jean-
Pierre Timbaud, pg. 792 — IT
Polaroid (France) S.A., 4 rue Jean Pierre Timbaud,
pg. 1314 — PB

Bois-Colombes

Detrey Dentsply S.A., 72, rue du General Leclerc,
pg. 500 — PB
DeZurik-France S.A.R.L., pg. 727 — PB
International Flavors & Fragrances I.F.F. (France) S.a.r.l.,
47 Rue Victor Hugo, pg. 899 — IT
Societe d'Exploitation des Materiels Martin Baker SEMMB
(SA), 20 Bld., Louis Seguin, pg. 1166 — IT

Boissy-Saint Leger

Fanuc France S.A., 10 rue de Valenton, pg. 477 — IT

Bon Encontre

SNT Calberson Agen, pg. 1164 — IT

Bonchamp-les-Laval

SNT Calberson, pg. 1164 — IT

Bondoufle

Cardo Door Production France S.A.S., 1/3 Rue Pierre
Josse, pg. 269 — IT
Soprelec SA, 27 rue Gustave Eiffel, pg. 803 — IT

Bondy

Dacem S.A.R.L., 129 Ave. Gallieni, pg. 734 — IT
Establissments Darty & Fils S.A., 129 Ave. Gallieni,
pg. 734 — IT
Le Groupe Darty, 129 Ave. Gallieni, pg. 734 — IT
MDR S.A., 129 av. Gallieni, pg. 734 — IT
Menacredit, 129 Ave. Gallieni, pg. 734 — IT

Bonneuil-sur-Marne

Cofrafer S.A., 8, route de Stains, pg. 79 — IT
DOM S.A.R.L., 2, Ave. des Roses, pg. 233 — PB
Knurr s.a.r.l., 4, Avenue des Violettes, pg. 739 — IT
Zippo Europe S.A., Z.A. des Petits Carreaux, pg. 1207 — PV
Zippo France S.A., Z.A. des Petits Carreaux, pg. 1207 — PV

Bonneval

Amortex, pg. 137 PB

Bonneville

Ascom HPF SA, Ave. de Savoie, pg. 87 IT

Bonvin

CREDIT AGRICOLE, 91-93, Boulevard Pasteur, pg. 341 IT

Boos

Thomson-CSF Airsys, Centre Electronique de Rouen-Ymare, pg. 1382 IT
Thomson-CSF Microelectronique, Z.I. du Mont-Jarret, pg. 1382 IT

Boossey

G. Leblanc S.A., 13 Rue Georges-Leblanc, pg. 657 PV

Bordeaux

A & R Barriere Freres S.A., 18, Rue Lafont, pg. 1322 IT
ALS Tonic, 43 cours de l'Intendance, pg. 116 IT
Ahlstrom-Hanssen S.A., 81 Boulevard Pierre 1er, pg. 34 IT
Banque de L'Aquitaine, 10, rue Vauban, pg. 548 IT
Bordeaux-Brazza, Quai de Brazza, pg. 784 IT
Bordeaux Office, 6 rue de Lajaunie, pg. 784 IT
Carclin S.A., pg. 612 IT
Domaines Codem S.A., pg. 467 IT
Grands Millesimes de France S.A., 43, Cours du Medoc, pg. 1322 IT
La Cornubia, 85 Quai de Brazza, pg. 852 IT
SHSO, Hotel Aquitania Quartier du Lac, pg. 20 IT
Societe Bordelaise de Cic, 42, Cours du Chapeau Rouge, pg. 565 IT
Societe Nouvelle des Etablissements Marly Freres SA, 24, rue des Terres de Borde, pg. 1172 IT
Somir, Rue Edouard-Faure, pg. 1172 IT
Somir Autover, Rue Edouard-Faure, pg. 1172 IT
Vickers Medical France S.A., Bat 3, Complexe Minipark, Avenue due Proffessuer Lavignol, pg. 1467 IT

Bordes

Turbomeca Division, pg. 787 IT
Turbomeca Microturbo Division, pg. 786 IT

Bornel

Levis Sapt. SA, 2 Rue Jeanne d'Arc, pg. 43 IT

Boucau

Ciments de l'Adour, rue Naurice Perse, pg. 292 IT
Socadour, Usine de Tarnos, pg. 964 IT

Boulay

Euroliners, Zone Industrielle de Boulay, Route de Metz, pg. 789 IT
Harris Moran Seed Company, Z.I. de Boulay, Route de Metz, pg. 789 IT

Boulazac

Bernis, pg. 1163 IT

Boulogne

Allen Automotive International (France) S.A.R.L., 112 Rue de Paris, pg. 1 PB
BERTRAND FAURE, 276, rue Louis Bleriot, pg. 192 IT
Bertrand Faure Equipements SA, 276, rue Louis Bleriot, pg. 192 IT
The Brand Company, 50/54 rue de Silly, pg. 116 IT
CCCE Nelson/Babylone, 50/54 rue de Silly, pg. 116 IT
CSAR France, 69 Rue d'Aguesseau, pg. 243 IT
Colorado, 52 rue Reinhardt, pg. 601 PV
Creep, 11, avenue Andre Morizet, pg. 1199 IT
Du Moulin S.C.I., rue Pierre Martin, pg. 463 IT
Steendy S.A., rue Pierre Martin, pg. 463 IT
Super JV S.A., rue Pierre Martin, pg. 463 IT
Transtar, 14 rue de la Ferme, pg. 316 IT
Vielle Colme S.C.I., rue Pierre Martin, pg. 463 IT

Boulogne-sur-Mer

Conte S.A., 6 rue Gerhard Hansen, pg. 1273 IT
Henkel Entretien S.A., pg. 612 IT
P.G. Group, Zone industrielle, de l'Inquetrie, rue Pierre Martin, pg. 463 IT

Boulogne-Billancourt

Agence Maritime et Conteneurs, 128, Rue Aguessean, pg. 682 IT
Alusuisse-Lonza France S.A., pg. 68 IT
Alusuisse Produits Speciaux Sarl, pg. 68 IT
BTU (France) SARL, 140 Rue d'Aguesseau, pg. 164 PB

D.L. Blair Europe, 69 bis, rued'Auguesau, pg. 148 PV
CPM & Compagnie, 50 rue de Silly, pg. 116 IT
Compagnie D'Etudes Et De Traitement De L'Information S.A., 1 Avenue Pierre Grenier, 92, pg. 776 PB
Defa S.A., 41 Rue Yves Kermen, pg. 1322 IT
Europcar International S.A., pg. 1475 IT
Forges de Bologne, pg. 62 PB
French Division, pg. 423 PB
Hakuhodo France S.A., 130, rue de Silly, pg. 588 IT
Henkel France S.A., 161 Rue de Silly, pg. 612 IT
ITMI, 86/90 rue Thies, pg. 263 IT
Janssen-Cilag S.A., 17, rue de'l Ancienne-Mairie, pg. 929 PB
Kanterbrau S.A., Tour Chenonceaux, 204, Rond Point du Pont de Sevres, pg. 381 IT
LA POSTE GROUP, 4 Quai du Point du Jour, pg. 785 IT
Lawson Mardon Packaging S.A., pg. 69 IT
Moore France SA, 22-24 Rue de Sevres, pg. 890 IT
Sophie Nerval S.A., 150, rue Gallieni, pg. 612 IT
Novo Nordisk Pharmaceutique S.A., 32-36, rue de Bellevue, pg. 988 IT
Oh!..Poivrier!, 98, rue du Chateau, pg. 1274 IT
Pathe Marconi EMI SA, 62 rue de Sevres, pg. 427 IT
RENAULT, 34 Quai du Point du Jour, pg. 1102 IT
Schneider Electric S.A., 40 Avenue Andre Norizet, pg. 1207 IT
SCHNEIDER S.A., 64-70 Ave. Jean-Baptiste Clement, pg. 1207 IT
Seagate Technology, 62 Bis Ave., Andre Morizet Ave., pg. 1450 PB
Teledyne France, L'Arche du Parc, 738 Rue Yves Kermen, pg. 44 PB
Unilaser, 86/90, rue du Dome, pg. 29 IT
Union Generale de Savonnerie (UGS), 150, rue Gallieni, pg. 612 IT
Watson Brown, 95, Rue de Billancourt, pg. 682 IT
Willis Faber (Middle East) S.A.L., 3 Ter. Avenue Jean-Baptiste Clement, pg. 1510 IT

Bourbourg

Trefileries de Bourbourg, Route Du Guindal 15, pg. 184 IT

Bourg-en-Bresse

Banque Regionale De L'Ain, 102, Boulevard Edouard Herriot, pg. 563 IT
Dupont-Bedu, pg. 1163 IT
Mutuelle de L'est, 8, avuenue Louis Jourdan, pg. 19 IT

Bourg-la-Reine

Volvic, 60, Boulevard du Marechal Joffre, pg. 381 IT

Bourg-les-Valence

ITW Spit, 150 Route de Lyon, pg. 869 PB

Bourges

Bernis, pg. 1163 IT
Rosinox, 23 rue Felix Chedin, pg. 260 IT
Usine de Bourges, 121, rue de Mazieres, pg. 570 IT

Bourron

Hepworth Minerals and Chemicals S.A., Route de Villiers, pg. 615 IT

Boussens

Societe des Produits Chimiques du Sidobre-Sinnova S.A., pg. 614 IT

Bouzonville

Plasanit SARL, pg. 838 IT

Brebieres

Perstorp S.A. Concrete Admixtures, 10 rue Comtesse, pg. 1037 IT
Perstorp S.A.-Div. Chemitec, 10, Rue Comtesse, pg. 1037 IT

Brest

Thomson-CSF Microelectronique, 10, avenue de la l'ere DFL, pg. 1382 IT
Thomson-CSF Radars & Contre-Mesures, Centre Electronique de Brest, 10, avenue de la l'ere DFL, pg. 1382 IT
Thomson-CSF Services Industrie, Rue Graham Bell-Plouzane, pg. 1383 IT
Thomson Sintra Activites Sous-Marines, Route de Sainte-Anne-du-Portzic, pg. 1383 IT

Bretigny-sur-Orge

CGA-HBS (Compagnie Generale d'Automatisme), Le Plessis Pate, pg. 53 IT
Clause, 1, avenue Lucien Clause, pg. 790 IT

Brive

Bernis, pg. 1163 IT

Thomson-CSF Communications, 6, rue Lieutenant Colonel Laporte, pg. 1382 IT

Bron

Bosam S.A., pg. 199 IT
Donaldson France, S.A., 4 Bis Rue Maryse Bastie, pg. 517 PB
Intergraph France S.A., Parc Saint Exupery-Bat.E, 6 Rue Maryse Bastie, 69500, pg. 892 PB

Brossac

Sarcal, Oriolles, pg. 662 IT

Brumath

Dominique Dutscher, S.A., pg. 448 PB

Brunoy

Unitol SA, Zone Industrielle, pg. 756 IT

Bruyers

Datec, pg. 571 IT

Bruz

Ouest Pare-Brise, ZI de la Diharbais, pg. 1172 IT

Buc

Antennes Andrew S.A.R.L., 320 Rue Helene Boucher Z.I. Centre, pg. 113 PB
Cerberus Guinard SA, 617, rue Fourny, pg. 1246 IT
Ranco France, S.r.l., pg. 1243 IT
StorageTek France, S.A., BP 73, 41, Rue Fourny, pg. 1523 PB
Syseca, Zone Industrielle Nord, 283, rue de la Minire, pg. 1384 IT
Thomson-CSF Services & Systemes sol Spatiaux, Z.I. Nord - 283, rue de la Miniere, pg. 1383 IT

Cachan

SEPHI, 7, avenue L'Eyrolles, pg. 20 IT

Caen

B.H.V. Caen, 2 rue de Vaucelles, pg. 181 IT

Cahors

Sylea Harness Assembly Plant, pg. 785 IT
Transquercy, pg. 1165 IT

Calais

Stena Line France, Car Ferries Stena Sealink, pg. 1300 IT
Tioxide Europe S.A., 1 rue des Garennes, pg. 666 IT
Travel Agency Calais, 2 Place d'Armes, pg. 1301 IT

Cambrai

H.M.Z. France s.a.r.l., 10, Rue du petit Seminaire, pg. 1134 IT
Sociafrance, 1461, Avenue de Cateau, pg. 1332 IT

Cande

Compagnie Industrielle de Materiels de Manutention, Route de Challain-la-Potherie, pg. 834 IT

Cannes

Lewmar Marine S.A.R.L., 284 Avenue Michel Jourdan, pg. 1462 IT

Carcassonne

Liferoca, pg. 1164 IT
Savim, 6, rue Coustoune, pg. 834 IT

Carignan

Ovako La Foulerie S.A., pg. 1157 IT

Carpiquet

MO Normandie, ZI de Caen Ouest, pg. 1172 IT

Carquefou

ATEA, rue de la Fonderie, pg. 503 IT
Aviatube, Z.I. Nantes-Carquefou, 15, rue de Grande-Bretagne, pg. 1028 IT
Hewlett-Packard France, Rue De L'Hotellerie, Allee du moulin Pinard, pg. 819 PB
Hewlett-Packard France, ru de l'Hotellerie, pg. 820 PB

Carrieres-sur-Seine

Smith Corona (France) S.A.R.L., pg. 1007 PV

PB - U.S. Public Companies Volume
PV - U.S. Private Companies Volume
IT - International Public & Private Companies Volume

1578

Geographic Index-Non U.S.

Carros

Paragerm France S.A., Zone Industrielle, Sectuer Bleu #17, pg. 612   IT
Soprover, ZI 5 Rue, pg. 1172   IT

Cassis

Societe Industrielle d'Automatisation Bancaire (SAIB), Quartier du Bregadan, pg. 316   IT

Castres

Castres Office, Z. I. du Melou, pg. 784   IT
PIERRE FABRE S.A., Burlats, pg. 1056   IT

Caudan

Flageul, pg. 1164   IT
MO Amorique, ZI de Kerpont, pg. 1172   IT

Cavaillon

Norton Materiaux Avances S.A.R.L., Rue Jean-Monnet, pg. 1175   IT

Cazouls-les-Beziers

Maraussan Office, Ave. de Cazouls, Maraussan, pg. 784   IT

Cely-en-Biere

Taisei (Deutscheland) GmbH, La Chateau Route de Saint-Germain, pg. 1347   IT

Cergy-Pontoise

AMP Export Ltd. S.a.r.l, pg. 8   PB
Aro Corporation S.A.R.L., B.P. 426, pg. 877   PB
Atlet France S.A., B.P. 7081, pg. 97   IT
BP France, 8 Rue des Gemeaux, pg. 220   IT
Braas France S.A.R.L., Immeuble Atrium, 3, Boulevard de l'Oise, pg. 1092   IT
CIBA Corning Diagnostics S.A., pg. 975   IT
Clarins Production Facilities, 31, chaussee Jules Cesar, pg. 295   IT
Clecim, Parc St. Christophe, pg. 774   IT
ESAB France S.A., Z.A. des Beaux-Soleils, 12, Chaussee Jules Cesar, pg. 282   IT
Electrolux & Cie SNC, pg. 441   IT
Fairchild Fasteners France, B.P. 14-95011, pg. 610   PB
FATA Industrie S.A., Les Cerclades, pg. 474   IT
Fenwick Kalmar SA, B.P. 501, pg. 1421   IT
Flymo-Husqvarna SNC, pg. 441   IT
Groupe ESAB S.A., ZA des Beaux-Soleils, 12, Chaussee Jules Cesar, pg. 283   IT
Grove Coles France, S.A., pg. 594   IT
Haden France S.A., Immeuble Athena, pg. 586   IT
Huber & Suhner France, BP 9060, pg. 637   IT
Hydro Agri Specialties France, 16, rue Traversiere, pg. 962   IT
Kalmar Kockum France SA, B.P. 501, pg. 1421   IT
Kammer Vannes S.A.R.L., B.P. No. 7059, pg. 659   PB
LIC Care S.A.R.L., Les 3 Fontaines, pg. 551   IT
La Johnson Francaise S.A., B.P. 606, pg. 593   PV
Les Pays Bas de 1845 SA, Immeuble les Cerclades, pg. 650   IT
Life Technologies SARL, 1 Rue du Limousim, pg. 505   PB
MSA de France, B.P. 617, 13 Rue De La Guivernone, pg. 1114   PB
Maxon S.A.R.L., Avenue Du Parc, pg. 717   IT
Mobrey SA, Boite Postale 675, pg. 854   PB
Raychem S.A., 2 Boulevard Du Moulin a Vent, pg. 1363   PB
Socrematic S.A., pg. 278   IT
Spie Batignolles, 10 avenue de L'Entreprise, pg. 16   IT
Synres-Almoco France S.a.r.l., Immeuble Ordinal, pg. 356   IT
TIFT SA, Eragny sur Oise, pg. 1223   IT
Thomson Training & Simulation, 1, rue du General de Gaulle, pg. 1383   IT
3M France, Boulevard de l'Oise, pg. 1606   PB
Tollens SA, 14/16, rue Saint-Hilaire, pg. 789   IT
Unisys France, La Palette Orange, Blvd. de L'Oise, pg. 1671   PB
Volvo Automobiles France S.A., Immeuble Le Montaigne, Blvd. de l'Oise, pg. 1477   IT
Watlow France S.A.R.L., Immeuble Somag, Z.I. Rue Ampere, pg. 1154   PV
Wilson Color, 7 Avenue des Oziers, Zone Industrielle du vert Galant, pg. 781   PB
Zeneca Pharma, Le Galien, 1 rue des Chauffours, pg. 1527   IT

Cergy-Saint-Christophe

Thomson-CSF Securite, 17, rue du Petit-Albi, pg. 1382   IT

Cernay

Du Pont de Nemours (France) S.A., Cernay Plant, Rue de l'Industrie, pg. 532   PB
Techlam SA, 1 Rue de L'Industrie, pg. 1166   IT

Cesson Sevigne

Metraille, pg. 1164   IT
Restaurel, 3, avenue des Peupliers, pg. 1274   IT

Cestas

Solectron France, S.A., Chemin Departemental 109, pg. 1483   PB

Ceyzeriat

Wilson-Fiberfil France SA, La Vavrette-Tossiat, pg. 46   IT

Chaillac

Barytine de Chaillac S.A., BP1, pg. 1279   IT

Chaille les Marais

Construction Mecanique et Hydraulique de Vendee, Sainte-Radegonde des Noyers, pg. 706   IT

Chalampe

Butachimie, Borte Postale 14, pg. 533   PB

Chalette-sur-Loing

Van Leeuwen Tubes SA, Le Pont A l'Ane, pg. 1450   IT

Chalon-sur-Saone

Kodak-Pathe, Zone Industrielle, pg. 554   PB
SEVA, 43, Rue du Pont de Fer, pg. 1176   IT
Simalu S.A., 9, rue Paul Sabatier, pg. 1028   IT
Sobotram, pg. 1164   IT
Socla S.a.r.l., 1, rue Paul Sabatier, pg. 378   IT

Chalons-sur-Marne

Gearhart France S.A.R.L., La Veuve, pg. 776   PB
LaBlanc, pg. 1164   IT
Mannesmann Demag SA, pg. 837   IT
Promo Industrie GV S.A., Av. du General-Patton, pg. 613   IT

Chambery

Danzas Voyages, 15, Blvd. de la Colonne, pg. 383   IT
Transrol S.n.c., Rue Felix Esclangon, Zone Industrielle de Bissy, pg. 1160   IT
Trinova S.A.-Aeroquip Div., 22 Rue Michael Faraday, pg. 25   PB
Vetrotex France, 130 avenue des Follaz, pg. 1177   IT
Vetrotex International, 767, quai des Allobroges, pg. 1177   IT

Champigny-sur-Marne

Electro Scientific Industries SARL, 1, Allee Lorentz, pg. 569   PB
Elpro S.A., 95, rue Alexandre Fourny, pg. 1246   IT
Gelman Sciences S.A., 10 Allee Lorentz, Cite' Descartes, pg. 1253   PB
Nikon France S.A., 191, rue du Marche Rollay, pg. 931   IT
Wander S.A., pg. 986   IT

Champillon

Provital, pg. 781   IT

Chantilly

Graines Franco-Suedoises S.A., 14, rue des Jardins, pg. 982   IT

Chapareillan

Proner Comatel, 3 RN 90, pg. 1242   IT

Chappes

GROUPE LIMAGRAIN, Boite Postale 1, pg. 566   IT

Charenta

Etablissements Rene Salomon, Gensac-la-Pallue, pg. 1171   IT

Charenton-le-Pont

Allianz Via Assurances, 2-4 avenue du General de Gaulle, pg. 60   IT
Allianz Via Vie-Compagnie d'Assurances sur la Vie, 8-12, avenue du General de Gaulle, pg. 60   IT
ELVIA Assurances Siege social, 2-4, avenue du General de Gaulle, pg. 60   IT
Gunnebo Entrance Control SARL, 82 ru de Paris, pg. 578   IT

ESSILOR INTERNATIONAL COMPAGNIE GENERALE D'OPTIQUE, 147 rue de Paris, pg. 462   IT
Lawter Intl. SARL, 7 rue Jean Pigeon, pg. 981   PB
Sopredis, 5, place des Marseilles, pg. 793   IT
Vellus SA, pg. 757   IT
Wang France S.A., 10, Place de la Coupole, pg. 1738   PB
Yamanouchi Pharma S.A., 10, Place de la Coupole, pg. 1519   IT

Charmeil

Sermeto, Les Martoulets, B.P. 1, pg. 1707   PB

Charquemont

Fresard Composants S.A., 2, Rue Cuiver, pg. 1161   IT

Chartres

EOC France SARL, BP 30, rue du Petit-Vau, pg. 75   IT
Echo Communication, 33 a 37, rue de Chateaudun, pg. 792   IT
Inter Regies Centre Ouesr (I.R.C.O.), 5-7, place de General de Gaulle, pg. 792   IT
Inter-Hebdo, 5.7, place du General de Galle, pg. 792   IT
Royneau, pg. 1164   IT

Chassagny

Hellion S.A., Zone Industrielle Richard Bloc, h Montargia, pg. 1028   IT

Chassieu

ABG-France S.A.R.L., 31, Av. des Freres Montgolfier, pg. 877   PB
Orchidis S.A., pg. 1461   IT

Chateau-du-Loir

Audax Industries, S.A., 2 Route de Tours, pg. 787   PB

Chateau-Gontier

Aztronic, pg. 1722   PB

Chateaufort

Sodeteg Formation, Aeroport de Toussus-le-Noble, pg. 1382   IT

Chateauroux

Bernis, pg. 1163   IT
Hydro Aluminium Chateauroux s.n.c., Zone Industrielle, Le Buxerioux, pg. 962   IT
Mead-Emballage S.A., Boulevard d'Anvaux, Zone Industrielle, pg. 1076   PB
Mead Europe Engineering, S.A.R.L., Boulevard d'Anvaux, Zone Industrielle, pg. 1076   PB

Chatellerault

Sextant Avionique, Centre de Logistique International, pg. 1382   IT
Sextant Avionique, 40, rue de la Brelandiere, pg. 1382   IT
Thomson-CSF Services Industrie, 21, rue Andre Boulle, pg. 1383   IT

Chatenay-Malabry

GEKA, S.A., 40 Ave. de Robinson, pg. 1722   PB

Chatillon

Avnet Composants and Avnet Time, 79, Rue Pierre-Semard, pg. 155   PB
Engins Tactiques Div., 2-18, rue Beranger, pg. 29   IT
FAG France, pg. 469   IT

Chatou

Auxilec, 41, boulevard de la Republique, pg. 1381   IT
IMR Finance S.A., 3 Avenue de l'Europe, pg. 1284   PB
Idmatics S.A., 41, boulevard de la Republique, pg. 1382   IT

Chaumont

Van Leer Maxemball S.A., pg. 1147   IT

Chaville

Volvo Vehicules Industriels France S.A., 140 Ave. Roger Salengro, pg. 1478   IT

Chazelles-sur-Lyon

Sibal S.A., Rue Joanny Desage, pg. 519   IT

Chelles

Moderne Mecanique SARL, pg. 1523   IT
Rexroth Pneumatic SA, pg. 839   IT

PB - *U.S. Public Companies Volume*
PV - *U.S. Private Companies Volume*
IT - *International Public & Private Companies Volume*

1579

Geographic Index-Non U.S.

Chemin-du-Petit-Bois

SEB Internationale, pg. 568   IT

Chenove

SNTR Calberson Dijon, pg. 1164   IT

Chepy

Sachs Industries SA, pg. 835   IT

Cherbourg

Intergraph France S.A., Immeuble Cherbourg Helios, 120
rue Roger Glinel B.P. 19, 50460, pg. 892   PB
Stena Line France, Gare Maritime, pg. 1300   IT
Thomson-CSF Services Industrie, 4 et 6, avenue Louis-
Lumiere, pg. 1383   IT

Chevilly Larue

Lancome Parfums et Beaute, 188 rue Paul Hochart,
pg. 818   IT
Techpack International-TPI, avenue de la Republique,
pg. 1029   IT

Chilly

Norelem S.A., Rue Blaise Pascal-Z.L., pg. 125   PB

Choisy-le-Roi

Jacobs Suchard France S.A., 16, Ave. Jean Jaures,
pg. 1289   PB

Cholet

CAIB SA - Composants Aluminium Industrialises Pour le
Batiment SA, pg. 68   IT
Nicoll, Rue Pierre et Marie Curie, pg. 430   IT
Thomson-CSF Communications, 110, avenue du Marechal-
Leclerc, pg. 1382   IT

Clairoix

C.U.P. SNC, pg. 328   IT

Clamart

BRI Group, Five, avenue Newton, pg. 52   IT
CPC France, 379, Avenue du General de Gaulle,
pg. 225   PB
Chambourcy Roche aux Fees & Cie, 361 Ave. de General
de Gaulle, pg. 920   IT
Controle Bailey Division, Five, avenue Newton, pg. 52   IT
ICI C & P France S.A., 1 Avenue Newton, pg. 664   IT
ICI France SA, 1 Avenue Newton, pg. 665   IT
SKF France S.A., Eight Avenue Reaumur, pg. 1158   IT

Claye-Souilly

WABCO Freinage de Vehicules S.A., 124 Avenue Aristide
Briand, pg. 92   PB

Clermont

BASF Peintures & Encres S.A., Zone Industrielle de Breuil
le sec, pg. 107   IT
**COMPAGNIE GENERALE DES ETABLISSEMENTS
MICHELIN**, 12, Cours Sablon, pg. 322   IT
Manufacture Francaise des Pneumatiques Michelin, Place
des Carmes Dechaux, pg. 322   IT
Queroy S.A., Breuil le Sec (Oise),Domaine de Bailly,
pg. 92   PB

Clermont-Ferrand

Economats du Centre, 55 Blvd. Cote Blatin, pg. 98   IT
Fuji Electric France S.A., 46, Rue Georges Besse,
pg. 522   IT
Hewlett-Packard France, Parc Techonologique de la,
Pardieu, 14 Avenue Leonard de Vinci, pg. 820   PB
Incognito, 31, Rue Gonod, pg. 601   IT
Rockwell Automation S.A., 158, avenue Leon Blum,
pg. 1400   PB
SMDA, Parc Helipolis, 40, rue Georges Berin, pg. 381   IT
Vitrages Isolants d'Auvergne, pg. 1172   IT

Clichy

Alcatel Submarine Networks S.A., 30 rue des Chasses,
pg. 52   IT
Bell & Howell France S.A., Espace Clichy-Immeuble Vega,
6 Allce Jean Prouve, pg. 201   PB
BIC Assemblage S.A.R.L., 11 rue Petit, pg. 1273   IT
BIC Commercial S.A., 11 rue Petit, pg. 1273   IT
BIC Marine S.A., 11 rue Petit, pg. 1273   IT
BIC Technique S.A.R.L., 11 rue Petit, pg. 1273   IT
Braun France S.A., 24/26, rue Henri Barbusse,
pg. 744   PB
Campenon Bernard, 92-98, Blvd. Victor Hugo, pg. 321   IT
Cebal S.A., 98 Boulevard Victor-Hugo, pg. 1028   IT
Checkpoint Systems France SARL, 42 Pue Mederic,
pg. 343   PB

Chep France SA, 51 Rue Pierre, pg. 212   IT
Ferembal S.A., 6 Boulevard General Leclerc, pg. 440   PB
Filergie S.n.c, 6 Blvd. Du General Leclerc, pg. 1059   IT
ITW Fixations, 15-17 rue Fournier, pg. 868   PB
Laboratoires Garnier Paris, 33 rue Martre, pg. 818   IT
Landis & Staefa Building Control (France) S.a.r.l, 16, Bd.
General Leclerc, pg. 800   IT
Landis & Staefa Energy Management (France) S.a.r.l., 16,
Bd. General Leclerc, pg. 800   IT
Les Cables de Lyon, 30 rue des Chasses, pg. 56   IT
L'OREAL S.A., Haut de Seine, pg. 818   IT
Pechiney Emballage Alimentaire, 16, boulevard du G
Leclerc, pg. 1028   IT
Programart France Incorporated, 92 Blvd. Victor Hugo,
pg. 390   PV
Rentokil SA, 84 all. Limite, pg. 1286   IT
SATAS - Societe pour l'Affranchissement et le Timbrage
Automatiques, 107, rue Henri-Barbusse, pg. 54   IT
Soblafror, Rue des Trois Pavillons, pg. 20   IT
SOCIETE BIC S.A., 8, Impasse des Cailloux, pg. 1272   IT
SOFREGAZ, 92-88, boulevard Victor Hugo, pg. 541   IT
Softal, boulevard du G Leclerc, pg. 1029   IT
Statoil France SA, c/o Gaz de France, 5, Rue des
Chasses., pg. 1298   IT
Taylor Instrument France, 65 Rue Henri Barbusse,
pg. 6   IT
Treficable Pirelli S.n.c., 6 Boulevard du General Leclerc,
pg. 060   IT

Clisson

La Crouzille Mining Division, Section geree de Vendee,
Usine de l'Ecarpiere, pg. 305   IT

Clos D' Asseville

Huck, Europe, pg. 1597   PB

Cluses

Decoupage Moulage de Savoie S.A., pg. 1122   PB
H F Securite S.A., pg. 590   IT
Somfy S.A., 8 Ave. de Margencel, pg. 376   IT

Cognac

Distillerie de la Groie, rue de la Groie, pg. 780   IT
Ja. Hennessy & Co., 1, rue de la Richonne, pg. 780   IT
Martell et Cie. S.A., Place Edouard-Martell, pg. 1217   IT
Pellisson, 58, ave. du General Leclerc, pg. 781   IT
Tonnellerie Taransaud, BP 187, ZI de Merpins, pg. 781   IT

Coignieres

EG & G Sealol-Callisto S.A., 2 Rue Lavoisier, pg. 544   PB
Suzuki France S.A., 25, Avenue De La Gare, pg. 1323   IT

Collegien

Barenbrug France SA, Parc d'Activites, Les Portes de La
Foret, pg. 167   IT
Morgan Matroc S.A., Alle de Clois des Charmes,
pg. 893   IT
Netstal-France SA, pg. 836   IT

Colmar

Freudenberg Spunweb S.A., pg. 506   IT
Liebherr-France S.A., 2, Avenue Joseph Rey, pg. 808   IT
Milupa S.A., pg. 992   IT
Societe Financiere et Commerciale de Cadillac, 10 Rue
Timken, pg. 1739   PB
Timken France, Succursale de The Timken Co., 2 Rue
Timken, pg. 1618   PB

Colombes

Channel 1, 4 et 6, rue Pierre-Brossolette 9, pg. 792   IT
Francaise d'Alimentation et de Boissons S.A., pg. 1437   IT
Gambro S.A., 1-3 Bd Charles de Gaulle, pg. 668   IT
Rene Garraud S.A., 18, rue de Plaisance, pg. 1490   IT
Johnson & Johnson S.A., 48/50 rue de Seine, pg. 931   PB
Gie LVMH Recherche, 50, rue e Seine, pg. 781   IT
Munters S.A., 142-176 Avenue de Stalingrad, pg. 669   IT
Olaer Group, 16 Rue de Seine, pg. 467   IT
Plantronics France S.A.R.L., Parc Technologique, 142-176
Avenue de Stalingrad, pg. 1308   PB
Richardson Franc SNC, 46 Avenue Kleber, pg. 1388   PB
Searle (France), 357 Rue d'Estienne d'Orves, pg. 88   IT
Skega SA, 142-176 Avenue de Stalingrad, pg. 1324   IT
Thomson-CSF Communications, Parc d'activites Kleber,
160, boulevard de Valmy, pg. 1382   IT

Combs-la-Ville

Barett S.A., rue Auguste Lumiere, pg. 1126   IT

Commentry

Pepinieres et Roseraies Geroges Delbard, Malicorne,
pg. 781   IT

Compiegne

Akzo Chemie France S.a.r.l., P.O. Box 52, pg. 47   IT
Hallmark Group France, S.A., Rue Eissel Zac de Mer
Cieres, pg. 496   PV
SNT Calberson, pg. 1164   IT

Conde-sur-Huisne

Soparco, pg. 430   IT

Conflans

Norton S.A., Rue de L'Ambassadeu, pg. 1175   IT
Sextant Avionique, Z.A. Les Boutries, pg. 1382   IT
Thomcast, 1, rue de l'Hautil, pg. 1382   IT
Thomson-LGT (Laboratoire des
Telecommunications), BP150, 78702, pg. 1385   IT
Thomson Training & Simulation, 5, rue Leonardo da Vinci,
Z.A. Les Boutries, pg. 1383   IT

Contamine-Sur-Arve

Parker Hannifin RAK, Z.A. E. La Foret, pg. 1261   PB

Contes

Mepps S.A., B.P. 09, pg. 992   PV

Coquelles

Servair Channel, Terminal Fret Zone 320, pg. 560   IT

Corbehem

Roval S.A.R.L., Rue de la Gare, pg. 1449   IT
Stora Corbehem S.A., Rue de Brebieres, pg. 1304   IT

Corbeil-Essonnes

Imprimerie Helio Corbeil, 1, rue Champlouis, pg. 792   IT
MoDo Paper Coupe Service, Rue de la Nacelle-Villabe,
pg. 887   IT

Cormeilles-en-Parisis

CiMatrix S.A., Chemin Du Travers des Champs Guillaume,
pg. 1395   PB

Correze

Van Leer Fibre & Plastique France S.A., pg. 1147   IT

Cosne-Cours-sur-Loire

SAIM Societe Les Adhesifs et Insonorisants Modernes, SA,
pg. 614   IT

Cote-d'Or

Chateau de Bligny, 21200, Bligny-Les-Beaune,
pg. 1322   IT

Coueron

Makita France S.A.-Nantes, Le Pan Loup, pg. 832   IT

Couhe

Target Technology France SARL, Aerodrome Couhe-Brux,
pg. 854   IT

Coulommiers

Brodard Graphique SNC, Boulevard de la Marne,
pg. 792   IT
Rexam Medical Packaging SA, 5 rue de Mohigny,
pg. 1106   IT

Courbevoie

Alliages Frittes Metafram, Tour Manhattan, 6 Place de l'Iris,
pg. 1028   IT
Astra-Calve S.A., pg. 1436   IT
BLC S.A. (France), 2 Boulevard Georges Clemenceau,
pg. 704   PV
Basic Chemicals Div., Quai Paul-Doumer, pg. 1109   IT
Canon Photo Video France S.A., Le Doublon, 11, Avenue
Bubonnet, pg. 263   IT
Cezus, Tour Manhattan, 6 Place de l'Iris, pg. 503   IT
Chiyoda Life Realty France S.A., 52-54, rue du Capitaine
Guynemer, pg. 287   IT
Colgate-Palmolive France, 55 Blvd. de la Mission
Marchand, pg. 398   PB
Comurhex, Tour Manhattan, pg. 305   IT
Courbevoie-Consumer Products Division, 23 Blvd. Georges
Clemenceau, pg. 673   PB
Crismatec, Les Miroirs, pg. 1174   IT
DASSAS COMMUNICATION, 37 rue Pierre Lhomme,
pg. 383   IT
Elf Aquitaine Angola, Tour Elf-2 place de la Coupole,
pg. 444   IT
Elf Lubricants, Tour Elf-2, place de la Coupole, pg. 445   IT
Fine Inorganic Chemicals, 25, quai Paul Donner,
pg. 1109   IT

PB - *U.S. Public Companies Volume*
PV - *U.S. Private Companies Volume*
IT - *International Public & Private Companies Volume*

1580

Geographic Index-Non U.S.

Framatome Connectors International, Tour Fiat, 1 place de la Coupole, pg. 503 — IT
GEFCO, 77-81 Rue du Mans, pg. 1021 — IT
Guigoz France S.A., 12 rue Industrie, pg. 920 — IT
Hoogovens Aluminium France SA, 2 Boulevard Georges Clemenceau, pg. 755 — IT
Ilco Unican France S.A., 16, rue Moulin des Bruyeres, pg. 1432 — IT
Isover Saint-Gobain, Les Miroirs, pg. 1176 — IT
John Crane France, 15 rue Laterale - BP42, pg. 1339 — IT
Kaysersberg S.A., 23, Boulevard Georges Clemenceau, pg. 673 — PB
KemRhone S.A.R.L., 25, Quai Paul Doumer, pg. 728 — IT
Kerlane, 18, avenue d'Alsace, pg. 1176 — IT
Laboratoires Pharmacia & Upjohn SARL, Tour Franklin, pg. 1049 — IT
Materiaux de Construction International, Les Miroirs, pg. 1170 — IT
Miroiteries de l'Ouest, Les Miroirs, pg. 1172 — IT
Nestle France, 17-19, Quai du President Paul Doumer, pg. 921 — IT
Norton Desmarquest Fine Ceramics, Les Miroirs, pg. 1175 — IT
Parke-Davis, 11 Avenue DuBonnet, pg. 1739 — PB
PECHINEY S.A., 10, place des Vosges, pg. 1027 — IT
Poliet, Les Miroirs, 18, avenue d'Alsace, pg. 1177 — IT
Polive/Tricosteril, 23 bd, G. Clemenceau, pg. 673 — PB
Quartz & Silice, Les Miroirs, pg. 1176 — IT
Raab Karcher France S.A., 10, Quai Paul Doumer, pg. 1458 — IT
Rhone-Poulenc Films, 25, Quai Paul Doumer, pg. 1109 — IT
RHONE-POULENC S.A., quai Paul-Doumer, 25, pg. 1108 — IT
Rhone-Poulenc Sante, 18 Boucle D'alsace, pg. 1109 — IT
Rhone-Poulenc-Textile, 25, Quai Paul Doumer, pg. 1109 — IT
SOCAP LTD Elf Trading SA, Tour Elf-2 place de la Coupole, pg. 445 — IT
SPAFI, Les Miroirs, pg. 1177 — IT
SAINT-GOBAIN, Les Miroirs, 18, avenue d' Alsace, pg. 1170 — IT
Saint-Gobain Desjonqueres, Les Miroirs, pg. 1171 — IT
Saint-Gobain Emballage, Les Miroirs, pg. 1171 — IT
Saint-Gobain Promotion et Participations Internationales, Les Miroirs, pg. 1177 — IT
Sepam, 35-41 Rue du Capraine, pg. 1501 — IT
Service Central de Propriete Industrielle, 50, rue Jean-Pierre Timbaud, pg. 1382 — IT
Societe de Distribution et d'Exportation Automobiles - SODEXA, 115 rue Danton, pg. 1020 — IT
Societe des Electrodes et Refractaires "Savoie" (SERS), Tour Manhattan, 6 Place de l'Iris, pg. 1028 — IT
Societe Europeenne des Products Refractaries (SEPR), Les Miroirs, pg. 1175 — IT
Societe Financiere des Miroirs SFM, Les Miroirs, pg. 1177 — IT
Societe Francaise de Protection Juridique (S.F.P.J.), Tour Gan, 16, place de l'Iris, pg. 565 — IT
Sogerap, Tour Elf, pg. 445 — IT
Specialty Chemicals Div., Quai Paul-Doumer, pg. 1109 — IT
Stesa, Bureau de liaison, 50, rue Jean-Pierre Timbaud, pg. 1382 — IT
Sulzer Infra S.A., pg. 1306 — IT
Tecnover, Les Miroirs, pg. 1172 — IT
Thomson Gestion Immobiliere, 50, rue Jean-Pierre Timbaud, pg. 1383 — IT
Trefimetaux S.A., 11 bis, rue de L'Hotel de Ville, pg. 720 — IT
Unilever Export France S.A., pg. 1439 — IT
VB Autobatterie S.A., 47, bd Geogres Cleueuceau, pg. 1452 — IT
VARTA S.A., pg. 1452 — IT
Vetrotex Finance, 18, avenue d'Alsace, pg. 1177 — IT
Wuhrlin-Soplamed S.A., pg. 673 — PB

Courcouronnes

Sphere SA, 6/8, rue du Bois Briard, pg. 21 — IT

Cournonterral

Cournonterral Office, Route de Murviel, pg. 784 — IT

Courtaboeuf

Optical Coating Laboratory EURL, Courtaboeuf 2, Centre Vie, pg. 1227 — PB
Telxon France S.A., Parc Hightec Apogee, 9 Avenue du Canada, pg. 1574 — PB

Coutras

Sivaq, ZI- BP 50, pg. 1172 — IT

Cran-Gevrier

Alp'Verre, 8, rue des Terrasses, pg. 1172 — IT

Craponne

S.A. MD Diffusion Sud Est, pg. 302 — IT

Crespin

Societe ANF-Industrie S.A., Place des Ateliers, pg. 201 — IT

Creteil

B.H.V. Creteil, C.C. Regional 210, pg. 181 — IT
Boge France SARL, pg. 835 — IT
Datascope SARL, Europure Creteil, 123, Chemin des Bassins, pg. 488 — PB
Gestetner S.A., Europarc, 5 Avenue Fernand Pouillon, pg. 1115 — IT
Linotype France SA, pg. 757 — IT
NRG France S.A., 70 Avenue du General-de-Gaulle, pg. 1116 — IT
OCE Graphics France S.A., 3, Rue des Archives, B.P. 138, pg. 994 — IT
Pernod, 120 av. du Marechal-Foch, pg. 566 — IT
Proser, 9/11, rue Georges-Enesco, pg. 503 — IT
S.E.P., 3/5, Voie Felix Eboue, pg. 20 — IT
Siliconix S.A.R.L., Centre Commercial De L'Echa, Place De L'Europe, pg. 367 — IT
Valeo-Electronical Systems, 2, rue Andre Boulle, pg. 240 — IT
Valeo-Electronics, Industrial Park Europorte, 2 Rue Fernand Poullion, pg. 240 — IT
Valeo-Friction Materials, 2, rue Andre Boulle, pg. 240 — IT

Crevant

Rennes, Parc d'Activities Ferchaud, pg. 1342 — IT

Crissey

Centre Est Vitrage, 40 Rue Paul Sabatier, pg. 1172 — IT
Centre Est Vitrage, 40, rue Paul-Sabatier, pg. 1172 — IT

Croissy-sur-Seine

Cogifer SA, 40 Quaide L'Ecluse, pg. 386 — IT
Disatec S.A., 101 chemin de Ronde, pg. 961 — IT
JEOL (Europe) S.A., Parc Technolgique Claude Monet, pg. 697 — IT

Croissy-Beaubourg

BetzDearborn S.A., Allee Du Ler Mai, pg. 227 — PB
Compagnie Hobart, S.A., Z.I. Paris-Est, Allee du ler Mai, pg. 1322 — PB
Herman Miller et Cie, Par d'activite de Paris Est., Rue Leon Jouhaux, pg. 1112 — PB
SNTR Calberson, pg. 1164 — IT

Croix

AUCHAN S.A., 40 Ave. de Flandres, pg. 98 — IT
3 Suisses France S.A., pg. 1015 — IT
3 Suisses International S.A., pg. 1015 — IT
VPC Promotion S.A., pg. 1015 — IT

Cruet

KOMPASS INTERNATIONAL NEUENSCHWANDER SA, St. Laurent, pg. 745 — IT

Cublize

Neste Color Compound S.A., 21, Rue Saint-Jean, pg. 914 — IT

Cuers

Thomson-CSF Services Industrie, 2, av. des Bousquets, pg. 1383 — IT
Vital Signs, Inc., pg. 1723 — PB

Custine's

PAV (Societe Industriele de Pre a Varois), pg. 570 — IT
Usine de Custines, pg. 570 — IT

D'Eppeville

Sucrerie D'Eppeville/Ham, pg. 549 — IT

D'Etrepagny

Sucrerie D'Etrepagny, pg. 549 — IT

Dammarie

Du Pont de Nemours (France) S.A., pg. 532 — PB
Sauer-Sundstrand Hydraulique S.A., 322, Rue de Seine, pg. 1198 — IT

Dardilly

Eurotherm Automation SA, Parc D'Affaires Dardilly, pg. 466 — IT

Daval

Daval, pg. 571 — IT

Davezieux

Binet Feutres, pg. 1473 — IT

Dax

Duverger, pg. 1163 — IT

Decize

Bois et Sciages de Sougy S.A., Z.I. de Teinte, pg. 1429 — IT

Descartes

Barbot Enterprise, pg. 571 — IT

Dieppe

Stena Line France, Quai Gaston Lalitte, pg. 1300 — IT
Travel Agency Dieppe, Quai G-Aston Lalitte, pg. 1301 — IT

Dijon

EURO RSCG Quartet, 6 rue Begnigne-Fremyot, pg. 601 — IT
Famicredit, pg. 379 — PB
International Flavors & Fragrances I.F.F. (France) S.a.r.l., pg. 899 — PB
Liebig Maille Amora, 48 Quai Nicholas Rollin, pg. 380 — IT

Diou

Pornon Et Cie, S.A.R.L., pg. 1488 — IT

Docelles

Papeteries de Docelles, pg. 1430 — IT

Dompierre-sur-Yon

Sovap, ZA de l'Eraudiere, pg. 193 — IT

Donchery

Harrison Radiator Division, B.P. 14 Zone Industrielle, pg. 725 — PB

Dordogne

Fromarsac SARL, Marsac Sur. Ile., Razac Sur Isle, pg. 201 — IT

Douarnenez

Star-Kist Europe, Inc., Zone Industrielle De Pouldavid, BPO 129, pg. 807 — PB

Dourdan

Calorstat Industries SA, pg. 1222 — IT
Lequeux S.A., 17 Rue de la Gaudree, pg. 552 — IT
Veeco S.A., Eleven Rue Marie Poussepin, pg. 1711 — PB

Douvrin

Societe Franco-Suedoise de Moteurs -PRV, Haisnes, B.P. 08, pg. 1476 — IT

Drancy

AlliedSignal Aerospace Service Corporation, 126, Rue de Stalingrad, pg. 52 — PB
AlliedSignal Aftermarket Europe S.A., 126, Rue de Stalingrad, pg. 53 — PB

Dreux

Banque Hieaux, 14, rue Godeau, pg. 548 — IT

Dunkirk

A.S.P. S.A., 676, rue Jean Zay, pg. 93 — IT
Det Norske Veritas, Tour de Reuze, Rue Docteur Louis Lemaire, pg. 397 — IT
Nacanco France S.A., 2 Route de Bergues, Couderque-Branche, pg. 1029 — IT
Stena Line France, Societe A.L.A., pg. 1300 — IT
Travel Agency Dunkirk, Societe A.L.A., B.P. 47, pg. 1301 — IT

Echirolles

S.A. Etablissements Bellue, pg. 302 — IT
Sogreah, 6 rue de la Lorraine, pg. 54 — IT

Ecouche

Verreries de l'Orne, pg. 1171 — IT

Ecouviez

Schleicher & Schuell France SARL, ZAI du Petit Parc, 5, Rue des Fontenelles, pg. 1206 — IT

Ecueille

Almet France, L'Oree d'Eouilly, 7, Chamin de la Forestiere, pg. 1028 — IT
EURO RSCG Quartet, 2 route de Champagne, pg. 601 — IT
GROUPE SEB, Les 4 M, Chemin-du-Petit-Bois, pg. 568 — IT
Hewlett-Packard France, Chemin des Mouilles 60, pg. 820 — PB
SEB Developpement S.A., B.P. 172, pg. 568 — IT

Elancourt

CRMA, rue Gay Lussac, pg. 560 — IT
Fenwick-Linde S.A.R.L., pg. 810 — IT
Flender S.A.R.L., 3, rue Jean Monnet, pg. 400 — IT
Matra Nokia Radiomobiles, 4, avenue Albert Einstein, pg. 793 — IT
Thomson-CSF Radars & Contre-Mesures, La Clef de St. Pierre, 1, boulevard Jean Moulin, pg. 1382 — IT

Elbeuf

Ets Asselin, rue Camille Randoing, pg. 1206 — IT

Epernay

Champagne Mercier, 75, avenue de Champagne, pg. 779 — IT
Champagne Moet & Chandon, 20 avenue de Champagne, pg. 779 — IT
France Champagne, 20, avenue de Champagne, pg. 780 — IT
Gie Moet Hennessy Distribution, 20, avenue de Champagne, pg. 781 — IT
Societe Commerciale du Champagne Mercier, 75, av. de Champagne, pg. 781 — IT
Virax, 39 Quai de La Marne, pg. 570 — IT

Epernon

Grace S.A., 53 rue St. Denis, pg. 756 — PB

Epinal

Trane Europe, B. P. 127, pg. 92 — PB

Epinouze

Sandvik Hard Materials S.A., Saint-en-valloire, pg. 1186 — IT

Epone

Duni SARL, Avenue des Paitis, pg. 421 — IT
Rescal S.A., pg. 673 — IT

Epuiseau

G.I.E. Pioneer France, pg. 1299 — PB

Eragny-sur-Oise

Senior Flexonics, pg. 1223 — IT

Esvres

Sourdillon SA, pg. 391 — IT

Etampes

Bertrand Faure Equipements SA, ZI de Brieres les Scelles, pg. 192 — IT

Etupes

Protek Synthes S.A., pg. 1307 — IT

Evian-les-Bains

Delco Products Division, 37, Avenue des Grottes, pg. 724 — PB
Evian, 22, Avenue des Sources, pg. 381 — IT
S.E.A.T., Chateau de Bionay, BP 8, pg. 381 — IT

Evreux

Minnesota Rubber Europe S.A., pg. 898 — PV
Parker Hannifin S.A., BP 3124, Rue Henri Becquerel, pg. 1261 — PB
Parker Hannifin S.A., Establishment d'Evreux, Rue Henri Becquerel, pg. 1263 — PB
SNT Calberson, pg. 1164 — IT

Evron

Bran & Luebbe S.a.r.l., 33 Bd. Renard-Benoit, pg. 1380 — IT
Ciral, Zone de la Presaie, pg. 213 — PV
Premier Industrial France S.A.R.L., Avenue de la Mauldre, pg. 1068 — IT

Evry

Academie Accor, 1, rue de la Mare-Neuve, pg. 20 — IT
ACCOR S.A., 2 rue de la Mare Neuve, pg. 20 — IT

Alcatel ISR, 523 Terrasses de l'Agora, pg. 56 — IT
ARIANESPACE SA, Boulevard de l'Europe, pg. 81 — IT
BMI, Parc techno. du Bois Chaland, 7, rue du Bois Chaland, pg. 1381 — IT
Belin/LU, Avenue Ambroise Croizat, pg. 380 — IT
Carrefour - France, ZAE Saint Guenault, pg. 272 — IT
Clever S.A., 1 a 5 Rue des Cevennes, pg. 269 — IT
Compagnie Brand et Associes S.A., 27, rue des Cerisiers, pg. 457 — IT
Crawford Door S.A., Parc Industriel Les Malines, Lisses CE No. 2701, pg. 269 — IT
Devimco, 4, rue de la Mar Nueve, pg. 20 — IT
Digital Equipment France, 9/13, Avenue du Lac, pg. 508 — PB
Dinol France S.A.R.L., pg. 981 — IT
Genus Europa SARL, Zac du Clos aux Pois, CE 4817, pg. 733 — IT
Hewlett-Packard France, Parc d'Activite du Bois Briard, pg. 819 — PB
Intech EDM SA, ZAC Les Aunettes Bat. C17, 10, Blvd. Louis Michel, pg. 489 — IT
Kennametal Hertel France, S.A., Z. I. DuBois De L'Epine, pg. 951 — PB
Lux International S.A., Z. I. La Maintiere, pg. 993 — IT
MBT France S.A., pg. 1465 — IT
MacDermid France S.A., Z.I. de L'Eglantier, 17, rue des Cerisiers, pg. 1030 — PB
MacNeal-Schwendler France, Immeuble L'EUROPEEN, 98, allee des Champs Elysees, pg. 1032 — PB
Micro-Controle S.A., P.A. de Saint Guenault, 3 bis rue Jean Mermoz, pg. 1179 — IT
Motorola S.A., 14, Allee du Cantal, Zone Industrielle, pg. 1140 — PB
Nicolitch, 1 Avenue du Bois de L'Epine, pg. 1722 — PB
PAIN JACQUET S.A., 2 rue Maryse Bastie, pg. 1021 — IT
Pullmar International Hotel, 2, rue de la Mare-Neuve, pg. 20 — IT
Resinter, 2, rue de la Mare-Neuve, pg. 20 — IT
Societe Hoteliere Paris Vanves, 2 rue de la Mare Neuve, pg. 20 — IT
Societe Internationale des Hotels Novotel, 2 rue de la Mare Neuve, pg. 21 — IT
Soderec International, 102 Place des Miroirs, pg. 803 — IT
Sumitomo Electric Hartmetall GmbH, pg. 1314 — IT
Wilson France SARL, Z.I. Petite Montagne Sud., 54 Rue du Cantal, pg. 73 — IT

Eybens

Hewlett-Packard France, 5, Avenue Raymond Chanas, pg. 819 — PB

Faches-Thumesnil

Electrification Charpente Levage (E.C.L.), 52, Rue Carnot, pg. 1028 — IT
Espace Jardin, 1 Route de Vendeville, pg. 276 — IT

Faremoutiers

Pechiney Batiment, Zone Industrielle Pechiney, pg. 1028 — IT

Fecamp

AEP France S.A.S., Boite Postale No.8, 76400, pg. 5 — PB

Feignies

SARL Distrisid, pg. 302 — IT

Feuquieres-en-Vimeu

Piole, 24 rue Saint-Saens, pg. 570 — IT
Swish France SA, 8 Rue Aristride Briand, pg. 925 — IT

Figeac

Ratier-Figeac, Route de Cahors, BP 2, pg. 192 — IT

Firminy

Clextral, Z.I. de Chazeau, pg. 503 — IT

Fixin

Serare, Restaurant Courte Paille, pg. 20 — IT

Flers

Bertrand Faure Equipements SA, Le Bois de Flers, pg. 192 — IT

Fleury-les-Aubrais

SNTR Calberson Orleans, pg. 1164 — IT
Thomson-CSF Airsys, 29, rue de Montaran, pg. 1382 — IT

Florange

GKN Florange SARL, Boite Postale No. 40, pg. 536 — IT
Someflor Societe Macanique de Florange SA, Z.I. d'Ebange Ste. Agathe, 3, rue Pascal, pg. 508 — IT

Fondettes

Poirier S.A., Les Roches, pg. 911 — PB

Fontaine

Bati Record, pg. 563 — IT

Fontaine-les-Luxeuil

ITW Gunther, rue de la Papeterie, pg. 868 — PB
Sonoco Gunther, S.A., pg. 1487 — PB

Fontenay-aux-Roses

Avenir Technologie International, 1-11 ave. du Val de Fontenay, pg. 315 — IT
Euromissle Dynamics Group, 12 rue de la Redoute, pg. 218 — IT

Fontenay-sous-Bois

Ficomet S.A.R.L., BP 100, pg. 103 — PV
Ludwig Metrologie, SA, 21, Ave. de Marechal, pg. 260 — PB
OMRON Electronics S.a.r.L., 19, Rue du Bois Galon, pg. 1006 — IT
OMRON Retail Systems France S.a.r.l., 174 Ave. du Marechal de Lattre, pg. 1006 — IT
Penarroya Metal Europe, Peripole 118, pg. 662 — IT
Pitney Bowes France Societe Anonyme (S.A.), 1 Avenue Louison Bobet, pg. 1304 — IT
SEMA Group Division, ISH Export, 56, Rue Roger Salengro, pg. 823 — PB
STV, pg. 1324 — IT
Saunier Duval Eau Chaude Chauffage SA, Le Technipole, 8 Ave. Pablo Picasso, pg. 615 — IT
Soditherm S.A., Le Technipole, Huit Ave. Pablo Picasso, pg. 615 — IT
Vibratechniques STV, 85 Avenue de Neuilly, pg. 1420 — IT

Fort-de-France

Caraibe Assurances S.A., 11, Rue Victor Hugo, pg. 90 — IT

Fosses

Ferro France-Eurostar, Z. I. Rue de la Ferme St. Ladre, pg. 619 — PB

Fourmies

Medtronic France S.A., Zone Industrielle Sud, Route d'Anor, pg. 1083 — PB

Fouy-aux-Arches

Sodem, 60 Rue de Metz, pg. 276 — IT

Fresnes

Arrow France S.A., Parc d'activite de Medicis, Batiment 63, pg. 135 — PB
Augat S.A., Ailee De La Vanne, 9 (Z.I. So filic), pg. 1598 — PB
Go Sport, 214 Ave. De La Cerisale, pg. 734 — IT
MSI France S.A.R.L., 2/4 Avenue de la Cerisaie, pg. 1546 — PB
Societe Kenwood France, 14-16 Ave. de Stalingrad, pg. 730 — IT

Fressenneville

Watts Eurotherm, 13, rue Jean Jacques Rousseau, pg. 1747 — PB

Futuroscope

Hewlett-Packard France, Futuropolis Avenue du Teleport, pg. 820 — PB

Gagny

Sucrerie De Cagny, pg. 549 — IT

Gaillac-d'Aveyron

Cimatarn, 19, Chemin Lapeyre, pg. 784 — IT

Gaillard

Laboratoires Roche Nicholas S.A., pg. 1121 — IT

Gaillon

Cinram France West, pg. 293 — IT

Garches

Electric Furnace France S.A.R.L., 1, Passage/du Clos, pg. 368 — PV

Garenne-Colombes

Mannesmann Tally SA, pg. 840 — IT

PB - *U.S. Public Companies Volume*
PV - *U.S. Private Companies Volume*
IT - *International Public & Private Companies Volume*

Garges-les-Gonesse

Nitto France S.A.R.L., Zone Industrielle De La Muette, Blvd. De La Muette, 1, pg. 951 IT

Gauchy

Hewlett-Packard France, Centre D'Entretien A 26, Route De Chauny, pg. 819 PB

Genay

Makita France S.A.-Lyon, Z.I. Est de Lyon, 5-7, Rue Jean Rostand, pg. 832 IT
SNTR Calberson, pg. 1164 IT

Gennevilliers

AC Rochester Division (Gennevilliers), 56/68 Avenue Louis Roche, pg. 724 PB
Citizen Watch France S.A., Parc des Barbanniers, 4 Allee du Carre, pg. 294 IT
Componenta International France S.A., 36 Avenue Louis Roche, pg. 1421 IT
Comptoir General des Glaces (CGG), 8, route des Champs-Fourgons, pg. 1172 IT
Coyne & Bellier S.A., Parc des Barbanniers-9, Allee des Barbanniers, pg. 1416 IT
Delco Moraine NDH Division, 56/68 Ave. Louis Roche, pg. 724 PB
Europ Assistance, #1 Promenade de la Bonett, pg. 91 IT
Europ Assistance S.A., 1, Promenade de la Bonnette, pg. 91 IT
General Motors France, 56/68 Ave. Louis Roche, pg. 724 PB
KSB S.A., pg. 721 IT
Krauss-Maffei France S.a.r.l., 5, Allee Des Berbaunniers, pg. 836 IT
Railtech Schlatter Systems, S.A.S., 119, Avenue Louis Roche, pg. 1206 IT
SAIA-Burgess, 10 Blvd. Louise Michel, pg. 1500 IT
SNT Calberson, pg. 1164 IT
Selas S.A., Parc des Barbanniers, 3/5 Place du Village, pg. 1455 PB
Settler International S.A., 1, Promenade de la Bonnette, pg. 92 IT
Thomintex, 135, rue des Caboeufs, pg. 1382 IT
Thomson-CSF Communications, 66, rue du Fosse-Blanc, pg. 1382 IT
Titan France SA, 119 Avenue Louis Roche, pg. 1619 PB
Twinner S.A., 1, Promenade de la Bonnette, pg. 92 IT

Gentilly

Mizuno (France) S.A.R.L., 102 Rue Gabriel Peri, pg. 885 IT
PPD Pharmaco Intl., 53 rue du Charles Frerot, pg. 1285 PB
VG Instruments SA, 5 Ave. Gallieni, pg. 1595 PB

Gerzat

Calberson Danzas, pg. 1163 IT
Societe Metallurgique de Gerzat, Rue de l'Industrie, pg. 1029 IT

Gevrey-Chambertin

SIMEL S.A., pg. 9 PB

Gien

Gien Mill, pg. 673 PB

Gif-sur-Yvette

Schering S.A., Les Algorithmes-Immeuble Thales, pg. 1204 IT

Gignac

Gignac Office, Route de Lodeve, pg. 784 IT

Gironde

Chateau Beychevelle, 33250, Saint-Julien-Beychevelle, pg. 1322 IT
Chateau Lagrange S.A., 33250, Saint-Julien-Beychevelle, pg. 1322 IT
Societe Anonyme Industrielle De Resines, 77096 Avenice Farvarque Belges (Girone), pg. 1580 PB

Givet

A. Schulman Plastics S.A., Rue Alex Schulman, pg. 1442 PB

Gonesse

SARL Robert Fret, pg. 302 IT
Hanimex (France) S.A., 18 Rue Ampere, pg. 1115 IT
Ets. Marshall S.A., Z.I. 35 Rue Gay Lussac, pg. 891 IT

Morgan Thermic S.A., Z.I. 35, rue Gay Lussac, pg. 894 IT
Rocol Limited, Succursale France,35 Rue Gay L, ussac sale France, pg. 893 IT
Societe Civile Immobiliere du Thillay, pg. 302 IT

Gouesnou

Cogin, pg. 563 IT
Distreco, pg. 563 IT
Gicquel, pg. 563 IT
Hewlett-Packard France, Zac Kergaradec, 8, Rue Fernand Forest, pg. 819 PB
Hyperallye, pg. 563 IT
Immodisque, pg. 563 IT
Marest, pg. 563 IT
Sodal, pg. 563 IT
Solodisque, pg. 563 IT
Somapem, pg. 563 IT

Goussainville

Rawl S.A., 11 avenue Ferdinand de Lesseps, pg. 925 IT
Yokohama France S.A., 2, Yue Le Corbusier, pg. 1521 IT

Gradignan

B.H.V. Gradignan, Avenue de l'hyppodrome, pg. 181 IT
Makita France S.A.-Bordeaux, 137, Rue de la Croix-de-Monjous, pg. 832 IT

Grand Couronne

Chapelle Darblay Grand Couronne, C.D. 3, pg. 1428 IT

Grand Quevilly

The Lincoln Electric Co. (France) S.A., Avenue Franklin Roosevelt, pg. 996 PB

Grande-Synthe

GTS Industries, pg. 571 IT

Grasse

C.A.L., 27, Avenue Sainte-Lorette, pg. 349 IT
ROBERTET S.A., Ave. Sidi Brahim, pg. 1119 IT

Graulhet

K.J. Quinn S. A., pg. 984 IT

Gravelines

Euro-Aspartame S.A., Z.I.P. des Huttes, route de la Grande Hernesse, pg. 41 IT
Nacanco S.A., Routes des Vignota, pg. 1029 IT

Greasque

Micropolish, 21 Des Pradeaux, pg. 803 IT

Gregy-sur-Yerres

SAS Institute S.A., Domaine de Gregy, pg. 967 PV

Grenoble

Caterpillar France S.A., 40-48 Ave. Leon Blum, Boite Postal 53 Centre de Tri, pg. 317 PB
Grenoble Mill, 25, rue Casimir Julhiet, pg. 673 PB
Hagglunds Drives SARL, 96, Cours de la Liberation, pg. 670 IT
Oxford Instruments, 11 a place Bir-Hakeim, pg. 1018 IT
Sinertech, 17, rue Denfert Rochereau, pg. 572 IT
Sogeti S.A., pg. 368 IT
Supradiamant S.A., B.P. n 4, pg. 1478 PB

Gron

Paperion Chimie S.A., Zone Industrielle, pg. 1086 IT

Grosbliederstroff

CB Sarreguemines, 61 Route Nationale, pg. 275 IT

Guayancourt

McDonald's France SA, 1 rue Gustave Eiffel, pg. 1069 PB

Guebwiller

ABS Production S.A.R.L., 2 Route D'Issenheim, pg. 270 IT
Nelco France, pg. 623 PV
N. SCHLUMBERGER & CIE, rue de la Republique, pg. 1206 IT

Gueret

Bernis, pg. 1163 IT

Guerville

Calcia, Les Technodes, pg. 292 IT

Ciments Francais Data Processing Center, Les Technodes, pg. 292 IT
Technodes S.A., Les Technodes, pg. 292 IT

Guilherand-Granges

Ascom Monetel SA, Rue Claude-Chappe, pg. 87 IT

Guyancourt

Bongrain - Gerard & Cie., Le Moulin-a-Vent, pg. 201 IT
CASI-RUSCO Europe, 2 Rue Helene Boucher, pg. 218 PV
DYNETCOM, Batiment Gaia, 9 parc Ariane, pg. 425 IT
Ericsson Composants S.A., 1, Parc Ariane, Rue Helene Boucher, pg. 1366 IT
Frank & Schulte (France) S.A.R.L., Parc club Ariane, Bat. n 3, Saturne, Saint Quentin En Yvelines, pg. 1458 IT
Nortel Matra Cellular SCA, 1, Place des Freres, pg. 970 IT
Pharmacia & Upjohn Biotech S.A., 1 Rue Antoine, pg. 1048 IT
Pharmacia & Upjohn S.A., 1 Rue Antoine Lavoiser, pg. 1050 IT
Thomson-CSF Optronique, Rue Guynemer, pg. 1382 IT
Thomson-TRT Defense, pg. 1383 IT

Hagondange

SAFE S.A., pg. 571 IT
Societe Mecanique Automobile de l'est, pg. 1020 IT

Haguenau

Mars Confectionery, pg. 707 PV
Robein S.A., 62, route de Soufflenheim, pg. 1459 IT

Haironville

Polytuil France S.A., pg. 302 IT

Haisnes

Francaise De Mecanique, B.P. 8, Zone Industrielle de Douvrin, pg. 1021 IT

Halluin

Etablissements Van Rullen, 16 Rue Emile Zola, pg. 1499 IT

Harfleur

Hydro Agri France Usine du Havre (S.N.A.), Usine du Havre Azote, pg. 962 IT

Harnes

Eda, Parc d'Enterprises de la Motte du Bois, pg. 1463 IT
McCain Alimentaire SA, pg. 850 IT

Hayange

Lormines (Societe des Mines de Sacilor), pg. 571 IT

Heillecourt

Thomson-CSF Services Industrie, 19, Grand Rue, pg. 1383 IT

Hellemmes-Lille

Castorama Diffusion, 4 Rue du Professeur Langeirn, pg. 275 IT

Henriville

Fort Securite, Zone Industrielle, pg. 419 PV

Herblay

DYWIDAG-Systems International S.A.R.L., Z.I.-14, avenue Paul Langevin, pg. 424 IT
Hydap S.A., Z1 2 Rue E. Branly, pg. 1285 IT

Hesingue

Cryostar France SA, Boite Postale 48, pg. 122 IT

Heyrieux

Dubois Materiaux Rhone Alpes, Z.I. les Cambergeres, pg. 275 IT

Hoenheim

Andros Service Inc., 27 Route de la Wantzenau, pg. 74 PV

Holtzheim

Bongard, 32 Route de Wolfisheim, pg. 570 IT

Hortes

Kalso S.A., 29, Rue Camille Perfertti, pg. 1428 IT

PB - *U.S. Public Companies Volume*
PV - *U.S. Private Companies Volume*
IT - *International Public & Private Companies Volume*

Huningue

Etablissements CIBA-GEIGY SA, 28, Rue de la Chapelle, pg. 982   IT
Laboratoires CIBA-GEIGY S.A., pg. 983   IT
Sandoz Huningue S.A., pg. 984   IT

Igny

Morton International S.A., Zone Industrielle, B.O. No.2, pg. 1136   PB

Illkirch-Graffenstaden

Flender-Graffenstaden S.A., Boite Postale 84, pg. 400   IT
Puma France S.A., 1, rue Louis Ampere, pg. 1072   IT
Schiesser International S.a.r.l., pg. 618   IT

Illzach

Danzas, pg. 1163   IT
Elevator Car System, pg. 1205   IT

Isle d'Espagnac

MO Charentes-Limousin, ZI N 3, pg. 1172   IT

Isle-sur-la-Sorgue

Lafarge Platreurope S.A., 5, Avenue de l'Egalite, pg. 788   IT

Isles-sur-Suippes

HYMECA Manutention S.A., 49, Rue de Boult, pg. 269   IT

Issoire

Forgeal, pg. 1028   IT

Issoudun

Polaroil S.A., Zone Industrielle, pg. 519   IT
Societe Petroliere Fuchs E.U.R.L., Zone Industrielle, pg. 519   IT
Valvoline Oil (France) S.A.R.L., Zone Industrielle, pg. 140   PB

Issy-les-Moulineaux

AGEMA Infrared Systems S.A.R.L., pg. 1289   IT
AGEMA Infrared Systems SRL, 18 rue Hoche, pg. 1289   IT
Gie Amadeus France, 2-8, avenue du Bas Meudon, pg. 560   IT
BGS Systems France, Technopolis, 175 Rue Jean Jacques Rousseau, pg. 161   PB
Carrefour - Picard Surgeles, 19, Pl. de la Resistance, pg. 272   IT
Dunlop France S.A., 62 rue Camille Desmoulins, pg. 1317   IT
EMI France, 41-43 rue Camille-Desmoulins, pg. 427   IT
Esterel, 2-8 Ave. du Bas Meudon, pg. 560   IT
EURO RSCG Opinions, 8 rue Rouget de Lisle, pg. 601   IT
Farallon Communications SARL, 2, rue du Docteur Lombard, pg. 1168   PB
Fiskars Power Systems, 30, Rue Guynemer, pg. 130   IT
Groupe Strategies, 15 bis, rue Ernest Renan, pg. 1099   IT
GROUPE ZODIAC, 48 Boulevard Gallieni, pg. 572   IT
ICIS LOR-Europe, 15 bis Ernest Renan, pg. 1094   IT
Laboratoires Stafford-Miller S.A.R.L., 18, rue Hoche, pg. 237   PB
LECLERC, 52 rue Camille Des Moulins, pg. 805   IT
Sumitomo Rubber Industries-Paris, 62 rue Camille Desmoulins, pg. 1317   IT
Voyage, 2 rue Rouget de Lisle, pg. 647   PV

Istres

Etablissement d'Istres, pg. 383   IT

Ivry-sur-Seine

Autologic Information International, Inc., 26 Rue Robert Witchitz, pg. 1724   PB
ELSAG, 200 Rue Marcel Hartmann, pg. 654   PB
Emhart S.A., 12,Ive Truillot, pg. 233   PB
Entrepot Ivry, 101 bld. P.V. Couturier, pg. 181   IT
IPC Corporation (France) S.A., 51-59, Rue Ledru-Rollin, pg. 651   IT
Jet Hotel, 23, rue raspail, pg. 560   IT
Jet Tours, 23, Rue Raspail, pg. 560   IT
Laboratoires des Produits Dentaires Odoncia S.A., 3, Rue Michelet, pg. 510   IT
Sodetif, 23 rue Raspail, pg. 560   IT

Janze

Trio-Kenwood Bretagne S.A., Rue Saint-Exupery, pg. 731   IT

Jarnac

Thomas Hine & Cie, 16, quai de l'Orangerie, pg. 780   IT
Louis Royer S.A., 27-29, Rud Chail, pg. 1322   IT

Jarrie

Fasson France S.a.r.l., Champ-sur-Drac, pg. 154   PB

Jarville

VDO Instruments SA, pg. 839   IT

Jaunay Clan

Chaveneau Bernis, pg. 1163   IT

Joigny

Stirn Industries S.A., 10 Rue Thibault, pg. 552   IT

Joinville-le-Pont

Forbo Parquet SA, pg. 498   IT
Societe Civile Immobiliere, pg. 618   IT

Joue-les-Tours

Charles-Andre S.A., 1-3, rue de Prony, pg. 1172   IT

Jouy-en-Josas

Adobe Systems France, Espace Jouy Technology, 21, rie Albert Calmette, pg. 20   PB
Campus Thomson, 67, rue Charles-de-Gaulle, pg. 1381   IT
Dionex S.A., 98, rue Albert Calmette, pg. 510   PB
Integrated Systems, Inc., S.A., 1 rue du Petit Robinson, pg. 886   PB
Xilinx, Sarl, Espace jouy Technology, 21, rue Albert Calmette Bt.C, pg. 1786   PB

Juarancon

Fromagerie des Chaumes S.A., Av. 155, Rausky, pg. 201   IT

Kaysersberg

Laboratoires P.O.S. S.A., pg. 920   IT

Kingersheim

Bricorev, 107 Route de Guebwiller, pg. 275   IT

L'Ile d'Elle

Societe des Emballages Keyes, pg. 1146   IT

L'Aigle-Orne

James Eurn International S.A., Boite Postale 134, pg. 1507   PB

L'Hay-les-Roses

Oki (France) sarl, 148 Rue De Chevilly, pg. 1000   IT
Oki Systemes (France) S.A., 44-50 Av. du General de Gaulle, pg. 1000   IT

L'Horme

Mavilor S.A., 24, Avenue de la Liberation, pg. 508   IT

L'Isle-sur-Sorgue

Lafarge Platre, Ave. de l'Egalite, 5, pg. 789   IT

La Chapelle

Hewlett-Packard France, Parc Tertiaire Helipolis, Route De Micy, pg. 819   PB
IDV France, B.P. 10, pg. 410   IT
Piat Pere & Fils, pg. 410   IT
Sodetrans, pg. 1165   IT

La Ciotat

Intervascular, S.A., Batiment-E, Voie Ariane, pg. 488   PB

La Courneuve

CSR Pampryl, 160 av Paul Vaillant Couturier, pg. 566   IT
Polyfilla SA, 24/26 avenue Louis Bleroit, pg. 1501   IT
Ets. Triaud Gauvain S.A., pg. 1202   IT

La Fere

S.A. Beautor, pg. 302   IT

La Ferte-sous-Jouarre

SOVIS, Societe de Verrerie Scientifique et Industrielle, pg. 1172   IT

La Fleche

Brodard et Taupin, Avenue Rhin et Danube, pg. 792   IT

La Garenne-Colombes

Societe Francaise des Amortisseurs de Carbon S.A., 8 Avenue Foch, pg. 725   PB

La Madeleine

Matra Communication Nord-Est, Rue Delesalle Z.A. du Pre-Catelan, pg. 793   IT
Matra Telecommunications Nord-Est, Rue Delesalle Z.A. du Precatelan, pg. 793   IT

La Madelure

Crompton & Knowles Intl. S.A.R.L., 28 Rue Saint Henri, pg. 460   PB

La Rivoire

Sovedys, 523, Emile Zola, pg. 1172   IT

La Roche-sur-Yon

Cime Bocuze, Les Digues, pg. 1028   IT
SNTR Calberson La-Roche-Sur-Yon, pg. 1164   IT

La Rochelle

C.F.I.T.R. S.A., Z.I. Chef de Baie, pg. 517   IT
Lewmar Marine S.A.R.L., La Ville en Bois, Avenue Marillac, pg. 1462   IT
Regie S.A. (Recherche, Etudes, Gestion des pour l'Informatisation de l'Entreprise, Village Informatique des Minimes 2, pg. 316   IT
Socofer, 357 Avenue Guiton, pg. 964   IT

La Teste

Base de Cazaux, Base aerienne 120, pg. 383   IT

La Verpilliere

L'Unite Hermetique S.A., pg. 1566   PB
Tylan SARL, 7-8 Place de L'Europe, pg. 1113   PB

La Verriere

Mikron France Sarl, BP 33, 6-10 rue de Panicale, pg. 867   IT
Sato Kogyo Co., Ltd.-Paris, 45 Ave. Du Bac, pg. 1197   IT
Valeo Climate Control, 8, rue Louis-Lormand -, pg. 240   IT
Valeo Engine Cooling, 8, rue Louis-Lormand, pg. 240   IT

Labastide Saint Pierre

Sylea Harness Assembly Plant, pg. 785   IT

Labatut

SERETRAM, pg. 411   IT

Labege

Thomson-CSF Services Industrie, ZAC de la Bourgade, rue Max Plank, pg. 1383   IT

Ladon

Stahl France S.a.r.l., 495 rue de la Motte Bezin, pg. 1526   IT

Lagny

Elitec S.A., 57 Rue Jacquard, pg. 1776   PB
Geotronics S.A.R.L., 2-4, Rue du Suffrage Universal, pg. 1290   IT
Nordson France, S.A., 2, rue Niels Bohr-L'Esplanda, pg. 1189   PB
Sieval, 2, rue de la Oaix, pg. 192   IT

Lamentin

Societe Martiniquaise de Carton Ondule, Boite Postale 201, pg. 906   PB

Landerneau

Quemeneur, rue du Calvaire-B.P. 33, pg. 206   IT

Landersheim

Adidas Sarragan France S.a.r.l., pg. 25   IT

Landivisiau

Rallye Super, pg. 563   IT
Sopradis, pg. 563   IT

Langres

Donnelly Euro Glas Systems, pg. 519   PB
PU, S.A., pg. 506   IT

PB - *U.S. Public Companies Volume*
PV - *U.S. Private Companies Volume*
IT - *International Public & Private Companies Volume*

1584

Geographic Index-Non U.S.

Lannemezan

Metclad S.A., Rte. des Usines, pg. 1258　　　PB

Lassay-les-Chateaux

Forbo 2MA SA, pg. 498　　　IT
2MA Centre S.a.r.l., pg. 498　　　IT

Latresne

EURO RSCG D 10, Chemin du port de l'homme, pg. 600　　　IT

Lattes

European Vacuum Interrupters S.A., Lotissement du Font do la Banquiere, pg. 1405　　　IT

Lauterbourg

Kemira Chimie S.A., BP 5, pg. 728　　　IT

Laval

COMPAGNIE LAITIERE BESNIER, 10a, 20 rue Adolphe Beck, pg. 322　　　IT
Dim S.A., 6 Rue Marius Aufan, pg. 1434　　　PB
Octel Communications S.A., 55-63, rue Anatole France, pg. 1018　　　IT
Societe de Transformation des Matieres Plastiques-S.T.M.P. S.A., Avenue d'Angers Zone, pg. 1279　　　IT
Thomson-CSF Communications, 83/85, rue Emile-Brault, pg. 1382　　　IT

Lavardac

Societe des Bouchages, Emballages et Conditionnement Modernes, Xaintrailles, pg. 919　　　IT

Lavaur

Sael Decors, Les Bories, pg. 421　　　IT

Laxou

Kleber Pneumatiques SA, 14 Rue du Mouzon, pg. 322　　　IT
Makita France S.A.-Nancy, 43, Rue du Colonel-Mol, pg. 832　　　IT

Le Beausset

Thomson-CSF Services Industrie, Atelier aeronautique, Aerodome du Castellet, pg. 1383　　　IT

Le Bourget

Dowty SA, Bat. No.55 Z1 Nord, pg. 1338　　　IT
EAI-Embraer Aviation International, Aeroport du Bourget, pg. 452　　　IT
Jet Chef, Aeroport du Bourget, pg. 560　　　IT
MB France S.A., 71 La Plaisse, pg. 798　　　PB
McNeil Akron Repiquet, 43 Rue Du CDT. Rolland, pg. 725　　　PV
Paris Learning Center, Bldg. 404, Zone d'Aviation d'Affaires, pg. 219　　　PB
SECA (Societe d'Exploitation et de Construction Aeronautiques), pg. 29　　　IT

Le Buisson

Dataproducts S.A.R.L., Zone D'Activities Batiment Evolic 2 Rout, pg. 621　　　IT

Le Chalard

Societe des Mines du Bourneix, pg. 305　　　IT

Le Chesnay

B.H.V. Parly II, Centre Commercial, pg. 181　　　IT
Litton Precision Products (France), 58, rue Pottier, pg. 1004　　　PB

Le Coudray-Montceaux

Bondioli & Pavesi-France S.A., 1 Rue Panhard, pg. 201　　　IT

Le Creusot

Schneider Jeumont Rail, 1, rue Baptiste Marcet, pg. 706　　　IT

Le Grand-Quevilly

Van Leer France S.A.R.L., pg. 1147　　　IT

Le Grau-du-Roi

Le Grau du Roi Office, Gare S.N.C.F., pg. 784　　　IT

Le Haillan

Valmet SARL, Bordeaux Technowest, Les Cinq Chemins, pg. 1448　　　IT

Le Havre

Agences Maritime Associes, Quoi George V, pg. 682　　　IT
Hydro Agri France Usine du Havre Complexes, Canal Central Maritime, Zone Industrielle SUD, pg. 962　　　IT
Oceangrais, pg. 964　　　IT
Societe de Maintenance et de Reparation de Containers S.A.R.L., pg. 596　　　IT
VGL Rail Cargo S.A.R.L., pg. 1145　　　IT

Le Mans

Compagnie des Dispositifs Semi-Conducteurs Westinghouse, 424, avenue Georges Durand, pg. 706　　　IT
Constructions Ferroviaires du Mans (CFM), 2, rue du Miroir, pg. 706　　　IT
Peintures Produits Plasdox, 19 rue de la Calandre, pg. 790　　　IT
Plasdox, 19, rue de la Calandre, pg. 789　　　IT
SNT Calberson, pg. 1164　　　IT
Skandia International Gestion de Reassurance Vie, 8 Rue Auvray, pg. 1258　　　IT

Le Mee-sur-Seine

Autotrol France, S.A., 230 rue Robert Schuman, pg. 1234　　　PB

Le Mesnil-Amelot

Centre de Production Alimentaire, 16, Rue de la Grande Barre, pg. 560　　　IT

Le Nouvion-en-Thierache

The West Company France, S.A., 38 Rue Robert Degon, B.P. 26, pg. 1756　　　PB

Le Pecq

Bull Ingenierie S.A., 12, rue de Paris, pg. 316　　　IT
Burmah Castrol France Holdings SA, 66 Route de Sartouville, pg. 235　　　IT
CETT (Compagnie Europeene de Teletransmission), Three Parc des Grillons, 60, Route de Sartrouville, pg. 53　　　IT
Habitat International, #1 Place Royale, pg. 659　　　IT
Scott S.N.C., Parc des Erables-Batiment 3, 66, Route de Sartrouville, pg. 960　　　PB
Sovap, Parc des Erables - Bat 3, pg. 193　　　IT

Le Pin

Omniplastic, Route de Claye-Souilly, pg. 789　　　IT

Le Plan-de-Grasse

Florasynth S.A., 45 Boulevard Marcel Pagnol, pg. 174　　　IT

Le Plessis-Robinson

Hewlett-Packard France, Parc Technologique, Bat Gay-Lussac, pg. 819　　　PB
Laboratoires Synthelabo France, 22 Ave. Galilee, pg. 818　　　IT
Synthelabo-Tanabe Chimie S.A., 22 Avenue Galilee, pg. 1354　　　IT
Technical Field Services International, Bureau de liaison, Centre d'affaires La Boursidiere, pg. 1382　　　IT
Thomson-CSF Services Industrie & Thomintex, 9, avenue Reaumur, pg. 1383　　　IT

Le Port

Compagnie Reunionaise d'Importation de Ciment, pg. 788　　　IT

Le Pre-Saint-Gervais

Endevco France S.A., 23 Rue Baudin, pg. 854　　　IT
Piher International SA, 23 Rue Baudin, pg. 854　　　IT

Le Puy

Vellave de Transports, pg. 1165　　　IT

Le Rheu

SSIG, Rue de la Romillais, pg. 316　　　IT

Le Tholy

BG SAS, B.P. 1, pg. 201　　　IT

Le Trait

H.B. Fuller France, Zone Industrielle, pg. 687　　　PB

Le Vesinet

Cognex-France, 131-135 Boulevard Carnot, pg. 394　　　PB
Pfauter France S.A.R.L., 131/135, Boulevard Carnot, pg. 617　　　IT
Sovcor, SA, 11, Chemin de Ronde, pg. 1722　　　PB
Steelweld France Sarl, 131, Blvd. Carnot, pg. 71　　　IT

Le Vigan

Cedimat S.A., Ave. Emmanuel d'Alzon, pg. 784　　　IT

Le-Gond-Pontouvre

Bernis, pg. 1163　　　IT

Le-Relecq-Kerhuon

SNT Calberson, pg. 1164　　　IT

Lens

Banque Regionale du Nord, 21-23, place Jean Jaures, pg. 548　　　IT
NAPS France S.A., Z.I. Nord-route de la Bassee, pg. 913　　　IT

Les Clayes-sous-Bois

Alfa-Laval S.A., B.P. 57, pg. 1379　　　IT
Diabolo-Manus S.A., B.P. 57, pg. 1379　　　IT

Les Milles

Hewlett-Packard France, Z.I. Mercure B, Rue Berthelot, pg. 819　　　PB

Les Mureaux

Pyroindustrie S.A., 139 Route de Verneuil, pg. 1207　　　PB
Space & Defense Division, Route de Verneuel, pg. 29　　　IT
VOAC Hydraulics S.A., pg. 1264　　　PB
Volvo Penta France S.A., pg. 1478　　　IT

Les Ponts-de-Ce

Les Graines Caillard S.A., pg. 983　　　IT
S & G Semences S.A., pg. 984　　　IT

Les Ulis

Acuson S.A.R.L., 6 Ave. Des Andes, pg. 18　　　PB
Advantest Europe R & D S.a.r.l., 5, Ave. du Quebec, pg. 25　　　IT
AlliedSignal Laminate Systems S.A., 4 Avenue de la Baltique, pg. 53　　　PB
Amersham France SA, BP144, pg. 993　　　IT
Apple Computer France SARL, Avenue de l'Oceanie, Z.I. de Courtaboeuf, pg. 121　　　PB
Bridgestone France S.A.R.L., Z.A. de Courtaboeuf, pg. 214　　　IT
Case Tracteurs, S.A., Z. A. De Courtaboeuf, pg. 1579　　　PB
Compaq Computer S.A.R.L., 5 Alle Gustav Eiffel, pg. 418　　　PB
Coutant Electronique SA, Azc Des Delaches, 91 Gometz le Chatel, pg. 1241　　　IT
DTV International, 31, avenue de la Baltique, pg. 792　　　IT
Eurotherm Mesures SA, 27 Avenue du Quebec, pg. 466　　　IT
Eurotherm Systemes SA, 27 Avenue de Quebec, pg. 466　　　IT
Eurotherm Vitesse Variable SA, 27 Avenue du Quebec, pg. 466　　　IT
Hewlett-Packard France, Z.A. De Courtaboeuf, 1, Avenue du Canada, pg. 819　　　PB
Hybrinova, avenue de la Baltique, 16, pg. 788　　　PB
IKOS Systems Inc., 6 Avenue des Andes, pg. 864　　　PB
Lambda Electronique SA, Zac Des Delaches, pg. 1242　　　IT
Motorola S.A., Zone Technopolis, Immeuble THETA, pg. 1140　　　PB
Nellcor Puritan Bennett France S.A.R.L., Parc D-Affaires Technopolis, 3, Avenure du Canada-Batiment Sigma, pg. 1040　　　PB
Nucletudes, Avenue du Hoggar, pg. 29　　　IT
Prologue S.A., Z.A. De Courtaboeuf, pg. 316　　　IT
Spectra-Physics S.A.R.L., Avenue de Scandinavie, pg. 1290　　　IT
Tektronix S.A., 6 Rue de la Terre du Feu, Zone Industrielle de Courtaboeuf, pg. 1568　　　PB
Viewlogic Systems, SARL, ZA de Courtboeuf, Batiment Le Narvik, pg. 1548　　　PB
Wind River Systems S.A.R.L., 19, Avenue de Norvege, pg. 1771　　　PB

Lescar

CGTM, Pau-Pyrenees Airport, pg. 787　　　IT

PB - *U.S. Public Companies Volume*
PV - *U.S. Private Companies Volume*
IT - *International Public & Private Companies Volume*

Lesquin

Dubois Materiaux, Rue de la Haie Plouvier, pg. 275   IT
Obi, Rue de la Voyette 12, pg. 534   IT
Societe Civile Immobiliere, Rue de la Haie Plouver, pg. 275   IT
Societe Verriere Francaise (SVF), Centre de Commerce de Gros, pg. 1172   IT

Levallois-Perret

A-L Services France S.N.C., pg. 68   IT
Aeroboutiques France, 126, rue Jules Guesde, pg. 791   IT
Affichage Centre Ville (A.C.V.), 149, rue Anatole France, pg. 791   IT
Alcatel ATFH, 55 rue Greffulhe, pg. 55   IT
Australie, 14 rue Aristide Briand, pg. 600   IT
Ayer France, 87 Rue de Villiers, pg. 104   **PV**
BASF France S.A., 49, avenue Georges Pompidou, pg. 106   IT
BRE Group, 13, rue Antonin-Raynaud, pg. 52   IT
Bordelais, Lemeunier-Leo Burnett Paris, 122 Rue Edouard Vaillant, pg. 184   **PV**
C.O.F.E.C., 126, rue Jules Guesde, pg. 792   IT
Cegelec, Aqua Michelel, pg. 52   IT
Champagnes et Spiritueux Associes, 22-24, rue du President-Wilson, pg. 780   IT
Compagnie Francais Buttner S.A., 90, rue Baudin, pg. 399   IT
Danone, Rue Jules Guesde, 126, pg. 379   IT
Delsey SA, 55, rue Raspail, pg. 192   IT
EDI 7, 149, rue Anatole France, pg. 792   IT
ERE P Division, Courcellor II, 35, rue d'Alsace, pg. 52   IT
ERE T Division, 13, rue Antonin-Raynaud, pg. 52   IT
Epson France S.A. (E.F.S.), 68bis rue Marjolin, pg. 1219   IT
EURO RSCG Audience, 84 rue de Villiers, pg. 600   IT
EURO RSCG Babinet, Erra, Tong Cuong, 84 rue de Villiers, pg. 600   IT
EURO RSCG France, 84 rue de Villiers, pg. 601   IT
EURO RSCG Gregoire, Blachere, Huard & Roussel, 84 rue de Villiers, pg. 601   IT
EURO RSCG Institutionnel, 84 rue de Villiers, pg. 600   IT
EURO RSCG Scher, Lefarge, 1 rue Kleber, pg. 601   IT
GGK Paris, 16 rue Antonin Raynaud, pg. 1335   IT
Gillette France, S.A., 92, rue Edouard Vaillant, pg. 744   **PB**
Hachette Filipacchi Presse, 149, rue Anatole France, pg. 794   IT
HAVAS ADVERTISING, 84 rue de Villiers, pg. 600   IT
Ketchum Public Relations/Paris, 39 Rue Anatole France, pg. 617   **PV**
L.A.D.V. (Laboratoires D'Applications Dermatologiques de Vichy), 39 rue Anatole France, pg. 818   IT
Laboratoires Knoll France, 49, avenue Geoges Pompidou, pg. 109   IT
Lever S.A., 32 rue Jacques Ibert, pg. 1438   IT
LEX Group, 16, rue P.V. Couturier, pg. 53   IT
Lonza France Sarl, pg. 69   IT
Mapa, 59, 61 rue Marius AuFan, pg. 1409   IT
Memorex Telex France S.A., 3-5 rue Maurice Ravel, pg. 857   IT
Navistar, 126, rue Jules Guesde, pg. 793   IT
NOTEMAT LEAU HELLIX S.A., 90, rue Baudin, pg. 399   IT
Parfums Givenchy S.A., 74, rue Anatole-France, pg. 781   IT
Publications France Monde, 149, rue Anatole France, pg. 793   IT
Publications Groupe Loisirs, 149, rue Anatole France, pg. 793   IT
Publiprox, 149, rue Anatole France, pg. 793   IT
Quillet S.A., 149, rue Anatole France, pg. 793   IT
Resteurop, 106, rue Danton, pg. 20   IT
S.E.A.V.T. SA, 106, rue Danton, pg. 20   IT
SFPTH SA, 106, rue Danton, pg. 20   IT
Sara Lee Personal Products Europe, 28 rue Jacques Ibert, pg. 1435   **PB**
Schweppes France S.A., 12-14 rue Selgrand, pg. 248   IT
Societe d'Etudie et de Development de la Presse Periodique, 10, rue Thierry Le Luron, pg. 793   IT
Sundstrand-Aerospace Europe, 68 Rue Anatole, pg. 1534   **PB**
Total Raffinage Distribution S.A., 84 rue de Villiers, pg. 1409   IT
WLFF SA, 106, rue Danton, pg. 21   IT
Ziff-Davis France SARL, Immeuble Omega, 10, Rue Thierry Le Luron, pg. 1276   IT

Liancourt

Avon Cosmetics, S.A., pg. 156   **PB**

Libourne

Lanvin Parfums, Zone Ind. Ballastiere, pg. 819   IT

Liffre

Canon Bretagne S.A., Les Landes de Beauge, pg. 262   IT

Lille

Banque Bruxelles Lambert France Succursale de Lille, Immeuble le Louis XIV, 7 Boulevard Louis XIV, pg. 148   IT
Banque Regionale du Nord, 84, rue Nationale, pg. 548   IT
Banque Scalbert Dupont, 33, Avenue Le Corbusier, pg. 563   IT

Bekaert-Stanwick Consultants, 104, rue Nationale, pg. 184   IT
Caisse Fraternelle D'Epargne, 57, Rue de Paris, pg. 563   IT
Caisse Fraternelle Vie, 57, Rue de Paris, pg. 564   IT
Delhaize "Le Lion" France S.A., Rue Marechal de Lattre de Tassigny 8, pg. 463   IT
Eaux du Nord, 217, Boulevard de la Liberte, pg. 823   IT
Gan Capitalisation, 57, Rue De Paris, pg. 564   IT
Ets. Frate S.A., 25, rue Augustin Drapiez, pg. 518   IT
Quinton Hazell PLC, Lille, pg. 561   **PB**
Rhenania Compagnie Europeenne de Transports et d'Affretement S.A.R.L., 76, Rue Jacquemars Gielee, B.P. No. 1343, pg. 1034   IT
Stena Line France, 9 Rue Tournai, pg. 1300   IT
Trave Agency Lille, 9 Rue Tournai, pg. 1301   IT

Limiel Brevannes

Thermo Electric S.A., 26 Rue Pasteur, pg. 1080   **PV**

Limoges

LEGRAND S.A., 128 Ave. du, Marechal-de-Lattre-de-Tassigny, pg. 805
Limoges Plant, 41, rue Barthelemy-Timonnier, pg. 305   IT
SNTR Calberson, pg. 1164   IT
SOTELEC, 22, avenue Louis de Broglie, pg. 793   IT

Limonest

B.H.V. Limonest, R.N. 6, pg. 181   IT
Darty Rhone-Alpes, pg. 734   IT
Thomson-CSF Services Industrie, Batiment Evolic 1, hall B1, pg. 1383   IT

Limoux

Limoux Office, Zone Industrielle, de Flassian, pg. 784   IT

Lingolsheim

Allergan France S.A., 4 Route de La Riviere, pg. 46   **PB**
Hewlett-Packard Sales, Parc Club Des Tanneries, Batiment B4, 4, Rue de la Faisanderie, pg. 821   **PB**

Linsellers

Peaudouce S.A. Baby Products, 59, rue de la Vignette, pg. 1326   IT

Lisieux

Knorr-Dahl Freinage S.A., 31, Rue Ferdinand Daulne, pg. 738   IT

Lisses

Check Technology France S.A., Europarc 1 Batiment 2, Avenue Du General de Gaulle, pg. 342   **PB**
Mallinckrodt Medical, 7 Avenue General de Gaulle, pg. 1040   **PB**

Lognes

American Power Conversion Corp., 4, Rue St. Claire Devi, pg. 39   **PB**
Christieensen, Rue de la Maison Rouge 10, pg. 534   IT
Goldstar France S.A.R.L., 12, Rue Lech Walesa Bat., Bat. B, pg. 779   IT
Jotun Polymer France S.A., Ctr. Evolie, 105 Rue des Campanules, pg. 714   IT

Lomme

SNTR Calberson, pg. 1164   IT
Siegling France S.A., pg. 498   IT

Longjumeau

Gould Instrument Systems, S.A., BP 115, pg. 1592   **PB**
Sekurit Saint-Gobain Vehicules Industriels (SSGVI), 1, allee d'Effiat, pg. 1172   IT

Longueville

Danrec, Route de Saint Loup de Naud, pg. 662   IT

Longvic

Sundstrand International S.A., Zone Industrielle de Longvic, pg. 1534   **PB**

Longwy

S.A. du Train Universel de Longwy, pg. 79   IT

Loos

FMC Food Machinery France, S.A., Centre Commercial des Oliveaux, pg. 606   **PB**

Lorgues

Novellus Systems, Ltd., 1488 Corniche de St. Ferreol, pg. 1204   **PB**

Lorient

Plastimo S.A., 15 Rue Ingenieur Verriere, pg. 933   **PB**

Loudun

Howard S.A., P.O. Box 33, pg. 1387   IT

Loue

Stic Hafroy S.A., pg. 422   IT

Loulay

Malvaux S.A., 21, rue de la Gare, pg. 1429   IT

Louveciennes

Bull Afrique, 68 rt. de Versailles, pg. 315   IT
Bull CP8, S.A., 68 route de Versailles, pg. 316   IT
Bull S.A., 68 route de Versailles, pg. 315   IT
COMPAGNIE DES MACHINES BULL, 68 Route de Versailles, pg. 315   IT
JS Telecommunications S.A., 36-38 Rue La Princesse, pg. 706   IT

Louviers

Alunord s.a., Parc Industriel d'Incarville, pg. 961   IT
Houndouville Mill, pg. 673   **PB**
NIFE France S.A., 43 av. W. Churchhill, pg. 54   IT

Louvres

IRD Mechanalysis France S.A.R.L., Zone Industriolle, Rue de la Briqueterie, pg. 790   **PB**

Luce

Hydro Aluminium Extrusion Services s.a.r.l., 42, rue de la Beauce, pg. 962   IT
Hydro Aluminium ITC s.n.c., 42, Rue de La Beauce, pg. 962   IT
Hydro Aluminium Luce s.n.c., 42, Rue de la Beauce, pg. 962   IT

Ludres

SNTR Calberson Nancy, pg. 1164   IT

Lunery

Rosieres S.A., Saint Florent sur Cher, pg. 260   IT

Lure

Bertrand Faure Equipements SA, 17, rue de la Metairie, pg. 192   IT

Luzenac

Talc de Luzenac S.A., Route Nationale 20, pg. 1119   IT

Lyon

ABH Lubrifants, 32, Rue Saint Romain, pg. 518   IT
Ateliers Sucre Liquide et Conditionnement de Lyon, 47, Quai Rambaud, pg. 549   IT
B.H.V. La Part Dieu, Rue du Dr. Bouchut, pg. 181   IT
Banca Nazionale del Lavoro, Rue du President Carnot, pg. 137   IT
Banque Veuve Morin-Pons, 177, rue Garibaldi, pg. 419   IT
Biocine S.a.r.l., 36 Quai Fulchiron, pg. 350   **PB**
Black & Decker (France) S.A.R.L., pg. 234   **PB**
Brossette BTI SA, pg. 1511   IT
C.R.L.F., 17-19, Av. Georges Pompidou, pg. 792   IT
CSB Bureautique, 180 rue Garibaldi, pg. 263   IT
Calor S.A., Place Ambroise Courtois, pg. 568   IT
Cellatex, Tour du Credit Lyonnail, pg. 1109   IT
Centre de recherche de l'Institut Merieux, Marcy l'Etolle, pg. 1109   IT
Chiron Domilens, 321 Avenue Jean Jaures, pg. 350   **PB**
Chloride France SA, 30 avenue des Freres Montgolfier, pg. 287   IT
COFATHEC, Siege Social, 26, rue Victor Lagrange, pg. 541   IT
Emerson Electric Indus. Controls, S.A., 5 rue Sports, pg. 576   **PB**
Euro RSCG Ensemble, 110 av Barthelemy Buyer, pg. 600   IT
Ferras, 28, rue Saint-Philippe, pg. 1028   IT
Filter Media, 15, Quai Tilsitt, pg. 636   IT
Fragema, 10, rue Juliette-Recamier, pg. 503   IT
Generale Traiteur, 41, quai Fulchiron, pg. 380   IT
HII, Les Jardins d'Entreprises, 213, rue de Gerlon, pg. 53   IT
Hogamed S.A., 48, Rue Pre-Gaudry, pg. 668   IT
Hospal International Marketing, 48, rue Pre-Gauday, pg. 668   IT
Hospal S.A., 188, Ave. Jean-Jaures, pg. 668   IT
Howmedica France S.A., 39 Boulevard Ambroise Pare, pg. 1283   **PB**
ICI Systems S.A.R.L., 213 rue de Gerland, pg. 665   IT
JEUMONT-SCHNEIDER TRENFORMETEURS, 84 Avenue Paul Santy, pg. 706   IT
Jump, 68 cours Albert Thomas, pg. 116   IT

Keller-Dorian Graveurs, Div. of Roehlen Industries/Europe, 10 Bis, Rue Saint Eusebe, pg. 1507 **PB**
La Lutece S.A., 52, Rue Duquesne, pg. 91 **IT**
La Suisse - Assurances (France), 30, Quai Claude-Bernard, pg. 1332 **IT**
La Suisse - Assurances-vie (France), 30, Quai Claude-Bernard, pg. 1332 **IT**
LeaRonal France, 3 Rue Sigmund Freud, pg. 982 **PB**
Linde Gaz Industriels S.A.R.L., pg. 811 **IT**
LIPHA CHEMICALS S.A., 34 rue Saint-Romain, pg. 812 **IT**
Lowara France, pg. 861 **PB**
Lyonnaise de Banque, 8, Rue de la Republique, pg. 565 **IT**
Merial SAS, 29 Avenue Tony Garnier, pg. 1114 **IT**
Metalair-Filliat SA, pg. 1065 **IT**
Oilgear Towler (Lyon), 76 Rue Cuvier, pg. 1215 **PB**
Pasteur Merieux Serums et Vaccins, 58 Ave. LeClerc, pg. 1109 **IT**
Rhone-Poulenc Agrochimie, 14, 20 Rue Pierre Baizet, pg. 1109 **IT**
Rhone-Poulenc Fibres, Tour du Credit Lyonnais, 129 rue Servie, pg. 1109 **IT**
Rhone-Poulenc Films, Rue Servient, pg. 1109 **IT**
Rhone-Silitec, 10 Rue du Commandant Faurax, pg. 1109 **IT**
SABM, Societe Africaine de Beton Manufacture S.A., 3, rue de l'arbre sec, pg. 425 **IT**
Sarelem, 128, rue de Crequi, pg. 706 **IT**
SepelCom, pg. 1097 **IT**
Simpson Industries E.U.R.L. (France), Dampers SAS, 33-35 Rue Roger Salengro, pg. 1475 **PB**
Simpson Techniparts E.U.R.L. (France), Techniparts SAS, 33-35 Rue Roger Salengro, pg. 1475 **PB**
Societe de Controle et de Management, 2, rue du President Carnot, pg. 824 **IT**
Sodily, Avenue du Marechal de Sape 163 B, pg. 534 **IT**
TPS Peyrard, 6/8, rue St. Nestor, pg. 1360 **IT**
Technip - Lyon Branch, 63-65, avenue Tony Garnier, pg. 1360 **IT**
Tektronix S.A.-LN, pg. 1568 **PB**
Vogtlin S.A., Z.A., de l'Arsenal, 41, Avenue de la Republique, pg. 551 **IT**
Wisaforest France S.A.R.L., Le Factory, 66 Cours Charlemagne, pg. 1429 **IT**
Woodward-Clyde International, 4, Rue du Viel Renverse, Immeuble Clement V, pg. 1658 **PB**
Zeneca SA, Z.I. La Pompelle, 11 rue Felix Brun, pg. 1527 **IT**

Machecoul

Novoferm France S.A., Z.I. Les Redoux, pg. 509 **IT**

Macon

Freudenberg LM Plast S.A.S., pg. 507 **IT**
Freudenberg S.A., pg. 505 **IT**
Simrit Distribution et CIE, pg. 507 **IT**
Simrit Distribution S.a.r.l., pg. 507 **IT**

Magny

Bertrand Faure Equipements SA, 17, rue de la Forge, pg. 192 **IT**

Maisons-Alfort

Retail Soft International (RSI), 13 rue Chevreuil, pg. 316 **IT**

Maizieres-les-Metz

France Transfo, Voie Romaine-Pont de Semcourt, pg. 706 **IT**
Refralor, Z.I. du Malambas Hauconcourt, pg. 789 **IT**

Malakoff

Barden SARL, 58, Rue Etienne Dolet, pg. 468 **IT**
Dumez Construction, 13, Voie d'Issy, pg. 823 **IT**
Syseca, 66-68, avenue Pierre Brossolette, pg. 1384 **IT**
Thomson-CSF Missile Electronics, 23-27, rue Pierre Valette, pg. 1382 **IT**
Thomson Software Products, 66/68, avenue Pierre Brossolette, pg. 1383 **IT**
Vishay Micro-Mesures, S.A., 98 Boulevard Gabriel Peri, pg. 1722 **PB**

Malaucene

Papeteries de Malaucene S.A., pg. 959 **PB**

Malemort

STEN, 66, avenue de la Liberation, pg. 793 **IT**

Mane-la-Vallee

De La Rue Systems SA, 40/42 Avenue de l'Europe, pg. 387 **IT**

Mantes-la-Jolie

APSYS (Aerospatiale Protection Systemes), 1, rue de Lorraine, pg. 29 **IT**
Compagnie de Construction Mecanique Sulzer, pg. 1305 **IT**

Elmo Semiconducteurs SARL, pg. 958 **PB**
Sulzer Pompes France S.A., Mantes-la-Jolie, France, pg. 1306 **IT**

Marconne

Financiere Ryssen, pg. 549 **IT**

Marcq-en-Baroeul

Nickel, 310, Boulevard Clemenceau, pg. 116 **IT**
Thomson-CSF Communications, Centre Electronique de Marcq-Baroeul, pg. 1382 **IT**
Thomson-CSF Microelectronique, 344, avenue de la Marne, pg. 1382 **IT**

Margaux

Chateau Beaumont, Cussac-Fort-Medoc, pg. 1322 **IT**

Marignier

Eurocopter France S.A., pg. 29 **IT**
Eurocopter Participations S.A., pg. 29 **IT**
Mitchell Sports SA, 396, Rue De La Precision, pg. 933 **PB**

Marle

Bently Nevada France S.A.R.L., 30 Ave. de L'Admiral Lemonnier, pg. 134 **PV**
Delsey SA, ZI Moimon - rue Jules Valles, pg. 192 **IT**
Disport, Z.A.C. d'Augny, pg. 534 **IT**
Vorwerk France SA, 30 ave. Am Lemonnier, pg. 1481 **IT**

Marmande

Expert Bois et Materiaux, Route de Bordeaux, pg. 784 **IT**

Marne la Vallee

Forbo Murs SA, pg. 497 **IT**
IRCON Pyrometers, Inc., B.P. 57, pg. 1209 **IT**
Kodak-Pathe, Zone Industrielle de Paris Est, pg. 554 **PB**
MTS Systems France (Marne la Vallee), 17, rue des Campanules, pg. 1029 **IT**
Martin Merkel France-Sarl, Parc Industriel de Torcy, Boite Postale, pg. 860 **IT**
Merloni Electromenagers S.A., Rue de la Maison Rouge, B.P. 120 Logne, pg. 860 **IT**
NAPS France S.A., Le Luzard 3, 35, Allee du 12 fevrier, pg. 913 **IT**
Oilgear Towler SA, Zone Industrielle de Paris, Allee Des Freres Montgolfier, pg. 1215 **PB**
Renishaw S.A., 74 Avenue de l'Europe, pg. 1103 **IT**
Rheometric Scientific France SARL, Espace Descartes, 7, rue Albert Einstein Champs sur Marne, pg. 1387 **PB**
SIMCI S.A., 74 Avenue de l'Europe, pg. 1103 **IT**
ScanData S.A., 47, Grande Allee du 12 Fevier, pg. 177 **PB**

Marseilles

Banque Bonnasse, 8, Allee Leon Gambetta, pg. 563 **IT**
Centre d'Importation et de Courtage Alimentaire, 513 Ave. du Prado, pg. 655 **IT**
Compagnie Europeenne des Peintures Julien SA, Chemin du Litoral, Mourepiane Port Activite, pg. 664 **IT**
Darty Province Mediterranne, Blvd. De La Valbarelle, pg. 734 **IT**
Det Norske Veritas, Impasse Blancard, pg. 397 **IT**
Eaux de Marseille, 25, rue Edouard Delanglade, pg. 823 **IT**
S.A. Etablissements A. Lafleur et F. Sicard, pg. 302 **IT**
EURO RSCG Novation, 515 av. du Prado, pg. 601 **IT**
Eurosud Publicite, 248, avenue Roger Salengro, pg. 792 **IT**
Le Nouveau Meridional, 4, rue Cougit, pg. 792 **IT**
Le Provencal, 248, avenue Roger Salengro, pg. 792 **IT**
MacGREGOR (FRA) S.A., Porte 4 Cap Janet, pg. 670 **IT**
MaK Mediterranee S.A.R.L., 38, Bd. Gay-Lussac, pg. 510 **IT**
Makita France S.A.-Marseille, 151, Avenue des Aygalades, pg. 832 **IT**
Mutuelle de Marseille, 31, rue Saint-Sebastien, pg. 19 **IT**
Raffinerie de Marseille, 336, rue de Lyon, pg. 549 **IT**
Ricard, 4 et 6 rue Berthelot, pg. 566 **IT**
SNTR Calberson Marseille, pg. 1164 **IT**
Select France, 4, rue Cougit, pg. 793 **IT**
Societe de Gestion de Restaurants-Bars Sur Les Auteoroutes SA, Burparc-Bat A, pg. 560 **IT**
Stolt Comex Seaway S.A., 36 Bd. des Oceans, pg. 1302 **IT**
Sud Presse Administration, 248, avenue Roger Salengro, pg. 794 **IT**
TSI France Inc., Technopole de Chateau Gombert, pg. 1559 **PB**
Watson Brown, 10, Place de la Joliette, pg. 682 **IT**

Martignas-sur-Jalle

Etablissement de Martignas, pg. 383 **IT**

Martin-Eglise

Davigel S.A., pg. 920 **IT**

Martiques

Enraf Sarl, 38 Ave. Jose Nobre, pg. 389 **IT**

Marvejols

Ollier Jacquot Bois et Materiaux, Route d' Antrenas, pg. 784 **IT**
Transports Rapides Lozeriens, pg. 1165 **IT**

Mas-Grenier

Barenbrug Tourneur Recherches SA, Negadis, Route de Bourret, pg. 167 **IT**

Massy

CGG GROUP, 1, rue Leon Migaux, pg. 241 **IT**
Cogitiel, 9, rue Ampere, pg. 53 **IT**
Compagnie Generale de Geophysique, 1, Rue Leon Migaux, pg. 241 **IT**
DEI Division, Nine, rue Ampere, pg. 52 **IT**
Elsag Bailey S.A., pg. 449 **IT**
Enerpac S.A., B.P. 200, Parc d'Activities du Moulin, pg. 125 **PB**
Genicom S.A., 17 Rue Ampere, pg. 729 **PB**
Hologic France, Parc du Moulin de Massy, pg. 831 **PB**
MET, 19, avenue Carnot, pg. 792 **IT**
MET Commutation, 19, avenue Carnot, pg. 792 **IT**
MLP France S.A., Parc d'Activites du Moulin de, Massy 17, rue du Saule Trapu 91882, pg. 874 **PB**
Micropolis S.A.R.L., 2 rue du Buisson aux Fraises, pg. 743 **PV**
Power-Packer France, B.P. 200, pg. 125 **PB**
Reckitt & Colman S.A., 15 Rue Ampere, pg. 1090 **IT**
Thomson-CSF Microelectronique, 29, avenue Carnot, pg. 1382 **IT**
Thomson-CSF Passive Components, 29, avenue Carnot, pg. 1382 **IT**

Matour

Sogri (Societe Guyanaise de Restauration Industrielle), Aeroport de Rochambeau, pg. 560 **IT**

Maubeuge

Societe de Maintenance Nucleaire, Z.I. de Grevaux les Guides, pg. 706 **IT**

Maurepas

Alpha Editions, 1, avenue Gutenberg, pg. 791 **IT**
Ampco Metal S.A., Rue Claude Bernard, pg. 67 **PV**
L-TEC France SARL, 25, rue Claude Bernard, pg. 283 **IT**
Mead Packaging Europe s.a.r.l., B.P. 131, 5 Allee Du Bourbonnais, pg. 1076 **PB**

Maurs

Auvergne Isolation, Montmurat, pg. 1172 **IT**

Maxeville

Pertuy, 8, rue de la Seille, pg. 206 **IT**

Mazingarbe

Nord Helioservice SA, pg. 69 **IT**

Meaux

Alme vis a Billes SA, pg. 838 **IT**
STILL & SAXBY S.A.R.L., pg. 811 **IT**

Melrand

Lydall Axohm, Saint-Rivalain, pg. 1021 **PB**
Lydall International, Inc., Saint-Rivalain, pg. 1021 **PB**

Melun

Etablissements Henri Peignen S.A., pg. 1205 **IT**
Parsons Chain Europe SA, 211 Rue Marinoni, ZI de Vaux Le Penil, pg. 473 **IT**

Mennecy

2AI Societe Nouvelle Automatisme et Avenir Informatique, 6 rue Champreux, pg. 316 **IT**

Merignac

Courbu Vitrage, ZI du Phare, pg. 1172 **IT**
Etablissement de Merignac, pg. 383 **IT**
Hewlett-Packard France, Parc d'Activite Cadera, Avenue du President Kennedy, pg. 819 **PB**
Merignac Office, rue Sarah Bernhardt, pg. 784 **IT**
Sogerma-Socea, B.P. 2, pg. 29 **IT**
Thomson-CSF Service Industrie, Parc Chateau Rouquey, 17 rue Thales, pg. 1383 **IT**

Meru

Auxilec, Zone Industrielle, 3, rue Emile Zola, pg. 1381 **IT**

Geographic Index-Non U.S.

Merville

Ecole de Pilotage Amaury de la Grange, Aerodrome de
Merville, pg. 560   IT
Samag, Aerodrome de Merville, pg. 560   IT

Merxheim

Reynolds Aluminium France, Rue du Ballon No. 1,
pg. 1387   PB

Mery-sur-Seine

Bourgey Montreuil, ZAC du Rebauchet, pg. 549   IT

Mesnil

ANGUS Chemie Gmbh, Le Bonaparte, pg. 75   PV

Metz

Banque Generale du Luxembourg S.A., 5 ave. Joffre,
pg. 162   IT
EURO RSCG Nord, 6 Place Saint Martin, pg. 601   IT
Hartmann & Braun France SA, pg. 835   IT
Herta S.A., pg. 920   IT
Hewlett-Packard France, Technolpole Metz 2000, 3, Rue
Graham Bell, pg. 819   PB
RTL9, 3, allee St. Symphorien, pg. 561   IT
Rothenberger France S.A.R.L., 24, Rue des Drapiers,
pg. 1129   IT
Unimetal, pg. 571   IT

Meudon

Balzers S.A., 47, Rue d'ArthElon, pg. 997   IT
Sciam S.N.C., pg. 506   IT
Sextant Avionique, Parc Tertiaire, 5/7 rue Jeanne
Braconnier, pg. 29   IT

Meudon de Foret

Data General Corp., pg. 486   PB
ESL S.N.C., 7 rue de l'Avenir, pg. 369   PV
Sodeteg, 18, avenue du Marechal Juin, pg. 1382   IT
TDA Armement, 18, avenue du Marechal Juin,
pg. 1382   IT
Thomson-CSF Airsys, 18, avenue du Marechal Juin,
pg. 1382   IT
Thomson Tubes Electroniques (Siege), 18, avenue du
Marechal Juin, pg. 1383   IT

Meylan

Becton Dickinson Vacutainer Systems Europe, Pre Pichat 5,
Chemin des Sources, pg. 200   PB
CAP Gemini Inovation, 86/90 rue Thiess, pg. 263   IT
Sames, S.A., Chemin de Malacher, pg. 230   PB

Meyzieu

Hospal Industrie S.A., Ave. Lionel Terray, pg. 668   IT
Tamrock Drills Secoma S.A., 19, Avenue de Lattre-de-
Tassigny, pg. 1353   IT
Tamrock France, 19, avenue de Lattre-de-Tassigny- Z.I.,
pg. 1353   IT
Van Leeuwen Tubes SA, 2, Avenue des Pays-Bas,
pg. 1450   IT
WEMCO EnviroTech Pumpsystems SA, Boite Postale 73,
pg. 1489   IT

Mezzavia

Corse Sud Express, pg. 1163   IT

Mielan

Laiterie de Villecomtal, 32730 Villecomtal sur Arros,
pg. 379   IT

Migennes

Kidde France, Zone Industrialle, pg. 594   IT

Mions

Roth SA, 43 Rue de Brosses, pg. 467   IT

Miramas

Miramas Plant, pg. 305   IT

Mirebeau

Biomet SA, 2-4 Synergiparc Avenue Jean Jaures,
pg. 232   PB
Gorcy S.A., Zone Industrielle, pg. 380   IT
Nelco S.A., Rte de Beze, pg. 1258   PB

Miserey-Salines

Virolle, pg. 1165   IT

Mitry-Mory

Elastogran France S.A., Z.I. Rue Decauville, pg. 108   IT
Groupacier, pg. 571   IT
ROR Rockwell S.A., Z.I. du Moulin a Vent, 9 rue des Freres
Lumiere, pg. 1399   PB

Moder

Ahlstrom-Hanssen S.A., Zone Industrielle, pg. 34   IT

Moirans

Thomson-LCD, Zone Industrielle Centr'Alp, pg. 1383   IT
Thomson Tubes Electroniques, Z.I. Voreppe-Moirans,
pg. 1383   IT

Moissac

Rieter Automotive Polymers S.A., pg. 1117   IT

Molieres-sur-Ceze

Societe Emballages des Cevennes S.A., pg. 20   IT

Molsheim

Millipore S.A., Zone Industrielle, pg. 1113   PB
Osram S.A., 1 Rue d'Altdorf, pg. 1244   IT

Mondeville

Rober Bosch Electronique SA, 15, Rue Charles-de-
Coulomb, pg. 205   IT
PROMODES SA, Zone Industrielle, Route de Paris,
pg. 1071   IT
SMN (Societe Metallurgique de Normandie), pg. 571   IT
SNT Noyon, pg. 1164   IT

Mondragon

Cie. Rhodanienne de Developpement, Quartier Le Pontet,
pg. 788   IT

Mont Louis

Bolquere/Font-Romeu, Col de la Perche, pg. 784   IT

Mont-Saint-Aignau

Hewlett-Packard France, P.A.T. Lavatine, 3, Rue Jacques
Monod, pg. 819   PB

Montaigu

Ordo, Route de Nautes, pg. 512   PV

Montaren

Uzes, Route d'Uzes, pg. 784   IT

Montataire

Dacral Europe, P.O. Box 4, Rue des Desportes, pg. 43   IT
Heidelberg Harris S.A., Square H. Marinoni, pg. 605   IT

Montauban

Chapel ier Bois-Materiaux-Quincaillerie, Z.I. Nord, Ave. de
Paris, pg. 784   IT
SNTR Calberson, pg. 1164   IT

Montbazon

Kami SA, Parc d'activites de la Grange-, Babier, 1, allee
des Vergers, pg. 781   IT

Montbron

Ets, Bricq & Cie S.A., pg. 1202   IT

Montdidier

Delsey SA, ZI de la Roseraie, pg. 192   IT
H&C Cereales S.A., Aux Sentiers d'Etelfay, pg. 752   IT

Montereau

Korf-Transport-France S.A.R.L., 36, rue de la grande,
pg. 759   IT
Micronyl-Wedco S.A., 3 Rte. de la Grande-Paroisse,
pg. 854   PB
SAM (Societe des Acieries de Montereau), pg. 571   IT

Montesson

AccuScan International, 8 Rue du Chateau D'Eau,
pg. 890   IT
White Cap France S.A.R.L., pg. 1207   IT

Montfort-le-Gesnois

Hygie France, pg. 672   PB

Monthyon

Salsi SA, 1, rue Chateau Gaillard, pg. 790   IT

Montigny-le-Bretonneux

Ascom Timeplex SA, 39, avenue des Trois Peuples,
pg. 87   IT
Automotive Wiring Systems Division - Sylea, Parc
d'Activites du Pas du Lac, 5, avenue Newton,
pg. 785   IT
Bouygues Offshore, 3 rue Stephenson, pg. 206   IT
Cablinal, Parc d'Activites du Pas du La, c, pg. 785   IT
Cinch Connector Division, Parc d'Activites du Pas du Lac,
8, square Newton, pg. 786   IT
Compagnie Versaillaise de Transports, 3, av. du Centre,
pg. 792   IT
Duquesne-Purina S.A., Place Charles de Gaulle,
pg. 1360   PB
Hewlett-Packard France, Pac De Bois D'Arcy, Buro Plus,
pg. 819   PB
KLA Instruments France, S.A., 25 Rue Michael Faraday,
pg. 939   PB
LABINAL SA, Parc D'Activites du Pas du Lac, 5, ave
Newton, pg. 785   IT
Moteurs Globe C/O Labinal, Parc d'activites du Pas du
Lac, 5, avenue Newton, pg. 787   IT
SKF Equipements S.n.c., 30-32 Ave. des trois Peuples,
pg. 1158   IT
Scori, 10, rue Ampere-Parc Technologique, pg. 788   IT
Scori Holding, Lorve Ampere, pg. 292   IT
SODEXHO S.A., Parc d'Activites du Pas du Lac, 3, avenue
Newton, pg. 1274   IT

Montlhery

B.H.V. Montlhery, 60 rue d'Orleans, pg. 181   IT
Nord France S.A., Rue de la Tourelle, pg. 634   IT

Montlouis-sur-Loire

Volumax S.A., Zone Industrielle du Saule-Michaud,
pg. 712   IT

Montmorency

Gachot S.A., 26, bis, Avenue de Paris, pg. 1650   PB

Montoir-de-Bretagne

Hydro Agri France Usine de Montoir, pg. 962   IT
MO Atlantique, Zone des Rochettes, pg. 1172   IT

Montpellier

ABX S.A., pg. 1120   IT
Dell Computer S.A., 1028 Rue de Vieille Post, pg. 496   PB
Hewlett-Packard France, BT 8 Parc Du Club Millenaire,
Avenue Albert Einstein, pg. 819   PB
Maurel & Calberson Montpellier, pg. 1164   IT
Meridionale de Travaux, 9,boulevard Sarrail, pg. 206   IT
Montpellier Office, 456, rue Mas-St.-Pierre, pg. 784   IT
SMS France, Batiment 8, Mini Parc, pg. 1463   PB

Montreuil

Imprimerie gauthier-Villars, 70 rue de Saint-Mande,
pg. 239   IT
SERV Trayvou Interverrouillage SA, 56-58 rue Brulefer,
pg. 590   IT

Montrouge

Armstrong World Industries-France S.A., 5 Rue Louis le
Jejune, pg. 132   PB
Babyliss. SA, 29, Rue Henri Ginoux, pg. 261   PV
CDZ, 17ter, rue de la Vanne, pg. 789   IT
Chryso, 17 ter, rue de la Vanne, pg. 789   IT
DSM France SA, Immeuble Perisud, 5, Rue Lejeune,
pg. 355   IT
Lafarge Materiaux de Specialites, 17, rue de La Vanne,
pg. 789   IT
Lafarge Nouveaux Materiaux, 17 ter, rue de las Vanne,
pg. 789   IT
Lafarge Refractaires Monolithiques, 17 ter st. de La Vanne,
pg. 789   IT
Lafarge Refractories Trading, 17 ter, rue de la Vanni,
pg. 789   IT
Parex (CDZ), 17 ter, rue de la Vanne, pg. 789   IT
Savima, pg. 563   IT
Schlumberger Industries, 50, avenue Jean Jaures,
pg. 1439   PB
Services Conselis Dowell, 50, Ave. Jean Jaures Bois
Postale 360, pg. 1439   PB

Morangis

Facom, 6-8 Rue Gustave Eiffel, pg. 570   IT
GROUPE STRAFOR FACOM, 6 Et, 8 Rue Gustave Eiffel,
pg. 569   IT
Traub-Heckert France S.A., 3, rue Dr. J. Charcot Z.I. Sud,
pg. 1419   IT

PB - *U.S. Public Companies Volume*
PV - *U.S. Private Companies Volume*
IT - *International Public & Private Companies Volume*

1588

Moulins

Chaussures Bally Moulins SA, 13, rue Henri Barbusse, pg. 997 **IT**
Darty Alsace Lorraine, Zone Commerciale De La Rotonde, pg. 734 **IT**
Fiskars S.a.r.l., 30 Rue Guynemer, pg. 492 **IT**
SNTR Calberson, pg. 1164 **IT**

Moutiers

Tamrock Loaders E.M. Franceloader S.A., 14 ru Clemenceau, pg. 1353 **IT**

Mouy

Sachs Allinquant SA, pg. 835 **IT**

Mulhouse

Baars France SA, pg. 752 **IT**
EURO RSCG Est, 25 place de la Reunion, pg. 601 **IT**
Gerrer, 4, rue des Verriers, pg. 1172 **IT**
Hewlett-Packard France, 11, Rue Gustave Hirn, pg. 819 **PB**
Mikron SA Mulhouse, 15, Rue de Quimper, pg. 867 **IT**
Naegelen S.A., 8, Rue de l-Ill, pg. 574 **PB**
SCPA, 2 Place du General de Gaulle, pg. 459 **IT**
Zellweger-Sauter-Energie S.A., pg. 618 **IT**

Muntzenheim

JA/MONT N.V. - Technology Office, pg. 673 **PB**
Kunheim Consumer Products Div., pg. 673 **PB**

Nancy

Espace 96, 4, rue du Moulin de Boudonville, pg. 792 **IT**
Pont-a-Mousson SA, 91, Avenue de la liberation, pg. 1176 **IT**
Societe Nanceienne Varin-Bernier, 4, Place Andre Maginot, pg. 565 **IT**

Nanterre

Alcatel Espace, 5 Rue Noel Pons, pg. 56 **IT**
Alcatel Telspace, 5, Rue Noel Pons, pg. 56 **IT**
Amtech International, 25 Boulevard des Bouvets, pg. 106 **PB**
Astor France S.a.r.l., pg. 185 **IT**
Auxisol, 81, av. du Mal-Joffre, pg. 1176 **IT**
Benckiser St. Marc S.A., pg. 186 **IT**
Biogen France SA, Le Capitole, 55 rue des Champs Pierreux, pg. 231 **PB**
Cogesal S.A., 1, Place De La Boule, pg. 1436 **IT**
DBLE, 72, Avenue de la Liberte, pg. 822 **IT**
Direct Assurance, Parc des Fontaines, pg. 18 **IT**
Dumez-GTM, 57 Ave. Jules Quentin, pg. 823 **IT**
Dumez-GTM, 57, avenue Jules Quentin, pg. 823 **IT**
Dun & Bradstreet France SA, 345 Avenue Georges Clemenceau, pg. 536 **PB**
Eau et Force, 72 avenue de la Liberte, pg. 822 **IT**
ELYO Corp., 235 Ave. G. Clemenceau, pg. 823 **IT**
Fifed, 32, Avenue Pablo Picasso, pg. 823 **IT**
GTM Construction, 61, avenue Jules Quentin, pg. 823 **IT**
Grace S.A., Le Clemenceau 11, 215 Ave. Georges Clemenceau, pg. 756 **PB**
Groupe GTM, 61, avenue Jules Quentin, pg. 823 **IT**
ITT Flygt S.A., 29, rue du Port, pg. 860 **PB**
Iota, 47, rue Sadi Carnot, pg. 792 **IT**
Isolmat, 81, av. du Mal Joffe, pg. 1176 **IT**
K.L.G. S.A., 1, rue Lavoisier, pg. 518 **IT**
Konica Bureautique S.A., 15 rue des Sorins, pg. 749 **IT**
Labo Industrie S.A., 1, rue Lavoisier, pg. 518 **IT**
Laboratoires Astra France, Avenir Quest 64, rue du 8 Mai 1945, pg. 94 **IT**
Les Techniques d'Interieur, 81, av. du Mal-Joffre, pg. 1176 **IT**
LYONNAISE DES EAUX S.A., 72, ave de la Liberte, pg. 822 **IT**
Materiaux Isolants Lillois, 81, av. du Mal-Joffre, pg. 1176 **IT**
Matival, 81, av. du Mal-Joffre, pg. 1176 **IT**
Media Informatique Service (M.I.S.), 47, rue Sadi Carnot, pg. 793 **IT**
Media Sud, 1-3, rue Sadi Carnot, pg. 793 **IT**
Midimat, 8, av. du Mal-Joffre, pg. 1176 **IT**
Nira S.A., 16, rue de Peupliers, pg. 1369 **IT**
Novo Nordisk Bioindustrie S.A., Immeuble Challenge 92, 79, Avenue Francois Arago, pg. 989 **IT**
Novo Nordisk Bioindustrie SA, Europe, Immeuble Challenge 92, pg. 989 **IT**
Olicom France, Immeuble Plein Ouest, 177, avenue Georges Clemenceau, pg. 1001 **IT**
Oracle France S.A., 65 rue des Trois Fontanot, pg. 1228 **PB**
Ositel Services, 151 rue de 1er Mai, pg. 316 **IT**
Peugeot-Citroen Moteurs (PCM), 49, rue Noel Pons, pg. 1021 **IT**
Promoref SA, 31, bd des Bouvets, pg. 1173 **IT**
Regma, 39, Boulevarde Des Bouvets, pg. 1109 **IT**
SAGEM Terminals & Telecommunications Division, 1, rue Louis Meunier, pg. 1273 **IT**
SDRC France S.A., Immeuble Le Capitole, 55, Avenue des Champs-Pierreux, pg. 1525 **PB**
SFIC, 81 au du Marischal Jaffre, pg. 1176 **IT**
SNET Materiaux, 81, av. du Mal-Joffre, pg. 1176 **IT**
Saab France S.A., pg. 687 **IT**

SmithKline Beecham Products France S.A., 5 Esplanade Charles de Gaulle, pg. 1266 **IT**
Solymat, 81,av. du Mal-Joffre, pg. 1176 **IT**
Stratus Computer S.A., Immeuble Le Vermont 119, Rue des Trois-Fontanot, pg. 1524 **PB**
Zenith Data Systems, Immeuble le Capitole, 55 ave. des Champs Pierreux, pg. 316 **IT**
Zenith Data Systems Europe, Immeuble le Capitole, 55 ave. des Champs Pierreux, pg. 316 **IT**

Nantes

Bateaux Nantais, Quai de la Motte-Rouge, pg. 1274 **IT**
Credit Industriel de L'Ouest, 2, avenue J.C. Bonduelle, pg. 564 **IT**
Etoile Bleue, 7 rue de Valmy, pg. 600 **IT**
Intergraph France S.A., Centre d'Affaires Nantais, 5 Boulevard Vincent Gache, 44062, pg. 892 **PB**
LM/Young & Rubicam, 1, re Du-guesclin, pg. 1199 **PV**
Matra Harris Semiconductors, La Chantrerie, pg. 793 **IT**
Matra-Harris Semiconductors S.A., pg. 791 **PB**
Matra M.H.S., La Chantrerie, Route de Gachet, pg. 793 **IT**
Medex Medical S.A.R.L., PA Antares, 12 Rue Antares, pg. 689 **PB**
Nouvelle Vague, 15 rue Lamoriciere, pg. 116 **IT**
Rockwell Automation S.A., Technoparc de L'Aubiniere, 16 Impasse des Jades, pg. 1400 **PB**
SCA Packaging France S.A., Three Blvd. des Martyrs Nantais, pg. 1326 **IT**
SNTR Calberson Nantes, pg. 1164 **IT**
Sunrise Medical (France), Village d'activite du Petit Chantelier, pg. 1536 **PB**
Tech-Atlan, 24, boulevard Vincent Gache, pg. 1360 **IT**
Unicom, 4 Chemin de l'Eraudiere, pg. 601 **IT**

Nassandres

Ateliers Sucre Liquide et Conditionnement-Laboratoire de Recherche de Nassandres, pg. 549 **IT**

Nerac

S.E.S. France S.A., Zone Industrielle, Route de Lavarac, pg. 1526 **IT**

Neuilly

Automobiles Citroen, 62 Blvd. Victor Hugo, pg. 1020 **IT**
Continental Can Distribution S.A.R.L., pg. 1207 **IT**
3i France, 168 Ave. Charles De Gaulle, pg. 1386 **IT**

Neuilly-sur-Marne

Hyster France, 29-39 Rue Des Freres Lumiere, pg. 1150 **PB**

Neuilly-sur-Seine

Alsthom-Jeumont, 157, avenue Charles de Gaulle, pg. 706 **IT**
Amgen S.A., 192 avenue Charles de Gaulle, pg. 101 **PB**
Cabot Europe Limited, 192 Avenue Charles de Gaulle, pg. 289 **PB**
Cereol S.A., 14 Blvd. du General Leclerc, pg. 324 **IT**
Chevron Chemical S.A., pg. 348 **PB**
CLARINS, 4 Commandant Pilot, pg. 295 **IT**
Clarins International Div., 5, rue du Commandant Pilot, pg. 295 **IT**
Comdisco France S.A./Promodata, 176, Avenue Charles DeGaulle, pg. 408 **PB**
Compagnie de Saint-Gobain-Pont-a Mousson, 62, boulevard Victor Hugo, pg. 313 **IT**
Compagnie Phonographique Francaise Barclay, 143 Ave. Charles de Gaulle, pg. 1053 **IT**
Conquest Europe S.A.R.L., 1 Rue Garnier, pg. 1484 **IT**
ECOM ET PARTENAIRE, 8, rue de l'Hotel-de-Ville, pg. 433 **IT**
Eridania Beghin-Say Group, 14, Boulevard du General-Leclerc, pg. 324 **IT**
Ethnor S.A., 192 Avenue Charles de Gaulle, pg. 929 **PB**
Fun Radio, 143, av. Charles de Gaulle, pg. 561 **IT**
Hoesch Systemes Batiment S.a.r.l., 3-5, Boulevard de Courbevoie, pg. 508 **IT**
Hydro Agri France, 46, rue Jacques Dulud, pg. 962 **IT**
Hydro Aluminium Primary Metal Sales, 46, rue Jacques Dulud, pg. 963 **IT**
Hydro Produits Chimiques, 46, rue Jacques Dulud, pg. 963 **IT**
IMS, 35 rue du Pont, pg. 571 **IT**
International Herald Tribune S.A., 181, Avenue Charles de Gaulle, pg. 1176 **PB**
International Herald Tribune, S.A., 181 Ave. Charles de Gaulle, pg. 1743 **PB**
Jotun France S.A., 88, Avenue Charles de Gaulle, pg. 715 **IT**
Kilometrage S.A., 11 Rue Bailly, pg. 650 **IT**
LMG (Lifestyle Marketing Group), 30 Boulevard Vital-Bouhot, pg. 1422 **PB**
Laboratoire Roger Bellon, 159 Avenue A. Peretti, pg. 1109 **IT**
MSD AGVET (EC Office), 43, Rue de Villiers, pg. 1092 **PB**
Matra Hachette Multimedia, 131, avenue du General-de-Gaulle, pg. 793 **IT**
Matra Hachette Multimedia Voyager, 131, avenue du General de Gaulle, pg. 793 **IT**
Thierry Mugler Parfums, 13 rue Madeleine Michelis, pg. 295 **IT**

Network Systems France S.A., 185, Ave. Charles de Gaulle, pg. 1523 **PB**
Outokumpu France S.A., 131 avenue Charles de Gaulle, pg. 1015 **IT**
Paco Rabanne Parfums, 6 Boulevard du Parc, pg. 1073 **IT**
Parfums et Beaute France & Cie., 6 rue Graviers, pg. 818 **IT**
Parfums Cachrel & Cie, 6 rue Graviers, pg. 818 **IT**
Parfums Ralph Lauren, 6 rue Graviers, pg. 818 **IT**
Paloma Picasso & Cie., 6 rue Graviers, pg. 818 **IT**
Prestige et Collections Inter. & Cie., 6 rue Graviers, pg. 818 **IT**
Procter & Gamble France, 96 Ave. Charles-De Gaulle, pg. 1332 **PB**
Produits Roche S.A., 52, Boulevard du Parc, pg. 1121 **IT**
Rainbow Technologies, 122 Ave. Charles de Gaulle, pg. 1359 **PB**
Rammer France, 168, avenue Charles de Gaulle, pg. 1352 **IT**
R.J. Reynolds Tobacco France, S.A., 171, Avenue Charles de Gaulle, pg. 1356 **IT**
Rhovyl, 47, Rue de Villers, pg. 1109 **IT**
Ricoh France S.A., 192 Ave. Charles de Gaulle, pg. 1116 **IT**
Roballo-France S.a.r.l., 13, Rue Madeleine Michelis, pg. 509 **IT**
Seagate Technology France, S.a.r.l., 31, Rue de Poissonniers, pg. 1450 **PB**
Societe Monsanto S.A., 120, avenue Charles-de-Gaulle, pg. 1126 **PB**
Yves Saint Laurent Parfums S.A., 28/34, blvd. du Parc, pg. 445 **IT**

Neuilly-Plaisance

Fuller-F.L. Smidth S.A., 2/4 rue Vincent van Gogh, pg. 475 **IT**
Radiometer S.A., ZA la Fontaine du Vaisseau, 8, rue Edmond Michelet, pg. 1084 **IT**

Neuvic

R.P. Scherer Production S.A., Theorat B.P. 24, pg. 1438 **PB**

Neuville-en-Ferrain

PCM France SA, Les Peupliers, pg. 356 **IT**

Neuville-sur-Saone

Valexy Rhone Alpes, pg. 571 **IT**

Nevers

SNTR Calberson Nievre, pg. 1164 **IT**

Nexon

Labinal Aero Plant, pg. 786 **IT**
Sofrance, Z.I. des Gannes, 6 et 8, rue Maryse Bastie, pg. 786 **IT**

Nice

Gelazur S.A., pg. 429 **PB**
Nica, pg. 563 **IT**
S-E-Banken Luxembourg S.A., Nice, 107, Quai des Etas Unis, pg. 1259 **IT**
SLE S.a.r.l., 179, bd Rene Cassin, pg. 1045 **PB**
SNTR Calberson Nice, pg. 1164 **IT**
Safare-Crouzet, 98, avenue Saint-Lambert, pg. 1382 **IT**
Sfernice S.A., 199, Blvd. de la Madeleine, pg. 1722 **PB**

Niederbronn-les-Bains

DE DIETRICH & CO., 23, route de Bitche, pg. 386 **IT**

Nimes

Eminence SA, pg. 618 **IT**
Nimes Office, Centre Commercial du Batiment, pg. 784 **IT**
SNTR Calberson Nimes, pg. 1164 **IT**
Serpo France S.A., Voie N 3, pg. 1200 **IT**

Niort

Dusolier, pg. 1163 **IT**

Nogent-sur-Marne

GESTRA S.A., 18, Rue Andre Pontier, pg. 550 **IT**

Nogent-sur-Oise

Eurand France S.A., 14 rue du Close Barrois, pg. 81 **PB**

Nogent-sur-Seine

Bertrand Faure Equipements SA, Av. de Beauregard, pg. 192 **IT**
Enco, Avenue du General de Gaulle, pg. 706 **IT**
Thrige Electric S.A., Avenue du General de Gaulle, pg. 1387 **IT**

PB - U.S. Public Companies Volume
PV - U.S. Private Companies Volume
IT - International Public & Private Companies Volume

1589

Geographic Index-Non U.S.

Noisy-le-Grand

Luwa Filtres Sarl, pg. 617 IT
Makita France S.A., 2 Allee des Performances, Zone Industrielle des Richardets, pg. 832 IT
Multanova France S.a.r.l., pg. 618 IT
OCE-France S.A., pg. 994 IT
Proner Comatel SA, 38-40 allee du Closeau, pg. 1242 IT
Pyral S.A., Marketing, Immeuble le SARI, Avenue du Levant, pg. 109 IT
qad.france eurl, 17-19 Bld du Mont d'Est, pg. 1345 PB
Schlatter France S.a.r.l., Immeuble Atria, pg. 1206 IT
Zellweger S.A., pg. 618 IT

Noyen

Societe Verriere d'Encapsulation, Rue de l'Europe, pg. 1172 IT

Nurieux

Perstorp S.A.-Div. Perstorp Stamp, Route en Doraise, pg. 1038 IT

Obernai

Hager Modulaire S.A., 22, rue du General-Leclerc, pg. 3 IT
Stoeffler, Zone Industrielle Boulevard de l'Europe, pg. 380 IT

Oissel

La Quinoleine et Ses Derives S.A., 3, rue Octave Fauquet, pg. 983 IT

Ollioules

La Republique, Route de la Seyne, pg. 792 IT

Oloron Sainte Marie

Messier-Dowty SAS, Establissement de Bidos, pg. 1340 IT

Onet-le-Chateau

Aveyron Express, pg. 1163 IT

Orange

Domaines Michel Bernard SA, pg. 752 IT

Orgeres en Beauce

Asbury Worldwide France, 4 Rue Du Gue Barrault, pg. 1110 PB

Orgeval

Habitat France SA, La Maison Blanche, pg. 659 IT

Orleans

ANTEA SA, P.O. Box 6119, pg. 607 IT
ARIOS SA, P.O. Box 6207, pg. 607 IT
CFG SA, P.O. Box 6429, pg. 608 IT
Dalla Vera, 9, quai du Roi, B.P. 1827, pg. 206 IT
Dormer Tools S.A., pg. 1186 IT
ESS-FOOD S.A., 1, Pl. Jean Monnet, pg. 429 IT
Komori-Chambon S.A., 6, Rue Aguste Rodin La Source, pg. 745 IT
Sandvik Aciers S.N.C., pg. 1186 IT
Sandvik Coromant S.N.C., pg. 1186 IT
Sandvik Outillage S.N.C., pg. 1186 IT
Sandvik S.A., B.P. 6209, pg. 1187 IT
Societe de Banque de l'Orleanais, 35, rue de la Bretonnerie, pg. 548 IT

Orsay

Bilfinger + Berger S.A.R.L., Freres S.A., 3, rue Rene Rozel, pg. 196 IT
Coherent S.A., Domaine Technologique de Saclay, pg. 396 PB
Finnigan MAT S.a.r.l., Parc Club Orsay Universite, pg. 1596 PB
Helly-Hansen France, 69, rue de Paris, pg. 1011 IT
Laboratoire Beral, S.A., c/o Pfizer S.A., 86 Rue de Paris, pg. 1283 IT
Laboratoire Central De Recherches, Domaine de Corbeville, pg. 1382 IT
Laboratoire de Recherche, Eurolysine, Parc Club Orsay Universite, Bat E, 1, rue Jean Rostand, pg. 41 IT
Orsim, S.A., 86, rue de Paris, pg. 1284 PB
Oxford Instruments, Parc Club-Orsay Universite, 27 rue Jean Rostand, pg. 1018 IT
Pfizer S.A., 86, Rue de Paris, pg. 1283 PB
Thomson-CSF Health Systems, Domaine de Corbeville, pg. 1382 IT
Thomson-CSF Semiconducteurs Specifiques, Route Departmentale 128, pg. 1383 IT
Thomson-CSF Technologies & Methodes, L'Oree de Corbeville, pg. 1383 IT

Osny

Invacare France, Z.A. Beau Soleis, 9, Chausse J. Cesar, pg. 311 PB
SAGEM, 18 Chaussee Jules Cesar, pg. 1273 IT

Ottmarsheim

Produits et Engrais Chimiques du Rhin S.A. (PEC-Rhin), pg. 109 IT

Ouillins

Societe Roannaise des Papiers S.A., 105 Ave. Jean-Jaures, pg. 567 IT
Soremap Henkel GV S.A., pg. 614 IT

Oyonnax

Sic Plastics France S.A., 57, Rue Rene Nicod, pg. 850 IT

Ozoir-la-Ferriere

CMIC SA, pg. 68 IT
Titleflex Europe SA, Zone Industrielle BP 73, 22 Maurice Chevalier Avenue, pg. 1341 IT

Palaiseau

Aladdin Industries, 5 Rue de LaCroix Martre, pg. 31 PV
Charmilles Technologies (France) S.A., 12, Avenue du 1 er Mai, pg. 489 IT
Georg Fischer Disa Sarl, 2 bis, rue Leon Blum, pg. 489 IT
Keithley Instruments S.A.R.L., 3 Allee des Garays, pg. 947 PB
L'Usinage Electrique Sarl, 17, rue Leon-Blum, pg. 489 IT
Pacific Scientific S.A.R.L., 2 Allee du 10 ru Ambroise Croizat, pg. 1250 IT
Societe Industrielle d'Automatisation Bancaire-SIAB S.A., Zone d'Activite de Courtaboeuf, Avenue de Quebec, pg. 316 IT

Pamiers

Delrieu Bois et Materiaux, Route de Toulouse, pg. 784 IT

Pantin

CIEMI, 13 Rue Auger, pg. 260 IT
Europe Auto Equipment, 32, rue Delizy, pg. 394 PB
ISS Net Inter S.A., 12 rue Hoche, pg. 657 IT
Pirelli Transmissions Industrielles, 110 bis Avenue du General Leclerc, pg. 1059 IT
SNT Calberson, pg. 1164 IT

Pardies

Hydro Agri France Usine de Pardies, Usine de Pardies, pg. 962 IT
L'Ammoniac Agricole, Route Des Usines, pg. 964 IT

Parempuyre

Consortium Vinicole de Bordeaux et de la Gironde SA, pg. 752 IT

Pargny-sur-Saulx

Huguenot-Fenal, Ave. de la Marne, pg. 661 IT

Paris

AGEFI, 48, rue Notre-Dame-des-Victoires, pg. 779 IT
AGF ASSURANCES, 87, rue de Richelieu, pg. 14 IT
AXA Asset Management Europe, 40, rue du Colisee, pg. 18 IT
AXA Assurances, La Grande Arche, pg. 18 IT
AXA Banque, 5-7, rue de Milan, pg. 18 IT
AXA Credit, 5-7, rue de Milan, pg. 18 IT
Gie AXA Gestion des Actifs, 40, rue du Colisee, pg. 18 IT
AXA Gestion Interessement, 5-7, rue de Milan, pg. 18 IT
AXA Re France, 39, rue du Colisee, pg. 18 IT
AXA-UAP, 9, place vendome, pg. 18 IT
Aberly, 121, avenue de Malakoff, pg. 791 IT
Abianne, 121, avenue de Malakoff, pg. 791 IT
Acclaim Entertainment, SA, 12/14 Rond Pt. des Champs-Elysees, pg. 15 PB
Acer Computer France S.A.R.L., pg. 22 IT
Aciers Krupp S.a.r.l., 50 Avenue de Wagram, pg. 515 IT
Action Municipale, 17 rue Uzes, pg. 239 IT
Administration d'Affichage et de Publicite, 152, rue de Picpus, pg. 791 IT
Aeroassurances, 37, boulevard e Montmorency, pg. 29 IT
AEROSPATIALE, 37 Blvd. de Montmorency, pg. 28 IT
Affimet, Immeuble Balzac, pg. 1028 IT
Ageris International, S.A., 93, Cours Des Petites Ecuries, pg. 438 PB
Agrotechnip S.A., La Defense 6, 170, place Henri Regnault, pg. 1360 IT
Air France C.S. Participation, 45 Rue de Paris, pg. 560 IT
AIR LIQUIDE S.A., 75, Quai d'Orsay, pg. 37 IT
Air Malta - Paris, 9 Boulevard de la Madeleine, pg. 38 IT
Air Products S.A., 78 Rue Championnet, pg. 32 PB
Ajinomoto Co., Inc., European Headquarters, 153, Rue de Courcelles, pg. 40 IT
Akerlunc & Rausing S.A.R.L., 2bd de Reuilly, pg. 33 IT

Album, 54, rue Etienne-Marcel, pg. 779 IT
Alcatel, 33 rue Emeriau, pg. 52 IT
ALCATEL ALSTHOM COMPAGNIE GENERALE D'ELECTRICITE, 54, rue La Boetie, pg. 52 IT
Alice, 10 rue de Clichy, pg. 678 PV
Alliance et Gestion Commerciale (Algeco) S.A., 16, Avenue de l'Opera, pg. 1071 IT
AlliedSignal International, Inc., 18, rue Marbeuf, pg. 52 PB
Alpha Assurances, Tour Franklin, 100-101, Terrasse Boieldieu, pg. 18 IT
Alphapage, 232 Blvd. Pereire 17th, pg. 503 IT
Alpnet, Interdoc, S.A.R.L., 62, rue Jean-Jacques Rousseau, pg. 58 PB
Alsi gestion, 15 Rue du Louvre, pg. 344 IT
Aluminum Dunkerque S.A., Immeuble Balzac, Cedex 68, pg. 1028 IT
Aluminum Pechiney, Immeuble Balzac, pg. 1028 IT
Amdahl France S.A., 1, Rond Point Victor Hugo, pg. 527 IT
Amerford France S.A., Aeroport Charles De Gaulle, pg. 1388 IT
Arisept, 61, rue des Belles-Feuilles, pg. 789 IT
Aritrois, 61, rue Ballu, pg. 790 IT
Arjo Wiggins SA, 3, rue du Pont de Lodi, pg. 567 IT
Armisse, 121, avenue de Malakoff, pg. 791 IT
Ascom Elsydel SA, 63, Boulevard Bessieres, pg. 87 IT
Assi France S.a.r.l., 1, rue de General Foy, pg. 966 IT
Assu-Vie, 26. Rue Laffitte, pg. 563 IT
Aticam, 12, rue de la Bourse, pg. 18 IT
ATLAS EDITIONS, 89 Rue La Boetie, pg. 96 IT
AtoHaas Europe S.C.A., pg. 1404 PB
AU BON MARCHE, Le Bon Marche, Rue de Babeelone, pg. 97 IT
Auditoire, 50/54 rue de Silly, pg. 116 IT
Audour, Soum, Larue/SMS, 38 Bis rue du Fer a Moulin, pg. 678 PV
Australia & New Zealand Banking Group Limited France, 6 rue de Berri, pg. 99 IT
Autoliv et Cie, 185, Ave. Charles de Gaulle, pg. 441 IT
Automobiles Peugeot S.A., Siege Social a Paris 16, pg. 1028 IT
Avions Div., 37, Boulevard de Montmorency, pg. 29 IT
Axiva, 58, Ave. Kleber, pg. 18 IT
Axson France, 14 rue de Prony, pg. 103 IT
AXSON S.A., 14 rue de Prony, pg. 102 IT
BAII, 12 Place Vendome, pg. 163 IT
BBGR SA, 22 rue de Montmorency, pg. 462 IT
BDDP, 162 rue de Billancourt, pg. 116 IT
BDDP Corporate, 50 rue de Silly, pg. 116 IT
BDDP GROUP, 162-164 rue de Billancourt, pg. 116 IT
BHF-Bank Representative Office, c/o CCF, 64, rue Galilee, pg. 120 IT
B.H.V. Flandre, 119-127 rue de Flandre, pg. 181 IT
B.H.V. Rivoli, 52 a 64 rue de Rivoli, pg. 181 IT
BMG Ariola S.A. (France), Immeuble Matignon-Mermoz, 9, avenue Mati, pg. 192 IT
BNP Arbitrage, 13 rue La Fayette, pg. 163 IT
BNP Finance, 9, Bvld. des Italiens, pg. 163 IT
BNPI, 20 blvd. des Italiens, pg. 163 IT
B.S.G.L., 147 rue de Coucelles, pg. 315 IT
BT France SNC, Immeuble Jean Monnet, 11 Place des Vosges, pg. 223 IT
BACCARAT (CIE DES CRISTALLERIES), Rue de Paridise, pg. 132 IT
Bacot-Allain S.A., 65 rue de Courcelles, pg. 1331 IT
Bail Equipement, 25 avenue Franklin Roosevelt, pg. 563 IT
Baltek S.A., 61 Rue la Fontaine, pg. 172 PB
Banca Nazionale del Lavoro, 26, Avenue des Champs Elysees, pg. 137 IT
Banco di Sicilia, 62, rue la Boetie, pg. 140 IT
Banco do Brasil S.A.-Paris, 4, Ave. de la Grande Armee, pg. 141 IT
Banco Santander, 30 Avenue de l'Opera, pg. 144 IT
BANEXI (Banque Pour l'Expansion Industrielle), 12, rue Chauchat, pg. 163 IT
Bank of America NT&SA, 43-47 Ave. de la Grande Armee, pg. 182 PB
The Bank of New York, 36 Boulevard Hausmann, pg. 179 IT
Bank of Tokyo-Mitsubishi Ltd., Paris Branch, pg. 158 IT
Bankers Trust New York Corporation, 12-14 Rond-Point des Champs-Elysees, pg. 186 PB
Banknote & Securities Division, 72, rue du Faubourg St-Honore, pg. 1517 IT
Banque Arjil, 7, rue de Cirque, pg. 792 IT
Banque De Boston S.A., 104, Ave. des Champs-Elysees, pg. 185 PB
Banque Bruxelles Lambert France, Immeuble Kupka B, pg. 148 IT
BANQUE DE FRANCE, 39 Rue Croix de Petit Chance, pg. 160 IT
Banque de Neuflize, Schlumberger, Mallet, 3 Avenue Hoche, pg. 12 IT
Banque d'Orsay, 33, Avenia de Wagram, pg. 1493 IT
Banque Dumenil-Leble, 2, Avenue Velasquez, pg. 240 IT
Banque Francaise Commerciale, 9 Rue Louis Murat, pg. 313 IT
BANQUE FRANCAISE DU COMMERCE EXTERIEUR, 21, Blvd. Haussmann, pg. 160 IT
Banque Franco Portugaise, SA, 8, Rue du Helder, pg. 251 IT
Banque Generale du Commerce S.A., 36 Rue Marbeuf, pg. 136 IT
Banque Hydro-Energie, 128, rue du Faubourg Saint-Honore, pg. 822 IT
Banque IBJ (France) S.A., Washington Plaza, 42, Rue Washington, pg. 676 IT
Banque Indosuez, 96 boulevard Haussmann, pg. 313 IT

PB - U.S. Public Companies Volume
PV - U.S. Private Companies Volume
IT - International Public & Private Companies Volume

1590

Geographic Index-Non U.S.

Banque Internationale de Placement S.A., 108, Boulevard Haussmann, pg. 419   IT
Banque Leumi France S.A., 100 Rue Reaumur, pg. 150   IT
Banque Nationale de Grece, pg. 907   IT
BANQUE NATIONALE DE PARIS, 16 Blvd. des Italiens, pg. 163   IT
Banque Nomura France, 164 rue de Rivoli, pg. 956   IT
Banque Paribas, 3, rue d'Antin, pg. 319   IT
Banque Parisienne de Credit, 56, rue de Chateaudun, pg. 548   IT
Banque Pour L'Industrie Francaise, 26, rue Laffitte, pg. 563   IT
Banque PSA Finance Holding, 75, ave. de la Grande-Armee, pg. 1021   IT
Banque Rivaud, 13, rue Notre-Dames des Victoires, pg. 1197   PB
Banque Saint Dominique, 45, rue Saint Dominique, pg. 344   IT
Banque Transatlantique, 17, boulevard Haussmann, pg. 563   IT
Banque Vernes et Commerciale de Paris, 52, Avenue Hoche, pg. 313   IT
Banque Veuve Morin-Pons, 1, rue de Tilsitt, pg. 419   IT
Barclays Bank SA, 24 Rue Laffitte, pg. 166   IT
Baring Asset Management (France), 34, Avenue Matignon, pg. 648   IT
Baring Capital Investors SARL, 148 Boulevard Haussman, pg. 648   IT
Baring Private Equity Partners, 23 Rue Vernet, pg. 648   IT
Barings (France), 49 Avenue d'Iena, pg. 648   IT
Bateaux Parisiens, Port de la Bourdonnais, pg. 1274   IT
Bati-Service, 44 rue de Washington, pg. 945   PB
Bayerische Landesbank - Succursale de Paris, 8, Ave. Delcasse, pg. 176   IT
Bayerische Vereinsbank S.A. (BV France), 34 rue Pasquier (Square Louis XVI), pg. 181   IT
BAZAR DE L'HOTEL DE VILLE, 55, rue de la Verrerie, pg. 181   IT
Bazars Alenconnais, 38, rue Sevres, pg. 97   IT
Bear Stearns Finance S.A., 21-25 Rue de Balzac, Eighth Fl., pg. 198   PB
Beaute Creaeurs S.A., pg. 1015   IT
Beghin-Meiji Industries, 54 Avenue Hoche, pg. 856   IT
Beissier S.A., pg. 423   IT
Bell Atlantic Financial France S.A., 89 Rue de Tocqueville, pg. 204   PB
Bensons, 32 rue Le Peletier, pg. 460   IT
Berlitz France S.A., 15 rue Louis le Grand, pg. 222   PB
Berluti, 26, rue Marbeuf, pg. 779   IT
Bernard Krief Motivation, S.A., Carlson Marketing Group, 115, rue du Bac, pg. 212   PV
Berriel Vittel France, Lieugit Rue de Courcelles, pg. 918   IT
BIDERMANN INTERNATIONAL S.A., 114, Rue de Turenne, pg. 918   IT
Bio-Rad S.A., 5 Bis Rue Maurice Rouvier, pg. 230   PB
Biscuiterie Vinchon-Jeanette S.A., c/o Pilstral, 21 rue Weber, pg. 1435   PB
Boeing International Corp., 2, Avenue Montaigne, pg. 242   PB
Boniface Thiem S.A., pg. 159   PV
Borden France S.A., 20 rue August Vacquere, pg. 159   PV
Bourns-Ohmic S.A., 21/23 Rue des Ardennes, pg. 161   PV
Braconnot, pg. 1138   IT
Bristol-Myers S.A., 17 Ave. Montaigne, pg. 255   PB
Buffet Montparnasse SA, 11, bd de Vaugirard, pg. 20   IT
SARL Bulow Bennet France, 28, rue de Belzunce, pg. 966   IT
C-E Europe, Tour Franklin Cedex 11, pg. 5   IT
CAP Sesa Finance, 79 avenue Kleber, pg. 263   IT
CAP Sesa Hoskyns, 5/7 avenue de Bouvines, pg. 263   IT
CAP Sesa Industrie, 86/90 rue Thiess, pg. 263   IT
CAP Sesa Informatique Hospitaliere, 129 rue de Yunivele, pg. 263   IT
CAP Sesa Tertiaire, 129, rue de l' Universite, pg. 263   IT
CCR-Titrisation, pg. 312   IT
CD Plus S.A., 2 Place La Defense, pg. 331   PB
CEA-INDUSTRIE (COMMISSARIAT À L'ENERGIE ATOMIQUE), 31-33, rue de la Federation, pg. 239   IT
CEGF, 29, Boulevard Malesherbes, pg. 606   PB
C.E.P. COMMUNICATION GROUP, 20, Avenue Hoche, pg. 239   IT
CERUS - COMPAGNIES EUROPEENNES REUNIES, 21 ave. George V, pg. 240   IT
CFM International SA, 2, Blvd. du General Martial Valin, pg. 1166   IT
CGEP (Cie Generale d'Electrolyse du Palais), 34, rue de Miromesnil, pg. 1028   IT
Cic Paris, 60, Rue de la Victoire, pg. 564   IT
CIP, 1 Bid Haussmann, pg. 163   IT
CNF S.A., pg. 1436   IT
CNP ASSURANCES, 4 Place Raoul Dautry, pg. 241   IT
CNT France S.A., Club Sari Affaires, pg. 421   PB
COGECOM, 20 Ave. Rapp, pg. 503   IT
CP8 - Microelectronique, 102 blvd. Malesherbes, pg. 316   IT
CP8 - Oberthur, 102 blvd. Malesherbes, pg. 316   IT
CTT Sceta, pg. 1163   IT
Cadillac Plastic France S.A., 77290 Mitry-Mory Cedex, 8 Rue Marc Sequin, pg. 781   PB
Caisse Central de Reescompte-Gestion, pg. 312   IT
Caisse Centrale de Reescompte, S.A., pg. 312   IT
Caisse Nationale de Credit Agricole International Division, 33, Avenue du Maine, pg. 341   IT
Caixa Geral de Depositos (France), 85, Avenue Marceau, pg. 251   IT
Calberson, 183 avenue de Clichy, pg. 549   IT
Calberson, 183 av. de Clichy, pg. 1163   IT
Calberson Freight Network Division, 183 av. de Clichy, pg. 1163   IT

Calberson International, B.P. 50082, pg. 1163   IT
Calmann-Levy, 3, rue Auber, pg. 792   IT
CAMP, Eight, rue de Torcy, pg. 53   IT
Canadian Imperial Bank of Commerce (International) S.A., 49 Avenue Hoche, pg. 257   IT
CAP GEMINI S.A., 11 Rue de Tilsitt, pg. 263   IT
Caprofem S.A., 11 Blvd. Pershing, pg. 734   IT
Cariane, pg. 1165   IT
Cariplo Banque S.A., 42 Rue La Boetie, pg. 275   IT
Carlton Cards France, pg. 78   PB
CarnaudMetalbox, pg. 463   PB
CARREFOUR, 6, avenue Raymond Poincare, pg. 272   IT
Case France S.A., 18 Place des Nympheas, pg. 1579   PB
Cegedur Pechiney, 23 rue Balzac, pg. 1028   IT
Celiv, 5, rue du Pont de Lodi, pg. 792   IT
Centrale G, pg. 312   IT
Centrale H, pg. 312   IT
Cerca, Tour Framatome, pg. 503   IT
CHARGEURS, 5, boulevard Malesherbes, pg. 280   IT
Chargeurs Fabrics, 5, boulevard Malesherbes, pg. 280   IT
Chargeurs Interlining, 5, boulevard Malesherbes, pg. 280   IT
Chargeurs Protective Films, 5, boulevard Malesherbes, pg. 280   IT
Chargeurs Wool, 5, boulevard Malesherbes, pg. 280   IT
The Chase Manhattan Bank, N.A., 18 Blvd. Malherbes, pg. 340   PB
Chase Manhattan, S.A., 18 Blvd. Malherbes, pg. 340   PB
Chaussures Bally-France S.A., 95 bis, Bld. Richard Lenoir, pg. 997   IT
Check Point Software Technologies SARL, CNIT Service Affaires, 2 Place e La Defense, B.P. 240, pg. 342   PB
Cherry SARL, 1 Av Des Violettes, pg. 346   PB
Chimique de la Mediterranee, pg. 1138   IT
Chlorure de Vinyle de Fos, pg. 1138   IT
Christian Dalloz, pg. 462   IT
Christian Dior S.A., 30, Ave. Montaigne, pg. 97   IT
Christian Lacroix Maroquinerie, 54, avenue Montaigne, pg. 780   IT
Christian Lacroix SNC, 73, rue du Fbg Saint-Honore, pg. 780   IT
Cigna Sicav I, 5, Rue de Turin, pg. 364   PB
CIMENTS FRANCAIS, Tour Ariane, pg. 292   IT
Cinram France, 130, rue Cardinet, 3rd Floor, pg. 293   IT
Citibank, N.A. Paris, 60, ave. des Champs-Elysees, pg. 378   PB
Clarify SARL-France, 35 Cours Michelet, pg. 382   PB
Club Mediterranee Investissements, 25 rue Vivienne, pg. 298   IT
CLUB MEDITERRANEE SA, 11, rue de Cambrie, pg. 298   IT
Codelco-France S.A.R.L., 174 Blvd. Haussmann, pg. 303   IT
Cofassur Vie, 26 rue Laffitte, pg. 564   IT
COFATHEC - Paris, 89, rue de Tocqueville, pg. 541   IT
COFLEXIP S.A., 23 Avenue de Neuilly, pg. 304   IT
Cognos SARL, Tour Aurore, 18 Place Des Reflects, pg. 306   IT
Columbia Pictures Television, 20 Rue Troyon, pg. 1282   IT
Combustion Engineering-Europe, Tour Winterthur Cedex N18, pg. 5   IT
Commerz Financial Products S.A., pg. 309   IT
Commerzbank AG Succursale de Paris, 3, Place de l'Opera, pg. 311   IT
Compagnie Auxiliare de Telecommunications, 9 rue 4 Septembre 20th, pg. 503   IT
Compagnie Bancaire, 5, Avenue Kleber, pg. 319   IT
Compagnie Continentale D'Assurances S.A., 5, Rue de Londres, pg. 90   IT
Compagnie Dakar Saint-Louis S.A., 15, Rue de Londres, pg. 90   IT
Compagnie de Participations Biochimiques (COPABIO), 61, rue Belles Feuilles, pg. 788   IT
COMPAGNIE DE SUEZ, 1, rue d'Astorg, pg. 313   IT
Compagnie des Gaz de Petrole Primagaz S.A., 64, Avenue Hoche, pg. 1155   IT
Compagnie des Immeubles des La Plaine Monceau, 23, avenue Matignon, pg. 18   IT
Compagnie des Sablieres de la Seine, 2, quai Henri IV, pg. 788   IT
Compagnie des Vernis Valentine SA, 185 Avenue des Gresillons, pg. 664   IT
Compagnie Fermiere de L'Etablissement Thermal de Vichy, 18, rue de Courcelles, pg. 919   IT
COMPAGNIE FINANCIERE DE PARIBAS, 3 Street D'Amtian, pg. 319   IT
Compagnie Financiere de Paris, 5-7, rue de Milan, pg. 18   IT
Compagnie Francaise d'Investissement, 121, Avenue de Malakoff, pg. 316   IT
Compagnie Francaise de Boissons Gazeuses, 18, rue de Courcelles, pg. 918   IT
Compagnie Francaise de Boissons Gazeuses, pg. 920   IT
Compagnie Francaise de l'Etain, pg. 1138   IT
Compagnie Francaise des Petroles (Algerie) CFP (A), Tour Total, pg. 1409   IT
Compagnie Francaise Philips, 50, av. Montaigne, pg. 1055   IT
COMPAGNIE GENERALE DES EAUX, 52 Rue d'Anjou, pg. 321   IT
Compagnie IBM France, S.A, 3 Place Vendome, pg. 897   PB
Compagnie Internationale Des Produits Sanitaires (CIPS) Jacob Delafon, 51 Rue Du Commandant, pg. 631   PV
Compagnie Parisienne de Reescompte, 59/61, rue Lafayette, pg. 313   IT
COMPAGNIE UAP, 9, place Vendome, pg. 323   IT
Compass Group, International, 188/193 Boulevard Malesherbes, pg. 325   IT
Conforama, 2, rue du Pont-Neuf, pg. 98   IT

The Continuum Company (France), 15-17 Rue Auber, pg. 423   PB
Continuum (France) SARL, Tour Winterthur, 7e etage, Cedex 18, pg. 423   PB
Copap, 18 bis rue d'Anjou, pg. 457   PB
Cordis S.A., Parc d'Activities de Viry, pg. 928   PB
Courcoux-Bouvet, 32, Avenue de l'Opera, pg. 319   IT
Cray Research France S.A., 7 Rue de Tilsitt, pg. 1474   PB
CREDIT COMMERCIAL DE FRANCE, 103, Avenue des Champs Elysees, pg. 341   IT
Credit de la Bourse S.A., 2, Rue du Quatre Septembre, pg. 1330   IT
Credit du Nord, 6/8 Boulevard Haussman, pg. 319   IT
Credit Industriel et Commercial, 66 rue de la Victoire, pg. 313   IT
CREDIT LYONNAIS S.A., 19 Boulevard des Italiens, pg. 343   IT
CREDIT MUTUEL, 88-90, rue Cardinet, pg. 344   IT
CREDIT NATIONALE, 45 rue Saint-Dominique, pg. 344   IT
Crehalet Pouget Poussielgues, 61 rue de Turenne, pg. 1152   PV
A.T. Cross (France) S.A., 11 Rue Laugier, pg. 461   PB
Crown Cork & Seal, European Division, Le Colisee 1, Rue Fructidor, pg. 464   PB
Crown Wallcoverings France, S.A., pg. 159   PV
Cupralex, 34, rue de Miromesnil, pg. 1028   IT
D & B Software France SA, Tour Franklin, pg. 532   IT
DG Bank-Paris, 112-114 Boulevard Haussmann, pg. 352   IT
Daewoo France S.A.R.L., 33-49, Ave. Du Bois De La Pie Zac, pg. 358   IT
Dai-Ichi Kangyo Bank, Ltd.-Paris, 50 Avenue Montaigne, pg. 361   IT
Dai-Ichi Life International Limited-Paris, 166, rue de Rivoli, pg. 362   IT
Daiwa Bank-Paris, 3rd Fl., Heron Bldg., pg. 374   IT
Daiwa Europe (France) S.A., 26, Avenue des Champs-Elysees, pg. 375   IT
Daiwa Finance Diffusion S.A., 26, Avenue des Champs-Elysees, pg. 375   IT
Daiwa France Gestion S.A., 26, Avenue des Champs-Elysees, pg. 375   IT
Damco Maritime France S.A.R.L., pg. 1144   IT
Danfoss S.A.R.L., pg. 377   IT
DANONE GROUP, 7-9 Rue de Teheran, pg. 379   IT
Danzas S.A., 15, rue de Nancy, pg. 382   IT
Dart Europe S.A., 12-14,rue Camille-Desmoulins, 92300 Levallais-Perret, pg. 1322   PB
Data General Europe, Inc., Tour Manhatta 5/6 Place de l'Iris, pg. 486   IT
Data General France SARL, La Borsidiere, Rn. 186, pg. 486   IT
DATAPOINT CORPORATION, 5-7 Rue Montalivet, pg. 384   IT
Datastream International (Paris) Ltd., 25 ave. Marceau, pg. 1326   IT
De Lage Landen Factors S.A., 112 ter, Rue Cardinet, pg. 1082   IT
De Neuflize, Schlumberger, Mallet S.A., 3 Avenue Hoche, pg. 12   IT
Georges Delbard S.A., 16, quai de la Megisserie, pg. 780   IT
Delegue de la Bayerische Vereinsbank aupres du Credit du Nord, 6-8, Boulevard Haussmann, pg. 181   IT
Delta Air Lines Marketing Officer, 4 Place des Vosges, pg. 497   PB
Dentsu Europe-Paris, 16, Avenue Kleber, pg. 393   PV
Desfosses International, 48, rue Notre-Dame-des-Victoires, pg. 780   IT
Desobry S.A., c/o Pilstral, 21 rue Weber, pg. 1435   PB
Deutsche Bank AG (Paris), 10, place Vendome, pg. 404   IT
Devarrieux Villaret, 164 rue de Rivoli, pg. 600   PV
Diffusion Assurance Conseil S.r.l., 32, Rue de Mogador, pg. 91   IT
The Walt Disney Company (France) S.A., 52 Ave. Champs Elysees, pg. 514   PB
Distriwax S.A., pg. 540   IT
Diversified Parcels Freight Division, 183 av. de Clichy, pg. 1163   IT
Dole Europe, S.A., 8 Avenue Kleber, pg. 515   PB
DOMIBAIL, 104, avenue du President Kennedy, pg. 344   IT
Domiequipment, 45 Rue St. Dominique, pg. 344   IT
Domlenz, pg. 462   IT
Dow Jones Markets France SA, 128 Rue de Faubourg St. Honore, pg. 525   PB
Driehoek, c/o Pilstral, 21 rue Weber, pg. 1435   PB
Du Pont de Nemours (France) S.A., 137, rue de l' Universite, pg. 532   PB
Dunkerque Electrometallurgie, Tour Manhattan, pg. 1028   IT
Durkopp Adler France S.A, 6 a 10 rue Riquet, pg. 469   IT
Dynisco Instrument Sarl., pg. 139   PV
Eagle Star Vie SA, 12r Torricelli 17e, pg. 112   IT
East Japan Railway Company - Paris Office, 24-26, rue de la Pepiniere, pg. 431   IT
Eclipse Combustion Sarl, 6-8 Avenue Salvador Allende, pg. 5   PV
Edelman-Rouet France, 24 rue Eugene Flachat, pg. 363   PV
Edition N 1, 79, boulevard Saint-Germain, pg. 792   IT
Editions Bordas, 17 rue Remy-Dumoncel, pg. 239   IT
Editions du Juris-Classeur, 141 rue de Javel, pg. 1095   IT
Editions du Moniteur, 17 rue d'Uzes, pg. 239   IT
Editions Garnier, 8 rue Garanciere, pg. 239   IT
Editions Gerard de Villiers, 79, boulevard Saint-Germain, pg. 792   IT
Editions Grasset-Fasquelle, 61, rue des Saints-Peres, pg. 792   IT

PB - *U.S. Public Companies Volume*
PV - *U.S. Private Companies Volume*
IT - *International Public & Private Companies Volume*

Geographic Index-Non U.S.

1591

Editions Jean-Claude Lattes, 17, rue Jacob, pg. 794   IT
Editions Lamy, pg. 1513   IT
Editions Musicales Francois I, 28, rur Francois I, pg. 792   IT
Editions Scientifiques et Medicales Elsevier, 141 rue de Javel, pg. 1099   IT
Editions Stock, 23, rue du Sommerard, pg. 792   IT
Eker, 24, rue du Chateau-Landon, pg. 1274   IT
Ekotech, 170, place Henri Regnault, pg. 1360   IT
ELECTRICITE DE FRANCE, 2 rue Louis-Murat, pg. 437   IT
Electro Protection Services/CEPS, 10 rue Alphonse de Neuville, pg. 1650   PB
Electrolux-Wascator S.A., 17, rue de l'Ancienne, pg. 441   IT
Elf Aquitaine (Production), Tour Elf 2, pg. 444   IT
ELF AQUITAINE, Tour Elf, 2, place de la Coupole, pg. 444   IT
Elf Atochem S.A., 4 cours Michelet, pg. 445   IT
Elf France, Tour Elf 2, pg. 445   IT
Elf Sanofi S.A., 32/34 Rue Marboeug, pg. 445   IT
Elida Faberge, 28 rue Jacque Ibert, pg. 1437   IT
Elkem s.a.r.l., 52 avenue de la Grande-Armee, pg. 447   IT
EMAP France, 43 Rue du Colonel Pierre Avia, pg. 451   IT
Endo-Services S.A.R.L., pg. 1005   IT
Enskilda S.A., 25, rue Balzac, pg. 1259   IT
Enso France S.A., 18 bis rue d'Anjou, pg. 457   IT
Enterprise Generale de Telecommunications, 66 Ave. Maine, pg. 503   IT
ENTREPRISE MINIERE ET CHIMIQUE, 62 rue Jeanne d'Arc, pg. 458   IT
Eramet-SLN, Tour Maine Montparnasse, pg. 661   IT
ESPACE Expansion, rue Saint George, pg. 1431   IT
Esselte SA, 192 rue Championnet, pg. 461   IT
Etablissements Bez S.A., pg. 62   IT
Etablissements Jean Salle, 14 Av. Edouard Vaillant, pg. 549   IT
Etablissements Vallaroche (SA), 2 Bld du General Martial Valin, pg. 1165   IT
EULER, 1, rue Euler, pg. 463   IT
Euralliance, Rue Blance 1, pg. 499   IT
Euro Synergies Management SA, 48 bis, Rue Fabert, pg. 181   IT
Eurocopter Holding S.A., 72 Boulevard de Courcelanes, pg. 29   IT
Eurocopter S.A., pg. 29   IT
Eurocoustic, Le Triangle, 14, rue du General-Audran, pg. 1176   IT
Eurolysine SA, 16 rue Ballu, pg. 41   IT
Euromezzanine Gestion, 50, rue Fabert, pg. 344   IT
Europe Audiovisuel, 26 bis, rue Francois I, pg. 792   IT
Europe Development International, 28, rue Francois I, pg. 792   IT
Europe Images Conseil, 28, rue Francois I, pg. 792   IT
Europe News, 26 bis, rue Francois I, pg. 792   IT
Europe 1 Communication, 32, rue Francois I, pg. 792   IT
Europe 1 Immobilier, 26 bis, rue Francois I, pg. 792   IT
Europe 1 Telecompagnie, 26 bis, rue Francois I, pg. 792   IT
Europe Presse et Radio, 26, rue Francois I, pg. 792   IT
Europe Regies, 28, rue Francois I, pg. 792   IT
Europe 2 Communication, 26 bis, rue Francois I, pg. 792   IT
Europe 2 Entreprises, 28, rue Francois I, pg. 792   IT
European Telecommunications Satellite Organization (EUTELSAT), 33 Ave. Du Maine, pg. 223   IT
Europeenne D'Intermediation Financiere et Boursiere, 12, rue Gaillon, pg. 564   IT
Europenne de Protection Jurdique S.A., 95, Rue Saint-Lazare, pg. 61   IT
Everite S.A., Les Miroirs, pg. 1170   IT
Ex Machina, 20-22, rue Hegesippe-Moreau, pg. 1381   IT
Excelsior Informatique sa, pg. 1445   IT
Execorp., 37, Boulevard de Montmorency, pg. 29   IT
Exide Electronics S.A., pg. 126   IT
Exor S.A., pg. 467   IT
The Export-Import Bank of Korea, 39, Avenue d'Iena, pg. 468   IT
Exxon Chemical Polymeres, SNC, Notre Dame-de-Gravenchon, pg. 602   PB
FBFC, Tour Framatome, pg. 503   IT
FCR (France Cables et Radio), 124 rue Reaumur 2nd, pg. 503   IT
FLS France s.a.r.l., rue de Messine, pg. 476   IT
FSP Laboratoires Pharmeurop S.A., pg. 1437   IT
Factofrance Heller, Tour Main Montparnasse, 33, Avenue du Maine, pg. 313   IT
FAR France Aluminium Recyclage S.A., pg. 68   IT
Faugere & Jutheau S.A., 13 Rue de la Ville L'Eveque, pg. 1049   PB
Faure Vadon Forest, 17 rue Jacques Bingen, pg. 601   IT
Feslente Boniface S.A., pg. 159   PV
Fevi-Promavent, 18, rue Pradier, pg. 706   IT
Fiat France, 140 Av. de Champs Elisees, pg. 483   IT
Fiat France SA, 140 Av. de Champs Elisees, pg. 484   IT
Films Paramount S.A., 1 Rue Meyerbeer, pg. 777   PV
Fimagest, 15 boulevard de l'Amiral Bruix, pg. 548   IT
Finances Conseil Interntional S.A., 11, Rue de Clichy, pg. 91   IT
Financial Security Assurance (U.K.) Limited, 116, Rue La Boetie, pg. 623   PB
Financiere Atlas S.A., 4, place Vendome, pg. 120   IT
Financiere Lafarge Coppee, 61, rue des Belles-Feuilles, pg. 788   IT
Financiere Saint Dominique, 48 bis, rue Fabert, pg. 344   IT
Finaxa, 23, avenue Matignon, pg. 18   IT
Fininvest, 96 Blvd. Haussmann, pg. 313   IT
First Marathon Securities, 2, rue Chauveau-Lagarde, pg. 487   IT

Fleishman-Hillard France, 69/71 rue Beaubourg, pg. 111   PV
Fleming Finance S.A., 39-41 Rue Cambon, pg. 493   IT
Robert Fleming (France) S.A., 39-41 Rue Cambon, pg. 494   IT
Fleurbourg, 54, rue Etienne-Marcel, pg. 780   IT
Fleurseille, 3, place des Victoires, pg. 780   IT
Fleurteuil, 99, rue de Passy, pg. 780   IT
Fleurus Boutique SA, 3, place des Victoires, pg. 780   IT
Floribilis, 54, rue Etienne-Marcel, pg. 780   IT
Forte France S.A., 10 Place des 5 Martyrs du lycee Buffon, pg. 556   IT
Foster Wheeler France S.A., 31 Rue Des Bourdonnais, pg. 677   PB
FoxVideo (France) S.A., Huit rue Bellini, pg. 926   IT
Fradis France Distributique, 121, avenue de Malakoff, pg. 792   IT
Framatome et Cie, Tour Fiat, pg. 52   IT
FRAMATOME SA, Tour Framatome, pg. 502   IT
France Assistance, 120 Avenue du General Leclerc, 8, pg. 334   IT
France Glaces-Findus S.A., Quatre, rue Brantome, pg. 920   IT
France Loisirs, 123 blvd. de Grenelle, pg. 239   IT
FRANCE TELECOM, 6 Pl. de'Alleray, pg. 503   IT
Franco-Belge De Fabrication De Combustibles (FBFC), Tour Manhattan, pg. 305   IT
Francomet S.A., 174 Blvd. Haussmann, pg. 303   IT
Fransabank (France) S.A., 104, avenue des Champs-Elysees, pg. 341   IT
Frantour Group, pg. 1165   IT
Fred S.A., Grue Royale, pg. 780   IT
Frigoscandia Food Process Systems S.A., 12, rue de l'Isly, pg. 607   PB
Fromagerie Perrault S.A., pg. 201   IT
Fromagerie Rambol S.A., pg. 201   IT
Fruisec S.A., pg. 201   IT
Fujisawa SARL, pg. 525   IT
GEC Alsthom, 38 Ave. Kleber, pg. 52   IT
GECI (Groupe d'Etudes et Conseils en Ingenierie), Tour Winterthur, pg. 1032   PB
GPRI, pg. 571   IT
Gama Services, 7, rue du Cirque, pg. 792   IT
Gan Holding Pacifique, 26, rue Laffitte, pg. 564   IT
Gan Incendie Accidents, 2, Rue Pillet-Will, pg. 564   IT
Gan International, 2, Rue Pillet-Will, pg. 564   IT
Gan Sa. 2, Rue Pillet-Will, pg. 565   IT
Gan Sante, 2, Rue Pillet-Will, pg. 565   IT
Gan Vie, 2, Rue Pillet-Will, pg. 565   IT
GAZ DE FRANCE, 23 rue Philibert Delmore, pg. 541   IT
Gefinor Finance S.A., 112 Avenue Kleber, pg. 542   IT
Andre Gelot Et Cie. S.r.l., 18, Rue Volney, pg. 91   IT
Generale de Banque Belge (France) SA, 22, rue de Londres, pg. 548   IT
Generale de Grandes Sources, pg. 920   IT
GENERALE SUCRIERE SNC, 23-25 Ave. Franklin D. Roosevelt, pg. 548   IT
General Finances S.A., 62, Rue de Caumartin, pg. 91   IT
S.N.C. Generali France Et Cie, 76, Rue Saint-Lazare, pg. 91   IT
General France S.A., 76, Rue Saint-Lazare, pg. 91   IT
General Gerance S.A., 11, Rue de Clichy, pg. 91   IT
General Gestion S.A., 62, Rue de Caumartin, pg. 91   IT
Gentleman Givenchy S.A., 9, avenue Marceau, pg. 780   IT
GEODIS, 183, avenue de Clichy, pg. 549   IT
Georg Jensen S.A.R.L., 239 rue Saint-Honore, pg. 1134   IT
Geosource S.A.R.L., 42 Avenue Gabriel, pg. 777   PB
Geris, 11, avenue Myron T. Herrick, pg. 1382   IT
Gestetner Services S.A., 1-7 Avenue d'Italie, pg. 1115   IT
Gestion et Patrimoine, 37, rue de la Victoire, pg. 19   IT
Gicel, 11 rue Hamlin, pg. 316   IT
Givenchy S.A., 3, avenue George V, pg. 780   IT
Glenco SA, 1565 Route de 40 Sous, pg. 536   IT
Gloria S.A., 14 rue de Bassano, pg. 920   IT
Go Voyages, 36, Rue du Chemin Vert, pg. 560   IT
Goldman Sachs Paris Inc. et Cie., 2, rue de Thann, pg. 432   PV
Goodyear S.A., 101 Avenue De La Chataignergie, pg. 753   PB
Grande Semoulerie de L'Ouest a Gond-Pontouvre, 44, rue de Beurlion, pg. 556   IT
Grandes Lignes International, pg. 1165   IT
GrandMet Foods Europe, 6, Rue Christophe Colomb, pg. 408   IT
GRANDS MOULINS DE PARIS S.A., 44, Rte. Principal Dupot, pg. 556   IT
Granges Aluminium S.A., 98 Avenue de Villiers, pg. 441   IT
Gray Tool Co. (Europe), Tour Franklin, pg. 5   IT
Griffine SA, Cedex 28, pg. 1278   IT
Groupe Abilis, 78 Rue de Crimee, pg. 1463   IT
Groupe DAFSA, 11 rue Robert de Flers, pg. 1326   PB
Groupe de La Cite, 264, rue du Faubourg St.Honore, pg. 53   IT
GROUPE DES CAISES D'EPARGNE, 29 rue de la Tombeissoire, pg. 563   IT
Groupe DMR S.A., 35 rue d'Artois, pg. 528   IT
GROUPE GAN, 2, Rue Pillet-Will, pg. 563   IT
Groupe L.S.A., 89 rue Faubourg St. Honore, pg. 239   IT
Groupe Origny S.A., 14/25, Boulevard de l'Amiral Bruix, pg. 629   IT
GROUPE PERNOD RICARD, 142 Blvd. Haussman, pg. 566   IT
GROUPE SAINT LOUIS, 23-25, avenue Franklin D. Roosevelt, pg. 567   IT
Groupe Systra, 5, Avenue du Coq., pg. 1165   IT
GROUPE USINOR, Pacific Bldg. TSA #10001, 13, cours Valmy, pg. 570   IT
Guerlain S.A., 125 Rue President Wilson, pg. 780   IT
HSBC James Capel S.A., 6 Rue Piccini, pg. 582   IT

Haagen-Dazs Europe, 69-71 Avenue Pierre Grenier, Boulogne, pg. 411   IT
Haagen-Dazs France, 69-71 Avenue Pierre Grenier, Boulogne, pg. 411   IT
Habib Bank Ltd., 123, Avenue Des Champs Elyees, pg. 584   PB
Hach France, S.A., pg. 773   IT
Hachette Distribution Services, 2, rue Lord Byron, pg. 792   IT
Hachette 5, 121, avenue de Malakoff, pg. 792   IT
Hachette Livre, 24, boulevard Saint-Michel, pg. 792   IT
Hachette Premiere SNC, 10, rue de Marignan, pg. 792   IT
Handelsbanken Markets France S.A., 1, rue Caumartin, pg. 1328   IT
Handi Thomson, 11, avenue Myron T. Herrick, pg. 1382   IT
Hapag-Lloyd (France) S.A., pg. 596   IT
Harman France, 33, avenue de lattre de tassigny, pg. 787   IT
Hasselblad France S.A., 5, Passage Piver, pg. 1468   IT
H.J. Heinz SARL, 89 Rue de la Boetie, pg. 806   PB
Hercules France S.A., 44 Av. Chatou, pg. 811   PB
HERMES INTERNATIONAL, 24, rue de Faubourg, pg. 617   IT
Hewlett-Packard France, 15 Avenue de L'Amiral-Bruix, pg. 819   PB
Hewlett-Packard France, 175, Rue Du Chevalaret, pg. 820   IT
Hewlett-Packard France, 28, Rue Jacques Ibert, pg. 820   IT
Hispano-Suiza S.A., 2 Bldg. du General Martial Valin, pg. 1165   IT
Hoche Friedland, 20, Avenue Hoche, pg. 239   IT
Holpa, 121, avenue de Malakoff, pg. 792   IT
Honda France S.A., Parc d'Activites de Paris-Est, pg. 635   IT
HOTEC, 33, Avenue du Maine, pg. 20   IT
Hoteltour, 25 rue Vivienne, pg. 298   IT
Hufvudstaden France S.A., 16, rue Chauveau-Lagarde, pg. 478   IT
Hugo Boss France S.A.R.L., pg. 638   IT
Hutchinson S.A., 2, rue Balzac, pg. 1409   IT
Hydromation France S.A.R.L., 3, rue du colonel Moll, pg. 484   IT
IAI-Europe-EAT-European Advanced Technologies S.A., 181, Ave. Charleg de Gaule, pg. 690   IT
IBL S.A., 33 Avenue Du Maine, pg. 21   IT
IBM Africa Middle East, S.A., pg. 897   PB
IBM Distribution and Support, S.A., pg. 897   PB
IBM Eurocoordination, S.A., pg. 897   PB
IBM France Diffusion, S.A, pg. 897   PB
IBM Trade Development, S.A., pg. 897   PB
IDC France, Immueble La Fayette, 2 Place des Vosges, pg. 571   PV
IDG Communications France, Immeuble La Fayette, pg. 569   PV
IFD, 40, rue de Colisee, pg. 19   IT
ING Bank Paris, 21, Boulevard de la Madeleine, pg. 649   IT
ING Baring Securities (France), 21, Avenue de la Madeleine, pg. 650   IT
ING Immobilier, 17 Avenue Hoche, pg. 650   IT
ING Lease France, 21, Boulevard de la Madeleine, pg. 650   IT
Iggesund Paperboard France SA, 3, Rue Christophe Colomb, pg. 886   IT
Ilva France, 54 Ave. Marceau, pg. 654   IT
IMETAL, Tour Maine-Montparnasse 33, pg. 661   IT
Immobiliere de La Distribution, 18, rue de Courcelles, pg. 919   IT
S.A. Immobiliere des 154/156 Bd. de La Gare, 15, Rue de Londres, pg. 91   IT
Immobiliere Saint Dominique, Tour Cristal 7-11, pg. 344   IT
Impact, Zone Industrial, pg. 1052   IT
Impell-France S.A.R.L., 10, rue du Colisee, pg. 6   IT
Inco Oceanie S.A., pg. 673   IT
The Industrial Bank of Japan, Limited (Paris Branch), Washington Plaza, 42, rue Washington, pg. 675   IT
Information et Technologies, 60 rue Hauteville, pg. 239   IT
Informatique Concorde Sisro S.A., 15, Rue de Londres, pg. 91   IT
Ingold France Sarl., 30, Bd Douaumont, pg. 983   IT
Initiative & Finance Investissement, 16, rue Chauveau Lagarde, pg. 344   IT
Instron S.A., Rue des Freres Forman, Z.I de Buc, pg. 883   PB
Integris Data Services France, 67-69 blvd. Bessieres, pg. 316   IT
Integris Data Services International, 67-69, blvd. Bessieres, pg. 316   IT
Inter Parfums-Selective Industrie, 90 rue de Miromesnil, pg. 924   PB
Interleaf France, S.A., pg. 893   IT
The International Commercial Bank of China, 131-133, Rue de Tolbiac, pg. 683   IT
International Nickel France S.A., 43 Avenue de Friedland, pg. 673   IT
Inverness France, 1 Rue Ambroise Thomas, pg. 574   PV
Investir Publications, 48, rue Notre-Dame-des-Victoires, pg. 780   IT
Investir Telecom, 48, rue Notre-Dame-des-Victoires, pg. 780   IT
Itoham Foods Inc., Bank of Tokyo Bldg. 6F, 4-8, Rue Sainte Anne, pg. 695   IT
Jaeger-LeCoultre France SA, pg. 839   IT
Jaeger SA, Rue Lavoisier 19, pg. 482   IT
Jet Loisirs, 10, Avenue Georges V, pg. 560   IT
Axel Johnson Minerais & Metaux S.A.R.L., 229 Rue Saint Honore, pg. 711   IT
Axel Johnson, 46/52 Rue Albert, pg. 712   IT

PB - *U.S. Public Companies Volume*
PV - *U.S. Private Companies Volume*
IT - *International Public & Private Companies Volume*

Jugobanka A.D. (Paris Rep.), 25, Rue Lauriston, pg. 716 **IT**
The Kansai Electric Power Co. - Paris Office, 3 Avenue Hoche, pg. 723 **IT**
Kaufman and Broad Developpement, 44 rue de Washington, pg. 945 **PB**
Kaufman and Broad, France, 44 rue de Washington, pg. 945 **PB**
Kaufman and Broad Maisons Individuelles, 4 rue de Washington, pg. 945 **PB**
Kaufman and Broad Renovations, 44 rue de Washington, pg. 945 **PB**
Kelly Services, 73 Boulevard Haussmann, pg. 949 **PB**
Kenner Parker Toys, Tour Essor 93, 14-16 Rue Scandicci, pg. 798 **PB**
Kenzo, 3, place des Victoires, pg. 781 **IT**
KEPCO Paris Office, Tour Framatone 92084, pg. 758 **IT**
Ketchum Advertising France, 6, rue Deodat de Severac, pg. 617 **PV**
Kimberly-Clark France S.A.R.L., 7 Avenue Ingres, pg. 959 **PB**
Kleinwort Benson France SA, 11 Avenue Myron T. Herrick, pg. 420 **PB**
Kodak Pathe S.A., 26 Rue Villiot, pg. 554 **PB**
Konica France S.A., Paris Nord 11, 305 rue de la Belle Etiole, pg. 749 **IT**
Korn/Ferry International, 166 Rue du Faubourg, pg. 633 **PV**
Korsnas France S.A., 79, Av. Raymond Poincare, pg. 759 **IT**
Kredietbank S.A. France, 203, rue du Faubourg Saint-Honore, pg. 760 **IT**
Kredietbank S.A. France Agence de Paris, 203, rue du Faubourg Saint-Honore, pg. 760 **IT**
Krupp Hoesch Aciers S.A.R.L., 21 Rue Royale, pg. 515 **IT**
KymTrans France, 104, avenue du President Kennedy, pg. 1430 **IT**
The Kyoei Life Insurance Co., Ltd.-Paris Office, 26, Avenue de Champs, pg. 777 **IT**
LCC S.A., BP13, 92403 Massy, pg. 1384 **IT**
LTR Industries, 7 Avenue Ingres, pg. 960 **PB**
LVMH MOET HENNESSY LOUIS VUITTON, 30 Avenue Hoche, pg. 779 **IT**
La Concorde S.A., 5, Rue de Londres, pg. 91 **IT**
La Federation Continentale Compagnie D'Assurances, 25, Rue Chaptal, pg. 91 **IT**
La Fonciere de Lavallois S.A., pg. 467 **IT**
La Fonciere Parixel, 2, rue Pillet Will, pg. 565 **IT**
LaBelle Jardiniere, 5 rue de Babylon, pg. 98 **IT**
Laboratoire Allard S.A., 10 Avenue De Messine, pg. 256 **PB**
Laboratoire Wellcome Glaxo S.A., 43 rue Vineuse, 16th Fl., pg. 553 **PB**
Laboratoires Bristol S.A., 32 Rue De L'Arcade, pg. 256 **PB**
Laboratoires Fison S.A., pg. 1111 **IT**
Laboratoires Sobio S.A., 15-25 bd. de l'Amiral Bruix, pg. 1265 **IT**
Laboratoires Wyeth France, 117, Rue de Chanteau des Rentiers, pg. 81 **PB**
Laboratoires Wellcome S.A., 159 Nationale 13, pg. 553 **IT**
Lafarge Aluminates, 28, rue Emile Menier, pg. 789 **IT**
LAFARGE S.A., 61 rue Belles Feuilleg, pg. 788 **IT**
LAGARDERE GROUPE, 121 Avinidimalkos, pg. 791 **IT**
LALIQUE S.A., 11 rue Royale, pg. 797 **IT**
Lancaster Group S.A., pg. 186 **IT**
Lancome Institut & Cie, 29 rue St. Honore, pg. 818 **IT**
Lanvin Parfums, 3 rue Tilsitt, pg. 818 **IT**
Guy Laroche SA, 6 rue de la Tremoille, pg. 1273 **IT**
Librairie Larousse, 17 rue du Montparnasse, pg. 239 **IT**
Laura Ashley SA, 94 Rue de Rennes, pg. 804 **IT**
Lazard Freres et Cie, 121 Blvd. Haussmann, pg. 1027 **IT**
Le Carbone Lorraine, Tour Manhattan, pg. 1028 **IT**
le Nouvel Eldorado, 104 Ave. des Champs-Elysees, pg. 600 **IT**
Legal & General Holdings (France) S.A., 68 rue Victoire, pg. 805 **IT**
Legion International SA, 121, avenue de Malakoff, pg. 792 **IT**
Leibinger S.A.R.L., c/o Salans Hertzfeld, Heilbronn 9, Rue Boissy d'Anglas, pg. 1282 **PB**
Lenotre, 44, rue d'Auteuil, pg. 20 **IT**
L'Equite S.A., 32, Rue de Mogadar, pg. 91 **IT**
Les Echos SA, 46 rue la Boetie, pg. 1027 **IT**
Les Editions Textuel, 7 rue Lacuee, pg. 116 **IT**
Les Grands Hotels Associes S.A., 25 Avenue Montaigne, pg. 556 **IT**
Les Laboratoires Beecham S.A., 15-25 Boulevard de l'Amiral Bruix, pg. 1265 **IT**
Les Presses de la Cite, 8, rue Garanciere, pg. 53 **IT**
Les Produits Siliceux and Constructions Thermiques Europeennes, 21 Avenue de Tourville, pg. 615 **IT**
L'Etoile Commerciale, 103, Blvd. Haussman, pg. 335 **IT**
Lexmark France, Immeuble Jean Monnet, 11, Place des Vosges, pg. 991 **PB**
Librairie Artheme Fayard, 75, rue des Saints-Peres, pg. 792 **IT**
Librairie des Champs-Elysees, 24, boulevard Saint-Michel, pg. 792 **IT**
Librairie Generale Francaise, 6, rue Pierre Sarrazin, pg. 792 **IT**
Lightnin France S.A., pg. 727 **PB**
Arthur D. Little International, Inc., 15 Rue Galvani, pg. 670 **PV**
Lloyds Bank SA, 43 Boulevard des Capucines, pg. 813 **IT**
Lockheed Corporation (International) S.A., 17, Ave. Hoche, pg. 1009 **PB**
Loewe France, 54, avenue Montaigne, pg. 781 **IT**
Loewe International, 54, avenue Montaigne, pg. 781 **IT**
Long-Term Credit Bank of Japan, Ltd. - Paris Branch, 55/57 Boulevard Haussmann, pg. 816 **IT**
Longman France SA, 95 Boulevard St., pg. 1025 **IT**

Louis Vuitton, 54, avenue Montaigne, pg. 781 **IT**
Louis Vuitton Malletier, 54, avenue Montaigne, pg. 781 **IT**
Lubrizol France S.A., Elysees la Defense 7, 19, pg. 1016 **PB**
Lucas France SA, 11 rue Lord Byron, pg. 820 **IT**
Lumiere, 7, Boulevard de la Madeleine, pg. 1199 **PV**
Lux de Morez, pg. 462 **IT**
Luxo-France, 96, Boulevard Auguste, pg. 821 **IT**
Luzzatto & Figlio (France) S.A., 10 Ave. Percier, pg. 166 **PB**
Lyonaise Communications, 18, rue de Prony, pg. 824 **IT**
M6, 16, Cours Albert Premier, pg. 561 **IT**
M.C.N. SAT Holding, 121, avenue de Malakoff, pg. 792 **IT**
M.C.N. SAT Service, 4, rue de Presbourg, pg. 792 **IT**
MID-FAG SA, pg. 757 **IT**
M.P. 55, 121, avenue de Malakoff, pg. 792 **IT**
M.P. 98, 121, avenue de Malakoff, pg. 792 **IT**
MP 65, 121, avenue de Malakoff, pg. 792 **IT**
M.P. 13, 121, avenue de Malakoff, pg. 792 **IT**
M.T.F., 48, rue Notre-Dame-des-Victoires, pg. 781 **IT**
MacGregor Golf France S.A., 11 Boulevard Ney, pg. 73 **IT**
Maison Lazard et Cie, 24 r La Fayette 9e, pg. 1027 **IT**
Mannesmann France SA, pg. 840 **IT**
Mannesmann Industries SA, pg. 838 **IT**
Mannesmann Scangraphic France SARL, pg. 840 **IT**
Manoir Industries, 207 rue de St. Petersbourg, pg. 570 **IT**
Marcam Europe, Middle East & Afica S.R.L., 6, cours Michelet, La Defense, pg. 1043 **PB**
Marcam France, 6, Cours Michelet, pg. 1043 **PB**
Marks & Spencer (France) S.A., 6-8, rue des Mathurins, pg. 843 **IT**
Masson-Williams & Wilkins, 4, Passage de la Main d'Or, pg. 1748 **PB**
Matec, 121, avenue de Malakoff, pg. 792 **IT**
Matra Automobile, 4, rue de Presbourg, pg. 792 **IT**
Matra Datavision S.A., 4, rue de Presbourg, pg. 793 **IT**
Matra Defense, 4, rue Presbourg, pg. 793 **IT**
Matra Defense-Espace, 4, rue Presbourg, pg. 793 **IT**
Matra Electronique, 4, rue Presbourg, pg. 793 **IT**
Matra Espace Participations, 121, avenue de Malakoff, pg. 793 **IT**
Matra Hachette General, 121, avenue de Malakoff, pg. 793 **IT**
Matra Hachette Multimedia On Line, 121, avenue de Malakoff, pg. 793 **IT**
Matra Marconi Space, 4, rue de Presbourg, pg. 793 **IT**
Matra Nortel Communication, 121, avenue de Malakoff, pg. 793 **IT**
Matra Participations, 4, rue de Presbourg, pg. 793 **IT**
Matra Telecommunications Ile-de-France, 96, avenue d'Ilena, pg. 793 **IT**
Matra Transfinex, 4, rue de Presbourg, pg. 793 **IT**
Matra Transport, 4, rue de Presbourg, pg. 793 **IT**
Matra Transport International, 4, rue de Presbourg, pg. 793 **IT**
Matrel, 121, avenue de Malakoff, pg. 793 **IT**
MATRIXX Phone Marketing Services, S.A., Rond Toint, Issy les Moulineux, pg. 368 **PB**
Mead Holdings S.A., 134, boulevard de Clinchy, pg. 1076 **PB**
Mead Johnson S.A., Tour Gale, pg. 256 **PB**
Mead Reassurance S.A., 134, boulevard de Clichy, pg. 1076 **PB**
Media PA, 50 rue de Silly, pg. 116 **IT**
Meeschaert-Rousselle, 16, Blvd. Montmarte, pg. 19 **IT**
Meijiseimei International France S.A., 21 Boulevard de la Madeleine, pg. 854 **IT**
Melitta Societe de Distribution Bentz & Cie, 60 Rue Hauteville, pg. 857 **IT**
Meridien S.A., 171 Blvd. Haussmann, pg. 556 **IT**
Merisel France, 124 Boulevard de Verdun, pg. 1096 **PB**
Merita Bank Ltd., Paris Representative Office, 25, Place Vendome, pg. 859 **IT**
Messages & Tequila, 50-54 rue de Silly, pg. 116 **IT**
Messier S.A., 2 Blvd. du General Martial Valin, pg. 1166 **IT**
Metaleurop S.A., 58, rue Roger Salengro, pg. 1071 **IT**
Metaux Speciaux, Tour Manhattan, pg. 1028 **IT**
Methodes et Informatique, 67-69 blvd. Bessieres, pg. 316 **IT**
Mettler Toledo Analyse Industrielle S.a.r.l., 30, Bd Douaumont, pg. 4 **PV**
Microsoft Europe, Tour Pacific, pg. 1108 **PB**
Microsoft France S.A.R.L., pg. 1108 **PB**
MIDIAL S.A., 7 Rue D'Atroises de Gaulle, pg. 865 **IT**
Midland Bank S.A., 6 Rue Piccini, pg. 580 **IT**
Midland International Trade Services (France) S.A., 6 Rue Piccini, pg. 583 **IT**
Minemet-France, Tour American International, Place Des Corolles, pg. 661 **IT**
Minemet Holding, Tour Maine-Montparnasse, 33 Ave du Maine, pg. 661 **IT**
Mircal, Tour Maine Montparnesse 33 Ave du Maine, pg. 662 **IT**
Mitsui & Co. Europe S.A., 37, Avenue Pierre Premier de Serbie, pg. 880 **IT**
Mitsukoshi Etoile, 3 Rue de Tilsitt, pg. 884 **IT**
Mitsukoshi France S.A., 25 Blvd., Des Capucines, pg. 884 **IT**
Mobil Oil Francaise, Tour Septentrion, pg. 1119 **PB**
Mobilier International, 162 Blvd. Voltaire, 75011, pg. 992 **PV**
MoDo Paper France, 31, rue Henri Rochefort, pg. 887 **IT**
MoDoCell France S.A.R.L., 31, rue Henri Rochefort, pg. 887 **IT**
Moody's France S.A., Services aux Investisseurs, 4, rue Auber, pg. 537 **PB**
Morgan Grenfell France S.A., 42 Ave. Montaigne, pg. 406 **IT**

Morgan Guaranty Trust Company, 14, Place Vendome, pg. 1130 **PB**
J.P. Morgan & Cie S.A., 21, Place du Marche St. Honore, pg. 1130 **PB**
Morgan Stanley Paris, 25, rue Balzac, pg. 1133 **PB**
Mugler Triumvirat, 416 rue aux Ours, pg. 295 **IT**
Multivision, 6 villa Thoreton, pg. 561 **IT**
Mutueel Saint-Christophe, 277, rue Saint-Jacques, pg. 19 **IT**
NATIO-VIE, Les Collines de l'Arche, pg. 163 **IT**
NLI International France S.A., 18 boulevard Malesherbes, pg. 936 **IT**
NLI Properties France S.A.R.L., 18 boulevard Malesherbes, pg. 936 **IT**
N.M.P.P., pg. 793 **IT**
NPI, Le Michelet, pg. 503 **IT**
NYK Line-Paris, 48/50, rue Notre-Dame des Victories, pg. 942 **IT**
Nacanco France S.A., pg. 1029 **IT**
Fernand Nathan, 9 rue Mechain, pg. 240 **IT**
National Bank of Pakistan-Paris, 90 Avenue des Champs Elysees, pg. 908 **IT**
National Utility Service, S.A., Tiur Fiat, Cedex 16, pg. 787 **PV**
National Westminster Bank s.a., 13 rue d'Uzes, pg. 911 **IT**
NationsBank (France), 22 Rue des Capucines, pg. 1166 **PB**
NatWest Sellier SA, 12 rue d'Uzes, pg. 911 **IT**
Nedlloyd Holding France S.A., pg. 1145 **IT**
Nedlloyd Lines France S.A., pg. 1145 **IT**
Nedlloyd Road Cargo S.A., pg. 1145 **IT**
NEPA, 8 Cite Paradis, pg. 239 **IT**
Nestle Sources International S.A., 18, rue de Courcelles, pg. 1074 **IT**
Neutrogena Corporation SARL, 5 rue Logelbach, pg. 928 **PB**
New Brunswick Scientific S.A.R.L., 3 Rues des Deux-Boules, pg. 1170 **PB**
Neyrpic Framatome Mecanique (NFM), Tour Fiat, pg. 503 **IT**
A.C. Nielsen Co., 44 Blvd. de Grenelle, pg. 1183 **PB**
Niger France S.A., pg. 540 **IT**
Nihon Keizai Shimbun Europe Ltd.-Paris, 32, avenue de l'Opera, pg. 930 **IT**
Nikko France SA, 21, Blvd. de la Madeleine, pg. 930 **IT**
Nippon Credit Bank Ltd.-Paris, Huit Place Vendome, pg. 933 **IT**
Nissho Iwai France S.A., Nissho Iwai Bldg., 21, pg. 948 **IT**
Nobel Electronique S.A.R.L., Z.A.C. Paris Nord II, Rue de la Perdrix, pg. 1290 **IT**
Nomura Bourse S.A., 164 rue de Rivoli, pg. 957 **IT**
NORD/LB - Paris, 4. Avenue du Docteur Brouardel, pg. 958 **IT**
Nord Rail, 116, rue de Maubeuge, pg. 560 **IT**
Noreco SA, 60, Rue de Caumartin, pg. 91 **IT**
NORIT France, Centre d'Affaires. 93153 Le Blanc-Mesnil, pg. 958 **IT**
Norske Skog France sarl. 37. rue de Acacias, pg. 966 **IT**
Norvista, 19, Rue de Choiseul, pg. 486 **IT**
NOUVELLES FRONTIERES, 87 Blvd. de Grenelle, pg. 971 **IT**
Nouvelles Messageries de la Presse Parisienne. 111, rue Reaumur, pg. 793 **IT**
Novell France, Tour Framatome. 1, Place de la Coupole, pg. 1204 **PB**
Nutricia France S.A., pg. 992 **IT**
OIP, 11 rue de Colonel Pierre-Avia. pg. 1097 **IT**
Obayashi Corporation-Paris. Washington Plaza. 44. Rue Washington, pg. 996 **IT**
Olivetti France S.A.. Siege Social. La Defense 9. Rue de l'Ancien Marche. pg. 1003 **IT**
Omnium Gestion Financier (OGF). 66 bd. Richard Lenoir. pg. 824 **IT**
154-Tesla, 56. rue de Londres. pg. 1377 **IT**
Ord Minnett Group Limited. 3 Rue de Gramont. pg. 1497 **IT**
ORIX Europe Limited-Paris Liaison Office. 38 rue Laffitte. pg. 1009 **IT**
ORLANE. 12-14 Rond Point Des Champs Elysees. pg. 1011 **IT**
Orlane Institut de Beaute. 163 av Victor Hugo. pg. 1011 **IT**
Orsan, 16. rue Ballu. pg. 791 **IT**
Orsem, 16. rue Ballu. pg. 790 **IT**
PHH France Arval Service Lease. 119/121 Grand Rue. pg. 321 **PB**
PR Europe. 2 rue de Solferino. pg. 566 **IT**
PSA PEUGEOT CITROEN. 75. ave. de la Grande Armee. pg. 1020 **IT**
Packinox. Tour Framatome. pg. 503 **IT**
Panalpina France Transports Internationaux S.A.. pg. 1023 **IT**
Panzalim, 7. rue de Teheran. pg. 381 **IT**
Pareco G.I.E.. pg. 201 **IT**
PAREXEL International. Societe d'etudes biomedicales. 48. boulevard des Batignolles. pg. 1258 **PB**
Parficom. 45. rue de Paris. pg. 560 **IT**
Parfinance S.A.. 1. Rond-Pointdes Champs-Elysees, pg. 562 **IT**
Parfums Christian Dior. 33. avenue Hoche. pg. 781 **IT**
PARI MUTUEL URBAIN. 83 Rue La Boetie. pg. 1023 **IT**
Paribas Asset Management S.A., 45, rue des Petits-Champs. pg. 321 **IT**
Parker Hannifin Instrumentation Division. 44 Avenue George Pompidou. pg. 1263 **PB**
Parvaland Gerance, 48 bis, rue Fabert. pg. 344 **IT**
Passiflore SA, 3. place des Victoires. pg. 781 **IT**
PATHE. 5. boulevard Malesherbes. pg. 1024 **IT**
Pechiney Electrometallurgie. Tour Manhattan. pg. 1028 **IT**

Pechiney Rhenalu, Tour Manhattan, pg. 1028　IT
Pechiney World Trade S.A., Immeuble Balzac, pg. 1028　IT
Pepsi-Cola de France, S.A.R.L., 41 Avenue Montaigne, pg. 1277　PB
Petrolite France S.A., 25 Rue Beranger, pg. 166　PB
Peugeot S.A., 75, av. de la Grande Armee, pg. 1020　IT
Phonogram S.A., 24, Bd. de l'Hopital, pg. 1052　IT
Pignone France S.a.r.l., 4 Boulevard Malesherbes, pg. 991　IT
PINAULT PRINTEMPS, 18, Place Henri-Bergson, pg. 1057　IT
Pinault Printemps, 18 Place O'Henry, pg. 1057　IT
Pipeline Sud-Europeen, pg. 1138　IT
Pirelli France S.A., 3, rue Scribe, pg. 1059　IT
Pneus Pirelli S.A., 173 Rue de Bercy, pg. 1059　IT
Polydor S.A., 2 Rue Cavallotti, pg. 1053　IT
POSSO S.A., 121 av. d'Italie, pg. 1064　IT
Praxair S.A., pg. 1320　PB
Pretabail-Sicomi, 82 Rue De Courcelles, pg. 1409　IT
Printemps Ginza S.A., c/o Printemps, 102, rue de Provence, pg. 364　IT
Prisma Presse & Cie, 6, rue Daru, pg. 191　IT
Prochimar S.A., 217 Rue du Faubourg, pg. 682　IT
Programmes Marketing Annuaires (PMA), 91 Avenue de la Republique, pg. 1065　IT
Promotion et Spectacles d'Europe 1, 26 bis, rue Francois I, pg. 793　IT
Prudence Vie, S.A., Le Monet, 9 Allee des Impressionnistes, pg. 16　IT
Quantum Media International, Inc., Paris Bureau, 71 Avenue Franklin D. Roosevelt, pg. 900　PV
Quarterdeck Office Systems S.A.R.L., 4, rue de General Lanrezac, pg. 1351　PB
RTL, 22, rue Bayard, pg. 561　IT
RTL 2, 22, rue Bayard, pg. 561　IT
RZB Paris, 112-114, Boulevard Haussmann, pg. 1085　IT
Rabobank France, 69, Blvd. Haussmann, pg. 1082　IT
Radex International S.A., 109 Rue du Faubourg St. Honore, pg. 904　PV
RADIO FRANCE, 116, av. du President Kennedy, pg. 1083　IT
Ram France, 63, Boulvard Hausmann, pg. 742　IT
Raschig AG　(France), 49, Avenue de Versailles, pg. 827　IT
Reafin, Immeuble SCOR, 1 avenue du President Wilson, pg. 1152　IT
Reed Exhibition Companies-Europe, 11 rue du Colonel Pietre Avia, pg. 1096　IT
Reed Expositions-France, 11 rue de Colonel Pierre-Avia, pg. 1097　IT
Reed MIDEM Organisation S.A., 11 rue de Colonel Pierre-Avia, pg. 1097　IT
Regional & Local Express Parcels Division, 183 av. de Clichy, pg. 1163　IT
Reichhold Chimie S.A., 103 Blvd. MacDonald, pg. 370　IT
REMY COINTREAU, 152, avenue des Champs-Elysees, pg. 1102　IT
Repsol Petroleo, Immeuble Kupka B, pg. 1105　IT
Reuters Services SARL, 101 rue Reaumur, pg. 1105　IT
REXEL, S.A., 25, rue de Clichy, pg. 1107　IT
Rhenane de Raffinage, pg. 1136　IT
Rhone-Poulenc Multi-Techniques, Tour Generale, Quartier Villon, pg. 1109　IT
Rhone-Poulenc Systemes, Tour Generale, Quartier Villon, pg. 1109　IT
Ringdex, 16, rue Ballu, pg. 790　IT
Road Transport, Warehousing & Distribution Division, 183 av. de Clichy, pg. 1163　IT
C.E.T. Robertshaw, 127-129 Ruede, pg. 1244　PB
Robinson Nugent, SARL, Zac de la Sabliere, 4, rue Maryse Bastie, pg. 1395　PB
Rockwell France, Tour GAN, pg. 1400　IT
Rockwell Light Vehicle Systems-France, Tour Gan, pg. 1401　PB
Rockwell Semiconductor Systems S.a.r.l., Tour Gan, pg. 1402　IT
Rohm & Haas France S.A., 185 Rue Bercy, pg. 1404　PB
Ross Systems France S.A., Espace 21, 31, Place Ronde, pg. 1406　PB
Rubson S.A.F., pg. 614　IT
Sade, 28, rue de la Baume, pg. 321　IT
SAGEM Allumage, Leponent 27, pg. 1273　IT
SAGEM Electronics and Industry Division, 27, rue Leblanc, pg. 1273　IT
SAGEM Navigation and Defense Division, 27, rue Leblanc, pg. 1273　IT
SBC Banque Warburg, 65 rue de Courcelles, pg. 1331　IT
SBS Gestion S.A., 112, avenue Kleber, pg. 1331　IT
SBS Valeurs S.A., 112, avenue Kleber, pg. 1331　IT
SCAC-Fisons S.A., pg. 1111　IT
S.C.I. Matra Toulouse, 47, rue de Monceau, pg. 793　IT
SCOR, Immeuble SCOR, 1 Ave. du President Wilson, pg. 1152　IT
SCOR Reassurance, Immeuble SCOR, 1 avenue du President Wilson, pg. 1152　IT
SCOR Vie, Immeuble SCOR, 1 avenue du President Wilson, pg. 1152　IT
SDIG, 17, rue Alfred Roll, pg. 541　IT
SFMRA, 4, rue de Presbourg, pg. 793　IT
S.F.T. Gongrand Freres, 95708 Charles de Gaulle CEDEX, pg. 1120　PV
SIAS - MPA, 142, Boulevard Haussmann, pg. 566　IT
S.I.E.F., 48, rue Notre-Dame-des-Victoires, pg. 781　IT
SIG Emballage France S.a.r.l., 31, Rue Desbordes-Valmore, pg. 1156　IT
SIP-Societe Immobiliere Prospection, 2 Quai Henri IV, pg. 790　IT
SKW France S.A., 16, av. de la Grande-Armee, pg. 1466　IT
SMH France S.A., 49, avenue Hoche, pg. 1161　IT

SNC-Lavalin Europe, 23, rue Vernet, pg. 1162　IT
SNC Sofrimat 4, 121, avenue de Malakoff, pg. 793　IT
SNCF, 88, Rue Saint Lazare, pg. 1163　IT
SNECMA Services International (SSI), 2 Bld du General Martial Valin, pg. 1166　IT
SNECMA - SOCIÉTÉ NATIONALE D'ETUDE ET DE CONSTRUCTION DE MOTEURS D'AVIATION, 2 Boulevard du General-Martial-Valin, pg. 1165　IT
SNTR Calberson Paris, pg. 1164　IT
SODIAAL, 170 bis, boulevard du Montparnasse, pg. 1166　IT
SPS, 40, rue de Colisee, pg. 19　IT
Sabliere du Ventoux, 18, rue de Courcelles, pg. 919　IT
Saint Dominique Finance, 45, rue Saint-Dominique, pg. 344　IT
Saint Dominique Participations, 48 bis, rue Fabert., pg. 344　IT
Ste. Europeenne de Restauration, 33, avenue du Maine, pg. 20　IT
Saint-Gobain Vitrage, Les Miroirs, pg. 1172　IT
Ste. Restaurants des Nouveaux Sites, 33, avenue du Maine, pg. 20　IT
The Sakura Bank - Paris Branch, 112, Avenue Kleber, pg. 1179　IT
Samin, Les Miroirs, pg. 1171　IT
Sandvik Process Systems S.A., 40, Rue Jean Jaures, pg. 1187　IT
Sandvik Tobler S.A., pg. 1187　IT
Satam S.A., pg. 846　IT
SCETA Voyageurs, pg. 1165　IT
Schlumberger Limited, 42, rue Saint-Dominique, pg. 1439　PB
A. Schulman S.A., 10/12 Rue Andras Beck, pg. 1441　PB
Science Applications International, Europe S.A., 2 Place de la Defense, pg. 976　PV
Sea Containers France S.A., 75 Ave. des Champs Elysees, pg. 1214　IT
Seagram Global Brands, 1719 Ave. Montaigne, pg. 1217　IT
Sedri, 33, avenue du Maine, pg. 20　IT
Sefranez, Immeuble Balzac, pg. 1028　IT
Segera, 4, rue de Presbourg, pg. 793　IT
SEIKO France S.A., 83 rue du Temple, pg. 1218　IT
SEITA, SOCIETE NATIONALE D'EXPLOITATION INDUSTRIELLE DES TABACS ET DES ALLUMETTES, 53, quai d'Orsay, pg. 1218　IT
Select Communications, Paris, 4 Passage Saint Avoye, pg. 982　PV
SEO Achat d'Espace, 3/5, Sente de la Pyramide, pg. 116　IT
SEPIC, 17 rue Uzes, pg. 239　IT
Septima S.A., 14 Rue Falguiere, pg. 451　IT
Serat, 7, rue Copernic, pg. 29　IT
SERES, 67-69 bd Bessieres, pg. 316　IT
Serese (Service de Restauration du Sud Est), 83, rue du Charolais, pg. 560　IT
Serie Club, 16, Cours Albert Premier, pg. 562　IT
Sers, Tour Manhattan, pg. 1028　IT
Services Petroliers Schlumberger S.A., France, 42, rue St. Dominique, pg. 1439　PB
Servirail, 9, bd de l'hopital, pg. 560　IT
Shandwick France, 5 rue de Rome, pg. 1227　IT
Shell Francaise, 29 Rue de Berri, pg. 1138　IT
Shell Recherche, pg. 1138　IT
Shimizu France S.A., 59 Rue de la Tour, pg. 1234　IT
Shiseido France S.A., 18, Avenue Matignon, pg. 1235　IT
Siemens Nixdorf Information Systems S.A., 14 Avenue des Beguines, B.P. 8298, pg. 1245　IT
Signode France, 3, rue de l'hopital St. Louis, pg. 869　PB
Simon Marketing International, 48 Rue Montmartre, pg. 1001　PV
Simura, Tour Maine Montparnasse, pg. 662　IT
Singapore Tourist Promotion Board - Paris, Centre d'Affaires Le Louvre, 2 Place du Palais-Royal, pg. 1254　IT
Siplast S.A., 12 Rue Cabanis, pg. 659　IT
Sita, 7, rue de Logelbach, pg. 824　IT
Scapi, 42, rue de Mathurins, pg. 565　IT
Socari, 2 rue de la Baume, pg. 1382　IT
Sochata, 2 blvd. du General Martial Valin, pg. 1166　IT
Ste. Socidoc, 142 rue Montmartre, pg. 239　IT
Societe Anonyme Formica (France), Rue de la Maison Rouge, Centres des Affaires de Paris, pg. 130　IT
Societe Anonyme Francaise de Reassurances, 153 rue de Courcelles, pg. 1024　IT
Societe Bancaire de Paris, 45, Avenue Georges Mandel, pg. 142　IT
Societe Centrale de Gestion, pg. 312　IT
Societe Civile de Gestion Immobiliere, 37, rue de la Victoire, pg. 19　IT
Societe Civile Immobiliere de Vergeze, 18, rue de Courcelles, pg. 919　IT
Societe Commerciale des Eaux Minerales du Bassin de Vichy Saint-Yorre, 18, rue de Courcelles, pg. 919　IT
Societe d'Application du Flockage, pg. 160　PV
Societe d'Agences et de Diffusion, 115, rue Reaumur, pg. 793　IT

SOCIETE D'APPLICATIONS GENERALES D'ELECTRICITE ET DE MECHANIQUE, 6, avenue d'Iena, pg. 1273　IT
Societe de Banque Suisse S.A., 112 avenue Kleber, pg. 1331　IT
Societe de Bourse J.P. Morgan S.A., 14, Place Vendome, pg. 1131　PB
Societe de Gestion d'Interets Petroliers (Sogedip), 41, ave. de l'Opera, pg. 319　IT
Societe de Produits Alimetaires et Dietetiques, SOPAD-Nestle S.A., Sept. rue Morand, 11e., pg. 922　IT
Societe des Ateliers Louis Vuitton, La Grande Arche, pg. 781　IT
Societe des Magasins Louis Vuitton-France, La Grande Arche, pg. 781　IT
Societe des Specialites Surgelees a Landevant, Zone Industrielle, pg. 556　IT
Societe d'Etudes et de Constructions Electroniques (SECRE), 214, rue du faubourg St. Martin, pg. 706　IT
Societe Europeenne des Melasses SA, 27, rue Chateaubriand, pg. 1357　IT
Societe Eurosucre S.N.C., 21/25 rue Balzac, pg. 549　IT
Societe Financiere d'Auteuil (SFA), Tour Total, 24 Cours Michelet, pg. 1409　IT
Societe Financiere de Depots et de Placements (Sofidep), 41, Rue de Chateaudun, pg. 1332　IT
Societe Financiere et de Developpement Alimentaire, 4, rue Montesquieu, pg. 557　IT
Societe Financiere pour la France et les Pays d'Outre-Mer (SOFFO), 23, rue de l'Amiral d'Estaing, pg. 313　IT
Societe Fonciere et Financiere de la Ville-l'Evegue, pg. 313　IT
Societe Francaise des Techniques Lummus, Tour Franklin Cedex No. 11, pg. 14　IT
Societe Francaise d'Organisation et de Participations, 25 Avenue Franklin D. Roosevelt, pg. 549　IT
Societe Francaise Laboratoire Abbott, 5, rue Anatole de la Forge, pg. 14　PB
SOCIETE GENERALE, 29 Boulevard Haussmann, pg. 1273　IT
Societe Generale de Grandes Sources Eaux Minerales, 18 rue de Courcelles, pg. 919　IT
Societe Generale D'Entreposage et de Manutention s.r.l., 95, Rue Saint-Lazare, pg. 92　IT
Societe Immobiliere du Parc de La Nque S.A., 15, Rue de Londres, pg. 92　IT
Societe Industrielle d'Exploration des Moyens de Transport SA, 36, rue Guersant, pg. 271　PV
Societe Industrielle du Titane S.A., 45 Rue de Courcelles, pg. 271　IT
Societe Lyonnaise des Eaux et de l'Eclairage, 45, rue Cortambert, pg. 313　IT
Societe Nouvelle Cellonite, pg. 160　PV
Societe Nouvelle des Pastilles de Vichy, 18, rue de Courcelles, pg. 919　IT
Societe pour la Conversion de l'Uranium en Metal et en Hexafluorure, Tour Manhattan, pg. 305　IT
Societe suisse accidents (France), 41, Rue de Chateaudun, pg. 1332　IT
Societe suisse-Banque (France), 41, Rue de Chateaudun, pg. 1332　IT
Societe suisse (France), 41, Rue de Chateaudun, pg. 1332　IT
Societe Toulousaine de Minoterie a Revel, pg. 557　IT
Society Francais Pour Le Development de la Porcelaine d'Art, 93-95, Ave. Daumesnil, pg. 1609　PB
Sodeva, 15, rue Croix des Petits Champs, pg. 557　IT
Sodiamex International SA, 22-26 Rue de Bitche, pg. 1269　IT
Sofimades, 4, rue de Presbourg, pg. 793　IT
Sofimo, 61, rue des Belles-Feuilles, pg. 790　IT
Sofineti, 48, rue Fabert, pg. 344　IT
Sofrimo, 121, avenue de Malakoff, pg. 793　IT
Softimage S.A.R.L., pg. 1108　PB
Sogemat Participations, 121, avenue de Malakoff, pg. 793　IT
Sogerem, Immeuble Balzac, pg. 1029　IT
Sogerisk/Egis, Immeuble SCOR, 1 avenue du President Wilson, pg. 1152　IT
Sogesval: Societe en Cours de Liquidation, 25 Rue Vivienne, pg. 298　IT
Solar Turbines S.A., pg. 317　PB
Solex S.A., Rue Lavoisier 19, 92002, pg. 482　IT
Solvay Interox S.A., Cours Albert Ier 12, pg. 1280　IT
SOMYCEL, 18, rue de Courcelles, pg. 919　IT
Soplachim S.A., rue Francois Ier, 5, pg. 1280　IT
Sorbus France S.A., 16 Boulevard du General Leclerc, pg. 204　PB
Sorenolif SA, 81-83, rue du Charolais, pg. 21　IT
Sotrimlo S.A., 15, Rue de Londres, pg. 92　IT
Sovedi France, 36 rue de Picpus, pg. 410　IT
Specia, 16 Rue Clisson, pg. 1109　IT
Spectral, 22, avenue des Nations, pg. 706　IT
Spontex S.A., 3 Blvd. Malesheives, pg. 1409　IT
Spur France, 46 Passage de Bureau, pg. 851　IT
Standard Chartered Leasing SARL, 34 Boulevard des Italiens, pg. 1297　IT
Owen Stanley Financial, 21, Boulevard de la Madeleine, pg. 651　IT
State Street Banque S.A., 21 Rue Balzac, pg. 1513　PB
Stena Line France, 19 Rue Louis Le Grand, pg. 1300　IT
Stena Line France, Paris Travel Shop, 38 Avenue de l'Opera, pg. 1300　IT
Stevens International, S.A., 72, rue du Faubourg St-Honore, pg. 1517　PB
Stevens Security Systems, 72, Rue du Faubourg St. Honore, pg. 1517　IT
Stolt Tank Containers Limited, pg. 1302　IT
Sucrerie et Distillerie de Souppes Ouvre et Fils S.A., pg. 549　IT
Sud Electra S.A., 72, rue Regnault, pg. 712　IT

PB - *U.S. Public Companies Volume*
PV - *U.S. Private Companies Volume*
IT - *International Public & Private Companies Volume*

Suisse de Reassurances (France), 5 rue de Logelbach, pg. 1333
Sulzer Industries France S.A., pg. 1306 — IT
The Sumitomo Bank, Ltd.-Paris Branch, 20, Rue de la Ville L'Eveque, pg. 1309 — IT
Symix Systems, Inc.-France, 173 Rue de la Croix Nivert, pg. 1547 — PB
Synergie Presse, 9-13 Rue du Colonel Pierre Avia, pg. 451 — IT
Synthelabo S.A., 58, Rue De La Glaciere, pg. 818 — IT
Systra-Sofretu-Sofrerail, 5 Ave. du Coq, pg. 1165 — IT
TBWA Paris, 25 rue du Pont-Neuf, pg. 1063 — PV
TRL S.A., pg. 160 — PV
TRT Lucent Technologies, 72 Rue du Faubourg St., pg. 1019 — PB
TSM (Telecom Systemes Mobiles), 66 Ave. Maine 14th, pg. 503 — IT
Tailleur Industrie, 44146 rue de la Bienfaisame, pg. 549 — IT
Taisei Europe, Ltd., 4-8 Rue Sainte Anne, pg. 1347 — IT
Takashimaya (France) S.A., 3, Rue de Castellane, pg. 1350 — IT
Tamaris SA, 3, place des Victoires, pg. 781 — IT
Tanabe Pharma S.A., 12 avenue d'Italie, pg. 1354 — IT
Tarif Media S.A., 5 Rue de la Boetie, pg. 451 — IT
TECHNIP, La Defense 6, 170, Place Henri Regnault, pg. 1360 — IT
Technip CLE, La Defense 6, 170, place Henri-Regnault, pg. 1360 — IT
Technip-Geoproduction, Tour Kupka C, La Defense 7, 14, rue Hoche, pg. 1361 — IT
Technip TPS, 24, boulevard de l'Hopital, pg. 1361 — IT
Tedeco S.A.R.L., pg. 1207 — IT
Tele Hachette, 32, rue Francois I, pg. 794 — IT
Telediffusion de France, 10, rue d'Oradour-sur-Glane, pg. 503 — IT
Telesystemes, 115 Rue Bac 7th, pg. 503 — IT
Teletec SARL, 13 Rue de Petites Ecuries, pg. 1074 — PV
Telxon Corporation, 23rd Floor, Tour Atlantique, 1 Place de la Pyramide, pg. 1574 — PB
Tesci, Tour Aurore, 18 Place des Reflets, pg. 976 — PV
Textuel, 29 bd Bourdon, pg. 116 — IT
Thermatome, Tour Atlantique, pg. 706 — IT
Thomson Competences, 11, avenue Myron T. Herrick, pg. 1382 — IT
Thomson-CSF S.A., Watson Haussmann, pg. 1383 — IT
Thomson Multimedia SA, pg. 1384 — IT
THOMSON S.A., 173 boulevard Haussmann, pg. 1381 — IT
3 Suisses Exemplaire S.A., pg. 1015 — IT
Tie Rack France SARL, Forum des Halles, 1 Pierre Lescot, pg. 1389 — IT
Time-Life International S.A., 17 Avenue Matignon, pg. 1615 — PB
The Tokio Marine & Fire Insurance Company (U.K.) Limited, 43, rue La Fayette, pg. 1392 — IT
Tolbiachim, 117, rue du Chateau des Rentiers, pg. 82 — PB
Top Tele, 25, rue Francois I, pg. 794 — IT
TOTAL S.A., 24, Cours Michelet, pg. 1408 — IT
Tourism Malaysia - Paris Office, 29 Rue de Pyramides, pg. 833 — IT
Transatlantic Holdings Inc., 92 Avenue de Wagram, pg. 84 — PB
Transbanque, 61, rue des Belles-Feuilles, pg. 790 — IT
Transmission Epargne Vie, Tour Franklin, 100-1-1 Terrasse Boieldieu, pg. 19 — IT
Transpac, 33 Ave. Maine, pg. 503 — IT
Transvet S.A., pg. 1144 — IT
Travel Agency Paris, 23 Rue Louis le Grand, pg. 1300 — IT
Travel Agency Paris, 3, Rue Ambroise Pare, pg. 1301 — IT
Tredi, 62 Rue Jeanne d'Arc, pg. 459 — IT
Tribune Desfosses, 48, rue Notre-Dame-des-Victoires, pg. 781 — IT
Trio-Kenwood France S.A., 13, Blvd. Ney, pg. 731 — IT
Trocadero Participations, 42 Ave. de Friedland, pg. 54 — IT
Ugefo, 5-7, rue de Milan, pg. 19 — IT
UNAT Re, S.A., 67 Blvd. Haussmann, pg. 85 — PB
UNAT, S.A., 67 Blvd. Haussmann, pg. 85 — PB
UPM-Kymmene France S.A., 104, avenue du President Kennedy, pg. 1430 — IT
Ufima S.A., Rue Lavoisier 19, pg. 482 — IT
Ugine Aciers de Chatillon et Gueugnon S.A., 4 Place de la Pyramide, pg. 571 — IT
Uni Europe, 24, rue Drouot, pg. 19 — IT
UNIBAIL, 108 rue de Richelieu, pg. 1431 — IT
Unic S.A., 10 rue Juliette Dodu, pg. 1273 — IT
Union de Banques Suisses, 69, Bd. Haussmann, pg. 1441 — IT
Union des Assurances Federales, 27, Avenue Claude Vellefaux, pg. 344 — IT
Union des Combustibles "UNICO" S.A., 15, Rue du Louvre, pg. 1457 — IT
Union Europeenne de Cic, 4, Rue Gaillon, pg. 565 — IT
Union Industrielle de Credit (UIC), 8, rue Lamennais, pg. 565 — IT
Union Pour Le Financement D'Immeubles Desouetes (UIS), 5, avenue Percies, pg. 565 — IT
Union Special-France, Inc., pg. 717 — IT
Union Technique Industrielle S.A., 32 Rue De L'Arcade, pg. 256 — PB
UREP, Tour Manhattan, pg. 305 — IT
Groupe Usine Nouvelle, 59 rue du Rocher, pg. 239 — IT
Utell International-France, Bercy Expo, 40 Avenue Des Tenoirs De France, pg. 1098 — IT
Utilisation Rationnelle des Gaz, pg. 1138 — IT
VG Emballage, 38, Rue Breguet, pg. 1171 — IT
VRG-Papier SA, pg. 757 — IT
Valeo Research Sooal, 43, rue Bayen, pg. 240 — IT
Valexy, 29 bis ave Laumiere 19th, pg. 571 — IT
Vedior France, 60-62, Rue de Hauteville, pg. 1463 — IT
Vertec, Les Miroirs, pg. 1171 — IT
Vicat S.A., Tour Gan, pg. 606 — IT

Victoire Telematique, 46, rue Notre-Dame-des-Victoires, pg. 781 — IT
Viking Direct S.A.R.L., Z.I. Mitry-Compans, 77294 Mitry Mory Cedex, pg. 1721 — PB
Vision 7, 28, rue Francois I, pg. 794 — IT
VISOFI S.A., pg. 1481 — IT
Voiles Gateff S.A., pg. 1273 — IT
Volvo European Corporate Office S.A., 6, rue Newton, pg. 1477 — IT
Vorwerk Textil France S.a.r.l., 30 Ave. Am Lemonnier, pg. 1481 — IT
WF Corroon-France, 18 Boulevard Malesherbes, pg. 1502 — IT
Warner's Aiglon, S.A., 66 Rue du Faubourg Saint-Honore, pg. 1738 — PB
Wattohm, 18-26 rue Goubet, pg. 662 — IT
West Japan Railway Company, 24-26, Rue de la Pepiniere, pg. 1491 — IT
WestLB (France) S.A., 15 Avenue de Friedland, pg. 1494 — IT
Willis Corroon France SA, 18 Boulevard Malesherbes, pg. 1509 — IT
Witco S.A., 20, Rue De La Ville L'Eveque, pg. 1774 — PB
Wolters Kluwer France, 187-189 Quai de Valmy, pg. 1513 — IT
The World Bank, 66, Avenue d'Iena, pg. 1189 — PV
Yamaichi France S.A., 51-53 Avenue des Champs-Elysees, pg. 1517 — IT
Yamazaki France S.A., 125 Rue du Faubourg, pg. 1519 — IT
Young & Rubicam France, 23 Allee Maillasson, pg. 1199 — PV
Zircotube, Tour Manhattan, pg. 503 — IT
Zurich Compagnie d'assurances sur la vie, 19 Rue Guillame Tell, pg. 1529 — IT
Zurich Epargne, 19 rue Guillaume Tell, pg. 1531 — IT
Zurich International (France) S.A., 19 rue Guillausme Tell, pg. 1532 — IT

Patricia

Albright & Wilson Patricia Srl, Strada Morolense Km 10, 100, pg. 49 — IT

Pau

Hewlett-Packard France, 242, Ter Avenue Jean, pg. 819 — PB
Usines Dehousse SA, Avenue Gaston Lacoste, pg. 1166 — IT

Perigny

Soferac-Francespar, Zone Industrielle, Rue Blaise Pascal, pg. 1462 — IT

Perigueux

EURO RSCG D 10, 2 rue A. Gadaud, pg. 600 — IT

Perpignan

Agricommerce SA, Marche St. Charles, pg. 491 — IT
Berlamont, Route de Pertus, pg. 275 — IT
Liferoca, pg. 1164 — IT
Perpignan Office, Docks du Vallespir, pg. 784 — IT

Perret

Rorer, S.A., 4 rue de la Gare, pg. 1112 — IT

Persan

ASEA S.A., 22 Rue du 8 Mai 1945, pg. 8 — IT

Pessac

Chantiers Modernes, 18, avenue Gustave Eiffel, pg. 823 — IT
Thomson-CSF Microelectronique, Avenue Gustave-Eiffel, Parc industriel de Pessac, pg. 1382 — IT
Thomson-CSF Radars & Contre-Mesures, Avenue Gustave-Eiffel, Parc industriel de Pessac, pg. 1382 — IT

Peyruis

Haute-Provence Express, pg. 1164 — IT

Pierrelatte

Pierrelatte Plant, pg. 305 — IT

Pierrepont

Bertrand Faure Equipements SA, 1, Place de la Victoire, pg. 192 — IT

Pithwiers

AEP/Borden Macaple S.A., Rue Marc Aangier, pg. 5 — PB

Plaisir

Wandel & Goltermann France, 46 bis, rue Pierre Curie, pg. 1486 — IT

Plancoet

Eau Minerale de Plancoet, pg. 919 — IT

Ploermel

Acieries De Ploermel, pg. 1711 — PB

Ploufragan

Laminoirs de Bretagne, pg. 571 — PB

Pluvigner

Hill-Rom/Le Couviour S.A., ZI de Talhoet, pg. 828 — PB

Podensac

Fines Specialites, Route de Balizac, Landiras, pg. 780 — IT

Pointe-a-Pitre

Societe des Ciments Antillais, ZI de Jarry, Baie Mahault, pg. 790 — IT
Sori (Societe de Restauration Industrielle), Aeroport du Raizet - Les Abymes, pg. 560 — IT

Poissy

GKN Glaenzer Cardan SA, Boite Postale No. 1, pg. 536 — IT
GKN Glaenzer Spicer SA, Boite Postale No. 1, pg. 536 — IT
GSM, 4 rue Freres Tissier, Carrieres-sous-Poissy, pg. 292 — IT
Locatel, Technoparc 2 a 10, Rue Charles Edouard Jeanneut, pg. 54 — IT
Parfums Rochas S.A., 75, rue d' Aigremont, pg. 1490 — IT

Poitiers

PGA Motors, Avenue du Teleport, pg. 807 — IT

Pons

Tonnellerie Garnier, Salignac S/Charente, pg. 781 — IT

Pont Audemer

Sacherie de Pont-Audemer S.N.C., pg. 1146 — IT

Pont-de-Claix

Becton Dickinson Pharmaceutical Systems, 11 Rue Aristide Berges BP 4, pg. 200 — PB

Pont-l'Eveque

Etablissements Debrise-Dulac & Cie, Route de Trouville, pg. 780 — IT

Pont-Saint Maxence

Ecocontainer S.A., pg. 1146 — IT
MoDo Paper PSM, 1225, rue Pasteur, pg. 887 — IT

Pont-Saint-Pierre

Dosapro-Milton Roy S.A., pg. 1534 — PB

Pont-sur-Yonne

La Verrerie Medicale SARL, pg. 1523 — IT
Lhomme S.A., pg. 1487 — PB

Pontarlier

Parker Hannifin RAK, S.A., 8 Rue Pierre Dechanet, pg. 1261 — PB

Pontcharra

Nordia S.A., ZI de Pre Brun, pg. 421 — IT

Ponte-Sainte Malense

Moore Lithorex Direct Marketing Services SA, pg. 890 — IT

Ponthierry

Henkel Nopco S.A., pg. 613 — IT

Pontoise

AMP de France, 29 Chausse Jules-Cesar, pg. 8 — PB

Port-de-Bouc

Ferro Chemicals S.A., Etang de la Gafette, pg. 619 — PB
Van Leeuwen Tubes SA, 7 Route de St. Mitre, pg. 1450 — IT

PB - *U.S. Public Companies Volume*
PV - *U.S. Private Companies Volume*
IT - *International Public & Private Companies Volume*

Geographic Index-Non U.S.

1595

Portes-les-Valence

Pavailler Equipement S.A., pg. 485   IT
Silkolene France S.A., Z.I. des Aureats, Rue Pierre Brossolette, pg. 519   IT

Pringy

Etablissement d'Argonay, pg. 383   IT
Mold-Tech S.a.r.L., RN 7, pg. 1507   PB

Pusignan

DIMA, ZAC de Mariage, pg. 1172   IT

Puteaux

Airforge S.A., pg. 571   IT
Ascometal, La Defense 7, 11/13 Cours Valmy, pg. 570   IT
BNP BAIL, 46.52 rue Arago, pg. 163   IT
Bayer France S.A., 49-51, Quai De Dion Bouton, pg. 175   IT
Bull Alpha, 1 Place Carpeaux Tour Bull, pg. 315   IT
Bull Europe Centrale et Orientale S.A., 1 Place Carpeaux, Tour Bull, pg. 317   IT
Bull Finanservices, 1 Place Carpeaux, Tour Bull, pg. 316   IT
Bull International S.A., 1, Place Carpeaux, Tour Bull, pg. 315   IT
Bull Omega, 1 place Carpeaux, pg. 316   IT
CAP Sesa Maintenence Tour Anjou, 33 quai de Dion-Bouton, pg. 263   IT
CAP Sesa Telecom, 30 quai de Dion Bouton, pg. 263   IT
Carel Fouche Industries (CFI), 31-32, quai de Dion Bouton, pg. 706   IT
Ceca S.A., 4/8 Cours Michelet, pg. 445   IT
Chavanne Kettin, pg. 571   IT
Cheque Restaurant, Sodetir, pg. 1274   IT
CISATOL, pg. 571   IT
Combustion Engineering Europe s.a.r.l., Tour Franklin, pg. 5   IT
Compagnie Francaise de Forges et Fondries (C3F), pg. 571   IT
Creusot-Loire Industrie, Immeuble La Pacifice, La Defense 7, pg. 571   IT
D.A.C. Systems/Micros France, 18-20, rue des Bas Rogers, pg. 1106   PB
Davum-Armatures, Immeuble La Pacific, pg. 571   IT
Dell Computer S.A., 12-12 Bis Rue Jean Jaures, pg. 496   PB
Fidelio-MICROS France S.A., 18-20 rue des Bas Rogers, pg. 1106   PB
Forecast International, pg. 571   IT
Francorail, 33, quai de Dion Bouton, pg. 706   IT
HFC Estamfor, pg. 570   IT
Huls France S.A., 49-51 Quai de Dion Bouton, pg. 1455   IT
IBM Europe, S.A., Tour Pascal, 22, route de la Demi-lune, pg. 897   PB
Imphy S.A., La Defense7, pg. 571   IT
Jistral, 31-32, quai de Dion Bouton, pg. 706   IT
Kendo, 11/15 quai de Dion Bouton, pg. 601   IT
La Fer Bouton, pg. 571   IT
Laboratoires Takeda, 15, Quai de Dion Bouton, pg. 1350   IT
Lagon, 11/15 quai de Dion-Bouton, pg. 601   IT
L'Esprit d'Equipe, 1 Place Carpeaux, Tour Bull, pg. 316   IT
MTE, 31-32, quai de Dion-Bouton, pg. 706   IT
Media-Polis/EURO RSCG Media, 40 quai de Dion Bouton, pg. 601   IT
Mediapolis France, Immeuble Galilee, 11, Square Leon Blum, pg. 1199   PV
Nipson International, 1 Place Carpeaux, pg. 316   IT
Omnium de Gestion des Valeurs Industrielles et Commerciales (OGIC), 1 Place Carpeaux, Tour Bull, pg. 316   IT
Promatel, 31-32, quai de Dion Bouton, pg. 706   IT
Promethee, 33, quai de Dion Bouton, pg. 706   IT
Research-Cottrell (France) S.A., pg. 30   PB
Safic Alcan & Cie S.A., rue Bellini, pg. 862   IT
Saric International, 1 Place Carpeaux, Tour Bull, pg. 316   IT
Sequent Computer Systems (France) S.A., Tour Chantecoq, 5 rue Chantecoq, pg. 1459   PB
SOFOM, 1, Place Carpeaux, Tour Bull, pg. 316   IT
Sollac, pg. 571   IT
Stanhome S.A., Tour Litwin, 10 Rue Jean Jaures, pg. 1508   PB
Stora Billerud Paper S.A., 56, Quai de Dion Bouton, pg. 1302   IT
Synergie, 11/15 Quai de Dion Bouton, pg. 601   IT
Texaco France S.A., 5, rue Bellinim Tour Arago, pg. 1584   PB
Toshiba Medical France S.A., 7, Rue Ampere, pg. 1407   IT
Toshiba Systems (France) S.A., 7, rue Ampere, pg. 1407   IT
Total Outre-Mer, Tour Total, pg. 1409   IT
Total Transport Maritime, 24 Cours Michelet, pg. 1409   IT
Totalgaz, 16 Rue de la Republique, pg. 1410   IT
Trefilunion, pg. 571   IT
Ugine ACG (Aciers de Chatillon et Gueugnon), pg. 571   IT
Valor, pg. 571   IT
Wacoal France, S.A., 46, Rue Arago, pg. 1484   IT

Puy-Guillaume

Verdome, 21, avenue Edouard Vaillant, pg. 381   IT

Quetigny

Soplachim S.A., Avenue de Tavaux, pg. 1280   IT
Syste Informatique, 18 rue du Cap Vert, pg. 316   IT

Quimper

Fleetguard International Corporation, Zone Industrielle due Grand Guelen, pg. 469   PB
Matra Communication, 50, rue du President-Sadate, pg. 793   IT
Matra Communication Distribution, 50, rue du President-Sadate, pg. 793   IT
Matra Communication Publique, 50, rue du President-Sadate, pg. 793   IT
Papeteries de Maudit S.A., Kerisole, pg. 959   PB

Rang-du-Fliers

Sofamor, S.N.C., 158, Rue de l'Eglise, pg. 1482   PB

Rantigny

Caterpillar Materiels Routiers, pg. 316   PB

Raon-l-Etape

Bertrand Faure Equipements SA, Place Robert Tisserand, pg. 192   IT

Razes

La Crouzille Mining Division, Route de St. Pardoux, pg. 305   IT

Redon

Siebre, ZI de Briangaud, pg. 192   IT

Reims

Champagne Pommery & Greno, 5, place du General Gouraud, pg. 780   IT
Champagne Pommery S.A., 5, place du General Gouraud, pg. 780   IT
Champagne Ruinart, 4, rue des Crayeres, pg. 780   IT
S.A. des Vignobles Henriot, 6, avenue du General Giraud, pg. 780   IT
Eau et Feu, 78-82 Rue Lesage, pg. 1500   IT
EURO RSCG Communicance, 30 rue Payen, pg. 600   IT
Europeenne de Surbouchage, 76, rue du Docteur Lemoine, pg. 1028   IT
Forbo Barlino SA, pg. 498   IT
Freinrail S.A., 47 49 Rue Gesset, pg. 738   IT
Henrio Distribution, 3, place des Droits de l'Homme, pg. 780   IT
Nairn Sol SA, pg. 498   IT
S.A. Plastiques Developpement, pg. 302   IT
S.A. Produits Metallurgiques de Champagne, pg. 302   IT
Rhenania Compagnie Europeenne de Transports et d'Affretement S.A.R.L., 124, Rue Ponsardin, pg. 1034   IT
Societe Civile Immobiliere Place de la Belgique, pg. 302   IT
S.A. Societe Industrielle de Souvigny, pg. 302   IT
TAITTINGER, 9, Place Saint Nicaise, pg. 1348   IT
VMC, 41, rue Pierre Maitre, pg. 381   IT
Veuve Clicquot Ponsardin, 12, Rue du Temple, pg. 781   IT
Walbaum, pg. 1165   IT

Remire

La Cimenterie Guyanaise, Zone Industrielle Degrad, des Cannes, pg. 788   IT

Remiremont

Ames Europe S.A., 3, Chemin Departemental, pg. 540   IT

Rennes

Canon Research Centre France S.A., Rue de la Touche-Lambert, 35510 Cesson-Sevigne, pg. 262   IT
Etoile Bleue, 17 rue de la Quintaine, pg. 600   IT
Hewlett Packard France, Rue Louis Kerautret-Botmelt, pg. 819   PB
Mindscape International, One Rue Victor Hugo, pg. 1027   IT
Tektronix S.A.-Rennes, pg. 1568   PB
Unicom 2A, rue du Bignon, pg. 601   IT

Revel

Dietitique et Sante S.A., pg. 981   IT
Nutrition et Sante S.A., pg. 983   IT

Revigny

SMR (Societe Metallurgique de Revigny), Route de Contuisson, pg. 571   IT

Ribeauville

S.A. des Eaux Minerales de Ribeauville, pg. 922   IT

Societe Anonyme des Eaux Minerales de Ribeauville, pg. 919   IT

Ribecourt

SECO S.A., B.P. 1, 1, rue Saverine, pg. 729   IT

Ribemont

GKN Ribemont SARL, 11 rue de la Briqueterie, pg. 536   IT

Riberac

Albany International S.A., pg. 37   PB
Compain Bois et Materiaux, 8, place du Palais, pg. 784   IT

Rilly-la-Montagne

Champagne Canard-Duchene, 1, rue Edmond-Canard, pg. 779   IT

Riom

Reti SA, Route de Marsat, pg. 45   IT

Riorges

SNTR Calberson Roanne, pg. 1164   IT

Rixheim

Schiedel S.A.R.L., Z.I. 56, rue de l'Ile Napoleon, pg. 1092   IT

Robaix

DAMART S.A., 25 Ave de La Fosse aux Chenes, pg. 376   IT
Damart Serviposte S.A., 25 Rue de La fosse aux Chenes, pg. 376   IT

Roche-Lez-Beaupre

BASF Horticulture et Jardin S.A., Zone Industrielle, pg. 106   IT

Rochecorbon

Sunrise Medical, pg. 1536   PB

Rochefort

Dusolier, pg. 1163   IT
Les Bois de la Baltique SA (Rochefort), Quai de l'Ecluse, Bassin no. 3, pg. 886   IT
Rochefort Plant, Z.I. Canal des Soeurs, pg. 673   PB

Rocquencourt

Mercedes-Benz France S.A., pg. 369   IT

Rodez

SocKalb G.I.E. France, 18 Rue de Sequret Saincric Siege Social, pg. 493   PB

Roissy

ACNA, Route du Midi, pg. 560   IT
Air France Finance, 45, rue de Paris, pg. 560   IT
Arenia, 45, rue de Paris, pg. 560   IT
Avesta Sheffield S.A., Le Done, 5, Rue de la Haye, pg. 222   IT
Barringer Europe, SARL, Villale Fret BAT-3435, pg. 192   PB
CESAF (Compagnie d'Exploitation des Services Auxiliaires Ferroviaires), 4, place de Londres Roissypole, pg. 560   IT
Calberson Overseas, 64 avenue de la Plaine de France, pg. 549   IT
Clarion France S.A., Z.I. Paris Nord II, 74, rue de la Belle Etoile, pg. 296   IT
Fuji Hunt Photographic Chemicals (France) S.A.R.L., 69 Rue de la Belle Etoile, pg. 524   PB
GROUPE AIR FRANCE, 45 Rue de Paris, pg. 559   IT
Groupe Servair (Compagnie d'Exploitation des Services Auxiliaires Aeriens), 4, place de Londres Roissypole, pg. 560   IT
Johnson Matthey SA, BP 50240, pg. 714   IT
Kintetsu World Express (France) S.A., Zone de Fret 4, 4 Rue du Te, pg. 735   IT
Ortho Clinical Diagnostic S.A., ZAC Paris Nord II, pg. 931   PB
Revima, Sogerma, Socca Logistic Center, pg. 560   IT
Ste Immobiliere Aeroportuaire, 45, rue de Paris, pg. 560   IT
Sharp Electronics France S.A., 22, Ave. des Nations, pg. 1230   IT
Sodetair, Rue du Tarteret, Zone Fret 1, pg. 560   IT
Sodexi, 14, rue des Voyelles, B.P. 10301, pg. 560   IT
Thomainfor, 167, rue de la Belle Etoile, pg. 1382   IT
Thomintex, Zone de fret 4, bat. 3447, 7, rue du Te, pg. 1382   IT

PB - *U.S. Public Companies Volume*
PV - *U.S. Private Companies Volume*
IT - *International Public & Private Companies Volume*

1596

Geographic Index-Non U.S.

Roissy Charles de Gaulle

BACOU S.A., OZI Paris North 2, 13 Rue de Perclerix, pg. 132
Circle Freight International France, S.A., Zone De Fret 4-Roissytech, 4, Rue Du Cercle, pg. 372 **PB**
Frionor France SARL, 4, Place De Londres, pg. 516 **PB**
Hewlett-Packard France, 45, Rue des 3 Soeurs, Centre d'Affaires Paris Nord II, pg. 820 **PB**
Livingston International Freight, Zone De Fret 4-Roisseytech, 4, Rue Du Cercle, pg. 373 **PB**
Nippon Express France, S.A., 20, rue du Trait d'Union, pg. 934 **IT**
OCG Microelectronic Materials S.A., ZAC Paris-Nord II, 209, avenue des Nations, pg. 1220
Olin S.A., ZAC Paris Nord 11-209, Ave. des Nations,B.P. 60019, pg. 1220
S.W. Airfreight, pg. 373 **PB**
WAGO Contact SARL, 214 Allee des Erables, Paris Nord 11, pg. 209 **IT**

Roissy-en-Brie

Binks International, France, ZAC de la Vallee 28, rue Antoine Lavoisier, pg. 229 **PB**

Romainville

Nokia Display Products, 97, Avenue de Verdun, pg. 951 **IT**
Nokia France S.A., 97, Avenue de Verdun, pg. 954 **IT**
Nokia Mobile Phones France, 97, Avenue de Verdun, pg. 952 **IT**
Nokia Telecommunications, 97, Avenue de Verdun, pg. 953 **IT**
Roussel UCLAF S.A., 102 Route de Noisy, pg. 626 **IT**
SAFT, 156 avenue de Reliz, pg. 54 **IT**

Romans

Moore Products Co. (France) SARL, Usine des Ors, pg. 1129 **PB**

Romilly-sur-Seine

CYCLES EUROPE, 193 rue Gabriel Peri, pg. 350 **IT**

Ronchin

E.C.L., 100, rue Chalant, pg. 1028 **IT**

Rosny-sous-Bois

ABS Pompes S.A., 14, Rue Montgolfier, pg. 270 **IT**
B.H.V. Rosny II, Centre Commercial, pg. 181 **IT**
Banninger France, Immeuble P H Spaak, 12 rue Jules Ferry, pg. 391 **IT**
Bohler Aciers Speciaux S.A.R.L., 13 Rue Montgolfier, pg. 1471 **IT**
Doret S.A., 8 Rue Montgolfier, pg. 154 **PB**
Kellogg's Produits Alimentaires, S.A., Bureaux de Rosny 2, pg. 948 **PB**
Ovako Acier S.A., rue de Rome, pg. 1157 **IT**
Panduit S.N.C., 91 Blvd. Alsace Lorraine, pg. 836 **PV**
Thermon France, 91 Boulevard d'Alsace Lorraine, pg. 1081 **PV**
Toshiba Electronics France S.A.R.L., Immeuble Robert Schumann, pg. 1406 **IT**

Roubaix

Banque Regionale du Nord, 50 boulevard du General de Gaulle, pg. 548 **IT**
Establis. Platt Freres S.A., pg. 268 **IT**
EURO RSCG Nord, 215 avenur Le Notre -BP 17, pg. 601 **IT**

Rouen

Credit Industriel de Normandie, 15, Place de la Pucelle, pg. 564 **IT**
Les Bois de la Baltique SA, pg. 886 **IT**
Lubrizol France S.A., B.P. 1062, pg. 1016 **PB**
Mutuelle Phoceenne Assurance, pg. 19 **IT**
SNTR Calberson Rouen, pg. 1164 **IT**

Rouillac

Renault Bisquit, Domaine de Ligneres, pg. 566 **IT**

Rousset

Fardem SA, Zone Industrielle, Reynier Rousset, pg. 353 **IT**

Roye

Sucrerie de Roye, pg. 549 **IT**

Rueil-Malmaison

AGA S.A., 140, avenue Paul Doumer, pg. 13 **IT**
Acheson France S.A., 4, Passage Saint-Antoine, pg. 12 **PV**
Agfa-Gevaert S.A., 274-276 av. Napoleon Bonaparte, pg. 174 **IT**
Alo-Jidac S.A., 81, rue de l'industrie, pg. 518 **IT**
Aqualon France B.V., Tour Corosa, 3 r Eugene et Armand Peugeot, pg. 810 **PB**
S.A. Arkovet, 8, rue Lionel Terray, pg. 974 **IT**
Chambourcy S.A., pg. 920 **IT**
CHARBONNAGES DE FRANCE, 100 Avenue Albert 1er, pg. 280 **IT**
CIBA Inter Marketing, 4, Allee Armand Camus, pg. 980 **IT**
CIBA Sante Amimale, 8, rue Lionel Terray, pg. 981 **IT**
Coverland S.A., Ariane, 2, rue Jacques Daguerre, pg. 1092 **IT**
Credit Ford S.A., 344 Ave. Napoleon Bonaparte, pg. 666 **PB**
DSI Group, 3, rue Eugene et Armand Peugeot, pg. 52 **IT**
Degremont Inc., 183, ave. du 18 juin 1940, pg. 822 **IT**
Det Norske Veritas, 10, rue Lionel Terray, pg. 397 **IT**
ENS Group, 3, rue Eugene et Armand Peugeot, pg. 52 **IT**
EPEX Group, 3, rue Eugene et Armand Peugeot, pg. 52 **IT**
EPPC Polyplastic S.A., 140 Ave. Paul Doumer, pg. 752 **PB**
Esso Societe Anonyme Francaise, 2 Rue des Martinets, pg. 602 **PB**
Fina France S.A., 8, rue Henri Ste-Claire Deville, pg. 1043 **IT**
Ford France S.A., 344 Ave. Napoleon Bonaparte, pg. 666 **PB**
Fuchs Lubrificants Industrie S.A., 81, rue de l'Industrie, pg. 517 **IT**
Holmen Papers, 118 Avenue Paul Doumer, pg. 885 **IT**
Hydro Aluminium France s.n.c., Neuf, Avenue Alexandre Maistrasse, pg. 962 **IT**
IPEDEX, 366, av. Napoleon Bonaparte, pg. 1361 **IT**
ITS Group, 3, rue Eugene et Armand Peugeot, pg. 53 **IT**
G.I.E. Ipedex International, 366, Ave. Napoleon Bonaparte, pg. 1361 **IT**
Kao Corporation (France) SARL, 2 rue Eugene et Armand Peugeot, pg. 718 **IT**
La Quinoleine et Ses Derives S.A., 4, Allee Armand Camus, pg. 983 **IT**
Laboratoires Alcon S.a.r.l., Rue henti Sainte-Claire Deville, pg. 920 **IT**
Laboratoires CIBA-GEIGY S.A., 2 & 4, rue Lionel Terray, pg. 983 **IT**
Laboratoires Sandoz S.a.r.l., pg. 983 **IT**
Laboratoires Zyma S.A., Tour Albert 1er, 65 Avenue de Colmar, pg. 983 **IT**
Makhteshim-Agan France S.a.r.l., 120 Avenue Paul Doumer, pg. 830 **IT**
NAT, 212, avenue Paul Doumer, pg. 1360 **IT**
Polysius S.A., 30, Boulevard Bellerive, pg. 512 **IT**
Produits Sandoz S.A., pg. 983 **IT**
RIBER, 133 Blvd. National, pg. 1114 **IT**
Sandoz Chimie S.A., pg. 984 **IT**
Sandoz France S.A., pg. 984 **IT**
Shell Chimie, 23-25 Ave. de la Republique, pg. 1138 **IT**
Sigma Coatings S.A., 10, rue Henri Ste-Claire Deville, pg. 1044 **IT**
Societe Anonyme CIBA-GEIGY, 2 & 4, rue Lionel Terray, pg. 983 **IT**
Societe d'Application des Techniques Linde S.A.R.L., pg. 811 **IT**
Societe des Petroles Shell, 89 Boulevard Franklin Roosevelt, pg. 1138 **IT**
Societe Internationale d'Ingenierie et de Maintenance S.A. (2IM), avenue de Colmar, pg. 1361 **IT**
Sodra France SA, 140 avenue Paul-Doumer, pg. 1276 **IT**
Sogebra S.A., 19 Rue des Deux Gares, pg. 608 **IT**
Thermal Ceramics de France S.A., 9-11 Rue du Colonel, pg. 894 **IT**
Valluy S.A.R.L., 87, rue de l'Industrie, pg. 518 **IT**
Werner & Pfleiderer France S.A.R.L., 30, Blvd. Bellerive, pg. 511 **IT**

Rumilly

Beaud-Challes-Solap S.A., 9, rue de l'industrie, pg. 430 **IT**
Lait Mont Blanc S.A., Cinq, rue Dumont Blanc, pg. 920 **IT**
Tefal S.A., pg. 569 **IT**

Rungis

Air Charter, 4, rue de la Couture, pg. 560 **IT**
B.H.V. Belle-Epine, C.C. Belle-Epine, pg. 181 **IT**
COBE S.A., 37 Place de la Loire, pg. 667 **IT**
Datapoint S.A., 1 Rue du Jura, pg. 384 **IT**
Emerson Electric (France) S.A., 1 Place des Etats Unis, pg. 576 **PB**
Gensym S.A., 22 rue Saarinen, pg. 731 **PB**
Graco S.A., 113-117 Rue des Solets, pg. 757 **PB**
Harris SARL-Scientific Calculations, 2 Place Gustave Riffel, pg. 791 **PB**
Honeywell-Measurex S.A.R.L., 8 Rue des Pyrenees, pg. 834 **PB**
Intercontrole S.A., 13 rue du Cabricaine, pg. 1361 **IT**
Intergraph Computer Systems, 95-101 Rue des Solets, pg. 891 **PB**
Jet Chandler International, 18 rue Saarinen, pg. 560 **IT**
Livingston S.A., 8 rue Esterel, pg. 212 **IT**
Mannesmann Kienzle S.A., pg. 839 **IT**
Materials Research S.A., Immeuble Berne, 3 Rue Le Corbusier, pg. 1283 **IT**
Mattel France S.A., 10 Bis Rue des Oliviers Senia 333, pg. 1059 **PB**
Moog S.A.R.L., 38 rue du Morvan, pg. 1128 **PB**
Neste Chemicals Holding France S.A., 3, place Gustav Eiffel, pg. 914 **IT**
RMC France S.A., 2, Rue du Verseau, pg. 1081 **IT**
Redland France S.A., 18 rue Saarinen-Silic 261, pg. 1093 **IT**
Redland Granulats SA, 18 rue Saarinen-Silic 261, pg. 1093 **IT**
Robinson Milling Systems S.A., pg. 232 **IT**
Rohm Electronics (France) S.A.S., 24 Rue Saarinen, Silic 224, pg. 1125 **IT**
Rosemount S.A.R.L., Cilip 265, 1, Place des Etats Unis, pg. 577 **IT**
Societe d'Exploitation Aeronautique, 4, rue de la Couture, pg. 560 **IT**
Sogelerg, 25 rue Pont des Halles, pg. 54 **IT**
Trinova Aeroquip Div., 14 Rue Du Morvan, pg. 25 **PB**
Zep Europe B.V., Batiment Dublin, Llot 6-Leretage 2, Rue Nicolas, pg. 1160 **PB**

Sable-sur-Sarthe

Sabim, pg. 563 **IT**

Saint Aignan

Georget S.A., Rue Rene Fonck, Zone D2A Nantes-Atlantique, pg. 371 **IT**

Saint Amand-les-Eaux

Produits Chimiques du Nord (PCN), 8, route de Lille, pg. 789 **IT**
Sienor, B.P. 89, ZAC 3 Parc Activities Jean Monnet, pg. 192 **IT**

Saint Aubin

Charles River France S.A., 59, rue de la Paix, pg. 195 **PB**
Herlitz S.A., 6, rue St. Louis, pg. 616 **IT**
Manopa Manufacture Normande de Papeterie, 6, rue Saint-Louis, pg. 616 **IT**
Nortech SA, Zac des Feugrais, Rue des Novalles, pg. 1242 **IT**
OREG, Z.I. des Barillettes, 200 Rue des Barillettes, pg. 378 **IT**
Protac, Route d'Ardon, pg. 1382 **IT**
TDA Armenents S.A.S., pg. 367 **IT**

Saint Berthevin

Etablissement Robert Bellanger S.A., B.P. 46-LaCroix des Landes, pg. 1579 **PB**

Saint Christol-les-Ales

Saint-Christol-Lez-Ales Office, Route de Montpellier, pg. 784 **IT**

Saint Clair

Benoist Girard & Cie S.C.A., 203 Boulevard del la Grande Delle, pg. 1283 **IT**

Saint Cloud

Auxitrol S.A., 168, Bureaux de la Colline, pg. 594 **PB**
BMC Software France, 260, Bureaux de la Colline Batiment E, pg. 162 **PB**
Etablissement de Saint-Cloud, 78 Quai Marcel Dassault, pg. 383 **IT**
Division Equipements Dassault (DED), 78, Quai Marcel Dassault, pg. 383 **IT**
Girpi, 12-18 Avenue de la Jonchere, pg. 430 **IT**
IVAC France S.A.R.L., 203 Bureaux de la Colline, pg. 35 **PB**
Kimberly-Clark Sopalin S.A., B.P. 201, pg. 959 **PB**
Lafarge Ciments, 5 blvd. Louis-Loucheur, pg. 788 **IT**
Lilly France S.A., 203 Bureaux de la Colline, pg. 994 **PB**
MAN GHH France Societe Anonyme, 119 Bureaux Colline, pg. 824 **IT**
NIFE France S.A., Avenue Caroline, pg. 53 **IT**
OCE-France Financement S.A., pg. 994 **IT**
Physio-Control S.A.R.L., 203 Bureaux de la Colline, pg. 1294 **PB**
Societe Mediterraneenne d'Emballages, 25, Rue Michel Salles, pg. 906 **PB**
Societe Normande de Carton Ondule, 25, Rue Michel Salles, pg. 906 **PB**
VCF (Video Communication France), 48 Quai Carnot, pg. 562 **IT**
Vulnax International Ltd., 321 Bureau de la Colline, pg. 47 **IT**

Saint Denis

Akzo Coatings SA, Tour Akzo 164, Rue Ambroise Croizat, pg. 43 **IT**
Akzo Zout Chemie France Sarl, Tour Akzo, 164 Rue Ambroise Croizat, pg. 44 **IT**
Arami France Sarl, Tour Akzo, 164 Rue Ambroise Croizat, pg. 45 **IT**
Bang & Olufsen France S.A., 19 Rue des Bretons, pg. 194 **IT**
Bausch & Lomb France S.A., Route de Levis Saint Nom, pg. 195 **PB**
Buss Waeschle Sarl, 103-113 rue Charles Michels, pg. 490 **IT**
Caterpillar Commercial S.A.R.L., 2, Blvd. de La Liberation, pg. 317 **PB**
Caterpillar Finance France S.A., 2 ave. de la Liberation, pg. 315 **PB**
Enka France SARL, Tour Akzo, 164 Rue Ambroise Croizat, pg. 46 **IT**

Geographic Index-Non U.S.

Insert France, 6 Boulevard de la Liberation, pg. 451 — IT
Laboratoires Fumouze S.A., 1 Rue Mechin, pg. 310 — PB
Mars Petfoods (UNISABI), Boite Postale No. 7, pg. 707 — PV
MONNOYEUR SCA, 117 rue Charles Michels, pg. 888 — IT
Nozal S.A., 132 Av. du Pdt. Wilson, pg. 570 — IT
Organon SA, Tour Akzo, 164 Rue Ambroise Croizat, pg. 45 — IT
Prodair, S.A., Tour Pleyel Centre Paris-Pleyel, pg. 32 — PB
S.E.M.T. Pielstick S.A., pg. 367 — IT
SLPM, pg. 571 — IT
SPCI Societe de Produits Chimiques Industriels SA, 43, Rue Christino Garcia, pg. 682 — IT
Siemens S.A., 39,47 Blvd. Ornano, pg. 1247 — IT
Tratel, 15 Quai de Chatelier, pg. 292 — IT
Unibeton, 15 Quai du Chatelier, pg. 292 — IT
Unimix, 15 Quai du Chatelier, pg. 292 — IT
Warner-Jenkinson France, B.P. 65, 2 Rue de la Montjoie, pg. 1696 — PB

Saint Didier

Electronic Arts S.A., Centre d'Affaire Telebase, 3 Rue Claude Chappe, pg. 569 — PB

Saint Die

Cinram France East, Z.I. des Paitoutes, Sainte Marguerite, pg. 293 — IT

Saint Dizier

Etilam-Gravigny, pg. 571 — IT
Ferro France S.a.r.l., 43 rue Jeanne D'Arc, pg. 619 — PB
Galle, pg. 1164 — IT
Sumitomo Chemical Agro Europe S.A., Parc d'Affaires de Telebase, 2, rue Claude Chappe, pg. 1311 — IT

Saint Egreve

SNTR Calberson, pg. 1164 — IT
Thomson-CSF Semiconducteurs Specifiques, Avenue de Rocheplaine, pg. 1382 — IT
Thomson Tubes Electroniques, pg. 1383 — IT

Saint Etienne

Ste. Andernoisienne de Distribution, pg. 563 — IT
Atomic France S.A., pg. 73 — IT
Auto-Service, pg. 563 — IT
Bonmets, pg. 563 — IT
Caf Casino, pg. 563 — IT
Carmag, pg. 563 — IT
Casino France, pg. 563 — IT
Casino-Guichard Perrachon & Cie, 24, rue de la Montat, pg. 562 — IT
Casino Rhone-Alpes, pg. 563 — IT
Chapelle Darblay Grand Couronne S.A., Rue Desire-Granet, pg. 1430 — IT
Claden, pg. 563 — IT
Cladevi, pg. 563 — IT
Dune, pg. 563 — IT
Dynamic S.A., B.P. 9, pg. 73 — IT
Euro-Bell S.A., Zone Industrielle du Galing, Rue Mathieu Vallat, pg. 207 — PB
Gem, pg. 563 — IT
Germinal, pg. 563 — IT
GROUPE CASINO, 24, Rue de la Montat, pg. 562 — IT
Houilleres de Bassin du Centre et du Midi, 4 Square Francois Margand, pg. 280 — IT
S.A. Immobiliere du Casino, pg. 563 — IT
La Ruche Meridionale, pg. 563 — IT
La Societe Stephanoise des Eaux, 28, rue Eugene Beaune, pg. 824 — IT
Messidor, pg. 563 — IT
Paradis, pg. 563 — IT
Pribas, pg. 563 — IT
Rockwell SVI S.A., 24, rue Scheurer Kestner, pg. 1402 — PB
Serca, pg. 563 — IT
Sodipra, pg. 563 — IT
Soreso, pg. 563 — IT
TPLM, pg. 563 — IT
Unimas, pg. 563 — IT

Saint Etienne-du-Rouvray

Chapelle Darblay Saint Etienne S.A., Rue Desire-Granet, pg. 1430 — IT
Comptoir Normand de Produits Verriers (CNPV), Z.I. secteur D, pg. 1170 — IT
Sodipan S.A., pg. 673 — PB

Saint Fargeau

Sidobre-Sinnova S.A., 185, Avenue de Fontainebleau, pg. 614 — IT

Saint Florentin

Alusuisse France Produits Industriels S.A., pg. 68 — IT

Saint Fons

CIBA-GEIGY SA, Usines de Saint-Fons, Boite Postale 47, pg. 979 — IT

Saint Gely-du-Fesc

Saint Gely Du Fesc Office, Zone Artisanale, pg. 785 — IT

Saint Genis Laval

B.H.V. St-Genis-Laval, C.C. 101 rue de Vourles, pg. 181 — IT

Saint Georges

NT Meridian S.A., 15 av. Alexander Graham Bell, pg. 970 — IT
Nortel France S.A., Parc Leonard de Vinci, 15 av. Alexander Graham Bell, pg. 793 — IT
Societe Cilile Immobiliere Demag, pg. 837 — IT

Saint Georges-de-Reneins

Societe Nouvelle Jules Pellerin SA, pg. 753 — IT

Saint Germain-en-Laye

Bose S.A.R.L., 6 Rue St. Vincent, pg. 161 — PV
Kamyr S.A., 32 rue du Vieil Abreuvoir, pg. 771 — IT
Kvaerner Pulping SA, 32 rue de Vieil Abrevoir, pg. 768 — IT
Lorentzen & Wettre S.A.R.L., 91, Rue Pereire, pg. 271 — IT
Pall Biomedical France, 3 Rue Des Gaudines, pg. 1254 — PB
Pall France S.A., 3, Rue Des Gaudines, BP 253, pg. 1254 — PB
Sandoz Agro S.A., pg. 984 — IT

Saint Germain-Lembron

Auda S.A., Le Breull-sur-Couze, pg. 430 — IT

Saint Gervais-d'Auvergne

Chateauneuf-les-Bains S.A., pg. 918 — IT

Saint Hippolyte-du-Fort

Jallatte S.A., rue du Fort, pg. 430 — IT

Saint Jean-de-Maurienne

Societe des Poudres et Produits Speciaux Hermillon, pg. 1029 — IT

Saint Jeoire

Societe Nouvelle de Chimie Industrielle (SNCI), pg. 986 — IT

Saint Julien de Peyrolas

Sefcal S.A., pg. 289 — IT

Saint Just

Matthey Beyrand & Cie S.A., pg. 714 — IT

Saint Just-Saint Rambert

Verreries de Saint-Just, pg. 1172 — IT

Saint Laurent-de-Mure

SAS, 15, avenue Jean Moulin, pg. 430 — IT

Saint Leu d'Esserent

Societe Specialisee dans le Materiel d'Imprimerie (SSMI), ZI du Sous-Biscain, pg. 1517 — PB

Saint Leu-la-Foret

Spirol S.A., 2, Rue Charles Cros -ZAE-, pg. 1026 — PV

Saint Louis

SNT Ncyon, pg. 1164 — IT

Saint Maur-des-Fosses

Dicalite France, S.A., Bvld. de Creteil,163, pg. 903 — PV
LTX France S.A., 50 Blvd. Rabelais, pg. 972 — PB
Lawson Mardon Cerlive S.A., pg. 68 — IT
Lawson Mardon Charmettes S.A., pg. 68 — IT

Saint Mesmin

Jade S.A., 7, Route d'Orleans, 45380 La Chapelle, pg. 859 — IT

Saint Michel-sue-Meurethe

Bertranc Faure Equipements SA, Nompatelize, pg. 192 — IT

Saint Mihiel

Albright & Wilson Saint Mihiel S.A., Boite Postale 19, pg. 50 — IT
Marchon France S.A., Hans-sur-Meuse, pg. 1580 — PB

Saint Nazaire

Det Norske Veritas, Quai des Fregates, pg. 397 — IT
Eaton S.A. Transmission Div., Zone Industrielle de Brais, Boite Postal 224, pg. 559 — IT
Fabrications Mecaniques de l'Atlantique (FAMAT SA), Zone Industrielle de Brais, pg. 1166 — IT

Saint Nicolas-de-Redon

Bertrand Faure Equipements SA, Rue de Tabago, pg. 192 — IT

Saint Ouen

Robert Bosch (France) SA, B.P. 170, pg. 205 — IT
Eldon France, Energy Park 4, 155-159 Rue du Dr. Bauer, pg. 436 — IT
Sonauto S.A., 1, Ave. Du Fief Z. A. des Bethunes, pg. 1063 — IT
TEMPO SANYS S.A., 4, rue Albert Dhalenne, pg. 1333 — PB
Valeo-Clutches, 15, rue des Rosiers, pg. 240 — IT
Valeo Distribution, 15, rue des Rosiers, pg. 240 — IT

Saint Ouen-l'Aumone

Airborne, 50 rue Andrion, pg. 569 — IT
Krupp Techniques Industrielles S.A., 3, allee Saint-Simon, pg. 510 — IT
Loc Manutention, Avenue de Vert Galant, pg. 834 — IT
NIKE France S.A.R.L., Ave. Fies Zi Des Bethens, pg. 1184 — PB
Scania France S.A., Zone Indus. Les Bethunes, Rue de Lequerre, pg. 687 — IT
Sealed Air Systems, Z.A. des Bethunes, 3, Avenue de la Mare, pg. 1451 — PB
Telma Plant, pg. 786 — IT
Telma Retarder Division, Parc Moderne d'Entreprises, 28, rue Paul Painleve, pg. 786 — IT
Valeo Security Systems, 15 rue des Rosaers, pg. 240 — IT
Vickers Systems Div., pg. 25 — PB

Saint Priest

ABB Petercem S.A., 61, route de Grenoble, pg. 2 — IT
Esco, S.A., Boite Postal 229, pg. 383 — PV
Ilford Anitec SA, pg. 906 — PB
Jielde S.A., Parc de la Bandonniere, pg. 821 — IT

Saint Quentin

Ancra International Sarl, 36, Rue De La Haye, pg. 71 — PV
Intel Europe, pg. 887 — PB
Lafarge Coppee Recherche-GIE, 95 rue du Montmurier, pg. 789 — IT
SACOC, Z1 de Rouvroy Morcourt, pg. 72 — IT
Societe Generale pour les Techniques Nouvelles S.A. (SGN), 1, rue des Herons, pg. 1361 — IT
Unelec S.A., Route de Guise, pg. 546 — IT

Saint Quentin-en-Yvelines

BOUYGUES, 1, Ave. Eugene Freyssinet, pg. 206 — IT
CITRA, pg. 1163 — IT
C.M.C. SA, Montigny le Bretonneux, pg. 792 — IT
Esselte Meto SNC, 1, rue Jean Pierre Timbaud, pg. 461 — IT
Honeywell, 4 avenue Ampere, pg. 834 — PB
Labinal Aero Systems Division, pg. 786 — IT
Laboratoires Terumo France S.A., Immueble Intl., pg. 1376 — IT
Lotus Development, SA, Blvd. de Chiens, pg. 896 — PB
Matra MS2i, BP 235, 38, boulevard Paul Cezanne, pg. 793 — IT
MERINOS, 2 bis rue Stephenson, pg. 858 — IT
PDA International France, pg. 1031 — PB
Siges, B.P. 140, pg. 1274 — IT
Societe Generale pour les Techniques Nouvelles (SGN), Reseau Eurisys-1, rue des Herons, pg. 305 — IT
Sodexho France Ecoles-Universites, pg. 1274 — IT
Sodexho France Entreprises-Administrations, pg. 1274 — IT
Sodexho France Hotellerie-Sante, pg. 1274 — IT
USSI Ingenierie, 15, Place Georges-Pompidou, pg. 305 — IT

Saint Remy-les-Chevreuse

Societe Chantilly, 12, Chemin de la Messe Saint Lambert Des, pg. 919 — IT
Source du Val Saint Lambert, 12, Chemin de la Messe Saint Lambert des, pg. 919 — IT

Saint Sauveur

Compagnie Europeenne de Dezingage "C.E.D." S.A., Zone Industrielle no. 4, pg. 754 — IT
Hilleshog NK S.A., pg. 982 — IT
Northrup King Semences S.A., pg. 983 — IT

Saint Sebastien

Georges Renoult S.A., 199, route de Clisson, pg. 96 — IT

Saint Seurin-sur-L'Isle

Papeteries R. Soustre & Fils S.A., pg. 458 — IT

PB - U.S. Public Companies Volume
PV - U.S. Private Companies Volume
IT - International Public & Private Companies Volume

1598

Saint Thibery

Saint Thibery, Zil du Causse, pg. 785   IT

Saint Valery-en-Caux

Vibratechniques, pg. 1324   IT
Vibratechniques STV, Route de Neville, pg. 1420   IT

Saint Vallier

SARMA, Parc Industruel La Brassiere, pg. 1158   IT

Saint Vulbas

Speichim-Processing, Parc Industriel Plaine, de l'Ain, Allee du Bois-des-Terres, pg. 1360   IT

Saint Yorre

France St.-Yorre, Avenue des Sources, pg. 919   IT

Saint-Andre-lez-Lille

Compagnie Generale De Chauffe, 37, ave. du Marechal de Lattre de Tassig, pg. 321   IT

Saint-Apollinaire

Thomson-CSF Passive Components, Avenue du Colonel-Prat, pg. 1382   IT

Saint-Barthelemy-d'Anjou

MO Pays-de-Loire, pg. 1172   IT

Saint-Brice-sous-Foret

Lista France S.A., pg. 812   IT

Saint-Brieuc

MO Semiver-Climaver, Rue d'Alembert, pg. 1172   IT

Saint-Germain-du-Puy

Castorama Bourges, 151 Route de la Charite, pg. 275   IT

Saint-Heand

Angenieux, pg. 1381   IT

Saint-Herblain

Defontaine S.A., 3, Rue Louis Renault, pg. 509   IT
Electro Navale Moteurs SAS, 334, Boulevard Marcel Paul, pg. 1387   IT
Entreprise Nouel, 125, rue Robert Schuman, pg. 788   IT
Matra Communication Ouest, Parc de l'Angeviniere, 10, rue Duguay-Trouin, pg. 793   IT
Matra Telecommunications Ouest-Normandie, Parc de l'Angeviniere, 10, rue Duguay-Trouin, pg. 793   IT
Waterman S.A., pg. 745   PB

Saint-Jean-Bonnefonds

SNTR Calberson St. Etienne, pg. 1164   IT

Saint-Jean-de-la-Ruelle

John Deere, 10 Rue du Paradis (Ormes), pg. 492   PB

Saint-Just-le-Martel

St. Just Mill, Usine de Sain Just, pg. 673   PB

Saint-Martin-du-Bosc

Herault Mining Division, pg. 305   IT

Saint-Martin-les-Boulogne

Communaute Boulonnaise de Developpement S.A., rue Pierre Martin, pg. 463   IT
Dhalenne Berguette S.C.I., rue Pierre Martin, pg. 463   IT
Dhalenne S.A., rue Pierre Martin, pg. 463   IT
Maes S.A., rue Pierre Martin, pg. 463   IT
Maes S.C.I., rue Pierre Martin, pg. 463   IT
Societe de Developpement des Supermarches P.G., rue Pierre Martin, pg. 463   IT
Societe D'Exploitation des Supermarches P.G. S.A., rue Pierre Martin, pg. 463   IT
Societe Vendinoise de Distribution, rue Pierre Martin, pg. 463   IT

Saint-Medard-en-Jalle

Sextant Avionique, Rue Toussaint-Castros, pg. 1382   IT

Saint-Menehould

Cotuplas S.A., Zone Industriele, pg. 1028   IT

Saint-Michel-sur-Orge

International Rectifier Company (Great Britain) Limited, 32, rue des Processions, pg. 907   PB

Saint-Nom-la-Breteche

P.C. Henderson (France) S.A., Parc D'Affairs, Trois rue de la Plaine, pg. 615   IT

Saint-Paul-les-Durance

Cadarache Fuel Fabrication Utility (CFCa), pg. 305   IT

Saint-Pierre-d'Allevard

Aimants Ugimag, BP 2, Avenue ol'Uriage, pg. 1028   IT

Saint-Pierre-des-Corps

Dusolier, pg. 1163   IT

Saint-Pierre d'Irude

Societe Industrielle et Salines de Bayonne S.A., Mouguerre, pg. 1279   IT

Saint-Remy-sur-Avre

TDA Armement, 15, rue Joliot Curie, pg. 1382   IT

Salaise-sur-Sanne

Eurofloat, Zone Industrielle et Portuaire, pg. 1172   IT

Salbris

SM5, Z.I. des Cousseaux, pg. 1382   IT

Salindres

La Chape liquide, 65, rue Henri Merle, pg. 788   IT
Skis Dynastar S.A., Route de Geneve, pg. 1127   IT

Saltatojo Furiani

Ersa, pg. 1164   IT

Santeny

Paretan Garoche, Route de Mandres, pg. 789   IT
SODAP-Ste d'application des syntheses techniques, Route de Mandres, pg. 789   IT

Sarcelles

Richard Hirschmann Electronique SA, 24, rue du Fer a Cheval, Z.I., pg. 1108   IT
Laboratoires Valdor SA, 13 bis. avenue de L'Escouvrier, pg. 1209   IT
Lance International S.A., 12 Ave. De L'Escouvrier, pg. 1116   IT
Rex-Rotary S.A., 12 Avenue de L'Escouvrier, pg. 1116   IT
Scholl SA, 13 Bis Avenue De L'Escouvrier, pg. 1210   IT

Sarrebourg

Lawson Mardon Morin S.A., pg. 68   IT
ETS Raffel Sarrebourg S.A., Zone Industrielle, pg. 88   IT
ETS Reinhard Raffel Galvanisation Sarl, Zone Industrielle, pg. 88   IT

Sarreguemines

Delco Remy Division, Rue de Sarreinsming, pg. 725   PB
Krupp Hazemag S.A., Z.I., Rue du champ de Mars, pg. 511   IT
Lagera S.a.r.l., 3, Av. de la Blies, B.P. No 112, pg. 1034   IT
Ondal-France S.a.r.l., rue du Champ de Mars, Terrain Industriel, pg. 1490   IT
SICUP SNC, pg. 328   IT

Sartrouville

Baasel Lasertech France SARL, pg. 836   IT
BRENNTAG FRANCE S.A., 1, Chemin du Pas de la Mule, pg. 1458   IT
Thomson-CSF Airsys, 17, quai Pierre-Brunel, pg. 1382   IT

Sassenage

GES, pg. 563   IT
Genty, pg. 563   IT

Sauitur

Royal Champignon, Chantemerle-Bagneux, pg. 567   IT

Saumur

Lucent Technologies BCS S.A., Zone Industrielle, Saint lambert de Levees, pg. 1019   PB

Sausheim

Bevaloid SA, Zone Indus. Napoleon, Ave. de Suisse, pg. 1113   IT

Sauveterre

Neste Polyester S.A., Quartier des Bonnelles, pg. 915   IT

Saverne

Precismeca S.A., pg. 399   IT

Savigny-le-Temple

Beiersdorf S.A., 1 rue des Sources, pg. 183   IT
DSM Engineering Plastic Products France, Zone Industrielle, Rue du Laiton, pg. 354   IT
Hydrogas France S.A., Zone Industrielle, (Parc d'activities), pg. 963   IT

Seclin

Autoliv S.A., B.P. 316-2.1., pg. 441   IT
Etablissement de Seclin, Zone Industrielle, pg. 383   IT
Gist-Brocades France S.A., 15, Rue des Comtesses, pg. 1143   IT
Gist-Brocades France S.A., 15 Rue des Comtesses, pg. 1142   IT

Selestat

Martel Catala et Cie, B.P. 88, pg. 37   PB

Selongey

Seb S.A., pg. 569   IT

Senlis

Asgrow France S.A., Avenue Felix Louat, pg. 1049   IT
Electrolux S.A., B.P. 139, pg. 441   IT
Lawson Mardon Packaging Sales SA, pg. 69   IT
Manelco S.A., pg. 69   IT
Tornado S.A., pg. 441   IT
Usines & Fonderies Arthur Martin S.A., "UFAM", B.P. 131, pg. 441   IT

Sens

Bayer Pharma S.A., Zone Industrielle, pg. 175   IT
Wella Paris Ets. Pelleray S.a.r.l., Bldg. du Pont Neuf, pg. 1490   IT

Serifontaine

Diosynth France SA, Usine Saint Charles, pg. 44   IT
Organon SA, Usine St. Charles, P.O. Box 6, pg. 45   IT

Serignan

Vendres, Embranchment route de Serignan, pg. 784   IT

Sermaises

Prochibat, ZI de Sermaises du Loiret, pg. 790   IT

Sete

Banque Dupuy de Parceval, 10, rue General de Gaulle, pg. 548   IT
EAC Timber (France) S.A., pg. 431   IT
Indubois S.A., pg. 431   IT
Omega Soufre, S.A., Manuelle Cancellut, 21 Les Eause Blanches, pg. 1279   IT
Sete Office, La Plagette, rue de la Claviere, pg. 785   IT

Seurre

Thomson-CSF Passive Components, 3, rue du Stade, pg. 1382   IT

Sevigne

Analog Devices SA, 2A, Rue de la Rigaudier, pg. 108   PB

Sevran

Enraf Nonius S.A., 15, Rue Paul Langevin, ZAC Les Beaudottes, pg. 389   IT
Nucletron Sarl, 15, Rue Paul Langevin, ZAC Les Beaudottes, pg. 389   IT
Pumpex S.A.R.L., 4-6 Boulevard Westinghouse, pg. 271   IT
SAB WABCO S.A., 4 Boulevard Westinghouse, pg. 271   IT
SAB WABCO Group Systems Centre, 4, Boulevard Westinghouse, pg. 271   IT
WABCO Westinghouse Equipements Ferroviaires S.A., 2 Blvd. Westinghouse, pg. 92   PB

Sevres

Hueppe SARL, Les Postillons Des Bruyeres, 65 Rue de la Galenne, pg. 1054   PB

Metsa-Serla Tissue S.a.r.l., 72-78 Grande Rue, pg. 864   IT
Tandem Computers S.A., 1 Avenue de la Cristallerie,
    pg. 418   PB

Seynod

Sadem, pg. 563   IT

Silic

Cyanamid France, 74 Rue d'Arcueil Centre, pg. 81   PB
Laboratories Lederle SA, 74 Rue d'Arcueil Centre,
    pg. 81   PB
Neste Chimie France S.N.C., 3, Place Gustave Eiffel,
    pg. 914   IT

Sines

Borealis Polimeros S.A., Monte Feio, pg. 914   IT

Sissonne

Sylea Harness Assembly Plant, pg. 785   IT

Soissons

Etirex S.A., Noyant Et Aconin, pg. 577   PB

Solesmes

Affival S.A., 70, Rue de l'Abbaye, pg. 1466   IT

Somain

Sotexo, ZI de la Renaissance, pg. 192   IT

Sophia Antipolis

Swedbank (Luxembourg) S.A., 2229 Route des Cretes,
    pg. 1328   IT
Thomson Microsonics, 399, route des Cretes, pg. 1383   IT
Thomson Sintra Activites Sous-Marines, 525, route des
    Dolines, 1383   IT
Thomson Sintra ASM, B.P. 57, pg. 1383   IT
Underwater Defense Systems International, 525, route des
    Dolines, pg. 1383   IT

Sorges

Lafarge PlatresInternational, 5 Avenue de l'Egalite,
    pg. 789   IT
Lafarge Prestia, 5 av. de l'Egalite, pg. 790   IT

Sorgues

Sorgues Office, ZI-Lot no 25-BP 63, pg. 785   IT

Sotteville

Plastilon France S.A., 4, rue Jean Sibelius, pg. 915   IT

Soultz

Gunther S.A., pg. 1186   IT
Sharp Manufacturing France S.A., Route de Bollwiller,
    pg. 1230   IT

Strasbourg

B.H.V. Strasbourg, C.C. - 24 Place des Halles, pg. 181   IT
Banque Leumi France S.A.-Strasbourg, One Rue du Vieux
    Marche aux Vins, pg. 150   IT
Banque Veuve Morin-Pons, 1, Avenue de la Liberte,
    pg. 419   IT
Blackhawk S.A., Centre Eurofiet Rue du Rheinfeld,
    pg. 805   PB
Calberson International Strasbourg, pg. 1163   IT
Carpap Libert SA, pg. 757   IT
Clestra Hauserman, 56 Rue Jean Giraudoux, pg. 569   IT
Compagnie Generale de Prevoyance, 1 rue des
    Arquebusiers, pg. 60   IT
Cosmeurop S.A., 21 rue de l'Elfterrain, pg. 295   IT
Credit Industriel D'Alsace et de Lorraine, 31, Rue Jean
    Wenger-Valentin, pg. 564   IT
Deutsche Bank AG (Strasbourg), 6, Avenue de la Liberte,
    pg. 405   IT
Dove Europe, pg. 707   PV
EURO RSCG Est, 4 rue Chatrian, pg. 600   IT
Gebhardt SARL, 33 Route Des Romains, pg. 1054   PB
Herbalife International Belgium S.A./N.V., 21 rue de
    Cherbourg, pg. 809   PB
Herbalife International-Czechoslovakia, 10, Rue Alexandre
    Dumas, pg. 809   PB
Herbalife International France, S.A., 10 rue Alexandre
    Dumas, pg. 809   PB
Huron - Graffenstaden S.A., 156 Route de Lyon, 67400
    Illkirch, pg. 481   IT
Hydra-matic Division, B.P. 33, pg. 725   PB
Kesser, 15, rue des l'Industrie, pg. 206   IT
Kronenbourg, 68 Rte. D'Oberhausbergen, pg. 381   IT
Maechler Freres S.A., 100, Rue de la Plain de Bouchers,
    pg. 1459   IT
Nielsen Sarl, 91 Route des Romains, pg. 462   IT
Rhin et Moselle Assurances Compagnie d' Assurances sur
    la vie Societe Anonyme, 1, rue des Arquebusiers,
    pg. 61   IT

Rockwell Automation S.A., Batiment Prisme, 9A rue du
    Parc, pg. 1400   PB
Roulement Service S.A., 15 Rue Schertz, pg. 212   IT
SIPEC Ste Internationale de Petrole et de Chimie a r.l., B.P.
    29/R/1, 11 a 15, rue de la Premiere Armee,
    pg. 1167   IT
STAC Societe Technique D'application Chimique S.A., Rue
    de L'Espansion, Zone Industrial, pg. 429   IT
Steelcase Strafor, 56 rue Jean Giraudoux, pg. 569   IT
Steelcase-Strafor, 56 Rue Jean Giradoux,
    pg 1038   PV
Tektronix S.A.-Strasbourg, pg. 1568   IT
Wartsila Diesel International Ltd. Oy, 12 Quai Saint-Jean,
    pg. 863   IT

Surbourg

Forbo Participations SA, pg. 498   IT
Helmitin SA, pg. 498   IT

Suresnes

CFEM, pg. 571   IT
Chiron France S.a.r.l., 10, Rue Chevreul, pg. 350   PB
Compagnie Generale Maritime, 22 Quai Gallieri,
    pg. 322   IT
COMPAGNIE GENERALE MARITIME ET FINANCIERE, 22
    Quai Gallieni, pg. 322   IT
Dassault Systemes, 22-28, Avenue Du General De Galle,
    pg. 383   IT
FCA!BMZ, 26, rue Salomon de Rothschild, pg. 469   IT
FCA!EMZ France, 26, rue Salomon de Rothschild,
    pg. 469   IT
FCA!EMZ Paris, 26, rue Salomon de Rothschild,
    pg. 469   IT
Laboratoires de Therapeutique Moderne LTM S.A., 42,
    Rue Rouget de Lisle, pg. 1279   IT
Micro Warehouse France SARL, 6 Boulevard Henri Sellier,
    pg. 1104   PB
P.N.B. SA, 4, rue Jean Mace, pg. 1604   IT
Placoplatre S.A., 34 Ave. Franklin Roosevelt, pg. 123   IT
Renault V.I., 40 rue Pasteur, pg. 1102   PV
SRA Europe, SA., pg. 958   PV
Sogitec, 4, Rue Marcel Monge, pg. 383   IT
Symantec SARL, 31-35 Rue Gambetta, pg. 1546   PB
Syntha S.A., Rue Rouget de Lisle 42, pg. 1280   IT

Survilliers

Owens-Corning Fiberglas France S.A., 10, rue des Fers,
    pg. 1237   IT

Tarbes

Danzas, pg. 1163   IT
Hughes Tool S.A.F., Allee des Forges, pg. 167   PB
S.O.C.A.T.A.(Societe de Construction d'Avions de
    Tourismes et d'Affaires), pg. 29   IT

Tassin-la-Demi-Lune

Rockwell Automation S.A., Les Bureaux du Parc, 56,
    Boulevard du 11 Novembre, pg. 1400   PB
Visea 'THORN, Immeuble 'Le Valvert', 46 bis, Chemin du
    Vieux Moulin, pg. 1386   IT

Taverny

Gerber France, 89, Rue Carnot, pg. 973   IT
SARL Valacier, pg. 302   IT

Templemars

Amiland SA, pg. 275   IT
Briker SA, Z.I., pg. 275   IT
CASTORAMA DUBOIS INVESTISSEMENTS S.C.A., Zone
    Industrielle, pg. 275   IT
GIE Castorama Transports, Z.I. de Templemars,
    pg. 276   IT
Castowest, Z.I., pg. 275   IT
GIE Gettinor, Z.I., pg. 276   IT
N.F.I. France, Z.I. De Templemars, 15-B Rue De Plouvier,
    59175, pg 797   PV
N.F.I. France, Z.I. De Templemars, 15-B Rue De Plouvier,
    59175, pg. 1396   IT
Sous Groupe Castorama, Z.I. de Templemars, pg. 275   IT

Tergnier

Saint-Gobain Produits Industriels, Z.I. de Condren,
    pg. 172   IT

Thann

Thann et Mulhouse, 95 Rue du General De Gaulle,
    pg. 1111   PB

Thaon-les-Vosges

AlliedSignal Turbo S.A., Route D'Oncourt-ZI, pg. 53   PB

Thiais

BSL Incustries S.A., Tour Europa 114/Belle Epine,
    pg. 1134   IT
Rockwell-Collins France, S.A., Centre Commercial Belle
    Epine, Tour Europa, pg. 1400   PB

Thionville

Cedest Ciments, pg. 788   IT
ETS Fringand, Chemip Linkling, B.P. 86, pg. 1240   IT
Rhenania Compagnie Europeenne de Transports et
    d'affretement, 27, Rue Joffre, B.P. No. 429,
    pg. 1034   IT
SNLFT (Societe Nouvelle des Laminoirs a Froid de
    Thionville), pg. 571   IT
Societe Civile Immobiliere Kuntzig, pg. 302   IT
Societe Scholtes S.A., Route De Luxemborg 44,
    pg. 860   IT

Thonon-les-Bains

Societe des Eaux Minerales de Thonon-Les-Bains, La
    Grangette, pg. 919   IT
Thomson Tubes Electroniques, pg. 1383   IT

Thourotte

Sekurit Saint-Gobain France (SSGF), Rue du Marechal
    Joffre, pg. 1172   IT

Tinteniac

Sanden Manufacturing Europe S.A., Le Quilliou,
    pg. 1184   IT

Torcy

EuroKasco, Zone Industrielle Nord, Bat 1, Allee Du Plateau,
    pg. 165   PB

Toulon

ASM Ingenierie, Z.E. de la Farlede, 101, rue Pasteur,
    pg. 1381   IT
Cetia, 150, rue Marcellin Berthelot, pg. 1381   IT
Marine Industrie S.N.C., pg. 506   IT
Neutrogena Provence SARL, Rue de Rome, Parc
    d'Activites de Signes, pg. 928   PB
Peintures et Vernis de la Mediterranee, 31, avenue du
    General Pruneau, pg. 790   IT
SMAC, Z.I. Toulon Est, pg. 1382   IT
SNTR Calberson Toulon, pg. 1164   IT

Toulouse

AGA S.A., B.P. 3084, pg. 13   IT
AIR Training Center, 316 route de Bayonne, pg. 29   IT
Alcan France, 171 route d'Espagne, pg. 51   IT
Als Conseil, Immeuble Le Sirius, 239 route de Saint Simon,
    pg. 116   IT
Analog Devices SA, Buroplis 1, 150, Rue Nicolas
    Vauquelin, pg. 108   PB
Ateliers Sucre Liquide et Depot de Toulouse/Colomiers, 4,
    Chemin d'El Pey, pg. 549   IT
Bisseuil, 131, Ave. de Lespinet, B.P. 4059, pg. 206   IT
CIBA Vision Ophthalmics, 8 rue Colomies, Site Industriel,
    pg. 981   IT
CIBA Vision S.A., 8, rue Colomies, pg. 981   IT
Editions Edouard Privat SA, 14 rue des Arts, pg. 239   IT
EURO RSCG D 10, 61 Blvd. Carnot, pg. 600   IT
Extand, 56 boulevard de l'Embouchure, pg. 549   IT
Hewlett-Packard France, Innoparc, Voie No. 7, pg. 820   PB
L'Union Office, 241, route d'Albi, pg. 784   IT
Labinal Aero Plant, pg. 786   IT
Liebherr-Aerospace Toulouse S.A., Av. des Etats-Unis 408,
    pg. 808   IT
Makita France S.A.-Toulouse, 15, Rue de Boudeville,
    pg. 832   IT
Materials Research France, Z. E. De Thibald, Blvd. de Thib,
    pg. 1283   IT
Matra Communication Sud-West, 23, avenue Champollion,
    pg. 793   IT
Matra Telecommunications Sud-Ouest, 23, avenue
    Champollion, pg. 793   IT
Medicornea S.A., 16 rue Rivoli de, pg. 920   IT
Microturbo Division, Chemin du Pont de Rupe, pg. 786   IT
Motorola Semi Conducteurs (Societe), Z.I. Du Mirail,
    pg. 1140   PB
Pioneer France Mais S.A., 4, Rue Paul Bernies,
    pg. 1299   PB
Poliesa France S.A.R.L., pg. 1207   IT
Raisio France S.A., c/o SNPE, Etablissement de Toulouse,
    pg. 1086   IT
Rohr Europe, 22 Chemin de La Crabe, pg. 752   PB
SNC Alfa-Laval & Cie, Ste. Nouvelle SAEEC, pg. 1379   IT
SNTR Calberson Toulouse, pg. 1164   IT
TSO (Telephone du Sud-Ouest), 73, boulevard de
    Strasbourg, pg. 794   IT
Tektronix S.A.-Toulouse, pg. 1568   IT
Thomson-CSF Communications, 36 bis, chemin de Liffard,
    pg. 1382   IT
Thomson-CSF Services & Systemes Sol Spatiaux, 105,
    avenue du General Eisenhower, pg. 1383   IT
Thomson-CSF Services Industrie, 105, avenue du General
    Eisenhower, pg. 1383   IT

Tourcoing

La Blanche Porte S.C.S., pg. 1015   IT
Lawson Mardon Trenteusax SA, 200 Rue du Pont-Rompu,
    pg. 69   IT
Peignage de la Tossee, pg. 1502   PB
Standard Wool France, SA, pg. 1502   PB

PB - *U.S. Public Companies Volume*
PV - *U.S. Private Companies Volume*
IT - *International Public & Private Companies Volume*

1600

Geographic Index-Non U.S.

Thibeau, rue des Cinq Voies, pg. 1206   IT

Tournan-en-Brie

Dynapac S.A., Rue de l'industri, pg. 1420   IT
Svedala France, pg. 1324   IT

Tournefeuille

Lancer S.A., 30 Bd de l'Industrie, pg. 552   IT

Tournon

Impressions et Teintures de Tournon S.A., RN86, pg. 807   IT

Tournus

Dexter S.A., 14 rue Chanay, pg. 505   PB
Puicouyoul, pg. 1164   IT

Tours

Docks de France S.A., 32-36 Avenue Charle Bedaux, pg. 98   IT
Etoile Bleue, 20-22 rue Clocheville, pg. 600   IT
ZURITEL Compagnie d'Assurances, 67 rue Fromentel, pg. 1532   IT

Trappes

AST Research France S.A.R.L., Miniparc du Manet, Rue Gaston Montmousseau, pg. 1182   IT
Boart Longyear S.A., 1 Rue Blaise Pascal, Parc D'Activites de, pg. 76   IT
Compagnie Ingersoll-Rand S.A., 5-7 Avenue A Einstein, pg. 878   PB
Constructions Entreprises Generales, Imprefer S.A., 6 Rue Nicolas Copernic, pg. 482   IT
Cramiques Techniques Desmarquest, 2 Avenue Albert Einstein, pg. 1028   IT
Hellermann France SA, Miniparc du Manet, pg. 209   IT
IVECO FRANCE S.A., 6, rue Nicolas Copernic, pg. 696   IT
Iveco-Unic S.A., 6, rue Nicolas Copernic, pg. 484   IT
Linde Froid et Climatisation S.A.R.L., pg. 810   IT
Manitou Tous Terrains et Industriels, 1, rue Enrico-Fermi, pg. 834   IT
Mather & Platt Wormald S.A., 29 Ave. George Politzer, pg. 1650   PB
Matra Systeme, 4, rue Edourd Branly, pg. 793   IT
Minemet Recherche, 1 Ave. Albert Einstein, pg. 661   IT
Newport Electronique, S.A.R.L., 9, rue Denis Papin, pg. 816   PV
Nicolet Instrument S.A.R.L., Z.I. de Pissaloup, pg. 1594   PB
Nissan France S.A., Zone d'Activites du Parc de Pissaloup, pg. 945   IT
Ohmeda SA, Parc de Pissaloup, 8 Avenue Jean d'Alembert, pg. 122   IT
Tecminemet, 1 Ave. Albert Einstein, pg. 662   IT

Tregueux

Sotrab, pg. 1165   IT

Trelaze

Societe Verriere d'Atlantique (SVA), Zone Industrielle, pg. 1172   IT

Tremblay

Amada Europe S.A., Avenue de la Pyramide, pg. 70   IT
Amada S.A., Avenue de la Pyramide, pg. 70   IT
Ofmi-Garamont SA, pg. 757   IT
Services et Systemes Logistique International (SSLI), 16 rue de l'Etang, pg. 316   IT
TKT Enterprise S.A., 52 Avenue Marcel Paul, pg. 400   IT

Trevoux

Maneurop S.A., B.P. 331, pg. 377   IT

Trith-Saint-Leger

Metalescaut (Societe Metallurgique de l'Escaut), pg. 571   IT

Troisfontaines

VTF Industries SARL, pg. 1523   IT

Troyes

Adidas Sarragen Sports E.u.r.l., pg. 25   IT
Etablissements Ventex SA, pg. 25   IT

Uckange

Lorfonte, pg. 571   IT

Ugine

Ugine-Savoie, pg. 571   IT

Ussel

Societe des Fonderies d'Ussel, Zone Industrielle, La Petit Borde, pg. 1028   IT

Vailly-sur-Aisne

Delsey SA, 9, Route de Soissons, pg. 192   IT

Val-de-Reuil

Selectpack SA, pg. 753   IT

Valbonne

Dow France S.A., Sophia Antipolis-Les Bouillides, pg. 524   PB
Hewlett-Packard France, Les Cardoulines Bat 2, Route Des Dolines, pg. 819   PB
Luxottica France S.a.r.l., 80 route des Lucioles, Les Espaces de Sophia, Batiment B, pg. 822   IT
Rockwell Semiconductor Systems Plc, Les Taissounieres-B.1, Route des Dolines, pg. 1402   PB

Valence

Barnier, S.A., 9-11 rue Edouard Branly, pg. 1202   IT
Crouzet Automatismes, 111, rue de la Foret, pg. 1381   IT
Hewlett-Packard France, Immeuble De Cime, 471, Avenue Victor Hugo, pg. 819   PB
ITW Finishing Systems & Products-Southern Europe, 163-171 Avenue des Aureats, pg. 868   IT
Kluber Lubrication France S.A., pg. 506   IT
Landis & Staefa SMART Sarl, 12 rue Jean Bertin, pg. 801   IT
SNTR Calberson Valence, pg. 1164   IT
Sextant Avionique, 25, rue Jules-Vedrines, pg. 1382   IT
Thomson-CSF Services Industrie, 18, allee Jean Bertin, Technoparc des Hautes Favantines, pg. 1383   IT

Valenciennes

Banque Regionale du Nord, 2 avenue des Dentellieres, pg. 548   IT
SNTR Calberson, pg. 1164   IT

Valente

FINANCIERE EQUIPMENT S.A., 54 rue Benoit Frachon, pg. 485   IT

Valmont

Perstorp S.A. Decorative Laminate, 1, Rue du General de Gaulle, pg. 1038   IT
Perstorp S.A.-Div. Perstorp Stamp, Rue du General de Gaulle, Zone Industriale, pg. 1038   IT

Valnor

Systems De Fermeture S.A., 21-23 rue des Jeunes Chiens, pg. 1462   IT

Vanves

E.D.I.C.E.F., 58 rue Jean Bleuzen, pg. 792   IT
Editions Rombaldi, 58, rue Jean Bleuzen, pg. 792   IT
Le Livre de Paris, 58, rue Jean Bleuzen, pg. 792   IT

Vaucresson

DASSAULT AVIATION GROUP, 27, rue du Professeur Pauchet, pg. 383   IT
Societe d'Importation et de Distribution des Automobiles Toyota S.A., 20 a 30 Bd. de la Republique, pg. 1413   IT
Toyota France S.A., 20 a 30 Bd. de la Republique, pg. 1414   IT

Vaujours

Sun Chemical S.A., 198 a 212 Route de Meaux, pg. 371   IT

Vaulx

Sulzer Metco (France) S.A., pg. 1308   IT
TRIAS SA, Parc d'Entreprises de Villefontaine, pg. 608   IT
Trischler/TRIAS S.A., Parc d'Entreprises de Villefontaine, pg. 608   IT

Vaux-en-Velin

CITEX, 13, avenue Bataillon C, Liberte, pg. 1360   IT
SLAPIS, 3, Rue Louis Saillant, pg. 790   IT

Vaux-le-Penil

La Teledynamique S.A., 550 Rue Saint Just, pg. 474   IT

Velizy

Cetia, 4, rue Latecoire, pg. 1381   IT
ECI Telematics SARL, Espace Velizy Le Nugesser, 13 Avenue Morane Saulnier, pg. 644   IT

QMS S.A.R.L., Velizy Plus, 1 Bis Rue Du Petit Clamart, pg. 1346   PB
Quantum France, 1 bis rue du Petit Clamart, pg. 1350   PB
Sextant Avionique, Aerodrome de Villacoublay, Zone aeronautique Louis Breguet, pg. 1382   IT
Thomainfor, 8, rue Grange Dame Rose, pg. 1382   IT
Thomson-CSF Applications Radar, 6, rue Nieuport, pg. 1382   IT
Thomson-CSF Services Industrie, 4, rue Dewoitine, pg. 1383   IT
Thomson Facilities Management, 3-5, avenue Morane Saulnier, pg. 1383   IT
Thomson Tubes Electroniques, 2, rue Latecoere, pg. 1383   IT

Velizy-Villacoublay

Alcatel CIT, 10 rue Latecoire, pg. 55   IT
ALCATEL CIT (S.A.), 10 rue Latecoire, pg. 56   IT
Bentone-Sud S.A., 11 Ave. Morane-Saulnier, pg. 271   PV
Borland France, Bois Postale 6, pg. 246   IT
COGEMA - COMPAGNIE GENERALE DES MATIERES NUCLEAIRES, 2 Rue Paul Dautier, pg. 304   IT
Commox, 2, rue Paul-Dautier, pg. 305   IT
Compagnie Francaise De Mokta (CFM), 4, rue Paul-Dautier, pg. 305   IT
Etablissement de Velizy, Zone Aeronautique Louis Breguet, pg. 383   IT
FORASOL S.A., 16 bis, rue Grange Dame Rose, pg. 496   IT
ICL (France) International Computers, 24 Avenue de l'Europe, pg. 529   IT
Matra Cap Systems, 6 rue Dewoitine, pg. 792   IT
Mentor Graphics (France) SARL, 8, Rue Nieuport, B.P. 22, pg. 1087   PB
Messier-Bugatti S.A., Zone Aeronautique Louis Breguet, pg. 1165   IT
Messier-Dowty International, Zone Aeronautique Louis Breguet, pg. 1340   IT
Messier-Dowty SAS, Zone Aeronautique Louis Breguet, pg. 1340   IT
Messier-Dowty SAS, Customer Support Centre-Velizy, pg. 1340   IT
Microtec Research S.A., 32 Aveune L'Europe B.P. 87, pg. 1087   PB
NEC Electronics (France) S.A., 9, rue Paul Dautier, pg. 901   IT
Rockwell Automation S.A., 36, avenue de l'Europe, pg. 1400   PB
Rockwell International S.A., Regional Head Office, Siege et Directio Commerciale, pg. 1401   PB
Roux Combaluzier Schindler, pg. 1205   IT
SMC International, S.A., 1 Bis, Rue Due Petit Clamart, pg. 1717   PB
Satcom International, 37 Ave. Louis Breguet BPI, pg. 218   IT
Schindler, pg. 1205   IT
Sepecat SA, Zone Aeronautique Louis Breget, BP No. 12, pg. 218   IT
Societe Industrielle des Minerals de l'Ouest (SIMO), 2, rue Paul-Dautier, pg. 305   IT
Societe pour le Perfectionnement des Materiels et Equipements Aerospatiaux SA (SOPEMEA), Zone Aeronautique Louis Breguet, pg. 1165   IT
Sodiema S.A., 13, rue Paul Dautier, pg. 986   IT
Stream International, 32 Avenue de l'Europe, pg. 518   PB
Sun Microsystems France, S.A., 13 Avenue Morane, pg. 1531   PB
Thomainfor, pg. 1383   IT
Zeneca Sopra SA, 18, rue Grange Dame Rose, pg. 1527   IT

Vendome

Sextant Avionique, Zone industriele Nord, 20, boulevard de l'Industrie, pg. 1382   IT

Venelles

Thomson-CSF Services Industrie, Z.I. Les Piboules, avenue des Ribas, pg. 1383   IT

Venissieux

Matra Communication Rhone-Alpes, Parc du Club du Moulin-a-Vent, 33, av. du Dr. G. Levy, pg. 793   IT
Matra Telecommunications Rhone-Alpes, Parc Club du Moulin-a-Vent, 33, avenue du Docteur G. Levy, pg. 793   IT
Rexroth Sigma SA, pg. 839   IT
Savoie Refractaires, 10, rue de l'Industrie, pg. 1176   IT
Woodward Governor France S.A.R.L., Parc Club du Moulin a, Vent/Bureau 115, 33 rue du, pg. 1777   PB

Vergeze

G.I.E. Perrier-Export, pg. 919   IT
Societe des Boissons Gazeuses de Vergeze (Gard), pg. 919   IT
Societe des Boissons Gazeuses de Vergeze, pg. 922   IT
Verrerie du Languedoc et Cie, pg. 919   IT

Verneuil en Halatte

Baldwin France Sarl, 30, Avenue de Bergoide, pg. 170   PB

Vernon

Rowenta France S.A., Rue du Virolet, pg. 569   IT

SEA, 14, avenue de l'Ile-de-France, pg. 430   IT

Vernouillet

ETEX, 3, rue d'Lamnamadier, pg. 430   IT
Eternit Industries, Rue de l'Amandier, pg. 430   IT
Gie ETEX Gestion, Rue de l'Amandier, pg. 430   IT
Hurel Arc, Aunay-sous-Crecy, pg. 962   IT
Induplast, Rue de l'Amandier, pg. 430   IT
Krupp Widia France S.A., 3, Rue Nicolas Robert, pg. 510   IT
Loiselet International S.A., 6 rue Nicolas Robert, pg. 570   IT
Meca 2000, pg. 1111   IT
Societe des Etablissements Schiffers, Boulevard de l'industrie, pg. 1500   IT

Verpilliere

Sigma Chimie S.a.r.L., Zone Industrielle, pg. 1472   PB

Versailles

Defense Civile, 1 ter, rue de la Porte de Buc, pg. 18   IT
Framatome Connectors France, 145 rue Yves Le Coz, pg. 503   IT
Frametal S.a.r.l., 73bis, Rue Du Marechal Foch, pg. 304   IT
Lloyd Instruments Ltd., pg. 100   PB
World Expo Corporation, 5A, rue de Bailliage, pg. 571   PV
SA 02 Technologie, 7 rue du Parc de Clagny, pg. 316   IT

Vesoul

Ferry Mougin, pg. 1164   IT

Vetraz

DAV, Rue Jules Verne, pg. 785   IT

Veurey Voroize

Gelalp, pg. 563   IT

Vichy

Imprimerie Wallon, Rue des Bourins, pg. 919   IT
KDG Houdec SA, Zone D'activites De la Tour, pg. 854   IT
Wallon Imprimeur S.A., pg. 922   IT

Vieil-Bauge

Jean-Pierre Girardeau SA, pg. 753   IT

Vierzon

Case France, S.A., 10, Rue Pierre Semard, pg. 1579   PB

Vieux Conde

Groupe Brenntag S.A., pg. 1458   IT

Village-Neuf

Societe Chimique Roche S.A., pg. 1121   IT

Villefontaine

Plasma-Technik S.A., pg. 1308   IT

Villefranche-sur-Saone

AxPro France S.A., 1117, Av. Edouard Herriot, pg. 710   IT
Diepal-N.S.A., 383, Rue Philipe Heron, pg. 380   IT
Le Clos de la Pellerie, pg. 781   IT
Materne-Fruibourg, 383 rue Philippe Heron BP466, pg. 619   IT
Produtec Houghton S.A., 259 Rue Benoit-Mulsant, pg. 541   PV

Villemeux-sur-Eure

Matincendie, pg. 1501   IT

Villemomble

Bettis France, 30-36 Allee Du Plateau, pg. 483   PB

Villemur-sur-Tarn

Labinal Aero Plant, pg. 786   IT

Villeneuve d'Ascq

Durco France S.A.R.L., 51, rue Tremiere, pg. 659   PB
Hewlett-Packard France, Parc d'Activite des Pres, pg. 819   PB
Makita France S.A.-Nord, Villa d'Entreprises, 51, pg. 832   IT
Norpac, Le Triolo 9, allee du Tennis, pg. 206   IT
Self Auto, 220 rue de la Convention, pg. 276   IT
Tech-Atlan - Villeneuve d'Ascq Branch, Miniparc, Rue Entre Deux Villes, pg. 1360   IT
3Com, S.A., City Parc, 3 rue Lavoisier, pg. 1604   PB

Villeneuve-la-Garonne

ACOR (Aciers de Constructions Rationalises), pg. 570   IT
Quaker Chemical S.A., 19-21 Avenue Nobel, pg. 1347   PB

Villeneuve-le-Roi

E.P.I., rue des Voeux-Saint-Georges, pg. 206   IT

Villeneuve-Loubet

EURO RSCG Novation, Les Twins 1, pg. 601   IT
Texas Instruments France SA, Siege Social Centre, Recherches et Usine, pg. 1586   PB

Villennes-sur-Seine

Ashland-Avebene, 136 Ave Gilbert de Voisins, pg. 139   PB

Villenoiy-Meaux

Meaux, Chemin d'en Bas, pg. 673   PB

Villeneve-la-Garonne

B.H.V. Villeneuve-La-Garenne, C.C. 20 rue de la Bongarde, pg. 181   IT
FIAT Chariots Elevateurs France S.A., pg. 811   IT
Glacauto, 92, Boulevard Gallieni, pg. 1172   IT

Villepinte

Battenfeld France S.A., Central Park, 255, Boulevard Robert Ballanger, pg. 825   IT
Frequence Plus, 9, allee des Impressionnistes, pg. 560   IT
Hewlett-Packard France, Centre d'Affairs Paris-Nord II, 45, Rue Des Trois Soeurs, pg. 819   PB

Viller-Saint-Paul

Lex Mamutention, ZA rue Albert Thomas, pg. 807   IT
NorsoHaas, S.A., pg. 1403   PB

Villers-Cotterets

Groupe Volkswagen France S.A., pg. 1475   IT
V.A.G. Financement S.A., pg. 1475   IT
V.A.G. France S.A., Boite Postal 62, pg. 1475   IT
V.A.G. Holding Financiere S.A., pg. 1475   IT
Volkswagen Finance s.a., pg. 1474   IT

Villers-la-Montagne

Batiroc, Zone Industrielle, pg. 430   IT

Villeurbanne

Avesta ABE SARL, 48, Rue Decomberousse, pg. 221   IT
Carrillon 12-14, rue Leon Blum, pg. 1028   IT
Chaussures Bally Villeurbanne SA, 12, rue du docten Papillon, pg. 997   IT
DSM Engineering Plastic Products S.A., Zone Industrielle Saint John, 60, Rue R. Desgrand, pg. 354   IT
G.F.C., 82, rue du Premier-Mars 1943, pg. 206   IT
Hexcel (Lyon) S.A., B.P. 1208, pg. 824   PB
Laboratoires Duphar S.A., Rue de Verdun 60, pg. 1279   IT
Levaillant SA, pg. 753   IT
Martin S.A., 22 rue, Decomberousse, pg. 199   IT
Radiometer Analytical S.A., 72, rue d'Alsace, pg. 1084   IT
Soprano S.A., 67, rue Frederic Fays, pg. 53   IT
Verreries Souchen Neuvesel, 64, Boulevard du, pg. 381   IT

Villiers-sur-Marne

Ceres, Immeuble Pascal, 11, bd Georges Melies, pg. 1274   IT

Vincennes

Astron S.A.R.L., 8 Rue Charles Pathe, pg. 411   PB
U.B.R., 10 Cours Louis Lumiere, pg. 565   IT

Vincey

Societe des Tubes de Vincey, pg. 571   IT

Vineuil

SNT Calberson, pg. 1164   IT

Vire

Labinal Aero Plant, pg. 786   IT
Sylea Harness Assembly Plant, pg. 785   IT

Viriat

Sandvik Rock Tools S.N.C., pg. 1187   IT

Viroflay

BONGRAIN S.A., L'Alliance, 42, rue Rieussec, pg. 201   IT

Mettler-Toledo S.A., BP 14 ZAE, 18-20 avenue de la Pepiniere, pg. 4   PV

Vitrolles

Cisigraph, pg. 792   IT
Matra Communication Mediterranee, La Bastide Blanche Centre Evolic, pg. 793   IT
Matra Telecommunications Mediterranee, La Bastide Blanche Centre Evolic, pg. 793   IT
Svedala France Vitrolles, pg. 1323   IT

Vitry-le-Francois

E & M Lamort, pg. 1596   PB

Vitry-sur-Seine

Beton de Paris, 7 Ave. du President S. Allende, pg. 788   IT
Carrefour - Erteco, 120, rue du General Malleret Joinville, pg. 272   IT
SCIAKY S.A., 119 Quai Jules Guesde, pg. 1211   IT
Vivagel, 42-54, rue Charles Heller, pg. 380   IT
Zimmer S.A., 68 70 Rue Malleret Joinville, pg. 257   PB

Vittel

Societe Generale des Eaux Minerales de Vittel, B.P. 43, pg. 920   IT
Vittel S.A., pg. 922   IT

Voiron

ROSSIGNOL S.A., pg. 1127   IT

Voisins-le-Bretonneux

Autoliasons France S.A., 15 bis, Rue aux Fleurs, pg. 190   PB
Bowman Distribution France, 15 bis, rue aux Fleurs, pg. 190   PB
Lee Company S.A., 24 rue Jean Bart, pg. 657   PV
NSK-RHP France S.A., Zone d'Activite du Merantais, Rue aux Fleurs, pg. 904   IT
Partner Relations, Europe, 13 Square Alfred de Musset, pg. 1032   PB

Voreppe

Stepan Europe, B.P. No. 127, pg. 1514   PB

Vulaines-sur-Seine

Britax (Geco) S.A., 1 et 3 Route d'Hericy, pg. 216   IT
Britax Puericulture S.A.R.L., One Rt. Phericy, pg. 216   IT

Wasquehal

Agora, Z.I. de la Pilaterie, 32 Rue de la Couture, pg. 789   IT
Banque Covefi S.A., pg. 1015   IT
Cofidis S.A., pg. 1015   IT
Kredietbank S.A. France Agence de Lille, 32 Avenue de la Marne, pg. 760   IT
Van Melle-France S.A., Z.I. de la Pilaterie, pg. 1451   IT

Wattignies

Cafe Grand Mere S.A., pg. 1289   PB
Vandamme - Pie Qui Chante, 300 rue Clememceau, pg. 380   IT

Wissembourg

Polyflex France S.A., Wissembourg Plant, Zone Industrielle Est, pg. 1261   PB

Wissous

D.I.A.L. Diffusion Internationale d'Arts et Loisirs S.A., 1, Boulevard Francois Arago, pg. 1052   IT
Eurodia Industrie S.A., 14/16 Voie de Montavas, pg. 1394   IT
Molex Eastern Europe S.A., 4 Blvd. Arago, pg. 1122   PB
Molex France S.A.R.L., Four Blvd. Arago, pg. 1122   PB
Orly Air Traiteur, 1, rue du Pont des Pierres, pg. 560   IT
RATP Val Service (RVS), Chemin de Fresnes, pg. 793   IT

Wittelsheim

MDPA, Avenue Joseph Else, pg. 459   IT

Wittenheim

Svedala France Wittenheim, pg. 1323   IT

Yffiniac

Laboratoires Neolait S.A., Boite Postale 1, pg. 1265   IT

PB - *U.S. Public Companies Volume*
PV - *U.S. Private Companies Volume*
IT - *International Public & Private Companies Volume*

Geographic Index-Non U.S.

Yutz

S.A. Compagnie des Produits Industriels C.P.I., pg. 302　IT
Societe Civile Immobiliere Basse-Yutz, pg. 302　IT

Yvelines

Intel Corporation S.A.R.L., 1 Rue Edison, pg. 887　PB

Yzuere

Transports Moulinois, pg. 1165　IT

FRENCH GUIANA

Cayenne

B.F.C. Antilles-Guyane, pg. 314　IT
Medicaraibe Guyane, 45 Rue du Lieutenant, pg. 822　PB

Kourou

Arianespace Kourou, pg. 81　IT
Dumez Guyane, ZI de Pariacabo, pg. 823　IT
Societe Shell des Antilles et da la Guyane Francaises, ZI
　Pariacabo, pg. 1142　IT
Sodexho Guyane, pg. 1275　IT
Thomson-CSF Services & Systemes Sol Spatiaux, Z.I. de
　Pariacabo, pg. 1385　IT

FRENCH POLYNESIA

Faaa

Electricite de Tahiti, Puurai, pg. 824　IT

Papeete

Banque de Tahiti, B.P. No. 1602, pg. 1248　PB
Banque Paribas Polynesie, Boulevard Pomare, pg. 320　IT
Polynesienne des Eaux, Vallee de TitioroBP, pg. 824　IT
Sodexho Polynesie, pg. 1275　IT
Westpac Banking Corp. - French Polynesia, Two Pl. Notre
　Dame, pg. 1497　IT

GABON

Libreville

Banque Internationale pour le Commerce et l'Industrie du
　Gabon (BICIG), Avenue du Colonel Parant, pg. 148　IT
Banque Paribas Gabon, Boulevard de l'Independance,
　pg. 320　IT
Bull Gabon, Immeuble Independance, Blvd. Bord de Mer,
　pg. 315　IT
CII-Honeywell Bull Gabon SARL, Immeuble Independance
　Boulevard Bord-de-, pg. 316　IT
Compagnie Des Mines D-Uranium De Franceville (COMUF),
　pg. 305　IT
Hatton et Cookson S.A., Routre D'oloumi Section Rue,
　Aristide Issembe, pg. 1437　IT
Helmerich & Payne (Gabon), pg. 808　PB
Societe Gabonaise de Produits Alimetaires (SOGAPRAL),
　pg. 922　IT
Total-Fina Gabon S.A., Quartier Ste.-Anne, Face College
　Bessieux, pg. 1044　IT

Port Gentil

Banque Paribas-Port-Gentil, Avenue Savorgnan de Brazza,
　pg. 320　IT
Elf Gabon, BP 525, pg. 446　IT
Milchem Gabon S.A.R.L., B.P. No. 668, pg. 167　PB
Panalpina Transports Mondiaux Gabon S.A., pg. 1023　IT
Shell Gabon, pg. 1137　IT
Sodexho Gabon, pg. 1275　IT

GAMBIA

Banjul

Shell Marketing Gambia Ltd., Shell Office, Independence
　Drive, pg. 1137　IT
Standard Chartered Bank Gambia Ltd., Box 259,
　pg. 1294　IT

GERMANY

Aachen

**AMB AACHENER UND MUENCHENER BETEILIGUNGS-
　AG**, Aachener und Munchener Allee 9, pg. 15　IT
Aachener und Muenchener Immobilien GmbH, Maria-
　Theresia-Allee 38, pg. 15　IT
Aachener und Muenchener Informatik Service, Anton-
　Kurze-Allee 16, pg. 15　IT
Aachener und Muenchener Lebensversicherung, Robert-
　Schuman-Strasse 51, pg. 15　IT
Aachener und Muenchener Versicherung
　Aktiengesellschaft, Aureliusstrasse 2, pg. 15　IT

Ascom Infrasys GmbH, Charlottenburger Alle 61,
　pg. 87　IT
Beton Union Aachen GmbH & Co. KG, pg. 422　IT
Caspar & Co. Handel GmbH & Co., pg. 838　IT
Caspar Verwaltungs GmbH, pg. 838　IT
Compagnie de Saint-Gobain Succ. Zweigniederlassung
　Deutschland, Viktoria-Allee 3-5, pg. 1177　IT
The Gates Rubber Company, Eisenbahnweg 50,
　pg. 1397　IT
Generale Bank & Co., Theaterstrasse 106, pg. 548　IT
Gevetex Textilglas GmbH, Viktoria-Allee,3-5, pg. 1177　IT
Hammermill Paper GmbH, Ederburgweg 137, pg. 905　IT
International Power Machines GmbH, Technologizentrum,
　am Europaplatz, Ste 105, pg. 126　PB
International Power Machines GmbH, Technologizentrum
　am Europaplatz, pg. 126　IT
Kingsoft GMBH, Gruner, Weg 29, pg. 569　PB
H. Krantz Textilmaschinen GmbH, pg. 399　IT
Munters Euroform GmbH, Susterfeldstr. 65, pg. 669　IT
Owens-Corning Eternit Rohre GmbH, Gutseeg 9B,
　pg. 1237　PB
Saint-Gobain & Glac. Saint-Roch OHG, Viktoria-Allee 3-5,
　pg. 1173　IT
Schumag AG, pg. 399　IT
Sekurit Saint-Gobain Deutschland Beteiligungen (SSGD)
　GmbH, Viktoria-Allee 3-5, pg. 1173　IT
Sekurit Saint-Gobain Deutschland (SSGD) KG, Viktoria-
　Allee 3-5, pg. 1173　IT
TSI GMBH, Zieglerstrasse 1, pg. 1559　PB
Takeda Pharma GmbH, Viktoriaallee 3-5, pg. 1351　IT
Uniroyal Englebert Reifen GmbH, Huettenstr. 7,
　pg. 327　IT
Vegla Vereinigte Glashandels-Gesellschaft mbH (VGG),
　Viktoria-Allee, 3-5, pg. 1173　IT
Vegla Vereinigte Glaswerke GmbH, Viktoria-Allee, 3-5,
　pg. 1173　IT
Waggonfabrik Talbot GmbH & Co. KG, Julicher Strasse
　213-237, pg. 201　IT

Aarbergen

Passavant-Werke AG, pg. 195　IT

Achern

ICOMA Packtechnik GmbH, pg. 759　IT
Lambda Electronics GmbH, Josef Hund Strasse 1,
　pg. 1242　IT
Lambda GmbH, P.O. Box 1367, pg. 1242　IT
Sud-West-Kamin GmbH, Neulandstrasse 8, pg. 1091　IT
Wilhelmstal-Werke GmbH Papiersackfabriken, Fauterbacher
　Strasse 24, pg. 759　IT

Achim

Hydro Aluminium Uphusen GmbH, Uphuser Heerstrasse 7,
　pg. 963　IT

Ahaus

Durco GmbH Atomac Division, Von-Braun-Strasse 19a,
　pg. 659　PB
Salzgewinnungsgesellschaft Westfalen mbH, Brook 9,
　pg. 1279　IT

Ahlen

BHA International GmbH, Filtrastr. 5-7, pg. 161　PB
Comforto Group, Bergstr. 1, pg. 512　PV
Nordiskafilt GmbH, Postfach 40, pg. 37　PB
Reflex-WellMate GmbH, Gersteinstr. 19, pg. 593　PB

Ahrensburg

Hasselblad Vertriebsgesellschaft m.b.H, Kurt Fischer
　Strasse 47, pg. 1468　IT

Aich

Bulthaup GmbH & Co., Kuchensystem, pg. 1410　IT

Albbruck

Papierfabrik Albbruck GmbH, Alte Landstrasse 49,
　pg. 864　IT

Albershausen

Georg Fischer Gmbh, Daimlerstrasse 6, pg. 489　IT

Aldersbach

Plant Aldersbach, Knorrstrasse 1, pg. 738　IT

Alf

Polarcup Germany, Bad Bertricher Strasse 6-9,
　pg. 638　IT

Alfeld

Knurr-Taunus GmbH, Brunker Stieg 7, pg. 739　IT
SPIRKA Maschinenbau GmbH & Co. KG, P.O. Box 16 44,
　pg. 399　IT

Alicante

Jimten, Ctra. de Ocana, 125, Junto a Plgo. Las Atalayas,
　pg. 430　IT

Allershausen

Svedala Deutschaland (Munich), pg. 1324　IT

Alpirsbach

Georg A. Brenner Arzneimittel-Fabrik GmbH, Postfach
　1140, pg. 80　PB
Kytta-Werk Sauter GmbH, Postfach 1260, pg. 81　PB

Alsbach-Hahnlein

Eurotherm Antriebstechnik GmbH, Birkenweg 8,
　pg. 466　IT

Altdorf

SUSPA COMPART AG, pg. 1322　IT
3 Pagen Versand Und Handelsgesellschaft mbH,
　pg. 1015　IT

Altenkirchen

Ferd. Jagenberg & Sohne GmbH & Co. KG, pg. 35　IT

Altenstadt

Wisaforest Deutschland GmbH, Zweigburo Altenstadt,
　Vogelsbergstrasse 43, pg. 1429　IT

Alzenau

Korf Transport GmbH, Brentanostrasse 2, pg. 758　IT
Lowara GmbH, pg. 861　PB
Nukem GmbH, pg. 1081　IT

Alzey

Real SB-Warenhaus GF-GmbH, Industristrabe 1,
　pg. 863　IT

Andernach

Curtis 1000 Europe GmbH, Rostocker Strasse 15,
　pg. 70　PB

Anklam

Danisco Sugar GmbH, Zuckerfabrik Anklam, Bluthsluster
　Strasse 24, pg. 378　IT

Ansbach

Crones Co. GmbH, Gutenbergstr. 4, pg. 867　PB
ITW Befestigungssysteme (Ansbach) GmbH, Durrnerstrasse
　1, pg. 868　PB
Schafft Fleischwerke G.m.b.H., Eyber Str. 81-85,
　pg. 1438　IT

Appenweier

E. Scheurich Pharmwerk GmbH, Postfach 1140, pg. 82　PB

Arnhem

Heidemij Computer Services, pg. 607　IT

Arnsberg

Eickel & Spindeldreher GmbH, Glosinger Strasse 150,
　pg. 1210　IT
Ruhr Pulverlack G.m.b.H., Postfach 2280, pg. 620　PB
Stora Carton Board GbmH, Werk Ansberg, pg. 1302　IT

Arnstein

Lompel-Bautenschutz GmbH & Co. KG, Wernstrasse 10-12,
　pg. 633　IT

Aschaffenburg

Linde AG Werksgruppe Gueldner Aschaffenburg,
　Schwinheimer Strasse 24, pg. 810　IT
Mikronwerk GmbH, Johann-Dahlem-Strasse 50,
　pg. 1157　IT

Aschau

Bayern-Chemie GmbH, Liebigstr. 1517, pg. 367　IT
Temic Bayern-Chemie Airbag GmbH, pg. 367　IT

Aschheim

DSI DYWIDAG-Systems International GmbH, Erdinger
　Landstr. 1, pg. 423　IT
DYWIDAG UMWELTSCHUTZTECHNIK GmbH, Erdlinger
　Landstrasse 1, pg. 423　IT
Micron Semiconductor (Deutschland) GmbH, Niederlassung
　Deutschland, Sternstrasse 20, pg. 1106　PB

PB - *U.S. Public Companies Volume*
PV - *U.S. Private Companies Volume*
IT - *International Public & Private Companies Volume*

Moet Hennessy Deutschland G.m.b.H., Max Planck Strasse 8, pg. 783   IT
Monopteros Werbeagentur GmbH, Erdinger Landstrasse 1, pg. 423   IT

Auerbach

Cherry Mikroschalter GmbH, Cherrystrasse, pg. 346   PB

Augsburg

Abieta Chemie GmbH, pg. 810   PB
Alpine Aktiengesellschaft, Peter-Dorfler-Strasse 13-25, pg. 636   IT
Augsburg Paper Mill, Georg-Haindl-Strasse 4, pg. 586   IT
Baldwin-Grafotec GmbH, Derchinger Strasse 137, pg. 170   PB
DG Bank - Augsburg, Halderstrasse 29, pg. 351   IT
Dialog Lebensversicherungs AG, Zeuggasse 7, pg. 89   IT
Die Betonknacker, Zusamstr. 21, pg. 1128   IT
Freudenberg Haushaltsprodukte Augsburg GmbH & Co, KG, pg. 505   IT
HAINDL PAPIER GMBH, Georg-Haindl-Strasse 5, pg. 586   IT
Hartmann & Flinsch GmbH, pg. 757   IT
Hasen-Brau AG, pg. 179   IT
LECH-ELEKTRIZITATSWERKE AG, Schaezlerstrasse 1-3, pg. 805   IT
MAN B & W Diesel AG, Stadtbachstrasse 1, pg. 824   IT
MAN Dezentrale Energiesysteme GmbH, Stadtbachstrasse 1, pg. 825   IT
PCI Augsburg GmbH, Postfach 102247, pg. 1464   IT
RENK Aktiengesellschaft, Goegginger Strasse 73, pg. 825   IT
Rohren und Sanitar GroBhandel GmbH, pg. 838   IT
Franz Silberhorn GmbH & Co. KG, pg. 838   IT
Franz Silberhorn Handel GmbH, pg. 838   IT

Babenhausen

Mattel GmbH, Ostheimerweg 37, pg. 1059   PB

Backnang

ANT Nachrichtentechnik GmbH, Gerberstr. 33, pg. 204   IT
Allcaps Weichgelatinekapseln GmbH, Gaildorferstrasse 6, pg. 1438   PB

Bad Abbach

Bertrand Faure Sitztechnik GmbH & Co. KG, Industriestrasse 1, pg. 193   IT

Bad Duben

Bad Duben Profilwalzmaschinen GmbH, pg. 1128   IT

Bad Gandersheim

Auer-SOG Glaswerke GmbH, pg. 1523   IT

Bad Harzburg

NORD/LB, Herzog-Wilhelm-Strasse 2, pg. 957   IT

Bad Hersfeld

Babcock-BSH AG, pg. 399   IT
Babcock-BSH Inc., pg. 399   IT
Design-Tuft DT GmbH, pg. 497   IT
Kupfermuhle Holztechnik GmbH, P.O. Box 16 53, pg. 399   IT

Bad Homburg

ALTANA AG, Seedammweg 55, pg. 65   IT
Commerz Beteiligungs GmbH, pg. 309   IT
Continuum (Deutschland) GmbH, Tannenwaldallee 76, pg. 423   PB
Criticare Systems, Inc.-Europe, c/o Medlog GmbH, Gotzenmuhlweg 66, pg. 459   PB
Deutsche Ges. fuer Immobilienanlagen "America" mbH, pg. 310   IT
Du Pont de Nemours (Deutschland) GmbH, Postfach 3000388, DuPont Str. 1, pg. 532   PB
FRESENIUS AG, Borkenberg 14, pg. 505   IT
Hewlett-Packard GmbH, Zone Office Central, Hewlett-Packard-Strasse, pg. 820   PB
Icore International GmbH, Hohenstrasse 31/33, pg. 1268   PB
Intermec Strichode Systeme GmbH, Saalburgstrasse, 157, pg. 1004   PB
International Rectifier GmbH, Saalburgstrasse 157, pg. 907   PB
Medlog GmbH, Gotzenmuhlweg 66, pg. 459   PB
Medtronic GmbH, Kisseleffstrasse 11a, pg. 1083   PB
Petrolite Europe, Kaiser-Friedrich Promenade 59, pg. 166   PB
THORN-Europe, Nehringstrasse 2, pg. 1386   IT
Verlag Dr. Max Gehlen GmbH & Co. KG, Daimlerstrasse 12, pg. 1479   IT
Vickers Systems GmbH (Aerospace-Marine-Defense Trinova GmbH), Frolingstrasse 41, pg. 25   PB

Bad Honnef

Frisch-Beton Aegidienberg GmbH & Co. KG, pg. 422   IT

Bad Honningen

Artus Mineralquellen GmbH & Co. KG, Im Strand 40, pg. 1279   IT
Kohlensaurewerk Deutschland GmbH, Im Strang 32, pg. 1278   IT

Bad Kostritz

Kostritzer Schwarzbierbrauerei GmbH & Co., pg. 197   IT

Bad Kreuznach

Niederlassung Bad Kreuznach, Weinkauffstrasse 8, pg. 194   IT
SASIB Beverage Deutschland Gmbh, Salinenstrasse 39A, pg. 1195   IT
Werk Bad Kreuznach, Planiger Strasse, 139-147, pg. 737   IT

Bad Lauterberg im Harz

Deutsche Baryt-Industrie Dr. Rudolf Alberti & Co., Bahnhofstrasse 21-39, pg. 1278   IT

Bad Mergentheim

AgroPlant SES Saatzucht GmbH, pg. 1525   IT

Bad Nauheim

TBG Nauheimer Lieferbeton GmbH & Co. KG, pg. 423   IT
Wetterauer Transportbeton GmbH & Co. KG, pg. 423   IT

Bad Nenndorf

SAB WABCO KP GmbH, Poststr. 1, pg. 271   IT

Bad Oeynhausen

Battenfeld Extrusionstechnik GmbH, Koenigstrasse 53, pg. 825   IT
Invacare Deutschland Fahrzeuge Korperbehinderte, Dehmer Str. 66, pg. 911   PB

Bad Oldesloe

HAKO-WERKE GMBH & CO., Hamburger Str. 209-239, pg. 587   IT
Minimax GmbH, Industriestrasse 10/12, pg. 1069   IT

Bad Salzuflen

Alba Moda GmbH, pg. 1014   IT
Gebruder Dippe Saatzucht G.m.b.H., pg. 982   IT
Heinz Essman GmbH, pg. 1261   IT
Hilleshog G.m.b.h., pg. 982   IT
Perstorp GmbH Verkaufsburo Compounds, Meierweg 1/B 239, pg. 1037   IT

Bad Schussenried

Liebherr-Mischtechnik GmbH, Im Elchgrund, pg. 808   IT

Bad Soden

Rothenberger Osteuropa GmbH, Konigsteiner Strasse 102, pg. 1128   IT
Eden Waren G.m.b.H., pg. 982   IT

Bad Soden am Taunus

Much Pharma, Prof. Much Strasse 2-34, pg. 81   PB

Bad Vilbel

Brother International G.m.b.H., Im Rosengarten 14, pg. 229   IT
Nippon Sanso Europe GmbH, Larchenstrasse 12, pg. 939   IT

Bad Wilbad

EG & G Berthold (HQ), Calmbacher Strasse 22, pg. 544   PB
Prontor-Werk Alfred Gauthier GmbH, pg. 1523   IT

Bad Wildungen

Correcta GmbH, Correcta Strasse 1, pg. 172   IT

Bad Wurzach

Oberland Glas AG, Oberlandstrasse, pg. 1171   IT

Bad-Wuertt

Thyssen Aufzuge GmbH, Bernhaeuser Stra. 45, pg. 1387   IT

Thyssen Industrie Aktiengesellschaft, Bernhaeuser Stra. 45, pg. 1387   IT

Baden Baden

Exide Electronics International-GmbH, pg. 126   IT
Fiskars Power Systems GmbH, Postfach 1014, pg. 492   IT
Jauch & Huebener, Lange Strasse 65, pg. 118   PB
Juvena Produits de Beaute GmbH, pg. 182   IT
R.P. Scherer GmbH, Gammelsbacherstrasse 2, pg. 1438   PB
Trinova Gmbh, Ruhrstrasse 11, pg. 25   PB

Bahratal

TBS Ges. fur Tank- und Bodenschutz mbH - Bahratal, Grenzlandstr., pg. 515   IT

Baienfurt

Stora Carton Board GmbH, Fabrikstrasse, pg. 1302   IT
Stora Carton Board GmbH, Werk Baienfurt, Fabrikstrasse, pg. 1302   IT

Balingen

Ballinger Schalttechnik G.m.b.H., Meisterstrasse 19, pg. 1366   PB

Bamberg

Bamberger Kaliko GmbH, pg. 327   IT
Rhenania-Friedrich Krauss Speditions Ges. mbH, Mainstrasse 10, pg. 1033   IT
Sand-und Kies-Kontor Gesellschaft mit beschrankter Haftung, Mainstrasse 10, pg. 1034   IT

Bargteheide

Susy Card GmbH & Co. KG, Am Redder 2, pg. 616   IT

Bautzen

Dyckerhoff Transportbeton Ostsachsen GmbH & Co. KG, pg. 422   IT

Beckum

Eisen Lothringen Stahlhandel GmbH (SSH), Westfaliaweg 1, pg. 1459   IT
Krupp Polysius AG, Graf-Galen Str. 17, pg. 512   IT

Beelitz

Bekina Lebensmittel GmbH, pg. 991   IT

Beibesheim

Praxair GmbH, pg. 1320   PB

Bellenberg

Hydro Aluminium Bellenberg GmbH, Am Muhlholz 1, pg. 962   IT

Benneckenstein

Plant Benneckenstein, Zollhauser StraBe 11b, pg. 738   IT

Benshausen

Thuringer Rexroth Pneumatik GmbH, pg. 838   IT

Bensheim

CIBA-GEIGY Marienberg GmbH, pg. 978   IT
Datascope GmbH, Zeppelinstrabe 2-4, pg. 488   PB
Deutsche Tiefbohr AG, Dalmannstrasse 1, pg. 1069   IT
Intervascular GmbH, Darmstadterstrasse 190, pg. 488   PB
Rheometric Scientific, Inc., pg. 1533   PB
Roell Pruefsysteme GmbH, Robert-Bosch Str. 32, pg. 1533   IT
TBG Lieferbeton GmbH & Co. KG Bergstrabe, pg. 423   IT

Berching

Schabmuller GmbH, Industriestrasse 8, pg. 1387   IT
Thrige Electric GmbH, Industriestrasse 8, pg. 1387   IT

Berge

RAFI GmbH & Co. Elektrotechnische Spezialfabrik, pg. 516   IT

Bergheim

Lawson Mardon Boxal Sales GmbH, Kolner Strasse 108, pg. 68   IT
Martinswerk GmbH fur chemische und metallurgische Produktion, pg. 69   IT
Rheinische Baustoffwerke GmbH & Co. KG, Fischbachstr. 51, pg. 623   IT

PB - *U.S. Public Companies Volume*
PV - *U.S. Private Companies Volume*
IT - *International Public & Private Companies Volume*

1604

Geographic Index-Non U.S.

Bergheim-Erft

Aluminum Industrie Wohmbau GmbH, pg. 68   IT

Bergisch Gladbach

Commercial Metals Deutschland GmbH, Braunsberger Feld 27, pg. 414   PB
H. Krantz-TKT GmbH, pg. 399   IT
METAPLAS IONON GmbH, pg. 400   IT
METAPLAS Oberdlachenveredelungstechnik GmbH, pg. 400   IT
Polypenco G.M.B.H., An der Zinkhutte 17, pg. 354   IT

Bergkamen

HTV Gesellschaft fur Hochtemperaturverbrennung mbH, Ernst-Schering-Strasse 14, pg. 1460   IT
Witco GmbH, Ernst Schering-Str. 14, pg. 1774   PB

Berhoepen

National-Oilwell Griffith Downhole Products GmbH, Eddesser Strasse 1, pg. 1158   PB

Berlin

ABB-Daimler Benz Transportation (Adtranz), Saatwinkler, pg. 8   IT
AEG Mobile Communications GmbH, Sickingenstrasse 20-28, pg. 795
AgrEvo GmbH, Miraustrasse 54, pg. 624   IT
Agrolinz Agrarchemikalien GesellschaftmbH Berlin, Postfach 79, Friedrichstr., pg. 356   IT
Akzo Coatings GmbH, 7-9 Oraniendamm, pg. 43   IT
Allianz Versicherungs-AG, Zweigniederlassung Berlin, Joachimstaler Strasse 10-12, pg. 58   IT
Analog Devices GMBH - Technisches Buero Berlin, Kantstrasse 54, pg. 108   PB
ARIDO Abdichtungs-Gesellschaft, Mockernstr. 25, pg. 423   IT
Auergesellschaft GmbH, pg. 1114   IT
AXEL SPRINGER VERLAG AG, Axel Springer Strasse 65, pg. 102   IT
BB-Asset Management Vermogensverwaltung GmbH, Kurfurstendamm 201, pg. 159   IT
BB-Betriebsservice GmbH, Brunnenstrasse 111, pg. 159   IT
BB-DATA Gesellschaft fur Informations-und Kommunikationssysteme mbH, Brunnenstrasse 111, pg. 159   IT
BB-Kapitalbeteiligungs gesellschaft GmbH, Fasanenstrasse 7-8, pg. 159   IT
BB-Privat Finanz-Service GmbH, Fasanenstrasse 7-8, pg. 159   IT
BFR GmbH, Cordesstrasse 9, pg. 657   IT
BHF-Bank, Franzosische Strasse 9-12, pg. 119   IT
BMW Maschinenfabrik Spandau GmbH, pg. 177   IT
BV-Consult, Karl-Liebknecht-Strasse 33, pg. 178   IT
Bank Hapoalim (Berlin), Europa Center 13, OG, pg. 149   IT
BANKGESELLSCHAFT BERLIN, Alexanderplatz 2, pg. 159   IT
Bankgesellschaft Berlin Investment GmbH, Kurfurstendamm 201, pg. 159   IT
Bankhaus Loebbecke & Co., Fasanenstrasse 76/77, pg. 275   IT
Banque Paribas-Representanz Berlin, Europa Center (13.0G), Tauentzienstrasse 8-9,1000, pg. 320   IT
Bayerische Landesbank Girozentrale - Berlin Branch, Unter den Linden 62-68, pg. 176   IT
BB Kartenservice GmbH, Gustav-Meyer-Allee 1, pg. 159   IT
Berlack Strassenmarkierungsfarben, Goethesstrasse 50-54, pg. 791   IT
Berlin Branch, Bismarckstrasse 105, pg. 645   IT
Berlin Representative Office, Eden Haus, Budapester Strasse 41, pg. 1517   IT
Berlin Works, Staakener Strasse 53-63, pg. 516   IT
Berliner Bank AG, Hardenbergstrasse 32, pg. 159   IT
Berliner Commerz Beteilgungs GmbH, pg. 309   IT
Berliner Hypotheken-und Pfandbriefbank AG, Budapester Strasse 1, pg. 159   IT
Berliner Kraft und Licht (Bewag) AG, pg. 1456   IT
Berliner Schmierstoffgesellschaft mbH, Nanmannstr. 33, pg. 517   IT
Bildungsakademie Berlin-Brandenburg GmbH, Maxstrasse 2-4, pg. 159   IT
BORSIG Kugelhahn GmbH, pg. 400   IT
Robert Bosch GmbH, Zitadellenweg 34, pg. 204   IT
Braas Berlin GmbH & Co., Holzhauser Strasse 102-106, pg. 1091   IT
Peter Breitenbach GmbH, pg. 838   IT
Peter Breitenbach Sanitar und Heizungsfachhandel GmbH, pg. 838   IT
CRSS Deutschland, Kurfurstendamm 26A, pg. 1415   IT
Max Cochius GmbH, Ziegrastr. 1, pg. 514   IT
Columbia Cosmetics GmbH, Postfach 61 02 98, Tempelhofer Ufer 8/9, pg. 609   IT
Commerz- und Industrie-Leasing Berlin GmbH, pg. 309   IT
Cosmed-Produktions GmbH, pg. 182   IT
DG Bank - Berlin, Friedrichstrasse 61, pg. 351   IT
DIC Berlin GmbH R & D Laboratory, Otisstrasse 39, pg. 371   IT
DKB Finance (Berlin), Kurfurstendamm 207/208, pg. 361   IT
D.W.M Copeland G.m.b.H., Eichborndamm 141-187, pg. 576   PB

Dai-Ichi Kangyo Bank, Ltd.-Berlin, Kurfurstendamm 207/208, pg. 361   IT
Daimler-Benz InterServices (debis) AG, Englerallee 40, pg. 367   IT
debis Gesellschaft fur Potsdamer Platz Projekt und Immobilienmanagement, Potsdamer Strasse 5, pg. 368   IT
debis Handel, Uhlandstrasse 7-8, pg. 368   IT
debis International Trading, pg. 368   IT
DeTeLine Deutsche Telekom Kommunikationsnetze GmbH, Rognitzstr. 8, pg. 407   IT
Deutsche Babcock Borsig AG, Egellsstrasse 21, pg. 399   IT
Deutsche Bank Berlin AG, Otto-Suhr-Allee 6/16, pg. 402   IT
Deutsche Bank-Kreditbank AG, Kurstrasse 40, pg. 402   IT
Deutsche Bank-Kreditbank AG (Berlin), Alexanderplatz 6, pg. 402   IT
Deutsche Girozentrale-Deutsche Kommunalbank, Bismarckstr. 101, pg. 406   IT
Deutsche Lebensversicherungs-AG, Breite Strasse 30/31, pg. 58   IT
Deutsche Post Beteiligungen GmbH, Dernburgstr. 50, pg. 407   IT
Deutsche Versicherungs-AG, Breite Strasse 30/31, pg. 58   IT
Die Betonknacker GmbH, Hans-Loch-Str.2, pg. 1128   IT
Dieter Hafemeister Erdbau GmbH & Co., Freiheit 20-21, pg. 623   IT
Dimeq Medizinelectronik GmbH, Nunsdorfer Ring 14, pg. 389   IT
Dr. Mann Pharma, Brunsbuttler Damm 165-173, pg. 196   PB
Dyckerhoff & Widmann Berlin GmbH, Mecklenburgische Strasse 57, pg. 423   IT
Electricite de France, Kurfurstendamm 184, pg. 437   IT
Electrolux GmbH, pg. 442   IT
Elektrowerke GmbH Holding, Einemstr. 1, pg. 1464   IT
ENERGAS Gesellschaft zur Energiegewinnung aus Mull und Kohle mbH, Gottlieb-Dunkel-Strasse 21, pg. 1128   IT
Energie und Umwelt Service GmbH, pg. 836   IT
Energieobjektgesellschaft mbH-EOG, Allee der Kosmonauten 29, pg. 1456   IT
FBT-Finance by Trade GmbH, Mommsenstr. 5, pg. 159   IT
FCM Unternehmensverwaltungs GmbH, pg. 1203   IT
FLASKAMP GMBH, Voltastr. 5, pg. 493   IT
Freudenberg Dichtungs- und Schwingungstechnik GmbH, pg. 505   IT
Joseph Frohlen Papiergrosshandlung GmbH, pg. 757   IT
GbR Leipziger Strasse/Quartier 108, pg. 309   IT
Gaz de France Deutschland GmbH, Internationales Handelszentrum, Friedrichstrasse 95, pg. 541   IT
Gebrueder Kemmer GmbH, Heerstrasse 24, pg. 632   IT
Gillette Deutschland G.m.b.H., Oberlandstrasse 75-84, pg. 744   PB
Gleisbau Hilbig und Ventzke GmbH & Co. KG, Tauentzienstrasse 16, pg. 632   IT
Goedecke A.G., Salzufer 16, pg. 1739   PB
Gottlieb Tesch GmbH Bauunternehmung, Breitenbachstrasse 10, pg. 195   IT
Graphischer Maschinenbau, Mertensstr. 127-131, pg. 742   IT
Guhl Ikebana GmbH, Mecklenburguische Str. 32, pg. 718   IT
Harbauer GmbH & Co. KG, Heerstrasse 24, pg. 632   IT
Carl Hasse & Wrede GmbH, Mohringer Allee 30-42, pg. 738   IT
Hauptniederlassung Berlin-Brandenburg Niederlassung Berlin, Breitenbachstrasse 10, pg. 194   IT
Herlitz Aktiengesellschaft Versand, Berliner Strasse 27, pg. 616   IT
Herlitz Falkenhoh GmbH, Berliner Str. 27, pg. 616   IT
HERLITZ PBS AKTIENGESELLSCHAFT, Berliner Strasse 27, pg. 616   IT
Hermann H.C. Starck Berlin GbmH & Co. KG, Eschenalle 36, pg. 174   IT
Hermann Leist GmbH & Co. KG, Teilestrasse 9-10, pg. 1459   IT
Hermes Versand Service Berlin GmbH, pg. 1014   IT
Hewlett-Packard GmbH, Lutzowllatz 15, pg. 820   PB
Holzmann Gleisbau GmbH, Marzahner Str. 28, pg. 632   IT
IAV Ingenieurgesellschaft fur Aggregatetechnik und Verkehrsfahrzeuge mbH, Carnotstrasse 1, pg. 1473   IT
IKB Leasing Berlin GmbH, Frankfurter Allee 71, pg. 645   IT
ING Lease, Storkower Strasse 139B, pg. 650   IT
IKON AG Prazisionstechnik, Goerzallee 299, pg. 18   IT
The Industrial Bank of Japan, Limited Berlin, Kurfurstendamm 195/196, 11. OG., pg. 675   IT
Jacobs Suchard Berlin GmbH & Co. KG, Prinzenstrasse 32-33, pg. 1288   PB
Jauch & Huebener, Ernst-Reuter-Platz 8, pg. 118   PB
Kappa Karton Vertriebs GmbH, pg. 757   IT
Knorr-Bremse Berlin, Landsberger Allee 399, pg. 738   IT
Kodak AG-Berlin, Schaperstrasse 30, pg. 552   PB
Kommunalconsult Gesellschaft fur die Beratung de Offentlichen Hand mbH, Uhlandstrasse 7-8, pg. 160   IT
KONE Sander Aufzug GmbH, Wackenbergstrasse 112-118, pg. 748   IT
Koralle Verlag GmbH, Kochstr. 50, pg. 102   IT
Kraft Versicherungs-AG, pg. 58   IT
Kraftwerks- und Netzgesellschaft mbH-KNG, Allee der Kosmonauten 29, pg. 1457   IT
Kredietbank-Bankverein AG, Wallstrasse 9-13, pg. 761   IT
Kroll Fahrzeugbau-Umwelttechnik GmbH, Otto-Franke-Strasse 77-97, pg. 1128   IT
Krupp Hoesch Stahl AG - Berlin, Bingerstr. 40, pg. 512   IT
Krupp Hoesch Stahlhandel GmbH, Gottliebdunkel Strasse 50-52, pg. 514   IT

Krupp Stahlbau Berlin GmbH & Co. KG, Gottlieb-Dunkel Str. 50-52, pg. 508   IT
Krupp Warmetechnik GmbH - Berlin, Gottlieb-Dunkel-Str. 50-52, pg. 514   IT
LBB Beteiligungsgesellschaft mbH, Bundesallée 184-185, pg. 160   IT
LBB Betriebsservice GmbH, Brunnenstrasse 111, pg. 160   IT
LBB Grundstucks-GesellschaftmbH der Landesbank Berlin, Rankestrasse 2, pg. 160   IT
LBB Immobilien-und Baumanagement Gesellschaft mbH, Berliner Strasse 44, pg. 160   IT
LBB Kartenservice GmbH, Gustav-Meyer-Allee 1, pg. 160   IT
LBB Service Gesellschaft mbH, Berliner Strasse 40/41, pg. 160   IT
LBS Immobilien GmbH Berlin, Kurfurstrasse 79, pg. 160   IT
Landesbank Berlin - Girozentrale, Bundesallee 171, pg. 160   IT
Landesbank Hessen-Thuringen-Berlin, Tauentzienstrasse 5, pg. 799   IT
Arthur D. Little International, Inc., Kurfurstendamm 66, pg. 670   PV
Logware Gesellschaft fur Entwicklung und Fertigung elektronischer Gerate mbH, Schwedenstrasse 9, pg. 1459   IT
Luwa LTA Luftechnische Anlagen GmbH, pg. 617   IT
MGB Medizinische Gerate GmbH Berlin, pg. 1523   IT
MSA Europe, pg. 1115   PB
MTS Systems GmbH, Hohentwielsteig 3, pg. 1029   PB
Malicha Brennstoffhandel GmbH, Residenzstrasse 32, pg. 1457   IT
Mannesmann Seiffert GmbH, pg. 836   IT
Mannesmann Seiffert Service GmbH, pg. 836   IT
McPaper GmbH, Berliner Strasse 27,-148, pg. 616   IT
MICROS-Fidelio Software Deutschland GmbH, Alt Mobit 89, pg. 1107   PB
Mitsui & Co., Ltd., Internationales Handelszentrum,18. ET., pg. 881   IT
Mitsukoshi Deutschland GmbH-Berlin Branch, Kufurstendamm 220, pg. 884   IT
Nichols Berlin, Oraniendamm 64-72, pg. 1263   PB
NIFE GmbH Stromversorgungssysteme, Naumannstrasse 33, pg. 54   IT
NORD/LB, Friedrichstrasse 95, pg. 957   IT
Obayashi Corporation-Berlin, Pariser Strasse 42-43, pg. 995   IT
Obayashi Projectbau GmbH, Pariser Strasse 42-43, pg. 996   IT
OEWA Wasser und Abwasser GmbH, Potsdam, Wallstrasse 17-20, pg. 1460   IT
104.6 RTL, Kurfurstendamm 207-208, pg. 561   IT
OSVAL Werkzeuge-Maschinen Handelsgesellschaft mbh, Potsdamerstrasse 90, pg. 1128   IT
Otis GmbH, Otis shr. 33, pg. 1690   PB
PLEcon Pipeline Engineering Consulting GmbH, pg. 1149   IT
Papierfabrik Melitta-Werk Bentz KG, pg. 857   IT
PAREXEL GmbH, Klinikum Westend, Haus 18, pg. 1258   PB
Willi Reddemann Import-Export GmbH, pg. 757   IT
REGINA Finanz- u. Versicherungsvermittlung, pg. 310   IT
Otto Reichelt GmbH, Daimlerstrasse 97-111, pg. 1156   IT
Reichs-Kredit-Gesellschaft mbH, Einemstr. 1, pg. 1464   IT
Respatex Vertrieb, Nostitzstrasse 20, pg. 966   IT
Rhenania Allgemeine Speditions-Gesellschaft mit beschrankter Haftung, Westhafenstrasse 1, pg. 1033   IT
Ross Systems Germany GmbH, Regus Business Centre, Kurfurstendamm II, pg. 1406   PB
Rowohlt Berlin Verlag GmbH, Einsteinufer 63a, pg. 1478   IT
SDRC Software & Services GmbH, Schonhauser Allee 163A, pg. 1525   PB
SKE Countertrade GmbH, Taubenstrasse 26, pg. 1458   IT
Sanorania GmbH, Dusterhaupstrasse 28-30, pg. 1049   IT
Sarotti GmbH, pg. 922   IT
SCHERING AG, Muellerstr. 178, pg. 1203   IT
Otto Scheurmann Bank-KG, Kurfurstendamm 52, pg. 418   IT
Schindler Aufzugefabrik GmbH, pg. 1205   IT
Dipl.-Ing Selzer Aufzuge GmbH, Wackenbergstrasse 112-118, pg. 747   IT
Sharp Electronics (Europe), Friedrichstrasse 130A, pg. 1230   IT
Shimizu GmbH-Berlin Office, Kaiserdamm 97, pg. 1234   IT
Skandia Leben Holding GmbH, Bismarckstrasse 101, pg. 1258   IT
Skandia Lebensversicherung AG, Bismarckstrasse 101, pg. 1258   IT
Skandia Versicherungs Mgmt und Serv GmbH, Postfach 127729, pg. 1258   IT
Spinnstoffabrik Zehlendorf AG, Wupperstrasse 10, pg. 626   IT
Springer-Verlag Barcelona, pg. 1291   IT
Springer-Verlag Budapest, pg. 1291   IT
SPRINGER-VERLAG GMBH & CO. KG, Heidelberger Platz 3, pg. 1291   IT
Springer-Verlag Hong Kong, pg. 1291   IT
Springer-Verlag London, pg. 1291   IT
Springer-Verlag Mailand, pg. 1291   IT
Springer-Verlag Paris, pg. 1291   IT
Springer-Verlag Tokyo, pg. 1291   IT
Springer-Verlag Vienna, pg. 1291   IT
Springer-Verlag GmbH & Co. KG, Heidelberger Platz 3, pg. 1291   IT
Statoil Mineraloel GmbH, Wallstrasse 17-22, pg. 1298   IT
TIG Technologie Investitions GmbH & Co. KG, pg. 180   IT
Taisei (Deutschland) GmbH, Dankelmannstrasse 32, pg. 1347   IT

PB - *U.S. Public Companies Volume*
PV - *U.S. Private Companies Volume*
IT - *International Public & Private Companies Volume*

Takenaka Europe GmbH, Berlin, Hauptstrasse 117, pg. 1351 — IT
Tandem Computers GmbH, Berliner Strasse 27, pg. 418 — PB
Tektronix GmbH-Berlin, pg. 1567 — PB
Telefunken Sendertechnik GmbH, Berlin-Mobalt, pg. 1563 — PB
Terrassenhaus-Bau GmbH, Heerstr. 24, pg. 633 — IT
Toys "R" Us Deutschland GmbH, pg. 1626 — PB
Tyler Berlin GmbH, Flankenschanze 28, pg. 592 — IT
UCB Umwelt Consult Berlin GmbH, pg. 837 — IT
Ullstein GmbH, Kochstr. 50, pg. 102 — IT
VEAG Vereinigte Energiewerke AG, Unter den Linden 38, pg. 1457 — IT
VW AUDI Vertrieb GmbH, pg. 1473 — IT
VW AUDI Vertrieb GmbH & Co. Vertriebszentrum Berlin KG, pg. 1473 — IT
VW Gedas Consult GmbH, Pascalstrasse 11, pg. 1474 — IT
VW-Gesellschaft fur Technische Datenverarbeitungssysteme mbH, Pascalstrasse 11, pg. 1474 — IT
Verlag Der Tagesspiegel, Potsdamer Strasse 87, pg. 1479 — IT
Voigt & Co. Baugesellschaft GmbH, Kitzingstr. 7-9, pg. 1261 — IT
Volkswagen Bordnetze Gmbh, pg. 1474 — IT
Weberbank Berliner Industriebank KGaA, Landecker Strasse 2-3, pg. 160 — IT
Wella Friseurbedarf GmbH, pg. 1489 — IT
Fritz Werner Machine Tools AG, pg. 1128 — IT
West Merchant Bank Limited, Kurfurstendamm 11, pg. 1493 — IT
WestLB Berlin Branch, Unter der Linden 26-30, pg. 1492 — IT
Winschermann Berlin GmbH, Quedlinburger Str. 11, pg. 1167 — IT
Wintershall Erdgas Handelshaus GmbH, Duesseldorfer Strasse 38, pg. 105 — IT
Zweigniederlassung der Rockwell International GmbH, Cicerostrasse 26, pg. 1402 — PB
Zyma GmbH, Neukollnische Allee 146, pg. 986 — IT

Besigheim

Watts MTR GmbH, Rudolph Dierd Strasse, pg. 1747 — PB

Bestensee

Perstorp Bauchemie, Motzener Strasse 111, pg. 1037 — IT

Betzdorf

ELCO Elektronik GmbH, Benjamin-Fox-Str. 1, pg. 775 — IT
Elco Eurpoe GmbH, Benjamin-Fox-Str. 1, pg. 1590 — PB

Beverungen

Kernkraftwerk Wurgassen-KWW, pg. 1456 — IT

Bexbach

Norton Hochtemperaturkeramik GmbH, In Der Kolling 6, pg. 1175 — IT

Biberach an der Riss

Liebherr-Gutsverwaltung GmbH, Hans Lieherr Str. 45, pg. 808 — IT
Liebherr-Holding GmbH, Hans Liebherr Str. 45, pg. 808 — IT
Liebherr-Werk Biberach GmbH, Hans Liebherr Str. 45, pg. 808 — IT
Liebherr-Wohnungbau GmbH, Hans Liebherr Str. 45, pg. 808 — IT

Bickenbach

ABS-Scanpump GmbH, Gewerbezentrum Jagdschloss, Darmstader Str. 3a-3b, pg. 270 — IT

Biebesheim

Ceilcote Korrosionstechnik G.m.b.H., pg. 975 — IT

Bielefeld

Adler Industrienahmaschinen Verkauf GmbH, pg. 468 — IT
Betriebsmittelbau GmbH, pg. 468 — IT
Deutsche Bank AG (Bielefeld), Herforder Strasse, 23, pg. 402 — IT
Durkopp Adler AG, Potsdamer Str. 190, pg. 468 — IT
Durkopp Maschinebau GmbH, pg. 468 — IT
Durkopp Systemtechnik GmbH, pg. 468 — IT
Jauch & Huebener, Oberntorwall 23 a, pg. 118 — PB
Optima Schneid und Losungsmittel Gesellschaft mbH, Ruckertstrasse 6, pg. 517 — IT
Parker Hannifin GmbH, Postfach 120206, pg. 1261 — PB
August Rabeneick GmbH, pg. 835 — IT
Rorer GmbH, Stieghorster Strasse 86, pg. 1111 — IT
Stora Carbonless Paper GmbH, Niedernholz 23, pg. 1303 — IT
WestLB Bielefeld Branch, Niederwall 26, pg. 1492 — IT

Bietigheim-Bissingen

Data Translation GmbH, Stuttgarter Str. 66, pg. 1079 — PB
HEINKEL INDUSTRIEZENTRIFUGEN GMBH & CO., Gottlob-Grotz-Str. 1, pg. 608 — IT

Parker Hannifin GmbH/Pradifa Packing Division, Postfach 1641, pg. 1262 — PB

Bindlach

Solar Fashion GmbH & Co. KG, pg. 618 — IT

Bingen

Balzers Verschleisschutz GmbH, pg. 997 — IT
A. RACKE GMBH, Stefan-George St. 20, pg. 1083 — IT
St. Ursula Weingut und Weinkellerei GmbH, pg. 922 — IT
Weinbrennerei Scharlachberg, Stefan-George Strasse 20, pg. 1083 — IT
Wurth Burobedarf & Organisation GmbH, pg. 758 — IT

Birkenfeld

LeaRonal GmbH, Gewerbestrasse 19, pg. 982 — PB

Birstein

Korf-Transport GmbH, Industriestrasse 9, pg. 759 — IT

Bischofsheim

Nortor Industrie Produkte GmbH, Neben Dem, pg. 1175 — IT

Bitburg

BITBURGER BRAUEREI TH. SIMON GMBH, Postfach 1164, pg. 197 — IT

Bitterfeld

Eastern Branch, Hallesche Strasse 18, pg. 401 — IT
HC Abbruch und Recycling GmbH, Strasse der Wissenschaften, pg. 513 — IT
Hoogovens Aluminium Profiltechnik Bitterfeld GmbH, Zorpigerstrasse, pg. 755 — IT
Industrie-und Kraftwerksrohrleitungsbau Bitterfeld GmbH, pg. 399 — IT
Krupp Warmetechnik GmbH - Bitterfeld, Strasse der Wissenschaften 4, pg. 514 — IT

Blaustein

Hefele GmbH, Mahringerstr. 19, pg. 511 — IT

Bleiche

Mannesmann Kienzle Instruments GmbH, pg. 839 — IT

Bobenheim-Roxheim

Bilfinger + Berger Vorspanntechnik GmbH, Indsutriestrasse, pg. 195 — IT

Boblingen

Hewlett-Packard GmbH, Zone Office South/West, Schickardstrasse 2, pg. 820 — PB
Moog GmbH, Hanns-Klemm-Str. 28, pg. 1128 — PB

Bocholt

A. Friedrich Flender AG, Alfred-Flender-Str. 77, pg. 400 — IT
Hepworth Mineralien und Chemicalien GmbH, Benztrasse 12, pg. 615 — IT
Red Band Susswaren Vertriebs GmbH, Ritterstr. 24, pg. 244 — IT

Bochum

Altpapier-Verwertung Wattenscheid GmbH, Coloniastrasse 13, pg. 1303 — IT
Aral AG, Sittener Strasse 45, pg. 1460 — IT
Bonifacius Kohle Transport und Handelsgesellschaft mbH & Co. KG, Lohrheidestrasse 1, pg. 1457 — IT
CGG Chemogas GmbH, pg. 811 — IT
Faltec Tore GmbH, Am Vorort 4, pg. 269 — IT
Dr. C. Otto Feuerfest GmbH, Dr. C. Otto Feuerfest Str. 222, pg. 1070 — IT
GEBR. EICKHOFF MASCHINENFABRIK UND EISENGIESSEREI MBH, Hunscheid, Strasse 176, pg. 542 — IT
Geschaftsstelle Bochum, Huestrasse 22, pg. 194 — IT
Haden GmbH, Hattinger Strasse 951, pg. 586 — IT
Heizol-Handelsgesellschaft mbH, Am Hain 2, pg. 1461 — IT
Krupp Hoesch Automotive GmbH, Alleestr. 165, pg. 507 — IT
Krupp Hoesch Stahl AG - Bochum, Alleestr. 165, pg. 513 — IT
Krupp Nirosta GmbH, Alleestr. 165, pg. 513 — IT
Nokia Mobile Phones Produktions GmbH, Meesmannstrasse 103, pg. 952 — IT
Nokia Mobile Phones R&D Center, Germany, Meesmannstrasse 103, pg. 952 — IT
ORM Eergold Chemie GmbH & Co., KG Daimlerstrasse 2-4, pg. 1426 — IT
Raab Karcher Warmetechnik GmbH, Lohrheidestrasse 1, pg. 1457 — IT
Thyssen Still Auto Anlagentechnik GmbH, pg. 1387 — IT
VEBA IMMOBILIEN AG, Philippstrasse 3, pg. 1460 — IT
VEBA URBANA AG, pg. 1460 — IT

Vereinigte Weichenbau GmbH, Stahlhauserstr. 20, pg. 513 — IT

Bodenheim

Costar GmbH, Am Kummerling 24-26, pg. 448 — PB

Boenningstedt

Senior Engineering TIFT GmbH, Nordriwa 17, pg. 1223 — IT

Bogen

Polyuretan-Element-Technik PURET GmbH, pg. 423 — IT

Bohlen

Borsig Service Bohlen GmbH, P.O. Box 4, pg. 399 — IT

Bohlitz-Ehrenberg

Werner & Pfleiderer Backtechnik Vertriebs-GmbH, Frauhoferstr. 8, pg. 511 — IT

Bonn

AVG Allgemeine Vertriebsgesellschaft fur Industrieerzeugnisse, pg. 835 — IT
Aluminum-Verwaltungs-Gesellschaft mbH, George-von-Boeselager-Str. 25, pg. 1466 — IT
Applied Technology (Germany), Theaterplatz 3, pg. 1004 — PB
Bofors Deutschland GmbH, Plittersdorfer Strasse 95, pg. 278 — IT
Boge GmbH & Co., pg. 835 — IT
Continental Can Europe GmbH Holding, Georg-von-Boeselager-Str. 25, pg. 1464 — IT
DEUTSCHE POST AG, Heinrich-von-Stephan-Str. 1, pg. 407 — IT
Deutsche PostConsult, Herbert-Rabius-Str. 24, pg. 407 — IT
DEUTSCHE TELEKOM AG, Godesberger Allee 87-93, pg. 407 — IT
EMS Kurierpost GmbH, Joseph-Wirmer-Str. 6, pg. 407 — IT
Elekluft Elektronik-und Luftfahrtgerate GmbH, pg. 367 — IT
Elekluft GmbH, P.O. Box 1509, pg. 367 — IT
Hewlett-Packard GmbH, Verbindungsstelle Bonn, Friedrich-Ebert-Allee 26, pg. 820 — PB
ILSE Bergbau-GmbH, Georg-von-Boeselager-Str. 25, pg. 1464 — IT
Ideal-Standard GmbH, Euskirchener Str. 80, pg. 92 — PB
Kautex Werke Reinold Hagen AG, pg. 310 — IT
KLOCKNER-MOELLER GMBH, Hein-Moeller-Strasse 7-11, pg. 736 — IT
Krupp Kautex Maschinenbau GmbH, Kautexstr. 54, pg. 510 — IT
LITEF (Litton Technische Werke), Poppelsdorfer Alle 102, pg. 1004 — PB
Lockheed International GmbH, Turmstrasse 10, pg. 1009 — PB
Maagh Leitungsbau GmbH, An den Markthallen 2, pg. 195 — IT
Niederlassung Bonn, Baumschulallee 9-13, pg. 194 — IT
Projektgesellschaft fur Kreislaufwirtschaft PK mbH, Friedrich-Wohler-Str. 56, pg. 1464 — IT
RTC Rostfrei-Technik-Center GmbH, Rudolf-Diesel-Strasse 10, pg. 1018 — IT
Reinhard Raffel Metallwarenfabrik GmbH, Pennefeldsweg 10, pg. 88 — IT
Rheinische Chamotte und Dinas GmbH, Drachenburgstr. 5, pg. 1464 — IT
Romantis Gesellschaft fir Satellitenkommunikation m.b.h., pg. 367 — IT
Shandwick Deutschland GmbH, Meckenheimer Allee 67-69, pg. 1227 — IT
Shandwick Europe Holding Co. GmbH, Bismarckstrasse 13, pg. 1227 — IT
T-Mobil Deutsche Telekom Mobil GmbH, Landgrabenweg 151, pg. 407 — IT
Thomson-CSF Deutschland GmbH, Godesberger Allee, 90, pg. 1385 — IT
Tractebel Ingenieur GmbH, Theaterplatz 18, pg. 1416 — IT
VAW Aluminum AG, Georg-von-Boeselager-Str. 25, pg. 1466 — IT
VIAG Aktiengesellschaft, Georg-von-Boeselager-Str. 25, pg. 1466 — IT
VIAG Konzernrevision und Beratung GmbH, Georg-von-Boeselager-Str. 25, pg. 1466 — IT
VIAG Verbindungsburo Bonn, Schaumburg-Lippe-Str. 2, pg. 1466 — IT
V.I.M.G. VIAG Immobilien-Management GmbH, Georg-von-Boeselager-Str. 25, pg. 1466 — IT
VIAG AG, George-von-Boeselager-Strasse 25, pg. 1464 — IT

Bopfingen

Dr. Rudolf Schieber Chemische Fabrik GmbH & Co. KG, pg. 610 — IT

Boppard

BOMAG, Hellerwald, pg. 1677 — PB

Borken

Spur Regal-Systeme SRS, Landwehr 25, pg. 851 — IT

PB - U.S. Public Companies Volume
PV - U.S. Private Companies Volume
IT - International Public & Private Companies Volume

1606

Geographic Index-Non U.S.

Bornheim

Abello Deutschland Pharma GmbH, Secundastrasse 8, pg. 288   IT

Bottrop

ABR Abfallbeseitigung und Recycling GmbH, pg. 1148   IT
ABR Handel GmbH, pg. 1148   IT
Bruno Fechner GmbH & Co. KG, Batenbrockstrasse 62-66, pg. 1454   IT
Hydro Magnesium Marketing GmbH, Industriestrasse 61, pg. 963   IT
Kohleol-Anlage Bottrop GmbH, Wilheimer Mark, pg. 1461   IT
Norsk Hydro Magnesium-gesellschaft mbH, Industriestrasse 61, pg. 964   IT
Region Europe Tamrock Europe GmbH, Industrietstrasse 36, pg. 1353   IT
Tamrock Deustchland GmbH, Industriestrasse 36, pg. 1353   IT

Botzingen

Eurotec Systemteile Gmbh, P.O. Box 11 51, pg. 737   IT

Bous

Rohrenwerke Bous/Saar GmbH, pg. 835   IT

Bramberg

Ferngas Nordbayern GmbH, Benzstrasse 9, pg. 1148   IT

Bramsche

Deutsche Duni GmbH, Robert Bosch-Strasse 4, pg. 421   IT

Brandenburg

Demag-Brandenburg Engineering, pg. 837   IT

Braunlingen

Coats Mez Industrieahfaden G.m.b.H., Hoefinger Strasse 24, pg. 300   IT
Dynacast Deutschland GmbH, Hoefinger Strasse 24, pg. 300   IT

Braunschweig

Amersham Buchler GmbH & Co. KG, Gieselweg 1, pg. 992   IT
Cebas Immobilienentwicklungs Gesellschaft mbH, Juliusstrasse 1-2, pg. 1134   IT
Cobelplast Trading Deutschland GmbH, pg. 1206   IT
Continental PET Europe GmbH, pg. 1206   IT
Heimbs & Sohn GmbH & Co KG, pg. 920   IT
NORD/LB, pg. 957   IT
NORD/LB, Dankwardstrasse 1, pg. 957   IT
Rhenania Transport GmbH, Am Hauptguterbahnhof, pg. 1033   IT
SLW-Versicherungsdienst GmbH, pg. 1206   IT
SCHMALBACH-LUBECA AG, Haupterwaltung Schmalbachstr. 1, pg. 1206   IT
Schmalback-Lubeca Unterstutzungskasse GmbH, pg. 1207   IT
Toshiba Semiconductor G.m.b.H., Grotrian-Steinwegstr. 10, pg. 1407   IT
V-Crest Systems GmbH, pg. 1473   IT
V.A.G. Marketing Management Institut GmbH, Klostergang 53, pg. 1473   IT
V.A.G. Synko GmbH, Zuckerbergweg 22, pg. 1473   IT
VW Finanz GmbH, Gifhorner Starsse 57, pg. 1474   IT
Volim Volkswagen Immobilien Vernietgesellschaft fur VW-Audi Handlerbetriebe mbH, pg. 1474   IT
Volkswagen Bank GmbH, Gifhorner Strasse 57, pg. 1474   IT
Volkswagen Financial Services AG, pg. 1474   IT
Volkswagen Leasing Anlagen GmbH, Gifhorner Strasse 57, pg. 1474   IT
Volkswagen Leasing GmbH, pg. 1474   IT

Brechen

Taunus-Beton GmbH & Co. KG, pg. 423   IT

Bremen

Assecuranz-Compagnie Mercur AG, pg. 58   IT
Bankhaus Neelmeyer AG, pg. 179   IT
Berag GmbH, Herrlichkeit 1, pg. 1502   IT
BONUM Anlage- und Beteiligungs GmbH, pg. 179   IT
Bregal, Bremer Galvanislerungs GmbH, Auf den Delben 35, pg. 79   IT
Bremer Reiseburo GmbH, pg. 596   IT
Bremer Schiffsvercharterungs AG, pg. 596   IT
Daimler-Benz Aerospace AG, Raumfahrt-Unfrastruktur, Hunefeldstrasse 1-5, pg. 367   IT
Deutsche Bank AG (Bremen), Domshof 22-25, pg. 402   IT
euroflamm GmbH, pg. 400   IT
Finnigan MAT GmbH, Barkhausenstrasse 2, pg. 1596   PB
Frionor Tiefkuhl-Produkte GmbH, Birkenstr. 15, pg. 516   IT
GESTRA GMBH, Hemmstrasse 130, pg. 549   IT
Max Grunhut GmbH, Martinstr. 33, pg. 1033   IT

Hapag-Lloyd Kreuzfahrten GmbH, pg. 596   IT
Hapag-Lloyd Reiseburo GmbH, pg. 596   IT
Hapag-Lloyd Tours GmbH, pg. 596   IT
Hapag-Lloyd Transport & Service GmbH, pg. 596   IT
Jacobs Suchard Erzeugnisse GmbH & Co. KG, Langemarckstrasse 4-20, pg. 1289   PB
Jacobs Suchard International Mfg. GmbH & Co. KG, Langemarckstrasse 4-20, pg. 1289   PB
Jacobs Suchard Service GmbH & Co. KG, Langemarckstrasse 4-20, pg. 1289   PB
Johann A. Krause, pg. 1387   IT
A. Johnson & Co. GmbH, Hermann-Bose-Strasse 35, pg. 711   IT
Kellogg (Deutschland) Gesellschaft mit beschrankter Hartung (GmbH), Auf der Muggenberg 30, pg. 948   PB
Knurr-Interplast GmbH, Am Waldeck 1, pg. 739   IT
Kredietbank-Bankverein AG, Wachtstrasse 16, pg. 761   IT
Krupp Hoesch Stahlhandel GmbH, Industriestrasse 6, pg. 514   IT
Krupp Warmetechnik GmbH - Bremen, Westerstr. 12-14, pg. 514   IT
Kuehne & Nagel (AG & Co.), Wilhelm-Kaisen Bruecke 1, pg. 763   IT
Kvaerner Brug (Deutschland) GmbH, pg. 771   IT
Kvaerner Ships Equipment GmbH, Wachtstrasse 17-24, pg. 768   IT
Lohmann & Company GmbH, Schwachauser, Heerstrasse 57, pg. 1502   PB
KG ms "Europa" der BRESCHAG Bremer Schiffsverch. AG & Co. KG, pg. 596   IT
MacGREGOR Conver GmbH, Fritz-Thiele Str. 4., pg. 670   IT
Mammoet-Hansa A.G., pg. 1144   IT
Meistermarken-Werke G.m.b.H., Spezialfabrik Back-und Grosskuchenbedarf, pg. 1438   IT
Melitta Kaffee GmbH & Co., Kommandit Gesellschaft, pg. 857   IT
Morton International G.m.b.H., Suedwestr. 17, pg. 1135   PB
Motor-Finanz GmbH, pg. 180   IT
NYK Line-Bremen, Martinistrasse 50, pg. 942   IT
Nestrans Seehafenspedition GmbH, Am Wall 96, pg. 514   IT
Niederlassung Bremen, Lloydstrasse 1, pg. 194   IT
Nor Holz Verkaufsgesellschaft, fur Holzprodukte mbH, Contrescarpe 53, pg. 966   PB
Orthoplant GmbH, pg. 256   PB
Panalpina Welttransport GmbH, pg. 1023   IT
Raffay Industrieprodukte GmbH, pg. 1474   IT
Ragal Feinblech-Vertriebs GmbH, Birkenstrasse 15, pg. 1088   IT
Rechenzentrum WESER GmbH, pg. 1474   IT
Wilhelm Sander Fertigung GmbH, Zum Panrepel 41, pg. 719   IT
Schiffsbetriebsgesellschaft Bremen mbH, pg. 310   IT
STAHLwerke Bremen GmbH, Auf den Delben 35, pg. 79   IT
Tastemaker Germany, pg. 811   PB
Uberlandwerk Nord Hannover AG, Stesemannstrasse 48, pg. 1457   IT
V.A.G. Vertriebszentrum Weser-EMS GmbH, Weser-Ems-Strasse 2, pg. 1474   IT
V.A.G. Vertriebszentrum Weser-EMS GmbH U Co. KG, Weser-Ems-Str. 2, pg. 1474   IT
WESER-EMS Vertriebsgesellschaft mbH, Weser-Ems-Strasse 2, pg. 1474   IT
Wisura Mineralolwerk Goldgrabe & Scheft GmbH & Co., Am Gaswerk 2-10, pg. 517   IT

Bremerhaven

Geestemunder Bank AG, pg. 179   IT
Geestemunder Verwaltungs- und Beteiligungsges mbH, pg. 179   IT
Grundstucksgesellschaft Geetbank-Haus, pg. 179   IT
Hans Huth Handel GmbH, pg. 838   IT
Hans Huth Handel GmbH & Co. KG, pg. 838   IT
Nordsee Deutsche Hochseefischerei G.m.b.H., Klussmannstr. 1-4, pg. 1438   IT

Bremervorde

Bebo-Plastik GmbH, pg. 1206   IT
GETI WILBA GmbH, pg. 1305   IT
MPB Folien Gesellschaft mbH, pg. 1206   IT
Maschinenverwertungsgesellschaft mbH, pg. 1206   IT

Brilon

Brima Mineralol-Vertriebs-Union GmbH, Nehdener Weg 9, pg. 1457   IT

Brinkum

Gerhard Prahm GmbH & Co., pg. 1288   IT

Brokdorf

Kernkraftwerk Brokdorf GmbH, pg. 1456   IT

Bruchkobel

Trimble Navigation Ltd. Deutschland, Innerer Ring 1b, pg. 1638   PB

Bruchsal

Asgrow GmbH, Lasshardstr. 6, pg. 1049   IT
Holzindustrie Bruchsal GmbH, Ernst-Blickle-Str. 21-25, pg. 368   IT

Huck Brennstoffe GmbH, Daimlerweg 6-8, pg. 513   IT
MacDermid GmbH, Postfach 2065, Industriegebiet West II, pg. 1030   PB
Sulzer Weise GmbH, Ernst-Blickle-Str. 29, pg. 1306   IT

Bruhl

DOM-Sicherheitstechnik GmbH & Co. KG, Wesselinger Str. 10-16, pg. 233   PB
Fisher-Price Spielwaren GmbH, Schildgesstrasse 71-163, pg. 1058   PB

Brunsbuttel

Hydro Agri Brunsbuttel GmbH, Hostendamm 2, pg. 962   IT
Kernkraftwerk Brunsbuettel Gmbh, Otto-Hahn-Strasse, pg. 1457   IT
Schelde Chemie Brunsbuttel GmbH, pg. 172   IT

Buchen

RuppKeramik GmbH, Ziegeleistrasse 10, pg. 1091   IT
Ruppkeramik GmbH, Ziegeleistrasse 10, pg. 1093   IT
TUCHENHAGEN GMBH, Am Industriepark 2-10, pg. 1426   IT

Buchholz

Analog Devices GMBH - Technisches Buero Nord, Hamburger Strasse 4A, pg. 108   PB
Merkel Kunststoff GmbH, pg. 859   IT
VARTA Recycling GmbH, Krautscheider Strasse 22, pg. 1452   IT

Buhl

A.u.P. Armbruster Bauunternehmung GmbH, Hurstrasse 4, pg. 195   IT

Bunde

Lawson Mardon Rotopack GmbH, pg. 69   IT
Revell AG, Henschelstrasse 20-30, pg. 926   PV

Burbach

Ingersoll Maschinen und Werkzeuge GmbH, pg. 562   PV
Thermon Deutschland GmbH, Dillenburger Strasse 26, pg. 1081   PV
Waldrich Siegen Werkzeugmaschinen GmbH, Postfach 1320, pg. 562   PV

Burgwedel

Wellcome GmbH, pg. 553   IT

Burscheid

AE Goetze GmbH, Burgermeister-Schmidt-Str. 17, pg. 1334   IT
Hugo Fassbender KG, pg. 505   IT

Burstadt

Perstorp Flooring GmbH, Industriestrasse 14, pg. 1039   IT
Perstorp GmbH, Industriestrasse 14, pg. 1040   IT
Perstorp GmbH Decorative Laminate, Industriestrasse 14, pg. 1038   IT
Perstorp GmbH-SBU Furniture (Unidur), Industriestrasse 14, pg. 1038   IT
Perstorp GmbH Verkaufsburo Chemitec, Industriestrasse 14, pg. 1037   IT

Buttenwiesen

Schuhle GmbH, Schuhlestrasse 8-9, pg. 1458   IT

Butzbach

Buss-SMS GmbH Verfahrenstechnik, Kaiserstrasse 13-15, pg. 490   IT
Sulzer Chemtech GmbH, pg. 1308   IT

Buxtehude

Babcock Holding (Deutschland) GmbH, Bahnhofstrasse 24, pg. 131   IT
Claudius Peters AG, Schanzenstrasse 40, pg. 131   IT
Pioneer Saaten, GmbH, Apenser Strasse 198, pg. 1299   PB

Calw-Hirsau

CALWER DECKEN-UND TUCHFABRIKEN AG, In der Insel 4, pg. 253   IT

Celle

Baker Oil Tools GmbH, Maschweg 9, pg. 167   PB
Boart Longyear GmbH, Grafftring 1, pg. 76   IT
Eastman Christensen GmbH, Postfach 309, Christensenstrasse, pg. 167   PB
Halliburton Company Germany GMBH, Bruchkampweg 7, pg. 777   PB
Sandoz Ernahrung G.m.b.H., pg. 984   IT

PB - *U.S. Public Companies Volume*
PV - *U.S. Private Companies Volume*
IT - *International Public & Private Companies Volume*

Smith International Deutschland GmbH, Grafftring 5-7, pg. 1478 — PB
Tuboscope Vetco (Deutchsland), pg. 1644 — PB
Wasa G.m.b.H., pg. 986 — IT

Cham

Scherbauer Spedition GmbH, pg. 1145 — IT

Chemnitz

DG Bank - Chemnitz, Bahnhofstrasse 24, pg. 351 — IT
Deutsche Bank-Kreditbank AG (Chemnitz), Fritz-Heckert-Platz 2, pg. 402 — IT
Heckert Chemnitzer Werzeugmaschinen GmbH, Otto-Scherbach Strasse 15-17, pg. 1419 — IT
KONE Garant Aufzug GmbH, Philippstrasse 7, pg. 748 — IT
Luwa Lufttechnische Anlagen GmbH, pg. 617 — IT
Motorenwerk Chemnitz GmbH, pg. 1474 — IT
NTG Netzwerk und Telematic GmbH I.L., Treffurthstr. 17, pg. 317 — IT
Niederlassung Chemnitz, Limbacher Strasse 111, pg. 194 — IT
Rexroth Hydraulikanlagen und service GmbH, pg. 838 — IT
Rexroth Vertriebs und Service GmbH, pg. 839 — IT
Volkswagen-Audi Vertriebs-GmbH Chemnitz, pg. 1474 — IT
Woodward-Clyde International, Lichtenwalder Strasse 9, pg. 1658 — PB

Cloppenburg

Derby Cycle Werke GmbH, Siemensstrasse 1-3, pg. 394 — IT

Coburg

Waldrich Coburg Werkzeugmaschinenfabrik GmbH, Postfach 3253, pg. 562 — PV

Coesfeld

Sperrholz Koch GmbH, pg. 1491 — IT

Cologne

Agrippina Lebensversicherung Aktiengesellschaft, Oppenheimstrasse 14, pg. 1531 — IT
Agrippina Rechtsschutzversicherung AG, Worringer Strasse 11-13, pg. 1531 — IT
Agrippina Ruckversicherung Aktiengesellschaft, Oppenheimstrasse 2, pg. 1531 — IT
Agrippina Versicherungs Aktiengesellschaft, Riehler Strasse 90, pg. 1531 — IT
Alcoa Fujikura GmbH, Robert-Perthel-Strasse 3, pg. 62 — PB
Allianz Versicherungs-AG, Zweigniederlassung, fur Nordrhein-Westfalen, pg. 58 — IT
Amro Handelsbank A.G., Gereonstrasse 5-11, pg. 10 — IT
Analog Devices GMBH - Technisches Buero West, Thielenbrucher Allee 5, pg. 108 — PB
Aponti GmbH, pg. 918 — IT
Beton Union Koln-Bonn, pg. 422 — IT
Bitburger Bier-GmbH Koln, Kirchbaguwirweg 19, pg. 197 — IT
Bosenberg Bauchemie GmbH, Welser Strasse 6A, pg. 790 — IT
Bull AG, Theodor-Heuss Str. 60-66, pg. 317 — IT
Bull Organisationssysteme GmbH I.L., Theodor Heuss Str. 60-66, pg. 317 — IT
CBG Chemie Beteiligungsgesellschaft m.b.H., Worthstrasse 34, pg. 682 — IT
CLT Deutschland, Im Mediapark 5b, pg. 561 — IT
Carbosulf Chemische Werke GmbH, pg. 47 — IT
Central Krankenversicherung AG, Hansaring 40-50, pg. 15 — IT
Chemische Fabrik Kalk GmbH, Vietorstr. 17, pg. 104 — IT
CLOUTH GUMMIWERKE AG, Niehler Strasse 102-116, pg. 297 — IT
D & B Software (Deutschland) GmbH, Neuenhofer Allee 49-51, pg. 532 — IT
DVM Datenverarbeitungsmaschinen und Time-Share GmbH, Theodor Heuss Str. 60-66, pg. 317 — IT
DVM GmbH, Theodor-Heuss Strasse 60-66, pg. 318 — IT
Delvag Luftfahrtversicherungs-AG, Von-Gablenz-Str. 2-6, pg. 407 — IT
Deutsche Bank AG (Cologne), An den Dominikanern 11-27, pg. 402 — IT
Deutsche Goodyear GmbH, Xantener Str. 105, pg. 753 — PB
Deutsche Krankenversicherung AG, Aachener Strasse 300, pg. 58 — IT
DEUTSCHE LUFTHANSA AG, Von-Gablenz-Strasse 2-6, pg. 407 — IT
DEUTZ AG, Deutz-Mulheimer-Str. 147-149, pg. 407 — IT
Dr. Ritter GmbH & Co., pg. 920 — IT
EC Erdolchemie GmbH, Neute Landstrasse, pg. 172 — IT
EMI Electrola GmbH, Postfach 303029, pg. 427 — IT
Eisenmetall Lager GmbH, Hanseki 3, pg. 514 — IT
Eurogroup SA, pg. 330 — IT
Ford Bank AG, Henry Ford Strasse 5, pg. 665 — PB
Ford Investitions GmbH & Co. oHG, Henry Ford Strasse 5, pg. 666 — PB
Ford Verischerungs-Vermittlungs GmbH, Henry Ford Strasse 5, pg. 666 — PB
Ford-Versorgungs-Und Unterstutzungseinrichtung GmbH, Henry Ford Strasse 5, pg. 666 — PB
Ford-Werke AG & Co., Henry Ford Strasse 5, pg. 666 — PB
Formica Vertriebs GmbH, Hanstetr. 61-63, pg. 130 — IT
Garten und Heim GmbH, Boltensternstr. 159, pg. 632 — IT
Generale Bank & Co., Christophstrasse 33-37, pg. 548 — IT
Geschaftsstelle Cologne, Ferdinand-Porsche-Str. 3, pg. 739 — IT
HK Asset Participation GmbH, pg. 1128 — IT

Hapag-Lloyd Reiseburo GmbH Koln, pg. 596 — IT
Hauptniederlassung Koln Niederlassung Koln, Horbellerstrasse 11, pg. 194 — IT
H.J. Heinz GmbH, Kaiser Wilhelm-Ring 34, pg. 806 — PB
Hewlett-Packard GmbH, Emil-Hoffmann-Strasse 1a, pg. 820 — PB
Honeywell Bull AG, Theodor-Heuss Strasse 60-66, pg. 318 — IT
Horst Brever GmbH, pg. 1055 — PB
Hosokawa MikroPul GmbH, 11 Welserstrasse, pg. 636 — IT
Interorgana Chemiehandel G.m.b.H., Worthstrasse 34, pg. 682 — IT
Axel Johnson Ore & Metals GmbH, Aachener Strasse 1187, pg. 711 — IT
KHD Humboldt Wedag AG, Wiersberg Str., pg. 408 — IT
Kodak AG-Koln, Xantener Strasse 105, pg. 552 — PB
Hermann Kolb Machinery AG, pg. 1128 — IT
Krupp Hoesch Metallhandel GmbH, Hanseki 3, pg. 514 — IT
Krupp Hoesch Stahlhandel Rheinland GmbH, Hansekai 3, pg. 514 — IT
Krupp Warmetechnik GmbH - Cologne, Kohlenstr. 2-6, pg. 514 — IT
Linde AG Werksgruppe Kalte- u. Einrichtungstechnik, Suether Haupstr. 178, pg. 810 — IT
Lufthansa Commercial Holding GmbH, Von-Gablenz-Str. 2-6, pg. 407 — IT
MSI Data GmbH, Horbellerstrasse 10-14, pg. 1546 — PB
The E.F. MacDonald Verkaufsforderung GmbH, Vorgeborgstrasse 1, pg. 212 — PV
METRO AG, Leonhard-Tietz-Str.1, pg. 863 — IT
Mettler-Toledo (Koln) GmbH, pg. 4 — PV
Montan Gesellschaft Warenhandel mbh, Vietorstr. 17, pg. 514 — IT
Moulinex GmbH, Amsterdamer Strasse 228, pg. 896 — IT
A. Nottermann & Cie GmbH, Nottermann Alle 1, pg. 1112 — IT
Francesco Parisi G.m.b.H., Friesenwall, 53, pg. 504 — IT
Parker Hannifin N.M.F. GmbH, Delmenhorster Str. 10, pg. 1261 — PB
Patria Versicherung Aktiengesellschaft, Riehler Strasse 90, pg. 514 — IT
Promwestorg Aussenhandel GmbH, Mauritiuswall 64-66, pg. 514 — IT
Protimeter Zweigniederlassung der Bowthorpe GmbH, Wilhelm Ruppert Strasse 38, pg. 209 — IT
RTL Television, Aachener Strasse 1036, pg. 561 — IT
Research-Cottrell (Deutschland) G.m.b.H., Kolner 195, pg. 29 — PB
REWE-HANDELSGRUPPE, Domstr. 20, pg. 1106 — IT
R.J. Reynolds Tobacco Co. GmbH, 3, Gulich Platz, pg. 1355 — PB
Rheinbraun AG, Lindenthal, Stuettgenweg 2, pg. 1081 — IT
Rherania Transport GmbH, Zweigniederlassung, Am Hansekaiserstrasse, pg. 1033 — IT
Rhocanid Chemie GmbH, 26 Geestemunderstr., pg. 47 — IT
Rhone-Poulenc Rorer GmbH, Nattermannallee 1, pg. 1113 — IT
Rohce & Schwarz GmbH, Graf-Zeppelin-Strasse 18, pg. 1124 — IT
SK EV Grundstucksentwicklungs GmbH & Co. KG, pg. 178 — IT
SK EV Grundstucksentwicklungs Verwaltung GmbH, pg. 178 — IT
Saarbach, Follerstrasse 2, pg. 796 — IT
Saar-Industrie, GmbH, Henry Ford Strasse 5, pg. 666 — PB
Sekurit Saint-Gobain Nutzfahrzeugglas KG, pg. 1173 — IT
Selkirk Europe, Postfach 1539, pg. 1795 — PB
Hch. Sieger GmbH und Co. Kg., Suntherstrasse 3, pg. 757 — IT
Sony Deutschland GmbH, Hugo-Eckener-Str. 20, pg. 1284 — IT
STADTSPARKASSE KOLN, Hahnenstrasse 57, pg. 1293 — IT
Sulzermedica GmbH, pg. 1307 — IT
Super RTL, Richard-Byrd-Str. 6, pg. 562 — IT
Tatung International (Deutschland) Gmbh, Max-Planch Strasse 42, pg. 1357 — IT
Tektronix GmbH, pg. 1567 — IT
TENSID Chemie Vertriebsgesellschaft mbH, Maarweg 163, pg. 104 — IT
Thermo Electric GmbH, Postfach 900 406, Fuggerstrasse 34A, pg. 1080 — PV
Total Walther Feuerschutz GmbH, Waltherstrasse 51, pg. 1651 — PB
Toyota Deutschland GmbH, Toyota-Allee 2, pg. 1413 — IT
Toyota Kreditbank GmbH, Max-Planck Strasse, pg. 1414 — IT
Toyota Leasing GmbH, Max-Planck Strasse, pg. 1414 — IT
Toyota Motor Corporation, Koln Representative Office, Bachemer Landstrasse 17, pg. 1413 — IT
Toyota Motorsport GmbH, Toyota-Allee 2, pg. 1414 — IT
Tropenwerke GmbH & Co., KG, Berliner Strasse 156, pg. 175 — IT
Universal Transport GmbH, Wilhelm-Ruppert-Str. 38, pg. 1034 — IT
VW AUDI Vertriebszentrum Koln GmbH, pg. 1474 — IT
VW AUDI Vertriebszentrum Koln GmbH & Co. KG, pg. 1474 — IT
Van Leer Verpackungen GmbH, Am Westhofer Berg 30, pg. 1147 — IT
WESTAG WERBEAGENTUR, Hulchrather Strasse 17-23, pg. 1491 — IT
WestLB Cologne Branch, Ludwigstrasse 2, pg. 1492 — IT

Cossebaude

Sachsenmetall Handelsgesellschaft Inhaber Max Cochius GmbH, Brietscheidstr. 45, pg. 514 — IT

Coswig

COSID GmbH, pg. 1148 — IT

Cottbus

LR Medienverlag GmbH, Strabe der Jurgend 54, pg. 1478 — IT
Lausitzer Rundschau Verlag und Druckerei GmbH, Strasse der Jugend 54, pg. 1478 — IT
Niederlassung Cottbus, Neustadter Strasse 13, pg. 194 — IT
TEVEBAU GmbH, pg. 1148 — IT

Crailsheim

Voith Turbo GmbH & Co. KG, Postfach 15 55, Voithstrabe 1, pg. 1473 — IT

Cuxhaven

Fishery Foods GmbH, Schillerstrasse 2, pg. 492 — IT

Dachau

MD Betriebswohnungen GmbH, Ostenstr. 5, pg. 864 — IT
MD Paper G.m.b.H., pg. 886 — IT
MD Papier GmbH, Ostenstrasse 5, pg. 864 — IT

Darmstadt

Acheson International S.A.-Equipment Div., Lerchenbergstrasse 23, pg. 12 — PV
AGEMA Infrared Systems GmbH, Siemensstrasse 20, pg. 1289 — IT
DBS Deutsche Bausparkasse AG, Heinrichstrasse 2, pg. 89 — IT
DBS Eigenheimbau G.m.b.H., Heinrichstrasse 2, pg. 89 — IT
Eisen Rieg Haustechnik-Handel GmbH, pg. 838 — IT
Flow Europe, Daimlerweg 6, pg. 656 — PB
Geschaftsstelle Darmstadt, Heidelberger Strasse 45, pg. 194 — IT
Goldwell AG, Zerninstrasse 10-18, pg. 717 — IT
Landesbank Hessen-Thuringen Girozentrale, Rheinstrasse 19-21, pg. 799 — IT
Lau GmbH & Co., pg. 1288 — IT
Livingston Services GmbH, Borsigstrasse 11, pg. 212 — IT
Newport GmbH, Bleichstrasse 26, pg. 1179 — PB
Parker Hannifin GmbH, Bunsenstrasse 15, pg. 1263 — PB
Quantronix, GmbH, Gross-Gerauer Weg 55, pg. 599 — PB
Rohm GmbH, Kirschenallee 45, pg. 1454 — IT
Rohm Holding GmbH, pg. 1454 — IT
SOFTWARE AG, Uhlandstrasse 12, pg. 1276 — IT
Spectra-Physics GmbH, Siemens Strasse 20, pg. 1290 — IT
Sun Chemical Pigments GmbH, Feldbergstrasse 38, pg. 371 — IT
Swedoor Bauelemente GmbH, Staudinger Strasse 4, pg. 1303 — IT
Trischler und Partner GmbH, pg. 608 — IT
WELLA GROUP, Berliner Allee 65, pg. 1489 — IT

Datteln

Deitermann Chemiewerk GmbH & Co. K.G., Lohstr., 61, pg. 606 — IT
Gesellschaft fur Wohnen Datteln mbh, pg. 1460 — IT

Debrecen

Curver kft, Kishegyesi ut, pg. 353 — IT

Deckenpfronn

Newport Electronics GmbH, Gaustrasse 28-30, pg. 816 — PV

Deggendorf

DFA Deggendorfer Freihafen Ansiedlungs GmbH & Co. Grundstucks KG, pg. 178 — IT
DFA Deggendorfer Freihafen Ansiedlungs GmbH, pg. 178 — IT
Deggendorfer Werft und Eisenbau GmbH, Werftstrasse 17, pg. 824 — IT
Dyckerhoff & Widmann Baugesellschaft mbH, Hauptstr. 26a, pg. 423 — IT
Interconnectron GmbH, Auwiesenstrasse 5, pg. 1268 — IT

Deggingen

Wilhelm Stahlecker GmbH, Degginger Str. 6, pg. 1290 — IT

Deisenhofen

Sigma Chemie GmbH, Grunwalder Weg 30, pg. 1472 — PB

Denkendorf

Dynex Technologies GmbH, Justinus-Kerner Strasse 32, pg. 1591 — PB

Detmold

Van Melle Deutschland GmbH, Van Mellestrasse 1, pg. 1451 — IT
Van Melle Holding GmbH, pg. 1451 — IT
Wilhelm Kanne GmbH & Co., pg. 1288 — IT

PB - *U.S. Public Companies Volume*
PV - *U.S. Private Companies Volume*
IT - *International Public & Private Companies Volume*

Deuna

Deuna Zement GmbH, pg. 422   IT

Dieburg

Coherent GmbH, Dieselstrasse 5b, pg. 395   PB
VW AUDI Vertriebszentrum Rhein Main GmbH & Co. KG, pg. 1474

Diemelstadt

C.D. Haupt Papier-und Pappenfabrik GmbH & Co., K.G., Orpethaler Strasse 50, pg. 1271   IT

Dietzenbach

Axson GmbH, Industriepark Steinberg, pg. 103   IT
Die Betonknacker GmbH, Justus-von-Liebig Strasse 30, pg. 1128
Ebara Pumpen GmbH, Philipp-Reis-Str. 15, pg. 432   IT
Excellon Europa GmbH, Justus-von-Liebig-Strasse 19, pg. 594
Frischmuth & Freitag GmbH, Justus-von-Liebig Strasse 30, pg. 1128
ITW Oberflachentechnk GmbH, Justus-Von-Liebig-Strasse 33, pg. 869   PB
Komori Deutschland GmbH, Waldstrasse 23/A3.6, pg. 745
Symbol Technologies GmbH, pg. 1546   PB
Volvo Deutschland GmbH, Postfach 2006, pg. 1477   IT
Volvo Nutzfahrzeuge Deutschland GmbH, pg. 1477   IT

Dillingen

Der Dillinger Huettenwerke AG, Postfach 1580, pg. 572   IT
Plasanit Haustechnik, pg. 838   IT

Dinkelsbuhl

Werner & Pfleiderer Lebensmitteltechnik GmbH, Eduard-von-Raumer-Str. 8-18, pg. 511   IT

Dinkelscherben

Korf Transport GmbH, Siefenwanger Strasse, pg. 758   IT

Dinslaken

ITW Signode System GmbH, pg. 869   PB
Mannesmann Stahlflaschen GmbH, pg. 835   IT
Signode Europa, Magnusstr. 18, pg. 869   PB

Ditzingen

Krupp Warmetechnik GmbH - Ditzingen, Maybachstr. 1, pg. 514   IT

Dohna

Graphit-Produkte Dohna GmbH, Braugasse 1, pg. 517   IT

Donzdorf

Maschinenfabrik Hoerauf, Mozartstr. 39-41, pg. 1290   IT

Dormagen

Bayer Faser GmbH, pg. 172   IT

Dorpen

Nordland Papier AG, Industriestrae 1, pg. 1430   IT
Nortrans Speditiongesellschaft mbH, pg. 1430   IT
UPM-Kymmene Deutschland GmbH, Postfach 1160, pg. 1430   IT

Dorstetten

Kault & Bux Commutator GMBH-Dorstetten, pg. 623   PV

Dortmund

Abfallverwertungsgesellschaft Westfalen mbH (AVW), Rheinlanddamm 24, pg. 1460   IT
Abwassersysteme GmbH, pg. 597   IT
Balster GmbH, pg. 506   IT
Deilmann-Haniel GmbH, Hanstenbeck 1-5, pg. 1069   IT
Dortmunder Eisenhandel Celler GmbH, Celler Scrap Processing Sector, Kohlenweg 1, pg. 513   IT
Dortmunder Eisenhandel Celler GmbH, Dortmund Iron Trading Sector, Riesestr. 12, pg. 513   IT
Dortmunder Shredder GmbH, Kohlenweg 1, pg. 513   IT
Entsorgung Dortmund GmbH, pg. 597   IT
Fasson Handelsgesellshaft GmbH, Alte Strasse 39, pg. 154   IT
Garny Sicherheitstechnik GmbH, Hannoversch Strasse 26-28, pg. 387   IT
Gensym GmbH, Technologiezentrum Dortmund, pg. 731   PB
Gesellschaft fur die Verwertund industrieller Reststoffe mbH, Mallinckrodtstr. 320, pg. 513   IT
Gesellschaft fur Gerotebau mbH, Hannoversche Strasse 72, pg. 594   IT

Gist-Brocades Bio-Specialties GmbH, Giselherstrasse 12, pg. 1142   IT
Givaudan-Roure GmbH, pg. 1120   IT
HARPEN AG, Vosskuhle 38, pg. 597   IT
Harpen AG & Co. Gewerbeimmobilien KG, Vosskuhle 38, pg. 597
Harpen AG & Co. Hotelbauten KG, Vosskuhle 38, pg. 597
Harpen AG & Co. Industriepark KG, Vosskuhle 38, pg. 597
Harpen AG & Co. Verbrauchermarkte KG, Vosskuhle 38, pg. 597
Harpen Immobilien verw.u. Beteilig Ges.mbH, Vosskuhle 38, pg. 597
Hewlett-Packard GmbH, Schleefstr. 28, pg. 820   PB
Hochtemperatur-Reaktorbau GmbH, Kanalstrasse 25, pg. 2   IT
Hoesch Platinen GmbH, Eberdhardstr. 12, pg. 512   IT
Hoesch Rothe Erde AG, Tremoniastrasse 5-11, pg. 509   IT
Hoesch Spundwand und Profil GmbH, Alte Ratstr. 27, pg. 512   IT
Hollinde & Boudon GmbH (SSH), Riesestrasse 20, pg. 1459   IT
Holstein and Kappert GmbH, Juchostrasse 20, pg. 737   IT
Krupp Hoesch Berufsbildung GmbH, Kirchdernerstr. 45, pg. 512   IT
Krupp Hoesch Coilex GmbH, Weidenstr. 60, pg. 512   IT
Krupp Hoesch Informationsverarbeitung GmbH, Nortkirchenstr. 101, pg. 512   IT
Krupp Hoesch Rohstoff und Recycling GmbH, Kohlenweg 1, pg. 513   IT
Krupp Hoesch Stahl AG - Dortmund, Eberdhardstr. 12, pg. 512   IT
Krupp Hoesch Stahlhandel GmbH, Bulowstr. 12, pg. 514   IT
Krupp Hoesch Tecna AG, Borsigstr. 22, pg. 509   IT
Krupp Hoesch Verbarbeitung, Eberhardstr. 12, pg. 508   IT
Krupp Warmetechnik GmbH - Dortmund, Lutge Heidestr. 116, pg. 514   IT
MicroParts Gesellschaft fur Mikrostrukturtechnik mbH, Hauert 7, pg. 1455   IT
Niederlassung Dortmund, Gutenbergstrasse 41-45, pg. 195   IT
Nuhse und Werner Guttges GmbH, pg. 838   IT
O&K Mining GmbH, Dortmund Works, Orensteinstr. 16-18, pg. 516   IT
O&K Orenstein & Koppel Aktiengesellschaft, Karl-Funke-Str. 30, pg. 516   IT
Oberlander Recycling Technik GmbH, Bransdschachtstr. 11, pg. 513   IT
Parker Hannifin, Paderborner Str. 19, pg. 1262   PB
Pohlschroder Gmbh & Co. KG, Steinbrinkstrasse 61, pg. 1038   PV
Rhenus Lager Und Umschlag AG, Mallinckrodtstrasse 320, pg. 1459   IT
Rhenus-Weichelt AG, Mallinckrodtstrasse 320, pg. 1459   IT
SCHENKER Eurocargo AG, Mallinckrodtstrasse 320, pg. 1459   IT
THF Technischer Handel Freudenberg Beteiligungsgesellschaft mbH, pg. 506   PB
Thermo Instrument Systems GmbH, Martenerstrausse 539, pg. 1596   PB
Touraine & Jacobi GmbH, Vosskuhle 38, pg. 597   IT
VEW Reststoffverwertungsgesellschaft mbH, pg. 597   IT
VEW Umwelt GmbH, pg. 597   IT
Wellman International GmbH, Alter Hellwig 111, pg. 1753   PB
Westfalenstadion, pg. 597   IT
WestLB Dortmund Branch, Kampstrasse 45, pg. 1493   IT
Wiemer und Trachte, Hauptverwaltung Markischestrasse 249, pg. 824   IT

Dransfeld

SECON GmbH, In der Dehne 10, pg. 669   IT

Dreieich

Sequent Computer Systems GmbH, An der Trift 65, pg. 1459   PB
Simon Marketing International GmbH - Frankfurt, Robert-Bosch-Strasse 18, pg. 1001   PV
WCI Umwelttechnik GmbH Frankfurt, Heinrich-Hertz-Strasse 3, pg. 1657   PB

Dreieichenhain

AZU Autoteile u. Zubehor Vertriebe GmbH, pg. 1474   IT
Curver Deutschland GmbH, An der Trift 63, pg. 353   IT
Dataproducts GmbH, Otto-Hahn-Strasse 49, pg. 621   IT
Dentsply GmbH, Eisenbahnstrasse 180, pg. 499   PB
Pall Biomedizin GmbH, Phillip Reis Strasse 6, pg. 1254   PB
Pall Filtrationstechnik GmbH, Phillip-Reis-Strasse -6, pg. 1254   PB
Pall Industrie-Hydraulik GmbH, Phillip-Reis-Strasse-6, pg. 1254   PB
SAIA-Burgess Electronics GmbH, Daimlerstrasse 1K, pg. 1501   IT
Spoerle Electronic Gmbh, Max-Planck-Strasse 1-3, pg. 135   PB
VOTEX GmbH, An der Trift 67, pg. 1474   IT

Drensteinfurt

Schulte Rohrearbeitung GmbH, Burener Str. 41, pg. 513   IT

Dresden

ACD Agro Consult Dresden GmbH, pg. 607   IT
AEG Starkstromanlagen, Industriegelande, Eingang G, pg. 367   IT
Ausbau Dresden GmbH, Strehlener Strasse 14, pg. 195   IT
Bull Systemhaus Dresden GmbH I.L., Grunaer Str. 2, pg. 317   IT
DG Bank - Dresden, Ferdinandplatz 1-2, pg. 351   IT
Deutsche Bank-Kreditbank AG (Dresden), Prager Strasse/Ecke Waisenhausstrasse, pg. 402   IT
Doring Industrietechnik BmbH, pg. 506   IT
Dresdner Bank Kreditbank AG, Ostra-Allee 9, pg. 418   IT
Dyckerhoff & Widmann Sachsen/Thuringen GmbH, Strehlener Strasse 24., pg. 423   IT
Dyckerhoff Transportbeton Sachsen GmbH, pg. 423   IT
Elbe-Flugzeugwerke GmbH, pg. 367   IT
Flugzeugwerft Dresden GmbH, pg. 367   IT
Geschaftsstelle Bautzen, Zwinglistrabe 11/13, pg. 194   IT
Hauptniederlassung Sachsen Neiderlassung Dresden Geschaftsstelle Spezialtiefbau, zwinglistrasse 11/13, pg. 194   IT
Ingenieurburo Antriebstechnik Dresden GmbH, Waldschlosschenstr. 10, pg. 400   IT
Krupp Warmetechnik GmbH - Dresden, Berthld-Haupt-Str. 37, pg. 515   IT
Linde-KCA-Dresden G.m.b.H, Ernst Thalmann Strasse 25-29, pg. 811   IT
MAIWALD BAUSTOFFE GmbH, Quohrener Strasse 73, pg. 1459   IT
Mannesmann Demag Logistic Consult GmbH, pg. 837   IT
SAIA-Burgess GmbH, Wilhelm-Liebknecht Strasse 6, pg. 1501   IT
Sachsen-Schwertransport GmbH, Schlacthofring 17, pg. 423   IT
SAXONIA BAUSTOFFE GmbH, Fritz Reuter Strasse 56, pg. 1459   IT
Siemens Microelectronics Center GmbH & Co., Konigsboucker Str. 180, pg. 1245   IT
TASTBAU Asphalt-Strassen- und Tiefbau GmbH, pg. 1148   IT
Tektronix GmbH-Dresden, pg. 1567   PB
VDO Adolf Schindling Beteteilungs GmbH, pg. 839   IT

Drolshagen

Ing. G. Klemm Bohrtechnik GmbH, Wintersohler Strasse 5, pg. 878   PB

Dueren

Dorries GmbH, Veldenerstrasse 52, pg. 1473   IT
Stamco-Depiereux GMBH, Albrecht-Bueren Str 9, pg. 1124   PB

Duingen

Lady Cake-Feine Kuchen GmbH, pg. 1305   IT

Duisburg

Allgemeine Assekuranz-Vermittlung GmbH, pg. 837   IT
Bremer & Leguil Handelsgesellschaft mbH, Am Burgaller 30-42, pg. 517   IT
Bunkerbetriebe Buchting KG, pg. 597   IT
Cargotrans Umschlags- und Speditionsgesellschaft mbH, pg. 597   IT
DSM Agarhandelen GmbH, Gallenkampstrasse 20, pg. 355   IT
Demag Unterstutzungskasse GmbH, pg. 837   IT
Duisburg Branch, Krabbenkamp 15, pg. 401   IT
ELG Haniel GmbH, Kremerskamp 16, pg. 591   IT
Erz und Stahl GmbH, Stein'sche Gasse 4, pg. 1458   IT
Frigoscandia GmbH, Postfach 29 01 40, pg. 607   PB
Galex Metall GmbH, Kremerskamp 16, pg. 710   IT
Grillo-Werke AG, Wesler Strasse 1, pg. 861   IT
HR Huttenwerksensorgung GmbH, Friedrich-Ebert Str. 134, pg. 513   IT
HR Industriemontage GmbH, Friedrich-Ebert-Str. 134, pg. 513   IT
HR Schlackenaufbereitung GmbH, Friedrich-Ebert-Str. 134, pg. 513   IT
Haniel Baustoff-Industrie GmbH, Franz-Haniel-Platz 6-8, pg. 592   IT
Haniel EnvirService GmbH, Moerser Strasse 149, pg. 592   IT
FRANZ HANIEL & CIE, GMBH, Franz-Haniel Platz 1, pg. 591   IT
Haniel Reederei Holding GmbH, Franz-Haniel-Platz 6-8, pg. 592   IT
Hansa Rohstoffe GmbH, Friedrich-Ebert Str. 134, pg. 513   IT
Harpen Transport AG, Kasteelstr. 2, pg. 597   IT
Hercules Oil Gesellschaft fur Hochleistungsschmier-Stoffe Mbh, Am Burgacker 30-42, pg. 517   IT
Huttenwerke Krupp Mannesmann GmbH, Ehringerstr. 200, pg. 512   IT
Hydro Chemtech GmbH, Wannheimer Strasse 429-431, pg. 963   IT
IGV Industrie-Grundstucksverwaltungs GmbH, pg. 837   IT
Interservice Gesellschaft fur Huttenweksanlagen mbH, pg. 837   IT
KLOCKNER-WERKE AG, Klocknerstrasse 29, pg. 736   IT
KLOECKNER & CO. AG, Neudorfer Strasse, 3-5, pg. 737   IT
Kloeckner Industrie-Anlagen Gmbh, Neudorfer Strasse 3-5, pg. 1081   IT

GERMANY DIRECTORY OF CORPORATE AFFILIATIONS

Krupp Anlagenbau GmbH, Friedrich-Alfred Str. 184, pg. 511 IT
Krupp Binnenschiffahrt GmbH, Dammstr. 19, pg. 515 IT
Krupp Fordertechnik GmbH, Franz-Schubert-Str. 1-3, pg. 511 IT
Krupp Montage- und Servicetechnik GmbH, Friedrich-Alfred-Str. 184, pg. 516 IT
Krupp Sigma-Stahl GmbH, Reichstr. 73, pg. 513 IT
Krupp VDM GmbH - Tubes & Components Division, Friedrich-Ebert-Str. 134, pg. 509 IT
Krupp Warmetechnik GmbH - Duisburg, Koloniestr. 86-88, pg. 515 IT
Lehnkering Montan Transport AG, Schifferstrasse 26, pg. 862 IT
Lowe & Jaegers GmbH, pg. 1450 IT
MHD Berzelius Duisburg GmbH, Richard-Seiffert-Strasse 20, pg. 861 IT
Makita Werkzeug GmbH, Keniastrasse 20, pg. 832 IT
Mannesmann Demag AG, Wolfgang-Reuter-Platz, pg. 837 IT
Mannesmann Fahrzeugteile GmbH, pg. 835 IT
Matthes & Weber GmbH, Werthauser Strasse 100, pg. 610 IT
Messo-Chemietechnik GmbH, pg. 836 IT
NESKA Schiffahrts- und Speditionskontor GmbH, pg. 597 IT
Nestrans Logistik GmbH, pg. 515 IT
Nestrans Logistik GmbH, Hombergerstr. 50, pg. 515 IT
Nestrans Seehafenspedition GmbH, Hombergerstr. 50, pg. 514 IT
Panopa Verkehrs-GmbH, Hombergerstr. 50, pg. 514 IT
RSG Rhenania Schiffahrts-Gesellschaft mit beschrankter Haftung, Zweigniederlassung Duisburg, pg. 1033 IT
Rautaruukki Stahlservice GmbH, Kiffward 34, pg. 1089 IT
Rhein-Weser Transport- und Handelsgesellschaft mbH, Dammstr. 19, pg. 514 IT
Rheinische Zinkgesellschaft GmbH, Richard-Seiffert-Strrasse 20, pg. 861 IT
Rutgers Kureha Solvents GmbH, pg. 1148 IT
Sachtleben Chemie GmbH, Dr. Rudolf-Sachtlebenstrasse, pg. 861 IT
Shimadzu Europa GmbH, Albert-Hahn-Strasse 6-10, pg. 1232 IT
Stinnes Reederei AG/Bayerischer Lloyd, August Hirsch Strasse 3, pg. 1459 IT
Stolt-Nielsen GmbH, pg. 1302 IT
Thyssen A.G., pg. 1388 IT
Thyssen Haniel Logistic GmbH, Beteiligung 331, pg. 1388 IT
Thyssen Haniel Logistic GmbH Rheinkraft, pg. 1388 IT
Thyssen Stahl AG, Kaiser-Wilhem-Strasse 100, pg. 1388 IT
Vft AG, Varziner Strasse 49, pg. 1148 IT
Vertex Antennentechnik GmbH, Baumstrasse 47, pg. 1718 PB
Walsum Paper Mill, Theodor-Heuss-Strasse 228, pg. 586 IT
Wambesco Rohstoffhandelsges. mbH, Stein'sche Gasse 4, pg. 1458 IT
Zellweger Energietechnik GmbH, pg. 618 IT

Dulmen

Donaldson Gesellschaft m.b.H., Postfach 1251, pg. 517 PB
HIG Holzleimbau-Industrie GmbH, Muensterstr. 200, pg. 632 IT
Hydro Agri Dulmen GmbH, Hanninghof 35, pg. 962 IT

Duren

Akzo Chemie GmbH, P.O. Box 641, 27 Philippstr., pg. 47 IT
Appleton Pohl GmbH & Co., pg. 1473 IT
Busch Gmbh, Albrecht-Bueren, Str. 9, pg. 1124 PB
Isola Werke AG, Isolastrasse 2, pg. 1148 IT
MAS Deutschland GmbH, pg. 1148 IT
Monarch Wetkzengmaschinen GmbH, Albrecht-Buren Str.9, pg. 1124 PB
Rappold, Hermann & Co. GmbH, Zollhausstr. 121, pg. 1464 IT
ZIMMERMANN & JANSEN GMBH, Bahnstrasse 52, pg. 1528 IT

Durmersheim

Baustoffwerke Durmersheim GmbH & Co. KG, Malscher Str. 17, pg. 606 IT

Dusseldorf

ADC Telecommunications GmbH, Prinzenpark, pg. 4 PB
ALA Vermietungs GmbH, pg. 310 IT
AOK-Nerval Cosmetics & Perfumes GmbH, pg. 609 IT
AST Research Deutschland GmbH, Schiess, Ste. 58, pg. 1182 IT
Accor Gastonomie AG, Grafenberger Allee 100, pg. 21 IT
AEGON Lebensversicherungs-AG, Kavalleriestrasse 2-4, pg. 28 IT
Aer Lingus, Berliner Allee 38, pg. 28 IT
Aglukon Spezialdunger GmbH, Heerdter Landstr. 199, pg. 1203 IT
Ahlstrom Alcore GmbH-Dusseldorf Core Plant, Marbacher Strasse 114, pg. 33 IT
Ahlstrom Machinery GmbH Ecomachinery, Niederrheinstrasse 42, pg. 35 IT
Albus Leasobjekt GmbH, pg. 310 IT
Almet Metall-Halbseug-Vertriebe-GmbH, Wiesenstrasse 51, pg. 1030 IT
Anritsu Elektronik GmbH, Grafenberger Allee 54-56, pg. 77 IT
Ansaldo Deutschland, 1, Worringer Str., pg. 654 IT
Applied Power GmbH, Mundelheimer Weg 51, pg. 125 PB
Aqualon GmbH, Paul-Thomas Strasse 58, pg. 810 PB
Atlas-Vermoegensverwaltungs-GmbH, Breite Strasse 25, pg. 309 IT
Aussenhandel-Foerderungsgesellschaft mbH, Breite Strasse 25, pg. 309 IT
Auto-trol Technology GmbH, Heltorter Strasse 6, pg. 148 PB
BB-AVAL Gesellschaft fur Aussenhandelsfinanzierungen mbH. Gereonstrasse 1-3, pg. 159 IT
BHF & IKB Baumanagement GmbH, Wilhelm-Botzkes-Str. 1, pg. 645 IT
BHF & IKB Immobilien-Leasing GmbH, Kasernenstrasse 36, pg. 119 IT
BHF-Bank, Pempelforter Strasse 11, pg. 119 IT
BHF & IKB Immobilien-Leasing GmbH, Wilhelm-Botzkes-Str. 1, pg. 645 IT
BMZ!FCA, Schirmerstrasse 76, pg. 470 IT
B/W WERBEAGENTUR GWA, Kennedydamm 1, pg. 130 IT
BWE Energietechnik GmbH, Werdener Strasse 3, pg. 398 IT
Bahntrans GmbH, pg. 1388 IT
Banca Nazionale del Lavoro, Konigsallee 28, pg. 137 IT
The Bank of Tokyo-Mitsubishi, Ltd. (Dusseldorf Branch), Konigsallee/Ecke Bahnstrasse, pg. 158 IT
Bankhaus Schliep & Co., pg. 179 IT
Banque Paribas-Dusseldorf, Konigsallee 13, pg. 320 IT
Barry Controls International GmbH, Mundelheimer Weg 51, pg. 125 PB
Bayerische Landesbank Girozentrale - Dusseldorf Branch, Wilhelm-Marx-Haus, Heinrich-Heine-Allee 53, pg. 176 IT
Bell Atlantic GmbH, Josephinestrasse 13, pg. 204 PB
Berag GmbH, Wahlerstrasse 32, pg. 1502 IT
Berendsen PMC GmbH, Muendelheimer Weg 48, pg. 1285 IT
Bestobell Mobrey GmbH, Nurnberger Strasse 22/24, pg. 854 IT
Beton Union Dusselforf GmbH & Co. KG, pg. 422 IT
Boehme Chemie Gesellschaft mbH, Henkelstrasse 67, pg. 609 IT
Bohler AG, Hansaallee 321, pg. 1471 IT
Brandeis Intsel Deutschland, c/o Pechiney Deutschland, Buropark Hansstern, pg. 1030 IT
C & D Leasingservice GmbH, pg. 309 IT
CAIB-Germany, Eva GmbH, Schillerstrasse 20, pg. 212 IT
CFB Commerz Fonds Beteiligungs GmbH, Ludwig-Erhard-Allee 5, pg. 309 IT
Carless Refining & Marketing B.V., Niederlassung Dusseldorf, Graf-Adolf-Platz, 3, pg. 1104 IT
CASIA Grundstuecks - Vermietungs- und Verwaltungs GmbH, pg. 310 IT
Cegelec GmbH, Marienstrasse 41, pg. 53 IT
Ceresit GmbH, Erkrather Strasse 230, pg. 609 IT
Churrasco Steak-Restaurant GmbH, Haffenstrasse 9, pg. 1499 IT
CIL Mietkauf GmbH, pg. 309 IT
Coba Vermoegensverwaltung GmbH, pg. 309 IT
Cockerill Sambre Beteiligungs GmbH, pg. 302 IT
Codelco-Kupferhandel GmbH, Beethovenstr. 21, pg. 303 IT
COGNIS Gesellscaft fur Biotechnologie mbH, pg. 609 IT
Commerz Baucontract GmbH, pg. 309 IT
Commerz Immobilien GmbH, pg. 309 IT
Commerz Immobilien Vermietungs GmbH, pg. 309 IT
Commerz- und Industrie-Leasing GmbH, pg. 309 IT
CommerzBaumanagement GmbH, pg. 309 IT
Commerzkommunalbau GmbH, pg. 309 IT
CommerzLeasing Anlagen-Vermietungs GmbH, pg. 309 IT
CommerzLeasing und Immobilien GmbH, Ludwig-Erhard-Allee 9, pg. 309 IT
DAVR - Deutsche Aluminium Verpackung Recycling GmbH, pg. 68 IT
DIC Europe GmbH, Immermann Strasse 65D, pg. 371 IT
DKB Finance (Dusseldorf), Konigsallee 60 D, pg. 361 IT
DMB&B Dusseldorf, Karlplatz 21, pg. 303 PV
DSM Deutschland GmbH & Co., Tersteegenstrasse 77, pg. 356 IT
Dai-Ichi Kangyo Bank, Ltd.-Dusseldorf, Konigsallee 60 D, pg. 360 IT
Dai Nippon Printing (Europa) GmbH, Steinstrasse 30, pg. 363 IT
Damixa Armaturen, GmbH, Aachener Strasse 81, pg. 1054 PB
DataCard Germany GmbH, Heerdter Lohweg 87, pg. 3[illegible]3 PV
De Lage Landen Leasing GmbH, Willstatterstrasse 15, pg. 1082 IT
Demag Komatsu GmbH, Buscherho Strasse 10, pg. 745 IT
Dentsu Europe-Dusseldorf, Konigsallee 60 B, pg. 393 IT
Desowag-Bayer Holzschutz GmbH, pg. 172 IT
Desowag GmbH, Robstrasse 76, pg. 1501 IT
Deutsche Bank AG (Dusseldorf), Konigsallee 45/47, pg. 402 IT
Deutsche Gamma GmbH, pg. 540 IT
Deutsche Post Wohnbau GmbH, Postfach 20 06 60, Karlplatz 18, pg. 407 IT
Development Company for TV-Program GmbH, Konigsallee 60B, pg. 394 IT
Disko Factoring Finanz GmbH, Goethestrasse 75, pg. 418 IT
Dow Vertriebsgesellschaft m.b.H., Georg-Glock-Strasse 3, pg. 524 PB
Dr. Tigges Incentives, Berliner Allee 47, pg. 515 IT
Durriesscharmann, AG, Schiess-Strasse 61, pg. 860 IT
Dusseldorf-Muenchener Beteiligungs-Gesellschaft mbH, Martin-Luther-Platz 32, pg. 179 IT
E-Plus Mobilfunk GmbH, pg. 1461 IT
E/B/D/Interpartners, Hallberg Strasse 28, pg. 1152 PV
Eisenbahn Verkehrsmittel A.G., Schillerstrasse 20, pg. 212 IT
Eisenstahl GmbH, pg. 302 IT
Elf Erdoel Underdgas Deutschland Gmbh, Berliner Allee 52, pg. 446 IT
Elimo Vermietungs GmbH, pg. 310 IT
Elkem Gmbh, Schirmerstrasse 76, pg. 447 IT
Encore Computer GmbH, Heerdter Landstrasse 191, pg. 580 PB
Epson Deutschland GmbH (E.D.G.), Zulpicher Strasse 6, pg. 1219 IT
Ericsson Business Communications GmbH, Heerdter Landstrasse 193, pg. 1366 IT
Ericsson GmbH, Fritz-Vomfelde-Strasse 14-18, pg. 1366 IT
Ericsson Mobilfunk GmbH, Werfsstrasse 16, pg. 1367 IT
EURO RSCG, Grafenberger Allee 125, pg. 602 IT
FPB Holding AG, Feldmuhleplatz 1, pg. 1303 IT
Forte Hotels (Deutschland) GmbH, pg. 556 IT
Fuji Bank, Berlin Representative Office, c/o Dusseldorf Branch, Immermannstrasse 3, pg. 520 IT
Fuji Leasing (Deutschland) GmbH, Immermannstrasse 3-5, pg. 521 IT
Fuji Photo Film (Europe) GmbH, Heesenstrasse 31, pg. 524 IT
GGK Communications, Immermannstr. 12, pg. 1335 IT
GGK Dusseldorf, Immermannstr. 6, pg. 1335 IT
GGK Europe, Immermannstr. 15, pg. 1335 IT
GIP Gewerbe im Park GmbH, Hildebrandt Str. 24, pg. 632 IT
GSI Europe-Import & Export GmbH, Friedrich-Ebert Strasse 54, pg. 579 IT
Generale Bank & Co., Graf-Adolf-Strasse 70, pg. 548 IT
Georgia-Pacific GmbH, Elisabethstrasse 51, pg. 739 PB
Gerresheimer Glas AG, Morsenbroicher Weg 191, pg. 1464 IT
Geschaftsbereich Schiess-Wotan, pg. 861 IT
Granges Aluminium GmbH, Malkastenstrasse 3; P.O. Box 320 466, pg. 442 IT
Grey Europe/Dusseldorf, Corneliusstr. 16-24, pg. 765 PB
Grundstucks- und Vermogensverwaltungsgesellschaft Geretsried mbH, pg. 309 IT
Grundstucksgesellschaft Simon beschrankt haftende Kommandigeseelschaft, pg. 179 IT
Hakuhodo Deutschland GmbH, Im Wehrhahn-Center, Oststrasse 10, pg. 588 IT
Halten GmbH & Co. KG, Harffstrasse 47-51, pg. 592 IT
Heidemij Deutschland GmbH, pg. 607 IT
Hein, Lehmann AG, Fichtenstrasse 75, pg. 80 IT
Henkel & Cie GmbH, Postfach 11 00, Henkelstrasse 67, pg. 609 IT
Henkel Bautechnik GmbH, Erkrather Strasse 230, pg. 609 IT
Henkel Cosmetic GmbH, Henkelstrasse 67, pg. 609 IT
Henkel-Ecolab GmbH & Co., Reisholzer Werfstrasse 42, pg. 610 IT
HENKEL KGAA, Henkelstrasse 67, pg. 609 IT
Henkel Waschmittel GmbH, pg. 610 IT
Hille & Muller, AM Tripplesbert 48, pg. 754 IT
Hitachi Zosen Dusseldorf, Graf-Adolf-Strasse 24, pg. 623 IT
Hoogovens Aluminium GmbH, Cecilienallee 6, pg. 755 IT
Hostra Beteiligungs GmbH, pg. 310 IT
IKB Beteiligungsgesellschaft mbH, Wilhelm-Botzkes-Str. 1, pg. 645 IT
IKB DEUTSCHE INDUSTRIEBANK AG, Wilhelm-Botzkes-Str. 1, pg. 645 IT
ILV Immobilien-Leasing Verwaltungs GmbH, pg. 310 IT
ING Lease Deutschland, Graf Adolf Strasse 63, pg. 650 IT
Ilva Deutschland, Grunerstrasse 133, pg. 654 IT
Inamed GmbH, Wehrhahncenter, Oststrasse 10, pg. 874 PB
Industriebank von Japan (Deutschland) Aktiengesellschaft, Deutsch-Japanisches Ctr., Immermannstr. 45, pg. 676 IT
Industrieschutz Assekuranz Vermittlung GmbH, pg. 836 IT
InfoCity NrW Informationsdienste GmbH & Co. KG, pg. 1461 IT
Inpec Engineering GmbH, pg. 1022 IT
Intergraph (Deutschland) GmbH, Paul-Thomas-Strasse 58, pg. 892 PB
International Nickel GbmH, Tallstrasse 32A, pg. 673 IT
IRIDIUM Services Deutschland GmbH, pg. 1461 IT
Italimpianti Intl.-Germany, Graf Adolfstrasse 18, pg. 655 IT
Jujo Paper GmbH, Cantadorstrasse 3, pg. 938 IT
KKB Bank KGAA, Kasernenstrasse 10, pg. 379 PB
Kao Corporation GmbH, Wanheimer Str. 57, pg. 718 IT
Kaufring Ag, pg. 310 IT
Kawasaki Heavy Industries GmbH, 5th Fl., Wehrhahn Center, Ostrasse 10, pg. 726 IT
Kawasaki Steel Co., Kreuzstrasse 20, pg. 726 IT
Keramik-Rohr Vertriebs-und Beratungs GmbH, Graf Adolph Strasse 43, pg. 615 IT
Kikkoman Trading Europe GmbH, Heerdter Lohweg 57-59, pg. 733 IT
Franz Kirchfeld GmbH & Co. KG, Moersenbroicher Weg 200, pg. 824 IT
Klaranlagen Winter & Co. GmbH, pg. 836 IT
Kobe Steel, Ltd. (Dusseldorf), pg. 741 IT
Korn/Ferry International, Koenigsallee 64, pg. 634 PV
Kossack Chemie GmbH, Bonner Strasse 117, pg. 610 IT
Kredietbank-Bankverein AG, Bahnstrasse 17, pg. 761 IT
Krupp Hoesch Stahl AG - Dusseldorf, Hildnerstr. 80, pg. 513 IT

PB - *U.S. Public Companies Volume*
PV - *U.S. Private Companies Volume*
IT - *International Public & Private Companies Volume*

1610
Geographic Index-Non U.S.

Kyowa Hakko Europe GmbH, Immermannstrasse 65C, pg. 778   IT
Kyowa Hakko Kogyo Co., Ltd., Immermannstrasse 65C, pg. 778   IT
L.I.A. Leasinggesellschaft fur Immobilien und Anlageguter mbH, pg. 310   IT
LLB Lurgi Lentjes Babcock Energietechnik GmbH, Hans-Allee 305, pg. 398   IT
Leasobjekt GmbH, pg. 310   IT
Legion Telekommunikation GmbH, Am Seestern 24, pg. 796   IT
Lentjes AG, Hansa-Allee 305, pg. 861   IT
Lixton Spezialreiniger GmbH, Henkelstrasse 67, pg. 610   IT
Louis Vuitton Deutschland G.m.b.H., Konigsallee 30, pg. 782   IT
Lowe & Partners, Heinrichstrasse 85, pg. 678   PV
MD Foods Deutschland GmbH, pg. 826   IT
MIPA Muller Verwaltungs GmbH, pg. 310   IT
M.L.&S. WERBEAGENTUR GMBH, Uhlandstr. 42, pg. 827   IT
Maerz Ofenbau GmbH, Corneliusstrasse 36, pg. 904   PV
Management Engineers GmbH, Niederkasseler Lohweg 8, pg. 162   PV
MANNESMANN A.G., pg. 834   IT
Mannesmann AG & Co. OHG, pg. 836   IT
Mannesmann Anlagenbau AG, Theodorstr. 90, pg. 836   IT
Mannesmann Eurokom GmbH, Mannesmannufer 2, pg. 838   IT
Mannesmann Handel AG, Niederkasseler Lohweg 20, pg. 838   IT
Mannesmann KTI GmbH, pg. 836   IT
Mannesmann Leichtbau GmbH, pg. 838   IT
Mannesmann Marktforschung GmbH, pg. 838   IT
Mannesmann Mobilfunk GmbH, Am Seestern 1, pg. 838   IT
Mannesmann Revision GmbH, pg. 838   IT
Mannesmann Webe GmbH, pg. 839   IT
Marcam Germany GmbH, Emanuel-Leutze-Strasse 4, pg. 1043   PB
Maritz GMBH (Germany), Rethelstrausse 38, pg. 704   PV
Marubeni Deutschland GmbH, Immermannstr. 45, pg. 845   IT
Matsubo GmbH, Liesegangstrasse 10, pg. 432   IT
Medical Graphics GmbH, Scheibenstrasse 61, pg. 1080   PB
Medtronic GmbH, Am Seestern 24, pg. 1083   PB
Metallgesellschaft Industrie AG, Moenchenwerther Strasse 15, pg. 861   IT
Metsa-Serla Tissue GmbH, Freligrathstrasse 13, pg. 864   IT
MICROS-Fidelio Software Deutschland GmbH, Volkardeyer Weg 14, pg. 1106   PB
Mitsubishi Chemical Europe GmbH, Niederkasseler Lohweg 8, pg. 871   IT
Mitsui & Co. Europe G.m.b.H., Konigsallee 92a, pg. 880   IT
Mitsukoshi Deutschland GmbH, Immermannstrasse 45, pg. 884   IT
Monsanto (Deutschland) GmbH, Immermanstrasse 3, pg. 1125   PB
Moore-Lithorex Direct Marketing Services N.V./S.A., Hildebrandtstrasse 24, pg. 889   IT
Morganite GmbH, Talstrasse 32A, pg. 892   IT
Mutoh Europe GmbH, Klosterstrabe 112, pg. 897   IT
NEC Electronics (Europe) GmbH, Oberratherstr. 4, pg. 901   IT
NEC Electronics (Germany) GmbH, Kanzlerstr. 2, pg. 901   IT
NETG Applied Learning GmbH, Pempelforterstrasse 52, pg. 784   PB
NKK Europe Ltd.-Dusseldorf Office, Immermannstrasse 43, pg. 903   IT
NUS Deutschland GmbH, Berliner Allee 52, pg. 787   PB
NYK Line (Deutschland)-Dusseldorf, Immermannstrasse 13, pg. 942   IT
NYK Line-Dusseldorf, Immemannstrasse 13, pg. 942   IT
National Bank of Greece Dusseldorf Branch, pg. 907   IT
Nedlloyd Deustchland Holding GmbH, pg. 1145   IT
Nedlloyd Districenters GmbH, pg. 1144   IT
Nedlloyd Lines Deutschland GmbH, pg. 1145   IT
Nedlloyd Road Cargo Division, Karlstrasse 76, pg. 1145   IT
Nedlloyd Road Cargo International, Karlstrasse 76, pg. 1145   IT
Nedlloyd Unitrans GmbH, Karlstrasse 76, pg. 1145   IT
Nedlloyd Unitras, Karlstrasse 76, pg. 1145   IT
Neste Chemicals GmbH, Monschaverstrasse 1, pg. 914   IT
NESTOR GVG mbH, pg. 309   IT
NESTOR GVG mbH & Co. Objekt Wiernelhausen KG, pg. 309   IT
NESTOR GVG mbH & Co. Objekt Erlangen KG, pg. 309   IT
NESTOR GVG mbH & Co. Objekt Hamme KG, pg. 309   IT
NESTOR GVG mbH & Co. Objekt ITTAE Frankfurt KG, pg. 309   IT
NESTOR GVG mbH & Co. Objekt Villingen-Schwennigen KG, pg. 309   IT
NEUTRALIS GVG mbH, pg. 309   IT
Nichimen Europe plc Dusseldorf Office, Wehrbahn Ctr., Am Wehrhahn 33, pg. 928   IT
Niederlassung Dusseldorf, Meineckestrasse 52, pg. 195   IT
Nikon GmbH, Tiefenbroicher Weg 25, pg. 931   IT
Nippon Steel Corporation-European Office, Konigsallee 30, pg. 940   IT
Nokia Mobile Phones GmbH, Opitzstrasse 12, pg. 952   IT
Nokia Telecommunications GmbH, Heltorferstrasse 22, pg. 953   IT
NOLICA GVG mbH, pg. 309   IT

NORA GVG mbH, pg. 309   IT
NORA GVG mbH & Co. Objekt Duesseldorf KG, pg. 309   IT
NORA GVG mbH & Co. Objekt Koblenz KG, pg. 309   IT
NORA GVG mbH & Co. Objekt Lampertheim KG, pg. 309   IT
NORA GVG mbH & Co. Objekte Plon und Preetz KG, pg. 309   IT
NORIT Deutschland, Adlerstrasse 54, pg. 958   IT
Norma Metallbau GmbH, Koppersstr. 17, pg. 509   IT
North Rhine Westphalia Branch, Wilhelm-Botzkes-Str. 1, pg. 645   IT
NOSCO GVG mbH, pg. 309   IT
NOTARIA GVG mbH, pg. 310   IT
Novell Germany, Monschauer Strasse 12, pg. 1204   PB
NUMERIA GVG mbH, pg. 310   IT
NUMERIA GVG mbH & Co. Objekt Huckelhoven KG, pg. 303   IT
NUMERIA GVG mbH & Co. Objekt Waldkraiburg KG, pg. 309   IT
o.tel.o Communications GmbH Co., Am Bonneshof 35, pg. 1082   IT
Oji Paper Co. Ltd., Immermann Str. 45, pg. 998   IT
OKI Systems (Deutschland) GmbH, Hansaalee 187, pg. 1000   IT
OLEANDRA GVG mbH & Co. Objekt Neptun KG, pg. 310   IT
OLEANDRA GVG mbH & Co. Objekt Pluto KG, pg. 310   IT
OLEANDRA GVG mbH & Co. Objekt Uranus KG, pg. 310   IT
OLEANDRA GVG mbH & Co. Objekt Jupiter KG, pg. 310   IT
OLEANDRA GVG mbH & Co. Objekt Venus KG, pg. 310   IT
OPTIO GVG mbH & Co. Objekt Hannover Hanomagstr. KG, pg. 310   IT
Outokumpu Deutschland GmbH, Grafenberger Allee 87, pg. 1015   IT
Panalpina Welttransport GmbH, pg. 1023   IT
Parfums Christian Dior G.m.b.H., Haus am Rhein, Rotterdamerstrasse 40, pg. 783   IT
Pechiney Deutschland GmbH, Buropark Hansstern, Fritz-Vomfelde-Str 12, pg. 1031   IT
Pharma-Waldhof GmbH, Hansa-Allee 159, pg. 331   IT
PLAVIS Vermietungsgesellschaft mbH, pg. 310   IT
Polydach-Dachsysteme GmbH, pg. 302   IT
POSCO Research Center Europe, Palladion, 3F Georg-Glock-Str. 18, pg. 1062   IT
Preussag Handel GmbH, Srwammstrasse 12, pg. 1069   IT
Prisma-Verlag GmbH & Co. KG, pg. 190   IT
Promoref GmbH, Corneliusstrasse 76, pg. 1175   IT
Quarterdeck Office Systems GmbH, Willstaetter Strasse 15, pg. 1351   PB
RIM - Rheinmetall Immobilien Management GmbH, Kennedydamm 17, pg. 1108   IT
RIS - Rheinmetall Informationssysteme GmbH, Kennedydamm 17, pg. 1108   IT
Reed Exhibition Companies-Germany, Heerdter Sandberg 32, pg. 1097   IT
Reed Travel Group-Germany, Heerdter Landstrasse 193, pg. 1097   IT
Reise-As GmbH, Duisburgerstr. 16-18, pg. 515   IT
Rentokil GmbH, Oberhausener Str. 11, pg. 1286   IT
RESIDIO GmbH, pg. 310   IT
Rheinmetall AG, Kennedydamm 17, pg. 1108   IT
Rheinmetall Elektronik AG, Kennedydamm 17, pg. 1108   IT
RHEINMETALL GROUP, Kennedydamm 17, pg. 1108   IT
Rigips GmbH, pg. 123   IT
Rivus Leasobjekt GmbH, pg. 310   IT
Rockwell International GmbH, Bublitzer Strasse 32, pg. 1401   PB
Rocol GmbH, Ungelsheimer Weg 7, pg. 892   IT
SAPA Aluminium Profile GmbH, Prinz Georg Strasse 126, pg. 442   IT
SIG Verpackungsmaschinen GmbH, Bendemannstrasse 11, pg. 1156   IT
SMS Aktiengesellschaft, P.O. Box 230229, pg. 825   IT
SMS Schloemann-Siemag AG, Eduard-Schloemann-Strasse 4, pg. 826   IT
The Sakura Bank - Dusseldorf Branch, Konigsallee 15, pg. 1179   IT
Sakura Finanz (Deutschland) GmbH, Konigsallee 15, pg. 1180   IT
Sandvik Coromant, pg. 1186   IT
Sandvik GmbH, Heerdtstrasse Landstrasse 229-233, pg. 1186   IT
Sandvik Hard Materials, pg. 1186   IT
Sandvik Rock Tools, pg. 1187   IT
Sandvik Steel, pg. 1187   IT
Sanwa Leasing (Deutschland) GmbH, Wehrhahn Center, Oststrasse 10, pg. 1190   IT
Schulverlag Vieweg GmbH, Corneiliussstrasse 9-11, pg. 190   IT
Scott Feldmuhle, Emanuel-Leutze Strasse-4, pg. 960   PB
SECUNDO GVG mbH, pg. 310   IT
SEIKO Deutschland GmbH, Zulpicherstrasse 5, pg. 1218   IT
Sensormatic GmbH, Am Schimmersfeld, pg. 1457   PB
Shimizu GmbH-Dusseldorf Office, Immermannstrasse 15, pg. 1234   IT
Shimizu Properties (Deutschland) GmbH, Immermannstrasse 15, pg. 1234   IT
Shionogi & Co. GmbH, Hansaallee 201, House I, pg. 1235   IT
Shionogi & Co., Ltd. - Dusseldorf, Hansaallee 201, House I, pg. 1235   IT
Shiseido Deuthchland GmbH, Monschauer Strasse 7, pg. 1235   IT

Showa Denko (Europe) GmbH, Uhlandstrasse 9, pg. 1237   IT
Simon AG, Martin-Luther-Platz 32, pg. 180   IT
Skandinaviska Enskilda Banken-Dusseldorf, Zweigstelle Dusseldorf, San Remo Strasse 15, pg. 1260   IT
Sorbus GmbH, Willstaetter Strasse 13, pg. 204   PB
STAHLEX GmbH, Friedrichstrasse 26, pg. 1459   IT
Standard Chartered Leasing GmbH, Dusselstrasse 26, pg. 1297   IT
GmbH Steelinter Deutschland, Graf Adolf Platz 12, pg. 302   IT
Stena Line, Hildebrandstrasse 4D, pg. 1300   IT
Stinnes Montanhandel GmbH & Co. KG, Friedrichstrasse 26, pg. 1459   IT
Stinnes Rohrunion GmbH, Friedrichstrasse 26, pg. 1459   IT
Stora Feldmuhle AG, Feldmuhleplatz 1, pg. 1303   IT
Stora Purchasing & Transport GmbH, Postfach 11 09 43, pg. 1303   IT
Stora Reisholz GmbH, Bonner Strasse 245, pg. 1303   IT
The Sumitomo Bank, Ltd.-Dusseldorf Branch, Immermannstr. 14-16, pg. 1309   IT
Sumitomo Chemical Deutschland GmbH, Nordstern Vershicherung Bldg., Georg-Glock-Strasse 14, pg. 1312   IT
Sumitomo Metal Industries, Ltd. (Dusseldorf Office), Worringer St. 1, pg. 1316   IT
Symantec GmbH, Grafenburger Allee 136, pg. 1545   PB
TBWA Dusseldorf GmbH, Wasserstrabe 6a, pg. 1063   PV
Taisei (Deutscheland) GmbH, Charlottenstrasse 15, pg. 1351   IT
Takenaka Europe GmbH, Dusseldorf, Oststrasse 10, pg. 1351   IT
Technip Anlagenbau GmbH, Grafenberger Allee 277, pg. 1361   IT
Tedeco Gmbh, pg. 1207   IT
TERTIO GVG mbH, pg. 310   IT
Thera Cosmetic GmbH, Henkelstrasse 67, pg. 610   IT
Thompson GmbH, Henkelstrasse 67, pg. 610   IT
Thompson-Siegel GmbH, Erkrather Strasse 230, pg. 610   IT
THYSSEN AG, August-Thyssen-Strasse 1, pg. 1387   IT
Thyssen Handelsunion AG, Hansguenthar Soch Strasse 1, pg. 1388   IT
Thyssen Telecom A.G., pg. 1388   IT
Thyssen Wohnstatten A.G., pg. 1388   IT
Tokuyama Europe GmbH, Wehrhahn Cedoer Bldg. 6, Oststrasse 10, pg. 1394   IT
Toppan Printing GmbH, Immermannstr. 14-16, pg. 1399   IT
Toshiba Electronics Europe GmbH, Hansaalle 181, pg. 1406   IT
Trans-Packet Service GmbH & Co. oHG, pg. 1145   IT
Kurt Trapp Ingenieurburo GmbH, Am Schuttenhof 5, pg. 514   IT
Trinkaus & Burkhardt Immobilien GmbH, Konigsallee 21/23, pg. 584   IT
Trinkaus & Burkhardt KGaA, Konigsallee 21/23,, pg. 584   IT
Trinkaus Capital Management, Konigsallee 21/23, pg. 584   IT
UBE Europe GmbH, Immermann Hof, Immermannstrasse 65B, pg. 1427   IT
Union Air Transport GmbH, Rather Str. 78-80, pg. 1120   PV
Utell International-Germany, Heerater, Landstrasse 191, pg. 1098   IT
VDI-Verlag GmbH, Heinrichstrasse 24, pg. 1479   IT
VEBA AG, Bennisgenplatz 1, pg. 1454   IT
VEBA Telecom Deutschland GmbH, Am Bonneshof 35, pg. 1461   IT
VEBA Vermogensanlage GmbH, pg. 1461   IT
VEBACOM GmbH, Am Bonneshof 35, pg. 1461   IT
Vectur GmbH, Voelklinger Landstr. 80, pg. 1129   PV
Vendo GmbH, Spanger Strasse 22, pg. 1184   IT
Verlagsgruppe Handelsblatt GmbH, Kasernenstrasse 67, pg. 1479   IT
W. & O. Bergmann GmbH & Co. KG, Wielandstrasse 27, pg. 1069   IT
WLP Wilhelm-Leuschner-Platz Beteiligungs-GmbH, pg. 310   IT
West Merchant Bank Ltd., Konigsallee 33, pg. 1493   IT
Westdeutsche Landesbank (Europa) AG, Friedrichstrasse 56, pg. 1493   IT
WESTDEUTSCHE LANDESBANK GIROZENTRALE, Herzogstrasse 15, pg. 1492   IT
Westdeutsche Wellpappenfabrik GmbH, pg. 1333   PB
Wisaforest Deutschland GmbH, Talstrasse 22-24, pg. 1429   IT
Yokohama Reifen GmbH, Hansaallee 201, pg. 1521   IT
The Yokohama Rubber Co., Ltd., Hansaallee, pg. 1521   IT

Eberswalde

AWE Abfallwirtschaft Eberswalde GmbH, Erich-Muhsam-Strasse 36, pg. 1460   IT

Ebingen

Mettler-Toledo (Albstadt) GmbH, Unter dem Malesfelsen 34, pg. 4   PV

Eching

Gleitmolybdan Schmierstoffe GmbH, Konigsberger Str. 2, pg. 517   IT
Kontron Messtechnik GmbH, Oskar von Miller Strasse 1, pg. 177   IT
Ross & Glas GmbH, Dieselstr. 24, pg. 509   IT
Soabar G.m.b.H., Ohm-Strasse 3, pg. 154   PB

PB - *U.S. Public Companies Volume*
PV - *U.S. Private Companies Volume*
IT - *International Public & Private Companies Volume*

Tylan GmbH, Kirchhoffstrasse 8, pg. 1113 — PB

Echterdingen

Debis Systemhaus, Fasanenweg 9, pg. 264 — IT
Sandoz-Quinn Producktie GmbH, pg. 985 — IT
Sprecher & Schuh GmbH, Dieselstrasse 28, pg. 1402 — PB

Eckental

Piher International GmbH, Orchideenstrasse 6, pg. 854 — IT

Eckernforde

J.P. Sauer & Sohn GmbH, Sauerstrasse 2-6, pg. 1156 — IT

Egelsbach

FLEISSNER GMBH & CO. MASCHINENFABRIK,
   Wolfsgartenstr. 6, pg. 493 — IT
Thomas & Betts GmbH, Theodor-Heuss-Strasse 7-9,
   pg. 1598 — PB

Eggenstein

Life Technologies GMbH, Dieselstrasse 5, pg. 505 — PB

Ehingen

Liebherr-Werk Ehingen GmbH, Munsinger Strasse 80,
   pg. 808 — IT

Ehrenburg

Bauchemie Leipzig GmbH, Ludwig Hupfeld Str. 19,
   pg. 791 — IT

Ehringshausen

Buderus Schleiftechnik GmbH, Am Bahnhof, Postfach 1141,
   pg. 1128 — IT

Eichstetten

Gould Electronics GmbH Foil Division, Postfach 20,
   pg. 1592 — PB

Eilenburg

Sachsen Papier Eilenburg GmbH, pg. 458 — IT

Einbeck

Hans Feierabend GmbH, Otto Hahn Str. 3-5, pg. 204 — IT
SCHLEICHER & SCHUELL GMBH, Grimsehlstrasse 23,
   pg. 1206 — IT

Eisenach

Zylinderkopffertigung Eisenach GmbH, pg. 1474 — IT

Eisenberg

Sanit, Klosterstrasse 5, pg. 430 — IT

Eitorf

Boge Handels GmbH, pg. 835 — IT
Fichtel & Sachs AG & Co., pg. 835 — IT

Elbe

Harz-Kalk GmbH, Suserbujo Strasse 14, pg. 1069 — IT
Woodward Governor Germany GmbH, Kothener Chaussee
   46, pg. 1777 — PB

Elchingen

Hydromatik GmbH, pg. 838 — IT
Mannesmann Tally GmbH, pg. 839 — IT

Elfsfleth

Nordenhamer Transportboten GmbH & Co. KG,
   pg. 422 — IT

Elgersburg

Sensycon Sensortechnik GmbH, pg. 835 — IT

Elmshorn

Autoliv GmbH, P.O. Box 108, pg. 442 — IT
Kohler Interconsult GmbH, Daimlerstrasse 9, pg. 1420 — IT

Emden

Thyssen Nordseewerke GmbH, pg. 1387 — IT

Emmendingen

Gasbetriebe GmbH, pg. 1456 — IT

Emmerich

BolsWessanen Beteilung GmbH, pg. 752 — IT
Brother Internationale Industriemaschinen G.m.b.H.,
   Dusseldorfer Str. 7-9, pg. 230 — IT
Eul & Gunther GmbH & Co KG, pg. 857 — IT
Gelderlander Fleischwaren GmbH, pg. 752 — IT
International Flavors & Fragrances I.F.F. (Deutschland)
   GmbH, Reeser Strasse 60, pg. 899 — PB
JOBST GmbH, pg. 182 — IT
Transit Kuhlhausgesellschaft mbH (TKG), Rotterdamer
   Strasse 2-6, pg. 607 — PB
Unichema Chemie G.m.b.H., Steintor 9, pg. 1438 — IT
Vink Kunststoffe GmbH & Co. K.G., Tackenweide 48,
   pg. 1210 — IT
Zippo Europe S.A., Tackenwide 54, pg. 1207 — PV

Emmerthal

Gemeinschaftskernkraftwerk Grohnde GmbH, pg. 1456 — IT

Engen

Ancra Jungfalk GmbH, Richard-Stocker-STR 19, pg. 71 — PV
Ericsson Components Europe GmbH, Industriestrasse 5,
   pg. 1366 — IT
Statoil Enden, Jannez Ohling Strassen, pg. 1298 — IT

Eningen

O.E. Runger Gebaudereinigung GmbH, pg. 1480 — IT
O.E. Runger KG, pg. 1480 — IT
WANDEL & GOLTERMANN GMBH & CO.,
   ELEKTRONISCHE MESSTECHNIK, Muehleweg 5,
   pg. 1485 — IT

Ennepetal

August Bilstein GmbH & Co. KG, August-Bilstein Str. 4,
   pg. 507 — IT
Traktor-Ersatzteil-Gesellschaft mbH, Hagener Strasse 256-
   270, pg. 511 — IT

Ennigerloh

Abfallwirtschaftsgesellschaft des Kreiss Warendorf mbH,
   pg. 597 — IT
Krupp Fordertechnik GmbH, Schleebergstr. 12, pg. 511 — IT

Epfenbach

Heinrich Lippert GmbH, Eschelbronner Str. 35, pg. 518 — IT

Eppingen

J. DIEFFENBACHER GMBH & CO., Heilbronner Str.,
   Postfach 162, pg. 413 — IT

Erding

Arrow Deutschland G.m.b.H., Robert-Koch-Str. 9,
   pg. 135 — PB

Erfstadt

Litton Precision International, Romerstrasse 14,
   pg. 1004 — PB

Erfurt

Brucken-, Strassen-und Tiefbau Gesellschaft mbH, An der
   Lache 3, pg. 195 — IT
DG Bank - Erfurt, Juri-Gagarin-Ring 160, pg. 351 — IT
Deutsche Bank-Kreditbank AG (Erfurt), Juri-Gagarin-Ring
   101, pg. 402 — IT
Die Betonknacker, Stotternheimer Str. 40, pg. 1128 — IT
Energiewerke Nordthuringen AG, Schwerborner Strasse 30,
   pg. 1456 — IT
Forbo Erfurt GmbH, pg. 497 — IT
Landesbank Hessen-Thuringen Girozentrale, Bonifaciusstr.
   16, pg. 798 — IT
Metall Rohstoffe Thuringen GmbH, Bogenstr. 3,
   pg. 513 — IT
Niederlassung Erfurt, Am RotenBerg 5, pg. 195 — IT

Erkelenz

Howden Germany, Kolnerstrasse 71/78, pg. 636 — IT

Erkrath

Amano Deutschland GmbH, Helen-Rubinstein Str. 2-4,
   pg. 71 — IT
BGS Systems GmbH, Steinhof 39, pg. 161 — PB
Dormer Tools GmbH, pg. 1186 — IT
Forbo Scanachrome GmbH, pg. 498 — IT
Forkardt International GmbH, Postfach 3442, pg. 1484 — IT
Hydro Aluminium Deutschland GmbH, Gruitener Strasse 23,
   pg. 962 — IT
ITW Dynatec-Macon, Max-Planck-Strasse 15, pg. 868 — PB
Intralox, Inc. GmbH, Heinrich-Hertz-Strasse 44, pg. 643 — PV
Klockner ER-WE-PA, Mettmanner Strasse 49-51,
   pg. 737 — IT
Lincoln Smitweld GmbH, pg. 997 — PB
Nordson Deutschland GmbH, Henrich-Hertz-Strasse 42,
   pg. 1189 — PB

Ovako Stahl GmbH, pg. 1157 — IT
SIS Sicherheits-Service fur Informations-Systeme GmbH,
   Max Planck Str. 17, pg. 317 — IT
Heinrich Scheven Anlagen- und Leitungsbau GmbH, Max-
   Planck-Strasse 77, pg. 195 — IT
Tomen Transportgeraete GmbH, Am Wimmersberg 14,
   pg. 1412 — IT
Toyota Gabelstapler Deutschland GmbH, Am Wimmersberg
   10-14, pg. 1414 — IT

Erlangen

Acuson GmbH, Michael-Vogel-Stasse 1C, pg. 18 — PB
CESIWID Elektrowarme GmbH, pg. 723 — IT
Pfrimmer Nutricia GmbH & Co. KG, pg. 992 — IT
Pharmacia & Upjohn GmbH, Hoffmannstrasse 26,
   pg. 1050 — IT
Wesgo Ceramics GmbH, Graf-Zeppelin-Str. 9-1,
   pg. 893 — IT

Erpel

Tonwerke Erpel Werner E. Gabler GmbH, Am Lisenberg 1,
   pg. 1278 — IT

Esch

DSD International Contractors S.A.R.L., pg. 310 — IT

Eschborn

Alphabet European Sales Office, pg. 1045 — PV
Autologic Information International Inc., Franfurterstrasse
   63-69, pg. 1724 — PB
Bosch Telecom Offentliche Vermittlungstechnik GmbH,
   Kolner Strasse 5, pg. 204 — IT
Brunswick GmbH, Mergenthalerallee 45-47, pg. 266 — PB
Bull Peripherals GmbH, Frankfurter Strasse 63 69,
   pg. 316 — IT
Clarion Deutschland GmbH, Rudolf-Diesel-Strasse 2,
   pg. 296 — IT
Clarion Europa GmbH, Mergenthaler Allee 19-21,
   pg. 296 — IT
DMR Gruppe GmbH, Rahmannstrasse 11, pg. 528 — IT
Delsey GmbH, Hauptstrasse 350, pg. 192 — IT
Diebold Deutschland GmbH, pg. 368 — IT
Hydro Magnesium Marketing Gesellschaft mbH,
   Rahmannstrasse 11, pg. 963 — IT
Interleaf GmbH, Mergenthalerallee 77-81, pg. 893 — PB
JVC Deutschland GmbH, JVC Haus, Mergenthaler Allee 31-
   33, pg. 847 — IT
Millipore GmbH, Haupstrasse 71-79, pg. 1113 — PB
Ricoh Deutschland GmbH, Mergenthaler Allee 38-40,
   pg. 1116 — IT
SKW Chemie - Technik GmbH, Mergenthaler Allee 79-81,
   pg. 1465 — IT
SMH Uhron und Mikroelektronik GmbH, Rudolf-Diesel
   Strasse 7, pg. 1161 — IT
Samna GmbH, Mergenthaler Alle 10-12, pg. 896 — PB
Stratus Computer GmbH, Mergenthaleralle 79-81,
   pg. 1524 — PB

Eschenbach

Curamik Electronics GmbH, Am Stadtwald 2, pg. 209 — IT

Eschershausen

Deutsche Schlauchbootfabrik Hans Scheibert GmbH & Co.,
   pg. 327 — IT

Eschwege

Prawema Berufsausbildung GmbH, Hessenring 4,
   pg. 1128 — IT
Prawema Machine Tools GmbH, pg. 1128 — IT
GEORG SAHM GMBH & CO. KG MASCHINENFABRIK,
   Sudetenladstr. 33, pg. 1169 — IT
Woelm Pharma GmbH & Co., Max Woelm Strasse,
   pg. 1112 — IT

Eschweiler

CEM Zementverkauf GmbH, Brunnenhof 7, pg. 605 — IT
Elektrowerk Weisweiler GmbH, Durener Strasse,
   pg. 735 — PV
The West Company Deutschland, Postfach 1419/1420,
   Stolberger Strasse 21-41, pg. 1756 — IT
The West Company Holding, G.m.b.H, Stolberger Strasse
   21-41, pg. 1756 — PB

Espenhain

Espla GmbH, Leipziger Str. 40, pg. 827 — PV

Essen

Agricultura GmbH, Freiheit 1, pg. 961 — IT
ALLVIA, Ing. Ges. fur Planung und Konstruktion,
   Schederhofstrasse 2, pg. 423 — IT
Aloverzee Handelgesellschaft mbH, Theodor-Althoff-Str. 1,
   pg. 515 — IT
Altenberg Zink AG, Hafenstrasse 280, pg. 1442 — IT
ANGUS Chemie GmbH, pg. 75 — PV
BTE Brauerei-Technik Essen GmbH, Fellenstrasse 5,
   pg. 400 — IT
Beton Union Essen GmbH & Co., pg. 422 — IT
Bonato GmbH, pg. 1148 — IT

PB - *U.S. Public Companies Volume*
PV - *U.S. Private Companies Volume*
IT - *International Public & Private Companies Volume*

1612

BRENNTAG Eurochem GmbH, Alfredstrasse 81, pg. 1458

BRENNTAG Interchem GmbH, Alfredstrasse 81, pg. 1458   IT

BRENNTAG Interplast GmbH, Alfredstrasse 81, pg. 1458   IT

Bruckner Grundbau GmbH, Zeche Ernestine 29, pg. 623   IT

Buckau-Walther AG, Altendorferstr. 30, pg. 516   IT

CVU-Consulting fur Versorgungsunternehmen GmbH, Praueweg 13-15, pg. 1148   IT

Capital Goods & Manufactured Products Business Group, pg. 1387   IT

Centrum Warenhaus Dresden GmbH, Theodor-Althoff-Strasse 2, pg. 724   IT

Centrum Warenhaus Gorlitz GmbH, Theodor-Althoff-Strasse 2, pg. 724   IT

Centrum Warenhaus Halle GmbH, Theodor-Althoff-Strasse 2, pg. 724   IT

Centrum Warenhaus Hoyerswerda GmbH, Theodor-Althoff-Strasse 2, pg. 724   IT

Centrum Warenhauser Leipzig GmbH, Theodor-Althoff-Strasse 2, pg. 724   IT

Coca-Cola G.m.b.H., Max-Keith Strasse 64, pg. 392   PB

Danieli Buro Deutschland, Krupstrasse 82, pg. 378   IT

Deminex-Deutsche GmbH, Dorotheenstrasse 1, pg. 1460   IT

Deminex Syria GmbH, Dorotheenstr. 1, pg. 1461   IT

Deutsche Bank AG (Essen), Lindenallee 29-45, pg. 402   IT

Deutsche Bau-und Siedlungs-Gesellschaft mbH, Huyssenallee 22-30, pg. 623   IT

Deutsche Industrieanlagengesellschaft mbH, Hohenzollernstrasse 24, pg. 824   IT

diga Gebaude - und Rohrtechnik GmbH, Eckenbergstrasse 54-58, pg. 1148   IT

diga Versorgungstechnik Holding GmbH, pg. 1148   IT

EES - Erdgas-Energiesysteme GmbH, Wolfsbankring 38, pg. 1148   IT

Erka Handelsgesellschaft mbH, Theodor-Althoff-Strasse 2, pg. 724   IT

Essener Hochdruck-Rohrleitungsbau GmbH, pg. 836   IT

Ferrocarbon GmbH, Westuferstrasse 10, pg. 1458   IT

Ferrostaal Aktiengesellschaft, Hohenzollernstrasse 24, pg. 824   IT

Frank & Schulte GmbH, Alfredstrasse 154, pg. 1458   IT

FRIED. KRUPP AG, Altendorfer Str. 103, pg. 507   IT

GFE Eicherheit Fuhrungsgesellschaft mbH, Bonsiepen 6, pg. 1457   IT

GKN Gelenkwellenbau GmbH, Westendhof 5-9, pg. 536   IT

Gaswerk Philippsburg GmbH, pg. 1148   IT

Generale Bank & Co., Am Waldthausenpark 4, pg. 548   IT

Gesellschaft fur Energiebeteiligung mbH, Kruppstrasse 5, pg. 1460   IT

Gesellschaft fur Kohle-Technologie mbH, Altendorferstr.120, pg. 511   IT

Gesellschaft zur Vermittlung von Bauversicherungen mbH, Rellinghauser Str. 53-57, pg. 623   IT

Grundstucksverwaltung LBH GmbH & Co., pg. 1148   IT

Grundstucksverwaltungsgesellschaft Ruhrgas AG & Co., pg. 1148   IT

HBE Grundbesitzverwaltungs- und Verwertungs GmbH, pg. 310   IT

HR Schrottaufbereitung GmbH, Weidkamp 115, pg. 513   IT

Hansa Rohstoff GmbH - IIa Trading Sector, Pferdebahnstr. 30, pg. 513   IT

Hartung, Kuhn, & Co., Maschinenfabrik GmbH, Altendorfer Str. 120, pg. 511   IT

Hauptniederlassung Essen/Niederlassung Essen/Niederlassung Warehausbau Essen, Schnabelstrasse 1, pg. 194   IT

Heinrich Industrie-und Handels-Aktiengesellschaft, Steeler Str. 529, pg. 597   IT

HOCHTIEF AG, Rellinghauser Str. 53-57, pg. 623   IT

Holter Group, Ruhrallee 185, pg. 101   IT

Hypothekenbank in Essen AG, pg. 310   IT

Industick GmbH, Alfredstrasse 81, pg. 1458   IT

Industrial Services, Business Park Essen Nord, Schnieringshof 10, pg. 398   IT

Joy Warenhandelsgesellschaft, Theodor-Althoff-Strasse 2, pg. 724   IT

Jung GmbH, Theodor-Althoff-Strasse 2, pg. 724   IT

KK-Service GmbH, Altendorfer Str. 104, pg. 515   IT

Kammer Ventile GmbH, Manderscheiderstrasse 19, pg. 659   PB

KARSTADT AKTIENGESELLSCHAFT, Theodor-Althoff-Strasse 2, pg. 724   IT

Karstadt Unterstutzungsfonds GmbH, Theodor-Althoff-Strasse 2, pg. 724   IT

Karstadt Versicherungs-Vermittlung GmbH, Theodor-Althoff-Strasse 2, pg. 724   IT

Kepa Kaufhaus GmbH, Theodor-Althoff-Strasse 2, pg. 724   IT

Kodak AG-Essen, Langemarckstrasse 13, pg. 552   PB

Krupp Corpoplast Maschinenbau GmbH, Helenenstr. 149, pg. 510   IT

Krupp Druckereibetriebe GmbH, Altendorfer Str. 1, pg. 513   IT

Krupp Energiehandel GmbH, Altendorfer Str. 104, pg. 513   IT

Krupp Entwicklungszentrum GmbH, Munchener Str. 100, pg. 512   IT

Krupp GfT Gesellschaft fur Anlagen-, Bau- und Gleistechnik mbH, Frohnhauserstr. 75, pg. 513   IT

Krupp Gft Gesellschaft fur Anlagen-, Bau- und Gleistechnik mbH, Theodor-Althoff-Str. 1, pg. 513   IT

Krupp GfT Gesellschaft fur Anlagen-, Bau- und Gleistechnik mbH, Altendorfer Str. 104, pg. 513   IT

Krupp Hoesch Berufsbildung GmbH, Altendorferstr. 102, pg. 512   IT

Krupp Hoesch Dienstleistungen GmbH, Martin-Luther-Str. 118, pg. 512   IT

Krupp Hoesch Immobilien GmbH, Martin-Luther Str. 118, pg. 512   IT

Krupp Hoesch Informationsverarbeitung GmbH, Altendorferstr. 103, pg. 512   IT

Krupp Hoesch International GmbH, Theodor-Althoff-Str. 1, pg. 513   IT

Krupp Hoesch Maschinenbau GmbH, Helenenstr. 110, pg. 509   IT

Krupp Koppers GmbH, Altendorfer Str. 120, pg. 511   IT

Krupp Maschinentechnik GmbH, Helenenstr. 149, pg. 510   IT

Krupp Medizintechnik GmbH, Harkortstr. 65, pg. 510   IT

Krupp Mineralolhandel GmbH, Altendorfstr. 104, pg. 513   IT

Krupp Stahl Wohnungsbau GmbH, Martin-Luther-Str. 118, pg. 512   IT

Krupp Warmetechnik GmbH, Altendorfstr. 104, pg. 514   IT

Krupp Warmetechnik GmbH - Essen, Theodor Althoff Str. 1, pg. 515   IT

Krupp Widia GmbH, Muenchener Str. 90, pg. 510   IT

LVE Verfahrenselektronik GmbH, pg. 1149   IT

Maxon GmbH, Ruttenscheider Platz 3, pg. 717   PV

MEGAL GmbH Mittel-Europaische-Gasleitungs-gesellschaft, pg. 1149   IT

METHA-Methanhandel GmbH, pg. 1149   IT

MICKE Reibbelag GmbH, pg. 1148   IT

Herman Miller Deutschland Inc., Worringstrasse 250, pg. 1112   PB

Montan-Entsorgung GmbH & Co., Rolandstrasse 5-9, pg. 1457   IT

NGT Neue Gebaudetechnik GmbH, Waudcheidtstr. 21-23, pg. 1149   IT

Norsk Hydro Deutschland GmbH, Freiheit 1, pg. 964   IT

Optic Point Warenhandels gesellschaft mbH, Theodor-Althoff-Strasse 2, pg. 724   IT

PLEdoc Gesellschaft fur Dokumentationserstellung und pflege mbH, Schnieringsliof 10-14, pg. 1149   IT

Pagolux Bausysteme GmbH, pg. 1148   IT

Panopa Reiseburo GmbH, Logenstr. 20-22, pg. 515   IT

Pico Bello Warenhandels gesellschaft mbH, Theodor-Althoff-Strasse 2, pg. 724   IT

Pipeline Engineering Gesellschaft fur Planung, Bau- und Betriebsuberwachung von Fernleitungen mbH, Kallenbergstrasse 5, pg. 1148   IT

Plettac-Plana GmbH, pg. 1061   IT

RWE AG, Operplatz 1, pg. 1081   IT

RWE Energie AG, Kruppstr. 5, pg. 1081   IT

RWE Entsorgung AG, Opernplatz 1, pg. 1081   IT

RWE Telliance AG, Gutenbergstrasse 3, pg. 1081   IT

Raab Karcher AG, Rudolf-u-Bennigsen-Foerder Platz 1, pg. 1457   IT

Raab Karcher Elektonik GmbH, pg. 1457   IT

Raab Karcher Energieservice GmbH, pg. 1457   IT

Raab Karcher Holz GmbH, Rudolf v. Bennigsen Foerder Platz 1, pg. 1457   IT

Raab Karcher Sicherheit GmbH, pg. 1457   IT

Railway Equipment Export, pg. 513   IT

RAM Mobile Data Network GmbH, Geschaftsfuhrung, GfD Gesellschaft fur Datenfunk mbh, pg. 208   PB

Rat und Tat Technischer Kundendienst GmbH, Theodor-Althoff-Strasse 2, pg. 724   IT

Reiseburo Dr. Tigges GmbH, Altendorfer Str. 104, pg. 515   IT

Rufas Rutgers Fahrzeug-Systeme AG, Westuferstrasse 7, pg. 1148   IT

Ruhr-Schwefelsaure GmbH & Co. KG, Alfredstrasse 81, pg. 1461   IT

Ruhrgas AG, Huttropstrasse, pg. 1149   IT

RUHRGAS AKTIENGESELLSCHAFT, Huttropstr. 60, pg. 1149   IT

Ruhrgas Energie Beteiligungs-Aktiengesellschaft, pg. 1149   IT

Ruhrgas Industrie Beteiligungsgesellschaft mbH, Huttropstrasse 60, pg. 1149   IT

Ruhrkohle-Umwelttechnik GmbH (RUT), Rellinghauser Strasse 1, pg. 1460   IT

Runners Point Warenhandelsgesellschaft mbH, Theodor-Althoff-Strasse 2, pg. 724   IT

Rutgers Pagid AG, pg. 1148   IT

Stefan Keith GmbH, Altendorfer Str. 104, pg. 513   IT

Stinnes Immobiliendienst Verwaltungsgesellschaft mbH, Gildehofstrasse 1, pg. 1460   IT

Stinnes Mineralolhandel GmbH, Alfredstrasse 81, pg. 1461   IT

Stinnes Stahlhandee GmbH (SSH), Stoppenberger Strasse 100, pg. 1459   IT

Teerbau GmbH, Prinz-Friedrich-Strasse 3, pg. 1148   IT

Tesch Industrie- und Rohrleitungsbau GmbH, Schnabelstrasse 1, pg. 195   IT

Theranostic Medizinelektronik GmbH, Huesstrasse 109, pg. 389   IT

Tiefenbach GmbH, pg. 47   IT

VEM Erz und Stahl GmbH, 40-42, Huyssenallee, pg. 682   IT

VEBA OEL VERTRIEB GmbH, pg. 1461   IT

VOAC Hydraulics GmbH, pg. 1264   PB

Westdeutsches Assekuranz-Kontor GmbH, Am Westbahnhof 2, pg. 513   IT

Westend Verlags- und Werbegesellschaft mbH, Westendstr. 1, pg. 513   IT

WestLB Essen Branch, pg. 1493   IT

Esslingen am Neckar

Boley G.m.b.H., Mettinger Strasse 11, pg. 294   IT

Citizen Machinery Europe G.m.b.H., Mettinger Strasse 11, pg. 294   IT

Deutsche Automobilgesellschaft mbH, Batterie-Forschungslaboratorium, pg. 1473   IT

FESTO AG & CO., Ruiter Str. 82, pg. 480   IT

Lawson Mardon Picopac GmbH, pg. 69   IT

Maschinenfabrik Esslingen AG, Emil-Kessler Str. 30, pg. 368   IT

Stinnes BauMarkt AG, Uhlandstrasse 1, pg. 1459   IT

Zeiss Industrielle Messtechnik GmbH, pg. 1523   IT

Ettlingen

Maschinenfabrik Lorenz GmbH, Hertzstrasse 9-15, pg. 808   IT

Molex Elektronik GmbH, Einstein Strasse 18A, pg. 1122   PB

Pharm-Allergan GmbH, Rudolf-Plank-Strasse 31, pg. 46   PB

Zeiss Messgeratebau GmbH, pg. 1523   IT

Euskirchen

Sulzer Papertec Euskirchen GmbH, pg. 1305   IT

Eutingen im Gau

Southern Branch, Hummelbergstrasse 2, pg. 401   IT

Falkensee

Herlitz Aktiengesellschaft Produktion, Str. der Einheit 142-148, pg. 616   IT

Feldkirchen

Francesco Parisi G.m.b.H., Am Kiesgrund, 2-4, pg. 504   IT

Intel GmbH, Dornacher Strasse 1, pg. 887   PB

Kohler Interconsult, Emeranstrasse 49-51, pg. 1420   IT

Fellbach

Charmilles Deutschland Maschinen Ges. mbH, Bruckmanstrasse 11, pg. 489   IT

Eisenmetall Rohstoff GmbH, Esslingerstr. 4, pg. 513   IT

Excentra GmbH Hydralische Antriebe, pg. 838   IT

Intech International, pg. 489   IT

Sandvik Process Systems GmbH, P.O. Box 4180, pg. 1187   IT

Sony-Wega Produktions GmbH, Stuttgarter Strasse 106, pg. 1284   IT

Filderstadt

Alarmcom Leutron GmbH, Raiffeisenstrasse 16, pg. 1246   IT

Alarmcom Loutron GmbH, Raiffeisenstrasse 27, pg. 1246   IT

Gebruder Sulzer Holding GmbH, pg. 1308   IT

Orga-Soft Organisation & Software GmbH, Weidacher Str. 26, pg. 317   IT

Parker Hannifin N.M.F. GmbH, Buro Stuttgart, Johann Strauss-Strasse-51, pg. 1263   PB

Rockwell International GmbH, Hornbergstrasse 35, pg. 1401   PB

Sulzer Holding GmbH, pg. 1308   IT

Universal Transport GmbH, Wolfsecker Str. 10, pg. 1034   IT

Veam GmbH, P.O. Box 1304, pg. 1005   PB

Flensburg

Danfoss Compressors GmbH, Mads-Clausen-Str. 7, pg. 377   IT

Fahrzeugwerke Nord GmbH, Werftstrasse 24, pg. 824   IT

Gebruder Dahl GmbH, Mergenthalerstrasse 8, pg. 359   IT

ISS Food Hygiene Service GmbH, Friesische Strasse 18, pg. 657   IT

Integral Technologie GmbH, Lise-Meitner-Str. 2, pg. 679   IT

Motorola Electronic GmbH, Eckenerstrasse 28, pg. 1139   PB

Stora Spezialpapiere GmbH, Husumer Strasse 12, pg. 1303   IT

Verwaltungsgesellschaft Friedrich Warnke mbH, pg. 838   IT

Friedrich Warnke GmbH & Co. KG, pg. 838   IT

Forchheim

4P Folie Forchheim GmbH, pg. 1146   IT

Mitsubishi Motor Marketing Research Europe GmbH, Schieferstein 11 A, pg. 876   IT

Frankenthal

Crown Cork Company (Germany) G.m.b.H., Postfach 1245, pg. 464   PB

KSB AKTIENGESELLSCHAFT, Johann Klein-Strasse 9, pg. 721   IT

KSB Service GmbH, pg. 721   IT

Frankfurt

AGIV GROUP, Mainzer Landstr 41, pg. 14   IT

AMS Management Systems Deutschland GmbH, Querstrasse 8-10, pg. 87   PB

PB - *U.S. Public Companies Volume*
PV - *U.S. Private Companies Volume*
IT - *International Public & Private Companies Volume*

Aer Lingus, An Der Hauptwache 7, pg. 28   **IT**
Alwin Schockemohle & Willenborg GmbH u. Co.
   Blechhandel KG, Kruppstr. 100-102, pg. 512   **IT**
Ascom GmbH, Victor-Slotosch-Str. 11, pg. 87   **IT**
Ascom Tateco GmbH, Flinschstrasse 67, pg. 87   **IT**
Ascom Timeplex GmbH, Edisonstrasse 11-13, pg. 87   **IT**
BHF-Bank, Neue Mainzer Strasse 76, pg. 119   **IT**
BHF-BANK AG, Bockenheimer Landstrasse 10,
   pg. 119
BHF Capital Management GmbH, Neue Mainzer Strasse
   80, pg. 119   **IT**
Banco Nacional de Mexico, Kettenhofweg, 220D-6000,
   pg. 574   **IT**
Bank of America NT&SA, Ulmenstrasse 30, pg. 182   **PB**
Bank of Ireland, Rathenauplatz 1a, pg. 153   **IT**
Bankenunion Aktiengesellschaft, Eschenheimer Anlage 23,
   pg. 504   **IT**
Bayerische Landesbank Girozentrale - Frankfurt Branch,
   Bockenheimer Landstrasse 19, pg. 176   **IT**
Berag GmbH, Burohaus am Seedamm, Wolf-Heidenheim-
   Strasse 12, pg. 1502   **IT**
CPF Deutschland GmbH, Dreieichstrasse 59, pg. 262   **IT**
CHEMAG Aktiengesellschaft, Senckenberganlage 10-12,
   pg. 104   **IT**
Chiron Behring GmbH & Co., pg. 350   **PB**
Chiron Behring GmbH & Co., pg. 624   **IT**
Christoph GmbH, Goldstrasse 134, pg. 513   **IT**
CIBA Additive GmbH, Hahnstrasse 40, pg. 975   **IT**
CIBA-GEIGY GmbH, Liebigstrasse 51/53, pg. 977   **IT**
CIBA-GEIGY GmbH, Medizin, Hahnstrasse 38, pg. 977   **IT**
CIBA-GEIGY GmbH, Hahnstrasse 40, pg. 977   **IT**
Classic GmbH, pg. 757   **IT**
Commerz Finanz-Management GmbH, Mainzer Landstr.
   225-227, pg. 309   **IT**
COMMERZBANK AG, Kaiser Platz, pg. 308   **IT**
DEA GmbH, Praunheimer Landstrasse 32, pg. 654   **IT**
Daiwa Bank (Deutschland) GmbH, Im Trutz Frankfurt 55,
   pg. 373   **IT**
Deutsche Telekom Medien GmbH, Wiesenhuettenstr. 18,
   pg. 407   **IT**
DyStar Textilfarben GmbH, pg. 174   **IT**
Energiewerke Frankfurt/Oder AG, Wilhelm-Pieck-Strasse
   333, pg. 1456   **IT**
Eurest Deutschland, Lyoner SR 23, pg. 21   **IT**
FABA Vermietungsgesellschaft mbH, pg. 309   **IT**
Faserwerk Kelheim GmbH, C 660, pg. 339   **IT**
FRANKFURTER SPARKASSE, Neue Mainzer Strasse 47-
   53, pg. 504   **IT**
GT Global Fondsservice GmbH, Bleichstrasse 60-62,
   pg. 809   **IT**
Haden Drysys GmbH, Ben Gurion Ring 21B, pg. 586   **IT**
Hartmann & Cie GmbH & Co KG, pg. 757   **IT**
Hewlett-Packard GmbH, Berner Strasse 117, pg. 820   **PB**
Hoechst Trevira GmbH & Co. KG, pg. 626   **IT**
Hostalen Polyethylen, pg. 626   **IT**
ING Lease Deutschland, Wiesenau 43, pg. 650   **IT**
ISS Servisystem GmbH, Glas-und Gebaudereinigung,
   Gutleutstrasse 320, pg. 657   **IT**
Immobiliengesellschaft der Frankfurter Sparkasse GmbH,
   Hamburgerallee 49-53, pg. 504   **IT**
Kanthal GmbH, pg. 724   **IT**
Ketchum Advertising GmbH, Mittlerer Hasenpfad 25,
   pg. 617   **PV**
Kreditbank-Bankverein AG, Mendelsohnstrasse 75-77,
   pg. 761   **IT**
Krupp Hoesch Stahlhandel GmbH, Gutleutstr. 363-365,
   pg. 514   **IT**
Krupp VDM GmbH - Semi-Finished Products & Systems
   Division, Zeilweg 42, pg. 509   **IT**
LGT Asset Management GmbH, Bleichstrasse 60-62,
   pg. 810   **IT**
LGT Bank in Liechtenstein (Deutschland) Gmbh,
   Bleichstrasse 60-62, pg. 810   **IT**
LGT Invest Kapitalanlagegesellschaft mbH, Bleichstrasse
   60-62, pg. 810   **IT**
Logica GmbH, Lyoner Strasse 14, pg. 814   **IT**
Lufthansa Cargo AG, Lufthansa Basis, pg. 407   **IT**
Luwa Anlagentechnik GmbH, pg. 617   **IT**
Luwa Fahrzeugklimatechnik GmbH, pg. 617   **IT**
Luwa Filtertechnik GmbH, pg. 617   **IT**
Luwa GmbH, pg. 617   **IT**
Luwa Service GmbH, pg. 617   **IT**
M & F Vermogens- und Grundstucksverwaltung GmbH,
   pg. 180   **IT**
McCain GmbH (Germany), Mergenthaler Allee 77,
   pg. 850   **IT**
The Meiji Life Insurance Company Frankfurt Office, Messe
   Turm, Friedrich-Ebert-Anlage 49, pg. 854   **IT**
Memorex Telex GmbH, Berner Strasse 38, pg. 857   **IT**
Merita Bank Ltd., Frankfurt Representative Office,
   Liebigstrasse 11, pg. 859   **IT**
METALLGESELLSCHAFT AG, Reuterweg 14, pg. 860   **IT**
Meuer GmbH, Konigstrasse Str. 88, pg. 513   **IT**
Mitsukoshi Deutschland GmbH-Frankfurt Branch,
   Kaiserstrasse 13, pg. 884   **IT**
Moody's Deutschland GmbH, Taunusanlage 11,
   pg. 537   **PB**
Morgan Stanley Frankfurt, Rahmhofstrasse 2-4,
   pg. 1133   **PB**
National Bank of Greece Frankfurt Branch, pg. 907   **IT**
Niederlassung Frankfurt/Oder, Logenstrasse 8,
   pg. 195   **IT**
Nortel Dasa Network Systems GmbH & Co. KG, Lyoner
   Strasse 15, pg. 970   **IT**
Nutrinova Nutrition Specialties & Food Ingredients GmbH,
   pg. 626   **IT**
OC Immobilienverwaltungs GmbH, pg. 178   **IT**
OC Orga Consult GmbH & Co. Baubetreuungs KG,
   pg. 179   **IT**
Oder-Spree Energieversorgung AG, pg. 1456   **IT**
Panalpina Welttransport GmbH, pg. 1023   **IT**

Parker Hannifin GmbH, Buro Frankfurt, Heimchenweg 8,
   pg. 1263   **PB**
Presstech Controls GmbH, Bolongarostrasse 59,
   pg. 790   **PB**
Pullman Hotels Deutschland, Karlstrasse 16, pg. 21   **IT**
Quantum GmbH, Berner Str. 28, pg. 1350   **PB**
Raab Karcher Sanitar Heizung Fliesen GmbH,
   pg. 1457   **IT**
Rockwell International GmbH, Hanauer Landstrasse 338,
   pg. 1401   **PB**
Rothenberger Werkzeuge Aktiengesellschaft, pg. 1128   **IT**
Sanpaolo-Frankfurt am Main Branch, Eschersheimer
   Landstrasse, 55, pg. 692   **IT**
Scan-Optics GmbH, Gervinusstrasse 17, pg. 1436   **PB**
Schindler Aufzuge GmbH, pg. 1205   **IT**
Georg Schlitt Werkzeuge und Werkzeugmaschinen GmbH,
   Voltenseestrasse 2, pg. 1128   **IT**
Singapore Tourist Promotion Board - Frankfurt,
   Hochstrasse 35-37, pg. 1254   **IT**
Svenske Handelsbanken Frankfurt/Main, Mittlerer
   Hasenpfad 25, P.O. Box 700955, pg. 1327   **IT**
Taisei (Deutscheland) GmbH, Bohmerstrasse 19,
   pg. 1347   **IT**
Takenaka Europe GmbH, Frankfurt, Friedrich-Ebert-Anlage
   56, pg. 1351   **IT**
Telxon rnde GmbH, Mergenthalerallee 77, pg. 1574   **PB**
Templeton Global Strategic Services, Taunusanlage 11,
   pg. 630   **PB**
Utell International-Germany, Gutleutstrasse 322,
   pg. 1098   **IT**
VW AUDI Vertriebszentrum Rhein Main GmbH,
   pg. 1474   **IT**
Vittel Mineralwasser Gmbh, pg. 922   **IT**
Von Ernst Deutschland Gesellschaft fur Vermogensplanug
   mbH, pg. 180   **IT**
Westdeutsch Max Cochius GmbH, Karl-Benz-Str. 21,
   pg. 514   **IT**

Frankfurt/Main

A.M.A. Asset Management Advisors of Dresdner Bank,
   Mainzer Landstrasse 11-13, pg. 418   **IT**
AMC, Bleichstrasse, 2-4, pg. 92   **PV**
Actium Leasobjekt GmbH, pg. 310   **IT**
AdPlus, Hamburger Allee 45, pg. 678   **PV**
Aeroquip Sterling GmbH, Eschborner Lanstr. 145-157,
   pg. 25   **PB**
Air Malta - Frankfurt, Munchener Strasse 49, pg. 38   **IT**
Alfa Romeo Vertriebsges m.b.H., Larchenstrasse 110,
   pg. 481   **IT**
Algemene Bank Nederland (Deutschland) A.G., Mainzer
   Landstrasse 39, pg. 12   **IT**
AlliedSignal Aerospace Service Corporation, Hahnstrasse
   40, pg. 52   **PB**
Asahi Bank (Deutschland) GmbH, Messe Turm, 24th Fl.,
   Friedrich-Ebert-Anlage 49, pg. 83   **IT**
Asahi Bank Frankfurt Representative Office, Messe Turm,
   24th Fl., Friedrich-Ebert-Anlage 49, pg. 83   **IT**
Asahi Chemical Industry - Frankfurt, Arabella Center,
   Lyonerstr. 44-48, pg. 84   **IT**
The Associated Press GmbH, 27 Mosel Strasse,
   pg. 92   **PV**
Australia & New Zealand Banking Group Limited Germany,
   Mainzer Landstr. 46, pg. 99   **IT**
BB-Leasing GmbH, Lyoner Str. 11 a, pg. 159   **IT**
BHF & CCF Leasing GmbH, Gruneburgweg 102,
   pg. 119   **IT**
BHF Asset Management GmbH, Neue Mainzer Strasse 80,
   pg. 119   **IT**
BHF Bank, Bockenheimer Landstrasse 10, pg. 342   **IT**
BHF - CCF Leasing, Gruneburgweg 102, pg. 342   **IT**
BHF Immobilien-GmbH, Bockenheimer Landstrasse 10,
   pg. 119   **IT**
BHF Trust Management Gesellschaft fur
   Vermoegensverwaltung mbH, Neue Mainzer Strasse 80,
   pg. 119   **IT**
BK Beteilgungsverwaltung GmbH, pg. 1148   **IT**
BMC Software GmbH, pg. 162   **PB**
B.U.S. Berzelius Umwelt-Service GmbH, Bockenheimer
   Landstrasse 24, pg. 860   **IT**
Bailey Germany, Graefstrasse 97, pg. 449   **IT**
Banca Nazionale del Lavoro, Neue Mainzer Str. 57,
   pg. 137   **IT**
Banco di Sicilia, Grunenburgweg 102, pg. 140   **IT**
Banco Santander, Zeppelinallee 35-37, pg. 144   **IT**
Bank Hapoalim (Frankfurt), Westendstrasse 24,
   pg. 149   **IT**
Bank of Boston, Fueerbachstrasse 26-32, pg. 184   **PB**
Bank of Ireland, Hochstrasse 29, pg. 153   **IT**
Bank of Ireland Asset Management, Hochstrasse 29,
   pg. 153   **IT**
Bank of Montreal - Germany, Ulmenstrasse 37-39,
   pg. 155   **IT**
The Bank of New York, Niedenau 61-63, pg. 179   **PB**
Bank of Tokyo-Mitsubishi (Deutschland) AG, Mainzer
   Landstrasse 16, pg. 158   **IT**
The Bank of Tokyo-Mitsubishi, Ltd. (Frankfurt Branch),
   Neue Mainzer Strasse 75, pg. 158   **IT**
Bankers Trust New York Corporation, Bockenheimer
   Landstrasse 39, pg. 186   **PB**
Bankhaus Gebruder Bethmann, Bethmannstr. 7-9,
   pg. 179   **IT**
Banque Generale du Luxembourg SA, Goethestrasse 10,
   pg. 162   **IT**
Banque Indosuez, Wilhelm-Leuschner Strasse 9-11,
   pg. 31   **IT**
Banque Internationale a Luxembourg S.A.-Represantanz fur
   die, Rhein-Main Ctr., Bockenheimer Landstr. 51-53,
   pg. 162   **IT**
Banque Paribas-BPB Capital Markets GmbH, Bockenheimer
   Landstrasse 51.53, pg. 319   **IT**

Banque Paribas Deutschland, Gruneburgweg 14,
   pg. 319   **IT**
Baring Brothers (Deutschland), Friedrichstrasse 26,
   pg. 648   **IT**
Baring Private Equity Partners, Friedrichstrasse 26,
   pg. 648   **IT**
Berlitz Schools of Languages GmbH, Kaiser Str. 66,
   pg. 222   **PB**
Berwein Wertpapierhandels-und Borsenmakler GmbH,
   Taunusanlage 11, pg. 1331   **IT**
Beteiligungsgesellschaft fuer Industrie und Handel mbH,
   pg. 309   **IT**
Beteiligungsgesellschaft fur die deutsche Wirtschaft GmbH,
   Gutleutstrasse 85, pg. 418   **IT**
Beteiligungsgesellschaft fur Industrie und Handel mbH,
   pg. 179   **IT**
Bethmann Liegenschafts KG, pg. 179   **IT**
Bethmann Vermogensbetreuung GmbH, pg. 179   **IT**
BeVerwal Beteiligungs und Verwaltungsgesellschaft mbH,
   pg. 179   **IT**
BORSCH, STENGEL & PARTNER GMBH, Eschersheimer
   Landstr. 60-62, pg. 203   **IT**
Brandeis Hauck & Partners, Kaiserstrasse 23, pg. 1030   **IT**
CB Beteiligungs Und Verwaltungsgesellchaft mbH,
   Ulmenstrasse 30, pg. 339   **PB**
CB Computer Services GmbH, Ulmenstrasse 30,
   pg. 339   **PB**
CIBC Holdings G.m.b.H., Erlenstrasse 2, pg. 257   **IT**
CTT Management GmbH, pg. 1186   **IT**
Canadian Imperial Bank of Commerce (Deutschland) AG,
   Erlenstrasse 2, pg. 257   **IT**
Cariplo (Frankfurt A/M), Taunusanlage 11, pg. 275   **IT**
Chase Bank, A.G., Alexanderstrasse 59, pg. 339   **PB**
Chase Manhattan Leasing GmbH, Ulmenstrasse 30,
   pg. 339   **IT**
CHEMETALL GMBH Gesellschaft fuer chemisch technische
   Verfahren, Reuterweg 14, pg. 861   **IT**
Chemische Fabrik Aubing GmbH, pg. 1148   **IT**
Cho Hung Bank (Deutschland) GmbH, MesseTurm,
   Friedrich-Ebert-Anlage 49, pg. 288   **IT**
Citibank A.G., Neue Mainzer Strasse 75, pg. 378   **PB**
Cognos GmbH, Lyoner Strasse 14, pg. 306   **IT**
Commerz Financial Products GmbH, Kaiserplatz,
   pg. 309   **IT**
Commerz International Capital Management GmbH,
   Kaiserstr. 16, pg. 309   **IT**
Commerz Service Gesellschaft fur Kundenbetreuung
   GmbH, pg. 309   **IT**
Commerz Unternehmensbeteiligungs AG, pg. 309   **IT**
Commerzbank Investment Management GmbH, Kaiserstr.
   16, pg. 309   **IT**
Conquest Europe, Bockenheimer Landstrasse 104,
   pg. 1484   **IT**
Michael Conrad & Leo Burnett GmbH, Alexanderstr. 65,
   pg. 184   **PV**
Conservenfabrik Eugen Lacroix GmbH, pg. 299   **PB**
Controlmatic GmbH, Genfer Strasse 11, pg. 615   **IT**
Credit Agricole (Deutschland) AG Handelsberatung, FBC
   Hochhaus, 17th Fl., Mainzer Landstr. 46, pg. 341   **IT**
DA Deutsche Allgemeine Leben Versicherung
   Aktiengesellschaft, Zurich-Haus am Opernplatz,
   pg. 1531   **IT**
DA Deutsche Allgemeine Versicherungs-Aktiengellschaft,
   Zurich-Haus am Opernplatz, pg. 1531   **IT**
DB Export Leasing G.m.b.H., Taunusanlage 12,
   pg. 402   **IT**
DEGI Deutsche Gesellschaft fur Immobilienfonds mbH,
   Bettinastrasse 53-55, pg. 418   **IT**
DG BANK, Am Platz der Republik, pg. 351   **IT**
DKB Finance (Frankfurt), Mainzer, Landstrasse 46,
   pg. 361   **IT**
DMB&B Frankfurt, Schaumainkai 87, pg. 303   **PV**
DMC Dresdner Management Consult GmbH, Theodor-
   Heuss-Allee 2, pg. 418   **IT**
DOWC Ost-West-Consult GmbH, Theodor-Heuss-Allee 2,
   pg. 418   **IT**
DPSA Deutsche Personensuch-Anlagen GmbH,
   Lyonerstrasse 14-7, pg. 1365   **IT**
D.R.S. Restaurant Scheck Sodexho GmbH, Lyoner Strasse
   12, pg. 1274   **IT**
DTZ Zadelhoff GmbH, Stephenstrasse 3, pg. 799   **IT**
Daewoo Handels GmbH, Hahnstrasse 31-35, pg. 358   **IT**
Dai-Ichi Kangyo Bank (Deutschland) AG, P.O. Box 10 06
   63, pg. 362   **IT**
Dai-Ichi Kangyo Bank, Ltd.-Frankfurt, P.O. Box 10 06 63,
   pg. 361   **IT**
Daiwa Europe (Deutschland) GmbH, FBC Frankfurter Buro
   Center, Mainzer Landstrasse 46, pg. 375   **IT**
DAMM Agentur Fur Marketing und Werbung,
   Alexanderstrasse 61, pg. 1152   **PV**
Datastream International (Frankfurt) Ltd., Triton-Haus,
   Taunusanlage 11, pg. 1326   **PB**
debis Marketing Services GmbH, Lyones Str. 9,
   pg. 368   **IT**
DEGUSSA AG, Weissfrauenstrasse 9, pg. 388   **IT**
Delta Air Lines Frankfurt, 360 Lyoner Strasse, 12th Fl.,
   pg. 497   **PB**
Deutsche Asset Management G.m.b.H., Bockenheimer
   Landstrasse 42, pg. 402   **IT**
DEUTSCHE BAHN, Zentrale, Hauptverwaltung,
   Stephensonstrasse 1, pg. 401   **IT**
DEUTSCHE BANK AG, Taunusanlage 12, pg. 401   **IT**
Deutsche Bank AG (Frankfurt), Rossmarkt 18, pg. 402   **IT**
Deutsche Carbone AG, Stadtteil Kalbach Talstrasse 112,
   pg. 1030   **IT**
**DEUTSCHE GIROZENTRALE-DEUTSCHE
   KOMMUNALBANK**, Taunusanlage 10, pg. 406   **IT**
Deutsche Hypothekenbank FrankfurtAG, Taunusanlage 9,
   pg. 418   **IT**
Deutsche ICI GmbH, Emil-von-Behring-Strasse 2,
   pg. 664   **IT**

PB - *U.S. Public Companies Volume*
PV - *U.S. Private Companies Volume*
IT - *International Public & Private Companies Volume*

Deutsche SB-Kauf AG, Hahnstrasse 72, pg. 863　IT
Deutsche Wagnisfinanzierungs-Gesellschaft mbH, Bockenheimer Landstrasse 42, pg. 179　IT
Deutscher Investment-Trust Gesellschaft fur Wertpapieranlagen mbH, Mainzer Landstrasse 11-13, pg. 418　IT
Diskus AG, Vilbeler Landstr. 36, pg. 1128　IT
The Walt Disney Company (Germany) GmbH, Savignystr. 76, pg. 514　PB
Dorfer Dialogue GmbH, Kennedyalle 111, pg. 304　PV
Dow Jones International Marketing Services GmbH, Gruneburgweg 149, pg. 525　PB
Dow Jones Markets G.m.b.H., Hungener Strasse 6-12, pg. 525　PB
Dow Vertriebsges.mbh, Gruneburgweg 102, pg. 524　PB
DRESDNER BANK AG, Juergen-Ponto-Platz 1, pg. 417　IT
Dresdner Bauspar AG, Mainzer Landstrasse 49, pg. 418　IT
Dresdner Vermogensberatungs-gesellschaft mbH, Theodor-Heuss-Allee 2, pg. 418　IT
Dresdnerbank Investment Management Kapitalanlagegesellschaft mbH, Mainzer Landstrasse 11-13, pg. 418　IT
Dun & Bradstreet Deutschland GmbH, Hahnstr. 31-35, pg. 536　PB
Eaton GmbH, Wielandstrasse 10-12, pg. 558　PB
Daniel J. Edelman GmbH, Bettianstrasse 64, pg. 363　PV
Emhart Deutschland GmbH, Postfach 940166, pg. 233　PB
Ericsson Paging Systems Zweigniederlassung Deutschland, Lyonerstrasse 14, pg. 1367　IT
FEC Consult Ges. f. Management- und Beteiligungsberatung mbH, Junghofstrasse 18-26, pg. 799　IT
Fiat Deutschland, Westendstrasse 60, pg. 483　IT
Fina Deutschland GmbH, Bleichstrasse 2-4, pg. 1043　IT
Fina Holding Deutschland GmbH, Bleichstrasse 2-4, pg. 1043　IT
Financiere Indosuez Beratungs-gesellschaft, Wilhelm Leuschner Strasse 9 11, pg. 314　IT
First Marathon Bank GmbH, Feuerbachstr. 26-32, pg. 487　IT
S. Fischer Verlag GmbH, Hedderichstrasse 114, pg. 1478　IT
Fischer Taschenbuch Verlag GmbH, Hedderichstrasse 114, pg. 1478　IT
Fleishman-Hillard Germany, Hanauer Landstrasse, 126-128, pg. 411　PV
Robert Fleming (Deutschland) GmbH, Im Trutz Frankfurt 55, pg. 493　IT
Flexibox GmbH, Schielestr. 45, pg. 426　IT
Forbo Novilon GmbH, Walter-Kolb-Str. 1-7, pg. 497　IT
Frankfurt Consult GmbH, Grueneburgweg 102, pg. 119　IT
Frankfurt Office, Feuerbachstrasse 26, pg. 1517　IT
Frankfurt-Trust Investment GmbH, Grueneburgweg 102, pg. 119　IT
Frankfurter Munzandlung GmbH, Grosse Bockenheimer Strasse 44, pg. 1330　IT
Frankfurter Versicherungs-AG, Taunusanlage 18, pg. 58　IT
Frega Vermogensverwaltungs GmbH, pg. 310　IT
Fuji Bank (Deutschland) AG, Mainzer Landstrasse 46, pg. 521　IT
Fuji Electric GmbH, Lyoner Strasse 26, pg. 522　IT
Fujitsu Mikroelektronik GmbH, Lyoner Strasse 44-48, Arabella Center 9, pg. 528　IT
GATX Financial Services GmbH, Wilhelm-Leuschner-Str 7, pg. 691　PB
GBB Gewerbebau-Beratung GmbH, pg. 310　IT
GGK Europe, Kennedyallee 111, pg. 1335　IT
GKH Gesellschaft fuer Kommunalbau in Hessen mbH, Myliusstr. 33-37,e 24, pg. 799　IT
GSG Siedlungsgesellschaft fuer Wohnungs-und Staedtebau mbH, Brueckhofstrasse 9, pg. 799　IT
Gas-Union GmbH, Kurmainzer Strasse 2, pg. 1148　IT
Generali Munchen Lebensversicherung AG, Kurt-Schumacher-Strasse 31, pg. 89　IT
Gesellschaft fur Industriebeteiligungen mbH, pg. 179　IT
Goldman, Sachs & Co. oHG MesseTurm, Friedrich-Ebert-Anlage 49, pg. 462　PV
Gotek GmbH, Gwinnerstr. 42/46, pg. 861　IT
Granges Metall GmbH, Schillerstrasse 15, pg. 442　IT
Grund- und Pfahlbau GmbH, Lyoner Strasse 38a, pg. 195　IT
Gunther & Co. GmbH, pg. 1186　IT
HSG-Holzmann Technischer Service GmbH, Eschborner Landstrasse 42-50, pg. 632　IT
Handelsblatt-Dow Jones GmbH, Gruneburgweg 149, pg. 1479　IT
Hardy & Co Privatbankiers, Necjarstrasse 7-9, pg. 418　IT
Harris GmbH, Rennbahnstrasse, 72-74, pg. 791　PB
Hartmann & Braun AG, Grafstr. 97, pg. 835　IT
Hartmann Druckfarben GmbH, Borsigallee 13, pg. 371　IT
Hauptniederlassung Rhein-Main Niederlassung Frankfurt Niederlassung Tied-und Industriebau, Lyoner Strasse 38a, pg. 194　IT
Helaba Invest Kapitalanlagegesellschaft mbH, Borsenstrasse 7-11, pg. 799　IT
Helaba Trust Beratungs-und Management Gesellschaft mbH, Borsenstrasse 7-11, pg. 799　IT
Hertie Waren-und Kaufhaus GmbH, Herriotstr. 4, pg. 724　IT
Hesse, Rhineland-Palatinate & Saar Branch, Zeppelinallee 38, pg. 645　IT
Hibernia Alpha Beteiligungs GmbH, pg. 310　IT
Hibernia Beta Beteiligungs GmbH, pg. 310　IT
Hibernia Delta Beteiligungs GmbH, pg. 310　IT
Hibernia Eta Beteiligungs GmbH, pg. 310　IT
Hibernia Gamma Beteiligungs GmbH, pg. 310　IT
Hibernia Omega Beteiligungs GmbH, pg. 310　IT
Hibernia Sigma Beteiligungs GmbH, pg. 310　IT

Hibernia Zeta Beteiligungs GmbH, pg. 310　IT
HOECHST AKTIENGESELLSCHAFT, pg. 624　IT
Hoechst Marion Roussel AG, pg. 624　IT
The Hokuriku Bank, Ltd.-Frankfurt Representative Office, 5 Obergeschoss, Freidenstrasse 5, pg. 627　IT
PHILIPP HOLZMANN AG, Taunusanlage 1, pg. 632　IT
IBP Armaturen GmbH, Friesstrasse 20-24, pg. 391　IT
ING Bank Frankfurt, Wiesenau 43, pg. 649　IT
IWC Uhren GmbH Deutschland, pg. 839　IT
Immobiliengesellschaft Beta von Burkersroda KG, pg. 309　IT
Immobiliengesellschaft Gamma von Burkersroda KG, pg. 309　IT
Immobiliengesellschaft Ost Bauer & Co. KG, pg. 310　IT
Immobiliengesellschaft von Burkersroda Objekt Zwei KG, pg. 309　IT
Indosuez Asset Management, Wilhelm Leuschner Strasse 9-11, pg. 314　IT
The Industrial Bank of Japan, Limited (Frankfurt), Niedenau 13-19, pg. 675　IT
Industrie-Beteiligungs Gesellschaftmbh, Bockenheimer Landstrasse 10, pg. 119　IT
Industriebank von Japan (Deutschland) Aktiengesellschaft, Niedenau 13-19, pg. 676　IT
Jauch & Huebener, Lyoner Strasse 15, pg. 118　PB
Jeppesen and Co. GmbH, P.O. Box 70-05-51, pg. 1617　IT
Gebr. Jung GmbH & Co. OHG, pg. 920　IT
KFW KREDITANSTALT FUR WIEDERAUFBAU, Palmengartenstrasse 5-9, pg. 718　IT
Kautschuk-Gesellschaft GmbH, Reuterweg 14, pg. 862　IT
Kleinwort Benson Deutschland GmbH, Wilhelm-Leuschner-Strasse 41, pg. 420　IT
Kodak AG-Frankfurt, Lyoner Strasse 36, pg. 552　PB
Konami (Deutschland) Gmbh, Berner Strasse 109, pg. 746　IT
Korn/Ferry International, Lyoner Strasse 15, ATRICOM, pg. 633　PV
Wolfgang Kruger Verlag GmbH, Hedderichstrasse 114, pg. 1478　IT
LBS Immobilien GmbH, Dreieichstrasse 59, pg. 799　IT
LANDESBANK HESSEN-THURINGEN GIROZENTRALE, Junghofstrasse 18-26, pg. 798　IT
Landesgirokasse an, Zeil 65-69, pg. 800　IT
Landis & Staefa Communications (Deutschland) GmbH, Friesstrasse 16, pg. 800　IT
Landis & Staefa (Deutschland) GmbH, Friesstrasse 20-24, pg. 800　IT
Landis & Staefa Energy Management (Deutschland) GmbH, Friesstrasse 20-24, pg. 800　IT
Lee Hydraulische Miniaturkomponenten, Berner Strasse 77, pg. 657　IT
Letraset Deutschland GmbH, Mergenthaler Str. 6, Postfach 630227, pg. 461　IT
Liegenschaft Hainstrasse GbR, pg. 310　IT
Long-Term Credit Bank of Japan (Deutschland) AG, Taunusstrasse 4, pg. 816　IT
Lowe & Partners, Hamburger Allee 45, pg. 678　PV
Lurgi AG, Lurgi-Allee 5, pg. 861　IT
MTBC Bank Deutschland GmbH, Eschersheimer Landstrasse 55, pg. 877　IT
Matra-Werke GmbH, Dieselstrasse 30-40, pg. 811　IT
McDonald's Deutschland Inc., Kennedyallee 109, pg. 1069　PB
The Meijiseimei Property Germany GmbH, Messe Turm, Friedrich-Ebert-Anlage 49, pg. 855　IT
Merian GmbH, Wohnungsunternehmen, Bruckhofstrasse 9, pg. 799　IT
Merloni Hausgerate GMBH, Landerweg 19, pg. 860　IT
Messer Griesheim GmbH, Corporate Office, Frankfurt Airport Center 1, C9, pg. 626　IT
Metallbank GmbH, Reuterweg 14, pg. 861　IT
Metallgesellschaft Services GmbH, Reuterweg 14, pg. 861　IT
Micchem Export/Import GmbH, Reineckstr. 11, pg. 716　IT
MLP Druckmaschinen GmbH, Eschersheimer Landstrasse 55, pg. 874　IT
Morgan Grenfell Deutschland GmbH, Grosse Gallustrasse 10-14, pg. 406　IT
Morgan Guaranty Trust Company, Borsenstrasse 2-4, pg. 1130　PB
J.P. Morgan GmbH, Borsenstrasse 2-4, pg. 1130　PB
J.P. Morgan Holding Deutschland GmbH, Borenstrasse 2-4, pg. 1131　PB
J.P. Morgan Investment GmbH, Borsenstrasse 2-4, pg. 1131　PB
J.P. Morgan Investment Management Inc., Borsenstrasse 2-4, pg. 1131　PB
NCNB National Bank, Frankfurt Representative Office, Kaiserhofstr. 10, pg. 1166　PB
National Bank of Pakistan-Frankfurt, Filiale Frankfurt, pg. 908　IT
National Westminster Bank AG, Natl. Westminster Haus, Feldbergstrasse 35, pg. 911　IT
National Westminster Bank Plc, Feldbergstrasse 35, pg. 911　IT
Naxos Union AG, pg. 1128　IT
Neckermann Versand AG, pg. 724　IT
Nestle Deutschland AG, Lyoner Strasse 23, pg. 921　IT
Network Systems GmbH, pg. 911　IT
A.C. Nielsen Co., GmbH, Ludwig-Landmann-Strasse 405, pg. 1183　PB
Nihon Keizai Shimbun Europe Ltd.-Frankfurt, Kettenhofweg 22, pg. 930　IT
Nikko Bank (Deutschland) GmbH, Kaiserstrasse 29, pg. 930　IT
Nippon Credit Bank AG, Messe Turm, Friedrich Ebert Anlage 49, pg. 933　IT
Nippon Credit Bank Ltd.-Frankfurt, FBC Frankfurter Buro Center, Mainzer Landstrabe 46, pg. 933　IT

Nippon Life (Deutschland) GmbH, Wilhelm-Leuschner-Strasse 41, pg. 936　IT
Nippon Shokubai GmbH, Niedenau 61-63, pg. 939　IT
Nira Deutschland Zweigniederlassung der Nira International B.V., Lyonerstrasse 14, pg. 1369　IT
Nomura Bank (Deutschland) GmbH, Hamburger Allee 2-10, pg. 956　IT
Norvista Reisen GmbH, Karlstrasse 12, pg. 486　IT
OfB Bauvermittlungs und Gewerbebau Gesellschaft mbH, Myliusstr. 33-37, pg. 799　IT
OfB Grundstuecksverwaltungs GmbH, Myliusstr. 33-37, pg. 799　IT
OTA Grundstiucks und Beteiligungsverwaltung GmbH, pg. 839　IT
Olivetti Germany, Lyoner Strasse 34, pg. 1003　IT
Omega Vermongensverwaltungs GmbH, pg. 310　IT
Oral-B Laboratories GmbH, Mailbox 19 03 40, Ruesselsheimer Strasse 22, pg. 745　PB
Ord Minnett Group Limited, Bockenheimer Landstrasse 51/53, pg. 1497　IT
Outokumpu Deutschland GmbH, pg. 1015　IT
PMC Personal Management Consult GmbH, pg. 310　IT
PTT Telecom Netherlands (Deutschland) GmbH, pg. 720　IT
Pedershaab Maschinenfabrik GmbH, Ziegelhuttenweg 30, pg. 475　IT
C. Portmann, pg. 310　IT
Prager Handelsbank AG, Gutleutstrasse 32, pg. 1085　IT
Pyrion-Chemie GmbH, pg. 1148　IT
Raab Karcher Baustoffe, Hanauer Landstrasse 150, pg. 1457　IT
Rabobank Deutschland AG, Solmsstrasse 2-26, pg. 1082　IT
Reichhold Chemie GmbH, Reuterweg 51-53, pg. 370　IT
Repsol Chemie Deutschland, Lyoner Strasse, 44-48, pg. 1105　IT
Reuters AG, Postfach 170465, pg. 1105　IT
RHEINHYP Rheinische Hypothekenbank, Taunustor 3, pg. 310　IT
Rhenania Umschlag und Lagerei GmbH, Zweigniederlassung, Schmickstrasse, pg. 1034　IT
Rohm & Haas Deutschland GmbH, Rheinstr. 29, pg. 1404　PB
Royal Bank of Canada AG, Lyoner Strasse 15, pg. 1131　IT
RUETGERS A.G., Mainzer Landstrasse 217, pg. 1147　IT
S-Beteiligungsgesellschaft Hessen- Thuringen mbH, Postfach 11 08 33, pg. 799　IT
SMS Zweigniederlassung der SMS Corp., Kolner Strasse 10b, pg. 1464　PB
Saab Deutschland GmbH, Postfach 560126, pg. 687　IT
Sakura Bank (Deutschland) GmbH, Im Trutz Frankfurt 55, pg. 1180　IT
Santander Direkt Bank A.G., Vilbeler Strasse, 29, pg. 144　IT
Sanwa Bank (Deutschland) AG, Bockenheimer Landstrasse 51-53, pg. 1190　IT
SCHENKER International AG, HainerWeg 13-15, pg. 1459　IT
Schweizerische Bankgesellschaft (Deutschland) AG, Bleichstr. 52, pg. 1440　IT
Schweizerischer Bankverein AG, Ulmenstrasse 30, pg. 1331　IT
Security Pacific Bank A.G., Ulmenstrasse 30, pg. 183　PB
Sextant Avionique, MerkurHauss, pg. 1385　IT
Shimizu GmbH-Frankfurt Office, Bockenheimer Landstrasse 83, pg. 1234　IT
Sigma Vermoegensverwaltungs GmbH, pg. 310　IT
Skadden, Arps, Slate, Meagher & Flom LLP, MesseTurm, 27th Fl., pg. 1004　PV
Skandinaviska Enskilda Banken AG, Rahmhofstrasse 2-4, pg. 1259　IT
Sopar Pharma GmbH, pg. 1148　IT
Storage Technology GmbH, Berner Strasse 35, Postfach 5600147, pg. 1523　PB
Suddeutsche Grossbauten GmbH, Taunusanlage 1, pg. 633　IT
Suedwestdeutsche Rohrleitungsbau GmbH, intzestr. 14-16, pg. 623　IT
The Sumitomo Bank, Ltd.-Frankfurt Branch, Hamburger Allee 2-10, pg. 1309　IT
Sumitomo Trust & Banking (Deutschland) AG, Eschersheimer Landstrasse 55, pg. 1318　IT
Synthomer GmbH, Reuterweg 51-53, pg. 370　IT
TBWA Germany, Hansaallee 30-32, pg. 1063　PV
Takeda Europe Research & Development Centre GmbH, Hamburger Allee 2-10, pg. 1350　IT
TELENORMA GmbH, Kleyer Str. 94, pg. 204　IT
Terumo (Deutschland) G.m.b.H., pg. 1376　IT
3i Germany, Bockenheimer Landstrasse 55, pg. 1386　IT
Tokai Bank (Deutschland) GmbH, Bockenheimer Landstrasse 51-53, pg. 1391　IT
TOP Prazisionswerkzeuge GmbH, pg. 1187　IT
Toray Deutschland GmbH, Nibelungenplatz 3, pg. 1400　IT
Tostmann & Domann, Windmuhlstrasse 1, pg. 1336　IT
Tourism Malaysia - Frankfurt Office, Rossmarkt 11, pg. 813　IT
Unisource Business Networks GmbH, pg. 721　IT
Unternehmensbeteiligungs-gesellschaft fur die deutsche Wirtschaft, Gutleutstrasse 85, pg. 418　IT
Unterstutzungs Gesellschaft MbH der Chemical Bank, Ulmenstrasse 30, pg. 341　PB
VDO Adolf Schindling AG, Sodener Strasse 9, pg. 839　IT
VDO Antriebstechnik GmbH, pg. 839　IT
VDO Kienzle Vertrieb und Service GmbH, pg. 839　IT
VDO-Luftfahrtgerate Werk Gmbh, And der Sandelmuhle 13, pg. 1385　IT
WESTBODEN-Bau und Verwaltungs GmbH, pg. 310　IT
WestLB Frankfurt Branch, Taunusanlage 3, pg. 1493　IT
Westpac Banking Corporation-Germany, Bockenheimer Landstrasse 51/53, pg. 1497　IT

PB - U.S. Public Companies Volume
PV - U.S. Private Companies Volume
IT - International Public & Private Companies Volume

Wohn-und Geschaeftsbauten GmbH, Taunusanlage 1, pg. 633   IT
F.W. Woolworth GmbH Co. (Germany), Buerostadt Niederrad, pg. 1778   PB
Yamaichi Bank (Deutschland) GmbH, Feuerbachstrasse 26, pg. 1517   IT
Young & Rubicam GmbH, Kleyerstrasse 25, pg. 1199   PV
Zeneca Agro GmbH, Emil-von-Behring-Strasse 2, pg. 1526   IT
Zurich International (Deutschland) Versicherungs-Aktiengesellschaft, Zurich-Haus am Opernplatz, pg. 1532   IT
Zurich Investmentgesellschaft mbH, Zurich-Haus am Opernplatz, pg. 1532   IT
Zurich Kautions-und Kreditversicherungs-Aktiengesellschaft, Zurich-Haus am Opernplatz, pg. 1532   IT
Zurich Lebensversicherungs-Gesellschaft, Zurich-Haus am Opernplatz, pg. 1529   IT
Zurich Rechtsschutzverischerungs-Aktiengesellschaft, Zurich-Haus am Opernplatz, pg. 1532   IT
Zurich Versicherungs-Aktiengesellschaft (Deutschland), Zurich-Haus am Opernplatz, pg. 1532   IT
Zurich Versicherungs-Gesellschaft, Zurich-Haus am Opernplatz, pg. 1531   IT

Frechen

Lawter Intl., GmbH, Koelner Str. 114, pg. 981   PB

Freden

Papiersackfabrik Junemann GmbH, pg. 759   IT

Freiburg

Alcon Pharma GmbH, Blankreutestrasse 1, pg. 918   IT
Bell & Howell GmbH, Gruener Weg 8, pg. 201   PB
Deutsche Bank AG (Freiburg), Rotteckring 3, pg. 402   IT
Howmedica Leibinger G.m.b.H., Boetzinger Strasse 41, pg. 1282   IT
Krupp Warmetechnik GmbH - Freiburg, Linnestra. 12, pg. 515   IT
Lafarge Gips Beteiligungs GmbH, Roeckring 4, pg. 791   IT
LITEF (GmbH), Loerracherstr. 18, pg. 1004   PB
Organon Teknika Medizinsche Produkte GmbH, 72 Tullastrasse, pg. 45   IT
Pharmacia & Upjohn Biotech GmbH, Munzinger Strasse 9, pg. 1047   IT
Pharmacia & Upjohn Deutschland GmbH, Munzinger Strasse 9, pg. 1050   IT
Protek GmbH, pg. 1307   IT
Rhodia A.G., Engesserstrasse O8, pg. 1112   PV
Stefansback Backwaren GmbH, pg. 160   IT
E. Stroh GmbH, Engesserstr. 5, pg. 514   IT
Tesa Leitz GmbH, Netzestrasse 32, pg. 260   PB
Trischler Consult GmbH, pg. 608   IT

Freiburg im Breisgau

Niederlassung Freiburg, Hans-Bunte-Strasse 12, pg. 195   IT

Freising

Sharplan Lasers GmbH, Am Lohmuhlbach 12a, pg. 429   IT
Texas Instruments Deutschland GmbH, Haggertystr. 1, pg. 1586   PB

Freudenberg

Werner & Pfleiderer Gummitechnik GmbH, Asdorfer Str. 60, pg. 510   IT

Frickenhausen

Ascom EBS Elektronische Bank Systeme GmbH, Siemenstrasse 11, pg. 86   IT

Frickingen

Eaton GmbH Controls Div.-Europe, pg. 558   PB

Friedrichsdorf

Bose GmbH, Postfach 1125, pg. 161   PV
CiMatrix GmbH, Otto-Hahn-Str. 40, pg. 1395   PB
Dynetcom GmbH, Max-Planck-Str. 22, pg. 425   IT
Kawasaki Motoren GmbH, Max-Planck-Strasse 26, pg. 726   IT
Kennametal Hertel GmbH, Max-Planck Strasse 13, pg. 951   PB
Koenig & Bauer-Albert, Koenig-Strasse 4, pg. 1341   PB
Milupa A.G., Bahnstrasse 14-30, pg. 991   IT
Milupa Gmbh & Co KG, pg. 991   IT
Nutricia Deutschland GmbH, pg. 992   IT
Nutricia Grundstucksverwaltungs GmbH, pg. 992   IT
Sealed Air G.m.b.H., Max-Planck Strasse 15, pg. 1451   PB

Friedrichshafen

Dornier GmbH, pg. 367   IT
Dornier GmbH Information & Communication, pg. 367   IT
Litton Precision International, Jahnstrasse 3, pg. 1004   PB
MTU Motoren-und Turbinen-Union Friedrichshafen GmbH, pg. 367   IT
ZF FRIEDRICHSHAFEN A.G., Postfach 25 20, Allmannsweilerstrasse 25, pg. 1522   IT

Fulda

John Crane GmbH, Werner-von-Siemens Strasse, pg. 1339   IT
Gummiwerke Fulda, Kunzeller Str. 59-61, pg. 753   PB
Helmke-Feuerstein Paketogistik GmbH, pg. 596   IT
KGM Kugelfabrik Gebauer GmbH, Johannistrasse 5, pg. 468   IT

Fuldabruck

Tchnoflow Tube-Systems GmbH, Postfach 1230, Industriestrasse 3, pg. 1341   IT

Furth

Flachglas AG, Siemestr. 1-3, pg. 1056   IT
ICL Deutschland International Computers GmbH, Ludwig-Quel en Stk 20, pg. 529   IT
Kennametal Hertel AG, Postfach 1751, pg. 951   PB
Milton Eradley GmbH, Fuerth/Bay, Waldstr. 49, pg. 798   PB
Plettac Electronic Security GmbH, pg. 1061   IT
QUELLE GROUP, Nuernberger Str. 91-95, pg. 1078   IT

Ganderkesee

Umweltschutz Nord GmbH & Co., Industriepark 6, pg. 633   IT

Garching

Dexter GmbH, Lilienthal Strasse 5, pg. 505   PB
Dexter Magnetic Materials GmbH, Dexter/Magnetic Technik, Lilienthal Strasse 5, pg. 505   PB
EDC European Excavator Design Center Verwaltungs Gmb H, Zeppelinstrasse 1-5, pg. 315   PB

Gartringen

Blount GmbH, Reinhardstrasse 23, pg. 239   PB

Gauting

Steelwe d Division-Zweigniederlassung Bonn der Ambac B.V., Starnbergerst. 22, pg. 71   IT

Geesthacht

Kernkra twerk Krummel GmbH, Elbuferstrasse 82, pg. 1456   IT
Kloeckner-Wilhelmsburger GmbH, Borsigstrasse 24, pg. 737   IT

Geisa

Fahrzeugbau GmbH, pg. 811   IT

Geiselhoring

Bertrand Faure Sitztechnik GmbH & Co. KG, Hadersbacher Strasse 16, pg. 193   IT

Geisenheim

Balzers Dunnschicht-Komponenten GmbH, Marienthaler Str. 2, pg. 997   IT
Fuji Hunt Photographic Chemicals (Deutschland) Gmbh, Untergasse 74, pg. 524   IT

Gelnhausen

K-Tron Germany, Soder Division, Im Steinigen Graben 10, pg. 938   PB

Gelsenkirchen

Allo Pro GmbH, pg. 1307   IT
Arnholdt Holding GmbH, pg. 1061   IT
Bitumen-Verkauf GmbH, Alexander-von-Humboldt-Strasse, pg. 1460   IT
Dahlbusch AG, Gruener Weg 1, pg. 1056   IT
Eisenmetall Lager GmbH, Ahlmannshof 22, pg. 514   IT
Eisenmetall Legierungen GmbH, Ahlmannshof 22, pg. 513   IT
Eisenmetall Rohr GmbH, Ahlmannsdorf 22, pg. 514   IT
Gelsenwasser AG, Galkenstrasse 26, pg. 1456   IT
Gipswerk Scholven GmbH, Bergmannsgluckstrasse 41-43, pg. 1460   IT
Hovelmann & Co. Eisengrosshandlung GmbH, Ahlmannshof 22, pg. 514   IT
KHT Kommissionier und Handhabungtechnik GmbH, pg. 837   IT
KOP Kohlensaure-Produktions-gesellschaft mbH, Alexander-von-Humboldt-Strasse, pg. 1461   IT
Kraftwerk Buer Betriebsgesellschaft mbH, Bergmannsgluckstrasse 41-43, pg. 1460   IT
Kraftwerk Buer GbR, Bergmannsgluckstrasse 41-43, pg. 1460   IT
Kraftwerk Schkopau GmbH, Bergmannsgluckstrasse 41-43, pg. 1460   IT
Krupp Hoesch Stahl und Metall GmbH, Ahlmannshof 22, pg. 514   IT
MUELLER'S MUEHLE GMBH, Am Stadhafen 42-50, pg. 896   IT

Nacanco GmbH & Co. KG, Emscherstrasse 46, pg. 1029   IT
RGV Rohol-Gewinnungs und Verarbeitungs GmbH, Alexander-von-Humboldt-Strasse, pg. 1461   IT
Rhenania Umschlag und Lagerei GmbH, Zweigniederlassung Werftst, pg. 1034   IT
RUHR OEL GmbH, Alexander-von-Humboldt-Strasse, pg. 1461   IT
Sanders Tapeten GmbH, pg. 540   IT
VEW-VKR Fernwarmeleitung Shamrock-Bochum GbR, Bergmannscluckstrasse 41-43, pg. 1460   IT
VEBA Fernheizung Castrop-Rauxel GmbH, Bergmannsgluckstrasse 41-43, pg. 1460   IT
VEBA Fernheizung Dattelm GmbH, Bergmannsgluckstrasse 41-43, pg. 1460   IT
VEBA Fernheizung Gelsenkirchen-Buer GmbH, Bergmannsgluckstrasse 41-43, pg. 1460   IT
VEBA Fernheizung Gladbeck GmbH, Bergmannsgluckstrasse 41-43, pg. 1460   IT
VEBA Fernheizung Recklinghausen GmbH, Bergmannsgluckstrasse 41-43, pg. 1460   IT
VEBA Fernheizung Wanne-Eickel GmbH, Bergmannsgluckstrasse 41-43, pg. 1460   IT
VEBA Kraftwerke Ruhr AG, Bergmannsglueckstrasse 41-43, pg. 1460   IT
VEBA OEL AG, Alexander-von-Humboldt-Strasse, pg. 1461   IT
VEBA OIL Technologie GmbH, Johannastrasse 2-8, pg. 1461   IT
VEBA WOHNEN AG, pg. 1460   IT
VESTOLEN GmbH, pg. 1461   IT
WWB Wasserwerks-Beteiligungs GmbH, pg. 1456   IT
Werk Horst, Johannastrasse 2-8, pg. 1461   IT
Werk Scholven, Pawikerstrasse 30, pg. 1461   IT

Genthin

Henkel Genthin GmbH, Ziegeleistrasse 56, pg. 610   IT

Georgensgmund

Emil Kiessling & Cie. G.m.b.H., pg. 1489   IT

Gera

DG Bank - Gera, Berliner Strasse 24, pg. 351   IT
Geschaftsstelle Gera, Platanenstrasse 7, pg. 194   IT
Union Werkzeugmaschinenfabrik Gera GmbH, Siemensstrasse 51, pg. 860   IT

Geretsried

DR. TH. BOEHME KG CHEM. FABRIK GMBH & CO., pg. 199   IT
Nissan Design Europe (NDE) GmbH, Brunnen Feldweg 1, pg. 945   IT

Gerlingen

ROBERT BOSCH GMBH, Robert-Bosch-Platz 1, pg. 203   IT
Kester Solder, Ganghoferstr. 45, pg. 1004   PB

Germering

Max Cochius GmbH - Germering Branch, Industriestr. 4, pg. 514   IT
Dispersa GmbH, Augenarzneimittel, pg. 982   IT
Keithley Instruments GmbH, Landsberger Strasse 65, pg. 987   PB
W. Schraml Softwarehaus GmbH, Burweg 6, pg. 317   IT

Gerolzhofen

Efesis Schleiftechnik, Georg Schafer Strasse 1, pg. 1174   IT

Gevelsberg

Intertractor Zweigniederlassung der Wirtgen GmbH, Hagener Strasse 325, pg. 1511   IT
Rockwell International GmbH, Heavy Vehicle Systems, Hagener Strasse 20, pg. 1401   PB
Steeb Software Service GmbH, In den Weiden 18, pg. 317   IT

Giessen

Canon Giessen GmbH, Canonstrasse 1, pg. 262   IT
CIBA Corning Diagnostics GmbH, Industriestrasse 11, pg. 975   IT
Franke Systemtechnik GmbH, Philosophenstrasse 116, pg. 389   IT
Garvens Automation GmbH, Kampstrasse 7, pg. 982   IT
Geschaftsstelle Giessen, Friedrich-List-Strasse 27, pg. 194   IT
Mettler-Toledo GmbH, Ockerweg 3, pg. 4   PV
Tucker GmbH, Postfach 111329, pg. 234   PB

Gifhorn

Bundy Systemwerk, Rockwellstr. 11, pg. 1342   IT

Gilching

Bang & Olufsen G.m.b.H., Rudolf-Diesel-Str. 8, pg. 146   IT
Sic Plastics GmbH, Roenerstrasse 23, pg. 850   IT

PB - *U.S. Public Companies Volume*
PV - *U.S. Private Companies Volume*
IT - *International Public & Private Companies Volume*

Verlegerdienst Munchen, Gutenbergstrasse 1, pg. 1748 **PB**

Gladbeck

Phenolchemie GmbH, Dechenstrasse 3, pg. 1454 **IT**

Glashutte

Lange Uhren, pg. 839 **IT**

Glindow

Havellandische Maschinenbau GmbH, Dr. Kulz Str. 134, pg. 587 **IT**

Gluckstadt

Heizkraftwerk Gluckstadt GmbH, Staststrasse 2-14, pg. 1456 **IT**

Glunanplan

Deutsche Spezialglas AG, Postfach 2032, pg. 1523 **IT**

Gnarrenburg

Brilliant AG, Brilliantstrasse 1, pg. 453 **IT**

Golsar

H.C. Starck GmbH, pg. 172 **IT**

Gommern

Erdol-Erdgas Gommern GmbH (E.E.G.), Magdeburger chaussee 21, pg. 541 **IT**

Goppingen

Albany International GmbH, Ulmerstrasse 41, pg. 37 **PB**
SKS TECHNIK Saure und Korrosionsschutz GmbH, Lehlestr. 15, pg. 1465 **IT**

Gosheim

Hermle AG, Industriestrasse 8-12, pg. 1419 **IT**

Goslar

Dr. Genthe GmbH & Co. KG, Glashuttenwerk Im Schleeke 27/31, pg. 1523 **IT**
Fels-Werke GmbH, Jeheimrat-Ebut-Strasse 12, pg. 1069 **IT**
MMG Division, Alte Heerstrasse 14, pg. 1227 **PB**
Mobel Unger GmbH, IM Schleeke 116, pg. 863 **IT**
TRINKS GmbH, pg. 922 **IT**

Gotha

Thuringer Gebaudetechnik GmbH, pg. 1149 **IT**

Gottingen

Bailey Fischer & Porter GmbH, Postfach 1843, pg. 449 **IT**
Raulf Bau GmbH, Maschmuhlenweg 101-109, pg. 630 **IT**
4P Rube Gottingen GmbH, pg. 1146 **IT**
Lambda Physik GmbH, Hans-Bockler Strasse 12, pg. 396 **PB**
SmithKline Beecham-Dauelsberg G.m.b.H & Co., Postfach 3333, pg. 1266 **IT**

Grafelfing

Alkor Markenhandels GmbH, Am Haag 8, pg. 1278 **IT**
Atomic Deutschland GmbH, Am Kirchenholzl 13, pg. 73 **IT**
Data I/O GmbH, Lochhamer Schlag 5A, pg. 486 **PB**
Microtec Research, GmbH, Lochhamer Schlag SA, pg. 1087 **PB**
Werk-Verlag, Hans-Cornelius-Strasse 4, pg. 1099 **IT**
Wilson Sporting Goods Europe, Am Kirchenholzl 13, pg. 73 **IT**
Wilson Sporting Goods GmbH, AM Kirchenholzl 13, pg. 73 **IT**

Grasbrunn

LTX (Deutschland) GmbH, AM Hochacker 5, pg. 972 **PB**
Sun Microsystems GmbH, Bretonischer Ring 3, pg. 1531 **PB**

Grefrath

GIRMES GMBH, Johs-Girmes-Str. 27, pg. 552 **IT**

Greifswald

Ericsson Netzbau GmbH, Guetzkower Landstr. 11a, pg. 1367 **IT**

Grenzach-Wyhlen

CIBA-GEIGY AG, Betriebsstatte Grenzach, Kochlinstrasse 1, pg. 975 **IT**
Forbo Beteiligungen GmbH, pg. 497 **IT**

Hoffmann-La Roche AG, pg. 1121 **IT**

Greven

Fricke GmbH & Co. KG, Eichendorffweg 10, pg. 719 **IT**

Grevenbroich

VAW Aluminum AG, Erftwerk, pg. 1466 **IT**

Gronau

Amoco Deutschland GmbH, Dupplestrasse, pg. 103 **PB**
MAN Uranit Gronau GmbH, pg. 825 **IT**
Uberlandwerk Leinetal GmbH, Am Eltwerk 1, pg. 1457 **IT**

Gross-Gerau

Bondioli & Pavesi GmbH Deutschland, Odenwaldstrasse, 7, pg. 201 **IT**
Case Poclain GmbH & Co., Odenwaldstrasse 16, pg. 1579 **PB**
Pantene GmbH, c/o Richardson GmbH, pg. 1331 **PB**
Simpson Industries, Inc. (Germany), Odenwaldstr 23, pg. 1475 **PB**
Wick Pharma, H. S. Richardson-Strasse, pg. 1333 **PB**

Gross-Umstadt

Resopal GmbH, Hans-Bockler-Str. 4, pg. 1322 **PB**

Grossenbrode

Pomosin GmbH, pg. 811 **PB**

Grossenhain

Ausbau Grossenhain GmbH, Waldaer Strasse 18, pg. 423 **IT**
Wolff Handelsgesellschaft & Co. GmbH, pg. 423 **IT**

Grossenlinden

Georg Fischer Disa GmbH, Industriestrasse 5, pg. 489 **IT**

Grossostheim

CVV Nelteg, Stockstadterstrasse 17, pg. 975 **IT**
CIBA Vision Vertriebs GmbH, Bauhofstrasse 16, pg. 981 **IT**
Rieter Automatik GmbH, pg. 1117 **IT**
Viking Direct Limited GmbH, Industrie Handelspark Nord, Babenhauser Strasse 50, pg. 1721 **PB**

Grosswallstadt

CIBA Vision GmbH, Industriering 1, pg. 981 **IT**
CIBA Vision Vertriebs GmbH-Eurologistics, Industriering 1, pg. 981 **IT**

Gruna

EOC Normalien Produktions und Vertriebs GmbH, An der Wiesenmuhle 19, pg. 75 **IT**

Grunberg-Queckborn

Parker Hannifin, Laubacher Weg 31, pg. 1260 **PB**

Grunwald

KG Allgemeine Leasing GmbH & Co., Tolzer Strasse 15, pg. 418 **IT**
RTL 2, Bavariafilmplatz 7, pg. 562 **IT**

Guenzberg

Wallace & Tiernan GmbH, pg. 61 **PB**

Gummersbach

SABO-Maschinenfabrik GmbH, pg. 493 **PB**
L. & C. Steinmueller GmbH, Fabrikstr. 1, pg. 633 **IT**

Gundelfingen

Henkos Cosmetic GmbH, pg. 610 **IT**

Gutersloh

BERTELSMANN AG, Carl Bertelsmann Strasse 270, pg. 189 **IT**
Bertelsmann Club GmbH, Carl-Bertelsmann-Strasse 270, pg. 189 **IT**
Bertelsmann Lexikothek Verlag GmbH, Carl-Bertelsmann-Strasse 105-107, pg. 189 **IT**
Electronic Arts GMBH, Verler Str. 1, pg. 569 **PB**
Gebr. Heimer GmbH, pg. 838 **IT**
Krauss-Maffei Kunststofftechnik Vertrieb & Service Nord, pg. 836 **IT**
MIELE & CIE, GMBH, Carl-Miele-Strasse, 29, pg. 865 **IT**
Pfleiderer Industrie GmbH Wirus-Werke Gutersloh, Holzstrasse 6-10, pg. 1047 **IT**

Haan

Alemite GmbH, Liechtmetallstr. 5, pg. 127 **IT**
Amada GmbH, Westfalenstrasse 6, pg. 70 **IT**
Cordis Medizinische Apparate GmbH, pg. 928 **PB**
DEJ datentechnik GmbH, Bahnhofstr. 6, pg. 317 **IT**
Fudickar Metall GmbH, Leichtmetallstr. 8-14, pg. 514 **IT**
Hagglunds Drives GmbH, Steinkulle 3, pg. 670 **IT**
Johnson Wax GmbH, Candstrasse 27-29, pg. 593 **PV**
Mittelrheinische Erdgastransport Gesellschaft mbH, pg. 1149 **IT**
MUKUSOL Kuffner GmbH, Schallbruch 53-55, pg. 423 **IT**
Rockwell International GmbH, Dusselberger Strasse 15, pg. 1401 **PB**
Timken Europa GmbH, Landstrasse 44/48, pg. 1618 **PB**
Unipol GmbH & Co., Rudolf-Harbig-Weg 10, pg. 519 **IT**

Haar

ADIG Allgemeine Deutsche Investment gesellschaftmbH, W. Richard-Reitzner Allee, pg. 180 **IT**
Adaptec GmbH, Munchner Strasse 17, pg. 19 **PB**
Zycad G.m.b.H., Bahnhofplatz 4A, pg. 703 **PB**

Hagen

Bergbaustahl GmbH, Spiekerstr. 7, pg. 513 **IT**
Eclipse Combustion GmbH, Profilstrasse 13, pg. 361 **PV**
Hoesch Federn GmbH, Voerder Str. 38, pg. 508 **IT**
Hoesch Hohenlimburg GmbH, Langenkampstrasse 14, pg. 508 **IT**
Konigswarter & Ebell Chemische Fabrik GmbH, pg. 1452 **IT**
Leaf Germany, Schillerstrasse 20-22, pg. 638 **IT**
Luhn & Pulvermacher, Voerder Str. 38, pg. 508 **IT**
Markantstahl GmbH, Volmarsteinerstrasse 1, pg. 79 **IT**
Panalpina Welttransport GmbH, pg. 1023 **IT**
Stora Kabel GmbH, Schwerter Str. 263, pg. 1303 **IT**

Haibach

Adler Modemarkte GmbH, Industriestrabe 1-5, pg. 863 **IT**
Firet, G.m.b.H., pg. 686 **PB**

Haiger

Pracht Spedition & Logistik GmbH, pg. 596 **IT**

Halle

BASF-Vertriebsstandort Agro, Wilhelm-Kuelz-Str. 13, pg. 104 **IT**
Braas Dachsteinwerke GmbH, Muhlweg 47, pg. 1091 **IT**
Cardiotron Medizintechnik GmbH, Leipziger Chaussee 191g, pg. 1083 **PB**
DG Bank - Halle, Grenzstrasse 21, pg. 351 **IT**
Deutsche Bank-Kreditbank AG (Halle), Hansaring 5, pg. 402 **IT**
Geologische Forschung und Erkundung - GFE GmbH, pg. 597 **IT**
Hochbau Halle-Seeben GmbH, Gruner Platz 1, pg. 195 **IT**
Niederlassung Halle, Rudolf-Breitschied-Strasse 6, pg. 195 **IT**
STORCK INTERNATIONAL GMBH, Paulinen Weg 12, pg. 1304 **IT**

Halstenbek

Crawford Tor GmbH, Gartnerstrasse 90, pg. 269 **IT**
KVH Kreditverwaltungsgesellschaft Hamburg mbH, pg. 310 **IT**
H. Krueger Maschinenfabrik GmbH, Gartnerstrasse 92, pg. 269 **IT**
Perstorp Pharma GmbH, Postfach 1155, Dockenhudener Chaussee, pg. 1037 **IT**

Hamburg

ADHOC, Paulstrasse 6, pg. 1463 **IT**
AFS Aviation Fuel Services GmbH, Sportallee 6, pg. 1460 **IT**
AGA-CRYO GmbH, Postfach 93 03 09, pg. 13 **IT**
AGA Gas GmbH, Postfach 20 19 54, pg. 13 **IT**
AON, Jauch & Huebener Gruppe, Katharinenstr. 10, pg. 118 **PB**
AVG Abfall-Verwertungs-Gesellschaft mbH, Grimm 8, pg. 1460 **IT**
Acer Computer GmbH, pg. 22 **IT**
Adecco Personaldienstleist Ungen GmbH, Pappelallee 33, pg. 24 **IT**
Adobe Systems GmbH, Hans-Henny-Jahnn-Weg 9, pg. 20 **PB**
AdvoCard Rechtsschutzversichereng AG, Heidenkampsweg 81, pg. 15 **IT**
Airbus Industrie Airspares, Weg Baeim Jaeger 150, pg. 39 **IT**
Ajinomoto Europe Sales G.m.b.H, Stubbenhuk 3, pg. 40 **IT**
Akerlund & Rausing Verpackung GmbH, In der Masch, pg. 33 **IT**
Alfa-Laval Agrar G.m.b.H., pg. 1377 **IT**
Alfa-Laval Industrietechnik G.m.b.H., Postfach 80 0329, pg. 1379 **IT**
Allianz Versicherungs-AG, Zweigniederlassung, fur Norddeutschland, pg. 58 **IT**
Allied Colloids Manufacturing GmbH, pg. 62 **IT**

AlliedSignal Bromsbelag GmbH, 2057 Reinbek/Hamburg, Glinder Weg 1, pg. 52   **PB**

Alsen-Breitenburg Zement- un Kalwerke GmbH, Ost-West-Strasse 69, pg. 629   **IT**

APOLLINARIS & SCHWEPPES GMBH & CO., pg. 78

Asche AG, Fischersalle 49-59, pg. 1203   **IT**

Asmussen GmbH, pg. 178   **IT**

Atmos Lebensmitteltechnik G.m.b.H., pg. 1379   **IT**

AURUM Beteiligungs- und Verwaltungs GmbH, pg. 178   **IT**

Avery Maschinen GmbH, Kollaustrasse 105, pg. 153   **PB**

B.A.T Cigarettenfabriken B.A.T., Alsterufer 4, pg. 111   **IT**

B.A.T (Deutschland) Export GmbH, Alstenrufer 4, pg. 112   **IT**

BEB Erdgas und Erdoel GmbH, Kapstadtring 2, pg. 601   **PB**

BHF-Bank, Paulstrasse 5, pg. 119   **IT**

Ballast Nedam Bau- und Bagger GmbH., Georg-Wilhelmstrasse 357, pg. 134   **IT**

Banque Paribas-Hamburg, Rathausmarkt 5, pg. 320   **IT**

Baring Capital GmbH, Heimhuder Strasse 72, pg. 648   **IT**

Bavaria Keytronic Technologie GmbH, Boschstrasse 23, pg. 940   **PV**

Beiersdorf AG, Unnastrabe 48, pg. 182   **IT**

BEIERSDORF GROUP, Unnastrasse 48, pg. 182   **IT**

Bekaert Deustchland GmbH, Dietrich-Bonhoeffer-Strasse 4, Postfach 12 61, pg. 184   **IT**

Joh. Berenberg, Gossler & Co., pg. 447   **PB**

Bergvik Chemie GmbH, Bahrenfelder Strasse 244, pg. 904   **IT**

Beteiligungs- und Handelsgesellschaft in Hamburg mbH, pg. 179   **IT**

Blohm + Voss AG, pg. 1387   **IT**

Blumenfeld Brennstoffe GmbH, Chilehaus C V, pg. 513   **IT**

Bode Chemie GmbH & Co., pg. 182   **IT**

Boehme Fettchemie GmbH, Hovestrasse 49, pg. 609   **IT**

Boeing International Corp., Glockengiesserwall 26 I, pg. 242   **PB**

Bon Prix Handelsgesellschaft mbH, pg. 1014   **IT**

Bonig & Yamaoka International Public Relations, Hoheluftchaussee 95, pg. 1210   **IT**

Bridgestone Reifen GmbH, Postfach 30 05 26, pg. 214   **IT**

British-American Tobacco (Germany) GmbH, Alsterufer 4, pg. 111   **IT**

James Burn International GmbH, Postfach 54 07 52, pg. 1507   **IT**

Carewood Transport Ltd., Postfach 100240, pg. 1165   **IT**

Chemische Fabrik Promonta GmbH, Postfach 260661, pg. 66   **IT**

Chemoflon GmbH, pg. 859   **IT**

Chr. Brouwer Schiffahrts- und Befrachtungskontor GmbH, Johannisbollwerk 20, pg. 515   **IT**

Christiania Bank-Hamburg Representative Office, ABC Strasse 12, pg. 289   **IT**

Citizen Computer Peripherals G.m.b.H., Hans-Duncker-Str. 8, pg. 294   **IT**

Citizen Uhrenfabrik G.m.b.H., Hans-Duncker-Str. 8, pg. 294   **IT**

Citizen Watch Europe G.m.b.h., Hans-Duncker-Str. 8, pg. 294   **IT**

Colgate-Palmolive A.B., Liebigstrasse 2-20, pg. 398   **PB**

Commercium Vermoegensverwaltung GmbH, pg. 309   **IT**

Commerzbank AG von 1870 i.L., pg. 309   **IT**

CONDEA CHEMIE GMBH, Weberseering 40, pg. 325   **IT**

Conoco Mineraloel GmbH, Uebersering 27, pg. 531   **PB**

Continentale Finanz Gesellschaft A. Asmussen GmbH & Co., pg. 179   **IT**

Corso Handelsgesellschaft mbH, pg. 1014   **IT**

DG Bank - Hamburg, Stephansplatz 10, pg. 351   **IT**

DMB&B Hamburg, Bleichenbruecke 10, pg. 303   **PV**

Daimler-Benz Aerospace Airbus, pg. 367   **IT**

Damco Maritime GmbH, pg. 1144   **IT**

Debis Systemhaus GmbH, pg. 368   **IT**

Delaware Computing Deutschland GmbH, Dietrich - Bonhoefferstrasse 4, pg. 184   **IT**

Demag-Jungheinrich Fahrerlose Transportsystems GmbH, pg. 837   **IT**

Det Norske Veritas, Albert Einstein Ring 21, pg. 397   **IT**

Deutsch-Sudamerikanische Bank AG, Neuer Jungfernstieg 16, pg. 418   **IT**

Deutsche Aerospace Airbus GmbH, pg. 367   **IT**

Deutsche Bank AG (Hamburg), Adolphsplatz 7, pg. 402   **IT**

Deutsche Grammophon Gesellschaft mbH, Hohe Bleichen 14-16, pg. 1052   **IT**

Deutsche Nyco GmbH, Adenauerallee 52, pg. 517   **IT**

Deutsche Schiffsbank AG, pg. 310   **IT**

Deutsche Shell AG, Uberseering 35, pg. 1138   **IT**

Deutsche Sinochem GmbH, Friedrich Ebert-Damm 160A, pg. 1255   **IT**

Deutsche Unilever Gmbh, Dammtorwall 15, pg. 1436   **IT**

Deutscher Container-Dienst GmbH, pg. 596   **IT**

Deutscher Press Vertrieb Buch-Hansa GmbH, Wenden 27/29, pg. 190   **IT**

Dialog Versicherungs AG, Dammtorstrasse 13, pg. 89   **IT**

Dinol GmbH, P.O. Box 630206, pg. 982   **IT**

Dolmar GmbH, Jenfelder Strasse 38, pg. 831   **IT**

EZL Hansa GmbH Entsorgungszwischenlager, Andreas-Meyer Strasse, pg. 423   **IT**

East-West Consultants GmbH, pg. 179   **IT**

EDEKA ZENTRALE AG, New York Ring 6, pg. 433   **IT**

Edelman/Heuer & Partner, GmbH, Deichstrasse 51, pg. 363   **PV**

Elbe Transport G.m.b.H., Trudensalle 333, pg. 1436   **IT**

Electrolux GmbH, Postfach 50 04 20, pg. 442   **IT**

Electrolux Kalte-und Warmetechnik GmbH, pg. 442   **IT**

Elida-Gibbs G.m.b.H., Hamburger Str. 23, pg. 1437   **IT**

Emsland-Raisio Chemie GmbH, Ballindamm 38, pg. 1086   **IT**

Enator Deustchland GmbH, Oberstrasse 14B, pg. 278   **IT**

Enskilda (Deutschland) GmbH, Esplanade 41, pg. 1259   **IT**

Enso (Deutschland) GmbH, Grosse Bleichen 30, pg. 457   **IT**

Enso Presse Druck Vertrieb GmbH, Grosse Bleichen 30, pg. 457   **IT**

Esso Aktiengesellschaft, Kapstadtring 2, pg. 601   **PB**

Europa Carton AG, Spitalerstrasse 11, pg. 20   **IT**

Europcar Autovermietung GmbH, Tangstedter Landstrasse 81, pg. 1473   **IT**

Euryza Reis GmbH, Oberwerder Damm 11-21, pg. 244   **IT**

Exled Warenhandelsgesellschaft mbH, pg. 506   **IT**

F & Z Baugesellschaft mbH, Billwerder Neuer, pg. 195   **IT**

F.A.A., Spaldingstrasse 218, pg. 1463   **IT**

Feron de Clebsattel, Postfach 100240, pg. 1165   **IT**

Fischer Imaging Europe, Alter Fischmarkt 11, pg. 647   **PB**

Flymo GmbH, Holstenstrasse 15, pg. 442   **IT**

Foster Electric (Europe) GmbH, Frankenstrasse 35, pg. 500   **IT**

Funai Electric Trading (Europe) GmbH, Bluecherstrasse 11, pg. 530   **IT**

Gemeinnutzige Wohnungs - Ges.mbH, Rledhofweg 23, pg. 172   **IT**

Gendex Dental Systems GmbH, Albert-Einstein Ring 13, pg. 500   **PB**

Gerlach-Werke GmbH, Industriegelande West, pg. 508   **IT**

German Bulk Chartering GmbH, Klosterwall 4, pg. 104   **IT**

Germapharm GmbH, Import, Export Spedition, 1 Spalding-210, pg. 1203   **IT**

Gesellschaft fur Wertpapieranlagen mbH, Hohe Bleichen 17, pg. 418   **IT**

Gilbarco GmbH, Schierenberg 74, pg. 545   **IT**

Givaudan-Roure GmbH, Flughafenstrasse 54, pg. 1120   **IT**

Globus Versicherungs AG, pg. 58   **IT**

Gluckslee Gesellschaft mbH, Mittelweg, 36, pg. 920   **IT**

Grammophon Spezialhaus Schallplatten-Einzelhandels-Gesellschaft mbH, Harvesthuder Weg 1-4, pg. 1052   **IT**

Max Gruenhut, GmbH & Co., Billhorner Deich 96, pg. 373   **PB**

Gruner + Jahr AG & Co., Am Baumwall 1120, pg. 190   **IT**

Gruner + Jahr AG & Co. Druck und Verlagshaus, Am Baumwall 11, pg. 190   **IT**

HDV Hamburger Datenverarbeitung GmbH, pg. 179   **IT**

Hakuhodo Deutschland GmbH, Neuer Wall 40, 3rd Fl., pg. 588   **IT**

HALTERMANN AG, Ferdinandstrasse 55/57, pg. 590   **IT**

Hamburger Abendblatt/DIE WELT Reiseburo GmbH, Kaiser Wilhelm Strasse 6, pg. 102   **IT**

Hamburger Aluminium-Werk Gesellschaft Mit Beschrankter Haftung, Firkenwerder Strasse, pg. 1387   **PB**

HAMBURGER SPARKASSE, Ecke Adolphsplatz, pg. 590   **IT**

Hamburgische Grundstuecks Gesellschaft mbH, Hasmaklen 11 Ness 1, pg. 310   **IT**

Hansa Melasse Handels GmbH, Kreusler, 10, pg. 1357   **IT**

Hansaport Hafenbetriebsgesellschaft mbH, Am Sandhafjen 20, pg. 1069   **IT**

Hanseatic Bank GmbH & Co., pg. 1014   **IT**

Hanseatic Versicherungs-Dienst GmbH, pg. 1014   **IT**

Hanseatische Investitions Bank GmbH, pg. 179   **IT**

Hanseatische Leasing GmbH, pg. 179   **IT**

HAPAG-LLOYD AG, Ballindamm 25, pg. 596   **IT**

Hapag-Lloyd Transport & Service GmbH, Baumwall 7, pg. 596   **IT**

Hapag-Lloyd Verwaltungs-gesellschaft mbH, pg. 596   **IT**

Hauptniederlassung Nord Niederlassung Hamburg, Karalstrasse 44, pg. 194   **IT**

Helly-Hansen GmbH, Grossmarkehre 1, pg. 1011   **IT**

Helly-Hansen Verakufs G.m.b.H., Grossmoorkehre 1, pg. 1011   **IT**

Hercules GmbH, Curslacker Neuer Deich 66, pg. 811   **PB**

Hermann Ludwig GmbH & Co., Postfach 100240, pg. 1165   **IT**

Hermes Technischer Kundendienst GmbH & Co., pg. 1014   **IT**

KG Hermes Versand Service GmbH & Co., pg. 1014   **IT**

Hesse Newman & Co., Ferdinandstrasse 25-27, pg. 137   **IT**

Hewlett-Packard GmbH, Vetriebszentrum Nord, Kapstadtring 5, pg. 820   **PB**

Hewlett-Packard GmbH, Oberseering 16, pg. 820   **PB**

Holmens Bruk G.m.B.H., Grosse Bleichen 8, pg. 885   **IT**

Husqvarna Vertriebs GmbH, Holstenstrasse 115, pg. 442   **IT**

Hydro Polymer GmbH, Airport Ctr., Flughafenstrasse 54 A, pg. 963   **IT**

Hypothekenbank in Hamburg AG, Hohe Bleichen 17, pg. 418   **IT**

IKB Leasing GmbH, Heidenkampsweg 79, pg. 645   **IT**

IMS Ingenieurgesellschaft mbH, Stadtdeich 5, pg. 633   **IT**

ING Bank Hamburg, Ballindamm 17, pg. 649   **IT**

ING Lease, Neuer Wall 50, pg. 650   **IT**

ING Lease Deutschland, Neuer Wall 50, pg. 650   **IT**

IQS Institut fur Qualitatssicherung, pg. 1288   **IT**

ISA Internationale Schiffahrts-Agentur GmbH, PO Box 103240, Brandsende 6, pg. 711   **IT**

ISI Insurance Service, pg. 596   **IT**

ISS Servisystem GmbH, Gebaudereinigung, Osterbekstrasse 90A, pg. 657   **IT**

IVO Energieanlagen GmbH, Neuer Dovenhof, pg. 661   **IT**

Iggesund Verkaufsgesellschaft G.m.b.H, Albert-Einstein-Ring 19, pg. 886   **IT**

Intergraph (Deutschland) GmbH, Osterbekstrasse 90b, pg. 892   **PB**

Interunfall Allgemeine Rechtsschutz-Schadenabwicklungs G.m.b.H., Johannisbollwerk 16, pg. 91   **IT**

Interunfall Allgemeine Versicherungs AG, Johannisbollwerk 16, pg. 91   **IT**

J.F. Jens Sohne Werkzeuge-Maschinen GmbH, Virchowstrasse 17-19, pg. 1128   **IT**

Japan Airlines Company, Ltd., 4th Floor, Spitalerstrasse 32, pg. 701   **IT**

Jauch & Huebener, Katharinenstrasse 10, pg. 118   **PB**

Jotun (Deutschland) GmbH, Winsbergring 25, pg. 715   **IT**

Juki (Europe) G.m.b.H., Garstedter Weg 14, pg. 717   **IT**

KG Maris Reisen GmbH & Co, pg. 1014   **IT**

Kansai Paint Europe Limited, Alstertor 18, pg. 723   **IT**

Kinetics Technology International GmbH, Kielerstrasse 163, pg. 836   **IT**

Kockums Computer Systems GmbH, Stubbenhuk 10, pg. 278   **IT**

Kodak AG-Hamburg, Steilshooper Allee 47, pg. 552   **PB**

Konica Business Machines Deutschland GmbH, Frankenstrasse 12, pg. 749   **IT**

Krupp Corpoplast Maschinenbau GmbH, Meinendorfer Str. 203, pg. 510   **IT**

Krupp Maschinentechnik GmbH, Harburg Seevestr. 1, pg. 510   **IT**

Krupp Seeschiffahrt GmbH, Chilehaus C V, pg. 514   **IT**

Krupp Warmetechnik GmbH - Hamburg, Billbrookdeich 207, pg. 515   **IT**

Kvaerner Brug (Deutschland) GmbH After Sales Service, Polhornbogen 8, pg. 771   **IT**

Kvaerner Ships Equipment GmbH After Sales Service, Pollhornbogen 8, pg. 768   **IT**

Langnese-Iglo G.m.b.H., pg. 1437   **IT**

Leafco Trading GmbH, 18 An Der Alster, pg. 1502   **PB**

Lever Sunlight G.m.b.H., pg. 1438   **IT**

Eli Lilly G.m.b.H., Marienbader Platz, pg. 994   **PB**

Litton Precision International, Alte Volksparkstrasse 24, pg. 1004   **PB**

Lowe & Partners GmbH, Schopenstehl 23, pg. 678   **PV**

Lubrizol GmbH, Kurze Muhren 3, pg. 1016   **PB**

Luft, Maack & Co. GmbH, Roedingsmarkt 39, pg. 966   **IT**

Lufthansa Technik AG, pg. 407   **IT**

Lutgens & Reimers GmbH, pg. 596   **IT**

M.S.C. Lebensmittel gmbH, Oberwerder Damm 11-21, pg. 244   **IT**

MacGREGOR (DEU) GmbH, Normannenweg 24, pg. 670   **IT**

MacGregor Golf GmbH, Steintorweg 4, pg. 73   **IT**

Manager Magazin Verlagsgesellschaft mbH, Brandswiete 19/Ost-West Strasse, pg. 190   **IT**

Marcard Stein & Co., Ballindamm 36, pg. 315   **IT**

Matzen & Timm Schlauchwerk, Grosse Bahn Strasse 11, pg. 1268   **IT**

Maxi-Papier Market GmbH, Klosterwall 2, pg. 1510   **PB**

Media Handelsgesellschaft mbH, pg. 1014   **IT**

Medic-Eschmann GmbH, Schnackenburgallee 116, pg. 1268   **IT**

Medtronic GmbH, Willhoop 1, pg. 1083   **PB**

MARTIN MERKEL GMBH & CO. KG, Sanitasstrasse 17-21, pg. 859   **IT**

MERKURHOF Grundstucks GmbH, pg. 180   **IT**

Carl G. Meyer Handel GmbH, pg. 838   **IT**

MICROS-Fidelio Software Deutschland GmbH, Borselstr. 16 a, pg. 1107   **IT**

Mitsui & Co., Ltd., Neuer Jungfernsteig 18, pg. 880   **IT**

Mobil ERDGAS-ERDOEL, Steinstrasse 5, pg. 1119   **PB**

Mobil Oil A.G., Steinstrasse 5, pg. 1119   **PB**

Josef Mobius Bau-Gesellschaft (GmbH & Co.), Brandstucken 18, pg. 633   **IT**

Moller Reiseburo, Grosse Bleichen 31, pg. 515   **IT**

Morgenpost Druck & Verlagsanstalt GmbH & Co., Grieg, 75, pg. 190   **IT**

Wm. H. Muller & Co. Bremen/Hamburg, Brook 6, pg. 682   **IT**

Mullverwertung Borsigstrasse GmbH, Uberseering 12, pg. 1460   **IT**

Munters GmbH, Hans Duncker Str. 14, pg. 669   **IT**

Munters Trocknungs Service GmbH, Postfach 261640, pg. 669   **IT**

NIB Norddeutsche Innovations- und Beteiligungsgesellschaft mbH, pg. 180   **IT**

NYK Line (Deutschland) GmbH, Gertrudenstr. 3, pg. 942   **IT**

NYK Line-Hamburg, Gertrudenstrasse 3, pg. 942   **IT**

National Rejectors, Inc., G.m.b.H., Zum Fruchtof 6, pg. 456   **PB**

Nedlloyd Schiffmakler GmbH, pg. 1144   **IT**

Neste Oel GmbH, Rodingsmarkt 9, pg. 915   **IT**

Neuma Vermoegsverwaltung GmbH, pg. 310   **IT**

Niedersachsen Versicherungs-AG, pg. 456   **IT**

Nissho Iwai Deutschland GmbH, Nagelsweg 47, pg. 948   **IT**

NORD/LB, Brodschrangen 4, pg. 957   **IT**

Norddeutsche Affinerie AG, Hovestrasse 50, pg. 861   **IT**

Norddeutsche Hypotheken und Wechselbank AG, Domstrasse 9, pg. 418   **IT**

Norddeutsche Immobilien- und Verwaltungs GmbH, pg. 310   **IT**

Nordinvest Norddeutsche Investment GmbH, pg. 180   **IT**

Norske Skog Deutschland GmbH, Niederlassung Hamburg, Teilfeld 5, pg. 966   **IT**

North German Branch, Heidenkampsweg 79, pg. 645   **IT**

Novacote International, Schnackenburgallee 62, pg. 1525   **IT**

Nur Hier GmbH, Niemdorfer Str. 25, pg. 160   **PV**

Oktavia Gesellschaft Fur Bekleidung mbH, pg. 1015   **IT**

Olympus Diagnostica GmbH, pg. 1005   **IT**

Olympus Optical Co. (Europa) GmbH, Wendenstrasse 14-16, pg. 1005   **IT**

Olympus Winter & Ibe GmbH, pg. 1005   **IT**

OMRON Europe G.m.b.H., Suederstrasse 16, pg. 1006   **IT**

OMRON Healthcare GmbH, Wendenstrasse 35-C, pg. 1006   **IT**

OMRON Systems Deutschland G.m.b.H., Suederstrasse 16, pg. 1006   **IT**

OMRON Systems Management G.m.b.H., Suederstrasse 16, pg. 1006   **IT**

Optimol Oelwerke GmbH, Esplanade 39, pg. 236   **IT**

Ortmann & Herbst GmbH, Alte Wohr 7, pg. 1240   **IT**

PB - *U.S. Public Companies Volume*
PV - *U.S. Private Companies Volume*
IT - *International Public & Private Companies Volume*

OTTO VERSAND (GMBH & CO.), Wandsbeker Strasse 3-7, pg. 1014   IT
Otto-Versand International GmbH, pg. 1015   IT
Panalpina Welttransport GmbH, pg. 1023   IT
Panasonic Deutschland GmbH, Winsbergring 15, pg. 847   IT
Panduit GMBH, Steinmuehlster 14, pg. 836   PV
Parafluid Mineralolgesellschaft mbH, Uberseering 9, pg. 517   IT
Peters Maschinenfabrik GmbH, Rodenbarg 9-17, pg. 199   IT
Phonogram GmbH, Roddingsmarkt 14, pg. 1052   IT
C. Plath, Gertigstrasse 48, pg. 1005   PB
Polydor International GmbH, Harvestehuder Weg 1-4, pg. 1052   IT
PolyGram Direct Marketing and Trading, Harvestehuter Weg 1-4, pg. 1053   IT
PROREMA An-und Vermietungsgesellschaft mbH, Gansemarkt 43, pg. 423   IT
RWE-DEA AG, Ueberseering 40, pg. 1081   IT
Raab Karcher Tankstellentechnik GmbH, Hamburg, Werner-Siemens-Strasse 70, pg. 1457   IT
REEMTSMA CIGARETTENFABRIKEN GMBH, HAMBURG, Parkstrasse 51, pg. 1100   IT
H.F. & Ph. F. Reemtsma GmbH, Parkstrasse 51, pg. 1101   IT
Otto Reisen GmbH, pg. 1015   IT
Rickmers-Linie GmbH, pg. 596   IT
Rohr Europe-Hamburg, Rohr Europe GmbH, Hein-Sass-Weg 17, pg. 752   PB
Rolf Butenschon GmbH, pg. 442   IT
Ruberoid AG, Billbrookdeich 134, pg. 1148   IT
S.F.T.C., Postfach 100240, pg. 1165   IT
STILL GmbH, Antriebsarten Berzeliusstrasse 10, pg. 811   IT
Sachsen Papier Eilenburg GmbH, Grosse Bleichen 30, pg. 458   IT
Salvia, pg. 922   IT
Wilh. Schauman GmbH, Kirchenallee 25, pg. 1429   IT
Scherax Arzneimittel GmbH, 52 Elbch. 336, pg. 1203   IT
Schindler Aufzuge GmbH, pg. 1205   IT
SCHOLZ & FRIENDS GMBH, Steinhoft 9, pg. 1210   IT
Schumann Sasol GmbH & Co KG, Worthdamm 13-27, pg. 1197   IT
Schumann Sasol International AG, Worthdamm 13-27, pg. 1196   IT
Hans Schwarzkopf GmbH, Hohenzollernring 127-129, pg. 610   IT
Sea Containers GmbH, Deichstrasse 1, pg. 1214   IT
Select Communications, GmbH, Hamburg, pg. 982   PV
Sequent Computer Systems GmbH, Wendenstrasse 379, pg. 1459   PB
Shandwick Lutz Bohme Public Relations GmbH, ABC-Strabe 1, pg. 1227   IT
Sharp Electronics (Europe) GmbH, Sonninstr. 3, pg. 1230   IT
Sinochem Trading Hamburg GmbH, Winterhuder Weg 29, pg. 1256   IT
Skandinaviska Enskilda Banken, Speersort 4, pg. 1260   IT
Skanska Property GmbH, Alsterufer 34, pg. 1260   IT
Sodra Cell GmbH, Ehrenbergstrasse 33, pg. 1276   IT
SPIEGEL-Verlag Rudolf Augstein GmbH & Co., Brandswiete 19, pg. 190   IT
Spraying Systems Deutschland GmbH, Grossmooring 9, pg. 1027   PV
Steinhoft-Pre-Press, pg. 1210   IT
Stinnes Interoil AG, Ballindamm 17, pg. 1459   IT
Stora Billerud Paper GmbH, Schillerstrasse 44, pg. 1302   IT
Stora Purchasing & Transport GmbH, Postfach 10 48 47, pg. 1303   IT
Svedala Deutschland (Hamburg) GmbH, pg. 1324   IT
Svedala-Scholtz Transportbandtechnik GmbH, pg. 1326   IT
TBWA Hamburg GmbH, Neuer Wall 50, pg. 1063   PV
Takeda Europe GmbH, Domstrasse 1, pg. 1350   IT
Takenaka Europe GmbH, Hamburg, Ohlsdorfer Strasse 1-3, pg. 1351   IT
Tektronix GmbH-Hamburg, pg. 1567   PB
Telxon mde GmbH, Gutenbergring 1-5, pg. 1574   PB
Dr. rer. nat. Peter Theiss Naturwaren, pg. 1489   IT
The Tokio Marine & Fire Insurance Company (U.K.) Limited, c/o Burmester, Dunker & Joly, Trostbrucke 1, pg. 1393   IT
Toyo Boseki (Europe) GmbH, Jungfernstieg 7, pg. 1411   IT
Transports Bernis, Postfach 100240, pg. 1165   IT
Transports Virolle, Postfach 100240, pg. 1165   IT
Tretorn GmbH, Rungedamm 33, pg. 1072   IT
Turbomeca GmbH, Geschaftsfliegerzentrum Gebaude 347, pg. 787   IT
Ufa Film und Fernseh GmbH, Alsterufer 33, pg. 190   IT
UPM-Kymmene Deutschland GmbH, Jessenstrasse 3, pg. 1430   IT
Union Deutsche Lebensmittelwerke G.m.b.H., 36 Dammontorwall, pg. 1439   IT
UNION Verwaltungs- und Treuhand GmbH, pg. 180   IT
V und B, Lohmuhlenstrasse 1, pg. 603   IT
VTG Paktank Hamburg GmbH, Brandsende 2-4, pg. 1459   IT
VTG Vereinigte Tanklager und Transportmittel GmbH, Warc Rabenstrasse 21, pg. 1070   IT
Valtec Mineraloel Vertriebs Gesellschaft, Uberseering 9, pg. 140   PB
Vattenfall AB, Neuer Wall 2-6, pg. 1453   IT
Vattenfall Deutschland GmbH, Neuer Wall 2-6, pg. 1453   IT
VEBA OIL INTERNATIONAL GmbH, Ballindamm 17, pg. 1461   IT
VEBA POSEIDON Schiffahrt GmbH, Ballindamm 17, pg. 1461   IT
Verein West Beratungsgesellschaft mbH, pg. 180   IT

Vereins- und Westbank AG, Geter Wall 1, pg. 180   IT
Vereinsbank Immobilien Verwaltungs GmbH, pg. 180   IT
Verwaltungsgesellschaft Katharinehof mbH, pg. 180   IT
Vital Signs Deutschland, Inc., pg. 1723   PB
Volksfursorge Deutsche Lebensversicherung AG, An der Alstet 57-63, pg. 16   IT
Volksfursorge Deutsche Sachversicherung, Besenbinderhof 43, pg. 16   IT
Volksfursorge Holding AG, An der Alster 57-63, pg. 15   IT
Volksfursorge Krankenversicherung AG, Besenbinderhof 43, pg. 16   IT
Walbaum, Postfach 100240, pg. 1165   IT
Werkhof GmbH, 18 An Der Alster, pg. 1502   PB
WestLB Hamburg Branch, Domstrasse 10, pg. 1493   IT
Yashica Kyocera GmbH, Eiffestrasse 76, pg. 776   IT
Zeitverlag Gerd Bucerius GmbH, Pressehaus, Speersort 1, pg. 1479   IT
Zweigniederlassung der Rockwell International GmbH, Grossmoorbogen 9, pg. 1402   PB

Hameln

AEG Zahler GmbH, Kuhbruckenstrasse 2-4, pg. 1439   PB
BHW BAUSPARKASSE AG, Lubahnstrasse 2, pg. 120   IT
OKA Teppichwerke GmbH., pg. 1480   IT
Vorwerk & Co. Teppichwerke GmbH. & Co. KG., Kuhlmannstr. 11, pg. 1480   IT

Hamm

Du Pont de Nemours (Deutschland) GmbH, Plant Uentrop, pg. 532   PB
Mannesmann Hoesch Prazisrohr GmbH, Kissinger Weg, pg. 513   IT
Raab Karcher Ambiente GmbH, pg. 1457   IT

Hanau

Dunlop GmbH, Dunlopstrasse 2, pg. 1317   IT
Ebara Germany GmbH, Donaustrasse 7, pg. 432   IT
HERAEUS HOLDING GMBH, Heraeusstrasse 12-14, pg. 615   IT
Heraeus Instruments GmbH, Heraeusstrasse 12-14, pg. 616   IT
Heraeus Kulzer GmbH, Gruner Weg 11, pg. 616   IT
Heraeus Med GmbH, Heraeusstrasse 12-14, pg. 616   IT
Heraeus Quarzglas GmbH, Quarztrasse, pg. 616   IT
W.C. Heraeus GmbH, Heraeusstrasse 12-14, pg. 616   IT
Kemira Chemidet GmbH, Nurnburger Strasse 4, pg. 729   IT
Rainbow Versandhandels-gesellschafr mbH, pg. 1015   IT
Roediger Anlagenbau GmbH, Kinzigheimer Weg 104, pg. 195   IT
Schwab Versand Aktiengesellschaft, pg. 1015   IT
Swift Klebstoffe GmbH, Am Freiheitsplatz 14, pg. 370   IT
Vacuumschmelze GmbH, Gruner Weg 37, pg. 1245   IT

Hannover

AVE Gesellschaft fur Horfunkbeteiligungen mbH, Goseriede 9, pg. 1478   IT
Allgemeine Privatkundenbank AG, Buchholzer Str. 98, pg. 159   IT
Auto-trol Technology GmbH, Fokenburger Str. 24, pg. 148   PB
BHF-Bank, Georgsplatz 9, pg. 119   IT
BOCM Silcock (N.I.) Ltd., Podbielshistrasse 134, pg. 440   IT
Bank GiroTel AG, Buchholzer Strasse 98, pg. 159   IT
Benecke-Kaliko AG, pg. 327   IT
Hans Berneburg GmbH & Co. KG, Strassenbau Berneburg, Hoefestr. 19-21, pg. 632   IT
CONTINENTAL AG, Vahrenwalder Strasse 9, pg. 327   IT
Curatio Versigherungs-Vermittlungs Gmbh, Hans-Bochlek Allee 20, pg. 1278   IT
DEUMU Deutsche Erz- und Metall-Union GmbH, Herrenstrasse 3-5, pg. 1069   IT
Deutsche Bank AG (Hannover), Georgsplatz 20, pg. 402   IT
Deutsche Hypothekenbank (Actien-Gesellschaft), Georgsplatz 8, pg. 119   IT
Deutsche van Rietschoten & Houwens GmbH, 12, Junkerstrasse, pg. 682   IT
DG Bank - Hannover, Berliner Allee 5/Andreas-Hermes-Platz, pg. 351   IT
Engelhard Catalysts GmbH, Hans-Bockler-Allee 20, pg. 582   PB
Ernst Siegling Beteiligungs GmbH, pg. 497   IT
Ernst Siegling GmbH & Co., pg. 497   IT
Esselte GmbH, Anderter Str. 99, pg. 461   IT
Geschaftsstelle Hannover, Liebenstrasse 60, pg. 739   IT
Gesellschaft fur Nuklear-Service mbH-GNS, Lange Laube 1, pg. 1457   IT
Giulini Pharma GmbH, Hans-Bockler-Allee 20, pg. 1278   IT
Hannover-Braunschweigische Stromversorgungs-AG, Humboldtstrasse 33, pg. 1456   IT
Otto Hansel GmbH, Lister Damm 19, pg. 737   IT
Hapag-Lloyd Fluggesellschaft mbH, Flughafen, pg. 596   IT
HASTRA Aktiengesellschaft, pg. 1456   IT
HERMANN BERSTORFF MASCHINENBAU GMBH, An Der Breiten Wiese 3-5, pg. 617   IT
Hewlett-Packard GmbH, Heidering 37-39, pg. 820   PB
Interkohle Beteiligungsgesellschaft mit beschrankter Haftung, Tresckowstrasse 5, pg. 1456   IT
Kali-Chemie Aktiengesellschaft, Hans-Bockler-Allee 20, pg. 1278   IT
Kali-Chemie Pharma GmbH, Hans-Bocker-Allee 20, pg. 1278   IT

Kavernen Bau- und Betriebs-Gesellschaft mbH, Karl-Wiechut-Allu 4, pg. 1069   IT
Kemira Deutschland GmbH, Sutelstrasse 63/64, pg. 728   IT
Kodak AG-Hanover, Hanomag Allee 2, pg. 552   PB
Komatsu Hanomag AG, Hanomag Strasse 9, pg. 744   IT
KONE Aufzug GmbH, Sudfeldstrasse 20, pg. 747   IT
KONE Aufzugwerke, Sudfeldstrasse 20, pg. 747   IT
Carl Gustav Krause GmbH, Schlorupfweg 9, pg. 514   IT
Krupp Fordertechnik GmbH, Hackethalstr. 4, pg. 511   IT
Krupp Hoesch Stahl AG - Hanover, Arnswaldstr. 18, pg. 512   IT
Krupp Warmetechnik GmbH - Hannover, Grambartstr. 28a, pg. 515   IT
Lyssia GmbH, Hans-Bockler-Allee 20, pg. 1278   IT
Mannesmann Rexroth Pneumatik GmbH, pg. 838   IT
Mikron Hannover GmbH, Wohlenbergstr. 6-8, pg. 867   IT
MINIRUF GmbH, pg. 1461   IT
NRG Office Systems GmbH, Grosser Kolonnenweg 18, pg. 1116   IT
NTO, Hacketalsstrasse 6, pg. 1145   IT
NTO Transport Organisation GmbH, Hacketalsstrasse 6, pg. 1145   IT
Niederlassung Hanover, Marienstrasse 45-47, pg. 195   IT
Nordcement AG, Warmbuechenstrasse 19, pg. 628   IT
Norddeutsche Gesellschaft zur Beratung und Durchfuehrung von Entsorgungsaufgaben bei Kernkraftwerken mbH, Postfach 48 49, pg. 1456   IT
NORDDEUTSCHE LANDESBANK (NORD/LB), Georgsplatz 1, pg. 957   IT
Objektverwaltungsgesellschaft Dampfkraftwerk Wet GbR, pg. 597   IT
Omnitechnic GmbH, Chemische Verbindungstechnik, Sichelstrasse 1, pg. 610   IT
Otto Eckhold GmbH + Co. KG Glas und Gebaudereinigung, pg. 1480   IT
Otto Eckhold Verwaltungsgesellschaft mbH, pg. 1480   IT
Prakla-Seismos AG, Buchholzer Str. 100, pg. 1439   PB
PREUSSAG AG, Karl-Wiechert-Allee 4, pg. 1069   IT
Preussag Anlagenbau GmbH, Karl-Wiedut-Allu 4, pg. 1069   IT
PreussenElektra Aktiengesellschaft, Tresckowstrasse 5, pg. 1456   IT
PreussenElektra-Kernbrennstoff GmbH, Tresckowstrasse 5, pg. 1457   IT
PreussenElektra Telekom GmbH, Tresckowstrasse 5, pg. 1456   IT
PreussenElektra/VKR, Treschowstrasse 5, pg. 1456   IT
PreussenElektra Windkraft Niedersachsen GmbH, Tresckowstrasse 5, pg. 1456   IT
PreussenElektra Windkraft Schleswig-Holstein GmbH, Tresckowstrasse 5, pg. 1456   IT
Pritt Produktionsgesellschaft mbH, pg. 610   IT
Reinfeldt & Trenschel Handel GmbH, pg. 838   IT
Rockwell International GmbH, Alter Flughafen 16b, pg. 1401   PB
S & W Elektromedizin GmbH, Rendsburgerstrasse 14, pg. 1467   IT
SCOR Deutschland, Seelhorststrasse 3, pg. 1153   IT
Schroedel Schulbuchverlag GmbH, Hildesheimer Str. 202-206, pg. 1478   IT
Sensycon Gesellschaft fur Industrielle Sensorsysteme und Prozeßleittechnik mbH, pg. 835   IT
Sichel-Werke GmbH, Sichelstrasse 1, pg. 610   IT
Siegling Gmbh, pg. 498   IT
Signum Arznelmittel GmbH, Hans-Bockler-Allee 20, pg. 1278   IT
Solvay Barium Strontium GmbH, Hans-Bockler-Allee 20, pg. 1279   IT
Solvay Enzymes GmbH & Co., Frundalle 20, pg. 1279   IT
Solvay Enzymes Verwaltungs GmbH, Freundallee 11, pg. 1280   IT
Solvay Pharma Deutschland GmbH, pg. 1280   IT
Solvay Umweltchemie GmbH, Hans-Bockler-Allee 20, pg. 1280   IT
TeleColumbus GmbH, pg. 1461   IT
Teleport Europe GmbH, pg. 1461   IT
Unterstutzungskasse der VDO MeB und Regeltechnik GmbH, pg. 839   IT
VB Autobatterie GmbH, pg. 1452   IT
VARTA AG, Am Leineufer 51, pg. 1451   IT
VARTA Batterie AG, Am Leineufer 51, pg. 1452   IT
WABCO Automotive Poducts Group, WABCO Fahrzeugbremsen, Am Lindener Hafen 21, pg. 92   PB
WABCO Westinghouse Fahrzeugbremsen G.m.b.H., Postfach 91 12 80, pg. 92   PB
White Cap Deutschland Vertriebsgesellschaft mbH, pg. 1207   IT
White Cap Europe GmbH, pg. 1207   IT
ZEXEL Corporation Hanover Representative Office, pg. 1528   IT
ZEXEL R&D Center, Ihmepassage 4, pg. 1528   IT

Harbarnsen

Biolac, Am Bahnhof 1, pg. 1278   IT

Harrislee

NOPI GmbH, pg. 182   IT

Hassloch

Perstorp Components, Fabrikstrasse 20, pg. 1040   IT

Hattersheim

Butler Newall GmbH, Auf Der Roos 4-12, pg. 449   IT
ITW Befestigungssysteme (Hattersheim) GmbH, Im Gotthelf 12-14, pg. 868   PB

Oilgear GmbH, Im Gotthelf, pg. 1215   PB
Sulzer Metco (Deutschland) GmbH, pg. 1307   IT

Hattingen

Air Products GmbH, Huttenstrasse 50, pg. 31   PB
O&K Antriebstechnik GmbH, Hattingen Works, Nierenhofer Str. 10, pg. 516   IT
O&K Rolltreppen GmbH, Hattingen Works, Nierenhofer Str. 10, pg. 516   IT

Hauzenberg

Graphitwerk Kropfmuehl AG, Langheinrich Str.l, pg. 1464   IT

Hechingen

Gambro Dialysatoren GmbH & Co KG, Holger Crafoord Strasse 26, pg. 667   IT

Heddesheim

Externa Handels- und Beteiligungsgesellschaft mbh, pg. 506   IT

Heidelberg

Bundy G.m.b.H., Postfach 103940, pg. 1341   IT
Endevco Vertriebs GmbH, Englestrasse 2, pg. 854   IT
Geschaeftsbereich Der AlliedSignal (Deutschland) GmbH (Enevco Germany), Schlosswolfsbrunnenweg 15, pg. 53   PB
Grau GmbH, Eppelheimer Strasse 76, pg. 561   PB
Hampshire Chemical GmbH, Waldhafer Strasse 17, pg. 498   PV
Heidelberger Daemmsysteme GmbH, Mittermaierstr. 18, pg. 606   IT
HEIDELBERGER DRUCKMASCHINEN A.G., Kurfuersten-Anlage 52-60, pg. 604   IT
HEIDELBERGER ZEMENT A.G., Berliner Strasse 6, pg. 605   IT
Heidelberger Zement International Holding GmbH, Berliner Str. 6, pg. 605   IT
Henkel Teroson GmbH, Hans-Bunte-Strasse 4, pg. 610   IT
Parker Hannifin GmbH, Waldhofer STR 102, pg. 1260   PB
Perstorp Components, Werk Heidelberg, Industriestrasse 61, pg. 1040   IT
SAS Institute GmbH, P.O. Box 10 53 07, Inder Neckarhelle 162, pg. 967   PV
Spektrum Akademischer Verlag GmbH, Vangerowstrasse 20, pg. 1478   IT
Spektrum der Wissenschaft Verlagsgesellschaft mbH, Vangerowstrasse 20, pg. 1478   IT
Springer-Verlag GmbH & Co. KG, Tiergartenstrasse 17, pg. 1291   IT
Steelcase Strafor Pohlschroder, Freiburger Strasse 21-23, pg. 1038   PV
Teldix GmbH, Grenzhofer Weg 36, pg. 204   IT
Yamanouchi Pharma GmbH, Hertzstrasse 2-4, pg. 1519   IT

Heideloh

Karstadt Heideloh GmbH, pg. 724   IT

Heidenau

Citax Klebetechnik GmbH, pg. 609   IT
ITW Heistrap GmbH, Haupstrasse 109a, pg. 868   PB

Heidenheim

F. Oberdorfer Siebtechnik GmbH, pg. 1202   IT
J.M. VOITH, GMBH, St. Poltener Str. 43, pg. 1472   IT
Voith-Novenco GmbH, pg. 1473   IT
Voith Sulzer Papiertechnik GmbH, pg. 1307   IT

Heilbronn

BLH SR-4 Sensoren GmbH, Wannenackerstrasse 24, pg. 1289   IT
CPC Deutschland GmbH, Knorrstrasse 1, pg. 225   PB
Deutsche Fiat AG, 140 Salzstrasse, pg. 484   IT
G. Drauz GmbH & Co., Weipertstr. 37, pg. 507   IT
Dynisco Gerate G.m.b.H., Ind. Geb. Bollinger Hofe, Postfach 1547, pg. 139   PV
Fiat Automobile AG, Salzstrasse 140, pg. 481   IT
Harman Deutschland GmbH, Huenderstrasse 1, pg. 787   PB
MAN GHH Logistics GmbH, Hans-Riesser-Strasse 7, pg. 824   IT
Molex GmbH, Felix-Wankel Strasse 11, pg. 1122   PB
Niederlassung Heilbronn, Bahnhofstrasse 7, pg. 195   IT
Rhenania Transport GmbH, Albertistrasse 16-20, pg. 1033   IT
Rhenania Umschlag und Lagerei GmbH, Zweigniederlassung Hafenstrass, pg. 1033   PV
Shure, GmbH, Lohtorstr. 24, pg. 997   IT
Temic Telefunken microelectronic GmbH, pg. 367   IT
ZEAG Zementwerk Lauffen-Elektrizitaetswerk Heilbronn AG, Badstrasse 80, pg. 605   IT

Heiligenhaus

Georg Fischer Disa GmbH, Hauptstrasse 297a, pg. 489   IT

Heitersheim

Hirtler GmbH, pg. 182   IT

Helmstedt

Braunschweigische Kohlen-Bergwerke AG, Schoninger Strasse 2-3, pg. 1456   IT
NORD/LB, Sudertor 8, pg. 957   IT
Uberland-Zentrale Helmstedt AG, pg. 1456   IT
Wohnungsbaugesellschaft niedersachsischer Braunkohlenwerke mbh, pg. 1456   IT

Hemer

FRIEDRICH GROHE ARMATURENFABRIK GMBH & CO., Haupstrasse 137, pg. 559   IT

Hemmingen

Michael Friess GmbH (SSH), Schlachtofstrasse 42, pg. 1459   IT
Hellma Gastronomie-Service GmbH, pg. 1305   IT
Union Special G.m.b.H., Schlosshaldenstrasse, pg. 717   IT

Hennef

Chronos Richardson GmbH, Reutherstrasse 3, pg. 1299   IT
Mallinckrodt Medical GmbH, Postfach 1462, Josef-Dietzgen-Strasse, pg. 1040   PB

Henningsdorf

ABB-Adtranz Henningsdorf, Am Rathenau Park, pg. 369   IT
Korf Transport GmbH, Finsterwalder Strasse 17a, pg. 759   IT

Heppenheim

Adrema Leasing Corporation, Tiergartenstrasse 7, pg. 1304   PB
Dany Club Sandwich GmbH & Co. Vertriebs KG, pg. 920   IT
Decision Data, Tiergartenstr. 12, pg. 645   IT
Esselte Meto, P.O. Box 1803, pg. 461   IT
Esselte Meto International GmbH, Westerwaldstrasse 3-13, pg. 461   IT
Peripherie & Netzwerke GmbH, Tiergartenstrasse 12, pg. 645   IT
Pharmacia & Upjohn GmbH, Humboldtstrasse 10, pg. 1049   IT
Pitney Bowes Deutschland G.m.b.H., Tiergartenstrasse 7, pg. 1304   PB
Suzuki Motor GmbH, Deutschland, Tiergartenstrasse 8, pg. 1323   IT

Herborn

Gerhard Collardin GmbH, pg. 609   IT

Herford

Richard Heinze Kunststoff Spritzgiesswerke GmbH & Co., Eupenerstrasse 35, pg. 1210   IT
Poggenpohl Mobelwerke GmbH, Poggenpohlstr. 1, pg. 1261   IT
Wilhelm Scheidt Bauunternehmung GmbH, Lockhauser Strasse 111, pg. 195   IT

Hermsdorf

Continental Can Europe Verpackungsgesellschaft Hermsdorf mbH, pg. 1206   IT

Herne

Chemische Betriebe Pluto GmbH, Thiesstrasse 61, pg. 1460   IT
Fernwarmeversorgung Herne GmbH, Grenzweg 18, pg. 1460   IT
Flender Engineering & Service Antriebstechnik GmbH, Sudstrasse 111, pg. 400   IT
SCHWING GMBH, Heerstr. 9-27, pg. 1211   IT
Warmetechnik Leickel GmbH, Dorstener Strasse 259, pg. 1460   IT

Herrenburg

Kault & Bux Commutator GMBH-Herrenberg, pg. 623   PV
Solectron GmbH, Solectronstrasse 2, pg. 1483   PB

Herten

BauMineral GmbH Herten, Hiberniastrasse 12, pg. 1460   IT

Herzberg

Herzberger Papierfabrik Ludwig Osthushanrich GmbH & Co. KG, Andreasberger Strasse 1, pg. 757   IT

Herzbrock-Clarholz

Perstorp Elemente GmbH, Dieselstrasse 94, pg. 1038   IT

Herzhorn

Namco Controls GmbH, Mittelfeld 10, pg. 482   PB

Herzogenaurach

ADIDAS AG, Adi-Dassler-Strasse 2, pg. 24   IT
Puma AG Rudolf Dassler Sport, Wurzburger Strasse 13, pg. 1072   IT

Herzogenrath

Ericsson Eurolab Deutschland GmbH, Ericsson Allee 1, pg. 1366   IT

Hessisch Lichtenau

Interlot GmbH, Lilienthalstrasse 11, pg. 1128   IT
ROWO-Rohr-und Kanalreinigungsgerate GmbH, Lilienthalstrasse 9, pg. 1128   IT

Hettingen

Medica GmbH, pg. 1523   IT

Heuchelheim

Schunk GmbH, pg. 310   IT

Heusenstamm

Kenwood Electronics Deutschland Gmbh, Rembrucker Strasse 15, pg. 731   IT
R-M Autolacke GmbH, Ernst-Leitz-Strasse 1, pg. 104   IT
Wirsbo Pex GmbH, P.O. Box 1128, pg. 442   IT

Hiddenhaen

Teutonia GmbH & Co. KG, pg. 217   IT

Hilden

Ashland-Suedchemie-Kernfest GmbH, Postfach 440, Reischolzstrasse 16, pg. 140   PB
ICI Lacke Farben GmbH, Duesseldorfer Strasse 102, pg. 665   IT
Notifier Deutschland GmbH, Hans-Sachs Strasse 10, pg. 1307   PB
OMRON Electronics GmbH, Itterpark 2-4, pg. 1006   IT
Pirelli Vertriebs G.m.b.H., Fabriciusstrasse 40, pg. 1059   IT
Shimano (Europa) GmbH, Kleinhulsen 1-3, pg. 1233   IT
Uddeholm GmbH., Westring 9, pg. 1472   IT
Ultra GmbH, Max-Volmer-Strasse 2, pg. 421   PB

Hildesheim

Blaupunkt-Werke GmbH, Robert Bosch Strasse 200, pg. 203   IT
Enesco Import, GmbH, pg. 1508   PB
Ericsson Fuba Telecom GmbH, Daimlerring 9, pg. 1366   IT
Kloth-Senking Metallgiesserei GmbH, pg. 1387   IT
Ledu GmbH, Feldstrasse 20, pg. 821   IT
Luxo Leuchten GmbH, Feldstrasse 18B-22, pg. 821   PB
Voi-Shan/Diessel GmbH, pg. 610   IT

Hirschberg

Simon-Lift GmbH, Carl Benz Strasse 10, pg. 1252   IT

Hirschhorn

Esselte Meto GmbH, Ersheimerstr. 69, pg. 461   IT
Esselte Meto International Produktions GmbH, Brentanostr. 27-29, pg. 461   IT

Hirtscheid

Klockner Maschinen - UND Anglagenbau GMBH, Grabenstrasse, 1-3, pg. 131   IT

Hochberg

ITW Devcon Ateco GmbH, Otto Hahnstrasse 15, pg. 868   PB

Hochheim

Akerlund & Rausing Verpackung GmbH, pg. 33   IT
Stora Beteiligungen GmbH, Postfach 1180, pg. 1303   IT

Hochst

Pirelli Deutschland A.G., Postfach 20, pg. 1059   IT
Pirelli Reifenwerke GmbH, Postfach 20, pg. 1059   IT

PB - U.S. Public Companies Volume
PV - U.S. Private Companies Volume
IT - International Public & Private Companies Volume

Hoehenkirchen

INKA PALETTEN GMBH, Bahnhofstr. 21, pg. 678   IT

Hof

Neue Baumwoll Spinnerei und Weberei Hof AG,
pg. 180   IT
NEUEBAUM WOLL-SPINNEREI UND WEBEREI HOF A.G., Fabrikzeile 21, pg. 922   IT

Hofheim

Matra Communications GmbH, Am Kreishams 16,
pg. 796   IT

Hohenbrunn

Konica Europe GmbH, Industriecenter X11, pg. 749   IT

Hohenhameln-Mehrum

Kraftwerk Mehrum GmbH, Triftstrasse 25, pg. 1456   IT

Hohenstein-Erntthal

Drauz Ingenieurbetrieb GmbH, Am Bahnhof 9, pg. 508   IT

Hohenzollern

EBE Edelstahl-Bauelemente GmbH, Langstadl 50,
pg. 508   IT

Holle

Titan Germany GmbH, Ziegeleis Strasse 29, pg. 1619   PB

Hollriegelskreuth

Linde AG Werksgruppe Technische Gase, Seitnerstr. 70,
pg. 810   IT
Linde AG Werksgruppe TVT, Dr. Carl-von-Linde-Str. 6-14,
pg. 811   IT

Holzgerlingen

RUKO GmbH Prazisionswerkzeuge, Robert-Bosch-Strasse,
pg. 1128   IT

Holzminden

Haarmann & Reimer GmbH, pg. 174   IT
NORD/LB, Bontalstrasse 9, pg. 957   IT

Hoppegarten

Porsche Zentrum Hoppegarten GmbH, pg. 1063   IT

Horb am Neckar

Brueninghaus Hydraulik GmbH, pg. 838   IT
Brueninghaus Hydraulik GmbH & Co., pg. 838   IT
PTG Plasma-Oberflachentechnik GmbH, pg. 400   IT

Hosbach

Matchbox Spielwaren GmbH, Siemensstrasse 23,
pg. 1059   PB

Hoxter

Zenker-Fenster GmbH & Co KG, Braunschweiger Str.,
pg. 633   IT

Hoyerswerda

UNION-BAU AG, pg. 423   IT

Huckelhoven

Lupos Gmbh, Rheinstrasse 12, pg. 430   IT

Hunfeld

Oreg Drayton Energietechnik GmbH, Zum Wolfsgraben S,
pg. 1242   IT
Oreg Ondal Regeltechnik GmbH, pg. 1489   IT

Hungen

Coleman (Deutschland) GmbH, Inheiden Ezetilstrasse,
pg. 691   PV

Hurth

Hurth Branch, Uraulastrasse 33-41, pg. 401   IT
Krautkramer G.m.b.H, Robert Bosch Strasse 3, pg. 577   PB
Plantronics GmbH, Postfach 71 01, pg. 1308   PB
Saarbach GmbH, Hans-Bockler-Str. 19, pg. 796   IT

Ibbenburen

ANGUS Chemie GmbH, Zeppelinstrasse 30, pg. 75   PV

Chemische Fabrik WIBARCO GmbH, Hauptstrasse 21,
pg. 104   IT
Elektro Chemie Ibbenburen GmbH, Hamptstrasse 47,
pg. 44   IT
Preussag Anthrazit GmbH, Osmabruchno Strasse 112,
pg. 1069   IT

Idar-Oberstein

Geschaftsstelle Idar-Oberstein, Langenfelder Strasse 11,
pg. 194   IT

Idstein

Black & Decker G.m.b.H., pg. 234   PB
Dionex GmbH, Am Woertzgarten, 10, pg. 510   PB
Nellcor Puritan Bennett GmbH, Black & Decker Strasse 28,
pg. 1040   PB
THERMOPLAST UND APPARATEBAU GMBH, Black & Decker Str. 25, pg. 1381   IT
Jack Wolfskin, Limburger Strasse 38-40, pg. 933   PB

Iffesheim

Pechiney Lebensmittelverpackungen, Josef-Hermann Strasse 1-3, pg. 1031   IT

Illertissen

Chemische Fabrik Grunau GmbH, Robert-Hansen-Str. 1,
pg. 609   IT
Grunau Illertissen GmbH, Robert-Hansen-Strasse 1,
pg. 609   IT
Tricosal GmbH, Robert Hansen Strasse 1, pg. 610   IT

Ingelfingen

SpeedFam GmbH, Schlosstrasse 5, pg. 1498   PB

Ingelheim

Boehringer Ingelheim, Bingerstrasse 173, pg. 199   IT
BOEHRINGER INGELHEIM GMBH, Bingerstrasse 173,
pg. 199   IT

Ingersleben

Krupp Warmetechnik GmbH - Erfurt, Karl-Marx-Str. 1,
pg. 515   IT

Ingolstadt

Audi AG, pg. 1473   IT
Elektro Metall Export Gmbh, Manchingerstrasse 116,
pg. 313   PV
Penny & Giles GmbH, Straussenlettenstr. 7B, pg. 209   IT
Rieter Deutschland GmbH & Co. OHG, pg. 1117   IT
Rieter Ingolstadt Spinnereimaschinenbau AG, pg. 1117   IT
Rieter Vertriebs GmbH, pg. 1117   IT

Iserlohn

Bakelite AG, Gennaer Strasse 2-4, pg. 1148   IT
ITW Befestigungssysteme, Liegnitzer Strasse 1 Postfach 7321, pg. 868   PB
OptiMel Schmelzgusstechnik GmbH & Co. KG, pg. 610   IT

Isernhagen

EFEKA Friedrich & Kaufmann GmbH & Co., Siemensstrasse, 1, pg. 81   PB
Krupp Hoesch Stahlhandel GmbH, Stahlstr. 2, pg. 514   IT
Pumpex GmbH, Tischler Strasse 10, pg. 271   IT

Ismaning

Biogen GmbH, Carl Zeiss-Ring 6, pg. 231   PB
Caterpillar Financial Services Holding GmbH, Carl-Zeiss-Ring 3-5, pg. 315   PB
Caterpillar Leasing GmbH (Ismaning), Carl-Zeiss-Ring 3-5,
pg. 315   PB
FSG Holding GmbH, Carl-Zeiss-Ring 17, pg. 1148   IT
Herlitz International Trading AG, Oskar-Messter-Str. 25,
pg. 616   IT
Hewlett-Packard GmbH, Fraunhofer Strasse 1, pg. 820   PB
Intergraph (Deutschland) GmbH, Adalperostrasse 26,
pg. 892   IT
NEC Deutschland GmbH, Steinheilstr. 4-6, pg. 901   IT
Network Systems GmbH, Carl-Zeiss ring 19-21,
pg. 1523   PB
Schlumberger Holding GmbH, Gutenbergstrasse 2-4,
pg. 1439   PB
Seagate Technology GmbH, Fraunhoferstrasse 9,
pg. 1450   PB
Sequent GmbH, Adalperostrasse 22, pg. 1460   PB
Steinheil Optronik GmbH, Osterfeldstrasse 82, pg. 218   IT
Vinnolit Kunststoff GmbH, pg. 626   IT
Wind River Systems GmbH, Freisinger Strasse 34,
pg. 1771   PB

Issleburg

Isselburger Hutte GmbH, Minervastrasse 1, pg. 1210   IT

Issum

DIEBELS PRIVATE BREWERY, Brauerei-Diebels-Str. 1,
pg. 413   IT

Itzehoe

SIHI GMBH & CO. KG, Lindenstrasse 170, pg. 1156   IT

Jena

Gustav Fischer Verlag Jena GmbH, Villengang 2,
pg. 1478   IT
IOT Integrierte Optik GmbH, pg. 1523   IT
Jenaer Glaswerk GmbH, pg. 1523   IT
Jena-Optronik GmbH, pg. 367   IT
Niederlassung Jena, Spitzweidenweg 107, pg. 195   IT
Carl Zeiss Jena GmbH, pg. 1523   IT

Julich

Uranit GmbH, Stetternicher Staatsforst, pg. 1457   IT
Wisapak Mertens GmbH, Alte Durener Strasse 3,
pg. 1430   IT

Kaarst

Funsoft Holding GmbH, Bruchweg 128-132, pg. 707   IT
Mindscape International Softwarevertrieb GmbH, Dainler Strasse 10A, pg. 1027   IT
Parker Hannifin N.M.F. GmbH, Gutenbergstr. 36,
pg. 1261   PB

Kaiserslautern

ASAL Ingenieure GmbH, Barbarostrasse 30, pg. 608   IT
Ferro (Deutschland) GmbH, Postfach 1032, pg. 619   PB
Landesbank Rheinland-Pfalz, Stiftsplatz 6-7, pg. 799   IT
Niederlassung Kaiserslautern, Flickerstal 5, pg. 195   IT
G.M. PFAFF AKTIENGESELLSCHAFT, Konigstrasse 154,
pg. 1046   IT
SBV Vermogensverwaltungs-gesellschaft mbH, pg. 596   IT
Stinnes Reifendienst GmbH, Mainzer Strasse 81,
pg. 1459   IT

Kaltenkirchen

Interturbine Germany GmbH, Industriegebiet Sud,
pg. 673   IT

Kamp-Lintfort

CEM GmbH, Carl-Friedrich-Gauf-Str. 9, pg. 277   PB

Karben

Dominion Vertriebs, G.m.b.H., Max-Planck-Str. 34,
pg. 938   PB
ESAB-Hancock GmbH, Robert-Bosch-Strasse 20,
pg. 282   IT
Krupp Warmetechnik GmbH - Frankfurt, Dieselstr. 27,
pg. 515   IT

Karlsbad

Becker, Im Stockmadle 1, pg. 787   PB

Karlsfeld

MAN Technologie AG, Liebigstrasse 5a, pg. 825   IT

Karlsruhe

Analog Devices GMBH - Technisches Buero Suedwest, Hermann-Weick-Weg 3, pg. 108   PB
Badenia Bausparkasse AG, Badeniaplatz 1, pg. 15   IT
Cerberus Ristow GmbH & Co., Killisfeldstrasse 72,
pg. 1246   IT
Georg Fischer Disa GmbH, Pfinztalstrasse 90, pg. 489   IT
Franz Pohl Metall- und Kunststoffwarenfabrik GmbH,
pg. 506   IT
Graner GmbH & Co., pg. 506   IT
Handelsgesellschaft Heinrich Heine GmbH, pg. 1014   IT
Heinrich Mack Nachf., Pfizerstrasse 1, pg. 1283   PB
Helline Beteiligungs GmbH, pg. 1014   IT
Isotech G.m.b.H., pg. 983   IT
KALAG Lagerhaus-und Speditions Ges. mbH, Werftstrabe 1a, pg. 1033   IT
Kemira Papierchemikalien, Postfach 210832, pg. 728   IT
Michelin Reifenwerke KGaA, P.O. Box 210951, Bannwaldallee 60, pg. 322   IT
Neef Elektrotechnik GmbH & Co., pg. 1306   IT
Niederlassung Karlsruhe, Beiertheimer Allee 22,
pg. 195   IT
Oberrheinische Mineraloelwerke GmbH, DEA-Scholven Strasse, pg. 533   PB
Pfizer G.m.b.H., Pfizerstrasse 1, pg. 1283   PB
Pfizer Holding Und Verwaltungs G.m.b.H., Pfizerstrasse 1,
pg. 1283   PB
Pharmaco GmbH, Karlstrasse 45B, pg. 1285   PB
Pohl GmbH & Co., pg. 505   IT
RAGOLDS SUSSWAREN GMBH & CO., Tullastrasse 60,
pg. 1084   IT
Suddeutsche Wohnungsbau GmbH, Klosestr 42,
pg. 623   IT
Taylor Kosmetik G.m.b.H., Pfizerstrasse 1, pg. 1283   PB

PB - *U.S. Public Companies Volume*
PV - *U.S. Private Companies Volume*
IT - *International Public & Private Companies Volume*

1621

Tektronix GmbH-Karlsruhe, pg. 1567 **PB**
Thomson Software Products, Kleinoberfled 7, pg. 1385 **IT**
Voith-Kleinwasserkraft GmbH, pg. 1473 **IT**
Winschermann Sued GmbH, Stephanienstr. 96, pg. 1167 **IT**

Karsdorf

Karsdorfer Zement Beteiligungs GmbH, Strasse der Einheit 25, pg. 789 **IT**

Kassel

DG Bank - Kassel, Standeplatz 1-3, pg. 351 **IT**
Deutscher Strassen-Dienst GmbH, Friedrich-Ebert-Str. 160, pg. 104 **IT**
Elektrizitaets-Aktiengesellschaft Mitteldeutschland, Scheidemannplatz 1, pg. 1456 **IT**
Energie-Aktiengesellschaft Mitteldeutschland EAM, pg. 1456 **IT**
Kali und Salz Beteiligungs AG, Friedrich-Ebert Strasse 160, pg. 104 **IT**
Kali und Salz Consulting GmbH, Friedrich-Ebert-Strasse 160, pg. 104 **IT**
Kali und Salz GmbH, Friedrich-Ebert-Strasse 160, pg. 104 **IT**
Kraftwerk Kassel GmbH, Dennhauser Strasse, pg. 1456 **IT**
Landeskreditkasse zu Kassel Niederlassung der Landesbank Hessen-Thuringen Girozentrale, Staendeplatz 17, pg. 799 **IT**
Monnich GmbH & Co. KG, pg. 1305 **IT**
Niederlassung Kassel, Hollandische Strasse 143, pg. 195 **IT**
Rhenania Umschlag und Lagerei GmbH, Zweigniederlassung, pg. 1034 **IT**
TGB Technisches Gemeinschaftsburo GmbH, pg. 836 **IT**
Wintershall AG, Friedrich-Ebert-Strasse 160, pg. 104 **IT**
Wintershall Erdgas Beteiligungs GmbH, Friedrich-Ebert-Strasse 160, pg. 105 **IT**
Wintershall Gas GmbH, Friedrich-Ebert-Strasse 160, pg. 105 **IT**

Kaufbeuren

Aktienbrauerei Kaufbeuren AG, pg. 178 **IT**

Kehl

Blackhawk GmbH, Sienibenstr 15, pg. 805 **PB**
Eaton GmbH Controls Div.-Europe Marketing Center, Honselstrasse, 8, pg. 558 **PB**
I-SPED Internationale Spedition GmbH, Weststrasse 30, pg. 759 **IT**
KORF-TRANSPORT-GMBH, Weststrasse 30, pg. 758 **IT**
Panalpina Welttransport GmbH, pg. 1023 **IT**
Rhenania Transport GmbH, Zweigniederlassung, pg. 1033 **IT**
Rhenania Umschlag und Lagerei GmbH, Haffenstr. 42, pg. 1034 **IT**
Dieter Scheel GmbH, Weststrasse 30, pg. 759 **IT**

Kelheim

Camloc Fastener GmbH, Industriestrasse 6, pg. 610 **PB**
Faserwerk Kelheim GmbH, Regensburger Strasse 109, pg. 339 **IT**
I.B.T. Ideal-Befestigungs-Technik und Industriebedarf GmbH, Industiestrasse 7, pg. 1128 **IT**
Nissin Foods GmbH, Am Hohenstein 305, pg. 950 **IT**
ROTHENBERGER GROUP GMBH, Industrie Strasse 7, pg. 1128 **IT**
Rothenberger Productions GmbH, Sodener Strasse 47, pg. 1128 **IT**
Rothenberger Rohrsanierung GmbH, Industriestrasse 7, pg. 1128 **IT**
Rothenberger Umwelttechnik GmbH, Industriestrasse 7, pg. 1128 **IT**
Rothenberger Werkzeuge Maschinen GmbH, Industriestrasse 7, pg. 1128 **IT**

Kelsterbach

Circle Freight International Speditionsgesellschaft mbH, Am Suedpark 10, pg. 373 **PB**
Condor Flugdienst GmbH, Am Grunen Weg 3, pg. 407 **IT**
Lufthansa Systems GmbH, Am Weiher 24, pg. 407 **IT**
Thyssen Haniel Logistic International GmbH, Langer Kornweg 36, pg. 1388 **IT**
Ticona Polymerwerke GmbH, pg. 624 **IT**
Universal Transport GmbH, Am Weiher 6, pg. 1034 **IT**

Kempenich

Fibrolith Dammstoffe Wilms GmbH, pg. 791 **IT**

Kempten

Allgauer Brauhaus AG, pg. 178 **IT**
DACHSER GMBH & CO., Memmingerstrasse 140, pg. 356 **IT**
Dixie Union Verpackungen GmbH, Romerstrasse 12, pg. 440 **PB**
EAB Deutschland Industrie-TV Anglen GmbH, Dieselstrasse 15, pg. 1129 **IT**
4P Nicolaus Kempten GmbH, pg. 1146 **IT**
4P Verpackungsgruppe B.V., pg. 1146 **IT**

General Biscuits GmbH (GBG), Arnoldstrasse 62, pg. 381 **IT**
Liebherr-Verzahntechnik GmbH, Kaufbeurer Strasse 141, pg. 808 **IT**
Rico Gesellschaft fur Microelectronik mbH, Dieselstrasse 15, pg. 1129 **IT**
Vemie-Vetrinar-Chemie GmbH, 69 St. Hubertstr., pg. 45 **IT**

Kerpen

Ascom GCT GmbH & Co., Gottlieb-Daimler-Strasse 19, pg. 87 **IT**
KA-RI-FIX Transportband-Technik GmbH, pg. 327 **IT**
Niederlassung Systembau Kerpen, Boelckestrasse 97-101, pg. 195 **IT**
A. Schulman GmbH, Huettenstrasse 211, pg. 1441 **PB**

Kiedrich

Weingut Robert Weil K.G., Muhlberg 5, pg. 1322 **IT**

Kiefersfelden

Francesco Parisi G.m.b.H., Autobahngrenzubergang, pg. 504 **IT**

Kiel

Anschutz & Co., pg. 1523 **IT**
DG Bank - Kiel, Raiffeisenstrasse 1, pg. 351 **IT**
ESS-FOOD Handels-GmbH, Sophienblatt 100, pg. 429 **IT**
GKN Gelenkwellenwerk Kiel GmbH, Rendsburger Landstrasse 191/197, pg. 536 **IT**
Gemeinschaftskraftwerk Kiel GmbH, Hasselfelde 40, pg. 1456 **IT**
Howaldtswerke-Deutsche Werft AG, Werftstrausse 112-114, pg. 1069 **IT**
Krupp Mak Maschinenbau GmbH, Falkensteiner Str. 2, pg. 509 **IT**
Niederlassung Kiel, Am Jagersberg 2, pg. 195 **IT**
Sonnichsen & Gortz Baugesellschaft mbH, Am Jagersberg 2, pg. 195 **IT**
Stena Line, Schwedenkai 1, pg. 1300 **IT**
Volvo Penta Deutschland GmbH, Postfach 9013, pg. 1476 **IT**

Kierspe

Ernst Backhaus & Co. GmbH, Waltheimstrasse 8, pg. 1210 **IT**

Kieve

S & G Samen G.m.b.h., pg. 984 **IT**

Kindsbach

Josef Skipiol Strassenbaustoffe GmbH & Co. KG, Industriestrasse 50, pg. 633 **IT**

Kipfenberg

SGD Glashuttenwerke GmbH, Altmuehlstrasse 2, pg. 1171 **IT**
SGD Glass Inc., pg. 1171 **IT**

Kirchdorf

Liebherr-Hydraulikbagger GmbH, Liebherrstrasse 12, pg. 808 **IT**
Liebherr-Mietpartner GmbH, Liebherrstrasse 12, pg. 808 **IT**

Kirchheim

A. Ahlstrom GmbH, Heinkelsstrasse 19-21, pg. 34 **IT**
KONE Wood Central Europe, Heinkelstrasse 19-21, pg. 14 **IT**
Liebert G.m.b.H., Dieselstrasse 3, pg. 577 **PB**
Rhenania Munchener Lagerhaus-und Transport-Ges.mbH, Weissenfelder Strasse 1, pg. 1033 **IT**
Temic MBB Mikrosysteme GmbH, pg. 367 **IT**
Zeidler & Wimmel GmbH & Co., Konsul-Metzing-Str. 7-9, pg. 633 **IT**

Kirchseeon

PVB Medizintechnik GmbH, Hauptstrasse 45-47, pg. 1268 **IT**

Kirkel-Neuhausel

Praktiker Bau- und Heimwerkermarkt AG, Am Tannenwald 2, pg. 863 **IT**

Kissing

Kissing Works, Munchner Strasse 18, pg. 516 **IT**

Kitzingen

Fichtel & Sachs & Co. Verwaltungsgesellschaft OHG, pg. 835 **IT**
Sachs-Gieberei GmbH, pg. 835 **IT**

Kleinostheim

Pirelli ATG Vertriebsgesellschaft m.b.H., Bruchtannenstrasse 7, pg. 1059 **IT**
Schmitt & Weitz Baustoffwerke GmbH & Co. KG, In der Heubrach 1-3, pg. 606 **IT**
Uta Finanz und Leasing, Mainparkstrasse 24, pg. 651 **IT**

Kleve

Electric Furnace Germany, GmbH, pg. 368 **PV**
Elefanten-Schuh GmbH, pg. 505 **IT**
Fuji Magnetics GmbH, Fujistrasse 1, pg. 524 **IT**
Ipsen Industries International G.m.b.H., pg. 1149 **IT**
Jela Schuh GmbH, pg. 506 **IT**
Rhenania Umschlag und Lagerei GmbH, Zweigniederlassung Neue Werft 1-9, pg. 1034 **IT**
Zwaan und Co. Samenzucht G.m.b.H., pg. 986 **IT**

Kliedrich

CSC Ploenzke, pg. 423 **PB**

Koblenz

Baustahl Schoder GmbH (SSH), Hans Bockler Strasse 8, pg. 1459 **IT**
Fuchs & Voss GmbH Co. KG., Industriegebiet Rheinhafen, Carl-Spaeter-Str. 9, pg. 1128 **IT**
Hoogovens Aluminium Bausysteme GmbH, pg. 755 **IT**
Hoogovens Aluminium GmbH, Carl Spaeterstrasse 10, pg. 754 **IT**
Hoogovens Aluminium Profiltechnik GmbH, Werk Koblenz, Carl-Spaeterstrasse 10, pg. 755 **IT**
Hoogovens Aluminium Walzprodukte GmbH, Carl-Spaeter-Strasse, pg. 755 **IT**
Kimberly-Clark GmbH, Carl Spaeter Str., pg. 959 **PB**
Landesbank Rheinland-Pfalz, Schloss-Strasse 1, pg. 799 **IT**
Lucas Automotive GmbH, P.O. Box 720, pg. 820 **IT**
Niederlassung Koblenz, Schloss Str. 34a, pg. 195 **IT**
Scania Deutschland GmbH, Postfach 2267, pg. 687 **IT**
Schultheis Brauerei GmbH & Co., pg. 197 **IT**
Select Communications, GmbH, Koblenz, pg. 982 **PV**
G.W. Sprinkler Gmbh, Wallersheimerweg 27, pg. 1500 **IT**
Stabilus GmbH, pg. 835 **IT**
Thermos GmbH, Lohrstrasse 87 a/b, pg. 938 **IT**
Thomson-CSF Elektronik GmbH, Fritz-Ludwig Strasse 1, pg. 1385 **IT**

Konigswinter

Didier Saurebau GmbH, pg. 1464 **IT**

Konstanz

AEG Electrocom GmbH, Konstanz, Bucklestr. 1-5, pg. 1244 **IT**
BYK Gulden-Lomberg GmbH, BYK-Gulden-Str. 2, pg. 66 **IT**
Dentsply Gmbh, DeTrey Strasse 1, pg. 499 **PB**
Siemens ElectroCom GmbH, Konstanz, Germany, Bucklestr. 5, pg. 1245 **IT**
Sudkurier GmbH, Max-Strohmeyer Strasse 178-180, pg. 1478 **IT**

Konz

Kuaggarn Textil AG, 1 Roscheiderstr., pg. 46 **IT**

Korschenbroich

Babcock Sempell AG, pg. 399 **IT**

Krauzau-Stockheim

Lawson Mardon Rotopack GmbH, pg. 69 **IT**

Krefeld

Canon Deutschland GmbH, Europark Fichtenhain A10, pg. 262 **IT**
Duewag AG, Duisburger Strasse 146, pg. 1244 **IT**
Guano-Werke H GmbH, Ohlendorffstrasse 29, pg. 104 **IT**
Werner Guttges GmbH, pg. 838 **IT**
Okuma Europe GmbH, Europark, Fichtenhain A20, pg. 1001 **IT**
Primagas Dusseldorf GmbH, Luisenplatz 9, pg. 1155 **IT**
Primagas GmbH, Luisenplatz 9, pg. 1155 **IT**
Standex International GmbH, Koelner Strasse 352-354, pg. 1507 **PB**
Standex International GmbH, Mold-Tech I North (Germany), Koelner Str. 352-354, pg. 1507 **PB**
Stockhausen GmbH & Co. kg, Bakerpfad 25, pg. 1454 **IT**
Sulzer Papertec GmbH, pg. 1305 **IT**
TPS, Hafelstrasse 237, pg. 1145 **IT**

Kreuztal

Blefa GmbH, Huttenstr. 43, pg. 508 **IT**
Krupp Hoesch Stahl AG - Kreuztal, Hammerstr. 11, pg. 513 **IT**
Siebau Siegener Stahlbauten GmbH, Heesstr. 5, pg. 509 **IT**

PB - U.S. Public Companies Volume
PV - U.S. Private Companies Volume
IT - International Public & Private Companies Volume

Kriftel

Ispo GmbH, pg. 422   IT
LSG Lufthansa Service Holding AG, Am Holzweg 26, pg. 407   IT
Lufthansa CityLine GmbH, Am Holzweg 26, pg. 407   IT
Wolters Kluwer Germany, Gutenbergstrasse 8, pg. 1513   IT

Kronau

Watlow Electric Mfg. Co. GmbH, Industriegebiet Heidig, Lauchwasenstrasse 1, pg. 1153   PV

Kronberg

Braun AG, Frankfurter Strasse 145, pg. 744   PB
Nederman GmbH, Niederhochstadter Strasse 62, pg. 283   IT

Kruft

TUBAG Trass- Zement- und Steinwerke GmbH, pg. 423   IT

Kulmbach

Dressin Kosmetik-u. Pharma GmbH, pg. 1333   PB
KKW, Am Goldenenfeld 18, pg. 554   IT
Turk & Kneitz GmbH, pg. 1480   IT
Vorwerk & Co. Mobelstoffwerke GmbH. & Co. KG, E.C.-Baumann-Str. 30-33, pg. 1480   IT
WABAG Wassertechnische Anlagen GmbH & Co. KG, pg. 399   IT

Kusel

SBV Vermogensverwaltungs-gesellschaft mbH, pg. 596   IT

Kvistgard

K. Loegager A/S, Hejreskovvej 10, pg. 859   IT
Martin Merkel Danmark A/S, Hejreskovvej 10, pg. 859   IT

Laatzen

Hesscon GmbH Walzlager und Industriebedarf, pg. 506   IT

Ladenburg

BK Ladenburg GmbH, Postfach 1180, pg. 626   IT
Benckiser Deutschland GmbH, pg. 185   IT
Benckiser Produktions GmbH, pg. 185   IT
Laporte ESD-Germany, Dr-Albert-Reimann-Strasse, pg. 803   IT
Propack Produkte fur Haushalt und Korperpflege GmbH, pg. 185   IT
Rhenania Transport GmbH, Zweigniederlassung Boveristras, pg. 1033   IT

Lagenfeld

VITS Maschinenbau GmbH, pg. 399   IT

Lahnstein

Erta Plastics GmbH, Koblenzer Strasse 25, pg. 354   IT

Lahr

Badische Tabakmanufaktur Roth-Handle GmbH, Industriehof 6, pg. 1101   IT
BERGER LAHR GmbH, Breslauer Strasse 7, pg. 1156   IT
SIG Positec, Breslauer Strasse 7, pg. 1156   IT

Lainz-Hechtsheim

BOD Datensystemem GmbH, Galileo Galiei Str. 14, pg. 317   IT

Lambrecht

Perstorp Components, Hauptstrasse 117, pg. 1040   IT
Perstorp Components Werk Lambrecht, Hauptstrasse 117, pg. 1040   IT

Lampertheim

Briggs & Stratton Germany, P.O. Box 1520, pg. 252   PB
CIBA Additive GmbH, Chemiestrasse, pg. 975   IT
CIBA-GEIGY Marienberg GmbH, Werk Lampertheim, pg. 977   IT
Polyflex Division, An der Tuchbleiche 4, pg. 1264   PB

Landau in der Pfalz

Pechiney Aluminium Presswerk GmbH, Industriegebiet Ost, Landkommissarstrasse 55, pg. 1031   IT

Landscheid

Schneider & Klein Metallwaren GmbH & Co. KG, pg. 423   IT

Landshut

Roederstein GmbH, Postfach 588, pg. 1722   PB

Langelsheim

MSW-Chemie GmbH, Seesener Strasse 19, pg. 104   IT

Langen

AMP Deutschland GmbH, Amperestrasse 7-11, pg. 8   PB
Alpha Therapeutic GmbH, Siemensstrasse 18, pg. 558   IT
BVZ GmbH, pg. 757   IT
Borland EMM, Robert-Bosch Strasse 11, pg. 246   PB
Dell Computer Gmbh, Monzastrasse 4, pg. 496   PB
Devilbiss Health Care (Europe) GmbH, Raiffeisenstrasse 10, pg. 1536   PB
NMB Minebea GmbH, pg. 868   IT
Nikon Precision Europe GmbH, Paul-Ehrlich Strasse 3-5, pg. 931   IT
Nipson Printing Systems GmbH, Robert Bosch Strasse 52, pg. 316   IT
Pittler Benevolent Fund GmbH, pg. 1128   IT
Pittler GmbH, pg. 1128   IT
Pittler Invention GmbH, pg. 1128   IT
Pittler Maschinenfabrik AG, Pittlerstrasse 6, pg. 1128   IT
Pittler Training GmbH, pg. 1128   IT
Spectris Messtechnik GmbH, Heinrich-Hertz Strasse 26, pg. 14   IT
Thomainfor, Otto Hahn Strasse 1-3, pg. 1385   IT
Zenith Data Systems GmbH, Robert Bosch Str. 52, pg. 317   IT

Langenfeld

CCI Crane Corporation International Handelsges. mbH, Helmholtzstr. 10-12, pg. 510   IT
Getinge GmbH, Bahnhofstrasse 43, pg. 551   IT
Mannesmann Edelstahlrohr GmbH, pg. 835   IT

Langenhagen

AMD GmbH, Marktplatz 3, pg. 21   PB
Hapag-Lloyd Fluggesellschaft GmbH, pg. 596   IT
ITT Flygt GmbH, Bayernstrasse 11, pg. 860   PB
MTU Maintenance GmbH, pg. 367   IT
Phonogram GmbH, In Den Kolkwiesen 44-48, pg. 1052   IT
PolyGram Record Service GmbH, Klusriede 26, pg. 1053   IT
Rekam Engineering GmbH, pg. 302   IT
Weatherford Oil Tool GmbH, Hainhauser Weg 150, pg. 1750   PB

Langweid

Ernst Michalke GmbH, pg. 624   IT
Pfersee Chemie GmbH, Rehlinger Str. 1, pg. 983   IT

Laubach

Dexion GmbH, Dexionstrasse 1-5, pg. 893   PB

Lauchheim

Sumitomo Electric Hartmetallifabrik GmbH, Industrie Strasse 2, pg. 1314   IT

Lauda

Walter Herzog G.m.b.H., pg. 1711   PB

Laudenbach

Freudenberg Anlagen-und Werkzeugtechnik KG, pg. 505   IT

Laupheim

ASSCO Gerustsysteme GmbH & Co. KG, pg. 1061   IT

Lautertal

CIBA Additive GmbH, Nibelungenstrasse 440, pg. 975   IT

Leck

Clausen & Bosse GmbH, Birkstrasse 10, pg. 1478   IT

Leer

Evert Heere GmbH & Co., Sagermuhlenstr. 102, pg. 513   IT

Lehrte

Chemische Fabrik Lehrte Dr. Andreas Kossel GmbH, Kothenwaldstrasse 2-6, pg. 1458   IT

Leimen

Heidelberger Baustofftechnik GmbH, Peter-Schuhmacher-Strasse 8, pg. 605   IT
Vulkan Verwaltungs-und Beteiligungsgesellschaft mbH, Peter-Schuhmacher-Str. 8, pg. 606   IT

Leingarten

KWG Kunststoffwerk Gessmann GmbH & Co., Dieselstrasse 27, pg. 355   IT

Leipzig

BHF-Bank, Kathe-Kollwitz-Str. 52, pg. 119   IT
Balcke-Durr Kuhlturmbau Leipzig GmbH, Ernst-Keil-Strasse 2, pg. 400   IT
Bilfinger + Berger Baustoffe GmbH, Reclamstrasse 52, pg. 195   IT
Caterpillar Leasing GmbH (Leipzig), Breuhl 76, pg. 315   PB
DG Bank - Leipzig, Markt 8, pg. 351   IT
Deutsche Bank-Kreditbank AG (Leipzig), Martin-Luther-Ring 2, pg. 402   IT
Die Betonknacker, Leipzig, Comeniusstr.13-15, pg. 1128   IT
Georg Fischer GmbH, Gerhardt-Ellrodt-Strasse 21, pg. 488   IT
GFW Gesellschaft zur Forderung von Wohneigentum mbH, pg. 310   IT
Geschaftsstelle Leipzig, Stohrerstrasse 17, pg. 739   IT
Hartmann & Braun Leipzig GmbH, pg. 835   IT
Hewlett-Packard GmbH, Nicolaistrasse 26, pg. 820   PB
Jauch & Huebener, Georg-Schumann-Strasse 79-81, pg. 118   PB
Krupp Hoesch Stahl AG - Leipzig, Arthur-Hoffman-Str. 120, pg. 512   IT
Leipzig Branch, Kathe-Kollwitz-Strasse 84, pg. 645   IT
MAN TAKRAF Fordertechnik GmbH, Theklaer Strasse 42, pg. 824   IT
Madler Passage Leipzig Grundstuck GmbH & Co KG, pg. 310   IT
Modern-Bau GmbH Leipzig, Erich-Zeigner-Allee 69-73, pg. 195   IT
Niederlassung Leipzig, Erich-Zeigner-Allee 69-73, pg. 195   IT
Pittler-Tornos GmbH, pg. 1128   IT
Schindler Aufzuge GmbH, pg. 1205   IT

Lemfoerde

Elastogran GmbH, Landwehrweg 9, pg. 104   IT

Lengerich

K-Tron Germany-Hasler Division, Munsterstrasse 69, pg. 938   PB
WINDMOELLER & HOELSCHER, Muensterstr. 50, pg. 1510   IT
Windmoeller & Hoelscher, pg. 1341   PB

Lenzkirch

Kadabell GmbH & Co. KG, Ludwig-Kegel-Strasse 15, pg. 1489   IT

Leonberg

Andrae Leonberg GmbH, Neve Ramtelstrasse 48, pg. 7   IT
Geschaftsstelle Stuttgart, Steinbeisstr. 4, pg. 739   IT
Leonberger Bausparkasse AG, Lindenstr. 21, pg. 310   IT
Leonberger Immobilien GmbH, pg. 310   IT
MotoMeter AG, Daimlerstrasse 6, pg. 204   IT
Pacific Scientific, GmbH, MollenbachStrasse 14, pg. 1250   PB
Wundrich-Meissen GmbH, Leonberger St. 99-101, pg. 1072   IT

Leuna

Hartmann & Braun Montage GmbH, pg. 835   IT

Leverkusen

Agfa AG, Kaiser-Wilhelm-Allee, pg. 172   IT
Agfa-Gevaert AG, Bayerwerk, pg. 174   IT
Babcock Industrierohrleitungsbau GmbH, pg. 399   IT
BAYER AG, pg. 171   IT
Bayer AG, pg. 172   IT
Bayer-Kaufhaus GmbH, pg. 172   IT
Bayer-Wohnungen GmbH, pg. 172   IT
EBE Edelstahl-Bauelemente GmbH, Friedrichstr. 3, pg. 508   IT
Hansa Beteiligungsgesellschaft mbH, pg. 172   IT
Kloeckner Ionon GmbH, Stauffenbergstrasse 14-20, pg. 737   IT
Kronos Chemie GmbH, Postfach 100720, pg. 271   PV
Kronos International, Inc., Postfach 100720, pg. 271   PV
Kronos Titan GmbH, Postfach 100720, pg. 271   PV
Krupp Stahl Kaltform GmbH, Friedrichstr. 3, pg. 508   IT
Land Infrarot GmbH, Daimlerstrasse 6, pg. 798   IT
Mazda Motors (Deutschland) GmbH, Weidenstrasse 2, pg. 849   IT
NL Industries Deutschland, GmbH, Postfach 100720, pg. 271   PV
Pallas Versicherung AG, pg. 172   IT
Raybestos Reibtechnik, pg. 1364   PB
SMS Schloemann GmbH, Josefstrasse 10, pg. 826   IT

Lichtenau

Widia Heinlein GmbH, An der Bruck 4, pg. 510   IT

PB - *U.S. Public Companies Volume*
PV - *U.S. Private Companies Volume*
IT - *International Public & Private Companies Volume*

Lichtenstein

Baumann GmbH, Friedrich-List-Str. 131, pg. 171   IT

Liederbach

Advanced Logic Research (Deutschland) GmbH, Hochsterstrabe 94, pg. 704   PB

Lilienthal

Gould Instrument Systems GmbH, Gutenbergstrasse 19, pg. 1592   PB

Limburg

BASF Aktiengesellschaft Unternehmensbereich Duengemittel, Carl-Bosch-Strasse 64, pg. 104   IT
BASF Aktiengesellschaft Unternehmensbereich Pflanzenschutz, Carl-Bosch-Strasse 64, pg. 104   IT
Eurotherm Messdatentechnik GmbH, Ottostrasse 1, pg. 466   IT
Eurotherm Regler GmbH, Ottostrasste 1, pg. 466   IT
Ridge Tool GmbH, Ottostrasse 20-22, pg. 577   PB
Scheid Strassenbaugesellschaft mbH, Grossbachstr. 4, pg. 633   IT

Lindau

Sulzer-Escher Wyss GmbH, Kemptener Str. 11-15, pg. 1307   IT

Linden

Arjo Wiggins Chemie GmbH, Im Boden 4, pg. 568   IT

Lindenberg im Allgau

Liebherr-Aerospace Lindenberg GmbH, Pfanderstrasse 50-52, pg. 808   IT

Lingen

Demag Schrader GmbH, pg. 837   IT
Preussag Energie GmbH, Waldstrasse 39, pg. 1069   IT
Svedala Strassenfertiger, pg. 1326   IT

Linnich

PKL VERPACKUNGSSYSTEME GMBH, pg. 1020   IT
PKL Verpackungssysteme GmbH, Rurstrasse 58, pg. 1156   IT

Lintorf

Frigoscandia Food Process Systems GmbH, Postfach 4114, pg. 606   PB

Lippstadt

Hoesch Rothe Erde GmbH, Lippstadt Works, Beckumer Str. 87, pg. 509   IT

Loffingen

Cleveland Precision Systems GmbH, P.O. Box 27, pg. 482   PB

Lohfelden

Wilfried Simon GmbH, pg. 838   IT

Lohmar

ABS Pump Center AG, Scheiderhohe Strasse 30-38, pg. 270   IT
ABS Pumpen GmbH, Scheiderhohe Strasse 30-38, pg. 270   IT
GKN Automotive International GmbH, Hauptstrasse 150, pg. 535   IT
GKN Walterscheid GmbH, Hauptstrasse 150, pg. 535   IT

Lohnberg

Molto GmbH, Industriestrasse 1, pg. 1501   IT

Lohne

ICI Pretechnik GGS Fuer Polyurethane-Rohstoffe MBH, Postweg 11, pg. 665   IT
Nordklima Luft-und Warmetechnik GmbH, Industriering 3, pg. 1222   IT
PAXAR Deutschland GmbH, Gewerbestrasse, 21-23, pg. 1266   PB
Stalo Chemicals GmbH, Gewerbering 25, pg. 610   IT

Lohra

Indramat GmbH, pg. 838   IT
Mannesmann Rexroth GmbH, Jahnstrasse 3-5, pg. 838   IT
Mannesmann Rexroth Grundbesitz GmbH, pg. 838   IT
Mannesmann Verwaltung GmbH, pg. 838   IT

Lommatzsch

Knurr-Lommatec GmbH & Co. KG, Raubaer Str. 1, pg. 739   IT

Lorch

Floordress Reinigungsgerate GmbH, Lorcher Strasse 30, pg. 609   IT

Lorrach

CIBA-GEIGY Versicherungsvermittlung GhbH, Luisenstrasse 1, pg. 980   IT
Sandoz Deutschland G.m.b.h., pg. 984   IT
Sandoz Verwaltungs G.m.b.H., pg. 985   IT

Loxstedt

Neynaber Chemie GmbH, Postfach 11 20, pg. 610   IT

Lubben

Stahlhochbau Lubben GmbH, Briesener Zergoweg, pg. 423   IT

Lubeck

APV Gaulin GmbH, Meklenburger Str. 223, pg. 1241   IT
Coherent Lubeck, Seelandstrasse 9, pg. 396   PB
Dataschalt Gesellschaft fur Industrielle Daten-Mess-Und Antriebstechnik mGH, Ander Hulshorst 7-9, pg. 473   IT
Deutsche Bank Lubeck AG, Kohlmarkt 7-15, pg. 402   IT
Enso Nord Transportgesellschaft mbH, Karlstr. 14, pg. 457   IT
Enso Papier Format GmbH, Leinweberstrasse 8, pg. 458   IT
Flexschlauch Produktions GmbH, Reepschlagerstrasse 10B, pg. 1268   IT
GrandMet Foods GmbH, Geniner Strasse 88-100, pg. 409   IT
Chr. Hansen G.m.b.H., Fackenburger Allee 67/69, pg. 289   IT
Krupp Fordertechnik GmbH, Einsiedelstr. 6, pg. 511   IT
Pillsbury GmbH, Geniner Strasse 88-100, pg. 411   IT
L. POSSEHL & CO. MBH, pg. 1063   IT
S & G Implants GmbH, Grapengiesser Strasse 34, pg. 255   PB
F.L. Smidth & Co. GmbH, Geniner Strasse 133-135, pg. 475   IT

Ludenscheid

Alcan Aluminium Folienwerk Verwaltungs GmbH, Wiesenstrasse 24-30, pg. 50   IT
Alcan Aluminiumfolienwerk GmbH & Co., Postfach 1190, pg. 50   IT
Busch-Jaeger Elektro GmbH, P.O. Box 1280, pg. 2   IT
Busch-Jaeger Ludenscheider Metallwerk GmbH, Altenaer Strasse 109, pg. 1427   IT
EOC Normalien GmbH & Co. KG, Hueckstrasse 16, pg. 75   IT
EOC Normalien und Verwaltungsgesellschaft mbH, Hueckstrasse 16, pg. 75   IT
PVD Beschichtungsservice GmbH, Hueckstrasse 17, pg. 75   IT

Ludwigsburg

AST Research Deutschland GmbH, Monreposstrasse 57, pg. 1182   IT
Bausparkasse Gemeinschaft der Freunde Wuestenrot gem.GnbH, Hohenzollernstr. 46, pg. 1514   IT
FILTERWERK MANN & HUMMEL GMBH, Hindenburgstrasse 45, pg. 484   IT
Gesellschaft fuer Markt- und Absatzforschung mbH, Hohenzollernstr. 12-14, pg. 1514   IT
Hausbau Wuestenrot GmbH, Hohenzollernstr. 12/14, pg. 1514   IT
HERMANN PFAUTER GMBH & CO., PO Box 820, Schwieberdinger Str. 87, pg. 617   IT
Mann & Hummel Hydromation GmbH, Gronerstrasse 44-50, pg. 484   IT
Porsche Classic GmbH, pg. 1063   IT
STAHL GMBH & CO., Austrasse 50, pg. 1293   IT
Tecnocar GmbH, Philip Reis Strasse 6, pg. 786   IT
Telma Retarder Deutschland GmbH, 23 Neckargroninger Strasse, pg. 786   IT
TINO Lebensmittel GmbH, pg. 922   IT
Unifranck Lebensmittelwerke GmbH, pg. 922   IT
VW AUDI Vertriebszentrum Sud-West GmbH & Co. KG, pg. 1474   IT
Wuestenrot Bank AG, Im Tambour 1, pg. 1514   IT
Wuestenrot Grundstuecksverwertungs-GmbH, Hohenzollernstr. 46, pg. 1514   IT
WUESTENROT HOLDING GMBH, Wuestenrot-Haus, Hohenzollernstrasse 46, pg. 1514   IT
Wuestenrot Immobilien GmbH, Im Tambour 3, pg. 1514   IT
Wuestenrot Lebensversicherungs-AG, Im Tambour 2, pg. 1514   IT
Wuestenrot Staedtebau- und Entwicklungsgesellschaft mbH, Hohenzollernstr. 12/14, pg. 1514   IT
Wustenrot Hypothekenbank Aktiengesellschaft, Im Tambour 5, pg. 1514   IT

Ludwigsfelde

MTU Motoren-und Turbinen-Union Ludwigsfelde GmbH, pg. 367   IT

Ludwigshafen

Alcoa Chemie GmbH, Guilini-Strasse 2, pg. 61   PB
Amsler Otto Wolpert Werke GmbH, Industriestrasse 19, pg. 883   PB
BASF AG, Carl-Bosch Strasse 38, pg. 103   IT
BASF Aktiengesellschaft, Carl-Bosch Strasse 38, pg. 104   IT
BASF Aktiengesellschaft Laenderbereich Vertrieb Deutschland, Benckiserplatz 1, pg. 104   IT
BASF Computer Services GmbH, Carl-Bosch-Strasse 38, Bau J 560, pg. 104   IT
JOH. A. BENCKISER GMBH, Ludwig-Bertram Strasse 8+10, pg. 185   IT
Die Betonknacker, Gartenstr.19, pg. 1128   IT
EMTEC Magnetics GmbH, Unterenhmensbereich, Informationssysteme, pg. 743   IT
Grunzweig & Hartmann und Glasfaser AG, Buergermeister-Grunzweig-Strasse 1, pg. 1176   IT
Knoll AG, Knollstrasse, pg. 104   IT
Knoll Deutschland GmbH, Rathausplatz 10-12, pg. 104   IT
Panalpina Immobilien Verwaltungs GmbH, pg. 1023   IT
Panalpina Welttransport GmbH, Hafenstr, 19, pg. 1023   IT
RUG-Rheinische Umschlag-Gesellschaft mbH, Lagerhausstrasse 32, pg. 1033   IT
Raschig GmbH, Mundenheimer Str. 100, pg. 827   PV
TBL Transportboten Ludwigshafen GmbH & Co. KG, pg. 423   IT
TV Kohlensaure Technik, pg. 811   IT
Ultrasorb Chemikalien GmbH, Carl-Bosch-Strasse 38, pg. 104   IT
Van Leeuwen Rohren GmbH, INdustriestrasse 47, pg. 1450   IT

Luisenthal

Mannesmann Demag Fordertechnik Kranbau Luisenthal GmbH, pg. 837   IT

Luneburg

H.B. Fuller Europe, Bei der Strasse Lambertikirche 8, pg. 687   PB
H.B. Fuller GmbH, An der Roten Bleiche 2-3, pg. 687   PB
Funai Electric (Europe) GmbH, Zeppelinstrasse 22, pg. 530   IT
Konica Business Machines Europe GmbH, Lilienthalstrasse 1, pg. 749   IT
Nordson Engineering GmbH, Lilienthalstrasse 6, pg. 1189   PB

Lunen

Innovatherm Gesellschaft zur innovativen Nutzung von Brennstoffen mbH, pg. 597   IT

Lunzenau

Metzeler Automotive Profiles GmbH, Bregenzerstrasse 133, pg. 130   IT

Lutherstadt

SKW Bauwerkstoffe Piesteritz GmbH, Coswiger Landstrasse 26, pg. 1465   IT
SKW Stickstoffwerke Piesteritz GmbH, Mollensdorfer Str. 13, pg. 1464   IT

Magdeburg

DG Bank - Magdeburg, Hegelstrasse 17, pg. 351   IT
Deutsche Bank-Kreditbank AG (Magdeburg), Domstrasse 1, pg. 402   IT
Dyckerhoff Transportbeton Elbe GmbH, pg. 422   IT
EVM AG, Editharing 40, pg. 1456   IT
Energiewerke Magdeburg AG, Editharing 40, pg. 1456   IT
Henkel Hartol GmbH, pg. 610   IT
Magdeburger Armaturenwerke MAW AG, pg. 400   IT
Niederlassung Magdeburg, Harnackstrasse 5, pg. 195   IT
NORD/LB Mitteldeutsche Landesbank, Breiter Weg 193, pg. 958   IT
Orga-Soft Organisation & Software GmbH, Schwiesaustr. 4, pg. 317   IT
Stinnes Stahlhandel GmbH (SSH), Saalestrasse 35, pg. 1459   IT
TESTRABAU GmbH Baugesellschaft, pg. 1148   IT

Mahlberg

EOC Formsystem GmbH, Industriestrasse 21, pg. 75   IT

Mainburg

Korf Transport GmbH, Gutenbergstrasse 10, pg. 759   IT
Sand- und Kieswerk Steinbach GmbH & Co. KG, Wolnzacher Strasse 40, pg. 1091   IT
Wolf Klimatechnik GmbH, Industriestrasse 1, pg. 1070   IT

Mainhausen

Geschaftsstelle Frankfurt, Jahnstrasse 27-29, pg. 739   IT

PB - U.S. Public Companies Volume
PV - U.S. Private Companies Volume
IT - International Public & Private Companies Volume

1624

Geographic Index-Non U.S.

Maintal

KS Klima-Service GmbH, pg. 617 — IT
Scholl Deutchland GmbH, Edisonstrasse 5, pg. 1209 — IT

Mainz

BHF-Bank, Schillerplatz 2, pg. 119 — IT
Cross (Deutschland) GmbH, Postfach 1220, pg. 461 — PB
Deutsche Bank AG (Mainz), Ludwigstrasse 8-10, pg. 402 — IT
EG & G GmbH Sealol, Gewerbepark Am Hemel, An Der Fahrt 13, pg. 544 — PB
Elsevier Thomas Fachverlag GmbH, Max-Hufschmidtstrasse 1, pg. 1100 — IT
ELSTER AG Mess- und Regeltechnik, Steinerstrasse 19-21, pg. 1148 — IT
ELSTER-HANDEL G.m.b.H. Mess- und Regeltechnik, Steinerstrasse 19-21, pg. 1148 — IT
ELSTER Produktion GmbH, Steinerstrasse 19-21, pg. 1148 — IT
GETAC Instrumentenbau GmbH, AM Obstmarkt 32, pg. 1111 — IT
Heller Bank A.G., pg. 521 — IT
LANDESBANK RHEINLAND-PFALZ, Grosse Bleiche 54-56, pg. 799 — IT
LIB Industrie Beteiligung GmbH, pg. 1523 — IT
Niederlassung Mainz, Heligkreuzweg 88, pg. 195 — IT
NOSCO GVG mbH & Co. Objekt Alzey KG, pg. 309 — IT
Novo Nordisk Biotechnologie GmbH, Gonsenheimer Strasse 56a, pg. 989 — IT
Novo Nordisk Pharma GmbH, Brucknerstrasse 1, pg. 988 — IT
Orga-Soft Organisation & Software GmbH, Carl von Linde Str. 12, pg. 317 — IT
Parker Bertea Aerospace, Lorenz-Schott - Strasse 9, pg. 1262 — PB
Procter & Gamble Health & Beauty Care Germany, Rheinallee 88, pg. 1332 — PB
Resart GmbH, Gassnerallee 40, pg. 104 — IT
Rhenania Transport GmbH, Zweigniederlassung, pg. 1033 — IT
Schott Glaswerke, Hattenbergstr. 10, pg. 1523 — IT
Schott-Zeiss Assekurantzkontor GmbH, pg. 1523 — IT
Syseca GmbH, Leittechnik, Peter Sander Strasse 41.a, pg. 1384 — IT
Targor GmbH, pg. 105 — IT
Westdeutsche ImmobilienBank, Wilhelm-Theodor-Romheld-Strasse 24, pg. 799 — IT

Maisach

Bax Burosysteme Vertriebsgesellschaft mbH, pg. 757 — IT
Rossignol Ski Deutschland GmbH, Frauenstrasse 26 28, pg. 1127 — IT
Sopur Medizintechnik GmbH, pg. 1536 — PB

Mannheim

ABB Isoprofil GmbH Stahlprofil-und Warmwalzwerk, P.O. 204, pg. 2 — IT
ABB Kabel und Draht GmbH, P.O. Box 1265, pg. 2 — IT
Achatz GmbH Bauunternehmung, Bergiusstrasse 19-21, pg. 195 — IT
Ascur Mannheim Versicherungsvermittlungsges. GmbH, Sandhofer Strasse 116, pg. 331 — IT
Asea Brown Boveri Aktiengesellschaft, P.O. Box 351, pg. 2 — IT
BGD Bodengesundheitsdienst GmbH, pg. 1305 — IT
BM Mannheim Beteiligungen GmbH, Sandhofer Strasse 116, pg. 331 — IT
bebit Informations-technik GmbH, Carl-Reiss-Platz 1-5, pg. 195 — IT
BILFINGER + BERGER BAUAKTIENGESELLSCHAFT, Carl-Reiss-Platz 1-5, pg. 194 — IT
Bilfinger + Berger Projektentwicklung GmbH, Carl-Reiss-Platz 3, pg. 195 — IT
Bilfinger + Berger Umweltverfahrenstechnik GmbH, Theodor-Heuss-Anlage 12, pg. 195 — IT
Boehringer Mannheim GmbH, Sandhofer Strasse 116, pg. 331 — IT
Braas Flachdachsysteme GmbH, Eisenbahnstrasse 6-8, pg. 1091 — IT
Brooks Instrument (Germany), Saarburger Ring 12, Friedrichfeid, pg. 576 — PB
Carl Fr. Cappel, Industriestrasse 2/L, pg. 104 — IT
Century Oils (Deutschland) GmbH, pg. 517 — IT
Clinicon Mannheim GmbH, Sandhofer Strasse 176, pg. 331 — IT
COMPAREX Informationssysteme GmbH, Gottlieb-Daimler-Strasse 10, pg. 105 — IT
Consulab Mannheim GmbH fur Laborberatung, Sandhofer Strasse 176, pg. 331 — IT
John Deere-Lanz Verwaltungs A.G., Steubenstrasse 36-42, pg. 493 — PB
Deutsche Bank AG (Mannheim), P-7, 10-15, pg. 402 — IT
Fuchs Finanzservice Gmbh, Friesenheimer Strasse 17, pg. 517 — IT
Fuchs Interlub Gmbh, Friesenheimer Strasse 15, pg. 517 — IT
Fuchs Interoil Gmbh, Friesenheimer Strasse 17, pg. 517 — IT
Fuchs Mineraloelwerke GmbH, Friesenheimer Str. 15, pg. 517 — IT
FUCHS PETROLUB AG OEL + CHEMIE, Friesenheimer Strasse 17, pg. 517 — IT
Fuchs Petrolub AG OEL & Chemie, Friesenheimer Str. 17, pg. 517 — IT

Galenus Chemicals GmbH, Sandhofer Strasse 176, pg. 331 — IT
Galenus Mannheim GmbH, Sandhofer Str. 176, pg. 331 — IT
Hestia-Pharma GmbH, Oppauer Strasse 130, pg. 331 — IT
Hewlett-Packard GmbH, Rosslauer Weg 2-4, pg. 820 — PB
Ista GmbH, Friedrich Koenig Strasse 3-5, pg. 1457 — IT
Kodak AG-Mannheim, Augusta-Anlage 59, pg. 552 — PB
Labora Mannheim GmbH fur Labortechnik, Sandhofer Strasse 116, pg. 331 — IT
Motoren-Werke Mannheim AG, Carl-Benz Str. 5, pg. 408 — IT
Niederlassung Mannheim, Theodor-Heuss-Anlagelz, pg. 195 — IT
Niederlassung Spezialtiefbau Mannheim, Harpener Strasse 1-3, pg. 195 — IT
OMRON Medizintechnik Handelsgesellschaft mbH, Rheinkaistrasse 30, pg. 1006 — IT
Palatinit Sussungsmittel GmbH, pg. 1305 — IT
Praemix Wirkstoff GmbH, Sandhofer Strasse 116, pg. 331 — IT
Propria Bautrager und Verwaltungsgesellschaft mbH, Carl-Reiss-Platz 3, pg. 195 — IT
Rhein-Chemie Rheinau GmbH, pg. 174 — IT
Rhenania Container GmbH, Zweigniederlassung, pg. 1033 — IT
Rhenania Schiffahrts-und Speditions-Gesellschaft mbH, Antwerpenelstrasse 24, pg. 1033 — IT
Rhenania Transport GmbH, B 6, 26 Postfach 19 80, pg. 1033 — IT
Rhenania Transport GmbH, Zweigniederlassung Rheinst, pg. 1033 — IT
Rhenania Umschlag und Lagerei GmbH, Zweigniederlassung, pg. 1034 — IT
Seitz Enzinger Noll, Maschinenbau Aktiengesellscraft, pg. 737 — IT
Stinnes Montanhandel GmbH & Co. KG, N 3, 12, pg. 1459 — IT
Suddeutsche Brennstoffhandelsgesellschaft mbH, Werderstrasse 31, pg. 1167 — IT
SudImmobilien Fonds, P.O. Box 10 03 52, pg. 1304 — IT
SudImmobilien GmbH, P.O. Box 10 03 52, pg. 1304 — IT
SudwestLB, P.O. Box 10 03 52, pg. 1304 — IT
SUDZUCKER AG MANNHEIM/OCHSENFURT, Maximilianstrasse 10, pg. 1305 — IT
Thomcast GmbH, Ohmweg 11-15, pg. 1385 — IT
Weyl GmbH, Sandhofer Strasse 96, pg. 1148 — IT

Marburg

Behringwerke AG, Postfach 1140, pg. 624 — IT
Deutsche Fernsprecher GmbH (DFG), Frauenbergstrasse 35, pg. 795 — IT
Edwards Hochvakuum GmbH, Postfach 1409, pg. 122 — IT

Marienheide

Berges Electronic, Gmbh, IndustriestrBe 13, pg. 1562 — PB
PFERD/AUGUST RUEGGEBERG, Hauptstrasse 13, pg. 1046 — IT
Square D Company (Deutschland) GmbH, Eichendorffstrasse, pg. 1209 — IT

Markdorf

Eaton GmbH Fluid Power Operations, Bruhlstrasse 14, pg. 558 — PB

Markkleeberg

WABAG Leipzig GmbH Wassertechnische Anlagen, Hauptstrasse 217, pg. 399 — IT

Marklkofen

Filterwerk Mann & Hummel GmbH, Kollbacher Strasse 31, pg. 484 — IT

Markt Schwaben

BDW - Bayerisches Druckguss-Werk Thurner GmbH & Co KG, pg. 68 — IT

Marl

Aethylen Rohrleitungs Gesellschaft mbH & Co. KG, pg. 356 — IT
BWH Koutschur GmbH, Paul-Baumann-Strasse 1, pg. 1454 — IT
GAF-Huls Chemie GmbH, Paul-Baumann-Strasse 1, pg. 1454 — IT
Huls AG, Paul Baumann Strasse, pg. 1454 — IT
IKO Industriekohle GmbH & Co. KG, Schmielenfeldstrasse 78, pg. 1455 — IT
Katalysatorenwerke Huls GmbH, Paul-Baumann Strasse 1, pg. 1454 — IT
Vestischer Vermittlungsdienst fur Versicherungen GmbH, Lipper Weg, pg. 1454 — IT
VESTOLIT GmbH, Paul-Baumann Strasse 1, pg. 1454 — IT
Westgas GmbH, Paul-Baumann-Strasse 1, pg. 1455 — IT

Martinsried

Corcom GmbH, Bunsenstrassel, pg. 446 — PB

Mayence

Allgemeine Bau- und Verietungs GmbH, pg. 839 — IT

Meerane

Meeraner Dampfkeeselbau GmbH, pg. 398 — IT

Meerbusch

Bobst GmbH, pg. 199 — IT
INTEGRAL HYDRAULIK & CO., Marienburgerstrasse 28, pg. 679 — IT
Kayaba Europe GmbH, Breite Strasse 10b, pg. 727 — IT
Kyocera Electronics Europe GmbH, pg. 776 — IT

Mehren

Kaolin-Und Tonwerke Seilitz-Lothain GmbH, Nummer 11, pg. 1488 — IT

Meinerzhagen

Battenfeld GmbH, Scherl 10, pg. 825 — IT
Battenfeld Service GmbH, Scherl 10, pg. 825 — IT

Melle

Star Mobelwerk GmbH, Oldendorfer Strasse 25-33, pg. 1303 — IT
Tetra Heimtierbedarf G.m.b.H., Herrenteich 70, pg. 1739 — PB

Melsungen

Michels Melsungen Haustechnik GmbH, Schwarzeuberger weg. 23, pg. 1149 — IT

Memmingen

ASF Thomas, Luitpoldstrasse 28, pg. 1599 — PB
Rohde & Schwarz Messgeraetebau GmbH, Riedbachstr. 58, pg. 1124 — IT

Menden

KME Schmole GmbH, Honnenwerth 13, pg. 719 — IT

Mendig

Continental PET Deutschland GmbH, pg. 1206 — IT

Meppen

DSM Kunstharze GmbH, Am Kreisforst 1, pg. 355 — IT

Merzdorf

Dyckerhoff Transportbeton Lausitz GmbH & Co. KG, pg. 422 — IT

Mettlach

Lands' End GmbH, In Der Langwiese, pg. 978 — PB
VILLEROY & BOCH AG, Saaruferstr., pg. 1468 — IT

Mettmann

Georg Fischer GmbH, Sudstrasse 18, pg. 488 — IT
Kleber Industrie GmbH, pg. 322 — IT
Sun Electric Deutschland, Auf Dem Huels 5, pg. 1481 — PB

Metzingen

HUGO BOSS AG, Dieselstrasse 12, pg. 637 — IT
Werner Baldessarini Design GmbH, pg. 637 — IT

Michelstadt

Cofa Cosmetik-Fabrikations GmbH, pg. 185 — IT
Howard Maschinenfabrik GmbH, Odenwald, pg. 1387 — IT
Zenker Hausbau GmbH & Co., Relystr. 20, pg. 633 — IT

Miehlen

Duroform-J. Fritz GmbH & Co KG, pg. 68 — IT

Minden

MELITTA UNTERNEHMENSGRUPPE BENTZ KG, P.O. Box 1126, pg. 856 — IT
Schoppe & Fraser GmbH, pg. 835 — IT
Strothmann Brennereien G.m.b.H., P.O. Box 3040, pg. 751 — IT
Toindustrie Heisterholz Ernst Rauch GmbH & Co. KG, pg. 1091 — IT
WAGO Kontakttechnik GmbH, pg. 209 — IT

Mittweida

Parker Hannifin GmbH, Buro Mittweida, Tzschirnerstr. 4, pg. 1261 — PB

Moers

Ferimpex GmbH, pg. 302 — IT
Svedala Flexowell Foerdersysteme, pg. 1324 — IT

Geographic Index-Non U.S.

Monchengladbach

Beton Union Monchengladbach GmbH & Co. KG, pg. 422 — IT
CC-Bank, A.G., Kaiserstrasse 74, pg. 144 — IT
Fardem Verpackungen GmbH, Stepgesstrasse 30, pg. 353 — IT
Generale Bank & Co., Bismarckstrabe 108, pg. 548 — IT
Heidemij Realisierung GmbH, Stresemanstrasse 30, pg. 608 — IT
Intech EDM GmbH, Dohrweg 23, pg. 489 — IT
Keystone G.m.b.H., Nobelstr. 14, pg. 1650 — PB
Konatec Nassbaggertechnik GmbH, Stresemannstrasse 30, pg. 608 — IT
Lorenz & Lihn Obst-Edel-Erzeugnisse GmbH, pg. 433 — IT
Nippon Express (Deutschland) GmbH, Marie-Bernays-Ring 23, pg. 934 — IT
Schiess Moweg GmbH, Postfach 2100 62, Egerstr. 73-75, pg. 860 — IT
Schneekoppe GmbH, Bottgerstr. 5, pg. 433 — IT
Sucker-Muller-Hacoba GmbH & Co., pg. 399 — IT

Monheim

Rheinische Presshefe - und Spirtwerke GmbH, Industriestrasse 2, pg. 1143 — IT
SCHWARZ PHARMA AG, Alfred Nobel Strasse 10, pg. 1211 — IT
Wilhelmstal-Werke GmbH Papiersackfabriken, pg. 759 — IT

Montabaur

Klockner-Pentaplast GmbH, pg. 737 — IT

Morbach

Raybestos Industrie-Produkte GmbH, Industriestrasse 7, pg. 1364 — PB

Morfelden

De La Rue Fortronic GmbH, Kurhessenstrasse 13, pg. 387 — IT
De La Rue Systems GmbH, Starkenburgstrasse 11-13, pg. 387 — IT
Garny AG, Starkenburgstrasse 11-13, pg. 387 — IT
Garny Sicherheitstechnik GmbH, Dreieichstrasse 12-16, pg. 387 — IT
Olicom GmbH, Hessenring 13a, pg. 1001 — IT
Seat Deutschland GmbH, pg. 1475 — IT

Mosbach

Electrolux-CR GmbH, Postfach 1206, pg. 442 — IT

Mosel

GKN Gelenkwellenwerk Mosel GmbH, Glauchauer Strasse 38, pg. 535 — IT
Sachsische Automobilbau GmbH, pg. 1473 — IT
Volkswagen Sachsen GmbH, Glauchauer Strasse, pg. 1474 — IT

Muchin-Haar-Slandorf

Augat GmbH, Buro Muchen, Johann Krgstrasse 30, pg. 1598 — PB

Mucke

Parker Fluid Verbindungstelle GmbH, Freiherr-Vom-Stein Strasse, pg. 1260 — PB

Muddersheim

Walter Patz OHG, Industriegebiet, pg. 1459 — IT

Muenchsmuenster

HEG Hopfenextraktion GmbH, P.O. Box 1113, pg. 1464 — IT

Muenster

DeTe Immobilien, Deutsche Telekom Immobilien und Service GmbH, Kaiser-Wilhelm-Ring 4-6, pg. 407 — IT

Muggensturm

Avesta Sheffield Rohr, Postfach 1164, pg. 222 — IT

Muhlacker

Bohlin Instruments Vetriebs GmbH, pg. 208 — IT
Skega GmbH, Lugwaldstr. 22, pg. 1323 — IT

Muhlhausen

Kodak AG-Muhlhausen, Werk Muhlhausen/Gruibingen, Breitwiesen, pg. 552 — PB

Muldenstein

RWM-Rohrwerke Muldenstein GmbH, Zur Luther-Linde, pg. 79 — IT

Mulheim

Bremin Mineraloel GmbH & Co., Reichsprasidentenstr. 21-25, pg. 517 — IT
BRENNTAG AG, Humboldtring 15, pg. 1458 — IT
DHC Solvent Chemie GmbH, Timmerhellstrasse 28, pg. 1461 — IT
DSM Chemicals Sales GmbH, Kaiserstrasse 86, pg. 353 — IT
Eisenmetall Rohstoff GmbH, Timmerhellstr. 7, pg. 513 — IT
Fragol Industrieschimierstoff GMBH, Reichsprasidentstrasse 21-25, pg. 517 — IT
HCM Intercoal Gmbh Import, Export, Transit, Humboldtring 15, pg. 1454 — IT
Mannesmannrohren-Werke AG, Wiesenstrasse 36, pg. 835 — IT
OCE-Deutschland GmbH, Solingerstr. 5-7, pg. 994 — IT
OCE-Deutschland Leasing GmbH, pg. 994 — IT
SCHENKER-RHENUS AG, pg. 1459 — IT
Stinnes AG, pg. 1458 — IT
Stinnes Agrar GmbH, Humboldtring 15, pg. 1458 — IT
Stinnes data Service GmbH, Humboldtring 15, pg. 1459 — IT
Stinnes Handel GmbH, pg. 1459 — IT
Stinnes Interfer GmbH, Humboldtring 15, pg. 1459 — IT
Stinnes Intertec GmbH, pg. 1460 — IT
Stinnes Organisationsberatung GmbH, Humboldtring 15, pg. 1460 — IT
Stinnes Technohandel GmbH, Humboldtring 15, pg. 1459 — IT
TENGELMANN WARENHANDELSGESELLSCHAFT, Wissollstrasse 5-43, pg. 1375 — IT
Thyssen Guss AG, pg. 1387 — IT

Mulheim an der Ruhr

Binks Deutschland GmbH, Lahnstrassee 31, pg. 229 — PB
Flexaust G.m.b.H., Weseler Strasse, 35, pg. 394 — PB
Jauch & Huebener, Luxemburger Allee 4, pg. 118 — PB
Koob & Partner/The Corporate Company, pg. 117 — IT

Mulsen Saint Jacob

Dyckerhoff Transportbeton Zwickau GmbH & Co. KG, pg. 422 — IT

Munderkingen

Neuweg Fertigung G.m.b.h., Ehinger Strasse 5, pg. 904 — IT

Munich

AES Airport Equipment & Services GmbH, pg. 836 — IT
AGIP Deutschland AG, Sonnenstr. 23, pg. 428 — IT
AMS Management Systems Europe, S.A./N.V., Bavariastrasse 7A, pg. 87 — PB
ARS Integrated Systems Gmbh, Starnberger Str. 22, pg. 886 — PB
AWG Abfallwirtschaft, Soldauer Strasse 14, pg. 1415 — IT
Abfallwirtschaft GmbH, Soldauer Strasse 14, pg. 1416 — IT
Acclaim Entertainment GmbH, Mohl Str. 10, pg. 15 — PB
Advanced Circuit Testing (ACT) GmbH, Suskindstrasse 4, pg. 25 — IT
Advantest (Europe) GmbH, Stefan-George-Ring 2, pg. 25 — IT
Agrarchemikalien Munchen GmbH., Arabellstrasse 4, pg. 356 — IT
Agrolinz Agrarchemikalien Munchen GesmbH, Arabellastr. 4, pg. 356 — IT
Ahlstrom Papiervertrieb GmbH, Brahmsstrasse 32, pg. 35 — IT
Air Malta - Munich, Maximilianplatz 9-10G, pg. 38 — IT
Akkurat Grundstucks GmbH, pg. 178 — IT
Akkurat Grundstucks GmbH & Co. Betriebs KG, pg. 178 — IT
Albrecht Knaus Verlag, Neumarkterstr.18, pg. 190 — IT
Alkor GmbH Kunststoffe, Morgansternstrasse 9, pg. 1278 — IT
Allgauer Alpenmilch A.G., Prinzregentenstrasse 155, pg. 918 — IT
ALLIANZ AKTIENGESELLSCHAFT, Koniginstrasse 28, pg. 58 — IT
Allianz Beteiligungsgesellschaft mbH, Koeniginstrasse 28, pg. 58 — IT
Allianz Versicherungs-AG, Koniginstrasse 28, pg. 58 — IT
AlliedSignal Aerospace Service Corporation, Munchener Freiheit 12, pg. 52 — PB
Alois Dallmayr Kaffee OHG, Dienerstr. 14, pg. 918 — IT
Alte Haice GmbH, pg. 836 — IT
Amdahl Deutschland GmbH, Balanstrasse 55, pg. 527 — IT
American Power Conversion, Firkenweg 1, pg. 89 — PB
Amgen GmbH, Riesstrasse 25, pg. 101 — PB
Analog Devices GmbH, Edelsbergstrasse 8-10, pg. 108 — PB
Apple Computer GmbH, Inolstaedter. 20, pg. 121 — PB
Aquila Beteiligungsgesellschaft mbH, Koeniginstrasse 28, pg. 58 — IT
Aufbaugesellschaft Bayern GmbH, pg. 178 — IT
Aupperle Aufzuge GmbH, Industriegebiet West, Dottinger Strasse 65, pg. 747 — IT
AUTARKA GmbH, Vermittlung von Versicherungen aller Art, Erdinger Landstr. 1, pg. 423 — IT

Auto-trol Technology GmbH, Joseph Dolinger-Bogen 12, pg. 148 — PB
Avnet E2000 GmbH, Stahlgruberring 12, pg. 155 — PB
BBG Betielingsgesellschaft m.b.H., Sonnenstrasse 31, pg. 89 — IT
BD Industrie Beteiligungsgesellschaft mbH, pg. 178 — IT
BFL Beteiligungsgesellschaft fur Flugzeug Leasing mbH, pg. 178 — IT
BGV Beteiligungsgesellschaft Fur Versicherungsagenturen m.b.H., Sonnenstrasse 31, pg. 89 — IT
BHF-Bank, Max-Joseph-Strasse 6, pg. 119 — IT
BHS-Bayer, Berg-, Huetten-, und Salzwerke AG, pg. 1464 — IT
BIL Burogebaude Verwaltungs GmbH, pg. 179 — IT
BIL Burogebaude Verwaltungs GmbH & Co. Leasing KG, pg. 179 — IT
BIL Burogebaude Verwaltungs GmbH & Co. Vermietungs KG, pg. 179 — IT
BIL Grundbesitzverwaltungs GmbH & Co. Lagergebaude, pg. 179 — IT
BIL Grundstucksverwaltungs GmbH, pg. 179 — IT
BIL Grundstucksverwaltungs GmbH & Co. Warenhaus KG, pg. 179 — IT
BIL Grundstucksverwaltungs GmbH & Co. Burogebaude KG, pg. 179 — IT
BIL Immobilien GmbH, pg. 179 — IT
BIL Immobilien GmbH & Co. Lagerhaus KG, pg. 179 — IT
BIL Immobilien GmbH & Co. Am Steinacker KG, pg. 179 — IT
BIL Immobilien GmbH & Co. Kellerei Am Schatzbogen KG, pg. 179 — IT
BIL Immobilien GmbH & Co. Lagerhallenvermietungs KG, pg. 179 — IT
BIL Immobilien GmbH & Co. Montagehallen Vermietungs KG, pg. 179 — IT
BIL Immobilien GmbH & Co. Speditionslagerhalle KG, pg. 179 — IT
BIL Immobilien GmbH & Co. UNI-DRUCK-KG, pg. 179 — IT
BIL Immobilien GmbH & Co. Vermietungs KG, pg. 179 — IT
BIL Immobilien GmbH & Co. Vertriebslager KG, pg. 179 — IT
BIL Immobilien GmbH & Co. Verwaltungsgebaude KG, pg. 179 — IT
BIL Immobilien GmbH & Co. Weberei-Lagerhaus KG, pg. 179 — IT
BIL Immobilien GmbH & Co. Bagrun KG, pg. 179 — IT
BIL Leasing GmbH, pg. 179 — IT
BIL Leasing GmbH & Co. Anturex KG, pg. 179 — IT
BIL Leasing GmbH & Co. ARATO KG, pg. 179 — IT
BIL Leasing GmbH & Co. ASTARI KG, pg. 179 — IT
BIL Leasing GmbH & Co. Balbex KG, pg. 179 — IT
BIL Leasing GmbH & Co. CANTARO KG, pg. 179 — IT
BIL Leasing GmbH & Co. ENTRO KG, pg. 179 — IT
BIL Leasing GmbH & Co. Gewerbegebaude KG, pg. 179 — IT
BIL Leasing GmbH & Co. Grundstucks KG, pg. 179 — IT
BIL Leasing GmbH & Co. Industriegebaude KG, pg. 179 — IT
BIL Leasing GmbH & Co. Industriehallen, pg. 179 — IT
BIL Leasing GmbH & Co. Kaufhaus KG, pg. 179 — IT
BIL Leasing GmbH & Co. Objekt Wacker Pensionskasse KG, pg. 179 — IT
BIL Leasing GmbH & Co. Textilhaus, pg. 179 — IT
BIL Leasing GmbH & Co. Verwaltungs KG, pg. 179 — IT
BIL Leasing GmbH & Co. Verwaltungsbauten KG, pg. 179 — IT
BLG Betonlieferungsgesellschaft gmbH, Zamila Strasse 9, pg. 606 — IT
BLG Betonlieferungsgesellschaft mbH Freising-Erding, Zamilastrasse 9, pg. 606 — IT
BLW Prazisionsschmiede GmbH, pg. 1387 — IT
BMW Bank GmbH, Heidemannstrasse 164, pg. 177 — IT
BMW Ingenieur Zentrum GmbH & Co., pg. 177 — IT
BMW Ingenieur Zentrum Verwaltungs GmbH, pg. 177 — IT
BMW Motorrad GmbH, Triebstr. 32, pg. 177 — IT
BMW Motorrad GmbH & Co., Trieb 32, pg. 177 — IT
BMW Motorsport GmbH, Preussenstrasse 45, pg. 177 — IT
BMW Technik GmbH, Hananer Strasse 46, pg. 177 — IT
BTU (Germany) Engineering GmbH, AM Mossfeld 27, pg. 164 — PB
BV Beteiligungs GmbH & Co. Verwaltungs KG, pg. 178 — IT
BV Beteiligungsgesellschaft mbH, pg. 178 — IT
BV Eastdil GmbH & Co. KG, pg. 178 — IT
BV Exportleasing GmbH, pg. 178 — IT
BV Financial Management GmbH, Am Tucherpark 1, pg. 178 — IT
BV Grundstuckentwicklungs GmbH, pg. 178 — IT
BV Grundstuckentwicklungs GmbH & Co., pg. 178 — IT
BV Grundstuckentwicklungs GmbH & Co. DELTA KG, pg. 178 — IT
BV Grundstuckentwicklungs GmbH & Co. ETA KG, pg. 178 — IT
BV Grundstuckentwicklungs GmbH & Co. GAMMA KG, pg. 178 — IT
BV Grundstuckentwicklungs GmbH & Co. LAMBDA KG, pg. 178 — IT
BV Grundstuckentwicklungs Gmbh & Co. OMIKRON KG, pg. 178 — IT
BV Grundstuckentwicklungs GmbH & Co. SIGMA KG, pg. 178 — IT
BV Immobilien Expertise GmbH, pg. 179 — IT
BV Immobilien GmbH, pg. 179 — IT
BV Informations Verabeitungs GmbH, pg. 179 — IT
BZV Zeitschriften Verlag GmbH & Co. KG, Arabellastrasse 23, pg. 233 — IT
Bally Deutschland GmbH, Winzererstrasse 106, pg. 997 — IT
Banca Nazionale del Lavoro, Oberanger 26, pg. 137 — IT
Bankhaus Reuschel & Co., Maximiliansplatz 13, pg. 418 — IT

PB - *U.S. Public Companies Volume*
PV - *U.S. Private Companies Volume*
IT - *International Public & Private Companies Volume*

1626

Geographic Index-Non U.S.

Barden Corporation GmbH, Georg Hallmaier Strasse 6, pg. 468   IT
Bavaria Filmkunst GmbH, pg. 179   IT
Bavaria Lloyd Reiseburo GmbH, Helene-Mayer-Ring 4, pg. 177   IT
Bavaria Wirtschaftsagentur GmbH, Helene-Mayer-Ring 4, pg. 177   IT
Bavarian Reinsurance Company Ltd., Sederanger 4-6, pg. 1333   IT
Bayerische-Bulgarische Handelsbank GmbH, Maffeistr. 3, pg. 179   IT
Bayerische Handelsbank AG, Von-der-Tann-Str. 2, pg. 179   IT
BAYERISCHE HYPOTHEKEN-UND WECHSEL-BANK AKTIENGESELLSCHAFT, Theatinerstrasse 11, pg. 175   IT
Bayerische Immobilien-Leasing GmbH, Theatinerstr. 1, pg. 179   IT
Bayerische Kapitalanlagegesellschaft mbH, Am Tucherpark 1, pg. 179   IT
BAYERISCHE LANDESBANK, Brienner Strasse 20, pg. 176   IT
Bayerische Manufactur fur Kluber Lubrication GmbH, pg. 506   IT
BAYERISCHE MOTOREN WERKE AKTIENGESELLSCHAFT, Petuelring 130, pg. 177   IT
BAYERISCHE VEREINSBANK GROUP, Kardinal-Faulhaber-Strasse 14, pg. 178   IT
Bayerische Versicherungsbank-AG, Ludwigstrasse 21, pg. 58   IT
Bayerische Wohnungsgesellschaft fur Handel und Industrie mbH, pg. 179   IT
Bayernwerk AG, Nymphenburger Str. 39, pg. 1464   IT
Bell Atlantic Mobilfunk GmbH, Briennerstrasse 28, pg. 204   PB
Berag GmbH, Schleissheimer Strasse 297, pg. 1502   IT
BIL Leasing GmbH & Co. Betriebsgebaude KG, pg. 179   IT
BIL Leasing GmbH & Co. DAKIA KG, pg. 179   IT
BIL Leasing GmbH & Co. Produktionsgebaude KG, pg. 179   IT
Bio-Rad Laboratories, GmbH, Dachauer Str. 364, pg. 230   PB
Blanvalet Verlag GmbH, Neumarkterstrasse 18, pg. 190   IT
Robert Bosch Hausgerate GmbH, Hochstr. 17, pg. 204   IT
Bosch-Siemens Hausgeraete GmbH, Hochstrasse 17, pg. 1245   IT
Bronborger & Kessler Handelsgesellschaft GmbH, Dreimibleustr. 43, pg. 428   IT
Brooktree Central Europe, Osterwald Strasse 10 Geb. 11, pg. 1398   IT
BURDA HOLDING GMBH & CO., KG, Arabellastrasse 23, pg. 233   IT
Caere GmbH, pg. 291   PB
Chiron Adatomed, Max-Planck Strasse 6, pg. 350   PB
CIBA Vision Kontaktlinsen-Pflegemittel GmbH, Schatzbogen 65, pg. 981   IT
CIBA Vision Ophthalmics GmbH, pg. 981   IT
Cinch Connectors GmbH, Aidenbachstrasse 137a, pg. 786   IT
Clarify GmbH-Germany, Weltenburger Strasse 70, pg. 382   PB
Comdisco Deutschland GmbH, Oskar-Messter-Strasse 24, pg. 408   PB
Compaq Computer GmbH, Arabella 30, pg. 418   PB
Compur-Electronic GmbH, pg. 172   IT
Computerwoche Verlag GMBH, Brabanter Strasse 4, pg. 569   PV
Cray Research GmbH, Perhamerstrasse 31, pg. 1474   PB
Creditanstalt Bankverein AG, Brienner Strasse 9, pg. 348   IT
DG Bank - Munich, Turkenstrasse 16, pg. 351   IT
DKB Finance (Munich), Prielmayerstrasse 1, pg. 361   IT
Dai-Ichi Kangyo Bank, Ltd.-Munich, P.O. Box 20 06 16, pg. 360   IT
Daimler-Aerospace AG Military Aircraft, pg. 367   IT
Daimler-Benz Aerospace AG, Postfach 801109, pg. 367   IT
Daimler-Benz Aerospace AG Dynamics, Abwer und Schutz, pg. 367   IT
Daimler-Benz Luft-und Raumfahrt Holding AG, pg. 367   IT
David, Landsburger Str. 87, pg. 787   PB
Delos Deutscher Lloyd Schulungszentrum G.m.b.H., Karlstrasse 10, pg. 89   IT
Delta Air Lines Munich, Maximillanspl. 17, pg. 497   PB
Deutsche Bank AG (Munich), Promenadeplatz 15, pg. 402   IT
Deutsche Industrie-Versicherungsstelle GmbH, Albrechtstr. 14, pg. 1464   IT
Deutscher Lloyd Lebensversicherung AG, Karlstrasse 10, pg. 89   IT
Deutscher Lloyd Versicherungs AG, Karlstrasse 10, pg. 89   IT
Digital Equipment G.m.b.H., Freischuetzstrasse 91, pg. 508   PB
Dornier Medizintechnik GmbH, pg. 368   IT
Dorsch Consult GmbH, Elsenheimerstrasse 63, pg. 1587   IT
Droemersche Verlagsanstalt Th. Knaur Nachf. GmbH & Co., Rauchstrasse 9-11, pg. 1478   IT
DYCKERHOFF & WIDMANN AG, Erdlinger Landstrasse 1, pg. 423   IT
Dyckerhoff & Widmann AG & Co. Grundstucks oHG, pg. 423   IT
EA Eisatzbetreuungs Und Auslandsdienste Gmbh, Karlstrasse 96, pg. 89   IT
EA-Generali Management-Consulting AG, Sonnenstrasse 31, pg. 89   IT
EA Rechtsschutz Versicherungs AG, Haberlstrasse 12, pg. 89   IT

EASAMS Systems Engineering GmbH, Freischutzstrasse 92, pg. 543   IT
EG & G GmbH Instruments Division, Hohenlindener Strasse 12, pg. 544   PB
EG & G Reticon, Hohenlindener Strasse 12, pg. 544   PB
Eiler & Riemel - Testa, Herzog Heinrich Str. 9, pg. 1377   IT
Elan Pharma GmbH, Freisinger Landstrasse 74, pg. 436   IT
Electro-Science Deutschland, 5, Stock, Sendlinger-Tor-Platz 8, pg. 369   PV
Electro Scientific Industries GmbH, Riesstrasse 17, pg. 569   PB
Encore Computer GmbH, Tegernseer Landstrasse 161/X OG, pg. 580   PB
EuraSpace Gesellschaft fur Raumfahrttechnik mbH, pg. 367   IT
EuroBayernwerk GmbH, Nymphenburger Str. 39, pg. 1464   IT
Eurofighter Jagdflugzeug GmbH, Arabellastrasse 16, pg. 218   IT
Eurojet Turbo GmbH, pg. 367   IT
Europ Assistance Verischerungs AG, Karlstrasse 96, pg. 89   IT
European Computer Industry Research Center GmbH, Arabellastr. 17, pg. 318   IT
Fidelio Software GmbH, Arabellastr. 17, pg. 1106   PB
Focus Magazin Verlag, Arabellastrabe 21, pg. 233   IT
Fromm, Mayer-Bass GmbH, pg. 1464   IT
Fujisawa Europe GmbH, Leveling-Strasse 12, pg. 525   IT
Fujisawa GmbH, Leveling-Strasse 12, pg. 525   IT
Fujitsu Deutschland GmBH, Rosenheimer Strasse 145, pg. 528   IT
GE Immobilienverwaltungs GmbH, pg. 178   IT
GE Immobilienverwaltungs GmbH & Co. Grundstucks KG, pg. 178   IT
GEFIL Gesellschaft fur Internationalen Laborservice mbH, pg. 174   IT
GIT Gesellschaft fur Ingeniieur-Technik mbH, pg. 836   IT
GLS Gesellschaft fur Logistischen Service mbH, Allacher Strasse 230 e, pg. 836   IT
GT Global Fondsservice Gmbh, Herzog-Wilhelm Strasse 19, pg. 809   IT
G.T. Management (Deutschland) GmbH, Herzog-Wilhelm-Strasse 19, pg. 809   IT
GTE Internetworking GmbH, Thomas-Wimmer-Ring 17, pg. 696   PB
GV Nestle GmbH fur Grossverbraucherzengnisse, Prinzregenten 155, pg. 920   IT
Generali Krankenversicherung AG, Leopoldstrasse 6, pg. 89   IT
GeoCenter Verlagsvertrieb GmbH, Neumarkter Strasse 18, pg. 190   IT
Gervais Danone AG, Heinrich Weiland Str. 170, pg. 380   IT
Gleason-Hurth, Maschinen und Werksuege, Nach F. GmbH, Moosacherstr. 36, pg. 746   IT
Wilhelm Goldmann Verlag GmbH, Neumarkter Strasse 18, pg. 190   IT
Granges Metalock GmbH, Eichenstrasse 3, pg. 442   IT
GretagMacbeth GmbH, Fraunhoferstrasse 14, pg. 966   IT
BV Grundstucksentwicklungs GmbH & Co. JOTA KG, pg. 178   IT
HAWA Grundsticks GmbH & Co. OHG Immobilienverwaltung, pg. 179   IT
HAWA Grundstuecks GmbH U. Co. OHG Hotelverwaltung, Kardinal-Faulhaber-Strasse 8 & 14, pg. 179   IT
H.F.&P. Munchen GmbH, Osterwaldstrasse 10, pg. 394   IT
HM1, HEUSER, MAYER & PARTNER DIRECT MARKETING GMBH, Bayerstr. 21, pg. 579   IT
HSBC Private Equity GmbH, Schleissheimer Strasse 4, pg. 583   IT
Hakuhodo Deutschland GmbH, Im Elisenhof, Prielmayerstr. 3, pg. 588   IT
Harris Semiconductor, Putzbrunner Strasse 69, pg. 791   PB
HATRIUM Grundstucks Beteiligungs GmbH, pg. 180   IT
HATRIUM Grundstuck GmbH & Co. KG, pg. 180   IT
Hauptniederlassung Munchen Niederlassung Munchen Niederlassung Tunnelbau Munchen, Kistlerhofstrasse 144, pg. 194   IT
Heimsoeth, Fraunhoferstr. 13, pg. 246   PB
Herkulesstraine GmbH, Erdinger Landstr. 1, pg. 423   IT
Philipp Holzmann-Held & Francke Bauaktiengesellschaft, Aschauer Str. 21, pg. 632   IT
Hosoft GmbH, pg. 465   PV
Humphrey Instruments GmbH, pg. 1523   IT
IDC Deutschland GmbH, Brabanter Strasse 4, pg. 571   PV
ISS Holding GmbH, Quagliostr. 9, pg. 657   IT
ISS Holzl GmbH Servisystem, Quagliostrasse 9, pg. 657   IT
IV Verwaltungsgesellschaft Gur Versicherungen m.b.H., Sonnenstrasse 31, pg. 89   IT
ILSE-Bayernwerk Energieanlagen GmbH, Nymphenburger Str. 39, pg. 1464   IT
AB Immobilienverwaltung GmbH, pg. 178   IT
GS Immobilienverwaltungs GmbH, pg. 178   IT
Indisco GmbH, Robert Busch 11, pg. 1286   IT
Ingenieur Beratungsgesellschaft Zur Risikound Schadensminderung m.b.H., Karlstrasse 10, pg. 89   IT
Innwerk AG, pg. 1464   IT
Intel Semiconductor GmbH, Seidl 27, pg. 887   PB
Internationales Immobilien Institut GmbH, pg. 180   IT
Isar-Seine Immobilien GmbH, pg. 180   IT
JK Lasers Deutschland GmbH, Bodenseestrasse 235, pg. 1315   IT
Jauch & Huebener, Augustenstrasse 40, pg. 118   PB
Julius Kleeman Werkzeugen Und Maschinen GmbH, Pelkovenstrasse 143, pg. 1128   IT
KHS Kunstoffmaschinen-Handels und Service GmbH, pg. 836   IT
KLA Instruments GmbH, Leonrodstrasse 58, pg. 939   PB

Ketchum Public Relations, GmbH, Schwanthalerstrasse 69, pg. 617   PV
Kindler Verlag GmbH, Rauchstrasse 9-11, pg. 1478   IT
Klinge Pharma GmbH, Berg-am-Laim-Strasse 129, pg. 525   IT
Kluber Lubrication Munchen KG, pg. 505   IT
KNORR-BREMSE AG, Moosacher Strasse 80, pg. 738   IT
Knorr-Bremse Electronic GmbH, Moosacher Strasse 80, pg. 738   IT
Knorr-Bremse Systeme Fur Nutzfahrzeuge GmbH, Moosacher Strasse 80, pg. 738   IT
Knorr-Bremse Systeme Fur Schienenfahrzeuge GmbH, Moosacher Strasse 80, pg. 738   IT
KNURR AG, Schatzbogen 29, pg. 739   IT
Knurr-Lommatec Beteiligungs-u. Verw Gmbh, Schatzbogen 29, pg. 739   IT
Kodak AG-Munich, Ingoldstadter Strasse 62, pg. 552   PB
Kraftverkehr Bayern GmbH, Bauberger Strasse 30, pg. 606   IT
Krauss-Maffei AG, Krauss Maffeistrasse 2, pg. 836   IT
Krauss-Maffei Automationstechnik GmbH, Krauss-Maffei-Str. 2, pg. 836   IT
Krauss-Maffei Dienstleistung GmbH, Krauss-Maffei Strasse 2, pg. 836   IT
Krauss-Maffei Gibtechnik GmbH, pg. 836   IT
Krauss-Maffei Kunststofftechnik GmbH, Krauss-Maffei Strasse 2, pg. 836   IT
Krauss-Maffei Kunstsofftechnik Vertrieb & Service Sud, pg. 836   IT
Krauss-Maffei Verfahrenstechnik GmbH, Krauss-Maffei-Str. 2, pg. 836   IT
Krauss-Maffei Verkehrstechnik GmbH, Krauss-Maffei-Str. 2, pg. 836   IT
Krauss-Maffei Versicherungsdienst GmbH, Krauss-Maffei Strasse 2, pg. 836   IT
Krauss-Maffei Wehrtechnik GmbH, Krauss-Maffei Strasse 2, pg. 836   IT
Krupp Hoesch Stahl AG - Munich, Briennerstr. 44, pg. 512   IT
Krupp Warmetechnik GmbH - Munich, Musenbertgstrasse 31, pg. 515   IT
Krupp Warmetechnik GmbH - Nuremburg, Giessener Str. 1, pg. 515   IT
LHI Leasing fur Handel und Industrie GmbH, Mannhardstrasse 6, pg. 160   IT
Labinal Components & Systems GmbH, Aidenbachstrasse 137a, pg. 746   IT
Lafarge GIPS GmbH, Ehrenbreitsteiner Str. 28, pg. 791   IT
Lafarge Gips Deutschland GmbH, Ehrenbreitsteiner Str. 28, pg. 791   IT
Lafarge Zement GmbH, Ehrenbreitsteiner Str. 28, pg. 791   IT
Lemo GmbH, Stahlgruberring 7, pg. 806   IT
Arthur D. Little International, Inc., Leopold Str. 11A, pg. 670   PV
Litton Precision Products International, Oberfoehringerstrasse 8, pg. 1004   PB
Lloyd-Immobilien G.m.b.H., Karlstrasse 10, pg. 89   IT
Loctite Deutschland G.m.b.H., Arabellastrasse 17, pg. 611   IT
Lorentzen & Wettre GmbH, Machtlfinger Strasse 24, pg. 271   IT
Lotus Development GmbH, Maximilianstrasse 40, pg. 896   PB
Lumonics Deutschland, GmbH, Plankenhof Strasse 33, pg. 1315   IT
Lupra Grundstucksgellschaft mbH, pg. 423   IT
Luxottica Fashion Brillen GmbH, Hans-Pinsel Str. 10A, pg. 822   IT
MAN AKTIENGESELLSCHAFT, Ungererstrasse 69, pg. 824   IT
MAN Nutzfahrzeuge AG, Dachauer Strasse 667, pg. 824   IT
MAN Nutzfahrzeuge Leasing GmbH, Am Neubruch 15, pg. 824   IT
MAN Verwaltungs-Gesellschaft mit beschraenkter Haftung, Dachauer Strasse 667, pg. 825   IT
MLV Munchener Leben Vermogensanlageund Vermittlungs G.m.b.H., Leopoldstrasse 6, pg. 89   IT
MTS Systems GmbH, Erchanbertstrasse 8, pg. 1029   PB
MTU Motoren-und Turbinen-Union Munchen GmbH, Postfach 50 06 40, pg. 367   IT
MTU Turbomeca Rolls-Royce GmbH, pg. 367   IT
MVT Magazin Verlag GmbH & Co. KG, Arabellastrasse 23, pg. 233   IT
MacNeal-Schwendler GmbH, Innsbrucker Ring 15, pg. 1032   PB
Mannesmann Pilotentwicklungs GmbH, pg. 838   IT
Marienplatz GroBgarage GmbH, pg. 180   IT
Materials Research GmbH, Elsenheimerstrasse 61-65, pg. 1283   IT
Matra Datavision GmbH, pg. 796   IT
McDonald's Deutschland GmbH, Drygalski Alee 51, pg. 1069   PB
Julius Meinl GmbH, pg. 856   IT
Mentor Graphics (Deutschland) GmbH, Westendstrasse 193, pg. 1087   PB
Merck Finck & Co., Firmenkundenbereich, Pacellistr 4, pg. 166   IT
Merides Grundbesitz- und Bebauungsgesellschaft mbH, pg. 180   IT
Merisel Germany, Peter Henlein Strasse, pg. 1096   PB
Metrologic Instruments GmbH, Dornierstrasse 2, pg. 1102   PB
Micropolis GmbH, Behringstrasse 10, pg. 742   PV
Microsoft GmbH, pg. 1108   PB
Microturbo GmbH, Aidenbachstrasse 137a, pg. 787   IT
Mitsui & Co. Europe G.m.b.H, Leopoldstrasse 19, pg. 880   IT
Mitsukoshi Deutschland GmbH-Munich Branch, Platzl 2, pg. 884   IT

PB - *U.S. Public Companies Volume*
PV - *U.S. Private Companies Volume*
IT - *International Public & Private Companies Volume*

Geographic Index-Non U.S.

1627

Mizuno Corporation Niederlassung Deutschland, Rosenheimer Str. 143d, pg. 885 IT
Molex Services GmbH, Dingolfinger Strasse 4, pg. 1122 PB
Monachia Grundstucks-Aktiengesellschaft, Nymphenburger Strasse 48, pg. 623 IT
Mosaik Verlag, Neumarkter Strasse 18, pg. 190 IT
Muenchener Lebensversicherung AG, Koeniginstrasse 28, pg. 61 IT
Multanova Verkehrsuberwachunsysteme GmbH, pg. 618 IT
Munchener Lebensversicherung AG, Leopoldstrasse 6, pg. 89 IT
MUNCHENER RUCKVERSICHERUNGS-GESELLSCHAFT, Koniginstrasse 107, pg. 897 IT
Munich Branch, Triebstrasse 14, pg. 401 IT
NatWest Securities GmbH, Kaufingerstrasse 12, pg. 911 IT
Nestle Erzeugnisse GmbH, Prinzregentenstrasse 155, pg. 921 IT
Nokia Monitors, Dachauer Strasse 124, pg. 951 IT
Olicom GmbH, Stefan-Georg-Ring 29, pg. 1001 IT
Omnia Grundstucks GmbH, pg. 180 IT
Omnia Grundstucks GmbH & Co. Betriebs KG, pg. 180 IT
OPTIMALGRUND Bautragergesellschaft mbH, Erdinger Landstr. 1, pg. 423 IT
OPTISCHE WERKE G. RODENSTOCK, Isartalstrasse 39-43, pg. 1007 IT
Oracle Deutschland GmbH, hauptverwaltung, Hanauer Strasse 87, pg. 1228 PB
Osram GmbH, Hellabrunner Str. 1, pg. 1244 IT
PDA International/Germany, Frankfurter Ring 224, pg. 1031 IT
PHH Deutschland, Inc., Stablistrasse 8, pg. 321 PB
PLE Systems Gesellschaft fur Entwicklung ung Vertrieb von Soft- und Hardware- Systemen nbH, 71 Fostenrieder, Allee 61, pg. 1149 IT
Panavia Aircraft GmbH, Arabellastr. 16, pg. 218 IT
Parker Hannifin GmbH, Buro Munchen, Freudstr. 1, pg. 1261 PB
Pepsi-Cola GmbH, Mars, 46-48, pg. 1277 PB
Philip Morris GmbH, Fallstr. 40, pg. 1290 PB
Picker International GmbH, pg. 545 IT
PictureTel GmbH, Denniger Strasse 116, pg. 1295 PB
Pond's G.m.b.H., Dachauer Str. 37, pg. 1436 IT
Prisma Verlag GmbH, Neumarkter Str. 18, pg. 190 IT
QMS International GmbH, Geigenberger Str. 18, pg. 1346 PB
Rechtsschutz Union Versicherungs-AG, Sonnenstr. 33, pg. 66 IT
Reise-und Verkehrs Verlag GmbH, Neumarkterstrasse 18, pg. 190 IT
Rentokil GmbH, 80 Kreiller, pg. 1286 IT
Resistance Technology GmbH, Arabellastrasse 17/4, pg. 1455 PB
Rockwell Semiconductor Systems, Paul-Gerhardt-Allee 50 a, pg. 1402 PB
ROHDE & SCHWARZ GMBH & CO. KG, Muehldorfstr. 15, pg. 1124 IT
Rohde & Schwarz Vertriebs GmbH, Muehldorfstr. 15, pg. 1124 IT
SAB WABCO GmbH, Ernst-Platz Strasse 2, pg. 271 IT
Sachs AG, pg. 839 IT
Salvatorplatz Grundstucksgesellschaft mbh & Co. OHG Saarland, pg. 180 IT
Salvatorplatz-Grundstucksgesellschaft mbH, Kardinal-Faulhaber-Strasse 1 & 14, pg. 180 IT
Sanpaolo-Monaco Branch, Ludwigstrasse 19, pg. 692 IT
Sanyo Fisher Vertriebs GmbH, Stahlgruberring 4, pg. 1192 IT
K.G. Saur, Ortlerstrasse 8, pg. 1099 IT
Schiedel GmbH & Co., Lerchenstrasse 9, pg. 1091 IT
Schindler Aufzuge GmbH, pg. 1205 IT
Schnurpfeil Bohr-GmbH, Erdinger Landstr. 1, pg. 423 IT
Schweizerische Rentenanstalt, Leopoldstrasse 8-10, pg. 1332 IT
Schweizerischer Bankverein (Deutschland) AG, Prannerstrasse 1, pg. 1331 IT
SERVICEPLAN GMBH, Prinzregentenstr. 50, pg. 1225 IT
Siecor GmbH, pg. 449 PB
SIEMENS AG, Wittelsbacherplatz 2, pg. 1244 IT
Siemens Finanzierungsgesellschaft fur Informationstechnik GmbH, Wittelsbacherplatz 2, pg. 1245 IT
Siemens Matsushita Components GmbH & Co. KG, Balaustrasse 73, pg. 1245 IT
Signalbau Huber AG, Paul Gerhardt Allee 48-50, pg. 204 IT
Walter Sohn G.m.b.H., Sonnenstrasse 31, pg. 89 IT
Speech Design, Landsberger Strabe 23, pg. 740 PB
Sport-Scheck GmbH, pg. 1014 IT
Squibb Medical Systems Europa GmbH, Dornach Karl Hammerschmidt 5, pg. 256 IT
STADTSPARKASSE MUNCHEN, Ungererstrasse 75, pg. 1293 IT
State Street GmbH, Nymphenburger Strasse 70, pg. 1513 PB
Stinnes-Ausbausysteme GmbH, Wilhelm Hale Strasse 42, pg. 1459 PB
Stream International, AM Moosfeld 11, pg. 518 PB
Suddeutsche Etna-Werk GmbH, pg. 617 IT
Sudkraft Suddeutsche Kraftwagen-Speditions GmbH, Bauberger Strasse 30, pg. 606 IT
Sudkraft Versicherungsvermittlungs GmbH, Gartnerstrasse 60, pg. 606 IT
Sudpetrol A.G., Sonnenstrasse 23/11, pg. 429 IT
Sueddeutsche Bodencreditbank AG, Ottostr. 21, pg. 180 IT
Systhema Verlag GmbH, Frankfurter Ring 224, pg. 1479 IT
TBS Ges. fur Tank- und Bodenschutz mbH, Musenbergstr. 33, pg. 515 IT

TBWA Munich, Linwurmstrasse 122, pg. 1063 PV
Technics Plasma GmbH Plasma- und Ionenstrahlsysteme, pg. 836 IT
Tektronix GmbH-Munich, pg. 1567 PB
Tela Versicherung AG, Pranner 8, pg. 58 IT
TELE-MUNCHEN FERNSEH GMBH & CO., Kaufingerstrasse 25, pg. 1362 IT
Thermo-Tank-Dienst GmbH, Musenbergstr. 33, pg. 515 IT
Thomson Bauelemente GmbH, pg. 1385 IT
Thomson-CSF Passive Components Gmbh, Perchtinger Strasse 3, pg. 1385 IT
Thuga Aktiengesellschaft, Mandlstrasse 3, pg. 1456 IT
Thuga-Konsortium Beteiligungs GmbH, pg. 1456 IT
Thuringia Versicherung AG, Adenauerring 7, pg. 15 IT
Thyssen Polymer GmbH, pg. 1387 IT
Time-Life International GmbH, Akadamiestrasse 7, pg. 1615 PB
TIVOLI Handels- un Grundstucks GmbH & Co. OHG Verwaltungszentrum, pg. 180 IT
TRIUMPH INTERNATIONAL GRUPPE DEUTSCHLAND, Marsstrasse 40, pg. 1424 IT
Universal Studios TV (Television) G.m.b.H., Ismaningerstrasse 98, pg. 1217 IT
Universal Transport GmbH, Postfach 870339, pg. 1034 IT
Unterstutzungskasse DYWIDAG GmbH, pg. 423 IT
Urban & Schwarzenberg GmbH, Landwehrstrasse 61, pg. 1748 PB
Urban & Vogel GmbH, Lindwurmstrasse 95, pg. 1748 IT
VB Ccnsult, Gesellschaft fur Mergers & Acquisitions, pg. 180 IT
VB Dialog Gesellschaft fur Direktmarketing mbH, pg. 180 IT
VLSI Technology GmbH, Rosenkavalienplatz 10, pg. 1703 PB
VVB Gesellschaft zur Vermittlung von Finanzdienstleistungen mbH, pg. 180 IT
VW AUDI Vertriebszentrum GmbH & Co. Sudbayern KG, pg. 1473 IT
VW AUDI Vertrienszentrum Sudbayern Verwaltungs-GmbH, pg. 1474 IT
Veeco GmbH, Wissenschaftliche Geraete, pg. 1711 PB
Verba Verwaltungsgesellschaft mbH, pg. 180 IT
Vereinsbank Victoria Bauspar AG, pg. 180 IT
Versicherungs-Planer-Vereinigung G.m.b.H., Schleissheimerstrasse 55, pg. 89 IT
Viag Interkom GmbH & Co., Eisenheimer Strasse 11, pg. 223 IT
VICTORIA Kapitalanlagegesellschaft mbH, pg. 180 IT
Viewlogic Systems, GmbH, Schatzbogen 50, pg. 1548 PB
Voest-Alpine GmbH, Eisenheimerstrasse 10, pg. 1472 IT
WBG-Wohnen, Grund, Gesellschaft fur Wohn-und Gewerbeimmobilien mbh, Maximiliansplatz 12b, pg. 1466 IT
W.U.G. Wohn- und Gewerbebau Beteiligungs GmbH, pg. 179 IT
W.U.G. Wohn- und Gewerbebau Gmbh & Co. Immobilien KG, pg. 179 IT
Wacker-Chemie GmbH, Hanns-Seidel-Platz 4, pg. 625 IT
Wavetek GmbH, Hans-Pinsel Strasse 9-10, pg. 1155 PV
Werk Munchsmunster, pg. 1461 IT
Xilinx GmbH, Dorfstr. 1, pg. 1786 PB
Zellweger Eco-Systeme GmbH, pg. 618 IT
Zellweger Uster GmbH, pg. 618 IT
ALOIS ZETTLER ELEKTROTECHNISCHE FABRIK GMBH, Holzstrasse 28-30, pg. 1528 IT
Ziff-Davis Germany, Ziff Verlag GmbH, Hanover Str. 85, pg. 1276 IT
Zyma GmbH, Zielstattstrasse 40, pg. 986 IT

Munster

Armstrong World Industries, G.m.b.H., Robert-Bosch-Strasse 10-12, pg. 132 PB
BASF Coatings AG, Glasuritstrasse 1, pg. 104 IT
COMPC GmbH Produktions und Vertriebsgesellschaft, Gildenstrasse 38, pg. 104 IT
Egon Lucas Medizin Technik GmbH, An der Kleinmannbrucke 13A, pg. 551 IT
Firma E. Lucas Med. Technik GmbH, pg. 551 IT
L. Stroetmann GmbH & Co., pg. 1288 IT
Titman GmbH., Wolberckerstrasse 118, pg. 232 IT
Westdeutsche Landesbank Girozentrale (WestLB), Friedrichstrasse 1, pg. 1492 IT
Wyeth-Pharma GmbH, Schleebrueggenkamp 15, pg. 82 PB

Nachrodt

Reynolds Aluminum Deutschland, Inc., Hagener Strasse 147, pg. 1387 PB

Namburg

Glaxo Wellcome GmbH, Industriestrasse 32-36, pg. 553 IT

Narsdorf

Narsdorfer Klinker GmbH, Hauptstrassse, pg. 1091 IT

Neckargemund

Ortho Diagnostic Systems G.m.b.H., Karl-Landsteiner-Strabe 1, pg. 932 PB

Neckarsulm

FIAT OM PIMESPO Fodertechnik GmbH, pg. 811 IT
Gentex GmbH, Heiner-Fleischmann-Str. 6, pg. 732 PB

Pieburg AG, Karl-Schmidt-Strasse, pg. 1108 IT

Neckartenzlingen

Richard Hirschmann GmbH & Co., Stuttgarter Strasse 45-51, pg. 1108 IT

Neitersen

Karl Georg Bahntechnik G.m.b.H., Postfach 12, Rheinstrabe 15, pg. 1711 PB

Nettetal

Knurr-Ercotec GmbH, Am Hotschgraf 3, pg. 739 IT
National Electrical Carbon GmbH, pg. 892 IT
REIN Elektronik GmbH, Lotscher Weg 66, pg. 1457 IT

Netzschkau

Nema Warmetauscher GmbH, pg. 399 IT
Verzinkerei Netzschkau GmbH, pg. 400 IT

Neu-Isenburg

Albright & Wilson GmbH (Germany), City Ctr., Frankfurterstr. 181, pg. 49 IT
Bently Nevada GmbH, Werner-von-Braun Str. 8-10, pg. 134 PV
Bristol-Myers G.m.b.H., Rathenstrasse 31, pg. 255 PB
Bytex GmbH, Hermannstrasse 54-56, pg. 1522 PB
Chemviron Carbon GmbH, Robert Koch Str. 507, pg. 293 PB
Clestra GmbH, Robert-Koch-Strasse 1, pg. 570 IT
Datapoint Deutschland GmbH, Hauptverwaltung, pg. 384 IT
Deutsche Asphalt GmbH, An der Gehespitz 20B, pg. 632 IT
Du Pont de Nemours (Deutschland) GmbH, Plant Neu-Isenburg, Schleussnerstrasse 2, pg. 532 PB
Ericsson Telekom GmbH, Schleussnerstrasse 56C, pg. 1368 IT
OHG Fegro/Selgros Gesellschaft Fur Grosshandel mbH & Co., pg. 1014 IT
FoxVideo (Germany) G.m.b.H., Postfach 2209, AM Forsthaus Gravenburch 7, pg. 926 IT
Hutec Holzmann Umwelttechnik GmbH, An der Gehespitz 50, pg. 633 IT
ISG Ingenieurbau + Schalungs-Baugesellschaft mbH, Dornhofstrasse 44-46, pg. 195 IT
Imbau Industrielles Bauen GmbH, An der Gehespitz LOD, pg. 633 IT
Interbrucke GmbH-Ram Deutschland, Hermannstrasse 54-56, pg. 742 IT
MTI GmbH, Am Forsthaus, Gravenbuch 5, pg. 1028 PB
Micro Warehouse (Deutschland) GmbH, Odenwaldstrasse 1, pg. 1104 PB
Niederlassung Spezialhochbau, Dornhofstrasse 69, pg. 195 IT
PAREXEL GmbH, Isenbug Park, Schleussnerstr. 90, pg. 1258 IT
Periphonics UPS Ltd., Martin-Behaim-Strasse 12, pg. 1279 PB
Plus Allgemeine, Am Forsthaus Gravenbruch 9-11, pg. 565 IT
Plus Leben, Am Forsthaus Gravenbruch 9-11, pg. 565 IT
qad.germany GmbH, City Center, Carl-Ulrich-Strasse 11, pg. 1345 PB
ReMo GmbH Renovieren und Modernisieren, Dornhofstrasse 44-46, pg. 195 IT
Wang Deutschland GmbH, Wang-Haus, Martin-Behaim-Strasse 20, pg. 1737 IT

Neu-Ulm

Hewlett-Packard GmbH, Messerschmittstrasse 7, pg. 820 PB
Reinz-Dichtungs-GmbH, Reinzstrasse 3-7, pg. 480 PB

Neubiberg

ICOS Systems, GmbH, Prof. Messerschmitt-Str.1, pg. 864 PB

Neubrandenburg

Energieversorgung Muritz-Oderhaff Aktiengesellschaft, Ihlenfelder Strasse 88, pg. 1456 IT
MTN Medizintechnik Neubrandenburg GmbH I.G., Gustav-Kirchhoff Strasse 2, pg. 669 IT
TEBABAU GmbH, pg. 1148 IT

Neuburg an dew Donau

Bertrand Faure Sitztechnik GmbH & Co. KG, Ruhrstrasse 5, pg. 193 IT

Neuenrade

MTN - Mineraloel-und Tanklager Gmbh, Bahnhofstrasse 59, pg. 517 IT

Neufahrn

Avon Cosmetics GmbH, pg. 156 PB

PB - *U.S. Public Companies Volume*
PV - *U.S. Private Companies Volume*
IT - *International Public & Private Companies Volume*

1628

Neuhausen

FANUC Europe GmbH, Bernhauser Strasse 22,
pg. 477
Fanuc Germany GmbH, Bernhauser Strasse 22,
pg. 477   IT

Neuisenburg

Skandia Sachsversicherung AG, Graf Folke Bernadotte
Strasse 23, pg. 1258   IT
Skandia Versicherungs-AG, Siemensstr. 9, pg. 1258   IT

Neumarkt

ECO Kunststoff GmbH, Dreichlinger Strasse 10,
pg. 436   IT
Jetbag GmbH, Dreichlinger Strasse 10, pg. 436   IT
PFLEIDERER AG, pg. 1046   IT
Thule Holding GmbH, Dreichlinger Strasse 10, pg. 436   IT

Neumunster

Lawson Mardon Hanse-Druck GmbH, pg. 68   IT
NEUMAG-Neumunstersche Maschinen-und Anlagenbau
GmbH, pg. 399   IT
SAUER SUNDSTRAND GMBH & CO., Krokamp 39,
pg. 1198   IT

Neunkirchen

Bendix Deutschland G.m.b.H., pg. 54   PB
Bundy Systemwerk, Zweibrucker Str. 109, pg. 1342   IT
Hoechst Trespaphan, pg. 339   IT

Neuss

Aluminum Norf GmbH, Postfach 100 353, pg. 51   IT
Beecham-Wulfing G.m.b.H. & Co. K.G., Stresemannallee 6,
pg. 1266   IT
Bienefeld-Peukert GmbH & Co. KG, pg. 505   IT
Buro Neuss, Europadamm 2, pg. 754   IT
Checkpoint Systems Deutschland GmgH, Forumstrasse 2,
pg. 343   PB
Eldon GmbH, Postfach 210263, pg. 436   IT
Franki Grundbau GmbH, Sperberweg 6A, pg. 632   IT
B.F. Goodrich Chemical Deutschland GmbH, Goerlitzer
Strasse 1, pg. 752   PB
Graco GmbH, Moselstrasse 19, pg. 757   PB
Hoogovens Aluminium Metall GmbH, Europadamm 2,
pg. 755   IT
Ikegami Electronics Europe, Ikegami Strasse 1,
pg. 660   IT
Inter-Beton GmbH, Siemensstrasse 8-10, pg. 606   IT
Jagenberg AG, Jagenbergstrasse 1, pg. 1108   IT
Jagenberg Papier Technik GmbH, Jagenbergstrasse 1,
pg. 1108   IT
Janssen Cilag GmbH, Postfach 210440, pg. 929   PB
Kyocera Europe GmbH, Hellersbergstrasse 2, pg. 776   IT
Network Systems GmbH, Geschaftsstelle Nord/West,
pg. 1523   PB
Nissan Bank GmbH, Hammer Landstrasse 87, pg. 945   IT
Nissan Motor Deutschland GmbH, Nissanstrasse 1,
pg. 945   IT
Oki Electric Europe GmbH, Hellersbergstrasse 2,
pg. 1000   IT
Heinz Peukert GmbH, pg. 506   IT
Schindler Aufzuge GmbH, pg. 1205   IT
Schuster & Partner, Breite Strasse 159, pg. 394   IT
SCHUSTER & PARTNER, Breitestrasse 159, pg. 1210   IT
Sequent Computer Systems GmbH, Hellersbergstr. 12,
pg. 1459   PB
3M Deutschland GmbH, Carl-Schurz Strasse 1,
pg. 1606   PB
Toshiba Europe (I.E.) G.m.b.H., Hammer Landstr. 115,
pg. 1406   IT
Toshiba Medical Systems GmbH, Hellerbergstr. 4,
pg. 1407   IT

Neustadt

Kendall GmbH, Raffineriestrasse 8, pg. 1648   PB
Siecor GmbH & Co. KG, 103 Austrasse, pg. 449   PB

Neustadt an der Donau

Erdoel-Raffinerie Neustadt GmbH & Co., oHG,
Raffineriestrasse 22, pg. 1461   IT

Neuwied

Baars Marketing GmbH, pg. 752   IT
Siegert & Cie GmbH, Beringstrasse 83/89, pg. 610   IT

Nidderau

Perrin GmbH, Siemensstrasse 1, pg. 1528   IT

Nieder-Olm

Chantre & Cie GmbH, pg. 433   IT
Chantre & Cie KG Mit Beschrankter Haftung, Ludwig-
Eckes-Allee 6, pg. 433   IT
ECKES AG, Ludwig-Eckes-Allee 6, pg. 432   IT
Eckes-Granini GmbH & Co., Ludwig-Eckes-Allee 6,
pg. 433   IT

Stromburg GmbH, pg. 433   IT

Niederaula

SAB-Profil GmbH, Industriestrasse 13, pg. 754   IT

Niederkruchten

Industrial Acoustics Company GmbH, pg. 875   PB

Nienburger

Henniges-Vehicle Sealing Div., 31547 Rehburg Loccum,
pg. 706   PB

Noerdlingen

Sanyo Industries Deutschland Gmbh, Nuernberger Strasse
64, 68, pg. 1192   IT

Nordenham

Bentone-Chemie GmbH, Titanstrasse, pg. 271   PV
MIDGARD Deutsche Seeverkehrs-AG, Midgardstrasse 50,
pg. 1459   IT

Norderstedt

Air Products GmbH, Werk Norderstedt, pg. 31   PB
Bran & Luebbe G.m.b.H., Postfach 1360, pg. 1379   IT
Casio Computer Co., G.m.b.H. Deutschland, Bornbarch 10,
pg. 274   IT
Customer Support Commercial Division, Bornbarch 5 Haus
F, pg. 1262   PB
Ethicon G.m.b.H. & Co. KG, Robert-Koch-Strasse 1,
pg. 929   PB
Florasynth GMBH, Oststrasse 104, pg. 173   IT
Geschaftsstelle Hamburg, Aspelohe 38, pg. 739   IT
Grace G.m.b.H., pg. 755   IT
ITW ATECO GmbH, Stormarnstrasse 43-49, pg. 868   PB
Johnson & Johnson G.m.b.H., pg. 930   PB
Johnson & Johnson Medical GmbH, Aspelohe 27,
pg. 931   PB
Johnson & Johnson Medical G.m.b.H., P.O. Box 1680,
pg. 931   PB
Pronova Biopolymer GmbH, Gutenbergring 1-5,
pg. 961   IT
SAT CHEMIE G.m.b.H., Oststrasse 92, pg. 1460   IT
Sumitomo Electric Schrumpf-Produkte GmbH, Oststrasse
89, pg. 1314   IT
Werk Hamburg, Robert Koch Str. 25, pg. 1298   IT

Nordhausen

Nordbrand Nordhausen, pg. 433   IT

Nordhorn

Sonoco Deutschland, Fennastrasse 94, pg. 1487   PB

Nordlingen

Burkhardt GmbH, pg. 836   IT

Nordrhein-Westfalen

Bols Strothmann Brennereien GmbH & Co. KG, Sollingweg
41, 32427 Minden, pg. 751   IT

Noremberg

Lucent Technologies Network Systems GmbH, Thurn-und-
Taxis Sts. 10, pg. 1018   PB

Northeim

Reiseland GmbH, pg. 1015   IT

Nottingen

H.F. Vogel Gmbh Elektrotechnische Fabrik, Remchingen 3,
pg. 1776   PB

Nottuln

ITW Meypack GmbH, Industriestr. 3, pg. 868   PB

Nufringen

OMRON Manufacturing of Germany G.m.b.H., Robert-
Bosch Strasse 1, pg. 1006   IT

Numbrecht

Homburger Papierfabrik Wilhelm Geldmacher GmbH & Co.
KG, P.O. Box 1240, pg. 35   IT

Nunchritz

Chemiewerk Nunchritz GmbH, Meissner Strasse 59,
pg. 1454   IT
Huls Silicone GmbH, Friedrich-von-Heyden-Platz 1,
pg. 1454   IT

Nuremberg

AEG Hausgerate AG, pg. 442   IT
Alka Nurnberger Warenhandelsgesellschaft mbH,
pg. 724   IT
Baustoff Union GmbH & Co. KG Baumarkt Franken, Leyher
Strasse 123, pg. 1459   IT
Bayerische Landesbank Girozentrale - Nuremberg Branch,
Lorenzer Platz 27, pg. 176   IT
BAYERNLAND GMBH & CO. KG, 90441 Nurnberg,
Platenstrasse 31, pg. 181   IT
Cebal Verpackungen GmbH & Co. KG, Schweinaur
Houpstrasse 80, pg. 1030   IT
DG Bank - Nuremberg, Konigstorgraben 11, pg. 352   IT
Diehl & Eagle-Picher GmbH, Bahnhofsplatz 6, pg. 355   PV
Florimex Worldwide GmbH, Ostenstrasse 132, pg. 510   PB
Franken WKV Bank GmbH, Faerberstr. 41, pg. 179   IT
FUNDUS Gesellschaft fur Grundbesitz und Beteilgungen
mbH, pg. 179   IT
Gebr. E. & O. Krause GmbH, pg. 506   IT
Geschaftsstelle Nurnberg, Bennostrasse 6, pg. 739   IT
Gesellschaft fur Elektrometallurgie m.b.H., pg. 735   PV
Grosskraftwerk Franken AG, Rudolphstr. 28, pg. 1464   IT
Hewlett-Packard GmbH, Emmericher Strasse 13,
pg. 820   PB
Hospal Med Tech GmbH, Brettergartenstrasse 16,
pg. 668   IT
Kluber Chemie KG, pg. 505   IT
MAUL-BELSER GMBH, Breslauer Strasse 300,
pg. 849   IT
Max Cochius GmbH - Nuremberg Branch, Isartrasse 12,
pg. 514   IT
Mechanische Weberei und Zwirnerei Rosenhammer GmbH,
Schoppershofstrasse 80, pg. 1333   PB
Mehnert und Veeck GmbH, Lochnerstrasse 12,
pg. 937   IT
Neumeyer Fliesspressen GmbH, Steiglehnerstrasse 10,
pg. 755   IT
Niederlassung Nurnberg, Sprottauer Strasse 51,
pg. 195   IT
Nurnberger Hercules-Werke GmbH, pg. 835   IT
Nurnberger Hypothekenbank AG, pg. 180   IT
Panalpina Welltransport (Deutschland) GmbH,
pg. 1023   IT
Philips Kommunikations Industrie AG, Thurn-und-Tasix Str.
10, pg. 1055   IT
Rhenania Transport GmbH, Zweigniederlassung
Neumeyerstra, pg. 1033   IT
Sandoz AG, Deutschherrnstr. 15, pg. 984   IT
Scholler Lebensmittel GmbH & Co. KG, pg. 1305   IT
SEMIKRON INTERNATIONAL, GMBH & CO. KG,
Sigmundstr. 200, pg. 1220   IT
TA Triumph-Adler Vertriebs GmbH, Fuerther Str. 212,
pg. 1004   IT
Technischer Handel Freudenberg Besitz GmbH,
pg. 506   IT
Temca Chemische Union GmbH, Aeussere Bayreuther Str.
35 b, pg. 1333   PB
TRIUMPH ADLER GROUP, SW Park 23, pg. 1424   IT
Tyco Toys (Deutschland) GmbH, Marienbergstr. 82,
pg. 1059   PB
Unterstutzungskasse der NHW GmbH, pg. 835   IT
VP-Schickedanz AG, Schoppershofstr. 80, pg. 1333   PB
Vereinsbank in Nuernberg AG, Marienstr. 3, pg. 180   IT
Wander Pharma G.m.b.H., pg. 986   IT
Zweirad Union Grundbesitz AG, pg. 835   IT

Nurtingen

AP & T GmbH, Hohes Gestade 14, pg. 620   PB
Fuchs NE-Metallhandel GmbH, Hohes Gestade 6,
pg. 514   IT
New Brunswick Scientific GmbH, In der Au 14,
pg. 1170   PB
Progress-Elektrogerate Mauz & Pfeiffer GmbH & Co.,
Postfach 41, pg. 442   IT
Progress VerKauf GmbH, Postfach 1004, pg. 442   IT
KARL M. REICH MASCHINENFABRIK GMBH, Kisslinstr.
1, pg. 1101   IT
Reich Spezialmaschinen GmbH, Plochinger Str. 65,
pg. 1101   IT

Oberhausen

Akzo Plastics GmbH, 162 Konigshardterstrasse, pg. 46   IT
Babcock BLK Giesserei GmbH, pg. 398   IT
Babcock Dienstleistungs-GmbH, pg. 398   IT
Babcock Feuerungssysteme GmbH, pg. 398   IT
Babcock Lentjes Kraftwerkstechnik, pg. 398   IT
Babcock Prozessautomation GmbH, pg. 398   IT
Babcock Rohrleitungsbau GmbH, pg. 399   IT
Babcock Sempell Armaturen-Service GmbH, pg. 400   IT
Babcock-Omnical-Industriekessel GmbH, pg. 398   IT
DVO-Datenverarbeitungs-Service Oberhausen GmbH,
pg. 401   IT
DEUTSCHE BABCOCK AG, Duisburger Str. 375,
pg. 398   IT
Deutsche Babcock Anlagen GmbH, pg. 398   IT
Deutsche Babcock Bau GmbH, P.O. Box 10 03 47/48,
pg. 401   IT
Deutsche Babcock-Beteiligung GmbH, pg. 401   IT
Deutsche Babcock Energie-und Umwelttechnik AG,
pg. 398   IT
Deutsche Babcock Handel GmbH, pg. 401   IT
Deutsche Babcock Industrie und Systemtechnik AG,
pg. 399   IT
Deutsche Babcock International Vetriebs-GmbH,
pg. 401   IT
Dresser-Rand GmbH, Brinkstrasse 21, pg. 877   PB

PB - *U.S. Public Companies Volume*
PV - *U.S. Private Companies Volume*
IT - *International Public & Private Companies Volume*

GHH BORSIG Turbomaschinen GmbH, Bahnhofstrasse 66, pg. 824 — IT
Hoogovens Aluminium Sidal GmbH, Fahnhorststrasse 3, pg. 755 — IT
Hydro Chemtech GmbH, Buschhaussener Strasse 153, pg. 963 — IT
MAN Gutehoffnungshuette AG, Bahnhofstrasse 66, pg. 824 — IT
Oberhausen Office, Allaestrasse 1, pg. 401 — IT
Carl Osmann GmbH, 29, Heinestrasse, pg. 682 — IT
Stollberg GmbH, Duisburger Str. 69-73, pg. 1465 — IT
Thyssen Immobilien GmbH, pg. 1388 — IT
YMOS AG, pg. 302 — IT

Oberkochen

Opton Feintechnik GmbH, pg. 1523 — IT
Carl Zeiss, Carl-Zeiss Str. 2-60, pg. 1522 — IT
CARL-ZEISS-STIFTUNG, Carl-Zeiss-Strasse 2-60, pg. 1522 — IT

Oberndorf

Heckler & Koch GmbH, pg. 217 — IT
Parker Hannifin GmbH, Romerweg 13, pg. 1263 — PB

Oberschleisheim

Organon GmbH, Mittenheimer Strasse 62, pg. 45 — IT

Obersulm

Snap-on Tools, GmbH, Rudolf-Diesel-Strasse 6, pg. 1481 — PB

Obertshausen

TAC Control Systems GmbH, Essenstrasse 5, pg. 670 — IT
Ymos A.G. Indstriepodukte, pg. 302 — IT

Oberursell

Alte Leipziger Rueckversicherung AG, pg. 66 — IT
ALTE LEIPZIGER VERSICHERUNG AKTIENGESELLSCHAFT, Alte Leipziger-Platz 1, pg. 66 — IT
Auto Direkt Versicherungs AG, John E. Fesher St. #1, pg. 789 — PV
BERG Electronics GmbH, Obere Zeil 2, pg. 213 — PB
Braas Dachsysteme GmbH, Frankfurter Landstrasse 2-4, pg. 1091 — IT
Braas Flachdachsysteme GmbH, Frankfurter Landstrasse 2-4, pg. 1091 — IT
Braas GmbH, Frankfurter Landstrasse 2-4, pg. 1091 — IT
The Braas Group, Frankfurter Landstrasse 2-4, pg. 1091 — IT
Columbus Versicherungs Vermittlungs, John E. Fesher St. #1, pg. 789 — PV
ECI Telecom GmbH, Buropark Oberusel, In der Au 27, pg. 643 — IT
IndustrieWerk Oberursel GmbH, pg. 839 — IT
Max Kammerer GmbH, pg. 839 — IT
Neckura Verischerungs AG, John E. Fesher St. #1, pg. 789 — PV
Nur Touristic GmbH, pg. 724 — IT
Redland (Deutschland) GmbH, Frankfurter Landstrasse 2-4, pg. 1093 — IT
UTIMACO SAFEWARE AG, pg. 1444 — IT
Zenith Versicherung AG, Alte Leipziger Platz-1, pg. 66 — IT

Ochsenhausen

Liebherr-Hausgerate GmbH, Memminger Strasse 77-79, pg. 808 — IT

Oderen

Lippert-Pelissier S.A., Zone Industrielle, pg. 518 — IT

Oer-Erkenschwick

ZK Hospital Bedarfs GmbH, Schachtstrasse 17, pg. 552 — IT

Offenbach/Main

Aramark Services, GmbH, Strahlenbergerstrasse 127, pg. 79 — PV
GKN Remanufacturing GmbH, Heinrich-Krumm-Strasse 1-3, pg. 536 — PB
Honda Deutschland GmbH, Sprendlinger Landshasse 166, pg. 635 — PB
Honeywell AG, Kaiserleistrasse 39, pg. 834 — PB
Instron International Ltd., Zweigniederlassung Deutschland, pg. 883 — PB
Lohr & Bromkamp GmbH, Postfach 101164, pg. 536 — IT
MAN Roland Druckmaschinen Aktiengesellschaft, Muehlheimer Strasse 341, pg. 825 — IT
NYK Line-Frankfurt, Gothering 56, pg. 942 — IT
Nicolet Instrument GmbH, Senefelderstrasse 162, pg. 1594 — PB
Polaroid GmbH, Sprendlinger Landstr. 109, pg. 1314 — PB
Rowenta Werke, Waldstrasse 202-256, pg. 569 — IT

Stahlbau Lavis Offenbach GmbH, Senefelderstr. 167, pg. 633 — IT
Stohr-Forderanlagen Salzer GmbH, pg. 837 — IT
Wackenhut Central Europe GmbH, Tulpenhofstrase 18, pg. 1731 — PB

Offenburg

Burda GmbH, Haupstrasse 130, pg. 233 — IT
Electromechanical Division, pg. 1263 — PB
Hobart GmbH, Am Holdenstock 4, pg. 1322 — PB
Tesa-Werke Offenburg GmbH, pg. 182 — IT

Ohringen

Eagle-Picher Wolverine Gmbh, Verrenberger Weg 20, pg. 355 — PV
Eagle-Picher Wolverine GmbH, Verrenberger WEG 20, pg. 355 — PV
Standex International GmbH, Mold-Tech South, P.O. Box 1444, pg. 1507 — IT

Olching

Ascom Hasler GmbH, Roggensteiner Strasse 19, pg. 87 — IT

Oldenburg

BUFA Baeuerle GmbH & Co., pg. 1464 — IT
Burgess GmbH, AM Kreyenhof 10-12, pg. 1500 — IT
DG Bank - Oldenburg, Raiffeisenstrasse 22/23, pg. 352 — IT
EWE Aktiengesellschaft, pg. 1456 — IT
Energieversorgung Weser-Ems AG, Tirpitzstrasse 39, pg. 1456 — IT
Frese & Wolff Werbeagentur, Donnerschweer Strasse 79, pg. 304 — PV
Micro-Tec Schalr-und Verbindungselemente Gmbh, Gebkenweg 51, pg. 1500 — IT
Oldenburgische Landesbank AG, Stau 15-17, pg. 418 — IT

Oldenzaal

Howden Group Europe B.V., Eekboerstraat 65, pg. 637 — IT

Osnabruck

Enichem Polyurethane Deutschland GmbH, Carl Stolcke Strasse 1, pg. 429 — IT
KM-EUROPA METAL AKTIENGESELLSCHAFT, Klosterstrasse 29, pg. 719 — IT
KME Rohstoff GmbH, Klosterstrasse 29, pg. 719 — IT
Kammerer GmbH, Romereschstrasse 33, pg. 35 — IT
Kapa GmbH Leichtsofftechnik, pg. 68 — IT
Kloeckner Durilit GmbH, pg. 737 — IT
G. Kromschroder Aktiengesellschaft, Strotheweg 1, pg. 1148 — IT
Reise-As GmbH, Neumarkt 12, pg. 515 — IT
Reise-Palette GmbH, Neumarkt-Passage, pg. 515 — IT
Reiseschrand GmbH, Am Neumarkt, pg. 515 — IT
Ticket-Palette GmbH, Neumarkt-Passage, pg. 515 — IT
Vereinigte Gaszahler-Werkstatten GmbH, pg. 1149 — IT

Osterode am Hartz

Ploychrome GmbH, Sessener Str. 11, pg. 370 — IT
Sun Chemical Druckfarben GmbH, Rolandsweg 22-24, pg. 371 — IT

Ostfildern

Hirose Electric Gmbh, Zepplinstr. 42, pg. 620 — IT
Kodak AG-Ostfildern, Plieninger Strasse 50, pg. 552 — PB

Osthofen

Wander G.m.b.H., Dr. Wander-Str. 11, pg. 986 — IT

Ostringen

Cytec Fiberite Europe GmbH, Industriestrasse, pg. 471 — PB

Oststeinbek

ING Leasing GmbH & Co. Fox oHG, pg. 1063 — IT

Ottenbach

Dieterle Edelstahl GmbH, Neuhofstrasse 22, pg. 222 — IT

Ottobrunn

Eurocopter Deutschland GmbH, pg. 369 — IT
Raychem GmbH, Haidgraben 6, pg. 1362 — PB

Paderborn

Forbo Werke GmbH, pg. 498 — IT
Guilford Kapwood GmbH, Kloechner Strasse 16, pg. 769 — PB
Nairn Bodenbelag GmbH, pg. 498 — IT
PESAG Aktiengesellschaft, Tegelweg 25, pg. 1456 — IT
Siemens-Nixdorf Informationssysteme AG, Heinz Nixdorf-Ring, pg. 1245 — IT

Pansdorf

Bertram & Graf GmbH, Bahnhofstrase 7, pg. 165 — PB

Parsberg

Niedermeier Vermogensverwaltungsgesellschaft mbH, pg. 1206 — IT
Philipp Niedermeier Metallwarenfabrik GmbH & Co. KG, pg. 1206 — IT

Passau

Niederlassung Passau, Regensburger Strasse 29, pg. 195 — IT

Peenemunde

Peenemunde Planungs und Projekt AG, pg. 597 — IT

Pegnitz

Bachmann GmbH, Am Berg 2, pg. 514 — IT
Norton Industrieprodukte GmbH, AM Winkelsteig 1, pg. 1175 — IT

Peine

TECO Schallschutz GmbH, pg. 1148 — IT

Penig

Flender Getriebewerk Penig GmbH, Thierbacher Strasse 24, pg. 400 — IT

Perneck

Neuper Beton Baustoffwerke GmbH & Co. KG, Am Kieswerke 4, pg. 606 — IT

Pfeffenhausen

Cerner Solutions Center -SNI Health Solutions Div., Am. Engelsberg 19, pg. 331 — PB

Pforzheim

ETA Uhrenwerke GmbH, Maximilianstrasse 46, pg. 1161 — IT
Flubb-und Schwerspatwerke Pforzheim GmbH, pg. 172 — IT
ITT Flygt Werk GmbH, Adolf-Richter-Strasse 4, pg. 860 — PB
Nokia (Deutschland) GmbH, Ostliche Karl-Friedrich-Strasse 132, pg. 954 — IT

Pfullendorf

ALNO AG, Heiligenberger Str. 47, pg. 65 — IT

Pfungstadt

KERI, Ostendstrasse 19, pg. 718 — IT
Valmet Service GmbH, Ostendstrasse 1, pg. 1449 — IT
Valmet Vertrieb Gmbh, Ostendstrasse 1, pg. 1448 — IT
Wilhelm Weber GmbH, Ostendstr 8, pg. 160 — PV

Pinneberg

Bergquist ITC, GmbH, Haderslebener St.19a, pg. 135 — PV
Bowthorpe GmbH, Prisdorfer Str. 99, pg. 208 — IT
Paul Hellermann GmbH, Siemensstrasse 5, pg. 209 — IT
Leca Deutschland GmbH, pg. 1200 — IT

Pirmasens

Forbo Helmitin GmbH, Weibrucker Str. 185, pg. 497 — IT

Planegg

COBE Laboratories GmbH, Lochhamer Strasse 15, pg. 667 — IT
EOS GmbH Electro Optical Systems, pg. 1523 — IT
Gambro Medizintechnik GmbH, Lochhamer Strasse 15, pg. 668 — IT

Plankstadt

Rhein-Pharma Arzneimittelwerk GmbH, Otto-Hahn Strasse, pg. 1525 — IT

Plattling

Kermi GmbH, Pankofen - Bahnhof 1, pg. 1069 — IT
MD Papier GmbH - Plattling Mill, Nicolausstrasse 7, pg. 864 — IT

Plauen

Julius Kleeman Handel mit Werkzeugen und Maschinen GmbH, Arndtstrasse 16, pg. 1128 — IT
MAN Plamag Druckmaschinen AG, Pausaer Strasse 284, pg. 825 — IT

PB - U.S. Public Companies Volume
PV - U.S. Private Companies Volume
IT - International Public & Private Companies Volume

1630

Geographic Index-Non U.S.

Pleidelsheim

Parker Hannifin GmbH, O-Ring Div. Europe, Stuifenstrasse 55, pg. 1263   PB

Plettenberg

Albert Biecker GmbH & Co. KG, pg. 1061   IT
PLETTAC AG, plettac Platz 1, pg. 1061   IT
Plettac Umformtechnik GmbH & Co. KG, pg. 1061   IT

Pliening

Disco Hi-tec Europe GmbH, Gewerbestrasse 11, pg. 413   IT

Pliezhausen

Renishaw GmbH, Karl-Benz Strasse 12, pg. 1103   IT

Plochingen

CeramTec Ag, Fabrikstr. 23-29, pg. 860   IT
Cerasiv GmbH, Fabrikstrasse 23-29, pg. 861   IT

Pocking

V.A.G. Leasing GmbH & Co. Besitz, pg. 1474   IT
Volkswagen Aktiengesellschaft & Co. Leasing, pg. 1474   IT
Volkswagen Financial Services AG & Co., pg. 1474   IT

Pohlheim

Rudolf Muller & Co. G.m.b.H., Giessener Strasse 94, pg. 289   IT

Poppendorf

Hydro Agri Rostock GmbH, pg. 962   IT

Porta Westfalica

Cordes & Co. GmbH, Hausberger Strasse 14-16, pg. 609   IT
Niemann Chemie G.m.b.H., Osterkamp 31, pg. 1426   PB

Potsdam

BAB IKON GmbH Schliesstechnik, Behlerstr. 29, pg. 18   IT
Bau-Union Potsdam GmbH, Am Luftschiffhafen 1, pg. 195   IT
DG Bank - Potsdam, Dortustrasse 68 a, pg. 352   IT
Energiewerke Potsdam AG, Berliner Strasse 10, pg. 1456   IT
Erdgas Mark Brandenburg GmbH - EMB, Glasmeisterstrasse 14-22, pg. 541   IT
Flaskamp GmbH, Behlerstr. 26, pg. 493   IT
Mannesmann Seiffert Industrieanlagen GmbH, pg. 836   IT
Markische Energieversorgung AG, pg. 1456   IT
Niederlassung Potsdam, Am Luftschiffhafen 1, pg. 195   IT

Prenden

TBS Ges. fur Tank- und Bodenschutz mbH - Prenden, Am Weinberg, pg. 515   IT

Puchheim

ASF Thomas, Seimenstrasse 4, pg. 1599   PB
ALLSPANN, Allgemeine Spannbeton GmbH, Benzstr. 7, pg. 423   IT
Amway GmbH, Benzstrasse 11 a-c, pg. 70   PV
Dale Electronics GmbH, Benzstrasse 28, pg. 1722   PB
K2 Ski-Sport & Mode GmbH, pg. 940   PB
Mary Kay Cosmetics, GMBH, Lilienthalstrasse 5, pg. 711   PV
Richardson Electronics GmbH, Benzstrasse 28, Bau B, pg. 1388   PB

Pullach

Selas-Kirchner GmbH, pg. 811   IT

Puttlingen

SKF Gleitlager GmbH, Muhlenstrasse 43, pg. 1158   IT

Quedlinburg

Geschaftsstelle Quedlinburg, Am Johannishain 3, pg. 194   IT

Quickborn

comdirect bank GmbH, Pascalkehre 15, pg. 309   IT
Miller Intl. Schallplatten G.m.b.H., Justus von Liebig-ring 2-4, pg. 1216   IT

Radebeul

Energie- und Umwelttechnik GmbH, Wasastrasse 50, pg. 1460   IT
KBA-Planeta AG, Friedrich List Strasse 47-49, pg. 742   IT
SSC Radebeul GmbH, Kotitzerstr. 110, pg. 512   IT
VEB POLYGRAPH DRUCKMACHINENWERK PLANETA RADEBEUL, Friedrich-List Strasse 47-49, pg. 1445   IT

Radevormwald

Beton Union Radevormwald GmbH & Co. KG, pg. 422   IT
Hartek Beverage Handling GmbH, Otto-Hahn Strabe 4, pg. 1445   PB

Ransbach-Baumbach

Fuchs' Sche Tongruben GmbH & Co. Ltd., Haus Petersberg, Hundsdorf, pg. 1488   IT
Wolf-Ton GmbH & Co., Ltd., Rheinstrasse 24, pg. 1488   IT

Ranstadt

Kloeckner-Pentapack GmbH, Bahnhofstr. 25, pg. 737   IT

Rastatt

BWR Werkstoffsysteme und Werkzeugbau GmbH, Werkstrasse 2, pg. 354   IT
DSM Compounds GmbH, Werkstrasse 2, pg. 355   IT
LLE, Am Oberwald 8, pg. 1045   PB
Landis & Staefa Deutschland Produktion GmbH, Berliner Ring 23, pg. 800   IT

Ratekau

Norfi Exhaust Extraction Systems GmbH, Zeiss-Strasse 3, pg. 283   IT

Ratingen

Aro GmbH, Kaiserwerther Strasse 49-51, pg. 877   PB
Asco G.m.b.H. & Co., Voisweg 5C, pg. 575   PB
BDAG Balcke-Durr AG, Homberger Str. 2, pg. 399   PB
Bekaert Deutschland GmbH, Zweigniederlassung Ratingen, Brandenburger Strasse 42, pg. 184   IT
Calor-Emag Elektrizitats-Aktiengesellschaft, P.O. Box 1220, pg. 2   IT
Chiron GmbH, Am Schmimmersfeld 5, pg. 350   PB
Componenta International Deutschland GmbH, Christinenstrasse 12, pg. 1421   IT
Ericsson Private Systems GmbH, Harkortstr. 25, pg. 1367   IT
Fluor Daniel GmbH, Daniel-Goldbach-Str. 17-19, pg. 660   PB
Hewlett-Packard GmbH, Vertriebszentrum Ratingen, Berliner Strasse 111, pg. 820   PB
Ingersoll-Rand GmbH, Harkortstrasse 35, Postfach 1362, pg. 878   IT
Kalmar Kockum GmbH, Postfach 2244, pg. 1421   IT
Karrena GmbH, Breitscheider Weg 34, pg. 398   IT
Kidde-Deugra GmbH, Halskestrasse 30, pg. 1500   IT
Kintetsu World Express (Deutschland) GmbH, Harkortstrasse 2-6, pg. 735   IT
MDS Mannesmann Demag Sack GmbH, pg. 837   IT
Mannesmann Datenverarbeitung GmbH, pg. 837   IT
Medex Medical GmbH, Alter Volksweg 68, pg. 689   PB
Michael & Co (MiCo) Tontrager Vertiebs-gesellschaft mbH, Am Sandbach 32, pg. 1052   PB
NSK-RHP Deutschland G.m.b.h., Harkortstrasse 15, pg. 904   IT
Nitto Deutschland GmbH, Am Sandbach 32, pg. 951   IT
OCG Microelectronic Materials GmbH, Harkorstrasse 32, pg. 1219   PB
Olin GmbH, Harkortstrasse 32, pg. 1220   PB
PRO Musica Musik-und Kunstversand GmbH, Am Sandbach 32, pg. 1053   IT
Readymix AG fur Beteiligungen, Readymix-Haus, Daniel-Goldbach-Strasse 25, pg. 1081   IT
Record Rack Schallplatten Vertriebsgesellschaft mbH, Am Sandbach 32, pg. 1053   IT
Rheinmetall Industrie AG, Pempelfurstrasse 1, pg. 1108   IT
Sanitec Ltd. Oy, Kreuzerkamp 11, pg. 863   IT
Selas Waermetechnik GmbH, Christinenstrauss 2, pg. 1455   PB
Stahlkontor Hahn GmbH, pg. 838   IT
Svedala Deutschland, pg. 1324   IT
TDK Electronics Europe GmbH, Christinenstrasse 25, pg. 1336   IT
Tioxide Europe GmbH, Am Brull 17, pg. 666   IT
Universal Transport GmbH, Broichhofstr. 5-7, pg. 1034   IT
VW AUDI Vertrienszentrum Rhein-Ruhr Gmbh, pg. 1474   IT
VW AUDI Vertrienszentrum Rhein-Ruhr GmbH & Co. KG, pg. 1474   IT

Raunheim

AlliedSignal Aerospace GmbH, Frankfurterstrasse 4165, pg. 52   PB
Rockwell International GmbH, Avionics Service Center, Kelsterbacher Strasse 20, pg. 1401   PB
Rockwell International GmbH, General Aviation Div., Kelsterbacher Strasse 20, pg. 1401   PB

Ravensburg

Sulzer Chemtech GmbH, pg. 1308   IT
Sulzer-Escher Wyss GmbH, pg. 1305   IT
Sulzer Hydro GmbH, pg. 1308   IT
Sulzer International (Deutschland) GmbH, pg. 1308   IT

Reckingen

Kraftwerk Reckingen AG, pg. 67   IT

Recklinghausen

Beton-und Monierbau GmbH, Karlstrasse 37-39, pg. 1069   IT
Grove Coles GmbH, Bochumer Strasse 1, pg. 594   IT
Winschermann West GmbH, Schaumburgstrasse 15-17, pg. 1167   IT

Rees

Novoferm GmbH, Isselburger Str.31, pg. 509   IT

Regensburg

DG Bank - Regensburg, Dreikronengasse 2, pg. 352   IT
DSM Andeno GmbH, Donaustaufferstrasse 378, pg. 355   IT
Kalkwerk D. Funk GmbH & Co. KG, Donaustaufer Str. 207, pg. 606   IT
Grau GmbH, pg. 561   PB
Niederlassung Regensburg, Siemensstrasse 3, pg. 195   IT
Scheu & Wirth AG, Dr. Gessler Str. 43, pg. 633   IT

Reichenbach

TRAUB AG, Ulmer Strasse 49-55, pg. 1419   IT
Traub Drehmaschinen GmbH, Ulmer Strasse 49-55, pg. 1419   IT
Traub-Heckert Vertriebs GmbH, Ulmer Strasse 49-55, pg. 1419   IT

Reinbek

DSG-Mecman Training Systems GmbH, pg. 838   IT
HERMAL KURT HERRMANN & CO., Scholtzstrasse 3A, pg. 616   IT
Kroll Fahrzeugbau Umwelttechnik GmbH, Guttenbergstrasse 26-30, pg. 1128   IT
Mecman GmbH, pg. 838   IT
Rowohlt Taschenbuch Verlag GmbH, Hamburger Strasse 17, pg. 1478   IT
Rowohlt Verlag GmbH, Hamburger Strasse 17, pg. 1478   IT
Wunderlich Verlag GmbH, Hamburger Strasse 17, pg. 1479   IT

Reinheim

OCLI Optical Coating Laboratory GmbH, Tilsiter Strasse 12, pg. 1227   PB

Rellingen

Weyburn-Bartel GmbH, 53-57 Adlerstrasse, pg. 1334   IT

Remagen

Morgan GmbH, pg. 891   IT

Rems

F.I.A.P. Deutschland GmbH, Walter Freitag Strasse 14, pg. 5   PB

Remscheid

Barmag Maschinenfabrik AG, 65 Lenerkuser Str., pg. 46   IT
Krupp Hoesch Stahl AG - Remscheid, Industriestr. 25 a, pg. 512   IT
Leschuplast Kunststoff-Fabrik GmbH, pg. 422   IT
Signode Bernpak GmbH, Greul 1A, pg. 869   PB
Thyssen Umformtechnik GmbH, pg. 1387   IT

Rendsburg

Grundstucksgesellschaft Jungfernstieg mbH, pg. 179   IT
HDW-Nobiskrug GmbH, Kielo Strasse 53, pg. 1069   IT
SCHLESWAG Aktiengesellschaft, Kieler Strasse 19, pg. 1456   IT

Renningen

Sandvik Kosta GmbH, P.O. Box 1209, pg. 1186   IT

Reutlingen

Erima GmbH & Co., pg. 24   IT
GUSTAV WAGNER MASCHINENFABRIK GMBH, Gustav-Wagner-Str. 11, pg. 579   IT
Hermann Wangner, Postfach 2952, pg. 1418   IT
Indumat GmbH & Co. KG, pg. 811   IT
Swiss Prestige, Wilhelmstrasse 12, pg. 1161   IT
Wagner Fordertechnik GmbH & Co. KG, St. Peterstrasse 5, pg. 811   IT

Rheda-Wiedenbruck

Nielsen Design GmbH, Rontgenstrasse 10, pg. 462   IT
WESTAG & GETALIT AG, Hellweg 15, pg. 1491   IT

Rheinberg

Solvay Alkali GmbH, Xantener Strasse 237, pg. 1279   IT
Solvay Kunststoffe GmbH, Xantener Strasse 237,
pg. 1280   IT
Solvay Salz GmbH, Karlstrasse 80, pg. 1280   IT

Rheine

Hohn & Hohn GmbH, 5657 Haan, pg. 81   PB

Rheinfelden

Cabot Huls GmbH, Friedrichstrasse 48, pg. 1454   IT
CIBA-GEIGY Holding Deutschland GmbH, Kirchplatz 1,
pg. 977   IT

Rhens

Blaue Quellen Mineral- und Heilbrunnen AG, Brunnen
Strasse 2-8, pg. 919   IT

Riedligen

Remington Products GmbH, Siemensstrasse 7,
pg. 921   PV

Riesa

Mannesmann Rohren und Stahlhandel GmbH, pg. 838   IT

Rocknitz

Sachsische Quarzporphyrwerke GmbH, Steinbergstrasse,
pg. 632   IT

Rodermark

Didier Misch- und Trenntechnik MUT GmbH, Max-Planck-
Str. 19, pg. 1464   IT

Rodgau

Alfa System Partner GmbH, pg. 835   IT
Funk Aluminum GmbH, Raiffeisenstr. 12, pg. 514   IT
Goss Graphic Systems Inc., Boschstrasse 8-10,
pg. 466   PV
Kenner Parker Toys International, Deutsche Niederlassung,
Klocknerstrasse 1, pg. 798   PB
Kubota Corp.-Frankfurt Office, Senefelder Strasse 3-5,
pg. 762   IT
Kubota (Deutschland) GmbH, Seneder Strasse 3-5,
pg. 763   IT
Oberflanchentechnik Wahl-CFR GmbH, Benzstr. 27,
pg. 517   IT
Perstorp Analytical GmbH, Ludwigstrasse 24-26,
pg. 1039   IT
Rockwell International GmbH, Boschstrasse 8-10,
pg. 1401   PB
Taylor Instrument GmbH, Diamlerstr. 11, pg. 6   IT

Rodolfzell

Schiesser AG, pg. 618   IT

Roedermark

Zimmer Chirugie G.m.b.H., Siemensstrasse 16, pg. 256   PB

Rohrdorf

Suedbayerisches Portland Simning Zementwerk Gebr.
Wiesboeck & Co. GmbH, pg. 605   IT

Ronsberg

4P Verpackungen Ronsberg GmbH, pg. 1146   IT

Rosbach

KEBE Ersatzteile GmbH, Beinhardsweg 9, pg. 283   IT

Rosdorf

Innovir GmbH, Olenhuser Landstrasse 20a, pg. 1703   PB

Rosenheim

Knurr-Heinzinger Electronic GmbH, Anton-Jakob-Strasse 4,
pg. 739   IT
Niedermayr Papierwarenfabrik AG, Bruckenstr. 1,
pg. 606   IT

Rosrath

GKN Distribution GmbH, Postfach 1169, pg. 536   IT
GKN Informatik GmbH, Postfach 1169, pg. 536   IT
GKN Service GmbH, Postfach 1169, pg. 536   IT

Rossdorf

Gelman Sciences (Deutschland) GmbH, Max-Arheilger Weg
6A, pg. 1253   PB

Rostock

DG Bank - Rostock, John-Brinckman-Strasse 9,
pg. 352   IT
Deutsche Bank-Kreditbank AG (Rostock), Lindenstrasse 7,
pg. 402   IT
Energiewerke Rostock AG, Bleicherstrasse 1, pg. 1456   IT
Hanseatische Energieversorgung Aktiengesellschaft
Rostock, pg. 1456   IT
Kvaener Warnow Werft GmbH, Werftalle 10, pg. 772   IT
Niederlassung Rostock, Industriestrasse 8, pg. 195   IT

Rott

Flender-ATB-Loher Systemtechnik GmbH, Hans-Loher-
Strasse 30-34, pg. 400   IT
Loher AG, pg. 400   IT

Rottweil

Mikrom Rottweil GmbH, Stadionstrasse 31, pg. 867   IT

Rudesheim

Asbach GmbH & Co., AM Rottland 2-10, pg. 412   IT

Rudisleben

Chema Balcke-Durr Verfahrenstechnik GmbH Rudisleben,
pg. 399   IT

Ruppach-Goldhausen

Martin & Pagenstecher Rohstoffbet Riebe GmbH & Co. KG,
pg. 1488   IT

Russelsheim

Adam Opel AG, pg. 721   PB
Convesco Vehicle Sales GmbH, Eisenstrasse 2, Postfach
1261, pg. 724   PB
General Electric Plastics GmbH, Eisenstrasse 5,
pg. 713   PB
General Motors Marketing Services Hellas AEE,
pg. 722   PB

Saal

MAHLO GMBH & CO. KG, Donaustrasse 12, pg. 830   IT

Saalfelden

PKL Verpackungssyteme Saalfelden GmbH,
Industriestrasse, pg. 1156   IT

Saarbruecken

Cogema Uran Services (Deutschland) MbH & CO KG,
Malstatter Makt 11, pg. 305   IT
Cosmos Krankenversicherung AG, Halbergstrasse 52-54,
pg. 15   IT
Cosmos Lebensversicherung AG, Halberstrasse 52-54,
pg. 15   IT
Cosmos Versicherung AG, Halbergstrasse 52-54,
pg. 15   IT
Daarberg-Oekotechnik GmbH, Hafenstr. 25, pg. 1167   IT
Deutsche Bank Saar AG, Kaiserstrasse 29-31, pg. 402   IT
GK Gesellschaft fuer Kohleverfluessigung mbH, Postfach
238, pg. 1166   IT
GVT Gesellschaft fuer Versorgungstechnik mbH, Postfach
238, Sulzbachstrasse 26, pg. 1167   IT
Halbergerhutte GmbH, pg. 1176   IT
INDUSTRIE-RING Sach-und Versicherungs-
Vermittlungsgesellschaft mbH, Postfach 1030, Trierer
Strasse 1, pg. 1166   IT
Interuran GmbH, Malstatter Markt 11, pg. 305   IT
Karl Vieh GmbH, Luisenthaler Str. 156, pg. 827   PV
Kohle-Kontor-Saar GmbH, Ursulinenstrasse 67,
pg. 1167   IT
LKS Daten-Service A.G., Haus der Datenverarbeitung,
Preussenstrasse 19, pg. 318   IT
LKS daten - service GmbH, Preussenstr. 19, pg. 317   IT
LAGERA Gesellschaft fur Lagerung und Spedition,
Zweigniederlassung der Rhenania, pg. 1033   IT
Modellkraftwerk Voelklingen GmbH, Postfach 1030, Trierer
Strasse 1, pg. 1167   IT
Modernbau GmbH, Eschberger Weg 59, pg. 195   IT
Rhenania-Saar Speditions-GmbH, An der Romerbrucke 5,
pg. 1033   IT
SBV Vermogensverwaltungs-gesellschaft mbH, pg. 596   IT
Saar Ferngas AG, pg. 1148   IT
Saarberg Brennstoffhandel GmbH, Ursulinenstrasse 67,
pg. 1167   IT
Saarberg-Fernwaerme GmbH, Postfach 238,
Sulzbachstrasse 26, pg. 1166   IT
Saarberg Handel GmbH, Postfach 503, Ursulinenstr. 67,
pg. 1167   IT
Saarberg-Hoelter-Lurgi GmbH, Hafenstrasse 6,
pg. 1167   IT
Saarberg-Hoelter Umwelttechnik GmbH, Hafenstrasse 6,
pg. 1167   IT

Saarberg-Interplan Gesellschaft fuer Rohstoff-, Energie-und
Ingenieurtechnik mbH, Postfach 73, Malstatter Markt 13,
pg. 1167   IT
SAARBERGWERKE AKTIENGESELLSCHAFT, Trierer
Strasse 1, pg. 1166   IT
Saarbrucker Zeitung Verlag und Druckerei GmbH,
Gutenbergstrasse 11-23, pg. 1478   IT
Saarlaendische Kraftwerksgesellschaft mbH, Postfach
1030, Trierer Str. 1, pg. 1167   IT
UNISPED Spedition und Transportgesellschaft mbH,
Postfach 728, Trierer Str. 1, pg. 1167   IT

Saarlouis

DSD Dillinger Stahlbau GmbH, pg. 310   IT

Saarnellingen

Feumas GmbH, pg. 659   IT

Sachsenheim

Velcro GmbH, Siemensstrasse 2, pg. 1462   IT

Sackingen

CIBA-GEIGY GmbH, Trottackerstrasse 26-28, pg. 977   IT

Saint Augustin

Makhteshim-Agan Deutschland GmbH, Sudstrasse 29,
pg. 830   IT
Maschinenfabrik Hennecke GmbH, Birlinghovener Strasse
30, pg. 172   IT
Steelweld Division Zweigniederlassung Bonn der Ambac
B.V., Frankfurterstrasse 59, pg. 71   IT

Saint Goar

Engel & Meier GmbH, Alte Heerstrasse 109, pg. 1152   IT

Saint Ingbert

Kleber Reifen und Technische Gummiwaren AG, P.O. Box
1560, pg. 322   IT
PWH Anlagen + Systeme GmbH, Erst-Heckel Str. 1,
pg. 511   IT

Salzgitter

Robert Bosch Eletronik GmbH, John-F.-Kennedy-Strasse
43-53, pg. 204   IT
Ferngas Salzgitter GmbH, Watenstedter Weg 75,
pg. 1148   IT
METAPLAS IONON Lohnharterei GmbH, John-F.-Kennedy-
Str. 52, pg. 400   IT
NORD/LB, In den Blumentriften 64, pg. 957   IT
P&S Filtration GmbH, Zur Finkenkuhle 40-42, pg. 1203   IT
PBG Preussag Bundelfunk Gmbh, Gottfried-Linke,
pg. 740   PB
Preussag Immobilien GmbH, Chemmtu Strasse 90-94,
pg. 1070   IT
Preussag Versicherrungsdienst GmbH, Albert-Schweitzer-
Strasse 51, pg. 1070   IT
Salzgitter GmbH, Eisenhittenstrasse 88, pg. 1070   IT
Salzgitter Oberflachentechnik GmbH, pg. 1308   IT
Sia-Handelsgesellschaft mbH, pg. 1207   IT
Verkehrsbetriebe Peine-Salzgitter GmbH, Am Hillenholz 28,
pg. 1070   IT
WAG Salzgitter Wohnungs-GmbH, Chemmitu Strasse 90-
94, pg. 1070   IT

Sandhausen

Gebhardt Ventilatoren Verwaltungs GmbH, Hinterm Haag
10, pg. 1055   PB
Hueppe GmbH, Hinterm Haag 10, pg. 1055   PB
Jung Pumpen Verwaltungs GmbH, Hinterm Haag 10,
pg. 1054   PB
Masco, GmbH, Hinterm Haag 10, pg. 1055   PB

Sarrebruck

C.E.R.T., 58-60 Richard Wagner Str., pg. 795   IT
Europa Plus Medien Beteiligungs, 58-60 Richard Wagner
Str., pg. 795   IT

Sarstedt

Landesgasversorgung Niedersachsen AG, pg. 1456   IT

Schenefeld

SPAR HANDELS AG, Osterbrooksweg 35245,
pg. 1288   IT

Schenklengsfeld

Forbo Uli-Chemie GmbH, pg. 498   IT

Scherwin

NORD/LB Landesbank fur Mecklenburg-Vorpommern, Graf-
Schack Allee 11, pg. 958   IT

PB - *U.S. Public Companies Volume*
PV - *U.S. Private Companies Volume*
IT - *International Public & Private Companies Volume*

1632

Geographic Index-Non U.S.

Schieder-Schwalenberg

Kanal-Muller-Gruppe, pg. 597   IT

Schleswig

Danfoss Schleswig, Heinrich-Hertz-Str. 2, pg. 377   IT

Schluctern

Immergut Milch Gmbh, pg. 991   IT
Nutricia Diatetik Gmbh, pg. 992   IT
Alfred Ziegler Molkerei Schluctern GmbH & Co. KG,
  pg. 992   IT

Schongau

Schongau Paper Mill, Friedrich-Haindl-Strasse 10,
  pg. 586   IT
Vatter, pg. 1435   PB

Schonkirchen

Hilekes G.m.b.H., Prof-Kuntscher-Str. 1-5, pg. 1282   PB
Wohlk Contact-Linsen GmbH, pg. 1523   IT

Schoppenstedt

Gurtec GmbH & Co., KG, pg. 1353   IT

Schorndorf

AGIE GmbH, Vorstadtstrasse 61-67, pg. 488   IT

Schrobenhausen

Daimler-Benz Aerospace AG, Entsorgung, pg. 367   IT

Schwabach

Spectrum Control, GmbH, Hansastrasse 6, pg. 1497   PB

Schwabhausen

Dyckerhoff Transportbeton Gotha GmbH & Co. KG,
  pg. 422   IT

Schwabisch Hall

Grau Werkzeug-und Formenbau Gmbh & Co.,
  Alemannenstrasse 65, pg. 755   IT
**KLAFS SAUNABAU GMBH & CO. KG MEDIZINISCHE
  TECHNIK**, Daimler Strasse 39, pg. 736   IT

Schwaig

Demag Kunststofftechnik GmbH, pg. 837   IT

Schwalbach

Danzas Holding GmbH, Am Kronberger Hang 3,
  pg. 382   IT
Data General GmbH, Am Kronberger Hang 3, pg. 486   PB
Procter & Gamble GmbH, Sulzbacher Str. 40, pg. 1332   PB

Schwalmtal

Berkmanns Antriebe GmbH, Danziger Str. 2, pg. 559   IT
Rosler Draht AG, Dulkener Strasse, Heerstrasse 3,
  pg. 185   IT

Schwarzheide

BASF Schwarzheide GmbH, Schipkauer Strasse 1,
  pg. 104   IT
Elastogran Schwarzheide GmbH, Schipkauer Strasse 6,
  pg. 104   IT

Schwedt

KSB Service GmbH, pg. 721   IT

Schwedt an der Oder

Petrolchemie und Kraftstoffe AG Schwedt, pg. 1461   IT

Schweinfurt

Deutsche Husqvarna GmbH, Postfach 4006, pg. 442   IT
Deutsche Star GmbH, pg. 838   IT
FAG Aircraft/Super Precision Bearings, GmbH, pg. 468   IT
FAG Automobiltechnik AG, pg. 468   IT
FAG GROUP, Georg-Schaefer-Str. 30, pg. 468   IT
FAG Komponenten AG, pg. 468   IT
FAG Kugelfischer Georg Schafer AG, pg. 468   IT
FAG OEM und Handel AG, pg. 468   IT
FAG Personaldienste u. Service GmbH, pg. 468   IT
Fichtel & Sachs AG, Ernst-Sachs-Str. 62, pg. 835   IT
KDJ-VmbH, Georg-Schafer Str., pg. 468   IT
PMT Prazisions-Mebtechnik GmbH, pg. 468   IT
SKF GmbH, pg. 1158   IT
SKF Linearsysteme GmbH, Hans-Bockler-Strasse 6,
  pg. 1159   IT

Schwelm

Titan Umreifungstechnik GmbH, Berliner Str. 51-55,
  pg. 509   IT

Schwenningen

Benzing Ventilatoren GmbH, Werastrasse 62, pg. 1268   IT
Swissmetal Deutschland Handelsgesellschaft mbH,
  Neuffenstrasse 23, pg. 1427   IT

Schwerin

DG Bank - Schwerin, Wismarsche Strasse 323,
  pg. 352   IT
Landesverlags und Druckgesellschaft mbH - Mecklenburg &
  Co. KG, Von Stauffenbergstrasse 27, pg. 233   IT
Niederlassung Schwerin, Am Margaretenhof 26,
  pg. 195   IT
Perstorp Norkun Kunstoffverarbeitung GmbH, Sacktannen,
  pg. 1038   IT

Schwerte

Flachform Stahl GmbH, Emil-Rohrmann-Strasse,
  pg. 79   IT
Waggonbau Bruninghaus GmbH, Bruninghausstr. 1,
  pg. 509   IT
Walter Hundhausen GmbH & Co KG, Ostendamm 23,
  pg. 508   IT

Schwetzingen

Hermann Bohler GmbH, Scheffelstrasse 34-35,
  pg. 616   IT
Konus-Kessel Gesellschaft fur Warmetechnik mbH,
  pg. 399   IT

Schwieberdingen

Sud Electra GmbH, Hermann Essig Strasse 13,
  pg. 712   IT

Seeheim

Neho Versand G.m.b.H., 6101 Seeheim, Berstasse
  Friedrich-Ebert, pg. 1216   IT

Seelow

Seelow Kasewerke GmbH, pg. 753   IT

Seelze

Case Traktoren GmbH, pg. 1579   PB
Riedel-de Haen AG, Postfach 100262, pg. 625   IT

Seesen

Hille Handel GmbH, pg. 838   IT
NORD/LB, Jacobsonstrasse 1, pg. 958   IT

Seevetal

Babcock Textilmaschinen GmbH, pg. 399   IT

Selb

Draloric Electronic GmbH, Postfach 1180, pg. 1722   PB
ROSENTHAL AG, Wittelsbacherstrasse 43, pg. 1127   IT

Seligenstadt

Gould Instrument Systems GmbH, Dieselstrasse 5-7,
  pg. 1592   PB

Senden

Maxitrol Company M.B.H., Industrie Strasse, pg. 716   PV

Senftenberg

Lausitzer Braunkohle Aktiengesellschaft (LAUBAG),
  pg. 1457   IT

Sennfeld

Franken Rohstoff GmbH, Schweinfurter Str. 6-8,
  pg. 513   IT

Shaftlach

Volland Telemetry GmbH, Krottenhaler Alm 2, pg. 209   IT

Shonkirchen

Howmedica G.m.b.H., Prof.-Kuentscher-Str. 1-5,
  pg. 1282   PB

Siegburg

Kepec Chemische Fabrik GmbH, Barbarastrasse 34,
  pg. 610   IT

Software Union Syseca GmbH, Hauptverwalting, Auf den
  Tongruben 3, pg. 1385   IT

Siegen

Eisen- und Stein-Gesellschaft mbH, Horn & Co.,
  Herrenfeldstr. 12, pg. 513   IT
Electrolux, Postfach 101001, pg. 442   IT
Electrolux-Constructor GmbH, Postfach 101001,
  pg. 442   IT
Electrolux-Cramer GmbH, Postfach 101001, pg. 442   IT
Electrolux Kuchentechnik GmbH, Postfach 10 10 01,
  pg. 442   IT
Electrolux Siegen GmbH, Postfach 101001, pg. 442   IT
Hoesch Renova GmbH, Konigstr. 22, pg. 508   IT
Hoesch Siegerlandwerke GmbH, Geisweider Str. 13,
  pg. 508   IT
KABELSCHLEPP GMBH, Marienborner Strasse 75,
  pg. 721   IT
Krupp Edelstahlprofile GmbH, Obere Kaiserstr.,
  pg. 512   IT
Krupp Hoesch Stahl AG - Siegerland, Geisweiderstr. 13,
  pg. 513   IT
Lowe & Jaegers GmbH, Industriestrasse 16, pg. 1450   IT
Rhenania Transport GmbH, Zweigniederlassung Siegen
  Hagener Strass, pg. 1033   IT

Siegsdorf

IPC Corporation (Germany), Reitweg 10, pg. 651   IT
Lang Apparatebau GmbH, Raiffeisenstrasse 7, pg. 610   IT

Simbach

Deutsche Heraklith A.G., pg. 903   PV

Simmerath

OTTO JUNKER GMBH LAMMERSDORF,
  Jagerhausstrasse 722, pg. 1014   IT

Sindelfingen

B & P Vermoegensverwaltungs GmbH, pg. 309   IT
Karl Baumgartner & Partner Consulting GmbH & Co. KG,
  pg. 309   IT
Carpenter Technology (Deutschland) GmbH, Waldenbucher
  Strasse 22, pg. 308   PB
Proner Comatel GmbH, Magstadter Strasse 36,
  pg. 1242   IT
Schlatter Gmbh, Max-Eyth-Strasse 12, pg. 1206   IT

Singen

Alusingen GmbH, pg. 68   IT
Alusuisse-Lonza GmbH, pg. 68   IT
Casino Moderne Menu Systeme GmbH, pg. 919   IT
Deutsche Libby GmbH, pg. 920   IT
Georg Fischer AG & Co., Julius-Buhrer-Strasse 12,
  pg. 491   IT
Georg Fischer Automobilguss GmbH, Julius-Buhrer-Strasse
  12, pg. 488   IT
Georg Fischer Beteiligungs GmbH, Julius Buhrer Strasse
  12, pg. 491   IT
Georg Fischer Geschaftsfuhrungs GmbH, Julius-Buhrer-
  Strasse 12, pg. 491   IT
Georg Fischer Rohrverbindungstechnik Gmbh,
  Freibuhlstrasse 18, pg. 490   IT
Georg Fischer Verkehrstechnik GmbH, Julius-Buhrer-
  Strasse 12, pg. 488   IT
Georg Fischer Wohnbau GmbH & Co., Julius-Buhrer-
  Strasse 12, pg. 491   IT
Lawson Mardon Singen GmbH, ALUSINGEN-Platz 1,
  pg. 69   IT
Maggi GmbH, Julius-Buehrer Str. 8, pg. 920   IT

Sinsheim

Dr. Wolmann GmbH, Dr.-Wolman-Strasse 31-33,
  pg. 104   IT
Moser-Bau GmbH, Neulandstrasse 25, pg. 195   IT
Polypenco GmbH, Niederlassung Sinsheim, Am Leitzelbach
  11, pg. 354   IT

Soest

CEAG Sicherheitstechnik GmbH, Senator-Schwartz-Ring
  26, pg. 444   PB
Entsorgungswirtschaft Soest GmbH, pg. 597   IT

Solingen

Wilhelm Boos jr., GmbH & Co., Postfach 10 11 06,
  pg. 492   IT
Delft Instruments - BRD GmbH, Obere Dammstrasse 10,
  pg. 389   IT
ESAB GmbH, Beethovenstrasse 135, pg. 282   IT
Enraf-Nonius GmbH, Obere Dammstrasse 8-10,
  pg. 389   IT
Franke Gmbh, Obere Dammstrasse 10, pg. 389   IT
Kieserling GmbH, Birkenweiher 66, pg. 399   IT
Krups GmbH & Co. KG, Heresbachstrasse 29, pg. 896   IT
Mannesmann Kronprinz, pg. 835   IT
Oldelft GmbH Medizingeratevertrieb, Obere Dammstrasse
  8-10, pg. 389   IT
Emil Schlemper G.m.b.H., P.O. Box 130239, pg. 17   PB
Tondeo-Werk GmbH, Hohscheider Weg 39-45,
  pg. 1489   IT

PB - *U.S. Public Companies Volume*
PV - *U.S. Private Companies Volume*
IT - *International Public & Private Companies Volume*

Sonneberg

Mann & Hummel Kunststofftechnik GmbH & Co. KG, Friedrich-Engels-Strasse 157, pg. 484   IT

Sonthofen

BHS-Voith Getriebetechnik Gmbh, pg. 1473   IT

Spaichingen

Precision Motors - Deutsche Minebea GmbH, Max Planck Str. 14, pg. 869   IT

Speyer

Deutsche Ranco GmbH, pg. 1243   IT
Filterwerk Mann & Hummel GmbH, Brunckstrasse 15, pg. 484   IT

Sprendlingen

Pall Deutschland GmbH, pg. 1254   PB

Stade

Aluminum Oxid Stade Gesellschaft Mit Beschrankter Haftung, Postfach 5160, pg. 1386   PB
Kernkraftwerk Stade GmbH, Postfach 17 80, pg. 1456   IT
Norddeutsche Salinen GmbH, One, Eisenbahnstrasse, pg. 44   IT
VAW Aluminum AG, Elbewerk, pg. 1466   IT

Stadland

Kernkraftwerk Unterweser GmbH, pg. 1456   IT

Stadthagen

Bertrand Faure Sitztechnik GmbH & Co. kg, Industriestrasse 3, pg. 193   IT
Bertrand Faure Sitztechnik GmbH & Co. KG, Nordsehler Strasse 38, pg. 193   IT

Stahnsdorf

Gottlieb Tesch Strassen-und Leitungsbau GmbH, Ruhlsdorfer Strasse 103, pg. 195   IT

Stapelburg

Beteiligungs-KG der DEFAG Deutsche Flugzeugv. AG & Co. KG, pg. 596   IT
DEFAG Deutsche Flugzeugv. AG & Co. KG, pg. 596   IT
Deutsche Flugzeugvermietungs AG, pg. 596   IT

Starnberg

Carl Baasel Lasertechnik GmbH, pg. 836   IT
Clarins GmbH, Petersbrunner Str. 3, pg. 295   IT
MHI Partners Werbeagentur GMBH, Gautinger Str. 10, pg. 1422   PB
PMB Elektronik Produktion GmbH, pg. 836   IT
Vermont GMBH, Gautinger Strasse 7A, pg. 578   PB

Steinau

Rewo Chemische Werke GmbH, Max Wolf Strasse 7, pg. 1774   PB

Steinbach

Ingold Messtechnik GmbH, Siemensstrasse 9, pg. 983   IT
Mettler-Toledo Prozessanalytik GmbH, Siemensstrasse 9, pg. 4   PV
Westerwalder Eisen-Rohstoffhandels-GmbH, Bindweide, Ladestr., pg. 514   IT

Steinfurt-Altenberge

Entsorgungsgesellschaft Steinfurt mbH, pg. 597   IT

Steinhagen

Jung-Pumpen GmbH, Industriestrasse 4-6, pg. 1054   PB

Steinheim

Aldrich Chemie Gmbh & Co. K.G., Riedstrasse 2, pg. 1472   PB

Stockach

Contraves GmbH, Winturspurerstrasse 17-19, pg. 998   IT

Stolberg

CAE Elektronik GmbH, Steinfurt 11, pg. 238   IT
Pharma-Metall GmbH, pg. 1755   PB
Schwermetall Halbzeugwerk GmbH & Co. KG, pg. 1220   PB
Stolberger Metallwerke GmbH & Co. KG, Frankentalstrasse 5, pg. 719   IT

The West Company (Custom & Specialty Services) G.m.b.H, Eschweiler Strass e 199, pg. 1755   PB
WILLIAM PRYM GMBH & CO. KG, Zweifaller Strasse 130, pg. 1499   IT

Stralsund

Continental Can Europe Beteiligungsgesellschaft mbH, pg. 1206   IT
Nordic Baumaschinenhandel GmbH, Richtenberger Chaussee 47, pg. 712   IT
Schmalback-Lubeca Stralsunder Metallverpackungen GmbH, pg. 1207   IT

Straubenhardt

gastechnic Produktions und Vertriebsgesellschaft m.b.H., Daimlerstrasse 7, pg. 1148   IT
Schroff, Langenalber Str. 96-100, pg. 1274   PB

Straubing

Nokia Audio Electronics GmbH, Schlesische Strasse 135, pg. 954   IT

Strehla

R.P. Scherer GmbH-Werk Strehla, Reussenerstrasse 1a, pg. 1438   PB

Strullendorf

Dr. Renger GmbH, Postfach 40, pg. 1135   PB

Stuttgart

AV Euromedia Gesellschaft fur Audiovision mbH, Gansheidestrasse 26, pg. 1478   IT
Aisin Deutschland GmbH, Boeblinger-Strasse 245, pg. 39   IT
Akzo Coatings GmbH, 26, Magirusstrasse, pg. 43   IT
Alcatel SEL, Lorenzstrasse 10, pg. 56   IT
Allianz Grundstuecks-AG, pg. 58   IT
Allianz Lebensversicherungs-AG, Reinburgstrasse 19, pg. 58   IT
Allianz Versicherungs-AG, Zweigniederlassung, fur Baden-Wurttemberg, pg. 58   IT
AlliedSignal Truck Brake Systems, Industriestrasse 20, pg. 54   IT
Alpnet, Schultz-Delitzsch-Str. 28, pg. 58   PB
BASF Drucksysteme AG, Sieglestrasse 25, pg. 104   IT
BHF-Bank, Theodor-Heuss-Strasse 21, pg. 119   IT
Baden-Wurttemberg Branch, Kronprinzstr. 24, pg. 645   IT
Badger Meter Europe GmbH, Karlstrasse 11, 72660 Beuren, pg. 165   PB
Bankhaus Bauer AG, Lautenschlager Str. 22, pg. 309   IT
Banque Faribas-Stuttgart, Augustenstrasse 7, pg. 320   IT
Bourns, GmbH, Breite Strasse 2, pg. 161   PV
Brush Wellman GmbH, Motorstrasse 34, pg. 266   PB
Buehler Net GmbH, Zeppelinstrasse 35, pg. 575   PB
Campina AG, Rosensteinstrasse 20, pg. 254   IT
Comdisco Deutschland GmbH, Rembrandt str. 15, pg. 408   IT
DAIMLER-BENZ AKTIENGESELLSCHAFT, MPC 0944, pg. 366   IT
Daimler-Benz InterServices (debis) AG, Epplestrasse 225, pg. 367   IT
Danfoss Fluidtechnik GmbH, Talstrasse 41, pg. 377   IT
debis Assekuranz Vermittlungs Gmbh, Epplestrasse 225, pg. 368   IT
debis Finanzdienstleistungen, Epplestrasse 225, pg. 368   IT
debis Industriehandel GmbH, pg. 368   IT
debitel Kommunikationstechnik GmbH & Co. KG, Schelmenwasenstrasse 37, pg. 368   IT
Deutsche Bank AG (Stuttgart), Theodor-Heuss-Strasse 3, pg. 402   IT
Dr. Tigges Geschaftsreisen GmbH, c/o Werner & Pfleiderer GmbH, Theodorstr. 10, pg. 515   IT
DURR AG, Otto-Durr-Str. 9, pg. 421   IT
E. Missel GmbH, pg. 1055   PB
EBG Verlegs GmbH, Wolfram Str. 36, pg. 190   IT
Eisen und Metall GmbH, Am Ostkai 15-17, pg. 514   IT
EvoBus GmbH, pg. 368   IT
FCB Freizeit-Club Betreuungs-GmbH & Co., pg. 1014   IT
Hans Fehr GmbH, pg. 837   IT
Gustav Fischer Verlag GmbH & Co. KG, Wollgrasweg 49, pg. 1478   IT
Hans Franke NE-Metallhandel GmbH, Turbinenstr. 51, pg. 514   IT
GEHE AG, Neckartalstrasse 155, pg. 591   IT
Genus Europa GmbH, pg. 733   PB
Gradmann & Holler & GmbH, pg. 1049   PB
HTH Haustechnische Handels Ges m.b.H, Industriestrasse 63, pg. 1054   PB
Hauptniederlassung Baden-Wurttemberg Niederlassung Stuttgart, Ernsthaldenstrasse 17, pg. 194   IT
Herzog Collex GmbH, Am Mittelkai 50, pg. 512   IT
Hetzel GmbH, P.O. Box 610, pg. 675   PB
Holy's Exclusive Herrenmoden GmbH, pg. 637   IT
IBD Informationssysteme Betriebs- und Dienstleistungs GmbH, pg. 1063   IT
IBM Deutschland GmbH, Pascalstrasse 100, pg. 897   IT
IBM Deutschland Kreditbank GmbH, pg. 897   PB
IBM Deutschland Produktvertrieb GmbH, pg. 897   PB
Intercord Tongesellschaft mbH, Aixheimer Strasse 26, pg. 428   PB
Intergraph Deutschland) GmbH, Zettachring 4, D-70567, pg. 892   PB

Jakob Trefz & Sohne, Am Mittelkai 25, pg. 1459   IT
Jauch & Huebener, Augustenstrasse 15, pg. 118   PB
Karl Jaus GmbH, pg. 159   PV
Karosseriewerk Porsche GmbH, Porschestrasse 42, pg. 1063   IT
Kodak AG, Hedelfinger Strasse, pg. 552   PB
Kodak AG-Stuttgart, Hedelfinger Strasse, pg. 552   PB
Krupp Hoesch Stahl AG - Stuttgart, Am Ostkai 15, pg. 512   IT
LANDESGIROKASSE BANK, Konigstrasse 3-5, pg. 799   IT
Lawson Mardon Packaging Gesellschaft fur Beteiligungen mbH, pg. 68   IT
Lawson Mardon Rotopack GmbH, pg. 69   IT
Life Sciences-Meissner & Wurst, Froelzheimerstrasse 6, pg. 317   PV
Luwa Bisinger Textiltechnik GmbH, pg. 617   IT
Manus Presse GmbH, Lieschingstrasse 6, pg. 1478   IT
Manus Presse GmbH Graphik International GmbH, Lieschingstrasse 6, pg. 1478   IT
Marwitz & Hauser GmbH, pg. 1523   IT
Maxon GmbH, Neiderlassung Stuttgart, pg. 717   PV
Mecatool GmbH, Pforzheimer Strasse 381, pg. 490   IT
Mercedes-Benz AG, Mercedesstr. 136, pg. 368   IT
Mercedes-Benz CharterWay GmbH, pg. 369   IT
Mercedes-Benz Finanz GmbH, Postfach 103262, pg. 368   IT
Mercedes-Benz Leasing GmbH, Nordbahnhofstrasse 147, pg. 368   IT
J.B. Metzler Verlag, Werastrasse 21-23, pg. 1478   IT
Milei GmbH, Sarweystrasse 5, pg. 895   IT
Morinaga Nutritional Foods Deutschland GmbH, Sarweystrasse 5, pg. 895   IT
Nadella Walzlager GmbH, Traenkestrasse 7, pg. 878   IT
Neckar-Getreide und Futtermittel Speditions Gesellschaft mbH, Am Westkai 25, pg. 1033   IT
Netstal Vertriebs GmbH, pg. 836   IT
Network Systems GmbH, Zettachring 10, pg. 1523   PB
Optimail/Direktwerbeservice GmbH, Augustenstrasse 1, pg. 1368   PB
Panalpina Welttransport GmbH, pg. 1023   IT
Francesco Parisi G.m.b.H., Wegengutbahnhof 10, pg. 504   IT
Pegasus Buch-und Zertschriften GmbH, Augustenstr. 1, pg. 1368   PB
PORSCHE AG, Porschestrasse, 42, pg. 1063   IT
Porsche Consulting GmbH, pg. 1063   IT
Rhenania Umschlag und Lagerei GmbH, Zweigniederlassung, pg. 1034   IT
Robinson-Nugent GmbH, Ziegelstrasse 28-1, pg. 1395   PB
ROMINGER REISEBUERO GMBH, Stephanstr. 33, pg. 1127   IT
Rotopack Sahre GmbH, Postfach 13117, Ulmer Strasse 184-188, pg. 69   IT
SKF Textilmaschinen-Komponenten GmbH, Lowentorstrasse 68, pg. 1159   IT
Saarlux Beteiligung, pg. 572   IT
Saarlux GMBH, pg. 572   IT
Schaffer-Poeschel Verlag, Werastrasse 21-23, pg. 1478   IT
Schweizerischer Bankverein AG, Lange Strasse 9, pg. 1330   IT
Siliconix GmbH, Johannesstrasse 27, pg. 367   IT
Soligar GmbH, Schulze-Delitzsch Strasse 7, pg. 6   PV
Spektrum Fachverlage GmbH, Werastrasse 23, pg. 1478   IT
Stinnes-Trefz AG, Am Mittelkai 25, pg. 1459   IT
Suddeutsche Rohprodukten GmbH, Innerer Nordbahnhof 40, pg. 514   IT
SudFactoring GmbH, Am Haupthos 2, pg. 1304   IT
SudKA, Am Haupthos 2, pg. 1304   IT
SudKB, Am Haupthos 2, pg. 1304   IT
SudKI, Am Haupthos 2, pg. 1304   IT
SudLeasing GmbH, Am Haupthos 2, pg. 1304   IT
SudLeasing Immobilien GmbH, Am Haupthos 2, pg. 1305   IT
SUDWESTLB, P.O. Box 10 6049, pg. 1304   IT
Sulzer Infra Deutschland GmbH., Furtbachstr. 4, pg. 1306   IT
Terrot Strickmaschinen GmbH, pg. 1307   IT
Tesa-Etikettendruckerei GmbH, pg. 182   IT
TosoHaas GmbH, Zettachring 6, pg. 1408   IT
Union Special G.m.b.H, Schwabstrasse 33, pg. 717   IT
VW AUDI Vertriebszentrum Sud-West GmbH, pg. 1474   IT
Verlag Das Beste GmbH, Augustenstrasse 1, pg. 1368   PB
Volta Electrogenerate Vertriebs GmbH, Postfach 41, pg. 442   IT
GEORG VON HOLTZBRINCK GMBH, Gaensheidestr. 26, pg. 1478   IT
Werner & Pfleiderer GmbH, Theodorstrasse 10, pg. 510   IT
Werner & Pfleiderer Lebensmitteltechnik GmbH, Theodorstr. 10, pg. 511   IT
Wurttembergische AG Versicherungs-Beteiligungsgesellschaft, Johannesstrasse 1-7, pg. 1333   IT
Wurttembergische Elektrizitats-Aktiengesellschaft, pg. 1456   IT

Suessen

SPINDELFABRIK SUESSEN, Dammstr. 1, pg. 1290   IT

Sulzbach

Ampex Europa GMBH, Otto-Volger Str. 7C, pg. 104   PB
BDDP Frankfurt, Limes Park, OttoVolger Str. 1, pg. 117   IT
Genicom GmbH, Oberliederbacher Weg 42, pg. 729   PB

PB - *U.S. Public Companies Volume*
PV - *U.S. Private Companies Volume*
IT - *International Public & Private Companies Volume*

Geographic Index-Non U.S.

Honeywell-Measurex G.m.b.H., Otto-Volger Strasse 7A, pg. 833 **PB**
Precismeca-Montan Gesellschaft fur Fordertechnik mbH, pg. 399 **IT**
Unisys Deutschland GmbH, Am Unisys Park 1, pg. 1672 **PB**

Sulzfeld

Charles River WIGA G.m.b.H., Sandhofer Weg 7, pg. 195 **PB**

Sundern

Carl Froh GmbH & Co., pg. 1088 **IT**

Tamm

Porsche Leasing GmbH, pg. 1063 **IT**

Tanna

Baasel-Rabe Lasertechnik GmbH, pg. 836 **IT**

Tauberbischofsheim

Weinig Intl. GmbH, Weinigstrasse 2-4, pg. 1488 **IT**
MICHAEL WEINIG AG, Weinigstrasse 2-4, Postfach 1440, pg. 1488 **IT**

Taufkirchen

Circon GmbH, Mehlbeerenstrasse 2, pg. 374 **PB**
Hewlett-Packard GmbH, Vetriebszentrum Munchen, Eschenstrasse 5, pg. 820 **PB**
Hewlett-Packard GmbH, Zone Office South, Eschenstrasse 5, pg. 820 **PB**
Nordic Synthesis GmbH, Wettersteinstrasse 4, pg. 297 **PB**
Suhner Elektronik GmbH, Mehlberenstrasse 6, pg. 637 **IT**

Taunusstein

Deutsche Owens-Corning Glasswool GmbH, Idsteiner Strasse 82, pg. 1237 **PB**
Gebr. Becker Sportanlagenbau GmbH, pg. 608 **IT**
Ircon GMBH, P.O. Box 1361 Grillparzerstrasse 40, pg. 1209 **IT**

Teisnach

Rohde & Schwarz GmbH, Kaikenrieder Strasse 27, pg. 1124 **IT**

Teningen

Ascom Frako GmbH, Tscheulinstrasse 21, pg. 87 **IT**

Thale

Mertik Maxitrol Gmbh & Co., KG, Klopstockweg 10, pg. 716 **PV**

Toging

Innkraftwerke GmbH, Werkstr. 1, pg. 1464 **IT**
VAW Aluminum AG, Innwerk, pg. 1466 **IT**

Tonisvorst

Daihatsu Deutschland GmbH, Industriestr. 5-11, pg. 365 **IT**

Torgau

Flachglas Torgau GmbH, Repitzer Weg 1, pg. 1172 **IT**
GIAG-Glasindustrie AG, Repitzer Weg 1, pg. 1172 **IT**
Sekurit Saint-Gobain Torgau GmbH, Repitzer Weg 1, pg. 1173 **IT**

Traunstein

BV Eastdil GmbH, pg. 178 **IT**

Travemunde

Stena Line, Skandinavienkai, pg. 1300 **IT**

Trebur

AKO Armaturen - Vertrieks GmbH, Beckerweg 6, pg. 710 **IT**
Asatsu (Deutschland) GmbH, Diamant Strasse 5, pg. 86 **IT**
Mitsubishi Motors R&D Europe GmbH, Diamantstr. 1, pg. 876 **IT**

Trier

GKN Walterscheid Presswerk GmbH, Hafenstrasse 41, pg. 536 **IT**
Leonard Kreusch GmBH & Co., Martinerfeld 61, pg. 635 **PV**
Mead Verpackung G.m.b.H., Schiffstrasse 1, pg. 1077 **PB**
TBM Transportboten GmbH & Co. KG, pg. 423 **IT**

Volksfreund-Druckerei Nikolaus Koch GmbH & Co. KG, Nikolaus-Koch-Platz 1-3, pg. 1479 **IT**

Triptis

Formembau und Kunststofftechmik GmbH, pg. 505 **IT**

Troisdorf

Augat Automotive GmbH, Postfach 1109, pg. 1598 **PB**
Battenfeld Anlagentechnik GmbH, Brusseler Str. 13, pg. 825 **IT**
Battenfeld Service GmbH, Gesschaftsfuhrung, Brussler Str. 13, pg. 825 **IT**
Dynamit Nobel AG, Kaiserstrasse 1, pg. 861 **IT**
HT Troplast, Kaiserstrasse 1, pg. 1148 **IT**
Morgan Matroc, Niederlassung Troisdorf, pg. 893 **IT**
NASSHEUER LOI Industrieofenanlagen GmbH, Lindenstrasse 75, pg. 1149 **IT**
REIFENHAUSER GMBH & CO. MASCHINENFABRIK, Spicher Strasse, 46-48, pg. 1101 **IT**
Sonoco Plastics Gmbh., Lindenstrasse 20, pg. 1487 **PB**
TNT Holding GmbH, Hauptverwaltung, Haberstrasse 2, pg. 1343 **IT**

Trostberg

SKW Trostberg Aktiengesellschaft, Dr.-Albert-Frank-Str. 32, pg. 1464 **IT**

Tubingen

Flender-Himmelwerk GmbH, pg. 400 **IT**
Himmelwerk GmbH & Co., pg. 400 **IT**
Humanpharmakologisches Institut CIBA-GEIGY GmbH, Waldhornlestrasse 22, pg. 982 **IT**

Tuttendorf

G.E.O.S. Freiberg Ingenieurgesellschaft mbH, Gewerbe Park, Schwartz Kiefern, pg. 632 **IT**

Tuttlingen

AESCULAP AKTIENGESELLSCHAFT, Am Aesculap-Platz, pg. 29 **IT**

Ueberlingen

Bodenseewerk Perkin-Elmer & Co. G.m.b.H., Postfach 1120, pg. 1279 **PB**

Uelzen

Bankgeschaft Heinrich Alten mbH, pg. 179 **IT**
Verwaltungsgesellschaft Atlten mbH, pg. 180 **IT**

Uetersen

Knoll AG Werk Uetersen, Pinnaualee 4, pg. 104 **IT**
Schmidt & Hagen GmbH & Co. KG, Deichstrasse 25a, pg. 610 **IT**
Stora Uetersen GmbH, Pinnau Allee 3, pg. 1303 **IT**

Ulm

Britax Autozubehor GmbH, Postfach Ulm 1450, Blaubeurer Str. 61, pg. 216 **IT**
Daimler-Benz Aerospace AG Sensor, pg. 367 **IT**
EvoBus GmbH Setra Omnibusse, Kaessbohrer Strasse 13, pg. 368 **IT**
Iveco Magirus A/G, Schillerstrasse 2, pg. 484 **IT**
Romer-Britax Autogurte GmbH, Postfach Ulm 3449, pg. 217 **IT**
Franz Spiegel Buch GmbH, Albstrasse 80, pg. 1478 **IT**
Wicona Bausysteme GmbH & Co. KG, Soflingerstrasse 70, pg. 964 **IT**
ZWICK/ROELL GROUP, August-Nagel-Str. 11, pg. 1532 **IT**

Unna

APV Rosista GmbH, Zechenstr. 49, pg. 1241 **IT**
Bertrand Faure Sitztechnik GmbH & Co. KG, Zechenstrasse 45, pg. 193 **IT**
V.A.G. Vertriebszentrum Westfalen GmbH, pg. 1473 **IT**
V.A.G. Vertriebszentrum Westfalen GmbH & Co KG., pg. 1473 **IT**

Unterfoehring

AVE Gesellschaft fur Fernsehproduktion mbH, Munchues Str. 14, pg. 1478 **IT**
Check Point Software Technologies GmbH, pg. 342 **PB**
Gensym GmbH, Firkenweg 1, pg. 731 **PB**
Litton Servotechnik, Feringastr. 14, pg. 1004 **PB**
Lucent Technologies Business Communications Systems & Microelectronics GmbH, Medien Allee 6, pg. 1019 **PB**
Motorola G.m.b.H., Muenchner Strasse 18, pg. 1139 **PB**

Unterhaching

Accor Hotellerie GmbH, Hauptstrasse 42, pg. 21 **IT**
Deutsche Wrigley G.m.b.H, Albrecht-Duerer-Strasse 2, pg. 1781 **PB**
Simon Marketing International GmbH - Munich, Leonhardswag 2, pg. 1001 **PV**

Unterschleissheim

EDC European Excavator Design Center GmbH & Co. KG, Carl-von-Linde-Strasse 12A, pg. 315 **PB**
Hoechst Veterinar GmbH, pg. 626 **IT**
Hydro Aluminium Automotive GmbH, Regenstrasse 3-5, pg. 962 **IT**
Linde Heimox GmbH, pg. 811 **IT**
Microsoft GmbH, Edisonstrasse 1, pg. 1108 **PB**
Rainbow Technologies, GmbH, Lise Meitner Strasse 1, pg. 1359 **PB**

Unterwellenborn

Stahlwerk Thuringen GmbH, Kronacherstrasse, Postfach 27, pg. 79 **IT**

Urmitz

Radex Deutschland, A.G., pg. 904 **PV**

Utting

i.m.b. Ingenieurtechnologien fur Materialprufung und Bauwerkserhaltung GmbH, Am Bernrieder Holz 3, pg. 423 **IT**

Vaihingen

Fairchild Technologies GmbH, pg. 610 **PB**
KSA Dichtsysteme G.M.b.H & Co. KG, Postfach 60, pg. 1323 **IT**

Vechta

Nowsco Well Service GmbH, pg. 990 **IT**

Veitshochheim

Demag Technica GmbH, pg. 837 **IT**

Velbert

Langenberg Kupfer und Messingwerke GmbH, Ziegeleiweg 20, pg. 1219 **PB**
Schrader Bellows GmbH, Heidestrasse 71, pg. 1264 **PB**

Verden

FOCKE & CO. (GMBH & CO.) VERPACKUNGSMASCHINER, Siemenstr. 10, pg. 496 **IT**

Vereingenstadt

Korf-Transport GmbH, Gunzenhofstrasse 9, pg. 759 **IT**

Vettelschoss

Streif AG, Erlenweg, pg. 623 **IT**
Streif Schalungsbau GmbH, Im alten Hohn, pg. 623 **IT**

Videbaek

BG Finans A/S, Sonderupvej 11, pg. 1279 **IT**

Viernheim

Alcoa Deutschland GmbH, Postfach 1140, pg. 61 **PB**
Cadillac Plastic GmbH, Alfred-Nobel-Strasse 17, Zeutrale, pg. 781 **PB**
Krupp Hoesch Stahl AG - Mannheim, Alfred-Noble-Str. 6, pg. 512 **IT**
WOB MARKETINGKOMMUNIKATION AG, Werner-Heisenberg-Str. 8-10, pg. 1482 **IT**
Walker Deutschland GmbH, P.O. Box 1480, Industrie Strasse 22, pg. 1580 **PB**
Wicona Deutschland GmbH, Max-Planck-Strasse 21, pg. 965 **IT**

Vierraden

Haindl Papier Schwedt GmbH, Kuhheide 1, pg. 586 **IT**

Viersen

GROSCHOPP & CO. GMBH EMW ELEKTROMOTOREN-FEINBAUWERK, Postfach 100561, pg. 559 **IT**
Kaiser's Kaffee-Geschaeft AG, Lichtenberg 44, pg. 1375 **IT**
Rhenania A.G., pg. 299 **IT**

Villingen-Schwenningen

Dr. Herbert Kienzle Untersstuzungskasse GmbH, pg. 839 **IT**
Mannesmann Kienzle Beteiligungs GmbH, pg. 838 **IT**
Mannesmann Kienzle Export GmbH, pg. 839 **IT**
Tanksysteme MKS GmbH, pg. 839 **IT**

Vilsbiburg

Flottweg GmbH, Industriestrasse 8, pg. 836 **IT**

PB - *U.S. Public Companies Volume*
PV - *U.S. Private Companies Volume*
IT - *International Public & Private Companies Volume*

Voelklingen

FernwaermeVerbund Saar GmbH, Bismarckstr. 11, pg. 1167 IT
Kohlbecher & Co. GmbH, Postfach 1680, Am Holzplatz, pg. 1166 IT

Voerde

Gemeinschaftskraftwerk West GbR, pg. 597 IT
Hoogovens Aluminium Huttenwerk GmbH, Schleusenstrasse, pg. 755 IT

Vogt

BUG Alutechnik GmbH, pg. 755 IT
Hoogovens Aluminium Profiltechnik GmbH, Werk Vogt, Bergstrasse 17, pg. 755 IT

Volperhausen

Square D Company (Deutschland) GmbH, Wissener Str., pg. 1209 IT

Wachtersbach

VARTA-Plastic GmbH, Industriestrasse, pg. 1452 IT

Wadern

Saar-Gummiwerk GmbH, pg. 1167 IT

Waiblingen

Emerson Electric GmbH, Heerstrasse 111, pg. 576 PB
ALBERT ROLLER GMBH & CO. KG, Schorndorferstr. 66, pg. 1126 IT
ANDREAS STIHL, pg. 1301 IT

Walchstadt

Walchstadt Kunststoff GmbH, pg. 423 IT

Waldbronn

Hewlett-Packard GmbH, Ermlis-All, pg. 820 PB

Waldeck

Mauser Waldeck AG, pg. 1108 IT

Waldfischbach-Burgalben

Convert Vliesveredelung GmbH & Co. KG, pg. 505 IT

Waldkrainburg

EMG Eisen-und Metallgusswerk GmbH, Teplitzerstrasse 22, pg. 400 IT
Nigu Chemie-Beteiligungs GmbH, Postfach 1620, pg. 1465 IT

Waldsassen

Franz Kassecker GmbH, Egerer Strasse 36, pg. 195 IT

Waldshut

Hammerli GmbH, Feldbergstrasse 9-11, pg. 1156 IT
Lonza-Werke GmbH, Konstanzer Strasse 15, pg. 67 IT
PKL Holding GmbH, Weilheimer Strasse 5, pg. 1156 IT
SIG Holding GmbH Deutschland, Weilheimer Strasse 5, pg. 1156 IT

Walldorf

Lincoln GmbH, Heinrich-Hertz Strasse, pg. 1274 PB
MICROM Laborgerate GmbH, pg. 1523 IT

Wallenfels

London Laboratories GmbH, pg. 995 PB

Walluf

Bauverlag GmbH, Pressehaus, Am Klingenweg 4A, pg. 451 IT
Media daten GmbH, Pressehaus, Am Klingenweg 4A, pg. 451 IT
Tefal Deutschland GmbH, Am Klingenweg 4, pg. 569 IT

Walsrode

International Bio-Research IBR Forschungs GmbH, Sudkampen 31, pg. 733 PB
Wolff Walsrode AG, pg. 175 IT

Waltrop

Deutsche Chefaro Pharma GmbH, 25 Im Wirrigen, pg. 44 IT
Diosynth Vertriebsgesellschaft mbH, 25 Im Wirrigen, pg. 44 IT
Thiemann Arzneimittel GmbH, 25 Im Wirrigen, pg. 45 IT

Walzbuchtal

Wossinger Zement, Bruchsalerstrasse 56, pg. 789 IT

Wardenburg

Dynapac GmbH, Ammerlander Strasse 93, pg. 1420 IT

Waren

Mowe Teigwarenwerk GmbH, Am Alten Bahndam, pg. 244 IT
SBV Vermogensverwaltungs-gesellschaft mbH, pg. 596 IT

Warstein

Haus Cramer Gaststatten Management GmbH & Co. KG, Domring, pg. 1486 IT
Haus Cramer GmbH & Co. Immobilien Management K.G., pg. 1486 IT
WARSTEINER BRAUEREI HAUS CRAMER GMBH & CO., pg. 1486 IT

Wasseralfingen

Schwaebische Huettenwerke GmbH, Wilhelmstrasse 67, pg. 826 IT

Wedel

Astra GmbH, Tinsdalerweg 183, pg. 93 IT
ESW Extel Systems Wedel, pg. 367 IT
International Copying Machines, pg. 836 IT
Mannesmann Scangraphic GmbH, pg. 839 IT

Wedemark

VW AUDI Vertriebszentrum GmbH, pg. 1473 IT
VW AUDI Vertriebszentrum GmbH & Co. Wedemark KG, pg. 1473 IT

Wehr

Dr. Christian Brunnengraber Chemische Fabrik GmbH, Oflinger Strasse 44, pg. 975 IT
CIBA-GEIGY GmbH, Oeflinger Strasse 44, pg. 977 IT

Weiden

Josef Witt GmbH & Co. KG., pg. 1015 IT

Weil am Rhein

Lonza-Folien GmbH, pg. 69 IT
Storage and Transport GmbH, pg. 866 IT

Weilerbach

Reiner Chemische Fabrik GmbH, Hans-Reiner Strasse 7-13, pg. 517 IT

Weilheim

Krauss-Maffei Kunstsofftechnik Vertrieb & Service Sud, pg. 836 IT

Weilmunster

Acco Platen GmbH, Dusseldorfer Strasse 2, pg. 473 IT
IndustrieWerk Weilmunster GmbH, pg. 839 IT

Weingarten

Buss Holding GmbH, Niederbiegerstrasse 9, pg. 490 IT
Nord-Ostsee Schiffahrt-und Transport GmbH, Danaiger Strasse 7, Postfach 1430, pg. 1303 IT
Waeschle Maschinenfabrik GmbH, Niederbiegerstrasse 9, pg. 491 IT

Weinheim

ASTO Beteiligungs-GmbH, pg. 506 IT
C.F. Boehringer & Soehne GmbH, Am Rollenbuckel, pg. 331 IT
Bongard GmbH, Schiledrnweg 53 A, pg. 570 IT
Conrad Tack Kommanditgesellschaft, pg. 506 IT
Convert Vliesveredelung GmbH, pg. 506 IT
Craner GmbH, pg. 506 IT
FHP Export GmbH, pg. 506 IT
FREUDENBERG & COMPANY, pg. 505 IT
Freudenberg Beteiligungsgesellschaft mbH, pg. 506 IT
Carl Freudenberg, P.O. Box 1369, pg. 505 IT
Carl Freudenberg GmbH, pg. 506 IT
Carl Freudenberg Wohnbauhilfe GmbH, pg. 506 IT
Freudenberg Haushaltsprodukte KG, pg. 506 IT
Freudenberg Haushaltsprodukte Verwaltungs-BmbH, pg. 506 IT
Freudenberg Versicherungsvermittlungs-GmbH, pg. 506 IT
Freudenberg Vertrieb Einlagestoffe KG, pg. 506 IT
Graner GmbH, pg. 506 IT
Kluber GmbH, pg. 506 IT
Pohl GmbH, pg. 506 IT
Prum-Turenwerk GmbH, Industriegelande, pg. 623 IT
Simflex Beteiligungs-GmbH, pg. 506 IT

Simflex GmbH & Co. KG, pg. 505 IT
Simplex Beteiliguns-GmbH, pg. 506 IT
Simrax GmbH, Gleitringdichtungen, pg. 505 IT
Technischer Handel Freudenberg KG, pg. 506 IT
Vileda GmbH, pg. 506 IT
Wiley-VCH, Pappelallee 3, pg. 1768 PB

Weinsberg

ASC Weinsberg Karosseriewerke Weinsberg GmbH, Lindichstrasse 11, pg. 8 PV

Weinstadt

BSB Nahrungsmittel GmbH, Postfach 12 20, Birkelstrasse, pg. 380 IT

Weitefeld

Mineralmahlwerk Westerwald Horn GmbH & Co. KG, Langenbacher Str. 21, pg. 514 IT

Weiterstadt

Danet, Gutenbergstrasse 10, pg. 976 PV
Geodimeter Gmbh, Feldstrasse 14, pg. 1290 IT
Herbalife International Deutschland GmbH, Rudolf Dieselstrasse 24, pg. 809 PB
C E Johansson GmbH, Feldstrasse 14, pg. 1290 IT
NIKE International Ltd., Feldstrasse 16, pg. 1184 PB
Pharos Holdings GmbH, Feldstrasse 14, pg. 1290 IT
SKODA Automobile Deutschland GmbH, pg. 1475 IT
Somos GmbH, Egerlander Strasse 2-4, pg. 484 IT

Wendlingen am Neckar

Procal GmbH, pg. 506 IT

Wennigsen

Woodward-Clyde, Hauptstrasse 45a, pg. 1657 PB

Werdohl

Bruninghaus Schmiede GmbH, Plettenberger Str. 12, pg. 508 IT
Walter Hundhausen GmbH & Co. KG, Industriestr. 20, pg. 508 IT
Krupp Bruninghaus GmbH, Plettenberger Str. 12, pg. 508 IT
Krupp VDM GmbH, Plettenbergerstr. 2, pg. 509 IT
Krupp VDM GmbH - Evidal Division, Plettenberger Str. 2, pg. 509 IT

Werl

Werler Drahtwerke GmbH & Co. KG, Runtestrasse 5-9 & 24, pg. 184 IT

Wermelskirchen

Bicron Vertriebes GmbH, Viktoriastrasse 5, pg. 1174 IT
Electrolux Wascherei und Service GmbH, Grune Strasse 12-24, pg. 442 IT
Forbo Glawo GmbH, pg. 497 IT
Lux GmbH & Co. KG, Industriestrasse 10, pg. 993 IT
Luxtronic Maschinen GmbH, Industriestr. 10, pg. 993 IT
OBI BAU-UND HEIMWERKERMAERKTE GMBH & CO. KG, Albert-Einstein-Strasse 7-9, pg. 993 IT

Wernau/Neckar

Robert Bosch GmbH Thermotechnik Division, Junkerstr. 20-24, pg. 204 IT

Werne

AB Elekronik GmbH, Klocknerstrasse 4, pg. 1344 IT
Icopal-Siplast GmbH, Capellerstrasse 150, pg. 659 IT
Klockner-Dowty, Pagensstrasse 2, pg. 1338 IT
Uniferm GmbH & Co., Brede 4, pg. 1143 IT
VEW-Harpen, pg. 597 IT

Wertheim

Glaskontor Mullheim GmbH, pg. 1523 IT
Schuller GmbH, pg. 927 PB
TOSOH Europe, Hospitalstrasse 8, pg. 1408 IT

Werther

Ravensberger Schmierstoffvertrieb GmbH, pg. 517 IT

Wesel

Bergemann GmbH Maschinen-und Apparatebau, pg. 398 IT
Kroll Fahrzeugbau Gmbh, Rudolf-Diesel-Strasse 85-89, pg. 1128 IT
Rhenania Umschlag und Lagerei GmbH, Zweigniederlassung Hafenstrasse 24, pg. 1034 IT

Wesseling

CIBA Vision Ophthalmics GmbH, Argelsrieder Feld 5, pg. 981 IT

PB - *U.S. Public Companies Volume*
PV - *U.S. Private Companies Volume*
IT - *International Public & Private Companies Volume*

1636

Geographic Index-Non U.S.

Fairchild Dornier Luftfahrt GmbH, P.O. Box 1103,
pg. 391 **PV**
Norton Advanced Materials GmbH, Vorgebirgsstrass 10,
pg. 1175 **IT**
Norton GmbH, Vorgebirgstr. 10, Postfach 100,
pg. 1175 **IT**
Norton Schleifmittel GmbH, Bruehler Strasse 101,
pg. 1175 **IT**
Rheinische Olefinwerke GmbH, Bruehler Strasse,
pg. 105 **IT**
Rosemount Engineering GmbH, Schulstrasse 29,
pg. 577 **PB**
Uranerzbergbau GmbH, Koelmo Strasse 38-44,
pg. 1070 **IT**

Westhausen

Deutsche Gardner-Denver GmbH & Co., D-73461,
pg. 444 **PB**

Wetter

Adronit GmbH & Co., pg. 1061 **IT**
Mannesmann Demag Fordertechnik AG, Ruhrstrasse 28,
pg. 837 **IT**
Thumann Stahl Service Gmbh & Co., pg. 754 **IT**
ZSA Zaun-und Sicherheitsanlagen GmbH, pg. 1061 **IT**

Wetzlar

Buderus AG, Sophienstrasse 30-32, pg. 861 **IT**
M. Hensoldt & Sohne Wetzlar, Optische Werke AG,
pg. 1523 **IT**
Leitz Messtechnik GmbH, P.O. Box 2060, Meline-Mueller-
Strasse, pg. 260 **PB**

Wiehe

Mannesmann Demag Kunststofftechnik, pg. 837 **IT**

Wiesbaden

AXA Leben, Hans-Bredow-Strasse 1, pg. 19 **IT**
abu Allgemeine Bau-Union GmbH & Co. KG, Gustav-
Nachtigal-Strasse 3, pg. 195 **IT**
AMETEK G.m.b.H., Dostojewskistrasse, 10, pg. 100 **PB**
BHF-Bank, Bahnhofstrasse 44, pg. 119 **IT**
Bauverlag G.m.b.H., Wittelsbacherstrasse 10, pg. 1124 **IT**
Carl Lotz Beton GmbH & Co., pg. 422 **IT**
Beton Union GmbH & Co. KG, pg. 422 **IT**
Betriebswirtschaft Licher Verlag Dr. Th. Gabler GmbH,
Taunusstrasse 54, pg. 189 **IT**
CCH Europe, Inc., Parkstr. 71-73, pg. 1513 **IT**
Cat Pumps Deutschland GmbH, Rostockerstr. 9,
pg. 336 **PV**
Chandon Sektkellerei GmbH, Sohnleinstr. 5, pg. 782 **IT**
Cognex-Germany, Weidenbornstrasse 8a, pg. 394 **PB**
Commerz Grundbesitz Investment Gesellschaft mbH,
Kreuzberger Ring 56, pg. 309 **IT**
Corning GmbH, 30 Abraham-Lincoln Strasse, pg. 449 **PB**
DBV-Winterthur AG, Frankfurter Str. 50, pg. 310 **IT**
Deutsche FATA GmbH, Hasengartenstr 15, pg. 474 **IT**
Didier-Anlagentechnik Holding GmbH, pg. 1464 **IT**
Diversa-Versicherungskontor GmbH, Victoriastr. 16,
pg. 1464 **IT**
DYCKERHOFF AG, pg. 422 **IT**
Dyckerhoff Ausbauprodukte GmbH, pg. 422 **IT**
Eduard Dyckerhoff GmbH, pg. 422 **IT**
Dyckerhoff Sopro GmbH, pg. 422 **IT**
Dyckerhoff Transportbeton GmbH, pg. 422 **IT**
Dyckerhoff Zement International GmbH, pg. 422 **IT**
EG & G Heimann Opto. Gmbh, Weher Koeppel 3,
pg. 544 **PB**
Elscint GmbH, Ostring 3, pg. 450 **IT**
Ferranti GmbH, Tanusstrasse 52, pg. 1384 **IT**
Fluor Daniel GmbH, Industrie-und Anlagenbau, Kreuzberger
Ring 13, pg. 660 **PB**
Forchem GmbH, Taunusstrasse 64, pg. 458 **IT**
Guerlain Parfumeur GmbH, Bierstadter Str. 9a, pg. 780 **PV**
Hoechst Roussel Vet GmbH, Rheingaustrasse 190,
pg. 626 **IT**
Hotel Nassauer Hof GmbH, Kaiser Friedrich Platz 3-4,
pg. 1459 **IT**
Jil Sanders Cosmetics G.m.b.H., Maunzerstrasse 15,
pg. 1265 **IT**
KARL KAUERMAN NASSAUISCHE SPARKASSE,
Rheinstrasse 42-44, pg. 724 **IT**
Kemira Katalysaforen GmbH, Friedrichstrasse 55,
pg. 729 **IT**
Korsnas GmbH, Taunusstrasse 5 A, pg. 759 **IT**
Lancaster Group Deutschland GmbH, pg. 185 **IT**
Lancaster Group Duty-Free GmbH, pg. 185 **IT**
Lancaster Group Export GmbH, pg. 185 **IT**
LINDE AG, Abraham-Lincoln-Strasse 21, pg. 810 **IT**
Arthur D. Little International, Inc., Delta Haus, Gustav-
Stresemann-Ring 1, pg. 671 **PV**
Media-Daten Verlagsgesellschaft, pg. 1124 **IT**
Mentor Graphics (Deutschland) GmbH, Bahnhofstrasse 27-
33, pg. 1087 **IT**
MoDo Paper AG, Hagenauer Strasse 55, pg. 887 **IT**
Morgan Thermal Ceramics GmbH, Alte Schmelze 18-20,
pg. 894 **IT**
Motorola G.m.b.H., Hagenauer Strasse 42, pg. 1139 **PB**
Niederlassung Wiesbaden, Gustav-Nachtigal-Strasse 3,
pg. 195 **IT**
Norske Skog Presspaier GmbH, Alwinenstrasse 24,
pg. 966 **IT**
Numetrix GmbH, Nerobergstrasse 13,EGL, pg. 990 **IT**

Owens-Corning Fiberglas Deutschland G.M.B.H., Aarstrasse
11-13, pg. 1237 **PB**
Oxford Instruments, Kreuzberger Ring 38, pg. 1018 **IT**
Parfums Givenchy G.m.b.H., Hagenauer Str. 53,
pg. 783 **IT**
Partner Immobiliendienst GmbH, pg. 310 **IT**
Q.V.F. Glastechnik GmbH, 11 Schossbergstrasse,
pg. 449 **PB**
R&D Systems GmbH, Boriigstrasse 7, pg. 1564 **PB**
Rammer Deutschland GmbH, Stielstrasse 3A, pg. 1352 **IT**
Roche Nicholas (Deutschland) GmbH, pg. 1121 **IT**
Salzgitter-Lummus G.m.b.H., Abraham Lincoln Strasse 1,
pg. 6 **IT**
Sciaky GmbH, Steinmetzstrasse 2, pg. 1211 **IT**
Sodexho Eiring, Siemensstrasse 8/9, pg. 1275 **IT**
Teac Deutschland GmbH, Bahnstrasse 12, pg. 1360 **IT**
Teledyne Germany, Abraham Lincoln Str. 38-42,
pg. 44 **PB**
VG Instruments GmbH, pg. 1595 **PB**
Veuve Clicquot Import G.m.b.H., Taunus Strasse 21,
pg. 783 **IT**
Friedrich Vieweg & Sohn Verlagsgesellschaft mbH,
Faulbrunnenstrasse 13, pg. 190 **IT**
Weltmarken Import Spirituosen und Weine GmbH,
Bahnstrasse 10, pg. 410 **IT**
Fritz Werner Machine Tools International GmbH,
pg. 1128 **IT**
Westdeutscher Verlag GmbH, Faulbrunnenstrasse 13,
pg. 190 **IT**
Westofen GmbH, Abraham-Lincoln-Str. 16, pg. 1466 **IT**
WinCom Versicherungs-Holding Aktiengesellschaft,
pg. 310 **IT**

Wiesmoor

Deutsche Hey'di Chemische GmbH, Pollerstrasse 161-169,
pg. 803 **IT**

Wildau

Geschaftsstelle Berlin, Am Kleingewerbegebiet 8,
pg. 739 **IT**

Wilhelmshaven

DFTG - Deutsche Flussigerdas Terminal Gesellschaft mbH,
pg. 1148 **IT**
ICI Atlantik GmbH, Inhauersieler Strasse 25, Postfach 660,
pg. 664 **IT**
ICI Wilhelmshaven GmbH & Co., pg. 665 **IT**
Krupp Mobilkrane GmbH, IndustriegebietWest, pg. 510 **IT**
Nord-West Oelleitung GmbH, Zum Olhafendamm 207,
pg. 1461 **IT**

Willich

Atlet Flurforderzeuge GmbH, Jacob-Kaiser-Strasse 3,
pg. 97 **IT**
Avesta Sheffield GmbH, pg. 221 **IT**
BetzDearborn GmbH, Siemensring 44, pg. 227 **PB**
Canon Euro-Photo Handelsgesellschaft mbH, Siemensring
90-92, pg. 262 **IT**
Goldstar Deutschland GmbH, Jakob-Kaiser Strasse 12,
pg. 779 **IT**
Micros Systems Deutschland, GmbH, Tibergraben 15,
pg. 1107 **PB**
Norton Beteiligungs GmbH, AM Nordkanal 37-43,
pg. 1175 **IT**
Norton GmbH Objekt Schiefbahn, Am NordKanal 37-43,
pg. 1175 **IT**
Norton Pampus GmbH, AM Nordkanal 37-43, pg. 1175 **IT**
PCM-EWP, pg. 356 **IT**
Pampus Vermogensverwalfungs GmbH & Co. KG.,
pg. 1175 **IT**
Plastilon, Daimlerstrasse 5-7, pg. 915 **IT**
Radiometer Deutschland GmbH, Am Nordkanal 8,
pg. 1084 **IT**
Radiometer GmbH, Linselestr. 142-156, pg. 1084 **IT**
Rohm Electronics GmbH, Kari-Arnold-Strasse 15,
pg. 1125 **IT**
Sumitomo Electric Hartmetall GmbH, Siemensring 84,
pg. 1314 **IT**

Wilnsdorf

ESTA Gesellschaft fur Edelstahlverarbeitung mbH,
Flocksdorfstr. 4, pg. 513 **IT**
Gunnebo GmbH, Essener Str. 1, pg. 578 **IT**
Ross Industrie- und Fassadenbau GmbH, Dortmunderstr. 6,
pg. 509 **IT**
TRP-Profile und Bauelemente GmbH, Essener Str. 1,
pg. 508 **IT**

Windhagen

WIRTEN GMBH, Hohner Str. 2, pg. 1511 **IT**

Winnenden

Atlas Copco Electric Tools, pg. 96 **IT**
Eclipse Combustion GmbH, Vertriebsburo Sud, pg. 361 **PV**

Wipperfurth

AlliedSignal Laminate Systems GmbH, pg. 53 **PB**
WAGO Contact i.Gr, Waldstr. 1, pg. 209 **IT**

Wirges

Westerwald AG, Siemenstrasse 1, pg. 1172 **IT**

Wissen

L-TEC Deutschland GmbH, Kottinger Weg 118,
pg. 283 **IT**

Witten

Amicon G.m.b.H., Salinger Feld 32, pg. 1113 **PB**
Dittman & Neuhaus GmbH, Schlossstr. 5-7, pg. 508 **IT**
Harterei VTN Witten GmbH, pg. 1149 **IT**
Lohmann & Stolterfoht GmbH, pg. 838 **IT**
Ruhrpumpen GmbH, Stockumer Strasse 28, pg. 395 **IT**

Wittgensdorf

Flender Guss GmbH, Obere Hauptstrasse 228-230,
pg. 400 **IT**
Schiesser Sachsen AG, pg. 618 **IT**

Wittlich

Franklin Electric Europa, GmbH, Rudolph Diesel Strasse,
pg. 679 **PB**

Wolfenbuttel

NORD/LB, Holzmarkt 20, pg. 958 **IT**

Wolfratshausen

FEODOR BURGMANN DICHTUNGSWERKE GMBH,
Aeussere Sauerlacher Str. 6-10, pg. 233 **IT**
Cyanamid GmbH, Pfaffenrieder Str. 7, pg. 81 **PB**
Schwarz Extrusionswerkzeuge GmbH, Hans-Urmiller-Ring
12a - 15, pg. 825 **IT**

Wolfsburg

NEULAND Wohnungsgesellschaft mbH, pg. 1474 **IT**
NORD/LB, Lange Strasse 19, pg. 958 **IT**
PREVAG Provinzialsachsische Energieversorgungs-GmbH,
pg. 1457 **IT**
Provinzialsaechsische Energie-Versorgungs GmbH,
Wolfsburg Fallersleben, pg. 1457 **IT**
V.A.G. Transport GmbH Co. DHG, Sudkopf-Center,
Porschestrasse 102, pg. 1473 **IT**
VW AUDI Vertriebszentrum Nord GmbH, pg. 1474 **IT**
VW AUDI Vertriebszentrum Nord GmbH & Co. KG,
pg. 1474 **IT**
VW Kraftwerk GmbH, Berliner Ring 2, pg. 1474 **IT**
VW-Versicherungsvermittlungs-GmbH, Oebisfelder Str. 34,
(BZ Nord), pg. 1474 **IT**
VW-Wohnungs Gesellschaft mbH, Poststrasse 28,
pg. 1474 **IT**
VOLKSWAGEN AG, Berliner Ring 1, pg. 1473 **IT**
Volkswagen AG PreussenElektra AG OHG, Berliner Ring 2,
pg. 1456 **IT**
Volkswagen Coaching Gesellschaft mbH, pg. 1474 **IT**
Volkswagen IFA Pkw. GmbH., Berliner Ring 1,
pg. 1476 **IT**

Worms

Alcoa Deutschland GmbH-Worms, Mainzer Strasse 185,
pg. 61 **PB**
CWW-GERKO Akustik GmbH & Co. KG, pg. 1148 **IT**
Chemie-Werk Weinsheim GmbH, pg. 1148 **IT**
Goldstar Europe GmbH, Hochrheinstrasse 12, pg. 779 **IT**
Rhenania Wormser Lagerhaus-und Speditions-AG, Am
Rheim 59, pg. 1034 **IT**

Wulfrath

Dolomitwerke GmbH, pg. 1388 **IT**
Rheinische Kalksteinwerke GmbH, pg. 1388 **IT**
Wulfrath Group, pg. 1387 **IT**

Wunstorf

Reiseburo Atlantis-Akademischer Reisedienst GmbH,
pg. 596 **IT**

Wuppertal

AKF KreditBank GmbH. & Co., Friedrioh-Ebert-Strabe 90,
pg. 1481 **IT**
AKF Leasing Beteiligungsgesellschaft m.b.H., Friedrich-
Ebert-Strabe 90, pg. 1481 **IT**
AKF Leasing GmbH & Co. KG, Friedrich-Ebert-Strabe 90,
pg. 1481 **IT**
ASF Thomas, Hahnerberger Strasse 173, pg. 1599 **PB**
Akzo Zout Chemie Deutschland GmbH, 9
Laurentiusstrasse, pg. 43 **IT**
Arami Faser-Vertrieb GmbH, Enka Haus, Kasinostrasse,
pg. 46 **IT**
Carl Bartsch KG, pg. 506 **IT**
Max Birngrube KG, pg. 506 **IT**
Brugman GmbH & Co., pg. 1480 **IT**
Brugman Verwaltungs GmbH, pg. 1480 **IT**
DBF Bundelfunk GmbH & Co. Betriebs KG, Uellendahler
Str. 353, pg. 740 **PB**

Geographic Index-Non U.S.

Deutsche Bank AG (Wuppertal), Friedrich-Ebert-Strasse 1, pg. 402   **IT**
Enka AG, Enka-Haus, Kasinostr., pg. 46   **IT**
Generale Bank & Co., Jagershofstrabe 43, pg. 548   **IT**
Gerlach & Co. GmbH, pg. 1144   **IT**
Hacoba-Textilmaschinen GmbH & Co. KG, pg. 399   **IT**
Herberts GmbH, pg. 625   **IT**
Hygienic Service Gebaudereinigung Betriebs-KG., Am Diek 52, pg. 1480   **IT**
Hygienic Service Gebaudereinigung und Gebaudedienste KG, Am Diek 52, pg. 1480   **IT**
Kabelwerke Reinshagen GmbH, Reinshagenstrasse 1, pg. 723   **PB**
Kuchenwelt Handels GmbH, pg. 1480   **IT**
Kuchenwelt System GmbH, pg. 1480   **IT**
LBE Beheizungseinrichtungen GmbH, Dieselstrasse 45, pg. 1149   **IT**
Lonza GmbH, pg. 69   **IT**
Membrana GmbH, 28 Oehder Strasse, P.O. Box 200916, pg. 46   **IT**
Moenus AG, pg. 399   **IT**
Rhenania Transport GmbH, In der Fleute 150, Postfach 22 02 30, pg. 1033   **IT**
Sandvik Belzer GmbH, pg. 1186   **IT**
Sandvik Belzer Produktion GmbH, pg. 1186   **IT**
Schmitz & Apelt LOI Industrieofenanlagen GmbH, Clausewitzstrasse 82-84, pg. 1149   **IT**
STOCKO METALLWAREN FABRIKEN HENKELS & SOHN, Kirchhofstr. 52, pg. 1301   **IT**
von der Heydt-Kersten & Soehne, Neumarkt 9, pg. 310   **IT**
VORWERK & CO., Muhlenweg 17-37, pg. 1480   **IT**
Vorwerk & Co. Elektrowerke KG., Muhlenweg 17-37, pg. 1480   **IT**
Vorwerk & Co. Interholding GmbH., Muhlenweg 17-37, pg. 1480   **IT**
Vorwerk & Co. Mobelstoff-Beteiligungsgesellschaft mbH., Muhlenweg 17-37, pg. 1480   **IT**
Vorwerk & Co. Teppich-Beteiligungsgesellschaft mbH., Muhlenweg 17-37, pg. 1480   **IT**
Vorwerk & Co. Thermomix GmbH, Muhlenweg 17-37, pg. 1480   **IT**
Woodward-Clyde, Kleiner Werth 34, pg. 1658   **PB**
ZEDA Beteiligungsgesellschaft mbH., Am Diek 52, pg. 1481   **IT**
ZEDA Gesellschaft fur Datenverarbeitung und EDV-Beratung mbH. & Co., Am Diek 52, pg. 1481   **IT**

Wurselen

Data Disc Systems GmbH, pg. 836   **IT**
Sekurit Saint-Gobain Modulartechnik GmbH, Jens-Otto-Kragstrasse 6, pg. 1173   **IT**
Torrington GmbH, Krefelder Strasse 22-26, pg. 878   **PB**

Wurzburg

Allen Codiergerate GmbH, Langes Grathlein 31, pg. 1268   **IT**
DG Bank - Wurzburg, Beethovenstrasse 1a, pg. 352   **IT**
HUNGER DFE GMBH, Alfred-Nobel-Strasse 26, pg. 639   **IT**
KOENIG & BAUER-ALBERT AG, Friedrich-Koenig Strasse 4, pg. 742   **IT**
Niederlassung Wurzburg, Sanderglacisstrasse 9a, pg. 195   **IT**
Noell GmbH, Alfred-Nobel-Strasse 20, pg. 1069   **IT**
Tega-Technische Gase und Gasetechnik GmbH, pg. 811   **IT**
VW AUDI Vertriebszentrum Franken GmbH & Co. KG, pg. 1473   **IT**
VW AUDI Vertriebszentrum Franken Verwaltungs-GmbH, pg. 1473   **IT**

Wurzen

WURZNER DAUERBACKWAREN GMBH, Am Muhlgraben 1, pg. 1514   **IT**

Zeithain

DYWIDAG Beton-und Umweltprodukte GmbH, Am See 12, pg. 423   **IT**
Mannesmannrohren Werke Sachsen GmbH, pg. 835   **IT**

Zeitz

SUDZUCKER Gmbh, pg. 1305   **IT**

Zell

Muller Zell GmbH, Fritz Muller Strasse 27, pg. 198   **IT**
Prototyp-Werke GmbH, pg. 1186   **IT**

Zeulenroda

Plan Object GmbH, AM Waldsadion 6-8, pg. 388   **IT**

Zirndorf

Jos. Rackl & Co. GmbH, Rothenburgerstr. 10, pg. 514   **IT**

Zweibrucken

Kubota Baumaschinen GmbH, Steinhauser Strasse 100, pg. 763   **IT**
Mannesmann Demag Fahrzeugkrane GmbH, pg. 837   **IT**
Turbo-Lufttechnik GmbH, pg. 399   **IT**

Zwickau

Metallaufbereitung Zwickau GmbH, Saarstr. 10, pg. 513   **IT**
Radsystem GmbH, pg. 835   **IT**
Schweisstechnisches Bildungszsntrum Zwickau GmbH, pg. 1474   **IT**
Volkswagen-Bildungsnstitut GmbH, pg. 1474   **IT**

GHANA

Accra

BASF (Ghana) Limited, Standard Chartered Bank Bldg., Kwame Nkrumah Ave., pg. 106   **IT**
Barclays Bank of Ghana Ltd., High St., pg. 165   **IT**
Battle Mountain Gold (Africa), 23 Senchi St., Airport Residential, Africa, pg. 193   **PB**
Blackwood Hodge (Ghana) Ltd., Ring Rd. W., P.O. Box 126, pg. 231   **IT**
Crusader Company (Ghana) Limited, Samlotte House, Kwame Nkrumah Avenue, pg. 363   **IT**
Crusader Insurance Company (Ghana) Limited, Samlotte House, Kwame Nkrumah Avenue, pg. 364   **PB**
Ghacem, Ltd., pg. 1201   **IT**
Ghana Cement Co. Ltd., pg. 1201   **IT**
Johnson's Wax Ltd., P.O. Box 5249, pg. 593   **PV**
Merchant Bank (Ghana) Limited, Merban House, 44 Kwame Nkrumah Avenue, pg. 1293   **IT**
Mobil Oil Ghana Ltd., Mobil House, pg. 1119   **PB**
Nestle Ghana Ltd., pg. 921   **IT**
Panalpina (Ghana) Limited, pg. 1023   **IT**
Pfizer Limited, 283/2 Ring Road Central, pg. 1282   **PB**
Shell Ghana Services Ltd., Nwawen House, High Street, pg. 1137   **IT**
Sodexho Ghana Ltd., Plot 525-8, Dadeban Road, pg. 1275   **IT**
Standard Chartered Bank Ghana Ltd., PO Box 768, High St., pg. 1294   **IT**
Svedala Ghana, pg. 1324   **IT**
Taysec Construction Limited, 4 Brewery Road, pg. 1359   **IT**
UAC of Ghana Ltd., pg. 1438   **IT**
West Coast Explosives, SRS029, 11th Lane, Osu R.E., pg. 1115   **PB**
The World Bank, 69 Eighth Avenue Extension, pg. 1189   **PV**

Osu

Taylor Woodrow of Ghana Limited, P.O. box 01010, 4 Brewery Road, pg. 1360   **IT**
Taysec Construction Ltd., P.O. Box 01010, 4 Brewery Road, pg. 1360   **IT**
Taysec Properties Ltd., P.O. Box 01010, 4 Brewery Road, pg. 1360   **IT**

Sekondi

Det Norske Veritas, pg. 397   **IT**

Tema

Food Specialties Ghana Ltd., pg. 920   **IT**
Ghana Sanyo Co., Ltd., pg. 1192   **IT**
Volta Aluminium Co. Ltd. (VALCO), pg. 1063   **PB**

GIBRALTAR

Gibraltar

Barclays Bank PLC, pg. 166   **IT**
Gibraltar Telecommunications International Limited, 31 Cannon Lane, pg. 223   **IT**
Gibraltar Telephone Company, pg. 204   **IT**
Hispanc Commerzbank (Gibraltar Ltd.), Don House, 30/38 Main St., 2nd Floor, pg. 140   **IT**
Inishtech plc, 57/63 Line Wall Rd., pg. 341   **IT**
Kvaerner Gibralter Ltd., The Dockyard, pg. 772   **IT**
Kvaerner Ships Equipment a.s Gibralter Branch, Main Wharf Road, pg. 768   **IT**
Republic National Bank of New York (Gibraltar) Ltd., Neptune House, pg. 1381   **IT**
The Royal Bank of Scotland (Gibraltar) Limited, 1 Corral Rd., pg. 1133   **IT**
Shell Co. of Gibraltar Ltd., Shell House, Linewall Rd., pg. 1138   **IT**
Taylor Woodrow of Gibraltar Limited, P.O. Box 126, Ellesmere House, pg. 1360   **IT**

GREECE

Acharne

Milupa Hellas EPE, pg. 991   **IT**

Aharnai

Estia Trading S.A., pg. 506   **IT**

Aharnes

Reemtsma Hellas S.A., Tatoiou Str. 307, pg. 1101   **IT**

Alimos Attikis

Alcon Laboratories Hellas E.P.E., pg. 918   **IT**

Amarousion

ISS Servisystem S.A., Amarousiou-Chalandriou 4, pg. 657   **IT**
Ilva Hellas S.A., 32 Kifissias Ave., pg. 654   **IT**
KSB TESMA AG, pg. 721   **IT**
Monsanto Chemical Products Hellas, E.p.E., 50 Kifissias Ave., pg. 1125   **PB**

Athens

ADT Greece, S.A., 46 Syngrou Ave., pg. 1649   **PB**
ANZ Grindlays Bank plc Greece, 7 Merlin St., pg. 99   **IT**
Alfa Agricultural Supplies Ltd., 13 Tim Filimonos, pg. 830   **IT**
Alfa-Beta Vassilopoulos S.A., 81 Spaton Ave., Gerakas, pg. 463   **IT**
Alfa-Laval AB Athens, 262, Messoghion Ave., pg. 1380   **IT**
Algemene Bank Nederland (Athens), 3, Paparigopoulou St., Klafthmonos Square, pg. 12   **IT**
Allianz General Insurance Company S.A., Kifissias Avenue 124, pg. 59   **IT**
Allianz Life Insurance Company S.A., Kifissias Avenue 124, pg. 59   **IT**
AlliedSignal Aerospace Service Corporation, 15410 Psychico, pg. 52   **PB**
Aluminum de Grece, 1, rue Sekeri, pg. 1030   **IT**
Amiga Computing/Gamepro Greece, Seven Diogenous & Chlois Street, pg. 569   **PV**
Amway Hellas, 2 Harokopou St. & 196 Syngrou, Ave, pg. 70   **PV**
Arrow Hellas AEE, Leoforos Kifisias 294 & Navarinon, pg. 135   **PB**
Asea Brown Boveri S.A., 9, Vissarionos St., pg. 3   **IT**
Astra Hellas S.A., pg. 93   **IT**
Athenian Brewery S.A., 107 Kifissou Avenue, pg. 608   **IT**
Athens Mill, 132 Iera Odos, pg. 672   **PB**
Audiotex S.A, 10-12, Kifissia Avenue, pg. 795   **IT**
Bank of America NT&SA, 39 Panepistimiou, pg. 182   **PB**
Banque Paribas-Grece, Panrepistimiou 39, pg. 320   **IT**
Barclays Bank PLC, 1 Kolokotroni St., pg. 166   **IT**
Baring Hellenic Ventures S.A., 17 Akadimias Street, pg. 648   **IT**
Bayerische Vereinsbank AG, 3, Valaortou S., pg. 180   **IT**
Beiersdorf Hellas AE, pg. 183   **IT**
Benckiser Hellas AG, pg. 185   **IT**
Biokat ATBE, pg. 836   **IT**
Bioton AG Industrieaktiengesellschaft fur Kosmetik und Friseurbedarf, Papadiamantopoulou 4, pg. 1489   **IT**
Robert Bosch SA, 162 Kifissos Ave., pg. 205   **IT**
Bristol Hellas A.E.B.E., 11 Km. Athinon Lamios National Rd., pg. 255   **PB**
Bull AE, 44 ave. Syngrou, pg. 317   **IT**
Bull Scion Services, 3 rue Skra, pg. 317   **IT**
Leo Burnett Athens, Sygrou Ave. 371, pg. 184   **PV**
CCF Athens, 20 Amalias Avenue, pg. 342   **IT**
Cariplo (Athens), 13, Panepistimiou Street, pg. 275   **IT**
Carmor Hellas Ltd., 31, rue Neou Falirou, pg. 1030   **IT**
Cartellas S.A., 132 Lera Odos, pg. 672   **PB**
Cartonpack S.A., 234, Syngrou Ave., pg. 864   **PB**
Century Oils Hellas A.B.E.E., 43, Tsendner Street, pg. 517   **IT**
The Chase Manhattan Bank, N.A., P.O. Box 3005, pg. 340   **PB**
Christie's Hellas, 27 Vassilisis Sophias Ave., pg. 290   **IT**
CIBA-GEIGY Hellas S.A., Anthoussas Ave., pg. 977   **IT**
Cigna Insurance Company (Hellas) S.A., Phidippidou No. 2, pg. 363   **IT**
Circle Freight International Greece S.A., Syngrou Ave. 226, pg. 372   **IT**
Citibank, N.A. Athens, 8 Othonos St., pg. 378   **PB**
Conquest Europe, Kifissias, 10-12, pg. 1484   **IT**
Copais Food & Beverage Company S.A., 161 Irakliou Ave., pg. 806   **PB**
DIN-S. Bakelas, 29, Cheldraich str., pg. 550   **IT**
DMB&B Athens, 3 Gyzi St. & Egialias, pg. 303   **PV**
Danzas A.E., Leoforos Kifissou & Ag. Annis 50, pg. 382   **IT**
Digital Equipment Hellas Ltd., 32 Kifissias Avenue, pg. 508   **PB**
Diorfil S.A., 7-9, ae. Halandriou, pg. 782   **IT**
Dr. D.A. Delis AG, Paleologou Benizelou 5, pg. 108   **IT**
Dresdner Bank AG, Panepistimiou St. 43, pg. 419   **IT**
EIB Athens Branch, 12 avenue Amalias, pg. 465   **IT**
Enka Hellas Ltd., 196 Kifissia Ave., pg. 46   **IT**
Ericsson (Hellas) Telecommunications Equipment S.A., 338, Vouliagmenis Ave., pg. 1366   **IT**
Eurofinn Services, N.A. Krokides-N.D. Tsoliakos, 44, Amalias Ave., pg. 458   **IT**
Fuchs Hellas S.A., 10, Vironos Street, pg. 517   **IT**
GEKE AE, pg. 836   **IT**
GGK Athens, 42 Antinoros St., pg. 1335   **IT**
Galileo Hellas, 31st St. & Mystra, pg. 1004   **IT**
Generali Hellas A.E. Asfaliseon Zimion, Merlin 5, pg. 91   **IT**
Generali Life A.E. Asfaliseon Zois, Michalakopoulou 75, pg. 91   **IT**
Geo-Young & Rubicam, 49, Vas Sofias Ave., pg. 1199   **PV**
Getinge/Castle International Limited, Areos 101, pg. 551   **IT**
Goodyear Hellas S.A.I.C., 94 Kifissou Ave., pg. 753   **PB**
Grace Hellas Industrial & Commercial L.L.C., 20 Lagoumitzi St., pg. 756   **PB**
Heinemann Hellas, 80 Kousidi Street, pg. 1094   **IT**

Hellamat, Avenue Mesogion 354, pg. 791   IT
Hellamco, 2, Sikcilanou St. & Kifissias Av., pg. 818   PB
Hellamco-Michael Cotoyannis, 2 Sikelianou St. & Kifissias av., pg. 818   PB
Hellas Can S.A., pg. 267
Hellenci Steel Co., 1 Mitropoleos St., pg. 654   IT
Henkel Hellas, S.A., Kiprou St. 23, pg. 612   IT
Hewlett-Packard Hellas, Atrina Center, 32, Kifissias Ave., pg. 820   PB
Honeywell Bull AE, 44, Avenue Syngrou 117-42, pg. 318   IT
Hydro Aluminium Systems Hellas S.A., 19 KM Leoforos Lavriou, pg. 963   IT
ING Bank Athens, 198 Syngrou Avenue, pg. 648   IT
ING Bank Greece, 198 Syngrou Avenue, pg. 649   IT
ING Barings Greece EPE, Voukourestiou 20, pg. 650   IT
Ideal-Standard S.A.I., 23 Alexandroupoleos St., pg. 92   PB
Inchcape Greece S.A., 168 Kifissou Ave., pg. 672   IT
Industrie Hellenique de Detergents S.A. (E.V.A.), pg. 1437   IT
Intergraph Hellas S.A., Patriarchou Ioakim, pg. 892   PB
International Marketing & Promotions, 3 Gyzi & Egialias, pg. 304   PV
Jacobs Suchard Pavlides S.A., pg. 1289   PB
Janssen/Cilag S.A.C.I., 56 Eirinis Ave., pg. 929   PB
Johnson & Johnson Hellas S.A., 4 Epidavrou Street, pg. 930   PB
Axel Johnson & Co. (Hellas) Ltd., 9, Ironda St., pg. 711   IT
S.C. Johnson & Son (Hellas) E.P.E., 479 Messogion Ave., pg. 593   PV
Kodak (Near East) Inc., Himaras St., Paradisos Maroussi, pg. 554   IT
Konica Athens Office, 250-254 Kifissias Ave., pg. 749   IT
Kosmobel AG Handelsaktiengesellschaft fur Kosmetik und Friseurbedarf, Papadiamantopoulou 4, pg. 1490   IT
Lambert Smith Hampton, 4 Sekeri Street, pg. 797   IT
Landis & Staefa Hellas AE, 5 Kolokotroni St., pg. 801   IT
Linde Hellas E.P.E., pg. 811   IT
Lockheed Corporation (International) S.A., 9 Giannitson St., pg. 1009   PB
Louis Vuitton Hellas SCA, 39 Voukourestiou St., pg. 782   IT
Luxottica Hellas AE, 8, Emm, Benaki St., pg. 822   IT
MAC BETON Hellas S.A., pg. 983   IT
MD Foods Caltsoyias Hellas S.A., 18, Matsa Street, pg. 826   IT
Macedonian Airlines, 120 Syngrou Ave., pg. 1004   IT
Marchon Hellas Limited, 45, Naiadon Street, Paleon Faliron, pg. 1580   PB
Medicare, 7, Katehaki Str., pg. 822   PB
Melissa, 1 Vionos Street, pg. 380   IT
Mercedes-Benz Hellas S.A., pg. 369   IT
Metaxa Distilleries, 6 Andrea Metaxa Str., pg. 410   IT
Metaxa Greece, 6,A. Metaxa Str., pg. 410   IT
Micronics Ltd., 46 Kritis St., pg. 822   PB
Microsoft Hellas S.A., pg. 1108   PB
Minos EMI, 51 Neo Psychico, pg. 427   IT
Mitsui & Co., Ltd., 6th Fl., Hermes Bldg., 56 Panepistimiou, pg. 881   IT
Mobil Oil Hellas A.E. Petroleum Co., pg. 1119   PB
NATIONAL BANK OF GREECE S.A., 86 Eolou Street, pg. 907   IT
Nationale-Nederlanden, 198 Syngrou Avenue, pg. 650   IT
Nedlloyd Road Cargo A.E., pg. 1145   IT
Novo Nordisk Ferment AG, Status Center, Athinas Avenue/ Areos 2, pg. 989   IT
Novo Nordisk Hellas Ltd., 518, Messoghion Avenue, pg. 988   IT
Novotel Hellenic, 4-8, rue Michael Voda, pg. 21   IT
Nutricia Hellas S.A., pg. 992   IT
Olivetti Hellas S.A., 236 Syngrou Ave., pg. 1003   IT
Olympic Airtours, 1st Syngrou Ave., pg. 1004   IT
OLYMPIC AIRWAYS, S.A., 96, Sygrou Ave., pg. 1004   IT
Olympic Aviation, Athens Intl. Airport, West Ter, Hellinikon, pg. 1004   IT
Olympic Catering, Eleftheriou Venizelou & 29th St., pg. 1004   IT
Oracle Hellas S.A., 30 Fokionos Negri Str., pg. 1228   PB
Palco A.E., pg. 618   IT
Pechiney World Trade (Hellas) S.A., 26, rue Mylopotamou, pg. 1031   IT
Petros Petropoulos SA, 96 Iera Odos, pg. 97   IT
Pfizer Hellas, A.E., 5 Alketou St., pg. 1282   PB
Pharmacia & Upjohn (Hellas) S.A., Marinou Antipa Street 62-66, pg. 1050   IT
Procter & Gamble Greece, 165 Fyngrou Ave., pg. 1332   PB
Producta-TBWA, Floias & Salaminos 4, pg. 1062   PV
Progress Advertising, 64 Apostolopoulou, 152 31 N. Halandri, pg. 470   IT
R.J. Reynolds Tobacco (Hellas) A.E.B.E., Athens Tower B, Suite 506, pg. 1356   PB
Rhone-Poulenc Hellas, 308 Messoghion Ave., pg. 1113   IT
Rhone-Poulenc Rorer A.E.B.E., 290 Messoghion Ave.,, pg. 1113   IT
Roche (Hellas) S.A., pg. 1121   IT
Roche Nicholas Health Products S.A., pg. 1121   IT
Rothenberger (Hellas) S.A., 41 Imitou, pg. 1129   IT
SKF Hellas S.A., Leoforos Athinon 46, pg. 1158   IT
Sandoz (Hellas) S.A.C.I., pg. 984   IT
Sanpaolo-Athens Representative Office, 11, Vasilissis Sofias Ave., pg. 691   IT
SASIB Hellas Signaling Systems I.C.S.A., 53 Solomou Street, pg. 1195   IT
Schiesser-Hellas S.r.l., pg. 618   IT
Schiesser-Pallas S.r.l., pg. 618   IT
Scholl Hellas SA, PO Box 17, pg. 1209   IT
Shell Company (Hellas) Ltd., 2 Eleftheriou Venizelou Ave., pg. 1138   IT
Siemens A.E., Artemidos 8, pg. 1247   IT

SmithKline Beecham C.I.S.A., 32 Xanthou St., pg. 1265   IT
Swift Adhesives Greece SAIC, 2, Bouboulinas Street, pg. 370   IT
TVX Hellas A.E., Koumbari 2, pg. 1345   IT
Thomson-CSF Hellas A.E., Tour d'Athenes, 2-4, avenue Messaghion, pg. 1385   IT
3M Hellas Limited, 20 Kifissias Ave., pg. 1606   IT
The Tokio Marine & Fire Insurance Company (U.K.) Limited, c/o Willis Corroon Kendriki, 44 Ermou St., pg. 1392   IT
Toyota Motor Corporation, Athens Representative Office, c/o Kassidopoulos S.A., 168 Kifissou Ave., 121-31, pg. 1413   IT
Z.N. Valmas & Co., 3, Stadio Street, pg. 458   IT
Vitamin, 12, Vikatou St., pg. 1377   IT
Wackenhut Security (Hellas), Ltd., 100, Kapodistriou St., pg. 1732   IT
Whitehall Greece, Chrysostomou Smyrnis 45 Kyprou, pg. 82   PB
Willis Corroon Hellas SA, 44 Ermou Street, pg. 1509   IT
Willis Corroon Kendriki SA, 44 Ermou Street, pg. 1509   IT
Wyeth Hellas EPE, Chrysostomou Smyrnis 45, pg. 82   PB
Zeneca Hellas S.A., 231 Syngrou Ave., pg. 1526   IT
Zurich Insurance Company, Atrina Center, Complex B, 32, Kifissias Ave., pg. 1531   IT

Chania

Omega Vision 2000 S.A., Dictinis 2, pg. 1032   PB

Corinth

Cartonpack S.A., Valtos, Glyfada, Ancient Korinthos, pg. 864   IT

Glyfada

Pharmacia & Upjohn Export AG, 14, Vouligmenis Ave., pg. 1048   IT

Halandri

Snap-on Tools International, Ltd. (Middle East/Africa Division), 4, Agias Varvaras, pg. 1481   PB

Ierapetra

Cretan Papermill S.A., pg. 864   IT

Kalamata

KARELIA TOBACCO COMPANY INC., Athinon St., pg. 724   IT

Kallithea

A.C. Nielsen Hellas Ltd., 2 Charokopou Str./196 Sygrou Ave., pg. 1183   PB

Kifissia

CPC (Hellas) A.B.E.E., Pigon 33, pg. 225   PB

Mandra-Attikis

Van Leer Elpack A.E.B.E., Local Rd. Mandra-Magoula, pg. 1146   IT

Maroussi

Carnation Hellas S.A.I., pg. 919   IT
EURO RSCG, 16 Kifissias Ave., pg. 602   IT
Forest Products S.A., 22 Kifissias Ave., pg. 458   IT
Nestle Hellas S.A.I., pg. 921   IT
Target Euro RSCG, 16 Kisfissias Ave., pg. 603   IT

Metamorphosis

Bohler Hellas A.E.B.E., 12 km National Road Athens-Lamia, pg. 1471   IT
Bristol-Myers Squibb, Athinon-Lamias National Rd., pg. 256   PB

Moschato

Henkel Hellas, 23 Kyprou St., pg. 612   IT

Nea Kifissia

Nutricia Hellas S.A., pg. 992   IT

Nea Smirni

Dow Hellas, Syngrou Ave., 213-215, pg. 524   PB

Neo Psichico

Eurosos, 249 Messogion Avenue, pg. 334   IT

Pallini

Pharmacia & Upjohn Inter-American Corporation-Greece, 16th Km., Marathonos Ave., pg. 1048   IT

Patras

Achoia Papermill S.A., Industrial Zone, pg. 672   PB

Peristeri

Loumidis S.A., pg. 920   IT
P. Papas & Co. O.E. Trading Company, Paparrigopoulou 7, pg. 109   IT

Piraeus

Algemene Bank Nederland (Piraeus), 59, Akti Miaouli &, 5-7 Philellinon St., pg. 12   IT
Castrol Hellas S.A., 14 Skouze St., pg. 235   IT
Colgate-Palmolive (Hellas) S.A., 89, Athinon St., pg. 398   PB
Det Norske Veritas, 26-28 Akti Kondyli, pg. 397   IT
Greek Salt Industrial Commercial EPE, 22 Flemingstreet, pg. 44   IT
Jotun Hellas Ltd., Branch Office Greece, 8, (Og-Tejn) Skouze 26, pg. 715   IT
MacGREGOR (GRC) E.P.E., 4-6 Efplias St., 6th Fl., pg. 670   IT
Makro Cash and Carry Wholesale S.A., Kifissou 98 & Petrou Ralli, pg. 1155   IT
The Royal Bank of Scotland plc, 61 Akti Miaouli, pg. 1133   IT
Willis Faber (Aegean) Limited, 8 Kanari Street, pg. 1510   IT

Psychiko

Texaco Greek Petroleum Company S.A., P.O.B. 65 030, pg. 1584   PB
Voest-Alpine Hellas A.E., Taygetou 25, pg. 1472   IT

Salonika

CIBA-GEIGY Hellas S.A., Constantinoupoleos 176, pg. 977   IT
Exelka S.A., 3 Tripotamou St. Stavroupolis, pg. 1502   PB

Sindos

Cartonpack S.A., pg. 864   IT

Stavoupolis

Transhellenic Tobacco S.A., 3 Tripotamou St., pg. 1502   PB

Thessaloniki

ABB Stotz-Kontakt Hellas S.A., Dodekanissou 21, pg. 2   IT
Credit Commercial de France, 9 rue Ionos Dragoumi, pg. 342   IT
Gretoba, S.A., pg. 1695   PB
Hansen Hellas Abee, 26th October 72 2 Limnou Str. 2, pg. 289   IT
Hewlett-Packard Hellas Service Center, 31, Papanastassiou Str., pg. 820   PB
Magnomin-General Mining S.A., 17 Agia Sophia St., pg. 904   PV
Tosoh Hellas A.I.C., Industrial Area of Sindos, pg. 1408   IT

Volos

IMAS S.A., pg. 298   IT

Vouliagmeni

Novo Nordisk A/S, Status Center, Athinas Avenue, pg. 988   IT

GREENLAND

Godthab

Det Norske Veritas, Augo Lyngesvej 8, pg. 396   IT

GUADELOUPE

Abymes

Air Guadeloupe, Reizet Airport, pg. 561   IT
B.F.C. Antilles-Guyane, P.O. Box 370, pg. 314   IT
Societe Shell des Antilles et de la Guyane Francaises, Immeuble Sodega, Route de l'Aeroport, pg. 1141   IT

Basse Terre

Societe Guadeloupeene de Carton Ondule, Boite Postale No. 2, pg. 906   PB

Petit Bourg

GTM Guadeloupe, Lotissement Vinci, N 10, pg. 823   IT

PB - *U.S. Public Companies Volume*
PV - *U.S. Private Companies Volume*
IT - *International Public & Private Companies Volume*

Pointe-a-Pitre

Gan Incendie Accidents Guadeloupe, 59/61 rue AR Boisneuf BP 694, pg. 564 **IT**
Gan Vie Guadeloupe, 59/61 rue AR Boisneuf BP 694, pg. 565 **IT**
Santipa S.a.r.l., 3, rue Euvremond Gene, pg. 985 **IT**

GUATEMALA

Guatemala

Alimentos Kern de Guatemala, S.A., Kilometro 6.5, Carretera al Atlantico, pg. 1392 **PB**
Amway de Guatemala, S.A., Avenida Las Americas 1881, pg. 69 **PV**
Arrow de Centro-America Ltda., 2a Calle 33-67 Zona 7, pg. 194 **IT**
Aseguradora General S.A., 10a Calle 3-17, pg. 90 **IT**
AVIATECA, Avda. Hincapie, 12-22 Zone 13, pg. 102 **IT**
BDF de CentroAmerica S.A., pg. 182 **IT**
BIC de Guatemala, 33 Calle 26-38, Zona 12, pg. 1273 **IT**
Bonifica-Guatemala, Col. Lomas de Prtugal Mixico, 5 Calle G - 147 Zona 1, pg. 655 **IT**
Leo Burnett Comunica S.A., 5TA Avenida 6-39, Zone 14, Colonia El Campo, pg. 185 **PV**
Ceramicas Termicas de Guatemala S.A., 12 Av. A, pg. 894 **IT**
CIBA-GEIGY SA (America Central y Caribe), pg. 979 **IT**
Citibank, N.A. Guatemala City, Edificio Buonafina, pg. 378 **PB**
Colgate-Palmolive (Central America) S.A., Avenida del Ferrocarril 49-65, pg. 398 **PB**
Cominco Resources International Limited, 18 Avenida 10-78, Zona 15, Apartamento No. 6, Vista Hermosa III, pg. 308 **IT**
Compania Farmaceutica Upjohn S.A., Aptdo. 991, pg. 1049 **IT**
Contabilidad Mecanizada, Sociedad Anonima, 6A. Ave. 20-25 Zona 10, pg. 364 **PB**
Crown Cork de Guatemala, S.A., Apartado Postal 2290, pg. 464 **PB**
Datum, 6ta Ave. 6-94, pg. 1228 **PB**
Discos de Centro America, 12 Calle 3-27 Zona, pg. 1052 **IT**
Dos:Puntos, 17 Avenida 42-26, pg. 304 **PV**
ECO, Young & Rubicam S.A., 8 Calle 2-38, Zona 9, pg. 1200 **PV**
Electrolux S.A., Edificio Vasil 3.0. Nivel 6a Calle 5-47, pg. 442 **IT**
Empresa Guatemaltica CIGNA de Seguros, Sociedad Anonima, 6A. Ave. 20-25 Zona 10, Edificio Plaza Maritima, pg. 364 **PB**
Ericsson de Guatemala, S.A., 6A. Ave. 7-39, Zona 10, pg. 1366 **IT**
Fertilizantes del Pacifico S.A., Anillo Periferico 17-39, Zona 2, pg. 108 **IT**
Formularios Moore de Guatemala, S.A., 49 Calle 18-65, pg. 889 **IT**
Grace Central America, Apartado Postal 2068-01901, pg. 755 **PB**
Gran Industria de Neumaticos Centroamericana, S.A., 50 Calle 23-70, 01012, pg. 753 **PB**
Guatemalteca Shell SA, 24 Avenida No. 35-81, Zona 12, pg. 1141 **IT**
Henkel Centroamericana S.A., pg. 612 **IT**
IBM de Guatemala, S.A., pg. 897 **PB**
Industria Centroamericana de Sanitarios, S.A., P.O. Box 2533, pg. 92 **PB**
Ipesa de Guatemala, Avenida Reforma 3-48, pg. 822 **PB**
Kativo de Guatemala, S.A., 14 Avenida 04-11, Zona 12, pg. 687 **PB**
Knoll Centroamericana S.A., Avenida Petapa 47-31, Zona 12, pg. 108 **IT**
Eli Lilly de Centro America, S.A., Apartado Postal 735, pg. 993 **PB**
Lucent Technologies de Guatemala S.A., 3a Ave. 14-30, Zona 10, pg. 1018 **PB**
Mitsui & Co., (Panama International, S.A.), Edificio Panamerican 4th Fl. 6a Avenida, pg. 882 **IT**
Molinos Modernos, S.A., 33 Calle 25-30 Zona 12, pg. 411 **IT**
Norsk Hydro Guatemala, S.A., Ruta 7, 4-54, Zona 4, pg. 964 **IT**
Olefinas, S.A., pg. 725 **PV**
ONCE, Calle 4, no. 7-73, pg. 334 **IT**
Productos Alimenticios Imperial, S.A., Apartado Postal 10-B, pg. 411 **IT**
Productos Avon de Guatemala S.A., Apartado Postal 198 A, pg. 156 **PB**
Productos de Maiz y Alimentos, S.A., Apartado Postal 1765, 46 Calle 20-56, pg. 447 **PB**
Productos Nestle (Guatemala) S.A., pg. 922 **IT**
Productos Roche S.A., pg. 1121 **IT**
Quimica Henkel Centroamericana S.A., 3 A. Azenida 11-18 Zona 9, Edificio El Acazar, Segundo Nivel, pg. 613 **IT**
Refractarios Multiples S.A., Calzada Aguilar Batres 15-38, pg. 894 **IT**
Rorer de Centro America (Guatemala) S.A., 12 Calle 1-25, Zena 10 Oficina 1502-03, pg. 1111 **IT**
Seguros Universales, S.A., Calle 4, no. 7, 73, pg. 334 **IT**
Texaco Guatemala Inc., Apartado Postal 336, pg. 1584 **PB**
3M Guatemala, S.A., KM13 Calzada Roosevelt 12-33, pg. 1606 **PB**
Triton Guatemala, pg. 1640 **PB**
Van Leer Envases de Guatemala, pg. 1147 **IT**
Wackenhut de Guatemala, S.A., Calle 14 8-51, Zona 10, pg. 1731 **PB**
Wandel & Goltermann Centroamerica y el Caribe, 6a. Calle 6-48 zona 9, pg. 1486 **IT**
Zeneca Panamericana S.A., Edificio Las Brisas, 5 nivel, 6a Avenida 7-39, Zona 10, pg. 110 **IT**

GUYANA

Cayenne

Banque Nationale de Paris-Guyane, 2 Pl. Vietor-Schoelcher, pg. 164 **IT**

Georgetown

Aroaima Mining Company Limited, Offices of E.Q. Luckhoo, Esq. N 1/2 Lot, pg. 1386 **PB**
Caribbean Molasses Co. Ltd., pg. 1357 **IT**
Colgate-Palmolive (Guyana) Ltd., R. 1 Ruimveldt, pg. 398 **PB**
Demerara Tobacco Co. Ltd., Bel Air, pg. 111 **IT**
OMAI Gold Mines Limited, 176-D, Middle Street, pg. 253 **IT**
Shell Antilles & Guianas Ltd., Lot BB Rome, pg. 1141 **IT**

HAITI

Laffiteau

Rice Corporation of Haiti, S.A., One Nationale Road, pg. 591 **PB**

Port-au-Prince

Walter Hirsch ADM, 12, Rue du Quai, pg. 108 **IT**
The Shell Company (WI) Ltd., Delmas 17-19, pg. 1141 **IT**

HONDURAS

Danli

Fabrica de Molduras y Cajas, S.A., pg. 1661 **PB**

San Pedro Sula

Certified Apparel Services of Honduras, S.A., Barrio La Guardia, 4 Y 5 Calle, 30 Y 31 Avenida, pg. 625 **PV**
Compania Hulera Sula, S.A. de C.V., pg. 69 **PB**
Inversiones Continental, S.A. de C.V., Edificio Continental, Segundo Piso, pg. 363 **PB**
Kativo Commercial S.A., Km.5 Carretera a Puerto Lortes, pg. 687 **PB**
Kativo de Honduras, S.A., Apartado 193, pg. 687 **PB**
Productos Avon, S.A., Apartado 1736, pg. 156 **PB**
Quimica Henkel Centroamericana de Honduras S.A. de C.V., pg. 613 **IT**
Refineria Texaco de Honduras, S.A., Apartado Postal 112, pg. 1584 **PB**
Shell Honduras SA, 8 Ave. Circunvalacion SE, No. 1701, pg. 1141 **IT**
T.R.C./Honduras, S.A. De C.V., Bldg. #7, Calle Sur-Este Segundo Annilo Periferico, pg. 1564 **PB**
Tabacalera Hondurenva SA, Carretera Chamelecon Zona El Cacao, pg. 111 **IT**

Tegucigalpa

Banco de Honduras S.A., Edificio Midence Soto, Plaza Morazan, pg. 378 **PB**
Colgate-Palmolive (Central America), Inc., Dos Cuadros al Norte de Granitos, pg. 398 **PB**
Delfos/Y&R, Blvd. Morazan Edificio Jarro's, pg. 1200 **PV**
Mass Publicidad, Colonia Palmira, pg. 1422 **PB**
Nestle Hondurena S.A., pg. 921 **IT**
P.A.Y.S.E.N., S.A. de C.V., Boulevard Morazan 2160, pg. 109 **IT**
SNC-Lavalin, Plaza San Jose,Bulevar Suyapa, No. 1402, 2 da Planta Oficina No 16, pg. 1162 **IT**

HONG KONG

Aberdeen

Bristol-Myers (Hong Kong) Limited, 8B Vita Towers, 29 Wong Chuk Hang Rd., pg. 255 **PB**
British American Tobacco Co. (Hong Kong) Ltd., Three Heung Yip Rd., pg. 111 **IT**
CIBA Vision (Hong Kong) Ltd., 21/F Gee Chang Hong Centre, 65 Wong Chuk Hang Road, pg. 981 **IT**
Dentsply Asia, 23/F Gee Chang Hong Centre, 65 Wong Chuk Hang Rd., pg. 499 **PB**
Eurotherm Ltd., Unit D-18/f Gee Chang Hong Ctr, 65 Wong Chuk Hang Road, pg. 466 **IT**
Hawley & Hazel Chemical Co., (Hong Kong) Ltd., 45 Wong Chuk Hang Rd., pg. 399 **PB**
Liebert Hong Kong, 1/F, Express Industrial Bldg., 43 Heung Yip Rd., pg. 577 **PB**
RHG Fishing Office Hong Kong, 71-73A Shek Pai Wan Rd., pg. 1152 **IT**
Thermo Instrument Systems (F.E.) Limited, Block A, 7th Fl., Gee Chang Hong Center, pg. 1596 **PB**

Causeway Bay

AST Asia, 29/F Citicorp Centre, 16 Whitfield Rd., pg. 1182 **IT**
Adecco Personnel Ltd., Unit B & C, 9th Floor, 38 Russell Street, pg. 24 **IT**
Amdahl Intl. Hong Kong, 701 B, Level 7, Caroline Ctr., 28 Yun Ping Rd., pg. 527 **IT**
Amway Asia Pacific Ltd-Hong Kong Branch, 38/F The Lee Gardens, 33 Nysan Ave., pg. 69 **PV**
Asatsu Hong Kong Ltd., 25/F, pg. 86 **IT**
Asia Pacific Capital Corp., Limited, 26/F Citicorp Centre 18, pg. 378 **PB**
Asian Food Industries (HK) Limited, 33rd Fl., Windsor House, 311 Gloucester Rd., pg. 703 **IT**
Asian Food Industries (Properties) Limited, 33rd Fl., Windsor Houe, 311 Gloucester Rd., pg. 703 **IT**
F.J. Benjamin Fashions (HK) Ltd., Suite 4501-45th Fl., Natwest Tower, pg. 187 **IT**
Borland (Hong Kong) Ltd., Rm. 2002, Cameron Commercial, Center, 458-468 Hennessy Road, pg. 246 **PB**
Robert Bosch Company Ltd., 2402 Caroline Ctr., 2-38 Yun Ping Rd., pg. 205 **IT**
C-E International, 906 Hanglung Centre, 2-20 Paterson St., pg. 5 **IT**
Colgate-Palmolive (Hong Kong) Ltd., 11/F Caroline Ctr., 28 Yun Ping Rd., pg. 398 **PB**
The Dairy Farm Company, Limited, 33rd Fl., Windsor House, 311 Gloucester Rd., pg. 703 **IT**
Dairy Farm International Finance Limited, 33rd Fl., Windsor House, 311 Gloucester Rd., pg. 703 **IT**
Dairy Farm Management Services Limited, 33rd Floor, Windsor House, 311 Gloucester Road, pg. 703 **IT**
EMC Computer Systems, 2001 AIA Plaza, 16-30 Hysan Ave., pg. 545 **PB**
ESS-FOOD (H.K.) Ltd., Unit 2202, 22/F, Causeway Bay Plaza 2, pg. 429 **IT**
Edelman Worldwide (Hong Kong) Limited, 3701-237F, Windsor House, 311 Glouchester Road, pg. 363 **PV**
Enso-Eurocan Hong Kong Ltd., World Trade Ctr., Rm. 1406, 14th Floor, pg. 457 **IT**
The Excelsior Hotel, Hong Kong, 281 Gloucester Rd., pg. 704 **IT**
Fidelio Software Ltd., 2805A Windsor House, 311 Gloucester Road, pg. 1106 **PB**
H.B. Fuller International, Inc., Sino Plaza, Ste. 2605, 255-257 Gloucester Rd., pg. 687 **PB**
Graco Hong Kong Ltd., Room 1203, The Goldmark, 502 Hennessy Road, pg. 757 **PB**
HSBC Investment Funds Hong Kong Limited, Suite 607, Citicorp Centre, 18 Whitfield Road, pg. 582 **IT**
Hayselton Enterprises Limited, 33rd Fl., Windsor House, 311 Gloucester Rd., pg. 703 **IT**
Hong Kong Convenience Stores Limited, 33rd Fl., Windsor House, 311 Gloucester Rd., pg. 704 **IT**
Hutchison Information Services Limited, 34/F Natwest Tower, Times Square, pg. 1139 **PB**
ICC (Hong Kong) Ltd., 20 th Flr., Universal House, 229-230 Gloucester Rd., pg. 554 **PV**
IHI (HK) Ltd., Room 501, 38 Russell Street, pg. 689 **IT**
Iceberg Properties Limited, 33rd Fl., Windsor House, 311 Gloucester Rd., pg. 704 **IT**
Imation Hong Kong Ltd., 15/F Citicorp Centre, 18 Whitfield Rd., pg. 870 **PB**
Intertec Limited, 20th. Flr., Universal House, 229-230 Gloucester Rd., pg. 554 **PV**
Kyowa Hakko (H.K.) Co., Ltd., Room 2303, Hang Lung Centre, 2-20 Paterson St., pg. 778 **IT**
Lowe & Partners/Live, S/F Eight Plaza, 8 Sunning Rd., pg. 678 **PV**
Lucent Technologies Asia/Pacific Ltd., 30th Fl., Shell Tower, Times Square, 1 Matheson St., pg. 1018 **PB**
Mandarin Oriental Hotel Group Limited, 281 Gloucester Rd., pg. 704 **IT**
Mitsukoshi Enterprises Co., Ltd., Hennessy Centre, 500 Hennessy Rd., pg. 884 **IT**
Motorola China Holding Limited, 41/F Natwest Tower, Times Square, pg. 1139 **PB**
NatWest Investment Management Asia Limited, 43/f NatWest Tower, Times Square, pg. 911 **IT**
Nikon Hong Kong Ltd., Rm. 304, 3rd Fl. Sunning Plaza, 10 Hysan Ave., pg. 931 **IT**
Olivetti Hong Kong Ltd., 9/f Citicorp Centre, 18 Whitfield Rd., pg. 1003 **IT**
Polaroid Far East Ltd., Windsor House, pg. 1314 **PB**
Rockwell Automation Asia Pacific Ltd., 27th Floor, Citicorp Center, 18 Whitfield Road, pg. 1399 **PB**
Ruthin Investments limited, 33rd Fl., Windsor House, 311 Gloucester Rd., pg. 704 **IT**
Sanderson Computers Hong Kong Ltd., c/o Hang Lung Bank Bldg., 14th Fl., pg. 1185 **IT**
Sanwa Housing Loan (Hong Kong) Limited, Room 502, Caroline Centre, pg. 1190 **IT**
ScotiaMocatta, Suite 2802-4, Sino Plaza, 256-257 Gloucester Rd., pg. 156 **IT**
Sime Darby Hong Kong Limited, Hennessy Centre, 16th Fl., East Wing, pg. 1251 **IT**
Simplex Sino Limited, Causeway Bay Commercial Bldg., Rm. 1103, 1-13 Sugar St., pg. 1002 **PV**
Sims Trading Company Limited, 33rd Fl., Windsor House, 311 Gloucester Rd., pg. 704 **IT**
Squibb (Far East) Ltd., Bank of America Tower, 1 Hysan Ave., Rm. 1701, pg. 256 **PB**
Sumitomo Electric Asia, Ltd., Room 3408, Windsor House, 311 Gloucester Rd., pg. 1314 **IT**
Taisei Properties (Hong Kong) Ltd., Room 1103, East Point Centre, 555 Hennessy Road, pg. 1347 **IT**
Teradyne Hong Kong Limited, 2310 Hang Lung Centre, Paterson Street, pg. 1581 **PB**
3M Hong Kong Limited, Victoria Centre, 5th Fl., pg. 1606 **PB**
Yale Electronics Asia - Pacific Limited, 1502A East Point Centre, pg. 1499 **IT**

PB - *U.S. Public Companies Volume*
PV - *U.S. Private Companies Volume*
IT - *International Public & Private Companies Volume*

NON-U.S. LOCATED COMPANIES HONG KONG

Yale Security Products (Hong Kong) Ltd., 1502A East Point Centre, 555 Hennessy Rd., pg. 1499 IT

Central

ABN Capital Markets Far East Ltd., Ste. 1609-1615 Swire House, 16th Fl., pg. 11 IT

ANZ Asia Limited, 27th Floor, One Exchange Square, 9 Connaught Place, pg. 98 IT

ANZ McCaughan Securities (Asia) Limited, 27th Floor, One Exchange Square, 8 Connaught Place, pg. 99 IT

Alexander & Alexander (Hong Kong) Holdings Ltd., 1302B Admiralty Centre, Tower 1, 18 Harcourt Rd., pg. 117 PB

AlliedSignal International, Inc., Ste. 1603, One Exchange Square, pg. 52 PB

Alpnet, Room 202, The Centre Mark, 287-299 Queen's Road, pg. 58 PB

Amro Finance and Securities (Asia) Ltd., 31st Fl., Edinburgh Tower, pg. 10 IT

Armstrong World Industries (H.K.) Limited, 2/F Harbour Comml. Bldg., pg. 132 PB

Asahi Life Investment Hong Kong Limited, Ste. 604, Two Exchange Sq., 8 Connaught Pl., pg. 85 IT

Asian Capital Partners Holdings Limited, 5th Fl., Jardine House, pg. 420 IT

Australia & New Zealand Banking Group Limited Hong Kong, 27th Fl., One Exchange Square, 8 Connaught Place, pg. 99 IT

BGL Finance (Asia) Ltd., Ste. 2310 Jardine House, pg. 162 IT

BHF-Bank, 55th Floor, Central Plaza, 18 Harbour Road, pg. 119 IT

BHP Minerals, Level 29, Bank of China Tower, 1 Garden Road, pg. 224 IT

BHP Steel Building Products Hong Kong Ltd., 29th Fl., Bank of China Tower, 1 Garden Road, pg. 226 IT

BHP Steel N Asia Ltd., 29th Floor, Bank China Tower, 1 Garden Road, pg. 227 IT

BIL Asia Holdings Ltd., 2306 Jardine House, 1 Connaught Place, pg. 215 IT

BT (Hong Kong) Limited, Suite 1301, Two Pacific Place, 88 Queensway, pg. 223 IT

Banco di Napoli-Hong Kong, 13 Fl., Two Exchange Sq., 8 Conaught Pl., pg. 140 IT

Banco Santander Switzerland, 3606 Gloucester Tower, The Landmark, pg. 144 IT

Bank Brussels Lambert Hong Kong Branch, 16/F Entertainment Building, pg. 148 IT

Bank Hapoalim (Hong Kong), Jardine House 1117-8, 1 Connaught Place, pg. 149 IT

The Bank of Bermuda Limited-Hong Kong Branch, 39/F Edinburgh Tower, The Landmark, 15 Queen's Road, pg. 151 IT

Bank of Yokohama Hong Kong, 36th Fl., Edinburgh Tower, 15 Queen's Road, pg. 159 IT

Banque Generale du Luxembourg S.A., Ste. 2310 Jardine House, 1 Connaught Pl., pg. 162 IT

Banque Indosuez, 44th Fl, One Exchange Square, 8 Connaught Road, pg. 314 IT

Baring Brothers, pg. 648 IT

Bayerische Hypotheken-und Wechsel-Bank AG (Hong Kong), 17th Fl., West Tower, Bond Centre, 89, Queensway, pg. 176 IT

Bayerische Landesbank - Hong Kong Branch, 19 F. Standard Chartered Bldg., 4A, Des Voeux Rd., pg. 176 IT

Bermuda Trust (Far East) Limited, 39/F Edinburgh Tower, The Landmark, 15 Queen's Road, pg. 151 IT

Bermuda Trust (Mauritius) Limited, c/o Bank of Bermuda Limited, Hong Kong Branch, 39/F Edinburgh Tower, pg. 151 IT

Brown Brothers Harriman (Hong Kong) Ltd., Gloucester Tower, 22nd Fl., The Landmark, pg. 173 PV

CA Capital Management Limited, Three Exchange Square, 28th Fl., Connaught Place, pg. 347 IT

CCF Asia Ltd, Jardine House, 39th Fl., One Connaught Place, pg. 342 IT

CCF Hong Kong, Jardine House, 39th Floor, One Connaught Place, pg. 342 IT

CCIC Finance Limited, 38th Fl. A, Bank of China Tower, 1 Garden Rd., pg. 676 IT

CPC/AJI (Asia) Ltd., Jardine House, Ste. 2301, 1 Connaught Pl., pg. 41 IT

CPC/AJI (Asia) Ltd., Jardine House, Ste. 2301, 1 Connaught Pl., pg. 225 PB

Cardo Door (Asia), Swedish Trade Council, 804, The Hong Kong Club Building, pg. 269 IT

Caterpillar Asia Limited, 88 Queensway, pg. 317 PB

Chemical Asia Ltd., Gloucester Tower, 43rd Fl., The Landmark, pg. 341 PB

Cho Hung Finance Limited, Ste. 512-520A, Jardine House, 5/F, 1 Connaught Pl., pg. 288 IT

Citibank, N.A. Hong Kong, Citibank Tower, 8 Queens Road, pg. 378 PB

Commonwealth Bank-Hong Kong, 1405-1408, Two Exchange Square, pg. 313 IT

Consilium Claudius Peters Babcock (HK) LTD, 21/F Fortune House, pg. 131 IT

Credit Agricole Asset Management - Southeast Asia, One Exchange Sq., 50th Fl., pg. 341 IT

Credit Lyonnais Hong-Kong, 25/F Three Exchange Square, 8 Connaught Place, pg. 344 IT

DB Capital Markets (Asia) Ltd. (Hong Kong), Hong Kong Head Office, pg. 404 IT

DBS Asia Capital Ltd., 32nd Floor, Alexandra House, 18 Chater Road, pg. 351 IT

DKB Asia Limited, 31th Floor, Gloucester Tower, 11 Pedder Street, pg. 361 IT

DKB Financial Products (Hong Kong) Limited, 32nd Fl., Gloucester Tower, 11 Pedder St., pg. 361 IT

Daewoo Hong Kong Ltd., 15th Fl., Peregrine Tower, Lippo Centre 89, pg. 358 IT

Daewoo Securities (Hong Kong) Ltd., Rm 902-4, 9/F, 8 Connaught Place, pg. 359 IT

Dai-Ichi Kangyo Bank, Ltd.-Hong Kong, 31st Floor, Gloucester Tower, 11 Pedder Street, pg. 360 IT

Daiwa Bank-Hong Kong, 12th Fl., The Hong Kong Club, Bldg., 3A Chater Rd., pg. 373 IT

Daiwa Overseas Finance Ltd., 11th Fl., The Hong Kong Club, Bldg., 3A Chater Rd., pg. 373 IT

Datastream International (Hong Kong) Limited, Printing House, 12th Fl., 6 Duddel St., pg. 1326 PB

Delft Instruments Far East, Ltd., 7/F Wang Kee Bldg., 34-37 Connaugh Rd., pg. 389 IT

Dentsu Hong Kong Office, Room 3201, tower 1, Admirality Centre, 18 Hardcourt Road, pg. 393 IT

Deutsche Bank AG (Hong Kong), New World Tower, pg. 404 IT

Dow Jones Markets (Hong Kong) Limited, 801, Two Exchange Sq., Eight Connaught Place, pg. 525 PB

Dresdner-ABD Securities Ltd., World-Wide-House, 4th Floor, 19 Des Voeux Road, pg. 419 IT

Dresdner Bank AG, World Wide House, 19 Des Voeux Road, pg. 419 IT

Electricite de France, 2114 Jardine House, 1 Connaught Pl., pg. 438 IT

Emhart (Asia) Ltd., Worldwide House, 19 Des Voeux Rd., Ste. 2401, pg. 233 PB

Equinox Capital (HK) Ltd., Jardine House, 25th Floor, One Connaught Place, pg. 343 IT

The Export-Import Bank of Korea, Ste. 502-3, 5th Fl., Three Exchange Square, pg. 467 IT

FPB Bank Holding Company Limited, 28F., First Pacific Bank Ctr., 56 Gloucester Rd., pg. 487 IT

First Pacific Davies Limited, 23rd Flr., Two Exchange Square, pg. 487 IT

Forum Asia Ltd., 18th Fl., EIE Tower, Bond Center, 89 Queensway, pg. 420 PV

Foster's China, 3901-6 Pacific Finance Tower, pg. 501 IT

Fuji Capital Markets (HK) Limited, 2502 Gloucester Tower, The Landmark, 11 Pedder Street, pg. 521 IT

Fuji International Finance (HK) Limited, 3301 Gloucester Tower, The Landmark, 11 Pedder St., pg. 521 IT

Gan Incendie Accidents Hong Kong, St. George's Building, 3737, 2 Ice House Street, pg. 564 IT

Goldman Sachs (Asia) Limited, Asia Pacific Finance Tower, pg. 462 PV

Guerlain (Asia Pacific) Ltd., 1202-3 Citibank Tower, Citibank Plaza, 3 Garden Road, pg. 780 IT

Guerlain Far East, 2507 Asia Pacific Fin. Twr., Citibank Plaza, 3 Garden Ctr., pg. 780 IT

HSBC Asset Management Asia Pacific Limited, 10/F, Citibank Tower, 3 Garden Road, pg. 582 IT

HSBC Futures (Singapore) Pte Limited, Universal Trade Centre, Suite 2401, 3-5A Arbuthnot Road, pg. 582 IT

HSBC Trustee (Hong Kong) Limited, Level 13, 1 Queen's Road, pg. 583 IT

Handelsfinanz-CCF Bank, Patzy TZE, Jardine House, 39th Floor, pg. 343 IT

Hang Seng Bank Limited, Level 9, 83 Des Voeux Road, pg. 583 IT

Hang Seng Bank Ltd., 83 Des Voeux Road, pg. 583 IT

Hanwa Co., Ltd.-Hong Kong Branch, Unit 3201-3203, 32nd Fl., Vicwood Plaza, 199 Des Voeux Rd., pg. 595 IT

Haw Par International Limited, United Overseas Bank Bldg., 54-58 Des Voeux Road, pg. 604 IT

Ja. Hennessy (Far East) Ltd, Rm. 1502, Wing On Ctr., 111 Connaught Road, pg. 782 IT

Hewlett-Packard Asia Pacific Ltd., 22nd Fl., EIE Tower, Bond Centre, pg. 818 PB

Hine Pacific, Room 1502, Wing On Center, 111 Connaught Road, pg. 782 IT

Hitachi Zosen Company (HK), Ltd., Room 1009, Tak Shing House, 20 Des Voeux Rd., pg. 623 IT

The Hokuriku Bank, Ltd.-Hong Kong, Ste. 706-8, 7th Flr., Two Exchange Square, pg. 627 IT

Hokuriku Finance (H.K.) Limited, Ste. 706-8, 7th Flr., Two Exchange Place, pg. 627 IT

Hong Kong Ltd., Bloomsbury Books, 22-28 Wyndham Street, pg. 1513 IT

Hong Kong Office, Two Pacific Place, 29th Fl., pg. 1517 IT

Hong Kong Office, 2303 Golden Centre, pg. 1519 IT

The Hongkong and Shanghai Banking Corporation Limited (HongkongBank), One Queen's Road, pg. 583 IT

Hongkong & Shanghai Banking Corporation (Nominees) Limited, BL1, 1 Queen's Road, pg. 583 IT

Hongkong and Shanghai Thomas Cook Ltd., 18/F, Vicwood Plaza, 199 Des Voeux Road, pg. 583 IT

IBJ Asia Limited, 41st Fl., Edinburgh Tower, Landmark, 15 Queen's Road, pg. 676 IT

ING Bank Greater China, 8, 10 & 11 Floors, Alexandria House, pg. 649 IT

ING Bank Hong Kong, 8,10, 11/F., Alexandra House, 18, Charter Road, pg. 649 IT

ING Capital Markets (Hong Kong), 8/F., Alexandra House, 16 Chater Road, pg. 650 IT

ING Financial Services International Asia, Room 260104, Alexandra House, pg. 650 IT

ING Trust (Hong Kong), 9/F Room 905, Alexandria House, 16 Charter Road, pg. 650 IT

The Industrial Bank of Japan, Limited (Hong Kong Branch), 41st Fl. Edinburgh Tower, Landmark, 15 Queen's Road, pg. 675 IT

Intel Semiconductor Ltd., 32/F Two Pacific Place, pg. 887 PB

JAFCO International (Asia) Limited, 20th Floor, 3 Garden Road, pg. 955 IT

Jardine Fleming Bank Limited, 45th Fl., Jardine House, One Connaught Pl., pg. 494 IT

Jardine Fleming Holdings Ltd., 46th Fl., Jardine House, One Connaught Pl., pg. 494 IT

Jardine Fleming Investment Management Limited, 47th Fl., Jardine House, One Connaught Pl., pg. 494 IT

Jardine Fleming Limited, 46th Fl., Jardine House, One Connaught Pl., pg. 494 IT

Jardine Fleming Securities Limited, 46th Fl., Jardine House, One Connaught Pl., pg. 494 IT

Jefferies Pacific Limited, Nine Queen's Road, pg. 925 PB

Kawasaki Heavy Industries (H.K.) Ltd., Room 1619, Jardine House, Connaught Road, pg. 726 IT

Kexim Asia Limited, Ste. 502-3, 5th Fl., Three Exchange Square, pg. 468 IT

Kim Eng Securities (Hong Kong) Limited, 8th Floor, Alexandra House, 16-20 Chater Road, pg. 733 IT

Kleinwort Benson Limited - Hong Kong Branch, 33rd Floor Jardine House, 1 Connaught Place, pg. 420 IT

Koh Wah Fashion Ltd., 4th Floor, Caxton House, Duddell Street, pg. 1350 IT

Korea-Japan Finance Company Limted (KJF), 38th Floor, Peregrine Tower, Lippo Centre, 89 Queensway, pg. 816 IT

Korn/Ferry International, 808 Gloucester Tower, pg. 633 PV

Kwong On Bank, Limited, 59-65 Asia Standard Tower, Queen's Rd., pg. 521 IT

LGT Asset Management Ltd., 12th Fl., Three Exchange Sq., 8 Connaught Place, pg. 810 IT

LGT Bank in Liechtenstein AG Hong Kong, Ste. 1001, One Exchange Square, pg. 810 IT

LGT Investment Management (Asia) Ltd., Ste. 1001, One Exchange Sq., 8 Connaught Place, pg. 810 IT

Lion Henkel (Hongkong) Ltd., 1910-1912 Wing on Centre 111, Connaught Road, pg. 614 IT

MIL (Far East) Limited, 39/F Edinburgh Tower, The Landmark, 15 Queen's Road, pg. 151 IT

Macmillan Publishers (China) Ltd., 111 Connaught Road, pg. 1480 IT

Mandarin Oriental, Hong Kong Limited, 5 Connaught Rd., pg. 704 IT

Mase Westpac Hong Kong Limited, 20th. Flr., Exchange Sq. III, 8 Connaught Place, pg. 1497 IT

Maxim's Caterers Ltd., 1728 Swire House, pg. 704 IT

Merita Bank Ltd., Hong Kong Representative Office, 3705 Pergrine Tower, pg. 859 IT

Mitsubishi Chemical Hong Kong Ltd., Unit 1901 & 06, 19th Fl., Peregrine Tower, Lippo Centre, pg. 871 IT

The Mitsubishi Trust & Banking Corporation, 34th Floor, Edinburgh Tower, 15 Queen's Road, pg. 876 IT

Mitsubishi Trust Finance (Asia) Limited, 34th Floor, Edinburgh Tower, 15 Queen's Road, pg. 877 IT

The Mitsui Trust and Banking Company - Hong Kong, 9th Fl., The Hong Kong Club, Bldg., 3A Chater Rd., pg. 883 IT

Mitsui Trust Finance (Hong Kong) Ltd., 9th Fl., The Hong Kong Club, Bldg., 3A Charter Road, pg. 883 IT

Mobile Data International Limited, Room 601, Prince's Bldg., Chater Road, pg. 1139 PB

J.P. Morgan Futures Hong Kong Ltd., Edinburgh Tower, 15 Queen's Road, 23rd Floor, pg. 1130 PB

NKK Corporation-Hong Kong, 402 Fairmont House, 8 Cotton Tree Drive, pg. 903 IT

NLI International Hong Kong Limited, Suite 3005, One Exchange Square, 8 Connaught Place, pg. 936 IT

N.N. Investment Limited, 20/F-21/F, 3 Garden Road, pg. 957 IT

Nanto Bank-Hong Kong Representative Office, Suite 2906-7, 29/F, Two Exchange Square, pg. 906 IT

Natcan Finance (Asia) Limited, Room 4001, Jardine House, 1 Connaught Place, pg. 907 IT

Nedship Bank, Two Exchange Square, 39th Fl., 8 Connaught Pl., pg. 1082 IT

New World Hotels (Holdings) Ltd., New World Tower, 30/F., 16-18 Queens Road, pg. 1048 PB

The Nikko Securities Co., (Asia) Limited, One Pacific Place, 19th Floor, pg. 931 IT

Nomura Asia Ltd., 20/F-21/F, 3 Garden Road, pg. 956 IT

Nomura Futures (Hong Kong) Limited, 20/F-21/F, 3 Garden Road, pg. 957 IT

Nomura International (Hong Kong) Limited, 20/F-21/F, 3 Garden Road, pg. 957 IT

Nomura Research Institute Hong Kong Limited, 20th Floor, Citibank Tower, 3 Garden Road, pg. 956 IT

Nomura Securities Hong Kong Limited, 20/F-21/F, 3 Garden Road, pg. 957 IT

Nomura Trust (Cayman) Limited, 20/F-21/F, 3 Garden Road, pg. 957 IT

Norwest Asia Limited, 3602 Edinburgh Tower, pg. 1203 PB

PPA Design Ltd., 69 Wyndham St., 7th Fl., pg. 118 IT

Paribas Asia, 39th Fl. Gloucester Tower, 11 Pedder Street, pg. 321 IT

Prudential Asia, Suites 901-2, Citibank Tower, Citibank Plaza, pg. 1073 IT

Prudential Corporation Asia Ltd., Ste. 901-2, Citibank Twr., Citibank Plaza, pg. 1073 IT

Quaker Chemical Limited, 26th Fl., E. Asia Tower, 308 Des Voeux Road, pg. 1347 PB

RNBNY Branch Office-Hong Kong, 6th Fl., Jardine House, 1 Connaught Place, pg. 1381 PB

Renaissance Hotel Group N.V., New World Tower, 17th Fl., 18 Queens Road, pg. 1048 PB

Republic Mase Hong Kong Ltd., 6th Fl., Jardine House, 1 Connaught Place, pg. 1380 PB

Rohm & Haas (Far East) Ltd., pg. 1404 PB

The Royal Bank of Scotland plc, Box 10130, 701-704 Two Exchange Sq., pg. 1133 IT

S.L. Realty Management Services (HK) Limited, 22nd Floor, pg. 1253 IT

SBC Warburg & Co. Ltd., 25th Fl., Alexandra House, 16-20 Chater Rd., pg. 1331 IT

PB - *U.S. Public Companies Volume*
PV - *U.S. Private Companies Volume*
IT - *International Public & Private Companies Volume*

1641

Geographic Index-Non U.S.

SBC Warburg Securities (Far East) Ltd., 25th Fl. Alexandra House, 16-20 Chater Rd., pg. 1331 **IT**
SBCM Limited Hong Kong Branch, 3202 Edinburgh Tower, 15 Queen's Road, pg. 1310 **IT**
The Sakura Bank - Hong Kong Branch, Level 24, One Pacific Place, 88 Queensway, pg. 1179 **IT**
Santander Investment Asia Ltd., New World Tower Two, 14th Floor, pg. 144 **IT**
Sanwa-DSP Credit Limited, Suite 1007, One Pacific Place, 88 Queensway, pg. 1190 **IT**
Sanwa Financial Products Co., L.P. Hong Kong, 9th Fl., Fairmont House, 8 Cotton Tree Drive, pg. 1190 **IT**
Sanwa International Finance Limited, 2101 Edinburgh Tower, The Landmark, pg. 1190 **IT**
Seattle-First Asia Ltd., Rm. 4104 Gloucester Tower, pg. 183 **PB**
Security Pacific Asian Bank, Ltd., 1 Connaught Place, 6 Des Voeux Rd., pg. 183 **PB**
Sedgwick Chartered Limited, Standard Chartered Bank Bldg., 25-26/F, 4-4A Des Voeux Rd., pg. 1297 **IT**
Shandwick Asia Pacific, 18/F, Dina House, Ruttonjee Centre, pg. 1227 **IT**
Shandwick Hong Kong Ltd., 18/F Dina House, 11 Duddell St., pg. 1227 **IT**
Shizuoka Finance H.K. Limited, Room 3305, Gloucester Tower, 11 Pedder Street, pg. 1236 **IT**
Shoko Chukin Bank, Rm. 3607, 36th Fl., Lippo Tower, Lippo Ctr., pg. 1236 **IT**
The Sincere Company (P.M.) Ltd., 173 Des Voeux Road, pg. 1252 **IT**
The Sincere Insurance & Investment Co. Ltd., 173 Des Voeux Road, pg. 1252 **IT**
The Sincere Life Assurance Co. Ltd., 173 Des Voeux Road, pg. 1252 **IT**
Skadden, Arps, Slate, Meagher & Flom LLP, 30/F Peregrine Tower, Lippo Ctr., pg. 1004 **PV**
Skandia Asia Ltd., 907-8 Hutchison House, 10 Harcourt Road, pg. 1258 **IT**
Ssangyong (Hong Kong) Co., Ltd., Rm. 609 Wing on Centre 111, Connaught Rd., pg. 1291 **IT**
The Standard Bank of South Africa Limited Representative Office, Citibank Tower, Citibank Plaza, pg. 1294 **IT**
Standard Chartered Bank (Hong Kong), Standard Chartered Bank Bldg., 4-4A Des Voeux Rd., pg. 1295 **IT**
Standard Chartered Equitor Group Limited, 8/F Edinburgh Tower, The Landmark, pg. 1296 **IT**
Standard Chartered Securities Limited, 23rd Fl., Bank of China Tower, 1 Garden Rd., pg. 1296 **IT**
Standard London (Asia) Limited, 36th Citibank Tower, Citibank Plaza, pg. 1294 **IT**
Steelcase International (Hong Kong), World Wide House, 19 Des Voeux Rd., pg. 1038 **PV**
The Sumitomo Bank, Ltd.-Hong Kong Branch, 2601 Edinburgh Tower, The Landmark, 15 Queen's Rd., pg. 1309 **IT**
Sumitomo Finance (Asia) Limited, 3205 Edinburgh Tower, 15 Queen's Rd., pg. 1310 **IT**
Sumitomo Life Hong Kong Limited, 3407 Two Exchange Square, 8 Connaught Place, pg. 1315 **IT**
Svenska Handelsbanken Hong Kong, 2008 Hutchinson House, 10 Harcourt Road, pg. 1327 **IT**
SWIRE PACIFIC LIMITED, 4th Fl., Swire House, 9 Connaught Rd., pg. 1328 **IT**
Swiss Bank Corporation, One Exchange Square, 8 Connaught Pl., 21st Fl., pg. 1330 **IT**
Taiyo Life International (H.K.), Ltd., Ste. 1008-1009, pg. 1349 **IT**
Takashimaya Hong Kong Enterprises Limited, Unit B2, 9th Fl., United Centre, 95 Queensway, pg. 1350 **IT**
Takenaka Hong Kong Ltd., 17th Floor, Sun House, 181, Des Voeux Road, pg. 1351 **IT**
Tatt Sing Sanyo Electric Company Limited, 12th Fl., Wing On House Bldg., pg. 1193 **IT**
TOHO Life International (HK) Ltd., Ste. 1704, One Exchange Sq., 8 Connaught Pl., pg. 1390 **IT**
Tokai Asia Limited, 28th Alexandra House, 16-20 Chater Rd., pg. 1391 **IT**
Universal Leaf Far-East, Ltd., 1435 Central Bldg., Queens Rd., pg. 1695 **PB**
Warburg Asset Management Hong Kong Ltd., 25th Fl., Alexandra House, pg. 1331 **IT**
Westpac Finance Asia Limited, 19th Flr., Exchange Sq. II, 8 Connaught Pl., pg. 1497 **IT**
World Standard Ltd., 14-16/F. St. John's Building, 33 Garden Road, pg. 92 **PB**
Worldsec International Limited, 11/F, Bank of America Tower, 12 Harcourt Rd., pg. 158 **IT**
Yamaichi Asset Management (Asia) Ltd., Two Pacific Pl., Ste. 2109, pg. 1517 **IT**
Yamaichi Capital Management (H.K.) Ltd., Two Pacific Pl., 29th Fl., pg. 1516 **IT**
Yamaichi International (H.K.) Ltd., Two Pacific Pl., 30th Fl., pg. 1518 **IT**
Yamaichi Securities (H.K.) Ltd., Two Pacific Pl., 30th Fl., pg. 1518 **IT**
Yasuda Life International (Hong Kong) Ltd., 31st Floor, Alexandra House, 16-20, Chater Road, pg. 1520 **IT**
Yokohama Asia Limited, 36th Fl., Edinburgh Tower, 15 Queen's Road, pg. 159 **IT**
Zeneca China Ltd., 14/F One Pacific Place, 88 Queensway, pg. 1526 **IT**

Chai Wan

Burgess-SAIA Hong Kong Limited, S/F Chai Wan Industrial Centre, pg. 1500 **IT**
Butterworths Asia (Hong Kong), 19F Eight Commercial Tower, pg. 1095 **IT**
Cahners Publishing-Hong Kong, 19th Floor, Eight Commercial Tower, pg. 1096 **IT**
Excerpta Medica Asia Limited-Hong Kong, 19th Floor, Eight Commercial Tower, pg. 1099 **IT**
Liebherr (HKG) Limited, Unit 6, 14th Floor, Paramount Building, 12 Ka Yip Street, pg. 809 **IT**
Reed Exhibition Companies-Hong Kong, 19th Floor, 8 Commercial Tower, 8 Sun Yip Street, pg. 1097 **IT**
Reed Travel Publishing-Hong Kong, 19th Floor, Eight Commercial Tower, pg. 1097 **IT**
Utell International-Hong Kong, 19th Floor, Eight Commercial Tower, pg. 1098 **IT**

Happy Valley

Kvaerner Fjellstrand (S) Pte Ltd., Hong Kong Representative Office, K2, 16/f, Beverly Hills, 6 Broadwood Road, pg. 767 **IT**

Hong Kong

AFE (Hong Kong) Ltd., Kingwin Industrial Bldg., pg. 129 **IT**
AGC Financial (H.K.) Limited, c.o. Coopers & Lybrand, Room 2301 Sunning Plaza, pg. 1497 **IT**
Accor Hong Kong Ltd., pg. 21 **IT**
Acer Computer (Far East) Ltd., pg. 22 **IT**
Action Instruments (China) Ltd., 9/F, Unit D, Gee Chang, Hog Centre, 65 Wong Chuck, pg. 15 **PV**
Acusor Hong Kong Ltd., pg. 18 **PB**
Adidas Hong Kong Ltd., pg. 25 **IT**
Aery Express Corporation Limited, pg. 1144 **IT**
Aetna Investment Management Limited, Suite 2106, Two Pacific Place, pg. 27 **PB**
Ajinomoto Co., (Hong Kong) Ltd., 21st Fl., 14-20 Bonham Strand West, pg. 40 **IT**
Allianz Asset Management (Hong Kong) Ltd., Ruttonjee House, 20th Floor, 11 Duddell Street, pg. 59 **IT**
Allianz Cornhill Insurance (Far East) Ltd., Ruttonjee House, 20th Floor, pg. 59 **IT**
American International Assurance Co. Ltd., pg. 85 **PB**
Amerom (Hong Kong) Ltd., Dominion Centre, pg. 99 **PB**
Amoco Chemicals Far East, Ltd., 16th Fl., Great Eagle Centre, pg. 103 **PB**
Apple Computer International Ltd., 14/F, Exchange Square Tower II, pg. 121 **PB**
Arabian Gulf Investments (Far East) Limited, 26/F, Bank of America Tower, 12 Harcourt Road, pg. 581 **IT**
Asahi Bank Hong Kong Branch, Level 32, One Pacific Pl., pg. 82 **IT**
Asahi Finance (Hong Kong) Ltd., Level 32, One Pacific Pl., pg. 83 **IT**
Ascom Hongkong Ltd., 3004 Windsor House, 30th Floor, 311 Gloucester Road, pg. 87 **IT**
Ascom Timeplex Far East Ltd., 3004 Windsor House, 30th Floor, 311 Gloucester Road, pg. 87 **IT**
Ashikaga Bank-Hong Kong Representative Office, 401 Far East Finance Center, 16 Harcourt Road, pg. 88 **IT**
Ashikaga Finance (H.K.) Limited, 401 Far East Finance Center, 16 Harcourt Road, pg. 88 **IT**
Asia Cit Enterprise (H.K.) Ltd., 12/F., Hong Kong Industrial Bldg., pg. 295 **IT**
Asia Equity Holding Limited, Two Exchange Square, 28/F 8 Connaught Pl., pg. 485 **IT**
Asian Qualiproducts Service Limited, 3 Ah Kung Ngam Village Rd., pg. 1368 **PB**
Asian Wall Street Journal, pg. 525 **PB**
BA Asia Ltd., Bank of America Tower 14th Floor, pg. 182 **PB**
BIL (Far East Holdings) Ltd., 2801 Three Exchange Square, pg. 215 **IT**
BNS International (Hong Kong) Limited, 25th Floor, United Centre, 95 Queensway, pg. 156 **IT**
BV Capital Markets (Asia) Ltd., pg. 180 **IT**
Baldwin Asia Pacific Ltd., Seaview Plaza, Unit A, 283 Shaukeiwan Rd., 26th Fl., pg. 170 **PB**
Baldwin Printing Controls Ltd., Seaview Plaza, Unit A, 283 Shaukeiwan Rd., 26th Fl., pg. 170 **PB**
Banca Nazionale del Lavoro, 6th fl., Three Exchange Square, 8 Connaught Place, pg. 137 **IT**
Banco Santander, 3606 Gloucester Tower, The Landmark, pg. 144 **IT**
Bank of America NT&SA, 12 Harcourt Rd., pg. 182 **PB**
The Bank of New York, New Henry House, 7th Floor, 10 Ice House Street, pg. 179 **PB**
Bankers Trust Asia Limited, G.P.O. 10098, 30th Fl., Admiralty Centre Tower 1, pg. 185 **PB**
Bankers Trust New York Corporation, Admiralty Centre Tower 1, 30th Fl., 18 Harcourt Rd., pg. 186 **PB**
Banque Generale de Luxembourg, Jardine House, Suite 2310, 1 Connaught Place, pg. 548 **IT**
Banque Paribas-Central Hong Kong, Gloucester Tower, 39th Fl., 11, Pedder St., pg. 319 **IT**
Banque Paribas (Suisse) S.A.-Hong Kong, The Landmark, 39 F Gloucester, pg. 320 **IT**
Barclays Bank PLC, pg. 165 **IT**
Bayerische Vereinsbank AG, 41/F Bank of China Tower, pg. 180 **IT**
Bear Stearns Asia Limited, 26th Fl., Citibank Tower, Citibank Plaza, pg. 198 **PB**
BenguetCorp. International Ltd., 6th Fl., Prince's Bldg., Chater Rd., pg. 187 **IT**
Bermuda Trust (Hong Kong) Limited, 8th Floor, Wheelock House, 20 Pedder Street, pg. 151 **IT**
Bio-Rad Pacific, 12/F Sincere Industrial, Western Bldg., pg. 230 **PB**
Bobst (Far East) Ltd., pg. 198 **IT**
Bobst Ko Ltd., pg. 199 **IT**
Leo Burnett Worldwide Asia/Pacific Hdqtrs., City Plaza 3, 6th Fl., 14 Taikoo Wan Rd., pg. 186 **PV**
Burroughs Wellcome & Co. (Hong Kong) Ltd., Sea View East, pg. 553 **IT**
CET Ltd., 10th Fl. F, Hua Asia Bldg., 64-66 Gloucester Rd., pg. 816 **PB**
CIBC (Hong Kong) Limited, China Bldg., 19th Floor, pg. 257 **IT**
CMC Fareast Limited, Unit C, 12th Fl., 128 Gloucester Road, pg. 413 **PB**
CPC Asia Consumer Foods Division, Ste. 1408, City Plaza 4, 12 Taikoo Wan Rd., pg. 224 **PB**
Carlingford Swire Assurance Ltd., Citicorp Centre, 18 Whitfield Rd., Rm. 502, pg. 581 **IT**
Carlton & United Breweries International, 3A Chater Rd., pg. 501 **IT**
Castrol China Ltd., Room 1301, Admiralty Centre, Tower 1, 18 Harcourt Rd., pg. 235 **IT**
Caterpillar China Limited, One Pacific Pl., Level 8, pg. 317 **PB**
Caxton Distributors Ltd., pg. 720 **IT**
Central Registration Hong Kong Ltd., 17/F & 19/F, Hopewell Centre, 183 Queen's Road East, pg. 581 **IT**
Chadwick-Miller Intl. Ltd., Hang Seng Bank Bldg., pg. 195 **PV**
The Chase Manhattan Bank, N.A., 1 Exchange Sq., pg. 340 **PB**
The Chase Manhattan Bank, N.A., Alexandria House, 7 Des Voeux Road, pg. 340 **PB**
The Chase Manhattan Bank, N.A., World Trade Center, 280 Gloucester Road, pg. 340 **PB**
Chase Manhattan Financial Services (Hong Kong) Ltd., World Trade Center, 280 Gloucester Road, pg. 340 **PB**
Chase Manhattan Investment Services (Hong Kong) Ltd., World Trade Center, 280 Gloucester Road, pg. 340 **PB**
Chase Manhattan Trust Company (Hong Kong) Ltd., Alexandra House, 7 Des Voeux Road, pg. 340 **PB**
Chekiang First Bank Ltd., 60 Gloucester Road, pg. 361 **IT**
Chiba Bank, Ltd.-Hong Kong Branch, Unit 2510, One Pacific Pl., 88 Queensway, pg. 283 **IT**
Christie's Hong Kong Ltd., 2804-6 Alexandra House, 16-20 Chater Road, pg. 290 **IT**
Chuo Trust Asia Limited, 2305-2308, Alexandra House, pg. 291 **IT**
CIBA Corning Diagnostics (HK) Ltd., 20/F Gee Chang Hong Centre, 65 Wong Chuk Hang Rd., pg. 975 **IT**
CIBA-GEIGY (Hong Kong) Limited, pg. 977 **IT**
Citicorp International Limited, 26th Fl., Citicorp Centre, pg. 378 **PB**
Colliers Jardine Holdings Ltd., 31/F, Two Pacific Place, pg. 705 **IT**
Commerzbank AG (East Asia) Ltd., 21, F Hong Kong Club Bldg., 3a Chater Road, pg. 311 **IT**
Compaq Computer Hong Kong Limited, pg. 418 **PB**
Continuum Asia, 2802 Admiralty Centre, Tower 1, 18 Harcourt Road, pg. 423 **PB**
Coop Switzerland Far East Ltd., pg. 330 **IT**
Cosky Co. Ltd., Blk. A. 11/F. Metropolitan, Fty & Warehouse Bldg., pg. 1455 **PB**
DBS Asia Ltd., 33-34th Fl., Two Pacific Pl, 88 Queensway, pg. 351 **IT**
DG Bank-Hong Kong, Tower II, 9th Floor, Admiralty Centre, 18 Harcourt Road, pg. 352 **IT**
Daihatsu Motor (H.K.) Ltd., 64-66 Gloucester Rd., pg. 365 **IT**
Daikin Airconditioning (Hong Kong) Ltd., Room 801, Block 8, Sea View Estate, Watson Rd., pg. 365 **IT**
Daiko Communications Asia Co., Ltd., 5/F, Sun Hung Kai Centre, 30 Harbour Rd., pg. 366 **IT**
The Daishi Bank, Ltd., 404 Far East Finance Ctr., 16 Harcourt Rd., pg. 373 **IT**
Daiwa Asset Management (H.K.) Ltd., 6F, One Pacific Place, 88 Queensway, pg. 374 **IT**
Daiwa Bank-United Centre Branch, Floor 32, United Centre, 95 Queensway, pg. 374 **IT**
Daiwa Futures (Asia) Ltd, Level 26, One Pacific Place, 88 Queensway, pg. 375 **IT**
Daiwa Institute of Research Hong Kong Ltd., Suite 3008-9, One Pacific Place, 88 Queensway, pg. 375 **IT**
Daiwa International Capital Management (H.K.) Limited, Level 30, One Pacific Place, 88 Queensway, pg. 375 **IT**
Daiwa Securities (Asia) Ltd, Level 26, One Pacific Place, 88 Queensway, pg. 375 **IT**
Daiwa Securities (H.K.) Limited, Level 26, One Pacific Pl., 88 Queensway, pg. 376 **IT**
Damco Maritime (HK) Ltd., pg. 1144 **IT**
Dana Asia/Pacific, 1602 Fairmont House, 8 Cotton Tree Dr., pg. 480 **PB**
Data General Hong Kong Sales & Service, Ltd., 5 Wheelock House, 20 Pedder St., pg. 486 **PB**
Dell Computer Asia Ltd., Suite 2204-7, Fortress Tower, 250 King's Road, North Point, pg. 496 **PB**
Dennison Trading Hong Kong Ltd., Regency Ctr., 12th Fl., 39 Wong Chuk Hang Rd., pg. 153 **PB**
Dentsu Young & Rubicam Limited (Hong Kong), 418 Mount Parker House, 1111 King's Rd., pg. 325 **PV**
Det Norske Veritas, Room 3204, Tower I, Admiralty Center, pg. 397 **IT**
Dixons Stores Group (Far East) Limited, 3rd Fl., V. Heun Bldg., 128-140 Queens Rd., pg. 414 **IT**
R.R. Donnelley Far East, Ltd., 1001 C. C. WU Bldg., 302-308 Hennessy Rd., pg. 519 **PB**
Dow Jones Markets (Asia Pacific) Limited, NatWest Tower, Times Square, One Matheson St., Causeway Bay, pg. 525 **PB**
Dow Jones Printing Company (Asia) Inc., A.I.A. Bldg., #1 Stubbs Road, pg. 525 **PB**
Dow Jones Publishing Co. (Asia), Inc., A.I.A. Bldg., 2nd floor, #1 Stubbs Road, pg. 525 **PB**

PB - *U.S. Public Companies Volume*
PV - *U.S. Private Companies Volume*
IT - *International Public & Private Companies Volume*

Dumez-GTM Hong Kong, Room 1103, Admiralty Centre, pg. 823   IT

Durable Electrical Metal Factory, Ltd., pg. 1771   PB

DYWIDAG-Systems International Far East, Ltd., CC WU Bldg., Rm. 1101-1102, 302-308 Hennessy Rd., pg. 424   IT

ELM Computer Technologies Limited, 14F, Bangkok Bank Building, 14-20 Bonham Strand West, pg. 243   IT

ESAB Far East Representative Office, Flat B, 19th Floor, Cheung Lee Industrial Bldg., pg. 282   IT

Eastern Harbour Crossing Co., Ltd., pg. 764   IT

Eastman Whipstock (China) Limited, 26F Great Eagle Centre, pg. 167   PB

Electrolux (Far East) Ltd., 9/F Sungib Industrial Centre, pg. 442   IT

Elkem Representative Office - Hong Kong, Room 1402, Beverly House, 93-107 Lockhart Rd., pg. 447   IT

Emerson Electric (Asia), 1501 Ruttonjee House, 11 Duddell St., pg. 576   PB

Ericsson Communications (Hong Kong) Ltd., 151 Gloucester Rd., 17th Fl., Wanchai, pg. 1366   IT

Ericsson Network Engineering Ltd., 151 Gloucester Rd., 17th Fl., pg. 1367   IT

Exide Electronics International/IPM, pg. 126   IT

FNCB Financial, Ltd., pg. 379   IT

Fiduciary Trust International Asia Limited, Suite 1903, Two Pacific Place, pg. 621   PB

First National Bank (Asia) LTD., 7th Floor, Alexandra House, 16-20 Chater Road, pg. 487   IT

First Pacific Bank, 22/F First Pacific Bank Centre, 56 Gloucester Rd., pg. 487   IT

FIRST PACIFIC COMPANY LIMITED, Tower 2, Exchange Square, 8 Connaught Place, 24th Fl., pg. 487   IT

FortWay Finance Limited, 18/F, Leighton Centre, 77 Leighton Road, pg. 581   IT

Fosroc Expandite Ltd., 4th Fl., Amber Comml. Bldg., 70-74 Morrison Hill Rd., pg. 236   IT

Freudenberg & Vilene Int. Ltd., pg. 507   IT

Freudenberg Trading (Hong Kong) Ltd., pg. 507   IT

F&S Alloys and Minerals Corp. Asian Branch, 4305 China Resources Bldg., 26 Harbour Rd., pg. 1458   IT

Fugro Hong Kong, Ltd., 11-F Park Commercial Centre, 2-12 Shelter St., pg. 430   PV

General Electric (USA) China Company, Ltd., 1301 Two Exchange Square, 13 F, pg. 713   PB

Generale Bank Overseas (Belgium) - Belgian Bank, 28th-32nd Fl. Belgian House, 77-79 Gloucester Rd., pg. 548   IT

Gist-Brocades IPPD Ltd., 1 Mathesonstreet, pg. 1142   IT

Givaudan-Roure Ltd., pg. 1120   IT

B.F. Goodrich Chemical (Far East) Ltd., Ste.1406 AIA Bldg., pg. 752   PB

Grand Generale Asia Ltd., 5/5 Tower 1, 18 Harcourt Road, pg. 548   IT

HSBC Asset Management Bahamas Limited, 10/F Citibank Tower, 3 Garden Road, pg. 582   IT

HSBC Asset Management Hong Kong Limited, 10/F Citibank Tower, 3 Garden Road, pg. 582   IT

HSBC Capital Limited, 7/F Hutchison House, 10 Harcourt Road, pg. 582   IT

HSBC Corporate Finance Limited, 7/F Hutchison House, 10 Harcourt Road, pg. 582   IT

HSBC Investment Bank Asia Holdings Limited, 7/F, Hutchison House, 10 Harcourt Road, pg. 582   IT

HSBC Investment Bank Asia Ltd., 6/F, Hutchison House, 10 Harcourt Road, pg. 582   IT

HSBC James Capel Asia Limited, 5/F, Hutchison House, Ten Harcourt Rd., pg. 582   IT

HSBC Life International Limited, Suite 602, Citicorp Centre, 18 Whitfield Road, pg. 582   IT

HSBC Nominees Asia Limited, 7/F, Hutchison House, 10 Harcourt Road, pg. 582   IT

HSBC Private Equity Management Limited, 10/F, Citibank Tower, 3 Garden Road, pg. 583   IT

HSBC Shipbrokers Limited, 4/F, Hutchison House, 10 Harcourt Road, pg. 583   IT

Hakuhodo Hong Kong Ltd., Admiralty Centre, Tower 1, Rm. 3018, 30th Fl., pg. 588   IT

Hakuhodo Inc., Room 3018, 30th Fl., Admiralty Center, Tower 1, pg. 588   IT

Hansen Far East Ltd., pg. 1144   IT

Harrisons & Crosfield (Hong Kong) Ltd., Wing On Centre, pg. 599   IT

Henkel Asia-Pacific Ltd., 30/F Dah Sing Financial Centre, 108 Gloucester Road, pg. 611   IT

Henkel Chemicals (H.K) Ltd., Wing On Centre, pg. 612   IT

Henkel China Ltd., pg. 612   IT

Henkel Cosmetics China Ltd., pg. 612   IT

The Hokkaido Takushoku Bank, Ltd. (Hong Kong), 28th Fl., Two Pacific Place, 88 Queensway, pg. 627   IT

The Hong Kong Land Property Company Ltd., 8th Fl., One Exchange Square, pg. 704   IT

Hong Kong Representative Office, Room 5503, Central Plaza, pg. 645   IT

Hong Kong Telecom International Limited, pg. 247   IT

Hong Kong Yamazaki Baking Co., Ltd., Tai Po Industrial Estate, 17 Dai Shing Street, pg. 1519   IT

Hsin Chong-Philipp Holzmann Civil Engineering Company Limited, 4th & 5th Fls., Devon House, 979 King's Rd., pg. 634   IT

Hugo Boss Hong Kong Ltd., pg. 638   IT

Hydro Magnesium Ltd., Bank of America Tower, 12 Harcourt Rd., pg. 963   IT

IBM Southeast Asia Services Ltd., pg. 897   PB

IDAB WAMAC Pacific Limited, Trinity House, 165-171 Wanchai Road, pg. 643   IT

ISC Systems Asia Pacific Ltd., 14/F Belgian House, 77-79 Gloucester Rd., pg. 1003   IT

Inchcape Pacific Ltd., 49th Floor, Exchange Sq. One, 8 Connaught Pl., pg. 672   IT

Inchcape (Vietnam) Ltd., 49th Fl., Exchange Sq. One., Eight Connaught Pl., pg. 672   IT

Innse-Hong Kong, Hutchison House 10, Harcourt Rd., pg. 655   IT

Intel Semiconductor Ltd., 13th Flr., Hong Kong Trade Center, pg. 887   IT

International Flavors & Fragrances (Hong Kong) Ltd., 11/F Watson Centre, 18-24 Kung Yip St., pg. 899   IT

International Rectifier Southeast Asia Pte. Ltd., Room 5, 20/F Pacific Plaza, 410 Des Voeux Road West, pg. 907   PB

InterPost Thailand Ltd., pg. 720   IT

Italimpianti Intl.-Hong Kong, Hutchinsong House, 10 Harcourt Rd., pg. 655   IT

Japan Airlines Company, Ltd., 20th Floor, Gloucester Tower, The Landmark, 11 Pedder St., pg. 700   IT

Japan Cosmo Securities (Hong Kong) Limited, Ste. 1910-1913, Two Pacific Pl., pg. 335   IT

Japan Universal Securities (Hong Kong) Limited, Lippo Tower,32nd Floor, Lippo Center #88-89, pg. 1444   IT

The Jardine Engineering Corporation Ltd., Jardine Engineering House, pg. 704   IT

Jardine Insurance Brokers Ltd., Evergo House, 18th Floor, 38 Gloucester Rd., pg. 705   IT

Jardine International Motor Holdings Ltd., 1st Fl, Bonaventure House, Leighton Rd., pg. 705   IT

Jinwoong Hong Kong Ltd., 3309 Bank of America Tower, 12 Harcourt Road, pg. 707   IT

KSB-Jebsen (China) Ltd., pg. 721   IT

Kansai P.H.K. Ltd., Unit 1803, 18th Fl., E. Point, Ctr. Extension, 30 Hennessy Rd., pg. 723   IT

Kao (Hong Kong) Limited, 1901-1923, 19th Fl., pg. 718   IT

Kawasaki Steel Co., 506, Three Exchange Square, 8 Connaught Place, pg. 726   IT

Kawasho International (H.K.) Ltd., 18 Harcourt Rd., pg. 727   IT

Kincheng-Tokyo Finance Co., Ltd., 16/F Tower 1, Admiralty Centre, pg. 158   IT

Kluber Lubrication (Hong Kong, China) Ltd., pg. 506   IT

Kmart Far East Ltd., 18 B United Center, 18th Floor, pg. 963   IT

Komatsu Huanan Ltd., Suite 1603A, Peregrine Tower, Lippo Centre, 89 Queensway, pg. 744   IT

Konica Hong Kong Ltd., Rm. 1818, Sung Hung Kai Centre, pg. 749   IT

Korea Orix Lease and Finance Limited, Rm. 3013 Shui On Centre, 6 Harbour Rd., pg. 1009   IT

Kraft Foods Asia/Pacific, Inc., 16/F One Pacific Place, 88 Queensway, pg. 1288   IT

The Kyoei Mutual Fire & Marine Insurance Company, Hong Kong Representative Office, 9th Fl., United Centre, 95 Queensway, pg. 777   IT

LBI Finance (Hong Kong) Ltd., 2901-4 Admiralty Centre, Tower 1, pg. 813   IT

LTCB Asia Limited, 45th Floor, Far East Finance Center, pg. 816   IT

Linde Refrigeration Systems Ltd., pg. 811   IT

Arthur D. Little Asia Pacific inc., 7th Flr, Bank of America Tower, 12 Harcourt Road, pg. 670   PV

Lockheed Aircraft (Asia) Ltd., Ste. 1907, Two Pacific Pl., pg. 1009   PB

Lonza Hongkong Ltd., pg. 69   IT

Ludgate Communications, 4th Floor, Capitol Plaza, pg. 1157   PV

Luwa Engineering (HK) Ltd., pg. 617   IT

MTV Asia, c/o Star TV, 12th Floor, Hutchison House, pg. 779   IT

MacGregor Golf Hong Kong Ltd., 22-C Floor Vulcan House, 21 Leighton Rd., pg. 73   IT

MacMillan Bloedel (Asia) Limited, 1401 Sunning Plaza, 10 Hysan Avenue, pg. 829   IT

Mannesmann Trading (Far East) Ltd., pg. 838   IT

Mannings Retail Limited, pg. 704   IT

The Manufacturers (Pacific Asia) Insurance Co. Ltd., 31/F, Manulife Tower, 169 Electric Rd., North Point, pg. 841   IT

Manulife Financial Systems (Hong Kong) Limited, 31/F, Manulife Tower, 169 Electric Rd., North Point, pg. 841   IT

ManuLife Holdings (Hong Kong) Limited, 31/F, Manulife Tower, 169 Electric Rd., pg. 841   IT

McDonald's Restaurants (Hong Kong) Ltd., Upper Ground Fl., Park Vale, 1060 King's Rd., pg. 1069   PB

MECO DEVELOPMENT LIMITED, Vulcan House, 3-4 Fl., 21-23 Leighton Rd., pg. 852   IT

Meco Engineering Co., 3-4/F Vulcan House, 21-23 Leighton Rd., pg. 852   IT

Meco Holdings Co. Ltd., 3-4/F Vulcan House, 21-23 Leighton Rd., pg. 852   IT

The Meijiseimei International Hong Kong, Ltd., Ste. 1508-09, 15th Fl., 2 Pacific Pl., pg. 854   IT

Melitta Hong Kong Ltd., 81F Blk. D, 58-66 Tai Lin Pai Rd., pg. 857   IT

Melitta Marketing (H.K.) Ltd., 81F, Block D., 58-66 Tai Lin Pai Road, pg. 857   IT

Melitta Pacific Ltd., 81F Blk. D, 58-66 Tai Lin Pai Rd., pg. 857   IT

Metropolitan Life Insurance Company of Hong Kong, Ltd., 11/F Bank of East Asia Building, pg. 738   PV

Mitsubishi Heavy Industries, (Hong Kong) Ltd., Room 2106, Hutchison House, 10 Harcourt Road, pg. 874   IT

Mitsui & Co., (Hong Kong) Ltd., 25th & 26th Fl., Far East Finance Centre, pg. 880   IT

Monsanto Far East Ltd., 1304-1308 Great Eagle Centre, 23 Harbour Rd., pg. 1125   IT

Moody's Asia Pacific, Ltd., 1503 Central Tower, 22-28 Queen's Road Central, pg. 537   PB

Morgan Grenfell (Hong Kong) Limited, 9th Fl., Hutchison House, 10 Harcourt Rd., pg. 406   IT

Morgan Guaranty Trust Company, Edinburgh Tower, 24th Fl., 15 Queen's Road Central, pg. 1130   PB

J.P. Morgan Securities Asia Ltd., Edinburgh Tower, 24th Fl., 15 Queen's Road Central, pg. 1131   PB

J.P. Morgan International Capital Corporation, 24th Fl., Edinburgh Tower, 15 Queen's Rd. Central, pg. 1131   PB

J.P. Morgan Securities Hong Kong Ltd., 24th Fl., Edinburgh Tower, 15 Queen's Road Central, pg. 1131   PB

Morgan Stanley Hong Kong, 30th Fl., 3 Exchange Sq., pg. 1133   IT

NEC Electronics Hong Kong Limited, 12F., Cityplaza 4, 12 Taikoo Wan Rd., pg. 901   IT

NIF International (Asia) Limited, Suite 3007, One Pacific Place, 88 Queensway, pg. 375   IT

NYK Line (Hong Kong) Ltd., 31st Floor, Admiralty Center, Tower 1, 18 Harcourt Road, pg. 942   IT

National Bank of Pakistan-Hong Kong, 324 Central Building 21-27, Queen's Road, pg. 908   IT

National Mutual Funds Management (Asia) Hong Kong, Level 37, 1 Pacific Place, 88 Queensway, pg. 909   IT

National Westminster Bank Plc, 43/f NatWest Tower, Times Square, pg. 911   IT

Nedlloyd Districenters Ltd., pg. 1144   IT

Nedlloyd (HK) Limited, pg. 1145   IT

Nestle China Ltd., Wing On Centre, pg. 921   IT

Nestle Dairy Farm Ltd., pg. 921   IT

New Hong Kong Tunnel Co., Ltd., pg. 764   IT

NEW WORLD DEVELOPMENT CO. LTD., New World Tower, 30th Fl., 18 Queens Road Central, pg. 923   IT

NextLevel Systems (Hong Kong), 29-F 38 Brussels St., pg. 716   PB

Nippon Credit Bank Ltd.-Hong Kong, Gloucester Tower, 17th Fl., The Landmark, 11 Pedder St., pg. 933   IT

Nippon Credit International (HK) Limited, 17th Fl., Gloucester Tower, The Landmark, 11 Pedder St., pg. 933   IT

Nissho Iwai Hong Kong Corporation Limited, 30/A Bank of America Tower, pg. 948   IT

Nomura Asset Management (Asia) Limited, 40th Floor, Peregrine Tower, Lippo Centre, pg. 955   IT

Norsk Hydro (Far East) Ltd., Bank of America Tower, Suite 1804, pg. 964   IT

OGE-Asia Ltd., pg. 994   IT

OCE (Hong Kong China) Ltd., pg. 994   IT

OPD Ltd. Hong Kong, pg. 1003   IT

Oakreed Financial Services Limited, 42nd Floor, Far East Finance Centre, pg. 817   IT

Olympus Asian Pacific Limited, pg. 1005   IT

Olympus Asset Management Ltd., pg. 1005   IT

Orion Research Far East Inc., 1702 Valley Centre, 80-82, pg. 1592   PB

ORIX Asia Limited, 30th Fl., United Centre, 95 Queensway, pg. 1009   IT

ORIX Auto Leasing Asia Limited, 30th Floor, United Centre, 95 Queensway, pg. 1009   IT

ORIX Hotels International Private Limited, c/o ORIX Asia Limited, Hotel Management & Development Dept., pg. 1009   IT

Outokumpu China Oy (Hong Kong Branch Office), Unit 3111, Level 31, Metroplaza Tower 2, pg. 1015   IT

P&O Asia, 1001 Tower Two, Exchange Square, pg. 1035   IT

Panalpina China Limited, pg. 1023   IT

Panduit Hong Kong, Unit 12, 3/F, Liadro Center, pg. 836   PV

Pechiney Far East Ltd., Room 1006, Fleet House, 38 Gloucester Rd., pg. 1031   IT

Pharmacia & Upjohn Company Hong Kong Branch, 1001 A.I.A. Bldg., pg. 1049   IT

Process Analytical Services (HK) Ltd., pg. 835   IT

Prudential Asia Capital Limited, Alexandra House, 16-20 Chater Rd., pg. 893   PV

Prudential Asia Investments Limited, Alexandra House, 32nd Fl., 16-20 Chater Road, pg. 893   PV

R.D. Properties, Ltd., 3 Ah Kung Ngam Village Rd., pg. 1368   PB

Ram & Kofisa Pacific, 66 Mody Road, Suite 811, pg. 742   IT

Reader's Digest Association Far East Ltd., 3 Ah Kung Ngam Village Rd., pg. 1368   PB

Reader's Digest (East Asia) Limited (Taiwan), 3 Ah Kung Ngam Village Rd., pg. 1368   PB

Reuters Hong Kong Limited, pg. 1105   IT

Review Publishing Company Ltd., 25/F Citicorp Centre, 18 Whitfield Rd., pg. 525   PB

Rexroth (China) Ltd., pg. 839   IT

R.J. Reynolds Tobacco Co. (Asia Pacific) Limited, 21st Flr., St. Georges Bldg., pg. 1355   PB

R.J. Reynolds Tobacco Co. (Hong Kong) Ltd., 401 Asian House, 1 Hennessy Rd., pg. 1355   PB

Rhone-Poulenc (Asia), 1302 Watson's Estate-Bloc, B-13th Fl., Watson Rd. N. Point, pg. 1111   IT

Rieter Asia (Hong Kong) Ltd., pg. 1117   IT

Royal Copenhagen (Hong Kong) Ltd., 122/123 Prince's Bldg., Chater Rd., pg. 1135   IT

Royal Skandia Life Assurance Ltd., Ste. 1201A, Admiralty Centre, Tower 1, pg. 1257   IT

SHK-Shimizu Co., Ltd., 45/F, Sun Hung Kai Centre, 30 Harbour Rd., pg. 1233   IT

SKF China Ltd., Unit A, 35/F Manulife Tower, 169 Electric Rd., pg. 1158   IT

Sakura Bank Hong Kong Trustee Limited, 41st Fl., Far East Finance Centre, pg. 1180   IT

Sakura Finance Asia Ltd., 41st Fl., Far East Finance Ctr, 16, Harcourt Rd., pg. 1180   IT

Sakura Global Capital Asia Limited, 41st Floor, Peregrine Tower Lippo Centre, pg. 1179   IT

Sandoz Industrial Chemicals Ltd., pg. 984   IT

Sandoz Pharmaceuticals Ltd., Rm. 1602 A, A Bldg., 1 Stubbs Rd., pg. 985   IT

Sandoz-Sodyeco Ltd., pg. 985   IT

Santa Fe Minerals (Asia) Inc., 1202 Alexandra House, pg. 766   IT

PB - *U.S. Public Companies Volume*
PV - *U.S. Private Companies Volume*
IT - *International Public & Private Companies Volume*

Scientific-Atlanta (H.K.) Limited, 4th Fl., Dian House, Ruttonjee, pg. 1443 **PB**
Scotiatrust (Asia) Limited, 25th Floor, United Centre, 95 Queensway, pg. 156 **IT**
Sea Containers Asia Ltd., 3201 Jardine House, pg. 1214 **IT**
Sea Containers Hong Kong Ltd., 2213 Jardine House, pg. 1214 **IT**
Sea-Land Orient Ltd., Berth No. 3, pg. 284 **PB**
Seagate Technology (Hong Kong) Limited, Unit 906, City Plaza 3, 14 Tai Koo Wan Road, pg. 1450 **PB**
Securair Ltd., HK International Airport, 672-674 Passenger Terminal Building, pg. 705 **IT**
SEIKO Hong Kong Ltd., 11/F Two Pacific Place, pg. 1218 **IT**
Semi-Tech (Global) Co., Ste. 3001-3004, Two Exchange Square, pg. 1220 **IT**
Sharp-Roxy (Hong Kong) Ltd., 1701-1711, Admiralty Center Tower 1, pg. 1230 **IT**
Shell Company of Hong Kong Ltd., 16F, Shell House, 24-28, Queen's Rd., pg. 1139 **IT**
Shell Developments (HK), 16F, Shell House 24-28, Queen's Rd., pg. 1139 **IT**
Shimizu Hong Kong Co., Ltd., Room 3302, Central Plaza, 18 Harbour Rd., pg. 1234 **IT**
Showpla Hong Kong Ltd., Unit 2111, 21 Telford House, 16 Wanf Hoi Road, pg. 1237 **IT**
THE SINCERE CO. LTD., 24th Floor, Leighton Centre, 77 Leighton Road, pg. 1252 **IT**
The Singer Company, 26th Fl., Two Chinachom Plaza, 68 Connaught Road Central, pg. 1220 **IT**
Skandinaviska Enskilda Banken Hong Kong, 2201 Jardine House, 1 Connaught Pl., pg. 1259 **IT**
Sodexho Hong Kong, Apt 7A, Winchester House, pg. 1275 **IT**
Sony Corporation of Hong Kong Ltd., St. George's Bldg., 22nd Fl., 2 Ice House St., pg. 1284 **IT**
Spectra-Physics Scanning Systems, 2802-2804 Admiralty Centre, Tower 1, pg. 1290 **IT**
Standard Chartered Asia Limited, 10F Standard Chartered Bank Bldg, pg. 1296 **IT**
State Street Bank-Hong Kong Branch, y, 2807 Alexandra House, pg. 1513 **PB**
Stratus Computer (HK) Ltd., 1201 Two Pacific Pl., pg. 1524 **PB**
Sulzer International (Hong Kong) Limited, pg. 1306 **IT**
The Sumitomo Trust & Banking Co., Ltd., 18th Fl., Three Exchange Sq., 8 Connaught Place, pg. 1318 **IT**
Sumitomo Trust Finance (H.K.) Limited, 18th Fl., Three Exchange Sq., 8 Connaught Place, pg. 1318 **IT**
Sunkist (Far East) Promotion, Ltd., Swire House, 11 Chater Rd., 12th Fl., pg. 1053 **PV**
Svedala Hong Kong, pg. 1324 **IT**
Swiss Reinsurance Company-Hong Kong Branch, 6107-08 Central Plaza, 18 Harbour Road, pg. 1333 **IT**
Takugin International (Asia) Ltd., 28th Fl., Two Pacific Place, 88 Queensway, pg. 627 **IT**
Tandem Computers Hong Kong Ltd., China Resources Bldg., Room 3701-6, pg. 418 **PB**
Templeton Investment Management (Hong Kong) Ltd., 2 Exchange Sq., Ste. 908, pg. 680 **PB**
Texaco Hong Kong Ltd., New World Tower,16-18 Queens Rd., pg. 1584 **PB**
Texas Instruments Asia Ltd., 1 Kai Hing Road, pg. 1586 **PB**
Thornton & Co. Ltd., 7/F Hutchinson House, 10 Harcourt Road, pg. 420 **IT**
Tiffany & Co. of New York Limited, 1301 The Hong Kong Club Bldg., 3A Charter Rd., pg. 1609 **PB**
Together Production Ltd., pg. 1015 **IT**
Tokio Marine Investment Services, Limited, 27th Fl., United Centre 95 Queensway, pg. 1393 **IT**
Tokyo-Mitsubishi International (HK) Ltd., 16/F, Tower 1, Admiralty Ctr., pg. 158 **IT**
Toronto Dominion-Hong Kong Branch, 18th Fl., Hutchinson House, 10 Harcourt Rd., pg. 1401 **IT**
Tourism Malaysia - Hong Kong Office, Malaysia Bldg., Ground Fl., 47-50 Gloucester Rd., pg. 833 **IT**
Toyo Trust Asia Limited, 15th Fl., Gloucester Tower, The Landmark, 11 Pedder St., pg. 1411 **IT**
Toyota Motor (China) Ltd., Unit 2702, Tower 1, Admiralty Centre, 18 Harcourt Road, pg. 1414 **IT**
Toys "R" US Lifung (Hong Kong) Ltd., pg. 1626 **PB**
Tractebel Pacific Ltd., Unit F 10th Floor, United Centre, 95 Queensway, pg. 1416 **IT**
Transatlantic Holdings Inc., 1001 AIA Building, 1 Stubbs Road, pg. 84 **PB**
Transformic Electronics Limited, 31-39 Wp Tong Tsui St., pg. 453 **IT**
UBS Securities (Hong Kong) Ltd., 7th Fl., Gloucester Tower, The Landmark, pg. 1440 **IT**
UPM-Kymmene Forest Products (HK) Ltd., 5/F., Tower 1, Admiralty Centre, pg. 1430 **IT**
UBE (Hong Kong) Ltd., Rooms 2622-4, Sum Hung Kai Centre, pg. 1427 **IT**
Union Bank of Switzerland, Hong Kong Branch, 12th Fl., Gloucester Tower, The Landmark, 11 Pedder Street, pg. 1440 **IT**
Union Special Far East Ltd., Watson Rd., pg. 716 **IT**
VG Instruments Asia Ltd., pg. 1595 **PB**
VRG Paper (Hong Kong) Ltd., pg. 757 **IT**
Velcro Hong Kong Ltd., Room 710 Watson's Estate Block B, pg. 1462 **IT**
Votra-Hymsun Ltd, pg. 757 **IT**
Wa Pei Finance Co. Ltd., 31st floor, Belgian House, 77-79 Gloucester Road, pg. 548 **IT**
Wako International (Hong Kong) Limited, Unit 1911-13, One Pacific Place, 88 Queensway, pg. 1485 **IT**
Wardley Data Services Ltd., 3/F, Hutchison House, Harcourt Road, pg. 584 **IT**
Wardley Financial Services Limited, 3/F, Hutchison House, 10 Harcourt Road, pg. 584 **IT**
Way Bo Finance Limited, 18/F, Leighton Centre, 77 Leighton Road, pg. 584 **IT**
Way Chong Finance Limited, 18/F, Leighton Centre, 77 Leighton Road, pg. 584 **IT**
Wayfoong Property Limited, 31/F, Hopewell Centre, 183 Queen's Road East, pg. 584 **IT**
Weatherford Inc., 2803 Admiralty Centre, Tower 1, 18 Harcourt Rd., pg. 1750 **PB**
Weatherford Inc. P.R.C., 2803 Admira Centre, Tower 1, 18 Harcourt Road, pg. 1750 **PB**
West Merchant Bank Limited, 32nd Floor, 3201 Bank of America Tower, pg. 1494 **IT**
Westpac Banking Corp. - Hong Kong, Level 20, Exchange Sq. III, 8 Connaught Pl., pg. 1497 **IT**
Westpac Banking Corporation-Asian Div., Level 19, Exchange Sq. III, 8 Connaught Pl., pg. 1497 **IT**
Westvaco Hong Kong, Ltd., Bank of America Tower, Ste. 3705, pg. 1763 **PB**
Wing Hang Bank Limited, 161 Queens Road Central, pg. 179 **PB**
Walter Wright Mammoet Ltd., pg. 1144 **IT**
The Wrigley Company (H.K.) Ltd., Rooms 3113-4, Hong Kong Plaza, 186-191 Connaught, pg. 1781 **PB**
Yamaichi Asset Management (Hong Kong) Ltd., Suite 2109, Two Pacific Place, 88 Queensway, pg. 1517 **IT**
Yamaichi Futures (H.K.) Ltd., 30th Floor, Two Pacific Place, 88 Queensway, pg. 1517 **IT**
Zung Fu Company Ltd., Bonaventure House, 85 Leighton Rd., pg. 704 **IT**

Kowloon

A & A Intl. (YICHI-HK) Ltd., 1406-1411 World Commerce Ctr., Harbour City Phase 1, pg. 1561 **PB**
AGRA (Hong Kong) Limited, 3/F, 320 Junction Road, pg. 31 **IT**
AMP Products Pacific Limited, Ocean Centre, Rm. 1301, pg. 9 **PB**
Ademco-Sontrix (Far East), Rm. 610, Silvercord Tower 1, pg. 307 **PB**
Advanced General Printing Inks Ltd., 10th Fl., Enterprise Centre, 4, Hart Avenue, Tsim Sha Tsui, pg. 370 **IT**
Alaron Asia Ltd., 2007-8, 20th Floor, Tower 1, 33 Canton Rd., Tsim Sha Tsui, pg. 31 **PV**
Albright & Wilson Asia (HK) Ltd., Rm. 1811, Star House, 3 Salisbury Rd., Tsim Sha Tsui, pg. 49 **IT**
AlliedSignal Chemicals, 1028/29 New World Office Bldg., East Wing, 24 Salisbury Rd., pg. 52 **PB**
AlliedSignal Laminate Systems, Unit 2506-2512, Level 25, Tower 1, Metroplaza 223, Hinj Funj Rd., pg. 53 **PB**
AlliedSignal Performance Additives, 1034/35 New World Office Bldg., East Wing, 24 Salisbury Rd., pg. 53 **PB**
Anju Jewelry Limited, Block G, 2-F, Kaiser Estate, Phase 2, pg. 1625 **PB**
Asahi Chemical Industry (H.K.) Ltd., Suite 23A 01, Tower 1, The Gateway, 25 Canton Road, pg. 84 **IT**
Asco General Supplies (Far East) Ltd., Room 602-3, pg. 1036 **IT**
Associated Engineers Ltd., Hong Kong Intl. Airport, 77 Concorde Road, pg. 705 **IT**
Astar Precision Co., Ltd., Flat M, 7/F., Kaiser Estate, Phase 3, 11, Hok Yen S., Ma Tau Wei Rd., pg. 294 **IT**
Autodesk Far East Ltd., Units 414-416, Hong Kong Indus. Ctr., pg. 149 **PB**
Avnet WKK Components, WKK Building, 10th Fl., Floor 1-8-A, pg. 155 **PB**
B + B Asia Limited, Franki Centre, 320 Junction Rd., Kowloon Tong, pg. 196 **IT**
BASF China Ltd., Tower I, 7th Fl., South Seas Centre, pg. 105 **IT**
Ballast Nedam Dredging (HK) Branch, Rm. 515 W. Wing, New World Office Bldg., pg. 134 **IT**
Ballast Nedam International B.V., New World Office Building, Rm. 515 W. Wing, pg. 134 **IT**
Bally Hong Kong Ltd., 20/F Tower 2, 33 Canton Rd., pg. 997 **IT**
Bel Fuse Ltd., Lok Hup Bldg., Eighth Fl., Lok Hup St., pg. 200 **PB**
BERG Electronics Hong Kong Ltd., Room 707, Tsim Sha Tsui Centre, (West Wing), 66 Mody Road, pg. 213 **PB**
Black & Decker Hong Kong Limited, c/o Tengis Ltd., 610 World Commerce Centre, pg. 234 **PB**
Body Drama (Far East) Ltd., Unit 4, 14/F, Fashion Centre, 51-53 Wing Hong Street, pg. 1182 **PB**
Branson Ultrasonics (Asia Pacific) Co. Ltd., Shop F., Ground Floor, Wei Chien Court, Wyler Garden, pg. 576 **PB**
Brother Corporation (Asia) Ltd., Unit 1201-2, 12/F, NewEast Ocean Center, pg. 229 **IT**
C & K Colours (H.K.) Limited, Unit 1206, 12 F, Tusen Wan Ind. Centre, pg. 460 **PB**
Canon Electronic Business Machines (H.K.) Co., Ltd., Chuan High Industrial Bldg.6F, 14, Wang Tai Rd., pg. 262 **IT**
Canon Hongkong Co., Ltd., 10F, Mirror Tower, 61 Mody Road pg. 262 **IT**
Casio Computer (Hong Kong) Ltd., Suite 921-24, Ocean Centre, Harbour City, pg. 274 **IT**
Chiaphua Shinko Copper Alloy Co., Ltd., No. 27, Ashley Rd., 5th Fl., Tsimshatsui, pg. 741 **IT**
Chubb Hong Kong Ltd., The Security Centre, 2/F., 481-483 Castlepeak Rd., pg. 705 **IT**
Citizen Tokuhan (H.K.) Co., Ltd., Flat B, 3/F., Hung Mou, Industrial Bldg., 62 Hung To Road, pg. 294 **IT**
Citizen Watches (H.K.) Ltd., Block, A.B., 8th Floor, Kaiser Estate, Man Yue Street, pg. 294 **IT**
Clarins Ltd., World Tech Center, Unit K, 12th Fl., pg. 295 **IT**
Clarion (H.K.) Co., Ltd., Rm. 908, Silvercord, Tower 1, 30 Canton Rd., pg. 296 **IT**
Clayorient Ltd., 1735 Park-In Commercial Centre, 56 Dundas Street, pg. 1488 **IT**
Cobra Electronics International (Hong Kong) Ltd., 1907 Tower One, pg. 391 **PB**
Coherent Pacific, Unit 1515-18, Lovel 15, Tower II, Grand Century Plaza, pg. 396 **PB**
Continental Conair, Ltd., Rm. 604, New World Centre, pg. 261 **PV**
Corex Technology (HK) Ltd., 25/F, Omega Plaza, 32 Dundas Street, pg. 651 **IT**
Crown Young Industries Ltd., Flat B, 3rd Floor, Hung Mou, Industrial Bldg., 62 Hung To Road, pg. 294 **IT**
CUNA Mutual Group-Asia/Africa, Flat A, Eliza Bldg., 12 Floor, 185-191 Sai Yee Street, pg. 296 **PV**
CUNA Mutual Group-Hong Kong, Flat 3, 6th Fl., Jade Mansion, 40 Waterloo Road, pg. 296 **PV**
Custom Accessories Asia Ltd., Room 1018, Peninsula Centre, pg. 298 **PV**
DSM Elastomers Asia Ltd., Suire 811, Tsimhatsui Centre, East Wing, 66 Mody Road, pg. 354 **IT**
Dainippon Ink & Chemicals (HK) Ltd., Room 1304, 13th Floor, East Ocean Centre, 98 Granville Road, pg. 372 **IT**
Data General Hong Kong Ltd., Kaiser Estate 41 Man Yue St., pg. 486 **PB**
Dataproducts (Hong Kong), Ltd., Sime Darby Indus. Centre, 420 Kwun Tong, pg. 621 **IT**
Dexter Asia Pacific Limited, Ste. 1201, Tower 6, China Hong Kong City, pg. 505 **PB**
Du Pont Asia Pacific Ltd., New World Office Bldg., pg. 532 **PB**
Du Pont Far East Inc., New World Office Bldg., pg. 532 **PB**
Durkopp Adler Far East Ltd., Room 604-605, Swire & Meclaine House, pg. 469 **IT**
EAO Far East, Unit 708, Towers II, Cheung Sha Wan Plaza, pg. 444 **IT**
EMI (Hong Kong) Ltd., P.O. Box 95263, Tsimshatsui Post Office, pg. 427 **IT**
Eaton Technologies Limited, Tung Ying Bldg., 100 Nathan Road, Room 1001, 101F, pg. 559 **PB**
Eclipse Combustion China Ltd., Unit 1026 Block B Focal Ind. Ctre., pg. 361 **PV**
Eltis Precision Printing Limited, 5/F, Block B2, Yau Tong Industrial City, pg. 581 **IT**
Emerson Radio Hong Kong Ltd., 1009-1015 World Shpng., Ctr. Harbor City Phase 1, pg. 578 **PB**
EMTEC Magnetics China Ltd., Room 904-5, South seas Centre, Tower 1, pg. 743 **IT**
Enesco International (Hong Kong) Ltd., Suite 1010, 10th Fl., P.O. Box 91405, Ocean Centre No. 5, pg. 1508 **PB**
Ertan J.V.-Hong Kong, Suite 1109 - Ocean Centre, pg. 823 **IT**
Ertl (H.K.) Ltd., 1107-9 World Shipping Centre, Seven Canton Rd., pg. 1684 **PB**
Fanuc Hong Kong Limited, Unit 1411, Sun Plaza, 28 Canton Road, pg. 477 **IT**
Far East Power Equipment Limited, c/o Tengis Ltd., 610 World Commerce Centre, Canton Rd., pg. 234 **PB**
Farah (Far East) Limited, 388 Castle Peak Rd., pg. 613 **PB**
Farbest Industries Ltd., Flat B, 3rd Floor, Hung Mou Industrial Building, pg. 294 **IT**
Ferro Far East Ltd., P.O. Box 98436, pg. 619 **PB**
Fuji Electric (Asia) Co., Ltd., 10th Fl., West Wing, Tsimshatsu Center, pg. 522 **IT**
Fuji Photo Film Co., Ltd., Hong Kong Office, Rm. 916, Sun Plaza, 28 Canton Road, pg. 525 **IT**
GSI Trading Hong Kong Limited, Room 1414, Lippo Sun Plaza, 28 Canton Rd., pg. 579 **IT**
Galco International Toys, N.V., Units 50 - 59, 12th Fl., Intl. Trademart, Wang Chin St., pg. 698 **PB**
Getinge/Castle Asia Limited, Room 1104, 11-F China Aerospace Technology Ctr., pg. 551 **IT**
B.F. Goodrich Aerospace, c/o Hong Kong Aircraft, Engineering Co., Rm. 10, China Traders, pg. 752 **PB**
Goodrington Co., Ltd., 44-50 Wang Wo Tsai Street, Harrington Bldg., 5/F., Flat A&B, pg. 295 **IT**
GretagMacbeth (UK) Ltd., 12A Wardley Centre, 9-11 Pratt Avenue, pg. 966 **PB**
Hanimex Vivitar (H.K.) Ltd., Units 1004-1005, Conic Investment Bldg., pg. 1061 **IT**
Hasbro Bradley Far East (1987) Ltd., Sands Bldg., 12th Flr., 17 Hankow Rd., pg. 797 **PB**
Hattori Overseas Hong Kong Ltd., Ying Tung Industial Bulding, 4th, pg. 1218 **IT**
Helen of Troy (Far East) Ltd., 408 Silvercord, Tower II, pg. 807 **PB**
Helly-Hansen (Far East) Ltd., Room 1012, 10th Fl., New Kowloon Plaza, pg. 1010 **IT**
Hong Kong Air Cargo Terminals Ltd., Cargo Terminal Bldg. Intl., San Po Kong, pg. 705 **IT**
Hong Kong Air Terminal Services Ltd., Hong Kong Airport, pg. 705 **IT**
Hong Kong Oxygen & Acetylene Co. Ltd., DD 234, Lot 317, Chun Yat Street, pg. 122 **IT**
Hong Kong Security Ltd., The Security Hse, Cheungshawan Kowloon, pg. 704 **IT**
Howden South East Asia, 1/F Sino Industrial Plaza, Nin Kai Cheung Rd., pg. 637 **IT**
IPC Corporation (HK) Ltd., 25/F, Omega Plaza, 32 Dundas Street, pg. 651 **IT**
IPM Pacific, Ltd., Unit C12, Eighth Fl., Block C, 489-491 Castle Peak Rd., pg. 126 **IT**
InterBold Pacific, Ltd., 1508 Towwer, Silvercord 30 Canton Road, pg. 506 **PB**
Intergraph Hong Kong Limited, Room 106-108, G/F Dfb Centre, Ker Kowloon Terminus-8 Cheong Wan Road, pg. 892 **PB**

PB - *U.S. Public Companies Volume*
PV - *U.S. Private Companies Volume*
IT - *International Public & Private Companies Volume*

JT International (HK) Ltd., 828 Ocean Ctr, Harbour City, Tsimshatsui, pg. 703 **IT**

Jardine Securicor Ltd., The Security Center, Cheung Sha Wan, pg. 705 **IT**

Johnson & Johnson International (Hong Kong), Room 1515-17, 15/F, Tower 1, Graud Century Place, pg. 930 **PB**

Johnson & Johnson Medical Hong Kong, Room 1816-19, 18F Tower 1, Grand Century Place, pg. 931 **PB**

S.C. Johnson, Ltd., P.O. Box 98450, pg. 593 **PV**

Jones International Ltd., Unit 804-6, Tower 1, Cheung Sha Wan Plaza, 833, pg. 933 **PB**

Juki (Hong Kong) Ltd., 6/F Park Lane Square, pg. 717 **IT**

Kanthal Electroheat (HK) Ltd., pg. 724 **IT**

Kellwood Asia Limited, 55 King Yip St., pg. 948 **PB**

Kenner Parker (H.K.) Ltd., 10/F Peninsula Centre, 67 Mody Rd., pg. 797 **PB**

Kenwood Electronics (H.K.) Ltd., Lippo Sun Plaza, Rm. 816 Fl. 8, 28 Canton Rd., Tsim Sha Tsui, pg. 735 **IT**

Kidde Consumer Durables Corp., World Finance Ctr., 19 Canton Rd., pg. 594 **IT**

King Pacific Ltd., 5/F Chuang's Bldg., 51 Hung To Rd., pg. 315 **IT**

Kintetsu World Express (H.K.) Ltd., G/F Sunshine Kowloon Bay, Cargo Centre, 59 Tai Yip St., pg. 735 **IT**

Kirkstone Company Ltd., Harbour Crystal Centre 605-607, 100 Granville Rd., pg. 336 **IT**

Konami (Hong Kong) Ltd., 11th Fl., Tower 2, The Gateway, pg. 746 **IT**

KONE Elevator (H.K.) Ltd., 9/F Tower II, Cheung Sha Wan Plaza, pg. 747 **IT**

KONE Elevators Asia Pacific, 9/F, Tower II, Cheung Sha Wan Plaza, pg. 747 **IT**

Krupp Hoesch Export, Units 1701-1702 Hong Kong, Pacific Center, pg. 515 **IT**

Kulicke & Soffa (Asia), Ltd., 21/F Yen Sheng Centre, pg. 969 **PB**

Kyocera Asia, Ltd., Rm. # 803, Tower 1, South Seas Centre, pg. 776 **IT**

Kyocera (Hong Kong), Ltd., Rm. # 803, Tower 1, South Seas Centre, pg. 776 **IT**

LeaRonal S.E. Asia Ltd., 207, 2/F Good Harvest Air Frt., Ctr., 70-78 Sung Wong Toi Rd., pg. 982 **PB**

Littelfuse HK Ltd., Suite 26, 16th Floor, pg. 1001 **IT**

Loewe Hong Kong Ltd, 807 Tower A, New Mandarin Plaza, pg. 782 **IT**

Louis Vuitton Hong Kong Ltd, 808 A, New Mandarin Plaza, 14 Science Museum Rd., pg. 782 **IT**

Louis Vuitton Pacific Ltd, Rm. 801-805, Mandarin Plaza Tower A, pg. 783 **IT**

MacGREGOR (HKG), Ltd., 7th Fl., May May Bldg., pg. 671 **IT**

Marsiling Ltd., Rm. 1414, Sun Plaza, pg. 579 **IT**

Mei Hoy Sports Co. Ltd., Rm. 601 World Shipping Centre, Harbor City, 7 Canton Rd., pg. 885 **IT**

Meto Far East, Unit 1111, No. 1 Hung To Road, pg. 462 **IT**

Millipore Asia Limited, Suite 3-6, 15/F, Tower 3, China Hong Kong City, pg. 1113 **PB**

Minebea Co. Ltd. - Hong Kong Branch, Room 1416, Star House, 3 Salisbury Road, pg. 869 **IT**

Mitsubishi Rayon Co., Ltd., Room 514-515, East Ocean Centre, pg. 876 **IT**

Mitsukoshi Enterprises Co., Ltd.-Tsim Sha Tsui Branch, Sun Plaza, 28 Canton Rd., pg. 884 **IT**

Mizuno Corporation of Hong Kong Ltd., 1025 Ocean Centre, 5 Canton Rd., pg. 885 **IT**

Mobil Oil Hong Kong Ltd., Canton Rd., pg. 1119 **PB**

Morganite Hong Kong Company Limited, Unit 4-6, 11th Fl., Siu Wai Industrial Ctr., pg. 892 **IT**

Moygashel Ltd., Suite 1501A, Tower 1, China Hong Kong City, 33 Canton Road, pg. 798 **IT**

Mr. Christmas Limited, 39 Chatham Rd. S. Ste. 901, pg. 765 **PV**

NCT Hong Kong Ltd., Room 1105, Wing on Plaza, 62 Mody Road, pg. 914 **IT**

NEC Hong Kong Limited, Room 1111-1120, Tower B, Mandarin Plaza, 14 Science Museum Rd., pg. 900 **IT**

Nalco Chemical (H.K.) Ltd., Room 1806, Tower 6, China Hong Kong City, pg. 1150 **PB**

National Bank of Pakistan-Kowloon, 1103 Fourseas Building, 208-212 Nathan Road, pg. 908 **IT**

Neste Chemicals South East Asia Ltd., Room 1105, Wing on Plaza, 62 Mody Road, pg. 914 **IT**

Nichimen Orient Wear Ltd., Rm. 1510-11, Ocean Ctr., Harbor City, No. 5 Canton Rd., pg. 928 **IT**

NIFE Silcon Ltd., 2/F Flat 8, Kinctic Industrial Centre, pg. 54 **IT**

NIKE Asia-Pacific, "The Gateway", 25 Canton Road, pg. 1184 **PB**

Nippon Express (H.K.) Co., Ltd., 1101 Chinachem Golden Plaza, 77 Mody Road, Tsim Sha Tsui East, pg. 934 **IT**

Nippon Paint (H.K.) Co., Ltd., Room 1101, Tower 1, Cheung Sha Wan Plaza, pg. 937 **IT**

Nishimatsu Construction Co., Ltd.-Hong Kong Branch, Room 508, Star House, Salisbury Rd., pg. 943 **IT**

Nitches (Far East) Ltd., Unit 4, 14/F, Fashion Centre, 51-53 Wing Hong Street, pg. 1182 **IT**

Noma (Hong Kong) Limited, Ste. 309, 3rd Fl., 77 Mody Rd., Tsimshatsui East, pg. 955 **IT**

Nordisk Aviation Products Asia Ltd., Highburgh House, Hunghom Bay Centre, A3, 2nd Fl., pg. 964 **IT**

Notifier Far East, pg. 1306 **IT**

Nucletron Far East (HK) Ltd., Tsimshatsui Centre, Room 406, 66 Mody Road, pg. 389 **IT**

O'Donnell Griffin (Hong Kong) Ltd., East Sun Industrial Centre, 16 Shing Yip St., pg. 1650 **IT**

Oki Electronics (Hong Kong) Ltd., Ste. 1901, Tower 3, China Hong Kong City, pg. 1000 **IT**

Olin Industrial (Hong Kong) Limited, 1111 Peninsula Centre, 67 Mody Rd., Tsim Sha Tsui E., pg. 1220 **PB**

Olympus Hong Kong Ltd., pg. 1005 **IT**

OMRON Electronics Hong Kong, Ltd., 601-9, Tower 2, The Gateway, pg. 1006 **IT**

OMRON Healthcare Ltd., Ste. 1010, China Hong Kong City, pg. 1006 **IT**

Osmonics Asia/Pacific, Ltd., Suite No. F, 15/F, Cameron Plaza, pg. 1234 **PB**

PAXAR Far East Limited, 210-212 Choi Hung Road, pg. 1267 **IT**

Plantronics Hong Kong, Ste. 1111, Tower II, Silvercord Bldg., Canton Rd., pg. 1308 **IT**

PLAYMATES HOLDINGS LTD., 21/F 100 Canton Road, pg. 1060 **IT**

Precision Moulds, Ltd., Lower Ground Floor, Wah Shun Industrial Bldg., pg. 1059 **IT**

Premier Precision Ltd., Block G-H 6th Floor Phase 2, Yip Fat Industrial Building, pg. 295 **IT**

Pulse Components Ltd.-Hong Kong, Unit 401-4, 410-2, 4/F, Hong Kong Industrial Ctr., pg. 1564 **PB**

RHG Yachting Office Hong Kong, Shop B7, pg. 1152 **PB**

Raychem (H.K.) Ltd., Unit 601 South Tower, World Finance Center, pg. 1362 **PB**

Reemtsma International China Ltd., Unit 1202, 12th Fl., Mirrow Tower, 61 Mody Rd., pg. 1101 **IT**

Respironics (HK), Ltd., 38 Hung To Rd, 3/F Microtron Bldg., pg. 1383 **IT**

Roche Pharmaceuticals & Chemicals Ltd., 12th Fl., Tower A, South Seas, Centre, Mody Rd., pg. 1121 **IT**

Rohm Electronics (H.K.) Co., Ltd., Rm. 1402-8, Tower 1, Silvercord, 30 Canton Rd., pg. 1125 **IT**

SEB Asia, Unit No. 1005, 10/F New kowloon Plaza, pg. 568 **IT**

Sandvik Hong Kong Ltd., 822 Lei Chi Kok Rd., pg. 1187 **IT**

Sanken Electric Hong Kong Co., Ltd., 615A Ocean Centre, Canton Rd., pg. 1188 **IT**

Sanyo Semiconductor (H.K.) Co., Ltd., Rm. 612, Harbour Crystal Centre, pg. 1192 **IT**

Sensormatic Hong Kong Limited, Room 904, Shui Hing Centre, 13 Sheung Yuez Road, pg. 1458 **PB**

Shakespeare (Hong Kong) Ltd., 175 Hoe Bun Road, 6th Fl., pg. 940 **IT**

Signode Hong Kong Limited, Unit B, 9th Fl., Kin Yip Factory Bldg., pg. 869 **PB**

Silicon Graphics, Ltd., Hong Kong Industrial Technology Center, pg. 1474 **PB**

Siliconix (H.K.) Ltd., 61-63 King Yip St., pg. 367 **IT**

Simmons Bedding & Furniture (HK) Ltd., Shop 24, 2/F China Hong Kong City, pg. 929 **IT**

The Sincere Company Ltd. (Kowloon Branch), 83 Argyle St., Mongkok, pg. 1252 **IT**

The Sincere Company Ltd., 73-81 Argyle St., Mongkok, pg. 1252 **IT**

Smart Shirts Ltd., 55 King Yip St., pg. 948 **IT**

Soundesign Corporation Hong Kong Ltd., 1103 E. Ocean Centre, 98 Granville Rd., pg. 956 **PV**

Spartus (HK) Ltd., World Finance Centre, Harbour City, pg. 595 **IT**

Strombecker (HK) Ltd., 926-7 East Wing, New World Office Bldg., pg. 1047 **PV**

Sumikin Bussan International (HK) Ltd., Suite 2001-6, Tower II, The Gateway, Harbour City, 25-27, pg. 1308 **IT**

The Sumitomo Bank, Ltd.-Kowloon Branch, 501-6 Tower II, 25 Canton Rd., pg. 1309 **IT**

Sumitomo Metal Mining Hong Kong Co., Ltd., Ste. 1501B Tower 6, China Hong Kong City, 33 Canton Rd., pg. 1316 **IT**

Sun Microsystems of California Ltd., Maxwell Industrial Bldg., 1st, Fl., Unit A 350 Kwun Tong Rd., pg. 1532 **IT**

Sunciti Manufacturers Ltd., 64 Hung To Road, Kwun Tong, pg. 295 **IT**

TDK Hong Kong Co., Ltd., 9F Lifung Tower (Tower 5), 33, Canton Rd., pg. 1337 **IT**

Thermalloy Ltd., B1 G/F Tuen Mun Industrial Centre, pg. 209 **IT**

Tien Lee Hong Co., Ltd., Room 606, The Hong Kong & Shanghai Bank Bldg., pg. 372 **IT**

TOMMY HILFIGER CORPORATION, 6/F, Precious Industrial Ctr., 18 Cheung Yue Street, pg. 1398 **PB**

Tonka Far East Limited, 610 World Commerce Ctr., pg. 798 **PB**

Tootal Thread Hong Kong Ltd., Yen Shing Indus. Bldg.; 4 Kin Fung Circu, pg. 299 **IT**

Toray Industries (H.K.) Ltd., 15th Fl., TAL Bldg., 49 Austin Rd., pg. 1400 **IT**

Toshiba Electronics Asia, Ltd., 10F, Lippo Sun Plaza, 28 Canton Road, Tsim Sha Tsui, pg. 1406 **IT**

Toyobo Hong Kong, Room 912, 9th Floor, Ocean Centre, Harbour City, Tsimshatsui, pg. 1411 **IT**

Trident Microsystems (Far East) Ltd., Unit 1, 18/F, Tower II, Enterprise Sq., 9 Sheung Yuet Rd., pg. 1637 **PB**

Union Carbide Asia Ltd., 15/F Prudential Assurance, Tower, 78 Chatham Road South, pg. 1667 **IT**

Union-Transport (HK) Ltd., 2-3/F Kowloon Godown, 1-3 Kai Hing Rd., Kowloon Bay, pg. 1120 **PV**

The Universal Hardware and Plastic Fty. Ltd., 82/86 Beech Street G/F, Tai Kok Isui, pg. 430 **IT**

Universal Optical Industries, Ltd., Rm. # 803, Tower 1, South Seas Centre, pg. 776 **IT**

VF Asia Limited, 528 Ocean Center, 5 Canton Rd., pg. 1702 **IT**

Van Melle Far East Limited, Suite 713A, Ocean Centre, Harbour City, Canton Rd., pg. 1451 **IT**

Vita-Wheel Company, Unit 7-11, 2/F, Hong Leong Industrial Complex, pg. 97 **IT**

Wackenhut Security (H.K.), Ltd., 1404 Argyle Centre I, pg. 1732 **IT**

Western Digital Hong Kong Ltd., 33 Canton, 807-809 Tower 3, pg. 1758 **PB**

Western Navigational Global Limited, 1201-1203 Wai Fung Plaza, 664 Nathan Rd., pg. 373 **PB**

WHARF HOTEL INVESTMENTS LTD., 16th Fl., Ocean Ctr., pg. 1497 **IT**

Wintai Food Manufacturers Ltd., 673 Nathan Rd., 11th Fl., pg. 950 **IT**

Woolkong, Ltd., 907-8 Po Lung Centre, pg. 1188 **PV**

World Cat Ltd., 18/F, Tower 2, 33 Canton Rd., pg. 1072 **IT**

World Fashion Hosiery Inc., Rm. 1414 Sun Plaza, pg. 579 **IT**

Wormald Engineering Services Ltd., Unit 801-802, Tower B, Hunghom Commercial Centre, pg. 1651 **IT**

Yashica Hong Kong Co., Ltd., Rm # 803, Tower 1, South Seas Centre, pg. 776 **IT**

Kowloon Bay

Amicon (H.K.) Ltd., Unit 9, 2/F Kenning Industrial Bldg., pg. 1113 **PB**

Amicon Polymers (H.K.) Ltd., Unit 9, 2/F Kenning Industrial Bldg., pg. 1113 **PB**

Catalina Industrial, Ltd., 6/F Kenning Indus. Bldg., 19 Wang Hoi Rd., pg. 314 **IT**

Go-Gro Industries, Ltd., 6/F Kenning Industrial Bldg., 19 Wang Hoi Rd., pg. 314 **PB**

Honeywell China Inc., 5/F, New Bright Bldg., 11 Sheung Yuet Rd., pg. 834 **PB**

Honeywell Limited, 5/F, New Bright Bldg., 11 Sheung Yuet Rd., pg. 835 **PB**

Kemet Electronics Asia Ltd., 4A, Chuan Hing Ind. Bldg., pg. 949 **PB**

Lamp Depot Limited, 6/F Kenning Industrial Bldg., 19 Wang Hoi Rd., pg. 314 **IT**

Renishaw (Hong Kong) Ltd., Unit 4A/3F New Bright Bldg., 11 Sheung Yuet Road, pg. 1103 **IT**

Kwai Chung

AST Research Far East Limited, 11/F, Vanta Industrial Centre, 21-33 Tai Lin Pai Road, pg. 1182 **IT**

Astra Pharmaceuticals (HK) Ltd., Rm. 2917-25, Metroplaza Tower 1, pg. 94 **IT**

Bevaloid Australia (Pty) Ltd., Unit 2, 4th Fl., Star Centre, Castle Peak Rd., pg. 1113 **IT**

Bowden Industries Limited, 1/F., Kam Bun Industrial Bldg., 13-19, K, pg. 537 **IT**

Clipsal Asia Limited, 1/F., Kam Bun Industrial Bldg., 13-19, K, pg. 537 **IT**

Corcom Far East Ltd., 2/F-4/F, 77-81 Container Port, Road, pg. 446 **PB**

DIC Colour (HK) Ltd., pg. 371 **IT**

DIC Express Co., Ltd., Flat A, G/F, Stage 1, Tung Chun Ind. Bldg., pg. 372 **IT**

Delta Electrical & Engineering Services Ltd., 6th Fl., MTL Warehouse, Phase II, pg. 390 **IT**

Freight-Trans International Co., Ltd., Unit 4618, Metroplaza Tower 1, 223 Hing Fong Road, pg. 704 **IT**

GP Battery Marketing (HK) Ltd., Gold Peak Building, 8/F, 30 Kwei Wing Road, pg. 537 **IT**

GP Electronics Limited, 4/F., FML Bldg., 30-34, Kwai Wing Road, pg. 537 **IT**

GPI International Limited, GPI Bldg., 8/F,30-34, Kwai Wing Rd., pg. 537 **IT**

Gold Peak Industries (Holdings) Limited, 8th Floor, Gold Peak Building, 30 Kwai Wing Road, pg. 537 **IT**

HBS Marketing (Asia) Limited, FML Building, 8/F, 30-34, Kwai Wing Road, pg. 537 **IT**

Krups Ltd., 66-72 lei Muk Road, 5th Floor, pg. 896 **IT**

Oxford Products International Ltd., Level 19, Metroplaza Tower 1, pg. 1239 **IT**

Parker Hannifin Hong Kong Ltd., Fluid Handling Headquarters, Unit A, 10th Floor, pg. 1263 **IT**

Prokit Electronics Company Ltd., Room 704-705, 7/F Star Ctr., 443-451 Castel Peak Rd., pg. 317 **IT**

Radio Holland Group Hong Kong, 806 Join-in Hang Sing Center, 71-75 Container Port Road, pg. 1152 **IT**

Sanyo Electric (Hong Kong) Limited, 14th Fl., Chuan Kei Factory Bldg., pg. 1192 **IT**

Sanyo Electronics (Hong Kong) Limited, 14th Fl., Chuan Kei Factory Bldg., pg. 1192 **IT**

Sigma Electronics Limited, 30-34 Kwai Wing Rd., 7/F, pg. 595 **IT**

Springbrau Testing & Research (Hong Kong) Limited, 1004, 10th Fl. Star Centre, 443-451 Castle Peak Rd., pg. 1027 **PV**

Sylva Industries Limited, 6th Fl., Wyler Ctr., 210 Tai Lin Pai, pg. 537 **IT**

Toledo Scale (Hong Kong) Limited, 61-69 Yau Ma Hom Rd., pg. 986 **IT**

Tyco (Hong Kong) Ltd., Roxy Industrial Bldg., 58-66 Tai Lin Pai Rd., pg. 1059 **PB**

Wellcome Company Limited, 7016-7025 East Roof Floor Atl, pg. 704 **IT**

Whitehall Properties Limited, GPI Bldg., 8/F., 30-34, Kwai Wing Rd., pg. 537 **IT**

Kwai Fong

Catalina Asia, Units 2619-2622, Level 26, Tower II, Metro Plaza, pg. 314 **IT**

Danzas Freight (H.K.) Ltd., Unit 3507-3519, Metroplaza, Tower 1, pg. 382 **IT**

Kenwood & Lee Electronics, Ltd., Unit 3712-3724, Level 37 Tower 1, pg. 730 **IT**

Nitto Denko (HK) Co. Ltd., Unit 4101-11, 23-25, 41st Fl., pg. 950 **IT**

Sharp Electronics (Malaysia) Sdn. Bhd., Room 4251-25, Metro Plaza Tower 1, pg. 1230 **IT**

PB - *U.S. Public Companies Volume*
PV - *U.S. Private Companies Volume*
IT - *International Public & Private Companies Volume*

1645

Geographic Index-Non U.S.

Trade World Industrial, Ltd., Units 2619-2622, Level 26, Tower II, Metro Plaza, pg. 314 **PB**
Woolkong Ltd., Tower 1 Metroplaza No. 223, Units 2513-19 Level 25, Hing Fong Road, pg. 1188 **PV**
Xilinx Asia Pacific, Unit No. 2520-2525, Tower 1, Metroplaza, Hong Kong Rd., pg. 1786 **PB**

Lan Tau Island

EMS Asia Pacific, Block 11, Discovery Bay La Vista, pg. 566 **PB**

North Point

Avesta Sheffield Asia Pacific Ltd., 6th Fl., Jardine Engrng. House, 260 King's Rd., pg. 221 **IT**
Bristol-Myers (Pacific) Limited, pg. 255 **PB**
Cherasia Limited, 14/F, Block B., North Point Industrial Bldg., pg. 346 **PB**
Dun & Bradstreet (HK) Ltd., 12/F, K. Wah Centre, 191 Java Rd., pg. 536 **PB**
Furukawa Electric Co., Ltd. Hong Kong, 1610, Fortess Tower 250, King's Road, pg. 530 **IT**
Hayes Microcomputer Products, Inc., 39/F Unit B. Manulife Tower, 169 Electric Rd., pg. 801 **PB**
Hutchison Paging Holdings Ltd., Citicorp Centre, G/F Whitfield Rd., pg. 1139 **PB**
Hutchison Telephone Company Ltd., Citicorp Centre, G/F, pg. 1139 **PB**
Kodak (Export Sales) Limited, Kodak House, 321 Java Rd., pg. 553 **PB**
Kodak (Far East) Limited, Kodak House, 321 Java Rd., pg. 553 **PB**
MLP Hong Kong Ltd. (MLPHK), G/F., 102 Wharf Road, pg. 874 **IT**
Mattel Asia Ltd., C-6 Watson Estate, pg. 1059 **PB**
Nokia Mobile Phones (H.K.) Ltd., Rm. 2502, K Wah Centre, 191 Java Road, pg. 952 **IT**
SMH Hong Kong Ltd., 40 F Manulite Tower, pg. 1161 **IT**
Sanyo Business Systems (Hong Kong) Limited, Unit 15, 8/F, Blk. B, Sea View Estate, No. 2-8, pg. 1192 **IT**
Stocker & Yale (HK) Ltd., Workingberg Commercial Bldg., Room 704, pg. 1518 **PB**
Terumo-Hong Kong, Fortress Tower, 250 King's Rd., pg. 1376 **IT**
THORN-EMI Hong Kong Ltd., 1/F Brock C, pg. 428 **IT**
THORN Hong Kong Ltd., Block C, First Floor, pg. 1386 **IT**
Tri-Russ International (Hong Kong) Limited, 5F & 6F Block C, Sea View Estate, pg. 223 **PB**
Vicon, Hong Kong, Room 804 Block A, 2-8 Watson Road, pg. 1719 **PB**
Woodward-Clyde International, Unit 910, 9th Fl., Stanhope House, pg. 1658 **PB**

Quarry Bay

Asia Computerworld, Mount Parker House, Ste. 1011-15, pg. 569 **PV**
Bull Information Systems (Hong Kong) Ltd., Suite 1801-1804 18/F, Chinachern Exchange Square, pg. 315 **IT**
Leo Burnett Greater China, City Plaza 3, 6th Fl., 14 Taikoo Wan Rd., pg. 185 **PV**
CIBA-GEIGY (Hong Kong) Limited, 13/F, Warwick House, 979 King's Road, pg. 977 **IT**
DMB&B Asia Pacific North, 6F, Deveon House, 979 Kings Road, pg. 303 **PV**
DMB&B/Hong Kong, 6/F Devon House, Taikoo Pl., 979 King's Rd., pg. 303 **PV**
Elle Hong Kong, 18 Hong on Street, pg. 795 **IT**
EURO RSCG Partnership, 21/F Devon House, 979 King's Rd., pg. 602 **IT**
Gammon Construction Ltd., 28/F, Devon House, Taikoo Place, 979 King's Road, pg. 775 **IT**
Gillette Far East Trading Limited, Rm. 1602-04 Westlands Ctr., 20 Westlands Rd., pg. 744 **PB**
Gillette (Hong Kong) Limited, Rm. 1602-04 Westlands Center, 20 Westlands Rd., pg. 745 **PB**
Glaxo Wellcome Hong Kong Ltd., 18/F Warwick House, pg. 553 **IT**
W.R. Grace (Hong Kong) Ltd., Devon House, 20th Floor, 979 King's Rd., pg. 756 **PB**
Grey Asia Pacific, 19F, Devon House, Taikoo Pl., 979 Kings Rd., pg. 765 **PB**
Hachette Magazine House H.K. Ltd., Shop A-8-9, 18 Hong on Street, pg. 795 **IT**
HAKING ENTERPRISES, 1401 Divine H, 979 King's Road, pg. 586 **IT**
Hong Kong Telecommunications Limited, 39th Fl, Hong Kong Telecom Twr, Taikoo Pl., 979 King's Rd., pg. 247 **IT**
I&S Corporation (Hong Kong Branch), Rm 1201-12/F, Stanhope House, 734-738 King's Rd., pg. 642 **IT**
International Distillers North Asia, 3806-11, 38th Floor, Dorset House, Taikoo Place, pg. 410 **IT**
Jardine Pacific Ltd., 25/F, Devon House, Taikoo Place, 979 King's Road, pg. 704 **IT**
Jardine Shipping Agencies (Hong Kong) Ltd., 18/F, Devon House, Taikoo Place, 979 King's Road, pg. 704 **IT**
Landis & Staefa Communications (HK) Ltd., 734-738 King's Rd., Rm. 1702 Stanhope House, pg. 800 **IT**
Landis & Staefa Hong Kong Co. Ltd., Room 1208, Stanhope House, pg. 801 **IT**
Landis & Staefa Management Corp., Hong Kong Branch, Room 1702, Stanhope House, pg. 801 **IT**
The MacNeal-Schwendler Company Ltd., Rm. 610, Kornhill Metro Tower, 1 Kornhill Rd., pg. 1032 **PB**
Memorex Telex (H.K.) Ltd., 1902-4 China Cham, pg. 857 **IT**
Namco Enterprises Asia Ltd., Unit 10, 9/F, Eastern Harbor, Ctr., 28 Hoi Chak St., pg. 905 **IT**
Oxford University Press (Hong Kong), 18th Fl., Warwick House, Taikoo Place, pg. 1019 **IT**
Parfums Christian Dior Hong Kong Co. Ltd., 23/F Devon House, Taikoo Pl., pg. 783 **IT**
Pharmacia & Upjohn Biotech Far East Ltd., 11/F South West Warwick House, pg. 1047 **IT**
Region Far East, 17A Somerset House, Taikoo Trading Estate, pg. 1353 **IT**
Schindler Lifts (Hong Kong) Ltd., 29/F, Devon House, Taikoo Place, 979 King's Road, pg. 1205 **IT**
Soabar Systems (Hong Kong) Ltd., 16 Westlands Rd., 14th Fl., Melbourne In, pg. 154 **PB**
The South China Morning Post, Limited, Morning Post Bldg., pg. 925 **IT**
Wacoal Hong Kong Co., Ltd., Unit 2, 2nd Fl., Westlands, Centre 20, Westlands Rd., pg. 1484 **IT**
Wang Pacific Limited, 15/F North, Somerset House, Taikoo Place, 979 King's Road, pg. 1738 **PB**
Wiggins Teape (Hong Kong) Ltd., Warwick House, 3rd Fl., West Wing, Taiko Trading Estate, pg. 567 **IT**
Zurich Insurance Company (Asia) Limited, 18/F Dorset House, pg. 1532 **IT**
Zurich Life Insurance Company Ltd., 18/F Dorset House, pg. 1530 **IT**

Queensway

Banco do Brasil S.A.-Hong Kong Representative Office, Unit 2103 B- 21/F Peregrine, Tower, Lippo Centre, pg. 142 **IT**
DBS Futures Hong Kong Ltd., 34th Floor, Two Pacific Place, pg. 351 **IT**
DBS Securities Hong Kong Ltd., 34th Floor, Two Pacific Place, pg. 351 **IT**
DBS Securities Nominees (HK) Ltd., 34th Floor, Two Pacific Place, pg. 351 **IT**
Premisys Communications Pte Ltd., Peregrine Tower, Lippo Centre, pg. 1323 **PB**

Sha Tin

Amersham Far East Trading Limited, 31F 2 Biotechnology Avenue, pg. 993 **IT**
Automated Systems (H.K.) Limited, 15/F, Topsail Plaza, No. 11 On Sum Street, pg. 242 **IT**
BASF Coatings & Inks Hong Kong Ltd., Unit C, 12th Floor, Unison Industrial Centre, pg. 105 **IT**
Dantas Holdings Ltd., Chiaphua Centre, 5/F, 12-14 Siu Lek Yuen Rd., pg. 704 **IT**
Griffith Laboratories (H.K.) Ltd., 8th Flr., Unit A-B, Supreme Industrial Bldg., pg. 481 **PV**
Kvaerner Hong Kong R O for Kvaerner Singapore Pte Ltd, Unit 35, 9/F, Block D, Phase 2, Wha Lok Indus. Ctr., pg. 772 **IT**
MacDermid Asia, Ltd., 2-12 Au Pui Wan St., pg. 1030 **PB**
Makita Power Tools (H.K.) LTD., 3F, Grandtech Centre, 8 On Ping Street, pg. 832 **IT**
Mentholatum Co. (Hong Kong) Ltd., 2-12 Au Pui Wan St., pg. 1126 **IT**
Microsemi (H.K.) Ltd., 5/F-7/F, Meeco Industrial Bldg., pg. 1107 **PB**
Moog Controls (Hong Kong) Ltd., Units 7-10, 6/F, Block New Trade Plaza, pg. 1128 **PB**
Most Crown Industries Ltd., 9/F., Units 913-916 Fo Tan, Industrial Center, 26-28 Au Pui Wan St., pg. 295 **IT**
NEC Technologies Hong Kong Limited, 6/F, Tower 1, Grand Central Plaza, pg. 900 **IT**
Nordson Application Equipment, Inc., Room 718, 7th Floor, Shatin Galleria, pg. 1189 **PB**
Power Conversion Asia-Pacific, 13-15 Shing Wan Rd., pg. 422 **PB**
Standard Motor Products Hong Kong Limited, San Miguel Bldg., pg. 1503 **PB**
Supreme Esteem Ltd., 15F, Topsail Plaza, No. 11 On Sum Street, pg. 243 **IT**
Systems Software Limited, 15/F, Topsail Plaza, No. 11 On Sum Street, pg. 243 **IT**
Tandy Electronics Asia, Block B, 9/F, Veristrong Indus, Ctr., 34-36 Au Pui Wan St., pg. 1561 **PB**
Vickers Systems Ltd., 2nd Fl., Chiaphua Centre, pg. 25 **PB**
Walop Ltd., Flat B&D, 5/F., Sha Tin, Industrial Center, 22-28 Wo Shui St., pg. 295 **IT**

Sham Tseng

San Miguel (Hong Kong), 13 Miles Castle Peak Rd., pg. 1183 **IT**

Shau Kei Wan

Mattel T Company Ltd., 4/F., Len Shing Industrial Bldg., pg. 1059 **PB**
Mattel Toys (H.K.) Ltd., Len Shing Ind. Bldg., 4A, Kung Ngam Village Rd., pg. 1059 **PB**

Sheung Shui

Bilfinger + Berger Bauaktiengesellschaft, Unit 19, Block A, Cambridge Plaza, pg. 196 **IT**

Tai No

Amoy, 11-15 Dai Fu Street, pg. 380 **IT**
Asea Brown Boveri Machinery Service Div., No. 7 Dai Shan St., pg. 2 **IT**
Britannia Brands (Hong Kong) Ltd., 11-15 Dai Fu Street, pg. 380 **IT**
CPC/AJI (Hong Kong) Ltd., Tai PO Industrial Estate, 6 Dai Fu St., pg. 41 **IT**
CPC/AJI (Hong Kong) Ltd., 6 Dai Fu Street, pg. 225 **PB**
Crown Can Hong Kong Ltd., Tai Po Industrial Estates, 8-10 Dia Kwai, pg. 464 **PB**
Thomas De La Rue (Hong Kong) Limited, 2-4 Dai Shing St., pg. 386 **IT**
Hong Kong Fujidenki Co., Ltd., 8 Dai Fu St., pg. 522 **IT**
JOHNSON ELECTRIC HOLDINGS LIMITED, Johnson Building, 6-22 Dai Shun Street, pg. 712 **IT**
Miracle Foods Co., Ltd., Tai Po Industrial Estates, 19 Dai Shing St., pg. 950 **IT**
Motorola Asia Ltd., Silicon Harbour Center, 2 Dai King Street, pg. 1139 **PB**
Motorola Asia Pacific Limited, Silicon Harbour Center, 2 Dai King Street, pg. 1139 **PB**
Motorola Semiconductors Hong Kong Ltd., Silicon Harbor Center, 2 Dai King Street, pg. 1140 **PB**
Nissin Foods Co., Ltd, Tai Po Industrial Estates, 21-23 Dai Shing St., pg. 950 **IT**
NITEC (H.K.), Ltd., 9-13, Dai Cheong Street, Tai Po Industrial Estates, pg. 950 **IT**
Wing On Foods Co., Ltd., Tai Po Industrial Estates, 9-13 Dai Cheong St., pg. 950 **IT**
Winner Food Products Ltd., Tai Po Industrial Estates, 9-13 Dai Shun St., pg. 950 **IT**

Tai Wan

Extensive Trading Co., Ltd., Flat A, 8/F,Chaiwan Industrial, Centre Building, 20 Lee Chung Street, pg. 550 **IT**
Simplex Time Recorder Co. Ltd., Honour Indus. Bldg., 22 Fl., 6 Sun Yip St., pg. 1002 **PV**

Taikoo Shing

CPC Asia Ltd. Operations, pg. 224 **PB**
Computasia Limited, 10/F, Cityplaza III, 14 Taikoo Wan Road, pg. 247 **IT**
Digital Equipment Hong Kong Limited, 15-22/F, Cityplaza 4, 12 Taikoo Wan Road, pg. 508 **PB**
East Asia Aetna Insurance Group, 10/F City Plaza 4, 12 Taikoo Wan Road, pg. 27 **PB**
Hong Kong Telecom CSL Limited, 22/F, Cityplaza III, 14 Taikoo Wan Road, pg. 247 **IT**
I&S Corporation (Hong Kong Office), Ogilvy & Mather, 7th Fl., Mount Parker House, pg. 642 **IT**
Nokia Telecommunications (H.K.) Ltd., Suite 1301, 13/F. Cityplaza 4, 12 Taikoo Wan Road, pg. 953 **IT**
SAS Institute Ltd., 14/F Cityplaza 4, 12 Taikoo Wan Road, pg. 967 **PV**

Teun Mun

China Thread Development Co. Ltd., Unit B, Yen Shing Ind. Bldg.; 7/F, 4 Kin, pg. 299 **IT**
QST Far East Limited, 110 Tin Haurd, pg. 897 **PV**

Tokwawan

Federal Express (Hong Kong) Ltd., World Shipping Center, 7 Canton Road, pg. 604 **PB**

Tsim Tsa Tsui

Fan Ling Machine & Mechanical Centre, P.O. Box 98612, pg. 943 **IT**
IDT Asia, Ltd., Tower 6, Ste. 1003, China Hong Kong City, pg. 884 **PB**
RZB Hong Kong, Room 507, Tower II, Silvercord, 30 Canton Road, pg. 1084 **IT**
Teledyne Hong Kong, RM 918 New World Centre, (East Wing), pg. 44 **PB**
Western Harbor Crossing Project Office, P.O. Box 98612, Tsim Tsa Tsui Post Office, pg. 943 **IT**

Tsuen Wan

Ademco Hong Kong Ltd., Flat A&B, 7th Fl., CDW Building, pg. 1307 **PB**
Asahi Metals (HK) Ltd., Rm. 2204 B, Nan Fung Centre, 264-298, Castle Peak Rd., pg. 710 **IT**
Asahi Optical (International) Ltd., Leader Indus. Centre, Phase 1, 7th Fl., Unit A & 8th Fl., pg. 85 **IT**
Cerberus Hong Kong Ltd., Units F.H.J. & K. 16/Fl., Leader Industrial Centre, pg. 1246 **IT**
Dai Nippon Printing Co. (Hong Kong) Ltd., 2-5/F, Tsuen Wan Indus. Centre, 220-248, pg. 363 **IT**
Donaldson Far East Ltd., CDW Building, Unit A, B and C, pg. 517 **PB**
Hagglunds Drives Ltd, Unit 3703 Wharf Cable Twr., 9 Hoi Shing Rd., pg. 670 **IT**
Marchon Toys, Ltd., Unit 3804 Space 38/F, Wharf Cable Tower, 9 Hoi Road, pg. 579 **PB**
Munters (HK) Pte. Ltd., Unit 3703 Wharf Cable Twr., 9 Hoi Shing Road, pg. 669 **IT**
Outboard Marine Asia Ltd., Tsing Yi Town Lot 54, P.O. Box 120, pg. 478 **PV**
Rocol (Hong Kong) Limited, Unit 9-10, 9th Fl., Technology Plaza, pg. 892 **IT**
Royal Doulton Hong Kong Limited, 15th Floor, Hale West Industrial Building, pg. 1135 **IT**
Sealed Air (Far East) Ltd., 9/F,Wing Kwai Industrial Bldg., 2-8 Wang Wo Tsai Street, pg. 1451 **PB**

Tuen Mun

VITASOY INTERNATIONAL HOLDINGS LTD., 1 Kin Wong Street, pg. 1468 **IT**

PB - *U.S. Public Companies Volume*
PV - *U.S. Private Companies Volume*
IT - *International Public & Private Companies Volume*

Victoria

WestLB Hong Kong Branch, BA Tower, 36th Fl., 12 Harcourt Rd., pg. 1493 IT

Wan Chai

AMD Far East, Ltd., 1201-2 Harcourt House, pg. 21 PB
Air Products Asia, Inc., Room 5507-10 Hopewell Centre, 183 Queen's Road East, pg. 31 PB
Allied Colloids (Asia) Ltd., pg. 62 IT
American Appraisal Hong Kong Ltd., 2901 Central Plaza, 18 Harbour Rd., pg. 50 PV
Amgen Greater China, Ltd., Ste. 4705 Central Plaza, 18 Harbour Rd., pg. 101 PB
Asea Brown Boveri Ltd., OTB Bldg., 19/F, 160 Gloucester Road, pg. 2 IT
ASTEC INTERNATIONAL LIMITED, 38th Fl., Central Plaza, 18 Harbor Rd., pg. 92 IT
Australian Mutual Provident Society, 19/F Sun Hung Kai Centre, pg. 100 IT
AxLamin Ltd., Rm. 1501, East Town Bldg., 41 Lockhart Rd., pg. 710 IT
AxTrade East Asia Ltd., Rm. 1801, East Town Bldg., 41 Lockhart Rd., pg. 710 IT
BFCE Hong Kong, 1818 Shui On Ctr., 8 Harbor Rd., pg. 161 IT
Barmag Far East Ltd., 1924, Sun Hung Kai Centre, pg. 45 IT
Batey Couldrey Jones Advertising, 25/F Fook Lee Commercial Ctr., Town Place, 33 Lockhart Rd., pg. 117 IT
Cambrex Hong Kong Ltd., 1607 Asian House, One Hennessy Rd., pg. 297 PB
Cariplo Hong Kong, 52/Fl., Central Plaza, pg. 275 IT
Circle Freight International (H.K.), 1401-2 Tung Wai Commercial Bldg., pg. 372 PB
Costain South East Asia, 2310 China Resources Bldg., 26 Harbor Rd., pg. 337 IT
Cyanamid (Far East) Ltd., 42nd Fl., Sung Hung Kai Centre, pg. 80 PB
DHL International (Hong Kong) Ltd., 23/F Shui on Center, 6-8 Harbor Rd., pg. 302 PV
Dai-ichi Life International (H.K.) Limited, Suite 6702, Central Plaza, 18 Harbour Road, pg. 362 IT
De La Rue Systems Asia Pacific Limited, Suite 5404-5, Central Plaza, 18 Harbor Road, pg. 387 IT
De La Rue Systems Ltd, Suite 5404-5, 54/F1, Central Plaza, 18 Harbour Road, pg. 387 IT
Dow Chemical Pacific Limited, 39th Fl., Sun Hung Kai Ctre., P.O. Box 711, pg. 523 PB
Dynapac Far East Ltd., Room Number 2502, 43-59 Queens Road East, pg. 1420 IT
ECI Telecom (HK) Ltd., 2806 China Resources Bldg., 26 Harbour Road, pg. 643 IT
East Asia Heller Limited, Suite 5904-07, Central Plaza, 18 Harbour Road, pg. 521 IT
Elscint (Asia Pacific) Ltd., Hong Kong Computer Center, 3rd Floor, pg. 450 IT
Epson Hong Kong Ltd., 20th Floor, Harbour Centre, 25 Harbour Rd., pg. 1219 IT
Esselte Asia Pacific, 22nd Floor, Shanghai Industrial Investment Building, pg. 460 IT
Esselte Ltd., 22nd floor, Shanghai Ind. Investment Bldg., pg. 461 IT
First Brands Asia, Room 2803 Central Plaza, 18 Harbour Road, pg. 627 PB
Formica Asia Limited, Dah Sing Fin. Center, Rm. 2409, 108 Gloucester Rd., pg. 129 IT
Franshin Company Ltd., Rm. 4611-4615, 46th Fl., Office Tower, Convention Plaza, pg. 1255 IT
The General Electric Company of Hong Kong Ltd., C C Wu Bldg., 062-308 Hennessey Rd., pg. 546 IT
Gestetner Office System (HK) Ltd., 15/F Tai Yau Building, 181 Johnston Road, pg. 1115 IT
Getinge Hong Kong Ltd., Flat B.2/F Lucky Plaza, pg. 551 IT
Glaxo Wellcome China Ltd., 30/F Shui On Centre, pg. 553 IT
Great Year Trading Co. Ltd., Room 1714, Sun Hung Kai Centre, 30 Harbour Road, pg. 558 IT
HSBC Gibbs (Asia-Pacific) Limited, 20/F Dah Sing Financial Centre, 108 Gloucester Road, pg. 582 IT
HSBC Insurance Limited, 40/F Sun Hung Kai Centre, 30 Harbour Rd., pg. 582 IT
Hale Engineering Ltd., 17th, East Town Bldg., 41 Lockhart Rd., pg. 711 IT
Hang Seng Life Ltd., 40/F, Sun Hung Kai Centre, 30 Harbour Road, pg. 582 IT
Herbalife International-Hong Kong, 1804-5, Tai Yau Bldg., pg. 809 PB
Herman Miller, Inc., 13/F Luk Kwok Centre, pg. 1112 PB
Honeywell Asia Pacific Inc., Suite 3213-25, Sun Hung Kai Centre, pg. 834 PB
Hong Kong Telephone Company Ltd., 26th Fl., Convention Plaza Office Tower, pg. 247 IT
Huber & Suhner (Far East), Harcourt House, 39 Gloucester Rd., pg. 637 IT
Huls Far East Co., Ltd., 23/F, CLI-Building, 313-317 B Hennessy Road, pg. 1455 IT
ICI Swire Paints Limited, 8/F Luk Kwok Centre, 72 Gloucester Rd., pg. 665 IT
Intergraph Asia Pacific Limited, Tai Yau Building, Rms. 901-910, 181 Johnston Road, pg. 891 PB
International Computers Hong Kong Limited, Sun Hung Kai Centre, 41st Floor, pg. 529 IT
International Paper (Asia) Limited, Room 2609-2618, 26th Floor, Shui On Centre, 6-8 Harbour Road, pg. 905 PB
JBA (HK) Ltd., 22/F Hennessey House, 313 317D Hennessey Rd., pg. 1527 PB
Jardine Riche Monde Ltd, 28th Floor, 108 Gloucester Road, pg. 782 IT
A. Johnson Corp (HK) Ltd., Rm. 1501, East Town Bldg., 41 Lockhart Rd., pg. 711 IT
Axel Johnson Corp. (HK) Ltd., Rm. 1201-1207, 12/F Tai Yau Bldg., pg. 711 IT
Kabi Pharmacia & Upjohn Far East, Room 1801, Allied Kajima Bldg., 138 Gloucester Road, pg. 1049 IT
Kemklen Industrial Suppl. Ltd., 17th Fl., East Town Bldg., 41 Lockhart Rd., pg. 712 IT
Keppel FELS China Ltd., 1906 Hopewell Centre, pg. 731 IT
Knorr-Bremse Rail Systems Far East Ltd., 1301 Everge House, 38 Gloucester Rd., pg. 739 IT
Kredietbank Hong Kong Branch, 60/F Central Plaza, 18 Harbour Road, pg. 760 IT
Krupp Plastics & Rubber Machinery, Far East, 19th Floor, 80 Gloucester Rd., pg. 510 IT
Leighton Asia, 18th Fl., Hopewell Centre, pg. 624 IT
Loctite Asia Ltd., Rm. 1207, Harbour Centre, 25 Harbour Rd., pg. 611 IT
Logica Limited, 4th Fl., Chung Nam Bldg., 1 Lockhart Road, pg. 814 IT
Lowlands Corporate Services Company Ltd., Unit B, 23rd Floor, One Capital Place, pg. 548 IT
Medtronic International, Ltd., 2002 CC Wu Bldg., 308 Hennessy Rd., pg. 1083 PB
Miller Freeman Asia Ltd, 44K Floor, 4401 China Resources Building, pg. 1443 IT
Mitel Far East Ltd., Room 803-5 Allied Kajima Bldg., 134-143 Gloucester Rd., pg. 870 IT
Modem Media Hong Kong, 2nd Fl., Harbour Centre, 25 Harbour Rd., pg. 1641 PB
NOF Jotun (H.K.) Ltd., Room 907, Dominion Centre, 37-59 A Queens Road East, pg. 716 IT
National Mutual Asia Ltd., National Mutual Centre, 151 Gloucester Rd., pg. 909 IT
Nellcor Puritan Bennett HK Ltd., Room 1602 Evergo House, pg. 1040 PB
Nichimen Co., (Hong Kong) Ltd., 16th Fl., Harbor Ctr., 25 Harbor Rd., pg. 928 IT
Nicoll Asia Ltd., Room 1910, C.C Wu Building, 302-308 Hennessy Road, pg. 430 IT
Northern Telecom (Asia) Limited, 34th Fl., Central Plaza, 18 Harbor Rd., pg. 970 IT
Novell Hong Kong, Rm. 4601-5, China Resource Bldg., 25 Harbour Rd., pg. 1204 PB
Novo Nordisk A/S, Room 2410, 24th Floor, China Resources Building, 26 Harbour Rd., pg. 989 IT
Nutricia (Asia-Pacific) Ltd., pg. 992 IT
Oracle Systems Hong Kong Ltd., Unit 2809-14, Office Tower, 1 Harbour Road, pg. 1228 PB
Orbotech Pacific Ltd., Room 3501,China Resources Bldg, 26 Harbor Road, pg. 1007 IT
Pall Asia International Ltd., Rm. 2806-7, Shui On Centre, 6-8 Harbour Rd., pg. 1254 PB
POSCO Asia Co., Ltd. (POA), Rm 6207, Central Plaza, pg. 1062 IT
POSCO Hong Kong Office, Rm. 3605, Central Plaza, 18 Harbour Road, pg. 1062 IT
Principal Insurance Company (Hong Kong) Ltd., Central Plaza, Unit 1002, Harbour Road, pg. 886 PV
Principal International Asia Limited, Unit 1002, Central Plaza 18 Harbour RD., pg. 886 PV
qad.asia-pacific, 3002 Office Tower, 1 Harbor Rd., pg. 1345 PB
Quantum Hong Kong Ltd., Suite 3201 Great Eagle Centre, 23 Harbour Road, pg. 1350 PB
Rhenania International Transport Services (H.K.) Limited, Tung Wai Commercial Bldg. Rm. 1401-1402, pg. 1034 IT
Riche Monde Ltd., 28th Fl., 108 Gloucester Rd., pg. 783 IT
Rillfung Company Ltd., Rm. 4601-4606, Office Tower, Convention Plaza, 1 Harbour Rd., pg. 1255 IT
River Wood International Corp., 1518 Shui On Center, 6-8 Harbour Road, pg. 927 PB
Sara Lee Corp.-Asia, Allied Kajima Building, 138 Gloucester Road, 17th Floor, pg. 1434 PB
SASIB Hong Kong Ltd., 17/F, Malaysia Building, 50 Glouchester Road, pg. 1195 IT
Sasol Chemicals Pacific Limited, 1111 Shui On Centre, pg. 1196 IT
Schmidt & Co. (Hong Kong) Ltd., 18th F., Great Eagle Center, 23 Harbour Rd., pg. 823 PB
Scholl (Asia) Limited, Stes. 503-5, Hong Kong Computer Company, pg. 1209 IT
Scotchbrook Communications Ltd., 28/F, Three Lockhart Rd., pg. 411 PV
Sequent Computer Systems (Hong Kong) Ltd., 2301 China Resources Bldg., 26 Harbour Rd., pg. 1460 PB
Simon Access Far East, 302-308 Hennessy Rd., pg. 1252 IT
Simon Marketing, Ltd., Everglo House, 3rd Fl., 38 Gloucester Rd., pg. 1001 PV
Singapore Petroleum Co. (HK) Ltd., Central Plaza, Ste. 5705, 5th Fl., 18 Harbour Rd., pg. 102 PB
Singapore Tourist Promotion Board - Hong Kong, Room 2003, Central Plaza, 18 Harbour Road, pg. 1254 IT
Sinochem International Chemicals (Hong Kong) Ltd., 47th Fl., Office Tower, Convention Plaza, 1 Harbour Rd., pg. 1255 IT
Sinochem International Oil (Hong Kong) Co., Ltd., 47th Fl., Office Tower, Convention Plaza, 1 Harbour Rd., pg. 1255 IT
Standard Chartered Finance Limited, 22nd Fl., Fleet House, 38 Gloucester Rd., pg. 1297 IT
SUN HUNG KAI PROPERTIES LTD., 45th Fl., Sun Hung Kai Centre, 30 Harbour Rd., pg. 1318 IT
Sun Microsystems of California Ltd., 29th Fl., Shul on Centre, 8 Harbour Rd., pg. 1532 PB
Takeda IMC Chemical Ltd., Rm. 1101, 11th Fl., Jubilee, Commercial Bldg., 42-46 Gloucester Rd., pg. 1351 IT
Tarmac Construction (Contracts) International Ltd., Room 2336, Sun Hung Kai Centre, pg. 1355 IT
Tektronix China Ltd., Dah Sing Financial Center, 22nd Floor, pg. 1567 PB
Tektronix Hong Kong Ltd., Dah Sing Financial Center, 22nd Floor, pg. 1567 PB
Toppan Moore Data Products Ltd., 12 F Hong Kong Computer Centre, pg. 313 PV
Toto Kiki (H.K.) Ltd., Rm. 1101, 11A, Inchcape AON Insurance Tower, pg. 1410 IT
URS Greiner International Ltd., Ste. 1502, Central Plaza, 18 Harbour Rd., pg. 1659 PB
Uni-Beauty Limited, Rm. 1201, Dominion Centre, 43-59 Queen's Rd. East, pg. 1490 IT
Van Melle Far East Ltd.-China Branch, 2101 Folk Lee Center, pg. 1451 IT
Volkswagen Asia-Pacific Ltd., Great Eagle Centre, 27th Fl., Stes. 2706-2710, 23 Harbour Rd., pg. 1475 IT
Wandel & Goltermann Ltd., Rm. 1501, Fook Lee Commercial Centre, pg. 1486 IT
Wayfoong Credit Ltd., 18/F, Leighton Centre, 77 Leighton Rd., pg. 584 IT
Wayfoong Finance Ltd., 18/F, Leighton Centre, 77 Leighton Rd., pg. 584 IT
Western Navigation Global Ltd., 1401-1 Tung Wau Commercial, Bldg., 109-11 Gloucester Rd., pg. 373 PB
Westrex Asia, Caltex House, 21st Fl., 258 Hennessey Road, pg. 1005 PB
Weyerhaeuser (Far East) Ltd., Rm. 1308, 13/F Harcourt House, 39 Gloucester Rd., pg. 1764 PB
Willis Faber Consulting (Far East) Ltd., 5108 Central Plaza, pg. 1502 IT
Willis Faber (Far East) Limited, 5108 Central Plaza, 18 Harbour Road, pg. 1510 IT
Wyeth (HK) Limited, 14/Fl., C.C. Wu Bldg., 302-308 Hennessy Rd., pg. 82 PB
XTRA Inc. Far East/Australasia, 20/F Centre Point, pg. 1787 PB

Yuen Long

BRC Weldmesh (FE) Ltd., Castle Peak Road, Fung Kut Heong, pg. 227 IT
DSM Kenkyo EPP Ltd., 108 Tai To Tsuen, Ping Shan, pg. 354 IT
Nikko Gould Foil (U.K.) Ltd., Yuen Long Industrial Estate, 36-38 Wang Lok St., pg. 702 IT
Nokia Mobile Phones (H.K.) Ltd., Man Kee Industrial Bldg., 129-149 On Lok Road, pg. 952 IT
Technophone Manufacturing (H.K.) Ltd., Man Kee Industrial Bldg., 129-149 On Lok Road, pg. 952 IT
Toppan Printing Co. (H.K.) Ltd., 1, Fuk Wang Street, Yuen Long Industrial Estate, pg. 1399 IT

HUNGARY

Bekescaba

Jamina Rt., Tegla-es Cserepgyarto, Reszvenytarsasag, Oroshazi ut 88, pg. 1092 IT

Beremend

Beremendi Cement-es Meszipari Rt., pg. 605 IT

Budaors

CPC Hungary Ltd., pg. 225 PB
ITT Flygt Kft, Stefania u.18, pg. 860 PB

Budapest

AC Bakony Kft., pg. 724 PB
AGA Gaz Kft., Illatos ut 7-9, pg. 13 IT
AGIP Hungaria R.T., Agip Komplex South, pg. 428 IT
AMP Hungary Trading Kft., Jaszberenyi ut 34/36, pg. 8 PB
Adecco Magyarorszagi Szemelyzeti Kozvetito Kft, Bajcsy-Zsilinszky ut 27, pg. 24 IT
Adidas Budapest Kft., pg. 24 IT
AB-AEGON Altalanos Biztosito Rt, Raday utca 42-44, pg. 28 IT
Aeroplex of Central Europe Ltd., pg. 834 IT
Agroferm Hungarian Japanese Fermentation Industry Ltd., Badacsonyi u. 9, pg. 778 IT
Akerlund & Rausing, Representation Office, Vorosmarty Ter 1, Office 407, pg. 33 IT
Algynvest, Vam Utca 5-7, pg. 1416 IT
Allied Colloids Magyarorszag Kft, pg. 62 IT
Alusuisse-Lonza Hungaria Kft., pg. 68 IT
American Appraisal Hungary Co. Ltd., Ganz U.16, 3rd Fl., 304, pg. 50 PV
Astra Pharmaceuticals Kft., Maros u. 19-21, pg. 94 IT
Autodesk Ltd., Szemlohegy u. 23/b, pg. 149 PB
BASF Hungaria Kft., Seregely u. 1-5, pg. 106 IT
BKD Bank Budapest, Honved utca 20, pg. 418 IT
BNP-Dresdner Bank (Hungaria) Rt., Honved utca 20, pg. 418 IT
Bayerische Landesbank Girozentrale, Rakoczi ut 1-3, pg. 177 IT
Beiersdorf KFT, pg. 183 IT
Benckiser Kft., pg. 185 IT
Berlitz KFT, Sommelweis Utca 2, pg. 222 PB
Boganyi es Fia KFT, XIV Amerikai-ut 39.EM 3, pg. 550 IT
Bohler Kereskedalmi KFT, Szep u. 6, pg. 1471 IT

PB - *U.S. Public Companies Volume*
PV - *U.S. Private Companies Volume*
IT - *International Public & Private Companies Volume*

Geographic Index-Non U.S.
1647

Bonifica-Hungary, East-West Bus. Center, Rakoczi Ut 1/3, pg. 655 **IT**
Borland Hungary Online/Delphi-Szoft Kft, Hungaria Krt 79-81, pg. 246 **PB**
Robert Bosch Kft, Budaorsi ut 31 C, pg. 205 **IT**
Brother International Hungary Kft., Gvadanvi ur, 87, pg. 229 **IT**
BUDAPEST MARRIOTT HOTEL, Apaczai U.4, pg. 232 **IT**
Bull Hungary, Szepvolgyi ut 35, pg. 317 **IT**
Bureau Rhone-Poulenc SA, Csorsz Utca, 35, pg. 1112 **IT**
Leo Burnett Budapest KFT, H-1036, pg. 185 **PV**
CCF Hungary, Ribary U. 12, pg. 342 **IT**
Csemege-Julius Meinl, pg. 856 **IT**
Cad Server Ltd., Vaci ut 168, pg. 1031 **PB**
Canon Hungria Kereskedelmi Kft., Vaci ut 37, pg. 262 **IT**
Central-European International Bank Ltd. (CIB), Medve utca 4-14, pg. 181 **IT**
Cerberus Hungaria Klt., Nimrod u. 3, pg. 1246 **IT**
Chemoldanzas GmbH, Gyori ut 18, pg. 382 **IT**
CIBA-GEIGY Services AG-Technical Advisory Office, pg. 979 **IT**
CIBA Hungaria Kft., pg. 980 **IT**
Commenda Hungaria Kpt., Zay u 1-3, pg. 1501 **IT**
Commerzbank AG-Budapest, Szechenyi rakpart 8, pg. 311 **IT**
Compack Douwe Egberts RT, Istva'n 23/25, pg. 1434 **IT**
Consulting and Engineering Agrober Company, Budafoki ut 79, pg. 607 **IT**
Creditanstalt Rt., Akademia utca 17, pg. 348 **IT**
DG Bank-Budapest, East-West Business Center, Rakoczi ut 1-3, pg. 352 **IT**
DMB&B/Budapest, Semmelweis u. 14 IV/20, pg. 303 **PV**
DSM Central Europe, Rath Gyorgy u. 56, pg. 355 **IT**
Daewoo Bank (Hungary) Ltd., 4th Fl., East-West Business, Center, 1088 Budapest VIII, pg. 359 **IT**
Daewoo Corp. - Budapest, pg. 358 **IT**
Daiwa-MKB (Hungary) Investment and Securities Co. Ltd., Rakoczi ut 1-3, pg. 376 **IT**
Deutsche Bank AG (Budapest), Vaci utca 7, pg. 404 **IT**
Digital Equipment Hungary Ltd., Nimetvvlgyi zt 97, pg. 508 **PB**
Dun & Bradstreet Hungaria Kft., Varmegye Utca 3-5, pg. 536 **PB**
Dunabest Kft., pg. 842 **IT**
Dunastyr Polystyr. Manufacturing Co. Ltd., Becsi ut. 4, pg. 429 **IT**
EA-Generali Epito es Tervezo Kft., Kuny Domokos Utca 13-15, pg. 91 **IT**
E/B/D-Interpartners Budapest KFT, Budafoki UT 9-11 f.em.1., pg. 1152 **PV**
ESAB KFT, Budafoki ut. 95-97, pg. 282 **IT**
ESS-FOOD Hungaria LLC, Puskin ut 4, pg. 429 **IT**
ETV-Eroterv Rt., Angyal u. 1-3, pg. 661 **IT**
EGIS-Nutricia Kft, pg. 991 **IT**
Electricite de France, Emke Building, Rakovci, pg. 437 **IT**
ENPAP KFT, Becsi ut 120-124 I em, pg. 457 **IT**
Erasmus Press Publishing kft., Dozsa Gyorgy ut 150, pg. 1445 **IT**
Ericsson Technika Kft., Venyige u. 3, pg. 1367 **IT**
EURO RSCG, Becsi Ut 83, pg. 602 **IT**
Europa-Gan Biztosito, Hamzsabegi Ut 37, pg. 564 **IT**
Fin.Co Budapest, pg. 654 **IT**
Fokusz Marketing Kommunikacio Kft., Nemetvologyi ut 114, pg. 1062 **PV**
Furukawa Electric Composite Insulators Co., Ltd., Cservenka Miklos ut 86, pg. 530 **IT**
Furukawa Electric Institute of Technology, Cservenka Miklos ut 86, pg. 530 **IT**
GGK Budapest, Gyarmat Utca 26, pg. 1335 **IT**
Gambro kft, Diosarok ut 5, pg. 667 **IT**
Gasztro-Lanc Kft, Cserhalom U.2, pg. 1274 **IT**
Gen-EA Befektetesi es Tanacsado Kft., Kuny Domokos Utca 13-15, pg. 91 **IT**
General Motors Hungary, pg. 722 **PB**
General Motors Hungary (Distribution) Ltd., pg. 722 **PB**
Generali Budapest Biztosito Rt., Kuny Domokos Utca 13-15, pg. 91 **IT**
Gerber Hungary Baby Products Trading, Nagyenyed U 6, pg. 973 **IT**
Global TH, Furg Utsa #18, pg. 1376 **IT**
Goldstar Magyar KET, pg. 779 **IT**
Groupe SEB Hungary, Rubin Apartment Hotel, Dayka Gabor u. 3, pg. 568 **IT**
Haegele Immobilien-Ost Ingatlanforgalmi Kft., pg. 310 **IT**
Henkel Budapest Chemische Gesellschaft mbH, pg. 612 **IT**
Henkel Magyarorszag Kft., pg. 613 **IT**
Herlitz Hungaria, Vasert Rt. Rakospalota, pg. 616 **IT**
Hewlett-Packard & Control Ltd., Erzebet kiralyne utja 1/c, pg. 818 **PB**
Hidepito, Andrassy UT 98, pg. 823 **IT**
Holderbank Ungarn GmbH, pg. 629 **IT**
Honeywell Kft, Gogol u., 13, pg. 835 **IT**
Huls Austria GmbH-Budapest Office, Intern, Trade Center Bldg. 3, Bajcsy-Zsilinszky ut 12, pg. 1455 **IT**
Hungaria Biztosito Rt., Vadasz u. 23-25, pg. 60 **IT**
Hungarofert Chemikalien HandelsgesmbH, Terez KRT. 9 III 4, pg. 356 **IT**
Hungary OBI Barkacsaruhaz, Kozpont Gitar u. 34, pg. 993 **IT**
IDG Communications/Hungary, pg. 570 **PV**
IDG Magyaroszagi Laplado Kft., Marvany V. 17., pg. 570 **PV**
IDV Central Europe, Office 302, Kapas U. 11-15, pg. 410 **IT**
ING Bank Budapest, Andrassy ut 9, pg. 649 **IT**
ING Bank Hungary, Bathory-u. 12, pg. 649 **IT**
IQSoft SZKI Intelligens-Software Co. Ltd., P.O. Box 73, H-1251, pg. 1228 **PB**
IR International Holdings, Inc., Szent Istvan Park 15, pg. 907 **PB**

ISS Servisystem Kft., Kevehaza U. 1, pg. 657 **IT**
Intergraph Hungary Ltd., Bosnyak ter 5, pg. 892 **PB**
International Flavors & Fragrances, Amerikai VT 11, pg. 899 **PB**
Iron-Lift Llc, Jaszbereny ut 24-36, pg. 97 **IT**
Jauch & Huebener, Zichy Geza u. 5, pg. 118 **PB**
KME Hungaria Szinesfem Kft., Andor u. 47-49, pg. 719 **IT**
KSB Szivattyu es Armatura Kft., pg. 721 **IT**
Kemira Kereskedelmi KFT, Nepfurdo u. 21/c, pg. 729 **IT**
Knorr-Bremse Vasuti Jarmu Rendszerek Hungaria Kft., Helsinki ut 86, pg. 739 **IT**
Kodak Kft. Hungary, Tartsay Vilmos u. 14, 3.em, pg. 553 **PB**
KONE Elevators Ltd., Hollan Erno utca 24-26, pg. 747 **IT**
KONE M-Lift Rt., Hollan Erno utca 24-26, pg. 747 **IT**
Kontaset Kft., Helsinki ut. 53, pg. 740 **IT**
Korn/Ferry International, pg. 633 **PV**
Kredietbank Representative Office (Budapest), Taltos u. 15/a, pg. 760 **IT**
Kyowa Hakko Kogyo Co., Ltd., 1st Flr., Madach Trade Center Bldg. B., pg. 778 **IT**
Landis & Staefa (Magyarorszag) Kft., Szuglo utca 9-15, pg. 801 **IT**
Lasbra Kavicsbanya Kft., Lossuth L. ut 49, pg. 1092 **IT**
Linde Kaltetechnik Hungaria GmbH, pg. 810 **IT**
Arthur D. Little International, Inc, Bajcsy-Zsilinszky, ut 57 III, ep.fszt 3, pg. 671 **PV**
MSA-AUER Hungaria, Biztonsaglechnikia Kft., pg. 1114 **PB**
Magyar Paribas R.T., 23-25 Ostrom, pg. 321 **IT**
MALEV HUNGARIAN AIRLINES, PLC., Roosevelt ter 2, pg. 833 **IT**
Mannesmann Anlagenbau Hungaria Kft., pg. 837 **IT**
Maresi Hungaria Kft., pg. 842 **IT**
Microsoft Kft, pg. 1108 **PB**
Milupa Kft., pg. 991 **IT**
Mitsui & Co., Ltd., Sallai U.28 II. 3, pg. 881 **IT**
Morgan Materials Hungary Limited, H-1103 Gyomroi St., pg. 891 **IT**
Morgan Trans Budapest Kft, pg. 895 **IT**
Moulinex Hungaria, Zold lomb u. 26-30/c., pg. 896 **IT**
Munters Kft, IV Komp utca 2, pg. 669 **IT**
NAP-TV, 1149 Budapest, pg. 394 **IT**
Nationale-Nederlanden, Magyarorszagi Biztosito Rt., pg. 650 **IT**
Nestle Hungaria Kft, pg. 921 **IT**
Nikon Kft, Devai utca 26-28, pg. 931 **IT**
Nokia Mobile Phones, Kiralyhago ter 8-9, Foldszint, pg. 952 **IT**
Nokia Telecommunications Kft, Kiralyhago ter 8-9, pg. 953 **IT**
Nomura Investment Bank Hungary Ltd., East-West Business Center, 7th Floor, Rakoczi ut 1-3, pg. 957 **IT**
NORD/LB - Budapest, Rakoczi ut 1-3, pg. 958 **IT**
Norsk Hydro a.s. Hungary, East West Trade Centre, Rakoczi ut 1-3, pg. 964 **IT**
Novell Hungary, East-West Business Center, Rakoczi ut 1-3, pg. 1204 **PB**
Novo Nordisk A/S, Felsoezoeldmali ut. 35, pg. 988 **IT**
Nutricia Hungary Kft, pg. 992 **IT**
Nutricia Kft., pg. 992 **IT**
OCE-Hungaria Kft., pg. 994 **IT**
Ole-Hungaria Kft, Karpat m. 54, pg. 995 **IT**
OMRON Electronics, KFT, Rokolya U. 1-13, pg. 1006 **IT**
Otto Katalogusaruhaz Kft, pg. 1015 **IT**
PCL, Napvirag Ut 17, pg. 1031 **IT**
PCL-Rep. Office of Pechiney Handelsgesellschaft in Hungary, Napvirag U, 17, pg. 1031 **IT**
Perstorp & Heinrich Puzeklik Ges.m.b.H.-Informations -und Serviceburo, Bercsenyi u. 9, pg. 1037 **IT**
Petroli Hungary KFT, Agip Complex South, pg. 428 **IT**
Pfizer Pharmaceutical Trading Limited Liability Company, Tabornuk u.2, pg. 1283 **PB**
Polifoam Plastic Processing Co., Ltd., Gyali ut 37, pg. 531 **IT**
Primagaz Hungaria Rt., Raday utca 42-44, V floor, pg. 1155 **IT**
Pro-Immo Vagyonkezelo es Szolgaltato Kft., Hungaria krt 178-186, pg. 92 **IT**
Promo, Rozsa u. 55, pg. 1377 **PB**
Providencia Osztrak-Magyar Biztosito Rt., Hungaria krt 178-186, pg. 92 **IT**
Purina-Hage Ltd., Moszkva ter 9, pg. 1360 **PB**
Reader's Digest KFT, XIV, Nezsider u.8., pg. 1368 **PB**
Recognita, Marvany U.17, pg. 291 **PB**
Reemtsma Hungary Kereskedelmi Kft., Lagos utca 48-66, pg. 1101 **IT**
Repeelacki Sajtyre, Vorosmarty U1, pg. 201 **IT**
Rexroth Danuvia Hajtastechnikai Kft., pg. 839 **IT**
Rothenberger (Hungary), Intl. Trade Center, Bajcsy-Zsilinsky ut 12/501, pg. 1129 **IT**
SKF Sved Golyoscsapagy Reszvenytarsasag, PF 52, pg. 1159 **IT**
SMS Hungary, Egeszeguqyi Informatikai Kft., pg. 1463 **PB**
Sandvik Magyarorszagon KFT, pg. 1186 **IT**
Schindler-Ganz Lift GmbH, pg. 1205 **IT**
Schleicher & Schuell, Paratrade, Kereskedelmi Bt., pg. 1206 **IT**
Scholl Kft, Varosligeti Fasor 47/49, pg. 1210 **IT**
Schrack Telecom RT, Koztarsasag ter 3, pg. 1369 **IT**
Scitel Telematics Ltd., Lehel ut 3/b, 1st Floor, pg. 1195 **IT**
Sensormatic kfi, Martirok Utja 245, pg. 1458 **PB**
Shell & Interag Kft., Csillaghegyi u 25, pg. 1138 **IT**
Shimizu Hungary Construction Ltd., Diosarok UT 26/B, pg. 1234 **IT**
Siemens Rt., Lajos M. 103, pg. 1247 **IT**
Sinochem Representative Office - Hungary, Zichy Geza U.5, pg. 1256 **IT**
Skanska Hungaria Ltd., East West Business Center, Rakocziut 1-3, pg. 1261 **IT**
Skanska Property Hungary, Rakoczi ut. 1-3, pg. 1261 **IT**

Sluis & Groot Vetomag Termelo es Kereskedo Kft., pg. 985 **IT**
Sodexho Pass Hungaria, Szuglo U.14, pg. 1275 **IT**
Sun Chemical Nyomdafestek Kereskedelmi Es Gyarto KFT, Csokako u. 27, pg. 371 **IT**
Svedala KFT, pg. 1325 **IT**
TA Wirsbo GmbH, Alvinci u Str 9, pg. 1324 **IT**
TA-Wirsbo Kft, Gogol utca 17, pg. 669 **IT**
Takenaka Hungaria kft, Akademia ut 1-3, pg. 1351 **IT**
Tatung Co., pg. 1357 **IT**
Teraglobus KFT, Hungaria Krt. 114, pg. 356 **IT**
3M Hungaria Kft., Vaci UT 110, pg. 1606 **PB**
Toyota Motor Hungary Kft., Szabadkikoto U. 4, pg. 1414 **IT**
UBS Representative Office, Szentkiralyi u. 18, pg. 1441 **IT**
UPM-Kymmene AG, Vertretung Budapest, 11 em, 1101 Kvassay, pg. 1430 **IT**
UPM-Kymmene kft, 11 em, 1101 Kvassay, Jeno ut 1, pg. 1430 **IT**
Unicbank Rt., Vaci Utca 19-21, pg. 1085 **IT**
Utell International-Hungary, C/O Skyline Tickets, KFT, Nagymezo u. 36, pg. 1098 **IT**
VARTA Kereskedelmi es Szolgaltato Kft., Konyves Gyorgy u. 5, pg. 1452 **IT**
Vorwerk Hungaria Kft., pg. 1481 **IT**
WestLB (Hungaria) Rt., Madach Imre Utca 13-14, pg. 1494 **IT**
Willis Corroon Hungary Kft, pg. 1509 **IT**
Wolters Kluwer Central & Eastern Europe, Prielle Kornelia u. 19-35, pg. 1513 **IT**
World Bank, Bank Center - Granite Towers, Szabadsag ter 5-7, pg. 1189 **PV**
Wrigley Hungaria, Ltd., Kiscelli Koy 30, pg. 1781 **PB**
Young & Rubicam Hungary, Szilagyi Erzsebet fasor 22/b, pg. 1199 **PV**
Zeneca Hungary Kft., pg. 1526 **IT**
Zurich Biztosito Rt., Karoly Krt. 11, pg. 1532 **IT**

Debrecen

Hajdutej Tejipari Rt., pg. 991 **IT**
Reemtsma Debreceni Dohanygyar Kft, Vagohid u. 2, pg. 1101 **IT**

Eger

Mecman Eger Kft., pg. 839 **IT**

Gyor

Audi Hungaria Motor Kft., pg. 1473 **IT**
EGAZ, Puskas Trvadar Ut. 35, pg. 541 **IT**
Ziegelwerke Gleinstatten Csorna-Beled Ceserepgyarto Rt., Turr Istvan ut 5, pg. 1092 **IT**

Hodmezovasarhely

Alucon Kft., pg. 1061 **IT**

Kecskemet

Knorr-Bremse Ungarn GmbH, Szegedi ut 49, pg. 738 **IT**
PKL Hungaria KFT, Arpad krt. 4, pg. 1156 **IT**

Komarom

Amstel Brewery Hungary Inc., Tuzolto U. 2., pg. 608 **IT**

Kornye

STILL Kft., pg. 811 **IT**

Mezokovacshaza

Dotto Mag Mezogazdasagi es Kereskedelmi Kft., Arpad Utca 20, pg. 91 **IT**

Mor

ESAB-Csepel Kft, Velegi ut 2, pg. 282 **IT**

Postafiok

Bundy Kft, Ipari ut 1, 5123 Jaszarokszallas, pg. 1342 **IT**

Repcelak

Linde Gas Ungarn AG, pg. 811 **IT**

Szazhalombatta

Montivo Kft, Olimpia U. 3, pg. 660 **IT**

Szeged

DEGAZ, Pulcz Ut. 44, pg. 541 **IT**

Szekesfehervar

Makita Kft., Seregelyesi ut 96, pg. 832 **IT**

Szentgotthard

General Motors Hungary (Manufacturing) Ltd., Haris dulo ut, pg. 722 **PB**

PB - *U.S. Public Companies Volume*
PV - *U.S. Private Companies Volume*
IT - *International Public & Private Companies Volume*

1648

Geographic Index-Non U.S.

Szombathely

Packard Electric Vas Kft, Zanati ut, pg. 723   **PB**

Vac

Duna-Drava Cement-es Meszmuvek Kft., Kohidpart dulo 2, pg. 605   **IT**

Vaciut

G.E. Tungstram Co., 11-1340 Budapeat IV, pg. 713   **PB**

Vaja

Continental Femcsomagolo Magyarorszag Kft., pg. 1207   **IT**
White Cap Magyarorszag Kft., pg. 1207   **IT**

Veszprem

Bramac Kft, Brusznyai Arpad U.24, pg. 1092   **IT**
Jotun Polymer Hungary Kft., pg. 715   **IT**
Schiedel Kemenygyar Kft., Kisto ut 12, pg. 1092   **IT**

ICELAND

Akranes

Icelandic Alloys, Grundartangi, Skilmannahreppur, pg. 448   **IT**
Mjolnir Wholesalers Ltd., pg. 966   **IT**

Hafnarfjordhur

ISAL Icelandic Aluminium Co. Ltd., pg. 68   **IT**

Novara

MEMC Electronic Materials, S.p.A., pg. 1456   **IT**

Reykjavik

Digital Equipment (Iceland), Ortolvutaekni ehf, pg. 508   **PB**
Eikin Ltd., Eftasund 10, pg. 966   **IT**
Fjarfestingarfelagid Skandia HF, Laugavegur 170, pg. 1257   **IT**
Hedinn Schindler Lyftur hf., pg. 1205   **IT**
Hewlett-Packard Iceland, Holdabakka 9, pg. 820   **PB**
ISAGA H.F., pg. 14   **IT**
ISS pjonustan hf., Stakkholti 4, pg. 657   **IT**
ICELANDAIR, Reykjavik Airport, pg. 658   **IT**
Johan Ronning HF, Sundaborg 15, pg. 1368   **IT**
Kvaerner Eureka Islandi, pg. 767   **IT**
LANDSVIRKJUN - THE NATIONAL POWER CO., Haaleitisbraut 68, pg. 801   **IT**
Sundagardar Ltd., Sundagardar 10, pg. 966   **IT**
Vatryggingarfelagid Skandia HF, Laugavegur 170, pg. 1258   **IT**

INDIA

Ahmedabad

Amol Dicalite Ltd., pg. 903   **PV**
Blue Star Ltd., B.D. Patel House, Near Sardar Patel Colony, pg. 816   **PB**
Presstech Controls Ltd., 211 Sampada, pg. 790   **PB**
TLT-Engineering India Pvt. Ltd., 64, G.I.D.C. Industrial Estate Vatva, pg. 401   **IT**

Ambarnath

Albright, Moraji & Pandit Ltd., MIDC Industrial Estate, pg. 50   **IT**

Ballabgarh

Woodward Governor India Pvt. Ltd., 23/6 Mathura Rd., pg. 1777   **PB**

Bandra

Imation India Representative Office, Mumbai, 201 Kakad Bhavan, 30th Rd. Opp Gaeity-Galaxy Cinema, pg. 870   **PB**

Bangalore

AMP India Private Limited, pg. 9   **PB**
Allen-Bradley India Limited, 204 & 205 2nd Floor,s, Parvati Plaza, pg. 1398   **PB**
ASEA Limited, pg. 8   **IT**
Astra-IDL Ltd., pg. 93   **IT**
Autodesk India, 206 Raheja Plaza, 17, Commissariat Rd., pg. 149   **PB**
BPL Sanyo Limited, 14 Church St., pg. 1191   **IT**
BetzDearborn India, Pvt., Ltd., 5th Floor Vayudhooth Chambers, Mahatma Gandhi Road, pg. 227   **PB**
Bicron Products Private Limited, SB Billimoria Co, 70/3 Miller Road, pg. 1174   **IT**
Birla 3M Ltd., Jubilee Bldg., 45 Museum Rd., pg. 1606   **PB**
Blue Star Ltd., 11 Magarath Rd., pg. 816   **PB**

Bowthorpe Thermometrics (India) Pvt. Ltd., 314 Raheja Arcade, pg. 208   **IT**
Ciba Vision, 210 Raheja Chambers, 12 Museum Road, pg. 982   **IT**
Dell Asia Pacific Sdn., India Liaison Office, No. 77, 1st & 2nd Floor, pg. 495   **IT**
Dentsply India, 7th Main, 4th Cross, pg. 499   **PB**
Deutsche Babcock Balcke-Durr Ltd., K.S.C.M.F., Bldg II, 2nd Fl., No. 8, Cunningham Road, pg. 401   **IT**
Digital Equipment (India) Ltd., Digital Park, 92 Industrial Suburb, II Stage, pg. 508   **PB**
Eskayef Ltd., Post Box No. 2, pg. 1265   **IT**
Fanuc GE Automation India Limited, Bo. 41 Electronics City, Keonics, pg. 478   **IT**
Fanuc GE Automation India Limited, Bo. 41 Electronics City, Keonics, pg. 714   **IT**
Fidelio India Private Ltd., 60, 4th Main, Domlur 2nd Stage, pg. 1106   **PB**
Fidelio STP, 83 Brigade Road, pg. 1106   **PB**
Georg Fischer Disa Ltd., 40/1A Basappa Complex, pg. 489   **IT**
Givaudan-Roure (India) PVT LTD., pg. 1120   **IT**
Hewlett-Packard India Pvt. Ltd., 29 Cunningham Rd., pg. 820   **PB**
Hinditron Tektronix Instruments Ltd.-Bangalore, pg. 1568   **PB**
Imation India Representative Office, Bangalore, 138 Raheja Arcade, pg. 870   **PB**
India Photographic Company Limited, 16 Saderamangala Industrial Area, pg. 552   **PB**
Indo Nissin Foods Ltd., Ranka Chambers 4th Fl., 31 Cunningham Rd., pg. 950   **IT**
Kanthal India Ltd., pg. 724   **IT**
Keithley Instruments India, Flat 2B, Wilocrissa, 14, Rest House Crescent, pg. 947   **PB**
Lucent Technologies Switching Systems (India) Ltd., Shubharam Complex, 144 M.G. Road, pg. 1019   **PB**
MAA Communications Bozell, MAA House, 6 Service Rd., pg. 1642   **IT**
Mitsui & Co., Ltd., No. 21/2B, Mahatma Gandhi Road, pg. 881   **PB**
Molex India Ltd., Plot #6A, Sadaramangala Industrial Area, pg. 1122   **PB**
Moog Controls Private Ltd., Poot 1,2,3, pg. 1128   **PB**
Motor Industries Co. Ltd., Hosur Road, pg. 206   **IT**
Motorola India Electronics Private Limited, No. 1, St. Mark's Road, pg. 1139   **PB**
Motorola Private Limited, 108 Gavipuram Guttahhalli, pg. 1140   **IT**
Novo Nordisk A/S, 101, 1st Floor, Shah Sultan, Cunningham Road, pg. 989   **IT**
Novo Nordisk (India) Pvt Ltd, Landmark 5th Floor, 21/15 M G Road, pg. 988   **IT**
PSI Data Systems Ltd., Shrutaa Complex, 19 Primrose Rd., pg. 316   **IT**
Rediffusion-Dentsu, Young & Rubicam (Bangalore), Swarnagiri 140, 2nd Main, 2nd Cross, pg. 326   **PV**
Rockwell International Overseas Corporation, 13E KIADB Industrial Area, pg. 1401   **IT**
Sealed Air (S) Pte. Ltd., 4/1 (122), Industrial Suburb, Chord Road, pg. 1451   **PB**
Seat Metal Components of India Pvt. Ltd., S-421 Manijal Center, South Block, pg. 193   **IT**
Svedala India (Bangalore), pg. 1324   **IT**
T B Wood's Enertec Limited, 14/15 Electronics City, Hosur Road, pg. 1562   **PB**
TVS BERG Ltd., 405, Prestige Meridian-I, 29, M G Rd., pg. 213   **PB**
Tekelec-India Pvt. Ltd., 3J 7th C Main, 3rd Cross, 3rd Block, 560-034, pg. 1566   **IT**
Tektronix Engineering Development (India) Private Limited, 11/5 Hays Road, pg. 1567   **PB**
Webb India Ltd., Khaleel Plaza, 32/1 RV Rd., pg. 1157   **PV**
Widaroc (India) Ltd., pg. 510   **IT**
Widia (India) Ltd., pg. 510   **IT**
Wipro-Acer Limited, pg. 22   **IT**
WIPRO Information Technology Limited, 88 Mahatma Gandhi Rd., pg. 1032   **PB**

Baroda

Blue Star Ltd., Kalyan, 19 Vishwas Colony, pg. 816   **PB**
Bundy India Ltd., 2 GIDC Estate, Makarpura, pg. 1341   **IT**
Keystone Valve (India) PVT. Ltd., 302-A Ivory Terrace, R.C. Dutt Road, pg. 1650   **PB**
Medtronic International, Ltd., A 919/2, G.I.D.C. Makarpura, pg. 1083   **PB**

Bhiwani

Hindustan Gum & Chemicals Ltd., Birla Colony, pg. 1113   **IT**

Bhubaneshwar

Mitsui & Co., Ltd., Plot No. 53, Saheed Nagar, pg. 881   **IT**

Bilaspur

South Eastern Coalfields Limited, Seepat Rd., pg. 299   **IT**

Burdwan

Eastern Coalfields Limited, Sanctoria, pg. 298   **IT**

Calcutta

ANZ Grindlays Bank plc Eastern India, 19 Netaji Subhas Rd., pg. 98   **IT**

Allen-Bradley India Limited, 3rd Floor, 3E, Shivam Chambers, 53 Syed Amir Ali Avenue, pg. 1398   **PB**
Arora-Matthey Limited, 166 Netaji Subhas, Chandra Bose Rd., pg. 714   **IT**
Assam Carbon Products Limited, Everest House, pg. 891   **IT**
BOC India Ltd., Oxygen House, P43 Tarkala Rd., pg. 122   **IT**
Belliss & Morcom India, Six Little Ruffle St., pg. 1065   **IT**
Blue Star Ltd., 7 Hare St., pg. 816   **PB**
Caristrap India, 31 Dalhousie Sq. Hongkong Hse., pg. 272   **IT**
Cemindia Company Limited, Anar Chambers, 5 Chowringhee Approach, pg. 774   **IT**
COAL INDIA LIMITED, 10, Netaji Subhas Rd., pg. 298   **IT**
Deutsche Babcock Limited, Four Mangoe Lane Surendra, Mohan Ghosh Sarani, pg. 401   **IT**
ESAB India Ltd., Oxygen House, P43, Taratala Rd., pg. 282   **IT**
Flender Macneill Gears Ltd., 34, Diamond Harbour Rd., pg. 401   **IT**
HCL Ltd., 45 Jhowtalla Rd., pg. 817   **PB**
Hewlett-Packard India Pvt. Ltd., DBS Executive Centre, 8 Acharya J.S. Bose Rd., pg. 820   **PB**
Hinditron Tektronix Instruments Ltd.-Calcutta, pg. 1568   **PB**
Hindustan CIBA-GEIGY Limited, Vardhan Building,4th Floor, 25 A Camac Street, pg. 982   **IT**
India Photographic Company Limited, 115 Park St., pg. 552   **PB**
Indian Aluminium Co. Ltd., P.O. Box 361, pg. 51   **IT**
Infar (India) Ltd., Saturday Club Bldg., 7 Wood St., pg. 45   **IT**
Axel Johnson & Co. (India) Ltd., 10 Princep Street, pg. 711   **IT**
MSA India Limited, P-25, Transport Depot Road, pg. 1115   **PB**
Metal Box India Limited, P.O. Box 2123, pg. 267   **IT**
Mitsui & Co., Ltd., 7th Fl., Poddar Centre, 50 Chowringhee R, pg. 881   **PB**
Nalco Chemicals India Limited, pg. 1150   **IT**
Oxford University Press of Calcutta, Elgin Road, 3rd Floor, 5 Lala Lajput Rai Sarani, pg. 1019   **IT**
Quaker Chemical India Ltd., 7B, Pretoria Street, pg. 1346   **PB**
Rediffusion-Dentsu, Young & Rubicam (Calcutta), 45 Jhowtalla Road, pg. 326   **PV**
Saha Woodall-Duckham (Private) Limited, Barick Bhawan 3rd. Fl., pg. 472   **IT**
Svedala India (Calcutta), pg. 1324   **IT**
Tega India Ltd, Unit House, 3rd & 4th Fl., P.40 B-Block, New Alipore, pg. 1324   **IT**
VXL Landis & Staefa Ltd., P.O. Jaka, pg. 801   **IT**
Wesalem Company, 1/2 Allenby Road, pg. 962   **PV**

Channo

Pepsi Foods Private Limited, pg. 1277   **PB**

Chennai

Citizen Watches (India) Ltd., 3H, Century Plaza, 560, Anna Salai, Teynampet, pg. 294   **IT**

Cochin

AMP Tools (India) Pvt. Ltd., pg. 9   **PB**
AVT-McCormick Ingredients, pg. 1067   **PB**
Accelerated Freeze Drying Co., Ltd., Amalgam House, Bristow Rd. Willingdon Island, pg. 950   **IT**
Kancor Flavours and Extracts Limited, Bazar Road, pg. 1067   **PB**
O/E/N India Ltd., Vyttila, P. B. No. 2 Cochin-682-019, pg. 1209   **PB**

Coimbatore

Lakshmi Machine Works Ltd., pg. 1117   **IT**

Dhaka

Organon (Bangladesh) Ltd., Alico Bldg., 2nd Fl., 18/20 Motijheel, pg. 45   **IT**

Dhanbad

Bharat Coking Coal Limited, Koyla Bhawan, pg. 298   **IT**

Faridabad

Knorr-Bremse Rail Systems India Pvt. Ltd., 14-6, Mathura Road, pg. 738   **IT**
Taylor Instrument Company (India) Ltd., 14 Mathura Rd., P.O. Amarnagar, pg. 6   **IT**

Ghaziabad

Allen-Bradley India Limited, C-11 Industrial Area, Site 4, pg. 1398   **PB**
Showpla (Delhi) Private Limited, B-135 & 206 Phase-II, pg. 1237   **IT**

Goa

Hindustan CIBA-GEIGY Limited, pg. 982   **IT**
Mitsui & Co., Ltd., 1st Fl. Aleluia Menezes House, Altinho, pg. 882   **IT**
Structural India Private, Limited, Verna Industrial Park, Pitase II, pg. 593   **PB**

PB - U.S. Public Companies Volume
PV - U.S. Private Companies Volume
IT - International Public & Private Companies Volume

Svedala India (Goa), pg. 1324   IT

Gujarat

Battenfeld India Ltd., Plot NO. 107-108 GIDC Kerala, Near Balva, pg. 825   IT

Hubli

Kirloskar Warner Swasey Ltd., c/o Mysore Kirloskar Ltd., Gokul Rd., pg. 1389   IT

Hyderabad

Allen-Bradley India Limited, Second Floor, Raj Bhavan Road,Somajiguda, pg. 1398   PB
Hewlett-Packard India Pvt. Ltd., 5-9-13 Taramandal Complex, 9th Fl. Saifabad, pg. 820   PB
ITW Signode India Limited, Lulla Centre, 5 S.P. Rd., pg. 869   IT
Intergraph (India) Private Ltd., 1-8-446 & 447, Begumpet, 500016, pg. 892   PB
Mitsui & Co., Ltd., 11-4-657-2/B, Lakdi-Ka-Pul, 1st. Fl., pg. 881   IT
Orient Longman Ltd., 5-9-41/1 Basheer Bagh, pg. 1026   IT
Voith India Private Ltd., pg. 1473   IT

Indore

Frigoscandia Winner Food Process Systems Pvt Ltd, Shreesh Chambers, 3rd Fl., 25/1 Yeshwant Niwas Rd., pg. 607   PB

Jaipur

BGE-NH 8 Project, Shy Am Colony Ward 12, pg. 823   IT

Jamshedpur

Tata Timken Limited, Bara, Agrico, pg. 1617   PB
Tata-Yodogawa Ltd., 3rd Floor, Tisco General Office Bldg., pg. 949   IT

Janakpur

Pioneer Biogene, Pvt. Ltd., 401/402 Suneja Towers, pg. 1299   PB

Jayanagar

Polyfluoro Private Limited, Ajay, 3rd Main Road, 6th Block, pg. 1175   IT

Kasarwadi

Moore Controls Pvt. Limited, Bombay-Poona Rd., pg. 1128   PB

Kerala

AKAY Flavours & Aromatics Ltd., No. 29A, Panampilly Nagar, pg. 288   IT

Kilpauk

Axles India Limited, 84 New Avadi Rd., pg. 558   PB

Madras

ANZ Grindlays Bank plc Southern India, 19 Rajaji Salai, pg. 99   IT
Blue Star Ltd., 133 Kodambakkam High Rd., pg. 816   PB
Circle Freight International India Pvt. Ltd., 2A First Floor, Wellington Estate, pg. 372   PB
Eurotherm India Limited, 152 Developed Plots Estate, pg. 466   IT
Fuller-K.C.P. Limited, Ramakrishna Building, No. 2, Bictoria Crescent, pg. 475   IT
Gambro India, Crown Court Complex II Fl., pg. 667   IT
HCL Ltd., 50-B Greams Rd., Murugesa Naiker Office Complex, pg. 817   IT
Hewlett-Packard India Pvt. Ltd., DBS Executive Ctr., 31-A Cathedral Garden Rd., pg. 820   PB
Hinditron Tektronix Instruments Ltd.-Madras, pg. 1568   PB
Hindustan CIBA-GEIGY Limited, Swathi Court, Type 4, Ground Floor, South Block, pg. 982   IT
Hindustan Powerplus Limited, Wellington Estate, 24 Commander-in-Chief Rd., 600105, pg. 316   IT
IDEA International Development and Engineering Associates Ltd., 4-5th Floor, Apex Plaza, 3, Nungambakkam High Road, pg. 401   IT
India Photographic Company Limited, Vijaya-Vauhini Complex, Vadapalani, Arcot Rd., pg. 552   PB
John Crane Engineered Sealing Systems Ltd., Post Box No. 5091, 1/173 Old Mahabalipuram Road, pg. 1339   IT
KONE Elevator India Ltd., 50 Vanagaram Road, pg. 748   IT
Mitsui & Co., Ltd., 2nd Floor, Arjay Apex Center, 24 College Rd., pg. 881   IT
Oxford University Press in Madras, Oxford House, Anna Salai, pg. 1019   IT
Pharmacia & Upjohn Biotech Far East Ltd., 3A, 1st Floor, Palani Towers, pg. 1047   IT
Redifussion-Dentsu, Young & Rubicam (Madras), 3A, Chaitanya Building, 12A, Khader Nawaz Road, pg. 326   PV

Skycell Communications Private Limited, Tarapore Towers, 826-827 Mount Rd., pg. 209   PB
Square D Software Limited, G R Complex, 407-408 Mount Rd., pg. 1043   PB
Zeneca ICI Agrochemicals, 17 Central Avenue, pg. 1526   IT

Madurai

TVS Cherry Private Limited, 7B, West Veli Street, pg. 346   PB

Mangalore

Svedala India (Mangalore), pg. 1324   IT

Mumbai

ACC-Babcock Ltd., Express Towers, 18th Fl., Nariman Point, pg. 474   IT
ANZ Grindlays Bank plc South Asia Headquarters, 90 Mahatma Gandhi Road, pg. 99   IT
ANZ Grindlays Bank plc Western India, 90 Mahatma Gandhi Road, pg. 99   IT
AIR INDIA, Air India Building, pg. 37   IT
Alfa-Laval India Ltd, P.O. Box 735, pg. 1380   IT
Algemene Bank Nederland, 14, Veer Nariman Rd., pg. 11   IT
Allen-Bradley India Limited, C-8 & 9 Minoo Minar, Veera Desai Road, Andheri West, pg. 1398   PB
Arms Communications P. Ltd., Blaze Business Centre, 134, Nagindas Master Rd., pg. 1642   PB
Arya Offshore Services Pvt Ltd., c/o The Ritz Hotel, Suites 202-205, Jarnshedji Tata Road, pg. 731   IT
Asahi Bank Bombay Representative Office, Room 1934, the Oberoi Towers, Narimon Point, pg. 83   IT
BASF India Ltd., Rhone-Poulenc House, Sudam Kalu Ahire Marg., pg. 106   IT
BHA Group International Pvt. Ltd., pg. 161   PB
BHF-Bank Representative Office, 107, Maker Chambers III, 10th Floor, 223 Nariman Point, pg. 120   IT
Ballast Nedam Dredging, Runwal Chambers, 1st Floor, 1st Road, pg. 134   IT
Balmer Lawrie-Fuchs Limited, Ballard Estate, 5, J.N. Heredia Marg, pg. 518   IT
Balmer Lawrie - Van Leer Ltd., pg. 1146   IT
Banca Nazionale del Lavoro, 67 Maker Chambers VI, 6th fl., pg. 137   IT
The Bank of New York, Express Towers, 13th Floor, pg. 179   PB
Bankers Trust New York Corporation, 702 Dalamal Hse., Plot 206 Nairman Point, pg. 186   PB
Barclays Bank PLC, pg. 165   IT
Baring Asset Management (India), 15th Floor, pg. 648   IT
Battenfeld India Ltd., 105, Trade Corner, pg. 825   IT
Bayer (India) Ltd., Pob. 1436, pg. 174   IT
Bharat Bijlee Ltd., pg. 1205   IT
BHARAT PETROLEUM CORPORATION LTD., 4 & 6 Currimbhoy Road, 400 038, pg. 194   IT
Birla Kennametal Ltd., Dalamal House, Ust Floor, 206 Nariman Point, pg. 951   PB
Blue Star Ltd., Unit 1, Probhadevi Industrial Estate, pg. 816   PB
Blue Star Ltd., Sahas, 414/2 Vir Savarkar Marg, pg. 816   PB
The Bookpoint (India) Pvt. Ltd., R. Kamani Marg, Ballard Estate, pg. 1026   IT
Burgmann India Pvt. Ltd, A.K. Industrial Estate, Madina Manzil Compound, pg. 234   IT
CCF Bombay, Harchandrai House, 6th Fl., 81 Queens Road, pg. 343   IT
CRB Daewoo Securities Ltd., 116, 11th Floor, Maker Chamber III, pg. 359   IT
Cambrex-India, Stanrose House, 2nd Fl. Appasaheb, Marathe Marg, pg. 297   PB
Cemindia Company Limited, Apeejay House, Dinshaw Vachha Rd., pg. 774   IT
Chaitra Leo Burnett Private Ltd., 9/11, N.S. Patkar Marg., Ardeshir B. Godrej Chowk, pg. 184   PV
The Chase Manhattan Bank, N.A., South Asia Management, New India Assurance Bldg., pg. 340   PB
Cho Hung Bank, Mumbai Branch, 63 Nariman Bharan, 6th Floor, pg. 288   IT
CIBA Pharma Purchase, Pattke Bapurao Marg, Falklands Bridge, Diana Cinema Lane, pg. 981   IT
Colgate-Palmolive (India) Ltd., 3 Dinshaw Vachha Rd., pg. 398   PB
Commerzbank AG-Mambai (Bombay), 12B, Free Press House, 13th Fl, 215, Free Press Journal Rd., pg. 311   IT
Corn Products Co. (India) Ltd., Shree Niwas House, H. Somani Marg, pg. 224   PB
Creditcapital Finance Corp., Ltd., Merchant Bankers, Allahabad Bldg., pg. 1440   IT
Cyanamid India Ltd., pg. 81   PB
DG Bank-Mumbai, 7th Floor, Unit # 3, Centre 1, World Trade, pg. 352   IT
Dai-Ichi Kangyo Bank, Ltd.-Bombay, 11/13 Botawala Bldg., 2nd Fl., pg. 361   IT
Det Norske Veritas, 96/98, 9th Fl., Maker Tower F, Cuffe Parade, pg. 398   IT
Deutsche Bank AG (Bombay), Post Bag 9995, Tulsiani Chambers, pg. 404   IT
Dinol-Shroff (India) Pvt. Ltd., Execel Estate, SV Rd., Goreagon (West), pg. 982   IT
Dresdner Bank AG, 126, 12th Fl., Maker Chambers VI, pg. 419   IT
Duchem Laboratories Limited, Express Towers, Nariman Point, pg. 1282   PB

Dun & Bradstreet (India) Pvt. Ltd., ICC Chambers, Saki Vihar Road, pg. 536   PB
ESAB India Ltd., Shivsagar Estate, G.Block, Poonam Chambers, N., pg. 282   IT
Elkem Metallurgy, 66/67 Mahavir Ctr., pg. 447   IT
Enterprise Nexus Communications, 367, Sane Guruji Mosq., pg. 678   PV
EURO RSCG-Bombay, CitiTower, 2nd Fl., 61 Dr. S. Rao Rd., Parel, pg. 602   PV
Georg Fischer Trenton Ltd., 401 Kakad Chambers, 123, Dr. Annie Besant Road, Worli, pg. 490   IT
Fuji Bank, Mumbai Branch, Maker Chamber III, 1st Floor, Jamnalal Bajaj Road, Nariman Point, pg. 520   IT
Generale Bank, Maker Chambers VI, Office 13, 1st Fl., pg. 547   IT
Godrej Makro PVT Ltd., Godrej Bhavan, 5th Floor, 4a Home Street, Fort, pg. 1155   PB
Goodlass Nerolac Paints Ltd., Ganpatrao Kadam Marg, Lower Parel, pg. 723   IT
Grindwell Norton Ltd., 148 Mahatma Gandhi Rd., pg. 1174   IT
Hanwa Co., Ltd.-Bombay Branch, c/o M.D. Jagat A/5 Kandar Bldg, S. Gokhale Rd. Dadar, pg. 595   IT
Henkel Chemicals (India) Ltd., pg. 614   IT
Herdillia Unimers Ltd., P.O. Box 100, pg. 460   PB
Hewlett-Packard India Pvt. Ltd., Sahas, 414/2 Vir Savarkar Marg, pg. 820   PB
Hewlett-Packard India Pvt. Ltd., Unit 1, B-Wing, Ground Fl., Neelam Centre, pg. 820   PB
Hinditron Tektronix Instruments Ltd.-Bombay, pg. 1568   PB
Hindustan CIBA-GEIGY Limited, pg. 982   IT
Hindustan CIBA-GEIGY Limited, Gangabawadi Road, pg. 982   IT
Hindustan CIBA-GEIGY Limited-Animal Health Division, pg. 982   IT
Hindustan CIBA-GEIGY Limited-Research Centre, Goregaon (East), pg. 982   IT
Hindustan CIBA-GEIGY Limited, pg. 982   IT
Hindustan Lever Ltd., Hindustan Lever House, 165/166, pg. 1437   IT
Humphreys & Glasgow Consultants Private Limited, Gammon House, Savarkar Marg, Prabhadevi, pg. 1587   PB
ICICI Asset Management Company Limited, Shanti Berlin, Walchand, Hirachand Rd., Ballard State, pg. 1130   PB
ICICI Securities & Finance Company Limited, 41/44 Minoo Desai Marg, pg. 1130   PB
ING Barings India Private Equity, 15th Floor, Nariman Bhavan, pg. 650   IT
IRD Mechanalysis (India) Limited, 47/48 Jolly Makers Chambers II, pg. 790   PB
IRD Mechanalysis, Ltd., B10/11, Ansa Industrial Estate, Saki Vihar Rd., pg. 790   PB
Inarco Limited, Advent, 1st. Fl., 12A Foreshore Rd., pg. 132   PB
India Photographic Company Limited, 222 Dr. Dadabhai Naoroji Rd., pg. 552   PB
India Photographic Company Limited, 483 S. Veer Savarker Marg, pg. 552   PB
Indian Oil Blending Limited, Badamia Manor, 3rd Fl., Keshavao Khadye Marg, pg. 673   IT
Indomag Steel Technology Private Ltd., pg. 837   IT
Infrastructure Leasing & Financial Services Limited, Mahindra Towers, 4th Fl., Rd. No. 13, Worli, pg. 1009   IT
Ing-Tech. Engineering Co., D-222/2 MIDC, TTC Industrail Area, pg. 550   IT
Ingersoll-Rand (India) Private Ltd., P.O. Box 9138, pg. 878   PB
Intalcable-India, c/o Taj Mahal Hotel (int. 622), pg. 655   IT
International Distillers India, Phoenix Mills Compound, 3rd fllor, 462 Senapati Bapat Marg, pg. 410   IT
Jardine Fleming India Securities Private Limited, c/o DBS Corporate Club, Raheja Chambers, pg. 494   IT
A. Johnson & Co. (India) Limited., Court Chambers 6th Flr., 35, Sir Vithaldas Thackersay Marg, pg. 711   IT
Johnson & Johnson India, 30 Forjett St., pg. 930   PB
KSB Pumps Limited, Pune (Bombay), pg. 721   IT
Kollmorgen Tandon India, Unit No. 2, SDF 1, SEEPZ, pg. 966   PB
Leema Chemicals & Cosmetics Pvt. Ltd., Express Towers, Nariman Point, pg. 1282   PB
Lubrizol India Limited, Leo House, 4th Fl., 88-C Old Prabhadevi Rd., pg. 1017   PB
Lubrizol India Limited, Thane Belapur Rd., pg. 1017   PB
Madison DMB&B Advertising, Koch House, Ground Fl., Jerbai Wadia Rd., pg. 305   PV
Madison DMB&B Advertising, PVT Ltd., Corp., Fin. & Media Office, Zoroastrian Bldg., Third Fl., pg. 304   PV
Geoffrey Manners and Co., Ltd., Magnet House, Narottam Morarjee Marg, pg. 81   PB
Mitsui & Co., Ltd., 5th Fl., Manek Mahal, 90, Vir Nariman Rd., pg. 881   IT
Monsanto Chemicals of India Limited, Wakefield House, 11 Sprott Rd., Ballard Estate, pg. 1125   PB
Morgan Stanley Bombay, 4/F, Forbes Bldg., Charanjit Rai Marg, pg. 1133   IT
NYK-Bombay, c/o Tata NYK Trans. Sys. Ltd., Badri Mahal 212-219, Dr. D.N. Rd., pg. 942   IT
Nordson India Private Limited, #3, Ground Floor, Maya Apartments, pg. 1189   PB
Novell India, Marwah Bhavan, Sakivihar Rd., Sakinaka, pg. 1204   PB
ORIX Auto Finance (India) Limited, Mahindra Towers, 4th Floor, Dr. G.M. Bhosale Marg, Worli, pg. 1009   IT
Oxford University Press of Bombay, Oxford House, Apollo Bunder, pg. 1019   IT
Parker Hannifin Corporation, 701 Gateway Plaza, Hiranandani Gardens Powai, pg. 1263   PB
Pfizer Limited, Express Towers, Nariman Point, pg. 1282   PB

PB - *U.S. Public Companies Volume*
PV - *U.S. Private Companies Volume*
IT - *International Public & Private Companies Volume*

Procter & Gamble India, Tiecicon House Dr. E. Moses Rd., pg. 1332 **PB**
RZB Bombay, Comtrade Corporate Centre, 5th Floor, Cambatta Bldg. N.W. Wing, pg. 1084 **IT**
Raychem RPG Limited, Ceat Mahal Annexe, 463 Dr. Annie Besant Rd., pg. 1363 **IT**
Rediffusion-Dentsu, Young & Rubicam (Mumbai), Readymoney Terrace, 1st Floor, 167, Dr. Annie Besant Road, pg. 326 **PV**
Rediffusion-DY&R Pvt. Ltd., Sterling Centre, 4th Fl., Dr. Annie Besant Rd., pg. 326 **PV**
Rhone-Poulenc Chemicals (India), Rhone-Poulenc House, S.K. Ahire Marg, pg. 1112 **IT**
Roche Scientific Company (India) Private Ltd., pg. 1122 **IT**
SKF Bearings India Ltd., Hoechst House, Nariman Point, pg. 1158 **IT**
The Sakura Bank - Mumbai Branch, 2-B, Mittal Court 224, Nariman Point, pg. 1179 **IT**
Sakura Capital India, Limited, 21 Mittal Chambers, 228 Nariman Point, pg. 1180 **IT**
Sandoz (India) Ltd., pg. 984 **IT**
Sanpaolo-Bombay Representative Office, 718, Dalamal Towers, 211, Nariman Point, pg. 1229 **IT**
Semcon Electronics Pvt. Ltd., Unit 13 & 16, SDF Bldg. 1, Santa Cruz Electrical Export Pr. ZN, pg. 1107 **IT**
Semiconductor Electronics Ltd., SDF Unit 23, SEEPZ Post Office, pg. 907 **PB**
Sidmark Sales, 146 Dewan Prakash, pg. 458 **IT**
Siemens Ltd., 130 Paudwrang Budhkar Marg Worli, pg. 1247 **IT**
Singapore Tourist Promotion Board - Mumbai, Unit No. 82, 8th Floor, Jolly Maker II, Nariman Point, pg. 1254 **IT**
Speer Communications, Eucharistic Congress, Bldg. III, pg. 1063 **PV**
Standard Chartered Bank, 4th Floor, New Excelsior Bldg., AK Naik Marg, pg. 1294 **IT**
Standard Chartered Bank (India), 4th Fl., New Excelsior Bldg., A.K. Naik Marg, pg. 1295 **IT**
STATE BANK OF INDIA, State Bank of India, International Division, pg. 1297 **IT**
Sulzer India Ltd., pg. 1306 **IT**
The Sumitomo Bank, Ltd.-Mumbai Branch, 15/F Jolly Maker Chamber No.2, 225, Nariman Point, pg. 1309 **IT**
Swiss Bank Corporation, Tulsiani Chambers, West Wing 11 floor, pg. 1330 **IT**
TVS BERG Ltd., 205, Madhava Bldg., Bandra-Kurla Complex, pg. 213 **IT**
Tandem Computers Asia, Ltd., Pharma House, 729/73 BGKher Road, pg. 417 **PB**
Tata Consultancy Services, Air India Bldg., 11th Fl., Nariman Point, pg. 1229 **IT**
Tata Engineering & Locomotive Co. Ltd (TELCO), Bombay House 24, Homi Mody St., pg. 369 **IT**
THE TATA IRON AND STEEL CO. LTD., Bombay House, 24 Homi Mody St., pg. 1356 **IT**
Tata Oil & Mills Company, Bombay House, 24 Homi Mody St., pg. 1437 **IT**
Tektronix (India) Limited, 69/A, L. Jagmohandas Marg., pg. 1568 **PB**
Toshbro Shimadzu Ltd., 198, Jamshedji Tata Rd., pg. 1232 **IT**
Tractor Engineers Limited, pg. 317 **PB**
Trans-India Network Systems Pvt. Ltd., 24 Homi Mody Street, pg. 1019 **PB**
Triton Communications, 202 Karimjee Building, pg. 118 **IT**
UBS Representative Office, 36 Maker Chambers VI, 3/F, pg. 1441 **IT**
Union Bank of Switzerland, 36 Maker Chambers VI, 3rd Floor, pg. 1441 **IT**
Verbatim-India, 141A Mittal Ct., 14th Fl., pg. 872 **PB**
Vickers Systems International Ltd., Akurli Rd., pg. 25 **PB**
Vulcan-Eclipse (PVT) Ltd., 427, Unique Ind. Estate, pg. 361 **PV**
Wander Ltd., pg. 986 **IT**
Weatherford Inc., OM Nivas 26, Tarun Bharat Society, pg. 1750 **PB**
John Wyeth (India) Limited, pg. 82 **PB**

Nagpur

Western Coalfields Limited, Coal Estate, Civil Lines, pg. 299 **IT**

New Delhi

ANZ Grindlays Bank plc Northern India, 'H' Block, Connaught Circus, pg. 99 **IT**
Ahlstrom Machinery, E-2 Saket, pg. 34 **IT**
Allen-Bradley India Limited, A-5, Second Floor, pg. 1398 **IT**
BHP Steel Building Products India, 4th Floor, World Trade Center, Bara Khamba Lane, Connaught Circus, pg. 226 **IT**
Bank of America NT&SA, DCM Bldg., 6th Fl., 16 Barakhamba Rd., pg. 182 **PB**
Banque Paribas-Inde, Le Meridien, West Tower, 7th Floor, pg. 320 **IT**
Bausch & Lomb India Ltd., 89, Hemkunt Chambers, 8th Fl., pg. 195 **PB**
Benckiser (India) Private Ltd., pg. 185 **IT**
Bharat Explosives Limited, 609 Devika Towers, 6, Nehru Place, pg. 1115 **PB**
BI Waverly Pvt. Ltd., 54 Janpath, pg. 1748 **IT**
Blue Star Ltd., 13 Community Center, New Friends Colony, pg. 816 **PB**
Butterworths India, G-2 Vardaan House, 7/28 Mahavir Street, pg. 1095 **IT**
CGG Pan India Ltd., 3rd Fl. C-1, pg. 241 **IT**

DBS-Capital Trust Securities India Pvt. Ltd., Capital Trust House, 47 Community Centre, Friends Colony, pg. 351 **IT**
DMC Toyota Limited, Kanchenjunga Bldg., 1st Fl., 18-Barakhamba Rd., pg. 1413 **IT**
Danzas Freight (India) Pvt. Ltd., Vasant Vihar F 8/5, pg. 382 **IT**
Deutsche Babcock-Borsig Ltd., 28, Kasturba Gandhi Marg, pg. 401 **IT**
Deutsche Bank AG (New Delhi), Tolstoy House, 15-17 Tolstoy Marg, pg. 404 **IT**
Donaldson Filter Systems Pvt. Ltd., B-22 Geetanjali Enclave, pg. 517 **PB**
Dowty Aerospace, A3 Apartment, Qutab Institutional Area, pg. 1337 **PB**
Ericsson India Ltd., Ericsson House, Pushp Vihar, pg. 1367 **IT**
Ericsson Telecommunications Pvt. Ltd., 20 Ericsson House, L.S.C. Madangir, Pushp Vihar, pg. 1368 **IT**
Food Specialties Ltd., pg. 920 **IT**
Goodyear-India Ltd., Godrej Bhavan (Third Floor), Mathura Road, pg. 753 **PB**
HCL Ltd., Bajaj House, 5th Fl., 97 Nehru Pl., pg. 817 **PB**
Hewlett-Packard India Pvt. Ltd., Meridian Commercial Complex, 6th Fl., 8 Windsor Pl., pg. 820 **PB**
Hewlett-Packard Pte. Ltd., B/8 Jangpura-B, Mathara Road, pg. 821 **PB**
Hinditron Tektronix Instruments Ltd., pg. 1568 **PB**
Hindustan CIBA-GEIGY Limited, 201, Palika Bhavan, pg. 982 **IT**
Howe (India) Private Ltd., Howe India House, 81 Nehru Place, pg. 31 **IT**
ICI India Limited, DLF Centre, 5th Fl., pg. 665 **IT**
India Photographic Company Limited, 22-A Jan path, pg. 552 **PB**
India Resident Mission, 37 Golf Links Rd., pg. 89 **IT**
INDIAN OIL CORPORATION LIMITED, Scrte Complex, Core 2, Lodhi Road, pg. 673 **IT**
Indian Shaving Products, Limited, 34, Okhla Industrial Estate, pg. 745 **IT**
International Nickel Services (U.K.) Limited, Rooms 302 & 304, Quatab Hotel, pg. 633 **IT**
Kinetics Technology India Ltd., Sheetla House, 73-74 Nehru Pl., pg. 837 **IT**
Knorrbrakes Ltd., 29, Community Centre, pg. 738 **IT**
LM Ericsson International AB India, New Delhi Liaison Office, Ericsson House, Pushp Vihar, pg. 1368 **IT**
Lucent Technologies India Pvt. Ltd., Mohan Dev House 13, Tolstoy Marg, pg. 1019 **IT**
Maadhyam Advertising Pvt. Ltd., Maadhyam House, pg. 304 **PV**
MAX-GB Ltd., Deviha Tower, 6, pg. 1143 **PV**
Media Transasia Pvt. Ltd., K-35 Green Park, pg. 570 **PV**
Microsoft Corporation (India) Private Limited, pg. 1108 **PV**
Mitsui & Co., Ltd., 6th Fl., Hindustan Times House, 18-20 Ka, pg. 881 **IT**
Modi Olivetti Ltd., Punj Lloyd House, 17-18 Nehru Pl., pg. 1003 **IT**
Motorola Singapore Pte. Ltd., Meridien Commercial Towers, 8th Fl., pg. 1140 **PB**
Nestle India Ltd., pg. 921 **PB**
New Delhi Representative Office, World Trade Centre, 5th Fl., Barakhamba Lane, pg. 520 **IT**
Nokia Mobile Phones (SEA) Pte. Ltd. (India) Liason Office, 14th Floor, International Trade Tower, Block E, pg. 952 **IT**
Nokia Telecommunications, 14th Floor, International Trade Tower, Block E, pg. 953 **IT**
Otto-Burlingtons Mail Order Pvt. Ltd., pg. 1015 **IT**
Owens-Corning (India) Limited, 16 Aradhana Ring Road, P.K. Puram xiii, pg. 1237 **PB**
Oxford University (India), YMCA Library Building, 1st Fl., Jai Singh Rd., pg. 1019 **IT**
Oxford University Press of New Delhi, 2/11 Ansari Rd., Daryaganj, pg. 1019 **IT**
Porritts & Spencer (Asia) Ltd., 308-309 Kanchenjunga, 18 Barakhamba Rd., pg. 1203 **IT**
Prentice-Hall of India Private Ltd., M-97 Connaught Circus, pg. 778 **PV**
Rediffusion-Dentsu, Young & Rubicam (New Delhi), Vashist House, 2nd Fl., 7/2 Kalu Sarai, pg. 326 **PV**
Rieter India Pvt. Ltd., pg. 1117 **IT**
Rockwell International Overseas Corporation, A-5, Kailash Colony, pg. 1401 **IT**
SAE (India) Ltd., 29 & 30 Community Commercial Centre, pg. 3 **IT**
SNC-Lavalin, JA Annexe, 54 Basant Lok, pg. 1162 **IT**
The Sakura Bank - New Delhi Branch, 28 Barakhamba Road, pg. 1179 **IT**
Samcor Glass Limited, Community Center, RFGD Office 50-51, pg. 449 **IT**
Shell Representative Office, 4 Vasant Marg, pg. 1139 **IT**
Standard Chartered Bank, Merchant Banking Division, c/o Hotel Samrat, Apt. 280, 2nd Fl., Chanakyapuri, pg. 1296 **IT**
Sulzer Flovel Hydro Ltd., pg. 1308 **IT**
Svedala India, pg. 1324 **IT**
TCIL BellSouth Ltd., 7th Fl., Mercantile House, 15 Kastruba Ghandi Marg, pg. 209 **IT**
TVS BERG Ltd., 806, Vikram Towers, 15, Rajehra Place, pg. 213 **PB**
Tata McGraw-Hill Publishing Co., Private Limited, 12/4 Asaf Ali Rd., pg. 1072 **PB**
Tefal India Household Appliances Pvt. Ltd., A-10 Green Park, pg. 568 **IT**
Toyota Motor Corporation, New Delhi Representative Office, b/o DCM Toyota Ltd., Kanchenjunga Bldg., 1st Fl., pg. 1413 **PB**
Trikona Services Ltd., Flat No. 2, 11, Aurangzeb Rd., pg. 303 **IT**

Triton Communications, M-26 Commercial Complex, 2nd Fl., Greater Kailash Part II, pg. 118 **IT**
Utell International-India, 1302 Ansal Towers, 38 Nehru Place, pg. 1098 **IT**
Voest-Alpine Ltd., 39, Golf Links, pg. 1472 **IT**
Waeschle Ideal Pvt Ltd., 402 Hemkunt Twr., 98 Nehru Pl., pg. 490 **IT**
Wandel & Goltermann Pvt. Ltd., 16-A Palam Marg, pg. 1486 **IT**
Windmoller & Holscher - Liason Office, 602 Hemkunt Tower, 98 Nehru Place, pg. 1511 **IT**
The World Bank, 70 Lodi Estate, pg. 1189 **PV**
Wrigley India Pvt. Ltd., Jeevan Vihar, pg. 1781 **PB**

Nolda

HVCL Ltd., A-10, 11 Sector III, pg. 818 **PB**
WAGO & Controls (India) Ltd., A-9, Sector 8, pg. 209 **IT**

Pimpri

Krupp Industries India Ltd., pg. 511 **IT**

Pune

Allen-Bradley India Limited, Flat No. D-2, Kaul Building No. 2, pg. 1398 **PB**
Autofield Engineers Private Ltd., 5-B Suchilia Apartments, pg. 469 **PB**
Bajaj Tempo Ltd., pg. 368 **IT**
BE-DELFT Electronics Ltd., El-30 'J' Block, Bhosari Industrial Area, pg. 389 **IT**
Blue Star Ltd., Mahendra Chambers, Thole Patel Rd., pg. 816 **PB**
Century Enka Ltd., pg. 46 **IT**
Dr. Beck & Co. (India) Ltd., Beck House, Damle Path, Off Law College Road, pg. 108 **IT**
FLO-TECH Welding & Cutting Systems Ltd., Block FX-11, Plot No. 71, pg. 283 **IT**
Fleetguard India Ltd., Murlidhar Apts., 129 C/E, pg. 469 **IT**
Hagglunds Hydraulic Drives (India) Pvt. Ltd., 18/4-19/4 Hadapsar Industrial Estate, pg. 670 **IT**
Indo Balzers Coating Ltd., pg. 997 **IT**
Kirloskar Cummins Ltd., Kothrude, pg. 469 **PB**
Kirloskar Ebara Pumps Ltd., 13-A, Karve Rd., pg. 432 **IT**
Kirloskar Electrodyne Ltd., 117, S Block, pg. 739 **IT**
Sandvik Asia Ltd., P.O. Box 40, pg. 1187 **IT**
Sempell Valves Pvt. Ltd., P.O. Box No. 29, Bombay-Pune Road, pg. 401 **IT**
Simpson Industries, Inc., Hodek Engineering Works, Private Limited, Gat. No. 767/769, pg. 1475 **PB**
Sudarshan Chemical Industries Ltd., 162 Wellesley Road, pg. 372 **IT**
Tata Honeywell Ltd., Hadapsar Industrial Estate, 55-A/8 & 9, pg. 835 **PB**
Thermax Fuji Electric Private Ltd., Plot N. 7, D-1 Block, MIDC Industrial Area, pg. 522 **IT**

Ranchi

Central Coalfields Limited, Darbhanga House, pg. 298 **IT**
Central Mine Planning & Design Institute Limited, Gondwana Pl., Kanke Rd., pg. 298 **IT**

Rewa

Biria Ericsson Optical Ltd., Udyog Vihar, pg. 1365 **IT**

Roha

Albright, Moraji & Pandit Ltd., MDC Area, Block 103 & 104, Village Dhatav Tal., pg. 50 **IT**

Sahibabad

SAB Electronic Devices Ltd., 64/2 Site IV. UPSIDC, Industrial Estate, pg. 1369 **IT**

Sambalpur

Mahanadi Coalfields Limited, Bishop's House, pg. 298 **IT**

Secunderabad

Blue Star Ltd., 2-2-47/1108 Bolarum Rd., pg. 816 **PB**
Computer Maintenance Corporation Ltd., 115, Sarojini Bevi Rd., pg. 817 **PB**
HCL Ltd., 92-93 A, Swapnalok Complex, Sarojini Devi Rd., pg. 817 **PB**
Hinditron Tektronix Instruments Ltd.-Secunderabad, pg. 1568 **PB**

Sidhi

Northern Coalfields Limited, P.O. Singrauli Colliery, pg. 299 **IT**

Sirur

Kalyani Sharp India Limited, Gat. No. 686/4, Koregaon Bhima, Tal., pg. 1229 **IT**

Thane

Khimline Pumps Limited, pg. 1305 **IT**

PB - U.S. Public Companies Volume
PV - U.S. Private Companies Volume
IT - International Public & Private Companies Volume

Precision Fasteners Ltd., Works & Marketing Head Office, 15, MIDC Industrial Area, pg. 1420 **PB**

Trivandrum

Blue Star Ltd., T.C. 7/603 Poornima, pg. 816 **PB**

Vadodara

Blue Star Ltd., Ramkrishna Chambers 7th Fl., Productivity Rd., pg. 816 **PB**

Vallabhipur

Eimco Elecon (India) Ltd., pg. 1353 **IT**

Valsad

Cibatul Ltd., Atul, pg. 981 **IT**

Vimanapura

Britannia Industries Ltd., Britannia Gardens, Airport Rd., pg. 380 **IT**

Visakhapatnam

Svedala India (Visakhapatnam), pg. 1324 **IT**

INDONESIA

Bali

Japan Airlines Company, Ltd., Ngurah Rai Airport, pg. 701 **IT**

Balikpapan

PT Arutmin Indonesia, BRI Bldg., 3rd. Floor, J1 Jend Sudirman No. 28, pg. 224 **IT**
PT Liebherr Indonesia Perkasa, JL Mulawarman No. 17, RT-19, RW-04, Kel. Manggar, pg. 808 **IT**

Bandung

P.T. Carlorindo Utama, jalan Banten No 1, pg. 1030 **IT**
PT. Fanuc Indonesia, Jl. Jend Gatot Subroto, pg. 478 **IT**
NSI (Nusantara Systems International Inc.), Jl. Pajajaran 154, pg. 1032 **PB**
P.T. Nowl Knitting Indonesia, Jalan Raya Bandung-Garut, Km., 23, Desa Linggar, Kecamatan Rancaekek, pg. 1350 **IT**
P.T. Tanabe-Abadi-Headquarters, Jl. Gedebage, Ujungberung, pg. 1354 **IT**

Bekasi

P.T. Burgmann Indonesia, Jl. Jababeka Blok J6-E, pg. 233 **IT**
PT Hanken Indonesia, Jalan Jababeka XII, Cikarang Industrial Estate, pg. 745 **IT**
PT Hokuriku United Forging Industries, Jalan Jababeka XI-H-11, Cikarang Industrial Estate, pg. 745 **IT**
PT Katsushiro Indonesia, Cikarang Industrial Estate, pg. 745 **IT**
P.T. Mazda Indonesia Manufacturing, JL. Diponegoro km 38, 2, Tambun, pg. 849 **IT**
P.T. NSK Bearings Manufacturing (Indonesia), Blok M-4, Kawasan Berikat, MM2100 Industrial Town, pg. 903 **IT**
PT OMRON Manufacturing of Indonesia, Ejip Industrial Park Plot 5C, pg. 1006 **IT**
PT Showpla Indo, Blk 1, 3-4 Kawasan Industri, pg. 1237 **IT**

Bogor

P.T. Ebara Indonesia, Jl. Raya Jakarta-Bogor km 32, pg. 432 **IT**
P.T. Goodyear Indonesia, pg. 753 **PB**

Buru

P.T. Irian Marine Product Development, Jalan Kemong 1A No. 11A, Kebayo-Ran, pg. 948 **IT**

Cibarusah-Bekosi

P.T. Ferro Mas Dinamika, Jl Raya Cikarang, Ds. Pasir Sari, pg. 619 **PB**

Cikajang

P.T. Nissinmas, Jababeka Industrial Estate, Jl. Jababeka Raya, pg. 950 **IT**

Cilegon

PT BHP Steel Indonesia, Krakatau Industrial Estate, Kav N2-02, J1.Raya Anyer Desa Warna Sari, pg. 227 **IT**
Pt. United Air Products Indonesia, Jl. Raya Merak Km 116, Desa Rawa Arum, pg. 32 **PB**

Jakarta

P.T. AGC Arta Leasing, 10th Fl., Summitmas Tower, pg. 1497 **IT**
PT AMP Panin Life, 2nd Floor, Panin Bank Plaza, pg. 100 **IT**
P.T. ANZ Panin Bank, 17th Floor, BNI Building, Jl. Jend., Sudirman No. 1, pg. 99 **IT**
Adwork! EURO RSCG Partnership, JL. Guntur 48, pg. 602 **IT**
P.T. Agra Monenco, Artha Graha Building, 23rd Floor, pg. 31 **IT**
P.T. Ajinex International, Jl. Laksda Yos Sudarso, 77-78 Sunter, pg. 40 **IT**
P.T. Ajinomoto Indonesia, Jl. Laksda Yos Sudarso 77-78, Sunter, pg. 40 **IT**
Amway Indonesia, Wisma SSK - 3rd Fl., Jl. Daan Mogot Km 11, pg. 70 **PV**
Asahi Bank Jakarta Representative Office, 7th Fl., Menara Cakrawala, Jl. M.H. Thamrin No. 9, pg. 83 **IT**
The Ascott Jakarta/Benchmark Service, The Golden Triangle, 2 Jalan Kebong, pg. 1212 **IT**
Asea Erown Boveri Sakati, 27, Menteng Raya, pg. 3 **IT**
P.T. Aseam Indonesia, Mulia Tower, Ste. 1211, Jl. Jend, Gatot Subroto Kav. 9-11, pg. 362 **IT**
P.T. Asian Development Securities, 21st Fl., JL. Jend Sudirman Kav. 1, pg. 1517 **IT**
P.T. Astra Daihatsu Motor, JL. Gaya Motor III, No. 5, pg. 365 **IT**
Astra Indonesia, P.O. Box 2249, pg. 94 **IT**
P.T. Asuransi Allianz Aken Life, New Summitmas, 20th Floor, pg. 60 **IT**
P.T. Asuransi Allianz Utama Indonesia, New Summitmas, 9th Floor, Jl. Jend Sudirman Kav. 61-62, pg. 60 **IT**
P.T. Asuransi Cigna Indonesia, The Landmark Centre, 9th Fl., Jala Jen Sudirman Kav. 70-A, pg. 363 **PB**
P.T. Asuransi Jiwa Dharmala ManuLife, JL. Pegangsaan Timur No. 1A, pg. 841 **IT**
Asuransi Jiwa Principal Egalita Indonesia, J1. Tanah Abang II No. 50, PT. Asuransi Jiwa Principal Egalita, pg. 886 **PV**
P.T. Asuransi Niaga Cigna Life, Jalan Jerderal Sudirman, Kav. 58, 8th Fl, pg. 363 **PB**
P.T. Asuransi Tokio Marine Indonesia, Wisma Kyoei Prince, 9th & 10th Fl., pg. 1392 **IT**
P.T. BASF Indonesia, P.O. Box 2431, pg. 106 **IT**
BFCE Indonesia, 8th Fl. Wisma Nusantara, 59 Jalan M.H. Thamrin, pg. 161 **IT**
PT BHP Steel Building Products Indonesia, Jalan Rawaterate 1, No 1 Pulogadung Industrial Estate, pg. 226 **IT**
PT BNF Lippo Utama Leasing, Menara Batavia, 20th Floor, Jl. KH Mas Mansyur 126, pg. 164 **IT**
P.T. BOC Gases Indonesia, The Raya Bekasi KM 21, pg. 121 **IT**
P.T. Ballast Indonesia Construction, Griya Ampera, pg. 134 **IT**
PT Bank BNP Lippo Indonesia, Menara Batavia, 20t Floor, Jl. KH Mas Mansyur 126, pg. 164 **IT**
Bank Brussels Lambert - Jakarta Representative Office, Tifa Bldg., 7th Fl., Ste. 701, JLN Kuningan Barat 26, pg. 148 **IT**
PT Bank DBS Buana, Ratu Plaza, Lantai 25, J1 Jend Sudirman No 9, pg. 350 **IT**
P.T. Bank Finconesia, pg. 312 **IT**
P.T. Bank LTCB Central Asia, 9th Foor, Wisma BCA, pg. 816 **IT**
P.T. Bank Merincorp, Plaza Exim, 27th Floor, Jl. Gatot Subroto Kav. 36-38, pg. 1310 **IT**
Bank of America NT&SA, 22/Fl Jakarta Stock Exchange, Bldg., Jl. Jend. Sudirman Kav. 52-53, pg. 182 **PB**
The Bank of New York, Mashill Plaza, #18-09, Jalan Jenderal Sudirman, Kav 25, pg. 179 **PB**
P.T. Bank Sakura Swadharma, 19th Fl., BNI Bldg., Jl Jendral, Sudirman Kav. 1, pg. 1180 **IT**
P.T. Bank Sumitomo Niaga, Summitmas II, 10th Fl., Jl. Jendral Sudirman Kav. 61-62, pg. 1310 **IT**
Bankers Trust New York Corporation, The Landmark Centre, 20th Fl., Ste. 2001, pg. 186 **PB**
Banque Paribas-Indonesie, Borobudur Intercontinental, Jalan Lapangan Banteng Selatan, pg. 320 **IT**
P.T. Barindo Loka Sentra Leasing, Summitmas Tower, 11th Fl., JL Jend, pg. 1391 **IT**
Barclays Bank PLC, pg. 166 **IT**
Battle Mountain Gold (Indonesia), Plaza Aminta, Ste. 601, JL Letjen T.B. Simatupang, pg. 194 **PB**
P.T. Bausch & Lomb Manufacturing, JL Pintu Air 36K-L, pg. 195 **IT**
P.T. Bayer Indonesia, Jl. Raya Cikini 97, pg. 174 **IT**
P.T. Beiersdorf Indonesia, pg. 183 **IT**
P.T. Bereca Hardayaperkasa, Wisma Dharmala Sakti 10th Fl., 32 JL Jendral Sudiman, Kav, pg. 816 **PB**
P.T. Bernadi Utama SK, 121, Jalan Letjen Suprapto, pg. 681 **IT**
P.T. Bridgestone Tire Indonesia, Nusantara Bldg., pg. 214 **IT**
P.T. Bristol-Myers Indonesia, Menara Duta Bldg., Th Hr Rasuna said Kav B9 Kuninggan, pg. 255 **PB**
P.T. Bukaka Fuji Electric, Plaza Bapindo, Menara 1, 24th Fl., pg. 522 **IT**
P.T. Bumi Daya-IBJ Leasing, 27th Fl., Bank Bumi Daya Plaza, Jalan Imam Bonjol 61, pg. 676 **IT**
Burmah Oil Indonesia Limited, Wisma Metropolitan II, 5th Flr., Jalan Jenderal, pg. 235 **IT**
P.T. Burroughs Wellcome Indonesia, pg. 553 **IT**
C-E International, 3rd Fl., Block B3 Setiaburg Bldg. Kuning, pg. 5 **IT**
CCF Jakarta, Wisma Antara 12 01, Jalan Medan Merdeka Selatan 17, pg. 343 **IT**

P.T. CSSL Indonesia, Wisma Dhamala Sakti, 9th Fl., pg. 1043 **PB**
California Energy International, Ltd., Bapindo Center, Bapindo Tower 1, 26th Floor, pg. 292 **PB**
P.T. Caltex Pacific Indonesia, Kotakpos 158, pg. 348 **PB**
P.T. Candra Sari, pg. 975 **IT**
P.T. Central Sari Finance Corporation (CSF), 12A Floor, Wisma BCA, Jalan Jendral Sudirman, pg. 816 **IT**
P.T. Chase Leasing Indonesia, Chase Plaza, 5th Fl., JL Jend Sudirman Kav 21, pg. 339 **IT**
The Chase Manhattan Bank, N.A., Chase Plaza, JL Jend Dudirman Kav 21, pg. 340 **PB**
P.T. CIBA-GEIGY Indonesia, Mampang Plaza, 5th Floor, pg. 977 **IT**
P.T. CIBA-GEIGY Indonesia, pg. 977 **IT**
P.T. Circle Freight International Indonesia, c/o Unipara Express, JL Kyai Caringin Blok A/6, pg. 372 **PB**
P.T. Cita Simas Artha, Gedung Sarinah 11th Floor Jl.M.H., pg. 243 **IT**
P.T. Citraguna Saranatama(CIBA Distributor), Mampang Plaza, 5th Floor, Jl Mampang Prapatan Raya No. 100, pg. 981 **IT**
Commerzbank AG-Jakarta Representative Office, Summitmas 11, 6th Floor, pg. 311 **IT**
Commonwealth Bank-Jakarta, 11th Fl., World Trade Centre, Jalan Jendral Sudirman, pg. 313 **IT**
Commonwealth Indonesia, Aspac Center, 7th Floor, Jl.H.R. Rasuna Said Kav. X-2 No.4, pg. 143 **PB**
Comstream, A Spar Company, WISMA BUDI, J. H.R. Rasuna Said, Kav. C-6, pg. 1288 **PB**
P.T. Coniplant Indonesia, 16th Fl., Wisma Kosgoro, Jl. M.H. Thamrin No. 53, pg. 196 **IT**
P.T. Crown Cork & Seal Indonesia, P.O. Box 3420/JKT, pg. 464 **IT**
CUNA Mutual Group-Indonesia, Jalan Gunung Sahari III, pg. 297 **PV**
P.T. DIC ASTRA Chemicals, Jl. Pulobuaran Raya Blok III, DD, 5-10, Kawasan Industri, pg. 371 **IT**
PT DIC Indonesia, 8th Fl., Bank Perdania Bldg., Jl. Jendral, Sudirman Kav. 40-41, pg. 372 **IT**
P.T. DSM KALTIM Melamine, Wisma Barito Pacific,4th Fl., Tower A, Jl. S. Parman Kav. 62-63, pg. 355 **IT**
Dai-Ichi Kangyo Bank, Ltd.-Jakarta, 6th Fl.,Wisma Rajawali Annex, Jalan Jenderal Sudirman Kav. 35, pg. 361 **IT**
P.T. Dai-Ichi Kangyo Panin Leasing, 6th Floor, Panin Bank Centre, Jl. Jendral Sudirman (Senayan), pg. 362 **IT**
P.T. Dai Nippon Printing Indonesia, Kawasan Industri Pulogadung, Jalan Pulogadung Kaveling II, pg. 363 **IT**
Daihatsu Diesel Mfg. Co., Ltd., 16th Fl., Wisma Antara Bldg., Jl.Medan Merdeka, pg. 364 **IT**
Dainippon Ink & Chemicals, Inc., 8th Fl., Bank Perdania Bldg., Jl. Jendral Sudirman Kav. 40-41, pg. 372 **IT**
Daiwa Bank-Jakarta, 5th Fl., Daiwa Perdania Bank, JL. Jend, Sudirman KAV. 40-41, pg. 373 **IT**
P.T. Daiwa Indonesia Securities, 14th Fl., Summitmas II Bldg., JL Jend Sudirman Kav. 61-62, pg. 375 **IT**
P.T. Daiwa Lippo Leasing Corporation, 5th Fl., Daiwa Perdania Bank, JL. Jend, Sudirman KAV. 40-41, pg. 374 **IT**
P.T. Daiwa Perdania Bank, JL. Jend, Sudirman KAV. 40-41, pg. 374 **IT**
P.T. Danzas Saranaperkasa, Lippo Plaza Suite 1202, Jl. Jend. Sudirman Kav. 25, pg. 382 **IT**
P.T. Darya-Varia Laboratoria, Graha Darya-Varia, 2-4/F, Jl. Melawai Raya No. 93, pg. 487 **IT**
Deminex Indonesia, P.O. Box 3021; Kantor Pos Pusat, pg. 1461 **IT**
P.T. Dentsu Young & Rubicam Indonesia (Jakarta), F15, MidPlaza 2, Jl. Jend., pg. 325 **PV**
Det Norske Veritas, Summarecon Plaza 6th Floor, Jalan Perintis Kemerdekaan 42, pg. 397 **IT**
Deutsche Bank AG (Jakarta), Deutsche Bank Bldg., 80 Jl. Imam Bonjol, pg. 404 **IT**
P.T. Dextam Contractors, 4th Fl., Midplaza Bldg., Jl. Jend Sudirman Kav. 10-11, pg. 1233 **IT**
Dharmala Manulife, 2-7th Floor, Jl. Pegaangsaan Timur No. 1A, pg. 841 **IT**
PT Digital Astra Nusantara, Standard Chartered Bank Bldg., Atria Square 21st Floor, pg. 507 **PB**
P.T. Dimet Indonesia, Jl. 129 **IT**
P.T. Dino Indonesia Industrial Ltd., Jl. M.T. Haryono 31-32, pg. 717 **IT**
PT Doulton Multifortuna, Wisma Bisnis, 11th Floor, Jl Let Jend S Parman Kav 12, pg. 1135 **IT**
Dresdner Bank AG, The Landmark Centre, 19th Fl., Jl. Jend. Sudirman, pg. 419 **IT**
Dumez-GTM Jakarta, Suite 502 Mulia Center, Jalan H.R. Rasuna Said KAV, pg. 823 **IT**
P.T. Dunkin do Lestari, pg. 64 **IT**
P.T. Eastern Polymer, J1. Cilincing Raya, Tanjung Priok, pg. 1394 **IT**
P.T. Easterntex, 3rd Floor, Summitmas Tower II, 61-62, Jalan Jenderal Sudirman, pg. 1400 **IT**
Edison Mission Energy International B.V., Gedung BRI II, Suite 2107, pg. 564 **PB**
Electricite de France, Wijaya Grand Center, Blok E 16-17, pg. 438 **IT**
Enso-Eurocan South East Asia Pte. Ltd., pg. 457 **IT**
Erindo Utama P.T., Wisma Anugraha, Jalan Taman, Kemang No 32 B, pg. 1368 **IT**
PT Esabindo Pratama, Jl. Rawagelam I/2, pg. 282 **IT**
P.T. Essence Indonesia, 74, Jalan Oto Iskandardinata, pg. 899 **PB**
The Export-Import Bank of Korea, Rm. 301, Korea Center Bldg., pg. 467 **IT**
Fidelio Indonesia, Wisma Aria 3rd Fl., Jalan HOS Cokroaminoto 81, pg. 1106 **PB**
Fluor Daniel Eastern, Inc., Plaza 89, Ste. 1101, JL. H.R. Rasuna Said Kav. x-7, No.6, pg. 660 **PB**
P.T. Food Specialties Indonesia, pg. 920 **IT**

PB - *U.S. Public Companies Volume*
PV - *U.S. Private Companies Volume*
IT - *International Public & Private Companies Volume*

1652

Geographic Index-Non U.S.

P.T. Fuji Bank International Indonesia, 24th Floor, BII Plaza Tower II, Jalan, M.H. Thamrin No. 51, pg. 521 IT
P.T. Fuji Dharma Electric, JL. Rawagelam 1/10, pg. 522 IT
Generale Bank, Panin Bank Centre, 9th Fl., Jalan Jend Sudirman/Senayan, pg. 547 IT
P.T. German Motor Mfg., P.O. Box 3769, pg. 368 IT
P.T. Gist-Brocades Indonesia, 7L Raya Cakung Cilincing, pg. 1143 IT
P.T. Givaudan-Roure, pg. 1120 IT
P.T. Goldstar Astra, JL Panjang No. 8 Kebon Ieruk, pg. 779 IT
P.T. Gray Indonesia, c/o PT Daya Alam, Tehnik Indonesia Jalan Sultan Hassanuddi, pg. 5 IT
Gulf Canada Resources - Jakarta, pg. 577 IT
P.T. HSBC Securities Indonesia, 5/F, World Trade Centre, Jalan Jeneral Sudirman, Kav 29-31, pg. 583 IT
Hanwa Co., Ltd.-Jakarta Branch, Skyline Bldg., 6th Fl., Jalan M.H. Thamrin 9, pg. 595 IT
P.T. Henkel Indonesia, pg. 614 IT
P.T. Hercules Mas Indonesia, pg. 811 PB
Hitachi Zosen Jakarta, 19th Fl., Mid Plaza 1 Bldg., Jl. Jenderal Sudirman Kav. 10-11, pg. 623 IT
The Hokkaido Takushoku Bank, Ltd. (Jakarta), Skyline Building, 17F, JL. M.H. Thamrin No. 9, pg. 627 IT
Honeywell Pte. Ltd., Wisma Abadi, Jalan Kyai Caringin No. 29 31 Room B4-b, pg. 835 PB
P.T. Hutama-Takenaka Corporation Indonesia, Summitmas Tower I, 7th FLoor, Jl. Jend. Sudirman Kav. 61-62, pg. 1351 IT
P.T. IBJ Indonesia Bank, BNI Bldg., 23rd Fl., Jl. Jenderal Sudirman Kav. 1, pg. 676 IT
P.T. ICI Farmasi Indonesia, Tifa Building, 6th Fl., JL.Kuningan Barat No. 26, pg. 666 IT
P.T. IKI Indah Kabel Indonesia, pg. 1313 IT
ING Bank Jakarta, New Summitmas, 14th Floor, Jl. Jendral Sudirman 6162, pg. 649 IT
ING Baring Securities Indonesia, Jakarta Stock Exchange Bldg., 21st Floor, pg. 650 IT
ING Insurance Indonesia, Lippo Centre, 10 Floor, Jl Jendral Gatot Subroto, pg. 650 IT
PT IPCindo SISKOMDATA, Wisma Bank Dharmala #1807, Jl Jendral Sudirman, pg. 651 IT
INDO RAMA SYNTHETICS P.T., Graha Irama, 17th Fl., Jalan H.R. Rasuna Said Block X-1, pg. 673 IT
P.T. Indofood Jaya Raya, pg. 920 IT
P.T. Indomobil Suzuki International, Central Plaza, JL. Jend. Sudirman Kav. 47-48, pg. 1323 IT
P.T. Indonesia Dai-Ichi Kangyo Bank, 3rd Fl., Wisma Rajawali Annex, Jalan Jenderal Sudirman Kav. 35, pg. 362 IT
Indonesia Resident Mission, Gedung BRI II, 7th Fl., Jl. Jend Sudirman Kav. 44-46, pg. 89 IT
P.T. Indonesia Steel Tube Works Ltd., J1 Rama Sumur 1, Block III AA, KAV 3-6, pg. 948 IT
Indonesia Wacoal Co., Ltd., Jl. Prof. Dr. Latumenten, pg. 1484 IT
Indosat, ATD Plaza 15th Fl., 3 Jalan M.H. Thamrin, pg. 1228 PB
P.T. Indotaisei Indah Development, Landmark Centre, 23rd Floor, Jl. Sudirman, No. 1, pg. 1347 IT
The Industrial Bank of Japan, Limited (Jakarta), BNI Bldg., 23rd Fl., Jl. Sudirman 1, pg. 675 IT
P.T. INFORMATICS OASE, pg. 777 IT
PT Inter Pacific Bank, Wisma Metropolitan 11, 9th Fl., Jalan Jenderal Sudirman Kav 31, pg. 343 IT
P.T. Inter-Pacific Bank, 8th-9th Fl., Wisma Metropolitan II, pg. 1190 IT
P.T. Inter-Pacific Securities, 8th Fl., Wisma Metropolitan II, Jl. Jenderal Sudiiirman Kav. 31, pg. 1190 IT
P.T. International Nickel Indonesia, Wisma Antara, 18th Fl., Jalan Medan, pg. 1316 IT
P.T. International Nickel Indonesia, Wisma Antara, Jalan Merdeka Selatan, pg. 947 IT
P.T. Jakarta Kyoei Medical Center, pg. 777 IT
Jakarta Office, Gedung Setiabudi Atrium, Suite 710, Setiabudi Office Park, pg. 871 IT
Jakarta Office, Chase Plaza Tower Lt. 14, J1. Jend, pg. 943 IT
Jalan Jenderal, Sudirman No. 5, pg. 1413 IT
Jalan Yos Sudarso, Sunter II Kel, Sungai-Bambu, Tanjung Priok, pg. 1413 IT
Japan Airlines Company, Ltd., Kyoei Prince Building, Ground Floor, Jl., Jenderal Sudirman, pg. 701 IT
P T Jardine Fleming Nusantara, 4th Fl., Wisma Dharmala Sakti, pg. 494 IT
P.T. Jardine Insurance Brokers Indonesia, World Trade Centre, 10th Fl., J1 Jendral Sudirman Kav 31, pg. 705 IT
Jardine Pacific Ltd Regional Representative Office, Level 10, World Trade Centre, 29/31, Jalan Jendral Sudirman, pg. 705 IT
P.T. Jaya Fuji Leasing Pratama, 9th Fl., Jaya Bldg., Jl. M.H. Thamrin 12, pg. 521 IT
P.T. Jaya Mandarin Agung, Jalan M H Thamrin, pg. 704 IT
P.T. Jaya Obayashi, J.L. Pancoran Timur II, 3, Pancoran, pg. 996 IT
PT John Crane Indonesia, Jl Agung Perkasa X, Blok KII/4, Sunter Agung Podomoro, pg. 1339 IT
P.T. Johnson & Johnson Indonesia, Wisma Kyoei Prince, Flr. 3A, pg. 930 PB
P.T. S.C. Johnson & Son (Indonesia) Ltd., P.O. Box 41/ JNG, pg. 593 PV
P.T. KADI International, pg. 764 IT
P.T. Kanebo-Nissho Iwai-Sahabat Textile Industries, Nusantara Bldg. 10th Fl., pg. 948 IT
P.T. Kangar Consolidated Industries, Jalan Raya, Bekasi Km. 24, 5-CA Kav, pg. 129 IT
Kansai Paint Jakarta Office, Gedung Galva, Lantai 3, pg. 723 IT

P.T. Kapo Kimia Kencana(CIBA Distributor), Mampang Plaza, 4th Floor, Jl Mampang Prapatan Raya No. 100, pg. 983 IT
P.T. Karya Yansantara Cakti, Pulogadung 45, KIP, pg. 283 IT
Kawasaki Steel Co., Ratu Plaza Building, 27th Flr., Jl. Jendral Sudirman No. 9, pg. 726 IT
P.T. Kayaba Indonesia, Jl. Rawaterate 1/4, Pulogadung Industrial Estate, pg. 727 IT
PT Kes Sinar Mas Securities, Wisma Kosgoro 7th Floor, JL M.H. Thamrin 53, pg. 733 IT
PT Kilborn Pakar Rekayasa, The Garden Centre, Suite 6- 06, Cilandak Commercial Estate, pg. 1162 IT
P.T. Kimballmas Sejati, pg. 1067 PB
P.T. Knorr Indonesia, pg. 224 PB
P.T. Komaritim, pg. 1302 IT
P.T. Komatsu Indonesia Tbk, Jalan Raya Bekasi Km 22 Cakung, pg. 744 IT
P.T. Konsultan Aktuaria Kyoeindo, pg. 777 IT
P.T. Krikras/BASF Department, P.O. Box 2431 Jbr., pg. 109 IT
Kreasindo Advertising & Marketing Consultants, Kreasindo Bldg., Pasar Baru Timur #9, pg. 184 PV
Kubota Corp.-Jakarta Office, Skyline Bldg., 17th Fl., No. 9, Jl. M.H. Thamrin, pg. 763 IT
Kvaerner a.s. Representative Office, Suite 1111 Mulia Center, pg. 771 IT
LASMO Companies Indonesia, Ratu Plaza Office Tower, 28th, Jalan Jenderal Sudirman No. 9, pg. 804 IT
LASMO Runtu Ltd., pg. 804 IT
P.T. Lautan Otsuka Chemical, Summitmas Tower 4th Floor, Jl.Jend. Sudirman Kav 61-62, pg. 1014 IT
P.T. Lucent Technologies Network Systems Indonesia, Gedung Menara DJTA, 1st Floor, JLN Rasuna Said #89, pg. 1019 PB
Makro in Indonesia, Jl. Lingkar Luar Selatan Kav. 6, pg. 1155 IT
Marathon Petroleum Indonesia, Ltd., JL.H.R. Rasuna Said, Kav.-B 10, Lippo Life Bldg., pg. 1662 IT
P.T. Maste Dayaa, Pondok Pinang Center Blok, Blok C No. 16-18, pg. 550 IT
Maxus Southeast Sumatra, Jakarta Stock Exchange Bldg., 6-11 Floors, J.L. Jendral Sudidrman, pg. 1515 IT
P.T. McCormick Indonesia, pg. 1067 PB
P.T. McDermott Indonesia, 24th Fl., Landmark Tower 1, P.O. Box 14281/JKT, pg. 1068 IT
P.T. Meiji Indonesian Pharmaceutical Industries, J1 Tanah Abang II No. 4, pg. 856 IT
P.T. Merapi Utama Pharma, Jl. Cilosari No. 23, pg. 1014 IT
P.T. Merincorp Securities Indonesia, Plaza Exim, 27th Floor, Jl. Gatot Subroto Kav. 36-38, pg. 1310 IT
PT Metrodata Electronics, pg. 22 IT
P.T. Milchem Indonesia, 4th Fl., Dl-5 Setiabudi Bldg., JL, H.R. Rasuna Said 62, pg. 167 IT
P.T. Mitrapermata Indah, Permata Plaza, 11th Floor, Jl. M.H. Thamrin 57, pg. 1347 IT
P.T. Mitsubishi Krama Yudha Motors & Manufacturing, Petukangan III, Raya Bekasi Km. 22J1, pg. 876 IT
Mitsui & Co., Ltd., 16th Fl., Nusantara Bldg., pg. 880 IT
Mobile Oil Indonesia, Inc., Ratu Plaza Bldg., 12-23 Flrs., Jl. Jend. Sudirman, pg. 1119 PB
P.T. Monier Indonesia, J.I. Melawai Raya, No. 165 Block C- 5, pg. 1091 IT
Morgan Guaranty Trust Company, Wisma Kosgro, 18th Flr, Jalan M.H. Thamrin 53, pg. 1130 PB
P.T. Multi Raga Agung, pg. 948 IT
P.T. Multicor Bank, World Trade Center, 13th & 15th Floors, pg. 817 IT
P.T. Multicor Securities, World Trade Center, World Trade Center, 13th Floor, pg. 817 IT
P.T. Multinational Finance Corporation, P.O. Box 730KBY, Wisma BCA, 12th. Flr., pg. 1133 IT
NKK Corporation-Jakarta Office, Midplaza II, 17th Fl., JL Jend. Sudirman, KAV 10-11, pg. 903 IT
NYK-Jakarta, 5th Fl., Nusantara Bldg., Jl. M.H. Thamrin No. 59, pg. 941 IT
P.T. Nalco Perkasa, Landmark Bldg., Tower B, 30th Fl., pg. 1151 PB
P.T. Natra Raya, P.O. Box 175/KBY, pg. 317 IT
P.T. Nestle Asean (Indonesia), pg. 920 IT
P.T. Nikko Securities Indonesia, 26th Fl., Land Mark Centre, JL. Jenderal Sudirman No. 1, pg. 931 IT
Nippon Paper Industries Company Limited Jakarta Office, Nusantra Bldg., 21st Fl., JL. M.H. Thamrin No. 59, pg. 938 IT
Nokia Representative Office, 4th Floor, Panin Building, Jalan Jendrae Sudiman 1, pg. 953 IT
P.T. Nomura Indonesia, 7th Fl., Daiwa Perdania Bank, Jl. Jend Sudirman Kav. 40-41, pg. 957 IT
North West Water Indonesia, Jalan Kemang Raya 18C, P.O. Box 236/KBY, pg. 1444 IT
Nowsco Well Service Ltd.-Asia & Pacific, Jl. Yos Sudarso No. 13, pg. 990 IT
P.T. Nutricia Indonesia Sejaharta, pg. 992 IT
Obayashi Corporation-Jakarta, JL. Pancoran Timur II No. 3, Pancoran, pg. 995 IT
P.T. O'Donnell Griffin Indonesia, J1 Margasatwa Raya No. 37, Jatipadang Pasar Minggu, pg. 1651 PB
P.T. Organon Indonesia, Jalan R. C. Veteran, Binatro- Kebayoran Lama, pg. 45 IT
P.T. ORIX Indonesia Finance, Wisma Kyoei Prince, 24th Fl., J1-Jend, Sudirman Kav 3-4, pg. 1009 IT
P.T. Otsuka Indonesia, Jl. Cilosari No. 25, pg. 1014 IT
P.T. Otsuka Jaya Indah, Jl. Cilosari No. 25, pg. 1014 IT
P.T. Praxair Indonesia, pg. 1320 PB
P.T. P.P. Taisei Indonesia Construction, Central Plaza Building, 47, Jl. Jenderal Sudirman, 7th Floor, pg. 1347 IT
PTDBS Securities Indonesia, Wisma Rajawali, 12th Floor, Jl. Jenderal Sudirman 34, pg. 351 IT

P.T. Pabrik Araya Indonesia, J1 Telepan Kota 14, pg. 949 IT
PT Panalpina Nusajaya Transport, pg. 1023 IT
P.T. Panata Tama Inter Instalasi Indonesia, 121, Jalan Letjen Suprapto, pg. 681 IT
P.T. Pardic Jaya Chemicals, Skyline Bldg. Jalan M.H., pg. 949 IT
P.T. Perjahl Leasing Indonesia, Mid Plaza Building Lt 9, Jl. Jend Sudirman Kav. 10-11, pg. 1181 IT
PT Perstorp Bumi Raya-Factory Melamine Ware, Jl. Agung Timur II, Block 01, pg. 1037 IT
PT Perstorp Bumi Raya, Jl. Let. Jen. S. Parman Kav. 12, pg. 1037 IT
P.T. Pertalenikki Engineering, Jl. Mampang Prapatan Raya, pg. 697 IT
Perwakilan Bureau Technique Rhone-Poulenc, J.L. H.R. Rasuna Said Kav B-34, pg. 1112 IT
Perwanal/D'Arcy Masius Benton & Bowles, JL. Buncit Raya Pejaten No. 25, pg. 305 PV
P.T. Pfizer Indonesia, Jalan Raya Bogor Km. 28, pg. 1282 PB
P.T. Pharmacia & Upjohn Indonesia, pg. 1049 IT
P.T. Pimaimas Citra, Kartika Plaza Bldg., 2nd Fl., Jln. N.H. Thamrin 10, pg. 1040 PB
P.T. Polekao Indonesia Chemicals, 16th Fl. Skyline Bldg., pg. 718 IT
POSTRADE Jakarta Office, #705 Mulia Towers, Jl. Jend, Gatot Subroto Kav. 9-11, pg. 1062 IT
P.T. Private Development Finance Company of Indonesia, Ja;am Abdul Muis 60, pg. 933 IT
RNBNY Representative Office-Indonesia, Sampoerna Plaza, JL. H.R. Rasuna Said, pg. 1381 IT
P.T. Rabo Finance Indonesia, Sampoerna Plaza, 10th Fl Jl.H.R. Rasuna Said Kav. X-7 No. 6, pg. 1082 IT
P.T. Rabobank Duta Indonesia, Sampoerna Plaza, 10th Fl., Jl.H.R. Rasuna Said Kav. X-7 No. 6, pg. 1082 IT
Reed Exhibition Companies-Indonesia, Level 15, Wisma Metropolitan 11, pg. 1097 IT
Renishaw's Representative Office, Jalan Permuda 44 Rawamangum, pg. 1103 IT
Representative of Ciba-Geigy-Crop Protection R+D, pg. 984 IT
Repsol Exploracion, Kunigan Plaza, South Tower, Ste. 506, pg. 1105 IT
Repsol Exploracion, Kuningan Plaza, South Tower, Ste. 506, pg. 1105 IT
P.T. Richardson-Vicks Indonesia, TIFA Bldg., 8th Fl., Jl Kuningan, pg. 1333 IT
Rockwell Automation Southeast Asia Pte. Ltd., Suite 2301, Gedung BRI II, 23rd Floor, pg. 1400 IT
SAIC Indonesia Limited, Kuningan Plaza, Ste. 401, South Tower, pg. 976 PV
P.T. SNC-Lavalin TPS, Exchange House, Suite 401, Jl. H.R. Rasuna Said Blok X-1, pg. 1163 IT
Saga Petroleum Indonesia AS, Bumi Daya Plaza 20th Fl., 61, Jl. Imam Bonjol, pg. 1169 IT
PT Sagita Dumez, Suite 502, Mulia Center, Jalan H.R. Rasuna Said KAV, pg. 823 IT
The Sakura Bank - Jakarta Representative Office, 19th Floor, BNI Building, Jl. Jendral, Sudirman Kav. 1, pg. 1179 IT
P.T. Sandoz-Biochemie Farma Indonesia, pg. 984 IT
Santa Fe Intl. Services Inc., P.O. Box 2351, Jalan Melawai IX/2, Kebayan Baru, pg. 766 IT
P.T. Sanwa-BRI Finance, Chase Plaza 10th Floor, pg. 1190 IT
P.T. Sanwa Indonesia Bank, 4th & 5th Fl., Bank Bali Tower, Building, Jl. Jenderal Sudirman Kav. 27, pg. 1190 IT
P.T. Sanyo Industries Indonesia, Jalan Laksda Yos Sudarso (By-Pass), pg. 1192 IT
P.T. Sarinitokyu Hotel Corp., Jalan, M.H., pg. 949 IT
PT Satomo Indovyl Polymer, UIC Building, 4th Floor, Jl. Jend. Gatot Subroto Kav. 6-7, pg. 1408 IT
P.T. Schering Indonesia, pg. 1204 IT
P.T. Semen Andalas Indonesia, PP Plaza Level 3, Jalan T.B. Simatupang n 57, pg. 791 IT
SERVOCORP (Triton Indonesia), pg. 1640 PB
P.T. Sharp Semiconductor Indonesia, Jalan Swadaya IV, pg. 1230 IT
P.T. Sharp Yasnota Antarnusa, Jl. Pinangsia Timur No. 20, pg. 1230 IT
P.T. Sharp Yasonta Indonesia, Jalan Swadaya IV, pg. 1230 IT
Shell Companies in Indonesia, S Widjojo Centre, Jl Jendral Sudirman 71, pg. 1139 IT
P.T. Shimizu-Lampiri Consultants, Setiabudi Atrium, 8th Fl., Ste. 801, Setiabudi Office Pk., pg. 1234 IT
P.T. Siemens Indonesia, Jalan Cikarang, Giaha Siemens, Jalan H.R. Rasuna Said Kav 3-4, pg. 1247 IT
Sinochem Representative Office - Indonesia, ATD Plaza, Ste. 1605, J.I.M.H. Thamrin Kav 3, pg. 1256 IT
Standard Chartered Bank (Indonesia), Wisma Standard Chartered Bank, Jl. Jendral Sudirman Kav. 33-A, pg. 1295 IT
P.T. Standard Chartered Leasing, Wisma Kosgoro 12th Fl., Jl. M.H. Thamrin No. 53, pg. 1297 IT
P.T. Standard Chartered Securities, Wisma Bank Dharmala, 9th Fl., Jalan Jenderal Sudirman Kav. 28, pg. 1296 IT
P.T. Standard Toyo Polymer, Permata Plaza Bldg., 9th Fl., Jl. M.H. Thamrin No.57, pg. 1408 IT
P.T. Stanvac Indonesia, Jalan H.R. Rasuna Said, Plaza 89, pg. 603 PB
P.T. Star Motors Indonesia, pg. 369 IT
P.T. Sumiden Serasi Wire Products, Tamara Centre, Ste. 1205 JL, pg. 1313 IT
The Sumitomo Bank, Ltd.-Jakarta Representative Office, Summitmas II, 11th Fl., Jl. Jend. Sudirman Kav. 61-62, pg. 1318 IT
The Sumitomo Trust & Banking Co., Ltd., Summitmas Tower, 11th Fl., JL. Jenderal Sudirman Kaveling 61-62, pg. 1318 IT

PB - U.S. Public Companies Volume
PV - U.S. Private Companies Volume
IT - International Public & Private Companies Volume

Geographic Index-Non U.S.

P.T. Surya Toto Indonesia, Jl., Tomang Raya No. 18, pg. 1410 — IT
Svedala International, pg. 1325
P.T. Takeda Indonesia, Mashill Tower 15th Tower, Jl. Jend. Sudirman Kav. 25, pg. 1351 — IT
Talisman (Asia) Ltd., Suite 802, Jl. H.R. Rasuna Said Kav. 62, pg. 1352 — IT
P.T. Tanabe-Abadi-Jakarta Office, Jl. Tanah Abang III/8, pg. 1354 — IT
PT Tandbam Jaya, Jalan Mercedes No. 105, Gunung Putri-Citeureup, pg. 603 — IT
P.T. Tembaga Mulia Semanan (TMS), KM-16 Jl, Daan Mogot Desa Semanan, pg. 531 — IT
P.T. Tempo National Life, Level 9, Bina Mulia I, Jl. H.R. Rasuna Said Kav. 10, pg. 909 — IT
Terumo-Jakarta, 10th Fl., Bunas Center, Jl. Senen Raya No. 135., pg. 1376 — IT
Texaco Natuna Inc., Jln. Keban Sirih 52, pg. 1584 — PB
P.T. 3M Indonesia, Wisma Bak Dharmala, 11th Fl., Jl Jend. Sudiman Kav. 28, pg. 1606 — PB
P.T. Tira Wahari Lestari, P.O. Box 4740, pg. 109 — IT
P.T. Tokai Lippo Bank, Bapindo Plaza Tower II, 25th Level, Jl. Jendral Sudirman, pg. 1391 — IT
P.T. Toppan Printing Indonesia, Jl. Gajah Mada 162-C, pg. 1399 — IT
Total Indonesie, Kunigan Plaza, North Tower, JL HR Rasuna Said Kav. 109, pg. 1409 — PB
P.T. Toyo Kanetsu Indonesia, Nusantara Bldg., 7th Fl., pg. 949 — IT
P.T. Toyota-Astra Motor, Jalan Jenderal Suidirman No. 5, pg. 1413 — IT
P.T. Tunggal Idaman, TIRA Building, Ground Floor, Jl. H.R. Rasuna Said, Blok X-2, pg. 109 — IT
P.T. Unilever Indonesia, pg. 1439 — IT
Union Carbide Indonesia PT, pg. 1667 — PB
Pt. United Air Products Indonesia, Gedung Sapta Mulia, Lt. IV, Jl. rawa Gelam V Kav. Or.3b, pg. 32 — PB
Unocal Geothermal of Indonesia Ltd., Ratu Plaza Tower, 5th Fl., J.L., Box 1264, pg. 1698 — PB
Unocal Indonesia, Ltd., Ratu Plaza Office Tower, 7th Fl. J.L., Box 1264, pg. 1698 — PB
Utell International-Indonesia, Wisma Bank, Dharmala, 19th Floor, Suite 04, Jalan Jenderal, pg. 1098 — IT
Van Leeuwen Pipe and Tube (Far East) Pte. Ltd., Wisma Dharmala Sakti, 4th Fl., J1. Jendral Sudirman 32, pg. 1450 — IT
P.T. Van Melle Indonesia, J1. Anggur III/33, pg. 1451 — IT
WestLB Jakarta, 17th Floor, Mid Plaza 2 Building, pg. 1493 — IT
Westpac Banking - Indonesia, 10th Flr., Summitras Tower, Bldg., Jalan Jend Sudirman, pg. 1497 — IT
P.T. Wisma Kyoei Prince Indonesia, Jl. Jend.Sudirman Kav. 3-4, pg. 777 — IT
P.T. Wisma Kyoei Prince Indonesia, pg. 777 — IT
Woodward-Clyde, Sudiman Tower, 7th Floor, Unit 7C, 12190, pg. 1657 — PB
The World Bank, Lippolile Building, 3rd Floor, Kav. B-10, pg. 1189 — PV
PT Zeneca Agri Products Indonesia, Niaga Tower 17th Fl., Jl Jenderal Sudinam Kav 58, pg. 1526 — IT
PT Zeneca Colours Indonesia, Niaga Tower 17th Fl., Jl Jenedral Sudinam Kav. 58, pg. 1526 — IT
ZEXEL Corporation Jakarta Representative Office, 17th Floor, Skyline Building, Jalan M.H. Thamrin 9, pg. 1528 — IT
P.T. Zurich Insurance Indonesia, 27th Fl., Jakarta Stock Exchange Bldg., pg. 1532 — IT
P.T. Zurich PSP Life Insurance Indonesia, Wisma Bank Dharmala, 4th Fl., Jl. Jend. Sudirman Kav. 52-53, pg. 1532 — IT

Java

PT KSB Indonesia, Jl. Raya Rungkut Menanggal 11, pg. 721 — IT
PT. KONE Indo Elevator, Jl. Berbek Industri I/23, pg. 747 — IT
P.T. Sumi Indo Wiring Systems, Kawasan Industri Bukit Indah, City Blok, All Lot 25-26 Ds, pg. 1313 — IT
P.T. Toppan Sampoerna Indonesia, Jl. Raya Cibitung, Desa Telaga Asih, pg. 1399 — IT

Jawa

P.T. Standard Toyo Polymer-Merak Plant, JL Raya Merak, pg. 1408 — IT

Medan

P.T. Atmindo, pg. 398 — IT
P.T. Kimsari Paper-Indonesia, P.O. Box 1317, pg. 959 — PB
Mitsui & Co., 6th Floor, Medan Jaya Bldg., Jalan Imam Bonjol No. 16-D, pg. 880 — IT

Mojokerto

P.T. Ajinex International, Mojokerto Factory, Mlirip Jetis, P.O. Box 10, pg. 40 — IT
P.T. Ajinomoto Indonesia, Mojokerto Factory, Mlirip Jetis, P.O. Box 10, pg. 40 — IT

Muka Kuning

P.T. Ciba Vision Batam, Jalan Beringin Kav 204 BIP, pg. 981 — IT
PT Quantum Peripherals Indonesia, Lot 209-01/02/03, Jalan Beringin, pg. 1350 — PB
P.T. Sumitomo Wiring Systems Battsm Indonesia, pg. 1314 — IT

Pondok Gede

PT. Valmet Indonesia, Jl. Raya Jatiwaringin No. 54, pg. 1448 — IT

Pontianak

PT Perstorp Bumi Raya-Factory Moulding Compounds, Jl. Adisucipto KM 8, pg. 1037 — IT

Pulau Batam

P.T. Petrolite Indonesia Pratama, Batu Ampar, pg. 166 — PB
P.T. Shimano Batam, Level 1 Lot. 10, Batamindo, Industrial Park, pg. 1232 — IT
P.T. VARTA Batteries Indonesia Ltd., pg. 1452 — IT

Semarang

P.T. Kubota Indonesia, JL. Setyabudi 279, pg. 763 — IT

Serang

P.T. Ebara Prima Indonesia, Kawasan Industri Modern, Cikande Jl. Modern Industri, I No 12, pg. 432 — IT

Sumatera Barat

JO DZ Int/Impregilo/Istaka Karya, Asampulau 25581, pg. 823 — IT

Surabaya

P.T. Ajinomoto Indonesia, Surabaya Branch, Jl. Gayungan PT.T. No.69, pg. 40 — IT
P.T. Bank Sumitomo Niaga-Surabaya Branch, Wisma BII, 8th Floor, Jl. Pemuda, pg. 1309 — IT
Deutsche Bank AG (Surabaya), 141, Jl. Jend. Basuki Rakhmat, pg. 405 — IT
InfoKomputer, Jalan Kayun No. 24, pg. 570 — PV
Mitsui & Co., 3rd Fl., Overseas Express Bank Bldg., pg. 880 — IT
P.T. Pioneer Hibrida Indonesia, Jalan Jemursari No. 240-A, pg. 1299 — PB
P.T. Toetal Thread Wdongsla, 43 Jalan Indrapura, pg. 299 — IT

Tangerang

P.T. Iron Wire Works Indonesia, Desa Batu Ceper Kabupaten, pg. 948 — IT
P.T. Mesin Isuzu Indonesia, JL. Pajajaran(Bumi Mas), Desa Gancasari-Jatiuwung, pg. 693 — IT
P.T. Mesin Isuzu Indonesia, JL. Pajajaran(Bumi Mas), Desa Gancasari-Jatiuwung, pg. 724 — IT
P.T. Multi Bintang Indonesia, Jalan Daan Mogot, Km 19, pg. 608 — IT
P.T. Tating BUDI Indonesia, Jl Paan Mogot KM. 18, pg. 1357 — IT

Ujung Pandang

P.T. Semiwa Steel Works, Tallo, pg. 949 — IT

IRAN

Tabriz

Iranian Diesel Engineering Manufacturing Co. (IDEM), pg. 368 — IT

Tehran

ANZ Grimdlays Bank plc Iran, 3rd Floor, No. 14, 4th Alley, Shahid Ahmad Ghasir, (ex Bucharest Ave.), pg. 99 — IT
Alfa-Laval Iran Co., P.O. Box 95-1626, pg. 1380 — IT
Aliaf-Public Joint Stock Co., 10 Moj St. Ebnesina Ave. Yousef Abad, pg. 174 — IT
Australia & New Zealand Banking Group Limited Iran, 3rd Floor, No. 14, 4th Alley, Shahid Ahmad Ghasir, (ex Bucharest Ave.), pg. 99 — IT
BASF Iran AG, Sohrevardi Shomali Ave., Kangavar Alley-No 5, pg. 106 — IT
BHP-Bark Representative Office, 2nd Floor, 14, Fourth Alley, Shahid Ahmad Ghasir Ave., pg. 120 — IT
Banca Nazionale del Lavoro, 131, Park Avenue, pg. 137 — IT
Banque Paribas-Iran, Immeuble Air France, 882, Av. Enghelab, pg. 320 — IT
Bayerische Vereinsbank AG, Dr. Ali Shariati Ave., pg. 180 — IT
Bridgestcne Trading Co., (Pte.) Ltd., No. 7, 7th St., Vozara (Park) Ave., pg. 214 — IT
Brown Boveri Iran (Private Joint Stock Company), Bukharest Ave., Ku 18 No. 14, pg. 3 — IT

CIBA-GEIGY Iran Ltd., 91, Ghem Magham Farahani Ave., pg. 977 — IT
Commerzbank AG-Teheran Representative Office, Argentine Square, Alvand Street, 35th Alley, No. 9, pg. 312 — IT
Daewoo Corp. - Tehran, pg. 358 — IT
AB S.A. des Roulements a Billes Suedois SKF, Vali Asr Ave., Daman Afshar Street, pg. 1158 — IT
Det Norske Veritas, 2th Fl., Apt. 15, No. 58 Maryam St., pg. 398 — IT
Deutsche Bank AG (Tehran), Ave. Boucharest, 5th St. No. 25, pg. 405 — IT
Dresdner Bank AG, 126 Ave. Nejatollahi, pg. 419 — IT
ESAB International AB, Tehran Office, 8th Fl., 135 Kheradmand Shomali, pg. 282 — IT
Generale Bank, Avenue Ahmed Ghassir, pg. 547 — IT
Hanwa Co., Ltd.-Teheran Branch, 6th Fl. Bldg. #10, 8th St., Mirzaye-Shirazi Ave., pg. 596 — IT
Henkel Industrie AG, 8th St. Block 13, pg. 612 — IT
Inter Alpha, 14 Fourth Alley, 2nd Fl., Shahid Ahmad Ghasi Avenue, pg. 343 — IT
Iran Henkel AG, pg. 613 — IT
Iran Schindler Lift Manufacturing Company Ltd., pg. 1205 — IT
Iran Steam Industries Equipment Co. Ltd., Apt. 8, Second Floor, No. 4 Yazdan panah Avenue, pg. 550 — IT
Italimpianti Intl.-Iran, Bucharest Ave. 15th St. 28, pg. 655 — IT
Italstrade-Iran, Africa Ave. 3 -E. Wahid St., pg. 655 — IT
Kredietbank Inter-Alpha Representative Office, 14, Fourth Alley, 2nd Fl., Shahid Ahmad Ghasir Ave., pg. 760 — IT
Krupp Iran Ltd., Ostad Motahri Ave. 368, pg. 511 — IT
MAN GHH (Iran) Sherkate Sahami Khass, pg. 824 — IT
Mitsui & Co., Iran Ltd., No. 25 Shahid Sara'raz St., Dr. Beheshti Ave., pg. 880 — IT
Monenco Iran, No. 17, 23rd Street, Gandi Avenue, pg. 31 — IT
NYK-Tehran, c/o Sea Express Co., 4th Fl., No. 4S, Negar Street, pg. 941 — IT
Nissho Iwai Corporation (Iran) Ltd., 3rd Floor, Argentine Square, No. 69, Ahmad Ghasir (Bokharest) Ave., pg. 948 — IT
Nokia Telecommunications, No. 10 and 12, Third Street, pg. 953 — IT
RZB Tehran, Africa Expressway 135, pg. 1085 — IT
Rhenania Commercial Delegation, c/o Daryabar Co. Ltd. Dr. Mofateh Ave., pg. 1034 — IT
A.H. Robins (Iran) Company, No. 109 12th St., Khadjeh Abdollah, pg. 82 — PB
A.H. Robins International Company, Gandi Ave., pg. 82 — PB
SIMCO Ericsson Ltd., 19, Bahara Shiraz St., Dr. Ali Shariati Ave., pg. 1370 — IT
SmithKline & French of Iran Limited, 17 Kargozat, pg. 1265 — IT
Spea-Iran, Kh. Khaled E. Eslamboki Park 14th, 5, pg. 655 — IT
Standard Chartered Bank (Iran), Kooshya Bldg., Apartment 2, pg. 1295 — IT
Sulzer Iran, pg. 1306 — IT
The Sumitomo Bank, Ltd.-Tehran Representative Office, 55, N. Palestine St., pg. 1310 — IT
Swiss Bank Corporation, 126 Ostad Nejatollahi Avenue, 5th Floor, 15997, pg. 1330 — IT
Telefonaktiebolaget LM Ericsson Iran, 74, Argentine Square, 1st floor, pg. 1370 — IT
UBS Representative Office Ltd., 126 Avenue Ostad Nejatolahi, pg. 1441 — IT

IRAQ

Baghdad

Mitsui & Co., Ltd., House No. 25, 903 Quarter, Lane No. 11, pg. 881 — IT
Rhenania Commercial Delegation, c/o HILAL Transport Co. Hay Babel929,Str., pg. 1034 — IT
Telefonaktiebolaget LM Ericsson Iraq Branch, Al Masbah No. 41, Sec. 929, St. 95, House No. 3B/8/35, pg. 1370 — IT

IRELAND

Abbeyleix

Manchester Tool Limited, Ireland, Balladine, pg. 617 — PB

Arklow

McGhan Limited, Kilbride Indus. Estate, pg. 874 — PB

Athlone

Elan Clinical Services Ltd., Monksland, pg. 436 — IT
Elan Pharma Ltd., Monksland, pg. 436 — IT
Elan/PRI Ltd., Monksland, pg. 436 — IT
Elan Transdermal Ltd., Monksland, pg. 436 — IT
Ericsson Systems Expertise Ltd., Cornamaddy, pg. 1367 — IT
The Institute of Biopharmaceutics Ltd., Monksland, pg. 436 — IT
M & C Specialties (Ireland) Limited, Athlone Business & Tech. Pk., pg. 684 — PV
Mallinckrodt Medical, Cornmaddy, pg. 1040 — PB
Utah Medical Products Ltd., Garrycastle Industrial Estate, pg. 1700 — PB

PB - *U.S. Public Companies Volume*
PV - *U.S. Private Companies Volume*
IT - *International Public & Private Companies Volume*

Ballina

A.T. Cross Ltd., One Cleaghmore, pg. 461 **PB**
Henniges-Vehicle Sealing Div., Crossmolina Road, pg. 706 **PB**

Ballivor

NEC Semiconductors Ireland Limited, pg. 900 **IT**

Ballytivnan

Abbott Ireland Ltd., pg. 13 **PB**

Bangor

NIIB Group Limited, 32 Central Avenue, pg. 152 **IT**
Oneida Silversmiths Limited, Rathgael Industrial Estates, pg. 1226 **PB**

Blackrock

BASF Ireland Limited, Enterprise House, Frascati Rd., pg. 106 **IT**
CLAI Limited, Canada Life House, Temple Rock, pg. 255 **IT**
The Canada Life Assurance Company of Ireland Limited, Canada Life House, Temple Rock, pg. 255 **IT**
Canada Life Assurance (Ireland) Ltd., Canada Life House, Temple Road, pg. 255 **IT**
Canada Life Financial Services Company of Ireland Limited, Canada Life House, Temple Rock, pg. 255 **IT**
Canada Life Ireland Holdings, Canada Life House, Temple Rock, pg. 255 **IT**
Canada Life Pension & Annuities (Ireland) Limited, Canada Life House, Temple Rock, pg. 255 **IT**
H.J. Heinz Company (Ireland) Limited, Stradbrook House, Stradbrook Rd., pg. 806 **PB**
Huls Ireland, Stradbrook House, Stradbrook Rd., pg. 1455 **IT**
Marathon Petroleum Ireland, Ltd., Mahon Industrial Estate, pg. 1662 **PB**

Bray

De La Rue Smurfit Limited, Pinewood Close, Bray Industrial Estate, pg. 386 **IT**
Dell Computer Corporation, pg. 496 **PB**
Roche Pharmaceutical (Ireland) Limited, pg. 1121 **IT**
A.O. Smith Electric Motors (Ireland) Ltd., Bog Hall Rd., Wicklow County, pg. 1477 **PB**

Carlow

Braun Ireland Ltd., Dublin Road, pg. 744 **PB**

Carrickmacross

Bose Ireland, Castleblaney Rd., pg. 161 **PV**

Casey Cross

M/A-Com Eurotech, Younglines Center, pg. 8 **PB**

Clarecastle

Syntex Ireland Limited, pg. 1122 **IT**

Cloghran

Lotus Development B.V., Unit 12, Airways Industrial Estate, pg. 896 **PB**

Clonmel

T.J. Carolan & Son Ltd., Annerville, pg. 63 **IT**
The Irish Mist Liqueur Co. Ltd., Annerville, pg. 63 **IT**
Merck Sharp & Dohme (Ireland) Ltd., Ballydine, Kilsheelan, pg. 1092 **PB**
Schiesser International (Ireland) Ltd., pg. 618 **IT**
Schiesser Ireland (Trading) Ltd., pg. 618 **IT**

Cork

Adidas (Ireland) Ltd., pg. 25 **IT**
Apple Computer Ltd., Holly Hill Industrial Estate, pg. 121 **PB**
Banta Global Turnkey Group, Hollyhill Industrial Estate, pg. 189 **PB**
Barley Exports Limited, One Victoria Rd., pg. 102 **IT**
Beamish & Crawford Plc, South Main St., pg. 1212 **IT**
CADCO Ltd., Trafalgar House, Montenotte, pg. 150 **PB**
Colborn-Dawes Ireland Ltd., pg. 1121 **IT**
Emerson Electric Ireland Limited, Bessboro Rd., pg. 576 **PB**
FMC (Ireland) Limited, Wallingstown, pg. 606 **PB**
Henry Ford & Son (Finance) Limited, Elm Court, Boreenmanna Rd., pg. 665 **PB**
Henry Ford & Son, Limited, Elm Court, Boreenmanna Rd., pg. 665 **PB**
Henry Ford & Son (Sales) Limited, Elm Court, Boreenmanna Rd., pg. 665 **PB**
Four-Phase Overseas Corp., Mahon Industrial Estate, pg. 1139 **PB**
Henkel Ireland Ltd., pg. 612 **IT**
Hickson PharmaChem Ltd., pg. 619 **IT**

The Irish Crown Cork Co., Ltd., Churchfield Indus. Estate, pg. 465 **PB**
Liebert International B.V., Model Farm Road, pg. 577 **PB**
Millipore Ireland, B.V. Tullagreen, pg. 1113 **PB**
Moog Ltd., Ringaskiddy, pg. 1128 **PB**
Motorola Ireland Ltd., Mahon Industrial Estate, Blackrock, pg. 1139 **PB**
Murphy Brewery Ireland Ltd., pg. 608 **IT**
Pepsi-Cola Manufacturing (Ireland), Little Island Industrial Estate, pg. 1277 **PB**
Sandoz Ringaskiddy Ltd., pg. 985 **IT**
Sifco Turbine Components, Ltd., Mahon Industrial Estate, Blackrock, pg. 1471 **PB**
Simon Aerials Ltd., Courtsdown Industrial Park, pg. 1252 **IT**
Summit Technology Ireland, Model Farm Road, Cork Business & Technology Park, pg. 1529 **IT**
Transistor Devices Europe Ltd., Carrigtwohill Indus. Estate, Carrigtwohill, pg. 1097 **PV**

Craigavon

Magheralin Cheese and Whey Products, 35 Steps Rd. Magheralin, pg. 102 **IT**

Donegal

Comhlucht Iascaireachta Fanad Teoranta (Fanad Fisheries), (Fanad Fisheries), Kindrum, pg. 961 **IT**

Drogheda

Brother Industries (Ireland) Ltd., Donore Rd., pg. 229 **IT**
Irish Flavors & Fragrances Limited, Industrial Estate, Donore Rd., pg. 900 **PB**

Dublin

ABN International Financial Services Co., 121/122, St. Stephen's Green, pg. 11 **IT**
AER Turas Teo, Corballis Park, Dublin Airport, pg. 28 **IT**
AIB Capital Markets plc, AIB International Centre, IFSC, pg. 64 **IT**
AIB Corporate Finance Ltd., 85 Pembroke Road, pg. 64 **IT**
AIB Finance & Leasing Ltd., Blackthorne Rd., Sandyford Business Ctr., pg. 64 **IT**
AIB International Consultants Ltd., Bankcentre, Ballsbridge, pg. 64 **IT**
AIB International Financial Services Ltd, AIB International Centre, IFSC, pg. 64 **IT**
AIB Securities Services Ltd., AIB International Centre, IFSC, pg. 64 **IT**
AMEV General Insurance Company Limited, AMEV House, Temple Rd., pg. 499 **IT**
AMP Ireland Limited, 65 Broomhill Rd., pg. 9 **PB**
Adecco Alfred Marks (Ireland) Ltd., 45 Grafton Street, pg. 24 **IT**
AER LINGUS, Head Office Building, Dublin Airport, pg. 28 **IT**
Air France Finance Ireland, 69/71 St. Stephen's Green, pg. 560 **IT**
Albright & Wilson Ireland, Ltd., Sandyford Industrial Estate, pg. 49 **IT**
Alfa-Laval (Ireland) Ltd., Kylemore Park West, pg. 1380 **IT**
Algemene Bank Nederland (Ireland), 121/122, St. Stephen's Green, pg. 12 **IT**
ALLIED IRISH BANKS, P.L.C., Bankcentre, Ballsbridge, pg. 64 **IT**
Amdahl Ireland Ltd., Balheary Industrial Park, pg. 527 **IT**
American International Managers Ltd., AIG House, Merrion Road, pg. 85 **PB**
Apple Computer (Sales) Ltd., Warrington House, pg. 121 **PB**
Applied Magnetics Ireland, Ltd., Clonshaugh Indus. Estate, pg. 123 **IT**
Ark Life Assurance Company Limited, 8 Burlington Road, pg. 64 **IT**
ARNOTTS PLC, 12 Henry St., pg. 81 **IT**
Asea Brown Boveri Ltd., pg. 8 **IT**
Asgard Financial Services Ltd, 104 Middle Abbey St., pg. 81 **IT**
Ashley Shops (Ireland) Ltd., pg. 804 **IT**
Astra Pharmaceuticals (Ireland) Ltd., 12 Upper Pembroke St., pg. 94 **IT**
Avery Label Ltd., Aalkinstown Ave., Long Mile Rd., pg. 153 **PB**
Avesta Sheffield Ireland Ltd., 57 Fairview Strand, pg. 221 **IT**
BBL Ireland, Harcourt Centre, Harcourt Rd., pg. 148 **IT**
BNP Capital Finance Limited - Ireland, 111 St. Stephen's Green West, pg. 163 **IT**
BNP (Ireland) Ltd., 111, St. Stephen's Green West, pg. 163 **IT**
BNY Fund Management (Ireland) Limited, AIB International Centre, I.F.S.C., 3531, pg. 179 **PB**
BOC Gases Ireland Ltd., P.O. Box 201, pg. 121 **IT**
BV Financial (Ireland) Ltd., 20 Upper Merrion St., pg. 180 **IT**
R & A Bailey & Co., Western Estate, pg. 409 **IT**
Bank Brussels Lambert - Dublin, Harcourt Centre, Harcourt Road, pg. 148 **IT**
Bank of America NT&SA, Russell Court, St. Stephen's Green, pg. 152 **PB**
BANK OF IRELAND, Lower Baggot St., pg. 152 **IT**
Bank of Ireland Asset Management Limited, 26 Fitzwilliam Place, pg. 152 **IT**
Bank of Ireland Commercial Finance Ltd., Colm House, 91 Pembroke Road, pg. 152 **IT**

Bank of Ireland Corporate Banking, Lower Baggot Street, pg. 152 **IT**
Bank of Ireland Credit Card Centre, 33/35 Nassau Street, pg. 152 **IT**
Bank of Ireland Finance Ltd., 6 Burlington Road, pg. 152 **IT**
Bank of Ireland International Finance Limited, La Touche House, International Financial Services Ctr., pg. 152 **IT**
Bank of Ireland International Services Limited, La Touche House, International Financial Services Centre, pg. 152 **IT**
Bank of Ireland Securities Services Limited, Andersen House, 1 Harbourmaster Place, pg. 152 **IT**
Bank of Ireland Trust Services, Head Office, Lower Baggot Street, pg. 152 **IT**
Bankgesellschaft Berlin (Ireland) plc, West Block Building, pg. 160 **IT**
Banta Global Turnkey, Sandyford Industrial Estate, pg. 188 **PB**
Banta Global Turnkey, Unit 14 Airways Industrial Estate, pg. 188 **PB**
Barclays Bank PLC, 47/48 St. Stephen's Green, pg. 166 **IT**
Batchelors (Ireland) Ltd., P.O. Box 88, pg. 968 **IT**
Bavarian Reinsurance Ireland Ltd., 54 Fitzwilliam Square, pg. 1333 **IT**
Bayer (Ireland) Ltd., Industrial Estate, Kill O The Grange, pg. 174 **IT**
Bear Stearns Bank plc, Eight Harcourt Centre, Fl. Three, pg. 198 **PB**
Bekaert (Ireland) Ltd., Jamestown Road, pg. 184 **IT**
Bermuda International (Dublin) Limited, First Floor, Europa House, Harcourt Centre, Harcourt Street, pg. 151 **IT**
Bermuda Trust (Dublin) Limited, First Floor, Europa House, Harcourt Centre, Harcourt Street, pg. 151 **IT**
Bewley's Manufacturing Ltd., 10-12 Westmorland St., pg. 254 **IT**
Bewley's Tea & Coffee Ltd., 10-12 Westmorland St., pg. 254 **IT**
Bewleys Hampers Limited, 23/29 Portland Street North, pg. 254 **IT**
Bewleys Hanover Street Limited, 7 Hanover Street East, pg. 254 **IT**
Boyers & Co. Limited, 20 N. Earl St., pg. 81 **IT**
Bradstock Insurance Brokers Limited, 38 Upper Fitzwilliam St., pg. 210 **IT**
Brinks-Allied, Clonshaugh Industrial Estate, pg. 81 **IT**
Broadcom Eireann Research Ltd., Kestrel House, Clanwilliam Place, pg. 1365 **IT**
Brother International Corporation (Ireland) Ltd., Boeing Rd., pg. 229 **IT**
Brown Brothers Harriman Trustee Services (Ireland) Limited, 80 Harcert St., pg. 173 **PV**
Bull Information Systems Ireland, 29/31 S. William St., pg. 318 **IT**
Bull Pension Trustees Ireland Ltd., 29/31 S. William St., pg. 318 **IT**
Burmah Castrol Ireland, Ltd., Alexandra Road, pg. 235 **IT**
Butterworths Ireland, 26 Upper Ormand Quay, pg. 1095 **IT**
CCG Ireland, 41-45 St., pg. 326 **IT**
CICM Fund Management Ltd., A.I.B. International Centre, pg. 309 **IT**
CICM (Ireland) Limited, A.I.B. International Centre, I.F.S.C., pg. 309 **IT**
C.M.I. International Ltd., pg. 302 **IT**
CPC Foods (Ireland) Ltd., Goldenbridge, Inchicore, pg. 225 **PB**
CRH, PLC, Belgard Castle, pg. 242 **IT**
Cadbury Ireland p.l.c., Coolock, pg. 248 **IT**
Cahill May Roberts Group plc., Pharmapark, Chapelizod, pg. 592 **IT**
Calor Teoranta, Long Mile Road, pg. 1155 **IT**
CAMPBELLS/BEWLEY GROUP, St. Johns Ct., pg. 253 **IT**
CANLIFE-IBI Investment Services Limited, 26 Fitzwilliam Pl., pg. 255 **IT**
Canon (Irl) Business Equipment Ltd., 294 Merrion Road, pg. 255 **IT**
Cantrell & Cochrane Group, Kylemore Park South, pg. 63 **IT**
P.J. Carroll Holdings p.l.c., Grand Parade, pg. 1130 **IT**
Celloglas Ireland Ltd., pg. 68 **IT**
Centre Reinsurance International Company, IFSC House, Custom House Quay, pg. 1531 **IT**
Chase Bank (Ireland) plc, 10/11 S. Leinster St., pg. 339 **PB**
CIBA-GEIGY Ireland Limited, Unit 60, Nore Rd., Dublin Industrial Estate, pg. 977 **IT**
CIBA-GEIGY Pharmaceuticals, Beech House, Beech Hill Office Campus, pg. 978 **IT**
CIBA Vision, Belgrave Road, United Drug House, pg. 981 **IT**
Clashfern Holdings Limited, 25 Fitzwilliam Sq., pg. 102 **IT**
Clintock Limited, Robin Hood Rd., pg. 262 **PB**
Cobra Electronics Europe, 2 Sydney Ave., pg. 391 **PB**
Colgate-Palmolive, Airport Industrial Estates, Swords Rd., pg. 398 **IT**
Combined Insurance Company of Ireland Ltd., Merrion House, Merrion Rd., pg. 118 **IT**
Commerzbank Europe (Ireland), AIB International Center, J.F.S.C., pg. 312 **IT**
The Concentrate Company of Ireland, Lagan Rd., pg. 1277 **PB**
Conoco Ireland Ltd., Conoco House, Deansgrange Blackrock, pg. 531 **IT**
Cornhill Insurance PLC, Russell Court, St. Stephen's Green, pg. 60 **IT**
Cow & Gate Nutricia (Ireland) Ltd., pg. 991 **IT**
JAMES CREAN PLC, Oakhouse, Leopards Town Office Park, pg. 340 **IT**

PB - *U.S. Public Companies Volume*
PV - *U.S. Private Companies Volume*
IT - *International Public & Private Companies Volume*

Geographic Index-Non U.S.

1655

Crosland Filters Ltd., 107 Dublin Industrial Estate, pg. 786 IT
Crush International (Overseas), Dublin Industrial Estate, Unit 70A,Moyle Road, pg. 248 IT
Daiwa Europe Bank plc-Dublin Branch, Level 2, Block 3, Harcourt Ctr., pg. 375 IT
Danisco Finance Plc, IFSC House, Ground Floor, Custom House Quay, pg. 378 IT
Dataproducts (Dublin) Ltd., Clonshaugh Industrial Estate, Coolock, pg. 621 IT
De La Rue Systems Ireland Ltd., Unit 206, Castleforbes Business Park, pg. 387 IT
De Lage Landen Leasing Ltd., Custom House Dock, 2, Harbourmaster Pl., pg. 1082 IT
Digital Equipment Ireland Limited, Park House, North Circular Road, pg. 508 PB
Edward Dillon & Co Ltd, 25 Mountjoy Sq. East, pg. 782 IT
Donohoe Lift Engineering Systems Ltd., pg. 1205 IT
Dow Jones Markets Ireland Limited, Longport House, First Fl., Lower Leeson St., pg. 525 PB
Dowdall, O'Mahoney & Company Limited, Unit 292, Beech Rd., pg. 1290 PB
Dresdner Asset Management Ireland Ltd., La Touche House, International Financial Services Centre, pg. 419 IT
Dresdner Bank (Ireland) plc, La Touche House, International Financial Services Centre, pg. 419 IT
Dresdner International Finance plc, Oracle House, Herbert St., pg. 419 IT
Dun & Bradstreet Ltd., Holbrook House Holles St., pg. 536 PB
EG & G Ireland, Instruments Division, Coolmine Industrial Estate, pg. 544 PB
EMI Records (Ireland) Ltd., 1 Ailesbury Road, pg. 427 IT
Daniel J. Edelman Ireland, Ltd., 5th Floor Huguenot House, pg. 363 PV
ELAN CORPORATION PLC, Lincoln House, Lincoln Place, pg. 435 IT
Electra Insurance Limited, Beech Hill Road, Clonskeagh, pg. 1365 IT
Elida Faberge (Ireland) Ltd., Belgard Industrial Estate, Mayberry Rd., pg. 1437 IT
Elsevier Reed Finance Ireland, First Floor, 1 FSC House, pg. 1093 IT
Ericsson Business Communications Ltd., 4th Fl., Harcourt Centre, Harcourt Rd., pg. 1366 IT
Ericsson I.F.S., Beech Hill, Clonskeagh, pg. 1367 IT
Eureko Ireland Holdings, Friends Provident House, 29-30 Adelaide Road, pg. 464 IT
Europ Assistance (Ireland) Ltd., 51 Donnybrook Road, pg. 91 IT
FCS Currency Management, 29 Earlsfort Terrace, pg. 219 IT
FSW Coatings Limited, Virginia Cavan, pg. 1466 PB
Fasson Ireland Ltd., Dublin Indus. Estate Fing, 37B Barrow Rd., pg. 154 PB
Fiat Auto Ireland Ltd., Hume House, Ballsbridge, pg. 481 IT
First Rate Bureau de Change Limited, 88 Lower Camden Street, pg. 152 IT
Fleishman-Hillard Saunders Limited, 35 Westland Sq., pg. 411 PV
Forbo Ireland Ltd., pg. 497 IT
Forte Holdings Ireland Limited, 1 Earlsport Centre, pg. 556 IT
William Freeman Limited, 12 Henry St., pg. 81 IT
Friends Provident Ireland, Friends Provident House, 29-30 Adelaide Road, pg. 464 IT
Fujitsu Microelectronics Ireland Ltd., Greenhills Centre, Greenhills Road, pg. 528 IT
G.E. Lighting (Ireland) Ltd., W. Industria Estates, 280 Holly Rd., pg. 713 PB
GEC Distributors (Ireland) Ltd., 15-19 Hendrick St., pg. 546 IT
GGK Dublin, 64 Lower Leeson St., pg. 1335 IT
Gartell Limited, One Earlsfort Ctr., pg. 102 IT
Gelman Ireland Ltd., Ashgrove House, Ashgrove Indus. Estate, Kill Ave., pg. 1253 PB
General Motors Distribution Ireland Ltd., Belgard Road Tallaght, pg. 722 PB
Gestetner (Ireland) Limited, Dublin Industrial Estate, 139 Slaney Close, pg. 1115 IT
Gilbey's of Ireland, Gilbey House, Belgard Rd., pg. 409 IT
Goodbody Stockbrokers, 122 Pembroke Road, pg. 64 IT
Green Isle Ltd., pg. 968 IT
Griffith Laboratories Ireland Limited, Pineview Industrial Estate, Firhouse Rd., pg. 481 PV
Guinness Ireland (Holdings) Ltd., St. James's Gate, pg. 412 IT
Gunnebo Ireland Ltd., Unit 32, Airton Terrace, Tallaght Industrial Estate, pg. 578 IT
Gypsum Industries plc., Clonskeagh Rd., pg. 123 IT
HB Ice Cream Ltd., pg. 1437 IT
Helaba Dublin-Landesbank International, AIB International Centre, pg. 799 IT
Helaba International Finance plc, 3 George's Dock, pg. 799 IT
Hellermann Ireland, 77 Cherry Orchard Industrial Estate, pg. 208 IT
P.C. Henderson (Ireland) Ltd., Westlink Industrial Estate, Kylemore Rd., pg. 615 IT
Henkel Chemicals (Ireland) Ltd., pg. 612 IT
Ja. Hennessy & Co Ltd, Central Hotel Chambers, Dame Ct., pg. 782 IT
Hewlett-Packard Ireland Ltd., Temple House, Temple Road, pg. 820 PB
Hodios (Ireland) Ltd., 11 Windsor Place, Lower Pembroke Street, pg. 1072 IT
Robert Horne Paper (Ireland) Limited, pg. 757 IT
IBI Corporate Finance Limited, 26 Fitzwilliam Place, pg. 152 IT
IBI Investment Services Limited, 26 Fitzwilliam Pl., pg. 152 IT
ICS Building Society, 25 Westmoreland Street, pg. 152 IT
IDV Operations Ireland Ltd., Nangor House, Western Estate, pg. 410 IT
IIB Finance Unltd., 93 Merrion Sq., pg. 760 IT
IIB International Finance Unltd., 93 Merrion Sq., pg. 760 IT
ISS Contract Cleaners Ltd., 14/17 Hanbury Lane, pg. 657 IT
ITT Flygt Ltd., 44 Broomhill Close, Airton Rd., pg. 860 PB
Incentive International Finance, 3 Harbourmaster Place, IFSC, pg. 669 IT
Industrial Detergents, Ltd., pg. 612 IT
Ingersoll-Rand Co. (Ireland) Ltd., John F. Kennedy Dr., pg. 878 PB
Intercontinental Finance Unltd., 93 Merrion Sq., pg. 761 IT
Intergraph Ireland Limited, Stadbrook House, Stadbrook Road, Blackrock Co., pg. 892 PB
INTERNATIONAL INVESTMENT & UNDERWRITING LTD., IFC House, Custom House Quay, pg. 684 IT
IRISH BISCUITS, Belgard Rd., Tallaght, pg. 688 IT
Irish Biscuits Experts Ltd., Belgard Road, pg. 688 IT
Irish Biscuits Ltd., Belgard Road, pg. 688 IT
Irish Biscuits Sales Ltd., Belgard Road, pg. 688 IT
Irish Biscuits-W & R Jacob, Belgard Road, Tallght, pg. 381 IT
Irish Distillers Ltd., Bow St., Smithfield, pg. 567 IT
Irish Flavors & Fragrances Limited, pg. 899 PB
Irish Intercontinental Bank, Ltd., 91 Merrion Square, pg. 761 IT
Irish Life Finance Group, 2 Hume Street, pg. 761 IT
Irish Life Finance Ltd., 2 Hume Street, pg. 761 IT
Irish Life Homeloans Ltd., 2 Hume Street, pg. 761 IT
Irish Sewing Ltd., Unit 56, Carriglea Industrial Estate, pg. 299 IT
Irish Shell Ltd., Shell House, Beach Hill, pg. 1138 IT
J & E Davy Holdings Limited, Davy House, 49 Dawson Street, pg. 152 IT
JC Distribution Limited, South City Executive Park, pg. 340 IT
JA/MONT Ireland Ltd., McKee Ave., Finglas W., pg. 673 PB
Jacobs International Limited, Inc., Merrion House, Merrion Rd., pg. 922 PB
Javelin/Young & Rubicam, Dawson House, 55 Dawson St., pg. 1199 PV
Jetphone Limited, 1 Earlsfort Centre, Hatch Street, pg. 223 IT
John Player & Sons Ireland, Box 286, pg. 595 IT
Johnson & Johnson (Ireland) Ltd., Belgard Road, pg. 930 PB
Jones Environmental (Ireland) Ltd., Richview, Clonskeagh, pg. 1444 IT
K-Tel Ireland Ltd., 30/32 Sir John Rogersons Quay, pg. 938 PB
KB Finance Dublin Unltd., 93 Merrion Sq., pg. 761 IT
KB Financial Services (Dublin) Unltd., 93 Merrion Square, pg. 761 IT
KB Financial Services (Ireland) Unltd., 93 Merrion Square, pg. 761 IT
Kabi Pharmacia & Upjohn Ireland Ltd., Pharmapak, Chapelizod, pg. 1049 IT
Kelly Temporary Services, Ltd.-Ireland, 21/22 Grafton St., pg. 949 PB
Kemira Ireland Ltd., 11 Merrion Sq., pg. 728 IT
KeyMed Ireland Ltd., pg. 1005 IT
Koratrade MTMC Ltd., Lifetime House, Earlsfort Center, pg. 742 IT
Kredietbank Dublin Branch, Kredietbank House, I.F.S.C., pg. 760 IT
LGT Asset Management Ltd., 5th Floor, Alexandra House, Earlsfort Centre, Earlsfort Terr., pg. 810 IT
LGT Finance Ireland Ltd, 5th Floor, Alexandra House, Earlsfort Centre, Earlsfort Terr., pg. 810 IT
LM Ericsson Holdings Ltd., Harcourt Centre, Harcourt Rd., 3rd Fl., pg. 1368 IT
LM Ericsson Ltd., Beech Hill, Clonskeagh, pg. 1369 IT
LMG Financial Services, pg. 68 IT
Label Art Limited, 72/74 Broomhill Rd., pg. 340 IT
Lambert Smith Hampton, 115 Lower Baggett Street, pg. 797 IT
Lawson Mardon Superior Packaging, Jamestown Rd., pg. 69 IT
Lever Brothers (Ireland) Ltd., Belgord Industrial Estate, Belgord Rd., Tallaght, pg. 1437 IT
Lifetime Assurance Co. Limited, Lifetime House, Earlsfort Terrace, pg. 152 IT
The Little Tikes Company (Ireland), Limited, Clonshaugh Industrial Estate, pg. 1411 PB
Livingston UK Limited, Unit 42, Airaways, pg. 212 IT
Loctite (Ireland) Ltd., Tallaght Business Park, Whitestown, Tallaght, pg. 611 IT
Lombard and Ulster Banking Limited, Ulster Bank Group Centre, George's Quay, pg. 911 IT
Lowara Ireland Ltd., pg. 861 PB
M&S Export (Ireland) Limited, 24-27 Mary St., pg. 843 IT
MTBC Ireland, 2 Harbourmaster Place, Custom House Dock, pg. 877 IT
MTI Ireland, Unit 8, Airways, Indus. Estate, pg. 1028 PB
MacGregor Golf Ireland, Ltd., Muirfield Dr., Naas Rd., pg. 73 IT
Management International (Dublin) Limited, First Floor, Europa House, Harcourt Centre, Harcourt Street, pg. 151 IT
Marks & Spencer (Ireland) Limited, 24-29 Mary St., pg. 843 IT
Masterfoods Ltd., 7-8 Harcourt St., pg. 707 PV
Mather & Platt (Ireland) Limited, 7 Ardee Rd., pg. 1650 PB
J.V. McDaniel Limited, Cookstown Industrial Estate, pg. 340 IT
W. & C. McDonnell Ltd., pg. 1438 IT
Memorex Telex Ireland, Ltd., Furze Road, pg. 857 IT
Merchants House, 27-30A Merchants Quay, pg. 321 PB
Martin Merkel Ireland Ltd., Cookstown Industrial Estate, pg. 860 IT
Merrymaid Limited, 12 Henry St., pg. 81 IT
Microsoft Manufacturing B.V., Blackthorn Road, Sandyford Industrial Estates, pg. 1108 PB
Midland International Financial Services (Ireland) Limited, 13-17 Dawson Street, pg. 583 IT
Milne Models Limited, 12 Henry St., pg. 81 IT
Mitsubishi Trust Finance (Ireland) Plc., 2nd Floor, Iveagh Court, 6-8 Harcourt Road, pg. 877 IT
Mitsui & Co., Ltd., BP House, 1 Setanta Place, pg. 881 IT
Monsanto Ireland Ltd., Ardeen House, 10-12 Marine Terrace, pg. 1125 PB
Motorola Ltd., Santry Village, Swords Road, pg. 1140 PB
National Irish Bank Limited, 7/8 Wilton Terrace, pg. 906 IT
Nevinar Ltd., 1 Sussex St., pg. 296 IT
Nicholas Laboratories Ltd., pg. 1121 IT
A.C. Nielsen of Ireland, Ltd., 36 Merrion Sq., pg. 1183 PB
Norske Skog (Ireland) Limited, 11, Anglesea St., pg. 966 IT
Novo Nordisk Pharmaceuticals Ltd., 3/4 Upper Pembroke Street, pg. 988 IT
Nutricia Financial Services Ltd., pg. 992 IT
Nutricia Ireland Ltd., 1B Sandyford Business Ctr., pg. 992 IT
OCE-Ireland Ltd., pg. 994 IT
Oki Systems (Ireland) Ltd., The Square Industrial Complex, pg. 1000 IT
Oracle Europe Manufacturing Ltd., Maretimo Court, Temple Road, pg. 1228 PB
Organon Ireland Ltd., Farnham Dr., Finglas Rd., pg. 45 IT
Organon Teknika Ireland Ltd., Farnham Dr., Finglas Rd., pg. 45 IT
ORIX Aviation Systems Limited, 2nd Fl., IFSC House, Intl. Financial Services Ctr., pg. 1009 IT
ORIX Ireland Limited, 2nd Fl., IFSC House, Intl. Services Center, pg. 1009 IT
Packard Electric Ireland Limited, Airton Rd., pg. 723 PB
Packwood Limited, One Earlsfort Ctr., pg. 102 IT
Paul & Vincent Ltd., pg. 1438 IT
Pfizer Holdings Ireland, La Touche House, International Financial Services Ctr., pg. 1283 PB
Pfizer International Bank Europe, La Touche House, International Financial Services Centre, pg. 1283 PB
Pfizer Research & Development Company, La Touche House, International Financial Services Centre, pg. 1283 PB
Pfizer Service Company Ireland, Alexandra House, Earlsfort Centre, pg. 1283 PB
Polycell Rawplug Ireland Limited, Furze Rd., Sandyford Industrial Estate, pg. 925 IT
Porsche Financial Management Services Ltd., pg. 1063 IT
Porsche International Financing Ltd., pg. 1063 IT
Porsche International Insurance Ltd., pg. 1063 IT
Premier Banking, Premier House, The Square, pg. 152 IT
QPI Financial Services, 2 Harbourmaster Pl., pg. 1078 IT
Quinn McDonnell Pattison DMB&B Dublin, 43 Lr. Leeson St., pg. 305 PV
Quinton Hazell PLC, Dublin, Dublin Industrial Estate, 101 Slaney Rd., pg. 561 PB
John G. Rathborne, East Wall Rd., pg. 1138 IT
Rayrock Finance Company, Irish Life Centre, Abbey Court, pg. 1089 IT
Readymix p.l.c., 5/23 East Wall Rd., pg. 1081 IT
Renishaw (Ireland) Limited, A1/2 Santry Ave., Industrial Estate, pg. 1103 IT
RHEINHYP Europe plc, pg. 310 IT
Riada & Co., One, College Green, pg. 12 IT
Rockwell Automation Limited, Naas Road Industrial Park, Naas Road, pg. 1399 PB
SMS Ireland Unlimited, SMS House, St. Johns Business Centre, pg. 1463 PB
STC (Northern Ireland) Limited, ICL House, Adelaide Rd., pg. 529 IT
Sandoz Products (Ireland) Ltd., pg. 985 IT
Sandoz Ringaskiddy Ltd., pg. 985 IT
Sandvik Ireland Limited, Indus. Park Stillorgan, pg. 1186 IT
Sanmina Ireland, Blanchardstown Industrial Park, pg. 1431 PB
Sanwa International (Ireland) PLC, I.C.L. House, Block 8, Harcourt Centre, Harcourt Street, pg. 1190 IT
Scotiabank (Ireland) Limited, I.F.S.C. House, 4th Floor, Custom House Quay, pg. 156 IT
Seven-Up Ireland Ltd., Lagan Road, Dublin Industrial Estate, pg. 1278 PB
Siemens Ltd., 8 Raglan Rd., pg. 1247 IT
SINSER (Ireland) Ltd., 11 Windsor Place, Lower Pembroke St., pg. 1258 IT
SmithKline Beecham Laboratories Ltd., Ferry House, 48-53 Lower Mount St., pg. 1266 IT
SmithKline Beecham of Ireland Ltd., Long Mile Rd., pg. 1266 IT
Smurfit Capital Funding plc, 4th Floor, IFSC House, IFSC, pg. 1269 IT
Smurfit Ireland Limited, Beech Hill, pg. 1269 IT
JEFFERSON SMURFIT GROUP P.L.C., Beech Hill, Clonskeagh, pg. 1269 IT
Smurfit-Paribas Bank Ltd., 94 St. Stephen's Green, pg. 321 IT
Softrans International, Ltd., 14, Carysfort Ave., pg. 222 PB
Spruce Insurance Ltd., Harcourt Centre, Harcourt Rd., pg. 729 IT

PB - *U.S. Public Companies Volume*
PV - *U.S. Private Companies Volume*
IT - *International Public & Private Companies Volume*

Statoil Ireland, Ltd., Sentanta Place, pg. 1298 — IT
Stratus Computer, Blanchardstown Industrial Park, pg. 1524 — PB
Strix Investments Ltd., pg. 310 — IT
Sumitomo Finance (Dublin) Limited, La Touche House I.F.S.C., pg. 1310 — IT
Sun Chemical Inks (Ireland) Ltd., 66 Lower Baggot Street, pg. 371 — IT
Swiss Life Investment Management, No. 1 Harbourmaster Place, International Financial Services Center, pg. 1332 — IT
Symantec Ltd., Bally Coolen Industrial Park, pg. 1546 — PB
Tektronix Ireland Limited, pg. 1568 — PB
TELECOM EIREANN, St. Stephen's Green West, pg. 1362 — IT
Tennant & Ruttle Distribution Limited, Greenhills Rd., pg. 340 — IT
Tennant & Ruttle Limited, Broomhill Rd., pg. 340 — IT
Texaco (Ireland) Ltd., Texaco House, Ballsbridge, pg. 1584 — PB
3M Ireland Ltd., 3M House, Adelphi Centre, pg. 1607 — PB
Tosara Group, Baldoyle Industrial Estate, Grange Rd., pg. 670 — PB
Toyota Motor Distributors (Ireland) Ltd., Toyota House, Killeen Rd., pg. 1413 — IT
TRUE LIFE, Wasdale House, Rathfarnham Road, pg. 1425 — IT
UPM-Kymmene Ireland, 3 Harcourt Terrace, pg. 1430 — IT
Ulster Bank Commercial Services Limited, Ulster Bank Group Centre, George's Quay, pg. 911 — IT
Ulster Bank Dublin Trust Company, 33 College Green, pg. 912 — IT
Ulster Bank Group Treasury (International) Limited, P.O. Box 3255, pg. 912 — IT
Ulster Bank Group Treasury Limited, IFSC House, International Financial Services Centre, pg. 912 — IT
Ulster Investment Bank Limited, Ulster Bank Group Centre, pg. 912 — IT
United Beverages Limited, Keeper Rd., pg. 340 — IT
Up-Right (Ireland) Ltd., Pottery Rd., pg. 1128 — PV
Utell International-Ireland, First Floor, Lincoln House, Lincoln Lane, Smithfield, pg. 1098 — IT
VB International Finance Ireland, pg. 181 — IT
Van Leer (Ireland) Ltd., pg. 1147 — IT
Vehicle Spares Ltd., Unit 410 Cherry Orchard Indust. Estate, pg. 861 — IT
Vent-Axia Ventilation Limited, 921 Western Industrial Estate, Naas Rd., pg. 1269 — IT
Volkswagen Investments Ltd., pg. 1475 — IT
Robert Wallace Limited, 12 Henry St., pg. 81 — IT
Robert Wallace (Shirts) Limited, 12 Henry St., pg. 81 — IT
Wang Ireland Limited, Business Centre, Ballymount Rd. Lower, pg. 1738 — PB
WATERFORD WEDGWOOD PLC, 1/2 Upper Hatch Street, pg. 1487 — IT
Wella Dublin, Kill Lane, pg. 1490 — IT
Wellcome Ireland Ltd., Clonard Rd. 12, pg. 553 — IT
Wessel Ind. Ltd., Whitestown Industrial Estate, pg. 3 — IT
WestLB (Ireland) Ltd., 2 Harbourmaster Pl., International Financial Services Centre, pg. 1494 — IT
Whitehall Laboratories Limited, 765 South Circular Rd., pg. 82 — IT
Wiggins Arjo Ireland (Holdings) Ltd., Gateway House, 74-112 East Wall Rd., pg. 567 — IT
Willis Corroon Ireland Limited, 80 Harcourt Street, pg. 1504 — IT
Willis Corroon Management Limited-Dublin, 80 Harcourt Street, pg. 1509 — IT
Woodchester Investments plc, Woodchester House, Golden Lane, pg. 712 — PB
X.L. Europe Insurance, pg. 467 — IT
Xlinx, Ireland, Logic Dr., Citywest Bus. Campus, pg. 1786 — PB
Yamanouchi Ireland Co., Ltd., Damastown, pg. 1519 — IT
Youghal Carpets (Yarns) Ltd., Unit 5B, Carriglea, Industrial Estate, pg. 301 — IT
Zeneca Ireland Ltd., College Park House, 20 Nassau St., pg. 1526 — IT
Zenith Data Systems Ireland Ltd., Unit 7 Airways Industrial Estate, pg. 317 — IT
Zurich Insurance Company, Europa House, Ground Floor, Harcourt Street, pg. 1531 — IT
Zurich International Services (Ireland) Limited, IFSC House, Custom House Quay, pg. 1532 — IT

Dun Laoghaire

Ericsson Treasury Ireland Ltd., Adelaide House, Adelaide St., pg. 1368 — IT
INTERMEC Group, 19/20 York Rd., pg. 1043 — PB
Kodak Ireland Limited, Kodak House, Pottery Rd., pg. 553 — PB
Parke-Davis/Elan Ltd., Pottery Rd., pg. 436 — IT
Quarterdeck International Limited, B.I.M. House, Crofton Terrace, pg. 1351 — PB
Stena Line Limited, Adelaide House, Haddington Terrace, pg. 1300 — IT

Dundalk

Custom Foods Limited, pg. 806 — PB
Quantum Peripheral Products (Ireland) Limited, Finnabair Industrial Park, pg. 1350 — PB

Dungarvan

Dungarvan Crystal Ltd., pg. 1487 — IT

Dunleer

Bi-Tech Engineering, pg. 554 — IT
Chilton Electric, pg. 554 — IT
THE GLEN DIMPLEX GROUP, Ardee Rd., pg. 553 — IT

Ennis

Microsemi Corp.-Ennis, Gort Rd., pg. 1107 — PB

Fermoy

HIVEC-Ireland, Rathealy Rd., pg. 528 — PV

Foxrock

Boole & Babbage Europe, Unit 5, Leopardstown Office Park, pg. 245 — PB

Foynes

Irish Bulk Liquid Storage Ltd., pg. 1252 — IT

Galway

Celtic International, Celtic House, pg. 464 — IT
Farah (Exports) Ireland, Ashe Road, pg. 613 — PB
Ireland Assistance Ltd., Celtic Court, pg. 334 — IT
Micromotors Groschopp Ireland Ltd., Industrial Estate Mervue - Galway, pg. 559 — IT
Square D Company Ireland, pg. 1209 — IT

Glasnovin

Computerscope Ltd., Prospect House, 1 Prospect Rd., pg. 569 — PV

Hillsborough

Irish Biscuits (N.I.), P.O. Box 3, pg. 688 — IT

Kells

BGB Finance (Ireland) plc, West Block Building, pg. 160 — IT
Wellman International Ltd., pg. 1753 — PB

Kilbarry

Waterford Crystal Gallery Ltd., pg. 1487 — IT
Waterford Crystal (Lightingware) Ltd., pg. 1487 — IT
Waterford Crystal Ltd., pg. 1487 — IT
Waterford Glass Research & Development Ltd., pg. 1487 — IT

Kilcock

Leaf Ireland Ltd., pg. 638 — IT

Kill

PDM Ltd., Old Milltown, pg. 864 — IT

Killarney

Killarney Hotels Ltd., pg. 809 — IT
Liebherr Container Cranes Ltd., pg. 809 — IT
Liebherr (Ireland) Holding Ltd., pg. 808 — IT

Killkenny

AVONMORE WATERFORD GROUP PLC, A.W. House, Main Street, pg. 102 — IT

Killorglin

Fujisawa Ireland Limited, pg. 525 — IT

Kilrush

Chemical Fabrics Limited, pg. 344 — PB

Laois

C & M Europe, Kylekiproe Ind. Est., pg. 192 — PV

Leitrim

Donnelly Vision Systems Europe Ltd., Park Rd., pg. 519 — PB

Limerick

AST Computer, National Technological Park, pg. 1182 — IT
Alcan Ireland Ltd., 5 Pery Square, pg. 51 — IT
Amicon Ireland Limited, Raheen Industrial Estate, Bay C-1, pg. 1113 — PB
Analog Devices BV, Bay F-1, Raheen Ind. Estate, pg. 108 — PB

Banta Global Turnkey, Raheen Industrial Estate, pg. 188 — PB
Dell Products (Europe) B.V., Raheen Industrial Estate, pg. 496 — PB
Essilor Ireland Ltd., Bay E1, Raheen Indus. Estate, pg. 462 — IT
Krups Sales Ltd., Roxboro Road, pg. 896 — IT
Wang Laboratories, Plassey Technical Park, Castleroy, pg. 1738 — PB
Wyeth (Ireland) Limited, Askeaton, pg. 82 — PB

Listowel

Imperial Stag Ltd., pg. 559 — PV
Stelrad Components Ltd., Clieveragh, pg. 268 — IT

Little Island

Chr. Hansen Ireland Limited, Rohan Industrial Estate, pg. 289 — IT
Henkel (Ireland) Ltd., pg. 612 — IT
Janssen Pharmaceutical Limited, pg. 930 — PB
Pegasus Engineering Ltd., Hexagon House, pg. 922 — PB

Maghera

Svedala Ltd. Maghera, pg. 1325 — IT

Mallow

The Borden Co., Limited, West End, pg. 159 — PV
Borden, Exports Limited, West End, pg. 159 — PV
Borden Foods Limited, West End, pg. 159 — PV
Borden Intl. Packaging, Ltd., West End, pg. 159 — PV
ITW Hi-Cone Ltd., Indus. Estate Quertertown, pg. 868 — PB

Meath

Atlantic 252, Mornington House, Summerhill Road, pg. 561 — IT

Mervue

Nellcor Puritan-Bennett Inc. (Ireland), New Mervue Indus. Park, pg. 1040 — PB
Northern Telecom (Ireland) Limited, Galway Industrial Estate, pg. 970 — IT

Mountmellick

Standex (Ireland) Ltd., Acragar Road, pg. 1508 — PB

Mullingar

EOC Normalien (IRL) Ltd., Streamstown House, Streamstown, pg. 75 — IT
Penn Racquet Sports, Lynn Road, pg. 706 — PB

Naas

Donnelly Mirrors, Limited, pg. 519 — PB
Eurotherm Ireland Ltd., IDA Industrial Estate, Monread Road, pg. 466 — IT
ROR Rockwell (Ireland) Limited, Newhall, pg. 1399 — PB

Navan

Tara Mines Limited, Knockumber House, Knockumber Rd., pg. 1016 — IT

Nenagh

R-V Chemicals Ltd., Gortlandroe Indus. Estate, pg. 1332 — PB
Rorer Ireland, Ltd., Linsbunny Industrial Estate, pg. 1112 — IT

New Ross

Lake Region Manufacturing Co., Ltd., pg. 643 — PV

Newtownards

Insoleq Semafour, Quarry Heights, North Rd., pg. 453 — PV

Palmerstown

Grassland Fertilisers (Kilkenny) Limited, pg. 102 — IT

Portarlington

Arlington, Ltd., Cooltederry, pg. 156 — PB

Portlaoise

Tretorn Sport Ltd., New Indus. Estate, pg. 1072 — IT
Tretorn Sport Sales Ltd., New Indus. Estate, pg. 1072 — IT

Ringaskiddy

BCB Beverages Limited, Raheens East, pg. 338 — IT
Pfizer (Ireland) Limited, pg. 1283 — PB
Pfizer Pension Trustees (Ireland) Limited, pg. 1283 — PB

PB - *U.S. Public Companies Volume*
PV - *U.S. Private Companies Volume*
IT - *International Public & Private Companies Volume*

IRELAND

Rosslare

Stena Line Limited, pg. 1300 — IT

Santry

Bewleys Oriental Cafes Limited, 4 St. Johns Court, pg. 254 — IT
Brenford, 4 St. Johns Court, pg. 254 — IT
Campbell Bewley Properties Ltd., 4 St. Johns Court, pg. 254 — IT
Dial A Hamper Limited, 14 St. Johns Court, pg. 254 — IT

Shannon

Aer Rianta Bewley Limited, Shannon Airport, pg. 254 — IT
Befab-Safeland, Ltd., Bay 15, Industrial Estates, pg. 313 — PV
Devcon Ltd., Shannon Indus. Estate, pg. 867 — PB
Elsevier Science Ireland Limited, Bay 15K, Shannon Industrial Estate, pg. 1100 — IT
GPA Group PLC, Shannon Airport Hse., pg. 37 — IT
Hypo Property Finance, Shannon Industrial Estate, pg. 176 — IT
International Aircraft Services, IAS House, pg. 340 — IT
Molex Ireland Ltd., Site 3, Shannon Indus. Estate, pg. 1122 — PB
Raychem International Ltd., 100/104 Industrial Estate, pg. 1362 — PB
Rothenberger (Ireland) Ltd., Shannon Industrial Estate, Bay.n. 119, pg. 1129 — IT
SPS International Ltd., Shannon Airport Industrial Estate, pg. 1420 — PB
Shannon Turbine Technologies Ltd., pg. 1308 — IT
Tellabs Ltd., Shannon Industrial Estate, pg. 1573 — PB

Skibbereen

Star Ball Retainer Company of Ireland Ltd., pg. 839 — IT

Sligo

Rexam Medical Packaging Ltd., Finisklin Industrial Estate, pg. 1106 — IT

Smithtown

Smithstown Light Engineering Ltd., Smithstown Indus. Estate, pg. 1123 — PB

Stillorgan

Irish Cement Ltd., Stillorgan Rd., pg. 242 — IT

Swords

Campbell Catering Limited, Leas Cross, pg. 254 — IT
Campbell Inflight Limited, Leas Cross, pg. 254 — IT
Campbell International Trading House Limited, Leas Cross, pg. 254 — IT
Campbell Management Services Limited, Leas Cross, pg. 254 — IT
Olin Chemicals, B.V., pg. 1220 — PB
Preplate Limited, Leas Cross, pg. 254 — IT

Tallaght

Gallaher (Dublin) Ltd., Virginia House, pg. 539 — IT
Nestle (Ireland) Ltd., pg. 921 — IT
Sony Ireland Ltd., 81 Broomhill Rd., pg. 1284 — IT
THORN EMI (Ireland) Limited, 27, Cookstown Industrial Estate, pg. 428 — IT

Tipperary

C & C (Wholesale) Ltd.., Brittas Rd., pg. 64 — IT

Tralee

Ansaldo Trasporti Signaling Ltd., Mona Valley Industrial Estate, pg. 78 — IT
KERRY GROUP PLC, Princes St., pg. 731 — IT

Tuam

Pulse Engineering-Ireland, pg. 1564 — PB

Tullow

Co-Operative Animal Health Limited, pg. 102 — IT

Walkinstown

Irish Driver-Harris Co., Ltd., Ballymount Trading Estate, pg. 530 — PB

Waterford

AlliedSignal Ireland Ltd., Unit 328, Western Extension Industrial Estate, pg. 53 — PB
Bausch & Lomb Ireland Limited, Waterford Industrial Estate, pg. 195 — PB
Brockmore Limited, Main St., pg. 102 — IT
CIBA-GEIGY Ireland Limited, Industrial Estate, pg. 977 — IT
Hughes Dairy Ltd., Main St., pg. 102 — IT

Lawter Intl. B.V., pg. 981 — PB
MB Ireland, Ballynaneashagh, Cork Rd., pg. 798 — PB
Nacanco Ireland Ltd., Waterford Industrial Estate, pg. 1029 — IT
Premier Dairies (Wexford) Limited, Main St., pg. 102 — IT
Stafford-Miller (Ireland) Limited, Clocherane, Youghal Rd., pg. 237 — PB
Virginia Milk Products Limited, Main St., pg. 102 — IT
Waterford Continental Cheese Limited, Main St., pg. 102 — IT
Waterford Co-Operative Dairy & Trading Society Limited, Main St., pg. 102 — IT
Waterford Foods Ireland Ltd., Main St., pg. 102 — IT
Waterford Pharmaceuticals Ltd., Industrial Estate, pg. 915 — PB

Westport

Allergan Pharmaceuticals (Ireland) Ltd., Inc., Castlebar Rd., pg. 46 — PB

Wexford

ABS Pumps Ltd., Industrial Estate, Clonard Road, pg. 270 — IT
CPM/Europe Ltd., Industrial Estate, pg. 705 — PB

Wicklow

Servtech Limited, Boghall Rd., pg. 316 — IT

Youghal

Power Conversion Europe, pg. 422 — PB

ISRAEL

Acre

Aircraft Division/BEDEK Aviation Group, Ben-Gurion Intl. Airport, pg. 690 — IT
BEDEK Aviation Group (IAI), Ben-Gurion Intl. Airport, pg. 690 — IT
Commercial Aircraft Group, Ben Gurion International Airport, pg. 690 — IT
Flight Operations/BEDEK Aviation Group, Ben-Gurion Intl. Airport, pg. 690 — IT
Geotek Israel, Geotek Yokneam, Bldg. Seven, Yokneam New Industrial Park, pg. 740 — PB
Geotek Technologies Israel Ltd., Geotek Yokneam, Bldg. Seven, Yokneam New Industrial Park, pg. 740 — PB
ISRAEL AIRCRAFT INDUSTRIES LTD., Ben-Gurion Intl. Airport, pg. 689 — IT
MHT Division, Ben Gurion Intl. Airport, pg. 690 — IT
Maman Division. Ben Gurion Intl. Airport, pg. 690 — IT
Military Aircraft Group, Ben-Gurion International Airport, pg. 690 — IT
Production Division/Commercial Aircraft Group, Ben-Gurion International Airport, pg. 690 — IT
SHL Division/Commercial Aircraft Group, pg. 690 — IT
Tambour Limited, P.O. Box 2238, Industrial Zone, pg. 644 — IT

Arad

Motorola South-Israel Limited, 16, Ha'Yotskim Street, pg. 1140 — PB

Ashdod

Elta Electronics Industries, Ltd., P.O. Box 330, pg. 690 — IT

Beer-Yaacov

MLM Division/Electronics Group, pg. 690 — IT

Beersheba

MAKHTESHIM CHEMICAL WORKS LTD., pg. 830 — IT
RAMTA Division/BEDEK Aviation Group, pg. 690 — IT

Bnei-Brak

AGIS INDUSTRIES LTD., 29 Lehi St., pg. 30 — IT
Astronautics C.A. Ltd., 23 Hayerarkon Street, 51261, pg. 93 — PV

Givatayim

Raychem Ltd., 5 Tefutzot Israel St., pg. 1362 — PB

Hadera

AMERICAN ISRAELI PAPER MILLS LTD., pg. 74 — IT
Amnir-Recycling Industries Ltd, Industrial Zone, P.O. Box 142, pg. 75 — IT

Haifa

Bio-Logic Systems Corporation Ltd., pg. 230 — PB
Det Norske Veritas, P.O. Box 7768, pg. 397 — IT
Elbit Computers Ltd., Advanced Technology Center, pg. 644 — IT
Elbit Ltd., pg. 644 — IT
Electrochemical Industries (Frutarom) Ltd., P.O. Box 1929, pg. 553 — PV

Elron Electronic Industries Ltd., pg. 644 — IT
ELSCINT LTD., Advanced Technology Center, pg. 450 — IT
Frutarom Ltd., pg. 553 — PV
International Paper USA Ltd, Starco Bldg., Stella Marris SQ, pg. 906 — PB
THE ISRAEL ELECTRIC CORPORATION LTD., 2 Hagana Ave., pg. 690 — IT
Jordan Investments Limited: Migrashi Hakablanim Limited, 2 Hagana Ave., pg. 691 — IT
Kulicke & Soffa (Israel) Ltd., P.O. Box 875, pg. 969 — PB
Lageen Box & Can Factory, Ltd., Kibbutz Meshek, pg. 1029 — IT
Ma'berot Hayarden Limited, P.O. Box 8810, pg. 691 — IT
Migrashi Hakablanim Limited, 2 Hagana Ave., pg. 691 — IT
Netwiz Ltd., Matam Post Office, pg. 645 — IT
Palestine Construction Company Limited, 2 Hagana Ave., pg. 691 — IT
Witco Ltd., P.O. Box 975, pg. 1774 — PB

Herzliyya

Bellsouth Israel, Inc. (CellCom Israel Ltd.), 2001 Merkazim Bldg., 29 Maskit St., pg. 208 — PB
Cott Beverages Israel Limited, 1 Mitspe Yam Street, Suite 16, pg. 338 — IT
General Engineers Limited, P.O. Box 557, pg. 645 — IT
Israel Edible Products Ltd., 91 Medinat Hayehudim St., pg. 225 — PB
KETER PLASTIC LTD., 2 Sapir Street, pg. 732 — PB
Kodak Israel, 16 Hagalim, pg. 553 — PB
Medtronic World Trade Corp., 11 Galgaleg Ha'Plada, pg. 1084 — PB
Veribest Israel, 20 Galgaley Haplada Industrial Area, 46106, pg. 892 — PB

Holon

Herbalife International Israel (1990) Ltd., 61 Hamelacha St., Industrial Zone, 58117, pg. 809 — PB
ICI (Israel) Limited, pg. 665 — IT
In Stent Israel, 5 Hazdref St., pg. 1083 — PB
Scitex Corporation Ltd., Industrial Zone, Herzlia B, pg. 644 — IT
Sigma Israel Chemical Co., Ltd., pg. 1472 — PB
Vishay Israel Ltd., 2 Haofan St., pg. 1722 — PB

Jerusalem

AVX Israel Ltd., P.O. Box 3108, pg. 776 — IT
Arab Medical Products, Shufat-Main Rd., pg. 816 — PB
BioMakor Ltd., pg. 1472 — PB
John Bryce (Glasgow) Ltd., Building D, 7 Hamarpeh St., pg. 1228 — PB
Eldan Electronics, 28 Pierre Konig, pg. 817 — PB
Jerusalem Post Publications Ltd., pg. 632 — IT
MIS, 11 Ben Gurion St., pg. 740 — PB
MATA (Helicopters) Division/Military Aircraft Group, pg. 690 — IT
Tel-Ad Jerusalem Studio Ltd., 20 Marcus St., pg. 644 — IT

Karmiel

Nemic-Lambda (Israel) Ltd., Karmiel Industrial Zone, pg. 1242 — IT

Kiryat Bialick

Power Spectrum Technology Ltd., Rafael Campus, Haifa-Acko Road, pg. 740 — PB

Kiryat Motzkin

Klil Industries Ltd., P.O. Box 210, Industrial Zone, pg. 644 — IT

Lod

EL AL AIRLINES LTD., P.O. Box 41, Mikoud, pg. 435 — IT

Migdal Ha'Emeq

KLA Instruments Israel, North Industrial Center, 4 Science Ave., pg. 939 — PB

Nahariyya

Iscar Blades Ltd., Industrial Zone, pg. 644 — IT
Iscar Ltd., North Industrial Zone, pg. 644 — IT

Or Yehud

Adanet Communications, 1C Yehounatan Netanyahu St., pg. 645 — PB
Fidelio MICROS Israel & Fidelio Ltd., 3a Yoni Netanyahu Street, pg. 1106 — PB

Pardis Hana

Harmonic Lightwaves (Israel) Ltd., 19 Alon Hatavor St., Zone 3, pg. 788 — PB

Petah Tiqwa

C.D. Packaging Systems Ltd., 2 Hashiloah St., Kiryat Matalon, pg. 75 — IT
Carmel Container Systems Ltd., 2 Chalamish Street, pg. 75 — IT

PB - U.S. Public Companies Volume
PV - U.S. Private Companies Volume
IT - International Public & Private Companies Volume

ECI Telecom Ltd., 30 Hasivim Street, pg. 643
ECI Telecom Ltd.-Israel, 30 Hasivim Street, pg. 643 **IT**
Hogla-Kimberly Ltd., 2 Hashiloa St., pg. 75 **IT**
Hogla-Kimberly Ltd., 2 Hashiloa St., pg. 959 **PB**
Memorex Telex Israel, Ltd., 15 Gonen Street, pg. 857 **IT**
Molett Marketing, 2 Hashiloah St., Kiryath Matalon, pg. 75
Shikma, 2 Hashiloah St., Kiryat Matalon, pg. 75 **IT**
TEVA PHARMACEUTICAL INDUSTRIES LTD., 5 Basil St., pg. 1380 **IT**

Ra'ananna

Analog Devices Ltd., Giron Center, Ste. 201-202, 3-5 Jabotinsky St., pg. 108 **PB**

Ramaliah

Arabian Computer Systems, Industrial Rd., pg. 816 **PB**

Ramat Gan

Autodesk Israel GmbH, 16 Aba Hilel Silver Street, pg. 149 **PB**
Autologic Information International Ltd., 6 Ahaliav St., pg. 1724 **PB**
Check Point Software Technologies Ltd., 3A Jabotinsky St., 24th Floor, pg. 342 **PB**
GITAM/BBDO, 1 Jabotinsky St., pg. 552 **IT**
Israel Distributor, Rimonet Information Systems Ltd., pg. 382 **IT**
Motorola Israel Information Systems Ltd., 6 Harakun Street, pg. 1139 **PB**
Motorola Semiconductor Israel Ltd., 147 Bialik Street, pg. 1140 **PB**
Natali, 17 Abba Hillel St., pg. 691 **IT**
Readymix Industries (Israel) Limited, 155/7 Bialik St., pg. 1081 **IT**
Wilhelm Rosenstein Ltd., 125, Bialik St., pg. 109 **IT**

Rehovot

MENNEN MEDICAL LTD., Kiryat Weizman, pg. 858 **IT**
Sapiens International, pg. 1193 **IT**

Rishon le Zion

Easy Move Handling & Industrial Equipment Ltd., 14 Sharet Street, pg. 97 **IT**
Servotronix Ltd., 12 Hachoma St., pg. 966 **PB**

Tel Aviv

Admon Advertising, 24 Se'adya Ga'on St., pg. 117 **IT**
Alexander Schneider Ltd., 16, Heim Hazaz Street, pg. 739 **IT**
Amerford Intl. Ltd., Gibor House, 6 Kaufman St., pg. 1388 **IT**
Ampal (Israel) Ltd., 111 Arlosorov Street, pg. 149 **IT**
Ariely Advertising, 140 Rothschild Blvd., pg. 678 **PV**
Ascot Cigarette Co. Ltd., 33 Lilienblum St., pg. 421 **IT**
BANK HAPOALIM, 50 Rothschild Blvd., pg. 149 **IT**
BANK LEUMI LE-ISRAEL B.M., 24-32 Yehuda Halevi St., pg. 150 **IT**
Barclays Discount Bank Ltd., 103 Allenby Rd., pg. 166 **IT**
Beeper Communications Israel Ltd., 116, Hayarkon Street, pg. 1139 **PB**
Christie's (Israel) Ltd., Asia House, 4 Weizman Street, pg. 290 **IT**
Computation & Measurement Systems (C.M.S.) Ltd., 11 Hashlosha Street, pg. 1139 **PB**
Delta Trading Co. Ltd., 50 Betzalel St., pg. 1003 **IT**
Discount Investment Corporation Ltd., 16 Beit Hashoeva Lane, pg. 644 **IT**
DUBEK LTD., 33 Lilienblum St., pg. 421 **IT**
Dubek Trade Ltd., 33 Lilienblum St., pg. 421 **IT**
Dun & Bradstreet (Israel) Ltd., City Palace, 27 Hamered St. Fl C-2, pg. 536 **PB**
EGGED ISRAEL TRANSPORT COOPERATIVE SOCIETY LTD., Petah Tikua Rd. 142, 61330, pg. 435 **IT**
GGK Tel Aviv, 25 Ben Yehuda St., pg. 1336 **IT**
Geller Nessis/DMB&B Tel Aviv, Moses Bldg., 76 Rothschild Ave., pg. 304 **PV**
Generali Properties (1977) Ltd., 2, Hagdud Haivri Street, pg. 91 **IT**
Gestetner (Israel) Limited, 110 Yigal Allon Street, pg. 1115 **IT**
Graffiti Office Suppliers and Paper Marketing Ltd., 19 Habarzel St., pg. 75 **IT**
Hadar Insurance Company Ltd., 1-3, Ben Yehuda Street, pg. 565 **IT**
ICC (Israel) Chemicals Ltd., 135 Dizengoff St., pg. 554 **PV**
IDB Development Corporation Limited, The Tower, 3 Daniel Frisch St., pg. 644 **IT**
IDB HOLDING CORPORATION, The Tower, 3 Daniel Frisch St., pg. 643 **IT**
I.L.D. Development & Construction Co. Ltd., 194 Hayarkon St., pg. 691 **IT**
I.L.D. Insurance Co. Ltd., 27 Montefiore St., pg. 691 **IT**
Inbar Computer Training Ltd., 10 Kehilat Venezia St., pg. 1007 **IT**
Intel Semiconductor Ltd., pg. 887 **PB**
IsLAMBDA Ltd., 14 Esser Tachanot St., pg. 1242 **IT**
The Israel Cigarette Co. Ltd., 33 Lilienblum St., pg. 421 **IT**
Israel Discount Bank Ltd., 27-31 Yehuda Halevi St., pg. 645 **IT**
THE ISRAEL LAND DEVELOPMENT CO., LTD., 194 Hayarkon St., pg. 691 **IT**
Israel Resort Hotels, 198 Hayarkon St., pg. 691 **IT**

The Israel Tobacco Corp. (M.T.) Ltd., 33 Lilienblum St., pg. 421 **IT**
The Jerusalem Co. Ltd., 33 Lilienblum St., pg. 421 **IT**
Laser Industries Ltd., Atidim Science Industrial Park, Neve Sharett, pg. 429 **IT**
Lewison Company Ltd., pg. 458 **IT**
Lod Cigarettes Ltd., 33 Lilienblum St., pg. 421 **IT**
MSI Engineering Software Ltd., 6 Asherman Street, pg. 1032 **PB**
Ma'ariv Modiin Publishing House Ltd., 2 Carlebach St., pg. 691 **IT**
MacDermid Israel Ltd., Deborah Street-End, pg. 1030 **PB**
Maliline Ltd, 28, Baruch Hirsh St., pg. 1120 **PV**
Microsoft Israel Ltd., pg. 1108 **PB**
Motorola Communications Israel Limited, 3, Kremenetsky Street, pg. 1139 **PB**
Motorola Israel Investments Limited, 3, Kremenetzky Street, pg. 1139 **PB**
Motorola Israel Ltd., 3 Kremenetski St., pg. 1139 **PB**
Motorola Telephone Cellular Communications Ltd., 16 Kremenetzky Street, pg. 1140 **PB**
Mul-T-Lock Group, pg. 644 **IT**
Nemic-Lambda Israel, Ltd., 14 Raoul Wallenberg St., pg. 1241 **IT**
New Media Communication, 10 Beit Shami St., pg. 788 **PB**
Onyx Interactive Multimedia Ltd., 10 Kehilat Venezia St., pg. 1007 **IT**
ONYX TECHNOLOGIES LTD., 10 Kehilat Venezia St., pg. 1007 **IT**
Paper Agents Ltd., 69 Frishman St., pg. 966 **IT**
People and Computers, 13 Yad Hrutzim St., pg. 570 **PV**
Pfizer Pharmaceutics Israel Ltd., City Towers, Fl. 13, 46-48 Derech Petach-Tikva, pg. 1283 **PB**
Reuveni Pridan Advertising Agency Ltd., 14 Wissotzky St., pg. 186 **PV**
Shalmor Avnon Amichay, 13 Rosanis St., pg. 1063 **PV**
Swiss Re (Israel) Ltd., Mozes House, Rothschild Boulevard 76, pg. 1333 **IT**
Teldan Information Systems, 7 Derech Hashalom, pg. 1180 **PB**
Teledyne Israel, America House, 35 Shaul Hamelech Boulevard, pg. 44 **PB**
Yavnir Trading Co. Ltd., pg. 75 **IT**

Yavne

ORBOTECH LTD., pg. 1007 **IT**

Yehuda

Octel Communications (Israel) Ltd., Yoni Netanyahu 1-C, pg. 1018 **PB**

Yokneam

ESC MEDICAL SYSTEMS LTD., P.O. Box 240, pg. 429 **IT**
IIS INTELLIGENT INFORMATION SYSTEMS LTD., New Industrial Zone, pg. 645 **IT**
Micro-Swiss Ltd., Israel, pg. 969 **PB**

ITALY

Abbiategrasso

D.I.W.S., pg. 1002 **IT**
Per Transport S.p.A, Via Redecesio, 5, 20090 Redecesio di Segrate (MI), pg. 1120 **PV**

Adro

Parker Seals SpA, Via Marzaghette 2, pg. 1264 **PB**

Aglie

Olivetti-Canon Industriale S.p.A., Via C. Olivetti, 8, pg. 262 **IT**

Agordo

LUXOTTICA GROUP S.P.A., Loc. Valcozzena, 10, pg. 822 **IT**

Alatri

Forte Italia Spa, Via Circonvallazione 87, pg. 556 **IT**

Albignasego

Swish Italiana Srl, Via S.Bellino 38, pg. 925 **IT**

Anagni

Novo Nordisk Bioindustriale Srl, Contrada-Fontana del Ceraso, pg. 989 **IT**

Ancarano

Collitex Srl, Prov. Bonifica, pg. 1266 **PB**

Ancona

Bulk Terminal Ancona S.p.A., Via 29 Settembre, 2/0, pg. 303 **IT**
Cesa S.p.A., Via Del Commercio 1/B, pg. 318 **IT**

Hewlett-Packard Italiana S.p.A., Via A. Coata, 30, pg. 821 **PB**

Anoro

Harris Europa, S.p.A., Via Nazionale 79, pg. 577 **PB**

Aprilia

Irvin Manifatture Industriali S.p.A., P.O. Box 19, pg. 640 **IT**
Pechiney Packaging Alimeniare, Via Nettunenae 120/122, pg. 1031 **IT**
R.P. Scherer S.p.A., Via Nettunense KM 20, 100, pg. 1438 **IT**
Yale Security Products S.p.A. (Italy), Via Dei Rutuli 74/76, pg. 1499 **IT**

Arcore

Knorr-Bremse Sistemi Per Autoveicoli Commerciali S.p.A., Via C. Battisti 68, pg. 738 **IT**

Arenzano

Square D Company Italia, S.P.A., Via Vel Lerone, 9, pg. 1209 **IT**

Arisate

Polaroid Italia S.A.R.L., Via Piave 11, pg. 1314 **PB**

Arluno

Componenta International S.P.A., Strada Provinciale Per Turbigo 64, pg. 1421 **IT**
Dynapac S.p.A., Via Santa Caterina 23, pg. 1420 **IT**
Svedala SpA, pg. 1325 **IT**

Arsago Seprio

Parker Hannifin SpA, Via Carducci 11, pg. 1263 **PB**

Atessa

Hydro Alluminio Atessa S.p.A., Contrada Saletti Z.I., pg. 962 **IT**

Avellino

Bull HN Sud S.p.A., Agglomerato Industriale, pg. 317 **IT**
Cavis S.r.l., Zona Industriale di Piandardin, Stabilimento, pg. 785 **IT**
Consorzio Inforsud, Strada Consortile--Agglomerato, Industriale de Pianodardine, pg. 317 **IT**
Rockwell Light Vehicle Systems Avellino s.r.l., Via Pianodardine, pg. 1401 **PB**

Avezzano

Fiamm-GS, Corso Liberta' 78, pg. 480 **IT**

Aviano

IN.F.A. S.p.A., Via De Zan, 54, pg. 442 **IT**

Bagnasco

Bagnasco S.R.L., Via Molino, 87, pg. 535 **PV**

Bari

Banca d'America e d'Italia S.p.A. (Bari), Via Calefati, 67, pg. 403 **IT**
Fiscambi Leasing Sud S.p.A., Via S. Matarrese, 10, pg. 138 **IT**
Fontana Sud Srl, Via f. de Blasio, 19, pg. 1172 **IT**
Hewlett-Packard Italiana S.p.A., Via Vitantonio Di Cagno, 34, pg. 820 **PB**

Battipaglia

F.O.S. Fibre Ottiche Sud S.p.A., Strada Provinciale 135 Km 4,500, pg. 1058 **IT**
Societa Meridionale Accessori Elastomerici S.p.A., Agglomerato Industriale, pg. 1058 **IT**

Beinasco

Gilardini S.p.A., V. le Risorgimento S, pg. 482 **IT**

Bergamo

ABB SACE S.p.A. Costrusioni Elettromeccaniche, Via Baioni 35, C.P. 218, pg. 2 **IT**
Ceprovip SpA, Via Roma n 61-63, pg. 790 **IT**
Luxo Italiana S.p.a., Via delle More, pg. 821 **IT**
Makhteshim-Agan Italia S.r.l., Via Giuseppe Verdi 12, pg. 831 **IT**
McCain Alimentari (Italia) Srl, Casella Postale 178, pg. 850 **IT**
Siad S.p.A., pg. 1320 **PB**
Zerowatt S.p.A., Via Busa, 19, pg. 260 **IT**

PB - *U.S. Public Companies Volume*
PV - *U.S. Private Companies Volume*
IT - *International Public & Private Companies Volume*

Bettolino di Pogliano

Frimont, S.p.A., Via Puccini 22, pg. 1445 — PB

Biella

Banca d'America e d'Italia S.p.A. (Biella), Via Losana, 22, pg. 403
Bloch & Behrens (Italia) S.r.l., pg. 431 — IT
FILA SPORT S.P.A., Viale Cesare Battisti, #26, pg. 484 — IT
Maglificio Bellia S.p.A., via C. Bellia, 34, pg. 1434 — PB

Bollate

Ausimont S.p.A., Viale Lombardia 20, pg. 324 — IT

Bologna

Aura S.R.L., Via Nobili 2, pg. 721 — PB
Banca d'America e d'Italia S.p.A. (Bologna), Via Marconi, 13, pg. 403 — IT
Biotec International S.R.L., Via dell' Arcoveggio, 70, pg. 1083 — PB
Brother Macchine Industriali S.R.L., Via Parini # 7, pg. 230 — IT
Gio. Buton S.p.a., Via Tomba Forella, 3, pg. 409 — IT
Castelli S.p.A., Via Olmatello, 21, Osano della Miglia, pg. 512 — PV
EL. BO. MEC. Thermalloy Srl., Via del Tipografo N 4, Zona Industriale Roveri, pg. 209 — IT
Fiat Componenti Autoveicolisti S.p.A., Via Delle Casse 4, pg. 481 — IT
G.D. S.P.A., Via Pomponia, 10, pg. 531 — IT
Gazzoni 1907 S.r.l., pg. 982 — IT
Graco S.r.l., Via Serra 22, 40012 Lippo Calderara Di Reno, pg. 757 — PB
Henkel Chimica S.p.A., Via Giambologna 18, pg. 612 — IT
Hewlett-Packard Italiana S.p.A., Via Emilia 51/C, pg. 821 — PB
Hospal S.p.A., Via Ferrarese 219/9, pg. 668 — IT
International Rectifier Corporation Italiana, S.p., pg. 907 — PB
KONE Elevators Overseas S.r.l., Via Emilia Ponente, 129, pg. 748 — IT
Lippert Italiana S.R.L., pg. 518 — IT
Logicasiel SpA, Via San Vitale 40/3, pg. 815 — IT
Mec-Track S.r.l., Via Muzza Spadetta 30, pg. 317 — PB
Pietro Costa & C Srl, pg. 69 — IT
Prinz Brau Italia S.p.A., Via A. Moro 38, pg. 680 — IT
Redi, Via Madonna dei Prati, 5/A, pg. 430 — IT
Sabiem S.r.l., Via Emilia Ponente 129, pg. 748 — IT
SASIB Railway S.p.A., Via Di Corticella, 75/87/89, pg. 1194 — IT
SASIB SPA, Via Di Corticella 87-89, pg. 1194 — IT
SASIB S.p.A.-Tobacco Division, Via di Corticella 75/87/89, pg. 1194 — IT
Sauer-Sundstrand S.p.A., Via Villanova 28, 40050 Villanova de Castenaso, pg. 1198 — IT
Sayerlack Industria Vernici Speciali S.p.A., pg. 619 — IT
Silectron SPA, Via Lombardia 2/c, pg. 287 — IT
Sirmac Officine Meccaniche SpA, Via Confortino, 2328, 40010 Crespellano Loc. Calcara, pg. 1619 — PB
Vista Multi National, Via C. Battisti, 2, pg. 222 — PB
VMark Software, Ltd., 102-104, Ave. Edouard Vallant, pg. 129 — PB
Volvo Italia SpA, Via Enrico Mattei, 66, pg. 1476 — IT
Weber S.p.A., Via del Timavo 33, pg. 483 — IT
Weber S.R.L., Via del Timavo 33, pg. 482 — IT

Bolzano

Braas Italia S.p.A., Via Velle Pusteria 21, pg. 1092 — IT
Braas Italia S.p.A., Via Valle Pusteria 17, pg. 1092 — IT
Cotto Coperture S.p.A., pg. 1092 — IT
INCAB S.p.A., pg. 856 — IT
Giulio Meinl S.p.A., pg. 856 — IT
Francesco Parisi S.p.A., Via Macello, 11/B, pg. 504 — IT

Borghetto

Aviocart S.p.A., Loc Campagnole, pg. 1076 — PB
Borghetto, Via Giacomo Ponassi 11, pg. 1341 — IT

Borromee

Alfatec SpA, 28 Via di Vittorio, pg. 442 — IT

Bottrighe

BIOITALIA-Biopro Italia S.p.A., Via A Gramsci 1, pg. 790 — IT

Brembate di Sopra

OPTICOS S.R.L., Via Giulio Terzi di Santa Agata 2, pg. 1007 — IT

Brescia

Data Translation S.r.l., pg. 1079 — PB
Flymo S.r.l., Via Viterbo 6, pg. 442 — IT
Locazioni Finanziarie S.p.A., Via Nicolo Tartaglia, 22, pg. 138 — IT
Oilgear SRL, Via Corfu 90, pg. 1215 — PB
Yokohama Italia S.p.A., 25013 Carpenedolo, Viale Santa Maria 48, pg. 1521 — IT

Brienza

ILRO SRL, Via Provinciale 5, pg. 646 — IT
George S. May International, S.P.A., Centro Direzionale Colleoni, pg. 717 — PV

Brindisi

Nuovi Tubi Brindisi SpA, Viale Arno 11, pg. 1341 — IT
Sud Est S.r.l., Via Pasquale Romano 13, pg. 303 — IT

Brugherio

CANDY S.P.A., Via Priv. Eden Fumagalli, pg. 259 — IT

Bruneck

GKN Birfield SpA, Reinzfeldstrasse 8, pg. 535 — IT

Brunico

Plettac Italy s.r.l., pg. 1061 — IT

Buccinasco

Linde K.T. Italiana S.p.A., pg. 810 — IT

Buguggiate

Linde Guldner Italiana S.p.A., pg. 810 — IT

Busalla

Bundy SpA, Via Pinan 2, pg. 1341 — IT

Busseto

I.B.I.S-S.P.A., Via Europa 14, pg. 642 — IT

Busto Arsizio

Baasel Lasertech Italia SRL, pg. 836 — IT

Cagliari

Fontana Sarda, Zona Industriale, Macchiareddu, pg. 1172 — IT
Hewlett-Packard Italiana S.p.A., Piazza Is Maglias, 8, pg. 820 — PB
Mediterranea Iniziative Turistiche Alberghiere Spa, Via Paoli 57, pg. 556 — IT

Caianello

WABCO Westinghouse Ferroviaria S.p.A., Via Ceraselle 30, pg. 271 — IT

Calderara di Reno

Allen-Bradley s.r.l., Via Persicetana, 12, pg. 1399 — PB

Calenzano

Calenzano Plant, Via Nuova di Pratignone 69, pg. 673 — PB

Caluso

Bull HN Information Systems Italia S.p.A., Via Martini D'Italia 3, pg. 317 — IT
Compuprint S.p.A., Via Martini d'Italia 26, pg. 317 — IT

Cameri

Rockwell CVC S.p.A., Strada Provinciale Cameri, pg. 1400 — PB

Campi Bisenzio

GKN Componenti Firenze SpA, Via Fretelli Cervi 1, pg. 536 — IT

Campoformido

Zeltron S.p.a., Via Principe di Udine, 114, pg. 443 — IT

Campoverde di Aprilia

Recordati Pharmaceutical Chemicals Productions, pg. 1090 — IT

Canale

BARBERO 1891 SPA, Frazione Valpone, pg. 164 — IT
Barbero S.p.A., pg. 64 — IT
Ottavio Riccadonna S.p.A., 25, Corso Liberta, pg. 751 — IT

Canosa di Puglia

S.I.A.P. S.r.l., Via Valli 10, pg. 271 — IT

Capua

Gist-Brocades Italy S.P.A., Strada Statale Appia 46/48, pg. 1143 — IT

Caronno Pertusella

Micromold SpA, Via 4 Novembre 228, pg. 1174 — IT

Carpi

Faxion Italy S.r.l., pg. 1144 — IT
ORVAC Spa, pg. 1266 — PB
SI Sealing Parts SpA, Via Della Ricerca Scientifica, pg. 1338 — IT

Carsoli

Tecnost-Mael, pg. 1002 — IT

Carugate

Yamanouchi Pharma SpA, Via Garibaldi 49, pg. 1519 — IT

Casale Monferrato

Valmet-Rotomec S.p.A. Automation, Strada Provinciale Casale-Valenza, pg. 1449 — IT
Vendo (Italy) S.p.A., Calella Postale 9, pg. 1184 — IT

Casalmorano

CIBA-GEIGY SpA-Seeds Division, SS per Soresina, pg. 980 — IT
Filodoro, Via Brescia 6, pg. 1434 — PB

Casalpusterlengo

Thermal Ceramics Italiana S.R.L., Via Delle Rogge, 6, pg. 894 — IT

Cascina

AGEMA Infrared Systems SRL, Centro Direzione Lombardo, Palazzo E/1, pg. 1289 — IT
CIBA Corning Diagnostics SpA, Centro Direzionale Lombardo, Palazzo E/1, Via Roma, 108, pg. 975 — IT
Esselte S.P.A., Centro Direzionale Lombardo, Via Roma 108, pg. 461 — IT
Forind Avio Elettronica SpA, Via Copernico, 6, pg. 739 — IT
Ghisalba S.P.A., Via Tevere, 15, pg. 559 — PB
S.E.I. Servizi Elicotteristici Italiani S.p.A., Via Giovanni Agusta 520, pg. 32 — IT
SKF Multitec, Corso Francia 155, pg. 1159 — IT
Siemens Nixdorf Informatica S.p.A., Via Roura, 108, pg. 1245 — IT
Spectra-Physics S.R.L., Centro Direzione Lombardo, Palazzo E/1, pg. 1290 — IT

Casella

Vickers Polymotor, Via Avosso 94, pg. 25 — PB

Casinalbo

Ferro (Italia) S.r.L., Via Radici in Piano, 312, pg. 619 — PB

Casoria

Allen-Bradley s.r.l., Via San Salvatore, 2, pg. 1399 — PB
Partenavia - Casoria Plant, Via Cava, pg. 653 — IT

Cassano Valcuvia

Viero SpA, Via Provinciale, 309, pg. 789 — IT

Cassina de Pecchi

BERG Electronics Srl, Via Roma, 108 E/1, pg. 213 — PB

Casteggio

Gist-Brocades S.p.A., Via Milano 42, pg. 1142 — IT

Castegnato

Simon-Cella S.r.l., Via Cavalleral Loc. Barco, pg. 1252 — IT

Castel Maggiore

Aqualon Italia S.p.A., Via Bondanello 15, pg. 810 — PB
Smith International Italia, S.p.A., Via Grandi 3/A, pg. 1478 — PB

Castelfranco Veneto

CastelMAC, S.p.A., Via del Lavoro 9, pg. 1445 — PB
FRAM Filter S.p.A., Via Borgo Treviso, 131, pg. 53 — PB

Castellanza

Agrolinz Melamin Italia S.r.l., Corso Sempione 13, pg. 356 — IT

PB - *U.S. Public Companies Volume*
PV - *U.S. Private Companies Volume*
IT - *International Public & Private Companies Volume*

Perstorp SpA-Div. Compounds, Via Sempione 13, pg. 1037   IT
Perstorp SpA-Polyols Div., Via Sempione 13, pg. 1038   IT

Castelli

Precision Rubber Sealings s.r.l., pg. 506   IT

Castiglione

MAZZUCCHELLI POLIMERI SRL, Via Sep Mazucchelli 7, pg. 850
Wella Italiana, Labocos s.a.s. di Rolf Kissing, Via Fontane, pg. 1490   IT

Castiglione delle Stiviere

Albright & Wilson Castiglione Srl, Via Cavour 50, pg. 49   IT
Marchon Italiana S.P.A., Casella Postale No. 36, pg. 1580   PB

Castiglione Olona

C & C - Coloring & Compounding SRL, Via S. e P. Mazzucchelli, 7, pg. 850   IT
MAZZUCCHELLI 1849 S.P.A., Via S. eP. Mazzucchelli, 7, pg. 849   IT

Catania

Air Malta - Catania, Corso Sicilia 71, pg. 38   IT
Banca d'America e d'Italia S.P.A. (Catania), Corso Sicilia, 52, pg. 403   IT
Citrus Machinery Italy, S.R.L., Contrada Bummacara 3, Box 281, pg. 606   PB
Cyanamid Italia S.p.A, XV Strada, Zona Industriale, pg. 81   PB
Hewlett-Packard Italiana S.p.A., Via Principe Nicola 43G/D/C, pg. 821   PB
Italiatour S.p.A., pg. 652   IT
Petrolite Italiana S.p.A., Via Sasari 86, pg. 166   PB
Takeda Italia Farmaceutici S.p.A., Via Giovannino, 7, pg. 1351   IT
Takeda Italia Farmaceutici S.p.A., Via Giovannino 7, pg. 1351   IT

Cava de Tirreni

Cartiera Del Tirreno Mill, Via Vittorio Venato 147, pg. 673   PB

Cavaglia

MacDermid Italiana SRL, Via Vercellone 54, pg. 1030   PB
Teknecomp, pg. 1002   IT

Cento

VM Motori S.p.A., Via Ferrarese 29, pg. 654   IT

Ceprano

Italtractor - Ceprano Plant, Via Pennea, pg. 654   IT

Cernusco

Hydromarine SRL, pg. 839   IT
Luwa Italia S.r.l., pg. 617   IT
Memorex Telex Italia S.P.A., Centro Summit, Via Brescia, 28/D, pg. 857   IT
Rapisarda Industries SrL, Strada Padana Superiore, pg. 317   PB
Rexroth SpA., pg. 839   IT
Star Mikron SpA, pg. 839   IT

Cesano di Senigallia

Societa Italo Svedese Seme S.p.A., pg. 985   IT

Cesano Maderno

BASF Italia Spa, Via Marconato, 8, pg. 106   IT
EMTEC Magnetics Italia Spa, Via Marconato 8, pg. 743   IT
Snia Fibre S.p.A., Via Friuli 55, pg. 482   IT

Chiavari

Banca d'America e d'Italia S.p.A. (Chiavari), Largo A.P. Giannini, 5, pg. 403   IT
Tirrenia Gas S.p.A., Via Trieste N. 2, pg. 428   IT

Ciserano-Zingonia

Mikron SpA Zingonia, Piazza Milano 12, pg. 867   IT

Cisterna di Latina

Algel S.p.A., pg. 1436   IT

Cittaducale

Texas Instruments Italia S.p.A., Viale Delle Scienze, pg. 1586   PB

Civate

Black & Decker Italia S.p.a., Via Broggi 16, pg. 234   PB
Coltellerie Montana S.r.L., Via Provinciale 15, pg. 492   IT

Cles

Ebara Italia S.p.A., Via Campo Sportivo 30, pg. 432   IT

Coggiola

BOZZALLA & LESNA S.P.A., via Garibaldi, 18, pg. 209   IT

Cogoleto

Tubi Ghisa SpA, Via Allegro 1, pg. 1177   IT

Colfosco di Susegana

Orion SpA., Via Mercatelli Sant Anna 6, pg. 1432   IT

Colico

Quinton Hazell PLC, Colico, pg. 561   PB

Colleferro

Construzioni Ferroviarie Di Colleferro S.p.A., Via Sabotino, pg. 481   IT

Cologno Monzese

Janssen-Cilag Farmaceutici S.p.A., Via Michelangelo BuonArroti 23, pg. 929   PB

Comerio

Whirlpool Europe B.V., E. Administrator Delgado, Viale 6, Borghi 27, pg. 1765   PB

Commessaggio

AIAL (Arimpex S.r.l. Industrie Alimentari), Via Alcide de Gasperi 2, pg. 807   PB
Heinz Food Service S.r.l., Via A De Gasperi 2, pg. 806   PB

Como

DSM Italia SrL, Via Silvio Pellico 12, pg. 355   IT
Eurotherm SpA, Via XXIV Maggio, pg. 466   IT
Francesco Parisi S.p.A., Via dei Cortili, 9, pg. 504   IT
Rockwell Light Vehicle Systems-Como S.p.A., Via Statale Briantea, 342, pg. 1401   PB

Comun Nuovo

Interbrew Italia S.p.A., Via Spirano 26, pg. 679   IT

Concorezzo

Costar Italia, s.r.l., pg. 448   PB
Schindler S.p.A., pg. 1205   IT

Copparo

Berco S.p.A., Via 1, pg. 511   IT

Cortine di Nave

Prodotti Baumann SpA, Via Brescia 261, pg. 171   IT

Cosenza

Ca. Tel S.p.A., Via D. Frugiuele 11, pg. 1365   IT
TEL-CA-Telecommunicazioni Calabrese S.p.A., Via D. Frugiuele 11, pg. 1370   IT
Unical S.p.A., Piazza Fera 50, pg. 1371   IT

Costa di Mezzate

Durco Europe S.R.L., 3 Via Generale Dalla Chiesa, pg. 659   PB

Crema

AlliedSignal Automotive Italia S.p.A., Via Cavalli 53/A, pg. 53   PB

Cremenaga

Mikron S.r.l. Luino, Via Provinciale 54, pg. 867   IT

Cremona

Lawter Intl. SRL, Via San Rocco 33, pg. 981   PB

Cuneo

Francesco Cinzano & C.ia Spa, Santa Vittoria D'Alba, pg. 409   IT
Eaton Controls S.p.A., Strada Berri-Regione Palice, pg. 558   PB

Cusago

Esselte S.P.A., Viale Europa 41, pg. 461   IT

Daggiovada

Tecnord @ Delta Power Co., Via Vittime Civil de Guerra 10, pg. 322   PV

Desio

Ragno Holding S.P.A., pg. 618   IT

Dormelletto

Brico SRL, Via C.Battisti 15, pg. 822   IT
Sikkens Linvea SpA, P.O. Box 72, 138, Via Cavour, pg. 43   IT

Enza

Polarcup s.r.l., Via XXV Aprile Ovest, 16, pg. 639   IT

Este

FKI FAI Komatsu Industries, S.p.A., Via Atheste 4, pg. 474   IT

Fabriano

Best S.p.A., 18, Via Euplo Natali, pg. 1194   PB
MERLONI ELETTRODOMESTICI S.P.A., Viale Aristide Merloni 71, pg. 860   IT

Felino

COBE Lab. Italia s.r.l., Via G. Galilei 4C, pg. 667   IT
Gambro S.p.A., Via Aldo Moro 1/A, pg. 668   IT

Felizzano

Cavis S.r.l., Stabilimento, Via Roma 31, pg. 482   IT

Fernetti

Francesco Parisi S.p.A., Autoporto Doganale, pg. 504   IT

Ferrara

Navale Assicurazioni S.p.A., Via Borgoleoni, 16, pg. 90   IT
Reynolds Wheels S.p.A., pg. 1387   PB

Filago

DSM Italia, Via Rodi 5, pg. 355   IT

Fiumefreddo di Sicilia

Keyes Italiana S.p.A., pg. 1146   IT

Florence

Agriline, Via G. di Vittorio 10, pg. 318   IT
Alberghiera Fiesolana S.R.L., pg. 1213   IT
Alkaline Batteries Volta S.r.l., Via Pisana 336, pg. 537   IT
Bally (Italia) S.r.l., pg. 997   IT
Banca C. Steinhauslin & C., S.p.A., Via dei Sassetti 4, pg. 347   IT
Banca d'America e d'Italia S.p.A. (Firenze), ViA Strozzi, 16/r, pg. 403   IT
Banca Mercantile S.p.A., Piazza Davanzati, 3, pg. 784   PB
Borri S.p.A., pg. 727   IT
Chemco Italia S.p.A., Via Pietro Tacca, 63, pg. 370   IT
Europa Metalli S.p.A., Borgo Pinti 97/99, pg. 719   IT
Finanziaria Media Italia, Piazza della Liberta, 13, pg. 784   IT
Fiorentina Gas S.p.A., Via De Neri N. 25, pg. 428   IT
FONDIARIA S.P.A., Piazza della Liberta, 6, pg. 496   IT
Frensistemi S.r.l., Via P. Petrocchi 24, pg. 738   IT
Gasline S.p.A., Via G. di Vittorio 10, pg. 318   IT
Hewlett-Packard Italiana S.p.A., Via Tevere, 92/2, pg. 821   PB
Hewlett-Packard Italiana S.p.A., Via Sacco e Vanzetti, 1, pg. 821   IT
LA FONDIARIA ASSICURAZIONI S.P.A., Via Lorenzo il Magnifico 1, pg. 784   IT
Line Informatica S.p.A., Via G. di Vittorio 10, pg. 318   IT
Nikon Instruments S.p.A., Via Tevere 54, pg. 931   IT
NUOVO PIGNONE S.P.A., 2 Via F. Matteucci, pg. 990   IT
SAB Sistemi S.p.A., Via E. Permi 24, pg. 271   IT
SAB WABCO Engineering S.r.l., Via E. Permi 24, pg. 271   IT
Sun Chemical S.p.A., Casella Postale 196, pg. 371   IT
Villa San Michele, pg. 1213   IT

Fossano

Audisio Industrie Alimentari SRL, Via Torino 53, pg. 244   IT

Funo di Argelato

ABS Pompe Srl, Via Degli Speziali Blocco 33, pg. 270   IT

PB - *U.S. Public Companies Volume*
PV - *U.S. Private Companies Volume*
IT - *International Public & Private Companies Volume*

Gaglianico

N. Schlumberger e C. Italia s.r.l., Via Cairoli, pg. 1206   IT

Gardone Riviera

P. BERETTA S.P.A., Via P. Beretta 18, pg. 187   IT

Gattatico

Nelsen S.p.A., Via Matteotti 80, pg. 1333   PB

Genoa

Adriafruit Italia S.r.l., Via Martin Piaggio, 17, pg. 303   IT
Agenzia Carboni S.r.l., Via Fogliensi 2/12, pg. 1461   IT
Ansaldo Componenti srl, Via N. Lorenzi 8 -, pg. 653   IT
Ansaldo Gie s.r.l., Via D'Annunzio 113 -, pg. 653   IT
Ansaldo Industria S.p.A., Via Pieragostini 50, pg. 653   IT
Ansaldo Ricerche Srl, Corso Perrone 25, pg. 653   IT
Archivo Storico Ansaldo, Villa Cattaneo dell'Olmo, pg. 653   IT
BNP SIM S.P.A., Piazza Borgo Pila 39, pg. 164   IT
Banca d'America e d'Italia S.p.A. (Genoa), Via Garibaldi, 5, pg. 403   IT
Bulk Terminal Torres S.p.A., Via Martin Piaggio, 17, pg. 303   IT
Bulkitalia S.p.A., Via Martin Piaggio, 17, pg. 304   IT
COECLERICI GROUP, Via Frnger 28, pg. 303   IT
Coeclerici Holding S.p.A., Via Martin Piaggio, 17, pg. 303   IT
Coeclerici Spedizioni S.p.A., Viale Padre Santo, 5, pg. 303   IT
Consorzio Pinacos, Viale E. Spalla 53, pg. 318   IT
COSTA CONTAINER LINES S.P.A., Via Sottoripa 1, pg. 336   IT
Divisione Ambiente, Via Pieragostini 50, pg. 653   IT
Divisione Nucleare, Corso Perrone 25-16161, pg. 653   IT
Finmare, Piazza Dante 7, pg. 652   IT
Fischer & Porter Italiana S.p.A., Via Puccini 2, pg. 449   IT
Forest S.p.A., Ponte Somalia Ponente, pg. 303   IT
Hapag-Lloyd (Italy) S.R.I., pg. 596   IT
Hewlett-Packard Italiana S.p.A., Viale Brigata Bisagno, 2, pg. 821   PB
Hewlett-Packard Italiana S.p.A., Via Rubaldo Merelio, 8, pg. 821   PB
Houghton Italia S.p.A., Casella Postale 669, pg. 541   PV
International Logistic Systems S.r.l., Viale Padre Santo, 5, pg. 303   IT
Iritecna, Via di Francia 1, pg. 654   IT
Italia Di Navigazione S.p.A., Via de Marini 1, pg. 653   IT
Italimpianti S.p.A., Piazza Piccapietra 9, pg. 654   IT
Lafarge Refrattari Monolitici Italia SRL, Via Carzino 2-16, pg. 791   IT
Lincoln Electric Italia SRL, Via Gelasio Adamoli 239 b/c, pg. 997   PB
Lotus Logistica S.r.l., Viale Padre Santo, 5, pg. 303   IT
MacGREGOR (ITA) S.p.A., Via Al Molo Giano, pg. 671   IT
Magazzini Frutta Salerno S.r.l., Via Martin Piaggio, 17, pg. 303   IT
Marconi S.p.A., Via A. Negrone 1A, pg. 546   IT
MUTUAMAR - Societa di Assicurazioni e Riassicurazioni per Azioni, Piazza S. Sabina n. 2, pg. 652   IT
NIFE Italia S.p.A., Viale Cembrano 11, pg. 54   IT
Novara Vita, Via Bartolomeo Bosco 15, pg. 464   IT
Francesco Parisi S.p.A., Via Amba Alagi, 5, pg. 504   IT
Promoport International S.r.l., Viale Padre Santo, 5, pg. 303   IT
Saiwa, Via Cecchi 6, pg. 381   IT
Sea Containers Italia SrL, Via de Marini 53, pg. 1214   IT
SIAMAR SaRL, pg. 1145   IT
Siat Vita, Via Bartolomeo Bosco 15, pg. 464   IT
Sidat S.r.l., pg. 506   IT
Sidermar Di Navigazione S.p.A., Via XX Settembre, 41, pg. 304   IT
Socoba S.r.l., Via Martin Piaggio, 17, pg. 303   IT
Solas Shipping Agency S.r.l., Viale Padre Santo, 5, pg. 303   IT
Somocar S.p.A., Via Martin Piaggio, 17, pg. 303   IT
Sosbam S.r.l., Via Martin Piaggio, 17, pg. 304   IT
Spedimatifa S.r.l., P. Le San Benigno, pg. 318   IT
Terminal Frutta Genova S.r.l., Via Martin Piaggio, 15, pg. 304   IT
Terminal Frutta Trieste S.r.l., Viale Padre Santo, 5, pg. 304   IT
Termoplastici Industria Ligure S.p.A., Via Romana della Castagna 20a, pg. 490   IT
Unikay S.r.l., Via Boccardo, 1, pg. 673   PB
Unione Mediterranea di Sicurta S.p.A., Via San Bartolomeo degli Armeni, 17, pg. 90   IT
Usag, Via Roma, 5, pg. 570   IT

Gerenzano

Guerlain Spa, Clerici 182/184, pg. 780   IT

Gessate

Nokia Telecommunications Italia S.r.l., Via della Fianda, 5, pg. 953   IT
Parker Hannifin SpA, Division SCEM SVD, Via E. fermi, 5, pg. 1263   PB

Ghislarengo

Adenax SpA, via per Carpignano, pg. 1202   IT

Gioia del Colle

Termosud S.p.A., Via Milano Km. 1,6, pg. 653   IT

Giovanne Milan

Morton International S.p.A., 12 Viale Regina, pg. 1136   PB

Giovinazzo

Meridionale Cavi S.p.A., Azienda ME.CA-Contrada Torre del Tuono, pg. 1058   IT

Giuliano di Roma

Mark S.R.L., 52. v. Monferrato fr. Sesto Ulteriano, pg. 1378   IT

Gorgonzola

Morgarite Italiana S.r.l., Via Primo Maggio 24, pg. 892   IT
Standex International S.r.L., Via 1 Maggio 20, pg. 1507   PB
Standex International S.r.L. (Mold-Tech Division), Via 1, pg. 1508   PB
Standex International S.r.L. (Procon Division), Via 1 Maggio, 20, pg. 1508   PB

Gorizia

Eaton EST S.p.A. Engine Components Operations, Via Nuovi Bagni Monfalcone, pg. 558   PB
Francesco Parisi S.p.A., Stazione Confinaria di S.Andrea, pg. 504   IT
Valmet-Gorizia S.p.A., Via A Gregorcic 46, pg. 1448   IT

Grandate

Gruppo Lepetit S.p.A., Via Vetreria 1, pg. 524   PB
Mecatool Italia Srl, Via Veteria 1, pg. 490   IT

Grassano

Heinemann Le Monnier, Via Antonio Meucci 2, pg. 1095   IT

Grisignano di Zocco

Esmach Spa, Via Vittorio Veneto 125, pg. 570   IT

Grugliasco

Comau Finanziaria S.P.A., Via Rivalta 30, pg. 480   IT
Comau S.p.A., Via Rivalta 30, pg. 480   IT
Sofinpa', Via Rivalta 30, pg. 482   IT
Unione Chimica Medicamenti-Difme-S.p.A., Via Marco Polo 38, pg. 1279   IT

Guardamiglio

Pulimat S.p.A., Localita' Novella Terza, pg. 442   IT

Gurizia

Keoma SRL, Zone Industrial Sant Andrea, pg. 1054   PB

Imperia

Agnesi SpA, Via T. Schiava, 80, pg. 380   IT

Ivrea

Baltea, Via Jervis 77, pg. 1002   IT
Decision Systems International SpA, pg. 1002   IT
Ing. C. Olivetti & C., Via Jervis 77, pg. 1002   IT
Olivetti Peripheral Equipment, Via Torino 603, pg. 1002   IT
Omnitel-Sistemi Radiocellai Italiani SpA, Via G. Jevis 77, pg. 204   PB
Sixtel, pg. 1002   IT
Syntax Processing, Via Jervis 77, pg. 1002   IT
Tecnost-Mael, pg. 1002   IT
Tecsinter, Via Jervis 77, pg. 1002   IT

L'Aquila

Ericsson Transmissions S.p.A., Strada Statale 17, KM. 96, 600, pg. 1368   IT

Lacchiarella

Oki Systems (Italia) S.p.A., Centro Commerciale Il Girasole, Palazzo Cellini-3.05/B, pg. 1000   IT

Lago di Patria

Il Carbonio Sud SpA, Via Morolense, km 2.600, pg. 1030   IT

Lainate

Lawson Mardon Seleprint Srl, pg. 69   IT
Lego S.P.A., Via Colombo, 10-12, pg. 805   IT
Lista Italia s.r.l., pg. 812   IT
Panduit S.A.S., Via Como 10, pg. 836   PV
Parke-Davis S.p.A., Via C. Colombo 1, pg. 1739   PB

Lallio

STILL Italia S.p.A., pg. 811   IT
Lanchem Spa, Via Madonna, pg. 791   IT

Lanuvio

Fontana Centro, Via Nettunense, pg. 1172   IT

Latina

Bristol Europe S.p.A., Pantanello, pg. 255   PB
Reynolds International, Inc., Via R.S. Reynolds, Sr., pg. 1387   PB

Latina Scalo

Gambro S.p.A., Via Appia km 65.934, pg. 668   IT
Uniroyal Chimica, S.P.A., Viale Delle Industrie, 40, pg. 460   IT

Lauriano

Persol S.P.A., Corso Torino 7, pg. 822   IT

Lecco

BONOMELLI S.R.L., Via Montecucoli 1, pg. 201   IT

Legnano

Ansaldo Componenti srl, Piazza Monumento 12 -, pg. 653   IT
SKW Italia S.R.L., Via Quasimodo, 28, pg. 1466   IT
VAW Italia S.r.l., Via Galta 8, pg. 1466   IT

Lenno

Kent-Tieghi S.p.A., Via Statale 113, pg. 3   IT

Lentate sul Seveso

Eurotherm Drives SpA, Via Gran Sasso 9, pg. 466   IT
Herman Miller Italia Spa, Via Gran Sasso 6, pg. 1112   PB

Limena

Celte S.p.A., Via IV Novembre 4/6, pg. 1365   IT
Hellerman Elettro Srl, Via Praimbole 9 Bis, pg. 207   IT

Limito

Hewlett-Packard Italiana S.p.A., Via Nuova Rivoltana 95, pg. 820   PB

Liscate

APV Pavailler Monziani, Via G. di Vittorio s.n., pg. 485   IT
Knoll Farmaceutici S.p.A., Via Fosse Ardeatine, 2, pg. 108   IT

Livorno

Banca d'America e d'Italia S.p.a. (Livorno), Via dei Carabinieri, 30, pg. 403   IT
Dowty Polypac Spa, Via G March 11 Venti, pg. 1338   IT
Francesco Parisi S.p.A., Via della Ferrovia, 15, pg. 504   IT
SPICA S.p.A., Via Enriquez 15, pg. 481   IT

Lodi

Condea Chimica D.A.C. S.p.A., Via E. Mattei 4, pg. 325   IT
R.P. Scherer S.p.A., Via Europa 3, pg. 1438   PB

Lomazzo

MD Foods Italia S.r.l., Via del Fossato 2, pg. 826   IT
Ranco Italian Controls, pg. 1243   IT

Lonigo

Vetrerie Italiane Vetr.I SpA, Via del Lavoro, 1, pg. 1171   IT

Lucca

Banca d'America e d'Italia S.p.A. (Lucca), Via Fillungo, 78, pg. 403   IT

Lugo di Vicenza

Burgopack-Stampa, Trasformazione, Imballaggi S.p.A., Via Dalmastro 2, pg. 1466   IT

Macchia di Ferrandina

Pirelli Nastri Tecnici S.p.A., Zona Industriale, pg. 1058   IT

Macherio

Bausch & Lomb Instituto Oftalmico Mediolanum, Via Pasubio 34, pg. 195   PB

PB - *U.S. Public Companies Volume*
PV - *U.S. Private Companies Volume*
IT - *International Public & Private Companies Volume*

Madignano

Hilleshog NK S.p.A., pg. 982 — IT
Northrup King Sementi S.p.A., pg. 983 — IT

Maggiore

Goldstar Iberna Italy S.R.L., Zona Industriale Volturno Nord, pg. 779 — IT

Mailand

Schering S.p.A., pg. 1204 — IT

Malcontenta

Nuova Sirma, Via della Chimica 4, pg. 1175 — IT
Sirma S.p.A., via Della Chimica 4, pg. 6 — IT

Malnate

Moog Italiana (SRL), Via Dei Tre Corsi, pg. 1128 — PB

Maniago

Zanussi Metallurgica S.p.A., Zona Industriale, Localita Campagna, pg. 442 — IT

Mantova

BANCA AGRICOLA MANTOVANA SARL, Corso Vittorio Emanuele, pg. 135 — IT
MARCEGAGLIA SPA, Via Bresciani 16, pg. 841 — IT
SASIB Labeling S.p.A., Z.I. Valdaro, pg. 1194 — IT

Marano Vicentino

Akzo Chemicals S.p.A., Via del Porto, pg. 46 — IT

Marcianise

Modinform, pg. 1002 — IT
Rieter Automotive Systems S.p.A., pg. 1117 — IT

Marcon

CIBA-GEIGY SpA-Divisione Additivi Italia, Via Pila 6/3, pg. 980 — IT
CIBA Vision Srl, Via Enrico Mattei, 17, pg. 981 — IT

Maremma

Azenida Agricola Perolla S.r.l., pg. 61 — IT

Mariano Comense

Sluis & Groot Italia S.p.A., pg. 985 — IT

Marostica

BELFE S.P.A., Via Roma 28, pg. 185 — IT

Martinengo

Siscat SpA, Via Savoldini 16, pg. 87 — IT

Maslianico

Valmet-Como S.p.A., Via Roma 8, pg. 1449 — IT

Massa

Eaton Engine Lifters S.p.A., Via Aurelia Ovest 99, pg. 558 — PB
Line Softeco S.r.l., Via Marina Vecchia 1/44, pg. 318 — IT
Olivetti Synthesis, pg. 1002 — IT
Societa Bario e Derivati, S.P.A., Via degli Uliveti n 84, pg. 1279 — IT

Mathi

Bosso Carte Speciali S.p.A., Via Stura 98, pg. 35 — IT

Mazzo di Rho

Valvoline Oil Company S.P.A., Via Risorgimento, 84, pg. 140 — PB

Medolla

Hospal Dasco S.p.A., Via Modenese, pg. 668 — IT

Melfi

Bundy SUD Srl, San Nicola di Melfi Z.I., pg. 1342 — IT

Melzo

Braas Italia S.p.A., Via S. Elia, 51, pg. 1092 — IT

Merate

Banca Briantea Spa, Via Vigano, 2/4, pg. 137 — IT

Mesero

FEMSA S.p.A., Via E. Mattei 24, pg. 283 — IT

Mestre

Banca d'America e d'Italia S.p.A. (Mestre), Mestre Riviera XX Settembre, 15, pg. 403 — IT

Mezzocorona

Refradige, Via del Teroldego, 1, pg. 1176 — IT

Milan

ABB Asea, 39, via Fara, pg. 8 — IT
ABB Tecnomasio S.p.A., Pizzale Lodi 3, pg. 2 — IT
ABN Finanziaria S.p.A., Via Mengoni 4, pg. 11 — IT
ABN Leasing Italia S.p.A., Via Mengoni 4, pg. 11 — IT
ADT Italiana, S.p.A., Via G. Di Vittorio 32, pg. 1649 — PB
AEI Italy, Via Eugenio Montale, 18/24, pg. 30 — PB
AGA S.R.L., Viale Monte Nero, 11, pg. 14 — IT
AGIP SpA, 20097 San Donato Milanese, pg. 428 — IT
ANIE-ASSOCIAZIONE NAZIONALE INDUSTRIE ELETTROTECNICHE ED ELETTRONICHE, Via Algardi 2, pg. 16 — IT
ARCA Merchant-ABK S.p.A., Largo Augusto, 7, pg. 420 — IT
AS. Co S.p.A., Via Tamburini 13, pg. 170 — IT
ATA S.p.A., Viale Tamburini 13, pg. 170 — IT
Acciai Krupp S.r.l., Via Milanese 20, pg. 515 — IT
Acer Italy s.r.l., pg. 22 — IT
Acheson Italiana s.r.l., Via G. Frua 18, pg. 12 — PV
Acuson S.p.A., Via Stadera, 18, pg. 1246 — PB
Ademco-Italia S.p.A., Via Cristoforo Colombo 1, pg. 1307 — PB
Adriatica Gestioni, Corso Italia 23, pg. 61 — IT
Aer Lingus, Galleria Passarrella 2, pg. 28 — IT
Aerimpianti S.p.A., Via Bergamo 21, pg. 653 — IT
AGEMA Infrared Systems SRL, Via Roma 18-20060 Cassina de Pecchi, pg. 1289 — IT
Agfa-Gevaert S.p.A., Viale De Gasperi Ang. Via., pg. 174 — IT
Agricoltura Assicurazioni, Via Montecuccoli, 20, pg. 89 — IT
Air Liquide Italy/SIO, via Capecelatro 69, pg. 37 — IT
Air Malta - Milan, Via Albricci 7, pg. 38 — IT
Ajinomoto Europe Sales G.m.b.H., Milano Representaive Office, Corso Venesia, pg. 40 — IT
Akzo Chemicals S.p.A., 80, Via E. Vismara, pg. 46 — IT
Akzo Coatings S.p.A., 11, Via Benedetto Croce, pg. 43 — IT
Alarmcom S.p.A., Via Stadera, 18, pg. 1246 — IT
Alcatel Cavi, S.p.A., Via Europa 40-42, pg. 55 — IT
Alcatel Face, Via Monterosa 15, pg. 55 — IT
Alcoa Italia S.p.A., Via Gioberti 3-5, pg. 62 — PB
Alcon Italia S.p.A., pg. 918 — IT
Alfa Lancia Industriale S.p.A., Viale Alfa Romeo, Centro Direzionale, pg. 481 — IT
Alinord S.p.A., Vial Tamburini 13, pg. 170 — IT
Alleanza Assicurazioni S.p.A., Viale L. Sturzo 37, pg. 89 — IT
Allen-Bradley s.r.l., Regional Headquarters, Viale de Gasperi, 126, pg. 1399 — PB
Allen-Bradley s.r.l., Via Cardinale Riboldi, 161, pg. 1399 — PB
Allianz RAS Tutela Guidiziaria S.p.A., Via Santa Sofia 27, pg. 60 — IT
AlliedSignal Automotive Italia S.p.A., Turbocompressori Garrett, via San Gregorio 6, pg. 53 — PB
Allo Pro Italia s.r.l., pg. 1307 — IT
Alluminio Alusuisse Spa, pg. 68 — IT
Alpine Center, s.r.l. (Berlitz), Via Mercadante, 17, pg. 221 — IT
Ambro Italia Societa di Intermediazione Mobiliare S.p.A., Strada 2, Palazzo D, pg. 138 — IT
Ambrofid Gestioni Fiduciarie S.p.A., Piazzale Cadorna, 5, pg. 138 — IT
American Appraisal Italia S.r.l., Centro Direzionale Colleoni, pg. 50 — PV
Amersham Italia Srl, Via Quintiliano 30, pg. 993 — IT
AMETEK Italia, Via De' Barzi, 20087 Robecco S/N, pg. 100 — PB
Amgen S.p.A., Via Vitruvio, 38, pg. 101 — PB
Amway Italia s.r.l., Palazzo Pitagora Milano 3 City, Via Ludovico il Moro, pg. 70 — PV
Anacomp Italia, Via Fantoli, 7, pg. 107 — IT
Analog Devices Italy, Via Galileo Galilei 2, pg. 108 — IT
Andrew S.R.L., Via Rombon, 11, pg. 113 — PB
Ansaldo Transporti-Milan Plant, Via Bergognone 34, pg. 653 — IT
Ansaldo Transporti S.p.A., Viale Sarca 336 -, pg. 653 — IT
Antibioticos S.p.A., Via Winckelmann, 1, pg. 324 — IT
Applied Power Italiana S.p.A., Via Canova 4-20094, pg. 125 — PB
Arami Italiana Srl, 259 Viale Monza, pg. 45 — IT
Asahi Chemical Industry - Milan, Via San Brunone, 21, pg. 84 — IT
Ascom Automation S.r.l., Via Leone Tolstoi 86, pg. 86 — IT
Ascom Hasler SpA, Via Rovetta 20, pg. 87 — IT
Ascom Safnat SpA, Via Garofalo, 31, pg. 87 — IT
Ashland Chemical Italiana S.p.A., Via Giacomo Watt 42, pg. 139 — PB
Asiservice S.R.L., Va Privata Mangili 2, pg. 334 — IT
Assi Italiana S.r.l., Via Mario Donati, 6, pg. 966 — IT
Assiba Distribuzione S.r.l., Corso Vittorio Emanuele, 37/B, pg. 89 — IT
Assiba Societa di Assicutazioni, Corso Vittorio Emanuele, 37/B, pg. 89 — IT
Assiprogetti S.p.A., Via Santa Tecla, 4, pg. 138 — IT
Astra Farmaceutici S.p.A., Via Messina 38, pg. 93 — IT

Ata Tonic, Via Filelfo, 10, pg. 602 — IT
Augat SRL, Centro Direzionale Colleoni, Via Colleni 5, pg. 1598 — PB
Aurora Assicurazioni S.p.A., Via Montecuccoli, 20, pg. 90 — IT
Ausiliare SpA, Via Leopardi 32, pg. 212 — IT
Avery Etichette Italia S.p.A., Viale dell'Industria 53, pg. 153 — PB
Avesta Sheffield SpA, pg. 222 — IT
Avnet EMG SRL, pg. 155 — PB
Azzura-International Marketing & Promotions, Via Correggio, 18, pg. 303 — PV
B Communications/GGK, Via Palermo 8, pg. 1335 — IT
BAC Financial Italia S.r.l., Corso Europa 12, pg. 203 — PB
BAI Factoring S.p.A., Via Tocqueville, 11, pg. 403 — IT
BAI Gest S.p.A., Via Manzoni, 5, pg. 403 — IT
BAI Leasing S.p.A., Via Trivulzio, 5, pg. 403 — IT
BASF Pitture Spa, Via Margherita De Vizzi, 51a, pg. 107 — IT
BDDP Milan, Via del Torchio, 7, pg. 117 — IT
BDDP S.p.A., Via del Torchio, 7, pg. 117 — IT
BFCE Milan, 5 Via Morigi, pg. 161 — IT
BFF Italia Srl, Centro Direzionale Milanofiori, Palazzo F1-4th Fl., pg. 798 — IT
BGS DMB&B Milan, Via Correggio, 18, pg. 303 — PV
BMC Software Srl, Via V. Forcella 3, pg. 163 — PB
BNP Leasing SPA, Via Meravigli 4, pg. 164 — IT
BRB, Via Benedetto Marcello 2, pg. 765 — PB
BTM Finanziaria (Italia) S.p.A., Pizza Luigi Einaudi 4, pg. 158 — IT
BV Finanziaria S.p.A., pg. 180 — IT
Baldini & Castoldi S.r.l., Via M. Pagano 36, pg. 888 — IT
Balzaretti Modigliani, Via E. Romegnoli 6, pg. 1176 — IT
Balzaretti Modigliani, Via E. Romanoli, 6, pg. 1177 — IT
Balzers-Silmax S.p.A., Via Caralcabo, 9, pg. 997 — IT
Banca Agricola Milanese S.p.A., Via Mazzini 9/11, pg. 137 — IT
BANCA COMMERCIALE ITALIANA, Piazza della Scala 6, pg. 135 — IT
Banca Commerciale Italiana S.p.A., Piazza della Scala, 6, pg. 652 — IT
Banca d'America e d'Italia S.p.A., Head Office, Via Borgogna, 8, pg. 403 — IT
Banca d'America e d'Italia S.p.A. (Milano), Via San Prospero, 2, pg. 403 — IT
BANCA POPOLARE DI MILANO, Piazza Filippo Meda 4, pg. 137 — IT
BANCO AMBROSIANO VENETO S.P.A., Piazza Paolo Ferrari, 10, pg. 138 — IT
Banco do Brasil S.A.-Milan, Via Baracchini, 2, pg. 141 — IT
Banco Santander, Via Pietro Mascagni, 1, pg. 144 — IT
Bank Brussels Lambert, Sede di Milano, 86 Corso Garibaldi, pg. 147 — IT
Bank of America NT&SA, Corso Matteotti, 10, pg. 182 — PB
The Bank of New York, Pazzale Cadorna 4, pg. 179 — PB
The Bank of Tokyo-Mitsubishi, Ltd. (Milano Branch), Via Filippo Turati, pg. 158 — IT
Bankers Trust Company, Via Turati, 16/18, pg. 186 — IT
Bankers Trust New York Corporation, Viaturati 16118, pg. 186 — IT
Banque Generale du Luxembourg S.A., Via Larga, 7, pg. 162 — IT
Banque Indosuez, Via Brera, 21, pg. 314 — IT
Banque Paribas-Milano, Casella Postale 1721, 14, via dell'Annunciata, pg. 320 — IT
Barclays Bank PLC, Via Della Moscova 18, pg. 166 — IT
Basinform-Bastogi Servizi Informatici S.p.A., Via Tamburini 13, pg. 170 — IT
BASTOGI-S.P.A., Via Tamburini 13, pg. 170 — IT
Bayer Italia S.p.A., V. Le Certosa 126, pg. 175 — IT
Bayerische Landesbank Girozentrale, Representative Office, pg. 177 — IT
Bayerische Vereinsbank AG, Filiale di Milano, Via Durini, 9, pg. 180 — IT
Beiersdorf SpA, pg. 183 — IT
Leon Bekaert S.p.A., Via Boccaccio 25, pg. 184 — IT
BIC Italia Spa, Via Quaranta 45, pg. 1273 — IT
Bio-Rad Laboratories S.R.L., Via Morandi, 66, pg. 230 — PB
Bio-Rad S.P.D., pg. 230 — PB
Biofin S.p.A., Via Laga, 13, pg. 1283 — PB
Biomet SpA, Via De Vecchi, 2, pg. 232 — PB
Bipiemme Fiduciaria Spa, Galleria De Cristoforis, 1, pg. 137 — IT
Bipiemme-Gestione Polizze di Assicurazione S.p.A., Via M. Gioia 127, pg. 137 — IT
Bobst Italiana SpA, 20099 Sesto San Giovanni, pg. 199 — IT
Robert Bosch Italia, Via M.A. Colonna 35, pg. 206 — IT
BRACCO S.P.A., Via Folli 50, pg. 209 — IT
Brandeis (Italia) s.r.l., Viali Restelli 5, pg. 1030 — IT
Branson Ultrasuoni S.p.a., Via Dei Lavoratori, 25, pg. 576 — PB
Braun Italia, S.r.l., Via G. Di Vittorio 10, pg. 744 — PB
BRENNTAG Italia S.p.A., Via Larga 23, pg. 1458 — IT
Bridgestone/Firestone Italia S.p.A., Direzione Commerciale, pg. 214 — IT
Brother Office Equipment S.p.A., Centro Direzionale Lombardo, Via Roma 108, pg. 230 — IT
Bugamor Pharma SRL Milan, Executive Center, Via V. Monti 8, pg. 1284 — PB
Leo Burnett Co., S.r.l., Via Fatebenefratelli 14, pg. 185 — PV
Buss S.r.l., Via Carpaccio 4, pg. 490 — IT
CAP Gemini (Italia), Via Cesare Lombroso 56, pg. 264 — IT
CCF Milan, Piazetta Bossi 1, pg. 342 — IT
CCP Positioning S.R.L., Piazza del Carmine 4, pg. 394 — PB
CEM S.r.l., Via Circonvallazione, 16, 24055, pg. 277 — PB
CEPSA Italia, S.p.A., Viale Milanofiori, Palazzo A/6, pg. 323 — IT
CPAC Italia, s.r.l./Chimifoto Ornano, Via Bolzano 29, pg. 282 — PB
CPC Italia S.p.A., Via 6. Gozzano 14, pg. 225 — PB

PB - U.S. Public Companies Volume
PV - U.S. Private Companies Volume
IT - International Public & Private Companies Volume

Geographic Index-Non U.S.

1663

C.S.O. Centrale Supporti Operativi S.p.A., Strada 2, Palazzo D, pg. 138 IT
CTIP S.p.A., Via Tamburini 13, pg. 170 IT
Caboto Gestioni Sim S.p.A., Piazzale Cardorna, 5, pg. 138 IT
Caboto Holding Societa di Intermediazione Mobiliare S.p.A., Piazzale Cadorna, 5, pg. 138 IT
Caboto Holding S.p.A., Piazzale Cardorna, 5, pg. 138 IT
Caboto Sim S.p.A., Piazzale Cadoma 5, pg. 138 IT
CAFFARO S.P.A., Via Friuli 55, pg. 248 IT
Canon Italia S.p.A., Via Mecenate, 90, pg. 263 IT
Canon Milano S.p.A., Via Zante, 16/2, pg. 263 IT
Carboghise S.p.A., pg. 303 IT
Carpenter Technology (Italy) s.r.l., Reporting s.r.l. Via Monte Rosa, 60, pg. 308 PB
Carrefour - Italy, Via della Pace 45, pg. 272 IT
CASSA DI RISPARMIO DELLE PROVINCIE LOMBARDE SPA (CARIPLO), Via Monte di Pieta, 8, pg. 274 IT
Cassina, pg. 570 IT
Castrol Italiana SpA, Via Aosta 4/A, pg. 236 IT
Cebal Italiana, Via Vincenzo Monti, 16, pg. 1030 IT
Cementeria di Merone S.p.A., Viale Jenner 56, pg. 629 IT
Cerberus Dati S.p.A., Via Milan, 141, pg. 1246 IT
Cerberus S.p.A., Via Caldera, 21/E, pg. 1246 IT
Charles River Italia S.p.A., Via Manzoni 31, pg. 195 PB
Charmilles Technologies (Italia) Srl., Via Monte Nevoso 2, pg. 489 IT
Chase Investimenti Mobiliari S.P.A., Piazza Meda 1, pg. 339 PB
The Chase Manhattan Bank, N.A., Piazza Meda 1, pg. 340 PB
Chasefin-Chase Finanziara, S.p.A., Piazza Meda No. 1, pg. 341 PB
Chem-Plast S.p.A., Piazza Verta 21, pg. 611 IT
Chemco Technologies North S.r.l., Via Buzzi, 16, pg. 371 IT
Chiron Italia S.r.l., Via Cimarosa 4, pg. 350 PB
CIBA-GEIGY SpA, Via Benadir, 5, pg. 980 IT
CID S.p.A., pg. 1015 IT
Cincinnati Milacron S.r.l., Via Lazzaro Palazzi, pg. 368 PB
Cinestella S.p.A., Via Tamburini 13, pg. 170 IT
Circle Freight International Italia-Eurolevant SRL, Via Francesco Baracca, 25/27, pg. 372 PB
Citizen Watch Italy S.p.a., Via G. de Vittorio, N 9-11, pg. 294 IT
Clarion Europa GmbH Filliale Italiana, Via Ravizza 40, pg. 296 IT
Clestra SRL, Via Alberto Mario 28, pg. 570 IT
Coats Cucirini S.p.A., Viale Restelli 3-7, pg. 300 IT
Coeclerici Holding S.p.A., Viale Brenta, 24, pg. 303 IT
Coeclerici Trading S.p.A., Viale Brenta, 24, pg. 303 IT
Cofina, Corso Italia 23, pg. 61 IT
Combibloc S.r.l., Galleria Pattari 2, pg. 1156 IT
Commerciale Finanziaria S.p.A., Via Gattamelala 45, pg. 481 IT
Commerzbank AG-Milan Representative Office, Via Passarella 4, pg. 311 IT
Compagnia di Genova, Corso Italia 23, pg. 61 IT
Compagnia Eurpoea d'Assicurazione, Corso Italia 23, pg. 61 IT
Compagnia Generale Elettromeccanica S.p.A. (COGEMEC), Via Tortona, 27, pg. 545 IT
COMPART SPA, Piazzetta Maurilio Bossi 3, pg. 324 IT
Condea Augusta S.p.A., Via Medici del Vascello, 26, pg. 325 IT
Conquest S.P.A., Corso Europa 13, pg. 1484 IT
Consorzio Inforturism, Via Frigia 27, pg. 318 IT
Consorzio Per Lo Sviluppo, Via Liri 8A, pg. 318 IT
Consorzio Resource Society, Via Vittor Pisani 6, pg. 318 IT
Consorzio Satsca, Via Boncompagni 60, pg. 318 IT
Continental Italia S.p.A., pg. 328 IT
Cordis Italia SpA, Piazza Don Mapelli n.1, pg. 928 PB
John Crane Italia SpA, Via Vesuvio, 1/3, pg. 1339 IT
Credit Agricole (CNCA) Milan, 11 Via San Pietro all Orto, pg. 341 IT
Creditanstalt Finanziaria S.p.A., Via Cordusio 2., pg. 348 IT
Credito Italiano, Piazza Cordusio, pg. 652 IT
Crespim S.p.A., Via Montebello, 27, pg. 90 IT
D & B Software Italy, P. Le Principessa Clotilde 8, pg. 532 IT
DG Bank-Milan, Piazza Castello, 16, pg. 352 IT
Daewoo Italia S.R.L., Via Parcelso 6, pg. 358 IT
Dai-Ichi Kangyo Bank, Ltd.-Milan, Via Dei Bossi, 4, pg. 360 IT
Daiwa Europe (Italia) SIM p.A., Via Turati 25, pg. 375 IT
Danone S.p.A., Via Fabio Filzi 25, pg. 379 IT
Danzas SPA, Via Vittor Pisani 8, pg. 383 IT
Data Base S.p.A, Via Tacito, 11, pg. 108 IT
Data General S.P.A., Via Folli Gracchi 36, pg. 486 PB
Datapoint Italia S.P.A., Via E. Tazzoli No. 6, pg. 384 IT
Datastream International (Milan) Ltd., c/o Dun & Bradstreet, International, pg. 1326 PB
DATEO IMPORT S.P.A., via Carlo Poma, 1, pg. 385 IT
DAVIDE CAMPARI, Via F. Turati 27, pg. 385 IT
Diana de Silva Cosmetiques S.p.A., pg. 210 IT
Defontaine Italia S.r.l., Via Marconi 28/1, pg. 509 IT
Del Bosco & C.S.R.L., Via Pietro Moscati 8, pg. 303 IT
Det Norske Veritas, Centro Direzionale Colleoni, Palazzo Sirio 2, pg. 397 IT
Digital Equipment S.p.A., Viala Fulvio Testi 280/6, pg. 508 PB
The Walt Disney Company (Italia), 3, via Hoepli, pg. 514 IT
Dival, Corso Italia 23, pg. 61 IT
Divisione Elettronica di Potenza e Macchine, Viale sarca 336, pg. 653 IT
Dodi S.p.A., Via San Francesco d'Assisi, 31, pg. 146 IT
Dormer Tools S.p.A., pg. 1186 IT
Dow Italia S.p.A., Reg. Hdqtrs., pg. 524 PB

Dresdner Bank AG, Piazza degli Affari 3, pg. 419 IT
Driver-Harris Italiana, Via Ospiate 51, pg. 723 IT
Du Pont de Nemours Italiana Sp.A., Casella Postale 17085, pg. 532 PB
Dun & Bradstreet Kosmos Spa, Via Dei Valtorta 48, pg. 536 PB
Durkopp Adler Italia S.r.l., Via J. Bach 13, pg. 469 IT
Dynisco S.r.L., Via 25 Aprile 49, pg. 139 PV
DYWIT S.p.A., Via Albricci 5, pg. 425 IT
EG & G S.p.A. Instruments Division, Via Bernardo Rucellai, 23, pg. 544 PB
EMI Italiana SpA, Via Bergamo 315, pg. 427 IT
ESAB Holding S.p.A., Piazza Martelli, 3/5, pg. 282 IT
ESAB Saldatura S.p.A., Piazza Martelli 3/5, pg. 282 IT
ESI Stampa Medica Srl, Largo Volontari del Sangue 10, pg. 1099 IT
Ebasco Italia S.r.l., Centro Direzionale, Lombardo, Via Roma 108, pg. 1587 IT
Edelman Gruppo D', Via Telesio, 25, pg. 363 PV
Edicom S.p.A., Via Montebello, 27, pg. 90 IT
Edison S.p.A., Foro Buonaparte 31, pg. 324 IT
Editrice Abitare Segesta S.p.A., C.so Monforte 15, pg. 888 IT
Editrice Portoria S.r.l., Via Chiossetto 1, pg. 888 IT
Edizioni Frassinelli S.r.l., Via Borgonuovo 25, pg. 888 IT
Edwards Alto Vuoto SpA, V. Carpaccio, 35, pg. 122 IT
Elemond S.p.A., Via Trentacoste 7, pg. 888 IT
Elga Ronal S.r.l., Via della Merlata 8,20014 Nerviano, pg. 982 PB
Elkem S.r.l., Centrl Direzionale Colleoni, Palazzo Taurus (A3), pg. 447 IT
Elscint Italia S.r.L. Via Rosa Massara de Capitani 13, pg. 450 IT
Emails S.p.A., pg. 175 IT
EMAP Publishing srl, Piazzale A Cantore 12, pg. 451 IT
Encore Computer Italia S.p.A., Via Volta N. 16, pg. 580 PB
Enichem S.p.A., Piazza della Repubblica, 16, pg. 428 IT
Eniricerche S.p.A., Via Felice Maritano 26, pg. 428 IT
Enka Italiana Srl., 259, Viale Monza, pg. 46 IT
Equipe, Via Crocefisso 12, pg. 602 IT
Ericsson Components S.r.l., Corso di Porta Romana, 121, pg. 1366 IT
ESSPA-Edilizia Siciliana S.p.A., Via Tamburini 13, pg. 170 IT
Euragrind S.r.l., Piazza Paolo Ferrari, 10, pg. 138 IT
Eurand International S.p.A., Via M. de Vizzi 60, pg. 81 PB
EURO RSCG Mezzano Costantini Mignani, Via Dante 7, pg. 603 IT
Eurocom Concato di Pace Srl, Via Dante 7, pg. 603 IT
EUROIPEX, S.p.A., Via Reisi Romoli, 4, pg. 593 IT
Europ Assistance Italia S.p.A., Piazza Trento, 8, pg. 90 IT
Europ Assistance Service S.p.A., Piazza Trento, 8, pg. 90 IT
Europ Assistance Trade S.p.A., Piazza Trento, 8, pg. 90 IT
Excelsior Hotel Gallia S.p.A., Piazza Duca Diaosta 9, pg. 556 IT
FAG Italia S.p.A., 44 via Aquileia, pg. 469 IT
FCA!BMZ, Corso Sempione, 65/A, pg. 470 IT
FHP di R. Freudenbert s.a.s., pg. 506 IT
FIAR-Fabbrica Italiana Apparecchiature Radioelectriche S.p.A., Via Montefeltro 8, pg. 1368 IT
Fanuc Italia S.p.A., Piazza Tirana, 24/4B, pg. 478 IT
Farmitalia Carlo Erba S.r.l., Via Carlo Imbonati, 24, pg. 1049 IT
Fiat Auto S.p.A., Viale Alfa Romeo, pg. 481 IT
Fiat OM Carrelli Elevatori S.p.A., pg. 811 IT
Ficut S.p.A., Via Fabio Filzi 10/14, pg. 994 IT
Fina Italiana SpA, Viale Premuda 27, pg. 1043 IT
Finanziaria Indosarez Italia SIM S.p.A., Via Brera, 21, pg. 314 IT
Finanziaria Sumitomo (Italia) S.p.A., Via Palestro 2, pg. 1310 IT
Finservizi S.p.A., Via Tamburini 13, pg. 170 IT
Firefin SrL, Via de Gasperi No. 44, pg. 1500 IT
Fiscambi Factoring S.p.A., Via Agnello, 12, pg. 138 IT
Fiscambi Leasing S.p.A., Via Agnello, 12, pg. 138 IT
Giorgio Fischer S.p.A., Via Sandrio 1, pg. 490 IT
Fleishman-Hillard, Italy, Via Palermo 8, pg. 411 PV
Robert Fleming Italia SpA, Via Manzoni 12, pg. 494 IT
Flender-Cigala S.p.A., Via Porpora 147, pg. 400 IT
Flexa Spa, 19, Viale Teodorico, pg. 280 IT
Flo-con Italiana S.r.l., Galleria S. Babila N. 4/A, pg. 1529 IT
Florasynth Italia S.R.L., Via F. LLI. Roselli, 5, pg. 173 IT
Forbo Resilienti S.r.l., pg. 498 IT
Forem S.p.A., Via Archimede, 22/24, pg. 46 PB
Formica Italia S.r.l., Via Sardegna 34 (M1), pg. 129 IT
Foster Wheeler Italiana S.P.A. (Italy), 1 Via Sebastiano Caboto, pg. 677 PB
Francesco Parisi S.p.A., Via Rosellini, 2, pg. 504 IT
Freudenberg S.p.A., pg. 506 IT
Frigoscandia Food Process Systems S.R.L., Via Beatrice D'Este 10, pg. 607 PB
Fuchs Lubrificanti S.R.L., pg. 517 IT
Fujisawa SRL, pg. 525 IT
Fujitsu Italia S.p.A., Via Melchiorre, Gioia No. 8, pg. 528 IT
GS Societa Generale Supermercati, via Caldera, 21, pg. 186 IT
Gaggiano S.r.l., Corso Italia 23, pg. 61 IT
Galbani, Via Fabio Filzi, 25, pg. 380 IT
Galstaff Industrie Chemiche S.p.A., pg. 619 IT
Gariboldi Parisi Verga/Interad, P. Le Biancamano 8, pg. 678 PV
Gavino Sanna Associati, Via Correggio, 18, pg. 304 PV
Gelman Italy S.R.L., Via Gioacchino Murat, 84, pg. 528 PB
Gema Volstatic Industrial Powder Systems (Italy), Via Spezia 35, pg. 868 PB
Gemeaz, Via Senato N 14/16, pg. 21 IT

Gendex Dental Systems, via Capelli, 12, pg. 500 PB
Generale Bank - Milano, Corso di Porta Romana, 3, pg. 547 IT
Genicom SpA, Via Achille Grandi 12, 20093 Cologno Monzese, pg. 729 PB
Genus Europa S.r.l., pg. 733 PB
Gerber Italy, Srl., Piazza Erculea N9, pg. 973 IT
Gescon 30 S.r.l., pg. 507 IT
Gestetner Italia SpA, Via Caviglia 11, pg. 1115 IT
Gestione Fondi Investimento Milano SpA, Galleria De Cristoforis 1, pg. 137 IT
Gestiras, Corso Italia 23, pg. 61 IT
Gillette Group Italy S.r.l., Via Baldissera 5, pg. 745 PB
Giuffre Editore S.p.A., Via Busto Arsizio 40, pg. 1095 IT
Givaudan-Roure S.p.A., pg. 1120 IT
Gleason Milano, Via Calera 21/B3, pg. 746 PB
Goldman Sachs S.I.M. SpA, Passaggio Centrale 2, pg. 462 PV
B.F. Goodrich Chemical Italia SRL, Viale Gian Galeazzo, 25/27, pg. 752 PB
Grace Italiana S.p.A., Via Trento 7, pg. 756 PB
Grolier Hachette Gestione Clienti SRL, 7 Via Salutati, pg. 795 IT
Grolier Hachette International, 7 Via Salutati, pg. 795 IT
Gruppo Editoriale Jackson srl, pg. 1445 IT
Guccio Gucci S.p.A., Piazza San Fedele, pg. 686 IT
Gulio Galavotti BV, Largo Augusto, 7, pg. 181 IT
Hagglunds Drives Srl, Via Pier Francesco Mola 39, pg. 670 IT
Chr. Hansen S.p.A., Viale della Liberazione 1/5, pg. 289 IT
Harlequin Mondadori S.p.A., C.so Consorida 7, pg. 888 IT
Harris Italiana, Inc., Viale Fulvio Testi, 126, pg. 791 PB
Hartmann & Braun Italia SpA, pg. 835 IT
Heineken S.p.A., 10 Via Maffucci, pg. 608 IT
Heinz Plasmon Dietetci Alimentari S.p.A., Via Cadolini 26, pg. 806 PB
Henkel Italiana S.p.A., pg. 613 IT
Henkel SpA, Via Barella, 6, pg. 613 IT
Henkel Sud S.p.A., Via Barrella 6, pg. 613 IT
Hepworth Refractories Italiana Srl, Via Toffetti 39/3, pg. 615 PB
Hercules Italia S.p.A., pg. 811 PB
Hewlett-Packard Italiana S.p.A., Via G. di Vittorio, 9, pg. 820 PB
Hewlett-Packard Italiana S.p.A., Via G. di Vittorio 10, pg. 820 PB
Hoechst Marion Roussel Italy, Via Le Gran Sasso 18, pg. 625 IT
Holmen MD S.r.l., Via Melchiorre Gioia 75, pg. 885 IT
Home Products Italiana SpA, Via Carlo Farini, 81, pg. 81 IT
Honeywell International, Management SpA, Via Vittor Pisani 13, pg. 835 PB
Honeywell-Measurex Italia S.R.L., Via Filargo 32, pg. 833 IT
Honeywell SpA, Via Vittor Pisani 13, pg. 835 PB
Hoogovens Aluminium Europe Srl., Via F. Russoli 1, pg. 755 IT
Hoogovens Aluminium Italia Spa, Via Pacinotti 50/50a, pg. 755 IT
Hoogovens Italia Srl, pg. 754 IT
Hotel Splendido, 4 Viale Doria, pg. 1213 IT
Hugo Boss Italia S.p.A., pg. 638 IT
Huls Italia S.p.A., Viale Marelli 165, pg. 1455 IT
Hyster Italia S.r.l., Via Gda Udine 34, pg. 1149 PB
IBM Italia S.p.A., Via G.B. Pirelli 18, pg. 897 PB
ICC Italia S.R.L., Via Cardano 8, pg. 554 PV
ICI Italia Milano S.p.A., pg. 665 IT
ICL Italia International Computers srl, Centro Direzionale E Commerciale, pg. 529 IT
IDC Italia S.R.L., Via G. Malipiero 14, pg. 571 PV
IDG Communications Italia Srl, Via G. Malipiero 14, 20138, pg. 570 PV
Ipsoa s.a.r.l., Strada 1, pg. 1514 IT
ITAS S.p.A., Via Metauro 5, pg. 361 PV
ITT Flygt S.p.A., Via Le Europa 30, pg. 860 PB
Ideal-Standard S.p.A., Via A.M. Ampere 102, pg. 92 IT
Il Carbonio SpA, Viale Lucania 6, pg. 1030 IT
Curt Georgi Imes, S.p.a., pg. 1696 PB
Immobiliare Maram S.r.l., Piazza Paolo Ferrari, 10, pg. 138 IT
Immobiliare Metanopoli S.p.A., Via Martiri di Cefalonia N. 67, pg. 428 IT
Immobiliare ML S.r.l., pg. 997 IT
Immobiliaro Sandoz S.p.A., pg. 982 IT
Impresit S.p.A., Via Crocefisso 10, pg. 482 IT
In Testa, Via Washington 17, pg. 1377 IT
The Industrial Bank of Japan, Limited (Milan), Via Senato 14/16, pg. 675 IT
Industrie Magneti Marelli S.R.L., Via Gozzano 14, pg. 482 IT
Infor-Team, Via Vittori Pisani 6, pg. 318 IT
Ingersoll-Rand Italiana S.R.L., Casella Postale 1232, pg. 878 PB
Intel Corporation Italia Spa, pg. 887 PB
Interbanca-Banca per Finanziamenti a Medio e Lungo Termine S.p.A., Corso Venezia, 56, pg. 136 IT
Intergraph Italia L.L.C., Strada 7, Palazzo R1, pg. 892 PB
International Chemical & Cosmetic Co. S.p.A., Via Tommasco Gulli 39, pg. 1436 IT
International Flavors & Fragrances I.F.F. (Italia) S.r.l., Via F. LLI Cervi, pg. 899 IT
International Paper Italia S.p.A., Via Ornago, 55, pg. 905 PB
International Rectifier Corporation Italiana, S.p.A., pg. 907 PB
Intochimica Marketing S.r.l., Piazza Belyiojoso 2, pg. 682 IT
Ionics Italba S.p.A., Piazza IV, Novembre 4, pg. 912 PB
Iriana S.r.l., Via Santa Maria Segreta, 7/9, pg. 90 IT

PB - U.S. Public Companies Volume
PV - U.S. Private Companies Volume
IT - International Public & Private Companies Volume

1664

Geographic Index-Non U.S.

Istituto delle Vitamine S.p.A., pg. 1121 **IT**
Itacard S.p.A., Piazza Paolo Ferrari, 10, pg. 138 **IT**
Itafinco S.p.A., Piazza Paolo Ferrari, 10, pg. 138 **IT**
Italfid Italiana Fiduciaria S.p.A., Via Algardi, 4, pg. 138 **IT**
Italgestra s.r.l., Via Carducci 125, pg. 550 **IT**
Italia S.p.A., Via Mauro Macchi 26, pg. 912 **PB**
S.p.A. Italiana Laboratori Bouty (Italy), Via Vanvitelli 6, pg. 310 **PB**
Italplan Srl, pg. 68 **IT**
Italsafety SrL, Viale de Gasperi No. 44, pg. 1500 **IT**
Italtel, Via A.Di Tocqueville 13, pg. 1363 **IT**
Itaservice S.p.A., Strada 2, Palazzo D, pg. 138 **IT**
Janssen-Cilag S.p.A., Via Michelangelo Buonarroti 23, pg. 929 **PB**
Johnson Wax S.p.A., P.le M. M. Burke 3, pg. 593 **PV**
Jugobanka A.D. (Milan Rep.), Via V. Monti 8, pg. 716 **IT**
KME Italia S.R.L., Piazza Giulio Cesare 9, pg. 719 **IT**
KSB Italia S.p.A., pg. 721 **IT**
Kao Corporation GmbH (Italy Branch), Via Giovanni da Unine, 34, pg. 718 **IT**
Keithley Instruments SRL, Viale S. Gimignano 38, pg. 947 **IT**
Kennametal Ca. Me. S., S.p.A., Via Corrado Il Salico, N. 50, 20141, pg. 951 **PB**
Kennametal Hertel S.p.A., Via Morivione, 5, pg. 951 **PB**
Kenwood Electronics Italia S.p.A., Via G. Sirtori, 7/9, pg. 731 **IT**
Kenwood Linear S.P.A., Via-Arbe, 50, pg. 731 **IT**
Ketchum Public Relations, SRL, Via Fatebenefratelli 19, pg. 617 **PV**
Kidde International Italy, Via De Gasperi 44, pg. 1500 **IT**
Kimberly-Clark (Italiana) S.r.l., Centro Direzionale Colleoni, Palazzo Cassiopea-Ing. 2, pg. 959 **PB**
Kluber Lubrication Italia S.r.l., pg. 506 **IT**
Knoll International Italia S.p.A., 11, v. M.te Napoleone, pg. 627 **PV**
Kodak S.p.A., Viale Matteoti 62, pg. 554 **PB**
Kofisa Italia S.R.L., 11 Via Giosue Carducci, pg. 742 **IT**
Komori Italia S.r.l., 94/12 Via B. Verro, pg. 745 **IT**
KONE Ascensori S.p.A., Via Figino 41, pg. 747 **IT**
KONE Elevators, BU 1, Via Figino, 41, pg. 747 **IT**
KONE Italia S.r.l., Via Figino, 41, pg. 747 **IT**
Konica Business Machines Italia, Via Bressanone N.10, pg. 749 **IT**
Korn/Ferry International, Sala dei Longobardi, Space 2, pg. 633 **PV**
Krauss-Maffei Chemiomeccanica S.r.l., Piazza Castello 2, pg. 836 **IT**
Kredietbank Representative Office (Milan), Foro Buonaparte 76, pg. 760 **IT**
Krupp Hoesch Acciai S.r.l., Via Milanese 20, pg. 515 **IT**
Krupp Widia S.p.A., Via Milano 42, pg. 510 **IT**
Krups S.P.A., Via Zuretti 61, pg. 896 **IT**
Kuehne & Nagel SpA, Largo Fratelli Cervi snc, pg. 763 **IT**
Kyowa Italiana Farmaceutici s.r.l., Viale Fulvio Testi 280, pg. 778 **IT**
L.P.B. Instituto Farmaceutico S.p.A., pg. 983 **IT**
LSB Europa Ltd., Via Vittor Pisani, 14, pg. 971 **PB**
LTX (Italia) S.r.l., Centro Colleoni, Palazzo Cassiopea-Scala 1, pg. 972 **PB**
La Centrale Consulenza S.p.A., Piazza Paolo Ferrari, 10, pg. 138 **IT**
La Centrale Fondi S.p.A., Via Andegari 4, pg. 138 **IT**
La Meccanoptica Leonardo S.p.A., Piazzale Lotto 2, pg. 822 **IT**
La Previdente S.p.A., Via Copernico, 38, pg. 784 **IT**
La Vittoria Riassicurazioni, Via della Moscova, 3, pg. 1152 **IT**
Lambda Electronics Srl, Via F.lli Gracchi, 36, pg. 1242 **IT**
Lancaster Group S.p.A., pg. 186 **IT**
Land Instruments Srl, Via dell'Industria, 2, pg. 798 **IT**
Landis & Staefa Building Control (Italia) S.p.A., Centro Direzionale Sein Felice, pg. 800 **IT**
Laura Ashley SrL, 4 via Brara, pg. 804 **IT**
Lavoro & Sicurta, Corso Italia 23, pg. 61 **IT**
Lee Sri, Via don Gnocchi 28, pg. 657 **PV**
Legion & Rusconi Srl, Via Vitruvio 43, pg. 795 **IT**
Letraset Italia Srl, Via Riccione 8, pg. 462 **IT**
Libreria Internazionale, Via Borgonuovo 25, pg. 888 **IT**
Liquigas SpA, Via Tucidide 56, pg. 1155 **IT**
L'Italia, Corso Italia 23, pg. 61 **IT**
L'Italica - Dival Vita, Corso Italia 23, pg. 61 **IT**
Arthur D. Little International, Inc., Via Serbelloni 4, pg. 671 **PV**
Litton Precision Products (Italy), Viale Fulvio Testi 126, pg. 1004 **PB**
Lloyd 1885, Corso Italia 23, pg. 61 **IT**
Loctite Italia S.p.A., Zona Industriale, Via Talete 56, pg. 611 **IT**
Loewe Italia S.r.l., Via Fratelli Gabba 3, pg. 782 **IT**
Logicasiel SpA, Via Leone XIII 14, pg. 815 **IT**
Longman Italia SRL, via Felice, Casati 20, pg. 1025 **IT**
Lonza Spa, pg. 69 **IT**
Lotus Logistica S.r.l., Via dei Pellegrini, 18, pg. 303 **IT**
Louis Vuitton Italia S.p.a., Via Fratelli Gabba 3, pg. 782 **IT**
Lubrizol Italiana S.p.A., Centro Direzionale, Milano Oltre-Palazzo Cimabue, pg. 1016 **PB**
Luigi Fontana S.p.A., Via E. Romagnoli, 6, pg. 1173 **IT**
M&A Societa di Mergers & Acquisitions S.p.A., Via Manzoni 43, pg. 1330 **IT**
MB Italy S.r.l., Centro Direzionale Milanofieri, Strada 2, Palazzo C1, pg. 798 **PB**
MCG Graficarbo Division, Via Di Vittorio 25/27, pg. 891 **IT**
MCG Morgan Carbon Graphite Srl, Via G. di Vittorio 25/27, pg. 891 **IT**
MR Srl, Palazzo Andromeda, pg. 1283 **IT**
MSI Data Italia S.R.L., Via Cristoforo Colombo, pg. 1546 **PB**
Mach 2 Libri S.p.A., Via B. Quaranta 40, pg. 888 **IT**
Maclean Hunter s.r.l., Piazzale A. Cantore 12, pg. 1124 **IT**

Magneti Marelli S.p.A., Via Gozzano 14, pg. 482 **IT**
Mannesmann Demag SpA, pg. 837 **IT**
Mannesmann Italiana SpA, pg. 838 **IT**
Mannesmann Tally SRL, pg. 840 **IT**
Marelli Autronica S.p.A., Via Gozzano 14, pg. 482 **IT**
Marquette Italia, Srl, pg. 1047 **IT**
Matra Communications ST PA, Via Richard I, pg. 796 **IT**
McDonald's Italia S.r.l., Via Anfossi, 36, pg. 1069 **PB**
McGraw-Hill Libri Italia, S.r.l., Piazza Emilia 5, pg. 1072 **PB**
Meda SIM Bipiemme S.p.A., Galleria de Cristofaris 1, pg. 137 **IT**
Medtronic Italia S.p.A., Piazza Duca D-Aosta 12, pg. 1084 **PB**
Mentor Graphics Italia S.p.A., Milanofiori Palafzzo Al, pg. 1087 **PB**
Meridian Diagnostics Europe s.r.l., pg. 1095 **IT**
METROPOLITANA MILANESE S.P.A., Via del Vecchio Politecnico, 8, pg. 863 **PV**
Mettler-Toledo SpA, Via Vialba, 42/44, pg. 4 **PB**
Micro-Controle Italia Srl, Via G. Pascoli 19, Cernusco Sul, Naviglio, pg. 1179 **IT**
Micropolis S.r.l., Via Stephenson 43/A, pg. 743 **PV**
Microsoft S.p.A., pg. 1108 **IT**
Miller Europa S.p.A., Via Privata Iseo, pg. 869 **PB**
Minemet Italia, Via Sigieri 14, pg. 661 **IT**
Minerva Assicurazioni S.p.A., Piazza Carlo Erba 6, pg. 1531 **IT**
Minerva Vita Assicurazioni S.p.A., Piazza Carlo Erba 6, pg. 1531 **IT**
Mira Lanza S.p.A., pg. 186 **IT**
Mito S.p.A., Via Filippo Turati 9, pg. 482 **IT**
Mitsui & Co. Europe (Italia) S.p.A., Piazza Del Liberty 2, pg. 880 **IT**
Mitsukoshi Ltd.-Milan Office, Via Monte Napoleone 19, pg. 884 **IT**
MoDoCell Italia s.r.l., Via Vittor Pisani 5, pg. 887 **IT**
Molding Compounds Spa, pg. 69 **IT**
Molex Elettronica S.r.l., Via Salomone 43, pg. 1122 **PB**
Molex Italia S.p.A., pg. 1122 **PB**
MOMO S.p.A., pg. 251 **IT**
Mondialcine S.p.A., Via Tamburini 13, pg. 170 **IT**
Monsanto Italiana S.p.A., Via Melchiorre Gioia-8, pg. 1125 **PB**
Montedison S.p.A., Piazzetta Bossi #3, pg. 324 **IT**
MONZINO S.P.A., Monza 22, pg. 888 **IT**
Moore Products Co. (Italia) S.r.l., Via Benedetto Marcello 5, pg. 1129 **PB**
Morgan Grenfell Italia S.p.A., Via A. Manzoni 12, pg. 406 **IT**
Morgan Guaranty Trust Company, Corso Venezia 54, pg. 1130 **IT**
J.P. Morgan Fondi Italia S.p.A., Corso Venezia 54, pg. 1130 **IT**
Morgan Matroc Srl, Centro Direzionale Milanofiori, Pal. A/2, pg. 893 **IT**
Morgan Stanley Milan, Palazzo Serbelloni, Corso Venezia, 16, pg. 1133 **PB**
Motorola S.p.A., Stabile A 1 C, Viale Milanofiori, pg. 1140 **PB**
Moulinex Italia SRL, Via Ernesto Breda 98, pg. 896 **IT**
Multi Language Center SrL, Via Larga, 8, pg. 222 **IT**
Multiass Assicurazioni S.p.A., Via Ripamonti 89, pg. 1256 **IT**
Munters SrL, Via Enrico Fermi 20, pg. 669 **IT**
Mutua Assicuratrice Cotoni, Corso Italia 23, pg. 62 **IT**
NEC Electronics Italiana s.r.l., Via Fabio Filzi, 25/A, pg. 900 **IT**
NMB Italia S.r.l., Via A, 39-41, pg. 868 **IT**
NRG Italia S.p.A., Via Caviglia 11, pg. 1116 **IT**
NSK-RHP Italia S.p.a., Via XX Settembre, 30, Garbagnate, pg. 904 **IT**
NUS Italia, s.r.l., Via Deruta 20, pg. 787 **PV**
NYK Line-Milan, Via XX Settembre 24, pg. 942 **IT**
National Westminster Bank Plc, Via Turati 18, pg. 911 **IT**
Nationale-Nederlanden Life, Via Tortona 33, pg. 651 **IT**
Nedlloyd Road Cargo SpA., pg. 1145 **IT**
Neste Chemicals Italia S.r.l., Corso Buenos Aires 92, pg. 914 **IT**
Nestle Italiana S.P.A., Viale Giulio Richard #5, pg. 921 **IT**
New York Language Center, Via delle Asole, 2, pg. 222 **IT**
A.C. Nielsen Italia S.p.A., Via Divittorio 10, pg. 1183 **PB**
Nikko Italia Societa Di Intermediazione Mobiliare S.p.A., Largo Augusto 7, pg. 931 **IT**
Nissho Iwai Italia S.P.A., Carso Italio 17, pg. 948 **IT**
Nitto Italia S.R.L., Via Aldo Moro, 45, pg. 951 **IT**
Noesis/The Corporate Company, Via Sant' Eusebio 26, pg. 117 **IT**
Nomura Italia S.p.A., Via Turati 16/18, pg. 957 **IT**
Nordica S.r.l., Via Tarvisio 6, pg. 35 **IT**
Nordson Italia SpA, Via Dei Gigli, 3/b, pg. 1189 **PB**
Norske Skog Italia Srl, Via Boscovich 14, pg. 966 **IT**
Norton S.p.A., Via per Cesano Boscone 4, pg. 1175 **IT**
Norvista S.R.L., Via Larga 2, pg. 486 **IT**
Notifier Italia S.r.l., Via Buozzi 55 San Donato Milanese, pg. 1307 **IT**
Novell Italy, Via San Vittore, 40, pg. 1204 **PB**
Novo Nordisk Bioindustriale Srl, Via Francesco Ferruccio 2, pg. 989 **IT**
Nutricia S.p.A., pg. 992 **IT**
OCE-Italia S.p.A., pg. 994 **IT**
OCG Microelectronic Materials S.r.l., Via dei Mille n.5/a, pg. 1220 **PB**
Occam S.r.l., Via A. Manzoni 43, pg. 318 **IT**
Olin Hunt Specialty Products S.r.l., Via Dei Mille 5/a, pg. 1220 **PB**
OMRON Electronics S.p.A., Viale Certosa 49, pg. 1006 **IT**
Ortho Clinical Diagnostic Systems S.p.A., Via Palmanova, 67, pg. 931 **PB**
Osram Societa Riunite Osram-Edison-Clerici S.p.A., Via Savona 105, pg. 1244 **IT**

Outokumpu Italia S.R.L., Via Cesare Cantu N. 19, pg. 1015 **IT**
PC Station S.r.l., Via Nuvolone 44, pg. 318 **IT**
PHH Italy Arval Service Lease Italia SPA, Milanfiori Strada 4, pg. 321 **PB**
PTT Telecom Netherlands (Italy) Srl, pg. 720 **IT**
Pall Italia S.R.L., Via G. Bruzzesi 38/40, pg. 1254 **PB**
Panalpina S.p.A. Transporti Internazionali, pg. 1023 **IT**
PAREXEL International, Via Guido d'Arezzo 4, pg. 1258 **PB**
Parfums Christian Dior S.p.a., Via dell'Unione 1, pg. 783 **IT**
Parfums Givenchy Italia S.r.l., Viale Teodorico 25, pg. 783 **IT**
Paribas Finanziaria SPA, 14 Via dell'Annunciata, pg. 321 **IT**
Parker Hannifin SpA, Via Privata Archimede 1, pg. 1263 **PB**
Passitalia, Piazza Principessa Clotilde 8, pg. 783 **IT**
Passlunch-Sodexho SRL, Via Gallarate 201, pg. 1275 **IT**
PAXAR Italia S.r.l., Via Rizzo 8, pg. 1267 **PB**
Pechiney Italia SpA, Viale Restelli 5, pg. 1031 **IT**
Pharmacia & Upjohn, Via Carlo Imbonati, 24, pg. 1049 **IT**
Pharmacia & Upjohn Biotech S.p.A., Via Alessandro Volta 16, pg. 1048 **IT**
Pharmacia & Upjohn Oncology Immunology, Via Carlo Imbonati, 24, pg. 1050 **IT**
Pharmacia & Upjohn GE2, Via Upjohn GE2, Casella Postale N.4, pg. 1049 **IT**
Pirelli Gottsche Lowe, P. Le Biancamano 8, pg. 678 **PV**
Pirelli Cavi S.p.A., viale Sarca, pg. 1058 **IT**
Pirelli Cavi S.p.A., Divisione Italia - Azienda Accessori Cavi, viale Sarca, pg. 1058 **IT**
Pirelli Coordinamento Pneumatici S.p.A., viale Sarca, pg. 1058 **IT**
Pirelli Informatica, viale Sarca 202, pg. 1058 **IT**
Pirelli Metzeler Motovelo S.R.L., Viale Sarca, pg. 1058 **IT**
Pirelli Sapsa S.p.A., Viale Rimembranza 62, pg. 1058 **IT**
Pirelli Sistemi Antivibranti S.p.A., via Caviglia 3, pg. 1058 **IT**
PIRELLI S.P.A., Viale Sarca 222, pg. 1058 **IT**
PLADA S.p.A., Via Cadolini 26, pg. 807 **PB**
Plantronics Acoustics Italia S.r.l., Centro Direzionale Lombardo, Palazzo E/2, Via Roma 108, pg. 1308 **PB**
Polygram Dischi S.p.A., Via Regina Giovanna 29, pg. 1053 **IT**
Polymetron Sieger S.r.l., pg. 618 **IT**
Polypenco S.r.L., Via Risorgimento 8, pg. 354 **IT**
POSTALMARKET, Via Triste #24, pg. 1064 **IT**
Premark Italia SpA, Via Pietro Mascagni 1, pg. 1323 **PB**
Presstech Controls Srl, Via Valtellina 20, pg. 790 **PB**
Previcommercio, Corso Italia 23, pg. 62 **IT**
Previndustria, Corso Italia 23, pg. 62 **IT**
Profarmaco Nobel S.r.l., Via Cucchiari, 17, pg. 297 **PB**
Publicfactoring S.p.A., Via Agnello 12, pg. 138 **IT**
Publifactoring S.p.A., Via Agnello, 12, pg. 138 **IT**
Purina Italia Spa, Viale Del Ghisallo 20, pg. 1360 **PB**
Quinton Hazell PLC, Milan, pg. 561 **PB**
R.C.S. EDITORI S.P.A., Via Angelo Rizzoli 2, pg. 1078 **IT**
RNBNY Branch Office-Milan, Via Dell'Orso 2, pg. 1381 **PB**
RZB Milan, Piazzetta Pattari 1/3, pg. 1084 **IT**
Rabofin Italia SpA, Via Spadari 3/5, pg. 1082 **IT**
Radiocor Telerate S.p.A., Via Degli Amedei, 15, pg. 525 **PB**
Rasfid, Corso Italia 23, pg. 62 **IT**
Raychem S.p.A., Centro Direzionale Milanofiori, pg. 1363 **PB**
Recordati Farma S.r.l., Via Matteo Civitali 1, pg. 1090 **IT**
RECORDATI INDUSTRIA CHIMICA E FARMACEUTICA S.P.A., Via M. Civitali 1, pg. 1090 **IT**
Recordati Pharmaceutical Chemicals Division:, Via Civitali, 1, pg. 1090 **IT**
Reed Travel Group-Italy, Via De Amicis 28, pg. 1097 **IT**
Reeves S.p.A., 20090 Lodivecchio, pg. 507 **PV**
Refrattari Italia S.R.L., Palazzo Pegaso 1, pg. 894 **IT**
Reglar Srl, pg. 69 **IT**
Repsol Italia SPA, Centro Uffici S. Siro, Via Caldera, 21, pg. 1105 **IT**
Repsol Quimica, Centro Uffizi, Via Caldera, 21, pg. 1105 **IT**
Resinmec Spa, pg. 69 **IT**
Resthotel International, Via Senato N 14/16, pg. 21 **IT**
Reuters Italia SpA, Viale Fulvio Testi, 280, pg. 1105 **IT**
Rhone-Poulenc Italia SpA, Via Winckelmann, 2, pg. 1113 **IT**
Riccardo Ricciardi Editore S.p.A., V.le di porta Vercellina 7, pg. 888 **IT**
Ricoh Italia S.p.A., Viale Suzzani, 287, pg. 1116 **IT**
Rieter Automotive Italiana S.p.A., pg. 1117 **IT**
Rieter Italiana S.R.L., pg. 1117 **IT**
RIMOLDI NECCHI S.R.L., 33 Via Montebello, pg. 1117 **IT**
Riunione Adriatica di Sicurta S.p.A., Corso Italia 23, pg. 61 **IT**
Riva Hydroart S.p.A., pg. 1473 **IT**
Robinson Nugent, s.p.a, Via Fidelina, 2, pg. 1395 **PB**
Roche S.p.A., Piazza Durante 11, pg. 1122 **IT**
Rockwell Semiconductor Systems, Via di Vittorio, 1, pg. 1402 **IT**
Roerig Farmaceutici Italiana S.r.l., Via Bernardino Zenale, n. 44, 20024 Garbagnate, pg. 1283 **PB**
Rognoni, pg. 506 **IT**
Rohm & Haas Italia, S.p.a, pg. 1404 **PB**
Rorer S.p.A., V.Le Europa, 11, pg. 1112 **IT**
Rothe Erde-Metallurgica Rossi S.p.A., Via Milanese, 20, pg. 509 **IT**
Rothenberger Italiana S.R.L., Via Reiss Romoli 17, pg. 1129 **IT**
Rotoink S.p.A., Galleria S. Babila 4-B, pg. 371 **IT**
Rotta Farmaceutici, S.p.A., San Fruttuoso di Monza, pg. 1112 **IT**
Rowenta Italia S.p.A., Via Caldera 21, pg. 569 **IT**

PB - *U.S. Public Companies Volume*
PV - *U.S. Private Companies Volume*
IT - *International Public & Private Companies Volume*

SAE-Società Anonima Electrificazione S.p.A., Piazzale Lodi
  3, pg. 3   IT
SAIA-Burgess SRL, Via Cadamosto 3, pg. 1501   IT
SAS Institute S.r.l., Via San Martino della Battaglia 17,
  pg. 967   PV
SBC Warburg Italia S.p.A., Via Gaetano Negri,
  pg. 1331   IT
SBS SIM S.p.A., Via Manzoni 43, pg. 1331   IT
SDRC Italia, Srl., Via Piero Portaluppi, 11/2, pg. 1525   PB
S.I.A, S.p.A., Via Tamburini 13, pg. 170   IT
SIE Systems SpA, pg. 835   IT
SIELTE Engineering S.p.A., Via Lattuada 20, pg. 1370   IT
SMET, Via P. Coletta, 59, pg. 1065   PV
SPF Promotio Sim SPA, Via Brera n. 19, pg. 341   IT
SACIT, S.p.a., Via Mecenate 87/2, pg. 577   PB
Sagit S.p.A., Via Paolo, pg. 1438   IT
Saint-Gobain Finanziaria SpA, Via E. Romagnoli, 6,
  pg. 1171   IT
Saipem S.p.A., Via Martiri di Cefalonia, San Donato
  Milanese, pg. 428   IT
The Sakura Bank - Milan Representative Office, Piazza San
  Babila 3, pg. 1180   IT
San Giorgio Servizi Distribuzione S.r.l., Via Montebello, 27,
  pg. 90   IT
Sandoz Agro S.p.A., pg. 984   IT
Sandoz Chimica S.p.A., Via Arconati, pg. 984   IT
Sandoz Prodotti Farmaceutici S.p.A., Via Arconalia,
  pg. 985   IT
Sandoz S.p.A., 26 Via Lainate-Bettolino, pg. 985   IT
Sandvik Coromant, pg. 1186   IT
Sandvik Hard Materials, pg. 1186   IT
Sandvik Italia S.p.A., Via Varesina 184, pg. 1186   IT
Sandvik Process Systems S.p.A., C.P. 16137, pg. 1187   IT
Sandvik Rock Tools, pg. 1187   IT
Sandvik Saws and Tools, pg. 1187   IT
Sandvik Steel, pg. 1187   IT
Santander Investment SpA, Via Olmetto, 17, pg. 144   IT
Sanyo Italiana S.p.A., Via Andrea Maffei 1, pg. 1192   IT
Saunier Duval Italia Srl, Via Ariberto 3, pg. 615   IT
Scab Elettronica Systems SpA, Viale de Gasperi No. 44,
  pg. 1500   IT
Scapa Italia, Via Senato N 14/16, pg. 21   IT
Schema S.p.A., Via Vittor Pisani 6, pg. 318   IT
SCHIAPPARELLI, Viale Sarca 223, 9th Fl., pg. 1204   IT
Schiesser International S.r.l., pg. 618   IT
Schlatter Italiana S.r.l., Centro Svizzero, pg. 1206   IT
Schleicher & Schuell Italia SRL, pg. 1206   IT
Sealed Air S.P.A., Via Per Ornago, pg. 1451   PB
SEARLE S.R.L., Via Tobagi 8, pg. 1217   IT
Sekurit Saint-Gobain Italia SRL, Via E. Romagnoli 6,
  pg. 1173   IT
Selas Italiana, S.r.l., Via Delle Tuberose 14, pg. 1455   PB
Selezione dal Reader's Digest S.p.A., Via Alserio 10,
  pg. 1368   PB
SelmaBipiemme Leasing SpA, Via M. Gidid 124,
  pg. 137   IT
Sensormatic E.C., S.r.l., Via Teocrito 36, pg. 1457   PB
Servizi Tecnici Swiss Re s.r.l, Via Brera 5, pg. 1333   IT
Shandwick Corporate Communications S.p.A., Foro
  Bonaparte 70, pg. 1227   IT
Shandwick Marketing Communication Srl, Piazza del
  Castello 26, pg. 1227   IT
Sharp Electronics (Italia) S.p.A., Via Lampedusa,
  pg. 1230   IT
Shell Italia SpA, Via F Londonio 2, pg. 1138   IT
Shimadzu Italia S.R.L., 20139, Via Gaggia 13, pg. 1232   IT
Shimizu Italia S.P.A., Via Vittor Pisani, 16, pg. 1234   IT
Shiseido Cosmetici (Italia) S.p.A., Centro Direzionale,
  Milano 2, pg. 1235   IT
Siagarage S.p.A., Via Tamburini 13, pg. 170   IT
Sicad S.r.l., Via Vittor Pisani 6, pg. 318   IT
SICIT IDE S.p.A., Via Vittori Pisani 6, pg. 318   IT
SICIT M.T. & T. S.p.A., Via Vittor Pisani 6, pg. 318   IT
SICIT (Società Iniziative Commerciali Industriali e Techniche)
  S.p.A., Via Vittor Pisani 6, pg. 318   IT
Sicom spa, Via S. Caboro 15a -, pg. 653   IT
Sicurta 1879 Assicuranzioni S.p.A., Piazza Carlo Erba 6,
  pg. 1531   IT
Siemens S.p.A., Via Fabio Filzi, 29, pg. 1248   IT
Silvani Antincendi spA, Via Redipuglia 8, pg. 1500   IT
Silverstar Ltd., S.p.A., Viale Fulvio Testi 280, pg. 135   PB
Singapore Tourist Promotion Board - Milan, c/o Theodore
  Trancu & Associates, pg. 1254   IT
Sinted S.p.A., Via G.B. Pirelli 20, pg. 318   IT
Sirma S.p.a., Via Tito Speri, 8, pg. 6   IT
Sirti, Via G.B. Pirelli 20, pg. 1362   IT
Skandia Vita S.p.A., Via Fatebenefratelli 3, pg. 1258   IT
SmithKline Beecham Italia S.p.A., Via Pirelli No. 19,
  pg. 1266   IT
Snam S.P.A., Vanone 1, St. Donato Milanese, pg. 428   IT
Snamprogetti S.p.A., Villa de Gasperi 16, San Donato
  Milanese, pg. 429   IT
Società Europea di Edizoni S.p.A., Via G. Negri 4,
  pg. 888   IT
Società Italiana per il Cynar S.p.A., Via Vittor Pisani 22,
  pg. 751   IT
Società Pneumatici Pirelli S.p.A., viale Sarca, pg. 1058   IT
Socla Italia (SRL), pg. 378   IT
Sodexho Italia Spa, Viale Stelvio 71, pg. 1275   IT
Sodiges S.r.l., Via Santa Maria Segreta, 7/9, pg. 90   IT
Sodra Italia S.r.l., Via Leopardi 3, pg. 1276   IT
Softimage S.R.L., pg. 1108   PB
Sogil, Aeroporto di Linate, pg. 1275   IT
Solplant, Via S. Sofia, 21, pg. 1524   IT
Solplant S.p.A. Via Santa Sofia 21, pg. 1526   IT
SOPASIN (Società di Partecipazione Sistemi Informativi)
  S.p.A., Via G.B. Pirelli 32, pg. 318   IT
Sotair Italia, Via Marradi 1, pg. 560   IT
Sperlari, S.R.L., 26100 Cremona, pg. 812   PB

Sperling & Kupfer Editori S.p.A., Via Borgonuovo 25,
  pg. 888   IT
Sperling & Kupfer S.r.l., Via Borgonuovo 25, pg. 888   IT
Sperling Paperback S.r.l., Via Borgonuovo 25, pg. 888   IT
Stabillus SRL, pg. 835   IT
Stafford-Miller S.r.l., Via Correggio 19, pg. 237   PB
Stahl Italia SRL, Via Lattuada, 40, pg. 1526   IT
Star S.p.A., Via Matteoti 142, pg. 380   IT
Steelinter Italia S.R.L., pg. 302   IT
Stinnes Interoil Italia S.r.l., Via P.L. da Palestrina 6,
  pg. 1459   IT
Stratus Italia, S.R.L., Via Emilia, 83, pg. 1524   PB
Studio Fiu, Via P. Cossa 2, pg. 1152   PV
Sulzer Italia S.p.A., Via San Senatore, 6/3, pg. 1306   IT
The Sumitomo Bank, Ltd.-Milan Branch, Via Palestro 2,
  pg. 1309   IT
Sun Microsystems Italia S.p.A., Centro Direzionale Colleoni,
  Andromeda (Ingresso 1), pg. 1531   PB
Swiss Life (Italia), Corso di Porta Romana, 2, pg. 1332   IT
Swiss Life (Italia) Infortuni e Malattie, Corso di Porta
  Romana, 2, pg. 1332   IT
Swissmetal Italia s.r.l., Via E. Bassini 27, pg. 1427   IT
Symantec Srl., Corso di Porta Vittoria, 32, pg. 1546   PB
Symbol Technologies S.R.L., Via Cristoforo Colombo 49,
  pg. 1546   PB
TBWA Italia S.p.A., Via Cusani 5, pg. 1063   PV
Takashimaya (Italia) S.P.A., Galleria del Corso N2,
  pg. 1350   IT
Tamalia, Piazza Principessa Clotilde 8, pg. 783   IT
Tandem Computers Italia S.p.A., Via Caldera 21,
  pg. 418   PB
Taylor Instrument, Via Trivulzio 18, pg. 6   IT
Teac Italiana S.p.A., Via C. Cantu 5, pg. 1360   IT
Tecnimont Spa, Viale Monte Grappa 3, pg. 324   IT
Tefal Italia S.p.A., Via Caldera 21, pg. 568   IT
Teledyne Italy, Corso di Porta Romana 2, pg. 44   PB
Telettra, Viale Testi 136, pg. 55   IT
Telxon Italia S.r.l., Palazzo Cimabue, Via Cassanese, 224,
  pg. 1574   PB
Tesa Italia SRL, Division Machine 3D, pg. 260   IT
Armando Testa S.p.A., Via Washington 17, pg. 1377   IT
TESTA INTERNATIONAL, Via Washington 17,
  pg. 1376   IT
Thermor Italia S.P.A., Via Lombellina 12A, pg. 1081   PV
3M Italia SpA, Via S. Bovio 3, pg. 1607   PB
3i Investors in Industry spa, Via Gaetano Negri 8,
  pg. 1386   IT
3i Italy, Via Orefici 2, pg. 1386   IT
Tiffany-Faraone, S.p.A. (Milan), Via Verri 10, pg. 1609   PB
Time-Life International S.r.l., Via Turati 29, pg. 1615   IT
Time/System Italia S.r.l., Via Cristoforo Colombo 7/9,
  pg. 73   IT
Timken Italia S.r.l., Viale delle Rimembranze di Greco 1,
  pg. 1618   PB
Tioxide Europe SRL, Via del Vecchio Politecnico,
  pg. 666   IT
Titanus Distribuzione S.p.A., Via Tamburini 13, pg. 170   IT
The Tokio Marine & Fire Insurance Company (U.K.) Limited,
  Piazza Cavour 5, pg. 1392   IT
Tonka Italia S.p.A., via Santa Sofia 10, pg. 798   PB
Toray Italia S.r.l., Via Mecenate 861, pg. 1400   IT
Toshiba Electronics Italiana S.R.L., Centro Direzionale
  Colleoni, Pallazzo Perseo Ingr.2-Piano 6, pg. 1406   IT
Total Italiana Srl, Via Santa Tecla 2, pg. 1409   IT
Tourism Malaysia - Milan Office, 2nd Floor, Piazza San
  Bablia, pg. 833   IT
Traub-Gioia S.R.L., via Vittorio Veneto, 4, pg. 1419   IT
Traub-Heckert Italia S.R.L., via Vittorio Veneto, 4,
  pg. 1419   IT
Tufira S.r.l., Via Brescia 8, pg. 490   IT
Tyco Toys (Italy) S.P.A., Centro Direzionale Colleoni,
  Palazzo Sirio - Ingresso 2, pg. 1059   PB
UBS Italia Investimenti e Finanza SpA, Via Salvini 10,
  pg. 1440   IT
UPM-Kymmene Italia S.r.l., Piazza Velasca 5,
  pg. 1430   IT
UTA Italiana SpA, Piazza Luigi di Savoia 24, pg. 1509   IT
Ufficio Affari Quebec Italia, Via Brisa, 5, pg. 249   IT
Unil-It S.p.A., Via Privata, Nino Bonnet # 10, pg. 1438   IT
Unisys Italia S.p.A., Via Benigno Crespi, 57, pg. 1671   PB
Unitecta Italiana SpA, Via Martelli 8, pg. 1501   IT
Utell International-Italy, Via de Amicis 28, pg. 1098   IT
Utras, Corso Italia 23, pg. 62   IT
VG Instruments Group Ltd., 20063, Cernusco Sul Naviglio,
  pg. 1595   PB
VRG Servizio Carta Srl., pg. 757   IT
Van Leer Italia SpA, Via Amerigo, pg. 1147   IT
Veam S.A., Via Statuto 2, pg. 1005   IT
Veglia Borletti S.R.L., Via Gozzano 14, pg. 482   IT
Velcro Italia S.R.L., Via Bellini 10/B, pg. 1462   IT
Vercolac S.p.A., 11, Via Benedetto Croce, pg. 43   IT
Vetrotex Italia, Via E. Romagnoli 6, pg. 1177   IT
Vickers Systems, Via Monzese, 34 20060 Vignate,
  pg. 25   PB
Viewlogic Systems SRL, Centro Direzionale Colleoni, Via
  Paracelso, 6, pg. 1548   PB
VOAC Hydraulics SpA, Casella Postale 10076,
  pg. 1264   PB
Voest-Alpine S.p.A., Via F. Turati 29, pg. 1472   IT
Vorwerk Contempora S.r.l., pg. 1481   IT
Vorwerk Folletto S.r.l., pg. 1481   IT
Wandel & Goltermann S.R.L.-Tecnologie di Misura
  Elettroniche, Via Pomponazzi 25, pg. 1486   IT
Wander S.p.A., pg. 986   IT
Wang Italia S.p.A, Centro Terziario, Strada Statale Padana
  Superiore, 1738   IT
Watlow Italy, Via Adige 13, pg. 1154   PV
Werner & Pfleiderer Italia S.R.L., via B. Eustachi, 45,
  pg. 1756   PB

Westdeutsche Landesbank-Milan Branch, pg. 1493   IT
WestLB Europa Finanziaria S.p.A., Via Canova 38,
  pg. 1494   IT
Wiggins Arjo Italiana Srl, 8, Via Maria Teresa, pg. 567   IT
Windmoller & Holscher Italiana S.r.L., Via G. da Procida 35,
  pg. 1511   IT
Witco Italiana, Viale Lunigaina, 40, pg. 1774   PB
Wolters Kluwer Italy, Strada 1, Palazzo F6, pg. 1513   IT
Wormald Italiana S.P.A., Via Ettore Ponti 55, pg. 1651   PB
Yamaichi Italia S.p.A. Società di Intermediazione Mobiliare,
  Corso Vittorio Emanuele II, 13, pg. 1518   IT
Young & Rubicam Italia, S.p.A., Piazza Eleonora Duse 2,
  pg. 1199   PV
Dr. Lo. Zambeletti S.p.A., Via Zambeletti, pg. 1266   IT
Zenith Data Systems Italia S.p.A., Milanofiori - Strada 4,
  pg. 318   IT
Zeta Finanza S.p.A., Via Maurizio Quadrio 17, pg. 1531   IT
Zurich International (Italia) S.p.A., Piazza Carlo Erba 6,
  pg. 1532   IT
Zurigo Compagnia di Assicurazioni, Piazza Carlo Erba 6,
  pg. 1531   IT
Zurigo Compagnia di Assicurazioni Sulla Vita, Piazza Carlo
  Erba 6, pg. 1530   IT

Modena

Ascom TCS SpA, Via Magellano 1, pg. 87   IT
Fiat Trattori S.p.A., Via Pico Della Mirandola 72,
  pg. 481   IT
FiatGeotech S.p.A., Viale delle Nazioni 55, pg. 484   IT
Officine A. Maserati S.p.A., Viale Ciro Menotti, 322,
  pg. 482   IT
Officine Alfieri Maserati, SpA, Viale Ciro, Menotti, 322,
  pg. 354   PB
Reed Exhibition Companies-Italy, Via Taglio 22,
  pg. 1619   IT
Siria Officine Meccaniche SpA, Via Miari, 2, pg. 1619   PB

Modugno

AlliedSignal France SpA, Zona Industriale, pg. 54   PB

Mogliano Veneto

Adriavita S.p.A., Bia Ferretto, 1, pg. 89   IT
Altinia S.p.A., Via Ronzinella, 186/15, pg. 89   IT
La Venezia Assicurazioni S.p.A., Via Ferretto, 1, pg. 90   IT
Risparmio Assicurazioni S.p.A., Via Ferretto, 1, pg. 90   IT
Risparmio Vita Assicurazioni S.p.A., Via Ferretto, 1,
  pg. 90   IT
Torcello S.r.l., Via Ferretto, 1, pg. 90   IT
Trieste E Venezia Assicurazioni S.p.A., Via Ferretto, 1,
  pg. 90   IT

Molinella

Diavia S.p.A., 2 v. Nobili, pg. 1691   PB

Monfalcone

Adriaplast S.p.A., Via Timavo 59, pg. 1278   IT
Liebherr Italia S.p.A., Via degli Schiavetti 11, pg. 809   IT
Meteor-Gorizia Plant, Stazione Ronchi Nord, pg. 653   IT
Francesco Parisi S.p.A., Via Duca d'Aosta 85, pg. 318   IT
Telesistemi S.p.a., Via Duca d'Aosta 85, pg. 318   IT

Monsano

IDEAL FORM TEAM S.R.L., Via Piemonte 14, pg. 659   IT

Montebelluna

Bauer Apparel Inc., Via Feltrina Sud, 172, pg. 1184   PB
LOTTO S.P.A., Via San Gaetano 200, pg. 819   IT

Montecchio Maggiore

FIAMM S.P.A., 63, VI. Europa, pg. 480   IT
Lowara S.p.A., 14 Via Dott Lomgardi, pg. 861   PB
Sumoto S.r.l., Via Tecchio 89, pg. 432   IT

Monticchio Bagni

S.I.A.M. Monticchio srl, pg. 753   IT

Montichiari

Duesse, Via Arturo Mercanti, 17, pg. 1172   IT

Monza

Air Products Italia, Via Silvio Pellico #48, pg. 31   PB
Comatel Srl, Via Sardegna, 39/c, pg. 1241   IT
Fidelio Italia Srl, Via Locarno, 1 Ang. Via Elvezia,
  pg. 1106   IT
Gendex Dental Systems S.r.l., via G. Casati, 23,
  pg. 500   PB
Marconi Automazione S.p.A., Via Marsala, 24, pg. 546   IT
Nuclital Srl, Via Elvezia 2, pg. 389   IT
Sapio, Via Silvio Pellico #48, pg. 32   IT
Società Alfa-Laval, S.p.A., C.P. 212, pg. 1378   IT

Mori

Dega S.r.l., Via Matteotti 50/8, pg. 807   PB

PB - U.S. Public Companies Volume
PV - U.S. Private Companies Volume
IT - International Public & Private Companies Volume

Mortara

Outokumpu Centro Servizi S.P.A., Via E. Fermi 52, pg. 1017 — IT

Mortegliano

Agrozoofarma S.p.A., Via Lavariano, 15, pg. 89 — IT
Sementi Dotto S.p.A., Via Lavariano, 15, pg. 90 — IT

Muggia

Jotun Brignola S.p.A., Via Petronio 8, Zona Industriale Noghere, pg. 715 — IT
Knoll Farmaceutici S.p.A, Via Europa 35, pg. 108 — IT

Naples

Aero Trasporti Italiani - A.T.I. S.p.A., Aeroporto Capodichino, pg. 652 — IT
Alenia, Piazzale Vincenzo Tecchip 51/A, pg. 653 — IT
Alfa Romeo Auto S.p.A., Via Medina, 40, pg. 481 — IT
Alfa Romeo Avio S.p.A., Via Medina 40, pg. 481 — IT
Alfa Romeo e Nissan Autoveicoli S.p.A., Via Medina, 40, pg. 481 — IT
Alfa Romeo Veicoli Comm. e Lav Mecc. S.p.A., Via Medina, 40, pg. 481 — IT
Also S.p.A., pg. 1436 — IT
Ansaldo Transporti spa, Via Nuova Della Brecce 260, pg. 653 — IT
Banca d'America e d'Italia S.p.A. (Napoli), Via Santa Brigida, 10, pg. 403 — IT
BANCO DI NAPOLI, Via Toledo 177-178, pg. 140 — IT
Hewlett-Packard Italiana S.p.A., Via Orazio, 16, pg. 821 — PB
Hewlett-Packard Italiana S.p.A., Centro Direzionale di Napoli, Via G. Przio, 4, pg. 821 — PB
Inca Investimenti SpA Alfa Romeo Alfasud, Via Medina, 40, pg. 481 — IT
Kodak S.p.A., Centro Direzionale, Isola F1, Viale della Constituzione, pg. 554 — PB
Partenavia Construzioni Aeronautiche, Piazzale Vincenzo Tecchio 51/A, pg. 653 — IT
S.I.C.A. S.p.A., Via Medina, 40, pg. 481 — IT
SME Societa Merdionale Finanziaria, Centro Direzionale di Napoli, pg. 655 — IT
Societa Italiana Assicurazioni Danni S.p.A., Via G. Ferraris, 119, pg. 90 — IT

Naturno

Berges Electronic, s.r.l., Via Zona Industriale, 11, pg. 1562 — PB

Nembro

MAF S.p.A., via Ronchetti, 37, pg. 1449 — IT

Nerviano

Mikron SNC Nerviano, Via Carducci 16, pg. 867 — IT
Pibiviesse SpA (PBVS), Via Bergamina, 24, pg. 1747 — PB

Nichelino

Gallino Plasturgia S.r.l., pg. 251 — PB

Nova Milanese

Agenzia Lombarda Distribuzione Giornali e Riviste S.r.l., Via Garibaldi 150, pg. 888 — IT

Novara

Akzo Chemicals S.p.A., Via L. Gherzi, 25, pg. 46 — IT
Akzo Salt Spa, 50 Via Fauser, pg. 47 — IT
Gruppo Dolciario Italiano S.p.A., pg. 920 — IT
Interappia Publicita S.p.A., Baluardo Partigiani 13, pg. 751 — IT
Mattel Toys, S.R.L., Via Vittorio Veneto 119 Oleggio, pg. 1059 — PB
Mondadori De Agostini Libri S.p.A., Via G. Da Verrazzano 15, pg. 888 — IT
SME International, Corso Vercelli 101, pg. 655 — IT
Societa Industrie Liquoristiche S.A.S., Baluardo Partigiani 13, pg. 751 — IT
Syremont S.p.A., Via Fauser 4, pg. 324 — IT
Terme di Crodo S.p.A., Baluardo Partigiani 13, pg. 751 — IT

Novegro di Segrate

A.I. OCEAN, Via Eugenio Montale, 20, pg. 14 — IT
Olpidurr S.p.A., Via G. Pascoli, 14, pg. 422 — IT

Novi Ligure

Jefferson Smurfit Italia. S.r.l., Strada Serravalle 40, pg. 1271 — IT

Oderzo

Zanussi Componenti Plastica S.p.A., Via G. Verdi, 30, pg. 442 — IT

Olgiate Comasco

Avon Cosmetics, S.p.A., 22077 Via XXV Aprile 15, pg. 156 — PB

Orbassano

Centro Ricerche Fiat, Strada Torino 50, pg. 480 — IT
Lear Corporation Italia S.p.A., Via San Luigi N. 18/20, pg. 982 — PB

Oriolo

AGIE Italia SpA, Via per Cantalupo 5, pg. 488 — IT

Ornago

Hydro Alluminio Ornago S.p.A., Via A. Ciucani no. 8, pg. 962 — IT

Ospiate di Bollate

Macchine e Accessori per l'Industria Grafica Macchingraf SpA, pg. 757 — IT
Neo Abello S.p.A., Via Falzarego 8, pg. 289 — IT

Ostiglia

Donaldson Italia s.r.l., Z.I. Strada A, 17, pg. 517 — PB

Paderno Dugnano

Pirelli Servocavi S.p.A., via Guido Rossa 4/6, pg. 1058 — IT
S.A.G.E. Serengi Azienda Grafica ed Editoriale S.p.A., Via C. Battisti 40, pg. 888 — IT
S.G.N. Societa Grafica Novarese S.p.A., Via C. Battista 40, pg. 888 — IT
Siegling Italia S.p.a., pg. 498 — IT
Societa Editrice Lombarda S.E.L. S.p.A., Via C. Battista 40, pg. 888 — IT
Societa Italiana Editrice Stampatrice S.I.E.S. S.p.A., Via C. Battista 40, pg. 888 — IT

Padua

Allen-Bradley s.r.l., Galleria Spagna, 35/3, pg. 1399 — PB
Banca d'America e d'Italia S.p.A. (Padova), Piazza Alcide De Gasperi, 34, pg. 403 — IT
Edilit, Lungargine Munson 5, pg. 430 — IT
Hewlett-Packard Italiana S.p.A., Via Pelizzo 15, pg. 821 — PB
Kodak S.p.A., Vicolo T. Aspetti 4, pg. 554 — PB
Porsche Italia S.p.A Padova, Via Castimabile, pg. 1063 — IT
SO.GE.AM S.p.a., pg. 922 — IT
SO.GE.PLAST S.r.l., pg. 922 — IT
Zetronic S.p.A., 27, Str. 1X Zona Industrial, pg. 1122 — PB

Pagani

Erisud S.p.A., Via Madonna di Fatima 2, pg. 1368 — IT

Palermo

El. Te. Siciliana S.p.A., Via Pietro Nenni 30/32, pg. 1365 — IT
MAPFRE Progress, S.P.A., Piazza A Gentili 3, pg. 333 — IT
S.I.Ga.T. S.p.A., Via Resuttana N. 360, pg. 428 — IT
Siciliana Electronica & Telecomunicazioni S.p.A., Via Pietro Nenno 30/32, pg. 1370 — IT

Parma

Banninger Italia Srl, via Raffaello Sanzio N. 16, pg. 391 — IT
FMC Food Machinery (Italy) S.p.A., Via Mantova 127, Box 333, pg. 606 — PB
FATA European Group S.p.A, Via Verdi 9, pg. 474 — IT
Italgel S.p.A., pg. 920 — IT
MB Holdings S.p.A., Casella Postale 429, pg. 267 — IT
PARMALAT S.P.A., via Oreste Grassi 26, pg. 1023 — IT
SASIB Beverage M.S. S.p.A., Via Fratelli Canvelli, 22, pg. 1194 — IT
SASIB Beverage S.p.A., Via La Spezia, 241/A, pg. 1194 — IT
SASIB Food S.p.A.-Food Processing Division, Via Paradigna, 94/A, pg. 1194 — IT
White Cap Italia S.r.l., pg. 1207 — IT

Pavia

Instant S.R.L., Via Montanari 7, S. Martino Siccomario, pg. 1128 — PV

Perni

Sigma Moore S.p.A., Via Barbarasa 23, pg. 890 — IT

Perugia

Buitoni SpA, Via Cortonese 4, pg. 919 — IT
Tatry Officina Meccanica S.r.l., Via Burno Buozzi, 12, pg. 234 — PB

Pescara

Banca d'America e d'Italia S.P.A. (Pescara), Via Tibullo, 5, pg. 403 — IT
Carbide & Graphite Technologies S.r.l., Zona Industriale, pg. 891 — IT

Peschiera del Garda

Grande Distribuzione Avanzata S.p.A., pg. 1015 — IT
Landis & Staefa (Italia) S.p.A., Divisione Daco Systems, pg. 801 — IT

Piacenza

Amada Schiavi S.r.l., Via Copernico 2/4., pg. 70 — IT
ASTRA VEICOLI INDUSTRIALI S.P.A., Via Caorsana 79, pg. 94 — IT
Biffi Italia S.r.l., Localita Caselle San Pietro, pg. 1650 — PB
Halliburton Italiana S.P.A, Casella Postale 86, pg. 777 — PB
Keystone Vanessa S.r.l., 29018 Lugagnano Val d'Arda, pg. 1650 — PB
MANDELLI INDUSTRIE S.P.A., Via Caorsana 35, pg. 834 — IT
Schiavi S.p.a., pg. 199 — IT
Sunrise Medical S.R.L., Via Riva, 20-Montale, pg. 1536 — PB

Pianezza

C.S.I., pg. 1002 — IT
FATA European Group S.p.A., Strada Statle 24 Km 12, pg. 474 — IT

Pieve Emanuele

Alcan Alluminio S.p.A., Via Bruno Buozzi 12, pg. 50 — IT
JEOL (Italia) S.p.A., Centro Direzionale Ripamonti, pg. 697 — IT

Pinerolo

Corfina S.p.A., pg. 507 — IT

Pino Torinese

FERRERO, Via Maria Cristina 47, pg. 480 — IT

Piossasco

WABCO Westinghouse Freni Veicoli Industriali S.p.A., Via Volvera 51, pg. 92 — PB

Pisa

Alpha Therapeutic Italia, S.p.A., Via Benedetto Croce, 13, pg. 558 — IT
Saint-Gobain Vetro Italia SpA, Via Ponte a Piglieri, pg. 1173 — IT
Saint-Gobain Vitro Italia, Via Ponte a Piglieri 2, pg. 1173 — IT
Toscana Glas S.p.A., Via Auvelia 1-Via Livornese, pg. 1173 — IT

Pistoia

SASIB Packaging Italia S.r.l., Via Traversa Della Vergine, pg. 1194 — IT

Poggio Rusco

Glo SpA, Via Pinzone 2, pg. 1055 — PB

Poirino

Borletti Climatizzazione S.R.L., Frazione Masio 24, pg. 482 — IT

Pomezia

Allergan S.p.A., Via Costarica 20/22, pg. 46 — PB

Pomigliano d'Arco

Alenia Aeronautica, pg. 653 — IT

Pont San Martin

Seagate Technology Europe S.p.A., Viale Carlo Viola, 65, pg. 1450 — PB

Pontebba

Francesco Parisi S.p.A., Via Pramollo, 4, pg. 504 — IT

Ponzano Veneto

BENETTON GROUP S.P.A., Via Villa Minelli 1, pg. 186 — IT

Porcari

Akzo Chemicals S.p.A., Via Ciarpi, 6, pg. 46 — IT
Bertelli SpA, 6 Via Ciarpi, pg. 47 — IT
SCA Italcarta S.p.A., Via del Frizzone, pg. 1326 — IT

PB - *U.S. Public Companies Volume*
PV - *U.S. Private Companies Volume*
IT - *International Public & Private Companies Volume*

1667

Geographic Index-Non U.S.

SCA Packaging Italia S.p.A., via Romana Ovest, 245, pg. 1326   IT

Pordenone

Electrolux International S.p.A., Via Giardini Cattaneo, 3, pg. 442   IT
Electrolux San Jose, Via Giardini Cattaneo 3, pg. 442   IT
Hewlett-Packard Italiana S.p.A., Via Udine, 13, pg. 821   PB
Jacuzzi Europe, S.p.A., S.S. Pontebbana Km. 97, pg. 1684   PB
P & O Centro Servizi S.p.A., Via Giardini Cattaneo, 3, pg. 442   IT
Propria s.r.l., Via Mazzini, 13, pg. 442   IT
Veneta Factoring S.p.A., Via Giardini Cattaneo, 3, pg. 442   IT
Zanussi Elettrodomestici S.p.A., Via Giardini Cattaneo, 3, pg. 442   IT
Zanussi Elettromeccanica S.p.A., Via G. Cattaneo, 3, pg. 442   IT
Zanussi Grandi Impianti S.p.A., Viale Treviso, 15, pg. 442   IT
Zanussi Italia S.p.A., Via G. Cattaneo, 3, pg. 442   IT

Potenza

Avigliano Mill, Localita Serra Ventaruli, pg. 673   PB
Banca Mediterranea S.p.A., Via N. Sauro s.n.c., pg. 135   IT
Italtractor ITM S.p.A., Zona Industriale, pg. 654   IT

Pozzuoli

Erven Lucas Bols Italia S.p.A., Strada Comunale Cerqueto, pg. 751   IT
Olivetti Ricerca, pg. 1002   IT
S.D.D. S.r.l., Strada Comunale Cerqueto, pg. 1466   IT

Prato

Banca d'America e d'Italia S.p.a. (Prato), Via Francesco Ferrucci, 41, pg. 403   IT
Italy OBI Systemzentrale SRL, Castella Postale 978, pg. 993   IT

Predosa

Mecup/Pfauter-Maag, Via Masetti 14/A, pg. 617   IT

Ravenna

Fermar S.p.A., Via XIII Giugno, 10, pg. 304   IT
NORIT Italia S.p.A., Via Negrini 9, pg. 958   IT
Weatherford Mediterranea S.p.A., Via Cherso, 19, pg. 1750   PB

Reggello

Boehringer Ingelheim Italia S.p.A., Localita I Prulli, pg. 199   IT

Reggio nell'Emilia

Abax Informatica S.r.l., Via Puccini 17/19/21, pg. 318   IT
Abax Service S.r.l., Via Puccini 17/19/21, pg. 318   IT
Apple Computer SpA, Via Bovio 5-Zone Ind. di Mancasale, pg. 121   PB
Intralox Italia s.r.l., Via Y Gagarin, pg. 643   PV
NIKE International Ltd.-Italy, Via Dell'Aeronaudica 22, pg. 1184   PB
Revetex, Via Gasparini 14, pg. 1177   IT
SASIB Food S.p.A.-Packaging Division, Via A. Volta 1, pg. 1194   IT

Resana

Settef SpA, Via Castellana 201, pg. 803   IT

Rescaldina

Shimano Italia S.R.L., Via Pisacane 7/9, pg. 1233   IT

Rivarolo Canavese

Eaton Automotive S.p.A. Engine Components Operations, Via Bicocca 28, pg. 558   PB

Rivoli

Castagnetti, Via Acqui 86, pg. 481   IT
Fataluminium, Via Chivasso, 15/17, pg. 474   IT
SKF Industrie S.p.A., Corso Francia 155, pg. 1158   IT

Rodano

Fisons Instruments, Strada Prov. Rivoltana, pg. 1111   IT
Ridge Tool Em. Elec. S.r.l., Via Kennedy 47, pg. 577   PB
Verind S.p.A., Via Papa Giovanni XXIII, 25/27, pg. 422   IT

Rome

AGIP Petroli, Via Laurentina 449, pg. 428   IT
AST Research Italia S.p.A., viale Castelle della Magliana 38/A, pg. 1182   IT

Aeroporti Di-Roma-Societa per la gestione del Aeroportuale della Capitale, Via dell'Aeroporto di Fiumicino, pg. 652   IT
Agrigest, pg. 61   IT
Air Malta - Rome, Via Barberini, 29, pg. 38   IT
Albacom SpA, Via Umberto Saba 11, pg. 223   IT
Alenia Spazio, Via Archimede 156, pg. 653   IT
Algemene Bank Nederland, Via Principessa Clotilde 7, pg. 11   IT
Aligame S.p.A., Via Uganda 41, pg. 652   IT
Alitalia Linee Aeree Italiane S.p.A., Palazzo Alitalia, via Alessandro Marchetti 111, pg. 652   IT
Allen-Bradley s.r.l., Via Ildebrando Vivanti, 151, pg. 1399   PB
Alps Institute s.r.l. (Berlitz), Via P.L. da Palestrina 19, pg. 221   PB
Amdah Italia S.p.A., Via Elio Vittorini 129, pg. 527   IT
American Power Conversion, Via Governo Vecchio 34, pg. 89   PB
Analog Devices SRL, Via Catalani 31, pg. 109   PB
Assicurazioni Generali S.P.A., Piazza Venezia #11, pg. 89   IT
BMG Ariola Musica S.p.A., Via S. Alessandro 7, pg. 92   IT
Banca d'America e d'Italia S.p.A. (Rome), Largo Tritone, 161, pg. 403   IT
BANCA DI ROMA, Via Marco Minghetti 17, pg. 135   IT
Banca Fideuran S.p.A., Piazzale Giulio Douhet, 31, pg. 692   IT
BANCA NAZIONALE DEL LAVORO SJA., Via Vittorio Veneto 119, pg. 136   IT
Banca Nazionale Dell'Agricoltura S.p.A., Via Salaria 231, pg. 135   IT
Banco di Roma, Viale Umberto Tupini, 180, pg. 652   IT
BANCO DI SICILIA, Via del Corso, 271, pg. 140   IT
Banco do Brasil S.A.-Rome, Leonida Bissolati 40, pg. 141   IT
Bankers Trust Finanzaria S.P.A., Via L. Bissolati 76, pg. 186   PB
Banque Indosuez, Via Condotti, 11, pg. 314   IT
Banque Paribas-Roma, 30 Piazzo di Monte Savello, pg. 320   IT
Bausch & Lomb International, Inc., Via Dei Prata Fiscali 215 Intl., pg. 195   PB
Bell Atlantic International-Italia S.r.l., Via del Quirinale 26, pg. 204   PB
Berlitz Language Centers, S.R.L., Via Cavour 256, pg. 222   IT
BetzDearborn S.p.A., Viale Gino Cervi 6, pg. 227   PB
Bioindustria Farmaceutici S.p.A., Via Valbondione, 113, pg. 1283   PB
Birra Peroni Industriale, Via Mantova 24, pg. 381   IT
Blue Cross S.r.l., c/o Restiva s.r.l., 00146 Roma, Via Valbondione 113, pg. 1283   PB
Boeing International Corp., Via Veneto 54/B, pg. 242   PB
Bose S.P.A., Via Luigi Capucci, 1Z, pg. 161   PV
Bristol Italiana (Sud), S.p.A., Via Angelo Bargoni 8/78, pg. 255   PB
BULGARI SPA, Via Lungo Teve Ari Marzo #11, pg. 232   IT
CESI Centro Elaborazioni e Studi Informatici S.p.A., Via Anagnina 203, pg. 1365   IT
CREA, Via Mario Bianchini 47, pg. 824   IT
CARACCIOLOSSIGENO s.r.l., pg. 811   IT
Cartiera di Subiaco S.p.A., Via Franco Sacchetti 16, pg. 567   IT
Caterpillar Commerciale S.r.L., Via Cassia 1778/F, pg. 317   PB
Christie's (International) S.A., Palazzo Massimo Lancellotti, Piazza Navona 114, pg. 290   IT
Cigna Italy - Societa a Responsabilita Limitata, Viale Mareschiallo Pilsudski 124, 00197, pg. 364   PB
Club Mediterranee Italia S.p.A., via Emilia No. 88, pg. 298   IT
Coeclerici Holding S.p.A., Via Parigi, 11, pg. 303   IT
Coeclerici Trading S.p.A., Via Parigi, 11, pg. 303   IT
Cofiri Societa ad Intermediazione mobiliare S.p.A., Via Boncompagni 26, pg. 652   IT
Colgate-Palmolive S.p.A., Via Palmolive 18 Loc., pg. 339   PB
Compagnia Finanziamenti E. Rifinanziamenti Cofiri S.p.A., pg. 652   IT
Consorzio Consac, Viale Marco Polo 59, pg. 317   IT
Consorzio Coresia, Via Cassiodoro 9, pg. 317   IT
Consorzio GESPIMV, Piazza di Tor Bella Monaca 3, pg. 317   IT
Consorzio Informatica A.T., Via dei Crociferi 19, pg. 318   IT
Consorzo SIMT, Piazza Borghese 91, pg. 318   IT
CREDICP-CREDITO PER LE IMPRESE E LE OPERE PUBBLICHE SPA, Via XX Settembre 30, pg. 341   IT
Crown Lance Italia Srl, Via dei Buonvisi, 61, pg. 155   PV
Danubio Compagnia di Assicurazioni e Riassicurazioni Generali S.P.A., Viale del Policlinico 149/b, pg. 1531   IT
Datamat SpA, Via Elio Vittorini 129, pg. 1228   PB
Delta Biologicals, S.r.l., pg. 915   PB
Deltafina S.p.A., Via Donzetti 10, pg. 1695   PB
Dentsply Italia, Via A. Cavaglieri, 26, pg. 499   PB
DeTrey/Dentsply S.r.l., Viale Delle Milizie, pg. 500   PB
Dionex S.r.l., Via della Maglianell, 65R, pg. 510   PB
Dresdner Bank AG, Via Nazionale, 230, pg. 419   IT
EIB Rome Branch, Via Sardegna 38, pg. 465   IT
ENI S.P.A., Piazzale Enrico Mattei 1, pg. 428   IT
Eisys S.p.A., Via Giulio Vincenzo Bona, 85, pg. 1385   IT
Electricite de France, via Abruzzi 25, pg. 437   IT
Elf Idrocarburi Italiana SPA, Via Aurelia 619, pg. 446   IT
ENTE NAZIONALE PER L'ENERGIA ELETTRICA SPA (ENEL), Via G.B. Martini 3, pg. 458   IT
Ericsson Sielte-International S.p.A., Via Campo Romano 71, pg. 1367   IT

Ericsson S.p.A., Via Anagnina 203, pg. 1367   IT
Ericsson Telecommunicatione S.p.A., Via Anagnina 203, pg. 1368   IT
Erifin Servizi Finanziari S.p.A., Via Campo Romana 71, pg. 1368   IT
Esso Italiana S.p.A., Viale Castello della Magliana, pg. 602   PB
Ethicon S.p.A., 00040 Practica di Mere, Pomezia, pg. 929   PB
Europe Language Center SrL, V. le Giulio Cesare, 207, pg. 222   IT
Farkemo S.r.l., c/o Restiva S.r.l., 00146 Roma, Via Valbondione, pg. 1283   PB
FATME Soc. per Az, Via Anagnina 203, pg. 1368   IT
Fidelio Italia Srl., Via della Frezza, 59, pg. 1106   PB
Finmeccanica S.p.A., Viale Maresciallo Pilsudski 92, pg. 653   IT
Finnigan MAT S.r.l., Via Valadier, 37B, pg. 1596   PB
Finsiel, Via Isonzo 21/B, pg. 654   IT
Fintecna - Soc. Per L'Impiantistica Industriale L'Assetto del Territorio S.p.A., pg. 654   IT
Ford Credit SpA, Viale Pasteur N. 8/10, pg. 666   PB
Ford Italiana S.p.A., Viale Pasteur N. 8/10, pg. 666   PB
Ford Leasing SpA, Viale Pasteur N. 8/10, pg. 666   PB
Gan Italia S.p.A., 45, Via Guidubaldo Del Monte, pg. 564   IT
Gan Italia Vita S.p.A., 45, Via Guidubaldo Del Monte, pg. 564   IT
General Motors Italia, S.p.A., Piazzale Dell Industria, 40, pg. 722   PB
Goodyear Italiana S.p.A., Piazza G. Marconi 25, pg. 753   PB
Griffith Laboratories Italia S.r.l., Via Cassia 640, pg. 481   PV
Herbalife Italia S.r.l., Via di Valle Lupara, G.R.A. Uscita N31, pg. 809   PB
Hewlett-Packard Italiana S.p.A., Viale del Tintoretto, 200, pg. 821   PB
I.M.I.B.J. S.p.A., Via Sardegna 14, pg. 676   IT
IRI ISTITUTO RICOSTRUZIONE INDUSTRIALE, Via Veneto 89, pg. 652   IT
Ilva, Viale Castro Pretorio 122, pg. 654   IT
International Forest Products, Viale della Tecnica, 205, pg. 966   IT
Iritech, P.za della Liberta 20, pg. 654   IT
Irkafarm S.r.l., c/o Restiva R.r.l., 00146 Roma, Via Valbondione, pg. 1283   PB
ISTITUTO MOBILIARE ITALIANO, Viale dell'Arte 25, pg. 692   IT
Italacquae, Via Appia Nuova 700, pg. 381   IT
Jenifer Srl, Via del Babuino 124/A, pg. 782   IT
Johnson & Johnson S.p.A., Via Ardeatina, 110, pg. 931   PB
Kodak S.p.A., Via Sambuca Pistoiese 55, pg. 554   PB
Korn/Ferry International, Via Nicolo' Tartaglia, 11, pg. 633   PV
Lafargessi SPA, Via Cornelia 498, pg. 789   IT
Landis & Staefa (Italia) S.p.A., Divisione Sacet, pg. 801   IT
LASMO International Limited, Viale Contro Pretoro 122, pg. 804   IT
LASMO Mineraria SpA, pg. 804   IT
Litton Italia S.p.A., Via Pontina km 27, 800, pg. 1004   PB
Litton Precision Products (Italy), Via Montauro 27, pg. 1004   PB
MSC (Italia) S.R.L., Viale America 93, pg. 1032   PB
Mercedes-Benz Italia S.p.A., Via Campo n'ell Elba 12-30, pg. 369   IT
Meteor Construzioni Aeronautiche ed Elettroniche S.p.A., Via Nomentana 146, pg. 653   IT
Meucci S.p.A., Via Aristide Leonoi 40/42, pg. 1369   IT
Mistukoshi Italia S.p.A., Via Torino 130-00184, pg. 884   IT
Mobil Oil Italiana Societa per Azioni, Piazzale Dell'Agricoltura 24, pg. 1119   PB
Moore Sigma, S.p.A, Via Delle Milizie, pg. 890   PB
Morgan Guaranty Trust Company, via Po No. 23, pg. 1130   PB
Nissan Finanziaria S.p.A., Via Tiberina KM15.740, 00060, pg. 945   IT
Nissan Italia S.p.A., Via Tiberina KM15.740, 00060, pg. 945   IT
Nittetsu Italiana S.p.A., Via Vittorio Veneto 84, pg. 940   IT
Nokia Mobile Phones Italia S.r.l., Via Emilio Bianchi 54, pg. 952   IT
Nokia Telecommunications Italia Srl, Via Salvini 2, pg. 953   IT
Nopco Italiana SpA, pg. 612   IT
Novo Nordisk Farmaceutici Srl, Via Elio Vittorini, pg. 988   IT
Oerlikon-Contraves S.p.A., Via Affile n. 102, pg. 998   IT
Office Leasing, P.le. G. Pastore n. 6, pg. 652   IT
Oldelft Electronic Instruments Srl, Via G. Armellini 20, pg. 389   IT
Perstorp Analytical, Via della Tenuta del, pg. 1039   IT
Pfizer Italiana S.p.A., Via Valbondione n. 113, pg. 1283   PB
Playtex Europe, Largo Lido Duranti 1-00128, pg. 1434   PB
Predil-Pertusola, Piazzale Flaminio, 9, pg. 662   IT
Procter & Gamble Health & Beauty Care So. Europe, Viale Cesare Pavese 385, pg. 1332   PB
Procter & Gamble Italia S.p.A., Viale Cesare Pavese 385, pg. 1332   PB
RNBNY Representative Office-Rome, Via Piemonte 39, pg. 1381   PB
Raffineria di Roma SpA, Via di Malagrotta 226, pg. 1043   IT
Rai - Radiotelevisione Italiana S.p.A., Viale Mazzini 14, pg. 655   IT
Rappresentanza Generale della Krupp MaK per L'Italia, Via Livorno 61 int. 9, pg. 510   IT
Reemstsa Distribution Company Italy S.r.L., Piazza Pio XI 53, pg. 1101   IT
Restiva S.r.l., 00146 Roma, Via Valbondione, pg. 1283   PB

Revlon S.p.A., pg. 690 — PV
Rockwell CVC S.p.A., Via Monte Giberto, 157, pg. 1400 — PB
S.A.G.A.R., Via Gradisca 29, pg. 21 — IT
SMS Italia, S.r.l., Piazza Sante Bargellini, pg. 1464 — PB
SOFID, Piazzale Mattei 1, pg. 429 — IT
SANGEMINI S.P.A., Via Fiume Giallo 3, pg. 1188 — IT
SASIB Railway Electrification S.p.A., Via Lago Dei Tartari, pg. 1194 — IT
Savafinbus S.p.A., Via Bellini 22, pg. 482 — IT
Scarfini S.p.A., Via di Vannina 80/82, pg. 1369 — IT
Sekur S.p.A., via Torrespaccata 140, pg. 1058 — IT
Setemer, S.p.A., Via Campo Romano 71, pg. 1369 — IT
Shandwick Rome Srl, Via XX Settembe 98/E, pg. 1228 — IT
SIELTE, S.p.A., Via Campo Romano, 71, pg. 1370 — IT
SIGMA-Societa Italiana Gestione Sistema Multi Accesso, Via Castello della Magliana 38, pg. 655 — IT
SIGMA-TAU FINANZIARIA S.P.A., Via Sudafrica, 20, pg. 1248 — IT
Societa Finanziaria di Partecipazioni - Sofinpar S.A., pg. 655 — IT
Societa Italiana Assicurazioni e Reassicurazioni S.p.A., Lungotevere dei Mellini 27, pg. 1531 — IT
Societa Italiana Servizi Aerei Mediterranei S.I.S.A.M. S.p.A., Via Castello della Tagliani 38, pg. 652 — IT
Spi Promozione E. Sviluppo Imprenditoriale S.p.A., Via Maurizio Bufalini 8, pg. 655 — IT
Squibb SpA, Via Paolo di Dono 73, pg. 256 — PB
Stabilimenti Chimico Farmaceutici Dott. R. Ravasini & Cia. SpA, 15 Via Ostilia, pg. 45 — IT
Stanhome S.p.A., Via Zoe Fontana 200, pg. 1508 — PB
Stet International, Via Aniene 23, pg. 1363 — IT
Storage Technology Italia S.p.A., Via Cina 413, pg. 1523 — PB
Stream, Via Salaria 1021, pg. 1363 — IT
T.V. Overseas, S.R.L., Via Sicilia N. 50, pg. 1282 — IT
Technipetrol, 68, Viale Castello della Magliana, pg. 1361 — IT
Tecnologie Progetti Lavori Spa, 38, Viale Castello della Magliana, pg. 1361 — IT
Telecom Italia Mobile, Via Flaminia 189, pg. 1363 — IT
TELECOM ITALIA S.P.A., Corso d' Italia 41, pg. 1362 — IT
TELECOM ITALIA S.p.A., Via Flaminia 189, pg. 1363 — IT
Terumo Europe-Rome, Viale Eriminio Spalla, pg. 1376 — IT
Armando Testa S.p.A., Via Tibullo 10, pg. 1377 — IT
Texaco Italiana SpA, Via Laurentina, 456, pg. 1584 — PB
Thomson-CSF, Via Ofanto n 18, pg. 1385 — IT
Thomson-CSF Passive Components Italy S.p.A., Via Sergio I, 32, pg. 1385 — IT
Toshiba Medical Systems S.R.L., Via Canton 115, pg. 1407 — IT
Toyota Motor Italia S.p.A., Via A. Allori No. 9, pg. 1414 — IT
Triton Mediterranean Oil & Gas N.V. (Italy), pg. 1640 — IT
Turbomotori Internazionale S.p.A., Via della Farnesina 269, pg. 481 — IT
Ufficio di Roma, Via di Villa Emillani, pg. 653 — IT
Uniass Assicurazioni S.p.A., Via Cristoforo Colombo 112, pg. 1256 — IT
Vista Multi Method, Via di Torre Argentina, 21, pg. 222 — PB
World Languages SrL, V. le Giulio Cesare, 207, pg. 222 — PB
Wyeth S.p.A., Via C. Colombo 112, pg. 82 — PB
Young & Rubicam Roma SRL, Via delle Montagne Rocciose 49, pg. 1199 — PV

Ronchi del Legionari

Francesco Parisi S.p.A., Aeroporto Friuli-Venezia Giulia, pg. 504 — IT

Rosignano Marittimo

Solvay Interox S.p.A., pg. 1280 — IT

Rovereto

Master Tools S.p.A., pg. 1186 — IT

Rozzano

Compaq Computer S.P.A., Milanofiori-Strada 7-Palazzo R, pg. 418 — PB
Fiatimpresit S.p.A., Strda 4, pg. 481 — IT
Impresit S.p.A., Strada 4, pg. 481 — IT
Linde Gas Italia S.r.l., pg. 811 — IT
MSA Italiana S.p.A., Via Po 13/17 Quinto de Stampi, pg. 1115 — PB
SMH Italia S.P.A., Centro Direzionale, Milano Fiori, pg. 1161 — IT
Sorbus Italia SpA, Strada 7, Palazzo T3, Centro Direzionale Milano Fiori, pg. 204 — PB

Saint Albano

Raiso Chemicals Italia S.R.L., Via Morozzo 27, pg. 1086 — IT

Salerno

Elkro gas S.p.A, Via Acquasanta, pg. 1149 — IT
Logadata Due S.p.A., Palazzo Ruggiero 41, Campagna loc. Quadrivio, pg. 318 — IT
Magazzini Frutta Salerno S.r.l., Molo Trapezio, pg. 303 — IT
National Can Italiana SpA, Via Piave 151, pg. 1031 — IT
Sosbam S.r.l., Molo Trapezio, pg. 303 — IT

Saluggia

Sorin Biomedica S.p.A., Strada per Crescentino, pg. 483 — IT

San Bernardo di Ivreta

SIAB Italia S.p.A., Stradale Torino 603, pg. 316 — IT

San Donato Milanese

Princeton Language Center, Via Pascoli, 9, pg. 222 — PB

San Giorgio

Boletti F.B. S.R.L., Via Verdi 33, pg. 482 — IT
Valmet-Rotomec S.p.A., Casale-Asti Km 5, pg. 1449 — IT

San Giovanni Teatino

C.R.T. S.p.A., Via Po 52, Zona Industriale di Sambuceto, pg. 1365 — IT

San Giuliano

Telma Retarder Italia srl, Via della Pace 41/41A, pg. 786 — IT

San Giuliano Milanese

Pirelli Cavi S.p.A., Divisione Italia - Azienda Cavi Speciali, via Giovanni XXIII 23, pg. 1058 — IT
Vickers Medical Italia S.p.A., Via Leone Tolstoi 86, pg. 1467 — IT

San Marco Evangelista

FATA Sud, Via Tagliatelle, Strada Statale 87, pg. 474 — IT

San Mauro Torinese

Cemit Direct Media S.p.A., Via Toscana 9, pg. 888 — IT

San Pellegrino Terme

F.I.R. Fabbrica Italiana Rele S.p.A., Via Viscardi, 5, pg. 546 — IT

San Polo di Piave

Jotun Itoc S.r.l., Via Romagnoli 19, pg. 716 — IT

San Vittore Olona

Makita S.p.A., Via Sempione 269A, pg. 832 — IT

Santena

ContiTech AGES S.p.A., pg. 328 — IT

Sarnico

Cantieri Riva S.p.A., pg. 1468 — IT

Saronno

Apparecchi di Controllo Ranco, S.r.l., pg. 1243 — IT
Axson-Italia, Via Morandi 13/15, pg. 103 — IT
Battenfeld Italia S.r.l., Via E.H. Greig, 9, pg. 826 — IT
CIBA-GEIGY SpA, pg. 980 — IT
D. LAZZARONI & C. S.P.A., Via 4, Novembri 4, pg. 804 — IT
Zyma S.p.A., pg. 986 — IT

Sarzana

Intermarine S.p.A., Via Alta Localita, pg. 324 — IT

Sassari

Bulk Terminal Torres S.p.A., Viale Italia, 53/b, pg. 303 — IT

Savigliano

Fiat Ferroviaria S.p.A., Piazza Galateri 4, pg. 481 — IT

Savona

Acquedotto di Savona S.r.l., Largo Folconi N. 3, pg. 428 — IT
Emhart S.r.l., Via Fratelli Canepa 1, Box 233, pg. 233 — PB
Lotus Logistica S.r.l., Largo Folconi, 3/5, pg. 303 — IT

Scafati

Eurogroup Italia SRL, Via Armando Diaz, pg. 534 — IT

Scarmagno

Ing. C. Olivetti & C., pg. 1002 — IT
Olteco, pg. 1002 — IT

Schio

De Pretto-Escher Wyss s.r.l., pg. 1305 — IT
Paper-Fin S.p.A., Via Lago di Varano 2, pg. 35 — IT

Sedico

Francesco Parisi S.p.A., Agenzia Doganale, Via Segusini 8, pg. 504 — IT

Segrate

AST Research Italia S.r.l., Centro Direzionale,Milano, Ohre, Pal Cimabue, pg. 1182 — IT
Club degli Editori S.p.A., Via Mondadori 1, pg. 888 — IT
Editoriale SORIT S.p.A., Via Mondadori 1, pg. 888 — IT
Edizioni di Comunita S.r.l., Via Mondadori 1, pg. 888 — IT
Ellemme S.R.L., Via Mondadori 1, pg. 888 — IT
Hydro Agricoltura S.r.d., Centro Direzionale e, Commerciale, Milano Oltre, pg. 962 — IT
Hydro Aluminium, Milano Oltre, Pal. Raffaello, pg. 962 — IT
IBM Italia-Distribuzione Prodotti S.r.l, v. Idroscala, pg. 897 — PB
Millipore S.p.A., Via Cassanese 218, pg. 1113 — PB
ARNOLDO MONDADORI EDITORE S.P.A., pg. 887 — IT
Mondadori Factor S.p.A., Residenza Portici 8, pg. 888 — IT
Mondadori Informatica S.p.A., Via Mondadori 1, pg. 888 — IT
Mondadori Leasing S.p.A., Palazzo Verrocchio, pg. 888 — IT
Mondadori Pubblicita S.p.A., Via Mondadori 1, pg. 888 — IT

Senago

GEDY S.P.A., via Mascagni 42, pg. 542 — IT

Sermoneta

Cebris S.p.A., Via Del Murillo, pg. 256 — PB

Sesto Calende

Lascor S.P.A., Via Piave 998, pg. 1161 — IT

Sesto Fiorentino

Elanco, Via Gramsci 731, pg. 993 — PB
Eli Lilly Italia, S.p.A., Via Gramsci 731/733, pg. 994 — PB
Richardson Electronics Italy, S.r.l., Viale L. Ariosto 492/G, pg. 1388 — PB

Settimo Milanese

Autodelta S.p.A., Via Enrico Fermi 7, pg. 481 — IT
Italiana Luce S.r.l., Via Edison 118, pg. 856 — PB
Uddeholm S.p.A., Via T. Edison 60, pg. 1472 — IT

Siena

BANCA MONTE DEI PASCHI DI SIENA S.P.A., Piazza Salimbeni 3, pg. 136 — IT
Biocine S.p.A., Via Fiorentina 1, pg. 350 — PB
Castello Banfi Srl, Tenuta Poggio All'oro, pg. 113 — PV

Silea

Quaker-Chiari & Forti S.P.A., Via Cendon 20, pg. 1348 — PB

Siracuse

Industrie Cavi Sud-Azienda Sotis, Quartiere Fusco, pg. 1058 — IT

Sissa

Pioneer Hi-Bred Italia S.p.A., Via Provinciale 42, pg. 1299 — PB

Sondalo

Biosol S.p.A., S.S. Stelvio, pg. 667 — IT

Sorrento

Banca d'America e d'Italia S.p.A. (Sorrento), Piazza Angelina Lauro, 27, pg. 403 — IT

Stagno

Livorno Marine Containers S.r.l., Via Aiaccia 8, pg. 1214 — IT

Sulmona

Crodo Sud S.p.A., Strada Statale N. 17-km 96, pg. 751 — IT

Suzzara

BONDIOLI & PAVESI S.P.A., Via 23 Aprile, 35/a, pg. 201 — IT

Taranto

Banca d'America e d'Italia S.P.A. (Taranto), Corso Umberto, 139, pg. 403 — IT

Tavazzano

Frigoriferi di Tavazzano s.p.a., Magazzini generali, Strada
per Pezzolo, pg. 606   PB

Teramo

Elettrolitica del Nera SpA, Via Roma, 338, pg. 891   IT
National Italia S.r.l., C.P. 50, Via Roma 338, pg. 892   IT

Termoli

Akzo Chemicals S.p.A., Zona Industriale, pg. 46   IT
Societa Italiana Prodotti Alcollci Naturali SpA, pg. 753   IT

Tesero

Officine Aeronavali Venezia S.p.A., Via Triestina 214,
pg. 653   IT
Francesco Parisi S.p.A., Aeroporto Marco Polo,
pg. 504   IT

Tombolo

Deutsche Babcock Italiana S.p.A., Via Vecchia Livornese,
600, pg. 398   IT

Torino

Flexider S.p.A., Corso Romania, 501/24, pg. 70   PV

Torre d'Isola

Mikron Pavia s.r.l., Via del Commercio 14, pg. 867   IT

Torre Annunziata

CIBA-GEIGY SpA, Via Provinciale Schito, 131, pg. 980   IT

Torreglia

CRIOSBANC S.p.A., pg. 810   IT

Torri di Quartesolo

C.S.O. Centrale Supporti Operativi S.p.A., Centro Torri, Via
dell'Industria, 1, pg. 138   IT

Torriana

Stock Libri S.p.A., Via Santarcangiolese 6, pg. 888   IT

Tortoreto

Metallurgica Adriatica S.p.A., Contrada Salinello 59,
pg. 185   IT

Trento

Banca Di Trento e Bolzano S.p.A., Via Mantova 19,
pg. 138   IT
Crawford Door S.r.l., Via Maccani 108.21, pg. 269   IT
Finanziaria BTB S.p.A., Via Grazioli 25, pg. 138   IT
I.S.A. Istituto Atesino di Sviluppo S.p.A., Via Grazioli, 25,
pg. 138   IT
Supradiamant S.p.A., 38050 Scurelle, pg. 1479   PB

Treviso

Dexter Aerospace Materials Division, Via Della Industrie,
22, San Zenone Degli Ezzelini, pg. 505   PB
Europlast, Via Gorizia 7, pg. 430   IT
MAC S.p.A., Modern Advanced Concrete, pg. 983   IT
Modolo Tecnologie Avanzate SRL, pg. 835   IT

Trezzano San Naviglio

Armstrong World Industries Halid S.r.l., Piazza 26,
pg. 132   PB
Vis, Via Boccaccio, 87, pg. 1173   IT
Volvo Penta Italia SpA, Via Copernico 20, pg. 1476   IT

Trezzo-sull Adda

Mikron Srl Trezzo Sull'Adda, Via Guido Rossa 8,
pg. 867   IT

Trichiana

Ceramica Dolomite S.p.A., 160, v. Cavassico Inferiore,
pg. 198   IT

Trieste

Adriafruit Italia S.r.l., Via della Geppa, 2, pg. 303   IT
Agricola San Giorgio S.p.A., Piazza Duca degli Abruzzi, 1,
pg. 89   IT
ASSICURAZIONI GENERALI S.P.A., Piazza Duca delle
Abruzzi, pg. 89   IT
A. Billitz S.r.l., Via della Geppa, 4, pg. 303   IT
Cantieri Italiani Navali (FINCANTIERI), Corso Cavour, 1,
pg. 652   IT
Casaletto S.r.l., Via Machiavelli, 4, pg. 90   IT
Fidras, pg. 61   IT

FRANCESCO PARISI S.P.A., Viale Miramare 5,
pg. 504   IT
Gambro Sales AB, Via Diaz 19/1, pg. 668   IT
Gefina, Via Machiavelli, 4, pg. 90   IT
Gefina Due S.p.A., Via Machiavelli, 4, pg. 90   IT
Genagricola S.p.A., Via Machiavelli, 4, pg. 90   IT
Generali - Austria, Piazza Duca degli Abruzzi, 2, pg. 89   IT
Generali - Germany, Piazza Duca degli Abruzzi, 2,
pg. 89   IT
Generali - Italy, Piazza Duca degli Abruzzi, 2, pg. 89   IT
Generali - North America, Piazza Duca degli Abruzzi, 2,
pg. 90   IT
Generali - U.K., Piazza Duc degli Abruzzi, 2, pg. 90   IT
Genimobil S.p.A., Via Machiavelli, 4, pg. 90   IT
Immobiliare Diciannove S.p.A., Via Machiavelli, 4,
pg. 90   IT
Jotun Italia S.p.A., Via Roma no. 20, pg. 715   IT
La Vigna, Piazza Duca degli Abruzzi, 1, pg. 90   IT
Lloyd Adriatico S.p.A, Largo Ugo Irneri 1, pg. 60   IT
Lotto Tre S.p.A., Via Machiavelli, 4, pg. 90   IT
Francesco Parisi S.p.A., Viale Miramare, 5, pg. 504   IT
Pittway Tecnologica S.p.A., Via Caboto 19, pg. 1307   PB
Prunus S.p.A., Via Machiavelli, 4, pg. 90   IT
S.A.S.A.-Assicurazioni Riassicurazioni Societa per Azioni,
Piazza Unita d'Italia n. 1, pg. 652   IT
SIELTE Data Net S.p.A., Via Flavia 23/I, pg. 1370   IT
Sofias, Largo Udo Irneri 1, pg. 62   IT
Tenuta S. Anna S.r.l., Piazza Duca degli Abruzzi, 1,
pg. 90   IT
Terminal Frutta Trieste S.r.l., Via della Geppa, 4,
pg. 304   IT
Transfruit S.r.l., Via della Geppa, 4, pg. 304   IT
Veneziani S.p.A., pg. 986   IT

Turate

DSM Italia, Via Isonzo 39, pg. 355   IT
F.I.A.P. SpA, Via Isonzo, 26, pg. 5   PB
Helene Curtis International Italia S.p.A., 120121 Milano,
pg. 1434   IT

Turin

AMP Italia S.p.A. Via Fratelli Cervi 15, pg. 9   PB
AXA Assicurazioni, Via Consolata, 3, pg. 19   IT
Acquedotto di Domodossola S.p.A., pg. 428   IT
Acquedotto Monferrato S.p.A., Corso Re Umberto N. 9 Bis,
pg. 428   IT
Alenia Sistemi Civili, Corso Marche41, pg. 653   IT
Alenia Systemi Difesa, Corso Marche 41, pg. 653   IT
Allianz Subalpina S.p.A., Societa di Assicurazioni e,
Riassicurazioni, pg. 60   IT
Analog Devices SRL, C. So. Raffaello 23, pg. 109   PB
Arte Film, Corso Quintino Sella 56, pg. 1377   IT
Aspera S.p.A., Via Bottiliai 6, pg. 480   IT
Auxilia Graphica S.r.l., Via Crevacuore, 48, pg. 370   IT
Azzura-International Marketing & Promotions, Via San
Quintino, 28, pg. 303   PV
BGS/DMB&B Turin, Corso Galileo Ferrari 24/a,
pg. 303   PV
BGS Systems s.r.l., Corso Francia 32, pg. 161   PB
Banca d'America e d'Italia S.p.A. (Torino), Via
Arcivescovado, 7, pg. 403   IT
Cselt, Via Reiss Romoli 274, pg. 1362   IT
Carello S.p.A., Corso Unione Sovietica 600, pg. 482   IT
Centro Ricerche, Strada Torino 50, pg. 480   IT
Centro Scientifico Internazionale, 57 Via Borgone,
pg. 1748   PB
Cinch Italia Srl, Corso Unione Sovietica, n 373,
pg. 786   PB
Cinzano International, via Principessa Felicita di Savoia 8/
12, pg. 409   IT
Claretta & C.S.p.a., Via Sismonda 26, pg. 782   IT
Comtest Italy, Via Emilio Brosa 20, pg. 1596   PB
Conquest Europe, Via Magenta 19, pg. 1484   IT
Cookson Matthey SpA, Via Magnenta 44/a, pg. 714   IT
Creativity, Via Figlie dei Militari 35, pg. 1377   IT
Danfoss S.r.l. Climatic Div., Via Gaspero Barbera 50,
pg. 377   IT
De Lage Landen Factors SpA, Corso Vittorio Emanuele II,
12, pg. 1082   IT
Editrice La Stampa S.p.A., Via Marenco 32, pg. 482   IT
Giulio Einaudi Editore S.p.A., Via M. Biancamano 2,
pg. 888   IT
Encore Computer Italia S.p.A., Corso Rosselli 71,
pg. 580   PB
Eurogenetics Italia SRL, Corso Susa No. 299, pg. 1408   IT
FATA-New Hunter Engineering S.p.A, Via Traversella 11,
pg. 474   IT
Fausto Carello S.p.A., Corso Unione Sovietica 600,
pg. 482   IT
FIAT AUTO SPA, Corso Agnelli 200, pg. 480   IT
Fiat Auto S.P.A., 45, c. Savona, pg. 481   IT
Fiat Aviazione S.p.A., Via Nizza 312, pg. 481   IT
Fiat Credit International S.R.L., Via Morgari 19, pg. 482   IT
Fiat Engineering S.p.A., Corso Ferrucci 112, pg. 481   IT
Fiat Ferroviaria Savigliano S.p.A., C. So. Ferrucci 112,
pg. 481   IT
Fiat TTG S.p.A., Via Cuneo 20, pg. 481   IT
Fiatsava S.p.A., Corso Ferrucci 112, pg. 482   IT
Fidis S.p.A., Via Morgari 19, pg. 482   IT
Fidis S.p.A.-Finanziaria di Sviluppo, Via Mazzini 51/53,
pg. 482   IT
Fincomau S.p.A., Grugliasco 100 95, pg. 482   IT
Fisat S.p.A., Via Torino 70, pg. 371   IT
Fitur S.p.A., Via Giacosa 38, pg. 482   IT
Framatome Connectors S.p.A., Strada Del Francese 137,
pg. 503   IT
Francesco Cinzano & C.IA SPA, Via Principessa Felicita di
Savoia, 8/12, pg. 409   IT

Gas Energia S.p.A., Via XX Settembre N. 41, pg. 428   IT
Ghia, S.p.A., 5 via al Montefeltro, pg. 666   PB
Gilardini S.p.A., Via Cuneo 20, pg. 482   IT
Hewlett-Packard Italiana S.p.A., Corso Svizzera 185,
pg. 821   PB
Itedi S.p.A., Corso Marconi 20, pg. 482   IT
ITW Fastex Italia, SpA, Strada Settimo, 344, pg. 868   IT
ITW Italia S.p.A., Lungo Dora Pietro Colletta, 95,
pg. 868   PB
Industrie Stampi e Stampaggio Lamiere Berto-Lamet-Impes
S.P.A., Strada del Portone 16, pg. 482   IT
International Rectifier Corporation Italiana, S.p.A., Via
Privata Liguria 49, 10071 Borgaro, pg. 907   PB
ISTITUTO BANCARIO SAN PAOLO DI TORINO S.P.A.,
Piazza San Carlo 156, pg. 691   IT
Isvor Fiat, Corso Dante 103, pg. 482   IT
Isvor S.p.A., Corso Dante 103, pg. 482   IT
Italgas S.p.A., Via XX Settembre N. 41, pg. 428   IT
Italmaceri, Strada Lanzo 237, pg. 1327   IT
Iveco Fiat S.p.A., Via Puglia 35, pg. 484   IT
L'Altra, Corso Quintino Sella 56, pg. 1377   IT
Logicasiel SpA, Corso Svizzera 185, pg. 815   IT
Logicasiel SpA, Via Corte d'Assise 8, pg. 815   IT
Matra Television S.p.A., pg. 796   IT
Media Italia, Corso Quintino Sella 56, pg. 1377   IT
Metalchimica srl, Via San Pio V, 36, pg. 735   PV
New Hunter Engineering, Via Servais 125, pg. 474   IT
OLIVETTI SPA, Via Jervis, 77, pg. 1002   IT
Owens Corning Polypan, SPA, Strada Settimo,399/11,
pg. 1237   PB
PDA International/Italy, Via Confienza, 15, pg. 1031   PB
Polisistem S.r.l., Via Pio VII, pg. 422   IT
Progest SPA (Impell/Fiat TTG J.V.), Via Cuneo, pg. 6   PB
Reinshagen Italia Srl., Via Della Brusa No. 28, pg. 723   PB
Renishaw S.p.A., Via Dei Prati 5, 10044 Pianezza,
pg. 1103   IT
Roltra-Morse S.p.A., 9 Via Albenga, pg. 857   PB
SAB WABCO S.p.A., Via Volvera 51, pg. 271   IT
SIELTE Padana S.p.A., Corso Cirie 18, pg. 1370   IT
San Bernardo S.p.a., pg. 922   IT
Sava Leasing S.p.A., Corso Ferrucci 112, pg. 482   IT
Savafactoring S.p.A., Corso Matteotti 39 bis, pg. 482   IT
Savara Purflux SRL, Via Servais 125, pg. 786   IT
Scott S.p.A., Via Bella Rocca 49, pg. 960   PB
Societa Assicuratrice Industriale Spa (SAI), Corso Galileo
Galilei, 12, pg. 565   IT
Societa Azionaria per la Condotta di Acque Potabili S.p.A.,
Corso Re Umberto N. 9 Bis, pg. 428   IT
Societa Iniziative Industriali S.r.l., Via XX Settembre N. 41,
pg. 428   IT
STET Societa Finanziaria Telefonica, Via Bertola, 28,
pg. 655   IT
Suzuki Italia S.p.A., pg. 1323   IT
TNT Traco S.p.A., Corso Romania 630, pg. 1343   IT
Tecnocar Plant, pg. 786   IT
Tecnocar SRL, Via Servais 125, pg. 786   IT
Tecumseh Europa, Casella Postale 1221, pg. 1566   PB
Teksid S.p.A., Via Pianezza 123, pg. 483   IT
Armando Testa S.p.A., Via Luisa Del Carretto, 58,
pg. 1377   IT
U.I.C.A. S.p.A., Corso Gulileo Ferraris, 61, pg. 481   IT
UTA, Via Padova 55, pg. 1502   IT
Unione Subalpina di Assicurazioni, Via Alfieri 22,
pg. 62   IT
Varian SpA, Via Flli Varian 54, pg. 1710   PB
WABCO Westinghouse Compagnia Freni S.p.A., Via Pier
Carlo Boggio n. 20, pg. 92   PB
Washington Language Center, Via Lagrange, 7,
pg. 222   PB
W.A. Whitney Italia Co., Strada del Francese 132/9,
pg. 594   PB
Zeneca Resins, Corso Piemonte 40, pg. 1527   IT

Udine

Birra Moretti S.p.A., V.LE Venezia, 9, pg. 680   IT
Carnation Italia S.p.A., pg. 919   IT
DANIELLI & C. OFFICINE MECCANICHE S.P.A., Via
Nazionale 41, pg. 378   IT
ELNI, S.p.A., pg. 727   PB
Encia S.p.A, pg. 920   IT
Friul-Venezia Giulia Assicurazioni, Viale Venezia, 99,
pg. 90   IT
Getinge AB Italia, V. le Ungheria 46, pg. 551   IT

Vado Ligure

Vitrofil S.p.A., Via Piave, 29, pg. 1177   IT

Valbrembo

Zanussi Vending S.p.A., Via Roma, 7, pg. 442   IT

Varese

Aermacchi S.p.A., C. P. 246, via Sanvito 80, pg. 653   IT
AGUSTA S.P.A., Viale Giovanni Agusta 520, pg. 32   IT
Bran & Luebbe S.r.l., Via Rainoldi 27, pg. 1380   IT
CS Cartiera del Nord S.R.L., Via 1 Maggio 2, pg. 567   IT
Fasson Italia S.p.A., Corso Italia 2, pg. 154   PB
Milupa S.p.A., pg. 992   IT
Rhone-Poulenc Rorer, Viale Europa 11, pg. 1113   IT

Vascigliano di Stroncone Terni

Asfalti Breitner S.p.A., Zona Industriale, pg. 1092   IT

PB - *U.S. Public Companies Volume*
PV - *U.S. Private Companies Volume*
IT - *International Public & Private Companies Volume*

Vedano Olona

LATI INDUSTRIA TERMOPLASTICI S.P.A., via Baracca 7,
pg. 804   IT

Venice

DeKalb Italia, S.p.A., Corso Del Popolo, pg. 493   PB
Eaton Controls S.p.A, Via F. del Vesco, 2 Belluno,
pg. 558   PB
Fincral - Finanziamenti Al Lavoro S.p.A., S. Marco, San
Samuele 3234, pg. 90   IT
Fincral Leasing S.p.A., S. Marco, San Samuele 3236,
pg. 90   IT
Hotel Cipriani S.p.A., Giudecca 10, pg. 1213   IT
Induplas SpA, Via Ugo Foscolo 21, pg. 1268   IT
Francesco Parisi S.p.A., Via Torino 65, pg. 504   IT
Venezia Nuova, Santa Croce 245, pg. 21   IT
Veneziana Gas S.p.A., S. Marco N. 4934, pg. 428   IT

Vercelli

Rossignol SC S.p.A., Formigliana, pg. 1127   IT

Vergiate

Sextant Avionique Italia S.p.A., Via F. Cavallotti n 38,
pg. 1385   IT

Verona

Autogerma S.p.A., Via G.R. Gumpert 1, pg. 1474   IT
BMW Italia S.p.A., pg. 178   IT
Banca d'America e d'Italia S.p.A. (Verona), Corso Porta
Nuov, 135, pg. 403   IT
Blackhawk Italia S.r.l., Via dell Industria 5, pg. 805   PB
Bontex Italia S.R.L., Viale de Commercio Villafranca,
pg. 734   PB
Dom Sementi S.r.l., Viale del Commercio, 16, pg. 90   IT
Fabbrica Accumulatori York S.p.A., Viale dell'Industria 21,
pg. 482   IT
FINGERMA S.p.A., pg. 1475   IT
Honda Automobili Italia S.p.A., Via Enrico Fermi 15,
pg. 635   IT
Inamed S.R.L., Via Leoncino, Space 10, pg. 874   IT
Martin Merkel Italia s.r.l., Via Silvestrini 30, Casella Postale
456, pg. 860   IT
MoDo Paper Italia Srl, Via San Mammaso 4, pg. 887   IT
Nacanco S.p.A., Via Molino di Sopra 48, pg. 1029   IT
ROR Rockwell Italia s.r.l., Via Monte Fiorino, 23, I-37057 S.
Giovanni Lupatoto, pg. 1399   PB
SASIB Bakery Italia S.p.A., Via Dell'Elettronica,
pg. 1194   IT
Seat Ricambi S.p.A., pg. 1474   IT
SOPOMA S.r.l., Via San Cosimo 6, pg. 109   IT
VARTA Batterie S.p.A., Stradone S. Ferma, 19,
pg. 1452   PB
VARTA Batterie S.p.A., Stradone S. Fermo, 19,
pg. 1452   IT

Viadana

CALEFFI S.P.A., Via Belfiore 24, pg. 252   IT

Viano

Speedline S.p.A., 3030 Tabina di S. Maria di Salva,
pg. 63   PB

Viareggio

Twin Disc Italia S.R.L., pg. 1647   PB

Vicenza

La Centrale Formazione S.r.l., Contra S. Corona, 23,
pg. 138   IT
SASIB Packaging Italia S.r.l.-Wrapper Division, Viale
Kennedy, pg. 1194   IT

Vigliano Biellese

Euronova s.r.l., pg. 1015   IT

Vignola

Aciom 1932 S.P.A., Azienda Commerciale Italiana Olii
Mieral, pg. 517   IT

Villanova d'Asti

Elastogran Italia S.p.A., Strada per Poirino, 38, pg. 108   IT
RFT S.p.A., Strada Per Poirini 41, pg. 1158   IT

Villanova di Castenaso

Monarimport S.p.A., Via di Vittorio, 13, pg. 295   IT
Pfauter Italia Spa, Via Tosarelli 340, pg. 617   IT

Villanova sull'Arda

VARTA Batterie Industriali S.p.A., Via E. Mattei 8,
pg. 1452   IT

Villaputzu

Meteor-Experimental Facility, Strada Statale 125 Km. 178,
pg. 653   IT

Villar Perosa

Sachs Boge Italia SpA, pg. 835   IT

Villastellone

Fiat Lubrificanti S.R.L., Via Santena 1/3, pg. 482   IT

Vimercate

Fuji Hunt Photographic Chemicals (Italia) Srl, Centro Torri
Bianche Edificio Larice, pg. 524   IT
Geotronics Italia S.P.A., Via Trento N. 66/C, pg. 1290   IT

Vinodrone

Luwa Filtri Srl, pg. 617   IT
Tektronix SpA, pg. 1568   PB

Vipiteno

Francesco Parisi S.P.A., Stazione Autodoganale, Campo di
Trens, pg. 504   IT

Visano

Rothe Erde-Metallurgica Rossi S.p.A., Viale Kennedy, 26,
pg. 509   IT

Voghera

Crown Cork Company (Italy) S.p.A., Via Lomellina 134,
pg. 464   PB

Volpiano

Italtest S.r.l., pg. 251   PB
Kleber Italiana S.p.A., Strada Brandizzo 150, pg. 322   IT
LMP Impianti Sri, Via Torino, pg. 1237   PB

Zingonia

Rubinetterie Mariani S.p.A., Via Berlino 214, pg. 1055   PB
Volvo Veicoli Industriali SpA, Via Enrico Mattei, 66,
pg. 1476   IT

JAMAICA

Arabi

Kaiser Jamaica Bauxite Co., 70032, pg. 1062   PB

Discovery Bay

Kaiser Jamaica Bauxite Co., pg. 1062   PB

Kingston

Alcoa Minerals of Jamaica, Inc., P.O. Box 241, pg. 62   PB
The Bank of Nova Scotia Jamaica Limited, Scotiabank
Centre, Duke & Port Royal Streets, pg. 156   IT
British Caribbean Insurance Company Limited, 36 Duke
Street, pg. 156   IT
CGR Communications, Guango Tree House, 29 Munroe
Rd., pg. 1422   PB
CIBC Jamaica Ltd., 53 Knutsford Blvd., pg. 258   IT
Caribbean Cement Co., Ltd., pg. 1201   IT
CIBA-GEIGY Foreign Sales Corporation Ltd, c/o Coopers &
Lybrand, pg. 976   IT
Colgate-Palmolive Co. (Jamaica) Ltd., 216 Marcus Garvey
Dr., pg. 398   PB
Computers & Controls, 18 Range Norman Garden,
pg. 817   PB
CUNA Mutual Group-Jamaica, 2A Manhattan Road,
pg. 297   PV
Dairy Industries (Jamaica) Ltd., 111 Washington Blvd.,
pg. 923   IT
Food Specialties Jamaica Ltd., pg. 920   IT
Goodyear Jamaica Limited, 8 Oliver Rd., pg. 753   PB
Henkel Chemicals (Caribbean) Ltd., 381/2 Red Hills Rd.,
pg. 614   IT
Industrial and Technical Supplies (I.T.S.) Jamaica, Ltd., 22
W. Kingshouse Rd., pg. 822   PB
Industrial Finance Corporation Limited, 36 Duke Street,
pg. 156   IT
Industrial Finance Holdings Limited, 36 Duke Street,
pg. 156   IT
Inter-Commercial Jamaica Ltd., 18 1/4 Lyndhurst Road,
pg. 108   IT
International Insurance Brokers Limited, 59 Half Way Tree
Road, pg. 156   IT
Jamaica Flour Mills, Ltd., 24 Trafalgar Rd., pg. 411   IT
Jamaica Match Holding Ltd., 10 East St., pg. 127   PV
Johnson & Johnson (Jamaica) Limited, 7-9 Norman Rd.,
pg. 930   PB
MB Jamaica Limited, P.O. Box 66, pg. 267   PB
Mead Johnson Jamaica Ltd., Box 159, pg. 256   PB
Moore Business Forms Caribean Ltd., 29 Slipe Pen Rd.,
pg. 890   IT
Nestle-JMP Jamaica Ltd., pg. 921   IT

Noel of Jamaica Ltd., 76 Marcus Garvey Dr., pg. 686   PB
Scotia Jamaica Insurance Agency Limited, Scotiabank
Centre, Duke & Port Royal Streets, pg. 156   IT
Scotiabank Jamaica Building Society, Scotiabank Centre,
Duke & Port Royal Streets, pg. 156   IT
Scotiabank Jamaica Trust and Merchant Bank Limited, 30
Duke Street, pg. 156   IT
Sherwin-Williams Company Resources Limited, White Marl,
P.O. Box 35, pg. 1466   PB
Sherwin-Williams (West Indies) Ltd., 164 Spanish Town
Road, pg. 1466   PB
Sigma Investment Management Systems Limited, 33
Harbour Street, pg. 156   IT
Sigma Unit Trust Managers Limited, 33 Harbour Street,
pg. 156   IT
3M Interamerica, Inc., 218 Marcus Garvey Dr.,
pg. 1606   PB
Van Leer Jamaica Ltd, pg. 1147   IT
The West India Company of Merchant Bankers Limited,
Scotiabank Centre, Duke & Port Royal Streets,
pg. 156   IT
The World Bank, Island Life Center, 6 St. Lucia Avenue,
pg. 1190   PV

Manchester

Alcan Jamaica Co., Kirkvine, Kirkvine Post Office, W.I.,
pg. 51   IT

Montego Bay

Akom Ltd., Montego Bay, pg. 1644   PB

Spanish Town

Comet Rice of Jamaica, Ltd., 36 Valdez Road, pg. 591   PB

Spurtree

Alumina Partners of Jamaica (ALPART), pg. 1062   PB

JAPAN

Abeno

Tanabe Plant, 22-22 Nagpike-cho, pg. 1228   IT

Ageo

Nissan Diesel Motor Co., Ltd., 1-1, Oaza, pg. 944   IT

Aichi

Otsuka Science Co., Ltd., 4 Sekitori-cho, pg. 1013   IT

Akashi

Kansai Caterpillar Mitsubishi Construction Equipment Sales,
Ltd., Ookubo 1, Ookubu-cho, pg. 317   PB

Akita

Akita Atorion Building Co., Ltd., 3-8, Nakadori 2-chome,
pg. 935   IT
Akita Shizuki Co., Inc., Minamida 35-2, Tarada, Ugo-machi,
pg. 1236   IT
Suzuki Parts Manufacturing Co., Ltd., 192-1 Hamaigawa,
Ikawamachi, pg. 1323   IT
Tohoku Electric Power Co., Ltd.-Akita Branch, 15-6, Sanno
5-chome, pg. 1390   IT
Toshiba Akita Denki Co., Ltd., 2-9-27 Sanno, pg. 1403   IT
Yokogawa-Hewlett-Packard Ltd., Nihonseimei-Akitachuodori,
Bldg., 4-2-7, Nakadori, pg. 824   PB
Zexel Corporation-Akita Office, pg. 1528   IT

Amagasaki

Amagasaki Mill, 1-4-1, Minamishinmachi Kuise,
pg. 1225   IT
Amagasaki Plant, 33-1 Kanzaki-cho, pg. 723   IT
Hitachi Kiden Kogyo, Ltd., 3-11-1, Shimosakabe,
pg. 621   IT
Kuise Plant, 1-3, Kuise Terajima 2-chome, pg. 1235   IT
Narita Giken Co., Ltd., Takeshima Bldg., 3rd & 4th Fl.,
pg. 1125   IT
SETTSU CORPORATION, 1-4-1 Kuise-Minamishinmachi,
pg. 1225   IT
Shimano Fishing Tackle Sales Co., Ltd., 85, Motohama 4
chome, pg. 1232   IT
Shinko Wire Co., Ltd., 10-1, Nakahama-cho, pg. 740   IT
Shinto Paint Co., Ltd., 6-10-73 Minamitsukaguchi-cho,
pg. 1311   IT
Sumitomo Bayer Urethane Co., Ltd., pg. 174   IT
SUMITOMO SITIX CORPORATION, 1 Higashihama-cho,
pg. 1317   IT

Anjo

Chubu Caterpillar Mitsubishi Construction Equipment Sales,
Ltd., 7-41 Higashimukaiyama, pg. 317   PB
MAKITA CORPORATION, 3-11-8 Sumiyoshi-cho,
pg. 831   IT

PB - *U.S. Public Companies Volume*
PV - *U.S. Private Companies Volume*
IT - *International Public & Private Companies Volume*

1671

Geographic Index-Non U.S.

Aomori

Aomori Hakuhodo Inc., 4th fl., Aomori Fukoku, Seimei Bldg., 2-10-3, pg. 587 IT
Citizen L.C. Tec Co., Ltd., 30-1, Tanosawagashira, Ichikawamachi, Hachinohe-shi, pg. 293 IT
Hirosaki Seiki, Inc., 5-2, Ishiwatari 3-chome, pg. 261 IT
JAE Hirosaki, Ltd., 5-5-1, Oaza Seinghukuro, pg. 701 IT
Tohoku Electric Power Co., Ltd.-Aomori Branch, 12-19, Minatomachi 2-chome, pg. 1390 IT
Toshiba Sound Systems Corporation, 3-31-2779, Minamicho, Misawa-shi, pg. 1405 IT
Tsugaru Toshiba Onkyo Co., Ltd., Goshogawara, pg. 1405 IT
Zexel Corporation-Aomori Office, pg. 1528 IT

Arao

AICHI STEEL WORKS, LTD., One, Wanowari, Arao-machi, pg. 35 IT

Arida

Tonen Corporation, 1000, Hama, pg. 1399 IT

Asahikawa

Asahikawa Mill, 505-01 Pulp-cho, pg. 938 IT
Hokuto Electronics Co., Ltd., 23-1975 Minamigojodori, pg. 1402 IT

Atsugi

Charles River Japan, Inc., Atsugi Breeding Center, 795 Shimofurusaw, pg. 195 PB
Feintool Engineering Co. Ltd., 260-53 Aza Yanagi-machi Hase, pg. 479 IT
Feintool Japan Co. Ltd., 260-53 Aza Yanagi-machi Hase, pg. 479 IT
Sony/Tektronix Corporation-Atsugi, pg. 1568 PB
Unisia JECS Corporation, pg. 944 IT

Ayase

Ikeda Bussan Co., 771, Kozono, pg. 944 IT
Met-Coil Ltd., #2647, Hayakawa, pg. 1100 PB
SpeedFam Co Ltd., No. 2647 Haykawa, pg. 1498 PB

Chiba

AEON GROUP, 1-5-1, pg. 28 IT
Applied Materials Japan, Inc., WBG Marivc W. 29F, Nakase 2-6, pg. 123 PB
Brighton Corporation, 1-7-106, Mihama, pg. 600 IT
Canon Sales Co., Inc., 7-2, Nakase 1-Chome, pg. 261 IT
THE CHIBA BANK, LTD., 1-2, Chiba-minato, pg. 283 IT
Chiba General Lease Co., Ltd., 1-17 Fujimi 1-chome, pg. 283 IT
Chiba Guarantee Service Co., Ltd., 4-5, Honchibacho, pg. 283 IT
Chiba Kogin Business Service Co., Ltd., 1-2 Saiwaicho 2-chome, pg. 284 IT
Chiba Kogin Computer Soft Co., Ltd., 1-2 Saiwaicho 2-chome, pg. 284 IT
Chiba Kogin Finance Co., Ltd., 1-17 Fujimi 1-chome, pg. 284 IT
Chiba Kogin Staff Services Co., Ltd., 1-2 Saiwaicho 2-chome, pg. 284 IT
Chiba Kogin UC Card Co., Ltd., 1-17 Fujimi 1-chome, pg. 284 IT
CHIBA KOGYO BANK, 1-2, Saiwaicho 2-chome, pg. 283 IT
Chiba Toyopet Co., Ltd., Inage Kaigan 4-5-1, pg. 1412 IT
Chiba Toyota Motor Co., Ltd., Shinden-cho 2-17, pg. 1412 IT
East Kanto Caterpillar Mitsubishi Construction Equipment Sales, 313 Toyofuta, pg. 317 PB
Hakuhodo Pro's, Inc., 6th Fl., Meiji Seimei Chiba Bldg., pg. 588 IT
Horikiri Spring Mfg. Co., Ltd., 1827-4 Kamikohya, pg. 901 IT
JUSCO Co., Ltd., 1-5-1, Nakase, pg. 28 IT
KIKKOMAN CORPORATION, 339, Noda, pg. 733 IT
Kinugawa Rubber Industrial Co., Ltd., pg. 944 IT
Matra Datavision Kk, pg. 796 IT
Narashino Sunpedec Co., Ltd., 16-1, Yatsu 1-chome, Narashino, pg. 935 IT
Nippon DPC Corp., 32nd Fl., W.B.G. Marivewest, 2-6 Nakase, Mihama-ku, pg. 369 IT
Novo Nordisk Bioindustry Ltd, Makuhari Techno Garden CB-6, 3, Nakase 1-chome, pg. 989 IT
PTK Limited, 217 Toyosuta, Kashiwa-Shi, pg. 878 IT
Seiko EG & G Co. Ltd., 563 Takatsukashinden, Matsudo-City, pg. 544 PB
SEIKO INSTRUMENTS INC., 8, Nakase 1-chome, Mihama-ku, Chiba-shi, pg. 1219 IT
Shin-Meito Co., Ltd., 2-16, Yahata-Kaigan-Dori, pg. 947 IT
Sord Computer Corporation, 5-20-7 Masago, Chiba, pg. 1403 IT
Sumitomo Chemical Engineering Co., Ltd., 7-1 Nakase 1-chome, pg. 1311 IT
Sungrain, Ltd., 16, Kitahama-cho, pg. 1321 IT
Toryu Cement Corp., 7-2,3-chome, Akanehama, pg. 1291 IT
Toyota Corolla Chiba Co., Saiwai-cho 1-6-3, pg. 1412 IT
Woodward Governor (Japan) Ltd., Tomisato P.O. Box 1, 251-1, Nakazawa, Tomisato-Machi, pg. 1777 PB

Yokogawa-Hewlett-Packard Ltd., WBG Maribu East 19F, 2-6, Nakase, pg. 823 PB

Chigasaki

Autech Japan, Inc., pg. 944 IT
Chigasaki Plant, 370, Enzo, pg. 871 IT
MIYATA INDUSTRY CO., LTD., 1-1-1 Shimomachiya, pg. 884 IT

Chita

Lubrizol Japan Limited, 1-1 Aza 5 Gochi Taketoyo-Cho, pg. 1016 PB

Fuji

DAISHOWA PAPER MFG. CO., LTD., 4-1-1 Imai, pg. 373 IT
JATCO Corporation, pg. 944 IT

Fujisawa

Fujisawa Research Laboratory, 2023-1, Endo, pg. 1394 IT
Koito Manufacturing Co.-Fujikawa Plant, 2270, Nakanogou, Ihara, pg. 743 IT
Koito Manufacturing Co.-Fujikawa Tooling Plant, 2340, Nakanogou, Ihara, pg. 743 IT

Fukui

Gunze Sangyo (Hokuriku), Mitani Bldg., 1-5, Chuo 3-chome, pg. 578 IT

Fukuoka

Apollo Electronics Co., Ltd., 883, Kamikitajima, Chikugo, pg. 1125 IT
THE BANK OF FUKUOKA, LTD., 13-1, Tenjin 2-chome, pg. 152 IT
Buzen Toshiba Electronics Corporation, Buzen, pg. 1402 IT
Daiko Advertising, Inc., 2-12, Tenjin 1-chome, pg. 365 IT
Dentsu Kyushu, 4-1-2 Tenjin, pg. 393 IT
Flender Ishibashi Co. Ltd., 4636-15, Oaza Kamitonno, pg. 400 IT
Fukuoka Sales Office, pg. 364 IT
Gunze Sangyo (Fukuoka), Sankou Bldg., 5-8, Hakata Ekimae 4-chome, pg. 578 IT
Hakuhodo Erg Inc., 9th Fl., Matsushita Watahabe Bldg., pg. 588 IT
Hakuhodo Inc., Matsushita Watanabe Bldg., 9th Fl., 4-10-10, Watanabe-dori, pg. 587 IT
Hitachi Zosen Fukuoka, 2-1, Hakata-ekimae 3-chome, pg. 522 IT
I&S Corporation (Fukuoka Branch), Nissei Bldg., 14-1, Tenin 1-chome, pg. 642 IT
I&S Corporation (Kyushu Regional Head Office), Nissei Bldg., 1-14-1 Tenjin, Chuo, pg. 642 IT
The Industrial Bank of Japan, Limited (Fukuoka Branch), 13-1, Tenjin 1-chome, Chuo-ku, pg. 674 IT
Kyodo Advertising Co., Ltd., Mainichi Fukuoka Kaikan, pg. 776 IT
Kyushu Central Kitchen, 10-7, Mizuki 2-chome, pg. 1262 IT
Kyushu Citizen Corporation, 8-18, Kamikawabatacho, Hakata-ku, Fukuoka-shi, pg. 294 IT
KYUSHU ELECTRIC POWER CO., INC., 1-82, Watanabe-dori 2 chome, pg. 778 IT
Kyushu Shizuki Co., Inc., Tachii 1915, Yamano, Inazuki-cho, pg. 236 IT
Kyushu Tokuyama Ready Mixed Concrete Co., Ltd., 82-2, Higashi-hama, 2-chome, Higashi-ku, pg. 1393 IT
Man Nen Sha, Inc., 16-1, Tenjin 1-chome, pg. 834 IT
Mitsui BASF Dyes Ltd., 2-65, Shinkai-machi, Omuta-shi, pg. 674 IT
Mitsui Matsushima Co., Ltd., 1-12, Ohtemachi 1-chome, pg. 877 IT
NYK-Kyushu (Hakata) Branch, 9th Floor, Hakata Fukoku Seimei Bldg., pg. 941 IT
The Nikkan Kogyo Shimbun-Seibu, 1-1, Komondomachi, pg. 930 IT
Nikkei Advertising Inc., 3-1-22 Maizuru, pg. 930 IT
Nippo Inc., Kyushu Branch, Sanyo Parking Bldg., 16-15, 3-chome Tenjin, pg. 932 IT
Nippon Shokubai-Sales Office, Hakata Building, 8-36 Chuogai Hakataeki, pg. 939 IT
Nippon Tungsten Co., Ltd., 2-20-31 Shimizu, Minamiku, pg. 1403 IT
Nogata Toshiba Electronics Co., Nogata, pg. 1403 IT
POSMETAL, 85-7 Hibikimachi 1-Chome, pg. 1062 IT
Rohm Amagi Co., Ltd., 258-1, Oguma, Amagi, pg. 1125 IT
Rohm Fukuoka Co., Ltd., 837-1, Hatakeda, Inado, pg. 1125 IT
Sanki Kansetsu Co., Ltd., 1-13-5, Tokoji-cho, Hakata-ku, pg. 1362 IT
Shionogi Fukuoka Office, Fukuoka Gion, Daiichi-Seimei Bldg. 5-35 Reisenmachi, pg. 1234 IT
Sogei Inc.-Kyushu Branch, Hinode Tokyo Kaijyo Bldg., 1-12-20, Tenjin, Chou-Ku, pg. 1277 IT
Sony/Tektronix Corporation-Fukuoka, pg. 1568 PB
Takenaka Corporation - Kyusyu Branch, 2-20, 4-chome, Tenjin Chuo-ku, pg. 1351 IT
Tokuyama Corporation-Fukuoka Branch, San-ei Bldg., pg. 1393 IT
Toshiba Control System Corporation, pg. 1403 IT
Toshiba Kyushu Consumer Electronics Co., Ltd., 2-4-1 Naganama, Chuo-ku, pg. 1404 IT

Toshiba Kyushu Denki Co., Ltd., 3-7-20 Tenjin, Chuo-ku, pg. 1404 IT
Toshiba Kyushu Services & Engineering Co., Ltd., 3-8-27 Gun no Tsu Chouo ku, pg. 1404 IT
Ube Industries Ltd.-Kyushu, Fukuoka Sanwa Building, pg. 1426 IT
Yokogawa-Hewlett-Packard Ltd., Daisan Hakata Kaisei Bldg., 1-3-6, Hakataeki-minami, pg. 823 PB

Fukushima

Fukushima Hakuhodo Inc., 8th Fl., Shokusan Ginko Fukoku Seimei Bldg., pg. 587 IT
Fukushima Sanken Co., Ltd., 15 Miyado, pg. 1188 IT
Hanawa Seiki, Inc., 35, Daijuku Sekisawa, pg. 261 IT
The Industrial Bank of Japan, Limited (Fukushima Branch), 6-5, Motomachi, pg. 674 IT
Kawamata Seiki Co., Ltd., 14 Aza-Hattanda, Kawamata-cho, Date-gun, pg. 1403 IT
Kitashiba Electric Co., Ltd., 9 Aza-Tennohara, Matsukawacho, pg. 1403 IT
Shirakawa Olympus Co., Ltd., pg. 1004 IT
Tama Seimitsu Co., Ltd., 11-1, Soribatake, Komagamine, Shinchimachi, Souma-gun, pg. 294 IT
Tohoku Electric Power Co., Ltd-Fukushima Branch, 2-35, Okitamacho, pg. 1391 IT
Tohoku Oki Electric Co., Ltd., 1 Utate Sasakino, pg. 999 IT
Toshiba Shomei Precision Corporation, 1-1 Machida Tsuchifane Aza, pg. 1404 IT
Toshiba Tohoku Denki Co., Ltd., 2-44-35 Shima, Kohriyama, pg. 1405 IT
Yokogawa-Hewlett-Packard Ltd., Nihondantaiseimei Kohriyama, Bldg., 21-10, Toramaru-machi, pg. 823 PB
York-Benimaru Co., Ltd., 18-2, Asahi 2-chome, pg. 693 IT

Fukuyama

Fukuyama Asahi Orikomi Center, 2-5 Asahicho, pg. 366 IT
Fukuyama Integrated Circuits Group, 1 Asahi, Daimon-cho, pg. 1228 IT
NKK-Fukuyama Works, 1, Kokan-cho, pg. 902 IT

Funibashi

Circle Freight International Japan Ltd., 11-7 Motonakayama 6-chome, pg. 372 PB

Gifu

Ad Daiko Gifu Inc., Sumitomo Seimei Bldg., 9-20 Kandamachi, pg. 366 IT
Ibiden Co., Ltd., 2-1, Kanda-cho, pg. 878 IT
Sanyo VLSI Engineering Co., Ltd., 180, Anapachi-cho Ohmori, pg. 1191 IT

Gotemba

International Flavors & Fragrances, pg. 899 PB

Gotsu

Gotsu Mill, 1280 Gotsu-cho, pg. 938 IT

Gunma

Fuji Heavy Industries, Ltd., Oizumi Plant, Tsukiji 3086-14, Oaza Kami, pg. 523 IT
Gunma Factory, 54-1, Shinozuka, Ohra-machi, Ohra-gun, pg. 25 IT
Japan Immunoresearch Laboratories Co., Ltd., 351-1 Nishi Yokote-machi, pg. 1013 IT
Oki Ceramic Industry Co., Ltd., 3344-1 Iyoku Oaza Sakai-cho, pg. 999 IT
Tokyo IC Co., Ltd., 414-1 Oaza Ohmana, pg. 1191 IT

Haibara

Koito Manufacturing Co.-Haibara Plant, 3407, Sakabe, Haibara-cho, pg. 743 IT

Hakataeki

Daewoo Fukuoka Corp., 3rd Fl. Sunlife 3rd Bldg., Fukuoka-Si Hakata-Ku, pg. 358 IT

Hakui

Nippon Slewing Ring Co., Ltd., pg. 509 IT

Hamamatsu

H.B. Fuller Japan Co. Ltd., 700 Matsushimacho, pg. 687 PB
KAWAI MUSICAL INSTRUMENTS MFG. CO., LTD., 200 Terajima-cho, pg. 725 IT
Takagi Chokoku Co., Ltd.-Hamamatsu Factory, 266 Kitajima-cho, pg. 1349 IT
YAMAHA CORPORATION, 10-1, Nakazawa-cho, pg. 1515 IT
Yamaha Credit Co., Ltd., 10-1 Nakazawa-Cho, pg. 1515 IT
Yamaha Plans Co., Ltd., 10-1 Nahazawa-Cho, pg. 1516 IT
Yamaha Recreation Co., Ltd., 10-1, Nahazawa-Cho, pg. 1516 IT

PB - U.S. Public Companies Volume
PV - U.S. Private Companies Volume
IT - International Public & Private Companies Volume

1672

Handa

Kinuura Laboratory, 110 Sunosaki-cho, 2-chome, pg. 697 — IT
MITSUKAN & NAKANO VINEGAR COMPANY LTD., 2-6 Nakamura-Cho, pg. 883
NAKANO VINEGAR CO., LTD., 6 Nakamura-cho, 2-chome, pg. 904

Hazaki

Specialty Products Center, 14, Sunayama, pg. 871 — IT

Himeji

Daiko: Himeji, Hanshin Bank & Daiiichi Seimei, Kyodo Bldg., 24 Shiroganecho, pg. 365 — IT
Display Technologies, Inc., pg. 1402 — IT
GLORY LTD., 3-1 Shimoteno 1-Chome, pg. 554 — IT
Himeji Asahi Orikomi Center, Ltd., 386 Nanjyo-Aza-Takada, pg. 366 — IT
Himeji Toshiba E.P. Corporation, 1000 Hamada, pg. 1402 — IT
Yumex/ILC, Daitoh Bldg., pg. 856 — PB

Hirano

Hirano Plant, pg. 1228 — IT

Hiratsuka

Moog Japan Ltd., 1532 Shindo, pg. 1128 — PB
Nihon Balzers K.K., 1510-2 Aza Shishimidoshita, pg. 997 — IT
Nissan Shatai Co., Ltd., 10-1, Amanuma, pg. 944 — IT
Technical Research Laboratory, 17-1, Higashi-Tawata 4-chome, pg. 723 — IT

Hiroshima

Bingo Express Co., Ltd., 16-18, Nishi-cho, 2-chome, pg. 934 — IT
Chugoku Citizen Corporation, 9-17, Mikawamachi, Naka-ku, Hiroshima-shi, pg. 293 — IT
THE CHUGOKU ELECTRIC POWER CO., INC., 4-33, Komachi, pg. 291 — IT
Communications & Audio Systems Group, 1484-6 Ida, Kachihon matsu-cho, pg. 1228 — IT
Daiko: Hiroshima Business Division, Hiroshima Asahi Bldg., 13-7, Motolcho, Naka-ku, pg. 365 — IT
Hakuhodo Inc., 7th Fl., Hiroshima Pk. Bldg., 3-7-5 Ohtemachi, Naka-ku, pg. 587 — IT
Hitachi Zosen Hiroshima, 13-14, Nobori-cho, Naka-ku, pg. 622 — IT
I&S Corporation (Hiroshima Branch), Churis Hachobori, 6-7 Hachobori, pg. 642 — IT
The Industrial Bank of Japan, Limited (Hiroshima Branch), 1-1, Kamiyacho 2-chome, Naku-ku, pg. 674 — IT
Innoshima Works, 2477-16, Habu-cho, pg. 623 — IT
Kyodo Advertising Co., Ltd., Hiroshima Sankei Bldg., 5-16 Teppo-cho, Naka-ku, pg. 776 — IT
Logicom Co., Ltd., 12009-3 Kitashinchi, pg. 901 — IT
Man Nen Sha, Inc., 8-5, Ohtemachi 2-chome, Naka-ku, pg. 834 — IT
MAZDA MOTOR CORPORATION, 3-1 Shinchi, Fuchu-cho, Aki-gun, pg. 849 — IT
Mukaishima Works, 14755, Mukaihigashi-cho, pg. 623 — IT
The Nikkan Kogyo Shimbun-Chugoku, 2-14, Inari-Cho, Minami-ku, pg. 930 — IT
Nippon Automotive Body Systems Co., Ltd., 722-35 Taguchi, pg. 1399 — PB
Pec Organic Co., Ltd., pg. 1024 — IT
Sogei Inc.-Hiroshima Branch, Hiroshima Shimizu Bldg., 8-2, Kami-Hatchobori, pg. 1277 — IT
Takenaka Corporation - Hiroshima Branch, 10-10, Hashimoto-cho Naka-ku, pg. 1351 — IT
Tokuyama Corporation-Hiroshima Branch, Hiroshima Chugin Bldg., 1506, Hatchobori, pg. 1393 — IT
Ube Industries Ltd.-Hiroshima, Hiroshima Kogin Bldg., 1-22, Kamiya-cho 2-chome, pg. 1426 — IT
West Chugoku Caterpillar Mitsubishi Construction Equipment Sales, Ltd., 1-7-1 Nakanohigashi Aki-ku, pg. 317 — PB
Yokogawa-Hewlett-Packard Ltd., Nissei Heiwakoen Bldg., 3-25, Nakajima-cho, pg. 823 — PB
Zexel Corporation-Hiroshima, pg. 1528 — IT

Hitachi

Hitachi Power Engineering Co., Ltd., 1-15-1, Higashionumacho, pg. 621 — IT

Hojo

Miura Techno Co., Ltd., 864-1 Tsuji, pg. 884 — IT

Hokkaido

Gunze Sangyo (Hidaka), 6-13, Sakai-machi higashi 2-cho, pg. 578 — IT
Hokkaido Caterpillar Mitsubishi Construction Equipment Sales, Ltd., 3-5, Satozuka 2-jo 6-chome, pg. 317 — PB
Hokkaido Citizen Corporation, 6, Nishi 2-Chome, Kita-Juyonjo, Kita-ku, Sapporo-shi, pg. 294 — IT
Hokkaido Shannon Co., Ltd., Toyokawa Bldg. 2 Fl., Kita, 1-31, Nango-dori 19-chome,Shiraishi-ku, pg. 1393 — IT

Hokuryu Cement Corp., 3rd Fl., Aisho Bldg., 4-184, 10-chome, Minami, Ichijo Nishi, Chuo-ku, pg. 1291 — IT
Medtronic Japan Co., Ltd., Technology Center, 1007-180 Izumisawa, Chitose-shi, pg. 1084 — PB
Novo Nordisk Biochemicals KK, 715-2, Minami 2-chome, Shinko, Ishikari-cho, pg. 989 — IT
Shin Hokken Ltd., 3-5, Salozuka 2-jo 6-chome, pg. 317 — PB
Yokogawa-Hewlett-Packard Ltd., Sumitomoseimei Sapporo Chuo, Bldg., 1-1-14, Minami, 2Jyo-higashi, pg. 823 — PB

Hyogo

Akoh Plant, 1125, Kariya, pg. 1235 — IT
Hikami Manufacturing Co., Inc., Isou 1767-7, Hikami-cho, pg. 1236 — IT
Kanebo Electronics Co., Ltd., 1-1-8 Shioya, pg. 722 — IT
Nippon Shokubai-Process Development Laboratory, 992-1 Aza Nishioki Okihama, pg. 939 — IT

Ichikawa

Komatsugawa Koki Co., Ltd., 14, Shiohama 2-chome, pg. 946 — IT

Ichinomiya

Makita Ichinomiya Corporation, 2-13, Kogane, Ashiyamada, pg. 831 — IT

Iiyama

Kanebo Iiyama, Ltd., 50 Ooaza-Kotobuki, pg. 722 — IT

Ikeda

DBS Co., Ltd., 1-1, Daihatsu-Cho, pg. 253 — PB

Imabari

Harrison Electric Co., Ltd., 5-2-1, Asahi-cho, pg. 1402 — IT

Ina

Uniflex Inc., 2445-4 Kitahara, pg. 902 — IT

Inashiki

Canon Chemicals Inc., 1888-2, Kukuzaki, pg. 261 — IT
Itoh Tekkosho Co. Ltd., 500 Machida Azuma-mura, pg. 317 — PB
Tsukuba Plant, 30 Kasuminosato, Amicho, pg. 1225 — IT

Iruma

Tonen Corporation, 3-1, Nishitsurugaoka 1-chome, pg. 1399 — IT

Isehara

Amada Butsuryu Co., Ltd., 200 Ishida, pg. 70 — IT
Amada Engineering Center Co., Ltd., 350 Ishida, pg. 70 — IT
Amada Franchise Center Co., Ltd., 200 Ishida, pg. 70 — IT
Amada Information Service Co., Ltd., 200 Ishida, pg. 70 — IT
Amada Metrecs Co., Ltd., 806, Takamori, pg. 70 — IT
Amada Sonoike Co., Ltd., 123 Ishida, pg. 70 — IT
NHK Precision Co., Ltd., 56 Suzukawa, pg. 901 — IT

Isesaki

Fuji Heavy Industries, Ltd., Bus. Div., 100, Suehiro-cho, pg. 523 — IT
Isesaki Mfg. Div., 100 Suehiro-Cho, pg. 522 — IT
Japan Electronic Control Systems Co., Ltd., pg. 944 — IT

Ishikawa

Dia Rental Hokiriku Co., Ltd., 54 Ro, Umeda-cho, pg. 317 — PB
Hokuriku Caterpillar Mitsubishi Construction Equipment Sales, Ltd., Ro 54 Umeda-cho, pg. 317 — PB
Ishikawa Sanken Co., Ltd., 10 Sueyoshi-Kosaki, Shika-machi, pg. 1188 — IT
Kaga Toshiba Electronics Company, 1-1 Iwauchi Aza, Tatsukuchi cho, pg. 1403 — IT

Itami

Itami Plant, 5-33 Higashi-Arioka, pg. 1225 — IT

Iwaki

Nakoso Mill, 1 Kubota-jujo, Nakoso, pg. 938 — IT

Iwakuni

Iwakuni Mill, 2-8-1 Iida-machi, pg. 938 — IT
Moralco Ltd., 1815-2, Naganojiri, pg. 62 — PB
TKM Limited, 1815-2, Naganojiri, pg. 62 — PB

Iwakura

Kanebo Soap Manufacturing Co., Ltd., 1-1 Nishide, Noyori-cho, pg. 722 — IT

Iwata

Snic Co., Ltd., No. 1403 Higashi Hiramatsu, pg. 902 — IT
Yamaha Motor Co., Ltd., 2500 Shingai, pg. 1516 — IT

Iwate

Ageo Seimitsu Mfg. Co., Ltd., 2-25, Kitakogyodanchi, Kitakami-shi, pg. 293 — IT
Citizen Iwate Co., Ltd., 2-15, 5-Chome, Mitake, Morioka-shi, pg. 293 — IT
Citizen Techno Co., Ltd., Kitakaminanbukogyodanchi, Hirabayashi, Aisarimachi, pg. 293 — IT
Grace Nanbu Ltd., 3-30 Ahyo, Towa-machi, Waka-gun, pg. 759 — IT
Iwate Toshiba Electronics Co., Ltd., 24 Aza-Murasakino, Iitoyocho, pg. 1402 — IT
Kanebo Kuji, Ltd., 22-13 Dai 2 Jiwari, pg. 722 — IT
Kanegasaki Plant, 7, Moriyama, Nishine, pg. 1235 — IT
Mikuni Adec., Takizawa-mura, pg. 867 — IT
Tohoku Electric Power Co., Ltd.-Iwate Branch, 1-25, Konyacho, pg. 1391 — IT
Tohoku Shanon Co., Ltd., Daiichi-chiwari 46-1, Kitayuguchi, Hanamaki, pg. 1394 — IT
Tohoku Yamanouchi Pharmaceutical Co., Ltd., 154-13, Dai-2 Chiwari, Obuke, Nishinecho, pg. 1518 — IT

Izumi-Otsu

Sunrack Oyodo Co., Ltd., 12 Rinkai-Machi 2-chome, pg. 947 — IT

Joetsu

Naoetsu Plant, 1, Fukuda, pg. 871 — IT

Kadoma

MATSUSHITA ELECTRIC INDUSTRIAL CO., LTD., 1006, Oaza Kadoma, pg. 846 — IT

Kagoshima

Daiko: Minami-Kyushu, Sunitomo Seimei Kagoshima Bldg, 3-22 Yamanokuchicho, pg. 365 — IT
Hakuhodo Inc., Mitsui Seimei Kagoshima Bldg., 6th fl., 18-8, Kajiya-cho, pg. 587 — IT
Nangoku Nissay Building Co., Ltd., 11-5, Chuocho, pg. 935 — IT

Kanagawa

AMADA CO., LTD., 200 Ishida-shi, pg. 70 — IT
AMANO CORPORATION, Mamedo-cho 275, pg. 70 — IT
Ayase Precision Co., Ltd., No. 1-13-6, Yoshioka higashi, pg. 901 — IT
BASF Nichiyu Coatings R&D Co., Ltd., 296, Shimokurata-cho, Totsuka-ku, pg. 106 — IT
CM Human Services Co. Ltd., Tanasagamihara-shi, pg. 317 — PB
CMEC Co., Ltd., 3700, Tana, Sagamihara-shi, pg. 317 — PB
Civil Engineering Instrument Center, 1-1-1 Katase, pg. 868 — IT
DEA KK, 879 Shimo Imaizuni, pg. 654 — IT
The Dai-ichi Mutual Life Insurance (Oi Office), Oi-machi, Ashigarakami-gun, pg. 362 — IT
Daikuma Co., Ltd., 62-1, Yuhigaoka, Hiratsuka, pg. 693 — IT
Dell Computer Japan, 2599-1 Nogawa, Miyamas-Ku, Kawaski-Shi, pg. 496 — PB
EXAR Japan Corporation, 3-18-9, Shin-Yokohama, Kohoku-Ku, Yokohama-Shi, pg. 598 — IT
Hitachi Seiko, Ltd., 2100, Kamiimaizumi, pg. 622 — IT
Hitachi Zosen Takamatsu, 3-17, Ban-cho 3 chome, Takamatsu, pg. 622 — IT
IZUMI MOTOR INDUSTRIES INC., 704-1 Kami-ichi Atsushi, pg. 696 — IT
Japan Whisker Co., Ltd., 3-3-5 Chigasaki, pg. 1013 — IT
Kanagawa Caterpillar Mitsubishi Construction Equipment Sales, Ltd., 2-1, Shinyokohama 1-chome, pg. 317 — PB
Kanagawa Works, 4-1, Mizue-cho, Kawasaki-ku, pg. 623 — IT
Kawasaki Tokuyama Ready Mixed Concrete Co., Ltd., 13-7, Ogi-machi, Kawasaki-ku, Kawasaki, pg. 1393 — IT
Kawasaki Works, 3-1, Yako 1-chome, pg. 84 — IT
Kenwood Devices Corporation, 180, Saedo-cho, Midori-ku, pg. 730 — IT
Kenwood Parts Center Corporation, 2-5032, Hironodai, pg. 730 — IT
Konami Service Co., Ltd., 2771-2, Shimotsuruma, pg. 746 — IT
Konica Odawara Industrial Center, 28 Horinouchi, pg. 748 — IT
Micro Warehouse, Japan KK, Mitsuhashi No.2 Bldg. 2F, 1-13-27 Okada, pg. 1104 — PB
Nippon R-M Co., Ltd., 1237 Nippa-cho, Kohoku-ku, pg. 109 — IT
NOK EG & G Optoelectronics Corporation, parale Mitsui Bldg., 18th Fl., 8, Higa Shida-cho, pg. 544 — PB
Ohara Inc., 15-30, Koyama 1-chome, pg. 261 — IT
Oki Electric Cable Co., Ltd., 2-12-8 Shimoodanaka, Nakahara-ku, pg. 999 — IT
SCM Operating Training co. Ltd., 3700, Tana, pg. 317 — PB
SCM System Service Co., Ltd., 3700, Tana, Sagamihara-shi, pg. 317 — PB
Sagami GS Co., Ltd., 3700, Tana, Sagamihara-shi, pg. 317 — PB
Terumo Res. & Devel Center, Nakai-machi, 1500 Inokuchi, pg. 1376 — IT

PB - *U.S. Public Companies Volume*
PV - *U.S. Private Companies Volume*
IT - *International Public & Private Companies Volume*

Tokyo Motor Vehicle Works, 10, Okura-cho, Nakahara-ku, pg. 875

Tokyo Motor Vehicle Works - Nakatsu Plant, 4001 Nakatsu Aza Sakuradai, pg. 875   IT

Topura Co., Ltd., 201 Soya, pg. 902   IT

Toshiba Automation Co., Ltd., 5-14-33, Higashihakugaya, Ebina, pg. 1403   IT

Toshiba Living Service Co., Ltd., 3-27 Nakasaiwaicho Saiwaiku, pg. 1404   IT

Truck & Bus Engineering Center, 10 Okura-cho, pg. 875   IT

Unirex Co., Ltd., Yanagida Bldg. 1F, 8-8, Tamura-cho, Atsugi, pg. 1394   IT

Xomox K.K., 403 Shin Yokohama, No.2 Hayama, Bldg.,13-12 Shin Yokohama, pg. 578   PB

Yamanouchi Sanicott Co., Ltd., Miyada 300, Kaiseimachi, pg. 1518   IT

Yokogawa-Hewlett-Packard Ltd., No. 2 Yasuda Bldg, 3-32-13 Tsuruya-Cho, pg. 824   PB

Yokogawa-Hewlett-Packard Ltd., 9-32, Tamura-cho, pg. 823   PB

Yokogawa-Hewlett-Packard Ltd., 100-3, Sakado, Takatsu-ku, pg. 824   PB

Yokogawa-Hewlett-Packard Ltd., 1-27-15, Yabe, pg. 824   PB

Kanazawa

Daiko: Hokuriko Inc., Sumitomo Seimei Kanazawa Takao, Kacho Bldg., 8th Fl., 1-39 Takaokacho, pg. 365   IT

Daiko Hokuriku Inc., Sunitomo Seimei Kanazawa Takao, Kacho Bldg., 8th Fl., 1-39 Takaokacho, pg. 366   IT

Hakuhodo Inc., 3rd Fl., Asahi-Seimei, Kanazawa-Daisan Bldg., pg. 587   IT

Kyodo Advertising Co., Ltd., Asahi Seimei Kanazawa Bldg., 1-8 Oyama-cho, pg. 776   IT

TSUDAKOMA CORP., No. 18-18, Nomachi 5-chome, pg. 1425   IT

Zexel Corporation-Kanazawa Office, pg. 1528   IT

Kariya

AISIN SEIKI CO. LTD., 2-1 Asahi-machi, pg. 39   IT

Nippondenso Co., Ltd., Showa-cho 1-1, pg. 1412   IT

Toyoda Automatic Loom Works, Ltd., Toyoda-cho 2-1, pg. 1412   IT

Toyoda Spinning & Weaving Co., Ltd., Toyota-cho 1-1, pg. 1412   IT

Kashima

Kashima Factory, 26 Sunayama, pg. 1394   IT

Kashima Sanken Co., Ltd., 8073 Yatabe, Hasaki-machi, pg. 1188   IT

Kashiwa

Hitachi Heating Appliances Co., Ltd., 3-1, Shintoyofuta, pg. 621   IT

Kasugai

Toyoda Gosei Co. Ltd., Nagahata 1, Ochiai, pg. 1412   IT

Kasukabe

Hirayama Manufacturing Ltd., pg. 1306   IT

Katsuta

HND Corporation, 1060 Takeda, pg. 620   IT

Hitachi Koki Co., Ltd., 1060 Takeda, pg. 620   IT

Kawaguchi

Dynapac Kenki KK, 1-1-8 Yanagisaki 1-chome, pg. 1420   IT

Hitachi Kenki Dynapac KK, 1-1-8 Yanagisaki 1-chome, pg. 1420   IT

Kawasaki

Asahi Electric Machinery Co., Ltd., 475, Hisamoto, Takatsu-ku, pg. 530   IT

Calpis Ajinmoto Danone, 2-1 Suzukicho, Kawasaki-Ku, pg. 379   IT

Dell Computer K.K., Solid Square East Tower 20F, 580 Horikawa-cho, pg. 496   PB

Fujitsu General Ltd., 1116, Svenaga, Takatsu-ku, pg. 526   IT

G.L.G. Corporation, 2-1-12 Kitakase, pg. 901   IT

Hirose Cherry Precision Company Ltd., No. 5-30-11 Shukugawara, Tama-ku, pg. 346   PB

IKOS Japan, KSP R&D Business Park, Bldg. D337, pg. 864   PB

Kawasaki Kizai Corporation, 8-2 Omiyacho, Saiwai-ku, pg. 1403   IT

Kawasaki Plant, pg. 364   IT

Kawasaki Terminal, No. 4, Chidori-Cho, pg. 693   PB

Kinseki, Ltd., 1-2-2 Mampuku-ji, Aso-ku, pg. 999   IT

KURODA PRECISION INDUSTRIES LTD., 239, Shimo-Hirama, Saiwai-ku, pg. 764   IT

Kuwano Electrical Instruments Co., Ltd., 890 Mizonokuchi, pg. 999   IT

LTX Co., Ltd., pg. 972   PB

Landis & Staefa Intersystem Corp., 4-3-1 Tsuchihashi, Miyamaeku, pg. 801   IT

MIKI PULLEY CO., LTD., 496, Imai-Minamicho, Nakaharaku, pg. 866   IT

NKK-Keihin Works, 1-1 Minamiwatarida, pg. 902   IT

Nisshc Iwai Delica Corp., 4157 Nogawa, Miyame-ku, pg. 946   IT

Showa Denko Kawasaki Works, 2-3, Chidori-cho, Kawasaki-ku, pg. 1236   IT

Showa Electric Wire & Cable Co., Ltd., 2-1-1 Oda-sakae, Kawasaki-ku, pg. 1403   IT

TOKICO LTD., 1-6-3 Fujimi, Kawasaki-ku, pg. 1391   IT

Tokyo Bankin Industries Co., Ltd., 5-12-18 Oda, Kawasaki-ku, pg. 1403   IT

Tonen Corporation, 7-1, Ukishima-cho, pg. 1399   IT

Toshiba Electronic Engineering Corporation, Saiwai-ku, pg. 1404   IT

Toshiba Engineering Co., Ltd., 66-2 Horikawa-cho, Saiwai-ku, pg. 1404   IT

Toshiba Information Systems (Japan) Corporation, 2-1 Nisshin-cho, Kawasaki-ku, pg. 1404   IT

Toshiba Logistic Support Corporation, 1 Komukai-Tosnibacho, pg. 1404   IT

Toshiba Microelectronics Corporation, Kawasaki-ku, pg. 1404   IT

Toshiba Steel Tube Co., ltd., 12-1 Minatocho, Kawasaki-ku, pg. 1405   IT

Toshiba Tungaloy Co., Ltd., 1-7 Tsukagoshi, Saiwai-ku, pg. 1405   IT

Kawauchi

Miura Seiki Co., Ltd., 2380 Oaza-Norinouchi, pg. 884   IT

Sunchemi Co., Ltd., 2323 Oaza-Norinouchi, pg. 884   IT

Kikkawa

Koito Manufacturing Co.-Kikkawa Plant, 1114, Shimizu, pg. 743   IT

Kitakami

Tohoku Nippatsu Co., Ltd., 18-25-2 Fujine, pg. 902   IT

Kitakyushu

I&S Corporation (Kita-Kyushu Branch), Sunshine Nangoku Bldg., 1-1-204 Konyacho, pg. 642   IT

Kurosaki Plant, Kurosaki, Yahatanishi-ku, pg. 871   IT

NYK-Kyushu (Moji) Branch, 8, Minatomachi 7-chome, pg. 941   IT

Sowa System Co., 502-1, Ohaza-haraikawa, pg. 317   PB

TOTO LTD., 1-1, Nakashima, 2-chome, pg. 1410   IT

Kobe

Acheson (Japan) Ltd., P.O. Box 538, pg. 12   PV

Akagane Kauin Sangyo Kabushiki Kaisha, Pearl Mansion, Rm. 401, No. 15-7, Tanakacho 1-chome, pg. 187   IT

Asco (Japan) Co. Limited, 89-1 Takahata-cho, Nishinomiya, pg. 575   PB

BANDO CHEMICAL INDUSTRIES, LTD., Sannomiya Migashi Building, 2-21, Isogami-Dori, pg. 145   IT

Chemipro Fine Chemical Kaisha Limited, 12 F, Kobe Harborland Bldg., 1-3-3, Higashikawasaki-cho, pg. 975   IT

THE DAIEI, INC., 4-1-1, Minatojima Nakamachi, pg. 354   IT

Det Norske Veritas, Sannomiya Chou Bldg., 9 Fl., 2-20, Goko-Dori, pg. 397   IT

Georg Fischer Disa K.K., 1, Mishi 6-chome, pg. 489   IT

Fujitsu TEN Ltd., 2-28 Goshodori 1-chome, pg. 526   IT

Hakuhoco Inc., 7th fl., Chukin-Daiichi Seimei Kobe Bldg., pg. 587   IT

Hyogo Toyota Motor Co., Ltd., Isobedori 4-2-12, pg. 1412   IT

The Industrial Bank of Japan, Limited (Kobe Branch), 1-1, Onoe-dori 7-chome, Chuo-ku, pg. 674   IT

International Reagents Corporation, 7F, Sannomiya Kokusai Bldg., 1-30 Hamabe-dori 2-chome, pg. 558   IT

Itoham Foods Inc., 3-2-1, Bingo-cho, pg. 695   IT

KAWASAKI HEAVY INDUSTRIES, LTD., Kobe Crysta Tower, 1-3, Higashikawasaki-cho, 1-chome, Chuo-ku, pg. 725   IT

Kobe Branch, pg. 1518   IT

KOBE STEEL, LTD., Kobe Head Office, 3-18, Wakinohamacho 1-chome, Chuo-ku, pg. 740   IT

Kobe Terminal, 1-43, Minami-Komaecho, pg. 693   PB

Kockums Computer Systems K.K., Nibon Seimei Sannomiya, Ekimae Building 5F, pg. 278   IT

Krupp Widia Japan Ltd., Sannomiya Building, 1-18, Onoe-dori, pg. 510   IT

Eli Lilly Japan K.K., 9th Fl., Kobe Kanden Bldg., 15, Kano-cho 4-chome, pg. 994   PB

NABCO Ltd., 7-1-12, Gokodori, pg. 740   IT

NYK-Kobe Branch, Yusen Terminal Bldg., 25, Kouyo-cho Higashi 4-chome, pg. 941   IT

Nestle Japan Ltd., 1-16, 7-chome, Goki-dori Chuo-ku, pg. 921   IT

Nippon Keystone Corporation, 1-5-1, Murotani, pg. 1650   IT

Nishishiba Electric Co., Ltd., 1000 Hamada, Amiboshi-ku, pg. 1403   IT

ORIX Baseball Club, No. 6 Kaigandori, pg. 1008   IT

PAREXEL International, Sanki Bldg., 3-1-15 Hachiman-Dori, pg. 1258   PB

Sandoz K.K., New Jarvis Bldg. 75, Kyo-machi, Chuo-ku, pg. 984   IT

Sandvik K.K., Sannpmiya Bldg., 7-1-18, Onoe-dori, pg. 1187   IT

Signode Kabushiki Kaisha, Sannomiya International Bldg., 1-30, Hamabe-Dori 2-chome, chuo-ku, pg. 869   PB

Simco Japan Inc., 12-12, 1-chome, Sumiyoshi, pg. 869   PB

SUMITOMO RUBBER INDUSTRIES LTD., 3-6-9, Wakinohama-cho, pg. 1316   IT

Taito Co., Ltd., 48, Fukae-Hamamachi, pg. 878   IT

Tioxide Japan KK, Shin Nanai Bldg., 1001, 10th Fl., pg. 666   IT

Yokogawa-Hewlett-Packard Ltd., Towa Bldg.,(Kobe Sales Office), 2-2-3 Kaigan-dori, pg. 824   PB

Kochi

Daiko: Kochi, Kataoka Bldg., 2-22 Sakaicho, pg. 365   IT

Kofu

Kofu Bell Foods, Ltd., 2-12-18 Yuda, pg. 722   IT

Kohnan

Kohnan Plant, 39, Aza-Higashihara, Oaza-Sendai, pg. 1528   IT

Training Center, 411-19, Aza-Minamikata, Oaza-Sendai, pg. 1528   IT

Komaki

Amada Wasino Co. Ltd., 158 Shimoobarinakashima 2-chome, pg. 70   IT

Komatsushima

Komatsushima Mill, 1 Toyoura-cho, pg. 938   IT

Koriyama

Fukushima Hakuhodo, Inc., 4th Fl., Nihon Dantai Seimei Koriyama Bldg., pg. 587   IT

Nara Liquid Crystal Display Group, 492 Minasho-cho, pg. 1228   IT

Kumagaya

Kumagaya Plant, 201-9, Oaza-miizugahara, pg. 931   IT

Kumamoto

Ariake Works, 1, Ariake, Nagasu-machi, pg. 623   IT

Kurashiki

Aisin Seiki Co. Ltd. (Okayama), 8-21, Higashikawa-cho, Mizushima, pg. 39   IT

Information Storage Products Center, 3-10, Ushiodori, pg. 871   IT

Mizushima Plant, 3-10, Ushiodori, pg. 871   IT

NAMBA PRESS WORKS CO., LTD., 8-3-8 Kojima-Ogawa, 8-chome, pg. 904   IT

Kusatsu

Metalart Corporation, 1350 Nozimachi, pg. 946   IT

Kushiro

Kushiro Mill, 2-1-47 Tottori-Minami, pg. 938   IT

Zexel Corporation-Kushiro Office, pg. 1528   IT

Kuwana

SAN-JIRUSHI, 1 chome Meisei-dori, pg. 1183   IT

Kyoei

AlliedSignal Turbochargers, Inc., Kodama-Machi, Saitama-Ken, pg. 53   PB

Kyoto

Ad Daiko Kyoto Inc., Kyoto Asahi Bldg., Oike-sagaru, Yanaginobanbadori, Nakagyo-, pg. 366   IT

Advanced Technology Center, c/o Kyoto Research Park, Science Ctr., Bldg. 3, pg. 1012   IT

Daiko Advertising, Inc., Daiwa Bank Kyoto Bldg., 82, Tachiuri-Nishimachi, Takakura-Nishi-, pg. 366   IT

The Fukoku Mutual Life Insurance Co.-Kyoto Branch, 33 Naginatakoko-cho, Hidashinotoin Nishi-iru, pg. 529   IT

Gunze Sangyo (Kyoto), 355 Enpukujicho, Muromachi-dori, pg. 578   IT

Hakuhodo Inc., 6th Fl., Kyoto Asahi Bldg., Yanagi-Yahatacho 65, Yanagino-Banba-dori, pg. 587   IT

The Industrial Bank of Japan, Limited (Kyoto Branch), 630 Shichikannon-cho, Rokkaku-sagaru, pg. 674   IT

KYOCERA CORPORATION, 5-22 Kitainoue-cho, Higashino, pg. 775   IT

Kyoto Branch, pg. 1518   IT

Kyoto Machinery Co. Ltd., 31, Oike-Cho, Kisshoin 601, pg. 1380   IT

Kyoto Works, 1 Uzumasa Tatsumi-cho, pg. 875   IT

MSC Japan Ltd., Karasuma Koizuimi Bldg., 626 Shichi-kannon-cho, pg. 1032   PB

Maizuru Works, 1180, Amarube-shimo, pg. 623   IT

Man Nen Sha Agency, Inc., 57, Masuyamachi, Takakura Higashiiru, pg. 834   IT

Man Nen Sha, Inc., 696-2, Osakazaimoku-cho, pg. 834   IT

MURATA MACHINERY, LTD., 136, Takeda-Mukaishiro-cho, pg. 897   **IT**
MURATA MANUFACTURING CO., LTD., 26-10 Tenjin, 2-chome, pg. 897   **IT**
Nanto Bank-Kyoto Branch, 566-1, Toraya-cho, pg. 905   **IT**
NINTENDO COMPANY, LTD., 60, Kami-Takamatsucho, Fukuine, pg. 932   **IT**
NIPPON DENSAN (NIDEC), 10 Tsutsumisoto-cho, pg. 933   **IT**
Nippon Jarrell-Ash Company, Ltd., 28 Joshungamae-cho, pg. 1596   **PB**
Ohkura Pharmaceutical, pg. 855   **PB**
OMRON CORPORATION, Karasuma Nanajo, pg. 1005   **IT**
ROHM CO., LTD., 21, Saiin Mizosaki-cho, Ukyo-ku, pg. 1124   **IT**
Rohm Mechatech Co., Ltd., 3-21-10, Ohi-cho, Tsutta, pg. 1125   **IT**
Sanyo Home Tech Co., Ltd., 1-2, Koaza Syoda, Oaza Hozono, pg. 1191   **IT**
SHIMADZU CORPORATION, 1, Nishinokyo-Kuwabaracho, Nakagyo-ku, pg. 1232   **IT**
Sogei Inc.-Kyoto Branch, Sumitomo Karasumarudori Bldg., 680 Oomandokoro-Cho, pg. 1277   **IT**
Steelcase Japan Ltd., 44 Asazi Iwataminami, pg. 1038   **PV**
Tsujicho Ltd., 12, Mameta-Machi, Nishi-Kyogoku, pg. 1321   **IT**
WACOAL CORPORATION, 29, Nakajima-cho, Kisshoin, pg. 1484   **IT**
Yokogawa-Hewlett-Packard Ltd., 518, Nijosaguru, Akino-cho, pg. 823   **PB**

Kyowa

Toyoda-Sulzer Manufacturing Ltd., pg. 1307   **IT**

Kyushu

Hanwa Co., Ltd.-Kyushu Branch, Nihon Seimei Hakataekimae 2nd, Bldg., 4-1-1, Hakataekimae Hakata-ku, pg. 595   **IT**

Maebashi

Maebashi Central Kitchen, 921-1, Kozakashimachi, pg. 1262   **IT**
Toshiba Electric Appliances Co., Ltd., 180, Furuichi-cho, pg. 1404   **IT**
Toshiba Elemec Corporation, pg. 1404   **IT**

Mariguchi

Matsushita Battery Industrial Co., Ltd., 1, Matsushitacho, pg. 846   **IT**

Matsudo

Komori Precision Co., Ltd., 313-6 Minamihanajima, pg. 745   **IT**

Matsue

Matsue Asahi Kokokusha, Ltd., Matsui Central Bldg., 88, Tonomachi, pg. 366   **IT**

Matsuyama

Daiko: Matsuyama, Nihon Dantai Seimei Matsuyama, Bldg., 5-3 Chifunecho 5-chome, pg. 365   **IT**
Hakuhodo Inc., 3-4, Sanban-cho, 6 Chome, pg. 587   **IT**
Higashi-Matsuyama Central Kitchen, 88-37-38, Shingo, pg. 1262   **IT**
Higashi-Matsuyama Plant, 3-13-26, Yaku-cho, pg. 1528   **IT**
Higashimatsuyama Mill, 1551 Higashidaira, pg. 938   **IT**
JKC Jidosha Kiki C., Ltd., Matsuvama Plant, 2-11-6 Shinmei-cho, pg. 738   **IT**
Japan Cargo Co., Ltd., 88-37, Ooaza-Shingo, pg. 1262   **IT**
Matsuyama Plant, 3-580, Ookaga, pg. 871   **IT**
MIURA CO., LTD., 7, Horie-cho, pg. 884   **IT**
Miura Institute of R & D Co., Ltd., 7 Horie-cho, pg. 884   **IT**
Miura Vider Co., Ltd., 2797 Minami-Yoshida Cho, pg. 884   **IT**
Z-System Co., Ltd., 7 Horie-Cho, pg. 884   **IT**

Mihana

BMW Japan Corp., 1-10-2 Navase, pg. 178   **IT**

Mino

Uster Datasystems KK, pg. 618   **IT**
Zellweger Uster KK, pg. 618   **IT**

Mito

Aichi Nikon Co., 2-1-2 Aza, Sawakihama, pg. 931   **IT**
Mito Plant, 276-6, Motoishikawa-cho, pg. 931   **IT**
Yokogawa-Hewlett-Packard Ltd., Mito Mitsui Bldg., 1-4-73, Sannomaru, pg. 824   **PB**
Zexel Corporation-Mito Office, pg. 1528   **IT**

Mitsukaido

Canon Aptex Inc., 5540-11, Sakaidemachi, pg. 261   **IT**

Miyagi

Advantest Laboratories, 48-2. Matsubara, Kami-Ayashi, pg. 25   **IT**
Denshi Giken Co., Ltd., pg. 634   **IT**
Hadsys, Inc., pg. 634   **IT**
Ishinomaki Mill, 2-2-1 Nanko-cho, Ishinomachi, pg. 938   **IT**
NMB Electro Precision Inc., 5-8-4 Ogi-machi, pg. 868   **IT**
Sendai Nikon K.K., 277 Aza-hara Tako, pg. 931   **IT**
Shannon Trading Co., Ltd., Hokushin Bldg., 4 Fl., 6-10, Uesugi 1-chome Aoba-ku, pg. 1393   **IT**
Tohoku Citizen Corporation, 4F, Sendai Jozenji Building, 4-33, 3-Chome, Kokubucho, Aoba-ku, pg. 294   **IT**
Tohoku Electric Power Co., Ltd.-Miyagi Branch, 5th Fl., Sumitomo Seimei, Sendai-Chuo Bldg., pg. 1391   **IT**
Yokogawa-Hewlett-Packard Ltd., Yamaguchi Bldg., 1-1-31, Ichiban-Cho, pg. 823   **PB**
Zao Nikon K.K., 20 Aza-shinoyoke, Miya, pg. 931   **IT**

Miyazaki

Asahi Chemical Industry Co., Ltd., 4100, Asahi-Machi, 6-chome, pg. 84   **IT**
Honda Lock Mfg., Co., Ltd., pg. 634   **IT**
Miyazaki Daishin Canon Co., Ltd., 4308-1, Ohaza Takajo, pg. 261   **IT**
Miyazaki Oki Electric Co., Ltd., 727 Oaza Kihara Kiyobe-cho, pg. 999   **IT**
Tsuriyoshi Co., Ltd., 1420, Kita-Harako Yoshimura-cho, pg. 1232   **IT**
Yokogawa-Hewlett-Packard Ltd., Miyazaki Nomura-Shoken Bldg., 4-1-2, Tachibana-dori-Higashi, pg. 824   **PB**

Mobara

FUTABA CORPORATION, 629 Oshiba, pg. 531   **IT**

Morioka

Morioka Hakuhodo Inc., 6th Fl., Nittetsukou Morioka Bldg., pg. 588   **IT**
Toshiba Iwate Denki Co., Ltd., pg. 1404   **IT**

Moriyama

Daihatsu Diesel Mfg. Co. Ltd., 45 Amura-cho, pg. 364   **IT**

Nagano

Asamagiken Co., Ltd., pg. 634   **IT**
Cimeo Precision Co., Ltd., 4107-5, Miyota, Miyotamachi, pg. 293   **IT**
Citizen Precision Machine Co., Ltd., 4107-6, Miyota, Miyotamachi, pg. 293   **IT**
Heiwa Tokei Manufacturing Co., Ltd., 435, Shimotonooka, Iida-shi, pg. 294   **IT**
JAE Shinshu, Ltd., 830 Kanikalaghi, Matsukawa-machi, pg. 701   **IT**
Kenwood Komagane Corporation, 8-32, Iizaka 2-chome, pg. 730   **IT**
Kenwood Nagano Corporation, 2676-1, nishiminowa, pg. 730   **IT**
Miyota Co., Ltd., 4107-5, Miyota, Miyotamachi, pg. 294   **IT**
Nagano Oki Electric Co., Ltd., 965 Mimitori, pg. 999   **IT**
Ohmachi Olympus Co., Ltd., pg. 1004   **IT**
Okaya Olympus Co., Ltd., pg. 1004   **IT**
Sakaki Olympus Co., Ltd., pg. 1004   **IT**
SEIKO EPSON CORPORATION, 3-5, 3-chome, Owa, pg. 1219   **IT**
Shinshu Pasco Bottling Co., pg. 1024   **IT**
Takano Co., Ltd., No. 137, Miyata-mura, pg. 902   **IT**
Yokogawa-Hewlett-Packard Ltd., Nagano-Tokyo-Kaijyo Bldg., 1081, Minami-Agata-machi, pg. 824   **PB**
Yokogawa-Hewlett-Packard Ltd., Daimon Bldg., 139-1, Yagi-nishi, pg. 824   **PB**
Zexel Corporation-Nagano Office, pg. 1528   **IT**

Nagaoka

KURAKI COMPANY LTD., 121 Joka, pg. 764   **IT**

Nagasaki

Aishin Co., 1647-1, Kuromaru-machi, pg. 317   **PB**

Nagoya

Ad Daiko Nagoya Inc., Fushimi It Bldg., 1-chome, 4-25 Nishiki Naka-ku, pg. 366   **IT**
Aichi-Emerson Electric Co., 2 Aichi-Cho, Kasugai-Shi, pg. 578   **PB**
Aichi Machine Industry Co., Ltd., 2-20, Kawanami-Cho, Atsuta-ku, pg. 943   **IT**
Aichi Nagoya Nissan Motor Co., Ltd., pg. 943   **IT**
Aichi Nissan Motor Co., Ltd., pg. 943   **IT**
Aichi Toyota Motor Co., Ltd., Takatsuji-cho 6-8, pg. 1412   **IT**
Allen-Bradley Japan Co. Ltd., Nagoya Nishiki Daiichi-Seimei, 6-5, Nishiki 1-chome, pg. 1398   **PB**
Brother Industrial Sewing Machines Div., 1-1-1, Kawagishi, pg. 229   **IT**
BROTHER INDUSTRIES, LTD., 15-1 Naeshiro-cho, pg. 229   **IT**
Brother International Corporation, 15-1, Naeshiro-cho, pg. 229   **IT**
Brothers Sales, Ltd., 15-1 Naeshiro-cho, pg. 229   **IT**

Bundy Japan Ltd., 2-14-4 Marunouchi, Exe-Marunouchi No. 807, pg. 1341   **IT**
CENTRAL JAPAN RAILWAY COMPANY, Sumitomo Seimei Bldg., 2-14-19, Meieki Minami, pg. 279   **IT**
Chubu Citizen Corporation, Fushimi Building, 22-23, 1-Chome, Osu, Naka-ku, Nagoya-shi, pg. 293   **IT**
CHUBU ELECTRIC POWER COMPANY, INC., 1, Higashi-shincho, pg. 946   **IT**
The Chuo Woollen Mills, Ltd., 5-13 Nisiki 1-chome, pg. 946   **IT**
Daewoo Corp. - Nagoya, pg. 358   **IT**
DAIDO STEEL CO., LTD., 11-18, Nishiki 1-chome, pg. 364   **IT**
Daiko Advertising, Inc., Nagoya Kokusai Center Bldg., 13th Fl., 47-1, Nagono 1-chome, pg. 366   **IT**
Daiko Seihan Inc., Zaikai Daini Marunouchii, Mansion Bldg., 2-chome, 16-5 Marunouchi, pg. 366   **IT**
Daiwa House Industry Co., Ltd.-Nagoya Office, 20-22, 1-chome, Aoi, pg. 374   **IT**
Dentsu Inc. Chubu (Nagoya), 4-16-36 Sakae, Naka-ku, pg. 393   **IT**
Deutsche Bank AG (Nagoya), Nagoya-AT Building 2 F, 1-18-22, Nishiki Naka-ku, pg. 404   **IT**
Eagle-Picher Far East, Inc., Nagoya Chogin Bldg., 4F, 460, pg. 355   **PV**
Hakuhodo Inc., 12th Fl., Nadia Park, Business Center Bldg., pg. 587   **IT**
Hanwa Co., Ltd.-Nagoya Branch, Chunichi Bldg., 4-1-1, Sakae, pg. 595   **IT**
Hitachi Zosen Nagoya, 10-27, Meiki 4-chome, Nakamura-ku, pg. 622   **IT**
I&S Corporation (Nagoya Regional Head Office), Lion Bldg., 19-1, Marunouchi 3-chome, pg. 642   **IT**
The Industrial Bank of Japan, Limited (Nagoya Branch), 11-18, Nishiki 1-chome, Naka-ku, pg. 674   **IT**
Kanebo, Ltd., Head Office Nagoya, 4-17-19 Meieki, pg. 722   **IT**
Kobe Steel, Ltd., Toyota Building, 7-23, Meieki 4-chome, pg. 740   **IT**
Konami Computer Entertainment Nagoya Co., Ltd., 13-3, Higashisakura 1-chome, pg. 745   **IT**
Kyodo Advertising Co., Ltd., Nihonseimei Sakae-cho Bldg., pg. 745   **IT**
Luwa Japan Ltd., pg. 617   **IT**
MTS Japan Ltd. (Nagoya), Kato-Kan Bldg., 1-512, Kami Yashiro, pg. 1029   **PB**
Makita Corporation-Nagoya Branch, 4-12-5, Meiekiminami, pg. 831   **IT**
Man Nen Sha, Inc., 7-35 Meieki 4-chome, pg. 834   **IT**
N Cor Ltd., 1-36, Noritake Shin-Machi, 3-chome, pg. 449   **PB**
NYK-Nagoya Branch, Meijiseimei Bldg., 1, Shinsakaemachi 1-chome, pg. 941   **IT**
Nagoya Branch, pg. 1518   **IT**
Nagoya Bus Works, 2 Oye-cho, pg. 875   **IT**
Nagoya Mitsukoshi, Ltd., 1-5 Sakae, pg. 883   **IT**
Nagoya Motor Vehicle Works, 2 Oya-cho, Minato-ku, pg. 875   **IT**
Nagoya Toyopet Co., Ltd., Oto-cho 2-22, pg. 1412   **IT**
Nambokusha Inc., Sakae-machi Bldg., 3-23-31 Nishiki, pg. 905   **IT**
NARUMI CHINA CORPORATION, 3 Denjiyama, Narumi-cho, Midori-ku, pg. 906   **IT**
Nichiyu Koki Co., Ltd., pg. 763   **IT**
The Nikkan Kogyo Shimbun-Naygoya, 2-21-28, Izumi, Higashi-ku, pg. 930   **IT**
Nikkei Advertising Co., 3-15-27 Sakae, pg. 930   **IT**
Nippo Inc., Nagoya Branch, Park Sakae Bldg., 9-26, 1-chome Higashi-Sakura, pg. 932   **IT**
Nippon Life Health Consultant, Nihon Seimei Sasajima Bldg., 27-2, Meiekiminami 1-chome, Nakamura-ku, pg. 935   **IT**
Nippon Shokubai-Sales Office, Mitsui Building, 1-24-21-Meiekiminami, pg. 939   **IT**
NORITAKE CO., LIMITED, 1-36, Noritake-Shinmachi 3-chome, pg. 958   **IT**
OKAYA & CO. LTD., 4-18, Sakae, Nakaku, pg. 999   **IT**
PALOMA INDUSTRIES LIMITED, 6-23 Momozono-Cho, Mizuho-ku, pg. 1022   **IT**
Regal Japan Co. Ltd., Taishoseimei Nishiki Bldg. 9F, 18-24 Nishiki-1-Chome Naka-ku, pg. 917   **PV**
Renishaw K.K., 6F, Ikko Imaike Central Bldg., 10-17 Uchiyama, 3-chome, pg. 1103   **IT**
RINNAI CORP., 2-26 Fukuzumi-cho Nakagawa-ku, pg. 1118   **IT**
Rogers Inoac Corporation, No. 2-70, Jinno-cho, pg. 1403   **PB**
Sankosha Advertising Agency, Ltd., Mori Bldg., 3-7-26, Nishiki, pg. 1189   **IT**
SHIKISHIMA BAKING CO., LTD., 1-28, Shirakabe, Higashiku, pg. 1231   **IT**
Shionogi Nagoya Office, 7-13, Haruoka 1-chome, pg. 1234   **IT**
Smiths Industries Medical Systems, Mednova, pg. 1268   **IT**
Sogei Inc.-Nagoya Branch, Nagoya Sakae Bldg., 5-1, Buhei-Cho, pg. 1277   **IT**
Sony/Tektronix Corporation-Nagoya, pg. 1568   **PB**
Takenaka Corporation - Nagoya Branch, 18-22, 1-chome, Nishiki Naka-ku, pg. 1351   **IT**
Tetsuna Kensetsu Co., Ltd., 5-12-18, Chiyoda Naka-ku, pg. 1362   **IT**
THE TOKAI BANK, LIMITED, 21-24, Nishiki 3-chome, Naka-ku, pg. 1391   **IT**
Tokuyama Corporation-Nagoya Branch, Nagoya AT Bldg., 18-22, Nishiki 1-chome, pg. 1393   **IT**
Toshiba Chubu Consumer Electronics Co., Ltd., Naka-ku, pg. 1403   **IT**
Toshiba Chubu Service & Engineering Co. Ltd., 2-5 Nakamiucho Kitaku, pg. 1403   **IT**

PB - *U.S. Public Companies Volume*
PV - *U.S. Private Companies Volume*
IT - *International Public & Private Companies Volume*

Geographic Index-Non U.S.

Toshiba Eletec Chubu Corporation, Nakamura-ku, pg. 1404   IT
Toyobo Nagoya, 5th Floor, Nikko Shoken Building, pg. 1411   IT
Toyota Corolla Aichi Co., Ltd., Izumi 1-6-1, pg. 1412   IT
Toyota Corolla Aiho Co., Ltd., Takikodori 2-2, pg. 1412   IT
Toyota Motor Corporation, 23-22, Izumi, 1-chome, pg. 1412   IT
Toyota Tsusho Corporation, Meieki 4-7-23, Nakamura-Ku, pg. 1412   IT
Ube Industries Ltd.-Nagoya, Nagoya Kogin Building, pg. 1426   IT
Yokogawa-Hewlett-Packard Ltd., Nagoya Kokusai Center Bldg., 1-47-1, Nagono, pg. 823   PB
Zexel Corporation-Nagoya, pg. 1528   IT

Nara

Daiko: Nara, Kintetsu Takama Bldg., 38-3 Takamacho, pg. 365   IT
Ibaraki Works, 4, Omiyamachi, Kogyo-danchi, pg. 623   IT
International Division (Nara), 16 Hashimoto-cho, pg. 905   IT
Makoto Sangoyo Co., Ltd., 1488 Hatakeda 8-chome, pg. 519   IT
Mito Nikon K.K., 4500 Sugaya, Naka-machi, pg. 931   IT
THE NANTO BANK, LTD., 16, Hashimoto-cho, pg. 905   IT
Nanto Business Service Co., Ltd., 16 Hashimoto-cho, pg. 905   IT
Nanto Card Services Co., Ltd., 2-1 Omiya-cho 6-chome, pg. 905   IT
Nanto Computer Service Co., Ltd., 93-2, Minamikyobate-cho 1-chome, pg. 905   IT
Nanto Corporation, 1-90 Sanjooji, pg. 905   IT
Nanto Credit Guarantee Co., Ltd., 2-1 Omiyacho 6-chome, pg. 905   IT
Nanto DC Card Co., Ltd., 2-1 Omiya-cho 6-chome, pg. 905   IT
Nanto Investment Management Co., Ltd., 28 Tsunofuri-cho, pg. 905   IT
Nanto Lease Co., Ltd., 52-1 Omori-cho, pg. 906   IT
Nanto Staff Service Co., Ltd., 2-1 Omiya-cho 6-chome, pg. 906   IT
Yokogawa-Hewlett-Packard Ltd., Nissei Naraekimae Bldg., 1-1-15, Omiya-Cho, pg. 824   PB

Naroshino

NDC Co., Ltd., pg. 944   IT

Niigata

Daiko: Niigata, Asahi Seimei Niigata Bldg., 1-1 Bandai 1-chome, pg. 366   IT
The Daishi Associated Finance Co. Ltd., 1-18, Higashi-ohdori 2-chome, pg. 372   IT
THE DAISHI BANK, LTD., 1071-1, Higashiborimae-dori, pg. 372   IT
The Daishi Cash Business Co. Ltd., 1-20, Horinouchi Minami 3-chome, pg. 372   IT
The Daishi Computer Service Co. Ltd., 1-17, Abumi 1-chome, pg. 372   IT
The Daishi Credit Service Co. Ltd., 1-18, Higashi-ohdori 2-chome, pg. 372   IT
The Daishi DC Card Co. Ltd., 1-18, Higashi-ohdori 2-chome, pg. 372   IT
The Daishi Factors Ltd., 1-18, Higashi-ohdori 2-chome, pg. 372   IT
The Daishi Guaranty Co. Ltd., 892-1, Nishibori-dori 6-chome, pg. 372   IT
The Daishi Information Systems Service Co. Ltd., 1-17, Abumi 1-chome, pg. 372   IT
The Daishi Investment Management Co. Ltd., 1-18, Higashi-ohdori 2-chome, pg. 373   IT
The Daishi Lease Co. Ltd., 2-10, Akashi 2-chome, pg. 373   IT
The Daishi Staff Service Co. Ltd., 892-1, Nishibori-dori 6-chome, pg. 372   IT
F.M.K. Co., Ltd., 53-1, Kawagishi-cho 1 chome, pg. 317   PB
G.M. Kenki Lease Co., 1-21, Adoumi 2-chome, pg. 317   PB
Hakuhodo Inc., 15th Fl., NEXT 21, pg. 587   IT
Hitachi Zosen Niigata, 2-25, Higashi-odori 1-chome, pg. 622   IT
Hokuetsu Caterpillar Mitsubishi Construction Equipment Sales, Ltd., 23-7-108 Ooazayamada, pg. 317   PB
The Industrial Bank of Japan, Limited (Niigata Branch), 5942 Rokubancho, Nishibori-dori, pg. 674   IT
Iwanohara Vineyard Co., Ltd., 1223, Oaza-Kitagata, pg. 1321   IT
Nemic Lambda KK, 2701 Togawa, pg. 1242   IT
Niigata Sales Office, pg. 364   IT
Niigata Sanyo Electronic Co., Ltd., 3000, Oaza-Chiyakoh, pg. 1191   IT
Tohoku Electric Power Co., Ltd.-Niigata Branch, 84, Gobancho, pg. 1391   IT
Toshiba Heating Appliances Co., Ltd., 2570-1 Oaza Ushirosuda, Kamo-shi, pg. 1404   IT
Yokogawa-Hewlett-Packard Ltd., Nagaoka St. Bldg., 2-5-11, Higashi, pg. 824   PB
Zexel Corporation-Niigata Office, pg. 1528   IT

Niihama

Nippon Ketjen K.K., 17-4 Isoura-cho, pg. 47   IT

Niiza

SANKEN ELECTRIC CO., LTD., 3-6-3, Kitano, pg. 1188   IT

Nishinomiya

The Japan Ramtite Co. Ltd., Nakabayashi Bldg., 7-12 Takamatsu-cho, pg. 6   IT
Kansai Central Kitchen, 5-7, Naruohama 3-chome, pg. 1262   IT
OZEKI CORPORATION, 4-9, Imazu Dezaike-Cho, pg. 1019   IT
SHIZUKI ELECTRIC CORPORATION, 10-45 Taisha-Cho, pg. 1236   IT

Niwa

OKUMA CORPORATION, 25-1 Shimoguchi, 5-chome, pg. 1000   IT

Oari

Nuclear Research Center, 2205 Narita-choti, pg. 697   IT

Odawara

Kasei Verbatim Corporation, 1060 Naruta, pg. 552   PB
Odawara Plant, 1060, Naruta, pg. 871   IT

Ogaki

Shinko Engineering Co., Ltd., 1682-2, Motoima-cho, pg. 740   IT

Ohsaka-City

BERG Electronics Japan K.K., 901 Room Hyougo Shin-Ohsaka, Building 9F, pg. 213   PB

Oita

Fuji Heavy Industries, Ltd., Automobile Div., 10-1, Higashi-honmachi, pg. 522   IT
Fuji Heavy Industries, Ltd., North Plant, 27-1, Kanayama-machi, pg. 523   IT
Fuji Heavy Industries, Ltd., Yajima Plant, 1-1, Shoya-machi, pg. 523   IT
Kitsuki Toshiba Electronics Corporation, Kitsuki, pg. 1403   IT
Nishi Nippon Electric Wire & Cable Co., Ltd., 2899, Dancharu, pg. 878   IT
Oita Canon Inc., 710-20 Shimohara Nakao, pg. 261   IT
Showa Denko Oita Works, 2, Nakanosu, Oaza, pg. 1236   IT
Taketa Toshiba Electronics Corporation, Taketa, pg. 1403   IT

Oji

Oji Plant, pg. 364   IT

Ojima

Ojima Plant, 3000, Oaza-Serada, Ojima-machi, pg. 1528   IT

Okayama

Asahi-CIBA Limited-Mizushima Plant, 3-13, Ushio-dori, pg. 975   IT
Daiko: Okayama, Okayama Daiichi Seimei Bldg., 1-3 Shimoishi 2-chome, pg. 366   IT
East Chugoku Caterpillar Mitsubishi Construction Equipment Sales Ltd., 40 Fujiwara, pg. 317   PB
Fukutake Publishing Co. Ltd., 3-7-17 Minamigata, pg. 222   IT
Hakuhodo Inc., New City Bldg., 8th Fl., Sumitomo Seimei Okayama, pg. 587   IT
Mizushima Motor Vehicle Works, 1-1 Mizushima Kaigandori, pg. 875   IT
Mizushima Works, 13 Ushiodori 3-chome, Kurashiki, pg. 875   IT
Okayama Factory, 33-2, Taiheidai Shoocho, pg. 1348   IT
Okayama Shizuki Co., Inc., Minobe 1626-2, Soja, pg. 1236   IT
Okayama Taiho Pharmaceutical Co., Ltd., 1775-1 Aza Oki, Kugui, pg. 1013   IT
Rohm Logistec Co., Ltd., 75, Masusaka, Kamogata-Cho, pg. 1125   IT
Sanyo Tokuyama Ready Mixed Concrete Co., Ltd., 759-1, Aza machida, Ikusaka, Kurashiki, pg. 1393   IT
Wako Electric Co., Ltd., 100, Tomioka, Kasaoka, pg. 1125   IT
Yokogawa-Hewlett-Packard Ltd., Nihonseimei Okayama Daini, Bldg., 1-1-3, Shimo-Ishii, pg. 824   PB
Zexel Corporation-Okayama Office, pg. 1528   IT

Okazaki

Nagoya Motor Vehicle Works - Okazaki Plant, 1 Nakashinkiri, Hashime-cho, pg. 875   IT
Okazaki Golf Club KK, 2-39, Aza-shimosktayama Ikegane-cho, pg. 1362   IT
Passenger Car Engineering Center, 1, Hashime-cho, pg. 875   IT

Polyurethane Engineering Co., Ltd., 1-15-10, Ohnishi, pg. 109   IT

Okinawa

Hakuhodo Inc., Nissei Naha Center Bldg., 5F, 1-12-12, Kumoji, pg. 587   IT
I&S Corporation (Okinawa Branch), Wako Bldg., 439 Minakawa, Urasoe, pg. 642   PB
Koyo Lindberg Co., Ltd., pg. 727   IT
Man Nen Sha, Inc., 8-13, Matsuyama 1-chome, pg. 834   IT
Nissay Okinawa Kogyo Co., Ltd., Nihon Seimei Azato Bldg., 102, Azato, Aza, pg. 935   IT
Okinawa Suntory Ltd., 628, Aza-Aja, pg. 1321   IT

Omiya

Fuji Heavy Industries, Ltd., Engine & Machinery Div., 9, Miyahara 1-chome, pg. 523   IT
Fuji Heavy Industries, Ltd., Omiya Parts Center, 1, Miyahara 1-chome, pg. 523   IT
Hakuhodo Pro's, Inc., 4th Fl., Meiji Seimei Omiya Nakamachi Bldg., pg. 588   IT
K.K. Geotronics, 10-2, 1-chome, Sakuragi-cho, pg. 1290   IT
Kansei Corp., 2-1910, Nisshin-Cho, pg. 944   IT
Omiya Factory and Research Center, 403, Yoshinocho 1-chome, pg. 1348   IT
Sony/Tektronix Corporation-Omiya, pg. 1568   PB

Ono

Ono Plant, 56 Hatacho, pg. 70   IT
Ono Plant, 21 Takumidai, pg. 1225   IT

Osaka

A.I. Ocean, Kansai Shinsaibashi Bldg., 304, 12-8 Minami Senba 4 - Chome, pg. 14   IT
Aisin Seiki Co. Ltd. (Osaka), Toyota Bldg., 3-11, Minami-Senba, pg. 39   IT
AG AJIKAWA CORPORATION, 4-11-88, Takeshima, Nishi-Yodogawaku, pg. 39   IT
Allen-Bradley Japan Co., Shin-Osaka IN Building, 14-5, Nishi-Nakajima 5-chome, pg. 1399   PB
Analytical Chemistry Research Laboratory, pg. 1354   IT
Aoki Corporation-Osaka, 4-15, Oyodo, Minami, Kita-ku, pg. 78   IT
Arrow Japan, Ltd.-Sales Office, Shin-Osaka Kita Bldg. 4F, 1-46 Miyahara 4-chome, pg. 135   PB
Asahi Advertising Inc., Asahi Bldg., pg. 81   IT
Asahi Chemical Industry Co., Ltd., Shin-Daibiru Building, 2-6, Dojimahama 1-chome, pg. 84   IT
Asahi-CIBA Limited-Osaka Sales Office, Shin-Osaka Yodogawa Bldg 5F, 4-13-22, Nishi-Nakajima, pg. 975   IT
Asahi Orikomi Center, Ltd., 1-chome, 14-9 Itachibori, Nishi-ku, pg. 366   IT
Astra Japan, 6-8, Kyutaromachi 3-chome, pg. 94   IT
Astra Japan Ltd., Midosuji Daiwa Bldg., 6-8, Kyutaromachi 3-chome, pg. 94   IT
BASF Japan Ltd., 1-7-20, Azuchimachi, pg. 106   IT
Bally Japan Ltd., pg. 997   IT
The Bank of New York, Nomura Fudosan Osaka Bldg., 8th Fl., 8-15, Azuchimachi 1-chome, pg. 179   PB
Bayer Yakuhin, Ltd., 10th. Fl., Nihon Seimei Sakaisuji Honmachi Bldg., pg. 174   IT
Bell Fashion, Ltd., 1-3-36 Minami Eguchi, pg. 722   IT
Bell Textile, Ltd., 4-6-8 Kawaramachi, Chuo-ku, pg. 722   IT
Cascade (Japan) Ltd., 8-10 1-chome Toyonaka-shi, pg. 311   PB
CENTRAL AUTOMOTIVE PRODUCTS, LTD., 2-30, Nakanoshima, 4-Chome, pg. 278   IT
The Chase Manhattan Bank, N.A., 47 Minami-Honmachi 4-chome, pg. 340   PB
Chiyoda Kogyo Co., Ltd., 4-8, Kasugade-Minami 1-chome, pg. 1321   IT
Cho Hung Bank, Osaka Branch, 6th Fl., Honmachi Mitsui Bldg., 4-25, Honmachi, 4-chome, pg. 288   IT
CHORI CO., LTD., 4-7, Kawaramachi 2-Chome, pg. 288   IT
Comdisco Japan Inc., Nomura Fudosan Bldg. 11F, 1-8-15 Azuchi-Machi, pg. 408   PB
Commerzbank AG-Osaka, Nichimen Building, 7th Fl., 2-2-2 Nakanoshima, pg. 311   IT
Coris Co., Ltd., 4-4-25 Shimo-Shinjo, pg. 322   IT
COSMO SECURITIES CO., LTD., 8-12, Imabashi 1-chome, pg. 335   IT
John Crane (Japan), Inc., 19-4 Higashi-Nakajima 1-Chome, Higashi-Yodogawa-ku, pg. 1339   IT
DAVC Inc., Daiko Shin-Osaka Bldg., 4-chome, 3-39 Miyahara, Yodogawa-ku, pg. 366   IT
Daewoo International (Japan) Corp., pg. 358   IT
Daicel Chemical Industries Ltd., 1, Teppo-cho, pg. 877   IT
Daido Hoxan Inc., 20-16, Higashi Shinsaibashi, 1-chome, pg. 363   IT
DAIDO LIFE INSURANCE COMPANY, 1-2-1 Edobori, Nishiku, pg. 363   IT
DAIHATSU DIESEL MFG. CO., LTD., Uno Bldg., 2-4-14, Tokui-cho, pg. 364   IT
DAIHATSU MOTOR CORPORATION, LTD., 1-1, Daihatsu-cho, pg. 364   IT
DAIKIN INDUSTRIES, LTD., Umeda Center Bldg., 2-4-12 Nakazaki-Nishi, 530, pg. 365   IT
Daiko Advertising, Inc., 4-3-39, Miyahara, pg. 366   IT
Daiko Mediax Inc., Osaka Green Bldg., 2-chome, 6-26 Kitahama, Chuo-ku, pg. 366   IT
Daiko P.C.A. Inc., Shin-Osaka Tensho Bldg., Annex, 3, 3-chome, 8-15 Nishinakanishima, pg. 366   IT

PB - *U.S. Public Companies Volume*
PV - *U.S. Private Companies Volume*
IT - *International Public & Private Companies Volume*

1676

Geographic Index-Non U.S.

Daiwa Bank International Business Division-Head Office, 2-1, Bingomachi 2-chome, pg. 373 **IT**
THE DAIWA BANK LIMITED, 2-1, Bingomachi 2-chome, pg. 373 **IT**
DAIWA HOUSE INDUSTRY CO., LTD., 5-16, 1-chome, Awaza, pg. 374 **IT**
Daiwa House Industry Co., Ltd.-Tokyo Head Office, 3-13, 1-chome, Nihonbashi, pg. 374 **IT**
Dentsu Inc. Kansai (Osaka), 2-4-5 Dojima, pg. 393 **IT**
Dentsu West Japan Inc., 2-4-5 Dojima, Kita-ku, pg. 393 **IT**
DESCENTE LTD., 1-11-3 Dogashiba, Tennoji-ku, pg. 395 **IT**
Deutsche Bank AG (Osaka), 1-18-21 Honmachi, pg. 404 **IT**
Developmental Research Laboratories, 1-1, Futaba-cho 3-chome, pg. 1235 **IT**
Distribution Engineering Center, 6-19-9, Torishima, pg. 1012 **IT**
DUSKIN CO., LTD., 1-33 Toyotsu-cho, pg. 422 **IT**
Earth Environmental Sanitary Service Co., Ltd., 1-1-2 Awaji-machi, pg. 1013 **IT**
Ellme Co., Ltd., 1-6-10 Kawaramachi, Chuo-ku, pg. 898 **IT**
Enso-Eurocan Far East Co. Ltd., Km Nishiumeda Bldg., 20-1, Fukushima, 7-chome, pg. 457 **IT**
Ferro Enamels (Japan) Ltd., 1-27 Oyodo, Kita 2-Chome, pg. 619 **PB**
Figaro Engineering Inc., 5-3, Senba Nishi 1-chome, Minoo, pg. 1393 **IT**
Fujisawa Fisons KK, Kawaramachi Bldg. 7F, 2-14 Kawaramachi 4-chome, pg. 1111 **IT**
Fujisawa Kashima, 1-6, Kashima 2-chome, pg. 525 **IT**
FUJISAWA PHARMACEUTICAL CO. LTD., 4-7 Doshomachi 3-Chome, pg. 525 **IT**
Fujiura Bolsuryu Center Co., Ltd., 116-3 Shiomi-Cho, pg. 1062 **IT**
The Fukoku Mutual Life Insurance Co.-Osaka Kita Branch, Fukoku Seimei Building, 2-4 Komatsubara-cho, pg. 529 **IT**
FUNAI ELECTRIC CO., LTD., 7-1, 7-chome, Nakagaito, pg. 529 **IT**
Fundamental Research Laboratories R&D Center, 1-1-3, Hokko Shiratsu, pg. 1012 **IT**
G-NET CORPORATION, 6-21, 3-chome, Itachibori, Nishi-ku, pg. 531 **IT**
GKN Japan Ltd., Sumitomo Seimei Shin-Osaka, Higashiguichi Building 8F, pg. 536 **IT**
GS-EE Co., Ltd., pg. 126 **IT**
Gigalex Co., Ltd., Ueno Toyo Bldg., 2nd Floor Shin-Osaka, pg. 1125 **IT**
Goldman Sachs (Japan) Ltd., K&K Shinsaibashi Bldg., 12-21, Nishi-Shinsaibashi, 1-chome, pg. 462 **PV**
THE GREEN CROSS CORPORATION, 3-3 Imabashi 1-chome, Chuo-ku, pg. 558 **IT**
Gunze Sangyo (Osaka), OMM Bldg., 7-31, Otemae 1-chome, pg. 578 **IT**
Hakuhodo Inc., OAP Tower Bldg., 8-30, Tenmabashil 1-chome, pg. 587 **IT**
Hanwa Co., Ltd-Osaka Branch, Hanwa Bldg., 4-3-9, Fushimi-machi, Chuo-ku, pg. 595 **IT**
Harima M.I.D., Inc., 4-2-18 Niranomachi, pg. 1077 **PB**
Haseko Corp.-Kansai Office, 5-7, 1-chome, Hirano-machi, pg. 600 **IT**
Haseko Development Inc., 1-5-7, Hirano-machi, pg. 600 **IT**
Henkel Hakusui Corporation, Izumi Bldg., 9-7, Toyosaki 3-chome, pg. 612 **IT**
HIT UNION COMPANY LTD., 4526 Ueshio Tennojiku, pg. 620 **IT**
Hitachi Maxell, Ltd., 1-1-88, Ushitora, pg. 621 **IT**
Hitachi Zosen Chikko, 2-11, Funamachi 2-chome, Taisho-ku, pg. 622 **IT**
HITACHI ZOSEN CORPORATION, 3-28, Nishi-kujo 5 chome, pg. 622 **IT**
Hitachi Zosen Kobe, 3-28, Nishikujo 5-chome, Konohana-ku, pg. 622 **IT**
HOSOKAWA MICRON CORPORATION, 5-14-2-Chome, Kawagamachi, pg. 635 **IT**
House of Lloyd Japan, Inc., Sekaicho Bldg., 6-24, Nakatsu 1-Chome, pg. 642 **IT**
I&S Corporation (Kansai Regional Head Office), Yomiuri Osaka Bldg., 5-9 Nozaki-Cho, pg. 642 **IT**
ITW Devcon Japan, 8-24 Koushiba-cho, pg. 868 **PB**
The Industrial Bank of Japan, Limited (Osaka Branch), 1-1, Koraibashi 4-chome, pg. 674 **IT**
Institute for Medical Science, 5-1, Mishima 2-chome, Settsu, pg. 1235 **IT**
The International Commercial Bank of China, 4-11, 3-chome, Doshomachi, pg. 683 **IT**
International Flavors & Fragrances, pg. 899 **PB**
International Rectifier Far East Company, Ltd., Shin-Osaka Ekimae Suehiro Bldg, 6-12 Nishi-Nakajima, pg. 907 **PB**
ISHIHARA SANGYO KAISHA, LTD., 3-15, Edobori 1-chome, Nishi-ku, pg. 689 **IT**
Ishihara Trading Co., Ltd., Ishihara Bldg., 3-22 Edobori, 1-Chrome, pg. 689 **IT**
Japan Maintenance Co., Ltd., 1-7-1 Hiranomachi, Chuo-ku, pg. 898 **IT**
Jitachi Zosen Systems, Inc., pg. 566 **PB**
Josephine Cosmetics, Inc., 3-8-26, Ueshio, pg. 1126 **IT**
Kaizuka Sanyo Industries Co., Ltd., 174, Asohnaka, pg. 1191 **IT**
Kanebo Bell Touch Co., Ltd., South Forest Bldg., 8F, 1-4-19 Minamimorimachi, pg. 722 **IT**
Kanebo Goshen Spinning Corporation, Ltd., Osaka Ekimae Daini Bldg. 16 F, 1-2-2 Umeda, Kita-ku, pg. 722 **IT**
Kanebo Kikuchi Electronics, Osaka Ekimae Daini Bldg., 15F, 1-2-2 Umeda, Kita-ku, pg. 722 **IT**
Kanebo, Ltd., Head Office Osaka, 105-90 Tomobuchi-cho, pg. 722 **IT**
Kanebo Silk Elegance, Ltd., Osaka Ekimae Daini Bldg., 16F, 1-2-2 Umeda, Kita-ku, pg. 722 **IT**

Kanebo Spinning Corporation, Osaka Ekimae Daini Bldg., 1-2-2 Umeda, Kita-ku, pg. 722 **IT**
Kanebo Stocking, Ltd., Osaka Ekimae Daini Bldg., 16F, 1-2 Umeda, Kita-ku., pg. 722 **IT**
Kanebo Synthetics Co., Ltd., South Forest Bldg., 8F, 1-4-19 Minmimorimachi, pg. 722 **IT**
Kanebo Textiles Co., Ltd., Osaka Ekimae Daini Bldg, 16F, 1-2-2 Umeda, Kita-ku, pg. 722 **IT**
Kanematsu Corporation, 2-15, Awaji-machi 4-chome, pg. 722 **IT**
Kansai Citizen Corporation, Citizen Osaka Building, 8-9, 3-Chome, Mimani-senba, Chuo-ku, pg. 294 **IT**
THE KANSAI ELECTRIC POWER CO., INC., 3-22 Nakanoshima, pg. 722 **IT**
KANSAI PAINT CO., LTD., 4-3-6 Fushimi-machi, pg. 723 **IT**
Kanzakigawa Laboratories, 1-1, Futaba-cho 3-chome, Toyonaka-shi, pg. 1235 **IT**
Kii Sangyo Co., Ltd., 1-3-20 Hon-machi, pg. 722 **IT**
Kinki Caterpillar Mitsubishi Construction Equipment Sales, Ltd., 1-23 Shimoi-cho, pg. 317 **PB**
Kinki Kokokusha, Ltd., 1-chome, 7-8 Kyomachibori, Nishi-ku, pg. 366 **IT**
Kinki Transportation Services Co., Ltd., 39-1, Takaida-Naka 1-chome, pg. 1321 **IT**
Kobayashi-Block Co. Ltd., 13-35, 3-chome, Mitsuya-minami Yodogawg-ku, pg. 237 **PB**
KOBAYASHI PHARMACEUTICAL CO., LTD., 3-6, Doshomachi, 4-Chome Chuo-ku, pg. 740 **IT**
Kobe Steel, Ltd., Midosuji Mitsui Building, 1-3, Bingomachi 4-chome, Chuo-ku, pg. 740 **IT**
Koei Chemical Company, Ltd., 6-17 Koraibashi 4-chome, pg. 1311 **IT**
Konami Computer Entertainment Osaka Co., Ltd., 15-10, Nishi-Tenman, pg. 745 **IT**
KOYO SEIKO COMPANY, LTD., 3-5-8-, Minami-Senba, pg. 760 **IT**
KUBOTA CORP., 2-47, Shikitsuhigashi 1-Chome, pg. 762 **IT**
Kubota George Fischer Ltd., 2-47, Shikitsu-Higashi 1-chome, pg. 490 **IT**
KURARAY CO., LTD., Higashi-Hankyu Building, 1-2-39 Umeda, Kita-ku, pg. 764 **IT**
Kyodo Advertising Co., Ltd., Mainichi Osaka Kaikan Kita-kan, pg. 776 **IT**
Kyowa Electric Wire Co., Ltd., 2-5, Kusunekitamachi, Neyagawa, pg. 530 **IT**
Land KK, 31-27 Toyotsuchou, Suita, pg. 798 **IT**
Makita Corporation-Osaka Branch, 1-26-8, Tenma, pg. 831 **IT**
Man Nen Sha Agency, Inc., 5-13, Awajimachi 1-chome, pg. 834 **IT**
MAN NEN SHA INC., 5-13 Awajimachi 1-chome, Chuo-ku, pg. 834 **IT**
Man Nen Sha, Inc., 5-13, Awajimachi 1-chome, pg. 834 **IT**
MARUBENI CORPORATION, 5/7, Hommachi 2-chome, pg. 844 **IT**
MATSUSHITA ELECTRIC WORKS, LTD., 1048 Kadoma, pg. 847 **IT**
Matsushita Refrigeration Company, 3-22, Takaida-Hondori, Higashi, pg. 846 **IT**
Matsushita Seiko Co., Ltd., 6-2-61, Imafuku-Nishi, Joto-ku, pg. 846 **IT**
Meiji Milk Products Co., Ltd., Kansai Br., Nishitenma Park Building, 3-gokan, 3-14-16 Nishitenma, pg. 855 **IT**
Mentor Graphics Japan Co., Ltd., Shin-Osaka Marusho Bldg., 3-2 Nishinakajima 4-chome Yodogawa-Ku, pg. 1087 **PB**
MINOLTA CO., LTD., Kokusai Bldg., 2-3-13, pg. 869 **IT**
MITA INDUSTRIAL COMPANY, LTD., 2-28, 1-chome, pg. 870 **IT**
Mitsubishi Estate Co., Ltd.-Osaka, 2-2-53 Shiromi, pg. 873 **IT**
Mitsubishi Rayon Co., Ltd., OAP Tower, 8-30 Tenmabashi 1-Chome, Kita-ku, pg. 876 **IT**
Miyakojima Mill, 2-2-7 Zengenji, miyojima-ku, pg. 938 **IT**
MIZUNO CORPORATION, 12-35 1-chome, Nanko-kita, pg. 884 **IT**
J.P. Morgan Securities Asia Ltd., Kotera Plaza, 2-5-23 Kitahama, pg. 1131 **PB**
Morganite Carbon Kabushiki Kaisha, 6-25, 3-chome, Tagawa, pg. 892 **IT**
MYCAL, CORP., 2-2-9 Awajimachi, Chuo-ku, pg. 897 **IT**
NFT Co., Ltd., 3-77, Oimatsu-cho, pg. 1232 **IT**
NHK Steel Co., Ltd., Nissho Iwai Bldg., 2F, 2-chome 5-8 Imabashi, pg. 902 **IT**
NIK Metal Corp., 6-9 Itachibori 4-chome, Nishi-ku, pg. 946 **IT**
NYK-Osaka Branch, 1-13 Honmachi 4-chome, pg. 941 **IT**
Nagase-Alfa K. K., San-ei Bldg., No. 6, pg. 1380 **IT**
Nagase-Ciba Ltd., 1-1-17, Shinmachi, Nishi-ku, pg. 983 **IT**
Nambokusha Inc., Osaka-Toyota Bldg., 4-3-11 Minami-Senba, pg. 905 **IT**
Nanto Bank-Osaka Branch, 7-2 Namba 4-chome, pg. 905 **IT**
Nanto Estate Co., Ltd., 7-2 Nanba, 4-chome, Chuo-ku, pg. 905 **IT**
Napa Inc., 5-chome, 5-17 Miyahara, Yodogawa-ku, pg. 366 **IT**
National Bank of Pakistan-Osaka, Baba Industry Building, 13-15, Nishi Shinsaibashi 1-Chome, pg. 908 **IT**
NICHIFU COMPANY LTD., 1-3-58 Tsurumi, Tsurumi-ku, pg. 927 **IT**
Nicolet Japan Corp.-Osaka, Ryokuchi-Eki, Bldg. 6-F, pg. 1594 **IT**
A.C. Nielsen Co., Higashi-Umeda Bldg., 9-6 Nozaki-cho, Kita-ku, pg. 1183 **PB**
Nihon Schering K.K., 6-64, Nishimiyahara, 2-chome, pg. 1204 **IT**

The Nikkan Kogyo Shimbun-Osaka, 2-16, Kitahamahigashi, pg. 930 **IT**
Nikkei Advertising Co., Nihon Seimei Bldg., 3-3 Doyama-cho, pg. 930 **IT**
Nippo Inc., Osaka Branch, Nihon Seimei Umeda Bldg., 3-3 Dozan-cho, Kita-ku, pg. 932 **IT**
Nippon Dionex K.K., Shin-Osaka GH Bldg., Ste. 205, 9-20, Nishi-Nakajima 6-chome-gu, pg. 510 **PB**
Nippon Dyneema Co., Ltd., 2-8, Dojima Hama 2-chome, pg. 354 **IT**
Nippon Insurance Service Co., Ltd., 6-12, Enokojima 1-chome, Nishi-ku, pg. 935 **IT**
NIPPON LIFE INSURANCE CO., 3-5-12, Imbashi, 3-chrome, pg. 934 **IT**
Nippon Life Insurance Foundation, Nihon Seimei Imabashi Bldg., 1-7, Imabashi 3-chome, Chuo-ku, pg. 935 **IT**
Nippon Life Lifesaving Society (Saisei-kai), 3-8, Itachibori 6-chome, pg. 935 **IT**
NIPPON MEAT PACKERS, INC., 3-6-14, Minami-Honmachi, pg. 936 **IT**
Nippon Monier Co. Ltd., 5F Daiwa Minami Morimachi Bldg, 2-6, 2-Chome Kita, pg. 1092 **IT**
NIPPON PAINT COMPANY LTD., 2-1-2, Oyodo-kita, pg. 937 **IT**
Nippon Paint Company Ltd.-Neyagawa Office, 19-17, Ikeda Nakamachi, pg. 937 **IT**
Nippon Paint Company Ltd.-Osaka, 2-1-2, Oyodo-kita, pg. 937 **IT**
Nippon Quaker Chemical, Ltd., 1-3, 2-chome, Shibukawa-Cho, pg. 1346 **PB**
NIPPON SHOKUBAI CO., LTD., Kogin Bldg., 4-1-1 Koraibashi, pg. 939 **IT**
Nippon Shokubai-Material & Functions Research Lab., 5-8 Nishi Otabi-cho, pg. 939 **IT**
Nippon Shokubai-Polymer Research Laboratory, 5-8 Nishi Otabi-cho, pg. 939 **IT**
Nippon Shokubai-Resins Research Laboratory, 5-8 Nishi Otabi-cho, pg. 939 **IT**
Nippon Vicks K.K., Higashi Hankyu Bldg., 1-1 Kakuda-Cho, pg. 1331 **PB**
Nippon Wellcome KK, 8th Fl., Sumitomo Seimei Shin, Osaka Kita Bldg., 1-14, Miyahara, pg. 553 **IT**
Nissay Athletics Co., Ltd., Kouan Nissay Building, 2-20, Imabashi 3-chome, Chuo-ku, pg. 935 **IT**
Nissay Business Service Co., Ltd., 3-24, Taiyuji-cho, Kita-ku, pg. 935 **IT**
Nissay Card Services Co., Ltd., 3-24, Taiyuji-cho, Kita-ku, pg. 935 **IT**
Nissay Computer Co., Ltd., 5-14, Kitahama 3-chome, Chuo-ku, pg. 935 **IT**
Nissay Credit Co., Ltd., Nissay Shinyo Bldg., 1-8, Koraibashi 3-chome, Chuo-ku, pg. 935 **IT**
Nissay New Creation Co., Ltd., 5-8, Chifune 2-chome, Nishiyodogawa-ku, pg. 935 **IT**
Nissay Seirei Health & Welfare Foundation, 3-24, Taiyuji-cho, Kita-ku, pg. 935 **IT**
Nissay Stadium Co., Ltd., 1-55, Morinomiyachuo 2-chome, Chuo-ku, pg. 935 **IT**
Nissay Trading Co., Ltd., Nissay Shinyo Bldg., 1-8, Koraibashi 3-chome, Chuo-ku, pg. 935 **IT**
Nissho Iwai Apparel Co., Ltd., 5-8, Imabasi 2-chome Chuo-ku, pg. 946 **IT**
Nissho Iwai Fiber & Yarn Ltd., 5-8, Imabasi 2-chome Chuo-ku, pg. 946 **IT**
Nissho Iwai Industrial Machinery Inc., 5-8, Imabashi 2-chome Chuo-ku, pg. 946 **IT**
Nissho Iwai Petroleum Corp., 3-7, Awajicho 3-chome Chuo-ku, pg. 947 **IT**
Nissho Iwai Textile Co., Ltd., 17-5 Shinmachi, pg. 947 **IT**
Nisshoku Schenectady Chemicals, Inc., pg. 970 **PV**
NISSIN FOOD PRODUCTS CO., LTD., 1-1, 4-Chome, Nishinakajima, pg. 949 **IT**
Nitta-Apitron Co., Ltd., 55-1, 2 chome, Honmachi, pg. 90 **PB**
NITTO DENKO CORPORATION, pg. 950 **IT**
Nomura Systems Kansai Co., Ltd., NRI Plaza, 1-1-23, Nankou-kita, Suminoe-ku, pg. 956 **IT**
O.S. Engines Mfg. Co., Ltd., 6-15, 3 Chome Imagawa, pg. 531 **IT**
Obayashi Corporation, 33, 4-chome, pg. 995 **IT**
The Ohtsu Tire & Rubber Co., Ltd., 9-1, Kawara-machi, pg. 1317 **IT**
Okumura Metals Co., Ltd, 6-5, Sakuragawa 2-chome Naniwa-ku, pg. 530 **IT**
Onkyo Corp., 2-1, Nisshinmachi, Neyagawa-shi, pg. 1403 **IT**
ORIX Estate Corporation, 1-2-30, Benten, Minato-ku, pg. 1008 **IT**
ORIX Interior Corporation, 3-2-30-201, pg. 1008 **IT**
Osaka Agency of Nippon Life Insurance Co., Ltd., Umeda NOA Building, 4-20, Taiyuji-cho, Kita-ku, pg. 935 **IT**
Osaka Beverage Bottling Co., Ltd., 3-20, Mitsuya-Kita 3-chome, pg. 1321 **IT**
Osaka Branch, pg. 364 **IT**
Osaka Chain & Machinery, Ltd., 4-16-1, Wakihama, pg. 740 **IT**
Osaka Distribution Center, 217-1, Takahama, Shimamoto-cho, Mishima-gun, pg. 578 **IT**
OSAKA GAS CO., LTD., 4-1-2, Hiranomachi, Chuo-ku, pg. 1011 **IT**
Osaka Mill, 7-1-24 Tsukuda, pg. 1225 **IT**
Osaka Toyopet Co., Ltd., Fukushima 5-17-2, pg. 1412 **IT**
Osaka Toyota Co., Ltd., Itachibori 3-1-1, pg. 1412 **IT**
Osaka Xerox Co., Ltd., Shimano Sumitomo Seimei Bldg., 9-8, Minami-senba 2-chome, pg. 1321 **IT**
Otsuka Chemical Co., Ltd., 3-2-27 Otedori, pg. 1013 **IT**
Otsuka Electronics Co., Ltd., 3-26-3 Shodaitajika, pg. 1013 **IT**
Otsuka Foods Co., Ltd., 3-2-27 Otedori, pg. 1013 **IT**
Otsuka Ohmi Ceramics Co., Ltd., 3-2-21 Ote-dori, pg. 1013 **IT**

Geographic Index-Non U.S.

Oxford Instruments, 2-7-38 Nishi-Miyahara, pg. 1018 IT

Pfauter Asia Leybold Machinery Co. Ltd., Shin-Osaka Daiichiseimei Bldg., 3-chome, 5-24, pg. 617 IT

Pharmaceutics Research Laboratory-Osaka, pg. 1354 IT

Polaroid Corporation of Japan (Osaka), Yagi Bldg., 10-1, Minami Kyutaro-cho 2-chome, pg. 1314 IT

POSCO International Osaka (PIO), Lions Otemae Bldg., 8th Floor, 3-14 Uchhirano-Machi, 2-chome, pg. 1062 IT

Production Technology Center, 1-1-16 , Hokko, pg. 1012 IT

Read-Rite SMI Corporation, Shimamoto-Cho, Mishima-Gun, pg. 1367 PB

The Research Institute of Life Insurance Welfare, Nihon Seimei Nakanoshima Bldg., 3-43, Nakanoshima 4-chome, Kita-ku, pg. 935 IT

Research Laboratory of Applied Biochemistry-Osaka, pg. 1354 IT

Rika-Hercules Inc., pg. 811 PB

Rock of Ages Asia Corp., 3-8, Uchihonmachi, 2-Chome, pg. 1396 IT

ROHTO PHARMACEUTICAL CO., 1-8-1, Tatsumi-Nishi, Ikuno-ku, pg. 1126 IT

Royal Tourist, Ltd., 5-5, Keihan-Hondori 2-chome, pg. 1191 IT

Safety Research Laboratory-Osaka, pg. 1354 IT

Saihara & Co., Ltd., 2-80, Honjo-Naka, pg. 1321 IT

Sakai Works, 5-1, Chikko-shinmachi 1-cho, pg. 623 IT

Sakata INX Corporation, 23-37, Edobori, 1-chome, pg. 1311 IT

Sambow Plastics Co., Ltd., 45-1, Minami-Shimamachi, pg. 947 IT

Sankosha Advertising Agency, Ltd., 1-11-4-1200, Umeda, pg. 1189 IT

THE SANWA BANK LIMITED, 5-6, Fushimamachi 3-chome, pg. 1189 IT

SANYO ELECTRIC CO., LTD., 5-5, Keihan-hondori 2-chome, pg. 1190 IT

Sanyo Electric Credit Co. Ltd., 2-27, Shiromi 1-chome, pg. 1191 IT

Sanyo Electric Trading Co., Ltd., 5-15, Hiyoshi-cho 2-chome, pg. 1191 IT

Sanyo Manufacturing Corporation, 18, Keihan-Hondori 2-chome, Moriguchi City, pg. 1191 IT

Saragen Japan K.K., pg. 25 IT

Schneider Japan K.K., 3-15, Awaza 1-chome, Nishi-Ku, pg. 1283 PB

Sealed Air Japan Ltd., Kano Building, 2-5-14 Nanbanaka, pg. 1451 PB

Seiko Building Maintenance Service Co., Ltd., 4-1, Fushimicho 4-chome, Chuo-ku, pg. 935 IT

SEKISUI CHEMICAL CO., LTD., 4-4, Nishi-Temma 2-chome, Kita-ku, pg. 1219 IT

SEKISUI HOUSE, LTD., Umeda Sky Building, 1-88 Oyodanaka, 1-Chome, pg. 1219 IT

Settsu Plant, 5-1, Mishima 2-chome, pg. 1235 IT

SHARP CORPORATION, 22-22, Nagaike-cho, Abeno-ku, pg. 1228 IT

SHIMA TRADING CO., 1-18 Kitahama, 3-chome, pg. 1231 IT

SHIMANO INC., 77, Oimatsu-cho, 3-chome, pg. 1232 IT

Shimano Rinkai Co., Ltd., 1-5-15, Chikko-Shinmachi, pg. 1232 IT

SHIN NIPPON KOKI CO. LTD., 2-4-1, Kita Kyuhoji-machi, pg. 1234 IT

Shinryu Cement Corp., 33, 1-chome, Rinkai-cho, Izumiootsu-city, pg. 1291 IT

Shinsho Corporation, 2-6-17, Kitahama, Chuo-ku, pg. 740 PB

SHIONOGI & CO., LTD., 1-8, Doshomachi 3-chome, Chuo-ku, pg. 1234 IT

Shionogi Research Laboratories, 12-4, Sagisu 5-chome, Fukushima-ku, pg. 1235 IT

Showa Products Co., Ltd., 8th Fl., Nittochi, Dojima Hama Bldg., No. 4-19, pg. 1487 PB

Singapore Tourist Promotion Board - Osaka, Osaka City Air Terminal, pg. 1254 IT

Sogei Inc.-Osaka Branch, Dai-Ni Kinkou Bldg., 2-6-6, Awaji-Machi, pg. 1277 IT

Sony/Tektronix Corporation-Osaka, pg. 1568 PB

Star Sangyo Co., Ltd., 3-22, Higashi-Koraibashi, pg. 1321 IT

Suita Institute, 36-27, Tarumicho 2-chome, pg. 1019 IT

Sumika A & L Inc., 2-4, Nakanoshima 3-Chome, pg. 1311 IT

Sumika-Hercules Co. Ltd., pg. 811 PB

SUMIKIN BUSSAN CORPORATION, 6-2, Hommachi 3-chome, pg. 1308 IT

THE SUMITOMO BANK, LIMITED, 6-5, Kitahama, 4-chome, pg. 1308 IT

Sumitomo Chemical-Osaka, Sumitomo Building, 5-33, Kitahama 4-chome, pg. 1311 IT

Sumitomo Dow Ltd., 2-4, Nakanoshima, 3-chome, pg. 1311 IT

SUMITOMO ELECTRIC INDUSTRIES, LTD., 5-33, Kitahama 4-chome, pg. 1313 IT

SUMITOMO LIFE INSURANCE COMPANY, 2-2-5 Nakanoshima, pg. 1315 IT

Sumitomo Osaka, 5-33, Kitahama, 4-chome, pg. 1316 IT

Sumitomo Pharmaceuticals Co., 2-8, Doshomachi 2-chome, pg. 1311 IT

Sumitomo Seika Chemicals Co., Ltd., 7-28, Kitahama, 4-chome, pg. 1311 IT

THE SUMITOMO TRUST & BANKING CO., LTD., 4-5-33, Kitahama, pg. 1317 IT

Sungrowth Co., Ltd., 9-2, Yamazaki 1-chome, pg. 1321 IT

Suntory Kosan Co., Ltd., Suntory Bldg., 2nd Fl., 1-40, Dojimahama 2-chome, pg. 1321 IT

SUNTORY LTD., 1-40, Dojimahama 2-chome, pg. 1321 IT

Swiss Bank Corporation, 5-13 Kyutaromachi 3-chome, pg. 1330 IT

TAD Daiho Inc., Nakao Royal Bldg., 2-chome, 14-10 Miyahara Yodogawa-ku, pg. 366 IT

Taiyo Chemical Industry Co., Ltd., 4-28, Imazu Minami 3-chome, pg. 947 IT

TAIYO KOGYO CORPORATION, 4-8-4 Kigawa Higashi, pg. 1348 IT

TAKARA BELMONT CO., LTD., 1322, 2-Chome, Shim Anouchi, pg. 1349 IT

Takara Standard Co., Ltd., 1-2-1, Shigino-Higashi, Joto-ku, pg. 1349 IT

TAKASHIMAYA COMPANY, LIMITED, 1-5, Namba 5-chome, Chuo-ku, pg. 1349 IT

TAKEDA CHEMICAL INDUSTRIES, LTD., 4-1-1 Doshomachi 4-chome, pg. 1350 IT

Takeda Food Products, Ltd., 20, Imoji 3-chome, pg. 1350 IT

TAKENAKA CORPORATION, 1-13, 4-chome Hommachi, Chuo-ku, pg. 1351 IT

TANABE SEIYAKU CO., LTD., 2-10, Dosho-Machi 3-chome, pg. 1354 IT

Tandem Computers Japan, Ltd., 2-2-3 Namb Chuo-ku, pg. 418 IT

Taoka Chemical Co., Ltd., 2-11, Nishimikuni, 4-chome, pg. 1311 IT

TEIJIN LIMITED, 6-7, Minami-hommachi 1-chome, pg. 1362 IT

Thermo Electron Nippon Co., Ltd., 3-5-11 Minami-Nakaburi, pg. 1596 PB

Tokuso Trading Co., Ltd., Kitahama Chuo Bldg. 10 Fl., 2-22, Kitahama 2-chome, pg. 1394 IT

Tokuyama Corporation-Osaka Branch, Kitahama Chuo Bldg., 2-22, Kitahama 2-chome, pg. 1393 IT

Tokuyama Ready Mixed Concrete Co., Ltd., 4-82, kaigan-dor 3-chome, Minato-ku, pg. 1394 IT

TOMEN CORPORATION, 6-7, Kawaramachi 1-chome, pg. 1395 IT

Toray Engineering Co., Ltd., 3-4-18, Nakanoshima, pg. 1399 IT

Toshiba Eletec Nishinihon Corporation, Nishi-ku, pg. 1404 IT

Toshiba Nishi Nihon Consumer Electronics Co., Ltd., 1-10-10 Nihonbashi Higashi, Naniwa-ku, pg. 1404 IT

Toshiba Nishi Nihon Service & Engineering Co., Ltd., 1-31-41 Esaka, Suita, pg. 1404 IT

Toshiba Osaka Building Co., Ltd., 4-2-12 Hon-cho, Chuo-ku, pg. 1404 IT

Tourism Malaysia - Osaka Office, Cotton Nissay Buidling, 10th Floor, pg. 833 IT

Towa Giken Co., Ltd., 28-1, Enoki-cho, Suita, pg. 1394 IT

Toyo Aluminium K.K., Midosuji-Daiwa Bldg., 14-F, 6-8, Kyutaromachi, pg. 52 IT

TOYO TIRE & RUBBER CO., LTD., 1-17-18,Edobori, Nishi-ku, pg. 1411 IT

TOYOBO CO., LTD., 2-8, Dojima Hama 2-chome, pg. 1411 IT

Toyode-Sulzer Sales Ltd., pg. 1307 IT

Toyota Corolla Nankai Co., Ltd., Hamadera Suwanomori-cho Nishi 1-7, pg. 1412 IT

TSUBAKIMOTO CHAIN CO., 17-96, Tsurumi 4-chome, pg. 1425 IT

Tunnel Rental Co., 2-19, Miyajima 3-chome, pg. 317 PB

Ube Industries Ltd.-Osaka, Sakurabashi Toyo Building, pg. 1426 IT

Unikis Japan Co. Ltd., 11-14 Minami-Senba, 4 Chome, pg. 1432 IT

Union Bank of Switzerland, Doukita Daibiru Bldg. 6F, 2-5, Dojima 1-chome Kita-Ku, pg. 1441 IT

Union Bank of Switzerland, Osaka, Doukita-Daibiru Building 6F, 2-5 Dojima 1-chome Kita-ku, pg. 1441 IT

Union Special-Japan Ltd., 5-17, Mikuni Hon-Machi, pg. 717 IT

UNITIKA LTD., 1-3, Kyutaro-machi, pg. 1444 IT

Utell International-Japan, Sumitomo Seimei Nishihommachi, Building 8F, pg. 1098 IT

Wako Pure Chemical Industries, Ltd., 1-2, Doshomachi 3-chome, pg. 1350 IT

West Japan Headquarters, 7-1, Kyomachibori 1-chome, pg. 363 IT

WEST JAPAN RAILWAY COMPANY, 4-24, Shibata 2-chome, pg. 1490 IT

WestLB Osaka, Ohbayashi Building, 4-33, Kitahama-Higashi, pg. 1493 IT

Whan Gong Co., Ltd., Suntory Annex, 5th Floor, 1-5, Dojima 2-chome, pg. 1321 IT

Yokogawa-Hewlett-Packard Ltd., Chuo Bldg., 5-4-20 Nishi-nakajima, pg. 823 PB

Yoshitomi-Astra Ltd., 6-9 Hiranomachi 2-chome, pg. 94 IT

Zeneca KK, Higashi, pg. 1527 IT

Zexel Corporation-Osaka, pg. 1528 IT

Ryugasaki

Hitachi Lighting, Ltd., 69, Wakashiba-cho, pg. 621 IT

Sagamihara

MARANTZ JAPAN INC., 35-1, 7-chome, pg. 841 IT

Sagamihara Plant, 1-10-1, Asamizodai, pg. 931 IT

Sagara

Koito Manufacturing Co.-Sagara Plant, 933-1, Sugegaya, Haibara, pg. 743 IT

Saipan

Pacific Engine Development & Consulting, Inc. (PEDC), Garapan, Annex II, pg. 873 IT

Saitama

Asahi Bank Business Service Co., Ltd., 4-10, Naka-cho, 1-chome, pg. 82 IT

Asahi Bank Kosei Service Co., Ltd., 9-15, Takasago, 2-chome, pg. 82 IT

Asahi Bank Supply Co., Ltd., 10, Fukai, 3-chome, pg. 82 IT

Asahi Trust and Banking Co., Ltd., 6-5, Takasago 2-chome, pg. 82 IT

Asahigin Guarantee Co., Ltd., 13-10, Tokiwa 10-chome, pg. 82 IT

Asahigin Software Co., Ltd., 5-5, Kitaurawa, 4-chome, pg. 82 IT

Canon Components, Inc., 3461, Nanahongi, pg. 261 IT

Canon Electronics Inc., 1248, Shimokagemori, pg. 261 IT

Citizen Mechatronics Co., Ltd., 818-1, Yamaguchi, Tokorozawa-shi, pg. 293 IT

Citizen Yoshimi Co., Ltd., 1006, Shimohosoya, Yoshimimachi, pg. 294 IT

Dynapac Hitachi Plant, pg. 1326 IT

Gyoda R&D Center, 1-16-1, Fujimi-cho, pg. 25 IT

Hanyu Sanyo Electronics Co., Ltd., 476, Oaza-Hideyasu, pg. 1191 IT

Honda Access Corp., pg. 634 IT

Honda Foundry Co., Ltd., pg. 634 IT

Honda Parts Sales Co. Ltd., pg. 634 IT

Honda Racing Corporation, pg. 634 IT

Honda R&D Co., Ltd., 8-1, Honcho Wako, pg. 634 IT

Kawaguchi Distribution Center, 4-1, Honbasu 1-chome, pg. 578 IT

Kenwood Saitama Corporation, 11-8, Sayamagahara, pg. 730 IT

Kumagaya Plant, 138-11 Miizugahara Kumagaya, pg. 1225 IT

Nikko Denki Seisakusho Co., Ltd., 3-12-15 Chuo Warabi, pg. 999 IT

North Kanto Caterpillar Mitsubishi Construction Equipment Sales, Ltd., 1-11-3 Hatara-cho, pg. 317 PB

Ogose Sanken Co., Ltd., 7 Naruse, Ogose-machi, pg. 1188 IT

Ohmiya Sonic City Co., Ltd., Sonic City Bldg., 7-5, Sakuragicho 1-chome, Ohmiya, pg. 935 IT

Ootone R&D Center, 1-5 Shin-tone, Ootone-machi, pg. 25 IT

SET Engineering Co., Ltd., 3-6-3 Kitano, pg. 1188 IT

Saiden Co., Ltd., 2787-1 Akiyama, Kodama-machi, pg. 1188 IT

Sanken-Airpax Co., Ltd., 5-6-3 Chiyoda, pg. 1188 IT

Sanken Densetsu Co., Ltd., 677 Shimoakasaka-Ohnohara, pg. 1188 IT

Sanken Kosan Co., Ltd., 3-6-3 Kitano, pg. 1188 IT

Sanyu Co., Ltd., 2-1, Ryutsudanchi 2-chome, pg. 1518 IT

Sayama Precision Industries Co., Ltd., 15-1, 2-Chome, Fujimi, Sayama-shi, pg. 294 IT

Shimano Adachi Co., Ltd., 27-15, Aoki 4-chome, pg. 1232 IT

Tokorozawa Seimitsu Co., Ltd., 818-1, Yamaguchi, Tokorozawa-shi, pg. 294 IT

Tokyo Computer Center, 2-18, Harigaya 4-chome, pg. 1348 IT

Tokyo Mill, 330 Nishibukuro, Yashio, pg. 1225 IT

Tokyo Plant, 512 Nishibukuro, Yashio, pg. 1225 IT

Toshiba Visual-Equipment Corporation, 2-29-8 Ueshibacho Higashi, Fukaya-shi, pg. 1405 IT

Waratoku Steel Co., Ltd., Kumagaya-Kogyodanchi 823, pg. 999 IT

Yokogawa-Hewlett-Packard Ltd., Nissei Kumagaya Bldg., 2-42, Miya-Cho, pg. 823 PB

Yokogawa-Hewlett-Packard Ltd., Mitsuiseimei Omiya Miya-Cho, Bldg., 2-96-1, Miya-Cho, pg. 824 PB

Sakai

Showa Aluminum Corp., 6-224, Kaisan-cho, pg. 1236 IT

Sakaide

Sakaide Plant, 1, Bannosu-cho, pg. 871 IT

Sanda

TABUCHI ELECTRIC CO., LTD., 5-4 Tetuno Park, pg. 1346 IT

Sapporo

Asahi Advertising Inc., Platinum Sapporo Bldg., 1-2, Higashi, pg. 81 IT

Daiko: Hokaido, Sankyo Bldg., 11-57, Nishi 3-chome, Kitanijyo, Chuo-ku, pg. 365 IT

Dentsu Hokkaido, 5-11-1 Kita Oodori Nishi, pg. 393 IT

Hakuhodo Inc., Yasuda-Semei Sapporo Bldg., 3rd Fl., 5-1, pg. 587 IT

The Haokkaido Takushoku Securities Co. (Sapporo), 2, Nishi 6-chome, Kita 5-jo, pg. 626 IT

Hitachi Zosen Sapporo, 3, Higashi 1-chome, Minami 1-jo, pg. 622 IT

Hokkaido Amada Co., Ltd., 1-21 Higashi 18-chome, pg. 70 IT

Hokkaido Coca-Cola Bottling Co., Ltd., 2-1, 1-chome, Ichi-jo,Kiyota Toyohira-Ku, pg. 363 IT

THE HOKKAIDO TAKUSHOKU BANK, LTD., 7, Odori-Nishi 3, pg. 626 IT

I&S Corporation (Sapporo Branch), Sapporo Kokusai Bldg., Nishi 4, Kita 4 Jo, Chuo, pg. 642 IT

The Industrial Bank of Japan, Limited (Sapporo Branch), 2, Kita 1-joh Nishi 5-chome, Chuo-ku, pg. 674 IT

PB - *U.S. Public Companies Volume*
PV - *U.S. Private Companies Volume*
IT - *International Public & Private Companies Volume*

1678

Geographic Index-Non U.S.

KABUTO DECOM INC., 1-Nishi 8, Minami-1-Jo, pg. 721 IT
Konami Computer Entertainment Sapporo Co., Ltd., 3-1, Nishi 4-chome, pg. 745 IT
Kyodo Advertising Co., Ltd., STV Kita Nijyo Bldg., 2-chome, Kita-Nijyo Nishi, pg. 776 IT
Man Nen Sha, Inc., 14-2, Minami-Ichijyo, Nishi 1-chome, pg. 834 IT
NYK-Sapporo Branch, Hokkaido Bldg. 1, Nishi 4-chome, Kita 2-jo, pg. 941 IT
Nippo Inc., Sapporo Branch, Minami Odori Bldg., 10-4 Minami Odori Nishi, pg. 932 IT
Nissho Propane Sekiyu Corp., 1, Kita Nijo Nishi 3-chome, pg. 947 IT
Nittsu Kiko Unyu Co., Ltd., 1-40 Higashi 1-Chome, Kita 30-jo, pg. 934 IT
Sapporo Branch, pg. 1518 IT
Shionogi Sapporo Office, Sapporo Toho-Seimei Bldg., 2-2, Kita Ichijo Nishi 4-chome, pg. 1234 IT
Snow Brand Milk Products Co. Ltd., 1-1, Naebo-cho, 6-chome, pg. 1272 IT
Sogei Inc.-Sapporo Branch, Kitasanjyou-Mitsui Bldg., 1-4, Nishi-3chome, pg. 1277 IT
Takenaka Corporation - Hokkaido Branch, 1, 4-chome, Odori-nishi Chuo-ku, pg. 1351 IT
Tokuyama Corporation-Sapporo Branch, Toyokawa Bldg., Kita 1-31, Nango-dori 19-chome, pg. 1393 IT
Toshiba E & S Hokkaido Corporation, Shiraishi-ku, pg. 1404 IT
Toshiba Hokkaido Service & Engineering Co., Ltd., 17-5-50 Tojo Tsukisamu Toyohiraku, pg. 1404 IT
Ube Industries Ltd.-Sapporo, Sapporo Kogin Building, 2, Kitaichijo Nishi 5-chome, pg. 1426 IT
Zexel Corporation-Sapporo, pg. 1528 IT

Sasayama

CIBA-GEIGY Japan Limited-Sasayama Factory, 25-1, Hioki, pg. 977 IT
Honda Engineering Co., Ltd., No. 10-1, 1-chome, Shin-sayama, pg. 634 IT
Sayama Plant, 1-5-14, Shinsayama, pg. 1528 IT

Sasima

Nippon Crown House Co., Ltd., 11,Okasato 11-chome, Sowamachi, pg. 946 IT

Sendai

Dac City Co., Ltd., 3-4-18 Tsutsuhigaoka, Miyagino, pg. 898 IT
Daiko: Sendai, Dalsan Aobu Bldg., 1-6, Omachi 1-chome, Aoba-ku, pg. 366 IT
Dentsu Tohoku Inc., 2-5-22 Ichibancho, Aoba-ku, pg. 393 IT
Hakuhodo Inc., 7th Fl., Sendai-Jyozenji Bldg., 4-33, pg. 587 IT
Hanwa Co., Ltd.-Tohoku Branch, Sendai Daiichi Seimei Tower Bl, dg., 4-6-1, Ichiban-cho Aoba-ku, pg. 595 IT
Hitachi Zosen Sendai, 6-1, Tsutsujigaoka 4-chome, pg. 622 IT
I&S Corporation (Sendai Branch), Daini Kawahoku Bldg., 1-10, Itsutsubashi, pg. 642 IT
The Industrial Bank of Japan, Limited (Sendai Branch), 4-1, Ichibancho 2-chome, Aoba-ku, pg. 674 IT
Kyodo Advertising Co., Ltd., Tohoku Ohji Fudosan Bldg., 1-6-8 Kokubu-cho, Aoba-ku, pg. 776 IT
The Nikkan Kogyo Shimbun-Tohoku, 1-17-18, Uesugi, Aoba-ku, pg. 930 IT
Pasco Restructuring Co., Ltd., pg. 1024 IT
Sendai Branch, pg. 1518 IT
Sogei Inc.-Sendai Branch, Yamaman Bldg., 1-12-12, Honcho, pg. 1277 IT
Sony/Tektronix Corporation-Sendai, pg. 1568 PB
Takenaka Corporation - Tohoku Branch, 4-33, 3-chome, Kokubu-cho Aoba-ku, pg. 1351 IT
TOHOKU ELECTRIC POWER CO., LTD., 7-1, Ichibancho, 3-chome, pg. 1390 IT
Tohoku Semiconductor Corporation, Izumi-ku, pg. 1403 IT
Tokuyama Corporation-Sendai Branch, Hokushin Bldg., 6-10, Uesugi 1-chome, pg. 1393 IT
Toshiba Ou Denki Co., Ltd., Wakabayashi-ku, pg. 1404 IT
Toshiba Tohoku Service & Engineering Co., Ltd., 7-2-40 Ougimachi Miyagiku, pg. 1405 IT
Zexel Corporation-Sendai, pg. 1528 IT

Shibukawa

Shibukawa Plant, pg. 364 IT

Shiga

Aburahi Laboratories, 1405, Ooaza-Gotanda, Koka-cho, Koka-gun, pg. 1235 IT
Asahi Chemical Industry Co., Ltd., 515, Kojima-cho, Moriyama, pg. 84 IT
Gambro K.K., P.O. Box 9, pg. 668 IT
John Crane (Japan) Inc., 2222 Oaza Kamitoyama, pg. 1339 IT
Kyoto Works - Shiga Plant, 2-1 Kosunacho, pg. 875 IT
Nagahama Canon, Inc., 1280, Kunitomomachi, pg. 261 IT

Shiki

Zexel Corporation-Shiki Office, 3-4-1, Kitano, pg. 1528 IT

Shimizu

Fuji Seito Co., Ltd., 4-10, Seikai 1-chome, pg. 947 IT
NKK-Shimuzu Works, 387-1 Miho, pg. 902 IT
Tonen Corporation, 1900, Sodeshi-cho, pg. 1399 IT

Shinjo

Electronics Components Group, 282-1 Majikami, pg. 1228 IT

Shinjuku

Gambro Medical K.K., Izumi Hishiichi Blgd., 7-23-12 Nishi-Shinjuku, pg. 668 IT

Shizuoka

Asahi Chemical Industry Co., Ltd., 2-1, Samejima, pg. 84 IT
Asahi Chemical Industry Co., Ltd., 632-1, Mifuku, Ohito-Cho, pg. 84 IT
Bailey Japan Company Ltd., pg. 449 IT
Corning Japan K.K., No. 35 Kowa Building, 14-14 Akasaka 1-chome, Minato-ku, pg. 449 PB
Elanco Ihara K. K., 582 Shio-Shinden, pg. 993 PB
Emerson Japan, Ltd., Fusite Division, 732 Fukasawa, Gotemba-Shi, pg. 576 PB
Fuji Bondstrand Co., Ltd., pg. 99 PB
Fuji Kiko Co., Ltd., pg. 944 IT
Fusite Japan, 732 Fukasawa, Gotemba-Shi, pg. 577 PB
Hakuhodo Inc., 18-1, pg. 587 IT
Hamamatsu Kohan Kako Co., Ltd., 585, Takaoko - Cho. Hamamatau, pg. 946 IT
Hamaoka Toshiba Electronics Corp., Sakura 4231, Hamaoka-cho, pg. 1402 IT
The Industrial Bank of Japan, Limited (Shizuoka Branch), 5-6, Miyukicho, pg. 674 IT
Koito Manufacturing Co.-Shizuoka Plant, 500, Kitawaki, Shimizu, pg. 743 IT
Kyodo Advertising Co., Ltd., Zoshin Bldg., 1-14-5 Takasho, pg. 776 IT
Minebea Electronics Co., Ltd., 1743-1 Asana, pg. 868 IT
Mishima Olympus Co., Ltd., pg. 1004 IT
Nikkei Advertising Co., 1-4-11 Tokiwa-Cho, pg. 930 IT
Rhythm Motor Parts Mfg. Co., Ltd., Hamamatsu, pg. 944 IT
Shizouka Caterpillar Mitsubishi Construction Equipment Sales, Ltd., 1200 Kaminishicho, pg. 317 PB
SHIZUOKA BANK, LTD., 10, Gofukucho 1 chome, Shizuoka-shi, pg. 1236 IT
Shizuoka Oki Electric Co., Ltd., 681-1 Azamihara Aza Osuwa, pg. 999 IT
Star Micronics Co., Ltd., 194, Nakayoshida, Shizuoka-shi, pg. 294 IT
SUZUKI MOTOR CORPORATION, 300 Takatsuka-cho, pg. 1322 IT
Suzuki Oil Co., Ltd., 300 Takatsuka-cho, Hamamatsu, pg. 1323 IT
Suzuki Real Estate Co., Ltd., 300 Takatsuka-cho, Hamamatsu, pg. 1323 IT
Suzuki Transportation and Packaging Co., Ltd., 2633 Kuramatsu-cho, pg. 986 IT
Tomono Agrica Co. Ltd., 12-25, 2-Chome Kasuga, pg. 993 IT
Usui Bundy Tubing Co. Ltd., No. 930 Nagasawa, Shimizu-Machi, pg. 1341 IT
Yamaha-Olin Metal Corporation, 2630, Shingai Iwata-shi, pg. 1220 PB
Yokogawa-Hewlett-Packard Ltd., Nissei Star Bldg., 3-8-23, Ohtemachi, pg. 824 IT
Yokogawa-Hewlett-Packard Ltd., Daiichiseimei Bldg., 219-21, Motoshiro-Cho, pg. 823 PB
Yutaka Giken Co., Ltd., pg. 634 IT
Zexel Corporation-Shizuoka Office, pg. 1528 IT

Suzuka

Suzuka Circuitland Co., Ltd., 7991 Ass Ikenoshita, pg. 634 IT

Takahagi

Takahagi Plant, pg. 1518 IT

Takahama

Sindai Co., Ltd., 3-3-6 Shinden-cho, pg. 902 IT

Takamatsu

Daiko: Takamatsu, Kinryo Bldg., 2-8 Kamaicho, pg. 366 IT
Hakuhodo Inc., 4th Fl. Daihyaku Seimei, Takamatsu Bldg., pg. 587 IT
The Industrial Bank of Japan, Limited (Takamatsu Branch), 6-8, Bancho 1-chome, pg. 674 IT
Matsushita Kotobuki Electronics Industries, Ltd., 2-2-10, Kotobuki-machi, pg. 846 IT
Takamatsu Branch, pg. 1518 IT
Takamatsu Orikomi Center, Ltd., 2-chome, 12-18 Nishikicho, pg. 366 IT
Tokuyama Corporation-Takamatsu Branch, Takamatsu Dai-ichi Seimei, Bldg., Shinkan, 1-1, Kotobuki-cho, pg. 1393 IT
Toshiba Shikoku Electric Co., Ltd., pg. 1404 IT
Zexel Corporation-Takamatsu, pg. 1528 IT

Takaoka

Fushiki Mill, 1-1-1 Fushiki, pg. 938 IT

Takarazuka

Asahi-CIBA Limited-R&D Department, 10-66, Miyuki-cho, pg. 975 IT
CIBA-GEIGY (Japan) Ltd., 10-66, Miyuki-cho, pg. 977 IT
CIBA-GEIGY Serviline Co. Ltd., c/o Ciba-Geigy Japan Limited, 10-66, Miyuki-cho, pg. 980 IT
Mettler-Toledo Pac Rim Limited-Japan Branch Office, c/o Ciba-Geigy Japan Limited, 10-66, Mikuyi-cho, pg. 4 PV
Nihon Medi-Physics Company Limited, pg. 1121 IT

Takasaki

Yokogawa-Hewlett-Packard Ltd., Takasaki Daiichiseimei Bldg., 116-1, Shin-machi, pg. 824 PB

Takatsuki

SUNSTAR INC., 3-1, Asahi-machi, pg. 1320 IT

Taki

Mie Liquid Crystal Display Group, 1177-1 Oaza Gosana, pg. 1228 IT

Tama

Sony/Tektronix Corporation-Tama, pg. 1568 IT

Tenri

Hikari Corporation, 220 Armaki-cho, pg. 185 IT
Nanto Bank-Tenri Branch, 303-1, Kawaharajo-cho, pg. 905 IT
Tenri Llquid Crystal Display Development & Group, 2616-1 Ichinomoto-cho, pg. 1228 IT

Tochigi

ASHIKAGA BANK, 1-25, Sakura 4-chome, Utsunomiya, pg. 88 IT
Circuit Foil Japan, Ltd., 601-2, Otorozawa, Imaichi City, pg. 80 IT
Hitachi Ohira Industrial Co., Ltd., 709-2, Oaza-Tomita, Ohira-machi, pg. 621 IT
Kanto Malting Co., Ltd., 2910-1, Aza-Naka-Okamoto, pg. 1321 IT
Kiriu Machine Mfg. Co., Ltd., pg. 944 IT
Kurobane Nikon Co., Ltd., 1434 Oaza-kurobanemuko-machi, pg. 931 IT
Nasu Nikon Co., Ltd., 1956-3 Oaza-kyono, Karasuyama-machi, pg. 931 IT
Tochigi Nikon K.K., 770 Midori Otawara, pg. 931 IT
Utsunomiya Mfg. Div., 1-11, Yonan 1-chome, pg. 522 IT
Yokogawa-Hewlett-Packard Ltd., Chiyodaseimei Utsunomiya Bldg., 2-3-1 Ohdori, pg. 824 PB

Tokorozawa

Toho Electronics Co., Ltd., 1 Kamiyamaguchi, pg. 999 IT

Tokushima

Daiko: Tokushima, Saiwaicho Bldg., 2-30 Saiwaicho, pg. 366 IT
Otsuka Packaging Industries Ltd., 1 Aza Higashi Tatsumi, pg. 1013 IT
Otsuka Techno Co., Ltd., 330 Aza Otsubo, Oaza Koniu, pg. 1013 IT

Tokyo

A & A Japan Ltd., 1-21-1 Nishi-Shinjuku, pg. 1561 PB
A&T Corporation, 30-28, Osakaue 1-chome, Hino, pg. 1393 IT
A Table Matsuya Co., Ltd., 3-9-11 Ginza, Chuo-ku, pg. 848 IT
AA Japan Co., Kabutocho Yachiyo Bldg., 20-5 Nihonbashi Kubatocho, pg. 50 PV
A.I. Ocean, Nakamachi Bldg., 2/13 Akasaka 6 - Chome, pg. 14 IT
AMP Technologies Japan, 1-1 Nikko-cho, J-Tower, 16th Fl., pg. 9 PB
ANZ Banking Group (Merchant Banking), 8th Fl., Yanmar Tokyo Building, 1-1 Yaesu 2-chome, Chuo-ku, pg. 98 IT
ANZ McCaughan Limited Japan, 8th Fl., Yanmar Tokyo Building, pg. 99 IT
AST Research (Japan) K.K., AST Building, 3-59-23 Izumi, Suginami, pg. 1182 IT
AXA Life Office, 48th Fl., Yebisu Garden Palace, Tower, 4-20-3 Ebisu, pg. 19 IT
Acclaim Japan, Ltd., 2F Meijiseimei-Kamata, Higashi Bldg. 5-28-4 Kamata, 144, pg. 15 PB
Acer Japan Corporation, pg. 22 IT
ACHILLES CORPORATION, 22 Daikyo-cho, pg. 22 IT
Actus Corporation, Bicks Shinjuku Bldg., 2-19-1 Shinjuku, pg. 868 IT
Acuson Nippon, K.K., pg. 18 PB
Adaptec - Japan, Kioicho Hills, 4F, pg. 19 PB
Addison-Wesley Publishers Japan Ltd., Nichibo Bldg., 1-2-2 Sarugaku-cho, Chiyoda-ku, pg. 1027 IT

PB - *U.S. Public Companies Volume*
PV - *U.S. Private Companies Volume*
IT - *International Public & Private Companies Volume*

Adecco Japan Ltd., 4th Fl., Kowa Bldg., No.45, 1-15-9, Minami Aoyama Minato-ku, pg. 24 IT
ADERANS CO., LTD., 1-6-3, Shinjuku, Shinjuku-ku, pg. 24 IT
Adobe Systems Co. Limited, City Plaza Shinjuku Bldg., 2-5-20, pg. 20 PB
Adobe Systems Japan, Swiss Bank House, 4-1-8 Toranomon, pg. 20 PB
ADVANTEST CORPORATION, Shinjuku-NS Bldg., 2-4-1, Nishi-Shinjuku, pg. 25 IT
Aero Asahi Corporation, Sunshine 60, 1-1, Higashijkebukura, 3-chome, pg. 1178 IT
Aesop Co., Ltd., 2-6-16 Komazawa, pg. 496 PV
Aetna Investment Management (Japan), K.K., Toranomon Mori Bldg. No. 45, 1-5 Toranomon 5-chome, pg. 27 PB
Agfa Copal Inc., pg. 173 IT
Agfa-Gevaert Japan, Ltd., No. 2 Kowa Bldg., 11-39, Akasaka 1-chome, Minato-ku, pg. 174 IT
Agrochemicals Div., P.O. Box 262, pg. 934 IT
Ahlstrom Daiichi Co., Ltd., 6th Fl., JBP Hakozaki Bldg., 5-14, Nihonbashi Hakozakicho, pg. 34 IT
Ahlstrom Sumiju K.K., 6th Fl., JBP Hakozaki Bldg., 5-14, Nihonbashi Hakozakicho, pg. 35 IT
Aim Services Co., Ltd., 1-15 Nishishinbashi 1-chome, pg. 79 PV
Air Products Asia, Inc., 3-18-19, Toranomon, pg. 31 PB
Air Products Japan, Inc., Shuwa No. 2, Kamiyache Bldg., 11th Fl., 3-18-19, Toranomon, pg. 31 PB
Airbus Industrie Tokyo, N9 Kowa Building, annex 4th Fl., pg. 39 IT
Aiwa Co., Ltd., 1-2-11, Ikenohata, Taito-ku, pg. 1280 IT
Aiya Co., Ltd., 1-25-8, Nishikubo, pg. 1262 IT
AJINOMOTO COMPANY INC., 15-1 Kyobashi, 1-chome, pg. 40 IT
Aksbono Brake Industry Co., Ltd., 19-5 Nihonbashi, Koami-Cho 1-Chome, Chuo, pg. 53 PB
Albright & Wilson Limited, Japan Branch, #2 Okamotoya Bldg. 6F, 1-24 Toranomon, 1-chome, pg. 49 IT
Alcoa Japan Limited, 427 Fuji Bldg., 2-3 Maranouchi, pg. 62 PB
Alcon Japan Ltd., Koraku Kokusai Bldg., 7th Fl., 5-3 Koraku 1-chome, pg. 918 IT
Alfa-Laval Engineering K.K., Okamoto Bldg., 3rd Fl., Nihonbashi, pg. 1380 IT
Alfa-Laval Service K.K., Okamoto Bldg.; 4th Fl.; Nihonbashi; Honc, pg. 1380 IT
ALL NIPPON AIRWAYS CO. LTD., Kasumigaseki Bldg., 3-2-5, Kasumigaseki, pg. 57 IT
All Nippon Airways World Tours Co., Ltd., Kasumigaseki Bldg., 3-2-5 Kasumigaseki, pg. 57 IT
Allegro MicroSystems Japan, Inc., Ikebukuro Chitose Bldg., 1-22-8 Nishi-Ikebukuro, pg. 1188 IT
Allen-Bradley Japan Co., Ltd., Shinkawa Sanko building, 8F, 1-3-17 Shinkawa,Chuo-ku, pg. 1398 PB
Allergan K.K., SBS Bldg., 5th Fl., 6 Sanbancho, pg. 46 PB
Allianz Fire and Marine Insurance Japan Ltd., Shibakoen Takahashi Building, 8th Floor, pg. 59 IT
AlliedSignal Aerospace Service Corporation, Mori Bldg.#43, 4th Fl., 13-16 Mita 3-chome, pg. 52 PB
AlliedSignal Inc. Asia, Mori Building #43, 13-16, Mita 3-chome, pg. 52 PB
Allstate Automobile & Fire Insurance Co., Ltd., Sunshine 60, 1-1, Higashijkebukura, 3-chome, pg. 1178 IT
Alpine Electronics, Inc., 1-1-8 NishiGotanda, pg. 65 IT
ALPS ELECTRIC CO., LTD., 1-7, Yukigaya-Ohtsuka-Cho Ohta-Ku, pg. 65 IT
Alron Chefaro KK, No. 1 Ueno Bldg., 1-19 1-chome, pg. 44 IT
Alusuisse Japan Ltd., Tsukiji MF Bldg., 26-go-kan, 12-10, Tsukiji 2-chome, pg. 68 IT
American Drug Corporation, No. 7 Chuo Bldg., 1-26-1, Hamamatsu-Cho, pg. 80 PB
Amersham K.K., Otsuka Diichi-Seimi Bldg., 32-22 Higashi Ikebukuro 2-chome, pg. 993 IT
Amgen Kabushiki Kaisha, Hamacho Ctr. Bldg. 13-F, 2-31-1 Nihonbashi Amacho, pg. 101 PB
Ampex Japan Limited, P.O. Box 15, Tokyo Ryutsu Center, pg. 104 PB
Amro International (Asia) Ltd., Fuji Building, 2-3, Marunouchi 3-chome, Chiyoda-ku, pg. 12 IT
Amtec Co., Ltd., 15-12 Tamagawa Denechofu 1-chome, pg. 70 IT
Amway (Japan) Limited, Arco Tower, 1-8-1 Shimomeguro Meguro-Ku, pg. 70 PV
Anacomp (Japan) Ltd., San Miyanaga Bldg., 7th Fl., 5-12 Motoakasaka, 1-chome, Minato-ku, pg. 107 PB
Analog Devices K.K., Daini Jibiki Bldg., 7-8 Kojimachi 4 chome Chiyoda-ku, pg. 108 PB
Andrew International Corporation, Rm. 305, Nagatacho TBR Bldg., 2-10-12 Nagata-cho, pg. 113 PB
Anheuser-Busch Asia, Inc., Akasaka Twin Tower, 17-22, Akasaka 2-chome, pg. 115 PB
ANRITSU CORPORATION, 5-10-27, Minamiazabu, pg. 77 IT
AOKI CORPORATION, 2-17-3 Shibuya-ku, pg. 78 IT
Apple Computer Japan, Inc., Akasaka Twin Tower, Main Bldg. 16F, pg. 121 PB
ARABIAN OIL COMPANY, LTD., Seiroka Tower, 8-1, Akashi-cho, pg. 78 IT
Area Headquarters-ASIA & OCEANIA, 1-11 Tsukiji, pg. 393 IT
Area Headquarters-CHINA, 1-11 Tsukiji, pg. 393 IT
Arianespace Tokyo, Hibiya Central Bldg., 1-2-9, Nishi-Shimbashi, pg. 81 IT
Armstrong (Japan) K.K., Onarimon Yusen Bldg., 23-5, Nishi Shinbashi 3-chome, pg. 132 PB
Arrow Japan, Ltd.-Main Office, 9-10F Chiyoda Asahi Building, 2-8-3 Iidabashi Chiyoda-ku, pg. 135 PB
ASAHI ADVERTISING INC., 2-16, Kyobashi 3-chome, Chuo-ku, pg. 81 IT
Asahi Bank Building Co., Ltd., 1-2, Otemachi, 1-chome, pg. 82 IT
Asahi Bank Building Maintenance Co., Ltd., 2-3, Kamimeguro, 3-chome, pg. 82 IT
Asahi Bank Career Service Co., Ltd., 2-6, Nihonbashi, Muromachi, 1-chome, pg. 82 IT
Asahi Bank Factoring Co., Ltd., 21-5, Minami-Ikebukuro, 1-chome, pg. 82 IT
Asahi Bank Finance Service Co., Ltd., 10-5, Nihonbashi, Kayabacho, 1-chome, pg. 82 IT
Asahi Bank Investment Co., Ltd., 2-6, Nihonbashi, Muromachi, 1-chome, pg. 82 IT
Asahi Bank Jimu Service Co., Ltd., 3-1, Kyobashi, 1-chome, pg. 82 IT
THE ASAHI BANK, LTD., International Banking Dept., 1-2 Otemachi, 1-chome, pg. 81 IT
Asahi Bank Loan Business Co., Ltd., 7-8, Kyobashi 3-chome, pg. 82 IT
Asahi Bank Property Co., Ltd., 14-6, Shiba Daimon 1-chome, pg. 82 IT
Asahi Bank Research Institute Co., Ltd., 3-1, Kyobashi, 1-chome, pg. 82 IT
Asahi Bank Sogo Service Co., Ltd., 2-6, Nihonbashi Muromachi 1-chome, pg. 82 IT
ASAHI BREWERIES LTD., 1-23-1, Azumabashi, pg 83 IT
Asahi Card Co., Ltd., 5-1, Marunouchi 1-chome, pg. 82 IT
ASAHI CHEMICAL INDUSTRY CO., LTD., Hibiya-Mitsui Bldg., 1-2, Yurakucho, pg. 83 IT
Asahi-CIBA Ltd., SVAX Nishi-Shimbashi Bldg 7F, 2-39-3, Nishi-Shimbashi, pg. 974 IT
Asahi Facility Management Inc., Toyocho Intesu, 5-14, Minamisuna2-chome, Koto-ku, pg. 1351 IT
ASAHI GLASS CO., LTD., 2-1-2, Marunouchi, pg. 84 IT
Asahi Industries Co. Ltd., Sunshine 60, pg. 1178 IT
Asahi Investment Management Co., Ltd., 38-9, Nihonbashi, Kakigara-cho, 1-chome, pg. 82 IT
ASAHI MUTUAL LIFE INSURANCE COMPANY, 7-3, Nishi-Shinjuku 1-chome, pg. 85 IT
Asahi Mutual Life Insurance Co.-Tama Home Office, 1-23, Tsurumaki, pg. 85 IT
Asahi-Olin Ltd., 25 Oasu Higashi Wada, pg. 1219 PB
ASAHI OPTICAL CO., LTD., 2-36-9, Maeno-cho, pg. 85 IT
Asahi-Penn Chemical Company Limited, Rm. 606, Shuwa Kioicho, TBR Bldg., 5-7, Koju-machi, Chiyoda-ky, pg. 1245 PB
Asahi Securities Co., Ltd., 2-15, Nihonbashi Muromachi, 3-chome, Chuo-ku, pg. 82 IT
Asahi Sogo Kanri Co., Ltd., 1-3, Kyobashi 3-chome, pg. 82 IT
Asahicin Leasing Co., Ltd., 13-7, Nihonbashi Koamicho, pg. 82 IT
Asahicin Systems Co., Ltd., 10-43, Minami-Aoyama, 3-chome, pg. 82 IT
ASATSU INC., 7-16-12 Ginza, Chuo-ku, pg. 85 IT
Asatsu International Inc., 7-17-14, Ginza, Chuo-ku, pg. 86 IT
Ascom Hasler (Japan) Ltd., 23-1 Oyama-Cho, pg. 87 IT
Ashikaga Bank-International Division, 3-2 Marunouchi 2-chome, pg. 88 IT
Ashikaga Bank-Treasury Division, 9-2 Nihonbashi 3-chome, pg. 88 IT
Asia Electronics Inc., 2-35-1, Yoga, Setagaya-ku, pg. 1402 IT
Australia & New Zealand Banking Group Limited Japan, 8th Fl., Yanmar Tokyo Building, 1-1 Yaesu 2-chome, Chuo-ku, pg. 99 IT
Autodesk Ltd., 24F1 Yebsiu Garden Place Tower, 4-20-3 Ebisu, pg. 149 PB
BASF Engineering Plastics Co., Ltd., 3-3, Kioicho, Chiyoda-ku, pg. 106 IT
BASF Japan Ltd., 3-3, Kioicho, pg. 106 IT
BHP Japan, 19th Fl, Hibayadai Bldg., 1-2-2 Uchisaiwai-cho, pg. 226 IT
BMC Software Japan Ltd., Yokoyama Bldg., 4-10, Higashi Nihonbashi, pg. 163 PB
BNP Securities (Japan) Limited, Shiroyama JT Mori Building, 3-1 Toranomon, pg. 164 IT
BP Japan KK, 12-32 Akasaka 1-chome, pg. 220 IT
BSN Tokyo, Akasaka Twin Tower, Main Building, 8th Floor, pg. 144 IT
Babcock-Hitachi K.K., Nippon Bldg., pg. 621 IT
Bain & Company Ltd. (Tokyo), ARK Mori Bldg., 22nd. Fl., 1-12-32 Akasaka, Minato-ku, pg. 406 IT
Baldwin Japan Ltd., 4-34 Toyo 2 Chome, pg. 170 PB
Ballast Nedam Dredging, Altus Shinjuku-Minami Bldg, 3F, nr. 33-7, 2-chome Yoyogi, pg. 134 IT
Ballast Nedam International B.V., Altus Shinjuku Minami 304, pg. 134 IT
Bamiyan Co., Ltd., 1-25-8, Nishikubo, pg. 1262 IT
Banca Nazionale del Lavoro, 510-511, Yurakucho Denki Bldg., pg. 137 IT
Banco do Brasil S.A.-Japan, New Kokusai Building, 4-1 Marunouchi 3-chome, pg. 141 IT
Banco Nacional de Mexico, Kokusai Bldg. No. 710, 3-1-1 Marunouchi, Chiyoda-ku, pg. 574 IT
Banco Santander, Akasaka Twin Tower Bldg., 8th Floor, 2-17-22 Akasaka, pg. 144 IT
BancTec Japan Inc., No. 6 Kowa Building 604 15-21, pg. 177 PB
BANDAI CO., LTD., 2-5-4, Komagata, Taito-ku, pg. 145 IT
Bang & Olufsen of Japan Ltd., Kudan-New Central Bldg. 4-5, pg. 146 IT
Bank Brussels Lambert Tokyo Representative Office, Landic Akasaka Mitsuke Bldg., 3-9-18 Akasaka, Minato-ku, pg. 148 IT
Bank of America NT&SA, 34/F, Ark Mori Bldg., 1-12-32 Akasaka 1-chome, pg. 182 PB
Bank of Boston, AIG Building, 7th Floor, 1-3, Marunouchi, 1-chome, pg. 184 PB
The Bank of Hiroshima-Foreign Dept., 1-13-1 Nihonbashi, pg. 620 IT
Bank of Ireland - Tokyo Representative Office, IEO Bldg., 4-6 10 Yotsuya, pg. 153 IT
Bank of Montreal - Japan, Mitsui Nigokan, 1-1 Nihonbashi, Muromachi 2-chome, pg. 155 IT
The Bank of New York, Fukoku Seimei Bldg. 6th Flr., pg. 179 PB
THE BANK OF TOKYO-MITSUBISHI, LTD., 7-1, Marunouchi, 2-chome, pg. 157 IT
Bankers Trust International (Asia) Ltd., Kishimoto Bldg., 21 Chiyoda-ku, pg. 186 PB
Bankers Trust New York Corporation, Kishimoto Bldg., 2-1 Marunouchi, 2-chome, pg. 186 PB
Banque Internationale a Luxembourg S.A.-Tokyo Representative Office, Madre Matsuda Bldg., 4F, 4-13 Kioicho, pg. 162 IT
Banque Paribas-Tokyo, Yurakucho Denki Building N., 1-7-1 Yurakucho Chiyoda-ku, pg. 320 IT
Barclays Bank PLC, pg. 165 IT
Barclays Trust & Banking Company (Japan) Ltd., IPO Box 5439, pg. 166 IT
Bausch & Lomb Japan Co., Ltd., Tamachi Nikko Bldg. 29-14, 5-1, Shiba 5-chome, pg. 195 PB
Bayer Japan Ltd., Seiwa Bldg., 12-15 Shiba Daimon, 1-chome Minato-ku, pg. 174 IT
Bayerische Landesbank Girozentrale, Yusen Building, 3-2, Marunouchi 2-chome, pg. 177 IT
Bayerische Landesbank - Tokyo Branch, Yusen Building, 3-2, Marunouchi 2-chome, pg. 176 IT
Bayerische Vereinsbank AG, Togin Bldg., 1-4-2, Marunouchi, Chiyoda-ku, pg. 180 IT
Bear Stearns (Japan), Ltd., Shiroyama Hills, 3-1 Toranomon 4-Chrome, pg. 198 PB
Beiersdorf Japan K.K., 14-17 Shibuya 2-chome, pg. 183 IT
Bekaert Asia, 934 Shin Tokyo Bldg., pg. 184 IT
Bell & Howell Japan Co. K.K., Otsuka Sts Building 32-1, Minami-Otsuka 3-chome, pg. 201 PB
Benckiser (Japan) Ltd., pg. 185 IT
BERG Electronics Japan K.K., 28-10 Minami Ohi 3-chome, pg. 213 PB
The Berlitz Schools of Languages (Japan) Inc., Kowa Bldg. No. 1, 5F, 1-11-41 Akasaka, pg. 222 PB
Berner International Co. Ltd., Nihon Jitensha Kaikan, 9-15 Akasaka 1-chome, pg. 669 IT
Bertrand Faure Japon KK, 1-3-12-6F, Chichibuya Bldg., Hirakawa-cho, pg. 193 IT
BetzDearborn K.K., R Bldg., &th Floor, 8-12, Kita-Shinagawa, 1-chome, pg. 227 PB
Binks Japan, Ltd., Shuwa Kioicho TBR Bldg., Rm. 919, No. 7, 5-chome, pg. 229 PB
Blount Japan Inc., Toranomon Kotohira Kaikan, 2-8, pg. 239 PB
Blue Pacific Tours, Room 109, Shin-Kokusai Bldg., 3-4-1, Marunouchi, Chiyoda-Ku, pg. 38 IT
BlueWave Inn Corporation, 2-33-7, Asakusa, Taitou-ku, pg. 1008 IT
Bobst Japan Ltd., 37-5 Minami-Otsuka 3-chome, pg. 199 IT
Boehringer Mannheim Japan K.K., 10-11, Toranomon 3-chome, pg. 331 IT
Boehringer Mannheim Yamanouchi K.K., 10-11, Toranomon 3-chome, pg. 331 IT
Boeing Japan, Fukokuseimei Bldg., 5th Fl., 2-2-2 Uchisaiwaicho Chiyoda-ku, pg. 242 PB
Boeing Japan, Ltd., Shin Toyo Akasaka Bldg. 9-25, pg. 242 PB
Bohler Steel Gomei Kaisha, 5th Fl. Shinbashi Pine Bldg., 5-11, Shinbashi 3-chome, pg. 1471 IT
Borland Company Ltd., Sasazuka South Building, 1-64-8 Sasazuka, pg. 246 PB
Bosch K.K., Bosch Ctr., 9-1, Ushikubo 3-chome, pg. 206 IT
Bose K.K., Bldg. 28-3, Shibuya YT, pg. 161 PV
Brain Forum Co., Ltd., 5-5-9, Akasaka, Minato-ku, pg. 1262 IT
BRIDGESTONE CORPORATION, 10-1, Kyobashi 1-chome, Chuo-ku, pg. 213 IT
Bridgestone Cycle Co., Ltd., Tomin-kogyo Nihonbashi Bldg., 5-14-, Nihonbashi 3-chome, pg. 213 IT
Bristol-Myers Lion Ltd., Nihon Seimei Akasaka No. 2, Bldg. 1-16, pg. 255 PB
Bristol-Myers Squibb K.K. (Japan), Nihon Seimei Akasaka No. 2, Bldg. 1-16, pg. 256 PB
Brooks Instrument (Japan), 362, Waseda, Tsurumaki-Cho, pg. 576 PB
Brown Brothers Harriman & Co., Tokyo, Daimatsu Bldg., 4th Fl., 8-14 Nihonbashi, 3-chome, pg. 173 PV
Brush Wellman (Japan) Ltd., Dai-Ichi Marusan Bldg., 9, Kanda Jimbocho 3-chome, pg. 266 PB
Building Management Division, 26-20 Sakuragaoka-cho, pg. 1395 IT
Bull Corporation of Japan, 911 Jino Bldg., 1-1, 2 chome, Uschisawaiwai, pg. 318 IT
Bull Kabushiki Kaisha, 4th Fl., Kojimachi Tsuruya Hachiman Bldg., pg. 316 IT
Leo Burnett Kyodo Co. Ltd., 18F Akasaka Twin Tower, 17-22, Akasaka 2-Chome, pg. 185 PV
Businessland Japan Company, Ltd., pg. 9 PB
Buss (Japan) Ltd., 8-1 Toyo 3-chome, pg. 490 IT
Butterworth & Co. Publishers Ltd.-Japanese Representation, 20-12, Yoshima, 3-Chome, pg. 1095 IT
CCF Tokyo, Hibiya Kokusai Bldg. 4th Floor, 2-2-3 Uchisaiwaicho, pg. 342 IT
CCH Japan Limited, Ginza Tk Bldg. 3F, pg. 1513 IT
CEC, Chuo Electronics Co., Ltd., Daiichi Siemei Bldg., 7 Fl., 3-20-6, Myojin-cho, pg. 739 IT

PB - *U.S. Public Companies Volume*
PV - *U.S. Private Companies Volume*
IT - *International Public & Private Companies Volume*

1680

Geographic Index-Non U.S.

COBE Laboratories, K.K., Nissei Otsuka 3, Chome Bldg 6F, pg. 667 IT
CPC Japan, Ltd., Yushima Sanyu Building, 2-31-1, Yushima, pg. 447 PB
CSO Division/CSK, Waseda University Nishi-Waseda, Building 5F, pg. 1043 PB
Cabot International Services Corp., 3-1-14 Shiba, Minato-ku, pg. 289 PB
Calgon Far East Co. Ltd., Inoue Akasaka Bldg., 6-8 Akasaka 1-Chome, Minato-ku, pg. 293 PB
Calpis Ajinomoto Danone Co. Ltd., Ebisu-minami, Shibuya-ku, pg. 380 IT
CALPIS FOOD INDUSTRY CO. LTD., 2-20-3, Ebisu-Nishi, pg. 252 IT
Calsonic Corp., 5-24-15 Minamidai, pg. 944 IT
Campbell Japan, Inc., 13-40 Konan, 2-chome, pg. 299 PB
Candela K.K., Nishii Bldg., 1st Fl., 4-27-12 Ryogo-ku, pg. 301 PB
Canon Copyer Sales Co., Ltd., Tokyo MI Bdlg., 2-4, Higashi Shinagawa 2-chome, pg. 261 IT
CANON INC., 30-2, Shimomaruko 3-chome, pg. 261 IT
Canon Precision Inc., 4-19 Nakane 2-chome, pg. 261 IT
Canon Software Inc., Mita Miyoshi Bldg., 9-7, Mita 3-chome, pg. 261 IT
James Capel Pacific Limited, Kokusai Bldg., 7F, 1-1, Marunouchi 3-chome, pg. 581 IT
Cariplo (Tokyo), Enokozaka Building, 12-12 Akasaka - 1-Chome Minato-Ku, pg. 275 IT
Carlson Marketing Group Japan Co. Ltd., Aoyama Bldg., Room 802, pg. 212 PV
Carlson Marketing Group Japan KK, 8F Helios Bldg., 5-1-3 Nishi-Gotanda, pg. 212 PV
Carroll Touch International, Ltd., pg. 9 PB
Cascade Design Automation Japan Co., Ltd., Kagurazaka Kitagawa Bldg. 9F, 6-42, Kagurazaka, Shinjuku-ku, pg. 999 IT
CASIO COMPUTER CO., LTD., Shinjuku-Sumitomo Bldg., 6-1-2 chome, pg. 274 IT
Castrol K.K., 7th Flr.,Izumiya Honcho, 4-21 Ohmori Honcho, pg. 236 IT
Caterpillar MHI Marketing Ltd., Utuma Kowa Bldg., 11-37 8-chome, pg. 317 PB
Central Japan Railway Company-Tokyo Head Office, International Section, Yaesu Center Bldg., 1-6-6, Yaesu, pg. 279 IT
Chase Leasing (Japan) Limited, New Tokio Kaijo Building, 1-2 Marunouchi 1-chome Chiyoda-ku, pg. 339 PB
The Chase Manhattan Bank, N.A., New Tokio Kaijo Building, 1-2 Marunouchi 1-chome Chiyoda-ku, pg. 340 PB
Chase Manhattan Securities (Japan), New Tokio Kaijo Building, 1-2 Marunouchi 1-chome Chiyoda-ku, pg. 340 PB
Chase Manhattan Trust and Banking Company (Japan) Limited, New Toyko Kailo Building, 1-2 Marunouchi 1-chome Chiyoda-ku, pg. 340 PB
Chase Trust Bank, Mitsubishi Shoji Bldg. Annex, pg. 341 PB
Check Point Software Technologies (Japan) Ltd., Horisho Bldg. 3F, 1-12-39 Taishido, pg. 342 PB
Chemie Linz Japan Ltd., PMC Bldg. 6 Fl., 1-23-5 Higashi Azabu, 106, pg. 356 IT
The Chiba Bank, Ltd.-International Divison, 5-3, Nihombashi Muromachi 1-chome, pg. 283 IT
Chiba Kogyo International Div., 11-2 Kyobashi 1-chome, pg. 283 IT
CHICHIBU ONODA CEMENT CORPORATION, 2-14-1 Nishi Shinbashi, pg. 284 IT
CHINON INDUSTRIES INC., 6-6-3 Nishi Shinjuku, pg. 286 IT
CHIYODA MUTUAL LIFE INSURANCE COMPANY, 19-18 Kamimeguro, pg. 286 IT
Cho Hung Bank, Tokyo Branch, 8-6, Nishi-Shimbashi, 2-chome, pg. 288 IT
CHUGAI BOYEKI CO., LTD., 2-15-13,Tsukishima, Chuo-ku, pg. 290 IT
CHUGAI PHARMACEUTICAL CO., LTD., 2-1-9, Kyobashi, Chuo-ku, pg. 290 IT
The Chugoku Electric Power Co., Inc., 8-2, Marunouchi 1-chome, pg. 291 IT
CHUO SENKO ADVERTISING CO., LTD., 2-6-1 Ginza, Chuo-ku, pg. 291 IT
Chuo Subaru Motors Co., Ltd., Subaru Bldg. 7-2, Nishishinjuku 1-chome, pg. 522 IT
THE CHUO TRUST & BANKING CO., LTD., 7-1 Kyobashi, 1-chome, pg. 291 IT
Churchill PPS-KK, 4th Fl., Zojirushi Bldg., 1-6-18 Minamazabu, Minato-ku, pg. 1025 IT
CIBA Corning Diagnostics KK, Unosawa Tokyo Bldg., 1-19-15, Ebisu, Shibuya-ku, pg. 975 IT
CIBA-GEIGY Japan Limited Pharmaceuticals Division, Tokyo Head Office, New Edobashi Building, pg. 977 IT
CIBA-GEIGY Japan Limited-Tokyo Branch, World Trade Center Bldg. 34F, 4-1, Hamamatsu-cho 2-chome, pg. 977 IT
CIBA Vision-Ricky Limited, Kamiyacho Mori Bldg 17F, 4-3-20, Toranomon, pg. 981 IT
Cigna International Investment Advisors K.K., Akasaka Eight-One Building, 8th Fl., 13-5 Nagata-Cho, pg. 357 PB
Cinch Japan KK, Tohsei Bldg. 4F, 3-8-2 Nishi-Shimbashi, pg. 786 IT
Cirrus Logic K.K., Shinjuku Green Tower Bldg. 26F, 6-14-1 Nishi Shinjuku, pg. 375 PB
Citizen Kohatsu Co., Ltd., 29-27, 4-Chome, Takadanobaba, pg. 293 IT
Citizen Trading Co., Ltd., 12F, Harmony Tower, 32-2, 1-chome, pg. 293 IT
CITIZEN WATCH COMPANY, LTD., 2-1-1, Nishi-Shinjuku, pg. 293 IT
City Bldg. Kanri Co., Ltd., 3-6-1 Ginza, Chuo-ku, pg. 848 IT
City Development Division, 26-20 Sakuragaoka-cho, pg. 1395 IT
Clarify Inc.-Japan, TE Bldg. 6F, 4-5-16 Yoga, Setagaya-ku, pg. 382 PB
Clarins KK, 6 8 10 Roppongi, pg. 295 IT
CLARION CO., LTD., 22-3, Shibuya, 2-chome, pg. 296 IT
Club Mediterranee Association Japan Co. Ltd., 9 Fl., Banque Indosuez Bldg., pg. 298 IT
Club Mediterranee K.K., 9 Fl., Banque Indosuez Bldg., pg. 298 IT
Cogema Japan, Urban Toranomon Bldg., 5F 1-16-4, pg. 305 IT
Cognex K.K., 5-4-7 Honkamagome, 113, pg. 394 PB
Cognos Japan KK, 6F, Green Life Building, 2-21-12 Sasazuka, pg. 306 IT
Coherent Japan Co., Ltd., Tokyo MK Building, 7-2-14 Toyo, pg. 395 PB
Colborn-Dawes Japan Ltd., pg. 1121 IT
Coleman Japan Ltd., 5th Fl., Eight Bldg., 4-5-9, Hachobori, pg. 691 PV
Cominco Japan K.K., 6 Fl. Hayabusa Toko Bldg., 3-19, Hayabusacho Chiyoda-ku, pg. 308 IT
Commerz International Capital Management (Japan) Ltd., Nippon Press Center Bldg., 2-2-1, Uchisai Waicho, pg. 309 IT
Commerz Securities (Japan) Company Ltd., pg. 312 IT
Commerzbank AG-Tokyo, Nippon Press Center Bldg., 2F, 2-2-1 Uchisaiwai-cho, pg. 311 IT
Commonwealth Bank-Tokyo, 8th Fl., Toranomon Waiko Bldg., 12-1 Toranomon 5-Chome, pg. 313 IT
Compaq Computer Japan KK, pg. 418 PB
ConAgra Nissui Inc., 2-6-2, Ohtemachi, Chiyoda-ku, pg. 429 PB
Consumer & Information Service Division, 26-20 Sakuragaoka-cho, pg. 1395 IT
The Continuum Company (Japan), Ltd., Muraki Building 3-7, Kanda-Kajicho, pg. 423 PB
Copyer Co., Ltd., 3-3, Shimorenjyaku 6-chome, pg. 261 IT
Cordis-Japan, Ltd., East 21 Tower, 10F, 6-3-2, Toyo, Koto-ku, pg. 928 PB
Corning International K.K., pg. 449 PB
Corporate Software Ltd., KK, East Roppongi Bldg., 3-16-35 Roppongi, pg. 519 PB
COSMO OIL CO., LTD., 1-1 Shibaura, 1 Chome, pg. 335 IT
Credit Agricole (CNCA) Representative Office-Tokyo, Ando Fukuyoschi Bldg., 10th Fl, 1-11-28 Akasaka, pg. 341 IT
Credit Lyonnais Japan, Hibiya Kokusai Bldg., 7th Fl., Chiyoda-Ku, 2-3 Ushisiawaicho, pg. 344 IT
Credit Saison Co., Ltd., Sunshine 60, 1-1, Higashijkebukuro, 3-chome, pg. 1178 IT
Criticare Systems, Inc.-Japan, Maruki Bldg., 3-6-11 Hongo Bunkyo-ku, pg. 459 PB
Cyanamid (Japan) Ltd., No. 30 Kowa Bldg., 4th Fl., 4-5 Roppongi, pg. 81 PB
DB Capital Markets (Asia) Ltd. (Tokyo), ARK Mori Bldg., 22nd Fl., 1-12-32, Akasaka Minato-ku, pg. 404 IT
DG Securities-Tokyo Branch, Toranomon Waiko Bldg., No. 2, pg. 352 IT
D.O.M. Ltd., 6-6-2, Nishi-shinjuku, pg. 317 PB
DSM Idemitsu Corp. Ltd., Koyo Building, 2nd Floor, 9-5, Shibakouen, 2-Chome, pg. 356 IT
DSM Japan KK, Hanai Building 7th Floor, 1-2-9 Shiba Koen, pg. 355 IT
D.S.P. Ltd., Shibashimizu Bldg., 2-chome, 3-11 Shibadaimon, Minato-ku, pg. 366 IT
Daewoo International (Japan) Corp., Rm. 404 Toranomon Mitsui Bldg., 3-8-1 Kasumigaseki, pg. 358 IT
Daewoo Securities - Tokyo Representative Office, Kyokuyo Bldg., 6th Fl., 2-8-11, Nihonbashi Chuo-ku, pg. 359 IT
THE DAI-ICHI KANGYO BANK, LIMITED, 1-1-5, Uchi-Saiwaicho, pg. 359 IT
Dai-Ichi Kikaku Co. Ltd., 9-11 Fls., Hibiya Kokusai Bldg, pg. 357 IT
DAI-ICHI MUTUAL LIFE INSURANCE COMPANY, 13-1 Yuraku-Cho 1-chome, pg. 362 IT
Dai Nippon Book Binding Co., Ltd., 39-3, 2 Chome, pg. 363 IT
DAI NIPPON PRINTING CO., LTD., 1-1, Ichigaya Kagacho 1-chome, pg. 363 IT
Dai Nippon Shoji Co., Ltd., 3, 3-chome Kanda-Jinbocho, Chiyoda-ku, pg. 363 IT
Daicel Huls Ltd., Mori Building, 7th Floor, 1-19-5 Toranomo, pg. 1455 IT
Daido Herr Engineering, 7-13 Nishi Shinbashi, 1-chome, pg. 962 PV
DAIDO HOXAN INC., 18-19, Toranomon 3-chome, pg. 363 IT
Daido Steel Co., Ltd.-Tokyo Head Office, pg. 364 IT
Daihatsu Diesel Mfg. Co., Ltd., 2-2-10 Nihonbashi-Honcho, pg. 364 IT
Daiichi Forging Co., Ltd., Subaru Bldg. 7-2, Nishishinjuku 1-chome, pg. 522 IT
Daikin Industries Ltd., -Tokyo Office, Shinjuki-Sumitomo Bldg., 6-1, Nishi-Shinjuku, pg. 365 IT
DAIKO ADVERTISING, INC., International Division, B-Khan, 2-chome, pg. 365 IT
Daiko Agency Inc., Daiichi Miyuki Bldg., 5-chome, 1-15 Ginza, Chuo-ku, pg. 366 IT
Daiko Denshi Tsushin, Ltd., 1, Ageba-cho, 2-Chome, pg. 374 IT
Daiko Intellect Inc., Shuwa Shiba Park Bldg., Annex B, 2-chome 4-1 Shiba-Koen, Minato-, pg. 366 IT
Daikyo Seiko Co., Ltd., 3-38-2 Sumida Sumida, Ku, pg. 1756 PB
DAINICHISEIKA COLOUR & CHEMICALS MFG. CO., LTD., 7-6 Nihonbashi Bakuro, 1-chome, pg. 369 IT
DAINIPPON INK & CHEMICALS, INC., DIC Building, 7-20, Nihonbashi 3-chome, Chuo-ku, pg. 369 IT
DAIO PAPER CORPORATION, 2-7-2 Yaesu, pg. 372 IT
The Daishi Bank, Ltd.-Tokyo, Yamamoto Bldg., 6-3, 1-chome, Nihombashi-Muromachi, pg. 372 IT
Daiwa Asset Management Co. Ltd., 10-5, Nihombashi-Kayabacho 2-chome, pg. 374 IT
Daiwa Bank-International Division, 1-1, Otemachi 2-chome, pg. 373 IT
Daiwa Bank-International Treasury Division, 1-1, Otemachi 2-chome, pg. 373 IT
The Daiwa Building Co., Ltd., 1-9, Kayabacho 1 Chome, Nihonbashi, pg. 374 IT
Daiwa Business Tourist Co. Ltd., 16-1, Shimbashi 2-Chome, pg. 374 IT
Daiwa Finance Co. Ltd., Gotanda Daiwa Building, 13-5, Nishi-Gotanda 7-chome, pg. 374 IT
Daiwa Institute of Research Ltd., Daiwa-Soken Building, 15-6, Fuyuki, pg. 374 IT
Daiwa International Capital Management Co., Ltd., 2-1, Kyobashi 1-Chome, pg. 375 IT
Daiwa International Trust Bank Limited, 2-1, Kyobashi 1-chome, pg. 375 IT
Daiwa Precious Metals Co., Ltd., 5-10, Sotokanda 2-chome, pg. 375 IT
The Daiwa Real Estate Co., Ltd., 3-11, Nihombashi 1-Chome, pg. 375 IT
Daiwa Sanko Co., Ltd., 5-9, Sotokanda 2-Chome, pg. 375 IT
Daiwa Securities Business Center Co. Ltd., 1-4, Edagawa 3-chome, pg. 375 IT
DAIWA SECURITIES CO. LTD., 6-4, Otemachi 2-chome, Chiyoda-ku, pg. 374 IT
Daiwa Software Research Co., Ltd., 5-2, Koji-machi 1-Chome, pg. 375 IT
Danzas K.K., Tateno Bldg., 4th Fl., 4-13 Kiba 6-chome, pg. 382 IT
Data I/O Japan Co., Ltd., Osaki CN, Bldg. 2F, 5-10-10 Osaki, pg. 486 PB
DataCard Japan Ltd, Svax Building 2-39-3 Nishi-Shinbashi, pg. 313 PV
Datastream International (Japan) KK, The Garden Ct. 7-F, 4-1 Kioicho, pg. 1326 PB
Dayton Progress of Japan, Shinjuku Shibata Bldg. 2-17, 2-Chome, pg. 617 PB
Dell Computer Corporation, F-Nissei Ebisu Bldg., 3-16-3, Higashi Gotanda Shibuya-Ku, pg. 496 PB
Delta Air Lines Tokyo, Kidicho Bldg.-9F, 3-12 Kioicho, pg. 497 PB
Denak KK, Sanshin Bldg., 4-1 Yuraku-Cho 1-chome, pg. 44 IT
Dengyosha Machine Works Corporation, 1-5-1, Omori-kita, Ota-ku, pg. 1402 IT
Denki Kagaku Kogyo Kabushiki Kaisha, Sanshin Bldg., 1-4-1, Yuraku-cho, pg. 877 IT
Dennison Transoceanic Corporation, Kojima Bldg., 4-1 Yotsuya Shinjuku-ku, pg. 154 PB
Denny's Japan Co., Ltd., 1-4, Shibakoen 4-chome, pg. 693 IT
Dentsply Japan, Tsunashima No. 2 Building, 20-12 Yushima 3-chome, pg. 499 PB
Dentsu East Japan Inc., 1-11 Tsukiji, Chuo-ku, pg. 393 IT
DENTSU INC., 1-11 Tsukiji, pg. 392 IT
Dentsu, Sudler & Hennessey Inc., Tsukiji MK Bldg., 2-11-26, pg. 325 PV
Dentsu Young & Rubicam Inc. (Tokyo), Kyobashi K-1 Bldg., 2-7-12 Yaesu, Chuo-ku, pg. 325 PV
Deutsche Bank AG (Tokyo), ARK Mori Building, 1-12-32, Akasaka, pg. 405 IT
Dexter Midland Co. Ltd., 37-2, 2-Chome Minamisuana, Koto-ku, pg. 505 PB
DIAMOND LEASE CO., LTD., 2-7-2, Yaesu, pg. 413 IT
Dicalite Orient Co. Ltd., Tachibana Bldg. 5, 4-Chome Kojimachi, pg. 903 PV
Digital Equipment Corporation Japan, 1-2-1, Kamiogi, Suginami-ku, pg. 507 PB
Dinol Japan, 3-12 Nishi Shimbasi, 1-chome, Minato-ku, pg. 982 IT
Diosynth International bv, Dai 2 Monami Bldg., pg. 44 IT
DISCO CORPORATION, 14-3 Higashi-Kohiya, 2-Chome, pg. 413 IT
Walt Disney Enterprises of Japan Ltd., No. 3 Toyo Kaiji Bldg., 7th Fl, 7th Fl., Nishi Shinbashi 2-chome, pg. 514 PB
Dohnan Shokuhin Co., Ltd., 2-4-16 Kyobashi, pg. 855 IT
Dole Asia, Sabokaikan-Bekkan, 4th Fl., 7-4 Hirakawa-cho, pg. 515 PB
Dow Chemical International Ltd., Office of Technology, Hiblya Chunichi Bldg., pg. 523 PB
Dow Chemical Japan Ltd., Hibiya Chunichi Bldg.,6th Fl., 1-4, Uchisaiwai-cho, pg. 523 PB
Dow Corning Toray Silicon Co., Ltd., AIG Building, 1-3, Marunouchi, pg. 1400 IT
Dow Kakoh Kabashiki Kaisha, 6-12 Toranomon, pg. 524 PB
Dresdner Bank AG, Ninonbashi Muromachi Ctr., Bldg., 2-15, pg. 419 IT
Dresdner Securities (Asia) Ltd., Shionogi Honcho Kyodo Bldg., 11th Floor, 7-2 Nihonbashi-, pg. 420 IT
Du Pont Japan Ltd., Du Pont Tower Toranomon Bldg., 10-1 Toranomon 2-chome, pg. 533 PB
Du Pont Mitsui Fluorochemicals Co., Ltd., Mitsui Seimei Bldg., 7th Fl., 2-3, Otemachi 1-chome, pg. 533 PB
Du Pont Mitsui Polychemicals Co., Ltd., P.O. Box 61, Kasumigaseki Bldg., Chiyoda-ku, pg. 533 PB
Du Pont-Showa Denko Co., Ltd., Shoko Bldg., 7-13 Shiba Park, 1-chome, Shinagana-ku, pg. 533 PB
Du Pont-Toray Company, Ltd., Toray Bldg., pg. 533 PB
Dumez-GTM Tokyo, 4F Sumitomo Fudosan Kameido Building, pg. 823 IT

PB - *U.S. Public Companies Volume*
PV - *U.S. Private Companies Volume*
IT - *International Public & Private Companies Volume*

Dun & Bradstreet Japan Ltd., 5F, Aobadai Hills, 4-7-7 Aobadai, pg. 536 **PB**
K.K. Dun & Bradstreet Software, Imperial Tower, 1-1, Uchisaiwaicho, 1-chome, Chiyoda-ku, pg. 532 **IT**
Dynac Co., Ohashi Gyoen Station Bldg., 7th Fl., 8-1, Shinjuku 1-chome, pg. 1321 **IT**
Dynapac Hitachi Construction Machinery, pg. 1326 **IT**
Dynapert Japan Ltd., 7-1 Nihonbashi Honcho Bldg., pg. 233 **IT**
Dynetcom, 54-5, Akabane 1-Chome, Kita-ku, pg. 425 **IT**
EG & G Japan, 401 Hiro-o Alpha Bldg., 4-5-48, Minami-Azabu, pg. 544 **IT**
EMI Music International Services Ltd., Toshiba-EMI Bldg., 2-17 Akasaka 2-chome, pg. 427 **IT**
ESL-Nippon Co. Ltd., Sukegawa Bldg., 1-3-4 Yanagi Bashi, pg. 369 **PV**
Eagle Industry, Ltd., 1-12-15, Shiba-Daimon, Minato-ku, pg. 544 **PB**
Earth Biochemical Co., Ltd., 2-9 Kanda Tsukasa-cho, pg. 1013 **IT**
Earth Chemical Co., Ltd., 2-9 Kanda Tsukasa-cho, pg. 1013 **IT**
East Japan Headquarters, 18-19, Toranomon 3-chome, pg. 363 **IT**
EAST JAPAN RAILWAY COMPANY, 6-5, Marunouchi 1-chome, pg. 431 **IT**
East Japan Toshiba Distributor Corporation, 1-1-8 Soto-Kanda, Chiyo-da-ku, pg. 1402 **IT**
Eastern Book Service, pg. 1291 **IT**
Eastman Kodak Asia Pacific Ltd., Gotenyama Mori Bldg., 4-7-35 Kita-Shinagawa, pg. 552 **IT**
Eastman Kodak (Japan) Ltd., Gotenyama Mori Bldg., 4-7-35 Kita-Shinagawa, pg. 552 **IT**
Eaton Japan Co., 3-3-3 Kasumigaseki, Chiyoda-ku, pg. 558 **IT**
EBARA CORPORATION, 11-1, Haneda Asahi-cho, pg. 431 **IT**
Eddie Bauer Japan Inc., pg. 1014 **IT**
Edelman Public Relations Worldwide, ARK Mori Bldg., 22nd Fl., Akusaka 1-12-32, pg. 363 **PV**
Edwards Japan Ltd., Shuwa Shiba Park, Bldg. A-3F, 4-1 Shibakoen, pg. 122 **IT**
Ehime Kanzume Co., Ltd., 2-4-16 Kyobashi, pg. 855 **IT**
EISAI CO., LTD., 4-6-10, Koishikawa, pg. 435 **IT**
Eizan Co., Ltd., Nihonbashi Kobunacho 3-2, pg. 1518 **IT**
Electro Scientific Industries KK, Denpa Bldg., 1st Fl., 1-11-15 Higashi Gotanda, pg. 569 **PB**
Electrolux (Japan) Ltd., Gadelius Bldg. 7-8 Moto Akasaka, 1-chome, pg. 443 **IT**
Electronic Arts Victor Inc., Fru X Gaien, 2-4-12 Jingumae, pg. 569 **PB**
Elkem International AS, Rm. No. 402, Nikko Sanno Bldg., 5-3 2-chome, Akasaka, pg. 447 **IT**
Elkem Materials Japan, Nikko Sanno Bld., No. 401, 5-3, 2-chome Akasaka, pg. 447 **IT**
Elsevier Science Japan, 9-15, Higashi-Azabu, pg. 1100 **IT**
Emerson Japan, Ltd., Dentsu Kosan, Daisan Bldg., 2-16-7 Ginza, Chuo Ku, pg. 576 **IT**
e'quipe, Ltd., 3-2-20 Kaigan, pg. 722 **IT**
Esso Sekiyu Kabushiki Kaisha, T.B.S. Kaikan Bldg. 3-3, Akasaka 5-chome, pg. 602 **PB**
Eurotherm (Japan) Limited, Matsuo Building 2F, 3-14-3 Honmachi, pg. 466 **IT**
Excellon Japan, 2-15-22 Hirakawa-Cho, pg. 594 **PB**
Excerpta Medica Limited-Japan, Higashi-Azabu 1-chome Bldg. 3F, 9-15 Higashi-Azabu 1-chome, pg. 1099 **IT**
Explosives Div., pg. 934 **IT**
The Export-Import Bank of Korea, Rm. 552, Yurakucho Denki Bldg., pg. 467 **IT**
FAG Japan Co. Ltd., pg. 469 **IT**
FFV Japan KK, Akasaka Chuo Bldg., 2-6 Akasaka 3-chome, pg. 278 **IT**
FLS Japan Ltd., Kyobashi, pg. 476 **IT**
Falconbridge (Japan) Ltd., Nihonbashi First Building 8F, 2-19, Nihonbashi Kabuto-cho, pg. 434 **IT**
Fallek Chemical Japan K.K., Teisen Kandabashi Bldg., 3rd Floor, pg. 553 **PV**
Famil Co., Ltd., 1-4, Shiba-Koen 4-chome, pg. 693 **PB**
Farah Japan Limited, No. 2 Mochizuki Bldg., 6-16, pg. 613 **PB**
Fashion House Train, 2-14-7, Ishihara, pg. 759 **PB**
Fasson-Sanyo Kokusaku Pulp Co. Ltd., Sanyo Kokusaku Pulp Bldg., 1-4-5 Marunouchi, pg. 154 **IT**
Ferrofluidics Japan Corporation, 1001 Chison Mansion, 24-8 Sakuragaoka-cho, pg. 620 **PB**
Fike Japan Corporation, 10-13 Minami Aoyama 5-Chome, Minato-Ku, pg. 404 **PV**
Fine Care Co. Ltd., Tamachi Kiyota Bldg., 3-4 Shibaura 4-chome, pg. 1490 **IT**
Finetech Co., Ltd., 16th Fl., pg. 1262 **IT**
Finmeccanica-Japan, Ark Mori Bldg.,W. 27 Fl., 1-12-32 Akasaka 1 chome, pg. 654 **IT**
Finnigan MAT Instruments, Inc., Shiozaki Bldg., 2-7-1 Hirakawa-cho, Chiyoda-ku, pg. 1596 **PB**
First Kitchen Co., Ltd., Ohashi Gyoen Station Bldg., 8th Fl., 8-1, Shinjuku 1-chome, pg. 1321 **IT**
First National Nippon Shinpan Co., Ltd., pg. 379 **PB**
Georg Fischer Japan Ltd., 8-1, Toyo 3-chome, pg. 490 **IT**
Flo Japon Co., Ltd., 1-25-8, Nishikubo, pg. 1262 **IT**
Florasynth-Lautier K.K., Kanda Shibasaki Bldg., No. 16-7, 1-Chome Higashi Kanda, pg. 173 **IT**
Fluke, Inc., Sumitomo Higashi Shinbashi Bldg., pg. 659 **PB**
Fluor Daniel (Japan) Inc., Sanno Grand Bldg., 2-14-2 Nagato-cho, pg. 660 **IT**
Ford Finance Company of Japan, Limited, Toranomon 37, Mori Bldg., 6F 5-1, Toranomon 3-chome Minato-ku, pg. 666 **IT**
Ford Motor Company (Japan) Ltd., Toranomon 37, Mori Bldg. 6F 5-1, pg. 666 **IT**
FOSTER ELECTRIC CO., LTD., 512, Miyazawa-cho, pg. 500 **IT**

Foster Wheeler k.k., JBP Hokozaki Building 5-14, Nishonbashi Hakozakicho, pg. 677 **PB**
FoxVideo (Far East) K.K., U.S. Hanzomon Bldg. 6S, 2-13 Hayabusa-cho Chiyoda-ku, pg. 926 **IT**
Framatome Japan, Ltd., Shuwa-Shinagawa Bldg., 5th Fl., pg. 503 **IT**
Frank & Schulte Group of Companies Japan, Excellent K Bldg. 3rd Fl., 10-5 Ningyo-cho, 2-chome, Nihonbashi, pg. 1459 **IT**
Fresh Matsuya Co., Ltd., 3-6-1 Ginza, Chuo-ku, pg. 848 **IT**
Fresh Skylark Co., Ltd., 2-8-13, Asahigaoka, pg. 1262 **IT**
Freudenberg NH Co. Ltd., pg. 506 **IT**
Frigoscandia Food Process Systems AB, Japan Branch, Sugizaki Bldg., 1-16-3 Hamamatsu-cho, pg. 606 **IT**
Fuchs Japan K.K., Kurosaki Building, 6F 5-2 Higashi Kanda 1-chome, pg. 517 **IT**
THE FUJI BANK, LIMITED, 5-5 Otemachi 1-chome, Chiyoda-ku, pg. 519 **IT**
FUJI ELECTRIC CO., LTD., 12-1 Yurakucho 1-chome, pg. 522 **IT**
Fuji Electrochemical Co., Ltd., 3611 Shinbashi 5-chome, pg. 526 **IT**
FUJI HEAVY INDUSTRIES, LTD., Subaru Bldg., 7-2, Nishi-Shinjuku, pg. 522 **IT**
Fuji Heavy Industries, Ltd., Mitaka Plant, 9-6, Osawa 3-chome, pg. 523 **IT**
Fuji Heavy Industries, Ltd., Transportation Equipment Div., Shinjuku-ku, pg. 522 **IT**
Fuji-Hunt Electronics Technology Co., 38th Kowa Building, 12-24 Nishiazabu, pg. 1219 **PB**
Fuji Kisen Kaisha, Ltd., Mitsui Bldg., 3-7, Nihonbashi-Muromachi, pg. 878 **IT**
FUJI PHOTO FILM CO., LTD., 2-26-30, Nishi-Azabu 2-chome, pg. 523 **IT**
Fuji Robin Industries, Ltd., Subaru Bldg. 7-2, Nishishinjuku 1-chome, pg. 523 **IT**
Fuji Xerox Company Ltd., 3, 5 Akaska 3-chome, pg. 1785 **PB**
FUJIKURA LTD., 1-5-1, Kiba, Koto-ku, pg. 525 **IT**
Fujisawa Synthelabo K.K., Dowa Bldg., 18-18 Roppongi 5-chome, pg. 818 **IT**
Fujisawa Tokyo, 2-1, Nihinbashi-Honcho 2-chome, pg. 525 **IT**
FUJITSU LIMITED, 6-1-1 Marunouchi, Center Bldg., Chiyoda-k, pg. 525 **IT**
Fujitsu Microdevices Ltd., 6-1 Marunochi 1-chome, pg. 526 **IT**
Fukada-Kidde Co., Ltd., No. 1-5, 3-chome Mita, pg. 594 **IT**
FUKOKU MUTUAL LIFE INSURANCE COMPANY, 2-2, Uchisaiwaicho 2-chome, pg. 529 **IT**
Funai Electric Research Institute Co., Ltd., 4-11-5 Soto-kanda, pg. 529 **IT**
Furukawa Aluminum Co., Ltd., 6-1, Marunouchi 2-chome, pg. 530 **IT**
THE FURUKAWA ELECTRIC CO., LTD., 6-1, Marunouchi 2-Chome, Chiyoda-Ku, pg. 530 **IT**
Furukawa Sangyo Kaisha, Ltd., 2-8, Muromachi, Nihonbashi, Chuo-ku, pg. 530 **IT**
Fushiman Co. Ltd., 6-2 Ohmori-Minami 4-chome, pg. 550 **IT**
Fuyo General Lease Co. Ltd., pg. 379 **IT**
GE Medical Systems Asia Ltd., 7-127 Asahigaoka, pg. 713 **IT**
GI-Yamanouchi, Inc., 10-13, Higashiazabu, 1-chome, pg. 1518 **IT**
GM Allison Japan Limited, Odakyu Minami Aoyama Bldg. 3F, 8-1, Minami Ayama 7-chome, Minato-ku, pg. 721 **PV**
GMOC Japan, Roppong, Fuji Bldg., 2-6 Nishrazaba 3-chome Minato-ku, pg. 723 **IT**
GPI (Japan) Limited, Room 401, Sanko Mori Bldg., 1-3-1, Atago, pg. 537 **IT**
GS-EE Co., Ltd., pg. 126 **IT**
GVG Japan, Ltd., 4F Sumitomo Higashi Ikebukuro, 3-13-2 Higashi-ikebukuro, pg. 1567 **PB**
GAEART Kumagai Co., Ltd., pg. 763 **IT**
Gambro K.K., Izumi Hoshiichi Bldg., pg. 668 **IT**
Gambro-Shimizu, 2F Izumi Hoshiichi Building, 7-22-12 Nishi Shinjuku, pg. 668 **IT**
Gan Incendie Accidents Japan, Yasuda Kasai Kaijo Building, 41st Floor, 1-26-1 Nishi-Shinjuku, pg. 564 **IT**
Gelman Sciences Japan Limited, 1-9-12, Kita-Ueno, pg. 1263 **IT**
Genentech, Ltd.-Japan, 8F Tohei Kudan Building, 1-4-5 Kudan-Kita, pg. 1120 **IT**
General Sekiyu K.K., TBS Kaikan Bldg., 8-6 Nishi-Shinbashi, 2 Chome, pg. 602 **PB**
Generale Bank, 9th Fl., Imperial Tower, 1-1-1, Uchisaiwaicho-Chiyoda-ku, pg. 547 **IT**
Genetics Institute Inc. of Japan, 1-10-13 Higashi Azabu, pg. 80 **IT**
Genzyme Japan, Izumiyamabuki-Cho Bldg., 333 Yamabuki-Cho, pg. 733 **IT**
Georgia-Pacific International Corp., Nihonbashi, Chuo-ku, pg. 759 **PB**
GEOSTR Corporation, pg. 763 **IT**
Getinge AB Japan, Sweden Ctr. Bldg. 6F, 6-11-9 Roppongi, pg. 551 **IT**
Giken Engineering Corporation, 21-5, Ogawahigashi 1-chome, pg. 730 **IT**
Gillette (Japan) Inc., Shinagawa NSS Bldg., pg. 745 **PB**
Givaudan-Roure K.K., 3-23 Shimomeguro, pg. 1120 **IT**
Givenchy KK (Japan), Sumitomo Hanzomon Building 1F, 3-16 Hayabusa-cho, Chiyoda-ku, pg. 782 **IT**
Globe-Meat Importers Co., Ltd., 6F Assend Jimbocho, 2-23 Kanda-Jimbocho, Chiyoda-ku, pg. 430 **IT**
Glory Ltd., 3-5-4-6 Ohsaki, 5-Chome, pg. 554 **IT**
Goldman Sachs (Japan) Limited, ARK Mori Bldg., 10th Fl., 12-32, Akasaka 1-chome, pg. 462 **PV**

Goldstar Japan, Hon-Kan 9F, Akasaka Twin-Tower Bldg., pg. 779 **IT**
Goldwin Inc., 20-6, 2-Chome, Shoto, pg. 1010 **IT**
Golf Sophisticates, 2-30-9 Eitai, Koto-ku, pg. 846 **IT**
Good Time Ltd., 6-15-21 Ohwada-cho, Hachioji-City, pg. 759 **IT**
Goodman Fielder (Japan) KK, 10th Floor, AADO Kyobashi, 3-6-6 Hatchobori, pg. 556 **IT**
Goss Graphic Systems-Japan Corporation, Mitsuya Toranomon Bldg., 2-F, 1-22-14, Toranomon, pg. 466 **PV**
Grace Japan K.K., Shinjuku Green Tower Bldg., 14-1. Nishi-Shinjuku 6-chome, pg. 756 **PB**
Gradco (Japan), Ltd., Toho Seimei Building 25-F, pg. 757 **PB**
Green Foods Service Co., Ltd., 3-6-1 Ginza, Chuo-ku, pg. 848 **IT**
Grey Daiko Advertising, Inc., Grey Daiko Building, 2-3-30 Motoazabu, pg. 366 **IT**
Griffith Laboratories, K.K., NSS Building, 13-31, Kohnan 2-Chome, pg. 481 **PV**
Guerlain KK, Kiocho Park Bldg., 7th Fl., 3-6, Kioi-cho, pg. 780 **IT**
GUNZE SANGYO, INC., 3-1 Kudan Minami, pg. 578 **IT**
HSBC Asset Management Japan KK, 6/F, No. 2 Tomoecho Annex, 3-8-27 Tornomon, Minato-ku, pg. 582 **IT**
Haagen-Dazs Japan, Inc., Arco Tower, 18th Fl., 8-1, Shimomeguro 1-chome, pg. 409 **IT**
Hachette Filipacchi Japan, Daini Sakae Building, 2-11-14 Otawa, pg. 795 **IT**
Hakuhodo Capco, Inc., SEC Bldg., 13-3 Shibaura 3 chome, pg. 587 **IT**
Hakuhodo Corporate Sound Design Co., Ltd., 3-22, Kanda-Nishikicho, pg. 587 **IT**
Hakuhodo Creative & Development, Inc., Tokyo Bldg., 4-1, Shibaura 3 chome, pg. 588 **IT**
Hakuhodo Foods Services Co., Ltd., 4-44, Shibaura 4 chome, pg. 588 **IT**
Hakuhodo I.O. Co. Ltd., YK Bldg., pg. 588 **IT**
Hakuhodo Incentive Promotions Inc., YK Bldg., 4-44, Shibaura 4 chome, pg. 588 **IT**
HAKUHODO INCORPORATED, Gran Park Tower, 4-1, Shibaura 3 chome, pg. 587 **IT**
Hakuhodo Institute of Life and Living, 3-22, Kanda-Nishikicho, pg. 588 **IT**
Hakuhodo Lintas, Granpark Tower, 4-1, Shibaura 3-chome, pg. 587 **IT**
Hakuhodo Office Services Co., Ltd., YK Bldg. 4-44, Shibaura 4 chome, pg. 588 **IT**
Hakuhodo Photo Creative Inc., 3-22, Kanda Nishikicho, pg. 588 **IT**
Hakuhodo Pro's, Inc., 4th Fl., Sakura Yotsuya Bldg., pg. 588 **IT**
Hakuhodo Services Co., Ltd., SEc Bldg., 13-3, Shibaura 3 chome, pg. 588 **IT**
Hakushian Co., Ltd., 2-20-19, Akasaka, pg. 1262 **IT**
Handy & Harman International, Ltd., pg. 780 **PB**
Hanimex Vivitar Japan K.K., 2F Kobayashi Honten Bldg., 8-6 Sakura Shinmach 1-chome, pg. 1061 **IT**
HANWA CO., LTD., 1-13-10 1-chome, pg. 595 **IT**
Hanwa Co.-Tokyo Branch, New Hanwa Bldg., 1-13-10, Tsukjii, Chuo-ku, pg. 595 **IT**
Hapag-Lloyd (Japan) Ltd., pg. 596 **IT**
Harman Japan, Hinoki Bldg. 3F 1-5 Azabudai 3 Chome, pg. 787 **PB**
Harris Trust & Savings Bank, Mitsui Nigokan 1-1, Nihonbashi-Muromachi 2-Chome, pg. 154 **IT**
Haseko Community Inc., 4-6-6 Shiba, pg. 600 **IT**
HASEKO CORPORATION, 2-32-1, Shiba, pg. 599 **IT**
Haseko Livenet Inc., 3-11-10, Higashi, pg. 600 **IT**
Haseko Real Estate Inc., 2-32-1, Shiba, pg. 600 **IT**
Haseko Urban Co., 32-1, Shiba 2-chome, Minato-ku, pg. 600 **IT**
Haseko Urbest Inc., 2-32-1, Shiba, Minato-ku, pg. 600 **IT**
Heinemann Japan, Shin Nichibo Building, 1-2-1 Sarugaku-cho, pg. 1094 **IT**
Heinz Japan Ltd., Koraku Intl. Bldg., 10th Fl., 5-3 Koraku 1-Chome, pg. 806 **IT**
Helene Curtis Japan Inc., 24th Floor, Shinjuku Daiichi Seimei Bldg., 7-1, pg. 1434 **IT**
Henderson International Japan KK, Shiba Koen Bldg., 6F, 2-22-22 Shiba Koen, pg. 609 **IT**
Herbalife of Japan K.K., Kudan Vigas, 1-10-9 Kudan Kita, pg. 809 **IT**
Hercules Japan Ltd., Pola Aoyama Bldg., 5th Fl., 5-17, Minami Aoyama 2-chome, pg. 811 **PB**
Hershey Japan Co., Ltd., 30-6, Shimbashi 4-chome, pg. 812 **IT**
Hexcel, Far East, 22-1, Ichiban-cho Chiyoda-ku, pg. 824 **PB**
Hibari Kaihatsu Co., Ltd., 1-25-8, Nishikubo, pg. 1262 **IT**
Hibino Real Estate Ltd., 20-3, Nihonbashi-Kodenma-cho, pg. 1321 **IT**
Hills Colgate Japan Ltd., Kakihara Asahi Eita, Bldg. 7F, 3-7-13, pg. 399 **IT**
HINO MOTORS, LTD., 1-1 Hinadai 3-chome, pg. 620 **IT**
HIROSE ELECTRIC CO., LTD., 5-5-23 Osaki 5-chome Shinagawa, pg. 620 **IT**
THE HIROSHIMA BANK, LTD., 1-13-1 Nihonbashi, pg. 620 **IT**
Hitachi-Borden Chemical Products, Inc., CN-2, Bldg. 6-F, 8-3 Kiba 2-Chome, pg. 622 **IT**
Hitachi Cable, Ltd., Chiyoda Bldg., pg. 621 **IT**
Hitachi Chemical Co., Ltd., Shinjuku Mitsui Bldg., pg. 621 **IT**
Hitachi Construction Machinery Co., Ltd., Nippon Bldg., pg. 621 **IT**
Hitachi Denshi, 4-1, Okisudamach Bldg., pg. 621 **IT**
Hitachi Electronics Engineering Co., Ltd., Nippon Bldg., 2-6-2, Otemachi, pg. 621 **IT**

PB - U.S. Public Companies Volume
PV - U.S. Private Companies Volume
IT - International Public & Private Companies Volume

1682

Geographic Index-Non U.S.

HITACHI KOKI CO., LTD., Nippon Bldg., 2-6-2 Ohtemachi, Chiyoda-ku, pg. 620
HITACHI, LTD., 6, Kanda-Surugadai 4-chome, pg. 621
Hitachi Medical Corporation, Hitachi Kamakurabashi Bekkan, pg. 621   IT
Hitachi Metals, Ltd., Chiyoda Bldg., pg. 621   IT
Hitachi Sales Corp., ATGO Bldg., 2-15-12, Nishi-Shinbashi, pg. 621   IT
Hitachi Zonsen Tokyo, 7th Fl., Palaceside Bldg., 1-1, Hitotsubashi 1-chome, pg. 622   IT
Hitachi Zosen Systems, Inc, pg. 566   PB
HOCHIKI CORPORATION, 10-43, Kami-Osaki, 2-chome, pg. 623   IT
Hokkaido Colliery & Steamship Co., Ltd., 3-7, Nihonbashi-Muromachi 3-chome, pg. 877   IT
Hokkaido Snow Brand Sales Co., Ltd., 13, Honshio-cho, Shinjuku-ku, pg. 1272   IT
The Hokkaido Takushoku Securities Co., Ltd., 14-8 Nihombashi-Ningyocho, 1-chome, pg. 626   IT
The Hokuriku Bank, Ltd.-International Dept., 2-10, Nihonhashi Muromachi 3-chome, pg. 627   IT
Honda Access Sales Corp., pg. 634   IT
Honda Clio Shin Tokyo Co., Ltd., No. 21-19, 4-chome, Shimo-Ochiai, pg. 634   IT
Honda Finance Co., Ltd., pg. 634   IT
Honda International Sales Corp., No. 1-1, 2-chome Minamiaoyama, pg. 634   IT
Honda Leasing Corporation, pg. 634   IT
HONDA MOTOR CO., LTD., 1-1, 2-chome, Minami-Aoyama, pg. 634   IT
Honda Motor Parts Service Co., Ltd., No. 27-8, 6-chome Jingumae, Shibuya-ku, pg. 634   IT
Honda Sogo Tatemono Co., Ltd., No. 1-1, 2-chome, Minamiaoyama, pg. 634   IT
Honda Trading Corp., No. 6-20, 2-chome, Yaesu Chuou-ku, pg. 634   IT
Honeywell-Measurex Japan, Ltd., 14-6 Shibaura, pg. 833   PB
Hongkong International Trade Finance (Japan) KK, Ginza Daiwa Building, 11-1, Ginza 8-chome, Chuo-ku, pg. 583   IT
Hoogovens Aluminium Japan Ltd., Takoh Building, Kudan 10F, 8-5 Lidabashi 2-chome, pg. 755   IT
Hospal Ltd., Roppongi First Building, 1-9-9, Roppongi, pg. 668   IT
HSBC James Capel Japan Limited, 8/F, AIU Building, 1-3 Marunouchi 1-chome, pg. 582   IT
Hugo Boss K.K., pg. 638   IT
Huls Japan Ltd. Chemical Division, Bancho Fifth Building, 5-5 Nibancho, pg. 1455   IT
Humphrey Co., Ltd., pg. 1523   IT
Hydro Magnesium Japan Office, Morimura Bldg., 3-1 Toranomon 1 Chome, pg. 963   IT
Hydron Japan K.K., 1-14-18 Shironganedai Minato-ku, pg. 695   PB
I&S CORP., 3-5, Nihombashi-Muromachi, pg. 642   IT
IBJ NW Asset Management Co., Ltd., 1-6-1, Marunouchi, Chiyoda-ku, pg. 1485   IT
IBM Japan, Ltd., 2-12, Roppongi 3-chome, Minato-ku, pg. 897   PB
IBM Japan Sales Company, Ltd., 10-10, Utsubo Hon-cho 1-chome, pg. 897   PB
ICI Japan Limited, Palace Bldg. 1-1-1, Marunouchi, Chiyoda-ku, pg. 665   IT
IDD Co., LTD., Nipporiekimaechuo Bldg, 10F, 6-60-10, Higashi Nippori, pg. 1125   IT
IDG Communications Japan, 1-2-27 Fujimi, 102, pg. 570   PV
I.E.D. Co., Ltd., Iwanoto-cho Toyo Bldg., 1-2, Iwanoto-cho 3 chome, pg. 1321   IT
IGT-Japan K.K., Iijima Bldg., 2-25-2, Nishi-Gotanda, Shinagawa-ku, pg. 900   PB
IMC Associates, Inc., Ginsho Bldg., 14-11 Ginza 1-chome, pg. 834   IT
INA Life Insurance Co., Ltd., Shinjuku Center Bld., 48th Fl., 1-25-1 Nishi-Shinjuku, Shinjuku-ku, pg. 362   IT
ING Life Insurance Company, New Otano Garden Court 26Fl., pg. 650   IT
IPI Corporation, Juzen Bldg., 96, 2-chome Nagata-cho, pg. 906   PB
ITT Flygt Ltd., Sumitomo Bldg., Shinjuku-ku, pg. 860   PB
ITW Dynatec KK, Minato Bldg., 21-4 Hamamatsuchou, l-chome, pg. 868   PB
ITW Industry Co., Ltd., Micro-Poise Asia Division, 5-3, 3-chome, Higashi Rokugo Ota-ku, pg. 868   PB
Ibaragi Snow Brand Milk Co., Ltd., 13, Honshio-cho, Shinjuku-ku, pg. 1272   IT
Ichikoh Industries, Ltd., pg. 944   IT
IDEMITSU KOSAN CO., 1-1, Marunouchi 3-chome, pg. 659   IT
Igaku-Shoin MYW Ltd., 3-23-14 Hongo, Bunkyo-ku, pg. 1748   IT
IKEGAMI TSUSHINKI CO., LTD., 5-6-16, Ikegami, Ohta-ku, pg. 660   IT
Ikegami Tsushinki Co., Overseas Sales Div., 4-1-23 HeiwaJima, Ohta-ku, pg. 660   IT
Ilva Tokyo, Premier 22, 160 Shinjuku-ku, pg. 654   IT
Imation Corp. Japan, Setagaya Bus. Sq., 10-2, Youga, 4-chome, pg. 870   PB
Inchcape Dodwell K.K., No. 35 Kowa Bldg., 14-14 Akasaka, pg. 672   IT
Inco Limited, Japan Branch, Shin Muromachi Bldg., 4-7, pg. 672   IT
The Industrial Bank of Japan, Limited (Akasaka Branch), 1-22, Akasaka 8-chome, Minato-ku, pg. 674   IT
The Industrial Bank of Japan, Limited (Ikebukuro Branch), 12-1, Higashi-Ikebukuro 1-chome, pg. 674   IT
The Industrial Bank of Japan, Limited (Machida Branch), 13-15, Morino 1-chome, Machida, pg. 674   IT
The Industrial Bank of Japan, Limited (Nihonbashi Branch), 2-16, Yaesu, Chuo-ku, pg. 674   IT

The Industrial Bank of Japan, Limited (Shibuya Branch), 24-10, Shibuya 1-chome, Shibuya-ku, pg. 674   IT
The Industrial Bank of Japan, Limited (Shinjuku Branch), 17-1, Nishi-Shinjuku 1-chome, Shinjuku-ku, pg. 674   IT
THE INDUSTRIAL BANK OF JAPAN, LIMITED, 3-3, Marunouchi 1-chome, pg. 674   IT
The Industrial Bank of Japan, Limited (Tokyo Branch), 11-1, Marunouchi, Chiyoda-ku, pg. 674   IT
The Industrial Bank of Japan, Limited (Toranomon Branch), 17-1, Toranomon 3-chome, Minato-ku, pg. 674   IT
Ingersoll-Rand (Japan) Ltd., Kowa Bldg. 17, 2-7 Nishi-Azabu 1-Chome, pg. 878   PB
Integrated Device Technology, KK, Sumitomo Fudosan, Sanbancho Bldg., pg. 884   PB
Intel Japan, pg. 887   PB
Inter-Tel Japan, Inc., 3-18-20 Minamiaoyama, pg. 888   PB
Interleaf Japan Inc., Center Building, Tokanodanobba, 1-31-18, pg. 893   PB
Intermedics Japan K.K., pg. 1307   IT
International Business Division (Toyko), 1-1, Otemachi 2-chome, pg. 373   IT
The International Commercial Bank of China, 4-2, 1-chome, Marunouchi, pg. 683   IT
International Distillers Japan, Madera Roppongi Bldg., 2-14, Roppongi 4-chome, pg. 410   IT
International Division, pg. 1235   IT
International Flavors & Fragrances (Japan) Ltd., IFF Building, 21-4, Higashi-Oh, pg. 899   IT
International Learning Systems (Japan) Ltd., 1-7-1 Nishi-Shinjuku, Shinjuku-ku, pg. 222   IT
International Paper Company (Japan) Ltd., pg. 905   PB
International Public Relations Co. Ltd., Shinbashi Fuji Bldg., 2-1-3 Shinbashi, Minato-ku, pg. 1227   IT
International Rectifier Far East Company, Ltd., K & H Bldg., 3-30-4 Nishi-Ikebukuro, pg. 907   PB
ISHIKAWAJIMA-HARIMA HEAVY INDUSTRIES CO., LTD., 2-2-1, Otemachi, pg. 689   IT
ISUZU MOTORS LIMITED, 6-26-1, Minami-oi, pg. 692   IT
Italian Tomato Ltd., 5-16-22, Roppongi, Minato-ku, pg. 905   IT
ITO-YOKADO CO., LTD., 1-4, Shibakoen 4-chome, pg. 693   IT
Itochu Cable T.V. Eng. Corp., 2-5-1 Kita Aoyma, pg. 1443   PB
ITOCHU CORPORATION, 5-1, Kita-Aoyama 2-chome, pg. 694   IT
ITOHAM FOODS INC., 1-6-21 Mita Meguro-ku, pg. 695   IT
Itoham Foods Inc., 1-6-21, Mita, pg. 695   IT
JAE Engineering, Ltd., 1-1, Musahino 3-chome, pg. 701   IT
JAE Foods, Ltd., 1-1, Musashino 3-chome, pg. 701   IT
JAE Services, Ltd., 1-1, Musashino 3-chome, pg. 701   IT
JCB INTERNATIONAL CO., LTD., 1-6, Kanda-Saragadai Chiyodaka, pg. 966   IT
JDAC, 303 Yotsuya Mansion, 1-22 Arakicho, Shinjuku-ku, pg. 1065   PV
JEOL, 3-1-2, Musashino, Akishima City, pg. 696   IT
JGC CORPORATION, New Ohtemachi Bldg., 2-1, pg. 697   IT
JT International Corp., 2-1, Toranomon 2-chome, pg. 703   IT
JTB Air Cargo Inc., 3-6 Minami-Shinagawa 2-Chome, pg. 1120   PV
Jacobs Suchard Japan Co., Ltd., pg. 1289   PB
JANOME SEWING MACHINE CO., LTD., 1-1 Kyobashi, 3-chome, Chuo-ku, pg. 699   IT
Janssen-Cilag K.K., Takanawadai Daiichi Semei, Bldg. 1-5, Higashi-Gotanda 3-chome, pg. 929   PB
Japan Acrylic Chemical Co., Ltd., Matsuoka Tamuracho Bldg., 22-10, Shinbashi 5-chome, pg. 1404   IT
JAPAN AIRLINES COMPANY, LTD., 4-11, Higashi-shinagawa 2 chome, pg. 699   IT
Japan Ajax Magnethermic Co. Ltd., 14-11,Ginze 4-chome, Chuo-ku, pg. 113   IT
Japan Alumoweld Co., Ltd., Okunomatsu Bldg., 31-16, pg. 662   IT
Japan Area, No. 2 Shuwa Shinbashi, Honcho, 3-2 Nihombashi Ohdemmacho, pg. 281   PB
Japan Associated Finance Co., Ltd., 1-8-2, Marunouchi, pg. 955   IT
JAPAN AVIATION ELECTRONICS INDUSTRY, LTD., 21-2, Dogenzaka, 1- Chome, pg. 701   IT
The Japan Bond Research Institute, 2-6-1 Kayabacho, pg. 929   IT
Japan Business Services Co., Ltd., 2-18, 1-chome, Nihonbashi-Kayabacho, pg. 702   IT
Japan CBM Corporation, 1-48, 1-Chome, Okubo, Shinjuku-ku, pg. 294   IT
THE JAPAN DEVELOPMENT BANK, 9-1 Otemachi 1-Chome, pg. 701   IT
Japan Encore Computer, Inc., 1st Fl., NKK Bldg., 18-2, Nishi Shinbashi 2-chome, pg. 580   PB
JAPAN ENERGY CORPORATION, 10-1 Toranomon, 2-chome, pg. 702   IT
Japan Fawick Co., Ltd., Shinjuku Mitsui Bldg., Mail Box 225, pg. 559   PB
Japan Gamma Asset Management Ltd, 1-5-2 Hatchobori, pg. 343   IT
Japan Information Processing Service Co. Ltd., 6-7 Nihonbashi-Kabutocho, pg. 702   IT
Japan International Enterprises, Inc., Hamamatsuco TS. Bldg. 9F, 8-14. 2-Chome, Hamamatsucho, pg. 1282   IT
Japan Lutravil Company, pg. 507   IT
Japan Marine Technologies Ltd., 5th Florr, Sigma Building, 3-7-12 Shibaura, pg. 1339   IT
Japan NUS Co., Ltd., 16th Floor, 7-1 Mishi, Shinjuku 2-chome, pg. 777   IT
Japan Pharmacia & Upjohn Limited, Sumitomo Bldg., pg. 1049   IT

Japan Polychem Corp., Palace Side Bldg., No.1-1, 1-chome, pg. 871   IT
Japan Securities Agents, Ltd., 2-14, 1-chome, pg. 702   IT
JAPAN SECURITIES FINANCE CO. LTD., 2-10, 1-chome, Nihonbashi-Kayabacho, pg. 702   IT
Japan Servo Co., Ltd., Kanda Daini Chuo Bldg., 7, pg. 622   IT
The Japan Steel Works, Ltd., Hibiya Mitsui Bldg., 1-2, Yurakucho 1-chome, Chiyoda-ku, pg. 878   IT
JAPAN STORAGE BATTERY CO., LTD., 8-1 Nishikshinbashi, 1-chome, pg. 702   IT
Japan Systems Corporation, Shinjuku, pg. 1403   IT
The Japan Times, Inc., Nifco Building, 4-5-4 Shibaura, pg. 928   IT
JAPAN TOBACCO INC., 2-1, Toranomon 2-chome, pg. 703   IT
Japan Vilene Company Ltd., pg. 507   IT
Japan Visual-Soft Network Co., 22, Kanda-Nishikicho, 3-chome, pg. 588   IT
Jardine Fleming Investment Advisers (Japan) Limited, Yamato Seimei Bldg., 2nd Fl., 1-7 Uchisaiwai-cho 1-chome, pg. 494   IT
Jardine Fleming Securities Limited, Yamato Seimei Bldg., 8th Fl., 1-7 Uchisaiwai-cho 1-chome, pg. 494   IT
Jardine Matheson K.K., Nisseki Honkan, 3rd Floor, 3-12 Nishi-Shinbashi 1-chome, pg. 705   IT
Jardine Wines & Spirits K.K., Ryuen Bldg., 3-1, Shiba Koen 1-chome, pg. 782   IT
JAX Ltd., pg. 1475   IT
Jefferies (Japan) Limited Tokyo Branch, Sumitomo Fudosan Hitotsubashi, Bldg. 7F, 3-29-1 Kanda-Jimbocho, pg. 925   IT
Johnson & Johnson K.K., 3-2 Toyo 6-chome, pg. 930   PB
Johnson & Johnson Medical K.K., 3-2 Toyo 6-chome, pg. 931   PB
Jonas & Co., Ltd., 1-6-14, Nishikubo, pg. 1262   PB
JUKI CORPORATION, 8-2-1 Kokryo-Cho, pg. 716   IT
K.G. System Construction Co., Ltd., pg. 763   IT
K-Lea Co. Ltd., 2-22-15 Minamiaoyama, pg. 317   PB
"K" LINE (KAWASAKI KISEN KAISHA, LTD.), Hibiya Central Bldg., 2-9, Nishi-Shinbashi 1-chome, pg. 726   IT
KAO CORPORATION, 14-10, Nihonbashi Kayabacho 1-chome, pg. 717   IT
KCK Co., Ltd., 8th Fl., Kobussha Bldg., 1631 Ikebukuro, 3-chome, pg. 875   IT
KLA Acrotec Company, Ltd., 20-16 Hikawadai, pg. 939   PB
KLA Japan, Ltd., Endo Dai-Ni Building, 1-3-11 Akebono-Cho, pg. 939   PB
KS Olympus Co., Ltd., pg. 1004   IT
KSB Ltd., pg. 721   IT
KAJIMA CORPORATION, 2-7, Motoakasaka 1-chome, pg. 721   IT
Kali-Duphar K.K., Ginza Wall Bldg., 8th Fl., 1316 Ginza 6-chome, pg. 1279   IT
Kamyr KK, 13-4, Shiba 2-chome, pg. 771   IT
Kanebo C fest Moii, Ltd., 3-2-20 Kaigan, pg. 722   IT
Kanebo Cosmetics, Head Office, 3-20-20 Kaigan, pg. 722   IT
Kanebo Cosmetie Co., Ltd., Kanebo Bldg. 9F, 3-2-20 Kaigan, pg. 722   IT
Kanebo Cosmillion, Ltd., Kanebo Bldg., 8F, 3-2-20 Kaigan, pg. 722   IT
Kanebo Elegance Family, Ltd., Kanebo Bldg. 5F, 3-20-20 Kaigan, pg. 722   IT
Kanebo Foods Co., Ltd., 1-42-13 Itabashi, pg. 722   IT
Kanebo Home Products Co., Ltd., Head Office, Kanebo Bldg. 7F, pg. 722   IT
KANEBO, LTD., The Kanebo Building, 20-20, Kaigan 3-chome, pg. 722   IT
Kanebo Pharmaceuticals Co., Ltd., Kanebo Bldg. 6F, 3-2-20 Kaigan, pg. 722   IT
KANEMATSU CORPORATION, SEAVANS NORTH, 2-1 Shibaura 1-chome, pg. 722   IT
Kanthal KK, pg. 724   IT
Kasai Paint Co., Ltd., 24-15, pg. 723   IT
Kawaguchiko Country Club Co., Ltd., 3-6-1 Ginza, Chuo-ku, pg. 848   IT
Kawasaki Heavy Industries, Ltd. (Tokyo), World Trade Center Bldg., 4-1, Hamamatsu-cho 2-chome, pg. 725   IT
KAWASAKI KISEN KAISHA, LTD., Hibiya Central Building, 2-9, Nishi-shinbashi 1-chome, pg. 726   IT
KAWASAKI STEEL CORPORATION, Hibiya Kokusai Bldg., 2-3, Uchi Saiwaicho, 2-chome, pg. 726   IT
KAWASHO CORPORATION, 2-7-1 Otemachi, pg. 726   IT
KAYABA INDUSTRY CO., LTD., World Trade Center Building, 2-4-1, Hamamatsu-cho, Minato-ku, pg. 727   IT
Kayaku-Noury K.K., c/o Nippon Kayaku Co. KK, Tokyo Fujimi Bldg., 11-12 Fujimi-cho, pg. 47   IT
Kellogg (Japan) K.K., Shinjuku Nomura Bldg., P.O. Box 3030, pg. 948   PB
Kemira-Ube Ltd., Ube Bldg., 3-11, Higashi-shinagawa 2-chome, pg. 728   IT
Kennametal Hertel Japan Ltd., Taiyo-Asakusabashi Bldg., 2-6-2, Yanagibashi, pg. 951   PB
Kentucky Fried Chicken Japan Ltd., Suyama Bldg., 8th Fl., 1-1-1 Ebisu Minam, pg. 1637   IT
Kenwood Agency Corporation, 16-7, Aobadai 3-chome, pg. 730   IT
Kenwood Business Corporation, 14-6, Dogenzaka 1-chome, pg. 730   IT
Kenwood Core Corporation, 16-7, Aobadai 3-chome, pg. 730   IT
KENWOOD CORPORATION, 14-6, Dogenzaka 1-chome, pg. 730   IT
Kenwood Engineering Corporation, 6-17, Aobadai 3-chome, pg. 730   IT
Kenwood Personnel Corporation, 16-7, Aobadai 3-chome, pg. 730   IT

PB - *U.S. Public Companies Volume*
PV - *U.S. Private Companies Volume*
IT - *International Public & Private Companies Volume*

1683

Geographic Index-Non U.S.

Kenwood Precision Corporation, 21-5, Ogawahigashi 1-chome, pg. 730 — IT

Kenzo Paris K.K., 6, 17, 15 Shimomeguro, Meguro-ku, pg. 782 — IT

KEPCO Tokyo Office, 23-5, 3 Chome Nishishimbashi Minato-Ku, pg. 758 — IT

KIBUN CO. LTD., 14-13 Ginza 7-chome, pg. 733 — IT

KINTETSU WORLD EXPRESS, INC., 3-6 Ohte-machi, 2-chome, pg. 734 — IT

KIRIN BREWERY CO., LTD., 10-1, Shinkawa 2-chome, pg. 735 — IT

Kiryu Industry Co., Ltd., Subaru Bldg. 7-2, Nishishinjuku 1-chome, pg. 523 — IT

Kleinwort Benson International Inc., 810 Kokusai Bldg., 1-1 Marunouchi, 3-chome, Chiyoda-ku, pg. 420 — IT

Kleinwort Benson Investment Management KK, 930 Kokusai Bldg., 1-1 Marunouchi, 3-Chome, pg. 420 — IT

Knoll Japan K.K., Hokuriku Seiyaku Bldg., 8F, pg. 108 — IT

Kodak Far East Purchasing Co. Inc., Gotenyama Mori Bldg., 4-7-35 Kita-Shinagawa, pg. 552 — PB

Kodak Imagica K.K. (KI), Gotenyama Mori Bldg., 4-7-35 Kita-Shinagawa, pg. 555 — PB

K.K. Kodak Information Systems (KKKIS), Gotenyama Mori Bldg., 4-7-35 Kita-Shinagawa, pg. 552 — PB

Kodansha International Ltd, 17-14 Otowa 1-chome, Bunkyo-ku, pg. 742 — IT

KODANSHA LTD., 12-21, Otowa 2 chome, pg. 742 — IT

Kodansha Scientific Ltd., Nisho Bldg. 4F, 9-25 Shin-Ogawa-Cho, pg. 742 — IT

KOITO MANUFACTURING CO., 4-8-3 Takanawa, pg. 743 — IT

KOKUSAI ELECTRIC CO., LTD., C-14-20 Higasi Nakano, pg. 743 — IT

KOMATSU LTD., Komatsu Building, 2-3-6 Akasaka, pg. 743 — IT

KOMORI CORPORATION, 3-11-1, Azumabashi 3-chome, pg. 745 — IT

Komori Realty Co., Ltd., 11-1, Azumabashi, 3-chome, Sumida-ku, pg. 745 — IT

KONAMI CO. LTD., 4-3-1 Toranomon, pg. 745 — IT

Konami Computer Entertainment Japan Co., Ltd., 20-3, Ebisu 4-chome, pg. 745 — IT

Konami Computer Entertainment Roppongi Co., Ltd., 4-30, Roppongi 1-chome, pg. 745 — IT

Konami Computer Entertainment Tokyo Co., Ltd., 3-25, Kanda Jimbocho, pg. 745 — IT

Konami Computer Games Aoyama Co., Ltd., 1-1, Minami-Aoyama, pg. 746 — IT

Konami Finance Co., Ltd., 3-1, Toranomon 4-chome, pg. 746 — IT

Konami Kosan Co., Ltd., 3-25, Kanda Jimbocho, pg. 746 — IT

Konami Music Entertainment Co., Ltd., 20-3, Ebisu 4-chome, pg. 746 — IT

Konami Parlor Entertainment Co., Ltd., 4-30, Roppongi 1-chome, pg. 746 — IT

KONE Japan Co. Ltd., Yz Building 7F, 4-4-12 Iidabashi, Chuyoda-ku, pg. 747 — IT

KONICA CORPORATION, Nomura Bldg., #26-2, Nishi-Shinjuku, 1-Chome, pg. 748 — IT

Konica Tokyo Industrial Center Hachioji, 2970 Ishikawacho, pg. 748 — IT

Konica Tokyo Industrial Center Hino, 1 Sakuramachi, pg. 748 — IT

Korn/Ferry International, AIG Bldg. 7th Fl., 1-3 Marunounchi 1-Chome, pg. 633 — PV

Koshin-Knorr Ltd., 12-3, Nukui 3-chome, pg. 738 — IT

KOSUGI SANGYO CO. LTD., 2-8-5 Horidome-cho, pg. 759 — IT

Kotobuki Corporation - International Division, 22-5, 1-chome, Sumitomo Seimei Bldg. 3/F, pg. 759 — IT

KOTOBUKI SEATING CO., 2-3-3 Shibokouen, pg. 759 — IT

Krautkramer-Foerster Japan Co., Ltd., Shintaisho Bldg. No. 3, 12-10 Dogenzaka-2-chome, Shibuya-Ku, pg. 577 — IT

Kubota Corp.-Tokyo Office, 3-1-3, Nihonbashi-Muromachi, 3-chome, pg. 762 — IT

Kulicke & Soffa (Japan), Ltd., No. 5, Koike Bldg., 3rd Fl., 1-3-12 Kita-Shinagawa, pg. 969 — PB

KUMAGAI GUMI CO., LTD., 2-1 Tsukudo-cho, pg. 763 — IT

Kure-Norton Co., Ltd., 1-5, 2-Chome, pg. 1174 — IT

Kvaerner Pulping KK, Mita 43 Mori Bldg., 16F, pg. 768 — IT

KYODO ADVERTISING CO., LTD., Hibiya Chunichi Bldg., 2-1-4 Uchisaiwai-cho, pg. 776 — IT

Kyodo Building Corporation, 6-4-4 Ginza, Chuo-ku, pg. 1403 — IT

Kyodo Mortgage Acceptance Co., Ltd., 1-7, Nihonbashi, Hon-cho, 2-chome, pg. 82 — IT

Kyodo TDI Limited Company, 2-5 Kasumigaseki 3-chome, pg. 1219 — PB

Kyodoh Haisoh Co., Ltd., 3-6-1 Ginza, Chuo-ku, pg. 848 — IT

The Kyoei Annuity Home Co., Ltd., 4-4-1 Hongoku-cho, pg. 776 — IT

Kyoei Kasai Business Service Co., Ltd., 18-6 Shimbashi 1-chome, pg. 777 — IT

Kyoei Kasai Claims Research Co., Ltd., 18-6 Shimbashi 1-chome, pg. 777 — IT

Kyoei Kasai Finance Co., Ltd., 18-6 Shimbashi 1-chome, pg. 777 — IT

Kyoei Kasai Investment Management Co., Ltd., 18-6 Shimbashi 1-chome, pg. 777 — IT

Kyoei Kasai Marine Service Co., Ltd., 18-6 Shimbashi 1-chome, pg. 777 — IT

Kyoei Kasai Training Center Management Co., Ltd., 18-6 Shimbashi 1-chome, pg. 777 — IT

Kyoei Kasai Training Service Co., Ltd., 18-6 Shimbashi 1-chome, pg. 777 — IT

THE KYOEI LIFE INSURANCE CO., LTD., 4-4-1 Hongoku-cho, pg. 776 — IT

Kyoei Loan Management Service Co., Ltd., 18-6 Shimbashi 1-chome, pg. 777 — IT

THE KYOEI MUTUAL FIRE & MARINE INSURANCE COMPANY, 18-6, 1-chome, Shimbashi, pg. 777 — IT

Kyoe Real Estate Co., Ltd., 18-6 Shimbashi 1-chome, pg. 777 — IT

Kyokuto Petroleum Industries Ltd., 7-2, Ohtemachi 1-chome, pg. 877 — IT

KYOKUYO CO. LTD., 2-1-2, Marunouchi, pg. 777 — IT

KYOTARU CO., LTD., 1-36-9, Nihonbashi-Kakigaracho, pg. 777 — IT

KYOWA HAKKO KOGYO COMPANY, LTD., 1-6-1 Ohtemachi Bldg., pg. 778 — IT

Kyowa Takken Kaihatsu Co., Ltd., pg. 763 — IT

Kyushu Electric Power Co., 7-1, Yurakucho 1-chome, pg. 778 — IT

LEC, Inc., 5-2-7 Koishikawa, pg. 929 — IT

LGT Asset Management Ltd., 3rd Fl., Kiocho Kelton Bldg., 4-5 Kiocho, pg. 810 — IT

LM Ericsson International AB Japan, Sweden Center Bldg., 11-9 Roppongi 6-Chome, pg. 1368 — IT

LSI Logic K.K., 4-1-8 Konan, pg. 971 — PB

LTCB International Leasing Co., Ltd., 1-2-4, Otemachi, pg. 816 — IT

LTCB Investment Management Co., Ltd., 1-2-4, Otemachi, pg. 816 — IT

LTCB Research Institute, Inc., 1-2-4, Otemachi, pg. 816 — IT

LTCB Securities Co., Ltd., 1-2-4, Otemachi, pg. 816 — IT

LTCB Consulting, Inc., 5-31-19, Shiba, pg. 816 — PB

LTX Co., Ltd., 3-4-57 Hisamoto, Tokatsu-Ku, pg. 972 — PB

LVMH- Moet Hennessy Louis Vuitton (Japan) KK, Sumitomo Hanzomon Bldg., 3-16 Hayobusa-cho, Chiyoda-ku, pg. 782 — IT

La Reine, Ltd., Kanebo Bldg. 9F, 3-2-20 Kaigan, pg. 722 — IT

Labinal Kabushiki Kaisha, Tohsei Building 4F, 3-8-2 Nichi-Shimbashi, pg. 786 — IT

Labinal Kabushiki Kaisha, Tohsei Bldg. 4F, 3-8-2 Nishi-Shimbashi, pg. 787 — IT

Landis & Staefa Japan Co., Ltd., Ebisu IS Bldg., 1-13-6 Ebisu Shibuya-ku, pg. 801 — IT

Le Carbone K.K., Shinjuku-ku Mitaui Bldg., 42nd Fl., pg. 1030 — IT

LeaRonal Japan Inc., 14-5, Nihonbashi-Bakurocho 1-chome, pg. 982 — PB

Lederle (Japan) Ltd., Hattori Bldg. 5th Flr., 1-10-3 Kyobashi, pg. 81 — PB

Lemo Japan, Kada-Yushima Bldg., Yushima 3-14-8, pg. 806 — PB

Letraset Japan Ltd., Sugita Building 6F, 6-5, Higashiyama 1-chome, pg. 462 — IT

Lion Akzo Co. K.K., 2-26 Yokoami 1-chome, pg. 47 — IT

Lion Henkel Corporation, 1-3-7, Honjo, pg. 614 — IT

Arthur D. Little (Japan), Inc., Fukide Bldg.,4-1-13 Toranomon, pg. 671 — PV

Litton-Westrex Company, Japan, Chiyoda Bldg. 2-1-2, Marunouchi, pg. 1046 — IT

Lockheed Aircraft (Asia) Ltd., Akasaka Twin Tower, 15th Fl., E., 2-17-22 Akasakam Minato-ku, pg. 1009 — IT

Loewe Japan K.K., Shin Aoyama Bldg., 1-1-1 Minami Aoyama, Minato-ku, pg. 782 — IT

THE LONG-TERM CREDIT BANK OF JAPAN, LIMITED, 1-8 Uchisaiwaicho, 2-chome, pg. 815 — IT

Longman Penguin Japan Co. ltd., Gyokureon Bldg., 1-13-19 Sekiguchi, Bunkyo-ku, pg. 1025 — PV

Lonza Japan Ltd., Tsujiki MF Bldg., 12-10, Tsukiji 2-chome, pg. 69 — IT

Lord Far East, Inc., 2F, Yoyogi Center Bldg., pg. 676 — PV

L'Oreal Japan Ltd., Masonic 39 Mori Bldg. 4-5, pg. 819 — IT

LOTTE COMPANY LTD., 3-20-1 Nishi Shinjuku-ku, pg. 819 — IT

Lotte Ice Cream Corp. Ltd., 2-3-6, Kyobashi, Chuo-ku, pg. 819 — IT

Lotus Development Japan Limited, Toranomon MF Bldg. No. 10, 3-10-11, Toranomon, pg. 896 — PB

Louis Vuitton Japan K.K., Shin Aoyama Bldg., W. 7th Fl., 1-1-1- Minami Aoyama, pg. 782 — IT

Lubrizol Japan Ltd., Toranomon 37 Mori Bldg., Eigth Fl., 5-1 Toranomon 3-Chome, pg. 1016 — IT

Lucent Technologies Semiconductor Marketing, Ltd., Sowa Gotando Bldg., 7-18, Higashi-Gatanda 2-Chrome, pg. 900 — IT

Lucent Technologies Semiconductor Marketing, Ltd., Sowa Gotando Bldg., 7-18, Higashi-Gatanda 2-Chrome, pg. 1019 — PB

Lucidol Yoshitomi Ltd., 955 Aza-Takahama, pg. 446 — IT

Lucky Goldstar-Honeywell Co. Ltd., 18th Fl., Kukje Center Bldg., 2-12-19 Shibuya-ku, pg. 835 — IT

Lummus-Japan Co. Ltd., 5-29 Akasaka, 8-chome, Minato-ku, pg. 6 — IT

Lumonics Pacific KK, P.O. Box 29, Nishi-Yubinkyoku, pg. 1315 — PB

Lydall International, Inc., Comodo Nishi-Azabu Bldg., 25-22, Nishi-Azabu 2-Chome, pg. 1021 — PB

MAN B & W Japan Ltd., pg. 824 — IT

MC BITOR Limited, New Pier Takeshiba, Noth Tower, 23rd Fl., pg. 1046 — IT

MDA Pacific, pg. 618 — IT

MSA Japan Ltd., 15-21 Roppongi 6-Chome, pg. 1115 — PB

MSC Japan Ltd., Entsuiji-Gadelius Bldg., 2-39, Akasaka 5-chome, pg. 1032 — PB

MTel International (Tokyo), 20-7 oi, 6-chome, pg. 1120 — PB

MTS Japan Ltd. (Tokyo), Jidosha Kaikan, 4-8-13 Kudan Minami, pg. 1029 — PB

MTV Japan, 6F Tango 33 Bldg. 3-25-11, pg. 779 — PV

MYU Planning and Operations Inc., 4-2, Moto Akasaka 1-chome, pg. 1321 — IT

MacGregor Golf (Japan) Ltd., Administration Office:, No 11 Mori Building 2-6-4, pg. 73 — IT

MacGregor Kayaba Ltd., 65 Tanaka Bldg., 2-1-25 Shiba, pg. 671 — IT

MacMillan Bloedel K. K., Sumitomo Toranomon Bldg. 6F, 6-12, Toranomon 1-chome, pg. 829 — IT

Macworld Communications Japan, Inc., 2F Shuwa Fujimicho Bldg., 1-2-27 Fujimi, Chiyoda-ku, pg. 570 — PV

MAKINO MILLING MACHINE CO. LTD., 3-19, Nakane 2-chome, pg. 831 — IT

Makita Corporation-Tokyo Branch, 3-5-3, Hongo, pg. 831 — IT

Man Nen Sha, Inc., 9-12 Ginza 1-chome, pg. 834 — IT

Manville Japan Ltd., Toranomon Asahi Bldg., 1-11-13, Nishi-Shinbashi, pg. 927 — PB

Marquette Electronics, Inc., Asia Pacific District, pg. 1047 — PB

Martin Marietta International, Inc., Kowa Bldg. No. 35, 5th Fl., 14-14 Akasaka, 1-Chome, pg. 1009 — PB

Marubeni Plasma Technik Co. Ltd., pg. 1307 — IT

MARUHA CORPORATION, 1-2, 1-chome, Otemachi, pg. 845 — IT

Maruzen Bookmates Co., Ltd., Shinkojimachi Bldg., 7th Fl., 4-3 Kojimachi, Chiyoda-ku, pg. 846 — IT

MARUZEN COMPANY LIMITED, P.O. Box 5050, pg. 845 — IT

Maruzen System Service Co., Ltd., Teiyo Bldg, 4th Fl., 2-3-10 Higashi Kanda, pg. 846 — IT

Mary Kay Cosmetics (Japan) K.K., Tokaido Ginza Bldg 7F, 6-4-1 Ginza, pg. 711 — PV

Matsushita Electric Works, Ltd.- Tokyo, 8-2, Shiba 4-chome, pg. 847 — IT

Matsushita Electronic Components Co., Ltd., 1-2, Shiba Koen, 1-chome, pg. 846 — IT

Matsushita Graphic Communication Systems, Inc., 3-8, Shimo Meguro 2-chome, Meguro-ku, pg. 846 — IT

Matsuya Asakusa, 4-1, Hanakawado 1-chome, pg. 848 — IT

MATSUYA COMPANY LTD., 3-6-1 Ginza, Chuo-ku, pg. 848 — IT

Matsuya Engineering Service Co., Ltd., 3-6-1 Ginza, Chuo-ku, pg. 848 — IT

Matsuya Fashion Service Co., Ltd., 3-6-1 Ginza, Chuo-ku, pg. 848 — IT

Matsuya Ginza, 6-1, Ginza 3-chome, pg. 848 — IT

Matsuya Shoji Co., Ltd., 3-6-1 Ginza, Chuo-ku, pg. 848 — IT

Matsuya Travel Service, 3-6-1 Ginza, Chuo-ku, pg. 848 — IT

Max Factor K.K., Daichi Seijitsu Bldg. 12-3, Nishi Gotanda 2-chome, pg. 1331 — PB

McCain Foods (Japan) Limited, Bois Hongo Building, 3-42-5 Hongo, Bunko-ku, pg. 850 — PB

McCormick-Lion Ltd., No. 3-7, 1 Chome, Honjo, pg. 1067 — IT

McGraw-Hill Publishing Co.-Japan Ltd., 77 Bldg., 4-14-11, Ginza, 104, pg. 1072 — IT

McGregor Golf Japan Ltd., San Toranomon Bldg., 22-17 Toranomon 1-chome, pg. 1321 — IT

Mead KK, 2-3, Hamamatsu cho, 1-chome, pg. 1076 — PB

Medicom Co., Ltd., pg. 1121 — IT

Medtronic Japan Co., Ltd., Shuwa Kioi-cho Park Bldg., 5th Floor, 3-6 Kioi-cho, pg. 1084 — IT

Meiji Baking Co., Ltd., 2-4-16 Kyobashi, pg. 855 — IT

Meiji Chewing Gum Co., Ltd., 2-4-16 Kyobashi, pg. 855 — IT

Meiji Engineering Co., Ltd., 2-4-16 Kyobashi, pg. 855 — IT

Meiji Frozen Dessert Corp., 2-4-16 Kyobashi, pg. 855 — IT

Meiji Information System Center Ltd., 2-4-16 Kyobashi, pg. 855 — IT

Meiji Jewelry, 2-4-16 Kyobashi, pg. 855 — IT

Meiji Kosan Corp., Ltd., 2-4-16 Kyobashi, pg. 855 — IT

MEIJI LIFE INSURANCE COMPANY, 2-1-1, Marunouchi, Chiyodaku, pg. 854 — IT

Meiji-McVitie, Ltd., 2-4-16 Kyobashi, pg. 855 — IT

MEIJI MILK PRODUCTS CO., LTD., 2-3-6 Kyobashi, 2-Chome, pg. 855 — IT

Meiji Sangyo Co., Ltd., 2-4-16 Kyobashi, pg. 855 — IT

MEIJI SEIKA KAISHA, LTD., 2-4-16 Kyobashi, pg. 855 — IT

Meiji Shokuhin Co., Ltd., 2-4-16 Kyobashi, pg. 855 — IT

Meiji Trading Corp., 2-4-16 Kyobashi, pg. 855 — IT

Meika Kosan Co., Ltd., 2-4-16 Kyobashi, pg. 855 — IT

Meito Warehouse Co., Ltd., 2-4-16 Kyobashi, pg. 855 — IT

MEITSU INC., 1-1-3, Nishi-shimbashi, pg. 856 — IT

Meiwa Trading Co., 3-3-1 Marunouchi, pg. 871 — IT

Memorex Telex Japan Ltd., Shiba park A-Bldg., 2-4-1, Shiba-Koen, pg. 857 — PB

Mentholatum Intl. Ltd., 802 Mori Bldg. No. 12, Nishikaido Sakuraguna, pg. 1126 — IT

Mentor Graphics Corporation, Asia Pacific Headquarters, Akasaka 2-chome Annex Bldg., pg. 1087 — PB

Mentor Graphics Japan Co., Ltd., Akasaka Twin Tower Bldg., 71-22, pg. 1087 — IT

Mercedes-Benz Japan Co., Ltd., Rappongi First Building, 3-11-15, Toranomon, Minato-ku, pg. 369 — IT

MERCIAN CORPORATION, 5-8, Kyobashi 1-chome, pg. 858 — IT

Merita Bank Ltd., Tokyo Representative Office, SF Kayabacho Bldg., 4th Fl., 10-5 Nihonbashi, pg. 859 — IT

Metallurg (Far East) Limited, P.O. Box 5221, Tokyo Int., pg. 735 — IT

Micron Technology Japan, K.K., Shiba Koen #32, Mori Building, pg. 1106 — PB

Micropolis Limited, Madre Matsuda Bldg. 3F-312, 4-13 Kioi-cho, Chiyoda-ku, pg. 743 — PV

Microsoft Company Limited, pg. 1108 — PV

Middleby Japan Corporation, Suntowers-B, 4F, 2-11-23 Sangenjaya, pg. 1110 — PB

K. MIKIMOTO & CO., LTD., 2-4-12 Ginza, pg. 866 — IT

MIKUNI CORPORATION, 13-11, Soto-kanda, 6-chome, pg. 867 — IT

Mikuni Industry Co., Ltd., 4-31-25 Nishinoujiya, pg. 999 — IT

Mikuni Shoko Corp., 11-5, Soto Kanda 1-chome, pg. 867 — IT

Mil Ltd., 1-2-21, Yaguchi, Ota-ku, pg. 905 — IT

Herman Miller Japan, Tokyo Design Center, 5th Floor, 5-25-19, pg. 1112 — PB

PB - U.S. Public Companies Volume
PV - U.S. Private Companies Volume
IT - International Public & Private Companies Volume

1684

Geographic Index-Non U.S.

Milton Roy (Japan) Ltd., Takanawa Dai-Ichi Bldg. 21-41, Takanawa, pg. 1534 **PB**
Minami-Hakone Dialand Co., Ltd., pg. 1024 **IT**
Minato Building Co., Ltd., 1-1-1 Shibaura, Minato-ku, pg. 1403 **IT**
MINEBEA CO., LTD., 19F Arco Tower, 1-8-1 Shimo, pg. 867 **IT**
Minebea Credit Co., Ltd., 9th Fl. Higashishinkanda Bldg., 14 Kanda, pg. 868 **IT**
Minemet Japan, Kokusai Shin Akasaka Bldg. West Bldg. 1-, pg. 661 **IT**
Mirari Japan Ltd., Aobadai Bldg., 8F 10-9 Aobadai 3-Chome, Meguro-ku, pg. 822 **IT**
Mitsubishi-Burlington Co., Daisho Bldg., Roppongi 13-chome, Minato-Ku, pg. 268 **PB**
MITSUBISHI CABLE INDUSTRIES, LTD., 3-4-1 Marunouchi, Chiyoda-ku, pg. 870 **IT**
MITSUBISHI CHEMICAL CORPORATION, 5-2, Marunouchi 2-chome, pg. 870 **IT**
Mitsubishi Chemical MKV Co., 1-23, Shiba 4-chome, pg. 871 **IT**
MITSUBISHI CORPORATION, 6-3, Marunouchi 2-chome, Chiyoda-ku, pg. 871 **IT**
MITSUBISHI ELECTRIC CORPORATION, Mitsubishi Denki Bldg., 2-3, Marunouchi 2-chome, pg. 872 **IT**
MITSUBISHI ESTATE CO., LTD., Tokyo Bldg., 7-3, Marunouchi, 2-chome, pg. 873 **IT**
Mitsubishi Estate Co., Ltd., 2-3-1 Marunouchi, pg. 873 **IT**
MITSUBISHI HEAVY INDUSTRIES LTD., 5-1 Marunouchi 2-chome, 72903, pg. 873 **IT**
MITSUBISHI LOGISTICS CORP., 1-19-1, Nihonbashi, pg. 874 **IT**
MITSUBISHI MATERIALS CORP., 5-1 Ohtemachi, pg. 874 **IT**
Mitsubishi Monsanto Chemical Co., Mitsubishi Bldg., 5-2, Marunouchi 2-chome, Chiyoda-ku, pg. 1125 **PB**
MITSUBISHI MOTORS CORPORATION, 33-8 Shiba 5-chome, pg. 875 **IT**
MITSUBISHI OIL CO. LTD., 6-41, Konan 1-chome, Minakto-ku, pg. 876 **IT**
MITSUBISHI RAYON CO., LTD., 2-3-19, Kyobashi, Chuo-ku, pg. 876 **IT**
Mitsubishi Real Estate Services Co., Ltd., 1-8-1 Yurakucho, pg. 873 **IT**
Mitsubishi Shindoh Co., Ltd., 1-6-2, Ginza, Chuo-ku, pg. 875 **IT**
THE MITSUBISHI TRUST AND BANKING CORPORATION, 4-5, Marunouchi 1-chome, pg. 876 **IT**
Mitsui Air & Sea Service Co., Ltd., Kyowa Shinbashi Bldg., 16-4, Shinbashi 1-chome, pg. 878 **IT**
Mitsui Aluminium Co., Ltd., Mitsui Bldg., 1, Nihonbashi-Muromachi, pg. 878 **IT**
MITSUI & CO., LTD., 2-1, Ohtemachi 1-chome, pg. 877 **IT**
Mitsui Coke Co., Ltd., 1-1, Nihonbashi-Muromachi 2-chome, pg. 877 **IT**
Mitsui Concrete Industries Co., Ltd., 10-1, Uchi-Kanda 1-chome, pg. 877 **IT**
Mitsui Construction Co., Ltd., 10-1, Iwamoto-cho 3-chome, pg. 877 **IT**
Mitsui Consultants Co., Ltd., 3-7, Nihonbashi-Muromachi 3-chome, pg. 877 **IT**
Mitsui Engineering & Shipbuilding Co., Ltd., 5-6-4, Tsukiji, pg. 878 **IT**
MITSUI FUDOSAN CO., LTD., 1-1, Nihonbashi-Muromachi 2-chome, pg. 882 **IT**
Mitsui Harbour & Urban Construction Co., Ltd., 2-11, Nishi-Shinjuku 3-chome, pg. 877 **IT**
Mitsui Home Co., Ltd., Shinjuku Mitsui Bldg., 1-1, Nishi-Shinjuku 2-chome, pg. 877 **IT**
Mitsui Kanko Development Co., Ltd., 1-1, Nihonbashi-Muromachi, pg. 878 **IT**
Mitsui Knowledge Industry Co., Ltd., 7-4, Kojimachi 3-chome, pg. 878 **IT**
Mitsui Leasing & Development Ltd., Hibiya Central Bldg., 2-9, Nishi-Shinbashi 1-chome, pg. 878 **IT**
Mitsui Liquefied Gas Co., Ltd., 1-1, Kyobashi 1-chome, pg. 877 **IT**
Mitsui Lumber Co., Ltd., 4-14, Toyo 2-chome, pg. 877 **IT**
Mitsui Marine & Fire Insurance Co., Ltd., 9, Kanda-Surugadai, pg. 878 **IT**
Mitsui Miike Engineering Corporation, 1-1, Nihonbashi-Muramachi 2-chome, pg. 878 **IT**
Mitsui Miike Machinery Co., Ltd., 1-1, Nihonbashi-Muromachi, pg. 878 **IT**
Mitsui Mining & Smelting Co., Ltd., Mitsui Bldg., 1-1, Nihonbashi-Muromachi, pg. 878 **IT**
Mitsui Mining Co., Ltd., 1-1, Nihonbashi-Muromachi, pg. 878 **IT**
Mitsui Mutual Life Insurance Company, 2-3, Ohtemachi 1-chome, pg. 878 **IT**
Mitsui Norin Co., Ltd., 1-1, Nihonbashi-Muromachi, pg. 878 **IT**
Mitsui Ocean Development & Engineering Co., Ltd., 3-1, Hitotsubashi 2-chome, pg. 878 **IT**
Mitsui Oil Co., Ltd., 3, Kanda-Surugadai 4-chome, pg. 877 **IT**
Mitsui O.S.K. Lines, Ltd., 1-1, Toranomon 2-chome, Minato-ku, pg. 878 **IT**
Mitsui Petrochemical Industries, Ltd., 2-5, Kasumigaseki 3-chome, pg. 877 **IT**
Mitsui Pharmaceuticals, Inc., Asahi Bldg., 12-2, Nihonbashi 3-chome, pg. 877 **IT**
Mitsui Precon Co., Ltd., 8-13, Nihonbashi-Horidome 1-chome, pg. 877 **IT**
Mitsui Real Estate Development Co., Ltd., 1-1, Nihonbashi-Muromachi, pg. 878 **IT**
Mitsui Road Co., Ltd., 10-1, Iwamoto-cho 3-chome, pg. 877 **IT**
Mitsui Seiki Kogyo Co., Ltd., 3-7, Nihonbashi-Muromachi, pg. 878 **IT**

Mitsui Sugar Co., Ltd., 6-5, Nihonbashi-Honcho, pg. 878 **IT**
Mitsui Toatsu Chemicals, Inc., 2-5, Kasumigaseki 3-chome, pg. 877 **IT**
THE MITSUI TRUST AND BANKING COMPANY, LIMITED, 1-1, Muromachi 2-chome, pg. 882 **IT**
The Mitsui Warehouse Co., Ltd., 13-12, Nihonbashi-Kayabacho 1-chome, pg. 878 **IT**
MITSUKOSHI, LTD., 4-1, Nihombashi Muromachi, pg. 883 **IT**
MITSUMI ELECTRIC CO., LTD., 882, Kokuryo-cho, pg. 884 **IT**
Mizuno Corporation (Tokyo Head Office), 22, Kanda Ogawa-Machi 3-chome, pg. 885 **IT**
Mizuno Handy Harman, Ltd., 11-12 Kitaueno, 2-chome, pg. 780 **PB**
Mizusawa Industrial Chemicals, Ltd., 1-21, Nihonbashi-Muromachi 4-chome, pg. 1350 **IT**
Mobil Kabushiki Kaisha, pg. 1119 **IT**
Molex Far East Management Ltd. (North), 4-21-1 Minami-Naruse, pg. 1122 **PB**
Molex-Japan Co., Ltd., pg. 1122 **PB**
Monsanto Japan Ltd., Rm. 520, Kokusai Bldg., 1-1 Marunouchi 3-Chome, Chiyoda-ku, pg. 1126 **PB**
Moody's Japan KK, Imperial Tower, 13th Fl., pg. 537 **PB**
Moore Products Co. (Japan) K.K., 5F, Mikuni Bldg., 6-14, Shibaurg 3-chome, pg. 1129 **PB**
Morgan Grenfell International Asset Management Co. Ltd. (Tokyo), Hibiya Kokusai Bldg., 4th Flr., 2-3 Uchisaiwaicho 2-chome, pg. 406 **PB**
Morgan Grenfell Japan Limited, Hibiya Kokusai Bldg., 4th Flr., 2-3 Uchisaiwaicho 2-chome, pg. 406 **PB**
Morgan Guaranty Trust Company, Akasaka Park Bldg., 2-20 Akasaka 5-chome, pg. 1130 **PB**
J.P. Morgan Investment Management Inc., Akasaka Park Bldg., 2-20 Akasaka 5-chome, pg. 1131 **PB**
J.P. Morgan Securities Asia Ltd., Alaska Park Bldg., 2-20 Akasaka 5-chome, pg. 1131 **PB**
J.P. Morgan Trust Bank Ltd., Akasaka Park Bldg., 2-20 Aksasaka 5-chome, pg. 1131 **PB**
Morgan Stanley Japan Ltd., Yebisu Garden Place Tower, 20-3, Ebisu, 4-chome, pg. 1133 **PB**
Morimura Badische Co., Ltd., 7 Floor, Okamotoya Bldg., 1-1-24, Toranomon, Minato-ku, pg. 109 **IT**
MORINAGA MILK INDUSTRY CO., LTD., 33-1, Shiba 5-chome, pg. 895 **IT**
Morton International K.K., 1-Bandi, Kanda Mikura-cho, pg. 1135 **PB**
Munters KK, Utoku Tamachi Bldg. 13-7, Shibaura 2-chome, pg. 669 **PB**
Muromachi Chemicals Co., Ltd., Tokyo Oroshiuri Bldg., 10F, 7-22-17 Nishi-Gotanda, pg. 722 **PB**
Musashino-Geigy Co. Ltd., Yaesu-Daibiru Bldg., 1-1-1, Kyobashi, Chuo-ku, pg. 983 **IT**
MUTOH INDUSTRIES LTD., 3, Ikejiri, Setagaya-ku, pg. 897 **IT**
N&T Co., Ltd., Isomura Bldg., 1-1-3, Toranomon, Minato-ku, pg. 905 **IT**
ND Communications Co. Ltd., 15-6, Fuyuki, pg. 375 **IT**
NDC Tokyo Representative Office, Uchisaiwaicho Osaka Building, Room 702, pg. 1156 **PB**
N.E. Chemcat, World Trade Center, pg. 583 **PB**
NEC CORPORATION, 7-1, Shiba 5-chome, pg. 899 **IT**
NFE Co., Ltd., Nissan Edobashi Bldg., 10-5 Nihonbashi, Honcho 1-chome, pg. 620 **IT**
NHK Sales Co., Ltd, 2-chome, 13-1 Edagawa, pg. 902 **IT**
NI Steel Products Co., Ltd., 13-7 Nisiki-Cho 3-chome, pg. 944 **IT**
NJC Engineering, No. 3-5, Uchikanda 3-Chome, pg. 361 **PV**
NKK CORPORATION, 1-1-2 Marunouchi, pg. 902 **IT**
NKU Investment Management Co., Ltd., 2-1, Kyobashi 1-chome, pg. 958 **IT**
NLI Research Institute, 1-1, Yurakucho 1-chome, Chiyoda-ku, pg. 935 **IT**
NOF Jotun Co. Ltd., Marumo Building, 2nd Fl., 24 Kanda Sudacho, pg. 716 **PB**
NOK Corp., pg. 507 **IT**
NOK-Kluber Co. Ltd., pg. 507 **IT**
NOK-Megulastik Co. Ltd., pg. 507 **IT**
NSK CO., 6-3, Ohsaki, 1-Chome, Shinagawa-ku, pg. 903 **IT**
Nacional Financiera, 1-1 Marunouchi 3-Chome, pg. 904 **IT**
Nagase-Landauer, Ltd., Saimo Bldg., 9-8, Kobuna-Cho, pg. 977 **PB**
Nalco Japan Co., Ltd., Ngashi-Nihonbashi Sky Bldg 6F, 1-Chame, Chuo-Ku, pg. 1151 **PB**
NAMBOKUSHA INC., 2-1-21, Hatchobori, pg. 904 **IT**
Nambokusha Inc., World Import Mart Bldg., 3-1-3 Higashi-Ikebukuro, pg. 905 **IT**
NAMCO LTD., 2-1-21, Yaguchi, pg. 905 **IT**
Nanbu Sen-i Kogyo Co., Ltd., 2-8-5 Horidome-cho, Nihonbashi, pg. 759 **IT**
Nanometrics Japan Ltd., Shin-izumi 34, pg. 1151 **PB**
Nanto Bank-Tokyo Branch, 7-3, Marunouchi 2-chome, pg. 905 **IT**
National Bank of Pakistan-Tokyo, Mori Building No. 18, 3-13 2-chome, Toranomon, Minato-Ku, pg. 908 **IT**
National Mutual Funds Management (Japan) Limited, 6/f Urban Toranomon Bldg., 16-4 Toranomon, 1-chome, pg. 909 **IT**
National Westminster Bank Plc, Riverside Yomiuri Bldg., 36-2 Nihonbashi-Hakozakichio, pg. 911 **PB**
NationsBank (Japan), 601 Yurakucho Bldg., 10-1 Yura-cho, pg. 1166 **PB**
Nature's Sunshine K.K. (Japan), pg. 1166 **PB**
NatWest Investment Management Japan Limited, Riverside Yomiuri Bldg., 36-2 Nihonbashi-Hakozakichio, pg. 911 **IT**
Nedlloyd Lines K.K., pg. 1145 **IT**
Nemic-Lambda KK, 1-11-15 Higashigotanda, pg. 1242 **IT**

Nesco Ltd., 5-27-7 Sendagaya, Shibuya-ku, pg. 443 **IT**
Neste Chemicals (Japan) Co., Ltd., Nichito Hatsuchobori Bldg. 10F, 3-11-8, Hatsuchobori, pg. 914 **IT**
Nestle KK, Nihonbashi Toho Seimei Bldg., 4-10, Nihonbashi Muro-machi 4-chome, pg. 921 **IT**
Nestle-Mackintosh K.K., pg. 921 **IT**
New Zealand Milk Products (North Asia) Ltd, 13th Floor, Atago Toyo Building, pg. 923 **IT**
NewsEdge, Saida Building, 4-6, Kandasakuma-Cho, pg. 1180 **PB**
NextLevel Systems (Japan), 7th Fl., Eltz 6, pg. 716 **PB**
NICHIMEN CORPORATION, Mita NN Bldg., 1-23, Shiba 4-chome, pg. 927 **IT**
NICHIREI CORPORATION, Nichirei Higashi-Ginza Bldg., 6-19-20 Tsukiji, Chuo-Ku, pg. 928 **IT**
NICHIRO CORPORATION, 1-12-1, Yuraku-cho, Chiyoda-ku, pg. 928 **IT**
Nicolet Japan Corp.-Tokyo, Nishi-Shinjuku, Toyokuni Bldg. ZF, pg. 1594 **PB**
Nicotec Co., 15-12, Tamagawa Denechofu 1-chome, pg. 70 **PB**
A.C. Nielsen Co., 1-1-71 Nakameguro, pg. 1183 **PB**
Nihon Building Co., 2-4, 1-chome, Nihonbashi-Kayabacho, pg. 702 **IT**
Nihon Exabyte K.K., pg. 597 **IT**
Nihon Ferras, 1-26-30, 1 Chome Higashi, pg. 1031 **IT**
NIHON KEIZAI SHIMBUN, INC., 1-9-5 Otemachi, pg. 929 **IT**
Nihon Kenall K.K., Usada Building, 36-5 Hongo, 4 Chome, pg. 1648 **PB**
Nihon Kyoei Securities Co. Ltd., 2-18, 1-chome, pg. 702 **IT**
Nihon Microtec Research, Kamiuma Central 4-2-5, pg. 1087 **PB**
Nihon Millipore Ltd.-Yonezawa, Dai-5 Koike Bldg., pg. 1113 **PB**
Nihon MRC Co. Ltd., 4F, Maurzen Bldg.,No. 3, pg. 1283 **PB**
Nihon-Pall Ltd., Gotanda Nomura Shoken Bldg., 1-5-1 Nishi-Gotanda, pg. 1254 **PB**
Nihon Pharmaceutical Co., Ltd., 9-8, Higashikanda 1-chome, pg. 1350 **IT**
Nihon Sara Lee, Sumitomo RE Hibiya Bldg. 3F, 2-8-6 Nishi-Shinbashi, pg. 1434 **IT**
Nihon Seiko Co. Ltd., 2, Shimo-Miyabi 3-chome, pg. 947 **IT**
Nihon Shokuhin Kako Co., Ltd., 8 Fl. Shinkokusai Bldg., 4-1, Marunouchi 3-chome, pg. 447 **IT**
Nihon Shortwave Broadcasting Co., Ltd., 1-9-15 Akasaka, pg. 929 **IT**
Nihon Silicon Graphics K.K., 31-F Yebisu Garden Place Tower, 4-20-3 Ebisu, pg. 1474 **PB**
Nihon Sun Microsystems K.K., Kowa Nibancho Bldg., 11-19 Nibancho, Chiyoda-ku, pg. 1531 **PB**
Nihon Sun Microsystems K.K., Ichibancho Kyodo Bldg., 16, Ichibancho Chiyoda-ku, pg. 1531 **PB**
Nihon Tokushu Noyaku Seizo K.K., 4 Nihonbashi Honcho 2-chome Chuo-ku, pg. 174 **IT**
Nihon Veeco K.K., 13-7 Rokuban-cho, pg. 1711 **PB**
Nihon Wang K.K., Nissho Bldg. 7F, 7-9 Kita Aoyama 2-Chome, pg. 1737 **PB**
Niigata Converter Co., Ltd., 27-9 Sendagaya, 5-chome, pg. 1646 **PB**
Niigata Technip Co., Ltd., 9-3 Kamata Honcho 1-chome, pg. 1361 **PB**
THE NIKKAN KOGYO SHIMBUN, LTD., 8-10, Kudan Kita 1-chome, pg. 930 **IT**
NIKKEI ADVERTISING CO., 3-6, Kanda Surugadai, pg. 930 **IT**
Nikkei Business Publications Inc., 2-7-6 Hirakawa-cho, pg. 929 **IT**
Nikkei Custom Publishing Services, Inc., 2-8-4 Kanda Tsukasa-cho, pg. 929 **IT**
Nikkei Home Publishing, Inc., Akasaka Oji Bldg., 8-1-22 Akasaka, pg. 929 **IT**
Nikkei International Inc., CRC Kita-Ohtemachi Bldg., 1-4-13 Uchikanda, pg. 929 **IT**
Nikkei Media Marketing, Inc., Nikko Kanda Bldg. 5th Fl., 1-1 Kanda-Ogawamachi, pg. 929 **IT**
Nikkei News Bulletin, Inc., Yamada Bldg. 4th Fl., 2-8-4 Uchikanda, pg. 929 **IT**
Nikkei Newspaper Marketing, Inc., Miyako Bldg. 1st Fl., 1-5-4 Uchikanda, pg. 929 **IT**
Nikkei Research, Inc., Parkside 1 Bldg., 2-2-7 Kanda Tsukasa-cho, pg. 929 **IT**
Nikkei Science, Inc., 14th Fl., Mitsubishi Research Institute Bldg., pg. 929 **IT**
Nikkei Visual Images, Inc., 2-1-2 Uchikanda, pg. 929 **IT**
Nikko International Capital Management Co., Ltd., Tokyo Bldg., 3-1, Marunouchi 3-chome, Chiyoda-ku, pg. 930 **IT**
Nikko Logistics Corp., 10-40 Musashino 2-chome, pg. 701 **IT**
THE NIKKO SECURITIES CO., LTD., 3-1, Marunouchi 3-chome, Chiyoda-ku, pg. 930 **IT**
Niko Co., Ltd., 33-31 Nishiochiai, 0161, pg. 883 **IT**
NIKON CORPORATION, Fuji Bldg., 2-3, Marunouchi 3-chome, pg. 931 **IT**
Nikon Geotecs Co., Ltd., 16-2 Minamikamata 2-chome, pg. 931 **IT**
Nikon Instech Co., Ltd., 4-25 Koraku 1-chome, pg. 931 **IT**
Nikon Life Co., Ltd., 1-3-3 Nishiohi, pg. 931 **IT**
Nikon Logistics Corporation, 1-6-3 nishiohi, pg. 931 **IT**
Nikon Optical Co., Ltd., 10-8 Ryogoku 2-chome, pg. 931 **IT**
Nikon Photo Products Inc., 23-1 Azumabashi 1-chome, pg. 931 **IT**
Nikon Sales Promotion Co., Ltd., 1-9-10 Hamamatsucho, pg. 931 **IT**
Nikon Tec Corporation, 1-5-20, Nishiohi, pg. 931 **IT**
Nilax Co., Ltd., 1-25-8. Nishikubo, pg. 1262 **IT**

Geographic Index-Non U.S.

Nippla Kasei Co., Ltd., 16-8, Taito 4-chome, pg. 946   IT
NIPPO CORPORATION, Nissan Bilnet-2, 6-17-2 Ginza, pg. 932
Nippo PR Co., Ltd., Nissan Bilnet-2, 17-2, 6-chome Ginza, pg. 932
Nippo Service Co., Ltd., Nissan Bilnet-2, 6-Chome Ginza, pg. 932
Nippon Alkyl Phenol Co Ltd., Kasumigaseki Bldg., 23rd. Fl., 3-2-5, Kasumigaseki, Chiyoda-ku, pg. 983   PB
Nippon Becton Dickinson Company Ltd., Akasaka DS Bldg., 5-26 Akasaka, 8-chome, Minato-ku, pg. 200   PB
Nippon Bio-Rad Laboratories K.K., Ato Bldg., 1-2-7 Shiba Daimon Minato-ku, pg. 230   PB
Nippon BOC KK, Shuwa Shiba Park, Bldg. A-3F, 4-1 Shibakoen, pg. 122   IT
Nippon BYK Gulden Co., Ltd., pg. 66   IT
Nippon Centocor, K.K., Land Mark Shiba Park, Bldg. 7F, 1-2-6, Shibaken, Minato-ku, pg. 323   IT
Nippon Chemical Handling, Ehara Bldg., 5-7 Kajicho, 1-Chome, pg. 693   PB
THE NIPPON CREDIT BANK, LTD., 13-10, Kudan-kita 1-chome, pg. 932   IT
Nippon Dome Structures Co., Ltd., pg. 763   IT
Nippon Donaldson Ltd., 13-2 5-chome, Imadera, pg. 517   IT
Nippon Electro Rent, Ltd., Shinagawa Operations Center, Shinagawa-ku, pg. 568   PB
Nippon ESS-FOOD, 6F Assend Jimbocho, 2-23 Kanda-Jimbocho, Chiyoda-Ku, pg. 430   IT
NIPPON EXPRESS CO., LTD., 12-9, 3-chome, Soto-Kanda, pg. 933   IT
Nippon Externa Corp., pg. 507   IT
Nippon Fisher Company, Ltd., 10th Fl. Empire Bldg., 23-1, Hatchobori 2-chome, Chuo-ku, pg. 1126   PB
Nippon Flour Mills Co., Ltd., 2715 Sendagaya Shibuya-ku, pg. 797   PV
Nippon Gasket Co., Ltd., 2-1-1 Kano, pg. 902   IT
Nippon Gatx Co., Ltd., Ehara Bldg., pg. 693   PB
Nippon Glaxo Ltd., P.O. Box 197, pg. 553   IT
Nippon Herr, Tamuracho Kaikan Bldg. 4-9, Nishi-Shimbashi, 1-chome, Minato-ku, pg. 962   PV
Nippon Homes Co., Ltd., Toyochointesu, 5-14, Minamisuna 2-chome, Koto-ku, pg. 1351   IT
Nippon Investment & Finance Co. Ltd., Daiwa Securities Kabuto-cho, 1-9, Nihonbashi-Kayabacho 1 chome, pg. 375   IT
NIPPON KAIJI KYOKAI, 4-7, Kioi-Cho, Chiyoda-Ku, 6th Floor, pg. 934   IT
NIPPON KAYAKU CO. LTD., Tokyo Fujimi Bldg., 11-2 Fujimi 1-chome, pg. 934   IT
Nippon Kayaku Pharmaceutical Div., Tokyo Fujimi Bldg., 11-2, Fujimi 1-chome, Chiyoda-ku, pg. 934   IT
Nippon Koshuha Steel Co., Ltd., 1-7-2, Otimachi, pg. 740   IT
Nippon Lever BV, pg. 1438
Nippon Light Metal Co. Ltd., P.O. Box 5, pg. 52   IT
Nippon Lincoln Electric K.K., Ikebukuro White House, 715, 1-20-2 Higashi Ikebukuro, pg. 997   PB
Nippon Magphane Company, 16 Kowa Bldg. Annex, pg. 1109   IT
Nippon Motorola Ltd., Minami Azabu, 3-20-1 Minato-ku, pg. 1140   PB
Nippon Motorola Micro Electronics, Takanawa 2-21-38, pg. 1140   PB
Nippon National Seikan Co., Ltd., 3-7-1 Kanda-Nishiki-cho, pg. 1029   IT
Nippon Novellus KK, 5 Fl. MS Center Bldg., 1-2-2 Minami-Naruse, 194 Machida, pg. 1204   PB
NIPPON OIL COMPANY, LIMITED (NISSEKI), 3-12, Nishi Shimbashi,1-chome, pg. 936   IT
Nippon Paint Company Ltd., 4-1-15, Minami Shinagawa, pg. 937   IT
NIPPON PAPER INDUSTRIES COMPANY LIMITED, 1-12-1, Yuaku-cho, Chiyoda-ku, pg. 937   IT
Nippon PDA Engineering K.K., Madre Matsuda Bldg. 4F, pg. 1031   PB
Nippon Phonogram Co. Ltd., Waco Bldg. PH/O 8-5, Roppong 4-Chome Min, pg. 1052   IT
NIPPON PISTON RING CO., LTD., 4-2-6, Kudan Kita, 4-chome, pg. 938   IT
Nippon Polaroid K.K., No. 30, Mori Bldg., 2-2, Toranomon 3-chome, pg. 1314   PB
Nippon Polypenco Ltd., 5-2, Marunouchi 2-Chome, pg. 356   IT
Nippon Roballo Co., Ltd., Atagoyama-Bengoshi Bldg. 6-7, pg. 509   IT
Nippon Roche K.K., 6-1, Shiba 2-chome, pg. 1121   IT
NIPPON SANSO CORPORATION, 1-16-7, Nishi-Shinbashi, Minato-ku, pg. 938   IT
Nippon Selas Co., Ltd., 4-3 Arakawa, 7-Chome, pg. 1455   PB
NIPPON SHINPAN CO., LTD., 33-5, 3-chome, Hongo, Bunkyo-ku, pg. 939   IT
Nippon Shipping Co., Ltd., 12-19, Sotokanda 3-chome, Chiyoda-ku, pg. 934   IT
Nippon Shokubai Co., Ltd., Hibiya Dai Bldg., 1-2-2 Uchisaiwai-cho, pg. 939   IT
NIPPON STEEL CORPORATION, 6-3, Ohtemachi, 2-chome, pg. 939   IT
NIPPON SUISAN KAISHA, LTD., 2-6-2, Otemachi, Chiyoda-ku, pg. 940   IT
NIPPON TELEGRAPH AND TELEPHONE CORPORATION, 19-2, Nishi-Shinjoku, 3-chome, pg. 940   IT
Nippon Truck Co., Ltd., 3-8, Komagome 1-chome, pg. 934   IT
Nippon Typewriter Co., Ltd., 11-2, Kyobashi 2-chome, pg. 261   IT
Nippon Univac Kaisha, Ltd., 17-51, Akasaka 2-chome, Minato-ku, pg. 879   IT
Nippon Vishay K.K., Machimoku Bldg., pg. 1722   PB

NIPPON YUSEN K.K., 3-2, Marunouchi, 2-chome, pg. 941   IT
NISHIMATSU CONSTRUCTION CO., LTD., 20-10, Toranomon 1-chome, pg. 942   IT
Nissan Altia Co., Ltd., pg. 944   IT
Nissan Car Leasing Co., Ltd., pg. 944   IT
Nissan Construction Co., Ltd., 1-2-6 Minami Aoyama, Minato-ku, pg. 898   IT
Nissan Credit Corporation, 17-1 Ginza, 6-chome, pg. 944   IT
Nissan Ferro Organic Chemical Co. Ltd., Nissan Edobashi Bldg., 10-5 Nihonbashi, Honcho, pg. 620   PB
Nissan Graphic Arts Co., Ltd., pg. 944   IT
Nissan Leasing Co., Ltd., pg. 944   IT
Nissan Motor Car Carrier Co., Ltd., 17-1 Ginza, 6-chome, pg. 944   IT
NISSAN MOTOR CO., LTD., 17-1 Ginza, 6-chome, pg. 943   IT
Nissan Motor Sales Co., Ltd., 6-17-1, Ginza, Chuo-ku, pg. 944   IT
Nissan Motorist Service Co., Ltd., Minato-ku, pg. 944   IT
NISSAN MUTUAL LIFE INSURANCE COMPANY, 6-30, Aobadai 2-chome, pg. 945   IT
Nissan Prince Motor Sales Co., Ltd., Shinagawa-ku, pg. 944   IT
Nissan Real Estate Co., Ltd., 17-1 Ginza, 6-chome, Chuo-ku, pg. 944   IT
Nissan Sunny Tokyo Motor Sales Co., Ltd., pg. 944   IT
Nissan Texsys Co., Ltd., pg. 944   IT
Nissan Trading Co., Ltd., 17-1 Ginza, 6-chome, Chuo-ku, pg. 944   IT
Nissay Asset Management Corporation, Nissay Kojimachi Bldg., 3-6, Kudanminami 3-chome, Chiyoda-ku, pg. 935   IT
Nissay Capital Co., Ltd., 2-2, Yurakucho 1-chome, Chiyoda-ku, pg. 935   IT
Nissay Culture Foundation, 1-1, Yurakucho 1-chome, Chiyoda-ku, pg. 935   IT
Nissay Green Foundation, 1-1, Yurakucho 1-chome, Chiyoda-ku, pg. 935   IT
Nissay Investment Co., Ltd., 2-2, Yurakucho 1-chome, Chiyoda-ku, pg. 935   IT
Nissay Investment Trust Management Co., Ltd., Nissay Kojimachi Bldg., 3-6, Kudanminami 3-chome, pg. 935   IT
Nissay Managament Co., Ltd., Kudan Center Building, 1-7 Kudankita 4-chome, pg. 935   IT
Nissay Mortgage Co., Ltd., Kudan Center Bldg., 1-7, Kudankita 4-chome, Chiyoda-ku, pg. 935   IT
Nissei Leasing Co., Ltd., 6-1 Hatchyobori 2-chome, Chuo-ku, pg. 935   IT
NISSEI SANGYO CO., LTD., 24-14, Nishi-Shimbashi 1-chome, pg. 945   IT
Nisshin Badische Co., Ltd., 19-12, Koamicho, Nihonbashi, Chuo-ku, pg. 109   IT
NISSHIN FLOUR MILLING CO., LTD., 19-12, Nihonbashi-Koamicho, pg. 946   IT
NISSHIN STEEL CO., LTD., Shinkokusai Bldg., 3-4-1, Marunouchi, 3-chome, pg. 946   IT
Nissho Electronics Corp., 3-1, Tsukiji 7-chome, pg. 946   IT
Nissho Iwai Aerospace Corp., 5-3 Akasaka 2-chome, pg. 946   IT
Nissho Iwai Building Materials Corp., 3-6, Kioi-cho, Chiyoda-ku, pg. 946   IT
NISSHO IWAI CORPORATION, 4-5 Akasaka 2-chome, pg. 946   IT
Nissho Iwai Foods Corp., 17-14, Kaami-cha, pg. 946   IT
Nissho Iwai Gas Co., Ltd., 38-4 Aoba-cho 2-chome, pg. 946   IT
Nissho Iwai General Merchandise Corp., 7-6, Shinbashi 1-chome, pg. 946   IT
Nissho Iwai Nonferrous Metals Corp., 15-15, /nishihira 1-chome, pg. 947   IT
Nissho Iwai Polymers & Products Corp., 4 Kanda Surugadai 3-chome, pg. 947   IT
Nissho Iwai Real Estate Corp., 19-4, Akasaka 2-Chome, pg. 947   IT
Nissho Iwai Steel Leasing Co. Ltd., 9-1, Hachobori 2-chome, pg. 947   IT
Nisso Master Builders Co. Ltd., Kawai Bldg., 8-15 Nihonbashi Hencho 4-chome, pg. 1466   IT
Nittan Valve Company Ltd., Yaesu Mitsui Bldg., pg. 559   PB
Nittetsu Shoji Co., Ltd., Nittetsu ND Tower, 5-7, Kameido, 1-chome, pg. 939   IT
Nittsu Real Estate Co., Ltd., 12-19, Sotokanda 3-chome, Chiyoda-ku, pg. 934   IT
Nittsu Shoji Co., Ltd., 12-9, Sotokanda 3-chome, Chiyoda-ku, pg. 934   IT
Nivea-Kao Co. Ltd., pg. 183   IT
Nokia Japan K.K. Ltd., Akasaka Eight-One Bldg, 6 F, 2-13-5, Nagata-cho, pg. 954   IT
Nokia Mobile Phones Japan K.K., Akasaka Eight-One Bldg 7F, 2-13-15 Nagata-cho, pg. 952   IT
Nomura Asset Management Co., Ltd., 2-1-14, Nihonbashi Chuo-ku, pg. 955   IT
Nomura Babcock & Brown Co., Ltd., 1-11-1, Nihonbashi, Chuo-ku, pg. 955   IT
Nomura Business Services Co., Ltd., 1-2-6, Nihonbashi-honcho, Chuo-ku, pg. 956   IT
Nomura China Investment Co., Ltd., 1-3-8, Nihonbashi-honcho, Chuo-ku, pg. 955   IT
Nomura Finance Co., Ltd., 1-11-1, Nihonbashi, Chuo-ku, pg. 955   IT
Nomura Human Resources Development Co., Ltd., 1-7-2, Nihonbashi-honcho, Chuo-ku, pg. 955   IT
Nomura Investment Management Co., Ltd. (NIMCO), 1-12-11, Nihonbashi, Chuo-ku, pg. 955   IT
Nomura Investor Relations Co., Ltd., 1-26-2, Nishi-Shinjuku, Shinjuku-ku, pg. 956   IT

Nomura Land & Building Co. Ltd., 1-3-8 Nihonbashi-honcho, Chuo-ku, pg. 956   IT
Nomura Real Estate Development Co., Ltd., 1-26-2, Nishi-Shinjuku, Shinjuku-ku, pg. 956   IT
Nomura Research Institute, Ltd., 1-10-1, Nihonbashi, Chuo-ku, pg. 956   IT
Nomura Satellite Communications Co., Ltd., 16-4, Nihonbashi-koamicho, Chuo-ku, pg. 956   IT
THE NOMURA SECURITIES CO., LTD., 9-1, 1-chome Nihonbashi, pg. 955   IT
Nomura System Services Co., Ltd., 4-16-3, Yotsuya, Shinjuku-ku, pg. 956   IT
Nomura Tourist Bureau, Inc., 1-5-3, Nihonbashi, Chuo-ku, pg. 956   IT
The Nomura Trust and Banking Co., Ltd., 1-1-1, Nihonbashi, Chuo-ku, pg. 956   IT
Nomura Wasserstein Perella Co., Ltd., 1-11-1, Nihonbashi, Chuo-ku, pg. 956   IT
Nordson K.K., 8th Floor Toshin Building, pg. 1189   PB
THE NORINCHUKIN BANK, 13-2 Yurakucho 1-chome, pg. 958   IT
Norinchukin Investment Trust Management Co., Ltd., 2-1, Kyobashi1-chome, pg. 958   IT
Norinchukin Securities Co., Ltd., 1-12, Uchikanda 1-chome, Chiyoda-ku, pg. 958   IT
The Norinchukin Trust & Banking Co., Ltd., 1-12, Uchikanda 1-chome, pg. 958   IT
NORIT Co. Ltd., Shiraimatsu Bldg. 4f, 11-Kaned Kitano rimano CHO, pg. 958   IT
Norsk Hydro a.s, Tokyo Representative Office, Room 1102, Shuwa Kioicho TWR Bldg., pg. 964   IT
Norske Skog (Japan) Ltd., 6F Shimbashi Tomite Bldg., pg. 966   IT
Northern Telecom Japan Inc., 3-19-23 Minami-Azabu, pg. 970   IT
Norton East Asia, Inc., 7 Kojimachi 3-chome, pg. 1175   IT
Norton Kabushiki Kaisha, 7, Kojimachi 3-chome, pg. 1175   IT
Norton KK, Noo. 33, Mori Bldg., 8-21 Toranomon 3-chome, Minato-ku, pg. 1175   IT
Novell Japan Ltd., Toei Mishuku Bldg., 1013-1 Mishuku, pg. 1204   PB
Novo Nordisk Pharma Ltd., Sumitomo Bank, Ningyocho Bldg., 5-7, Nihonbashi Ohdenma-cho, pg. 988   IT
NOZAKI & COMPANY LTD., 2-6 Nihonbashi Bakurocho, pg. 990   IT
Nutritec K.K., pg. 1121   IT
OBAYASHI CORPORATION, 3, 2-chome, Kanda Tsukasa-cho, pg. 995   IT
ODAKYU ELECTRIC RAILWAY CO., LTD., 1-8-3, Nishishinjuku, pg. 996   IT
Ohi Plant, 1-6-3, Nishiohi, pg. 931   IT
Ohkura-Rosemount Co., Ltd., 161 Iguchi Mitaka-Shi, pg. 577   PB
Ohmeda Ltd., Shuwa Shiba Park, Bldg., A-3F, 4-1 Shibakoen, pg. 122   IT
OJI PAPER CO., LTD., 7-5 Ginza 4-chome, pg. 998   IT
OKABE COMPANY LIMITED, 21-15, Mukojima 4-chome, Sumida-ku, pg. 999   IT
Okayamaken Shokuhin Co., Ltd., 2-4-16 Kyobashi, pg. 855   IT
Oki Electric Industry Co., Ltd., 3-36-1 Inadaira Musashimurayama-City, pg. 999   IT
Oki Electric Industry Co., Ltd., 7-5-25 Nishishinjuku, pg. 999   IT
OKI ELECTRIC INDUSTRY COMPANY, LTD., 7-12, Toranomon 1-chome, pg. 999   IT
Oki Unisys Kaisha, Ltd., 2-3-13 Toranomon, pg. 999   IT
OKURA & CO., 3-6, Ginza, 2-chome Chuo-ku, 104, pg. 1001   IT
Oldelft Japan Ltd., Kowa Bldg., 5th Fl., nr. 6, 4-15-21 Nishi-Azabu, pg. 389   IT
Olin Japan, Inc., Shiozaki Bldg. 7-1 Hirawaka-Cho 2 Chome, pg. 1220   PB
Olivetti Corporation of Japan, 1-24, 1 chome, Himonya Meguro-ku, pg. 1003   IT
Olympus Japan Co., Ltd., pg. 1004   IT
OLYMPUS OPTICAL CO., LTD., 3-1 Nishi-Shinjuku 2-chome, pg. 1004   IT
Olympus Opto-Electronics Co., Ltd., pg. 1004   IT
Olympus Systems Corporation, pg. 1004   IT
Optrex Corporation, 3-14-9 Yushima, Bunkyo-ku, pg. 84   IT
Oracle Corporation Japan, C. Sano, No. 15 Arai Bldg., pg. 1228   PB
Ord Minnett Group Limited, 8th Flr., Imperial Towers, 1-1-1 Uchisaiwai-Cho, pg. 1497   IT
Organic Chemistry Research Laboratory-Tokyo, pg. 1455   IT
ORIENTAL MOTOR CO., LTD., 16-17 Ueno 6 Chome Taito-Ku, pg. 1008   IT
ORIX Aircraft Corporation, World Trade Center Bldg., 2-4-1, Hamamatsu-cho, Minato-ku, pg. 1008   IT
ORIX Alpha Corporation, Karuko-Zaka MN Bldg., 4F, 2-1, Ageba-cho, pg. 1008   IT
ORIX Auto Leasing Corporation, TOC Osaki Bldg., 1-6-1, Osaki, pg. 1008   IT
ORIX Capital Corporation, TOC Osaki Building, 1-6-1, Osaki, pg. 1008   IT
ORIX Club Corporation, 1-3-8 Nishi-Gotanda, pg. 1008   IT
ORIX COMMODITIES Corporation, Fujiwara Bldg., 4F, 1-10-11, Ebisu Nishi, Shibuya-ku, pg. 1008   IT
ORIX Computer Systems Corporation, Osaki CN Bldg., 5-10-10, Osaki, Shinagawa-ku, pg. 1008   IT
ORIX CORPORATION, World Trade Center Bldg., 35th Floor, 2-4-1, Hamamatsu-cho, pg. 1008   IT
ORIX Credit Corporation, HI Gotanda Bldg., 2-11-17 Nishi-Gotanda, pg. 1008   IT
ORIX Insurance Services Corporation, World Trade Center Bldg., 2-4-1, Hamamatsu-cho, Minato-ku, pg. 1008   IT

PB - *U.S. Public Companies Volume*
PV - *U.S. Private Companies Volume*
IT - *International Public & Private Companies Volume*

1686

Geographic Index-Non U.S.

ORIX Life Insurance Corporation, BYGS Shinjuku Bldg., 12F-3F, 2-19-1, Shinjuku, Shinjuku-ku, pg. 1009 IT
ORIX Maritime Corporation, 1-31-8, Kakinokizaka, Meguro-ku, pg. 1009 IT
ORIX Rent-A-Car, Nikko-Gotanda Bldg., 2-29-5, Nishi-Gotanda, Shinagawa-ku, pg. 1009 IT
ORIX Rentec Corporation, 5-7-21, Kita-Shinagawa, Shinagawa-ku, pg. 1009 IT
ORIX Securities Co., Ltd., 2-26-9, Hachobori, Chuo-ku, pg. 1009 IT
Ortho Clinical Diagnostic Systems K.K., 3-2 Toyo 6-chome, pg. 931 PB
Osaka Gas Co., 2-2-1, Otemachi, Chiyoda-ku, pg. 1011 IT
OTARI, INC., 4-33-3, Kokuryocho, Chofu-shi, pg. 1013 IT
Otsuka Beverage Co., Ltd., 2-9 Kanda Tsukasa-cho, pg. 1013 IT
OTSUKA PHARMACEUTICAL CO., LTD., 2-9, Kanda Tsukasa-cho, pg. 1013 IT
Otsuka Tokyo Assay Laboratories Inc., 1-26-8 Nakaikegami, pg. 1013 IT
Otto Sumisho Inc., Sumitomo Kanda Bldg., 3-24-4, Kandanishi-cho, pg. 1015 IT
Otto-Sumisho Inc., pg. 1015 IT
Our Design Corporation, Seventh Minami-Aoyama Bldg., 2nd Fl., 12-14, Minami-Aoyama 7-chome, pg. 1321 IT
Outokumpu Japan K.K., Izumi Ningyo-cho Bldg., 4th Fl., pg. 1015 IT
Oversea Courier Service Co., Ltd., 2-9 Shibaura, pg. 929 IT
Owens-Corning (Japan) Ltd., Yusen Building 5F, 3-2 Marunouchi 2-Chome, pg. 1237 PB
Oxford Instruments, No. 2 Funato Building, 8th Floor, pg. 1018 IT
Oxford University Press K.K., 2-4-8 Kanamecho 2-chome, pg. 1019 IT
OYO CORPORATION, 2-6, Kudan-kita 4-chome, pg. 1019 IT
PDA International/Japan, Hiax Hirakawa-cho Bldg., 1F, 2-10-10, Hirakawa-cho, pg. 1031 PB
PPG Industries Asia/Pacific Ltd., Takanawa Ct., 5th Fl., 13-1 Takanawa 3-chome, pg. 1245 PB
Pacific Engineering Co., Ltd., pg. 1024 IT
Pacific Golf Co., Ltd., pg. 1024 IT
Pacific Resort Co., Ltd., pg. 1024 IT
Pall Asia, No. 7 Koike Bldg., 3-6 Minami-Shinagawa, 2-chome, pg. 1254 PB
Panalpina World Transport (Japan) Ltd., pg. 1023 IT
Panduit Corp. Japan Branch, 31-5, Omori Kita 6-chome, pg. 836 PV
PARCO Co. Ltd., 28-2 Minamiikubukiro, 1-chome, pg. 1178 IT
Parfums Christian Dior Japan KK, Sumitomo Hanzomon Bldg., 3-16 Hayabusha-cho, Chiyoda-ku, pg. 783 IT
Parfums Givenchy K.K., Sumitomo Hanzomon Bldg. annex, 2-1-2 Hirakawa-cho, pg. 783 IT
Paribas Asset Management Japan Ltd., Yurakucho Denki Bldg., North 18th Fl., pg. 321 IT
Paribas Capital Markets-Tokyo Branch, Yurakucho Denki Bldg., 18th Fl. North, 1-7-1 Yurakucho, pg. 321 IT
Parker Pen Japan K.K., Shinjuku Mitsui Bldg., 42nd Fl., pg. 745 PB
Pasco Computer-Mapping Center Co., Ltd., pg. 1024 IT
PASCO CORPORATION, 7-10-20, Akasaka, Minato-ku, pg. 1024 IT
Pasco Engineering Co., Ltd., pg. 1024 IT
Pasco Estate Co., Ltd., pg. 1024 IT
Pasco International Inc., pg. 1024 IT
Pearson KK, 13th Floor, AIG Building, 1-3 Marunouchi 1-chome, pg. 1027 IT
Pechiney Food Packaging Japan, Shinjuku Mitsui Bldg., 43 Fl., 2-1-1 Nishi Shinjuku, pg. 1031 IT
Pechiney Japan, Shinjuku Mitaul Bldg., 43rd Fl, 2.1.1 Nishi-Shinjuku, pg. 1031 IT
PENTEL CO., LTD., 7-2, Koami-cho, pg. 1035 IT
People Co., Ltd., 8-5-30 Akasaka, Minato-ku, pg. 898 IT
Perrier Japon K.K., pg. 922 IT
Petrofina Japan Office, Nishikawa Building 2F, 3-5-19 Kojimachi, pg. 1044 IT
Pfizer Pharmaceuticals Inc., Shinjuku Mitsui Bldg., 2-1-1, Nishi Shinjuku, Shinjuki-ku, pg. 1283 PB
Pfizer Shoji Co. Ltd., Shinjuku Mitsui Bldg., 1, Nishi Shinjuku, pg. 1283 PB
Pharmaceutical, Salon & Food Products Division, pg. 1236 IT
Pharmaceuticals and Diagnostics Company, 2-24, Higashi-Shinagawa, 2-chome, Shinagawa-ku, pg. 871 IT
Pharmacia & Upjohn Biotech K.K., Honda Denki Bldg., 5-37, Kami-Osaki 4-chome, pg. 1048 IT
Pharmacia & Upjohn Group, Shuwa Kamiyacho Bldg., 3-13, Toranomon, 4-chome, pg. 1050 IT
Pharmacological Research Laboratory-Tokyo, pg. 1354 IT
Philip Morris K.K., Akasaka Twin Tower, Main Tower, 7th Fl., pg. 1290 PB
Phoenix Technologies K.K., Nishisando Yamaki Building,4-F, 3-28-6, Yoyogi, Shibuya-ku, pg. 1292 PB
PictureTel Japan KK, ABS Bldg. (#707), 2-4-16 Kudan Minami, pg. 1295 PB
THE PILOT CORPORATION, 8-1 Nishi-Gotanda, 2-chome, pg. 1057 IT
PIONEER ELECTRONIC CORPORATION, 1-4-1, Meguro, Meguro-ku, pg. 1057 IT
Pioneer Hi-Bred Japan Co. Ltd., Landic Toranomon Building 7F, 3-7-10 Toranomon, pg. 1299 PB
Pitney Bowes Japan, Kowa No. 1 Bldg. 14-14, Akasaka 1-Chome, pg. 1304 PB
Plantronics K.K., 1-22-7, Naka-Cho, pg. 1308 PB
PLAZA CREATE, 2F Ichigaya Daigo Bldg. 1-10, pg. 1060 IT
Polydor K.K., 8-4 Ohashi 1-chome Meguro-ku, pg. 1052 IT
PolyGram Record Service K.K., 1000 Kamisukiahara, Showa-machi, Nakakom, pg. 1053 IT
Polystar Co. Ltd., 6 F Ellie Bldg., 5-1-2 Minamiaoyama, pg. 1053 IT
Porsche Engineering Japan Co.. Ltd., pg. 1063 IT
POSCO Tokyo Office, POSCO Tokyo Bldg., 4 Fl., 11-14, Ginza 5-chome Chuo-ku, pg. 1062 IT
POSCO Tokyo Research Lab, POSCO Tokyo Bldg. 4 Fl., 11-14, Ginza 5-Chome Chuo-Ku, pg. 1062 IT
Pozzolith Bussan Co. Ltd., pg. 983 IT
Prap Japan, Inc., Shibuya R. Sankei Bldg., 3-10-13 Shibuya, pg. 617 PV
Praxair K.K., pg. 1320 PB
Prentice Hall Regents Japan, Inc., Nishi-Shinjuku KF Bldg. 602, 8-14-24 Nishi-Shinjuki, pg. 778 PV
President Inc., Aoyama Bldg., 1-2-3 Kita Aoyama Manato-ku, pg. 1615 PB
The Prudential Life Insurance Company, Ltd., Sogo Hanzomon Bldg., 1-7 Kojimachi, pg. 893 PV
Q.P. CORPORATION, 1-4-13 Shibuya Shibuya-ku, pg. 1074 IT
Quaker State Japan Co., Ltd., Kairaku Bldg., 6-5-12 Soto Kanda, pg. 1348 PB
Quantum Japan Procurement Center, Inc., 2-25-15 Minami Otsuka, pg. 1350 PB
Quantum Peripherals Japan Corporation, Shinjuku Square Tower 4F, 6-22-1 Nishi-Shinjuku, pg. 1350 PB
Quest Japan Inc., Room 102, Colins-34, 3-6-1, Tamagawa-Gakuen, pg. 707 IT
Quick Corp., 8th Fl., Otemachi Bldg., 1-6-1 Otemachi, pg. 929 IT
RNBNY Branch Office-Tokyo, Fuji Bldg., 3-2-3 Marunouchi, 3-Chome, pg. 1381 PB
RTZ-CRA Japan Limited, 7th Fl., Shiroyama JT Mori Bldg., pg. 307 IT
Radiometer K.K., MT2 Building, 1-12-23, Mita, pg. 1084 IT
Radiometer Trading K.K., MT2 Building, 12-23, Mita 1-chome, pg. 1084 IT
Ransburg Industrial Finishing, 5-3, 3 chome, Higashi Rokugo Ota-Ku, pg. 869 PB
Reader's Digest Global Advertising, Ltd., Shiba Matsushita Building, 4th Floor, 3-3-12, Shiba, pg. 1368 PB
Reed Exhibition Companies-Asia North, 18th Floor, Shinjuku Nomura Building, pg. 1096 IT
Reed Travel Publishing-Japan, U & M Akasaka Building, B1F 7-5-47 Akasaka, pg. 1097 IT
Reemtsma Japan Ltd., ITO Building, 20-7 Hakozaki-cho, pg. 1101 IT
Renishaw K.K., 6F & 7F Anzai Bldg., 1-12, Hatagaya 1-chome, pg. 1103 IT
Rentokil Japan Ltd, pg. 1286 IT
Research Laboratory of Drug Metabolism-Tokyo, pg. 1354 IT
Resort Development Division, 26-20 Sakuragaoka-cho, pg. 1395 IT
Reuters Japan Kabushiki Kaisha, Shuwa Kamiyacho Bldg., 5th Fl., pg. 1105 IT
Rexroth Kabushiki Kaisha, pg. 839 IT
Rheometrics Scientific Far East Ltd., 1-7-6 Higashi Gotanda, Shinagawa-ku, pg. 1387 PB
Rhone-Poulenc Japan, Ltd., Roppongi First Bldg., Central 1649, pg. 1113 IT
Richardson Electronics Japan Co., Ltd., Tachibana Bldg., 1-22, 3 Chome, Negishi, pg. 1388 PB
Ricky Contact Lens Inc., 7, Yotsuya 3-chome, Shinjuku-ku, pg. 984 IT
RICOH COMPANY, LTD., 15-5, Minami-Aoyama 1-chome, pg. 1114 IT
Riken Electric Wire Co., Ltd., 12-22, Tsukiji 1-chome, Chuo-ku, pg. 530 IT
A.H. Robins International Company, Dai 7 Chuo Bldg., No. 26-1 chome, pg. 82 PB
Robinson Nugent, Inc., Selon Building, 11-7 Shinsen-cho, pg. 1395 PB
Rockwell International Japan Co., Limited, Shimomoto Building, 1-46-3 Hatsudai, Shibuya-ku, pg. 1401 PB
Rockwell International Japan Co., Ltd., Shinkawa Sanko Building, 9F, 1-3-17 Shinkawa, Chuo-ku, pg. 1401 PB
Rodic Co., Ltd., pg. 1122 IT
Rogers Japan Inc., Seventh Floor, ST Bldg., 2-26-9, Nishi Nippori, pg. 1403 PB
Rohm & Haas Japan K.K., pg. 1404 PB
Rohm Co., Ltd. - Tokyo Branch, 3-14-31, Takanawa, pg. 1125 IT
Rollins Burdick Hunter Intl. Inc., Tokyo Bldg. East No. 3, 2-16-8 Minami-Ikebukuro, pg. 119 PB
Ronde Corp., 2-4-16 Kyobashi, pg. 855 IT
Rorer Japan, Inc., Nihon Seimei Mita Bldg., 9-11, Mita 3-chome, pg. 1112 IT
The Royal Bank of Scotland plc, Dai-Ichi Seimei Sogo Kan, 7-1 Kyobashi 3-chome, pg. 1133 IT
Royal Copenhagen Japan Ltd., 10th Fl., Mita Kokusai Bldg., pg. 1135 IT
Royal Doulton Japan KK, Meguro Higashiyama Bldg., 7th Floor, pg. 1135 IT
RYOBI LTD., 3-15-1, Soto-Kanda, Chiyoda-ku, pg. 1151 IT
Rythm Watch Co., Ltd., 27-7, 2-chome, Taito, pg. 294 IT
SAS Institute Japan Ltd., Inui Bldg., Kachidoki 8th Flo, 1-13-1 Kachidoki, pg. 967 PV
SBC Portfolio Management International K.K., Kamiyacho Mori Building, 3-20 Toranomon 4-chrome, pg. 1330 IT
SBC Warburg Securities (Japan) Inc., New Edobashi Bldg., 1-7-2 Nihombashi-Honcho Chuo-ku, pg. 1331 IT
SDRC Japan K.K., Roppongi Yamada Building, 5-27, Roppongi 3-chome, pg. 1525 PB
SDS Biotech K.K., Sumitomo Higashi Shinbashi Bld, 2-go-kan 12-7, pg. 984 IT
SEB Japan Co. Ltd., Gotanda HS Bldg., 4F, 7-1-9 Nishigotanda, pg. 568 IT
SEC (Soft, Event & Promotion) Planning, Inc., 4-1, Shibaura 3 chome, pg. 588 IT
SIA Co., Ltd., 1-20-5, Ginza, pg. 1189 IT
SKF Japan Ltd., 9-1, 1-chome, Shiba Daimon, pg. 1159 IT
SKW East Asia Ltd., Tug Building, 1-10, Jidabashi 2-chome, Chiyoda-ku, pg. 1466 IT
SMH Japan KK, Dai-ni Marutakak Bldg., 9th Floor, pg. 1161 IT
SMI Co., Ltd., Sanyo Electric Tokyo Bldg., 1-10, Uemachi 1-chome, pg. 1191 IT
SPS/Unbrako K.K., Ogawa 2-25-4, Machida, pg. 1420 PB
THE SAISON GROUP, Sunshine 60 Bldg., 32nd Fl., pg. 1178 IT
The Sakura Bank, 1-2, Yurakucho 1-chome, pg. 1179 IT
THE SAKURA BANK, LIMITED, 3-1 Kudan Minami 1-Chome, pg. 1178 IT
Samsung Japan Corporation, 15F Hamacho Center Bldg., pg. 1183 IT
San Nopco Ltd., pg. 614 IT
SANDEN CORPORATION, 31-7 Taito, pg. 1184 IT
Sandoz Japan K.K., pg. 984 IT
Sandoz Yakuhin K.K., Nishi Azabu Mitsui Bldg., 17-30, Nishi Azabu 4-chome, pg. 985 IT
Sanki Engineering Co., Ltd., 4-1, Yurakucho 1-chome, pg. 877 IT
Sanko-Stevens Chemical, Inc., Tameike Meisan Bldg., 1-12, 1-chome Akasaka, Minato-ku, pg. 1466 PB
SANKOSHA ADVERTISING AGENCY, LTD., 3-13-1, Ginza, pg. 1189 IT
SANKOSHA CORPORATION, 3-8 Osaki 4-chome, pg. 1189 IT
SANKYO COMPANY LIMITED, 5-1, Nihonbashi Honcho, 3-Chome, pg. 1189 IT
Sanofi-Meiji Pharmaceuticals Co., Ltd., Yowa Bldg., 6th Fl., 7-13, Nihonbashi Tomozawa-cho, pg. 855 IT
Sanofi Yamanouchi Inc., Gotenyama Mori Bldg., 11th Fl, 7-35, Kitashinagawa 4-chome, pg. 1518 IT
Sanshin Electric Co., Ltd., 1-8-14 Toyotama-Kami, pg. 1188 IT
Sanwell Co., Ltd., Aquatellus UII Bldg., 20-3, Kaminarimon 2-chome, Taito-ku, pg. 1518 IT
Sanyo Tourist Sales Co., Ltd., 2-1-10 Yushima, Bunkyo-ku, pg. 1191 IT
SAPPORO BREWERIES LTD., 20-1, Ebisu 4-chome, pg. 1193 IT
SATO KOGYO CO., LTD., 12-20, Nihonbashi-Honcho 4-chome, pg. 1197 IT
Savory Co., Ltd., 3-6-1 Ginza, Chuo-ku, pg. 848 IT
R.P. Scherer K.K., Shin Toyo Akasaka Building, 4-9-25 Akasaka, pg. 1438 PB
Schindler Elevator K.K, pg. 1205 IT
Scholl Japan Limited, Ayoma White Adobe Building, 2-2-6 Shibuya, pg. 1210 IT
Seagate Technology K.K., Fonte Nishi-Harajuku, Bldg. 2F, 1-13-9 Tomigaya, pg. 1450 PB
Sealed Air Japan Ltd., 1-14-2 Saga, Koto-ku, pg. 1451 PB
Sealed Air Japan Ltd., 1-14-2 Saga, Koto-Ku, pg. 1451 PB
SECOM CO., LTD., 1-26-2, Nishi-Shinjuki, Shinjuku-ku, pg. 1217 IT
Security Pacific National Bank, Tokyo, ARK Mori Bldg., 15/F 12-32 Akasaka, 1-Chome, pg. 183 PB
SEGA ENTERPRISES LTD., 2-12 Haneda, pg. 1218 IT
Seibu Allstate Life Insurance Co., Ltd., Sunshine 60, 1-1, Higashijkebukura, 3-chome, pg. 1178 IT
Seibu Department Stores, Ltd., 28-1 Minamiikebukuro, 1-chome, pg. 1178 IT
SEIKO CORPORATION, 2-6-21 Kyobashi, pg. 1218 IT
Seiwa Kaikan Co., Ltd., 1-1, Yurakucho 1-chome, Chiyoda-ku, pg. 935 IT
Seiyo Corporation, Sunshine 60, pg. 1178 IT
Seiyo Food Systems, Ltd., Sunshine 60, 1-1, Higashijkebukuro, 3-chome, pg. 1178 IT
Seiyo, Ltd., Sunshine 60 Bldg., 1-1, Higashi-Ikebukuro 3-chome, pg. 1178 IT
Sequent Computers Japan, Ltd., Marumasu Kojimachi Bldg., 3-3 Kojimachi, pg. 1460 PB
Seven-Eleven Japan Co., Ltd., 1-4, Shibakoen 4-chome, pg. 693 IT
Shaklee Japan K.K., Roppongi Fuji Bldg., pg. 1518 IT
Shell Japan Ltd., Kasumigasiki Bldg., 2-5, Kasumigasiki 3-chome, pg. 1139 IT
Shell Kagaku K.K., Kasumigaseki Bldg., 2-5, Kasumigaseki 3-chome, pg. 1139 IT
Shibaura Engineering Works Co., Ltd., 1-1-12 Akasaka, Minato-ku, pg. 1403 IT
Shibazaki Seisakusho Limited, 17-12 Ishihara-Cho 2-Chome, pg. 62 PB
Shimex Ltd., Terao Bldg. 8-4, Nishi-Shimbashi 2-chome, pg. 303 IT
SHIMIZU CORPORATION, Seavans South, No. 2-3, Shibaura 1-chome, pg. 1233 IT
Shimoda Electric Co., Ltd., 2-34-2 Higashi-mukojima, pg. 1188 IT
Shimura Kako Company, Ltd., 3-1-1, Marunouchi, pg. 673 IT
SHIN-ETSU CHEMICAL CO. LTD., 6-1,2 chome, Otemachi, Chiyoda-ku, pg. 1234 IT
Shin-Etsu Handotai Co. Ltd., 4-2, Marunouchi 2-chome, pg. 1234 IT
Shin-Etsu Polymer Co. Ltd., 4-3-5, Nihonbashi-Honcho, pg. 1234 IT
Shin Nippon Air Conditioning Engineering Co., Ltd., Mitsui Bldg., Annex No. 2, 2, Nihonbashi-Hongokucho 4-chome, pg. 877 IT
Shin-Wako Securities Investment Trust and Management Co., Ltd., 1-12-2, Kayaba-cho, Nihonbashi, pg. 1485 IT
Shinjuku NS Building Co., Ltd., Shinjuku NS Bldg., 4-1, Nishishinjuku 2-chome, pg. 935 IT
Shinko Electric Co., Ltd., 3-12-2, Nihonbashi, Chuo-ku, pg. 740 IT

PB - *U.S. Public Companies Volume*
PV - *U.S. Private Companies Volume*
IT - *International Public & Private Companies Volume*

Shinko Telecommunications Construction Co., Ltd., 12-13, Shiba 5-chome, Minato-ku, pg. 530   IT

Shionogi Tokyo Office, Shionogi Shibuya Bldg., 17-5, Shibuya 2-chome, pg. 1234   IT

Shipley Far East Limited, pg. 1404   PB

SHISEIDO COMPANY LTD., 7-5-5, Ginza, pg. 1235   IT

Shobisha Co., Ltd., 3-6-1 Ginza, Chuo-ku, pg. 848   IT

SHOKO CHUKIN BANK, 2-10-17, Yaesu 2-chome, pg. 1236   IT

Showa Aircraft Industry Co., Ltd., 3-7, Nihonbashi-Muromachi, pg. 878   IT

Showa Bussan Co., 13, Honshio-cho, Shinjuku-ku, pg. 1272   IT

SHOWA DENKO K.K., 13-9 Shiba Daimon 1-chome, pg. 1236   IT

Showa GATX Company, Ltd., Ehara Bldg., 5-7 kajicho, 1-Chome, pg. 693   IT

Showa High-Tech-Rent Co., Ltd., Meguro Center Bldg., 2-1, Kamiosaki 3-chome, pg. 730   IT

Showa Leasing Co., Ltd., 10-43, Minami-Aoyama, 3-chome, pg. 82   IT

Showa Savoie, P.O. Box 242, Mitsui Building, pg. 1032   IT

Showa Shell Sekiyu KK, 3-2-5, Kasumigaseki, 3-Chome, pg. 1140   IT

SHUWA CORPORATION, Shuwa Kioicho TBR Bldg., 5-7 Kojimachi, pg. 1237   IT

Siemens K.K., Siemens Fujikura Bldg., 11-20, Nishi Gotanda 2-chome, pg. 1247   IT

Sigma Aldrich Japan, Kyodo Bldg., Shinkanda, pg. 1472   PB

Simon Marketing, Inc., Excel Ty Bldg., 2nd Fl., 1-16-13 Ebisu-Minami, pg. 1001   PV

Singapore Petroleum Co (Japan) Ltd., Rm. 308, Zenkoku Nenryo Bldg., 8-12-15 Ginza, Chuo-ku, pg. 102   PB

Singapore Tourist Promotion Board - Tokyo, 1st Floor, Yamato Seimei Bldg., 1 Chome, 1-7 Ucisaiwai-cho, pg. 1254   IT

Sinochem Japan Co. Ltd., 7th Fl., Onarimon Bldg., 17-1, 6-chome, Shinbashi, pg. 1255   IT

Sinochem Representative Office - Japan, 7th Fl., Onarimon Bldg., 17-1, 6-chome, Shinbashi, pg. 1256   IT

Skadden, Arps, Slate, Meagher & Flom, 16F, Shiroyama JT Mori Bldg., 4-3-1, Toranomon, 105, pg. 1005   PV

Skandia International Insurance Co., Fukuoku Seimei Building, 16th Floor, pg. 1258   IT

Skandia Life Insurance Co. (Japan) Ltd., Sweden Center Building, 6-11-9 Roppongi, Minato-ku, pg. 1258   IT

Skandinaviska Enskilda Banken, Shin Tokyo Bldg., Rm. 425, 3-3-1 Marunouchi, pg. 1259   IT

Skandinaviska Enskilda Banken, Tokyo Branch, Rm 425, Shin Tokyo Building, 3-3-1 Marunouchi, pg. 1259   IT

Sky Sangyo Co., Ltd., 20-3, Funabashi 6-chome, pg. 1321   IT

SKYLARK CO., LTD., Shinjuku Green Tower Bldg., 14-1 Nishishinjuku 6-chome, pg. 1262   IT

SmithKline Beecham Pharmaceuticals, SKB Bldg., 6 Sanbancho, pg. 1266   IT

SmithKline Beecham Yakuhin K.K., Shin-Nanpeidai Tokyu Bldg., 21-22 Dogenzaka-chome, pg. 1266   IT

Smiths Industries (Japan) Limited, Hongo-km Yumicho Bldg., 38-3 Hongo 2-chome, pg. 1268   IT

Snap-on Tools Japan K.K., 8-10, Shikiba 1-Chrome, pg. 1481   PB

Snow Brand Food Co., Ltd., 1-7-10, Narihira, Sumida-ku, pg. 1272   IT

SNOW BRAND MILK PRODUCTS CO. LTD., 13, Honshio-cho, Shinjuku-ku, pg. 1271   IT

Snow Brand Pillsbury Inc., No. 13, Honshio-Cho Shinjuku-ku, pg. 411   IT

Snow Brand Rolly Co., Ltd., 13, Honshio-cho, Shinjuku-ku, pg. 1272   IT

Snow Brand Seed Co., Ltd., 13, Honshio-cho, Shinjuku-ku, pg. 1272   IT

Snow Brand Shoji Co., Ltd., 13, Honshio-cho, Shinjuku-ku, pg. 1272   IT

Sodegaura Chemical Ltd., Shibuya Konno Bldg., 3-1, Shibuya 3-chome, pg. 1393   IT

Sodex, Nissei Waseda Bldg. 6F, 1, Babashita cho 1-chome, pg. 1275   IT

SOFTBANK CORPORATION, 3-42-3, Nihonbashi-Hamacho, pg. 1276   IT

SOGEI INC., 1-15-7, Tsukishima, pg. 1277   IT

Sogei Inc., Daihyakuseimei Kyobashi Bldg., 3-2-11, pg. 1277   IT

Solectron Japan, Inc., Yurakucho Denki Building, 1-7-1 Yurakucho Chiyoda-Ku, pg. 1483   PB

SONY CORPORATION, 7-35 Kitashinagawa 6-chome, pg. 1280   IT

Sony Music Entertainment (Japan) Inc., 1-4 Ichigaya-Tamachi, Shinjuku-ku, pg. 1281   IT

Sony/Tektronix Corporation, 9-31, Kitashinagawa-5 Shinagawa-ku, pg. 1568   PB

Sophisticated Products Div., P.O. Box 262, pg. 934   PV

South East Asia Petroleum Exploration Co., Ltd., 5-13, Nishi-Shinbashi 1-chome, pg. 877   IT

Spalding Japan Inc., Izumi Shinkawa Building, 6F-7F, 5-18 Shinkawa 1-Chome, pg. 630   PV

Spectra-Physics KK, 1-1-2 Higashiyama Meguro-ku, pg. 1290   IT

Spectra-Physics KK, 15-8 Nanpeioaicho, pg. 1290   IT

SPOM Kabushiki Kaisha, Yokoi Bldg., 2nd Fl., 26-8 Nandocho, Shinjuku-Ku, pg. 316   IT

Spraying Systems Co. Far East, Dai Ichi Iwata Bldg., 8f-5-10-18, Higashi Gotanda, pg. 1027   PV

Ssangyong Japan Corporation, 7th Fl., Matsuoka Tamuracho, Bldg., 22-10, 5-chome, Shimbashi, pg. 1291   IT

Standard Chartered Asia Limited, Fuji Bldg., 3-2-3 Marunouchi, pg. 1296   IT

Standard Chartered Bank (Japan), Fuji Bldg., 3-2-3 Marunouchi, pg. 1295   IT

Stange (Japan) K.K., 5-3 Kayabacho, 3-Chome, Nihonbashi, pg. 1067   PB

State Street Trust & Banking Company, Ltd., New Diamond Bldg., 1-4-4 Kasumigaseki, pg. 1513   IT

Stauffer Japan, Ltd., Tokyo Fujimi Bldg., 11-12 Fujimi-Cho, pg. 47   IT

Stolt-Nielsen Shipping A/S, pg. 1302   IT

Stone Container Japan Company Limited, Kabutocho Wachiyo Bldg.,20-5 Kabutocho, pg. 1522   PB

Storage Technology of Japan Ltd., Entsuji Gadelius Bldg., pg. 1523   PB

Stratus Japan Co. Ltd., Shoei Rokubancho Bldg. 4F, 6 Rokubancho, pg. 1524   PB

Subway Japan Inc., Akasaka Floral Plz. Bldg., 4th Floor, pg. 1321   PV

Sulzer (Japan) Ltd., Asahi-Tokai Bldg., 23rd Fl., 6-1, 2-chome, pg. 1308   IT

Sulzer Metco (Japan) Ltd., pg. 1308   IT

Sulzermedica Japan K.K., pg. 1307   IT

Sumihatsu Co., Ltd., 3-chome, 5-5 Iwamoto-cho, pg. 902   IT

Sumikin Bussan Corporation, 8-5-27 Minato-ku, pg. 1308   IT

Sumitomo Bakelite Co., Ltd., 2-2, Uchi-Saiwaicho 1-chome, pg. 1311   IT

The Sumitomo Bank, LTD.-Tokyo, 3-2, Marunouchi 1-chome, pg. 1308   IT

SUMITOMO CHEMICAL COMPANY, LTD., Tokyo Sumitomo Twin Building, 27-1 Shinkawa 2-chome, pg. 1310   IT

SUMITOMO CORPORATION, 2-2, Hitotsubashi, 1-chome, pg. 1312   IT

Sumitomo Densetsu Co., Ltd., 3-12, Moto-Akasaka 1-chome, pg. 1313   IT

Sumitomo Eaton Hydraulics Co. Ltd.-Hydraulics Div., Shin-Kanda Bldg., 8-5, pg. 559   IT

Sumitomo Eaton Nova Corporation, Mita 43 Mori Bldg., pg. 559   PB

SUMITOMO HEAVY INDUSTRIES, LTD., Sumitomo Heavy Industries Bldg., pg. 1314   IT

Sumitomo Life Insurance Company, 7-18-24, Tsukiji, pg. 1315   IT

SUMITOMO METAL INDUSTRIES, LTD., Tokyo Head Office, 1-8, Otemachi, 1-chome, pg. 1315   IT

SUMITOMO METAL MINING CO., LTD., 11-3, Shimbashi 5-chome, pg. 1316   IT

Sumitomo Rubber Industries-Tokyo Head Office, Toyosu Center Bldg., 3-3-3, Toyosu, Koto-ku, pg. 1317   IT

Sumitomo 3M Limited, P.O. Box 43 Tamagawa, 33-1 Tamagawadai 2-chome, pg. 1606   PB

Sumitomo-Yale Co., Ltd., 2-75 Daitoh-Cho, pg. 1150   PB

Sun-Ad Co., Ltd. Palace Bldg., 9th Fl., 1-1, Marunouchi 1-chome, pg. 1321   IT

SUN WAVE INDUSTRIAL CO., Daitokyo Kasai Shinju-ku, 3-25-3 Yoyogi, Shibuya-ku, pg. 1320   IT

Sunkist Pacific, Ltd., 4F Izumiya Tokyo Bldb No 2, pg. 1053   PV

Sunland Co., Ltd., 1, Kanda-Sakumacho 2-chome, pg. 878   IT

Suntory Allied Limited, 1509 New Aoyama Building East, 1-1 Minami Aoyama 1-chome, pg. 63   IT

Suntory Allied, Ltd., 2-3, Moto-Akasaka 1-chome, pg. 1321   IT

Suntory Allied Limited, 1509 New Aoyama Building East, 1-1 Minami Aoyama 1-chome, pg. 1321   IT

Suntory Food Manufacturing Co., Ltd., 2271, Omaru, pg. 1321   IT

Suntory Foods, Ltd., Southgate Shiryui Bldg., 6th/7th Floor, pg. 1321   IT

Suntory Publicity Service Co., Ltd., NNK Bldg., 1-12, Shinjuku 1-chome, pg. 1321   IT

Suntory Service Ltd., Shin-Nihon Bldg., 3rd Fl., 21-4, Akasaka 3-chome, pg. 1321   IT

Suntory Shopping Club, Ltd., Kyodo Bldg., 8th Fl., 10-12, Nihonbashi-Horidome-cho 1-chome, pg. 1321   IT

Super Channel Joint Enterprise, 5th Fl. Kikyo Bldg., 11-15, Akasaka 3-chome, Minato-ku, pg. 588   IT

Super Dining Corporation, Akasaka Alto Bldg. 7th Fl., 8-1, Akasaka 3 Chome, pg. 1321   IT

Svenska Handelsbanken Tokyo, Komai Building 9th Fl., 2-9 Nihonbashi Muromachi, pg. 1327   IT

Swedbank, Sweden Center Building, 6-11-9 Roppongi, pg. 1328   IT

Sweden Center Japan K.K., Sweden Center Bldg., 6-chome, 11-9 Roppongi, pg. 478   IT

Swiss Bank Corporation, Swiss Bank House, 1-8, Toranomon 4-chome, pg. 1330   IT

Swiss Bank Corporation, Swiss bank House, 1-8, Toranomon 4-chome, pg. 1330   IT

Swiss Bank Corporation, Swiss Bank House, 1-8 Toranomon 4-chome, pg. 1330   IT

Swiss Reinsurance Company-Representative Office Tokyo, Otemachi First Square 9F, pg. 1333   IT

Symantec K.K., Pine Bdlg. 6F, 3-11-2 Shibuya, pg. 1545   PB

Synthelabo Pharmaceuticals K.K., Dowa Bldg., 18-18 Roppongi 5-chome, pg. 818   IT

Systems Development Ltd., 2-12, Roppongi 3-chome, pg. 897   PB

TBS-Britannica Co., Ltd., 24-12, Meguro 1-chome, pg. 1321   IT

TDK CORPORATION, 1-13-1, Nihonbashi, Chuo-ku, pg. 1336   IT

T.I.C.-Citizen Co., Ltd., Daiichikangin Inagaki Building, 2-1, Shimomiyabicho, Shinjuku-ku, pg. 294   IT

T.K.K. Co., Ltd., 2-4-7, Misako-cho, pg. 1362   IT

TU-KA Cellular Tokyo Inc., pg. 944   IT

TYK CORPORATION, Tekko Bldg., 1-8-2, pg. 1345   IT

Tachi-S Co., Ltd., pg. 944   IT

Taiko Electric Work, Ltd., 6-10-13 Nakanobe, pg. 999   IT

Taisei Building Maintenance Service Co., Ltd., Nissay Edobashi Bldg., 13-12, Nihonbashi 2-chome, Chuo-ku, pg. 935   IT

TAISEI CORPORATION, 1-25-1, Nishi-Shinjuku, Shinjuku-ku, pg. 1347   IT

Taisei Rotec Corp., 3-13-1, Kyobashi, Chuo-ku, pg. 1347   IT

TAISHO PHARMACEUTICAL CO., LTD., 24-1, Takata 3-chome, pg. 1348   IT

THE TAIYO MUTUAL LIFE INSURANCE CO., 11-2, Nihonbashi 2-chome, pg. 1348   IT

The Taiyo Mutual Life Insurance Co., 7, Nibancho 7-chome, pg. 1348   IT

TAIYO YUDEN COMPANY LTD., 16-20 Ueno, pg. 1349   IT

Takeda Badische Urethane Industries Ltd., 3-3, Kioicho, Chiyoda-ku, pg. 109   IT

Takeda Chemical Industries, Ltd., 12-10, Nihonbashi 2-chome, pg. 1350   IT

Takeda Kagaku Shiryo Co., Ltd., 8-7, Kameido 1-chome, pg. 1350   IT

Takenaka Civil Engineering & Construction Co., Ltd., Hamarikyu Building, 21-1, Ginza 8-chome, Chuo-ku, pg. 1351   IT

Takenaka Corporation - Tokyo Office, 21-1, 8-chome, Ginza Chuo-ku, pg. 1351   IT

Takenaka Real Estate Development Co., Ltd., Toyocho Intesu, 5-14, Minamisuna 2-chome, Koto-ku, pg. 1351   IT

Tanabe Seiyaku Co., Ltd.-Tokyo, 26, Sanban-cho, Chiyoda-ku, pg. 1354   IT

Tandem Computers Japan Div., Tennoz Central Tower 2-2-24, Higashi-Shinagawa, pg. 417   PB

Tastemaker K.K., pg. 811   PB

Tatekawa Distribution Center, 14-6, Tatekawa 2-chome, Sumida-ku, pg. 578   PB

Tatung of Japan, Inc., Sanko Bldg., Honkan, 2f, 10-5, Ginza, 4-Chome, Chuo-ku, pg. 1357   IT

Taylor Instrument K.K., 4F Kokusai Hamamatsucho Bldg. 9-18,Kaiga, pg. 6   IT

TEAC CORPORATION, 3-7-3 Naka-Cho, pg. 1360   IT

Technical Research Institute, 640, 4-chome, Shimokiyoto, Kiyose-shi, pg. 995   IT

Techno Matsuya Co., Ltd., 3-6-1 Ginza, Chuo-ku, pg. 848   IT

Teijin-Hercules Ltd., pg. 811   PB

Tekelec, Ltd., Daiichi Ogikubo Bldg., 27-8 Ogikubo 5-chome, pg. 1566   PB

TEKKEN CORPORATION, 2-5-3 Misaki-cho, pg. 1362   IT

Teledyne Japan, Nihon Seimei Akasaka Bldg., 3rd Flr., pg. 44   PB

Television Tokyo Channel 12 Ltd., 4-3-12 Toranomon, pg. 929   IT

Telxon Japan, 6th Fl., Oxson Building,1-2-13, pg. 1574   PB

Teradyne, K.K., 5-4 Higashiyama 1-chome, pg. 1581   PB

TERUMO CORPORATION, 44-1, 2-chome, pg. 1375   IT

Terumo Japan Co. Ltd., 44-1, 2-chome, pg. 1376   IT

Tesa Seimitsu Co. Inc., Muranaka Bldg., 23-1, 2 Chome, pg. 261   PB

Tetsudo Sharyo Kogyo Co., Ltd., pg. 764   IT

Texas Instruments Japan Ltd., Aoyama Fuji Bldg., 6-12, Kita Aoyama 3-chome, pg. 1586   PB

Thermometrics Japan Co. Ltd., OT Building, 28-24 Hongo, pg. 209   PB

Tiffany & Co. K.K. (Japan), 3-1-31 Minami-Aoyama, pg. 1609   PB

Tipness, Ltd., 16-25, Nampeidai, pg. 1321   IT

Tohei Co., Ltd., 3-6-1 Ginza, Chuo-ku, pg. 848   IT

Toho Kagaku Kenkyusho Co., Ltd., Tatekawa 2-chome, Sumida-ku, pg. 540   PB

TOHO MUTUAL LIFE INSURANCE COMPANY, 15-1, Shibuya 2-chome, pg. 1390   IT

Tohoku Electric Power Co., Ltd.-Tokyo Branch, 5th Fl., Daini-Tekko Bldg., 8-2, Marunouchi 1-chome, pg. 1391   IT

The Tokai Bank, Limited, 6-1, Otemachi 2-chome, Chiyoda-ku, pg. 1391   IT

Toki Electric Co., Ltd., 4-3-1, Higashi-Shinagawa, pg. 1403   IT

THE TOKIO MARINE & FIRE INSURANCE COMPANY, LTD., 2-1, Marunouchi 1-chome, pg. 1391   IT

TOKO INC., 1-17, 2 Chome, Higashi, pg. 1393   IT

TOKUYAMA CORPORATION, Shibuya Konno Bldg., 3-1, Shibuya 3-chome, pg. 1393   IT

Tokyo Agency of Nippon Life Insurance Co., Ltd., Nihon Seimei Higashiikebukuro, Bldg., 11-1, Higashiikebukuro 1-chome, pg. 935   IT

Tokyo Calpis Beverages Co., Ltd., Higashi-Kurume, pg. 253   IT

Tokyo Caterpillar Mitsubishi Construction Equipment Sales, Ltd., 2968-6, Ishikawa, machi, pg. 317   PB

Tokyo Citizen Corporation, 18-7, 1-Chome, Ueno, Taito-ku, pg. 294   IT

Tokyo Electric Co., Ltd., 1-14-10, Uchikanda, Chiyoda-ku, pg. 1403   IT

THE TOKYO ELECTRIC POWER CO., INC., 1-1-3, Uchisaiwai-cho, pg. 1394   IT

Tokyo Electronic Industry Co., Ltd., 4-7-1 Asahigaoka, Hino, pg. 1403   IT

Tokyo Fashion Institute, 3-6-1 Ginza, Chuo-ku, pg. 848   IT

TOKYO GAS CO., LTD., 1-5-20 Kaigan, Minato-ku, pg. 1394   IT

Tokyo Iyakuhin Co., Ltd., 7-35, Horinouchi 1-chome, pg. 1350   IT

Tokyo Kinzoku Co., Ltd., pg. 1004   IT

Tokyo Lifestyles Institute, Inc., 3-6-1 Ginza, Chuo-ku, pg. 848   IT

Tokyo Motor Vehicle Works - Maruko Plant, 21-1 Shimomaruko 4-chome, pg. 875   IT

Tokyo Nissan Motor Co., Ltd., pg. 944   IT

PB - U.S. Public Companies Volume
PV - U.S. Private Companies Volume
IT - International Public & Private Companies Volume

1688

Geographic Index-Non U.S.

Tokyo Plant, 12-1 Minami-Rokugo 3-chome, pg. 723 **IT**
TOKYO PRINTING INK MANUFACTURING CO., LTD., 2-7-15, Tabata-Shinmachi, Kita-ku, pg. 1394 **IT**
Tokyo Reine, Ltd., Ginza Daihachi Kanai Bldg 7F, 5-15-18 Ginza, Chuo-ku, pg. 722 **IT**
TOKYO SENKO INTERNATIONAL INC., 6F NOA Bldg., 2-3-5, Azabudai, pg. 1394 **IT**
Tokyo Snow Brand Sales Co., Ltd., 13, Honshio-cho, Shinjuku-ku, pg. 1272 **IT**
Tokyo Subaru Motors Co., Ltd., pg. 523 **IT**
Tokyo Toyo-Pet Motor Sales Co., Ltd., Takanawa 3-23-10, pg. 1412 **IT**
Tokyo Toyota Motor Co., Ltd., Mita 3-11-34, pg. 1412 **IT**
TOKYU AGENCY INC., 4-8-18, Akasaka, pg. 1394 **IT**
Tokyu Agency International/DMB&B Japan, Shibuya TOD Bldg., 1-21-14 Dogenzaka, pg. 305 **PV**
TOKYU CORPORATION, 5-6 Nanpeidai-cho, pg. 1394 **IT**
Tokyu Hospital, 1-45-6 Kita-Senzoku, pg. 1395 **IT**
TONEN CORPORATION, Palace Side Bldg., No 1-1, 1-chome, pg. 1398 **IT**
Topcon Corporation, 75-1 Hasunumacho, Itabashi-ku, pg. 1403 **IT**
Toppan Moore Company Ltd., 1-6 Surugadai, Kanda, Chiyoda-ku, pg. 890 **IT**
TOPPAN PRINTING COMPANY, LTD., 1, Kanda Izumi-cho, Chiyoda-ku, pg. 1399 **IT**
TORAY INDUSTRIES, INC., 2-1, Nihonbashi-Muromachi 2-chome, pg. 1399 **IT**
Toray Research Center, Inc., Miyako Bldg., 1-8, Nihonbashi, Muro-machi 3-chome, pg. 1399 **IT**
Toronto Dominion Japan, Kamiyacho Mori Bldg., 16th Flr., 3-20 Toranomon 4-chome, pg. 1401 **IT**
Toshiba Air Conditioning Co., Ltd., 2-25-2 Kanda-sudacho, Chiyoda-ku, pg. 1403 **IT**
Toshiba AVE Co. Ltd., Hankyu Kotsusha Bldg. 3-3-9, pg. 1403 **IT**
Toshiba Ballotine Co., Ltd., 3-3-10 Shiba, Minato-ku, pg. 1403 **IT**
Toshiba Battery Co., Ltd., 7-13-10 Ginza, Chuo-ku, pg. 1403 **IT**
Toshiba Builders Appliance Co., Ltd., 1-11-15 Higashigotanda, Shinagawa-ku, pg. 1403 **IT**
Toshiba Building Corporation, 2-2-15 Soto Kanda, Chiyoda-ku, pg. 1403 **IT**
Toshiba Ceramics Co., Ltd., 1-26-2 Nishi Shinjuku, Shinjuku-ku, pg. 1403 **IT**
Toshiba Chemical Corporation, 3-3-9, Shinbashi, pg. 1403 **IT**
Toshiba Chuo Consumer Electronics Co., Ltd., 1-1-8 Soto Kanda, Chiyoda-ku, pg. 1403 **IT**
TOSHIBA CORPORATION, 1-1, Shibaura 1-chome, pg. 1402 **IT**
Toshiba Credit Corp., 1-8-5 Shinjuku, Shinjuku-ku, pg. 1403 **IT**
Toshiba Device Corporation, 7-25-2 Nishi Gotanda, pg. 1403 **IT**
Toshiba East Japan Life Electronics Co., Ltd., 1-1-8, Sotokanda, Chiyoda-ku, pg. 1404 **IT**
Toshiba Electronic Systems Co., Ltd., 2-5-1 Akasaka, Minato-ku, pg. 1404 **IT**
Toshiba Eletec Higashi Nihon Corporation, 3-4-7 Honcho, Chuo-ku, pg. 1404 **IT**
Toshiba Elevator & Escalator Service Co., Ltd., 7-9-5 Nishi Gotanda, Shinagawa-ku, pg. 1404 **IT**
Toshiba Elevator Sales Corporation, 2-31-19 Shiba, Minato-ku, pg. 1404 **IT**
Toshiba-EMI Limited, 2-17 Akasaka, 1-Chome, pg. 427 **IT**
Toshiba Engineering & Construction Co., Ltd., 3-7-1, Nishi-Shinbashi, Minato-ku, pg. 1404 **IT**
Toshiba Glass Co., Ltd., 5-35-10 Shinbashi, Minato-ku, pg. 1404 **IT**
Toshiba Information Equipment Co., Ltd., 1-4-28 Mita, Minato-ku, pg. 1404 **IT**
Toshiba Insurance Service Corporation, 5-2-1 Ginza, Chuo-ku, pg. 1404 **IT**
Toshiba KN System Co., Ltd., 4-9-11 Nihonbashi-honcho, pg. 1404 **IT**
Toshiba Leasing Corporation, 1-1-1 Shibaura, Minato-ku, pg. 1404 **IT**
Toshiba Lighting & Technology Corporation, 1-4-28 Mita, Minato-ku, pg. 1404 **IT**
Toshiba Logistics Corporation, 3-3-9 Shinbashi, Minato-ku, pg. 1404 **IT**
Toshiba Machine Co., Ltd., 4-2-11 Ginza, pg. 1404 **IT**
Toshiba Medical Systems Co., Ltd., 3-26-5 Hongo, Bunkyo-ku, pg. 1404 **IT**
Toshiba OA Consultants Ltd., 2-8-1 Toranomon, Minato-ku, pg. 1404 **IT**
Toshiba Physical Distribution Co., 3-3-9, Shinbashi, Minato-ku, pg. 1404 **IT**
Toshiba Shutoken Service & Engineering Co., Ltd., pg. 1404 **IT**
Toshiba Silicone Co., Ltd., 6-2-31 Roppongi, Minato-ku, pg. 1405 **IT**
Toshiba Technical Services International Corporation, 7-10-18 Ginza, Chuo-ku, pg. 1405 **IT**
Toshiba Telecommunication Field Engineering Corporation, 3-14 Asahigaoka, Hino, pg. 1405 **IT**
Toshiba Tourist Corporation, 1-1-1 Shibaura, Minato-ku, pg. 1405 **IT**
TOSHOKU LTD., Shimmuromachi Bldg., 4-3 Nihonbashi-Muromachi, pg. 1407 **IT**
TOSOH CORPORATION, 7-7, Akasaka 1-chome, pg. 1407 **IT**
TOSTEM CORPORATION, 1-1, Ojima 2-chome, pg. 1408 **IT**
Tourism Malaysia - Tokyo Office, 5 Fl., Chiyoda Building, 1-6-4, Yurakucho Chiyoda-ku, pg. 833 **IT**
Towa Kensetsu Co., Ltd., Kiya Bldg. 2F, 4-3-2, pg. 1362 **IT**

TOYO CORPORATION, 1-1-2 Nihonbashi-Hongokucho, pg. 1410 **IT**
Toyo Engineering Corp., 2-5, Kasumigaseki 3-chome, pg. 878 **IT**
Toyo-Morton, Ltd., TOIN Bldg., 8th Flr., pg. 1136 **PB**
Toyo Petrolite Co. Ltd., TOIN Bldg. 12-15, 2-chome, Shinkawa, Chuo-ku, pg. 166 **PB**
TOYO SEIKAN KAISHA, LTD., 1-3-1, Uchi-Saiwaicho, Chiyoda-ku, pg. 1411 **IT**
THE TOYO TRUST AND BANKING COMPANY, LIMITED, 4-3, Marunouchi 1-chome, pg. 1411 **IT**
Toyobo Tokyo, Toyobo Building, 17-9, Nihonbashi, Koami-cho, pg. 1411 **IT**
TOYOTA MOTOR CORPORATION, 1, Toyota-cho, pg. 1411 **IT**
Toyota Motor Corporation, 4-18, Koraku, 1-chome, Bunkyo-ku, pg. 1412 **IT**
Toyota Tokyo Auto Co., Ltd., Shinjuku 7-27-19, pg. 1412 **IT**
Toyota Tokyo Corolla Co., Ltd., Aobadai 3-1-1, pg. 1412 **IT**
Train Kogyo Co., Ltd., 2-8-5 Horidome-cho, Nihonbashi, pg. 759 **IT**
Transatlantic Holdings, Inc., Yurakucho Denki Building S., 7-1, Yuraku-cho 1 chome, pg. 84 **IT**
Transatlantic Holdings, Inc.-Tokyo, Yurakucho Denki Building, 7-1, pg. 85 **PB**
Transport Division, 26-20 Sakuragaoka-cho, pg. 1395 **IT**
Trimble Navigation Japan, Believe Mita Building, 11th Fl., Shiba 3-43-16, Minato-ku, pg. 1638 **PB**
Trio Labo Corporation, 14-6, Dogenzaka 1-chome, pg. 730 **IT**
Tsuchiya Mfg. Co., Ltd., 4-6-3, Higashi-Ikebukuro, pg. 944 **IT**
TSUMURA & CO., 12-7 Nibancho, Chiyoda-ku, pg. 1425 **IT**
UBE INDUSTRIES LTD., UBE Bldg., 3-11, Higashi-Shinagawa 2-chome, pg. 1426 **IT**
UBS Phillips & Drew Intl. Ltd., Yamato Seimei Bldg. 19F, 7, Uchisaiwai-cho, pg. 1440 **IT**
UBS Securities Limited, Tokyo Branch, Urbannet Otemachi Building 11F, 2-2-2 Otemachi Chiyoda-ku, pg. 1440 **IT**
UBS Securities Ltd., Urbannet Building 11F, 2-2-2 Otemachi, pg. 1441 **IT**
UBS Trust & Banking Ltd., Urbannet Building 12F, 2-2-2 Otemachi, pg. 1441 **IT**
Uddeholm KK, #2 Hibiya Osaka Bldg., 1-2-2, Uchisaiwai-cho, pg. 1472 **IT**
UNIDEN CORPORATION, 2-10-9 Hatchobori, pg. 1433 **IT**
Union Bank of Switzerland, Tokyo Branch, Urbannet Otemachi Building 12F, 2-2-2 Otemachi, pg. 1440 **IT**
Union Bank of Switzerland (Trust and Banking) Limited, Urbannet Otemachi Building 12F, 2-2-2 Otemachi, pg. 1441 **IT**
Union Carbide Japan K.K., Hiroo SK Bldg., 36-13, Ebisu 2-chome, pg. 1667 **PB**
Union Medical Supply Company, Mita Bldg., 29-10, Shiba 5-chome, Minato-ku, pg. 986 **PB**
Uniroyal Chemical Japan, Parkside Annex, 5th Fl., Banchi, Sanbancho, Chiyoda-ku, pg. 460 **PB**
United Asset Management (Japan), Inc., Sumitomo Toranomon Bldg., 1-6-12, Toranomon, pg. 1674 **PB**
United Media Japan, Mitsui Nishi Azabu Bldg., 17th Fl., 4 Chome 17-30, pg. 1448 **PB**
Universal Public Relations Inc., Matsu-ura Bldg., 18-3 Ebisu-minami 1 chome, pg. 1228 **IT**
UNIVERSAL SECURITIES CO., LTD., 4-2, Marunouchi 3-chome, pg. 1444 **IT**
Universal Studios Japan, Ltd., 5-2, Hirakawa Cho, 2-Chome, Chiyoda-ku, pg. 1216 **IT**
Universal Studios Music KK, 4-3, 3-Chome Akasada Minaid-Ku, pg. 1217 **IT**
UNUM Japan Accident Insurance Company Limited, Sanbancho UF Bldg.,2nd Floor, 6-3, Sanban-Cho, pg. 1700 **PB**
Upxon, Inc., A-Z Building, 1-12-6 Higashinakano, pg. 1435 **IT**
Utell International-Japan, 11F Nihon Seimei, Akasaka Dai 2 Building, pg. 1098 **IT**
V-One, Inc., Shibashimizu Bldg., 2-chome, 3-11 Shibadaimon, Minato-ku, pg. 366 **IT**
Valmet Japan Co., Ltd., Sumitomo Jukikai Bldg., 9-11, Kitashinagawa, 5-Chome, pg. 1448 **IT**
Van Leer Japan, Ltd, pg. 1147 **IT**
Vaubel & Partners Ltd., ARK Mori Bldg., 22nd Fl., pg. 405 **IT**
Veratec Japan, Ltd., Shichijushichi Bldg. 14-11, Ginza 4-chome, pg. 906 **PB**
Viacom Japan, Inc., 4F, Mitsuwa Bldg., pg. 779 **PV**
Victor Company of Japan, Ltd., 4-8-14, Nihonbashi-Honcho, Chuo-ku, pg. 846 **IT**
Viewlogic Asia Corporation, King Hills Hakusan 9F, 2-25-10, Hakusan 9F, pg. 1548 **PB**
Vitt Corporation, 2-62-6 Nihonbashi-hamacho, pg. 1405 **IT**
Volvo Japan Corporation, West Wing 16F, Ark Mori Bldg., 12-32, Akasaka 1-chome, pg. 1476 **IT**
Volvo Penta Asia Pacific Corporation, Sweden Center Bldg. 7F, 6-11-9 Roppongi, Minato-ku, pg. 1477 **IT**
Vorwerk Nippon K. K., Akasaka, Minuto-ku, pg. 1481 **IT**
Wackenhut Keibi K.K., Ginza-Matsuyoshi Bldg., Ginza 7-17-8, pg. 1731 **PB**
WAGO Company of Japan Limited, Kanda Center Building, 3-2 Kaji-cho 2-chome, pg. 209 **IT**
Wako Computer System Co., 2-4-14, Toyo, Koto-ku, pg. 1485 **IT**
Wako Finance Co., Ltd., 1-12-2, Kayaba-cho, Nihonbashi, pg. 1485 **IT**
The Wako Research Institute of Economics, Inc. (WRI), 1-16-3, Nishikawa, Chuo-ku, pg. 1485 **IT**
WAKO SECURITIES CO., LTD., 6-1, Koami-cho, Nihonbashi, pg. 1485 **IT**

Wall Data Japan K.K., Okayasu Biru 6F, 7-14, Shibaura 1-chome, pg. 1734 **PB**
Warburg Asset Management Japan Ltd., Hibiya Kokusai Bldg., 7th Fl., 2-2-3 Uchisaiwaicho, Chiyoda-ku, pg. 1331 **IT**
Warburg Investment Trust Management Company Ltd., Hibiya Kokusai Bld., 4th Fl., 2-2-3 Uchisaiwaicho, Chiyoda-ku, pg. 1331 **IT**
Warner-Lambert K.K., No. 31 Kowa Bldg. 19-1, pg. 1739 **PB**
Weber Marking Systems (Far East) Co. Ltd., 3-6-1 chome Tsukiji Chuo-ku, pg. 1157 **PV**
Werner & Pfleiderer Asia Ltd., 1-11, Shimabashi 3-Chome, pg. 511 **IT**
WestLB Securities Pacific Ltd., Fukoku Seimei Building, 2-2-2 Udisai Waicho, pg. 1494 **IT**
WestLB Tokyo Branch, Fukoka Seiruni Building, 2-2-2 Uchinsai Waicho, pg. 1493 **IT**
Westpac Banking Corp. - Japan, 8th Flr., ImperiaL Tower, 1-1-1 Uchisaiwai-Cho, pg. 1497 **IT**
Westvaco Asia, K.K., Shoyu Kaikan Bldg., 3-3-1 Kasumigaseki, Chiyoda-ku, pg. 1762 **PB**
Weyerhaeuser Japan Ltd., c/o William E. Franklin, pg. 1764 **PB**
Willis Corroon Japan Limited, Onarimon BN Building 6-F, 16-10 Shinbashi 6-Chome, pg. 1509 **IT**
Wilson Japan, Inc., Pola Bldg., 12F, 9-5, Nishigotanda 8-Chome, pg. 73 **IT**
Wind River Systems Japan/Asia-Pacific, Pola Ebisu Bldg. 11F, 3-9-19 Higashi, pg. 1771 **PB**
Woodhead Japan Corporation, 30 Sankyo Building, 3F, 1-30-4 Takadanobaba, pg. 1776 **PB**
The World Bank, Kokusai Bldg., Rm. 916, 1-1, Marunouchi 3-chome, pg. 1189 **PV**
Wrigley Company, Ltd., Japan, 1-2-1 Ohtemachi, pg. 1781 **PB**
Wyeth (Japan) Corporation, Central P.O. Box 975, pg. 82 **PB**
Xilinx K.K., Daini-Nagaoka Bldg. 2F, pg. 1786 **PB**
YKK CORPORATION, 1 Kanda Izumi-cho, Chiyoda-ku, pg. 1514 **IT**
Y.O. Machinery Leasing Co., Ltd., World Trade Center Bldg., 2-4-1, Hamamatsu-cho, pg. 1009 **IT**
Yamaha Hall Co., Ltd., 9-18, Ginza, 7-chome, pg. 1515 **IT**
Yamaha Kyohan Co., Ltd., 9-18, Ginz, 7-chome, pg. 1516 **IT**
Yamaichi Business Services Co., Ltd., 20-1 Shiohama 2-chome, pg. 1516 **IT**
Yamaichi Echo & Co., Ltd., 5-1, Kabuto-cho Nihombashi, pg. 1516 **IT**
Yamaichi Enterprise Co., Ltd., 1-5-1, Hatchobori, Chuo-ku, pg. 1516 **IT**
Yamaichi Finance Co., Ltd., 20-1, Shiohama 2-chome, pg. 1516 **IT**
Yamaichi Information Systems Co., Ltd., 20-1, Shiohama 2-chome, pg. 1516 **IT**
Yamaichi International Capital Management Co., Ltd., 14-8, Ningyo-cho Nihombashi, 1-chome, pg. 1516 **IT**
Yamaichi Investment Trust Management Co., Ltd., 3-4, Nihombashi, 2-Chome, Chuo-ku, pg. 1516 **IT**
Yamaichi Real Estate Inc., 16-1, Nihombashi Kayabacho, pg. 517 **IT**
Yamaichi Research Institute of Securities & Economics, Inc., 20-1, Shiohama, 2-chome, pg. 1517 **IT**
YAMAICHI SECURITIES CO., LTD., 4-1, Yaesu 2-chome, Chuo-ku, pg. 1516 **IT**
Yamaichi Trust & Bank, Ltd., 4-3, Nihombashi Kabutocho, pg. 1517 **IT**
Yamaichi World Tourist Inc., 9-15, Kabuto-cho Nihombashi, pg. 1517 **IT**
Yamako Electric Manufacture Co., Ltd., 4-3-3 Higashishinagawa, pg. 999 **IT**
Yamamoto Mfg. Co., Ltd., 4-4, Shimizucho, Itabashi-ku, pg. 294 **IT**
Yamanouchi Health and Beauty Co., Ltd., 3-11, Nihonbashi-Honcho 2-chome, pg. 1518 **IT**
Yamanouchi Medical Co., Ltd., 3-11, Nihonbashi-Honcho 2-chome, pg. 1518 **IT**
YAMANOUCHI PHARMACEUTICAL CO. LTD., 3-11, Nihonbashi-Honcho, 2-chome, pg. 1518 **IT**
Yamanouchi Real Estate Co., Ltd., 3-11, Nihonbashi-Honcho 2-chome, pg. 1518 **IT**
Yamatake-Honeywell Company Ltd., Totate-International Bldg., pg. 835 **PB**
YAMATO TRANSPORT CO., LTD., 16-10, Ginza 2-chome, pg. 1519 **IT**
YAMAZAKI BAKING CO., LTD., 3-10-1 Iwamoto-cho, pg. 1519 **IT**
THE YASUDA FIRE & MARINE INSURANCE COMPANY LIMITED, 26-1, Nishi-Shinjuku 1-chome, pg. 1519 **IT**
YASUDA MUTUAL LIFE INSURANCE CO., 1-9-1, Nishi-Shinjuku, pg. 1519 **IT**
THE YASUDA TRUST AND BANKING CO., LTD., 2-1 Yaesu, 1-chome, Chuo-ku, pg. 1520 **IT**
Yatsugatake Snow Brand Milk Co., Ltd., 13, Honshio-cho, Shinjuku-ku, pg. 1272 **IT**
YAZAKI CORPORATION, Mita Kokusai Bldg., 17th Flr., pg. 1520 **IT**
YOKOGAWA ELECTRIC CORPORATION, 2-9-32 Nakacho, Musashino-shi, pg. 1520 **IT**
Yokogawa-Hewlett-Packard Ltd., 3-8-21, Takaido-higashi, pg. 824 **PB**
Yokogawa-Hewlett-Packard Ltd., Shinjuku Daiichiseimei Bldg., 2-7-1, Nishi-shinjuku, pg. 824 **PB**
Yokogawa-Hewlett-Packard Ltd., 9-1, Takakura-Cho, pg. 823 **PB**
Yokogawa-Hewlett-Packard Ltd., Tokyo Nissan Minato Bldg., 1-6-34, Konan, pg. 823 **PB**
Yokogawa-Hewlett-Packard Ltd., 3-8-20, Takaido-Higashi, pg. 823 **PB**

PB - *U.S. Public Companies Volume*
PV - *U.S. Private Companies Volume*
IT - *International Public & Private Companies Volume*

Yokogawa-Hewlett-Packard Ltd., Japan Marketing Center, 4-15-7, Nishi-Shinjuku, pg. 824 **PB**
Yokogawa-Hewlett-Packard Ltd., Tokyu Sakuragaoka Bldg., 31-2, Sakuragaoka-Cho, pg. 824 **PB**
Yokogawa-Kitz-Valtek Corp. (Y-K-V), Gotanda San Haitu 2F, 1-26-2 Nishi-gotanda, pg. 659 **PB**
Yokohama Aeroquip KK, Dowa Bldg., 10-5 Shimbashi 5-chome, pg. 1521 **IT**
THE YOKOHAMA RUBBER CO., LTD., 36-11, Shimbashi 5-chome, pg. 1521 **IT**
YOMIKO ADVERTISING INC., 8-14, Ginza, 1-Chome, pg. 1522 **IT**
YONEX CO., LTD., 23-13, Yushima 3-chome, pg. 1522 **IT**
York Mart Co., Ltd., 1-4, Shibakoen 4-chome, pg. 693 **IT**
YUASA CORPORATION, NT Building, 47-1, Oh-1, 1-Chome, pg. 1522 **IT**
Yuasa-Ionics Co., Ltd., No. 12-11 2-chome, pg. 912 **PB**
Zao Shokuhin Co., Ltd., 2-4-16 Kyobashi, pg. 855 **IT**
Zeneca KK, 9th Fl. Akasaka Ohji Bldg., pg. 1526 **IT**
THE ZENSHINREN BANK, 8-1, Kyobashi 3-chome, pg. 1527 **IT**
ZEXEL CORPORATION, Zekusuru Building, Shibuya, 6-7, 3-Chome, pg. 1528 **IT**
Zexel Corporation-Tokyo, pg. 1528 **IT**
Zurich Insurance Company, Shinanomachi Rengakan, 35, Shinanomachi, pg. 1531 **IT**

Tomakomai

Yufutsu Mill, 143 Yufutsu, pg. 938 **IT**

Tomioka

Tomioka Plant, 1-1, Tajino, pg. 1528 **IT**

Toride

Optron Inc., 5-16, Hakusan 7-chome, pg. 261 **IT**

Tottori

Tottori Asahi Kokokusha, Ltd., Tauda Bldg., 2-109 Nishimachi, pg. 366 **IT**
Tottori Sanyo Electric Co., Ltd., 201, Minami-Yoshikata 3-chome, pg. 1191 **IT**

Toyama

Hakuhodo Inc., 7th fl., Urban Place Bldg., 18-7 Ushijima-cho, pg. 587 **IT**
THE HOKURIKU BANK, LTD., 2-26, Tsutsumicho-dori 1-chome, pg. 627 **IT**
HOKURIKU ELECTRIC INDUSTRY CO., LTD., 3158, Shimo-okubo, Osawano-machi, pg. 627 **IT**
The Industrial Bank of Japan, Limited (Toyama Branch), 5-13, Sakurabashi-dori, pg. 674 **IT**
NKK-Toyama Works, 2-9-38, Shosei-machi, pg. 902 **IT**
Richell Corporation, 136 Sakuragi Mizuhashi, pg. 1411 **PB**

Toyohashi

Asahi Kogyo Co., Ltd., 88, Zosha, pg. 621 **IT**
Kabushiki Kaisha TMK, 1 Ishizu, Aotake-cho, pg. 831 **IT**
VANS Finance Corporation, pg. 1475 **IT**
Volkswagen Audi Nippon K.K., 5-11 Akemi-cho, pg. 1475 **IT**

Toyokawa

Sampo Techno Construction Co., Ltd., pg. 764 **IT**
Suzuki Special Products Manufacturing Co., Ltd., 2-30 Kaiun Douri, pg. 1323 **IT**

Toyonaka

Japan Power Fastening Co., Ltd., 1-5-3 Shinsenrihigashi-machi, pg. 901 **IT**
TIGERS POLYMER CORPORATION, 4-1,1, Shinsenri-Higashimachi, pg. 1390 **IT**

Toyota

Takashimaya Nippatsu Kogyo Co., Ltd., No. 1-1 Maihata, pg. 902 **IT**
Yokogawa-Hewlett-Packard Ltd., Toyota Tokyokaijou Bldg., 1-179, Miyukihonchou, pg. 823 **PB**

Tsu

NKK-Tsu Works, 1 Kumozu-kokan-cho, pg. 902 **IT**

Tsuchiura

Cocos Japan, Kantochiiki-Spar, pg. 724 **IT**
KASUMI CO., LTD., 1-3 Higashi-Nakannkimachi, pg. 724 **IT**
Sony/Tektronix Corporation-Tsuchiura, pg. 1568 **PB**

Tsukuba

Intel Japan K.K., 5-6 Tokodai, pg. 887 **PB**
LSI Logic Japan Semiconductor Inc., 10 Kitahara, pg. 971 **PB**

Nihon Sun Microsystems K.K., Tsukuba Techinical Center, 5-6 Tokodai, pg. 1531 **PB**
Nihon Sun Microsystems K.K., Tsukuba Technical Center, 278-1, Onozaki, pg. 1531 **PB**
Nippon Shokubai-Tsukuba Research Laboratory, 1-25-12 Kannondai, pg. 939 **IT**
Oxford Instruments, Nunokawa Building, 2nd Floor 8-1 Inarimae, pg. 1018 **IT**
Tsukuba Research Laboratory, 40, Wadai, pg. 1394 **IT**
Yokogawa-Hewlett-Packard Ltd., Tsukuba Mitsui Bldg., 1-6-1, Takezono, pg. 823 **PB**

Ube

Ube Machinery & Engineering Works, 1980, Okinoyama, Kogushi, pg. 1427 **IT**
Ube Office, 12-32 Nishi-honmachi 1-chome, pg. 1426 **IT**

Ushiku

Tsukuba Plant, 1000, Higashimamiana, pg. 871 **IT**

Utsunomiya

Calsonic Harrison Co., Ltd., 11-6, Kiyohara Kogyo-Danchi, pg. 724 **PB**
Fuji Heavy Industries, Ltd., Rolling Stock Div., 1-11, Yonan 1-chome, pg. 523 **IT**
Kyodo Advertising Co., Ltd., Tochigi Chuo Bldg., 2-3-6 Haniwada, pg. 776 **IT**

Uwae

Miura Koki Co., Ltd., 4020 Oaza-Kakio, pg. 884 **IT**

Wakayama

Daiko: Wakayama, Taiyo Seimei Wakayama Daini, 39-1 Misonocho 2-chome, pg. 366 **IT**
Rental Sanwa Co., Ltd., 775, Iwahashi, pg. 317 **PB**
TAKAGI CHOKOKU CO., LTD., 1525 Nakanoshima, pg. 1349 **IT**

Yaita

T.V. & Video Systems Group, 174 Hayakawa-cho, pg. 1228 **IT**

Yaizu

Yaizu Plant, pg. 1518 **IT**

Yamagata

Asahi Komag Company Limited, 2837-9 Hachimanpara, pg. 966 **PB**
JAE Yamagata, Ltd., Oaza Izumida, Stanjo-shi, pg. 701 **IT**
Kenwood Yamagata Corporation, 15-80, Takarada 1-chome, pg. 730 **IT**
Komori Electronics Co., Ltd., 2589-15, Oaza-Nukanome, Takahatamachi, Higashiokitama-gun, pg. 745 **IT**
Komori Machinery Co., Ltd., 300, Oaza-Fukuzawa, Takahatamachi, Higashiokitama-gun, pg. 745 **IT**
Komori Precision Yamagata Co., Ltd., 6, Fukuzawa, Takahatamachi, Higashiokitama-gun, pg. 745 **IT**
Marcor Electronics Co., Ltd., 1-1, Saiwai-cho, pg. 1403 **IT**
Tohoku Electric Power Co., Ltd.-Yamagata Branch, 1-9, Honcho 2-chome, pg. 1391 **IT**
Yamagata Sanken Co., Ltd., 5600-2 Higashine-Ko, pg. 1188 **IT**

Yamaguchi

Kemira-Ube, Ltd., Ube Plant, 2575 Ohaza Fujimagari, pg. 729 **IT**
MTT Ltd., 1-1, Mikage-cho, Tokuyama, pg. 1393 **IT**
Seibu Tokuyama Ready Mixed Concrete Co., Ltd., 1-1, Mikage-cho, Tokuyama, pg. 1393 **IT**
Shimano Yamaguchi Co., Ltd., 4-7, Ozuki Kojima 1-chome, pg. 232 **IT**
Sun Arrow Chemical Co., Ltd., 1-2, Harumi-cho, Tokuyama, pg. 1394 **IT**
Tokuyama Factory, 1-1 Mikage-cho, pg. 1394 **IT**

Yamanashi

Citizen Electronics Co., Ltd., 23-1, 1-Chome, Kamikurechi, pg. 293 **IT**
FANUC LTD., 3580, Shibokusa Aza-Komanba, pg. 477 **IT**
JAE Fuji, Ltd., 1035, Uenohara, Denohara-machu, pg. 701 **IT**
Kawaguchiko Seimitsu Co., Ltd., 6663-2, Funatsu, Kawaguchikomachi, pg. 294 **IT**
Koshin Caterpillar Mitsubishi Construction Equipment Sales, Ltd., 427 Shimoimai, pg. 317 **PB**
Minebea Onkyo Co., Ltd., 753 Nakadate, pg. 868 **IT**
Rohm Fuji Co., Ltd., 4453, Kamiyoshida, pg. 1125 **IT**
Showa Kanko Kaihatsu Co., Ltd., 3859, Ushiku, pg. 1321 **IT**
Tesco Co., Ltd., 881, Mami-Imai-cho, pg. 1262 **IT**
Yamanashi Jozo Co., Ltd., pg. 855 **IT**

Yamato

Molex Ltd., 1-5-4 Fukami-Higashi, pg. 1122 **PB**

Yamatotkada

Nanto Bank-Takada Branch, 12-28 Katashio-cho, pg. 905 **IT**

Yao

Appliance Systems Group, 3-1-72 Kita Kamei-cho, pg. 1228 **IT**
HOSIDEN CORPORATION, 1-4-33, Kitakyuhoji, pg. 635 **IT**
Koyo-Mattison, 34, 2-Chome, pg. 715 **PV**

Yatsushiro

Yatsushiro Mill, 1-1 Jujo-machi, pg. 938 **IT**

Yawata

Yawata Plant, pg. 364 **IT**

Yokkaichi

Daiko: Mio, Yokkaichi-Sanko Bldg., 12-3 Hamada-cho, pg. 365 **IT**
Mitsubishi Chemical BASF Co., Ltd., 1000 Kawajiri-cho, pg. 106 **IT**

Yokohama

AMP (Japan), Ltd., 87 Hisamoto, Takatsu-Ku, pg. 9 **PB**
AGIE Nippon Ltd., 27-10 Hayabuchi 1-chome, pg. 488 **IT**
Ancra Japan, Kan-nai-Kowa Bldg., 9F-2-9-4 Minato-Cho, pg. 71 **PV**
Asahi Advertising Inc., Yokohama Asahi Kaikan, pg. 81 **IT**
Atsugi Motor Parts Co., Ltd., Atsugi, pg. 944 **IT**
BANK OF YOKOHAMA, 1-1, Minatomirai 3-chome, pg. 158 **PB**
Braun Japan K.K., 891 Siber Hegner Bldg., pg. 744 **IT**
Charmilles Technologies (Japan) Ltd., 1-14-11, Shin Yokohama, Kohoku-Ku, pg. 489 **IT**
Cherry Automotive-Japan, 20-20 Hiradai,Midori-Ku, pg. 346 **PB**
Eastman Kodak (Japan) Research & Devel. Ctr., 1-2 Ninomaru, Midori-ku, pg. 552 **PB**
ELCO International K.K., 1794 Nippa-cho, Kohoku-ku, pg. 775 **IT**
Ericsson Toshiba Telecommunication Systems K.K., Hayama, Dai-4 Building, 1-2-1, Shin-Yokohama, Kohoku-ku, pg. 1368 **IT**
ESTECH Corporation, Siber Hegner Building, 5F, 89-1 Yamashita-cho, pg. 1525 **IT**
The Furukawa Battery Co., Ltd., 16-1 Hoshikawa 2-chome, Hodogaya-ku, pg. 530 **IT**
Genus KK, Shin Yokohama W. Bldg., 8th Fl, 2-3-3 Shin Yokohama, pg. 733 **PB**
Goldstar Japan C/S, Saedo 140-1, Midori-ku, pg. 779 **IT**
Graco K.K., 1-26-10 Hayabuchi, Tsuzuki-ku, pg. 757 **PB**
Hagglunds Drives Ltd, Higashi-totsuka West Bldg., 9F, 90-6 Kawakami-cho, pg. 670 **IT**
Hagglunds Ltd. Dept. Drives, West Bldg. 902, Higashi-Totsuka, pg. 670 **IT**
Hakuhodo Pro's, Inc., 10th Fl., Yokohama Fukoku Seimei Bldg., pg. 588 **IT**
Hysol Japan Limited, 2050 Kamiyabe-Cho, pg. 505 **PB**
The Inctec Inc., 450 Aoto-cho Midori-ku, pg. 363 **IT**
The Industrial Bank of Japan, Limited (Yokohama Branch), 4-1, Kitasaiwai 1-chome, Nishi-ku, pg. 674 **IT**
K.K. Japan Helium Center, 6-2 Kojima-Cho, pg. 122 **IT**
Johnson Company, Ltd., Ninomiya P.O. Box 7, pg. 593 **PV**
K and M Co., Ltd., pg. 1024 **IT**
Kanagawa Toyota Motor Sales Co., Ltd., Sakae-cho 7, pg. 1412 **IT**
Kenex Corporation, 16-2, Hakusan 1-chome, pg. 730 **IT**
Kodak Japan Industries Ltd., 18-2, Hakusan 1-chome, pg. 552 **PB**
Kodak Japan Ltd.-Technical Center, 1-2 Ninomaru, Midori-ku, pg. 552 **PB**
Lambda Physik Japan Co., Ltd., German Industry Center, 1-18-2, Hakusan-Midori-ku, pg. 396 **PB**
Lands' End Japan, K.K., Shinyokohama Tobu AK Bldg. 5F, 3-23-3 Shinyokohama, pg. 978 **PB**
Liebherr Japan Co. Ltd., 5-39, Daikoku-Cho, pg. 809 **PB**
Littelfuse KK, KC Building 6F, 3-16-1 Shinyokohama Kouhoku-ku, pg. 1001 **PB**
Loctite (Japan) Corp., 15-13 Fukuura 1-chome, pg. 611 **IT**
MacGREGOR Hagglunds, Higashitotsuka, West Bldg. 9F, 90-6 Kawakami Cho, pg. 671 **IT**
Matsushita Communication Industrial Co., Ltd., 4-3-1, Tsunashima-Higashi, Kohoku-ku, pg. 846 **IT**
Mikron Ltd. Tokyo, Nisso 11, Bldg. 2-3-4, Shin-Yokohama, Kohoku-ku, pg. 867 **IT**
Mitsui Wharf Co., Ltd., 9-1, Ohgi-machi, Kawasaki-ku, pg. 878 **IT**
NHK Morse Co., Ltd., 3-21-10 Shinyokohama, pg. 901 **IT**
NHK SPRING CO., LTD., 3-10, Fukuura, Kanazawa-ku, pg. 901 **IT**
NHK Spring R&D Center Inc., 3-10 Fukuura, pg. 902 **IT**
NHK Transport Co., Ltd., 3-10 Fukuura, pg. 902 **IT**
NKK-Tsurumi Works, 2-1 Suehiro-cho, pg. 902 **IT**
NYK-Yokohama Branch, 9, Kaigandori, 3-chome, pg. 941 **IT**
NIFCO INC., 184-1, Maioka-cho, pg. 928 **IT**
Nihon Robinson Nugent K.K., 2F, Bldg. No. 1, 1 Higashikata-cho Midori-ku, pg. 1395 **PB**
Nihon Timken K.K., 89-1 Yamashita-Cho, pg. 1617 **PB**
Nikkei Advertising Co., 2-11-5, Tsuruya-Cho, pg. 930 **IT**
Nippatsu Amemity Co., Ltd., 3-10 Fukuura, pg. 902 **IT**

PB - *U.S. Public Companies Volume*
PV - *U.S. Private Companies Volume*
IT - *International Public & Private Companies Volume*

1690

Geographic Index-Non U.S.

Nippatsu Service Co., Ltd., 3-chome, 32-1 Tsuruya-cho, pg. 902 — IT
Nippon MacDermid K.K., 35-5 Sakuradai, pg. 1030 — PB
Nippon Shaft Co., Ltd., 2-1-15 Sachivra, pg. 902 — IT
Nissan Koei Co., Ltd., pg. 944 — IT
Nissan Rikuso Co., Ltd., pg. 944 — IT
Nissan Transport Co., Ltd., pg. 944 — IT
Olicom Japan, 4F, Shin-yokohama Daisan Tosho Bldg., pg. 1001 — IT
Osram-Melco Ltd., Tobu Yokohama Bldg. No. 3 (4F), 8-29, Kitaisawai 2-Chome, Nishi-ku, pg. 1244 — IT
Parker Bertea Aerospace, 1-15-19 Hirato, Totsuka-ku, pg. 1262 — PB
Parker Hannifin Japan Ltd., 626 Totsuka-cho, Totsuka-ku, pg. 1263 — PB
Pasco Retail Co., Ltd., pg. 1024 — IT
Pasco Road Technology Center Co., Ltd., pg. 1024 — IT
qad.japan k.k., Landmark Tower 43/F, Minato-mirai 2-2-1 Nishi-ku, pg. 1345 — PB
Rammer Oy Japan Office, 202 4-19-1 Edahigashi, Midori-ku, pg. 1352 — IT
K.K. Raychem, 1-12-17 Eda-nishi, pg. 1362 — IT
SAKATA SEED CORPORATION, 2-7-1 Nakamachidai-Tsuzuki-Ku, pg. 1178 — IT
Shin Caterpillar Mitsubishi Ltd., 3700 Tana Sagamihara-shi, pg. 317 — IT
Siegling (Japan) Ltd., pg. 498 — IT
Suntory Sports System, Ltd., 1588-1, Shinano-machi, pg. 1321 — IT
Thermon Far East, Ltd., 2-17-1 Tsuruya-cho, pg. 1081 — PV
Tokyo Ryuki Seizo Co., Ltd., 50-1 Kawawa-cho, Midori-ku, pg. 878 — PB
Tokyo Sokuhan Co., Ltd., pg. 944 — IT
Toshiba Components Co., Ltd., 450 Nakayama-cho, Midori-ku, pg. 1403 — IT
Toyota Corolla Kanagawa Co., Ltd., Kariba-cho 65, pg. 1412 — IT
Tri-Sure Japan Ltd., pg. 1146 — IT
Wandel & Goltermann K.K., Kyorisu Shin-Yokohama Bldg. 6, 2-15-12 Shin-Yokohama, Kouhoku-ku, pg. 1486 — IT
Wells Japan Ltd., Shin Yokohama Hayama Bldg. #6, 1-28-9 Shin Yokohama, pg. 1242 — IT
Yokohama Branch, pg. 1518 — IT
Yokohama Creative Center, 1-1-32, Shinurashima-cho, pg. 905 — IT
Yokohama Kiko Co., Ltd., 2-chome, 11-1 Fukuura, pg. 902 — IT
Yokohama Mirai-Kenkyusho, 15-1, Shinei-cho, Tsuzuki-ku, pg. 905 — IT
Yokohama Plant, 471 Nagaodai-machi, pg. 931 — IT
Yokohama Toyopet Co., Ltd., Higashi-cho 14, pg. 1412 — IT
Yokohama Transportation Co., Ltd., pg. 944 — IT
Yokoyu Vantec Corporation, pg. 944 — IT
Zycad Japan K.K., Toshin 24 Shin Yokohama Bldg., B-8F, 2-3-8, Shin-Yokohama, Kohoku-ku, pg. 703 — PB

Yokosuka

Hitachi Machinery & Engineering, Ltd., 1-284-5, Funakoshicho, pg. 621 — IT
Japan Nuclear Fuel Co., Ltd., 2-3-1, Uchikawa, pg. 1403 — IT
Kanto Auto Works, Ltd., Taura-Minatomachi, pg. 1412 — IT

Yono

Saitama Toyopet Co., Ltd., Kami-Ochiai 2-2-1, pg. 1412 — IT
Saitama Toyota Motor Sales Co., Ltd., Shimo-Ochiai 6-1-18, pg. 1412 — IT

Yorii

Yorri Plant, 1744-1, Aza-Minamiotsuka, Oaza-Orihara, pg. 1528 — IT

Yubari

Shanon Co., Ltd., 1-63, Asahidai, Kuriyama-cho, pg. 1393 — IT

Zama

Simmons Co., Ltd., 4-6259 Hibarigaoka, pg. 929 — IT

JORDAN

Amman

ANZ Grindlays Bank plc Jordan, pg. 99 — IT
Bailey Controls Jordan for Process Controls Services, Ltd., pg. 449 — IT
Best Foods Jordan, pg. 224 — IT
CIBA-GEIGY Services Limited-Scientific & Advisory Office, pg. 980 — IT
Computer & Engineering Bureau (CEB), pg. 1228 — PB
Electrolux Jordan Trading Company Ltd., P.O. Box 925229, pg. 443 — IT
Intermarkets Jordan/Jerusalem Ad. Agency, Shmeisani Area, Abdul Hamid Sharaf St., pg. 680 — IT
Lockheed Corporation (International) S.A., Housing Bank Complex Bldg., pg. 1009 — PB
Mechanical Engineers & Contractors (MEC), Jabal Amman, Prince Moh'd Str., Tower Building, 10th Floor, pg. 550 — IT
Middle East Can Manufacturing Company, pg. 465 — PB
Mitsui & Co., Ltd., Salim Awad Bldg. Malfoof El Gharbi, 4th, pg. 881 — IT

Notifier Middle East, pg. 1307 — PB
OMNITRADE EST., pg. 458 — IT
SKF Intertrade S.A. Amman, pg. 1158 — IT
Schauman Wood Oy-Regional Office, pg. 1429 — IT
Scientific and Medical Supplies Co., P.O. Box 1387, pg. 823 — PB
Sharikat al Asmida al Muttahida Ltd. (Unifert), pg. 109 — IT
Shell Chemical Distributing Co. Ltd., Opposite Ministry of Industry, & Commerce, pg. 1140 — IT
United Telecom Services Co. Ltd., pg. 1371 — IT
Yordan Obegi & Co. Ltd., Smeisani Road, pg. 110 — IT

Aqaba

Det Norske Veritas, pg. 397 — IT

KAMPUCHEA

Phnom Penh

Dumez-GTM Cambodge, 1, rue 150, pg. 823 — IT
Pochentong Airport Construction JV, 1, rue 150, pg. 823 — IT
Standard Chartered Bank (Cambodia), 95-A Sihanouk Avenue, pg. 1295 — IT

KAZAKHSTAN

Akmola

CIBA-GEIGY Limited-Representative Office, ul. Monina 7, pg. 978 — IT

Almaty

CCF Kazakhstan, 48 Karasay Batir, Apt. 2, pg. 342 — IT
CIBA-GEIGY Limited-Representative Office, ul. Naurysbaj Batyra 58, pg. 978 — IT
CIBA-GEIGY Limited-Representative Office, ul. Bogenbaj Batyra 152, pg. 978 — IT
Coeclerici Trading S.p.A., Zhibek Zholi, 64-Room 603, pg. 303 — IT
EurAsia Consult, 52, Amangeldi (3rd floor), pg. 606 — IT
Novo Nordisk A/S, Seiphulina Str. 534, Apt. 28,30, pg. 987 — IT
Ram Representative Office-Kazakhstan, Prospect Lenina DOM 19 KB 1, pg. 741 — IT
SNC-Lavalin, 157 Abai Street, 7th Floor, pg. 1162 — IT
Sodexho Kazakhstan, 7, rue Tchaikovski, pg. 1275 — IT
Sogecred S.A., Kazakh Business Center Office, n.208, Prospect Lenina 85, pg. 137 — IT
Styx & Leo Burnett, 39 Gogol Str., 3rd. Floor, pg. 186 — PV
Vertretung der BASF in Kasachstan, ul. Tole bi 69, pg. 110 — IT
The World Bank, Samal-1 Bldg. No. 36, 3rd Floor, pg. 1189 — PV
Zeneca Almaty, Ul. Abaya, pg. 1526 — IT

KENYA

Mombassa

Bamburi Portland Cement Co Ltd, pg. 789 — IT
Det Norske Veritas, Laxmi House, Moi House, pg. 398 — IT
Kodak (Kenya) Limited, Meru Rd., pg. 553 — PB
Nedlloyd (E.A.) Limited, pg. 1144 — IT
Van Leer East Africa Ltd, pg. 1146 — IT

Nairobi

Access Advertising Limited, Bishop Gardens Towers, 6th Fl., pg. 303 — PV
Adcom Ltd., Inc., Kenya, P.O. Box 30070, pg. 816 — PB
Ashcott Ltd., Nationwide House, Koinange St., pg. 816 — PB
Ayton Young & Rubicam Ltd., 5th Fl., Longonot Place, Kijabe St., pg. 1198 — PV
BASF East Africa Ltd., Nacico Co-op Chambers, Mondlane St., pg. 106 — IT
BDF East Africa Ltd., pg. 183 — IT
BOC Kenya Ltd., Kitui Rd., Indus. Area; P.O. Box 18010, pg. 122 — IT
Barclays Bank of Kenya Ltd., P.O. Box 30120, Bank House, Moi Ave., pg. 165 — IT
BarclayTrust Investment Services Limited, Queensway House, Kaunda St., pg. 166 — IT
Bissett & Rogers, pg. 1502 — IT
Blackwood Hodge (Kenya) Ltd., Enterprise Rd., pg. 607 — IT
CEGP, Consulting Engineers Grabowsky & Poort), pg. 607 — IT
CPC Industrial Products, Outer Ring Rd., pg. 225 — PB
CPC Industrial Products (Kenya) Ltd., Outer Ring Road, pg. 447 — PB
CPC Kenya Ltd., pg. 225 — IT
Cadbury Kenya Limited, OL Kalou Rd., pg. 248 — IT
CIBA-GEIGY Trading and Marketing Services Co. Ltd.-Regional Office, pg. 980 — IT
Colgate-Palmolive (E. Africa) Ltd., Mogadishu Rd., Plot L.R. 209/6554, pg. 398 — PB
The Crown Cork Company (East Africa) Ltd., Funzi Rd., pg. 464 — PB
CUNA Mutual Group-Africa, Ralph Bunche/Valley Roads, pg. 296 — PV
D.I.C. (UK) Ltd., 4th Fl., Kimati House, Kimati Street, pg. 372 — IT
Daewoo Corp.- Nairobi, Posta Sacco Plaza, 11th Fl., University Way, pg. 358 — IT

Thomas De La Rue (Kenya) Limited, Noordin Rd., pg. 386 — IT
East Africa Industries Ltd., pg. 1436 — IT
East African Cables Ltd., Kitui Rd., pg. 390 — IT
Gailey & Roberts Ltd., pg. 1437 — IT
General Motors Kenya Ltd., Mombasa & Enterprise Rds., pg. 724 — PB
Gestetner Limited, Bunyala Road Junction, Uhuru Highway, pg. 1115 — IT
Guiness Kenya Limited, c/o Queensway Trustees Ltd., Barclays Bank Bldg., Kayunda St., pg. 412 — IT
Habib Bank Ltd., Clyde House, Kimathi St., pg. 584 — IT
Henkel Kenya Ltd., Outer Ring Rd., pg. 613 — IT
ICL Kenya Limited, 8th Floor, Bruce House, pg. 529 — IT
Interfreight (Kenya) Limited, pg. 1022 — IT
International Flavors & Fragrances I.F.F. (East Africa) Ltd., Lavington Green Shopping Centre, pg. 899 — PB
Johnson & Johnson (Kenya) Ltd., Industrial Area, Nanyuhi Road, pg. 930 — PB
Johnson's Wax (East Africa) Ltd., Lunga Lunga Road, pg. 593 — PV
Kenya Shell Ltd., Shell & BP House, Harambee Ave., pg. 1136 — IT
Kenya-Swiss Chemical Co. Ltd., pg. 983 — IT
Kodak (Kenya) Limited, Funzi Rd., pg. 553 — PB
Longman Kenya Limited, Funzi Road, pg. 1027 — IT
MB Kenya Limited, Nanyuki Rd., pg. 267 — IT
MCL, MCL House, pg. 1422 — PB
Middle East Bank Kenya Ltd., Kenyatta Avenue, pg. 548 — IT
Mitsui & Co., Ltd., 2nd Fl., South Wing in Utali House, Uhur, pg. 882 — IT
Morgan Grenfell (Kenya), 4th Ngong Ave., pg. 405 — IT
NAPS Kenya, Box 19533, pg. 913 — IT
Nestle Foods Kenya Ltd., pg. 921 — IT
Norsk Hydro U.K. Ltd. Kenya Branch, Liaison Office for East Africa, Shell BP House, 5th Floor, pg. 964 — IT
Novo Nordisk A/S, Mageso Chambers, Moi Avenue, pg. 987 — IT
The Old East African Trading Co. Ltd., pg. 431 — IT
Old East Graphics (Kenya) Limited, pg. 431 — IT
Oxford University Press (Kenya), ABC Place, Waiyaki Way, pg. 1019 — IT
PC World East Africa, Gilgil House, Monrovia Street, pg. 570 — PV
Panalpina East Africa Limited, pg. 1023 — IT
Panalpina Kenya Limited, pg. 1023 — IT
Pfizer Laboratories Limited, Isiolo Rd., pg. 1282 — PB
Resources Interlink Ltd., 3rd Fl., Kenindia House, pg. 1228 — PB
Rhone-Poulenc Kenya Ltd., Kahawa Station, pg. 1113 — IT
SKF Kenya Ltd., Lusaka Rd., pg. 1159 — IT
SNC-Lavalin, 2nd Floor, Museum Hill House, pg. 1162 — IT
Sandvik Kenya Ltd., P.O. Box 18264, pg. 1187 — IT
Sanyo Armco (Kenya) Limited, Hughes Bldg. 2nd Floor, pg. 1192 — IT
Schindler Ltd., pg. 1205 — IT
Signode Packaging Systems Limited, 01 Kalou Rd., Industrial Area, pg. 869 — PB
Stanbic Bank Kenya Limited, Kenyatta Avenue, pg. 1293 — IT
Standard Chartered Bank Kenya Limited, Moi Avenue, pg. 1294 — IT
Standard Chartered Financial Services Limited, International House, Mama Ngina St., pg. 1296 — IT
TAC The Advertising Company Limited, Bruce House Standard Street, pg. 389 — PV
Technical Engineering Services Ltd., Nacico Coop Chambers, 4th floor, Moi Avenue, pg. 1370 — IT
3M Kenya Ltd., P.O. Box 48567, pg. 1607 — PB
Wellcome Kenya Ltd, pg. 553 — IT
The World Bank, Hill Park Building, Upper Hill, pg. 1189 — PV
The Wrigley Co., (East Africa) Ltd., Bamburi Rd., pg. 1781 — PB

Thika

Standard Chartered Estate Management Limited, pg. 1295 — IT

KOREA

Ansan

Bundy Systems Korea, 401-5Ra Shihwa Complex, Seong Kok-Dong, pg. 1341 — IT
Holset Korea, Ltd., B-609-2 Banwol Industrial, Complex, pg. 469 — PB
Hyun Dai Terminal Co., Ltd., 726-3, Wonsi-dong, pg. 1122 — IT
KOHAP Engineering Plastics Ltd., 631-3 Sunggok-dong, pg. 742 — IT
Molex Korea Co., Ltd., 726-3, Wonsi-dong, pg. 1122 — PB
Unikor Chemical, Inc., #433 Moknaedong, pg. 460 — PB

Anyang

Dong-A Otsuka Co., Ltd., 450-1, Suksoo-Dong, pg. 1014 — IT

Buchon

Applied Power Korea Ltd., 163-12, Dodang-dong, Choong-Ku, pg. 125 — PB
Carbone-Lorraine Korea Co. Ltd., 161, 12 Dodang Dong, pg. 1030 — IT

Busan

Bontex Korea, Rm. 303, Song Nam Bldg., 76-1, 4Ga, Chung Ang-Dong, pg. 734 **PB**
Dongseong Express Tourists Co., Ltd., 265-25 Bujeon-dong, Busanjin-gu, pg. 1292 **IT**

Changwon

Citizen Precision of Korea Co., Ltd., 853-9, Ye-Dong Changwon, Industrial Complex, pg. 294 **IT**
Fanuc Korea Corporation, 42 Ungnam-Dong, pg. 478 **IT**
Korea Sanyo Electric Co., Ltd., Mok Dong Area, 2nd Block, Chang Won Industrial Complex, pg. 1192 **IT**
Lucas Diesel Korea Ltd., 853-3 Oe- Dong, Changwan Industrial Complex, pg. 820 **IT**

Cheonan

Advantest Korea Co., Ltd., 6F, Youngduk Bldg., 109-2, Munhwa-Dong, pg. 25 **IT**
Cheonan Technical Center, 6f, Youngduk Bldg., 109-2, Munhwa-Dong, pg. 25 **IT**

Cheongju

Hanseo Food Co. Ltd., pg. 920 **IT**
Nestle Korea Ltd., pg. 921 **IT**
Newmax Co., Ltd., 27-15 Song Jeong-Dong, pg. 1347 **IT**

Choongnam

Hyundai Oil Refinery Co., Ltd., 640-6 Daejuk-ri, pg. 642 **IT**
Hyundai Petrochemical Co., Ltd., 679 Daejuk-ri, pg. 642 **IT**

Choryang

Kvaerner Korea Ltd., 14th Floor, Hyundai Bldg., pg. 767 **IT**

Chung Nam

Crown Snack Co., Ltd., 5, Nam-dong, OnYang-City, pg. 348 **IT**
Union Polymer Co., Ltd., 32-1 Doosan-Dong, Chun-an-Shi, pg. 949 **IT**

Chunwon

FKL Dong Hwa Ltd., 338-13 Dae Hong-RI Sunghwan-Eub, pg. 528 **IT**
Rocol Korea Limited, 147-2 2nd Fl., Ha dae won Dong, pg. 892 **IT**

Daechi-Dong

ANGUS Korea, Rm 910, Building A, Champs Elysees Center 889-5, pg. 75 **PV**

Daegu

Kluber Lubrication (Korea) Ltd., pg. 507 **IT**
Korea Sintered Metal Co., Ltd., 29-10, Bonri-Dong, Nongong-Myeon, pg. 1313 **IT**
Open Systems Consulting, 79-6 Susung-3GA, pg. 566 **PB**

Euiwang

KOHAP Fine Chemical Ltd., 122-1 Ojon-dong, pg. 742 **IT**

Gumi

Delkor Battery Company, pg. 724 **PB**

Gyungbuk

Korea Electronics Inc., 171 Gongdan-dong, Gumi, pg. 1236 **IT**

Gyunggi

PSK Tech, Inc., 430-3, Mogok-Dong Songtan-City, pg. 939 **IT**

Inchon

Daewoo Heavy Industries, Ltd., 6, Mansok-Dong, Tong-Gu, pg. 357 **IT**
Daewoo Motor Company, Ltd., 199, Chungchon-dong, Puk-gu, pg. 357 **IT**
DONG-SUH FOODS CORPORATION, 404-8 Cheung Chen, 2 clong bupyung, pg. 416 **IT**
Grace Korea, Inc., 17-1 Namdong Indstrl Cmplx430, Nonhyun-Dong, pg. 756 **PB**
Inchon Iron & Steel Co., Ltd., 1 Songhyun-dong, pg. 642 **IT**
Korag Company, Ltd., 401-48, Hagig-dong, Nam-gu, pg. 1126 **PB**
Royal Toto Metal Co., Ltd., 414-3 Chongchon 2-Dong, pg. 1410 **IT**
Seoul-Heinz Ltd., 62-3 Shinheung Dong 3 GA, pg. 807 **PB**
Sharp Korea Corporation (Inchon), 418, Chung Cheon-Dong, pg. 1230 **IT**

Kangnung

Novo Nordisk A/S, Room 302, Sang Min Bldg., pg. 988 **IT**

Kumi

Cheil CIBA-GEIGY Co, Ltd., 288-11, Kongdan-dong, pg. 975 **IT**
Ssangyong Uni-Charm Co., Ltd., 155 Kongdan-dong, pg. 1291 **IT**

Kun Po

MULTITEK, #505 Jeil Industrial Bldg., pg. 740 **IT**

Kwangju

Daewoo Electric Motor Industries, Ltd., 988-1, Changdok-Dong, pg. 357 **IT**

Kwangsan

Mitsui & Co., Ltd., 2nd Fl., Kwangyang Bldg., Control Office, 615, Gumho-ri, pg. 881 **IT**

Kwangyang

Kwangyang Works, 700 Kumho-dong, pg. 1061 **IT**

Kyongbuk

POHANG IRON & STEEL CO., LTD., 1, Koedong-dong, pg. 1061 **IT**

Kyonggi-do

Daewoo Metal Co., Ltd., 345-6, Hoejong-Ri, Hoechon-Up, pg. 357 **IT**
Dong-Myung Industrial Co., Ltd., 415, Suksu-Dong, pg. 856 **IT**
Hyundai Electronics Industries Co., Ltd., San 136-1, Ami-ri, pg. 641 **IT**
Hyundai Elevator Co., Ltd., San 136-1, pg. 641 **IT**
KNC (Korea Network Corporation), 339-10 Dangjung-dong, pg. 742 **IT**
Kefico Corporation, 410 Dangjung-dong, pg. 642 **IT**
Keystone Valve (Korea) Ltd., 270-4 Kerug-ri, pg. 1650 **PB**
Korea Green Pharm. Co. Ltd., 903-4, Sangsin-ri, pg. 558 **IT**
Moog Korea, 505-4 Yeolmi-Ri, Shilcon-Myon Kuang Ju-Kun, pg. 1128 **PB**
Nipsea Chemical Co., Ltd., 407-7, Mokne-Dong, pg. 937 **IT**
Nordson Sang San Engineering Co., 324-2 Gosan-Ri, pg. 1190 **PB**
OMRON Automotive Electronics Korea Co., Ltd., 272-2 Kyerukri, pg. 1005 **IT**
Oriental Telecommunication Company Ltd., pg. 1369 **IT**
SUNKYONG INDUSTRIES CO., 600 Chongja-Dong, pg. 1320 **IT**
Varian Korea Ltd., 433-1 Mogok-Dong, Songtan, pg. 1710 **PB**

Kyongki

Karahm Company Limited, 147-2 2nd Fl., Hadaewon Dong, pg. 891 **IT**
Korea Bundy Corporation, 206-1 Shin-Ri, Jinwi-Myun, Pyongtaek-Gun, pg. 1341 **IT**
Polypenco Korea Co. Ltd., San 18-3, Chupalri-Paengsung, pg. 354 **IT**
Tosoh SMD Korea Ltd., 433 Mogok-Dong, pg. 1408 **IT**
Unbrako Inc., 754-10 Jowon-Dong, Jangen-ku, pg. 1420 **PB**

Kyung Buk

Kelim Toto Co., Ltd., 167, Kongdan Dong, pg. 1410 **IT**

Kyunggi-do

BERG Korea Electronics Ltd., 345-1 Sooha-ri, Shindoon-Myon, pg. 213 **PB**

Masan

Casio Korea Co., Ltd. (South), 654-4, Bongam-Dong, pg. 274 **IT**
Citizen of Korea Co., Ltd., Masan Free Export-Zone, Bong Am Dong, pg. 294 **IT**
Korea Sanken Co., Ltd., BG-2 Free Export Zone Masan, 974-17 Yong Duck-Dong, pg. 1188 **IT**
Korea Tokyo Electronic Co., Ltd., 410-47, Yangduk-Dong, pg. 1192 **IT**
Korea Tokyo Silicon Co., Ltd., 973-4, Yangduk-Dong, pg. 1192 **IT**
Korea T.T. Co., Ltd., 658-7, Bongam-Dong, pg. 1192 **IT**
The Masan Steel Tube Works Co. Ltd., 1-974, Yang-Duk-Dong, pg. 948 **IT**
TMC Company Ltd., Masan Free Export Zone, 973-6 Yangduk-dong, pg. 952 **IT**

Pohang

Jinbang Steel Co., Ltd., 605, Ho-dong, pg. 1291 **IT**
Mitsui & Co., Ltd., 2nd Fl., POSCO Co-operators Bldg. 171-18, pg. 881 **IT**
Pohang Works, 5 Dongchon-dong, pg. 1062 **IT**

Pusan

Alloy Rods Korea Corporation, 65 Kamman-Dong, pg. 281 **IT**
The Bank of New York, Chosun Ilbo Bldg., 9th Fl., 1198-7 Choryang-dong, Dong-ku, pg. 179 **PB**
Chokwang Jotun Ltd., 379-1, Samrak-Dong, pg. 715 **IT**
Deutsche Bank AG (Pusan), Korea Development Bank Bldg., 44, 2-ka, Chungang-Dong, Chung-Ku, pg. 404 **IT**
Dong Hoo Trading Co. Ltd., Daerim Bldg. 33rd Floor, (Rm. 302), 55-1. 4 KA, pg. 550 **IT**
Korea Nippon Sanso Engineering Co., Ltd., Sun Officetel #1103, 830-42, Pomil-dong, Dong-ku, pg. 939 **IT**
Kvaerner Korea Ltd., Hyundai Bldg.., 14th Fl., 1193-5 Choryang 3 dong, pg. 772 **IT**
MacGREGOR (Kor) Ltd., Rm. 601, Dong Ju Bldg., 13-5 Ka, Jungang-dong, Jung-Ku, pg. 671 **IT**
Mitsui & Co., Ltd., 10th Fl., K.E.B. Pusan Branch Bldg., No.89, pg. 881 **IT**
C. Plath, 1196-1, Choryang-3 Dong, pg. 1005 **PB**
Pusan Office, 10 F Dongbang Bldg., 25, pg. 1062 **IT**
Rexroth Seki Co. Ltd., 839 **IT**
SKF Korea Ltd., Rm. 1135, 11th Fl., Ocean Tower, pg. 1159 **IT**
Woo Yun Co., Ltd., 161-5, Gamjeon-Dong Puk-ku, pg. 1233 **IT**

Seoul

A & A International-Seoul Branch, 5th Fl., Han Hyo Bldg., Yong Dong Pu-Ku, pg. 1561 **PB**
AMP Korea Limited, 11F B-Block Samho, Ctr. Bldg., 275-6, Yangjae-Dong, pg. 9 **IT**
AST Korea, 17/F Taemon Bldg., 143-40/41, pg. 1182 **IT**
Acer Korea, pg. 22 **IT**
Acheson Korea Ltd., 1305-6 Seocho-Dong, pg. 12 **PV**
Aekyung Chemical Co., Ltd., 5th Fl., Second Seoul Misung, #106-3, Guru-5 Dong, Guro-ku, pg. 371 **IT**
Ahlstrom Korea Co., Ltd., 3rd Fl. Chongju Spinning Bldg., 154-6 Samsung-dong, pg. 35 **IT**
Ahlstrom Korea Co., Ltd.-Hyun Poon Mill, 7, Keumdong-Li, pg. 35 **IT**
Air Products Korea Inc., 15th Floor Chung Am Building, 129-11 Chungdam-Dong Kangnam-Ku, pg. 31 **PB**
Ajinomoto Co., Inc., Seoul Office, Seoul Center Bldg., 91, Sokong-Dong, pg. 40 **IT**
AlliedSignal International, Inc., 6th Fl., Sambo Mutual Savings, & Finance Bldg., 441-1 Banpo-dong, pg. 53 **PB**
Amano Korea Corporation, DBM Building, 8F, 200-30 Donggyo-Dong, pg. 71 **IT**
Amway Korea, Ltd., Dong Sung Bldg., 12th Fl., 158-24 Samsung-dong, pg. 70 **PV**
Analog Devices Korea, Ltd., 3rd Fl., Unori Bldg. 961-3, Dae Chi-Dong, pg. 108 **PB**
Applied Magnetics Korea, Ltd., pg. 123 **PB**
Asahi Bank Seoul Branch, 18th Fl., Kyobo Life Insurance Bldg., pg. 82 **IT**
Asbury Worldwide Korea Co., Ltd., Site 503 Samkwang Building, 255-53 Yongdoo-Dong, pg. 1110 **PB**
Astra Korea Ltd., 1600-3, Seocho-Dong, pg. 94 **IT**
Australia & New Zealand Banking Group Limited Korea, 18th Fl., Kyobo Building, 1 Chongro 1, pg. 99 **IT**
Autodesk Korea Limited, Samboo Building, 17th Fl., 676 Yuksam-dong, pg. 149 **PB**
AxTrade Korea Ltd., Rm. 311, Chung Dam Bldg., 52 Chung Dam-Dong, pg. 710 **IT**
BASF Korea Ltd., 11th Fl., Korea Chamber of Commerce & Industry, 45, pg. 106 **IT**
BHP Steel N Asia Ltd. - Korea Branch, 1310 13th Fl., Kyobo Bldg., 1 Chongro Ika, Chongro-ku, pg. 227 **IT**
BMC Software Korea Ltd., Hongwoo Bldg., Fourth Floor, 945-1 Daechi-dong, pg. 163 **PB**
Banco Di Napoli-Seoul, Doosan Bldg. #1101, 101-1, Ulchi-Rol-I-Ka, pg. 140 **IT**
Bank Brussels Lambert-Seoul Representative Office, 14th Floor, Koran Bank Head Office Bldg., pg. 148 **IT**
Bank of America NT&SA, 9/F, Hanwha Bldg., No. 1 Jangkyo-dong, Chung-ku, pg. 182 **PB**
Bank of Boston, Kyobo Building, 15th Floor, 1 Chongro, 1-Ka, Chongro-ku, pg. 184 **PB**
Bank of Montreal - Korea, Suhrin Bldg., 88 Suhrin-Dong, Chongro-ku, pg. 155 **IT**
The Bank of New York, Young-Poong Bldg., 23rd Fl., 33 Seolin-dong, Chongro-ku, pg. 179 **PB**
The Bank of Tokyo-Mitsubishi, Ltd. (Seoul Central Branch), The Seoul Shinmun and Press, Center Bldg., 11th Fl., 25, pg. 158 **IT**
Bank of Yokohama Seoul, 5th Floor, Hyonam Bldg., 1 Jangkyo-Dong, Chung-ku, pg. 159 **IT**
Bankers Trust New York Corporation, Center Bldg. 10th Fl., 91-1 Sokong Dong, pg. 186 **PB**
Banque Paribas - Korea, Kyobo Bldg - 21st., 1 chongo, 1-ka, chongro-ku, pg. 320 **IT**
Barclays Bank PLC, pg. 165 **IT**
Bausch & Lomb Korea, Ltd., 5th Fl., Young Han Bldg., 1475-8 Seocho-3 Dong, Seocho-Gu, pg. 195 **PB**
BetzDearborn Korea, Ltd., Rm. 1105, Dongwha Bldg., 25-5, Yoido-Dong Youngdeungpo-ku, pg. 227 **PB**
Boeing International Corp., Daeham Bldg., Ste. 1605, 51-1 Namchang-Dong, pg. 242 **PB**
Bosch Korea Ltd., Bongwoo Bldg., 31-7, 1-ka, pg. 205 **IT**

Ssangyong Investment & Finance Co., Ltd., 77-3, Jooan 1-dong, pg. 1292 **IT**
Ssangyong Precision Industry Co., Ltd., 219, Hyosung-don, Puk-ku, pg. 1292 **IT**

PB - *U.S. Public Companies Volume*
PV - *U.S. Private Companies Volume*
IT - *International Public & Private Companies Volume*

1692

Geographic Index-Non U.S.

Bull Information Systems (Korea) Ltd., 10/F Dong Gyong Bldg., 824-19 Yeoksam-dong, pg. 315 **IT**

Bum-A Petroleum Co., Ltd., 117-1, Samsung-dong, Yeogsam-gu, pg. 1292 **IT**

Burgmann Korea Ltd., 3F, Cheong Lim Building, 38-30 Samsung-dong, pg. 233 **IT**

Leo Burnett Sonyon Inc., 6th Fl., Kwanhoon Bldg., 198-42 Kwanhoon-Dong, pg. 185 **IT**

C-E International, Hotel Schilla, Rm. 527 202, 2-6a Jang Ch, pg. 5 **IT**

Canon Semiconductor Engineering Korea Inc., 8F, Seung Kwang Bldg., 143-8 Samsong-dong, pg. 263 **IT**

Cariplo (Seoul), Oriental Chemical Bldg., 50, Sogong-dong Chung-Ku, pg. 275 **IT**

Carrefour Korea Ltd., 3F, Samyoon Building, 17-5, Nonhyun-dong, pg. 272 **IT**

Cascade (Korea) Ltd., pg. 311 **PB**

Castrol Korea Limited, Han Seo Bldg., 62-2 Yoeuido-dong, pg. 236 **IT**

The Chase Manhattan Bank, N.A., Chase Plaza, 34-35 Chung-Dong, Choong-Ku, pg. 340 **PB**

Cheil CIBA-GEIGY Co., Ltd, 21st Floor, Samsung Life Bldg, 150, 2-Ka, Taepyung-Ro, pg. 975 **IT**

Cheil Communications, Inc., Institute of Marketing, Kuk Je Bldg., 13F, pg. 588 **IT**

Cheil Foods & Chemicals Inc., C.P.O. Box 1155, 18th Fl. Samsung Life Insurance Bldg., pg. 1181 **IT**

Cheil Industries Inc., Samsung Life Ins. Bldg. 19 Fl., 250, 2-ka, Taepyong-ro, Chung-ku, pg. 1181 **IT**

Cheil Synthetics Inc., 19th Fl., Samsung Life Insurance Bldg., pg. 1181 **IT**

CHO HUNG BANK, 14, 1-ka, Namdaemun-ro, Chung-ku, pg. 287 **IT**

Chonju Paper Mfg. Co., Ltd., 150, 2-ka Taepyong-ru, Chung-ku, pg. 1181 **IT**

CIBA Corning Marketing Services (HK) Limited KB, Kukjo Center, 11th Fl., 191, Hanang-Ro, 2-Ka Yongsan-ku, pg. 975 **IT**

CIBA-GEIGY Korea Ltd., 13th Floor, Haesung Bldg. II, 942-10, Daechi-dong, Kangnam-Ku, pg. 977 **IT**

CIBA-GEIGY Korea Ltd., 13th Floor, Haesung Bldg. II, 942-10, Daechi-dong, pg. 977 **IT**

Circle Airfreight International Korea, Room 903, Kumjung Bldg., 192-11 Chung-ku, pg. 372 **PB**

Citibank, N.A. Seoul Branch, 1-1, 1-ga, Jong-ro, Jongro-gu, pg. 378 **IT**

Clestra Hauserman Korea, KOTEF Bldg., 35-3 Yoido-Dong, Youngdong po-Gu, pg. 569 **IT**

Commerzbank AG Representative Office-Seoul, Hanway Bldg., 8th Floor, pg. 312 **IT**

John Crane (Korea) Co., Ltd., Room 602- Sungji Building, 538 Dohwa-Dong, Mapo-ku, pg. 1339 **IT**

Credit Lyonnais S.A., Youone Bldg. 75-95, Seosomun-Doug-Chung-ku, pg. 344 **IT**

CROWN CONFECTIONERY CO., LTD., 241-20, Muk-dong, pg. 348 **IT**

Crown Engineering Co., Ltd., 241-20, Muk-dong, Choong Rang-ku, pg. 348 **IT**

Cummins Korea Ltd., 5th Fl., Hye Sung Bldg., 36-26 Sam Sung Dong, Kang Nam Ku, pg. 469 **IT**

CUNA Mutual Group-Korea, NACUFOK Building, 5th Floor, 874-1 Bangbae-dong, pg. 297 **PV**

Cyanamid Korea, Inc., C.P.O. Box 3436, pg. 81 **PB**

DIC KOREA Corp., Room 752, KCCI Bldg., 45, 4-ka, Namdaemun Road, Chung-ku, pg. 372 **IT**

Daehan Chemical Machinery Mfg. Co., Ltd., Dae-Jun Bldg. 1318-5, Seocho-Dong, pg. 741 **IT**

DAEHONG ADVERTISING INC., 7th Fl., Hanmi Bldg., #1 Gongpyong-Dong, pg. 357 **IT**

Daewoo Automotive Components, Ltd., 34-3, Yoido-Dong, Yongdungpo-Gu, pg. 357 **IT**

Daewoo Capital Management Co., Ltd., 34-3, Youido-dong, pg. 359 **IT**

DAEWOO CORPORATION, 541, Namdamunno, 5-GA, Chung-ku, pg. 357 **IT**

Daewoo Electronics Co., Ltd., 541, 5-Ga, Namdaemun-ro, Chung-Ku, pg. 357 **IT**

Daewoo Engineering Company, 12-3, Youido-dong, pg. 357 **IT**

Daewoo Precision Industries, Ltd., 34-3, Youido-dong, Yongdungpo-gu, pg. 357 **IT**

Daewoo Research Institute, 34-3, Youido-dong, Yongdungpo-ku, pg. 359 **IT**

Daewoo Sang Sa, 194, Wonnam-Dong, Chongno-Gu, pg. 357 **IT**

DAEWOO SECURITIES CO., LTD., Daewoo Securities Bldg., 34-3, Youido-dong, pg. 358 **IT**

Daewoo Shipbuilding & Heavy Machinery, Ltd., 541, 5-Ga, Namdaemun-ro,Chung-ku, pg. 357 **IT**

Daewoo Telecom Co., Ltd., 541, 5-Ga, Namdaemun-ro, Chung-Gu, pg. 357 **IT**

Dai-Ichi Kangyo Bank, Ltd.-Seoul, Nae Wei Bldg., 6, 2-ka, Eulji-ro, pg. 361 **IT**

Daihan Swiss Chemical Corporation, 5th floor, AhTae Bldg., 1337-20, Seocho-Dong, pg. 977 **IT**

Daiwa Bank-Seoul, 8th Fl., Shinhan Bank Bldg., 120, 2-ka, Taepyung-ro Chung-ku, pg. 373 **IT**

Daiwa Securities (Seoul), 6th Fl., DITC Building, #27-3, Youido-dong, pg. 376 **IT**

Daltrading Limited, Wooduk Bldg. Sixth Fl., 832-2 Yoksamdong, pg. 414 **PB**

Deasung-Henkel Chemical Co., Ltd., pg. 614 **IT**

Dell Computer Corporation, Han Kook Keum Bak Bldg., 182-1, Booam-Dong, pg. 496 **IT**

Dentsu Inc. Seoul Office, 275 Gongdeok-dong, pg. 393 **IT**

Dentsu Young & Rubicam/Seoul, Chungho Bldg., 2nd Fl., 97-7, Nonhyun-Dong, pg. 325 **IT**

Det Norske Veritas, pg. 397 **IT**

Deutsche Bank AG (Seoul), Daehan Fire & Marine Insurance Bldg., pg. 404 **IT**

Diamond Advertising Ltd., 136 Hanhyo Building, 10th Floor, Seorin-Dong, pg. 1422 **PB**

Digital Equipment Korea Inc., 12-14/F Boram Securities Bldg., 23-3 Yoido-Dong, pg. 508 **PB**

Dinol Korea Ltd., Chung Dam Bldg., Rm. 611, 52 Chung Dam-Dong,Kangnam-ku, pg. 982 **IT**

Dong Bang Communications, Sungam Bldg., 114 Nonhyun-Dong, pg. 117 **IT**

DONG BU INSURANCE CO., Ja Bo Bldg., 21-9, Cho-Dong, Chung-gu, pg. 416 **IT**

Dong Hoo Trading Co. Ltd., Dong Hoo Bldg., 394-41, Shindorim-Dong, pg. 550 **IT**

Dong-Hwa Advantest Co., Ltd., Naray Bld. 6th Fl., 719-1, pg. 25 **IT**

Dong Yang Elanco Co., Ltd., 50 Sokong-dong, pg. 993 **PB**

Dongbang Healthcare Products Co. Ltd., 3/F, Unicon Bldg., 140-17, Samsung-dong, pg. 817 **PB**

Dongbo Express Co. Ltd., 118 Namdaemun-Ro 2Ga, Chung-Gu, pg. 383 **IT**

Dongbu Aetna Life Insurance Co., Ltd., 12th Fl. Hyun-Am Bldg., #1 Jangkyo-Dong, Jung-ku, pg. 27 **PB**

Doosan Crown Can Mfg. Co. Ltd., 270 Yonji-Doug, pg. 465 **PB**

Dresdner Bank AG, Samsung Life Bldg. 1202, 150, 2-ka Taepyung-ro, pg. 419 **IT**

Dun & Bradstreet International Ltd., Korea Branch, KLI63 Bldg., Yoido-Dong, Yungdung Po-Ku, pg. 536 **IT**

DYWIDAG-Systems International Co., Ltd.., Duckham Bldg. 401, pg. 424 **IT**

ESS-FOOD Korea, Room 904-1 Kangnam Building, 1321 Seocho-Dong, Seocho-ku, pg. 429 **IT**

Eaton International Corporation, Korea, 7th Fl., Woo Duk Bldg., pg. 558 **IT**

Ebara Precision Machinery Korea Incorporated, 15th Fl., Kangnam Building, 1321 Seocho-dong, Seocho-ku, pg. 432 **IT**

Electro Scientific Industries Korea, So-Mang Bldg., Second Floor, pg. 569 **PB**

Elsevier Science-Korea, South-East Asia, Marketing, Room 705, Hanaro Building, pg. 1100 **IT**

Enso-Eurocan-Bumjin Co. Ltd., 6F Bupmusa Bldg., 151-31 Nonhyung-Dong, Kangnam-ku, pg. 457 **IT**

Ericsson Korea Ltd., Room 705 Leema Bldg., 146-1 Soosong-Dong, Chongro-ku, pg. 1367 **IT**

AB Erifon Korea Branch, Room 705, Leema Bldg., 146-1, Soosong-Dong, Chongro-ku, pg. 1368 **IT**

EURO RSCG Korea, #602 Namhan Bldg., 76-42, Hannam-dong, Yongsan-ku, pg. 602 **IT**

Eurotherm Korea Ltd., Ste. 903, Daejoo Bldg., 132-19 Chungdam-Dong, pg. 466 **IT**

THE EXPORT-IMPORT BANK OF KOREA, Youngpong Bldg., 16-18th Fl., 33 Seorindong, pg. 467 **IT**

FCN Corporation, Ryukung Bldg. 239-1, Nonhyun-dong, pg. 742 **IT**

First RepublicBank Dallas, N.A. Representative Office, 12th Fl Sung HWA Bldg., pg. 1165 **PB**

Fleetguard Korea Ltd., 143-11 Doksan-Dong, pg. 469 **PB**

Fuji Electric Korea Co., Ltd., 16th Fl., Shinsong Bldg., 25-4 Youido-dong, pg. 522 **IT**

Fuji Photo Film Co., Ltd., Seoul Office, Samduck Building 6F, 144-1, Samsung-Dong, pg. 525 **IT**

Fujisawa Pharm Korea Ltd., Youngpung Bldg., 9th Fl., 142, Nonhyon-dong, pg. 525 **IT**

Fujitsu Korea Ltd., 9th Fl., Korean Reinsurance Bldg. 80, pg. 528 **IT**

Gambro Korea Co., Ltd, 3rd Floor, Daeyang Bldg., 198-7, Jamshil Bon-Dong, pg. 668 **IT**

Genus Korea, Inc., 3F, KEC Building, #275-7, Yangjae-Dong, pg. 733 **IT**

Givaudan-Roure Ltd., pg. 1120 **IT**

Global Rental Corporation, 13th Floor, Dong-A Building, 88 Da-dong, Choong-Gu, pg. 1009 **IT**

Goldman, Sachs & Co., Samsung Insurance Bldg., 6th Fl., 87, Ulchiro 1-Ga, pg. 462 **PV**

Goldstar Cable Co. Ltd., Chung Ku/Kai Bldg., 6th Fl., 120 Namdaemunno 5-ga, pg. 778 **IT**

Goldstar Co. Ltd., Youido, pg. 778 **IT**

Goldstar Electric Co. Ltd., 11th Fl. Sahaknyunkem Bldg., pg. 779 **IT**

Goldstar Instrument & Electric Co. Ltd., 20, Youido-dong, pg. 779 **IT**

Goldstar Precision Industries Ltd., 20-7 Youido-dong, pg. 779 **IT**

Goldstar Semiconductor Ltd., 60-1 3-GA Chungmu Ro Jung Ku, pg. 779 **IT**

Goldstar Telecommunications Co. Ltd., 20, Youido-dong, pg. 779 **IT**

Graco Korea, Dae-A Building, 3rd Floor, 707-7/8, Yoksam-Dong, Gangnam-Ku, pg. 757 **PB**

Green Giant Company, pg. 411 **PB**

Han Ryuk Electronics Co., LTD., 459-14 Gasan-Dong, pg. 628 **IT**

Han Wha Pharma Co. Ltd., Dongdaemun, pg. 44 **IT**

Hanguke Gensym, Korea World Trade Ctr., 27th Fl., pg. 731 **IT**

Hanil Development Co. Ltd., Hanjin Shipping Bldg., 25-11 Yoido Dong,Young Deungepo-ku, pg. 592 **IT**

Hanil Leasing Company Limited, 51 Sogong Dong, pg. 1391 **IT**

Hanjin Shipping Co., Hanjin Shipping Bldg., 25-11 Yoido Dong, Young Deungepo-ku, pg. 592 **IT**

HANJIN SHIPPING COMPANY LTD., Hanjin Shipping Bldg., 25-11 Yoido Dong, Young Deungeip-ku, pg. 592 **IT**

Hanjin Transportation Co. Ltd., Hanjin Shipping Bldg., 25-11 Yoido Dong, Young Deungepo-ku, pg. 592 **IT**

Hankook Ilbo Time-Life Ltd., 14, Chunghak-dong, Chongno-gu, pg. 1615 **IT**

Hankook Otis Elevator Company, 13-5, Youido-dong, Yongdungpo-gu, pg. 1691 **PB**

Hankuk Safety Glass Limited, 45-1, Youido-dong, pg. 1057 **IT**

Hanwa-NSK Precision Co., Ltd., 5f, Samhee Bldg. (7th), 530-12 Dapsipri 5-dong, pg. 903 **IT**

Hee Sung Co. Ltd., 120 Namdaemun-ro, 5-GA Chung-gu, pg. 779 **IT**

Henkel-Daesung Co., pg. 612 **IT**

Henkel Korea Ltd., pg. 613 **IT**

Hercules Korea Chemical Co. Ltd., 44-21 Yeoido-Dong, pg. 811 **IT**

Hirose Korea Co. Ltd., 472-5, Mok Nae-Dong, pg. 620 **IT**

Hitachi Zosen Seoul, 21st Floor, Lotte Bldg., 1, Sogong-Dong, Chung-Ku, pg. 623 **IT**

Honam Oil Refinery Co. Ltd., CPO Box 2467, pg. 779 **IT**

Hotel Shilla Co. Ltd., 202, Jang Chong Dong 2-GA, pg. 947 **IT**

Hyosung ASC, 52-1 Samsung-Dong, pg. 8 **PV**

Hyosung Aluminum Co., Ltd., Dongsung Bldg., 11-14, pg. 640 **IT**

Hyosung-BASF Co., Ltd., 4/5th Floor Kongduk Building, 450 Kongduk-Dong, Mapo-ku, pg. 108 **IT**

Hyosung-Ebara Company Ltd., 450, Gongduk-Dong, pg. 432 **IT**

Hyosung-Ebara Environment Engineering Co., Ltd., 53-5, Wonhyoro-3ga, Yongsan-ku, pg. 432 **IT**

HYOSUNG GROUP, Dongsung Bldg., 17-7, 4KA, pg. 640 **IT**

Hyosung Industries Co., Ltd., 4, Tangsang-dong 5-ga, Yongdun-gu, pg. 640 **IT**

Hyosung Metal Products Co., Ltd., 11-14, Youido-Dong, Yongdun-gu, pg. 641 **IT**

Hyundai Construction Equipment Service Co., Ltd., 2724 Bangbae 2-dong, pg. 641 **IT**

Hyundai Engineering & Construction Co., Ltd., 140-2, Kye-dong, pg. 641 **IT**

Hyundai Engineering Co., Ltd., 140-2, Kye-dong, pg. 641 **IT**

Hyundai Housing & Industrial Development Co., Ltd., 603-2 Sinsa-dong, pg. 641 **IT**

Hyundai Marine & Fire Insurance Co., Ltd., 178 Sejong-ro, pg. 641 **IT**

Hyundai Merchant Marine Co., Ltd., 92 Mukyo-dong, pg. 641 **IT**

HYUNDAI MOTOR COMPANY, Hyundai Building, 140-2 Kye dong, pg. 641 **IT**

Hyundai Motor Company, 140-2, Kye-dong, pg. 641 **IT**

Hyundai Motor Service Co., Ltd., 113-25 4ka, Wonhyo-ro, pg. 641 **IT**

Hyundai Precision & Industry Co., Ltd., 140-2, Kye-dong, pg. 642 **IT**

Hyundai Securities Co., Ltd., 34-4 Yuido-dong, pg. 642 **IT**

Hyundai Wood Industries Co., Ltd., 450 Apkujung-dong, pg. 642 **IT**

IBM Korea, Inc., 25-11, Youido-dong, pg. 897 **IT**

IBM Korea Systems Corporation, 25-11, Youido-dong, pg. 897 **PB**

ICI Korea Ltd., 889-5 Daechi-Done, pg. 665 **IT**

IPC Corporation (Korea) Ltd., Samsong Bldg 997-10, Daechi-Dong, pg. 651 **IT**

ITW Korea Incorporated, Room 501 Moksan Bldg., 156, Chokson-Dong, Chongro-ku, pg. 868 **IT**

Imation Korea, Kookmin Life Insurance Bldg., 6th Fl., 168 Gongduk-dong, pg. 870 **IT**

The Industrial Bank of Japan, Limited (Seoul), Samsung Marine & Fire Insurance Bldg., pg. 675 **IT**

Intel Semiconductor Asia Ltd., pg. 887 **PB**

Intergraph Korea, Ltd., Young Dong P.O. Box 6, 135-600, pg. 892 **PB**

INTERNATIONAL AERO-SEA FORWARDERS, LTD., 35-22, Tongeui-Dong, Chongro-ku, pg. 682 **IT**

International Flavors & Fragrances (Korea) Inc., 3rd Fl. Daesung Bldg., 775-3 Daerim-Dong, pg. 899 **PB**

International Paper Korea Ltd., IP House, 552-19 Shinsa-Dong, pg. 906 **IT**

JEOL Korea Ltd., Nonhyundong Bldg., 7th Fl., 59-8, Chongdam-Dong, pg. 697 **IT**

JAENEUNG EDUCATION CO., LTD., 55-5 Hyehwa-dong, Chongno-gu, pg. 697 **IT**

Janssen Korea, Ltd., Kangman, pg. 929 **PB**

Jardine Fleming Securities Limited, Ste. 2211, Kyobo Bldg., 1 1-Ka Chong-Ro, pg. 494 **IT**

JINWOONG INC., 228-2 Kueui-Dong, Kwangjin-ku, pg. 706 **IT**

KKBC International Ltd., 77 Mukyo-dong, pg. 642 **IT**

KLA Instruments Korea, 4th Floor, Chunil Bldg., 961-1 Daechi 3-Dong, pg. 939 **IT**

K.S., Rm. 607 Shinhwa Bldg., 34-1, Mapo-Dong, Mapo-ku, pg. 303 **IT**

KSB Korea Ltd., pg. 721 **IT**

Kang Nam Chemical Co., Ltd., 9th Fl., Kangnam Bldg., 1355-21 Seocho-Dong, Seocho-ku, pg. 372 **IT**

Kanthal Korea Ltd., pg. 724 **IT**

Kennametal GTS GmbH Korea Branch, New Seoul Bidg. #202, 618-3 Shinsa-Dong, 135, pg. 951 **PB**

Keum Kang Development Industrial Co., Ltd., 456 Apkujung-dong, pg. 642 **IT**

KIA MOTORS CORP., 15-21 Yoito, pg. 732 **IT**

Kidde Consumer Durables Corp., World Vision of Korea Bldg., 24-21, Yoido-Dong, pg. 594 **IT**

Kleinwort Benson Limited, 14th Fl., Leema Bldg., 146-1, Soosong-Dong, pg. 420 **IT**

Knorr-Bremse Rail Systems Korea Ltd., Room 501, im-Sung Bldg., 788-2 Yeok Sam-Dong, pg. 738 **IT**

Kodak Korea Ltd., 7F, Yonkang Bldg., 270, Yonji-dong, pg. 555 **IT**

KOHAP Chemical Corporation, KOHAP Bldg, 89-4 Kyungun-dong, pg. 742 **IT**

KOHAP Eng. & Const. Co., Ltd., 88, Kyungun-dong, pg. 742 **IT**

KOHAP GROUP, Kohap Building, 89-4 Kyungun-dong, pg. 742 **IT**

KOREA DIRECTORY OF CORPORATE AFFILIATIONS

KOHAP Inc., KOHAP Bldg., 89-4 Kyungun-dong, pg. 742 IT
KOHAP-New York Life Insurance Ltd., 14th Fl., Textile Center, 944-31 Daechi-dong, pg. 742 IT
KOHAP Petrochemical Corporation, KOHAP Bldg., 89-4 Kyungun-dong, pg. 742 IT
KOHAP Textile Co., Ltd., 46 Haknam-ri, Onsan-myun, pg. 742 IT
Kolon-Met Life Insurance Company Limited, 141 Samsung-Dong, Kangnam-Ku, Sungwon B/D 6,7,8th Fl., pg. 738 PV
Konami (Korea) Co., Ltd., 10th Fl., Korea Press Ctr. Bldg., pg. 746 IT
Kookmin Leasing Co., Ltd., 7th Floor, Golden Tower Bldg., 191, 2-ka, Chungjong-ro, pg. 1180 IT
Korea & Pharmacia Upjohn Limited, C.P.O. Box 5816, pg. 1049 IT
Korea Development Leasing Corporation, Suhrin Bldg., 11th & 20th Fl., 88 Suhrin Dong, pg. 1010 IT
KOREA ELECTRIC POWER CORPORATION (KEPCO), 167 Samsong-dong, Kangnam-ku, pg. 758 IT
Korea FA Systems Co., Ltd., Keum Kang Bldg., 3rd Fl., #1545-5, pg. 522 IT
KOREA HEAVY INDUSTRIES & CONSTRUCTION CO., LTD., 87 Samsung-dong, Kangnam-ku, pg. 758 IT
Korea High Polymer Company Limited, 126-4 Gugi-Dong, pg. 32 PB
Korea High Precision Co., Ltd., 5F Samhee Bldg., 7th Fl., 530-12, Dapsipri 5-dong, pg. 903 IT
Korea Industrial Gases Ltd., 6-4 Yi-Tae Won Dong Yong Sangu, pg. 32 PB
Korea Industrial Gases Ltd., Han IL Building 10th Floor, Chung Mu-Ro, pg. 32 PB
The Korea Industrial Leasing Co., Ltd., Lotte Building, 17th Fl., 1 Sogong-dong, pg. 933 IT
Korea International Merchant Bank, Hanway Bldg. 4th-8th Flrs., 70 Da-dong, pg. 312 IT
Korea Investment & Finance Corp., pg. 447 PB
Korea Johnson Co., Ltd., Sungdong P.O. Box 39, pg. 593 PV
Korea Makro Company Ltd., 4th Fl., Poonglim Bldg., Yeoksam-dong, pg. 1155 IT
Korea Master Builders Co. Ltd., pg. 1465 IT
Korea Otsuka Pharmaceutical Co., Ltd., 5F Chunji Bldg., 809 Yeoksam-Dong, Kangnam-Ku, pg. 1014 IT
Korea TDK Co. Ltd., 670, Garibong-Dong, Guro-Ku, pg. 1336 IT
Korea Transformer Co. Ltd., 237 Kuro-Dong, Kuro-Ku, pg. 1346 IT
Korea Yamanouchi Pharmaceutical Co., Ltd., Duckmyung Bldg., 170-9, Samsung-Dong, pg. 1519 IT
KOREAN AIRLINES CO., LTD., 351 Gonghang-dong, pg. 758 IT
Korloy Inc., Dongin Bldg., 3rd Fl., 1606-2, Seocho-Dong, pg. 1313 IT
Koryeo Industrial Development Co., Ltd., 178 Sejong-ro, pg. 642 IT
Krupp Widia Korea Ltd., Baek Am Building 703, 1303-34, Seocho-Dong, pg. 510 IT
Kyobo Information & Communication Co., Ltd., pg. 777 IT
LG GROUP, 20, Youido-Dong, pg. 778 IT
LG Owens Corning, 17th Floor, Han Shin Securities Bldg. 34-7, pg. 1237 PB
Lambda-Korea K.K., Rm. 402 Taekun Bldg. 822-5, Yoksam Dong, pg. 1242 IT
Landis & Staefa Korea Co., Ltd., Hyunjin Building 10F, pg. 801 IT
LeaRonal Korea, Dong-Ah Bldg., Sixth Fl., 14-6 Youido-Dong Youngdungpo-Gu, pg. 982 PB
LITKOR Litton Korea Ltd., Kuro Industrial Estates, 345-15 Garibong Dong, pg. 1004 PB
Littelfuse Triad, Inc., 277-105 2KA, pg. 1001 PB
Arthur D. Little Korea, Inc., 13th Floor, Kyobo Bldng., 1-1 Chongro, pg. 671 PV
Lockheed Aircraft (Asia) Ltd., Rm. 1406, Leema Bldg. 146-1, Soosong-Dong, Chongro-ku, pg. 1009 PB
Lord Korea Ltd., Seventh Floor, Sung-Bo Bldg., 19, Nunyun Dong, Kanyram-ku, pg. 676 PV
Lotte Canon Co., Ltd., Tae Hwa Bldg., 996-16, Daechi-3 Dong, pg. 262 IT
Lotte Shopping Co. Ltd., 1 Sokong-Dong, Chung-ku, pg. 819 IT
Louis Vuitton Korea, Ltd, Rm 604 Moksan Bldg., 156 Chukoun-Dong, Chongro-Gu, pg. 782 IT
Lucky Advanced Materials Inc., Rm. 1703 Kukdong Bldg., pg. 779 IT
Lucky Development Co. Ltd., 35-3 Youido-Dong, Youngdengpo-Gu, pg. 779 IT
Lucky Goldstar International Corp., 537, 5-ka, Namdaemun-ro, Chung-ku, pg. 779 IT
Lucky Ltd., 20, Youido-Dong, Yongdungpo-Gu, pg. 779 IT
MacDermid Korea Ltd., 752-8 Bang-Bae Dong, Ste. 303, Bae Yoo Bldg., pg. 1030 PB
Macworld/PC World Korea/Hi-Tech Information, 3 F Woosung Bldg., 333 Chang Jeon-Dong, pg. 570 PV
Makita Korea Co., Ltd., Suite 1707, Seocho Plaza, 1573-1, pg. 832 IT
Martin Marietta International, Inc., Korea World Trade Ctr., 27th Fl., 159 Samsung-Dong, pg. 1010 PB
Matheson Gas Products Korea, Inc., Room #303, Kum Moon Building, pg. 938 IT
Mead Packaging Korea, Inc., pg. 1076 PB
Medtronic Asia, Ltd., 3rd Floor Peter Bldg., 570-6 Shinsa-Dong Kangram-ku, pg. 1083 PB
The Meiji Life Insurance Company Seoul Office, 8th Fl., Kwanghwamun Building, pg. 854 IT
Mentor Graphics (Korea), 7th Fl. Chungdam Bldg., 52, Chungdam-dong Kangnam-Ku, pg. 1087 PB
Merck Korea, Ltd., 10th Fl., Woonam B/D, 824-22 Yukam-Dong, Kangnam-Gu, pg. 1092 PB
Merck Sharp & Dohme Intl., Sok C. Chongh, Dae Kyung Bldg. #501-B, pg. 1092 PB
Michelin Korea Tire Company Limited, Ste. 400, Leema Bldg., 146-1, Susong-dong, Chongno-gu, pg. 322 IT
Microsoft CH, pg. 1108 PB
Millipore Korea, Ltd., Room #202, Junwha Bldg., 157-10, Samsung-Dong, pg. 1113 PB
The Mitsubishi Trust & Banking Corporation, 10th Floor, Kwanghwamun Bldg., 211-1 Sejong-ro, Chongro-ku, pg. 876 IT
Mitsui & Co., Ltd., 9th Fl., The Korea Press Center Building, pg. 881 IT
Mitsukoshi Ltd.-Seoul Office, Rm. 65 Unesco House, 2-50 Myung-Dong, pg. 884 IT
Morgan Guaranty Trust Company, Kyobo Bldg., 22nd Flr., No. 1, Chongro, 1-Ka, pg. 1130 PB
J.P. Morgan Securities Asia Ltd., 22nd Fl., Kyobo Bldg., 1 Chongro, 1-Ka, pg. 1131 PB
Morgan Stanley Seoul, Ste. 1903, Kwanghwamoon Bldg., 211-1, 1-Ka, Sejong-Ro, pg. 1133 PB
Motorola Electronics & Communications, Inc., 80-6, Soosong-dong, pg. 1139 PB
Motorola Korea Ltd., 445 Kwangjang Dong, pg. 1139 PB
NCH Corporation Korea, 6th Fl., Cheungkwun Haikwan Bldg., 34, pg. 1145 PB
NMB Korea Co., Ltd., 9th Fl., Woo Duck Building, 832-2, Yeok Sam-Dong, pg. 868 IT
NYK-Seoul, c/o Soyang Shipping Co. Ltd., 3rd Floor, Sejong Bldg., pg. 941 IT
Nalco Korea Co., Ltd., 47th Fl., Dli 63 Bldg., 60 Yoido-Dong, pg. 1151 PB
Namkwang Engineering & Construction Co., Ltd., 87, Samsung-dong, Kangnam-gu, pg. 1291 IT
Nanometrics Korea Ltd., 2nd Floor, Keunkwang Bldg., 943-9 Daechi-Dong, pg. 1151 PB
National Bank of Pakistan-Seoul, 12/F, Kyobo Building, 1-Chongra IKA, Chongro-Ku, pg. 908 IT
National Westminster Bank Plc, 18th Floor, Dong Ah Life Insurance Building, pg. 911 IT
The Netherlands Life Ins Co, 2nd Floor, Leema Building, #146-1 Soosung-Dong, pg. 651 IT
New Computer Service Co., Ltd. (NCS), 8-14 Nonhyun-Dong, pg. 1043 PB
Nhong Shim Kellogg Co. Ltd., 1007, Suh-Woo Building, 17-10, Yoido-dong, pg. 948 PB
A.C. Nielsen Company of Korea, 6th. Fl, Sungbo Bldg., 90-2 Nonhyuh-Dong, pg. 1183 PB
Nikon Precision Korea Ltd., Clock Tower Bldg., 820-11 Yoeksam-Dong, pg. 931 IT
Nippon Credit Bank Ltd.-Seoul, Daekyung Building 120, 8th Fl., 2-ka, Taepyung-ro, Chung-ku, pg. 933 IT
Nissho Iwai Korea Corporation, Samkoo Building, 15F, 70, Sogong-Dong, Chung-ku, pg. 948 IT
Nokia Mobile Phones (Korea) Ltd., Room 902, Dae Dong Bldg, 587-21, Sinsa Dong, Kangnam Ku, pg. 952 IT
Norton Co. Ltd., Samwon Building, 210-1 Nonhyun-Dong, pg. 1175 IT
Novell Korea, 11th Fl., Kunja Bldg., 942-1, Daechi-dong, pg. 1204 PB
Novellus Systems Korea, 2F Suh Won Bldg. 57 KaRak-Dong, Song Pa-Ku, pg. 1204 PB
Novo Nordisk Bioindustrial, Korea, Room 201, Namsong Building, 260-199, Itaewon-dong, pg. 989 IT
Novo Nordisk Pharma Korea Limited, 3rd Fl., Haesung 2nd Bldg., 942-10 Daechi-dong, pg. 988 IT
NURI Enterprise, 126-1, ChoongMoo-ro, Choong-ku, pg. 348 IT
OMRON Korea Co., Ltd., 3F, New Seoul Bldg., #618-3 Shin Sa-dong, pg. 1006 IT
Open Systems Consulting, #516 Teheran Officetel, pg. 566 PB
Oracle Korea, Ltd., KLI 63, 41st Fl., #60 Yoido-Dong, pg. 1228 PB
ORICOM INC., 105-7, Doosan Bldg., Nonhyun-Dong, Kangnam-Ku, pg. 1008 IT
Oriental Processors & Exporters of Korea, Ltd., pg. 1695 PB
ORIX Maritime Corporation-Seoul Representative Office, Suhrin Bldg., 11th Fl., 88 Suhrin-Dong, Chongro-ku, pg. 1010 IT
Oyang ESI, Inc., So-Mang Bldg., 2nd Floor, 99-16 Itaewon-Dong, pg. 569 PB
Pall Korea Limited, Orida Building 3rd & 4th Fl., 1023-6, Daechi Dong, Kangnam-Gu, pg. 1254 PB
Pan Korea Insurance Co., Taiwa Bldg., 194-27 Insa Dong, pg. 779 IT
Panalpina Korea Ltd., pg. 1023 IT
Panduit Korea Ltd., Third Fl., Insung, 10,2,9 Sanjun-Doug, pg. 836 PV
Parfums Christian Dior Korea Co. Ltd., 12th Fl., Youwha Bldg., 1305-2 Seocho-Dong, pg. 783 IT
Parker Hannifin Asia Pacific Co., Ltd., 902 Dae Heung Bldg., 648-23 Yeoksam-Dong, 135-080, pg. 1263 PB
Pechiney AIM Korea Branch, Leema Bldg., Room 904, 146-1 Scosong-Dong, Chongro-ku, pg. 1031 IT
Perstorp Flooring, Korea World Trade Center, 27th Floor, pg. 1039 IT
Pfauter Korea, 3F. Myungsen Bldg., pg. 617 IT
Pfizer Healthcare Ltd., 6th Fl., Wooduk Bldg. 8322, Yeoksam-Dong., pg. 1283 PB
Pfizer Korea Limited, 427, Kwangjang-Dong, pg. 1282 PB
Pfizer Limited, 427 Kwangjang-Dong, pg. 1282 PB
Pharmacia & Upjohn Dong-il Co, Ltd., 6F Dong-il B/D, 58-6 Nonhyun-dong, pg. 1048 IT
Pohang Iron & Steel Co., Ltd.-Seoul, Kum-se-ki Bldg., 16 Eulchiro 1-ga, pg. 1061 IT
Praxair Korea, pg. 1320 PB
Purina Korea Inc., International Insurance Bldg., 5Ka, Namdaemun Rd., Choong-ku, pg. 1360 PB
Pusan Precision Industries, Ltd., No. 172, pg. 230 IT
Quantum Korea, Dong Gyung Bldg. #1401 824-19, Yeaokam-dong, pg. 1350 PB
Raychem Korea Limited, 831-45 Yeuksam-Dong, pg. 1362 PB
Regal Korea, Third Fl., Wooduk Bldg. 770-20, Yeoksam Dong, Kangnam Ku, pg. 917 PV
Rhone-Poulenc Chemicals Ltd., 7-22 Dongbinggo-Dong, pg. 1109 IT
Roche Korea Company Ltd., pg. 1121 IT
Roche Products Ltd. Korea, pg. 1122 IT
Rockwell Automation, 4th Floor, KEC Building, 275-7 Yangjae Dong, pg. 1399 PB
Rockwell International Korea Ltd., 6th Floor, KEC Building, 275-7 Yangjae-dong, Seocho-ku, pg. 1401 PB
Rockwell Semiconductor Systems, Room 1508, Textile Centre, 944-31, Daechi-3 Dong, Kangnam-ku, pg. 1402 PB
Rohm Electronics Korea Corporation, Chung-Ang Circulation Complex, Business A B/D 8F, pg. 1125 IT
Rohm Korea Corporation, 371-11, Kasan-Dong, pg. 1125 IT
SAS Software Korea Ltd., #503 Wonchang Bldg., 26-3 Yoido-Dong, pg. 967 PV
SDRC Korea Limited, 11th Floor, Shinbong Building, 736-6, Yeoksam-dong, Kangnam-ku, pg. 1525 PB
SDS (Samsung Data Systems Co. Ltd.), 194-15 Insong Bldg., 8th Fl., Hwaihyun-Dong, 1-Ga Chung-Gu, pg. 1032 PB
SMH (Korea) Ltd., Uno Bldg., 3 F, 787-13 Yeoksam-dong, pg. 1161 IT
SAB WABCO AB, Yeonhap Building, 314 Yangje-Dong, pg. 271 IT
Saehan Merchant Banking Corporation, Samsung Insurance Bldg., 87, 1-Ga, Ulchiro, Chung-Gu, pg. 676 IT
The Sakura Bank - Seoul Branch, 7th Floor Young Poong Building, 33, Sorin-Dong, Chongro-ku, pg. 1179 IT
Samsung Aerospace Industries, Ltd., 24 Fl. Samsung Life Ins. Bldg., 150, 2-ka, Taepyong-ro, Chung-ku, pg. 1181 IT
Samsung-Corning Company Ltd., 472 Shin-ri, Taean-up, Hwasong-GUN, pg. 449 PB
Samsung Electron Devices Co., Ltd., 10-14th Fl., Daekyung Bldg., 120, 2-ka, Taepyung-ro, pg. 1181 IT
Samsung Electronics Co., Ltd., Samsung Main Bldg., Taepyungro, pg. 1181 IT
SAMSUNG GROUP, 250, 2-Ka, Taepyung-ro, Chung-Ku, pg. 1181 IT
Samsung Hewlett-Packard, Dongbang Yeoeuldo Bldg., 12-16th Fls., pg. 823 PB
Samsung Life Insurance Co. Ltd., 1st - 8th Fl., Samsung Life Insurance Bldg., pg. 1183 IT
Samsung Petrochemical Co. Ltd., 10th Fl., Samsung Life Bldg., 150, 2-Ka, Taepyong-Ro, Chung-ku, pg. 102 PB
Samsung Shipbuilding & Heavy Industries Co. Ltd., 15-18th Fl., Daekyung Bldg., 120, 2-ka, Taepkong-ro, Chung-ku, pg. 1183 IT
Sandoz Dongkook Ltd., pg. 984 IT
Sandoz Korea Ltd., pg. 985 IT
Sandvik Korea Ltd., pg. 1187 IT
SangAm Communications Co., Ltd., 78 Chu-Dong, 2-Ga, pg. 765 PB
Saniserv-Korea, Rm. 303 Myung-Jong B/D, 1500-8, Seocho-Dong (#3), pg. 965 PV
R.P. Scherer Korea Limited, Room 1001, Youngdong Bldg., 832 Yeogsam-Dong, pg. 1438 PB
Schering Korea Ltd., pg. 1204 IT
Seagate Technology Korea, Inc., 9th Floor, Dongshin Bldg., 141-28 Samsung-Dong, pg. 1450 PB
Seagate Technology Korea, Ltd., 609 City Air Terminal Bldg., 159-6 Samsung-Dong, pg. 1450 PB
Sealed Air Korea Ltd., Na-Hyun Bldg./3F, 587-12, Shin-Sa-Dong, pg. 1451 PB
Searle CIBA-GEIGY Korea Ltd., pg. 985 IT
Security Pacific National Bank, Seoul, KIFC Bldg., 101-1 1-Ka Ulchiro, Chungku, pg. 183 PB
Sejong - AMC Corp., Ltd., 203-4, Dongkyo Dong, pg. 1149 IT
Seoul DMB&B, Inc., 15/F Dong-hwa Bldg., 58-7 Sesomoon-dong, Jung-Gu, pg. 305 PV
SEOUL DMB&B, INC., 14-15th Fl. Donghwa Bldg., #58-7, Sesomoon-dong, pg. 1223 IT
Seoul Finance Corporation, Fantom Tower Bldg, 4th Fl., 705-18 Yeoksam-dong, pg. 743 IT
Seoul Liaison Office, Office 417, Korea Air Terminal Bldg., pg. 305 IT
Seoul Office, Rm. 702, Hyo Ryung Bldg., pg. 578 IT
Seoul Office, Duckmyung Bldg., 170-9, Samsung-Dong, pg. 1519 IT
Shell Pacific Enterprises Ltd, 368, 3-Ka, Choongjeongro, pg. 1140 IT
Shinyoung Wacoal Inc., 345-54, Ka San Dong, pg. 1484 IT
Simpson Industries, Inc., Banwol Industrial Complex, B609-2 Banwol, pg. 1475 PB
Singapore Tourist Promotion Board - Seoul, 9th Floor, Young Poong Bldg., 33 Sorin-Dong, Chongro-ku, pg. 1254 IT
Sinochem Seoul Office, 1 100-200 1103 Chang-Kyo b/d, 1 Chang-Kyo Dong, pg. 1256 IT
Sodexho Korea Co., Ltd., Rm. No. 401, Woolim Building, 90-10 Banpo 4 Dong, pg. 1275 IT
SORAK Co., Ltd., KOHAP Bldg., 89-4 Kyungun-dong, pg. 743 IT
SSANGYONG BUSINESS GROUP, 24-1, Jeo-dong, 2-ga, Jung-ku, pg. 1291 IT
Ssangyong Cement Industrial Co., Ltd., 24-1, 2-ga, jeo-dong, jung-gu, pg. 1291 IT
Ssangyong Corporation, 24-1, 2-ga, Jeo-dong, Jung-gu, pg. 1291 IT
Ssangyong Engineering & Construction Co., Ltd., 87, samsung-dong, kangnam-gu, pg. 1291 IT

PB - U.S. Public Companies Volume
PV - U.S. Private Companies Volume
IT - International Public & Private Companies Volume

1694

Geographic Index-Non U.S.

Ssangyong Engineering Co., Ltd., 823-1, Yoksam-dong, Kangnam-gu, pg. 1292 **IT**
Ssangyong Finance Inc., 60-1, 3-ga, Chungmu-ro, pg. 1292 **IT**
Ssangyong Fire & Marine Insurance Co., Ltd., 60, Doryun-dong, Chongro-gu, pg. 1292 **IT**
Ssangyong Heavy Industries Co., Ltd., 60-1, 3-ga, Chungmu-ro, Jung-gu, pg. 1292 **IT**
Ssangyong Information & Communication Corporation, 60-1, 3-ga, Chungmu-ro, Jung-gu, pg. 1292 **IT**
Ssangyong Investment & Securities Co., Ltd., Ssangyong Tower, 23-2, Youido-dong, pg. 1292 **IT**
Ssangyong Investment Management Co., Ltd., Ssangyong Tower, 23-2, Youido-dong, pg. 1292 **IT**
Ssangyong Motor Company, 150-3, Chil Kei-dong, Pyungtaek-So, pg. 1292 **IT**
Ssangyong Oil Refining Co. Ltd., Ssangyong Tower, 23-2, Yoido-dong, pg. 1292 **IT**
Ssangyong Paper Co., Ltd., Ssangyong Tower, 23-2, Youido-dong, pg. 1292 **IT**
Ssangyong Research Institute, Ssangyong Tower, 23-2, Youido-dong, pg. 1292 **IT**
Ssangyong Shipping Co. Ltd., Ssangyong Tower, 23-2, Youido-dong, pg. 1292 **IT**
Standard Chartered Bank (South Korea), 13th Fl., Nae Wei Bldg. 6, 2-Ka, Ulchi-ro, Chung-ku, pg. 1296 **IT**
Sulzer Korea Ltd., pg. 1306 **IT**
Sumikin Bussan International (Korea) Co., Ltd., Room No. 1007, Marine Center, Bldg., No. 118, Namdaemunro, 2-ka, pg. 1308 **IT**
The Sumitomo Bank, Ltd.-Seoul Branch, 21st Flr., Kyobo Bldg. 1, Chongro 1-ka, Chongro-ku, pg. 1309 **IT**
The Sumitomo Trust & Banking Co., Ltd., 100-716 23rd Fl., Samsung Life, Bldg., #150 2-Ka, Taepyung-Ro, pg. 1318 **IT**
Sun Microsystems of California Ltd., 7th Floor, Chui Am Bldg., 1001, Deachi-Dong, pg. 1532 **PB**
Swiss Bank Corporation, 8th Fl., Young Poong Building, 33, Seorin-dong, pg. 1330 **IT**
Swiss Bank Corporation (Luxembourg) Ltd., Securities Rep. Office, 8th fl., Young Poong Building, pg. 1330 **IT**
Swiss Reinsurance Company-Korea Liason Office, 7th Floor Kwanghwamun-Building, 211 Sejang-ro, Chongro-ku, pg. 1333 **IT**
TAI-IL MEDIA CO., Tai-Il Building, 333 Yangjae -Dong, 18/ Seocho, pg. 1347 **IT**
Tektronix Korea Ltd., 13th Floor, Il-Song Bldg., 153-37 Samsung-Dong, pg. 1568 **PB**
Teledyne Korea, Room 403, Nam Song Mansion, pg. 44 **PB**
Thermon Korea Ltd., Ste., 2602, KWTC Bldg. 159-1, Samsung-Dong, Kangnam-Ku, 135-729, pg. 1081 **PV**
3M Korea Ltd., Daehan Investment Trust Bldg., 22nd Floor, 27-3 Yoido-Dong, pg. 1607 **PB**
Tiffco Korea, Ltd., 726-173 Hannam-dong, pg. 1609 **PB**
Tong Yang SHL Corp., Kwanhoon Bldg., 5F, 198-42, Kwanhoon-dong Chongro-ku, pg. 1154 **IT**
Toray Industries, Inc.-Seoul Office, 7th Fl., Kolon Bldg., 45 Mugyo-Dong, Chung-ku, pg. 1400 **IT**
Toto Seoul Branch, Rm2503, Chang-Gyo Building, 1-2 Chang Gyo Dong, Chung-ku, pg. 1410 **IT**
Tourism Malaysia - Seoul Office, Han Young Bldg., 1st Floor, 57-9 Seosomun-dong, pg. 833 **IT**
UBS Securities Branch Office, 18F, Kwanghwamoon Building, pg. 1440 **IT**
Union Carbide Chemicals Korea Ltd., 3rd Fl., Hong Woo Bldg., 945-1, Dsechi-Dong, pg. 1667 **PB**
Union Corporation, 107 Industry Matl. Distrib. Ctr., pg. 361 **PV**
Utell International-Korea, Jin Hyung Building, 2nd Floor, Kang Nam Ku, Shin-Sa Dong 536-16, pg. 1098 **IT**
VG Instruments Korea Ltd., pg. 1595 **PB**
Valmet Korea Inc., 3rd Fl., Woonam Bldg., 294, Chamsil-Dong, Songpa-Gu, pg. 1448 **IT**
Van Leeuwen Pipe & Tube, Daiha Building 825, 14-11 Yoido-Dong, Yongdeungpo-Gu, pg. 1450 **IT**
Van Leeuwen Pipe and Tube Korea Ltd., Room 204, Namjoong Building, #13-19, Yoido-dong, pg. 1450 **IT**
Vicon, Korea, Sam Jung Bldg., 11th Floor, 237-11 Non-Hyun-Dong Kangnam-Ku, pg. 1719 **PB**
Votra (Korea) Ltd., pg. 757 **IT**
Voyungsa Ltd, pg. 757 **IT**
Wandel & Goltermann Ltd., Yehsung Building, 2nd Floor, 150-3 Samsung-dong, pg. 1486 **IT**
Wang Computer Korea, Ltd., 25th Fl., First Securities Bld, 23-5, Yoido-Dong, pg. 1737 **PB**
Watlow Korea, Samsung Bldg., St. 302, 945-3 Daechi-Dong, Kangham-ku, pg. 1154 **PV**
West Company of Korea Limited, 98-3, Karakbon-dong, Songa-Ku, pg. 1756 **PB**
Westpac Banking Corp. - Korea, 7th Flr., Dong Bang Plaza, Bldg., 150 Taepyong Rd., pg. 1497 **IT**
Willis Faber & Dumas Limited, Room 601, Leema Building, 146-1 Soosong-Dong, pg. 1510 **IT**
Young-In Scientific Co., Ltd., Youngwha Bldg., 547 Shinsa-Dong, pg. 824 **PB**
Young Poong Manulife, Young Poong Building 8/F, 142 Nonhyon-Dong, pg. 841 **IT**
Young Poong Manulife Insurance Company, 8/F, Young Poong Bldg., 142 Nonhyon-Dong-Kangnam-gu, pg. 841 **IT**
YuHan-Kimberly, Ltd., CPO Box 2537, pg. 960 **PB**
Yukong Fuchs Ltd., 26-4, Yoido-dong, pg. 518 **IT**
ZEXEL Corporation Seoul Representative Office, 150-30 Samsung-Dong, pg. 1528 **IT**

Taegu

Sung San Company, Ltd., 436-41, Songso Industrial Complex, Talso-Gu, pg. 724 **PB**

Tonghae

Ssangyong Resources Development Co., Ltd., 200, Samhwa-dong, Kangqon-do, pg. 1291 **IT**

Ulsan

Aluminum of Korea Ltd., 1 Yeocheon-dong, pg. 641 **IT**
Daihan Swiss Chemical Corporation, 272-2, Yeochon-dong, Nam-ku, pg. 292 **IT**
Hyundai Aluminum Industry Co., Ltd., 1 Gilchun-ri, pg. 641 **IT**
Hyundai Construction Equipment Industrial Co., Ltd., 1-8 Ilsan-dong, pg. 641 **IT**
Hyundai Electrical Engineering Co., Ltd., 337 Ilsan-dong, pg. 641 **IT**
Hyundai Heavy Industries Co., Ltd., 1 Cheonha-dong, pg. 641 **IT**
Hyundai Mipo Dockyard Co., Ltd., 251-1 Yeompo-dong, pg. 641 **IT**
Hyundai Pipe Co., Ltd., 265 Yumpo-dong, pg. 642 **IT**
Kum Yang Otsuka Chemical Co., Ltd., 749-4 Hwa Sanri Onsanup Uljugu, pg. 1014 **IT**

Yangsan

Hanil Can Co., Ltd., 11-1, Yoosan-Ri, pg. 1029 **IT**
TrefilARBED Korea Co. Ltd., 134, Usan-Ri, Yangsan-Eup, pg. 80 **IT**

KUWAIT

Ahmadi

Kuwait Drilling Co., Plot 142, E.Ahmadi Industrial Area, pg. 765 **IT**
Kuwait Oil Company K.S.C., P.O. Box 22, pg. 765 **IT**

Kuwait

A.A. al-Qatami's Sons Trading Co., Ltd., pg. 928 **IT**
PromoPub/DMB&B Kuwait, pg. 305 **PV**
Tariq Alghanim Catering Division, pg. 1275 **IT**

Safat

Arabian Oil Company, Ltd. (Kuwait), Kuwait Airways Bldg., Al-Hilali St., pg. 78 **IT**
The Blue Sea Company W.L.L., P.O. Box 28554, pg. 357 **IT**
Business Machines Company W.L.L., Fahad Al Salem Street, pg. 107 **IT**
John Crane Kuwait, Regional Office, c/o, Al-Julaiah Trading & Contracting Co. WLL, pg. 1339 **IT**
Det Norske Veritas, Awqaf Complex, Mubarak Al-Kabeer Street, pg. 398 **IT**
Hanwa Co., Ltd.-Kuwait Branch, c/o Al-Sabih Engineering Co., pg. 595 **IT**
House of Trade & Construction Co., Plod 25, Block 7, East Ahmedi, pg. 550 **IT**
Intergraph Technical Services MIddle East Limited, c/o M.A. Kharafi, 13009, pg. 892 **PB**
Intermarkets Kuwait, AlaWadi Towers, 3rd Tower, 6th Fl., Ahmed Al-Jaber Str., Al-Sharq, pg. 680 **IT**
International Marine Construction Co. S.A.K., pg. 948 **IT**
KUWAIT AIRWAYS CORP., Kuwait Intl. Airport, pg. 764 **IT**
Kuwait Aviation Fuelling Company K.S.C., pg. 765 **IT**
Kuwait Aviation Services Co., P.O. Box 24417, pg. 764 **IT**
Kuwait Foreign Petroleum Exploration Co. KSC, Fahed Al-Salem Str., pg. 765 **IT**
Kuwait National Petroleum Company K.S.C., Ali Al-Salem, pg. 765 **IT**
KUWAIT PETROLEUM CORPORATION, P.O. Box 26565, pg. 764 **IT**
Kuwait Shipbuilding & Repair Yard Company K.S.C., P.O. Box 21998, pg. 765 **IT**
Kuwait Swedish Cleaning Services Co. S.A.K., pg. 443 **IT**
Magasin Louis Vuitton, Kuwait, Sahlia Commercial Complex, pg. 783 **IT**
Mazidi Trading Company W.L.L., Al Naki Building, Ali Al Salem Street, pg. 109 **IT**
Morad Yousuf Behbehani, Shuwaikh Industrial Area, Behbehani Building, pg. 1369 **IT**
Petrochemical Industries Company K.S.C., Khalid Ebn Al Waleed Str., pg. 765 **IT**
Telefonaktiebolaget LM Ericsson Technical Office Kuwait, Awadi Building, Mubarak al Kabir St., pg. 1370 **IT**

KYRGYZSTAN

Bishek

The World Bank, Koskovskaya & K. Akieva Streets, pg. 1190 **PV**

LAOS

Vientiane

Mitsui & Co., Ltd., House No. 123 Chanthakoummane Rd., pg. 880 **IT**
Prakit/FCB, 108/2 Baan Anu, Samaenthai Road, pg. 389 **PV**

LATVIA

Riga

AGA SIA, Pulkveza Brieza 15, pg. 14 **IT**
AS Latvijas Krasas, Kruzes Str. 3, pg. 729 **IT**
Algol-Latvija SIA, Cruzes iela 3, pg. 15 **IT**
Baltic Power (Latvia) Ltd., L. Ganibu Dambis 12, pg. 1453 **IT**
Robert Bosch Limited, Riga-Centrs, Pk 70, pg. 205 **IT**
CIBA-GEIGY Services AG-TAO Riga, ul Lielvardes 36/38, pg. 979 **IT**
KONE Lifti Latvija Oy, Dzerbenes iela 27a, pg. 747 **IT**
LM Ericsson International AB Latvia, 41/43 Elizabetes Str, 4th floor, pg. 1369 **IT**
Latvian Traffic Service, Pernavas iela 78, pg. 914 **IT**
Latvijas Lifts-Schindler, pg. 1205 **IT**
Neste Oil Latvia, 2A Elizabetes Street, pg. 915 **IT**
Nokia Telecommunications, Kronvalda Blvd. 10, 2nd Fl., pg. 953 **IT**
Norrkoping AxTrade AB, Repr. Office, Lacplesa iela 13-12, pg. 712 **IT**
Norvista, Kr. Barona 13/15, pg. 486 **IT**
Pakenso Baltica SIA, Ritausmas iela 2, pg. 458 **IT**
Quadra Pack, Basteja Bulv. 4, pg. 458 **IT**
Rannila Steel Latvia Sia, Grecinieku 22/24, pg. 1088 **IT**
SKF Riga, Elizabetes 2, Room 147, pg. 1159 **IT**
Statoil, Riga Latvia, Aspazijas Bulv 36-38, pg. 1298 **IT**
Vattenfall Latvia SIA, Pulkveza Brieza 12, pg. 1453 **IT**
The World Bank, Kalku Street, 15, pg. 1189 **PV**

Strassen

KONE Luxembourg S.a.r.l., 128, rue du Kiem, pg. 747 **IT**

Talsi

Talsi Building Materials Ltd., Kr. Valdemara 17, pg. 1201 **IT**

Tukums

SIA Baltic Feed, P.O. Box 194, pg. 349 **IT**

LEBANON

Beirut

The Bank of New York, Avco Center, 2nd Floor, Autostrade Jdeideh, pg. 179 **PB**
Banque Libano-Francaise S.A.L., Rue de Rome, pg. 315 **IT**
Bull S.A.L., Immeuble Marie, pg. 315 **IT**
CCF Finance Moyen-Orient, Immeuble SNA, Place Tabaris, pg. 342 **IT**
CIBA-GEIGY Services Limited, Weavers Center, 7th Floor, Clemenceau Street, pg. 979 **IT**
Commerzbank AG Representative Office-Beirut, Liberty Tower, 7th Floor, pg. 311 **IT**
Computer Information Systems, Chammas Bldg., P.O. Box 11-6274, pg. 817 **PB**
Dresdner Bank AG, pg. 419 **IT**
Electrolux Middle East S.a.r.l., P.O. Box 11-7507, pg. 443 **IT**
Fouad & Toufic Fadel & Co., pg. 458 **IT**
Fuchs Petroleum S.A.R.L., Gargour Building, pg. 517 **IT**
GAM/DMB&B Beirut, Palm Center, Rond Point Chevrolet, pg. 304 **PV**
Gefinor Finance S.A., Gefinor Center, pg. 542 **IT**
H&C, Leo Burnett, Sofil Center, 5th Fl., pg. 184 **PV**
Habib Bank Ltd., 4th Flr., Sabbag Centre, Al-Hamra St., pg. 584 **IT**
Honeywell Bull SAL, Immeuble Union des Assurances de Paris, pg. 318 **IT**
ING Bank Beirut, Fouad Boutros Building, Sursock Street, pg. 648 **IT**
INTERMARKETS ADVERTISING, Mirna Chalouhi Ctr., pg. 680 **IT**
Intermarkets Advertising/Lebanon, Mirna Chalouhi Comm. Center, Blvd. Sin el Fil, pg. 680 **IT**
Intermarkets Lebanon, Mirna Chalouhi Centre, pg. 1062 **PV**
Kodak (Near East) Inc., Hetco Bldg., Bauchrien, pg. 554 **PB**
Mephico SAL, pg. 983 **IT**
Mitsui & Co., Ltd., Sadat Tower, Sadat St., Block No. 2342, pg. 881 **IT**
Obegi Chemicals S.A.L., Obegi Building, pg. 109 **IT**
RNBNY Representative Office-Lebanon, Ryad Bank Bldg., Ryad El Solh, pg. 1381 **PB**
Societe des Ciments Libanais, pg. 629 **IT**
Societe Libanaise des Telephones Ericsson S.A.R.L., Hayek Round About, Sin El Fil 82, pg. 1370 **IT**
Societe Nouvelle de Banque, pg. 321 **IT**
Societe pour l'Exportation de Produits Nestle S.A., pg. 922 **IT**
UBS Representative Office, Starco South 1001-1004, pg. 1441 **IT**
Unifert S.A.L., pg. 109 **IT**
Union Bank of Switzerland, Starco South 1001-1004, pg. 1441 **IT**
Willis Faber (Middle East) S.A.L., Intra Investment Co. Building, Abdel Aziz Street, pg. 1510 **IT**

PB - *U.S. Public Companies Volume*
PV - *U.S. Private Companies Volume*
IT - *International Public & Private Companies Volume*

Sin El-Fil

Assurex, Immeuble Fattal, Jisr El Wati, pg. 564　IT

LESOTHO

Maseru

Stanbic Bank Lesotho Limited, 1st Floor, Bank Building, P.O. Box 115, pg. 1293　IT
Standard Chartered Bank Lesotho Limited, 1st Fl., Standard Bank Bldg., Kingsway, pg. 1295　IT

LIBERIA

Monrovia

Inagua Transports, Inc., pg. 1135　PB
Insurance Company of Africa, Pan African Plaza, 80 Broad Street, pg. 364　PB
Lamco J.V. Operating Co., Alt Buchanan/Yekepa/Monrovia, pg. 443　IT
Liberia Cement Corp., pg. 1201　IT
Liberia Telecommunications Corporation, Telecommunications Building, Lynch Street, pg. 1369　IT
Libmar Four, Inc., c/o The Intl. Trust Co. of Liberia, pg. 341　PB
Libmar Six, Inc., c/o The Intl. Trust Co. of Liberia, pg. 341　PB
Mobil Oil Liberia Incorporated, Bushrod Island, pg. 1119　PB
NEB Shipping Co., pg. 312　IT
Nesstra (Liberia) Inc., 14 Randall Street, pg. 109　IT
Shell Liberia Ltd., Bushrod Island, pg. 1137　IT
Ssangyong International Ltd., 80 Broad St., pg. 1292　IT

LIBYA

Banghazi

Bilfinger + Berger Bauaktiengesellschaft Benghazi, S.P.L.A.J., Benghazi Branch Office, pg. 196　IT

Tripoli

Air Malta - Benghazi, 18 Benina International Airport, pg. 37　IT
Arab Drilling & Workover Company, P.O. Box 680, pg. 765　IT
Bilfinger + Berger Bauaktiengesellschaft Tripoli, S.P.L.A.J., Tripoli Branch Office, Swani Camp, pg. 196　IT
Braspetro Libya, Hai-Al-Handalus, Alghiran Zone, pg. 1042　IT
Daewoo Corp. - Tripoli, P.O. Box 15070, pg. 358　IT
Fina Exploration Libya S.A., Zat Al-Imad Complex, Tower 1, Floors 10 & 11, pg. 1044　IT
LASMO Grand Maghreb Limited, Dhat Al-Imad Towers, Tower No. 4, Floor 14, pg. 804　IT
Mitsui & Co., Ltd., 6th Flr., Gargani Bldg., Side Eissa St., pg. 881　IT
Saga Petroleum ASA - Libya, Zat el Imad Complex, Tower No. 5, Floor 13, pg. 1169　IT
Sodexho North Africa, P.O. Box 91364, pg. 1275　IT
Telefonaktiebolaget LM Ericsson Libya Branch, Quaser Benghashir, P.O.B. 5307, pg. 1370　IT
VEBA OIL LIBYA GmbH, Zubeida St. 7, pg. 1461　IT

LIECHTENSTEIN

Balzers

Merck Balzers AG, pg. 997　IT

Eschen

Press- und Stanzwerk AG, Essanestr., pg. 508　IT

Schaan

HILTI AG, pg. 619　IT

Triesen

Rheintal Werkstoff-Technik AG, pg. 998　IT

Vaduz

ABN Management Services A.G., 18 Stadtle, pg. 11　IT
Allianz Lebensversicherung (Schweiz) AG, An der Landstrasse 5, pg. 59　IT
Allianz Versicherung (Schweiz) AG, An der Landstrasse 5, pg. 60　IT
BILTRUST Management Aktiengesellschaft, Stadtle 18, pg. 809　IT
Black & Decker (Overseas) A.G., Staedtle 36, pg. 234　PB
LGT Bank in Liechtenstein Aktiengesellschaft, Herrengasse 12, pg. 809　IT
LGT Finanz Aktiengesellschaft, Herrengasse 12, pg. 809　IT
LGT Treuhand Aktiengesellschaft, Stadtle 18, pg. 809　IT
LGT Trust Management Limited, Stadtle 18, pg. 809　IT

LIECHTENSTEIN GLOBAL TRUST LIMITED, Herrengasse 12, pg. 809　IT
Repsol Oil International (ROIL), Schwefelstrasse, 33, pg. 979　IT
Riunione Adriatica di Sicurta, Toniaule 10, pg. 61　IT
Trans-Continental Leaf Tobacco Corp., P.O. Box 21851, Staedtle 22, pg. 1502　PB
Zurich Versicherungs-Gesellschaft, Aeulestrasse 80, pg. 1531　IT

LITHUANIA

Litovskaya

AB Akerlund & Rausing, pg. 33　IT

Vilnius

AGA UAB, Didlaukio 69, pg. 14　IT
CIBA-GEIGY Services AG-TAO Vilnius, pr Gediminas 19, pg. 979　IT
LM Ericsson International A/S Lithuania, Traku 9/1, pg. 1369　IT
Litfinn Service, Aguonu Gatve 24, pg. 914　IT
Litfinn Service, Aguono Gatve 24, pg. 914　IT
Nerisena, Pilies 23/15, pg. 317　IT
Neste Oil LT, Labdariu 5, pg. 915　IT
Pan-Lit Service AO, pg. 1022　IT
Schindler Liftas AG, pg. 1205　IT
Uab Rannila Steel Vilnius, T. Sevcenkos 19, pg. 1088　IT
Vattenfall Lithuania UAB, Jouzapavicius St 13, pg. 1453　IT
The World Bank, Vilnius Str. 28, pg. 1189　PV

LUXEMBOURG

Bascharage

ADIG Servicegesellschaft S.A., pg. 312　IT
European Technical Center, Rte. de Luxembourg, pg. 721　PB
General Motors Luxembourg Operations S.A., Rte. de Luxembourg, pg. 723　PB
Norton S.A., Rue J. F. Kennedy, pg. 1175　IT
TDK Recording Media Europe S.A., pg. 1337　IT

Bertrange

MILLICOM INTERNATIONAL CELLULAR SA, 75 Route de Longwy, pg. 867　IT
Shell Luxembourgeoise SA, Rue de L'Industrie 7, pg. 1138　IT

Bettembourg

TrefilARBED Bettembourg S.a.r.l., pg. 80　IT

Bissen

TrefilARBED Bissen S.a.r.l, pg. 80　IT

Capellen

Morganite Luxembourg S.A., pg. 892　IT

Charlotte

WestLB International S.A., 32-34 Boulevard G.-D., pg. 1305　IT

Colmar

Goodyear-Luxembourg, Avenue Gordon Smith, L-7750, pg. 753　PB

Contern

Chaux de Contern S.A., pg. 423　IT

Diekirch

Barentrug Luxembourg SA, pg. 167　IT
Commercial Intertech S.A., Rte. d'Ettelbruck, pg. 411　PB

Dudelange

Ewald Giebel Luxembourg G.m.b.H., pg. 79　IT
Galvalange S.a.r.l., Zone Industrielle Wolser, B.P. 92, pg. 79　IT
Laminoir de Dudelange S.a.r.l., pg. 79　IT
MecanARBED Dommeldange S.a.r.l., B.P. 5034, pg. 80　IT

Echternach

Fanuc Robotics Europe S.A., Zone Industrielle, pg. 478　IT
GE Fanuc Automation Europe S.A., pg. 478　IT

Ehlange

Astra Luxembourg S.A.R.L., P.O. Box 62, pg. 94　IT

Esch-sur-Alzette

Ciments Luxembourgeois S.A., pg. 80　IT

S.A. des Ciments Luxembourgeois, pg. 423　IT
ISSCO Luxembourg S.A., 66, rue de Luxembourg, pg. 80　IT
ProfilARBED, 66, rue de Luxembourg, pg. 79　IT

Howald

Digital, 23, Rue des Bayeres, pg. 507　PB
Fleming Fund Management (Luxembourg) S.A., 45, rue des Scillas, pg. 493　IT
Robert Fleming & Co. Limited, 45, rue des Scillas, pg. 493　IT

Luxembourg

ABN (Luxembourg) S.A., 3 Place de Clairefontaine, pg. 11　IT
ABN Trustcompany (Luxembourg) S.A., 2, Rue de l'Eau, pg. 11　IT
AC Rochester Luxembourg S.A., Route de Luxembourg, 4901 Bascharage, P.O. 29, pg. 723　PB
ADIG Investment Luxembourg S.A., pg. 181　IT
AIT - Arbed International Trading S.A., 19, Avenue de la Liberte, pg. 79　IT
AXA Assurances Luxembourg, 4-6 rue Adolphe, pg. 19　IT
Adecco Luxembourg SA, Grand'Rue 70, pg. 24　IT
ARBED S.A., 19, Avenue de la Liberte, pg. 78　IT
Audiofina S.A., 1 rue de Namur, pg. 561　IT
Autostrade Intl.-Luxembourg, 19/21 Bd. de Prince Henry, pg. 655　IT
BHF-BANK International S.A., 283, route d'Arlon, pg. 119　IT
BHF Investment Management AG, 283, route d'Arlon, pg. 120　IT
BIL Participation S.A., 69, Rte. d'Esch, pg. 162　IT
BNL International Investments, 51, Rue de Glacis, pg. 136　IT
BNP Luxembourg SA, 24 Blvd. Royal, pg. 164　IT
Bally-Biver S.a.r.l., Avenue de la Liberte 44, pg. 997　IT
Banca Nazionale del Lavoro, 51, Rue des Glacis, pg. 137　IT
Banco Di Napoli International S.A., 10-12 Ave. Pasteur, pg. 140　IT
Banco di Sicilia International S.A., 14, Ave. Marie Therese, pg. 141　IT
Bank for Europe Ltd., 13, rue Beaumont, pg. 419　IT
Bank Hapoalim (Luxembourg) Ltd., 18 Blvd. Royal, pg. 149　IT
Bank of Bermuda (Luxembourg) S.A. 13 rue Goethe, pg. 151　IT
Bank of Boston S.A., 41 Boulevard Royal, pg. 185　PB
The Bank of Tokyo-Mitsubishi (Luxembourg) S.A., 1-3, rue de St. Esprit, pg. 158　IT
Bankgesellschaft Berlin International S.A., 60 Grand Rue, pg. 159　IT
Banque Continentale Du Luxembourg, 2, Blvd. E. Servais, pg. 319　IT
Banque de Luxembourg, 80, Pl. de la Gare, pg. 406　IT
Banque Ferrier Lullin (Luxembourg) SA, 26 av. Monterey, pg. 480　IT
BANQUE GENERALE DU LUXEMBOURG SA, 50, Ave. J.F. Kennedy, pg. 161　IT
Banque Generale du Luxembourg SA, 50, avenue J F Kennedy, pg. 548　IT
Banque Indosuez Luxembourg, 39, allee Scheffer, pg. 314　IT
Banque International a Luxembourg, Route-d'esch 283, pg. 343　IT
BANQUE INTERNATIONALE A LUXEMBOURG S.A., pg. 162　IT
Banque IPPA & Associates, Boulevard de la Foire 15, pg. 562　IT
Banque Paribas (Luxembourg) S.A., 10A Boulevard Royal, pg. 320　IT
Banque pour L'Europe S.A.-Europa Bank AG, 13, rue Beaumont, pg. 419　IT
Barclays European Investment Holdings SA, pg. 166　IT
Bayer Finance S.A., pg. 172　IT
Bayerische Landesbank International S.A., 3, rue Jean Monnet, pg. 176　IT
Bayerische Vereinsbank International S.A., 38-40 av. Monterey, B.P. 481, pg. 181　IT
Brasilux S.A., 4, rue Pierre de Coubertin, pg. 79　IT
Brown Brothers Harriman (Luxembourg) S.A., 33, Blvd. Prince Henri, pg. 173　PV
CB German Index Fund Management Company S.A., pg. 311　IT
CCF (Luxembourg) S.A., 8 Avenue Marie-Therese, pg. 342　IT
CLT-UFA, 45, Boulevard Pierre Frieden, pg. 561　IT
Caisse Hypothecaire du Luxembourg, Blvd. de la Petrusse, pg. 162　IT
Captive Management Company SA (Captima), Rue des Glacis 1, pg. 548　IT
Cariplo Bank International S.A., 12 Rue Goethe, pg. 275　IT
Cash Invest Management S.A., Rue Aldringen 14, pg. 1416　IT
Casiopea Reaseguradora, S.A., 5 Pza. de la Gare, pg. 1371　IT
Chase Manhattan Bank Luxembourg, S.A., 5 Rue Plaetis, pg. 340　PB
Cheque Repas Luxembourg S.A., 8, boulevard Royal, pg. 1274　IT
Chiyoda Life Investment Luxemburg S.A., 1-3 rue du St. Esprit, pg. 287　IT
Cho Hung Bank Luxembourg S.A., 25B, Boulevard Royal, pg. 288　IT
Christiania Bank Luxembourg S.A., 16, Avenue Pasteur, pg. 289　IT

PB - *U.S. Public Companies Volume*
PV - *U.S. Private Companies Volume*
IT - *International Public & Private Companies Volume*

1696

CitiCorp Bank (Luxembourg) S.A., pg. 378   **PB**
Cofhylux SA, 50, Ave. J.F. Kennedy, pg. 162   **IT**
S.A. Comeci Holding, pg. 302
Commerzbank International, S.A., 11 rue Notre Dame, pg. 311   **IT**
Compagnie Europeenne de Financement S.A. Boulevard Royal 2bis, pg. 1415   **IT**
Comptoir des Fers et Metaux SA, pg. 838   **IT**
Considar Europe S.A., 6-12, rue du Fort Wallis, pg. 79   **IT**
Credit Agricole (CNCA) Luxembourg, 13, Avenue de la Porte-Nueve, pg. 341   **IT**
Credit Europeen, 52 Rte. D'Esch, pg. 148   **IT**
Cregelux SA, 27, Ave. Monterey, pg. 162   **IT**
DG Bank-Luxembourg, 4, rue Thomas Edison, pg. 352   **IT**
Dai-Ichi Kangyo Bank (Luxembourg) S.A., 2, Boulevard de la Foire, pg. 362   **IT**
Dai-ichi Life Luxembourg S.A., pg. 363   **IT**
Datastream International (Luxembourg) Ltd., c/o Price Waterhouse, 24-26 Avenue de la Liberte, pg. 1326   **PB**
DERBY INTERNATIONAL CORPORATION S.A., 5, Boulevard de la Foire, pg. 394   **IT**
Deutsche Bank Luxembourg S.A., 25, Blvd. Royal, pg. 405   **IT**
Deutsche Girozentrale-Deutsche Kommunalbank (Luxembourg), 16, Boulevard Royal, pg. 406   **IT**
Deutsche Girozentrale International S.A., 16, Boulevard Royal, pg. 407   **IT**
Dow Jones Markets Luxembourg SARL, 16 Avenue Pasteur, 4th Fl., pg. 525   **PB**
Dresdner Bank Luxembourg S.A., 26, rue du Marche-aux-Herbes, pg. 419   **IT**
Du Pont Photolux S.A., P.O. Box 1703, pg. 533   **PB**
Ericsson Reinsurance S.A., 65, Avenue de la Gare, pg. 1367   **IT**
Eskimo Europ S.a.r.l., 16, Boulevard d'Avranches, pg. 592   **PB**
Eureko RE, 5, rue Emile Blan, pg. 464   **IT**
Eurolease Factor SA, 26, boulevard Royal, pg. 162   **IT**
Eurolease-Factor (Elfa) SA, Boulevard Prince Henri 3A, pg. 548   **IT**
Europ Assistance Societe D'Assistance Aux Voyageurs S.A., 6, Rue Albert Borschette, pg. 91   **IT**
Europa Bank AG, 13, rue Beaumont, pg. 420   **IT**
Europaische Hypothekenbank der Deutschen Bank, 25A, Blvd. Royal, pg. 405   **IT**
Europartners Holding S.A., pg. 312   **IT**
EUROPEAN INVESTMENT BANK, 100 Blvd. Konrad Adenauer, pg. 465   **IT**
EXOR GROUP, 2 Blvd. Royale, pg. 467   **IT**
Fides Trust Company Ltd., pg. 312   **IT**
Fina Road Services, Route d'Esch 310, pg. 1043   **IT**
S.A. Frecolux, pg. 302   **IT**
Fuji Bank (Luxembourg) S.A., Centre Financier, 29 Ave. de la Porte-Nueve 2227, pg. 521   **IT**
GB International, Boulevard de la Foire, pg. 534   **IT**
Gaviota Re, S.A., 65, Avenue de la Gare, pg. 1104   **IT**
GEFINOR S.A. LUXEMBOURG, 23 Avenue de la Porte Neuve, pg. 542   **IT**
Generale Finance Luxembourg SA, 14, rue Aldringen, pg. 162   **IT**
GeneraLife, Rue Beck 4, pg. 548   **IT**
HSBC Investment Funds Luxembourg SA, Maison Gilly, 7 Rue du Marche-aux-Herbes, pg. 582   **IT**
Handelsgest S.A.R.L., pg. 312   **IT**
HANSA-NORDLUX Managementgesellschaft, pg. 181   **IT**
Helaba Luxembourg Landesbank Hessen-Thuringen International S.A., 2, Place de Paris, pg. 799   **IT**
Henderson International Luxemborg SA, 6D, Route de Treves, pg. 609   **IT**
Hypobank International S.A., 27, Blvd. du Prince Henri, pg. 176   **IT**
ICL Luxembourg S.A., 21 Blvd. Grande-Duchesse Charlotte, pg. 529   **IT**
ISS Luxembourg S.A., Avenue de la Faiencerie 121, pg. 657   **IT**
IKB International, 2, rue Jean Monnet, pg. 646   **IT**
Imasca S.A., Royal Rome 1, pg. 112   **IT**
Indugest S.A.R.L., pg. 312   **IT**
The Industrial Bank of Japan (Luxembourg) S.A., 6, rue Jean Monnet, pg. 676   **IT**
International Investment Management Gesellschaft S.A., pg. 405   **IT**
Internationale Leasing Gesellschaft, pg. 312   **IT**
Korn/Ferry International, 19 Cote d' Eich, pg. 633   **PV**
Kredietbank SA Luxembourgeoise, Boulevard Royal 43, pg. 65   **IT**
Kredietbank S.A. Luxembourgeoise, 43, Boulevard Royal, pg. 761   **IT**
Kredietcorp SA, Rue Notre Dame 37, pg. 65   **IT**
Kredietrust SA, Rue Aldringen 11, pg. 65   **IT**
Kyoei Fire & Marine Investment (Luxembourg, S.A.), 9, Boulevard F.D. Roosevelt, pg. 777   **IT**
Kyoei Life Investment Luxembourg S/A, pg. 777   **IT**
LGT Asset Management PLC Luxembourg, 9A, Boulevard de Prince Henri, pg. 809   **IT**
LGT Bank in Liechtenstein Vaduz, Bureau d'information Luxembour, 9A Boulevard du Prince Henri, pg. 810   **IT**
Landesbank Rheinland-Pfalz, 10-12 Boulevard Roosevelt, pg. 799   **IT**
Landesbank Rheinland Pfalz International S.A., 10-12 Boulevard Roosevelt, pg. 799   **IT**
Luxlife, 4, Rue Du Fort Rheinsheim-BP 723, pg. 565   **IT**
Management International (Luxembourg) S.A., 13 rue Goethe, pg. 152   **IT**
Mannesmann Finanz-Holding SA, pg. 840   **IT**
Maplux Reinsurance Company Ltd., Immeuble, Centre Europe, pg. 335   **IT**
Materiaux S.A., pg. 423   **IT**
Merita Bank Luxembourg S.A., 189 Ave. de Faiencerie, pg. 859   **IT**
Minorco, 9 rue Sainte Zithe, pg. 77   **IT**

Nedlloyd Road Cargo S.A., pg. 1145   **IT**
Nikko Bank (Luxembourg) S.A., 16, Boulevard Royal, pg. 930   **IT**
NOBIS Societe des Banques Privees, 2, rue Jean Monnet, pg. 119   **IT**
Nomura Advisory Company S.A., 2, Boulevard Royal, L-2449, pg. 955   **IT**
Nomura Bank (Luxembourg) S.A., 6 Avenue Emile Reuter, pg. 956   **IT**
Northern Telecom (Luxembourg) S.A., 3, Boulevard Royal, pg. 970   **IT**
Olivetti International S.A., pg. 1003   **IT**
PanEuroLife, pg. 323   **IT**
Paneurolife, Rue de la Chapelle 7, pg. 562   **IT**
RTL4, 45 Boulevard Pierre Frieden, pg. 561   **IT**
RTL Radio-Die Grossten Oldies, 45 boulevard Pierre Frieden, pg. 561   **IT**
RTL Radio Letzebuerg, 45, boulevard Pierre Frieden, pg. 561   **IT**
RTL Tele Letzebuerg, 45 Boulevard Pierre Frieden, pg. 561   **IT**
Rabobank Luxembourg S.A., 283, Route d'Arlon, pg. 1082   **IT**
Rabobank Trust Company, 283, Route d'Arlon, pg. 1082   **IT**
Redelcover S.A., Avenue de la Gare 65, pg. 463   **IT**
Risk & Insurance Services, 5, Rue Emile Bian, pg. 464   **IT**
Royale UAP IARD, Rue de la Chapelle 7, pg. 562   **IT**
Royale UAP VIE, Rue de la Chapelle 7, pg. 562   **IT**
S-E-Banken Luxembourg S.A., 16, Boulevard Royal, pg. 1259   **IT**
SBC Warburg Asset Management Luxembourg S.A., 14 rue Leon Thyes L-2636, pg. 1331   **IT**
SCEM Reinsurance S.A., pg. 1331   **IT**
SME International, 1921 Vd. du Prince Henry, pg. 655   **IT**
SMH Finance (Luxembourg) S.A., 29, avenue Monterey, pg. 1161   **IT**
Safe Reinsurance, Allee Marconi 16, pg. 534   **IT**
The Sakura Bank (Luxembourg) S.A., Central Parc 33, Boulevard du Prince Henri, pg. 1180   **IT**
Schindler S.a.r.l., pg. 1205   **IT**
SINSER (Luxembourg) Sarl, b p 593, 11 rue Beaumont, pg. 1258   **IT**
Skandia Advisory Company SA, 69, route d'Esch, pg. 1258   **IT**
Skandinaviska Enskilda Banken, 15 rue Notre Dame, pg. 1259   **IT**
Societe de Banque Suisse (Luxembourg) S.A., 26, route d'Arlon, pg. 1331   **IT**
Softe-Luxembourg, 33 Blvd. du Prince Henri, pg. 656   **IT**
Sopade S.A., Boulevard Joseph II 28, pg. 1416   **IT**
State Street Bank (Luxembourg) S.A., 47 Boulevard Royal, pg. 1513   **PB**
Sumitomo Trust & Banking (Luxembourg) S.A., 18, Blvd. Royal, pg. 1318   **IT**
Svenska Handelsbanken Luxembourg, 146 Blvd. de la Petrusse, pg. 1328   **IT**
Swedbank (Luxembourg) S.A., 8-10, avenue de la Gare, pg. 1328   **IT**
Swiss Life (Luxembourg), 1, Rue du Potager, pg. 1332   **IT**
Taiyo Life Investment Luxembourg, S.A., Central Parc, 33 Bouldvard du Prince Henri, pg. 1349   **IT**
TechnoARBED Luxembourg S.a.r.l., 16a, Avenue de la Liberte, pg. 80   **IT**
Templeton Global Strategic Services S.A., Centre Nueberg, 30 Grand Rue, pg. 680   **PB**
TOHO Life Luxembourg S.A., 1-3 Rue du St. Esprit, pg. 1390   **IT**
The Tokio Marine International Fund (Luxembourg) S.A., 3B Boulevard de Prince Henri, pg. 1393   **IT**
Tractebel Engineering Luxembourg S.A., Rue Glesner 58, pg. 1416   **IT**
TradeARBED S.A., Ave. de la Liberte, pg. 79   **IT**
TrefilARBED Luxembourg/Saarbrucken S.a.r.l., 16a, Ave. de la Liberte, pg. 80   **IT**
Trinkaus & Burkhardt (International) S.A., 1-7, Rue Nina et Julien Lefevre, pg. 584   **IT**
Unico Financial Services S.A., 12-14 Blvd. G.D. Charlotte, pg. 1085   **IT**
Unico Investment Fund, 12-14 Blvd, G.D. Charlotte, pg. 1085   **IT**
Union Bank of Norway International S.A., 22, rue Jean-Pierre Brasseur, pg. 1439   **IT**
Union de Banques Suisses (Luxembourg) S.A., 36-38, Grand-rue, pg. 1441   **IT**
Vereins- und Westbank Beteiligungsgesellschaft S.A., pg. 181   **IT**
Vereinsbank International S.A., pg. 181   **IT**
Von Ernst Capital Management S.A., pg. 181   **IT**
Wagofi SA, 6, rue Aldringen, pg. 22   **IT**
WestLB International S.A., 32-34 Blvd. Grande-Duchesse Charlotte, pg. 1494   **IT**
Willis Corroon Management SA-Luxembourg, Galerie Kons-3e, 24-26 Place de la Gare L-1616, pg. 1509   **IT**
Wuestenrot International Management-Gesellschaft AG, 69, route d'Esch, pg. 1514   **IT**
Paul Wurth S.A., 32, rue d'Alsace, pg. 80   **IT**
Zellweger Finanz AG, pg. 618   **IT**
Zurich Compagnie d'Assurances, 48 Rue de Bragance, pg. 1531   **IT**
Zurich Compagnie d'assurances sur la vie, 48 Rue de Bragance, pg. 1529   **IT**
Zurich Eurolife S.A., 48 rue de Bragance, pg. 1531   **IT**
Zurich International Services (Luxembourg) S.A., 48 rue de Bragance, pg. 1532   **IT**

Mersch

SISTO Armaturen S.A., pg. 721   **IT**

Petange

S.A. John Steel International, pg. 302   **IT**

Rodange

Ares S.A., pg. 79   **IT**
MMRA Metallurgique et Miniere de Rodange-Athus S.A., pg. 80   **IT**

Rumelange

Intermoselle S.a.r.l., pg. 80   **IT**

Senningerberg

Amdahl Luxembourg Succursale d'Amdahl Belgique S.A./N.V., Regus Luxembourg, pg. 527   **IT**
Bank Leumi (Luxembourg) S.A., 60 Route de Treves, pg. 150   **IT**
Banque Belge Guernsey Luxembourg SA, Airport Center, 5, rue Heienhaff, pg. 547   **IT**
Banque Cogeba-Gonet Luxembourg SA, Airport Center, 5, rue Heienhaff, pg. 547   **IT**
Den norske Bank (Luxembourg) S.A., 6A, route de Treves, pg. 392   **IT**
Dresdnerbank Asset Management S.A., 6A, route de Treves, pg. 420   **IT**
Elsevier SA, Route de Treves 6, pg. 1093   **IT**
Morgan Stanley Luxembourg, 6C, Rte. de Treves, pg. 1133   **PB**
Niederlassung Luxembourg, Frankfurter Sparkasse, European Bank & Business Center, pg. 504   **IT**
Societe de Reassurance Vallaroche SA (SOREVAL), 6B Route de Treves, pg. 1165   **IT**

Steinfort

Uniroyal Englebert Textilcord S.A., pg. 328   **IT**

Steinsel

Bay State SA, Rue J.F. Kennedy 1, pg. 1174   **IT**

Strassen

ING Bank Luxembourg, Route d'Arlon 224, pg. 649   **IT**
Sodexho Luxembourg S.A., 255, route d'Arlon, pg. 1275   **IT**

Vianden

Electrolux S.a.r.L., 4, Rue de la Frontiere, pg. 443   **IT**

Wecker

Usine de Wecker S.r.l., pg. 1529   **IT**

Wiltz

Circuit Foil Luxembourg S.A., pg. 80   **IT**

MACAU

Macau

Banco Espirito Santo do Oriente SARL (Besor), Av. Dr. Mario Soares, 323, pg. 142   **IT**
Bela Vista Limitada, 8, Rua do Comendador, pg. 704   **IT**
CSA Automated (Macau) Ltd., No. 126 Rua DE Paquim, Edif. Comercial 1 Tak, 17-Andar F, pg. 243   **IT**
Companhia de Construcao e Engenharia Kin Sun (Macau), Limitada 5, Andar, Nos 60-64 Avenida,Infante D. Henrique, pg. 196
Deutsche Bank AG (Macau), 7/F, Nam Wah Commercial, Edificio, 1L-1LB Avenida Aleida Ribeiro, pg. 404   **IT**
Excelsior Hoteis E Investimentos Limitada, Avenida de Amizade, pg. 704
National Mutual Macao, Rua de Xanghai, No. 175, Edif da Associacao Commercial de, pg. 908   **IT**
Standard Chartered Bank (Macao), 16/17 F, Edif. Centro, Commercial Central, 60-64 Avenida, pg. 1295   **IT**

MACEDONIA

Kavadarci

SKF Maktrade d.o.o., Marsal Tito b.b., pg. 1159   **IT**

Skopje

Hemomak Export-Import c.o., Dane Grujev 5, pg. 108   **IT**
Novo Nordisk A/S, ul 11 Oktomvri Br 36 i Kat, pg. 988   **IT**

MADAGASCAR

Antananarivo

BMOI, Place de l'Independance, pg. 163   **IT**
Banque Malgache de l'Ocean Indien S.A. (BMOI), Place de l'Independance, pg. 149   **IT**
Banque Mondiale, 1, Bis Rue Patrice Lumumba, pg. 1189   **PV**

PB - U.S. Public Companies Volume
PV - U.S. Private Companies Volume
IT - International Public & Private Companies Volume

Bull Madagascar S.A., 12 rue Indira Ganhi, pg. 315   IT
CIBA-GEIGY Trading and Marketing Services Co. Ltd., pg. 980   IT
Cimelta-Jeumont, Oest Ambohijanahary, pg. 706   IT
Honeywell Bull Madagascar S.A., 12, rue de Nice, pg. 318   IT
Shell Exploration & Development Madagascar BV, 26-28 Rue Patrice Lumumba, pg. 1137   IT
Union Commercial Bank S.A., Rue Solombavambahoaka, pg. 1294   IT

MALAWI

Blantyre

Gestetner Limited, Gestetner House, Kamuzu Highway, pg. 1115   IT
ICL (Malawi) Limited, Plantation House, Ground Floor, pg. 529   IT
Industrial Gases Ltd., pg. 122   IT
National Bank of Malawi, Victoria Avenue, pg. 1296   IT
Shell Malawi Ltd., off McLeod Rd, Industrial Area, pg. 1136   IT

Kanengo

Stancom Tobacco Packers (Malawi) Ltd., P.O. Box 48, pg. 1502   PB

Lilongwe

The World Bank, Development House, Capital City, pg. 1189   PV

Limbe

Lever Brothers (Malawi) Ltd., Cnr Tsirana Rd. & Citrona Ave., pg. 1437   IT
Stancom Tobacco Co. (Malawi) Ltd., P.O. Box 5360, pg. 1502   PB
Tobacco Processors (Malawi) Ltd., Churchill Rd., pg. 1502   PB

MALAYSIA

Ampang

Raychem S.A. Industrial Y Commercial, Ste. 703, 3rd Fl., Wisma Chinese Chawer, pg. 1363   PB

Bahau

KGV Lambert Smith Hampton, Suite 2, 17th Floor, Kompleks Tun Abdul Bazak, pg. 797   IT

Balakong

NSK Micro Precision (M) Sdn. Bhd., 43, Jalan Taming Dua, Taman Taming Jaya, Selangor, pg. 904   IT

Batu Pahat

Sharp Manufacturing Corporation Sdn. Bhd., PLO-225 Kawasan Perindustrian, Sri Gading, pg. 1230   IT
Sharp-Roxy Electronics Corporation (M) Sdn. Bhd., PLO-1 Kawasan Perindustrian, Sri Gading, Industrial Estate, pg. 1230   IT

Bayan Baru

LeaRonal (SEAsia) Ltd., Representative Office, 56, 1st Floor, Jalan Mahsuri, pg. 982   PB

Ehsan

Weatherford (Malaysia) Sdn. Bhd., Lot C12 B-1 Jalan Selaman 1, Palm Square, pg. 1750   PB

Ipoh

Great Eastern Life Assurance Company-Ipoh, Great Eastern Life Building, 119 Jalan Sultan Idris Shah, pg. 557   IT
Harta Wangsa Sdn. Bhd., 4th Floor, Wisma Wan, Mohamed, Kalan Panglima Bukit GangTang, pg. 1293   IT
Micromechanics (Malaysia) Sdn. Bhd., PT 51660 Kawasan Perindustrian, pg. 1161   IT

Jalan Merdeka

Labuan Branch, Level 12D, Main Officer Tower, Financial Park Labuan, pg. 82   IT

Johor Baharu

ALPHA Industries Sdn. Bhd., No. 37 Jalan Kangkar Tebrau, Karung Berkunci No. 744, pg. 530   IT
Beiersdorf (Malaysia) SDN. BHD., pg. 183   IT
Brother Industries (Johor) Sdn. Bhd., No. 6 Jalan Firma 1, Kawasan Perindustrian Tebrau, pg. 229   IT
Brother Industries Technology (M) Sdn. Bhd., 17, Jalan Firma 2, pg. 229   IT
Crown Cork of Malaysia SDN BHD, P.O. Box 252, pg. 465   PB

Fujitsu Component (Malaysia) SDN. BHD., No. 1, Lorong Satu Kawasan, Perindustrian Parit Raja, pg. 528   IT
Great Eastern Life Assurance Company-Johor Bahru, Oversea Chinese Bank Building, 2nd Floor, pg. 557   IT
Johore Mining & Stevedoring Co., P.O. Box 188, pg. 52   IT
KLA Instruments Malaysia, 60 Jalan Timah 7, pg. 939   PB
MTPB - Southern Region, No. 1, 4th Floor, Kompleks Tun Abcul Razak, pg. 833   IT
Medical Latex (DUA) SDN. BHD., pg. 183   IT
Outokumpu Copper Products (Malaysia) Sdn. Bhd., No. 3-01, Jalan Permas 10/8, Bandar Baru Permas Jaya, pg. 1017   IT
Shimano Components (Malaysia) Sdn. Bhd., Lot 4550, Lorong A-16, pg. 1233   IT
Shimano (Malaysia) Sdn. Bhd., No. 4059, Pekan Nanas, pg. 1233   IT
Showp atronics (M) Sdn. Bhd., 77 Jalan Langkasuka Kawasan, Perindustrian, pg. 1237   IT
Solectron Technology, Sdn. Bhd., Lot 7963, Jalan Air Hitam, pg. 1483   PB
Sumitomo Electric Interconnect Products (M) Sdn. Bhd., No. 1, Jalan Angkasa Mas Utama, pg. 1314   IT
TWP Sendirian Berhad, 89, Jalan Tampoi, pg. 363   IT
Tiger Balm (Malaysia) Sdn Bhd, PLO 95 No. 6, Jalan Firma 1/1, pg. 604   IT
Trio-Kenwood Electronics Engineering (M) Sdn. Bhd., No. 7, Jalan Tahana, Kawasan, pg. 731   IT
Willis Faber (Malaysia) Sdn Bhd, Lot 1A, Tingat 20, pg. 1510   IT

Kangar

Mediquip SDN. BHD., Padang Lati, Mukin Paya, pg. 648   PB

Kauntan

Nemic-Lambda (Kanutan) Sdn. Bhd., Lot 2 & 3, Kawasan Perindustrian, pg. 1242   IT

Kedah

Great Eastern Life Assurance Company-Alor Setar, 66 & 68 Jalan Teluk Wan Jah, pg. 557   IT
Kedah Sato Sdn. Bhd., Tingkat 4, Wisma PKNK, pg. 1197   IT

Keluang

Casio (Malaysia) Sdn. Bhd., No. 7, Jalan Keluli 1, Kawasan Perindustrian Bukit Raja, pg. 274   IT
FE Magnet Wire (Malaysia) Sdn. Bhd., Lot 2, Persiarann Waja Bukit, Raja Indusrial Estate, pg. 530   IT
Great Eastern Life Assurance Company-Keluang, Wisma Tanjong, 7 Jalan Stesen, pg. 557   IT
Pamol Plantations Sdn. Bhd., pg. 1438   IT
Ssangyong Eng. & Const. (M) Sdn. Bhd., Suite 16 03B, 16th Floor, Wisma Spk, pg. 1292   IT
Van Lee Cylinders Sdn. Bhd., pg. 1146   IT
Van Lee Packaging Sdn. Bhd., pg. 1147   IT

Kluang

Asahi Industries (Malaysia) Sdn. Bhd., Plo 1, Kawasan Perindustrian, Mengkibol Off Jalan Batu Pahat, pg. 274   IT
Great Eastern Life Assurance Company-Kluang, No. 1 (1st & 2nd Floor), Lorong Yayasan, pg. 557   IT
Lilly Industries (Malaysia) Snd. Bhd., Lot No. 4963, Jalan Teratai, 5.5 Miles, Meru Industrial Zone, pg. 995   PB
NS Thermo (Malaysia) SDN. BHD., Lot 9906, 4 1/2 Miles, Jalan Kebun, pg. 938   IT
Top Thermo Mfg. (Malaysia) SDN. BHD. Lot 9906, 4 1/2 Miles, Jalan Kebun, pg. 939   IT

Kota Baharu

Great Eastern Life Assurance Company-Kota Bharu, Oversea Chinese Bank Building, 1st Floor, pg. 557   IT
Rohm-Wako (Kelantan) Sdn. Bhd., Lot 1320 Kawasan Perindustrian, pg. 1125   IT

Kota Kinabalu

BHP Steel Building Products (Sabah) Sdn Bhd, pg. 226   IT
Hanwa Co., Ltd.-Kota Kinabalu Branch, pg. 595   IT
MTPB - Sabah Region, Ground Floor, Wisma Wing Onn Life, pg. 833   IT
Mitsui & Co., Ltd., 5th Fl., Central Bldg. Jalan Sagunting, pg. 880   IT

Kuala Langat

Henkel Oleochemicals (Malaysia) Snd. Bhd., pg. 613   IT
Kayaba (Malaysia) Sdn. Bhd., Lot 4, Jalan Perak, Kawasan Perindustrian, pg. 727   IT
Lovytex SDN. BHD., Lot 8, Jalan Suasa, 42500 Telok Panglima Garang, pg. 1648   PB
NEC Semiconductors (Malaysia) Sdn. Berhad, Telok Panglima Garang, Free Trade Zone, pg. 900   IT
Toshiba Electronics Malaysia Sdn. Bhd., 42507 Telok Panglima Garang, pg. 1406   IT

Kuala Lumpur

AMMB Holdings Berhad, 22nd Fl., Bangunan Arab-Malaysian, pg. 1391   IT
AMP Products (Malaysia) SDN. BHD., Lot 11.3, 11th Fl., pg. 9   PB
ANZ Grindlays Bank plc Malaysia, Suite 1, 4th Floor, Wisma Genting, Jalan Sultan Ismail, pg. 99   IT
AST Computer & Services, (M) Sdn. Bhd., 8A Floor Wisma Genting, pg. 1182   IT
Acer Sales & Service Sdn. Bhd., pg. 22   IT
Aetna Universal Insurance SDN. BHD., Menara Aetna Universal, 84, Jalan Raja Chulan, pg. 27   PB
Ajinomto (Malaysia) Berhad, Lot 5710, Jl. Kuchai Lama, pg. 40   IT
Alfa-Laval (M) Sdn Bhd, P.O. Box 2062, pg. 1380   IT
Antah Sedgwick Chartered Insurance Brokers Sdn Berhad, Bangunan MAS, 23rd Fl., Jalan Sultan Ismail, pg. 1297   IT
Arab-Malaysian Merchant Bank Berhad, 21st-26th Fl, Bangunan Arab-Malaysian, pg. 1391   IT
Asahi Bank Kuala Lumpur Representative Office, 12th Fl., Pernas International, Jalan Sultan Ismail, pg. 83   IT
The Ascott Kuala Lumpur, Jalan Pinang, pg. 1212   IT
Asea Brown Boveri Sdn. Bhd., pg. 8   IT
Aseambankers Malaysia Berhad, 33rd Fl., Menara Maybank, 100 Jalan Tun Perak, pg. 362   IT
Associated Pan Malaysia Cement Sdn. Berhad, 20th Fl., Plaza Lee Hoy Chan, pg. 198   IT
Astra Pharmaceuticals (Malaysia) Sdn Bhd., pg. 94   IT
Australia & New Zealand Banking Group Limited Malaysia, Suite 1, 4th Floor, Wisma Genting, Jalan Sultan Ismail 50250, pg. 99   IT
Ballast Nedam Groep N.V. (Malaysia) Sdn. Bhd., 28th Floor, Menara Tun Razak, pg. 134   IT
Ballast Nedam International (Malaysia) Sdn. Bhd., 28th Floor, Menara Tun Razak, pg. 134   IT
Bangkok Bank Berhad, 105 Jalan Tun H.S. Lee, pg. 146   IT
Bank of America Malaysia Berhad, Wisma Goldhill, 18th Fl., Jalan Raja Chulan, pg. 182   PB
Bank of Commerce (M) Berhad, 22nd Floor, 6 Jalan Tun Perak, pg. 1190   IT
The Bank of Nova Scotia Berhad, Menara Boustead, 69 Jalan Raja Chulan, pg. 156   IT
Banque Paribas-Malaisie, 17th Floor, Mui Plaza, Jalan P. Ramlee, pg. 320   IT
Barclays Bank PLC, pg. 166   IT
Barringer Asia-Pacific, No. 25-1 Jalan 3176D, pg. 192   PB
Batey Ads Malaysia Sdn. Bhd., 12 Jalan 1/71, Off Jalan Tun Mohd Fuad, pg. 117   IT
Baymont Malaysia SDN BHD, 54 Jalan SS 21/39, Damansara Utama, pg. 31   IT
F.J. Benjamin Fashions (M) Sdn. Bhd., Menara Sabre, Ste. 12.1 & 12.2, 12th Fl., No. 8 Lorong P Ramlee, pg. 187   IT
Berjaya General Insurance Sdn. Bhd., Shahzan Prudential Tower, Level 11, 30 Jalan Sultan Ismail, pg. 1392   IT
Bilfinger + Berger (M) Sdn Bhd., 3rd Fl., Menara 2, Faber Towers, pg. 196   IT
Robert Bosch (South East Asia) Pte Ltd., Blocks 1 & 2, Lot 1989, pg. 206   IT
Bull Information Systems (Malaysia), Suite 2205, 22nd Floor, Plaza Pengkalan Jalan Ampang, pg. 315   IT
Leo Burnett Advertising SDN.BHD., 10th Fl., MCB Plaza, pg. 184   PV
CCF Kuala Lumpur, Pernas International Bldg., Ste. 310, 3rd Fl., pg. 342   IT
C.I. Holdings Berhad, Wisma M, 3rd Fl., 66 Jalan Ampang, pg. 1092   IT
C.M.I. Malaysia, pg. 302   IT
CPC/AJI (Malaysia) Sdn. Berhad, Lot 1989, Block C, Jalan Segambut, pg. 41   IT
CPC/AJI (Malaysia) Sdn. Berhad, Lot 1989, Block C, Jalan Segambut, pg. 225   PB
CSSL (M) Sdn Bhd, 13F Menara TR Tower, 161B Jalan Ampang, pg. 1043   IT
CT Paging Sdn. Bhd., 12 Jalan 1/82B Bangsar Utama, pg. 1365   IT
CT Radioset Sdn. Bhd., 12 Jalan 1/82B Bangsar Utama, pg. 1365   IT
Carrefour - Malaysia, Magnificient Diagraph SDN BHD, 3rd Floor Wisma Socfin, pg. 272   IT
Cegelec (M) Sdn Bhd, Peti 35-36, Tingkat 4-West Block, pg. 53   IT
CelsiusTech Systems AB, Trading Sdn Bhd, 9th Floor, Menara Bank Pembangunan, pg. 278   IT
The Chase Manhattan Bank, N.A., Pernas International, Jalan Sultan Ismail, pg. 340   PB
Chemical Company of Malaysia Berhad, 9th Fl., Wisma Sime derby, pg. 664   IT
Clarins SDN BHD, Annexe Block, Level 5, Amoda Bldng., pg. 295   IT
Clearways Drilling (M) SDN BHD, 332A-11A, 11th Fl., Ampang City, Jalan Ampang, pg. 146   PB
Colgate-Clorox (Far East) Ltd., pg. 387   PB
Commerce International Merchant Bankers Berhad, 10-12th Fl., Commerce Square, Jalan Semantan, Damansara Heights, pg. 1190   IT
Control Instruments (M) Sdn. Bhd, Lot 7732 (PT 207), Kampong Baru Balakong, pg. 361   PV
Credit Corporation (Malaysia) Berhad, Jalan Sultan Ismall, pg. 1297   IT
Crest Engineering (Malaysia) Sbn. Bhd., Ste.12.06, 12th Fl., Wisma Stephens, No., pg. 5   IT

PB - *U.S. Public Companies Volume*
PV - *U.S. Private Companies Volume*
IT - *International Public & Private Companies Volume*

1698

Geographic Index-Non U.S.

NON-U.S. LOCATED COMPANIES MALAYSIA

Dai-Ichi Kangyo Bank, Ltd.-Kuala Lumpur, 5th Floor, Mui Plaza, Jalan P. Ramlee, pg. 361 IT
Dai-Ichi Kangyo Bank, Ltd.-Kuala Lumpur, 5th Fl., Mui Plaza, Jalan P. Ramlee, pg. 360 IT
Daiwa Bank-Kuala Lumpur, Unit 13.04 (B), 13th Fl., Menara Promet, Jalan Sultan Ismail, pg. 373 IT
Daiwa Securities Adviser Sdn. Bhd., Letter Box No. 131, 35th Fl., UBN Tower, 10 Jalan P. Ramlee, pg. 375 IT
De La Rue Systems Ltd., Suite 19.03, Level 19, Menara Lion, pg. 387 IT
Dell Asia Pacific Ltd., 805 HLA Building, Jalan Raja Chulan, pg. 495 PB
Dentsu Mandate (Malaysia) Sdn. Bhd., 54-1 Medan Setia 2, pg. 393 IT
Dentsu Young & Rubicam Sdn. Bhd. (Kuala Lumpur), 6th Fl., WISMA MBSB, 48 Jalan Dungun, pg. 325 PV
Det Norske Veritas, 5th Fl., Menara Aik Hua, pg. 397 IT
Deutsche Bank AG (Kuala Lumpur), Apera-ULG Centre, 84, Jalan Raja Chulan, pg. 404 IT
Dumez-Jaya Sdn Bhd, Suite 12.06-12th Floor, Wisma HLA, pg. 823 IT
Dun & Bradstreet Information Services (M) Sdn. Bhd., Suite 50/D, 50th Floor, Empire Tower, Jalan Tun Razak, pg. 536 PB
EMI (Malaysia) Sdn Bhd, Suite 10-01, 10th Floor, Exchange Square off Jalan Semantan, pg. 427 IT
Ebara Engineering (Malaysia) Sdn. Bhd., Lot 7.01, 7th Floor, MCB Plaza, pg. 432 IT
Daniel J. Edelman Sdn. Bhd., Wisma Damansara, 2nd Fl., Jalan Semantan, Damansara Heights, pg. 363 PV
Empresas ICA Sociedad Controladora (Malaysia), Floor 28.15, Menara Haw Par 651, pg. 454 IT
Enso-Eurocan South East Asia Pte. Ltd., No. 1 Jalan Chengkeh, pg. 457 IT
Esselte Meto (Malaysia) SDN BHD, Lot 29-A, Mukim Batu Ind. Area, pg. 461 IT
Esselte Meto SDN BHD, Lot 29-A, Mukim Batu Ind. Area, Jalan Kepong Batu 6 1/2 miles, pg. 461 IT
Esso Malaysia Berhad, Kompleks Antarabangsa, pg. 602 PB
Esso Production Malaysia Inc., Kompleks Antarabangsa, pg. 602 PB
Fluor Daniel (Malaysia) Sdn. Bhd., Menara Maybank-44th Fl., Suite, 8-15-1, Level 15, Plaza Raja Chulan, pg. 660 PB
Fuji Electric (Malaysia) Sdn. Bhd., 19th Fl., Wisma Cyclecarri 288, pg. 522 IT
Furukawa Electric Cables (Malaysia) Sdn. Bhd., 4th Floor, Wisma Pahlawan, Jalan, pg. 530 IT
GEC-Marconi Projects (Malaysia) Sdn. Bhd., Level 15, Bangunan Tabung Ha ji, pg. 544 IT
GTMI (M) Sdn Bhd, Suite 12.01 & 12.02-12th Floor, Wisma HLA, pg. 823 IT
Golden Donuts SBN. BHD., pg. 63 IT
Goodyear Malaysia Berhad, 40914 Shah Alam, Selangor, pg. 753 PB
Great Eastern Life Assurance Company, Semua House, Lorong Bunus 6, pg. 557 IT
Great Eastern Life Assurance Company-Malaysia, Great Eastern Life Bldg., 40 & 44 Jalan Ampang, pg. 557 IT
Guerlain (Malaysia) Sdn Bhd, Ste. 14.6 Level 16, Menara IMC-Jalan Sultan Ismail, pg. 780 IT
HP Sales Malaysia Sdn Bhd, 9th Fl. Chung Khian Bank Bldg., 46, Jalan Raja Laut, pg. 818 PB
HSBC Finance (Malaysia) Berhad, 3/F, Plaza See Hoy Chan, Jalan Raja Chulan, pg. 582 IT
HSBC (Kuala Lumpur) Nominees Sdn Bhd, 2 Leboh Ampang, pg. 582 IT
HSBC (Malaysia) Trustee Berhad, 2 Leboh Ampang, pg. 582 IT
Hakuhodo Malaysia Sdn. Bhd., 4th Flr., Wisma Socfin, Jalan Semantan, pg. 588 IT
Hakuyo Construction Sdn. Bhd., c/o Management Advisory Servic, es Sdn. Bhd., Wisma Selangor Dredging, pg. 996 IT
Hanwa Co., Ltd.-Kuala Lumpur Branch, 18th Fl., Ste. 1802A, Plaza See Hoy Chan, pg. 595 IT
Haw Par Land (Malaysia) Sdn. Bhd., 9th Floor, Menara, Haw Par, Lot 242, pg. 604 IT
Heller Factoring (M) Sdn. Bhd., Suite 08.04, Level 8, Menara Lion 165 Jalan, pg. 521 IT
Henkel Chemicals (Malaysia) Sdn. Bhd., pg. 612 IT
Henkel Kimianika (M) Sdn. Bhd., pg. 614 IT
Henkel Rika (M) Sdn. Bhd., pg. 613 IT
Hewlett-Packard Sales (Malaysia) Sdn. Bhd., Wisma Mirama, 13/F, Jalan Wisma Putra, pg. 821 PB
Highway Toll Systems Sdn. Bhd. (HTS), Regent Office Block 4F, 160 Jalan, Bukit Bintang, pg. 874 IT
Hong Leong Assurance Sdn. Bhd. (Non-Life Div), Tingkat 18, Wisma HLA, pg. 60 IT
Hongkong Bank Malaysia Berhad, 2 Leboh Ampang, pg. 583 IT
Hume Industries (Malaysia) Berhad, 3rd Fl., Bangunan Hong Leong, 117 Jalan Tun H.S. Lee, pg. 475 IT
Humphreys & Glasgow (Malaysia) Sdn. Bhd., c/o Messrs. Skrine & Co., P.O. Box 987, pg. 1587 PB
Hwang-DBS Asset Management (Malaysia) Sdn. Bhd., 1st Floor, Plaza MBF, Jalan Ampang, pg. 351 IT
ICI Agrochemicals (Malaysia) SDN BHD, Tingkat 9 Wisma Sime Darby, pg. 664 IT
ICI Fertilizers (Malaysia) SDN Berhad, 9th Fl., Wisma Sime Darby, Jalan Raja Laut, pg. 665 IT
ICI Industrial Chemicals (Malaysia) SDN BHD, 9th Fl., Wisma Sime Darby, Jalan Raja Laut, pg. 665 IT
IVO Sendi Prima Sdn Bhd, Suite 27.03, Level 27, Menara Lion, pg. 661 IT
The Industrial Bank of Japan (Kuala Lumpur), Ste. 1403, 14th Fl., Pernas Intl., Jalan Sultan Ismail, pg. 675 IT
Industrial Resins (Malaysia) Sdn. Bhd., 5th Fl., Rumah Rohas 61, Jalan Raja Abdullah Kg Baru, pg. 1408 IT
Intergraph Systems (Malaysia) Sdn BHD, 46-1 Jalan Telawi, Bangsar Baru, 59100, pg. 892 PB
International Computers (Malaysia) SDN.BHD, Wisma Damansara, 7th Floor, pg. 529 IT
JGC (Malaysia) Sdn. Bhd., Kompleks Antarbangsa, Jalan Sultan Ismail, 2nd Fl., pg. 697 IT
James Hardie Asia, 24/1 Jalan Telawi Tiga, pg. 597 IT
Japan Airlines Company, Ltd., Ste. 20, 03 Level 20 Menama Lion 145, pg. 701 IT
Jardine Matheson (Malaysia) Sdn Bhd, Level 6 Wisma Inai, 241, Jalan Tun Razak, pg. 705 IT
KGV Lambert Smith Hampton, Ikt 3, 1-2 Menara Aikhua, Cangkat Raja Chulan, pg. 797 IT
KLCC Picnic Food court, Level 2, Suria KLCC, pg. 1213 IT
Kenwood Electronics (Malaysia) Sdn. Bhd., 10th Fl., Block B, Wisma Semantan No. 12, pg. 731 IT
Kintetsu Integrated Air Services Sdn Bhd, Block A Lots 4 & 5, Kompleks Kargo Udara, pg. 735 IT
Kleinwort Benson Limited, Ste. 9.4, 9th Fl., Menara IMC, pg. 420 IT
KONE Elevator (M) Sdn. Bhd., 122-124, 3rd Fl., pg. 747 IT
Korn/Ferry International, 6th Fl., UBN Tower, 10 Jalan P. Ramlee, pg. 633 PV
Kuala Lumpur City Centre Project Office, c/o Nishimatsu-Corpro., Lot D,Section 58, pg. 943 IT
Kuala Lumpur Golf & Country Club Berhad, 21st Floor, Wisma Sime Darby, pg. 1250 IT
Kvaerner Engineering Sdn Bhd, 2004-2009, 20th Fl., Wisma HLA, Talan Raja Chulan, pg. 766 IT
Lever Brothers (Malaysia) Sdn. Bhd., pg. 1437 IT
Arthur D. Little (Malaysia) Sdn Bhd, Ste 19-16-3A, 16th Fl., UOA Centre, pg. 671 PV
Loewe Fashion Sdn. Ehd, No. 2 Benteng, pg. 782 IT
Logica (Malaysia) Sdn. Bhd., 5th Fl., Bangunan Getah Asli, 148 Jalan Ampang, pg. 814 IT
Louis Vuitton Malaysia Sdn Bhd, Lot 8 Main Lobby Fl., Arcade Hotel, Kuala Lumpur Hilton, pg. 782 IT
MBT (Malaysia) Sdm. Bhd., pg. 1465 IT
MDK Consultants (Malaysia), 22 A Jalan Tun Mohd Fuad, Taman Tun Dr Ismail, pg. 117 IT
MMC-GTM Bina Sama, 35th Floor, Menara PNB 201A, Jalan Tun Razak, pg. 823 IT
Mailway Sdn. Bhd., pg. 720 IT
Mal Pacific Technology Sdn. Bhd., 18th Fl., Wisma Sime Darby, Jalan Raja Laut, pg. 1293 IT
Malayan Cement Berhad, Wisma Damansara, JLN Semantan, pg. 198 IT
Malayan Law Journal, Suite 1001-1002, 10th Floor, pg. 1095 IT
Malaysia Packaging Industry Berhad, 6 1/2 Miles, Simpang Salak, South Bharu (Jalan Kuchai Lama), pg. 41 IT
MALAYSIA TOURISM PROMOTION BOARD (MTPB), Menara Dato'Onn, Putra World Trade Center, pg. 832 IT
Malaysian Oxygen Berhad, P.O. Box 10633, pg. 122 IT
Malaysian Roofing Industries Sdn. Bhd., pg. 129 IT
Mannesmann Steel & Pipe SDN.BHD., pg. 838 IT
Mastrak Sdn Bhd, No. 7 Jalan 5/76 B, Desa Pandan, pg. 1199 IT
Microsoft (Malaysia) Sdn. Bhd., pg. 1108 PB
Minebea Co., Ltd. - Kuala Lumpur Branch, 4th Fl., West Tower, Wisma Consplant No. 2, pg. 869 IT
Mitsui & Co., Ltd., 17th Fl., Menara Promet, Jalan Sultan Is, pg. 880 IT
Mobil Oil Malaysia Sendirian Berhad, 10th Fl., Pernas Intl. Bldg., Jalon Sulton Ismail, pg. 1119 PB
Morgan Grenfell (Malaysia), P.O. Box 112, 10th Fl., UBN Tower, 10 Jalan P. Ramlee, pg. 405 IT
Morinaga Milk Industry Co., Ltd., Malaysia Regional Office, Suite 4.03, 4th Floor, Regent Office, pg. 895 IT
NYK Agencies (M) Sdn. Bhd., 16th Floor, Ste. 16.3W, Wisma Sime Darby, Jalan Raja Laut, pg. 941 IT
Nedlloyd (Malaysia) Sdn Bhd, pg. 1145 IT
Neste Representative Office, Letter Box 116, UBN Tower, pg. 915 IT
NIFE Power Systems Sdn. Bhd., No. 37, Jalan 10/91, Taman Shamelin Perkasa, Batu 3 1/2, pg. 54 IT
Nippon Oil Exploration (Malaysia), Ltd., Letter Box 74, 34th Fl., U8N Tower, No. 10 Jalan P. Ramlee, pg. 937 IT
Nishimatsu Construction Co., Ltd.-Malaysia Office, Suite 1803, 18th Floor, Plaza See Hoy Chan, Jalan Raja Chulan, pg. 943 IT
Nishimatsu - Corpro Construction (M) Sdn. Bhd., Suite 1803, 18th Fl., Plaza See Hoy Chan, pg. 943 IT
Nishimatsu (Malaysia) Sdn. Bhd., Suite 1803, 18th Floor, Plaza See Hoy Chan, pg. 943 IT
Nokia (Malaysia) Sdn. Bhd., 31st Fl. Empire Tower, 182, Jalan Tun Razak, pg. 953 IT
Nomura Advisory Services (Malaysia) Sdn Bhd, Suite Np. 16.3, Level 16, Letter Box 46, Menara IMC, pg. 956 IT
Norse Crown (M) Sdn. Bhd., 38 Jalan Tun Sambanthan 3, pg. 1390 IT
Norsk Hydro Malaysia Sdn Bhd, Suite E, 19th Fl., Bangunan Angkasa Raya, pg. 964 IT
North West Water (Malaysia) Ltd., 36th Floor, Empire Tower, 182 Jalan Tun Razak, pg. 1444 IT
Novell Malaysia, Ste. 26-00, 26th Fl., Menara IMC, No. 8, Jalan Sultan Ismail, pg. 1204 PB
Novo Nordisk A/S, Suite 7 4-5, 7th Floor, Plaza See Hoy Chan, pg. 989 IT
Obayashi Corporation-Kuala Lumpur, Peti #5, Wisma Selangor Dredging, pg. 995 IT
Olivetti Malaysia Sdn Bhd, Wisma Tong Ah, 1 Jalan Perak, pg. 1003 IT
Oracle Systems Malaysia, Level 35 Shahzan, Prudential Tower, pg. 1228 PB
ORIX Car Rentals Sdn. Bhd., 16-1, Jalan 6/91, Taman Shamelin Perkasa, pg. 1009 IT
PSD Holdings Bhd., 19th Flr., Wisma Sime Darby, Jalan Raja Laut, pg. 1250 IT
Pacline (M) Sdn. Bhd., No. 26, Jalan 13/91, Taman Shamelin Perkasa, pg. 550 IT
Paragon Communications Sdn. Bhd. (Kuala Lumpur), 57, Medan Setia Satu, Plaza Demansara, pg. 325 PV
Pempena Consult Sdn. Bhd., 9-2A, 9th Fl., Menara Aik Hua, Cangkat Raja Chulan, pg. 833 IT
Penerbit Fajar Bakti Sdn Bhd, 19-25 Jalan Kuchai Lama, pg. 1019 IT
Perstorp-Mah Sing Sdn Bhd., Wisma Mah Sing, Penthouse Suite 1, pg. 1038 IT
Perwira Habib Bank Malaysia Berhad, Wisma SPK, Golan Sultan Ismail, pg. 585 IT
Pesaka Jardine Fleming Sdn. Bhd., Level 32, Shahzan Prudential, Tower, 30 Jalan Sultan Ismail, pg. 494 IT
PETROLIAM NASIONAL BERHAD (PETRONAS), Menara Dayabumi, Kompleks, Dayabumi, Jalan Sultan Hishamuddin, pg. 1046 IT
Petrolite (Malaysia) Sdn. Bhd., 2.12, 2nd Floor, Angkasa, Raya Building, pg. 166 PB
Pumpex AB, 27-2 Jalan Desa, Taman Desa, pg. 271 IT
RHB Capital Berhad, Level 8, DCB 1&2, RHB Centre, 426, Jalan Tun Razak, pg. 1180 IT
Rakyat Merchant Bankers Berhad, 9th Floor, bangunan, Angkasa Raya, Jalan Ampang, pg. 1085 IT
Reader's Digest (Malaysia) Sdn. Bhd, No. 2 Benteng, pg. 1368 PB
Reed Exhibition Companies-Malaysia, No 3, 6th Floor, Block G Central, Damansara Town Centre, pg. 1097 IT
Rexroth SDN BHD, pg. 839 IT
Riche Monde Sdn Bhd, Inc., 8th Fl., Menara Boustead, 69 Jalan Raja Chulan, pg. 783 IT
Robertson, Wilson, Jamil (M) Sdn Bhd., 9th Floor, Menara Haw Par, Lot 242, pg. 604 IT
Roche Malaysia Sdn. Bhd., pg. 1121 IT
Rockwell-Collins International, Inc., Ste. 14.01, 14th Fl., Wisma Stephens, pg. 1400 PB
SAS Institute Sdn. Bhd., Plaza Raja Chula, Level 12, Suite 8-12-2, 8 Jalan Raja Chulan, pg. 967 PV
SKF Malaysia Sdn. Bhd., 432 Jalan Ipoh, pg. 1159 IT
SMH Trading Sdn. Bhd., 65, 17th Floor/Wisma Goldhill, pg. 1161 IT
Sachs Malaysia SDN.BHD., pg. 835 IT
The Sakura Bank - Kuala Lumpur Representative Office, 9th Floor, Mui Plaza No. 3, Jalan P. Ramlee, pg. 1180 IT
Sandvik Malaysia Sdn. Bhd., P.O. Box 213, pg. 1187 IT
Sapura-Nokia Telecommunications Sdn. Bhd., Lot 23434, Section 10, pg. 954 IT
SASIB Pacific SDN BHD, Amoda Building, 11th Level, 22 Jalan IMBI, pg. 1195 IT
Sato Amoy Construction (Malaysia) Sdn. Bhd., Level 31, Menara Dato'Onn, Putra World Trade Center, pg. 1197 IT
Sato Kogyo Co., Ltd.-Kuala Lumpur, Level 31, Menara Dato'Onn, Putra World Trade Center, pg. 1197 IT
Sato Kogyo (M) Sdn. Bhd., Level 31, Menara Dato'Onn, Putra World Trade Center, pg. 1197 IT
SCANLAB Sdn. Bhd., Resource Complex, 4049-4058 Block D, pg. 1390 IT
Shandwick Sdn. Bhd., Letter Box 81, 4th Floor, pg. 1228 IT
Shell Malaysia Ltd, Bangunan Shell, off Jalan Semantan, pg. 1140 IT
Shimizu-Peremba Sdn. Bhd., No. 15 Jalan, 3/82B Bangsar Utama, pg. 1234 IT
Sime Bank Berhad, 2nd Floor, UMBC Bldg., Jalan Sultan Sulaiman, pg. 1250 IT
SIME DARBY BERHAD, 21st Flr., Wisma Sime Darby, Jalan Raja Laut, pg. 1249 IT
Sime Darby Berhad Insurance Services Division, 15th Fl. Wisma Sime Darby, Jalan Raja Laut, pg. 1250 IT
Sime Darby Berhad Malaysia Region, 19th Flr., Wisma Sime Darby, Jalan Raja Laut, pg. 1250 IT
Sime Diamond Leasing (Malaysia) Sdn. Bhd., 3rd Floor, Wisma Sime Darby, Jalan Raja Laut, pg. 158 IT
Smith International Sdn. Bhd., 7 IA, 7th Floor, Pertama Complex, pg. 1478 PB
Solus Oceaneering (Malaysia) Sdn. Bhd., Unit No. 19A-12-3A, Level 12, UOA Centre, pg. 1211 PB
Standard Chartered Bank Malaysia Berhad, 2 Jalan Ampang, pg. 1295 IT
Standard Chartered Securities Asia Limited, Ste. 25, 1A, 25th Fl., Menara Haw Par, pg. 1296 IT
Steel Service Center (Malaysia) S.B., Room 1304-6, 13th Fl., Wisma Mpi, pg. 949 IT
Subang Jaya Medical Centre Sdn. Bhd., 21st Floor, Wisma Sime Darby, Jalan Raja Laut, pg. 1250 IT
The Sumitomo Bank Ltd.-Labuan Marketing Office, 3rd Fl., MUI Plaza, Jalan P. Ramlee, pg. 1309 IT
The Sumitomo Bank, Ltd.-Kuala Lumpur Representative Office, 3rd Fl., MUI Plaza, Jalan P. Ramlee, pg. 1310 IT
Svedala Malaysia, pg. 1325 IT
Swiss Reinsurance Company Kuala Lumpur Branch, Suite 27-01 Menara Keck Seng, 203 Jalan Bukit Bintang, pg. 1333 IT
Taisei (Malaysia) SDN. BHD., UBN Tower, No. 10, Jalan P. Ramlee,24th Floor, pg. 1347 IT
Takenaka (Malaysia) Sdn. Bhd., Kuala Lumpur, Room 1208, 12thFloor, Wisma HLA, Jalan Raja Chulan, pg. 1351 IT
Teamwork Corporation Sdn Bhd, Peti No 19, Wisma Selangor Dredging, Tingkat 5, pg. 1360 IT
Teamwork Malaysia Sendirian Berhad, P.O. Box 12556, Room 1706, Wisma Foo Young, 86 Jalan Raja Chulan, pg. 1360 IT
Technip Malaysia, 2nd Floor Wisma Inai, 241, Jalan Tun Razak, pg. 1361 IT

PB - *U.S. Public Companies Volume*
PV - *U.S. Private Companies Volume*
IT - *International Public & Private Companies Volume*

Geographic Index-Non U.S.
1699

Triton Oil Company of Thailand (Malaysia), pg. 1640 **PB**
Turboservices SDN BHD, No. 42, Jalan 1/82B, Bangsar Utama, pg. 316 **IT**
UBS Research (Malaysia) Sdn Bhd, Suite 22.1, Level 22, Menara IMC, Letter Box No. 53, pg. 1440 **IT**
Union Bank of Switzerland, Representative Office, Suite 22.1, Level 22, Menara IMC, Letter Box 53, pg. 1441 **IT**
Uniphone Ushasama Sdn. Bhd., 280 & 281, Bangunan Metro Jalan, pg. 1314 **IT**
United ORIX Leasing Berhad, 12th Fl., Menara Promet, Jalan Sultan Ismail, pg. 1010 **IT**
Van Leeuwen Pipe and Tube (Malaysia) SDN. BHD., 38-2 Jalan Tun Sambanthan 3, pg. 1450 **IT**
Vorwerk (Malaysia) SDN BHD, pg. 1481 **IT**
Votra (Malaysia) Sdn Bhd, pg. 757 **IT**
Westpac Banking Corp.-Malaysia, 13th. Flr., Chung Khiaw, Bank Bldg., Jalan Raja Laut, pg. 1497 **IT**
Willis Faber (Malaysia) Sdn Bhd, 6th Floor, Wisma Harwant, 106 Jalan Tuanku Abdul Rahman, pg. 1510 **IT**
The Wrigley Company (Malaysia) Sdn. Bhd., No. 105, Jalan 1191, Taman Shamelin Perkasa, pg. 1781 **PB**
Yamaichi Advisory Services (Malaysia) Sdn. Bhd., UBN Tower, 33rd Fl., 10 Jalan P. Ramlee, pg. 1517 **IT**
Yu Hua Loong Trading Sdn. Bhd., Ste. 1505, 15th Fl., Plaza See Hoy Cham, pg. 1256 **IT**
Zurich Insurance (Malaysia) Sdn. Bhd., Peti #14, Wisma Selangor Dredging, pg. 1532 **IT**

Kuala Terengganu

MTPB - East Coast Region, 2243, Ground Floor, Wisma MCIS, pg. 833 **IT**

Kuantan

Sitt Tatt Industrial Gases Sdn. Bhd,, Lot HS (D) 3831, Mukim Sungai Karang, pg. 32 **PB**

Kuching

BHP Steel Building Products (Sarawak) Sdn Bhd, Lot 610, Section 66, Pending Industrail Area, pg. 226 **IT**
Hexza-Neste Chemicals Sdn. Bhd., GPO L/B No. 3113, pg. 914 **IT**
Kuching Stadium Project Office, c/o Nishimatsu-Corpro Construc, New Sarawak Outdoor Stadium, pg. 943 **IT**
MTPB - Sarawak Region, 2nd Floor, Bangunan Rugayah, pg. 833 **IT**
Mitsui & Co., Ltd., 4th Fl., Rm. No. 402, Wisma Bukit Mata, pg. 880 **IT**
Van Leer (Sarawak) Sdn. Bhd., pg. 1147 **IT**
Veritas DGC INC, Room 107, Lanka Bldg., Khoo Hun Ycany St., pg. 1137 **PV**

Labuan

Bank Brussels Lambert, Labuan, Level 4H, Main Office Tower, Financial Park Labuan, pg. 148 **IT**
Bayerische Landesbank - Labuan Branch, Lot E-2, Level 11, Wisma Oceanic, pg. 176 **IT**
Commerzbank AG-Labuan, Loc. Offshore Bazik, No. 968048C, Level 6 E, Main Office Twr., pg. 311 **IT**
Dai-Ichi Kangyo Bank, Ltd.-Labuan, 1st Fl., Ste. 115, Jalan Merdeka, pg. 360 **IT**
Fuji Bank, Labuan Office, Level 10A Main Office Tower, Financial Park Labuan, Jalan Merdeka, pg. 520 **IT**
ING Bank Labuan, Yen Room, 2nd Floor, Waterfront Labuan Financial Hotel, pg. 649 **IT**
The Sakura Bank, Labuan Branch, Level 15A(1), Main Office Tower, pg. 1179 **IT**
Skandia AFS Southeast Asia (L) Ltd., Level 14 D, Main Office Tower, Financial Park Labuan, pg. 1258 **IT**
The Sumitomo Bank, Ltd.-Labuan Branch, Level 12 (B&C), Main Office Twr., Financial Park Labuan, pg. 1309 **IT**

Melaka

Contraves Advanced Devices, Sdn. Bhd., Batu Berendam, pg. 998 **IT**
Great Eastern Life Assurance Company-Melaka, Bangunan Bank Rakyat, 6th Floor, pg. 557 **IT**
Mardec-Yokohama Fertlizer Corp. Sdn. Bhd., 76100, Durian Tunggal, pg. 1521 **IT**
Siemens Components Snd. Bhd., Tree Trade Zone, pg. 1247 **IT**
Tootal Thread Malacca Sdn Bdn, P.O. Box 317, pg. 299 **IT**

Miri

Safemal Drilling Sdn. Bhd., CDT No. 187, P.O. Box 98009, pg. 765 **IT**
Sarku Comex Sdn. Bhd., pg. 1302 **IT**

Nilai

SKF Bearing Ind. (Malaysia) Sdn. Bhd., Lot 7910, Kawasan Perindustrian Nilai, pg. 1158 **IT**
Showpla (M) Sdn. Bhd., Lot 8, Nilai Industrial Estate, pg. 1237 **IT**
TDK (Malaysia) Sdn. Bhd., Nilai Industrial Estates, pg. 1337 **IT**

Pahang

W.R. Grace (Malaysia) Sdn. Bhd., 9/F, Ste. 908, Kompleks Triuntum, pg. 756 **PB**

Great Eastern Life Assurance Company-Kuantan, B-16 Lorong Tun Ismail Satu, pg. 557 **IT**
MTBE Malaysia Sdn. Bhd., Lot 11 1, Gebeng Industrial Estates, pg. 914 **IT**

Pasir Gudang

Grand Banks Yachts Sdn. Bhd., pg. 531 **IT**

Pasir Panjang

Iwaki-Corning (Malaysia) Sdn. Bhd., PLO 315, Jalan Perak, Kawasan Perindustrian Pasir Gudang, pg. 449 **PB**
Laporte (Malaysia) Sdn Bhd, PLO 228, pg. 803 **IT**
Sitt Tatt Industrial Gases Sdn. Bhd., Kawasan Perusahaan Pasir Gudan, Jalan Perak Dua, pg. 32 **PB**

Pekan

Automotive Manufacturers (Malaysia) Sdn. Bhd., Kawasan Perindutrian, Peramu Jaya, pg. 692 **IT**

Penang

Advartest - Eng(M) Sdn. Bhd., Plot 5, Technoplex, Medan Bayan Lepas, pg. 25 **IT**
Applied Magnetics (Malaysia) Sdn. Bhd., Plot 201, FTZ Phase 3, pg. 123 **IT**
Robert Bosch (Malaysia) Sdn Bhd, Phase I, Free Trade Zone, 11900 Bayan Lepas, pg. 205 **IT**
Circle Freight (Maylaysia) SDN BHD, B7 MAS Cargo Complex, pg. 373 **PB**
Dell Asia Pacific Sdn., Plot P27, Bayan Lepas Industrial Zone, pg. 495 **PB**
Escoy Smelting Sendirian Bhd., Birch House, 73, Jalan Daur Keramet, pg. 1071 **IT**
Great Eastern Life Assurance Company-Penang, Ground, 1st & 2nd Floor, Wisma Hai Thong, pg. 557 **IT**
ITW Meritex SDN BHD, Bayan Lepas, FTZ Phase 3, pg. 868 **PB**
Jabil Circuit, Sdn Bhd, Plot 63, Pesara Kampung Jawa, Mukim 12, Bayan Lepas Indus. Park, pg. 920 **PB**
Ke-Zen Securities Sdn Bhd, Wisma Ke-Zan, 64 Bishop Street, pg. 733 **IT**
MTPE - Northern Region, 10, Jalan Tun Syed Sheikh Barakbah, pg. 833 **IT**
Motorola Malaysia Sdn. Bhd., Bayan Lepas Free Trade Zone, pg. 1140 **IT**
Northern Telecom Industries Sdn., Phase 1, Free Incustrial Zone, pg. 970 **IT**
Pentabric Sdn. Berhad, Block B, Plot 117-119 & 200-202, pg. 1400 **IT**
Quantum Peripherals (Malaysia), Sdn, Bhd, Plot 21, Phase IV, pg. 1350 **IT**
Read-Rite (Malaysia), Sdn. Bhd. Plot 2580, Tingkat, Zon Perdagangan Bebas Perai 2, pg. 1367 **PB**
Robinson Nugent, Inc., 12th Fl., Merlin Office Block, pg. 1395 **PB**
Sandez Products (Malaysia) Sdn. Bhd., pg. 985 **IT**
Sitt Tatt Industrial Gases Sdn. Bhd., Plot No. 386, Lorong Perusahaan Dua Belas, pg. 32 **PB**
Solectron Technology Sdn. Bhd, Prai Industrial Estate, Plot 13 Phase IV, pg. 1483 **IT**
Takemaka (Malaysia) Sdn. Bhd., Penang, 11-4-1 & 2, New Bob Centre, No. 11, Jalan Gottlieb, pg. 1351 **IT**

Perai

BASF Chemdyes Sdn. Bhd., Lot 254 Lorong Perusahaan 10 Kawasan Perindustrian Perai, pg. 105 **IT**
DIC Compounds (Malaysia) Sdn. Bhd., Plot 481, Lorong Perusahaan Baru2, pg. 371 **IT**
Molex (Malaysia) Snd. Bhd., 2607 Jalan Perusahaan, Kawasan Perindustrian Perou, pg. 1122 **PB**
VDO Components SDN.BHD., pg. 839 **IT**
VDO Instruments SDN.BHD., pg. 839 **IT**

Perak

Chunghwa Picture Tubes SDN. BHD., Lot 181723, Kawasan Perindustrian, Taman Bandar, pg. 1357 **IT**
Makdin Electronics SDW. BHD., Lot 181723, Taman Baru Industrial Zone, pg. 1357 **IT**
Perak Hanjung Sinien Sdn. Berhad, 33700 Padang Regas, pg. 758 **IT**
Scapa Scandia (Asia) Sdn. Bhd., 4 Jalan Woodward, pg. 1203 **IT**

Petaling Jaya

Adhesives (Malaysia) Sdn. Bhd., pg. 129 **IT**
Albright & Wilson (Malaysia) Sdn. Bhd., 15th Fl. Menara MPPJ, pg. 49 **IT**
Aluminum Co. of Malaysia Berhad, P.O. Box 1096, pg. 51 **IT**
Amano Cleantech Malaysia Sdn. Bhd., No-11, Jalan PJS11/16, Bandar Sunway, pg. 71 **IT**
Amway (Malaysia) Sdn. Bhd., P.O. Box 84, Jalan Sultan, pg. 70 **IT**
Avon Cosmetics (Malaysia) Sdn. Bhd., P.O. Box 322, Jalan Sultan, pg. 156 **IT**
BASF Coatings & Inks Hong Kong Ltd. Malaysia, Lot 7, Jalan 225/51A, pg. 105 **IT**
BASF (Malaysia) Sdn. Bhd., 15th Floor West Wing, Wisma Tractors, 7 Jalan 16/1, pg. 106 **IT**
Berkat-Honeywell Sdn Bhd Honeywell Eng Sdn Bhd, No. 4, 2nd Floor, Wisma CSA, Jalan Bersatu 13/4, pg. 834 **PB**

BetzDearborn (Malaysia) Sdn. BHD, No. 10-A Jalan SS25/34, Tamang Mayang, pg. 227 **PB**
Bobst (Malaysia) SDN. BHD, pg. 199 **IT**
Bristol-Myers (Malaysia) Sdn. Bhd., Jalan Semahgat, pg. 255 **PB**
Burgmann Malaysia SDN BHD, 6 Subang Jaya Indus. Estate, No. 7 Lorong SS 13 6B, pg. 233 **IT**
Butterworths Malaysia, No. 3 Jalan PJS 11/20, Bendar Sunway, pg. 1095 **IT**
CSA Distribution (M) Sdn. Bhd., Wisma CSA, 3rd Floor Jalan Bersatu Section 13, pg. 243 **IT**
Canon Marketing (Malaysia) Sdn. Bhd., 13A, Jalan 219, pg. 263 **IT**
CIBA-GEIGY (Malaysia) Sdn. Bhd., pg. 978 **IT**
CIBA Vision Malaysia, No 37 and 37A, Jalan SS 21/60, pg. 981 **IT**
Colgate-Palmolive (Malaysia) Sdn. Bhd., Jalan Semangat/Jalan Bersato, pg. 398 **IT**
Computer Systems Advisers (M) Bhd, Wisma CSA, Jalan Bersatu Section 13, pg. 243 **IT**
DIC (Malaysia) Sdn. Bhd., No. 1, Lorung 223A, pg. 372 **IT**
Danzasmal Sdn. Bhd., No. 6, 1st floor, Jalan MJ/2, Medan Maju Jaya, pg. 383 **IT**
De La Rue Services (Malaysia) Sdn Bhd, 6th Flor, Wisma MCIS, Main Tower Block, No. 4 Jalan Barat, pg. 387 **IT**
Digital Equipment (Malaysia) Sdn Bhd, pg. 508 **PB**
ESAB (Malaysia) Sdn, Bhd, Lot 8238, pg. 282 **IT**
Electrolux Malaysia Sdn. Bhd., No. 20A, Jalan 223, pg. 443 **IT**
Electroscon Network Engineering Sdn. Bhd., No. 9A Jalan 51A/223, pg. 1366 **IT**
EURO RSCG Malaysia, 801C, Level 8, Tower C, Uptown 5, pg. 602 **IT**
Fanuc Mechatronics (Malaysia) Sdn. Bhd., Fujitsu Plaza, Suite 1, Level 2B, No. 1A Jalan Tandang 204, pg. 478 **IT**
Fidelio Software GmbH, Suite 501, Menara Choy Fook On, 1B Jalan Yong Shook Lin, pg. 1106 **PB**
Fima Metal Box Berhad, pg. 267 **IT**
Fima Metal Box Holdings Sendirian Berhad, Wisma, MCIS Jalan Barat, pg. 267 **PV**
Fugro Malaysia, 98 Jalan SS 15/4, pg. 430 **IT**
Fuji Photo Film (Malaysia) Sdn. Bhd., Letter Box 3, 3rd Floor, Office Block 1, Crystal Plaza, pg. 524 **IT**
The General Electric Company of Malaysia Sdn. Bhd., Wisma GEC, Jalan 215-Templer, pg. 546 **IT**
Gestetner Malaysia Sdn Bhd, 3rd Floor, Lot 1, Jalan 13/6, pg. 1115 **IT**
Hydro Aluminium Automotive, No. 16-A, Jalan SS 5B/2, pg. 962 **IT**
ICI Paints (Malaysia) SDN BHD, pg. 665 **IT**
IPC Systems (M) Sdn Bhd, No. 75 Jalan SS 23/15, pg. 651 **IT**
Imation Malaysia Representative Office, Glomac Bus. Centre, Unit A306, Block A, pg. 870 **PB**
Johnson & Johnson Sdn. Bhd., P.O. Box 8017, pg. 931 **PB**
Kao (Malaysia) Sdn., Bhd., 5, Jalan 51 A/24I, pg. 718 **IT**
Kimberly-Clark Malaysia Sendirian Berhad, P.O. Box 198, pg. 960 **PB**
Kodak (Malaysia) Sendirian Berhad, Jalan Semangat, pg. 554 **PB**
Kuala Lumpur Glass Manufacturers Co. Sdn. Bhd., pg. 129 **IT**
Kyowa Hakko (Malaysia) SDN BHD., 20, Jalan SS 19/5, pg. 778 **IT**
Laporte Chemicals (Malaysia) Sdn Bhd, 19G Hwy. Centre, Jalan 205, pg. 803 **IT**
Longman Malaysia Sdn. Bhd., No. 3 Jalan Kilang A, pg. 1025 **IT**
Malayan Fibre Containers Sdn. Bhd., pg. 129 **IT**
Malayan Law Journal, No. 3 Jalan PJS 11/20, Bendar Sunway, pg. 1095 **IT**
Malaysia Cocoa Manufacturing, Sdn. Bhd., pg. 920 **IT**
Maruzen Nihonbashi Sdn., 2F Jaya Jusco Bandar Utama Store, pg. 846 **IT**
Martin Merkel-I.M.S., 12, Lorong SS 13/3 B, pg. 860 **IT**
MICROS Systems, Inc., Suite 501, Menara Choy Fook On, 1B Jalan Yong Shook Lin, pg. 1107 **PB**
MICROS Systems, Inc. & Fidelio Software GmbH, Suite 501, Menara Choy Fook On, 1B Jalan Yong Shook Lin, pg. 1107 **PB**
Minolta Marketing (M) SDN BHD, No. 12 Jalan 558/2, pg. 869 **IT**
Monsanto (Malaysia) Sendirian Berhad, 116, Jalan Semangat, pg. 1126 **IT**
NSK Bearings (Malaysia) Sdn. Bhd., 1st Floor, Kompleks Kemajuan, No. 2, Jalan 19/1B, pg. 903 **IT**
NSSP Malaysia Sdn. Bhd., pg. 1166 **PB**
Nestle Asean (Malaysia), pg. 1022 **IT**
Nestle (Malaysia), Sdn. Bhd., NESMAL, 4 Lorong Pesiavan Barat, pg. 921 **IT**
Nippon Express (Malaysia) Sdn. Bhd., A504 & A505, 5th Fl., West Wing, Wisma Tractors, pg. 934 **IT**
Novo Nordisk A/S, 5 Jalan Bersatu 13/4, pg. 988 **IT**
OCE Systems (Malaysia) Sdn. Bhd., pg. 995 **IT**
OMRON Business Systems Malaysia Sdn. Bhd., No. 6, Jalan SS 17/16 Damansara Utama, pg. 1005 **IT**
OMRON Electronics Sales and Service (M) Sdn. Bhd., 10F, Block B Menara Pkns-Pj No. 17, pg. 1006 **IT**
OMRON Malaysia Sdn. Bhd., Lot 15, Jalan Ss 8/4 Sungei Way, pg. 1006 **IT**
ORIX Rentec (Malaysia) Sdn. Bhd., 1st Floor, Wisma Domain, 18A (Lot 318) Jalan 51A/223, pg. 1010 **IT**
Parfums Christian Dior (Malaysia) Sdn Bhd, Lot 7.2, 7th Fl., Menara Cold Storage, Section 14, pg. 783 **IT**
Parker Hannifin Malaysia, 16B Jalan SS21/35 Damansara Utama, pg. 1263 **PB**
Pfizer (Malaysia) Sendirian Berhad, pg. 1282 **PB**

PB - U.S. Public Companies Volume
PV - U.S. Private Companies Volume
IT - International Public & Private Companies Volume

Pharmacia & Upjohn Biotech Asean Support Centre, 2nd Floor No. 68, Jalan SS 15/4D, Subuang Jaya, pg. 1047 — IT

Procter & Gamble (Malaysia), Lot 16B Jalan 225, pg. 1332 — PB

RH Communications (M) SDN BHD, No. 95A, 1st Floor, pg. 1152 — PB

Raychem SDN Berhad, 3rd Fl. Wisma Ali Bawal, Lot 11 Jalan Tandang, pg. 1363 — PB

Rhone-Poulenc Malaysia Sdn, Bhd, Lot. 8-Jalan 19/1, pg. 1113 — IT

Rockwell Automation (Malaysia) Sdn. Bhd., No. 7 Jalan SS 21/37, pg. 1400 — IT

Rohm Electronics (Malaysia) SDN. BHD., Ste. 9-4, 9th Fl., Jaya Shopping Center, pg. 1125 — IT

SCSM (SCS Computer Systems Sdn.Bhd.), Lot 3, Jalan 51A/219, pg. 1032 — PB

Georg Sahm Singapore Pte. Ltd., 8.5, 8th Flr., Men. Cold Storage, pg. 1169 — PB

Sanyo Sales & Service Sdn. Bhd., Lot 15 Jalan 13/6, pg. 1192 — IT

Scholl (Malaysia) SDN Bhd., No 5 B, 2nd Floor, Jalan SS 21/60, pg. 1210 — IT

Shaklee Products (Malaysia) Sdn. Bhd., 7 Jalan USJ 10/1, UEP Subang Jaya, pg. 1519 — IT

Sharp-Roxy Appliances Corp. (M) Sdn. Bhd., Lot 4 & 6, Jalan 225, Section 51-A, pg. 1230 — IT

Sharp-Roxy Sales & Service Company (M) sdn. Bhd., #11B, Jalan 223, Section 51-A, pg. 1230 — IT

Sime Chemical Products Sdn. Bhd., 4 Jalan Tandang, pg. 1250 — IT

Sime Darby Berhad Tyre Manufacturing Division, 4, Jalan Tandang, pg. 1250 — IT

Sime Darby Commodity Trading & Plantations Division, 1st Floor, Wisma Consplant, No. 2, Jalan SS 16/1, pg. 1250 — IT

Sime UEP Properties Berhad, 3rd Fl. Wisma Tractors, pg. 1250 — IT

Sirah Sdn. Bhd., pg. 995 — IT

SmithKline Beecham Consumer Brands Sdn. Bhd., Jalan Berstau/Jalan Kemajuan, pg. 1265 — IT

Sodexho Malaysia Sdn. Bhd., 19, Jalan PJS 11/18, pg. 1275 — IT

South-East Asian Publishing Services Unit, 7 Jalan Semangat, pg. 1019 — IT

Spider/DMB&B, Glomac Business Centre, 210 Bloc C, pg. 305 — PV

Stamford Food Industries Sdn. Berhad, 112 Jalan Semangat, pg. 447 — IT

Teledyne Malaysia, 4th fl., Wisma Consplant, No2 Jalan SS16/4, pg. 44 — PB

3M Malaysia Sdn. Berhad, Lot 16, Jalan 225, Setion 51A, pg. 1607 — PB

Toshiba Sales and Services Sdn. Bhd., No. 40 Jalan Penchala, pg. 1407 — IT

Tractors Malaysia Berhad, 11th Fl., Wisma Tractors, No. 7, Jalan SS16/1, pg. 1250 — IT

UMW Toyota Motor Sdn. Bhn., Lot 5, Jalan 219, Federal Highway, pg. 1414 — IT

Uniphone Cables Sdn. Bhd., 10, Jalan Tandang, pg. 1314 — IT

VRG Paper Malaysia Sdn. Bhd., pg. 757 — IT

Van Leer (Malaysia) Sdn. Bhd., 10 Jin Kilang, pg. 1147 — IT

Vickers Systems Sendinian Berhad, Lot 5 Lorang 51A/227B, pg. 25 — IT

Wadkin Robinson (Malaysia) Sdn Bhd, 29 Jalan SS14/1, pg. 232 — IT

Wilson Sporting Goods (Malaysia) Sdn. Bhd., 40 & 42 Jalan BM1/2, pg. 73 — IT

Woodward-Clyde, 34B, Jalan SS 21/62, Damansara Utama, pg. 1657 — PB

Port Kelang

IPI Sdn. Bhd., Lot 2, Jalan Simpanan, Kaw Miel Ind. Est., Pandamaran, pg. 108 — IT

Mattel (K.L.) Sdn. Bhd. (Maylaysia), Lot 7 Jalan Hishamuddin 2, Kawasan 20Kawasan Perusahaan, pg. 1059 — PB

Mead Coated Board (Malaysia) Sdn. Bhd., Lot 23, Lorong Sultan Hishamuddin 3, pg. 1076 — IT

Nortonmas Sdn. Bhd., Lot 2, Solok Sultan Hishamudin 7, pg. 1175 — IT

R.J. Reynolds Tobacco Company Sdn. Bhd., Jalan Perbadanan 3/5 Syah A, pg. 1355 — PB

Prai

Century Chemical Works Sdn. Bhd., MK. 1, No. 1026, Prai Industrial Complex, pg. 1350 — IT

Fatty Chemical (Malaysia) Sdn., Bhd., Wisma Palmex, Prai Industrial Complex, pg. 717 — IT

Mattel (Malaysia) SDN. BHD., Plot 206 Prai, Free Zone, pg. 1059 — PB

Seagate Technology Malaysia Sdn. Bhd., 2610, Tingkat Perusahaan Tiga, Kawasan Perusahann Prai, pg. 1450 — PB

Pulau Penang

Clarion (Malaysia) Sdn. Bhd., Free Trade Zone One, 11900 Bayan Lepas, pg. 296 — IT

Crystal Precision (M) Sdn. Bhd., Phase 3, Free Trade Zone, 11900 Bayan Lepas, pg. 296 — IT

Raja Chulan

Kvaerner Engineering Sdn Bhd, Lot 2004-2009, 20th Floor, Wisma HLA, pg. 767 — IT

Kvaerner Process Systems Asia Pacific Sdn Bhd., Lot 2004-2009, 20. Floor, pg. 768 — IT

Senai

Matsushita Industrial Corporation (Sdn. Bhd.), P.L.O. No.1, Kawasan Perdaag Anga, pg. 847 — IT

Nemic Lambda (M) Sdn. Bhd., PLO 33 Kawasan Perindustrian, pg. 1242 — IT

Seremban

Great Eastern Life Assurance Company-Seremban, No. 36 & 37, Jalan Dato Lee Fong Yee, pg. 557 — IT

Motorola Electronics Sdn. Bhd, Lot 55 Senawang Ind. Estate, Negri Sembilan, pg. 1139 — PB

Motorola Semiconductors Sdn. Bhd., Lot 122 Senawang, Industrial Estate, pg. 1140 — PB

Semiconductor Miniature Products (M) Sdn. Bhd., Lot 122-123, Senawanr Industrial Estate, pg. 1140 — PB

Totokiki (Malaysia) Sdn.Bhd., Lot 74(Part), 76 (Part), 80, 81, 84 & 85, pg. 1410 — IT

Seri Kemangan

Symix Malaysia-Sdn Bhd, Sin Heap Lee Bus. Ctr., No. 352, Jalan Sr 8/1, pg. 1547 — PB

Shah Alam

BHP Steel Building Products (Malaysia) Sdn Bhd, 16/9 Jalan Gudang, Shah Alam Industrial Estate, pg. 226 — IT

BHP Steel (Malaysia) Sdn Bhd, Lot 7.2, Tkt 7, Wisma MPSA, Persiaran Perbandaran, pg. 227 — IT

Bensons Metal Products Sdn Bhd, pg. 460 — IT

Canon Camera (Malaysia) Sdn. Bhd., Jalan Seliski, Sek. 26, pg. 262 — IT

Canon Opto (Malaysia) Sdn. Bhd., Jalan Selisik, Sek. 26, pg. 262 — IT

Chunghwa Picture Tubes SDN. BHD., Lot 1, Subang Hi-Tech Industrial Park, pg. 1357 — IT

Corro-Coat (Malaysia) Sdn. Bhd., PT 3 Lot 6 Sek 16/9, Jalan Gudang, pg. 715 — IT

Daihatsu Malaysia Sdn. Bnd., Lot 1, Jalan Keluli., pg. 365 — IT

Eastman Christensen (M) Sdn. Bdh, c/o Morgan Inks Complex, Jalan Pengapit 15/19, pg. 167 — PB

Ericsson Telecommunications Sdn Bhd, Jalan Sepana 15/3, pg. 1368 — IT

Fuchs Chemicals Trading SDN.BHD., Lot 1179, 2 km Jalan Subang, Bata Tiga, pg. 517 — IT

Gunong Printing Ink (M) Sdn. Bhd., PT 501 & 502, Persiaran Sabak Bernam, pg. 372 — IT

Hokuriku (Malaysia), Sdn. Bhd., Lot 8090, Persiaran Kemajuan, Seksyen, pg. 628 — IT

Inchcape Timuran Bhd, Inchcape House, Lot 6, Persiaran Perusahaan Seksyen 23, pg. 672 — IT

Johnson & Johnson Medical Mfg., Sdn. Bhd., P.O. Box 8017, pg. 931 — IT

Jotun (Malaysia) Sdn. Bhd., Lot 7, Persiaran Perusahaan, pg. 715 — IT

M-SMM Electronics Sdn. Bhd., Lots 7 & 9, Jalan Ragum 15/17, pg. 1316 — IT

Makro Cash & Carry Distribution (M) Sdn. Bhd., No. 1 Persiaran Sukan, Section 13, pg. 1155 — IT

Malaysian Electronics Materials SDN. BHD, Lots 7 & 9, Jalan Ragum 15/17, pg. 1316 — IT

Nippon Paint (Malaysia) Sdn. Bhd., Lot I-17, Taman Perindustrian, pg. 937 — IT

Nissan-Industrial Oxygen Incorporated Sdn. Bhd., Lot 2, Persiaran Sabak Bernam, Section 26, pg. 939 — IT

Nitto Denko Electronics (Malaysia) Sdn. Bhd., No. 2, Persiaran Budiman, Seksyen 23, pg. 950 — IT

Nitto Denko (Malaysia) Sdn. Bhd., No. 2, Persiaran Budiman, Seksyen 23, pg. 950 — IT

Nitto Denko Materials (Malaysia) Sdn. Bhd., No. 2, Persiaran Budiman, Seksyen 23, pg. 950 — IT

Nordson (Malaysia) Sdn. Bhd., Subang Jaya Industrial Estate, pg. 1189 — IT

Paint Marketing Company (M) Sdn. Bhd., 63 Jalan Sesiku 15/2, pg. 937 — IT

Pelago Marketing Corp. Sdn. Bhd., Lot 4 Jalan Ragum 15/17, pg. 1490 — IT

Perwira Ericsson Sdn. Bhd., Jalan Sepana 15/3, pg. 1369 — IT

PROTON, Hicom Industrial Estate, pg. 1071 — IT

Rohm-Wako (Malaysia) Sdn. Bhd., Lot 58, Jalan 26/6, pg. 1126 — IT

Sealed Air (Malaysia) Sdn Bhd, 25 Jalan PS 1/11, pg. 1451 — PB

Sitt Tatt Industrial Gases Sdn. Bhd., Lot 54, Jalan Jitra 26/7, Section 26 (Hicom Sector B), pg. 32 — IT

Sumitomo Electric Magnet Wire (M) Sdn. Bhd., Lot 499 & 500, Persiaran Sabak Bernam, pg. 1314 — IT

Sumitomo Electric Sintered Components (M) Sdn. Bhd., Lot Pt 5086-5091, Jalan Jenjarum (28/39), pg. 1314 — IT

Swedish Motor Assemblies Sdn. Bhd., Peti Surat 7009, Bangunan Pej Pos Besar, pg. 1477 — IT

T&K Autoparts Sdn. Bhd., pg. 1413 — IT

Subang

Advantest Malaysia Sdn. Bhd., No. 21-1, pg. 25 — IT

Sulang Jaya

Liebert Malaysia Sdn. Bhd., No. 17 Jalan SS 18/6, pg. 577 — PB

Sungai Petani

NEC Home Electronics (Malaysia) Sdn. Bhd., Lot 9, Kawasan Perusahaan Tikam Batu, pg. 900 — IT

Robinson Nugent, Plot 10.16, Jalan Pknk 1/2, Sungai Petani Industrial Estate, pg. 1395 — IT

Robinson Nugent (Malaysia) Sdn. Bhd., Plot 10,15, Jalan Pknk 1/2, Sungai Petani Industrial Estate, pg. 1395 — PB

Sharp-Roxy Corporation (M) Sdn. Bhd., Lot 202, Bakar Arang Industrial Estate, pg. 1230 — IT

Taiping

Sanyo Industries (Malaysia) Berhad, Kamunting Industrial Estate, pg. 1192 — IT

Tampoi

Britannia Brands (Malaysia) SON BHD, 126 A Batu 4, 3/4 Jalan Skudai, pg. 380 — IT

Terengganu

Roteq Services Sdn. Bhd., pg. 1305 — IT

Tioxide (Malaysia) SDN BHD, Kawasan Perindustrian Telok, Kalong, pg. 666 — IT

MALDIVES

Male

Habib Bank Ltd., Ground Fl., Ship Plaza, 1/6 Orchid Magu, pg. 584 — IT

MALI

Bamako

BHP Minerals Mali Inc., pg. 224 — IT

CIBA-GEIGY Services SA, Bureau d'assistance technique, pg. 980 — IT

Petromali-Shell, Rue Mare Diagne, pg. 1136 — IT

Shell Mali, Rue Mare Diagne, pg. 1137 — IT

The World Bank, Immeuble SOGEFIH, Centre Commercial Rue 321, pg. 1189 — PV

MALTA

Attard

Baron Technical Services Ltd., Everton House, Triq It-Torba, pg. 739 — IT

Luqa

AIR MALTA CO. LTD., pg. 37 — IT

Air Supplies & Catering Co. Ltd., Luqa Airport, pg. 37 — IT

Marsa

Dowty Tecmold, Industrial Estate, pg. 1338 — IT

Mriehel

Megabyte Ltd., Notabile Rd., pg. 1228 — PB

Merit-Malta Methode Ltd., Mriehel Industrial Estate, pg. 1101 — PB

Msida

Powerserv Limited, Victor Denaro Street, pg. 246 — PB

Qormi

Dowty O Rings & Actuation Polymers, Industrial Estate, pg. 1338 — IT

Sliema

De Mattos & Sullivan Limited, 47-1 Tigne Seafront, pg. 108 — IT

Oswald Arrigo Limited, Finnish Consulate General, 63/64 Graham Street, pg. 458 — IT

Valetta

Crown Advertising Ltd., Regency House, Republic St., pg. 303 — PV

Det Norske Veritas, Flat K, Blk. B, Dolphin Court, pg. 397 — IT

Zejtun

Thomas De La Rue (Malta) Limited, B40/43 Bulebel Industrial Estate, pg. 386 — IT

MARTINIQUE

Fort-de-France

GTM Caraibes, ZI de la Jambette, pg. 823 — IT
Gan Incendie Accidents Martinique, 30, boulevard du General de Gaulle, pg. 564 — IT
Gan Vie Martinique, 30, boulevard du General de Gaulle, pg. 565 — IT
Raffinerie des Antilles, Box 705, pg. 1141 — IT
Rentokil Martinique SARL, pg. 1286 — IT

Guadeloupe

CBM Guadeloupe Immeuble EVC, Rue Henri Becquerei, pg. 816 — PB

Lamentin

Cohiba, ZI. La Lezarde, Immeuble des Amandiers, pg. 117 — IT

MAURITIUS

Nouakchott

Generale de Banque de Mauritanie pour l'Investissement et le Commerce, Avenue de l'Independance, pg. 548 — IT
The World Bank, Villa No. 30, Lot A, pg. 1189 — PV

Port Louis

Coroi Maurice Ltee., 3, Leoville l'Homme St., pg. 108 — IT
Det Norske Veritas, 4, Edith Cavell St., pg. 398 — IT
Dominion Nonwovens Sudamericana, Third Floor, Cerne House, La Chassee, pg. 415 — IT
Dominion Textile Mauritius Inc., Third Floor, Cerne House, La Chausse, pg. 415 — IT
Ericsson Network Engineering AB, 1 Military Road, pg. 1367 — IT
HSBC Trustee (Mauritius) Limited, 4th Floor, Moorgate House, 29 Sir William Newton Street, pg. 583 — IT
Habib Bank Ltd., Sir William Newton St., pg. 584 — IT
MICROS Fidelio Maurice Ltee, Angle des Rues Brown Sequard, et St. Louis, pg. 1106 — PB
Nestle Products (Mauritius) Ltd., pg. 921 — IT
Shell Mauritius Ltd., Shell House, 5 St. George's St., pg. 1137 — IT

MEXICO

Acuna

Barry of Ciudad Acuna, Ciudad Acuna Industrial Park, pg. 192 — PB
Barton Nelson De Mexico, Parque Ind. L Cid, Cantetdra Internacional KM 7.5, pg. 120 — PV
Douglas y Lomason de Mexico S.A. de C.V., Km. #5, Carretera Presa La Amistad, pg. 830 — PV
Equipos de Acuna, S.A. de C.V., Parque Industrial Modelo, pg. 356 — PV

Agua Prieta

Velcromex S.A. de C.V., Calle 8-No.2601, pg. 1462 — IT

Aguascalientes

Donaldson Micro Pore S.A. de C.V., Angel Dorronsoro Gandaia No. 106, pg. 517 — PB

Apodaca

Danfoss Compressors S.A. de C.V., Carr. Miguel Aleman #162, Col. El Milagro, pg. 377 — IT
Hylsa S.A.-North Plant, Ant. Carr. Miguel Aleman y Mezquital, pg. 56 — IT
Parker Automotive de Mexico SA de CV, Calle Segunda Oriente, No. 101 Parque Industrial, Monterrey, 66600, pg. 1263 — IT
SM-Cyclo de Mexico, S.A. de C.V., Calle RCS No. 506A, pg. 1315 — IT

Atlacomulco

Peliculas Plasticas, S.A. de C.V., Lote 1, Manzana 3, 1A. Seccion, Parque Industrial Atlacomulco, pg. 1346 — IT

Baja California

Kenworth Mexicana, S.A. de C.V., Kilometro 10.5 Carratera a San Luis, pg. 1246 — PB

Campeche

Molinos Del Sudeste, S.A. de C.V., Km. 8.5 Carr. Campeche-Hampolol, pg. 1346 — IT

Celaya

Alimentos Deshidratados del Bajio, S.A. de C.V., pg. 1067 — PB

INDUSTRIAS BACHOCO S.A. DE C.V., Avda. Tecnologico 401, Col. Industrial, pg. 677 — IT
Sakata Seed De Mexico, S.A. de C.V., Guillermo Prieto 202-201, pg. 1178 — IT

Chapulepa

Biosenal, S.A. de C.V., Pedro Antonio de los Santos, pg. 816 — PB

Chapultepec

Fleishman-Hillard, Mexico, S.A. de C.V., Monte Caucaso 915-502, pg. 411 — PV

Chicoloapan

Tube Turns de Mexico, S.A., K.M. 22.5 Carretera Federal Mex-Puebla, pg. 1533 — PB

Chihuahua

Ademco de Juarez, Avenue Fuentes Sur #7151, Complejo Industrial Fuentes, pg. 1307 — PB
Alphabet de Mexico, Ave. Las Americas S/N, Parque Industrial Las Americas, pg. 1045 — PV
Altec Electronica de Chihuahua S. A. de C. V., Av De La Juventud S/N, pg. 665 — IT
Cable Productos de Chihuahua, S.A. de C.V., Parque Indus., Las Americas Prolongacion, pg. 1790 — PB
Data General de Mexico S.A. de C.V., pg. 486 — PB
GRUPO CEMENTOS DE CHIHUAHUA S.A. DE C.V., Av. Vicente Suarez y Calle 6a s/n, pg. 573 — IT
INTERNACIONAL DE CERAMICA S.A. DE C.V., Prol. Av. Pacheco y Vias FFCC CH-P, pg. 680 — IT
Kenwood Electronics (Mexico) S.A. de C.V., Parquet Industrial Fernandez, Calle Tomas Becket 2200, pg. 731 — IT
Minera del Norte, Abasolo e Indepencia #508 Co. Centro, pg. 66 — IT
Papelera de Chihuahua S.A. de C.V., Plaza de Ferrocarril Kansas 1, pg. 330 — IT
Proctor-Silex, S.A. de C.V., pg. 1150 — PB
Security Plastics de Mexico, William Shakespeare #1, Local 3-4 Complejo Indl. Chihuahua, pg. 981 — PV
Svedala Mexico, Cd. Juarez, pg. 1325 — IT
System Sensor de Mexico S.S. de C.V., Calle Intermex #1250, Parque Industrial Intermex, pg. 1307 — PB
TDK de Mexico S.A. de C.V., Juarez-Porvenir, Cd. Juarez, pg. 1337 — IT
Taloquimia, S.A., pg. 811 — PB
Touche Industrial, S.A. de C.V., Pino 2307 Col Unidad Satelite, pg. 613 — PB
Zenco de Chihuahua, S.A. de C.V., Carretera Pan Americana No. 9225, pg. 1790 — PB

Churumucu

Avesta Sheffield S.A. de C.V., Callijon Catita No. 10, pg. 222 — IT

Ciudad Camargo

Domicilio Conocido Hercules, Independencia 508 Centro, pg. 572 — IT

Ciudad Juarez

Camisus de Juarez, S.A. de C.V., Parque Industrial, pg. 933 — PB
SISTEMA ARGOS S.A., Simona Barba 6515, Fracc Villahermosa, pg. 1256 — IT

Coahuila

Refractarios Mexicanos S.A. de C.V. (REFMEX), Carretera Saltillo, Monterrey Km. 9, pg. 748 — PB

Coatzacoalcos

Albright & Wilson Troy de Mexico, S.A. de C.V., Coatzcoalcos Plant, Complejo Industrial Pajaritos, pg. 50 — IT
Otis Mexicana, S.A., 16 Deseptiembre N606, pg. 777 — PB

Codigo

John Crane Latin America, Poniente 152 No. 679-Col. Ind., Delegacion Azcapotzalco, pg. 1339 — IT

Colonia

ADI Mexico, Calle Doctor Vertiz, No. 95 & 97, pg. 1307 — PB
CTD de Mexico, S.A., 8 Avenida Juarez, Ste. 1602, pg. 950 — PB
EA Engineering, Science & Technology de Mexico, S.A. de C.V., Newton 53, Suite 11, pg. 541 — PB
Herramientas Cleveland, S.A., 8 Avenida Juarez, Ste. 1602, pg. 950 — PB

Coyoacan

ADC de Mexico, S.A. de C.V., Belsario Dominguez 40A, pg. 4 — PB
PolyGram S.A. de C.V., Apartado Postal 21069, pg. 1053 — IT
Willis Faber & Dumas Limited, Viena #71 - 2o. Piso, pg. 1510 — IT
Woodward-Clyde de Mexico, S.A. de C.V., Calle Paris 1900, pg. 1658 — PB

Cuajimalpa

Arrendadora Bancomer, Carr. Libre Mexico-Toluca 5714, pg. 145 — IT

Cuauhtemoc

Electronica Condor De Mexico, S.A., Costa Rica #14, pg. 1419 — PB
Hylsa S.A.-Mining and Pelletiing Division, Domicilio Conocido, Estacion Alzada, pg. 56 — IT
INDUSTRIAS PENOLES S.A. DE C.V., Rio de la Plata, Piso 15, pg. 677 — IT
Merisel Mexico, Rio Lerma 196 Bis, Torre B, 70 Piso, pg. 1096 — PB
Mobil Oil De Mexico S.A., Apartado 22 BIS, pg. 1119 — PB

Cuautitlan

Albany International S.A. de C.V., Km 18.5 Carr, Tlaincpatla-Cuautitlan, pg. 37 — PB
Florasynth S.A. de C.V., pg. 174 — IT
Griffith Laboratories Worldwide, Guillermo Gonzalez Camarena No. 15, pg. 481 — PV
Polymer Chemicals Additives Group, Calle Guadalupe No. 410, pg. 1774 — PB
Sulzer (Mexico) S.A. de C.V., pg. 1306 — IT
Whitehall-Robins de Mexico, S.A. de C.V., Autopista Mexico Queretaro, pg. 82 — PB

Cuautla

Disogrin Mexicana S.A. de C.V., pg. 505 — IT
Freudenberg-Nok de Mexico, Km 1, Carr Cuautla, Las Estacas, pg. 428 — PV

Cuernavaca

ATAPCO Azteca, S.A. de C.V., Calle 21 Este No. 305, pg. 64 — PV
Consorcio Industrial Packsa, S.A. de C.V., pg. 1146 — IT
Laboratorios Julian de Mexico, S.A., pg. 1265 — IT

Culiacan

COPPEL S.A. DE C.V., Avda. Alvaro Obregon 728 Sur, pg. 330 — IT

Durango

Fama de Durango, S.A. de C.V., Cia. 1320 Victoria Sur, pg. 613 — PB
GRUPO INDUSTRIAL DURANGO S.A. DE C.V., Potasio 150, pg. 575 — IT
Neste Resinas S.A. de C.V., Carretera, Panamericana Km 959, pg. 915 — IT

El Salto

Crown Cork de Mexico, S.A., pg. 464 — PB
Honda de Mexico, S.A. de C.V., Carr. a El Castillo 7250, pg. 635 — IT
Quimi-Kao S.A. de C.V., Km 22.5 Carr., Guad., pg. 718 — IT
Roche Mexicana de Farmacos, S.A. de C.V., pg. 1121 — IT

Garza Garcia

ALFA, S.A. DE C.V., Ave. Gomez Morin 1111, pg. 56 — IT
Alpek, S.A. de C.V., Ave. Gomez Morin 1111, pg. 56 — IT
CYDSA S.A., Ave. Ricardo Margain Zozaya No. 325, pg. 246 — IT
Celulosa y Derivados, S.A. de C.V., Ave. Ricardo Margain Zozaya No. 325, pg. 246 — IT
Consorcio Intermex S.A. de C.V., Ave. Ricardo Margain Zozaya No. 325, pg. 246 — IT
COPAMEX INDUSTRIAS S.A. DE C.V., Montes Apalach 101, Col. Residencial Zona San Austin, pg. 330 — IT
Cydsa S.A. Chemical Div., Ave. Ricardo Margain Zozaya No. 325, pg. 246 — IT
Cydsa S.A. Fibers Div., Ave. Ricardo Margain Zozaya No. 325, pg. 246 — IT
Cydsa S.A. Packaging Div., Ave. Ricardo Margain Zozaya No. 325, pg. 246 — IT
Cydsa S.A. Treament Div., Ave. Ricardo Margain Zozaya No. 325, pg. 246 — IT
Derivados Acrilicos, S.A. de C.V., Ave. Ricardo Margain Zozaya No. 325, pg. 246 — IT
Fordath S.A. de CV, Avenida Humberto Lobo Sur 820, pg. 615 — IT
Grupo Cydsa, S.A. de C.V., Ave. Ricardo Margain Zozaya No. 325, pg. 246 — IT
GRUPO IMSA S.A. DE C.V., Av. Batallon de San Patricio 111-26, pg. 575 — IT
Hewlett-Packard de Mexico, S.A. de C.V., Calzada del Valle Oriente 409-440, pg. 819 — PB

PB - *U.S. Public Companies Volume*
PV - *U.S. Private Companies Volume*
IT - *International Public & Private Companies Volume*

Industria Quimica del Istmo, S.A. de C.V., Ave. Ricardo Margain Zozaya No. 325, pg. 246 **IT**
Industrias Cydsa Bayer, S.A. de C.V., Ave. Ricardo Margain Zozaya No. 325, pg. 246 **IT**
Masterpak, S.A. de C.V., Ave. Ricardo Margain Zozaya No. 325, pg. 246 **IT**
Onexa, S.A. de C.V., Ave. Gomez Morin 1111, pg. 56 **IT**
Plasticos Rex. S.A. de C.V., Ave. Ricardo Margain Zozaya No. 325, pg. 246 **IT**
Policyd, S.A. de C.V., Ave. Ricardo Margain Zozaya No. 325, pg. 246 **IT**
Quimica Organica de Mexico, S.A. de C.V., Ave. Ricardo Margain Zozaya No. 325, pg. 246 **IT**
Sales del Istmo, S.A. de C.V., Ave. Santa Engracia n325, pg. 247 **IT**
Sigma Alimentos, S.A. de C.V., Ave. Gomez Morin 1111, pg. 56 **IT**
Versax, S.A. de C.V., Ave. Gomez Morin 1111, pg. 56 **IT**
Video Electronics de S.A., Calle Zinc 99, 66210, pg. 1720 **PB**
VITRO, SOCIEDAD ANONIMA, Apardo Postal 103, Suc. B, pg. 1469 **IT**
Vitro, Sociedad Anonima - Capital Goods, Ave. Ricardo Margain #400, pg. 1469 **IT**
Vitro, Sociedad Anonima - Chemical, Fibers & Mining, Ave. Ricardo Margain Zozaya #400, pg. 1469 **IT**
Vitro, Sociedad Anonima - Containers Div., Ave. Ricardo Margain Zozaya #400, pg. 1469 **IT**
Vitro, Sociedad Anonima - Flat Glass Div., Ave. Ricardo Margain Zozaya #400, pg. 1469 **IT**
Vitro, Sociedad Anonima - Glassware Div., Ave. Ricardo Margain Zozaya #400, pg. 1469 **IT**
Vitromatic, S.A. de C.V., Ave. Ricardo Margain Zozaya #400, pg. 1765 **PB**

Guadalajara

Adelantos de Tecnologia S.A. de C.V., Apartado Postal 1-1874, pg. 1417 **PB**
Aralmex, S.A. de C.V., pg. 724 **PB**
Arancia CPC Industrial S.A. de C.V., pg. 448 **PB**
CIBA-GEIGY Mexicana SA de CV, Planta Atotonilquillo, Apartado Postal 1-130, pg. 978 **IT**
Compania Siderurgia de Guadalajara, Lazaro Cardenas 601, pg. 576 **IT**
Everest & Jennings de Mexico S.A. de C.V., Calle 3 No. 631, Zona Industrial, pg. 758 **PB**
Fabrica de Valvulas, Calle 5 No. 1906, pg. 686 **IT**
Grupo Agrogen S.A. de C.V., Mexico, Av. Hidalgo 2375,1-5-6th Flrs., pg. 493 **IT**
GRUPO EMBOTELLADORAS UNIDAS SA DE CV, Severo Diaz 17, Col. Ladron de Guevara, pg. 574 **IT**
GRUPO SIDEK, S.A. DE C.V., Agustin Yanez 2343, Piso 1, pg. 576 **IT**
Grupo Simec, S.A. de C.V., Colz. Lazaro Cardenas 601, pg. 576 **IT**
Grupo Sitra, S.A. DE C.V., AV. Oledoducto No. 2780, pg. 775 **IT**
Grupo Situr SA de CV, Circ. Agustin Yanez 2343, pg. 576 **IT**
Grupo Termoindustrial ECA, S.A. de C.V., Av. Washington 1576, pg. 361 **PV**
Herbalife International de Mexico, S.A.D.C.V., Av. Washington No. 200, Sector Reforma, pg. 809 **PB**
Herman Miller Mexico, Av. Pablo Neruda No. 2886, pg. 1112 **IT**
Hewlett-Packard de Mexico, S.A. de C.V., Monte Morelos No. 299, pg. 819 **PB**
Hibridos Pioneer De Mexico S.A. DE C.V., Carretera Guadalajara, Morealia Km. 21 #8601, Poblado de, pg. 1299 **PB**
Industria Fotografica Interamericana S.A. de C.V., Prol. Mariano Otero #408, pg. 554 **PB**
Investigaciones Pioneer S de R.L. de C.V., Avenida Americas 1297, Piso 7, pg. 1299 **PB**
Lawson Products de Mexico, S.A., Av Washington #1103, Col. Moderna, CD 44190, pg. 980 **PB**
Cia. Minera Constelacion S.A. de C.V., Pablo Neruda No. 2886, pg. 308 **IT**
Molex de Mexico S.A. de C.V., Productividad Ote #305, Parque Industrial Guadalajara, pg. 1122 **PB**
Northrup King y Compania, S.A. de C.V., Circunvalacion Agustin, Yanez 2895, 3er Piso, pg. 983 **IT**
Panduit Mexico S. EN N.C., Lazaro Cardenas 2785, pg. 836 **PV**
Productos de Maiz S.A., Arancia CPC Industrial, Lopez Cotilla #2030, pg. 448 **PB**
Publicidad Ferrer de Occidente, S.A. de C.V., pg. 1073 **IT**
Real de Tennis S.A. De C.V., Calle 22 No. 2760, pg. 1072 **IT**
SASIB Beverage Mexicana S.A., Pedro de Alarcon, 45, pg. 1195 **IT**
Tamrock EJC de Mexico S.A. de C.V., Gonzalez Gallo 2050-2070, Sector Reforma, pg. 1353 **IT**
Tecnologias NEC de Mexico, S.A. de C.V., Carretera Guadalajara, El Castillo Kilometro 9 No. 8200, pg. 901 **IT**
Tulon de Mexico, S.A. de C.V., Calle 32 No. 2715, pg. 594 **PB**
Valvulas Keystone de Mexico S.A. de C.V., Apartado Postal 1-736, pg. 1650 **PB**

Guadalupe

Kaydon S.A. de C.V., Parque Industrial La Silb, Avenue Sierra con Pablo Livas, pg. 946 **PB**

Guaymas

INVERSIONES DE GUAYMAS S.A. DE C.V., Av. A.L. Rodriguez No. 99 Orient, pg. 685 **IT**

Hermosillo

Battle Mountain Gold (Mexico), Galeria Cinemark, Desp. 7, Blvd. Luis Donaldo Colosio, pg. 194 **PB**
Hewlett-Packard de Mexico, S.A. de C.V., Plaza Ejecutiva Las Torres, Av. Nayarit 131-316, pg. 819 **PB**
Mexicoro S.A. de C.V., Norwalk No. 1-A Esq. Estadio, Col. Centro C.P. 83000, pg. 169 **IT**
Cia. Minera Constelacion S.A. de C.V., Campodonico No. 68, pg. 308 **IT**
Minera Hecla S.A. de CV, Concepcion L. de Soria #70, pg. 804 **PB**

Irapuato

Gigante Verte S.A., Km. 337 Carraterra Pan Americana, Aparta, pg. 409 **IT**
Harinera La Montana S.A. de C.V., Boulevard Solidaridad #10781, pg. 1346 **IT**
Skega Mexicana SA de CV, Apdo Postal 455, pg. 1324 **PB**
Skega SA de CV, Apdo, pg. 1324 **IT**

Ixtapalapa

Catalina Lighting Mexico, S.A. de C.V., Calle de las Palmas No. 43, pg. 314 **PB**
Square D Company Mexico, S.A. de C.V., Calz. Javier Rojo, Gomex No. 1121, pg. 1209 **PB**
Unbrako Mexicana, S.A. de C.V., Colonia Lomas Estrella, Paseo De Antioquia #14, pg. 1420 **PB**
Widisa Metal S.A., Vincente Guerroro 53, Col. Guadalupe, pg. 474 **IT**

Juarez

Autovidrio, S.A. de C.V., pg. 665 **PB**
Boss de Mexico, S.A., pg. 1142 **PV**
Breed Technologies, Parque Industrial Gema, Calle Chamizal, San Numero, pg. 251 **PB**
Cableados S.A. de C.V., C/O P.O. Box 20027, El Paso, Texas 79998, pg. 721 **PB**
Coclisa S.A. de C.V., pg. 665 **PB**
Corcom S.A. de C.V., Camino Antiguo A, Las Parcelas S/N, pg. 446 **PB**
Diesel ReCon de Mexico, S.A. de C.V., Parque Ind. A.J. Bermudez, Ave. Recinto de la Oracion y Cal. Fulton, pg. 469 **PB**
Electronia Dale de Mexico S.A. de C.V., Calle Ohm Ave de la Industria, Parque Industrial A.J., pg. 1722 **PB**
Falcon de Juarez, S.A. de C.V., Apartado Postal 2519 E. CD., pg. 611 **PB**
Herman Miller Mexico, Edificio Zurich No. 102, Centro Ejcutivo Plaza, pg. 1112 **IT**
Hewlett-Packard de Mexico, S.A. de C.V., Rio Nio No. 4049 Desp. 12, pg. 819 **PB**
Juver Industrial S.A. de C.V., Prolongacion Avenida Hermanos Escobar, pg. 1065 **PV**
Kelly de Mexico, Paseo Triunfo de la Republica No. 215, 32320, pg. 949 **PB**
Mexico Plant, pg. 443 **PB**
Outboard Marine de Mexico S.A. de C.V., pg. 479 **PV**
Tonka Corp., pg. 798 **PB**
Woodhead de Mexico, Manuel Quinones Ponce #3, pg. 1776 **PB**

Leon

Bandag de Mexico S.A. de C.V., Calle Guadelupe Oriental #901, pg. 178 **PB**
Bontex De Mexico S.A. De C.V., Boulevard Mariano Escobedo #801, pg. 734 **PB**
Broad Steel Construction-Mexico Operations Office, Calle de las Gardenias 101, desp. 4, Jardines de Jerez Sector 1, pg. 170 **PV**
Hewlett-Packard de Mexico, S.A. de C.V., Rocio No. 117-D, pg. 819 **PB**
KSB Controladora S.A. de C.V., pg. 721 **IT**
KSB Mexicana S.A. de C.V., pg. 721 **IT**

Lerma

Dart S.A. de C.V., Apartado Postal No. 9, pg. 1322 **PB**
Durakon Mexicana, S.A. de C.V., Av. Sta Ana Lotes, 19 y20 Mzna, 3, pg. 537 **PB**

Los Reyes

Hexaquimia SA, Km. 20.7 Carretera,Mexico-Texcoco, pg. 47 **IT**
Itapsa, S.A. de C.V., pg. 561 **PB**

Manzana V11

Martin Sprocket & Gear de Mexico, S.A. de C.V., Km 52.8 Carretera, Naucalpan-Toluca, CP 50200, pg. 709 **PV**

Matamoros

Asgrow Mexicana S.A. de C.V., Bravo y Calle 7, pg. 1049 **IT**

CTS De Mexico, S.A., AV LauraVillar Esquina N., pg. 286 **PB**
Condura, S.A. de C.V., Lauro Villar 378 Ote., pg. 558 **PB**
Electro Partes de Matamoros, S.A. de C.V., General Lauro Villar KM4, NUM 700 H, pg. 1790 **PB**
Kemet De Mexico De S.A. De C.V., Bldg. A, Plan De Ayutlay Leyes, pg. 949 **PB**
Maquiladora General de Matamoros, S.A. de C.V., pg. 1403 **PB**
Porta Systems S.A. de C.V., pg. 1317 **PB**
Ranco de Mexico, S.A. de C.V., pg. 1243 **IT**
Trico Componentes, S.A., pg. 1397 **IT**

Matehuala

Bemis Craftil, S.A., Boulevard Carlos Lago No. 201, pg. 210 **PB**

Merida

Industrias Oxford de Merida, S.A. de C.V., Parque Industrial Yucatan, KM. 12.5 Carr Merida-Progresso, pg. 1239 **PB**
Infra Del Sur, S.A. de C.V., Calle 15 N 312 Mza, 4A, CD Industrial, pg. 32 **PB**
Infra Del Sur, S.A. de C.V., Calle 60 X 35 No. 337, pg. 32 **PB**

Metepec

Papeles Corrugados, S.A. de C.V., Ignacio Lopez Rayon S/ N, pg. 1346 **IT**

Mexicali

AlliedSignal Turbos Automatrices, S.A. de C.V., Calle Ind. del Papel No. 30, Parque Ind. El Vigia Gonzalez Ortega, pg. 54 **PB**
Bicomp, S.A. de C.V., Calle Jupiter 182, pg. 576 **PB**
Calavo Foods de Mexico S.A. de C.V., 1099 Calle Electra, pg. 200 **PV**
Coast Cast Corporation S.A., Parque Industrial Mexicali, Calle Mercurio #70, 21210, pg. 391 **PV**
Emerex S.A. de C.V., Calle Industrial Del Papel No. 34, pg. 576 **PB**
Expo Partes S.a. de C.V., Mercurio 46, pg. 1709 **PB**
Hewlett-Packard de Mexico, S.A. de C.V., Av. Argentino no. 855, pg. 819 **PB**
Insteel Panel-MEX S.A. de C.V., pg. 882 **PB**
Maxon Industries, S.A. de C.V., pg. 717 **PV**

Mexico

ABC Instrumentacion Analitica, S.A. de C.V., Tepeji No. 88 Colonia Roma, pg. 816 **PB**
AFIA Sociedad Anonima, c/o Basham, Ringe y Correa, Liverpool 123-1 Piso, pg. 363 **PB**
AST Research, Av. Insurrgentes S.A. de C.V., pg. 1182 **IT**
Abbott Laboratories de Mexico S.A., Ave. Coyoacan, 1622, pg. 13 **PB**
Acciones y Valores de Mexico, S.A. de C.V., Reforma 398, Col. Juarez, pg. 1 **IT**
Aceites Lubricantes Y Grasas Castrol S.A., Lago Alberto 375-A, pg. 235 **IT**
Acer Computec Latino America, Berruguete No. 25, pg. 22 **IT**
Aceros Camesa S.A. de C.V., Margarita Maza de Juarez 154, pg. 575 **IT**
Adidas de Mexico S.A. de C.V., pg. 24 **IT**
Aero-Boutique de Mexico S.A. de C.V., Aeropuerto International, pg. 796 **IT**
Aeroboutiques de Mexico, Aeropuerto Internacional, pg. 795 **IT**
Aeromexpress S.A. de C.V., Ave. Texcoco, pg. 332 **IT**
Aeroquip Mexicana S.A. De C.V., Ingenieros Militares 105 1 Er. Piso, pg. 25 **IT**
Air Products and Chemicals de Mexico S.A. de C.V., World Trade Center, Avenida de las Naciones No. 1, pg. 31 **PB**
Aire Sellado, S.A. de C.V., Calzada Mexico Xochimilco, #16, Colo. Huipulco-Halpan, pg. 1451 **PB**
Ajinomoto U.S.A., Inc., Mexico Representative Office, Homero No. 404, Desp. 102, Colonia Polanco C.P. 11570,Deleg., pg. 41 **IT**
Alambrados Automotrices, S.A. de C.V., Lago Victoria 74 Col. Granada, pg. 721 **PB**
Alambrados y Circuitos Electricos, S.A. De C.V., Lago Victoria 74, Col. Granada, pg. 721 **PB**
Alberto-Culver de Mexico S.A. de C.V., Alce Blanco 11, pg. 38 **PB**
Alcatel Indetel, Bosque de Duranzos, No. 127, Aparatado, pg. 56 **IT**
Alcon Laboratorios S.A. de C.V., Jose Ma. Rico #418, pg. 918 **IT**
Alfa-Laval S.A. de C.V., Circunvalacion Norte 406, pg. 1380 **IT**
Alimentos Findas S.A. de C.V., Jose lillo 3, Naucalpan, Conmutador, pg. 918 **IT**
Allergan S.A. de C.V., Homero 1425-101, Col. Los Morales, pg. 46 **PB**
Allianz Mexico S.A. Compania de Seguros, Boulevard Manuel Avila Camacho 164, pg. 19 **IT**
Allied Colloids de Mexico S.A. de C.V., pg. 62 **IT**
AlliedSignal de Mexicano, S.A. de C.V., Ejercito Nacional 579-6 Piso, pg. 54 **PB**
Almacenadora Bancomer, Virginia Fabregas 80, pg. 145 **IT**
American Appraisal Mexico, Avenida Colonia del Valle 615, pg. 50 **PV**

PB - *U.S. Public Companies Volume*
PV - *U.S. Private Companies Volume*
IT - *International Public & Private Companies Volume*

1703

Geographic Index-Non U.S.

Anderson, Clayton & Co. S.A., Blvd. M. Avila Camacho, No. 1 5o Piso, Lomas de Chapultepec, pg. 1436　IT

Anglo Mexicana de Seguros S.A., Calle Chicontepec 63, pg. 90　IT

Ansaldo de Mexico, 14 Calle Rousseau, pg. 654　IT

Apasco S.A. de C.V., Campos Eliseos No. 345 Piso 18, pg. 629　PB

Apple de Mexico, Blvd. M. Avila Camacho #1, pg. 121　PB

Arrendadora Comermex S.A. de C.V., Paseo del la Reforma #116, pg. 182　PB

Arrendadora Gorvac S.A. de C.V., Canela 277, pg. 1621　PB

Arrow de Mexico S.A. de C.V., pg. 194　PB

Arrow Internacional de Mexico S.A., De C.E. Blvd. Adolfo Ruiz Cortines #379-, pg. 135　PB

Asahi Bank Mexico Representative Office, Paseo de la Reforma 199-505, pg. 83　IT

Ascomatica S.A. de C.V., Bosques De Duraznos, No. 65-1003A, Fraccionamiento Bosques, pg. 576　PB

Ase Rent, S.A. de C.V., Arquimedes 199, 3 A Polanco, pg. 334　IT

Asea Reguladores S.A. de C.V., pg. 8　IT

Aseguradora Cuauhtemoc S.A., Blvd. Manuel Avila, pg. 61　IT

Ashland de Mexico S.A. de C.V., Darwin 32-2nd Flr., Anzures, Dellegacion, pg. 139　PB

Asset Defensa Legal Mexicana, S.A. de C.V., M.M. de Llano 140, pg. 334　IT

Astra Chemicals S.A., Urbina No. 15, Parque Industrial, pg. 93　IT

Atlas De Mexico, S.A. De C.V., San Lorenzo No. 1009, pg. 664　IT

Australia & New Zealand Banking Group Limited Mexico, Andes Bello #10, 7th Floor, Chapultepec Polanco, pg. 99　IT

Autodesk Mexico, Monte Pelivoux 111 Piso 4, pg. 149　PB

Avantel, S.A., Reforma 265-6 piso, Col. Cuaohtemoc, pg. 574　IT

Avicola Pilgrim's Pride de Mexico, S.A. de C.V., Oklahoma #112, Piso 3, pg. 1296　PB

Avon Cosmetics, S.A. de C.V., Apartado Postal 591, pg. 156　PB

BASF Mexicana S.A. de C.V., Insurgentes sur 975, Col. Ciudad de los Deportes, pg. 106　IT

BBC Brown Boveri S.A. de C.V., Apartado Postal M-10 726, pg. 3　IT

BDF Mexico S.A. de C.V., pg. 183　IT

BHF-Bank Representative Office, Edificio Parque Reforma, Campos Eliseos 400, Oficina 203, pg. 120　IT

BMG Ariola S.A. de C.V. (Mexico), Avenida Cuitlahuac, pg. 192　PV

BNP (Mexico) SA, Edificio Arcos Oriente, Bosques de Alisos 47-B, pg. 164　IT

BTgraphic SA de CV, pg. 757　IT

BYK Gulden, S.A. de C.V., Av. 1o. de Mayo No. 130, pg. 66　IT

Bailey Mexico S.A. de C.V., Calle 3, Nr. 1-C, pg. 449　IT

Banca Hipotecaria, Ave. Universidad 1200, Col. Xoco, pg. 145　IT

Banca Patrimonial, Hamburgo 190, Col. Juarez, pg. 145　IT

BANCA SERFIN, S.N.C., Padre Mier Corriente No. 134, 9th Floor, pg. 137　IT

Banco J.P. Morgan, S.A., Avenida de las Palmas 405, Torre Optima Pisos 14, 15 y 16, pg. 1130　PB

Banco Mundial, Plaza Nafin, Insurgentes Sur 1971, pg. 1189　PV

Banco Nacional de Mexico, S.A. (Banamex), Isabel la Catolica 44, pg. 574　IT

Banco Santander, Presidente Masaryk 490, 5 Piso, pg. 144　IT

BANCOMER, S.A., Avda. Universidad 1200, pg. 145　IT

Bank Hapoalim (Mexico City), Homero 109, Oficina 1603, Esq. Mariano Escobedo 375, pg. 149　IT

Bank of America NT&SA, Paseo de la Reforma #116, 12th Fl., pg. 182　IT

Bank of Montreal - Mexico, Horacio No. 1855-301, Colonia Los Morales, Polanco, pg. 155　IT

The Bank of New York, The Forum Bldg., 10 Andreas, Bello, 6th Fl., Colonia Chapultepec, pg. 179　PB

Bankers Trust New York Corporation, Paseo de la Reforma 199-1201, pg. 186　PB

Banque Paribas-Mexique, Paseo de la Reforma 359, pg. 320　IT

Bayer de Mexico, S.A. de C.V., Blvd. Miguel De Cervantes, Saavedra 259, pg. 175　IT

Berlitz de Mexico, S.A. de C.V., 530 Ejercito Nacional, pg. 221　PB

Betancourt Barba EURO RSCG, Galilieo 13, pg. 603　IT

Bienes Rentables Morelos, S.A. de C.V., Rio Tiber 51 Colonia Cuaihetemoc, pg. 1436　IT

Binks de Mexico, S.A. de S.V., Floresta No. 104, Colonia Claveria, pg. 229　IT

Bitumex S.A. de C.V., Calle Oso No. 127-406, pg. 717　IT

Black & Decker S.A. de C.V., Jupiter 26, Avenue Central 186, pg. 234　PB

Boart Longyear S.A. de C.V., Apartado Postal 325, pg. 76　IT

Bombardier-Concarril, S.A. de C.V., Paseo de la Reforma, 369, pg. 200　PB

Bombas Goulds de Mexico, S.A. de C.V., Cincinnati, 40, Firat Fl., pg. 861　PB

Robert Bosch SA de CV, Dr. Lucio 270, pg. 206　IT

Bralemex S.A. de C.V., Paseo de las Palmas 765, pg. 515　IT

Brandeis US Division-Rep. Office in Mexico, Avenida Paseo de Las Palmas 558, pg. 1030　IT

Braun de Mexico y Compania de C.V., Victoria No. 25, Fracc. Industrial Alce Blanco, Naucalpan Estado, pg. 744　PB

Bridgestone/Firestone de Mexico, S.A. de C.V., Darwin 74, Col Anzures del Rep, M. Hidalgo, Apartado Postal 53-1000, pg. 214　IT

Bristol-Myers de Mexico, S.A. de C.V., Poniente 150 765 Col., pg. 255　PB

Brother International de Mexico, S.A. de C.V., Arquimedes No. 219-A 1er Piso, pg. 229　IT

Bucyrus Blades de Mexico, pg. 383　PV

Bufete de Ingenieria Clinica, S.A., Avenida Ejercito Nacional No. 254, pg. 816　IT

BUFETE INDUSTRIAL S.A. DE C.V., Moras 850, Col. del Valle, pg. 232　IT

Bujias Champion de Mexico S.A. de C.V., Poniente 150 #956, pg. 444　PB

Bull HN Sistemas de Informacion S.A. de C.V., Col. San Miguel Chapultepec, pg. 317　IT

Burgmann Mexico SA de C.V., Calzada de Guadelupe, Num. 350-6, Co. El Cerrito, pg. 233　IT

Leo Burnett S.A. de C.V., Bosque de Duraznos 65-8P, pg. 185　PV

CCL Label de Mexico S.A. de C.V., Pino 588 G Colonia el Arenal, pg. 238　IT

CIFRA, S.A. DE C.V., Jose Maria Castorena No. 470, Col. San Jose de los Cedros, pg. 241　IT

Cafe Continental S.A. de C.V., pg. 919　IT

Canon Mexicana, S. de R.L. de C.V., Calzada de Tlapan 479, pg. 263　IT

Carbide Condo, S.A. de C.V., Lomas de Sotelo 1102, Col. Loma Hermosa, pg. 1368　PB

Carbono-Lorena de Mexico S.A. de C.V., Av. Francisco I. Madero, 28, pg. 1030　IT

Caristrap de Mexico S.A. de C.V., Insurgentes Sur 58-50, pg. 272　IT

Carnation de Mexico S.A. de C.V., Mariano Escobedo No. 748, pg. 919　IT

Carrefour Mexico, Av. Presidente Masarik, 219, pg. 273　IT

Carter-Wallace, S.A., Blvd. M De Cervantes Saavedra 193, pg. 310　PB

Casa de Bolsa Bancomer, Hamburgo 190, Col. Juarez, pg. 145　IT

Casa de Cambio Bancomer, Bolivar 24, Col. Centro, pg. 145　IT

Casa Ley S.A., Carretera Int. y Calle Deportiva km 1434, pg. 1426　PB

Casio Electromex S.A. de C.V., Sor Juana Ines de la Cruz, 19602, Fraccionamiento Neuva Tijuana, pg. 274　IT

Cegelec de Mexico, Rio Nilo 90, Piso # 9, pg. 53　IT

Cemex, S.A de C.V. - Mexico City, Av. Presidente Mazarik 101, Floor 18, pg. 278　IT

Central de Industrias, S.A., Ave. Tiahuae No. 6732, Col. Santiago Zapotitlan, pg. 982　PB

Centro de Servicio de Computo, S.A. de C.V., Avenida via Lactes No. 43, pg. 816　PB

The Chase Manhattan Bank, N.A., Apartado Postal 37-477, pg. 340　IT

Checkpoint De Mexico, Or Barragan No. 785, Col Narvorte, pg. 343　IT

Chicle Adams, S.A. De C.V., Ave. Division Del Norte 3443, pg. 1739　PB

Chr. Hansen de Mexico, S.A. de CV, Calle 8 Num. 220, pg. 289　IT

Chrysler Comercial, S.A. de C.V., Paseo de las Palmas 755, 11th Fl., pg. 354　PB

Chrysler de Mexico, S.A., P.O. Box 53-951, pg. 354　PB

CIBA Corning Diagnostics de Mexico, S.A. de C.V., Vito Alessio Robles 68, 1er Piso, pg. 978　IT

CIBA-GEIGY Mexicana SA de CV, Calzada de Tlalpan 3058, pg. 978　IT

CIBA-GEIGY Mexicana SA de CV, Apartado Postal 21-993, pg. 978　IT

Cigarros la Tabaccalera Mexicana SA de CV, Manuel Salazar 132, pg. 572　IT

Cilag de Mexico, S.A. de C.V., M.A. de Quevedo 247, pg. 929　IT

Cinram Latino Americana, S.A. de C.V., av. Tlahuac no. 6710, pg. 293　IT

Circle Airfreight International de Mexico S.A. de C.V., Av. Texcoco #18, Col. Penon De Los Banos, pg. 372　PB

Citizen de Mexico, S.A. de C.V., Gabriel Mancera No. 327, Col. del Valle, Deleg. B. Juarez, pg. 294　IT

Clarins de Mexico Sade CV, Edificio Ex 2 No. 301, Fracto. Industrial Alce Blanco, pg. 295　IT

Clevite de Mexico, Monte Caucaso No. 915-6 Piso, pg. 1577　IT

Cliffs Neddrill Central Turnkey International, pg. 1144　IT

Clorox de Mexico SA de C.V., Avenida de Henry Ford, No. 31, 54030, pg. 387　PB

COBE de Mexico, S.A. de C.V., C.P. 14050, pg. 667　IT

Coca-Cola FEMSA, S.A. de CV, Rio Amazonas #43, 8 Piso, pg. 496　IT

Coca-Cola North Latin America, Apartado Postal 57-211, pg. 392　PB

Colgate-Palmolive, S.A. De C.V., Presa De La Angostura 225, Irrigacion, pg. 399　PB

Columbia Pictures International Television, Darwin 68, Office 301, pg. 1282　IT

Commerzbank AG-Mexico Representative Office, 390-1304 Paseo de la Reforma, pg. 311　IT

Compania Distribuidora Del Centro S.A. de C.V., Horacio 1855, 4th fl., esq. Periferico, pg. 1283　PB

Compania Hulera Goodyear-Oxo Sociedad Anonima, Km. 14.5 Carretera Puente de Vigas a Cua, pg. 753　PB

Compania Medicinal La Campana, S.A. de C.V., Av. Division del Norte 3443, pg. 1739　PB

Compania Mexicana de Geofisica, Ave. Revolucion 468, pg. 241　IT

Compania Mexicana Tri-Sure, S.A. de C.V., pg. 1146　IT

COMPANIA MINERA AUTLAN S.A. DE C.V., Mariano Escobedo No. 510-9, pg. 324　IT

Compania Nacional De Direcciones Automotrices, S.A. De C.V., Calle del F.C. No. 5, pg. 724　PB

Compania Sherwin-Williams, S.A. de C.V., Apartado Postal 35-Bis, pg. 1466　IT

Componentes Mecanicos de Matamoros S.A. de C.V., Lago Victoria 74, Col. Granada, pg. 721　PB

Comunicaciones Mtel, S.A. de C.V., Tiber 85-5, Piso, pg. 1120　PB

Conductores Componentes Electricos de Juarez S.A. de C.V., Lago Victoria 74, Col. Granada, pg. 721　PB

Conductores Latincasa S.A. de C.V., Cafetales 39 A, Col. Ex. Hacienda de Coapa, pg. 1365　IT

Consolidacion Comercial Infra, S.A. de C.V., Felix Guzman No. 16, Col. El Parque, pg. 32　PB

CONSORCIO G. GRUPO DINA, S.A. DE C.V., Tlacoquemecatl 41, pg. 326　IT

Consorcio Industrial Packsa, S.A. de C.V., pg. 1146　IT

Constructora ALMEX S.A., Bosques de los Duraznos 65, despacho 1007, piso 13, pg. 424　IT

CONTROLADORA COMERCIAL MEXICANA, S.A. DE C.V., Fernando de Alva, Ixtlixochitl 27, pg. 328　IT

CORPORACION INDUSTRIAL SANLUIS, Monte Pelvoux 220 Piso 4, Lomas de Chapultepec, pg. 332　IT

CORPORACION INTERNACIONAL DE AVIACION (CINTRA), Xola 535-16, Col. del Valla, pg. 332　IT

Credit Commercial de France, Gutenberg S. 143, Col. Anzures, pg. 343　IT

Crown Cork de Mexico, S.A., pg. 464　PB

CryoInfra S.A. de C.V., Felix Guzman No. 16, Colonia El Parque, pg. 32　PB

Cummins de Mexico S.A., Norte 35 No. 1015, pg. 468　PB

Cutler Hammer Mexicana, S.A., Javier Rojo Gomez 1300, pg. 558　PB

Cyanamid Mexico, Calzada de Tlalphan 3092, pg. 81　IT

DMB&B S.A. de C.V., Constituyentes 908, pg. 304　PV

DMC de Mexico, S.A. de C.V., pg. 508　IT

Daewoo Corp. - Mexico, pg. 358　IT

Dai-Ichi Kangyo Bank, Ltd.-Mexico City, Campos Eliseos No. 345-12, Col. Chapultepec Polanco, pg. 361　IT

Daisytek De Mexico S.A. de C.V., Av. Michoucan No. 20, Nave 8-B, pg. 477　PB

Daiwa Bank-Mexico, Edificio Omega, Campos Eliseos No. 345, 9 Piso, pg. 374　IT

Danone de Mexico, Circuito Civico 27, pg. 379　IT

Danzasmex S.A., Av. Rio Consulado No. 2983, Col. Pensador Mexicano, pg. 383　IT

Dell Computer de Mexico S.A. de C.V., Rio Lerma 302, 4o. Piso, pg. 496　PB

Delmex de Juarez S.A. de C.V., Lago Victoria 74, Col. Granada, pg. 721　PB

Delnosa, S.A. De C.V., Lago Victoria 74, Col. Granada, pg. 721　PB

Delredo S.A. de C.V., Lago Victoria 74, Col. Granada, pg. 721　PB

Deltronicos de Matamoros S.A. de C.V., Lago Victoria 74, Col. Granada, pg. 721　PB

Dentsply Mexico, S.A. de C.V., Calz. Vallejo 846, Col. Industrial Vallejo, pg. 499　IT

DESC, S.A. DE C.V., Bosque de Ciruelos 304-9, pg. 395　IT

Det Norske Veritas, pg. 397　IT

Deutsche Bank AG (Mexico), Campos Eliseos 345, 11' Piso, Col. Polanco Chapultepec, pg. 404　IT

Devcon de Mexico, S.A., Calz., Echegaray No. 16, pg. 867　PB

DeZurik-Mexico, S.A. de C.V., pg. 727　PB

Dicaser S.A. de C.V., Lafayette #121, pg. 903　PV

Diebold Mexico, S.A. de C.V., Durango 199, pg. 506　PB

Dietzgen de Mexico S.A. de C.V., Belisario Dominquez No. 151-A, pg. 332　PV

Digital Equipment de Mexico S.A. de C.V., Colonia Napoles, pg. 507　PB

Dispositivos de Precision Electronica, S.A. de C.V., Fulton 96, Zona Industrial, San Juan Del Rio, pg. 296　IT

Dow Jones Markets Financial Information Services, Inc., Edificio Anahuac, Paseo de la Reforma 51, Piso 9, pg. 525　PB

Dresdner Bank Mexico S.A., Bosque de Alisos, No. 47-B, 4. piso, pg. 419　IT

Du Pont S.A. de C.V., Apartado Postal 5-831, pg. 533　PB

Du Pont, S.A. de C.V. Div. Pigmentos y Productos Quimicos, Homero 206, 14o. Piso, pg. 531　PB

Dun & Bradstreet S.A. de C.V., Durango 263, 4th & 5th Fls., Col. Roma, pg. 537　PB

Durkopp Adler Mexico S.A. de C.V., pg. 469　IT

Duro-Test de Mexico, S.A., Paseo de la Reforma 195-10O Piso 5, pg. 349　PV

Durr de Mexico S.A. de C.V., Calle Utbina #6, Parque Industrial, pg. 422　IT

EMI Capitol de Mexico SA de CV, Rio Balsas 49, pg. 427　IT

Echlin Mexicana S.A. de C.V., Calz Vallejo #1874, Col. Santa Rosa Deleg. G.A. Madeno, pg. 561　PB

Edelman PR Worldwide, Rincon del Bosque #12, pg. 363　PV

Editorial Alhambra Mexicana S.A. de C.V., Prolongacion Amores 2027, pg. 1025　IT

Editorial Diana, S.A. de C.V., Roberto Gayol 1291 del Valle, pg. 304　IT

EL PUERTO DE LIVERPOOL S.A., Avenida Mariano Escobedo No. 425, pg. 435　IT

Electricite de France, Calle Rio 23 bis, pg. 437　IT

Electro Quimica Mexicana S.A. de C.V., Salamanca 102, pg. 606　PB

Electrolux S.A. de C.V., Apartado Postal 17-722 Col Tacuba, pg. 443　IT

Electronica Clarion, S.A. de C.V., Tata Vasco No. 77, Col. Villa Coyoacan, pg. 296　IT

Elevadores Kone Sabiem S.A. de C.V., Calle Clavel No. 227, pg. 747　IT

Elevadores Otis, S.A. de C.V., Abedules 75, pg. 1691　PB

PB - *U.S. Public Companies Volume*
PV - *U.S. Private Companies Volume*
IT - *International Public & Private Companies Volume*

1704

Geographic Index-Non U.S.

Elevadores Schindler Suwis, S.A. de C.V., Eje Central Lazaro Cardenas 1150, pg. 1205 **IT**

Elizabeth Arden de Mexico, S.A., Pestalozzi 578, Apartado Postal 12671, pg. 1437 **IT**

Elscint de Mexico S. de R.L. de C.V., Ave. Polanco No. 65, Colonia Polanco, pg. 450 **IT**

EMBOTELLADORES DEL VALLE DE ANAHUAC S.A. DE C.V., Av. Vasco de Quiroga, pg. 452 **IT**

Empaques Ponderosa SA, Paseo de las Palmas 405-103, pg. 454 **IT**

Empresas Frisco SA de CV, Jaime Balmes II, pg. 572 **IT**

EMPRESAS ICA SOCIEDAD CONTROLADORA S.A.C.V., Minera 145, Col. Escandon, pg. 454 **IT**

Ensamble de Cables & Componentes, S.A. de C.V., Lago Victoria 74, Col. Granada, pg. 721 **PB**

Envases de Acero, S.A. de C.V., Y/O Ava. San Luis Tlatilco, Avenida 1 de Mayo N 151, pg. 32 **PB**

Especialidades Nutritivas S.A. de C.V., pg. 920 **IT**

Especialidades Quimicas SA de CV, Colonia Portales, pg. 1113 **IT**

Esselte de Mexico, S.A. de C.V., Av. Nuevo Leon 253-703, pg. 461 **IT**

Estelar SA de CV, Tlaxcoque 8 Col. Centro, pg. 1434 **PB**

Evenflo Mexico S.A., Apartado 18939, pg. 630 **PV**

Eveready de Mexico S.A. de C.V., Floresta 65, pg. 1360 **IT**

Exide Electronics de Mexico, pg. 126 **IT**

Eyelet Mexicana S.A. de C.V., Rey Maxtla 213, Fraccionamiento Industrial San Antonio, pg. 464 **PB**

FMC Agroquimica de Mexico Si de R.L. de C.V., Gauss 12 Piso, pg. 606 **IT**

Factoraje Bancomer, J. Balmes 11, Torre C. Mezzanine, pg. 145 **IT**

Farmitalia Carlo Erba S.A., Apartado 21-909, Miguel Angel de Quevedo 555, pg. 1049 **IT**

Fasson de Mexico, S.A., Ave. Circunvalacion Pte. No. 53-F, pg. 154 **IT**

Felicitaciones Nacionales de C.V., Calzada, Mexico - Tulyehualco 4513, pg. 78 **IT**

Fermentaciones Mexicanas, S.A. de C.V. (FERMEX), Edificio Torre Diamante, Insurgentes Sur #1685-Piso 14, pg. 778 **IT**

Ferro Mexicana S.A. de C.V., Oriente 171,No. 450, pg. 619 **PB**

Fianzas Monterrey S.A., Presidente Masaryk 8, Floor 6, Col. Polanco, pg. 27 **PB**

Fibro Tambor, 16 DE Septiembre 200, pg. 1487 **PB**

Fideicomisos, Ave. Universidad 1200, Col. Xoco, pg. 145 **IT**

Ford Motor Compania Commercial, S.A. de C.V., pg. 666 **PB**

Ford Motor Company S.A. de C.V., (Mexico), Apartado Postal 39, pg. 666 **PB**

Foxboro, S.A., Durango 247, Apartado Postal 7-938, pg. 1243 **PB**

Frenos Lusac S.A. de C.V., Canela 379, pg. 561 **PB**

Fuji Bank (Mexico) SA., Arquimedes #130, Plaza Arquimedes, Piso 9, pg. 521 **IT**

H.B. Fuller Mexico, S.A. de C.V., 07720, pg. 687 **PB**

Fundacion GCN S.A., Av. Coyoacan 1878-504, pg. 1043 **PB**

Fundiciones Metalicas, S.A., Av. del Trabajo No. 6 Zimpan, HGO, pg. 1244 **PB**

GATX Logistics de Mexico, S.A. de C.V., Km 43 Au tapista, Parque Industric La Luz, pg. 692 **PB**

GR do Mexico, Lago Rodollo 29 colonia Grana, pg. 21 **PB**

GSI de Mexico S.A. de C.V., Rio Rhin No. 22-7 Col. Cuaupemoc, pg. 776 **PB**

General Electric de Mexico, S.A. de C.V., Marlano Escobedo 456, 12 Piso, Col. Anzuares, pg. 713 **PB**

General Motors de Mexico, S.A. de C.V., Lago Victoria 74, Col. Granada, pg. 722 **PB**

Generale Bank, Florencia No. 39 Desp. 601-602, pg. 547 **IT**

Gillette de Mexico S.A. de C.V., Atomo. No. 3, Parque Industrial Naucalpan, 53370, pg. 744 **PB**

Gist-Brocades Food Specialties Mexicana S.A. de C.V., A. de Las Torres 75, pg. 1142 **PB**

Gist-Brocades Industrial Pharmaceuticals Mexicana, Av. A. de Lavoisier 22, pg. 1143 **PB**

Givaudan-Roure, S.A. de C.V., Av. Universidad 902, Piso 4, Col. Santa Cruz Atoyac, pg. 1120 **PB**

Goldman Sachs Mexico Casa de Bolsa, S.A. de C.V., Torre Optima Bldg., Paseo de las Palmas 405, 18th Fl., pg. 462 **PV**

Goldstar Mexicana, S.A. de C.V., Call San Andres Atoto No. 8, pg. 779 **IT**

Gran Auto Express, S.A. de C.V., pg. 1475 **IT**

Gray Tool Company, c/o EPN-Gray S.A., Avenida Central n235, Unidad Industrial, pg. 5 **IT**

Griffin Bacal Publicidad, 2nd Floor, Col. Florida, pg. 480 **PV**

Grinnell Sistemas de Proteccion Contra Incendio S.A. de C.V., Poniente 116 No. 494, pg. 1651 **PB**

GRUPO ACERERO DEL NORTE S.A. DE C.V. (GAN), Rincon del Bosque 63, Piso 8, pg. 572 **IT**

GRUPO CARSO S.A. DE C.V., Insurgentes Sur # 3500, pg. 572 **IT**

GRUPO CASA AUTREY, Netzahualcoyotl 79, Col. Centro, pg. 573 **IT**

Grupo Celanese, Ave. Revolucion 1425, pg. 625 **IT**

Grupo Condumex, Paseo del Rio 186, pg. 572 **PV**

Grupo ECA S.A. de C.V., Rodriguez Saro 424, pg. 361 **PV**

Grupo Echlin Automotriz, Calz Vallejo No. 1874, Col. Santa Rosa, pg. 561 **PB**

GRUPO ELEKTRA S.A. DE C.V., Insurgentes sur 3579, pg. 573 **IT**

GRUPO FINANCIERO BANAMEX/ACCIVAL, S.A. DE C.V., Reforma 420, 44 Col. Ivarez, pg. 574 **IT**

Grupo Financiero Santander Mexico, Monte Pelvoux, 220 - 2 Piso, pg. 144 **IT**

GRUPO GIGANTE S.A. DE C.V., Av. Ejercito Nacional 769-A, pg. 574 **IT**

Grupo ICI de Mexico, S.A. de C.V., San Lorenzo No. 1009, 3rd Piso, pg. 664 **IT**

GRUPO INDUSTRIAL BIMBO S.A. DE C.V., Paseo de la Reforma, pg. 575 **IT**

GRUPO INDUSTRIAL CAMESA S.A. DE C.V., Margarita Maza de Juarez 154, pg. 575 **IT**

Grupo Industrial Minera Mexico, S.A. de C.V., Av. Baja California No. 200, pg. 138 **PB**

Grupo Industrial Morgan, S.A. de C.V., Calle 17 Lote 1, pg. 891 **IT**

Grupo inmobiliario Caisse, Lope de Vega 117, pg. 249 **IT**

Grupo Iusacell SA de CV, Monte Urales 460, Col Lomas de Chapultepec, pg. 204 **PB**

GRUPO MEXICANO DE DESARROLLO, Carretera Mexico-Toluca 4000, pg. 575 **IT**

Grupo Mexico S.A. de C.V., Av. Baja California 200, pg. 138 **IT**

Grupo Modelo S.A., Campos Eliseos 400, Piso 4, Col Lomas de Chapultepec, pg. 115 **IT**

GRUPO PALACIO DE HIERRO S.A. DE C.V., Salamanca 102, Col. Roma, pg. 576 **IT**

GRUPO POSADAS S.A. DE C.V., Reforma Lomas, 155-2, Col. Lomas de Chapultepec, pg. 576 **IT**

Grupo Siemens S.A. de C.V., Poniente 116 No. 590, pg. 1247 **IT**

GRUPO SYNKRO, S.A. DE C.V., Blvd. Manuel Avila Camacho 191-2 Piso, pg. 576 **IT**

GRUPO SYR, S.A. DE C.V., Presidente Masaryk 169, Col. Chapultepec Morales, pg. 576 **IT**

GRUPO TELEVISA, S.A. DE C.V., Av. Chapultepec 28, 1er Piso, pg. 576 **IT**

Grupo Termoindustrial ECA S.A. de C.V., Poniente 126 A No. 62, pg. 361 **PV**

GRUPO TRIBASA S.A. DE C.V., Bosque de Cidros 173, Bosques de las Lomas, pg. 577 **IT**

GRUPO VIDEO VISA S.A. DE C.V., Acoxpa 444, pg. 577 **IT**

Guerlain de Mexico S.A., Av. Rio San Joaquin n820, pg. 780 **IT**

HSBC James Capel Research Mexico S.A de C.V., Edificio Omega, Campos Eliseos 345-Piso 12, pg. 582 **IT**

Hachette Latino America S.A. de C.V., Calle Presidente Yazaruk, nr 4to friso, pg. 796 **IT**

Halliburton de Mexico S.A. de C.V., Apartado Postal 32-950, pg. 777 **PB**

Hallmark Mexicana, S. de R.I. de C.V., Escape #10, Fraac Industrial, Aice-Blanco, Naucalpan edo de, pg. 496 **PV**

Health-Mor Mexicana S.A. de C.V., pg. 771 **IT**

Helene Curtis Mexico, Homero 1933 9 Piso, pg. 1434 **IT**

Henkel Mexicana S.A. de C.V., Calz. de la Viga s/n, pg. 614 **IT**

Herman Miller Mexico, Bosques de Chapultepec, pg. 1112 **IT**

Herman Miller Mexico, Recursos Petrolcras No.14, Tlalnepantla Edo de Mexico, 54060, pg. 1112 **PB**

HERMI Ingenieria de S.A. de C.V., Ave. Nuevo Leon No. 80 Col., pg. 874 **PB**

Herramientas Klein S.A. de C.V., Avenida 1 No. 3, Parque Indus. Cartagena, pg. 625 **PV**

Herramientas Snap-on de Mexico, S.A., Insurgentes Norte 514 D, Col. Sta. Maria, pg. 1481 **IT**

Hewlett-Packard de Mexico S.A. de C.V., Monte Pelvoux No. 111, pg. 819 **PB**

Hewlett-Packard de Mexico, S.A. de C.V., Av. Periferico Sur 6501, pg. 819 **PB**

Holophane, S.A. de C.V., pg. 725 **PV**

Honeywell-Measurex S.A. de C.V., Mazatlan No. 43, pg. 834 **IT**

Honeywell S.A. de C.V., Av. Constituyentes 900, Col Lomas Altas, pg. 835 **IT**

Hoover Mexicana S.A. de C.V., Calle Norte 45-802 Col., pg. 1065 **IT**

Hovomex S.A. de C.V., Ruben Dario #13, 6th Fl., pg. 535 **PB**

Hughes Tool Company de Mexico, S.A. de C.V., Apartado Postal 14-102, pg. 167 **IT**

IBM de Mexico, S.A., Blvd. M. Avila Camacho 389, pg. 897 **IT**

IDC Mexico, Gonzalez de Cossio #334, Colonia del Valle, pg. 571 **PV**

IDG Communicaciones S.A. de C.V., Gonzalez de Cossio #334, pg. 570 **PV**

ING Insurance Mexico, Bosque de Alisos 45B, Piso 2, pg. 650 **IT**

Ideal-Standard, S.A. de C.V., Apartado Postal 291, pg. 92 **IT**

INAMEX S.A., Viena #71, 2 Piso, pg. 364 **IT**

The Industrial Bank of Japan, Limited (Mexico), Edificio Omega, Campos Eliseos, No.345-11 Piso, Col.Chapultec, pg. 675 **IT**

Industrias Alimenticias Club S.A., Ave. de Las Fuentes 41, Piso 5, Z.P. 10, pg. 920 **IT**

Industrias Kolmex, S.A., Calle del Rio No.u, pg. 690 **IT**

Industrias Nacobre SA de CV, Poniente 134, No. 719, pg. 572 **IT**

Industrias Purina, S.A. de C.V., Avenida Constituyentes 956, pg. 1360 **PB**

Industrias Pyrolas, S.A., Vainilla 186, Colonia Granjas, pg. 371 **PB**

Industrias Resistol, S.A., Bosque de Ciruelos 99, Col Bosques de las Lomas, pg. 1125 **IT**

Industrias Sola Basic, P. O. Box 92007, pg. 727 **IT**

Inmobiliaria Wackenhut, S.A. de C.V., Mar Mediterraneo #133, pg. 1731 **PV**

Instumentos Bristol S.A., Parque Rio Frio No. 6 Col Del Parque, pg. 473 **IT**

Intergrah de Mexico S.A. de C.V., Durango #263 Col. Roma, Piso 7, pg. 892 **PB**

Intervet Mexico SA de CV, Col del Carmen, pg. 45 **IT**

Itsemap Mexico, S.A. de C.V., Porfirio Diaz 102, pg. 333 **IT**

JEOL de Mexico S.A. de C.V., Av. Amsterdam # 46 DEPS, 402, pg. 697 **IT**

JWG Asociados Mexico, Col. Ciudad de las Deportes, Holbein 21A, #804, 03710, pg. 579 **PV**

Janssen Farmaceutica, S.A. de C.V., Apartado Postal No. 20-759, Col. San Angel, pg. 929 **IT**

Japan Airlines Company, Ltd., Paseo de la Reforma, 295, pg. 701 **IT**

Jeumont-Schneider de Mexico, Darwin n 32, 8 Piso, pg. 706 **IT**

Johnson & Johnson de Mexico SA de CV, Apartado Postal 74062, pg. 930 **PB**

Axel Johnson de Mexico SA de CV, Apartado Postal 21-313, Col. Del Carmen, pg. 711 **IT**

S.C. Johnson & Son, S.A. de C.V., Poniente 140 No. 717, pg. 593 **PV**

JUGOS DEL VALLE, S.A. DE C.V., Av. Ejercito Nacional 904-15, pg. 716 **IT**

Kaufman y Broad de Mexico SA de CV, Andres Bello #45 Piso 22, Col. Polanco CP, pg. 945 **IT**

Kendall de Mexico S.A. de D.V., Poniente 44, No. 3401 Col. San Salvador, pg. 1648 **PB**

Walter Kidde de Mexico S.A., Geramio #336, Esq. Tilos, pg. 594 **IT**

Kienzle Argo de Mexico SA de C.V., pg. 839 **IT**

Kimberly-Clark de Mexico, S.A. de C.V., Jose Luis Lagrange No. 103-3, pg. 960 **PB**

Kluber Lubrication Mexicana S.A. de C.V., pg. 507 **IT**

Kobe Steel, Ltd., Rio Danubio No. 69, 9-Piso, pg. 741 **IT**

Kodak Mexicana SA de C.V., Calzada de Tlalpan, pg. 554 **PB**

Kohler de Mexico, S.A. de C.V., Calle Norte 45 No. 766, pg. 631 **PV**

Komatsu Mexicana S.A. de C.V., Corredor Industrial S/N, CD. Sahagun, pg. 744 **IT**

Korn/Ferry International, Montes Urales 641, Lomas De Chapultepec, pg. 633 **PV**

Kvaerner S.A. de C.V., La Placita, Fuente de la Templanza no 6 Desp 204, pg. 767 **IT**

Kyowa Hakko Kogyo Co., Ltd., Edificio Torre Diamante, Insurgentes Sur #1685-Piso 14, pg. 778 **IT**

La Dominica, S.A. de C.V., Apartado Postal 5-831, pg. 333 **IT**

La Hacienda S.A. de C.V., Homero 1804, Piso 11, Los Morales Polanco, pg. 460 **IT**

Labinal Electronica de Reynosa, SA de CV, Carretera Riberena, Kilometro 9-Parque Industrial, pg. 786 **IT**

Lamiforma S.A. de C.V., pg. 614 **IT**

Ediciones Larousse S.A. de C.V., Marsella 53, pg. 240 **IT**

Eli Lilly y Compania de Mexico, S.A. de C.V., Apartado Postal 864, pg. 994 **IT**

Lincoln Electric Mexicana S.A. de C.V., Colonia Industrial Vallejo, Calz. Azcapotzalco La Villa No. 869, pg. 997 **IT**

Arthur D. Little Mexicana, S.A. de C.V., Av. Sinola No. 149-10 Piso, Col. Roma, D.F., pg. 671 **PV**

Loctite Co. de Mexico, S.A. de C.V., Bosques De Ciruelos No 130, 11 piso, pg. 611 **IT**

Louis Vuitton Mexico sarl de CV, Alejandro Dumas no. 4, Colonia Polanco, pg. 782 **IT**

Lowe & Partners/SMS de Mexico, Lafayette 88, pg. 678 **PV**

Lubrizol Servicios Tecnicos S. de R.L., Paseo de la Reforma, 381-601, pg. 1017 **IT**

Lucent Technologies Consumer Products Mexico, S.A. de C.V., Avenida Jardin No. 257 Col., pg. 1018 **IT**

Lucent Technologies de Mexico S.A. de C.V., Bosque de Cidros No. 18-5to., Piso Bosque de las Lomas, pg. 1019 **PB**

Lucent Technologies Holdings de Mexico S.A. de C.V., Bosque de Cidros, No. 19-5to. Piso, pg. 1019 **PB**

Luxottica Mexico SA de C.V., Monte Elbruz 132-9 Piso, Entre Mollere y Blvd. M.Avila Camacho, pg. 822 **IT**

MSA de Mexico, S.A. de C.V., Francisco I., Madero No. 84, Apartado 168, pg. 1114 **IT**

Makita Mexico, S.A. De C.V., Av. 1 de Mayo #231, pg. 832 **IT**

Manufacturas Gargo, 16 De Septiembre, Apartado Postal 615, pg. 1487 **IT**

Manufacturas Mallorca S.A., Via dr. Gustavo Baz, #142, pg. 1434 **IT**

Manville Mexicana S.A. de C.V., Apartado Rental No. M-7879, pg. 927 **IT**

Maritz De Mexico S.A. de C.V., Tamaulipas No. 30-2 y 3 Floor, Col. Hipodromo Condesa, pg. 704 **IT**

Marli de Mexico S.A. de C.V., Mexico D.F., Aparto Postal M-9072, pg. 613 **IT**

Marubeni Mexico S.A. de C.V., P. Reforma, 116-1101, pg. 845 **IT**

McCormick de Mexico, S.A. de C.V., Apartado Postal 17540, pg. 1067 **PB**

McCormick Pesa, S.A. de C.V., pg. 1067 **PB**

McGraw-Hill/Interamericana de Mexico, S.A. de CV, Atlamulco 499-501, Fraccionamiento Int'l San Andres, pg. 1072 **PB**

Mead Empaques S.A. de C.V., pg. 1076 **PB**

Mead Johnson de Mexico S.A. de C.V., Calz de Tlalpan 2996, Co. Santa Ursula Coapa, pg. 256 **PB**

Medidores Bailey S.A., Felix Guzman 15, Col. El Parque, pg. 474 **IT**

Medtronic, S. de R.L. de C.V., Adolfo Prieto 1521-1 er Piso, Col. del Valle, pg. 1084 **IT**

Memorex S.A. de C.V., Angel Urraza No. 1439, pg. 858 **IT**

Mentholatum de Mexico, Insurgents Sur., Np. 4120, Col. da, pg. 1126 **IT**

Mercedes-Benz Mexico, S.A. de C.V., Km 23.7 Carretera La Marquesa a, pg. 369 **IT**

PB - *U.S. Public Companies Volume*
PV - *U.S. Private Companies Volume*
IT - *International Public & Private Companies Volume*

Geographic Index-Non U.S.

1705

Metallurg Mexico, S.A. de CV, Eucken 16-501 & 502, pg. 735 **PV**

Mettler-Toledo S.A. de C.V., pg. 4 **PV**

Mexalit Industrial SA de CV, Horacio, Numero 1855-502, pg. 1171 **IT**

Mexalit S.A., Horacio, pg. 1171 **IT**

Mexicana de Aviacion S.A. de C.V., P.O. Box 12-813, Xola 535, Edificio de Mexicana, pg. 332 **IT**

Mexicana De Biene De Capital, S.A. c/o Campos Hermanos, S.A., Apdo. Postal M-29-B1S, pg. 6 **IT**

Mexico Asistencia, S.A., Porfirio Diaz, pg. 334 **IT**

Micro Warehouse, S.A., Circuito Vovelistos 129, pg. 1104 **PB**

Microsoft Mexico S.A. de C.V., pg. 1108 **PB**

Millipore S.A. de C.V., Ingenieros Militares No. 85-P.B., pg. 1113 **PB**

Mitsui de Mexico, S.A. de C.V., Campos Eliseos 400, 14th Fl. Col. Lomas, pg. 882 **IT**

Mojonnier de Mexico, S de R.L. de C.V., Miguel Angel de Quevedo 320-10, pg. 1194 **IT**

Monsanto Commercial, S.A. de C.V., 3R. Piso, Bosque de Dura ZNOS 61, pg. 1125 **IT**

Moore Products de Mexico, S.A. de C.V., Giorgione No. 6, Col. Mixcoac, pg. 1129 **IT**

Morgan Guaranty Trust Company, Avenida de las Palmas 405, Torre Optima Pisos 14, 15 & 16, pg. 1130 **PB**

J.P. Morgan Casa de Bolsa S.A. de C.V., Avenida de las Plamas, 405, Torre Optima Pisos 14, 15 y 16, pg. 1130 **PB**

J.P. Morgan Grupo Financiero, S.A. de C.V., Avenida de las Palmas 405, Torre Optima Pisos 14,15 y 16, pg. 1130 **PB**

Morton Thiokol S.A. de C.V., Ave. 16 de Septiembre No. 445, pg. 1136 **PB**

Mosler SA de C.D., Calle 2 No. 257, pg. 763 **PV**

Motorola de Mexico, S.A. de C.V., Tonala 59, pg. 1139 **PB**

Movilidad Moderna, S.A. de C.V., pg. 308 **IT**

NEC de Mexico, S.A. de C.V., Av. Ejercito Nacional No. 418, Piso 10, Col. Chapultepec Morales, pg. 901 **IT**

NKK Corporation de Mexico SA de C.V., Homero 136-703, pg. 903 **IT**

NRG Mexico S.A. de C.V., Insurgentes Sur 664,11 Piso, pg. 1116 **PB**

NSK Rodamientos Mexicana, S.A. de C.V., Minas Palacio No. 42-6, Col. San Antonio Zomeyucan, pg. 904 **IT**

NYK-Mexico City, c/o Mar Servicios S.A. de C.V., Londres No. 40, Piso 3, pg. 941 **IT**

NACIONAL FINANCIERA, Colonia Guadelupe Inn, Insurgentes Sur 1971, pg. 904 **IT**

Nadro S.A. de C.V., Londres 107, 8 Piso, pg. 1073 **PB**

Nalcomex S.A. de C.V., Av. Lomas Verdes 750, pg. 1151 **PB**

Nature's Sunshine de Mexico, Alvaro Obregon 89, pg. 1166 **PB**

Nichimen de Mexico SA de CV, 4th Fl., Temistocles No. 10, pg. 928 **IT**

A.C. Nielsen Co., Blvd. Avila Camacho 191, pg. 1183 **PB**

Nissan Mexicana, S.A. de C.V., Av. Insurgentes Sur No. 1457, pg. 945 **IT**

No Sabe Fallar S.A., KM 41.5 Carr Mexico-Queretaro, pg. 1273 **IT**

Nobiles-Lees S.A. de C.V., Blvd. A. Lopez Mateos 2601, pg. 268 **PB**

Nokia Telecommunications, Camino al Ajusc0 124-2, pg. 953 **IT**

Nomon S.A. de C.V., Paseo de las Palmas No. 765-3, pg. 512 **IT**

Nopco Industrial S.A. de C.V., pg. 614 **IT**

Nordson de Mexico, S.A. de C.V., Prolongacion 5 de Mayo # 27, Parque Industrial Nacalpan, pg. 1189 **IT**

North West Water (Mexico), Insurgentes Sur 1787, 01020, pg. 1444 **IT**

Northern Telecom de Mexico, S.A. de C.V., Insurgentes Sur, 1685 piso 30, pg. 970 **IT**

Nova Plast S.A. de C.V., Trigo No. 37, pg. 1530 **PB**

Novaquim S.A. de C.V., Insurgentes Sur, 1106 Col. Nochebuena, pg. 460 **IT**

Novell Mexico, Periferico Sur 4124, Piso 8, Torre Zafiro II, pg. 1204 **PB**

Novo Nordisk A/S, Paseo de las Palmas 735-807, pg. 988 **IT**

Novo Nordisk de Mexico S.A. de C.V., Paseo de las Palmas 735-807, pg. 989 **IT**

Novo Nordisk de Mexico S.A. de C.V., Edificio Forum, Abdres Bello No. 10, Piso 15, pg. 989 **IT**

OfficeMax De Mexico, Nueva York No. 280 A, Col. Napoles, pg. 1212 **PB**

Oilgear Mexicana S.A., Manuel E Izaquirre 29-203, pg. 1215 **PB**

Olin Quimica, S.A. de C.V., Campos Eliseos No. 385, Piso 9, Torre A, Col. Polanco, Delg., pg. 1220 **PB**

Olivetti Mexicana S.A., Poniente 152 n. 649, Col. Indus. Vallejo, pg. 1003 **IT**

Optima Industrial S.A. de C.V., Prolongacion Sanctorum 5, Col. Lomas de Sotelo, pg. 196 **PB**

Oral-B Laboratories S.A. de C.V., Jose Maria Rico 221, pg. 745 **PB**

Organizacion Roberts S.A. de C.V., Tejocotes # 164, pg. 796 **PB**

Organon Mexicana SA, 134 Calzada de Camarones, pg. 45 **PB**

Outokumpu Copper Kenosha, Inc., Goethe No 72, Col. Anzures, pg. 1017 **IT**

Outokumpu Mexicana S.A. DE C.V., pg. 1017 **IT**

PHH Mexican Corporation, Andres Bello, 10 Piso 7, pg. 321 **PB**

Packard Electric Division Mexican Operations, Lago Victoria 74, Col. Granada, pg. 723 **PB**

Panalpina Transportes Mundiales S.A., pg. 1023 **IT**

Parfums Christian Dior de Mexico S.A. de C.V., Nicolas San Juan 1641, pg. 783 **IT**

Parker Amchem S.A. de C.V., pg. 614 **IT**

PAXAR De Mexico, S.A. de C.V., Norte 45 #805 "BYC", pg. 1266 **PB**

Pechiney Mexicana S.A. de C.V., Avenida Paseo de Las Palmas 55, 5-Piao 4, pg. 1031 **IT**

Pemex Exploracion y Produccion, Ave. Marina Nacional 329, Piso 41, pg. 1046 **IT**

Pemex Gas y Petroquimica Basica, Ave. Marina Nacional 329, Piso 39, pg. 1046 **IT**

Pemex Petroquimica, Ave. Marina Nacional 329, pg. 1046 **IT**

Pemex Refinacion, Ave. Marina Nacional 329, Piso 40, pg. 1046 **IT**

PEPSI-GEMEX SA DE CV, Calzada de la Viga, No. 891, pg. 1036 **IT**

Pepsico de Mexico, S.A. de C.V., Basco de Quiroga 3000, 4th Fl., pg. 1277 **PB**

Perfumes Christian Dior de Mexico S.A. de C.V., Nicolas San Juan 1641, Col del Valle, pg. 783 **IT**

Periphonics S.A. de C.V., San Francisco No.1626-301, pg. 1279 **PB**

PETROLEOS MEXICANOS, Ave. Marina Nacional 329, pg. 1046 **IT**

Pfizer Holding Mexico, S. de R.L. de C.V., Damas 120, Colonia San Jose Insurgentes, pg. 1283 **PB**

Pfizer S.A. de C.V., Damas No. 120, Colonia San Jose Insurgentes, pg. 1284 **PB**

Pfizer Servicios de Mexico, S.A. de C.V., Damas 120, Colonia San Jose Insurgentes, pg. 1283 **PB**

Pharmacia & Upjohn S.A. de C.V., Calzada de Tlapan 2962, pc. 1049 **IT**

Plasticos de Mantenimiento SA de CV, pg. 356 **IT**

Polaroid de Mexico S.A. de C.V., Paseo DeLaReforma, pc. 1314 **IT**

Polioes S.A. de C.V., Calle Fernando Montes, de Oca 71, Col. Condesa, pg. 109 **IT**

Porcelanite SA de CV, Bosques de Ceruelos, pg. 572 **IT**

Precision S.A., Calle San Juan 763, Col. Aragon, pc. 1244 **IT**

Preformados De Mexico SA, Poniente 140, 526 Fracc Ind. Vellejo, pg. 1321 **PB**

Prentice-Hall Hispanoamericana, S.A., Enrique Jacob no. 20, pg. 778 **PV**

Prestaciones Mexicanas, Shakespeare no. 30, pg. 1275 **IT**

Principal Internacional, S.A. Compania de Seguros, Ave. Universidad 1571-2 Piso, pg. 886 **PV**

Producciones Automotrices , S.A. de C.V., 379-2, pg. 561 **PB**

Productora de Cosmeticos S.A., Patriotisimo 587, Piso 7, pg. 1490 **IT**

Productora Industrial, S.A. de C.V., Ings. Militares N 4, pg. 32 **IT**

Productos de Maiz S.A., Av. Rio Consulado N721, pg. 447 **PB**

Productos Industriales S.A. de C.V., pg. 422 **PB**

Productos Modificados, S.A. de C.V., pg. 448 **PB**

Productos Roche, S.A. de C.V., Av. de la Universidad 902, pg. 1121 **IT**

Profimex, S.A. de C.V., pg. 458 **IT**

Promotora De Partes Electricas Automotrices, S.A. De C.V., pg. 724 **PB**

PUBLICIDAD FERRER Y ASOCIADOS, S.A. DE C.V., Miguel Angel de Quevedo, No. 8, Octavo Piso, pg. 1073 **IT**

Publisiana/BDDP, Amores # 26, pg. 118 **IT**

qad.mexico S.A. de C.V., Newton 27-101, pg. 1345 **PB**

Quimica del Rey S.A. de C.V., Rio de La Plata 48, 13ero Piso, pg. 677 **PB**

Quimica Esteroidal SA de CV, P.O. Box M-9469, pg. 45 **IT**

Quimica Fluor, S.A. de C.V., Apartado Postal 5-831, pg. 533 **PB**

Quimica Hercules, S.A. de C.V., pg. 811 **PB**

Quimica Knoll de Mexico, S.A. de C.V. BASF Pharma, Calle La Candelaria 186, Col. Atlantida Delegacion Coyoacan, pg. 109 **IT**

Quimica Parker S.A. de C.V., pg. 614 **IT**

Quimica S.A. de C.V., Bosques de Ciruelos 180, Piso No. 7, Col. Bosques de las Lomas, pg. 614 **IT**

RNBNY Representative Office-Mexico, Avenida Juarez, 4, pg. 1381 **IT**

Rapistan Demag SA de CV, pg. 838 **IT**

Reader's Digest Mexico S.A. de C.V., Lomas de Sotelo 11C2, pg. 1368 **PB**

Reichhold Quimica de Mexico, S.A. de C.V., Norte 45 No. 731, Col. Industrial Vallejo, pg. 370 **PB**

Representacion Deutsch-Sudamerikanische Bank AG y Dresdner Bank AG, Edificio Plaza Comermex, Blvd. Manuel Avila Camacho, No. 1-603, pg. 420 **IT**

Repso Mexico, S.A. de C.V., Arquimedes, 199, 5o, Colonia Polanco, pg. 1105 **IT**

Repso S.A. de C.V. Mexico, Arquimedes, 199-5, Colonia Polanco, pg. 1105 **IT**

Resortes Mecanicos, S.A., P.O. Box 756, Del Cuauhtemoc, pg. 190 **PB**

Resortes y Productos Metalicos-Mexico City Plant, Privado de Rio Pilcomayo 183-A, pg. 857 **PV**

Rexroth Mexico SA de CV, pg. 839 **IT**

Rhone Poulenc de Mexico, S.A. de C.V., Matias Romero 216 Esquina martin Mendalde, pg. 1112 **IT**

Rhone Poulenc de Mexico S.A. de C.V., Josa Ma. Ibarraran 84, Piso 10, pg. 1113 **IT**

Richardson-Vicks S.A. de C.V., San Andres Atoto No. 326, pg. 1333 **PB**

Rimir, S.A. de C.V., Lago Victoria 74, Col. Granada, pg. 723 **PB**

Rinbros, S.A., Av. Del Taller, No. 174, pg. 1434 **PB**

Rio Brevo Electricos, S.A. de C.V., Lago Victoria 74, Col. Granada, pg. 724 **PB**

Roche Mexicana de Farmacos, S.A. de C.V. El Salto (Jalisco), pg. 1121 **IT**

Rockwell Automation de Mexico S.A. de C.V., Bosques de Ciruelos no. 160, C.P. 11700, pg. 1399 **PB**

Rocol Mexicana S.A. de C.V., Czda. Azcapotzalco, La Villa 882-2, pg. 893 **IT**

Rodamientos FAG S.A. de C.V., pg. 469 **IT**

Rohm & Haas Mexico S.A. de C.V., Av. Insurgentes Sur 670, Piso 2 ZP 12, pg. 1404 **PB**

Rorer de Mexico, S.A. de C.V., Ave. Division del Norte 3315, Apartado Postal 69-169, pg. 1111 **IT**

Roussel Quimica Mexicana S.A. de C.V., Paseo de Las Palmas, 555-1/2/3 Pisos, pg. 625 **IT**

Rubbermaid de Mexico, pg. 1411 **PB**

Ryerson de Mexico/Mexico, D.F., Av. de las Granjas 972, pg. 66 **IT**

SAIC de Mexico, S.A. de C.V., Ejercito Nacional 926, pg. 976 **PV**

SKF de Mexico, S.A. de C.V., Col. Nueva Industrial Vallejo, Eje Central Lazaro Cardenas No. 869, pg. 1158 **IT**

SNC-Lavalin, Calle Lope de Vega No 117, Piso 10, pg. 1162 **IT**

Sabritas S.A. de C.V., Ind. Vallejo, Norte 45, No. 740, Z.P. 16, pg. 1278 **PB**

Sachs Mexico SA de CV, pg. 835 **IT**

The Sakura Bank - Mexico Representative Office, Paseo de la Reforma 382-301, pg. 1180 **IT**

Sanborn Hermanos, Calvario 106, pg. 573 **IT**

Sandoz de Mexico S.A. de C.V., Ave. Gustavo Baz 352, pg. 984 **IT**

Sandoz Quimicos S.A. de C.V., pg. 985 **IT**

Sandvik de Mexico S.A. de C.V., Apartado Postal 512 Centro, pg. 1188 **IT**

Sanitaria Mexicana S.A. de C.V., Manuel Dublan 53, Col. Tacubaya, pg. 614 **IT**

Sara Lee Knit Products-Mexico, Cjon. Ressurreccion No. 4, pg. 1435 **PB**

Schenectady Mexico, S.A., Zettina 16, ZPEM, pg. 970 **PV**

Schering Mexicana SA, Apartado Postal no. 22-111, pg. 1204 **IT**

Schrader-Bellows Parker S.A. de C.V., Calle 9 No. 6 Alce Blanco, pg. 1261 **PB**

A. Schulman de Mexico, S.A. de C.V., Manuel E. Izaguirre # 13, pg. 1441 **PB**

Sears del Mexico, Vasco de Qurga 3800, pg. 573 **IT**

Seguros Banamex-Aegon, S.A. de C.V., Av. Periferico sur 4605 - 2o Piso, pg. 574 **IT**

Seguros Cigna, S.A., Arquimedes 199-10th Fl., pg. 363 **PB**

Seguros Genesis, S.A., Boulevard Manuel Avila Camacho, 40, Colonia Lomas de Chapultapec, pg. 738 **PV**

Seguros Monterrey, S.A., Presidente Masaryk 8, Floor 6, pg. 27 **PB**

Seguros Tepeyac, S.A., Humboldt, 56, pg. 334 **IT**

Selecciones Mercantiles, S.A. de C.V., Ave. de Las Torres 233, Naucalpan Juarez, pg. 256 **PB**

Sensormatic S.A. de C.V., Curretera Picacho AJusco #236, Torre Bosques Del Pedregal V, pg. 1458 **IT**

Servicios Especiales de Ventas Automotrices, S.A. de C.V., pg. 1475 **IT**

Shaklee Mexico, S.A. de C.V., Boulevard Avila Camacho No. 40, pg. 1518 **IT**

Sharp Electronics Corporation, Jose Antonio Torres No. 694, pg. 1229 **IT**

Shell Mexico, SA de CV, Av. Insurgentes Sur 954, Piso 5, pg. 1141 **IT**

Simpson Industries S.A. de C.V. (Mexico), Apartado Postal 55-472, pg. 1475 **PB**

Sinochem Mexico S.A. de C.V., Sierra Vertientes No. 406, Esq. SierraTorrecillas, pg. 1255 **IT**

Sinochem Representative Office - Mexico, Sierra Vertientes No. 406, Esq. SierraTorrecillas, pg. 1256 **IT**

Sistema de Ahorro para el Retiro, Ave. Universidad 1200, Col. Xoco, pg. 145 **IT**

Sistemas Electricos Y Conmutadores, S.A. de C.V., Lago Victoria 74, Col. Granada, pg. 724 **PB**

Sistemas Ericsson S.A. de C.V., Via Dr. Gustavo Baz 2160, Tlalnepantla, Edo. de Mex., pg. 1370 **IT**

Sistemas NIFE S.A. de C.V., Parque Industrial Naucalpan, San Luis Tlatilco No. 25, pg. 54 **IT**

Skandia S.A., Bosque de Ciruelos 162, 3rd Fl., pg. 1256 **IT**

Skandia Vida, S.A., Bosque de Ciruelos No. 162, 1er.piso, pg. 1258 **IT**

SmithKline & French, S.A., Avenida Univeridad 1449, pg. 1265 **IT**

SmithKline Beecham de Mexico S.A. de C.V., Jose Luis LaGrange 103, 9th Fl., pg. 1266 **IT**

Smurfit Carton y Papel de Mexico, Jaime Balmes 11, Piso 7, pg. 1271 **IT**

Sodexho Mexico, Shakespeare no. 30, pg. 1275 **IT**

Soilax de Mexico S.A., Av. Norte Sur 8 Alce, pg. 562 **PB**

Sonoco Latin America, Centro de la Ciudad, Delegacion Cuauhtemoc, pg. 1487 **PB**

Spicer S.A., pg. 480 **PB**

Springs de Mexico, S.A. de C.V., Benjamin Franklin No. 161, Piso 4, pg. 1500 **PB**

Stafford-Miller de Mexico S.A. de C.V., Calle 1 No. 129, Col. Pantitlan, Del. A. Obrego, pg. 237 **PB**

Stahl de Mexico, S.A. de C.V., Prolongacion Gonzalez Ortega 1737, pg. 1526 **IT**

Standard Chartered Bank (Mexico), Ave. Paseo De Las Palmas, 239 Piso 4, Col. Lomas De Chapultepec, pg. 1295 **IT**

Stanhome de Mexico, S.A. de C.V., Apartado Postal No. 877, pg. 1508 **PB**

Star Paper Tube de Mexico, S.A. de C.V., Av. Independencia #13-A, Col. Independencia, pg. 304 **PB**

Suiza Re Mexico, S.A. de C.V., Av. Insurgentes Sur No. 1685, Piso 13-B, Colonia Guadelupe Inn, pg. 1333 **IT**

PB - *U.S. Public Companies Volume*
PV - *U.S. Private Companies Volume*
IT - *International Public & Private Companies Volume*

The Sumitomo Bank, Ltd.-Mexico Representative Office, Campos Eliseos #345 Piso 11, Col. Chapultepec Polanco, pg. 1310 **IT**
Sun Chemical S.A. de C.V., Apartado Postal M-7186, pg. 371 **IT**
Sun Electric de Mexico S.A. de C.V., Apartado 525, pg. 1481 **PB**
Suntory Mexicana, S.A. de C.V., Magdelena No. 226 Col. Del Valle, pg. 1322 **IT**
Swequipos, S.A., Ave. Ejercito National N. 752, pg. 578 **PB**
Swiss Bank Corporation, Paseo de la Reforma No. 390, pg. 1330 **IT**
Swiss Bank Corporation, Campos Eliseos 345-19, pg. 1330 **IT**
Symix Systems Inc., Galileo No. 13, pg. 1547 **PB**
Syntex S.A. de C.V., pg. 1122 **PB**
Syseca de Mexico S.A. de CV, Quetzalcoatl 10 bis, pg. 1384 **IT**
Systemhouse de Mexico S.A. de C.V., Avenida Jalisco No. 180, 1er Piso, pg. 1154 **IT**
T-Fal de Mexico S.A. de C.V., Calle Jose Ramon Albarran, No. 110, pg. 568 **PB**
Tandem Computers de Mexico S.A. de C.V., Moras No. 313, pg. 417 **PB**
Tarjeta de Credito, Bolivar 38, Piso 5, Col. Centro, pg. 145 **IT**
Tastemaker S.A., pg. 811 **PB**
Taylor Instrument S.A. de C.V., Calle 4 No. 34-A Apartado Postal 84, pg. 6 **IT**
Teac Mexico S.A. de C.V., Privada Corina No. 18, pg. 1360 **IT**
Tecnocreto S.A. de C.V., pg. 986 **IT**
Tektronix S.A. de C.V., Col. Insurgentes Cuiculco, Periferico Sur 5000, 8 Piso, pg. 1568 **PB**
Teledyne Mexico, Andres Bello No. 10, Piso 5, pg. 44 **IT**
TELEFONOS DE MEXICO S.A. DE C.V., Parque via 198, Edificio 701, pg. 1373 **IT**
Teleindustria Ericsson, S.A. de C.V., Via Gustavo Baz 2160, Tlalnepantla, Edo. de Mexico, pg. 1371 **IT**
Telemontaje Ericsson S.A. de C.V., Antonio Caso No. 205, Col. San Rafael, Del. Cuahtemoc, pg. 1371 **IT**
Teran TBWA Publicidad, Durango No. 274-4 piso, pg. 1063 **PV**
Terumo Medical-Mexico, Rio Lerma No. 196, pg. 1376 **IT**
Tetraetilo de Mexico, S.A., Apartado Postal 5-83, pg. 533 **PB**
Texaco Mexicana S.A. de C.V., Insurgentes SUR 1822, pg. 1584 **IT**
Textiles Morelos S.A. de C.V., Blvd. A. Lopez Mateos 2601, pg. 268 **PB**
Thermos De Mexico S.A. de C.V., Lope De Vega 117, Despacho, 401 Y 402 Colonia Chapultepec, pg. 938 **IT**
3M Mexico S.A. de C.V., Calzada San Juan De Aragon 516, Colonia Carrera Lardizabal, pg. 1607 **PB**
Tiffany & Co. Mexico, S.A. de C.V., El Palacio de Hierro, pg. 1609 **PB**
Time-Life International de Mexico S.A. de C.V., Leibnitz 13-8, pg. 1615 **PB**
Tlalnepantla Estado De Mexico Mexicana De Bienes De Capital, S.A., Combustion Engineering, Inc., Juan De La Barrera N 2, Apdo 75-353, pg. 6 **IT**
Toastmaster de Mexico, pg. 1619 **IT**
Tokio Marine Compania de Seguros, S.A. de C.V., Col. Guadalupe Inn, Insurgentes Sur 1787 Piso 12, pg. 1393 **IT**
Tokio Marine Internacional Sociedad Anonima, Privada Horacio, 22 Penthouse, Colonia del Bosque, pg. 1393 **IT**
Toledo Scale Co de Mexico, SA De CV, pg. 986 **IT**
Topps Mexico, S.A. de C.V., Alborada 136, 9 Piso, Col. Parques del Pedregal, pg. 1622 **PB**
Tork Electro Sistemas S.A. de C.V., Calle Hortensia #97, Local 2, Col. Los Angeles Femina, pg. 1092 **PV**
Toronto Dominion Bank, 15th Fl., Torre Diana, Avenida Paseo de la Reforma, pg. 1401 **IT**
Toshiba de Mexico, S.A. de C.V., Paseo de Reforma No.30, 4 Piso, pg. 1406 **IT**
TRANSPORTACION MARITIMA MEXICANA S.A. DE C.V., Av. de la Cuspida 4755-9, pg. 1418 **IT**
Troquelados Especiales S.A. de C.V., pg. 8 **IT**
Tubetec, Calle Mayas, No. 12, Sta. Cruz Acatlan, pg. 873 **PV**
TUBOS DE ACERO DE MEXICO, S.A., Campos Eliseos No. 400 1er piso, pg. 1426 **IT**
Tusti S.A. de C.V., Canela 277, pg. 1621 **PB**
UBS Representative Office, Andres Bello 10, Piso 19A, pg. 1441 **IT**
Unidad Movil de Diagnostico, Humboldt 56 P.B., Centro, pg. 334 **IT**
Union Air Transport De Mexico, S.A. DE C.V., Notre 186 No.674, Colonia Pensador Mexicano, pg. 1120 **PV**
Union de Bancos Suizos, Andres Bello 10, Piso 19-A, Col. Polanco Deleg. Miguel Hidalgo, pg. 1441 **IT**
Utell International-Mexico, Hermosillo 16-4 Piso, pg. 1098 **IT**
Vaessen Shoemaker de Mexico, pg. 1067 **PB**
Van Leeuwen Pipe and Tube Corporation, Calle Eucken 8 Despacho 403, pg. 1450 **IT**
VARTA S.A. de C.V., pg. 1452 **IT**
Vestiduras Fronterizas, S.A. de C.V., Lago Victoria 74, Col. Granada, pg. 724 **IT**
Vistar S.A. de C.V., Bd Adolfo Ruiz Cortines 4152, Col Jardines del Pedregal, pg. 896 **PB**
Vitro-Fibras, S.A., Ingenieros Militares 85, pg. 1238 **PB**
Voest-Alpine Mexicana S.A. de C.V., Paseo de la Reforma 509-801, pg. 1472 **IT**
Vorwerk Mexiko, pg. 1481 **IT**
WWF de Mexico, S.A. de C.V., Cipres No. 426, Col. Sta. Maria Insurgentes, pg. 1145 **PV**

Wacker Mexicana, S.A. de C.V., Apartado Postal 99-070, pg. 625 **IT**
Wal-Mart Holding Co., Antiguo Camino a San Mateo 2, Col. Anexo Coamilco, pg. 241 **PB**
Wal-Mart Holding Co., Antiguo Camino a San Mateo 2, Col. Anexo Coamilco, pg. 1733 **IT**
Wallace & Tiernan de Mexico SA de CV, Av. Jose Lopez Portillo No. 321, pg. 61 **PB**
Wandel & Goltermann de Mexico S.A. de C.V., San Francisco No. 6, pg. 1486 **IT**
Wang de Mexico, S.A. de C.V., Avenida Constituyentes, #117,Col. San Miguel, pg. 1737 **PB**
Wang de Mexico, S.A. de C.V., Av. Constituyentes, No. 117, pg. 1737 **PB**
Warner-Jenkinson S.A. de C.V., Ave. Lomas Verdes, pg. 1696 **PB**
Warner's de Mexico S.A. de C.V., Londres 75, pg. 1738 **PB**
Werner & Pfleiderer de Mexico S. de R. L. de C.V., Av. Insurgentes, pg. 511 **PB**
The West Company Mexico, SA.de C.V., NVA Sto Domingo 139, pg. 1756 **PB**
West Merchant Bank Limited, Av. Insurgentes Sur 1991, Torre B, Despacho 201, pg. 1494 **IT**
WestLB-BEAL - Mexico City, Montes Urales 723-402, pg. 1494 **IT**
Wilson Sporting Goods Co. de Mexico, 1000 Constituyentes, Planta Baja, pg. 73 **PB**
T B Wood's (Mexico) S.A. de C.V., Oriente 237 No. 171, Colonia Agricola Oriental, pg. 1562 **PB**
Woodward Governor de Mexico S.A. de C.V., Insurgentes SUR No. 18, pg. 1776 **PB**
Woolworth Mexicana S.A. de C.V., Sudermann No. 250, pg. 1778 **PB**
Wyeth S.A. de C.V., Poniente 134, #740, pg. 82 **PB**
Xerox Mexicana S.A., Bosque De Duraznos No. 61, pg. 1785 **PB**
Yeso Panamericano, S.A. de C.V., Providencia 334, pg. 1660 **PB**
Young & Rubicam, S.A. de C.V., Bosques de Duraznos, No. 61-5, pg. 1200 **PV**
Zeneca Mexicana S.A. de C.V., Super Avenida Lomas Verdes 67, pg. 1527 **IT**
Zeneca Mexicana SA de CV, San Lorenzo 1009, pg. 1527 **IT**
Zurich Chapultepec, Guillermo Prieto No. 76, pg. 1532 **IT**
Zurich Compania de Seguros S.A., Guillermo Prieto No. 76, pg. 1531 **IT**
Zurich Vida Compania de Seguros S.A., Guillermo Prieto No. 76, pg. 1532 **IT**
Zwanenberg de Mexico S.A., Estacas 34 Esq. Primavera, pg. 1439 **IT**

Miguel Hidalgo

Tefal Mexicana S.A. de C.V., Goldsmith 38-103, Col. Polanco, pg. 568 **IT**

Monclova

ALTOS HORNOS DE MEXICO, S.A., Prolongacion Juarez s/n, pg. 66 **IT**
Procarsa, Av. Francisco y Madero S/N, Prolongacton Sur, Zona Industrial, pg. 677 **IT**
Ryerson de Mexico, Monclova Div., Prolongacion Fertilizantes No. 1900, pg. 66 **IT**

Monterrey

ACS Internacional S.A. de C.V., Ruiz Cortines 1855 Pte., pg. 4 **PV**
Adhesivos Swift de Mexico S.A. de C.V., Calle Felix U Gomez 2818, Col. Norte Moderna entre las calles de, pg. 370 **IT**
Amway de Mexico, S.A. de C.V., Washington #539 Ote piso 10, C.P. 64000, pg. 69 **PV**
Cadena Comercial Oxxo, S.A. de CV, Edison #1235 Nte., pg. 496 **PB**
Carplastic S.A. de C.V., Carr Apodaca Villa De Juarez, pg. 665 **PB**
CEMEX, S.A. DE C.V., Av. Constitucion 444 Pte., pg. 278 **IT**
Cigarrera la Moderna, SA de CV, Av. Francisco I. Madero Pte. 2750, Apartado 092, pg. 112 **IT**
Compania de Motores Domesticos, S.A. de C.V., Apartado Postal 1941, pg. 576 **IT**
Corporacion E.G., S.A. de C.V., Diaz Ordaz 3937 PTE, Col. Santa Maria, pg. 395 **IT**
John Deere S.A. de C.V., Apartado 1153, pg. 493 **PB**
Dimemn, S.A., Avenida Celulosa 2940, pg. 817 **PB**
Electrodos Monterrey S.A. de C.V., Av. Diego Diaz de Berlanga 130, Col. Nogcalar C.P. 66480, pg. 281 **IT**
EMPRESSA LA MODERNA SA DE CV, Av. Francisco Madera Pte. 2750, pg. 454 **IT**
FAR-BEN S.A. DE C.V., J. Cantu Leal 1528 Sur, pg. 478 **PB**
Femsa Cerveza SA de CV, Ave. Alfonso Reyes 2202 Nte., pg. 496 **IT**
FEMSA Empaque, S.A. de CV, General Anaya 601 Pte., Col. Bella Vista, pg. 496 **IT**
Fersinsa Gist-Brocades SA de CV, Ricondel Gato s/n, pg. 1143 **IT**
Fibras Quimicas SA, Ave. Ruiz Cortines y Privada Roble, pg. 46 **IT**
FOMENTO ECONOMICO MEXICANO, S.A. DE CV, General Anaya 601 Pte., pg. 496 **IT**

Gist-Brocades Mexicana, S.A. de CV, Rincon del Gato s/n, pg. 1142 **IT**
Grupo Termoindustrial ECA, S.A. de C.V., Av. Madero Pte. 3534, pg. 361 **PV**
Hewlett-Packard de Mexico, S.A. de C.V., Trevino 1233 Poniente, pg. 819 **PV**
Hickman, Williams de Mexico S.A. de C.V., Blvd. Puerta del Sol # 502-11, pg. 525 **PV**
Immobiliaria Conek S.A., Apartado Postal 2781, pg. 316 **IT**
Industrias Lubrizol S.A. de C.V., Camino Apodaca, Huinala 431, pg. 1017 **PB**
Intergraph de Mexico S.A. de C.V., Kalos-Centro Financiero, Zaragoza 1300 Sur 254y255-Piso A2, pg. 892 **IT**
Jacuzzi Universal, S.A., Km.339-Carretera Monterrey-Saltillo, pg. 1684 **PV**
KCS Villanueva S.A. de C.V., Prol. Pino #2620, Colvella Vista C.P., pg. 188 **PB**
Kir Alimentos, S.A. de C.V., Avenue Conductores No. 600, pg. 1434 **PB**
Korn/Ferry International, Daniel Zambrano 525, pg. 633 **PV**
Laboratorios Griffith de Mexico, S.A. de C.V., Apartado Postal 1832, pg. 482 **PV**
Arthur D. Little Mexicana, S.A. de C.V., Ave. San Pedro 400, pg. 671 **PV**
Lubrizol de Mexico, S. de R.L., Apartado Postal 972, pg. 1016 **IT**
Manufacturera Thermon de Mexico, S.A., Edif. Santos Despacho 415, pg. 1081 **PV**
Mary Kay Cosmeticos de Mexico Pty., S.A. de C.V., Zaragoza 1300 Sur, pg. 711 **PV**
Metalsa, S.A. de C.V., Ave. Churubusco Nte. 3890, pg. 1477 **IT**
Mitsui de Mexico, S.A. de C.V., Venustiano Carranza 627-Sur 3 Piso, pg. 882 **IT**
Montoi S.A. de C.V., A. V. Raul Rangel Frias #5625, pg. 1059 **PB**
Motor Wheel de Mexico, Platon #100, Parque Industrial Kalos, pg. 513 **PV**
Munters de Mexico Sa De CV, Calle E, 214, pg. 669 **IT**
Nylon de Mexico, S.A., Apartado Postal 800, pg. 533 **PB**
ORGANIZACION SORIANA S.A. DE C.V., Alejandro de Rodas 3102A, Col Cumbres, pg. 1008 **IT**
Parker/Zenith, Av. Morones Prieto, pg. 1264 **PB**
Perstorp Xytec, Inc., Eugenio Garza Sada, pg. 1038 **IT**
Publicidad Clave, S.A. de C.V., pg. 1073 **PV**
Quimobasicos, S.A. de C.V., Ave. Ruiz Cortines 2333 Pte, pg. 247 **IT**
Rockwell Automation de Mexico S.A. de C.V., Avenida Pablo A. Gonzalez, No. 130 Poniente, C.P. 64640, pg. 1399 **PB**
A. Schulman, Camino del Lago #4517, Sector 4, pg. 1441 **PB**
TecniQuimia Mexicana S.A. de C.V., Apartado Postal 4425, pg. 1347 **PB**
Tiendas de Descuento Sultana S.A. de C.V., Alejandro de Rodas 3102-A, pg. 1008 **IT**
Tolmex S.A. de C.V., Av. Constitucion 444 Pte., pg. 278 **IT**
Wellcome Mexico SA de CV, pg. 553 **IT**

Morelia

Sulzer Hydro S.A. de C.V., pg. 1308 **IT**
Turbinas y Equipos Industriales, S.A. de C.V., pg. 1306 **IT**

Morelos

AMS Management Systems Mexico S.A. de C.V., 1 Homero 203, Piso 10, pg. 87 **PV**
Aluplast S.A. de C.V., Calle 40-S con 13-E CIVAC, 62500 Jiutepec, pg. 1756 **PB**
Alustar, S.A. de C.V., Lote No. 2 Manzana XIII, Parque Industrial Cuautla, pg. 239 **IT**
Henkel Comercial S.A. de C.V., pg. 612 **IT**
Len S.A., Km. 20-1/2, pg. 613 **IT**
Pharma-Tap S.A. de C.V., Calle 21-E con 36 sur, pg. 1756 **PB**
Quimica Henkel S.A. de C.V., Carr. Mexico-Laredo Km. 20.5, Col. Tulpetlac, pg. 613 **IT**

Naucalpan Estado de Mexico

Asbury Worldwide Mexico S.A. de C.V., Parque Industrial Naucalpan, Electron #10, pg. 1110 **PB**

Nogales

Avent, S.A. de C.V., pg. 959 **PB**
Badger Meter de Mexico, S.A. de C.V., Parque Industrial de Nogales, KM 6, pg. 165 **PB**
Minebea Electronics Mexico S.A. de C.V., Carrebera International Km 5.5, pg. 868 **IT**
Systemes y Connexiones Integrados S.A. de C.V., pg. 955 **IT**

Nuevo Laredo

Barry of Nuevo Laredo, Cesar Lopez de Lara Ave., pg. 192 **PB**
Lamosa S.A. de C.V., (Mexico), pg. 667 **PB**
Planta Kodak, Parqie Industrial de America, pg. 554 **PB**
Productos para Escuela y Oficina, S.A. de C.V., Calle Industrios #6060, Bay 3 #, pg. 1077 **PB**
Repsol Gas Nuevo Laredo, pg. 1105 **IT**
Tecnologia Modificado S.A. de C.V., Paseo Loma Real #34, Parque Industrial Rio Bravo, pg. 317 **PB**

Geographic Index-Non U.S.

Nuevo Leon

Aerolitoral, Carretera Miguel Aleman Km 22, pg. 332 IT

Piedras Negras

Coopermex, Victoria Norte, 2707, pg. 445 PB
Littelfuse S.A. de C.V., Poder Judicial 1005, pg. 1001 PB
Rassini-NHK Torsion Bars S.A. de C.V., Prolongacion Calle, Puerto Arturo S/N Col. Bravo, pg. 902 IT

Piso

Explosivos Mexicanos S.A. De C.V., San Lorenzo No. 1009 3ER, pg. 664 PB
Grupo Sitra, S.A. DE C.V., Mexico City Office, Londres 212 - 5, pg. 775 IT
Servicios Westinghouse de Mexico, S.A. de C.V., Ave Homero 1804-9, pg. 273 PB

Polanco

Aquaconsult S.A. de C.V., Blas Pascal 111, Los Morales, pg. 474 IT
Babcock & Wilcox de Mexico SA de CV, Blas Pascal 111, Los Morales, pg. 474 IT
Babcock Mexico SA de CV, Blas Pascal 111, Los Morales, pg. 474 IT
Construcciones Instalaciones Babcock S.A. de C.V., Blas Pascal 111, Los Morales, pg. 474 IT
Heller Financial (Mexico), S.A. de CV, Monte Elbruz No. 124-8 Piso, pg. 521 IT
Pohang Iron & Steel Co., Ltd., Privada No.22 Desp. No. 1, pg. 1062 IT

Puebla

Aero Tecnica SA, pg. 617 IT
CIBA-GEIGY Mexicana SA de CV, Planta Puebla, Apartado Postal 62, pg. 978 IT
Compania de Chicle Adams, Inc., Carretera Mexico-, Veracruz No. 1028, pg. 1739 PB
Flender de Mexico, S.A. de C.V., Apdo. Postal 2-85, pg. 400 IT
Freudenberg Telas sin Tejer S.A. de C.V., pg. 507 IT
Grupo Termoindustrial ECA, S.A. de C.V., Blvd. Hnos. Serdan 143, pg. 361 PV
Herman Miller Mexico, Puebla Office, 5 Poniente 2109-3, pg. 1112 PB
Hylsa S.A.-Bar and Rod Division, Carr. Mexico-Puebla Km. 108, pg. 56 IT
Nokia Mobile Phones (Mexico) S.A. de C.V., 47 Poniente 703-300, pg. 952 IT
Scapa de Mexico S.A. de C.V., Calle Resurrection Oriente 44, Parque Industriel La Resurrection, pg. 1203 IT
Telecomunicaciones e Informatica para Concesionarios S.A. de C.V., pg. 1475 IT
Temesa Tecnoindustrial Mexicana SA de CV, pg. 837 IT
Volkswagen Comercial S.A. de C.V., Autopista Mexico-Puebla Km 116, pg. 1475 IT
Volkswagen de Mexico S.A. de C.V., pg. 1475 IT
Volkswagen Financial Services, S.A. de C.V., pg. 1475 IT
Volkswagen Leasing S.A. de C.V., Autopista Mexico-Puebla Km 116, pg. 1475 IT

Queretaro

Air Products Resinas, S.A. de C.V., Calle 4, No. 3, Nuevo Parque Industrial, pg. 32 PB
Alimentos Balanceados Pilgrim's Pride, Avenida 5, Defebrero #1048, pg. 1296 PB
Carvel Print Grupo Serigraph, Calle 2, No.117 Fracc. Benito Juarez, pg. 985 PV
Gerber Products, S.A. de C.V., Lafontaine 57, Colonia Polanco, pg. 973 IT
Graficas Monte Alban, S.A., Fraccionnamiento Agro, Industrial La Cruz, pg. 1078 IT
Graficas Monte Alban, S.A., Apartado Postal 512, Villa del Marquez, pg. 1078 IT
Grupo Termoindustrial ECA, S.A. de C.V., Morelos 195, pg. 361 PV
Hewlett-Packard de Mexico, S.A. de C.V., Circuito del Mezon No. 186, Desp. 6, Condominio Cadereyta, pg. 819 PB
Kellogg de Mexico S.A. de C.V., Km. 1 Carretera, pg. 948 PB
Lubricantes Fuchs De Mexico, S.A. De C.V., Manzana 1, Acceso C no. 101, pg. 519 IT
Marvin de Mexico, S.A. de C.V., km. 9.5 Carretera Constitucion, pg. 137 PB
Productos Gerber S.A. de C.V., pg. 983 IT
Resortes y Productos Metalicos-Queretaro Plant, Acceso 11 No. 3, Parque Ind. Benito Juarez, pg. 857 PV
Rockwell Mexicana, S.A. de C.V., Av. de las Fuentes No. 17, Parque Industrial Bernardo Quintana, pg. 1402 PB
Watlow de Mexico S.A. de C.V., Colon No. 6, pg. 1153 PV

Ramos Arizpe

Forjacero, Carretera a los Pinos km. 2.5 B, pg. 66 IT
General Motors de Mexico, S.A. de C.V., Carr. Monterrey-Saltillo, Km. 7.5, pg. 722 PB
Wohlert De Mexico, Carretera a Los Pinos, 25900, pg. 1185 PV

Reynosa

Datacomm de Mexico, S.A. de C.V., Apartado Postal 775, Carretera a Matamoros con Brecha E-99, 88780, pg. 729 PB
Especialidades de Reynosa S.A. de C.V., Carretera A Matamoros y Brecha E.99, pg. 1174 IT
Foarsa Forjas Y Aceros De Reinosa, S.A., P. de Alejandro Canonje, 1, pg. 1225 IT
Impresora Donneco Internacional, S.A. de C.V., pg. 519 PB
Kimball Electronics Group, Carretera Matamoros, Brecha 99, Parque Industrial Norte, pg. 958 PB
Lambda Electronica de Mexico, S.A., Carretera Matamoros KM 9, pg. 1242 IT
Norton Company de Mexico SA de CV, Carretera a, Matamoros y Brecha, pg. 1175 IT
Otis Mexicana, S.A., Acuario 1400 Col. Resendez Sierro, pg. 777 IT
Partes de Television de Reynosa S.A. De C.V., Matamoros y Erecha E-99, Carretera A, pg. 1790 PB
Semtech Corpus Christi S.A. de C.V., pg. 1456 PB
Stuart Entertainment, S.A. de C.V., Avenida Industrial Falcone, pg. 1526 PB
Wells Manufacturera de Mexico S.A. de C.V., Carretera Laredo, Km. 9, pg. 1113 PV
West Bend/Mexico, pg. 1323 PB

Salamanca

Harinera Los Pirineos, S.A. de C.V., Km: 11 Carr. Pan Americana, pg. 1346 IT

Saltillo

Douglas y Lomason de Coahuila S.A. de C.V., Blvd. Nazario Ortiz Garza 4021 Pte., pg. 830 IT
Grupo Industrial Saltillo, Apto. Postal 29, Chiapas #375, pg. 1469 IT
Pace Industries of Mexico, L.L.C., Blvd. Vito Allessio Robles NO 2451, 25230, pg. 578 IT
VITROMEX, S.A., Blvd. Isidro Lopez Certuche 4103, pg. 1469 IT

San Juan del Rio

Neumatica Hidraulica S. de RL de CV, pg. 839 IT
Ultra ndustrial S.A. De C.V., Queretaro, Dom. Betania #13 Infonavit, pg. 296 IT

San Luis Potosi

Bemis Maral, S.A. de C.V., Av. Industrias & Eje 100, Zona Industrial, pg. 210 PB
Compania Minera Las Cuevas S.A. de C.V., Eje 106 s/n, Zona Industrial, pg. 575 IT
Cummins S.A. de C.V., Zona Industrial, Eje 122 Asq. Avenida Industrias, pg. 469 PB
Grupo Termoindustrial ECA, S.A. de C.V., Injuve III, Locs. 35-36, pg. 361 PV
Long de Mexico, Zona Industrial del Potosi, pg. 815 IT
MACtac Mexico, S.A., Av. Industrias y Eje 100, Zona Industrial, pg. 210 IT
Oficina Tecnica San Luis, Av. Industrias Esq. Eje 120, Zona Industrial, pg. 1369 IT
Rockwell Fumagalli, S.A. de C.V. Light Vehicle Systems, Eje 130, No. 175, Zona Industrial del Potosi, C.P.78395, pg. 1400 PB
A. Schulman de Mexico, S.A. de C.V., Avenida CFE, 730, Entre Eje 134 y Eje 136, pg. 1442 PB
Simpson Industries S.A. de C.V. (Mexico), Eje 122 No. 200, Zona Industriale, pg. 1475 IT

San Miguel Xoxlta

Perstorp Components S.A. DE C.V., KM. 108 autopista, pg. 1040 IT

San Nicolas

Acerex S.A., Nogalar Ave. 330, pg. 56 IT
Galvak S.A., Paseo de la Juventud Ave. 340, pg. 56 IT
Hylsa S.A.-Flat Rolled Division, Cd. de los Angeles Ave. 235, pg. 56 IT
Hylsa S.A.-Technology Division, Munich Ave. 101, pg 56 IT
Hylsa S.A.-Tubular Division, Guerrero Ave., pg. 56 IT
Hylsamex, S.A. de C.V., Ave. Munich 101, pg. 56 IT
Ryerson de Mexico, Ave. Conductores #313, pg. 66 IT

Santa Catarina

Caterpillar Mexico S.A. de C.V., Carr Monterrey-Villa de Garcia y, pg. 316 PB
GRUPO PROTEXA S.A. DE C.V., Km. 399 Carr Monterrey-Saltilla, pg. 576 IT
Perforaciones Maritimas Protexa S.A. de C.V., Carr Monterrey-Saltillo Km. 339, pg. 576 IT
Protexa Industrias S.A. de C.V., Carr Monterrey-Saltillo Km. 339, pg. 576 IT

Santa Clara

American Textil, S.A. de C.V., Via Morelos, pg. 769 PB
Grupo Termoindustrial ECA, S.A. de C.V., Km. 11.5, pg. 361 PV

Liberty Mexicana S.A. de C.V., Km. 15, 100 Carretera, Mexico-Laredo, pg. 39 IT

Sonora

Autopartes de Precision de Santana, S.A. de C.V., Avenida Serna y Calle 13 Santa Ana, pg. 750 PV
Bose S.A. de C.V., Av Miguel de la Madrid, y Calle de la Industria KM 9.5, pg. 161 PV
Breed Technologies, Plant 1, Calle 16 Avenidas 10, pg. 251 PB
CE Sonora S.A. de C.V., 83250 Hermosillo, pg. 468 PB
Cambior de Mexico S.A. de C.V., Boulevard Navarrete no. 86, pg. 253 IT
Camisas Bahia Kino S.A. de C.V., Argua Prieta, pg. 1239 PB
Grafito Superior SA, pg. 1055 PV
Molex S.A. de C.V., Parque Industrial, Apdo, pg. 1122 PB
S.I. De Mexico S.A. de C.V., Calle Primera 2550 Agua Prieta, pg. 1507 PB
Virsan S.A. de C.V., Calzada Constitution Calle Rio Mayo, San, pg. 1721 PB

Tampico

GRUPO CONTINENTAL S.A., Avenida Hidalgo No. 2303, Col. Smith, pg. 573 IT
Novaquim S.A. de C.V., Caretera Mante-Tampico Km. 139, pg. 460 PB

Tecamachalco

Especialidades Quimicias Grace de Mexico S.A. de C.V., Ave. de las Fuentes 41-A, Piso 8, pg. 755 PB

Telepan

Sandoz Agricola S.A. de C.V., pg. 984 IT

Tepetlacalco

Aceromex-Atlas S.A. DE C.V., Calle E. Zapata No. 21, pg. 1118 IT

Tepic

Casa Export, Ltd., Apartado Postal 490, Predio Las Sauces, pg. 1695 PB

Tijuana

Artesanias Baja, S.A., Blvd. Alivio Norte 25, pg. 594 IT
COBE Renal Care, Inc., Boulevard Pacifico #10014, pg. 667 IT
Canon Business Machines de Mexico S.A. de C.V., C. Conchenacar No. 6459, pg. 262 IT
Deltec S.A., Avenida Ensenada 14, pg. 492 IT
Dowty O Rings North America, Insurgentes, 19802-4, Parque Industrial Cerro Colorado, pg. 1338 IT
Falcon de Baja California, S.A. de C.V., La Campina # 19511, Colonia La Mesa, pg. 611 PB
Hewlett-Packard de Mexico, S.A. de C.V., Dr. Atl No. 1, Desp. 402, pg. 819 PB
Hitachi Consumer Products de Mexico, Ave. Industrial No. 105, pg. 622 IT
Industria Mexicana de Fotocopiadoras, S.A. de C.V., Av. Universidad Edificio 7/A, Parque Industrial Internacional Tijuana, pg. 554 IT
Industrias Universales Unions de Mexico SA, Calle Intl. No. 130.1, pg. 1539 PB
Kelsar, S.A., Blvd. Insurgentes Parcela 37, pg. 81 PB
Keystone Automotive Industries, Inc.-Tijuana, Paseo Reforma #123, pg. 955 PB
Kyocera Mexicana S.A. de C.V., Blvd. Buenavista-Otay, pg. 776 IT
Levimex de Baja California S.A. de C.V., Blvd. Los Insurgentes 20004, pg. 663 PV
Mabamex S.A., Calle 29 Firall La Goya, pg. 1059 PB
Matsushita Industrial de Baja California, S.A., Blvd. Alivio No. E-2 Eje Oriente, pg. 847 IT
Maxell de Mexico S.A. de C.V., Calle Maquiladoras S/N, pg. 621 IT
Maxon Industries, S.A. de C.V., Calle Centenario, pg. 717 PV
Muebles Fino Bueno, Blvd. San Martin Y Calle La. Sin, pg. 463 PV
Nellcor de Mexico, S.A. de C.V., La Mesa Parque Industrial, Avenida Reforma S/N, pg. 1040 PB
Oficina Tecnica Tijuana, Av. Mision San Javier, No. 10611, Col. Zona del Rio, pg. 1369 IT
Parker Seal de Baja, S.A. de C.V., Calle Siete Norte No. 111, Esquina Con Calle Uno Poniente, pg. 1262 PB
Plamex, S.A. de C.V., Parque Industrial Internacional, pg. 1308 PB
Plasticos Maraton, S.A., Calle 29 Fracc, La Joya, pg. 1059 PV
Productos Maestros, Central Industrial Arboleda, pg. 341 PV
Raychem Technologias, S.A. DE C.V., Calle 11 Norte Y 1 Poniente No. 110, C.P. 22500, pg. 1363 PB
Rectificadores Internacionales, S.A., Durazno No. 30, Centro Industrial, pg. 907 PB
Sanmex, S.A. de C.V., Calle 9 Norte No. 102, Ciudad Industrial, pg. 1192 PB
Switchcraft de Mexico, S.A., Calle Uno Oriente No. 117, pg. 1306 PB
Tabuchi Electric de Mexico S.A. de C.V., Calle Ensambladores No. 180, Ciudad Industrial Mesa de Otay, pg. 1346 IT

Temati S.A. de C.V., Calle Siete Norte No. 108, pg. 1278 **PB**
Turbo Technologia de Reparaciones S.A. de C.V., Cuidad Indus. Mesa de Otay, Calle 7, Sur. No. 1409, pg. 316 **PB**

Tlalnepantla

AGA de Mexico S.A. de C.V., Apartado 284x, pg. 13 **IT**
AGA S.A. de C.V., Apartado Postal 284, pg. 14 **IT**
AMP de Mexico, S. A., Alfredo Nobel No. 28 La Loma, pg. 8 **IT**
ATS Omega de Mexico, S.A. de C.V., Presidente Juarez No. 2023, Francc. Industrial Los Reyes, pg. 1222 **IT**
Aceromex Atlas, S.A. de C.V., Cerrada de Nino Flavio Zavala No. 108-2, 54090, pg. 308 **IT**
Amercoat Mexicana S.A. de C.V., Dr. Gustavo Baz 3999, 54030, pg. 99 **IT**
Anyl-Mex SA DE CV, Rio Lerma no. 32, pg. 1525 **IT**
ASEA S.A. de C.V., Gustavo Baz y Henry Ford, pg. 8 **IT**
Briggs & Stratton Mexico S.A. de C.V., Boulevard Manuel Avila Comache No. 29, pg. 252 **IT**
Chromalox, S.A., c/o A. B. Chance de Mexico, S.A. de C.V., pg. 576 **PB**
DeVilbiss Ransburg Mexico, Via Dr. Gustavo Baz 3990, pg. 868 **PB**
Dixon Ticonderoga Company de Mexico, S.A. de C.V., Apartado Postal M-9531, pg. 515 **PB**
Empresa Tecnologica Ericsson S.A. de C.V., Via Gustavo Baz Prada, No. 2160, pg. 1366 **IT**
Ensueno-Tyco (Mexico) S.A. de C.V., Munecas Y Jugetes Ensueno S.A., pg. 1059 **PB**
Envases Multipac S.A. De C.V., Emilio Cardenas 166, pg. 868 **IT**
Fabrica de Botes Casari, Juan Fernandez Albarran No. 30, pg. 66 **IT**
Filtros Mann S.A. de C.V., Apartado Postal No. 465, pg. 484 **IT**
Flakt, S.A. de C.V., Via Gustavo Baz 166, Col. San Jeronimo Tepetlacalco, pg. 5 **IT**
Gates Rubber de Mexico, Cerrada de Galeana No. 5, pg. 1397 **PB**
Gemisa S.A. de C.V., Via Ejercito del Trabajo 14, Col. La Blanca, pg. 614 **IT**
Grupo Carpenter S.A. de C.V., Av. Lic. Juan Fernandez Albarran No. 31, pg. 308 **PB**
Hoesch Suspensiones Automotrices S.A. de C.V., Calle Marconi No. 9, pg. 508 **IT**
Ilco Unican Mexico S.A. de C.V., Calle 8 de Boulevard, Queretare #5, pg. 1432 **IT**
INDUSTRIAS CH, S.A. DE C.V., Agustin Melgar No. 23, Frac. Industrial Ninos Heroes, pg. 677 **IT**
International Flavors & Fragrances (Mexico) S.A. de C.V., San Nicholas No. 5, pg. 899 **PB**
Kolmar de Mexico, S.A., Apartado Postal 553, Calle Lateral No. 20, pg. 239 **IT**
Moore Business Forms de Mexico S.A. de C.V., Cerrada de Galeana No. 26, pg. 889 **IT**
Pardue via IPM, Via Gustavo Baz Prada 2160, pg. 1369 **IT**
Parker Seal de Mexico SA, Rio Lerma 221, pg. 1262 **PB**
Securitas ISM, Via Gustavo Baz Prada 2160, pg. 1369 **IT**
Siegling Mexico S.A. de C.V., pg. 498 **IT**
Sunbeam Mexicana S.A. de C.V., A.V. Dr. Gustavo Baz, pg. 1533 **IT**
Telecomponentes Ericsson S.A. de C.V., Calle Fulton S/N, Fraccionamiento La Loma, pg. 1370 **IT**
Temple y Forja Fortuna S.A. de C.V., Prolongacion Fulton No.2, Col. LaLonne, pg. 308 **IT**
Timken de Mexico S.A. de C.V., J. Fdz. Albarran 38, pg. 1617 **PB**
Xomox S.A. de C.V., Apartado Postal 113Y319, Camino Real A Santa Monica 238, pg. 578 **PB**

Tlaquepaque

IBM de Mexico, S.A., Carr. a El Castillo Km. 2, Apartado Postal 172, pg. 897 **PB**

Toluca

Comercializadora La Moderna de Toluca, S.A. de C.V., Leandro Valle No 404-201, Col. Reforma y FFCC. Nales, pg. 1346 **IT**
Compania Nacional de Harinas, S.A. de C.V., Boulevard Isidro Fabela #1000, pg. 1346 **IT**
Corporativo Tablex, S.A. de C.V., Leandro Valle No 404-317, pg. 1346 **IT**
Eaton Ejes, S.A. de C.V., A. Einstein e Industrias Quimicas, pg. 558 **PB**
Eaton Manufacturera, S.A. de C.V., A. Einstein e Industrias, Quimicas, pg. 559 **PB**
Fabrica de Galletas La Moderna, S.A. de C.V., Vialidad Naucalpan #110, pg. 1346 **IT**
Fabrica de Pastas Alimenticias La Moderna, S.A. de C.V., Leandro Valle N# 404, Col. Reforma y FFCC. Nales., pg. 1346 **IT**
Grupo Celanese, Av. Hidalgo Oriente 1350, pg. 625 **IT**
Impulsora de Bienes Inmuebles de Toluca, S.A. de C.V., Leandro Valle No 404-317, Col. Reforma y FFCC Nales, pg. 1346 **IT**
Inemex S.A. de C.V., A. Einstein e Industrias, pg. 559 **PB**
Oneida Mexicana, S.A., pg. 1226 **PB**
Parker Fluid Connectors de Mexico, Av. San Antonio No. 102, Parque Ind. San Antonio Buena Vista, pg. 1261 **PB**

TABLEX, S.A. DE C.V., Leandro Valle No 404, Col. Reforma y FFCC. Nales., pg. 1346 **IT**
Tonermex S.A. de C.V., Parque Ind. Exportec, Manzana, pg. 1116 **IT**

Torreon

Hewlett-Packard de Mexico, S.A. de C.V., Blvd. Independencia No. 2000, pg. 819 **PB**

Tultitlan

BASF Pinturas S.A. de C.V., Avenida No. 9, Parque Industrial Cartagena, pg. 107 **IT**
Bundy Mexico SA, Via Jose Lopex Portillo No. 8-A, pg. 1342 **IT**
Consorcio Industrial Packsa, S.A. de C.V., pg. 1146 **IT**
Dynacast de Mexico, S.A. de C.V., Via Jose Lopez Portillo #8, pg. 300 **IT**
Hylsa Bekaert, Autopista Mexico-Queretaro Km. 32.5, pg. 56 **IT**
Hylsa DAD, Km. 32.5 Autopista Mexico-Queretaro, pg. 185 **IT**
Osram de Mexico S.A. de C.V., Camino a Tepalxaga No. 8, pg. 1244 **IT**
Rassini S.A. de C.V., Avenida Via Jose Lopez Portillo 1, pg. 332 **IT**
Total Mexicana, Carretera Tlainepantla Cuautitlan 1100, pg. 1651 **PB**

Uruapan

Industrial Papelera Mexicana S.A. de C.V., Carretera Uruapan-Taretan Km 3.5, pg. 330 **IT**

Veracruz

Federal-Mogul Services, Domicilio Conocido, pg. 778 **IT**
GRUPO COMERCIAL CHEDRAUI S.A. DE C.V., Privada de Antonio Chedraui s/n, pg. 573 **IT**
Tiendas Chedraui S.A. de C.V., Privada de Antonio Chedraui s/n, pg. 573 **IT**
Turbina Solar S.A. de C.V., Apartado Postal 218, pg. 316 **PB**

Veronica Anzures

Raychem Technologias, Melchor Ocampo 193-A-13, 11300, pg. 1363 **IT**

Villagran

Campbell's de Mexico, S.A. de C.V., Km. 292 Carr Mexico CD Juarez, pg. 299 **PB**
Opisec, S.A. de C.V., Km. 282.4 Carr. Panamericana, pg. 1346 **IT**

Villahermosa

Guardian Inspection, S.A.C.V., 151 Rosendo Taracena, pg. 1231 **IT**
Herramientas Varco S.A.C.V., Av. Del Hierro No. 20, pg. 1709 **PB**
Petrolite de Mexico S.A. de C.V., Mercurio 126, Fracc. Galaxia, pg. 166 **IT**
Smith Internacional, S.A. de C.V., Paseo de Las Flores, #255 C.P. 86010, pg. 1478 **PB**

Xochimilco

Seguros Azteca, S.A., Av. 20 de Noviembre 700, pg. 363 **IT**

Zapopan

Andrew Corporation (Mexico) S.A. de C.V., Chimalhuacan No. 3569, Terces Piso, Int. 4, pg. 113 **PB**
Electronica Pantera, S.A. de C.V., Montemorelos No. 121, pg. 919 **IT**
La Moderna de Occidente, S.A. de C.V., Km. 3 Carr. A Nogales, pg. 1346 **IT**
Ryerson de Mexico/West Division, Av. Soleras No. 130, pg. 66 **IT**

Zaragoza

Fleetguard Mexico S.A. de C.V., Circuito Gustavo Baz 2, pg. 469 **PB**
Toshiba Electromex, S.A. de C.V., Ave. Rio Bravo 1540, pg. 1406 **IT**

MICRONESIA

Saipan

S.C. Corporation of Micronesia, Ltd., P.O. Box 529, pg. 1233 **IT**
S.C. Properties (Saipan), Inc., P.O. Box 529, pg. 1233 **IT**

MONACO

Fontvieille

Schindler Monaco, pg. 1205 **IT**

Monaco

ALPHA OMIKRON LIMITED, Ermanno Palace, 27 Boulevard Albert Premiere, pg. 65 **IT**
Banque Internationale de Credit et de Gestion Monaco, 27, Bd. Princesse Charlotte, pg. 180 **IT**
Chiltem Group SAM, Ermanno Palace, 27 Boulevard Albert Premiere, pg. 65 **IT**
Credit Foncier de Monaco, 11, boulevard Albert-Ier, pg. 314 **IT**
Eaton s.a.m-Controls Div.-Europe, 14, Avenue Prince Hereditaire Albert, pg. 559 **PB**
Lancaster S.A.M., Stadte De Fontvielle, pg. 186 **IT**
Loews Monte Carlo, B.P. 179, Ave. De Spelvges, pg. 1011 **PB**
Louis Vuitton Monaco SA, 6, avenue des Beaux-Arts, pg. 782 **IT**
Rust Craft International, S.A., 12, Quai Antonine 1, pg. 78 **PB**
Sodexho Monaco, 5, rue Gabian, pg. 1275 **IT**
TBG MANAGEMENT S.A.M., 29 Blvd. Francaise Princess Charlotte, pg. 1335 **IT**

Monte Carlo

Ansaldo International Services, 13 blvd. Princesse Charlotte, pg. 654 **IT**
BNL Services S.A.M., 7 Rue du Gabian 98000, pg. 137 **IT**
Bulkitalia Overseas N.V., 7, Rue du Gabian, pg. 304 **IT**
CCF (Monaco) S.A.M., 2 bis, boulevard des Moulins, pg. 342 **IT**
CGRM, Immeuble le Montaigne, 6, Blvd. des Moulins, pg. 19 **IT**
Christie's Monaco S.A.M., Park Place, pg. 290 **IT**
Coeclerici Holding Overseas N.V., 7, Blvd. des Moulins, pg. 304 **IT**
Italimpianti Intl.-Monaco, 20 Blvd. de Suisse, Bloc C, pg. 655 **IT**
Societe de Banque Suisse (Monaco), 2, av. de Grande-Bretagne, pg. 1331 **IT**
Somocar Overseas N.V., 7, Blvd. des Moulins, pg. 304 **IT**
Union de Banques Suisses, 20, Boulevard de Suisse, pg. 1441 **IT**

MOROCCO

Agadir

Ciments Dunaroc, Route d'Essaouira, pg. 292 **IT**

Casablanca

Adecco Industry, 125, BD Zerkyouni, pg. 24 **IT**
Al Watania, 83, Ave. de L'Armee Royale, pg. 564 **IT**
Algemene Bank Marokko S.A., Tour des Habous 11, 5th Fl., pg. 11 **IT**
American Appraisal Maroc, Boulevard Mouley Yussef, 2, pg. 252 **IT**
Attijari Credit, Boulevard Mouley Yussef, 2, pg. 252 **IT**
BASF Maroc S.A., 7, rue des Orchidees, pg. 106 **IT**
BDF Maroc S.A., pg. 183 **IT**
BMCI Morocco, 26 place Mohammed V, pg. 163 **IT**
Bayer Maroc S.A., pg. 175 **IT**
Bull Maroc, 644 Blvd. Mohamed V, pg. 315 **IT**
CPC Maghreb S.A., Lotissement Fadioullah No. 3, 9 Rte. d'El Sadida, pg. 225 **PB**
Cabelec, Bouskoura, pg. 785 **IT**
Carlor Maroc, 118 allee du Phoenix, pg. 1030 **IT**
Casa Madrid Developpement, Boulevard Mouley Yussef, 2, pg. 252 **IT**
CIBA-GEIGY Maroc SA, 82, Bd Chefchaouni, pg. 978 **IT**
CIBA-GEIGY Pharma Maroc SA, pg. 978 **IT**
Cimenterie Nouvelle de Casablanca-CINOUCA, 239, bld Moulay-Ismail, pg. 790 **IT**
Cinemapresse Agence Conseil en Communication, 93 bd Massira Khadra, pg. 1198 **PV**
Colgate-Palmolive, 11 Ave. de L'Armee Royal, pg. 398 **IT**
Crown Cork Company (Morocco) S.A., Boite Postale 13998, pg. 464 **PB**
Danzas Maroc SA, 18, rue Chaoula, pg. 382 **IT**
ETCD, 95-97, bd de la Gare, pg. 823 **IT**
Fonciere Casamadrid, Boulevard Mouley Yussef 2, pg. 252 **IT**
Framlington Asset Management Maghreb, 28, Avenur des Far, pg. 343 **IT**
General Tire & Rubber Co. of Morocco, Boite Postale 2608, pg. 327 **IT**
Goodyear Maroc S.A., Autoroute Casablanca-Rabat, pg. 753 **PB**
Henkel Maroc S.A., pg. 613 **IT**
Henkomar S.A., pg. 613 **IT**
Honeywell Bull Maroc S.A., 644, Boulevard Mohamed-V, pg. 318 **IT**
Italstrade-Morocco, 63 Blvd. d'Anfia, pg. 655 **IT**
Johnson & Johnson Morocco S.A., Boite Postale 15979, pg. 931 **PB**
Klem EURO RSCG, 25 Bd Mohamed Abdouh, pg. 603 **IT**
La Garantie Generale Marocaine (G.G.M.), 106, Rue Abderrahman Sehraoui, pg. 1531 **IT**
Laboratoires Nicholas (Maroc) S.A., pg. 1121 **IT**
Laboratoires Pfizer S.A., 280, Blvd. Yacoub El Mansour, pg. 1283 **PB**
L'Alliance Africaine, 63, Boulevard Moulay Youssef, pg. 565 **IT**
Le Soleil S.A., 45, Rue Doumit, ex St. Loubes, pg. 613 **IT**
Makro Morocco S.A., Route secondaire 1029, pg. 1155 **IT**
SA Marocaine des Peintures Astral Celluco (SAMPAC), 13 Ruede Provinson, pg. 43 **IT**

PB - *U.S. Public Companies Volume*
PV - *U.S. Private Companies Volume*
IT - *International Public & Private Companies Volume*

Merck Sharp & Dohme Intl., Immeuble Oceania,
 pg. 1092 **PB**
Microsoft Maroc S.A.R.L., pg. 1108 **PB**
Mitsui & Co., Ltd., Tour Habous 16eme etage, avenue des
 F.A., pg. 881 **IT**
Nokia Telecommunications, Complexe des Habous, Tour C,
 Avenue des F.A.R., pg. 953 **IT**
Novo Nordisk Maroc, 2 Rue Souktani, Residence Bellevue,
 4eme Etage, pg. 988 **IT**
Outokumpu Espana, S.A., Inmeuble Grey D'Albion,
 pg. 1015 **IT**
Produits Roche S.A., pg. 1121 **IT**
Repsol Quimica, 131 Blvd., D'Anfa 13 eme etage,
 pg. 1105 **IT**
Rhone-Poulenc Maroc, 92, boulevard de la Resistance,
 pg. 1113 **IT**
Sacem, 5, Avenue de l'Armee Royale, pg. 662 **IT**
SAGA Communications, 6 Rue de la Fraternite,
 pg. 305 **PV**
Sandoz-Maroc S.A., pg. 985 **IT**
Sciom S.A., pg. 614 **IT**
Seprob, 7, rue Mohamed-Diouri, pg. 207 **IT**
Serinfor, 31, Bd Claude Perrault, pg. 823 **PB**
Sherazade Conseil, 6 rue Al Araar, pg. 118 **IT**
Sicotel, Complexe des Habous, Tour C, Avenue des Far,
 pg. 823 **PB**
Societe Marocaine de Depot et de Credit, 79, Ave. Hassan-
 II, pg. 321 **IT**
Societe Marocaine de Montage et d'entretien des
 Ascenseurs "MOENA" S.A., Rue de Province-Angel,
 Boulevard Emile Zola, pg. 1370 **IT**
Societe Marocaine des Ascenseurs Schindler S.A.,
 pg. 1205 **IT**
Societe Shell du Maroc, 36 Rue d'Azilal, pg. 1137 **IT**
Sodipi(t), 242-246 Boulevard Emile Zola, pg. 1155 **IT**
Wafabank, 1, avenue Hassan II, pg. 314 **PB**
Wafabank Casablanca, 163, avenue Hassan II, pg. 314 **IT**
Zeneca Agrochemicals Maroc S.A., Route 110, Bd Aicha
 Bent, Haimond, pg. 1526 **IT**

El Jadida

Nestle Maroc S.A., pg. 921 **IT**

Larache

Lukcor, S.A., BP 13 Zone Portuaire, pg. 1067 **PB**

Maghreb

Citibank-Maghreb, pg. 378 **PB**

Meknes

Ciments Artificiels de Meknes-CADEM, KM8 route de Fez,
 pg. 790 **IT**

Mohammedia

Afrisports SA, pg. 25 **IT**
Manufacture Marocaine d'Aluminium, Rue Fatima Zhara,
 pg. 1031 **IT**

Rabat

Compagnie Africaine de Geophysique, 88 Zankat Oued Ziz,
 pg. 241 **IT**
Enso (Morocco), Care of Embassy of Finland, 6, rue
 Demnate, pg. 457 **IT**
Les Ciments de l'Oriental (CIOR), 22, Rue Jabal Ayachi -
 Agdal, pg. 629 **IT**
Societe Nationale de Telecommunications, 43, Zankat Al
 Mansour Addahbi, pg. 1370 **IT**
Telefonaktiebolaget LM Ericsson Delagation Technique du
 Projet au Maroc, 24 Charia Fransa, pg. 1370 **IT**
Telefonaktiebolaget LM Ericsson Morocco, Delegation
 Technique du Projet, au Maroc, 24 Charia Fransa,
 pg. 1370 **IT**
Wackenhut Morocco, Inc., Ex. Villa Bouabid, Lot 3, Bir
 Kacem, pg. 1731 **PB**

Tangiers

Cementos Tanger, 17 rue El Jabha El Ouatania,
 pg. 791 **IT**

Tetouan

Cementos Marroquies, pg. 790 **IT**

MOZAMBIQUE

Maputo

Banco Standard Totta de Mocambique, SARL, Box 2086,
 Praca 25 de Junho No. 1, pg. 1296 **IT**
Banco Totta & Acores, Praca 25 de Junho, 1C,
 pg. 145 **IT**
Bonifica-Mozambique, Avenida Kim Il Sung, pg. 655 **IT**
Brithol Michcoma Mocambique Limitada, Av. Mao Tse Tung
 346, pg. 107 **IT**
CIBA-GEIGY Trading and Marketing Services Co Ltd,
 pg. 980 **IT**
Companhia Exportadora de Melacos Ltda., pg. 1357 **IT**
Det Norske Veritas, Embaixada Real da Noruega,
 pg. 397 **IT**

Mitsui & Co., Ltd.- Maputo Liason Representative, Avenue
 Romao Fernandes Farinha, pg. 882 **IT**
Shell Chemical Mozambique (Pty.) Ltd., Av Martires
 Inhaminga 170-5, pg. 1136 **IT**
Societa Ital. per Condotte D'Acqua-Mozambique, Ave.
 Kenneth Kaunda 524, pg. 655 **IT**
The Standard Bank of South Africa Limited Representative
 Office, Praca 25 de Jullo N 01, 7 andar, n 713,
 pg. 1294 **IT**
World Bank, Ave. Kenneth Kaunda, 1224, pg. 1189 **PV**

MYANMAR

Rangoon

Mitsui & Co., Ltd., Natl. Insurance Bldg., No. 654/666,
 Merchant St., pg. 881 **IT**
Myanma Shell B.V., No. 57, 6 1/2 Miles, pg. 1140 **IT**

Yangon

BFCE Myanmar, 42, Pyidaungsu Yeiktha Rd., pg. 161 **IT**
Myanmar Daewoo International Ltd., No. 22, Yawmingyi
 Rd., pg. 358 **IT**
NKK Corporation-Yangon, 2nd Floor, Red Cross Building,
 42 Strand Road, pg. 903 **IT**
POSCO Yangon Office, 32 A, 6 1/2 Mile, Pyay Road,
 pg. 1062 **IT**
The Sakura Bank - Yangon Representative Office, Room
 No. 605, FMI Centre, No. 380 Bogyoke Aung San St.,
 pg. 1180 **IT**
The Sumitomo Bank, Ltd.-Yangon Representative Office,
 Room No. 603-604, 6th Fl., FMI Centre, 380 Bogyoke
 Aung San Street, pg. 1310 **IT**

NAMIBIA

Arandis

Hospitality, 707 Parrot Street, pg. 1274 **IT**

Steinhausen

Landis & Staefa Schweiz AG, Sennweidstrasse 47,
 pg. 801 **IT**

Windhoek

Allianz Insurance of Namibia Ltd., 4th Floor, Sanlam
 Centre, Independence Avenue, pg. 59 **IT**
The Commercial Bank of Namibia Limited, 12-20 Bulow
 Street, pg. 149 **IT**
First National Bank of Nambia LTD., First National Bank
 Bldg 2nd, Cnr Post Stree & Independence Avenue,
 pg. 487 **IT**
Norsk Hydro Namibia a.s., Sanlam Ctr., 10th Fl.,
 Independence Ave., pg. 964 **IT**
Rossing Uranium, Saniam Centre, 12th Fl., 154
 Independence Avenue, pg. 1115 **PB**
Rossing Uranium Ltd., 12th Floor, Sanlam Centre,
 Independence Avenue, pg. 1119 **IT**
Schindler Lifts (Namibia) (PTY) Ltd., pg. 1205 **IT**
Schindler Lifts (PTY) Ltd., pg. 1205 **IT**
Shell Namibia Ltd., 119 Independence Ave., pg. 1137 **IT**
Sonnex Investments (Pty) Ltd, pg. 167 **IT**
Stanbic Bank Namibia Limited, Mutual Platz, Post Street
 Mall, pg. 1293 **IT**

NEPAL

Kathmandu

M/s. Amaravati International, c/o Soaltee Hotel Limited,
 pg. 109 **IT**
Mitsui & Co., Ltd., Himalayan Height, Tahachal, Cosy
 Cottage, pg. 882 **IT**
Nepal Grindlays Bank Limited, Kantipath, pg. 100 **IT**
Nepal Resident Mission, Srikunj Kamaladi Ward No. 31,
 Block 2/597 ka.Na.Pa., pg. 89 **IT**
Standard Chartered Bank (Nepal), pg. 1295 **IT**
The World Bank, Lal Dubar, Yak & Yeti Hotel,
 pg. 1189 **PV**

NETHERLANDS

s Gravendeel

Wedco Holland B.V., Mijlweg 7, P.O. Box 5187,
 pg. 854 **PB**

s Gravenhage

AMS Management Systems Netherlands B.V.,
 Koninginnegracht 14J, pg. 87 **PB**
AXA Equity & Law Levensverzekeringen NV, Korte
 Voorhout 20, pg. 19 **IT**
Elf Petroland, Mariahoeveplein 6, pg. 446 **IT**
Gekru B.V., pg. 540 **IT**
HVR/BMZ La Haye, Alexanderstraat 4, pg. 470 **IT**
IRIBV-International Refractory Investment B.V., 27,
 Konninginnegracht, pg. 791 **IT**

s Hertogenbosch

AMP-Holland B.V., Rietveldenweg 32, pg. 8 **PB**
Acer Computer B.V., Europalaan 89, pg. 22 **IT**
Adecco Personnelsdiensten B.V., Hambakenwetering 1,
 pg. 24 **IT**
Brabant Pers bv, Emmaplein 25, pg. 1445 **IT**
Crosland Filters BV, Ketelaarskampweg 17, pg. 786 **IT**
Dynadro bv, Sluisweg 200, pg. 681 **IT**
ENCI N.V., Sint Teunislaan 1, pg. 605 **IT**
Interpharm bv, 151, Parallelweg, pg. 681 **IT**
Interpharm Groep B.V., 151, Parallelweg, pg. 682 **IT**
Koudijs-Wouda Voeders B.V., Tramkade 24, pg. 555 **IT**
Krups B.V., Ketelaarskampweg 9, pg. 896 **IT**
L.C.G. Malmberg BV, Leeghwaterlaan 16, pg. 1445 **IT**
MEBIN B.V., Saint Teunislaan 1, pg. 605 **IT**
Medica bv, 1, Lederstraat, pg. 1063 **PB**
NRG Benelux B.V., Utopialaan 25, pg. 1116 **IT**
Nellcor Puritan Bennett Europe B.V., Hambakenwetering 1,
 pg. 1040 **PB**
OCE Nederlandse Verkoopmaatschappij B.V., Brabantlaan
 2, pg. 994 **IT**
Olicom Benelux, Bolduc Office Centre, Utopialaan 35-N,
 pg. 1001 **IT**
Possehl Electronic Nederland bv, pg. 1064 **IT**
Robinson Nugent, Inc., Pettelaarpark 24, pg. 1395 **PB**
Schleicher & Schuell Nederland BV, pg. 1206 **IT**
Skala Home Electronics, pg. 1386 **IT**
F van Lanschot Bankiers NV, Hooge Steenweg 29,
 pg. 911 **IT**
Wander (Nederland) B.V., pg. 986 **IT**

Aalsmeer

Florigene BV, Legmeerdijk 313, pg. 982 **IT**
Perry Sport, Onsteinderweg 247 B, pg. 1462 **IT**

Aalten

Koomaf-Aalten B.V., pg. 222 **IT**
Sonoco Nederland B.V., Damstraat 25, 7121 AW Aalten,
 pg. 1487 **PB**

Aason

SOBEL NV, P.O. Box #9, pg. 1272 **IT**

Alkmaar

Benckiser B.V., pg. 185 **IT**
General Cosmetics B.V., pg. 186 **IT**
Kentucky Fried Chicken Netherlands B.V., 69 Gedempte
 Neluwe Sloot, pg. 1637 **PB**
Ravo International, Otterkoog 1, pg. 617 **PB**
Recycling Maatschappij Feniks B.V., Bergerweg 150,
 pg. 134 **IT**
S.I. Nederland, B.V., Hermelynkoog 2-4, pg. 1478 **PB**

Almelo

Cirex BV, Bornsestraat 365, pg. 753 **IT**
Fusite, B.V., pg. 577 **PB**
Polypenco B.V., Anthony Fokkerweg 2, pg. 354 **IT**
Texas Instruments Holland BV, Kolthofsingel 8,
 pg. 1586 **PB**

Almen

Novoferm Nederland B.V., Scheggertdijk 54, pg. 509 **IT**

Almere

Al-Techniek Benelux B.V., De Steiger 24, pg. 710 **IT**
Babyhallen B.V., pg. 750 **IT**
Ballast Nedam Bouwmaterieel B.V., Damsluisweg 61,
 pg. 133 **IT**
Beiersdorf NV, pg. 183 **IT**
C-Cor Europe, B.V., pg. 272 **PB**
Cascade Europe, P.O. Box 50086, pg. 311 **PB**
Cinevideo Enterprises BV, pg. 720 **IT**
Johnson & Johnson GABA B.V., Postbus 1039,
 pg. 930 **PB**
MHI Equipment Europe B.V. (MEE), Damsluisweg 2,
 pg. 874 **IT**
Mailprofs Uitzendbureaux BV, pg. 720 **IT**
Mitsubishi Caterpillar Forklift Europe B.V., Hefbrugweg 77,
 pg. 316 **PB**
NewsEdge Corp., Randstad 21-09, pg. 1180 **IT**
Pont Packaging B.V., pg. 1345 **IT**
Prenatal B.V., pg. 750 **IT**
Radio Holland Electronics, Microfoonstraat 5, pg. 1151 **IT**
Synres-Almoco B.V., Zekkenstraat 23-29, pg. 354 **IT**
Teleprofs BV, pg. 720 **IT**
Vedior, Marktgracht 48-62, pg. 1463 **IT**
Vedior Compuhelp, pg. 1463 **IT**
Vedior International, De Paal 1-6, pg. 1463 **IT**

Alphen aan den Rijn

Alpha Muurverffabrieken BV, 15 Van Foreestlaan,
 pg. 43 **IT**
Componenta International B.V., Produktieweg 5,
 pg. 1421 **IT**
Munters BV, pg. 669 **IT**
Munters Droogtechniek BV, Energieweg 69, pg. 669 **IT**
Munters Nederland BV, pg. 669 **IT**
Novo Nordisk Farma B.V., Flemingweg 18, pg. 988 **IT**

Robot Pompen B.V., Produktieweg 5, pg. 1421 — IT
Svedala Robot, pg. 1325 — IT

Amerongen

H.B. Fuller Netherlands B.V., pg. 687 — PB

Amersfoort

AST Computer Netherlands BV, Computerweg 12e, pg. 1182 — IT
Akzo Chemicals B.V., 48 Stationsstraat, pg. 42 — IT
Akzo Chemie Nederland bv, 48, Stationsstraat, P.O. Box 247, pg. 46 — IT
Albank B.V., Stadsring 65, pg. 9 — IT
Cordis, a Johnson & Johnson Company Europa N.V., pg. 928 — PB
Delamine B.V., Barchman Wuytierslaan 10, pg. 1408 — IT
Greenock Engineering BV, pg. 756 — IT
Hapam-Goldbach b.v., 3, Neonweg, pg. 681 — IT
High Voltage Engineering B.V., Amsterdamseweg 61, pg. 528 — PV
ISS Servisystem B.V., Drentsestraat 4, pg. 657 — IT
Johnson & Johnson Medical N.V., Postbus 188, pg. 931 — PB
Liebherr-Nederland B.V., Beeldschermweg 2, pg. 809 — IT
Morton International B.V., Kleine Koppel 31, P.O. Box 32, pg. 1135 — IT
Nettenbouw B.V., Amersfoort, 11, Hardwareweg, pg. 681 — IT
NORIT N.V., P.O. Box 105, pg. 958 — IT
Procter & Gamble Health & Beauty Care Scandinavia, P.O. Box 255, Vanadiumweg 16, pg. 1332 — PB
Service Centrale voor Koeltechniek B.V., 22, Argonweg, pg. 681 — IT
Sun Microsystems Nederland, B.V., Computerweg 1, pg. 1532 — PB
3M/ECC Europa BV, pg. 209 — IT
Turnkiek Holding B.V., Henri Dunantstrowt 38, pg. 682 — IT
Warner-Jenkinson Netherlands, Kleine Koppel 39-40, pg. 1696 — PB

Ammerzoden

Alabastine Holland BV (Manufacturing), Industrieterrein 1, pg. 1501 — IT

Amstelveen

Admedia bv, Startbaan 8, pg. 1445 — IT
Algemene Levensherverzekering Maatschaapij nv, Burgemeester Rijnderslaan 28, pg. 1333 — IT
Ballast Nedam Beton en Waterbouw B.V., Laan van Kronenburg 2, pg. 133 — IT
Ballast Nedam Engineering B.V., Laan van Kronenburg 2, pg. 133 — IT
Ballast Nedam Equipment Services B.V., Laan van Kronenburg 2, pg. 133 — IT
Ballast Nedam Grond en Wegen B.V., Laan van Kronenburg 2, pg. 133 — IT
Ballast Nedam Grond en Wegen Projecten B.V., Laan v. Kronenburg 2, pg. 133 — IT
Ballast Nedam IGB B.V., Laan van Kronenburg 2, pg. 133 — IT
Ballast Nedam Industriebouw B.V., Laan van Kronenburg 2, pg. 133 — IT
Ballast Nedam International B.V., Laan van Kronenburg 2, pg. 133 — IT
Ballast Nedam Milieutechniek B.V., Laan van Kronenburg 2, pg. 134 — IT
BALLAST NEDAM NV, Laan Van Kronenburg 2, pg. 133 — IT
Ballast Nedam Services B.V., Laan van Kronenburg 2, pg. 134 — IT
Ballast Nedam Telecom Infrastructures, Laan van Kronenburg 2, pg. 133 — IT
Beecham Research Laboratories, Sportlaan 198, pg. 1265 — IT
Bencard, Sportlaan 198, pg. 1265 — IT
Benjamens, Van Doorn EURO RSCG, Burg A Colijnweg 2, pg. 602 — IT
BolsWessanen International BV, pg. 751 — IT
BolsWessanen Nederland BV, pg. 751 — IT
BolsWessanen Transatlantic Holdings BV, pg. 751 — IT
Borland International B.V., Van Heuven Goedhartlaan 935, pg. 246 — PB
Brother International (Nederland) B.V., P.O. Box 600, pg. 229 — IT
Canon Europa N.V., Bovenkerkerweg 59-61, pg. 262 — IT
Food Products Management BV, pg. 751 — IT
Hewlett-Packard Nederland B.V., Country Response Center, Van der Hooplaan 241, pg. 821 — PB
Hewlett-Packard Nederland B.V., Startbaan 16, pg. 821 — PB
Hoogovens Aluminium BV, Uilenstede 475, pg. 753 — IT
Hoogovens Technische Dienstverlening BV, Uilenstede 475, pg. 754 — IT
Huhtamaki Finance B.V., Burgemeester Rijnderslaan 26, pg. 639 — IT
Infonet Nederland BV, pg. 720 — IT
KLM ROYAL DUTCH AIRLINES, 55 Amsterdamseweg, pg. 719 — IT
KONINKLIJKE BOLSWESSANEN NV, Prof. E.M. Meijersiaan 2, pg. 750 — IT
NSK-RHP Nederland B.V., Bouvwerij 81, pg. 904 — IT
Newport Electronics B.V., Postbus 8034, pg. 816 — PV
Raychem (Nederland) BV, Benelux Bldg., Van Heuven Goedhartlaan 121, pg. 1362 — PB
Reassurantie Maatschappij Nederland nv, Burgemeester Rijnderslaan 28, pg. 1333 — IT

Rhone-Poulenc Nederland B.V., Bovenkerkerweg 6-8, pg. 1113 — IT
Ricoh Europe B.V., Groenelaan 3, pg. 1116 — IT
ROYAL PACKAGING INDUSTRIES VAN LEER B.V., Amsterdamseweg 206, pg. 1145 — IT
SmithKline Beecham Consumer Brands BV, Sportlaan 198; Postbus 394, pg. 1266 — IT
TBWA/H NETH-work, Dr. Willem Dreesweg 2, pg. 589 — PB
Tenneco Automotive Europe, Inc., Prof. J. H. Bavincklaan 5, pg. 1580 — PB
Tenneco Nederland B.V., Prof. J. H. Bavincklaans 5, pg. 1580 — PB
Unisource Satellite Services BV, pg. 721 — IT
VNU Tijdschriftengroep Nederland Bv, Startbaan 8, pg. 1445 — IT
Van Leer Services B.V., pg. 1146 — IT
Wella Netherlands N.V. van Ravensberg, pg. 1490 — IT

Amsterdam

A-Partners, Willem de Zwijgerlaan 17-19, pg. 1463 — IT
ABN-AMRO HOLDING N.V., Foppingadreef 22, pg. 8 — IT
ABN Auto Lease B.V., 32 Vijzelstrast, pg. 9 — IT
ABN (Head Office), Vijzelstraat 32, pg. 11 — IT
ABN Trustcompany (Nederland) B.V., Nieuwe Weteringstraat 38, pg. 9 — IT
AGA Gas B.V., P.O. Box 37601, pg. 13 — IT
AGIP International B.V., Strawinskylaan 845, pg. 429 — IT
AGIP Petroli International B.V., Strawinskylaan 1041, pg. 429 — IT
A.S.I. (Computer Training) Netherlands B.V., c/o Applied Learning Int., Hettenheuvelweg 41, pg. 784 — PB
Addison-Wesley Publishers B.V., DeLairessestraat 90, pg. 1027 — IT
Aer Lingus, Heiligeweg 14, pg. 28 — IT
Air Malta - Amsterdam, Singel 540, pg. 37 — IT
Alcan Finances B.V., Museumplein 11, pg. 51 — IT
Alcatel A.V., World Trade Center, Strawinskylaan 341, pg. 55 — IT
Alfa-Laval N.V., Postbus 341, pg. 1380 — IT
Algemene Bank Nederland N.V., Vijzelstraat 32, pg. 9 — IT
Algemene Lease Maatschappij B.V., Keizersgracht 560-562, pg. 9 — IT
Algemene Participatiemaatschappij B.V., Vijzelsracht 50, pg. 9 — IT
Allianz Nederland N.V. (Stock Exchange Office), Assurantie Beurs, pg. 60 — IT
Amerford Intl. Nederland B.V., Vrachstation Km 511 Schiphol-C, pg. 1388 — IT
American Express Service Europe Ltd., 166 Amstecdijk, pg. 74 — PB
Amro Effectenbewaarbedrijf N.V., Foppingadreef 20-22, 1102 BS, pg. 9 — IT
Amstel Lease N.V., Foppingadreef 20-22, pg. 9 — IT
Amsterdam Depositary Co. N.V., Spuistraat 127, pg. 9 — IT
Amsterdam-Rotterdam Bank N.V., Foppingadreef 20-22, pg. 9 — IT
Anamet Europe BV-Amsterdam, Transformatorweg 30, pg. 70 — PV
ANSALDO SIGNAL N.V., Strawinskylaan 3051, pg. 77 — IT
Apollo Hotel B.V., Apollaan 2, pg. 556 — IT
Asahi Bank (Nederland) N.V., Strawinskylaan 3029, pg. 83 — IT
Asahi Glass Europe B.V., World Trade Center, Strawinskylaan 1525, pg. 85 — IT
Asahi Trust (Nederland) B.V., Strawinskylaan 3029, pg. 83 — IT
Atlantic West B.V., World Trade Center, Tower B, 17th Fl., Strawinskylaan 1725, pg. 203 — PB
AUDI Finance N.V., pg. 203 — IT
AudioSonic, Tijnmuiden 15-19, pg. 1463 — IT
Aurum France BV, Hoekenrode 6, pg. 1269 — PB
Automatiseringcentrum Ideta B.V., Frankemaheerd 6, pg. 750 — IT
Avesta Sheffield B.V., pg. 221 — IT
BAC Financial B.V., c/o Caron & Stevens, Hirsch Gebouw, Leidseplein 29, pg. 203 — PB
BHF-Bank Representative Office, Haaksbergweg 27, pg. 120 — IT
BHF Finance (Netherlands) B.V., Atlas Complex, pg. 119 — IT
BNP Bank N.V., Herengracht 477, pg. 163 — IT
BancTec Benelux B.V., Buikslotermeerplein 418 NL-1025 WP, pg. 177 — PB
Bank Mendes Gans NV, Herengracht 619, pg. 647 — IT
Bank of America NT&SA, Herengracht 469, pg. 182 — PB
The Bank of Tokyo-Mitsubishi (Holland) N.V., Keizersgracht 603, pg. 158 — IT
Banque de Suez Nederland NV, Herengracht 320/324, pg. 314 — IT
Banque Paribas Nederland N.V., Herengracht 539-543, pg. 320 — IT
Barclays Bank PLC, pg. 166 — IT
Bavarian Finance Company B.V., pg. 180 — IT
Bayer Capital Corporation N.V., pg. 172 — IT
Bayernhypo Finance N.V., Hoekenrode 6, pg. 176 — IT
Belgelectric Finance B.V., Nieuwe Zijds Voorburgwal 326-328, pg. 1416 — IT
JOHN BENJAMINS BV, Amsteldek 44, pg. 187 — IT
Bercum Boender Cardozo & Werkendam B.V., Maassluisstraat 2, pg. 1198 — PV
F. Berger & Co. B.V., Vijzelstraat 32, pg. 9 — IT
Berlitz Schools of Languages B.V., Robin 87-89, pg. 222 — PB
Bifin B.V., pg. 467 — IT
Biofin Holding International BV, Klizersgracht 253, pg. 483 — IT
Bohler B.V., Isolatorweg 30-32, pg. 1471 — IT
Bonaventura, Van de Sande Bakhuyzenstraat 4, pg. 1099 — IT
Robert Bosch BV, Karlspeldreef 19, pg. 205 — IT

British Land Investments N.V., Atrium Bldg., Strawinskylaan 3037, pg. 219 — IT
Brother Finance (Netherlands) B.V., Hoekenrode 6, pg. 229 — IT
Bulkitalia International N.V., Drentestraat, 24, pg. 304 — IT
Bull Benelux N.V., Hoogooddreef 66-68, pg. 317 — IT
Bull Data Systems N.V., Hooggoorddreef 66-68, pg. 317 — IT
Bull International N.V., Hoofdoorddreef 66-68, pg. 317 — IT
Bullal B.V., Hoogoorddreef 66-68, pg. 317 — IT
Bullcol B.V., Hoogoorddreef 66-68, pg. 317 — IT
Bulldom B.V., Hoogoorddreef 66-68, pg. 317 — IT
Bullinvest B.V., Hoogoorddreef 66-68, pg. 315 — IT
Buro Britain, Vijzelgracht 17, pg. 1300 — IT
Buro Scandinavia, Vijzelgracht 17, pg. 1300 — IT
CB Finance Company B.V., pg. 312 — IT
CIBC Finance B.V., Vizelstraat 79 B, pg. 257 — IT
CII-Honeywell Bull Finance BV, 26 Vliegtuigstraat, pg. 318 — IT
CPM Europe B.V., pg. 705 — PB
Cemex, S.A. de C.V. - Amsterdam, Riverstaete Building, Amsteldijk 166, pg. 278 — IT
Chase Bank NV, Weteringsschaus, P.O. Box 15,545, pg. 339 — PB
Christie's Amsterdam B.V., Cornelius Schuystraat 57, pg. 290 — IT
Cinema International Corp., N.V., Rijswijkstraat 175, pg. 1216 — IT
Coeclerici Holding International B.V., Drentestraat, 24, pg. 304 — IT
Coeclerici Logistic International B.V., Drentestraat, 24, pg. 304 — IT
Coeclerici Shipping N.V., Drentestraat,20, pg. 304 — IT
Coeclerici Trading International B.V., Drentestraat, 24, pg. 304 — IT
Combined Terminals Amsterdam V.O.F., 10 Corsicaweg, pg. 1144 — IT
Commerzbank (Nederland) N.V., Herengracht 571-579, pg. 311 — IT
Compagnie CII-HB Internationale N.V., Vliegtuigstraat 26, pg. 319 — IT
Computer Task Group Europe B.V., Weerdestein 21, pg. 423 — PB
B.V. Container Service, pg. 1144 — IT
Cyanamid-Ketjen Katalysator bv, 1-3 Nieuwendammerkade, pg. 47 — IT
DG Bank-Amsterdam, Herengracht 386, pg. 352 — IT
DG Finance Company B.V., Herengracht 386, pg. 352 — IT
DMB&B/Worldwide Communications, 81 G-N, pg. 304 — PV
DMB&B/Worldwide Communications Amsterdam, Cronenburg 2, pg. 304 — PV
Daewoo Corp. - Amsterdam, pg. 358 — IT
Daewoo Corp. Amsterdam B.V., Berghausgebouw 3N, pg. 358 — IT
Dai-Ichi Kangyo Bank Nederland N.V., Apollolaan 171, pg. 362 — IT
Daiwa Europe Limited - Amsterdam, pg. 375 — IT
Data General Holland BV, Gebouw De Admiraal Baarsjesweg 224, pg. 486 — PB
H. Albert de Bary & Co. N.V. (Amsterdam), Herengracht 450-458, pg. 404 — IT
de Bijenkorf B.V., Frankemaheerd 4, pg. 1099 — IT
B.V. De Factorij, Factorbedrijf Algemene van de Bank Nederland, Vyzelsracht 50, pg. 9 — IT
De Geillustreerde Pers bv, pg. 1445 — IT
De Geillustreerde Pers/MC, Haaksbergweg 75, pg. 1445 — IT
DeBoer's Fabrieken B.V., P.O. 4105, pg. 594 — IT
Dell Computer BV, Zekeringstraat 45B, 23, pg. 496 — PB
Dentsu Europe-Amsterdam, Honthorststraat 9, pg. 393 — IT
Dentsu Holdings B.V., Honthorststraat 9, pg. 393 — IT
Distilleerderijen Erven Lucas Bols BV, pg. 751 — IT
Distrimedia Services B.V., Hogehilweg 17, pg. 1368 — PB
Dow Jones Markets Netherlands BV, Papenbroekssteeg, 2, pg. 525 — PB
DRAKA KABEL B.V., Hamerstraas 2//4, pg. 417 — IT
Drukkerij Jacob van Campen, Kollenbergweg 80, pg. 386 — IT
Drukkerijen de Bussy Ellerman Harms, Naritaweg 14, pg. 386 — IT
Drukkerj van Roessel, Marifoonweg 3, pg. 386 — IT
Duracell Holdings B.V., Leidseplein 29 2HG, pg. 744 — PB
ECP - Enichem Polymers Netherlands B.V., Museumplein, 11, pg. 429 — IT
ENI International Holding, Strawinskylaan 1041, pg. 429 — IT
ESH Netherlands Holding B.V., Office 1, 2nd Fl., De Boelelaan 7, pg. 432 — IT
East Asiatic Timber (Holland) B.V., pg. 431 — IT
Eastern Sugar, pg. 549 — IT
Efthor Holding BV, Stationsplein 61, pg. 21 — IT
Eland-Brandt, B.V., Distelwg. 78, pg. 895 — PB
Elsevier Business Information, Van de Sande Bakhuyzenstraat 4, pg. 1099 — IT
Elsevier NV, Van de Sande Bakhuyzenstraat 4, pg. 1093 — IT
Elsevier Reed Finance BV, Van de Sande Bakhuyzenstraat 4, pg. 1093 — IT
Elsevier Science-Excerpta Medica Base, Molenwerf 1, pg. 1099 — IT
Elsevier Science (International), Sara Burgerhartstraat 25, pg. 1099 — IT
Elsevier Science (The Netherlands), Sara Burgerhartstraat 25, pg. 1099 — IT
ELVIA Levenverzekeringen N.V., Weesperzijde 150, pg. 60 — IT
ELVIA Schadeverzekeringen N.V., Weesperzijde 150, pg. 60 — IT
Enichem International Holdings B.V., Strawinskylaan 1041, pg. 429 — IT
Enso (Holland) B.V., Meer En Vaart 318, pg. 457 — IT

PB - *U.S. Public Companies Volume*
PV - *U.S. Private Companies Volume*
IT - *International Public & Private Companies Volume*

1711

Geographic Index-Non U.S.

NETHERLANDS DIRECTORY OF CORPORATE AFFILIATIONS

Ericsson Business Mobile Networks BV, World Trade Center, D-Tower, 12th Floor, pg. 1366 IT
Eufidis, De Lairessestraat, 109, pg. 534 IT
EUREKO B.V., pg. 464 IT
Eurest Nederland BV, Paasheuvelweg 40, pg. 21 IT
Euro Makita Corporation B.V., De Boelelelaan 7, pg. 831 IT
EuroCetus, Paasheuvelweg 30, pg. 350 PB
European Vinyls Corp. (Holdings) B.V., Strawinskylaan 1041, pg. 429 IT
Excerpta Medica Medical Communications BV, Van de Sande Bakhuyzenstraat 4, pg. 1099 IT
FCA!BMZ Amsterdam, A.J. Ernststraat 199, pg. 470 IT
Fabian Holdings BV, Herengracht 257, pg. 795 IT
Farmacas B.V., Jesselschadestreet, 18-12, pg. 1126 IT
Faxion B.V., Pelikaanweg 1, pg. 1144 IT
Fiat-Allis B.V., pg. 483 IT
Finata Bank N.V., Rembrandtplein 43, pg. 9 IT
Finland Vakanties Westerman, Keizergracht 628, pg. 485 IT
Fins Verkoopkantoor, Fins Verkoopkantoor, pg. 458 IT
Ford Credit B.V., pg. 665 PB
Ford Export Services B.V., P.O. Box 795, pg. 665 PB
Forte Finance N.V., Apollolaan 2, pg. 556 IT
Fotolabo Club BV, Paasheuvelweg 17, pg. 501 IT
Fuji Bank Nederland N.V., Rivierstaete Amsterdam 166, pg. 521 IT
Fujisawa Holland B.V., Officia I, De Boelelaan 7, pg. 525 IT
Fuller Offshore Finance Corp., B.V., C/O Intra Baheer, B.V., pg. 475 IT
Furukawa Finance Netherlands B.V., Office Centre, Josef Israelskade 48B, pg. 531 IT
GD Express Worldwide NV, Centerpoint II, Hoogoorddreef 62, pg. 1343 IT
GEC Alsthom N.V., World Trade Center, pg. 56 IT
Geldnet BV, pg. 720 IT
Geo-Marktprofiel BV, pg. 720 IT
Gerlach Art Packers & Shippers B.V., Pelikaanweg 8, pg. 1144 IT
Graphic Lease, Karlspeldreef 14, pg. 647 IT
Groninger Industrieele Crediet Bank N.V., Brouwerswapen, Rembrandtplein 43, pg. 9 IT
HKS Hoogovens Klockner Scrap Metals BV, Kwadrantweg 12, pg. 754 IT
HLPB, De Boelelaan 411, pg. 1377 IT
HLPB, De Boelelaan, 411, pg. 1377 IT
HSBC Holdings BV, 3/F, Atlas Building, Hoogoorddreef 9, pg. 582 IT
Hachette Magazine VDB, Herengracht 247, pg. 795 IT
Hanson Overseas Finance, Amsterdam De Lairessestraat 127, pg. 594 IT
HEINEKEN N.V., Tweede Weteringplantsoen 21, pg. 608 IT
Hema B.V., Frakemaheerd 2, pg. 750 IT
Henderson International Europe BV, Jan Willem Brouwersstraat 12, pg. 609 IT
Will Henko BV, pg. 614 IT
Hickson Coatings Holland BV, pg. 619 IT
Hillen & Roosen B.V., Mesinge 78, pg. 633 IT
Hollandse Disconteringsmaatschappij Mundus N.V., Brouwerswapen, pg. 9 IT
Honeywell BV, Laarderhoogtweg 18, pg. 834 PB
Hoogovens Handel BV, pg. 754 IT
Hoogovens Metals BV, pg. 754 IT
Hosokawa Micron International B.V., World Trade Center, Strawinskylaan 249, pg. 636 IT
Hufvudstaden Nederland B.V., P.O. Box 1469, pg. 478 IT
IBM Nederland N.V, Postbus 9999, pg. 897 PB
ICBC (Europe) N.V., World Trade Center, Strawinskylaan 1203, pg. 684 IT
ICC Industries, B.V., Amteldijk 166, P.O. Box 7000, pg. 554 PV
ICL Nederland B.V., Zwaansvliet 20, pg. 529 IT
IDM Bank N.V., Kabelweg 37, pg. 9 IT
IKB Finance B.V., Hoekenrode 8, pg. 646 IT
ING GROEP N.V., Strawinskylaan 2631, pg. 647 IT
ING Lease Vastgoed, Karspeldreef 14, pg. 647 IT
IKEA HOLDINGS AB, Karsteldreef 16, pg. 659 IT
Imasco B.V., Herengracht 495, pg. 112 IT
INCSTAR B.V., De Ruyterkade 125, pg. 483 IT
Independent Mail BV, pg. 720 IT
Indisco Nederland BV, Antillenstrasse 33/a, pg. 1286 IT
Industrie-en Handelsonderneming Bernard Reijn B.V., pg. 540 IT
Interadvies (NNFD, Regiobank, NVB/Vola), Europahuis, James Wattstraat 79, pg. 647 IT
The International Commercial Bank of China, World Trade Center, Strawinskylaan 1203, pg. 684 IT
International Media Holding BV, Zwaansvliet, 20, pg. 795 IT
International Publications Holding, Zwaansvliet, 20, pg. 795 IT
Intralox Inc., Postbus 23280, Lemelerbergweg 2D, pg. 643 PV
KKBR/Conquest, Postbus 7849, pg. 1484 IT
KHI Europe Finance B.V., Hoekenrode 6, pg. 726 IT
KLM Cityhopper, P.O. Box 7700, pg. 719 IT
KLM/ERA Helicopters, Postbus 7700, pg. 719 IT
KNP BT Nederland B.V., Paalbergweg 2, pg. 756 IT
KNP Financieringen B.V., Paalbergweg 2, pg. 756 IT
KNP International B.V., Paalberweg 2, pg. 756 IT
KNSM Group B.V., pg. 1144 IT
Kaukas Nederland B.V., Backershagen 97a, pg. 1429 IT
Kawasaki Heavy Industries (Europe) B.V., 7th Fl., Rivier Staete, Amsteldijk 166, pg. 726 IT
Keithley Instruments B.V., Avelingen-West 49, pg. 947 PB
Kenner Parker Toys, Koninginneweg 6, pg. 798 PB
Kiekens B.V., Amsterdam, 360, Kadoelenweg, pg. 681 IT
Knoll Pharma, Hettenheuvelweg 41-43, pg. 109 IT
Komcri International Finance B.V., Foppingadreef 22, pg. 745 IT
Konica Nederland B.V., Kuiperbergweg 44, pg. 749 IT
N.V. KONINKLIJKE BIJENKORF BEHEER KBB, Hoekenrode 8, pg. 750 IT
Koninklijke Eduard Van Leer B.V., pg. 966 IT
N.V. KONINKLIJKE KNP BT, Teniersstraat 1, pg. 756 IT
Korn/Ferry International, Strawinskylaan 545, pg. 633 PV
Kredietbank (Nederland) N.V., Hoogoorddreef 9, pg. 761 IT
LB Rheinland Pfalz Finance B.V., Strawinskylaan 3111, pg. 799 IT
LGT Asset Management PLC, Concertgebouwplein 15, pg. 810 IT
Labouchere N.V., 617 Keizergracht, pg. 26 IT
Lancaster Group B.V., pg. 186 IT
Leaf Holland B.V., Paul van Vlissingenstraat 8, pg. 638 IT
Lloyds Eurofinance NV, Hirsch Building, Leidseplein 29, pg. 813 IT
Lowe Kuiper & Schouten, Koningslaan 42, pg. 678 PV
M&S Mode, Hoekenrode 8, pg. 750 IT
M.M.H. SA, Kantooretage Kamer, pg. 22 IT
Maatschappij Tot Financiering Van Bedrijfspanden N.V., Foppingadreef 20-22, pg. 9 IT
Magedoma B.V., Mr. S.J.M. Ackermans, Walgemoed 2 Moore, pg. 1126 IT
Makro Zelfbedieningsgroothandel C.V., Spaklerweg 53, pg. 1155 IT
Mammoet Transport B.V., pg. 1144 IT
Mammoet Transport Div. B.V., De Ruyterkade 7, pg. 1144 IT
Markgraaf, Markgraaf House, Hgoehilweg 3, pg. 1463 IT
Martinair Holland, Martinair Building, P.O. Box 7507, pg. 719 IT
Mattel B.V. (Netherlands), Amstelveste, Joan Muyskenweg 22, pg. 1059 PB
Meiji Seika Europe B.V., De Beelelaan 7, pg. 856 IT
Memorex Telex Netherland BV, Hoogoorddreef 9, pg. 857 IT
MEMOREX TELEX N.V., Hoogoorddreef 9, pg. 857 IT
Mercantile Canada Finance B.V., Hoekenrode 6-8, pg. 907 IT
Midor Europe B.V., World Trade Center, Tower D 3rd, pg. 558 IT
Herman Miller BV, Teilingen 3-5, pg. 1112 PB
Minebea Europe Finance B.V., pg. 868 IT
Mirovoy Global Parts B.V., pg. 467 IT
Mitsui & Co. International (Europe) B.V., Herengracht 566, pg. 880 IT
Mitsui & Co., Ltd. (Amsterdam Branch), Herengracht 566, pg. 882 IT
Mizuno Finance Netherlands B.V., Hoekenrode 6, pg. 885 IT
Mobil Oil B.V., pg. 1119 PB
MoDc Van Gelder, pg. 886 IT
Monicata VOF, pg. 720 IT
Moore Nederland B.V., Karperstraat 10, pg. 890 IT
J.P. Morgan Nederland N.V., Appollolaan 171, pg. 1131 PB
MultiCopy International B.V., Weesperstraat 65, pg. 890 IT
Music & Media, pg. 1446 IT
NVS Salland Verzekeringen N.V., Rokin 75, pg. 61 IT
Nationale Bank voor Middellang Krediet N.V., Foppingadreef 20-22, pg. 9 IT
N.V. Nationale Borg-Maatschappij, pg. 647 IT
Nationale Maatschappij voor Vliegtuigfinanciering B.V., Foppingadreef 20-22, pg. 9 IT
Nationale Trust Maatschappij N.V., Foppingadreef 20-22, pg. 9 IT
Nederlandsche Trust-Maatschappij B.V., Nieuwezijds Voorburgwal 326-328, pg. 9 IT
Nedlloyd Districenters B.V., pg. 1144 IT
Nedlloyd Districenters International, Lemelerbergweg 32, pg. 1144 IT
Nedlloyd Districenters Westpoort B.V., pg. 1144 IT
Nestle Nederland B.V., Hilversumstraat 316, pg. 921 IT
Netherlands Management Company BV, Herengracht 320, pg. 314 IT
Netway BV, pg. 720 IT
Nikko Europe Plc.-Amsterdam Branch, 12th Floor, Parnassustoren, Locatellikade 1, pg. 930 IT
Nippo Corporation, Europe Branch, Johan Huizingalaan 400, pg. 932 IT
Nissan Europe N.V., Johan Huizingalaan 400, pg. 945 IT
Nissan International Finance (Netherlands) B.V., Johan Huzingalaan 400, pg. 945 IT
Nissan Motor Parts Centre (Europe) B.V., Hornweg 32, pg. 945 IT
Nokia Finance International B.V., Hoekenrode 8, pg. 954 IT
Nomura Bank Nederland N.V., De Boelelaan 7, pg. 957 IT
Noordervliet & Winninghoff/Leo Burnett B.V., Buitenveldertselaan 106, pg. 186 PV
Noord-Europese Houtimport BV, pg. 886 IT
NORD/LB - Amsterdam, Herengracht 469, pg. 958 IT
Norske Skog Holland B.V., pg. 966 IT
Norta Timber B.V., Backershagen 97A, pg. 458 IT
Norvista B.V., World Trade Center, Schiphol Boulevard 185, pg. 486 IT
Oscar Film NV, pg. 720 IT
BV Oscar Productions, pg. 720 IT
Overslagbedrijf De IJbunker bv, 100 James Walstraat, pg. 43 IT
PCT EV, pg. 720 IT
PMSVW/Young & Rubicam B.V., Frans van Mierisstraat 92, pg. 1199 PV
Panalpina World Transport B.V., pg. 1023 IT
Paramount Pictures International, Postus 9255, pg. 777 PV
Pechiney Verkoop B.V., Ottho Heldringstraat 41, pg. 1031 IT
Pierson, Heldring & Pierson N.V., 214 Herengracht, pg. 9 IT
Playboy Products & Services International, B.V., Museumplein 11, pg. 1310 PB
PolyGram Record Service B.V., Vander Madeweg 12-14a, pg. 1052 IT
Postbank Funds Transfer Operations, Haarlemmerweg 520, pg. 647 IT
Postbank Insurance, Haarlemmerweg 520, pg. 647 IT
Postbank Lease, Karspeldreef 14, pg. 647 IT
Postbank Retail Banking, Haarlemmerweg 520, pg. 647 IT
B.V. Projectontwikkelingsmaatschappij Amro, Amsteldijk 166 8th Floor, pg. 9 IT
Proost en Brandt nv, pg. 756 IT
Proost-VRG Paper International, pg. 757 IT
RBC France B.V., Keizergracht 604, pg. 1131 IT
Radio-Holland AV Systems Group, Jan Rebelstraat 14, pg. 1151 IT
Radio Holland Group-Defense Staff Div., Jan Rebelstraat 20, pg. 1151 IT
Radio-Holland Security Systems, Jan Rebelstraat 14-20, pg. 1151 IT
The Reader's Digest N.V., Hogehilweg 17, pg. 1368 PB
Reed Elsevier Nederland BV, Van de Sande Bakhuyzenstraat 4, pg. 1100 IT
Reed Exhibition Companies-The Netherlands, Van de Sande Bakhuyzenstraat 4, pg. 1097 IT
Bernard Reijn B.V., pg. 540 IT
Renishaw International B.V., Koningslaan 34, pg. 1103 IT
Rentokil BV, Antillenstrasse 33/a, pg. 1286 IT
BV Rentokil Chemie, Antillenstrasse 33/a, pg. 1286 IT
Repsol Intl. Finance B.V., Prinses Irenestraat 59A, pg. 1104 IT
RetailNet B.V., Postbus 75355, pg. 750 IT
Revere Transducers BV, Ramshoorn 7, pg. 790 PB
RHEINHYP Finance, N.V., pg. 310 IT
Rovin Rotterdamse Vinylunie vof, P.O. Box 140, pg. 43 IT
SGS-Thomson Microelectronics Netherlands, World Trade Center, Strawinskylaan 1025, pg. 654 IT
SKF Multitec B.V., Zekeringstraat 36, pg. 1159 IT
Sandoz Holding Netherlands B.V., pg. 984 IT
Sandoz International Participations B.V., pg. 984 IT
Sanpaolo-Amsterdam Branch, Herengracht, 446-1017 CA, pg. 692 IT
Saroph Holdings B.V., c/0 Holland Intertrust Corporation B.V., pg. 1290 IT
Schick Nederland B.V., Postbus 8166, pg. 1739 PB
Selandia Finance and Investment B.V., pg. 431 IT
Sharp Finance Netherland B.V. (Amsterdam), Hoekenrode 6, pg. 1230 IT
Shimizu Benelux S.A., Office 1, 2nd Fl., De Boelelaan 7, pg. 1234 IT
Shimizu Europe B.V., Office 1, 2nd Fl., De Boelelaan 7, pg. 1234 IT
Shionogi Europe B.V., Emmaplein 5, pg. 1235 IT
Smurfit International B.V., Stibbetoren, Strawinskylaan 2001, pg. 1271 IT
Solvay Chemie B.V., Vlaardingenlaan 11, pg. 1279 IT
Solvay Duphar B.V., Ankerweg 16, pg. 1279 IT
Somocar International N.V., Drentestraat, 24, pg. 304 IT
Sorbus B.V., World Trade Center, Strawinskylaan 1725, pg. 204 PB
SPAR Internationale Financiering B.V., pg. 1288 IT
Suez Nederland Securities N.V., Nieuwezijds Voorburgwal 162, pg. 314 IT
The Sumitomo Bank, Ltd.-Amsterdam Representative Office, 4F Kantoorgebouw Atrium, pg. 1309 IT
Sumitomo Chemical Nederland B.V., Officia I, De Boelelaan 7, pg. 1312 IT
Sumitomo Electric Finance Netherlands B.V., Strawinskylaan 3127, pg. 1314 IT
Sumitomo Rubber Europe B.V., Official 1-de Boelelaan 7, pg. 1317 IT
Sun Electric Nederland, B.V. (SEN) Varodo B.V. (VRD), Spaklerweg 69, pg. 1481 PB
Svenska Skum B.V., Postbus 8236, pg. 595 IT
Swado Grafigroep, Marifoonweg 1, pg. 386 IT
Swiss Bank Corporation Nederland N.V., Hoogoorddreef 5, pg. 1332 IT
TBWA Campaign Company, Reclamebureau B.V., Van Eeghenstraat 94, pg. 1063 PV
TBWA International, 20 Nachtwachtlaan, pg. 589 IT
TNT Logistics Europe, Hessenbergweg 8-10, pg. 1343 IT
Tab Products Europa B.V., Hettenheuvelweg 8-10, pg. 1559 PB
Taisei Holland B.V., World Trade Center, Amsterdam Tower B, 4th Floor, pg. 1347 IT
Takashimaya International Finance B.V., Hoekenrode 6, pg. 1350 IT
Takenaka Netherlands B.V., Kabelweg 21, pg. 1351 IT
Tanabe Finance (Holland) B.V., Officia 1, De Boelelaan 7, pg. 1354 IT
Televisie-Unit BV, pg. 720 IT
bv Televizier, pg. 1445 IT
Tenneco Holdings B.V., De Lairessestraat 133, pg. 1580 PB
Tetterode-Nederland BV, pg. 757 IT
Tiffany & Co. Overseas Finance B.V., Baker & McKenzie, Liedseplein 29, pg. 1609 PB
Time-Life Books B.V., Ottho Heldring-Stratt 5, pg. 1615 PB
Time-Life International B.V., Otto Heldringstraat 5, pg. 1615 PB
Tokai Bank Nederland N.V., Keizersgracht 452, pg. 1391 IT
The Tokio Marine & Fire Insurance Company (U.K.) Limited, c/o Delta Lloyd Schadeverzeker, Sparklerweg 4, pg. 1392 IT

PB - *U.S. Public Companies Volume*
PV - *U.S. Private Companies Volume*
IT - *International Public & Private Companies Volume*

Tosoh Europe B.V., Crown Building South, Hullenbergweg 359, pg. 1408 **IT**
Toyota Motor Finance (Netherlands) B.V., Officia 1 De Boelelaan 7, pg. 1414 **IT**
TRICOM Paper International B.V., pg. 756 **IT**
Trifin B.V., pg. 467 **IT**
UPM-Kymmene (Nederland) B.V., Backershagen 99 B, pg. 1430 **IT**
Ubel B.V., Kabelweg 22, pg. 550 **IT**
Uddeholm Tooling B.V., H. J. E.Wenckebachweg141, pg. 1472 **IT**
Uitgeversmaatschappij The Reader's Digest N.V., Hogehilweg 17, pg. 1368 **PB**
Underlining BV, pg. 720 **IT**
Unico Banking Group, Standing Secretariat Herengracht 386, pg. 1085
Uniroyal Chemical B.V., Ankerweg 18, pg. 460 **PB**
Unisource NV, pg. 720 **IT**
Unisys Nederland N.V., Hoogoorddreef 11, pg. 1671 **PB**
United Media Europe/Scripps, Strewinskylaan 1135, pg. 1448 **PB**
Universal Studios International B.V., Rijswijkstraat 175, pg. 1216 **IT**
VDO Nederland BV, pg. 839 **IT**
VNU Business Publications bv, pg. 1445 **IT**
VRG Holding BV, Centerpoint II, Hoogoorddreef 62, pg. 757 **IT**
Van Leer Metallized Products B.V., pg. 1146 **IT**
Van Leer Nederland B.V., pg. 1146 **IT**
Vemedia B.V., Drentestraat 11, pg. 1279 **IT**
VENDEX INTERNATIONAL N.V., De Klencke 6, pg. 1462 **IT**
Volkswagen Intl. Finance N.V., Herengracht 495, pg. 1475 **IT**
Volvo Group Finance Europe B.V., WTC Amsterdam, Strawinskylaan 665, pg. 1477 **IT**
Vroom & Dreesman B.V., Spaklerweg 52, pg. 1463 **IT**
Warner-Lambert Verkoop B.V., Postbus 8166, pg. 1740 **PB**
Westland/Utrecht Hypotheekbank, Mr. Treublaan 7, pg. 647 **IT**
Westmin Talc BV, Coengebouw, Kabelweg 37, pg. 1494 **IT**
Whitehall Laboratoria B.V., Sophialaan 25, pg. 82 **PB**
Wieden & Kennedy-Amsterdam, Keizersgracht 125-127, pg. 1175 **PV**
Wijkertunnel Beheer III B.V., pg. 312 **IT**
Willis Corroon Scheuer, Havengebouw, De Ruyterkade 7, pg. 1502 **IT**
Willis Corroon Scheuer, De Ruyterkade 7, pg. 1509 **IT**
Windmoller & Holscher BV, Gebouw Rivierstaete, Amsteldijk 166, pg. 1511 **IT**
WOLTERS KLUWER N.V., Stadhouderskade 1, pg. 1512 **IT**
WoodCommerz N.V., pg. 312 **IT**
Wrigley N.V., Hogehilwegis, pg. 1781 **PB**
Wuestenrot Finance B.V., c/o Premier Trust N.V., De Boelelaan 7, pg. 1514 **IT**
Yamaichi Bank Nederland Custody N.V., World Trade Center, Tower D 10th, Strawinskylaan 1057, pg. 1517 **IT**
Yamaichi Overseas Finance N.V., World Trade Center, Tower D 10th, Strawinskylaan 1057, pg. 1518 **IT**
Yokohamagomu Finance Europe N.V., Officia 1, De Boelaan 7, pg. 1522 **IT**
Zenith Data Systems B.V., Hoogoorddreef 66-68, pg. 317 **IT**
ZwitserLeven, Apollolaan 153, pg. 1332 **IT**

Apeldoorn

AEP/Borden B.V., pg. 5 **PB**
Asea Brown Boveri Industrie B.V., pg. 8 **IT**
BTU (Netherlands), Bas Backerlaan 15, pg. 164 **PB**
Banta Global Turnkey, Europaweg 224, pg. 188 **PB**
Bordex (Nederland), B.V., pg. 159 **PV**
Clarins B.V., Laan Van Westenenk 64, pg. 295 **IT**
Eureko Benefits Service, pg. 464 **IT**
Eureko Sales Support, pg. 464 **IT**
Iveco B.V., Europaweg 212, pg. 483 **IT**
Koninklijke Talens bv, 46, Sophialalaan, pg. 42 **IT**
Loher Benelux B.V., Lage Brink 5-7, pg. 401 **IT**
Machinefabriek Werklust B.V., Postbus 159, pg. 1133 **IT**
Nemef B.V., P.O. Box 13, pg. 235 **PB**
Owens-Corning Veil Netherlands B.V., Laan Van Westenenk 5, pg. 1237 **PB**
Pollux BV, pg. 756 **IT**
Talboom B.V., Laan Van Westenenk 64, pg. 296 **IT**
Thompack B.V., pg. 5 **PB**
Vectur B.V., Zwolseweg 335, pg. 1129 **PV**

Appingedam

Kartonfabriek "De Eendracht" N.V., Woldweg 18, pg. 123 **IT**

Arnhem

Akzo Nobel Fibers B.V., Velperweg 76, pg. 43 **IT**
AKZO NOBEL N.V., Velperweg 76, pg. 42 **IT**
Akzo Plastics B.V., 76, Velperweg, pg. 45 **IT**
Aramide Maatschappij vof, 76 Velperweg, P.O. Box 60, pg. 45 **IT**
Ascom Hasler BV, Blankenweg 22, pg. 87 **IT**
Audet Tijdschriften, Kronenburgsingel 8-01, pg. 1099 **IT**
BASF Finance Europe N.V., Jansbuitensingel 29, pg. 106 **IT**
BASF Nederland B.V., Kadestraat 1, pg. 106 **IT**
BMB Management Consulting for Development BV, pg. 606 **IT**
BV Boreon, pg. 607 **IT**

CIBA-GEIGY BV, Raapopseweg 1, pg. 976 **IT**
Colbond bv, 76, Velperweg, pg. 45 **IT**
Enka bv, 76 Velperweg, pg. 45 **IT**
Enka Household Products B.V., pg. 505 **IT**
Enka International bv, 76 Velperweg, P.O. Box 60, pg. 45 **IT**
Euroconsult BV, pg. 606 **IT**
Heidemij Advies BV, pg. 607 **IT**
Heidemij Europe BV, pg. 607 **IT**
Heidemij Nederland BV, Lovinklaan 1, pg. 607 **IT**
HEIDEMIJ N.V., Utrechtseweg 68, pg. 606 **IT**
Heidemij Realisatie BV, pg. 607 **IT**
Heidemij Realisatie Lelystad BV, pg. 607 **IT**
ILIS International Land Information Services CV, pg. 606 **IT**
Ilaco BV, pg. 606 **IT**
Ilis/Ilaco BV, pg. 606 **IT**
KAFI BV, pg. 607 **IT**
KLM Aerocarto BV, P.O. Box 7002, pg. 607 **IT**
Koninklijke PBNA BV, Ijssellaan 82, pg. 1100 **IT**
LB&P ecologisch advies BV, pg. 607 **IT**
N.V. Maxon International S.A., Groningensingel 1, pg. 776 **PV**
Nederlandse Hardmetaal Fabrieken B.V., Nieuwe Havenweg 29, pg. 951 **PB**
Neproma Textiel Service B.V., 2 Pieter Calandweg, pg. 1285 **IT**
Unit Precisiebuis, Westervoortsedijk 65, pg. 754 **IT**

Asperen

SASIB Bakery Holland N.V., 2E Industrieweg 8, pg. 1194 **IT**

Assen

Analytisch Biochemisch Laboratorium B.V., pg. 991 **IT**
Nederlandse Aardolie Maatschappij B.V., Shepersmaat 2, pg. 603 **PB**

Baarn

Chemie Linz Benelux B.V., Oude Utrechtseweg 16, pg. 356 **IT**
Foxboro Nederland N.V., pg. 1243 **IT**
Koninklijke De Ruyter BV, Oude Utrechtseweg 38, pg. 244 **IT**
Luwa BV, pg. 617 **IT**
Phonogram International B.V., Gerrit Va Der Veenlaan, pg. 1052 **IT**
Polygram N.V., Gerrit Van Der Veenlaan 4, pg. 1051 **IT**

Badhoevedorp

Costar Europe, Ltd., pg. 448 **PB**
Henkel Oleochemicals Nederland B.V., pg. 613 **IT**
Ivacon B.V., Sloterweg 321, pg. 134 **IT**
Nikon Europe B.V., Schipholweg 321, pg. 931 **IT**
Rowen Drilling & Aviation B.V., Akerdijk 150A, pg. 1410 **PB**

Barendrecht

John Crane Holland B.V., Zuideinde 49, pg. 1339 **IT**
ODS/Hoogovens Handel BV, Donk 6, pg. 754 **IT**

Barneveld

AKAPP Electro Industries B.V., Nijverheidsweg 14, pg. 1776 **PB**
Ferrosan Benelux B.V., Gildeweg 42, pg. 989 **IT**
IMd Micon BV, pg. 607 **IT**
Tastemaker B.V., pg. 811 **PB**

Beek

DSM Transport Maatschappij B.V., DSM Kantoor Urmond, St. Antoniusplein 21, pg. 353 **IT**

Beesd

De Lampenier, Bedrijfsweg 43, Postbus 241, pg. 750 **IT**
Van Leeuwen Stainless, Industrieweg 26, pg. 1449 **IT**

Belfeld

De Globe BV, Witveldweg 40, pg. 753 **IT**
BV Hepworth-NGI, Stationstraat 9, pg. 615 **IT**

Bergen-op-Zoom

Eurolec BV, 1 Plasticslaan, pg. 546 **IT**
G.E. Plastics Europe, Plasticlaan 1, pg. 713 **PB**
Lawson Mardon Brabant BV, pg. 68 **IT**
Synthese bv, 5, Ringersweg, pg. 43 **IT**
Waco-Liesbosch Beton B.V., Lelyweg 23, pg. 134 **IT**

Bergschenhoek

HAWE Holding B.V., Oosteindsepad 8, pg. 1133 **IT**
Rothenberger Nederland B.V., Burgemeester v. Oostenweg 13, pg. 1129 **IT**

Berkel

Tradinco Instrumenten-Apparaten B.V., P.O. Box 37, pg. 590 **IT**

Best

Marcam European Support Centre, BV, DeWaal 20, pg. 1043 **PB**
Marcam Nederland B.V., DeWaal 20, pg. 1043 **PB**
Motorola B.V., De Waal 26, pg. 1139 **PB**
Philips Medical Systems International B.V., pg. 1051 **IT**

Beverwijk

Ceta-Bever bv, 152 Grote Houtweg, pg. 43 **IT**
Hoogovens Aluminium BV, Vondellaan 10, pg. 753 **IT**
Hoogovens Aluminium Primary Products, Vondellaan 10, pg. 753 **IT**
Hoogovens Corporate Services BV, Vondellaan 10, pg. 753 **IT**
Hoogovens Scrap Processing BV, Vondellaan 10, pg. 754 **IT**
LASMO Nederland B.V., Beaver Base, Nijuerheidsweg 50, pg. 804 **IT**
CV Scheuer Verzekeringen, Koude Horn 3, pg. 755 **IT**
Weatherford Oil Tool Nederland B.V., Wijkermeerweg 7, 1951 AH Velsen-Noord, pg. 1750 **PB**

Bilthoven

Ohmeda BV, Jan van Eycklaan, 2, pg. 122 **IT**

Bladel

Henderson (Nederland) BV, pg. 615 **IT**
Roche Nicholas B.V., pg. 1121 **IT**

Bleiswijk

FTK Holland B.V., Klappolder 191-193, pg. 710 **IT**

Bloemendaal

Hoogovens Staalverwerking en Handel BV, Mollaan 1a, pg. 754 **IT**
McCormick Ingredients Europe, Inc., pg. 1067 **PB**

Bodegraven

Best'Ware BV, pg. 756 **IT**
Info'Products BV, pg. 756 **IT**
Info'Products Holding BV, pg. 756 **IT**
Info'Products Services BV, pg. 756 **IT**

Boekelo

Texoprint B.V., pg. 540 **IT**

Boesingheliede

Snap-on Tools Netherlands B.V., Schipholweg 1003, pg. 1481 **PB**

Born

Netherlands Car B.V., Dr. Hub van Doorneweg 1, pg. 876 **IT**

Boxmeer

Intervet International bv, 35, Wim de Korverstraat, pg. 44 **IT**
Intervet Nederland bv, One Kleine Broekstraat, pg. 44 **IT**

Boxtel

Ancra CHS, Schouwrooy 26-5281 RE, pg. 71 **PV**
Hydraudyne Beheer BV, pg. 838 **IT**
Hydraudyne Cylinders BV, pg. 838 **IT**
Hydraudyne Hydrauliek BV, pg. 838 **IT**
Hydraudyne Systems & Engineering BV, pg. 838 **IT**
Hydrocare BV, pg. 838 **IT**
Mannesmann Holding Nederland BV, pg. 840 **IT**
Organon Teknika bv, Eight Boseind, pg. 44 **IT**
Organon Teknika Nederland bv, Eight Boseind, pg. 44 **IT**
Robinson Milling Systems B.V., Van Salmstraat46, pg. 231 **IT**

Breda

AIP B.V., Postbus 3260, pg. 1133 **IT**
Aartsenfruit Breda BV, meilaarstraat 240, pg. 491 **IT**
Alusuisse-Lonza Europe, pg. 68 **IT**
Alusuisse-Lonza Nederland B.V., pg. 68 **IT**
Alusuisse Nederland B.V., pg. 68 **IT**
AMBAC B.V., Terheijdenseweg 169, pg. 71 **PB**
Amgen B.V., Elleboog 56, pg. 101 **IT**
Arkel Management Group B.V., Postbus 2189, pg. 1133 **IT**
Bank Brussels Lambert, Breda, 4G-4H Prinsenkade, pg. 148 **IT**
Breda Sugar Factory, Markkade 29, pg. 244 **IT**
Breemars Assurantien B.V., Postbus 3143, pg. 1133 **IT**
Campina Melkunie, Butter Division, Veilingkade 4, pg. 254 **IT**
Cebas B.V., Postbus 2189, pg. 1133 **IT**
Chemferm VoF, De Bijster 18, pg. 354 **IT**
CIBA Vision Optics b.v., Prinsenkade 4, pg. 981 **PB**
Dionex B.V., Takkebijsters, 65, pg. 510 **IT**
Directview bv, pg. 1445 **IT**

PB - *U.S. Public Companies Volume*
PV - *U.S. Private Companies Volume*
IT - *International Public & Private Companies Volume*

1713

Durco B.V., Elleboog 52, pg. 659
Gambro B.V., pg. 667 — IT
Generale Bank - Breda, Prinsenkade 9C, pg. 547 — IT
Hydro Aluminium, Zandhovenstraat 12, pg. 962 — IT
Inamed N.V., Takkebijsters 17A, pg. 874 — PB
Interbrew Netherlands, P.O. Box 3212, pg. 679 — IT
Investment Fund Breda B.V., Postbus 2189, pg. 1133 — IT
JNI Investments N.V., Postbus 2189, pg. 1133 — IT
Kameleon Beheer IV, pg. 1133 — IT
Keystone Valve (Europa) B.V., Mijkenbroek 22, pg. 1650 — PB
Knurr Nederland B.V., Nikkelstraat 3, pg. 739 — IT
Kredietbank (Nederland) N.V., Seeligsingel 6-7, pg. 761 — IT
Lekturama, Goldina, Mijkenbroek 31, pg. 1463 — IT
Lignac & Levison BV, pg. 756 — IT
Liquied Molking Resins B.V., pg. 811 — PB
Lonza Benelux B.V., pg. 69 — IT
Lonza Europe BV, pg. 69 — IT
B.V. Machinefabriek Breda, Postbus 2189, pg. 1133 — IT
Mammoet Stoof B.V., pg. 1144 — IT
NCT Holland N.V., Wilhelminasingel 19, pg. 914 — IT
Neste Chemicals Benelux Holding B.V., Wiheminasingel 19, pg. 914 — IT
Neste Finance B.V., Paardeweide 4, pg. 915 — IT
Outokumpu Benelux B.V., Baronielaan 63, pg. 1015 — IT
Peco Suikerwerken B.V., Lunestraat 158, pg. 1451 — IT
Raab Karcher Bouwstoffen B.V., pg. 1458 — IT
Red Band Venco, Takkebijsters 11, pg. 244 — IT
Rosemount B.V., Konijnenberg 60, pg. 577 — PB
ROYAL BEGEMANN GROUP, Speelhuislaan 173, pg. 1133 — IT
SDRC Nederland B.V., Druivenstraat 3, pg. 1525 — PB
Schlatter Benelux B.V., Essendonk 7, pg. 1206 — IT
Skil Nederland B.V., Konijnenberg 60, pg. 577 — PB
Square Wheels B.V., pg. 1133 — IT
Steelweld BV, Postbus 338g, pg. 71 — IT
Sulzer Metco (Benelux) B.V., pg. 1308 — IT
Thermo Instrument Systems B.V., Heerbaan 220, pg. 1596 — PB
Uitgeversmaatschappij De Stem bv, pg. 1445 — IT
Van Melle Export B.V., pg. 1451 — IT
Van Melle International Holding B.V., pg. 1451 — IT
Van Melle International Trust B.V., pg. 1451 — IT
Van Melle Nederland B.V., Zoete Inval 20, pg. 1451 — IT
Van Melle Nederland Holding B.V., pg. 1451 — IT
Van Melle Nederland Services B.V., Zoete Inval 20, pg. 1451 — IT
Van Melle Nederland Verkoop B. V., Zoete Inval 20, pg. 1451 — IT
VAN MELLE N.V., Zoete Inval 20, pg. 1450 — IT
Vimarc, P.O. Box 3316, pg. 71 — IT
Willebroek Vastgoed B.V., pg. 1133 — IT
Windfonds Van Melle B.V., Zoete Inval 20, pg. 1451 — IT
Zyma-Nederland, pg. 986 — IT

Breskens Kreek

Gebr. Verduijn's Suikerwerkenfabriek B. V., Deltahoek 110, pg. 1451 — IT

Breukelen

Huls Nederland B.V., Straatweg 62, pg. 1455 — IT

Brunssum

Enraf-Nonius B.V., Boschstraat 6, P.O. Box 75, pg. 389 — IT
VEPO Aannemingsbedrijf B.V., Wijenweg 137, pg. 134 — IT

Bunnik

NMB Heller N.V., Runnenburg 30, pg. 521 — IT
Newport B.V., Regulierenring 9, pg. 1179 — PB
Sara Lee Processed Meats-Europe, pg. 1435 — PB
Sensormatic B.V., Regulierenring 11, pg. 1457 — PB

Bunschoten

Automotive Tailored Blanks BV, Amersfoortseweg 9, pg. 753 — IT
De Graaf's Bakkerijen BV, pg. 752 — IT

Bussum

Cadsand Medica B.V., Groot Hertoginnelaan 34, pg. 1284 — PB
C. de Groot Houtagenturen, pg. 966 — IT
Schauman B.V., Brediusweg 33, pg. 1429 — IT
Seven-Up Nederlands N.V., Habenstraat 122, pg. 1278 — PB
Van Cadsand Beheer B.V., Groot Hertoginnelaan 34, pg. 1284 — PB

Buurse

Ter Huurne, Alsteedseweg 64, pg. 749 — IT

Capelle

Novell Netherlands, Barbizonlaan 25, pg. 1204 — PB

Capelle aan den Ijssel

Brugman Beheer B.V., pg. 1481 — IT
Brugman Keukens B.V., pg. 1481 — IT
Framatome Connectors Nederland B.V., Essebaan 7, pg. 503 — IT
Grace B.V., Essenbaan 19 a/b, pg. 755 — PB

Hoogovens Aluminium Geveltechniek BV, Vierbaan 19, pg. 753 — IT
Hoogovens Aluminium Sales BV, Vlierbaan 19, pg. 753 — IT
Hydro Aluminium Netherlands, Kanaalweg 33-35, pg. 962 — IT
Letraset Nederland BV, Vlierbaan 13, pg. 462 — IT
Pfizer B.V., Roer 266, pg. 1283 — PB
Roerig B.V., Roer 266, pg. 1283 — PB
Uitgeverij Gebr, Spanjersberg B.V., pg. 496 — PV
Van Rietschoten & Houwens Zuid-West bv, Rivium Boulevard 122, pg. 681 — IT
Van Swaay Toegangstechniek bv, Hooldweg 22, pg. 680 — IT
Veenman Kantoormachines BV, pg. 757 — IT
Veenman Office Management BV, pg. 757 — IT
WABCO Westinghouse B.V., Mient 12-16, Postbus 26, pg. 92 — PB

Coevorden

Componenta Benelux, pg. 1326 — IT
Componenta Benelux B.V., Monierweg 9, pg. 1421 — IT
Corepro B.V., pg. 497 — IT
Forbo Novilon produktiebedrijven bv, pg. 497 — IT
Imtech Projects Noord-Oost bv, Ing Arjan von Kweg 4, pg. 681 — IT
Vonk Systems, Ing Arjen Vonkweg 4, pg. 681 — IT
VonkData bv, Inj. Arjen Vonkweg 2, pg. 681 — IT

Culemborg

Logion B.V., pg. 1144 — IT
Wang Netherland B.V., Costerweg 12, pg. 1738 — PB

Cuyk

Celtona B.V., Lange Linden 22, pg. 672 — PB
Cuyk Mill, Lange Linden 22, pg. 672 — PB
Nutricia Cujik B.V., pg. 991 — IT

Dalfsen

Zuivelfabriek 'Salland' BV, pg. 752 — IT

De Lier

Horticom BV, Hoofdstraat 88, pg. 1099 — IT

De Meern

bv Aldipress, pg. 1445 — IT
European Technology Centre, Rijnzathe 6, pg. 1228 — PB
Sequent Computer Systems, B.V., Rijnzathe 7A2n, pg. 1459 — PB
Sovedi Benelux-Nederland, De Dompelaar 1, pg. 410 — IT
VNU Verkoopgroep BV, Burgemeester Verderlaan 11, pg. 1445 — IT

Dedemsvaart

Rollepaal B.V., pg. 1136 — IT

Delden

SERVO Delden B.V., Lange Straat 167, pg. 1456 — IT

Delft

Bakery Ingredients Division, Wateringseweg 1, pg. 1142 — IT
Calve-De Betuwe B.V., pg. 1436 — IT
Corporate New Business Development Div., pg. 1142 — IT
Cosmoferm B.V., Wateringseweg 1, pg. 1143 — IT
De Boo Beheer B.V., pg. 1200 — IT
Delft Instruments Defense BV, Mercuriusweg 1, pg. 388 — IT
Delft Instruments Electro-Optics B.V., Rontgenweg 1, pg. 389 — IT
Delft Instruments International B.V., Mercurinsweg 1, pg. 389 — IT
Delft Instruments Nederland B.V., Mercuriusweg 1, pg. 389 — IT
DELFT INSTRUMENTS N.V., Mercuriusweg 1, pg. 388 — IT
Devoe Coatings, B.V., Rotterdamseweg 144A, pg. 663 — PB
Enraf B.V., Rontgenweg 1, pg. 389 — IT
Enraf-Nonius B.V., Rontgenweg 1, P.O. Box 810, pg. 389 — IT
Genencor International B.V., A. Fleminglaan 1, pg. 349 — IT
Gist-Erocades B.V., Wateringseweg 1, pg. 1142 — IT
Gist-Erocades Food Specialties, Wateringseweg 1, pg. 1142 — IT
Gist-Erocades International BV, Wateringseweg 1, pg. 1142 — IT
Hartmann & Braun Nederland BV, pg. 835 — IT
Industrial Pharmaceutical Products Division, Wateringseweg 1, pg. 1142 — IT
Kadee Delft BV, Buitenwatersloot 335, pg. 461 — IT
Nonius BV, Rontgenweg 1, pg. 389 — IT
Oldelft B.V., Rontgenweg 1, pg. 389 — IT
ROYAL GIST-BROCADES N.V., Wateringseweg 1, pg. 1142 — IT

Delfzijl

Aluminium Delfzijl, Oosterhorn 20-22, pg. 755 — IT
Aluminium Delfzijl BV, Oosterhorn 20-22, pg. 753 — IT
Delamine B.V.-Delfzijl Plant, Oosterhorn 8, pg. 1408 — IT
Delesto bv, 4 Oosterhorn, pg. 43 — IT
Lafarge Gips BV, pg. 791 — IT
Methanol Chemie Nederland vof, 32 Rijksstraatweg, pg. 43 — IT
Methanor vof, 4 Oosterhorn, pg. 43 — IT
Neste Resins B.V., P.O. Box 109, pg. 915 — IT
Norgyps BV, pg. 791 — IT

Demeern

A.B. Dick Holland B.V., European Distribution &, Support Centre, pg. 791 — PV

Den Bosch

CW Lease Nederland, Pettelaarpark 80, pg. 647 — IT
Dixons, Goudenheuvel 47, pg. 1462 — IT
Electro-Jacobs, Guco, Heijmans, Rovato and Valkenberg, Goudenheuvel 47, pg. 1462 — IT
Klick, Goudenheuvel 47, pg. 1462 — IT
OMRON Manufacturing of the Netherlands B.V., Zilverenberg 2, pg. 1006 — IT
Pet's Place, Kobaltweg 17, pg. 1463 — IT

Denekamp

Petrolite Nederland B.V., De Gervelink 21, pg. 166 — PB

Deurne

Fastfood International BV, pg. 751 — IT
Makro N.V., Bisschoppenhoflaan 643-645, pg. 1155 — IT
Technostaal Schouten BV, pg. 1357 — IT

Deventer

Beleggingsmaatschappij Zaandijk B.V., pg. 1207 — IT
Continental Can Company of Europe B.V., pg. 1207 — IT
Continental Can Europe Services B.V., pg. 1207 — IT
De Vereenigde Blikfabrieken B.V., pg. 1207 — IT
Handelsmaatschappij V/H Kortman B.V., pg. 1207 — IT
Maatschappij tot Verwaarding van "Ducaat" Verwarmings en Kookapparaten, pg. 1207 — IT
Metaalfabriek Drenthina B.V., pg. 1207 — IT
Metaalwarenfavriek Pielkenrood B.V., pg. 1207 — IT
Tedeco B.V., pg. 1207 — IT
Thomassen & Drijver-Verblifa N.V., pg. 1207 — IT
Van Leeuwen Precision BV, Hamburgweg 6, pg. 1449 — IT
White Cap Benelux B.V., pg. 1207 — IT
Wolters Kluwer Business Publishing, Welle 39, pg. 1513 — IT
Wolters Kluwer Law and Taxation, Staverenstraat 32015, pg. 1513 — IT
YRSU B.V., pg. 1207 — IT

Didam

Vink Kunststoffen B.V., Bergvredestraat 7, pg. 1210 — IT

Diemen

B.V. Algemene Holding en Financierings Mij., Wildenborch 1, pg. 90 — IT
Beleggingsmaatschappij de Grachten B.V., Wildenborch 1, pg. 90 — IT
B.V. Beleggingsmaatschappij Nedasinvest, Diemerhof 42, pg. 90 — IT
CSM Food Division, Nienoord 13, pg. 243 — IT
CSM Ingredients Division, Nienoord 13, pg. 243 — IT
CSM N.V., Nienoord 13, pg. 243 — IT
CSM Sugar Division, Nienoord 13, pg. 243 — IT
CSM Suiker BV, Nienoord 13, pg. 243 — IT
DB Reclame Services, Wildenborch 2, pg. 386 — IT
DaVinci B.V., Wildenborch 2, pg. 386 — IT
De Bussy, pg. 386 — IT
DE BUSSY HARMS N.V., Wildenborch 2, pg. 386 — IT
De Bussy Participaties, Wildenborch 2, pg. 386 — IT
De Bussy Uitgeverij, Wildenborch 2, pg. 386 — IT
Electrolux Constructor B.V., Postbus 188, pg. 443 — IT
Electrolux Nederland B.V., Postbus 188, pg. 443 — IT
Exploitatiemaatschappij Transportbeton B.V., Op de Sniep 20, pg. 134 — IT
Financierings Maatschappij Nedasfimij B.V., Diemerhof 42, pg. 91 — IT
GME Generali-Midi Expansion B.V., Diemerhof 42, pg. 91 — IT
Generali Levensverzekering MIJ. N.V., Diemerhof 42, pg. 91 — IT
Generali Schadeverzekering Maatschappij N.V., Diemerhof 44, pg. 91 — IT
Generali Verzekeringsgroep N.V., Diemerhof 42, pg. 91 — IT
Gestetner Holding BV, pg. 1115 — IT
Gestetner Securities B.V., P.O. Box 163, pg. 1115 — IT
Hubbard Europa B.V., Dalsteindreef 2, pg. 1091 — PB
NV Levensverzekering Mij. Eerste Hollandsche, Diemerhof 44, pg. 91 — IT
NV Schadeverzekering Maatschappij N.V., Diemerhof 44, pg. 92 — IT
Nederlands Algemeen Verzekeringskantoor B.V., Diemerhof 42, pg. 91 — IT
A.C. Nielsen (Nederland) B.V., Diemerhof 2, pg. 1183 — PB

PB - *U.S. Public Companies Volume*
PV - *U.S. Private Companies Volume*
IT - *International Public & Private Companies Volume*

Onroerend Goed Exploitatie Mij. Lepaka B.V., Diemerhof
  42, pg. 91   IT
The PFH Group, Wildenborchg, pg. 750   IT
Participate Maatschappij Transhol B.V., Diemerhof 42,
  pg. 92   IT
Participatie Maatschappij Graafschap Holland N.V.,
  Diemerhof 42, pg. 92   IT
Praxis Doe-het-Zelf Center B.V., Wildenborchg, pg. 750   IT
Redoze Holding N.V., Diemerhof 42, pg. 92   IT
N.V. Schadeverzelering Mij. De Nederlanden Van 1870,
  Diemerhof 42, pg. 92   IT
Claudia Strater, Stammerhove 1, pg. 1462   IT

Dieren

Albany International B.V., Postbus 32, pg. 37   PB
Koninklijke Gazelle BV, Wilhelminaweg 8, pg. 394   IT
Te Hennepe LIN-PACK B.V., pg. 498   IT

Dodrect

Svedala Netherlands, pg. 1325   IT

Doesburg

Hermedico BV, Leigraafseweg 2, pg. 987   IT

Doetinchem

Century Oils Holdings (Nederland) B.V., pg. 517   IT
Drankenhandel De Graafschap B.V., pg. 559   IT
Elsevier Bedrijfinformatie B.V., Hanzestraat 1, pg. 1099   IT
Hein de Windt B.V., Fabriekstraat 14, pg. 517   IT
Hosokawa Micron B.V., Industriestraat 25, pg. 636   IT
Misset, Hanzestraat 1, pg. 1099   IT
Nederlandse Ijzergieterij Vulcanus B.V., Keppelseweg 347-
  353, pg. 1210   IT
Vredestein Fietsbanden B.V., Broekweg 29, pg. 1481   IT

Dokkum

Delta-Bouw BV, pg. 607   IT

Dongen

Tentler & Co., B.V., pg. 1502   PB

Dordrecht

Ballast Nedam Funderingstechnieken B.V., Donker
  Duyvisweg 25, pg. 133   IT
Bekaert Nederland B.V., Kamerlingh Onnesweg 14,
  pg. 184   IT
Du Pont de Nemours (Nederland) B.V., Baanhoekweg,
  pg. 532   PB
Gist-Brocades Benelux B.V., Mijlweg 77, pg. 1143   IT
ITT Flygt S.V., Kamerlingh Onnesweg 35, pg. 860   PB
Internatio Hout B.V., 213, Weeskinderendijk, pg. 682   IT
JGC Dordtse Engineering B.V., 3300 AJ Dordrecht,
  pg. 697   IT
KME Nederland B.V., Stationweg 4, 1e etage, pg. 720   IT
Kemira Color B.V., Mijlweg 65, pg. 729   IT
Kemira Color Europe B.V., pg. 729   IT
Marathon Petroleum Netherlands, Ltd., Wolwevershaven
  24, pg. 1662   PB
Raab Karcher Nederland B.V., pg. 1458   IT
Ubel B.V., Kamerlingh Onnesweg 18, pg. 551   IT
Valvoline Oil Nederland B.V., Wieldrechtseweg 39,
  pg. 140   PB
Villares Steel International BV, pg. 23   IT
Wolters Kluwer Academic Publishers, Spuiboulevard 50,
  pg. 1512   IT

Dosterhort

Analog Devices Nederland B.V., Beneluxweg 27,
  pg. 108   PB

Drachten

Eldon N.V., Postbus 38, pg. 436   IT
LeoReitsma B.V., pg. 1146   IT

Driebergen-Rijsenburg

Van Gend & Loos B.V., Odijkerweg 2-B, pg. 1145   IT

Drunen

Alcoa Nederland Holding B. V., Lipsstraat 40, pg. 62   PB
John Crane Marine-Lips, P.O. Box 176, 5150 AD, Lipstraat
  52, pg. 1339   IT
Lips B.V., Lipsstraat 52, pg. 812   IT
LIPS UNITED B.V., Lipsstraat 52, pg. 812   IT

Duiven

Modipack BV, Postbus 216, pg. 983   IT

Edam

BOON EDAM B.V., Ambachstraat 4, pg. 202   IT
Bose B.V., Nijuerheidstratt, pg. 161   PV
Es+Es Verpakkingen B.V., pg. 1146   IT
Fardem BV, Nijverheidstraat 55, pg. 352   IT

Ede

Grootverbruik Ahold bv, Frankeneng 18, pg. 749   IT
Kimberly-Clark Benelux Operations B.V.-West Office,
  Pascalstraat 15, pg. 959   PB
RVS Levensverzekering, Loevestein 33, pg. 647   IT
Verkerke Reprodukties, N.V., Morsestraat 9-11,
  pg. 496   PV

Eemnes

Genzyme B.V., Seldenrijkweg 2, pg. 733   PB

Eerbeek

PSG Pillo-Pak Maatschappij BV, pg. 756   IT
SCA De Hoop, pg. 1326   IT
SCA De Hoop Recycling, Harderwijkerweg 41,
  pg. 1327   IT
SCA Packaging Benelux, Coldenhovenseweg 130,
  pg. 1326   IT
Watts Industries Europe B.V., Kollergang 14, pg. 1747   PB

Eersel

B.A.T Netherlands B.V., Nieuwstraat 75, pg. 111   IT
Henri Wintermans' Sigarenfabrieken B.V., Nieuwstraat 75,
  pg. 111   IT

Eibergen

De Haes Holland B.V., De Kiefte 18, pg. 198   IT
Verosol Fabrics B.V., De Kiefte 18, pg. 198   IT

Eindhoven

Ballast Nedam Woningbouw B.V., Gebouw Vierlander,
  Fellenoord 27, pg. 134   IT
Beamix Holding B.V., Hastelweg 161, pg. 605   IT
BERG Electronics BV, Aalsterweg 183, pg. 213   PB
Candela Europe, Vestdijk 9, pg. 300   PB
DAF Trucks N.V., Hugo van der Goeslaan 1, pg. 1247   IT
Evoluon-Philips Competence Centre, pg. 1051   IT
Generale Bank - Eindhoven, Fellenoord 220, pg. 547   IT
Grabowsky & Poort eta ingenieurs, pg. 607   IT
Grabowsky & Poort Schiebroeck-Struik BV, Parklaan 60,
  pg. 607   IT
Grabowsky & Poort Zuid BV, P.O. Box 330, pg. 607   IT
Hewlett-Packard Nederland B.V., Boschdijk 131,
  pg. 821   PB
Hydrowa B.V., 6 Hoppenkuil, pg. 1285   IT
Ingenieursbureau Schiebroek-Struik BV, Parklaan 60,
  pg. 607   IT
International Kendix Textiles B.V., pg. 540   IT
Laura Ashley BV, Luchthavenweg 24, pg. 804   IT
Laura Ashley CER Countries BV, Luchthavenweg 24,
  pg. 804   IT
Multicom TBWA Advertising B.V., Dillenburgstraat 5A,
  pg. 1062   PV
Novellus Systems, B.V., Dillenburgstraat 5B, pg. 1204   PB
Pharmacia & Upjohn Holding Nederland BV,
  Luchthavenweg 38, pg. 1050   IT
Pharmacia & Upjohn International NV, Luchthavenweg 38,
  pg. 1050   IT
Philips Communication Systems B.V., pg. 1051   IT
Philips Communications & Processing Services B.V.,
  pg. 1051   IT
Philips Components B.V., Hurksestraat 9, pg. 1051   IT
Philips Consumer Electronics International B.V,
  pg. 1051   IT
PHILIPS ELECTRONICS N.V., Groennewoudseweg 1,
  pg. 1051   IT
Philips Industrial Electronics International B.V.,
  pg. 1051   IT
Philips International B.V., Bldg. VO, pg. 1051   IT
Philips Lighting B.V., pg. 1051   IT
Philips Machinefabrieken B.V., Building TAM 106,
  pg. 1051   IT
Philips PMF International B.V., pg. 1051   IT
Philips Semiconductors B.V., pg. 1051   PB
Pulsarr, Marinus von Meelweg 20, pg. 20   IT
Redland Holding BV, Stratumsedijk 29-D, pg. 1093   PB
Robinson Nugent (Europe) B.V., pg. 1395   PB
Leo Schellens B.V., pg. 540   IT
Signaal USFA, Meerenakkerweg 1, pg. 1385   IT
Spectra-Physics B.V., Prof. Dr. Dorgelolarn 20,
  pg. 1290   IT
VDL GROEP BV, Hoevenweg 1, pg. 1444   IT
Van Zandbeek/The Corporate Company, Tramstraat 72,
  pg. 118   IT
Videotex Oost-Brabant BV, pg. 720   IT
Wandel & Goltermann B.V., Teleport Science Park,
  pg. 1486   IT

Elst

H.J. Heinz B.V., Stationstraat 50, pg. 806   PB

Emmeloord

Geesink B.V., P.O. Box 52, pg. 1066   IT

Emmen

Ericsson Mobile Networks B.V., Nieuw Amsterdamsestraat
  40, pg. 1367   IT

Ericsson Radio Systems B.V., Nieuw Amsterdamsestraat
  40, pg. 1367   IT

Enkhuizen

Draka Polva B.V., Flevolann 1-5, pg. 1278   IT
Koninklijke Zaadteelt en Zaadhandel Sluis en Groot B.V.,
  pg. 983   IT
C.W. Pannevis Zaadteelt en Zaadhandel B.V., pg. 975   IT
S & G Seeds B.V., pg. 984   IT
Sandoz Holding Netherlands B.V., pg. 984   IT
Zaadunie B.V., pg. 986   IT

Enschede

AMEV V-A Ardanta, M.H. Tromplaan 52, pg. 499   IT
Ames Europe B.V., pg. 539   IT
Ames Europe Enschede B.V., pg. 539   IT
Atlet-Multicar BV, Oljeslagweg 7, pg. 97   IT
Boekelo Folien B.V., Bockelosestraat 300, pg. 1278   IT
Esta Behang B.V., pg. 540   IT
FREDESTEIN BANDEN, P.O. Box 27, pg. 504   IT
GROLSCH N.V., Brouwerijstraat 1, pg. 559   IT
HiChem Diagnostics B.V., Zomerweg 147, pg. 436   IT
Machinenfabriek Roberine B.V., pg. 493   PB
McKechnie Investments, Postbus 6366, pg. 852   IT
Polaroid (Europa) B.V., 24 Market, pg. 1314   IT
Polaroid (Europa) B.V., Hoge Bothofstraat 45, pg. 1314   PB
Verosol Nederland B.V., Strootsweg 22, pg. 198   IT
Vredestein Banden B.V., ir E.L.C. Schiff Sr. Straat 370,
  pg. 1481   IT
Vredestein Consulting B.V., ir E.L.C. Schiff Sr. Straat 370,
  pg. 1481   IT

Epe

Georg Fischer Holding (N.V.), Lange Veenteweg 19,
  pg. 489   IT
Georg Fischer N.V., Lange Veenteweg 19, pg. 489   IT
Georg Fischer WAGA N.V., Lange Veentweg 19,
  pg. 490   IT

Erp

Gis Munsters B.V., Postbus 2, pg. 1133   IT

Etten-Leur

Bakker Continental, Florijnstraat 20, pg. 1463   IT
Black & Decker (Nederland) B.V., Florijnstraat 10,
  pg. 234   PB
Boart Longyear B.V., P.O. Box 56, Nijverheidsweg 47,
  pg. 76   PB
Gamko Holdings, Mon-Plaisir-75, pg. 1497   PB
Isover BV, Parallelweg 20, pg. 1176   IT
Millipore B.V., Penningweg 33, pg. 1113   PB
Varco BJ Oil Tools B.V., P.O. Box 17, Nijverheidsweg 45,
  pg. 1709   PB

Europoort

Van Leer Nederland B.V., pg. 1146   IT

Farum

Bull A/S, Ryttermarken 15-21, pg. 317   IT

Fijnaart

Escher Holland B.V., Postbus 34, pg. 1133   IT
Mannesmann Nederland BV, pg. 838   IT
Timac B.V., Indus. area dintelmond, 1e Februariweg 13,
  pg. 712   IT

Franeker

Leopack B.V., pg. 1146   IT
Leotech B.V., pg. 1146   IT

Geertruidenberg

B.V. Ashland-Suedchemie V.H. Necof, P.O. Box 6,
  pg. 140   PB

Geldermalsen

Ameron B.V., Fiberglass Pipe Division-Europe, J. F.
  Kennedylaan 7, pg. 99   PB
Ameron B.V., Protective Coatings Division-Europe, J. F.
  Kennedylaan 7, pg. 99   PB

Geldrop

Baldwin Europe Consolidated, Inc., Heuvel 6, pg. 170   PB
Baldwin Graphic Equipment BV, pg. 170   PB
SP Aerospace & Vehicle Systems B.V., Eindhovenseweg
  120, pg. 809   IT

Geleen

DSM Kunststoffen B.V., pg. 353   IT
DSM Limburg B.V., Mijnweg 1, pg. 353   IT
DSM Research B.V., Koestraat 3, pg. 353   IT
DSM Special Products B.V., pg. 353   IT
DSM Transportmaatschappij BV, pg. 354   IT
Engineering-Stamicarbon, pg. 354   IT

Geographic Index-Non U.S.

Holland Sweetener Company, Production Dept.,
  pg. 1408   IT
Intercai Holding BV, pg. 720   IT
Reko B.V., De Asselen Kuil 15, pg. 354   IT
Stamicarbon BV, 6160 AB Geleen, pg. 354   IT

Genderen

Forbo Genderen B.V., pg. 497   IT

Gent

Finero B.V., pg. 1018   IT
Outokumpu Steel Processing B.V., pg. 1018   IT

Giesbeek

Bell & Howell Nederland B.V., Nijverheidsstraat 22,
  pg. 201   PB
Pretec Precisie Techniek B.V., Kuyperlan 28, pg. 201   PB

Giessen

Hak B.V., Jagerspad 7, pg. 244   IT

Gieten

Exportslachterij Udema B.V., Stationstraat 36, pg. 1437   IT

Goirle

Curver B.V., Edisonstraat 8, pg. 352   IT
Forbo Bonaparte B.V., pg. 497   IT
B.V. Tapijveredelingsindustrie, pg. 498   IT

Goor

Lakatex B.V., D.J. Bunschotenstraat 14, pg. 198   IT

Gorcum

PURAC Group, Arkelsedijk 46, pg. 244   IT

Gorinchem

Bailey-Fischer & Porter B.V., Avelingen West 3,
  pg. 449   IT
Carnation Nederland B.V., pg. 919   IT
Hagglunds Drives GmbH, Stephensonweg 8, pg. 670   IT
Ingenieursbureau van der Mast B.V., pg. 607   IT
Axel Johnson Steel International B.V., Business Center,
  pg. 712   IT
MERCON STEEL STRUCTURES B.V., Krinkelwinkel 6-8,
  pg. 858   IT
Oxford Instruments, Avelingen West 1, pg. 1018   IT
Oxford Instruments-Medical Systems, Avelingen West 1,
  pg. 1018   IT
Robbe Radiatoren B.V., Ijsbaan 45, pg. 267   IT
Veebman Direkt, pg. 757   IT

Gouda

Albro Bakkerijen Zwanenburg B.V., Groningenweg 8,
  pg. 555   IT
Auto Lease Holland B.V., Kampenringweg 49, pg. 9   IT
Blikman & Sartorius B.V., Muidenweg, pg. 682   IT
Compaq Computer B.V., Hanzeweg 14, pg. 418   PB
DMR Groep B.V., Harderwijkweg 7, pg. 528   IT
Datapoint Nederland B.V., 1 Kampenringweg 47,
  pg. 384   IT
Eclipse Combustion B.V., Zwolleweg 5, pg. 361   PV
HBW, Hollandsche Beton en Waterbouw B.V., H.J.
  Nederhorststraat 1, pg. 630   IT
Landis & Staefa (Nederland) B.V., Kampenringweg 45,
  pg. 801   IT
The MacNeal-Schwendler Co. B.V., Groningenweg 6,
  pg. 1032   PB
Moulinex B.V., Doesburweg 4, pg. 896   IT
PDA International/Netherlands, Agnietenstraat 66-A,
  pg. 1031   PB
Quality Bakers Nederland B.V., Groningenweg 8,
  pg. 555   IT
Unichema-Chemie B.V., Buurtje 1, pg. 1438   IT

Gravenhage

Thomson-CSF, c/o Signaal, Lange Voorhout 62,
  pg. 1385   IT

Groenlo

Polarcup Benelux B.V., Houtwal 3, pg. 638   IT

Groningen

ALK Benelux BV, Moesstraat 28, pg. 288   IT
KPN KONINKLYKE PTT NEDERLAND NV, Stationsplein 7,
  pg. 720   IT
Logica B.V., Brugstraat 32B, pg. 814   IT
MOC BV, pg. 720   IT
NVG Levensverzekeringmaatschappij NV, 5 Queridolaan,
  pg. 26   IT
NVG Schadeverzekeringmaatschappij NV, 5, Queridolaan,
  pg. 26   IT
NVG Uitaartverzekeringmaatschappij NV, 5 Queridolaan,
  pg. 26   IT

N.V. Nederlandse Gasunie, Laan Corpus den Hoorn 102,
  pg. 602   PB
Nederlandse Verzekerings Groep NV, 5 Queridolaan,
  pg. 26   IT
Norplast-Lamaf B.V., Sontweg 1, pg. 1210   IT
PTT Finans BV, pg. 720   IT
PTT Vastgoed BV, pg. 721   IT
Philips Domestic Appliances and Personal Care B.V.,
  pg. 1051   IT
Telecourt BV, pg. 721   IT
Vierverlaten Sugar Factory, Fabrieklaan 12, pg. 244   IT
Wolters Kluwer Educational Activities, Bisonspoor 2016,
  pg. 1513   IT

Groot-Ammers

Koninklijke Brink/Molyn B.V., PO Box 4, 33
  Schoodhovenseveer, pg. 42   IT

Haaksbergen

Reobijn B.V., Industriestraat 28, pg. 1210   IT
Textiel Techniek Haaksbergen B.V., Goorestraat 17,
  pg. 1203   IT

Haarlem

A.P. De Assurantiepartners Amsterdam B.V., Jansweg, 42,
  pg. 90   IT
AtoHaas B.V., pg. 1403   PB
AtoHaas Holding C.V., pg. 1403   PB
AtoHaas Pacific B.V., pg. 1403   PB
AtoHaas Technologies B.V., pg. 1403   PB
Donaldson Torit, Waardewag 45, pg. 517   PB
Fluor Daniel B.V. Haarlem, pg. 660   PB
IDC Benelux, Schipholwegl, pg. 570   PV
IDC Nederland, Schipholweg 1, pg. 571   PV
IDG Communications Nederland BV, Schipholwegl,
  pg. 570   PV
Ideal-Standard, Lange Herenstraat 45-47, pg. 92   PB
MCMC Corrugating Machinery Co. Holland B.V., Hendrik
  Figeeweg 5L, pg. 874   IT
Medianet bv, Stationsplein 112-118, pg. 1445   IT
Merck Sharp & Dohme-Holland, Waarderweg 39,
  pg. 1092   PB
NEC Industries Netherlands B.V., Grote Houtstraat 95,
  pg. 900   IT
NIFE B.V., Zijlweg 156, pg. 53   IT
Oud Wijnkopers & Hustinx BV, pg. 751   IT
Pfizer Hospital Products (Netherlands) B.V., Claus
  Sluterweg 125, pg. 1284   PB
Schiphol Telematics BV, pg. 720   IT
Schiphol Telematics CV, pg. 720   IT
Top Sante vof, pg. 1445   IT
Toshiba International Finance (Netherlands) B.V., Zijlstraat
  7C, pg. 1406   IT
Uitgeverij Spaarnestad bv, Ceylonpoort 5-25, pg. 1445   IT
VNU Business Information Europe, Ceylonpoort 5-25,
  pg. 1445   IT
VNU Magazine Group International bv, Ceylonpoort 5-25,
  pg. 1445   IT
**VNU VERENIGDE NEDERLANDSE
UITGEVERSBEDRIJVEN B.V.**, Ceylonpoort 5-25,
  pg. 1445   IT
VERMEULEN HOLLANDIA BV, Kuppersweg 89,
  pg. 1463   IT
Witco B.V., Spaarndamseweg 466, pg. 1774   PB

Haastrecht

Tableau Fine Arts Magazine bv, Grote Haven 1,
  pg. 1445   IT

Hague

ASB, Herengracht 23, pg. 1463   IT
AEGON International B.V., Mariahoeveplein 50, pg. 25   IT
AEGON Levensverzekering NV, 50, Mariahoeveplein,
  pg. 25   IT
AEGON Nederland N.V., 50, Mariahoeveplein, pg. 26   IT
AEGON Nevak Holding N.V., pg. 26   IT
AEGON N.V., Mariahoeveplein 50, pg. 25   IT
AEGON Reinsurance N.V., 50, Mariahoeveplein, pg. 26   IT
AEGON Schadeverzekering N.V., Mariahoeveplein 50,
  pg. 26   IT
Alcatel Netherland, Plantinaweg 10-20, pg. 55   IT
Amoco Netherlands Petroleum Co., Stichthage (Central
  Station), pg. 102   PB
BAC Financial Services International B.V., Carnegielaan 10-
  14, pg. 203   PB
BAC International-The Netherlands B.V., Room ST 730,
  Koningin Julianaplein 15, pg. 203   PB
BMW Finance N.V., pg. 178   IT
Bally Schoenhandel B.V., Venestraat 54-56, pg. 997   IT
Bank Mees & Hope NV, pg. 9   IT
NV Casema, pg. 720   IT
Chevron Oil Company of Netherlands, Eisenhowerlaan 110,
  pg. 348   PB
CLAM Petroleum Co., Parkstramt 31, pg. 1662   PB
Clyde Petroleum - Netherlands, Mauritskade 35,
  pg. 578   IT
Consulting Engineers Grabowsky & Poort BV, pg. 607   IT
Cres Netherlands Inc., Kalvermarkt 9, pg. 5   IT
Daval Nederland, pg. 572   IT
Ebasco B.V., Verrijn Stuartlaan 7, pg. 1587   PB
Elts BV, pg. 720   IT
Encompass Europe NV, pg. 720   IT
Esso Nederland B.V., 129-131 Jan van Nassaustraat,
  pg. 602   PB

Gebr. Eijffinger B.V., pg. 540   IT
B.F. Goodrich Chemical Sales Co., B.V., Paviljoensgracht 1,
  pg. 752   PB
Grabowsky & Poort BV, P.O. Box 84319, pg. 607   IT
Grabowsky & Poort BV, pg. 606   IT
Grabowsky & Poort International Consultants, P.O. Box
  84319, pg. 607   IT
H-Partners, Kerkeminenweg 18, pg. 1463   IT
Hovanes B.V., pg. 1205   IT
ING Verzekeringen N.V., pg. 647   IT
Ingenieursbureau Grabowsky & Poort BV, pg. 607   IT
International Satellite Services BV, pg. 720   IT
JGC Corporation, Scheveningseweg 58, pg. 697   IT
Kelly Uitzendburo, De Horst 2, pg. 949   PB
Kluwer Law International, Carnegieplein 5, pg. 1512   IT
Konmar, De Werf 13, pg. 1463   IT
Leerdams Vervoers Centrum BV, pg. 720   IT
Luigi Lucardi, Spui 3, pg. 1462   IT
Lummus Nederland B.V., Kalvermarkt 9, pg. 6   IT
Marconi Space Systems Participations BV, pg. 796   IT
Matra Espace Holding BV, pg. 796   IT
Matra Marconi Space BV, pg. 796   IT
Meneba N.V., Koninginnegracht 15, pg. 555   IT
Milchem International Limited, Eisenhowerlann 108-110,
  pg. 167   PB
Mobile Producing Netherlands Incorporated,
  Kantoorgebouw Babylon, Koning Julianaplein 30,
  pg. 1119   PB
Monsanto B.V., Jan van Nassaustraat 53-55, pg. 1125   PB
Nationale-Nederlanden Schaadeverzekering Maatschappij
  N.V., pg. 647   IT
Nationale-Nederlanden Zorgverzekering N.V., pg. 647   IT
Nederlandse PersDataBank BV, pg. 720   IT
O.O.M. Onderlinge Molestverzekering-Maatschappij U.A., 5
  Carnegieplein, pg. 26   IT
O.O.M. Onderlinge Verzekering-Maatschappij U.A, 5,
  Carnegieplein, pg. 26   IT
O.O.M. Onderlinge Ziektekostenverzekering-Maatschappij
  U.A., 5, Carnegieplein, pg. 26   IT
PTT Autolease BV, pg. 720   IT
PTT Contest BV, pg. 720   IT
PTT Post Beheer BV, pg. 720   IT
PTT Post BV, pg. 720   IT
PTT Post Logistiek Maarssen BV, pg. 720   IT
PTT Post Logistiek Nijmegen BV, pg. 720   IT
PTT Telecom BV, pg. 720   IT
Raadgevend Ingenieursbureau voor Bouwcontrole BV,
  pg. 607   IT
N.V. Rotterdam Rijn Pijpleiding, Borweg 7, pg. 1461   IT
ROYAL DUTCH/SHELL GROUP OF COMPANIES, Carel
  Van Bylandtlaan 16, pg. 1135   IT
Royal Gold, Spui 3, pg. 1462   IT
SHL Systemhouse Nederland B.V., Koninginnegracht 23,
  pg. 1154   IT
Satellite Business Television BV, pg. 720   IT
Schaap & Citroen, Spui 3, pg. 1462   IT
Schinac B.V., pg. 1205   IT
Schindler Liften B.V., pg. 1205   IT
Schlumberger B.V., Netherlands, 181, Bezuidenhoutseweg,
  pg. 1439   PB
Shandwick Van de Meeberg PR, Koninginnesaracht 23,
  pg. 1227   IT
Shell Internationale Petroleum Mij BV, Carel van
  Bylandtlaan 30, pg. 1135   IT
Siebel, Spui 3, pg. 1462   IT
Siemens Nederland N.V., Postbus 16068, pg. 1247   IT
Sodra Nederland B.V., Kettingstraat 2, pg. 1276   IT
Tebodin BV Consultants & Engineers, Laan van Nieuw
  Oost Indie 25, pg. 630   IT
Telematch BV, pg. 720   PV
Titania A/S, Dolane, pg. 271   PV
Total Oil & Gas Nederland B.V., Alexanderstraat 10,
  pg. 1409   IT
Unisource Business Networks Nederland BV, pg. 720   PB
Unocal Netherlands, pg. 1698   IT
VEBA OIL NEDERLAND B.V., Bezuidenhoutseweg 1,
  pg. 1461   IT
Verebus Engineering B.V., The Hague, Duinweg 37,
  pg. 680   IT
Voest-Alpine Nederland B.V., Hartogstraat 13,
  pg. 1472   IT
Wintershall Nederland B.V., Eisenhowerlaan 142/146,
  pg. 110   IT
Wintershall Noordzee B.V, Eisenhowerlaan 142,
  pg. 110   IT
Zurich Levensverzekering-Maatschappij,
  Bezuidenhoutseweg 111, pg. 1529   IT

Halfweg

Mentor Graphics (Netherlands) N.V., Haarlemmerstraatweg
  133-137, pg. 1087   PB

Hardenberg

Cetra Metaal B.V., Nieuwe Haven 20, pg. 1210   IT

Harderwijk

California B.V., Verkeersweg 75, pg. 243   IT
Deni Distributiecentrum B.V., Lorentzstrat 41,
  pg. 1144   IT
Reynolds Aluminium Holland B.V., Industrieweg 15,
  pg. 1387   PB

Haren

Holmen Nederland B.V., pg. 885   IT
Iggesund Benelux B.V., pg. 886   IT
KNP Oud Papier B.V., Rijksstraatweg 240, pg. 756   IT

PB - *U.S. Public Companies Volume*
PV - *U.S. Private Companies Volume*
IT - *International Public & Private Companies Volume*

1716

Kappa B.V., Rijksstraatweg 240, pg. 756 — IT
Schering Agro B.V., pg. 1203 — IT

Hazerwoude

Fasson Producten Verkoopmaatschappij B.V., Rijndijk 86, pg. 154 — PB

Heemstede

Bausch & Lomb B.V., Nijverheidsweg 41, pg. 195 — PB
Big Balloon bv, Raadhuisstraat 27, pg. 1445 — IT
Dactylo, Kerklaan 21, pg. 1463 — IT
EMI Music Holland BV, Bronsteeweg 49, pg. 427 — IT
Luxottica Nederland B.V., Van de Eijndekade 2, pg. 822 — IT

Heerde

Ventilex Milieutechniek B.V., Heerde, 8, Europaweg, pg. 681 — IT

Heerenveen

Algemene Friese Onderlinge Schadeverzekeringmaatschappij 'Zevenwouden' U.A., 22, Van Maasdijkstraat, pg. 26 — IT
Tektronix Holland N.V., pg. 1567 — PB
Tektronix Holland N.V.-Heerenveen, pg. 1567 — PB

Heerhugowaard

Ammeraal Conveyor Belting B.V., pg. 540 — IT
Cardo Door Continental B.V., Marconistraat 18, pg. 269 — IT
Cardo Door Logistics B.V., P.O. Box 120, pg. 269 — IT
Crawford Deur B.V., Costerstraat 20, pg. 269 — IT
SAB WABCO Holdings B.V., Marconistraat 18, pg. 271 — IT

Heerlen

Akrosil Europe B.V., pg. 904 — PB
Braden-Metrio, pg. 924 — PB
DSM Energie B.V., Het Overloon 1, pg. 353 — IT
DSM Engineering Plastic Products BV, pg. 353 — IT
DSM High Performance Fibers B.V., Eisterweg 3, pg. 353 — IT
DSM N.V., Het Overloon 1, pg. 352 — IT
DSM Plastic Products, Het Overloon 1, pg. 353 — IT
Dow Jones Courrier, B.V., In de Cramer 37, pg. 525 — PB
Energie Beheer Nederland B.V., Het Overloon 1, pg. 353 — IT
Hallmark Cards Nederland, B.V., Imstenraderweg 21, pg. 496 — PV
Laura Metaal B.V., Gebouw op de Geer, pg. 754 — IT
Muva Greetings B.V., Imstenraderweg 21 6422 PM, pg. 78 — PB
NV Pensioenverzekeringsmaatschappij, pg. 354 — IT
Sulzer Keuls B.V., pg. 1306 — IT
Wisaforest Benelux B.V., Emmastraat 722/2A, pg. 1429 — IT

Heithuizen

Omni Films International, pg. 916 — PB

Helden

Werner & Pfleiderer Haton B.V., Industrieterrein 13, pg. 511 — IT

Helmond

Avesta Sandvik Tube B.V., pg. 221 — IT
Avesta Sheffield Trading B.V., pg. 222 — IT
Edah, Kanaaldijk N.O. 82, pg. 1463 — IT
Expeditiebedrijf Gamex B.V., pg. 540 — IT
Gamma Holding Nederland N.V., pg. 540 — IT
GAMMA HOLDING N.V., Hoogeindsestraat 47, pg. 539 — IT
Golfkartonfabriek Van Dam B.V., Kanaaldijk NW 129, pg. 756 — IT
HTM Onroerend Goed B.V., pg. 540 — IT
Handelmij. Roestvrij B.V., pg. 222 — IT
Hatema-Distributie B.V., pg. 540 — IT
Hatema Retail Beheer B.V., pg. 540 — IT
Parabeam Industrie-en Handelsonderneming B.V., pg. 540 — IT
Planox B.V., pg. 540 — IT
ROR Rockwell B.V., Middendijk 40, pg. 1399 — PB
Robur Buizenfabriek B.V., Englesweg 173, pg. 513 — IT
Sandvik Saws and Tools Benelux B.V., pg. 1187 — IT
Silicon Materials Services B.V., Achterdijk 8, pg. 1456 — PB
Van Vlissingen-Ankersmit Export Maatschappij B.V., pg. 540 — IT
Vendex Food Groep, Julianalaan 2, pg. 1463 — IT
Vlisco B.V., pg. 540 — IT

Hendrik-Ido-Ambacht

STILL Intern Transport B.V., pg. 811 — IT
Zwijsen B.V., Nyverheidsweg 40, pg. 754 — IT

Hengelo

Akzo Zout Chemie B.V., 20 Boortorenweg, pg. 43 — IT

Akzo Zout Chemie Nederland B.V., 20, Boortorenweg, pg. 43 — IT
Bevrachtingskantoor Twenthe-Rijn bv, 60 Havenkade, P.O. Box 53, pg. 43 — IT
BLYDENSTEIN-WILLINK N.V., Amarilstraat 30, pg. 198 — IT
Centralebouw Combinatie B.V., Bornsestraat 5, pg. 1133 — IT
Eljssink, Wegterweg 33, pg. 1463 — IT
Hepworth Minerals and Chemicals B.V., Markt 307, pg. 615 — IT
Holec Projects B.V., Bornsestraat 5, pg. 1133 — IT
Hollandse Signaalapparaten B.V., Zuidelijke Havenweg 40, pg. 1385 — IT
Stork Ketels B.V., pg. 398 — IT
Sulzer Pompen Benelux B.V., pg. 1306 — IT

Hertogenbosch

BERG Electronics BV, Helfthenuelweg 11, pg. 213 — PB

Hilversum

AT&T Network Systems International, pg. 11 — PB
ATT Network Sistems International, B.V., Larenseweq 50, pg. 1373 — IT
Boeing International Corp., Graaf Florislaan 2A, pg. 242 — PB
CPC Benelux B.V., Rading 1, pg. 225 — IT
EMI Music Publishing (Holland) B.V., pg. 427 — IT
Hunkemoller, Liebergerweg 28, pg. 1462 — IT
INDIVERS B.V., Arena Office Park, Marathon 9H, pg. 673 — IT
International Flavors & Fragrances I.F.F. (Nederland) B.V., Liebergerweg 72-98, pg. 899 — PB
N.V. Interturbine, Marathon 9H, pg. 673 — IT
Kreymborg, Liebergerweg 28, pg. 1462 — IT
Lucent Technologies EMEA B.V., Larenseweg 50, pg. 1018 — IT
NIKE European Headquarters, Marathon 7, pg. 1184 — PB
Phonogram B.V., Catharina Van Renneslaan, pg. 1052 — IT
Polydor B.V., Albertus Perkstraat 35, pg. 1052 — IT
R.J. Reynolds Tobacco B.V., Larensweg 30, pg. 1355 — PB
Utell International-Benelux, Stationsraat 30, pg. 1098 — IT
Vendex Fashion Group, Liebergerweg 28, pg. 1462 — IT

Hoek van Holland

Air Products Nederland B.V., Willemskerkeweg 3, pg. 31 — PB
DSM Desotech B.V., Slachthuisweg 30, pg. 353 — IT
DSM Resins Benelux B.V., Slachthuisweg 30, pg. 353 — IT
DSM Resins International B.V., Slachthuisweg 30, pg. 353 — IT
Stena Line Holland BV, Staionsweg 10, pg. 1300 — IT

Hoensbroek

Norton B.V., Wijngaardsweg 73, pg. 1175 — IT
Norton (FSC) B.V., Winjngaardsweg 73, pg. 1175 — IT

Hoevelaken

Datascope B.V., Drs. W. Van Royenstraat 8, pg. 488 — PB
Prodetis B.V., Hogebrinkweg 9-11, pg. 317 — IT

Honselersdijk

Electro West B.V., Postbus 23, pg. 1133 — IT

Hoofddorp

AAR Allen Airmotive, Inc., 705 Kruisweg, pg. 1 — PB
Akzo Coatings B.V., 115 Planetenweg, pg. 42 — IT
Asatsu Europe B.V., Hoeksteen 80, pg. 86 — IT
Bilfinger + Berger Bouwmaatschappij B.V., Planetenweg 80c, pg. 196 — IT
Binter Finance, B.V., Planetenweg, 80-j, pg. 1225 — IT
Canon Benelux N.V., Neptunusstraat 1, pg. 262 — IT
Circle Freight International (Holland) B.V., Hoeksteen 115-117, Avio Trade Park, pg. 372 — PB
GD Net BV, pg. 720 — IT
Gall & Gall, Wijkermeerstraat 3, pg. 749 — IT
Gandalf Nederland B.V., Kruisweg 609, pg. 540 — IT
Herbalife International (Netherlands) B.V., Transpolis Schiphol Airport, Polaris Ave. 83D, pg. 809 — PB
IGT-Europe b.v., Bijlmermeerstraat 30, pg. 900 — PB
ITW Bevestigingssystemen B.V., Bijlmermeer Straat 62, pg. 868 — PB
Insurance Systems Nederland B.V., 791a, Kruisweg, pg. 26 — IT
Intergraph (Benelux) B.V., Siriusdreef 2, pg. 891 — PB
InterPost Group of Companies BV, pg. 720 — IT
Intrax BV, pg. 720 — IT
Kawasaki Motors Netherlands N.V., Diamantlaan 14, pg. 726 — IT
Kien, J.C. Beetslaan 153, pg. 1462 — IT
Life Technologies B.V., Starnmeerstraat 5-7, pg. 505 — PB
B.V. Machinefabriek Spaans, P.O. Box 4, pg. 472 — IT
McCain Foods Holland B.V. (The Netherlands), Rijnlanderweg 766, pg. 850 — IT
Microsoft B.V., pg. 1108 — PB
Mitsubishi Motor Sales Europe B.V., Hoeksteen 74-84, pg. 876 — IT
Mitsubishi Motors Europe B.V., Hoeksteen 74-84, pg. 876 — IT
Montell Polyolefins, Montell Polyolefins Hoeksteen 66, pg. 1136 — IT

Northern Telecom International Finance B.V., Siriusdreef 17-27, pg. 970 — IT
Obayashi Corporation-Amsterdam, 2nd Floor Building 4, Holland Office Center Kruisweg 815A, pg. 995 — IT
Obayashi Finance International (Netherlands) B.V., 2nd Floor Bldg. 4, Holland Office Ctr. Kruisweg 815A, pg. 996 — IT
Oki Systems (Holland) B.V., Kruisweg 765, pg. 1000 — IT
OMRON Electronics B.V., Wegalaan 61, pg. 1005 — IT
OMRON Europe B.V., Wegalaan 67-69, pg. 1006 — IT
PDS Handling CV, pg. 720 — IT
Plantronics B.V., Antareslaan 9, pg. 1308 — PB
qad.europe b.v., Neptunusstraat 23-25, pg. 1345 — PB
Rockwell-Collins (U.K.) Limited, Antareslaan 43, pg. 1400 — PB
Rorer B.V., Jupiterstaat 196, pg. 1111 — PB
Saunier Duval Nederland BV, Avio Trade Park, Hoeksteen 155, pg. 615 — IT
Signode B.V., Graftermmerstraat 18, pg. 869 — PB
Tandem Computers B.V., Kocksteen 26, pg. 417 — PB
Tandem Computers European Div., Antareslaan 11, pg. 417 — PB
Technish Handelskantoor Lloyd B.V., Kruisweg 703, pg. 2 — PB
Transpolis Schiphol Diensten BV, pg. 720 — IT
Uitgeverij Veldhuis bv, Wijkermeerstraat 35, pg. 1445 — IT
Unifix (Nederland) B.V., Bijlmermeerstraat # 1, pg. 232 — IT
Woodward Governor Nederland B.V., Hoofdweg 601, pg. 1777 — IT
Wyeth Laboratoria B.V., pg. 82 — PB

Hoogerheyde

Fokker Aircraft Services B.V., Avialandalaan 31, pg. 1304 — IT

Hoogeveen

Kappa Golfkarton B.V., Industrieweg 17, pg. 756 — IT
Lucas Aardenburg B.V., pg. 1438 — IT
Vedena B.V., Industrieweg 17, pg. 757 — IT

Hoogezand

Parker Hannifin Hoogezand B.V., Foxham 59, 9601 LE Hoogezand, pg. 1263 — PB

Hoogezand-Sappeemeer

Armstrong World Industries-A.C.I. B.V., pg. 132 — IT
Scandex Aluminium N.V., Postbus 102, Nijverheidsweg 9, pg. 443 — IT
Trelleborg Fabrieken B.V., Postbus 33, pg. 1423 — IT

Hoorn

Konijn Baggertechniek BV, P.O. Box 118, pg. 607 — IT
MSA Nederland B.V., pg. 1115 — PB
National Electrical Carbon B.V., Kernweg 32, pg. 892 — IT

Hornelaan

Smith's Chewing Sweets Mij. B.V., Graafschap, pg. 1451 — IT

Houten

Amici, Meidoornkade 12, pg. 750 — IT
Artland Nederland B.V., pg. 918 — IT
Brinks-Nedlloyd v.o.f., pg. 1144 — IT
Ciba Corning Diagnostics NV, pg. 975 — IT
Comfort Financieringen Nederland BV, De Molen 10-14, pg. 911 — IT
Essex Electric BV, Peppelkade 56, pg. 651 — IT
Inspectrum BV, pg. 607 — IT
Nordson Nederland B.V., Peppelkade 40, pg. 1189 — PB
Sharp Electronics Benelux B.V., Meidoornkade 10, pg. 1229 — IT

Huizen

Bergvik Chemie B.V., De Molenberg, Hellingstraat 22h, pg. 904 — PB
Kalkzandsteenfabriek Rijsbergen B.V., pg. 1199 — IT
SAS Institute B.V., Flevolaan 69, pg. 967 — PV
Signaal, Communications, Botterstraat 45, pg. 1385 — IT

Ijmuiden

Goulds Pumps Europe B.V., pg. 861 — PB
HTD Verzekeringen & Transport BV, pg. 753 — IT
Hoogovens Groep B.V., pg. 753 — IT
Hoogovens Hylite BV, pg. 753 — IT
Hoogovens Ijmuiden, Kesslerplein 1, pg. 753 — IT
Hoogovens Ijmuiden Verkoopkantoor B.V., Kesslerplein 1, pg. 754 — IT
Hoogovens Packaging Steel, pg. 756 — IT
Hoogovens Research & Development, pg. 754 — IT
Hoogovens Staal BV, Kesslerplein 1, Velsen-Noord, pg. 754 — IT
Hoogovens Steel Primary Products, pg. 756 — IT
Hoogovens Steel Products, pg. 756 — IT
Hoogovens Steel Strip Mill Products, pg. 754 — IT
Hoogovens Technical Services BV, Kesslerplein 1, pg. 755 — IT
Hoogovens Technical Services Energy & Environment BV, pg. 755 — IT

Hoogovens Technical Services Iron & Steel BV,
  pg. 755   IT
Hoogovens Technical Services Technological & Operational
  Assistance BV, pg. 755   IT
KONINKLIJKE HOOGOVENS N.V., Kesslerplein 1, Velsen
  Noord, pg. 753   IT
NEBAM Nederlandse Bevrachting en Agentuur
  Maatschappij, Rooswijkweg Velsen Noord, pg. 754   IT
Radio Holland Group-Fishery Equip., Trawlerkade 98,
  pg. 1151   IT
Radio Holland Group-Survey Equip., Trawlerkade 64,
  pg. 1151   IT
Stuwadoorsbefrijf Velserkom BV, pg. 754   IT

Ijsselstein

Brugman Badkamers B.V., pg. 1481   IT
Deutschmann & Roelants BV, pg. 756   IT
Litton Precision Products (Netherlands), Griendstraat 10,
  pg. 1004   PB
SAB Profiel B.V., pg. 754   IT

Jaeindhoven

B.V. Europese Tabak Maatschappij, Kanaaldivk Noord 123,
  pg. 1695   PB

Kampen

Lyempf/Van Heel B.V., pg. 752   IT
Pack-o-Med Medical Supply Systems B.V., pg. 991   IT
Van Heel B.V., P.O.B. 22, pg. 751   IT

Katwijk

Duif Convenience Foods BV, pg. 751   IT

Kerkrade

Caddock Electronics Europe B.V., Jupiterstraat 2,
  pg. 198   PV
Medtronic B.V., Wenckebachstraat 10, pg. 1083   PB

Kesteren

Van Soest BV, Meezendreef 5, pg. 491   IT

Klazienaveen

Rademakers Gieterij B.V., Langestraat 2, pg. 134   IT

Koboltn

A/S Direct, Soensterudveien 26, pg. 1052   IT

Koog aan de Zaan

Cacao de Zaan B.V., Stationsstraat 76, pg. 128   PB
Honig Foods-B.V., Lagedijk 3, pg. 244   IT
Honig Merkartikelen B.V., Lagedijk 3, pg. 244   IT
Witco B.V., Wezelstraat, pg. 1774   PB

Krimpen aan der Ijssel

Clestra Hauserman B.V., Industrieweg 2, pg. 570   IT
Litton Business Systems Holland B.V., Van Utechtweg 25,
  pg. 1004   PB

Krommenie

Forbo Krommenie B.V., pg. 497   IT

Kruisweg

Nissin Foods B.V., Holland Office Ctr. Bldg. 4, pg. 950   IT

Kwintsheul

Babcock Duiker B.V., Bovendijk 39, pg. 472   IT

Landgraaf

Mayfran Limburg, B.V., Edisonstraat 7, pg. 1398   IT
Perstorp Analytical Lumac B.V., Amperestraat 13,
  pg. 1039   IT

Le Spijkenisse

Jotun Nederland B.V., pg. 715   IT

Leerdam

Akerlund & Rausing, Statiionsweg 27, pg. 33   IT
Ballast Nedam Grond en Wegen Specialiteiten B.V.,
  Nyverheidstraat 12, pg. 133   IT
Zuivelonderneming De Vijfheerenlanden B.V., pg. 751   IT

Leeuwarden

AEGON Levensverzekering N.V. (Life), 11, Lange
  Marktstraat, pg. 26   IT
AEGON Schadeverzekering N.V., Lange Marktstraat 11,
  pg. 26   IT
B.V. Lyempf, P.O.B. 406, pg. 752   IT
Nutricia LYEMPF B.V., pg. 991   IT

Oldelf vestiging Leeuwarden, Branch Edisonstraat 22,
  pg. 389   IT
SAB WABCO B.V., Harlingerstraatweg 115, pg. 271   IT

Leiden

Centocor B.V., pg. 323   PB
Fasson (Nederland) B.V., Lammenschansweg 140,
  pg. 154   PB
Gensym B.V., Schipholweg 85, pg. 731   PB
NEM Nederlandsche Elektrolasch Maatschappig B.V.,
  pg. 633   IT
Nalco Europe, 2342 BV Oegstgeest, pg. 1151   PB
Olivetti Nederland B.V., Verbeekstraat 19/21, pg. 1003   IT
Symantec Ltd., Kanaalpark 145, pg. 1546   PB

Leiderdorp

Electro Scientific Industries B.V., Elisabethhof 21,
  pg. 569   PB
Gamma Biologicals, B.V., Splinterlaan 154B, pg. 698   IT
Yamanouchi Europe B.V., Elisabethhof 19, pg. 1519   IT
Yamanouchi Europe B.V.-Research Laboratories,
  Elisabethhof 1, pg. 1519   IT
Yamanouchi Pharma B.V.-Leiderdorp, Elisabethhof 17,
  pg. 1519   IT

Leidschendam

Continental Netherlands Oil Company, Weigelia 251,
  pg. 532   PB
KONE Starlift B.V., Rijh 10, pg. 748   IT
Nokia Telecommunications B.V., Loire 148, pg. 953   IT
Restoplan, Dillenburgsingel 69, pg. 1463   IT
Zurich International (Nederland) N.V., Veurse Achterweg
  26, pg. 1532   IT
Zurich Verzekeringen, Veurse Achterweg 26, pg. 1531   IT

Leidssenhage

PDVSA Services B.V., Kantorencomplex, pg. 1046   IT

Leislen

Moore International B.V., Schipholweg, pg. 889   IT

Lelystad

Van Campen Bending Technics B.V., Kolkweg 1,
  pg. 1387   PB
Windmaster Nederland B.V., Zuiveringweg 26,
  pg. 1134   IT

Leusden

ISS Food B.V., Olmenlaan 2, pg. 657   IT

Liessel

Kalkzandsteenfabriek Hoogdonk B.V., Hoogdonkseweg 15,
  pg. 1199   IT

Lisse

Nissan Finance, B.V., Vennestraat 13-15, pg. 945   IT
Nissan Motor Nederland B.V., Vennestraat 13-15,
  pg. 945   IT

Lochem

Dedert Europe Holding Co, pg. 320   PV
Simco (Nederland) B.V., Aalsvoort 5, pg. 869   PB

Lomm

Dayton Process B.V., Industrieterrein Spikweien,
  pg. 673   IT
Elbar B.V., Industrieterrein Spikweien, pg. 673   IT
Eldim B.V., Industrieterrein Spikweien, pg. 673   IT
Intech EDM BV, Spikweien 21, pg. 489   IT
Interturbine Holland B.V., Industrieterrein Spikweien,
  pg. 673   IT
Interturbine Paton B.V., Industrieterrein Spikweien,
  pg. 673   IT

Loosdrecht

B.V. w/h FIRMA L.J. VOLKERS, Industrieweg 1,
  pg. 1458   IT

Maarheeze

Kiggen Afvaltechniek, pg. 1066   IT
Nolte Mastenfabriek, Dr. A. Philipsweg 2, pg. 1707   PB

Maarssen

Balzers Process Systems Eurpoe N.V., pg. 997   IT
Comdisco Nederland B.V., Planetenbaan 15, pg. 408   PB
DSM Andeno Maarssen B.V., Sportparkweg 6, 3604 AW
  Maarssen, pg. 353   IT
Haitsma Beton B.V., Computerweg 5, pg. 134   IT
Iggesund Paper & Board Service B.V., Ruimteweg 5,
  pg. 886   IT
Lever Industrial B.V., pg. 1437   IT
Polarcid Nederland B.V., Zonnebaan 45, pg. 1314   PB

PontMeyer NV, Bisonspoor 356, pg. 864   IT
RAM Mobile Data (Netherlands) B.V., Planetenbaan 26,
  pg. 208   PB
Reisrevue and Medical Journals, Planetenbaan 100,
  pg. 1099   IT
Stratus Computer B.V., P.O. Box 1300, pg. 1524   PB
Sybase Inc.-European Headquarters, Planetenbaum 25,
  pg. 1544   PB

Maastricht

ABS Pompen B.V., pg. 270   IT
Bakken Research Center B.V., P.O. Box 1220,
  Endepolsdomein 5, pg. 1083   PB
Bovil, Gaetano Martinolaan 85, pg. 117   IT
CIBA-GEIGY Maastricht B.V., Sortieweg 39, pg. 978   IT
Cookson Matthey B.V., Postbus 23, pg. 714   IT
DSM Rim Nylon VoF, Karveelweg 3, pg. 353   IT
ENCI Nederland B.V., Lage Kanaaldijk 115, pg. 605   IT
Faltec Benelux B.V., pg. 269   IT
Generale Bank - Maastricht, Bouillonstraat 8-10,
  pg. 547   IT
Grabowsky & Poort Hameleers BV, pg. 607   IT
Holland Sweetener Company V.O.F., Blekerij 52,
  pg. 1408   IT
KNP Leykam B.V., Erasmusdomein 50, pg. 756   IT
KNP Maastricht B.V., Biesenweg 16, pg. 756   IT
Kennametal Hertel Nederland, B.V., Postbus 460,
  pg. 951   PB
Kredietbank (Nederland) N.V., St. Annalaan 21,
  pg. 761   IT
M.T.C. Interiors B.V., pg. 540   IT
Nordson European Distribution B.V., Bergerstraat 10,
  pg. 1189   PB
Papeteries Libert BV, pg. 756   IT
Royal Doulton Benelux bv, Abdissenweg 1, pg. 1135   IT
Tenneco Transicol B.V., Ankerkade 81, 6202 NA,
  pg. 1580   PB
Uitgeversmaatschappij De Limburger bv, pg. 1445   IT
Vredestein Rubber Recycling B.V., Lage Frontweg 2a,
  pg. 1481   IT

Malden

Dubbers Malden Groep B.V., De Horst 10, pg. 633   IT

Marum

KNP Secondary Fibres B.V., pg. 756   IT

Meern

Merloni Huishoudapparten B.V., Veldzigt 22, pg. 860   IT

Mepissant

Den Hertog B.V., pg. 752   IT

Meppel

Krips Repro B.V., Kaapweg 6, pg. 1100   IT
Northprint B.V., Industrieweg 1B, pg. 1100   IT
Yamanouchi Europe B.V.-Manufacturing Meppel, Hogemaat
  2, pg. 1519   IT

Middelburg

Algemene Zeeuwse Verzekering Maatschappij N.V.,
  Houtkaai 11, pg. 647   IT

Mijdrecht

Bayer B.V., Energieweg 1, pg. 175   IT
BetzDearborn B.V., Energieweg 4, pg. 227   PB
Indesit Nederland N.V., Nijverheideweg 13, pg. 860   IT
Johnson Nederland B.V., P.O. Box 22, pg. 593   PV
MB Europe B.V., Energieweg 33, pg. 267   IT
MB International B.V., Postbus 164, Energieweg 33,
  pg. 267   IT
Roche Nederland B.V., pg. 1121   IT
SKF Maintenance Products B.V., Constructieweg 7,
  pg. 1159   IT

Moerdijk

Namascor B.V., Industriegebied Moerdijk,
  OostelijkeRandweg 44-46, pg. 754   IT
Nedlloyd Road Cargo FTL, Middenweg 6, pg. 1145   IT
VGL Rail Cargo B.V., Middenweg 6, pg. 1145   IT

Monster

PKF/Jongekrijg Holding B.V., pg. 756   IT

Montfoort

Hoogovens Wapeningsstaal BV, Willeskop 94, pg. 754   IT
Redland Dakprodukten B.V., Heeswijk 155, pg. 1093   IT

Muiden

Gray Tool Co. (Europe), 5 Cornwallstraat, pg. 5   IT
Muiden Chemie International BV, pg. 217   IT

Naaldwijk

Swift Adhesives B.V., Energiestraat 2-4, pg. 370   IT

PB - *U.S. Public Companies Volume*
PV - *U.S. Private Companies Volume*
IT - *International Public & Private Companies Volume*

1718

Geographic Index-Non U.S.

Naarden

Accres Uitgevers bv, L. Hortensiuslaan 30-32,
pg. 1445 **IT**
Boertien & Partners, Gooimeer 5, pg. 1094 **IT**
Cott Benelux, Beethovenlaan 10, pg. 338 **IT**
Freudenberg Simrit B.V., pg. 506 **IT**
Hagemeyer N.V., Rijksweg 69, pg. 487 **IT**
Kopele Beheen B.V., Gooimeer 1b, pg. 1133 **IT**
LVMH B.V., Jan Ter Gouwweg 147, pg. 782 **IT**
Melitta-Nederland B.V., pg. 857 **IT**
Perstorp Flooring BV, Rijksweg 81 C, pg. 1039 **IT**
Quest International, Huizerstraatweg 28, pg. 1438 **IT**
Reemtsma Nederland B.V., Comeniuslaan 10,
pg. 1101 **IT**
STORK N.V., P.O. Box 5004, pg. 1304 **IT**
Technisch Handelsbureau Wemex B.V., Gooimeer 1b,
pg. 1133 **IT**
Uitgeverij Woudestein bv, Kootjesbuurt 9, pg. 1445 **IT**
Wilmerink & Muller, Jan ter Gouwweg 147, pg. 783 **IT**

Nederhorst den Berg

Shakespeare Hengelsport B.V., Reeweg 16, pg. 940 **PB**

Nieuw-Vennep

Bols International B.V., Lucas Bolsstraat 7, pg. 751 **IT**
Bols Royal Distilleries, Lucas Bolsstraat 7, pg. 751 **IT**
B.V. Distillerderij 'De Fransche Kroon' v/h Hartevelt en
Zoon, Lucas Bolsstraat 7, pg. 751 **IT**
Exploitatiemaatschappij Leliegracht B.V., Lucas Bolsstraat
7, pg. 751 **IT**
Exploitatiemaatschappij Rozengracht B.V., Lucas Bolsstraat
7, pg. 751 **IT**
Grands Terroirs Associes BV, pg. 751 **IT**
Pezziol B.V., Lucas Bolsstraat 7, pg. 751 **IT**
Praxair B.V., pg. 1320 **PB**
Spur Holland, Vlasstraat 6, pg. 851 **IT**
Zuiderhout B.V., Lucas Bolsstraat 7, pg. 751 **IT**

Nieuwegein

Aannemingsbedrijf Van Oudbroekhuizen B.V., Nieuweglin,
Veldwade 14-16, pg. 681 **IT**
Ascom Teletron B.V., Edisonbaan 23, pg. 87 **IT**
BMC Software B.V., Coltbaan 7, pg. 162 **PB**
Biozim B.V., pg. 975 **IT**
Cognos B.V., Fultonbaan 52, pg. 306 **IT**
COMPAREX Information Systems B.V., Binnenwal 2,
pg. 108 **IT**
D & B Software Nederlander B.V., Luifelstede 46,
pg. 532 **IT**
Delaware Computing Nederland B.V., Meentwal 1,
pg. 184 **IT**
Esselte Meto BV, Archimedesbaan 19, pg. 461 **IT**
G&P Starke Diekstra BV, P.O. Box 1075, pg. 607 **IT**
Henkel Nederland B.V., Bruwal 11, pg. 613 **IT**
Holland Novochem B.V., Villawal 15, 3432 NX Nieuwegein,
pg. 962 **IT**
Eli Lilly Nederland B.V., Raadstede 15, pg. 994 **IT**
Meto B.V., P.O. Box 1330, pg. 462 **IT**
NEDCO (Newport European Distribution Co.), Krijtwal 9,
pg. 1179 **PB**
SKF Engineering & Res. Centre B.V., Kelvinbaan 16,
pg. 1158 **IT**
SMS Nederland b. v., Nevelgaarde 4, pg. 1464 **PB**
Spaarbeleg N.V., 60, Nevelgaarde, pg. 26 **IT**
Sunrise Medical B.V., Pascalbaan 3, pg. 1536 **PB**
Travel-Net BV, pg. 720 **IT**
Videotex Nederland BV, pg. 720 **IT**
Zwolsche Algemeene N.V., pg. 795 **PB**

Nieuwkoop

Vicker Medical Nederlands, pg. 1467 **IT**

Nijkerk

Piher Benelux International BV, Ambachsstraat 13B,
pg. 854 **IT**

Nijmegen

Eurasem B.V., Postbus 566, pg. 1133 **IT**
Euratec B.V., Postbus 566, pg. 1133 **IT**
Hickson-Garantor Nederland BV, pg. 619 **IT**
Honig Merkartikelen B.V., Waalbandijk 20, pg. 244 **PB**
Hyster B.V., Nijverheidsweg, 26 6541, pg. 1149 **PB**
Intergraph Services B.V., 6503 GB, pg. 891 **PB**
KNP Leykam B.V., Ambachtsweg 2, pg. 756 **IT**
Latenstein Zetmeel B.V., pg. 752 **IT**
Lincoln Smitweld BV, Nieuwe Dukenburgseweg 20,
pg. 997 **PB**
New Brunswick Scientific Benelux B.V., Kerkenbos 1101,
6546 BC Nijmegen, pg. 1170 **PB**
Sealed Air B.V., Lindenhoutseweg 45, pg. 1451 **PB**
USB Pharma B.V., Lagelandsweg 78, pg. 1681 **PB**
Uitgeversmaatschappij De Gelderlander bv, Voorstadslaan
2, pg. 1445 **IT**
V&D Projectinrichting, Oostkanaaldijk 110, pg. 1462 **IT**
VNU Dagbladengroep B.V., Meijhorst 6010, pg. 1445 **IT**

Nuenen

Berson Milieutechniek B.V., pg. 590 **IT**

Nunspeet

Shimano Benelux B.V., Industrieweg 24, pg. 1233 **IT**
Ultegra Nederland B.V., Postbus 180, pg. 1233 **IT**

Nuth

Performance Polymers B.V., Thermiekstraat 2, pg. 236 **IT**
Stelrad B.V., Kathagen 30, pg. 268 **IT**

Odijk

Kodak Nederland B.V., Zeisterweg 1, pg. 554 **PB**

Oirschot

American Power Conversion, Schoonoord 1, pg. 89 **PB**

Oldemarkt

Banta Global Turnkey, pg. 188 **PB**

Oldenzaal

Parker Hannifin B.V., Edisonstraat 1, pg. 1263 **PB**
Power-Packer Europa B.V., pg. 125 **PB**

Ommen

Taltron B.V., Ommen, 15, Slagenkampweg, pg. 1063 **PB**

Oosterhout

Analog Devices Nederland B.V., Beneluxweg 27,
pg. 108 **PB**
BARENBRUG HOLLAND BV, P.O. Box 4, pg. 166 **IT**
Hoogovens Buizen B.V., Wilhelminakanaal Zuid 150,
pg. 754 **IT**
Houghton-Benelux B.V., Mechelaarstraat 12, pg. 541 **PV**
Jamin, Krombaak 2, pg. 749 **IT**
Overspecht, B.V., Wilhelminakanaal Noord 2, pg. 812 **PB**
Traub-Heckert Benelux B.V., Mechelaarstraat 8,
pg. 1419 **IT**
Unit Conduit & Construction, Souvereinstraat 35,
pg. 754 **IT**
Unit Contiflo, Souvereinstraat 33, pg. 754 **IT**
Van Neerbos-PCI B.V., Karolusstraat 2, pg. 1466 **IT**

Oosterwolde

Pieterman Glas B.V., pg. 1523 **IT**

Oss

Akzo Pharma B.V., One Weth. van Eschstraat, pg. 44 **IT**
Akzo Pharma Nederland B.V., One Weth. van Eschstraat,
pg. 44 **IT**
Brabant Alucast International BV, Rijnstraat 19,
pg. 753 **IT**
Chefaro International B.V., 46 Kloosterstraat, pg. 44 **IT**
Diosynth bv, Six, Kloosterstraat, pg. 44 **IT**
Nourypharma Nederland B.V., One Weth. van Eschstraat,
pg. 44 **IT**
Organon International B.V., 6, Kloosterstraat, pg. 44 **IT**
Organon Nederland B.V., One Weth. van Eschstraat,
pg. 44 **IT**
UVG Nederland B.V., pg. 1438 **IT**
VPF B.V., One Weth. van Eschstraat, pg. 44 **IT**
Wim Vos Internationale Transporten B.V., pg. 1145 **IT**

Ossendrecht

Steenfabriek Boudewijn B.V., pg. 1199 **IT**

Oud-Beijerland

Perstorp Analytical B.V., Rontgenstraat 18, pg. 1039 **IT**
Perstorp Nederland B.V., Rontgenstraat 18, pg. 1038 **IT**
Perstorp Nederland B.V. Decorative Laminate,
Rontgenstraat 18, pg. 1038 **IT**

Oude Pekela

GSF Verpakkingen, H. Westerstraat 20-22, pg. 756 **IT**

Oude Tonge

Trencon Vuurvast BV, Dabbestraat 67, pg. 894 **IT**

Petten

Mallinckrodt Medical B.V., Westerduinweg 3, pg. 1040 **PB**

Pijnacker

Bently Nevada Europa B.V., Weterinweg 14, pg. 134 **PV**
Sanders Behang B.V., pg. 540 **IT**
Thermon Europe B.V., Korteweg 1, pg. 1081 **PV**

Prinsenbeek

Saval B.V., Prinsenbeek, 17, Westrik, pg. 681 **IT**

Pufmerend

Security House, 41 Amperestraat, pg. 1307 **PB**
Toeristiek BV, Corslaan 10, pg. 1099 **IT**

Putte

Van Niftrik B.V., Bosweg 2, pg. 1210 **IT**

Putten

Smits' Reform B.V., pg. 991 **IT**
Zonnatura/Pharmafood B.V., pg. 991 **IT**

Raalte

Durisol Raalte B.V., Almelosestraatweg 83, pg. 134 **IT**
Hevea B.V., Kanaalstraat O.Z. 21, pg. 1481 **IT**
Uitgeverij Veldhuis bv, Kaagstraat 10, pg. 1445 **IT**

Raamsdonksveer

Clarion Europa Liaison Office (NL), Elftweg 50, pg. 296 **IT**
Clarion Nederland, Elftweg 50, pg. 296 **IT**
Fluorplast Nederland B.V., Postbus 61, Lissenveld 65,
pg. 1174 **IT**
HOLMATRO INDUSTRIAL & RESCUE EQUIPMENT,
Zalmweg 30, pg. 632 **IT**
Laporte Absorbents-Holland, Weegbree 27, pg. 803 **IT**
Norton Fluorplast Nederland BV, Lissenveld 65,
pg. 1175 **IT**
Sandvik Process Systems B.V., pg. 1186 **IT**

Renkum

Parenco B.V., Industrieterrein Erweg, pg. 586 **IT**
Vredestein Extrusions, Beukenlaan 50, pg. 1481 **IT**
Vredestein Icopro B.V., Beukenlaan 50, pg. 1481 **IT**

Rheden

Thomassen International Holding B.V., Havelandsweg 8,
pg. 401 **IT**
Thomassen Stewart & Stevenson International B.V.,
pg. 1518 **PB**

Ridderkerk

Holec Machines & Apparaten B.V., Postbus 4050,
pg. 1133 **IT**
Honda Nederland B.V., pg. 635 **IT**
Kvaerner Rotterdam bv, Dokwerkerstraat 1, pg. 772 **IT**
Kvaerner Ships Equipment b.v., Dokwerkerstraat 1,
pg. 768 **IT**
Look-o-Look BV, Klompenmalerstraat 12, pg. 1451 **IT**
Moore Products Co. B.V., Wagenmarkerstraat 3,
Industrieterrein Donkersloot-Noord, pg. 1129 **PB**
Zeneca Agro, Voorn 47, pg. 1526 **IT**
Zeneca b.v., Voorn 47, pg. 1526 **IT**
Zeneca Farma, Voorn 47, pg. 1526 **IT**

Rijen

Buss (Benelux) B.V., pg. 490 **IT**
Curver BV, Spoorlaan Noord 92, pg. 352 **IT**
Ericsson Data Services Nederland B.V., Haansbergseweg
1, pg. 1366 **IT**
Ericsson Finance Holding B.V., Haansbergseweg 1,
pg. 1366 **IT**
Ericsson Holding International B.V., Hannsbergseweg 1,
pg. 1367 **IT**
Ericsson Holding Nederland B.V., Haansbergseweg 1,
pg. 1367 **IT**
Ericsson Property Company B.V., Haansbergseweg 1,
pg. 1367 **IT**
Ericsson Telecommunicatie B.V., Haansbergseweg 1,
pg. 1367 **IT**

Rijssen

Baukje Beheer bv, Galvanistraat 11, pg. 243 **IT**
Sakata Seed Europe B.V., Kruizemuntweg 27,
pg. 1178 **IT**

Rijswijk

Agfa-Gevaert B.V., Polakweg 10, pg. 174 **IT**
BMW Holding B.V., pg. 178 **IT**
BMW Nederland B.V., pg. 178 **IT**
Berendsen PMC B.V., Polakweg 6, pg. 1285 **PB**
Braun Nederland B.V., Visseringlaan 22, pg. 744 **PB**
CEF Safety Systems B.V., pg. 590 **IT**
COMSIP Nederland B.V., Koopmanstraat 7, pg. 53 **IT**
Communication Services Nederland BV, pg. 720 **IT**
Core Laboratories (Netherlands), Heulweg 28-30,
pg. 1004 **PB**
Gillette Finance B.V., Visseringlaan 22, pg. 744 **PB**
HBM, Hollandsche Beton Maatschappij bv, Generaal
Spoorlaan 489, pg. 630 **IT**
HCG industrieservice bv, Cobbenhagenstraat 7,
pg. 630 **IT**
HDM, Hollandsche Delfstoffen Maatschappij bv, Generaal
Spoorlaam 489, pg. 630 **IT**

PB - *U.S. Public Companies Volume*
PV - *U.S. Private Companies Volume*
IT - *International Public & Private Companies Volume*

HMI, Hollandsche Maatschappij Installatietechniek bv, De Bruin Kopsstraat 4, pg. 630   IT
Hercules B.V., pg. 810   PB
HOLLANDSCHE BETON GROEP NV, Generaal Spoorlaan 489, pg. 630
Interbeton B.V., Generaal Spoorlaan 489, pg. 630   IT
Intervam B.V., General Spoorlaan 489, pg. 630   IT
Maatschappij van Berkel's Patent NV, Van Ginjnstraat 17, pg. 546   IT
Mabon B.V., Generaal Spoorlaan 489, pg. 630   IT
Sedneth, Sea Drilling Netherlands bv, Generaal Spoorlaan 489, pg. 630   IT
SmithKline & French B.V., Postbus 1928, pg. 1265   IT
SmithKline Beecham Farma B.V., pg. 1266   IT
Taylor Instrument B.V., Van Gijn Straat 28, pg. 6   IT

Roden

BV Delft Electronic Products, Dwazziewegen 2, pg. 388   IT
Sissing Elektrotechniek B.V., Kanaalstraat 61, pg. 1133   IT

Roermond

ARI Group Europe, pg. 1650   PB
Harcros Chemicals, pg. 599   IT
Imtech Projects Zuit B.V., 503, Keulsebaan, pg. 681   IT
Limox Chemie B.V., pg. 599   IT
RP Europe B.V., Mijnheerkensweg 18, pg. 757   IT
Snijbrandcentrum Roermond, pg. 754   IT

Roosendaal

Brabants Nieuwsblad BV, Molenstraat 7-11, pg. 1445   IT
CIBA-GEIGY Agro BV, pg. 976   IT
General Biscuits Nederland (GBNL), Molenstraat 4, pg. 381   IT
Herlitz Benelux BV, Hoge Bergen 10/212, pg. 616   IT
Mead Verpakking B.V., pg. 1076   PB
Pharmacia & Upjohn Biotech Benelux, Bergrand 230, pg. 1047   IT
Red Band, Spoorstraat 51, pg. 244   IT
Rust-Oleum Nederland B.V., Braak 1, pg. 1358   PB
Style Keukens B.V., pg. 1481   IT

Rosmalen

Alabastine Holland BV (Sales), P.O. Box 307, pg. 1499   IT
Ballast Nedam Petrol Stations, Kloosterstraat 1-3, pg. 133   IT
Getinge-D.S.E. BV, pg. 551   IT
Graseby Medical BV, pg. 1268   IT
Panduit Nederland, Eikenburglan 11 E, pg. 836   PV

Rotterdam

ABN Assurantie Holding B.V., Centraal Kantoor, pg. 9   IT
ABN Assurantien B.V., Centraal Kantoor, pg. 9   IT
ADT Security Systems, Vijverhofstraat 47, pg. 1649   IT
ARA/BDDP, World Trade Center Rotterdam, Beursplein 37, pg. 117   IT
AVR Chemie, Prof. Gerbrandyweg 10, pg. 754   IT
Air Products Nederland B.V., Merseyweg 8, 3197 K6, Botlek-Rotterdam, pg. 31   PB
Alcoa Chemie Nederland B.V., Theemsweg 30, pg. 61   PB
Algemeen Vrachtkantoor B.V., pg. 1436   IT
Allianz Finance B.V., Schadeverzekeringsmaatschappij, pg. 59   IT
Allianz Nederland N.V. (Rotterdam Office), Schadeverzekeringsmaatschappij, Beurs-World Trade Center, pg. 60   IT
Aluminum & Chemie Rotterdam B.V. - (ALUCHEMIE), pg. 68   IT
Antoine Petit, Twentestraat 58-60, pg. 1463   IT
Asea Brown Boveri Nederland B.V., Postbus 301, pg. 2   IT
Autodesk Benelux B.V., Rivium Quadrant 81, 2909 LC Capelle a/d IJssl, pg. 149   IT
Automobielbedrijven Hoogenboom B.V., Geyssendorfferweg 5/15, pg. 216   IT
Baasel Lasertech Benelux BV, pg. 836   IT
Ballast Nedam Projectontwikkeling B.V., K.P. van der Mandelelaan 32, pg. 134   IT
Bicker Caarten en Obreen N.V., pg. 9   IT
Bowthorpe BV, Rotterdam Bldg., 4th Fl., Rm. 23, Aert van Nesstraat 45, pg. 208   IT
Britax Autolease B.V., Geyssendorfferweg 5/15, pg. 216   IT
Brown & Root Nederland B.V., P.O. Box 125, pg. 776   PB
Brugman Administratie en Distibutiecentrum B.V., pg. 1481   IT
Bulkhendl Holding B.V., 40, Boompjes, pg. 304   IT
C.A.I.B./EVA Nederland B.V., Waalhaven ZZ2, pg. 212   IT
Carless Refining & Marketing B.V., Oosterhof Bldg., Entrance A, Schorploenstraat 274, pg. 1104   IT
Carrefour Nederland B.V., Coolsingel 139, pg. 273   IT
Center Parcs N.V., Admiraliteiskade 40, pg. 1212   IT
Chefaro Nederland B.V., Eight Keileweg, pg. 44   IT
Citronas BV, Keilweg 80, pg. 491   IT
City Com B.V., 190, Innsbruckwey, pg. 681   IT
Cliffs Neddrill Turnkey International v.o.f., pg. 1144   IT
Coastal Financial B.V., Bouwcentrum, pg. 390   PB
Coastal (Rotterdam) B.V., Hofplein 33, 3rd Fl., pg. 390   PB
Continental European Representative Office, Weena 290, pg. 692   PB
Crowcon Instruments B.V., Vlambloem 129, pg. 590   IT
Crown Cork Company (Holland) B.V., SluisJesdijk 119-121, pg. 464   PB
DSM Chemicals Rotterdam, Montrealweg 15, pg. 353   IT
Damco Maritime B.V., pg. 1144   IT

Damco Maritime International B.V., Albert Plesmanweg 161, pg. 1144   IT
Datastream International Limited, Hofplein 19, pg. 1326   PB
H. Albert de Bary & Co. N.V. (Rotterdam), Westblaak 212, pg. 404   IT
Delhaize "The Lion" Nederland B.V., Weena 618, 10th fl., pg. 463   IT
N.V. Deli-Universal, pg. 1695   PB
Det Norske Veritas, Haastrechtstraat 7, pg. 397   IT
Dicalite Holding B.V., pg. 903   PV
Dun & Bradstreet B.V., Westblaak 138, pg. 536   PB
Dutch Parcel Distribution Zuid B.V., pg. 1145   IT
Elf Atochem Rotterdah B.V., pg. 446   IT
B.V. ERMAF, pg. 1149   IT
Europe Combined Terminals B.V., 7, Seattleweg, pg. 682   IT
FAG Nederland B.V., pg. 469   IT
Fergusson Wild Nederland B.V., Calandstraat 41, pg. 1458   IT
Ferro (Holland) B.V., P.O. Box 6088, Van Helmontstraat 20, pg. 619   PB
Fransen Transport B.V., pg. 1144   IT
Frigoscandia Transport B.V., pg. 607   PB
FURNESS BV, pg. 530   IT
Generale Bank Nederland, Coolsingel 63, pg. 548   IT
HAM, Hollandsche Aanneming Maatschappij B.V., Rivium Quadrant 2, Capelle a/d IJssel, pg. 630   IT
Habib Bank Ltd., Westblaak 127, pg. 585   IT
Handelmaatschappij Noorda B.V., pg. 1437   IT
Hansa Industrial Insurance N.V., K.P. van der Mandelehan 90, pg. 1425   IT
Hapag-Lloyd Nederland B.V., pg. 596   IT
Health-Mor B.V., pg. 771   PB
Hendrik Veder B.V., pg. 1144   IT
Hobart B.V., Gustoweg 45, pg. 1322   PB
HUNTER DOUGLAS N.V., 2 Piekstraat, pg. 639   IT
Hydraudyne Bruinhof B.V., pg. 838   IT
Hydraudyne Pneumatiek B.V., pg. 838   IT
IHI Marine B.V., Glashaven 10A, pg. 689   IT
Ilva Benelux B.V., Gebouw Willemswerf Bldg., Boompjes 40, pg. 654   IT
Intel Semiconductor B.V., pg. 887   IT
Internatio Minerals & Chemicals, Wilhelminaplein 32, 15th Fl., pg. 682   IT
INTERNATIO-MULLER N.V., 1, Westerlaan, pg. 680   IT
International Factors Nederland B.V., P.O. Box 604, pg. 9   IT
Intis BV, pg. 720   IT
Intis Enterprise BV, pg. 720   IT
Intis Research & Development VOF, pg. 720   IT
Jewo Ferrous B.V., Droogdokweg 84, pg. 514   IT
Jotun Protective Coatings B.V., pg. 715   IT
KNSM-Kroonburgh B.V., pg. 1144   IT
Kelvin Hughes Observator B.V., Nieuwe Langeweg 41, pg. 1268   IT
Kemira Agro Pernis B.V., Vondelingenplaat 17, pg. 729   IT
Kemting Neddrill v.o.f., pg. 1144   IT
Keukenstel B.V., pg. 1481   IT
KONINKLIJKE BUNGE B.V., Aert v. Nesstraat 45, pg. 753   IT
KONINKLIJKE VAN OMMEREN NV, Westerlaan 10, pg. 758   IT
Kredietbank (Nederland) N.V., Westersingel 88, pg. 761   IT
KROMOS B.V., pg. 1149   IT
Krupp Scheepvaart B.V., Konigin Emmaplein 8, pg. 515   IT
Kuehne & Nagel N.V., Lloydstraat 35, pg. 763   IT
Le Carbone-Lorraine (Nederland) B.V., Breevaartsraat, 50, pg. 1030   IT
Lipoma B.V., pg. 1438   IT
Arthur D. Little International, Inc., Willemswerf, pg. 670   PV
Logica B.V., Wijnhaven 69, pg. 814   IT
Logistic Services Division, Boompjes 40, pg. 1144   IT
MacGREGOR (NLD) B.V., Rietdijk 12, pg. 671   IT
Mammoet Ferry Transport B.V., pg. 1144   IT
Marga B.V., pg. 1438   IT
Marine Safety Rotterdam B.V., Wilhelminakade 701, pg. 219   PB
Maritima Services, 6 Stelle, pg. 682   IT
Mavibel (Maatschappij voor Internationale Beleggingen) B.V., pg. 1438   IT
Mead Holdings B.V., pg. 1076   PB
Mead Packboard B.V., pg. 1076   PB
Mecman International BV, pg. 838   IT
Medimatica Groep BV, pg. 720   IT
Meneba Meel B.V., Brielselaan 115, pg. 555   IT
Monterey Management B.V., P.O. Box 4298, Max Euwelaan 61, pg. 162   IT
Motorola Finance B.V., Coolsingel 139, pg. 1139   PB
Wm. H. Muller & Co. Nederland B.V., Stelle 2, pg. 682   IT
NKK Netherlands B.V.-Rotterdam Office, 9th Fl., Rm. 913, Calandstraat 66, pg. 903   IT
NYK Line (Benelux) B.V., Rotterdam Bldg., Aert Van Nesstraat 45, pg. 941   IT
National Bank of Greece Rotterdam Branch, pg. 907   IT
Nationale-Nederlanden, Weena 505, pg. 647   IT
Navar BDDP, World Trade Center Rotterdam, Beursplein 37, pg. 117   IT
Neddrill Holding B.V., pg. 1144   IT
Neddrill Nederland B.V., Coolsepoort, Coolsingel 139, pg. 1144   IT
Nederlandse Unilever Bedrijven B.V., pg. 1438   IT
Nedlloyd Bedrijfsgebouwen c.v., pg. 1144   IT
Nedlloyd Beheer B.V., pg. 1144   IT
Nedlloyd Bulk B.V., Willemswerf, Boompjes 40, pg. 1144   IT
Nedlloyd Computer Serices B.V., pg. 1144   IT
Nedlloyd Distribution Systems, pg. 1144   IT

Nedlloyd Energy B.V., Willemswerf, Boompjes 40, pg. 1144   IT
Nedlloyd Fleet Services, Willemswerf, Boompjes 40, pg. 1145   IT
Nedlloyd Flowmasters, Boompjes 40, pg. 1145   IT
Nedlloyd Lijnen B.V., pg. 1145   IT
Nedlloyd Lines B.V., Willemswerf, Boompjes 40, pg. 1145   IT
Nedlloyd Lines Nederland B.V., pg. 1145   IT
Nedlloyd Rijn- en Binnenvaart B.V., Van Weerden Poelmanweg 25, pg. 1144   IT
Nedlloyd Road Cargo B.V., pg. 1145   IT
Nedlloyd Vastgoed Beheer B.V., pg. 1145   IT
Netto Bouwmarkt Beheer B.V., pg. 1481   IT
Nieuw Rotterdam Knight Schippers, Blaak 16, pg. 562   IT
Nijgh Interpartners, Weena 695, pg. 1152   PV
Noble Neddrill, Coolsingel 139, pg. 1187   PB
Noordzee Veerdiensten B.V., Luxemburgweg 2, pg. 1145   IT
Novotel Nederland BV, Orangeboom straat 28, pg. 21   IT
Outokumpu Copper Resources B.V., Terwenakker 42/44, pg. 1016   IT
Outokumpu Zinc Commercial B.V., Terwenakker 42/44, pg. 1016   IT
Paktank International B.V., Blaak 33, pg. 1147   IT
Parfums Christian Dior BV, Max Euwelaan 55-57, pg. 783   IT
Penguin Huis B.V., pg. 715   IT
Pluspoint, pg. 750   IT
R. & H. Systems B.V., Sluisjedijk 155, pg. 680   IT
R-Partners, Heemraadssingel 100, pg. 1463   IT
RDM Technology Investments B.V., pg. 1133   IT
RVS Schadeverzekering N.V., pg. 647   IT
Rhenania Transport B.V., Wilhelminakade 33, pg. 1034   IT
Rhenus Nordic B.V., Strevelsweg 700/6001-605, pg. 447   IT
Royal Nederland Schadeverzekering, Coolsingel 139, pg. 16   IT
ROYAL NEDLLOYD GROUP N.V., Willemswerf, Boompjes 40, pg. 1143   IT
ROYAL PAKHOED NV, Blaak 333, pg. 1147   IT
SSM Coal B.V., Rochussenstraat 125, pg. 1155   IT
Safial B.V., pg. 1438   IT
Saponia B.V., pg. 1438   IT
Schilperoort Beheer, B.V., pg. 1306   IT
Senior TIFT B.V., Abraham van Stolkweg 102, pg. 1223   IT
Shell Nederland Verkoop MIJ B.V., Hofplein 20, pg. 1135   IT
Shell Tankers B.V., F. Elsingastraat 34, pg. 1135   IT
Skandia Insurance Company Ltd., Boompjes 410, pg. 1258   IT
Smit Internationale N.V., Zalmstraat 1, pg. 1449   PB
Solar Scheepsbouw B.V., Postbus 913, pg. 1133   IT
B.V. Somef-Daher Rotterdam, pg. 302   IT
Stolt-Nielsen B.V., pg. 1302   IT
TFA - Trans-maritime Freight Agencies B.V., Stelle 10, pg. 682   IT
TOTAL Exploitatie en Produktie Maatschappij B.K. (TEPMA), Baan 2, pg. 1409   IT
Total Marine Exploitatie N.V.-TME, Baan 2, pg. 1409   IT
Transport Uitgeverij, pg. 1099   IT
UAP-Nieuwrotterdam Schade, Blaak 16, pg. 562   IT
Unilever Export B.V., pg. 1439   IT
Unilever Financierings Maatschappij B.V., pg. 1439   IT
Unilever N.V., Weena 45, pg. 1434   IT
Unisource Network Partners B.V., pg. 720   IT
VB Autobatterien B.V., Bovendijk 137, pg. 1452   IT
Van den Bergh en Jurgens B.V., Nassaukade 3, pg. 1439   IT
J. Th. van der Cammen B.V., Waalhaven N.Z. 57-59, pg. 400   IT
Wemado B.V., pg. 1439   IT
Westdeutsche Landesbank-Rotterdam Branch, Veerhaven 17, pg. 1493   IT
Willemswerf v.o.f., pg. 1145   IT

Rozenburg

Kemira Holding B.V., pg. 729   IT
Kemira Peroxides B.V., P.O. Box 1015, pg. 728   IT
Kemira Pigments B.V., pg. 729   IT
Kemwater B.V., P.O. Box 1015, pg. 728   IT

Saint Maartensdijk

I.F.F. (Nederland) B.V., pg. 899   PB

Sappemeer

Kappa Eskaboard B.V., pg. 756   IT
Kappa Scholten B.V., Noorderstraat 394, pg. 756   IT

Sas-van-Gent

Cerestar Holding B.V., Nijverheidsstraat 1, pg. 324   IT
Glasfabrick Sas van Gent B.V., Westkade 20, pg. 1173   IT
Internationale Maatschappij Voorhet Beheer Van Glasmaatschappijen BV, Westkade 20, pg. 1173   IT
Saint-Gobain Nederland, Westkade 20, pg. 1177   IT

Sassenheim

Akzo Coatings Nederland B.V., 31 Rijksstraatweg, pg. 42   IT
Sikkens B.V., 31, Rijksstratweg, pg. 42   IT

PB - *U.S. Public Companies Volume*
PV - *U.S. Private Companies Volume*
IT - *International Public & Private Companies Volume*

Schalkhaar

Agrarische Unie-Vulcaan BV, pg. 353   IT

Scheemda

Acheson Colloiden B.V., Postbus 1, pg. 12   PV

Scherpenzeel

Asco Controls B.V., Industrielaan 21, pg. 575   PB
Interface Europe B.V., Postbus 16, pg. 889   PB

Schiedam

nv W.A. Hoek's Machine- en Zuurstoffabriek, pg. 811   IT
Sandvik Benelux B.V., P.O. Box 248, pg. 1186   IT
N.V. Vereenigde Glasfabrieken, Buitenhavenweg 114-116, pg. 381   IT

Schiphol

AIRVO B.V., pg. 278   IT
Amaco B.V., Amstelveen, Gebouw 72 Room 454, pg. 682   IT
Applied Materials Europe BV, Airport Office Ctr., pg. 123   PB
ELSAG BAILEY PROCESS AUTOMATION N.V., Schiphol Boulevard, pg. 449   IT
JOEL (Europe) B.V., Tupolevlaan 28-A, pg. 697   IT
J.P. Janssen International Freight Forwarders B.V., pg. 1144   IT
Kintetsu World Express (Benelux) B.V., Valkweg 2, pg. 735   IT
Nippon Express (Nederland) B.V., Maraboeweg 1, pg. 934   IT

Schoonrewoerd

Baars Kaas B.V., pg. 752   IT
Dairy Projects BV, pg. 751   IT
Zuivelonderneming De Vijfherenlanden' B.V., pg. 752   IT

Sevenum

Montair Andersen B.V., Heuvelsestraat 14, pg. 462   PB

Sittard

ACN Product Group, Poststraat 1, pg. 353   IT
Computer Centrum Sittard, Plakstraat 51, pg. 1463   IT
DSM Agro BV, pg. 353   IT
DSM Chemicals & Fertilizers, Poststraat 1, pg. 353   IT
DSM Elastomers, Poststraat 1, pg. 353   IT
DSM Elastomers Europe B.V., Poststraat 1, pg. 353   IT
DSM Fine Chemicals, Poststraat 1, pg. 353   IT
DSM Hydrocarbons, Poststraat 1, pg. 353   IT
DSM Melamine Limburg, Poststraat 1, pg. 353   IT
DSM Meststoffen B.V., Poststraat 1, pg. 353   IT
DSM Polymers, Poststraat 1, pg. 353   IT
DSM Polymers International, pg. 353   IT
DSM Thermoplastic Elastomers B.V., pg. 353   IT
Eurocarbon Tilburg B.V., Dr. Nolenslaan 119a, pg. 354   IT
Forton B.V., Paardestraat 31, pg. 354   IT
Hatema Contract B.V., pg. 540   IT
Helly-Hansen Distributie B.V., Nieuwstadterweg 21, pg. 1010   IT

Sliedrecht

OPEL Nederland B.V., Baanhoek 188, pg. 723   PB

Sluiskil

Hydro Agri Sluiskil B.V., Industrieweg 10, pg. 962   IT

Sneek

Flexa Fabrieken B.V., 62 Oppenhuizerweg, pg. 43   IT
Tonnema B.V., Oude Oppenhuizerweg 6, pg. 244   IT

Soest

Ballast Nedam & Industrie & Toelevering B.V., Koningsweg 30, pg. 133   IT
Branson (Europa) B.V., Energieweg 2, pg. 576   PB
Bruil Specialistische Bouwtechnieken B.V., Koningsweg 28, pg. 134   IT
Forbo NL Holding B.V., pg. 497   IT
Forbo Parade Tapijt B.V., pg. 497   IT
Forbo Stamoid B.V., pg. 498   IT
Hermans Groep B.V., Laatstrasse 2, pg. 1375   IT
Ingenieursbureau voor Systemen en Octrooien Spanstaal B.V., Koningsweg 28, pg. 134   IT
Smurfit Mercurius Verpakking B.V., Koningsweg 26, pg. 1271   IT
TBS Soest, Koningsweg 30, pg. 134   IT

Son

Makita Benelux B.V., Ekkersrijt 4086, pg. 832   IT

Steenbergen

BAC COLOR FRANSEWEG, P. Bost 16, pg. 131   IT

Stellendam

Jotun Polymer B.V., Delta Industrieweg 9, pg. 714   IT

Stramproy

Gusto Geleen B.V., Postbus 3107, pg. 1133   IT

Strawinskylaan

Yamaichi Bank Nederland N.V., World Trade Center Tower D, pg. 1517   IT

Ter Aar

Conserverifabriek L.P. Ugttewaad BV, Westkanaalweg 1, pg. 491   IT

Ter-Apel

Glucona vof, 13M/0 Weg, pg. 47   IT
Kjellbergs Successors B.V., P.O. Box 17, Kapelweg 13, pg. 712   IT
MB International B.V., Nomdenweg 2, pg. 798   PB

Terborg

Kimball Systems BV, Akkersmansbeekweg 12, pg. 461   IT
Meto Kimbal Systems b.v., P.O. Box 55, pg. 462   IT

Terneuzen

Association Cooperative Zelandaise de Carbonisation, pg. 572   IT
Dow Benelux (Nederland) B.V., pg. 523   PB

Tiel

Amway Nederland Ltd., Edisonstraat 18, pg. 70   PV
BASF Coatings & Drukinkt B.V., Papesteeg 102, pg. 105   IT
Danone B.V., Panovenweg 10, pg. 379   IT
Honeywell-Measurex B.V., Stephensonstrat 4, 4004, pg. 833   PB
Koninklijke Maatschappij De Betuwe B.V., pg. 1437   PB
Lowara Nederland B.V., pg. 861   PB
MassGlas B.V., Panovenwet 21, pg. 85   IT
Metawa-Tray B.V., pg. 1307   IT
Mettler-Toledo B.V., Franklinstraat 5, pg. 4   PV

Tilburg

Brekelmans BV, pg. 751   IT
Campina Melkunie, Cheese Division, Jules Verneweg 87, pg. 254   IT
Crompton & Knowles Tertre B.V., Dr. Hub. van Doornewag 91, pg. 460   PB
Dailycer BV, pg. 751   IT
Danzas B.V., Industrieterrein Katsbogten, Aletta Jacobsweg 4, pg. 382   IT
Delicia B.V., pg. 752   IT
Favory Convenience Food BV, pg. 751   IT
Fuji Photo Film B.V., Oudenstaart 1, pg. 524   IT
International Flavors & Fragrances, pg. 899   PB
Janssen/Cilag B.V., Dr. Paul Janssenweg 150, pg. 929   PB
N.V. Kaardenfabriek "Nederland", pg. 268   IT
Otto B.V., pg. 1015   IT
Sulzer Caliqua B.V., pg. 1306   IT
Sulzer Infra Nederland B.V., pg. 1306   IT
Sulzer Netherlands Holding B.V., pg. 1308   IT
Taxandria Pharmaceutica B.V., Dr. Paul Janssenweg 150, pg. 932   PB

Tolbert

Impex Walchar B.V., Feithspark 19, Industrieterrein Olde Bert, pg. 869   PB

Tolkamer

Wellman Recycling, pg. 1753   PB

Uden

EMI Compact Disc (Holland) BV, P.O. Box 333, pg. 427   IT
Hospal B.V., Loopkantraat 23, pg. 668   IT
Sandoz B.V., pg. 984   IT
Sandoz Pharma B.V., pg. 985   IT
Tennant Holding B.V., Industrielaan 6, pg. 1577   PB

Udenhout

Nordson Walcom B.V., Nijverheidsweg 23, pg. 1189   PB
Thermal Ceramics Nederland BV, Brabantcorner, pg. 894   IT

Uithoorn

Cindu Chemicals B.V., Amsteldijk, Noor 35, pg. 754   IT
Hitma BV, Anton Philipsweg 1, pg. 678   IT
Kenwood Electronics Europe B.V., Amsterdamseweg 37, pg. 731   IT
Kenwood Electronics Nederland B.V., Amsterdamseweg 35, pg. 731   IT

Ulft

Ampro Handelsonderneming B.V., Huttweg 24, pg. 1210   IT
Dru Industrial Products & Services BV, Frank Daamenstraat 4, pg. 1210   IT
Dru Stainless Steel Products B.V., Huttweg 24, pg. 1210   IT
Dru Verwarming B.V., Huttweg 24, pg. 1210   IT

Utrecht

AMEV Beleggingsconsortium N.V., Archimedeslaan 6, pg. 499   IT
AMEV Financieringen N.V., Archimeslaan 10, pg. 499   IT
AMEV Hypotheekbedrijf, Archimedeslaan 6, pg. 499   IT
AMEV Levensverzekering N.V., Archimedeslaan 10, pg. 499   IT
AMEV Nederland N.V., Archimedeslaan 6, pg. 498   IT
AMEV Ontwikkeling Maatschappij N.V., Archimedeslaan 10, pg. 499   IT
AMEV Praktijkvoorziening N.V., Archimedeslaan 6, pg. 499   IT
AMEV Schadeverzekering N.V., Archimedeslaan 6, pg. 499   IT
Air Products Nederland B.V., pg. 31   PB
Algemene Sein Industrie B.V., 100, Moeder Teresalaan, pg. 1194   IT
Amdahl Nederland B.V., Weg der Verenigde Naties 1, pg. 527   IT
Bensons International Systems BV, Positronweg 12, pg. 460   IT
Bobst Benelux N.V., pg. 198   IT
CAP Volmac, Daltonlaan 300, pg. 264   IT
Cemsto, Atoomweg 466, pg. 1463   IT
CETECO N.V., Beneluxlaan 909, pg. 279   IT
Compu'Train BV, pg. 756   IT
The Continuum Company, Inc. (Netherlands), pg. 423   PB
Copijn Utrecht Holding BV, pg. 607   IT
Crediet en Effecten Bank, Herculesplein 5, pg. 647   IT
DSM Verkoopkantoor Polymeren Nederland, pg. 353   IT
Dagmarkt, Reactorweg 263, pg. 1463   IT
Digital Equipment (Holdings) B.V., Eurogalaan 44, pg. 508   PB
Dyas B.V., Rijnkade 1, pg. 1155   IT
ESAB International Holding B.V., Kernkade 8, pg. 282   IT
ESAB Nederland B.V., P.O. Box 8183, pg. 282   IT
ESTA B.V., Kernkade 8, pg. 282   IT
ESTA Vastgoed B.V., Kernkade 8, pg. 283   IT
FGH Bank N.V., 50, Leidseveer, pg. 26   IT
FILARC Welding Industries B.V., Kernkade 14, pg. 283   IT
FORTIS, Archimedeslaan 6, pg. 498   IT
Fortis International N.V., Archimedeslaan 6, pg. 499   IT
Generale Bank - Utrecht, Newtonlaan 57, pg. 547   IT
Geytenbeek B.V., Rutherfordweg 51, pg. 1144   IT
HTS Inspection Systems BV, pg. 753   IT
HWZ, Hollandsche Wegenbouw Zanen B.V., Winthontlaan 28, pg. 630   IT
Hasselblad BV, Savannahweg 69, pg. 1468   IT
Hoogovens BV, Uraniumweg 27, pg. 754   IT
Hoogovens Technical Services Inspection Systems BV, Uraniumweg 27, pg. 753   IT
ISS Hospital Service B.V., Atoornweg 350, pg. 657   IT
Iglo-Ola B.V., pg. 1437   IT
Industar B.V., c/o Esab Nederland B.V., Kernkade 14, pg. 283   IT
Komori Benelux B.V., Reactorweg 151, pg. 745   IT
Komori International (Europe) B.V., Reactorweg 151, pg. 745   IT
Littelfuse B.V., pg. 1001   PB
Maxis B.V., Kobaltweg 11, pg. 1156   IT
Mercedes-Benz Nederland B.V., Reactorweg 25, pg. 369   IT
Nieuw Welgelgen B.V., Admiraal Helfrichlaan 1, pg. 91   IT
Nira Nederland B.V., Savannahweg 31, pg. 1369   IT
OWAT Assurantie B.V., pg. 1145   IT
Parcom Ventures B.V., pg. 647   IT
Quinton Hazell PLC, Utrecht, pg. 561   PB
RABOBANK NEDERLAND, Croeselaan 18, pg. 1082   IT
Ross Systems Nederland B.V., pg. 1406   PB
Royal Nederland Levensverzekering N.V., Europalaan 280, pg. 16   IT
SHV Energy N.V., Rijnkade 1, pg. 1155   IT
SHV HOLDINGS N.V., Rijnkade 1, pg. 1154   IT
SHV Makro, Rijnkade 1, pg. 1155   IT
Sailtron B.V., Croeselaan 163, pg. 1151   IT
Samas Universal Office Supplies, Atoomweg 103, pg. 707   IT
Sara Lee/DE, Vleutensevaart 100, pg. 1434   PB
Schiesser International Nederland BV, pg. 618   IT
Selektvracht B.V., Kernweg 1, pg. 1145   IT
Servonsite International BV, pg. 720   IT
Surfnet B.V., pg. 720   IT
Tiel Utrecht, Uniceflaan 1, pg. 647   IT
Tiel Utrecht Schadeverzekering N.V., pg. 647   IT
Tiel Utrecht Verzekerd Sparen N.V., pg. 647   IT
UAP-Nieuwrotterdam Leven, Sint-Jacobusstraat 200, pg. 562   IT
UAP-Nieuwrotterdam Schade, Sint-Jacobusstraat 200, pg. 562   IT
UAP-Nieuwrotterdam Zorg, Sint-Jacobusstraat 200, pg. 562   IT
UBO Levensverzekeringen N.V., 251, Euclideslaan, pg. 26   IT

Quaker Chemical B.V., Industrieweg X, 1-13, pg. 1346   PB
Quaker Chemical Europe B.V., P.O. Box 579, pg. 1346   PB
Rockwell Automation B.V., Amsterdamseweg 15, pg. 1399   PB
Sigma Coatings B.V., Amsterdamseweg 14, pg. 1044   IT

PB - *U.S. Public Companies Volume*
PV - *U.S. Private Companies Volume*
IT - *International Public & Private Companies Volume*

UBO Schadeverzeheringen N.V., 251, Euclideslaan, pg. 26   IT
UBO Verzekeringen, 251, Euclideslaan, pg. 26   IT
VGL Internationale Expeditie B.V., pg. 1145   IT
Van Leer Nederland B.V., pg. 1146   IT
VARTA B.V., Savannahweg 53, pg. 1452   IT
Vendopolis, Europalaan 30, pg. 1463   IT
Vicorp, N.V., Europalaan 542, pg. 1321   PB
Wellcome Pharmaceuticals BV, pg. 553   IT
Wolters Kluwer Trade Publishing, St. Jacobsstraat 127, pg. 1513   IT

Vaals

Bioplex Medical B.V., Selzerbeeklaan 9, pg. 487   PB

Vaassen

Droste B.V., Zwarteweg 31, pg. 243   IT
Vassen Aluminium BV, pg. 753   IT

Veenendaal

Ames Europe Veenendaal B.V., pg. 540   IT
Arrow Holland Medical Products B.V., pg. 135   PB
Benelux Periodieken bv, pg. 1445   IT
Bio-Rad Laboratories BV, Fokkerstraat 10, pg. 230   PB
Brooks Instrument B.V., Groenveldselaan 6, pg. 576   PB
COBE Laboratories Europe N.V., Kernreactorstraat 36, pg. 667   IT
Central Service Group BV, pg. 756   IT
Codi International B.V., Verlaat 22, pg. 686   PB
Corrugated Europe BV, pg. 756   IT
Dormer Tools B.V., pg. 1186   IT
DYWIDAG Aquaschutz B.V., Vendelier 55c+d, pg. 424   IT
Enerpac B.V., Storkstratt 25, pg. 125   PB
Finnigan MAT Benelux, Landjuweel 7, pg. 1596   PB
Firet, B.V., Verlaat 22, pg. 686   PB
Kimberly-Clark Benelux Operations B.V., Groeneveldselaan 41, pg. 959   PB
Kimberly-Clark Sales Corporation, P.O. Box 72, pg. 959   PB
Kortman Intradal, pg. 1434   PB
Lawson Mardon Boxal Nederland B.V., pg. 68   IT
Melitta Nederland B.V., pg. 857   IT
Nucletron BV, Waerdgelder 1, pg. 389   IT
Reforma-Dianata B.V., pg. 984   IT
Rowenta Nederland B.V., Generatorstraat 6A, pg. 569   IT
SKF Kogellagerindustrie B.V., Groeneveldselaan 25, pg. 1159   IT
SKF Nederland B.V., Schietboom 2, pg. 1159   IT
Sandoz Nutrition B.V., pg. 985   IT
Tefal Nederland B.V., Generatorstraat 6, pg. 568   IT
Wasa Wander B.V., pg. 986   IT

Veghel

Campina Melkunie International Division, NCB-laan 80, pg. 254   IT
DMV International, NCB-laan 80, pg. 254   IT
Mars BV, Taylorweg 5, pg. 707   PV

Veldhoven

eta Ingenieurs BV, Luchthavenweg 67, pg. 607   IT
Fardem International B.V., De Run 1150, pg. 352   IT
Fardem Packaging B.V., De Run 1150, pg. 352   IT
Molex (Benelux) B.V., Dommelstraat-Zuid 47, pg. 1122   PB
A.O. Smith-Water Products Co., 27 Industrie Weg., pg. 1477   PB

Velp

Copem Compagnie de Participation Europeenne Meinl B.V., pg. 856   IT
Vitatron Medical B.V., Reigerstraat 30, pg. 1084   PB
VREDESTEIN N.V., President Kennedylaan 104, pg. 1481   IT

Velsen-Noord

Hoogovens Beheermaatschappij Industriele Produkten BV, Gebouw Nieuw Transwijk, Rooswijkweg, pg. 753   IT

Venlo

CMV Crediet Maatschappij Venlo N.V. Steegh Assurantien B.V., Spoorstraat 1, pg. 9   IT
DSM Andeno B.V., Noorderpoort 9, pg. 353   IT
EnviroTech Pumpsystems Netherlands BV, pg. 1489   IT
Eurotapijt Nederland B.V., pg. 540   IT
Gerlach & Co. Internationale Expediteurs B.V., Horsterweg 217, pg. 1144   IT
J.P. Janssen B.V., pg. 1144   IT
Mead Coated Board Europe B.V., pg. 1076   PB
NITEC (Europe) B.V., Trade Port West Columbusweg, pg. 950   IT
OCE Direct Export, pg. 994   IT
OCE-Nederland B.V., pg. 994   IT
OCE-VAN DER GRINTEN N.V., St. Urbanusweg 43, pg. 993   IT
Viking Direct B.V.I.O., Venlo Trade Port, Celsiusweg 40/42, pg. 1721   PB
Winter-Bouts B.V., Jachthavenweg 9, pg. 729   IT

Vianen

American Power Conversion, Middelmolen 27, pg. 89   PB

Daihatsu Holland B.V., Witboom 2, 4131 PL, pg. 365   IT
De La Rue Systems BV, Stuartweg 27, pg. 387   IT
Foot Locker Europe B.V., Hagenstaete, Langedreff 8, pg. 778   PB
Kawasaki Motors N.V., Marconiweg 5, Industrie Park, pg. 726   IT

Vlaardingen

Cincinnati Milacron B.V., pg. 368   PB
Helene Curtis Europa B.V., pg. 1434   IT
Hydro Agri Benelux B.V., 103 Maasluissedijk, pg. 962   IT
Hydro Agri Rotterdam B.V., 103 Maasluissedijk, pg. 962   IT
Hydrogas Holland B.V., Maasluissedijk 103, 3133 KA Vlaardingen, pg. 963   IT
Lever Sunlight B.V., pg. 1438   IT
Nederlands Studiecentrum, Schiedamseweg 34, pg. 1100   IT
Raadgevende Ingenieurs Jongen BV, pg. 607   IT
Van Eijle B.V., 30, Industrieweg, pg. 682   IT

Vlijmen

Shimano Center Bicy B.V., Postbus 144, pg. 1233   IT

Vlissingen

Houtopslag Maatschappij Vlissingen B.V., pg. 431   IT
Pechiney Nederland NV, Frank Rijkweg, 2, pg. 1031   IT

Vondelingenplaat

Air Products Nederland B.V., 3196 KL Vondelingenplaat-Rt, pg. 31   PB
Kemira Agro Rozenburg B.V., Vondelingenplaat 17, pg. 729   IT
Kemira International Finance B.V., Vondelingenplaat 17, pg. 729   IT
Kemira Services Holland B.V., Vondelingenplaat 17, pg. 729   IT

Voorburg

Bourns Benelux B.V., Van Tuyl Van Serooskerkestraat 81-85, pg. 161   PV
Fina International N.V., Nieuwe Havenstraat 2, pg. 1044   IT
Fina Nederland B.V., Nieuwe Havenstraat 2, pg. 1043   IT
Mafina E.V., Nieuwe Havenstraat 2, pg. 1044   IT

Voorschoten

Formica Nederland B.V., Dobbeweg 15, pg. 129   IT
PKF/STEUN B.V., pg. 756   IT

Vreeland

Van Lee Nederland B.V., pg. 1146   IT

Vriezenveen

Eshuis Bouwmaterialen Groep, pg. 1458   IT

Waalre

B.V. Linnenweverijen v/h v Dijk en Zonen, pg. 540   IT

Waalwijk

Henningsen Nederland B.V., Slvisweg 20, pg. 1074   IT
Henningsen-Van den Burg, Slvisweg 20, pg. 1074   IT
ICI Resins B.V., pg. 665   IT
Internationale Gas Apparaten B.V., pg. 1149   IT
Levis B.V., 9 Industrieweg, P.O. Box 319, pg. 42   IT
Serasea BV, pg. 607   IT
Stahl Holland b.v., Sluisweg 10, pg. 1526   IT
Stahl International b.v., Sluisweg 10, pg. 1526   IT
Zeneca Resins bv, Sluisweg 12, pg. 1527   IT

Waddinxveen

Air Products Nederland B.V., P.O. Box 56, Noordkade 100, pg. 31   PB
Volvo Bedrijfswagens B.V., Postbus 30, pg. 1476   IT

Wageningen

Selectpack BV, pg. 751   IT

Wamel

Lancer Holland BV, pg. 552   IT

Wapenveld

Berghuizer-Enso Formaatfabriek B.V., pg. 458   IT

Warmond

Halm Industries International, Veerpolder II, pg. 496   PV
Thermo Electric Intl. B.V., P.O. Box 65, pg. 1080   PV

Waspik

Keizer B.V. (Waspik), Industrieweg 3-5165, pg. 850   IT

Wassemaar

Communicatie & Design, Rijksstraantweg 426, pg. 1335   IT

Weert

Frencken De Bruyn B.V., Straevenweg 1, pg. 354   IT
Presco International B.V., pg. 752   IT
Projecta B.V., pg. 306   PV
Rieter Automotive Nederland B.V., pg. 1117   IT

Weesp

Bristol-Myers B.V., Flevolaan 50, pg. 255   PB
Colgate-Palmolive Nederland, Postbus 437 NL, Amstellandlaan 84, pg. 398   PB
Ivec Handelsonderneming bv, pg. 1445   IT
Multipharma BV, pg. 983   IT
Nederlandsche Kali-Import Maatschappij B.V. (N.K.I.M.), Kantoorgebouw, De Muiderpoort, Leeuwenveldsweg 3, pg. 109   IT
Network Systems Nederland B.V., Pampuslaan 1, pg. 1523   PB
Plavina Benelux B.V., Nyverheidslaah 2-8, pg. 1279   IT
Process Analytics Benelux, Pampuslaan 89, pg. 6   IT
Richard Hirschmann Electronica Nederland B.V., Postbus 92, Saint Martins Business Centre, pg. 1108   IT
Schering Nederland B.V., Van Houten Industriepark 1, Postbus 116, pg. 1204   IT
Sun Electric Systems B.V. (SES), Nijverheidslaan 15-17, pg. 1481   PB
VG Instruments B.V., pg. 1595   PB

Weurt

Draad Nijmegen B.V., Postbus 10, pg. 1133   IT

Wijhe

Meester Wijhe bv, Stationsweg 27, pg. 749   IT

Wijk

Siegling Nederland B.V., pg. 498   IT

Willemstad

Long-Term Credit Bank of Japan Finance N.V., Pietermaai 15, pg. 816   IT

Winschoten

Winpac B.V., Papierbaan 50, pg. 864   IT

Winterswijk

BW Industrial Products B.V., pg. 198   IT
Cirex Machining BV, pg. 753   IT

Woerden

Ampco Metal Nederlands B.V., pg. 67   PV
Certanium B.V., P. O. Box 106, pg. 1068   IT
Esselte BV, Ampereweg 17, pg. 461   IT
Harris Corp. B.V., Houttinlaan 18, pg. 791   PB
Intochem B.V., Pelmolenlaan 17b, pg. 682   IT
Krupp Widia Nederland B.V., Vijzelmolenlaan 3, pg. 510   IT
Logica B.V., Het Kasteel, pg. 814   IT
Melkunie, De Bleek 1, pg. 254   IT
Mona, De Bleek 1, pg. 254   IT
Nedsafe, Ohmweg 11A, pg. 1463   IT
Pharmacia & Upjohn Nederland B.V., Houttuinlaan 4, pg. 1050   IT
Premier Industrial Holland B.V., P. O. Box 106, pg. 1068   IT
Receptionelle, Ohmweg 11A, pg. 1463   IT
Sauer-Sundstrand Benelux BV, Rietdekkersweg 12, pg. 1198   IT
Telematics International B.V., Houttuinlaan 18, pg. 644   IT
Tukkers Milieu-onderzoek BV, pg. 607   IT

Wolfheze

Barenbrug Research Wolfheze, Duitsekampweg 60, pg. 166   IT

Wormer

Storm van Bentem & Kluyver B.V., Veerdijk 4-9, pg. 756   PB

Wormerveer

Ahlstrom Papier B.V., Bruynsvisweg 14, pg. 35   IT
Croklaan B.V., Zaandj Kerweg 36, pg. 1436   IT
Eurocol B.V., pg. 497   IT
Van Heusden, Industrieweg 120, pg. 1463   IT
Wessanen Meel B.V., P.O.B. 11, pg. 751   IT

Zaandam

Ahold Vastgoed B.V., Ebbehout 31, pg. 749   IT

PB - *U.S. Public Companies Volume*
PV - *U.S. Private Companies Volume*
IT - *International Public & Private Companies Volume*

1722

Geographic Index-Non U.S.

Ballast Nedam Grondstoffen B.V., Sluispolderweg 67, pg. 133 — IT
Bolding Verpakkingen B.V., Postbus 1037, pg. 1466 — IT
Etos bv, Vredeweg 46, pg. 749 — IT
Eurometaal Holding N.V., pg. 998 — IT
Gist-Brocades Savoury B.V., Gerrit Bolkade 10, pg. 1142 — IT
Albert Heijn B.V., Ankersmidplein 2, pg. 749 — IT
KONINKLIJKE AHOLD NV, Albert Heijnweg 1, pg. 749 — IT
Marvelo B.V., Hoofdtocht 3, pg. 749 — IT
Transinko B.V., P.O. Box 630, pg. 751 — IT
Van Rietschoten & Houwens Noord-West bv, c.van Uikgeest Straat 1, pg. 681 — IT
Wessanen Flour International B.V., P.O. Box 630, pg. 751 — IT

Zaltbommel

Basismarkt, Toepadweg 12 A, pg. 1463 — IT
CAMPINA MELKUNIE BV, Hogeweg 9, pg. 254 — IT
DYWIDAG-Systemen Nederland B.V., Veilingweg 2, pg. 424 — IT
HODY B.V., Veilingweg 2, pg. 754 — IT
Kijkshop/Best-sellers, Schimminck 12, pg. 1462 — IT
Sugro B.V., pg. 991 — IT

Zeewolde

Hillshog Holland B.V., pg. 982 — IT

Zeist

Achmea, Handelsweg 2, pg. 464 — IT
Apple Computer B.V., Huis ter Heideweg 50, pg. 121 — PB
Ballast Nedam Dredging, Utrechtseweg 62, pg. 133 — IT
Dynartail bv, Griffensteijnselaan 202, pg. 681 — IT
Micro Warehouse Holding B.V., Prof. Lorenzianan 3A, pg. 1104 — PB
SCHUTTERSVELD HOLDING N.V., Utrechtseweg 46, pg. 1210 — IT
Wemex Technology B.V., pg. 1133 — IT
Zickenhuis Diensten Groep, Huis ter Heideweg 14, pg. 1463 — IT

Zelhem

Zelhem Plant, Brinkweg, 38, pg. 672 — PB

Zenlo

Breyer Chemie B.V., pg. 599 — IT

Zevenaar

B.F. Goodrich Aerospace, Voltastraat 33, pg. 752 — PB

Zoetermeer

Astra Pharmaceutica B.V., Louis Pasteurlaan 5, pg. 94 — IT
BS-Service B.V., Zoetermeer, 24, Bredewater, pg. 682 — IT
Bestuurcentrum der Verenigde Bedrijven Nutricia B.V., pg. 991 — IT
Bols Benelux B.V., Wattstraat 61, pg. 751 — IT
Coherent Benelux, Argonstraat 136, pg. 395 — PB
Flender Nederland B.V., Platinstraat 133, pg. 400 — IT
Installatiegroep Van Buuren-Van Swaay bv, Bredewater 24, pg. 681 — IT
KTI Group B.V., 26 Bredewater, pg. 837 — IT
Kaagro B.V., pg. 991 — IT
Kathabar Systems Europe, Zoetermeer, 24, Bredewater, pg. 681 — IT
Kinetics Technology International BV, 26 Bredewater, P.O. Box 86, pg. 837 — IT
Kulk & Kramer Kantoorsystemen B.V., Wiltonstraat 7-9, pg. 1116 — IT
Noordgastransport BV, pg. 354 — IT
NUTRICIA BV, Rokkeveenseweg 49, pg. 991 — IT
Nutricia Export B.V., pg. 991 — IT
Nutricia International B.V., pg. 991 — IT
Nutricia Medical Devices B.V., pg. 991 — IT
Nutricia Nationaal B.V., pg. 991 — IT
Nutricia Nederland B.V., pg. 991 — IT
Nutricia Nederlander Beheermaatschappij B.V., pg. 991 — IT
N.V. Nutricia, pg. 991 — IT
Nutricia Poland B.V., pg. 991 — IT
BV Papiergroothandel v/h Riem & Honig, pg. 756 — IT
Pfizer Animal Health B.V., Franklinstaat 1, pg. 1283 — PB
Puma Benelux B.V., Edelgasstraat 250, pg. 1072 — IT
Radiometer Nederland B.V., Chroomstraat 6-8, pg. 1084 — IT
Siemens Nixdorf Informatiesystemen BV, Postbus 609, pg. 1245 — IT
Signaal Special Products, Bleiswijkseweg 55, pg. 1385 — IT
SmithKline Beecham Diergeneeskundige Producten B.V., pg. 1266 — IT
Sulzer Nederland B.V., pg. 1306 — IT
Toshiba Medical Systems Europe B.V., Zilverstraat 1, pg. 1407 — IT
Van Buuren-Van Swaay Marine Airconditioning, Zoetermeer, 24, Bredewater, pg. 681 — IT
Van Swaay International Contracting B.V., 24, Bredewater, pg. 681 — IT
Van Swaay Trading B.V., 24, Bredewater, pg. 681 — IT

Zoeterwoude-Rijndijk

Ascom Zarli BV, Energieweg 10, pg. 87 — IT

Comtest Instrumentation B.V., Industrieweg 12, pg. 1596 — PB
Eurotherm BV, Johan Frisostraat 1, pg. 466 — IT
Heineken Nederland BV, Burgemeester Smeetsweg 1, pg. 608 — IT
Thermo Voltek Corp., Industrieweg 12, pg. 1596 — PB
3M Nederland B.V., Industrieweg 24, pg. 1607 — PB

Zundert

Luijckx BV Chocolade, pg. 751 — IT

Zutphen

Buhrmann-Ubbens Papier BV, pg. 756 — IT
Buhrmann-Vromen Verpakking BV, pg. 756 — IT
Lawson Mardon Picopac BV, pg. 69 — IT
Outokumpu Copper B.V., pg. 1017 — IT
Outokumpu Copper Strip B.V., P.O. Box 2, pg. 1017 — IT
Primagaz Nederland B.V., Industrieweg 102, pg. 1155 — IT

Zwaanshoek

Enthoven B.V., Bennebroekerweg 880, pg. 555 — IT

Zwanenburg

AMRI Nederland B.V., pg. 721 — IT
KSB Nederlander B.V., pg. 721 — IT

Zwijndrecht

Aqualon B.V., pg. 810 — PB
CBBM BV, Westelijke Parallelweg 54, pg. 1100 — IT
Duni Nederland B.V., P.O. Box 1095, pg. 421 — IT
Elsevier Opleidingen BV, Westelijke Parallelweg 54, pg. 1094 — IT
Euryza bv, Ringdijk 468, pg. 243 — IT
Parker Pneumatic, Merwedeweg 7, pg. 1264 — PB
Quaker Oats B.V., pg. 1348 — PB
TEMPO ROPARKO B.V., Stationsplein 4, pg. 1333 — PB
UniMills B.V., pg. 1439 — IT
Van Leeuwen Buizen Europa BV, Lindsedijk 20, pg. 1449 — IT
P. Van Leeuwen Jr's Buizenhandel B.V., pg. 1449 — IT
VAN LEEUWEN PIPE AND TUBE GROUP B.V., Lindtsedijk 20, pg. 1449 — IT

Zwolle

Advanced Metal Forming CV, Ceintuurbaan 15, pg. 753 — IT
Agrarisch Dagblad, Dr. D R Stoltenweg 11-15, pg. 1099 — IT
Amefo BV, Ceintuurbaan 30, pg. 753 — IT
Checkpoint Systems Nederland BV, Branderweg 11, pg. 343 — PB
N.V. Consultants & Assistants "Consultass", P.O. Box 70, pg. 9 — IT
DSM Resins B.V., Ceintuurbaan 5, pg. 353 — IT
Lewmar Mid-Europe BV, Branderweg 19, pg. 1462 — IT
Scania Nederland B.V., Postbus 618, pg. 687 — IT

NETHERLANDS ANTILLES

Bonaire

Antilles International Salt Company NV, pg. 44 — IT
Bonaire Petroleum Corp. N.V. (BOPEC), Plantage Brasil, pg. 1046 — IT

Curacao

ANR Finance N.V., De Ruyterkade 62, pg. 391 — PB
Ahold Finance Company (Nederlandse Antillen) NV, International Trade Center-Placade, pg. 750 — IT
Antillean Telematics NV, pg. 720 — IT
Banque de Suez Nederland International N.V., Kaya Flamboyant, Plaza Rooi Catootje 3C, pg. 314 — IT
Bayer International Finance N.V., pg. 174 — IT
Bekaert Trade Latin America N.V., ITC Building, P.O Box 6065, pg. 184 — IT
Bulkitalia Investments N.V., De Ruyterkade, 62, pg. 304 — IT
Bulknedlloyd Antilles N.V., De Ruyterkade, 62, pg. 304 — IT
Canadian Maas River Investment N.V., De Ruyterkade 62, pg. 829 — IT
Carib Teleconsult NV, pg. 720 — IT
Caterpillar Financial Services N.V., c/o ABN Trustcompany (Curacao), N.V., 15 Pietermaai, pg. 316 — PB
Cigna Overseas Finance N.V., Handelskade 8, pg. 364 — PB
Coeclerici Holding Overseas N.V., De Ruyterkade, 62, pg. 304 — IT
Coeclerici Logistic Overseas N.V., De Ruyterkade, 62, pg. 304 — IT
Coeclerici Trading Overseas N.V., De Ruyterkade, 62, pg. 304 — IT
Commerzbank Overseas Finance N.V., pg. 312 — IT
Crowncen Intl. N.V., Handelskade 8, pg. 462 — PB
CUNA Mutual Group-Netherlands Antilles, Curacaostraat 50, pg. 297 — PV
Curacao Oil Terminal, pg. 1141 — IT
Deutsche Bank Finance N.V., pg. 405 — IT
Enserch Finance N.V., 16A Pietermaai, pg. 1587 — PB
Eurobull Overseas N.V., 15 Pietermaai Willemstad, pg. 318 — IT
Ford Credit Overseas Finance N.V., pg. 665 — PB

Gefina International N.V., 6, John B. Gorsiraweg, pg. 91 — IT
Georgia-Pacific Finance N.V., pg. 739 — PB
Gist-Brocades N.V., Willemstad, pg. 1142 — IT
Hippocrene Holdings, 15 Pietermaai, pg. 1269 — PB
Holdux Curacao N.V., Handelskade, 8, pg. 91 — IT
Household Finance Intl. N.V., De Ruyterkade 6Z, pg. 842 — PB
International Mail Handling NV, pg. 720 — IT
Moore Holdings Curacao N.V., pg. 890 — IT
NS Holdings NV, Prof. Kernkampweg 1, pg. 1082 — IT
N.V. Nutricia Americas, pg. 992 — IT
Occidental International Finance N.V., P.O. Box 812, pg. 1210 — PB
ORTHOFIX INTERNATIONAL N.V., 7 Abraham de Veerstraat, pg. 1011 — IT
PTT Post Caribbean NV, pg. 720 — IT
PTT Telecom Carribean NV, pg. 720 — IT
Pensioen ESC, pg. 1332 — IT
Pepsi-Cola N.V., Mecakgan Zealandia, pg. 1277 — IT
Prudential Overseas Funding Corp. N.V., Labadera Plaza, Santa Rosaweg 129 E, pg. 893 — PV
Rabobank Curacao NV, Prof. Kernkampweg 1, pg. 1082 — IT
Rabobank Trustmaatschappij, Prof. Kernkampweg 1, pg. 1082 — IT
Refineria Isla (Curazao), S.A., Emmastad, pg. 1046 — IT
R.J. Reynolds Overseas Finance Co. N.V., Schottegatweg-Oost, Salinjay, P.O. Box 3, pg. 1355 — PB
Richardson-Vicks (Overseas) Finance N.V., De Ruyterkade 62, pg. 1333 — PB
S.E.L. Maduro & Sons (Curacao) Inc., Merchandise Dept., Emancipatie Boulevard 19, pg. 1369 — IT
Sandoz Finance N.V., pg. 984 — IT
Sandoz Investment N.V., pg. 984 — IT
Sandoz Overseas N.V., pg. 985 — IT
SAPIENS INTERNATIONAL CORPORATION N.V., De Ruiterkad 58-A, pg. 1193 — IT
Schlumberger Antilles N.V., CITCO, de Ruyterkade 62, pg. 1439 — IT
Schlumberger Offshore Services Limited, CITCO, de Ruyterkade 62, pg. 1439 — IT
Sedco Forex Offshore International Limited, CITCO, de Ruyterkade 62, pg. 1439 — IT
Somocar Overseas N.V., De Ruyterkade, 62, pg. 304 — IT
Tokai Finance (Curacao) N.V., 6 John B Gorsiraweg, pg. 1391 — IT
Van Melle Latin America NV, P.O. Box 3998, pg. 1451 — IT
Velcro Industries N.V., 22-24 Castorweg, pg. 1462 — IT

Oranjestad

BOC Gases Anba NV, pg. 121 — IT

Philipsburg

The Chase Manhattan Bank, N.A., Soualiga Bldg., Cannegieter Straat, pg. 340 — PB
Chase Manhattan Overseas Finance Corporation, N.V., Soualiga Bldg., Cannegieter Straat, pg. 340 — PB
RHG St. Maarten, P.O. Box 2546, A. Th. Illidge Rd., pg. 1152 — IT

Salinja

Moore International Holdings N.V., Schottegatweg Oost 130, pg. 890 — IT

San Nicolas

RHG Aruba, P.O. Box 20, pg. 1152 — IT

Willemstad

ABN Trustcompany (Curacao) N.V., Pietermaai 15, pg. 11 — IT
Amro Bank Overseas N.V., John B. Gorsiraweg 6, pg. 9 — IT
Amro Bank Overseas N.V., Pietermaai 17, pg. 12 — IT
Amro Beheers-Maatschappij N.V., John B. Gorsiraweg 6, pg. 9 — IT
N.V. Antradex Nutricia Americas, pg. 991 — IT
BMW Overseas Enterprises N.V., pg. 178 — IT
Bellast Nedam Caribbean N.V., pg. 134 — IT
Bols Latin America N.V., pg. 751 — IT
Cormagic N.V., Kaya Willem (Jombi), pg. 751 — IT
Crisson Securities NV, International Trading Center, BC IV 04, P.O. Box 6349, pg. 1115 — IT
Ennia Caribe N.V., J.B. Gorsiraweg 6, pg. 28 — IT
Grabowsky & Poort Caribbean NV, pg. 607 — IT
Kredietbank International Finance N.V., Zeelandia Office Park, 14, Kata W.F.G. (Jombi) Mensing, pg. 761 — IT
Lamic nv, 11, Sorsaca, pg. 682 — IT
Mavibel International N.V., pg. 1438 — IT
Nationale Trust Maatschappij (Nederlandse Antillen) N.V., John B. Gorsiraweg 6, pg. 10 — IT
Occidental Overseas Finance N.V., P.O. Box 812, pg. 1210 — PB
Oldelft International Trading Cy. N.V., International Trade Center, B1V/06, pg. 389 — IT
Pierson, Heldring & Pierson (Curacao) N.V., John B. Gorsiraweg 6, pg. 10 — IT
Radio Holland Group Carribbean, P.O. Box 3894, Pletterijweg z/n, pg. 1152 — IT
Ralston Purina Overseas Finance N.V., De Ruyterkade 62, pg. 1360 — PB
Soveper NV, Banco Di Caribe, Schottegatweg Oost 205 C, pg. 919 — IT

PB - *U.S. Public Companies Volume*
PV - *U.S. Private Companies Volume*
IT - *International Public & Private Companies Volume*

Geographic Index-Non U.S.

Telefonaktiebolaget LM Ericsson Technical Office, Maduro Plaza, pg. 1370 IT
Unilever Becumij N.V., pg. 1439 IT
VELCRO INDUSTRIES N.V., 15 Pietermaai, pg. 1462 IT
Volkswagen Overseas Finance N.V., 15 Pietermaai, pg. 1475 IT

NEW CALEDONIA

Noumea

BHP Steel Building Products New Caledonia SA, Perimetre Ducos, Baie De Numbo, pg. 226 IT
BNP-Nouvelle Caledonie, 37 Ave. Henri-Lafleur, pg. 164 IT
Banque de Nouvelle Caledonie, B.D.L. 3, pg. 1248 PB
Banque Paribas Pacifique, 33, rue de l'Alma, pg. 320 IT
Dumez Caledonia, B.P. 2086, pg. 823 IT
Gan Pacifique Iard, 58 bis avenue de la Victoire BP 223, pg. 564 IT
Gan Pacifique Vie, 58 bis avenue de la Victoire, pg. 564 IT
Goro Nickel S.A., pg. 672 IT
Minniti, Im. Carcopino, pg. 823 IT
Mitsui & Co., Ltd., Immeuble Lafleur, Avenue Marechal Foch, pg. 882 IT
Nestle Nouvelle-Caledonia S.A., pg. 921 IT
Restauration Francaise, 3, rue Henri-Simonin, pg. 1275 IT
Societe des Emulsions du Pacifique, Rue Eiffel prolongee, pg. 824 IT
Societe Shell Pacifique, Route de La Digue, pg. 1138 IT
Sodexho Nouvelle-Caledonie, pg. 1275 IT
Westpac Banking Corp. - New Caledonia, 44 Rue de L'alma, pg. 1497 IT

NEW ZEALAND

Albany

Hanimex (NZ) Limited, Cnr. William Pickering Dr. & Bush Rd., pg. 1116 IT
Transworld Publishers (Nz) Ltd., 3 William Pickering Rd., pg. 191 IT

Ashburton

Five Star Beef Ltd., Seaside Rd., Wakanui, pg. 695 IT

Auckland

A.I. Ocean (New Zealand) Ltd., Airport Oaks, 1st Fl., 42 Richard Pearce Dr., pg. 14 IT
ANZ McCaughan (NZ) Limited, 21st Fl. ASB Building, 165 Albert Street, pg. 99 IT
ASB Bank Limited, ABB Bank Centre, Corner Albert & Wellesley Square, pg. 313 IT
AST New Zealand Limited, 8 Arthur Brown Place, pg. 1182 IT
Abbott Laboratories NZ Ltd., 1/24 Eric Paton Way, pg. 14 PB
Acer Computer New Zealand, pg. 22 IT
Adecco New Zealand, Level 3, 10 O'Connell St., pg. 24 IT
Aetna Health (New Zealand) Limited, Aetna House, pg. 27 PB
Air New Zealand Cargo Services, Private Bag 92007, pg. 38 IT
Air New Zealand Catering Services, Private Bag 92007, pg. 38 IT
Air New Zealand Engineering Services, Private Bag 92007, pg. 38 IT
Air New Zealand Information Services, Private Bag 92007, pg. 38 IT
Air New Zealand International, Private Bag 92007, pg. 38 IT
AIR NEW ZEALAND LTD., Quay Tower, 29 Customs Street West, pg. 38 IT
Air New Zealand National, Private Bag 92007, pg. 38 IT
Air New Zealand Terminal Services, Private Bag 92007, pg. 38 IT
Alexander & Alexander Holdings NZ Limited, Quay Tower, 16th Fl., 29 Customs St. W., pg. 117 PB
Allied Colour (N.Z.) Ltd., 12 Silver Place, Takapuna, pg. 371 IT
Amway of New Zealand Limited, 15 Lady Ruby Dr., pg. 70 PV
Ancra New Zealand, 174 Maura Rd., pg. 71 PV
Asea Brown Boveri Ltd., pg. 2 IT
Astra Pharmaceuticals (New Zealand) Ltd., pg. 94 IT
Australian Guarantee Corporation (NZ) Limited, Agc House, 52-64 Victoria St., West, pg. 1497 IT
Autocrat Sanyo Holding (N.Z.) Limited, 24 Allright Place, pg. 1191 IT
Avnet VSI Electronics (N.Z.) Ltd., 274 Church St., pg. 155 PB
BASF New Zealand Ltd., 38 Mahunga Dr., pg. 106 IT
B.J. (N.Z.) Limited, pg. 905 PB
BMW New Zealand Ltd., Pacific Business Ctre., 7 Pacific Rise, pg. 178 IT
Babcock Engineering Ltd., 26 Walmsley Rd., pg. 474 IT
Babcock International (NZ) Ltd., 26 Walmsley Rd., pg. 474 IT
Baker Perkins (NZ) Limited, 63 Tidal Rd., Mangere, pg. 1240 IT
Bandag New Zealand Ltd., 8 Nandina Ave., pg. 178 PB
Bausch & Lomb (New Zealand) Limited, 16 H Saunders Place, pg. 195 PB
Bell Atlantic Holdings Limited, The Shorland Centre, Level 17, 51-53 Shorland St., pg. 204 PB
BellSouth New Zealand, Level 6, Regional House, 21 Pitt Street, Private Bag, pg. 208 PB
Benckiser New Zealand Ltd., pg. 185 IT
Bermuda Trust (New Zealand) Limited, Level 25, ASB Bank Centre, 135 Albert Street, pg. 151 IT
Best-Wood Limited, 195 Browns Rd., pg. 905 PB
BestFriend Pet Foods Limited, 89 Carbine Rd., pg. 807 PB
Biomet Orthopaedics Ltd., 98 Carlton Gore Rd., Ste. Five, pg. 232 PB
Boart Longyear Ltd., P.O. Box 43-030 Mangere, pg. 76 IT
Borland International (New Zealand) Ltd., pg. 246 PB
Brambles Industries (N.Z.) Ltd., Downtown House, 21-29 Queen St., pg. 212 IT
Bristol-Myers (N.Z.) Limited, 234 Khyber Pass Rd., P.O. Box 9175, pg. 255 PB
Donald Brown & Co. Ltd., 6-10 South St., pg. 1030 IT
Bundy Tubing (New Zealand) Ltd., 88 Harris Road, pg. 1341 IT
Buttle Wilson Group Ltd., Level 23, Stock Exchange Ctr., 191 Queen St., pg. 1331 IT
CCH New Zealand Limited, 17 Kahika Rd., pg. 1513 IT
CFS New Zealand Ltd., 12 Brigade Road, pg. 372 PB
CIBC New Zealand Holdings Limited, Stock Exchange Centre, 15th Fl., Queen St., pg. 258 IT
CIBC New Zealand Limited, Stock Exchange Centre, 15th Fl., Queen St., pg. 258 IT
CSP Pacific, 306 Neilson St., Onehunga, pg. 495 IT
Cadillac Plastic (New Zealand) Ltd., 32 Saleyard Rd., P.O. Box 22747, pg. 781 PB
Camera House Limited, 4-10 Alma Street, pg. 1115 IT
Canon Finance New Zealand Ltd., Fred Thomas Drive, pg. 262 IT
Canon New Zealand Ltd., Fred Thomas Drive, pg. 263 IT
Capral NZ Limited, Wiri Station Road, pg. 266 IT
Carlton Brewery New Zealand, 60 Khyber Pass Rd., pg. 501 IT
Carter Holt Harvey Forests Limited, 322 Great South Rd., pg. 905 PB
Carter Holt Harvey Garage Doors, pg. 904 PB
Carter Holt Harvey Limited, 640 Great South Rd., pg. 904 PB
Carter Holt Harvey Plastic Products-Beverage Division, 100 Carbine Rd., pg. 904 PB
Carter Holt Harvey Roofing International, 90-104 Felton Mathew Ave., pg. 904 PB
Carter Holt Harvey Timber Limited, 640 Great South Rd., pg. 904 PB
The Caxton Group of Companies, pg. 905 PB
Cellphone Sales Ltd., 52 Cook St., pg. 1365 IT
CelsiusTech New Zealand, North City Center, 4th Floor, pg. 278 IT
Cemac Commercial Interiors Ltd., 11a Tawari St., pg. 905 PB
Centaine Investments Ltd., pg. 1024 IT
Challenge Properties Limited, Challenge Propertie House, 666 Great South Rd., Penrose, pg. 495 IT
CIBA-GEIGY New Zealand Ltd., 43-53 Patiki Rd., pg. 978 IT
Cigna Insurance New Zealand Limited, CIGNA House, 345 Queen St., pg. 364 PB
Cigna Reinsurance New Zealand Limited, Quay Tower, 29 Customs St., pg. 363 PB
Circle International (N.Z.) Ltd., 12 Brigade Rd., Airport Oaks, pg. 373 PB
Citizen Watches New Zealand Ltd., 10 Eden Street, pg. 294 IT
Clear Communications Limited, 11th Floor, Clear Tower, 49 Symonds Street, pg. 223 IT
Comalco-CHH Aluminum, 30-32 Bowden Rd., pg. 905 PB
Combined Ins. Co. of America, Tudor House, 105 Great South Rd., Remuera, pg. 118 PB
Compaq Computer New Zealand LTd., Level 9, Sil House, 44 Wellesley St. W., pg. 418 PB
Concrete Industries Sector, 302 Great South Rd., Greenlane, pg. 495 IT
Continuum (NZ) Limited, Continuum Building, 105 Symonds Street, pg. 423 PB
Daihatsu New Zealand Ltd., Crn. Sturdee & Parkham Sts., pg. 365 IT
Dell Computer Ltd., Level 8, Kensington Swan Bldg., 22 Fanshawe Street, pg. 496 PB
Denstree Corporation Ltd., 47-51 Fort Street, pg. 703 IT
Det Norske Veritas, pg. 398 IT
Digital Equipment Corporation (New Zealand) Ltd., 162-164 Grafton Rd., pg. 507 PB
Dimond Industries, 119 Carbine Rd., Mt. Wellington, pg. 495 IT
Doubleday New Zealand Ltd., 1 Parkway Dr., Mairangi Bay, pg. 192 IT
Dow Chemical (N.Z.) Limited, 6th Fl., Feltrax Ctr., 145 Symonds St., pg. 523 PB
Dow Jones Markets (New Zealand) Ltd., P.O. Box 2129, Level 4, Tower 1, Lobby Area, pg. 525 PB
Du Pont (New Zealand) Ltd., 41 Shortland St., pg. 533 PB
Dulmison (NZ) Limited, 107-111 Harris Rd., pg. 893 IT
Dun & Bradstreet (New Zealand) Ltd., Level 3, pg. 536 PB
EAC Graphics (New Zealand) Ltd., pg. 431 IT
EMI (New Zealand) Ltd., P.O. Box 864, pg. 427 IT
Ecolab New Zealand Ltd., 16 Clonbern Rd., pg. 562 PB
Ericsson Cellular Ltd., 6 Pacific Rise, Pacific Business Centre, pg. 1366 IT
Esselte New Zealand, Druces Road, Wiri, P.O. Box 76-221, pg. 461 IT
Events Marketing Limited, P.O. Box 6463, pg. 38 IT
Feltrax International, Inc., 145 Symonds St., pg. 130 IT
Fibre Products New Zealand Limited, pg. 905 PB
Firestone Tire & Rubber Company of New Zealand Limited, 110 Symonds St., Level 6, pg. 214 IT
FLETCHER CHALLENGE LIMITED, Fletcher Challenge House, 810 Great South Rd., pg. 494 IT
Fletcher Challenge Methanol Limited, 583 Great South Rd., Penrose, pg. 495 IT
Fletcher Homes Limited, 666 Great South Rd., Penrose, pg. 495 IT
Fletcher Merchants Limited, 150 Marua Rd., Mt. Wellington, pg. 495 IT
Fletcher Wood Panels Limited, 289 Great South Rd., Greenlane, pg. 495 IT
Focus Travel, P.O. Box 148, pg. 38 IT
FoxVideo (New Zealand) Limited, pg. 926 IT
Fujitsu New Zealand Ltd., Grafton 3, pg. 528 IT
H.B. Fuller Co. (N.Z.) Ltd., 64 Tidal Rd., Mangere, pg. 687 PB
GF Pacific Exports (NZ) Ltd., Level 15, 66 Wynhan St., pg. 556 IT
Gambro Pty Ltd., 5B, Target Court, pg. 668 IT
Givaudan-Roure Ltd., Richard Pearse Dr., pg. 1120 IT
Golden Bay Cement Ltd., 303 Greath South Rd, Greenlane, pg. 495 IT
Goodman Fielder Mills (NZ) Ltd., 65 Fort Street, pg. 556 IT
Goodman Fielder New Zealand, Level 15, 66 Wyndham Street, pg. 555 IT
Griffins Foods Ltd., 52/54 Grafton Rd., pg. 381 IT
Guerlain (Asia Pacific) Ltd.-New Zealand Branch, Unit 1, 4 Rennie Dr.-Airport Oaks, pg. 780 IT
HMC Division, 447-449 Rosebank Road, pg. 851 IT
Hardware Manufacturing, 447-449 Rosebank Rd., pg. 851 IT
Heidelberg Graphic Equipment Ltd.-Heidelberg New Zealand, 13th Fl., Quay Tower, pg. 605 IT
Heinz-Wattie's Australasia, 46 Parnell Rd., pg. 807 PB
Hewlett-Packard (N.Z.) Ltd., Ports of Auckland Bldg., Princess Wharf, Quay St., pg. 821 PB
Honeywell Limited, 264 Mount Eden Rd., pg. 835 PB
Horizon Aluminium Prods. Ltd., pg. 51 IT
Hotpac Reservations (NZ) Ltd., pg. 38 IT
Husqvarna Chainsaws Ltd., pg. 443 IT
ICI New Zealand Limited, Gm. Khyber Pass & Nugent St., pg. 665 IT
IDC New Zealand, Level 8, 246 Queen Street, pg. 571 PV
IDG Communications Ltd., Level 8,246 Queen Street, pg. 570 PV
Imation New Zealand, 41 E. Sale St., pg. 870 PB
Intergraph Corp. (NZ) Limited, Level 3, Sequent House, 8-10 Whitaker Pl., pg. 891 PB
S.C. Johnson New Zealand Ltd., Private Bag, pg. 594 PV
Kanthal Trading Australasia Ltd., pg. 724 IT
Kenner Parker (N.Z.) Ltd., 16 Akepiro St., pg. 798 PB
Kodak New Zealand Ltd., 70 Stanley St., pg. 554 PB
Kvaerner Boving (ANZ) Pty Ltd, Pier 21, Building 11, Westhave Drive, pg. 772 IT
Letraset New Zealand Ltd., 42 Lunn Avenue, pg. 462 IT
Louis Vuitton New Zealand, 99 Queen Street, pg. 783 IT
MMI General Insurance (N.Z.) Ltd., 45 Queen Str., pg. 60 IT
MacDermid New Zealand, Ltd., 60, The Concourse, pg. 1030 PB
Madison Systems Ltd., 22 Dundonald St., pg. 1043 PB
Makita (New Zealand) Ltd., 7 Atlas Place, pg. 832 IT
Marubeni New Zealand Ltd., Southern Cross Bldg., Corner of High St. & Victoria St. East, pg. 845 IT
Mattel Toys (NZ) Limited (New Zealand), Ideal House, CNR Gillies Ave., Eden St., pg. 1059 PB
Matua Finance Limited, Level 2, Windsor Court, 136 Parnell Rd., pg. 500 IT
Medtec Products Pty. Ltd., 129 Onewa Rd., pg. 822 PB
Microsoft New Zealand Limited, pg. 1108 PB
Milton Bradley (N.Z.) Ltd., Private Bag, Glenfield, pg. 798 PB
Mitsui & Co. (N.Z.) Ltd., Princes Court, Princes St., pg. 882 IT
Moore Business Forms & Systems Ltd., pg. 889 IT
Morganite Carbon NZ Ltd, 58 Tidal Rd., pg. 892 IT
Motorola New Zealand Limited, Unit 3/750 Great South Road, pg. 1140 PB
Multiwall Packaging Limited, pg. 905 PB
NSK-RHP Bearings New Zealand Ltd., 3 Te Apunga Pl., Mt. Wellington, pg. 904 IT
NYK Shipping (NZ) Ltd., Level 22, 151 Queen Street, pg. 942 IT
The Nestle Company, New Zealand Ltd., 177-187 Parnell Road, pg. 921 IT
Nestle New Zealand Ltd., pg. 921 IT
New Zealand AMP Ltd., 57 Mahunga Dr., pg. 9 PB
New Zealand Fibre Glass Company-Imported Products Division, 38 Olive Rd., pg. 904 PB
New Zealand Forest Products Limited, Private Bag, Symonds St., pg. 905 PB
New Zealand Milk Products (Pacific) Ltd., 114 Dominion Rd., pg. 923 IT
New Zealand Starch, 319 Church Street, pg. 555 IT
A.C. Nielsen (N.Z.) Limited, 107 Great South Rd., pg. 1183 PB
Nippon Meat Packers, New Zealand Ltd., 18th Fl., 44 Emily Pl., pg. 936 IT
Nissan Datsun Holdings Ltd., 261 Roscommon Rd., pg. 945 IT
Nissho Iwai New Zealand Limited, Level 17, ASB Bank Centre, 133-135 Albert Street, pg. 948 IT
Norton (New Zealand) Limited, Te Atatu, pg. 1175 IT
Norton New Zealand (Operat) Ltd., 248 Archers Road, PO Box 100-646, pg. 1175 IT
Novo Nordisk Pharmaceuticals Ltd., 642 Great South Road, pg. 988 IT
Nu-Way Energy (N.Z.) Ltd., 116 Harris Road, pg. 361 PV
OMRON Electronics Ltd., 65 Boston Road, pg. 1006 IT
Oracle New Zealand, Level 16, Lumley House, pg. 1228 PB

PB - *U.S. Public Companies Volume*
PV - *U.S. Private Companies Volume*
IT - *International Public & Private Companies Volume*

1724

Geographic Index-Non U.S.

ORIX New Zealand (NZ) Limited, 32 Manakau Road, Level 3, pg. 1010 **IT**
Pacific Coilcoaters Limited, 968 Great South Rd., Penrose, pg. 495 **IT**
Pacific Steel Ltd., James Fletcher Dr., Otahuhu, pg. 495 **IT**
Packaging House NZFP limited, pg. 905 **PB**
Parker Chemical Corp. Ltd., pg. 613 **IT**
Parker Enzed New Zealand Pty. Limited, 3 Bowden Rd., pg. 1261 **PB**
Parker Hannifin (NZ) Limited, 103 Harris Road, East Tamaki, pg. 1261 **PB**
Pasco Development New Zealand Ltd., pg. 1024 **IT**
Pegler Hattersley NZ, pg. 550 **IT**
Pharmacia & Upjohn New Zealand, Level 3 Building 5, Central Park, 666 Great South Road, pg. 1050 **IT**
Printpac-UEB Carton Group, 630 Great South Rd., pg. 905 **PB**
Printpac-UEB Case Group, pg. 905 **PB**
Propak, pg. 904 **PB**
Quality Bakers New Zealand Ltd., 44 Kerwyn Ave., pg. 556 **IT**
The Radio Network, 54 Cork St., pg. 386 **PB**
Radiometer Pacific Ltd., Unit A, 10/20 Sylvia Park Road, pg. 1084 **IT**
Raychem New Zealand Limited, 4 Arthur Brown Pl., pg. 1362 **PB**
Rayonier New Zealand Limited, Level 5, Symonds Centre, 49 Symonds St., pg. 1363 **PB**
The Reader's Digest Association (New Zealand) Limited, 8 College Hill, pg. 1368 **PB**
Red Seal Laboratories Ltd., pg. 1490 **IT**
Rentokil Laboratories Ltd., Engrng. Hwy. 16, pg. 1286 **IT**
Rexroth Hydraulics Ltd., pg. 839 **IT**
Richardson-Vicks Ltd., 47 St. Paul St., pg. 1333 **PB**
Roche Products (New Zealand) Ltd., 8 Henderson Place, pg. 1122 **IT**
Rockwell Automation (N.Z.) Ltd., Mt. Wellington, 118A Carbine Road, pg. 1400 **PB**
Rohm & Haas New Zealand Ltd., pg. 1404 **PB**
S.C. Properties (NZ) Ltd., c/o Pan Pacific Properties Ltd, Room 219-220, Cnr. of Mayoral Dr. and, pg. 1233 **IT**
SKF New Zealand Ltd., 23 Ra Ora Dr., East Tamaki, pg. 1159 **IT**
Schindler Lifts NZ Ltd., pg. 1205 **IT**
Sealed Air (New Zealand) Packaging Products Division, Dock 1, 24 Bancroft Crescent, Glendene, pg. 1451 **PB**
Senior New Zealand Limited, #5 Industry Rd., pg. 1223 **IT**
Sensormatic New Zealand Ltd., 31 Cheshire St., pg. 1458 **PB**
Sequent Computer Systems (New Zealand) Ltd., Sequent House, Level 6, 8-10 Whittaker Pl., pg. 1460 **PB**
John Shaw (N.Z.) Limited, pg. 268 **IT**
Shiseido N.Z. Ltd., 114 Felton Mathew Ave., Glenn Innes, pg. 1235 **IT**
Singapore Tourist Promotion Board - Auckland, 3rd Floor, 43 High Street, pg. 1254 **IT**
Sky Network Television Limited, 10 Panorama Road, pg. 204 **PB**
Smith & Smith Glass Ltd., pg. 904 **PB**
SmithKline Beecham (New Zealand) Ltd., 950 Great So. Rd., Penrose, pg. 1266 **IT**
Sonata Laboratories Ltd., 391 Rosebank Rd., pg. 1490 **IT**
Sphinx Manufacturing Company, Ltd., 31 Olive Rd., Penrose, pg. 53 **PB**
Stafford-Miller (N.Z.) Limited, 95 Felton Mathew Ave., pg. 237 **PB**
Sulzer New Zealand Limited, pg. 1306 **IT**
TN Media Inc., 4th Fl., Textile Centre, Kenwyn St., pg. 1642 **PB**
TNT New Zealand Limited, Level 11, Patent House, 57 Fort Street, pg. 1343 **IT**
Tasman Lumber Company Limited, 7-9 Alpens Avenue, Newmarket, pg. 495 **IT**
Tasman Pulp & Paper Company Limited, 11th Flr., National Mutual, Centre, 41-43 Shortland St., pg. 495 **IT**
Tastemaker Ltd., pg. 811 **PB**
Taylor Instrument Ltd., 58 Huia Road, P.O. Box 22-143 Otahuhu, pg. 6 **IT**
Taylor Woodrow International NZ Limited, c/o Price Waterhouse, 18th Fl., Quay Tower, pg. 1359 **IT**
Te Papapa Paper Mill, pg. 905 **PB**
THORN EMI New Zealand, Private Bag, pg. 428 **IT**
3M New Zealand Ltd., Box 33-246, pg. 1607 **PB**
Tip Top Ice Cream Co. Limited, 113 Carbine Rd. Mount Wellington, pg. 1040 **IT**
Tradcor International Limited, pg. 904 **PB**
Transport Fuel Systems (N.Z.) Limited, pg. 905 **PB**
Utell International-New Zealand, Level 4, 8 Commerce Street, pg. 1098 **IT**
Valtek New Zealand, Ltd., North Shore Mail Centre, pg. 659 **PB**
Wang New Zealand Limited, Wang Terraces, 9 City Rd., pg. 1738 **PB**
Western Staff Services (N.Z.) Ltd., Level 2, Quay Tower, CNR Customs & Albert Sts., pg. 1760 **PB**
Willis Corroon Limited, Level 16, Tower Two, The Shortland Centre, pg. 1509 **IT**
Winstone Aggregates Limited, 302 Great South Rd., Greenlane, pg. 495 **IT**
Winstone Wallboards Limited, 37 Felix St., Penrose, pg. 495 **IT**
Wiremakers Limited, 21 Beach Rd., Otahuhu, pg. 495 **IT**
Wood Export New Zealand (1986) Limited, Mount Maunganui, pg. 905 **PB**
Woodward-Clyde, 8th Fl., 385 Queen St., pg. 1657 **PB**
Woolworths (New Zealand) Limited, 47-51 Fort St., pg. 704 **IT**
The Wrigley Company (N.Z.) Ltd., 45 Banks Rd., pg. 1781 **PB**

John Wyeth & Brother (N.Z.) Ltd., P.O. Box 47-303, Ponsonby, pg. 82 **PB**
Wynn Oil (N.Z.) Limited, 69 St. Georges Bay Rd., pg. 1783 **PB**
Young & Rubicam, 2 Augustus Terrace Corner, Parnell Rise, 3rd Floor, pg. 1198 **PV**
Young & Rubicam Mattingly, Retail Group, 3rd Fl., Cnr. Augustus Terrace & Parnell Rise, pg. 325 **PV**
Zellweger Ltd., pg. 618 **IT**
Zimmer New Zealand Limited, 6 Crawley St., pg. 257 **IT**
Zurich Australian Insurance Ltd., Level 10, pg. 1531 **IT**

Avondale

Embecon (New Zealand) Limited, 138 St. Georges Road, pg. 982 **IT**
Henkel New Zealand Ltd., pg. 613 **IT**
ITW New Zealand, Ltd., Seven Charann Pl., pg. 868 **PB**
MBT (New Zealand) Ltd., pg. 1465 **IT**
Selleys Chemical Co NZ Ltd., 495 Rosebank Rd., pg. 665 **IT**

Birkenhead

Reed Publishing (NZ) Ltd., 39 Rawene Road, pg. 1094 **IT**

Blenheim

Cloudy Bay Vineyards Ltd, pg. 782 **IT**

Christchurch

Bloch & Behrens (New Zealand) Limited, pg. 431 **IT**
Bowthorpe (NZ) Limited, 46 Disraeli St., pg. 208 **IT**
Crown Crystal Glass, pg. 129 **IT**
The East Asiatic Co. (New Zealand) Limited, pg. 431 **IT**
Firestone Tire & Rubber Co. of New Zealand, Ltd., P.O. Box 5012 Papanui, pg. 214 **IT**
A.W. Fraser, 39 Lunns Rd., pg. 852 **IT**
Helene Curtis New Zealand Ltd., 171 Main N. Road, pg. 1434 **IT**
Kodak New Zealand Ltd., 204 Hereford St., pg. 554 **PB**
Makita (New Zealand) Ltd.-Christchurch, 49 Phillips Street, pg. 832 **IT**
Milburn New Zealand Ltd., 106 Hansons Lane, pg. 629 **IT**
The Mount Cook Group Limited, 47 Riccarton Rd., pg. 38 **IT**
NYK Shipping-Christchurch, Hong Kong Bank House, 141 Cambridge Street, pg. 942 **IT**
PGF New Zealand Limited, 130b Shortland Street, pg. 604 **IT**
Rockwell Automation (N.Z.) Ltd., Unit C, 480 Moorhouse Avenue, pg. 1400 **PB**
Senior Christchurch Limited, 86 Falsgrave St., pg. 1223 **IT**
Willis Corroon Limited, BNZ Building, 137 Armagh Street, pg. 1509 **IT**
Woodward-Clyde, Amuri Courts, 293 Durham St., pg. 1657 **PB**
Woodward Governor Company (New Zealand) Ltd., Unit 1, 9 Vulcan Place, pg. 1776 **PB**

Drury

Rentokil Pest Control Ltd., 54 Firth St., pg. 1286 **IT**

Dunedin

Methven Tapmakers, 374 Andersons Bay Rd., pg. 851 **IT**

East Tamaki

AHI Roll-A-Door, 70 Allens Rd., pg. 904 **PB**
Johnson & Johnson Pacific Pty. (New Zealand) Ltd., Locked Mail Bag 5, pg. 931 **PB**
Van Leer New Zealand Ltd., pg. 1147 **IT**

Ellerslie

Cutler-Hammer New Zealand Limited, 6 Findlav St., pg. 558 **PB**
K.F.C. (N.Z.) Ltd., 22 Kalmia St., pg. 1637 **PB**
J. Wattie Foods, Block 2, Ground Fl., Central Park, 666 Great South Rd., pg. 807 **PB**

Elsdon

GEC (New Zealand) Ltd., P.O. Box 50 244, Prosser St., pg. 546 **IT**
W.R. Grace (N.Z.) Ltd., Prosser St., pg. 756 **IT**

Freeman's Bay

McDonald's System of New Zealand Ltd., 61 Wellington Street, pg. 1069 **PB**

Gisborne

Optipak Systems, pg. 1146 **IT**

Glenbrook

BHP New Zealand Steel Ltd., Mission Bush Road, pg. 226 **IT**

Greenmont

Ashton/Scholastic Ltd., 21 Lady Ruby Drive, pg. 1440 **PB**

Hamilton

Alfa-Laval (N.Z.) Ltd., P.O. Box 10241, pg. 1380 **IT**
Carter Holt Harvey Plastic Products, 696 Te Rapa Rd., pg. 904 **PB**
Carter Holt Harvey Plastic Products Group Limited, 696 Te Rapa Rd., pg. 904 **PB**
Eagle Aviation Ltd., pg. 38 **IT**
NZ Aluminum Franchising, pg. 905 **PB**
Scapa Scandia (Australasia) Ltd., Avalon Drive, pg. 1203 **IT**
Sealed Air (New Zealand) Food Packaging Division, Corner Avalon Drive & Foreman Road, pg. 1451 **PB**
South Pacific Aluminum, pg. 905 **PB**

Hastings

Plix Packaging Limited, pg. 904 **PB**

Henderson

Polarcup (N.Z.) Limited, 30 Keeling Road, pg. 638 **IT**

Huntly

Heat Containment Industries Limited, 24 Rayner Rd., pg. 894 **IT**

Invercargill

New Zealand Aluminium Smelters Ltd., Tiwai Rd., pg. 307 **IT**

Johnsonville

Toyota New Zealand Ltd., 125-137 Johnsonville Road, pg. 1414 **IT**

Kawerau

Caxton Paper Limited, pg. 905 **PB**

Levin

Bevaloid Chemicals Ltd., pg. 1113 **IT**

Lower Hutt

Ford Motor Co. of New Zealand Ltd., P.O. Box 30012, pg. 666 **PB**
Ford Motor Credit Company of New Zealand Limited, P.O. Box 30012, pg. 663 **PB**
ICI New Zealand Limited, 36-42 Sea View Rd., pg. 665 **IT**
IGT-(New Zealand) Limited, Birchwood Park, Unit 4, 483 Hutt Road, pg. 900 **PB**
Landis & Staefa (NZ) Ltd., Level 1, Autopoint House, 20 Daly St., pg. 801 **IT**
SM-Cyclo New Zealand, 421-423 Cuba Street, pg. 1315 **IT**

Mairangi Bay

Briggs & Stratton New Zealand Limited, 2/8 Constellation Dr., pg. 252 **PB**

Mangere

Hallmark Cards New Zealand Ltd., 59 Mahunga Dr., pg. 496 **PV**
Sharp Corporation of New Zealand Ltd., Cnr. Mahunga Dr. & Hastie Ave., pg. 1229 **IT**

Manukau

Bluebird Foods Ltd, 124 Wiri Station Rd., pg. 556 **IT**
Dominion Television Rentals Limited, CNR Puhinui & Great South Roads, pg. 1386 **IT**
Kiwi Packaging, 33 Lambie Drive, pg. 72 **IT**
Olin Corporation N.Z. Limited, 9 Joval Place, pg. 1220 **PB**
Pfizer Laboratories Ltd., Level 4, AMI Bldg., Cnr. Osterly Way & Ronwood Ave, pg. 1282 **IT**
Quik Stik International Ltd., P.O. Box 76-221, pg. 462 **IT**

Masterton

New Zealand Controls Ltd., pg. 1244 **IT**
Pharmacia & Upjohn Inter-American Corporation-New Zealand, Akura Rd., pg. 1048 **IT**
Robertshaw Controls New Zealand, P.O. Box 511, pg. 1244 **IT**

Matamata

Svedala New Zealand, pg. 1325 **IT**

Mataura

Mataura Paper Mill, pg. 905 **PB**

Geographic Index-Non U.S.

NEW ZEALAND DIRECTORY OF CORPORATE AFFILIATIONS

Miamar

Audio Club of New Zealand Ltd., Wexford Rd., pg. 1052 IT

Napier

Ericsson Communications Ltd., 12 Wakefield St., Onekawa, pg. 1366 IT
Pan Pacific Forest Industries (N.Z.) Limited, pg. 938 IT

Nelson

Air Nelson, pg. 38 IT
Baigent Forest Industries Limited, pg. 905 PB

New Lynn

Ure Pacific Ltd., pg. 1203 IT
Wormald Holdings N.Z. Limited, 6 Portage Rd., pg. 1651 PB

New Plymouth

McKechnie Metal Products, Paraite Rd., Bell Block, pg. 852 IT
Petrocorp Exploration Limited, Connett Rd., Bell Block, pg. 495 IT
Weatherford Inc.-New Zealand Branch, P.O. Box 4033, pg. 1750 PB

Newmarket

Tegel Foods Limited, 11-13 George St., pg. 807 PB
Wattie Frozen Foods Limited, Level Four, 277 Broadway, pg. 807 PB

Newton

KONE Elevators (Australia) Pty. Ltd., 81 Union Street, pg. 747 IT

Onehunga

Guest International (New Zealand) Ltd., 31 Princess St., pg. 768 PB

Pakuranga

Accord Industries, 71 Ben Lomond Crescent, pg. 851 IT
Avon Cosmetics Ltd., P.O. Box 1828, pg. 156 PB
Sandvik New Zealand Ltd., P.O. Box 51-154, pg. 1187 IT
Vickers Systems Ltd., 77-79 Ben Lomond Crescent, pg. 25 PB

Palmerston

Sunbeam Corporation Ltd., 1043 Tremaine Ave., pg. 539 IT

Palmerston North

Howard Engineering Ltd., 7 Downing Street, pg. 1387 IT
Howard Pacific Ltd., 7 Downing Street, pg. 1387 IT
Howard Rotavator Co., 7 Downing Street, pg. 1387 IT

Panmure

AEP Industries (NZ) Ltd., 100 Carbine Rd., pg. 5 PB

Papatoetoe

Eli Lilly and Company (N.Z.) Limited, pg. 993 PB

Parnell

DuraCell New Zealand Limited, 33 Falcon St., pg. 744 PB
A.C. Hatrick (N.Z.) Ltd., 22 York St., pg. 811 PB
Nokia Telecommunications NZ Limited, Level 4, 60 Stanley Street, pg. 953 IT
PolyGram Records Ltd., P.O. Box 37-611, pg. 1053 IT
Wattie's Limited, 46 Parnell Rd., pg. 807 PB

Penrose

ACI New Zealand Ltd., 752 Great S. Rd., pg. 129 IT
Black & Decker (New Zealand) Ltd., 483 Gt. South Rd., pg. 234 PB
Boral Acrow Ltd. (New Zealand), 930 Great S. Rd., pg. 203 IT
Dominion Seal Ltd., 428 Church St., pg. 129 IT
The Fletcher Construction Company Limited, Fletcher Challenge House, 810 S. Great Road, pg. 495 IT
Herbalife (N.Z.) Limited, Unit K, 665 Great South Road, pg. 809 PB
New Zealand Fibre Glass, Aranui Rd., pg. 904 PB
New Zealand Glass Manufacturers Co., 752-754 Great S. Rd., pg. 129 IT

Petone

Brother International (NZ) Limited, Car Victoria St. & Railway Ave, Corner Hutt, pg. 229 IT
Colgate-Palmolive Ltd., Nevis St., pg. 398 PB
Gray Tool Company, c/o Lordco (New Zealand), Ltd., pg. 6 IT
Lever Brothers (New Zealand) Ltd., pg. 1437 IT
Unilever New Zealand Ltd., 458 Jackson St., pg. 1439 IT

Ponsonby

Gestetner Office Systems New Zealand Limited, 13-15 College Hill, pg. 1115 IT
Sanderson Computers New Zealand Ltd., 100 Ponsonby Rd., pg. 1185 IT
Symix Systems-New Zealand, 33 College Hill, Level Three, pg. 1547 PB

Porirua

Graseby Goring Kerr (N2) Ltd., 47 Kenepuru Drive, pg. 1268 IT
Mitsubishi Motors New Zealand Ltd., Todd Park, Heriot Dr., pg. 876 IT

Rangiora

Canterbury Timber Products Limited, Upper Sefton Rd., pg. 905 PB

Rotorua

Honeywell-Measurex Systems N.Z. Ltd., P.O. Box 1547, pg. 834 PB
Tasman Forestry Limited, Ngahere House, Vaughan Road, pg. 495 IT

Takapuna

AlliedSignal Chemicals N.Z. Ltd., P.O. Box 33-1461, ASDA Plaza, 2nd Fl. Ste. 9, pg. 52 PB
Longman Paul Ltd., Private Bag, pg. 1025 IT
The Macmillan Co. of New Zealand Ltd., 86 Wairau Road, pg. 1480 IT
Southcorp Wines New Zealand, 1st Fl., Asda Plaza Two, Fred Thomas Dr., pg. 1287 IT

Tauranga

BHP Steel Building Products (NZ) Ltd., 67 Korimiko Street, pg. 226 IT

Te Papapa

Danbrand Products Australasia, 298 Neilson St., pg. 904 PB

Timaru

McCain Foods (NZ) Ltd., Meadows Road, pg. 850 IT

Tokoroa

Kinleith Mill, pg. 905 PB

Upper Hutt

General Motors New Zealand Ltd., Trentham Plant No. 1, Private Bag, pg. 722 PB

Wanganui

Suzuki New Zealand Ltd., Pacific Commercial Site, No. 1 Heads Rd., pg. 1323 IT

Wellington

ANZ Banking Group (New Zealand) Ltd., 215-229 Lambton Quay, pg. 98 IT
AST Research, Level 5, 197-201 Willis St., pg. 1182 IT
Amdahl New Zealand, ASB Bank Tower, Level 8, 2 Hunter St., pg. 527 IT
Ascom Timeplex Ltd. (New Zealand), 14th fl., Kirkaldies Rise, Cnr Lambton Quai & Johnston Str., pg. 87 IT
Australian Mutual Provident Society, 86-90 Customhouse Quay, pg. 100 IT
BOC Gases New Zealand Ltd, 133-137 The Terrace, pg. 121 IT
Bain & Company New Zealand Ltd., Level 8, Barclays House, pg. 406 IT
Bank of New Zealand, BNZ Ctr., 1 Willis St., pg. 906 IT
Banque Indosuez New Zealand Limited, Indosuez House, 114 The Terrace, pg. 315 IT
Barclays Bank PLC, pg. 165 IT
Bell Atlantic New Zealand Limited, Barclay House, Level 12, 36 Customhouse Quay, pg. 204 PB
Bridge Pacific Ltd., Level 6 Coal Corp House, 17-21 Dixon St., pg. 317 IT
BRIERLEY INVESTMENTS LIMITED, Level 28, Majestic Centre, 100 Willis Street, pg. 215 IT
Robert Bryce & Co., Ltd., Barnes St., Seaview, Lower Hutt, pg. 682 IT
Bull HN Information Systems New Zealand Ltd., Level 6, Coal Corp. House, 17-21 Dixon St., pg. 317 IT
Butterworths New Zealand, Level 14, Data Central House, pg. 1095 IT
Castrol NZ Ltd., pg. 236 IT
Cigna Life Insurance New Zealand Limited, 40 Mercer St., 30762, pg. 364 PB
Comalco New Zealand, 16th Fl., ASB Bank Tower, 2 Hunter St., pg. 307 IT
D & B Software New Zealand Ltd., Maritime House 4th Fl., 2-10 Customhouse Quay, pg. 532 IT
DMR Group New Zealand Ltd., City Tower, 95 Customhouse Quay, pg. 528 IT
Data General New Zealand Ltd., 24 Fl., Williams Centre, pg. 486 PB
Datapoint Corp. (N. Z.) Ltd., Box 27-172, pg. 384 IT
Electrolux Ltd., P.O. Box 1336, pg. 443 IT
Ericsson Communications Ltd., 121 Adelaide Road, Newtown, pg. 1366 IT
Fletcher Challenge Petroleum Limited, Natural Gas Corporation House, 22 The Terrace, pg. 495 IT
Goldsack Harris Thompson Advertising, Level 2, Korea House, 29 Tory St., pg. 184 PV
Haines Recruitment Advertising, Head Office, Level 2, Woolstore,262 Thorndon Quay, pg. 389 PV
Harrisons & Crosfield (N.Z.) Ltd., 2-18 Branson St., pg. 599 IT
Hewlett-Packard (N.Z.) Ltd., 186-190 Willis St., pg. 821 PB
ICL New Zealand Limited, ICL House, pg. 529 IT
Intergraph Corp. (N.Z.) Limited, Level 1, Walsh Wrightson Twr., 94 Dixon Street, pg. 891 PB
International Correspondence Schools (New Zealand) Limited, 1st Fl., Athenic Bldg., 45 Courtenay Pl., pg. 784 PB
International Public Relations (NZ) Ltd., Level 5, 2 Woodward St., pg. 1227 IT
Jardine Fleming New Zealand Limited, Level 8, Trust Bank Centre, 125 The Terrace, pg. 494 IT
Kodak New Zealand Ltd., 184-190 Willis St., pg. 554 PB
Logica New Zealand Limited, Level 14 Microsoft House, 49 Boulcott Street, pg. 815 IT
Lucent Technologies (NZ) Limited, Riddiford St., pg. 1019 PB
Marine Underwriting Agencies (NZ) Ltd. (Cornhill), 17th Floor, Aurora House, 54-64 The Terrace, pg. 60 IT
Medtec Products Pty. Ltd., 1/125 Naenae Rd., pg. 822 PB
Mitsui & Co. (N.Z.) Ltd., Investment Centre, 9th Flr., Featherstone, pg. 882 IT
Mobil Oil New Zealand Ltd., Aurora House, 54-64, The Terrace, pg. 1119 PB
Monsanto New Zealand, Ltd., Suite C, Broderick Office Pk., 19-21 Broderick Road, pg. 1126 PB
NYK Shipping-Wellington, Level 8, Castrol House, 36 Customhouse Quay, pg. 942 IT
National Bank of New Zealand Ltd., 170-186 Featherston St., pg. 814 IT
National Bank of New Zealand Savings Bank Ltd., 170-186 Featherstone St., pg. 814 IT
National Mutual Funds Management NZ Limited, 80 The Terrace, pg. 909 IT
National Mutual New Zealand, 80 The Terrace, pg. 908 IT
Nedlloyd (New Zealand) Limited, pg. 1145 IT
NEW ZEALAND DAIRY BOARD, Pastoral House, 25 The Terrace, pg. 923 IT
Ord O'Connor Grieve Limited, Level 12, BNZ Center, 1 Willis St., pg. 1497 IT
P&O (New Zealand) Ltd., P.O. Box 1699, 2-10 Customhouse Quay, pg. 1035 IT
Pilkington (New Zealand) Limited, Peterkin St., pg. 1057 IT
Post Office Bank Limited, 215-229 Lambton Quay, pg. 100 IT
Precision Office Industries, pg. 904 PB
William Press Engineering Services (NZ) Ltd., 24-26 Kingsford Smith St., pg. 16 IT
Prudential Assurance Co.-New Zealand Ltd., 332-340 Lambton Quay, pg. 1073 IT
Rhone-Poulenc New Zealand Ltd., Lower Hut, Peterkin Street Wingate, pg. 1113 IT
SAS Institute (NZ) Ltd., Andersen Consulting Tower Fl13, 45 Johnston Street, pg. 967 PV
Senior Wellington Limited, 112 Hutt Rd., pg. 1223 IT
Sequent Computer Systems (New Zealand), Level 7, M.W. Marshall House, 142-146 Wakefield St., pg. 1460 PB
Sharp Corporation of New Zealand Ltd., 264 Cuba Street, pg. 1229 IT
Shell New Zealand Holding Company Ltd, Shell House, 96-102 The Terrace, pg. 1137 IT
South Pacific Merchant Finance Ltd., 170-186 Featherstone St., pg. 814 IT
Statham Industries, pg. 905 PB
Stolt-Nielsen Pty. Ltd., pg. 1302 IT
Stratus Computer (NZ), Ltd., c/o Simpson Grierson Butler, White Unisys House, pg. 1524 PB
Sumitomo Chemical Company, Ltd.-Wellington Office, Level 7, BNZ Centre, 1 Willis St., pg. 1312 IT
Tandem Nonstop Pty. Ltd., 8 Pacific Rise, pg. 418 PB
Tektronix N.Z. Limited, Level 15, BN2 Center, 1 Willis Street, pg. 1568 PB
Telecom Corporation of New Zealand Limited, 13-27 Manners St., pg. 204 PB
D.W. Thorpe-New Zealand, 205-207 Victoria Street, pg. 1095 IT
Tranzrail Limited, Bunny St., pg. 1773 PB
UDC Group Holdings Limited, 113-119 The Terrace, pg. 100 IT
Vehicle Assemblers New Zealand Limited, pg. 666 PB
Westpac Banking Corporation-New Zealand, 318-324 Lambton Quay, pg. 1497 IT
Willis Corroon Limited, Level 9, Willis Corroon House, 58-66 Jervois Quay, pg. 1509 IT

Whakatane

Whakatane Board Mill, pg. 905 PB

PB - *U.S. Public Companies Volume*
PV - *U.S. Private Companies Volume*
IT - *International Public & Private Companies Volume*

NICARAGUA

Managua

Formularios Moore de Nicaragua S.A., Bello Horizonte R-1-7, Apartado 2112, pg. 890 **IT**
IMASA, Edificio Malaga, Modulo No. A15, Plaza Espana, pg. 108 **IT**
Inacap - Reaseguros, Sociedad Anonima, Oficina Legal Dr., Heraldo Zuniga M., KM. 8, pg. 364 **PB**
Inacap Sociedad Anonima, Oficina Legal Dr., Hernaldo Zuniga M., KM. 8, pg. 364 **PB**
Industria Ceramica Centroamericana, S.A., Apartado Postal 2551, pg. 92 **PB**
JB/Young & Rubicam, Planes de Altamira, pg. 1200 **PV**
Kativo Nicaragua, S.A., Km 7.5C, Norte, pg. 687 **PB**
Mitsui & Co., (Panama International), 2da Avenida Sur Oeste, Entre el Palmar y, pg. 882 **IT**
Productos Alimenticios Imperial de Nicaragua, S.A., pg. 411 **IT**
Productos Nestle (Nicaragua) S.A., pg. 922 **IT**
Publiciaa Cuadra Chamberlain, Colonial Los Robles #173, pg. 186 **PV**
Quimica Nicaraguense, pg. 1141 **IT**
Shell Nicaragua S.A., Cuesta de los Martires, pg. 1141 **IT**
Tabacalera Nicaraguense S.A., pg. 111 **IT**
Van Leer Envases de Centro America S.A., pg. 1147 **IT**
Zeneca Nicaragua, Edifico Malaga, pg. 1527 **IT**

NIGER

Namey

BIAO Niger, Av de la Mairie, pg. 547 **IT**
Banque Mondiale, Rue des Dallols, pg. 1189 **PV**
Bull Niger, Ave. Charles de Gaulle, pg. 315 **IT**
CII-Honeywell Bull Niger SARL, Avenue Charles-de-Gaulle, pg. 316 **IT**
Citibank, N.A. Niger S.A., pg. 378 **PB**
Compagnie Miniere D'Akouta (COMINAK), pg. 305 **IT**
Niger-Afrique S.A., pg. 540 **IT**
Shell Niger, Route de L'Aeroport, pg. 1137 **IT**
Societe des Mines de l'air (SOMAIR), pg. 305 **IT**

NIGERIA

Abuja

Julius Berger Nigeria PLC, Regional Office Abuja Area, pg. 196 **IT**

Apapa

Bayer Pharmaceuticals (Nigeria) Ltd., pg. 175 **IT**
Metal Box Nigeria Limited, Private Mail Bag 1179, pg. 267 **IT**
Van Leer Containers (Nigeria) Plc, pg. 1146 **IT**

Enugu

Anambra Motor Mfg. Co. Ltd., Emene Industrial Layout, pg. 368 **IT**

Ibadan

Heinemann Educational Nigeria Limited, Private Mail Bag 5202, 1 Ighodaro Road, pg. 1094 **IT**
Nigerian Wire and Cable Co., Ltd., Industrial Estate, Kilometer 9, Ibadan-Abeokuta Rd., pg. 1313 **IT**
SEI Nigeria Ltd., PMB 0018, Agodi Post Office, Plot 12+13 Ashi Rd., pg. 1313 **IT**

Iganmu

Taylor Woodrow of Nigeria Limited, 10, Abebe Village Rd., pg. 1360 **IT**

Ikeja

Cadbury Nigeria PLC, Lateef Jakande Rd., pg. 248 **IT**
Canmakers Nigeria Ltd., pg. 463 **PB**
Crown Cork & Seal Company (Nigeria) Ltd., pg. 464 **PB**
Johnson Wax Nigeria Limited, Plot 5, Block H, Isolo Industrial Estate, pg. 593 **PV**
Roche (Nigeria) Ltd., pg. 1121 **IT**
SKF Nigeria Limited, 3 Fl., Elephant Cement House, Assbifi Road, Alausa, pg. 1159 **IT**
Sandoz (Nigeria) Ltd., pg. 985 **IT**
SmithKline & French Nigeria, Ltd., Musuru House 1st Fl., 33 To Yin St., pg. 1265 **IT**

Kaduna

Peugeot Automobile Nigeria Ltd., Kakuri Industrial Estate, pg. 1021 **IT**
Van Leer Containers (Nigeria) Plc, pg. 1146 **IT**

Kano

Mentholatum Nigeria Ltd., Plot 50, Sharada Industrial Estate, pg. 1126 **IT**

Koko

Van Leer Containers (Nigeria) Plc, pg. 1146 **IT**

Lagos

Aluminum Smelting Co. of Nigeria, Cowrie Tower, Adeyemo Alakija Street, pg. 1386 **PB**
Ashland Oil (Nigeria) Co., Ltd., #10 Bishop Aboyade-Cole St., pg. 140 **IT**
B + B Gas and Oil Services (Nigeria) Limited, 27/29 Adeyemo Alakija Street, pg. 196 **IT**
BASF (Nigeria) Limited, 21, Mobolaji Bank, pg. 106 **IT**
BOC Gases Nigeria plc, Apapa-Oshodi Expressway, pg. 121 **IT**
Bouygues Nigeria Limited (B.N.L.), Idejo St., Plot 932, pg. 207 **IT**
R.T. Briscoe (Nigeria) PLC, pg. 431 **IT**
Bull Information Systems Nigeria Ltd., 89 A Ajose, Adeogun St. (401 Rd.), pg. 315 **IT**
Costain (West Africa) Ltd., 174 Western Ave.; P.O. Box 88, pg. 337 **PB**
Cutler-Hammer Nigeria Limited, Isolo Expwy. (Itire Junction), Ilasumaja Scheme, Isolo, pg. 558 **PB**
Daewoo Nigeria Limited, Plot 1608, Adeola Hopewell St., pg. 358 **IT**
Daewoo Nigeria Ltd., pg. 358 **IT**
Deutsche Babcock (Nigeria) Ltd., pg. 399 **IT**
Deutsche Bank AG (Nigeria) Ltd., Plot 78 B, 3rd Ave., pg. 404 **IT**
DYWIDAG Nigeria Ltd., Tiamiyu-Savage Street, Off. Ahmadu Belloway, pg. 424 **IT**
Elf Nigeria, 35, Kofo Abayomi Str., pg. 446 **IT**
Fire, Equity & General Insurance Company Limited, 13-15 Lake Street, pg. 363 **PB**
First Bank of Nigeria PLC, 35 Marina, pg. 1296 **IT**
Food Specialties (Nigeria) Ltd., pg. 920 **IT**
Granges Nigeria Ltd., 45, Saka Tinubu Street Plot 1282, Victor, pg. 443 **IT**
Gray Tool Company, c/o SASCO (West Africa) Ltd., 10A Ibiyinka Olorunnimbe Close Victoria, pg. 5 **IT**
Habib Nigeria Bank Ltd., 6th Fl., Marble House, One KIngsway Road, Falomo, pg. 585 **IT**
Halliburton Nigeria Ltd., P.O. Box 3694, pg. 777 **PB**
Henkel Chemicals (Nigeria) Ltd., pg. 614 **IT**
Philipp Holzmann (Nigeria) Ltd, 2 First Ave., Ismail Estate, pg. 634 **IT**
IDC Africa, House 2, C Close, pg. 570 **PV**
International Computers (Nigeria) Limited, 178 Awolowo Rd., pg. 529 **IT**
JGC Nigeria Ltd., 188 Awolowo Rd., Swikoyi, pg. 697 **IT**
Julius Berger Nigeria PLC, Ijora Causeway, pg. 196 **IT**
Keydril Nigeria Limited, 10 Waziri Ibrahim, Flat 1, pg. 765 **IT**
LM Ericsson (Nigeria) Ltd., 9 Kingsway Rd., Ikoyi, pg. 1369 **IT**
Livestock Feeds PLC, No. 1 Henry Carrl St., Ikeja Industrial Estate, pg. 1282 **PB**
Longman Nigeria Ltd., 52 Oba Akran Ave., PMB 21036, Ikeja, pg. 1027 **IT**
MB Toyo Glass Nigeria Limited, P.O. Box 2515, pg. 267 **IT**
MBK Nigeria Ltd., 5th Fl., 138/146 Broad St., pg. 880 **IT**
Management Information Systems Co. Ltd. (MIS), 3, Gerard Rd., pg. 822 **IT**
May & Baker Nigeria Ltd., PMB 21049, 3/5 Sapara St., pg. 1112 **IT**
Merchant Banking Corporation Nigeria Ltd., 16 Keffi St. - S.W. Ikoyi, pg. 321 **IT**
Minnesota Nigeria Limited, Isolo Expresswway, Mushin, P.O. Box 10380, pg. 1606 **PB**
Mobil Oil Nigeria Ltd., Mobil House Lekki Expressway, pg. 1119 **PB**
Mobil Producing Nigeria, Mobil House Lekki Expressway, pg. 1119 **PB**
Monenco Nigeria Limited, 711 Road A Close, pg. 31 **IT**
Nestle Foods Nigeria PLC, pg. 921 **IT**
Nigbel Merchant Bank (Nigeria) Ltd., 77 Awolowo Road, PO Box 52463, pg. 548 **IT**
Nigerian-American Merchant Bank Ltd, Boston House, 10-12 McCarthy St., pg. 185 **IT**
Nigerlec Contractors Ltd., 311 Apapa Rd., pg. 53 **IT**
Noble Drilling (West Africa) Ltd., 18 Thompson Ave., pg. 1187 **PB**
Otis Nigeria, Ltd., P.O. Box 3694, pg. 777 **PB**
Ovaltine (West Africa) Ltd., pg. 983 **IT**
Pamol (Nigeria) Ltd., Calabar Itu Highway, pg. 1438 **IT**
Panalpina World Transport (Nigeria) Limited, pg. 1023 **IT**
Pfizer Products PLC, One Henry Carr St., pg. 1282 **PB**
Pfizer Specialties Limited, No. 1 Henry Carr St., Ikeja Industrial Estate, pg. 1284 **PB**
SNC-Lavalin Nigeria Ltd., Unit 3, 17 Mekuwen Road, pg. 1163 **IT**
Savannah Bank of Nigeria Ltd., Alpha Tower, Catholic Mission St., pg. 183 **PB**
The Shell Petroleum Development Company of Nigeria Ltd., Freeman House, 21/22 Marina, pg. 1137 **IT**
Stanbic Merchant Bank Nigeria Limited, 188 Awolowo Road, Ikoyi, pg. 1294 **IT**
Statoil (Nigeria) Limited, P.O. Box 56190, pg. 1298 **IT**
Sunrise Marketing Communications Ltd., Sunrise DMB&B House, 21 Balogun Street, pg. 305 **PV**
Swiss Nigerian Chemical Co. Ltd., 387, Agege Motor Road, pg. 986 **IT**
Taisei (West Africa) Ltd., Flat 3, 24A, Cameron Road, pg. 1347 **IT**
Tara Consulting Nigeria, Ltd., 25 Bishop Oluwole St., pg. 1229 **PB**

Texaco Overseas (Nigeria) Petroleum Co., Western House 8/10, Yakubo Gowon St., pg. 1584 **PB**
United Bank for Africa, Ltd., Stock Exchange Bldg., 17th Fl., 2-4 Customs St., pg. 186 **PB**
Volkswagen of Nigeria Ltd., P.M.B. 12663 G.P.O., pg. 1475 **IT**
Wellcome Nigeria Ltd., pg. 553 **IT**
George Wimpey & Co. (Nigeria) Ltd., 1st Fl., 3 Hospital Rd., P.O. Box 2049, pg. 1510 **IT**
The World Bank, Plot PC-10, Engineering Close, pg. 1189 **PV**

Maiduguri

Geosource Nigeria Ltd., P.M.B. 1315, pg. 777 **PB**

Port Harcourt

Det Norske Veritas, 5th Floor, Orosi House, 28, Forces Avenue, pg. 397 **IT**
Eastern Bulkcem Co. Ltd., Rumuolumeni, pg. 1201 **IT**
Gearhart Middle East S.A., Plot 75 Trans Amadi Ind. Layout, pg. 776 **PB**
Gearhart Nigeria Limited, Plot 75 Trans Amadi Ind. Layout, pg. 776 **PB**
Gearhart West Africa S.A., Plot 75 Trans Amadi Ind. Layout, pg. 776 **PB**
Noble Drilling (Nigeria) Ltd., Staff House, KM 14 PH/ABA Expressway N., pg. 1187 **PB**
Service & Supply Co. of West Africa, Plot 52, Transamadi, P.O. Box 387, pg. 6 **IT**
Sodexho Nigeria Ltd., Plot 226-Bodo Road, pg. 1275 **IT**
Weatherford Services S.A., C/O Weatherford Nigeria Ltd., pg. 1750 **PB**

Victoria Island

Krupp Steel & Engineering (Nigeria) Ltd., 3 Goriola St., pg. 513 **IT**
Nissho Iwai (Nigeria) Ltd., 6th Floor C and C Towers, Plot 1684, Sanusi Fabunwa Street, pg. 948 **IT**

Warri

Otis Nigeria, Ltd., P.N.B. 1069, pg. 777 **PB**

Yaba

Macmillan Nigeria Publishers Ltd., Ilupeju Estate, Four Industrial Ave., pg. 1480 **IT**

NORWAY

Agotnes

Kvaerner Energy, Agotnes, pg. 767 **IT**
Kvaerner Installasjon, Agotnes Division, pg. 769 **IT**

Alesund

Den norske Bank - Central Norway, Commercial Banking, Kongensgt. 15, pg. 392 **IT**
Kvaerner Eureka, Alesund Division, pg. 767 **IT**
Kvaerner Fish Process Technology a.s - Kvaerner Kulde, Skarbovik, pg. 768 **IT**
LONGVA GROUP, Gangstoevik, pg. 817 **PB**
Parker Hannifin A/S, Postveien 12, Breivika, pg. 1263 **PB**

Alvik

Bjolvefossen, pg. 448 **IT**

Andenes

Andenes Helikopterbase a.s., P.O. Box 20, pg. 1298 **IT**

Ardalstangen

Hydro Energi Sogn, pg. 960 **IT**

Asker

AST Research-Norway, pg. 1182 **IT**
Acer Computer Norway A/S, pg. 22 **IT**
BASF Norge AS, Leangbukta 40, pg. 106 **IT**
Forbo A/S, pg. 497 **IT**
Honeywell AS, Askerveien 61, pg. 834 **PB**
Norsk Forkonservering (NOFO), pg. 960 **:T**
Norske Fina A/S, Johan Drengsrudsvei 52, pg. 1043 **IT**

Askim

A/S Norlett, Box 187, pg. 443 **IT**

Avaldsnes

Hydro Aluminium Structures a.s., pg. 960 **IT**

Ballangen

Nikkel OG Olivin A/S, Arnesfjellet, pg. 1016 **IT**

Bergen

Bailey Norge AS, pg. 449 **IT**

PB - *U.S. Public Companies Volume*
PV - *U.S. Private Companies Volume*
IT - *International Public & Private Companies Volume*

1727

Geographic Index-Non U.S.

Den norske Bank, Retail Banking, Torgalm. 2, pg. 392   IT
Den norske Bank, Commercial Banking, Lars Hillesgt. 30, pg. 392   IT
Hydro Bergen, Lars Hillesgt 30, pg. 960   IT
Kvaerner Fjellstrand Shipping A/S, pg. 768   IT
Mitsui & Co. Europe (Scandinavia), c/o Coast Center Base Ltd., 5363 Agotnes, pg. 880   IT
Norsk Blikkvalseverk A/S, pg. 754   IT
Pronova Biocare a.s., Sandviksboder 75c, pg. 961   IT
Statoil, Bergen, pg. 1298   IT
Stolt Sea Farm A/S, pg. 1302   IT
Storage Technology Norway, Lars Hillsg. 20B, pg. 1523   PB
Vesta Forsikring A/S, Folke Bernadottesvei 50, pg. 1257   IT
Vesta Forvaltning AS, Folke Bernadottesvei 50, pg. 1258   IT
Wormald Signalco A/S, Tjaereviken, pg. 1651   PB

Billingstad

CPC Foods A/S, Bilingstadsletta 25, pg. 225   PB
Ericsson A/S, Olav Brunborgs vei 6, pg. 1366   IT
Ericsson Radar A/S, Olav Brunborgsv. 6, pg. 1367   IT
Ericsson Telecom A/S, Olav Brunborgsvei 6, pg. 1367   IT
Intergraph Norge A/S, Nesoyveien 4, pg. 892   PB
Kvaerner Process Systems A/S, pg. 766   IT
Kvaerner Process Systems a.s, Billingstadsletta 38, pg. 769   IT
NFT Ericsson Communications ANS, Bergerveien 12, pg. 1369   IT
Nordic Electronic Systems A/S, Bergerveien 8, pg. 1369   IT

Biri

Madshus A/S, pg. 940   PB

Birkeland

Owens-Corning Fiberglas Norway AS, pg. 1237   PB

Bodo

Svedala A/S Bodo, pg. 1324   IT

Braskereidfoss

Chipboard Mill Braskereidfoss, pg. 965   IT
Valer Skurlag, pg. 965   IT

Brattholmen

Svedala A/S Brattholmen, pg. 1324   IT

Brevik

Norsk Hydro A/S Brevik Packaging Dept., Stromtangvn. 21, pg. 960   IT

Bronnoysund

Algea Produkter A/S, Biskopholmen, pg. 959   IT

Brumunddal

Langmoen AS, pg. 965   IT
Norske Skogindustrier Business Area Building Materials, pg. 965   IT
Sealed Air Norge A S, pg. 1451   PB

Bryne

ABB Trallfa Robot A/S, Postboks 265, pg. 8   IT
Kvaerner Eureka, Bryne Division, pg. 767   IT
Kvaerner Hetland a.s, Herikstadvn 25, pg. 769   IT

Drammen

AWA A/S, Gronland 81, pg. 965   IT
Ahlstrom A/S Ahlstrom Machinery, Nedre Eikervei 26, pg. 34   IT
Akerlund & Rausing A/S, P.O. Box 893, pg. 33   IT
Algea Produkter A/S, Tomtegaten 36, pg. 959   IT
Bang & Olufsen A/S, Ingvald Ludvigsensgate 14, pg. 146   IT
Bauda A/S, Svelvikveien 59B, pg. 1413   IT
J.I. Case Norge A/S, O Storgt 9, pg. 1579   PB
Henkel Nopco A/S, pg. 613   IT
A/S Ingenior Gran, 75 Rosenkrantzgate, P.O. Box 1, pg. 359   IT
Lasgruppen a.s., Hamborggatan 21, pg. 18   IT
Mannesmann Demag Materialhandtering A/S, pg. 837   IT
Nodest A/S, pg. 715   IT
Norsk Virke Norske Skogindustrier BA Fibre, Gronland 81, pg. 966   IT
Pronova Biopolymer a.s., Havnegata 59, pg. 961   IT
Pronova Biopolymer a.s., Tomtegaten 36, pg. 961   IT
Pronova Biopolymers A/S, Tomegaten 36, pg. 961   IT
Prosess-Styring A/S, Syretarnet 39, Gulskogens Industriomrade, pg. 1040   IT
A/S Sunland-Eker Papirfabrikker, pg. 1420   IT
Toyota Norge A/S, Svelvikveien 59, pg. 1414   IT

Dreggen

Mowi A/S, pg. 960   IT

Drobak

Jobu A/S, Postboks 57, pg. 443   IT

Egersund

Kvaerner Rosenberg A/S Kvaerner Egersund, pg. 769   IT

Eggedal

Stora Byggprodukter Norge A/S, pg. 1303   IT

Eidanger

Componenta International A/S, Moheim, pg. 1421   IT

Elnesvagen

Moxy Trucks AS, pg. 745   IT

Elverum

Borregaard Skoger AS, pg. 1011   IT

Etterstad

Saab Norge A/S, Postboks 6179, pg. 688   IT

Eydehavn

Arendal Smelteverck A.S., Postboks 38, pg. 1174   IT

Farsund

Elkem Aluminium Lista, pg. 446   IT

Fjellhamar

Fasson Norge A/S, Elveveijen 26/28, P.O. Box 70, pg. 154   PB
Fjeldhammertak Nord A/S, pg. 659   IT
Fjeldhammertak Ost A/S, pg. 659   IT
Fjeldhammertak Sor A/S, pg. 659   IT
Fjeldhammertak Vest A/S, pg. 659   IT
Folldal Gjenrinning A/S, pg. 659   IT
Martin Haraldstad A/S, pg. 659   IT
Icopal as, Fjellhamarveien 52, Postboks 55, pg. 659   IT
Kanthal Norden AB, pg. 723   IT
Norfolier A/S & Co., pg. 659   IT

Flatasen

Svedala A/S Flatasen, pg. 1324   IT

Flesberg

Numedal Bruk, pg. 965   IT

Floro

Ewos Aqua A.S, Floro, Gunfildvagen, pg. 349   IT
Kvaerner Floro a.s., pg. 769   IT
Kvaerner Floro Consult a.s., pg. 769   IT
Kvaerner Kleven Floro A/S, pg. 769   IT
Saga Petroleum Floro, Botnaneset, pg. 1169   IT
Statoil, Floro, P.O. Box 223, pg. 1298   IT
Weatherford Norge A/S, Fjordbase, pg. 1750   PB

Follafoss

Folla CTMP A/S, pg. 966   IT

Forde

Kvaerner Kleven Forde A/S, pg. 769   IT

Fortun

Hydro Energi Kraftverk, pg. 960   IT

Forus

Saga Petroleum ASA, Godesetdalen 8, pg. 1169   IT
Saga Petroleum Stavanger, Godesetdalen 8, pg. 1169   IT

Fredrikstad

Brodrene Bockmann A/S, Harbornveien 50, Ora, pg. 1172   IT
Den norske Bank, Commercial Banking, Farmannsgt. 2, pg. 392   IT
Gyproc Gipsplatefabrikk A/S, pg. 1200   IT
Jotul a.s., pg. 42   IT
Kemwater A/S, Box 1177, pg. 728   IT
Kronos Norge A/S, Ostfold, pg. 271   PV
Kronos Titan A/S, Fredrikstad Plant, pg. 271   PV
Kvaerner Eiendom a.s, Ostfold Fredrikstad Division, K G Meldahlsvei 9 Krakeroy, pg. 766   IT
Norcem Betong A/S, pg. 42   IT

Gardermoen

Shell of Gardermoen, Oslo Gardermoen Airport, pg. 1139   IT

Gjettum

Norsulfid A/S, Baerumsveien 373, pg. 1016   IT
Outokumpu Norge A/S, Baerumsveien 373, pg. 1016   IT

Gjeving

Kvaerner Incineration A/S, pg. 769   IT

Gjovik

Adidas Sarragan Norge A/S, pg. 25   IT
Borden Kjemi Norge A/S, Postboks 195, pg. 159   PV
Den norske Bank, Commercial Banking, Hunnsvn. 5, pg. 392   IT

Glomfjord

Hydro Agri Glomfjord, pg. 959   IT
Permipipe Titanium A/S (PTI), pg. 1662   PB

Grubhei

Norske Skogindustrier A.S., I-Bjelker, pg. 965   IT

Hagan

DYWIDAG Systems Norge A/S, Industrieveien 7A, pg. 424   IT

Halden

Saugbrug Trelast A/S, Walkers gate 1, pg. 966   IT

Hamar

Den norske Bank, Strandgt. 41, pg. 392   IT
Ideal Wasa A/S, pg. 982   IT
Kvaerner Thune A/S, pg. 769   IT

Harstad

Den norske Bank - Northern Norway, Retail Banking, Sjogt. 5, pg. 392   IT
Hydro Harstad, Storakern 11, pg. 960   IT
Saga Petroleum Harstad, Torvet 7, pg. 1169   IT
Statoil, North Norway, Medkila, pg. 1298   IT

Haugesund

Den norske Bank, Haraldsgt. 125, pg. 392   IT
K/S Markedet Haugesund, pg. 41   IT
Norpipe Oil A/S, c/o Statoil, pg. 1043   IT
Norsea Gas A/S, c/o Statoil, pg. 1043   IT
Pronova Biopolymer a.s., Vormedal, pg. 961   IT
Statoil, Transport Division Bygnes, P.O. Box 308, pg. 1298   IT
Statoil, Transport Division Karsto, P.O. Box 308, pg. 1298   IT
Stolt Comex Seaway A/S, pg. 1302   IT
Stolt-Nielsen Ruderi A/S, pg. 1302   IT

Havik

Hydro Aluminium Hydal, pg. 960   IT
Hydro Aluminium Karmoy Fabrikker, pg. 960   IT
Hydro Aluminium Karmoy Rolling Mill, pg. 960   IT
Hydro Aluminium Profiler A/S Karmoy Extrusions, pg. 960   IT
Norcable A/S, pg. 960   IT

Herre

Hydro Rafnes, pg. 960   IT

Holmestrand

Hydro Aluminium A/S Rolled Products, pg. 959   IT
Hydro Aluminium ETP Holmestrand, pg. 959   IT
Hydro Aluminium Formtech A/S, pg. 959   IT
Hydro Aluminium Holmestrand Laquered Products, pg. 959   IT
Hydro Aluminium Holmestrand Rolling Mill, pg. 959   IT
Hydro Aluminium Nordisk Aviation Products A/S, pg. 960   IT
Hydro Aluminium Vik Verk A/S, Sales Office Holmestrand, pg. 960   IT

Holmsbu

Intralox A/S, P.B. 40, pg. 643   PV

Honefoss

Follum Fabrikker, P.O. Box 220, pg. 965   IT
Kato Kraner Norge A/S, Hensmoen, pg. 1420   IT
Keyes Norway A/S, pg. 1146   IT

Horten

Gambro A/S, pg. 667   IT
Nordisk Feral A/S, pg. 960   IT
SIMRAD NORGE AF, Strandpromenaden 50, pg. 1252   PB
Sonoco Norge A/S, Postboks 32, pg. 1487   IT
Vingmed Sound A/S, Strandpromenaden 52, pg. 644   IT

PB - *U.S. Public Companies Volume*
PV - *U.S. Private Companies Volume*
IT - *International Public & Private Companies Volume*

1728

Hovik

DET NORSKE VERITAS, Veritasveien 1, pg. 396 — IT
Det Norske Veritas Eiendom A/S, Veritasveien 1, pg. 396 — IT
Det Norske Veritas Industry, Veritasveien 1, pg. 396 — IT
Extratec AS, Veritasveien 16, pg. 959 — IT
Kvaerner Concrete Construction a.s., Sandviksveien 22, pg. 766 — IT
Monsanto Norge A/S, Sandviksveien 58 A, pg. 1126 — PB
Oracle Norge A/S, Sandviksveien 26, pg. 1228 — PB

Hoyanger

Hydro Aluminium Fundo A/S, pg. 959 — IT
Hydro Aluminium Hoyanger Verk, pg. 960 — IT
Hydro Aluminium Slugfabrikken, pg. 960 — IT
Hydro Energi Hoyanger, pg. 960 — IT

Hoyden

TrioVing a.s., Varnaveien 32a, pg. 18 — IT

Hundvag

Kvaerner Hydrotech a.s., Skipsbyggergt 16, pg. 769 — IT
Kvaerner Installasjon a.s., Skipsbyggergt 12-16, pg. 769 — IT
Lysaker Reisebyra. Stavanger, Skipsbyggergt. 12, pg. 770 — IT

Husnes

Sor-Norge Aluminium a.s., pg. 961 — IT
SORAL - Sor-Norge Aluminum A/S, pg. 69 — IT

Hvalstad

Nortec Electronics A/S, P.O. Box 123, Smeddsvingen 4B, pg. 712 — IT
Plast-Teknik Curver AS, Torstadbakken 4 Boks 150, pg. 356 — IT

Jarpen

Norske Skog AB, pg. 965 — IT

Kirkenes

Kvaerner Kimek a.s., Storgaten 4, pg. 770 — IT

Klofta

Albright & Wilson A/S, P.O. Box 170, pg. 49 — IT

Kokstad

Parker Hannifin A/S, Kokstadflaten 19B, pg. 1263 — PB

Kolbjoernsvki

Semafor A/S, pg. 1369 — IT

Kolbotn

Ford Motor Norge A/S, Trollasveien 34, pg. 666 — PB
Kodak Norge A/S, Trollsveien 6, pg. 554 — PB
SAS Institute A/S, P.O. Box 713, pg. 966 — PV
Saetre AS, pg. 1011 — IT
Vink Plast AS, Sam Edesvei 7a, pg. 1211 — IT
Volvo Lastebiler og Busser Norge AS, pg. 1477 — IT
Volvo Norge A/S, Pb 1, pg. 1477 — IT

Kongsberg

Ciba Vision Norge A/S, pg. 981 — IT
Danfoss Esco AS, Gamle Gormsrudvej 40, pg. 377 — IT

Kongsvinger

Svedala A/S Plant, pg. 1324 — IT

Kopervik

Hydro Aluminium Extrusion Tools, Ostrem Industiomrade, pg. 959 — IT
Hydro Aluminium Hydro Trans, pg. 960 — IT

Koppang

Osterdalsbruket AS, pg. 965 — IT

Koppera

Meraker Naeringspark, pg. 448 — IT

Kristiansand

Air Products A/S-Gardner Cryogenics Div., Lumberveien 49, pg. 31 — PB
Den norske Bank - Southern Norway, Commercial Banking, Markensgt. 25, pg. 392 — IT
Elkem Carbon, pg. 447 — IT
Elkem Fiskaa Silicon, pg. 448 — IT

Elkem Materials, pg. 447 — IT
Elkem Research, pg. 448 — IT
Falconbridge Nikkelverk A/S, pg. 434 — IT
Hydro Kristiansund, Verkstedveien 11, pg. 960 — IT
Kvaerner Installasjon, Kristiansund Division, pg. 769 — IT
Maritime Protection A/S, Lumberveien 43-51, pg. 1125 — PB
Saga Petroleum ASA, Omagata 122, pg. 1169 — IT
Statoil, Kristiansund, P.O. Box 2123, pg. 1298 — IT

Kroderen

Tyri A/S, pg. 421 — IT

Kvam

Chipboard Mill Kvam, pg. 965 — IT

Kystbasen

Statoil, Bergen Base, P.O. Box 25, pg. 1298 — IT

Laksevag

Norwegian Underwater Technology Center a.s.-Nutec, P.O. Box 6, pg. 1298 — IT

Langesund

Jotun Cathodic Protection A/S, pg. 714 — IT

Langhus

Parker Hannifin A/S, Handverksveien, Berghagan, pg. 1263 — PB
Rammer Norge A/S, Berghagan, pg. 1352 — IT
Rexroth A/S, pg. 839 — IT

Larvik

Black & Decker (Norge) A/S, Lagavn, pg. 234 — PB
Corro-Coat A/S, Hegdal, pg. 714 — IT
AS ESAB, Frankendalsveion 97, pg. 281 — IT
Kvaerner Kleven Leirvik A/S, pg. 769 — IT
Neste Kjemi A/S, Lagaveien 9 A, P.O. Box 2022, pg. 915 — IT

Lauvsnes

A/S Namdalens Traesliperi, pg. 965 — IT

Lier

Algea Produkter A/S, pg. 959 — IT
Kvaerner Eureka A/S, Tranby, Joseph Kellers vei, pg. 766 — IT
Kvaerner Fish Process Technology a.s - Kvaerner Kulde, Joseph Kellers vei, pg. 768 — IT
Kvaerner Pulp Equipment a.s, Joseph Kellers vei, pg. 769 — IT
Kvaerner Ships Equipment a.s, Joseph Kellers vei, pg. 770 — IT
Kvaerner Ships Equipment a.s Marine Automation, Joseph Kellers vei 20, pg. 770 — IT
Kvaerner Ships Equipment a.s Tranby, Joseph Kellers vei 20, pg. 770 — IT

Lierstranda

Elopak A/S, Industrigt. 4, Frydenlund, pg. 1389 — IT
Polarcup Norway, pg. 638 — IT

Lillehammer

Kvaerner Mesna A/S, Sliperiervn 2, pg. 769 — IT
Swix Sport, pg. 1390 — IT

Lillesand

Den norske Bank - Southern Norway, Retail Banking, Vestregt. 7, pg. 392 — IT
Norton A/S, Nordheim, pg. 1174 — IT

Lillestrom

Norsk Michelin Gummi A/S, Leiravn 13B, pg. 322 — IT
Pharmacia & Upjohn Biotech, Svelleveien 27, pg. 1047 — IT
Pharmacia & Upjohn Biotech AS, Svelleveien 27, pg. 1047 — IT
A/S SAPA, Storgatam 11, P.O. Box 48, pg. 443 — IT

Limingen

Norsulfid A/S, Avd. Grong Gruber, pg. 1016 — IT

Loddefjord

Gray Tool Co. (Norway) A/S, P.O. Box 31, pg. 5 — IT

Lommedalen

Graco Norge A.S., Lommedalsveien 281, pg. 757 — PB

Lorenskog

Ewos Aqua A.S., Luhrtoppen 2, pg. 349 — IT

Lyngdal

Fibo-Trespo, pg. 965 — IT

Lysaker

Borregaard NEA, pg. 1011 — IT
Dell Computer AS, Lysaker Torg 8, pg. 496 — PB
Digitale Kartsystemer, Fornebuveien 3, pg. 766 — IT
Forsikringsaksjeselskapet Allianz Nordeuropa, Arnstein Arnebergsvei 30, pg. 60 — IT
Frigoscandia A/S, Drammensveien 302, pg. 606 — PB
FRIONOR A/S, Lysaker Torg 8, pg. 516 — IT
Hydro Olje A/S, Strandveien 6, pg. 960 — IT
A/S IVARAN REDERI, P.O. Box 175, pg. 696 — IT
Ivaran Shipping A/S, pg. 696 — IT
Kvaerner Arctic Offshore A/S, pg. 769 — IT
KVAERNER A.S.A., Prof. Kohtsu #5, pg. 766 — IT
Kvaerner Concrete Construction a.s., Elveveien 25B, pg. 766 — IT
Kvaerner Doris Offshore Concrete A/S, pg. 766 — IT
Kvaerner Engineering A/S, Professor Kohts vei 5, pg. 766 — IT
Kvaerner Moss Technology a.s., Strandveien 4, pg. 769 — IT
Lysaker Reisebyra a.s., Strandveien 5, pg. 769 — IT
Neste Petroleum A/S, Strandveien 50, pg. 915 — IT
NIKE International Ltd.-Norway, Vollsveien 13-J, pg. 1184 — PB
Nordic Bull Net, Drammensvein 302-304, pg. 318 — IT
Norske Skog Sales AS, Vollsvn. 9-11, pg. 965 — IT
Norske Skogindustrier A.S., Vollsveien 9-11, pg. 965 — IT
Norske Skogindustrier A.S-Paper, Vollsvn. 9-11, pg. 965 — IT
Orkla Media A.S, pg. 1011 — IT
Pfizer A.S., Strandveien 4, pg. 1282 — PB
Pronova A/S, Strandveien 50, pg. 961 — IT
Pronova Biocare a.s., Strandveien 5, pg. 961 — IT
SAS Park Royal Hotel, Fornebuparken, P.O. Box 185, pg. 1202 — IT
Tandem Computers-Noway, Fornebuveien 46-48, pg. 418 — PB

Magnor

Hydro Aluminium Magnor A/S, pg. 960 — IT
Hydro Aluminium Sverige AB, pg. 960 — IT
Wicona Scandinavia AB, pg. 961 — IT

Mandal

Huls Nordic AB, Taljegardsgatan 4, pg. 1455 — IT
Kvaerner Mandal A/S, Gismeroya, pg. 769 — IT

Minde

TINE-VESTLANDSMEIERIET, Minde Alle 10, pg. 1390 — IT

Mjoendalen

Viking Mjoendalen A/S, Postboks 55, pg. 1423 — IT

Mo

Elkem Rana, pg. 447 — IT

Molde

Linjebygg AS, Fannestrandvn. 54, pg. 660 — IT

Mongstad

Statoil, Mongstad, pg. 1298 — IT

Mosjoeen

Elkem Aluminium Mosjoen, pg. 447 — IT
Norsk Alcoa A/S, c/o Mosal Aluminum, pg. 62 — PB

Moss

Aker Elementbygg a.s., Peer Gynts vei 1, pg. 41 — IT
Continental MG Plast A.S., pg. 1207 — IT
Den norske Bank, Retail Banking, Ibsensgt. 2, pg. 392 — IT
Helly-Hansen A/S, Solgaard Skog 139, pg. 1010 — IT
Helly-Hansen A/S, Carlbergveien 6, pg. 1010 — IT
Helly-Hansen A/S, Solgaard Skog 139, pg. 1010 — IT
Helly-Hansen Spesialprodukter AS, Solgaard Skog 139, pg. 1010 — IT
Helox AS, Solgaar Skog 139, pg. 1010 — IT
Hiko Byggplast A/S, Skredderveien 6, pg. 1037 — IT
Kvaerner Eiendom a.s, Ostfold Moss Division, Vaerftsgt 13, pg. 766 — IT
Kvaerner Eureka, Moss Division, Verftsgt 15, pg. 767 — IT
Kvaerner Moss Stal a.s, Verftsgt 13, pg. 766 — IT
Kvaerner Moss Technology a.s., Moss Division, Vaerftsgt 13, pg. 769 — IT
Kvaerner Ships Equipment a.s, Kvaerner Moss, Vaerfsgt 13, pg. 770 — IT
Stena Line A/S, Varlebrygga, pg. 1300 — IT

Myre

Biomar a.s., pg. 959 — IT

Naersnes

CGG Norge A/S, Baarsrudveien 2, pg. 241   IT

Namsos

Namsenbygg, pg. 965   IT
Van Severen, Tiendeholmen, pg. 965   IT
A/S Van Severen & Co. Ltd., pg. 965   IT

Nesbru

Ericsson Business Communications A/S, Nesbruveien 75, pg. 1366   IT
Ericsson Holding A/S, Nesbruveien 75, pg. 1367   IT
Ericsson Radio Systemer A/S, Nesbruveien 75, pg. 1367   IT
Kvaerner Professional Services Ltd., Arengveien 2, pg. 767   IT
Perstorp A/S Decorative Laminate, Fekjan 15, pg. 1038   IT
Perstorp Gulv A/S, Fekjan 13, pg. 1039   IT

Nesflaten

Hydro Energi Roldal-Suldal, pg. 960   IT

Nesoddtangen

Norsk Rehab AS, Rehabsenteret, pg. 1536   PB

Notodden

Hydro Notodden Industripark, pg. 960   IT
Kurssenteret Bratterein, Brattreinsgt. 9, pg. 960   IT

Nygardsjoen

Sundsfjord Kraftlag I/S, pg. 961   IT

Odda

Odda Smelteverk A/S, P.O. Box 63, pg. 122   IT

Omastrand

Kvaerner Fjellstrand A/S, pg. 768   IT

Orkanger

Elkem Thamshavn, pg. 448   IT
Norsk Exolon A/S, pg. 600   PB
K/S Orkla Exolon A/S & Co., pg. 600   PB

Oslo

AGA Progas A/S, P.O. Box 42, pg. 13   IT
Adecco Norge AS, Karl Johans Gate 5, pg. 24   IT
Agronova A/S, Joh.H.Andresens vei 5, pg. 1389   IT
Aker Betong a.s., Brobekkvn 84, pg. 42   IT
Aker Brygge Drift A/S, Fjordalleen 16, pg. 41   IT
Aker Building and Cement Materials, Fjordalleen 16, pg. 42   IT
Aker Eiendom, Standen 1, pg. 41   IT
Aker Engineering a.s. (AE), Tjuvholmen, pg. 42   IT
Aker ExClay A/S, Brobekkvn 84, pg. 42   IT
Aker Oil and Gas Technology, Fjordalleen 16, pg. 41   IT
AKER RAJ ASA, Fjordalleen 16, pg. 41   IT
Akzo Chemie Norge AS, Postbox 3183 Elisenberg, pg. 47   IT
Amdahl Norge A/S, Brynsveien 13, pg. 527   IT
Amerada Hess Norge A/S, Langkaia 1, pg. 65   PB
Aquatic Animal Health, Harbitzalleen 3, pg. 58   PB
Ascom Tateco A/S, Kakkelovnskroken 2, pg. 87   IT
ASEA Skandia A/S, Postboks 49 Leirdal, pg. 7   IT
The Associated Press A/S, Fridtiof Mansens Plass 5, pg. 92   PV
Ebbe C Astrup AS, Tidemandsgt. 5, pg. 731   IT
Avesta Sheffield A/S, pg. 221   IT
AxTrade Scandinavia A/S, Sorkedalsveien 106, pg. 710   IT
BASF Norge A/S, Glasurit Center, Persveien 32, pg. 106   IT
BBDO Oslo, Dronningens Gate 3, pg. 1224   PB
BNP Finans A/S - Norway, Biskop Gunnerus Gate 2, pg. 163   IT
Bakers AS, pg. 1010   IT
Basberg Papir AS, Postbox 144, pg. 886   IT
Bausch & Lomb Norway A/S, PB2562 Solli, pg. 195   PB
Beiersdorf Norge A/S, Stromsun. 314, pg. 183   IT
Bekaert Norge A/S, Linstowgate 6, pg. 184   IT
Berendsen Components A/S, 8 Konowsgate, pg. 1284   IT
BERGESEN D.Y. A.S., Drammensveien 106, pg. 188   IT
Berlitz A/S, Lille Grensen 5, pg. 221   PB
AS Bofors Norge, pg. 278   IT
Bold, Thunes Vei 2, pg. 678   PV
Brodrene Dahl A/S, 65-67 Grenseveien, P.O. Box 6146, pg. 359   IT
Brother Norge A/S., P.O. Box 93, pg. 230   IT
Bull A/S, Fyrstikkalleen 3A, pg. 317   IT
Leo Burnett A/S, Drammensveien 130, pg. 184   PV
CCB Stal AS, Professor Birkelands vei 21, pg. 1089   IT
Castrol Norge A/S, Drammensveien 175, pg. 236   IT
Caterpillar Financial Services Norway A/S, Brobekkv 62B, pg. 315   PB
Cerberus AS, pg. 1246   IT

CHRISTIANIA BANK OG KREDITKASSE ASA, Middelthuns gate 17, pg. 289   IT
CIBA-GEIGY A/S, Ensjoveien 18, pg. 976   IT
Cinet A/S, Sagveien 17, pg. 710   IT
Clarion I.M.P. A/S, Drammensveien 145, pg. 303   PV
Coca-Cola Norge A/S, pg. 392   PB
Compaq Computer Norway A/S, Brynsengvn 2, pg. 418   PB
The Continuum Company, Inc. (Norway), pg. 423   PB
Crawford Door A/S, Stromsveien 179, pg. 269   IT
Daewoo Corp. - Oslo, pg. 358   IT
Dagens Naeringsliv A/S, pg. 958   IT
D'Arcy Masius Benton & Bowles, Drammensveien 145, pg. 304   PV
Data General A/S, pg. 485   PB
Datateam Norge A/S, Stromsveien 323, pg. 712   IT
Deminex Norge AS, P.O. Box 1767, pg. 1461   IT
Den norske Bank, Retail Banking Div., Kirkegt. 21, pg. 392   IT
Den norske Bank, Commercial Banking Div., Kiregt. 21, pg. 392   IT
DEN NORSKE BANK ASA, Stranden 21, pg. 392   IT
A/S Denofa og Lilleborg Fabriker, pg. 1010   IT
Det Beste A/S, Hovfaret 11, pg. 1368   IT
DIAL Forsikring A/S, Ulvenveien 75A, pg. 1257   IT
Digital Equipment Corporation A/S, Olaf Helsets vei 6, Skullerud, P. Boks 6401 Etterstad, pg. 507   PB
Diners Club Nordic A/S, Langkaia 1, pg. 1202   IT
Dinol Norge A/S, Verkseier Furlunds vei 5, pg. 982   IT
Dow Jones Markets Norway AS, Rosenkrantzgaten 20, pg. 525   PB
A/S Drommekjokkenet, Grenseveien 109, pg. 443   IT
Dun & Bradstreet Norge AS, pg. 536   PB
Duni A/S, Enebakkeveien 150, pg. 421   IT
Dynapac A/S, Alfaset, 1 Industrivei 6, pg. 1420   IT
DYWIDAG-Systems International A/S, pg. 424   IT
EB Installasjon A/S, Postboks 263 Sentrum, pg. 3   IT
EMI Norsk A/S, P.O. Box 42 Korsvoll, pg. 427   IT
Eklow Scandinavia A/S, pg. 710   IT
Electrolux Constructor A/S, Ostre Aker vei 203, pg. 443   IT
Electrolux Industrier A/S, Postbox 246, Okern, pg. 443   IT
Electrolux Rengjo/ringsmaskiner A/S, Postboks 6645, Roddelokka, pg. 443   IT
Elkem Aluminium ANS, Hoffsvienen 65B, pg. 446   IT
ELKEM ASA, Hoffsveien 65B, pg. 446   IT
Elkem ASA Energy, Hoffsveien 65 B, pg. 447   IT
Elkem ASA Ferrosilicon Division, Hoffsveien 65B, pg. 448   IT
Elkem ASA Manganese/Chrome Division, Hoffsveien 65B, pg. 447   IT
Elkem Chartering, Hoffsveien 65B, pg. 447   IT
Elkem Mangan, Hoffsveien 65B, pg. 447   IT
Elkem Technology Services, Nydalsveien 26 B, pg. 448   IT
Emil Moestue as, P.O. Box 22rlSLOKKA, pg. 460   IT
Ericsson Components A/S, Brobekkveien 38, pg. 1366   IT
Erling Sande A/S, Ryensvingen 3, pg. 1390   IT
Esselte A/S, Postboks 11 Rislokka, pg. 460   IT
Esselte Meto A/S, Rosenbergveien 15, pg. 461   IT
Esso Norge a.s., Drammensveien 149, pg. 602   PB
EURO RSCG, Sagbeien 21A, pg. 602   IT
Euroclean A/S, Postboks 6645, Roddelokka, pg. 443   IT
Eurotherm A/S, pg. 466   IT
FAG Norge A/S, pg. 469   IT
FPS Power Systems A/S, pg. 492   IT
Fiber Kemi A/S, Nedre Slottsgt. 4, pg. 355   IT
Fidelio Nordic Norge A/S, Konghellegata 3, pg. 1106   PB
Fine Chemicals, Harbitzalleen 3, pg. 58   PB
Georg Fischer A.S., Bygdoey Alle 23, pg. 489   IT
Fiskars Norge A/S, Postboks 4215 Torshov, pg. 492   IT
Freudenberg A/S, pg. 506   IT
GGK Oslo, 8 Egertorvet, pg. 1335   IT
Gasell Profil AS, Brobekkveien 80, pg. 1088   IT
Geonor a.s., Grinidammen 10, pg. 959   IT
Getinge Vaxjo A/S, P.O. Box 61, Alnabru, pg. 552   IT
Gorud, pg. 18   IT
W.R. Grace A/S, Sofiemyrveien 6, N-1412 Sofiemyr, pg. 755   PB
Gregersen Male-og Prosessteknikk A/S, pg. 710   IT
Gunnebo A/S, pg. 578   IT
Hakon Gruppen AS, pg. 643   IT
Handelsbanken Oslo, Radhusgatan 27, pg. 1327   IT
Chr. Hansen AS, Spireavn, 6, pg. 289   IT
Hellermann Norge A/S, pg. 209   IT
Henkel Norge A/S, pg. 613   IT
Honeywell-Measurex Norway A/S, c/o Resident Agent, Thommessen and Krefting, pg. 833   PB
Husqvarna A/S, Postboks 85, Bryn, pg. 443   IT
Hydro Aluminium Vekst, Bygdoy Alle 2, pg. 960   IT
Hydro Chemicals Norge a.s., Persveien 30, pg. 960   IT
Hydro Seafood A/S, c/o Industriens og Eksportens Hus, pg. 960   IT
Hydrogas A/S, Ringnesveien 50, pg. 960   IT
Hydrogas A/S Markedsseksjon, Karoline Kristiansens vei 18, pg. 960   IT
IBM Norge Produkt Distribusjon A/S, Dronnengg Maudsgt 10, pg. 898   PB
IDC Norge A/S, Toyenbekken 21, pg. 571   PV
IDG Communications Norge AS, Toyenbekken 21, pg. 570   PV
ISI AS, pg. 278   IT
ISS Catering A/S, Ostensjoveien 18, pg. 656   IT
ISS Darenas a.s., Ulvenveien 92 B, pg. 656   IT
ISS Norge a.s., Ulvenveien 83, pg. 656   IT
ITT Flygt A/S, Staalfjaera 14, pg. 860   PB
Igloo Pool, Kronprinsesse Marthas pl. 1, pg. 766   IT
Industriforsikring A/S, Bogdoy alle 2, pg. 960   IT
International Business Machines A/S, Dronnengg Maudsgt 10, pg. 898   PB

International Flavors & Fragrances I.F.F. (Norge) A/S, pg. 899   PB
International Pharmaceuticals, Harbitzalleen 3, pg. 58   PB
Axel Johnson A/S, PO Box 98, Mustads vei 1, pg. 711   IT
Axel Johnson Lab Systems A/S, P.O. Box 98, pg. 711   IT
Carl Jonsson Papir A/S, Tvetenv. 12, pg. 864   IT
JORDAN A/S, Haavard Martinsens vei 30, pg. 714   IT
A/S Jotul Industrier, Grenseveien 97, pg. 42   IT
Kalmar Kockum A/S, Postboks 10, Bryn, pg. 1421   IT
Kalmar LMV A/S, Postboks 10, Bryn, pg. 1421   IT
Kelley Bemanningslosninger, Karl Johansgate 35, pg. 949   PB
Knurr-Norge AS, Gjerdrums vei 16, pg. 739   IT
Kockums Computer Systems A/S, pg. 277   IT
KONE A/S, Frysjaveien 40, pg. 747   IT
Korn/Ferry International, Haakon VII's Gate 2, pg. 634   PV
Krupp MaK Scandinavia A/S, Oslo Kontor, pg. 510   IT
Kvaerner a.s, Hoffsveien 1, pg. 766   IT
Kvaerner Eiendom a.s, Hoffsveien 1, pg. 766   IT
Kvaerner Energy a.s., Kvaernerveien 10, pg. 767   IT
Kvaerner Hilnor a.s., Hoffsveien 1, pg. 769   IT
Kvaerner Insurance A/S, Hoffsveien 1, pg. 769   IT
Kvaerner Invest a.s., pg. 769   IT
Kvaerner Prosjekt a.s., Hoffsveien 1, pg. 769   IT
Kvaerner Shipping a.s., Hoffsveien 1, pg. 770   IT
Kvaerner Venture a.s, Hoffsveien 1, pg. 770   IT
Kvaernerkonsernets Pensjonskasse, pg. 770   IT
Landbruk/Agriculture, Bygdoy Alle 2, pg. 960   IT
Landis & Staefa (Norge) A/S, pg. 801   IT
Linde K.T. Norge A/S, pg. 810   IT
Lorentzen & Wettre A/S, Ensjoveien 8, pg. 271   IT
LUXO A/S, Enebakkveien 117, pg. 821   IT
MAN B & W Norge A/S, pg. 824   IT
MD Foods Norge A/S, Jerikovejen 10, pg. 826   IT
MacGREGOR (NOR) A/S, pg. 671   IT
Marathon Petroleum Company (Norway), Tollbodgaten 27, pg. 1662   PB
Maskin A/S Zeta, Postboks 7553, pg. 1380   IT
Mecman A/S, pg. 839   IT
Megon a.s., Forskningsparken, Gaustadalleen 21, pg. 960   IT
Mettler-Toledo A/S, Professor Birkelandsvei 24 C, pg. 4   PV
Micro Warehouse, Norway AS, Waldemar Thranesgate 98B, pg. 1104   PB
Microsoft Norge AS, pg. 1108   PB
Mitsui & Co. Europe (Scandinavia) AB, Haakon VII's, Gate 5, pg. 880   IT
Mobil Oil A/S Norge, Fyrstikkforget, Karoline Kristiansense V.7, pg. 1119   IT
Molex-G. Knutsen A/S, Akersbakken 12, Post Box 2714, pg. 1122   IT
Moore Paragon Norge A/S, P.O. Box 67, pg. 889   IT
Motorola Norway A/S, Prof. Birkelandsvei 27, pg. 1140   PB
Munters Dry Air AB, Enebakkvn 307, pg. 669   IT
NIFE A/S, Drammensveien 130, pg. 54   IT
NAPS Norway A/S, Brobekkveien 101, pg. 913   IT
Nautisk Forlag A/S, pg. 958   IT
Nederman A/S, Haavard Martinsensvei 19, pg. 283   IT
A/S Nestle Norge, pg. 921   IT
Network Systems Norge A/S, Gjerdrumsvei 12, pg. 1522   PB
Nielsen Norge, Kjelsasveien 160, pg. 1184   PB
Nobel Elektronikk A/S, Haavard Martinsens vei 19, pg. 1290   IT
Nokia Telecommunications, Stromsveren 96, pg. 953   IT
NorBetong a/s, pg. 1199   IT
Norcem a.s., Beddingen 8, pg. 42   IT
Norcem a.s., pg. 1199   IT
Norcem Cement A/S, Fjordalleen 16, pg. 42   IT
Norcem Industrier, Fjordalleen 16, pg. 42   IT
Norden Banking Group, Kirkegatan 14-18, pg. 1328   IT
Nordson Norge A/S, Stromsveien 125, pg. 1189   PB
THE A/S NORGES HANDELS OG SJOEFARTSTIDENDE GROUP, pg. 958   IT
NORGRO A.S, pg. 1011   IT
NORSK HYDRO A.S, Bygdoy alle 2, pg. 959   IT
a.s. Norsk Leca, pg. 960   IT
Norsk Texaco A/S, P.O. Box 7000 H, Homansbyen, pg. 1199   PB
NORSK VEKST ASA, pg. 965   IT
A/S Norske Shell, Pilestredet 33A, pg. 1139   IT
Novell Norway, Sinsenveien 53 A, Postboks 6779 Rodelokka, pg. 1204   PB
Nycomed Amersham. Slemdalsveien 37, pg. 993   IT
Nycomed Imaging AS, Nycoveien 2, pg. 993   IT
Nycomed Pharma AS, Slemdalsveien 37, pg. 993   IT
OCE-Norge A/S, Gjerdrumsveg 8, pg. 994   IT
OTD&C A/S (Offshore Technology Development & Consulting), Ravnasveien 3, pg. 1032   FB
OMRON Electronics Norway A/S, Ole Deviks Vei 4, pg. 1006   IT
ORKLA A.S.A., pg. 1010   IT
Orkla Finans A.S, pg. 1011   IT
AS OSLO SPORVEIER, OekrnVeien 9, pg. 1012   IT
Partrederiet Nemo A/S, Havtor Management, P.O. Box 1374, Vika, pg. 915   IT
Pechiney Norge A/S-Rep. Office of Pechiney Sverige in Norway, Sorkedalsvej 6, pg. 1031   IT
Perstorp Form, Postboks 92, Roa, pg. 1038   IT
Petrokjemi/Petrochemicals, Bygdoy Alle, pg. 960   IT
Pharmacia & Upjohn A/S, Gjerdrums vei 10 B, pg. 1049   IT
Plastic Padding A/S, Sandakerveien 102, pg. 611   IT
A/S Polygon, Enebakkvn 307, pg. 669   IT
Pripps Ringnes a.s., pg. 1011   IT
Provona A/S, Gaustadalleen 21, pg. 961   IT
Roche Norge A/S, pg. 1121   IT
Royal Copenhagen Norge A/S, Pilestredet 15, pg. 1135   IT
SKF Multitec A/S, Jerikoveien 14, pg. 1159   IT

PB - *U.S. Public Companies Volume*
PV - *U.S. Private Companies Volume*
IT - *International Public & Private Companies Volume*

1730

Geographic Index-Non U.S.

SKF Norge A/S, Jerikoveien 14, pg. 1159 — IT
Sameiet Aker Brygge A/S, Bryggegt 3, pg. 41 — IT
Sandoz Pharma A/S, pg. 985 — IT
Sandvik Norge A/S, P.O. Box 54, pg. 1186 — IT
Scan Control Services, Ostre Aker vei 33, pg. 53 — IT
Scancem International ANS, Munkedamsvn 45, pg. 1201 — IT
A/S Scandia Kjemiske, pg. 715 — IT
Scanvest Olivetti A/S, pg. 1004 — IT
Scholl (Norge) A/S, Ostenjoveien 44, pg. 1210 — IT
Sensormatic A/S, Ole Deviksvei 6, pg. 1457 — PB
Siemens A/S, Oestre Aker Vei 90, pg. 1247 — IT
Simrad Optronics, Ensjoveien 18, pg. 770 — IT
Skandinaviska Enskilda Banken Oslo, Rosencrantzgate 22, pg. 1259 — IT
Skil Norge A/S, Enebakkveien 36B, pg. 578 — PB
Sodra Cell A/S, Vitaminv 11A, pg. 1276 — IT
Sporveis-Annonsene A/S, Oekernveien 9, pg. 1012 — IT
Standard Marine A/S, John G. Matteson svei 4, pg. 1152 — IT
Statoil Norge AS, Sorkedalsveien 8, pg. 1298 — IT
Stena Line A/S, Jernbanetorget 2, pg. 1300 — IT
Stolt Sea Farm A/S, Nedre Slottsgate 15, pg. 1302 — IT
Store Norske Stinnes Intercoal A/S, Munkedamsveien 45, pg. 1461 — IT
Sulzer Norge A/S, pg. 1306 — IT
Sun Chemical A/S, Saqueier 21A, pg. 371 — IT
Jan Sundt AS, Haakon VII's gt 1, pg. 731 — IT
Svedala A/S, pg. 1324 — IT
TA Control System A/S, Hans Nielsen Haugesgt 50B, pg. 670 — IT
TBWA Oslo, Stortingsgt 4, pg. 1063 — PV
TDN Nyhetsbyra A/S, pg. 958 — IT
TTS International AS, Bjornegarden, pg. 283 — IT
Tamrock Norge A/S, Verkseier Furulunfsvei 11, pg. 1353 — IT
Taugbol & Overland A/S, Etterstad, pg. 42 — IT
Tektronix Norge A/S, Brobekkveien 40, pg. 1568 — PB
Telecom Scandinavia A.S., Pilestredet 17, pg. 796 — IT
Texaco Exploration Norway A/S, P.O. Box 7000 H, pg. 1584 — PB
THORN Norge A/S, P.O. Box 40, pg. 1386 — IT
J.L. Tiedemanns Tobaksfabrik, Joh. H. Andresens vei 5, pg. 1390 — IT
TIEDEMANNS - JOH.H.ANDRESEN ANS, P.O. Box 6086, Etterstad, pg. 1389 — IT
Time/System Norge a/s, Storgaten 32, pg. 73 — IT
Titech-Autosort, Grensevn. 65-67, pg. 1390 — IT
The Tokio Marine & Fire Insurance Company (U.K.) Limited, Prinsens gt. 14-16, pg. 1392 — IT
Toledo Norge A/S, Professor Birkelandsvei 24C, pg. 986 — IT
Total Norge AS, Haakon VII's Gate 1, pg. 1409 — IT
Tradewinds A/S, pg. 958 — IT
Trelleborg Atlas A/S, Postboks 14, Leirdal, pg. 1423 — IT
Uddeholm A/S, pg. 1472 — IT
UNION BANK OF NORWAY, Kirkegt. 18, pg. 1439 — IT
VB Autobatteri A/S, Postboks 4473 Torshov, Hans-Nielsen Hauges gt. 39, pg. 1452 — IT
VARTA Batteri A/S, Postboks 4473 Torshov, Hans Nielsen Hauges gt. 39, pg. 1452 — IT
Vattenfall A/S, Radhusgata 1-3, pg. 1453 — IT
Vel-Vask Tekstil Service A/S, Hjalmar Brantingsvei 8, pg. 1286 — IT
Vesta Dial Forsikring A/S, Ulvensveien 75A, pg. 1257 — IT
Vicon, Norway, pg. 1719 — PB
Viking Fottoy A.S., pg. 1011 — IT
Voest-Alpine Norge A/S, Majorstua, pg. 1472 — IT
Wellcome Norge AS, pg. 553 — IT
Wrigley Scandinavia A/S, pg. 1781 — PB
Zeneca A/S, Drammensveien 126A, pg. 1526 — IT
Zimmerlund & Co., Bernt Ankersgt, 10B, pg. 72 — IT
Zurich Forsikring, Ruselokkveien 6, pg. 1531 — IT

Osteras

Ferrosan Norge AS, Grini Naeringspark 1, pg. 989 — IT
Hewlett-Packard Norge A/S, Oesterndalen 16-18, pg. 821 — PB

Ovre Ardal

Hydro Aluminium Aluserv A/S, pg. 959 — IT
Hydro Aluminium Ardal Verk, pg. 959 — IT
Hydro Aluminium Equipment A/S, pg. 959 — IT
Hydro Energi Ardal, pg. 960 — IT

Porsgrunn

Elkem Mangan PEA, pg. 447 — IT
Grenland Industriutvikling A/S, Hydrovn. 50, pg. 959 — IT
Hydro Magnesium Norge, Heroya, pg. 960 — IT
Hydro Porsgrunn, Heroya, pg. 960 — IT
Hydroship A/S, Storgt. 96, pg. 960 — IT

Randaberg

Petrolite Norge A/S, Harestadvika, pg. 166 — PB

Raufoss

Hydro Aluminium Profiler A/S, pg. 960 — IT

Rjukan

Hydelko KS, pg. 959 — IT
Hydro Energi Telemark, pg. 960 — IT
Hydro Rjukan Naeringspark, pg. 960 — IT

Norsk Kraftrevisjon A/S, Hydro Haeringspark, Saheimsv., pg. 960 — IT

Rovde

Kvaerner Kleven Rovde A/S, pg. 769 — IT

Rud

AMP Norge A/S, Rudssletta 97, pg. 9 — PB
Frionor-Produkter A/S, Olav Ingstads vei 12, pg. 516 — IT
Henkel KeNord AS, pg. 613 — IT
Novo Nordisk Pharma A/S, Hauger Skolevei 16, pg. 988 — IT

Sagvag

Aker Elektro a.s., pg. 41 — IT

Sande

Sande Paper Mill A/S, pg. 965 — IT

Sandefjord

Beaumont-Bennett A/S, P.O. Box 2097, pg. 714 — IT
Den norske Bank, Retail Banking, Radhusgt. 11-13, pg. 392 — IT
JOTUN A/S, pg. 714 — IT
Jotun Polymer A/S, pg. 714 — IT
Kvaerner Engineering, Miljo, Hindervn. 5, pg. 766 — IT
Pronova Biocare a.s., Framnesveien 54, pg. 961 — IT
Pronova Oleochemicals a.s., Framnesvn. 54, pg. 961 — IT
Veroc Technology A/S, pg. 714 — IT

Sandnes

Air Products A/S Permia Maritime Div., Stavangerveien Lure, pg. 31 — PB
Aker Singel & Grus a.s., Langgt 41-43, pg. 42 — IT
Den norske Bank, Lannggt. 1, pg. 392 — IT
A/S Dikema Stal, pg. 302 — IT
Norsk Hydro A/S-Development & Commercialization, Postboks 2053 Hana, pg. 960 — IT
NorStone a.s, pg. 1199 — IT

Sandsli

Hydro Bergen, Sundsliveien 90, pg. 960 — IT
Kvaerner Engineering, Bergen, Sandslimarka 55, pg. 766 — IT
Kvaerner Installasjon, Bergen Division, pg. 769 — IT
Stord International a.s., Sandslimarka 51, pg. 42 — IT

Sandvika

ABS Pumper A/S, Industriveien 34, pg. 270 — IT
Hagglunds Drives A/S, pg. 670 — IT
Ingeniorfirma Sigurd Sorum A.S., Jongsasveien, pg. 550 — IT
LIC Hygien A/S, Eyvind Lyckesvei 19A, pg. 551 — IT
LIC Nordenta A/S, Eyvind Lychesvei 19A, pg. 551 — IT
LIC Rehab Care A/S, Eyvind Lychesvei 19A, pg. 551 — IT
SAGA PETROLEUM ASA, Kjoerboveien 16, P.O. Box 490, pg. 1169 — IT
Soren Berner A/S, Lokketangen 12B, pg. 189 — IT
Statoil, Hamang, P.O. Box 910, pg. 1298 — IT
Statoil, Methanol & MTBE Division, P.O. Box 910, pg. 1298 — IT
Western Staff Services, Eyvind Lyches vei 13 B, pg. 1760 — PB

Sarpsborg

Borregaard Industries Limited, pg. 1011 — IT
Borvi AS, pg. 1040 — IT
Husqvarna Elektro A/S, Postboks 321, Tunborg, pg. 443 — IT
Swede Rescue, Kamoenes Naeringspark, pg. 712 — IT
Tunborg A/S, Postboks 10, pg. 443 — IT

Sauda

Elkem Mangan Sauda, pg. 447 — IT
Elkem Saudefaldine, pg. 447 — IT

Saudasjoen

Si-Glas A/S, pg. 1173 — IT

Sem

Hydro Aluminium Packaging A/S, pg. 960 — IT
Scandi-Glass A/S, Aasbakken 83, pg. 1173 — IT

Skare

Acuson A/S, pg. 18 — PB
Alarmcom AS, pg. 1246 — IT
Astra Norge A/S, pg. 94 — IT
Canon A/S, Industrieun 6, pg. 262 — IT
Esmi A/S, Tunveien 8, pg. 33 — IT
Eldon A/S, Postboks 414, pg. 436 — IT
Forslid A/S, Solheimsveien 62, pg. 1368 — IT
Huls Norge A/s, pg. 1455 — IT
Leaf Norway A/S, Solheimsveien 112, pg. 638 — IT
Norwesco A/S, Tunveien 8, pg. 33 — IT

Optiroc AS, pg. 1200 — IT
Polaroid (Norge) A/S, Industrivein 8 B, pg. 1314 — PB
A/S Scancem Chemicals, pg. 1199 — IT

Skarnes

Interconsult Norge A/S, Slomarka, pg. 1420 — IT

Skedsmokorset

Nordiskafilt A/S, pg. 37 — PB
Opel Norge AS, Kjeller Vest 6, pg. 723 — PB

Ski

Alfa-Laval Agri Scandinavia A/S, Postboks 250, pg. 1377 — IT
Berendsen PMC A/S, 2 Haugenveien, pg. 1285 — IT
GPA Plast A/S, Verkstedsvn. 23, pg. 678 — IT

Skien

Stabburet A/S, pg. 1011 — IT

Skjetten

Intel Norway, Hvamveien 4, pg. 887 — PB
Oki Systems (Norway) A/S, Hvamsvingen 9, pg. 1000 — IT
3M Norge A/S, Hvamveoen 6, Postboks 100, pg. 1607 — PB

Skogmo

TreNova AS, pg. 965 — IT

Skogn

NORSKE SKOGINDUSTRIER A.S., Fiborgtangen, pg. 965 — IT

Skytta

Bayer A/S, Postboks 114, Brennavn 18, pg. 174 — IT
S.C. Johnson, Postboks 34, pg. 593 — PV

Slemmestad

Zanda A/S, pg. 1092 — IT

Slependen

ICL Data A/S, Billinstadsletta 19, pg. 529 — IT

Sokna

Soknabruket, pg. 965 — IT

Sola

Shell Aviation Service, pg. 1139 — IT

Solheimsvik

Hewlett-Packard Norge A/S, Bohmergt. 44, pg. 821 — PB
Kvaerner Energy, Damsgard, Damsgardsveien 106, pg. 767 — IT

Sorumsand

Kvaerner Energy, Sorumsand, Industrivein 7, pg. 767 — IT

Spydeberg

Norak A/S Le Carbone-Lorraine, Lovestad Industrifelt, pg. 1031 — IT

Stabekk

Hydro Aluminium A/S, Drammensveien 264, pg. 959 — IT
Hydro Aluminium Fundo A/S, Drammensveien 264, pg. 959 — IT
Hydro Energi, Drammensveien 264, pg. 960 — IT
Hydro Magnesium, Drammensveien 246, pg. 960 — IT
Norsk Schering A/S, Gml. Drammensv. 48, pg. 1439 — PB
Norwegian Contractors A/S, Holtet 45, pg. 42 — IT
Raffinering & Markedsforing, Drammensveien 264, pg. 961 — IT
Teknologi & Utbygging/Technology & Projects, Drammensveien 264, pg. 961 — IT
Utforskning & Produksjon, Drammensveien 264, pg. 961 — IT

Stange

JIFFY PRODUCTS INTERNATIONAL LTD., Svensrudbegen 8, pg. 706 — IT

Stathelle

Borealis A/S, pg. 914 — IT
Statoil, Borealis, Bamble, pg. 1298 — IT

Stavanger

Aker Contracting a.s., Verven 2, pg. 41 — IT
Amoco Norway Oil Co., Bergjelandsgata 25, pg. 102 — PB

Caravelle Technology AS, Gramgarden, Tangen 4,
  pg. 731   IT
Conoco Norway, Inc., Finnestadveien 28, pg. 531   PB
Elf Aquitaine Norge A/S, Postboks 168, pg. 445   IT
GECO A.S., Bjergstedveien 1, pg. 1439   PB
Gray Tool Co. (Norway) A/S, P.O. Box 4, pg. 5   IT
Hanco A/S, pg. 711   IT
Hewlett-Packard Norge A/S, Dadegt. 2, pg. 821   PB
A. Johnson & Co. A/S, Offshore, P.O. Box 138,
  pg. 711   IT
Kvaerner Engineering, Stavanger Division, Haugasstubben
  8, pg. 766   IT
Kvaerner Rosenberg a.s., Skipsbyggergt 20, pg. 769   IT
Kvaerner Rosenberg a.s. International Developments,
  pg. 770   IT
Kvaerner Rosenberg A/S Rosenberg Verft, Skipsbyggergt.
  20 Buoy, pg. 769   IT
Mobil Exploration Norway, Inc., P.O. Box 510, pg. 1119   PB
Oceaneering A/S, Lagerveien 20, Forus, pg. 1211   PB
Parker Hannifin A/S, Auglendsmyra 2, pg. 1263   PB
STATOIL, pg. 1297   IT
Stolt Comex Seaway A/S, pg. 1302   IT
Weatherford Norge, A/S, pg. 1750   PB
Weatherford Norge, A/S, P.O. Box 5053, pg. 1750   PB

Stavern

Lincoln Norweld AS, Risoyaveien 14, pg. 997   PB

Stjoerdal

Shell of Stjoerdal, Trondheim Airport, Vaernes,
  pg. 1139   IT

Stord

Aker Stord a.s., pg. 42   IT
Aker Subsea a.s., pg. 42   IT

Straume

A/S Bergen Stal Dikema, pg. 302   IT
A/S Dikema Norge, pg. 302   IT

Straumen

Elkem Salten, pg. 448   IT
Siso Power Plant, pg. 447   IT

Sunndalsora

Hycast a.s., Industriveien 25, pg. 959   IT
Hydro Aluminium Hycast A/S, Industriveien 25, pg. 960   IT
Hydro Aluminium Sunndal Verk, pg. 960   IT

Svelgen

Bremanger Power Plant, pg. 447   IT
Elkem Bremanger, pg. 448   IT

Tana

Elkem Tana, pg. 448   IT

Tananger

Aker Base a.s., pg. 41   IT
Coppee Engineering A.S., J.M. Building, Tankatvegen,
  pg. 1162   IT
Phillips Petroleum Co. Norway, P.O. Box 220, pg. 1291   PB
Smith International Norway A/S, Risavikveien 5,
  pg. 1478   PB

Tiller

Hewlett-Packard Norge A/S, Vestre Rosten 81,
  pg. 821   PB

Tofte

Hurum Papirfabrikk, pg. 965   IT
Tofte Industrier, pg. 966   IT

Tonsberg

Bulklift A/S, pg. 965   IT
Den norske Bank, Retail Banking, Storgt. 24, pg. 392   IT
K/S Kaldnes de Groot A/S, pg. 965   IT
Kaldnes Heavy Lift Trucks, Postboks 2011-Postterminalen,
  pg. 965   IT
Kaldnes Heavy Lift Trucks A/S, pg. 965   IT
Kaldnes Industri A/S, pg. 965   IT
Kaldnes Miljoteknologi A/S, pg. 965   IT
Jac. O. Lyngaas & Co. A/S (Cornhill), Ovre Langgate 69,
  pg. 60   IT

Trollasen

Robert Bosch A/S, Postboks 10, pg. 205   IT
Orkla Foods AS, pg. 1011   IT
Raychem A/S, Trollaasveien 36, pg. 1362   PB

Tromso

Den norske Bank - Northern Norway, Commercial Banking,
  Gronnegt. 48, pg. 392   IT

Kvaerner Eureka, Tromso Division, pg. 767   IT
Kvaerner Fish Process Technology a.s - Kvaerner Kulde,
  Stakkevold, pg. 768   IT

Trondheim

Den norske Bank - Central Norway, Retail Banking,
  Veritsgt. 2, pg. 392   IT
FOKUS BANK A/S, Vestre Rosten 77, pg. 496   IT
Frionor Fabrikker A/S, Brattora, P.O. Box 2117,
  pg. 516   IT
Hewlett-Packard Norge A/S, Sluppenvn. 5, pg. 821   PB
Kvaerner Engineering, Trondheim, Nygata 6, pg. 766   IT
K/S Nedre Elvehavn Trondheim, pg. 41   IT
Nidar AS, pg. 1011   IT
Rishaug Maskin A/S, Postboks 1813, pg. 97   IT
Statoil, Research Centre, Sorskingsenter, pg. 1298   IT
TiMar Seafood A/S, Pirsenteret, pg. 1390   IT

Ulsteinvik

Kvaerner Kleven a.s., pg. 769   IT

Valderoy

Kvaerner Fodema a.s., Saetra, pg. 769   IT

Vennesla

Reber-Schindler Heis A/S, pg. 1205   IT

Verdal

Aker Verdal a.s., Oppland, pg. 42   IT

Vestby

A/S Mulva Grafiske Produkter, Stottumvejen 7, pg. 78   PB
Uni-Cardan Norge A/S, Postboks 40, pg. 536   IT

Vestre Gran

Swedcor A/S-Gran, Avd. Gran, pg. 1303   IT

Vika

Hydro Aluminium Vik Verk A/S, pg. 960   IT

Vikersund

Vikersund Trelast, pg. 965   IT

Voyenenga

Carmeda A/S, Ringeriksvn. 147, pg. 959   IT

Vraliosen

Skafsa Kraftverk I/S, pg. 961   IT

OMAN

Muscat

Circle Freight International LLC, pg. 372   PB
Imtac (Industrial Mgmt. Technology & Contracting), P.O.
  Box 51196, pg. 822   PB
C. Jayant Bros. (Oman) Co., pg. 108   IT
Jotun L.L.C., pg. 716   IT
Mitsui & Co., Ltd., Essaco Building, Bait-Al-Falaj St.,
  pg. 882   IT
Muscat (Overseas) Agriculture Co. LLC., 115 Madinat
  Qaboos, pg. 109   IT
Oman ORIX Leasing Saog, pg. 1009   IT
Petroleum Development Oman LLC, Mina al Fahal,
  pg. 1141   IT
Read-Mix Muscat LLC & Premix LLC, pg. 1092   IT
Reem Scientific & Energy Technologies LLC, Building No.
  1339, Way No. 9342, Waljat Street, pg. 109   IT
Shell Markets (Middle East) Ltd., Mina al Fahal,
  pg. 1141   IT
Telefonaktiebolaget LM Ericsson Technical Office Oman,
  Bait Al-Hanna, Al-Khuwait, pg. 1371   IT
Utell International-Oman, pg. 1098   IT

Ruwi

ANZ Grindlays Bank plc Oman, pg. 99   IT
Banque Dhofar Al-Omani Al-Fransi, Al Buri St., pg. 319   IT
Habib Bank Ltd., Central Branch, pg. 584   IT
Laing Oman LLC, P.O. Box 6006, pg. 797   IT
Omar International Development Co. (LLC) P.O. Box 5868,
  Shopping Centre, pg. 1359   IT
Power Development Company, pg. 1415   IT
Santa Fe Intl. Services Inc., P.O. Box 8404, pg. 765   IT
Standard Chartered Bank (Oman), pg. 1295   IT
Taylor Woodrow-Towell Co. (LLC), Dhofar House, Medinat
  Al Sultan Qaboos West, pg. 1360   IT
Wimpey Alawi LLC, P.O. Box 4436, pg. 1355   IT
Yahya Costain LLC, P.O. Box 5282, pg. 337   IT

PAKISTAN

Faisalabad

CPC Rafhan Ltd., pg. 224   PB
CPC Rufhan Limited, Rakh Canal East Road, pg. 225   PB

Islamabad

Ericsson Telecom AB, 61-A Saudi Park Towers, 2nd floor,
  Jinna Avenue, pg. 1367   IT
Mitsui & Co., Ltd., House No. 1-A, Street 56, Shalimar 6/4,
  pg. 881   IT
Pakistan Resident Mission, Overseas Pakistanis Foundation
  Bldg., pg. 89   IT
Panasian Marketing Services (Pvt) Limited, U.N. Boulevard,
  Diplomatic Enclave, G-5, pg. 1369   IT
Shell Company of Pakistan Ltd., House no. 4, Street 24,
  pg. 1140   IT
The World Bank, 20 A, Shahrah-e-Jamhuriat, Rama 5,
  pg. 1189   PV

Karachi

ANZ Grindlays Bank plc Pakistan, I.I. Chundrigar Rd.,
  pg. 99   IT
AST Research Inc. (Pakistan), 509 5th Floor Clifton Centre,
  Block 5, pg. 1182   IT
BASF Pakistan (Private) Limited, 46-A, Block 6,
  pg. 106   IT
BOC Pakistan Ltd., W. Wharf Rd.; P.O. Box 4845,
  pg. 122   IT
Bank of America NT&SA, Jubilee Insurance House, Ismail
  Ibrahim Chundrigar Rd., pg. 182   PB
Blackwood Hodge (Pakistan) Ltd., 19 W. Wharf Rd.,
  pg. 231   IT
The Burmah Oil Company (Pakistan Trading) Limited,
  P.I.D.C. House, Moulvi Tamizuddin Khan Rd.,
  pg. 235   IT
The Chase Manhattan Bank, N.A., Shaheen Commercial
  Complex, pg. 340   PB
CIBA-GEIGY (Pakistan) Limited, S-53, SITE, Hawksbay
  Road, pg. 978   IT
CIBA-GEIGY (Pakistan) Ltd., 15 West Wharf, pg. 978   IT
Continental Biscuits Limited, Mezzanine Fl., PIDC House,
  Dr. Ziauddin Ahmad Rd., pg. 380   IT
Daewoo Corp. - Karachi, 10th Floor, Sheheen Complex
  Bldg., pg. 358   IT
Det Norske Veritas, Bahria Complex, 24 M.T. Khan Rd.,
  pg. 398   IT
Deutsche Bank AG (Karachi), pg. 404   IT
Eastern Technological Services Pte. Ltd., New Block 111,
  Hockey Stadium, Liaquat Barracks, pg. 817   IT
Gestetner (Private) Limited, Ground Floor, P & D Plaza, I.I.
  Chundrigar Road, pg. 1115   IT
HABIB BANK LTD., Habib Bank Plaza, I-I Chundrigar Rd.,
  pg. 584   IT
Habib Bank Limited, Karachi Export Processing, Landhi
  Indus. Area Extension, pg. 584   IT
Habib Credit & Exchange Bank Ltd., I-I Chundrigar Rd.,
  pg. 584   IT
Johnson & Johnson Pakistan (Private) Ltd., pg. 931   PB
Kodak Pakistan Ltd., 4th Fl: Bahria Complex, Mavlvi
  Tamizuddin Khan Rd., pg. 554   PB
LASMO Oil Pakistan Limited, Sasi Arcade, No. BC5, Block
  No. 7, Clifton, pg. 804   IT
Lever Brothers Pakistan Ltd., Avari Plaza Fatiman, Jinnah
  Rd., 2nd Fl., pg. 1437   IT
Lipton Pakistan Ltd., pg. 1438   IT
Mackinnon Mackenzie & Co. of Pakistan (Private) Ltd.,
  Mackvolk Bldg., II Chundrigar Rd., pg. 1035   IT
Manhattan Pakistan (Private) Limited, Manhattan Center,
  6A/45 DCHS, Dr. Mahmood Hussain Rd., pg. 186   PV
Mitsui & Co., Ltd., 8th Fl. of Sheikh Sultan Trust Bldg. 10,
  pg. 881   IT
Mushko Electronics (Pvt) Limited, Oosman Chambers,
  Abdullah Haroon Rd., pg. 822   PB
NATIONAL BANK OF PAKISTAN, I.I. Chundrigar Rd.,
  pg. 907   IT
National Bank of Pakistan, Export Processing Zone,
  Offshore Banking Branch EPZ, pg. 908   IT
NATIONAL REFINERY LIMITED, P.O. Box 4557, 75530,
  pg. 909   IT
Novo Nordisk A/S, 113, Main Clifton Road, pg. 988   IT
Ora-Tech Systems (pvt.) Ltd., 8-9 Qamar House, M.A.
  Jinnah Rd., pg. 1228   PB
Organon Pakistan (Private) Limited, 39-K, Block 6,
  pg. 45   IT
ORIX Leasing Pakistan Limited, 3rd Floor, PIC Towers, 32-
  A, Lalazar Drive, pg. 1010   IT
Otsuka Pakistan Ltd., 30-B Sindhi Muslim Coop. Housing
  Society, pg. 1014   IT
PC World Pakistan/MICRO Publications, Lotia Building,
  First Floor, Club Road, pg. 570   PV
Pakistan Gum & Chemicals Ltd., pg. 1113   IT
Pakistan Gum Industries Limited, pg. 811   PB
PAKISTAN INTERNATIONAL AIRLINES CORPORATION,
  PIA Bldg., Karachi Airport, pg. 1021   IT
Parke-Davis & Company, Limited, B-2, S.I.T.E.,
  pg. 1739   PB
Pfizer Laboratories Limited, 12 Dockyard Rd., W.Wharf,
  pg. 1282   PB
Rhone-Poulenc Pakistan (Pvt.) Ltd., B-11, KDA Scheme n
  1, pg. 1113   IT
Roche Pakistan Ltd., pg. 1121   IT
Sandoz (Pakistan) Ltd., pg. 985   IT
Siemens Pakistan Engineering Co. Ltd., Ilaco House,
  Abdullah Haroon Rd., pg. 1247   IT

Sinochem Representative Office - Pakistan, No. 43/1 E(A) Block 6 P.E.C.H., Society, pg. 1256 **IT**
SmithKline & French Pakistan, Ltd., P.O. Box 157, pg. 1265 **IT**
SmithKline Beecham Pakistan (Private) Limited, P.O. Box 2802, pg. 1266 **IT**
Standard Chartered Bank (Pakistan), Box 4896, Ismail Ibrahim, pg. 1295 **IT**
Suzuki Motorcycles Pakistan Ltd., pg. 1323 **IT**
3M Pakistan (PVT) Ltd., Baria Comlex II, 1st Floor, Mt. Kahn Road, pg. 1607 **PB**
Toyota Motor Corporation, Karachi Liaison Office, 5th Fl., Shaheen Commerical, Complex, M.R. Kayani Rd., pg. 1413 **IT**
Wahedna/DMB&B, 239, Staff Lines, pg. 305 **PV**
Wellcome Pakistan Ltd, pg. 553 **IT**
Wyeth Laboratories (Pakistan) Ltd., Fifth Fl. Avari Plaza, Fatima Jinnah Rd., pg. 82 **PB**

Lahore

CPC Refhan Ltd., pg. 224 **PB**
The Chase Manhattan Bank, N.A., 70 Sharah-e-Quaid E-Azam, pg. 340 **IT**
Deutsche Bank AG (Lahore), Escourts House, 26 Davis Road, pg. 404 **IT**
Euroconsult Pakistan, 175 A Abu Baker Block, New Garden Town, pg. 606 **IT**
Jardine Fleming Pakistan Limited, 26-B Sarwar Rd., pg. 494 **IT**
KSB Pumps Co. Ltd., Lahore, pg. 721 **IT**
Milkpak Ltd., pg. 920 **IT**
Mitsui & Co., Ltd., 49-D-1, Gullberg 3, pg. 881 **IT**
Pakistan Mobile Communications (Pvt.) Ltd., Empire Center, 1st Floor, Main Blvd., Gullberg II, pg. 1140 **IT**
Techno-Commercial, 24 Farid Plaza/65,Shadman, pg. 550 **IT**

Sharae Faisal

Oxford University Press, 5 Bangalore Town, pg. 1019 **IT**

PANAMA

Colon

Bristol Laboratories International, S.A., Edificio 9 Y 27, Local 1, pg. 255 **PB**
CIBA-GEIGY Sociedad Anonima de Venta y Distribucion, Zona Libre de Colon, pg. 980 **IT**
Circle Freight International de Panama S.A., Colon Free Zone, pg. 372 **PB**
Daewoo International - Colon, P.O. Box 3018, pg. 358 **IT**
The International Commercial Bank of China, Calle 16 Colon Free Zone Local, Nr. 4 Edificio Nr. 49, pg. 683 **IT**
Pharmacia & Upjohn Company S.A., P.O. Box 536, pg. 1049 **IT**

El Dorado

Amway de Panama S.A., Apartado 6-4200, pg. 69 **PV**
Black & Decker International Corp., Via Espana Con Via Porras, pg. 234 **PB**

Final

Prisma Panama S.A., Calle 15 Rio Abajo, pg. 371 **IT**

Paitilla

Toyota Motor Corporation, Panama Representative Office, Edif, Bank of Tokyo, Piso #2, Via Espana y Calle, pg. 1413 **IT**

Panama

Aracruz Trading, P.O. Box 85116, pg. 78 **IT**
Aztec Trading Company, S.A., pg. 739 **PB**
BASF Panama S.A., Edificio Aero Peru, Calle 51 E., Campo Alegre, pg. 106 **IT**
Bamburi Tankers Holding (Nauru) Corp., 53rd Street-Urbanizacion Obarrio, pg. 789 **IT**
Banco do Brasil S.A.-Panama, Calle Elvira Mendez, 10, Edificio Interseco, pg. 141 **IT**
Bank Hapoalim (Panama City), Edificio Global, Intervalores 50, pg. 150 **IT**
Bank Leumi Le-Israel B.M., Grobman Bldg., Manuel Maria Icaza Street No. 10, pg. 158 **IT**
The Bank of Tokyo-Mitsubishi (Panama Branch), Apartado 1313, pg. 158 **IT**
Banque Nationale de Paris (Panama) SA, Edificio Omanco N 200 via Espana, pg. 164 **IT**
Canon Panama, S.A., Apartado 7022, pg. 263 **IT**
Cemex, S.A. de C.V. - Panama, Calzada Larga Chi Libre, pg. 278 **IT**
Centrobanco (Panama), S.A., Edificio Banco Central, Calles Samuel Lewis y Gerardo Ortega, pg. 140 **IT**
The Chase Manhattan Bank, N.A., Plaza Chase Headquarters, pg. 340 **PB**
Cia. Chiricana de Leche, S.A., pg. 159 **PV**
Cigna Compania de Seguros de Panama S.A., Torre Banco Union, Ave. Samuel Lewis, pg. 364 **PB**
Cigna Reaseguros, S.A., Ave. Samuel Lewis, pg. 364 **PB**
Citicorp International Bank S.A., Via Espana 124, pg. 378 **PB**
Citizen Latinamerica Corp., Balboa Avenue, Plaza Balboa, Commercial Center, Floor 4 Offices, pg. 294 **IT**

Colgate-Palmolive (Central America), Apartado 860, pg. 398 **PB**
Compania Internacional de Ventas, S.A., pg. 159 **PV**
Comunica Leo Burnett Panama, S.A., Edificio Global Bank, Calle 50, Piso 16, pg. 184 **PV**
Cosmeticos, S.A., Edificio A. J. Alfaroto, pg. 1436 **IT**
Daewoo International (Panama) S.A., Banco Exterior Piso 21, Avenida Balboa y Calle 43, pg. 358 **IT**
Dai-Ichi Kangyo Bank, Ltd.-Panama, Plaza Internacional, Via Espana, pg. 360 **IT**
Defover, S.A., Aquilino de la Guardia, 8, pg. 1224 **IT**
Delpanama S.A., C/O Arias, Fabrega Y Fabrega, pg. 364 **IT**
Det Norske Veritas, Edificio Sonesta, Apt. 13-B, Ave. Winston Churchill, pg. 397 **IT**
Dow Jones Markets (Panama) Inc., Apartado 83-0375, Zona 3, La Almeda, pg. 525 **PB**
Electronico Republica, S.A., Calle Samuel Lewis, pg. 817 **PB**
Empresas ICA Sociedad Controladora (Panama), Calle Primera, Nuevo Campo Alegre, pg. 454 **IT**
Financiera Bamerical S.A., Edificio Centro Transistmica Avenida Bol, pg. 183 **IT**
Foto Internacional, S.A., Centro Comercial Bal Harbour, Apdo. 55-0055 Punta Paitilla, pg. 817 **PB**
GO International South America, S.A., pg. 776 **PB**
Galp International Corporation, Calle Aguilino de la Guardia, No 8, pg. 1045 **IT**
Goldstar Panama S.A., pg. 779 **IT**
Griffith Panama S.A., via Argentina, Balmoral Bldg., 10th Flr., Apt. 10A, pg. 481 **PV**
Gulf Offshore Marine International, Inc., Eduardo Valdes, pg. 769 **PB**
Hapag-Lloyd International S.A., pg. 596 **IT**
The Industrial Bank of Japan, Limited (Panama), Swiss Bank Tower, 13th Floor, 53rd Street East, Urbanizacion Obarrio, pg. 675 **IT**
The International Commercial Bank of China, Edificio ICBC, No. 74, Calle 50, pg. 683 **IT**
Johnson & Johnson Panama S.A., P.O. Box 10569, pg. 931 **PB**
Kativo de Panama S.A., Via Simon Bolivar, Transistmica, pg. 687 **PB**
Kendall S.A., P.O. Box 55-0739 Paitilla, pg. 1648 **PB**
Kenwood Electronics Latin America S.A., Piso 6 Plaza, Chase C1, 47 y Aquilino de la Guardia, pg. 731 **IT**
Kimberly-Clark International, S.A., pg. 959 **PB**
Kodak Panama Limited, Via Israel No. 96, pg. 554 **PB**
Marpan One, Inc., c/o Arias, Fabrega & Fabrega, Bank of America Bldg., pg. 341 **IT**
Marpan Two, Inc., c/o Arias, Fabrega & Fabrega, Bank of America Bldg., pg. 341 **IT**
Mitsui & Co., (Panama International) S.A., Edificio Banco de Boston, Via Espana y C, pg. 882 **IT**
Monsanto Overseas, S.A., pg. 1126 **PB**
Moore International SA (Panama), pg. 890 **IT**
Nestle Caribbean, Inc., pg. 921 **IT**
Nestle Panama S.A., 1 Avenida 5a, No. 5-05, pg. 921 **IT**
Nissho Iwai Panama International S.A., Banco General Tower 14th Floor, 47 Street and Aquilino de la Guardia St., pg. 948 **IT**
Onyx Latinoamerica, Calle 61 Obarrio y Calle 50, pg. 822 **PB**
PC World Panama/Edicomouto, S.A., Urbanizacion Marbella, Calle 53 Este, pg. 570 **PV**
Panalpina S.A., pg. 1023 **IT**
Pfizer Corporation, Calle 41 Este Avenidas, Mexico Y Chile, Edificio Davivienda, pg. 1282 **PB**
Pfizer International Corporation, Calle 41 Este Avenidas Mexico Y Chile, pg. 1282 **PB**
Private Investment Co. for Asia S.A., Edificio Interseco, 3rd Fl., pg. 949 **IT**
Productos Roche Interamericana S.A., pg. 1121 **IT**
Productos Roche Panama S.A., pg. 1121 **IT**
Punto Aparte Publicidad, S.A., Ave. Samuel Lewis, Edificio Plaza Obarrio Piso 2, pg. 305 **PV**
Refineria Panama S.A., Apartado 3104, pg. 1584 **PB**
Rorer Panama S.A., Avenida Samuel Lewis y Calle 65 E, pg. 1112 **IT**
SKF Latintrade, Inc., Torre Banco Union, Piso No. 17, Ave. Samuel Lewis, pg. 1159 **IT**
SKF Panama Region, Torre Banco Union, 17th, Avenida Samuel Lewis, pg. 1159 **IT**
Sandoz Latinoamericana (Panama) S.A., pg. 985 **IT**
Schlumberger Overseas, S.A., Icaza, Gonzalez-Ruiz & Aleman, pg. 1439 **PB**
Schlumberger Surenco, S.A., Icaza, Gonzalez-Ruiz & Aleman, 8 Calle Aquilino de la Guardia, pg. 1439 **PB**
Sequridad Tecnica, S.A., Calle 38 #2-42, pg. 1731 **PB**
Sharp Electronics Corporation, Torre Global Bank, pg. 1229 **IT**
The Shell Company (WI) Ltd., Edificio Plaza Obarrio, Calle Samuel Lewis y Calle Santa Rita, pg. 1142 **IT**
Solusoft, Torre Swiss Bank, Piso 3, pg. 1228 **IT**
Sonitel S.A., Esq. Via Brasil y, Calle 1a C-Sur, Urbanizacion Obarrio, pg. 1370 **IT**
Sony Corporation of Panama, ViaSimon Bolivar, Zona 5, pg. 1284 **IT**
Sun Chemical de Panama, S.A., Apartado 6-896, pg. 397 **PB**
Swiss Bank Corporation (Overseas) S.A., Torre Swiss Bank, Calle 53 Este Marbella, pg. 1332 **IT**
TPA Latin America, Officina 701-702(7Piso) Calle, Aquilino de la Guardia y Calle 54, pg. 1406 **IT**
Tabacalera Istmena SA, Vie Fernandez de Cordoba, pg. 111 **IT**
Telefonaktiebolaget LM Ericsson Technical Office, Via Brazil, Edificio Julieta, Calle 1ra, pg. 1370 **IT**
Telequipos, S.A. Via Brazil Edificio Julieta, Calle 1ra, pg. 1371 **IT**
Texaco Panama Inc., Via Simon Bolivar, pg. 1584 **PB**

3M Panama S.A., Calle D Y Alberto Navarro, pg. 1607 **PB**
Toshiba de Panama, S.A., Officina 701-702(7 Piso) Calle, Aquilino de la Guardia y Calle 54, pg. 1406 **IT**
Union Bank of Switzerland (Panama) Inc., Edificio UBS, Calles 50 & 56, pg. 1441 **IT**
Wackenhut Internation (Panama), S.A., Icaza, Gonzalez Ruiz y Aleman, Edificio IGRA Piso 4 y 5, pg. 1731 **PB**
The Yokohama Rubber Co., Ltd., Edifico Banco Central, 4 Piso, Av. S, Lewis, Y Calle G Ortega, pg. 1521 **IT**

Punta Paitilla

Parfums Christian Dior de Panama S.A., pg. 783 **IT**

PAPUA NEW GUINEA

Bata

Promomar S.L., Apartado 133, pg. 304 **IT**
Promoport Guinea S.A., Puerto de Bata, pg. 304 **IT**

Boroko

Hastings Deering (PNG) Pty Ltd, P.O. Box 6308, pg. 1250 **IT**
Moore Business Systems Pty. Ltd., Waigini Drive Port Moresby, pg. 889 **IT**

Conakry

Banque Internationale pour L'Afrique en Guinee (BIAG), Boulevard du Commerce, pg. 548 **IT**
Banque Internationale pour le Commerce et l'Industrie de la Guinee (BICI-GUI), Avenue de la Republique, pg. 149 **IT**
Friguia, 9th Avenue, pg. 1030 **IT**
Shell Aviation Guinea, pg. 1136 **IT**
Societe Generale de Banques en Guinee, Avenue de la Republique, pg. 548 **IT**

Kimbe

Stettin Bay Lumber Co., Pty., Ltd., P.O. Box 162, pg. 949 **IT**

Kiunga

Ok Tedi Mining Limited, pg. 228 **IT**

Lae

BHP Steel Building Products Papua New Guinea Pty Ltd., Montoro Street, pg. 226 **IT**
BOC Gases Papua New Guinea Pty Ltd., pg. 121 **IT**
Dulux Papua New Guinea Pty Ltd, Aircorps Rd., pg. 664 **IT**
Nestle (PNG) Ltd., pg. 921 **IT**
Pacific Paints Pty Ltd., Aircorps Rd., pg. 665 **IT**

Madang

United Pacific Drilling P/L, Fikus St., pg. 666 **IT**

Port Moresby

Australia & New Zealand Banking Group (PNG) Limited, 2nd Floor, Defens Haus, Cnr. Champion Parade & Hunter St., pg. 100 **IT**
Helmerich & Payne Invest Ltd., Invesmen Haus, 6th Fl., No. 4, pg. 808 **PB**
Misima Mines Pty. Ltd., pg. 1060 **IT**
Mitsui & Co. (Australia), 8th Fl. A.N.G. House Hunter St., pg. 880 **IT**
Porgera Joint Venture, pg. 1060 **IT**
Port Moresby BHP Papua New Guinea, Pacific Place, Corner Musgrave & Champion, pg. 228 **IT**
Westpac Bank - PNG Limited, 5th. Flr., Mogoru Moto Bldg., Champion Parade, pg. 1497 **IT**
The Wrigley Company (P.N.G.) Pty. Ltd., pg. 1781 **PB**
Zurich Pacific Insurance Pty. Ltd., Cuthbertson House, 5th Fl., Cuthbertson Street, pg. 1532 **IT**

Rabaul

BHP-RMI Holdings Pty Ltd., Malaguna Road, pg. 226 **IT**

Tabubil

Ok Tedi Mining Limited, Dakon Road, pg. 228 **IT**

PARAGUAY

Asuncion

BASF Paraguaya S.R.L., Independencia Nacional No. 811, Esquina Fulgencio R. Moreno, Edificio El, pg. 107 **IT**
Banco de Asuncion, Calle Palma esquina a 14 de Mayo, pg. 140 **IT**
Banco do Brasil S.A.-Paraguay, Calle Oliva Y Nuestra, pg. 141 **IT**
Bilbao/Y&R, Pte. Franco esq. Nuestra, Sra. de la Asuncion, pg. 1200 **PV**
CIBA-GEIGY Services SA, Sucursal Paraguay, pg. 980 **IT**
El Chaco S.A. Financiera, pg. 379 **PB**

PB - *U.S. Public Companies Volume*
PV - *U.S. Private Companies Volume*
IT - *International Public & Private Companies Volume*

1733

Geographic Index-Non U.S.

La Rural del Paraguay S.A. , Paraguaya de Seguros, 15 de Agosto 608, pg. 1392 **IT**
Maizena, S.A., pg. 447 **PB**
MAPFRE Paraguay Cia de Seguros, S.A., Avda. Mariscal Lopez 910, pg. 333 **IT**
Mass Publicidad S.R.L., Estados Unidos 961, 3rd Floor, pg. 186 **PV**
Mitsui & Co., Ltd., Edificio Inter-Exp., Piso 16, Calle Luis, pg. 881 **IT**
Nivel Publicidad, Av. Mariscal Lopez 1851, pg. 389 **PV**
Senior Publicidad S.R.L., Celsa Speratti 3706, pg. 305 **PV**
Shell Paraguay Ltd., Calle Presidente Franco ESQ, Ayolas, Edificio Ayfra, pg. 1142 **IT**
Wackenhut Paraguay S.R.L., Nevy Quevedo 315, pg. 1732 **PB**

Ciudad del Este

Banco do Brasil S.A.-Paraguay, Calle Nanawa nr., pg. 141 **IT**

PERU

Callao

AGA S.A., pg. 13 **IT**
Alimentos y Productos de Maiz S.A., Av. Elmer Faucett 3825, pg. 447 **PB**
Kolana S.A., Omicron 218, pg. 81 **PB**
Prolansa S.A., Nestor Gambetta 6429, pg. 185 **IT**

Lauitus

Geosismo S.A., Raymondi 439, pg. 777 **PB**

Lima

Cia. AGA del Peru S.A., Casilla 2067, pg. 13 **IT**
Aceros Boehler Del Peru S.A., Luis Castro Ronceros No. 777, pg. 1471 **IT**
Adolphus S.A., Jiron Napo 126, pg. 549 **IT**
Ajinomoto del Peru S.A., Av Republica de Panama 2455, pg. 40 **IT**
Ajinomoto del Peru S.A., Plant, Av. Coronel Gambetta Km. 8, pg. 40 **IT**
Alfa-Laval S.A., Casilla 1083, pg. 1380 **IT**
ALICORP S.A., Chinchon 980, 12th Fl., pg. 57 **IT**
Ascensores Schindler del Peru S.A., pg. 1205 **IT**
Asea Brown Boveri Industrial S.A., Apartado 3846, pg. 3 **IT**
Asea Brown Boveri S.A., Apartado 2493, pg. 3 **IT**
Asea Brown Boveri S.A., pg. 7 **IT**
BASF Peruana S.A., Av. Oscar R. Benavides, No. 5915, Callao, pg. 107 **IT**
BCTS, German Schreiber 271, pg. 1043 **PB**
Banco Santander, Avenida Central 643, 2 B, pg. 144 **IT**
Banco Santander Peru, pg. 144 **IT**
Banque Paribas-Perou, Piso 9 - San Isidro, Avenida Central 643, pg. 320 **IT**
Barrick Gold Peru S.A., Avenida 28 de Julio, No. 1120, pg. 169 **IT**
Bayer Industrial S.A., Av. Bolivar 163-165, Piso 3, pg. 175 **IT**
Bayer Quimicas Unidas S.A., Av. Bolivar 165 Pueblo. Libre, pg. 175 **IT**
Bonifica-Peru, Malecon Costa Sur 240, pg. 655 **IT**
Brainco del Peru S.A., Avenida Larco 743, pg. 1030 **IT**
Bristol-Myers Peruana S.A., Av. Colonial 1560-1562, pg. 255 **PB**
CEPER-Conductores Electricos Peruanos S.A., Panamerican Norte Km 10,700, Apartado 23, pg. 1059 **IT**
CEPER-Conductores Electricos Peruanos S.A., Carretera Panamericana Nortekm. 18,200, pg. 1059 **IT**
Castrol del Peru SA, Camino Real III of 216, pg. 235 **IT**
Causa Publicidad, Parque Armendariz 159, pg. 184 **PV**
Christensen Diamond Products del Peru S.A., P.O. Box 5788, pg. 1174 **IT**
CIBA-GEIGY Peruana S.A., Apartado 3777, pg. 978 **IT**
Cominco (Peru) S.R.L., Calle Uno No. 873, pg. 307 **IT**
Compania de Petroleo Shell del Peru SA, Av Nicholas Arriola 740, pg. 1141 **IT**
Compania de Seguro Atlas S.A., Jr. Antonio Miro Quesada 191, pg. 90 **IT**
Compania Ericsson S.A., Av. Jorge Chavez No. 275, pg. 1365 **IT**
Compania Goodyear Del Peru, S.A., Avenida Argentina 6037, pg. 753 **PB**
Compania Peruana de Alimentos S.A., Avenida Paseo de la Republica, pg. 920 **IT**
Corporacion Electronica Metropolitana S.A., Av. Maquinarias 2460-2414, pg. 1192 **PV**
Creativity/Young & Rubicam Asociados, Victor Andres Belaunde 370, pg. 1200 **PV**
Crown Cork del Peru, S.A., Av Minerales 487, pg. 464 **PB**
Data General del Peru S.A., 80 Paseo de la Republica, pg. 486 **PB**
Dun & Bradstreet SA, Apt. 3571, Republica de Chile 388, pg. 537 **PB**
Edificios Aurora, pg. 61 **IT**
El Sol Compania de Seguros Generales, av. 28 de Julio n. 873, pg. 61 **IT**
Electrolux S.A., Casilla 1455, pg. 443 **IT**
Cia. Electromedica, S.A., Los Flamencos 145, Oficina 301/2, pg. 817 **IT**
Empresas ICA Sociedad Controladora (Peru), Av. Camino Real No. 390, pg. 454 **IT**
H.B. Fuller Peru, Km 10.9 Carretera Central, Sta. Clara, pg. 687 **PB**

GO Well Services, Inc., Ricardo Rivera Navarrate 765, pg. 776 **PB**
Gillette de Peru S.C., Las Begonias 441, Of. 502, pg. 744 **PB**
Gray Tool International, Inc., c/o Indasa S.C.R.L., Casilla Postal 657, pg. 6 **IT**
Humanasegur SA, Las Begonias 441 90 Piso, pg. 1502 **IT**
ICI (Peru) S.A., AV. Arequipa 660-7o Piso, pg. 665 **IT**
Industrial Minera SA, pg. 1323 **IT**
Industrias Pacocha S.A. (Unilever), Francisco Grana 155 La Victoria, pg. 1437 **IT**
International Wire Line Services, Inc., Ricardo Rivera, Navarrate 765, pg. 777 **IT**
Kilborn Peru S.A., Calle Morelli 181, Office 402, pg. 1162 **IT**
Kodak America, Ltda., Nicolas Arriola 480, pg. 554 **PB**
La Positiva, Compania Nacional de Seguros S.A., Esquina Javier Prado (Este), pg. 363 **PB**
Lucent Technologies del Peru S.A., Paseo de la Republica 3245, pg. 1018 **PB**
MSA cel Peru S.A., Los Telares 139, pg. 1115 **PB**
Mathieu Peru, Calle Daniel Hernandez 639, pg. 846 **IT**
Minera Sunshine Del Peru, S.A., Jr. Chinchon #901, 3er, y 4to, piso, pg. 1536 **IT**
Mitsui del Peru S.A., Avenida Central 717, 9 Piso, San Isidro, pg. 882 **IT**
Mobil Oil Del Peru (Compania Commercial) S.A., Apartadie 1272, pg. 1119 **IT**
Nestle Peru S.A., pg. 921 **IT**
Nissan Motor del Peru S.A., Av. Tomas Valle No. 601, pg. 945 **IT**
Olivetti Peruana S.A., Calle Las Camelias 750, pg. 1003 **IT**
Outokumpu Tecnica Peru S.A., pg. 1017 **IT**
Panalpina Transportes Mundiales S.A., pg. 1023 **IT**
Park Advertising & Direct Marketing, Santa Isabel 194, pg. 389 **PV**
Peruana de Seguridad y Vigilancia, S.A. (Pesevisa), Avenida Arequipa 4856, pg. 1731 **PB**
Petrodata S.A., Ricardo Rivera, Navarrate 765, pg. 777 **IT**
Pfizer S.A., Av. Paseo de la Republica, No. 3074, 7th Fl., Piso, pg. 1282 **PB**
Pharmacia & Upjohn Inter-American Corporation-Peru, Natalio Sanchez 220-1202, pg. 1048 **IT**
Pragma/DMB&B, Avenida Salaverry 3328, pg. 305 **PV**
Procte & Gamble of Peru, Av. Pardo y Alliaga 695, pg. 1332 **PB**
Productos Avon, S.A., Apartado Postal 9-01-3, pg. 156 **PB**
Productos Roche Quimica Farmaceutica S.A., pg. 1121 **IT**
Quorum Publicidad, Parque Guatemala 165, San Isidro, pg. 1422 **PV**
Refineria de Cajamarquilla, Carretera Central, Altura Km 9.5, pg. 308 **IT**
SKF del Peru S.A., Av. Nicolas Arriola 654, pg. 1158 **IT**
Sandoz Peru S.A., pg. 985 **IT**
Sandvik del Peru S.A., Casilla 6183, pg. 1188 **IT**
Scania-Vabis del Peru S.A., Casilla 3190, pg. 687 **IT**
Servicios Avanzados De Metodos Y Sistemas, S.A. (Sams), Avenida Republica de Panama 3534, pg. 823 **PB**
Servicios Expeciales de Edicion, A. Miro Quesada 247-702, pg. 570 **PV**
Smithkline & French Inter-American Corp., Apartado 5242, Las Flores #334, pg. 1265 **IT**
Sociedad Minera La Granja S.A., Av. Jose Casimiro Ulloa #312, pg. 253 **IT**
Standard Chartered Bank (Peru), Francisco Masias 370, Piso 13, Edificio La Positiva, pg. 1295 **IT**
Sulzer del Peru S.A., pg. 1306 **IT**
Svedala Fima, pg. 1324 **IT**
Swiss Bank Corporation (Overseas) S.A., Camino Real 348, Edificio Torre el Pilar, pg. 1330 **IT**
TVX Minera del Peru S.A., Av. Jose Galvez, pg. 1345 **IT**
Tamrock EJC Ltd., Sucirsal del Peru, pg. 1353 **IT**
3M Peru S.A., Av. Canaval y Moreyra 641, pg. 1607 **PB**
Toyota del Peru S.A., Edificio del Banco Continental, Av. Republica de Panama 3055, pg. 1414 **IT**
Utell International-Peru, Bolognesi #599, pg. 1098 **IT**
Volvo del Peru S.A., Casilla 815, pg. 1477 **IT**
Volvo Distribuidora S.A., Casilla 815, pg. 1477 **IT**
Volvo Penta Latinoamerica S.A., Casilla 815, pg. 1478 **IT**
Willis Faber & Dumas Ltd., Ricardo Rivera Navarrete 765, Of. 52 San Isidro, pg. 1510 **IT**
Xerox del Peru, S.A., Ave. Canaval Morey Ra 562, pg. 1785 **PB**

San Isidro

Banco do Brasil S.A.-San Isidro Representative Office, Av. Camino Real 348-Torre El Pilar, pg. 142 **IT**
Gestetner S.A., Javier Prado Oeste 1358, pg. 1115 **IT**

PHILIPPINES

Aroroy

Masbate Gold Operation, pg. 95 **IT**

Bacolod

Mitsui & Co., Ltd., Rm. 5-6, Virgen San Barangay Bldg., Lacs, pg. 880 **IT**

Bago

Distileria Bago, Inc. (DBI), pg. 785 **IT**

Baguio

BMC Forestry Corporation, Wagner Rd., pg. 186 **IT**

Moog Controls Corp., Philippine Branch, BCEPZ Loakan Rd., pg. 1128 **PB**

Batangas

EEI-Construction Fabrication Shop, Bo. Sta. Maria, pg. 426 **IT**

Binan Laguna

Middleby Philippines Corporation, 113 Technology Avenue, pg. 1110 **PB**

Bulacan

Arrow Freight Corporation, Santiago St., Veinte Reales, pg. 186 **IT**

Cabuyao

Nestle Philippines, Inc., pg. 921 **IT**

Cainta

Philippine Automotive Manufacturing Corporation, Ortigas Avenue Extension, pg. 876 **IT**

Cavite

Clarion Manufacturing Corporation of the Philippines, Phase II Block 7, Cavite Export Processing Zone, pg. 296 **IT**
Clarion-Mitsuwa Philippines, Inc., Phase II Block 7, Cavite Export Processing Zone, pg. 296 **IT**
Pulse Engineering-Philippines, pg. 1564 **PB**
Rohm Electronics Philippines, Inc., People's Technology Complex, pg. 1125 **IT**
Rohm Electronics (Philippines) Sales Corporation, People's Technology Complex, pg. 1125 **IT**
Rohm Mechatech Philippines, Inc., People's Technology Complex, pg. 1125 **IT**

Cebu

Cebu Mining Operation, pg. 95 **IT**
EEI-Machinery Division (Cebu Regional Office), 103104 Orient Bldg., pg. 426 **IT**
NEC Technologies Philippines, Inc., Philippine Economic Zone, Mactan Export Processing Zone, pg. 900 **IT**
Pilmico, P.O. Box 318 183 Osmena Blvd., pg. 411 **IT**

Davao

Davao Central Chemical Corporation, Bunawan, pg. 1350 **IT**
Philippine Cocoa Estates Corporation, Upper Catitipan, pg. 187 **IT**

Laguna

Benguet Ebara Real Estate Corp., Terelay Phase, Canlubang Industrial Estate, pg. 187 **IT**
CIBA-GEIGY (Philippines) Inc, Silangang Canlubang Industrial Park 1, pg. 978 **IT**
Ebara-Benguet, Inc., Terelay Phase, Canlubang Industrial Estate, pg. 187 **IT**
Fuji Electric Philippines, Inc., Carmelray Industrial Park, Canlubang, pg. 522 **IT**
Nippon Paint (Philippines) Inc., Kologram Street, Light Industry & Science Park, pg. 937 **IT**
Read-Rite (Philippines), Inc., Lots 5, 6 & 7, pg. 1367 **PB**
Toyota Autoparts Philippines Inc., Barangay Pulong, pg. 1413 **IT**

Legaspi

Induplex, Inc., pg. 904 **PV**

Libis

Kao (Philippines) Inc., 108-A E. Rodriguez, Jr. Ave., pg. 718 **IT**
Pilipinas Kao Inc., 108-A E. Rodriguez, Jr. Ave., pg. 718 **IT**

Makati

ACI Systems, Inc., 4th Floor, Majalco Building, Benavidez cor. Trasierra Sts., pg. 242 **IT**
Amway Philippines, 23rd Floor, Multinational Bancorporation Centre, pg. 70 **PV**
Asahi Bank Manila Representative Office, 26th Floor, Citibank Tower, 8741 Paseo de Roxas, pg. 83 **IT**
Digital Equipment Filipinas Inc., 18/F Citibank Tower, Valero corner Villar Streets, pg. 508 **PB**
ECI Telecom (Philippines) Ltd., Country Space 1 Condo Corp., 4th/F Unit B Sen. Gil Puyat Ave. Ext., pg. 643 **IT**
Imation Philippines Representative Office, Ste. 1603 Cityland, Condominium 10., Tower 1, pg. 870 **PB**
The International Commercial Bank of China, 3rd Floor, Pacific Star Bldg., Sen. Gil Puyat Avenue Cor., pg. 683 **IT**
KPI Elevators, Inc., Suite 903, King's Court 1, 2129 Pasong Tamo Corner dela, pg. 747 **IT**
Mabuhay Philippines Satellite Corp., 22/F Rufino Pacific Tower, 6784 Ayala Avenue, pg. 1051 **IT**

PB - *U.S. Public Companies Volume*
PV - *U.S. Private Companies Volume*
IT - *International Public & Private Companies Volume*

Malayan Zurich Insurance Company, Inc., Grepalife Bldg., 2nd. Floor, 221, Sen. Gil J. Puyat Ave., pg. 1532　**IT**
Nippon Life Insurance Company of the Philippines, Inc., Citibank Twr., Citibank Plaza, 21st Fl., 8741 Paseo de Roxas, pg. 936　**IT**
Obayashi Corporation-Manila, 7th Floor, Corinthian Plaza, 121 Paseo do Roxas, pg. 995　**IT**
Obayashi Philippines Corporation, 7th Floor, Corinthian Plaza, 121 Paseo de Roxas, pg. 996　**IT**
Pfizer, Inc., 14F Citibank Tower, 8742 Paseo de Roxas, pg. 1282　**PB**
Rizal Commercial Banking Corporation, 333 Sen Gil Puyat Avenue Extension, pg. 1190　**IT**
Sealed Air Philippines, Inc., 23/F Unit D Trafalgar Plaza, H.V. Dela Costa Street, Sakedo Village, pg. 1451　**PB**
Standard Chartered Bank (Philippines), Bankmer Building, 6756 Ayala Ave., pg. 1295　**IT**
Summa Kumagai Inc., 7th Floor, Sage House, 110 Herrera Street, pg. 764　**IT**

Manila

AEA Development Corp., pg. 447　**PB**
AGP INDUSTRIAL CORPORATION, 6760 Ayala Ave., pg. 14　**IT**
AMP Phillippines Inc., 4th Fl., Kings Court, 2129 Pasong Tamo St., pg. 9　**IT**
AVC Chemical Corporation, 7th Fl., Padilla Bldg., Emerald Avenue, pg. 689　**IT**
Alamag Processing Corporation, pg. 174　**IT**
Allegro MicroSystems Philippines, Inc., Marimar Village, Sampaguita St., pg. 1188　**IT**
Allergan Div., P.O. Box 229 MCC, pg. 1265　**IT**
Allied Thread Co. Inc., Maybunga Pasig, pg. 299　**IT**
Alsons Cement Corporation, Alson Building, 2286 Pasong Tamo Extension, pg. 629　**IT**
Analog Devices (PHILS), Inc., Km.-14 Edison Ave., South Expressway, pg. 108　**PB**
Analytical Technology & Research Corporation, Room 201 Accra Bldg., Salcedo Cor., Gamboa St., pg. 816　**IT**
APEX Motor Mfg. Corp., Shaw Blvd. Corner Oranbo Dr., pg. 947　**IT**
Asea Brown Boveri Inc., pg. 8　**IT**
ASIAN DEVELOPMENT BANK, Six ADB Ave., Mandaluyong, pg. 88　**IT**
Asian Transmission Corp., P.O. Box 371, Makati Central, pg. 947　**IT**
Astra Pharmaceuticals (Philippines) Inc., P.O. Box 7689, Domestic Airport Post Office, pg. 94　**IT**
Atkinson Construction, Unit #1404E, Tektite Towers 1, PSE Centre Exchange Road, Ortigas Center, pg. 143　**PB**
Atlas Cement Corporation, Kalayaan Bldg., 164 Salcedo St., pg. 475　**IT**
ATLAS CONSOLIDATED MINING & DEVELOPMENT CORPORATION, 2/F Phelps Dodge Annex 6, 2 Pioneer St., pg. 95　**IT**
Australia & New Zealand Banking Group Limited Philippines, 6th Floor, Salustiana Dee Ty, Tower, 104 Paseo de Roxas, Cnr Perea St., pg. 99　**IT**
Avia EURO RSCG, 3/F Metro House Bldg., 345 Sen. Gil J. Puyat Ave., pg. 602　**IT**
Avon Products Manufacturing, Inc., MIA-ADC 3120, P.O. Box 7593, pg. 156　**PB**
BASF Coatings & Inks Philippines, Inc., 101 Marcos Alvarez Avenue, Talon, pg. 105　**IT**
BASF Philippines, Inc., Emerald Bldg., 14 Emerald Ave., Ortigas Center, pg. 107　**IT**
BHP Trading Philippines Inc., Unit C, 9th Floor, ACT Tower, 135 Sen Gil J. Puvat Avenue, pg. 227　**IT**
BT Brokerage (Philippines) Inc., 12 /F Pacific Star Bldg., pg. 185　**PB**
Ballast Nedam International B.V.-Philippine Branch, 16F, One Magnificent Mile Building, pg. 134　**IT**
Banco Santander, 24th Floor, 6750 Ayala Avenue, pg. 144　**IT**
Banco Santander Philippines Ltd., 6750 Ayala Ave., pg. 144　**IT**
Bank of America NT&SA, 2/F BA Lepanto Bldg., 8747 Paseo de Roxas, pg. 182　**PB**
Bank of Boston of the Philippines, Boston Bank Center, 23rd Floor, 6750 Ayala Ave., pg. 184　**PB**
The Bank of New York, 15th Fl., China Bank Bldg., Paseo de Roxas, pg. 179　**PB**
Bankers Trust New York Corporation, Corinthian Plz. 3rd. Fl., 121 Paseo de Roxas, Legaspi Village, pg. 186　**PB**
Banque Paribas-Philipines, 5th Floor, APMC Bldg., 136 Amorsolo St., c/o UNEFICO, pg. 320　**IT**
Barclays Bank PLC, pg. 165　**IT**
Bataan Optical Inc., Singapore Airlines Bldg., 8th, pg. 462　**IT**
Bayer Philippines, Inc., 3rd. Fl., Equitable Bank Bldg., Ortigas Ave. Greenhill, pg. 175　**IT**
BENGUET CORPORATION, Benguet Centre, 12 ADB Avenue, pg. 186　**IT**
Benguet Ebara Real Estate Corporation, 10th Fl, Sage House, 110 Herrera St., pg. 432　**IT**
Benguet Management Corporation, 391 J. P. Rizal St., pg. 186　**IT**
Block Drug Co. (Philippines) Inc., Central Post Office, (Marsman, Bldg.), pg. 237　**PB**
Boart Longyear Inc., pg. 76　**IT**
Boie-Takeda Chemicals, Inc., 3rd Fl., King's Court II Bldg., 2129 Pasong Tamo St., pg. 1350　**IT**
Borden Intl. Philippines, Inc., Filipinas Life Bldg., 10th Fl., Ayala Ave., pg. 159　**PV**
Bristol Laboratories (Philippines), Inc., 2309 Pasong Tamo, pg. 255　**PB**
California Manufacturing Co., Inc., Las Pinas Plant, Barrio Talon, pg. 41　**IT**

California Mfg. Co., Inc., Km. 18 East Service Rd., pg. 225　**PB**
Capital international CDPQ - Manila, 22/F, PCI Bank Tower II, Makati Ave. Cor. H.V. de la Costa St., pg. 249　**IT**
The Chase Manhattan Bank, N.A., 15/F Pacific Star Bldg., Makati & Se. Gil J. Puyat Ave., pg. 340　**PB**
Chemo-Technische Manufacturing, Inc., 8531 West Service Rd., km 14, pg. 1490　**IT**
CIBA-GEIGY (Philippines) Inc., Asian Reinsurance Bldg., Corner Gamboa & Salcedo Sts., pg. 978　**IT**
Circle Freight International (Philippines) Ltd., Ninoy Aquino Ave., Cor. Barrio Ibayo, pg. 373　**PB**
City Trust Banking Corp., pg. 379　**PB**
Colgate-Palmolive Philippines Inc., 1049 J.P. Rizal Ave., pg. 398　**IT**
Columbia Pictures International Television, Room 307, President Lines Bldg., pg. 1282　**PB**
Consolidated Industrial Gases Inc., CIGI Building, Sheridan St., pg. 122　**IT**
Consolidated Industrial Gases, Inc., CIGI Bldg., Sheridan Cor Pioneer St., pg. 817　**PB**
Consolidated ORIX Leasing and Finance Corporation, 19th Fl., Solidbank Bldg., 777 Paseo de Roxas, pg. 1009　**IT**
Cyanamid Philippines, Inc., Makati Commercial Center, pg. 81　**PB**
DBP - Daiwa Securities (Philippines), Inc., 18th Fl., Citibank Tower, 8741 Paseo de Rexas, pg. 375　**IT**
DBS Securities Philippines, Inc., 11/F Sage House, 110 Herrera Street, pg. 351　**IT**
Dainippon Ink & Chemicals, Inc., Room 1402, Sage House, 110 Herrera Street, pg. 372　**IT**
Davao Union Cement Corporation, Phimna Bldg., 166 Salcedo St., pg. 475　**IT**
Dentsply Philippines, Trans-Phil House 3-F, 1177 Pasong Tamo, col. Bagitkan Flr., pg. 500　**PB**
Dentsu Young & Rubicam-Alcantara Inc. (Manila), 704 Pablo Ocampo Sr. St., pg. 325　**PV**
Det Norske Veritas, G-5, Velco Center, Myers Bldg., pg. 397　**IT**
Deutsche Bank AG (Manila), 17/f BPI Paseo de Roxas Condominium, pg. 404　**IT**
Dumez GTM, Expocrafts Building, 1008 Metropolitan Avenue, pg. 823　**IT**
EEI-Construction Div., #12 Manggahan St., Brgy. Bagumbayan, Libis, pg. 426　**IT**
EEI CORPORATION, Felina Building, 188 E. Rodriguez Jr. Ave., pg. 425　**IT**
EEI Limited, 188 E. Rodriguez Jr. Ave. Bgy., pg. 426　**IT**
EEI-Machinery Division, 186 E. Rodriguez Jr. Ave., pg. 426　**IT**
EEI-Marine Corp., 12 Manggahan St., pg. 426　**IT**
EEI Power Corp., 188 E. Rodriguez Jr. Ave., pg. 426　**IT**
EEI-TOEI Animation Corporation, 128 West Ave., pg. 426　**IT**
Elan Pharma Philippines, Inc., 9th Fl., Country Space 1, Sen. Gil J. Puyat Ave. Ext., pg. 436　**IT**
Elasco International Corp., 4514 Casind St. Palanan, pg. 361　**PV**
Electrolux Philippines, Inc., Electrolux Bldg. East Cloverleaf Bldg., pg. 443　**IT**
Equipment Engineers, Inc., 188 E. Rodriguez Jr. Ave., pg. 426　**IT**
Ericsson Networks, Inc., 7th Fl., Sterling Centre, De La Rosa cor. Esteban St., pg. 1367　**IT**
Ericsson Telecommunications, Inc., 3rd floor, Goodwill Building, 393 Sen. Gil J. Puyat Ave., pg. 1367　**IT**
Evenflo, 3/F, Done Narcisa Bldg., 8751 Paseo de Roxas, pg. 630　**PV**
Exchange Capital Corporation, 151 aseo de Roxas, 3rd Floor Corporate Business Centre, pg. 493　**IT**
Fanuc Philippines Corporation, 2nd Floor, United Life Building, pg. 478　**IT**
Far East Bank and Trust Company, Far East Bank Center, Senator Gil Puyat Avenue, pg. 1180　**IT**
Filipinas-Iseki Corp., Diamond Motors Bldg., No.44, Bonnie Seranno St., pg. 947　**IT**
First Brands Philippines, 622 Shaw Blvd., pg. 627　**PB**
First Nationwide Assurance Corporation, Yuchengco Bldg., 484 Q. Paredes St., pg. 1532　**IT**
First Philippine Industrial Corp., Producers Bank Centre, 8737 Paseo De Roxas, pg. 1140　**IT**
Fluor Daniel Pacific, Inc., 9th Fl., Pacific Star Bldg., Makati Avenue, pg. 660　**IT**
Food Ingredients (Phillipines) Inc., pg. 606　**IT**
H.B. Fuller (Philippines) Inc., KM 18 Barrio Talon, Las Pinas, pg. 687　**PB**
General Electric Philippines Inc., 2291 Pasong Tamo Ext., pg. 713　**PB**
Gillette (Philippines), Inc., Villonco Rd., Bo., San Dionisio, Sucat, pg. 745　**IT**
Goldstar Collins Phils Inc., Francisco Legaspi Street No. 15 BO, pg. 779　**IT**
Goldstar Phils. Sales Co., Ltd., No. 167 Edsa. Collins Bldg., pg. 779　**IT**
Goodyear Philippines Inc., 790 Pasay Road, pg. 753　**PB**
Goulds Pumps (Phil.) Inc., pg. 861　**PB**
Gray Tool International, Inc., c/o Medcophil Services, Raha, Sulayman Bldg. 7th Fl., pg. 6　**IT**
Griffith Laboratories (Phils.) Inc., Building No. 2, Honeydew Rd., pg. 481　**PV**
Gulf Asia International Corporation, 99 E. Rodriguez Ave., pg. 426　**IT**
Gulf Asia Travel Corporation, Hanston Bldg., Emerald Ave., pg. 426　**IT**
HSBC James Capel Securities (Philippines), Inc., 13/F, Royal Match Building, 6780 Ayala Avenue, pg. 582　**IT**
Hemisphere-Leo Burnett, Inc., Planters Products Inc., 2nd Fl., Esteban St., pg. 184　**PV**
Henkel Philippines Inc., pg. 614　**PV**
Herbalife International Philippines, 2301 Pasong Tamo Ext., pg. 809　**PB**

The Hi-Daiei Trading Co., Ltd., R.M. 209/2 Flr.Cityland Condo, 10 Tower 2, 6817 H.V. Delacosta St., pg. 364　**IT**
Hi-Eisai Pharmaceuticals, Inc., 4th Fl., Reliable Bldg., 7230 Maleegarg St., pg. 435　**IT**
IBM Philippines, Incorporated, pg. 897　**PB**
ICI (Philippines) Inc., 3rd Fl. Corinthian Plaza, 121 Paseo de Roxas, pg. 665　**IT**
Iligan Cement Corporation, 3rd Floor, Alson Building, 2286 Pasong Tamo Extension, pg. 629　**IT**
Ingersoll-Rand Philippines, Inc., MCPO 1299, pg. 878　**PB**
Intercon Garments Inc., 1231 MCC P.O. Box 158, pg. 1434　**IT**
The International Commercial Bank of China, 277 Edsa, Balintawak, pg. 683　**IT**
International Distillers Philippines, 2306 Kayamanan C, Pasong Tamo Extension, pg. 410　**IT**
International Flavors & Fragrances (Philippines) Inc., Unit No. 9, First Avemue, Bo. Bagong Bayan, pg. 899　**PB**
Investors' Finance Corp., pg. 379　**PB**
Isuzu Pilipinas Corporation, Penafrancia Ext. Paco, pg. 693　**IT**
Japan Airlines Company, Ltd., Hotel Nikko Manila Garden, Ayala Center, pg. 701　**IT**
Jardine Davies Inc., Jardine Davies Bldg., 222 Sen. Gil J. Puyat Ave., pg. 705　**IT**
Jardine Fleming Exchange Capital Securities Inc., 2nd Fl., Corp. Business Ctr., 151 Paseo de Roxas, pg. 494　**IT**
Jimenez/DMB&B, 23rd Fl., Pacific Star Bldg., Sen. Gil J. Puyat Ave. Corner, pg. 304　**PV**
Johnson & Johnson Medical (Philippines), Inc., P.O. Box 2007, pg. 931　**PB**
Johnson & Johnson (Philippines) Inc., P.O. Box 2007, pg. 931　**PB**
S.C. Johnson & Son, Inc., pg. 593　**PV**
KENG HUA PAPER PRODUCTS CO., INC., 516 Neuva St., pg. 729　**IT**
Keppel FELS Energy Incorporated, 2nd Floor, Benguel Center, #12 ADB Avenue, pg. 731　**IT**
Kim Eng Securities Philippines Inc., Unit 506, Plaza Tower 1, Ayala Triangle, pg. 733　**IT**
Kimberly-Clark Philippines Inc., P.O. Box 1467, pg. 959　**PB**
Kodak Philippines Ltd., 2247 Pasong Tamo Ext., pg. 554　**PB**
Kraft Foods Inc., pg. 1290　**PB**
Krupp Maschinentechnik GmbH, 5/f, Sterling Center, Dela Rosa Corner, Esteban Sts., pg. 510　**IT**
Kvaerner Shipping Manila, Representative Office, Suite 300, Velco Center, 13th Corner Chicago Street, pg. 772　**IT**
LA TONDENA DISTILLERS, INC., Don Carlos Palanca Bldg., 453 Carlos Palanca Sr. St., pg. 785　**IT**
Eli Lilly (Philippines), Incorporated, Dona Narcisa Bldg., 8751 Paseo de Roxas St., pg. 994　**IT**
MHI Technical Services Corporation (MTS), 11th Floor, Producer's Bank, Building, 8737 Paseo de Roxas, pg. 874　**IT**
Malayan Insurance Company, Inc., Yuchengco Tower, 500 Q. Paredes St., pg. 1484　**IT**
Manila Mandarin Hotel Incorporated, Makati Avenue, pg. 704　**IT**
Manulife - Philippines Branch, Manulife Centre, Tordesillas Cor. Gallerdo, pg. 841　**IT**
Marketforce Advertising Philippines Inc., 704 Pablo Ocampo Sr. Street, pg. 325　**PV**
Mead Johnson Philippines, Inc., Commercial Center, 2309 Pasong Tamo Ext., pg. 256　**PB**
Microsoft Philippines, Inc., pg. 1108　**PB**
Millworks Industries, Inc., Country Space 1 Bldg., 3rd Floor, Unit 3-C, pg. 1347　**IT**
Minebea Technologies Pte. Ltd. - Manila Branch, 1601, 1 Magnificent Mile Bldg., San Miguel Avenue, pg. 869　**IT**
Mitsui & Co., Ltd., 17th Fl., Citibank Center Bldg., pg. 880　**IT**
Mobil Philippines, Inc., P.O. Box 246, pg. 1119　**PB**
Monarch Insurance Company, Monarch Bldg., 101 Herrera/ De La Rosa St., pg. 363　**PB**
Monsanto Philippines Inc., Comm. Center, pg. 1126　**PB**
Morgan Guaranty Trust Company, Ayala Ave. & Paseo de Roxas, pg. 1130　**PB**
Motorola Philippines Inc., KM 17 South Super Highway, pg. 1140　**IT**
NYK-Manila, TDG-NYK Harbor Center, Rairoad Corner 23rd & 24th Streets, pg. 941　**IT**
Nalco Chemical Co. (Philippines), Inc., Bankmer Bldg., 8th Fl., 6756 Ayala Ave., pg. 1150　**PB**
Nokia Mobile Phones, 24th Floor, 6750 Ayala Avenue, pg. 952　**IT**
Nokia Telecommunications (Philippines) Inc., 24th Floor, 6750 Ayala Avenue, pg. 954　**IT**
Norsk Hydro Philippines Inc., Suite 102, Gammon House, 110 Rada St., pg. 964　**IT**
Online Advanced Systems Corp., 2nd Fl., Electra House, 115-117 Esteban St., pg. 822　**IT**
Oracle Systems (Philippines) Inc., 5/F, The Athenaeum Bldg., 160 Alfaro St., pg. 1228　**PB**
Orient Leaf Tobacco Co., Ltd., Manila International Airport, pg. 1695　**IT**
Pan-Malayan Insurance Corporation, 6th & 7th Fls., Y Tower II, Alfaro Cor. Gallardo St., pg. 1392　**IT**
Parsons International Inc., P.O. Box 2188, pg. 842　**PV**
Pasco-Certeza Computer Mapping Corporation, pg. 1024　**IT**
Pechiney Philippines Inc., Room 306, ITC Building, 337 Sen Gil Puyat Avenue, pg. 1031　**IT**
Pepsi-Cola Far East Trade Development Co., Inc., pg. 1277　**PB**
Petrofields Exploration & Development Co., Inc., 7th Floor, JMT Bldg., ADB Ave., Ortigas Ctr., pg. 187　**IT**
PHILAM Life Holding Co., P.O. Box 1152, pg. 85　**IT**
PHILIPPINE AIRLINES, INC., Allied Bank Ctr., Ayala Ave., pg. 1050　**IT**

PB - *U.S. Public Companies Volume*
PV - *U.S. Private Companies Volume*
IT - *International Public & Private Companies Volume*

The Philippine American Accident Insurance Co., Inc., 4th Fl., Philamlife Bldg., U.N. Ave. Ermita, pg. 85 **PB**
The Philippine American Management & Financing Co., Inc., 4th Fl., Philamlife Bldg., U.N. Ave. Ermita, pg. 85 **PB**
Philippine Geothermal Incorporated, 15/F Pacific Star Bldg., Sen. Gil Puyat Ave., pg. 1698 **IT**
PHILIPPINE LONG DISTANCE TELEPHONE COMPANY, Ramon Cojuangco Bldg., Makati Ave., pg. 1051 **IT**
Philippine Refining Company Inc., pg. 1438 **IT**
Philippine Sunsystems Products, Inc., 2nd Floor Union Bank Bldg. II, 843 Pasay Road, pg. 1531 **PB**
Philippine Wacoal Corp., 5F, Centro Bldg. No. 180, Saleedo St., pg. 1484 **IT**
The Philippines American Assurance Co., Inc., 4th Fl., Philamlife Bldg., U.N. Ave. Ermita, pg. 85 **PB**
Philippines Dairy Products Corp., 5th Level, OAC Building, San Miguel Avenue, pg. 923 **IT**
Philippines Explosives Corporation, 7th Fl., Citytrust Bldg., Mandaluyong, pg. 665 **IT**
Philnet Ericsson Inc., 7th Fl., Sterling Centre, De La Rosa cor. Esteban St., pg. 1369 **IT**
Pilipinas Makro Inc., 9F Merchants Center, pg. 1156 **IT**
Pilipinas Shell Petroleum Corporation, Shell House, 156 Valero St., Salcedo Village, pg. 1140 **IT**
Plant Design & Management Corp., 188 E. Rodriguez Jr. Ave., pg. 426 **IT**
Procter & Gamble Philippines Inc., 777 Paseo de Roxas, pg. 1332 **PB**
Raco Trading Phils., Inc., Mezzanine, Jaka 1 Bldg., 6794 Ayala Ave., pg. 303 **IT**
Reynolds Philippine Corporation, 11th Fl., Combank Bldg., Ayala Ave., pg. 1387 **PB**
Rhone-Poulenc Philippines Inc., 3rd Floor-Gammon House, Legaspi Village, 110 Rada St., pg. 1113 **IT**
Rhone-Poulenc Rorer Philippines Inc., 3/F Gammon House, 110 Rada St., pg. 1111 **IT**
Right Computer Systems, 118 Perea St., Legaspi Village, pg. 1043 **PB**
RIO-TUBA Nickel Mining Corp., 2nd Fl., Solid Mills Bldg., De La Rosa St.,Mills Bldg., pg. 949 **IT**
Roche (Philippines) Inc., 2252 Don Chino, Rocas Ave., pg. 1121 **IT**
Rohm & Haas Philippines, Inc., 19th Fl., Metrobank Plaza, G.J. Puyat Ave., pg. 1404 **IT**
SAS Institute Ltd. (Philippines), Strata 100 Emerald Ave., pg. 967 **PV**
SKF Philippines Inc., G2 Kodak Bldg., 2247 Pasong Tamo Extension, pg. 1160 **IT**
SPA/FCB, Room 502, Greenbelt Mansion, 106 Perea Street, pg. 389 **PV**
The Sakura Bank - Manila Representative Office, Far East Bank Center, Senator Gil Puyat Avenue, pg. 1180 **IT**
SAN MIGUEL CORP., 40 San Miguel Ave., pg. 1183 **IT**
Sandoz (Philippines) Inc., pg. 985 **IT**
Sandvik Philippines, Inc., pg. 1187 **IT**
Sanitary Wares Mfg. Corp., pg. 92 **PB**
Sanyo Marketing Corporation, 1624 Dart St., pg. 1192 **IT**
Sanyo (Philippines), Inc., Barrio Tanyag, Bagumbayan, Taguig, pg. 1192 **IT**
SARMIENTO RAPPAN INDUSTRIES, Sarmiento Bldg. II, 2316 Pasong Tamo Extension, pg. 1194 **IT**
Security Pacific National Bank, Manila, 11/F Metrobank Plaza, pg. 183 **PB**
Seven-Up Philippines, Inc., Ricogen Bldg., 113 Aguirre St., pg. 1278 **PB**
Shaklee Philippines, Inc., Renaissance Center, Ground Floor, 215 Salcedo Street, pg. 1518 **IT**
Sharp (Philippines) Corporation, KM23, West Service Rd., South Superhighway, pg. 1230 **IT**
Shimizu Philippine Contractors, Inc., 3rd Fl., Prince Bldg., 117 Rada St., pg. 1234 **IT**
Siam Mariwasa Toto, Inc., pg. 1410 **IT**
Sime Darby Philipinas, Inc., Sime Darby Bldg., Ayala Ave., Cor. Malugay St., pg. 1251 **IT**
Stolt-Nielsen Inc., pg. 1302 **IT**
Sumigin Metro Investment Corp., 20/F Rufino Pacific Tower, 6784 Ayala Avenue, pg. 1310 **IT**
The Sumitomo Bank, Ltd.-Manila Representative Office, 20th Floor, Rufino Pacific Tower, pg. 1310 **IT**
Sun Life of Canada, Interbank Building-6th Floor, 111 Paseo de Roxas, pg. 1319 **IT**
Superior Metal Printing Philippines, Inc., Unit 3, Richgold Warehouse, Manalac Avenue, pg. 1322 **IT**
Suzuki Philippines, Inc., Canley Road, Bagong ILOG, pasig, pg. 1323 **IT**
Swiss Reinsurance Company Manila, 19D Tower One, Ayala Triangle, pg. 1333 **IT**
Tas Plan, Inc., Hong Kong Bank Centre, 9th Floor, San Miguel Avenue, pg. 1348 **IT**
Technoserve International Co., 1606 Trade St., Corner Investment Dr., pg. 697 **IT**
Telecommunications & Computer Technologies, Inc., 2nd Flr Kalaw-Ledesma, Condomiknium, 117 Gamboa St., pg. 1370 **IT**
3M Philippines, Inc., PCIB Tower 2-18th Fl., Makati Ave., pg. 1607 **PB**
Tiger Balm (Philippines) Inc., EDSA Corner, Pioneer Street, pg. 604 **IT**
Toyota Motor Philippines Corp., Km. 15, South Superhighway Pranaque, pg. 1414 **IT**
Union Ajinomoto, Inc., Union Ajinomoto Bldg., 331, Sen. Gil J. Puyat Ave., pg. 41 **IT**
Union Ajinomoto , Inc., Plant, Barrio Ugong, Eulogio Rodriguez Ave., pg. 41 **IT**
Union Carbide Philippines (Far East) Inc., 15th Fl. Royal Match Bldg., pg. 1667 **PB**
Upson International Corp., pg. 22 **IT**
Van Melle-(Phils.) Inc., No. 4 Pioneer St., pg. 1451 **IT**
Velsicol Chemical Corp., 4th Fl., Marsman Bldg., Buendia Ave. & Washington St., pg. 1135 **PV**

Votra (Philippines) Inc, pg. 757 **IT**
WS Publishing Company, Inc., Room 704 Sedcco Building, Rada Street, Corner Legazpi Street, pg. 570 **PV**
Warner-Lambert Philippines, Inc., National Life Insurance Bldg., Ortigas Ave., pg. 1740 **PB**
Wellccme Philippines Inc, pg. 553 **IT**
Westinghouse Asia Controls Corp., 3rd Fl., Adamson Centre Bldg., 121 Alfaro St., Salcedo Village, pg. 273 **PB**
Woodward-Clyde International, Alcco Bldg., Ste. 106, Ortigas Ave., pg. 1658 **PB**
The World Bank, Multi-Storey Bldg., Rm. 200, Roxas Blvd., pg. 1189 **PV**
Wrigley Philippines, Inc., Pioneer & United Sts., pg. 1781 **IT**
Wyeth-Suaco Laboratories, Inc., 2236 Pasong Tamo, pg. 82 **IT**
Zeneca Pharma, 5th Fl, Solid Mills Bldg., 143 Dela Rosa corner Adelantado St., pg. 1527 **IT**

Paranaque

California Manufacturing Co., Inc., Km. 18 East Service Rd., pg. 41 **IT**

Pasay

Avon Cosmetics, Inc., P.O. Box 7059, pg. 156 **PB**
Geotronics AB, pg. 1290 **IT**
W.R. Grace (Philippines) Inc., Domestic Airport Lockbox, 1300 Domestic Rd., pg. 756 **PB**
Pharmacia & Upjohn, Inc., P.O. Box 7063, Domestic Airport Post Office Lock Box, pg. 1049 **IT**

Pasig

Infoccm Technologies, Inc., P/H Padilla Building, Emerald Avenue, pg. 1051 **IT**
Ingasci Inc., Phil. Stock Exchange Centre W., 8th Floor Exchange Road, pg. 939 **IT**
KEPCO Philippines Corporation, Suite 2501-A 25th Floor, Textile Tower 1, Exchange Road, pg. 758 **IT**
SNC-Lavalin, 28 Ste. Maria St., pg. 1162 **IT**
SmithKline Beecham Research Limited, 5/F JMT Corporate, Condominium, ADB Ave., pg. 1266 **IT**
Vitacolor Industries, Inc., Emerald Building, 14 Emerald Avenue, Ortigas Center, pg. 110 **IT**
Wander (Philippines) Inc., pg. 986 **IT**

Quezon City

Bauer Machineries & Industrial Corporation, Suite 405-408 R&G Tirol Bldg., Cor. Scout Albano, EDSA, pg. 549 **IT**
Golden Donuts, Inc., Tuscan Bldg., 14 Visayas Ave.,Proj. Village, pg. 63 **IT**
Kubota Agri-Machinery Philippines, Inc., 1031 Edsa, pg 763 **IT**
McCormick-Philippines, Inc., 145 Panay Ave., pg. 1067 **PB**
Nissir-Universal Robina Corporation, 110 E. Rodriguez Jr. Ave. Libis, pg. 950 **IT**
Reader's Digest (Philippines) Inc., Rm. 301, VIR Bldg., No. 1840 E. Rodriguez Ave., pg. 1368 **PB**

Rizal

Batangas Bay Terminal, Inc., C-J Yulo Bldg., Pasong Tamo Ccr., Don Basco, pg. 947 **IT**
Joffko Philippines, Inc., 11 Emerald Dr., pg. 589 **PV**

Subic Bay

The International Commercial Bank of China, Subic Bay Industrial Park, Argonaut Highway, Corner Rizal Highway, pg. 683 **IT**

POLAND

Bielsko-Biala

Makita Sp. Z O.O., UL. Strazacka 81, SKR. Pozt. 81, pg. 832 **IT**
Savia S.A., Przedsiebiorstwo Handlowe, pg. 1376 **IT**
TI Poland sp zo.o., pg. 1341 **IT**

Bydrossez

Lucent Technologies Poland S.A., Vl. Pilicka 6, pg. 1019 **PB**

Chelmec

4P Rube Polska, pg. 1146 **IT**

Dabrowa Gornicza

PolFloat Saint-Gobain, SP Z.O.O., Ul. Arm II Krajowej 12, pg. 1173 **IT**

Gdansk

Det Norske Veritas, Ul. Heweliusza 11, pg. 396 **IT**
PZ Gestra Polonia Sp. z o.o., Ul. Oplotki nr. 1, pg. 550 **IT**
Krupp Hoesch Stahlexport GmbH, Krzysztof Kurjanski Waly Piastowski 1, pg. 515 **IT**
Olicom Poland Sp. z.o.o., ul. Uphagena 27, pg. 1001 **IT**
Plettac-rem Spolka zo.o., pg. 1061 **IT**

Gdynia

ENA Line Limited, ul. Kwiatkowskiego 60, pg. 1300 **IT**
Gunnebo Baltic Sp z o o, Al. Zjednoczenia 1, pg. 578 **IT**
MacGREGOR (POL) Sp. z.o.o., Ul. Polska 1D, pg. 671 **IT**

Grodzisk

Ewos Polfarm Ltd., ul. Swieza, pg. 349 **IT**

Katowice

Business Management & Finance International Ltd., Ul. PCK 10/14, pg. 1332 **IT**
Elektrody Baildon, u. Zelazna 9, pg. 282 **IT**
Fuchs Oil Co. (PL) SP ZO.O., ul Rozdzienska 41, pg. 518 **IT**
Hoogovens Technical Services Poland, ul. 1 Maja 11, pg. 755 **IT**
Krupp Hoesch Stahlexport GmbH, Damian Trocha, Al. W. Korfantego 83A/P.405, pg. 515 **IT**
Svedala Polska, pg. 1325 **IT**
Svensk Teknisk Byra AB, Oddzial w Katowicach, pg. 712 **IT**

Koluszki

Magazyn Szwedzkiego Biura Technicznego, ul. Budowlanych 51, pg. 712 **IT**

Kostrzyn

Novoferm Polska GmbH, Skalovo 5, pg. 509 **IT**

Kotlarnia

Bekaert Kotlarnia Sp.z.o.o., Wyroby z drutu, Ki Bierawy Woy, pg. 184 **IT**

Kozienice

Esselte Polska Sp.z.o.o., ul. Warszawska 34, pg. 461 **IT**

Krakow

Electricite de France, Ul Michalowskiego 4, pg. 437 **IT**
Linde Gaz Polska spolka z.o.o., pg. 811 **IT**
White Cap Sp.z.o.o., pg. 1207 **IT**

Legionowo

Leaf Poland Sp.z.o.o., ul. Olszankowa 49, pg. 638 **IT**

Lodz

CIBA-GEIGY AG, Oddzial w Warszawie, Filia u Lodzi, pg. 975 **IT**
Freudenberg Vilene Sp. z.o.o., pg. 507 **IT**
Otto Sp. Z O.O., pg. 1014 **IT**
Swisscolor, ul Wilenska 38, pg. 986 **IT**

Mloty

Centrale de Mloty, pg. 1415 **IT**

Nowy Dwor

Benckiser S.A., pg. 186 **IT**

Opole

Cementownia Gorazdze S.A., W. Choruli, skr. poczt. 220, pg. 605 **IT**
Cementownia Strzelce Opolskie S.A., ul. 1-go Maja 50, 47-100 Strzelce Opolskie, pg. 605 **IT**
Ovita Nutricia Sp. z o.o., pg. 992 **IT**

Piaseczno

IR International Holdings, Inc., Teren Zakladu Lamina, pg. 907 **PB**

Police

Kemipol Ltd., ul. Walki Mlodych 1, pg. 729 **IT**

Poznan

AMP Polska Sp. Z.o.o., V.L. Gronowa 22, pg. 9 **PB**
Adidas Polen Sp. z.o.o., pg. 25 **IT**
Barenbrug Polska Sp. z.o.o., ul Gronowa 22, pg. 167 **PB**
CPC Amino S.P. ZO.O., UL Baltycka 43, pg. 225 **PB**
IBP Installfittings Sp zoo, Ul Obodrzycka 61, pg. 391 **IT**
Kali und Salz Polska Sp.z.o.o., Bulgasska 9, pg. 108 **IT**
WWT (Wytwornia Wyrobow Tytoniowych) S.A., ul. Wojskowa S, pg. 1101 **IT**
Wrigley Poland, Sp. z.o.o., ul. Libeltz 34, pg. 1781 **PB**

Prague

Pragoplettac Spol. s.r.o., pg. 1061 **IT**

PB - *U.S. Public Companies Volume*
PV - *U.S. Private Companies Volume*
IT - *International Public & Private Companies Volume*

Pruskow

Rexroth Sp.Zoo, pg. 839   **IT**

Przedstawickel

Perry Machinery Poland, Ul. Duchnicka 36, pg. 855   **PV**

Przezmierowo

Herlitz Spolka z.o.o., ul. Szamotulska 2, pg. 616   **IT**

Rybnik

Van Leer Silesia Sp. z.o.o., pg. 1147   **IT**

Rzeszow

Alima-Gerber SA, ul Siemienskiego 19, pg. 973   **IT**
Continental Can Polska Sp.zo.o., pg. 1207   **IT**

Siedlce

Plettac Distribution Spolka zo.o, pg. 1061   **IT**

Siemianowice

Polarcup Poland Sp. z.o.o., ul. Budowlana 6, pg. 638   **IT**

Sosnowiec

Foster Wheeler Energy Fakop, Ltd., ul. Staszica 31, pg. 677   **PB**

Szczecin

Bosman Browar Szczecin S.A., pg. 197   **IT**
Elgro Sp z.o.o., ul. Nadodrazanska 14, pg. 559   **IT**
Fibo ExClay Polska Sp.z.o.o., ul. Wiosenna 1, pg. 1200   **IT**
Hydro Poland Sp.Z.O.O., Filia W. Szczecinie, ul. 3 Maja 1, pg. 963   **IT**

Varsovie

Rhone-Poulenc Polska, 80/82, rue Grzybowska, pg. 1113   **IT**

Warsaw

AGA Gaz Sp.z.o.o., Ul. Muszynska 35, pg. 13   **IT**
Adecco Poland Sp. Z.o.o., UL. Koszykowa 59/4, pg. 24   **IT**
Akerlund & Rausing, Ul. Mariensztat 8, pg. 33   **IT**
American Appraisal Poland Sp. z.o.o., ul. Filtrowa 43, pg. 50   **PV**
American Power Conversion, pg. 89   **PB**
Amway Poland, ul. Mangalia 4, pg. 70   **PV**
BNP-Dresdner Bank (Polska) S.A., LIM Center, 6th Floor, Al. Jerozolimskie 65/79, pg. 418   **IT**
Bank Brussels Lambert, Warsaw, FIM Tower, 5th Floor, 81 Yerozolimskie, pg. 148   **IT**
Bank Creditanstalt S.A., ul. Nowy Swiat 6/12 V Pietro, pg. 347   **IT**
Bank Rozwoju Eksportu SA, Pl. Bankowy 2, pg. 312   **IT**
Bayerische Landesbank Girozentrale, ul. Emilii Plater 28, pg. 177   **IT**
Benckiser Cosmetics Sp.z.o.o., pg. 185   **IT**
Benckiser Polen Sp.z.o.o., pg. 186   **IT**
Berlitz-Polska Limited Liability Company, UL. Wiejska 12A, pg. 222   **PB**
Bonifica-Poland, Ul. Swietokrzyska 31/33 A, pg. 655   **IT**
Robert Bosch Sp.z.o.o., Ul. Samsonowska 1, pg. 206   **IT**
Bosta Beton Sp.z.o.o., ul. Swiderska 15, pg. 1200   **IT**
Bull Polska Sp. Z.O.O., Srebrna 16, pg. 317   **IT**
Leo Burnett Warsaw SP.Z.O.O., UL. Karmelicka 9, pg. 186   **PV**
Business Management & Finance International Ltd., Al. Jerozolimskie 53, pg. 1332   **IT**
Canon Polska spol z.o.o., Office Center Hotel Sobieski, Place A. Zawiszy 1, pg. 263   **IT**
Capital International CDPQ - Poland, Atrium Tower, Aleja Jana Pawla II 25, pg. 249   **IT**
Cerberus Poland S.p.z.o.o., Al W Wilosa 31/224, pg. 1246   **IT**
Ciba Corning Diagnostics Ltd, P1 Konstylucji 5, pg. 975   **IT**
CIBA-GEIGY AG, Oddzial w Warszawie, Aleja W Witosa 31, pg. 975   **IT**
CIBA-GEIGY Poland Sp. z.o.o., Al. W. Witosa 31, pg. 978   **IT**
Commerzbank AG Representative Office-Warsaw, ul. Jasna 24, pg. 312   **IT**
DG Bank-Warsaw, Al. Jerozolimskie 51/3, pg. 352   **PB**
DMB&B/Warsaw, ul. Goraszewska 7, pg. 304   **PV**
DSM Poland Sp.z o.o, Ul. Ursynowska 64, pg. 355   **IT**
Daewoo Corp. - Warsaw, pg. 358   **IT**
Danfoss Poland Sp. z.o.o., ul. Obozowa 20, pg. 377   **IT**
Danzas Sp.z.o.o., Mochnackiego ul. 3, pg. 383   **IT**
Data serwis Sp. Z.O.O., Pruszkowska 19, pg. 317   **IT**
Dell Computer Poland, Sp.zo.o.ul. Srebrna 16, pg. 496   **PB**
Dun & Bradstreet Poland SP. Z.O.O., Krzywickiego 34 Street, pg. 536   **PB**
Durrpol Sp.z.o.o., Al. Yjadowskie 33/35, pg. 422   **IT**
E/B/D/Interpartners Warszawa, Agencja Marketingu i Promocji Sp. z.o.o., pg. 1152   **PV**

ESAB Przedstawicielstwo w. Polsce, ul. Nowy Swiat 19, pg. 282   **IT**
EMTEC Magnetics Polska Sp. z.o.o., ul. Emailowa 28, pg. 743   **IT**
Enso (Poland), Ul. Dzika 19/23 m. 54, pg. 457   **IT**
Epstein Engineering Export (Warsaw), Ltd., Biuro Nadzora w Warszawie, AI 1 Armii Wojska Polskiego, 16 M 3, pg. 379   **PV**
Ericsson Business Systems AB - Warsaw Branch Office, Nowy Swiat 57/59 m14, pg. 1366   **IT**
EURO RSCG, Ul. M. Gandhiego, pg. 602   **IT**
EURO RSCG Poland, Ul. M. Gandhiego 3, pg. 603   **IT**
FHP Vileda Sp. z.o.o., pg. 506   **IT**
Failure Analysis Associates, Naleczowska 62/21, pg. 1032   **PB**
Ferrosan International A/S, Oddzial w Warszawie, ul. Lucka 11, pg. 989   **IT**
GGK Warsaw, u. Bagatela 10/10, pg. 1336   **IT**
Gambro Poland sp. z.o.o., Ul Floriana 5, pg. 668   **IT**
Gaspol Sp. z o.o., Al. Jerozolimskie 184, pg. 1155   **IT**
Gerber Polska, Ul. Obserwatorow 3, pg. 973   **IT**
Getinge Poland Sp.zo.o., Ul Walecznych 44, pg. 551   **IT**
Gist-Brocades Sp. z o.o., Nalkowskiego 2b/12, pg. 1143   **IT**
Groupe SEB Polska, ul. Tykoniowa 22, pg. 568   **IT**
Handlowy-Heller S.A., U1 Kasprzaka 18/20, pg. 521   **IT**
Chr. Hansen Poland Sp. z.o.o., ul. Dunskas, pg. 289   **IT**
Heinz Polska Sp., Ul. Kredytowa 6M 20/21, pg. 806   **PB**
Herbalife Polska sp.z.o.o., ul. Kadlubka, 13, pg. 809   **PB**
Hewlett-Packard Polska Sp.z.o.o., Ul.Newelska 6, pg. 821   **PB**
Honeywell Ltd., Augustowka 3, pg. 835   **PB**
Hydrobudowa-6 S.A., ul. Skoczylasa 4, pg. 196   **IT**
IDG Poland S.A., 20 Tytoniowa Street, pg. 570   **PV**
IDV Poland, Ul. Domaniewska 39a, pg. 410   **IT**
IR International Holdings, Inc., Ul. Gwiazdzisla, pg. 907   **PB**
ITT Flygt Sp.z.o.o., pg. 860   **PB**
IVO Polska Sp. z.o.o., 4 Migdalowa Street, 2nd. Floor Suite 27, pg. 660   **IT**
Icopal Poland Sp.z.o.o., pg. 659   **IT**
Intercell Co. Ltd. Paper Sack Division, ul. Niecala 4a IIIp., pg. 1429   **IT**
Intergraph Europe (Polska), Wisniowa 38, pg. 892   **IT**
Juki (Europe) G.m.b.H.-Warsaw Office, AL, Jerozolimskie, pg. 717   **IT**
KSB Pumpy i Armatura Sp. zo.o, pg. 721   **IT**
Kanthal Warsaw, pg. 723   **IT**
KONE Elevators Poland Sp.zo.o., Ul. Cybernetyki 13, pg. 747   **IT**
Korn/Ferry International, Frascati 3/6, pg. 634   **PV**
Kredietbank Representative Office (Warsaw), Vl. Kasprozaka 2/8, pg. 760   **IT**
Landis & Staefa (Polska) Sp.z.o.o., ul. Jubilerska 10, pg. 801   **IT**
Arthur D. Little/TMBK Partners, U1 Adolfa Pawi'skiego 5a, pg. 671   **PV**
Lucent Technologies Sp. Z.o.o., Ulica Senatorska 12, pg. 1019   **PB**
MSA-AUER Polska, Sp. zo.o., pg. 1114   **PB**
Makro Cash and Carry Poland Ltd. Sp. z.o.o., Aleje Jerozolimskie 184, pg. 1155   **IT**
Mannesmann Anlagenbau Polonia Sp. Zoo, pg. 837   **IT**
Market Link, ul. Powsinka 12, pg. 1062   **PV**
Mead Packaging Poland Sp.z O.O., pg. 1076   **PB**
Merita Bank Ltd., Warsaw Representative Office, Jana Pawla II 73, pg. 859   **IT**
Mettler-Toledo Sp. z.o.o., Aleja W Witosa 31, pg. 4   **IT**
Microsoft sp z.o.o., pg. 1108   **PB**
Mitsui & Co., Ltd., UL. Poznanska 16M.3 and 4, pg. 881   **IT**
J.P. Morgan Polska, LIM Ctr., 19th Fl., Ste. 1911, pg. 1131   **PB**
Neste Oil Poland Ltd., Bagatela 14, pg. 915   **IT**
Neste Oy Chemicals - Warsaw, Bagatela 14, pg. 915   **IT**
Nokia Telecommunications Sp.z.o.o., Ul. Stawki 2, pg. 954   **IT**
NORD/LB - Warsaw, ul. Emilii Plater 28-IX p., pg. 958   **IT**
Nordson Polska Sp.z.o.o., W/. Lektykarska 29/8, pg. 1189   **PB**
Norsk Hydro a.s. Poland, Plac Bankowy 2, pg. 964   **IT**
Novell Poland, ul. Sienna 64, pg. 1204   **PB**
Novo Nordisk A/S, Oddzial w Warszawie, ul. Lucka 11, pg. 988   **IT**
Novo Nordisk A/S, Oddzial w Warszawie, ul Messynska 16, pg. 989   **IT**
OCE-Poland Limited, Sp. z o.o., pg. 995   **IT**
Olicom Poland Sp.z.o.o., ul. Koscielna 12, pg. 1001   **IT**
OMRON Electronics Sp.Z.O.O., Ul Fortaczna 6, pg. 1006   **IT**
Optiroc Group Sp.z.o.o., Al. Wilanowska 277, pg. 1200   **IT**
Oracle Poland, Towarowa 28, pg. 1228   **PB**
ORIX Polska S.A., Ul. Stawki 2, XXXV Floor, pg. 1010   **IT**
Outokumpu Poland Sp.zo.o., Ul. Filtrowa 59/2, pg. 1016   **IT**
Pall Poland Ltd., UL Kasprowicza, 151 pok.315, pg. 1254   **PB**
PAXAR Polska Sp.zo.o., UL Syrokomli 6, pg. 1267   **PB**
Perstorp Sp.z o.o., ul Ostrobramska 101, pg. 1038   **IT**
Perstorp Sp.z o.o. Decorative Laminate, ul Ostrobramska 101, pg. 1038   **IT**
Perstorp Sp.z o.o. Industrial Flooring, ul Ostrobramska 101, pg. 1037   **IT**
Pharmaco Intl. Sp., ul. Mieroslawskiego 24, pg. 1285   **PB**
Pol Krusz S.A., ul. Gorezewska 179 A, pg. 1200   **IT**
Poland OBI Centrala Systemowa, ul. Pulawska 12A/4, pg. 993   **IT**
POLSKIE LINIE LOTNICZE LOT S.A., 39, 17 Stycznei Str., Apt. 106, pg. 1062   **PV**
Polskie Towarzystwo Prywatyzacyjne Kleinwort Benson, 5 Dluga Str., pg. 420   **IT**

Przedstawicielstwo Knoll AG w Polsce, Aleje Jerozolimskie 154, pg. 109   **IT**
R.F.R./ARIP, ul. Rozana 53, pg. 1377   **IT**
Raiffeisen Centrobank S.A., Ul. Nowogrodzka 50, pg. 1085   **IT**
Raisio Polska Foods Sp. z.o.o., ul. Sienna 64, pg. 1085   **IT**
Reader's Digest Przeglad Sp.z.o.o., pg. 1368   **PB**
Roche Polska Sp. z.o.o., pg. 1121   **IT**
SKF Centr. Handlowo-Techn. Sp. z.o.o., ul. Jaktorowska 3, pg. 1158   **IT**
Sandvik Polska Ltd., pg. 1186   **IT**
Scholl (Polska) Sp zoo, ul. Bobrowiecka 3, pg. 1210   **IT**
Schrack-Ericsson Sp. z.o.o., 17 Stycznia 32, pg. 1369   **IT**
Sealed Air Polska Sp. Z.O.O., ul. Niedzwiedzia 10A, pg. 1451   **IT**
Sodexho Polska, ul. Przasnyska 6, pg. 1275   **IT**
Statoil Poland Ltd., ul Chopina 1, pg. 1298   **IT**
Sulzer Polska GmbH, pg. 1306   **IT**
Sun Chemical Sp. (z.o.o) (Ltd.), Wal Miedzeszynski 646, pg. 371   **IT**
Svenska Teknisk Byra AB, Oddzial w Warszawie, pg. 712   **IT**
Tampella Power Corp., Natpoll Bldg., 4 Migdalowa St., 2nd Fl., pg. 1354   **IT**
3M Poland Sp. z.o.o., Bema str. 57a, pg. 1607   **IT**
Toyota Motor Poland Co., Ltd. Sp. zo. o., 5-Konstruktorska, pg. 1414   **IT**
UBS Representative Office, 81, Al. Jerozolimskie, pg. 1441   **IT**
Urban & Partner, Marii Sklodowskiej-Curie Str. 55/61, pg. 1174   **IT**
Van Melle Polska SP. z.o.o., ul. Lektykarska 29 (p 17/18), pg. 1451   **IT**
Vattenfall Poland Sp.z.o.o., ul. Krakowskie, pg. 1453   **IT**
WWT (Wytwornia Wyrobow Tytoniowych) S.A., ul. Kasprzaka 29/31, pg. 1101   **IT**
Warsaw Branch Office, ul. Ostrobramska 101, pg. 1519   **IT**
Westendorski Landesbank Polska S.A., Warsaw Corporate Centre, ul. Emilii Plater 28, pg. 1494   **IT**
Willis Corroon Polska Spolka Akeyjna, Reinsurance Department, ul. Jana Pawla II 34/12, pg. 1509   **IT**
Woodward Governor Poland Sp.z.o.o., u.1 Chmielna 8, pg. 1777   **PB**
The World Bank, INTRACO I Bldg., 17th Fl., 2 Stawki St., pg. 1189   **PV**
Wydawnictwa Prawnicze PWN, Ul. Bagatela 10/5p, pg. 1095   **IT**
Young & Rubicam Poland, ul. Madalinskiego 101 A, pg. 1199   **PV**
Zeneca Poland Sp. z.o.o., ul. Nieklanska 23, pg. 1527   **IT**
Zurich Ubezpieczenie Service Sp. z o.o., Ul. Marszalkowska 82, pg. 1532   **IT**

Wegrow

Ovita Nutricia Wegrow Sp. z o.o., pg. 992   **IT**

Wroclaw

Durkopp Adler Polska Spolka zo.o., ul. Powstancow Sl. 20/22, pg. 469   **IT**
Ekokonrem Spolka z o.o., Ul. Tarnogajska 18, pg. 608   **IT**
Parker Hannifin Sp. z.o.o., ul Grabiszynska 268, pg. 1263   **PB**

Zyrardow

Rautaruukki Polska Sp. Z.O.O., ul. Jaktorowska 13, pg. 1088   **IT**

PORTUGAL

Abrantes

AlliedSignal Automotive Portugal Ltda., Olho de Boi, pg. 53   **PB**

Abrunheira

Mercedes-Benz Portugal-Comercio de Automoveis, S.A., pg. 369   **IT**

Agueda

Haworth Portugal-Cortal, Mobiliario De Escritorio, SA, pg. 512   **PV**

Alcamena

Stahl Portuguesa, LDA, Cha do Rabacal, pg. 1526   **IT**

Alges

BetzDearborn Portugesa, L.D.A., Rua General Ferreira Martins, pg. 227   **PB**
NeoCom Publicidade, Av. General Norton De Matos 65A, pg. 678   **PV**

Geographic Index-Non U.S.

Tagus-Dragagens Lda., Avienda des Tulipes 43, pg. 135 **IT**

Almada

GESTRA Portuguesa Valvulas Ltda., Rua do Clube Recreativo, da Ramalha No. 9/R/ch B, pg. 550 **IT**
Jotun-Tinco Tintas Maritimas Lda., Rua Antonio Nobre 3 A/B, pg. 716 **IT**
MacGREGOR (PRT) Lda., Av. Alianca Povo MFA, pg. 671 **IT**

Almancil

Lusotel Industria Hoteleira Ltda., Hotel Dona Filipa, pg. 556 **IT**

Amadora

Chloride Portugal Limitada, Rua Eng Lucio de Azevedo 27, pg. 287 **IT**
Roche Farmaceutica Quimica Limitada, Estrada Nacional 249-1, pg. 1121 **IT**
SKF Portugal Rolamentos, Lda., Casal de Alfragide, Lote 1, pg. 1159 **IT**
Siemens S.A., Estrada Nacional 117, km 2,6, pg. 1248 **IT**

Arruda dos Vinhos

Euroseel Equipamentos Metalicos, SA, Estrada Nacional 115-4, pg. 569 **IT**

Avelar

Leca Portugal Argilas Expandidas S.A., pg. 1200 **IT**

Azambuja

Impormol Industria Portuguesa de Molas S.A., Vale do Cardal, pg. 508 **IT**

Azeitao

Lancers, J.M. da Fonseca Intl. Vinhos, Vila Nogueira de Azeitao, pg. 411 **IT**
Sileno, SOC Distribuidora de Bebidas, Quinta Da Bassaqueira, pg. 410 **IT**

Caldas da Rainha

Cerapasta-Pastas Para Ceramica Lda., Apartado 294, Lote 19, Zona Industrial, pg. 1488 **IT**
ROL Rolamentos Portugueses S.A., pg. 469 **IT**

Carnaxide

Amway de Portugal, Inc., Av. do Forte, 10C, pg. 69 **PV**
Bricodis, Estrada da Outorela, Lotes 2021, pg. 534 **IT**
Bricogal, Estrada da Outorela, Lotes 20-21, pg. 534 **IT**
Brother International (Portugal) Distribuidores de Equipamentos Electricos LDA., Rua Da Garagem 7, Urbanizacao Industrial Da Barruncheira, pg. 230 **IT**
Ericsson de Portugal, Lda, Rua de Barruncheira, 4, pg. 1366 **IT**
Honeywell Lda, Edificio Suecia II, Av. do Forte n 3, pg. 835 **PB**
Axel Johnson (Acose Equipamentos) Lda, Rua da Barrancheira 6, Carnaxide, pg. 711 **IT**
Kodak Portugal, Ltd., Edificio KODAK, Rua Alexandre Herculano, pg. 554 **PB**
Neste Chemicals S.A., Praceta das Fabricas, 2/2A, pg. 914 **IT**
Nestle Portugal, S.A., Apartado 2, pg. 921 **IT**
Sociedade Ericsson de Portugal Lda., Edificio Ericsson, Rua da Barruncheira, 4, pg. 1370 **IT**
TOFA- Torrefaccao de Cafes de Portugal, s.a.r.l., pg. 922 **IT**
VPC Portugal Lda., Linda-a-velha, pg. 1015 **IT**

Cascais

Alcatel Portugal, Apartado 80, pg. 56 **IT**
Vorwerk Portugal, pg. 1481 **IT**

Coimbra

Central de Cervejas-Loreto Factory, Estrada Nacional n 1, pg. 279 **IT**
Transmeca Transmissoes Mechanica Lda., pg. 835 **IT**
Zeneca Produtos Biociencia, LDA, Rua Joao Machado, 100-7, Sala 706, pg. 1527 **IT**

Covilha

Zeneca Produtos Biociencia, LDA, Rua Marques d'Avila e Bolama, pg. 1527 **IT**

Figueira da Foz

Celbi SA, Leirosa, pg. 1303 **IT**
SOPORCEL-Sociedade Portuguesa de Celulose S.A., Apartado 5, pg. 567 **IT**
Vidreria do Mondego, pg. 1172 **IT**

Funchal

Madeira Offshore, Av. Arriaga 17/19-3, pg. 250 **IT**

Guimaraes

J. Bonifacio & CIA., LDA., Lugar da Cruz-Brito, pg. 517 **IT**
Repergal LDA., Apart. 8, Caldas das Taipas, pg. 519 **IT**

Joao do Estoril

Bilfinger + Berger Portugal Construcoes Lda., Avenida Marques Leal, 9, pg. 196 **IT**

Leiria

Neste Quimica Comercial, S.A., Delegacao de Leiria, R. Capitao Mouzinho de, pg. 915 **IT**

Linda-a-Velha

AXIMS Acos Especiais Lda, Apartado 140, Rua da Barrancheira 6, pg. 710 **IT**
Fidelio Portugal, Lda., Alameda Antonio Sergio, pg. 1106 **PB**
ISS Servisystem Ltda., Rua Moinho Da Barrunchada 4, pg. 657 **IT**
Milupa Portuguesa L.D.A., pg. 991 **IT**
Repsol Portugal Petroleo e Denvados Lda., Rua Mario Dionisio, 2, 2a-3a Planta, pg. 1105 **IT**

Lisbon

ADT Prosegur, Avenida Joao XXI 6, pg. 1649 **PB**
AF Investimentos, Av. Jose Malhoa, pg. 464 **IT**
AMP Portugal, Lda., pg. 9 **PB**
AMS, Rua Tomas da Fonsca, Torre A-8B, pg. 86 **IT**
Adecco Recursos Humanos, AVa Duque de Loule, N 47A, pg. 24 **IT**
Alcantara, 1357 **IT**
ALUVETICA Lda., pg. 68 **IT**
Amdahl International Corporation Sucursal em Portugal, Av. Marques de Tomar, 35-4 Esq., pg. 527 **IT**
American Appraisal Consultores De Avaliacoa Limitada, Av. Miguel Bombarda, 36-11, pg. 50 **PV**
Amgen-Biofarmaceutica, Lda., Rua Alexandre Herculano, 5, pg. 101 **PB**
Asea Brown Boveri Lda., pg. 8 **IT**
Astra Portuguesa Lda., Apartado 30265, pg. 94 **IT**
Avon Cosmeticas, Lda., Av. Fontes Pereira de Melo 14-50, pg. 156 **PB**
BASF Portuguesa, Lda., Largo Jean Monnet, 1-7, pg. 107 **IT**
BCP, Rua Augusta 61/74, pg. 464 **IT**
BCP Investimentos, Av. Jose Malhoa, pg. 464 **IT**
BNU, Av. 5 de Outubro, 175, pg. 250 **IT**
BNU Capital - Sociedade de Capital de Risco, SA, Rua do Comerico, 78, pg. 250 **IT**
BSN Portugal, Avd. Ingenieor Duarte Pacheco-, pg. 144 **IT**
Banco de Comercio E Industria, S.A., Marques de Pombal, 2-4 piso, pg. 144 **IT**
Banco do Brasil S.A.-Portugal, Praca Marques de Pombal, 16, pg. 141 **IT**
BANCO ESPIRITO SANTO E COMERCIAL DE LISBOA SA, Avenida da Liberdade #195, pg. 142 **IT**
Banco Hispano de Investimento, S.A., Avenida da Liberdade, 144-156, pg. 140 **IT**
Banco Internacional de Credito SA., Av. Fontes Pereira de Melo. 27, pg. 142 **IT**
Banco International de Credito SA (Portugal), Av. Fontes Pereira de Melo, 27, pg. 341 **IT**
BANCO TOTTA & ACORES, Rua do Ouna, 88, pg. 144 **IT**
Banque Paribas Portugal, Rua dos Ferreiros a Estrela N 2, pg. 320 **IT**
Barclays Bank PLC, Avenida da Republica 50-3rd Fl., pg. 166 **IT**
Barro Marketing & Publicidade, Av. Duque de Loule, 86, pg. 1377 **IT**
Bausch & Lomb Espana S.A., Rua Soeira Pereira Gomes, pg. 195 **PB**
Bayer Portugal S.A.R.L., Sociedade Farmaceutica 3, pg. 175 **IT**
Joh. A. Benckiser (Portugal) Lda., pg. 185 **IT**
Betao Liz S.A., Av. Infante Don Henrique 341, pg. 790 **IT**
Robert Bosch Lda, Apartado 8058, Av. Infante D. Henrique, pg. 205 **IT**
BRENNTAG PORTUGAL Produtos Quimicos Lda., Avenida Infante Santo 52, pg. 1458 **IT**
Bull Portugal Computadores Lda., Av. 5 de Outubro, 35-6, pg. 318 **IT**
CCF Lisbon, Torres das Amoreiras, Torre 2, 10 andar n12, pg. 342 **IT**
CEPSA Cia. Portuguesa de Petroleos, Lda., Avda. Columbano Bordalo Pinheiro 108 3o, pg. 323 **IT**
C.P.C. Instrumentacao, Torre de Santo Antonio, Rua Gregorio Lopez, pg. 816 **PB**
CAIXA GERAL DE DEPOSITOS, Av. Joao XXI, 63, pg. 250 **IT**
Caixa-Imobiliario-Sociedade de Gestao e Investimento Imobiliario S.A., Av. Joao XXI, 63, pg. 250 **IT**
Caixa Participacoes, SGPS. S.A., Av. Joao XXI, 63, pg. 250 **IT**
Caixa - Sistemas de Informacao, SA, Rua Padre Antonio Vieira, 32, pg. 250 **IT**
Caixagest, Joao XXI, 63, pg. 250 **IT**

Carbogal-Carbonos de Portugal, S.A., Rua Latino Coelho, pg. 1045 **IT**
Carrefour - Portugal, Piso II, Ave. das Nacoes Unidas Telheira, pg. 273 **IT**
CENTRAL DE CERVEJAS, S.A., Av. Almirante Reis 115, pg. 279 **IT**
Cerberus-Engenharia de Seguranca Lda., Rua Sarmento de Beires, Lote 35, pg. 1246 **IT**
The Chase Manhattan Bank, N.A., Rua Alexandre Herculano 50, pg. 340 **PB**
CIBA-GEIGY Portuguesa Lda., Ave 5 de Outubro, 48, pg. 978 **IT**
Cineponto/Leo Burnett Publicidade Lda., Av. Da Republica, 139-D-Alges, pg. 184 **PV**
Circle Freight International (Portugal) Ltda., Rua C, Edificio 124 Gabinete 8-Segundo, pg. 373 **PB**
Circulo de Leitores, Edificio Circulo, Rua Professor Jorge DaSilva, pg. 192 **IT**
Companhia de Seguros Metropole S.A., Rua Barata Salguiero 41, pg. 1531 **IT**
Companhia Paribas de Portugal SGPS S.A., Rua dos Ferreiros, pg. 321 **IT**
A.S. Companhia Portuguesa de Seguros, Rua Braamcamp, 11, pg. 784 **IT**
The Continuum Company, Inc. (Portugal), Praca Marques de Pombal, pg. 423 **PB**
Crown Cork & Seal (Portugal) S.A., P.O. Box 8034, pg. 464 **PB**
Cyanamid Portugal Ltd., Rua Dos Anjos 68, pg. 81 **PB**
DMB&B Lisbon, Av. Eng Duarte Pacheco, pg. 304 **PV**
Danone Portugal, S.A., Rua dos Arneiros, 64-Benfica, pg. 379 **IT**
Danzas LDA, Av. Infante D. Henrique 332-3, pg. 382 **IT**
De La Rue Systems Limited, Sucursal Portuguesa, Rua Professor Fernando da Fonseca, 26, pg. 387 **IT**
Det Norske Veritas Portugal, Lda., Av. Infante Santo 23-9 B, pg. 398 **IT**
Deutsche Bank de Investimento, S.A. (Lisbon), Av. da Liberdade, 144-156-6o, pg. 405 **IT**
Digital Equipment Portugal, Lda, Empr. Torres das Amoreiras, Av. Eng. Duarte Pacheco, pg. 508 **PB**
Dow Jones Markets Informacao Financeira, Lda., Praca da Alegria, 58-4A, pg. 525 **PB**
Dresdner Bank AG, Av. Fontes Pereira de Melo 14, pg. 419 **IT**
Dumez-GTM Portugal, Rua Do Salitre N 139, pg. 823 **IT**
Dun & Bradstreet Portugal Lda., Rua Barata Salgueiro 28-5 o, pg. 398 **PB**
EIB Lisbon Branch, Avenida da Liberdade 144-156, pg. 465 **IT**
EMI-Valentini de Carvalho Musica Lda., Rua Cruz Dos Poiais 111, pg. 427 **IT**
EPG/TBWA, Avenida de Libertad, 38-6th Floor, pg. 1062 **PV**
Esa Portugal, Avenue Elias Garo 49-6, pg. 21 **IT**
ESAB Lda., Ave. Infante D. Henrique, pg. 282 **IT**
EIVAL, S.A., Rua Braamcamp, pg. 1045 **IT**
Electrolux Lda., Rua Palmira 23, pg. 443 **IT**
EMDEME SA, Rua Rosa Araujo, 2-6/7, pg. 608 **IT**
Europ Assistance Companhia Portuguesa de Seguros de Assistencia, S.A., Avenida Alvares Cabral, 41, pg. 91 **IT**
Europ Assistance Servicos de Assistencia Personalizados, S.A., Avenida Alvares Cabral, 41, pg. 91 **IT**
Euroseleccors-Publicacoes & Artiges Promocionas, Lda (Portugal), Rua D. Francisco Manuel de Melo 21, pg. 1368 **PB**
FCA/BMZ Park, Travessa Cova Da Moura, pg. 470 **IT**
FIMA-PRODUCTOS ALIMENTARES, LDA, Largo Monterroio Mascarenhas 1, pg. 471 **IT**
Fiat Auto Portuguesa SA, Av. Engo. Durarte Pacheco 15, pg. 481 **IT**
Fidelidade, Largo do Corpo Santo, 13, pg. 250 **IT**
Ford Lusitana, Rua Rosa Araujo, No. 2-2-3, pg. 666 **PB**
Fundimo, Joao XXI, 63-2, pg. 250 **IT**
Galpgeste, Lda., Av. Marechal Gomes da Costa, pg. 1045 **IT**
Gan Portugal Seguros, Edificio Gan, 24 D, Avenida De Berna, pg. 564 **IT**
Gan Portugal Vida, Edificio GAN, 26A, Avenida de Berna, pg. 564 **IT**
General Motors de Portugal, Sociedade Anonima, pg. 722 **PB**
Generale Bank - Lisboa, Rua Alexandre Herculano, 50, pg. 547 **IT**
Generali Vida Companhia de Seguros S.A., Avenida Duque d'Avila, 114, pg. 91 **IT**
Gestao e Publicidade, Rua Filipe Folque n. 40.A, pg. 795 **IT**
Guerlain de Portugal, Perfumaria e Cosmetica Lda., Avenida 24 de Julho, pg. 780 **IT**
Hachette Filipacchi Publicacoes, Duque de Palmela 37, pg. 795 **IT**
Heller Factoring Portuguesa S.A., Edificio Castil, Rua Castilho, 39-14th Fl., pg. 521 **IT**
Henkel Portuguesa Productos Quimicos Lda., pg. 613 **IT**
Herbalife International, S.A.-Portugal, Edificios Segres, 3oC, Quinta Da Francelha, pg. 809 **PB**
Hoogovens Aluminium Portugal Lda., Avenida Alvares Cabral 5, 1, pg. 755 **IT**
Hoover Electrica Portuguesa Ltda., Rua de Estefania 90A, pg. 260 **IT**
Huls Portugal-Produtos Quimicos, Lda., Avenida da Republica, 56-8 Esq., pg. 1455 **IT**
ICL Computadores Limitada, Av Duque D'Avila 120, pg. 529 **IT**
IDAL-Benavente, Apartado 6, 2131 Benavente Codex, pg. 807 **PB**
IDAL(Industrias de Alimentacao, Lda.), Avenida de Republica 52-70, pg. 807 **PB**
Iberoasistencia Portugal, Avda. Liberdade, 40, pg. 334 **IT**

PB - *U.S. Public Companies Volume*
PV - *U.S. Private Companies Volume*
IT - *International Public & Private Companies Volume*

1738

Geographic Index-Non U.S.

Iberphone Portugal Telemarketing, Rua Bradmcamp, 52, pg. 252 IT
Iglo Industrias de Gelados, Lda., Av. Consilheiro Ternando De, Sousa 19-14, pg. 1437 IT
Imocascais Gestao Mobiliaria e Immobiliaria, Avda. Liberdade, 40, pg. 333 IT
Imoleasing, Av. Joao XXI, 63-2, pg. 250 IT
Industrias Lever Portuguesa, Lda., Largo Monterroio Mascarenhas 1, pg. 1437 IT
Instituto Pasteur de Lisboa, Av. Marechal Gomes da Costa, 9, pg. 81 PB
International Flavors & Fragrances I.F.F. (Portugal) Lda., Av. Fontes Pereira De Melo, pg. 899 PB
Investil - Sociedade Gestora Fundos Investimento Imobiliario, SA, Campo Grande, 46D - 1 Esq., pg. 250 IT
Iofil, S.A., Rua dos Arneiros, 64-Benfica, pg. 380 IT
Italstrade-Portugal, Ave. Antonio Augusto De Aguiar 126/2, pg. 655 IT
JERÓNIMO MARTINS, Rua Lusiadas 25, pg. 705 IT
KSB Bombas e Valvulas S.A., pg. 721 IT
Kabi Pharmacia & Upjohn S.A., Av. do Forte 3, Carnaxide, pg. 1049 IT
Knoll Lusitana, Lda., Rua Alfredo da Silva 3 C e D-2, pg. 109 IT
Knorr Portuguesa-Productos Alimentares S.A., Avenida Antonio Augusto de Aguiar 108-2, pg. 225 PB
Krups, Urbinizacao da Matinha, rua 3, Edificio Altego, 6 andar, sola 5, pg. 896 IT
Laboratorios Wellcome de Portugal Lda, pg. 553 IT
Landis & Staefa Lda., Rua Filipe de Mata Nr. 66-1/2a, pg. 801 IT
Lilly-Farma Produtos Farmaceuticos, Lda., Av. Duque de Loule, pg. 994 PB
Linde Sogas, LDA, pg. 811 IT
Arthur D. Little International, Inc., Edifico Monumental, 2 C, Av. Praia Da Vitoria, 71-A, pg. 671 PV
Locapor - Companhia Portuguesa Locacao Financeira Mobiliaria, SA, Av. da Republica, 35-2, pg. 250 IT
Comp. Logistica Combustiveis, S.A., Av. Da Republica, 90, 1, pg. 1045 IT
Louis Vuitton Portugal Maleiro Limitada, Rua Augusta 196, pg. 783 IT
Lusoceram-Empreendimentos Ceramicos, S.A., Rua Castilho, 39-8 C/D, pg. 1092 IT
Lusofactor - Sociedade de Factoring, SA, av. Joao XXI, 63-2, pg. 251 IT
Lusotecna, Rua Padre Antonio Vieira, 26, 5, pg. 1361 IT
Luxottica Portugal S.A., Rua Joao de Freitas Branco,32-C, pg. 822 IT
MBT Portugal Lda., pg. 1465 IT
Mac-In/Macworld Portugal, Av. dos E.U.A. 110-B, pg. 570 PV
Makro Autoservico Grossista, S.A., Estrada da Circunvalacao, Quinta da Cabreira, pg. 1155 IT
McGraw-Hill Interamericana de Portugal, Ltda, Avenida Almirante Reis 59-6, pg. 1072 PB
Minnesota (3M) de Portugal, Lda., Rua Conde de Redondo, 98, pg. 1606 PB
Mitsui & Co. Europe (Portugal) Lda., Edificio Mobil Rua Castilho 165-3, pg. 880 IT
Mobil Oil Portuguesa Lda., Rua Castillo 165, pg. 1119 PB
Motorola Portugal Comunicacoes, Lda., Avenida da Republica 90-96 1 Fraccao 3, pg. 1140 PB
Moulinex, pg. 896 IT
Movifil-Movimentacao Industrial Lda., pg. 838 IT
MSFT Software Para Microcomputadores, LDA, pg. 1108 PB
Mundinter Intercambio undial de Commercio, Avenida Antonio 2761, pg. 822 PB
Nacionalgas, Avenida Antonio Aug de Aguiar, pg. 1416 IT
Nedlloyd Lines Navegacao S.A., pg. 1145 IT
Nedlloyd Road Cargo Transitarios Lda., pg. 1145 IT
A.C. Nielsen Company of Portugal, Rua D. Filipa De Vilhena, 38, pg. 1183 PB
Nokia Telecomunicacones Portugal S.A., Rua Soeiro Pereira Gomes, pg. 954 IT
Norske Skog Portugal, LDA, Rua Sampaio e Pina 50, pg. 966 IT
Novell Portugal, Rua Latino Coelho 1, Edificio Aviz, Bloco A3-9 Dto, pg. 1204 PB
OCE-Lima Mayer S.A., pg. 994 IT
Ocidental, Avenida da Republica 26, pg. 464 IT
Olivetti Portuguesa S.A., Praca Marques de Pombal 14-4, pg. 1003 IT
Oracle Soft Informatica, Lda., Praga de Damao 9, pg. 1228 PB
Panalpina Transportes Mundiais Lda., pg. 1023 IT
Pantrans Transitarios S.A., pg. 1023 IT
Pechiney Portugal Lda., Avenida da Liberdade 190-8 Esq, pg. 1031 IT
PETROGAL, S.A., Rua das Flores, 7, pg. 1044 IT
Pharmacia & Upjohn Farmoquimica, LDA., Rua Gregorio Lopes, pg. 1049 IT
Pharmacia & Upjohn Laboratorios S.A., Avenida do Forte No. 3, pg. 1048 IT
Portugal Previdente Companhia de Seguros (RAS), Rua Andrade Corvo, 32, pg. 61 IT
PORTUGUESE RAILWAYS (CP), Calcada do Duque, 20, pg. 1063 IT
Produtos SANDOZ Lda., pg. 983 IT
Promindustria - Sociedade de Investments, Av. Joao XXI, 63-2, pg. 251 IT
Publiter/BDDP, rua Gregorio Lopes, pg. 118 IT
Quimifar, Lda., Av. Marechal Gomes da Costa 33, pg. 1279 IT
Raychem (Portugal) Produtos Quimicos Lda., Rua Viriato, pg. 1363 PB
Rentokil (Portugal) Desinfestacoes Limitada, pg. 1286 IT
R.J. Reynolds (Portugal) Limitada, Rua do Proletariado No. 14, Portela de A, pg. 1355 PB

Sacor Maritima, S.A., Av. 24 De Julho, No 42, pg. 1045 IT
Sandvik Portuguesa Lda., pg. 1186 IT
Sapropur, S.A.R.L., Rua Dr. Antonio Candido, 10-40, pg. 429 PB
Secil S.A., Av. Conselheiro Fernando de Sousa 19, 18, pg. 476 IT
Seguros e Pensoes, Avenida da Republica, 26, pg. 464 IT
Seguros Genesis, S.A., Edificio Monumental, Av. Fontes Pereira de Melo, pg. 738 PV
Seleccoes do Reader's Digest (Portugal) S.A., Rua Francisco Manuel de Melo 21, pg. 1368 PB
Sensormatic Lda., Rua Jose de Melo e Castro, 17 A/B, pg. 1458 PB
Shell Portuguesa SA, Sede. Av de Liberdade, 249, pg. 1139 IT
Shimizu Construcao (Portugal) S.A., Av. Bombeiros Voluntarios, pg. 1234 IT
Sistemas de Informatica e de Medida, S.A., Rua Gregorio Lopes, pg. 823 IT
Skandia Portugal Propriedades S.A., Rua de Sao Jose 93-2, pg. 1258 IT
SmithKline & French Portuguesa, Productos Farmaceuticos Lda, pg. 1265 IT
Sociedad Gestora de Fundos de Pensoes SA, Rua Gastilho, 39-11 B, pg. 565 IT
Sociedade Portuguesa de Desenvolvimento-Quimico De Monsanto, Limitada, R. D. Joao 25, 1 Esq., pg. 1126 PB
Sociedad Portuguesa Honeywell Bull, Av. 5 Outubro 35-6, pg. 319 IT
Sociedade Gestora de Fundos de Pensoes da CGD, SA, Rua de Santa Catarina, 71-A, pg. 61 IT
Sociedade Portuguesa de Produtos Wander Lda., pg. 985 IT
Sociedade Portuguesa dos Ascensores Schindler Lda., pg. 1205 IT
Sociedade Zickermann S.A., Rossio, 3, Apartado 2115, pg. 740 IT
Societa Ital. per Condotte D'Acqua-Portugal, Ave. Conselheiro Fernando de Sousa 19/11, pg. 655 IT
Sofin - Dealers, S.A., Avda. Eugenio Duarto Pacheco, pg. 252 IT
Soltegio Portugal, Avenue Rose Malhoa, Lote 1642, pg. 21 IT
Solvay Interox, Ave. Marechal Gomes da Costa 33, pg. 1280 IT
Solvay Portugal Productos Quimicos S.A., Ave Marechal Gomes da Costa 33, pg. 1280 PB
Soquimica, Av. da Liberdade, 220-2, pg. 823 PB
Sulzer Infra Portugal, Ltda., pg. 1306 IT
Sulzer Portugal, Lda., pg. 1306 IT
The Sumitomo Bank, Ltd.-Lisbon Representative Office, Av. Antonio, Augustode Aguiar, pg. 1310 IT
TLT Iberphone, Avda. Eng. Arantes e Oliviera, pg. 252 IT
Tefal Rowenta Portugal, Av. da Republica 90-96-4 DTO, pg. 568 IT
Tima SA, Av. Defensores de Chaves 48-B, pg. 97 IT
TRANSPORTES AEREOS PORTUGUESES, Apartado 50 194, pg. 1418 IT
UPM-Kymmene Papel Lda., Rua Viriato 25-2o Dto, pg. 1430 IT
Uniao de Bancos Suicos, Rua Barata Salgueiro 30, Piso 7, pg. 1441 IT
Utell International-Portugal, Almitante Reis N 113, pg. 1098 IT
VB Autobaterias Lda., Apartado 8058, pg. 1452 IT
Wander (Portugal) Alimentocao Lda., pg. 986 IT
Warner-Lambert (Portugal) Comercio e Industria Limitada, Rua Gregorio Lopes Lote 1512, 1st Fl., pg. 1740 PB
Whitehall Portugal, Av Marechal Gomes Da Costa 9, pg. 81 PB
Willis Faber Limitada, Rua Vitor Cordon 7-3, pg. 1510 IT
YMR, Largo Das Fontainhas 5, pg. 750 IT
Yamanouchi Pharma Lda., Avenida Ferreira Godinho, Cruz Quebrada, pg. 1519 IT
Young & Rubicam (Portugal), Av. Eng. Duarte Pacheco 19, 10th Fl., pg. 1199 PV
Zeneca Agro-Produtos para a Agricultura LDA, Av. D. Carlos 1, 42.3, pg. 1526 IT
Zeneca Produtos Biociencia, LDA, Av dos Combatentes, pg. 1527 IT
Zurich Life Insurance Company, Rua Barata Salgueiro 41, pg. 1530 IT

Loures

Autodesk Software Lda., Apartado 152, pg. 150 PB

Madeira

Adriafruit Produtos Alimentares Florestais E Derivados Lda, Avenida Arriaga, 30, pg. 304 IT

Maia

CIBA-GEIGY Portuguesa, Lda., Apartado 7, pg. 978 IT
Companhia Nacional de Oxigenio S.A., pg. 1320 PB
Fuchs Lubrificantes LDA, Zona Industrial, Maia 1- Sector VII, pg. 518 IT
INAC Industria Nacional de Produtos Quimicos Lda., Rua de Custio, pg. 982 IT
Mold-Tech Portugal, Rua Da Estrada, 266, pg. 1507 PB
Nordson Portugal Equipamento Industrial, Lda., Rua Sidonio Pais 30-34, pg. 1189 PB
Teledinamica LDA., Rue De Cavaro No. 115, pg. 474 IT

Mamede de Infesta

Neste Quimica Comercial, S.A., Delegacao do Porto, Apartado 9, pg. 915 IT
UNICER-UNIAO CERVEJEIRA, S.A., Via Norte, Leca do Balio, pg. 1432 IT

Matosinhos

Bekaert Portugal-Importacao Comercializacao de Arames e Seus Derivados, Ltda., Av. D. Afonso Henriques, n 930-1, B2, pg. 184 IT
Gist-Brocades, Lda., Rue Herois Franca 846, pg. 1143 IT
Axel Johnson (Acose Equipamentos) Ltd., Apartado 294, Av. D. Afonso Henriques, 1208, pg. 711 IT
Longa Vida S.A., pg. 920 IT
Marie Elisabeth Produtos Alimentares S.A., Rua Sousa Aroso 648, pg. 807 PB
Procter & Gamble Portugal, Rua Monte dos Pipos, 109, pg. 1332 PB
Zeneca Produtos Biociencia, LDA, Rua Antero de Quental, pg. 1527 IT

Mem Martins

CIBA-GEIGY Portuguesa, Lda., Estrada Casais, Alto do Forte, pg. 978 IT
Laboratorio Normal Productos Farmaceuticos, Lda., Est Casais, Alto do Forte, pg. 983 IT
Moore Portuguesa Limitada, Estrada Nacional 250-1 km6, pg. 890 IT

Moita

Helly-Hansen Confeccoes Lda., Estrada National, 37-43, pg. 1010 IT

Noqueira

Raisio Portugal - Produtos Quimicos Lda., Rio-Noqueira, Apt. 7-Vermoim, pg. 1086 IT

Oeiras

Apliventil, Lda., Apartado 92, Sto. Amaro de Oeiras, pg. 710 IT
Betecna, Rua des Palmeiras, Torre Palmeiras-lote 69-P-1Q A-B-C, pg. 789 IT
Ceras Johnson de Portugal, Lda., Rua Maestro Raul Portela, 1, pg. 592 PV
Esselte, P.O. Box 1075, pg. 460 IT
Esselte Meto Portugal LDA, Estrada de Paço d'Arcos, 6E, pg. 461 IT
EURO RSCG, Estrada Marginal, Edificio Parque Oceano, 4th Fl., pg. 602 IT
KME Europa Metal Portugal, Lda., Rua Brito Camacho 15, Quinta, pg. 719 IT
Perstorp Ltda., Quinta da Fonte, pg. 1037 IT
Rockwell Automacao, Lda., Taguspark Edificio Inovacao, pg. 1399 PB
Zyma Farmaceutica Portuguesa Lda, pg. 986 IT

Olhao

Timar (Culturas em Agua), Lda., Apartado 49, pg. 1390 IT

Oporto

Enka Portuguesa Lda, 276-2 Rua do Coampo Alegre, pg. 46 IT
Willis Faber Limitada, Rua Julio Dinis 825, 2o, pg. 1510 IT

Palmela

AutoEuropa Automovels Lda., Quinta de Marqueza, pg. 1474 IT
Vanpro Assentos Lda., Parque Industrial Autoeuropa, IPOB 10206, pg. 193 IT

Parede

Gambro Lda., Parque Industrial Cotai, Estrada de Matos Cheirinhos, pg. 668 IT
Nutricia Portugal L.D.A., pg. 992 IT
Soplacas Lda, Estrada para Polima, pg. 1199 IT
Wormald Services De Proteccao Contra Incendios Limitada, Quinta Sao Miguel Das Encostas, pg. 1651 PB

Pinhal Novo

Frigoscandia Food Process Systems S.A., Delegacao Portugal, Praca de Independencia No 11-3, pg. 607 PB

Ponte de Sor

INLAN-Industria de Componentes Mecanicos, S.A., Apartado 40, pg. 723 PB

Portimao

Sociedade Turistica Da Penina Sarl, Penina Golf & Resort Hotel, pg. 556 IT
Willis Faber Limitada, Rua do Colegio 46-1C, pg. 1510 IT

PB - *U.S. Public Companies Volume*
PV - *U.S. Private Companies Volume*
IT - *International Public & Private Companies Volume*

Porto

ABB Stotz-Kontakt (Portugal) Lda., Rua do Rio, pg. 2 — IT
Aliada Quimica de Portugal Lda., Rua Jose Fulcao, 199, pg. 728 — IT
Ampco Metal Portugal Ltda., Rua de Recarei 312, 4465 S. Mamede de Infesta, pg. 67 — PV
BNP Factor - Portugal, Edificio Aviz, Avenida da Boavista 3523, pg. 163 — IT
Banco Portugues de Investimento, S.A., Rua Tenente Valadim, 284, pg. 1190 — IT
C.P.C.S.I., Rua de Costa Cabral 575, pg. 816 — PB
Caixa Geral de Depositos, Rua de Camoes, 155, pg. 250 — IT
Central de Cervejas-Porto Supply Center, Rua Manuel Pinto de Azevedo 414, pg. 279 — IT
CIBA-GEIGY Portuguesa, Lda., Apartado 1136, pg. 978 — IT
COMCAFE Comercial de Cafe, Ltda., pg. 920 — IT
Deutsche Bank de Investimento, S.A. (Porto), Av. da Boa Vista, 1361-2o, pg. 405 — IT
Forbo Pergol Revestimentos SA, pg. 498 — IT
Freudenberg Trading Portuguesa Lda., pg. 506 — IT
Generale Bank - Porto, Rua Nossa Senhora de Fatima 177, pg. 547 — IT
GESTRA Portuguesa Valvulas Lda., Av. Dr. Antunes Guimaraes, 1159, pg. 550 — IT
Kodak Portuguesa, Ltd., ACTIFOTO, Lda., Rua de Santa Catarina, 677, pg. 554 — PB
Lowara Portugal, pg. 861 — PB
Outokumpu (Portugal) Ltda., Rua Caldas Xavier, pg. 1016 — IT
PORTGAS, Rua de Sabrosa, 71, pg. 541 — IT
Sistemas de Informatica e de Medida, S.A., Rua Dorm Manuel II, pg. 823 — PB

Povoa de Santa Iria

Embalagens de Portugal - Van Leer, Ltda, pg. 1146 — IT
Solvay Portugal Productos Quimicos S.A., Rue enq Clement Dumoulin, pg. 1280 — IT

Queluz

Beiersdorf Portuguesa Lda, pg. 183 — IT
Central de Cervejas-Belas Factory, Quinta Aqua Fonte Cedro, pg. 279 — IT
Colgate-Palmolive Portuguese Ltda, Rua Mario Castelhano, Apartado 14, pg. 398 — PB
Enso Portugal Lda., Av. Dr. Fernando Ricardo, Ribeiro, Leitao, No. 8, pg. 457 — IT
Johnson & Johnson Limitada, Apartado 17, pg. 930 — IT
SmithKline Beecham Portuguesa Productos Farmaceuticos e Quimicos Lda., Rua Sebastio E Silva 56, Massama, pg. 1266 — IT

Rio de Mouro

Novo Nordisk Comercio de Produtos Farmaceuticos, Lda, Parque Industrial Meramar II, pg. 988 — IT

Sacavem

Central de Cervejas-Prior Velho Supply Center, Rua de Guine, pg. 279 — IT
Fina Portuguesa-Oleos E Carburantes, S.A., Quita do Figo Maduro, Apartado 105, pg. 1043 — IT
OMRON Electronics Lda., Edificio OMRON, Rua de Sao Tome, Lote 131, pg. 1006 — IT
Tintas Robbialac S.A., Vale de Lide, S. Joac da Talha, pg. 1501 — IT
Triumph International, R. Vasco de Gama, 36-3, pg. 1424 — IT
Wella Portugal Sociedade de Cosmeticos Luso-Alema Lda., Quinta da Francelha de Baixo, Lote 9, pg. 1490 — IT

San Joao da Madeira

Bertrand Faure Equipamentos para Automoveis SA, R. Comendador Rainho, Apartado 61, pg. 193 — IT
SPAV Lta., Avenida dos Chapeleiros, pg. 192 — IT

Santa Iria de Azoia

Companhia Vidreira Nacional SA, Ugar De Dom Pedro, pg. 1172 — IT

Santo Tirso

VERCOOPE-UNIAO DAS ADEGAS COOPERATIVAS DA REGIAO DOS VINHOA VERDES, U.C.R.L., Gandra, Agrela, pg. 1463 — IT

Savcavem

Grace Portuguesa Lda., Apartado 1401, pg. 756 — PB

Seixal

Delco Remi-Componentes Electronicos, Lda., Centro de Formaco, Profissional do Seixal, pg. 721 — PV
Farminova Produtos Farmaceuticos de Inovacao, Lda., Porto Zemouto, Coina, pg. 1283 — PB
Laboratorios Pfizer Lda., Porto Zemouto, Coina, pg. 1283 — PB
Lusosider Acos Planos SA, Aldeia de Paio Pires, pg. 755 — IT
Pfizer S.G.P.S. Lda., Porto Zemouto - Coina, pg. 1283 — PB

Seixezelo

Elefanten Portuguesa Lda. Industria de Calcado, pg. 505 — IT

Serzedo

Sun Chemical Portugal-Tintas Graficas S.A., Poligorno Industrial Vila Nova de Gaia, pg. 371 — IT

Setubal

Honeywell-Measurex (Portugal) Sistemas de Controle Ltda., Av. 22 de Dezemnbro, 21-7c, pg. 833 — PB
Merloni Electrodomesticos Lda., Praias do Sado, Apartado 99, pg. 860 — IT
Polarcup Portugal, Parque Industrial, Da Mitrena Hote 27, pg. 639 — IT
Rieter Componentes para Veiculos Lda., pg. 1117 — IT
Sasal, Vale de Ana Gomes, pg. 193 — IT

Sintra

CABLESA-Industria de Componentes Electricos Sociedade Anonima, Tapada Nova, pg. 721 — PB
Sondagens RODIO LDA., Avenida Dos Combatientes No. 52, pg. 454 — IT

Vendas

Bundy SA - Sucursal Portugesa, Estrada Nacional 4, Foros da Misericordia, pg. 1341 — IT

Viana do Castelo

Cablinal Portuguesa, Zona Industrial-Neiva, pg. 785 — IT

Vila do Conde

Sandvik Obergue-Limas e Mecanica Lda., pg. 1186 — IT

Vila Franca de Xira

Central de Cervejas-Vialonga Factory, Estrada daAlfarrobeira, pg. 279 — IT
Cimianto Sth SA, Alhandra, pg. 430 — IT
Metal Portuguesa S.A., Apartado 10, Castanheira do Ribatejo, pg. 619 — PB
Mitsubishi Motors de Portugal, S.A., Povos-2601, pg. 876 — IT

Vila Nova de Famalicao

Continental Mabor Industria de Aneus S.A., Lousado, pg. 328 — IT

Vila Nova de Gaia

Delaforce Sons & Ca Vinhos Lda., Apartado 6, pg. 409 — IT
Rozes Limitada, Rua Candido dos Reis 526-532, pg. 783 — IT
Salvador Caetano I.M.V.T., S.A.R.L., Apartado 51, pg. 1413 — IT
Toyota Motor Corporation, Porto Representative Office, Apartado 51, pg. 1413 — IT

QATAR

Doha

ANZ Grindlays Bank plc Qatar, pg. 99 — IT
Banque Paribas-Qatar, Rayyan Rd., pg. 320 — IT
British Aerospace BNI B.V. - Qatar, D Ring, Jn. Hassan Bin Thabit Street, pg. 134 — IT
Darwish Trading Company, pg. 550 — IT
Det Norske Veritas, no. 8, Bilas Villas, Al Qagila Street, pg. 398 — IT
Dukhan Service, pg. 1141 — IT
Fugro Peninsular Geotechnical Services, P.O. Box 318, pg. 431 — PV
Kassem Darwish Fakhroo & Sons, Government Road, pg. 1368 — IT
Nasser Trading & Contracting, P.O. Box 1563, pg. 822 — PB
Norsk Hydro A.S. Middle East Repr., pg. 964 — IT
Qatar Datamation Systems, KDS Bldg. 2, Mezzanine Fl., Chartered Bank Bldg., Al-Sudd St., pg. 823 — PB
Qatar Drilling Co., P.O. Box 4396, pg. 765 — IT
Qatar Shell Service, pg. 1141 — IT
Readymix Qatar WLL & The Quatar Quarry Co. WLL, pg. 1092 — IT
Standard Chartered Bank (Qatar), Abdullah Bin Jasim St., pg. 1295 — IT
Teyseer Services, pg. 1275 — IT

Umm Said

Qatar Fertiliser Co. S.A.Q., P.O. Box 50001, pg. 964 — IT
Qatar Steel Co. Ltd., P.O. Box 10090, pg. 741 — IT

REUNION

Le Port

Coroi-Negoce, pg. 108 — IT

Saint Denis

Brasseries de Bourbon S.A., 60 Quai Ouest, pg. 608 — IT
Sogeho-Reunion, 26, Rue de la Bourdonnais, pg. 823 — PB

ROMANIA

Bucharest

AGA Gaz S.R.L., Str. Frunzei, Nr 41, pg. 13 — IT
BASF SRL, 155, Calea Victoriei, Bl. D1, pg. 107 — IT
BASF SRL Abt. Knoll Pharma, 155, Calea Victoriei, Bl. D1, pg. 107 — IT
Robert Bosch S.R.L., Bl. 13, Bvd. Unirii Nr. 23, pg. 206 — IT
Brandeis Ltd.-Rep. Office of Pechiney Handelsgesellschaft in Romania, Apt. 8, 3rd Fl., 37 Mendeleev St., pg. 1030 — IT
Leo Burnett & Target, Pasajul Victorici 48, pg. 184 — PV
CCF Romania, Calea Dorobanti, 172, pg. 342 — IT
CPC Romania, pg. 225 — PB
CIBA-GEIGY Agro International SRL, 14B Feleacu Str., sector 1, pg. 976 — IT
CIBA-GEIGY Services AG, 36 Polona Street ap. 10, pg. 979 — IT
Danzas Romania, Calea Dorobantilor No. 111-131, Bloc 9B, pg. 382 — IT
Digital Equipment Romania S.R.L., Eminescu Street 124, pg. 508 — PB
Generala Asiigurari S.A., Str. Ion Ghica, 13 Sector 3, pg. 91 — IT
Henkel Romania SRL, pg. 613 — IT
Hepardimpex S.R.L., Str. Apusului nr. 35 Bl. D3, pg. 818 — IT
Honeywell Bucharest, St. Aurel Vlaicu, pg. 834 — PB
IDG Communications Publishing Group SRL, Bdul. Maresal Averescu, pg. 570 — PV
IIRUC, Blvd. Dimitrie Pompei 6, pg. 822 — PB
Korn/Ferry International, World Trade Center, Bd Expozitiei 2, pg. 634 — PV
Krupp Hoesch Stahlexport GmbH, Bloc 60A, Ap. 1, Rodica-Maria Ruhrig, pg. 516 — IT
Makhteshim-Agan Romania S.r.l., 9 Arjesului Street, pg. 831 — IT
Mitsui & Co., Ltd., c/o Hotel Inter-Continental, 4 Blvd. N., pg. 881 — PV
Monopoly International S.A., Bld N. Titulescu 1, bl A7, ap 8, pg. 1152 — PV
Norsk Hydro a.s. Romania, Hotel Diplomat, pg. 964 — IT
Novo Nordisk A/S, Str. Ion Calin 24, pg. 988 — IT
OFC/DMB&B Bucharest, Strada Aviator Mircea Zorileanu, #26, pg. 305 — PV
RZB Bucharest, Str. Brezoianu. 26-32 bl. 20, sc. A-B, et 5 ap. 53, Sect. 1, pg. 1084 — IT
Ram Representative Office-Romania, Calea Victoriei 32-34, pg. 741 — IT
Rhone-Poulenc Bucarest, Str. Sipotul Fintinilor no. 8, pg. 1112 — IT
AB Sandvik International, pg. 1186 — IT
Shell Romania SRL, Diplomat Hotel, Apt. 110B, Sevastopol Str. 13-17, pg. 1139 — IT
Sirom Graphic Trading, str. Av. Radu Beller nr. 25, pg. 1032 — PB
Swisscolor SRL, str Jean Texier No. 5, pg. 986 — IT
The World Bank, Boulevard Dacia 83, pg. 1189 — IT
Young & Rubicam Bucharest, 2 Logofat Luca Stroici Street, 1st Floor, pg. 1199 — PV
Zeneca Romania, 29 Tache Ionescu Street, pg. 1527 — IT

Timisoara

CIBA-GEIGY Services Ltd, Timisoara, Str Piatra Craiului, pg. 979 — IT

RUSSIA

Arkhangelsk

Kvaerner Kimek a.s, Arkhangelsk Office, Voskresenskaya Street 87B, pg. 772 — IT

Beloyarskiy

Van Leer Ural, pg. 1147 — IT

Chudovo

Chudovo-RWS, Novgorodskaja Obl., pg. 1429 — IT

Engels

Sovhenk, pg. 614 — IT

Ilyichevsk City

MacGREGOR (UKR) A/O, Ilyichevsk Shipyard, Rm. 401-404, pg. 671 — IT

Istra

OAO Istra-Nutricia, pg. 992 — IT

Ivanteevka

Polarcup Russia, Zheleznodorozhnaya Ulitsa 1, pg. 638 — IT

PB - *U.S. Public Companies Volume*
PV - *U.S. Private Companies Volume*
IT - *International Public & Private Companies Volume*

1740

Geographic Index-Non U.S.

Kommunar

OAO Komsomolets, Ul. Sovjetskaja, D.1., pg. 864 IT

Konstantinova

Fuchs-Janos, pg. 517 IT

Krasnodar

CIBA Kuban Ltd, ul im Shaumyana, 329, pg. 981 IT
Sedin-Schiess, Sacharow-Strasse 1, pg. 860 IT
Zeneca Kubanj, Ul. Pochtovaya, 78, pg. 1527 IT

Kromtau

Donax J/V, 25 Pl. Mira, pg. 710 IT

Mitischtehi

Kvaerner Hymac, Moscow Office, 22 4th Parkovaya St., Apt. 23, pg. 770 IT

Moscow

AMT, Khoroshevskoe Shosse 42-a, pg. 954 IT
AO Enercon, Mamonovskij per. 4/1, pg. 660 IT
A.O. Krokha, pg. 991 IT
A/O Pfizer, 129223 Russian Federation, Prospect Mira, VVC, pg. 1283 PB
AO UNOC Equipment & Supply, Bolshoi Gnezdikovsky per., 10, Room 108, pg. 316 IT
AO Zeneca Russia, Office 201, Bolshoi Strochenovski Per. 22/25, pg. 1525 IT
Abbott Laboratories-Moscow Sales Office, pg. 14 PB
Acuson CIS, pg. 18 IT
Adidas Russia, pg. 25 IT
Agro Barter United AB, Kutuzovskij Pr 13, Apt. 131-132, pg. 710 IT
Ahlstrom Representation in Moscow, Pokrovskij Bulvar, pg. 33 IT
Amercard, 3rd Cherepkovskaya St 15A, pg. 993 IT
American Bank Note Company, Maroseyka, 3/13, pg. 68 PB
American International Group-Moscow Representative Office, Radisson Hotel Slavyanskaya, 2 Berezhkovskaya Naberezhnaya, pg. 85 PB
Anser, 171, 54 2nd Tverskaya-Yamskaya, pg. 76 PV
Arthur D. Little International, Inc., 3rd Khoroshevsky Proyezd, 3V, Bldng. 2, pg. 670 IT
Autodesk Russia, 2 Baumanskaya, dom 9/23, pg. 149 PB
AUTOTRACTOREXPORT, 43 Lesnaja St., pg. 101 IT
BHP Group Resources Pty Ltd., Nororyazanskaya Street 38, pg. 225 IT
Bailey Automatisatzija, pg. 449 IT
Baker Trading Co., Rm. 422, Hotel Metropole, pg. 5 IT
Banca Nazionale del Lavoro, Intl. Trade Center, 16th, 12 Krasnesnenskaja Nab.- Office 1602, pg. 137 IT
Banco Di Napoli-Moscow, Voznesensky Pereulok, (Ul. Stankentcha), 20 - Bldg. 3, pg. 140 IT
Bank of America NT&SA, Krasnopresnenskaya Na 12, 15th Fl., Office 1503A, pg. 182 IT
The Bank of New York, Posledny Pereulok 17, 3rd Fl., No. 4, pg. 179 PB
Banque Paribas, Pokrovskij Blvd. 4/17, pg. 319 IT
Becema, Ilinskoye Shosse, 143400 Krasnogorsk-5, pg. 1134 IT
Berlitz Sovincenter, 12, Krasnopresenskaya NAB, pg. 222 PB
Bestrom, Illinskoye Shosse, 143400 Krasnogorsk, pg. 1134 IT
BHF-Representative Office, Ulanski Perevlok 4, 5th Floor, pg. 120 IT
Borland Representative Office, 1st Khvostov Pereulok 11-a, pg. 246 PB
Robert Bosch t.o.o., Novotscherjomuschkinskaja, pg. 205 IT
John Brown/Davy International, Pokrovsky Blvd., 4/17, pg. 772 IT
Bul A/O, Potapovsky Lane 5 Buil 3, pg. 317 IT
Bureau Rhone-Poulenc SA, Mytnaja UL. 1, pg. 1112 IT
Leo Burnett & Moradpour/Moscow, Sofitel Residence, Korovinskoya Chausse 10, pg. 184 PV
CIS, Yuzhinskiy Pereulok 13/1, pg. 654 IT
CPC Foods Company Ltd., pg. 225 PB
Cariplo (Moscow), Sajmonovskij Pr. 7, pg. 275 IT
Caterpillar Commercial A/O, 4/17 Pokrovsky Blvd., pg. 316 IT
CESIWID Refractories J.S.C., pg. 723 IT
The Chase Manhattan Bank, N.A., WTC/Krasnopresnenskaya Embankment 12, pg. 339 PB
Cho Hung Bank, Moscow Representative Office, Moscow Olympic Penta Hotel, Olympijskij Prospekt 18/1, pg. 288 IT
CIBA-GEIGY, Pokrowskij b-r, 4/17, kw 37, pg. 975 IT
CIBA-GEIGY Limited-Representative Office, Yuzhinsky Pereulok 15/A, pg. 977 IT
Coeclerici Trading S.P.A., 4, Dobryninskij Pereulok 6/9, pg. 304 IT
Commerzbank AG-Moscow Representative Office, Mamonovskij Pereulok 4-9, pg. 311 IT
Credit Commercial de France, Konushkovskaya Witsa 30, pg. 343 IT
DG Bank-Moscow, Ul. Mytnaja 3, pg. 352 IT
DMB&B Moscow, 20 Usievitcha St., pg. 304 PV
DSM Eastern Europe, VVC Building 5 Off. 52, Prospekt Mira, pg. 355 IT
Daewoo Corp. - Moscow, pg. 358 IT

Danzas Delegation, Ul. Dubininskay 94 a,4th Fl., pg. 382 IT
Deminex Moscow Office, P.O. Box 121, pg. 1461 IT
Dentsply Stomadent, Garshina Street, House #1, pg. 500 PB
Dentsu Moscow Office, E9, Entresol Floor, Business Ctr. S. Wing, Hotel Slavyanska, pg. 393 PV
Deutsche Bank AG (Moscow), ul. Ostoshenka 23, pg. 404 IT
Dumez Moscou, 14, bolchaia Dorogonilovskaia, pg. 823 IT
Dun & Bradstreet CIS, 3 Khoreshevski Proezd, Building 1/1, 4th Floor, pg. 536 PB
Durkopp Adler R. Ltd., Tichorezkij Bilvar, 1, pg. 469 IT
E/B/D/Interpartners - Moscow GmbH, Bolschoi Gnezdnikovskij pereulok 10/604, pg. 1152 PV
ESAB Representative Office, ul. Usacheva 35, pg. 282 IT
Electricite de France, 2e Spasonalivkovski per., 8, pg. 438 IT
Elkem Representative Office - Russia, P.O. Box 148, Krzhyzhanovskogo str. 14, bld 3, pg. 447 IT
EURO RSCG Media, c/o Maxima, 2 Sheremetievskaya St., pg. 603 IT
Falconbridge International Russia, 50 Ulitsa Bolshaya Ordynka, ap.3-4, pg. 434 IT
FATA USSR, Dobryninskaia 7-Office No. 6, pg. 474 IT
Fin.Co-Moscow, Yuzhinskiy Pereulok Pal 13/1, pg. 654 IT
Framlington Asset Management Russia, Konushkovskaya Witsa 30, pg. 343 IT
Frigoscandia Food Process Systems International AB, Danilovskij Business Centre, Gostinichnij Komplex, 5, Bolshio, pg. 607 PB
GDIVC (Glavni Demonstratciono-Ispytalelnjy Vychesliteinjy Center), Prospect Mira, pg. 817 PB
Generale Bank, International Trade Center, Krasnopresnenskaya Naberejnaya 12, pg. 547 IT
Hewlett-Packard Co. Representative Office, Pokrovsky Blvd. 4/17, pg. 819 PB
H.J. Heinz Company C.I.S., Dom Seven, Korpus One, Office 57, pg. 806 PB
Honeywell Inc., Tryokprudny per 11/13, pg. 835 PB
Honeywell Sterch Industrial Automation, Partizanskaya ul 27, pg. 835 IT
Hydro Aluminium Moscow, 35 Ulitsa Usatcheva, pg. 962 IT
Hydro Aluminium Nordisk Aviation Products Russia, Sheremetyevo-2, K-340, pg. 962 IT
IDC Russia, Prospekt Mira, VDNH, Pav. 4, Room 105-107, pg. 571 PV
INCOM J.V., Zubovsky Bulvar 27/26, pg. 1368 IT
ING Bank Eurasia, 45 Krasnaya Presna Street, pg. 649 IT
IR International Holdings, Inc., Ussievicha 24/2, UL, pg. 907 PB
Innse-Moscow, Yuzhinskiy Pereulok 11/2, pg. 655 IT
International Moscow Bank, 516 Pushkinskaya St., pg. 181 IT
Interturbine Moscow Rep. Office, c/o Energotechnocenter, 13/19 Tzhorskayastr., pg. 673 IT
Iritecna-Moscow, Yuzhinskiy Pereulok 13/1, pg. 655 IT
Axel Johnson Resources AB, Kutuzovskij Prospekt 13, 131-132, pg. 712 IT
Kemira Oy, Korovy Val 7/12, pg. 729 IT
Kidde-Graviner Moscow, 9 Ubking St., pg. 1500 IT
Kleinwort Benson Limited, 21/16 Bolshaya Ordnyka Street, pg. 420 IT
Kobe Steel, Ltd. (Moscow), Rm. No. 808, International Hotel No. 2, pg. 741 IT
KONE Representative Office, Chistiy Pereulok 11/7, pg. 747 IT
Korn/Ferry International, 20 Voznesensky per, pg. 634 PV
Kreditbank Representative Office (Moscow), Ulansky Per 4, 5th Fl., pg. 760 IT
Krupp Hoesch International GmbH, c/o Office of Fried.Krupp AG, International Trading Center, pg. 515 IT
Krupp Hoesch Stahlexport GmbH, Uliza Gubkina 14, 9th Floor, pg. 516 IT
Kvaerner Masa-Yards Inc., Moscow, Ul Lunacharskogo 7, kv 13-14, pg. 771 IT
LogoVAZ Systems, Kosinski Rojdestvenkij, pg. 1228 PB
Lotus Logistica S.r.l., 4, Dobryninskij Pereulok 6/9, pg. 304 IT
MKTS, pg. 1186 IT
MacNeal-Schwendler GmbH, ul. 26 Bakinskich, Komissarow 11, Vhg. 96, pg. 1032 IT
Merisel CAT, Ltd., 3 Kroutitskiy Val St., pg. 1096 PB
Merita Bank Ltd.- Moscow Representative Office, Pokrovsky Bldg. 4/17, Bldg. 4B, pg. 859 IT
Microsoft ZAO, pg. 1108 IT
Mitsui & Co., Ltd., Trade Center Krasnopresne, pg. 881 IT
Morgan Grenfell (Soviet Union), Ste. 34, Pokrovsky Blvd. 4/17, pg. 406 IT
Morgan Stanley Moscow, Ducat Pl., 8/10 Gasheka St., pg. 1133 PB
Moscow Printing Ink, 35 Volnaya Street, pg. 371 IT
Moscow Representative Office, Sarinskyi proezd 13, pg. 1519 IT
Motorola Mobile Communications, Narodnogo Opolchenia Str. 34, pg. 1140 IT
Moulinex, Representation a Moscou, KOROVY VAL, 7, APP.74, pg. 896 IT
NOKO-Nokia Representative Office, Chistyj Pereulok 11/7, pg. 953 IT
National Bank of Greece Moscow Branch, pg. 907 IT
National-Oilwell/Dreco Eastern Europe, Pereulok Building 1, 8 Maly Znamensky, Suite A, pg. 1158 PB
New Zealand Milk Products (CIS) AO, 2nd Fl., 6 Brigadersky Pereulok, pg. 923 IT
Norsk Hydro Moscow, 35 Ulitsa Usatcheva, pg. 964 IT
Novell Russia, Radisson Slavyanskaya Hotel, American Business Ctr., Ste. 509, pg. 1204 PB

Novo Nordisk A/S, Lomonosovskiy Prospect 38-11, pg. 987 IT
Novotruck, Avtozavodskaya 19, pg. 317 PB
Ost-West Allianz, 3rd Samotechny, Pereulok, 3, pg. 61 IT
Pall Filtrationstechnik GmbH, 5 Myakininskaya Ulitsa, Poselok-Rublewo 2, pg. 1254 PB
Panalpina World Transport AO, pg. 1023 IT
Parker Hannifin Corporation, Komsomolsky Prospect 42, Office 407, pg. 1263 PB
Pechiney Moscow, Oulitsa Guilisrovskogo, 65, pg. 1031 IT
Pepper, Hamilton & Scheetz, 19-27 Grokholsky Per., 129010, pg. 851 PV
Pepsi International Bottlers, 11-A Novinsky Boulevard, pg. 990 IT
Pharmacia & Upjohn Biotech AO, UL. Gobkane 14, Ext. KV 35, pg. 1047 IT
Pizza Hut (USSR), pg. 1637 PB
Plenum Publishing Corporation, 26 Vavilov St., pg. 1311 PB
POSTRADE Moscow Office, Leninsky prosp., 49, pg. 1062 IT
Power Conversion, P.O. Box 102, pg. 90 IT
Predstavitelstvo firmy "Enso", Pokrovskij buljvar 4/17,Kv. 11, pg. 458 IT
RNBNY Representative Office-Moscow, 9/5 Vesnina St., Ste. 9, pg. 1381 PB
RZB Moscow, Mytnaja 3, pg. 1085 IT
Ram Representative Office-Russia, Sadovaya-Samotechnaya Str. 24/27, pg. 742 IT
RECON, Building 1, Baumanskaya 43/1, pg. 608 IT
Reemtsma International GmbH - Russia, Office Russia/CIS, Armyansky Pereulok 6, pg. 1101 IT
Reprasentanz OMV AG, ITC-1 106, Krasnopresnenskaja nab. d 12, pg. 356 IT
Repres. Off. Intern. Trade Center, Ul. bolshaya Pionerskaya 4a, pg. 1004 IT
Repsol Exploracion, Groholsky, per., 19-27, Section 3, Fl. 1, pg. 1105 IT
Roche Moscow Ltd., pg. 1121 IT
Rockwell International Overseas Corporation, Suite 403, Bolshoi Strochenovski, pg. 1401 IT
Rosh Telecom Ltd., Technopark, V V C Mira Avenue, pg. 644 IT
SAIC-MIR/SAIC Global Technology, Moscow Ballet Theater, pg. 976 PV
SKF Moscow, Leninskaja Sloboda, 26, pg. 1159 IT
SNC-Lavalin, Centre International, Krasnopresnenskaia Nab. 12, Suite 608, pg. 1162 IT
SNC Lavalin - Moscow, Krasnopresnenskaia Nab. 12, Suite 608, pg. 1162 IT
SV Information Computer Enterprise, Ulitsa Gubkina, pg. 570 PV
Sandvik Russia A/O, pg. 1187 IT
Sanpaolo-Moscow Representative Office, Ul. Mosfilmovskaya 54, pg. 692 IT
Sayanal, 662793, Autonomous District of Zakhassk-, pg. 1387 PB
Schindler-Mosmontash-Lift, pg. 1205 IT
Shcherbinka Otis Lift, pg. 1691 IT
Shimadzu Moscow Office, Hotel Slavyanskaya Bus. Center, Berezhkovskaya Naberezhnaya 2, pg. 1232 IT
Sinochem Moscow Co., Ltd., Ste. 1647, Hotel, Wezhdunarodnaya-2, pg. 1256 IT
Sinochem Representative Office - Russia, Hotel Orekhovo, Korpus 2, Ul. Shipilovsky Proezd 43/1, pg. 1256 IT
Skadden, Arps, Slate, Meagher & Flom LLP, Pleteshkovsky Pereulok 3/2, pg. 1004 IT
Skandinaviska Enskilda Banken - Moscow, 22/25 Bolshoy, Strochenovskiy Pereulok, pg. 1259 IT
Sodexho A.O., c/o Societe Technologia, Ulitsa Tatiana Macarova No. 14-Bat .1, pg. 1275 IT
Sogecred S.A., Intl. Trade Center, 14th Floor, Office 1402, 12 Krasnopresnenskaja Nab., pg. 137 IT
Statoil CIS Moscow, Malayaordynka, pg. 1298 IT
STET-Moscow, Yuxhinskiy Pereulok Pal. 11/1, pg. 656 IT
Svedala Russia (Moscow), pg. 1325 IT
Svenska Handelsbanken Moscow, Pokrovskij Boulevard 4/17, pg. 1327 IT
Symantec, 1 Khvostov Pereulok 11A, pg. 1545 PB
Symtronix Corporation, Senezhskaya Street 1/9, Ste. 507, pg. 1563 PB
TBWA Moscow, 31 Staromonetny Per, pg. 1063 PV
Tampella-Metra, ul. Lunacharskogo kv. 2+13, pg. 1354 IT
Tamrock Moscow Office, Ul. Lunacharskogo 7, kv. 2, pg. 1353 IT
Teledyne Russia, Leningradsky Prospekt 55, pg. 44 PB
3M Russia (East), Samarsky Per, 3, pg. 1607 PB
UBS Representative Office, Pokrovskij Bulvar 4/17, kv. 4, pg. 1441 IT
Union Bank of Switzerland, Pokrovskij Bulvar 4/17 kv 4, pg. 1441 IT
Utell International-Russia, (VEI) Krasnokazarmennaja, pg. 1099 IT
Valmet Trade Promotion Office, Ul. Solyanka, 7, pg. 1449 IT
Van Melle Moscow Representative Office, Ulitsa Vavilova 69, pg. 1451 IT
Vertretung der BASF in der Russischen Foederation, B. Gnezdnikovskij per. 7, pg. 110 IT
Vertretung der BASF in der Russischen Foederation Abt. Knoll Pharma, Ul. Malaja Trubezkaja, 8, pg. 110 IT
Werner & Pfleiderer Backtechnik AG, Ul. Uljanowskaja 57/1, pg. 511 IT
Westdeutsche Landesbank Moscow, A/O Westdeutsche Landesbank Vostok, pg. 1494 IT
Willis Corroon & Willis Faber & Dumas Limited, ul. Spiridonovka (Alekseia Tolstogo) 16, pg. 1509 IT
Windmoller & Holscher -Buro Moskau, Kasatschi Pereulok, Haus 5/2, pg. 1511 IT

PB - *U.S. Public Companies Volume*
PV - *U.S. Private Companies Volume*
IT - *International Public & Private Companies Volume*

The World Bank, Moscow Office, Sadovo-Kudrinskaya No. 3, pg. 1190 **PV**
Young & Rubicam/Sovero, 801 Sovincenter, 12 Krasnopresnenskaya Nab., pg. 1199 **PV**
ZAO Outokumpu Moskva, Ul. Arhitektora Vlasova, Dom. 51, 6th Floor, pg. 1016 **IT**
ZAO Russia, Mytnaya Str. 1, & lat 15, pg. 638 **IT**
ZAO Danfoss, Marksistskaya ul. 34, pg. 378 **IT**
ZAO KONE Lifts, Ul. Giljarovskogo, 4, pg. 748 **IT**
ZAO Norvista - Moscow, Spiridonevski Pereulok 5 kv 5, pg. 486 **IT**

Murmansk

Kvaerner Kimek a.s, Murmansk Office, Tralovaya str. 12 A, pg. 772 **IT**
OAO Kola Mining, Lenin Str. 75, pg. 1016 **IT**

Novgorod

CIBA-GEIGY Limited-Representative Office, ul. Uljanowa 11, pg. 977 **IT**
Vera Co., Ltd., Russian Federation, M. Gorkiy St.. 147-A, pg. 697 **IT**

Novosibirsk

CIBA-GEIGY Limited-Representative Office, Novosibirsk p/o Krasnoobsk, pg. 977 **IT**
Commerzbank AG Representative Office-Novosibirsk, Krasny Prospekt 42, 4th Floor, pg. 312 **IT**
SAIC in Novosibirsk, The American Business Center, Ulitsa Lenina 21, Hotel Sibir 7th Floor, pg. 976 **PV**
Silbertech, Monocrystal Institute, 43 Russkay Street, pg. 1115 **PB**

Orenburg

CIBA-GEIGY Limited-Representative Office, ul. Turkestanskaja 5, kw. 413, pg. 977 **IT**

Petrozavodsk

Gemeinschaftsunternehmen Petrovoith, pg. 1473 **IT**
A/O Kivijarvi Oy, Uritsky Ul. 65, pg. 1016 **IT**

Podolsk

BLK-SIO Energie-und Umwelttechnik AG, Zheleznodoroznaya, 2, pg. 398 **IT**
Balacke-Durr SIO AG, Zheleznodoroznaya, 2, pg. 400 **IT**
Bergemann-SIO, Zhelznodorozhnayn, 2, pg. 398 **IT**

Saint Petersburg

A/O Ahlstrom, (Institut Gipronikel), Grazhdanskji Prospekt 11, pg. 34 **IT**
AO Finncolor, Lesnoj pr. 61 k l, pg. 729 **IT**
Akerlund & Rausing, Ahlstrom Eurapak, Lermontovskij pr. 44, kv. 83, pg. 33 **IT**
American Appraisal (AAR), Inc., pg. 50 **PV**
Amerpap East Ltd., Nevskij prospeckt 93, 2nd Floor, pg. 863 **IT**
BNP-Dresdner Bank (Rossija), Isaak Place 11, pg. 418 **IT**
Benckiser AG, pg. 185 **IT**
Betomix AO, Grazhdansky Ave. 11, pg. 1200 **IT**
Charmilles Technologies Ltd. Spb St. Petersburg, 1 Krasnoarmeiskaya ul. 13, pg. 489 **IT**
CIBA-GEIGY Limited-Representative Office, B. Podjatscheskaja 30, pg. 977 **IT**
CIBA-GEIGY Limited-Representative Office, Lermontowskij pr. 44, pg. 977 **IT**
Commerzbank AG Representative Office-St. Petersburg, Bolschoj Prospekt 10, pg. 312 **IT**
DMB&B St. Petersburg, 19, ul Smoliatchkova, pg. 304 **PV**
Energosofin, Serebristyj bulvar, dom 38, kv. 138, pg. 1354 **IT**
Honeywell Home & Buiiding Control, Ulitsa Zakharevskaya 31, pg. 834 **PB**
ZAO KONE Lifts St. Petersburg, Lisichanskaya ul. 19, pg. 748 **IT**
Korn/Ferry International, Office 5, Bolshaya Morskaya 57, pg. 634 **PV**
Leaf Russia, V.O. 13th, Liniya 14, pg. 638 **IT**
Lucent Technologies Manufacturing of St. Petersburg, 17 Tchapaeva St., pg. 1018 **PB**
MacGREGOR (RUS) A/O, Ul. Zvenigorodskaja 3, pg. 671 **IT**
Merita Bank Ltd. - St. Petersburg Representative Office, Nevsky Prospekt 57, 4th Fl., pg. 859 **IT**
A/O Mineral Processing Engineers, 21 Line, 8a, pg. 1017 **IT**
Neste Chemicals, pg. 914 **IT**
Neste St. Petersburg, 160, Leninskij prospekt, pg. 915 **IT**
A/O Nevamash, pr Stachek 47, pg. 317 **PB**
Nokia Switching Systems, Pr. B. Sampsonievsky 60, pg. 954 **IT**
Nordson Deutschland GmbH Representative Office, 37 Energetikov Ave., 6th Fl., pg. 1189 **PB**
Ost-West Allianz (St. Petersburg Office), ul. Divenskaja 3, pg. 61 **PB**
Len Otis Lift, pg. 1691 **IT**
Predstavitelstvo firmy "Enso", Lermontovskij pr., pg. 458 **IT**
Svedala Russia (St. Petersburg), pg. 1325 **IT**
Tampella Power St. Petersburg Ltd., Serebristyj bulvar, dom. 38 kv. 157-158, pg. 1354 **IT**
Technip C.I.S., 20, rue Galernaya, pg. 1361 **IT**

Tefal et KV Saint Petersburg, Sverdlovskaya Nab 12, pg. 568 **IT**
Valmet Trade Promotion Office, P.O. Box 208, pg. 1449 **IT**
Vink ZAO, Ul. Karavannaja 1, 3rd Floor, pg. 1211 **IT**
WestLB St. Petersburg, Bolschoj Prospekt 10, W.O., pg. 1493 **IT**
ZAO Norvista - St. Petersburg, Hotel Astoria, Boljshaja Morskaja 39, pg. 486 **IT**
ZAO Outokumpu St. Petersburg, 18 Line dom 47, pg. 1016 **IT**

Saratov

CIBA-GEIGY Limited-Representative Office, ul. Babuschkin Wswos 1, pg. 977 **IT**
TANTEL-EOC Normalien GU, Burovaja Uliza 6, pg. 75 **IT**

Taldom

Rannila Taldom A/O, Moskovskoj oblasti, ul. zagoroduajala, pg. 1088 **IT**

Tosno

A.O.O.¨. Henkel era Tosno, pg. 611 **IT**

Ufa

CIBA-GEIGY Limited-Representative Office, ul. Sowetskaja 18, pg. 978 **IT**

Uljanowsk

CIBA-GEIGY Limited-Representative Office, ul. Lenina 9, pg. 977 **IT**

Vladivostok

ING Bank Vladivostok, Svetlanskaya Street 11, pg. 649 **IT**

Wolgograd

CIBA-GEIGY Limited-Representative Office, ul. Mira 15, pg. 977 **IT**

Woronesh

CIBA-GEIGY Limited-Representative Office, ul. Serafimowitscha 26, pg. 977 **IT**

RWANDA

Kigali

BP-Fina Rwanda S.A.R.L., Parc Industriel Gikondo, B.P. 144, pg. 1044 **IT**
Banque Commerciale du Rwanda S.A., Avenue de la Revolution, 11, pg. 148 **IT**
Banque de Kigali, Avenue du Commerce 63, pg. 548 **IT**
Brasseries et Limonaderies du Rwanda "Bralirwa" S.A.R.L., Centre de Gestion, pg. 608 **IT**
Interfreight Investissements Rwanda S.A., pg. 1022 **IT**
R.T.I. Infotech, Avenue Kansambi, pg. 823 **PB**
The World Bank, SORAS Bldg., Blvd. de la Revolution, pg. ¨190 **PV**

SAINT KITTS AND NEVIS

Basseterre

Harowe Servo Controls, Bourkes Rd., pg. 90 **PB**
Reed Data Services Limited, Ponds Industrial Estate, pg. ¨096 **IT**
Shell Antilles, P.O. Box 215, St. Kitts Intl. Airport, pg. ¨141 **IT**

SAMOA

Apia

BOC Gases (Samoa) Ltd., P.O. Box 1862 Vaitele, pg. ¨21 **IT**
Bank of Western Samoa, pg. 100 **IT**
Bermuda Trust (Western Samoa) Limited, Level 2, Gold Star Building, Beach Road, pg. 151 **IT**
Pacific Commercial Bank Limited, P.O. Box 192, pg. ¨248 **PB**
Westpac Banking Corp. - Western Samoa, c/o Pacific Commercial, Bank Limited, pg. 1497 **IT**

SAUDI ARABIA

Al-Khobar

Arabian Paper Products Company (APPCO), P.O. Box 1520, pg. 639 **IT**
Arabian Pipecoating Company Ltd., P.O. Box 106, pg. 1231 **IT**
John Crane Saudi Arabia Ltd., pg. 1339 **IT**
Crest Arabia Ltd., Dhahran Airport, pg. 5 **IT**
Ebasco Arabia Limited, Hilal Bldg., Al Khobor 28th Street, pg. 1587 **PB**
JGC Arabia Ltd., P.O. Box 2414, pg. 697 **IT**

Mannesmann Anlagenbau Arabia Ltd., pg. 837 **IT**
Mantech Computer & Education Aids, P.O. Box 710, pg. 822 **IT**
Mitsui & Co., Ltd., 2nd Fl., ACE Bldg., 28th St., pg. 881 **IT**
Modern Electronic Establishment (M.E.E.), pg. 822 **PB**
NKK Corporation-Al-Khobar, pg. 903 **IT**
Pool Arabia Ltd., Dhahran Airport, pg. 1316 **PB**
Saudi SNC-Lavalin Company Limited, Fluor Daniel Arabia Office Complex, pg. 1163 **IT**
Taisei Saudi Arabia Co., c/o Rezayat Trading Co., pg. 1347 **IT**
Technip Saudi Arabia Ltd., pg. 1361 **IT**

Al-Krabiyah

Weatherford Saudia Arabia Ltd., Al Rushaid Grp. Bldg., P.O. Box 623, pg. 1750 **PB**

Dammam

Abdulla Fouad Corporation Ltd., P.O. Box 806, pg. 502 **IT**
Ameron Saudi Arabia, Ltd., P.O. Box 589, pg. 99 **PB**
Amiantit Fibreglass Indus., Ltd., P.O. Box 589, pg. 1237 **PB**
Arabian Fiberglass Insulation Co., P.O. Box 1289, pg. 1237 **PB**
Bondstrand, P.O. Box 589, pg. 99 **PB**
Computer & Electronic Division, P.O. Box 257, pg. 501 **IT**
Continental Can of Saudi Arabia, Dammam Industrial Park 2, pg. 465 **PB**
Corro-Coat Saudi Arabia Ltd., pg. 715 **IT**
Abdulla Fouad Auctioneers, P.O. Box 257, pg. 502 **IT**
ABDULLA FOUAD CO. LTD., P.O. Box 257, pg. 501 **IT**
Abdulla Fouad Impalloy Ltd. Co., P.O. Box 257, pg. 502 **IT**
Abdulla Fouad-Testrade Middle East, P.O. Box 257, pg. 502 **IT**
Fouad Supply & Services Division, P.O. Box 257, pg. 502 **IT**
Fouad Travel & Cargo Agency, P.O. Box 257, pg. 502 **IT**
Gray Tool International, c/o Drilling Equipment, & Chemicals Co., pg. 6 **IT**
Honeywell Turki Arabia Ltd., King Khalid Str., pg. 835 **PB**
Iscosa Industries & Maintenance, Ltd., Box 1032, pg. 1198 **PB**
Mantech Co., Ltd., P.O. Box 257, pg. 502 **PV**
McClelland-Suhaimi, Ltd., pg. 431 **IT**
Medical Supplies Division, P.O. Box 257, pg. 502 **IT**
Nalco Saudi Co. Ltd., Old Damman Industrial Estate, pg. 1151 **IT**
National Cleaning Products Ltd., P.O. Box 5952, Abudawood Bldg., pg. 387 **PB**
Oasis-Ameron, Ltd., P.O. Box 589, pg. 99 **PB**
Petrolite Saudi Arabia Ltd., P.O. Box 1940, pg. 166 **PB**
Qanbar Steetley (Saudi) Limited, pg. 1092 **IT**
Saudi Arabia Concrete Products Ltd., pg. 99 **PB**
Saudi Electro-Mechanical Construction Co. (Petcon), P.O. Box 1664, pg. 1122 **PB**
Yusuf Bin Ahmed Kanoo, via Dhahran Airport, pg. 110 **IT**

Dhahran

Al Rushaid Eastman Arabia Limited, Dhahran Airport, pg. 1174 **IT**
Awabed - Ssangyong Contracting Co., P.O. Box 1058, pg. 1292 **IT**
Christensen Saudi Arabia Limited, P.O. Box 244, Dhahran Airport, pg. 1174 **IT**
Fluor Daniel Arabia Limited, Dhahran Airport 31932, pg. 660 **IT**
Santa Fe Braun Inc., Riyadh Towers Bldg., 9th Fl., King Abdul Aziz & 28th St., pg. 765 **IT**
Texaco Arabia Inc., Box 5000, pg. 1584 **PB**

Jeddah

Al-Osama Co., Ltd., pg. 105 **IT**
Alahamrani-Fuchs Petroleum Products Co. Ltd., pg. 518 **IT**
Arabian Elevator & Escalator Co. Ltd. (AREECO), P.O. Box 14326, pg. 748 **IT**
Arabian Environmental Services Company Limited, pg. 777 **PB**
Atlas Mammoet Co. Ltd., pg. 1144 **IT**
Banque Indosuez, Medina Rd., P.O. Box no1, pg. 315 **IT**
Best Foods Saudi Arabia Co. Ltd., Ali-Reza Tower, Medina Rd., pg. 225 **PB**
Det Norske Veritas, 2nd Fl., Pearl of Jeddah Bldg., Hail St., pg. 398 **IT**
Farouk Advertising, Al-Tahlia Street, pg. 304 **PV**
Furukawa Saudi Arabia, Ltd. (FSA), pg. 531 **IT**
Hanwa Co., Ltd.-Jeddah Branch, Office #219, Kaki Ctr., pg. 595 **IT**
Intermarkets Saudi Arabia, Al Esayt Plaza, Madinah Road, pg. 680 **IT**
The International Commercial Bank of China, C/O Commercial Division, Taipei Economic & Cultural Rep. Office, pg. 683 **IT**
JGC Arabia Ltd., P.O. Box 1077, pg. 697 **IT**
Jeddah Beverage Can Making Company Ltd., St. 33, Rd. 31, pg. 465 **PB**
Litton Saudi Arabia Ltd., pg. 1004 **PB**
Mining Services Co. Minserco, P.O. Box 3199, pg. 443 **IT**
Mitsui & Co., Ltd., Saico Bldg., Medina Rd., pg. 881 **IT**
Modern Electronic Establishment (M.E.E.), pg. 822 **PB**
NYK Line-Jeddah, c/o Haji Abdullah Alireza & Co, King Abdul Aziz Street, pg. 942 **IT**
Nesma-Costain Process Co. Limited, P.O. Box 6967, pg. 337 **IT**
Saudi Arabian Parsons Ltd., P.O. Box 3087, pg. 842 **PV**

PB - *U.S. Public Companies Volume*
PV - *U.S. Private Companies Volume*
IT - *International Public & Private Companies Volume*

Geographic Index-Non U.S.

1742

Saudi Building Systems, Ltd., pg. 271   **PB**
Saudi Factory for Electrical Appliances Company Ltd.,
 Industrial City Phase II, pg. 874   **IT**
Saudi Food Industries Ltd. Liability Co., pg. 922   **IT**
Saudi Industrial Resins Ltd., pg. 140   **PB**
Saudi Liebherr Company Ltd., pg. 809   **IT**
Saudi National Insurance Company EC (SNIC), New Juffali
 Head Office Bldg., pg. 1532   **IT**
Sherwin-Williams Saudi Arabia Ltd., pg. 1466   **PB**
Sumitomo Rubber Industries-Jeddah, pg. 1317   **IT**
Targets-Leo Burnett Advertising, Shinkar Commercial
 Center, 2nd Fl., Medina Rd., pg. 186   **PV**
Toyota Motor Corporation, Jeddah Representative Office,
 P.O. Box 248, pg. 1413   **IT**
Utell International-Saudi Arabia, Medina Road,
 pg. 1099   **IT**
Voest-Alpine Saudi Arabia Ltd., Sharafia Road,
 pg. 1472   **IT**
The Yokohama Rubber Co., Ltd., C/O Abdulaziz &
 Mohammed A., Alijomaih, P.O. Box 467, pg. 1521   **IT**
Yusuf Bin Ahmed Kanoo BASF Division, Medina Road km
 9, pg. 110   **IT**

Jubail

Qanbar Dywidag Precast Concrete Ltd., P.O. Box 515,
 pg. 425   **IT**

Khamis Mushayt

Boeing Services, Inc., Unit 61901, Box R, pg. 242   **PB**

Mubarraz

Banque Indosuez, Al Hazm St., pg. 315   **IT**

Riyadh

Al-Bab Care of Daewoo, pg. 357   **IT**
Al Bank Al Saudi Al Franki, Ma'ther Road, pg. 315   **IT**
Alrashid-Abetong Co. Ltd., P.O. Box 6058, pg. 1199   **IT**
Ansaldo Saudia Ltd., pg. 654   **IT**
Arabian Plastic Manufacturing Company, pg. 489   **IT**
Arthur D. Little International, Inc., pg. 670   **PV**
BBC Brown Boveri Saudi Arabia Ltd., P.O. Box 4441,
 pg. 3   **IT**
Ballast Nedam Groep N.V., Al Akariyah Commercial
 Complex, Olaya Road, pg. 134   **IT**
Boeing Middle East Limited, B4 Tower, Fl. 7, Abunumay
 Comml. Center, Sitteen St., pg. 242   **PB**
CRSS Arabia Ltd., pg. 1415   **IT**
Cerner Arabia Ltd., c/o El Seif Development Co., P.O. Box
 15665, pg. 331   **PB**
CIBA-GEIGY Services Limited, pg. 979   **IT**
Electrolux Saudi Services, Ltd., P.O. Box 7210, pg. 443   **IT**
GETCO General Enterprises and Trading Corp.,
 pg. 550   **IT**
General Dynamics International Corporation, pg. 709   **PB**
Hanwa Co., Ltd.-Riyadh Branch, pg. 595   **IT**
Harris Saudi Arabia Ltd., P.O. Box 3750, pg. 791   **PB**
Hawa Munters Co. Ltd., c/o Hawa Cooling System Co Ltd,
 pg. 669   **IT**
Intalcable-Saudi Arabia, pg. 655   **IT**
Intergraph Saudi Arabia Ltd., Al Mousa Bldg., 2nd Tower, Al
 Olaya Street, pg. 892   **PB**
JGC Arabia Ltd., P.O. Box 17781, pg. 697   **IT**
KSB Pumps Arabia Ltd., pg. 721   **IT**
Litton Saudi Arabia, P.O. Box 7529, pg. 1004   **PB**
Lockheed Corporation (International) S.A., c/o Lockheed
 Middle East Services, pg. 1009   **PB**
Lockheed Middle East Services, P.O. Box 2811,
 pg. 1010   **IT**
Lummus Alireza Ltd. Co., P.O. Box 245, pg. 6   **IT**
Mansour General Dynamics Ltd., M60 Conversion,
 pg. 709   **PB**
Martin Marietta International, Inc., Eastern Corporation
 Bldg., 4th Fl., Dhabab St., pg. 1010   **PB**
Martin Marietta International, Inc., c/o Safari Co., Ltd.,
 Khurais Rd., pg. 1010   **PB**
Mitsui & Co., Ltd., Al-Sitten Trading Center, Riyadh Sitten
 St., pg. 881   **IT**
Modern Electronic Establishment (M.E.E.), P.O. Box 22015,
 pg. 822   **PB**
Neste Arabia Oil Co., P.O. Box 61134, pg. 914   **IT**
Pechiney Baker, P.O. Box 2985, pg. 1031   **IT**
Peninsular Aviation Services, pg. 1141   **IT**
Raychem Saudi Arabia Limited, Al Khaleej Commercial
 Center, 2nd Fl., Flat No. 207, Olaya St., pg. 1363   **PB**
Rockwell Systems International, Inc., P.O. Box 2375,
 pg. 1402   **PB**
Saduc, pg. 823   **IT**
Saudi American Bank, P.O. Box 833, pg. 379   **PB**
Saudi American General Electric, pg. 713   **PB**
Saudi Arabian Biokat Ltd., pg. 837   **IT**
The Saudi British Bank, Al Amir Abdul Aziz Ibn Mossaad,
 Ibn Jalawi Street, pg. 583   **IT**
Saudi Crawford Doors Factory Ltd., P.O. Box 259 60,
 pg. 270   **IT**
Saudi Ericsson Communications Co. Ltd., Sitteen St.,
 pg. 1369   **IT**
Saudi TKT Air Conditioning Company Ltd., pg. 400   **IT**
Shell Overseas Services Ltd., P.O. Box 16996,
 pg. 1141   **IT**
Stolt-Nielsen Inc., pg. 1302   **IT**
Sumitomo Electric Industries, Ltd., pg. 1314   **IT**
Teamwork Saudi Arabia Limited, P.O. Box 10747,
 pg. 1360   **IT**
Telefonaktiebolaget LM Ericsson Saudi Arabia,
 pg. 1370   **IT**

The World Bank Resident Mission, UNDP Bldg., King Faisal
 St., pg. 1190   **PV**
The Yokohama Rubber Co., Ltd., C/O Mitsubishi
 Corporation, Services, pg. 1521   **IT**

Tareet

Al-Jubail Petrochemical Company, Industrial Area,
 pg. 601   **PB**

Yanbu

Jotun Saudia Co. Ltd., pg. 716   **IT**

SENEGAL
Dakar

Africaine de Raffinage, pg. 1136   **IT**
Banque Internationale pour le Commerce et l'Industrie du
 Senegal (BICIS), 2 Av. Roume, pg. 149   **IT**
Bull Senegal, Extension Immeuble Kebe 99, ave. Andre
 Peytavain, pg. 315   **IT**
CII-Honeywell Bull Senegal SARL, Extension Immeuble
 Kebe, 99, Avenue Adnre-Peytavin, pg. 316   **IT**
Det Norske Veritas, 43 Ave. Albert Sarraut, pg. 397   **IT**
Iransen et Shell, pg. 1136   **IT**
Nestle Senegal, pg. 921   **IT**
R.T.I. Senegal Services, 150, Av. President Lamine Gueye,
 pg. 823   **PB**
Rhone-Poulenc Senegal-SSPT, 14, avenue B. Desbordes,
 pg. 1114   **IT**
Senmatel, 9-11, allees Robert Delmas, pg. 706   **IT**
Shell Senegal, Route des Hydrocarbures, pg. 1137   **IT**
Soc. Africaine d'Expansion Chimique (SAEC) SA, Ave. Felix
 Eboue, pg. 43   **IT**
Societe Generale de Banques Au Senegal, Avenue Roume
 19, pg. 548   **IT**
The World Bank, Immeuble S.D.I.H., 3 Place de
 l'Independance, pg. 1190   **PV**

SERBIA
Belgrade

Bull HN Jugoslavia D.O.O., St. Mite Ruzica 28, pg. 318   **IT**
CIBA-GEIGY Services AG, Bulevar Nikole Tesle 3,
 pg. 979   **IT**
CIBA-GEIGY Services AG, p fah 941, pg. 979   **IT**
Comercio Exterior de Chile Ltda., E.C.E. Belgrado, Sremska
 4/A, Fl. 3 & 4, pg. 303   **IT**
Daewoo Corp. - Belgrade, pg. 358   **IT**
Electronska Industrija Kft., Preduzec El Bull HN, Masankova
 15/19, pg. 317   **IT**
Hermes, Zrmanjska 10, pg. 818   **PB**
JUGOBANKA BANKING GROUP, 7 Jula 19-21,
 pg. 716   **IT**
Mitsui & Co., Ltd., Palata Jadran Parter, pg. 881   **IT**
Novo Nordisk A/S, Generala Zdanova 76, pg. 988   **IT**
Zeneca International Ltd., Pharmaceuticals Division,
 Interncionalnih Brigada 54, pg. 1526   **IT**

Zrenjanin

IPOK, Pancevacka 70, pg. 447   **PB**

SEYCHELLES
Mahe

Habib Bank Ltd., Francics Rachel St., pg. 584   **IT**
Seychelles International Mercantile Banking Corporation
 Limited, State House Ave., pg. 1296   **IT**

SIERRA LEONE
Freetown

Barclays Bank of Sierra Leone Ltd., Siaka Stevens St.,
 pg. 165   **IT**
Blackwood Hodge (Sierra Leone) Ltd., Kissy Works,
 Pilgrims Way, pg. 231   **IT**
Lazare Kaplan (Sierra Leone) Ltd., pg. 981   **PB**
Mobil Oil Sierra Leone Limited, pg. 1119   **IT**
Shell Sierra Leone Ltd., Kissy Installation, Kissy Dockyard,
 pg. 1141   **IT**
SIEROMCO Sierra Leone Ore & Metal Co. Ltd., pg. 69   **IT**
Sierra Leone Cement Corp. Ltd., pg. 1201   **IT**
Sierra Leone Petroleum Refining, pg. 1137   **IT**
Standard Chartered Bank Sierra Leone Ltd., 9-11 Lightfoot
 Boston St., pg. 1295   **IT**
UAC of Sierra Leone Ltd., pg. 1438   **IT**

SINGAPORE
Alexandra Point

Acer Computer International Ltd., 438 Alexandra Rd., #17-
 00, pg. 22   **IT**
SAS Institute Pte. Ltd., 438 Alexandra Road, 0511,
 pg. 967   **PV**

Belait

The Netherlands Insurance, Shop Lot No. 86, 2nd Floor,
 Jalan Bunga Raya Kuala, pg. 651   **IT**

Chinatown Point

Vertex Asia, 133 New Bridge Rd. #25-03/05, 059413,
 pg. 1718   **PB**

Hougang

MEC International Pte. Ltd., pg. 1122   **PB**

Jurong

Adhesives (Far East) Pte. Ltd., 107 Neythal Rd.,
 pg. 129   **IT**
Aeracom Technologies Pte. Ltd., 17 Pioneer Crescent,
 pg. 1293   **IT**
AlliedSignal (Ltd.) Singapore, 161 Gul Circle, pg. 53   **PB**
American Marine Pte. Ltd., 26 Jalan Terusan, pg. 531   **IT**
Asea Brown Boveri Pte. Ltd., 2 Sixth Lok Yang Rd.,
 pg. 8   **IT**
Associated Spring-Asia, 28 Tuas Ave. 2, pg. 190   **PB**
BHP Steel Building Products Singapore Pte Ltd., 18 Benoi
 Sector, pg. 226   **IT**
BHP Steel Engineering Services Singapore Pte Ltd., 18
 Benoi Sector, pg. 227   **IT**
BRC Weldmesh (SEA) Pte Ltd., 350 Jalan Boon Lay,
 pg. 227   **IT**
BetzDearborn Pte. Ltd., 10, Tanong, Penjuru Crescent,
 608973, pg. 227   **PB**
Black & Decker Housewares (Pte.) Ltd., Two Pioneer Rd.,
 pg. 234   **PB**
The Crown Company (Singapore) Ltd., pg. 464   **PB**
Dainippon Ink & Chemicals Singapore Pte., Ltd., 80
 International Road, pg. 372   **IT**
Eastman Whipstock (Far East) Pte. Ltd., 11 Gul Ln.,
 pg. 167   **PB**
Ecolab Pte. Ltd., 7 Fourth Lok Yang Rd., pg. 562   **PB**
Enercon Engineering Private Limited, 29 Gul Lane,
 pg. 550   **IT**
Fosroc Expandite (Pte) Ltd., 61 Gul Drive, pg. 236   **IT**
GATX Private Ltd., 59 Penjuru Rd., pg. 693   **PB**
GB HOLDINGS, 26 Jalan Terusan, pg. 531   **IT**
General Electric (USA) Hermetic Motor Operation (Pte) Ltd.,
 251 Jalan Ahmad Ibrahim, pg. 714   **PB**
Gerrard Signode Pte. Ltd., No. 2 Joo Koon Circle,
 pg. 868   **IT**
Glaxo Development Pte. Ltd., 1 Pioneer, Sec. 1,
 pg. 553   **IT**
Goulds Pumps Singapore PTE, Ltd., No. 3 Tuas Ave. 2,
 pg. 861   **PB**
Grinnell Supply Sales Asia Pte Ltd., 35 Tuas Basin Link,
 pg. 1651   **PB**
Handy & Harman Manufacturing (Singapore) Pte. Ltd., 20,
 Tuas Ave. 5, pg. 780   **PB**
Harricros Chemicals Pte. Ltd., 10-12 Third Lockyang Road,
 pg. 599   **IT**
Hi-P Tool & Die Pte. Ltd., Jurong Indus. Estate, 8 Chia Ping
 Rd. #01-11, pg. 1122   **IT**
Jade Technologies Singapore Pte. Ltd., 10 Gul Crecent,
 pg. 1684   **PB**
Jotun NOF Singapore Pte. Ltd., 11-15, Sixth Lok Yang
 Road, pg. 715   **IT**
Kennametal Hertel (Singapore) Pte. Ltd., No. 11 Gul Link,
 pg. 951   **IT**
Keystone Southeast Asia Pty. Ltd., No. 45, Tuos Ave. 9,
 pg. 1650   **PB**
Kobe Welding (Singapore) Pte. Ltd., No. 20 Pandang Ave.,
 Off Pandang Rd., pg. 741   **IT**
Komatsu Asia & Pacific Pte. Ltd., 1 Gul Avenue,
 pg. 744   **IT**
Lawter Intl. Products Pte. Ltd., 24 Tuas Avenue 9,
 pg. 981   **PB**
Longman Singapore Publishers (Pte.) Ltd., 25 First Lok
 Yang Road, pg. 1025   **IT**
M/D Totco Instrumentation, No. 8, Sixth Lok Yang Rd.,
 pg. 1709   **PB**
MSC Pte. Ltd., No. 20 Benoi Sector, pg. 1232   **IT**
McCormick Ingredients Southeast Asia Pvt., Ltd., 4
 Enterprise Rd., pg. 1067   **PB**
Methode Electronics FarEast PTE, Ltd., No. 1 Tuas Lane,
 pg. 1101   **PB**
Molex Singapore Pte. Ltd., 3, Fourth Lok Yang Rd.,
 pg. 1122   **PB**
Molex Singapore Pte. Ltd., 110 International Road,
 pg. 1122   **PB**
NHK Gasket Singapore Co., (Pte) Ltd., No. 7 Pioneer Rd.,
 pg. 902   **IT**
NHK Gasket Singapore Co. (Pte.) Ltd., No. 7, Pioneer Rd.,
 pg. 948   **IT**
Nakano Metal Press (Singapore) Pte. Ltd., 70 Joo Koon
 Circle, pg. 1232   **IT**
Nalco Pacific, 21 Gul Lane, pg. 1151   **IT**
National Oxygen Pte. Ltd., 21, Tanjong Kling Road,
 pg. 903   **IT**
Nelco Products Pte. Ltd., pg. 1258   **PB**
Nestle Singapore Pte. Ltd., 50 International Road,
 pg. 921   **IT**
Parker Chemical Company Pte. Ltd., 9 Tanjong Penjuru
 Crescent, pg. 613   **IT**
Parker Hannifin Singapore Pte. Ltd., No. 11-4th Chin Bee
 Rd., pg. 1263   **PB**
Petrolite Pacific Pte. Ltd., 2 Tanjong Penjuru Crescent,
 pg. 166   **PB**
Possehl Sumiko Electronics Singapore Pte. Ltd., No. 11
 Tues Avenue 4, pg. 1316   **IT**

PB - *U.S. Public Companies Volume*
PV - *U.S. Private Companies Volume*
IT - *International Public & Private Companies Volume*

Geographic Index-Non U.S.

Rising Paper Products Private Limited, 12 Kwong Min Rd., pg. 1251   IT
S.E.A. Glass Ind. Pte. Ltd., 6 Tuas Ave. 16, pg. 1348   IT
Sandvik South East Asia Ltd., 111 Nsythal Rd., pg. 1187   IT
SEMBAWANG MARITIME LIMITED, 59 Shipyard Road, pg. 1219   IT
Senior TIFT Pte. Ltd., 14 Soon Lee Rd., pg. 1223   IT
Shimano (Singapore) Pte. Ltd., No. 20 Benoi Sector, pg. 1233   IT
Singapore Electrical Steel Services Private Ltd., 2, Benoi Crescent, pg. 949   IT
Singapore Glass (1974) Ltd., 30 Tuas Rd., pg. 129   IT
Singapore Kobe Private Limited, No. 3, Lok Yang Rd., pg. 741   IT
Soss of Singapore Pte. Ltd., 3rd Chin Bee Rd., pg. 1677   PB
Sumitomo Electric Interconnect Products (Singapore) Pte., Ltd., 19 Neythal Rd., pg. 1314   IT
Sumitomo Electric (Singapore) Pte. Ltd., 15, Gul Way, pg. 1314   IT
Tatung Electronics (Singapore) PTE Ltd., No. 4, 1st Cokyang Rd., pg. 1357   IT
Toppan Printing Co. (Singapore) Pte. Ltd., 38 Liu Fang Rd., pg. 1399   IT
Toyota Motor Corporation, Singapore Representative Office, c/o UMW Industries Pte., Ltd., 47-C Jalan Buroh, pg. 1413   IT
United Paper Industries Pte. Ltd., 20, Liu Fang Road, pg. 1444   IT
UNITED PULP & PAPER COMPANY LIMITED, 20 Liu Fang Road, pg. 1444   IT
Van Leer Singapore Pte. Ltd., 2 Lor Tukang Sata, pg. 1147   IT
Varco BJ Drilling Systems, No. 8, Sixth Lok Yang Rd., pg. 1709   PB
Varco BJ Oil Tools, No. 8, Sixth Lok Yang Rd., pg. 1709   PB

Loyang Crescent

Weatherford Oil Tool (Pte.) Ltd., Loyang Offshore Supply Base, 1750, pg. 1750   PB

Ngee Ann City

Autodesk Asia Pte. Ltd., 391B Orchard Road, pg. 149   PB
BERG Electronics Singapore Pte. Ltd., 391B Orchard Road, #18-00, pg. 213   PB

Pulau Bukom

Van Leer Singapore Pte. Ltd., pg. 1147   IT

San Centre

CIBA-GEIGY SE Asia (Pte) Limited, 171 Chin Swee Road, #02-03 & #02-04, pg. 979   IT
Kvaerner Pulping Pte. Ltd., 171 Chin Swee Road, pg. 768   IT

Singapore

AAR Pacific Pte. Ltd., No. 1 Loyang Street, 1750, pg. 1   IT
ABB Regional Product Centre Pte. Ltd., Block C 2, Ayer Rajah Crescent, pg. 2   IT
ABS Pump AB, Far East, Orchard Plaza, 150 Orchard Rd., 07-05, pg. 270   IT
ABS Pumps International AB, 170 Upper Bukit Timah Road #13-01, pg. 270   IT
ACAP Chemicals Pte. Ltd., 19 Tanglin Rd., #09-03, pg. 61   PV
A.C.E. Daikin (Singapore) Pte., Ltd., No. 10, Ang Mo Kio Industrial, Park, 2, pg. 365   IT
ADC Telecommunications Singapore PTE Limited, 70 Shenton Way, pg. 4   PB
AES Transpower, # 16-05, Six Battery Rd., pg. 5   PB
A.I.F. Investments Pte. Ltd., 36 Robinson Rd., #15-00, pg. 40   IT
ALR International (Pte.) Ltd., 140 Paya Lebar Rd., pg. 704   PB
AMD Intl. Ltd., 512 Chai Chee Lane, #07-01/07-15 Bedok Industrial Estate, pg. 21   PB
AMP Singapore PTE. Ltd., 26 Ang Mo Kio Industrial Park 2, pg. 9   PB
AMRI Pte. Ltd., pg. 721   IT
ANZ International Pte Limited, Ocean Building, 10 Collyer Quay, No 17 02/05, pg. 99   IT
ANZ Singapore Limited, Ocean Building, 10 Collyer Quay, No 17 02/05, pg. 99   IT
AST Research Inc., 150 Beach Rd., #17-08, pg. 1182   IT
AST Singapore Pte. Limited, 401 Commonwealth Drive, pg. 1182   IT
AXA Re Asia, 152 Beach Rd., pg. 19   IT
Acacia Technologies Asia, #10-01/03 Suntec City Tower 2, 9 Temasek Boulevard, pg. 420   IT
Accor Asia Pte, c/o Business Advisory, Singapore Pte Ltd., Japankayu, pg. 21   IT
Adaptec Mfg. (Singapore) Pte. Ltd., Block 1003, Bukit Merah Central, #07-09, pg. 19   PB
Addison-Wesley (Singapore) Pvt. Ltd., 15 Beach Rd., No. 05-09/10, pg. 1027   IT
Adecco Personnel Services Pte. Ltd., Blk. 502 Jurong West St., pg. 24   IT
Advantest Asia Pte. Ltd., 438 A Alexandra Road, #08-03/06, pg. 25   IT
Advantest (Singapore) Pte. Ltd., 438 A Alexandra Road #08-03/06, pg. 25   IT

Aeroquip Singapore Private Limited, 83 Tagore Lane, pg. 25   PB
Aerospace Operations Asia Pacific, 21 Loyang Crescent, pg. '337   PB
AGIE Singapore, 130 Joo Seng Road #14-01, pg. 488   IT
Ahlstrom Machinery (Asia-Pacific) Pte Ltd., 10-01/03 Pacific Plaza, 9 Scotts Rd., pg. 35   IT
Air Express International Singapore (Pte.) Ltd., 115 Airport Cargo Rd., pg. 30   PB
Air Products Singapore Pte Ltd., #28-01 Suntec Tower 2, 9 Temasek Boulevard, pg. 32   PB
Aisin Asia Pte. Ltd., 10 Anson Rd., No. 3107, pg. 39   IT
Ajinomoto (Singapore) Pte. Ltd., No. 6, Senoko Ave., pg. 40   IT
Ajitrade Pte. Ltd., No. 6, Senoko Ave., pg. 41   IT
Albright & Wilson (Marchon) Pte. Limited, 6, Jalan Besut, pg. 49   IT
Alfa-Laval South East Asia Pty Ltd., 11, Too Koon Circle, pg. 1380   IT
Allianz Asia Pacific, #20-06/13 Shaw Towers, pg. 59   IT
Allianz Insurance (Singapore) Pte. Ltd., #20-06/13 Shaw Towers, 100 Beach Road, pg. 59   IT
Allied Colloids Chemicals (Far East) Pte. Ltd., pg. 62   IT
AlliedSignal Aerospace Service Corporation, Shaw Centre 15-09, 1 Scotts Rd., pg. 52   PB
AlliedSignal General Aviation Avionics, 512 Chai Chee Ln., pg. 52   PB
AlliedSignal Laminate Systems, 101 Gul Circle, pg. 53   PB
Alpnet, 71 Robinson Rd., #05-01, pg. 58   PB
Alucobond Far East Pty Ltd, pg. 68   IT
Amada Singapore (1989) Pte. Ltd., 5611, N. Bridge R., pg. 70   IT
Amcor Fibre Packaging - Asia, 17 Senoko Loop, Woodlands East Industrial Estate, pg. 72   PV
Amdahl Singapore, 152 Beach Rd., pg. 527   IT
American Biltrite Far East, Inc., 26 Tuas Ave. 3, pg. 69   PB
American Fine Wire Ltd., Block 5002, Ang Mo Kio Avenue 5, pg. 969   PB
American Power Conversion, 03-10 Holland Hill Park, 7A Holland Hill, pg. 89   PB
American Power Conversion, 22 Scotts Rd., Apt. 535, pg. 89   PB
Ameron (Pte) Ltd., No. 7A Tuas Ave. 3, pg. 99   PB
Amro Bank (Asia) Ltd., 18 Church St., pg. 12   PV
ANGUS Chemical (Singapore) Pte. Ltd., 150 Beach Rd., 0718, pg. 75   PV
Asahi Bank Singapore Branch, #25-01/06 Shell Tower, 50 Raffles Pl., pg. 82   IT
Asahi Electronics (Singapore) Pte. Ltd., 16, Ang Mo Kio Industrial Park 2, pg. 274   IT
Asahi Financial Futures (Singapore) Pte. Ltd., #25-01/06 Shell Tower, 50 Raffles Pl., pg. 83   IT
Asahikasei Asia Pte. Ltd., 6 Battery Road #13-01, pg. 84   IT
Asama Pte. Ltd., Asia, 06-11 545 Orchards Rd., pg. 1046   PV
Ascott International Management Pte. Ltd., 391B Orchard Road, pg. 1212   IT
The Ascott Singapore, 6 Scotts Road, pg. 1212   IT
Asea Brown Boveri (S.E.A.) Pte. Ltd., P.O. Box 95 Pasir Panjang, pg. 3   IT
Asia Cable Engineering Co., Pte. Ltd. (ACECO), 623 Aljunied Road #03-09, Aljunied Industrial Complex, pg. 530   IT
Asia Computerworld Communications, 80 Marine Parade Road, pg. 569   PV
Asia/Pacific Area, 7 Changi South Street 2, pg. 281   PB
Asia Pacific Breweries Ltd., 438 Alexandra Road, pg. 608   IT
Asia-Pacific Operations, #28-08 Tong Eng Building, 101 Cecil Street, pg. 1795   PB
Asia-Pacific Training & Simulation Limited, 4 Loyang Crescent, pg. 218   IT
Asia Representative Office, 101 Thomson Road, pg. 693   PB
Asian-American Merchant Bank Ltd., 78 Shenton Way, pg. 362   IT
Asian Computer Services Pte. Ltd., #07-01 Setron Building, 10 Dundee Road, pg. 603   IT
Associated Merchandising-Singapore, Odeon Towers14-01, 331 North Bridge Rd., pg. 92   PV
Associated Merchant Bank Ltd., 9 Battery Rd.,08-03 Straits, pg. 1133   IT
Astra Pharmaceuticals (Singapore) Pte. Ltd., 51 Goldhill Plaza, Penthouse II, pg. 94   IT
Astra Southeast Asia Area Office, Robinson Rd., pg. 94   IT
Atex Asia, 305 Alexandra Rd., pg. 551   PB
Augat Pte. Ltd., Woodlands E. Industrial State, pg. 1598   PB
Australia & New Zealand Banking Group Limited Singapore, Ocean Building, 10 Collyer Quay, No 17 02/05, pg. 99   IT
Avesta Sheffield (SEA) Pte Limited, 1123 Serangoon Rd., No. 1-2, pg. 222   IT
Avex Electronics Pte. Ltd., 510 Thomson Rd. # 14-03, pg. 545   PV
Avimo Group Limited, 14 Fifth Lokyang Road, pg. 70   IT
BASF Singapore Pte. Ltd., 7 Temasek Boulevard, pg. 107   IT
BASF South East Asia Regional Headquarters Pte. Ltd., 7 Temasek Boulevard, pg. 107   IT
BASF Textile & Leather Dyes & Chemicals Pte. Ltd., 7 Temasek Boulevard, pg. 107   IT
B.B.H. Asia Pacific, 28 Duxton Hill, pg. 169   IT
BBL Asset Management (Singapore) Pte. Ltd., 1 Raffles Place #57-02, pg. 148   IT
BCS Information Systems Private Limited, 10 Shenton Waya, #09-01/09 MAS Building, pg. 581   IT
BHF-Bank, 150 Beach Road #03-00, pg. 119   IT

BHF-Bank Representative Office, 150 Beach Road # 03-00, Gateway West, pg. 120   IT
BHP Steel SE Asia Pte Ltd., 10 Collyer Quay, #10-01 Ocean Bldg., pg. 227   IT
BICC Cables Asia-Pacific Pte. Ltd., 435 Orchard Road, 17-02 Wisma Atria, pg. 120   IT
BMI Pte. Ltd., Singapore, 6-B Orange Grove Road, pg. 187   IT
Bain & Company Pte. Ltd. (Singapore), Clifford Centre, 24 Raffles Pl. #20-01, pg. 406   IT
Baker Oil Tools Far East (Pty) Ltd., #23-05 Orchard Towers, pg. 167   PB
Ballast Nedam Equipment Services Pte. Ltd., 11 Tanjong Penjuru Crescent, pg. 134   IT
Ballast Nedam Far East Pte. Ltd., Dredging Division, 11 Tanjong Penjuru Crescent, pg. 134   IT
Bally Singapore (Pte) Ltd., 45-C Brach Rd., 4th Fl., pg. 997   IT
Banca Nazionale del Lavoro, 111 Somerset Road, Hex 09-07, 0923, pg. 137   IT
Banco do Brasil S.A.-Singapore, 1, Philip Street 09-00, pg. 141   IT
Banco Santander, 20 Raffles Place #27-00, Ocean Towers, pg. 144   IT
Bank Brussels Lambert, Singapore Branch, 1 Raffles Pl. 42-00, pg. 148   IT
Bank Brussels Lambert (Singapore) Ltd., OUB Centre, 1 Raffles 42-00, pg. 148   IT
Bank of America NT&SA, 78 Shenton Way, #20-00, pg. 182   PB
Bank of Boston, 150 Beach Road #07-00, pg. 184   PB
Bank of Montreal - Singapore, 150 Beach Rd., #26-01, Gateway W., pg. 155   IT
The Bank of New York, #02-01 Millenia Tower, 1 Temasek Avenue, pg. 179   PB
The Bank of Nova Scotia Asia Limited, #15-01, Ocean Building, 10 Collyer Quay, pg. 156   IT
The Bank of Tokyo-Mitsubishi, Ltd. (Singapore Branch), 9 Raffles Pl, #01-01, pg. 158   IT
Bank of Yokohama Singapore, 50 Raffles Place, #30-04/05 Shell Tower, pg. 159   IT
Bankers Trust International (Asia) Ltd., Shell Tower, 50 Raffles Place, pg. 186   IT
Bankers Trust New York Corporation, Shell Tower, 50 Raffles Place, pg. 186   IT
Banking Computer Services Private Limited, 10 Shenton Way, #09-01/09 MAS Building, pg. 581   IT
Banque Internationale a Luxembourg BIL (Asia) Ltd., Hex 22-01 Republic Plaza, 9, Raffles Place, pg. 162   IT
Barclays Bank PLC, pg. 165   IT
BATEY ADS SINGAPORE, Batey House 28, Ann Siang Road, pg. 170   IT
Baumann Spring Co. (S) Pte. Ltd., 5 Wan Shih Rd., pg. 171   IT
Bausch & Lomb (Singapore) Private Limited, 10 Anson Rd., Ste. 20-07, International Plaza, pg. 195   PB
Bayerische Landesbank - Singapore Branch, The Concourse, 300 Beach Rd., #37-01, pg. 176   IT
Baymont Technologies (PTE) Ltd., 510 Thompson Road, pg. 31   IT
Bear Stearns Singapore Pte. Limited, 21-00 Caltex House, 30 Raffles Pl., pg. 198   PB
Becton Dickinson Singapore, pg. 200   PB
Behn, Meyer & Co. (Pte.) Ltd., 100, Pasir Panjang Rd., pg. 107   IT
Bekaert Singapore Pte. Ltd., 350 Orchard Road, #21-04/05 Shaw House, pg. 184   IT
F. J. BENJAMIN HOLDINGS LTD., 6-B Orange Grove Rd., pg. 187   IT
F.J. Benjamin Multimedia Pte Ltd., 6-B Orange Grove Road, pg. 187   IT
F.J. Benjamin Fashions (Singapore) Pte. Ltd., 583 Orchard Rd., pg. 187   IT
Benmark Pte. Ltd., 583 Orchard Road, #16-02 Forum, pg. 187   IT
Bensons Metal Products Pte. Ltd., No. 9 Sungei Kadut Avenue, pg. 460   IT
Bently Nevada Sales & Service Singapore Pte. Ltd., #3 Duxton Hill, pg. 134   PV
Bermuda Trust (Singapore) Limited, 20 Raffles Place, pg. 151   IT
Bobst (SEA) Pte Ltd, pg. 199   IT
Robert Bosch (South East Asia) Pte. Ltd., 38 C-38D, pg. 206   IT
Brani Ready Mix Pte. Ltd., 17 Pioneer Crescent, Jurong Town, pg. 1293   IT
Bristol-Myers (Singapore) Pte. Ltd., Cideco Industrial Complex, 50 Genring Lane No. 04-01/05, pg. 256   PB
British-American Tobacco Co. (Singapore) Ltd., 57 Senoko Dr., pg. 111   PB
Brooktree Pte., 1 Kallang Sector, pg. 1398   PB
Brother International (Singapore) Pte. Ltd., No. 1 Phillip St. # 06-00, pg. 230   IT
Brunswick Haw Par Holdings Pte Ltd., #07-02 Setron Building, 10 Dundee Road, pg. 604   IT
Bull Far East Ltd., 15-00 BP Tower, 395 Alexandra Rd., pg. 315   IT
Bull Far East Pte. Ltd., 16 Raffles Quay 0104, Unit 3105, pg. 318   IT
Bull Information Systems Pte. Ltd., #15-00 BP Tower, 395 Alexandra Rd., pg. 315   IT
Leo Burnett Pte. Ltd., 100 Beach Rd., #34-00 Shaw Towers, pg. 185   PV
Butterworths Asia, No 1 Temasek Avenue, #17-01 Millenia Tower, pg. 1095   IT
C-E International, 2403-2404 Shaw Ctr., One Scotts Rd., pg. 5   IT
CAM INTERNATIONAL HOLDINGS LTD., 35 Jalan Pemimpin, 05-01 Wedgent, pg. 238   IT
CCF Singapore, 150 Beach Road, pg. 343   IT
CCH Asia Limited, 139 Cecil St., #02-00, pg. 1513   IT

PB - U.S. Public Companies Volume
PV - U.S. Private Companies Volume
IT - International Public & Private Companies Volume

1744

CIBC Asia Limited, Level 23, OUB Centre, pg. 257 **IT**
CMC International (S.E. Asia) Pte. Limited, 302 Orchard Rd., pg. 413 **PB**
CMS Enhancements, Pte. Ltd., pg. 96
COBE Laboratories, Inc., 19 Tanglin Road, 12-07 Tanglin Shopping Center, pg. 667
CPC/AJI (Singapore) Pte. Ltd., No. 6, Senoko Ave., pg. 41 **IT**
CPC/AJI (Singapore) Pte. Ltd., 6 Senoko Ave., pg. 225 **PB**
CSA Automated Private Limited, 221 Henderson Road, pg. 242 **IT**
CSA Distribution Pte. Ltd., 221 Henderson Road, pg. 242 **IT**
CSA HOLDINGS LTD., 221 Henderson Rd., #08-01, pg. 242 **IT**
CSA Private Limited, 221 Henderson Road, pg. 242 **IT**
CSA Research Pte. Ltd., 221 Henderson Road, pg. 242 **PB**
CTI Singapore, Pte, 22 Tuas West Road, pg. 781 **PB**
CTS Singapore Pte., Ltd., Box 502, 14 Ang Mo Kio Central Pl., pg. 286 **PB**
CWT DISTRIBUTION LIMITED, 47 Jalan Buroh, pg. 246 **IT**
Cabletron Systems, Inc.-Asia, 85 Science Park Drive, #03-03/04, pg. 288 **PB**
Candela Singapore, c/o Blk. 209, New Upper, pg. 301 **IT**
Canon Singapore Pte. Ltd., 79 Anson Road, #09-01/06, pg. 263 **PB**
Carrier Singapore (Pte.) Ltd., 28 Teban Gardens Crescent, pg. 1691 **PB**
Casio Asia Pte. Ltd., 16, Ang Mo Kio Industrial Park 2, pg. 274 **IT**
Castrol Singapore Pte. Ltd., Castrol House, 6 Hill View Road, pg. 236 **PB**
Caterpillar Asia Pte. Ltd., 150 Beach Rd. #11-00, pg. 316 **PB**
Caxton Services Company Pte. Ltd., pg. 720 **IT**
CelsiusTech Systems AB Far East Branch, Cintech Bldg. 01-22, 73 Science Park Dr., pg. 278 **IT**
Cemex, S.A. de C.V. - Singapore, 40-01, Suntec Tower 2, pg. 278 **PB**
Central Spraysafe Company PTE LTD, 45 Genting Ln. #07-02, pg. 327 **IT**
Cerberus Singapore Pte. Ltd., 5000 Ang Mo Kio Avenue 5, pg. 1246 **PB**
Cerebos Pacific Ltd., #20-03/04, Liat Towers, 541 Orchard Rd., pg. 1322 **IT**
Cerner Singapore Pte Ltd., Taman Warna P.O. Box 141, pg. 331 **PB**
Champion Motors (1975) Pte. Ltd., 2 Pandan Crescent, pg. 672 **IT**
Char Yong Gardens, 1/3 Hullet Road, pg. 1212 **IT**
Charmilles Technologies (South East Asia) Pte., 01-00 & 04-01 Olivine Building, 130 Joo Seng Road, pg. 489 **IT**
Chase Investment Bank Limited, Shenton Way, pg. 339 **PB**
The Chase Manhattan Bank, N.A., Shell Tower, 50 Raffles Place, pg. 340 **IT**
Chase Manhattan Futures Corp., Shell Tower, 50 Raffles Place, pg. 340 **PB**
Check Point Software Technologies (Singapore) Ltd., 02-06 RiverSide Piazza, pg. 342 **IT**
Chiron Vision Singapore PTE Ltd., International Plaza, 10 Anson Rd. #19-16, pg. 358 **PB**
Cho Hung Bank, Singapore Branch, 9-1/5 Shing Kwan House, 4 Shenton Way, pg. 288 **IT**
Christiania Bank-Singapore Branch, #21-01 Odeon Towers, 331 North Bridge Road, pg. 289 **IT**
Christie's International Singapore Pte. Ltd., Unit 3, Park Ln., Goodwood Park Hotel, pg. 290 **IT**
Chubb Singapore Private Limited, 207 Kallang Bahru, pg. 1250 **PB**
CIBA Corning Marketing Services (HK) Ltd, 15 McCallum St. #12-04, pg. 975 **PB**
CIBA-GEIGY SE Asia (Pte) Limited, 400 Orchard Road #19-07, pg. 979 **IT**
CIBA-GEIGY S.E. Asia (Pte.) Ltd., 4, Fourth Lok Yang Road, pg. 979 **IT**
CIBA Vision (Singapore) Pte Ltd, 171 Chin Swee Rd., pg. 981 **IT**
Cinch Microfits Pte Ltd., 63 Loyang Way, pg. 786 **IT**
Circle Freight International Pte., Ltd., 97/100 Duxton Rd., pg. 373 **PB**
CitiCorp Investment Bank (Singapore) Ltd., #29-01 UIC Bldg., pg. 379 **IT**
Clarins Pte Ltd., 06-00 Pacific Bldg., 627 Aljunied Road, pg. 295 **IT**
Clarion Asia Pte. Ltd., Performance Ctr., 315 Alexandra Rd. 04-03, pg. 296 **IT**
Clarion Electronics (S) Pte. Ltd., 05-01/02 Boon Siew Bldg., 75 Bukit Timah Rd., pg. 296 **IT**
Coastal Belcher Petroleum Pte. Ltd., 3805 O.C.B.C. Centre, 65 Chulia St., pg. 390 **PB**
Coastal Petroleum (Far East) Pte Ltd., 3805 O.C.B.C. Center, 65 Chulia St., pg. 390 **PB**
Codelco-Asia, 14-03 UIC Bldg., No. 5 Shenton Way, pg. 303 **PB**
Cognos Far East Pte. Limited, 750-D Chai Chee Road, pg. 306 **PB**
Colgate-Palmolive (Eastern) Pte. Ltd., P.O. Box 35, pg. 398 **PB**
Comdisco Asia Pte. Ltd., No. 2 Handy Rd., #14-05 Cathay Bldg., pg. 408 **PB**
Cominco Metals Pte. Ltd., 268 Orchard Road, pg. 308 **IT**
Commerz Asset Management Asia Ltd., pg. 312 **IT**
Commerzbank AG (South East Asia) Ltd., Temasek Tower, 8, Shenton Way #32-01, pg. 311 **IT**
Commonwealth Bank-Singapore, Level 22, 50 Raffles Place, pg. 313 **IT**

Communications Services Pte. Ltd., Units 04-02, 3rd Fl., Alpha Bldg., 45 Kallang Pudding Rd., pg. 1365 **IT**
Compagnie Generale de Geophysique (Far East), 268 Orchard Rd., pg. 241 **IT**
Compaq Computer Asia Pte Ltd., 50 Tagore Lane #03-07, pg. 418 **PB**
Componenta International Marketing (F.E.) Pte. Ltd., Ruby Warehouse Complex, Hex. 04-38, pg. 1421 **IT**
ConAgra Asia-Pacific, #27-04 Raffles City Tower, pg. 429 **PB**
ConAgra International, Inc., #27-04 Raffles City Tower, pg. 429 **PB**
Continuum Asia, 139 Cecil St., pg. 423 **PB**
Core Laboratories (Singapore), 24-A Lim Teck Boo Rd., pg. 1004 **IT**
Corex Technology (S) Pte Ltd., #04-01/02 Corex Building, No. 10 Tannery Lane, pg. 651 **IT**
Corning Trading (Singapore) Pte. Ltd., 39A Jln Pemimpin #04-01, pg. 448 **IT**
Cosmetiques de France Pte. Ltd., 04-20 Tg Katong Complex, pg. 819 **IT**
CPM/Pacific Private Ltd., 17 Liu Fang Road, pg. 705 **PB**
John Crane Singapore Pte. Ltd., 21 Tuas Ave 11, pg. 1339 **IT**
Crawford Door (Far East) Pte Ltd., 13-279 Selegie Complex, 257 Selegie Rd., pg. 269 **IT**
Credit Corporation (Singapore) Ltd., 1 Scotts Road, Shaw Centre #18-07/14, pg. 1297 **IT**
Credit Lyonnais Singapour, 65 Chulia St. 37-01, pg. 344 **IT**
Creditanstalt (Singapore) Ltd., 1, Finlayson Green, 12th Floor, pg. 348 **IT**
Crown Cork & Seal, Asia-Pacific Division, c/o CarnaudMetalbox Asia Ltd., 750-D Chai Chee Industrial Park, pg. 464 **PB**
Cyborg Systems Asia, Ltd., 73 Science Park Dr., pg. 299 **PV**
CYCLE & CARRIAGE INDUSTRIES (1986) PTE. LIMITED, 239 Alexandra Rd., 4th Fl., pg. 303 **IT**
D & B Software (Singapore) Pte. Ltd., 4 Shenton Way, Unit 19-05, pg. 532 **IT**
DBS Asset Management Ltd., 24 Raffles Place, pg. 350 **IT**
DBS Asset Management (United States) Pte. Ltd., #10-00 Clifford Centre, 24 Raffles Place, pg. 350 **IT**
DBS BANK LTD., DBS Bldg., Tower 1, 6 Shenton Way, pg. 350 **IT**
DBS Capital Investments Ltd., 6 Shenton Way, pg. 350 **IT**
DBS Card Centre Pte. Ltd., 1 Kim Seng Promenade, pg. 350 **IT**
DBS China Square Ltd., 6 Shenton Way, DBS Building, pg. 350 **IT**
DBS Computer Services Pte. Ltd., DBS Buidling, 6 Shenton Way, pg. 350 **IT**
DBS Factors Pte. Ltd., 112 Robinson Road, #09-00 DBS Finance Building, pg. 350 **IT**
DBS Finance Ltd., 112 Robinson Rd., DBS Finance Bldg., pg. 350 **IT**
DBS Finance Nominees Pte. Ltd., 112 Robinson Road, DBS Finance Bldg., pg. 350 **IT**
DBS Investment Research Pte. Ltd., 22 Malacca St., DBS Securities Bldg., pg. 350 **IT**
DBS Nominees Pte. Ltd., 24 Raffles Place, B1-00 Clifford Centre, pg. 350 **IT**
DBS Pte. Ltd., 6 Shenton Way, pg. 351 **IT**
DBS Securities Holding Pte. Ltd., 22 Malacca St., pg. 351 **IT**
DBS Securities Malaysia Pte Ltd., DBS Securities Building, 22 Malacca Street, pg. 351 **IT**
DBS Securities Nominees Pte. Ltd., 22 Malacca Street, pg. 351 **IT**
DBS Securities Singapore Pte. Ltd., 22 Malacca St., DBS Securities Bldg., pg. 351 **IT**
DBS Trading Pte. Ltd., 6 Shenton Way, DBS Bldg., pg. 351 **IT**
DBS Trustee Ltd., 24 Raffles Place, pg. 351 **IT**
DBSF Holdings Pte Ltd., DBS Finance Building, 112 Robinson Road, pg. 351 **IT**
DBSF Investments Pte. Ltd., 112 Robinson Road, pg. 351 **IT**
DHL International (Singapore) Pte. Ltd., No. 1 Tai Seng Dr., pg. 302 **PV**
DIC Polymer & Chemicals Asia, Pte., Ltd., 78 Shenton Way, #13-03, pg. 372 **IT**
DKB Futures (Singapore) Pte Ltd., 1 Raffle Place, #47-00 OUB Centre, pg. 361 **IT**
DKB Merchant Bank (Singapore) Limited, 1 Raffles Place, #18-1 OUB Centre, pg. 361 **IT**
DMB&B Singapore, 30 Prinsep St., #09-01, pg. 304 **PV**
DSM Elastomers Asia Pacific Pte Ltd., 152 Beach Road, #12-01, pg. 354 **IT**
DSM Elastomers Asia Pacific Pte. Ltd., 152 Beach Road, #12-01, pg. 355 **IT**
Daewoo Securities - Singapore Representative Office, 6 Battery Road Unit 17-08, pg. 359 **IT**
Daewoo Singapore Pte. Ltd., #15-08/09 M.A.S. Bldg., 10 Shenton Way, pg. 358 **IT**
Dai-Ichi Kangyo Bank, Ltd.-Singapore, 1 Raffles Place, #47-00 OUB Centre, pg. 361 **IT**
Dai-Ichi Life International Limited-Singapore, Hitachi Tower, 16 Collyer Quay #33-02, pg. 362 **IT**
Dai Nippon Printing Co. (Singapore) Pte. Ltd., 896 Dunearn Rd., pg. 363 **IT**
Daihatsu Diesel (Singapore) Pte. Ltd., 15 Joo Yee Rd., pg. 364 **IT**
Daiwa Asset Management (Singapore) Ltd., DBS Building Tower Two, 6 Shenon Way #24-09, pg. 374 **IT**
Daiwa Bank-Singapore, 8 Shenton Way, No. 30-01, Treasury Bldg., pg. 373 **IT**
Daiwa BK Financial Futures Singapore Pte. Ltd., 8 Shenton Way, No.-30-01, Treasury Bldg., pg. 373 **IT**

Daiwa Futures Pte Ltd, DBS Building Tower Two, 6 Shenton Way, #26-08, pg. 375 **IT**
Daiwa Institute of Research Singapore Pte Ltd, DBS Buiding, Tower Two, 6 Shenton Way, #25-08, pg. 375 **IT**
Daiwa International Capital Management (Singapore) Limited, 152 Beach Road, #6-01/02, pg. 375 **IT**
Daiwa Merchant Bank (Singapore) Limited, 8 Shenton Way, No. 30-03, Treasury Bldg., pg. 373 **IT**
Daiwa Securities (Singapore) Pte Ltd, DBS Building Tower Two, 6 Shenton Way, #26-08, pg. 376 **IT**
Daiwa Singapore Limited, 6 Shenton Way, pg. 376 **IT**
Damco Maritime Pte. Ltd., pg. 1144 **IT**
Danielli & C. Far East, 16 Raffles Quay, pg. 378 **IT**
Danone Brands (Singapore) Pte. Ltd., 4 Chin Bee Drive, pg. 380 **IT**
Danzas (Singapore) Pte Ltd., 138 Robinson Road Nr. 11-00, pg. 382 **IT**
Data General International Manufacturing Ltd., Market St., 702 Harapan Bldg., pg. 486 **PB**
Data General Singapore Pte. Ltd., Market St., 702 Harapan Bldg., pg. 486 **PB**
Michael de Kretser Consultants, 100 Amoy St., pg. 117 **IT**
De La Rue Systems Ltd., 1 Joo Koon Way 13-01, pg. 387 **IT**
Thomas De La Rue (Singapore) Pte. Limited, 1 Joo Koon Way, pg. 386 **IT**
De Zaan Far East Pte. Ltd., 342 Jalan Boon Lay, pg. 128 **IT**
Dell Computer Asia Pte Ltd., Level 37 Shell Tower, 50 Raffles Pl., pg. 496 **IT**
Dell Computer Asia Pte Ltd., #02-00 Dell Building, 913 Bukit Timah Road, pg. 496 **IT**
Den norske Bank AS, Singapore Branch, 8 Shenton Way #48-02, pg. 392 **IT**
Dentsu Mandate Singapore Pte. Ltd., 5 Pereira Road, #03-02, Asiawide Industrial Building, pg. 393 **IT**
Dentsu Young & Rubicam brand communications (Network Center), 300 Beach Road, #36-05/06 The Concourse, pg. 325 **PV**
Dentsu Young & Rubicam/Singapore, 300 Beach Road #30-00, The Concourse, pg. 325 **PV**
Det Norske Veritas (Asia Pacific), DNV Technology Ctr., 10 Science Park Dr., pg. 398 **IT**
Deutsche Bank AG (Singapore), Treasury Bldg., 8, Shenton Way, #20-01, pg. 404 **IT**
Deutsche Bank (Asia Pacific) Ltd., Treasury Bldg., 8 Shenton Way, #19-02/03, pg. 405 **IT**
A.B. Dick/Itek Graphix International Division Distributor Operations-Far East, Magnet House, 985 Bukit Timah Rd., pg. 791 **PV**
Digiphonic Systems Pte. Ltd., 70 Bendemeer Rd., pg. 1000 **IT**
Digital Equipment Singapore (PTE) Limited, 152 Beach Road, #36-00 Gateway Road, pg. 508 **PB**
Disco Hi-Tec (Singapore) Pte., Ltd., A-Z Bldg., 140 Paya Lebar Rd #07-03, pg. 413 **IT**
R.R. Donnelley Far East Limited, 50 Raffles Place #05-05, pg. 519 **IT**
Dow Jones Markets (Asia Pacific) Singapore Pte Ltd., 02-03 New Tech Pk., 151 Lorong Chuan, pg. 525 **IT**
Dow Jones Markets (Asia Pacific) Pte Ltd., Six Battery Rd., #23-03, 0104, pg. 525 **PB**
Dowty Aerospace Aviation Services Pte Ltd, 21 Loyang Crescent, pg. 1337 **IT**
Dresdner (S.E. Asia) Ltd., 20 Collyer Quay, pg. 420 **IT**
Dresdner (South East Asia) Ltd., 20 Collyer Quay No. 22-00, pg. 419 **IT**
Drug Houses of Australia (Asia) Pte. Ltd., Tiger Balm Building, 2 Chia Ping Road, pg. 603 **IT**
Du Pont (Singapore) Electronics Pvt. Ltd., 6 Gul St. 5, pg. 531 **PB**
Dumez-GTM, 20, Bideford Road, pg. 823 **IT**
Dun & Bradstreet (Singapore) Pte. Ltd., 6 Temasek Boulevard, #06-05/06, Suntec Tower 4, pg. 537 **PB**
Dunearn Distribution Services Private Limited, Sime Darby Center, 896 Duncan Rd. #01-02, pg. 1250 **IT**
Duracell (S.E.A.) Pte. Ltd., 34 Boon Leat, pg. 744 **PB**
Durco-Valtek (Asia Pacific) Pte. Ltd., 12 Tuas Ave. 20, pg. 659 **IT**
Dynachem Singapore Pte. Ltd., 03-07 Ruby Warehouse Complex, pg. 1135 **PB**
Dynamar International Ltd., 109 Defu Lane 10, pg. 817 **PB**
ECI Telecom (Singapore), 150 Beach Road, pg. 643 **IT**
EMI (Singapore) Pte Ltd., 213 Henderson Road, pg. 427 **IT**
ESAB Asia/Pacific Pte Ltd., 38 Joo Koon Cir., Jurong, P.O. Box 241, Jurong Town Post Office, pg. 282 **IT**
ESAB Singapore Pte. Ltd., 38 Joo Koon Cir., P.O. Box 241, Jurong Town Post Office, pg. 282 **IT**
Earth Development (S) Pte. Ltd., Lorong Kanching, off Bedok Reservoir Rd., pg. 741 **IT**
Eastman Kodak Company-Singapore, Godown P8, Pasir Panjang Wharves, pg. 552 **PB**
Eaton Corporation Singapore Representative Office, 101 Thompson Rd., No. 07-05, pg. 558 **PB**
Ebara Engineering Singapore Pte. Ltd., No. 1 Tuas Link 2, pg. 432 **PB**
Ebasco Services Singapore Pte. Ltd., 119A Kallang Road, pg. 1587 **PB**
Edelman Public Relations Worldwide Pte. Ltd., Cathay Bldg., Ste. 13-04, 11 Dhoby Ghaut, pg. 363 **PV**
Edison Mission Energy Asia Pte. Ltd., 391-B Orchard Road, pg. 564 **PB**
Electric Component of PTE. Ltd., 105 Boon Keng Rd. #03-01, pg. 713 **PB**
Electricite de France, 34-01 The Concourse, pg. 437 **IT**
Electrode/Ore, 10 Pioneer Rd., pg. 1360 **PB**
Electrolux S.E.A. Private Ltd., 240 MacPherson Road; Units 03-01/04, pg. 443 **IT**
Elsag Bailey Pte. Ltd., 152 Beach Road, pg. 449 **IT**

PB - *U.S. Public Companies Volume*
PV - *U.S. Private Companies Volume*
IT - *International Public & Private Companies Volume*

Geographic Index-Non U.S.

1745

Emerson Pacific Pte. Ltd., 2 Tuas Drive, pg. 576   **PB**

Emhart Singapore Pte. Ltd., 19 Jookoon Cir., pg. 233   **PB**

EMTEC Magnetics Singapore Pty. Ltd., 1, Rochor Canal Road #05-15, pg. 743   **IT**

Encore Computer (Asia) Ltd., Level 36 Hong Leong Bldg., 16 Raffles Quay, pg. 580   **PB**

Enso-Eurocan South East Asia Pte. Ltd., Shaw Ctr., 1 Scotts Rd. Hex 15-10/11, pg. 457   **IT**

Enso Surya Pte. Ltd., Shaw Ctr., 1 Scotts Rd. #22-12, pg. 457   **IT**

Epson Singapore pte., Ltd. (ESP), No. 1 Raffles Place, #26-00 OUB Centre, pg. 1219   **IT**

Equinox Capital (Singapore) Ltd., 9 Raffles Place, pg. 343   **IT**

Ericsson Network Engineering (B) Sdn Bhd, 510 Thomson Road, 18-00 SLF Complex, pg. 1367   **IT**

Ericsson Network Engineering Pte. Ltd., 510 Thomson Road, pg. 1367   **IT**

Ericsson Telecommunications Pte Ltd., 510 Thomson Road, 18-00 SLF Complex, pg. 1368   **IT**

ESPAN Corporation, 197 Ubi Avenue 4, pg. 1358   **PB**

Esso Singapore Private Limited, 1 Raffles Place, pg. 602   **PB**

Euclid Technologies Pte. Ltd., 17 Pioneer Crescent, Jurong Town, pg. 1292   **IT**

EURO RSCG Partnership, 180 Clemenceau Ave., pg. 602   **IT**

Eutech Cybernetics Pte. Ltd., 55 Ayer Rajah Crescent #04-05, pg. 242   **IT**

Eveready Singapore Pte. Ltd., 25 Gul Way, pg. 1360   **PB**

Exide Electronics International/IPM, pg. 126   **IT**

Exxon Trading Asia Pacific Private Limited, 1 Raffles Pl., pg. 602   **PB**

FAG South East Asia Pte. Ltd., pg. 469   **IT**

FCB Singapore, 70 Anson Road, pg. 389   **PV**

FMC Southeast Asia Ltd., 2102 Shaw Centre, Scotts Rd., pg. 606   **PB**

Fanuc GE Automation Singapore Pte. Ltd., No. 1 Teban Gardens Crescent, pg. 478   **IT**

Fanuc GE Automation Singapore Pte. Ltd., No. 1 Teban Gardens Crescent, pg. 714   **PB**

Fanuc Singapore Pte. Ltd., No. 1 Teban Gardens Crescent, pg. 478   **IT**

Fedders Asia Pte. Ltd., Utech Industrial Bldg., 128 Joo Seng Rd., #05-01, pg. 615   **PB**

Ferrier Lullin & Cie SA, 80, Raffles Place, #28-02, UOB Plaza 1, pg. 480   **IT**

Fidelio Software (Pte) Ltd., SLF Building 12-05, 510 Thomson Rd., pg. 1106   **PB**

Fike Southeast Asia Pte Ltd, 81 Loyang Way, pg. 404   **PV**

Fina Far East Pte. Ltd., 19, Pioneer Sector 1, pg. 1044   **IT**

Georg Fischer Pte. Ltd., 15 Kaki Bukit Road 2, pg. 490   **IT**

Fiserv (ASPAC), Pte. Ltd., 80 Raffles PL., #56-02UOB Plaza, pg. 647   **PB**

Fleetguard International Corporation, Jurong Industrial Estate, 8 Tanjong Penjuru, pg. 469   **PB**

Flender Singapore Pte. Ltd., Block 2033 #01-302 Bukit Batok Street 23, pg. 401   **IT**

Florasynth Singapore Pte Ltd., The Curie, Singapore Science, Park, 83 Science Park Dr. #04-01, 0511, pg. 174   **IT**

Food and Snack Holdings (Singapore), pg. 159   **PV**

Forbo Siegling Singapore Pte. Ltd., pg. 498   **IT**

Foseco (Singapore) Pte. Ltd., 33 Gul Lane, pg. 236   **IT**

Foster Electric (Singapore) Pte. Ltd., 158 Kallang Way, pg. 500   **IT**

Foster Wheeler Asia, 32 Maxwell Rd., #02-03, pg. 677   **IT**

Foster Wheeler Eastern Private Limited, 32 Maxwell Rd. #02-03, pg. 677   **PB**

Frionor Asia Pacific Pte. Ltd., 400 Orchard Road, No. 10-03 Orchard Towers, pg. 516   **IT**

Fuchs Chemicals Pte. Ltd., No. 6 Tuas Avenue 10, pg. 517   **IT**

Fugro-Singapore, Ltd., 510 Thomson Rd., pg. 431   **PV**

Fuji Electric Singapore Private Limited, 401 Commonwealth Drive, pg. 522   **IT**

The Fuji Futures (Singapore) Pte., Limited, 1 Raffles Pl. #20-00, pg. 521   **IT**

Fuji/GE Private Ltd., #12-01/04 San Center, 171, Chin Swee Rd., pg. 522   **IT**

Fuji/GE PTE Ltd., 896 Durean Rd., #04-06, pg. 713   **PB**

Fuji Hunt Photographic Chemicals Pte. Ltd., 15 Tuas Ave., pg. 524   **IT**

Fuji Photo Film (Singapore) Pte. Ltd., 10 New Industrial Rd., pg. 524   **IT**

Fujitsu (Singapore) Pte. Ltd., 200, Cantonment Road, pg. 528   **IT**

Furukawa Electric Co., Ltd. Singapore, International Plaza, 10 Anson Road, #13-15, pg. 530   **IT**

Furukawa Electric Singapore Pte. Ltd., 10 Anson Road, #13-15, pg. 530   **IT**

GATX Leasing (Pacific) LTD., 11 Collyer Quay, pg. 691   **PB**

GATX Terminals (Pte.) Ltd., 59 Penjuru Road, pg. 693   **PB**

G.C. Pharmaceutical (Singapore) Ltd., 1 Maritime Square #09-53, pg. 558   **PB**

G.E. Asia, Hong Leong Bldg., 16 Raffles Quay-Bldg. 44-02, pg. 713   **PB**

G.E. Plastics Pacific Ltd., 150 Beach Rd., pg. 713   **PB**

G.E. Technical Services, Cathay Bldg., Dhoby Ghaut 08-04, pg. 713   **PB**

GE Toshiba Appliances Company Pte. Ltd., 38 Robinson Rd., #18-01, City House, pg. 1405   **IT**

G.E. (U.S.A.) Aviation Service Operation Pte. Ltd., 23 Loyang Way, pg. 713   **PB**

GM Singapore Pte. Limited, 501 Ang Mo Kio Industrial Park 1, pg. 721   **PB**

GP BATTERIES INTERNATIONAL LTD., 50 Gul Crescent, pg. 537   **IT**

GP Battery Marketing (Singapore) Pte Ltd., 50 Gul Crescent, pg. 537   **IT**

GTM Wan Soon Pte Ltd., 20 Bideford Road, pg. 823   **IT**

Gateway Land Private Limited, 5 Shenton Way, #02-11, pg. 1253   **IT**

Gearhart (Malaysia) Sdn. Bhd., 20-05 Orchard Towers, 400 Orchard Rd., pg. 776   **PB**

General Datacom Industries, Inc., 05-05/07 Lane Crawford Place, 501 Orchard Road, pg. 708   **PB**

The General Electric Co. of Singapore Private Ltd., No. 3 Tai Seng Dr., pg. 546   **IT**

General Electric (USA) Asia Co., 2 Pioneer Sector 3, pg. 713   **PB**

General Electric (USA) Aviation Service Operation Pte. Ltd., 23 Loyang Way, pg. 714   **PB**

General Electric (USA) Consumer Electronics (Pte) Ltd., 100 Toa Payoh North, pg. 714   **PB**

Gerber Products Co Singapore, 05-04 International Building, 360 Orchard Road, pg. 973   **IT**

Gestetner Private Limited, 211 Henderson Road, #04-02 Henderson Industrial Park, pg. 1115   **IT**

Givaudan-Roure Pte. Ltd., pg. 1120   **IT**

Glaxo Far East Pte. Ltd., Gateway West-21st fl., 150 Beach Rd., 0718, pg. 553   **PB**

Glaxo Wellcome Singapore Pte. Ltd., Gateway West, 21st Fl., pg. 553   **IT**

Glaxochem Pte. Ltd., 101 Thompson Rd., #25-26, pg. 553   **IT**

Goldman Sachs (Singapore) Pte., 50 Raffles Pl., 29-01 Shell Tower, pg. 462   **PV**

Goodman Fielder Asia Holdings Ltd., 2 Enterprise Road, pg. 529   **IT**

B.F. Goodrich Aerospace, c/o Singapore Airlines, Airlines House (Sin ALH 7A), 1781, pg. 752   **PB**

W.R. Grace (Singapore) Pte., 25 Tanjong Penjuru, pg. 756   **PB**

Gray Service Co., A.G., Loyang Offshore Base, Loyang Crescent, pg. 5   **IT**

THE GREAT EASTERN LIFE ASSURANCE COMPANY LIMITED, 65 Chulia Street, pg. 557   **IT**

Griffith Laboratories Pte. Ltd., 1, Defu Ln. 10, #03-567 Defu Industrial Park, pg. 481   **PV**

Guerlain (Asia Pacific) Ltd., 435 Orchard Rd., pg. 780   **IT**

Gulf Canada Resources - Singapore, pg. 577   **IT**

Gulf Marine Far East Pte. Ltd., pg. 769   **PB**

HSBC Asset Management Singapore Limited, 21 Collyer Quay, #20-02 HongkongBank Building, pg. 582   **IT**

HSBC Capital (Asia) Pte Limited, 6 Claymore Hill, 03-02 Claymore Plaza, pg. 582   **IT**

HBSC Forfaiting Asia Pte. Limited, 21 Collyer Quay, #19-03 HongkongBank Building, pg. 582   **IT**

HSBC Gibbs Singapore Pte Ltd, 10 Collyer Quay, #03-03A Ocean Building, pg. 582   **IT**

HSBC International Trustee (Singapore) Limited, 10 Collyer Quay, #03-02 Ocean Building, pg. 582   **IT**

HSBC (Singapore) Nominees Private Limited, 21 Collyer Quay, #02-00 HongkongBank Building, pg. 583   **IT**

HSBC Trustee (Singapore) Limited, 10 Collyer Quay, #03-02 Ocean Building, pg. 583   **IT**

Habit Bank Ltd., Inno-Pacific Bldg., 141 Market St., pg 584   **IT**

Hagglunds Drives Ltd, 11 Lorong Tukang Dua, pg. 670   **IT**

John Hagley Communications, 255A Bukit Timah Rd., pg. 117   **IT**

HAI SUN HUP GROUP LTD., 200 Cantonment Road #90-01 pg. 586   **IT**

Hakuhodo Singapore Pte. Ltd., Pub Building, 111 Somerset Rc., #10-06, pg. 588   **IT**

Halma Asia Pte. Limited, 54 Genting Lane, #05-02 Hiang Kie Complex II, pg. 590   **IT**

Hanwa Co., Ltd.-Singapore Branch, 11-02 The Exchange, 20 Cecil St., pg. 595   **IT**

Hapag-Lloyd (Asia) Pte. Ltd., pg. 596   **IT**

Hapag-Lloyd Holding Pte. Ltd., pg. 596   **IT**

Hapag-Lloyd (Singapore) Pte. Ltd., pg. 596   **IT**

Happland Singapore Private Ltd., Namco Wonder Park, 200 Victoria St., pg. 905   **IT**

HAW PAR BROTHERS INTERNATIONAL LIMITED, 180 Clemenceau Avenue, pg. 603   **IT**

Haw Par Leisure International Pte. Ltd., #07-02 Setron Building, 10 Dundee Road, pg. 604   **IT**

Haw Par Properties (Singapore) Private Limited, 180 Clemenceau Avenue, pg. 604   **IT**

Haw Par Securities (Private) Limited, 180 Clemenceau Avenue, pg. 604   **IT**

Heller Factoring (Singapore) Ltd., DBS Bldg., Tower 2, 6 Shenton Way, #20-08, pg. 521   **IT**

Henkel Chemicals (Singapore) Pte. Ltd., 11 Tg Penjuru Cres., pg. 612   **IT**

Henkel Singapore Pte., Ltd., 11 Tg Penjuru Cres, pg. 613   **IT**

Hercules Singapore Pte Ltd., pg. 811   **PB**

Hewlett-Packard Singapore Pte. Ltd., 150 Beach Rd. # 29-00, pg. 822   **PB**

Hewlett-Packard Singapore (Sales) Pte., Ltd., 1150 Depot Rc., pg. 822   **PB**

Hillard Scotchbrook Communications Pte. Ltd., 03-00 Pacific Can Bldg., 19 Cecil St., pg. 411   **PV**

Hirakawa Singapore Pte. Ltd., 47 Pandan Road, pg. 531   **IT**

Hitachi Zosen Engineering Singapore (Pte.) Ltd., UOB Bldg., 325 Boon Lay Pl., pg. 623   **IT**

Hitachi Zosen Singapore Limited, No. 15, Benoi Rd., pg. 623   **IT**

Hoei Electronics (S) Private Limited, 51 Goldhill Plaza, #14-09/10 Newton Rd., pg. 627   **IT**

The Hokkaido Takushoku Bank, Ltd. (Singapore), 65 Chulia Street, #48-01, pg. 627   **IT**

Hokuriku (Singapore) PTE., LTD., 3A Joo Koon Circle, pg. 628   **IT**

Honeywell Pte. Ltd., Southeast Asia Block 750E, Chai Chee Rc. 06-01, pg. 835   **PB**

HONG FOK CORPORATION LTD., 300 Beach Road #41-00, The Concourse, pg. 635   **IT**

Hong Fok Land Pte. Ltd., 300 Beach Road #41-00, The Concourse, pg. 635   **IT**

Hoover Stainless Pte Ltd., No. 521 Yishun Industrial Park A, pg. 1322   **IT**

Hotel Plaza Limited, 101 Thomson Road, pg. 1443   **IT**

Huber & Suhner (Singapore) Pte. Ltd., 24 Kian Teck Rd., pg. 637   **IT**

Hughes Tool Company (Far East) Pte. Ltd., 20 Gul Way, Jurong P.O. Box 333, pg. 167   **PB**

Hunter Douglas Singapore Pte. Ltd., 3 Tuas Ave. 1, pg. 640   **IT**

Hutchinson Technology Asia, 20 Jalan Afifi 05-07., pg. 851   **PB**

I&S Corporation (Singapore Branch), 229A Bugis Village, Victoria St., pg. 642   **IT**

IBJ Futures Pte. Limited, DBS Bldg., 6 Shenton Way, #14-01, pg. 676   **IT**

IBJ Merchant Bank (Singapore) Limited, 16 Collyer Quay, #14-00, Hitachi Tower, pg. 676   **IT**

IBM Singapore Pte Ltd., pg. 897   **PB**

ICI Paints (Singapore) Private Limited, 22, Soon Lee Rd., 2262, pg. 665   **IT**

ICI (Singapore) Private Limited, 152 Beach Rd., pg. 665   **IT**

ICIS LOR-Asia/Pacific, 1 Maritime Square, #12-06A World Trade Centre, pg. 1094   **IT**

ICL Singapore Private Limited, 1 Maritime Square, pg. 529   **IT**

IHI Marine Engineering (Singapore) Pte. Ltd., 11 Jurong Pier Road, pg. 689   **IT**

ING Insurance, 80 Raffles Place #17-20, pg. 650   **IT**

INS Communications Pte Ltd., 55 Amoy Street, pg. 1253   **IT**

IPC CORPORATION LTD., IPC Building, 23 Tai Seng Drive, pg. 651   **IT**

IPC Interactive Pte Ltd., #03-02 Corex Building, No. 10 Tannery Lane, pg. 651   **IT**

IPC Peripherals Pte Ltd., 21 Tai Seng Drive, pg. 651   **IT**

I.R.E. Corporation Pte. Ltd., Block 1004, Toa Payoh Industrial Park, pg. 937   **IT**

ISK Singapore Pte Ltd., 39 Tuas West Dr., pg. 689   **IT**

ITW Asia (Pte) Ltd., 8, Kaki Bukit Rd. 2 N02-34, pg. 868   **PB**

Ideal Homes Pte., Limited, 5 Shenton Way #02-11, pg. 1253   **IT**

Imation Singapore Pte. Ltd., Century Indus. Bldg., 23 New Industrial Red. #03-01, pg. 870   **PB**

Inchcape Bdh, 11 Keppel Rd. #09-01, pg. 672   **IT**

Inchcape Berhad, Inchcape House, 450/452 Alexandra Rd., pg. 672   **IT**

Industrial & Offshore Computer Services (S) Pte. Ltd., 71 Ayer Rajah Crescent #05-24/26, pg. 242   **IT**

The Industrial Bank of Japan, Limited (Singapore Branch), 16 Collyer Quay, pg. 675   **IT**

Ingersoll Rand S.E. Asia (Private) Limited, Jurong Town, pg. 878   **PB**

Inoue-Nissei Engineering Pte Ltd., 7 Benoi Sector, pg. 1322   **IT**

Intel Singapore Ltd., Block 26, Ayer Rajah Crescent, No. 03/01/10, pg. 887   **PB**

Intergraph Systems South-East Asia (Pte.) Ltd., 85 Science Park Drive, pg. 891   **PB**

The International Commercial Bank of China, 6 Battery Road, Unit 36-03, pg. 683   **IT**

International Distillers South Asia, 08-232 Faber House, pg. 410   **IT**

International Factors Leasing Pte Ltd., 7 Temasek Boulevard, pg. 684   **IT**

INTERNATIONAL FACTORS (SINGAPORE) LTD., #10-01 Suntec Tower One, 7 Temasek Boulevard, pg. 684   **IT**

International Flavors & Fragrances (Singapore) Pte. Ltd., #10-01 LKN Bldg., 135 Cecil St., pg. 899   **PB**

International Rectifier Southeast Asia Pte Ltd., 315 Outram Rd., pg. 907   **PB**

International Video Products Pte. Ltd., 190 Yishun Ave. 7, pg. 1405   **PB**

Interpex Services Private Limited, 5 Shenton Way, #02-11, pg. 1253   **IT**

Interturbine Compressor Technology Pte. Ltd., 18 Loyang Crescent, pg. 1690   **PB**

Interturbine Singapore Pte. Ltd., 18 Loyang Crescent, pg. 1690   **PB**

InterVoice, Inc., 20 Cecil St. #25-07, pg. 910   **PB**

Intraco Asia Singapore, 15 Catonment Road, pg. 1205   **PB**

JEOL Asia Pte. Ltd., #05-17, Henderson Building, 221 Henderson Road, pg. 697   **IT**

JGC Singapore Pte. Ltd., 78 Shenton Way, #29-01, pg. 697   **IT**

JT International (Singapore) Pte. Ltd., 96 Somerset Road, pg. 703   **IT**

JACKS INTERNATIONAL LIMITED, 7500E Beach Road #03-201, pg. 697   **IT**

Japan Energy (Singapore) Pte., Ltd., #33/04-07 Hong Leong Bldg., 16 Raffles Quay, pg. 702   **IT**

Jardine Fleming International Securities Ltd., Representative Office, 4 Shenton Way No 17-02, pg. 494   **IT**

Jardine Fleming International Securities Limited, Shell Tower, #14-01, 50 Raffles Place, pg. 494   **IT**

Jardine Matheson (Singapore) Ltd, 4 Shenton Way #17-00, pg. 705   **IT**

John Crane Asia Pacific, 21 Loyang Crescent, pg. 1339   **IT**

Johnson & Johnson Asia Pacific, 5 Temasek Blvd., pg. 930   **PB**

Axel Johnson & Co. (SEA) Pte. Ltd., 453 Tagore, Ave., pg. 711   **IT**

Axel Johnson (SEA) Pte. Ltd., PO Box 3250, pg. 712   **IT**

Geographic Index-Non U.S.

S.C. Johnson & Son Pte. Limited, 23, Playfair Road, pg. 593 — PV

Juki (Hong Kong) Ltd.-Singapore Branch, 122 Middle Rd., #09-01, pg. 717 — IT

Jurong Engineering Limited, 25 Tanjong Kling Road, pg. 689 — IT

K-Tron Asia Pacific Pte, 2 Havelock Road #03-09, pg. 938 — PB

KE-Burgmann Singapore Pte. Ltd., Blk 7 Pioneer Road North No. 10-51, pg. 234

KLA Instruments Singapore, Pte Ltd, BLK 3A Woodlands Centre Road, pg. 939 — PB

KME Asia Pte. Ltd., 09-13 Pasadir Centre, One Selegie Rd., 0718, pg. 719 — IT

KSB Pumps Asia Pacific Pte. Ltd., pg. 721 — IT

Kwe-Kintetsu World Express(S)Pte Ltd., Cargo Agents Bldg. C., 115 Airport Cargo Rd., #04-12, pg. 735 — IT

Kalmar LMV East Asia Pte. Ltd., 605A MacPherson Rd. #06-04, pg. 1421 — IT

Kansai Paints (Singapore) Pte. Ltd., 57, Penjuru Rd., pg. 723 — IT

Kanthal Electroheat (SEA) Pte. Ltd., pg. 724 — IT

Kao (Singapore) Private Limited, 247 Alexandra Rd., pg. 718 — IT

Kao (Southeast Asia) Pte., Ltd., 247 Alexandra Rd., pg. 718 — IT

Kawasaki Heavy Industries (Singapore) Pte. Ltd., Six Battery Road, #18-04, pg. 726 — IT

Kawasaki Steel Co., Hong Leong Building, 16 Raffles Quay, No. 15-03, pg. 726 — IT

Kay Hian Private Ltd., 80 Raffles Place, #30-01 UOB Plaza 1, pg. 583 — IT

Kelvin Hughes (Singapore) Pte. Limited, 4 Loyang Drive, pg. 1268 — IT

The Kendall Co.-Singapore Representative Office, 1 Selegie Road, pg. 1647 — IT

Kenwood Electronics Singapore Pte. Ltd., Kenwood Bldg., No. 1, Genting Ln., #07-00, pg. 731 — IT

KEPPEL CORPORATION LIMITED, 325 Telok Blangah Road, pg. 731 — IT

Keppel-Fels Ltd., 31 Shipyard Road, pg. 731 — IT

KHONG GUAN FLOUR MILLING LIMITED, 2 MacTaggart Road (Level 3), pg. 732

Kidde International Protection Systems Pre. Ltd., 143 Ceal Street, pg. 1500 — IT

Kikkoman (S) Pte. Ltd., 7, Senoko Crescent, pg. 733 — IT

KIM ENG HOLDINGS LIMITED, 9 Temasek Boulevard, pg. 733

Kim Eng Securities (Private) Limited, 9 Temasek Boulevard, pg. 733 — IT

Kimberly-Clark Far East Pte. Ltd., Pasir Panjag, pg. 959 — PB

Kinetics Technology (Singapore) Pte. Ltd., pg. 837 — IT

Kleinwort Benson Research (Asia) Pte. Limited, 6 Battery Road, The Chartered Bank Building, #10-05, pg. 420 — IT

Knurr-Spectra (S.E.A.) Pte. Ltd., #04-05 Ayer Rajah Ind. Estate, 26 Ayer Rajah Crescent, pg. 739 — IT

Kobe International (S) Co., Pte. Ltd., 60, Pandan Rd., Jurong, pg. 741 — IT

Kobe Steel Asia Pte Ltd., 6 Shenton Way, #22-02 DBS Building Tower 1, pg. 741 — IT

Kockums SE Asia Pte Ltd., Forum Galleria #09-02, 583 Orchard Rd., pg. 277 — IT

Kodak (Singapore) Pte. Limited, 305 Alexandra Rd., pg. 554 — PB

Kollmorgen International Logistics, Block 203, #03-53, Hougang St. 21, pg. 966 — PB

Konami Asia (Singapore) Pte. Ltd., 13th Fl., 200 Cantonment Road, pg. 746

Konami (Singapore) Pte. Ltd., 13th Fl., 200 Cantonment Road, pg. 746 — IT

KONE Elevator Pte. Ltd., 510 Thomson Rd., pg. 747 — IT

Konica Singapore Pte. Ltd., 401 Commonwealth Dr., pg. 749 — IT

Korn/Ferry International, 28-06 Shell Tower, 50 Raffles Pl., pg. 633 — PV

Krauss-Maffei Asia Pacific Pte. Ltd., pg. 836 — IT

Kredietbank Singapore Branch, 1 Raffles Place, pg. 760 — IT

Krupp Polysius Asia Pacific (Pty.) Ltd., Shaw Center, 1 Scotts Rd. 16-06, pg. 512 — IT

Krupp Widia S.E. Asia (Pte.) Ltd., 16-06 Shaw Center, 1, Scotts Rd., pg. 510 — IT

Kubota Corp.-Singapore Office, CPF Bldg, 79 Robinson Rd., pg. 763 — IT

Kubota Supplies & Engineering (Asia) Pte. Ltd., CPF Building, 79 Robinson Rd., 20-06, pg. 763 — IT

Kulicke & Soffa Singapore, Inc., Block 5012, Ang Mo Kio Ave 5, pg. 969 — PB

Kureha Chemicals (Singapore) Pte. Ltd., pg. 1404 — IT

Kvaerner Energy a.s Southeast Asia Representative Office, 15 Benoi Cresent, Jurong, pg. 767 — IT

Kvaerner National Division of Kvaerner Singapore Pte. Ltd., 17 Gul Way, pg. 768 — IT

Kvaerner R J Brown Pte. Ltd., 73, Science Park Drive, #02-14 Cintech 1, pg. 767 — IT

Kvaerner Singapore Pte Ltd, 15 Benoi Crescent, pg. 768 — IT

Kyodo Printing Co. Pte., Ltd., 112 Neythal Road, Jurong, pg. 372 — IT

Kyowa Hakko Industry (Singapore) Pte. Ltd., 300 Orchard Rd., #06-02, pg. 778 — IT

L & N Singapore, Pte., Ltd., pg. 727 — IT

LGT Asset Management Pte. Ltd., 20 Raffles Pl., 21-07/08, Ocean Towers, pg. 809 — IT

LM Ericsson International AB Singapore, 921 Bukit Timah Rd., TCB Bldg., 2nd Fl., pg. 1369 — IT

LTCB Futures (Singapore) Pte. Ltd., 80 Raffles Place, #27-01, pg. 816 — IT

LTCB Merchant Bank (Singapore) Limited, 80 Raffles Pl., #26-01, pg. 816 — IT

Lancashire Dairies (Overseas) Pte. Ltd., Blk. 3016, #03-145 Ubi Road 1, pg. 798 — IT

Landis & Staefa (Sea) Pte Ltd., 2D Ayer Rajah Crescent, pg. 803 — IT

Laporte Industries (Singapore) Pte Limited, 13 Tuas Ave., 1, pg. 803 — IT

LASMO - Singapore Representative Office, 545 Orchard Road, # 1304 Far Eastern Shopping Ctr., pg. 804 — IT

LeaRonal Singapore Pte. Ltd., 23 Joo Koon Rd., pg. 982 — IT

Legacy Storage Systems Corp., Blk. 35 Marsiling Industrial, Estate Road 3 #05-01/06, pg. 805 — IT

Leong Jin Corporation Pte. Ltd., 11 Benoi Crescent, pg. 516 — IT

Lever Brothers Singapore Sdn. Bhd., pg. 1437 — IT

LIANG COURT HOLDINGS LTD., 298 Tiong Bahru Road, pg. 807 — IT

Liebert Far East Ltd., 896 Duneam Rd. No. 04-06, pg. 577 — PB

Liebherr-Singapore Pte. Ltd., No. 8 Pandan Avenue, pg. 809 — IT

Lilly Industries, Inc., Level 36, Hong Leong Bldg., 16 Raffles Quay, pg. 995 — PB

The Lincoln Electric Company (Asia Pacific) Pte. Ltd., Blk 219 Henderson Indus. Park, #02-01 Henderson Rd., pg. 996 — PB

Lips Asia Pte Ltd., 8A Tuas Avenue 12, pg. 812 — IT

Littelfuse Fareast, PTE Ltd., A-Z Building, 140 Paya Lebar Rd., #08-01/04, pg. 1001 — IT

Arthur D. Little Far East, Inc., The Gateway, East Tower #13.06, 152 Beach Rd., pg. 670 — PV

Litton Components Private Ltd., 500 Chai Chee Lane, pg. 1004 — IT

Loewe Fashion Pte Ltd, 2208, F Twr. A, 391 Orchard Rd., pg. 782 — IT

Logica Pte Ltd, PIL Bldg., 140 Cecil St. #16-04, pg. 815 — IT

Louis Vuitton (Singapore) Pte Ltd, 01-09 The Shopping Gallery, Hilton Intl.-391 A Orchard Rd., pg. 783 — IT

Lubrizol Southeast Asia (Pte.) Ltd., 44 Tanjong Penjuru, pg. 1017 — IT

Lucent Technologies Consumer Products Ptd. Ltd., 3014A Ubi Rd. 1, Kampong Ubi Industrial Estate, pg. 1018 — PB

Lucent Technologies Microelectronics Pte. Ltd., 3, Kallang Sector, Kolam Ayer Industrial Park, pg. 1019 — PB

Lucent Technologies Singapore Pte. Ltd., 77 Science Park Dr., #03-18 Cintech III, pg. 1019 — PB

Lummus Overseas Corp., Ste. 2403-4 Shaw Centre, One Scotts Rd., pg. 6 — IT

Luwa Engineering (Pte.) Ltd., pg. 617 — IT

M/S Fischbein Packaging (Singapore) Pte. Ltd., No. 37, Lorong 23, pg. 103 — PV

MBT (Singapore) Pte. Ltd., 11 Tuas Ave. 20, pg. 1465 — IT

MD Biomedical Engineering Pte. Ltd., Blk 1004 Toa Payoh Indus Park, Lorong 8, #07-1497, pg. 822 — PB

MEZ Power Industries Pte. Ltd., No. 1 A, Tuas Ave. 16, pg. 712 — IT

MHE Demag Pte. Ltd., pg. 838 — IT

MHI South East Asia Pte Ltd (MHIS), No. 2 Tuas Avenue 20, pg. 874 — IT

MSA S.E. Asia Pte. Ltd., 51 Ayer Rajah Crescent #02-03, pg. 1115 — PB

MSP Steel Works Ltd., 30, Jalan Buroh, pg. 948 — IT

MacDermid Singapore Pte. Ltd., 80 Marine Parade Rd., pg. 1030 — PB

MacGREGOR (SGP) Pte. Ltd., No. 1 Lokyang Way 01-6A, pg. 671 — IT

Mag-E Furnaces Pte Ltd., No. 20, Benol Place, pg. 361 — PV

Magdel Services Pte. Ltd., pg. 720 — IT

Makita Singapore PTE. LTD., 7, Changi South Street, 3, pg. 832 — IT

Mann & Hummel Pte. Ltd., 25 International Business Park, No. 02-59/60 German Centre, pg. 484 — IT

Mannesmann Handel (SEA) Pte. Ltd., pg. 838 — IT

ManuLife (Singapore) Pte. Ltd., IBM Tower, 80 Anson Rd., # 27-01, pg. 841 — IT

Marcam Asia-Pacific Pte., Ltd., #30-04 IBM Towers, pg. 1043 — PB

Mardev-Singapore, 10 Anson Road, 32-02 International Plaza, pg. 1094 — IT

Marina Bay Hotel Private Limited, 5 Raffles Avenue, pg. 704 — IT

Martin Marietta International, Inc., 250 North Bridge Road, #30-10, Raffles City Tower, pg. 1010 — PB

Martin Marietta International, Inc., 150 Beach Rd., Gateway West, pg. 1010 — PB

Maruzen Asia Private Ltd., Takashimaya Dept. Store, 391 Orchard Road #04-08, pg. 846 — IT

Matsushita Refrigeration Industries (S) Pte. Ltd., 1 Bedok South Road, pg. 847 — IT

McDermott Southeast Asia Pty. Ltd., 1 Science Center Rd., pg. 1068 — PB

Mecomb Singapore Limited, Sime Darby Center, 896 Duncan Rd. #04-02, pg. 1251 — IT

Meiji Seika (Singapore) Pte. Ltd., 36, Quality Rd., Jurong Town, pg. 856 — IT

The Meijiseimei Investment Singapore Pte. Ltd., 6 Battery Rd #10-02, pg. 854 — IT

Memorex Telex Pte. Ltd., 47 Scotts Road, pg. 857 — IT

Mentor Graphics (Singapore) Pte. Ltd., Unit 53, Block 2 Science Park Dr., pg. 1087 — PB

Merita Merchant Bank Singapore Ltd., Shell Tower, 50 Raffles Pl. 15-01, pg. 859 — IT

Messier-Dowty Customer Support Centre-Asia Pacific, 21 Loyang Crescent, pg. 1340 — IT

Metal Box Singapore Limited, P.O. Box 7, Marsiling Post Office, pg. 267 — IT

Mettler-Toledo (SEA) Pte Ltd, 26 Ayer Rajah Crescent, #02-04 Ayer Rajah Industrial Estate, pg. 4 — PV

Micron Semiconductor Asia Pacific Pte. Ltd., Cititech Industrial Bldg., 629 Aljunied Rd. #07-21, pg. 1105 — PB

Micropolis Limited, Block 5002, Ang Mo Kio Ave., pg. 742 — PV

Micropolis Limited, Block 5004, Ang Mo Kio Ave. 5 #01-11, pg. 742 — PV

Mikron Machine Tool Asia Pte Ltd, Midlink Plaza, 122 Middle Road #06-02, pg. 867 — IT

Milk Products Holdings (SEA), 218 Pandan Loop, pg. 923 — IT

Miller Freeman PTE Ltd., 26-00 Shaw Towers, 100 Beach Rd., pg. 1443 — IT

Minebea Investment (Pte) Ltd., 1, Chai Chee Avenue, pg. 868 — IT

Minebea Technologies Pte. Ltd., PSA Building, 460 Alexandra Road, #34-02, pg. 868 — IT

Minolta Singapore (Pte.) Ltd., 10 Teban Gardens Crescent, pg. 869 — IT

Mitsubishi Caterpillar Forklift Asia Pte., 36 Robinson Rd., pg. 316 — IT

Mitsubishi Chemical Singapore Pte Ltd, 78 Shenton Way, #23-01, pg. 871 — IT

The Mitsubishi Trust & Banking Corporation, 6 Battery Road #08-01, pg. 876 — IT

Mitsui & Co., Ltd., Hong Leong Bldg., 16 Raffles Quay No. 28-00, pg. 882 — IT

The Mitsui Trust and Banking Company - Singapore, 6 Shenton Way, #35-01 DBS Building, pg. 883 — IT

Mitsui Trust Futures (Singapore) Pte. Ltd., 6 Shenton Way, pg. 883 — IT

Mobil Oil Singapore Pte. Ltd., 18 Pioneer Rd., pg. 1119 — PB

Modern Packaging Industries Pte. Ltd., No. 8, 2nd Chin Bee Road, pg. 1444 — IT

Moet-Hennessy (Asia) Pte Ltd, 33.02 PSA Bldg., 460 Alexandra Rd., pg. 783 — IT

Monsanto Singapore Company (Pte.) Ltd., 101 Thomson Rd., 19-00, 20-03 105, pg. 1126 — PB

Moody's Singapore Pte. Ltd., Offfice Suite 15, Level 37, Shell Tower, pg. 537 — IT

Moog Singapore Pte Ltd., The Maxwell, Singapore Science Park, pg. 1128 — PB

Moore Products Co. (S) Pte. Ltd., No. 03-01 Corex Bldg., 10 Tannery Lane, pg. 1129 — PB

Morgan Grenfell Asia Limited (Singapore), 36 Robinson Rd., #13-01 City House, pg. 406 — IT

Morgan Guaranty Trust Company, 32-08 DBS Bldg., Tower 2, 6 Shenton Way, pg. 1130 — IT

J.P. Morgan Investment Management Inc., 32-08 DBS Bldg., Tower 2, 6 Shenton Way, pg. 1131 — IT

J.P. Morgan Securities Asia Ltd., 32-08 DBS Bldg., Tower 2, 6 Shenton Way, pg. 1131 — IT

J.P. Morgan Futures Inc., 32-08 DBS Bldg., Tower 2, 6 Shenton Way, #30-01, pg. 1130 — IT

J.P. Morgan International Capital Corporation, 32-08 DBS Bldg., Tower 2, 6 Shenton Way, pg. 1131 — IT

Morgan Stanley Singapore, 80 Raffles Pl., UOB Plaza 1, Unit 42-01, pg. 1133 — IT

Morganite Carbon of Singapore Pte. Limited, 155, Kallang Way, pg. 892 — IT

Motorola Electronics Pte., Ltd., No. 10 Ang Mo Kio Street 64, pg. 1139 — IT

Motorola Electronics Pte. Ltd., Components Div., 14 Tuas Ave. 5, pg. 1139 — IT

Motorola Singapore Pte., Ltd., 100 Beach Rd., Shaw Towers 35-00, pg. 1140 — IT

AB Carl Munters (SEA), Hex 02-02, Poh Leng Bldg., 21, Moonstone Ln., pg. 669 — IT

Munters Pte Ltd., Jubilee Industrial Bldg., 6 Genting Rd., Hex 04-00, pg. 669 — IT

Myanmar Computer Systems Pte. Ltd., Blk 998, Toa Payoh North #03-05/07, pg. 242 — IT

NCT Singapore Pte. Ltd., 152 Beach Rd., pg. 914 — IT

NDC Merchant Bank Ltd., 6 Shenton Way, #41-00, DBS Bldg., pg. 351 — IT

NDC Merchant Bank Nominees Ltd., DBS Building Tower One, 6 Shenton Way, #41-00, pg. 351 — IT

NEC Electronics Singapore Pte. Ltd., 101 Thomson Road, #04-02/5 United Square, pg. 901 — IT

NEC Semiconductors Singapore Pte. Ltd., 38, Ang Mo Kio Industrial Park 2, pg. 900 — IT

NEC Singapore Pte. Ltd., One Maritime Square, #12-10 World Trade Centre, pg. 900 — IT

NIF Management Singapore Pte Ltd, 6 Shenton Way, #21-11, DBS Building Tower Two, pg. 375 — IT

NKK Corporation-Singapore, 78 Shenton Way, pg. 903 — IT

NLI International Singapore Pte. Ltd., Tung Centre, 20 Collyer Quay, #15-02/03, pg. 936 — IT

NMB Precision Tool & Die (Pte) Ltd., 6 Gul Avenue, pg. 868 — IT

NMB Singapore Limited, pg. 868 — IT

NSK Singapore (Private) Ltd., 03-02 World Trade Centre, One Maritime Square, pg. 904 — IT

NYK Bulkship (Asia) Pte. Ltd., 150 Beach Road, #24-00, pg. 941 — IT

NYK Line (Singapore) Pte. Ltd., 150 Beach Road, #25-00, pg. 942 — IT

National Bank of Canada (Asia) Ltd., 331 North Bridge Road, #11-04/06, pg. 907 — IT

National Industrial Gases Pte. Ltd., 1 Shipyard Road, pg. 766 — IT

National Westminster Bank Plc, 5th Floor, Shell Tower, 50 Raffles Place, pg. 911 — IT

NationsBank (Singapore) Branch, Bank of East Asia Building 137 Market St, pg. 1166 — PB

Nedlloyd Districenters Pte. Ltd., pg. 1144 — IT

Nedlloyd (Singapore) Pte. Ltd., pg. 1145 — IT

Nemic-Lambda Pte. Ltd., Block 1008, pg. 1242 — IT

PB - *U.S. Public Companies Volume*
PV - *U.S. Private Companies Volume*
IT - *International Public & Private Companies Volume*

1747

Geographic Index-Non U.S.

NEPTUNE ORIENT LINES LTD., 456 Alexandra Road, pg. 912 IT
Neste Petroleum (Singapore) PTE. Ltd., 78, Shenton Way, 26-03, 26th Fl., pg. 915 IT
Neste Singapore Holdings Pte. Ltd., 152 Beach Rd. 08-01/04, pg. 915 IT
Nestle Asean Singapore (Pte) Ltd., pg. 920 IT
Netstal Singapore Pte. Ltd., pg. 836 IT
Ngee Ann Development Pte. Ltd., 391A Orchard Road, pg. 1350 IT
NIFE Power Systems Pte Ltd., Unit 211 Intrepid Warehouse Complex, pg. 54 IT
Nihon Keizai Shimbun Singapore Pte. Ltd., 331 North Bridge Rd., pg. 930 IT
The Nikko Merchant Bank (Singapore) Ltd., 6 Battery Road, #28-01, pg. 931 IT
Nikko Petroleum (Asia) Pte. Ltd., #33/04-07 Hong Leong Bldg., 16 Raffles Quay, pg. 702 IT
Nippon Credit Bank Ltd.-Singapore, 6 Battery Rd., #25-01, pg. 933 IT
Nippon Express (Singapore) Pte., Ltd., 541 Orchard Road #21-00, Liat Towers, pg. 934 IT
Nippon Meat Packers Singapore Pte. Ltd., 16th Raffles Quay, #42-08, Hong Leong Building, pg. 936 IT
Nippon Oil (Asia) Pte. Ltd., 6 Banery Rd., #29-02/03, pg. 937 IT
Nippon Paint (Singapore) Co., Pte. Ltd., No. 1, First Lokyang Road, pg. 937 IT
Nippon Shokubai-Representative Office, 138 Cecil Street, pg. 939 IT
Nippon Steel Corporation-Singapore Rep. Office, Hong Leong Bldg., 16 Raffles Quay #11-01, pg. 940 IT
Nipsea Paint Research Pte. Ltd., No. 1, First Lokyang Road, pg. 937 IT
Nishimatsu Construction Co., Ltd.-Singapore Office, 150 Beach Rd., pg. 943 IT
Nishimatsu Lum Chang JV Pte. Ltd., 38 Kim Tian Road #02-07 Kim Tian Plaza, pg. 943 IT
Nissin Foods (S) Pte. Ltd., 3, Senoko Crescent, pg. 950 IT
NITEC (South Asia) Pte. Ltd., 3, Senoko Crescent, pg. 950 IT
Nitto Denko (Singapore) Pte. Ltd., 315 Outram Rd., pg. 950 IT
Nokia Mobile Phones, S.E.A. Pte. Ltd., 15 Tai Seng Drive #04-00, pg. 952 IT
Nokia Telecommunications (Singapore) Pte. Ltd., 501 Orchard Rd., #14 Lane Crawford Pl., pg. 954 IT
Nomura Asset Management (Singapore) Limited, No. 6 Battery Road, #29-04, pg. 955 IT
Nomura Capital Management (Singapore) Ltd., No. 6 Battery Road, #42-03, pg. 956 IT
Nomura Futures (Singapore) Pte. Ltd., 6 Battery Rd., 39-02, pg. 957 IT
Nomura/JAFCO Investment (Asia) Ltd., 6 Battery Road, #42-01, pg. 957 IT
Nomura Research Institute (Singapore) Private Limited, No. 6 Battery Road, #35-03, pg. 956 IT
Nomura Securities Singapore Pte. Ltd., 6 Battery Road, #39-04, pg. 957 IT
Nomura Singapore Limited, 6 Battery Rd., 39-01, pg. 957 IT
NORD/LB Singapore, 6 Shenton Way, #16-08, pg. 958 IT
Nordisk Aviation Products Pte. Ltd., Room No. 272 SATS Airfreight, Terminal 4, pg. 964 IT
Nordson S.E. Asia (Pte.), Ltd., 16A, Science Park Drive, #01-01, pg. 1189 PB
NORIT Singapore PGE Ltd., 401 Bldg. Unit 11-03-04, 97 Sommerset Rd., pg. 958 IT
Norske Skog Trading Far East Pte. Ltd., 38 Medway Dr., pg. 966 IT
Norton Pte. Ltd., 51 Goldhill Pte Ltd., pg. 1175 IT
Novell Singapore, 300 Beach Rd., #28-00, The Concourse, pg. 1204 PB
Novellus Singapore Pte Ltd., 101 Thomson Rd., 21-01/02 United Sq., pg. 1204 PB
Novo Nordisk A/S, So. East Regional Office, 10 Shenton Way, MAS Building #17-03/05, pg. 987 IT
Novo Nordisk A/S, Asia Pacific Center, 10 Shenton Way, pg. 987 IT
Novo Nordisk A/S, Far East Regional Office, 10 Shenton Way, pg. 987 IT
Nypro Singapore Pte. Ltd., pg. 836 IT
O.C.B.C. Centre East Project, Robinson Road, pg. 943 IT
OCE (Singapore) Pte. Ltd., pg. 995 IT
OUB Manulife Pte. Ltd., 10 Anson Rd., International Plaza #6-18, pg. 841 IT
Obayashi Corporation-Singapore, 6 Shenton Way #16-09, pg. 996 IT
Obayashi Singapore Pte. Ltd., #16-10 DBS Bldg., 6 Shenton Way, pg. 996 IT
Oceaneering International Sdn. Bhd., No. 1 Kwong Min Rd., pg. 1211 PB
Oerlikon Singapore Pte. Ltd., 12 Tuas Ave. 7, pg. 998 IT
Offshore Logistics Far East (PTE) Ltd., P. O. Box 24, Changi Post Office, pg. 1213 PB
Oki Electronics (Hong Kong) Ltd.-Singapore Branch, 78 Shenton Way, No. 09-01, pg. 1000 IT
Oki Electronics (Singapore) Pte Ltd., 78 Shenton Way, #09-01, pg. 1000 IT
Olicom Singapore, 10 Anson Road, pg. 1001 IT
Olin Pte., Ltd., Singapore, 9, Tuas Ave.10, pg. 1220 PB
Olivetti Singapore Pte. Ltd., Eight Ayer Rajah Crescent, pg. 1003 IT
Olympus Singapore Pte Ltd., pg. 1005 IT
OMRON Asiapacific Pte. Ltd., 510 Thomson Road, #13-03 SLF Building, pg. 1005 IT
OMRON Business Systems Singapore Private Limited, 1 Marine Parade Central, #13-04/05/06 Parkway Builders Centre, pg. 1005 IT
Onoda Singapore Pte. Ltd., 16 Raffles Quay, #15-01, Hong Leong Building, pg. 284 IT
Oracle Systems Southeast Asia (S) Pte. Ltd., 8 Shenton Way, #22-02, pg. 1228 PB
ORCHARD PARADE HOLDINGS LIMITED, 1 Tanglin Road #05-01, pg. 1007 IT
ORIX Car Rentals Pte Ltd., 30, Bukit Batok East Ave. 6, pg. 1009 IT
ORIX Commodities Singapore Pte Limited, 331 North Bridge Rd., pg. 1009 IT
ORIX Investment and Management Private Limited, 250 North Bridge Road, 17/02 Raffles City Tower, pg. 1009 IT
ORIX Leasing Singapore Limited, 331 North Bridge Rd., 19-01/06 Odeon Towers, pg. 1010 IT
ORIX Rentec (Singapore) Pte. Limited, 140 Paya Lebar Road, #05-09 A-Z Bldg., pg. 1010 IT
Osaka Gas Co.-Asia Representative Office, 10 Shenton Way, #12-03 MAS Building, pg. 1012 IT
Outokumpu (S.E.A.) PTE Ltd., International Plaza, 10 Anson Road 33-10, pg. 1016 IT
Owens-Corning (Singapore) Pte Ltd., 9, Temasek Boulevard, #19-02 Suntec Tower 2, pg. 1237 PB
Oxford Instruments, #22-02, Suntec City Tower One, 7 Temasek Boulevard, pg. 1018 IT
Oxford University Press Pte. Ltd., Block A, #03-03 Union Industrial Bldg., pg. 1019 IT
Pak Pacific (South East Asia) Pte. Ltd., Ten Pandan Rd., pg. 129 IT
Pacific Beauty Care Pte. Ltd., 76 Playfair Rd., pg. 1490 IT
Pacific Technology Private ltd., 17 Pioneer Crescent, Jurong Town, pg. 1292 IT
PacifiComp Pte. Ltd., 221 Henderson Road, pg. 242 IT
Pall Fluid Filtration Pte. Ltd., 15 Kallang Way, pg. 1254 PB
Palm Courtt Singapore, 15 Cairnhill Road, pg. 1212 IT
Pan Malaysia Cement Works (Singapore) Pte. Ltd., 17 Tg Kilding Road, pg. 198 IT
Panalpina World Transport (Singapore) Pte. Ltd., pg. 1023 IT
Panduit Singapore Pte. Ltd., 5 Gul Lane, pg. 836 PV
Parfums Christian Dior (Singapore) Pte Ltd, 06-18 Trademart Singapore, 60 MArtin Rd., pg. 783 IT
Paribas South East Asia, 39-01 Hong Leong Bldg., 16, Raffles Quay, pg. 321 IT
PARKWAY HOLDINGS LIMITED, 80 Marine Parade Road, pg. 1023 IT
Parsons Brinckerhoff International, Pte. Ltd. 585 North Bridge Road, pg. 841 PV
Pechiney Singapore Pte. Ltd., 78 Shenton Way 05-01, pg. 1031 IT
Pelmec Industries (Pte.) Limited, 28 Gul Way, pg. 868 IT
Periphonics Corporation, 152 Beach Rd. #04-06/08, pg. 1279 PB
Perstorp Asia-Pacific Ltd. Concrete Admixtures, 1 Shenton Way #10-08, Robina House, pg. 1037 IT
Perstorp Asia-Pacific Ltd.-Div. Specialty Chemicals, 1 Shenton Way #10-08, pg. 1038 IT
Perstorp Asia-Pacific Pte. Ltd.-Div. Chemitec, 1 Shenton Way #10-08, Robina House, pg. 1037 IT
Perstorp Asia-Pacific Pte. Ltd. Div. Flooring, 1 Shenton Way #10-08, Robina House, pg. 1039 IT
Perstorp Asia-Pacific Pte Ltd., 1 Shenton Way # 10-08, Robina House, pg. 1039 IT
Perstorp Asia-Pacific Pte Ltd., 1 Shenton Way #10-08, Robina House, pg. 1040 IT
Pfizer Private Limited, 18 Pasir Panjang Rd. #11, 17, PSA Multi-Storey Complex, pg. 1282 PB
AB Pharos Marine Pte. Ltd., Tannery Blk, Ruby Ind Complex, 35 Tannery Rd. 05-05, pg. 1290 IT
Phillips Petroleum Singapore Chemicals Pte. Ltd., 80 Anson Rd. #35-00, IBM Towers, pg. 1291 PB
Pioneer Electronics Asia Centre Pte. Ltd., 501 Orchard Road, #10-00, Lane Crawford Place, pg. 1058 IT
Plantronics Singapore, 391 A Orchard Rd., #12-01 Ngee Ann City, Tower A, pg. 1308 PB
Plasma Technik Coating Systems S.E.A. PTE Ltd., pg. 1307 IT
Pohang Iron & Steel Co., Ltd., Hong Leong Bldg., 16 Raffles Quay #27-04, pg. 1062 IT
Pol Baltic International Pte. Ltd., pg. 596 IT
Pol Gulf International Pte. Ltd., pg. 596 IT
Polacup Singapore Pte. Ltd., 42 Senoko Rd., pg. 639 IT
Polaroid Singapore (Pte) Ltd., Suite 1104, 11th Fl., pg. 1314 PB
Pothonier Singapore Pte Ltd., 5 Shenton Way, #02-11, pg. 1253 IT
Praxair Asia, Inc., pg. 1320 PB
Premisys Communications Pte Ltd., 8, Ang Mo Kio Industrial Park, pg. 1323 PB
Printronix, AG, No. 42 Changi S. St. One, pg. 1330 PB
Process Analytical Services Pte. Ltd., pg. 835 IT
Procter & Gamble (Singapore) Pte. Ltd., 80 Anson Road #36-00, pg. 1332 PB
Pulse Engineering-Singapore, pg. 1564 PB
Purac Far East, 138 Cecil Street, pg. 245 IT
qad.inc., 105 Cecil St., pg. 1345 PB
Quality Bakers (Asia) Pte Ltd., 2 Senoko Ave., pg. 555 IT
Quantum Asia-Pacific Pte. Ltd. Logistics Center, No. 2 Corporation Road, #01-01/06 Corporation Place, pg. 1350 PB
Quantum Asia-Pacific Pte. Ltd., 9 Temasek Blvd. #24-01, pg. 1350 PB
RMA - Land Development Private Ltd., 5 Shenton Way, #02-11, pg. 1253 IT
RNBNY Branch Office-Singapore, 143 Cecil St., pg. 1381 PB
RZB Singapore, 50 Raffles Place 27-04, Shell Tower, pg. 1085 IT
Rabobank Asia Ltd., Shell Tower, 50 Raffles Pl. 32-07, pg. 1082 IT
Radio Holland Group Singapore, 900 Dunearn Rd., pg. 1152 IT
Raychem Singapore Pte Ltd, 438 Alexandra Road, pg. 1363 PB
Read-Rite International, #28-02 Suntec City Tower 2, No. 9 Temasek Boulevard, pg. 1367 PB
Reader's Digest Asia, Ltd., #03-04 Union Bldg., 37 Jalan Pemimpin, pg. 1368 PB
Reader's Digest Asia, Ltd. (Singapore), #03-04 Union Industrial Building, pg. 1368 PB
Realty Management Services (Pte) Ltd., 5 Shenton Way #02-11, pg. 1253 IT
Reed Asian Information, No 1 Temasek Avenue, #17-01 Millenia Tower, pg. 1094 IT
Reed Elsevier (Singapore) PTE Limited, No 1 Temasek Avenue, #17-01 Millenia Tower, pg. 1095 IT
Reed Exhibition Companies-South Asia/Pacific, 1 Maritime Square, 12-01 World Trade Centre, pg. 1097 IT
Reed International (Singapore) PTE Limited, Union Industrial Bldg., 37 Jalan Pemimpin, pg. 1095 IT
Reed Travel Publishing-Asia/Pacific, No 1 Temasek Avenue, pg. 1097 IT
Reel-Tech Singapore Pte. Ltd., Sindo Building, 66 Tannery Lane, pg. 486 PB
Reemtsma International Far East Pte. Ltd., 101B-109B, Telok Ayer Street, pg. 1101 IT
Regent Motors Limited, 475 Tanglin Halt Rd., pg. 1251 IT
Regina Haw Par Private Limited, Tiger Balm Building, 2 Chia Ping Road, pg. 603 IT
Reliability Singapore Pte Ltd., 5004 Ang Mo Kio Ave. 5 #04-01, pg. 1374 PB
Renishaw's Representative Office, 171 Chin Swee Road, pg. 1103 IT
Republic National Bank of New York (Singapore) Ltd., 143 Cecil St., pg. 1381 PB
Reuters Singapore Pte Limited, pg. 1106 IT
Reuters South East Asia Ltd., 16A Science Park Dr., 0511, pg. 1106 IT
G.L. Rexroth Private Ltd., pg. 838 IT
Rhenania International Transport Services Pte. Ltd., 1203 Cathay Bldg.; 11 Dhoby Ghaut, pg. 1034 IT
Rhone-Poulenc Singapore Pte. Ltd., 14 Chin Bee Rd., pg. 1114 IT
Riche Monde Pte Ltd, 33.03 PSA Bldg., 460 Alexandra Rd., pg. 783 IT
Robinson Nugent, Inc., 268 Orchard Road, #08-07, pg. 1395 PB
Roche Singapore Pte. Ltd., Roche Bldg., 30 Shaw Rd., pg. 1122 IT
Rockwell Automation Southeast Asia Pte. Ltd., Singapore Science Park, 77 Science Park Drive, pg. 1400 PB
Rockwell International Manufacturing Pte. Ltd., No. 1, Gul Way, pg. 1401 PB
Rockwell Sales & Support Services, No. 10-230/232 Faber House, 230 Orchard Rd., pg. 1402 PB
Rohm & Haas (Singapore) Pte. Ltd., pg. 1404 PB
Rohm Electronics Asia PTE. LTD., Investment Div., 9 Temasek Boulevard, #20-02 Suntec, pg. 1125 IT
Rohr Aero Services-Asia, 1 Loyang Way 2, pg. 752 PB
Rorer Pharmaceutical (Singapore) Pte. Ltd., 10 Anson Rd. #27-10/11, pg. 1112 IT
Rothenberger Tools (Far East) PTE Ltd., 1298 Siong Hoe Bldg., No. 03-01, Rm. 1, pg. 1129 IT
Rothmans Industries Ltd., 905 Bukit Timah Rd., pg. 1130 IT
Royal Bank of Canada (ASIA) Limited, 140 Cecil street, #01-00, pg. 1131 IT
The Royal Bank of Scotland plc, 6 Battery Road, #18-01, pg. 1133 IT
Royal Copenhagen Singapore Pte. Ltd., 16-17 Duxton Hill, pg. 1135 IT
S.L. Building Investments Pte Limited, 5 Shenton Way, #02-11, pg. 1253 IT
S.L. Civic Investments Pte Limited, 5 Shenton Way, #02-11, pg. 1253 IT
S.L. Class Investments Pte Limited, 5 Shenton Way, #02-11, pg. 1253 IT
S.L. Development Management Pte Limited, 5 Shenton Way, #02-11, pg. 1253 IT
S.L. Earn Investments Pte Limited, 5 Shenton Way, #02-11, pg. 1253 IT
S.L. Home Loans Pte Ltd., 5 Shenton Way, #02-11, pg. 1253 IT
S.L. Management Services Pte Limited, 5 Shenton Way, #02-11, pg. 1253 IT
S.L. Marina Centre Development Private Limited, 5 Shenton Way, #02-11, pg. 1253 IT
S.L. Prime Development Pte Ltd., 5 Shenton Way #02-11, pg. 1253 IT
S.L. Prime Securities Pte Ltd., 5 Shenton Way, #02-11, pg. 1253 IT
S.L. Properties Limited, 5 Shenton Way, #02-11, pg. 1253 IT
S.L. Realty Services Pte Limited, 5 Shenton Way, #02-11, pg. 1253 IT
SATS Apron Services Pte., Ltd., SATS Bldg., 55 Airport Blvd., pg. 1374 IT
SATS Passenger Services Pte. Ltd., SATS Bldg., 55 Airport Blvd., pg. 1374 IT
S.B. Merchant Bank (Singapore) Limited, 6 Shenton Way # 27-08, pg. 1309 IT
SBC Warburg Securities (Singapore) Pte. Ltd., 16 Collyer Quay, pg. 1331 IT
S.C. Properties (Singapore) Pte. Ltd., 10 Anson Rd., #26-01, pg. 1233 IT
SCOR Asia-Pacific Pte. Ltd., 143 Cecil Street, 20-01, pg. 1152 IT
SCSG (SCS-Grumman Systems Pte Ltd.), Chai Chee Industrial Park, 750D Chai Chee Rd., #03-01, pg. 1032 PB

PB - U.S. Public Companies Volume
PV - U.S. Private Companies Volume
IT - International Public & Private Companies Volume

SDRC Singapore Pte. Ltd., 24 Raffles Place, #15-00 Clifford Centre, pg. 1525   **PB**
SICO Asia Pte Ltd., 115 A Commonwealth Dr., pg. 997   **PV**
SIG Asia Pte. Ltd., No. 1 Tannery Road 01-00, pg. 1156   **IT**
SKF Mfg. Singapore (Pte.) Ltd., 151 Gul Circle, pg. 1159   **IT**
SKF Singapore, 153 Gul Circle, Jurong, pg. 1159   **IT**
SKF Vehicle Parts Asia (Pte) Ltd., Block 1 no 01-06 Pasir Panjang Rd., pg. 1159   **IT**
S.L. Prime Properties Pte. Ltd., 5 Shenton Way #02-11, pg. 1253   **IT**
S.L. Prime Realty Pte. Ltd., 5 Shenton Way 02-11, pg. 1253   **IT**
SMH S.E.A. (S) Pte. Ltd., North Bridge Road 15, Raffles City Tower, pg. 1161   **IT**
SNC-Lavalin, 8 Shenton Way, pg. 1162   **IT**
ST Mobile Data Pte. Ltd., 19 Tai Seng Dr., 6th Storey, pg. 208   **PB**
STB Financial Futures (Singapore) Pte Limited, Five Shenton Way, pg. 1318   **IT**
Sachs (Far East) Pte. Ltd., pg. 835   **IT**
Safire Private Limited, 24 Raffles Pl., pg. 363   **PB**
The Sakura Bank - Singapore Branch, 16, Raffles Quay No. 01-04, pg. 1179   **IT**
Sakura Financial Futures (Singapore) Pte. Ltd., 16, Raffles Quay No. 35-01, pg. 1180   **IT**
Sakura Merchant Bank (Singapore) Ltd., 16, Raffles Quay #02-06, pg. 1180   **IT**
Samsung Asia Headquarters, 80 Robinson Road, pg. 1183   **IT**
Sanden International (Singapore) Pte. Ltd., Sanden House, 25 Ang Mo Kio Street 65, pg. 1184   **IT**
Sanderson Computers Pte. Ltd., 21-15 International Plaza, 10 Anson Rd., pg. 1185   **IT**
Sandoz Chemicals Pte. Ltd. Singapore, 34 Boon Leat Terrace, pg. 984   **IT**
Sanken Electric Singapore Pte. Limited, 150 Beach Rd., #14-03, pg. 1189   **IT**
Sankosha Engineering Singapore Pte. Ltd., 102E Pasir Panjang Road, pg. 1189   **IT**
Santa Fe International Services, Inc., P.O. Box 89, pg. 765   **IT**
Sanwa Futures (Singapore) PTE Limited, 6 Raffles Quay, #24-01 John Hancock Tower, pg. 1190   **IT**
Sanwa Singapore Limited, 6 Raffles Quay, #23-06 John Hancock Tower, pg. 1190   **IT**
Sanyo Airconditioners (Singapore) Pte. Ltd., 03-03 Bylands Bldg. 135, Middle Rd., pg. 1192   **IT**
Sanyo Electronics (Singapore) Pte. Ltd., No. 160, Kallang Way, pg. 1192   **IT**
Sanyo Industries (Singapore) Private Limited, No. 117/119, Neythal Rd., pg. 1192   **IT**
Sanyo Malaysia Sdn. Bhd, 1, Sophia Road #05-01, pg. 1192   **IT**
Sara Lee/DE Asia, No. 1 Shenton Way, pg. 1435   **PB**
Sato Kogyo Co., Ltd.-Singapore, Fu Lu Shou Complex, #04-14/15, 149 Rochor Rd., pg. 1197   **IT**
A. Schulman, Inc., pg. 1441   **PB**
Scientific-Atlanta, Inc., 15-02/4 Far East Shopping Center, pg. 1443   **PB**
ScotiaMocatta, 6 Battery Rd., #14-08, pg. 156   **IT**
Scott & English Limited, No. 2 Sixth Lok Yang Road, pg. 603   **IT**
Scott Paper (Singapore) Pte. Ltd., 450/452 Alexandra Road, pg. 960   **IT**
Scotts Centre Management Pte Ltd., 391B Orchard Road, pg. 1213   **IT**
Scotts Development (Saraca) Pte. Ltd., 391B Orchard Road, pg. 1213   **IT**
SCOTTS HOLDINGS LIMITED, 391B Orchard Road, pg. 1212   **IT**
Scotts Shopping Centre, 6 Scotts Road, pg. 1213   **IT**
Sea Containers Asia Pte. Ltd., 12 Gul Rd.,Jurong, pg. 1214   **IT**
Seagate Technology International, 151 Lorong Chuan #06-01, pg. 1450   **PB**
Seagate Technology (Singapore) Development Centre, Block 1, Science Park Dr., #02-63, pg. 1450   **PB**
Seagate Technology (Singapore) PCB Assembly Operations, 61 Senoko Dr., pg. 1450   **PB**
Seagate Technology (Singapore) Pte. Ltd., 16 Kallang Place, #02-35, pg. 1450   **PB**
Sealed Air (Singapore) Pte. Ltd., No.2, Tuas Ave. 6, pg. 1451   **PB**
Secureware International Privat Ltd., Blk 211, Henderson Road, pg. 18   **PB**
Security Pacific National Bank, Singapore, 50 Raffles Place, pg. 183   **PB**
Sedgwick Chartered Private Limited, 51 Bras Basah Rd., Plaza by the Park, pg. 1297   **IT**
Sensormatic Asia/Pacific, 10 Jalan Kilang Timor, pg. 1457   **PB**
Sequent Computer Systems (Singapore), 5 Shelton Way, pg. 1460   **PB**
Shandwick PTE Ltd., 12-04 Raffles City Tower, 250 N. Bridge Rd., pg. 1227   **IT**
Sharp Electronics (Singapore) Pte. Ltd., 100, Beach Road, pg. 1230   **IT**
Sharp-Roxy Sales (Singapore) Pte. Ltd., 100G Pasir Panjang Rd., pg. 1230   **IT**
Shell Eastern Petroleum, 50 Raffle Pl., pg. 1140   **IT**
Shell Eastern Petroleum (PTE) Ltd., 31 Pandan Road, pg. 1140   **IT**
Shenton Holdings Private Limited, 5 Shenton Way, #02-11, pg. 1253   **IT**
Shimadzu (Asia Pacific) Pte. Ltd., 16 Science Park Dr. #01-01, pg. 1232   **IT**
Shimizu Precon Pte. Ltd., Lots 113-11, 217 & 1079, Off Admiralty Rd. W., pg. 1234   **IT**

Shing Kwan Realty (Pte) Limited, 5 Shenton Way, #02-11, pg. 1253   **IT**
Showa Denko Singapore (Pte.) Ltd., 230 Orchard Road, #12-232 Faber House, pg. 1237   **IT**
SHOWPLA ASIA LIMITED, No. 8 Jurong Pier Road, pg. 1237   **IT**
Showpla International Pte. Ltd., 8 Jurong Pier Road, pg. 1237   **IT**
Siemens Components (Pte) Ltd., 65A Jalan Tenteram #04-14, pg. 1247   **IT**
Silk Air, 55 Airport Blvd., pg. 1374   **IT**
Sime Diamond Leasing (Singapore) Pte. Ltd., 20 Collyer Quay #09-01, pg. 1251   **IT**
Sime Rengo Packaging Singapore Limited, 20 Chin Bee Dr., pg. 1251   **IT**
Sime Singapore Limited, Sime Darby Centre #04-01, 896 Dunearn Rd., pg. 1251   **IT**
Sime Travel (Singapore) Private Limited, Goldbell Towers, 47, Scotts Rd. #04-01, pg. 1251   **IT**
Simon & Schuster (Asia) Pte. Ltd., 317 Alexandra Rd. #04-01, pg. 778   **PV**
Sims Pte. Limited, 7500A Beach Rd., pg. 1268   **IT**
Singalab Pte. Ltd., 81 Science Park Drive, pg. 242   **IT**
Singapore Airlines Ltd., Airline House, 25 Airline Road, pg. 1374   **IT**
Singapore Airport Terminal Services, P.O. Box 3, Singapore Changi Airport, pg. 1374   **IT**
Singapore Bankers Club Pte. Ltd., 6 Shenton Way, DBS Building, pg. 351   **IT**
Singapore British Engineering Pte. Limited, 78 Shenton Way, Apt. 15-01, pg. 218   **IT**
Singapore Engine Overhaul Centre (Pte.) Ltd., 51 Calshot Rd., pg. 1374   **IT**
Singapore Factory Development Ltd., 6 Shenton Way, DBS Bldg., pg. 351   **IT**
SINGAPORE LAND LIMITED, 5 Shenton Way #02-11, Podium Block, pg. 1252   **IT**
Singapore Office, Hong Leong Centre, 138 Robinson Rd. #21-01, pg. 1517   **IT**
Singapore Oil Seal Co. (Private) Ltd., pg. 507   **IT**
Singapore Oxygen Air Liquide Pte. Ltd., P.O. Box 323, pg. 122   **IT**
Singapore Polymer Corporation (Pte.) Ltd., 10 Jalan Buroh, Jurong, pg. 964   **IT**
SINGAPORE PRESS HOLDINGS LTD., 82 Genting Lane, pg. 1253   **IT**
SINGAPORE REINSURANCE CORPORATION LIMITED, 85 Amoy Street, pg. 1253   **IT**
Singapore Representative Office, 38 Tuas Avenue 9, pg. 363   **IT**
SINGAPORE TECHNOLOGIES PTE. LTD., 83 Science Park Drive, pg. 1253   **IT**
Singapore Technologies Shipbuilding & Engineering Limited, 7 Benoi Road, pg. 1253   **IT**
Singapore Tobacco Co. (Private) Co., 57 Senoko Dr., pg. 111   **IT**
SINGAPORE TOURIST PROMOTION BOARD, Tourism Court, 1 Orchard Spring Lane, pg. 1253   **IT**
Sinochem International Oil (Singapore) Pte. Ltd., Shing Kwan House, 4 Shenton Way 09-08/12, pg. 1255   **IT**
Sinochem Representative Office - Singapore, Shing Kwan House, 4 Shenton Way, Hex 16-01/03, pg. 1256   **IT**
Sinochem Trading (Singapore) Pte. Ltd., Shing Kwan House, 4 Shenton Way, Hex 16-01/03, pg. 1256   **IT**
Skadden, Arps, Slate, Meagher & Flom International, 9 Temasek Boulevard, Suite 29-01, pg. 1004   **PV**
Skandia International Insurance Co., 10 Collyer Quay, pg. 1258   **IT**
Skandinaviska Enskilda Banken, Singapore Branch, 50 Raffles Place #36-01, pg. 1259   **IT**
Skandinaviska Enskilda Banken South East Asia Limited, Shell Tower, 50 Raffles Pl. #36-01, pg. 1260   **IT**
Skega Far East Pte. Ltd., P.O. Box 190, pg. 1323   **IT**
Skega South East Asia Ltd., Circuit Rd., pg. 1324   **IT**
Smith Corona (PTE) Ltd., pg. 1007   **PV**
SmithKline Beecham Animal Health (Singapore) Private Limited, 190 Middle Rd., #09-03-05, Fortune Centre, pg. 1282   **IT**
SmithKline Beecham Pharmaceuticals (Pte.) Ltd., Quality Rd., Jurong Indus. Estate, pg. 1266   **IT**
Software AG Asia/Pacific, 151 Lorong Chuan No. 04-01C/02, pg. 1277   **IT**
Software Technology (Singapore) Pte. Ltd., 111 North Bridge Road, pg. 242   **IT**
Sony International (Singapore) Pte. Ltd., 203 Henderson Rd. #03-03/04, pg. 1284   **IT**
Sony Logistics (Singapore) Pte. Ltd., 201 Henderson Rd., #02-01 A, pg. 1284   **IT**
Sony Precision Engineering Center (Singapore) Pte. Ltd., 52 Tuas Ave. 9, pg. 1284   **IT**
Sony Singapore Pte. Ltd., 2 Alexandra Rd. #02-01, pg. 1284   **IT**
South East Asia Fertilizer Comp. (Pte.) Ltd. (SEAFCO), 78 Shenton Way 12-02, pg. 109   **IT**
Southcorp Wines Asia, Goldhill Plaza Podium Block, 1 Goldhill Plaza 02-31, pg. 1287   **IT**
Springborn Testing & Research (Singapore) Pte Ltd., #04-04 Lipo Factory Bldg., 621 Aljunied Rd., pg. 1027   **PV**
Square D Company Singapore Pte. Ltd., 896 Dunearn, #04-08, pg. 1209   **PB**
Ssangyong Cement (Singapore) Ltd., 17 Pioneer Crescent, Jurong Town, pg. 1293   **IT**
Ssangyong Developments Pte. Ltd., 16 Raffles Quay, No. 12-04, pg. 1292   **IT**
Ssangyong Singapore PTE., Ltd., 7 Temasek Boulevard, pg. 1291   **IT**
Stahl Asia Pte Ltd, 14 Tanjong Penjuru Crescent, pg. 1526   **IT**
Standard Chartered Equitor Trustee Singapore Limited, 6 Battery Rd, #04-00, pg. 1296   **IT**

Standard Chartered Finance Limited, 90 Cecil St. #01-01 Carlton Bldg., pg. 1297   **IT**
Standard Chartered Futures (Singapore) Pte Limited, 6 Battery Road, pg. 1295   **IT**
Standard Chartered Merchant Bank Asia Limited, 6 Battery Rd. #22-01, pg. 1296   **IT**
Standard Chartered Securities Investment Pte Limited, 24 Raffles Pl., #28-02/03A, pg. 1296   **IT**
Statoil Far East Pte. Ltd., 435 Orchard Rd., #10/04-05, pg. 1298   **IT**
Stenhouse (S.E. Asia) Pte. Ltd., Capitol Bldg., 4th Fl., 11 Stamford Rd., pg. 118   **PB**
Stolt Comex Seaway (S), pg. 1302   **IT**
Stolt-Nielsen Pte. Ltd., pg. 1302   **IT**
Stora Treasury Asia Pte. Ltd., 100 Beach Road #32-01, pg. 1303   **IT**
Stratus Computer (Singapore) Pte, Ltd., 26-08 UIC Bldg., 5 Shenton Way, pg. 1524   **PB**
Sullair Asia Ltd., 74, Joo Koon Circle, Jurong, pg. 1534   **PB**
Sulzer Chemtech Pte. Ltd., 11 Tuas Ave. 18, pg. 1308   **IT**
Sulzer Metco (Singapore) PTE Ltd., pg. 1308   **IT**
Sulzer Pumps (PTE) Ltd., pg. 1306   **IT**
Sumikin Bussan International Pte. Ltd., Hex 14-07/08, 1 Shenton Way, pg. 1308   **IT**
Sumitomo Chemical Asia Pte Ltd., 150 Beach Rd., #19-05/06 Gateway W., pg. 1311   **IT**
Sumitomo Electric Automotive Products (Singapore) Pte., Ltd., Shaw Towers, #24-07, 100 Beach Rd., pg. 1314   **IT**
Sumitomo Electric International (Singapore) Pte. Ltd., Shaw Towers, #24-07, 100 Beach Rd., pg. 1314   **IT**
Sumitomo Financial Futures (Singapore) pte. Ltd., 6 Shenton Way, #27-08, pg. 1310   **IT**
Sumitomo Life Investment Singapore Limited, 16 Collyer Quay #27-02, pg. 1315   **IT**
Sumitomo Metal Industries, Ltd. (Singapore Office), DBS Bldg., Tower 2, 6 Shenton Way #25-01, pg. 1316   **IT**
Sumitomo Metal Mining Electronics Parts Pte., Ltd., No. 6 Tues Avenue 20, pg. 1316   **IT**
Sumitomo Metal Mining Singapore Pte., Ltd., Nos. 35 & 41, Kallang Pl., pg. 1316   **IT**
The Sumitomo Trust & Banking Co., Ltd., Five Shenton Way, pg. 1318   **IT**
Sumitomo Trust Merchant Bank (Singapore) Ltd., Five Shenton Way, pg. 1318   **IT**
Sun Microsystems of California Ltd., Standard Chartered Bank Bldg., 24-03, 6 Battery Rd., pg. 1532   **PB**
Sundstrand Pacific Aerospace (Pte) Ltd., 18 Bedok South Rd., pg. 1534   **PB**
SUPERIOR METAL PRINTING LIMITED, 135 Cecil Street #15-00, pg. 1322   **IT**
Svenska Handelsbanken Singapore, 65 Chulia Street, Units 21-00, pg. 1328   **IT**
Swensen's of Singapore Pte. Ltd., 141 Middle Rd., pg. 884   **PB**
Swiss Bank Corporation, 6 Battery Road #34-01, pg. 1330   **IT**
SwissRe Advisers (Singapore) Pte. Ltd., 1 Raffles Place, pg. 1333   **IT**
Symbol Technologies Asia, Inc., 04-05, Bugis Junction Office Tower, pg. 1546   **PB**
Symix Systems Inc., Marina House, 70 Shenton Way, #15-01, pg. 1547   **PB**
Syntron Asia Pte. Ltd., 68 Loyang Way, pg. 1563   **PB**
TAC Control Pte. Ltd., 04-10 Sindo Bldg., 66 Tannery La., pg. 670   **IT**
TCE Television Singapore Pte. Ltd., 164 Callagpny, pg. 1384   **IT**
TDK Singapore (Pte.) Ltd., PSA Building, 460 Alexandra Rd., 04-00, pg. 1383   **IT**
TNT Logistics Asia Pte Ltd., 12 Prince Edward Road, #06-03, Podium B, Bestway Building, pg. 1343   **IT**
LEE KIM TAH HOLDINGS LTD., 20 Jalan Afifi #07-01, pg. 1346   **IT**
Takashimaya (Singapore) Ltd., 391A Orchard Rd., #10-01, pg. 1350   **IT**
Takeda Vitamin & Food Asia Pte. Ltd., Shaw Towers, 100 Beach Rd., #30-01/03, pg. 1351   **IT**
Takenaka Singapore Pte. Ltd., Euro-Asia Centre, 15 Hoe Chiang Road #12-04, pg. 1352   **IT**
Tampella Power Asia Pacific Pte. Ltd., Faber House, 230 Orchard Road, pg. 1354   **IT**
Tanabe Seiyaku Singapore Pte. Ltd., 10 Hoe Chiang Road, pg. 1354   **IT**
Tandem Computers Asia/Pacific Div., 300 Beach Rd., pg. 417   **PB**
Tandem Computers International Inc., Gateway East Tower, 152, Beach Rd., #26-00, pg. 418   **PB**
Tankstore Pte Ltd., Standard Chartered Bank Bldg., 6 Battery Rd. #15-08, 0104, pg. 693   **PB**
Tastemaker Pte. Ltd., pg. 811   **PB**
Taylor Instrument Pte. Ltd., 5000 Ang Mo Kio Ave. 5 N01-11, pg. 6   **PB**
Tech Group Singapore, Inc., 51 Joo Koon Circle, pg. 1071   **PV**
TECH Semiconductor Singapore Pte., Ltd., No. 1 Woodlands Indus. Park D, Street 1, pg. 262   **IT**
Technomer (Private) Ltd., pg. 129   **IT**
Tektronix Singapore Pte. Ltd., United Square, 101 Thomson Road #02-02, pg. 1568   **PB**
Teledyne Singapore, 11 Dhoby Ghaut, #09-06, pg. 44   **PB**
Telma Retarder, 63 Loyang Way, pg. 786   **IT**
Telxon Corporation, Singapore Branch, Block 1020, Tai Seng Avenue, pg. 1574   **PB**
TEMASEK HOLDINGS PTE. LTD., Temasek Tower #38-03, pg. 1374   **IT**
Templeton Asset Management (Singapore) PTE Ltd., 20 Raffles Pl. #10-03, pg. 680   **PB**
Terumo-Singapore, 11-06 International Plaza, Anson Rd., pg. 1376   **IT**

PB - *U.S. Public Companies Volume*
PV - *U.S. Private Companies Volume*
IT - *International Public & Private Companies Volume*

Texas Instruments Singapore (Pte.) Ltd., 990 Bendemeer Road, pg. 1586 — PB
The Norinchukin Bank, UOB Plaza 1, 80 Raffles Place, pg. 958 — IT
3M Singapore Pte. Ltd., 9 Tagore Lane, pg. 1607 — IT
Tien Wah Press (Pte.) Ltd., 4 Pandan Crescent, pg. 363 — IT
Tiffany & Co. Pte. Ltd., Millenia Tower, 1 Temasek Ave., No. 27-01, pg. 1609 — IT
Tiger Medicals Ltd., #09-00 Haw Par Tiger Balm Building, pg. 603 — IT
TIMES PUBLISHING LIMITED, Times Centre, 1 New Industrial Road, pg. 1390
Tokai Financial Futures (Singapore) Pte. Ltd., 80 Raffles Place, #1601, pg. 1391 — IT
Tokio Management Services (Asia) Pte. Ltd., DBS Bldg., 6 Sheton Way # 23-08, Tower Two, pg. 1392 — IT
The Tokio Marine & Fire Insurance Company (Singapore) Pte. Limited, DBS Bldg., 6 Shenton Way # 23-08, Tower Two, pg. 1392 — IT
Tokyo-Mitsubishi International (Singapore) Ltd., 9 Raffles Pl., pg. 158 — IT
Top Mix Concrete, 17 Pioneer Crescent, Jurong Town, pg. 1293 — IT
Toray Industries (Singapore) Pte. Ltd., Comcentre, 31st Story, pg. 1400 — IT
Toronto Dominion (Southeast Asia) Limited, 65 Chulia St., 25-08 OCBC Centre, pg. 1402 — IT
Toshiba Data Dynamics Pte. Ltd., 10 Kallang Sector, Data Dynamics Bldg., pg. 1406 — IT
Toshiba Electronics Asia (Singapore) Pte. Ltd., 460 Alexandra Rd., #21-00 PSA Bldg., pg. 1406 — IT
Toshiba Singapore Pte., 460 Alexandra Rd., #26-02, pg. 1407 — IT
Toto Singapore Branch, UIC Building, 5 Shenton Way #21-08, pg. 1410 — IT
Tourism Malaysia - Singapore Office, 10, Collyer Quay, #01-06; #18-02 Ocean Bldg., pg. 833 — IT
Toyota Motor Management Services Singapore Pte. Ltd., Hong Leong Bldg., 16 Raffles Quay #40-01, pg. 1414 — IT
Toys "R" Us-Metro (Singapore) Pte. Ltd., pg. 1626 — PB
Tractors Machinery International Pte. Ltd., 26 Benoi sec. Off Pioneer Rd., pg. 1251 — IT
Tradewinds Far Int'l., SATS Bldg. #03-00, 55 Airport Blvd., pg. 1374 — IT
TRANSMARCO LIMITED, 11 Collyer Quay, pg. 1417
Traub-Heckert Tech. Centre (s) Pte. Ltd., 110 Paya Lebar Rd. #01-01, pg. 1419 — IT
Trio-Kenwood Singapore (Pte.) Ltd., No. 1, Ang Mo Kio St. 63, pg. 731 — IT
Turbomeca Asia Pacific Pte Ltd., 63 Loyang Way, pg. 787 — IT
Twin Disc (Far East) Ltd., 40 Lok Yang Way, pg. 1646 — PB
Tyco Laboratories Asia Pacific (S) Pte Ltd., 25 McCallum St., pg. 1651 — PB
Tyton Hellermann Asia Pacific Ltd., 545 Industrial Park A, Yishun Avenue 7, pg. 209 — IT
UBS (East Asia) Ltd., 80 Raffles Place, pg. 1440 — IT
UBS Securities (Singapore) Pte. Ltd., 80 Raffles Place, pg. 1441 — IT
UFE Pte Ltd, No. 5 Joo Koon Way, pg. 1112 — PV
UPM-Kymmene Far East Pte. Ltd., 350 Orchard Road, pg. 1430 — IT
Ugimagnetics Pte. Ltd., Block 1020, Hougang Avenue 1, pg. 1032 — IT
Unbrako Products (Singapore) PTE Ltd., 627 Aljunied Road, Pacific Building, pg. 1420 — PB
Underwater World Singapore Pte. Ltd., 80 Siloso Road, pg. 604 — IT
Union Bank of Switzerland, Singapore Branch, 80 Raffles Place, 36-00 UOB Plaza One, pg. 1440 — IT
Union Carbide Asia Pacific Inc., 227/F, Treasury Bldg., 8 Shenton Way, pg. 1667 — PB
Uniroyal Chemical Company, Inc. (Singapore), 101 Thompson Road, pg. 460 — PB
United Overseas Bank Ltd., UOB Building, 1 Bonham Street, pg. 1443 — IT
UNITED OVERSEAS LAND LIMITED, 101 Thomson Road, pg. 1443 — IT
Universal (Hong Kong Teakwood), 19 Kranji Way, Kranji Industrial Estate, pg. 432 — PV
Up-Right (Far East) Ltd., Unit 243, Ubi Ave. 4, pg. 1128 — PV
Utell International-Singapore, No 1 Temasek Avenue, #17-01 Millenia Tower, pg. 1099 — PV
VDO South East Asia Pte. Ltd., pg. 839 — IT
VL Bus Asia (Pte) Ltd., 20-00 Shing Kwan House, 4 Shenton Way, pg. 1477 — IT
VRG ASIA PACIFIC Ltd., pg. 757 — IT
VRG Paper (Singapore) Pte Ltd, pg. 757 — IT
Valley Park Condominium Project, Alexandra P.O. Box 0023, pg. 943 — PV
Valley Point Commercial Development, Alexandra, pg. 943 — IT
Valley Point Commericial Development, Alexandra P.O. Box 0256, pg. 943 — IT
Valmet (SEA) Pte Ltd. Paper Machinery Division, 152 Beach Road, pg. 1448 — IT
Van Leeuwen Pipe and Tube (Far East) Pte. Ltd., 1 Jalan Terusan, pg. 1450 — IT
VARTA Batteries Pte. Ltd., 750-C Chai Chee Road, pg. 1452 — IT
Vermiculite Industries Ltd., 17 Pioneer Crescent, Jurong Town, pg. 1293 — IT
Vickers Systems Pte. Ltd., 01-420 Indus Rd., Block 79A, pg. 25 — PB
Vicon, Singapore, Swee Hong Ind. Bldg., 320 Circuit Road, pg. 1719 — PB
Villa Begonia, Begonia & Saraca Roads, pg. 1213 — IT

Volvo Car Asia (Pte) Ltd., 20-00 Shing Kwan House, 4 Shenton Way, pg. 1477 — IT
Volvo East Asia (Pte.) Ltd., 20-00 Shing Kwan House, 4 Shelton Way, pg. 1477 — IT
Votra (Singapore) Pte Ltd, pg. 757 — IT
WBB Pacific Clays Ltd., 1 Phillip Street, pg. 1488 — IT
Wacoal Singapore Pte. Ltd., Henderson Industrial Park #01-08, pg. 1484 — IT
Wadkin Robinson Asia Pte. Ltd., 88 Tagore Ln., pg. 232 — IT
Waeschle Pte Ltd., 122 Middle Rd., No. 08-08, pg. 491 — IT
Wako Merchant Bank (Singapore) Limited, 16 Collyer Quay, Suite 27-01, Hitachi Tower, pg. 1485 — IT
Wander (Singapore) Pty. Ltd., Third Chin Bee Rd., pg. 986 — IT
Wang Computers (Pte.) Limited, 1020 Tai Seng Avenue, #06-3508, pg. 1737 — PB
Warburg Asset Management Singapore Pte. Ltd., Six Battery Rd. #14-06, pg. 1331 — IT
Wardley Broking Services Private Limited, 21 Collyer Quay, #17-01 HongkongBank Building, pg. 584 — IT
Watlow Singapore Pte. Ltd., Ayer Rajah Industrial Estate, 55 Ayer Rajah Crescent, pg. 1154 — PV
Wayfoong Mortgage and Finance (Singapore) Limited, 6 Claymore Hill, #03-01 Claymore Plaza, pg. 584 — IT
Wellcome Singapore Private Ltd., 33 Quality Rd., pg. 553 — IT
Wells Electronics Asia Pte Ltd., 1, Marine Parade Central, #C4-09 Parkay Builder's Center, pg. 1242 — IT
Wemex Engineering Asia (Pte) Ltd., 453 Tagore Ave., pg. 712 — IT
The West Company Singapore Pty. Ltd., 15 Joo Koon Circle, pg. 1756 — IT
West Merchant Bank Limited, 21 Collyer Quay #08-00, pg. 1494 — IT
Western Digital Singapore Ltd., 750 B Chai Chee Road, pg. 1758 — PB
Western Geophysical (Singapore), 37 Jalan Pemimpin, pg. 1005 — IT
Westinghouse Industry Services Asia Pte. Ltd., 10 Gul Avenue, Jurong Industrial Estate, pg. 275 — IT
WestLB Singapore Branch, 21 Collyer Quay #10-00, Hong Kong Bank Bldg., pg. 1493 — IT
Westpac Banking Corp. - Singapore, 4301 OCBC Center, 65 Chulia St., pg. 1497 — IT
Wickland International Asia, Ltd., #15-01 MAS Building, 10 Shenton Way, pg. 1175 — PV
Willis Corroon Asia Pacific Limited, 78 Shenton Way, #23-03, pg. 1509 — IT
Robert Wilson (Singapore) Limited, #07-02 Setron Building, 10 Dundee Road, pg. 604 — IT
Window Furnishings Singapore Pte. Ltd., 9, Third Lok Yang Road, Turong, pg. 640 — IT
Windsor Airmotive Asia Pte. Ltd., No. 21 Loyang Lane, pg. 190 — IT
Woodhead Asia Pte. Ltd., JTC Flatted Factory, 8 Chia Ping Rd #5-09/10, pg. 1776 — IT
Woodward Governor Asia-Pacific Pte. Ltd., No. 03-02A Delta House, 2 Alexandra Road, pg. 1776 — IT
Wunderman Cato Johnson Singapore, 300 Beach Rd., pg. 326 — PV
The Wuphoon Insurance Company Limited, 27th Fl., Union Centre, 95 Queensway, pg. 1393 — IT
Yamaichi Asia Venture Capital Pte Ltd., 138 Robinson Road #17-08/09, Hong Leong Centre, pg. 1516 — IT
Yamaichi Asset Management (Singapore) Pte Ltd., 138 Robinson Road #16-03, pg. 1517 — IT
Yamaichi Capital Management (Singapore) Ltd., Hong Leong Centre, 138 Robinson Rd. #16-01, pg. 1516 — IT
Yamaichi Futures Pte. Ltd., Hong Leong Centre, 138 Robinson Rd. #21-01, pg. 1517 — IT
Yamaichi Merchant Bank, Hong Leong Centre, 138 Robinson Rd. #21-01, pg. 1518 — IT
Yamaichi Securities (Singapore) Pte. Ltd., Hong Leong Centre, 138 Robinson Rd. #21-01, pg. 1518 — IT
Yasuda Life International (Singapore) Ltd., 79 Anson Road, #1-04, pg. 1520 — IT
Yat Yuen Hong Company Limited, 300 Beach Road #41-00 The Concourse, pg. 635 — IT
Yeo Hiap Seng Limited, 950 Dunearn Road, pg. 1008 — IT
The Yokohama Rubber Co., Ltd., 50 Raffles Place, pg. 1521 — IT
Zeneca Resins Pte. Ltd., 135 Pioneer Road, pg. 1527 — IT
Zimmer Pte Ltd., Sanford Bldg., 15 Hoe Chiang Rd., #04-02 pg. 257 — PB
Zurich Insurance Company Regional Reinsurance, 1 Temasek Avenue, pg. 1532 — IT
Zurich Insurance (Singapore) Pte. Ltd., Robinson Towers, 30 Robinson Rd., No. 11-01, pg. 1532 — IT

SLOVAKIA

Bratislava

AGA GAS Spol.s r.o., Mytna 15, pg. 13 — IT
Allianz poistovna a.s., Kosicka 37, pg. 60 — IT
Amway Slovensko, s.r.o., P.O. Box 36, Pribinova 25, pg 70 — PV
BASF Slovensko spol. s r.o., Frana Krala 35, pg. 107 — IT
Benckiser Slovakia spol.s.r.o., pg. 186 — IT
Bull Slovakia S.R.O., Frana Krala 5, pg. 317 — IT
CIBA-GEIGY Services AG, Zahradnicka 21, pg. 979 — IT
CIBA-GEIGY Services AG, Trencianska 47, pg. 979 — IT
Creo Young & Rubicam, Kosicka 52, pg. 1199 — PV
Danzas AG, Opavska No. 22, pg. 382 — IT
EuroTel Bratislava Ltd., Jarosova 1, pg. 204 — IT
Groupe SEB Slovensko, Stolarska 35, pg. 568 — IT
Henkel-Palma spol, s.r.o., pg. 613 — IT
Hewlett-Packard Ceskoslovensko spol.s.r.o., Polianky 5, pg. 818 — PB

Honeywell GmbH, Trnavska 3, pg. 834 — PB
Hydro Czechoslovakia s.r.o., Medena 35, pg. 963 — IT
ING Bank Bratislava, Kolarska6, pg. 649 — IT
ISS Marischka spol.s.r.o., Trnavska Cesta 3, pg. 657 — IT
Impax Trading A.S., ul. Cervenej Armady 6, pg. 669 — IT
Istropolitana/DMB&B Bratislava, Liscie Nivy 11, pg. 304 — PV
Isys spol SRO, pg. 720 — IT
Jauch & Huebener, Mozartova 21, pg. 118 — PB
KONE Lifts s.r.o., Puchovska 16, pg. 747 — IT
Korn/Ferry International, Dubravska Cesta 2, pg. 634 — PV
Landis & Staefa (Slovensko) s.r.o., Mileticova 5, pg. 801 — IT
Medata Czechoslovakia spol.s.r.o., Pobocka: Lubinska 4, pg. 712 — IT
Julius Meinl Baliarne a.s., pg. 856 — IT
Microsoft S.R.O., pg. 1108 — PB
Novo Nordisk A/S, Stefanikova 22, pg. 987 — IT
Perstorp Plastic Systems, Spol. S.R.O., Horarska Str. 12, pg. 1038 — IT
Probugas a.s., Mlynske Nivy 42, pg. 1155 — IT
Roche Slovakia spol.s.r.o., pg. 1122 — IT
Sandvik Slovakia s.r.o., pg. 1187 — IT
Schrack Ericsson spol. s.r.o. Slovakia, Mileticova 23, pg. 1369 — IT
SkoFIN s.r.o., pg. 1475 — IT
Slovak International Tabak, a.s. (S.I.T.), Mlynske Nivy c.54, pg. 1101 — IT
Tatra banka, a.s., Vajanskeho nabrezie c. 5, pg. 1085 — IT
Volkswagen Bratislava spol. s.r.o., Devinska Nova Fes, pg. 1475 — IT
Zeneca Slovakia s.r.o., Resetkova 15, pg. 1527 — IT
Zurich Poistovna sluzby s.r.o., Palarikova 13, pg. 1532 — IT

Galanta

Tos Galanta a.s., Esterhazyovcov 1407, pg. 1419 — IT

Kosice

ING Bank Kosice, Komenskeho 3, pg. 649 — IT

Nemecke

Fuchs-Petrochema SPOL, S.R.O., n.p. Dubova, pg. 518 — IT

Piestany

Avent de Honduras, S.A. de C.V., Vrbovska Cesta 2617/102, pg. 959 — PB

Pivovarska

Elefanten-Slowakei, spol.sr.o., pg. 507 — IT

Povazska

Sauer-Sundstrand CS, P.O. Box 54, pg. 1198 — IT

Prievidza

Nestle Food S.r.o., pg. 921 — IT

Svit

Sun Chemical s.r.o., Sturova Ulica C. 101, pg. 371 — IT

Trencin

CIBA TF/CH Vertretung, c/o Swisscolor, Kozusnicka 2, pg. 981 — IT

Trnava

Sachs Trnava SRO, pg. 835 — IT

SLOVENIA

Crnomelj

Danfoss Compressors d.o.o., Heroja Starihe 24, pg. 377 — IT

Kikinda

Industrija Delova Automobila, Kikinda, pg. 724 — PB

Kranj

Sandvik International, Representative Office, pg. 1186 — IT

Litija

Hartmann d.o.o., Dusana Kvedra 7, pg. 371 — IT

Ljubljana

Amway Slovenia, Leskoskova 4, First Floor, pg. 70 — PV
BASF Slowenija d.o.o., Kersnikova 5, pg. 107 — IT
Banka Creditanstalt d.d., Kotnikova 5, pg. 347 — IT
Bull Computer & Services D.O.O., Trebinjska 15, pg. 317 — IT
CIBA-GEIGY Agro d.o.o., Einspielerjeva 6, pg. 976 — IT
CIBA-GEIGY Services AG, Trzaska C 132, pg. 979 — IT
Danfoss Trata d.d.., Jozeta Jame 16, pg. 377 — IT
Hartmann d.o.o., Dunajska 123, pg. 371 — IT

PB - *U.S. Public Companies Volume*
PV - *U.S. Private Companies Volume*
IT - *International Public & Private Companies Volume*

1750

Geographic Index-Non U.S.

Hermes, Celovska 73, pg. 818 — PB
MARAND d.o.o., Cesta v. Mestni log, 55, pg. 246 — PB
MarinTeS D.o.o. Ltd., Bratovzeva pl. 18, pg. 1032 — PB
Microsoft d.o.o. Ljubljana, pg. 1108 — PB
Moj Mikro, Celovska 43, P.P. 354, pg. 570 — PV
MONITOR Magazine, Calovska 43, p.p. 354, 570 — PV
Novo Nordisk A/S, Dunajska 7, pg. 988 — IT
Oracle d.o.o., World Trade Center, pg. 1228 — PB
Robert Bosch d.o.o., Celovska 228, pg. 205 — IT
SKF Trgovina d.o.o., Roznadolina c. XV/9, pg. 1159 — IT
Tobacna Ljubljana d.o.o., Tobabcna Ulica 5, pg. 1101 — PV
Vision Factory Productions, pg. 305 — PV
Votan Leo Burnett, Resljeva 20, pg. 186 — PV
Wrigley Ljubljana, Ltd., Wrigley d.o.o., pg. 1781 — PB
Zeneca International Ltd., Einspielerjeva 6, pg. 1526 — IT

Maribor

Henkel Zlatorog d.o.o., pg. 613 — IT
ISS Servisystem d.o.o., Kopitarjeva 5, pg. 657 — IT
Schiess-Metalna Gmbh, Zagrebska 20, pg. 860 — IT

Murska Sobota

IPC Corporation Racunalniki in Pos Sistemi D.O.O., Plese 5, pg. 651 — IT

Sisenska

Daewoo Corp. - Slovenia, pg. 358 — IT

Skocjan

Bramac D.O.O., Dobruska vas 45, pg. 1092 — IT

SOLOMON ISLANDS

Honiara

Australia & New Zealand Banking Group Limited Solomon Islands, Mendana Avenue, pg. 99 — IT
Hastings Deering (Solomon Islands) Limited, Kukum Estate, Industrial Ave., pg. 1250 — IT
National Bank of Solomon Islands, pg. 1248 — PB
Westpac Banking Corp. - Solomon Islands, 721 Mendana Ave., pg. 1497 — IT
Woodward-Clyde International, pg. 1658 — PB

Yandina

Lever Solomons Ltd., pg. 1438 — IT
Shell (Pacific Islands), pg. 1137 — IT

SOMALIA

Mogadishu

Intalcable-Somalia, pg. 655 — IT

SOUTH AFRICA

Alrode

Ingersoll-Rand Co., South Africa (Proprietary) Ltd., P.O. Box 3720, pg. 878 — PB
Sasol Fuel Oil, crn Garfield & Clarke Street, pg. 1197 — IT

Atlantis

Van Leer South Africa (Pty.) Ltd., pg. 1147 — IT

Bedfordview

Dorbyl Automotive Products (Pty) Ltd., P.O. Box 1451, pg. 416 — IT
Dorbyl Light & General Engineering (PTY) Limited, 4 Skeen Blvd., pg. 416 — IT
DORBYL LIMITED, P.O. Box 1451, pg. 416 — IT
FOODCORP LIMITED, Block C, Pellmeadow Park, 60 Civin Drive, pg. 496 — IT
Gillette South Africa Limited, Riverwoods Office Park, Johnson St., St. Andrews, pg. 745 — PB
Sinochem R.S.A. (Pty.) Ltd., 5 Skeen Blvd., pg. 1256 — IT
Stewarts & Lloyds Trading (Pty) Limited, pg. 416 — IT

Bellville

Crown Cork Company S.A. (Pty.) Ltd., pg. 464 — PB

Benmore

Conshu Holdings Ltd., pg. 1287 — IT

Benoni

Ahlstrom South Africa (Pty) Ltd., 3rd Fl., General Bldg., 90 Elston Ave., pg. 35 — IT
Ilco Unican (SA) (PTY) Ltd., P.O. Box 13017, North Meade 1511, pg. 1432 — IT
Sandvik (Pty.) Ltd., P.O. Box 206, pg. 1187 — IT

Bergville

Technor Pty. Limited, pg. 1123 — PB

Toyota Motor Corporation, Johannesburg Representative Office, c/o Toyota South Africa Motors (Pty) Ltd, pg. 1413 — IT

Boksburg

Air Express International (S.A.) (Pty), Ltd., Patrick Rd., Stand 10, Jet Park, pg. 30 — PB
Barlows Equipment Manufacturing Co. SA, pg. 167 — IT
Blackwood Hodge (South Africa) (Pty.) Ltd., Griffiths Street, P.O. Box 2, Jet Park, pg. 231 — IT
Colgate-Palmolive Ltd., P.O. Box 213, 528 Commissioner St., pg. 398 — PB
Dorbyl Transport Products (Pty) Ltd., P.O. Box 229, pg. 416 — IT
SKF South Africa (Pty.) Ltd., 47 Jones Road, Witkoppie, pg. 1159 — IT

Booysens

P&S Filtration S.A. (Pty) Ltd., pg. 1203 — IT

Braamfontein

Amalgamated Retail Ltd., pg. 1286 — IT
Elscint (Pty) Ltd., Metal Box Centre, 25 Owl Strasse, pg. 450 — IT
Nokia Telecommunications Parktown Office Suites, 23 Wellington Road, Parktown 2193, pg. 954 — IT
Rennies Group Limited, 19 Amershof St., pg. 76 — IT
SAPPI LIMITED, 48 Ameshoff St., pg. 1193 — IT

Brakpan

Baldwins Steel (Pty) Limited, 9 Molecule Rd., pg. 416 — IT

Bramley

MacDermid S.A. (PTY) Ltd., 767 Sixth St., pg. 1030 — PB

Bromhof

Ensign-Bickford, pg. 1196 — IT

Bryanston

African Amines (Pty) Ltd., pg. 1196 — IT
Astra Pharmaceuticals (Pty.) Ltd., Private Bag X49, pg. 94 — IT
Bulk Mining Explosives, pg. 1115 — PB
Dell Computer S.A., Northdown Office Park, 17 Georgian Crescent, pg. 496 — PB

Cape Town

AA The Motorists Publications (Pty.) Limited, Reader's Digest House, 130 Strand St., pg. 1368 — PB
Adidas South Africa Ltd., pg. 25 — IT
African Life Assurance Company Limited, Great Westerford, Main Rd., pg. 77 — IT
Amway South Africa, 16 Esso Road, Moantague Gardens, pg. 70 — PV
Bull Calvert Pace, 15 Pepper Street, pg. 678 — PV
Butterworths South Africa, 3 Gardens Business Village, pg. 1095 — IT
Cape Town Iron and Steel Works (Pty) Ltd., pg. 689 — IT
Coates Brothers (South Africa) Ltd., 18th Ave., Maitland, pg. 1409 — IT
Coates Chemie Compounds (Pty.) Ltd., 18th Ave., Maitland, pg. 1410 — IT
Donaldson Filtration Systems (Pty.) Ltd., P.O. Box 149 Eppindust, pg. 517 — PB
Freudenberg Nonwovens (Pty.) Ltd., pg. 505 — IT
Hi Performance Systems (Pty.) Ltd., pg. 822 — PB
Hunt Lascaris/TBWA, Block C, 2nd Floor, Portswood Square, pg. 1062 — PV
Knowledge Systems International, Howard Studios, Sheldon Dr. & Howard Dr., pg. 1228 — PB
Modern Hairdressing Supplies (Pty) Ltd., 65 Bofors Circle, Epping 3, pg. 1490 — IT
Mount Nelson Hotel Ltd., 76 Orange St., pg. 1214 — IT
Ondelle S.A. (Pty.) Ltd., pg. 1490 — IT
Oxford University Press (South Africa), pg. 1019 — IT
R&R Tobacco Limited, pg. 1129 — IT
The Reader's Digest Association South Africa Pty. Limited, Reader's Digest House, 130 Strand St., pg. 1368 — PB
Reader's Digest Investments (Pty) Limited, Reader's Digest House, 130 Strand St., pg. 1368 — PB
Shell South Africa (Pty) Ltd., Shell House, 9 Riebeek St., pg. 1136 — IT
The Southern Life Association Limited, Great Westerford, Main Rd., pg. 77 — IT
U.D. Imports (Proprietary) Limited, 11th Fl., Metcliffe Centre, 7 Cosn Steytler Avenue, pg. 412 — IT
Utell International-South Africa, 3rd Floor, 62 Strand Street, pg. 1099 — IT
Warner-Lambert S.A. (Proprietary) Limited, P.B.x6, pg. 1740 — PB
Young & Rubicam Tholet, Two Long Street, pg. 1198 — PV

Cascades

Scapa Scandia S.A. (Proprietary) Ltd., pg. 1203 — IT

Claremont

South African Mining Company (SAPCO), P.O. Box 23601, pg. 388 — IT

Cleveland

Rotek Industries (Pty) Ltd., pg. 459 — IT

Craighall

OUP Transvaal, pg. 1019 — IT

Cramerview

Appletiser South Africa (Pty) Ltd., pg. 1286 — IT

Crown Mines

Barprop Ltd., 5 Handel Road, pg. 1081 — IT
Edgars Stores Ltd., pg. 1287 — IT
RMP PROPERTIES LTD., 5 Handel Road, pg. 1081 — IT

Dunswart

SM-Cyclo South Africa, Cnr. Van Dyk Rd. & Falkirk St., pg. 1315 — IT
Skega (PTY) Ltd., P.O. Box 1508, pg. 1324 — IT

Durban

Butterworths South Africa, P.O. Box 4, pg. 1095 — IT
Det Norske Veritas, 2305 Embassy Building, 199 Smith Street, pg. 397 — IT
Dorbyl Marine (Pty) Ltd., P.O. Box 932, pg. 416 — IT
Elida-Gibbs (Pty.) Ltd., pg. 1437 — PB
Hi Performance Systems (Pty.) Ltd., pg. 822 — PB
Jenesis Advertising, 17/19 Aisla Avenue, Glenwood, pg. 1422 — PB
Lever Brothers (Pty.) Ltd., pg. 1437 — IT
The Lion Match Company Limited, pg. 1287 — IT
Lipton (SA) (Pty.) Ltd., pg. 1438 — IT
Morganite Refractory Industries (MRI), 23 Brooklyn Rd., pg. 895 — IT
Natal Thread Co. (Pty) Ltd., P.O. Box 4773, pg. 299 — IT
Nedlloyd Lines SA (Proprietary) Limited, pg. 1145 — IT
PD Terminals (Pty) Limited, P.O. Box 21030, pg. 1065 — IT
The Pure Cane Molasses Co. (Durban) (Pty.) Ltd., pg. 1357 — IT
The Tongat-Hulett Group Limited, 1001, Umblanga Rocks Dr., pg. 76 — IT
Unilever South Africa (Pty.) Ltd., pg. 1439 — IT
Valvecraft (PTY) Ltd., 84/88 Berea Road, pg. 551 — IT
Van den Bergh & Jurgens (Pty.) Ltd., pg. 1439 — IT

East London

Da Gama Textile Company, pg. 1287 — IT
Hyde Pharmaceuticals (Pty.) Ltd., 80 Bonza Bay Rd., pg. 1126 — IT

Edenvale

R.A.R.E. (Pty) Ltd., pg. 1306 — IT

Elandsfontein

Flender Power Transmission (Pty.) Ltd., pg. 400 — IT
Sulzer South Africa Ltd., pg. 1306 — IT

Epindust

CIBA-GEIGY (Pty) Limited, pg. 978 — IT
Van Leer South Africa (Pty.) Ltd., pg. 1147 — IT

Evendale

Burgmann Seals South Africa (Pty) Ltd., P.O. Box 1210, pg. 234 — IT

Ezakheni

Van Leer South Africa (Pty.) Ltd., pg. 1147 — IT

Fairland

S.C. Johnson & Son of South Africa (Pty.) Ltd., 192 Smith St., pg. 593 — PV

Ferndale

IT Media, Thomson House, 2194, pg. 570 — PV
Munters (Pty) Ltd., pg. 669 — IT

Gauteng

Weir EnviroTech (Pty.) Ltd., pg. 1489 — IT

Germiston

Bandag Inc. of S.A. (Pty.) Ltd., Corner North Reef Rd. & Makro Pl., pg. 178 — PB
Dorbyl Structural Engineering (Pty) Ltd., P.O. Box 68, pg. 416 — IT
KSB Pumps (S.A.) (Pty.) Ltd., pg. 721 — IT
OK Bazaars (1929) Ltd., pg. 1287 — IT

PB - U.S. Public Companies Volume
PV - U.S. Private Companies Volume
IT - International Public & Private Companies Volume

Geographic Index-Non U.S.

SOUTH AFRICA DIRECTORY OF CORPORATE AFFILIATIONS

Glenrista

Finwood Papers (Pty.) Ltd., pg. 757 IT

Halfway House

Chemrite Southern Africa (Pty) Ltd., pg. 1358 PB
MUSC (Pty.) Ltd., 16 Alphen Square North, pg. 1032 PB
Outokumpu Mintec South Africa (Pty) Ltd., pg. 1017 IT
Rhone-Poulenc Chemicals SA (PTY) Ltd., P.O. Box 819, 238 Old Pretoria Road, pg. 1112 IT

Howick

Howard Machinery (Pty.) Ltd., 11 Campbell Road, pg. 1387 IT

Industria

Kenwood (S.A.) (Pty.) Ltd., 28 Blumberg Street, pg. 730 IT

Isando

Amquip (Proprietary) Limited, Cnr. Diesel & Isando Rd., pg. 76 IT
Barlow Handling (Pty) Ltd., P.O. Box 251, pg. 167 IT
Bayer South Africa (Pty.) Ltd., pg. 175 IT
J.I. Case South Africa (Pty.) Ltd., P.O. Box 347, pg. 1580 PB
Caterpillar (Africa) (Proprietary) Limited, pg. 317 PB
CIBA-GEIGY (Pty.) Ltd., 72/74 Steel Road, Spartan, pg. 978 IT
Crown Cork Company S.A. (Pty.) Ltd., P.O. Box #4, pg. 464 PB
Fuchs Lubricants (S.A) Pty., Ltd., pg. 518 IT
Givaudan-Roure (Pty.) Ltd., 4 Brewery St., pg. 1120 IT
Pharmacia & Upjohn (Proprietary) Limited, 44 Monteer Road, pg. 1049 IT
RHP South Africa Pty Ltd., pg. 904 IT
RIH Group (Pty) Limited, P.O. Box 263, pg. 167 IT
The Simba Group, Andre Greyvensteyn Ave., pg. 496 IT
SmithKline & French (Proprietary) Ltd., P.O. Box 38, pg. 1265 IT
SmithKline Beecham Consumer Brands (Pty) Ltd., 21 Wrench Rd., pg. 1265 IT

Isipingo

Cray Valley Products, 2 Baltex Rd., pg. 1410 IT

Isipingo Beach

Lubrizol South Africa (Pty.) Limited, P.O. Box 26025, pg. 1017 PB
Toyota Motor Corporation, Durban Representative Office, c/o Toyota South Africa Motors (Pty) Ltd, pg. 1413 IT

Jacobs

Quaker Chemical South Africa (Pty.) Ltd., 188 Lansdowne Rd., pg. 1347 PB

Jet Park

Ritasa Freight Services Pty. Ltd., Stand 10, Patrick Rd., pg. 14 IT
Tamrock Africa Pty. Ltd., Unit 5, Old Mutual, Jet Park Industrial, pg. 1353 IT
Triplejay (Pty) Ltd., Babcock Triplejay House, 21 Pretoria Rd., pg. 474 IT

Johannesburg

Accident & Miscellaneous Acceptances (Pty.) Ltd., 17, Empire Road, Parktown, pg. 90 IT
Acer Africa Pty. Ltd., pg. 22 IT
African Oxygen Ltd., pg. 121 IT
Allianz of South Africa (Pty.) Ltd., Allianz House, 13 Frazer Street, pg. 60 IT
Amerford Intl. (PTY) Ltd., Corner Innes & Bismuth St., Jet Park Ext, pg. 1388 IT
Anamint, 44 Main St., pg. 76 IT
ANGLO AMERICAN CORPORATION OF SOUTH AFRICA LIMITED, 44 Main St., pg. 76 IT
Apron Services (Pty) Ltd., Johannesburg International Airport, pg. 1417 IT
The B-M Group (Pty.) Ltd., Total Centre, Harrison St., 6th Fl., pg. 255 PB
Babcock Africa (Pty) Ltd., pg. 131 IT
Babcock Ames Crosta Div., 10th Fl., Longsbank, 187 Bree St., pg. 474 IT
Babcock Bristol Africa Div., 13th Fl., 87 Risik St., pg. 474 IT
Babcock Claudius Peters Div., 13th Fl., 87 Rissik St., pg. 474 IT
Babcock Engineering Contractors (Pty) Ltd., 6th Fl., 87 Rissik St., pg. 474 IT
Babcock Industrial Contractors (Pty) Ltd., 13th Fl., 87 Rissik St., pg. 474 IT
Babcock Metstep Div., Lower Jupiter Rd., Heriotdale, pg. 474 IT
Babcock Moxey Div., 13th FL. 87, Rissik St., pg. 474 IT
Babcock Tripplejay, pg. 131 IT
Babcock TVW Div., 13th Fl., 87 Rissik St., pg. 474 IT
Banque Commerciale Zairoise, Norwich Life Towers, Corner Fredman Drive & Bute Lane, pg. 547 IT
Banque Indosuez-South Africa, 1st. Fl., 4 Ferreira St., pg. 314 IT
Bayer-Miles (Pty.) Ltd., pg. 175 IT
Bayerische Landesbank Girozentrale, 3rd Fl., 158 Jan Smuts Ave, pg. 177 IT
Bayerische Vereinsbank AG, 11 Eton Rd., Parktown, pg. 180 IT
Boart MSA (Pty.) Ltd., pg. 1114 PB
Robert Bosch (Pty) Ltd., 56-58 Rosettenville Rd., Newcentre, pg. 206 IT
Bowthorpe-Hellermann (Pty.) Ltd., P.O. Box 27063, pg. 208 IT
Bucyrus (Africa) Proprietary Ltd., 415 Wrench Rd., pg. 177 PV
Butterworths South Africa, 108 Elizabeth Avenue, pg. 1095 IT
Cadbury Schweppes South Africa Ltd., pg. 248 IT
Carlton Paper Corp. Ltd., P.O. Box 6473, pg. 959 PB
Cascade (Africa) Pty. Ltd., 60A Steel Rd., pg. 311 PB
Chrome Chemicals (South Africa) (Pty.) Ltd., pg. 175 IT
Citibank, N.A. Ltd., pg. 378 PB
Coca-Cola Southern Africa (Pty) Ltd., 9 Junction Ave., pg. 392 PB
Comazar (Pty) Ltd., pg. 1417 IT
Commerzbank AG Johannesburg Office, 4301 Carlton Intl. Trade Ctr., Commissioner St., pg. 311 IT
Commerzbank Properties South Africa Pty. Ltd., pg. 312 IT
Connex Travel (PTY) Ltd., pg. 1417 IT
Consolidated Share Registers Limited, First Flr., Edura, 40 Commissioner St., pg. 77 IT
Construction & Engineering Underwriters (Pty.) Ltd., 12, Harrison Street, pg. 91 IT
Daewoo Corp. - Johannesburg, pg. 358 IT
Deutsche Bank AG (Johannesburg), 25th Floor, Southern Life Centre, pg. 404 IT
Domestic Liability Underwriters (Pty.) Ltd., 17, Empire Road, Parktown, pg. 91 IT
Dow Jones Markets (South Africa) (Pty) Limited, African Life Bldg., 19th Fl., 111 Commisioner St., pg. 525 PB
Drescner Bank AG, No. 88 Fox St., pg. 419 IT
EAC Graphics (S.A.) (Pty.) Ltd., pg. 431 IT
EMI Music South Africa (Pty) Ltd., P.O. Box 11254, pg. 427 IT
The East Asiatic Company (S.A.) (Pty.) Limited, pg. 431 IT
Ericsson Project Services (Pty) Ltd, 158 Jan Smuts Avenue, pg. 1367 IT
Europ Assistance Worldwide Services (South Africa) Ltd., 12, Harrison Street, pg. 91 IT
FAG South Africa (Pty.) Ltd., pg. 469 IT
FBC Holdings (Pty.) Ltd., pg. 1204 IT
Fasson Products (Pty) Ltd., Seven Sherwell St. Doornfontein, pg. 154 PB
First Bowring Insurance Brokers Holdings (Pty.) LTD., 15th Floor, Southern Life Ctr., 45 Commissioner Street, pg. 487 IT
First Brands Africa (Pty) Ltd., Sloane Siuare, pg. 627 PB
First National Asset Management & Trust Company (Pty) Ltd., Mezzanine Floor, 1 First Place, pg. 487 IT
FIRST NATIONAL BANK HOLDINGS LIMITED, 6th Floor, 1 First Place, pg. 487 IT
Firstcorp Merchant Bank Limited, 4 First Place, pg. 487 IT
Robert Fleming (South Africa) (Pty) Limited, 5th Fl. First National Bank, House, Corner West St. & Fredmon Dr., pg. 494 IT
Franklin Electric South Africa, pg. 679 PB
Gestetner (Pty) Limited, 12-14 Bonanza Street, pg. 1115 IT
Grupo Santander, Hamlet Bldg., West Wing, 3rd Floor, pg. 144 IT
Hartmann & Braun (Pty.) Ltd., pg. 835 IT
Heinemann Publishers (Pty) Ltd., Office Block B2, Old Mutual Business Park, pg. 1094 IT
Henkel South Africa (Pty.) Ltd., P.O. Box 3933, Potgieter Street 1450 Alrode Ext. 4, pg. 614 IT
Honeywell Southern Africa Ltd., 34 Harry St., pg. 835 PB
Howden Group South Africa Limited, 151 Kimberlet Rd., pg. 637 IT
ICI (South Africa) Limited, pg. 665 IT
Information Trust Corporation (Pty.) Ltd., 8 Junction Avenue, pg. 537 PB
International Bank of Southern Africa SFOM Ltd. (IBSA-SFOM), 32 Princess of Wales Terrace, pg. 149 IT
JCI LIMITED, pg. 696 IT
Joy Manufacturing Company (Africa) (Pty) Ltd. Johannesburg Plant, 1 Steele St., pg. 789 PB
K.C.S.A. Holdings (Pty.) Ltd., P.O. Box 3955, pg. 959 PB
Kent Instruments South Africa Pty. Ltd., P.O. Box 7396, pg. 3 IT
Kent Meters S.A. (Pty.) Ltd., P.O. Box 43174, Industria 2042, pg. 3 IT
Kleinwort Benson Limited, P.O. Box 651414, Benmore 2010, 7th Fl.,Norwich Towers, pg. 420 IT
KLOOF GOLD MINING COMPANY LIMITED, 75 Fox Street, pg. 738 IT
Kopp Electronics Ltd., pg. 155 PB
LM Ericsson International AB South Africa, Office 302, 158 Jan Smuts Avenue, Rosebank, pg. 1369 IT
Le Carbone (South Africa) Pty. Ltd., pg. 1031 IT
MAN Automotive (South Africa) (Proprietary) Ltd., pg. 825 IT
Mannesmann Demag Plastic Technical Services (Pty.) Ltd., pg. 837 IT
Mannesmann Demag (Pty.) Ltd., pg. 837 IT
Mannesmann Pty. Ltd., pg. 840 IT
Mannesmann Trading (Pty.) Ltd., pg. 838 IT
Metal Box South Africa Limited, P.O. Box 7752, pg. 267 IT
Microsoft (S.A.) (Proprietary) Ltd., pg. 1108 PB
Mitsui & Co., Ltd., 14th Fl., Total Hse., 209 Braamfontein, pg. 881 IT
Morgan Stanley Johannesburg, 11th Fl., Ten Sixty Six, 35 Pritchard St., pg. 1133 PB
Morganite South Africa (Pty) Limited, 149 S. Rand Rd., pg. 895 IT
NYK Line-Johannesburg, 2nd Floor, 5 Sturdee Avenue, pg. 942 IT
Novell South Africa, Morning View Office Park, 214 Rivonia Rd., Morningside, pg. 1204 PB
Olin (Proprietary) Limited, 15 Spartan Crescent Eastgate Ext. 3, pg. 1220 PB
Olivetti Africa Pty. Ltd., 15 Stiemens St., pg. 1003 IT
Owner Driver Management (Pty) Ltd., pg. 1417 IT
PCI Properties (ONE) (Pty.), pg. 835 IT
PCI Properties (Three) (Pty.) Ltd., pg. 835 IT
PCI Properties (Two) (Pty.) Ltd., pg. 835 IT
P.I. Acceptances (Pty.) Ltd., 17, Empire Road, Parktown, pg. 91 IT
PTH Trading (Pty) Ltd., pg. 469 IT
PERMARK INTERNATIONAL (PTY.) LTD., pg. 1036 IT
Plascon (Pty) Ltd., P.O. Box 1227, pg. 167 IT
Polypenco (PTY) Ltd., 1725 Roodepoort, pg. 354 IT
Pretoria Portland Cement Co. Ltd., P.O. Box 3811, pg. 167 IT
Roche Products (Proprietary) Limited, pg. 1122 IT
Rockwell Automation (Proprietary) Limited, 42, Webber Street, Selby, pg. 1400 PB
S.G.I. Properties (Pty.) Ltd., 12, Harrison Street, pg. 92 IT
Sabiem Elevators (Pty.) Ltd., Cor Hilliard & Earp Streets, pg. 748 IT
Sachs SA (Pty.) Ltd., pg. 835 IT
Sasol Ammonia, pg. 1196 IT
SASOL LIMITED, 1 Sturdee Ave., pg. 1196 IT
Sasol Minchem, pg. 1196 IT
Sasol Technology Division, pg. 1197 IT
Scaw Metal Ltd., 45 Main St., pg. 76 IT
Schindler Lifts (S.A.) (PTY) Ltd., pg. 1205 IT
Siemens Ltd., pg. 1247 IT
The South African Bank of Athens Ltd., pg. 907 IT
SOUTH AFRICAN BREWERIES, LTD., 2 Jan Smuts Ave., pg. 1286 IT
South African Hosiery Company Ltd., 1st Floor Building, No. 3, Albury Park Dunkeld West, pg. 1435 PB
Stalker Hutchinson & Associates (Pty.) Ltd., 17, Empire Road, Parktown, pg. 92 IT
Stalker Hutchinson Systems (Pty.) Ltd., 17, Empire Road, Parktown, pg. 92 IT
STANDARD BANK INVESTMENT CORPORATION LIMITED, 9th Fl., Standard Bank Centre, 5 Simmonds Street, pg. 1293 IT
The Standard General Insurance Company Ltd., 12, Harrison Street, pg. 92 IT
STEELEDAG (PTY) Ltd., 8, Nansen Place, Tulisa Park, pg. 425 IT
Sumitomo Electric Industries, Ltd., pg. 1314 IT
Svedala Skega (Johannesburg), pg. 1325 IT
Svedala South Africa, pg. 1325 IT
Swiss Bank Corporation, 1st Floor, Swiss Park, 10 Queens Road, pg. 1330 IT
Swiss Re Southern Africa Ltd., 10 Queens Road, pg. 1333 IT
Symbol Technologies Africa, Inc., 387 Devereux Avenue, pg. 1546 PB
Taylor Instrument Pty. Ltd., Stand 215, Diesel Road 1 Sando, Kempton, pg. 6 IT
3M South Africa (Pty.) Ltd., 181 Barbara Rd., pg. 1607 PB
Total South Africa (Pty.) Ltd., 209 Smit Str., pg. 1409 IT
Tourism Malaysia - Johannesburg Office, 1st Floor, Hutton Court, CNR Jan Smuts Ave. & Summit Rd., pg. 833 IT
Twin Disc (South Africa) (Pty.) Ltd., 2047 Gardenview, pg. 1647 PB
UBS Representative Office Ltd., Bank of Lisbon Building, 22/F, 37 Sauer Street, pg. 1441 IT
Union Carbide South Africa (Pty.) Ltd., P.O. Box 75943, pg. 1667 PB
Utell International-South Africa, Suite 220, pg. 1099 IT
Van Leer South Africa (Pty) Ltd, pg. 1147 IT
Werner & Pfleiderer South Africa (Pty.) Ltd., pg. 511 IT
West Merchant Bank Limited, Corporate Place, 23 Fredman Drive, pg. 1494 IT
The World Bank, Grosvenor Gate, First Floor, Hyde Park Lane, pg. 1190 PV
Young & Rubicam South Africa, 68 Grayston Place, pg. 1198 PV
Zeneca Agrochemicals, Private Bag X8, pg. 1526 IT
Zeneca Pharmaceuticals, Private Bag X7, pg. 1527 IT

Kelvin

Arrow Africa (Pty.), Ltd., 7 Sandton Commercial Village, Marlboro Drive Sandton, pg. 135 PB
Deutsche Babcock (S.A.) (Pty.) Ltd., pg. 399 IT

Kempton Park

Air Chefs (PTY) Ltd., pg. 1417 IT
Anikem (Proprietary) Ltd., One Plane Rd., Spartan, pg. 1150 PB
Aquachlor (Proprietary) Limited, Plantation Rd., Chloorkop, pg. 1219 PB
Knorr-Bremse S.A. (Pty.) Ltd., 3, Derrick Rd., pg. 738 IT
MSA (Africa) (Pty) Ltd., CNR. Kelvin St. & Steel, Rd. Spartan, pg. 1114 PB
Parker Hannifin Africa Pty Ltd., pg. 1263 PB

Kimberley

CDM (Proprietary) Limited, 27 Stockdale St., pg. 77 IT

PB - *U.S. Public Companies Volume*
PV - *U.S. Private Companies Volume*
IT - *International Public & Private Companies Volume*

1752

Geographic Index-Non U.S.

De Beers Consolidated Mines Limited, 27 Stockdale St., pg. 76   IT
De Beers Industrial Diamond Division (Proprietary) Limited, 27 Stockdale St., pg. 77   IT

King Williams Town

Bundy South Africa, King Williams Town Works, 13 Buffalo Road, pg. 1341   IT

Kloof

Royal Beech-Nut Pty Ltd., pg. 388   IT

Knights

GEC South Africa (Pty) Ltd., Two Magnet Rd., pg. 546   IT

Kramerville

Luwa (South Africa) (Pty) Ltd., pg. 617   IT

Krugersdorp

Internatio (Pty.) Ltd., 6, Jacobsstreer, Chamdor, pg. 682   IT

Maitland

Enso South Africa, pg. 457   IT

Midrand

BASF South Africa (Pty.) Ltd., 852, 16th Road, pg. 107   IT
Knoll Pharmaceuticals South Africa (Pty.) Ltd., 852, 16th Road, pg. 109   IT
Marcam Southern Africa, Halfway House, Fedlife Park, pg. 1043   PB
McCormick Glentham (Pty), pg. 1067   PB
Schering Pty. Ltd., pg. 1204   IT

Mobeni

Van Leer South Africa (Pty) Ltd., pg. 1147   IT

Natal

Kiwi Brands South Africa, 15 Trotter Road Pinetown, pg. 1434   PB
Playtex South Africa, pg. 1434   PB

Nelspruit

Nelspruit Brewery, P.O. Box 888, pg. 909   IT

Nigel

John Deere (Pty.) Ltd., P.O. Box 198, pg. 493   PB
Unaform South Africa (Pty) Ltd., 3rd Avenue, pg. 1203   IT

Northcliff

Chemag South Africa Ltd., pg. 107   IT

Onderstepoort

Rhone-Poulenc Agrichem S.A. (Pty) Ltd, pg. 1112   IT

Parklands

Bally South Africa Ltd., pg. 997   IT
S.A. Paper Chemicals (Proprietary), Limited, P.O. Box 47002, pg. 1580   PB

Parktown

Standard Chartered Bank (South Africa), Suite 202, 2nd Fl., 31 Princess of Wales Terrace, pg. 1295   IT

Parkview

Esselenpark Developments (Pty) Ltd., pg. 1417   IT
TRANSNET LTD., 8 Hillside Road, pg. 1417   IT
Transtrade (Pty) Ltd., pg. 1417   IT

Phalaborwa

Palabora Mining Co. Ltd., P.O. Box 65, pg. 1119   IT

Pinelands

Lawter Intl. (Proprietary) Ltd., pg. 981   PB

Pinetown

Automould (Pty) Limited, 23-28 Cherry Rd., pg. 895   IT

Port Elizabeth

Algoa Oil & Pipeline (Pty) Ltd., Box 1916, Kendle St., pg. 5   IT
Van Leer South Africa (Pty) Ltd., pg. 1147   IT

Pretoria

Air Products South Africa (Proprietary) Limited, 4th Fl., Prudential Bldg., Church Square, pg. 32   PB
BMW (South Africa) (Pty.) Ltd., 31 3rd Rd., Raudjos Park Ext. 17, pg. 178   IT
ISCOR, Iscor Head Office Bldg., Roger Dyason Rd., pg. 688   IT
Kredietbank Representative Office (Arcadia), The Ramd Street 308, pg. 760   IT
Mercedes-Benz of South Africa (Pty.) Ltd., P.O. Box 1717, pg. 369   IT
South African Motor Corporation Proprietary Limited (Samcor), Vermooten Rd., pg. 76   IT

Primrose

Angus Fire Armour (S.A.) Limited, pg. 1500   IT

Randburg

Amdahl South Africa (Pty) Ltd., pg. 527   IT
CCF Randburg, 312 Kent Avenue, 3rd Floor, pg. 342   IT
CIBA-GEIGY (Pty) Limited, pg. 978   IT
Danzas (Southern Africa) Transport (pty) Ltd., 5th fl., Oak Park, 352 Oak Ave., pg. 383   IT
Food & Nutritional Products (Pty.) Ltd., 192 Hendrik Verwoerd Drive, pg. 920   IT
Huls Southern Africa (Pty.) Ltd., 275 Oak Avenue, pg. 1455   IT
Kluber Lubrication (Pty.) Ltd., pg. 506   IT
Krupp South Africa (Pty.) Ltd., Corner of Bond & Surrey St., pg. 511   IT
Laser Optronic Technologies (Pty.) Ltd., pg. 836   IT
Nestle (South Africa) (Pte) Ltd., pg. 921   IT
Polifin Limited, 156 Hendrik Verwoerd Road, pg. 1197   IT
Polysius Division of Krupp South Africa Pty. Ltd., Corner of Bond & Surrey Streets, pg. 512   IT
S.G.I. Guarantee Acceptances (Pty.) Ltd., 726, Pretoria Avenue, pg. 92   IT
Sandoz Products (Pty.) Ltd., pg. 985   IT
Sasol Fertilizers, 32 Hill Street, pg. 1196   IT
Sasol Gas, 32 Hill Street, pg. 1197   IT
Sasol Mining Explosives (SMX), Surrey Place, 291 Surrey Avenue, pg. 1196   IT
Sasol Oil (Pty) Ltd., 32 Hill Street, pg. 1197   IT
TML Reed Exhibitions (Pty) Ltd.-Africa, Thomas House, 83 Hendrik Verwoed Drive, pg. 1097   IT

Randfontein

Rolling Mill Supplies & Eng. (Pty.) Ltd., pg. 1455   PB

Reunion

Sasol Fibres, Fibres Road, pg. 1196   IT

Rhodepoort

International Flavors & Fragrances, pg. 899   PB

Rivonia

BRL Leasing (Pty) Ltd., pg. 167   IT
Barlow Information Systems (Pty) Ltd., pg. 167   IT
Barlow Motor Investments Ltd., P.O. Box 2031, pg. 167   IT
CIBA-GEIGY (Pty) Ltd., pg. 978   IT
Danfoss (Pty) Ltd., pg. 377   IT
DEL MONTE ROYAL CORPORATION, pg. 388   IT
Fuller-F.L. Smidth (Pty) Ltd., 363 Rivonia Blvd., pg. 475   IT
Hospitality, 360 Rivonia Road, pg. 1274   IT
NewsEdge S.A., P.O. Box 4500, pg. 1180   PB
SAB International Inc., pg. 1287   IT

Rosebank

BHF-Bank Representative Office, 1st Floor, Cradock Heights, 21 Cradock Avenue, pg. 120   IT
NUS-South Africa, 5 Cradock Pl., pg. 787   PV
Sasol Alpha Olefins, 2 Baker Street, pg. 1196   IT
Sasol Carbo-Tar, 2 Sturdee Avenue, pg. 1196   IT
Sasol Oil, 13 Baker St., pg. 1197   IT
Sasol Petroleum International (Pty.) Ltd., 1 Sturdee Avenue, pg. 1197   IT
Sasol Phenolics, 2 Sturdee Avenue, pg. 1196   IT
Sasol Solvents, 2 Sturdee Avenue, pg. 1196   IT
Sasolchem, 2 Sturdee Ave., pg. 1196   IT

Sandton

A S Ruffel (Mozambique) Limitada, c/o SmithKline Animal Health, East Block, Southern Life Park, pg. 1282   PB
A S Ruffel (Private) Ltd., c/o SmithKline Animal Health, East Block, Southern Life Park, pg. 1282   PB
Anglo-Alpha Ltd., 94 Rivonia Road, pg. 629   IT
Autodesk Ltd. (Africa), Hurlingham Office Park, Block A, pg. 149   IT
Bank of America NT&SA, Price Waterhouse Bldg., Cnr Rivonia Rd. & Katherine St., pg. 182   PB
BARLOW LTD., P.O. Box 782248, pg. 167   IT
Barlows Equipment Co., P.O. Box 781291, pg. 167   IT
Bilston Investments, 2nd. Fl., Sandton City Office, Tower, Riviona Rd., pg. 392   IT
Boart International Limited, 4th Flr., Boart Pl., Freedman Dr., pg. 76   IT

Brandeis Africa-Lutece Division Agency, 6th Fl., Norwich Life Towers, Center Fredman Drive, pg. 1030   IT
Brandeis (Pty) Ltd., 6th Fl., Norwich Life Towers, Center Fredman Drive, pg. 1030   IT
Bull Computers South Africa Pty. Ltd., 115 West St., pg. 315   IT
Bull Information Technology (Southern Africa) Pty. Ltd., 115 West St., pg. 315   IT
Butterworths South Africa, 1st Floor, Grayston Sixty Six 2 Norich Close, pg. 1095   IT
Cyborg Systems South Africa, Ltd., Block E, Hurlington Office Park, pg. 299   PV
Derby Industries (Pty.) Ltd., 7 Carey Street, pg. 394   IT
Electricite de France, Norwich Towers Life, 7th Fl., CNR Fredman Drive & Bute Lane, pg. 437   IT
Escap Limited, Megawatt Park, Maxwell Drive, pg. 459   IT
ESKOM, Maxwell Drive, pg. 459   IT
Federated-Blaikie Ltd., P.O. Box 782250, pg. 167   IT
Fidelio Southern Africa (Pty) Ltd., Wierda Mews, Block B 41, Wierda Road West, Wierda Valley, pg. 1106   PB
First Net (Pty.) LTD., 5th Floor, First National Bank House, pg. 487   IT
Fondarge (Pty.) Ltd., Dartfield Rd., Eastgate Ex. 12, pg. 790   IT
Fondarge Pty. Ltd., Dartfield Rd. Eastgate Ext. 12, pg. 791   IT
Hi Performance Systems (Pty.) Ltd., 9, Eastern Service Rd., Eastgate Ext. 3, pg. 822   PB
Hunt Lascaris/TBWA, Fika Futi, 51 Wierda Valley Road West, pg. 1062   PV
ING Barings Southern Africa (Proprietary), West Crescent, pg. 650   IT
Information Technology (South Africa) Pty. Ltd., 115 West St., pg. 315   IT
Inter Carbon (Pty.) Ltd., 14th Fl., Sandton City Tower, Rivonia Rd., pg. 1461   IT
International Computers (South Africa) (Proprietary) Limited, ICL Park, 3 Alice Lance, pg. 529   IT
Janssen/Cilag (Pty) Limited, Fifth St. & Norwich Close, pg. 929   PB
McKechnie Delta Holdings (Pty.) Ltd., Sandton 2146, 2nd Fl., Sandton, City Office Tower, Rivonia Rd., pg. 392   IT
Mohawk Media Supplies Pty. Ltd., 115 West St., pg. 315   IT
Monsanto South Africa (Pty.) Limited, Sandton City Office, 4th Fl., P.O. Box 78025, pg. 1126   PB
Pfizer Laboratories (Proprietary) Limited, East Block, Southern Life Pk., 102 Rivonia Rd., pg. 1282   PB
REUNERT LTD., Lincoln Wood Office Park, Woodlands Dr., pg. 1105   IT
Rio Tinto South Africa Ltd., Rio Tinto House, 1 Pybus St., pg. 1119   IT
C G SMITH LTD., P.O. Box 784525, pg. 1263   IT
SmithKline Animal Health (Proprietary) Limited, East Block, Southern Life Park, pg. 1282   IT
SmithKline Beecham Pharmaceuticals (Pty.) Ltd., 476 7th St. Ext. 4, pg. 1266   IT
Southern Sun Hotel Holdings Limited, pg. 1287   IT
The Sumitomo Bank, Ltd.-Johannesburg Representative Office, 3rd Floor, South Tower, Sandton Square, Sandown, pg. 1310   IT
Tampella Power South Africa, 12 Autumn Street, pg. 1354   IT
Voest-Alpine South Africa (Pty.) Limited, Brookhouse, Norwich Park, 5th St., pg. 1472   IT
Wynn Oil (South Africa)(Pty.)Ltd., 702 Main Pretoria Rd., pg. 1783   PB

Sasolburg

Natref, pg. 1197   IT
Orchem (Pty) Ltd. (Plant), Sunsen St., pg. 460   PB
SCI Operations Division, pg. 1196   IT
Sasol Chemical Industries Ltd., P.O. Box 1, pg. 1196   IT
Sasol Synthetic (Operating Division), pg. 1197   IT
Sasol Technology (Pty) Ltd., P.O. Box 1, pg. 1197   IT
Schumann Sasol (South Africa) Pty Ltd., pg. 1197   IT

Satonwold

Plate Glass & Shutterprufe Industries Limited, pg. 1287   IT

Secunda

Sasol Akrylo, pg. 1196   IT
Sasol Engineering Division, pg. 1197   IT
Sasol Mining, pg. 1197   IT
Sasol Mining (Pty) Ltd., Private Bag X1015, pg. 1197   IT
Sasol Synthetic Fuels (Pty) Ltd., Private Bag X1000, pg. 1197   IT
Sasol Three Div., pg. 1197   IT
Sasol Two Div., pg. 1197   IT

Sloane Park

Associated Furniture Companies Ltd., pg. 1286   IT
Traditional Beer Investments, pg. 1287   IT

South Hills

THORN EMI South Africa (Pty.) Limited, pg. 428   IT

Springs

Amalgamated Plastic Industries (Pty) Limited, pg. 1146   IT
Kellogg Company of South Africa (Proprietary) Limited, Stand 190 Steel Rd., pg. 947   PB

Liebherr-Africa (Pty.) Ltd., Vlakfontein Road, Fulcrum Ind. Township, pg. 808   **IT**
Owens Corning South Africa Pty Ltd., Iron Rd., New Era Springs, pg. 1238   **PB**
Van Leer South Africa (Pty) Ltd., pg. 1147   **IT**

Standerton

Standerton Brewery, P.O. Box 349, pg. 909   **IT**

Stellenbosch

Distillers Corporation S.A., Aan-de-Wagenweg, pg. 1129   **IT**
International Distillers Africa, P.O. Box 137, pg. 410   **IT**
W & A Gilbey SA, P.O. Box 137, 16 Stellentia Ave., pg. 409   **IT**

Sunninghill

Sonnenberg Murphy Leo Burnett, Leo Burnett House, 3 Simba Rd., pg. 186   **PV**

Transvaal

G.C. Baars (Pty.) Ltd., 42, Rand Road, Georgetown, Germiston, pg. 549   **IT**
John Crane (Pty.) Ltd., P.O. Box 890, Jansen Road, Nuffield Springs, pg. 1339   **IT**
Johnson Matthey (Pty.) Limited, Cnr Henderson & Premier, Germiston South Ext. 7, pg. 714   **IT**
Roche Products (Pty.) Ltd., 4, Brewery St., pg. 1122   **IT**

Uitenhage

SKF Bearing Mfrs. Pty. Ltd., Brickfield Rd., pg. 1158   **IT**
Volkswagen of South Africa (Pty.) Ltd., Algoa Rd., pg. 1475   **IT**

Umbogintwini

Tioxide Southern Africa (PTY) Ltd., Lodestar Ave., pg. 666   **IT**

Vanderbijlpark

Dorbyl Heavy Engineering, P.O. Box 8, pg. 416   **IT**
Van Leer South Africa (Pty) Ltd., pg. 1147   **IT**
Zimmermann & Jansen S.A. (Pty) Ltd., P.O. Box 1335, pg. 1529   **IT**

Vereeniging

Senior Engineering (Pty) Limited-South Africa, pg. 1223   **IT**

Wadeville

Crown Cork Company S.A. (Pty.) Ltd., pg. 464   **PB**
Tosas (Pty) Ltd., 12 Commercial Rd., Ext. 2, Wadeville, pg. 1197   **IT**

Wandsbeck

GKN Chep SA (Pty) Ltd., P.O. Box 1053,3631, pg. 536   **IT**

Wendywood

Amalgamated Beverage Industries, pg. 1286   **IT**
Avroy Shlain Cosmetics (Pty.) Ltd., Avroy Shlain House 23, Appel Road Kramerville, pg. 1434   **PB**

Westmead

CIBA-GEIGY (Pty) Limited, pg. 978   **IT**

Westville

Hunt Lascaris/TBWA Durban, Ste. 1, Southend Essex Gardens, Nelson Road, pg. 1062   **PV**

Witbank

NATIONAL SORGHUM BEER BREWERIES PTY. LTD. HIGHVELD DIVISION, Justisie St., pg. 909   **IT**
Witbank Brewery, P.O. Box 124, pg. 909   **IT**

Woodmead

Novo Nordisk (Pty) Ltd., Lincoln Wood Office Park, Woodland Drive, pg. 988   **IT**

SPAIN

Abrera

Sealed Air Espana, S.A., Hostal Del Pi, S/N, pg. 1451   **PB**

Agoncillo

ACG Componentes, S.A., Poligono El Seguero, pg. 724   **PB**

Alaquas

Toval Japon S.A., Camino Viejo de Torrente, 28, pg. 1399   **IT**

Alcala de Henares

Aeroquip Iberica S.A. (Automotive Group), Carretera, Madrid, pg. 25   **PB**
The West Company Hispania, S.A., Carretera de Meco, KM 1,100, pg. 1756   **PB**

Alcantara

S-E-Banken Luxembourg S.A., San Pedro, Avenida Las Mimosas, pg. 1259   **IT**

Alcobendas

Amercoat Espana, S.A., Poligono Industrial, C/Los Calabozos, 5, pg. 99   **PB**
Applied Power International S.A., C/La Granja, s/n. Poligono Industrial, pg. 125   **PB**
Bausch & Lomb Espana S.A., Avda. Valdelaparra 4, pg. 195   **PB**
ESAB Iberica S.A., Calle Aragoneses, 17, Zona Industrial, Apartado 61, pg. 282   **IT**
ESAB Soldadura S.A., Calle Aragoneses 17, Zona Industrial, pg. 282   **IT**
Grima Quimica, S.A., Avda. de la Industria, 30, pg. 994   **PB**
Hispano Sueca de Soldadura S.A. (Hissol), Calle Aragoneses 17, pg. 283   **IT**
Raychem SA, CTRA Antigua de Francia, KM 15, 100, pg. 1363   **PB**

Alcover

Albright & Wilson Espana S.A., Carretera de Montblanc Km 2,4 pg. 49   **IT**

Alicante

AEP Industries Packaging Espana, S.A., Valencia KM 117, pg. 5   **PB**
Prakoll, S.A., Calle Los Cincuenta 36-38, pg. 687   **IT**

Allo

Prat de Allo Mill, pg. 673   **PB**

Almeria

Sluis & Groot Semilas S.A., pg. 985   **IT**

Alonsotegui

Mure S.A., Pertxeta, 22, pg. 508   **IT**

Andoain

Krafft, S.A., Crta. Urrieta, s/n, pg. 323   **IT**

Andorra

Banca Privada D'Andorra, Carlemany Avenue, 119, pg. 250   **IT**

Aranjuez

Krupp Gruas Hidraulicas, S.A. Aranjuez, Carretera de Ancalucia km. 44, pg. 510   **IT**

Arazuri

Volkswagen Navarra, S.A., pg. 1475   **IT**

Argentona

Beiersdorf S.A., pg. 183   **IT**
Velcro Europe S.A., Ctra. Mataro a Granollers KM. 5, 8, pg. 1462   **IT**

Artajona

Calsec S.A., Ctra Puente La Reina, pg. 430   **IT**

Asturias

HULLERAS DEL NORTE, S.A. (HUNOSA), Avenida de Galicia, pg. 639   **IT**

Badalona

De La Rue Lerchundi Personalizacion SA, Ctra. de Mataro (N-11), 121 al 133/Ctra. Tiana, 1-7, pg. 386   **IT**
ICI Paints Espana SA, C/Industria 328, Apartado 107, pg. 565   **IT**

Barbera del Valles

ABB Industria AB, pg. 7   **IT**

Barcelona

ABN, Sucursal en Espana (Barcelona), Avenida Diagonal 427 bis-429,6, pg. 11   **IT**
AMP Espanola, S. A., Apartado de Correos 5294 Muntaner 249-5A, pg. 8   **IT**
Abello Linde, S.A., pg. 811   **IT**
Aceros Phoenix-Bohler S.A., Gran Via 604, 8, pg. 1471   **IT**
Acheson Colloiden B.V., Sucursal en Espana, pg. 12   **PV**
Adams, S.A., 88 Apartado de Correos No. 88, pg. 1739   **PB**
Aferfrans S.A., 463 bis, avenida Diagonal, pg. 782   **IT**
Agfa-Gevaert, S.A., Provenza 392, pg. 174   **IT**
Ahlstrom Pulp & Paper Engineering S.A., Ronda General Mitre 86, 4-2, pg. 35   **IT**
Aki Bricolage, Centro Commercial Baricenres, pg. 534   **IT**
Akzo Coatings SA, Feixa Llarga, s/n (Zona Franca), pg. 43   **IT**
Alarmcom Seguridad S.L., Francisco Tarrega 26, pg. 1246   **IT**
Albright & Wilson Iberica S.A., Pollgono Zona Franca, pg. 49   **IT**
Aliada Quimica S.A., pg. 728   **IT**
Allianz-RAS Seguros y Reaseguros, S.A., C/ Aragon, 332, pg. 60   **IT**
AlliedSignal Materiaux de Friction S.A., Balmes 243, pg. 54   **PB**
AlliedSignal Materiaux de Friction S.A. Zona Franca, IZ Franca, pg. 54   **PB**
Alpnet, Travesera de Gracia 17-21, 6 4, pg. 58   **PB**
Alusuisse Espana S.A., pg. 68   **IT**
American Power Conversion, Calvet 59, (Planta 3), pg. 89   **PB**
Amgen S.A., Avda. Diagonal, 429, 4, pg. 101   **PB**
Amway de Espana, S.A., C/Industria, 101-115, Poligono Gran Via, Zona 22A, pg. 69   **PV**
Ancra Espana, C/Portugal 25, pg. 71   **PV**
Dr. Andreu S.A., pg. 1120   **IT**
APLI Combustion, S.A., Santander, 71, pg. 361   **PV**
Apple Computer Espana S.A., Balmes 150 atico, pg. 121   **PB**
Arcadia Internacional S.A., pg. 1015   **IT**
Ascat Vida, S.A. de Seguros y Reaseguros, Doctor Ferran, 3-5, pg. 250   **IT**
Asland Catalunya y del Mediterraneo S.A., C/Corcega 325, pg. 790   **IT**
Atevi S.A., pg. 1523   **IT**
Autologic Information International, Inc., Gran Via de les Corts, Catalanes 774, pg. 1724   **PB**
Axson Espana, Ramon Turro 100, pg. 103   **IT**
Ayra Servicio SA, Pol. Ind. Can Salvatella, Avenida Arrahona 54-56, pg. 535   **IT**
BASF Espanola S.A., Paseo de Gracia 99, pg. 106   **IT**
BBL Sucursal de Barcelona, Edificio Heron Barcelona, Avda. Diagonal, 605-8, 5 planta, pg. 148   **IT**
Banca Jover, Paseo de Gracia 103, pg. 344   **IT**
Banca March S.A., Tuset 2, pg. 136   **IT**
Banca Nazionale del Lavoro, Avinguda Diagonal 468-3a, pg. 137   **IT**
Banco Comercial Transatlantico, S.A. (BANCOTRANS) (Barcelona), Avenida Diagonal 446, pg. 403   **IT**
Banco di Napoli-Barcelona, Paseo de Gracia 54-3C, pg. 140   **IT**
Banco Mercantil de Tarragona, Gran Via de les Corts Catalanes, 613, pg. 139   **IT**
Banco Vitalicio de Espana Compania Anonima de Seguros, Paseo de Garcia, 11, pg. 90   **IT**
Banque Paribas-Barcelone, Avenida diagonal 427, pg. 319   **IT**
Barcelona Terminal, Muelle de Inflamables, pg. 692   **PB**
Bayer Hispania Comercial S.A., Via Layetana 196, pg. 175   **IT**
Bayer Hispania Industrial, S.A., Pau Claris, 196, pg. 175   **IT**
Bekaert Iberica, S.A., Traversera de Gracis 30, 3C, pg. 184   **IT**
Belassi S.A., pg. 507   **IT**
Benckiser S.A., pg. 186   **IT**
BERG Electronics, Travessera de Gracia 62, 4-3A, pg. 213   **PB**
Bertrand Faure Componentes SA, Sector A-Calle 2- n 20-22, Zona Franca, pg. 193   **IT**
Bettor S.A., Basters 13-15, pg. 1465   **IT**
Beyela S.A., pg. 1015   **IT**
Bimbo S.A., Provenza, 388-58 Planta, pg. 548   **PB**
Biochemie S.A., pg. 975   **IT**
B. Braun-Dexon SA, Calle Marti I, pg. 80   **PB**
Brooks-TODO, Secretario Coloma 48, pg. 172   **PV**
Bundy SA, Mutaner, 374-376, pg. 1341   **IT**
CEDIPSA, Autovia de Castelldefels, Km. 7.5, pg. 323   **IT**
COBE Iberica S.A., Josep pla, 82-84, pg. 667   **IT**
CPC Spain, S.A., Via Augusta 59, 1, pg. 225   **PB**
Cables Pirelli S.A., Rambla Pirelli 2, pg. 1059   **IT**
Caila y Pares SA, PoligonoIndustrial Zona Franca, pg. 47   **IT**
Caixa Catalunya Gestio, Fontanella, 5-7, pg. 250   **IT**
CAIXA D'ESTALVIS DE CATALUNYA, Plaza de Antoni Maura 6, pg. 249   **IT**
Caja de Prevision y Socorro S.A., Josep Tarradellas, 34, pg. 90   **IT**
S.A. Camp and Group, pg. 186   **IT**
Candy Iberica S.A., Pasaje Tasso 8, pg. 260   **IT**
Capsulas Metalicas S.A., Partida Del Pont 352, pg. 62   **PB**
S.E. Carburos Metalicos S.A., Consejo de Ciento, 365, pg. 32   **PB**
S.A. Cardoner, pg. 984   **IT**
S.A. Casmitjana Mensa, pg. 612   **IT**
Catalana D'Iniciatives, C.R., S.A., Passeig de Gracia, 2, pg. 1372   **IT**
CCF Barcelona, Balmes 89-91, pg. 342   **IT**

PB - *U.S. Public Companies Volume*
PV - *U.S. Private Companies Volume*
IT - *International Public & Private Companies Volume*

1754

Cebal Entec S.A., Calle Alfonso XII 687-697, pg. 1030   **IT**

Cemenland S.A., Avda. Joseph Tarradellas 123, pg. 790   **IT**

Cementos Nolins Financera Minera, Carretera Nacional 340, pg. 292   **IT**

Central, Ave Meridiana, 350, pg. 21   **IT**

Central Nuclear Vandellos II A.I.E., Travessera de les Corts, pg. 1224   **IT**

Centre Ludic Diagonal, Ganduxer, 25-27, pg. 250   **IT**

Cerberus Proteccion SA, Calle Peru 186, pg. 1246   **IT**

Chandon S.A., Masia Chandon, Sant Cugat Sesgarrigues, pg. 782   **IT**

Charles River Espana S.A., Mejia Lequerica 34, pg. 195   **PB**

Chemag Iberica S.A., Avda. Diagoual, 593-595, 2o2o, pg. 107   **IT**

Chiron Vision Domilens Spain, Bori I Fontesta 39-41, pg. 350   **PB**

CIBA-GEIGY S.A., Carrer de la Marina, 202, pg. 979   **IT**

CIBA-GEIGY S.A., Carrer de Balmes, 117, pg. 979   **IT**

CIBA-GEIGY S.A., Passeig de Gracia, 16, pg. 979   **IT**

CIBA-GEIGY S.A., Ronda de Santa Maria, 160, pg. 979   **IT**

CIBA Vision SA, Bertran 140, pg. 981   **IT**

Circulo de Lectores S.A., Calle Valencia 344, pg. 192   **IT**

Citizen Watch Espana S.A., C/Guitard, 43, 1 08014, pg. 294   **IT**

Coemco-Sodexho, Recinto Mercabarna, c/Longitudinal, 8, Parcela 23 b, pg. 1274   **IT**

COISSA Correduris Internacional de Suguros, pg. 1475   **IT**

Commercial Henkel S.A. (Cohesa), Balmes 105, pg. 611   **IT**

Commerzbank AG-Barcelona, Oficina de Barcelona, Consejo de Ciento 357-359, pg. 311   **IT**

Commestsa, Sector A-Calle 2-n 20-22, Zona Franca, pg. 193   **IT**

Compania General de Esencias Grupo Florasynth S.A., Poligono Industrial Congost, Ave. San Julian 154, pg. 173   **IT**

Compania General de Tabacos de Filipinas, S.A., pg. 1345   **IT**

COMPAREX Sistemas Informaticos S.A., Paseo de Gracia, 99, pg. 108   **IT**

Comunicacion y Publicaciones, Diagonal 437, pg. 795   **IT**

Condal Corner, S.A., Paseo de Gracia, 11, pg. 91   **IT**

Construcciones Radio Electro Mecanicas S.A., c/ Manbesa-Gerona, pg. 265   **IT**

Corbero S.A., Baronesa de Malda 56, Esplugues De, pg. 443   **IT**

Cosmeticos Astor S.A., pg. 186   **IT**

Courtaulds Espana S.A., Apartado de Correos 193, pg. 339   **IT**

Cresa Aseguradora y Reaseguradora Iberica S.A., Calle Aragon 332, pg. 61   **IT**

DIC Europe GmbH, Penedes, 42-44, 08820 El Prat de Llobregat, pg. 371   **IT**

DSM Engineering Plastic Products S.A., pg. 354   **IT**

DSM Espana, S.A., Edificio EURO-3, c./ Frederic Mompou, 5, pg. 355   **IT**

DSM Resins Espana SA, Edificio EURO-3, c/. Frederic Mompou, 5, pg. 355   **IT**

DSM Resins Espana S.A., Pol. Ind. Can Jane, Coll de la Manya, pg. 355   **IT**

Danone S.A., Buenos Aires 21, pg. 379   **IT**

D'Arcy Masius Benton & Bowles, S.A., Avda. Diagonal 512, pg. 304   **PV**

Dentsu Espana S.A., Av. Diagonal, 593-595, 7-1, pg. 393   **IT**

B. D'etudes Moulinex, Calle Caballero No 89-Bajos, pg. 896   **IT**

Dieter Hase BV, Rbla. de Catalunya, 115, pg. 181   **IT**

Dietisa S.A., pg. 981   **IT**

Cia. Distribuidora de Petroleos, S.A. (CEDIPSA), Autovia de Castedefeld, Km. 7.5, pg. 323   **IT**

Domar S.A., Pologino Indus., Roca Verneda, pg. 443   **IT**

Dresdner Bank AG, Avenue Diagonal 427-429, pg. 419   **IT**

Du Pont Iberica S.A., Calle Tuset 23,3, pg. 533   **PB**

ENHER - E.N. Hidroelectrica Del Ribagorzana, S.A., Po. de Gracia, 132, pg. 1224   **IT**

EPFSA, pg. 795   **IT**

ESS-FOOD Espana S.A., Avenida de l'eix Macia, 46-50, 4-2 do, pg. 429   **IT**

Eclipse Combustion S.A., Santander, 71, pg. 361   **PV**

EDITORIAL PLANETA - DEAGOSTINI, S.A., Aribav 1851, pg. 433   **IT**

Electronica Basica, S.A. (ELBASA), Carretera Nal 2, KM 577'3, pg. 1199   **PB**

Elscint Espana S.A., Tusel 5 la Planta, pg. 450   **IT**

Elsevier Prensa SA, Avenida Paral-lel 180, pg. 1100   **IT**

Envases y Alimentacion, S.A., Viladomat, 319, First Attic, pg. 1387   **PB**

Esselte S.A., Via Augusta 20-26, pg. 461   **IT**

EURO RSCG Barcelona, Planella 39, pg. 603   **IT**

Exisa Construcciones S.A., Passaje Marsal, pg. 790   **IT**

Explotacion y Comercializacion de Aguas Minerales S.A., pg. 920   **IT**

FAG Espanola S.A., pg. 469   **IT**

FCA!BMZ Barcelona, C/Entenza, N 332-334, pg. 470   **IT**

FCA!BMZ CID Barcelona, Avda. Diagnol 464, pg. 469   **IT**

Fabricacion Nacional de Colorantes, S.A., pg. 175   **IT**

Factorcat, Establecimiento Financiero de Credito, S.A., Fontanella, 5-7, pg. 250   **IT**

Famesa S.A., Poligono Urbasa, Carreterra Caldas Km. 3, pg. 43   **IT**

Fiberpachs S.A., Poligono Industrial 'La Xarmada, pg. 355   **IT**

Fibroco S.A., Calle Llobregat 4, pg. 1368   **IT**

Flexiplas SA, Vial Centro Tecnico, pg. 1268   **IT**

Font Vella, Avenida Diagonal 615, pg. 381   **IT**

Forbo Pavimentos SA, pg. 498   **IT**

Framatome Connectors Espana S.A., Poligono Industrial, pg. 503   **IT**

Freudenberg Espana S.A., pg. 507   **IT**

Freudenberg Iberica S.A., pg. 505   **IT**

Freudenberg Telas sin Tejer S.A., pg. 506   **IT**

Frigo S.A., Peru 84, pg. 1437   **IT**

Fuji Film Espana, S.A., Aragon, 180, pg. 524   **IT**

GGK Barcelona, Calle Roger, 65-67/5, pg. 1335   **IT**

Gallina Blanca Purina, Paseo San Juan 189, pg. 159   **PV**

Gallina Blanca S.A., Avenida Infanta Carlota 38, pg. 159   **PV**

Gates Spain Automotive Products Division, Avenida de la Riera, 3-5, pg. 1397   **IT**

Gedy Iberica, Bernat Metge 110, Sabadell, pg. 542   **IT**

General Biscuits Espana (GBE), Coll de la Manya, pg. 381   **IT**

Generale Bank - Banco Belga, Paseo de Gracia, 85-6A, pg. 547   **IT**

Geresa, Ave Meridiana, 350, pg. 21   **IT**

Gescat, Entidad Gestora de Fondos de Pensiones, S.A., Fontanella, 5-7, pg. 250   **IT**

Gist-Brocades S.A., Ponsich 22, pg. 1142   **IT**

Givaudan-Roure S.A., pg. 1120   **IT**

Grace S.A., Calle Riera de Fonollar 12, 08830 Sant Boi de Llobrequat, pg. 756   **PB**

Grali, Servicios Contables y Administrativos, S.A., Josep Tarradellas, 34, pg. 91   **IT**

Gran Distribucion Avanzada Espanola S.A., pg. 1015   **IT**

Grijalbo Mondadori S.A., Arago 385, pg. 888   **IT**

Grupo Barro Testa, C. Sabino de Arana 38-2, pg. 1377   **IT**

Grupo Grifols, S.A., Torre Mapfre, piso 27, Calle de la Marina, 16-18, pg. 558   **IT**

Guerin S.A., Ronda San Pedro 52-7, pg. 1059   **IT**

Hallmark Cards Iberica, S.A., Gran via de les Cortes, Catalanes 630, 40, pg. 496   **PV**

Hammerite Productos Especiales, Poligono Industrial, Santa Rita S/N, pg. 1501   **IT**

Harrod Devitt Sociedad Anonima, Avad. Diagonal,601,5.A., pg. 1459   **PV**

Hebron S.A., Avenida Estacion 61, La Llagosta, pg. 1014   **IT**

Heller Factoring Espanola, S.A., Urgel, 240-8 D, pg. 521   **IT**

Henkel-Eytesa S.A., pg. 612   **IT**

Henkel Iberica S.A., Corcega 480-492, pg. 612   **IT**

Hewlett-Packard Espanola, S.A., Avda. Diagonal, 605, pg. 819   **PB**

Hispacement S.A., Avda. Joseph Tarradellas 123, pg. 790   **IT**

Hispano Olivetti Office, Ronda Universidad 18, pg. 1003   **IT**

Hispavic Industrial S.A., Mallorca 269, pg. 1278   **IT**

Hoogovens Aluminium Espana SA, Avenida Puerta del Angel 40, pg. 755   **IT**

Hosokawa Micron Espana S.A., Avda. Conflent, s/n Nave 26, Poligono Ind. Pomar de Dalt, pg. 636   **IT**

Hospal S.A., Napoles, 249 1:a planta, pg. 668   **IT**

Howard S.A., Carretera Granollers A Gerona, pg. 1387   **IT**

Huls Espanola S.A., Passeig de Gracia, 54, pg. 1455   **IT**

Hydro Aluminium Systems Iberica-Domal Division, Avda. Generalitat 96, pg. 963   **IT**

Hydro Aluminium Systems Iberica-Wicona Division, Poligono Industrial Polisur, Nave 21 Zona A, pg. 963   **IT**

ICI Espana SA, Gran Via Sur, pg. 665   **IT**

ICI Resins SA, CTRA. Nacional 152, KM. 23, pg. 665   **IT**

ITW Espana, S.A., Ctra. de Ribas, Km. 31.7, Las Franquesas, pg. 868   **IT**

ITW Espana S.A. SPIT, Traversera Juan de la Cierva, N-4 POL. Ind. Can Castells, pg. 868   **PB**

ITW Nexus Europe, Ctra. de Ribas, Km. 31,7, Les Franquesas del Valles, pg. 868   **PB**

Iberphone Cataluna, S.A., Entonza, 114, pg. 252   **IT**

Icart S.A., pg. 310   **PB**

Industrial Bruger SA, 383-405 Alfonso XII, pg. 43   **IT**

Industrias de Tableros Y Derivados De La Madera, S.A., Sicilia 93-97, 4, pg. 905   **IT**

Ingenieria y Gestion de Redes, S.A., Ciencias 153, pg. 252   **IT**

INPAU, S.A., Fontanella, 5-7, pg. 250   **IT**

Intergraph (Espana) S.A., Edificio Uniber, C/Aribau 197-199, pg. 892   **IT**

International Marketing & Promotions Barcelona, Avenida Diagonal, 512, pg. 304   **PV**

International Paper (Espana), S.L., Muntaner 200, pg. 905   **IT**

Interox Solvay, Mallorca 269, pg. 1278   **IT**

Interservicios y Tecnologia S.A., Barcelona, 354, Avenida Meridiana 13', pg. 681   **IT**

Inverban Gestion, S.G.I.I.C., S.A., Avenida Diagonal 530, pg. 251   **IT**

Invercartera, S.A., Fontanella, 5-7, pg. 250   **IT**

Johnson & Johnson Productos, Comte d'Urgell, pg. 928   **PB**

Jotun S.A.E., Corcega 663 E-B, pg. 715   **IT**

KME Ibertubos S.A., Pujadas, 118, pg. 719   **IT**

Kali-Chemie Iberia, S.A., Av. Diagonal 507, pg. 1279   **IT**

Kalifarma S.A., Av. Diagonal 507, pg. 1279   **IT**

Kanthal Spain S.A., Molins de Rei, pg. 724   **IT**

Kao Corporation S.A., Puig dels Tudons, pg. 718   **IT**

Kemira Iberica S.A., Gran Via Corts Catalanes, 641, pg. 728   **IT**

Kentucky Fried Chicken, Espana S.A., Infanta Carlota, 40 Entlo, pg. 1637   **PB**

Kenwood Iberica S.A., Bolivia, 239, pg. 731   **IT**

Klippan Espana, Poligna Ind. Can. Baliarda Ctra., pg. 443   **IT**

Kluber Lubrication GmbH Iberica S. en C., pg. 506   **IT**

Kluber Lubrication Iberica S.A., pg. 506   **IT**

Kodak S.A., Avda. Diagonal, 662-664, pg. 554   **IT**

Kodak S.A., Trav. Industrial de Barcelona, 159, 08907, pg. 554   **PB**

Kofisa Trading Espana S.L., C/Bergara, 3-3 B, pg. 742   **IT**

Korn/Ferry International, Avenida Diagonal, 484, pg. 634   **PV**

Krups, Plaza Wagner 5, 6, pg. 896   **IT**

LA CAIXA, Avda. Diagonal 621-629, pg. 784   **IT**

La Familia, Frederic Mompou 5, pg. 380   **IT**

La Seda de Barcelona, 47-49 C/Major, pg. 46   **IT**

La Seda de Barcelona S.A., Carretera de Camara, S/U, pg. 46   **IT**

Laboratorio Astra Espana, S.A., Mestre Joan Corrales, 95-105, pg. 94   **IT**

Laboratorio Padro SA, Ronda de Santa Maria, 16, pg. 983   **IT**

Laboratorios Miquel, S.A., Santanyi, 16, pg. 1014   **IT**

Lancaster Group S.A., pg. 186   **IT**

Lawter Intl. S.A., Polizono Ind. Can Volart, pg. 981   **PB**

Leaf Iberia S.A., 10-12, 2a 1a, Edificio Oceano, c/ Garrotxa, pg. 638   **IT**

Leasing Catalunya, Establecimiento Financiero de Credito S.A., Fontanella, 5-7, pg. 250   **IT**

Lincoln KD S.A., Ctra. Laurea Miro, 396-398, Sant Feliu de Llobregat, pg. 997   **PB**

Linde-Confrio, S.A., pg. 810   **IT**

Lista sistemas de almacenaje, S.A., pg. 812   **IT**

Lonza Iberica S.A., pg. 69   **IT**

Lowe MBAC, Paseo de los Tilos, 3-9, pg. 678   **PV**

Lucas Automotive SA, Spain, Carretera de Cerdanyola s/n, pg. 820   **IT**

Luwa Espanola SA, pg. 617   **IT**

Luxo Espanola, Sugranyes 39/41, pg. 821   **IT**

Luxottica Iberica S.A., C/Silici, 79-81, 08940 Cornella de Llobregat, pg. 822   **IT**

MSA Espanola, S.A., C/Narciso Monturiol, 7, Apartado de Correos 104, pg. 1115   **PB**

MacDermid Espanola S.A., Avda. Barcelona, 6 & 8, pg. 1030   **IT**

Maices Hibridos y Semillas SA, Carrer de la Marina, 202, pg. 983   **IT**

Marcam Spain, Diagonal Business Centre, Sabino de Arana, 32, pg. 1043   **PB**

Matra de Comunicaciones Espana, Cornella de Llobregat, Citypard ronda de dalt, Edificio 7, pg. 796   **IT**

Mattel Espana, S.A., Aribau 200, 8th Fl., pg. 1059   **PB**

Mead Sistemas Embalaje S.A., Lincoln 11, atico 2A, pg. 1077   **IT**

Medibarna, S.L., Av. Josep Tarradellas, 110, pg. 250   **IT**

Mettler-Toledo SAE, Carrer Motores 178, pg. 4   **PV**

Mitsui & Co. Europe (Espana), San Elias, 29-35, 3rd Floor B-4A, pg. 880   **IT**

Mitsukoshi Espana S.A.-Barcelona Branch, Rambla de Catalunya No.8 & No. 10, pg. 884   **IT**

Mold-Tech S.A., Calle Cromo, pg. 1507   **PB**

Molex Overseas Inc. dba Molex Espana, Valencia, 307, 1-4, pg. 1122   **IT**

Monsanto Espana S.A., Avenida Diagonal 615.4, B, pg. 1125   **IT**

Morgan Matroc S.A., Carretera de Sabadell a, Granollers km. 15, pg. 893   **IT**

Moulinex Espana S.A., Diagonal 622 7 Etage, pg. 896   **IT**

Multinacional Aseguradora S.A., de Seguryos y Reaseguros, Dr. Ferran, 3-5, pg. 250   **IT**

NRG Comunicaciones S.A., Av. Alcade Barnils, s/n, pg. 1116   **IT**

NRI Iberica, S.A., Avenido Francisco Combo, pg. 457   **PB**

NSK-RHP Iberica S.A., Calle de la Hidraulica, Nave 6, pg. 904   **IT**

Navinca, S.A., Diagonal, 490, pg. 1447   **IT**

Nedlloyd Roque S.A., pg. 1145   **IT**

Neste Chemicals Iberica S.L., c/Garrotxa 10-12, Planta Baja 4D, pg. 914   **IT**

Nezel S.A., Apartado de Correos 35347, pg. 1279   **IT**

Nissan Financiacion, S.A., Paseo de Gracia 45,4, pg. 945   **IT**

Nissan Motor Iberica S.A., Calle Panama 7, pg. 945   **IT**

Notifier Espana S.A., C/Pallars, 459, pg. 1307   **PB**

OCE-Espana S.A., Mas Blau, Osona 2, pg. 994   **IT**

OCE-Renting S.A., pg. 995   **IT**

Oracle Iberica SA, Avda. Diagonal 615, pg. 1228   **PB**

Outokumpu Rawmet S.A., C/Gran Via de Carlos III, 86 2-I, pg. 917   **IT**

Owens Corning Building Materials Espana SA, Santa Perpetua de La Mogoda, pg. 1237   **PB**

PAGSA, pg. 796   **IT**

PAMCO Espana Sociedad Anonima de Seguros, Diagonal, 601, 5-D, pg. 893   **PV**

Panalpina Transportes Mundiales S.A., pg. 1023   **IT**

Parke-Davis S.A., Apartado de Correos No. 86, pg. 1739   **IT**

Pavimentos Ceramicos S.A., Corcega 325, pg. 790   **IT**

PAXAR Iberia, S.A., Pol. Cova Solera, C/Athens Nave 3, pg. 1267   **IT**

Pechiney Celograf, Avenida 11 Septiembre S/N, pg. 1031   **IT**

Pechiney Espana, Calle Jose Tarradellas, 36, pg. 1031   **IT**

Peritaciones Tecnicas de Seguros, S.A., Paseo de Gracia, 11, pg. 92   **IT**

Pharmacia & Upjohn Biotech S.A., Paseo de Rubi 29-31 Valldoreix, pg. 1048   **IT**

Pharmacia & Upjohn S.A., Ctra. de Gracia a Manresa Km.15, pg. 1050   **IT**

Philips Informatica Communicaciones SA, Provenza 20, pg. 1055   **IT**

Plastrom S.A., Ave. del Maresme, s/n, pg. 612   **IT**

Plaza y Janes S.A., calle Enrique Granados, No. 86-88, pg. 192   **IT**

Portcemen S.A., Avda. Josep Tarradellas 123, pg. 790   **IT**

PRENATAL, S.A., Botanica St. 29, pg. 1068   **IT**

Productos Eaton Livia S.A. Engine Components Operations, Poligono Indus. Congost Apartado 24, pg. 559   **PB**

Productos Electroliticos, S.A., pg. 175   **IT**

Productos Pirelli, S.A., Av. Diagonal 662, planta 4A, pg. 1059   **IT**

PB - *U.S. Public Companies Volume*
PV - *U.S. Private Companies Volume*
IT - *International Public & Private Companies Volume*

Productos Pirelli S.A., Grupo Metzeler Pendelastica, Carretera Can Bros s/n, pg. 1060   IT
Productos Pirelli S.A.- Grupo Moltex, Calle San Fernando S/N, pg. 1059   IT
Produimica, S.A., Muelle De Inflamables, pg. 693   PB
Prolimper S.A., Corcega 480-492, pg. 612   IT
Promocio De Ciutat Vella, Ramblas, 77, pg. 1372   IT
Promotora Catalunya Mediterranea, S.A., Rossello, 257, pg. 250   IT
Promsa, Carretera Nacional 340, KM 242,300, Santo Vincenco dels, pg. 292   IT
Proner Comatel Espagne, C/Jaine Roig 20, pg. 1242   IT
Proyectos y Construcciones Catalunya, S.A., Rossello, 257, pg. 250   IT
ANTONIO PUIG SA, Travesera de Gracia 9, pg. 1073   IT
Pujol Y Tarrago S.A., Gran Via Carlos 111 No. 98, pg. 474   IT
Pulcra X.A., Avda. de Roma 157, pg. 612   IT
Quaker Chemical, S.A., Poligono Industrial Urvasa, Calle Maresme Esquina Ripolles, pg. 1347   PB
Quimica Farmaceutica Bayer, S.A., Calabria 268, pg. 175   IT
Quinton Hazell PLC, Barcelona, pg. 561   PB
ROR Rockwell Espana S.A., Ctra. de Granollers a Sabadell km 13,3, pg. 1399   PB
RV Clima-TKT S.A., c/Sepulveda, 143 5., pg. 400   IT
Reliance Electric S.A., Muntaner 270, pg. 1400   PB
Renishaw Iberica S.A., Edificio Oceano, Calle Garroxta 10-12, Parque Mas Blau, pg. 1103   IT
Resinas Sinteticas, S.A. (RESISA), Ctra. de Olzielles, s/n, pg. 323   IT
Reuters Espana S.A., Diagonal 429 bis, pg. 1105   IT
Ricoh Espana, S.A., Guitard 45, pg. 1116   IT
Rimoldi Espanola S.A., Poligono 2nd. Este - Cobalto 13-15, pg. 1118   IT
Risexo S.A., pg. 507   IT
Rockwell Automation S.A., Avda. Gran Via, 8-10, pg. 1400   PB
Rockwell Light Vehicle Systems-Espana, S.A., Dr. Robert No. 13, 08460 Santa Maria de Palautordera, pg. 1401   PB
Rohm & Haas Espana, S.A., pg. 1404   PB
Ross Systems Iberica, Frederic Mompou 5, Ed Euro 3, pg. 1406   PB
Rowenta Espana S.A., Calle Betlem 2y6, pg. 569   IT
Rubson Iberica S.A., pg. 612   IT
S.A.E. Wander, Gran Via. Corts Catalanas 764, pg. 984   IT
SAEL, Ramon Turro 153, pg. 657   IT
SAIFA-Keller S.A., pg. 1117   IT
SDP, Sociedad de Desarrollo Postal, Colle Bonsoms 15/17, pg. 654   IT
SKF Productos Industriales S.A., C/Cobalto 68, Cornella de Llobrega, pg. 1159   IT
S.L. de Gestion Mobiliaria, Avenida Diagonal 530, pg. 252   IT
Sabel Serveis, S.A., Pl. Espanya, 6-8, pg. 250   IT
The Sakura Bank - Barcelona Branch, Paseo de Gracia, 85, 7A, pg. 1179   IT
Salvat Editores S.A., 45 Calle Mallorca, pg. 796   IT
Salvat SA de Distribucion, pg. 796   IT
San Miguel, Urgel, 240, pg. 381   IT
Sandoz Agro S.A.E., pg. 984   IT
Sandoz Hispania S.A., pg. 984   IT
Sandoz Nutrition S.A., pg. 985   IT
Sandoz Pharma S.A.E., Gran Via. Corts Catalanas 764, pg. 985   IT
Sandoz Productos Quimicos S.A., pg. 985   IT
Sandoz Quimica S.A.E., pg. 985   IT
Sans, S.A., Carretera de Ciera S/N, pg. 1434   PB
Sanyo Espana S.A., Casal de Santa Coloma 6, pg. 1119   IT
Sarrio Tisu S.A., Vallespir, 24 Poligono Font Santa, pg. 673   PB
SASIB Beverage Iberica S.A., Provenza, pg. 1195   IT
Scapa Scandia (Espana) S.A., Secretario Coloma 64-68, pg. 1203   IT
R.P. Scherer S.A., Avenida Diagonal 615 4E, pg. 1438   PB
A. Schulman, Oficina de Representation en Espana, pg. 1441   PB
SEAT, S.A., pg. 1475   IT
Segurcat, S.A., Passatge Centelles, 10-20, pg. 250   IT
Senalizacion y Accesorios Del Automovil Yorka, S.A., Venezuela 76, pg. 724   IT
Servair Espagne, Avenida de Septembre, S/N 08820 El Prat Del Llobregat, pg. 560   IT
Servicat, S.A., Fontanella, 5-7, pg. 250   IT
Servicios y Suministros, S.A., Paseo de Gracia, 11, pg. 92   IT
Shandwick Barcelona, Via Augusta, 18, pg. 1227   IT
Sharp Electronica Espana S.A. (Barcelona), Pligon Can Sant Joan, Parcela No. 8, 08190 Sant Cugat, pg. 1229   IT
Shimizu Espana, S.A.-Barcelona Office, Provenza 281, 2-4, pg. 1234   IT
Signode Spain, Poligono Industrial, Els Bellots, Avenida del Valles 320, pg. 869   PB
R.J. Simpson International, SL (Spain), Damper Iberica S.A., C/L 'Energia No. 18, pg. 1475   PB
Siplast Espana S.L., pg. 659   IT
Sirma Iberica, S.A., Apartado de Correos 5040, pg. 6   IT
Skis Rossignol de Espana S.A., Santa Maria de Artes, pg. 1127   IT
Slogan Publicidad, Avda. Diagonal 463 bis 9o, pg. 1152   PV
Sociedad Catalana de Talleres Artesanos, Avenida Torre d'en Mateu S/N, 08210 Barbera del Valles, pg. 783   IT
Sociedad Espanola de Automoviles de Turisme, S.A. (SEAT), Pau Claris, 162-164, 7, pg. 1475   IT
Sociedad Nestle A.E.P.A., Avda. de los Paises Catalanes 33 al 49, pg. 922   IT

Soder S.A., Avenida Diagonal 672, pg. 966   IT
Sofazel S.A., Calle Ramon de Trinchoria, pg. 1032   IT
Solis Industrias de Alimentacion S.A., pg. 922   IT
Sonoco Espana, S.A., pg. 1487   PB
Square D Company Espana S.A., c/Villarroel, 177-179 entl 2, pg. 1209   IT
Stahl Iberica, S.A., C/Llevant 7, Poligono Llevant Industrial, pg. 1526   IT
Standex International S.A., Carretera Del Medio 251 Hospitalet, pg. 1507   PB
Stanhome S.A., Calle Tuset 32, 2, pg. 1508   IT
Starlux, Via Congost, pg. 225   PB
STILL S.A., pg. 811   IT
The Sumitomo Bank, Ltd.-Barcelona Branch, Avenida Diagonal 615, 7th Fl., pg. 1309   IT
Sun Chemical S.A., pg. 371   IT
Supergrif SL, Poligono Industrial El Pla, c/ Ramon de Trincheria, 1 08980, pg. 391   IT
Swift Adhesifs S.A., Carretera Nacional II Km. 593, Poligono Industrial Torre Bovera, pg. 370   IT
Syntex Latino S.A., pg. 1122   IT
TBWA Barcelona, Avda. Diagonal, 604, pg. 1063   PV
Takenaka (U.K.) Ltd., Spain, Edificio Macia, Plaza Francesc Macia, 7 8-B, pg. 1352   IT
TAVCOM, S.A., Avenida Diagonal, 530, pg. 252   IT
Tecpant Ingest, Gran Via Carlos III, 97 J, pg. 1361   IT
Tefal Espana SA, Calle Betlem, 2y6, pg. 568   IT
Tektronix Espanola S.A.-Barcelona, pg. 1567   PB
Telesincro S.A., Avda. Universitat Autonoma 29, pg. 317   IT
Terminals Portuarias, S.A., Muelle de Inflamables, pg. 693   PB
Texsa S.A., Poligono can Pelegri, pg. 791   IT
The Tokio Marine & Fire Insurance Company (U.K.) Limited, c/o Commercial Union Assurance, Via Augusta, 21-23, pg. 1393   IT
3i Iberia de Inversiones Industriales SA, Paseo de Garcia 125, 4-12, pg. 1386   IT
Thyssen Haniel Logistics, pg. 1388   IT
Torne-Jotun S.A., pg. 716   IT
Torre Collserola, S.A., Ctra. Vallvidrera-Tibidabo, s/n, pg. 1372   IT
TRADICION TEXTIL, S.A., Avenida de Madrid 133, pg. 1416   IT
Transfashion SA, pg. 1144   IT
Travisa Transformadora del Vidrio S.A., pg. 1523   IT
Turovalles, S.A., Diagonal, 490, pg. 1447   IT
Tyco Toys Espana, pg. 1059   PB
Uddeholm S.A., Giufre 690-692, pg. 1472   IT
Union Naval de Levante, S.A. (Talleres Nuevo Vulcano), Muelle Nuevo 23, pg. 1442   IT
Utell International-Spain, Consell de Cent, 474 Entl A, pg. 1099   IT
VDO Instrumentos SA, pg. 839   IT
V.F. Consultores de Seleccion y Formacion, S.A., Paseo de Gracia, 11, pg. 92   IT
VRG-Papel Iberica, S.A., pg. 757   IT
Valorcat, Agencia de Valores, S.A., Fontanella, 5-7, pg. 250   IT
Vendo Iberia, S.A., C/Sant Ferran, No. 92, pg. 1184   IT
Vickers Systems S.A., Poligono Industrial Zona, Franca Sector C, Calle D, pg. 25   PB
Vileda Espana S.A., pg. 507   IT
Vileda Iberica S.A., pg. 507   IT
Vileda Iberica S.A., S.en C, pg. 506   IT
Vinizius/Young & Rubicam, S.A., Diagonal 652-656, Edificio A-Planta 2A, pg. 1099   PV
Vitalico Agencia de Seguros S.A., Paseo de Gracia, 11, pg. 92   IT
Vitalico Asesoria de Pensiones, S.A., Paseo de Gracia, 11, pg. 92   IT
Vitalico Servicios Informaticos, S.A., Calle San Eusebio, 58, pg. 92   IT
Vitruvio/Leo Burnett, Avda. General Mitre, pg. 186   PV
Whitehall Spain, Calle Baronesa de Malda 73, pg. 82   PB
Wilsor Sporting Goods Espana, S.A., Calle Casanova 173, pg. 73   IT
Witco Espana S.L., Poligono Industrial de Congost, pg. 1774   PB
Woodward-Clyde/Limnos, S.A. Barcelona, Bruc, 168, entlo 2, pg. 1658   PV
Wormald Mather & Platt Espana S.A., Gran Via 322-324, 7a Planta, pg. 1651   PB
Wyeth-Orfi S.A., Calle Baronesa De Malda 73, 08950, pg. 82   PB
Zellweger S.A., pg. 618   IT
Zeneca Resins SA, Apartado de Correos 5, Poligono Llevant Industrial, pg. 1527   IT
Zeneca Specialties SA, Avda. de la Granvia 179, pg. 1527   IT
Zurich Compania de Seguros, Via Augusta 200, pg. 1529   IT
Zurich Compania de Seguros sobre la Vida, Via Augusta 200 pg. 1529   IT
Zurich International (Espana) Compania de Seguros y Reaseguros, S.A., Via Augusta 200, pg. 1532   IT
Zyma Pharmaceutica SA, Apartado 6149, pg. 986   IT

Basauri
Cavexsa, Barrio Ugarte, pg. 694   PV

Benicarlo
Du Port Iberica S.A., Apartado Correos 13, pg. 533   PB

Berga
Mayc S.A., Ahumategui 3, pg. 260   IT

Bilbao
Arte y Cemento SA, Calle Zancoeta, pg. 1099   IT
BWE-Babcock & Wilcox Espanola, S.A., Alameda de Recalde, 27, pg. 1224   IT
BANCO BILBAO VIZCAYA, S.A., Gran Via #1, pg. 138   IT
Bekaert Consulting, C/Henao n 7, 6, DCHA, pg. 184   IT
DMB&B Bilbao, Gran Via 81, 5th Fl., pg. 303   PV
De La Rue Lerchundi SA, Barrio Elotxelerri, 64, 48150 Loiu (Vizcaya), pg. 386   IT
Derivados del Fluor, S.A., San Vicente 8, pg. 175   IT
Distribuidores Concesionarios S.A., Calle Jose Luis Goyoaga 36, pg. 615   IT
FCA/BMZ CID Bilbao, Cale Luchana 4, pg. 469   IT
Formica Espanola S.A., Guadalcano Vizcaya, pg. 129   IT
IBERDROLA, S.A., Cardinal Gardoqui 8, pg. 657   IT
Iberica de Crisoles, Poligono Industrial, Erletxe Nave, 7, pg. 894   IT
Kodak S.A., Guepro Arta Patti, 4, pg. 554   PB
Lippert S.A., Begonalde, 9-1, pg. 518   IT
Lubriner (Lubricates Del Nervion, S.A.), Plaza de Espania 4, pg. 323   IT
MAPFRE Servicios Maritimos, Comisariado y Liquidacion de Averias, Avda. Sabino Arana, 4, pg. 333   IT
Outokumpu Copper Tubes S.A., pg. 1017   IT
Rodamientos USA SA, Ma Diaz De Haro 28, pg. 212   IT
Sachs Iberica SA, pg. 835   IT
Talleres Uribarri, S.L., Poligono Bakiola 41, Arrankudiaga, pg. 1536   PB

Burgos
Constel S.A., Poligono Gam. Villimar, pg. 1365   IT
Industrias del Ubierna, S.A., Poligono Industrial de Villalonquejar, pg. 184   IT
McCain Espana S.A. (Spain), Poligono Indo de Villa Longuejar, pg. 850   IT

Burlada
Industrias Cousin Freres, Poligono Industrial Burlada, pg. 193   IT

Caceres
Banco de Extremadura, S.A., Calle Pintores, 8, pg. 251   IT
SODIEX - Sociedad Para el Desarrollo Industrial de Extremadura, S.A., Doctor Maranon, 2, Torre 3, pg. 1225   IT

Cadiz
Alcaidesa Costain Developments S.A., Cortijo Las Aguzaderas', 125 San Roque, pg. 337   IT
Banco de Jerez, Alameda Cristina, 11-12, pg. 139   PB
Cadiz Electronics, S.A., pg. 665   IT
Costain Developments SA, Cortijo 'Las Aguzaderas', Apdo De Correo's, 125 San Roque, pg. 337   IT
Darsa Gaditana, S.A., Avda. Marconi, 34, pg. 1372   IT
Iberica AGA S.A., Apartado 2252, pg. 14   IT

Carboneras
Central Termica Litoral de Almeria A.I.E., Carretera Faro Mesa Roidan, s/n., pg. 1224   IT

Castellbisbal
BetzDearborn Iberica, S.A., Carrer Forjadors, s/n, Polig, Industriale Comte de Sert, pg. 227   PB
Cartiberia S.A., Ctra. Nacional II, Km. 592,6, pg. 458   IT
Norton Iberica, Poligono Industrial., pg. 1175   IT

Castellon de la Plana
Ferro Enamel Espanola, S.A., Apt. 232, pg. 619   PB
Proquimed S.A., pg. 1427   IT
Thermal Ceramics Espana, S.L., Avenida Hermanos Bou, pg. 894   IT
UBE Europe (Espana), S.A., c/o Proquimed S.A., pg. 1427   IT

Ceuta
Acuicultura de Ceuta, S.A., Independencia, 5, pg. 252   IT
Exportadora de tabaco de Ceuta y Melilla, S.A., pg. 1345   IT
Heliceuta, S.A., Independencia, 5, pg. 252   IT

Ciudad Real
Alcoholes Y Vinos, S.A., Carretera Zancara, pg. 1322   IT

Claris
Netstal-Maquinas SA, pg. 836   IT

Colmenar
International Flavors & Fragrances, pg. 899   PB

Cornella
DEA Iberica, Carretera del. Mig. 37, pg. 654   IT
Maquinaria Artes Graficas Hartmann SA, pg. 757   IT

PB - U.S. Public Companies Volume
PV - U.S. Private Companies Volume
IT - International Public & Private Companies Volume

Correos

Hughes Microelectronics Europa Espana S.A., Parque Tecnologico de, Andalucia, Parcela P-1, Carretera MA-401, pg. 725 **PB**

Coslada

CACESA - Compania Auxiliar Al Cargo Expres, S.A., Juan de la Cierva, 7 y 9., pg. 1224 **IT**
Compania Ingersoll Espanola, S.A., Poligono Industrial de Coslada, Ave. de Fuentemar 26 & 28, pg. 878 **PB**
Continental Industrieas del Caucho SA, pg. 328 **IT**
Mannesmann Demag S.A., Ave. de la Industria 38, pg. 837 **IT**
Tedec-Meiji Farma S.A., Poligono Industrial de Coslada, Camino de Carriles, pg. 856 **IT**

Crevillente

VICENTE PUIG OLIVER S.A., C/. Oscar Espla, 14, pg. 1001 **IT**

Deba

GKN Ayra Cardan SA, Apartado 72, pg. 535 **IT**

Duenas

Ewos S.A., Apartado de Correos 16, pg. 349 **IT**

Durango

Super Ego Tools S.A./Rothenberger Espana, Carretera de Durango, Elorrio Km 2, Abadiano, pg. 1129 **IT**

Eibar

Alfa-Cercast Microfusion de Aluminio S.A., Avenida Otoala 13, pg. 1030 **IT**

El Astillero

ASTANDER - Astilleros de Santander S.A., Fernandez Hontoria, 24, pg. 1223 **IT**

Escatron

ELECBRO - Termoelectrica del Ebro, S.A., Extramuros, s/n., pg. 1224 **IT**

Fene

Renosa - Remolcadores del Noroeste, S.A., Perlio, pg. 1223 **IT**

Fuengirola

Christiania Bank Luxembourg S.A.-Representacion en Espana, Edificio Tres Coronas, pg. 289 **IT**

Gava

Barnasud, S.A., Progres, 69, pg. 250 **IT**
Dampers Iberica, S.A., Riera de las Parats, S/N, pg. 469 **PB**
MD Foods Espana, c/Premia 1, pg. 826 **IT**
Sociedad General de Hules S.A., pg. 1279 **IT**

Getafe

ABB Stotz-Kontakt S.A., Apartado de Correos 33, pg. 2 **IT**
CESA - Compania Espanola de Sistemas Aeronauticos, S.A., Diesel, s/n. Poligono Industrial, pg. 1224 **IT**

Gibraltar

CEPSA Gibraltar, Ltd., Waterport House, Waterport, pg. 323 **IT**

Gijon

Armstrong Amortiguadores S.A., P.O. Box 87, pg. 265 **IT**
Juliana Constructora Gijonesa, S.A., Avda. Galicia, 60, pg. 1223 **IT**
Praxair Iberica S.A., pg. 1320 **PB**
Suzuki Motor Espana S.A., pg. 1323 **IT**

Granada

Aguas de Lanjaron, c/Nueva de la Virgen, 25, pg. 381 **IT**

Guadalajara

Liebherr Iberica, S.A., Carretera Nacional 2, km 41, Parcela 7, pg. 808 **IT**
SODICAMAN - Sociedad Para el Desarrollo Industrial de Castilla-La Mancha, S.A., Avda. de Castilla, 12, 1., pg. 1225 **IT**

Guechoa

Hewlett-Packard Espanola, S.A., Avda. Zugazarte, 8, pg. 819 **PB**

Guisona

AGROPECUARIA DE GUISSONA, S. COOP. LTDA., Avenida Vergel del Claustro 32, pg. 31 **IT**

Hernani

Oilgear Towler SA, Entidad Zicunaga 62, pg. 1215 **PB**

Hospitalet

BASF Curtex S.A., Carretera del Medio, 219, pg. 105 **IT**
Erie Controls Iberica S.A., C/Independencia 98, pg. 1241 **IT**

Huelva

Portumbria, S.A., pg. 1447 **IT**
Tioxide Europe S.A., Poligono Nuevo Puerto, pg. 666 **IT**

Huesca

Eurotron S.A., Poligono Industrial No. 8, pg. 1192 **IT**

Irurzun

Industria Navarria Del Aluminio, S.A., Victoria Rd, Aralar 9, pg. 1387 **PB**

Jerez de la Frontera

Croft Sherry, Rancho Croft, pg. 409 **IT**
Williams & Humbert Ltd., Nuno de Canas, pg. 751 **IT**

La Cartuja Baja

Rothe Erde Iberica S.A., Ctra. Castellon, Km 7, pg. 509 **IT**

La Coruna

Banco Gallego, Anda Linares Riuas, 30, pg. 145 **IT**
ConAgra Spain, Avenida del Ejercito, 2-2, pg. 429 **PB**
Genosa, Zona Industrial de la Grela, S/N, pg. 1030 **IT**
Prodemar, 15126 Merexo, pg. 964 **IT**

La Moraleja-Alcogendas

Nokia Telecommunications S.A., Miniparc 1 - Edificio F, Azalea, 1, pg. 954 **IT**

Lamiaco

Agra S.A., pg. 1436 **IT**

Laroca

Hydro Alluminio La Roca S.A., Sta. Agnes de Malanyanes, Pol. Ind. Can Font de la Parera, pg. 962 **IT**

Las Arenas

Hewlett-Packard Espanola, S.A., Edificio El Abra 4, Av. de Zugazarte, 8, pg. 819 **PB**
MacGREGOR (ESP) S.A., C/Ibaigane no. 15-5, pg. 670 **IT**
Petronor, Avda. Zugazarte, 29, pg. 1104 **IT**
Rockwell Automation S.A., Villa de Plencia, 4, pg. 1400 **PB**

Las Palmas

Banca March S.A., Francy y Roca, 10, pg. 136 **IT**
Binter Canarias, Aprtdo. Correos 50, pg. 574 **IT**
Binter Canarias, S.A., Alcalde Jose Ramirez Bethencourt, 8, pg. 1224 **IT**
Electrolux Canarias S.A., Jesus Ferrer Jimeno 4, pg. 443 **IT**
Hanwa Co., Ltd.-Las Palmas Branch, Frigorificos Agasa, Explanada, Del Castillo S/N, pg. 595 **IT**
Kodak S.A., Profesor Lozano, 10, pg. 554 **PB**
MAPFRE Guanarteme Cia. de Seguros Generales y Reaseguros de Canarias, S.A., Leon y Castillo, 57, pg. 333 **IT**
Mitsui & Co. Europe (Espana), Albareda; 3-2, pg. 880 **IT**
Petroleos De Canarias, S.A. (PETROCAN), Explanada de Tomas, Quevedo s/n, pg. 323 **IT**
UNELCO - Union Electrica de Canarias, S.A., Alcalde Jose Ramirez Bethencourt, 83, pg. 1224 **IT**

Las Rozas

Hewlett-Packard Espanola, S.A., Carretera de la Coruna, km. 16,500, pg. 819 **PB**
Kodak S.A., Ctra. Nal. VI, km 23, pg. 554 **PB**
Schauman Iberica S.A., Edificio Burgo Sol, Oficinas 36-37, Comunidad de Madrid, pg. 1429 **IT**

Lasarte

S.A.V. Moulinex, Urdaneta, 11, pg. 896 **IT**

Leganes

Ericsson Radio, S.A., Poligono Industrial, Severo Ochoa, 9, pg. 1367 **IT**
Industrias de Telecommunicacion S.A. (Intelsa), c/o Torres Quevedo 2, pg. 1368 **IT**

Legazpia

GKN Forjas de Precision de Legazpia SA, c/- Urola No. 10, pg. 536 **IT**

Legutiano

Baumann Muelles, S.A., Poligono Industrial Gojain, C/ Padurea s/n, pg. 171 **IT**

Llers

Ilco Orion S.A., Ctra. de Figueres a Albanya, pg. 1432 **IT**

Llica de Vall

FATA SA, Carretera DeSabadel La Gronollers, pg. 474 **IT**
Perstorp Evanplas S.A., C/Maresme s/n., P.I. Palaudaries Nave 13, pg. 1038 **IT**

Llobregat

Braun Espanola, S.A., Enrique Granados, 46, pg. 744 **PB**
Gearbox del Prat, S.A., pg. 1475 **IT**

Logrono

Arteaga, Sociedad Anomima, "Arteaga, S.A.", Carretera de Laguardia, 98, pg. 1386 **PB**
GM Espana Fisher Guide, P.O. Box 281, pg. 724 **PB**
Industrias del Lacado, S.A. (Indulacsa), Poligono Cantabria I, Parcela 44, pg. 1387 **PB**

Lorqui

Perstorp Evanplas S.A., Ctra. Nac. 301. Km. 377, pg. 1038 **IT**

Madrid

ABG-Iberica, Plaza Castilla, 3-17 D1, pg. 877 **PB**
ABN Leasing Espana, S.A., Serrano 55, 2nd Fl., pg. 11 **IT**
ABN, Sucursal en Espana (Madrid), Serrano 55, pg. 11 **IT**
ABS Bombas Ltda, Carretera Vicalvaro a Rivas, pg. 270 **IT**
ABS Bombas S.A., c/o Madera, 14-16, Pol. Ind. Santa Ana, Urb., pg. 270 **IT**
ADT/Proegur, S.A., Menendez Pelayo, 87, pg. 1649 **PB**
AEG Radiocomunicaciones SA, Carmino de Hormigueras 146, pg. 795 **IT**
AESA Astilleros Espanoles, S.A., Ochandiano, 12-14, pg. 1223 **IT**
AF Sistemas SA, Antonio Lopez 243, pg. 569 **IT**
AGA S.A., Avenida Burgos 16-E 1, pg. 13 **IT**
A.H.V. Ensidesa Capital, S.A., pe de la Castellana, 91, pg. 1223 **IT**
AMS Management Systems Espana, S.A., Avenida de Europa, Parque Empresarial, La Moralega, pg. 87 **PB**
AMVI S.A., pg. 721 **IT**
AST Research Spain, S.L., Plaza Picasso, a/n Edif. Serantes, pg. 1182 **IT**
ASTANO - Astilleros y Talleres del Noroeste, S.A., Orchandiano, 12-14, pg. 1223 **IT**
AXA Seguros y Reaseguros, Calle O'Donnel 17, pg. 19 **IT**
Aceros Krupp Hoesch S.A., Plaza de Manuel Gomez Moreno, pg. 515 **IT**
Adecco ETT, SA, Hermosilla 11-1, pg. 24 **IT**
Ademco-Sontrix Espana, S.A., Vivero 5, pg. 1307 **PB**
Adriatica-Sociedad Anonima de Seguros y Reaseguros, Paseo de la Castellana 39, pg. 61 **IT**
AEGON-Union Aseguradora, S.A. de Seguros y Reasequros, Principe de Vergara 154-156, pg. 28 **IT**
Aer Lingus, Edificio Espana, Group 3 Planta 10-No. 2, pg. 28 **IT**
Agencia EFE, S.A., Espronceda, 32, pg. 1372 **IT**
Agrolaser S.A., Av. Camino de lo Cortao, 24-Nave 4, pg. 1289 **IT**
Alcatel Standard Electrica, S.A, Ramirez de Prado 5-6, pg. 1372 **IT**
Alcon Iberhis S.A., pg. 918 **IT**
Alergia e Inmunologia Abello S.A., Miguel Fleta 19, pg. 288 **IT**
Alfa-Laval S.A., Apartado 31015, pg. 1380 **IT**
Alfa Romeo Espana, pg. 481 **IT**
Alfer Consulting Immobiliario, S.A., P.o. de la Castellana, 83-85, pg. 1447 **IT**
Alhambra Longman S.A., Fernandez de la Hoz. 9, pg. 1025 **IT**
Allergan S.A.E., Avenida de la Industria #24, Poligono Industrial de Tres Cantos/, pg. 46 **PB**
AlliedSignal Aerospace Service Corporation, Princesa 47-3A, pg. 52 **PB**
Amdahl Computer Systems Sucursal en Espana, Edifico Iberia Mart 1, pg. 527 **IT**
American Appraisal Espana, S.A., Principe de Vergara, 9, pg. 50 **PV**

Geographic Index-Non U.S.

Amersham Iberica SA, c/ Bambu 8, pg. 993   IT
Amoco Espana Exploration Co., Paseo de la Castellana 91, pg. 102   PB
Amper, S.A., Maria de Molina, 37 bis, pg. 1372   IT
Antibioticos S.A., Avenida De Burgos, 8A, pg. 324   IT
Arapiles, S.A., Ventura Rodriguez 7, pg. 1447   IT
ARGENTARA CORPORACION BANCARIA DE ESPANA, S.A., Paseo de Recoletos 10, pg. 80   IT
Arrow Iberia, S.A., Avenida De Valgrande 14, pg. 135   PB
Ascom Hasler SA, C/ Manuel Luna 12, pg. 87   IT
Asea Brown Boveri S.A., Apartado 36127, pg. 3   IT
Asemap, Asesoramiento e Inversiones, S.A., Paseo de Recoloetos, 23, pg. 332   IT
Asfaltos Espanoles, S.A. (ASESA), c/Juan Bravo 3B, pg. 323   IT
Asland S.A., pg. 788   IT
Asland S.A., Orense, 81, pg. 790   IT
Asland Tecnologia S.A., Orense 81, pg. 790   IT
Asociacion Telefonica Para Asistencia A Minusvalidos (A.T.A.M.), Avda. Del Monte, s/n, pg. 1371   IT
ATECSA, Paseo de La Habana 14, pg. 424   IT
Atenea Comunicacion Y Mecenazgo, S.A., Duque de Liria 6, pg. 251   IT
Aurora Polar, Po Recoletos, 4, pg. 19   IT
Auseco, S.A., San Bernardo, 123, pg. 252   IT
Auxitrol Iberico S.A., C/Caucho 18, Poligono Industrial, Apartado 30, pg. 594   PB
Avalmadrid, S.G.R., S.A., General Oraa, 64, pg. 252   IT
Aviacion y Comercio, S.A., Maudes, 51, pg. 1224   IT
Aviaco, C/Maudes, 51, pg. 574   IT
Avon Cosmetics, S.A., Apartado de Correos 14.875, pg. 156   PB
AxTrade LIC Medica S.A., Avenida de Burgos, 16E, pg. 710   IT
BAC International-The Netherlands B.V. Sucursal en Espana, Calle Princessa 3, Planta 4, pg. 203   PB
BDDP Mancebo Kaye, Calle Fortuny 39, pg. 117   IT
BHF-Bank Representative Office, Marques de Cubas 21, pg. 120   IT
BMC Software, S.A., c/Gobelas, No. 25-27 Urbanizacion La Florida, pg. 163   IT
BMW Iberica S.A., Paseo Dela Castellana 149, pg. 178   IT
BNP Espana S.A., Calle Genova 27, pg. 163   IT
BSN S.A. Sociedad de Valores y Bolsa, Paseo de Castellana 75, pg. 143   IT
BSN Vidrio Espana, Carretera de Villaverde Km.8,200, pg. 381   IT
BT Telecomunicaciones S.A., Edificio Herre, Salvador de Madariaga,1, pg. 223   IT
Bailey-Fischer & Porter Espana S.A., Sanchez Pacheco 79, pg. 449   IT
Bally Moda SA, pg. 997   IT
Banca March S.A., Nunez de Balboa, 70, pg. 136   IT
Banca Nazionale del Lavaro, Calle Cedaceros 10, pg. 137   IT
Banco Banif de Gestion Privada, Juan Bravo, 2, pg. 139   IT
BANCO CENTRAL HISPANOAMERICANO S.A., Plaza Canalejas 1, pg. 139   IT
Banco Comercial Transatlantico, S.A. (BANCOTRANS) (Madrid), Paseo de la Castellana, 18, pg. 403   IT
Banco de Credito Local, Paseo de Recoletos 10, pg. 80   IT
Banco de Formento, Paseo de la Castellana, 92-96, pg. 139   IT
Banco di Napoli-Madrid, Torre Picasso, Plaza Pablo Ruiz Picasso, pg. 140   IT
Banco do Brasil S.A.-Madrid, Calle Serano, 73, pg. 141   IT
Banco Espanol de Credito SA, Alcala, 14, pg. 143   IT
Banco Espirito Santo Sa. (Bessa), Calle Velazquez, 108-110, pg. 142   IT
Banco Hipotecario de Espana, Paseo de Recoletos 10, pg. 80   IT
Banco Internacional de Comercio, Jose Ortega y Gasset, 56, pg. 139   IT
Banco Luso Espanol S.A., Maria de Molina 39, pg. 251   IT
Banco Mapfre, S.A., Gobelas 41-43, pg. 332   IT
Banco Nacional de Mexico, Serrano No. 41, 60. piso, pg. 574   IT
Banco NatWest Espana SA, 125 Principe De Vergara, pg. 911   IT
Banco Popular Hipotccario, Maria de Molina 43, pg. 176   IT
BANCO SANTANDER, Paseo de la Castellana, 24, pg. 143   IT
Banco Santander de Negocios, Paseo de Castellana 75, pg. 143   IT
BANCO 21, Henri Dunant 17, pg. 145   IT
Banco Urquijo S.A., Principe de Vergara 131, pg. 136   IT
BancTec Iberica S.A., Paseo Castellana 45, pg. 177   PB
Bang & Olufsen Espana S.A., Avda. Europa 2, pg. 146   IT
Bank Brussels Lambert Sucursal en Espana, Paseo de la Castellana 95, pg. 148   IT
Bank of America S.A., Capitan Haya 1, Apartado 1168, pg. 182   PB
The Bank of New York, Plaza de Colon, 2, Torre Colon 1, 13th Fl., pg. 179   PB
The Bank of Tokyo-Mitsubishi, Ltd. (Madrid Branch), Jose Ortega y Gasset 29, pg. 158   IT
Bankers Trust New York Corporation, Paseo de la Castellana 31, pg. 186   PB
Banque Indosuez Espana S.A., Paseo de la Castellana, 1, pg. 315   IT
Banque Paribas-Spain, Hermanos Becquer 3, pg. 320   IT
Bansafina, Plaza de Manuel Gomez Moreno 2, pg. 143   IT
Bansaleasing, Plaza de Manuel Gomez Moreno 2, pg. 143   IT
Barclays Bank SA-Madrid, Apartado de Correos 1075, pg. 166   IT
Bayerische Vereinsbank AG, Plaza de Colon 2, Torre de Colon II, 19B, pg. 180   IT

Beiersdorf Espanola S.A., pg. 183   IT
Bertrand Faure Componentes SA, Calle Resina 18, pg 193   IT
Beter S.A., pg. 1207   IT
Bilfinger y Berger Espana S.A., Calle Costa Rica, 13 bajo, pg. 196   IT
BINESA-Bioquimica Industrial Espanola, S.A., Principe de Vergara, 109, pg. 1283   PB
Binter Mediterraneo, S.A., P. de la Castellana, 52, 7. pl., pg. 1224   IT
Bioter-Biona S.A., Bioter-Biona Bldg., Emilio Vargas 7, pg 1224   PB
Boart Longyear S.A., Avda de los Metales, S-N Leganes, pg. 76   IT
Boeing International Corp., Calle Alcala 87-7 Derecha, pg. 242   PB
Robert Bosch Espana SA, Hermanos Garcia Noblejas 19, pg. 205   IT
Robert Bosch SA, Hermanos Garcia Noblejas, 19, pg. 206   IT
Bridgestone/Firestone Hispania S.A., c/Fuerteventura, 9, Po/igno Industrial Norte,S. Sebastian, pg. 214   IT
Bristo-Myers S.A.E., Isala De Java 1, pg. 255   PB
Bull (Espana) S.A., Paseo Doce Estrellas, No. 2, pg. 317   IT
CAM, Paseo de Recoletos, 27, pg. 662   IT
CAP Gemini Espana, Condesa de Venadito 7, pg. 264   IT
CARBOEX - Sociedad Espanola de Carbon Exterior, S.A., Manuel Cortina, 2, pg. 1224   IT
CASA - Construcciones Aeronauticas, S.A., Avda. Aragon, 404, pg. 1224   IT
CCF Madrid, Paseo de la Castellana No. 91, pg. 342   IT
CEPSA Estaciones de Servicio, S.A., Avda. del Partenon, 12, pg. 323   IT
CIREX - Cia. de Representaciones, Inversiones y Exportac, S.A., General Peron, 38, pg. 1224   IT
COFIR (Corporacion Financiera Reunida), Plaza de Ruiz Picasso, S/N, Edificio Torre Picasso, Planta 12, pg. 240   IT
C.S.I. Corporacion Siderurgia Integral, S.A., Po de la Castellana, 91, pg. 1224   IT
CTE - Compania Trasatlantica Espanola, S.A., General martinez Campos, 46, pg. 1224   IT
Cabinas Telefonicas, S.A. (Cabitel), Pl. Carlos Trias Bertran, 7, (Edificio SOLLUBE), pg. 1371   IT
Cafes La Estrella S.A., pg. 919   IT
Caja ce Madrid de Seguros Generales, S.A. de Seguros y Reaseguros, Eloy Gonzalo, 10, pg. 251   IT
CAJA DE MADRID GROUP, Plaza de Celenque n. 2, pg. 251   IT
Caja Madrid de Pensiones, E.G.F.P., S.A., Eloy Gonzalo, 10, pg. 251   IT
Caja Madrid Vida, S.A. de Seguros y Reaseguros, Eloy Gonzalo, 10, pg. 251   IT
Caja Salud, S.A. de Seguros y Reaseguros, Eloy Gonzalo, 10, pg. 251   IT
Campos Velazguez, S.A., Velazquez,134, pg. 1224   IT
Candela Iberica, S.A., Parque Empresarial, San Fernando de Henares, pg. 300   PB
Canon Espana, S.A., C/Joaquin Costa, No. 41, pg. 262   IT
James Capel-Midland Agencia de Valores S.A., Calle Jose Ortega y Gasset 29, pg. 581   IT
Cargosur, S.A., edificio Iberfreight, Avda. de la Hispanidad, 13, pg. 1225   IT
Cariplo Madrid, Calla Alcala 44, pg. 275   IT
Cartorajes International, S.A., Apartado 632, Avenida De Brasil, 7-6, pg. 905   IT
Caterpillar Financial Leasing, S.A., Cuesta de San Vincente, 4-2 pg. 315   PB
Caterpillar Logistics Services Spain S.A., Castellana 164, pg. 316   PB
Cauda S.A. de Seguros y Reaseguros, Nunez de Balboa 118, pg. 1531   IT
Cedosa, S., 1384   IT
Celulosas de Asturias, Jose Lazaro Galdiano, pg. 567   IT
Cementos Asland S.A., Orense 81, pg. 790   IT
Cementos HISPANIA S.A., pg. 423   IT
Cemex, de S.A. de C.V. - Madrid, Hernandez de Tejada No. 1, pg. 278   IT
Central Hispano Generali, Holding de Entidades de Seguros, S.A., Calle Alcala, 21, pg. 90   IT
Central National Espanola S.A., Joaquin Costa 36, pg. 966   IT
Centro de Informacion y Servicios del Mercado Inmobiliario, S.A., Eloy Gonzalo 10, pg. 251   IT
Centro de Tratameinto de la Documentacion, S.A., San Romualdo, 26, pg. 252   IT
Centro Inmobiliare Caja de Madrid, S.A., Eloy Gonzalo 10, pg. 251   IT
Centro Medico de Chequeos de MAPFRE Vida, Cardenal Herrera Oria, 11, pg. 334   IT
Centro Superior de Marketing, S.A., Villanueva, 10, pg. 252   IT
Centros Commerciales Pryca, Campezo 16, Carretera de Barcelona, km. 11 300, pg. 273   IT
Ceras Alex S.A., Crta. si Irun-km. 12, pg. 611   IT
Ceselsa-Inisel, S.A., Avda. de Burgos, 8 bis, pg. 1224   IT
Cesvimap Internacional, S.A., P. de Recoletos, 23, pg. 333   IT
Charmilles Technologies Iberica S.A., Pol Industrial de tres cantos, pg. 489   IT
Chase Leasing (S.A.E.), Maria de Molina 39, pg. 339   PB
Chase Manhattan Bank Espana S.A., Maria de Molina 39, pg. 340   PB
The Chase Manhattan Bank, N.A., Maria de Molina 39, pg. 340   PB
Chase Manhattan Securities S.A., Maria de Molina 39, pg. 340   PB
Cheque Restaurant, Boresa, Calle Santisima Trinidad 32, 4, pg. 1274   IT

Chiron Iberia S.A., Edificio Dublin, Parque Empresarial San Fernando, pg. 350   PB
Chr. Hansen-Lacta S.L., Alcala, 178, pg. 289   IT
Cimex-Nor S.A., Plaza de Manuel Gomez Moreno, pg. 515   IT
Circle Espana S.A., C/Ferrocarril 25 Nave 18, pg. 372   PB
Citibank Espana S.A., pg. 378   PB
Citilease Internacional, S.A., pg. 379   PB
Citroen Hispania S.A., Doctor Ezquerdo 62, pg. 1020   IT
Claudius Peters (Iberica) S.A., Avda. Alberto Alcocer 46, pg. 131   IT
Club Vida Agencia de Viajes, S.A., Sor Angela de la Cruz, 6, pg. 334   IT
Coca-Cola de Espana, Josefa Valcarcel, 36, pg. 392   PB
Codimesa S.A., Goya 115, pg. 1123   IT
Cognos Espana S.A., Calle Orense, 34 Planta 9, pg. 306   IT
Colborn-Dawes Iberica SA., pg. 1121   IT
Combibloc S.A., C./Caleruega 102-6 dcha., pg. 1156   IT
Comercial Papelera Aldi S.A., Antonio Lopez 67, Portal 1, pg. 886   IT
Commercio Intl. Luso Espansol s.a., Calle Alcala 95, pg. 655   IT
Commerzbank AG Sucursal en Espana, Paseo de la Castellana 110, pg. 311   IT
Compania de Financiacion Case, S.A., Poligono Industrial de Coslada, pg. 1579   PB
COMPANIA ESPANOLA DE PETROLEOS, S.A. (CEPSA), Avenida del Partenon 12, pg. 323   IT
Compania Espanola de Tabaco en Rama, S.A., pg. 1346   IT
Compania Espanola de Tecnologia, S.A., Paseo de la Castellana, 83-85, pg. 1371   IT
Compania Espanola para la Fabricacion de Acero Inoxidable S.A., Doctor Fleming 51, pg. 947   IT
Compania General de Geofisica S.A., Passeo de la Castellana 140, pg. 241   IT
Compania Gestora de Servicio Mensatel, S.A., C/Manuel Tower, 35-3, pg. 1372   IT
Compania Importadora de Maquinas Copladores SA, pg. 757   IT
Compania Logistica de Hidrocarburos - CLH, S.A., Capitan Haya, 41, pg. 1104   IT
Compania Radio Aerea Maritima Espanola, S.A., Barajas Park, La Rioja, pg. 1152   IT
Compania Scholl S.A., Infanta Mercedes, 90, 7th Fl., pg. 1209   IT
Compaq Computer S.A., Gobelas No. 19, pg. 418   PB
COMSIP Automacion S.A., Avenida del Mediterraneo 9, Planta 2, pg. 53   IT
Condepols S.A., Ramirez Arellano 37, pg. 323   IT
Conexiones Telematicas Iberica, S.A., Leganitos, 9, pg. 252   IT
Conquest Europe, Av. Brasil, 7-10, pg. 1483   IT
Construcciones Aeronauticas, SA, Avda John Lennon S/N, pg. 242   PB
Construcciones Aeronauticas, S.A. (CASA), Calle del Rey Francisco, 4, Apartado 193, pg. 1199   PB
Construcciones Telefonicas S.A., Embajadores 189/191, pg. 1365   IT
Consulting Informatico S.A. (CINSA), c/Rosario Pino, #14 4-4A Planta, pg. 1043   PB
Consultora Actuarial y de Pensiones MAPFRE Vida, S.A., Avda. General Peron, 40, pg. 334   IT
Consultores de Pensiones, S.r.l., Gran Via, 20, pg. 91   IT
Continental PET Espana S.A., pg. 1207   IT
Corporacion Financiera Alba S.A., Castello 77, pg. 136   IT
Corporacion Financiera Caja de Madrid, S.A., Eloy Gonzalo, 10, pg. 251   IT
CORPORACION MAPFRE, COMPANIA INTERNACIONAL DE REASEGUROS, S.A., Paseo de Recoletos 25, pg. 332   IT
Covadonga S.A. de Seguros y Reaseguros, Paseo de Castellana, 130, pg. 91   IT
John Crane Iberica S.A., Cemento 1, pg. 1339   IT
Crawford Door S.A., Camino de Rejas, 1, pg. 269   IT
Credit Agricole (CNCA) Madrid, Edisico Sinanco Paseo da La Habana 101, pg. 341   IT
Credit Lyonnais Espana SA, Paseo de la Castellana, 35, pg. 344   IT
Cresan, S.A., Leganitos, 9 y 11, pg. 252   IT
Cresan II, S.A., Leganitos, 9 y 11, pg. 252   IT
Cristaleria Espanola SA, Edificio Ederra, Centro Azca, pg. 1172   IT
Cristaleria Espanola S.A., Edificio Ederra, Centro Azca, Paseo de la Castellana No. 77, pg. 1176   IT
A.T. Cross Espana S.A., Calle Lanuza 14, Bajo, pg. 461   PB
Crown Cork Company (Spain) S.A., Apartado 23, pg. 464   PB
Cyanamid Iberica, S.A., Apartado 471, pg. 81   PB
D & B Software Iberica S.A., Paseo de Eduardo Dato 3, pg. 532   IT
Daewoo Corp. - Madrid, pg. 358   IT
Dai-Ichi Kangyo Bank, Ltd.-Madrid, 5th Floor, Maria de Molina 4, pg. 360   IT
Daiwa Bank-Madrid, Plaza Pablo Ruiz Picasso, S/N, Torre Picasso, 2a Planta, pg. 373   IT
Daiwa Europe (Spain) Sociedad de Valores S.A., Paseo de la Castellana 51-3, pg. 375   IT
Danzas SA, C. Orense, 4-8a, pg. 382   IT
D'Arcy Masius Benton & Bowles, S.A., Lagasca 88, 7th Fl., pg. 304   PV
Data General Spain S.A., Condesa de Venadito 27, pg. 486   PB
Datapoint Iberica S.A., Costa Brava 13, pg. 384   IT
Datasystem S.A., Paseo Doce Estrellas No. 2, pg. 317   IT
De La Rue Lerchundi SA, Hermosilla. 13-3, pg. 386   IT
De La Rue Systems SA, San Severo, s/n, Edificio A-1 Modulo C, pg. 387   IT

PB - *U.S. Public Companies Volume*
PV - *U.S. Private Companies Volume*
IT - *International Public & Private Companies Volume*

1758

Geographic Index-Non U.S.

John Deere Iberica S.A., Apartado de Correos 14.412, pg. 493 **PB**

Defex, S.A., General Peron, 38. Edificio Master-1,9, pg. 1224 **IT**

Dell Espana S.A., Calle San Severo s/n, pg. 496 **PB**

Delsey Espana SA, Calle Luisa Fernanda 27, pg. 192 **IT**

DELTA - Desgasificacion y Limpieza de Tangques, S.A., Padilla, 17, pg. 1223 **IT**

Derivados Del Propileno, S.A. (DERPROSA), Ctra. Montefrios, s/n, pg. 323 **IT**

Derly, S.A., Avda. de la Industria 30, pg. 993 **IT**

Desarollo del Vidrio (Devisa), Edificio Ederra, Centro Azca, pg. 1172 **IT**

Desarrollo de Sistemas de Informacion, S.A., Km. 16,4 Nac. VI-Las Rozas, pg. 91 **IT**

Desarrollo y Comercializacion de Inmuebles, S.A., Eloy Gonzalo, 10, pg. 251 **IT**

Desarrollos Urbanos Ci., Paseo de Recoletos, 25, pg. 334 **IT**

Det Norske Veritas, Campus Empresarial Jose M. de, Churruca, Edificio III, C/Almansa, 397 **IT**

Deutsche Babcock S.A., pg. 398 **IT**

Deutsche Bank AG (Madrid), Paseo de la Castellana, 42, pg. 404 **IT**

Diagonal Sarria, S.A., Eloy Gonzalo, 10, pg. 251 **IT**

Digital Equipment Corporation Espana S.A., C/ Cerro del Castagar, 72, pg. 507 **PB**

DISEL (Diseno e Ingenieria de Sistemas Electronicos S.A.), Ave. de Burgos, 8 Bis, Edificio Genesis, pg. 1032 **PB**

Dista, S.A., Avda. de la Industria, 993 **PB**

Distribucion Quelle, S.A. y Cia SEC, pg. 1346 **IT**

Distribuidora de Productos Petroliferos SA (DISPESA), Corazon de Maria 6, pg. 323 **IT**

Dow Chemical Iberica S.A., Avenida de Burgos 109, pg. 524 **PB**

Dow Jones Markets Espana S.A., Edificio Eurocentro, Ave. General Peron, 29, pg. 525 **PB**

Dresdner Bank AG, Calle Del Pinar 2-4, pg. 419 **IT**

Dun & Bradstreet S.A., Salvador de Madariaga, 1-2o, pg. 537 **PB**

Dynapac S.A., Carretera C-501, km 4,300, Poligono Industrial No 6 de Mostoles, pg. 1420 **IT**

DYWIDAG-Systems International S.A., Poligono Industrial, Matagallegos, pg. 424 **IT**

ECI Telematics International S.A., Barajas Park, San Severo, 20, pg. 644 **IT**

EIB Madrid Branch, Calle Ortega y Gasset 29, pg. 465 **IT**

EMI Music Group, Torrelaguna 64, pg. 427 **IT**

E.N. Bazan de Construcciones Navales Militares, S.A., Paseo de la Castellana, 55, pg. 1224 **IT**

ENCASUR - E.N. Carbonifera del Sur, S.A., Monte Esquinza, 24, pg. 1224 **IT**

ENCE - E.N. de Celulosas, S.A., Avda. de Burgos, 8 bis, pg. 1224 **IT**

ENDESA - Empresa Nacional de Electricidad, S.A., Principe de Vergara, 187, pg. 1224 **IT**

ENSA - Equipos Nucleares, S.A., Plaza Marques de Salamanca, 3, pg. 1224 **IT**

ENUSA - E.N. del Uranio, S.A., Santiago Rusinol, 12, pg. 1224 **IT**

Eastman Christensen de Espana S.A., Orense, 4-8, pg. 167 **PB**

Ebara Espana Bombas S.A., Poligono Los Arenas, C/ Alameda 1, pg. 432 **IT**

Ebasco Espana, S.A., c/o Mendosa Servicios S.A., Niguel Angel No. 1, 1587 **PB**

Ebco Agricolas, Compania de Alimentacion, S.A., pg. 1346 **IT**

Ecogest AIE, Arapiles, 14, pg. 607 **IT**

Edelman Espana S.A., Torre Europa, Paseo Castellana 93-2 1/2, pg. 363 **PV**

Edificaciones en Madrid y Provincia, S.A., P.o. de la Castellana, 83-85, pg. 1447 **IT**

El Aguila S.A., Edificio Eje Sur, c/ Retama no. 3, pg. 608 **IT**

EL CORTE INGLES SA, Calle Hermosilla 112, pg. 435 **IT**

Elanco Premezclas, S.A., pg. 993 **PB**

Elanco, Veterinaria, S.A., pg. 993 **PB**

E.N. Elcano de la Marina Mercante, S.A., P. General Martinez Campos, 46, pg. 1224 **IT**

Electricite de France, Calle Rodriguez Marin, 21, pg. 438 **IT**

Electrolux S.A., Apartado 627, pg. 443 **IT**

Electronics Arts Software S.A., C/Moratin, 52, 4 DCHA, pg. 569 **PB**

Elquiber, S.A., pg. 994 **IT**

ELVIAseg S.A., Edificio Gorbea 3, Jose BardasanoBaos, 9-5to Izda., pg. 60 **IT**

EMESTA Empressa Espanola de Tabacos S.L., Edificio Link, C/Gobelas, 25-27 3a Planta, pg. 1101 **IT**

Empresa Auxiliar de la Industria, Auxini, S.A., Padilla, 46, pg. 1224 **IT**

EMTEC Magnetics Iberica SA, Velazques, 140 Bis, pg. 743 **IT**

Encore Computer Espana S.A., Augustin de Foxa, 25-2nd Planta, pg. 580 **PB**

Enraf-Nonius Iberica S.A., Avda del Llano Castellano 43, pg. 389 **IT**

Enskilda Espana S.A., Zurbano 17, pg. 1259 **IT**

Enso Iberica S.A., Paseo de la Castellana 135, pg. 457 **IT**

Envases y Alimentacion Madrid, S.A., Number 1, 14 Floor, pg. 1386 **PB**

Eptisa SA, Arapiles 14, pg. 608 **IT**

Epysa, Calle Alcala, 95, pg. 790 **IT**

Equipos Agricolas Alfa-Laval S.A., Apartado 31015, pg. 1377 **IT**

Ericsson Redes S.A., Av. Burgos, 12-20, pg. 1367 **IT**

Ericsson, S.A., Calle Maria de Molina, 41-43, pg. 1367 **PV**

Ericsson Sistemas Avanzados S.A., Rosario Pino 14-16, Piso 2, 1367 **IT**

Ericsson Telecomunicaciones S.A., c/Torres Quevedo 2, Poligono Industrial, 1368 **IT**

Ericsson Terminales Moviles S.A., Calle Silva 6-10, pg. 1368 **IT**

Eritel, S.A., Paseo De La Castellana, 141, pg. 1372 **IT**

Escuelas de Idiomas Berlitz de Espana, S.A., Gran Via 80-4, pg. 222 **PB**

Cia. Espanola de Petroleos Atlantico, S.A., Avda. America 32, pg. 323 **IT**

Esselte S.A., Tomas Redondo S/N, Edificio Luarca, pg. 461 **IT**

Estacionamientos Subterraneos Montevideo, S.A., Orense, 11, pg. 252 **IT**

Estado Solido, S.A., Hortaleza, 106, pg. 252 **IT**

Estrategias Telefonicas, S.A. (Estratel), Principe de Vergara, 110, pg. 1371 **IT**

Eurest Espagne, Princessa 5, pg. 21 **IT**

EURO RSCG, Zurbano 46/48, pg. 602 **IT**

Eurofip (Madrid), Calle Serrano 67, pg. 163 **IT**

Euroforum Escorial, S.A., Arroyo del Fresno, 19, pg. 252 **IT**

Euroforum Torrealta, S.A., Arroyo del Fresno, 19, pg. 252 **IT**

Europ Assistance Espana S.A., Calle Orense, 4, pg. 91 **IT**

Europ Assistance Servicios S.A., Calle Orense, 4, pg. 91 **IT**

Eurotherm Espana SA, C/La Granja 74, Pol. Ind. Alcobendas, pg. 466 **IT**

Eurovida S.A. (Allianz-RAS/Banco Popular), c/Jose Ortega y Gasset, 29, pg. 60 **IT**

Expandite S.A., Avenedia General Peron 8-3B, pg. 236 **IT**

Eyelet Iberica, S.A., Torrejon de Ardoz, KM 21400, Calle Ebro, pg. 464 **PB**

FCA!BMZ CID, Carbonero y Sol # 12, pg. 469 **IT**

FCA!BMZ Madrid, Carbonero y Sol, 12, pg. 470 **IT**

Fanuc Iberia, S.A., C/Alfonso Gomez, Planta 1, pg. 478 **IT**

Felguera-IHI S.A., Esplandin 11-5, pg. 689 **IT**

Fernando Roque TISA, pg. 1145 **IT**

Fiat Auto Espana S.A., Paseo de la Habana 74, pg. 481 **IT**

Fiat Iberica, S.A., Calle Serrano 67, pg. 483 **IT**

Figueroa, Avenida Jose Antonio, pg. 662 **IT**

Fina Iberica S.A., c/Sepulveda 7B, Poligono Industrial, pg. 1043 **IT**

Finadis S.A., pg. 1015 **IT**

Financial Security Assurance (U.K.) Limited, Paseo de la Castellana 36-38, Edificio Castellana, pg. 623 **PB**

Finanmadrid Entidad de Financiacion, S.A., Eloy Gonzalo, 10, pg. 251 **IT**

Finanz Charterhouse Iberica, SA, Paseo de la Castellana, 110, pg. 343 **IT**

Finex Espana, E.F., S.A., Paseo de Recoloetos, 33, pg. 332 **IT**

Georg Fischer S.A., Calle Isla de la Palma, 32 Nave 1, pg. 490 **IT**

Robert Fleming Spain SA, Paseo de la Castellana 40 Bis, pg. 494 **IT**

Flender Iberica S.A., Avda. General Perron 8, 8b Apartado 3159, pg. 400 **IT**

Flowmax S.A., Avenida de Burgos, 16E, pg. 710 **IT**

Fomento de Obras Urbanas Europeas, S.A., Ortega y Gasset, 22 y 24, pg. 252 **IT**

Fonditel Entidad Gestora de Fondos de Pensiones, S.A., Pedro Teixeira, 8, pg. 1371 **IT**

Fonogram S.A., Avenida de America y Hernandez de Tejada, pg. 1052 **IT**

Food Premier, S.A., pg. 1345 **IT**

Ford Credit S.A., Paseo de la Castellana 135, pg. 665 **PB**

Ford Espana S.A., Paseo de la Castellana 135, pg. 665 **PB**

Ford Leasing S.A., Paseo de la Castellana 135, pg. 665 **IT**

Foster Wheeler Energia, S.A., Parque Empresarial Madrid-, Las Rozas, NVI Ctra. de la Corvna, pg. 677 **PB**

Foster Wheeler Iberica S.A., Calle Gabriel, pg. 677 **PB**

FoxVideo (Espanola) S.A., Pl. de la Castellana 141, pg. 926 **IT**

Frigoscandia Food Process Systems S.A., Sucursal Espana, C/Julian Camarillo, 26-4 Local 2, pg. 607 **PB**

Fujisawa SA, pg. 525 **IT**

Fujitsu Espana, SA, P de la Castellana, pg. 528 **IT**

GESTRA Espanola S.A., Luis Cabrera, 86-88, pg. 550 **IT**

GGK Madrid, Conde de Aranda 24-30, pg. 1335 **IT**

Gambro S.A., Principe de Vergara, 43-2A, pg. 668 **IT**

Gan Espana Seguros Generales y Vida, Edificio Gan, Calle Ramirez De Arellano, 37, pg. 564 **IT**

Generale Bank - Banco Belga, Jose Ortega y Gasset 29-6A, pg. 547 **IT**

Geninver S.A., Paseo de la Castellana, 130, pg. 91 **IT**

Gensegur, Agencia de Seguros Grupo Generali, S.A., Calle Nunez de Balboa, 46, pg. 91 **IT**

Geotronics S.A., Av. Camino ce lo Cortao, 24-Nave 4, Poligono Industrial Sur, pg. 1290 **IT**

Gesbansander, Plaza de Manuel Gomez Moreno 2, pg. 143 **IT**

Gesmadrid Patrimonios, S.G.C., S.A., Eloy Gonzalo, 10, pg. 251 **IT**

Gesmadrid S.G.I.I.C., S.A., Eloy Gonzalo, 10, pg. 251 **IT**

Gestion de Centros Culturales, S.A., Preciados, 44, pg. 251 **IT**

Gestion Moda Shopping S.A., Avenida General Peron, 40, pg. 334 **IT**

Gestora de Seguros de MAPFRE Diversos, Sociedad de Agencia, S.A., Francisco de Rojas, 12, pg. 332 **IT**

Gillette Espanola, S.A., Agustin de Foxa, 27, 10, pg. 744 **PB**

Goldman Sachs International, Paseo de la Castellana, 21, 2nd Fl., pg. 462 **PV**

Graco S.A. Succursale Espagnole, Avenida de Castilla No. 32, Nave 82, pg. 757 **PB**

Gran Circulo de Madrid, S.A., Eloy Gonzalo 10, pg. 251 **IT**

GrandMet Foods Southern Europe, C/Cochabamba, 2, pg. 409 **IT**

Granges Essem Iberica S.A., Calle Dr. Flemming 51,2, pg. 443 **IT**

Group Accor Espana, Avenida de Burgos 10, pg. 21 **IT**

Groupo Caja Postal, Paseo de Recoletos 10, pg. 81 **IT**

Gruner + Jahr (Espana) Distribuidora S.A., Marques de Villamagna 4, pg. 190 **IT**

Grupo Banco Exterior, Paseo de Recoletos 10, pg. 80 **IT**

Grupo Barro Testa, C. Pedro de Valdivia 36, pg. 1377 **IT**

GRUPO IBERIA, Velasquez 130, pg. 574 **IT**

Grupo Iberphone Inversiones, S.A., Plaza de Santo Domingo, 1, pg. 252 **IT**

Guerlain S.A.E., Ant. Ctra. de Burgos, pg. 780 **IT**

HISALBA - Hornos Ibericos Alba S.A., Nunez de Balboa 35 A, pg. 629 **IT**

Hachette Filipacchi SA, 23 Santa Engracia, pg. 795 **IT**

Hachette Interdeco SA, Calle Tormes, 7, pg. 795 **IT**

Halesa Ltd., pg. 982 **IT**

Hartmann & Braun S.A., pg. 835 **IT**

Hebra Promocion e Inversiones, S.A., pg. 1345 **IT**

Heinemann Iberia SA, Calle Almagro, 2-2 dcha., pg. 1094 **IT**

Heinz Iberica, S.A., Plaza de Las Cortes 2-4, pg. 806 **PB**

Herbalife International Espana, S.A., Calle Marconi 5Y7, Poligono de Coslada, pg. 809 **PB**

Hercules Aerospace Espana, S.A., pg. 810 **PB**

Hidro Nitro Espanola, Calle Castello 128, pg. 1030 **IT**

Hipotebansa, Plaza de Manuel Gomez Moreno, pg. 143 **IT**

Hirschmann Espana S.A., Calle Albala, pg. 1108 **IT**

Hispaland, S.A., P.o. de la Castellana, 83-85, pg. 1447 **IT**

Hispasat, S.A., Gobelas, 41-45, 2nd Fl., pg. 1372 **IT**

Hoesch Industria Espanola de Suspensiones, S.A., Avda. San Martin de la Vega n 24, pg. 508 **IT**

Holmen Espana S.A. (MoDo Iberica SA), Principe de Vergara, 33-20 Izq., pg. 885 **IT**

Philipp Holzmann Iberica, S.A., Velazquez, 140-21, pg. 633 **PB**

Honeywell SA, Josefa Valcarcel 24, pg. 835 **PB**

Hotel Ritz Madrid S.A., c/o B Plaza De La Lealtad 5, pg. 556 **IT**

Howmedica Iberica S.A., Manuel Tovar, 25, pg. 1283 **PB**

Hydro Agri Espana S.A., Villanueva 13, pg. 962 **IT**

IBJ Espana, Torre Picasso Planta 9, pg. 676 **IT**

IBM Espana Distribuidora de Productos, S.A., Paseo de la Castellana, 4, pg. 898 **PB**

ICA - RODIO, Paseo de la Castellana, pg. 454 **IT**

ICC Iberica S.A., Paseo de la Castellana 115, pg. 554 **PV**

ICI-Mevisa, Calle Costa Brava 13, Edificio Mirasierra, pg. 665 **IT**

ICL Espana International Computers S.A., Luchana 23, pg. 529 **IT**

I.C.S.A. - Internacional de Composites, S.A., Julian Camarillo, 32, pg. 1224 **IT**

IDG Communications, S.A., Fortuny, 18-4, pg. 570 **PV**

INESPAL - Industria Espanola del Aluminio, S.A., Jose Abascal, 2 y 4, pg. 1225 **IT**

Ini Medioambiente, S.A., Zurbaran 29, 1. y 2. pl., pg. 1225 **IT**

INITEC - E.N. de Ingenieria y Tecnologia, S.A., Padilla, 17, pg. 1225 **IT**

Iber-Swiss Catering, S.A., Carretera de la Munoza, s/n., pg. 1225 **IT**

Iberia, Velasquez 130, pg. 574 **IT**

Iberia Cargo, Velazquez 130, pg. 574 **IT**

Iberia Lineas Aereas de Espana, S.A., Velazquez, 130, pg. 1224 **IT**

Iberia - Spain, Velazquez 130, pg. 575 **IT**

Iberia Tecnologia, S.A., Velazquez, 130, pg. 1225 **IT**

Iberoasistencia, S.A., Claudio Coello, 123, pg. 334 **IT**

Iberphone, S.A., Plaza de Santo Domingo, 1, pg. 252 **IT**

Igemisa, Fernandez de la Hoz,58, Semisoto C, pg. 608 **IT**

Indumob, S.A., P.o. de la Castellana, 83-85, pg. 1447 **IT**

The Industrial Bank of Japan, Limited (Madrid Branch), Torre Picasso Planta 9, Plaza Pablo Ruiz Picasso, s/n. AZCA, pg. 675 **IT**

Industrias Transformadoras del Cemento Eternit SA, Mejia Lequerica 10, pg. 1092 **IT**

Industrias Traterh, S.A., Rufino Gonzalez 46, pg. 1222 **IT**

Infoinvest, S.A., Avda. Burgos, 8 bis, pg. 1225 **IT**

Infoleasing SAF, S.A., Avda. Burgos, 8 bis, pg. 1225 **IT**

Infoservicios, S.A., Emilio Munoz, 31, pg. 251 **IT**

Ingeniera de Telecomunicaciones e Instalaciones, S.A., Calle Eduardo Torroja, 15-17 Poligono Industrial de Caslada, pg. 1368 **IT**

Iniberica, S.A., P.o. de la Castellana, 83-85, pg. 1447 **IT**

Inmobiliaria Calvo-Barbara, Paseo de Recoletos, 25, pg. 335 **IT**

Instalaciones y Proyectos de Telecomunicaciones, S.A., P.o de la Castellana, 83-85, pg. 1447 **IT**

Intel Iberia SA, Yuelines, pg. 887 **PB**

Intercaser S.A. de Seguros y Reaseguros, EDP Ctr., Parador del Sol 3, pg. 1256 **IT**

Intercontinental Quimica, S.A. (INTERQUISA), Avda. del Partenon, 12, pg. 323 **IT**

Intergraph (Espana) S.A., Calle Gobelas, 47-49, La Florida, pg. 892 **PB**

International Business Machines, S.A.E., Paseo de la Castellana, 4, pg. 898 **PB**

International Flavors & Fragrances (Espana) S.A., Paseo De La Castellana, pg. 899 **PB**

International Marketing & Promotions Madrid, Lagasca 88, 7th Fl., pg. 304 **PV**

Interprestige, S.A., pg. 1345 **IT**

Inverban, S.V.B., S.A., Serrano 39, pg. 251 **IT**

Inversion y Comercializacion de Immuebles, S.A., Eloy Gonzalo 10, pg. 251 **IT**

PB - *U.S. Public Companies Volume*
PV - *U.S. Private Companies Volume*
IT - *International Public & Private Companies Volume*

Cia. de Investigacion y Explotaciones Petroliferas, S.A. (CIEPSA), Auda America, 32, pg. 323 IT
Italstrade-Spain, Celle Orense 16, pg. 655 IT
Itsemap Iberica, S.A., Paseo de Recoletos, 25, pg. 332 IT
JOTSA, S.A. Empressa Constructor, Edificio Vega Velazquez 157, pg. 634 IT
Jacobs Suchard Espana S.A., Paseo de la Castellana 149, pg. 1289 PB
Janssen-Cilag, Edificio Johonson & Johnson, Passeo de las Doce Estrellas 57-5 Planta, pg. 929 PB
Japan Airlines Company, Ltd., c/Luchana, 23 6-2, pg. 701 IT
Jaramiel Sociedad de Inversion Mobiliaria S.A., Pedro de Valdivia, 10, pg. 334 IT
Jauch & Huebener KGaA, Corredores de Reaseguro, pg. 118 PB
Johnson & Johnson S.A. Consumer, Apartado 79, pg. 931 PB
Johnson's Wax Espanola, S.A., Calle Orense 4-6.a, pg. 593 PV
KME Iberica S.L., Zurbano 34 3 dcha, pg. 719 IT
KSB-AMVI S.A., pg. 721 IT
Kleinwort Benson Espana S.A., Paseo de la Castellana, 151, pg. 420 IT
Kleinwort Benson Iberfomento Funciones & Adquicisiones S.A., Paseo de la Castellana, 151, 6th Fl., pg. 420 IT
Kodak S.A., Laboratorio Fotografico, Poligono Industrial, pg. 554 PB
Komatsu Espana S.A., Avenida de la Constitucion s/n, pg. 744 IT
KONE Elevadores, S.A., Enrique Larreta, 5-1, pg. 747 IT
Korn/Ferry International, Calle Felipe IV, #9, pg. 633 PV
Kredietbank Oficina de Representacion, Paseo de la Castellana 95, pg. 760 IT
Krupp Iberica, S.A., Antonio Cabezon 71, pg. 510 IT
Kubota Servicios Espana S.A., Ctra. del Barrio de la Fortuna, s/n Cuatro Vientos, pg. 763 IT
Kvaerner Eureka Espanola S.A., Parque Empresarial Las Rozas, Complejo Europa Empresarial, pg. 767 IT
LGT Asset Management PLC Spain, Torre de Colon II, Planta 20, pg. 809 IT
LA BANDA DE AGUSTIN MEDINA S.A., Espronceda, 40, pg. 783 IT
La Estrella S.A. de Seguros y Reaseguros, Gran Via, 7, pg. 91 IT
La Veneciana S.A., Edificio Ederra, Centro Azca, pg. 1173 IT
Labinal Espana, 3 Calle, Zacarias Homs, pg. 787 IT
Laboratorios Knoll, S.A., Avda. de Burgos, 91, pg. 109 IT
Laminados Oviedo-Cordoba S.A., Zurbano, 34 3 dcha, pg. 720 IT
Landis & Staefa BC, S.A., Batalla del Salado 25, pg. 800 IT
Laura Ashley Espana SA, Calle Antonio Maura No. 10, Piso 3, pg. 804 IT
Lever Iberica S.A., Manuel de Falla, pg. 1437 IT
Liberia Arte y Cultura, S.A., Avda. General Peron, 40, pg. 334 IT
Arthur D. Little S.R.C., General Peron 40A, pg. 671 PV
Litton Precision Products (Spain), Condes de Val 8, pg. 1004 PB
LLoyd Adratico Espana, Orense 81, pg. 60 IT
Loctite Espana, S.A., Poligona Industrial Alparrache, pg. 611 IT
Louis Vuitton Espana S.A., Calle Jose Ortega y Gasset 17, pg. 782 IT
Lowe RZR, Calle Carbonero y Sol 15, pg. 678 PV
Lubricantes Del Sur, S.A. (LUBRISUR), Avda. America 32, pg. 323 IT
Lubrizol Espanola, S. A., Paseo Castellana 50, 4, pg. 1016 PB
Lucent Technologies Microelectronica S.A., Albadete 1, Apartado 190, pg. 1019 PB
Lucent Technologies Network Systems Espana S.A., Ronda de Valdecarnzo, 14-N2, pg. 1018 PB
Lurgi Espanola S.A., Edificio Eurocentro, Planta 9, pg. 861 IT
MacNeal-Schwendler Iberica S.A., Castellena 141, pg. 1032 PB
Madrid Hipotecaria, S.C.H., S.A., Eloy Gonzalo, 10, pg. 251 IT
Madrid Leasing Corporation, S.A.F., S.A., Eloy Gonzalo, 10, pg. 251 IT
Madrid Representative Office, Paseo del la Castellana, 50, pg. 1517 IT
Mahou S.A., Paseo Imperial, 32, pg. 381 IT
Makita, S.A., Avenida de la Canada, 64-66, pg. 832 IT
Makro Autoservicio Mayorista, S.A., Calle Campezo, 7, pg. 1155 IT
Mannesmann Importacion y Exportcation SA, pg. 838 IT
Mannesmann Kienzle SA, pg. 839 IT
Mantequerias Arias S. A., Orense 2, pg. 201 IT
MAPFRE Asistencia Cia. Internacional de Seguros y Reaseguros, S.A., Claudio Coello, 123, pg. 334 IT
MAPFRE Caucion y Credito Cia Internacional de Seguros y Reaseguros, S.A., Paseo de Recoletos, 29, pg. 335 IT
MAPFRE Consultores de Seguros y Reaseguros, S.A., Paseo de Recoletos, 25, pg. 333 IT
MAPFRE Factoring E.F., S.A., Gobelas 41-43, pg. 332 IT
MAPFRE Finanzas Entidad de Financiacion, S.A., Gobelas 41-43, pg. 332 IT
MAPFRE Hipotecaria S.C.H., S.A., Gobelas 41-43, pg. 332 IT
MAPFRE Industrial, S.A. de Seguros, Paseo de Recoletos, 23, pg. 333 IT
MAPFRE Inmuebles, S.A., Prieto Urena, 6, pg. 334 IT
MAPFRE International S.A., Paseo de Recoletos, 25, pg. 333 IT
MAPFRE Inversion S.V., S.A., Avda. General Peron, 40, pg. 334 IT
MAPFRE Inversion 2, Soc. Gestora de Instituciones de Inversion Colectiva, Pedro de Valdivia, 10, pg. 334 IT
MAPFRE Leasing S.A., Gobelas 41-43, pg. 332 IT
MAPFRE Re Cia Reaseguros, S.A., Paseo de Recoletos, 25, pg. 334 IT
MAPFRE Seguros Generales Cia. de Seguros y Reaseguros, S.A., Paseo de Recoletos, 23, pg. 332 IT
MAPFRE Servicios de Caucion, S.A., Paseo de Recoletos, 25, pg. 335 IT
MAPFRE Servicios Informatica, S.A., pg. 333 IT
Mapfre Soft, S.A., Ctra. Pozuelo-Majadahonda, pg. 335 IT
MAPFRE Vida Pensiones Entidad Gestora de Fondos de Pensiones S.A., Avda. General Peron, 40, pg. 334 IT
Mapfre Vida, S.A. de Seguros y Reaseguros sobre la Vida Humana, Avda. General Peron, 40, pg. 334 IT
MAPFRE Video y Comunicaion, S.A., Sor Angela de la Cruz, 6, pg. 334 IT
Mapte, S.A, c/Orense, 11, 1st Fl., pg. 1372 IT
Maritz Espana S.A. (Spain), Calle Pinar 7, pg. 704 PV
Marquette Espana S.A., pg. 1047 PB
McDonald's Sistemas de Espana, c/Jose Bardasano Baos, 9, Edificio Gorbea, 3-1, pg. 1069 PB
McGraw Hill Interamericana de Espana S.A., Edificio A, Ctra. de la Coruna Km. 12, pg. 1072 PB
Medelec Espana S.A., Avd Matapinoneras 2, pg. 1467 IT
Mediacion y Diagnosticos, S.A., Eloy Gonzalo 10, pg. 251 IT
Medtronic Hispania S.A., Traverisia de Costa Brava 6, pg. 1083 PB
Melitta Iberica S.A., pg. 857 IT
Memorex Telex, S.A., Gobelax, 15-La Florida, Ctra. La Coruna, km. 13, pg. 858 IT
Menalvaro, S.A., P.o. de la Castellana, 83-85, pg. 1447 IT
Mercedes-Benz Espana, S.A., Jose Ortega y Gasset 22/24, pg. 369 IT
Merloni Elettrodomestici S.A., San Sebastian de Los Reyes, Aven. Da Fuente Nueva 4, pg. 860 IT
MICROS-Fidelio Hispania S.L., Calle Diego De Leon, 31-1B, pg. 1106 PB
Micros Systems Hispania S.L., Calle Diego De Leon 31, pg. 1107 PB
Microsoft Iberica S.R.L., pg. 1108 PB
Millipore Iberica S.A., Avda. del Llano Castellano, 13 3A, pg. 1113 PB
Milupa S.A., Carretera de Andalucia, pg. 991 IT
Minas De Gador S.A., General Zabala 24, pg. 803 IT
Minco Iberica, pg. 1326 IT
Minemet SA-Spain, Calle Alfonso XII, pg. 661 IT
Miraceti, S.A., Avda. General Peron, 40, pg. 334 IT
Mitsui & Co. Europe (Espana) S.A., Calle Orense 4, 7/A Planta, pg. 880 IT
Mitsukoshi Espana S.A., Gran Via, 74, pg. 884 IT
Mobil Oil Espana, S.A., Maria de Molina 40, pg. 1119 PB
MoDo Iberica SA, Principe de Vergara 33-2o, pg. 887 IT
Moody's Investors Service Espana, S.A., pg. 537 PB
Morgan Gestion S.A., Jose Ortega y Gasset, 29, pg. 1130 PB
Morgan Grenfell (Spain), Jose Abasca; 55, pg. 406 IT
Morgan Guaranty Trust Company, Jose Ortega y Gasset, 29, pg. 1130 PB
J.P. Morgan Espana S.A., Jose Ortega y Gasset, 29, pg. 1130 PB
J.P. Morgan Iberica S.L., Jose Ortega y Gasset, 29, pg. 1131 PB
J.P. Morgan Sociedad de Valores y Bolsa, S.A., Jose Ortega y Gasset, 29, pg. 1131 PB
Morgan Stanley Madrid, Fortuny 6, Ala Norte-Zona B, pg. 1133 PB
Motorola Espana S.A., Alberto Alcocer 46, pg. 1139 PB
Munters Spain SA, C/Almansa 62, pg. 669 IT
Musini, Sociedad Mutua de Seguros y Reaseguros a Prima Fija, Padilla, 46, pg. 1225 IT
NAVINTEC - Naval de Investigacion y Tecnologia, S.A., Ochandiano, 12,El Plantio, pg. 1223 IT
NIFE Espana S.A., Avda. Llano Castellano 13, pg. 53 IT
Nacional Hispanica, S.A. de Seguros y Reaseguros, Paseo de la Castellana, 52, pg. 91 IT
National Can Iberica SA, Ctra. Comarcal 600, pg. 1029 IT
National Westminster Bank Plc, Principe de Vergara, 125, pg. 911 IT
Nationale-Nederlanden Spain, Calle Severo Ochoa 2, pg. 651 IT
Naviera Castellana, S.A., Padilla, 17, pg. 1223 IT
Nederman Iberica S.A., C/. Buganvilla, 2, pg. 283 IT
A.C. Nielsen Company S.A., C/Salvador de Madariaga, 1, pg. 1183 PB
Nikko Espana Sociedad de Valores, S.A., Paseo de la Castellana 31-7, pg. 930 IT
Nissho Iwai Iberia S.A., Plaza de Colon N., 2 Edeficio Torres de Colon, pg. 948 IT
Nokia Mobile Phones, Miniparc 1, Edificio F, Azalea, 1, pg. 952 IT
Nomura Espana Sociedad de Valores, S.A., Alcala 44, 3-A, pg. 957 IT
Norsk Hydro Espana S.A., Villanueva 13, pg. 964 IT
Norsk Hydro Handelsselskap A/S, Villanueva 13, pg. 964 IT
Norske Skog Espana S.A., Paseo de la Castellana, 143, pg. 966 IT
Northern Telecom S.A., Avenida de las, Dos Castillas 33-1, pg. 970 IT
Novell Spain, Paseo de la Castellana 40 bis, 5a, pg. 1204 PB
Novo Nordisk Bioindustrial S.A., P de la Castellana, 153-8B, pg. 989 IT
Novo Nordisk Pharma S.A., C/Calerueja 102, pg. 988 IT
Novoferm Espana S.A., Travesia de Navaluenga 27, pg. 509 IT
Nucleron S.A., C. Montera 33, pg. 389 IT
Nutricia S.A., pg. 992 IT
OCLI Optical Coatings Espana S.A., 7th Floor Suite D, Antonio Leyva, 92, pg. 1227 PB
OUP Espana, Edificio E, Parque Empresarial, San Fernando, Esc. B Planta 2a, AVDA. de, pg. 1019 IT
Oki Systems (Iberica) S.A., C/Goya 9, pg. 1000 IT
OMRON Electronics S.A., C/Arturo Soria 95, pg. 1006 IT
Onduladores Del Norte S.A., Azufre 8-10, Poligono Industrial Sur, pg. 287 IT
Orange Info 'Products, pg. 757 IT
Otresa, Poligono Industrial Urtinsa, Calle de las industrias, pg. 789 IT
Outokumpu Espana S.A., C/Jazmin, 66 Piso 4l, pg. 1015 IT
Outokumpu Minera Espanola S.A., Agustin de Foxa, 25-60 B, pg. 1016 IT
Outokumpu Rawmet S.A., C/Jazmin, 66-4 Izquierda, pg. 1017 IT
P.C. Henderson (Espanola) S.A., Capitan Haya, 56-2.C, pg. 615 IT
PRESUR - Prerreducidos Integrados del Suroeste de Espana, S.A., Claudio Coello, 20, pg. 1224 IT
PUCARSA - Puerto de Carboneras, S.A., Principe de Vergara, 187, pg. 1224 IT
P.Y.C.A.S.A.-La Cocinera, Apartado 54, Carretera de Loeches, 49, pg. 380 IT
Pabellon de Operadores Europeos de Telecomunicaciones, S.A. (P.O.E.T.), Gran Via, 28, pg. 1372 IT
Pall Espana S.A., Corcega 2, pg. 1254 PB
Panalpina Transportes Mundiales S.A., pg. 1023 IT
Parker Hannifin Espana S.A., Parque Industrial Las Monjas, Calle de las Estaciones 8, pg. 1263 PB
Pechiney Espana, Calle Castello, 128, pg. 1031 IT
Pefipresa S.A., San Usamo 22-24, pg. 1071 IT
Penarroya Espana, Calle Alfonso XII, 30, pg. 662 IT
Pepsi-Cola de Espana, S.A., Plaza de la Lealtad, 4, pg. 1277 PB
RICARDO PEREZ ASOCIADOS, Lagasca 92, 1st Fl., pg. 1036 IT
Perstorp Flooring Iberia, c/ Padilla 19 1 l, pg. 1039 IT
Petrogal Espanola, S.A., Plaza Descubridor Diego de Ordas, pg. 1045 IT
Petrolite Iberica, S.A., Marques de Urquijo 8, pg. 166 PB
Petroquimica Espanola, S.A. (PETRESA), Avda. Partenon, 12, pg. 323 IT
Peugeot Talbot Espana, Carretera Madrid Getafe por Villaverde, pg. 1021 IT
Pfizer S.A., Principe de Vergera, 109, pg. 1284 PB
Pharmacia & Upjohn Farmoquimica, S.A., Albacete 5-7o Edificio Adf., pg. 1049 IT
Pignone Espanola S.A., Oficina Commercial, Calle Velazquez 100, pg. 991 IT
Playa De Madrid, S.A., Paseo De La Castellana, 83-85, pg. 1371 IT
Pleyade Peninsular Correduria de Seguros, S.A., Avenida General Peron, 38, pg. 1371 IT
Pluritel de Comunicacaiones, S.A., Eloy Gonzalo 10, pg. 251 IT
Poclain Hispana S.A., Poligono Industrial de Coslada, Avenida Jo, pg. 1580 PB
Polaroid (Espana) S.A., Nunez De Balboa, 56, pg. 1314 PB
Poligono de Actividades Logisticas, PAL - Coslada, S.A., Garcia de paredes, 92, pg. 252 IT
Polydor S.A., Avenida de America y Hernandez de Tejada, pg. 1053 IT
Polysius S.A., Pl. Manuel Gomez Moreno, pg. 512 IT
Porsche Espana S.A., Edificio Cuzco IV, pg. 1063 IT
Portfolio Inmobiliario, S.A., Eloy Gonzalo 10, pg. 251 IT
Potasas de Llobregat, S.A., Nunez de Balboa, 108, pg. 1225 IT
Praxair Espania S.A., Orense 11, pg. 1320 PB
Principal International Espana S.A. de Seguros de Vida, C/ Alcala Galiano 4, pg. 886 PV
Procoter, S.A., P.o. de la Castellana, 83-85, pg. 1447 IT
Procter & Gamble Espana S.A., Av Del Partneon, 16-18, pg. 1332 PB
Productos Asfalticos, S.A. (PROAS), Avda. America 32, pg. 323 IT
Productos Cosmeticos S.A., Av. Constitucion, 2, pg. 1490 IT
Productos Pepsi Co., S.A., Plaza de la Lealtad, pg. 1278 PB
Productos Roche S.A., Carretera de Carabanchel a la Andalucia, pg. 1121 IT
Promapf, S.A., C/Prieto Urena, 6, pg. 333 IT
Proyectos y Desarrollos Urbanisticos, S.A., Plaza de Celenque, 2, pg. 252 IT
Proyectos y Programas Inmobiliarios, S.A., Paseo de la Castellana 66, pg. 251 IT
Quavitae, S.A., Serrano, 23, pg. 252 IT
R.J. Reynolds Tobacco Espana, S.A.E., Alcala No. 115, pg. 1355 PB
RAD (Rose Abascal SA), Marques de Villamejnz, pg. 394 IT
Radiometer Espana S.A., C/Caramuel 38, pg. 1084 IT
Radiored Uno, S.A., Manuel Torres, 35, pg. 1372 IT
Rail Europe Espana, pg. 1165 IT
Reader's Digest Selecciones S.A., Golfode Salonica 27-4 A, pg. 1368 PB
Readymix Asland S.A., Avenida de Brasil 13-20, pg. 791 IT
Recoletos Compania Editorial SA, 14 Paseo Recoletos, pg. 1027 IT
Recordati-Elmu S.L., Carr.ra Nacional III, Km 23, pg. 1090 IT
Red Electrica de Espana, S.A., Paseo Conde de los Gaitanes, 179, Urbanizacion La Moraleja, pg. 1224 IT
Redland Iberica S.A., Plaza de la Independencia 5, pg. 1093 IT
Reemtsma Espana S.A., Edificio Link, C/Gobelas, 25-27 3a Planta La Florida, pg. 1101

PB - *U.S. Public Companies Volume*
PV - *U.S. Private Companies Volume*
IT - *International Public & Private Companies Volume*

Refractarios Norton, S.A., Calle San Fernando, 8, pg. 1175 IT
Registro de Prestaciones Informaticas, S.A., Capitan Haya, 51, pg. 252 IT
Relecmap, S.A., Paseo de Recoletos, 25, pg. 333 IT
Repsol Butano S.A., Arcipreste de Hita, 10, pg. 1104 IT
Repsol Comercial de Productos Petroliferos, S.A., P. de la Castellana, 278-280, pg. 1104 IT
Repsol Derivados, Orense, 34, pg. 1104 IT
Repsol Distribucion, S.A., Orense, 34, pg. 1104 IT
Repsol Exploracion, Paseo de la Castellana, 280, pg. 1104 IT
Repsol Petroleo, Paseo de la Castellana, 278, pg. 1104 IT
Repsol Quimica, Paseo de la Castellana, 278-280, pg. 1104 IT
REPSOL S.A., Paseo de la Castellana 278, pg. 1104 IT
Retail Brands SA, Goya 115 1, pg. 338 IT
R.J. Reynolds Espana, S.L., pg. 1346 IT
Rhone-Poulenc Delegation Generale, Calle de Capitan Haya 1-6e Piso, pg. 1113 IT
Richardson Electronics Iberica S.A., Calle Hierro 9, 1a Planta, Nave 10, Edificio Lagazpi, pg. 1388 PB
Richardson-Vicks S.A., Jose Lazaro, Galdiano 6, 5th Fl., pg. 1333 PB
A.H. Robins Farmaceutica, S.A., c/Rufino Gonzalez No 50, pg. 82 PB
Rockwell Automation S.A., Belmonte de Tajo, 31, pg. 1400 PB
Rorer, S.A., Calle Francisco Sanecha, Inc., pg. 1112 IT
Ross Systems S.L. Iberica, pg. 1406 PB
Rovifarma S.A., Rufino Gonzalez 50, pg. 1283 PB
Royal Guest, S.A., Jose Abascal, 58, pg. 252 IT
Ruiz Nicoli Group, c/ Plaza de Manuel Gomez Moreno, s/n, pg. 603 IT
S&C Willis Corroon Correduria de Seguros y Reaseguros S.A., C/ Rafael Calvo 18, pg. 1509 IT
SAB Iberica S.A., Mar Tirreno, 7 y 9, pg. 271 IT
SAB WABCO S.A., Mor Tirreno, 7 y 9, pg. 271 IT
SAFA, Virgen de Los Peligros 2, pg. 1114 IT
SAS Institute S.A. (Madrid), C/Marbella 19, pg. 967 PV
SBC Warburg Espana S.A., Alfonso XII, 30 6th Fl., pg. 1331 IT
SBS Espanan S.A., Paseo de la Castellana 31, 20th Fl., pg. 1331 IT
SBS Ibersuizas S.A., Paseo de Catellana 31, pg. 1332 IT
SBS Sociedad de Valores S.A., Paseo de la Castellana 31, 20th Fl., pg. 1331 IT
SDRC Espana, S.A., Edificio Francia, 2B, pg. 1525 PB
S.I.G., S.A. Polig. Ind. Jumapi, Suecia 8, pg. 740 IT
SKF Espanola S.A., Avda de Manoteras 20, pg. 1158 IT
SMH Espana S.A., Avda de Aragon, 334, pg. 1161 IT
SMS Corp y Cia S.R.C., Avenida de los Encuartes No. 4, pg. 1463 PB
SAB WABCO Dimetal Equipos Ferroviarrios, Antigua Carretera Barcelona, km. 18.8, Apartada 14.485, pg. 271 IT
The Sakura Bank - Madrid Branch, Paseo de la Castellana 89-9, pg. 1179 IT
San Juva, S.A., P.o. de la Castellana, 83-85, pg. 1447 IT
Sandvik Espanola S.A., Avenida San Pablo 36, Apartado 92, Coslada, pg. 1186 IT
Santa Barbara Empresa Nacional de Industrias Militares, S.A., Julian Camarillo, 32, pg. 1224 IT
Santander de Factoring, Plaza de Manuel Gomez Moreno, pg. 143 IT
Santander de Leasing, Plaza de Manuel Gomez Moreno, pg. 143 IT
Santander de Patrimonios, Plaza de Manuel Gomez Moreno, pg. 143 IT
SASIB Railway Iberica S.A., c/estudiantes, 5, pg. 1195 IT
Sauer-Sundstrand Iberica S.A., C Sierra de Guadarrama, 35 Naves 6 y 7,San Fernando de Henares, pg. 1198 IT
Schering Espana S. A., Mendez Alvaro, 55, pg. 1204 IT
Schweppes S.A., Sor Angela de la Cruz 3, pg. 248 IT
Scott Iberica, S.A., c/Juan Esplandia, 11-13, pg. 960 PB
Segurcaja, Correduria de Seguros, S.A., Eloy Gonzalo, 10, pg. 252 IT
Seguridad MAPFRE, S.A., Francisco de Rojas, 12, pg. 333 IT
Seguros De Vida Y Pensiones Antares, S.A., General Peron, 38, pg. 1371 IT
Seguros Genesis, S.A., Paseo de Las Doce Estrellas, 4th Fl., pg. 738 PV
Seguros Orbita S.A., po de la Castellana 140, pg. 499 IT
Sensormatic E.C., S.A., Las Rozas, pg. 1457 PB
SEPI, Plaza del Marques de Salamanca, 8, pg. 1223 IT
Sepi, Plaza del Marques de Salamanca, 8, pg. 1224 IT
Servicio de Venta Automatica, S.A. (S.V.A.), pg. 1345 IT
Servicios Financieros MAPFRE, Avda. General Peron, 40, pg. 334 IT
Servicios Logisticos Integrados S.A., Avda. Senda Galiana, pg. 1120 PV
Servicios Teledistribucion, S.A. (St-Hilo), C/Luchana, 23-1a Pl., pg. 1371 IT
Shandwick Madrid, Paseo de la Castellana, pg. 1227 IT
Shandwick Spain, Paseo de la Castellana, pg. 1228 IT
Shell Espana S.A., Barquillo 17, pg. 1139 IT
Shionogi Qualicaps, S.A., Calle de la Granja, 49, pg. 1235 IT
Siemens Nixdorf Sistemas de Informacion S.A., Madrid, Ronda de Europa, 5, pg. 1245 IT
Siemens S.A., Edificio Triesle, Oreuse 2, pg. 1248 IT
Sifasa Sales Office, pg. 786 IT
Sigma, Avenida de Valdelaparra, 29 Poligono Industrial, pg. 796 IT
Simago, S.A., Cartagena, 36, pg. 704 IT
Sistemas Tecnicos Loterias Del Estado (S.T.L.), Manuel Tovar, 9-4th Fl., pg. 1372 IT
Skandia Compania de Administracion Inmobilaria S.A., Principe de Vergara 108-12, pg. 1258 IT
Skandia Correduria de Reaseguros SA, Pseo de General Martinez Campos 46, pg. 1256 IT
SmithKline Beecham Division Veterinaria, Paseo de la Castellana, 83-85 11, pg. 1266 IT
SmithKline Beecham Pharmaceuticals, Costa Brava, 14, pg. 1266 IT
Smurfit Espana, S.A., Calle Capitan Haya 38, pg. 1271 IT
Sociedad de Almacenaje y Transportes S.A., Doctor Esquerdo, 138-6, pg. 212 IT
Sociedad de Participacion y Promocion Empresarial Caja de Madrid, Eloy Gonzalo, 10, pg. 252 IT
Sociedad Espanola de Frenos, Calefaccion Y Senales, S.A., Calle Nicolas Fuster 2, pg. 738 IT
Sociedad General Espanola de Libreria, Avenida de Valdelaparra, 29 PoligonoIndustrial, pg. 796 IT
Sodexho Espana S.A., Calle Santisima Trinidad, 32, 1, pg. 1275 IT
Sofres AM, S.A., Pza. Carlos Trias Bertran, 7, pg. 1372 IT
Sopra Bull, Paseo Doce Estrellas No. 2, pg. 317 IT
Spanish Executive Information Services (SEIS), Miguel Angel, 24,4 Exterior, pg. 617 PV
Spectra-Physics S.A., Avda. Camino de lo Corao, 24-Nave 4, pg. 1290 IT
Stafford-Miller De Espana, Capitan Haya, 49 1 C Y D, pg. 237 PB
Steelcase Strafor S.A., Antonio Lopez, 243, pg. 1038 PV
Suiza de Reaseguros (Iberica) Agencia de Reaseguros, S.A., de la Cia. Suiza de Reaseguro, Paseo de la Castellana, 135, pg. 1333 IT
Sulzer Espana S.A., pg. 1306 IT
Sulzer Sistemas e Instalaciones S.A., pg. 1306 IT
The Sumitomo Bank, Ltd.-Madrid Branch, Paseo de la Castellana 51, 6th Fl., pg. 1309 IT
Sun Microsystems Iberica S.A., Plaza Pablo Ruiz Picasso S/N, Torre Picasso Planta 25, pg. 1531 PB
Suria K, S.A., Nunez de Balboa, 108, 1., pg. 1225 IT
Swiss Bank Corporation, Paseo de Castellana 31, pg. 1330 IT
Swiss Life (Espana), Calle Velazquez, 50, pg. 1332 IT
Symbol Technologies S.A., Calle Peonias No. 2, Sexta Planta, pg. 1546 PB
TBWA Madrid, S.A., Alfonso XI, 12, pg. 1063 PV
T.G.I. - Tecnologia del Grupo INI, S.A., Pza. Marques de Salamanca, 3 y 4, pg. 1225 IT
TMP Worldwide, Inc., Principe DeVergara 112, pg. 1065 PV
T.S. Telefonica Sistemas, S.A., Sor Angela de La Cruz, 3, pg. 1372 IT
TABACALERA, S.A., pg. 1345 IT
Tabapack, S.A., pg. 1346 IT
Tabapress, S.A., pg. 1346 IT
Taetel, S.L., Beatriz de Bobadilla, 3, pg. 1371 IT
Taisei Europe, Ltd., Calle Velazques 59, 4-izq., pg. 1347 IT
Tamrock Espana S.A., Avenida San Pablo 36, pg. 1353 IT
Tandem Computers Iberica S.A., Calle Cardenal, pg. 418 PB
Tasaciones Madrid, S.A., Velazquez, 150, pg. 252 IT
Taylor Control S.L., 6 Plaza Ciudad de Viena, Planta 2, pg. 6 IT
Tecla, S.A., Goya, 47, pg. 252 IT
Tektronix Espanola S.A.-Madrid, Calle Procion 1-3, La Florida, pg. 1567 PB
Telcel S.A., Plaza Pablo Ruiz Picasso s/n, Torre-Picasso - Planta 37, pg. 1140 PB
Telecartera, S.A., Beatriz de Bobadilla, 3, pg. 1371 IT
Telecomunicaciones Marinas, S.A. (Temasa), C/Silva, 1-4th Fl., pg. 1372 IT
Teledyne Spain, Pedro de Valdivia #10, pg. 44 PB
Telefonia y Finanzas, S.A. (Telfisa), Paseo de la Castellana, 151, pg. 1372 IT
TELEFONICA DE ESPANA, S.A., Gran Via, 28, Planta No. 4a, pg. 1371 IT
Telefonica Fiat Factoring, S.A., Paseo de la Castellana, 83-85, pg. 1372 IT
Telefonica Internacional De Espana S.A., Jorge Manrique, 12, pg. 1372 IT
Telefonica Investigacion Y Desarrollo, S.A. (Tidsa), c/Emilio Vargas, 6, pg. 1372 IT
Telefonica Publicidad e Informac., Avda. de Manoteras, No. 12, pg. 1372 IT
Telefonica Servicios Moviles, S.A., Plaza de la Independencia, 6, pg. 1372 IT
Telefonica Servicios Multimedia, S.A., Paseo de la Castellana, 9-11, pg. 1372 IT
Telefonica Telecomunicaciones Publicas, S.A., Paseo de Recoletos, 41, pg. 1372 IT
Telefonica Transmision de Datos, S.A., Beatriz de Bobadilla, 3, pg. 1372 IT
Teleinformatica Y Comunicaciones, S.A., Raimundo Fernandez Villaverde, pg. 1372 IT
Telma Retarder Espana Sales, pg. 786 IT
Telxon Corporation Systems Espana, S.A., Golfo de Salonica N 27 1 A, pg. 1574 PB
Tempo Espana S.A. y Cia S.e.C., Cl Estebanez Calderon 5, 6, pg. 1333 PB
Tenel, S.A., Embajadores 189/191, pg. 1371 IT
Terumo Europe-Madrid, Edificio Euromex, Avda. de Burgos, pg. 1376 IT
THORN, C/Tellez 24, pg. 1386 IT
3i Spain, Calle Ruiz de Alarcon 12-1, pg. 1386 IT
3M Espana S.A., Juan Ignacio Luca de Tena, 19-25, pg. 1606 PB
Thyssen Boetticher S.A., pg. 1387 IT
Toshiba Electronics Espana S.A., Parque Empresarial, San Fernando, Edificio Europa, pg. 1406 IT
Toshiba Medical Systems S.A., Carretera de Fuencarral, 100 Poligono Industrial de Alcobendas, pg. 1407 IT
Toyota Espana, S.L., Plaza Canovas del Castillo, 4-6, pg. 1414 IT
Tractebel Espana S.A., Calle Alcala 61-5, pg. 1416 IT
Traub-Heckert Iberica, S.A., Jardin de San Federico 13, 1. izda., pg. 1419 IT
Twin Disc Spain, S.A., pg. 1647 PB
UPM-Kymmene Papel S.A., Calle Almagro 23, pg. 1430 IT
Umar-Union Maritima Internacional S.A., Torre Picasso, Plaza de Pablo Ruiz Picasso s/n., pg. 629 IT
Unilever Espana S.A., Manuel de Falla, pg. 1439 IT
Union de Bancos Suizos, Maria de Molina 4-4, pg. 1441 IT
UNION NAVAL DE LEVANTE, S.A., Alcala 73, pg. 1442 IT
Uniseguros Vida y Pensiones (UNIVYP), Calle Ramirez de Arellano 37, pg. 565 IT
Unisys Espana S.A., Avda. del Partenon, 4, pg. 1671 PB
Unitros, Eduardo Dato 2 Dpdo., pg. 603 IT
Urbana Iberica, S.A., Paseo de la Castellana, 151, pg. 1372 IT
Utell International-Spain, Santa Engracia 31 6-B, pg. 1099 IT
VNU Business Publications Espana sa, pg. 1445 IT
Valle Agora S.A., P.o. de la Castellana, 83-85, pg. 1447 IT
Vallehermoso - Centro Inmobiliario Caja de Madrid, U.T.E., Eloy Gonzalo 10, pg. 252 IT
VALLEHERMOSO, S.A., Paseo de la Castellana, 83-85, pg. 1447 IT
Valquimica, S.A., Paraje de la Cruz, pg. 994 PB
Van Leeuwen Tubos Espana S.A.E., Crta. de Alcala a Camarma de Esteruelas, pg. 1450 IT
VARTA Autobaterias S.A., Serrano 16, pg. 1452 IT
Verisol, S.A., P.o. de la Castellana, 83-85, pg. 1447 IT
Vetrotex Espana SA, CTRA, Nacional II, Km. 32,500, pg. 1177 IT
Viajes Ecuador, Marques de Urguijo 41, pg. 22 IT
Vicasa SA, Edificio Ederra, Centro Azca, pg. 1171 IT
Vidrierias Espanolas Vicasa, Paseo de la Castellana 77, pg. 1176 IT
Viniclor S.A., Avenida de Burgos, 12-6, pg. 1280 IT
Vitalicio Pensiones, S.A. Seguros y Reaseguros, Paseo de la Castellana, 52, pg. 92 IT
Vitruvio-Leo Burnett, Duque De Sevilla, 3, pg. 186 PV
Viva, C/Zurbano, 41, pg. 575 IT
Viva, Vuelos Internacionales de Vacaciones, S.A., Zurbano 41, 3, pg. 1225 IT
VOAC Hydraulics S.A., Paseo de Arroyomolinos, 45, Poligono No.1 Calle A, pg. 1264 PB
Voest-Alpine Espanola S.A., Basilica 19, 8-A, pg. 1472 IT
Volkswagen Finance, S.A., pg. 1474 IT
Volvo Espana, S.A., Paseo de la Castellana 130, pg. 1477 IT
Volvo Penta Espana, S.A., Paseo de la Castellana 130, pg. 1478 IT
Volvo Vehiculos Industriales Espana, S.A., Gobelas 45-49, Urbanizacion La Florida, pg. 1478 IT
Vorwerk Espana S.A., pg. 1481 IT
Wandel & Goltermann S.A., Arturo Soria, No 343-3, pg. 1486 IT
Wang Espana, S.A., Avenida del Partenon, 16-18 1 loc. 4, pg. 1737 PB
Wanner y Vinyas, Hermonos Buquer 10, pg. 1176 IT
Wanner y Vinyas, Edificio Ederra, Centro Azca, pg. 1176 IT
Weatherford/Espana, S.A., c/o COEMSA Antonio Acuna, No. 25, pg. 1750 PB
Wellcome Farmaceutica SA, pg. 553 IT
Westdeutsche Landesbank-Madrid Branch, Edificio Torre Picasso, Piso 34, Plaza Pablo Ruiz Picasso s/n, pg. 1493 IT
Willis Faber S.A., Zurbano 45,3 Planta, pg. 1510 IT
Wintershall Petroleum Iberia S.A., c/o Abogado Aranegui van Ingen, Fuente del Romero, 29, pg. 110 IT
Wolters Kluwer Spain, C/Albacete, 5-2, pg. 1514 IT
Wynn's Espana, S.A., Paseo de la Castellana No. 210, 12th Fl, pg. 1783 PB
Yamanouchi Pharma, S.A., Centro Empresarial, El Plantio, Calle Ochandiano 6, pg. 1519 IT
Yesos Ibericos, Calle Alcala, 95, pg. 791 IT
Young & Rubicam, S.A., Avenida de Burgos, 21 Planta 9a, pg. 1199 PV
Zardoya Otis SA, Plaza Del Liceo, Sn, pg. 1691 PB
Zeneca Agro SA, Calle Costa Brava 13, pg. 1526 IT
Zeneca-Pharma S.A., C/ Josefa Valcarcel 3 y 5, pg. 1527 IT
Zenith Data Systems Espana S.A., Paseo Doce Estrellas No. 2, pg. 317 IT

Malaga

Flottweg Iberica SL, pg. 836 IT
Malaga Comercial S.A., pg. 920 IT

Mallorca

Club del Mar, Avenida de Jaime III no 17, pg. 560 IT

Marbella

Svenska Handelsbanken Marbella, Centro Plaza 2, Nueva Andalucia, pg. 1327 IT

Martigues

Albright & Wilson Lavera, Route de Ponteau Lavera Sud, pg. 49 IT

PB - *U.S. Public Companies Volume*
PV - *U.S. Private Companies Volume*
IT - *International Public & Private Companies Volume*

Martorell

Enso Espanola, S.A., Apartado 76, pg. 458   IT

Martos

Eldon Espana S.A., Poligono Industrial s/n, pg. 436   IT

Massanes

Tybor, S.A., Barri Marques, 2, pg. 769   PB

Mollerusa

Granja Castello S.A., pg. 920   IT

Montcada

Battenfeld Iberica S.A., Polig. Ind, La Ferreria, pg. 826   IT
Critesa S.A., Manzana 3, Pasaje 1-J, pg. 108   IT
Siegling Iberica S.A., pg. 498   IT

Montmelo

Purac Bioquimica S.A., Gran Vial 19, pg. 244   IT

Montornes del Valles

Bundy SA, Carretera San Adrian a La Roca Km 15,9, pg. 1341   IT

Munguia

Bremen S.A., Barrio Atela 6, Aptdo. 71, pg. 185   IT
Serpo Onena S.A., Poligono Industrial Belako, Apartado de Correos 79, pg. 1200   IT

Navarra

Eguzkia-NHK, S.A., 31,800 Alsasua, pg. 902   IT
Kayaba Arvin S.A., Poligono Indistrial de Ipertequi, pg. 727   IT

Neguri

BILBAO Compania Anonima de Seguros y Reaseguros, Rosales, Paseo del Puerto 20, pg. 499   IT
Cement Equipment Company S.A., Amann No. 2, pg. 475   IT

Nules

Iberica de Suspensiones, S.A., Poligono Industrial, Sector 2, pg. 902   IT
Polarcup S.A., Ctra. Nacional 340 Km 955.5, pg. 638   IT

Orense

Labauto Iberica, Poligono Industrial, San Ciprian de Vinas, pg. 785   IT

Orio

Moog Spain, Pabellon Altxerri, pg. 1128   PB

Oviedo

HUNOSA - E.N. Hulleras del Norte, S.A., Avda. galicia, 44, pg. 1224   IT
Minas de Figaredo, S.A., Cervantes, 27-2, pg. 1224   IT
Syseca Cantabrico, Gonzalez Besada 7, pg. 1384   IT

Oyarzun

Sifasa, Poligono Industrial de Ugaldetxo, pg. 786   IT
Sifasa Plant, pg. 786   IT

Palafrugell

Armstrong World Industries, S.A., pg. 132   PB

Palau de Plegamans

Herpu S.A., Carreterra Sabadell, pg. 43   IT

Palencia

Bundy SA, Poligono Industrial Villalobon, Avda Comunidad Europea s/n Parcela 29, pg. 1341   IT

Palleja

Linde Carretillas e Hidraulica S.A., pg. 810   IT

Palma de Mallorca

BANCA MARCH S.A., Avda. Alejandro Rossello, 8, pg. 136   IT
GESA - Gas y Electricidad, S.A., Juan Maragall, 16, pg. 1224   IT
Kodak S.A., Cabo Alomar Blanes, 29, pg. 554   PB
MAPFRE Balear, Cia. de Seguros Generales y de Reaseguros, Avda. Jaume III, 20, pg. 333   IT

March Correduria de Seguros S.A., Avda. A. Rossello 8, pg. 136   IT
March Inversiones S.A., Avda. A. Rossello, 8, pg. 136   IT
March Patrimonios S.A., Avda. A. Rossello, 8, pg. 136   IT
Poto Fi, S.A., San Jaime, 6 A, pg. 1447   IT
Prebetong Ibiza S.A., Camino Vecinal de Jesus 12, pg. 790   IT
SOL MELIA, Gremio Toneleros, 24, pg. 1277   IT

Pamplona

AP Amortiguadores, S.A., Ororbia (Navarra), pg. 727   IT
Asientos del Norte SA (ANSA), Poligono Industrial Lardaben - Calle F, pg. 193   IT
Comercial Norton, S.A., Apartado de Correos 162, pg. 1174   IT
Conexionados Electricos Tarazona S.A., Poligono Industrial de Landaben, pg. 724   PB
Eaton S.A. Axle Div., Poligono Industrial Landaben, Calle E/Apartado 1012, pg. 559   PB
Gorvi S.A., Poligono Industrial de Landaben, Calle A, pg. 1278   IT
Industrias Quimicas de Navarra S.A., Avda. Arostegui s/n, pg. 982   IT
La Vasco Navarra S.A. de Seguros y Reaseguros, Avenida sar Ignacio, 7, pg. 91   IT
Liebherr Industrias Metalicas, S.A., Apartado 4096, pg. 808   IT
Norton S.A., Km 7,5, Apartado de Correos, pg. 1175   IT
Onena Bolsas de Papel, S.A., pg. 440   IT
Tecnoconfort SA, Carretera Guipuzcoa s/n, Poligono Santa Lucia (Agustinos), pg. 193   IT
Telma Retarder Espana Plant, pg. 786   IT
Unicables, S.A., Poligono Industrial de Landaben, pg. 724   PB
V.N. Sociedad de Agencia de Seguros de la Vasco Navarra, S.A., Avenida San Ignacio, 7, pg. 92   IT

Parets del Valles

Kalifarma S.A., Apartado de Correos Nr.1, pg. 1279   IT
Nezel S.A., Calle en Proyecto s/no, pg. 1279   IT

Pasajes

Beissier S.A., pg. 423   IT

Pontevedra

Citroen Hispana S.A., Avda. de Citroen 395, pg. 1020   IT

Porrino

Wellcome Biofarma SA, pg. 553   IT

Pozuelo de Alarcon

Anglo Espanola de Distribucion, AED SA, Avda. dos Castillas, 33, Atica 7-Edif 2, 2 y 3, pg. 409   IT

Quart de Poblet

MB Espana, S.A., General Lobo, Montero 1, pg. 798   PB

Reus

Productos Brasilia S.A., pg. 922   IT
Van Leer Espana S.A., pg. 1147   IT

Ripollet

Boge Caucho Metal SA, pg. 835   IT
Boge Espana SA, pg. 835   IT
Sachs Auto SA, pg. 835   IT
Sintermetal SA, pg. 835   IT

Riveira

Stolt Sea Farm (Spain) S.A., pg. 1302   IT

Rubi

Branson Ultrasonidos, S.A.E., Poligono Industrial, Can Roses, pg. 576   PB
Cosmonogar, S.A., Apartado Correos 52, pg. 1508   PB
Elastogran S.A., Poligono Industrial can Jardi, pg. 108   IT
Euroresins S.A., Poligono Cova Solera, Avenida Can Suzarrats 114, pg. 355   IT
Grafita Sociedad Anonima, Carretera de Sam Cignat 14, pg. 1387   PB

Sagunto

AHM ALTOS HORNOS DEL MEDITERRANEO, S.A., Avda, 9 de Octubre, 7, pg. 1223   IT

Saint Quirze del Valles

ABB Motores S.A., pg. 8   IT
Unidad Hermetica S.A., Calle Antoni Forrellad, pg. 443   IT

Salamanca

Laboratorios Intervet S.A., Poligonos Industrial, El Montalvo, pg. 45   IT

Salcedo

S.A. Alavesa de Productos Quimicos BAYQUISA, pg. 174   IT

San Feliu de Llobregat

Inminsa SA, pg. 617   IT

San Fernando de Henares

CMT DASCO S.A., Avda. Ntra. Sra. de Montserrat, pg. 107   IT
Telma Retarder Espana, Avda de Castilla, 41, pg. 786   IT

San Sebastian

Behr Iberica S.A., pg. 422   IT
European Safety & Health Consultants (ESC), C/Renteria 10 2, pg. 1503   IT
Koipe S.A., Paseo del Urumea 23, pg. 324   IT
Vizdurr S.A., Avda de Zaruz 82, Edificio Lotea, pg. 422   IT

Sant Joan Despi

Baasel Lasertech Espana SA, pg. 836   IT

Sant Just Desvern

Cruz Verde-Legrain, 143 Carretera Real, pg. 1434   PB

Santa Ana

Extract-oil, S.A., Finca La Almazara, pg. 288   IT

Santa Cruz de Tenerife

Banca March S.A., La Marina, 15, pg. 136   IT
Wrigley Co. S.A., pg. 1781   PB

Santa Perpetua de Mogoda

Chemferm Industrial Pharmacueticals S.A., Calle Ripoles s/n, pg. 1143   IT
Rexroth SA, pg. 839   IT

Santander

Banco Santander, Pasco de Pereda, 9-12, pg. 143   IT
Electra de Viesgo, S.A., Calle Medio, 12, pg. 1224   IT
Funditubo, Paseo de Perez Galdos, 59, pg. 1176   IT

Santurce

Avesta Sheffield S.A., Iparraguirre, 59-1, pg. 222   IT

Segovia

Robinson Milling Systems Espana, Calle Cervantes 30, pg. 231   IT

Seville

CID FCA!BMZ Sevilla, Avda. Republica Argentina 3/B Primero, pg. 469   IT
FCA!BMZ Sevilla, Av. Republica Argentina 29 2, pg. 470   IT
Grupo Cruzcampo S.A., Avenida de la Innovacion, S/N, pg. 412   IT
Hewlett-Packard Espanola, S.A., Luis Morales, 32, Edifico Forum 3rd, Fl., No. 1, pg. 819   PB
Iberphone Andalucia, S.A., Castillo Aroche- Edificio Octogono s/n, pg. 252   IT
Kodak S.A., Louis Morales s/n, Edificio Forum, 3a. Pl., pg. 554   PB
Landis & Staefa Espana S.A., Estornino 3, pg. 801   IT
SODIAN - Sociedad Para el Desarrollo Industrial de Analucia, S.A., Avda. Republica Argentina, 29, B, 2., pg. 1225   IT
Urlocer, S.A., Avda. de la Constitucion, 7, pg. 1447   IT
Van Leeuwen Tubos Espana S.A.E., Avda. San Francisco Javier 24, Edificio Sevilla 1, pg. 1450   IT

Soria

Eagle-Picher Espana, S.A., Poligono Las Casas, 42080, pg. 355   PV

Tarragona

Black & Decker de Espana S.A., Carreterra Accesso Roda De Bara Km 0.700, pg. 234   PB
Ceratonia S.A., pg. 810   PB
Cogrami S.A.E., Apartado de Correos 258, pg. 751   IT
Duni Iberica S.L., Zona Industrial La Drecera, pg. 421   PB
Kellogg Espana, S.A., Apartado Postal 40, pg. 948   PB
Marchon Espanola S.A., Carretera de Montblanc Km 2, 4, pg. 1580   PB
Owens-Corning Tubs, S.A., Poligon Industrial, La Venta Nova 91, pg. 1238   PB
Robinson Nugent, Inc., Vileta de mar, No 17-bis, pg. 1395   IT
Tarragona Terminal, Muelle de Inflamables-, pg. 693   PB

PB - *U.S. Public Companies Volume*
PV - *U.S. Private Companies Volume*
IT - *International Public & Private Companies Volume*

Geographic Index-Non U.S.

Tauste

Technoflow Iberica SA, Avdo Cinco Villas No 17-19, pg. 1341　IT

Telde

Tissu Canarias S.A., Poligono Industrial El Goro, Calle C. s/n, pg. 864　IT

Tenerife

CITA Tabacos de Canarias, S.A., pg. 1346　IT
Grupo Tabaquero Canario, S.A., pg. 1346　IT
Philip Morris Espana, S.A., pg. 1346　IT

Terrassa

BASF Labiana S.A., Poligono Industrial, Can Parellada, Calle Venus 26, pg. 106　IT
Esselte S.A., Poligono Industrial can Parellada, pg. 461　IT

Toledo

Reto 2000, S.A., Pza. San Vicente, 3, pg. 1372　IT

Tolosa

Voith Tolosa S.A., P. Larramendi 9, pg. 1473　IT

Torrejon de Ardoz

Sistemas y Technicas de Seguridad, S.A., Calle Sierre de Segura, 4, pg. 233　PB

Torrelavega

Minas de Torrelavega S.A., pg. 1279　IT

Torrijos

Power-Packer Espana, S.A., Apartado 27, pg. 125　PB

Tres Cantos

BGS Spain, Centro Empresarial Euronova, Ronda de Poniente, 16-Bajo J, pg. 161　PB

Tudela

Navarra de Componentes Electronicos SA (NACESA), Poligono Industrial S/N, pg. 854　IT
Xantoflor, S.A., pg. 289　IT

Valdemoro

Milupa Productora S.A., pg. 991　IT

Valencia

Altae Banco S.A., Pintor Sorolla, 21, pg. 251　IT
Banco de Valencia, Pintor Sorolla, 2 y 4, pg. 139　IT
Binter Mediterraneo, Bloque Tecnico, pg. 574　IT
Brother Industrial Espana S.A., Calle dels Traginers, 3, pg. 229　IT
Cementos Peyland S.A., Avda. Marques del Turia 75, pg. 790　IT
Envases Valencianos, S.A., Calle Olta, No. Four, pg. 1386　PB
FCA!BMZ CID/Valencia, San Vicente, 81, pg. 469　IT
Generale Bank - Banco Belga, Calle Perez Pujol 4, puerta 3, pg. 547　IT
Hewlett-Packard Espanola, S.A., Isabel La Catolica 8, pg. 819　PB
Iberphone Levante, S.A., Albacete, 9, pg. 252　IT
Industrias Quirurgicas de Levante, S.A., Calle Islas Baleres, #50, P.O. Box 96, pg. 232　PB
Kodak S.A., Plaza Puerto del Mar, 6, pg. 554　PB
Lawson Mardon Suner SA, Alzira, pg. 69　IT
Makhteshim-Agan Espana S.L., Periodista Azzati 5, pg. 830　IT
Nordson Iberica S.A., Carretera de Torrente 225, pg. 1189　PB
Perstorp Railite S.A. Decorative Laminate, Ctra. Valencia-Alicante, (CN 332) km. 280 (Pista De Silla), pg. 1038　IT
Union Naval De Levante, S.A. (Madrid), Paseo de Caro, pg. 1442　IT
Valencia Terminal, Nuevo Dique, pg. 693　PB
White Cap Espana S.L., pg. 1207　IT

Valladolid

Asientos de Castilla Leon SA, Poligono Industrial El Berrocal, pg. 193　IT
Hillshog Espanola S.A., pg. 982　IT
Productores de Semillas S.A., pg. 983　IT
SODICAL - Sociedad Para el Desarrollo Industrial de Castilla y Leon, S.A., Doctrinos, 6, 4., pg. 1225　IT

Valls

Griffith Laboratories Iberia S.A., Apartado de Correos 78, pg. 481　PV

Viana

Defontaine Iberica S.A., Polygono Lagranja, pg. 509　IT
Rollix-Defontaine S.A., Polygano Lagranja, pg. 509　IT

Vicalvaro

Made Sistemas Electricos, S.A., Rivas, s/n., pg. 1224　IT

Vigo

Barreras Hijos De J. Barreras, S.A., Avda Belramar, 2, pg. 1223　IT
Cablinal Espana, Camino del Caramuxo, 37-39 San Andres de Comesana, pg. 785　IT
Estampaciones Noroeste S.A., Apartado 5130, pg. 265　IT
GKN Indugasa SA, Apartado 1586, pg. 536　IT
Hijos de J. Barreras, S.A., Avda. Beiramar, 2, pg. 1224　IT
Union Cristalera, 108, Avenue de Madrid, Apartado 267, pg. 1176　IT

Viladecans

Derivados Lacteos y Alimenticios S.A., Crta. de Villa S/N, pg. 920　IT

Vilanova

BASF Sistemeas de Impresion, S.A., Carretera de Valldeoriolf Km 5,5, pg. 107　IT
Venta Catalogo S.A., pg. 1015　IT

Vilches

Ceramica Syre S.A., Avda. de Almeria s/n, pg. 790　IT

Villagarcia de Arosa

Kvaerner Eureka Espanola S A, Poligono Industrial de Bamio, pg. 767　IT
Pechiney Envasse Iberica S.A., Carretera Pontevedra, Villagarcia de Arosa, km 13.8, pg. 1031　IT

Villarreal

Muelles y Ballestas Hispano-Alemanas S.A., Camino Viejo de Castellon, A Onda, S/N, pg. 902　IT

Vitoria

Fuchs Lubricantes S.A., Portal de Bergara 4, pg. 518　IT
Guardian Espanola S.A., Calle Larragana 16, pg. 1030　IT
Krupp Hispania S.A., Apartado 322, pg. 510　IT
Krupp Widia Iberica, Apartado 322, pg. 510　IT
Perstorp Components S.A., c/ Mendigorritxu, s/n, pg. 1040　IT

Vizcaya

Asbury Worldwide, Europe, C/Las Acacias, 39-bajo, 48990-Neguri-Guecho, pg. 1110　PB
Bilbao Terminal, Explanadas Punta Ceballos, pg. 693　PB
Danielli Morgardshammar SA, Avenida Zugazarte, 8, 2 Depto. 2, pg. 378　IT
Intergraph (Espana) S.A., C/Las Mercedes, 8 1oo.A, 48930 Las Arenas-Getxo, pg. 892　IT
Morganite Espanola SA, Av. Sabino Arana, 10, pg. 892　IT
Productos Tubulares, S.A., Valle de Trapaga, Carretera de Ugarte a Galindo, pg. 1224　IT

Zaragoza

Adidas Espana, S.A., 6A Planta, pg. 25　IT
Bondioli y Pavesi Iberica S.A., Poligono De Malpica II, Calle F, Parcela 1/a, pg. 201　IT
Construcciones Agrometalicas Levante, S.A. (Calsa), Apartado 200, San Juan de la Pena 230, pg. 1579　PB
Curver Rodex S.A., Carretera de Logrono, km 4,5, pg. 353　IT
ERZ - Electricas Reunidas de Zaragoza, S.A., San Miguel, 10, pg. 1224　IT
Filtros Mann S.A., pg. 484　IT
Manufacturas Rodex S.A., Carrera de Logrono, Km 4,5, pg. 355　IT
Metalagrafica de Aragon S.A., Poligono de Coaullada, pg. 1222　IT
Nurel S.A., CTRA. De Barcelona, KM 329, pg. 665　IT
Opel Espana, Apartado 375, pg. 724　PB
SES Iberica SA, Poligono Industrial Malpica, pg. 1526　IT
SODIAR - Sociedad Para el Desarrollo Industrial de Aragon, S.A., Plaza Roma F-1, planta 1, of. 12, pg. 1225　IT
Schindler S.A., pg. 1205　IT

Zumaya

GKN Ayra Durex SA, Apartado 37, pg. 535　IT

SRI LANKA

Colombo

ANZ Grindlays Bank plc Sri Lanka, 37 York St., pg. 99　IT
BASF-Finlay (Pvt.) Ltd., Finlay House, pg. 106　IT
Bankers Trust New York Corporation, Cargo Boat Devel. Co. Bldg., 5th Fl., 41 Janadhipathi Mawatha, pg. 186　PB
Blackwood Hodge (Ceylon) Ltd., Bandaranahce Memorial Intl. Conf. Hall, pg. 231　IT
CPC (Lanka) Ltd., pg. 224　PB
Ceylon Nutritional Foods Ltd., pg. 919　IT
Ceylon Oxygen Limited, 50, Sri Pannananda Mawatha, pg. 961　IT
The Commercial Bank of Ceylon Limited, 57 Sir Baron Jayatillaka Mawatha, pg. 1296　IT
Data Management Services (DMS), 159 Dharmapala Mawatha, pg. 1228　IT
Thomas De La Rue Lanka (Pte) Limited, GCEC Industrial Promotion Zone, pg. 386　IT
Det Norske Veritas, 3rd Floor, 103, R.A. de Mel Mawatha, pg. 398　IT
Deutsche Bank AG (Columbo, Sri Lanka), 86, Galle Rd., pg. 404　IT
HDF Securities PVT Limited, 27-1/I, York Arcade Bldg., York Arcade Rd., pg. 494　IT
Habib Bank Ltd., 140-142, Second Cross St., pg. 584　IT
Lever Brothers (Ceylon) Ltd., pg. 1437　IT
Metropolitan Communications Ltd., 85, Braybrooke Place, pg. 1369　IT
Mitsui & Co., Ltd., 2nd Fl. of Premises, 315 Vauxhall St., pg. 881　IT
Nestle Lanka Ltd., pg. 921　IT
Nokia Telecommunications, Liasion Office, 5 Palmyrch Avenue, pg. 953　IT
Precision Tech Services (Pvt.) Ltd., 65/14 Park St., pg. 822　PB
The Shell Company of Sri Lanka Ltd., 161 Sri Gnanendra Mwawatha, pg. 1140　IT
Smart Shirts (Lanka) Limited, pg. 948　PB
Standard Chartered Bank (Sri Lanka), PO Box 27, 17 Janadhipathi Mawatha, pg. 1296　IT
Tootal Thread (Pte.) Ltd., P.O. Box 1122, 33/1 Staples St., pg. 299　IT
The World Bank, DFCC Bldg., 1st Fl., 73/5 Galle Rd., pg. 1190　PV

Ja-Ela

Jinwoong Lanka (Pvt) Ltd., No. 21, Temple Road, Ekala, pg. 707　IT

Rajagirya

Lanka ORIX Leasing Company Limited, No. 100/1-1/1, Sri Jayawardenapura Mawatha, pg. 1009　IT

SUDAN

Khartoum

CIBA-GEIGY Services Limited-Technical Office Agrochemicals, pg. 980　IT
Daewoo Corp. - Khartoum, Plot No. 21, Block 2, Mogran, pg. 358　IT
Habib Bank Ltd., pg. 584　IT
Kenana Sugar Co., Ltd., Plot 2, Block 11 1E St. 29, pg. 948　IT
Mitsui & Co., Ltd., Sudanese Kuwaiti Ctr., pg. 881　IT
Mobil Oil Sudan Limited, pg. 1119　PB
Shell Company of the Sudan Ltd., Aboulela New Building, Barlman Ave., pg. 1136　IT

Omdruman

Nlle. Corp. Construction Corp., Hara 5, Ruva 2 Sinnat St., pg. 358　IT

SURINAME

Paramaribo

Ballast Nedam Suriname N.V., Mirandastraat 9, pg. 134　IT
De Surinaamsche Bank N.V., Gravenstraat 26, pg. 12　IT
Eerste Surinaams-Nederlandse Levensverzekering Maatschappij ENNA nv, pg. 28　IT
Ilaco Suriname NV, pg. 606　IT
Shell Suriname Verkoop Mij NV, Sir Winston Churchilweg, Suhoza-Livorno, pg. 1142　IT
Van Romondt Trading Company Ltd., Waterkant 40-42, pg. 1371　IT

SWAZILAND

Malkerns

Swaziland Fruit Canners (Pty.) Ltd., pg. 922　IT

Manzini

Hospitality, 2nd Floor, Liqhaga House, pg. 1274　IT
Longman Swaziland (Pty) Ltd., Eyartto Bldg., Nkoseluhlaza St., pg. 1026　IT
Macmillan Boleswa Publishing (Pty) Ltd., P.O. Box 1235, pg. 1479　IT
Macmillan Swaziland National Publishing Co., pg. 1480　IT

Mbabane

Barclays Bank of Swaziland Ltd., pg. 165　IT

PB - *U.S. Public Companies Volume*
PV - *U.S. Private Companies Volume*
IT - *International Public & Private Companies Volume*

Stanbic Bank Swaziland Limited, Stanbic House, pg. 1293   IT
Standard Chartered Bank Swaziland Limited, 21 Allister Miller St., pg. 1295   IT

SWEDEN

Ahus

Svenska Foder AB, Steffen Sohstagatan, pg. 350   IT

Akersberga

Fiskars Power Systems AB, Box 543, pg. 492   IT

Alingsas

Electrolux Storkok AB, pg. 438   IT
Luna AB, Sandbergsvagen 3, pg. 188   IT
Platluna AB, pg. 1422   IT

Almhult

Almhults Gjuteri, pg. 1323   IT
Ikea Svenska AB, Box 701, pg. 660   IT
Ikea Svenska Forsaljnings AB, 343 00, pg. 660   IT

Alvesta

Alvesta Gjuteri AB, Agatan 14, pg. 1323   IT

Alvkarleby

CX-Grus, pg. 1200   IT
Vattenfall Utveckling AB, pg. 1453   IT

Alvsjo

Celsius Information System AB, pg. 276   IT
Dialog AB, pg. 277   IT
Ericsson Utvecklings AB, Armborstvagen 14, pg. 1364   IT
Svenska Elgrossist AB SELGA, Armborstvagen 1, pg. 1363   IT

Amal

AMAL AB, pg. 170   PB
Electrolux Cleaning Equipment AB, Box 127, pg. 438   IT
GKN Nordiska Kardan AB, pg. 536   IT
Mecel AB, pg. 686   IT

Amotfors

Perstorp Components, pg. 1040   IT

Aneby

Sealed Air Svenska A.B., Stigbergsvagen 12, pg. 1451   PB

Angelholm

HemoCue AB, Munka Ljungbyvagen 77, pg. 1040   PB

Angered

Courtaulds Nippon Paint AB, Box 100 Asperdsgatan 2, pg. 937   IT
Wilson-Fiberfil Sweden AB, 6A Asperedsgatan, pg. 46   IT

Anneberg

Sektionsbyggarna AB, pg. 1260   IT

Arboga

FFV Aerotech AB, pg. 277   IT
FFV Matteknik AB, pg. 277   IT
Telub Teleanlaggningar AB, pg. 278   IT
Volvo Aero Support Corporation, pg. 1476   IT

Arlandastad

Acuson AB, pg. 18   PB

Arlov

Bengtssons Maskin AB, Foretagsvagen 14, pg. 678   IT
ICA Handlarna Syd AB, pg. 643   IT
Jimek, pg. 170   PB
PolyGram Direct Marketing Scandinavia Organization, Foretagsvagen 14, pg. 1053   IT

Arnasvall

Converflex AB, pg. 1429   IT

Arsta

ICA Handlarna Ost AB, pg. 642   IT
Saba Trading AB, pg. 709   IT

Arvika

Electrolux Commercial Refrigeration AB, P.O. Box 138, pg. 438   IT
Ovako Arvika AB, pg. 1157   IT

Asarum

Outokumpu Copper Tubes AB, Granefors Works, pg. 1017   IT

Aseda

Wicona Scandinavia AB, Jarnvagsgatan 45, pg. 965   IT

Askim

CIBA Vision AB, Datavagen 24, pg. 981   IT
Kodak AB, Box 1006, pg. 552   PB
MTS Systems Norden AB, Datavagen 3, pg. 1029   PB
Moog Norden AB, Datsvagen 18, pg. 1128   PB
Rintekno Oy - Sweden, Datavagen 14 A, pg. 1361   IT
Tampella Power AB, Askims Verkstadsvag 1A, pg. 1354   IT
Vitactiv AB, pg. 1536   PB

Astorp

Swedoor AB-Astorp, pg. 1303   IT

Atvidaberg

Euroclean AB, P.O. Box 249, pg. 439   IT

Avesta

Avesta Prefab AB, pg. 221   IT
Avesta Press Plate AB, pg. 221   IT
Avesta Sheffield AB, pg. 221   IT
Avesta Welding AB, pg. 221   IT
Bagheera & Haglofs AB, Industrigatan 18, pg. 708   IT
Granges Aluminium AB, Avestaverket, pg. 439   IT

Balsta

Gyproc Balsta Plant, pg. 1200   IT
Philipssons Grav & Schakt AB, Tegelbruksvagen 6, pg. 1364   IT

Bandhagen

FRAM Europe A.B., Box 85, pg. 53   PB
Tele-ekonomi AB, Hardemogatan 1, pg. 29   IT

Barkakra

Hydro Hagebruk a.s., Sverstad Gard, pg. 963   IT

Bastad

Ahlstromforetagen Svenska AB-Eljo, pg. 33   IT

Bengtsfors

Skapafors Paper Mill, pg. 421   IT

Billesholm

Gullfiber AB, pg. 1176   IT

Bjorneborg

Bjorneborgs Jernverks AB, pg. 708   IT

Bjuv

Consilium CMH-Babcock AB, Gunnarstorp, pg. 131   IT
AB Findus, Box 500, pg. 920   IT
Svenska Nestle AB, pg. 922   IT

Bohus

Chemtronics AB, pg. 1289   IT
Ledu International AB, pg. 821   IT

Boliden

Boliden Mineral AB, Kontorsvagen 1, pg. 1422   IT

Bollnas

AB Sandvik Hand Tools, pg. 1185   IT

Boras

Borens AB, Box 44093, pg. 821   IT
Ellos AB, pg. 643   IT
Freudenberg A.B., pg. 506   IT
Industrifilter AB, pg. 1422   IT
Monsanto (Scandinavia) AB, Yxhammarsgaten 27, pg. 1126   PB
VOAC Hydraulics AB, pg. 1264   PB

Borlange

Honeywell-Measurex Sweden AB, P.O. Box 5091, Cirkelgatan 14, pg. 834   PB
AB Kaffebonans Rosteri, pg. 920   IT
Mecman Gillberg Hydraulic AB, pg. 839   IT
Stora Kvarnsveden, Box 733, pg. 1304   IT

Boxholm

Boxholms Skogar AB/Skanska Forestry Group, P.O. Box 101, pg. 1260   IT

Bromma

AKA Industriprodukter AB, pg. 666   IT
Analog Devices AB, Mariehallsvagen 42, pg. 108   PB
Auto-Products AB, pg. 708   IT
CAP Programmator, Gustavlundsvagen 131, pg. 264   IT
Dotcom AB, pg. 277   IT
DuraCell-Daimon Svenska, Archimedesv. 2, pg. 743   PB
EMI Music Publishing (Sweden) AB, pg. 427   IT
Ericsson Radio Messaging AB, Gardsfogdevagen 18A, pg. 1364   IT
Fiat Auto Sverige AB, pg. 481   IT
Gambro Engstrom AB, Karlsbodavagen 18, pg. 667   IT
ICA Meny Foretagen AB, pg. 643   IT
Komori Sweden AB, Ulvsundavaven 106, pg. 745   IT
Magnetic AB, Gardsfogdevagen 18A, pg. 1364   IT
Motorola AB Communications Group, Enighetsv. 5, pg. 1139   PB
Rimi Svenska AB, pg. 643   IT
Rohm & Haas Nordiska AB, Karlsbodav 9-11, Box 11045, pg. 1404   PB
Sauer-Sundstrand Svenska AB, Mariehallsvagen 44, pg. 1198   IT
Tektronix AB, pg. 1567   PB
Toshiba Electronics Scandinavia AB, pg. 1406   IT
Vipac Vibrator AB, Johannesfredsvagen 11, pg. 1420   IT

Charlottenberg

Fundo Aluminium AB, pg. 961   IT

Danderyd

AGEMA Direct Sales AB, Box 3, pg. 1289   IT
Agema Infrared Systems AB, Rinkebyvagen 19, pg. 1289   IT
Amdahl International Corporation Filial, Sverige, pg. 527   IT
Braas Scandinavia AB, Svardvagen 23, pg. 1092   IT
Broderna Berner HAB, Enebybergsvagen 10, pg. 189   IT
Bull AB, pg. 317   IT
Caterpillar Financial Nordic Services A.B., Svarovagen 3B, pg. 315   PB
Cementa AB, Box 144, pg. 1198   IT
Euroc Recycling AB, pg. 1199   IT
Forslid AB, Rinkebyvagen 21 B, pg. 1363   IT
Geotronics Scandinavia AB, Rinkebyvagen 17, pg. 1289   IT
Krupp Hoesch Stahl AB, Morbyleden 20, pg. 515   IT
Lubrizol Scandinavia AB, Berga Backe 2, pg. 1017   PB
Mobile Oil AB Sweden, P.O. Box 502, pg. 1119   PB
Ovako Steel AB, Svardvagen 3A, pg. 1157   IT
Pirelli Scandinavia AB, Box 29, Svardvagen 11, pg. 1059   IT
SKANSKA AB, Vendevagen 89, pg. 1260   IT
Skanska Bygg AB, pg. 1260   IT
Skanska Capital AB, pg. 1260   IT
Skanska Data AB, pg. 1260   IT
Skanska Fastigheter Riks AB, pg. 1260   IT
Skanska Fastigheter Stockholm AB, pg. 1260   IT
Skanska International Civil Engineering AB, pg. 1260   IT
Skanska Maskin AB, pg. 1261   IT
Skanska Stockholm Malardalen, Vandevagen 89, pg. 1260   IT
Stabilator AB, pg. 1261   IT
Tampella Power AB, Box 69, Svardvagen 3A, pg. 1354   IT
Time/System Sverige AB, Svardvagen 11, pg. 73   IT
Trigon Informatik AB, pg. 278   IT
Yokohama Scandinavia AB, pg. 1521   IT
ZDS Groupe AB, pg. 317   IT

Degerfors

Avesta Sheffield AB, pg. 221   IT

Degerhamn

Cementa AB (Degerhamn), pg. 1199   IT

Djursholm

Carlson Marketing Group Scandinavia Motivation Service AB, Box 225, pg. 212   PV

Domsjo

Domsjo Sawmill, pg. 886   IT

Edsbyn

SP-Snickerier AB, Snickarvagen 1, pg. 1302   IT

PB - *U.S. Public Companies Volume*
PV - *U.S. Private Companies Volume*
IT - *International Public & Private Companies Volume*

1764

Geographic Index-Non U.S.

Eksjo

IDAB WAMAC INTERNATIONAL, pg. 643   IT

Emmaboda

Emmaboda Glas AB, pg. 1173   IT
Scandifloat AB, pg. 1173   IT

Enkoping

AB Bahco Ventilation, Stockholmsvagen, pg. 7   IT
AB Nordenta, Verkmastaregatan 1, pg. 709   IT
Sandvik Bahco Norden AB, pg. 1185   IT

Enskede

Svenska Allen Coding AB, pg. 1269   IT
Wormald Fire Systems AB, Skoniksvagen 245,
    pg. 1650   PB

Ersmark

Skega AB, pg. 1323   IT

Eskilstuna

ASSA AB, Kungsgatan 71, pg. 17   IT
ASSA Industrie AB, Kungsgatan 71, pg. 17   IT
Billing Metal Trading AB, pg. 221   IT
Bofors Carl Gustaf AB, pg. 276   IT
Celsius Industries Corp., Tullgatan 8, pg. 276   IT
Celsius Invest AB, Tullgatan 8, pg. 276   IT
Dataliner AB, Pressargatan 11, pg. 1289   IT
EME-Norlett AB, pg. 438   IT
AB FAS Lasfabrik, Hejargatan 20, pg. 17   IT
C E Johansson AB, Fraktgatan 6, pg. 1289   IT
Lundbergs-Malardalen Region, Nysforgatan 27,
    pg. 821   IT
Market Sweden, pg. 1422   IT
NCC Eskilstuna, pg. 899   IT
Nordic Service Center AB, pg. 221   IT
Svetsprodukter AB, pg. 388   IT
Sweden Table Tennis AB, Box 642, Skjulstagatan 10,
    pg. 591   PB
Tedak AB, Svista 1561, pg. 281   IT
Valmet Svenska AB, pg. 1449   IT

Eslov

Sekurit Saint-Gobain Scandinavia AB, pg. 1173   IT
Travaru AB A. Moberg & Co., pg. 1199   IT
Trempex AB, Fack, pg. 1173   IT
Volvo Excavators AB, Bruksgatan 5, Box 115,
    pg. 1477   IT

Fagersta

Avesta Sandvik Tube AB, P.O. Box 510, pg. 221   IT
FAGERSTA STAINLESS AB, P.O. Box 508, pg. 476   IT
Traco AB, Box 103, Vinthundsvagen 157, pg. 709   IT
Uniroc AB, pg. 96   IT

Falkenberg

Componenta Transport AB, Sanddynevegen, pg. 1420
FALKEMA AB, Sandgatan 5A, pg. 477   IT
Interconsult i Falkenberg, pg. 1323   IT
Precon AB, Vinsbergs Hed, pg. 1199   IT
Preconal, Box 173, pg. 477   IT
Svedala Superstructures, pg. 1325   IT

Falun

Dala Sanering AB, pg. 669   IT
J.S. Hemkopskedjan AB, Norra Jarnvagsgatan 25,
    pg. 272   IT
Industriskog AB, pg. 886   IT
J S Hemkopskedjan AB, pg. 708   IT
Saab-Scania AB, Box 4700, pg. 687   IT
Stora Corporate Research, Sodra Mariegatan 18,
    pg. 1303   IT
Stora Forest AB, Asgatan 22, pg. 1303   IT
STORA KOPPARBERGS BERGSLAGS AB, pg. 1302   IT
Stora Power AB, Gruvvagan 36, pg. 1303   IT
Stora Purchasing & Transport, Asgatan 22, pg. 1303   IT
Stora Timber AB, Linslagarvagen 2, pg. 1303   IT

Farsta

Maskinaktiebolaget AXAB, pg. 709   IT
Nortelco AB, pg. 709   IT
TELIA AB, pg. 1373   IT
Telia Holding AB, pg. 1374   IT
Telia Nattganster Division, pg. 1373   IT

Fellingsbro

Stora Fors AB, Oppboga, pg. 1302   IT

Filipstad

Chips-OLW AB, pg. 975   IT
OLW-Snacks AB, pg. 983   IT
Sandoz Svenska AB, pg. 985   IT
Svenska Knacke AB, pg. 986   IT

Wasabrod AB, Fack, pg. 986   IT

Finspang

ABB Stal AB, pg. 7   IT
Igelfors Portsystem AB, pg. 269   IT
Outokumpu Copper Strip AB, pg. 1017   IT

Flen

De La Rue Cash Handling Product Group, pg. 387   IT
De La Rue Inter Innovation AB, pg. 387   IT

Forserum

Stora Fors AB, Kopparforsvagen 3, pg. 1302   IT
Swedoor AB-Forserum, pg. 1303   IT

Forslov

Interdock, Akagardsvagen, pg. 269   IT

Fristad

Fibo-Trespo-Langmoen, Postboks 134, pg. 966   IT

Frolunda

Bauer Hiss AB, Gruvatan 37, pg. 747   IT
H.B. Fuller Sverige AB, Lona Knapes Gata 5, pg. 687   PB
Millipore Scandinavia AB, Box 233, S-421 23 Vastra,
    pg. 1113   PB
Svenska BOC AB, P.O. Box 140, S-421 22 Vastra,
    pg. 122   IT

Gallivare

Trellex AB, pg. 1324   IT

Gavle

Euronord WTM AB, Tredbe Tvargatan 3, pg. 678   IT
Gasell Profil AB, pg. 1088   IT
Karskar Energi, pg. 759   IT
KORSNAS AB, pg. 759   IT
Kvaerner Eureka Gaevle AB, Utmarksvagen 1, pg. 767   IT
Kvaerner Pulp Equipment AB, Utmarksvagen 1,
    pg. 768   IT
Leaf Sweden, S. Skeppsbron 26, pg. 638   IT
Stora Cell AB, Ruddammsgatan 32, pg. 1303   IT

Genevad

Genevad Cellplast, pg. 1199   IT

Getinge

Getinge AB, pg. 551   IT
GETINGE INDUSTRIER AB, P.O. Box 69, pg. 551   IT

Goteborg

AGA-Cryo AB, Box 8887, pg. 12   IT
ALNAB Armatur AB, Ogaerdet Vagen, pg. 549   IT
Adtec AB, P.O. Box 8415, pg. 276   IT
Akzo Zout Chemie Svenska AB, 142 Kajplats
    Sannegardshamnen, pg. 44   IT
Ascom Tateco AB, Grimbodalen 2, pg. 87   IT
Autodesk AB, Moelndalsvagen 24, pg. 149   PB
Avfallsteknik AB, pg. 276   IT
BASF Svenska AB, Haraldsgatan 5, pg. 107   IT
BTL AB, Falkenbergsgatan 3, pg. 123   IT
BTL Sweden AB, Falkenbergsgatan 3, pg. 123   IT
Ballast Vast AB, pg. 899   IT
Ballograf BIC AB, Klangfargsgatan 6, pg. 1273   IT
Bang & Olufsen Svenska AB, Gullbergs Strandgatr 4,
    pg. 146   IT
Bayer Sverige AB, P.O. Box 5237, pg. 175   IT
Leon Bekaert Svenska A/B, Stigbergsliden 5, pg. 184   IT
Brukens Hardverkstader AB, Box 110, pg. 1471   IT
Carlander-Dialysen AB, Carlandersplatsen, pg. 667   IT
AB Celsius Finance, pg. 276   IT
Componenta Kranlyft AB, Gullbergs Strandgata 40,
    pg. 1419   IT
Continental Gislaved Dack, pg. 327   IT
DAB Dental AB, Erik Dahlbegsgaten 9, pg. 711   IT
Det Norske Veritas, Lilla Bommen 1, pg. 396   IT
Drott AB, pg. 1260   IT
Esab AB, Herkulesgatan 72, pg. 281   IT
ESAB International AB, Herkulesgatan 72, pg. 281   IT
ESAB Sverige AB, Herkulesgatan 72, pg. 281   IT
ESAB Treasury AB, Herkulesgatan 72, pg. 281   IT
ESTA Fastighets AB, c/o T. Alexandersson, Fastighets AB,
    pg. 281   IT
Edmeston AB, pg. 1185   IT
Enator Vast AB, pg. 277   IT
Enka Sverige AB, 7A Kungsgatan, P.O. Box 2180,
    pg. 46   IT
Ericsson Emergency Control Systems AB, pg. 1363   IT
Ericsson Microwave Systems-Gothenburg, pg. 1363   IT
Eriksbergs Forvaltnings AB, pg. 277   IT
Fastighetsaktiebolaget Hufvudstaden, Drottninggatan 56,
    pg. 478   IT
Fix AB, Bruksgatan 17, pg. 17   IT
Flex-Links Systems AB, pg. 1157   IT
Forbo Forshaga AB, pg. 497   IT
Forsakringsaktiebolaget Volvia, pg. 1476   IT

GVA Consultants AB, pg. 277   IT
GVA Industriservice AB, pg. 276   IT
GVA Materialverkstader AB, pg. 277   IT
W. Gebhart, Aktiebolag, Vasagatan 43A, pg. 1054   PB
Gotaverken Arendal AB, pg. 277   IT
Gotaverken Cityvarvet AB, pg. 277   IT
Gotaverken Energy AB, pg. 771   IT
Gotaverken Miljo AB, pg. 276   IT
Gotaverken Motor AB, pg. 276   IT
Gothia Pulp & Paper AB, pg. 708   IT
Gothia-Wellmabolagen AB, pg. 708   IT
Granges Metalock AB, pg. 439   IT
Chr. Hansen AB, Flygfaltsgatan, pg. 288   IT
ELOF HANSSON AB, Forsta Landdatan 17, pg. 595   IT
Hasselblad Svenska AB, Torggatan 4, pg. 1468   IT
Henkel Nopco AB, pg. 613   IT
Hercules AB, pg. 810   PB
Hoechst-Perstorp AB, pg. 1039   IT
Hoogovens Aluminium NV filial Sverige, Odinsgatan 13,
    pg. 755   IT
ICA Banan AB, pg. 643   IT
ICA Butiksfinans AB, pg. 643   IT
ICA Specialvaror AB, pg. 643   IT
IDAC Bilfarger Svenska Aktiebolag, pg. 665   IT
ITW Fixfast AB, Lantvarnsgatan 4, pg. 868   PB
ITW Fixlock AB, Bruksgatan 17, pg. 868   PB
Iggesund Paperboard Norden, Kungsgatan 12, pg. 886   IT
John Crane Sverige AB, Ruskvadersgatan 8, pg. 1339   IT
Jotun Midex AB, Jotun Middle East Export, pg. 715   IT
KSB Morck AB, pg. 721   IT
KappAhl AB, pg. 718   IT
Kodak AB, Banehagsgatan 6, pg. 552   PB
Korn/Ferry International, Ostra Hamngatan 5, pg. 634 PV
Kranlyft, pg. 1323   IT
AB Kranlyft, Gullbergs Strandgata 40, pg. 1420   IT
Kvaerner EnviroPower AB, Anders Carlssons gata 14,
    pg. 767   IT
Kvaerner Gotfab AB, Elin Svendssons Gata 2, pg. 767 IT
Kvaerner Pulping Technologies AB, Regnbagsgatan 6,
    pg. 768   IT
Kvaerner Ships Equipment AB, Kilsgatan 4, pg. 768   IT
Kvaerner Ships Equipment AB, Kampegatan 3, pg. 771   IT
Kvarn AB Juvel, pg. 718   IT
S Lennart Larsson AB, pg. 709   IT
Larsson & Sundqvist Paper AB, pg. 709   IT
Arthur D. Little, A.B., Lilla Bommen 1, pg. 670   PV
Lundbergs-Goteborg Region, Molndalsvagen 26,
    pg. 821   IT
Luxottica Sweden A.B., Britthagsvagen 2-Tralasvagen 14,
    pg. 822   IT
MacGregor (SWE) AB, Fiskhamnsg 2, pg. 670   IT
Molnlycke AB, Backstensgatan 5, pg. 1326   IT
Molnlycke AB Consumer Products, Kvarnbacken 2,
    pg. 1326   IT
Molnlycke AB Research, Chalmers Teknikpark,
    pg. 1326   IT
Molnlycke Tissue AB, Backstensgatan 5, pg. 1326   IT
Molnlycke Toiletries AB, Mobelgatan 4, pg. 1326   IT
NCC Building, Gullsberg Strandgata 2, pg. 898   IT
NCC Building - Goteborg, Gullbergs Strandgata 2,
    pg. 898   IT
NCC Goteburg, pg. 899   IT
NCC HUS, pg. 899   IT
NYK Line (Sverige) AB, Forsta Langgatan 16, pg. 942 IT
NOBEL BIOCARE, pg. 951   IT
Panalpina AB, pg. 1022   IT
Precon Teknik AB, Prinsgatan 12, pg. 1199   IT
Region Goteborg, Molndalsvagen 85, pg. 23   IT
Royal Copenhagen Svenska AB, Vestre Hamngatan 12,
    pg. 1135   IT
AB SKF, Hornsgatan 1, pg. 1156   IT
SKF Dataservice AB, Hornsgatan 1, pg. 1157   IT
SKF Eurotrade AB, Hornsgatan 1, pg. 1157   IT
SKF Nova AB, Chalmers Teknikpark, Sven Hultinsgata 9,
    pg. 1157   IT
SKF Reinsurance Co. Ltd., Hornsgatan 1, pg. 1157   IT
SKF Specialty Products AB, Hornsgatan 1, pg. 1157   IT
SKF Sverige AB, Hornsgatan 1, pg. 1157   IT
SKF Treasury Centre, Hornsgatan 1, pg. 1157   IT
Saab Marine Electronics AB, Box 13045, pg. 686   IT
Saab Space AB, pg. 687   IT
Safe Partners AB, pg. 277   IT
Safe Service AB, pg. 277   IT
Scandinavian Heart Center AB, Carlanderplatsen,
    pg. 670   IT
Scansped Group, Falkenbergsgatan 3, pg. 123   IT
Skanska Fastigheter Goteborg AB, pg. 1260   IT
Skanska Vast, pg. 1261   IT
Stena Data Line IT Services A.B., Andreegatan 9,
    pg. 1300   IT
STENA LINE AB, Stena Terminalen, pg. 1300   IT
Stena Line Scandanavia A.B., pg. 1300   IT
Stora Purchasing & Transport AB, Box 2556, pg. 1303 IT
Svedala Cranes, pg. 1324   IT
Travel Agency Nordstadstorget, Gotgatan 14, pg. 1300 IT
Uddeholm Tooling Svenska AB, pg. 1471   IT
VICTOR HASSELBLAD AB, Ostra Hamngatan 3,
    pg. 1468   IT
Viking Fruit AB, pg. 643   IT
AB VOLVO, pg. 1476   IT
Volvo Bus Corporation, pg. 1476   IT
Volvo Car Corporation, pg. 1476   IT
Volvo Cars Intercontinental AB, pg. 1476   IT
Volvo Data Corporation, pg. 1476   IT
Volvo Group Finance Sweden AB, pg. 1476   IT
Volvo Group Insurance Forsakrings AB, pg. 1476   IT
Volvo International Development Corp., pg. 1476   IT
Volvo Lastvagner Sverige AB, pg. 1476   IT
Volvo Parts Corp., pg. 1476   IT
AB Volvo Penta, pg. 1476   IT
Volvo Penta Industry Corporation, pg. 1476   IT

PB - *U.S. Public Companies Volume*
PV - *U.S. Private Companies Volume*
IT - *International Public & Private Companies Volume*

Volvo Personvagnar Norden AB, pg. 1476 — IT
AB Volvo, Technological Development, pg. 1476 — IT
Volvo Transport Corporation, pg. 1476 — IT
Volvo Truck Corporation, pg. 1477 — IT
Willis Faber Gothia AB, Lilla Torget 1, pg. 1510 — IT
Wilson Group, Falkensbergsgatan 3, pg. 123 — IT
Zeneca AB, Drakegatan 10, pg. 1526 — IT

Grums

Stora Gruvon, pg. 1302 — IT

Grycksbo

Stora Grycksbo AB, pg. 1303 — IT

Guldsmeds-hyttan

Guldsmedshytte Bruks AB, pg. 1185 — IT

Gumligen

Nissen Trampoline AG, pg. 595 — IT

Gunnebo

GUNNEBO INDUSTRIER AB, pg. 578 — IT

Gusum

Bruza Gusum Viror AB, pg. 1202 — IT

Hagersten

Adidas-Sarragan Svenska AB, pg. 25 — IT
Finnigan MAT AB, Vastertorpsvagen 135, pg. 1596 — PB
Flender Svenka AB, Elektravagen 49, pg. 401 — IT
AB Formverktyg, Electravagen 5, pg. 439 — IT
Wandel & Goltermann AB, Ellen Keys gata 60, pg. 1486 — IT

Hagfors

Componenta Vagstal AB, Hagfors Jarnverk, Box 710, pg. 1421 — IT
Hagfors Mekaniska Verkstads AB, Bryggerivagen, pg. 1471 — IT
Hagfors Tooling AB, pg. 1471 — IT
Uddeholm Tooling AB, pg. 1471 — IT

Hallefors

Electrolux Gjuteriprodukter AB, pg. 438 — IT

Hallstahammar

KANTHAL AB, Box 502, pg. 723 — IT
Precon Hus AB, Eriksbergsvagen 15, pg. 1199 — IT

Hallstavik

Hallsta Paper Mill, pg. 885 — IT

Halmstad

Battenfeld Svergie AB, Ryttarevargen 18A, pg. 825 — IT
Dormer Tools AB, pg. 1185 — IT
Duni AB-Nordic Division, Vastervallvagen, pg. 421 — IT
Eurotherm Drivteknik AB, Box 9084, pg. 466 — IT
Lion Ferry AB, Kattegatthamnen, pg. 1300 — PB
Nomafa, pg. 37 — PB
Nordiskafilt AB, Box 510, pg. 37 — PB
Pilkington Floatglas AB, pg. 1057 — IT
Waco Jonsereds AB, P.O. Box 41, pg. 1421 — IT
Wallbergs Fabriks Aktiebolag, pg. 37 — PB

Handen

Grindex AB, Hantverkarvagen 25, pg. 860 — PB
Melitta AB, BFX 514, pg. 857 — IT

Haninge

General Motors Nordiska AB, Armaturvaegen 4, pg. 722 — PB
Mannesmann Demag Materialhantering AB, pg. 837 — IT
Telemobitel, Rudsjoterassen 2, pg. 1373 — IT
Telia Research AB, pg. 1374 — IT

Haparanda

KOPO AB, pg. 1353 — IT

Harnosand

ASEA Truck AB, pg. 7 — IT
YDAB i Harnosand AB, Solumnsvagen 6, pg. 278 — IT

Hassleholm

Dinol AB, Spangatan 3, pg. 981 — IT
Microbas AB, Tippvagen, pg. 1289 — IT
Silver-Weibull AB., Industrigatan 15, pg. 705 — PB

Hedemora

Hedemora AB, pg. 898 — IT

Helsingborg

ASK-Centralen AB, Torbornavagen 13, pg. 708 — IT
Akron AB, Jarnvagsgatan 14, pg. 1072 — IT
Alufluor Aktiebolag, pg. 69 — IT
Aritmos AB, Ronnoscatan 10, pg. 1072 — IT
BOC Ohmeda AB, P.O. Box 631, pg. 122 — IT
BetzDearborn AB, Box 622, Industrigatan, pg. 227 — PB
Blomstercentralen AB, Torbornavagen 13, pg. 708 — PB
Carbotrade International AB, pg. 1201 — IT
AB Carlsson & Moller, Garnisonsgatan 45, pg. 678 — IT
Domilens AB, Drottninggatan 62, pg. 350 — PB
Eaton Svenska AB, Florettgatan 37, pg. 559 — PB
Ekomat Sweden AB, Landskronavagen 9, pg. 920 — IT
AB Elektrokoppar, pg. 7 — IT
Fraktarna AB, Kungsgatan 2, pg. 476 — IT
Frigoscandia AB, Box 912, pg. 606 — PB
Frigoscandia Food Process Systems AB, Box 913, pg. 606 — PB
Frigoscandia Svenska AB, Box 912, pg. 606 — PB
Grace (Sweden) AB, pg. 756 — PB
W.R. Grace AB, Industrigatan 125, pg. 755 — PB
Hydro Supra KemiService AB, Morsaregatan 19, pg. 963 — IT
Hydro Sydplast AB, Gevarsgt. 4, pg. 963 — IT
Indra AB, Landskronavagen 9, pg. 920 — IT
Kemira Kemi AB, Industrigatan 83, pg. 728 — IT
Laporte Kemwood AB, Lastgatan 9, pg. 803 — IT
John Martensson Elmaterial AB, Bergavagen 17, pg. 1363 — IT
NCC Building - Helsingborg, pg. 898 — IT
NYK Line-Helsingborg, Hamntorget 5, pg. 942 — IT
AB Ph. Nederman & Co., Sydhamnsgatan 2, pg. 281 — IT
AB Novum, Mosaregatan 8, pg. 678 — IT
Perstorp Analytical AB-Distribution HQ, Sodra Storgatan 7, pg. 1039 — IT
Pharmacia & Upjohn Consumer Pharma, Norrbroplatsen 2, pg. 1048 — IT
SKF Multitec AB, Ekslingan 3, pg. 1157 — IT
Salen Coal AB, pg. 1201 — IT
Swedish Tyre Tube AB, pg. 1422 — IT
Travaru AB A. Thomee, pg. 1199 — IT
Tretorn AB, Ronnowsgatan 10, pg. 1072 — IT
Tretorn Forsaljnings AB, Ronnowsgatan 6, pg. 1072 — IT
Zeneca Agro, Kullagatan 30, pg. 1526 — IT
AB Zoegas Kaffe, pg. 922 — IT

Hestra

Isaberg Rapid AB, Metallgatan 15, pg. 678 — IT

Hillared

Bergis Textil Service AB, 55, Centralvagen, pg. 1285 — IT

Hillerstorp

Industri AB Thule, Box 69, pg. 436 — IT

Hisings Backa

Bicapa-Bjoernklaeder AB, Importgatan 23-33, pg. 1285 — IT
Contronic Development ab, S:t Jorgens Vag 10, pg. 1039 — IT
Histocenter-Skandinaviskt Centrum for Histoteknik AB, Arods Industrivag 40, pg. 708 — IT
AB Nobel Plast, Salsmastaregatan 32, pg. 48 — IT
Outokumpu Stal & Metall AB, Exportgatan 81, pg. 1016 — IT
Plast-Teknik Curver AB, Exportgatan 59 Box 4158, pg. 356 — IT
Statoil EuroParts AB, Salsmastaregatan 32, pg. 1298 — IT

Hisings Karra

Machinery West, Tagenevagen 25, pg. 899 — IT

Hjarnarp

GPA Plast AB, Brovagen 5, pg. 678 — IT

Hjo

Hydro Aluminium Packaging AB, Tubgatan 2, pg. 962 — IT

Hofors

Ovako Couplings AB, pg. 1157 — IT

Hoganas

AB Iwan Paulson, Brannerigatan 2, pg. 1199 — IT
Mataki Heltackande Tak, pg. 1422 — IT
Perstorp Analytical Tecator AB, Litteratervagen 8, pg. 1040 — IT

Hogsater

Perstorp Components, Annerudsvagen 2, pg. 1040 — IT

Hogsjo

Scandiafelt IT AB, pg. 1203 — IT
Scapa Scandia AB, pg. 1203 — IT

Hoor

AB Hoors Plat, P.O. Box 76, pg. 439 — IT

Horby

Atos Medical AB, pg. 1036 — IT
Medical Rubber AB, Lyby 309, pg. 1036 — IT

Hova

WABCO Westinghouse AB, Industriegatan, pg. 92 — PB

Huddinge

Bevinggruppen AB, pg. 188 — IT
Jirva AB, pg. 1422 — IT
Landis & Staefa AB, Elektronwagen 4-6, pg. 800 — IT
Landis & Staefa Energy Management AB, Elektronwagen 4-6, pg. 800 — IT
Mannesmann Kienzle AB, pg. 839 — IT
Mastsystem AB, Regulatorv. 21, pg. 914 — IT
Werner & Pfleiderer AB, Patron Pehrsvag 6 11, pg. 511 — IT

Hudiksvall

Iggesund Sawmill, pg. 886 — IT
Iggesund Timber AB, pg. 886 — IT
Voith Safeset AB, pg. 1473 — IT

Huskvarna

Electrolux Motor AB, P.O. Box 1010, pg. 438 — IT
Husqvarna AB, pg. 439 — IT
Husqvarna Svenska Forsaljnings AB, pg. 439 — IT
Saab Training Systems AB, Box 2049, pg. 687 — IT

Husum

Husum Mills, pg. 886 — IT

Hyllinge

Ecophon AB, pg. 1176 — IT

Hyltebruk

Stora Hylte AB, Box 300, pg. 1304 — IT

Iggesund

Iggesund Paperboard AB, pg. 886 — IT
Iggesunds Bruk, pg. 886 — IT
MoDo Data, Box 15, pg. 886 — IT
MoDo Skog AB - Iggesund, Box 15, pg. 887 — IT

Jakobsberg

AMP Svenska AB, Data ragen 5, pg. 9 — PB
Kodak AB, Nettovagen 2, pg. 552 — PB

Jarfalla

ABB Hafo AB, Box 520, pg. 7 — IT
CelsiusTech AB, pg. 276 — IT
CelsiusTech Electronics AB, pg. 276 — IT
CelsiusTech IT AB, pg. 277 — IT
CelsiusTech Systems AB, pg. 277 — IT
Dynapac Norden AB, Saldovagen 20, pg. 1420 — IT
Hellermann Scandinavia AB, Datavagen 4, pg. 209 — IT
Hydro Aluminium Hydro Trans, Spjutvagen 5-7, pg. 962 — IT
Irvin Fallskarms AB, Girovagen 9, S-175, pg. 640 — IT
Machinery Stockholm, Box 909, pg. 899 — IT
Micropolis A.B., Aprilvagen 3, pg. 742 — PV
Mitel Semiconductor AB, Box 520, pg. 870 — IT
Norton Scandinavia AB, Kontovagen 1-5, pg. 1175 — IT
Robator AB, Bruttovagen 6, pg. 1199 — IT

Johanneshov

Ampco Metal Nordiska AB, Mockelv, pg. 67 — PV
Mobrey AB, Box 5056, pg. 854 — IT
AB Nynas Petroleum, Huddingevagen 107, 1 tr, pg. 915 — IT
Pumpex AB, Rokerigatan 10, pg. 270 — IT

Jonaker

JonakerPannan AB, pg. 1092 — IT

Jonkoping

Emulsio AB, Tomtebogatan 2, pg. 370 — IT
GD-Golvdepan i Sverige AB, pg. 498 — IT
Gisebo Vagnindustri AB, Industrigatan 16, pg. 436 — IT
AB Huskvarna Elektrolytpolering, Barrsatragatan 16, pg. 221 — IT
JONKOPINGS LANTMAN EK. FOR., Solasvag 4, Box 1018, pg. 714 — IT

PB - *U.S. Public Companies Volume*
PV - *U.S. Private Companies Volume*
IT - *International Public & Private Companies Volume*

1766

Geographic Index-Non U.S.

Munksjo AB, P.O. Box 624, pg. 1423 — IT
Munksjo Hygien AB, Box 624, pg. 1423 — IT
Munskjoe Paper AB, Box 624, pg. 1423 — IT
NCC Building - Jonkoping, pg. 898 — IT
Region Jonkoping, Vedtorget 3, pg. 23 — IT
SKF Transmission AB, Osterangsvagen 2, pg. 1157 — IT
Saab Automation AB, Box 1017, pg. 686 — IT
Saab Instruments, Box 1017, pg. 686 — IT
Saab-Scania Combitech, Box 1017, pg. 686 — IT
Stifab, pg. 1422 — IT
Stora Building Products AB, Slottsgatan 14, pg. 1302 — IT
Sydved AB, Skolgatan 2, pg. 887 — IT
Tambox AB - Jonkoping Factory, pg. 458 — IT

Kallered

Sabema Material AB, pg. 1199 — IT
Siegling Svenska A.B., pg. 498 — IT

Kalmar

Kalmar Industries AB, Torsagatan 5, pg. 1420 — IT
Kalmar Verkstad AB, Box 943, pg. 1421 — IT
Skanska Stalteknik AB, P.O. Box 803, pg. 1261 — IT
Ventim AB, Flygplatsvagen 19, pg. 678 — IT

Karlshamn

Karlshamns AB, Vaestra Kajen, pg. 718 — IT

Karlskoga

Bofors Explosives AB, pg. 276 — IT
Bofors Norabel AB, pg. 276 — IT
Celsius Materialteknik Karlskoga AB, c/o Bofors AB, pg. 276 — IT
Componenta Tools AB, Kilsta Industriomrade, Box 700, pg. 1421 — IT
Nobel Elektronik AB, Skrantahojdsvagen 40 A, pg. 1289 — IT
Nordic Synthesis AB, pg. 297 — PB
Wikers AB, Boforsvagen, pg. 278 — IT

Karlskrona

Dynapac Heavy Equipment AB, Industrivagen 2, pg. 1420 — IT
E-P Consulting Group AB, Ostra Hamngatan 7B, pg. 1363 — IT
Karlskronavarvet AB, pg. 277 — IT
Lion Ferry AB, Farjeterminalen, pg. 1300 — IT
Maxcimator AB, Ostra Kopmansgatan 1, pg. 1364 — IT
Svedala Dynapac Heavy, pg. 1324 — IT
Uddcomb Sweden AB, P.O. Box 523, pg. 1421 — IT

Karlstad

Avesta Valbruna AB, Kungsgatan 8, pg. 221 — IT
Ericsson Infocom Consultants, Kanikenasbanken 4A, pg. 1363 — IT
Ericsson Programatic Sweden AB, Industrigatan 1, pg. 1363 — IT
GG Ws Gross, Tynasgatan 6, P.O. Box 338, pg. 359 — IT
Glashuset I Karlstad AB, Sagvaggsgatan 28, pg. 1173 — IT
Kamfab AB, pg. 771 — IT
Kamyr AB, pg. 771 — IT
Kamyr Engineering AB, pg. 771 — IT
Kvaerner Kamfab AB, Axel Johnsons vag 6, pg. 767 — IT
Kvaerner Pulping Technologies, Knud Dahls vag, pg. 772 — IT
LBI Luftbehandling AB, pg. 1261 — IT
Lundbergs-Varmland Region, Drottninggatan 27, pg. 821 — IT
NCC Building - Karlstad, pg. 898 — IT
Stora Purchasing & Transport, Box 5026, pg. 1303 — IT
Uddeholm Kraft AB, pg. 1471 — IT
Valmet-Karlstad AB, Axel Johnsons Vag 6, pg. 1448 — IT
Valmet Skandinavien AB, Axel Johnsons vag 6, P.O. Box 1034, pg. 1448 — IT

Katrineholm

SKF Mekan AB, Fredsgatan 3, pg. 1157 — IT
Scania-Bussar AB, Box 366, pg. 687 — IT
Yttec AB, pg. 278 — IT

Kil

Outokumpu Wenmec AB, P.O. Box 175, pg. 1017 — IT

Kinna

NEK/CDT, pg. 287 — PB

Kiruna

J.W. Andersson Maskin AB, pg. 1422 — IT

Kisa

Duni/Finess Hygiene, pg. 421 — IT
Langasjonas Paper Mill, pg. 421 — IT

Kista

Adobe Systems Nordic PB, pg. 20 — PB
B & W Stormarknader AB, Kistagangen 21, pg. 708 — IT

AB BINAB, Box 65, pg. 899 — IT
Robert Bosch AB, Isafjordsgatan 15, pg. 205 — IT
CCS Deskpro Computer AB, Norgegatan 2, pg. 418 — PB
Colly Company AB, Raseborgsgatan 9, pg. 678 — IT
Datateam Sverige AB, Electrum 228, pg. 708 — IT
De La Rue Cash Handling Product Group, Kronborgsgrand 11, pg. 387 — IT
Dialog CRS AB, pg. 277 — IT
Enator AB, pg. 708 — IT
Ericsson Radio Access AB, Borgarfjordsgatan 14, pg. 1364 — IT
GA Lindberg AB, Raseborgsgatan 9, pg. 678 — IT
Hercules Grandlaggning AB, pg. 899 — IT
Hewlett-Packard Sverige AB, Skalholtsgatan 9, pg. 822 — PB
Indutrade AB, Raseborgsgatan 9, pg. 678 — IT
Ingersoll-Rand AB, Isafjordsgatan 19, Box 1029, pg. 878 — PB
Axel Johnson Fastighetsforvaltning AB, Electrum 229, pg. 709 — IT
Axel Johnson International AB, pg. 709 — IT
Knurr Sverige AB, Finlandsgatan 16-18, pg. 739 — IT
KONE Hissar AB, Haukadalsgatan 3, pg. 747 — IT
KONE Rulltrappor A.B., Haukadalsgatan 3, pg. 748 — IT
AB Lorentzen & Wettre, Viderogatan 2, pg. 271 — IT
A.C. Nielsen Company AB, Borgarfjordsgatan 13, pg. 1183 — PB
Nokia Mobile Phones AB, Torshamnsgatan 30B, pg. 952 — IT
Nokia Monitors, Torshamngatan 39, pg. 951 — IT
Nokia Telecommunications AB, Torshamnsgatan 30B, pg. 953 — IT
Nordisk Elektronik AB, pg. 709 — IT
Novell Sweden, Farogatan 7, pg. 1204 — PB
OMRON Electronics A.B., Norgegatan 1, pg. 1005 — IT
Oracle Corporation Svenska AB, Kottbygatan 7, pg. 1228 — PB
Philips Kistaindustrier AB, pg. 1055 — IT
Priab AB, pg. 709 — IT
Radiosystem Sweden AB, Borgarfjorsgatan 14, pg. 1364 — IT
Reader's Digest AB, Skalholtsgatan 2, pg. 1368 — PB
Rockwell Automation AB, Finlandsgatan 52, pg. 1399 — PB
Sandvik Stal Forsaljnings AB, pg. 1185 — IT
Tandem Computers AB, Norgegatan 1, pg. 417 — PB
Ventilizationunion AB, pg. 1422 — IT

Klippan

Duni AB-Finess Forsaljning, pg. 421 — IT
Vera Klippan AB, pg. 715 — IT

Kolsva

Kohlswa Jernverk AB, pg. 439 — IT

Koping

Hydro Supra AB, Nya Hamnvegen, pg. 963 — IT
AB H. Karlstrom, pg. 709 — IT
Krupp Stahl AB, Stora Gatan 21, pg. 516 — IT

Kopparberg

Dexter Nonwovens AB, S-714 03 Stalldalen, pg. 505 — PB

Kristianstad

CPC Foods AB, Tegelbruksvagen 18, Box 2126, pg. 225 — PB
Coherent Scandinavia, Bjorkhemsvagen 19, pg. 396 — PB
Mactec AB, Industriagatan 41, pg. 860 — PB
Novia Livsmedelsindustrier AB, pg. 1438 — IT

Kristinehamn

Albin Komponenter AB, Hantverkaregatan 3, pg. 1323 — IT
Componenta Wear Parts, pg. 1323 — IT
Kamewa AB, pg. 1341 — IT
Kvaerner Turbin AB, Eldaregatan, 681 35 Kristinehamn, pg. 770 — IT
Siluett Nordia AB, Box 199, pg. 421 — IT

Kuidinge

J.D. Stenquist AB, pg. 421 — IT

Kumla

Aminkemi AB, Narkes Kvarntorp, pg. 728 — IT
Ferriklor AB, Kvarntorp, pg. 728 — IT

Kungalv

Evert Larsson Industri AB, Box 4, pg. 439 — IT
ICA Handlarna Vast AB, pg. 643 — IT
Svenska Skumslacknings Aktiebolaget, Box 32, Byggmastaregatan 1, pg. 595 — IT

Kungsbacka

ALK Sverge AB, Energigatan 12, pg. 288 — IT
Nordiska Balzers AB, Lilla Verkstadsgatan 2, pg. 998 — IT
Scancables AB, Energigatan 10, pg. 1363 — IT

Kunsgatan

Novotel Goteborg AB, c/o Advolcafirma Carlers, pg. 21 — IT

Kvanum

Consilium Bulk-Babcock, Kvanum AB, pg. 131 — IT

Kvillsfors

Metsa-Serla AB (Nyboholm Mill), pg. 864 — IT

Laholm

John O. Butler Company (Sweden), P.O. Box 29 Industrigatan 32, pg. 1321 — IT
Kalmar Lagab AB, Box 209, pg. 1421 — IT

Landskrona

Besam AB, Lodjursgatan 10, pg. 678 — IT
Bofors S A Marine AB, pg. 276 — IT
Boliden Bergsoe AB, pg. 1422 — IT
DSM Scandinavia AB, Varvsvagen, pg. 355 — IT
Hilleshog AB, Sabyholm, Box 302, pg. 982 — IT
Hilleshog Forestry AB, pg. 982 — IT
Hilleshog Research AB, pg. 982 — IT
Hilleshog Skogar AB, pg. 982 — IT
Hilleshog Sugar Beet Seed AB, pg. 982 — IT
Hydro Supra AB, Storgatan 24, P.O. Box 516, pg. 963 — IT
Oresundsvarvet AB, pg. 277 — IT
SAB WABCO AB, Instrumentgatan 15, pg. 271 — IT
SIA Lustgarden AB, Norra Kyrkogranden 9, pg. 439 — IT
ScanDust AB, pg. 1157 — IT

Langshyttan

Avesta Sheffield AB, pg. 221 — IT

Laxa

ESAB Welding Equipment AB, Walter Edstroms vag, pg. 281 — IT

Lidingo

AGA AB, pg. 12 — IT
AGA Industrial Gas Engineering AB, pg. 12 — IT
AGA RE, pg. 13 — IT
AGA SpecialGas AB, pg. 13 — IT
AB Lidingo Verkstader, pg. 1377 — IT

Lidkoping

Hagglunds Lidan AB, Fiskaregatan 3, pg. 670 — IT
Lincoln Svetshuset AB, pg. 997 — PB
Rockwell Automation AB, Konvaljvagen 35, pg. 1399 — PB
AB Sandvik Metal Saws, pg. 1185 — IT
Svenska Foder AB, Kinnegatan 23, pg. 350 — IT

Lindesberg

Bofors LIAB AB, pg. 276 — IT

Lindome

Nitto Scandinavia AB, Heljesvagen 9, pg. 951 — IT

Linkoping

Applied Composites AB, pg. 276 — IT
BBB Bildedelhandling AB, Tanneforsvagen 96 B, pg. 1289 — IT
Ballast Ost AB, Skyttegatan 2C, pg. 899 — IT
Bundy AB, pg. 1341 — IT
Celsius Materialteknik AB, pg. 276 — IT
ETP Transmission AB, Roxtorpsgatan 14, pg. 678 — IT
FFV Aerotech AB, pg. 276 — IT
FFV AvioComp AB, pg. 276 — IT
GV Emission Technology AB, pg. 277 — IT
Lidkoping Machine Tools AB, Fabriksgatan, pg. 1157 — IT
Lovene Dorr AB, Lovene, pg. 1302 — IT
Machinery East, pg. 899 — IT
NAF AB, pg. 1422 — IT
NCC Building, pg. 898 — IT
NCC Linkoping, pg. 899 — IT
Saab AB, Broderna Ugglas Gala, pg. 686 — IT
Saab Aircraft Division, pg. 686 — IT
Saab Missiles AB, pg. 686 — IT
AB Svensk Leca, pg. 1200 — IT

Ljungby

Bentone-Electro Oil AB, pg. 1422 — IT
CTC Parca AB, pg. 1422 — IT
Componenta Gjuterier AB, Stalgatan 2, pg. 1419 — IT
Componenta Industri, pg. 1323 — IT
Dynapac Concrete Equipment AB, Gangesvagen 4, pg. 1420 — IT
Dynapac Light Equipment AB, Gangesvagen 4, pg. 1420 — IT
Electrolux-Wascator AB, P.O. Box 305, pg. 439 — IT
Enertech Industries AB, pg. 1422 — IT
Kalmar LMV AB, Box 308, pg. 1421 — IT
AB Ljungby Stalgjuteri, Stalgatan 2, Box 320, pg. 1419 — IT

PB - *U.S. Public Companies Volume*
PV - *U.S. Private Companies Volume*
IT - *International Public & Private Companies Volume*

Geographic Index-Non U.S.

1767

Ljungby Stalgjuteri Ljungby, pg. 1323 — IT
Svedala Dynapac Light, pg. 1324 — IT

Lodose

B. Johanssons Pappersforadling AB, pg. 439 — IT

Ludvika

ABB HV Switchgear AB, pg. 7 — IT
ABB Transformers AB, pg. 7 — IT
National Electrical Carbon A.B., pg. 892 — IT
Vasterbergslagens Elnat AB, pg. 1453 — IT
Vattenfall Hydropower AB, pg. 1453 — IT

Lulea

Erisoft AB, Laboratoriegrand 11, pg. 1364 — IT
NCC Building, pg. 898 — IT
Saab-Scania AB, Box 815, pg. 687 — IT
Vattenfall Norrnat AB, pg. 1453 — IT
Vattenfall Vattenkraft, Box 807, pg. 1453 — IT

Lund

AB Akerlund & Rausing Group, pg. 33 — IT
Alfa Laval AB, Ruben Rausings gata, pg. 1378 — IT
Alfa Laval Agri AB, Ruben Rausings gata, pg. 1378 — IT
Alfa-Laval Food Engineering AB, pg. 1378 — IT
Alfa-Laval Thermal AB, Rudeboksvagen, pg. 1378 — IT
Astra Draco AB, pg. 93 — IT
AU-System Radio AB, pg. 1363 — IT
Bioinvent International AB, pg. 961 — IT
Draco Lakemedel AB/Tika Lakemedel AB, pg. 93 — IT
Excorim AB, Emdalavagen, pg. 667 — IT
Gambro AB, Magistratsvagen 16, pg. 666 — IT
Gambro Sales AB, Magistratsvagen 10, pg. 667 — IT
Gambro Svenska Forsaljnings AB, Scheelevagen 30, pg. 667 — IT
Medical Data Intelligence AB, Emdalavagen, pg. 667 — IT
Park Dialys AB, S:t Lars vag 45, pg. 667 — IT
Perstorp Pharma AB, Ideon, Scheelegatan 17, pg. 1036 — IT
Scandinavian Bellyloading Co. AB, pg. 1570 — PB
Tetra Laval Food, Ruben Rausings gata, pg. 1378 — IT
TETRA LAVAL GROUP, Rubon Rausings gata, pg. 1377 — IT
Tetra Laval International AB, Landerigranden, pg. 1378 — IT
Tetra Pak, Ruben Rausings gata, pg. 1378 — IT

Lycksele

MoDo Skog AB - Lycksele, Vilhelminavagen 3, pg. 887 — IT

Malmkoping

Zig-Zag Fabriks AB, P.O. Box 50, pg. 439 — IT

Malmo

ABS Pump AB, Kattsundsgatan 15, pg. 270 — IT
ACTIVE BIOTECH AB, Stora Nygatan 61, pg. 23 — IT
Agency at Malmo, Frederiksbergsgatan 7, pg. 1030 — IT
Athena AB, Roskildevagen 1 B, pg. 666 — IT
B & W Stormarknader AB, Gygersro 151, pg. 708 — IT
BSD Teknik, Bjelkhult 1, pg. 361 — PV
Ballast Syd AB, pg. 899 — IT
Baltic Cable AB, Carl Gustafs VAG 4, pg. 1457 — IT
Biogram AB, Borrgatan 31 a, pg. 961 — IT
Broderna Edstrand AB, Spadegatan 1, pg. 1422 — IT
James Burn International AB, P.O. Box 4093, Engelbrektsgaten 15, pg. 1507 — PB
CARDO AB, Roskildevagen 1B, pg. 268 — IT
Cardo Door AB, Roskildevagen 1B, pg. 269 — IT
Cardo Door Export AB, Roskildevagen 1B, pg. 269 — IT
Cardo Railway AB, Roskildevagen 1B, pg. 271 — IT
J.I. Case Sweden AB, Hakegatan 1, Box 27 088, pg. 1580 — PB
G Cederholms Verkstad AB, Stora Varvsgatan 11E, pg. 281 — IT
Cementa AB (Malmo), pg. 1198 — IT
Crawmator AB, Roskildevagen 1B, pg. 269 — IT
DAB Dental AB, Sodra Skolgatan 37, pg. 711 — IT
Danisco Sugar AB, Sockerbruksgatan, Arlov, pg. 378 — IT
Electrolux Mecatronik AB, Industigatau 26, pg. 438 — IT
Enator Syd AB, Slagthuset, pg. 277 — IT
Esselte Wensbo AB, Box 9083, pg. 459 — IT
Euroc Reinsurance S.A., pg. 1199 — IT
Euroc Trade AB, Box 60081, pg. 1199 — IT
Eurotherm AB, Lundavagen 143, pg. 466 — IT
Fasson AB, Kosterogatan 5, pg. 154 — PB
Ferrosan AB, Grynbodgatan 14, pg. 989 — IT
GCE, Box 21044, pg. 14 — IT
GCE-Gas Control Equipment AB, Flygfaltsvagen 1, pg. 281 — IT
Gyproc AB, Jurgen Kocksgatan 9, pg. 122 — IT
Huls Sverige AB, Norra Vallgatan 64, pg. 1455 — IT
Hydro Pharma A/S, Baergatan 31 A, pg. 963 — IT
Icopal ab, 11 Skeppsbron, Box 848, pg. 659 — IT
Icopal Entreprenad AB, pg. 659 — IT
AB Jan Ralling, pg. 1261 — IT
Axel Johnson Chemicals AB, Norra Vallgatan 64, pg. 708 — IT
Axel Johnson Instrument AB, Stenyxegatan 21, pg. 709 — IT
Lars Jonsson AB, Fosievagen 8, pg. 922 — IT
AB Karosseritillbehor, pg. 709 — IT
Knorr-Bremse System for Tunga Fordon AB, Hemsogatan 20, pg. 738 — IT

Kockums AB, pg. 277 — IT
Kockums Computer Systems AB, pg. 277 — IT
Kockums Engineering AB, pg. 277 — IT
Kockums Holdings AB, pg. 277 — IT
Kockums Industrier AB, pg. 277 — IT
Kockums Submarine Systems AB, pg. 277 — IT
Kockums Verkstader AB, pg. 277 — IT
Linde Kylteknik Svergie AB, pg. 810 — IT
Lundbergs-Malmo Region, Sodra Tullgatan 3, pg. 821 — IT
MD Foods Sverige AB, von Troils Vag 1, pg. 826 — IT
Machinery South, pg. 899 — PV
Maste' Foods AB, Box 4138, pg. 707 — PV
AB Mataki, pg. 1422 — IT
NCC Building, Thomsons vag 40, pg. 898 — IT
NCT Norden AB, Scheelegatan 32, pg. 915 — IT
NVS Nordiska Varme Sana AB, pg. 899 — IT
A.C. Nielsen Company AB, Sodergatan 3, pg. 1183 — PB
Nordisk Elektra AB, PO Box 50344, Bjurogatan 42, pg. 709 — IT
Novo Nordisk Pharma AB, Murmansgatan 126, pg. 988 — IT
Pfizer Hospital Products A.B., Krossverksgatan 3, pg. 1284 — PB
Pierre Robert AB, pg. 1438 — IT
Prestige AB (Scandinavian Music Club), Ronnviksgatan 13, pg. 1053 — IT
PreussenElektra Scandinavia AB, pg. 1457 — IT
Procordia Food AB, pg. 1011 — IT
AB SANI-Maskiner, Jagersrovagen 202, pg. 444 — PB
SATTControl AB, pg. 1378 — IT
SCANCEM AB, Annetorpsvagen 100, P.O. Box 600 66, pg. 1198 — IT
Scancem Fastigheter AB, Box 60066, pg. 1200 — IT
Scancem Service AB, pg. 1200 — IT
AB Skane-Reportage, Azngelholmsgatan 1-3, Box 7069, pg. 29 — IT
Skanska Anlaggning AB, pg. 1260 — IT
Skanska International Building AB, pg. 1260 — IT
Skanska Oresund AB, pg. 1261 — IT
Skanska Prefab AB, pg. 1261 — IT
Skanska Syd, pg. 1260 — IT
Skanska Teknik AB, pg. 1261 — IT
Sonesson Inredningar AB, Sturkogatan 9, pg. 23 — IT
Spectra-Physics Laserplane AB, Sporregatan 12, pg. 1289 — IT
Sveda a Compaction & Paving, pg. 1324 — IT
Sveda a Conveyor Belting, pg. 1324 — IT
Sveda a Crushing & Screening, pg. 1324 — IT
Sveda a Foundries, pg. 1324 — IT
SVEDALA INDUSTRI AB, pg. 1323 — IT
Sveda a International, pg. 1324 — IT
Sveda a Pumps & Process, pg. 1325 — IT
Sveda a Wear Protection, pg. 1325 — IT
Svenska Polystyren Fabriken AB, Norra Vallgatan 64, pg. 1456 — IT
Sydkreft AB, Carl Gustafs VAG 4, pg. 1457 — IT
TAC Control AB, Jagershillg 18, pg. 670 — IT
AB Tegma, Kopparbergsgatan 29, pg. 1114 — PB
AB Tvattman Textil Service, 108 Limhamnsvagen, pg. 1286 — IT
Vattenfall AB, Stortorget 3, pg. 1453 — IT
White Cap Inc. Nordiska AB, pg. 1207 — IT
Yamanouchi Pharma AB, Hans Michelsengatan 1B, pg. 1519 — IT

Malung

Byggs Sprutbetong AB, pg. 899 — IT

Mariestad

Metsa-Serla AB (Katrinefors Mill), Hollandaregatan 4, pg. 864 — IT

Markaryd

Ahlstromforetagen Svenska AB-Markaryd Core Plant, Harnabadsvagen 15, pg. 33 — IT

Marsta

Atlas Copco Craelius AB, pg. 96 — IT
Harper Freight International (Sweden) AB, Soderbyagen 4, pg. 373 — PB

Matfors

Ahlstromforetagen Svenska AB-Matfors Core Plant, pg. 33 — IT

Mellansel

Hagglunds Drives AB, pg. 669 — IT

Mellbystrand

Intralox A/S, 8, Strandvagen 29b, pg. 643 — PV

Mjolby

BT INDUSTRIES AB, Svarvargatan 8, pg. 123 — IT
Danfoss AB, Industrigatan 7, pg. 377 — IT
Danfoss AB Plumbing Controls Div., Industrigatan 9, pg. 377 — IT
Forss-Parator, Albacken, pg. 1420 — IT
Gusab Stainless AB, pg. 1185 — IT

Molkom

Avesta Calamo AB, pg. 221 — IT
Avesta Nords AB, pg. 221 — IT

Molndal

ABS Pump AB, Taljegardsgatan 11, pg. 270 — IT
ABS Pump Production AB, Krokslatts Parkgata 4, pg. 270 — IT
ABS Pumps International AB, Krokslatts Parkgata 4, pg. 270 — IT
Astra Hassle AB, pg. 93 — IT
Astra Tech AB, pg. 93 — IT
Cardo Pump AB, Krokslatts Parkgata 4, pg. 270 — IT
Danzas AB, Flojelbergsgatan 11, pg. 382 — IT
Ericsson Microwave Systems-Molndal, pg. 1363 — IT
Ericsson Radar Electronics AB, Bergfotsgatan 2, pg. 1363 — IT
Glaxo Wellcome AB, pg. 553 — IT
Hassle Lakemedel AB, pg. 93 — IT
Henkel Kemi AB, pg. 613 — IT
Hydro Supra AB, Specialkemi, pg. 963 — IT
Jac Jacobsen AB, Kraketorpsgatan 10 A, pg. 821 — IT
Lewmar Marine AB, Argongatan 8, pg. 1462 — IT
Stora Merchant, Box 1004, pg. 1303 — IT
Stora Molndal AB, Box 213, pg. 1302 — IT
Stora Papyrus AB, Kvarnbygatan 2B, pg. 1303 — IT
Stora Papyrus International AB, Box 183, pg. 1303 — IT
Stora Papyrus Network AB, Box 183, pg. 1303 — IT
Vader Vast AB, Goteborgsvagen 97, pg. 1364 — IT

Molnlycke

ATLET AB, Metallvagen 7, pg. 97 — IT
AB Kaj Mandorf, Metallvagen 20, pg. 678 — IT
Molnlycke AB New Markets Development, Fibervagen 8, pg. 1326 — IT
Molnlycke Absorbant Products Supply AB, Kvarnbacken 2, pg. 1326 — IT

Mora

AB Wibe, Wibevagen 1, pg. 678 — IT

Morgongava

Vittinge Tegel AB, pg. 1092 — IT

Motala

Bofors Underwater Systems AB, pg. 276 — IT
Fiskars Konsumentprodukter AB, Ringtrastvagen 4, pg. 492 — IT
Fiskars Sverige AB, pg. 492 — IT
Fogelsta Industri AB, Fagelsta, pg. 436 — IT
Hycop AB, pg. 328 — IT
Motala Hissar A.B., Myntgatan 1, pg. 748 — IT
Motala Tank, Skenasverkstaden, pg. 1420 — IT
Nokia Audio & Electronics AB, Mederivagen 55, pg. 954 — IT
Nokia Satellite Systems AB, Luxorgatan 1, pg. 954 — IT
Vattenfall Eastern Sweden, Box 940, pg. 1453 — IT
Vattenfall Energimatning AB, pg. 1453 — IT
Vattenfall VatterNat AB, pg. 1453 — IT

Nacka

Atlas Construction Tools, pg. 96 — IT
Atlas Copco Berema AB, pg. 96 — IT
Nordic Business Management Systems AB, Varmdovagen 84, pg. 87 — PB

Nassjo

ELDON AB, Egnahemsgatan 39, pg. 436 — IT
Eldon Electronics AB, pg. 436 — IT
Eldon Elmateriel AB, pg. 436 — IT
Eldon Rental Trailer, Box 908, pg. 436 — IT
AB Skandinaviska Elverk, pg. 670 — IT

Njurunda

SCABA Production AB, Verkstadsvagen 12, pg. 270 — IT

Nol

AB Axel Christiernsson, P.O. Box 19, pg. 708 — IT

Nordmaling

Pumpex AB, Asgatan 15, pg. 270 — IT

Norrkoping

Ahlstrom Machinery AB Process Equipment, Lindovagen 77, pg. 34 — IT
Ahlstromforetagen Svenska AB-Norrkoping Core Plant, Lindovagen 77, pg. 33 — IT
AB Akerlund & Rausing, pg. 33 — IT
Braviken Paper Mill, pg. 885 — IT
CAE ScreenPlates AB, Lindovagen 73, pg. 238 — IT
FHP, Freudenberg Household Products AB, pg. 505 — IT
Flavoring AB, Koppargatan 10, pg. 349 — IT
Holmen Paper AB, Vattengranden 2, pg. 885 — IT

PB - U.S. Public Companies Volume
PV - U.S. Private Companies Volume
IT - International Public & Private Companies Volume

1768

Landegrens Mekaniska Verkstad AB, Hanholmsvagen 61, pg. 1419   IT
Lundbergs-Norrkoping & Gotaland Region, S:t Persgatan 105, pg. 821   IT
MoDo Data, Vattengranden 2, pg. 886   IT
MoDo Skog AB - Norrkoping, Vattengranden 2, pg. 887   IT
Norrkoping AxTrade AB, pg. 709   IT
Norrkopings Sand AB, Finspangsv, 490, pg. 1200   IT
Outokumpu WTT AB, pg. 1017   IT
Philips Norrkoepengsindustrier AB, pg. 1055   IT
AB Profila, Lindovagen 75, pg. 1377   IT
STAL Refrigeration AB, Butangsgatan 14-16, pg. 7   IT
Tenokron AB, pg. 507   IT
Vattenfall Varmekraft, Drottninggatan 36, pg. 1453   IT
Wettex AB, pg. 506   IT

Norrsundet

Stora Cell Norrsundet AB, pg. 1303   IT

Norrtalje

Neste Cellplast AB, Braxenvagen 8, pg. 914   IT

Nybro

AB Gustaf Kahr, pg. 1260   IT
Munksjoe Forpackningar AB, Box 824, pg. 1423   IT
Nybro Smide, Tegelvagen 1, pg. 1421   IT
AB Sture Ljungdahl, Box 823, pg. 1423   IT

Nykoping

ABB Selfa AB, pg. 7   IT
Fabriken Odin AB, Idbacksvagen 8B, pg. 1378   IT
Leverindus AB, Lager Dantorpsv. 17, pg. 1438   IT
Mecman Engineering AB, pg. 839   IT
Saab Automobile AB, pg. 687   IT
Saab Automobile AB, pg. 725   PB
Saab Sweden AB, pg. 687   IT
AB Sunlight, pg. 1438   IT
Thorsman & Co. AB, Tillverkarvagen 2, Arno, pg. 678   IT
Vattenfall Ostnat AB, pg. 1453   IT

Nyland

Ahlstrom Machinery AB-Hammars, Strandvagen 64, pg. 34   IT

Nymolla

Stora Nymolla AB, pg. 1303   IT

Nynashamn

Amdent AB, pg. 708   IT
LM Ericsson i Nynashamn AB, Industrivagen 4, pg. 1364   IT

Obbola

SCA Nordliner AB, Linjevagen 33, pg. 1326   IT

Olofstrom

ESAB Tele-Comp AB, Agrasjovagen, pg. 281   IT

Orebro

Emhart Teknik AB Machinery Division, P.O. Box 246, pg. 233   PB
Fundo Aluminium AB, pg. 962   IT
Hewlett-Packard Sverige AB, Elmentvagen 16, pg. 822   PB
Johnson Metall AB, Stalgatan 15, P.O. Box 1513, pg. 439   IT
NCC Building, pg. 898   IT
Orebro Kartongbruck AB, pg. 791   IT
Plantronics Nordic, Oskarsvagen 10, pg. 1308   PB
RECI Industri AB, Radiatorv. 11, pg. 1200   IT
Roxon AB, Norrgatan 15 A, pg. 1353   IT
Sigma AB, Stalgatan 2, pg. 1422   IT

Ornskoldsvik

Avesta ABE AB, pg. 221   IT
Domsjo Mills, Horneborgsvagen, pg. 886   IT
MacGREGOR Cranes AB, Bjornavagen 14, pg. 670   IT
MoDo Data, Hornettvagen 1, pg. 886   IT
MoDo Paper AB, Horneborgsvagen 6, pg. 886   IT
MoDo Research & Development, Horneborgsvagen 12, pg. 887   IT
MoDo Skog AB, Horneborgsvagen 6, pg. 887   IT
MoDo Skog AB - Ornskoldsvik, Modovagen 27, pg. 887   IT
Ornskoldsviks Mekaniska Verkstad (OMV), pg. 221   IT

Osby

Armaturteknik i Osby AB, Vintervagen 1, pg. 1323   IT
Osby Armatur AB, Vintervagen 1, pg. 1323   IT
Osby Parca AB, pg. 1422   IT
Osby Tvattutrusiningar AB, pg. 439   IT

Oskarshamn

NIFE AB, Jungnergatan, pg. 53   IT

SAFT Nife AB, pg. 54   IT
Saab-Scania AB, Box 903, pg. 687   IT

Ostersund

Permanova Lasersystem AB, Fagerbacken 28, pg. 1290   IT

Osthammar

Forsmarks Kraftgrupp AB, pg. 1453   IT

Overum

AB Overums Bruk, P.O. Box 100, pg. 439   IT
AB Overums Fonsterfabrik, P.O. Box 100, pg. 439   IT

Partille

Alnab Armatur AB, Orgardesvagen 4, pg. 678   IT
Binks-Bullows Sweden AB, Box 90, Ogardesvagen 6C, pg. 229   PB
Jonsereds Godsskydd AB, pg. 439   IT
Kvaerner Generator AB, Laxfiskevagen, pg. 767   IT
Network Systems AB, Brodalsvagen 7, pg. 1522   PB
Nordic Forestry Equipment AB, pg. 439   IT
Pharmacia & Upjohn AB, pg. 1049   IT

Paulistrom

Metsa-Serla AB (Paulistrom Mill), pg. 864   IT

Perstorp

Advanced Polymers, pg. 1036   IT
ESAB AB, Elektrodvagen, pg. 281   IT
Hoechst-Perstorp AB, pg. 1039   IT
Metfoils AB, pg. 1039   IT
Pernovo, pg. 1036   IT
PERSTORP AB, pg. 1036   IT
Perstorp AB Decorative Laminate Northern Europe, pg. 1038   IT
Perstorp Chemitec, pg. 1037   IT
Perstorp Construction Chemicals, pg. 1036   IT
Perstorp Energie AB, pg. 1039   IT
Perstorp Form, pg. 1037   IT
Perstorp Formox, pg. 1038   IT
Perstorp Pharma AB, pg. 1037   IT
Perstorp Plastic Systems, pg. 1037   IT
Perstorp Polyols, pg. 1038   IT
Perstorp Pressmassor, pg. 1037   IT
Perstorp Regeno, pg. 1039   IT
Perstorp Resins, pg. 1037   IT
Perstorp Specialty Chemicals, pg. 1038   IT
Perstorp Surface Materials, pg. 1038   IT
Perstorp Treasury AB, pg. 1039   IT
Rubsteel AB, Verkstadsgatan 2, pg. 1146   IT
SBU Decorative Laminate, pg. 1038   IT
SBU Flooring Laminate, pg. 1038   IT

Pitea

ABB Plast AB, pg. 7   IT

Rattvik

Siljans Knacke AB, Stora Industriomradt, pg. 349   IT

Robertsfors

MoDo Skog AB - Robertsfors, Herrgardsvagen 14, Box 66, pg. 887   IT

Ronneby

AB Best Matic, V. Industrigatan 3C, pg. 877   PB
Cascade Djupagow AB, pg. 274   IT

Ronninge

Framatome Connectors Sweden AB, Forradsvagen 18, pg. 503   IT

Rydaholm

Horda Packingsindustri AB, pg. 1422   IT

Ryds

RYDS Batindustri AB, pg. 479   PV

Saffle

Electrolux Constructor AB, Saterivagen 1-3, P.O. Box 122, pg. 438   IT
Stora Billerud Research, Box 601, pg. 1302   IT
Stora Cell AB, Box 601, pg. 1303   IT
Svenska Hylsfabriken AB, pg. 1146   IT

Saltsjobaden

Ipsen Industries Nordiska AB, Domnarvsgatan 33, pg. 1149   IT

Sandarne

Bergvik Kemi AB, pg. 906   PB

Sandviken

SANDVIK AB, pg. 1185   IT
AB Sandvik Belts, pg. 1185   IT
Sandvik Benelux B.V., pg. 1185   IT
AB Sandvik Coromant, pg. 1185   IT
AB Sandvik Information Systems, pg. 1185   IT
AB Sandvik Rock Tools, pg. 1185   IT
Sandvik Rock Tools Svenska Forsaljnings AB, pg. 1185   IT
AB Sandvik Saws & Tools, pg. 1185   IT
AB Sandvik Service, pg. 1185   IT
AB Sandvik Steel, pg. 1185   IT

Savsjo

Savsjo Falgar AB, pg. 1422   IT
Sorensens Livs AB, Vastra Jarnsvagsgatan 33, pg. 922   IT

Sennan

Zanda AB, pg. 1092   IT

Sibbhult

Saab-Scania AB, pg. 687   IT

Silverdalen

Silverdalen Paper Mill, pg. 886   IT

Skanor

Iggesund Timber AB Scandinavia, Tarepilsvagen 4, pg. 886   IT

Skara

Perstorp Components, Erik Jarnakers gata 11, pg. 1040   IT
Svenska Foder AB, Erik Jarnakersgatan 3, pg. 350   IT

Skarhamn

Getinge Skarhamm AB, Industrivagen 5, pg. 551   IT

Skarholmen

Ahlsell Kyl AB, pg. 1422   IT
Canon Svenska AB, Stensatravagen 13, pg. 263   IT
Cerberus AB, Varbergstorget 1-3, pg. 1246   IT
Clarion Svenska AB, Stensatravagen 4, pg. 296   IT
Kungsfoto AB, pg. 709   IT
Mitrex AB, stensatravagen 9, pg. 1420   IT
NAPS Sweden AB, Stensatravagen 3, pg. 913   IT
Raychem Aktiebolag, Box 2054, pg. 1362   PB
Roche AB, pg. 1121   IT
Sharp Electronics (Svenska) AB, Stensatravagen 2, pg. 1230   IT
Tremix AB, Stensatravagen 9, pg. 1324   IT

Skelleftea

AB Arv Anderson, pg. 1422   IT
Ericsson Anslutningssystem AB, pg. 1363   IT
Hydrauto AB, Svedjevagen 4, pg. 678   IT
Hydro Supra AB, Supra Kemi, pg. 963   IT
Ing Fa Kjell Lidstrom AB, Sodra Jarnvagsgatan 50, pg. 277   IT
Megadoor AB, Servicegatan 6, pg. 269   IT
Stifab Plat AB, pg. 1422   IT

Skene

Tambox AB - Skene Factory, pg. 458   IT

Skoghall

Stora Billerud AB, pg. 1302   IT
Stora Skoghall, Box 501, pg. 1302   IT

Skovde

Cementa AB (Skovde), pg. 1199   IT
AB Svenska Uno-X, Hertig Johans Torg 4, pg. 236   IT
Volvo Car Components Corporation, pg. 1476   IT
Volvo Truck Components Corp., pg. 1476   IT

Skutskar

Stora Skutskar AB, P.O. Box 100, pg. 1303   IT

Slite

Cementa AB (Slite), pg. 1199   IT
Gotlands Energiverk AB, pg. 1453   IT
Scancem Research AB, pg. 1200   IT

PB - U.S. Public Companies Volume
PV - U.S. Private Companies Volume
IT - International Public & Private Companies Volume

Geographic Index-Non U.S.

Smedjebacken

Morgardshammar AB, pg. 378 IT

Soderhamn

Soderhamns Verkstader AB, P.O. Box 56, pg. 1421 IT

Sodertalje

Alfa-Laval Agri Scandinavia AB, Hantverksvagen 1, pg. 1377 IT
ASTRA AB, pg. 93 IT
Astra Arcus AB, pg. 93 IT
Astra Export & Trading AB, pg. 93 IT
Astra Lakemedal AB, pg. 93 IT
Astra Pain Control AB, pg. 93 IT
Astra Pharmaceutical Production AB, pg. 93 IT
Astra Production Chemicals AB, pg. 93 IT
Astra Production Liquid AB, pg. 93 IT
Astra Production Tablets AB, pg. 93 IT
Componenta International Scandinavia AB, Bergaholmsvagen 1, pg. 1421 IT
AB Mikro-Verktyg, Box 281, pg. 686 IT
Outokumpu Stal & Metall AB, pg. 1016 IT
Rammer Svenska AB, pg. 1352 IT
Scania Division, pg. 687 IT
V.A.G. Sverige AB, Fack 15188, pg. 1474 IT
Weda Pump AB, Bergaholmsvagen 1,Box 621, pg. 1421 IT
AB Werba, pg. 686 IT

Sollentuna

ABB ASEA Skandia AB, pg. 7 IT
AST Sweden, AB, pg. 1183 IT
Ahlsell AB, Bagarbyvagen 61, pg. 1422 IT
Auto-trol Technology AB, pg. 148 PB
Autologic Information International AB, Bergkallavagen 34, pg. 1724 PB
BERG/CBOS Electronics AB, Turebergsvaegen 3, pg. 213 PB
Dynapac AB, Lastbilsvagen 14, pg. 1420 IT
H. Eigenbrodt AB, pg. 708 IT
ESSVE Produkter AB, Box 770, pg. 188 IT
Ewos AB, Box 431, pg. 349 IT
Fuji Hunt Photographic Chemicals (Sverige) AB, Box 321, pg. 524 IT
ISS Darenas AB, Hammarbacken 6, pg. 656 IT
Janssen-Cilag AB, Rotebergsvagen 1, pg. 929 PB
Johnson & Johnson AB, Staffans Vag 2, pg. 930 PB
Lagercrantz Elektronik AB, P.O. Box 981, pg. 188 IT
Merck Sharp & Dohme (Sweden) AB, Rotebergsvagen 3, pg. 1092 PB
AB Carl Munters, Kung Hans vag 8, pg. 669 IT
Munters Dry Air AB, Kung Hans vag 8, pg. 669 IT
Munters Sverige, Kung Hans vag 8, pg. 669 IT
Munters Torkteknik AB, Kung Hans vag 8, pg. 669 IT
NCC Prefab AB, pg. 899 IT
NIFE AB, Tingsvagen 17, pg. 52 IT
Nielsen Design AB, Box 951, pg. 459 IT
OCE Graphics Svenska AB, pg. 994 IT
Optiroc AB, pg. 1200 IT
Optiroc Group AB, pg. 1200 IT
Perstorp Analytical Sweden, Turebergshuset, Turebergs Torg 1, pg. 1040 IT
Pharmacia & Upjohn Biotech Norden, Djupdalsvagen 20-22, pg. 1047 IT
PLUS Grossist AB, pg. 709 IT
qad.ab, Turebergs torg, pg. 1345 PB
SAS Institute AB, Silverdals Gard, pg. 966 PV
Skil Sverige AB, Lastbilsvaegen 6B, pg. 578 PB
Strabruken AB, pg. 899 IT
3M Svenska AB, Bollstanasvagen 3 Rotebro, pg. 1607 PB
Veribest Nordic, Hammarbacken 12, pg. 892 PB
Vink Plast AB, Sidensvansvagen 8, pg. 1211 IT
Wind River Systems Scandanavia, Turebergs Torg 1, pg. 1771 PB
Wyeth Nordiska AB, pg. 82 PB

Solna

Amersham Sweden AB, pg. 993 IT
Apple Computer AB, Industrivagen 7, pg. 121 PB
Avnet Nortec AB, Huvudstagatan 1, pg. 155 PB
AxTrade Care AB, Svetsarvagen 20, pg. 708 IT
AxTrade Dental AB, Svetsarvagen 20, pg. 708 IT
BASF Svenska AB Agro Nordenl Baltikum, Rasundavagen 166, pg. 107 IT
BMW Sverige AB, Gardsvagen 9-M, pg. 178 IT
Betoma AB, pg. 708 IT
Bjornklader AB, Box 1331, pg. 438 IT
Bristol-Myers AB, Hufvudsa Gard. Solna, pg. 255 PB
D-gruppen AB, Parkvagen 2A, pg. 708 IT
Dagab Snabbgross AB, pg. 708 IT
Distribution AB Dagab, Anderstorpsvagen 22, pg. 272 IT
Dun & Bradstreet Sverige AB, Box 1506, pg. 537 PB
EMI Svenska AB, P.O. Box 1289, pg. 427 IT
Effka Information AB, pg. 708 IT
ESSELTE AB, Sundbybergsvagen 1, pg. 459 IT
Esselte Chrono AB, Box 1375, pg. 459 IT
Esselte Meto AB, Box 1505, pg. 459 IT
Esselte Sverige AB, Box 1377, pg. 459 IT
Fri Kopenskap Forlags AB, pg. 708 IT
Fidelio Nordic Sverige AB, Englundavagen 7, 3 tr, pg. 1106 PB
Fujitsu Nordic AB, Torggatan 8, S-171, pg. 528 IT
ICA HANDLARNAS AB, Vallgatan 7, pg. 642 IT
ITT Flygt AB, Svetsarvaegen 12, pg. 860 PB
Intel Sweden, pg. 887 PB
Axel Johnson Instrument AB, Pyramidvagen 2B, pg. 709 IT
Axel Johnson Lab System AB, PO Box 1488, I Pyramidvagen 2B, pg. 709 IT
LIC Care AB, pg. 551 IT
LIC Hygien AB, pg. 551 IT
LIC Ortopedi AB, pg. 551 IT
Logica Svenska AB, Solna Torg 19, pg. 815 IT
Martin Merkel Svenska AB, Vintervagen 17, pg. 860 IT
Moore Business Forms (Scandinavia) AB, pg. 890 IT
Motorola AB, Dalv. 2, pg. 1139 PB
NCC AB, Vallgatan 3, pg. 898 IT
NCC Civil Engineering, Vallgatan 3, pg. 899 IT
NCC Finans, Vallgatan 3, pg. 899 IT
NCC Industry, Vallgatan 5, pg. 899 IT
NCC Invest, Vallgatan 3, pg. 899 IT
NCC Real Estate, Vallgatan 3, pg. 899 IT
NCC Stora Projelet, Vallgatan 3, pg. 899 IT
NIKE International Ltd.-Sweden, Dalvagen 14, pg. 1184 PB
Nortec AB, pg. 709 IT
Nortec Electronics AB, Parknagen 2A, pg. 709 IT
Otis Hiss AB, Englundwagen 9, pg. 1691 PB
Pitney Bowes Svenska Aktiebolag, pg. 1304 PB
Polarcup Sweden, Dalvagen 14, pg. 639 IT
Polydor AB, Dalvagen 4, pg. 1052 IT
PolyGram Records AB, Dalvagen 4, pg. 1053 IT
Pronesto, Box 1358, pg. 687 IT
AB Restaurangfrys, Ankdammsgatan 35, pg. 920 IT
S Invest AB, pg. 709 IT
SSH Svensk ServiceHandel AB, pg. 709 IT
Saab TechTrade AB, pg. 687 IT
SCANDINAVIAN AIRLINES SYSTEM (SAS), Frosundaviks Alle 1, pg. 1201 IT
Siemens-Elema AB, Rontgenvagen 2, pg. 1247 IT
Skanska Bostader Stockholm AB, P.O. Box 1535, pg. 1260 IT
Stora Project, Vallgatan 3, pg. 899 IT
Sun Microsystems AB, Hemvarnsgatan 9, pg. 1531 PB
Systecon AB, pg. 277 IT
THORN Svenska AB, P.O. Box 1362, pg. 1386 IT
Vattenfall Central Sweden, Englundav 13, pg. 1453 IT
VEXA Svenska AB, Smidesvagen 10-12, pg. 278 IT
Wang Svenska AB, Dalvagen 10, pg. 1738 PB
Warner-Lambert Scandinavia Aktiebolag, Box 4130, pg. 1740 PB
Wasa, Hemvarnsgatan 9, pg. 464 IT

Solvesborg

Dayco Europe AB, pg. 1045 PB
AB Halleviks Rokeri, pg. 920 IT
Mark IV Automotive, Gesallvagen-2, pg. 1045 PB

Spanga

Abbott Scandinavia AB, Torshamnsg 24, pg. 14 PB
Gestetner AB, Stormbyvagon 6, pg. 1115 IT
Helly-Hansen AB, Stormbyvagen 2-4, pg. 1010 IT
International Rectifier Company (Great Britain) Limited, pg. 907 PB
M.G. (Scandanavia) AB, Farogatan 6, pg. 1087 PB
Motorola AB Information Systems Group, Kistagangen 2, pg. 1139 PB
Parker Hannifin (Sweden) AB, Fagerstagatan 51, pg. 1263 PB
Robinson Nugent Nordic, Fagerstagatan 9, pg. 1395 PB
Traub Heckert AB, Fagerstagatan 2, pg. 1419 IT
Vickers Systems AB, P.O. Box 65, Fagerstagatan 19 A, pg. 25 PB

Spangenas

Ahlsell El AB, pg. 1422 IT
Dahl Sverige, Kistagangen 2, P.O. Box 1144, pg. 359 IT
Dickursby Farg AB, Arrendevagen 36, pg. 729 IT
LIC Rehab Care AB, pg. 551 IT
Oki Systems (Sweden) AB, Stormbyvagen 2-4, Spanga Center, pg. 1000 IT

Stenungsund

Borealis Petrokemi AB, pg. 914 IT
Borealis Polyeten AB, pg. 914 IT
Hydro Plast AB, pg. 963 IT
Neste Kemi Forsaljnings AB, S-444 86, pg. 915 IT
Neste Oxo AB, pg. 915 IT
Nordson Sverige AB, pg. 1189 PB
Statoil Marknad Plaster, pg. 1298 IT
Statoil Petrokemi AB, Olefins Division, pg. 1298 IT

Stockholm

ABB AB, pg. 7 IT
ABB Cables AB, pg. 7 IT
ABN-AMRO Bank (Sverige) AB, Engelbrektsgatan 711, pg. 11 IT
ALM & Company, Nybrokajen 1, Box 1366, pg. 1422 PB
ASAB Serviceforetaget AB, P.O. Box 34046, pg. 438 IT
ASSA ABLOY AB, Klarabergsviadukten 90, pg. 17 IT
Abloy AB, Textilvagan 1, pg. 17 IT
AFTONBLADET AB, Arenavagen 63, pg. 29 IT
Agfa-Gevaert AB, pg. 174 IT
Agro Barter United AB, pg. 708 IT
Ahlens AB, Torshamnsgatan 33, pg. 708 IT
Ahlsell VVS AB, Hammarbyv. 37, pg. 1422 IT
Ahlstrom Machinery AB, Norra Stationsgatan 75-77, pg. 34 IT
Ahlstrom Machinery AB-Fiber Processes, Norra Stationsgatan 75-77, pg. 34 IT
Ahlstrom Machinery AB-Recovery Processes, Norra Stationsgatan 75-77, pg. 35 IT
Ahlstrom Machinery AB-Sawmill Machinery, Norra Stationsgatan 75-77, pg. 35 IT
Ahlstromforetagen Svenska AB, Norra Stationsgatan 75-77, pg. 33 IT
Akademibokhandelsgruppen, pg. 718 IT
Aktiebolaget LM Ericsson Finans, Telefonplan, pg. 1363 IT
Akzo Nobel AB, P.O. Box 11500, pg. 48 IT
Alarmcom AB, Liljeholmsvagen 8, pg. 1246 IT
Amdahl Svenska AB, Box 150, Svardvagen 11, pg. 527 IT
American Power Conversion, Brahegatan 48, pg. 89 PB
Andren & Werne Leo Burnett AB, Kungsgatan 49, pg. 184 PV
Jan Arbman EURO RSCG, Kungsgatan 2, pg. 602 IT
AROS Fondkommission AB, pg. 7 IT
The Associated Press AB, Vattugatten 12, pg. 92 PV
Assurance & Financial Services, Sveavagen 44, pg. 1256 IT
ATLAS COPCO AB, Sickla Industrivag 3, Nacka, pg. 95 IT
Atlas Copco Industrial Tools & Equipment, pg. 96 IT
Atlas Copco Rockdrilling Equipment, pg. 96 IT
Attendor Industri och Handel AB, pg. 708 IT
Autotank AB, pg. 839 IT
Avesta AB, pg. 708 IT
Avesta Sheffield AB, Vasagatan 8-10, 6TR, pg. 221 IT
Axtec AB, pg. 708 IT
AxTrade AB, World Trade Center, Klarabergsviadukten 70, pg. 708 IT
AxTrade East AB, pg. 708 IT
AxTrade East Asia Ltd., pg. 708 IT
AxTrade Flow AB, pg. 708 IT
AxTrade Scandinavia AB, pg. 708 IT
B&W Stormarknader AB, pg. 718 IT
Balzers Sandvik Coating AB, Larkrogsvagen 19, pg. 997 IT
AB Banan-Kompaniet, pg. 708 IT
BancTec Sverige A.B., Arstaangsvagen 1C, pg. 177 PB
Banque Paribas Sverige AB, Norrlandsgaten 16, pg. 320 IT
Bauer Sverge AB, Skogsbovagen 15, pg. 1184 PB
Bausch & Lomb Svenska AB, Soder Malarstrasse 45, pg. 195 PB
Berendsen Components AB, 14 Hammarby Kajvaeg, pg. 1284 IT
Berendsen PMC AB, Hammarby Kajvag 14, pg. 1285 IT
Alfred Berg Fondkommission AB, pg. 12 IT
BERGMAN & BEVING AB, P.O. Box 10024, pg. 188 IT
Bernhard M. Bergman AB, Rosenlundsgatan 54, pg. 708 IT
Berlitz Schools of Languages AB, Vasgatan 52, pg. 222 PB
Betongindustri AB, pg. 1199 IT
Bino (Societe Civile Immobiliere), pg. 317 IT
Boliden AB, Norra Stationdgatan 75-77, pg. 1422 IT
Boliden Contech AB, Norra Stationdgatan 75-77, pg. 1422 IT
Boliden Intermarket AB, Norra Stationsgatan 75-77, pg. 1422 IT
Boliden International Mining AB, Norra Stationsgatan 75-77, pg. 1422 IT
Boliden Ore & Metals, Hammarbyvagen 37, pg. 1422 IT
Boliden WP-Contech AB, pg. 1422 IT
CA II Pantbelaning AB, Bib Lir Teksgatan 3, 11146, pg. 312 PB
CM Materials AB, pg. 276 IT
CRS Data AB, pg. 708 IT
CRS Databuilding AB, Electrum 229, pg. 708 IT
CRS Datasystem AB, pg. 708 IT
CW/Communications AB, Sodra Hamnvagen 22, pg. 569 PV
D. Carnegie AB, Gustav Adolf Torg 18, pg. 272 IT
CARNEGIE HOLDING AB, Gustav Adolf Torg 18, pg. 272 IT
Casco Nobel AB, pg. 48 IT
Castrol AB, Wallingatan 20-22, pg. 235 IT
AB Celleco, P.O. Box 12109, pg. 1378 IT
CELSIUS AB, P.O. Box 7214, pg. 276 IT
Celsius Industries Corp., Birger Jarlsgatan 33, pg. 276 IT
Cementa AB (Stockholm), pg. 1198 IT
AB Centralsug, pg. 276 IT
Chase Manhattan Overseas Corporation, Biblioteksgatan 11, pg. 340 PB
Checkpoint Systems Scandinavia AB, Hammarby Fabriksvag 21A, pg. 343 PB
Christiania Bank-Stockholm Branch, Birger Jarlsgatan 26, pg. 289 IT
City Stormarknad, pg. 718 IT
Colgate Palmolive AB, Norra Stationsgatan 79-81, S-113, pg. 398 PB
Comdisco Sweden AB, Rungsgatan 44, pg. 408 PB
Conquest Europe, Kungsgaten 27, pg. 1483 IT
AB Custodia, Gustav Adolf Torg 18, pg. 272 IT
DAHL INTERNATIONAL AB, Drottninggatan 2, pg. 359 IT
D'Arcy Masius Benton & Bowles AB, Igeblammsgatan 22, pg. 304 PV
Data General AB, Armegiatan 38 Box 1290, pg. 485 PB
DataCard Sweden AB, Box 42015, pg. 313 PV
Datafast AB, pg. 277 IT
Datapoint Svenska AB, Box 114 12523, pg. 384 IT
De La Rue Systems AB, Arstaangsvagen 1A, pg. 387 IT
Detaljinvest/Vivo-Favor, Parkvaegen 2A, Solna, pg. 272 IT

PB - *U.S. Public Companies Volume*
PV - *U.S. Private Companies Volume*
IT - *International Public & Private Companies Volume*

Deve Schindler AB, pg. 1205 — IT
Diskomat AB, Ingenjorsvagen 3, pg. 270 — IT
Dow Jones Markets Sweden AB, Kungsgatan 8, 5TR, pg. 525 — PB
Dow Sverige AB, pg. 524 — PB
Du Pont Scandinavia AB, Torshamnsgatan 35-39, pg. 533 — PB
Dun & Bradstreet Soliditet AB, pg. 537 — PB
DUNI AB, Kungsgatan 74, pg. 421 — IT
EAC Graphics Nordic AB, pg. 431 — IT
Eklow Scandinavia Group AB, pg. 708 — IT
ELECTROLUX, AB, Luxbacken 1, Lilla Essingen, pg. 438 — IT
Electrolux Aterforsakrings AB, pg. 438 — IT
Electrolux Autoliv, pg. 439 — IT
Electrolux International Sales AB, pg. 438 — IT
Electrolux Svenska Forsaljinings AB, pg. 439 — IT
AB Elektro Helios, pg. 438 — IT
AB Elektroservice, pg. 439 — IT
Elkem Sverige, Kungsgatan 18, pg. 447 — IT
Empatica AB, Nybrogatan 39, pg. 1047 — IT
Enskilda Securities, Nybrokajen 5, pg. 1259 — IT
Ericsson Components AB, Isafjordsgatan 16, Kista, pg. 1363 — IT
Ericsson Components Power Division, Dialoggatan 2, Huddinge, pg. 1363 — IT
Ericsson Electronic Distr. AB, pg. 1363 — IT
Ericsson Hewlett-Packard Telecommunications AB, Vastberga Alle 9, pg. 1363 — IT
Ericsson Mobile Communications AB, Torshamnsgatan 27, pg. 1364 — IT
Ericsson Network Constructions AB, Masholmstorget 3, pg. 1363 — IT
Ericsson Paging Systems AB, Arstaangsvagen 13, pg. 1364 — IT
Ericsson Procomp, Isafjordsgatan 16, pg. 1363 — IT
Ericsson Radio Systems AB, Torshamnsgatan 21-23, pg. 1363 — IT
Ericsson Signal Systems AB, Vastberga alle 32, pg. 1364 — IT
Ericsson Standard Components AB, Isafjordsgatan 16, pg. 1363 — IT
Ericsson Telecom AB, pg. 1364 — IT
Ericsson Traffic Systems AB, Arstaangsvagen 19, pg. 1364 — IT
Ericsson Treasury Services AB, Telefonplan, pg. 1364 — IT
Erifocas AB, pg. 1364 — IT
Erlang Systems AB, pg. 1363 — IT
ERVACO GRUPPEN AB, Sveavagen 90, pg. 459 — IT
Eurocard AB, Stockholm, Master Samuelsgatan 34, pg. 1259 — IT
European International Holding, Kungsgatan 9, pg. 464 — IT
Europeiska Forsakring (Sweden), Kungsgatan 9, pg. 464 — IT
FAG Svenska AB, pg. 469 — IT
FFV Test Systems AB, pg. 277 — IT
Fakta, pg. 718 — IT
Fastighets AB Fundament/Real Estate Operations, Brunnsgrand 4, pg. 678 — IT
FASTIGHETSAKTIEBOLAGET HUFVUDSTADEN, Norrmalmstorg 14, 5th Floor, pg. 478 — IT
FERMENTA AB, Kungsgatan 4A, pg. 480 — IT
AB Ferrolegeringar, Box 7163, pg. 735 — PV
Fischer & Porter AB, Malmgardsvagen 16-18, pg. 449 — IT
Georg Fischer AB, pg. 489 — IT
Flakt AB, Sickla Alle 13, Nacka, pg. 7 — IT
Fokab AB, Sturegatan 32, pg. 708 — IT
Ford Credit AB, pg. 666 — PB
Ford Motor Co. Aktiebolag, pg. 666 — PB
Ford Vagnskadegaranti AB, pg. 666 — PB
Forsakringsaktiebolaget Allianz Nordeuropa (RAS), Hantverkargatan 21, pg. 60 — IT
Forsakringsaktiebolaget Sirius, Nybrokajen 15, pg. 7 — IT
Forsvarsmedia AB, pg. 277 — IT
FORVALTNINGS AB RATOS, Drottninggatan 2, pg. 500 — IT
Freudenberg Simrit A.B., pg. 506 — IT
AB Frionor, Arstaangsvagen 1A, pg. 516 — IT
Fuji Film Sverige AB, pg. 708 — IT
Georg Jensen Silver AB, 13, Birger Jarlsgatan, pg. 1134 — IT
Gibbs AB, Unilever Sveav 9-11, pg. 1437 — IT
AB Goman-Produkter, pg. 718 — IT
AB Gosta Backstrom, Alstromergatan 22, pg. 1363 — IT
Granges AB, pg. 439 — IT
Granges Hedlund AB, Hammarbyvagen 40, pg. 439 — IT
Granges International Mining, pg. 439 — IT
Grona Konsum Stockholm AB, pg. 718 — IT
Gunnar Olsson Transportkonsult AB, Nybrogatan 71, pg. 966 — IT
AB Gust Carlsson & Co., pg. 431 — IT
HAB Mercator, World Trade Center, Klarabergsviadukten, 70, pg. 708 — IT
Hachette Sverige HB, Saltamgatan, 8, pg. 795 — IT
Hall & Cederquist/Young & Rubicam, Kaptensgatan 6, pg. 1198 — PV
Handelsbanken Finans, Master Samuelsgatan 42, pg. 1327 — IT
Handelsbanken Fonder AB, Blasieholmstorg 12, pg. 1327 — IT
Handelsbanken Liv, Torsgatan 12, pg. 1327 — IT
Handelsbanken Markets, Blasieholmstorg 11 and 12, pg. 1327 — IT
Hartmann Tryckfarger AB, Box 29067, pg. 371 — IT
Hector & Co. A.B., Drottninggatan 25, pg. 904 — PV
Helene Curtis Scandinavia AB, pg. 1434 — IT
Henkel Norden AB, Gustavslundsvogen 129, pg. 613 — IT
Herbalife Sweden AB, pg. 809 — PB
Honeywell AB, Storsatargrand 5, pg. 834 — PB
Honeywell Bull AB, Sveagen 163, pg. 318 — IT

Husdjurforsakrings AB Sleipner, Englundavagen 7, pg. 1256 — IT
IBM Svenska Aktiebolag, Oddegatan 5, pg. 897 — PB
IBM Svenska Produkt Distribution Aktiebolag, Oddegatan 5, pg. 897 — PB
ICA Handlarnas AB, pg. 642 — IT
ICA Kort AB, pg. 643 — IT
IDG Sweden, Sturegaten 11, 5-10678, pg. 570 — PV
IL RETURPAPPER, Box 5388, pg. 646 — IT
ISS Sverige AB, Arstaangsvagen 25, pg. 656 — IT
IVO Energi AB, Svarvargatan 11, pg. 661 — IT
IL Sekretess, pg. 646 — IT
INCENTIVE AB, Hamngatan 2, pg. 666 — IT
Incentive Credit AB, Hamngatan 2, pg. 670 — IT
Incentive Financial Services AB, pg. 669 — IT
Inductus/Industrial Operations, Storgatan 10, pg. 678 — IT
Industrforvaltnings AB Kinnevik, Skeppsbron 18, pg. 759 — IT
Industrigruppen JAS AB, pg. 1364 — IT
AB INDUSTRIVARDEN, Storgatan 10, pg. 678 — IT
Interdental AB, Brannkryrkagatan 66 70, pg. 708 — IT
International Flavors & Fragrances, pg. 899 — PB
INVESTOR AB, Arsenalgatan 8C, pg. 686 — IT
JM Byggnads och Fastighets AB, P.O. Box 27319, pg. 1260 — IT
AXEL JOHNSON AB, Villagatan 6, pg. 707 — IT
Axel Johnson Credit AB, Jakobsbergsgatan 7, pg. 708 — IT
Axel Johnson Ore & Metals AB, Villagatan 6, pg. 709 — IT
Axel Johnson Petroleum AB, Villagatan 6, pg. 709 — IT
Axel Johnson Resources AB, pg. 709 — IT
Axel Johnson Servicehandelsgruppen AB, pg. 709 — IT
Johnson Matthey AB, Box 17129, pg. 714 — IT
Jugobanka (Skandinavska Reprsentationskontor), Kungsgatan 55/3 TR, pg. 716 — IT
Juvelbagerierna AB, pg. 718 — IT
KF Fastigheter AB, pg. 718 — IT
KF/KONSUM COOP GROUP, pg. 718 — IT
KF Stormarknader AB, pg. 718 — IT
Kemetyl AB, pg. 1011 — IT
Korn/Ferry International, Norrmalmstorg 14, pg. 634 — PV
LM Ericsson Data Services AB, Gotalandsvagen 230, pg. 1364 — IT
LM Ericsson Fastigheter AB, Telefonplan, pg. 1364 — IT
AB LM Ericsson Finans, Telefonplan, pg. 1364 — IT
Lauderdale Computer AB, Albygatan 109 F, S-171 54 Solna, pg. 580 — PB
Eli Lilly Sweden AB, pg. 994 — PB
Litton Precision Products (Sweden), Warfvinges Vag 32, pg. 1004 — PB
Lowe Brindfors, Regeringsgatan 45, pg. 678 — PV
L E LUNDBERGFORETAGEN AB, Hovslagargatan 5B, pg. 820 — IT
Lundbergs-Stockholm Region, Hovslagargatan 5 B, pg. 821 — IT
Mannesmann Sverige AB, pg. 838 — IT
Marcusan AB, Stureplan 19, 111 45, pg. 783 — IT
Margarinbolaget AB, Strandbergsgatan 20, pg. 922 — IT
Marquette Scandinavia, pg. 1047 — PB
Marubeni Scandinavia AB, Regeringsq. 30, pg. 845 — IT
Mecman Svenska AB, pg. 839 — IT
Medata AB, pg. 709 — IT
AB Mekanprodukter, pg. 838 — IT
Mellansvenska Elektriska AB, Sveavagen 136, pg. 1363 — IT
Merita Bank Ltd. - Stockholm Branch, Master Samuelsgatan 3, pg. 859 — IT
Mettler-Toledo AB, pg. 4 — PV
Micro Warehouse, Sweden AB, Midskogsgrand 1-3, pg. 1104 — IT
Microsoft Aktiebolag, pg. 1108 — PB
Mitsui & Co. Europe (Scandinavia) AB, Stureplan 2, 114, pg. 880 — IT
MO OCH DOMSJO AB, Strandvagen 1, pg. 885 — IT
MoDo Merchants AB, Strandvagen 1, pg. 886 — IT
Morgan Grenfell (Sweden), Birger Jarlsgatan 15, pg. 406 — IT
NCC Building, pg. 898 — IT
NUS Scandinavia AB, Fatbursgatan 1, pg. 787 — PV
NYK Line-Stockholm, Frejgatan 91 S-102, pg. 942 — IT
Neste Polymer Compounds AB, Vastberga Alle 60, pg. 915 — IT
Neste Sverige AB, Villagatan 13B, pg. 915 — IT
Nobel Consumer Goods AB, pg. 718 — IT
NORDBANKEN AB, Smalandsgatan 17, pg. 957 — IT
Norden Banking Group, Brunkebergstorg 8, pg. 1328 — IT
Nordfor Training & Consultation AB, pg. 439 — IT
Nordic Power Invest AB, Vasag 15-17, pg. 1453 — IT
Nordiska Kompaniet (NK) AB, NK 100, pg. 899 — IT
Norsk Hydro Olje AB, Tegeluddsvagen 76, pg. 964 — IT
Norsk Hydro Sverige AB, Biblioteksgatan 12, pg. 964 — IT
North Coal AB, pg. 709 — IT
Norvista Travel AB, Fatburgs Kvarngatan 10, pg. 486 — IT
Nutricia Nordica AB, pg. 992 — IT
Obs! Stormarknaden AB, pg. 718 — IT
OCE Svenska AB, pg. 995 — IT
Objectory AB, pg. 1364 — IT
PLD Nordic AB, P.O. Box 3176, pg. 188 — IT
Pechiney Sverige, Norr Malarstrand 22, pg. 1031 — IT
Pharmacia & Upjohn BioScience Center, Strandbergsgatan 49, pg. 1047 — IT
Pharmacia & Upjohn Hospital Care, Franzengatan 9, pg. 1048 — IT
Pharmacia & Upjohn Peptide Hormones, Linhagensgatan 133, pg. 1048 — IT
Pharmacia & Upjohn Plasma Products, Lindhagensgatan 133, pg. 1048 — IT
Pharmacia & Upjohn Risk Management Service AB, Frosundaviks alle 15, pg. 1048 — IT
Pharmacia & Upjohn Sverige AB, Gardsvagen 8, pg. 1048 — IT

Pharmacia & Upjohn Treasury Services AB, Frosundaviks alle 15, pg. 1048 — IT
AB Pharos Marine, Funckens grand 2, pg. 1289 — IT
Philips Norden AB, Kontorstid 8-30-17, pg. 1055 — IT
Philips Toersaelynings AB, Kontorstid 8-30-17, pg. 1055 — IT
Polaroid AB, Ekholmsvagen 34, pg. 1314 — PB
PREEM PETROLEUM AB, Sandhamnsgatan 51, pg. 1066 — IT
PriFast AB, Strandbergsgatan 61, pg. 709 — IT
Prosec Forsakingsaktiebolag, Frosundaviks alle 15, pg. 1048 — IT
PROVENTUS AB, P.O. Box 1719, pg. 1072 — IT
RM Ravarumaklarna AB, pg. 709 — IT
Raben & Sjogren AB, pg. 718 — IT
Rantaruukki Holding AB, Fatbursgatan 7, pg. 1089 — IT
Region Stockholm, Warfvinges vag 28, pg. 23 — IT
AB Reportagebild, Vattugatan 12, Box 325, pg. 29 — IT
AB Rexroth Mecman, pg. 838 — IT
Rhone-Poulenc Sverige AB, Folkungagatan 122, pg. 1114 — IT
Richardson-Vicks AB, P.O. Box 7515, Kungsgatan 33, pg. 1333 — PB
Rikskuponger, Brunkebergstorg 6, pg. 21 — IT
Robur, Brunkebergstorg 8, pg. 1328 — IT
S-E-Banken BoLan AB, Regeringsgatan 65, pg. 1259 — IT
S-E-Banken Custody Service, Sergels Torg 2, pg. 1259 — IT
S-E-Banken Foretagsinvest, Hamngatan 24, pg. 1259 — IT
S-E-Banken Forsakring, Regeringsgatan 45, pg. 1259 — IT
SAS Airline, pg. 1201 — IT
SAS Financial Services, pg. 1201 — IT
SAS Mediapartner AB, Gavlegatan 18, pg. 1202 — IT
SAS Trading, pg. 1202 — IT
SBC Arbitech AB, Regeringsgatan 38, 7th Floor, pg. 1330 — IT
SDRC Svenska AB, Isafjordsgatan 30A, pg. 1525 — PB
S-E-Banken Fonder AB, Regeringsgatan 45, pg. 1259 — IT
S-E Banken Kapitalforvaltning, Sergels Torg 2, pg. 1259 — IT
SMH Sweden AB, pg. 1161 — IT
SMS Telecom AB, Solkraftsvagen 18 A, pg. 277 — IT
Saba Fastighets AB, Regeringsgatan 42, pg. 272 — IT
Saba Foretagshalsovard AB, pg. 709 — IT
Sand & Grus AB Jehander, pg. 1200 — IT
Sandvik Coromant Skandinavien AB, Box 12, pg. 1185 — IT
AB Sandvik Hard Materials, pg. 1185 — IT
Sandvik Hard Materials Norden AB, pg. 1185 — IT
AB Sanera, pg. 277 — IT
Sanpaolo-Stockholm Representative Office, World Trade Center, Klarabergsviadukten 70, pg. 692 — IT
Scandinavian Leisure Group AB, Sveavagen 25, pg. 39 — IT
Schauman Wood AB, Arstaangsvagen 17, pg. 1429 — IT
Schindler Scandinavian Holding AB, pg. 1205 — IT
Scholl (Sverige) SA, Solna Torg 19, pg. 1210 — IT
Sensormatic AB (Sweden), Roslagsvagen 101, pg. 1457 — PB
Servera R & S AB, pg. 709 — IT
Siemens AB, Johanneslundsvaegen 12-14, pg. 1247 — IT
Signal System, 22 Spagna, pg. 654 — IT
Silja Line AB, Positionen 8, pg. 899 — IT
SINSER Holding AB, Grev Turegatan 9, pg. 1256 — IT
Skandia Capital Services, Sveavagen 44, pg. 1256 — IT
Skandia Holding AB, Sveavagen 20, pg. 1256 — IT
SKANDIA INSURANCE COMPANY LIMITED, pg. 1256 — IT
Skandia International Consulting (SICON) AB, Sveavagen 44, pg. 1256 — IT
Skandia International Insurance Corporation, Barks vag 15, pg. 1256 — IT
Skandia Investment AB, Sveavagen 38, pg. 1256 — IT
Skandia Investment Management, Sveavagen 44, pg. 1257 — IT
Skandia Life Insurance Company Ltd., Sveavagen 44, pg. 1257 — IT
SkandiaBanken AB, Hamngatan 15, pg. 1257 — IT
SkandiaBanken Fonder AB, Hamngatan 15, pg. 1257 — IT
Skandialink Livforsakrings AB, Sveavagen 44, pg. 1258 — IT
SKANDINAVISKA ENSKILDA BANKEN, Kungstradgardsgatan 8, pg. 1258 — IT
Solid AB, Strandsbergsgatan 57, 2 tr, pg. 17 — IT
Sparbanken Fastighetsbyra, Regeringsgatan 13, pg. 1328 — IT
Sparbanken Finans, Regeringsgatan 25, pg. 1328 — IT
Sparbanken Sverige AB, Brunkebergstorg 8, pg. 1328 — IT
SparLiv och SparFond, Drottninggatan 29, pg. 1328 — IT
Specialservice AB, pg. 277 — IT
SPECTRA-PHYSICS AB, Box 5226, pg. 1288 — IT
Spintab, Regeringsgatan 13, pg. 1328 — IT
Statoil AB, P.O. Box 5833, pg. 1298 — IT
AB Stockholms-Brandskyddskonsulenter, Vretensborgsvagen 21, pg. 35 — IT
Stockholms Byggplat, pg. 1422 — IT
Stor & Liten AB, pg. 718 — IT
Stora Finance Stockholm AB, Box 16100, pg. 1303 — IT
Stora Financial Services, Vastra Tradgardsgatan 15, pg. 1303 — IT
Storage Technology Sweden, pg. 1523 — PB
Stratus Computer AB, Isafjordsgatan 11, pg. 1524 — PB
Sulzer Metco (Norden) AB, pg. 1308 — IT
The Sumitomo Bank, Ltd.-Stockholm Representative Office, Norrlandsgatan 11, pg. 1310 — IT
Sun Chemical AB, Box 502, pg. 371 — IT
Sundstrand International Corp., Pampar U.S.-Filial, Box 5063, pg. 1534 — PB
Svensk Teknisk Byra AB, World Trade Center, Klarabergsviadukten 70, pg. 709 — IT
SVENSKA CELLULOSA AKTIEBOLAGET (SCA), Box 7827, pg. 1326 — IT
SVENSKA HANDELSBANKEN, Kungstradgardsgatan 2, pg. 1327 — IT

PB - U.S. Public Companies Volume
PV - U.S. Private Companies Volume
IT - International Public & Private Companies Volume

Svenska Handelsbanken International, Kungstradgardsgatan 2, pg. 1327 — IT
Svenska Johnson's Vax AB, Postbox 28, pg. 594 — PV
Svenska Le Carbone A/B, Karlsbodavagan 45, pg. 1032 — IT
AB Svenska Pressbyran, pg. 709 — IT
AB Svenska Shell, Armegatan 38, S-171 79 Solna, pg. 1139 — IT
Svenska Unilever Forvaltnings AB, Sveav. 9-11, pg. 1438 — IT
Svenska Voest-Alpine AB, Nybrogatan 44, pg. 1472 — IT
Svenskt Papper AB, Box 20093, pg. 886 — IT
SWEDBANK, Brunkebergstorg 8, pg. 1328 — IT
Swedbank Markets, Regeringsgatan 13, pg. 1328 — IT
SWEDISH MATCH S.A., Rosenlundsg 36, pg. 1328 — IT
SwedPower AB, Vasag 15-17, pg. 1453 — IT
Synectics Medical AB, Renstiernas Grata 12, 3 tr., pg. 1084 — PB
TBWA Stockholm, Kungsgatan 38, 3tr, pg. 1063 — PV
Tegner & Son AB, Narvavagen 22, pg. 412 — IT
TELEFONAKTIEBOLAGET LM ERICSSON, HF-LME-DM, pg. 1363 — IT
Telenordia A.B., Arstaansvagen 11A, pg. 223 — IT
Telephone Bank Sesam, pg. 1259 — IT
Texas Instruments International Trade Corporation, Sverigefilial N. Hamnv. 3, pg. 1586 — PB
Thule-Konsult AB, Stureplan 4, pg. 1257 — IT
AB Tidningen Vi, pg. 718 — IT
Topcomp Elektronik, Isafjordsgatan 16, pg. 1363 — IT
Tornet, Malmskillnadsg 32, pg. 1328 — IT
Tourism Malaysia - Stockholm Office, Ground Floor, Sveavagan 18, pg. 833 — IT
Transelectric AB, Svarvargatan 11, pg. 660 — IT
Travel Agency Stockholm, Kungsgatan 12-14, pg. 1300 — IT
TRYGG-HANSA, Fleminggatan 18, pg. 1425 — IT
Trygg-Hansa Insurance Co. Ltd., Fleminggatan 18, pg. 1425 — IT
U.K. Division, Klarabergsviadukten 90, pg. 17 — IT
UniTimber AB, Box 12166, pg. 886 — IT
Utell International-Sweden, Sveavagen 90, pg. 1099 — IT
Utvecklings AB, pg. 1364 — IT
V.A.G. Stockholm AB, 72-76 Lindhagensplan S, pg. 1476 — IT
VB Autobatteri AB, Kommendorsgatan 16, pg. 1452 — IT
VG Instruments AB, pg. 1595 — PB
VARTA Batteri AB, Kommendorsgatan 16, pg. 1452 — IT
VATTENFALL AB, Jamtlandsgatan 99, pg. 1452 — IT
Vattenfall AB, pg. 1453 — IT
Vattenfall Energisystem AB, pg. 1453 — IT
Vattenfall Engineering AB, Box 529, pg. 1453 — IT
Vattenfall Generation Services AB, pg. 1453 — IT
Vattenfall Naturgas AB, pg. 1453 — IT
Vattenfall Regionnat AB, pg. 1453 — IT
Vattenfall Transmission AB, pg. 1453 — IT
Vattenfall Treasury AB, pg. 1453 — IT
AB Volta, Luxgatan 23, pg. 439 — IT
WOW, Westermark och, Wistmar Reklmabyra, pg. 470 — IT
Whitehall Sweden, pg. 82 — PB
Wisaforest Sverige AB, Arstaangsvagen 17, pg. 1429 — IT
Wolters Kluwer Sweden, Halsingegatan 49, pg. 1514 — IT
Wrigley Scandinavia AB, Nasby, Alle 6, pg. 1781 — PB
Zurich Forsakring, Zurich-Huset, Linnegatan 5, pg. 1531 — IT

Storfors
Avesta Sandvik Tube AB, pg. 221 — IT

Storvik
Stora Fors AB, Hammarby, pg. 1302 — IT

Strangnas
Gist-Brocades AB, Mancefzedsvagen 35, pg. 1142 — IT
MoDo Skog AB - Strangnas, Sundby Park 654, pg. 887 — IT

Stromsnabruk
Stroms Bruk, pg. 886 — IT
Traryds Metall AB, Gransvagen, Industricenter, pg. 1323 — IT

Stromstad
International Door Automation AB, Prastangvagen 30, pg. 269 — IT
Perstorp AB Flooring Laminate, Prastangsvagen 2, pg. 1038 — IT

Sundbyberg
ABS Pump AB, Starrbacksgatan 1, pg. 270 — IT
AGA Gas AB, pg. 12 — IT
Digital Equipment (BCFI) AB, Allen 6, pg. 507 — PB
Ericsson Business Networks AB, Landsvagen 66, pg. 1363 — IT
Ericsson Cables AB, Landsvagen 66, pg. 1363 — IT
Ericsson Radio Systems Sverige AB, Rissneleden 138, pg. 1364 — IT
JEOL (Skandinaviska) A.B., Vegagatan 19, pg. 697 — IT
Skanska Installation AB, pg. 1260 — IT
Toyota Motor Svenska AB, pg. 1414 — IT

Sundsvall
ABS Pump AB, Storgatan 1, pg. 270 — IT
DAB Dental AB, Kopmangatan 32, pg. 711 — IT

Emhart Sweden Aktiebolag, Fabriksgatan 1, P.O. Box 710, pg. 233 — PB
NCC Building, pg. 898 — IT
NCC Sundsvall, pg. 899 — IT
Neste Gas AB, Kolvagen 17, pg. 915 — IT
Parker Hannifin Sweden AB, Bulgatan 9, pg. 1264 — PB
Regam Medical Systems International AB, Regementsvagen 5, pg. 6 — PB
Region Sundsvall, Forradsgatan 11, pg. 23 — IT
Skanska Norr AB, pg. 1260 — IT
Sundsvalls Verkstader AB, P.O. Box 710, pg. 233 — PB
Superior Graphite Europe, Ltd., pg. 1055 — PV
Vattenfall, pg. 1453 — IT
Vattenfall Northern Sweden, pg. 1453 — IT

Surte
EKA Nobel AB, pg. 48 — IT
Raisio Svenska AB, P.O. Box 2203, pg. 1086 — IT

Svedala
Svedala Arbra, pg. 1324 — IT

Svenljunga
Bergis Produktions AB, pg. 438 — IT

Taby
Carmeda AB, Nytorpsvagen 10, pg. 961 — IT
Componenta Parts AB, Reprovagen 3, pg. 1421 — IT
Gunnar F. Hoglund AB, pg. 708 — IT
Intercosmetic AB, pg. 1490 — IT
Master Builders Scandinavia AB, Slottsv. 1, pg. 1465 — IT
Pfizer AB, Nytorpsvagen 36, pg. 1282 — PB
R.J. Reynolds Scandinavia AB, Kemistvagen 10A, pg. 1355 — PB
Rima AB, Mallslingan 13, pg. 270 — IT
Roerig A.B., c/o Pfizer A.B., Nytorpsvagen 36, pg. 1282 — PB
SUAB Svensk Undervattenselektronik AB, Nytorpsvagen 9, pg. 277 — IT
Sandoz AB, Slottsv. 1, Box 3047, pg. 984 — IT
SCABA AB, Enhagsvagen 12, pg. 270 — IT

Tanumshede
Tanum Komponent AB, Storemyrsvagen, pg. 1040 — IT

Tibro
Forbo Parkett AB, pg. 497 — IT

Tidaholm
Stora Byggprodukter AB, pg. 1302 — IT

Timra
Outokumpu Stal & Metall AB, Terminalvagen 9, pg. 1016 — IT

Tobo
Munters Component AB, Garjovagen 8, pg. 669 — IT

Tocksfors
Tockfors Verkstads AB, Industrivagen, pg. 1364 — IT

Torshalla
Avesta Sandvik Tube AB, pg. 221 — IT
Avesta Sheffield AB, pg. 221 — IT

Torslanda
Cardo Door Production AB, Gamla Flygplatsvagen 2-4, pg. 269 — IT
Crawford Garage Door Systems AB, Hangarvagen 3, pg. 269 — IT

Tranas
Akvamatik AB, pg. 1422 — IT
IVT Graphics, pg. 170 — PB

Trelleborg
Boliden Allis AB, Nygatan 102, pg. 1423 — IT
AB Joh Kock, pg. 1199 — IT
Minco International AB, pg. 1423 — IT
Perstorp AB Decorative Laminate Furniture, Strandridaregatan 8, pg. 1038 — IT
Perstorp Flooring AB, Strandridaregatan 8, pg. 1039 — IT
Trellborg Industri AB, Nygatan 49A, pg. 1422 — IT
TRELLEBORG AB, Nygatan 102, pg. 1419 — IT
Trelleborg Mining & Metals Div., Nygatan 102, pg. 1422 — IT
Trelleborg Rubber & Plastics Div., Nygatan 102, pg. 1422 — IT
Trelleborgdack AB, Nygatan 102, pg. 1422 — IT

Trollhattan
AB Cerbo, pg. 1423 — IT
Kalmar Nohab AB, Box 903, pg. 1421 — IT
Saab Automobile AB, pg. 687 — IT
Saab Automobile AB, pg. 720 — PB
Vattenfall AB, pg. 1453 — IT
Vattenfall Western Sweden, pg. 1453 — IT
Volvo Aero Corporation, pg. 1476 — IT

Tumba
Alfa-Laval Agri International AB, pg. 1377 — IT
Alfa-Laval Separation AB, pg. 1378 — IT

Tyreso
Contronic Development ab, Mediavagen 7, pg. 1039 — IT
Hydro Aluminium Sverige AB (Tyreso), Skogsangsvagen 54, pg. 963 — IT

Uddevalla
Arvid Hogstrom AB, Schillersvag 4, pg. 1172 — IT
Glashuset Uddevalla AB Participacoes Ltda., Schillersvag 4, pg. 1173 — IT
NCC Uddevalla, Junogatan 2, pg. 899 — IT

Ulricehammn
Jarnia AB, Karlsnas Ind. Omr., pg. 188 — IT
Parker Pneumatic AB, Karlin AS Vagen 19, pg. 1264 — PB

Umea
Ballast Nord AB, pg. 899 — IT
ICA Handlarna Norr AB, pg. 642 — IT
Machinery North, pg. 899 — IT
NCC Building - Umea, pg. 898 — IT
NCC Umea, pg. 899 — IT
Pharmacia & Upjohn Biotech AB, Umea Plant, Mariehemsvagen 12, pg. 1047 — IT
Symbicom AB, pg. 93 — IT

Upplands Vasby
Ballast Stockholm AB, pg. 899 — IT
Cederroth International AB, Box 715 S-194 27, pg. 38 — PB
DAB Dental AB, Finvids vag 8-10, pg. 708 — IT
DAB Ortodonti AB, Finvids vag 8-10, pg. 711 — IT
Dell Computer AB, Kanalvagen 12, pg. 496 — PB
Ericsson Electronic Services, Kanalvagen 1B, pg. 1363 — IT
Fundia AB, Kanalvagen 12, pg. 1088 — IT
ICL Data AB, Kanalvagen 18, pg. 529 — IT
Axel Johnson Dental AB, Finvidsvagen 8-10, pg. 709 — IT
LIC Dental AB, pg. 551 — IT
Nikon Svenska AB, Antom Tammsvag 3, pg. 932 — IT
Olicom Sweden, Kanalvagen 10 C-12, 9 van, pg. 1001 — IT
Olivetti A/B, Truckvagen 14, pg. 1003 — IT
Seimens Nixdorf Informationssystem AB, Solna (Stockholm), Johanneslundsvaegen 12-14, pg. 1247 — IT
Svenska Dentalinstrument AB, pg. 709 — IT

Uppsala
Enso Trading AB, Skolgatan 43, pg. 457 — IT
Gensym, Gluten, pg. 731 — PB
NCC Building - Uppsala, pg. 899 — IT
Pharmacia & Upjohn Biosensor AB, Rapsgatan 7, pg. 1047 — IT
Pharmacia & Upjohn Biosystems AB, Rapsgatan 7, pg. 1047 — IT
Pharmacia & Upjohn Biotech AB, Bjorkgatan 30, pg. 1047 — IT
Pharmacia & Upjohn Data AB, Ragsgatan 7, pg. 1048 — IT
Pharmacia & Upjohn Diagnostics, Inc., Ragsgatan 7, pg. 1048 — IT
Pharmacia & Upjohn Management Centre AB, Krusenberg Herrgard, pg. 1048 — IT
Pharmacia & Upjohn Ophthalmics, Rapsgatan 7, pg. 1048 — IT
Pharmacia & Upjohn Therapeutics, Rapsgatan 7, pg. 1048 — IT
TSI Aktiebolag, Halinasgatan 3, pg. 1559 — PB
Vattenfall Malarnat AB, pg. 1453 — IT
Zonex AB, pg. 1364 — IT

Vadstena
ABS Pump Production AB, Kvarnbacksvagen, pg. 270 — IT
Perstorp ByggKemi-Pelplast, Box 77, pg. 1036 — IT

Vallingby
Grafiskt Paper & Norden AB, Siktgatan 2, pg. 864 — IT

Vanersborg
Infrarodteknik AB, Regementsgatan 39, pg. 661 — IT
Precon VA System AB, Grunnebo, pg. 1199 — IT
Teknosan AB, Industrigatan 9, pg. 349 — IT

Varberg
Lion Ferry AB, Farjelaget Hamnen, pg. 1300 — IT
Svenska Blount AB, Box 1104, pg. 239 — PB

PB - *U.S. Public Companies Volume*
PV - *U.S. Private Companies Volume*
IT - *International Public & Private Companies Volume*

Geographic Index-Non U.S.

1772

NON-U.S. LOCATED COMPANIES — SWITZERLAND

Vargarda

Ancra ABT AB, pg. 71 PV
Autoliv Development AB, P.O. Box 104, pg. 438 IT
Autoliv Stil AB, P.O. Box 124, pg. 438 IT

Vargon

Wargon Mill, pg. 885 IT

Varnamo

Maskin AB Rapid, pg. 678 IT
SCA Emballage AB, pg. 1326 IT
Varnamo Isolerduk, Norregard, pg. 1422 IT

Varnersborg

Vattenfall Bohus-Bal Elnat AB, pg. 1453 IT

Varobacka

Vattenfall Ringhals, pg. 1453 IT

Vasby

Molex Svenska A.B., Travgatan 88, pg. 1123 PB
Network Systems AB, Business Campus, pg. 1522 PB

Vasteras

ABB Atom AB, pg. 7 IT
ABB Distribution AB, pg. 7 IT
ABB Drives AB, pg. 7 IT
ABB Generation AB, pg. 7 IT
ABB Metallurgy AB, pg. 7 IT
ABB Motors AB, pg. 7 IT
ABB Relays AB, pg. 7 IT
ABB Robotics AB, pg. 7 IT
ABB Service AB, pg. 7 IT
ABB Traction AB, pg. 7 IT
Avesta Information Systems AB, Pilgatan 8, pg. 221 IT
Babcock-Bristol AB, Box 20015, Fallhammagatan 2A, pg. 473 IT
Enator Malardalen AB, pg. 277 IT
GA Feral AB, Ostra Ringvagen 4, pg. 962 IT
Grav & Schakt Vasteras AB, Jonas Wenstromsgatan 11, pg. 1200 IT
ICA Ekonomibyra AB, pg. 643 IT
ICA Fastighets AB, pg. 643 IT
ICA Forlaget AB, pg. 643 IT
ICA Handlarna Mellansverige AB, pg. 642 IT
ICA Kopmannatjanst AB, pg. 643 IT
ICA Utbildningar AB, pg. 643 IT
Outokumpu Copper Brass Rod AB, Kopparbergsvagen 28, pg. 1017 IT
Outokumpu Copper Partner AB, Kopparbergsvagen 28, pg. 1017 IT
Outokumpu Copper Tubes AB, Kopparbergsvagen 28, pg. 1017 IT
Outokumpu Financial Services AB, Kopparbergsvagen 28, pg. 1015 IT
SMT Machine Company AB, P.O. Box 800, pg. 1421 IT

Vasterhaninge

Van Leer Svenska AB, pg. 1147 IT

Vastervik

Moore Paragon Svenska AB, Baumansgatan 4, pg. 890 IT
Simia AB, Kvistrum, pg. 1199 IT

Vastra Frolunda

Albright & Wilson AB, Halleflundregatan 12, pg. 49 IT
Black & Decker AB, pg. 234 PB
Brother International Sweden A.B., Holda Lindgrensg. 6B, pg. 230 IT
CIBA-GEIGY AB, J A Wettergrens Gata 5, pg. 975 IT
Componenta Dynapac AB, F.O. Petersons Gatan 24, pg. 1419 IT
Crawford Door Forsaljnings AB, Redegatan 7, pg. 269 IT
ESAB Tech AB, Langebergsgatan 4, pg. 281 IT
Edwards, Datavagen 29, Box 159, pg. 661 IT
Eritel AB, Radiovagen 2, pg. 1364 IT
FOGA SYSTEM INTERNATIONAL AB, Box 4080, pg. 496 IT
Hewlett-Packard Sverige AB, Topasgatan 1A, pg. 822 PB
Jotun Sverige A.B., pg. 715 IT
Perstorp Components, Otto Elanders gata 6, pg. 1040 IT
Perstorp Components Europe, Otto Elanders gata 6, pg. 1040 IT
AB Pharos Marine, Halleflundregatan 24, pg. 1289 IT
Svenska Emissionsteknik AB, Victor Hasselblads gata 8, pg. 713 IT
Volvo Penta Norden AB, pg. 1476 IT

Vaxholm

Dial Forsakrings AB, pg. 1256 IT

Vaxjo

Abetong Miljo AB, pg. 1199 IT
Abetong Prefab AB, pg. 1199 IT
Abetong Teknik AB, Box 24, pg. 1199 IT
Ascom Energy Systems AB, pg. 87 IT
Euroc Beton AB, pg. 1199 IT
ICA Handlarna Sydost AB, pg. 643 IT
Industriventilation Produkt AB, pg. 1260 IT
Industriventilation Svenska AB, pg. 1261 IT
NCC Building - Vaxjo, Arabygatan 11, pg. 899 IT
NCC Vaxjo, pg. 899 IT
SODRA CELL AB, Skogsudden, pg. 1275 IT
Sodra Skogagarna, Skogsudden, pg. 1275 IT
Telub AB, pg. 277 IT
Telub Inforum AB, pg. 277 IT
Telub Teknik AB, pg. 278 IT
Vaxjo Rostfritt AB, P.O. Box 1505, pg. 551 IT

Veddesta

Kodak AB, Veddesta Foretagscentrum, Veddestavagen 13, pg. 552 PB

Vejbystrand

ANA KALTO AB, Magnarp, pg. 188 IT

Vessigebro

AB Tomal, Bohl, pg. 1377 IT

Vetlanda

Elit Fonster AB, pg. 1260 IT
Elitfonster AB, pg. 678 IT
Myresjo AB, pg. 1260 IT
Swedoor AB-Vetlanda, pg. 1303 IT

Vidsel

Telub Miltest AB, pg. 278 IT

Vikingstad

Svenska Foder AB, Vasterlosa, pg. 350 IT
Tambox AB - Vikingstad Factory, pg. 458 IT

Virsbo

Wirsbo Stalrør AB, pg. 1088 IT

Viskafors

Viskafors AB, pg. 1423 IT

Vittaryd

AB Starla-Werken, Box 38, pg. 1580 PB

Volketswil

Battenfeld Schweiz AG, Brunnenstrasse 7, pg. 826 IT

Ystad

Swedish Rail System SRS, pg. 1199 IT

SWITZERLAND

Aarau

The Continuum Company, Inc. (Switzerland), Igelweid 22, pg. 423 PB
Coop Rechtsschutz, Bleichemattstrasse 43, pg. 330 IT
Elcalor AG, Postfach, pg. 443 IT
Lonstroff-BTR AG, pg. 130 IT
Schweizerischer Bankverein, Beim Bahnhof, pg. 1329 IT
Sprecher + Schuh AG, Buchserstrasse 7, pg. 1402 PB

Aargan

HERO, Niederlenzer Kirchweg 3, pg. 617 IT

Adelboden

Mineral und Heilquellen AG, Adelboden, pg. 751 IT

Affoltern

AST Research Switzerland S.A., pg. 1182 IT
Bill Getranke AG, Zurichstrasse 179, pg. 479 IT
Gebauer AG, pg. 1204 IT

Allschwil

Bilger Getranke AG, Binningerstrasse 112, pg. 479 IT
Hartmann & Braun AG, pg. 835 IT
MDL Information Systems AG, Muhlebachweg 9, pg. 1100 IT
OK Coop AG, Hegenheimermattweg 65, pg. 330 IT
Oracle Software (Schweiz) AG, Paradiesrain 10, pg. 1228 PB
Wella (Suisse), Binningerstr. 123, pg. 1490 IT

Altendorf

DOM AG Sicherheitstechnik, Breite Str. 11, pg. 233 PB
Elliott Turbomachinery S.A., Zucherstrasse 4, pg. 373 PV
Transver AG, Zurcherstrasse 42, pg. 1156 IT

Altstatten

Greiter AG, Industriestrasse 12, pg. 929 PB

Arbon

NAW Nutzfahrzeuggesellschaft Arbon & Wetzikon AG, pg. 369 IT
SAURER AG, Schlossgasse 2, pg. 1198 IT

Arnegg

Lista Arnegg, pg. 812 IT

Avenches

Fag S.A., pg. 198 IT

Baar

Allo Pro A.G., pg. 1307 IT
Bourns AG & Bourns (Schweiz) AG, Zugerstrasse 74, pg. 161 PV
EMI Records (Interton) AG, Oberdorfstrasse 4, pg. 427 IT
Framatome Connectors Schweiz A.G., Sihlbruggstrasse 144, pg. 503 IT
Herbol Farben & Lacke AG, Laettichstr. 4, pg. 108 IT
Honeywell-Measurex AG, Laehichstrasse II, pg. 833 PB
Janssen-Cilag Pharmaceutica AG, Sihlbraggstrasse 111, pg. 929 PB
KONE Elevator GmbH, Rathausstrasse 1, pg. 748 IT
Lego AG, Sihlbriggstrasse 3, pg. 805 IT
Raychem AG, Oberneuhofstrasse 8, pg. 1362 PB
Rosemount AG, Arbachstrasse 2, pg. 577 PB
Rosemount Holding AG, Blegistrasse 21, pg. 577 PB
SASIB Support Service (SSS), Zugerstrasse 8/A, pg. 1195 IT
SIKA FINANZ AG, Zugerstrasse 50,, pg. 1248 IT

Bachenbulach

Andrew AG, Postfach 51, Bachliwis 2B, pg. 113 PB

Baden

Asea Brown Boveri AG, Hasel Street, pg. 1 IT
Bekaert (Schweiz) AG, Mellingerstrasse 1, pg. 184 IT
Brother (Schweiz) A.G., Taefernstrasse 30, pg. 230 IT

Ballaigues

Dentsply Maillefer, Maillefer Instruments SA, pg. 499 PB

Balterswil

Walter & Bruynzeel AG, Werkstrasse, pg. 444 IT

Balzers

Balzers, c, pg. 997 IT

Basel

Algemene Bank Nederland (Schweiz) Basle, Dufourstrasse 5, pg. 12 IT
BOC AG, Wasgenning 90-94, pg. 121 IT
Banque Bruxelles Lambert (Suisse)-Basel, 1 Gerbergasse-Am Marktplatz, pg. 148 IT
Banque Nationale de Paris (Suisse) S.A., Aeschengraben 26, pg. 164 IT
BASEL TRADING COMPANY LTD., Petersgraben 35, pg. 169 IT
Bell AG, pg. 329 IT
Bell-Gruppe, Elsasserstrasse 174, pg. 329 IT
Birkhauser + GBC AG, pg. 329 IT
Blendax-Richardson AG, Holbeinstrasse 91, pg. 1331 PB
CAG Anlagefondsleitung, pg. 329 IT
CCB Co-op Bank Limited, Aechenplatz 3, pg. 329 IT
Caliqua AG, pg. 1306 IT
Cantrade Private Bank Ltd., Gellerstrasse 18, pg. 1440 IT
CIBA-GEIGY AG Pharma Schweiz, Reinacherstrasse 115, pg. 972 IT
CIBA-GEIGY International AG, Klybeckstrasse 141, pg. 972 IT
CIBA Industrial Marketing Ltd, Webergasse 34, pg. 972 IT
CIBA SPECIALTY CHEMICALS HOLDING INC., Klybeckstrasse 141, pg. 291 IT
CIBA Vision Holding AG, Klybeckstrasse 141, pg. 972 IT
Clestra Holding AG, St. Jakobsstrasse 25, pg. 570 IT
Coop Bank, Aeschenplatz 3, pg. 329 IT
Coop Basel, pg. 329 IT
Coop Hostellerie AG, pg. 330 IT
Coop Lebensversicherungs Genossenschaft, Aeschenvorstadt 67, pg. 330 IT
COOP SWITZERLAND, Thiersteinerallee 12, pg. 329 IT
Crossair Ltd., pg. 1334 IT
DCD (Schwiez) GmbH, pg. 596 IT
DMR Gruppe AG, Innere Margarethenstrasse 5, pg. 528 IT
DANZAS HOLDING LTD., Leimenstrasse 1, pg. 382 IT
Danzas Management Ltd., Leimenstr. 1, pg. 382 IT
Duracell AG, Kirchgartenstrasse 12-14, pg. 743 PB
Frionor AG, Peter Merian Str. 45, Postfach, pg. 516 IT
Genentech Europe Limited, pg. 1120 IT

PB - U.S. Public Companies Volume
PV - U.S. Private Companies Volume
IT - International Public & Private Companies Volume

Geographic Index-Non U.S.

Hapag-Lloyd (Schweiz) AG, pg. 596 — IT
Hewlett-Packard (Schweiz) AG, Clarastrasse 12, pg. 821 — PB
Hilton International (Switzerland) AG, Aeschengraben 31, pg. 788 — IT
F. Hoffmann-La Roche Ltd., Grenzacherstrasse 124, pg. 1119 — IT
HOLAD Holding & Administration AG, St. Jakobs-Strasse 7, pg. 1475 — IT
Holdux Beteilgungsgesellschaft, St. Alban-Vorstadt, 17, pg. 91 — IT
Holmen (Schweiz) AG, Neubadstrasse 7, pg. 885 — IT
Hospal Ltd., Dornacherstrasse 8, pg. 668 — IT
Krupp Hoesch Basel AG, Engelgasse 43, pg. 515 — IT
Life Technologies A.G., Bruderholdztrasse 45, pg. 505 — PB
Mobil Oil Switzerland, Picassoplatz 4, pg. 1119 — PB
Munters AG, Birsigstrasse 18, pg. 669 — IT
Nedlloyd Lines (Switzerland) A.G., pg. 1145 — IT
Nedlloyd Road Cargo AG, pg. 1145 — IT
Novartis, pg. 972 — IT
NOVARTIS AG, Lichtstrasse 35, pg. 971 — IT
Novartis AG, FI 3.4, pg. 972 — IT
OCG Microelectronic Materials AG, pg. 973 — IT
OCG Microelectronic Materials AG, pg. 1220 — PB
Panalpina Ltd., Reinacherstrasse 261, pg. 1022 — IT
Pardux Anlagesellschaft, St. Alban-Vorstadt, 17, pg. 92 — IT
Pechiney Bale, 25 rue Saint-Jacques, pg. 1031 — IT
Pent Holding AG, pg. 330 — IT
Prognos AG, Missionstrasse 62, pg. 1480 — IT
Roche Finanz AG, pg. 1120 — IT
ROCHE HOLDING LTD., Grenzacherstr. 124, pg. 1119 — IT
Rudolphe Haller AG, pg. 1022 — IT
SOFITEC, Societe Financiere et Technique SA, Sevogelstrasse 52, pg. 634 — IT
St. Johann Lagerhaus & Schiffahrts-Gesellschaft, Rheinhafer Str Johann 6, pg. 330 — IT
Sandoz Biosciences Ltd., pg. 972 — IT
Sandoz Holding Ltd., Lichtstrasse 35, pg. 972 — IT
Sandoz International Ltd., Lichtstrasse 35, pg. 972 — IT
Sandoz Pharma Ltd., Lichtstrasse 35, pg. 972 — IT
Sandoz Pharma Services Ltd., pg. 972 — IT
Sandoz Produkte (Schweiz) AG, Missionstr. 62, pg. 974 — IT
Sandoz Technology Ltd., Lichstrasse 35, pg. 972 — IT
Sanyo (Europe) International AG, Steinengraben 40, pg. 1192 — IT
Schachenmann & Co. AG, pg. 1306 — IT
Schweizerischer Bankverein, Gartenstrasse 9, pg. 1329 — IT
Schweizerischer Bankverein, Aeschenvorstadt 1, pg. 1329 — IT
Schweizerischer Bankverein, Aeschenplatz 6, pg. 1329 — IT
Servipharm Ltd., pg. 972 — IT
Societe Internationale Pirelli S.A., 54 St. Jakob-Strasse, pg. 1060 — IT
Sodra AG, Henric Petri-Strasse 19, pg. 1276 — IT
Spectra-Physics AG, Schweizergasse 39, pg. 1290 — IT
Steelcase Strafor AG, Auberg 2, pg. 569 — IT
Sulzer-Burckhardt Engineering Works Ltd., pg. 1305 — IT
Sulzer-Burckhardt Engineering Works ltd., Dornacherstrasse 210, pg. 1307 — IT
SWISS BANK CORPORATION, Aeschenplatz 6, pg. 1329 — IT
Swiss Shipping and Neptune AG, pg. 866 — IT
Thomi & Franck AG, Horburgerstrasse 105, pg. 916 — IT
Thyssen Haniel Logistics, pg. 1388 — IT
Tornado AG, pg. 1481 — IT
Tuflin AG, Holeestrasse 87, pg. 578 — PB
Wyeth AG, Dufourstrasse 49, pg. 82 — PB

Bassecourt

Georges Ruedin SA, Rue de la Combe 10, pg. 1160 — IT

Bassersdorf

Bang & Olufsen AG, Grindelstrasse 15, pg. 146 — IT
Compaq Computer AG, IM Grindel, Grindelstrasse 6, pg. 418 — PB
MBA-KONE AG, Zurichstrasse 46, pg. 748 — IT

Bazenheid

Micarna AG, pg. 865 — IT

Beil

Pfauter Schweiz, Alleestrasse 23, pg. 617 — IT

Belfaux

Lawson Mardon Boxal Suisse SA, pg. 67 — IT

Bellevue

Marsh Company M.C.S.A., 36 Chemin des Mollies, CH-1293, pg. 708 — PV

Bellinzona

B.F. Goodrich Aerospace, Via Visconti 1, pg. 752 — PB

Bergdietikon

Bandfix AG, pg. 183 — IT

Bern

AMS Management Systems (Switzerland) AG, Laupenstrasse 19, pg. 87 — PB
Ascom Energy Systems, Murtenstrasse 133, pg. 86 — IT
Ascom Ericsson Transmission AG, Belpstrasse 37, pg. 86 — IT
Ascom Finanz AG, Belpstrasse 37, pg. 86 — IT
Ascom Hasler AG, Belpstrasse 37, pg. 86 — IT
Ascom Hasler Mailing Systems AG, Brunnenstrasse 66, pg. 86 — IT
ASCOM HOLDING AG, Belpstrasse 37, pg. 86 — IT
Ascom Immobilien AG, Belpstrasse 37, pg. 86 — IT
Ascom Installationen AG, Sudbahnhofstrasse 1, pg. 86 — IT
Ascom Tech AG, Morgenstrasse 129, pg. 86 — IT
Bank von Ernst & Cie AG, pg. 180 — IT
Bauer Apparel Inc., Talgut-Zentrum 19, pg. 1184 — PB
Bausch & Lomb AG/SA, Langmauerweg 19A, pg. 195 — PB
Bess Hygiene AG, pg. 1333 — PB
Coop Bern, Kasparstrasse 7 + 9, pg. 329 — IT
Impuls Advertising, Maulbeerstr. 8, pg. 666 — IT
Le Carbone S.A., Ostermundigenstrasse 34 A, pg. 1030 — IT
MSA Switzerland Ltd., Grubenstrasse 24-26, pg. 1115 — PB
Radio TV Steiner AG, Winterholzstrasse 55, pg. 330 — IT
Reisburo Popularis AG, pg. 330 — IT
Rex-Rotary AG, Kramgasse 33, pg. 1116 — IT
Sandoz Nutrition Ltd., pg. 972 — IT
Sandoz Nutrition Trading Ltd., pg. 972 — IT
Sandoz Research Institute Berne Ltd., pg. 972 — IT
Sandoz-Wander Pharma AG, Monbijoustrasse 115, pg. 972 — IT
Scherz Verlag GmbH, Theaterplatz 4-6, pg. 1480 — IT
SCHWEIZERISCHE BUNDESBAHNEN - SBB AG, Hochschulstrasse 6, pg. 1211 — IT
SCHWEIZERISCHE KASEUNION AG, Monbijoustrasse 45, pg. 1211 — IT
Schweizerischer Bankverein, Barenplatz 8, pg. 1329 — IT
SmithKline Beecham A.G., Weltpoststrasse 4, pg. 1265 — IT
Sulzer Ruti Group, pg. 1307 — IT
SWISSCOM, Viktoriastr. 21, pg. 1334 — IT
Tobler Chocolat AG, Riedbachstrasse 150, pg. 1288 — PB
UMS Swiss Metalworks Ltd., Kollerweg 32, pg. 1427 — IT
Vidmar AG, pg. 812 — IT
Von Roll AG Departement Maschinen & Fordertechn, Fabrikstrasse 2, pg. 1480 — IT
Wandel & Goltermann (Schweiz) AG, Postfach 254, pg. 1486 — IT
Wandel & Goltermann (Schweiz) AG, Postfach 779, pg. 1486 — IT
Wander AG, Monbijoustr. 115, pg. 972 — IT
Wander Ltd., pg. 972 — IT

Berneck

Verin S.A., P.O. Box 85, pg. 1322 — IT

Bevaix

KLA Instruments, S.A., Chemin de Buchaux 38, pg. 939 — PB

Biel

Asulab S.A., pg. 1160 — IT
Citizen Watch (Switzerland) AG, Zurichstrasse 17, pg. 294 — IT
DTC - Dynamic Test Center, pg. 998 — IT
Endura SA, pg. 1160 — IT
MIKRON HOLDING AG, Muhlebrucke 2, pg. 866 — IT
Puma (Switzerland) AG, Solothurnstrasse 44, pg. 1072 — IT

Bienne

Concord Watch Company, S.A., 35 rue de Nidau, pg. 1140 — PB
General Motors Suisse S.A., Salzhausstrasse 21, pg. 723 — PB
Houghton A.G. Switzerland, Furstenlandstrasse 7, pg. 541 — PV
MC Micro Compact Car AG, Mattenstrasse 149, pg. 368 — IT
Montres Movado, S.A., 35 rue de Nidau, pg. 1140 — PB
Omega Electronics SA, Mattenstrasse 149, pg. 1161 — IT
Omega SA, J Stampflistrasse 96, pg. 1160 — IT
SMH Automobile AG, Mattenstrasse 149, pg. 1161 — IT
SMH SWISS CORPORATION FOR MICRO ELECTRONICS & WATCHMAKING INDUS. LTD., Faubourg du Lac 6, pg. 1160 — IT
Mido G. Schaeren & Co., SA, Bozingenstrasse 9, pg. 1161 — IT
Swatch S.A., J. Stampflistrasse 94, pg. 1161 — IT
Swatch Telecom AG, Neumarkstrasse 64, pg. 1161 — IT
Von Roll Eisen & Stahlgiesserei AG, Johan Renferstrasse 51-55, pg. 1480 — IT

Binningen

Air Sea Broker AG, pg. 1022 — IT
Panalpina Management AG, pg. 1022 — IT
PANALPINA WELTTRANSPORT (HOLDING) AG, Huebweg 25, pg. 1022 — IT
Pantainer AG, pg. 1022 — IT

Bioggio

Electroform S.A., CH-6934, pg. 1598 — PB

Birmenstorf

Leu & Gygax AG, Fellstrasse 1, pg. 356 — IT

Birsfelden

Migros Enterprises Birsfelden AG, pg. 866 — IT
Zurich Shipping Company AG, pg. 866 — IT

Bischofszell

Bischofszell Canning Factory AG, pg. 865 — IT

Bonaduz

Hamilton Bonaduz AG, pg. 497 — PV

Bottens

Vectur S.A., pg. 1129 — PV

Bottmingen

John Crane (Switzerland) AG, Wuhrmattstrasse 13a, pg. 1339 — IT

Boudry

Mikron SA Boudry, Route du Vignoble 17, pg. 866 — IT
New Ingenia SA, Route du Vignoble 17, pg. 866 — IT

Breganzona

Ticino Societa d'Assicurazzioni Sula Vita, Via Camera 17, pg. 85 — PB

Brugg

Bank Aufina, Badenerstrasse 9, pg. 1439 — IT
UBS Leasing AG, Badenerstrasse 11, pg. 1440 — IT

Brunnen

Reismuhle Brunnen AG, Industriestrasse 1, pg. 330 — IT

Bruttisellen

Ericsson AG, Stationsstrasse 5, pg. 1366 — IT
Ericsson Finanz AG, Stationsstrasse 5, pg. 1366 — IT
Rieter Automotive Management AG, pg. 1116 — IT
SAS Institute S.A. (Geneve), Ruchstuckstr, 6, pg. 967 — PV

Bubikon

Teleinform-Gruppe, pg. 618 — IT

Buchrain

A.C. Nielsen Management Services S.A., Nielsen House, pg. 1183 — PB

Buchs

Chocolat Frey AG, pg. 865 — IT
Fluka Chemie AG, Industriestrasse 25, pg. 1472 — PB
Mibelle AG, pg. 865 — IT
OWL AG Logistik-Systeme, Webereiweg 3, pg. 490 — IT
Vink Kunststoffe AG, Fabrikweg 93, pg. 1210 — IT

Bulach

CIBA Vision Management AG, Grenzstrasse 10, pg. 972 — IT
Dow Chemical Export S.A., Grenzstrasse 10, pg. 523 — PB
Schneider (Europe) AG, Ackerstrasse 6, pg. 1283 — PB
Sulzer Bulachguss AG, pg. 1307 — IT

Bulle

Liebherr-Industrieanlagen AG, Rue de l'Industrie 19, pg. 808 — IT
LIEBHERR-INTERNATIONAL AG, Rue de L'industrie 19, pg. 807 — IT
Liebherr-Intertrading AG, Rue de l'Industrie 19, pg. 808 — IT
Liebherr-Investment AG, 19, rue de l'Industrie, pg. 807 — IT
Liebherr Machines Bulle S.A., Rue de l'Industrie, pg. 808 — IT
Liebherr-Swissholding AG, Rue de l'Industrie 19, pg. 808 — IT
Mariso Bulle S.A., Rue de l'Industrie 19, pg. 808 — IT
Waelzlager Industriewerke Bulle AG, Rue Champ-Barby 23, pg. 904 — IT

Burgdorf

Mauerhofer, Lanz & Co. AG, pg. 330 — IT

Busswil

Nutrex AG, Juraweg 5, pg. 330 — IT

Buttikon

Rexroth AG, pg. 839 — IT

PB - *U.S. Public Companies Volume*
PV - *U.S. Private Companies Volume*
IT - *International Public & Private Companies Volume*

1774

Geographic Index-Non U.S.

Capolago

Monte Generoso Railway AG, pg. 866   IT

Carouge

Naville, 38, avenue Vibert, pg. 796   IT
Nokia Finance International B.V., Geneva Branch, Geneva Branch, 21, rue des Caroubiers, pg. 954   IT

Cham

Abbott AG, Gewerbestrasse 5, pg. 13   PB
Alcon Pharmaceuticals Ltd., Singerstrasse 47, pg. 916   IT
Fisons AG, Alte Steinhouserstrasse 35, pg. 1111   IT
Perstorp Vertriebs AG, Riedstrasse 7, pg. 1039   IT
Perstorp Vertriebs AG, Riedstrasse 7, Postfach 5267, pg. 1039   IT
Sensormatic AG, Gewerberstrasse 8, pg. 1457   PB

Chatel Saint Denis

C.M.D. Chatel Medical Devices S.A., pg. 991   IT
Nutraco S.A., pg. 992   IT

Chiasso

Algemene Bank Nederland (Svizzera), Via Livio 5, pg. 12   IT
Danzas S.p.A., Via Motta 6, pg. 383   IT
ESS-FOOD Meatimex S.A., Via Bossi 4, pg. 429   IT
Francesco Parisi S.a.g.l., Via Soldini 13, pg. 504   IT
SA Magazzini Generali, pg. 330   IT

Choindez

Von Roll AG Departement Druckrohre, pg. 1480   IT

Chur

Albula Verwaltungs-und Beteiligungs-AG, Zedernweg, 1, pg. 90   IT
Coop Graubunden-Sarganserland, Alexanderrstrasse 2, pg. 329   IT
Fit Container AG, pg. 67   IT
Makro International AG, Aspermonstrasse 24, pg. 1155   IT
Schweizerischer Bankverein, Bahnhofstrasse 9, pg. 1329   IT
Sporic AG, Lindenquai 10, pg. 1280   IT

Claro

Lubrizol AG (Switzerland), pg. 1016   PB

Colombier

K-Tron Switzerland-Hasler Division, Chemin de la Scierie, pg. 938   PB

Corcelles

Yokohama (Suisse) SA, La Maladaire, pg. 1521   IT

Courtepin

Micarna S.A., pg. 865   IT

Crissier

Metallica SA, Route de Marcolet 37, pg. 1427   IT

Cully

IKON Cully S.A., Route de Grandvaux 22, pg. 18   IT

Dallenwil

Color Media AG, pg. 501   IT
FLC Shop AG, pg. 501   IT
Junior Discount Service AG., pg. 501   IT

Dallikon

CRUSPI S.A., Muttenwiesenstraase 10, pg. 348   IT
Sharp Electronics (Schweiz) AG, Langwiesenstrasse 7, pg. 1230   IT

Degersheim

Lista Degersheim AG, pg. 812   IT

Deitingen

ABB Maschinenfabrik Meyer AG, Oeschbachstrasse 428, pg. 1   IT

Delemont

Black & Decker (Switzerland) S.A., Communance 26, pg. 234   PB
Robinson-Nugent S.A., 6, rue Saint-Georges, pg. 1395   IT
Von Roll Machinery & Handling Systems, Route de Moutier 109, pg. 1480   IT

Dielsdorf

BMW (Schweiz) AG, pg. 178   IT
Dr. R. Maag AG, pg. 972   IT

Dietikon

AGIE Verkauf Schweiz AG, Neue Winterthurerstrasse 30, pg. 488   IT
Astra Pharmaceutica AG, KanalStrasse 6, pg. 94   IT
E. Brandle AG, pg. 506   IT
Bridgestone (Schweiz) AG, Postfach 52, Lerzenstrasse 11, pg. 214   IT
Canon (Schweiz) AG, Industriestrasse 12, pg. 263   IT
CIBA Corning Diagnostics AG, Neue Winterthurerstrasse 15, pg. 972   IT
Divino AG, Aegertstrasse 5, pg. 479   IT
ESAB AG, Riedstrasse 7, pg. 282   IT
Ex Libris AG, pg. 865   IT
Fehr Demag AG, pg. 837   IT
Getranke-Dienst AG, Bestellungen Aegertstr. 5, pg. 479   IT
Heinrich Heine Handelsgesellschaft AG, pg. 1014   IT
Johnson Wax AG, Ried Strasse, pg. 593   PV
Linde Lansing Fodertechnik AG, pg. 810   IT
M-Informatics AG, pg. 865   IT
Mannesmann Finanz AG, pg. 840   IT
Reliance Electric AG, Industriestrasse 9 + 11, pg. 1400   PB
Rio-Getrankemarkt AG, Riedwiesenstrasse 6, pg. 479   IT
Texas Instruments (Switzerland) AG, Riedstrasse 6, pg. 1586   PB

Dittingen

Novo Nordisk Ferment Ltd., Neumatt, pg. 989   IT

Domdidier

Milupa S.A., pg. 991   IT
WAGO Contact SA, Zone Industrielle C, pg. 209   IT

Dornach

Swissmetal Plant Dornach, Weidenstrasse 50, pg. 1427   IT
UMS SWISS METALWORKS HOLDING LTD, Weidenstrasse 50, pg. 1427   IT

Dubendorf

Agfa-Gevaert AG, pg. 174   IT
Analog Devices SA, Rosenstrasse 13, pg. 108   PB
Ascom Telematic AG, Stettbachstrasse 6, pg. 86   IT
Bestobell Mobrey AG, Birch Lenstrasse 46, pg. 854   IT
Digital Equipment Corporation AG, pg. 507   PB
Fasson Vertriebs, AG, Stettbachstrasse 8, pg. 154   PB
Ferrolegeringar AG, Zuerichstrasse 131, pg. 735   PV
Givaudan-Roure Flavours Ltd., Ueberlandstrasse 138, pg. 1119   IT
Givaudan-Roure Research Ltd., Ueberlandstrasse 138, pg. 1119   IT
Kabi Pharmacia & Upjohn AG, Lagerstrasse 14, pg. 1049   IT
Keithley Instruments S.A., Kriesbachstrasse 4, pg. 947   PB
Medtronic (Schweiz) AG, Bahnhofstrasse 60, pg. 1084   PB
Moulinex, Stettbachstrasse, 10, pg. 896   IT
Nokia Telecommunications AG, Auenstrasse 10, pg. 953   IT
Noralu AG, Zurichstrasse 79, pg. 964   IT
Pharmacia & Upjohn Biotech AG, Lagerstrasse 14, pg. 1047   IT
Tyco Toys (Schweiz/Suisse) AG/SA, Neugutstrasse 66, pg. 1059   PB

Dudingen

Perchem SA, Bonnstrasse, pg. 47   IT

Ebikon

Schindler Aufzuge AG, Zugerstrasse 13, pg. 1204   IT
Schindler Immobilientreuhand und-Verwaltungs AG, pg. 1204   IT
Schindler Informatik AG, pg. 1204   IT
Schindler Management AG, pg. 1204   IT

Ebmatingen

Allen-Bradley AG, Lohwisstrasse 50, pg. 1398   PB

Ecublens

LEMO SA, Chemin des Champs-Courbes 28, pg. 806   IT
SAPAL SA, Av. du Tir Federal 44, pg. 1156   IT

Effretikon

Pitney Bowes (Switzerland) AG, Vogelsangstrasse 17, pg. 1304   PB
Schaltag AG, pg. 1116   IT

Egerkingen

Melitta Bentz & Co, Melittawerk, pg. 857   IT
Melitta GmbH, pg. 857   IT

Eglisau

Forbo Finanz SA, pg. 497   IT
FORBO HOLDING SA, pg. 496   IT
Forbo Immob SA, pg. 497   IT
Forbo International SA, pg. 497   IT
Forbo-Stamoid SA, pg. 497   IT

Embrach

Curver (Schweiz) AG, pg. 353   IT
Herlitz AG, Postfach 48, pg. 616   IT

Emmen

Manitec AG, Buhlozstrasse 36, pg. 1205   IT
Manitec Consulting AG, Buholzstrasse 36, pg. 1205   IT
Rhone-Poulenc Viscosuisse, pg. 1114   IT
Viscosuisse S.A., pg. 1114   IT

Engelberg

Tefina Holding AG, pg. 1116   IT

Ennenda

Forbo Teppichwerke SA, pg. 497   IT

Erlen

Lista AG, Fabrikstr., pg. 812   IT
LISTA HOLDING AG, Fabrikstrasse 1, pg. 812   IT

Erlenbach

Laesser Klebstoffe AG, pg. 613   IT

Estavayer le Lac

Conserves Estavayer S.A., pg. 865   IT

Ettingen

Nexstar, Inc., pg. 1180   PB

Fallanden

Knurr AG, Bruggacherstrasse 16, pg. 739   IT
Reed Exhibition Companies-Switzerland, Bruggacherstrasse 26, pg. 1097   IT

Feldmeilen

Jauch & Huebener, General-Wille-Strasse 201, pg. 118   PB

Flawil

Mecatool AG, Wilerstrasse 98, pg. 489   IT

Forch

Aritron Instrument A.G., pg. 1114   PB

Frauenfeld

Fuchs Petrolub AG, Thundorferstr. 1, pg. 517   IT
Great Lakes Chemical (Europe) Ltd., Juchstrasse 45, pg. 760   PB
Hess Engineering AG, Langfeldstrasse 88, pg. 524   PV

Frenkendorf

Mifa AG, pg. 866   IT

Fribourg

Ampco Metal S.A., 9 Route de Chesalles, pg. 67   PV
Bausch & Lomb Fribourg S.A., pg. 195   PB
Dyna S.A., Route de la Fonderie 18, pg. 916   IT
Ilford SA, Industriestrasse 15, pg. 906   PB
Imasco B.V.-Fribourg Branch, 34, rue de Lausanne, pg. 112   IT
International Saint-Gobain, 10, rue Saint-Pierre, pg. 1177   IT
Novotel International, One, rue Fries, c/o Me Andrey, pg. 21   IT
O.L.F., Z.I.-3, Corminboeuf, pg. 796   IT
Payot Naville Distribution, Z.I.-3, Corminboeuf, pg. 796   IT
Schweizerischer Bankverein Reprasentanz, Merianstrasse 31, pg. 1330   IT
Societe de Banque Suisse, Rue de Romont 35, pg. 1329   IT
Sodipress, Z.I.-3, Corminbouef, pg. 796   IT
Sogecred S.A., Bvd. de Perolles 55, pg. 137   IT
Tradisco, Route des Daillettes 21, pg. 534   IT
Wella Beteiligungen AG, Case Postale, pg. 1490   IT

Fruthwilen

Semilab AG, Seepanorama, pg. 803   IT

PB - *U.S. Public Companies Volume*
PV - *U.S. Private Companies Volume*
IT - *International Public & Private Companies Volume*

1775

Gampel

Lonza AG, pg. 67 — IT

Gattikon

Unifridge AG, Dreikonigstrasse 35, pg. 444 — IT

Gelterkinden

Bose AG, Runenbergerstrasse 13A, pg. 160 — PV
Maloya Fredestein, 58 Ergolzstrasse, pg. 505 — IT

Genesterio

Societe Pour La Vente Des Produits Cinzano SA, Via Prella, pg. 410 — IT

Geneva

ABB Secheron S.A., 14, Ave de Secheron, B.P. 40, pg. 1 — IT
ABN Trustcompany (Suisse) S.A., Rue du Rhone 80, pg. 12 — IT
ANZ Grindlays Bank plc Switzerland, 7 Quai du Mont Blanc, pg. 99 — IT
Abbott Laboratories S.A., 2, rue Thalberg, pg. 14 — IT
Algemene Bank Nederland (Suisse), 12 Quai General-Guisan, pg. 12 — IT
AlliedSignal Engines, Geneva Airport, P.O. Box 422, pg. 52 — PB
Amoco Chemical (Europe) S.A., 15, rue Rothschild, pg. 103 — PB
Analog Devices SA, 9, Rue de Berne, pg. 108 — PB
Applied Power International S.A., 47, Avenue Blanc, pg. 125 — PB
ARES-SERONO S.A., Ch. des Mines 15b, pg. 80 — IT
Autodesk (Europe) S.A., Case Postale 766, 20 Route de Pre-Bois, pg. 149 — PB
B.A.T (Suisse) SA, Route des Acacias 43, pg. 111 — IT
BvE Capital Management S.A., pg. 180 — IT
Balair/CTA Ltd., Case postale, pg. 1333 — IT
Balboa Finance S.A., Rue Ceard 6, pg. 136 — IT
Banco Santander (Suisse), S.A., 2-4 Place des Alpes, pg. 144 — IT
Banco Santander-Suiza, 2-4 Places des Alpes, pg. 143 — IT
Bank Hapoalim (Switzerland) Ltd., Seven Pl. du Molard, pg. 150 — IT
Bank Leumi Le-Israel (Switzerland), 80 Rue du Rhone, pg. 150 — IT
Bank SBC Warburg Soditic AG, 118 rue du Rhone, pg. 1331 — IT
Banque Bruxelles Lambert (Suisse), 30, Avenue De Frontenex, pg. 148 — IT
Banque Cantrade, Ormond Burrus SA, 12, rue Ami-Lullin, pg. 1439 — IT
Banque Diamantaire Anversoise (Suisse) SA, 12 rue Bellot, pg. 548 — IT
Banque du Credit Agricole (Suisse) SA, 12 place de la Fusterie, pg. 341 — IT
Banque Indosuez, 4, quai General Guisan, pg. 314 — IT
Banque Indosuez, 19, rue du Rhone, pg. 314 — IT
Banque Kleinwort Benson SA, Place du Rhone 2, pg. 420 — IT
Banque Lavoro S.A., 7, Rue Versonnex, pg. 137 — IT
Banque Morgan Grenfell en Suisse S. A. (Switzerland), 4 Pl. Des Alpes, pg. 406 — IT
Banque Paribas (Suisse) S.A., 2, place de Hollande, pg. 320 — IT
Barclays Bank SA, pg. 166 — IT
Bear, Stearns & Co. Inc., Geneva, 30 Rue de Rhone, pg. 198 — PB
BERG Electronics S.A., 2, Chemin du Pavillon, pg. 213 — PB
Berlitz Schools of Languages AG, 1, Carrefour de Rive, pg. 222 — PB
Borealis S.A., 20, Route de Pre-Bois, pg. 914 — IT
Branson Sonic Power, S.A., 9 Chemin Faubourg-De-Cruseilles, pg. 576 — IT
CAP Gemini Suisse, 2, chemin du Beau-Soleil, pg. 264 — IT
CAP Rechtsschutz, Avenue de Champel 8 c, pg. 60 — IT
Canadian Imperial Bank of Commerce (Suisse) S.A., 6, Cours de Rive, pg. 258 — IT
Canon S.A., 1, Rue de Hesse, pg. 263 — IT
Caterpillar Overseas Credit Corporation S.A., 76 route de Frontenex, pg. 316 — PB
Caterpillar Overseas S.A., P.O. Box 456, 76 route de Frontenex, pg. 316 — PB
CCF (Suisse) SA, 1 Place Longemalle, pg. 342 — IT
The Chase Manhattan Bank, N.A., 63 Rue du Rhone, pg. 340 — PB
Chase Manhattan Bank (Switzerland), 63 Rue du Rhone, pg. 340 — PB
Chesebrough-Pond's (Geneve) S.A., 89-91 Rue Servette, pg. 1436 — IT
Christie's (International) S.A., 8 Place de la Taconnere, pg. 290 — IT
Citroen (Switzerland), 27, rue des Acacias, pg. 1020 — IT
Club Mediterranee (Bureau Suisse) S.A., 28, Quai General Guisan, pg. 298 — IT
Comimet, 8c Avenue de Champel, pg. 661 — IT
Commerzbank AG, 86, Rue da Rhone, pg. 311 — IT
Compagnie de Gestion et de Banque Gonet SA, 8, place de L'Universite, pg. 548 — IT
Coutts & Co. (Trustees) SA, 13 Quai de l'Ile, pg. 911 — IT
Credit Lyonnais Suisse SA, Place Bel Air, pg. 344 — IT
Daiwa Securities Bank-Geneva Branch, Rue de Rhone, 19, pg. 376 — IT
Dell Computer SA, 46 Chemin de l'Etang, pg. 496 — PB

Deutsche Bank (Swiss) S.A., Place des Bergues 3, pg. 405 — IT
Dow Jones Markets (Switzerland) AG, 20 Route de Pre-Bois, ICC, Immeuble C, Case Postale 706, pg. 525 — PB
Dresdner Bank (Switzerland) Ltd., 9,Quai des Bergues, pg. 419 — IT
Du Pont de Nemours International S.A., 2, Chemin du Pavillon, pg. 532 — PB
Dynapresse, 7, rue Levrier, pg. 795 — IT
Elanco S.A., pg. 993 — PB
Elf Suisse S.A., Pery-Reucherette, pg. 446 — IT
ELVIA Leben, Avenue du Bouchet 2, pg. 60 — IT
FTI-Banque Fiduciary Trust, 15 World Trade Center, pg. 621 — PB
FERRIER LULLIN & CIE SA, 15, rue Petiot, pg. 480 — IT
Fiat Auto Suisse SA, 108 Rue de Lyon, pg. 481 — IT
Finagrain, Cie Commerciale Agricole et Financiere S.A., P.O. Box 327, 16, Avenue Eugen-Pittard, pg. 268 — PV
FIRMENICH S.A., 1 rue de Jeune, pg. 486 — IT
Robert Fleming (Switzerland) S.A., 1 Rue Etienne Dumont, pg. 494 — IT
Gefinor Finance S.A., Gefinor Building, 30 Quai Gustave-Ador, pg. 542 — IT
Geneva General Insurance Company, Avenue Eugene-Pittard 16, pg. 1529 — IT
Geneva Life Insurance Company, Avenue Eugene-Pittard 16, pg. 1529 — IT
Guerlain S.A., 4, chemin de la Graviere, pg. 780 — IT
Guyerzeller Bank AG, 12 Rue Charles-Galland, pg. 582 — IT
Handelsfinanz-CCF Bank, 3 bis Place de la Fusterie, pg. 343 — IT
Hein-Werner (Europe) S.A., 2, Promenada des Artisan, pg. 805 — PB
Hyposwiss Schweizerische, 12, rue Ceard, pg. 1440 — IT
ISS Holding S.A., Rue Lecht 29, pg. 657 — IT
Interavia Publishing Group, Intl. Center Cointrin, Route de Pre-Bois 20, pg. 1601 — PB
International Fibre Sales, S.A., 59, Rue de la Servette, pg. 1077 — PB
Jacquet Orthopedie S.A., 5, Chemin des Aulx, 1228 Plan-Lex-Ouates, pg. 1282 — IT
Japan Airlines, 42, Rue De Lausanne, pg. 700 — IT
Kemet Electronics SA, 15 Chemin Des Mines, pg. 949 — PB
Kofisa Trading Company SA., 54, Rue de Lausanne, pg. 742 — IT
Korn/Ferry International, 61 Rue du Rhone, pg. 633 — PV
Kredietbank (Suisse) S.A., 7, boulevard Georges-Favon, pg. 761 — IT
Laboratoires Sauter S.A., Chemin de l'Etang 46, pg. 1120 — IT
Landis & Staefa Communications SA, 70, Grand-Pre, pg. 800 — IT
Larousse (Suisse) SA, pg. 240 — IT
Eli Lilly S.A., 6 Route des Jeunes 1227, pg. 994 — PB
Lockheed Corporation (International) S.A., 1, Pl. Longemalle, pg. 1009 — PB
Logica Informatique SA, Rue du Tir 3, pg. 814 — IT
Louis Golay S.A., 33C, avenue de Miremont, pg. 782 — IT
MSI Switzerland, 81 Avenue Louis Casai, pg. 1546 — PB
MAUS FRERES S.A., CB 1880, pg. 849 — IT
Minemet S.A., 8c Avenue de Champel, pg. 661 — IT
Mobim, pg. 61 — IT
Moet & Chandon (Suisse) S.A., 26, rue du Mont-Blanc, pg. 783 — IT
J.P. Morgan (Suisse) S.A., 3, Place des Bergues, pg. 1131 — PB
Motorola Suisse S.A., 16 Chemin de La Voie-Creuse, pg. 1140 — PB
Nikko Bank (Switzerland) Ltd., 65, rue du Rhone, pg. 930 — IT
Orca Bank Ltd., 65, rue du Rhone, pg. 1440 — IT
PSA International S.A., 62, quai Gustave Ador, pg. 1021 — IT
Pullman Suisse SA, 18-20, rue du Cendrier, pg. 21 — IT
Quantum Peripherals (Europe) SA, ICC-Bldg. D, Route de Pre-Bois 20, pg. 1350 — PB
Reed Travel Publishing-Switzerland, Rue Cornavin 11, pg. 1097 — IT
Reuters SA, Geneva Centre, pg. 1105 — IT
R.J. Reynolds Finance S.A., 12-14 Chemin Rieu, pg. 1355 — PB
R.J. Reynolds Tobacco International S.A., 12-14 Chemin Rieu, pg. 1356 — PB
R.J. Reynolds Tobacco Intl., Inc., Chemin Riev 12-14, pg. 1355 — PB
Roche Consumer Health (Worldwide) S.A., 5, chemin de la Parfumerie, pg. 1121 — IT
ROLEX WATCH CO. SA, pg. 1126 — IT
SGS SOCIETE GENERALE DE SURVEILLANCE HOLDING S.A., 8, rue des Alpes, pg. 1153 — IT
Saudi-Swiss Bank, 31, route de l'Aeroport, pg. 1440 — IT
Sensore S.A., Rue Bellatte 6, pg. 777 — PB
Silicon Graphics S.A. Intl., 18, Ave. Louis Casai, pg. 1474 — PB
Snamprogetti International S.A., 4, Cours de Rive, pg. 429 — IT
Societe de Banque Suisse, Rue de la Confederation 2, pg. 1329 — IT
Societe Financere de Geneve, 28 boul. du Pont D'Arve, pg. 240 — IT
S.A. Socometaux, pg. 302 — IT
Spierer Freres & Cie S.A., 12 rue Le Corbusier, pg. 1502 — PB
Standard Chartered Bank (Switzerland), 18 rue de la Pelisserie, pg. 1295 — IT
Stauffer Chemical B.V., 8 Rue Jacques-Grosselin, pg. 1526 — IT
Tractebel Finance S.A., Rue Jargonnant 2, pg. 1416 — IT
Union Suisse Compagnie Generale D'Assurances, 1, Rue de la Fontaine, pg. 92 — IT
Volvo Finance S.A., pg. 1476 — IT

Yamaichi Bank-Geneva, 18-20 Rue Plantamour, pg. 1517 — IT
Young & Rubicam Business Communications S.A., 2, Rue Thalberg, pg. 1199 — PV

Gerlafingen

Roth Geruste AG, pg. 1061 — IT
VON ROLL AG, pg. 1480 — IT
Von Roll AG Departement Stahlprodukte, pg. 1480 — IT

Giubiasco

Forbo-Giubiasco SA, Via Industrie 16, pg. 497 — IT
Swifloor SA, pg. 497 — IT

Givisiez

Coop Broye-Fribourg-Moleson, Rte du Tir Federal 18, pg. 329 — IT

Gland

Sun Microsystems (Suisse) SA, Route des Avouillons 12, pg. 1532 — PB
Zyma Healthcare, pg. 972 — IT

Glaris

HOLDERBANK FINANCIERE GLARIS LTD., pg. 628 — IT

Glarus

Bull Holding, Spielhof 3, pg. 318 — IT
Erlen Getrankedienst AG, Auf Erlen 16, pg. 479 — IT

Glattbrugg

Avis Autovermietung AG, Flughofstrasse 61, pg. 321 — PB
Bio-Rad Laboratories AG, Kanalstrasse 17, pg. 230 — PB
CWS International A.G., Industriestrasse 20, pg. 592 — PB
EDS (Switzerland) Ltd., Thalackerstr. 7, pg. 570 — PB
Eurotherm Produkte (Schwiez) AG, Kanalstrasse 17, pg. 466 — IT
General Motors (Europe) AG, Stelzenstrasse 4, pg. 721 — PB
ICI (Switzerland) AG, Aircenter, Stelzenstrasse 6, pg. 665 — IT
Letraset AG, Kanalstrasse 15, pg. 461 — IT
A. Messerli AG, pg. 995 — IT
SIG Bautechnik, Flughofstrasse 51, pg. 1156 — IT
Zurich Insurance Company, Ambassador House, Talackerstrasse 1, pg. 1529 — IT

Gossau

Camelia Werk AG, Schlachthofstrasse 6-8, pg. 959 — PB
Cerbex AG, Industriestrasse 149, pg. 1246 — IT
Coop Ostschweiz, Industriestrasse 109, pg. 329 — IT

Granges

Asitrade AG, pg. 198 — IT

Greifensee

Mettler-Toledo AG, pg. 4 — PV
Mettler-Toledo (Schweiz) AG, pg. 4 — PV

Grenchen

Certina Gebr. Kurth AG, pg. 1160 — IT
Commercial Bank of Soleure, Marktplatz 6, pg. 1440 — IT
ETA S.A. Fabriques D'Ebauches, Schild-Ruststrasse 17, pg. 1160 — IT
Littelfuse AG, Lengnaustrasse 13, pg. 1001 — PB
Meco S.A., Schutzengasse 30, pg. 1160 — IT
Movado Watch Company, S.A., Bettlach Strasse 8, pg. 1140 — PB
N.A. Trading Ltd., Bettlach Strasse 8, pg. 1140 — PB
SMH Automation, Schmelzistrasse 16, pg. 1160 — IT

Gruningen

Vernicolor A.G., Lack-und Farbenfabrik, pg. 505 — PB

Gumligen

Ascom Autelca AG, Worbstrasse 201, pg. 86 — IT

Hausen

Reichhold Chemie AG, Haupstrasse 96, pg. 370 — IT

Hergiswil

ALSO Holding AG, pg. 1204 — IT
Inventio AG, pg. 1204 — IT
Pars Handel AG, pg. 1204 — IT
SCHINDLER HOLDING AG, Seestrasse 55, pg. 1204 — IT
Schindler Trading AG, pg. 1205 — IT

Herisau

Huber & Suhner AG, pg. 637 — IT

PB - *U.S. Public Companies Volume*
PV - *U.S. Private Companies Volume*
IT - *International Public & Private Companies Volume*

1776

Geographic Index-Non U.S.

Herrliberg

Isco Instruments (Europe) AG, Heckenweg 3, pg. 914   PB

Hettlingen

CIBA Vision AG-Hettlingen, pg. 972   IT
Dispersa AG, Riethofstrasse 1, pg. 972   IT

Hinwil

Coop Zurichsee-Linth, Zurichstrasse 55, pg. 329   IT
Ferag AG, Zurichstrasse 74, pg. 1484   IT

Hombrechtikon

Ascom Zelcom AG, pg. 86   IT
NeoTecha Ag, Fabrikweg 2, pg. 1651   PB

Horgen

Dow Europe SA, Bachtobelstrasse 3, pg. 523   PB

Horn

Springborn Testing & Inspection (Europe) AG, Amperestrasse 5, pg. 1027   PV

Hunenberg

Ameda AG, Boesch 106, pg. 535   PV
Gambro AG, pg. 667   IT

Itingen

Flik Flak, pg. 1160   IT
Renata AG, Kreuzenstrasse 30, pg. 1160   IT
Renata SA, Kreuzenstrasse 30, pg. 1161   IT

Jona

EWU-Aktiengesellschaft, Meienbergstrasse 80, pg. 1411   PB

Jongny

Centre de Formation, pg. 329   IT

Kaisten

CIBA-GEIGY Werke Kaisten AG, pg. 972   IT

Kemptthal

Maggi AG, pg. 916   IT

Kersers

Schweizerische Genpssenschaft fur Gemusebau, pg. 330   IT

Kestenholz

Amway (Schweiz) AG, IndustrieStrasse 444, pg. 70   PV

Killwangen

Dictaphone International AG, P.O. Box Ch-8956, pg. 1045   PV

Kirchberg

Nyffeler Corti AG, Solothurnstrasse, pg. 755   IT

Kloten

Alfa-Laval Industriegesellschaft AB, Postfach 1485, pg. 1380   IT
Clestra Hauserman A.G., Steinackerstrasse 25, pg. 570   IT
Millipore AG, Steineckerstrasse 11, pg. 1113   PB
Morganite AG, Steinackerstr 25, pg. 891   IT
Siemens Nixdorf Informationssysteme AG, Obstgartenstrabe 25, pg. 1245   IT

Klus

SF Air Filtration AG, pg. 161   PB

Kolibrunn

Henry Berchtold AG, pg. 637   IT

Koppigen

Floordress Reinigungsmaschinen AG, pg. 611   IT
J.U.L. Seilaz AG, pg. 613   IT

Kreuzlingen

Lawson Mardon Neher AG, pg. 67   IT
Meyhall Chemical AG, Sonnenwiesenstr., pg. 1113   IT
Schiesser + Scherrer AG, pg. 618   IT

Kriens

Bell-Escher Wyss Ltd., pg. 1305   IT
Coop Zentralschweiz, Nidfeldstrasse 1, pg. 329   IT
Sulzer Hydro AG, pg. 1307   IT

Kusnacht

Burkhalter Holding AG, pg. 618   IT
Editor AG Multimedia und Design, pg. 666   IT
Huls (Schweiz) AG, Kohlrainstrasse 1, pg. 1455   IT
IMPULS ADVERTISING AG, Freihofstrasse 22, pg. 666   IT
Impuls Direct, Freihofstr. 22, pg. 666   IT
Nikon AG, Kasper-Fenner Strasse 6, pg. 931   IT
Novo Nordisk Pharma AG, Untere Heslibachstrasse 46, pg. 988   IT
Publik AG, Freihofstr. 22, pg. 666   IT

La Chaux de Fonds

Coop La Chaux-de-Fonds, Rue du Commerce 100, pg. 329   IT
Kammer Vannes, Allee du Quartz 1, pg. 658   PB

La Plaine

DSM Andeno S.A., 4, Chemin du Chalet-Du-Bac, pg. 355   IT

La Tour de Peilz

Nestle World Trade Corporation, pg. 922   IT
Societe Immobiliere La Mandragore S.A., pg. 808   IT

Lachen

Bandag AG, St. Galler Str. 31, pg. 178   PB
Coron Verlag Monika Schoeller & Co., Markstrasse 2, pg. 1479   IT
Mesotex S.A., pg. 497   IT
Transammonia AG, Muelistrasse 3, pg. 1096   PV

Lagenthal

Coop Oberaargau-Thal/Gau, St. Urbanstrasse 3, pg. 329   IT

Lalden

Teranol AG, pg. 1120   IT

Lamone

COMARSA s.a. Agno, pg. 655   IT

Landquart

Georg Fischer Kunststoffarmaturen AG, pg. 489   IT
Georg Fischer Plastik A.G., pg. 489   IT

Langenthal

Baumberger-Getranke AG, pg. 479   IT
Luxottica (Switzerland) A.G., Wiesenstrasse 16, pg. 822   IT
Motorex AG, Bern-Zurich Strasse 31, pg. 518   IT

Langnau

Ing. Bureau Sonvico AG, Sihltalstrasse 67, pg. 399   IT

Laufenburg

Siegling (Schweiz) A.G., pg. 497   IT

Lausanne

AGIP (Suisse) S.A., Rue Caroline 7 Bis, pg. 428   IT
AMS Medinvent S.A., 4 Rue Etraz, pg. 1283   PB
Adecco Resources Humaines SA, Grand-Pont 12, pg. 24   IT
ADECCO S.A., Rue de Laugallerie 11, pg. 23   IT
AGIE AG (Fur Industrielle Elektronik), Via dei Pioppi 2, pg. 488   IT
Alcoa S.A., Avenue d'Ouchy 61, pg. 62   PB
Arkas A.G., c/o Moore Paragon (Suisse) S.A., pg. 890   IT
Banque Bruxelles Lambert (Suisse)-Lausanne, 20 Rue de Bourg, pg. 148   IT
BANQUE CANTONALE VAUDOISE, 14, Place St. Francois, pg. 160   IT
Banque Cantrade Lausanne S.A., 20, ave. de Rumine, pg. 1439   IT
Banque Internationale a Luxembourg BIL (Suisse) S.A., 4 Ave. Sainte-Luce, pg. 162   IT
BOBST S.A., Route des Flumeaux 50, pg. 198   IT
Brite Holding AG, c/o Visura Societe Fiduciaire, Rue Saint-Martin 9, pg. 257   PB
Brown Boveri-York Suisse, 10, chemin de la Colline, pg. 1   IT
Cedigraph S.A., Route des Flumeaux 50, pg. 198   IT
Clestra Hauserman Overseas, Ave. de Cour 32, pg. 570   IT
Cocler S.A., Avenue de Villamont, 19, pg. 304   IT
Columna S.A., pg. 1160   IT

Dana Europe Industrial, pg. 480   PB
Diffusion Payot, 1, rue du Bourg, pg. 795   IT
EIBA Lausanne Branch, Rue du Grand-Chene 1, pg. 1440   IT
Elsevier Science SA, Avenue de la Gare 50, pg. 1100   IT
Externa S.A., pg. 507   IT
Fag-VRG SA, pg. 757   IT
Fina Aviation-Chemicals S.A., Route d'Oron 2, pg. 1043   IT
Fotolabo Club S.A., pg. 501   IT
FOTOLABO S.A., pg. 501   IT
Gan Incendie Accidents Switzerland, Avenue CF Ramuz 70, pg. 564   IT
Gaznat SA (GAZNAT), pg. 67   IT
Hewlett-Packard (Schweiz) AG, Chemin de Rionzi 59, pg. 821   PB
Huhtamaki Finance B.V., Lausanne Branch, Rue Langallerie 1, pg. 639   IT
Hydro Aluminium S.A., Route de Chavannes 31, pg. 963   IT
Isover S.A., Chemin de Mornex 3, pg. 1176   IT
Kodak S.A., 50 Ave de Rhodanie, pg. 554   PB
SA La Tourelle Place St. Francois, pg. 996   IT
Leaf Switzerland, 1, Rue Langallerie, pg. 638   IT
Louis Vuitton (Suisse) S.A., 30, rue du Bourg, pg. 783   IT
Medtronic Europe S.A./N.V., c/o World Trade Ctr., 2, Avenue Gratta Paille, pg. 1083   PB
Metallica S.A., pg. 67   IT
Moore Paragon (Suisse) S.A., 74 rue de Geneve, pg. 890   IT
Nilo Holding, S.A., Rue d'Etraz 4, pg. 1283   PB
Nouvelle Societe Victoria, Chemin des Charmettes, 7, pg. 298   IT
Optigal S.A., pg. 866   IT
Payot SA, 1, rue du Bourg, pg. 796   PB
Philip Morris EEC, Brillancourt 4, pg. 1290   IT
Philip Morris EFTA, (Eastern Europe, Middle East & Africa), Avenue de Cour 107, pg. 1290   PB
S.I. Grand Pont No 1, pg. 997   IT
Santino, 78, chemin de Montelly, pg. 796   IT
Societe d'assurances sur la vie et contre les accidents, Avenue de Rumine 13, pg. 1332   IT
Societe de Banque Suisse, 16, Pl. St-Francois, pg. 1329   IT
Societe Pour la Vente des Produits Cinzano SA, Rue du Grand-Chene 8, pg. 410   IT
Sunkist (Europe) S.A., Rue du Valentin 29, pg. 1053   PV
UBS Leasing, 2, rue Caroline, pg. 1440   IT
Votra SA, pg. 757   IT
Woodward-Clyde, One Bd. de Grancy, pg. 1657   PB

Le Brassus

Blancpain S.A., pg. 1160   IT
Frederic Piguet S.A., Le Rocher 12, pg. 1160   IT

Le Locle

Comadur S.A., Rue Girardet 55, pg. 1161   IT
Intermedics S.A., Chemin Blanc 36, pg. 1307   IT
Nivarox-FAR S.A., Avenue du College 10, pg. 1161   IT
Technocorp Holding S.A., Rue Girdardet 57, pg. 1161   IT

Le Sentier

JAEGER-LE COULTRE, Rue de la Golisse 8, pg. 697   IT
Manufacture Jaeger-LeCoultre SA, pg. 839   IT

Lengnau

Rado Uhren AG, Bielstrasse 45, pg. 1160   IT

Lenzburg

Coop Aargau, pg. 329   IT
Frismat AG, pg. 916   IT
Hammerli Ltd., pg. 1156   IT

Les Plans

Clarins SA, 2, Route de la Galaise, pg. 295   IT

Liebefeld

Ascom Ericsson Transmission Ltd., Schwarzenburgstrasse 73, pg. 1365   IT

Liestal

Knoll AG, Oristalstrasse 65, pg. 108   IT
Marklin AG, pg. 443   IT
Prometheus AG, Industriestrasse 15, pg. 443   IT

Littau

LeaRonal AG, Grossmatte 4, pg. 982   PB
Netlab A.G., Luzerne Str. 127, pg. 317   IT

Locarno

Schindler Ascensori e Motori S.A., pg. 1204   IT

Lorient

NOUVELLE LEMANIA S.A., 2 Rue Alfred Lugrin, pg. 971   IT

Lotzwil

Step-Tech AG, Alleeweg 6-8, pg. 866　　IT

Lucerne

Adidas-Handels AG, pg. 25　　IT
Amgen (Europe) AG, Alpenquai 30, pg. 101　　PB
Axflow International Ltd., Robstockhalle 30, pg. 710　　IT
BRAUEREI EICHHOF, Obergrundstr. 110, pg. 213　　IT
De Beers Centenary AG, pg. 77　　IT
Frigorex AG fur Kaltetechnik, Tribschenstrasse 61, pg. 1306　　IT
ISL Marketing A.G., P.O. Box 3339, pg. 394　　IT
Linde Holding AG, pg. 811　　IT
Santrade Ltd., pg. 1187　　IT
Schweizerischer Bankverein, Bahnhofplatz 2, pg. 1329　　IT
SmithKline & French Switzerland Ltd., Obergrundstrasse 70, pg. 1265　　IT
TRANSWORLD INTERWEAVING AG (TIAG), Moorgartenstrasse 9, pg. 1418　　IT
Valfix Finanz AG, Stauffacherweg 8, pg. 1177　　IT
Wirsbo AG, Seefeldstrasse 21, pg. 444　　IT
Zeneca AG, pg. 1526　　IT

Lugano

BDL Banco di Lugano, Piazzetta San Carlo 1, pg. 1439　　IT
Banca Cantrade Lugano SA, Viale Stefano Franscini 22, pg. 1439　　IT
Banca del Gottardo, Viale S. Franscini 8, pg. 1310　　IT
Banque Bruxelles Lambert (Suisse)-Lugano, 5 Via Nassa, pg. 148　　IT
Banque Indosuez, 3, via Monte Ceneri, pg. 314　　IT
Bear Stearns, Corso Elvezia 14, pg. 198　　PB
Caboto International S.A., Riva Caccia, 1, pg. 138　　IT
Cantrade Banca Privata Lugano SA, Viale Stefano Franscini 22, pg. 1439　　IT
Daiwa Securities Bank Switzerland-Lugano, Via d'Alberti 1, pg. 376　　IT
Deutsche Bank (Svizzera) S.A. (Lugano), Via Monte Ceneri 1, pg. 405　　IT
Handelsfinanz-CCF Bank, 8 Piazza Dante, pg. 343　　IT
Hewlett-Packard (Schweiz) AG, Via A. Vanoni 3a, pg. 821　　PB
I.H.F. S.A., Via Pretorio 13, pg. 483　　IT
Internazionale Holding Fiat SA, Via Pretorio 3., pg. 483　　IT
Interplas SA, 6805 Mezzovico, pg. 1268　　IT
Axel Johnson Ore & Metals AG, Via Ceresio57, pg. 711　　IT
Kofisa Trading Company, 9, Via Balestra, pg. 742　　IT
LGT Asset Management AG Rappresentanza di Lugano, Via Serafino Balestra 12, pg. 810　　IT
Lacona SA, pg. 997　　IT
Mikron SA Agno, Casella Postale 115, pg. 866　　IT
Nikko Bank (Switzerland) Ltd., Piazza Monte Ceneril 13, pg. 930　　IT
Societa di Banca Svizzera, International & Finance Div., Via Balestra 7, pg. 1329　　IT
Societa di Banca Svizzera, Via Nassa 11, pg. 1329　　IT
UBS Leasing, Via L. Caninica 4, pg. 1440　　IT
Yamaichi Bank (Lugano), Via Magatti 1, pg. 1517　　IT

Lupfig

Ugimag Recoma AG, Industriestrasse 297, pg. 1032　　IT

Lyss

Arni AG, Zeughausstrasse 55, pg. 329　　IT
Feintool AG Lyss, Industriering 3, pg. 479　　IT
FEINTOOL INTERNATIONAL HOLDING AG, Industriering 8, pg. 479　　IT
Volvo Automobile (Schweiz) AG, pg. 1477　　IT
Volvo Trucks (Schweiz) AG, pg. 1478　　IT

Magenwil

Ascom Systec AG, Gewerbepark, pg. 86　　IT
Sprecher & Schuh Verkauf AG, Gewerbepark, Hintermattlistrasse 3, pg. 1402　　PB

Mannedorf

Cerberus AG, pg. 1246　　IT

Marin

EM Microelectronic-Marin S.A., Rue des Sors 3, pg. 1160　　IT
ICB Ingenieurs Conseils, Rue des Sors 7, pg. 1160　　IT

Marly

CIBA-GEIGY AG Forschungszentrum Marly, pg. 972　　IT
Cosmital S.A., pg. 1490　　IT

Meggen

Ahlstrom Paper AG, Huobmattstrasse 9, pg. 35　　IT

Meilen

Production AG Meilen, pg. 866　　IT

Mendrisio

Diantus Watch SA, Via Angelo Mapoli, pg. 1160　　IT
Ventomatic SA, Via Carlo Pasta 3/a, pg. 475　　IT

Meyrin

Charmilles Technologies SA, 8-10 rue du Pre-de-la-Fortaine, pg. 489　　IT
Hewlett-Packard (Schweiz) AG, Rue de Vegrot 39, pg. 821　　PB
MacDermid Suisse S.A., la, Rue de la Bergere, pg. 1030　　PB
Mazda (Suisse) S.A., pg. 849　　IT
Union Carbide (Europe) S.A., 7 rue du Pre-Bouvier, pg. 1667　　PB

Mohlin

Argo AG, Baumlimattstrasse, pg. 329　　IT

Monchaltorf

Metrocontrol AG, pg. 618　　IT
Sinomec AG, pg. 618　　IT

Monthey

CIBA-GEIGY SA, Usine de Monthey, Usine de Monthey, pg. 972　　IT

Morat

Floridor S.A., pg. 972　　IT

Morel

Aletsch AG, pg. 67　　IT

Morges

Cereal Partners Worldwide, Avenue de la Gottaz 36, pg. 718　　PB
Cereal Partners Worldwide, Avenue de la Gottaz 36, pg. 916　　IT
Comdisco, S.A., Baarerstr 20, pg. 408　　PB
LOGITECH INTERNATIONAL SA, Moulin DuChoc, pg. 815　　IT
Pasta Gala SA, Rue du Dr-Yersin 10, pg. 330　　IT
Tiffany & Co. Watch Center S.A., pg. 1609　　PB

Moutier

Tornos-Bechler S.A., pg. 1128　　IT

Munchenstein

Beiersdorf AG, Aliothstrasse 40, pg. 183　　IT
Nordson Schweiz AG, Pumpwerkstrasse 25, pg. 1189　　PB

Munchwilen

CIBA-GEIGY Munchwilen AG, Breitenloh 180, pg. 972　　IT
A. Sutter AG, Avenue de Lignon 41, pg. 1438　　IT

Munsingen

Protek Group, Erlenauweg 17, pg. 1307　　IT

Muri

Otto Wild AG, pg. 617　　IT
Sunrise Medical AG, Luckhalde 14, pg. 1536　　PB

Murten

Henkel Nopco AG, pg. 613　　IT
Menalux S.A., Route de Fribourg 25, pg. 443　　IT
Roland Murten AG, Route de Frieborg, pg. 972　　IT
SAIA AG, Bahnhofstrasse 18, pg. 1500　　IT

Mutschellen

MB (Switzerland) AG, Alte Bremgartenstr. 2, pg. 798　　PB

Muttenz

Clariart International Ltd., Rothausstrasse 61, pg. 624　　IT
Clariart (Schweiz) AG, Rothausstrasse 61, pg. 624　　IT
Coop Bildungszentrum, Seminarstrasse, pg. 330　　IT
Pall (Schweiz) AG, Hofackerstr. 73, pg. 1254　　PB
Sandoz Agro Ltd., pg. 972　　IT
Sandoz Chemicals Ltd., pg. 972　　IT
Sandoz Products (Switzerland) Ltd., pg. 972　　IT
Sandoz Seeds Ltd., pg. 972　　IT

Nafels

NM-Beteiligungen AG, pg. 836　　IT
Netsta-Maschinen AG, pg. 836　　IT

Neuchatel

Autodesk Developement BV (Technical & Operations), Rue du Puits-Godet 6, pg. 149　　PB
Coop Neuchatel, 55 av. des Portes-Rouges, pg. 329　　IT
Elsevier SA, Rue du Seyon 5, pg. 1093　　IT
Elslux Holding SA, Rue du Seyon 5, pg. 1093　　IT
Euroc Capital B.V., pg. 1200　　IT
Fabriques de Tabac Reunis SA, Quai Jeanreaud 5, pg. 1290　　PB
Jacobs Suchard Tobler AG, pg. 1288　　PB
O.K. Personnel, 51 Rues des Moulins, pg. 949　　PB
Oscilloquartz SA, Rue des Brevards 16, pg. 1161　　IT
Quantum Peripherals (Europe) SA, Champs-Montants 16a, pg. 1350　　PB
SMH Immobilien S.A., Faubourg de l'Hopital 1, pg. 1161　　IT
Societe de Banque Suisse, Fbg. de l'Hopital 8, pg. 1329　　IT
Westvaco Worldwide Distribution, S.A., pg. 1763　　PB

Neuendorf

Migros Distribution Center Neuendorf AG, pg. 866　　IT
Profidata AG, pg. 489　　IT
Projidata A.G., Industriestrasse 7, pg. 489　　IT
SAB NIFE (Suisse) S.A., Poststrasse 4, pg. 54　　IT
Statron AG, Eichstrasse 18, pg. 54　　IT

Neuhausen

A-L Packaging Services Ltd., pg. 67　　IT
Alusuisse Holdings Ltd., pg. 67　　IT
Alusuisse-Lonza Services Ltd., pg. 67　　IT
Lawson Mardon Packaging Services AG, pg. 67　　IT
RKN Rheinkraftwerk Neuhausen AG, pg. 67　　IT
SIG Schweizerische Industrie-Gesellschaft, pg. 1156　　IT
SIG SCHWEIZERSICHE INDUSTRIE-GESELLSCHAFT HOLDING AG, pg. 1156　　IT

Neuheim

Beringer Hydraulik GmbH, pg. 46　　IT

Nidau

Mikron AG Biel, Ipsachstrasse 14, pg. 866　　IT
Mikron AG Nidau, Ipsachstr. 14-16, pg. 866　　IT

Niederglatt

Metallwerke Refonda AG, pg. 67　　IT

Niederhasli

Oerlikon-Knorr Eisenbahntechnik AG, Mandachsh 50, pg. 738　　IT

Niederlenz

K-Tron Switzerland-Soder Division, Lenzhard, pg. 938　　PB

Niederwangen

CIBA Vision AG, Freiburgstrasse 572, pg. 972　　IT
Hewlett-Packard (Schweiz) AG, Meriedweg, pg. 821　　PB

Nussbaumen

Liebherr-Export AG, General Guisanstrasse 14, pg. 808　　IT
Liebherr-Service AG, General Guisanstrasse 14, pg. 808　　IT

Nyon

Aracruz Europe S.A., Av. Reveril 12-14, pg. 78　　IT
Bell Atlantic Financial S.A., 36, Rue de la Gare, pg. 204　　PB
Compagnie de Gestion et de Banque Gonet SA, 9,Place Bel-Air, pg. 548　　IT
La Metaire Clinic, pg. 1036　　PB
Merisel Switzerland, Chemins des Rosiers, pg. 1096　　PB
PROVIDENTIA, Chemin de la Redoute 54, pg. 1072　　IT
Swedish Match S.A., 5, Chemin du Canal, pg. 1328　　IT
Willi Voegtlin S.A., pg. 551　　IT
Wolters Kluwer Professional Training, 31, Chemin de la Vuarpilliere, pg. 1514　　IT
Zyma SA, Case postale 269, pg. 972　　IT

Oberentfelden

ISS Hasco Management AG, Ausserfeldstrasse 9, pg. 657　　IT
ISS Hospital Service AG, Ausserfeldstrasse 9, pg. 657　　IT
Sprecher Energie, Kirchfeld 3, pg. 55　　IT
TopTip (R. Muller AG), Kollikerstrasse 80, pg. 330　　IT

Oberglatt

FAG (Schweiz), pg. 469　　IT

Oberwil

Golf de la Largur Management AG, pg. 181　　IT

PB - U.S. Public Companies Volume
PV - U.S. Private Companies Volume
IT - International Public & Private Companies Volume

1778

Oensingen

Von Roll AG Departement Armaturen, pg. 1480   IT

Oftringen

PLUESS-STAUFER AG, Baslerstrasse 42, pg. 1061   IT

Olten

Commercial Bank of Soleure, Baslerstrasse 30,
pg. 1440   IT
Dionex (Switzerland) AG, Solothurnerstr. 259, pg. 510   PB
ELEKTRO-APPARATEBAU OLTEN AG, Tannwaldstrasse
88, pg. 444   IT
Sunlight, AG, Tannwaldstrasse 117, pg. 1438   IT

Otelfingen

Robert Bosch AG, Industriestr. 31, pg. 205   IT
STILL GmbH, pg. 811   IT
Svedala Switzerland, pg. 1325   IT

Petit-Lancy

Societe de Banque Suisse, 47, route de Saint-Georges,
pg. 1329   IT

Pfaffikon

Baltec Maschinenbau AG, Obermattstr. 65, pg. 479   IT
Enso AG, Bahnhofstrasse 13, pg. 457   IT
HUBER & SUHNER AG, Tumbelenstrasse 20, pg. 637 IT
Nordic Fibres AG, Bahnhofstasse 13, pg. 458   IT
Renishaw A.G., Postrasse 5, pg. 1103   IT

Pfungen

Linde Kryotechnik AG, pg. 811   IT

Pratteln

AGA AG, Industriestrasse 30, pg. 13   IT
Buss AG, Hohenrainstrasse 10, pg. 490   IT
CIBA-GEIGY Werke Schweizerhalle AG, pg. 972   IT
Faxion-Oeschger A.G., pg. 1144   IT
Georg Fischer Anlagenbau Holding AG, Hohenrainstrasse
10, pg. 490   IT
Henkel & Cie AG, Hardstrasse 55, pg. 611   IT
Linde Kaltetechnik AG, pg. 810   IT
Schenectady Pratteln, AG, Kastelliweg 7, pg. 970   PV
Schenectady Pratteln A.G., Kastelliweg 7, pg. 970 PV
Schindler Waggon AG, pg. 1205   IT

Prilly

Bobst Participations SA, pg. 198   IT
Inspectorate (Suisse) S.A., Route De Cossonay 28B,
pg. 679   IT

Puidoux

Minoterie Coop Rivaz, pg. 330   IT

Pully

Nespresso S.A., pg. 916   IT
Zenith Vie, Avenue C.F. Ramuz, 70, pg. 565   IT

Quartono

Fatati-BTR S.A., Tappeti per I,Industria, pg. 130 IT

Rebstein

Zuco Burositzmobel AG, pg. 812   IT

Reconvilier

Swissmetal Plant Boillat, pg. 1427   IT

Regensdorf

Eurodis AG, Barnstrasse 5816, pg. 1247   IT
GretagMacbeth AG, Althardstrasse 70, pg. 966   PB
McCormick S.A., Pumpwerkstrasse 32, pg. 1067   PB
Studer, Althardstrasse 30, pg. 788   PB

Reiden

Sphinx Chemicals, pg. 614   IT

Reinach

Crown Obrist AG, Roemerstrasse 83, pg. 465   PB
International Flavors & Fragrances I.F.F. (Switzerland) A.G.,
Europstrasse 15, pg. 899   PB
Meto, Kagenstrasse 17, pg. 462   IT
Reemtsma Cigaretten AG, Bahnhofstrasse 5, pg. 1101 IT
Roche Pharma (Switzerland) Ltd., Schonmattstrasse 2,
pg. 1120   IT
Scholl AG, Christoph Merian-Ring 23, pg. 1209   IT
Wellcome AG, pg. 553   IT

Willi Voegtlin Aktiengesellschaft, Kagenstrasse 12,
pg. 551   IT

Reinich

HABISAT SVERGIE AB, Roemerstrasse 1, pg. 585   IT

Renens

Coop Vaud Chablais Valaisan, Ch. du Chene 5,
pg. 329   IT
Kodak S.A., Laboratoire, Ave. de Longemalle, pg. 554 PB
Lange International S.A., Chemin de la Rueyre 120,
pg. 1127   IT
Tesa, S.A., Bugnon 38, pg. 260   PB

Reussbuhl

Salvis AG, Hauptstr. 49, pg. 213   IT

Rhaeninfelden

FELDSCHLOSSCHEN HURLIMANN HOLDING,
pg. 479   IT

Rheinau

ERAG Elektrizitatswerk Rheinau AG, pg. 67   IT

Rickenbach

Rentsch Ltd., Industriestrasse West 6, pg. 72   IT

Riehen

Schleicher & Schuell AG, pg. 1206   IT

Rolle

P. Roch, Ltd., PO Box 77, pg. 260   PB

Romont

Tetra-Pak Romont SA, pg. 1380   IT

Rorschach

Alcan Rorschach AG, Industriestrasse 35, pg. 51   IT
Frisco-Findus AG, Industriestr. 71, pg. 916   IT

Rossdorf

Rieter Automotive Germany GmbH, pg. 1117   IT

Rothrist

Armstrong World Industries (Schweiz) AG, Postfach 86,
pg. 132   PB
Liebherr-Baumaschinen AG, Industrieweg 31, pg. 808 IT

Rotkreuz

Cardo Door International AG, Industriestrasse 11,
pg. 269   IT
Duni AG, Lettenstrasse 5, pg. 421   IT
Tegimenta AG, Forrenstrasse, pg. 1120   IT
3M (East) AG, Grundstrasse 14, pg. 1606   PB

Rumlang

Formica Switzerland AG, Riedackerstr. 7, pg. 129   IT

Ruschlikon

Meteor AG, Moosstrasse 7, pg. 2   IT
3M (Schweiz) AG, P.O. Box CH-8803, pg. 1607   PB
UPM-Kymmene AG, Seestrasse 78, pg. 1430   IT

Ruthi

Insteik AG, pg. 839   IT
LMH Les Manufactures Horlogeres SA, pg. 839   IT
Sulzer Ruti Limited, pg. 1307   IT
VDO Technik AG, pg. 839   IT

Ruti

BAUMANN FEDERN AG, Postfach, pg. 171   IT

Saas-Grund

Kraftwerke Mattmark AG, pg. 67   IT

Sachseln

Swift Adhesives AG, Spis 7, pg. 370   IT

Saint Antonino

Coop Ticino, Via Serrai, pg. 329   IT
Knoll-BioResearch S.A., pg. 108   IT

Saint Aubin

CIBA-GEIGY SA Centre de recherches agricoles,
pg. 972   IT

Saint Gallen

Bank Rohner Ltd., Neugasse 26, pg. 1439   IT
Dietiker AG, pg. 865   IT
Gema Volstatic Industrial Powder Systems (Switzerland),
Moevenstrasse 17, pg. 868   PB
Gist-Brocades Holding A.G., Zuercherstrasse 202,
pg. 1142   IT
Hausmann Transport AG, pg. 1022   IT
LEICA A.G., Post Straffe 28, pg. 806   IT
SCHWEIZER VERBAND DER RAIFFEISENBANKEN,
Vadianstrasse 17, pg. 1211   IT
Schweizerischer Bankverein, Multertor, pg. 1329   IT

Saint Imier

Pierre Balmain, pg. 1160   IT
Swiss Timing, pg. 1161   IT

Saint Maurice

Decolletage S.A. St.-Maurice, pg. 9   PB

Saint Prex

Rolls-Royce Motor Cars International S.A., Au Glapin,
pg. 1467   IT

Saint Sulpice

Diffulivre, 41, rue des Jordils, pg. 795   IT

Schaffhausen

Aufzuge AG Schaffhausen, pg. 1204   IT
Charmilles Technologies Maschinenbau AG, Ebnatstrasse
91, pg. 489   IT
Cilag AG, Hochstrasse 201, pg. 929   PB
Georg Fischer Amasteel S.A., Muhlenstrasse 105,
pg. 382   PV
Georg Fischer Disa AG, Solenbergstrasse 5, pg. 488 IT
Georg Fischer Disa Engineering AG, Solenbergstrasse 5,
pg. 488   IT
Georg Fischer Disa Holding AG, Solenbergstrasse 5,
pg. 488   IT
Georg Fischer Fahrzeugtechnik AG, Muhlentalstrasse 65,
pg. 488   IT
Georg Fischer Forwarding Logistics Ltd., Amsler-Laffron-
Strasse 9, pg. 490   IT
Georg Fischer Immobilien AG, Solenbergstrasse 5,
pg. 491   IT
Georg Fischer Leichtmetall AG, Muhlentalstrasse 260,
pg. 490   IT
GEORG FISCHER LTD., Amsler-Laffon-Strasse 9,
pg. 488   IT
Georg Fischer Logimatics Ltd., Ebnatstrasse 91,
pg. 490   IT
Georg Fischer Piping Systems Ltd., Amsler-Laffon-Strasse
9, pg. 489   IT
Georg Fischer Real Estate Services Ltd., Solenbergstrasse
5, pg. 490   IT
Georg Fischer Risk Management Ltd., Amsler-Laffon-
Strasse 9, pg. 491   IT
Georg Fischer Rohrleitungssysteme (Schweiz) A.G.,
Amsler-Laffon-Strasse 9, pg. 489   IT
Georg Fischer Treuhand A.G., Amsler-Laffon Strasse 9,
pg. 490   IT
Georg Fischer Verkehrstechnik AG, Muhlentalstrasse 65,
pg. 488   IT
IDC Switzerland, c/o MSM AG, /hypark-Rheinweg 4,
pg. 571   PV
IWC International Watch Co. AG, pg. 839   IT
Rhenum Metall Ltd., Amsler-Laffon-Strasse 9, pg. 491 IT
Schweizerischer Bankverein, Schwertstrasse 2,
pg. 1329   IT
Wohnbaugesellschaft Niklausen, Solenbergstrasse 5,
pg. 491   IT

Schindellegi

KUEHNE & NAGEL INTERNATIONAL AG, Kuehne &
Nagel House, P.O. Box 67, pg. 763   IT

Schlieren

Gas Control Polymetron AG, pg. 618   IT
Gillette (Switzerland) AG, Rutistrasse 26, pg. 745 PB
Isotech AG, pg. 972   IT
Memorex Telex AG, Ruetlstrasse 16, pg. 857   IT
Micros Systems AG (Ltd.), Wiesenstrasse 10A,
pg. 1107   PB
Newport Instruments AG, Giessenstrasse 15, pg. 1179 PB
Phonogram AG, Bahnhofstrasse 6, Postfacaps 8,
pg. 1052   IT
Rheno Umwelttechnik AG, Brandstrasse 24, pg. 1205 IT
Ruf AG, pg. 618   IT
Schering (Schweiz) AG, Grabenstr. 3, pg. 1204   IT
H.A. SCHLATTER AG, Brandstrasse 24, pg. 1205   IT
Tandem Computers AG, Ifangstrasse 1-5, pg. 417   PB

Geographic Index-Non U.S.

Schonenwerd

Bally Management AG, Parkstrasse 1, pg. 996   IT
Bally Schuhfabriken S.A., Parkstrasse 1, pg. 996   IT
Bally Trading AG, pg. 996   IT
Forbo CTU SA, pg. 497   IT

Schwanden

Swandisc AG, pg. 836   IT
Therma AG, pg. 444   IT

Schwerzenbach

Mettler-Toledo AG-Abt. Analytical Instruments, pg. 4   PV
SKF (Schweiz), Eschenstrasse 5, pg. 1159   IT
Sun Microsystems (Schweiz) AG, P.O. Box 263, Eschenstrasse 8, pg. 1532   PB

Schwyz

ISO Holding, AG, pg. 132   PB
Van Melle AG, Hauptplatz 7, pg. 1451   IT

Sevelen

Rieter Automotive Heatshields, pg. 1116   IT

Sierre

Alusuisse Swiss Aluminium Ltd., pg. 67   IT
Kraftwerke Gougra AG-(GOUDRA), pg. 67   IT

Sins

Airex AG (AIREX), pg. 67   IT

Sion

Coop Valais/Wallis, pg. 329   IT
Electricite de la Lienne SA-(LIENNE), pg. 67   IT
Gazoduc SA, pg. 67   IT
Seba Aproz S.A., pg. 866   IT
Societe de Banque Suisse, Avenue de la Gare 36, pg. 1329   IT

Sisseln

Roche AG, pg. 1120   IT

Solothurn

Ascom Business Systems AG, Ziegelmattstrasse 1, pg. 86   IT
Ascom Infrasys AG, Glotz-Blotzheimstrasse 1, pg. 86   IT
Commercial Bank of Soleure, Stalden 1, pg. 1440   IT
Scintilla AG, Postfach 632, pg. 206   IT

Spreitenbach

Ascom Zeag, Pfadackerstrasse 10, pg. 86   IT
Johnson & Johnson AG, Rotzenbuehistrasse 55, pg. 930   PB
Limmatdruck AG, pg. 865   IT
Microsoft AG, Geschaefpshaus Limmatpark, Pfabackerstrasse 6, pg. 1108   PB

Stabio

Diffucap-Eurand S.A., Via Ai Mulini, pg. 81   PB
Koss Europe, Centro Commerciale, pg. 966   PB

Stans

CIBA-Pilatus Aerial Spraying Co. Ltd., pg. 998   IT
EKN Bank in Nidwalden, Buochserstrasse 2, pg. 1440   IT
Pilatus Flugzeugwerke AG, pg. 998   IT
Rossignol Ski AG, pg. 1127   IT

Steckborn

BERNINA HOLDING AG, Seestrasse, pg. 189   IT
Bernina Naehmaschinenfabrik AG, Seestrasse, pg. 189   IT

Steffisburg

Astra Fett-und Oelwerke AG, pg. 1436   IT

Steg

Kraftwerk Lotschen AG-(LOTSCHEN), pg. 67   IT

Stein

CIBA-GEIGY AG Werke Stein, Schaffhauserstrasse, pg. 972   IT
Schiesser Eminence Holding AG, Chirchhofplatz 5, pg. 618   IT

Steinach

AMP (Schweiz) AG, Amperestrasse 3, pg. 9   PB

Steinhausen

OMRON Electronics AG, Sennweldstrasse 44, pg. 1005   IT

Sursee

Alfa-Laval AG, Postfach 221, pg. 1380   IT
Therma Grosskuchen AG, Postfach 253, pg. 444   IT

Taegerwilen

Dow Plastics Development AG, Konstanzerstrasse 19, pg. 524   PB

Tagelswangen

Adidas Sport GmbH, pg. 25   IT

Taverne

Riseria Taverne S.A., pg. 866   IT

Thalwil

Arthur D. Little, A.G., Seestr. 185, pg. 670   PV
Radiometer RSCH GmbH, Zurcherstrasse 68, pg. 1084   IT
Unisys (Schweiz) A.G., Zuercherstrasse, 59, pg. 1672   PB

Thayngen

Knorr-Nahrmittel Aktiengesellschaft, Bahnhofstrasse 19, pg. 225   PB

Thorishaus

Rexroth Pneumatik AG, pg. 839   IT

Thun

Coop Bern Oberland, pg. 329   IT
Lasag AG, Mittlere Strasse 52, pg. 1161   IT

Trubbach

Balzers Hochvakuum AG, pg. 997   IT

Ulrichen

Kraftwerk Aegina AG (AEGINA), pg. 67   IT

Unterengstringen

Schaffner-Behrend AG, Dorfstr 55, pg. 536   IT

Urdorf

Dun & Bradstreet Schweiz AG, In der Luberzen 1, pg. 537   PB
Ingold Messtechnik AG, Industrie Nord, pg. 972   IT
Mettler-Toledo AG -Bereich Process, pg. 4   PV
Nissan Motor (Schweiz) AG, Bergermoostrasse 4, pg. 345   IT

Ursy

Mifroma S.A., pg. 866   IT

Uster

Biwag-Getranke AG, Brauereistr. 11, pg. 479   IT
Multanova AG, pg. 618   IT
SMM Spindel AG, Seestrasse 102, pg. 1160   IT
Zellweger Luwa, pg. 618   IT
Zellweger Uster AG, pg. 618   IT

Uznach

Mettler-Toledo AG Production Uznach, Buchbergstrasse 4, pg. 4   PV

Vernayaz

Salanfe SA, pg. 67   IT

Vernier

AST Research Switzerland S.A., 42 Route de Sating Y, pg. 1182   IT
Coop Geneve, 5, rue des Moulieres, pg. 329   IT
Givaudan-Roure (International) S.A., Case Postale 655, pg. 1119   IT
Givaudan-Roure S.A., Chemin de la Parfumerie 5, pg. 1119   IT

Vevey

NESTLE S.A., Avenue Nestle 55, pg. 915   IT
Nestle World Trade Corporation, Case Postale 353, pg. 916   IT
ORIOR HOLDING S.A., Rue du College 3, pg. 1008   IT
Pommery Distribution S.A., 58, avenue du General Guisan, pg. 783   IT
Societe des Produits Nestle S.A., pg. 916   IT

Viganello

Luganella S.A., pg. 916   IT

Villars

Food Ingredients Specialties S.A., pg. 916   IT

Villmergen

Braas Schweiz AG, Nordstrasse 10, pg. 1092   IT
Molto AG, c/o Puag AG, Durisolstrasse 8, pg. 1501   IT
Montana Bausysteme AG, Durisolstrasse 11, pg. 754   IT

Visp

Alusuisse-Lonza Energie AG, pg. 67   IT

Volketswil

Alarmcom AG, Industriestrasse 1, pg. 1246   IT
Cerberus AG, Industriestrasse 22, pg. 1246   IT
Jowa AG, pg. 865   IT
Juvena (International) AG, pg. 183   IT
Marmoran AG, Industriestr. 10, pg. 606   IT

Vouvry

CIBA-GEIGY SA, Station d'essais les Barges, pg. 972   IT

Vuadens

Guigoz S.A., pg. 916   IT

Wabern

Rena-Ware GmbH, Seftigenstrasse 300B, pg. 922   PV

Waedenswil

BASF (Schweiz) AG, Appital, pg. 107   IT
EMTEC Magnetics (Schweiz) GmbH, Appital, Postfach 99, pg. 743   IT

Wallbach

Transelastic A.G., pg. 497   IT

Wallisellen

Coop Versicherungs-Gesellschaft, Birgistrasse 4a, pg. 330   IT
Gebruder Bohler & Co. AG, Guterstr. 4, pg. 1471   IT
Halba AG, Alte Wintenthurstrasse 1, pg. 330   IT
Helly-Hansen (Suisse) SA, Oberwiesenstrasse 5, pg. 1011   IT
Honeywell AG, Hertistrasse 2, pg. 834   PB
ICL (Switzerland) International Computers AG, Hertistrasse 29, pg. 529   IT
Olivetti (Schweiz) AG, Industriestrasse 50, pg. 1003   IT
Panofina AG, Alte Winterthurerstrasse 1, pg. 330   IT
Wang (Schweiz) AG, Birgistrasse 4A, pg. 1738   PB
Windmoller & Holscher AG, Opfikonerstr. 3, pg. 1511   IT

Wangen

Diana, Industriestrasse, pg. 330   IT
Hewlett-Packard (Schweiz) AG, Punten 4, pg. 822   PB
Leisi AG Nahrungsmittelfabrik, Industriestrasse 16, pg. 916   IT

Wettingen

Lamb AG, Landstrasse 15, pg. 378   PV

Wetzikon

Elma Electronic Ltd., Hofstrasse 93, pg. 1305   IT

Widen

Hewlett-Packard (Schweiz) AG, Allmend 2, pg. 822   PB

Wil

Wiler Aktienbrauerei, pg. 479   IT

Windisch

Kunz & Dietfurt, Dorfstrasse 69, pg. 998   IT
Kunz Spinning Mills Ltd., Dorfstrasse 69, pg. 998   IT

Winterthur

Benckiser (Schweiz) AG, pg. 186   IT
Bertschinger Textilmaschinen AG, pg. 1116   IT
CWK AG, St-Galler-Strasse 180, pg. 329   IT
Calanda Haldengut AG, Haldenstrasse 69, pg. 608   IT
Coop Winterthur, Rudolf-Diesel-Strasse 25, pg. 329   IT
Maschinenfabrik Rieter AG, pg. 1116   IT
Neef AG, pg. 1306   IT
Neuwiesen Immobilien AG, pg. 1305   IT
Outokumpu Rawmet (Switzerland) Ltd., pg. 1016   IT
Outokumpu Zinc Commercial B.V., pg. 1016   IT

PB - *U.S. Public Companies Volume*
PV - *U.S. Private Companies Volume*
IT - *International Public & Private Companies Volume*

1780

Geographic Index-Non U.S.

Repoxit SA, pg. 497 — IT
RIETER HOLDINGS, Klostir Str. 20, pg. 1116 — IT
Rieter Immobilien AG, pg. 1116 — IT
Rieter Management AG, pg. 1116 — IT
SLM Immobilien AG, pg. 1305 — IT
Schweizerischer Bankverein, Bahnhofplatz 12, pg. 1329 — IT
Steinfels Cleaning Systems AG, St.-Galler-Strasse 180, pg. 330 — IT
Sulzer Betriebsliegenschaften AG, pg. 1307 — IT
Sulzer Chemtech AG, pg. 1307 — IT
Sulzer Electronics Ltd., pg. 1305 — IT
Sulzer Energy Consulting Inc., pg. 1306 — IT
Sulzer Friotherm Ltd., pg. 1306 — IT
Sulzer Immobilien AG, pg. 1306 — IT
Sulzer Informatik AG, pg. 1306 — IT
Sulzer Infra (Schweiz) AG, pg. 1306 — IT
Sulzer Innotec Ltd., pg. 1306 — IT
Sulzer International Ltd., pg. 1306 — IT
SULZER LTD., Zurcherstrasse 14, pg. 1305 — IT
Sulzer Medical Technology Ltd., pg. 1307 — IT
Sulzer Pumps Ltd., pg. 1306 — IT
Sulzer Thermatec Ltd., pg. 1307 — IT
Sulzer Triebwerke AG, pg. 1307 — IT
Sulzer Wintec Ltd., pg. 1307 — IT
Sulzer-Winterthur Group, pg. 1307 — IT
SulzerMedica Group, pg. 1307 — IT
Swiss Locomotive and Machine Works, pg. 1307 — IT
Winterthur Lebensversicherungs-Gesellschaft, Paulstrasse 9, pg. 345 — IT
Winterthur Schweizerische Versicherungs Gesellschaft, General Guisan-Strasse 40, pg. 345 — IT

Wohlen

Sulzer Metco AG, Rigackerstrasse 16, pg. 1307 — IT

Wollerau

Vorwerk International AG., pg. 1481 — IT

Worb

Bernische Grossmosterei, pg. 329 — IT

Yverdon

Banque Piguet & Cie S.A., rue de la Plaine 14, pg. 160 — IT
HPI HOLDING S.A., Avenue des Sports 18, pg. 579 — IT

Zolikerberg

Legion AG, Buhlstrasse 1, pg. 795 — IT

Zollikon

Bosch & Butz, Werbeagentur AG BSW, Alte Landestrasse 88, pg. 678 — PV

Zug

AGIE Charmilles Group, Kolinplatz 9, pg. 488 — IT
Margaret Astor Cosmetics AG, pg. 185 — PB
Augat AG, Aegeristr. 58, pg. 1598 — PB
BASF Intertrade AG, Grafenauweg 6, pg. 106 — IT
BS Building Sevices AG, Gubelstrasse 22, pg. 800 — IT
BolsWessanen AG, pg. 752 — IT
Bristol-Myers Products S.A., Lorethohoe 3, pg. 255 — PB
Bristol-Myers S.A., Reidstrasse 3, pg. 255 — PB
R.J. Brown and Associates Corporation AG, Bahnhhosstrasse 11, pg. 766 — IT
CMC Trading AG, Baaerstrasse 14, pg. 414 — PB
Cat Pumps AG, Loretohohe 5, pg. 336 — PV
Cemland Investment AG, Baaerstrasse 12, pg. 790 — IT
Cilag AG International, Chollerstrasse 38, pg. 929 — IT
Comdisco Switzerland S.A., Baarerstr. 20, pg. 408 — IT
Commercial Metals (International) AG, Baarerstrasse 14, pg. 414 — PB
DEC AG, Poststrasse 14, pg. 301 — PV
Danubia Holding AG, Baarerstrasse 2-6, pg. 790 — IT
Dentsply Switzerland, Weinreben 9, pg. 500 — PB
Dominion Textile International B.V., Industriestasse 11, pg. 415 — IT
Effems AG, Hertizentrum 6, pg. 707 — PV
Engelhard Metals AG, Baarerstrasse 94, pg. 582 — PB
Euryza International AG, Kollerstrasse 3, pg. 244 — IT
Ferranti Syseca, Grienbachstrasse 11, pg. 1384 — PB
Georgia-Pacific S.A., pg. 739 — IT
Handel und Finanz Warmond AG, 69, Ageristrasse, pg. 682 — IT
Healds AG, Baarer Strasse 101, pg. 102 — IT
HESTA TEX AG, Baarerstrasse 101, pg. 617 — PV
ICC Handels AG, Chamerstr. 12, pg. 554 — IT
Icopal AG, pg. 659 — PB
Intairdril Ltd., Bundesplatz 18, pg. 1316 — PB
Intech EDM AG, Sumpfstrasse 24, pg. 491 — IT
Interstoff AG, pg. 181 — PB
Intrafin S.A., Loretohohe 3, pg. 256 — IT
Jacobs Suchard Finanz AG, Kollerstrasse 4, pg. 1288 — PB
Joseph Dawson AG, Baarerstrasse 73, pg. 386 — IT
Ka-Tee-Ka AG, Kollerstrasse 4, pg. 1288 — PB
Kulicke & Soffa, Zeughausgasse 9A, pg. 969 — PB
Lancaster Group AG, pg. 186 — IT
LANDIS & STAEFA AG, Gubelstrasse 22, pg. 800 — IT
Landis & Staefa Europe AG, Gubelstrasse 22, pg. 800 — IT
Landis & Staefa Immobilien AG, Gubelstrasse 22, pg. 800 — IT
Landis & Staefa Management AG, Grafenauweg 10, pg. 800 — IT

Landis & Staefa Technology Innovation Inc., Grafenauweg 10, pg. 800 — IT
Mees & Hope Finanzgesellschaft AG, Untermuhleweg 7, pg. 12 — IT
Mees & Hope Management AG, Untermuhleweg 7, pg. 12 — IT
National Chemsearch (Switzerland) AG, Loberenstrasse 49, pg. 1145 — PB
NutraSweet AG, Innere Guterstrasse 2-4, pg. 41 — PB
Nutrasweet Europe, Innere Guterstrasse 2-4, pg. 1126 — PB
Pechiney Trading Company (PTC), Chamerstrasse 52, pg. 1031 — IT
SAPA S.A., Baarerstrasse 59, pg. 443 — IT
R.P. Scherer (Europe) AG, Baarerstrasse 77, pg. 1438 — PB
Sonotron Holding AG, Steinhauserstrasse 74, pg. 644 — IT
Sopra S.A., Kollerstrasse 4, pg. 1288 — PB
Sorbus AG, pg. 204 — PB
Stinnes International AG, Grienbachstrasse 36, pg. 1461 — IT
Stinnes Steel AG, Grienbachstrasse 36, pg. 1459 — IT
Taloca AG, Kollerstrasse 4, pg. 1288 — IT
Tanabe-Glaxo S.A., Baaerstrasse 18, pg. 1354 — IT
Technip International AG, Industriestrasse 13c, pg. 1361 — IT
Techotel AG, Sumpfstrasse 26, pg. 1527 — PB
Tektronix International AG, Gubelstrasse 11, pg. 1568 — PB
Viacom S.A., Chamerstrasse 18, pg. 779 — PV
Wessanen AG, pg. 753 — IT
Westwood Products, S.A., Riedstrasse 3, pg. 256 — PB
Wintershall Erdgas Handelshaus Zug AG, Grafenauweg 6, pg. 110 — IT
Wintershall Oil AG, Grafenauweg 6, pg. 110 — IT

Zumikon

MCMC European Office, Im Geissacher 6, pg. 874 — IT

Zurich

ABB ASEA BROWN BOVERI (HOLDING) LTD., Affolternstrasse 44, pg. 1 — IT
ABB Asea Brown Boveri Ltd., pg. 8 — IT
Advico Young & Rubicam AG, Werbeagentur BSW, pg. 1198 — PV
Aemtlerhalle AG, Brandschenkestrasse 150, pg. 479 — IT
Aer Lingus, Lintheschergasse 17, pg. 28 — IT
Air Malta - Zurich, 1-216 Terminal B, pg. 38 — IT
Alesa Alusuisse Engineering Ltd.-(ALESA), Max-Hoggerstrasse 6, pg. 67 — IT
Algemene Bank Nederland (Suisse), S.A., Talstrasse 41, pg. 12 — IT
Allega Ltd.-(ALLEGA), Fedeggstrasse 4, pg. 67 — IT
Allianz Versicherung (Schweiz) AG, Seestrasse 356, pg. 60 — IT
Alpina Insurance Company, Seefeldstrasse 123, pg. 1529 — IT
Alstadt Insurances, Albisriederstrasse 164, pg. 1529 — IT
Aluminum-Metall Almet AG, Militarstrasse 90, pg. 1030 — IT
ALUMOB Alusuisse Real Estate Ltd., Fledeggstrasse 4, pg. 67 — IT
Alusuisse-Lonza A.G. fur Kreislaufwirtschaft, pg. 67 — IT
ALUSUISSE-LONZA HOLDING LTD., Feldeggstr. 4, pg. 66 — IT
Alusuisse-Lonza Trading Ltd., pg. 67 — IT
Alusuisse Road & Rail Ltd., pg. 67 — IT
Amdahl (Schweiz) AG, World Trade Center, Leutschenbachstrasse 95, pg. 527 — IT
American Express Bank (Switzerland) S.A., Bahnhofstrasse, pg. 74 — PB
American Home Assurance Company New York, Swiss Branch, Kappelstrasse 7, pg. 85 — PB
Amro Bank & Finance, Bleicherweg 21, pg. 9 — IT
Anlage-und Kreditbank AKB, Zurich, Muhlebachstrasse 23/25, pg. 176 — IT
Asahi (Schweiz) AG, Talacker 41, pg. 83 — IT
Audatex Holding AG, Seestrasse 315, pg. 150 — PB
BHF-BANK Representative Office, Schulhausstrasse 6, pg. 120 — IT
BHF-BANK (Switzerland) Ltd., Schulhausstrasse 6, pg. 119 — IT
BMW Holding AG, pg. 178 — IT
Bally (Schweiz) S.A., pg. 996 — IT
Bank Hapoalim (Switzerland) Ltd., Stockerstrasse 33, pg. 150 — IT
Bank Leumi Le-Israel (Switzerland), Claridenstrasse 34, pg. 150 — IT
Bank of America NT&SA, Giesshubelstrasse 45, pg. 182 — PB
Bank of Tokyo-Mitsubishi, Zurich Representative Office, Lowenstrasse 1, pg. 158 — IT
Bank of Tokyo-Mitsubishi (Switzerland) Ltd., Bahnhofplatz 1, pg. 158 — IT
Bank of Yokohama (Schwiez) AG, Wiesenstrasse 9, pg. 159 — IT
Bank SBC Warburg Soditic AG, Gartenstrasse 26, pg. 1331 — IT
Bankers Trust AG, Dreikonigstrasse 6, pg. 185 — PB
Bankers Trust New York Corporation, Dreikonigstrasse 6, pg. 186 — IT
Banque Generale du Luxembourg (Suisse) SA, Rennweg 57, pg. 162 — IT
Banque Indosuez, Bahnhofstrasse 18, pg. 314 — IT
Bayer-Schweiz AG, Grubenstrasse 6, pg. 175 — IT
Bayerische Landesbank (Schweiz) AG, Munstergasse 2, pg. 175 — IT
Bols-Cynar, AG, 29, Weinbergstrasse, pg. 751 — IT
Brauerei AG, Brandschenkestr. 150, pg. 479 — IT
Brown Brothers Harriman Services AG, Stockerstr. 38, pg. 173 — PV
Bull (Schweiz) AG, Wenigstr. 28, pg. 318 — IT

CCF (Suisse) SA, Theaterstrasse 12, pg. 342 — IT
CIBC Finanz AG, Bleicherweg 39, pg. 257 — IT
CPC Export (Africa/Middle East) AG, Steinackerweg 8, pg. 225 — PB
CS Life, Tessinerplatz 5, pg. 345 — IT
CW Publikationen AG, Witkonerstrasse no.15, pg. 569 — PV
Cantrade Private Ltd., Morgartenstrasse 1, pg. 1439 — IT
CAREAL HOLDING AG, P.O. Box 5073, pg. 271 — IT
Cash Werbeagentur AG/DMB&B Zurich, Wasserwerkstrasse 129, pg. 303 — PV
Cementia Engineering & Consulting Ltd., Nuschlerstr. 45, pg. 791 — IT
Cementia Holding AG, Nuschelerstrasse 45, pg. 790 — IT
Cementia Planungs und Beratungs AG, Nuschelerstrasse 45, pg. 790 — IT
Cementia Trading, Nuschelerstrasse, pg. 790 — IT
Certas AG, Militarstrasse 24, pg. 1246 — IT
Chase Manhattan Bank (Switzerland), Genferstrasse 24, pg. 340 — PB
Circle-ATS AG, Buero 0-363, Frachthof West, pg. 372 — PB
Citicorp Bank (Switzerland), pg. 378 — PB
Colgate-Palmolive AG, Postfach 8022, pg. 398 — PB
Commerzbank (Switzerland) AG, Lintheschergasse 7, pg. 311 — IT
Comsof AG, pg. 181 — IT
Conquest Europe, Limmattalstrasse 184, pg. 1484 — IT
Continental Caoutchouc (Suisse) S.A., pg. 327 — IT
Continental Lebensversicherungsgesellschaft, Seestrasse 356, pg. 61 — IT
Continentale Allgemeine Versicherungs-AG, Seestrasse 356, pg. 61 — IT
Coop Zurich, Turbinenstrasse 30, pg. 329 — IT
Cosmo (Switzerland) Ltd., Bahnhofstrasse 67, pg. 335 — IT
Coutts & Co AG, Talstrasse 59, pg. 911 — IT
Credit Suisse, Paradeplatz 8, pg. 345 — IT
Credit Suisse First Boston, Paradeplatz 8, pg. 345 — IT
CREDIT SUISSE GROUP, Paradeplatz 8, pg. 345 — IT
DG Bank (Switzerland) Ltd., Muensterhof 12, pg. 352 — IT
Daewoo Securities - Zurich Representative Office, Bahnhofstr. 18, pg. 359 — IT
Dai-Ichi Kangyo Bank (Schweiz) AG, Lowenstrasse 32, pg. 362 — IT
Daiwa Bank (Schweiz) AG, Bahnhofstrasse 69, pg. 373 — IT
Daiwa Securities Bank (Switzerland) Head Office, Rennweg 38, pg. 376 — IT
Danbeer AG, Brandschenkestrasse 150, pg. 479 — IT
Das Beste aus Reader's Digest AG, Raffelstrasse 11, pg. 1368 — PB
Data General AG, Neugasse 247, pg. 485 — PB
Datacolor AG, Brandbachstr. 10, pg. 213 — PB
Datapoint (Schweiz) AG, Albulastrasse 57, pg. 384 — IT
Datastream International (Zurich) Ltd., Lowenstrasse 17, pg. 1326 — PB
Davum Stahl, Geroldstr. 28, pg. 572 — IT
DESCO DE SCHULTHESS LTD., Brandschenkerstrasse 2, pg. 396 — IT
Det Norske Veritas, Querstrasse 4, pg. 397 — IT
Detrey Dentsply AG, Nordstrasse 89, pg. 500 — PB
Deutsche Bank (Schweiz) AG (Zurich), Bleicherweg 50, pg. 405 — IT
Dourthe Freres AG, pg. 752 — IT
Dr. Muller Feindraht AG, pg. 969 — PB
Dresdner Asset Management (Schweiz) AG, Farberstrasse 6, pg. 419 — IT
Dresdner Forfaitierungs Aktiengesellschaft, Farberstrasse 6, pg. 419 — IT
EDS Fides, Feldstrasse 42, pg. 570 — PB
EIBA, Bleicherweg 30, pg. 1440 — IT
EMI Records (Switzerland) AG, Buckhauserstrasse 24, pg. 427 — IT
E.Z. Editions Zurich AG, pg. 1288 — PB
Eisenbahn-Transportmittel AG, Lavaterstrasse 40, pg. 212 — IT
Electrolux AG, pg. 443 — IT
Electrowatt Ltd., Bellerivestrasse 36, pg. 1246 — IT
Elida Cosmetic AG, Postjack 319, pg. 1437 — IT
ELVIA Reiseversicherungen, Todstrasse 65, pg. 60 — IT
ELVIA Versicherungen, Bleicherweg 19, pg. 60 — IT
Emhart Glass S.A., pg. 233 — PB
Eurad RSCG, pg. 602 — IT
European Reinsurance Company of Zurich, Mythenquai 50/60, pg. 1332 — IT
Ewotra SA, 36 Birschmatt Strasse, pg. 21 — IT
Robert Fleming (Switzerland) A.G., Roschibachstrasse 22, pg. 494 — IT
Ford Credit S.A., Kurvenstr. 35, pg. 666 — PB
Ford Motor Co. (Switzerland) S.A., Kurvenstr. 35, pg. 666 — IT
Freudenberg Simrit AG, pg. 506 — IT
Fuji Bank (Schweiz) AG, Paradeplatz/Tiefenhofe 6, pg. 521 — IT
GGK Basel, Talstrasse #80, pg. 1335 — IT
GGK Zurich, Seefeldstrasse 229, 8L34, pg. 1335 — IT
G.T. Management PLC Zurich, Todstrasse 36, pg. 809 — IT
G.T. Management PLC Zurich, pg. 809 — IT
AG Gambrinus, Brandschenkestrasse 150, pg. 479 — IT
Geschaftshaus Seilbahn AG, Brandschenkestrasse 150, pg. 479 — IT
Goldman, Sachs & Co. Bank, Munsterhof 4, pg. 462 — PV
Gruner + Jahr AG (Schweiz), Germaniastrasse 47, pg. 190 — IT
HandelsBank NatWest, Talstrasse 59, pg. 911 — IT
Handelsfinanz-CCF Bank, 44 Todstrasse, pg. 343 — IT
Helaba Switzerland Ltd., Boersenstrasse 16, pg. 799 — IT
F. Heusser AG, pg. 1306 — IT
Hewlett-Packard (Schweiz) AG, Schwamendingenstrasse 10, pg. 822 — PB
Hobart AG, Farbhofstrasse 20, pg. 1322 — PB
Holderchem Ltd., Baumackerstrasse 24, pg. 628 — IT
Honeywell Bull (Schweiz) A/G, Wengistrasse 28, pg. 318 — IT

PB - U.S. Public Companies Volume
PV - U.S. Private Companies Volume
IT - International Public & Private Companies Volume

Geographic Index-Non U.S.

1781

Hotel Zurich AG, Neumuhlequai 42, pg. 996 **IT**
Hotelplan International Travel Organization AG, pg. 865 **IT**
Hurlimann Immobilien AG, Brandschenkestrasse 150, pg. 479 **IT**
Hydro Aluminium Metal Sales s.a., Seefeldstrasse 162, pg. 962 **IT**
Hydrocarbons International Holding Co., Bahnhofstrasse 18, pg. 429 **IT**
Hyposwiss (Swiss Mortgage & Commercial Bank), Schutzengasse 4, pg. 1440 **IT**
IAE International Aero Engines AG, pg. 367 **IT**
IBM Switzerland, Gen. Guisan-Quai 26, pg. 897 **PB**
ING Bank Zurich, Glarnischstrasse 36, pg. 649 **IT**
ISS Servisystem, Hernstrasse 57, pg. 657 **IT**
Ideal-Standard, Dohlenweg 28, pg. 92 **PB**
Iggesund AG, pg. 886 **IT**
Immobiliengesellschaft, Brandschenkestrasse 150, pg. 479 **IT**
Impo Import Parfumerien AG, Turbinenstrasse 24, pg. 330 **IT**
The Industrial Bank of Japan Limited (Zurich), Bahnhofstrasse 82a, pg. 675 **IT**
The Industrial Bank of Japan (Switzerland) Limited, Bahnhofstrasse 82a, pg. 676 **IT**
Intel Switzerland, Talackerstrasse 17, pg. 887 **PB**
Interallianz Bank Zurich AG, Stadthausquai 1, pg. 933 **IT**
Intergraph (Switzerland) AG, Thurgauerstrasse 40, pg. 892 **PB**
International Paper Company (Europe) Limited, Talacker 41, pg. 905 **IT**
International Rectifier GmbH, Cherstrasse 4, pg. 907 **PB**
Intrag, Bahnhofstrasse 45, pg. 1440 **IT**
Jacobs Suchard Management & Consulting AG, Klausstrasse 4-6, pg. 1288 **PB**
Jacobs Suchard Service AG, pg. 1288 **PB**
Japan Airlines, Pelikan str. 37, pg. 700 **IT**
Jefferies (Switzerland) Ltd., Uraniastrasse 12, pg. 925 **PB**
JELMOLI AG, St. Annagasse 18, pg. 705 **IT**
Johnson Matthey & Brandenberger AG, Glattalstrasse 18, pg. 714 **IT**
Jugobanka (Zurich Rep.), Zweierstr. 169/1, pg. 716 **IT**
KME (Suisse) SA, Thurgauer Strasse 76, pg. 720 **IT**
KSB Zurich AG, pg. 721 **IT**
Kamyr Holding AG, Utoquai 43, pg. 770 **IT**
Kluber Lubrication AG (Switzerland), pg. 506 **IT**
Knight Wendling AG, Forrlibuckstrasse 66, pg. 627 **PV**
Kodak S.A., Forrlibuckstrasse 150, pg. 554 **PB**
Konsum Verein Zurich AG, Baslerstrasse 52, pg. 330 **IT**
Korn/Ferry International, C.F. Meyer - Strasse 14, pg. 633 **PV**
Kraft Jacobs Suchard AG, Klausstrasse 4, pg. 1288 **PB**
Kulling & Partner Identity, Muhlebachstrasse 20, pg. 1199 **PV**
Kvaerner Pulping AG, c/o Dr. Kurt Mueller, Utoquai 43, pg. 768 **IT**
LGT Asset Management AG, Gladbachstrasse 105, pg. 810 **IT**
LGT Services AG, Gladbachstrasse 105, pg. 810 **IT**
Lagerhaus Zurich-Altstetten AG, pg. 617 **IT**
Lavoro Bank A.G., Talacker 21, pg. 137 **IT**
Lintapharm AG, Siewerdtstr. 105, pg. 356 **IT**
Litton International S.A., Gubelstrasse 28, pg. 1004 **PB**
Litton Precision Products (Switzerland), Gubelstrasse 28, pg. 1004 **PB**
Litton World Trade Corporation, Gubelstrasse 28, pg. 1005 **PB**
Logica Informatik AG, pg. 814 **IT**
Long-Term Credit Bank of Japan (Schweiz) AG, Dreikonigstrasse 21, pg. 816 **IT**
Lowenbrau Zurich AG, Limmatstr. 264, pg. 479 **IT**
Luwa AG, pg. 617 **IT**
MBT Environmental Engineering Ltd., pg. 1465 **IT**
MBT Holding, Ltd., Vulkanstr. 110, pg. 1465 **IT**
MBT (Switzerland) Ltd., pg. 1465 **IT**
Maerz Ofenbau AG, Richard Wagnerstrasse 28, pg. 904 **PV**
Matter Leo Burnett, Werbeagentur, RotbuchStrasse 46, pg. 186 **PV**
Mead Management Services S.A., Gallusstrasse 4, pg. 1076 **PB**
Media Daten AG, Kanzleistrasse 80, pg. 451 **IT**
Meina Holding AG, pg. 1438 **IT**
Mentor Graphics (Schweiz) AG, Leutschenbachstr. 45, pg. 1087 **PB**
Mercedes-Benz (Schweiz) AG, Zuerichstrasse 109, pg. 369 **IT**
Metsa-Serla AG, Wiesenstrasse 7-9, pg. 864 **IT**
Meynadier AG, Vulkanstr. 110, pg. 1465 **IT**
Micafil AG, Badenerstrasse 780, pg. 2 **IT**
Microsoft A.G., pg. 1108 **PB**
MIGROS, Limmatstrasse 152, pg. 865 **IT**
Migrol Cooperative Society, pg. 866 **IT**
Migros Bank, pg. 866 **IT**
Mitsui Trust Bank (Switzerland) Ltd., Othmarstrasse 8, pg. 883 **IT**
MoDo Paper AG, Sternenstrasse 12, pg. 887 **IT**
Monaval Finanz AG, Talstrasse 39, pg. 12 **IT**
Monsanto Finance AG, Tiefenhoefe 10, pg. 1125 **PB**
Monsanto (Suisse) S.A., Tiefenhofe 10, pg. 1126 **PB**
Moore Special Tool AG, Hohlstrasse 608, pg. 889 **PV**
Morgan Guaranty Trust Company, Stockerstrasse 38, pg. 1130 **PB**
J.P. Morgan Securities Ltd., Stockerstrasse 38, pg. 1131 **PB**
J.P. Morgan (Switzerland) Ltd., Stockerstrasse 38, pg. 1131 **PB**
Morgan Stanley Zurich, Bahnhofstrasse, 92/3rd Fl., pg. 1133 **PB**
NatWest Securities Limited, Limmatquai 112, pg. 911 **IT**

Network Systems (Schweiz) AG, Hohlstrasse 536, pg. 1523 **PB**
Nikko Bank (Switzerland) Ltd., Utoquai 55, pg. 930 **IT**
Nippon Credit (Schweiz) AG, Seidengasse 16, pg. 933 **IT**
Nomura Bank (Switzerland) Ltd., Kasernenstrasse 1, pg. 957 **IT**
Norinchukin Bank (Schweitz) AG, Utoquai 55, pg. 958 **IT**
Norske Skog (Schweiz) AG, pg. 966 **IT**
Novelair-Sifrag AG, pg. 1306 **IT**
Novell Switzerland, Vor Ort 21, pg. 1204 **PB**
OERLIKON-BUHRLE HOLDING AG, Hofwiesenstrasse 135, pg. 996 **IT**
Oerlikon Buhrle Immobilien AG, Hofwiesenstrasse 135, pg. 998 **IT**
Oerlikon-Contraves AG, Birchstrasse 155, pg. 998 **IT**
Oerlikon-Contraves Pyrotec AG, pg. 998 **IT**
Oil-Dri S.A., P.O. Box 47, Place du Four, 1296 Coppet, pg. 1215 **PB**
PBZ Privatbank Zurich, Barengasse 29, pg. 1440 **IT**
Parfums Christian Dior AG, Buckhauserstrasse 32, pg. 783 **IT**
Francesco Parisi G.m.b.H., Norastrasse 5, pg. 504 **IT**
Pendia Pension Fund Services, Todistrasse 38, pg. 1332 **IT**
Pfizer AG, Fluelastrasse 7, pg. 1283 **PB**
Philips AG, Allmendstr. 140, pg. 1055 **PB**
PictureTel AG, Lowenstrasse 17, pg. 1295 **PB**
Polaroid AG, Hardturmstrasse 133, pg. 1314 **PB**
The Private Bank Group, CS Holding, Nuschelerstrasse 1, pg. 345 **IT**
Pucci Sulzer, Stauffacherstrasse 45, pg. 1377 **IT**
Rabobank (Schweiz) AG, Steinentischstrasse 5, pg. 1082 **IT**
Rank Xerox AG, Airgate, Thurgauestrasse 40, pg. 1785 **PB**
Reinsurance Derivatives Holding AG, Mythenquai 50/60, pg. 1332 **IT**
Reinsurance Finance Consultants Limited, Freigutstrasse 16, pg. 1332 **IT**
RINGIER AG, Dufourstrasse 23, pg. 1118 **IT**
Rothenberger (Schweiz) AG, Albisriederstr. 232, pg. 1129 **IT**
The Royal Bank of Scotland AG, Talstrasse 82, pg. 1133 **IT**
Rud, Blass & Cie Ltd. Bankers, Selnaustrasse 32, pg. 1529 **IT**
Sais, Forribuskstr. 10, pg. 1438 **IT**
SAMC Acieres, Geroldstr. 28, pg. 572 **IT**
SDRC AG, Ruchstuckstrasse 19, pg. 1525 **PB**
SEI Corporation, Claridenstrasse 36, pg. 1417 **PB**
SIHI International AG, Lowenstrasse 1, pg. 1156 **IT**
Saipem International A.G., Bahnhofstrasse 18, pg. 429 **IT**
Sakura Bank (Schweiz) AG, Lintheschergasse 10, pg. 1180 **IT**
Sandvik (Schweiz) AG, Limmatstrasse 2, pg. 1187 **IT**
Sanwa Bank (Schweiz) AG, Badenerstrasse 6, pg. 1190 **IT**
A. Schulman AG, Kernstrasse 10, pg. 1441 **PB**
Schweizerischer Bankverein, Barengasse 16, pg. 1329 **IT**
Schweizerischer Bankverein, Paradeplatz 6, pg. 1329 **IT**
Secura Insurance Companies, pg. 866 **IT**
ServiceMaster AG, pg. 1462 **PB**
Shell (Switzerland), Bederstrasse 66, pg. 1139 **IT**
Siemens Schiez AG, Freikigershr 28-40, pg. 1248 **IT**
Singapore Tourist Promotion Board - Zurich, Lowenstrasse 51, pg. 1254 **IT**
Skandia Leben AG, Bellerivestrasse 44, pg. 1258 **IT**
Snam International Holding A.G., Banhofstrasse 18, pg. 429 **IT**
Solvay Schweiz S.A., Seefeldstrasse 214, pg. 1280 **IT**
Squibb AG, Melitarstrasse 90, pg. 256 **PB**
Stadtmuhle CMZ Zurich, Sihlquai 306, pg. 330 **IT**
Storage Technology Switzerland AG, Wallisellerstr. 114, pg. 1523 **PB**
Stratus Computer AG, c/o Rohner & Knecht, Ramistrasse 8, pg. 1524 **PB**
Sulzer-Escher Wyss AG, Hardstrasse 319, pg. 1305 **IT**
Sulzer Turbo Ltd., pg. 1305 **IT**
Sumitomo Bank (Schweiz) AG, Seidengasse 20, pg. 1310 **IT**
Sumitomo Trust & Banking (Switzerland) Limited, Stockerstrasse 55, pg. 1318 **IT**
Sun Chemical AG, Neunbrunnenstrasse 41, pg. 371 **IT**
Svenska Handelsbanken Zurich, Gotthardstrasse 21, pg. 1327 **IT**
Swiss Air Transport Company Ltd., Hirschengraben 84, pg. 1334 **IT**
Swiss Life Holding, General Guisan-Quai 40, pg. 1332 **IT**
Swiss Life Portfolio Management, General Guisan-Quai 40, pg. 1332 **IT**
THE SWISS LIFE/RENTENANSTALT GROUP, General-Guisan-Quai 40, pg. 1332 **IT**
SWISS REINSURANCE COMPANY, pg. 1332 **IT**
Swissair Associated Companies Ltd., pg. 1334 **IT**
THE SWISSAIR GROUP, Zurich Airport, pg. 1333 **IT**
Switzerland Reprasenlanz Zurich, Borenstrasse 14/3, pg. 504 **PV**
TBWA/GGK, pg. 1063 **PV**
TBWA GGK ZURICK, Seefeldstrasse 229, pg. 1335 **IT**
Takugin Bank (Schweiz) AG, Utoquai 29, pg. 627 **IT**
Teepak, Inc., Zurich Branch, P.O. Box 8025, Zahringerstrasse 32, pg. 408 **PB**
Tiffany & Co. AG, Bahnhofstrasse 14, pg. 1609 **PB**
Tokai Bank (Switzerland) Ltd., Nuschelerstrasse 30, pg. 1391 **IT**
Toyo Trust & Banking (Schweiz) AG, Falkenstrasse 23, pg. 1411 **IT**
Transatlantic Holdings, Inc., Trans Re Zurich, Seestrasse 121, pg. 84 **PB**
Trinkaus & Burkhardt (Schweiz) AG, Florastrasse 7, pg. 584 **IT**
Turegum Insurance Company, Mythenquai 2, pg. 1529 **IT**

UBS Swiss Life Ltd., Geroldstrasse 20, pg. 1440 **IT**
Ueberseebank AG, P.O. Box 268, pg. 85 **PB**
Ultralin AG, pg. 519 **IT**
Unilever AG, pg. 1439 **IT**
UNION BANK OF SWITZERLAND, Bahnhofstr. 45, pg. 1439 **IT**
Union Bank of Switzerland, Head Office, Bahnhofstrasse 45, pg. 1439 **IT**
Union Reinsurance Company, Geferstrasse 27, pg. 1332 **IT**
Utell International-Switzerland, 4th Floor, Badenerstrasse 808, pg. 1099 **IT**
Uto Albis AG, Hofwiesenstrasse 135, pg. 998 **IT**
Valvoline Oil Co. Ltd., Hardsturmstrasse 175, pg. 140 **PB**
Voest-Alpine AG, Siewerdstr 105, pg. 1472 **IT**
Von Roll AG Departement Umwelttechnik, Hardturmstrasse 133, pg. 1480 **IT**
WM Wirtschafts-Medien AG, Forrlibuckstrasse 10, pg. 1484 **IT**
WRH WALTER REIST HOLDING AG, Ueberlandstr. 74, pg. 1484 **IT**
Wako Bank (Schweiz) AG, Schutzengasse 4, pg. 1485 **IT**
Warner-Lambert (Schweiz) AG, C.P. 8040, pg. 1740 **PB**
Westdeutsche Landesbank (Schweiz) AG, Bleicherweg 50, pg. 799 **IT**
WestLB (Schweiz) AG, Stockerstrasse 43, pg. 1305 **IT**
Wicona Bausysteme AG, Badenerstrasse 816, pg. 964 **IT**
Widag AG, Badenerstrasse 580, Postfach, pg. 444 **IT**
Willis Faber AG (Zurich), Lavaterstrasse 83, pg. 1510 **IT**
Wirtschafs-und Privatbank, Stauffacherstr. 45, pg. 181 **IT**
Yamaichi Bank (Switzerland), Bahnhofstrasse 92, pg. 1517 **IT**
Young & Rubicam Europe, Binzaenstrasse 1, pg. 1199 **PV**
ZUERCHER LAGERHAUS AG, Giesshuebelstrasse 62, pg. 1529 **IT**
AG Zum alten Zeughaus, Brandschenkestrasse 150, pg. 479 **IT**
ZURICH INSURANCE COMPANY, Mythenquai 2, pg. 1529 **IT**
Zurich Insurance Company Reinsurance, General Guisan-Quai 26, pg. 1529 **IT**
Zurich Investment Management Ltd., Mythenquai 2, pg. 1529 **IT**
Zurich Life Insurance Company, Austrasse 46, pg. 1529 **IT**
Zurich Pension Fund Consultants & Investments Mngmt. Ltd., Austrasse 44, pg. 1530 **IT**

SYRIA

Aleppo

Bechara Obegi, pg. 107 **IT**

Damascus

CIBA-GEIGY Services Limited-Animal Health Division, pg. 979 **IT**
CIBA-GEIGY Trading and Marketing Services Co Ltd-Scientific Office, pg. 980 **IT**
Kirakinian Engineering and Technical Supplies Center, Al Abed Street 58, pg. 550 **IT**
Middle East Electronics, P.O. Box 2308, pg. 822 **PB**
Mitsui & Co., Ltd., 6th Fl., Amin Abdrabuh Bldg., Bizm St., pg. 881 **IT**
SAA Intermarkets, pg. 680 **IT**
Syria Shell Petroleum Development BV, Cham Complex, Maysaloon St., pg. 1141 **IT**

TAIWAN

Chiayi

Ajinomoto Tong Hsing Foods, Inc., Chia-Yi Plant, 692-1, Chung Hsiao Rd., pg. 40 **IT**
Refining & Manufacturing Research Center, 239, Min-Sheng S. Rd., R.O.C., pg. 286 **IT**

Chu Dong

Electro Scientific Industries Taiwan, 3F, No. 548, Chung Hsing Rd. Sec.4, pg. 569 **PB**

Chung Li

Ebara Densan Taiwan Manufacturing Co., Ltd., No. 7 Nan Yuen, 2nd Rd., pg. 432 **IT**
Fung Yong Co., Ltd., Chung Li Industrial Zone, No. 12 Ding Ning Rd., pg. 1413 **IT**
Kuozui Motors, Ltd., Ching Li Industrial Zone, No. 73 Ding Ning Rd., pg. 1413 **IT**
Motorola Electronics Taiwan, Ltd., 550 Chung Hua Road, Section 1, pg. 1139 **PB**
Sandvik Titan Pty. Ltd., pg. 1187 **IT**
Shieh Chi Industrial Company Ltd., No. 99 Hsi Yuan Rd., pg. 1580 **IT**
Sony Video Taiwan Co. Ltd., 24-1 Sung Kang N. Rd., pg. 1284 **IT**

Hsin Chuang

Rockwell Automation Taiwan, Sixth Floor, No. 11, Wu Gong 5th Road, pg. 1400 **PB**

PB - *U.S. Public Companies Volume*
PV - *U.S. Private Companies Volume*
IT - *International Public & Private Companies Volume*

1782

Geographic Index-Non U.S.

Hsin-chu

AST Taiwan Ltd., No. 46 Park Ave. 2, Science-Based Industrial Park, pg. 1183   IT
Advantest Taiwan, Inc., 14F, 307, Pei-Da Rd., pg. 25   IT
Ambit Microsystems Corp., pg. 22   IT
CPC/AJI (Taiwan) Plant, 150 Hsin Ho Rd., pg. 41   PB
Comdisco Trade, Inc., 15F-4 Empire Commercial Building, pg. 408   PB
Eaton Limited Aerospace & Commercial Controls, 2nd Fl., 51 Park Ave. 2, Hsin Chu, pg. 559   PB
Elastogran Headway Urethanes Co., Ltd., Hsinchu County, No. 11, Jen Cheng Road, Hsinchu, pg. 108   IT
Flow Asia, #2 Third Technology Rd., pg. 656   IT
H.B. Fuller Taiwan Co., Ltd., Hsin Chu Industrial Park, No. 79, Koung-Fu Rd., ROC, pg. 687   IT
Gold Peak Industries (Taiwan) Ltd., 18,16 Chung Su, Hukow, pg. 537   IT
KLA Instruments Taiwan, Fifth Floor, 115 Ming Sheng Rd., pg. 939   PB
MacDermid Taiwan Ltd., 77, Kuang Fu, N. Road, pg. 1030   IT
Novellus Systems Taiwan, 5F-2, No. 295, Sec 2, Kuong Ku Rd., pg. 1205   IT
Southern Information Systems, Inc., No. 4, R&D Road III, Science Based Industrial Park, pg. 970   IT
TI-Acer Incorporated, pg. 22   IT
Taisil Electronic Materials Corporation, 8F, No.11 Park Ave. II, Science-Based Industrial Park, pg. 286   IT
Taiwan JSP Chemical Co., Ltd., Factory, Hsin Chu Industrial Park, No. 43 Kuang Fu South Rd., pg. 41   IT
Wha-Yo Electronic Materials Corporation, No. 2 Kon Ye 5 Rd., pg. 1314   IT

Hsin-Ying

Miura Boiler Co., Ltd. (Taiwan), No. 18, Hsin-Kung Road, pg. 884   IT

Kao-hsiung

Asia Pacific Resin Corporation, 42 Ta-Yeh Street, Ta-Liao Hsiang, pg. 975   IT
BHP Steel N Asia Ltd. - Taiwan Branch, Unit B, 5th Fl, Duke Bldg., 80 Suwei 3rd Road, pg. 227   IT
C.S. Aluminium Corporation, No. 17, Tong Lin Road, pg. 285   IT
CTS Components Taiwan, Ltd., 7, Central 6th Rd., (Chung Liu Rd.), P.O. Box 26-20, pg. 286   IT
China Ecotek Corporation, 8F, No. 8, Ming-Chuan 2nd Rd., pg. 285   IT
China Hi-Ment Corp., 10F-1, No. 243, pg. 285   IT
China Steel Chemical Corp., pg. 286   IT
CHINA STEEL CORPORATION, 1 Chung Kang Rd., Hsiao Kang, pg. 285   IT
China Steel Express Corporation, 1 Chung-Kang Road, pg. 285   IT
China Steel Global Trading Corporation, No. 8, Ming-Chuan Second Road, pg. 285   IT
China Steel Structure Co., Ltd., 1 Chung Kang Rd., pg. 286   IT
CIBA-GEIGY (Taiwan) Ltd, No. 6, Kwang-Hwa Rd., Ta-Liao, Hsiang, Ta-Fa Industrial District, pg. 980   IT
Clarion (Taiwan) Manufacturing Co., Ltd., 2 N. Nei-Huan East Rd., N.E.P.Z., pg. 296   IT
John Crane (Taiwan) Co. Ltd., No. 324-4 Feng-Jen Rd. W, pg. 1339   IT
Dai-ichi Kangyo Bank, Ltd.-Kaohsiung Branch, 12th Fl., No. 2, Chung Cheng 3rd Rd., pg. 360   IT
FORMOSA PLASTICS CORPORATION, 39, Chung Shan 3rd Rd., pg. 498   IT
Foster Electric Co. (Taiwan), Ltd., A-8 61, KEPZ, pg. 500   IT
Gains Investment Corporation, 30 Floor, No. 6, Ming-Chuan Second Road, pg. 285   IT
Hewlett-Packard Taiwan Ltd., 11F, 456, Chung-Hsiao 1st Rd., pg. 822   PB
Hitachi Television (Taiwan) Ltd., 11, S. First Road, pg. 622   IT
Hwan Chong Enterprise Co., Ltd., No. 201, Wan Dan Road, pg. 868   IT
ITW Switches-Asia, Box 26140 A4-52, pg. 868   IT
Kaohsi Corporation, R. 501, No. 168, Chung Cheng 4 Rd., pg. 1233   IT
Kaohsiung Monomer Co Ltd, 1 Hsin-Kung Rd., Ta She, pg. 665   IT
Kaohsiung Refinery, Tso-Ying, pg. 286   IT
LNG Project & Construction Division, 41, Yung-An Rd., pg. 286   IT
Lilly Industries (Far East), Ltd., No. 1 Kung Yeh First Road, pg. 995   PB
Mitsui & Co., Ltd., 7th Fl., A Room, Cathay Life Chung Cheng Bldg., No. 2, pg. 880   IT
Morganite Taiwan Limited, 25 Hsin-Yeh Rd., pg. 892   IT
NYK-Kaohsiung, 7th Floor, Land Bank Bldg., No. 131 Dah Yung Road, pg. 941   IT
Nitto Denko (Taiwan) Corporation, No. 50, Chin 5th Rd., N.E.P.Z., pg. 950   IT
Premier Chemical Plant, 3-1 Hsing Kung Rd., pg. 460   PB
Pulse Engineering-Taiwan, pg. 1564   IT
Sharp Electronics (Taiwan) Co., Ltd., # 1 N. Nei-Huan E. Rd., Nantze Export Processing Zone, pg. 1230   IT
Shin Kong Mitsukoshi Department Store Co. Ltd. - Kao Hsiung San Tuo, 213 Santuo 3rd Rd., pg. 884   IT
Shin Taiwan Agricultural Machinery Co., Ltd., 16, Fengping 2nd Rd., pg. 763   IT
Siliconix (Taiwan), Nan-tze Export Processing, Zone, pg. 367   IT

Sumiko Electronics Taiwan Co., Ltd., 36, Chin 3 Rd., Nan-Tze E.P.Z., pg. 1316   IT
Taiwan Branch Office, 11F-1, No. 206, Kwan Huwa First Road, pg. 871   IT
Taiwan Brother Industries, Ltd., Kai Pa Road, pg. 230   IT
Taiwan Kansai Paint Co., Ltd., 6 Yungkong 2nd Rd., pg. 723   IT
Taiwan Nisseki Co., Ltd., 149, Chien Kuo 4th Rd., pg. 937   IT
Tektronix Taiwan Ltd.-Kaohsiung, pg. 1568   PB
Watlow Taiwan, 10F-1 No. 189, pg. 1154   PV
Wilson Sporting Goods Asia, Ltd., 14F-2, 6 Min-Chuan 2nd Road, pg. 73   IT

Miao-li

Exploration & Production Research Center, 1, Da Yen, R.O.C., pg. 286   IT
Taiwan Petroleum Exploration Division, 140, Chung Cheng Road, R.O.C., pg. 286   IT
Union and NHK Auto Parts Corp., No. 40-10, Po Kung Kun, pg. 902   IT

Neihu

Axel Johnson Corp. (Taiwan) Ltd, 7th Fl., No. 7, Ln. 30, Sec. 4, Chengkung Rd., Neihu Dist., pg. 711   IT

Ping-tung

DSM Resins (Far East) Ltd., No. 27, Yung-Hsiang Road, Ping-Nan Industrial Zone, pg. 355   IT
Ferro Toyo Co. Limited, 515 Ma Tzuu Road, R.O.C., pg. 619   PB
Lafarge Eastern Monolithic Refractories, 6-6 Hsing-Tien Road, Hsin-Nan Tsun Kao-Shu Shiang, pg. 791   IT
President Foods Co., Ltd., 1 Kong Yang 2nd Rd., ROC, pg. 1069   IT
Ta Ching Motors Co., Ltd., 337 Ta Hsi Road, pg. 523   IT

Tai-chung

BASO Precision Optics, 14, Chien Kuo Rd., pg. 551   PB
Catalina Industrial, Ltd., Unit 2, 8th Floor, No. 123, Sec. 3, pg. 314   IT
CUNA Mutual Group-Taiwan, 33, Section 1, Pei Ping Road, pg. 297   PV
Ebara - Elliott Service (Taiwan) Co., Ltd., 1,42 Road, Industrial Zone, pg. 432   IT
Elite Sewing Machine Mfg. Co. Ltd., 3, 3rd Rd., Taichung Indus. Park, pg. 39   IT
Fanuc Taiwan Limited, No. 4, 17th Rd., pg. 478   IT
Hewlett-Packard Taiwan Ltd., 10F, 540, Sec. 1, Wen-Shin Rd., pg. 822   PB
JAE Taiwan, Ltd., 35.20RD Industrial Park, pg. 701   IT
Rockwell International Taiwan Co., Ltd., Room 1, Fifth Floor, No. 68, Chung-Kong 1st Road, pg. 1401   PB
Sanyo Electronic (Taichung) Co., Ltd., No. 5-3, Nan 2nd Rd, pg. 1192   IT
Shiang Pao Precision Co., Ltd., No.6-1, Alley 106 Lane 399, Sec. 3, Chung Shan Road, pg. 295   IT
Signode International Trading Corporation, No. 132 Sec. 3, Taichung Kang Rd., pg. 869   PB
TWI International Taiwan, Inc., Industrial Park, No. 10, 7th Rd., pg. 1749   IT
Taiwan Autoglass Industries Corp., 222-1, Tzu-Li 3rd, pg. 1348   IT
3M Taiwan Limited, 2F-3 #306 Wen Sin Road, Sec. 1, pg. 1607   PB
Wilson Sporting Goods Asia, 2F, No. 25, Road 18, pg. 73   IT

Tai-nan

PRESIDENT ENTERPRISES CORP., 301, Chung-Cheng Rd., ROC, pg. 1068   IT
President Frito-Lay Corp., 181 Ching-Shan Rd., ROC, pg. 1069   IT
Shin Chun Precision Co., Ltd., 7, Kuo Chi Road, Kang Chien Tsun, Hsin Shih Hsiang, pg. 295   IT
Taho Engineering Co., Ltd., 249 Chung Shan Rd., Kuan-Miao Hsiang, pg. 531   IT
TAINAN SPINNING CO., LTD., Tung District, pg. 1347   IT
Taiwan Green Cross Co. Ltd., 73 Industry West Road, pg. 558   IT

Taipei

A & A International-Taipei Branch, Shen Hsing Tandy Bldg., 10th Fl., No. 148, Sung Chiang Rd., pg. 1561   PB
AMP Taiwan B.V., No. 136 Jen Ai Rd., Rm. 1404, pg. 9   IT
AST Taiwan Limited, 10th Fl., No. 100, Section 3, Chiang Hsiao East Rd., R.O.C., pg. 1183   IT
ACER INCORPORATED, 156 Min Sheng E. Rd., Sec. 3, 6F, pg. 22   IT
Acer Incorporated, Information Products Business Unit, 6F, 156 Min Sheng E. Rd., Sec. 3, pg. 22   IT
Acer Labs, pg. 22   IT
Acer Property Development Inc., pg. 22   IT
Acer Sertek Incorporated, 135 Chien Kuo N. Rd., Sec. 2, pg. 22   IT
Acer TWP Corporation, pg. 22   IT
Aetna Life Insurance Co. of America (ALICA), 8F, 176, Section 1, pg. 27   PB
Air Products Asia Electronics, 2f, 21 Chung Shan N. Rd., Sec. 2, pg. 31   PB
Ajinomoto Tong Hsing Foods, Inc., 5th Fl., 32 Chung Yang South Rd., pg. 40   IT

Alcon Pharmaceuticals Ltd., pg. 918   IT
Amway Taiwan, Ltd., 11/F, No 168, Tun Hwa North Road, pg. 70   PV
Anping Distributors Ltd., pg. 918   IT
Asbury Worldwide, North Asia, G/F No. 15, Lane 28, Sec. 1, Huan-Shan Road, pg. 1110   PB
Asia Industries, Ltd., 24, Tung-Yuan Road, pg. 937   IT
Astra Pharmaceuticals (Taiwan) Ltd., 4th Fl., No. 9 Sec. 2, Roosevelt Rd., pg. 94   IT
Australia & New Zealand Banking Group Limited Taiwan, 8F, 44 Chung Shan North Road, pg. 99   IT
Autodesk, Inc. Taiwan, 403 Bank Tower, 205 Tun Hwa N. Road, pg. 149   PB
Avon Cosmetics (Taiwan) Ltd., 127 Chung Hsing North St., pg. 156   PB
BASF Taiwan Ltd., Empire Bldg., 16th Fl., No. 87, Sung Chiang Rd., pg. 107   IT
BHA Group International, Inc., pg. 161   PB
BHP Steel Building Products Taiwan Ltd., Room 401, Lotus Bldg., 136 Jen-Ai Road, pg. 226   IT
BOC Lien Hwa Industrial Gases Co. Ltd., 44 E Chng Teh Rd., 6th Fl., pg. 122   IT
Banco Santander, 602 Tun Hwa South Road, 14 Fl. 1, ROC, pg. 144   IT
Bank of America NT&SA, 3/Fl, Bank Tower, 205 Tun Hwa North Rd., pg. 182   IT
Bank of Boston, United Commercial Building, 137 Nanking East Road, 5th Floor, pg. 184   PB
Bank of Montreal - Taiwan, 685 Minsheng E. Rd., R.O.C., pg. 155   IT
The Bank of New York, Section 1, 4th Floor, 245 Tun Hwa South Rd., pg. 179   PB
Bankers Trust New York Corporation, Bankers Tower, 8th Fl., 205 Tun Hwa N. Rd., pg. 186   PB
Banque Paribas-Taiwan, Bank Tower - 11th Floor, 205 Tun Hwa North Rd., pg. 320   IT
Barclays Bank PLC, 14th Floor, Bank Tower, 205 Tun Hwa North Rd., pg. 165   IT
Batey Ads Taiwan, 16F-2, No. 51 Keelung Rd., Sec. 2, pg. 117   PV
Bausch & Lomb Taiwan Limited, Chung Hsiao East Rd., Sec. 4, 11F, No. 16, Alley 56, Lane 181, pg. 195   PB
BetzDearborn Taiwan, Ltd., 5f, 155 Kang Ning Street, pg. 227   PB
Bilfinger + Berger Bauaktiengesellschaft, 12th Floor, 168, Tun Hwa N. Road, pg. 196   IT
Bista (Taiwan) Co. Ltd., Rm. 607, No. 136, Sec. 3, Jen-Ai Road, pg. 295   IT
Bobst (Taiwan) Ltd., pg. 199   IT
Bontex Taiwan, 8F1, No. 52, Sec. 2, Chung Shan N. Rd., pg. 734   IT
Borland Taiwan Ltd., 7F-4, 207, Tun Hua N. Road, pg. 246   PB
BRENNTAG (Taiwan) Co. Ltd., Rm. 808 No. 142, Ming Chuan E. Rd., R.O.C., pg. 1458   IT
Bridgestone Taiwan Co., Ltd., Chung Lung Bldg. 261, Sung Chiang Rd., pg. 214   IT
Bristol-Myers (Taiwan) Limited, 7F 125 Nanking E. Rd., Sec. 5, pg. 256   IT
Bull Information Systems Taiwan Ltd., 11th Floor, Chan Kwo Bldg., 350 Min Sheng E. Rd., pg. 315   IT
Leo Burnett Company, Ltd.-Taiwan Branch, 9th Floor, Taipei Metro, 207 Tun Hwa S. Road, Section 2, pg. 185   PV
Burroughs Wellcome (Far East) Ltd, pg. 553   IT
C-E International, Ste. 3 11/F, 235 Hsin Y Road, Sec. 4, pg. 5   IT
CPA/AJI (Taiwan) Ltd., 2nd Fl., No. 180, Section 4, Nanking East Rd., pg. 41   IT
CPC/AJI (Taiwan) Ltd., 7/F, No. 108, Section 5, Section 4, Nanking East Road, pg. 225   PB
CRSS International, Inc. (Taiwan), 9F, Kuan Fu Building, 310, Chung Hsiao East Road, pg. 1415   IT
Capital Investment Trust Corporation, pg. 312   IT
Cariplo (Taipei), Room 620, 4F, 25, Sec. 1, Tun Hua South Rd., pg. 275   IT
Carpenter Technology Corp. (Taiwan) Ltd., 333 Keelung Rd., Sec. 1, Ste. 2202, pg. 308   PB
Carrefour-Taiwan, Presicarre Corp. 6 F, pg. 273   IT
Castrol (Taiwan) Limited, Shin Kong Commercia; Bldg., 287 Section 3, pg. 236   IT
Chang Shing Electric Co., Ltd., 3rd Fl., 27, Chang An East Rd. Sec. 1, pg. 522   IT
Charmilles Taiwan Engineering Services Co., Ltd., No. 18-17 Lane 609 Sec. 5, pg. 489   IT
The Chase Manhattan Bank, N.A., 9th Fl. Walsin Lihwa Bldg., #115 Min Sheng East Rd., ROC, pg. 340   PB
Chia Lung Chemical Industrial Corp., 10th Fl., Chang An Building, No. 18 Chang An East Road, pg. 371   IT
CHINA AIRLINES LTD., 131 Nanking East Road, Section 3, R.O.C., pg. 284   IT
China American Petrochemical Co., 12th Fl., Taipei Business Bank, 36 Nanking E. Road, Sec. 3, pg. 102   IT
China Management Systems (CMS), No. 1120 Cheng TEh Rd., pg. 1043   IT
CHINA SYNTHETIC RUBBER CORPORATION, 122 Tung Hwa North Rd., 7th Fl., pg. 286   IT
CHINESE PETROLEUM CORPORATION, 83 Chunghwa Road, Section 1, R.O.C., pg. 286   IT
Chips and Technologies, Inc., 7F, 133 Ming Sheng E. Rd., pg. 349   PB
Christie's Taiwan, 6th Fl., 369 Fu Hsing North Rd., pg. 290   IT
Chronicle Sit Co., Ltd., Nanking East Road, pg. 343   IT
Chugai Pharmaceutical Co., 4F, No. 180, Sec. 2,, pg. 291   IT
Chung Huey Pharmaceutical Co., Ltd., 4F, No. 180, Sec. 2, pg. 291   IT
CIBA-GEIGY (Taiwan) Limited, PO Box 24-562, Fu Key Building, 11/F, #99, pg. 980   IT

PB - *U.S. Public Companies Volume*
PV - *U.S. Private Companies Volume*
IT - *International Public & Private Companies Volume*

Geographic Index-Non U.S.

1783

CIBA-GEIGY (Taiwan) Limited, Dyes & Chemicals Division, 7th Fl., Taiwan Glass Bldg., No. 261 Nanking E. Rd., Sec 3, R.O.C., pg. 292 **IT**

CIBA Vision Taiwan Co Ltd, 14th Fl., 296 Hsin Yi Rd., pg. 981 **IT**

Circle Airfreight Intl. (Taiwan) Ltd., No. 25, 10th Flr. Setion 1, R.O.C., pg. 372 **PB**

Cirrus Logic International Ltd., pg. 375 **PB**

Clairol (Taiwan) Ltd., P.O.Box 22659, pg. 256 **PB**

Combibloc Ltd., Taiwan Branch, Suite 603, 6th Floor, 236 Tun Hwa North Road, pg. 1156 **IT**

Commerzbank AG Representative Office-Taipei, Taipei Metro Bldg., 14th Floor, 207 Section 2, pg. 312 **IT**

Corowan Taiwan Corporation, 9F, No. 31 Chung Shan N. Rd., pg. 296 **IT**

Croslene Chemical Industries, Ltd., 11th Fl., No. 22, Nanking West Rd., pg. 1350 **IT**

Crown Manufacturing Corp., Room No. 2, 6F No. 87 Sung Ching Road, pg. 939 **IT**

Cyanamid Taiwan Corp., 8/F Union Comml. Bldg., 137, Nanking E. Rd., Sec. 2, pg. 81 **PB**

DIC (Taiwan) Ltd., 8th Fl., Chang An Bldg., No. 18, Chang An East Road, pg. 372 **IT**

DMB&B Taiwan, 15/F, 88 Chung Hsiao E. Rd., R.O.C., pg. 304 **PV**

Daewoo Corp. - Taiwan, P.O. Box 34-58, pg. 358 **IT**

Dai-Ichi Kangyo Bank, Ltd.-Taipei, Hung Kuo Building, 167 Tun Hua North Road, pg. 361 **IT**

Dai-Ichi Life International Limited-Taipei, 6th Floor, 123 Nanking East Road, Sec. 2, pg. 362 **IT**

Daiasia Motor Co., Ltd., 2nd Floor, No. 98, Sect. 2, Jen-Ai Rd., pg. 365 **IT**

Daiko HWG Advertising Corp., 13/F No. 89, Sec. 5, Nanking E. Rd., pg. 366 **IT**

Daiwa Securities (Taipei), 14th Fl., 200, Keelung Road, pg. 376 **IT**

Damco Intermodal Systems (Taiwan) Inc., pg. 1144 **IT**

Danzas Taiwan Ltd., 4th Fl., No. 72, pg. 383 **IT**

Data Systems Consulting Co., Ltd., 8F, 52 Ming Chuang Road, Hsin Tine, pg. 243 **IT**

Dayeh Takashimaya Department Store, Inc., No. 55, Sec. 2, Cheng Cheng Road, pg. 1350 **IT**

Dell Computer Corporation, No. 8, Lane 6 Hang Chou S. Rd. Sec. 1, pg. 496 **PB**

Dell Products (Asia) B.V., Taiwan Branch 7F-1, No. 200 Kee Lung Road, pg. 496 **PB**

Dentsu Inc. Taipei, 11F, 167 Tun Wua North Rd., pg. 393 **IT**

Dentsu (Taiwan) Inc., 13F, 68, Nanking, E. Road, pg. 394 **IT**

Dentsu Young & Rubicam/Taipei, 17th Fl., 207 Tun Hwa South Rd., pg. 325 **PV**

Det Norske Veritas, 21 st Fl., Room 2102, International Trade Bldg., pg. 397 **IT**

Deutsche Bank AG (Taipei), Cathay Life Insurance Bldg. 10/F, pg. 405 **IT**

Digital Equipment Corporation, Taiwan, 7/F, 245 Tuang-Hua South Road, Section 1, pg. 507 **PB**

Diodes Co. Ltd., 510-16 Chung-Cheng Rd., 5th Fl., pg. 510 **PB**

Dresdner Bank AG, 19th Fl., 30 Chungking S. Rd. Sec.1, pg. 419 **IT**

Du Pont Taiwan Limited, 7th Fl., 8 Tun Hwa, North Road, R.O.C., pg. 533 **PB**

Dun & Bradstreet International, Ltd. Taiwan Branch, 12/F Ntional Enterprises Ctr., No. 188 Nanking E. Rd., Sec. 5, pg. 536 **PB**

Durco Valtek (Asia Pacific) Pte. Ltd., Taiwan Office, 3rd Fl., Room No. 3, pg. 659 **PB**

DYWIDAG-Systems International Co., Ltd., pg. 424 **IT**

DYWIDAG Systems Taiwan Co. Ltd., Room 1102, 11th Floor, pg. 425 **IT**

Ebara Kailay Environmental Engineering Co., Ltd., Room # 1402, Chia Hsin Bldg., No. 96, Sec. 2, Chung Shang N. Rd., R.O.C., pg. 432 **IT**

Ebasco-CTCI Corporation, 19th Fl., 77, Tun Hwa South Road, Sec. 2, R.O.C., pg. 1587 **IT**

Eclipse Combustion Taiwan., 2/F, No. 15-3, pg. 361 **PV**

Electrolux (Far East) Ltd., pg. 444 **IT**

Encore Computer (Asia) Ltd., Min Hwa Bldg., 150 Fu Hsing N. Rd., pg. 580 **PB**

Epson Electronics Trading, Ltd., Taiwan Branch (E.T.T.), 10th Floor, No. 287, Nanking E Rd., Sec. 3, pg. 1219 **IT**

Ericsson Taiwan Ltd., 14/F B 18 Nanking, East Rd. sec. 4, pg. 1367 **IT**

EURO RSCG Partnership, 3F, 69 Min Sheng E. Rd., pg. 602 **IT**

FSQ Taiwan Co. Ltd., 186 Yung Chi Rd., R.O.C., pg. 1157 **IT**

Fa Hua Fragrance & Cosmetic Co Ltd, Taiwan Branch, 6th Floor, No. 148 Chung Hsiao East Road, Sec. 4, pg. 782 **IT**

Far Eastern Electric Industry Co., Ltd., 6th Floor, No. 111, pg. 1000 **IT**

First RepublicBank Dallas, N.A. Representative Office, Worldwide House, SUite 803, pg. 1165 **PB**

Fora International Corp., pg. 22 **IT**

Ford Enterprise Company Taiwan, Ltd., pg. 665 **PB**

Ford Lio Ho Motor Co., Ltd., P.O. Box 12, Chung Le, pg. 665 **PB**

Formica Taiwan Corporation, Sixth Fl., 68-70, Sect. 3, Nanking East Rd., R.O.C., pg. 130 **IT**

Freudenberg Far Eastern Spunweb Comp. Ltd., **IT**

Fubon Insurance Co. Ltd., 237 Chien Kuo S. Rd. Sec. 1, pg. 60 **IT**

Fuchs Lubricants Taiwan Corp., 8 F-2 No. 7 Ta-Cheng Strasse, pg. 517 **IT**

Fuji/GE (Taiwan) Co., Ltd., 12F, No. 70, Cheng Teh N. Rd., pg. 522 **IT**

Fuji Photo Film Co., Ltd., Taipei Office, Rm. 601, Hung Chang Bldg., No. 38, Sec. 6, pg. 525 **IT**

GP Battery Marketing (Taiwan) Ltd., Rm 1200, International Trade Building, pg. 537 **IT**

Gambro Taiwan Co., 4th floor, no 8, Alley 83, Sec. 1, Kuang-Fu Road, pg. 668 **IT**

General Motors Taiwan, Inc., 333 Keelung Rd., R.O.C. pg. 723 **PB**

Generale Belgian Bank, Room 501 Worldwide House, 131 Min Sheng East Rd., pg. 547 **IT**

Goldman, Sachs & Co., Hung Kuo Bldg., 7th Fl., No. 167, Tun Hua, North Rd., pg. 462 **PV**

Goodyear Taiwan Limited, pg. 753 **PB**

Graco Hong Kong Limited (Taiwan Liaison Office), 8F, No. 37 Min Chuan East Rd. Sec. 3, pg. 757 **PB**

Green Giant Company, pg. 411 **IT**

Guerlain Taiwan Co. Ltd., 9th Fl, Tun Hua Financial Bldg, 214 Tun Hua North Rd., pg. 780 **IT**

H&Y Communications Inc., 11th Fl., 180 Chung Hsiao E. Rd., pg. 588 **IT**

HBS Marketing (Asia) Limited Taipei Branch Office, 9/F, Rm. 905, Chung-Nan Bldg., 63 Chung, pg. 537 **IT**

HSBC James Capel Taiwan Limited, Taipei World Trade Center, Room 1610, 333 Keeling Road, Section 1, pg. 582 **IT**

HY Marketing Inc., 5th Fl., 180 Chung hsiao E. Rd., Sec. 4, pg. 588 **IT**

Hachette Interculture Inc., N 62 Jen Ai Road, pg. 795 **IT**

Hakuho Communications, Inc., 5th Fl., 180 Chunghsiao Eas Rd., pg. 588 **IT**

Hanwa Co., Ltd.-Taipei Branch, Rm. 303, 3FL, 79 Chuan Shan North Rd., pg. 595 **IT**

Hapag-Lloyd (Taiwan) Shipping Agencies Ltd., pg. 596 **IT**

Henkel Nopco Taiwan, pg. 613 **IT**

Henkel Taiwan Ltd., pg. 613 **IT**

Hewlett-Packard Taiwan Ltd., 8th Fl., Hewlett Packard Bldg., pg. 822 **PB**

Hitachi Zosen Taiwan Office, Room 902, Chia Hsin Bldg., 96 Sec. 2, Chung Shan N. Rd., pg. 623 **IT**

Honeywell Taiwan Limited, 11th Floor, 4, Sec. 3, Ming-Sheng East Rd., pg. 835 **PB**

Hsin-feng Chemical Corp., #57 Ho-Pin Road, Lu Chou Hsiang, pg. 924 **IT**

Huls Taiwan Co., Ltd., 9/F., 158 Hsin Sheng S. Rd., pg. 1455 **IT**

Hwacheng General Contractor Co., Ltd., 10th Floor, No. 146, Song Chiang Road, pg. 1347 **IT**

Hwaching Construction Co., Ltd., 6-3F, Sun Plaza Bldg., No. 57, Fu Hsing N. Rd., pg. 1233 **IT**

I&S Corporation (Taiwan Branch), 8F-1, No. 15, Lane 3, Sec 2, Chien-kuo N. Rd., pg. 642 **IT**

ICC Trading (Taiwan) Ltd., 6th Fl. No. 8 Lane 22, pg. 554 **PV**

ICI Taiwan Limited, 5th Fl., No. 2, Tun Hwa S. Rd., pg. 665 **IT**

IDG Communications, Inc., 12F No. 4, Min Sheng E Rd., 10639, pg. 570 **PV**

ISK Taiwan Co., Ltd., 3rd Fl., 112, Section 2, Chung Shan North Road, pg. 689 **IT**

Imation Taiwan Ltd., 6F TFIT Bldg., 85 Section 4, Jen Ai Rd., pg. 870 **PB**

Inco Pacific Sales Limited, R.O.C., pg. 673 **IT**

Integrity Life Insurance Company, 12B No. 44, Chung Shan N. Fd., pg. 908 **IT**

Intel Technology Far East Ltd., pg. 887 **PB**

Intergraph Corporation Taiwan, 11th Fl., 21st. Century Bldg., 207, Tung HWA N. Rd., 10592, pg. 892 **PB**

International Auto Co., Ltd., 363 Sung Chiang Road, pg. 693 **IT**

THE INTERNATIONAL COMMERCIAL BANK OF CHINA, 100 Chi Lin Rd., pg. 683 **IT**

International Paper Taiwan Ltd., 7th Fl., Walsin Fin. Building, 117, Section 3, Min Sheng East Road, pg. 905 **PB**

Interworld Enterprises Ltd., 17 Hsin Hsin St., pg. 594 **IT**

Ito-Yokado Taipei Liaison Office, Sun Plaza Building, 9S 3 # 57 Fuhsing N. Road, pg. 694 **IT**

JT International Taiwan Corp., 1810 International Trade Bldg., 3333 Keelung Road, pg. 703 **IT**

Jardine Fleming Taiwan Investment Management Limited, 17th Fl., No. 2, Hsin-yi Rd., pg. 494 **IT**

Jardine Fleming Taiwan Securities Limited, 2nd Fl., Bl 65 Tun Hwa S. Rd., pg. 494 **IT**

Jardine, Matheson & Co., Ltd., 13, 14/F World Trade Bldg., 50 Hsin Sheng South Rd., pg. 704 **IT**

Jeep Construction Co., Ltd., 6-3F, Sun Plaza Bldg., No. 57, Fu Hsing N. Rd., pg. 1233 **IT**

Johnson & Johnson Taiwan Ltd., 4F #319 Sec. 2, Tun Hwa South Rd., ROC, pg. 931 **PB**

S.C. Johnson & Son Taiwan Ltd., P.O. Box 87-300, pg. 593 **PV**

KSB Taiwan Co. Ltd., pg. 721 **IT**

Kao (Taiwan) Corporation, 10F No. 363 Fu Hsing N. Rd., pg. 718 **IT**

Karneval Cosmetic Co., Ltd., pg. 1490 **IT**

Kennametal Hardpoint (Taiwan) Inc., P.O. Box 91-226, No. 10, 1st Floor, Lane 56, pg. 951 **IT**

Kidde Consumer Durables Corp., No. 2 Fu Hsing North Rd. 5F6, pg. 594 **IT**

King Car Otsuka Co., Ltd., 6F No.261 Sec. 3, Roosevelt Road, pg. 1014 **IT**

Kintetsu Intermodal (Taiwan), Inc., 3rd Fl., No. 99, Sec. 2, Chang An E. Rd., pg. 735 **IT**

Kintetsu World Express (Taiwan), Inc., 3rd Fl., No. 99, Sec. 2, Chang An E. Rd., pg. 735 **IT**

Knoll Pharmaceuticals Taiwan, Empire Building, 16th Floor, No. 87, Sung Chiang Road, pg. 109 **IT**

Kodak Taiwan Limited, 35, Chung Yang South Rd. Section 2, pg. 555 **PB**

Kodak Taiwan Limited, Chemical Dept., 35, Chung Yang South Rd. Section 2, pg. 555 **PB**

KONE Elevators C&N Products Corporation, 3rd Floor, No. 7 Sec. 2, Nanking East Road, pg. 747 **IT**

Kredietbank Taipei Branch, 99, Fu Hsing North Road, 15th fl., pg. 760 **IT**

Kuo Hua Inc., 9th Floor, No. 109, Tung Hsing Street, pg. 394 **IT**

LGT Asset Management Ltd., Rm. 1205B, 12G, Lotus Bldg., 136 Jen Ai Road, Sec. 3, pg. 810 **IT**

Land Win Electronic Corporation, No. 2 & 3, 2 & 4, Alley 39, Lane 246, pg. 1123 **PB**

Landis & Staefa SMSTAR Co., Ltd., 9F, 356, Section 5, pg. 801 **IT**

Laporte (Taiwan) Limited, 3 F.82, Sec. 2, Fu-Hsing S. Rd., pg. 803 **IT**

Lidye Chemical Co., Ltd., 10th Fl., The Lidye Commercial Bldg., 22, pg. 372 **IT**

Life Insurance Company of Georgia, Chant World Building, 11th Fl., No. 120 Chien Kuo North Rd., pg. 650 **IT**

Life Investors Insurance Co., Taipei International Business Center, pg. 28 **IT**

Lin & Roe Company, Taiping & First Bldg., 550 Chung Hsiao East Rd., Section 4, pg. 187 **PV**

Lion Henkel Taiwan Ltd., pg. 614 **IT**

Lockheed Aircraft (Asia) Ltd., Bank Tower, Ste. 808, 205, Tun Hwa North Rd., pg. 1010 **PB**

Loewe Taiwan Ltd, 3rd Fl., 47 Chung San N. Rd. Sec. 2, pg. 782 **IT**

Louis Vuitton Taiwan Ltd, 1 & 2F-47, Chung Shan North Rd., pg. 783 **IT**

Luwa (Taiwan) Ltd., pg. 618 **IT**

MBT (Taiwan) Co. Ltd., pg. 1465 **IT**

MDK Consultants, A2/6F, Number 51 Keelung Road, pg. 117 **IT**

MacGregor Golf (Taiwan) Ltd., 16 Lane 194, pg. 73 **IT**

Makita (Taiwan) LTD., 2F No. 4, Lane 83, Kuang-fu Rd., pg. 832 **IT**

Makro Taiwan Ltd., 8th Fl., Lucky Star Building, 97, sec. 2, Nan Kang Road, pg. 1156 **IT**

Malayan Overseas Insurance Corporation, No. 56, Tun Hwa N. Rd., pg. 1532 **IT**

Manamerica - Taiwan Branch, International Trade Bldg., Ste. 3201, 333 Keelung Rd., R.O.C., pg. 841 **IT**

Mandarin Airlines, 14F, #134, Sec. 3, Minsheng E. Road, pg. 284 **IT**

Martin Marietta International, Inc., Formosa Plastics Bldg., 7th Fl., 201 Tun-Hua North Rd., pg. 1010 **PB**

Memorex Telex Taiwan Ltd., Rm 501, 5th Floor, 125 Nanking E. Road, Sec. 5, pg. 858 **PB**

Mentholatum Taiwan Ltd., Fifth Fl., 45 Section 1, Hankow St., pg. 1126 **IT**

Mentor Graphics (Taiwan) Ltd., Room 1201 No. 136, Lotus Bldg. Section 3 Jen-Ai Road, pg. 1087 **PB**

Merck Balzers Ltd., pg. 997 **IT**

Metropolitan Insurance & Annuity Company, Taiwan Branch, 11th Fl., 85 Jen Ai Road, Sec. 4, pg. 738 **PB**

Micron Semiconductor Asia Pacific Inc., Ste. 1010 10F, 333 Keeling Rd., Sec. 1, pg. 1105 **PB**

Micropolis Limited, Rm. 1111, 11F, No.333, Keelung Road, Sec. 1, pg. 742 **PV**

Microsoft Taiwan Corporation, pg. 1108 **PB**

Mighty Exim Corporation, 10 Fl., 213, Sec. 2, Hsin I Rd., pg. 1032 **PB**

Minebea Technologies Pte. Ltd. - Taipei Office, Room C, 13th Fl. Sanhsin Bldg., 167, Fu-Hsing N. Road, pg. 869 **IT**

Mitsui & Co., Ltd., 11th Fl., Chang Hwa Commercial Bank, Taipei, pg. 880 **IT**

Mizuno (Taiwan) Corporation, 11th Fl., International Union, Bldg. No. 363, Sung Chiang Rd., pg. 885 **IT**

Molex Taiwan Ltd., 100-3 Shia-Kwei-Rou-Shan, pg. 1123 **IT**

Morgan Guaranty Trust Company, Bank Tower, 10th Fl., 205 Tun Hwa North Rd., pg. 1130 **IT**

J.P. Morgan Securities Asia Ltd., Bank Tower, 10th Fl., 205 Tun Hwa North Rd., pg. 1131 **PB**

Morgan Stanley Taipei, Rm. 1503, Chia Hsin Bldg., 96 Chung Shan N. Rd., Sec. 2, pg. 1133 **PB**

Morganite Thermal Ceramics Taiwan Limited, 35 Hankow St., R.O.C., pg. 894 **IT**

NEC Electronics Taiwan Ltd., 7F, No. 363, Fu Shing North Rd., pg. 901 **IT**

NEC Taiwan Ltd., 12F, No. 37, Sec. 3, pg. 900 **IT**

NKK Corporation-Taipei, 502B, 5th Fl., Chia Hsin Bldg., No. 96, Sec. 2, Chung Shan North Rd., pg. 903 **IT**

NYK-Taiwan, c/o Lien Ho Co., Ltd, 9th Floor, No. 83, pg. 941 **IT**

Nan Shan Life Insurance Company, Ltd., 302, Min Chuan East Rd., R.O.C., pg. 85 **IT**

Nestle Taiwan Ltd., pg. 921 **IT**

New Tai Milk Products Co. Ltd., 345 Ting Hu Road, pg. 923 **IT**

A.C. Nielsen Company-Taiwan Branch, 8/F-2, 87, Sung Chiang Rd., pg. 1183 **IT**

Nippon Life - Taipei Representative Office, 12th Floor, 296, 296, Jen Ai Road, Sec. 4, pg. 936 **IT**

Nippon Meat Packers (Taiwan), Inc., Room No. D. 15F, No. 125, Section 2, Nanking, East Rd., pg. 936 **IT**

Nippon Sanso Taiwan, Inc., 2F, No-176, Sec. 2, Min-Seng East Road, pg. 939 **IT**

Nitto Formosa Co., Ltd., 4th Fl., No. 124 Mintsu W. Road, pg. 951 **IT**

Nittobo Norplex Oak Co., Ltd. (NNO), P.O. Box 3192, 59 Chung Yang Rd., pg. 53 **PB**

Nomura Financial Advisory Co., Ltd., 14th Floor, 109 Min-Sheng East Road Sec 3, R.O.C., pg. 957 **IT**

Nomura Securities Investment Advisory Co., Ltd., 14th Floor, 109 Min-Sheng East Road, Sec. 3, R.O.C., pg. 957 **IT**

Nopco Trading Corp., pg. 613 **IT**

PB - U.S. Public Companies Volume
PV - U.S. Private Companies Volume
IT - International Public & Private Companies Volume

Geographic Index-Non U.S.

1784

Northern Storage and Transportation Project and Construction Div., 9f, #110, Yen-Pin S. Rd., R.O.C., pg. 286 **IT**

Norton Performance Plastic Co. Ltd., Suite 1203-MO 147, Chien Ruo North RD-Sect 2, pg. 1175 **IT**

Novell Taiwan, Rm. E-F, 5th Fl., 168 Tun-Hwa North Rd., pg. 1204 **PB**

Novo Nordisk Pharma (Taiwan) Ltd., 7F-1, 216 Tun Hua South Road, pg. 988 **IT**

Nutricia (Hong Kong) Ltd.-Taiwan Branch, pg. 992 **IT**

OCE (Taiwan) Ltd., pg. 995 **IT**

OPIC (Overseas Petroleum Investment Group), 83 Chunghwa Rd., Sec. 1, R.O.C., pg. 286 **IT**

Offshore & Overseas Petroleum Exploration Division, 3, Pei-King E. Rd., Fl. 4, R.O.C., pg. 286 **IT**

Oki Electronics (Hong Kong) Ltd.-Taipei Branch, 7th Floor, No. 260, Somitomo-Flyson Building, pg. 1000 **IT**

OMRON Taiwan Electronics Inc., 6F, Home Young Bldg., #363, pg. 1006 **IT**

Oracle Taiwan Inc., Ste. 804, 129 Ming-Sheng E. Rd., Sec. 3, ROC, pg. 1228 **PB**

ORIX Taiwan Corporation, 10th Floor, 217, Nan King E. Road, Sec. 3, pg. 1010 **IT**

Panalpina Taiwan Ltd., pg. 1023 **IT**

Panalpina World Transport Ltd., pg. 1023 **IT**

Panduit International Corp.-Taiwan Branch, Rm. 901, #20 Nan King, East Road, Section 2, pg. 836 **PB**

Parker Hannifin Taiwan Co. Ltd., 8F-1, No. 102, Sung Lung Road, R.O.C., pg. 1264 **IT**

Pechiney Taiwan Inc., Chia Hsin Bldg., Rm. 1008, 96 Chung-Shan North Road, pg. 1031 **IT**

Pfizer Trading Corp., 177 Chung Cheng E. Rd., Sec. 2 Tansui, pg. 1282 **IT**

Pharmacia & Upjohn Biotech Far East Ltd., 6F No. 99-Chung Cheng Rd., pg. 1047 **IT**

Pharmacia & Upjohn Laboratories Limited, Rm. N-811, Chia Hsin Bldg. 11, 9 Lane 3, Min Shen W. Rd., ROC, pg. 1049 **IT**

Phoenix Technologies (Taiwan) Ltd., 14F, No. 363 Fu Hsing N. Road, pg. 1292 **IT**

Premier Chemical Co. Ltd., Bank Tower, Ste. 704, 205, Tun Hwa North Rd., pg. 460 **PB**

Presicarre Corp., 6F-1, 137, Nanking East Rd., Section 2, pg. 273 **IT**

Prince Housing Development Corp., 3F, 560, Chung-Shiao E. Rd., Sec. 4, pg. 1347 **IT**

Quantum Corporation Taiwan Branch, A 26F, Taipei Intl. Building, 216, Sec. 2, Tun-Hwa S. Rd., pg. 1350 **PB**

RNBNY Representative Office-Taiwan, Ste. 606, Bank Tower, pg. 1381 **PB**

Raw Materials Ltd., 3rd. Fl., 141 Tun Hua North Rd., pg. 303 **IT**

Raychem Taiwan Limited, 8F, 2, Lane 94, Tsao Ti Wei Road, pg. 1363 **IT**

Rhenania Trading Corp., pg. 613 **IT**

Rhone-Poulenc Taiwan Ltd., 7F, 70 Nanking East Rd., Sec. 3, pg. 1114 **IT**

Rieter Asia (Taiwan) Ltd., pg. 1117 **IT**

A.H. Robins International Company, 309-3 Tun Hua North Rd., pg. 82 **PB**

Roche Products Ltd., Cosmos Bldg. 9/F, No. 134, Min Sheng East Rd., Sec. 3, pg. 1121 **IT**

Rockwell International Taiwan Company, Ltd., Rm. 2808, International Trade, Bldg., pg. 1401 **PB**

Rohm & Haas Taiwan, Inc., pg. 1404 **PB**

Rohm Electronics Taiwan Co., Ltd., 11F No. 6, Sec. 3, Min Chuan E. Rd., pg. 1125 **IT**

Royal Copenhagen (Taiwan) Ltd., Suite 905, 9F, 136 Den-Ai Road, pg. 1135 **IT**

SAS Software Taiwan Ltd., Ming Sheng E. Road #149, Section 2 11F., R.O.C., pg. 967 **PV**

SKF Bearing Services Taiwan Ltd., Rm. B, 13th Fl., No. 129, Section 3, R.O.C., pg. 1158 **IT**

SMH (Asia) Inc., Taiwan, 200 Nanking East Road, pg. 1161 **IT**

SNC-Lavalin, 8F-7, 51 Keelung Road, Esc. 2, pg. 1162 **IT**

The Sakura Bank - Taipei Representative Office, 4th Floor-D, Hung-tai Center, No. 170, Tun-hwa North Road, pg. 1180 **IT**

Sampo Corporation (Taipei), 2F1, 217 Section 3, Nanking E. Rd., pg. 1229 **IT**

San Fu Chemical Co., Ltd., 5th Fl., Shankong Bldg. 21, Sec. 2, pg. 32 **IT**

Sanden International Taiwan Corporation, 2F, No. 21-16, Section 1, Tun Hwa S., Road, pg. 1184 **IT**

Sandvik Taiwan Ltd., Litung Tower, 6th Fl., No.1 Nanking E. Rd., Sec. 4, pg. 1187 **IT**

Sanyo Electric (Taiwan) Co., Ltd., 266, Sung Chiang Rd., pg. 1192 **IT**

Sato Engineering Consultants, Inc., Tong Fang Bldg., 11th Fl.-7, No.2, Chung Hsiao E. Rd., pg. 1197 **IT**

Seagate Technology Pte. Ltd. (Taiwan Branch), Rm A, 12th Floor #138, Sec. 3, Ming-Sheng East Road, pg. 1450 **PB**

Sealed Air (Taiwan) Ltd., No. 20, Lane 238, pg. 1451 **PB**

Security Pacific National Bank, Taipei, 62 TUN HWA North Rd., pg. 183 **PB**

SEIKA ELECTRIC CO., LTD., No. 34, Lane 387, R.O.C., pg. 1218 **IT**

Shaklee (Asia) Inc., Taiwan Branch, 3F, No. 99, Sec. 2, Tun-Hwa South Road, pg. 1518 **IT**

Sharp Corporation (Taiwan), 8F, 45, Sec. 3, Shunshan N. Rd., pg. 1229 **IT**

Sharp Electronic Components (Taiwan) Corporation, 8F, No 16, pg. 1229 **IT**

Sharp Technology (Taiwan) Corporation, 7F, No. 16, SEC 4 Nanking E. Rd., pg. 1230 **IT**

Shell Taiwan Ltd., International Trade Bldg., Room 2001, 20th Floor, pg. 1140 **IT**

Shin Kong Mitsukoshi Department Store Co. Ltd., 12, Nanking West Rd., pg. 884 **IT**

Shin Kong Mitsukoshi Department Store Co. Ltd. - Taipei Station Front, 66 Chung Hsiao West Rd. Sec. 1, pg. 884 **IT**

Shionogi & Co., Ltd. - Taipei, Transworld Commercial Center, 2, Sec. 2, Nanking E. Rd., pg. 1235 **IT**

Singapore Tourist Promotion Board - Taipei, Unit H, 6th Floor, Hung Tai Center, pg. 1254 **IT**

Sino-American Great Wall Food Industries Co., Ltd., 8th Floor, Kuang Fu Bldg., 310 Chung Hsi, pg. 411 **IT**

Snow Brand Milk Products Co., Ltd., 4th Fl., 237 Chien Kuo S. Rd., pg. 1272 **IT**

Sound Bell Enterprises Co. Ltd., No. 9, Alley 9, Lane 250, Sec. 2, Cheng Kong Road, pg. 550 **IT**

Springborn Testing & Research (Taiwan) Ltd., 3F-1, No. 135, Roosevelt Rd. Sec. 3, R.O.C., pg. 1027 **PV**

The Standard Bank of South Africa Limited, 14th Floor, Hong-Tai, Century Bldg., 156 Minsheng East Road, pg. 1294 **IT**

Standard Chartered Asia (Taiwan) Limited, 6/F The Waisin Lihwa Bldg., 117 Ming Sheng E. Rd., Sec. 3, pg. 1296 **IT**

Standard Chartered Bank (Taiwan), 337 Fu Hsing North Rd., pg. 1296 **IT**

Standard Chartered Securities Asia Limited, 6/F, The Waisin Lihwa Bldg., 117 Ming Sheng E. Rd., Sec. 3, pg. 1296 **IT**

Sullair Taiwan Ltd., 6th Fl., #90, Chen Kuo N Rd., pg. 1534 **PB**

Sumi-Pac Electro-Chemical Corporation, 3rd Fl., Pacific Commercial, Bldg., 285, Chung Hsiao E. Rd., pg. 1313 **IT**

Sumitomo Chemical Taiwan Co., Ltd., 6F-3, No. 369, Fu-Shing North Road, pg. 1312 **IT**

Sun Microsystems of California Ltd., 385, Tun Hwa South Rd., Ste. 705, R.O.C., pg. 1532 **PB**

Svenska Handelsbanken Taipei, Room 0813, International Trade Building, pg. 1327 **IT**

Swiss Bank Corporation, 8A, 133 Min Sheng East Road, pg. 1330 **IT**

Swiss Reinsurance Company-Taipei Liason Office, 10th Floor, Suite C, Hung Tai Century Tower, pg. 1333 **IT**

Swisspharma Taiwan Ltd., pg. 986 **IT**

TDK Taiwan Corp., 6th Floor, 21st Century Bldg., 207 Tun-Hwa, North Rd., pg. 1337 **IT**

Tai Tien Pharmaceuticals Co., Ltd., 11F, No.108, Nanking East Road, pg. 1354 **IT**

Taipei Branch, Shin Kong World Bldg.,5th Fl, No. 287, Sec. 3, Nanking East Road, pg. 1519 **IT**

Taipei Representative Office, 11th Floor, Area B, Hung Kuo Bldg., pg. 1485 **IT**

Taipei Takashimaya International Co., Ltd., Rm. 1503, 13th Fl., I.T. Bldg., No. 205, Sec. 1, Tun-Hua S. Rd., pg. 1350 **IT**

Taiso Commerce Inc., 4th Fl., 148 Sung-Chiang Rd., pg. 41 **IT**

Taiwan Autogalss Industries Corp., 261, Section 3, Nanking E. Road, pg. 1348 **IT**

Taiwan Engineering & Mngmt. Consultant (Te & mc), 11, Lane 78, Chien-Kuo North Rd., pg. 321 **IT**

TAIWAN GLASS INDUSTRY CORP., 11th Fl., 261 Nanking East Rd. Sec. 3, pg. 1348 **IT**

Taiwan Hercules Chemicals, Inc., pg. 811 **PB**

Taiwan Kumagai Co., Ltd., Room No. 1408, 12th Floor, International Trade Building 205, pg. 764 **IT**

Taiwan Marketing & Transportation Div., 71, Kuan-Chien Rd., R.O.C., pg. 286 **IT**

Taiwan Meiji Co., Ltd., 10F. Hsieh Ho Commercial Bldg., pg. 856 **IT**

Taiwan Morinaga Nutritional Foods Inc., 6th Fl., No. 153 Sec. 2, pg. 895 **IT**

Taiwan NSK Precision Co. Ltd., Room A, Fifth Fl., 34, Chung Shan N. Rd., Sec. 3, pg. 904 **IT**

Taiwan Nalco Chemical Co Ltd., Taiwan Glass Bldg., 8th Fl., 261 Sec. 3, pg. 1151 **IT**

Taiwan Obayashi Corporation, 6F-2, 57, Fu-Hsing N. Rd., pg. 996 **IT**

Taiwan Otsuka Pharmaceutical Co., Ltd., 18/F. No. 88, Sec. 2, pg. 1014 **IT**

TAIWAN POWER COMPANY, 242, Roosevelt Rd., Sec. 3, pg. 1348 **IT**

Taiwan Scott Paper Corp., 4th Fl. Bank Tower, 205, Tun Hwa North Road, pg. 960 **PB**

Taiwan Shionogi & Co., Ltd., Transworld Commercial Center, 2, Sec. 2, Nanking E. Rd., pg. 1235 **IT**

Taiwan Takagi Chokoku Co., Ltd., 186, Hshin-shu Rd., Hsin-chuang, pg. 1349 **IT**

Taiwan Takenaka Co., Ltd., Taipei International Building, A2, 7F, No. 216, Sec. 2, Tun-Hwa, pg. 1351 **IT**

Taiwan Takenaka Engineering Co., Ltd., Taipei International Building, A2, 7F, No. 216, Sec. 2, Tun-Hwa, pg. 1351 **IT**

Taiwan Tanabe Seiyaku Co., Ltd., 11F, No.108, Nanking East Road, pg. 1354 **IT**

Taiwan Toto Co., Ltd., 9th Fl. No. 46, Sec. 2, Chung Shan North Road, pg. 1410 **IT**

Taiwan Vilene Nonwovens Comp. Ltd., pg. 507 **IT**

Taiwan Yamanouchi Pharmaceutical Co., Ltd., Shin Kong World Bldg., 5th Fl, No. 287, Sec. 3, Nanking East Road, pg. 1519 **IT**

Taiwan Yamazaki Co., Ltd., 3F, 35-1, Section 1, Cheng Kuo N. Rd., pg. 1519 **IT**

Takeda Chemical Industries (Taiwan) Ltd., 7th Fl., Great China Bldg., No. 217, Sec. 3, Nanking East Rd., pg. 1350 **IT**

Tally Industrial & Trading Co. Ltd., 7 F. 5 Tun Kwa South Road, pg. 1455 **IT**

TARGET ADVERTISING AGENCY LIMITED, 9th Fl., No. 1, Fu Hsing N. Rd., pg. 1355 **IT**

TATUNG CORPORATION, 22 Chungshan, pg. 1357 **IT**

Tatung-Fanuc Robotics Company, 22 Chungshan N. Road, pg. 477 **IT**

Tektronix Taiwan Ltd.-Taipei, 6th Floor, CDC Tower, 125 Nanking East Road, Section 5, R.O.C., pg. 1568 **PB**

Teledyne Taiwan, Formosa Plastic Bldg., B 10th Floor, pg. 44 **PB**

Terumo-Taipei, 7-A, No. 170, Tun-Hwa Norte Rd., pg. 1376 **IT**

Thorsen Trading Co., 70-3, Pa Shih Li Chu Wei, Tam Shui, pg. 842 **IT**

Tiffany & Co. International (Taiwan), B-1 No.3, Lane 39, Chung Shan North Road, Sec. 2, pg. 1609 **PB**

Tong Shing Inc., Shinkong Life Ins. Bldg., # 123 Nanking E. Rd., Section 2, R.O.C., pg. 1400 **IT**

Tongling General Contractor Co., 10th Floor, No. 146, Song Chiang Road, pg. 1348 **IT**

Toronto Dominion-Taipei Branch, 13th Fl. Hewlett-Packard Bldg., pg. 1402 **IT**

Toshiba Electronics Taiwan Corp., 17F. Union Enterprise Plaza Bldg. 629, pg. 1406 **IT**

Toto Taipei Branch, 6th Fl., No. 46, Sec. 2, Chung Shan North Road, pg. 1410 **IT**

Tourism Malaysia - Taiwan Office, Unit C, 8 Floor, Hing Tai Center, No. 170, Tan Hwa, pg. 833 **IT**

Toyota Motor Corporation, Taiwan Office, 2213, 22F. No. 333, Keelung Rd., pg. 1413 **IT**

Trident Microsystems (Far East) Ltd., 6F, No. 2, Sec. 3, Pa Teh Road, pg. 1637 **PB**

Union Bank of Switzerland, Taipei Branch, 15/F, Hung Kuo Building, 167, Tun Hua North Road, pg. 1441 **IT**

United-Asatsu International Ltd., 14th Fl., No. 7, pg. 86 **IT**

Utell International-Taiwan, 34-3, 148 Chung Hsiao, East Road Sec. 4, pg. 1099 **IT**

Van Leeuwen Pipe and Tube (Far East) Pte. Ltd., 7th Floor 3, no. 207, Tung HWA N. Road, pg. 1450 **IT**

Votra Taiwan, pg. 757 **IT**

Wang Industrial Co., Ltd., 8th Fl., 56, Tun Hwa North Rd., R.O.C., pg. 1738 **PB**

WEI-CHUAN FOODS CORPORATION, 125, Sungchiang Rd., pg. 1488 **IT**

Wellcome Taiwan Limited, 2F, 175 Hua Ling St., pg. 704 **IT**

WestLB Taipei, 7th Floor, Hung Tai Centre, 7D, pg. 1493 **IT**

Westpac Banking Corp. - Taiwan, World Financial Center, 15th. Flr., 99 Fu Hsing, pg. 1497 **IT**

Willis Corroon (Taiwan) Limited, 2nd Floor, 114 Sec. 2, Chung Shan N Road, pg. 1510 **IT**

World Lock Co. Ltd., 135, Sec. 1, Nan Kan Road, pg. 548 **IT**

Wormald Engineering Systems Taiwan Limited, 4F, No. 394, Sec. 1, Keelung Rd., pg. 1651 **IT**

Wrigley Taiwan Ltd., 9th Fl.-1, No. 112, Sec. 2, pg. 1781 **IT**

Wyeth-Ayerst (Asia) Ltd., Lotus Bldg., 15th Fl., 136 Jen Ai Rd., Section 3, pg. 82 **PB**

Yamaichi Securities Co., Ltd.-Taipei Branch, 5th Floor, CDC Tower, 125 Nanking East Road, Sec. 5, pg. 1517 **IT**

Zeneca Pharma, 51, No. 2 Sec, 1 Tun Hwa South Road, pg. 1527 **IT**

ZEXEL Corporation Taipei Representative Office, 86, Sec 3, Cheng Teh Road, pg. 1528 **IT**

Ziff-Davis Taiwan, 12 F-7, No.1 Futtsin N. Rd., R.O.C., pg. 1276 **IT**

Zurich Life Insurance Company of America, 6th Fl., No. 56, Tun Hwa North Road, pg. 1532 **IT**

Tamsui

Pfizer Limited, 177 Chung Cheng East Rd. Sec. 2, pg. 1282 **PB**

Tanzte

Canon Inc., Taiwan, Taichung Export Processing Zone, pg. 262 **IT**

Tao-yuan

Acer Peripherals, Inc., 157 Shan-Ying Road, pg. 22 **PB**

AlliedSignal Laminate Systems, pg. 53 **PB**

Amada Taiwan Inc., 21, Wenming St., pg. 70 **PB**

BERG Electronics Taiwan Ltd., No. 7-1 Tsu-Chiang 1st Road, Chungli Industrial Zone, pg. 213 **IT**

Casio Taiwan Ltd., No. 171-1, Shan Ying Road, Kwei Shan, Industrial Park, pg. 274 **IT**

CIBA-GEIGY Animal Health (Taiwan) Limited, No. 12, Tung Yuan 2nd Road, R.O.C., pg. 976 **IT**

Du Pont Taiwan Limited-Hsien Plant, 7 Tun Chiang 1st Rd., pg. 533 **PB**

Ferro Industrial Products Ltd., No. 239, Hsia Chung Tzu Road, 32707, pg. 619 **PB**

Grace Taiwan, Inc., #84-1, Kwah Yeh West Rd., pg. 756 **PB**

Hewlett-Packard Taiwan Ltd., 20, Kao-Shuang Rd., pg. 822 **PB**

LeaRonal (S.E. Asia) Ltd. Taiwan Branch, 722, Kuang Fu Rd., pg. 982 **IT**

Eli Lilly and Company (Taiwan), Inc., 2 Kuo Kuang Lane, ROC, pg. 993 **IT**

RTE Far East Corporation, 2-7 Nan Yuan Road, R.O.C., pg. 445 **IT**

Siemens Telecommunication Systems Ltd., No. 6 Wenming 1st Street, Kueishan Hsiang, pg. 1248 **IT**

Snap-on Worldwide, Inc., 824 Min Sheng Road, pg. 1481 **IT**

Sumi-Pac Construction Co., Ltd., 1671, Sec. 1 Wan-Shou Road, pg. 1313 **IT**

Taiwan Hokuriku Co., LTD., No. 8-10, Wu-Chuan, Tsun Tayuan, Shiang, pg. 628 **IT**

Taiwan Wacoal Co., Ltd., 15, Jingkwo Rd., R.O.C., pg. 1484 **IT**

PB - *U.S. Public Companies Volume*
PV - *U.S. Private Companies Volume*
IT - *International Public & Private Companies Volume*

1785

Geographic Index-Non U.S.

Taoyuan Refinery, 50, Min-Sheng N. Road, R.O.C., pg. 286 IT
Toppan Chunghwa Electronics Co., Ltd., 1127-1 Hopin Road, pg. 1399 IT
Toshiba Compressor (Taiwan) Corp., No 3, Kong-Yeh 6th Rd., Kuan-yin, pg. 1406 IT
Yung Hwa Machinery Industrial Co., Ltd., No. 493, Kuang Hsing Road, Kuang Hsing Tsun, pg. 727 IT

TANZANIA

Arusha

General Tyre East Africa Ltd., P.O. Box 554, pg. 327 IT

Dar es Salaam

Blackwood Hodge (Tanzania) Limited, Oyster Bay, pg. 231 IT
CIBA-GEIGY Sales and Distribution Co. Ltd., pg. 980 IT
Det Norske Veritas, c/o Tanzania Coastal Shipping, pg. 398 IT
Eurafrican Bank (Tanzania) Ltd., NDC Development House, Kivukoni/Ohio Street, pg. 548 IT
Henkel Chemicals East Africa Ltd., Pugu Rd., pg. 612 IT
Interfreight Investments Limited, pg. 1022 IT
Interfreight Tanzania Limited, pg. 1022 IT
Kamyn Industries (Tanzania) Ltd., 112-113, MBO 21 Rd., pg. 948 IT
MB Tanzania Limited, P.O. Box 618, pg. 267 IT
Mitsui & Co., Ltd., P.O. Box 9613, pg. 882 IT
Ocelot International Tanzania Ltd., 1st Fl., Maarifa House, Ohio Street, pg. 996 IT
The Old East African Trading Co. (T) Ltd., pg. 431 IT
Oxford University Press (Dar Es Salaam), Maktaba St., pg. 1019 IT
Shell Tanzania Ltd., TDFL Building, Ohio Street, pg. 1137 IT
Songas, Maarifa House, Ohio Street, pg. 1417 IT
Standard Chartered Bank Tanzania Limited, NIC Life House, Corner Sokoine Dr. & Ohio St., pg. 1295 IT
Tanzania Portland Cement Company Ltd., pg. 1201 IT
UAC of Tanzania Ltd., pg. 1438 IT
The World Bank, N.I.C. Bldg., 7th Fl., B, pg. 1190 PV

THAILAND

Ayutthaya

Ajinomoto Frozen Foods (Thailand) Co., Ltd., Plant, 59 Mu 5, pg. 41 IT
Hana Semiconductor (BKK) Co., Ltd., Hi-Tech Industrial Estate, Asia-Nakhon Sawan Road, Km. 59-60, pg. 943 IT
Hana Semiconductor (Hi-Tech) Plant, High-Tech Industrial Estate, Asia-Nakhon Sawan Road, Km. 59-60, pg. 943 IT
NMB Thai Limited, 18 Moo 3, Asia Road, Km. 72, pg. 868 IT
Nikon (Thailand) Co., Ltd., 1/42 Moo 5, Rojana Indus. Pk., Rojana Rd., pg. 932 IT
Oki (Thailand) Co., Ltd., Rojana Industrial Park, 1/39 Rojana Rd., Tambol Kanham, pg. 1000 IT
P.I.B.F. Ayutthaya Branch, Krungsri River Hotel 27/2 Moo, 11 Rojchana Road, Kamang, pg. 1310 IT
Read-Rite SMI (Thailand) Co. Ltd., 140 Moo 2, Udomsorayuth Road, pg. 1367 PB
Read-Rite (Thailand) Co. Ltd., 140 Moo 2, Udomsorayuth Road, pg. 1367 PB
Royal Time Citi Co., Ltd., 69 Phaholyothin Road, Sanubtube, pg. 295 IT
Thai Nippon Foods Co. Ltd., 1/21 Rojana Industrial Park, Moo 9 Kanham Village, pg. 936 IT

Ban Si Racha

Michelin Siam Co., Ltd., Laem Chabang Industrial Estate, 87/11 Moo 2, Sukhumvit Rd., pg. 1238 IT
Siam Asahi Technoglass Co., Ltd., Laem Chabang Industrial Estate, 87/12 Moo 2, Sukhumvit Rd., pg. 1238 IT
Siam Compressor Industry Co., Ltd., Laem Chabang Industrial Estate, 87/10 Moo 2, Sukhumvit Road, pg. 1238 IT
Thai CRT Co., Ltd., Laem Chabang Industrial Estate, 87/9 Moo 2, Sukhumvit Rd., pg. 1238 IT

Bang Pakong

Molex (Thailand) Ltd., No. 7 1/4 Moo 5, Bangpakong Ind. Pk., pg. 1123 PB

Bangkok

AGC (Thailand) Finance & Securities Co., Limited, Asoke Tower, 219 Sukhumvit 21, pg. 1497 IT
AMP Thailand, 10F Thansettakij Bldg., 222 Viparadee-Rangsit Rd., pg. 9 PB
ARS Chemical (Thailand) Co., Ltd., 27 Soi Phiphat Silom Road Bangrak, pg. 1014 IT
Adhesives (Thailand) Ltd., pg. 129 IT
Aggregate Supply Co., Ltd., 1516 Pracharaj 1 Rd., Bangsue, pg. 1237 IT
Air Products Industry Co., Ltd., 35/9 Moo 5, Soi Petkasem 69, Bangborn III Road, pg. 939 IT
Ajinomoto Co., (Thailand) Ltd., 487/1 Si Ayutthaya Rd., pg. 40 IT
Akzo Coatings (Thailand Ltd.), 1-7 Quellig Bldg., 7th Fl., Silom Rd., pg. 43 IT
Alcan Siam Limited, pg. 51 IT
AlliedSignal Laminate Systems Thailand Co., Ltd., Suriwong Business Center, 8th Floor, Panjaphat Bldg., pg. 53 PB
Amdahl Pacific Basin Operations (Thailand), Lake Rajada Office 35th Fl., 193-195 Ratchadapisek Rd., pg. 527 IT
American Appraisal Thailand Ltd., Room 313-319, 3 W. Fl., Thai C C Tower, pg. 50 PV
American Standard Sanitaryware (Thailand) Ltd., 392 Piyatanee Bldg., Sukhumvit Rd., SCI 1, pg. 92 PB
Amway (Thailand) Limited, 52/183 Ramkhamhaeng Rd., pg. 70 PV
Arabian Shaw Pipecoaters (Thailand) Limited, Level 23, CP Tower, 313 Silom Road, pg. 1231 IT
Asahi Bank Bangkok Representative Office, 33/115 22nd Fl., Rm. No. 2203, Wall Street Tower Bldg., pg. 83 IT
Asea Brown Boveri Ltd., pg. 8 IT
Asia Shinwa Engineering Co., Ltd., 3rd Floor, ACME Building, 125 Phetchburi Road, Rajthevee, pg. 432 IT
Asian Bleaching Earth Co., Ltd., 12th Fl., Sino-Thai Tower, 32-33 Asoke Rd., pg. 803 IT
Asian Honda Motor Co., Ltd., Bangkok Investment Bldg., pg. 635 IT
Asset Development Co., Ltd., IFCT Building 3, 2nd Fl., 1770 New Petchburi Road, pg. 677 IT
Astra (Thai) Ltd., P.O. Box 43, Bangna Post Office, pg. 94 IT
Australia & New Zealand Banking Group Limited Thailand, 9th Floor, Tower A, Diethelm Towers, 93/1 Wireless Road, pg. 99 IT
Ayudhya Investment and Trust Public Co., Ltd., 3rd Floor, Ploenchit Tower, 898 Ploenchit Rd., pg. 1180 IT
B.A. Resources Co., Ltd., 7/3 Soi Suwansawasdi, Rama IV Rd., pg. 414 PB
BASF (Thai) Ltd., 17th Fl., Asoke Towers, 219/56-59 Sukhumvit 21 Rd., pg. 107 IT
BASF Vita Limited, 17th Floor, Asoke Towers, 219/56-59 Sukhumvit 21 Road, pg. 107 IT
BBLP Drill Company Limited, 4th Floor, K.C.C. Building, 2 Soi Suksawitthaya, pg. 196 IT
BFCE Thailand, Dusit Thani Office Bldg., 8th Fl., pg. 161 IT
BTM Finance and Securities (Thailand) Ltd., 4th Fl., Harindhorn Tower, 54 N. Sathorn Rd., pg. 157 IT
Bangkok Athletic Co., Ltd., 611/210-213 Soi Rajuthit 2, pg. 146 IT
BANGKOK BANK OF COMMERCE LTD., 99 Surasak Rd., pg. 146 IT
BANGKOK BANK PUBLIC COMPANY LIMITED, 333 Silom Rd., pg. 146 IT
Bangkok Central Leasing Co., Ltd., 9th Fl., Sethiwan Tower 139, Pan Rd., pg. 1391 IT
Bangkok First Tokai Company Limited, C.P. Tower Bldg., 25th Fl., 313 Silom Rd., pg. 1391 IT
Bangkok Industrial Gas Co., Ltd., 518/5 Maneeya Centre, 14th Fl., pg. 32 PB
Bangkok International Banking Facility, 11th Floor, Diethelm Towers B, Room No. 1101, 93/1 Wireless Rd., pg. 1190 IT
Bangkok OA Coms Co., Ltd., 199/82-84 Vipavadee Rangsit Hwy., pg. 816 PB
Bangkok Office, c/o Thai Nishimatsu Con. Co., 19th Floor, Sino-Thai Tower, pg. 942 IT
Bangkok Representative Office, 18th Floor, Ramaland Building, 952 Rama IV Road, Bangrak, pg. 1517 IT
BANGKOK RUBBER PUBLIC CO., LTD., 611/40, Watchan Nai (Rajuthit 2), pg. 146 IT
Bangkok Sakura Leasing Co., Limited, 19th Floor, Sathorn City Tower, 175 South Sathorn Road, pg. 1180 IT
Bangkok Steel Industry Co. Ltd., United Flour Mill Bldg., pg. 947 IT
Bangkok Telecom Co., Ltd. (BTC), 460/1-9 Siam Square, Section 4, Rama 1 Road, Kwaeng Patumwan, pg. 531 IT
Bangkok Waste Water Project, Site Office BMA, 2, Mitrmaitree Road, pg. 942 IT
Bangkok Waste Water Project-Stage 1, Site Office BMA 2, Mitrmaitree Road, pg. 943 IT
Bank Brussels Lambert-Bangkok Representative Office, C.P. Tower, 19th Fl., 313 Silom Rd., pg. 148 IT
Bank of America NT&SA, Bank of America Center, 2/2 Wireless Rd., pg. 182 PB
The Bank of New York, Sino-Thai Tower, 18th Fl., 32/47 Sikhumvit 21 (Asoke), pg. 179 PB
Bank of Yokohama Bangkok, 22nd Fl., C.P. Tower Bldg., 313 Silom Road, pg. 159 IT
Bankers Trust New York Corporation, Boon-Mit Bldg., 12th Fl., 138 Silom Rd., pg. 186 PB
Banque Indosuez, Indosuez House, 152 Wireless Road, pg. 314 IT
Banque Paribas-Thailande, 9th Fl., Maneeya Center Bldg., 518/5 Ploenchit Rd., pg. 320 IT
Barclays Bank PLC, 102 Soi Aree, pg. 166 IT
Batey Ads Thailand, 9 Sukhumvit Rd. (Soi 4), pg. 117 IT
Beiersdorf (Thailand) Co. Ltd., 437 Soi Sirijulsawak Silom Rd., pg. 183 IT
BENETONE LAND & HOUSES CO., LTD., Benetone Building, 6th Floor, 16/23-24 Surhumvit Road, pg. 186 IT
Berli Jucker Public Co. Ltd., 99 Soi Rubia, Sukhumvit 42 Rd., pg. 487 IT
Berlitz Thailand Ltd., Silom Complex 22F, 191 Silom Rd., pg. 222 PB
Bilfinger + Berger Bauaktiengesellschaft Bangrak, 4th Floor, K.C.C. Building, 2 Soi Suksawitthaya, pg. 196 IT
Bilfinger + Berger (Thai) Construction Company Limited, 4th Floor, K.C.C. Building, 2 Soi Suksawitthaya, pg. 196 IT
The Book Club Finance and Securities Public Company Ltd., 3rd-6th Floors, The Siam Commercial Bank, Building 2, pg. 816 IT
Bristol-Myers (Thailand) Ltd., 294/8 Soi Somprasong 3, Petchburi Rd., pg. 256 PB
Bull HN Information Systems (Thailand) Ltd., 946 Dusit Thani Bldg., Rama IV Rd., pg. 316 IT
Leo Burnett Ltd. Thailand, 2nd Floor, USOM Bldg., 37 Soi Somprasong 3, pg. 185 PV
The CPAC Ready Mixed Concrete Co., Ltd., 1516 Pracharaj Rd., Bangue, pg. 1237 IT
CPAC Roof Tile Co., Limited, 1365 Pracharat Road, pg. 1092 IT
The CPAC Roof Tile Co., Ltd., 1365 Pracharaj 1 Rd., Bangsue, pg. 1237 IT
CPC/AJI (Thailand) Ltd., 84 Soi Samarnmitr, Ramkhamhaeng Rd., pg. 41 IT
CPC/AJI (Thailand) Ltd., 84 Soi Samarnmitr, Ramkhamhaeng Rd., pg. 224 PB
CPC/AJI (Thailand) Ltd., Bangpoo Plant, 470 Bangpoo MAi, pg. 40 IT
Canon Marketing (Thailand) Co., Ltd., 2F Indosuez House No. 152, pg. 263 IT
Capital Nomura Securities Public Company Limited, 21/3 Thai Wah Tower, Ground Fl, South Sathorn Road, pg. 957 IT
Carnation Manufacturing Co. (Thailand) Ltd., pg. 919 IT
W.I. Carr Indosuez Capital Asia Ltd., 11th Floor, Nava Finance Building, pg. 314 IT
W.I. Carr Ltd., 9th Floor, Nava Finance & Securities Building, pg. 314 IT
Cencar Limited, Golden Pavilion Bldg., 603, 153/3 Soi Mahatlek Luang 1, pg. 273 IT
Chada Thong Consultants Co., Ltd., 9th Fl., 1101 New Petchburi Rd., pg. 1239 IT
Chada Thong Properties Co., Ltd., 11th Fl., 1101 New Petchburi Rd., pg. 1239 IT
Chao Phaya Finance & Securities Co., Ltd., 1091/213-214 New Petchburi Rd., pg. 1239 IT
Charoen Seeds Company Ltd., 36 Soi Yenchit, Chan Rd, Yannawa, pg. 493 PB
The Chase Manhattan Bank, N.A., Siam Center, 965 Rama 1 Road, pg. 339 PB
Chichibu Onoda Cement Corporation-Bangkok, 5 Sitthivorakit Building, 9th Flsoi Pipat, pg. 284 IT
CIBA-GEIGY (MPL) Limited, pg. 978 IT
CIBA-GEIGY Services Limited-Technical Advisory Office, pg. 980 IT
CIBA-GEIGY (Thailand) Ltd., Ciba-Geigy Building, 159/30 Vibhavadi Rangsit Road, pg. 980 IT
CIBA Vision (Thailand) Limited, 10th Floor, Unit 1003-4, Monterey Tower, 2170 New Petchburi Rd, pg. 981 IT
Cigna Thai Company Limited, Sinthon Bldg., 12th fl., 132 Wireless Road, pg. 363 PB
Circle Airfreight Intl. (Thailand) Ltd., Rm 301-302, 3rd Floor, Ruamrudee 3 Bldg., 5 1/2 Soi Ruamrudee, pg. 372 PB
Club Andaman Beach Resort Co., Ltd., 1st Fl., Rart Xalerm Bldg., 319/15-19 Wiphawadi Rangsit Rd., pg. 1239 IT
Colgate-Palmolive (Thailand) Ltd., 19 Off Sunthorn Kosa Rd., Klong Toey, pg. 399 PB
Commerzbank AG Representative Office-Thailand, 13th Floor, Regent House, 183 Rujadamri Road, pg. 312 IT
Comstream, A Spar Company, Olympia Thai Tower, 444 Rachadaphisek Rd., 15th Floor, pg. 1288 IT
The Concrete Products and Aggregate Co., Ltd., 1516 Pracharaj 1 Road, Bangsue, pg. 1238 IT
The Concrete Products and Aggregate Industry Co., Ltd., 123 Moo 5, Romklao Rd., Khlong Samprawet, pg. 1237 IT
Corro-Coat (Thailand) Ltd., 5th Fl. Okakarn Bldg., 26/15 Soi Chidlom Ploenchit Rd., pg. 715 IT
Credit Agricole (CNCA) Representative Office-Bangkok, Kian Gwan House, 8th Fl., 140 Wireless Rd., pg. 341 IT
Credit Commercial de France, c/o Franco-Pacific, 8th Floor, Mahatun Plaza., pg. 343 IT
CUNA Mutual Group-Thailand, 56/2 Moo 3, pg. 297 PV
DIC Trading Co., Ltd., 21st Fl., Sermmit Tower, 159 Soi Asoke, Sukhumvit 21 Road, pg. 372 IT
DKB Leasing (Thailand) Co., Ltd., 10th Floor, Bubhajit Bldg., 20 North Sathorn Rd., pg. 362 IT
Dai-Ichi Kangyo Bank, Ltd.-Bangkok, 11th Fl., Bubhajit Bldg., 20 North Sathorn Rd., pg. 361 IT
Daihatsu-Phranakorn Motor Co., Ltd., 108 Vipawadi Rangsit Road, pg. 365 IT
Dainippon Ink & Chemicals (Thailand) Co., Ltd., 21st Fl., Sermmit Tower, 159 Soi Asoke, Sukhumvit 21 Road, pg. 372 IT
Daiwa Bank-Bangkok, 13th Fl., Regent House Bldg., 183 Rajdamri Rd., Pathumwan, pg. 373 IT
Danzas (Thailand) Limited, 89/2 Viphawadee Rangsit Road, Don Muang-Airport Mini Office, pg. 383 IT
Dell Computer Co., Ltd., One Pacific Place, 140 Sukhumvit Road, pg. 496 PB
Dentsply (Thailand) Limited, 13th Floor Panjathani Tower, pg. 500 PB
Dentsu (Thailand) Ltd., 6th Floor, Boonmitr Bldg., 138 Silom Road, pg. 394 IT
Dentsu Young & Rubicam Ltd. (Bangkok), 19th-20th Fls., Grand Amarin, Tower, 1550 New Petchburi Rd., pg. 325 PV
Det Norske Veritas, Unit C, 14th Fl., Ocean Twr. 1, 170/43 New Rachadapisek Rd., pg. 397 IT
Deutsche Bank AG (Bangkok), 21, South Sathorn Rd., pg. 404 IT
Dimeq South East Asia Ltd., 1st Floor Bank of America Bldg, 2/2 Wireless Road, pg. 389 IT
Dimet (Thailand) Ltd., pg. 129 IT
Dow Jones Markets (Thailand) Ltd., 942/151-2 Charn Issara Tower, Rama IV, Suriyawong, Bangrak, pg. 525 PB

PB - *U.S. Public Companies Volume*
PV - *U.S. Private Companies Volume*
IT - *International Public & Private Companies Volume*

Dresdner Bank AG, 33/88 Suriwong Rd., Ste. 1706, pg. 419 **IT**
Dulmison (Thailand) Co. Ltd., 133/2 Thai Military Bank Bldg., pg. 893 **IT**
Dumez-GTM Representative Office, 4/F Kian Gwan Building, pg. 823 **IT**
DYWIDAG-Systems International Co., Ltd., 408/150 Phaholyothin Place, 35th Floor, pg. 424 **IT**
ECI Telecom (Thailand), Ban Chang Glas Haus 11th Fl., pg. 643 **IT**
EMI (Thailand) Limited/Audiovision Limited, 1090/183 New Petchburi Rd., pg. 427 **IT**
ESAB (Thailand) Ltd., 889 Srinakarin Rd., pg. 282 **IT**
Eastern Sea Laem Chabang Terminal Co., Ltd., Alongside Express Way, 250 New Rd., pg. 1239 **IT**
Ebara (Thailand) Limited, 3rd Fl., Acme Bldg., 125 Petchburi Rd., pg. 432 **IT**
Electrolux Thailand Co. Ltd., Electrolux Bldg., pg. 444 **IT**
Energy Technology Co. Ltd., 70/11 Srinakarin Road, Nongbon, Prakanong, pg. 550 **IT**
Ericsson Communications (Thailand) Ltd., 99/349 Chaengwatana Rd., Don Muang, pg. 1366 **IT**
Ericsson Telephone Corporation Far East AB, 99/349 Chaengwatana Rd., Don Muang, pg. 1368 **IT**
Ericsson Thai Networks Company Ltd., 15th Fl., Chokchai Bldg., 690 Sukhumvit Rd., pg. 1368 **IT**
Esso Standard Thailand Ltd., 3195/17-29 Rama IV Road, pg. 602 **PB**
EURO RSCG Partnership, 8th Fl., Sino-Thai Tower, 32/29 Sukhumvit 21, pg. 602 **IT**
Eyecare (Thailand) Limited, pg. 982 **IT**
Fanuc Thai Limited, 8th Fl., Platong Karat Bldg., 448 Rachada Rd., pg. 478 **IT**
Fidelio Thailand Co. Ltd., 1525 Fidelio Building, Srivara in Town, pg. 1106 **IT**
FINANCE ONE PUBLIC COMPANY LIMITED, One Sathorn Bldg., 119 S. Sathom Rd., pg. 484 **IT**
First Asia Securities Limited, 7th Fl., Bank of Asia Bldg., 191 S. Sathom Rd., pg. 485 **IT**
Fluor Daniel Thailand Ltd., BB Bldg., Ste. 2108, 54 Asoke Rd., pg. 660 **IT**
Frigoscandia Food Process Systems AB, Level 23, C.P. Towere, 313 Silom Rd., pg. 606 **PB**
Frionor (Thailand) Ltd., 1, Soi Klueynamtai, Rama 4, pg. 516 **IT**
Fruehling Cosmetics Co. Ltd., 10/12-13 Soi Daeng Udom, pg. 1490 **IT**
Fuchs Lubricants (Thailand) Ltd., 5th Floor Nai Lert Tower, 2/4 Wireless Road, pg. 517 **IT**
Fuji Photo Film (Thailand) Ltd., S.P. Bldg., 8th Fl., 388 Phaholyothin Rd., pg. 525 **IT**
Furukawa Metal (Thailand) Co., Ltd., 121 Mahaton Plaza 12th 888, Ploenchit Road, pg. 531 **IT**
GCMP (Thailand) Ltd., 5/F, Asoke Towers, 219/14-15 Sukhumvit 21 Road, pg. 108 **IT**
Generale Bank, C.P. Tower 22nd Fl., 313 Silom Rd., pg. 547 **IT**
Givaudan-Roure Ltd., pg. 1120 **IT**
Glory Kawasaki Motors Co., Ltd., 222/1 Asok-Din Daeng, pg. 947 **IT**
Goldman, Sachs & Co., 2nd Floor, Montathip Ct., The Regent Bangkok, pg. 462 **PV**
Goodyear-Thailand Ltd., Sirinee Bldg., 518/4 Ploenchit Road, pg. 753 **PB**
B. Grimm, 164314 Phetburi Rd., 10310, pg. 713 **PB**
HSBC Capital (Thailand) Limited, 7/F, HongkongBank Bldg., 64 Silom Rd., pg. 582 **IT**
HSBC Finance & Securities (Thailand) Limited, 7/F, Hong Kong Bank Building, 64 Silom Road, pg. 588 **IT**
Hakuhodo Bangkok Co., Ltd., Ocean Tower II, 39F, Soi Wattna, Sukhumvit 21 Rd., pg. 588 **IT**
Hanwa Co., Ltd.-Bangkok Branch, Rm. 907 Kasemkij Bldg., 120 Silom Rd., pg. 595 **IT**
Haworth Thailand Company Ltd., 10th M. Thai Tower, All Seasons Place, Ste. 1005-6, pg. 512 **PV**
Henkel Thai Ltd., pg. 613 **IT**
Hewlett-Packard (Thailand) Ltd., 11th Fl., Pacific Pl., 140 Sukhumvit Rd., pg. 822 **PB**
Hitachi Zosen Bangkok, 7th Fl., Harindhorn Tower, 54 North Sathorn Rd., pg. 623 **IT**
The Hokkaido Takushoku Bank, Ltd. (Bangkok), Diethelm Towers, Tower A, Ste., 1502, 93/1 Wireless Rd., pg. 627 **IT**
Philipp Holzmann (Thai) Ltd, 23rd Fl. Lake Rajada Complex, 193 Ratchadapisek Rd., pg. 634 **IT**
Home Electronics Ltd., China-roj Building, 27 Soi Prachanukul Ratchadapisek Road, pg. 1239 **IT**
Honeywell Systems (Thailand) Ltd., Unit 15-02 Times Square Bldg., 246 Sukhumvit Rd., pg. 835 **PB**
Hospitality Int. Thailande, 33/JJ6 Wall St. Tower, Surawongse Rd., pg. 21 **IT**
Hydro Thai Ltd., 630/32-34 Phapinklao Road, pg. 963 **IT**
IBM Thailand Company Limited, IBM Building, 1 Silcom Road, pg. 897 **PB**
ICI ASIATIC (Agriculture) Co. Ltd., 1168/94 31st Fl., Lumpini Tower, pg. 664 **IT**
IDC Thailand, 14th Fl., Orakarn Bldg., 26 Chidlom Rd., pg. 571 **PV**
IFCT Finance & Securities Co. Ltd., 10th-12th Floors, IFCT Bldg. 2, 1770 New Petchburi Road, Bangkapi, pg. 677 **IT**
IFCT Nomura/JAFCO Holdings Co., Ltd., IFCT Bldg., 3rd Floor, 1770 New Petchburi Road, pg. 677 **IT**
ING Bank Bangkok, Silom Complex Building, 24th Floor, 191 Silom Road, pg. 648 **IT**
ITW (Thailand) Co. Ltd., 3rd Fl. Tanjasri Bldg., 1091/82-83 Nakornluang Shopping Center, pg. 869 **IT**
Imation Representative Office, 9th Fl., Na-Nakorn Bldg., 99/439 Chengwatana Rd., pg. 870 **PB**
Inchcape Thailand Ltd., Inchcape House, 2160 Ramkhamhaeng Rd., pg. 672 **IT**

The Industrial Bank of Japan, Limited (Bangkok), Thai Obayashi Bldg. 15th Fl., Rajdamri, 161 Rajdamri Rd., Lumpini, pg. 675 **IT**
THE INDUSTRIAL FINANCE CORPORATION OF THAILAND, 1770 New Petchburi Rd., pg. 677 **IT**
The International Commercial Bank of China, 36/12 P.S. Tower, Asoke, pg. 683 **IT**
INTERNATIONAL COSMETICS CO., LTD., 757/10 Soi Pradoo 1, pg. 684 **IT**
International Flavors & Fragrances (Thailand) Ltd., 10th Fl., Kasemku Bldg., 120 Silom Rd., pg. 899 **PB**
Island Resort Hotel Co. Ltd., 134/5-6 Silom Rd., pg. 1239 **IT**
Isuzu Engine Manufacturing co., (Thailand) Ltd., Lad Kiabang Indus. Est., 122 Moo Four, pg. 693 **IT**
Isuzu Technical Center (Thailand) Co., Ltd., 23rd Floor, Rasa Town, 555 Paholyothin Rd., pg. 693 **IT**
Italthai Carbone CY. Ltd., 2 Soi Soonvijai-3, pg. 1030 **IT**
Ito-Yokado Bangkok Liaison Office, 8th Floor, Kian House, pg. 694 **IT**
Janssen Pharmaceutical Ltd., P.O. Box 31, pg. 930 **PB**
Jardine Fleming Thanakom Securities Limited, 29th Fl. Silom Complex, 191 Silom Rd., pg. 494 **IT**
Jardine Matheson (Thailand) Ltd., 21st Fl., Times Square Bldg., 246 Sukhumvit Road, pg. 705 **IT**
Johnson & Johnson Medical Thailand, pg. 931 **PB**
Johnson & Johnson Ltd., Chalongkrung Rd., pg. 931 **PB**
S.C. Johnson & Son, Ltd., P.O. Box 11-1140, pg. 593 **PV**
Jotun Thailand Ltd., 8th Fl. Orakarn Bldg., 26/24-25 Soi Chidlom, Ploenchit Road, pg. 715 **IT**
KSB Pumps Co. Ltd., pg. 721 **IT**
Kao Commercial Company Limited, 161 Thai Ohbayashi Bldg., pg. 718 **IT**
Kao Industrial Company, (Thailand), Ltd., 161 Thai Ohbayashi Bldg., pg. 718 **IT**
Kawasaki Steel Co., Room 504, Dusit Thani Bldg., Rama 4 Road, pg. 726 **IT**
Kemira Thai Ltd., Metro Bldg., 7th Fl., 180-184 Rajawongse Rd., pg. 728 **IT**
Kendall-Gammatron Ltd., 882/87-88 Krungthon Juri Road, pg. 1648 **IT**
Kimberly-Clark Thailand Ltd., 41st Floor, United Center, 323 Silom Road, pg. 959 **PB**
Kintetsu World Express (Thailand) Co., Ltd., Talomsin Bldg., 6th Fl., 227/73 Rama 3 Rd., pg. 733 **IT**
Kodak (Thailand) Ltd., 197 Vipavadi Rangsit Rd., pg. 555 **PB**
Konica (Thailand) Co., Ltd., 11th Fl., Sermmit Tower, 159 Assoke Rd., Sukhumvit 21, pg. 749 **IT**
Korn/Ferry International, 12th Fl. Rajapark Bldg., 163 Soi Asoke (21), pg. 633 **PV**
Kredietbank Representative Office (Bangkok), Thaniya Plaza Bldg., 23rd Fl., 52, Silom Road, pg. 760 **IT**
Krung Thai IBJ Leasing Co., 15th Fl., Thai Obayashi Bldg., Rajdamri, 161 Rajdamri Rd., Lumpini, pg. 676 **IT**
Kubota Corp.-Bangkok Office, Thaniya Bldg., 4th Fl., 62 Silom Rd., pg. 762 **IT**
Kyowa Hakko (Thailand) Ltd., 101/11 Srinakarintra Rd., pg. 778 **IT**
Laporte Industries (Singapore) Pte Limited, 12th Fl., Sino-Thai Tower, Sukhumvit Rd., pg. 803 **IT**
Laporte (Thailand) Ltd., 12th Fl., Sino-Thai Tower, 32/33 Asoke Rd., pg. 803 **IT**
Lat Krabang Pumping Facilities Project, On-Nuch Road, Lat Krabang, pg. 943 **IT**
Lever Brothers (Thailand) Ltd., 1037 Pleonchit Arcade, Pleonchit Rd., 5th Fl., pg. 1437 **IT**
Liebherr-Thailand Co., Ltd., 19th Floor-Wall Street Tower, 33/96 Surawong Road, pg. 809 **IT**
Lucent Technologies Thailand Inc., 21th Fl., Silom Complex Bldg., 191 Silom Rd., pg. 1019 **PB**
MHI-Mahajak Air Conditioners Co., Ltd. (MACO), Lat Krabang Industrial Estate, Phase 3, 200 Moo 4, Lamplatiew, pg. 874 **IT**
MMC Sittipol Company, Ltd., 1990 Ramkhamhaeng Rd., pg. 876 **IT**
Mahajak International Electric Co., Ltd., Mahajak Bldg., 4th Fl., #46 Soi 3, Sukhumvit Rd., pg. 522 **IT**
McCormick Thailand, Inc., pg. 1067 **PB**
Media Transia Thailand Ltd., 14th Fl. Orakaarn Bldg., 26 Chidlom Rd., 10330, pg. 570 **PV**
Microsep International Thailand, Ltd., 6th Floor, Kongboonma Building, 699 Silom Road, pg. 143 **PB**
Microsoft (Thailand) Limited, pg. 1108 **PB**
Mirano (Thailand) Limited, 4th Fl., K.C.C. Bldg., 2 Soi Suksawitthaya, Silom 9, pg. 196 **IT**
Mitsiam International, Ltd., 6th Fl. Boon-Mit Bldg., pg. 880 **IT**
Mitsubishi Chemical (Thailand) Co., Ltd., 9th Floor, Regent House, 183, Rajdamri Road, pg. 871 **IT**
Mitsui & Co. (Thailand) Ltd., 6th Fl., Boon-Mit Bldg., pg. 882 **IT**
Mitsukoshi Ltd.-Bangkok Office, Rm. No. 942/135A Charn Issara, Tower, Rama IV Rd., pg. 884 **IT**
Mobil Oil Thailand Limited, pg. 1119 **IT**
Modular Samco Co., Ltd., 70/9 Soi Ekamai Sukhumvit Rd., pg. 1239 **IT**
Monsanto Thailand Ltd., P.O.Box 2316,17th Flr., Silom Center Building, pg. 1118 **IT**
J.P. Morgan Securities Asia Ltd., 130 Sindhorn Tower III, 27th Fl., Unit 3273, pg. 1131 **PV**
Motorola (Thailand) Limited, 140 Pacific Place Bldg., 10th Floor, pg. 1140 **PB**
Multi-Credit Corporation of Thailand Ltd., 18th Floor, Kian Gwan Bldg. 2, 140/1 Wireless Rd., pg. 374 **IT**
The Mutual Fund Co., Ltd., Lake Rajada Bldg.,30th-32nd Fl, 193-195 Tarchadaphisek Road, pg. 677 **IT**
NIM Co., Ltd., 41 Fl. UFM New Bldg., 205, pg. 948 **IT**
NKK Corporation-Thailand, 11th Floor, Ramaland Bldg., 952 Rama IV Road, Bangrak, pg. 903 **IT**

NSK Bearings (Thailand) Co., Ltd., 25th Fl., RS Tower, 121/76-77, Rachadaphisek Rd., pg. 903 **IT**
NYK Shipping Service (Thailand) Co., Ltd., 10th & 11th Floors, Ocean Insurance Bldg., pg. 942 **IT**
NAKORNTHON BANK PUBLIC COMPANY LIMITED, 90 N. Sathorn Rd., pg. 904 **IT**
Nalco Chemical Co. (Thailand) Ltd., 60/19-20 Soi Amonpunnivet 4, Vibhavadee-Rangsit Road, pg. 1150 **PB**
The Navakij Insurance Co., Ltd., 18th Fl., Sathorn Thani Bldg., 90 North Sathorn Rd., pg. 61 **IT**
Nestle Asean (Thailand) Ltd., pg. 920 **IT**
Nestle Products (Thailand), Inc., pg. 921 **IT**
Nestle (Thailand) Ltd., 18/F, Amarin Tower, 502 Ploenchit Rd., pg. 921 **IT**
Nissho Iwai (Thailand) Limited Partnership, 17th Floor, Thaniya Plaza Bldg, 52 Silom Road, pg. 948 **IT**
Nokia Telecommunications (Thailand) Ltd., 108 Bangkok Thai Tower Bldg., 16th fl., pg. 954 **IT**
Nordic Power Invest-South East Asia Office, Times Square Building 25th Fl., 246 Sukhumvit Road (Soi 12-14), pg. 1453 **IT**
North West Water (Thailand) Ltd., 19th Floor, Pacific Tower. 21 Vibhavadi Rangsit Road, pg. 1444 **IT**
Novo Nordisk Pharma (Thailand) Ltd., 139 Sethiwan Tower, 9th Floor, Pan Road, Bangrak Area, pg. 988 **IT**
Nutritional Products (Thailand) Ltd., pg. 922 **IT**
OCE (Thailand) Ltd., pg. 995 **IT**
Obayashi Corporation-Bangkok, 16th Floor, Thai Obayashi Building, pg. 995 **IT**
Oracle Systems Thailand, 23rd Fl., CP Tower, 313 Silom Rd., pg. 1228 **PB**
The Oriental Hotel (Thailand) pcl, 48 Oriental Avenue, pg. 704 **IT**
Osmonics Asia/Pacific Ltd., 1044/8 Soi Sukhumvit 44/2, pg. 1234 **IT**
M.E. Otsuka Co., Ltd., 665 Soi Onnuch Sukhumvit Road, pg. 1014 **IT**
Outokumpu (Thailand) Co., Ltd., 22nd Fl. Silom Complex Bldg., 191 Silom Rd., Silom, Bangrak, pg. 1016 **IT**
PDTL Trading Co., Ltd., 6th Fl., Panunee Bldg., 518/3 Ploenchit Rd., pg. 1313 **IT**
Pacific Plastics (Thailand) Ltd., 75 Soi Rubia, Sukhumvit 42 Rd., pg. 1238 **IT**
Paiboon Watana Co., Ltd., 9/1, Dejo Rd., pg. 1350 **IT**
Palm Courtt Bangkok, 27 Soi Saladaeng 1, pg. 1212 **IT**
Panalpina World Transport (Thailand), pg. 1023 **IT**
PATRA CERAMICS CO., LTD., 5A Floor, 91/1 Rama II, pg. 1024 **IT**
Pechiney Singapore, Wall Street Tower, 17th Fl., 88/84 Surawongse Rd., pg. 1031 **IT**
PETROLEUM AUTHORITY OF THAILAND, 555 Vibhavadi Rangsit Rd., pg. 1046 **IT**
Pfizer Limited, Ocean Insurance Bldg.,17th Fl., 163 Surawongse Rd., pg. 1282 **IT**
Pharmacia & Upjohn Company Limited, P.O. Box 245, pg. 1049 **IT**
Phelps Dodge Thailand Ltd., 6th Fl., Panunee Bldg., 518/3 Ploenchit Rd., pg. 1313 **IT**
Pioneer Hi-Bred (Thailand) Co., Ltd., 60/1 Monririn Building, 5th, Floor, Phaholyothin 8 Road, pg. 1299 **PB**
Pornpat Chemicals Co., Ltd., 787 Sukhumvit Rd. (SOI 43), Bangkok Bank Branch Bldg., 4 Fl., pg. 1394 **IT**
POSTRADE Banhkok Office, 14th Fl., Sino-Thai Tower, No. 32/35, Sukhumvit Road 21, pg. 1062 **IT**
Quality Coffee Products Ltd., pg. 922 **IT**
Raychem Thai Limited, 3rd Fl., Vanissa Bldg., 29 Chidlom Rd., pg. 1363 **PB**
Reader's Digest (Thailand) Limited, 175 Sathorn City Tower, 18th Floor, South Sathorn Road, pg. 1368 **PB**
Rentokil (Thailand) Ltd, pg. 1286 **IT**
Rhone-Poulenc Chemicals Thailand (Ltd.), 3rd Fl., VTT 1, 3195 Rama IV Rd., pg. 1112 **IT**
Richardson-Vicks Ltd., White Group Bldg., 75 SOi Rubia, pg. 1333 **PB**
Riche Monde (Bangkok) Ltd, 10th-11th Fl., Diethel Towers, 93/1 Wireless Road, pg. 783 **IT**
Robert Bosch Ltd., 32 Saladaeng Rd., pg. 205 **IT**
Roche Thailand Ltd., 280 New Rd., pg. 1122 **IT**
Rovithai Limited, pg. 1122 **IT**
SBCS Company Limited, 12th Floor, Ramaland Bldg. 952, Rama IV Road, Bangrak, pg. 1181 **IT**
SCF Finance & Securities Co., Ltd., 2922/209 Charnissara Tower2, 12A, 15-17th Floor, New Petchburi, pg. 1239 **IT**
SCT Co., Ltd., 1 Siam Cement Rd., Bagsue, pg. 1238 **IT**
SKF (Thailand) Ltd., 72/70 Rama III Road, pg. 1159 **IT**
SNC-Lavalin, 1045/5 Soi Nai Lert, 3rd Floor, pg. 1162 **IT**
SR Risk Management Services Ltd., 24th Floor, Tower 2, Muang Thai-Phatra Complex, pg. 1333 **IT**
SV-Acer Co. Ltd., pg. 22 **IT**
Sahakol Chassis Co., Ltd., 1677/4 Phaholyothin Rd., pg. 1239 **IT**
SAHAPATHANAPIBUL PUBLIC COMPANY LIMITED, 2156 New Petchburi Road, pg. 1169 **IT**
The Sakura Bank - Bangkok Branch, Boon-Mitr Bldg., 138 Silom Rd., pg. 1179 **IT**
Sandoz Chemicals (Thailand) Ltd., pg. 984 **IT**
Sandoz Pharmaceuticals Ltd., pg. 985 **IT**
Sanpaolo-Bangkok Representative Office, Thaniya Plaza, 27th Fl., 52 Silom Rd., pg. 691 **IT**
Sanyo (Thailand) Co., Ltd., Sanyo Bldg. 601, Asoke-Dindaeng Rd., pg. 1193 **IT**
Sanyo Universal Electric Public Co., Ltd., 19 Sukhumvit Rd., Soi 103, pg. 1192 **IT**
Sato Co., Ltd.-Bangkok, 19th Floor, Thai Wah Tower 2, 21/135-136, South Sathorn Rd., pg. 1197 **IT**
Schering Chemicals Ltd., pg. 1204 **IT**
Securities One Limited, Bldg. One,, 99 Wlreless Rd., pg. 485 **IT**

PB - U.S. Public Companies Volume
PV - U.S. Private Companies Volume
IT - International Public & Private Companies Volume

Shandwick/Presko Ltd., 20th Fl., TST Tower, 21 Vibhavadi-Rangsit Rd., pg. 1227 **IT**
Sharp Thebnakorn Co., Ltd. (Bangkok), 664 Siphraya Rd., pg. 1230 **IT**
Shell Company of Thailand Ltd, Shell House, 10 Soonthornkosa Rd., pg. 1140 **IT**
Siam Algae Co., Ltd., 21st Fl., Sermmit Tower, 159 Soi Asoke, Sukhumvit 21, pg. 372 **IT**
Siam Cellulose Co., Ltd., 1 Siam Cement Rd., Bangsue, pg. 1238 **IT**
THE SIAM CEMENT PUBLIC COMPANY LIMITED, 1 Siam Cement Road, Bangsue, pg. 1237 **IT**
Siam Chemical Industry Co., Ltd., 17th Fl., Thai Ohbayashi Bldg., Rajdamri, 161 Rajdamri Road, pg. 372 **IT**
SIAM CITY BANK PUBLIC COMPANY LIMITED, 1101 New Petchburi Rd., pg. 1239 **IT**
Siam City Credit Finance & Securities Co., Ltd., 518/5 7th Fl. Maneeya Center Bldg., pg. 1239 **IT**
Siam City Factoring Co., Ltd., 2922/205-206 Charnissara Tower, 11th Floor, New Petchburi Road, pg. 1239 **IT**
Siam City-Showa Leasing Co., Ltd., 1091/179-181 New Petchburi Rd., pg. 1239 **IT**
Siam City Syndicate Finance & Securities Co., Ltd., 333 United Tower Soi Thonglor, Sukumvit Road, pg. 1239 **IT**
The Siam Construction Steel Co., Ltd., 1 Siam Cement Rd., Bangsue, pg. 1238 **IT**
The Siam Fibre-Cement Co., Ltd., 1 Siam Cement Rd., Bangsue, pg. 1238 **IT**
Siam Furukawa Co., Ltd., 85/2 Moo 13, Sukhapibarn 2 Rd., Bangchan, pg. 1238 **IT**
The Siam Gypsum Industry Co., Ltd., 1 Siam Cement Road, Bangsue, pg. 1238 **IT**
The Siam Iron and Steel Co., Ltd., 1 Siam Cement Rd., Bangsue, pg. 1238 **IT**
Siam Kiki Co., Ltd., 2236/1 New Petchburi Road, pg. 1528 **IT**
Siam Kraft Industry Co., Ltd., 1 Siam Cement Rd., Bangsue, pg. 1238 **IT**
The Siam Kubota Industry Co., Ltd., 1 Siam Cement Rd., Bangsue, pg. 763 **IT**
Siam Magotteaux Co., Ltd., 1 Siam Cement Rd., Bangsue, pg. 1238 **IT**
Siam Makro Ltd., 3498 Lardprao Rd., pg. 1156 **IT**
The Siam Nawaloha Foundry Co., Ltd., 1 Siam Cement Rd., Bangsue, pg. 1238 **IT**
Siam Perstorp Co., Ltd., 51 Moo 2 Poochao Road, Bangyaprak, Prapradaeng, pg. 1039 **IT**
Siam Perstorp Co Ltd., 947 Thotsaphol Land 3 Building, 8th Floor, pg. 1039 **IT**
The Siam Pipe Industry Co., Ltd., 1 Siam Cement Rd., Bangsue, pg. 1238 **IT**
The Siam Pipe Products Co., Ltd., 1 Siam Cement Rd., Bangsue, pg. 1238 **IT**
The Siam Pulp and Paper Co., Ltd., 1 Siam Cement Rd., Bangsue, pg. 1238 **IT**
The Siam Sanitary Fittings Co., Ltd., 30th Fl., Tower A, Muang Thai Prathara Complex, pg. 1410 **IT**
Siam Sanitary Ware Co., Ltd., 30th Fl., Tower A, Muang Thai Prathara Complex, pg. 1410 **IT**
The Siam Sanwa Industrial Credit Co., Ltd., 1st-4th Fl., Sintorn Tower II, 130-132 Wireless Road, Lumpini, pg. 1190 **IT**
The Siam Sanwa Trilease Co., Ltd., 15th Fl., Sino-Thai Tower 32/39, pg. 1190 **IT**
Siam Synthetic Latex Co., Ltd., 75 Soi Rubia, Sukhumvit 42 Rd., pg. 1238 **IT**
Siam Toyota Manufacturing Co., Ltd., Lamplatiew Sub-District, No. 102 Group 4, pg. 1239 **IT**
Siam Yamato Steel Co., Ltd., 1 Siam Cement Rd., Bangsue, pg. 1238 **IT**
Signetics Thailand Co., Ltd., 303 Changwatana Rd., pg. 1055 **IT**
Singapore Tourist Promotion Board - Bangkok, c/o Burson-Marstellar, 16/F, 25 Alma Link Building, pg. 1254 **IT**
Singkee Co., Ltd., 25/9 Pibulsongkram Road, pg. 764 **IT**
Sinochem Representative Office - Thailand, Asoke Tower, 14th Fl., 219/47, Sukhumvit 21 Rd., pg. 1256 **IT**
Snow Brand Milk Products Co., Ltd., 2nd Flr., Jetro Bldg., 159 Rajadamri Rd., pg. 1272 **IT**
Spar Business Development, Olympia Thai Tower, 444 Rachadaphisek Road, 15th Fl., pg. 1288 **IT**
The Sri Muang Insurance Co., Ltd., Kamolsukosol Bldg., 10th & 11th Fls., pg. 1392 **IT**
Standard Chartered Bank (Thailand), 990 Rama IV Road,e Bldg., pg. 1296 **IT**
Standard Chartered Securities Asia Limited, SNC Tower, 8th Fl., 33 Sukhumvit Soi 4, Klong Toey, pg. 1296 **IT**
Standard Chartered Thailand Limited, 13th Fl., Q. House Convent, Bldg., 946 Rama IV Rd., pg. 1296 **IT**
Statoil (Thailand) Ltd., BB Bldg., Ste. 2106, 54 Asoke Rd., Sukhumvit 21, pg. 1298 **IT**
Steelcase International Bangkok (Thailand), Ste. 1502, 15th fl, Modernform, Tower, pg. 1038 **PV**
Sulzer (Thailand) Ltd., pg. 1307 **IT**
Sumikin Bussan International (Thailand) Ltd., 10th Fl., Thaniya Bldg., 62 Silom Rd., pg. 1308 **IT**
The Sumitomo Bank, Ltd.-Bangkok International Banking Facility, 11th Floor, Ramaland Building, No. 952 Rama IV Rd., Kwaeng Suriyawong, pg. 1309 **IT**
Sumitomo Electric Communications Engineering (Thailand), Ltd., 1524/1-3 Phiboonsongkram Rd., pg. 1314 **IT**
Sumitomo Electric (Thailand) Ltd., 15th Fl., B.B. Bldg., 54 Sukhumvit 21 Rd., pg. 1314 **IT**
Sumitomo Electric Wiring Systems (Thailand) Ltd., pg. 1314 **IT**
Sun Microsystems of California, 18/F Sathorn Thani Tower II, 92 North Sathorn Road, pg. 1532 **PB**
Svenska Thailand Ltd., pg. 1187 **IT**
SwedPower (Thailand) Ltd., 39/1 Ladprao 124 Road, pg. 1453 **IT**

Swiss Bank Corporation, Alma Link Building, 18th Floor, 25 Soi Chidlom, pg. 1330 **IT**
Symix Systems Inc., Nai Lert Bldg., 71F, 87 Sukhumvit Rd., pg. 1547 **PB**
Synercie Tokyu DMB&B Ltd., 7/F Ban Chang-Glas Haus Bldg., 1 Sukhumvit 25, Sukhumvit 48, pg. 305 **PV**
Toa-Uni Chemicals Ltd., 107 Sulchumirt 63 Ekamai Rd., pg. 460 **PB**
Taisei (Thailand) Co., Ltd., Grand Amarin Tower Building, 1550 New Petchburi Road, 8th Floor, pg. 1347 **IT**
Takashimaya (Thailand) Co., Ltd., 24th Fl., Charn Issara Twr. II, 2922/281 New Petchburi Rd., Huay Khwang, pg. 1350 **IT**
Takeda Chemie Thai Co., Ltd., Chamnan Phenjati Business Ctr. 15th Fl., 65/125 Rama IX Rd., pg. 1350 **IT**
Takeda (Thailand), Ltd., 8th Fl., Si Ayutthaya Bldg., 487/1 Si Ayutthaya Rd., pg. 1351 **IT**
Tatung Thailand Company Ltd., Tower, Soi Wathong, 17th Floor, 89/24-25 Amornphan 205, pg. 1357 **IT**
Telefon AB LM Ericsson Thailand, 14th Floor, Thansetthakij Bldg, 222 Vibhavadee Rangsit Rd., pg. 1370 **IT**
Telefonaktiebolaget LM Ericsson Thailand Branch, 15th Fl., Chokchai Bldg., 690 Sukhumvit Rd., pg. 1371 **IT**
Terumo-Bangkok, B.B. Bldg. #1206, 54 Asoke Rd., pg. 1376 **IT**
THAI AIRWAYS INTERNATIONAL LTD., 89 Vibhavadi Rangsit Rd., pg. 1381 **IT**
Thai Bridgestone Co., Ltd., 2nd Fl., pg. 214 **IT**
Thai Caprolactam, Ltd., 17F., LPN Tower, 216/73-75 Nanglinchee Rd., pg. 1427 **IT**
Thai Ceramic Co., Ltd., 1 Siam Cement Rd., Bangsue, pg. 1238 **IT**
Thai Chemical & Engineering Co. Ltd., 7th Fl., UFM New Bldg., 205 Rajawongse Road, pg. 949 **IT**
Thai Compressor Manufacturing Co., Ltd., 212/62 Pattanakarn Road, pg. 874 **IT**
Thai Containers Industry Co., Ltd., 1 Siam Cement Rd., Bangsue, pg. 1238 **IT**
Thai Containers Ltd., 1 Siam Cement Rd., Bangsue, pg. 1238 **IT**
Thai Containers Ratchaburi (1989) Co., Ltd., 1 Siam Cement Rd., Bangsue, pg. 1238 **IT**
Thai Copper Rod Co., Ltd., 6th Fl., Panunee Bldg., 518/3 Ploenchit Rd., pg. 1314 **IT**
Thai Engineering Products Co., Ltd., 1 Siam Cement Rd., Bangsue, pg. 1238 **IT**
Thai Farmers Heller Factoring Co., Ltd., Phatra Insurance Building, 1st Floor, 252 Ratchadapisek Rd., pg. 521 **IT**
Thai Foods International Co., Ltd., 9th Fl., Regent House, 183 Rajdamri Rd., pg. 1351 **IT**
Thai Fuji Finance and Securities Company Ltd., Q House Convent Bldg., 7th Fl., 38 Convent Rd., pg. 521 **IT**
Thai Furukawa Unicomm Construction Co., Ltd., 68 Moo-5, Soi Sangsri,Phayasuren Road, pg. 531 **IT**
Thai Glass Industries Ltd., pg. 129 **IT**
Thai Hakuhodo Co., Ltd., 12th Fl., Diethelm Tower Bldg., pg. 589 **IT**
Thai Industrial Gasses Public Co. Ltd., P.O. Box 1026, pg. 122 **IT**
Thai Investment & Securities Co. Ltd., 9th Fl., Boonmitr. Bldg., 138 Silom Rd., pg. 362 **IT**
Thai Kraft Paper Industry Co., Ltd., 1 Siam Cement Rd., Bangsue, pg. 1238 **IT**
Thai Master Builders Co. Ltd., pg. 986 **IT**
Thai Meiji Pharmaceutical Co., Ltd., Grand Fl., Regent House 183, Rajdamri Rd., pg. 856 **IT**
Thai Metal Processing Co., Ltd., 460/1-7 Siam Square, Section 4, Rama 1 Road, Pathumwan, pg. 531 **IT**
Thai Nippon Meat Packers Co., Ltd., Jetro Bldg. 3rd Floor, 159 Rajadamri Rd., pg. 936 **IT**
Thai Nishimatsu Construction Co., Ltd., 19th Fl., Sino-Thai Tower, 32/48 Sukhumvit 21 (Soi Asoke), pg. 943 **IT**
Thai NOK Company Ltd., pg. 507 **IT**
Thai Obayashi Corporation Limited, 12th Floor, Thai Obayashi Building 16, pg. 996 **IT**
Thai Orix Leasing Co., Ltd., 24th Floor, C.P. Tower Bldg., 313 Silom Road, Bangkok, pg. 677 **IT**
Thai Otsuka Pharmaceutical Co., Ltd., 11th Fl., Regent House 183, Rajdamri Rd., pg. 1014 **IT**
Thai Paper Co., Ltd., 1 Siam Cement Rd., Bangsue, pg. 1239 **IT**
Thai Polyethylene Co., Ltd., 1 Siam Cement Rd., Bangsue, pg. 1239 **IT**
Thai Sakura Finance & Securities Co., Ltd., 952 Rama IV Road, pg. 677 **IT**
Thai Sato Kogyo Co., Ltd., 19th Floor, Thai Wah Tower 2, 21/135-136, South Sathorn Rd., pg. 1198 **IT**
Thai Shimizu Co., Ltd., 11th Fl., Sethiwan Tower, 139 Pan Rd., pg. 1234 **IT**
Thai Soluble Coffee Company Ltd., 18/F, Amarin Tower, 500 Ploenchit Rd., pg. 922 **IT**
Thai Sports Garment Co., Ltd., 1024/90 Soi Jaturamitr, Rama 3 Rd., pg. 885 **IT**
Thai Sumiden Engineering and Construction Co., Ltd., 72/6-8 Srinakarintara Rd., pg. 1314 **IT**
Thai-Swedish Assembly Co. Ltd., 283 Sukhumvit Rd., pg. 1476 **IT**
Thai Takenaka International Ltd., Silom Complex, 26th Floor, 191 Silom Road, pg. 1352 **IT**
Thai Toray Textile Mills Public Company Limited, 10th Fl., Thaniya Building, 62 Silom Rd., pg. 1400 **IT**
Thai Toshiba Electric Industries Co., Ltd., 181/1 Tivanon Rd., pg. 1406 **IT**
Thai Wacoal Co., Ltd., 930/1 Soi Pradoo 1, pg. 1484 **IT**
Thai Yamazaki Co., Ltd., 1091/40 Soi Jaruat, New Petchburi Rd., pg. 1519 **IT**
Thana One Finance and Securities Limited, One Sathom Bldg., 119 S. Sathom Rd., Thungmahamek, pg. 485 **IT**
The Siam Fiberglass Co., Ltd., 1 Siam Cement Rd., Bangsue, pg. 1238 **IT**

Thoon Ruam Karn Co., Ltd., 9th Fl., Siam Thanakarn Bldg. 2, pg. 1239 **IT**
3M Thailand Limited, 12th Fl., Serm-mit Tower, 159 Asoke Rd., pg. 1607 **PB**
Tokio Marine South-East Servicing Company Limited, Kamolsukosol Bldg., 10th & 11th Fls., pg. 1393 **IT**
Tomco Co. Ltd., 133-137 Chakrawat Road, pg. 361 **PV**
Toray Fibers (Thailand), Ltd., 6th Fl Bubhajit Bldg., 20 North Sathorn Road, pg. 1400 **IT**
Toshiba Thailand Co., Ltd., 201 Viphavadi Rangsit Rd., pg. 1407 **IT**
Tourism Malaysia - Bangkok Office, Ground Floor, 315, South East Insurance Bldg., pg. 833 **IT**
Toyota Leasing (Thailand) Co., Ltd., 898 Ploenchit Tower, 18th Floor, Ploenchit Road, Lumpini, pg. 1414 **IT**
Tri Petch Isuzu Sales Co., Ltd., 1705 Phaholyothin Road, pg. 693 **IT**
Triton Oil Co. of Thailand (Bangkok), Shell House, 140 Wireless Rd., pg. 1640 **IT**
Tyco Grinnell Asia Pacific (Thailand) Limited, Ste. 4, Level 23 C.P. Tower, 313 Silom Rd., pg. 1651 **PB**
UBS Securities (East Asia) Limited Representative Office, Sintorn Building, Tower 3, 15th Floor Room 3152, pg. 1440 **IT**
Ua Withya Equipment Co., Ltd., 99 Surasak Rd., pg. 146 **IT**
UBE (Thailand) Co. Ltd., 18F, Thaniya Plaza Building, pg. 1427 **IT**
UNICORD PUBLIC CO. LTD., 606-608 Luang Road, pg. 1432 **IT**
Unimesa Co. Ltd., 2540 Sukumwit Rd., pg. 823 **PB**
Union Bank of Switzerland, Representative Office, Sindhorn Building, Tower III, 15th Floor, Room 3151, pg. 1441 **IT**
Union Daewoo Engineering & Construction Co., Ltd., 63/92 28th Fl., P.S. Tower, Sukhumvit 21, Asoke Rode, pg. 358 **IT**
Unocal Thailand, 5th Floor Tower III, 19 Ratahadaphisek Road, Chatuchak, pg. 1698 **PB**
Utell International-Thailand, Suite 2110, 21st Floor, B.B. Building, 54 Asoke Road, pg. 1099 **IT**
Van Leeuwen Pipe and Tube Thailand Ltd., 18th Floor, K.S.L. Tower, 503/34 Sri Ayudhya Road, pg. 1450 **IT**
Veritas DGC INC, C/OThai Shell Exploration &, Production Co., pg. 1137 **PV**
Viking Fertilizer Ltd., 630/32-34 Phapinklao Rd., pg. 964 **IT**
Volvo Thailand Ltd., SMC Bldg. 3/F, 283 Sukhumvit Rd., pg. 1476 **IT**
Votra (Thailand) Co Ltd., pg. 757 **IT**
Wackenhut Thailand Co., Ltd., 952 Sukhumvit, 71 Klong-Ton, 10110, pg. 1732 **IT**
Wan Thai Foods Industry Co., Ltd., Bangchan IndustrialEstate, Plan No. B-1, pg. 41 **IT**
Wander (Thailand) Ltd., pg. 986 **IT**
Wang Thailand Ltd., Alma Link Bldg., 10th Fl., 25 Soi Chidlom, pg. 1738 **PB**
Wellcome Thailand Ltd., 64/1-4 Pan Rd., Silom, pg. 553 **IT**
WestLB Bangkok, 18th Floor, Sintorn Building Tower III, pg. 1493 **IT**
Williams & Wilkins Asia Pacific Ltd., 5th Fl., The Seri Ctr., 12/90 M006, Srinakarin Rd., pg. 1748 **PB**
Witthayu Complex Project, Wireless Road, pg. 943 **IT**
The World Bank, 14th Fl., Tower A, Diethelm Towers, pg. 1189 **PV**
Wunderman Cato Johnson, 19th Grand Amarin Tower, 1550 New Petchburi Rd., pg. 326 **PV**
Xovic Co. Ltd., Thosapol Bldg., F1-5B, 200 Ratchadapisek Rd., pg. 823 **IT**
ZEXEL Corporation Bangkok Representative Office, pg. 1528 **IT**
Zurn Thailand, 119/17 Bangna-Thani Bldg., 8th Fl., Moo 8, Bangna-Trad KM.3, pg. 1795 **IT**

Bangpa-in

Canon Engineering (Thailand) Ltd., Hi-Tech Industrial Estate, 56, Moo, 1, pg. 262 **IT**
Canon Hi-Tech (Thailand) Ltd., Hi-Tech Industrial Estate, 89 Moo-1, pg. 262 **IT**
Minebea Thai Limited, 1 Moo 7, Phaholyothin Road, Km. 51, Tambol Chiang Rak-Noi, pg. 868 **IT**
Pelmac Thailand, 1 Moo 7, Phaholyothin Road, pg. 868 **IT**

Chachoengsao

Asian PVS Chemical Co., Ltd., Wellgrow Industrial Estate, 85/1 M.5 T. Bangsamark, pg. 828 **PV**
CPC/AJI (Thailand) Ltd., Gateway Plant, Gateway City, 181 Moo 7, KM 10, Highway No. 331 Tambol Huasamrong, pg. 41 **IT**
Sukosol and Mazda Engineering Co., Ltd., Wellgrow Industrial Estate, K.M. 36 Bangna-Trad Road, Bangpakong, pg. 849 **IT**

Chiang Mai

Piboon Concrete Co., Ltd., 49/24 Moo 5 Chiangmai-Lampang Rd., pg. 1239 **IT**
Siam Tobacco Export Corp. Ltd., Yarn Nemg, pg. 1502 **PB**
Siegra, pg. 429 **PB**
Thai-Am Tobacco Limited, pg. 1695 **PB**

Chon Buri

Arabian Shaw Pipecoaters (Thailand) Limited, P.O. Box 30, Samae San Port Road, pg. 1231 **IT**

PB - U.S. Public Companies Volume
PV - U.S. Private Companies Volume
IT - International Public & Private Companies Volume

1788

Geographic Index-Non U.S.

Bangkok Komatsu Co., Ltd., Bangpakong Industrial Park 2, 700/21 Moo 5 T. Nongmaidaeng, pg. 745 **IT**
Daikin Industries (Thailand) Ltd., 700/11 Bangpakong Industrial, Estate, Bangna-Trad Rd., pg. 365 **IT**
FDK Tatung Co. Ltd., Bangpakong Industrial Estates II, pg. 1357 **IT**
Foster Wheeler (Thailand) Limited, Scirarha Engineering Office, 217 Moo 12, Sukhaplban 8 Rd., pg. 677 **PB**
ING Bank Chonburi, Bangkok Bank Bldg., 6th Fl., 98 Sukhumvit Road, pg. 648 **IT**
Nissin Foods (Thailand) Co., Ltd., 999 M0011 Sukapiban 8RD, pg. 950 **IT**
P.I.B.F. Chon Buri Branch, 9th Floor, Talay-Thong Tower, 53 Moo 9 Opp., Laem Chabang Deep Seaport, pg. 1310 **IT**
Prestia Thailande, N. 29 Moo 72, National Highway 331-km 50, pg. 791 **IT**
Siam NEC Co., Ltd., 38/7 Moo 5 Sukhunvit Road, Laem Chabang Industrial Estate, pg. 1239 **IT**
Thai Kabaya Industries Co., Ltd., 700/460 Moo 7, pg. 727 **IT**

Hatyai

Mitsiam International, Ltd., House No. 9/4, Niyomrat Rd., pg. 880 **IT**
Teck Chem Company Limited, 157, Niphat Uthit 2 Rd., pg. 1256 **IT**

Kaohsiong

Sharp Electronics (Thailand) Ltd., No. 1 North Nei-Huan East Road, pg. 1230 **IT**

Nakhon Ratchasima

Shonan Gousei (Thailand) Ltd. New Factory, Plot No. 3019, 3020, 3021, Suranaree Industrial Zone, pg. 943 **IT**

Nakornpathom

Sharp Thebnakorn Manufacturing (Thailand), 58 Moo 3, Tambol Sampatuan, pg. 1230 **IT**

Nong Khae

Siam Cement Industrial Land Co., Ltd., Siam Cement Industrial Estate, 111 Moo 7, Nong Pla Kradi Rd., pg. 1238 **IT**
Siam Guardian Glass Co., Ltd., Siam Cement Industrial Estate, 43 Moo 8, Nong Plakradi Rd., pg. 1238 **IT**
Siam Tyre Industry Co., Ltd., Siam Cement Industrial Estate, 57 Moo 6, Nongplakradee Rd., pg. 1238 **IT**

Nonthaburi

The CPAC Concrete Products Co., Ltd., 181/10 Moo 4, Sanambinnam Rd., pg. 1237 **IT**
Reed Exhibition Companies-Thailand, Reed Tradex, 323 Bond Street, Office Villa, pg. 1097 **IT**
Rockwell Automation Thai Co., Ltd., Fourth Floor, Sailom Building, 50/89 Changwattana Road, pg. 1400 **PB**

Pailing

The Sakura Bank - Ayudhya Branch, 3rd Floor, Bank of Asia Bldg., pg. 1179 **IT**

Pathum Thani

Ajinomoto Co., (Thailand) Ltd., Pathum Thani Plant, 99 Mu 1, Wat Daowadoeng-Pathum Thani Rd., pg. 40 **IT**
Asahi Electronics (Thailand) Co., Ltd., 60/70 Moo 19 Klong Luang, Nava Nakorn Industrial Estate, pg. 274 **IT**
BHP Steel Building Products (Thailand) Ltd., 279/2 Moo 2, Soi Tongpoon U-Tid, Km 22 Phaholyothin Road, pg. 226 **IT**
Clays & Minerals (Thailand) Ltd., Management (Astl. Plant), Banuadee Industrial Estate, pg. 1488 **IT**
Micropolis Corporation (Thailand) Ltd., 733/1-8 Moo 8, Phaholyothin Rd., pg. 742 **PV**
NEC Technologies (Thailand) Co., Ltd., 101/75 Nava Nakorn Indus. Est., Paholyothin Rd., pg. 900 **IT**
Nitto Denko (Thailand) Co., Ltd., Bangkadi Industrial Park, Unit No. F. 1-B TFD Bldg., pg. 950 **IT**
Rangsit Machine & Material Center, Tambol Ban Klang, pg. 943 **IT**
Rohm Apollo Electronics (Thailand) Co., Ltd., 102 Navanakorn Indus. Estate, Moo 20, Tambol Khlong-Nung, pg. 1125 **IT**
SCI (Thailand) Ltd., 90 Tiawan Rd., pg. 1417 **PB**
Sealed Air (Thailand) Ltd., 9/29 Rangsit Prosper Estate, Unit B12, Phaholyothin Road, Klong 1, pg. 1451 **PB**
The Siam Sanitary Fittings Co., Ltd., Nava Nakorn Industrial Estate, 60/57 Moo 19, Paholyothin Rd., pg. 1239 **IT**
Toshiba Consumer Products (Thailand) Co., Ltd., 144/1 Moo 5, Bangkadi Industrial Park, pg. 1406 **IT**
Toshiba Display Devices (Thailand) Co., Ltd., 142 Moo 5 Bangkadi Industrial Park, pg. 1406 **IT**
Toshiba Semiconductor (Thailand) Co., Ltd., Bangkadi Industrial Park, 135 Moo 5, Tivanon Road, pg. 1407 **IT**
Weiser Thailand, 101/47/8 Nava Nakorn, Industrial Estate, pg. 1055 **PB**

Rayong

BetzDearborn (Thailand) Co., Ltd., 267/214 Sukhumvit Road, pg. 227 **PB**

Burgmann Thailand Co. Ltd., 17, 17/1-3 Soi Sophon, 6, Wat Sophon Road, pg. 234 **IT**

Samutprakan

Ajinomoto Co., (Thailand) Ltd., Phra Pradaeng Plant, 6 Mu 2, Suksawasdi Rd., pg. 40 **IT**
Crown Cork & Seal (Thailand) Co., Ltd., 405 Bangpoo Industrial Estate, pg. 464 **PB**
Digital Equipment Corporation (Thailand) Limited, Bagna Tower, 2/3 Moo,14 Bangna-Trad Rd. Km. 6.5, pg. 507 **PB**
ETA (Thailand) Co. Ltd., 439 Bangplee Industrial, Estate II, Moo 17 Bansautong, pg. 1161 **IT**
Goldstar Electronics (Thailand) Co., Ltd., 84 Moo 12 Phetkasem, K.M. 22, pg. 779 **IT**
Goldstar MITR Co. Ltd., 84 Moo 12, Phetkasem Road, K.M. 22, pg. 779 **IT**
W.R. Grace (Thailand) Ltd., 253, 2 Bangpoo Indus. Estate, Sukhumvit Rd., Km 34, pg. 756 **PB**
Griffith Laboratories Limited, 482 Mu 19 Soi Pookmitr, pg. 481 **PV**
Heinz Win Chance Ltd., 134 Moo 17 Teparak Rd., pg. 807 **PB**
ICI Asiatic Chemical Co. Ltd., 303 Moo 4 Bangpoo, Industrial Estate, pg. 664 **IT**
IT Forging (Thailand) Co., Ltd., 38 Puchaosming-Prai Road, pg. 693 **IT**
Isuzu Motors Co., (Thailand) Ltd., 38, Poochao Saming Prai Road, pg. 693 **IT**
NHK Gasket (Thailand) Co., Ltd., Barng-Poo Indus. Estate, 549 Moo 4 Tambol Phragsa, pg. 902 **IT**
NHK Spring (Thailand) Co., Ltd., No. 72 Samrongtai, Sukumvit Rd., pg. 902 **IT**
Nippon Paint (Thailand) Co., Ltd., 101 Moo3 Soi Suksawad 76, pg. 937 **IT**
Siam Electric Industries Co., Ltd., 209 Poochaosaming-prai Rd., pg. 1313 **IT**
Siam-Hitachi Construction Machinery Co., Ltd., 406 Sukhumvit Rd., pg. 1238 **IT**
Siam Kabaya Co., Ltd., 380 Moo 2, pg. 727 **IT**
Siam Printing & Packaging Co., Ltd., 543 Soi 9, Moo 4, Bangpoo Industrial Estate, pg. 1399 **IT**
Siam Tyre Co., Ltd., 32 Moo 4, Poochaosamingprai Rd., pg. 1238 **IT**
Square D Company Manufacturing (Thailand), 540 SOI 9, Bangpoo Indus. Est., Sukhumvit Rd., Village Grp. No. 4, pg. 1209 **IT**
Strong Pack Co., Ltd., 91 Moo 13 Kingkaew Rd., pg. 1239 **IT**
Thai Food Coatings, Industrial Estate, 139/11 Moo 17, Bang Plee, pg. 797 **PV**
Thai International Die Making Co., Ltd. (TDI), 331-332 Bangpoo Industrial Estate, pg. 693 **IT**
Thai Kansai Paint Co., Ltd., 180 Moo 3 Taparuk Rd., pg. 723 **IT**
Thai Kobe Welding Co., Ltd., 36, Suksawad Rd., pg. 741 **IT**
Thai Polyphosphate & Chemicals Co. Ltd., Poochao Saming Prai Rd., 77 Moo 12 Soi Wat Mahawong, pg. 1578 **PB**
Thai Union Paper Co., Ltd., 131 Moo 6, Poochaosamingprai Rd., pg. 1239 **IT**
Thai Union Paper Industry Co., Ltd., 131 Poochaosamingprai Rd., pg. 1239 **IT**
The Thai Wanaphan Co., Ltd., 36 Moo 2, Poochaosamingprai Rd., pg. 1239 **IT**
Toyota Motor Thailand Co., Ltd., 186/1 Mu 1, Old Railway Rd., pg. 1414 **IT**

Sara Buri

Ferro (Thailand) Co. Ltd., 46/4 Rim Klong Rapeepat Rd., pg. 619 **PB**
The Nawaloha Industry Co., Ltd., 19 M003 Suwannasorw Road, Bualoy, Nonkhae District, pg. 1238 **IT**
Pacific Seeds (Thai), PO Box 15, 1 Moo Phaholyothin Road, pg. 1525 **IT**
Pioneer Overseas Corporation (Thailand), Ltd., P.O. Box 16, pg. 1299 **PB**
Siam Lemmerz Co., Ltd., Kasemsap Building, 89/1 Vibhavadirangsit Rd., 8th Floor, pg. 1238 **IT**

Songkhla

Siam City Charoen Hire-Purchase (Hat Yai) Co., Ltd., 1-3 Jutianusorn Rd., pg. 1239 **IT**
Weatherford Inc.-Thailand, 29 Suan Mark Road, pg. 1750 **PB**

Sri Racha

Van Leeuwen Pipe and Tube (Thailand) Ltd., Chonburi Industrial Estate, 341 Moo 6, Highway no. 331 KM 91, pg. 1450 **IT**

Surat Thani

Siam City Surat Leasing Co., Ltd., 32/2-3 Karunrath Road, pg. 1239 **IT**

Tambol

Showpla (Thailand) Co. Ltd., Bangpakong Industrial Estate 2, 700-46 Moo. 6, pg. 1237 **IT**
Tanaka (Thailand) Co., Ltd., 1/10 Moo 5 Rojana Road, pg. 939 **IT**

TOGO

Lome

BIAO Togo, Rue du Commerce 13, pg. 547 **IT**
Banque Tongolaise pour le Commerce et L'Industrie (BTCI), 169 Boulevard du 13 Janvier, pg. 149 **IT**
Ciments du Togo, S.A., pg. 1201 **IT**
Societe Africaine de Promotion, B.P. 4150, pg. 823 **PB**
TOBETON, Societe Togolaise de Beton, S.A., pg. 425 **IT**
U.A.C.-Togo S.A., pg. 540 **IT**
The World Bank, 169 Boulevard du 13 Janvier, pg. 1190 **PV**

TONGA

Nuku'alofa

Australia & New Zealand Banking Group Limited Tonga, Cnr Railway & Salote Roads, pg. 99 **IT**
Bank of Tonga, P.O. Box 924, pg. 1248 **PB**
Westpac Banking Corp. - Tonga, c/o Bank of Tonga, Taufa'ahau Rd., pg. 1497 **IT**

TRINIDAD & TOBAGO

Arima

Geddes Grant Sprostons Indus., Ltd., 41 O'Meara Industrial Estate, pg. 52 **IT**

Champs Fleurs

Lever Brothers West Indies Ltd., Eastern Main Road, pg. 1437 **IT**

Couva

PCS Nitrogen-Trinidad, Goodrich Bay Road, pg. 1064 **IT**
Tarmac Construction (Caribbean) Ltd., Southern Main Rd., pg. 1355 **IT**

Port of Spain

Amoco Trinidad Oil Co., Tatil Bldg., 11 Maraval Rd., pg. 103 **PB**
Bank of Commerce Trinidad and Tobago Limited, 72 Independence Sq., pg. 257 **IT**
The Bank of Nova Scotia Trinidad and Tobago Limited, Scotia Centre, Park and Richmond Streets, pg. 157 **IT**
The Bank of Nova Scotia Trust Company of Trinidad and Tobago Limited, Scotia Centre, Park and Richmond Streets, pg. 157 **IT**
Colgate-Palmolive (Caribbean), Inc., pg. 398 **PB**
Computers & Controls Ltd., 80-82 Edward St., pg. 817 **PB**
Crown Cork & Seal (West Indies) Ltd., Tumpuna Rd., pg. 464 **PB**
Electrolux Ltd., 1 Jerningham Av, Belmont, pg. 444 **IT**
Farmland MissChem, Ltd., 11-13 Victoria Ave., pg. 1117 **PB**
Hydro Agri Trinidad Ltd., Point Lisas Plant, pg. 962 **IT**
Lange Ballast Contractors Ltd., 43 Charles Street, pg. 135 **IT**
Maritime General Insurance Company Limited, 1 Chancery Lane, pg. 364 **PB**
Metal Box Trinidad Limited, P.O. Box 1297, pg. 267 **IT**
Mitsui & Co., Ltd., L. J. Williams Bldg., 122 St. Vincent St, pg. 881 **IT**
Nestle Trinidad and Tobago Limited, pg. 921 **IT**
Nucor Iron Carbide, c/o Trinidad Hilton, Rm. 154, Lady Young Road, pg. 1206 **PB**
Offshore Logistics Caribbean, S.A., P.O. Box 843, pg. 1213 **PB**
Premiums Intl. Ltd., Park & Charlotte St., pg. 212 **PV**
Shell Chemicals & Services (East Caribbean) Ltd, Chic Bldg., 3rd Floor, 63 Park St., pg. 1141 **IT**
Texaco Trinidad, Inc., 29 St. Vincent St., Colonial Life Bldg., pg. 1584 **PB**
3M Interamerica, Inc. (Trinidad & Tobago Div.), One Jerningham Ave., W.I., pg. 1606 **PB**
Trinidad Food Products Ltd., pg. 922 **IT**

San Fernando

Halliburton Trinidad Ltd., Coconut Dr., Cross Crossing, pg. 777 **PB**
Helmerich & Payne Finco, 21 Scott St., pg. 808 **PB**
Oil Patch & Industrial Services, Ltd., 34 Todd St., pg. 6 **IT**

Siparia

Tri-Can Perforators Limited, Coora Camp, Coora Rd., pg. 777 **PB**

TUNISIA

Ben Auros

Defontaine Tunisie, Z.I. Bata, pg. 509 **IT**

Bougrine

Societe Miniere de Bougrine S.A., pg. 862 **IT**

Jebel Jeloud

Sicoac, pg. 430 — IT

Kebili

Bonifica-Tunisia, Rue Salah Ben Josuef 4200, pg. 655 — IT

La Marsa

CIBA-GEIGY Services SA-Bureau de consultation techn, 1 bis, rue Salammbo, pg. 980 — IT

Menzel Bourguiba

Sotuves SA, pg. 25 — IT

Monastir

Somoves SA, pg. 25 — IT

Sfax

Instrumentation Medicale & Maintenance, 65 Avenue Habib Mazzoun, pg. 822 — PB

Sousse

Sinutex S.a.r.l., pg. 25 — IT

Tunis

Afrique Assistance, Rue Charles Nicole, 54, pg. 334 — IT
Arabtel, 92, avenue Hedi Chaker, pg. 706 — IT
BASF Tunisia S.A., Villa Essaada, Rue 8710, No. 10, pg. 107 — IT
Bobst (Africa & Middle East). Ltd, pg. 198 — IT
Compagnie de Faisceaux Tunisian International S.A., pg. 723 — PB
Det Norske Veritas, 10 Rue du Mali, pg. 397 — IT
Ericsson Tunisie S.A., 44, Avenue Khereddine, Pacha, pg. 1368 — IT
Gray Tool International, Inc., c/o Starep Immeuble Saadi, P.O. Box 232, pg. 6 — IT
Groupe des Assurances de Tunisie (GAT), 92/94, avenue Hedi Chaker, pg. 565 — IT
Impol SA, Route de L'Ariana, pg. 429 — IT
Industrien Chimiques Maghrebines Company, 20 Nahj Al-Iraq, pg. 766 — IT
Industries Mecaniques Maghrebines, pg. 693 — IT
Mitsui & Co., Ltd., 8eme etage, 25, avenue Jean Jaures, pg. 881 — IT
Nestle Tunisie, pg. 921 — IT
Precision Electronique, 5 Rue de Chypre, pg. 822 — PB
Produits Alimentaires et Dietetiques (SIDPAD), pg. 922 — IT
SCOGAT S.A. (Societe pour la Construction du Gazoduc Transt.), Immeuble Saadi Route, pg. 429 — IT
SNC-Lavalin, 80 bis, rue Palestine, pg. 1162 — IT
STER, 2, rue Abdelaziz Thaalbi, pg. 1163 — IT
S.T.I.M.A. S.a.r.l., 48, Av. Kamel Attaturk, pg. 109 — IT
SERGAZ S.A. (Societe de Service du Gazoduc Transt.), pg. 429 — IT
Societe d'Etudes et d'Installations Telphoniques, Cite Olympique, Imm. 41, Cite el Khadra 3, pg. 1370 — IT
Societe Shell de Tunisie, 24/26 Place du 7 Novembre 1987, pg. 1137 — IT
Societe Tunisienne d'Assurances et de Reassurances, Square de l'Avenue de Paris 1, pg. 61 — IT
STITELE S.p.A., Rue Farhat Hached, 68, pg. 1370 — IT
TECI, 15, rue Abderrahmene - El Jaziri, pg. 1361 — IT
TH Com, 53, Rue Azzouz Rebai, pg. 305 — PV
Tanit International, 5, rue Mahomed-Badra, pg. 21 — IT
Telefonaktiebolaget LM Ericsson Bureaux Techniques de Tunisie, 7, Rue Mohamed Ali Annabi, pg. 1370 — IT
Tunisie Electronique Sarl, 94, Rue Jugurtha, pg. 823 — PB
UBCI (Tunisia), 7 et 9 rue Jamal Abdel Nasser, pg. 163 — IT

TURKEY

Ankara

Ankara Metro Consortium, Ahmet Refik Sokak No. 13, pg. 1162 — IT
Aydin Yazilim ve Elektronik Sanayii A.S. (AYES AS), Mustafa Kemal Mahallese, 19 uncu Sokak, Eskisehir Yolu Km. 7, pg. 158 — PB
Cominco Madencilik Sanayi A.S., Farabi Sokak 3/3, pg. 307 — IT
Dardanel Madencilik Sanayi ve Ticaret S.A., pg. 672 — IT
Dumez Mesa, Abidin Daver Sokak No 12/A, pg. 823 — IT
E.M.A., Schit Ersan Caddesi 30/8, pg. 817 — IT
Ericsson Cukorova Telekom A.S., Cinnah Caddesi No. 41/9, pg. 1366 — IT
Intergraph Computer Services Industry & Trade, A.S., Abidin Daver Sokak No.3/6-7, pg. 891 — PB
Kredietbank Representative Office (Ankara), Kizkulesi Solak 3/5, pg. 760 — IT
Martin Marietta International, Inc., Cevre Sokak No 16/24, pg. 1010 — IT
Mediterranean Fertilizer Industries Company, Ataturk Bulvari No. 127/3, pg. 766 — IT
Mitsui & Co., Ltd., Ataturk Bulvari No. 219/13, Bulvar Apt., pg. 881 — IT
Nokia Telecommunications, Ataturk Blvd. 223/18, pg. 953 — IT

Noksel A.S., Sanayi Cad. 35 Kat:5, pg. 954 — IT
Weatherford Oil Tool Middle East Ltd., C/O Galip Oymar, Murnessillik ve Musaurlik, pg. 1750 — PB
The World Bank, Gama-Guris Bldg. Kat 6, Ataturk Bulvari, No. 211, pg. 1190 — PV
Yibitas Lafarge Hazir Beton San. ve Tic. A.S., Portakal Cicergi Sokak 33, pg. 791 — IT
Yibitas Lafarge Orta Anadolu Cimento San.ve Tic. A.S., Portakal Cicegi Sokak 33 Cankaya, pg. 791 — IT

Armatur Sanayi ve

KSB Pompa, pg. 721 — IT

Bursa

Robert Bosch Motorlu Araclar Yan Sanayi ve Ticaret AS, Yesil Cad. No. 27, pg. 206 — IT
ITC Inland Teknik Oto Yan Sanayi Limited Sirketi, pg. 723 — PB
Teknik Malzeme, Ticaret Ve Sanayi AS, pg. 193 — IT

Cankaya

Amway Turkiye Ltd., Sair Esref Bulvari, No 6 Kat. 7, pg. 70 — PV
CIBA-GEIGY Ilac ve Kimya Urunleri Sanayi ve Ticaret AS, Ahmet Mithat Efendi Cad 11/1, pg. 977 — IT

Cayeli

Cayeli Bakir Isletmeleri, pg. 862 — IT

Esentepe

Novo Nordisk Ferment AG, Maya Akar Center, Buyukdere Cad. No. 100-102, pg. 988 — IT

Gebze

BASF-Suemerbank Tuerk Kimya Sanayii A.S., Dilovasi Mevkii P.K. 1, pg. 107 — IT
Van Leer Mimaysan Ambalaj Sanayi A.S., pg. 1147 — IT

Iskenderun

Oysa Iskenderun Cimento Sanayi Ve Ticaret A.S., Adana Karayolu Karayilan Beldesi, pg. 1168 — IT

Istanbul

A4 Reklamcilik, Turizm ve Seyahat Ltd.Sti, Tesvikiye Cad No 137/5, pg. 1062 — PV
ABS Pompalaei Ltd., Karman Ciftligli Cad. Yakut 1/9, pg. 270 — IT
AMP Elektrik-Elektronik, Baglanti Sistemieri Ticaret, Ltd., Buyukdere Cad. Yapi Kredi Plaza, pg. 8 — IT
AMP Turkey, pg. 9 — PB
Acer Computer Turkey, pg. 22 — IT
Agretas Agrega Insaat San.ve Tic. A.S., Barbados Plaza Is Merkezi, Rahiman Cad., pg. 791 — IT
Akcansa, Maya Meridien is Merkezi, pg. 605 — IT
Anadolu Otomotiv Sanayii ve Ticaret A.S., Ankara Asfslti Uzeri 81412 Kartal, pg. 692 — IT
Arcelik A.S., Cayirova, pg. 741 — IT
Ardem Pisiriciler Ve Isitici San. A.S., Unalan Mh. Ayazma Cd., Camlica Is Mrk., pg. 741 — IT
Aslan Cimento AS, Emiran Cad., Barbaros Plaza Is, pg. 788 — IT
Asland Cimento A.S., Barbaros Plaza Is Merkezi, Emizhan Cad., No. 145 Blok kat 13, pg. 790 — IT
BASF Tuerk, P.K, 424, pg. 107 — IT
BNP-AK, Dresdner Bank A.S., Tak'i Zafer Cad., Vakif Han C Blok pg. 420 — IT
BNP-AK, Dresdner Finansal Kiralama A.S., Inonu Cad. Vakif Is Hani No. 2/12, pg. 1167 — IT
The Bank of New York, BJK Plaza, Spor Caddesi, No. 92, Kat 6, pg. 186 — IT
Bankers Trust New York Corporation, Yapi Kredi Plaza B/11, pg. 186 — PB
Banque Indosuez Generale Euro Turk AS, Bujukdere Caddesi, Yapi Kredi Plaza Block C, pg. 548 — IT
Baring Securities International, Buyukdere Caddesi, Yapi Kredi Plaza, pg. 648 — IT
Bayer Turk Kimya Sanayi Ltd. Sti, Kemankes Cadd Ici Han No. 231-233, pg. 195 — IT
Beko Elektronik A.S., Buyukcekmece Beylik Duzu Mevkii, pg. 741 — IT
Beksa Celik Kord Sanayi ve Ticaret A.S., Sabanci Ctr., 80745, pg. 185 — IT
Benckiser Turkei A.S., pg. 186 — IT
Bilar Bilgi Araclari Ticaret A.S., Buyukdere Caddesi, Onur Ishani No. 118/8-9, pg. 1115 — IT
Birikim FCA!, Mevlut Pehlivan Sokak, Yilmaz Han, pg. 470 — IT
Birlesik Alman Ilac Fabrikalari Turk A.S., pg. 175 — IT
Bizimgaz A.S., Buyukdere Cad., pg. 1155 — IT
Brisa Bridgestone Sabanci Lastik Sanayi ve Ticaret A.S., Sabanci Ctr., pg. 213 — IT
Bundy SpA, Izzettin Cahslar Caddesi 48/4, pg. 1341 — IT
Burgmann Endustriyel Sizdirmalik San Ve Tic Ltd Sti, Yukari Dudullu Imes, Yani Gamak Sapagi, pg. 233 — IT
Carrefour Ticaret Merkezi A.S., Hal Binasi Yani, pg. 270 — IT
The Chase Manhattan Bank, N.A., Yildiz Posta Caddesi 52, Dedeman Ticaret Merkezi, Kat II, pg. 339 — PB

CIBA-GEIGY Ilac ve Kimya Urunleri Sanayii ve Ticaret A.S., Yildiz Posta Caddesi, Dedeman Is Hani, No. 48, pg. 977 — IT
CIBA-GEIGY Ilac ve Kimya Urunleri Sanayi ve Ticaret AS, Kosuyolu, Veliefendi, pg. 977 — IT
CIBA-GEIGY Ilac ve Kimya Urunleri Sanayi ve Ticaret AS, pg. 977 — IT
Cignasa Sigorta A.S., Meclis-I Mebusan Cad., pg. 363 — PB
Cignasa Sigorta A.S., Meclis-I Mebusan Cad., pg. 1167 — IT
Commerzbank AG-Istanbul Representative Office, Bueyuekdere Caddesi, Yapi Kredi Plaza, pg. 311 — IT
Corro-Coat Toz Boya San.ve Tic. A.S., Eski Buyukdere Cad., Yunus Emre Sok. No. 1, pg. 715 — PB
Credit Commercial de France, c/o Iktisat Bankasi, Buyukdere Caddesi 165, pg. 343 — IT
Daewoo Corp. - Istanbul, pg. 358 — IT
Danko Gida Ticaret A.S., Piyalepasa Bulvari, Kastel is Merkezi B-Block Kat. 2, pg. 288 — IT
Det Norske Veritas, Ciragan Asariye Cad., pg. 397 — IT
Deutsche Bank AG (Istanbul), Mete Caddesi 34, Necip Akar Is Hani Kat 2, pg. 404 — IT
Dow Jones Markets Finansal Sistemler A.S., Buyukdere Cad No. 54/9, pg. 525 — PB
Dresdner Bank AG, Inonu Caddesi No. 70, Tumsah Han, pg. 419 — IT
Dusa Endustriyel Iplik Sanayi Ve Ticaret A.S., Sabanci Center, 80745, pg. 533 — PB
Dusa Endustriyel Iplik Sanayi Ve Ticaret A.S., Sabanci Center, 80745, pg. 1167 — IT
EBC Eczacibasi-Beiersdorf, pg. 183 — IT
Ege Ferro Kimya Sanayi ve Ticarret, Cedere yolu 18, pg. 619 — PB
Ekmel Lafarge Beton AS, Buyukdere Caddesi Noramin Is, Merkezi Kat, pg. 790 — IT
Elektrik Komurleri Anonim Sirketi, Davutpasa Cad. Salhane, pg. 1030 — IT
Ericsson Telekomunikasyon A.S., Buyukdere Caddesi No. 49/4, pg. 1368 — IT
Eterplast Plastik Sanayi, Ayazma Caddesi Otim Yani, Aliye Meric Konak 7 is Merkesi Kat: 6, pg. 430 — IT
European Turkish Merchant Bank, Bujukdere Caddesi, Yapi Kredi Plaza Block C, pg. 548 — IT
FANUC Turkey LTD, Kusbakisi Sok. No. 21, pg. 478 — IT
Foster Wheeler Bimas, Yolbulan Plaza, Kozyatagi Sari Karanya S.K. 22, pg. 677 — PB
Foster Wheeler Bimas, Kozyatagi-Sari Kananya Sok. zz, pg. 677 — PB
Freudenberg Household Products Evici Kullanim Araglari Ticaret A.S., pg. 506 — IT
Frigoscandia Food Process Systems International AB, Istanbul Irtibat Burosu, Selamicesme, Bagdat Cad. No. 186/1, pg. 607 — PB
Garanti-Koza Insaat, Baglarbasi Kisikli Cad. 28, pg. 624 — IT
Generale Bank, Cumhuriyet Caddesi, pg. 547 — IT
Generali Sigorta A.S., Bankalar Caddesi 31-33, pg. 91 — IT
Gillette Bosphorus Sanayi A.S., Ulus Yolu No. 17/7, pg. 744 — PB
Goodyear Lastikleri Turk Anonim Sirketi, Buyukdere Caddesi, pg. 753 — IT
Gunes Sigorta A.S., Meclisi Mebusan Caddesi, Setustu N 5 Kabatas, pg. 565 — IT
Habib Bank Ltd., Abide-i-Hurriyat Cad., pg. 585 — IT
Heinemann ELT-Turkey, Inkilap Cad., pg. 1479 — IT
Heller Factoring Anonim Sirketi, Buyukdere Caddesi No:101, Lalezar Han. Kat:3, pg. 521 — IT
Hewlett-Packard Biiglsayar Ve Olcum Sistemleri AS, 19 Mays Cad. Nova/Baran Plaza K.12, pg. 818 — IT
Holantse Bank-Uni, Inonu Caddesi 13-17, Gumussuyu, pg. 12 — IT
Honeywell AS, Emirhan Cad 145, Barbaros Plaza C/18, pg. 834 — IT
Huls Stockhausen Kimya Ticaret A.S., Ankara Asfalti Uzeri, Kanli Mandira Mevkii, pg. 1455 — IT
I-Bimsa Uluslararasi Is Bilgi Veyonetim Sistemleri A.S., Sabanci Ctr., 80745, pg. 898 — PB
I-Bimsa Uluslararasi Is Bilgi Veyonetim Sistemleri A.S., Sabanci Ctr., 80745, pg. 1167 — IT
IBM Turk Limited Sirketi, Buyukdere Caddesi, pg. 1043 — PB
IDC Turkey, Sanayi Mah Eski/Suyukder Cad., pg. 571 — PV
IDG/UFT, Eski Boyokodere Caddesi, Ucar Sokak No 25 B Kat 5, pg. 570 — PV
ING Bank Istanbul, Spor Caddesi No 92,9, pg. 649 — IT
Intergraph Computer Services Industry & Trade, Zeytinoglu Cad., Yonca Sok., Metropol Apt., D.3, Akadlar-Etiler, pg. 891 — PB
Interim, Necatibey Cad 151 Karakoy, pg. 1455 — PB
International Flavors & Fragrances, pg. 899 — PB
Ipek Kagit Sanayi ve Ticaret A.S., Buyukdere Cad. 193, pg. 673 — PB
Ipragaz A.S., Nova Baran Plaza, 19 Mayis Cad. N 4, pg. 1155 — IT
John Crane Turkey, Izzettin Calislar Caddesi 48/4, pg. 1339 — IT
Jotun Boya San. ve Ticaret A.S., Cilekli Cad. No. 18, pg. 715 — IT
Jotun Polisan Boya Tic A.S., Cilekli Cad. No. 18, pg. 715 — IT
Kanthal Besikatas, pg. 723 — IT
Karbon Grafit Sanayi A.S., Siracevizier Caddesi, No. 14/16 D, pg. 890 — IT
Kimyateks Dis Ticaret A.S., pg. 614 — IT
Kluber Lubrication Yaglama Urunleri Sanayi Ve Ticaret A.S., pg. 506 — IT
KOC HOLDING A.S., Nakkastepe, Azizbey Sok, No:1, pg. 741 — IT
Kocbank A.S., Barbaros Bulvari Morbasan, SK. Koza Is Merkezi, pg. 741 — IT
Kodak (Near East), Inc., Buyukdere Cad. 80/6, pg. 554 — PB
KONE Asansor Sanayi ve Ticaret A.S., Bulgurlu Cad 32, pg. 747 — IT

PB - *U.S. Public Companies Volume*
PV - *U.S. Private Companies Volume*
IT - *International Public & Private Companies Volume*

1790

Geographic Index-Non U.S.

Linz Kimya Ticaret Ltd. Sirketi, pg. 356   IT
Lowe Adam, Buyukdere Caddesi 57, pg. 678   PV
MAN Kamyon Ve Otobues Ticaret Ltd. Sirketi, pg. 825   IT
Markom/Leo Burnett A.S., Buyukdere Caddesi No. 22, pg. 186   PV
Marsa Kraft Jacobs Suchard Sabanci Gida Sanayi Ve Ticaret A.S, Kisikli Cad. No. 90, pg. 1168   IT
Marsa Kraft Jacobs Suchard Sabanci Gida Sanayi Ve Ticaret A.S, Kisikli Cad. No. 90, pg. 1290   PB
Mercedes-Benz Turk A.S., Burmali Cesame Sokak Askeri, pg. 369   IT
Microsoft Bilgisayar Yazilim Hizmetleri Limited Sirketi, pg. 1108   PB
Midland Bank AS, Cumhuriyet Caddesi No. 8, Elmadag Han Kat. 2, 80200 Elmadag, pg. 580   IT
Mitsui & Co., Ltd., Buyukdere Caddesi 85, pg. 881   IT
Mobil Oil Turk AS, Pegasus Evi, Cumhuriyet Caddesi No. 26, pg. 1119   PB
Momentum Inc., Zincirlikuyu CAd. Dag Apt. 72/, Ulus 80600, pg. 1032   PB
Nedlloyd Road Cargo Ltd. Sti., pg. 1145   IT
Nestle Turkiye Gida Sanayi A.S., pg. 921   IT
Netas-Northern Electric Telekomunikasyon A.S., Alemdag Caddesi, pg. 970   IT
Olivetti Sanay Ve Ticaret A.S., Cemal Sahir SoK, 26-28, pg. 1003   IT
OMRON Electronics Ltd., Acibadem Caddesi, pg. 1006   IT
Outokumpu Istanbul Dis Ticaret Limited Sirketi, pg. 1015   IT
Owens-Corning Yapi Merkezi Boru Sanayi Ve Ticaret A.S., Cemil TopuzluCad., Is. Bankasi C Blok, D.6, pg. 1238   PB
Packard Elektrik Sistemleri Limited Sirketi, 81260 Omrani, pg. 723   PB
Pardior Kozmetik Tic. Ve San A.S., Kore Sehitleri Caddesi, Mithat Unlu Sok. 23 K. 3-4, pg. 783   IT
Pechiney AIM-Rep. Office in Turkey, Setustu, Engin Apt. No. 25/4, pg. 1031   IT
Penajans DMB&B Ticaret, Korukent Sitesi, pg. 305   PV
Peyma Chr. Hansen's A.S., Piyale Pasa Bulvari, pg. 289   IT
Pfizer Ilaclari, A.S., Muallim Naci Caddesi Bostan Cikmazi, pg. 1282   IT
Philip Morris Sabanci Pazalarma Ve Satis A.S., Maya Akar Center, Buyukdere Cad. No. 100-102, pg. 1168   IT
Philip Morris Sabanci Pazalarma Ve Satis A.S., Maya Akar Center, Buyukdere Cad. No. 100-102, pg. 1290   PB
Philsa Philip Morris Sabanci Sigara Ve Tutunculuk A.S., Maya Akar Ctr., Buyukdere Cad. #100-102, pg. 1168   IT
Philsa Philip Morris Sabanci Sigara Ve Tutunculuk A.S., Maya Akar Ctr., Buyukdere Cad. #100-102, pg. 1290   PB
Pioneer Tohumculuk A.S., Mehmet Akif Cad. 1. Sok, pg. 1299   PB
Prodalim Gida Mamulleri Imalat Ve Pazarlama Anonim Sirketi, pg. 922   IT
Pronova Biopolymer Kimyevi, Balmumcu Plaza 3, Sakir Kesebir, Cd. 34/8, pg. 964   IT
RPM/Radar-CDP Europe, Akaretler Spor Caddesi, BJK Plaza B Blok No. 92, pg. 394   IT
Raychem Elektro Yalitim Sistemleri Limited Sirkety, Buyukdere Cad Arzu Apt 99/3, pg. 1362   PB
REMSAN, Buyukdere Caddesi, Bor Apt. 79/7, pg. 6   IT
Rexroth Hidropar AS, pg. 839   IT
Rhone-Poulenc Kimyevi Maddeler Ltd., Buyukdere Caddesi 15/A, pg. 1113   IT
Roche Kimyasal Urunler ve Teknik Cihazlar Ltd., pg. 1121   IT
Roche Mustahzarlari Sanayi Limited Sirketi, pg. 1121   IT
Rockwell Otomasyon Ticaret a.s., Maya-Akar Center, Kat 14, D.55 Esentepe, pg. 1402   IT
SEM Ltd., Kalfa Cesme Sokak, Levazin Sitesi 4 Block, D6, pg. 823   PB
SKF Turk Sanayi ve Ticaret, Buyukdere Caddesi 12/2, pg. 1159   IT
STS Binasi Ankara, Asfalti Uzeri, Yeni Yol Sok. 80010, pg. 550   IT
SABANCI HOLDING A.S., Sabanci Center, pg. 1167   IT
Sandoz Urunleri Ltd., pg. 985   IT
Sandvik Ticaret Ltd. AS, P.O. Box 111, 80622 Levent, pg. 1187   IT
Sanpaolo-Istanbul Representative Office, Edin & Suner Plaza, pg. 691   IT
Sark Hayat Sigorta T.A.S, Baglarbasi, Kisikli Cad. No. 9, pg. 61   IT
Sark Sigorta T.A.S. (RAS), Baglarbasi Kisikli Cad. No. 9, pg. 62   IT
Schauman Wood Oy-Istanbul Office, Bagdat Cad. Yesilbahar Sok #1, pg. 1429   IT
Schering Alman Ilac ve Ecza Ticaret Ltd., pg. 1204   IT
Schindler Turkeli Asansor san a.s., pg. 1205   IT
Serpo AS, Ulus Yolu, pg. 1200   IT
Shell Company of Turkey Ltd., Buyukdere Caddesi No 32, pg. 1141   IT
Sodexho-Istek Toplu Yemek, Baglarbasi, Tophanelioglu Cad. No. 28, pg. 1275   IT
Sodexho Restoran Servisleri, Halaskargazi Cad. Cankaya, pg. 1275   IT
The Sumitomo Bank, Ltd.-Istanbul Representative Office, Buyukdere Cad. Yapi Kredi, Plaza, B Blok K. 7, 80620 4, pg. 1310   IT
Tefal Istanbul, Spor Cad N. 92, pg. 568   IT
Tekimal Asanor Sanayi ve Ticaret A.S., Kosuyolu, Ankara asfalti 1. Km., pg. 748   IT
3M Sanaii ve Ticaret, Nespetiye Cad. Akmerkez, Blok 3, pg. 1607   PB
Toyotasa A.S., Gulsuyu Mevkii Ankara Asfalti, pg. 1168   IT
Transkimya Ticaret ve Sanaye A.S., Kurtulus Deresi Cad. 13/I, pg. 1490   IT

Turk Elektrik Endustrisi A.S., Davutpasa Cd. Litros Yolo No:1, pg. 741   IT
Turk Henkel A.S., Kore Sehitleri Cad. 39, pg. 614   IT
Turk Philips Aydinlatma Sanayi Ve Ticaret A.S., Talatpasa Cad. #5, pg. 1055   IT
Turk Philips Sanayi A.S., Talatpasa Cad. #5, pg. 1055   IT
Turk Philips Ticaret A.S., Talatpasa Cad. No. 5, pg. 1055   IT
Turk Pirelli Lastikler A.S., Buyukdere Caddesi 117, pg. 1060   IT
Turk Sakura Bank A.S., Buyukdere Caddesi, Enka Han, pg. 1180   IT
Turkeli Ticaret A.S., pg. 1205   IT
Unilever Is Ticaret ve Sanayi Turk Limited Sirketi, pg. 1439   IT
Wellcome Ilac Urunleri Ltd Sirketi, pg. 553   IT
Westdeutsche Landesbank-Istanbul Branch, Akasyali Sokak No. 6, pg. 1493   IT
Windmoller & Holscher Dis Ticaret A.S., Seher Yildizi Sokak No. 33 D4, pg. 1511   IT
Wyeth Laboratuvarlari A.S., P.K. 67, Aksaray, pg. 82   PB
Yapkim Yapi Kimya Sanayi A.S., Davutpasa Caddesi No. 145, pg. 1466   IT
Young & Rubicam Turkey, Suleyman Nazif Sokak, No. 20, pg. 1200   PV
Zeneca Turkiye, Ihlamur, Yildiz Caddesi, pg. 1527   IT
Zeneca Turkiye Ltd. (Agrochemicals), Bagdat Caddesi, Goksei Is Merkezi, pg. 1527   IT

Izmir

CIBA-GEIGY Ilac ve Kimya Urunleri Sanayi ve Ticaret AS, Halit Ziya Bulvari 74/7, Halk Sigorta Is Merkezi Kat 7, pg. 977   IT
Etitas Elektrik Techizati, pg. 706   IT
General Motors Turkiye Limited Sirketi, pg. 723   PB
Habetas Hazir Beton San. ve Tic. A.S., 515 Sok, pg. 791   IT
Henkel Turyag A.S., Turkiye Yag Ve Mamulati A.S., Sair Esref Bulvari No. 48, pg. 613   IT
Izmir Branch, Ataturk Caddesi, No. 40, pg. 1180   IT
Lawson Mardon Bak Grayure Baskili Karton Sanayi ve Ticaret AS, pg. 68   IT
Ortadogu-KVK, P.O. Box 594, pg. 371   IT
Sandoz Kimya Sanayii Ltd. Sirketi, pg. 984   IT
Spierer Tutun Ihracat Sanaui Ticaret AS, pg. 1502   PB
Turyag Turklye Yag ve Mamulati A.S., pg. 614   IT

Izmit

Celikord A.S., Devlet Karayolu 1, P.K. 40, pg. 1059   IT
Karamursel Mill, Karamursel, pg. 673   PB
Mannesmann Sumerbank Boru Endustrisi TAS, pg. 835   IT
Turkkablo A.O., Cenesuyu Karsisi P.K. 53, pg. 954   IT

Karakoy

Banque Ottomane, Voyvoda Caddesi 35 37, pg. 319   IT
Simko Ticaret ve Sanayi A.S., pg. 1248   IT

Kirikkale

STS Tesisat Armatuerler Pazarlama A.S., Ankara yolu, 10 km, pg. 550   IT

Manisa

Nacanco Paketleme Sanayi A.S., Ve Ticaret, pg. 1029   IT

Nigde

Oysa Nidge Cimento Sanayi Ve Ticaret A.S., Adana Yolu Uzeri, pg. 1168   IT

Sakarya

Yazaki Sabanci Otomotiv Kablo Donanimi San. Ve Tic A.S., Topcu Sirti Mah., pg. 1168   IT

Sisli

Besan-Besin Sanayi ve Ticaret A.S., Perihan Sokak no. 126, pg. 224   PB

Spea Tecnic

Spea-Turkey, Turhan Cemal Beriker Bulvari 201, pg. 655   IT

Tophane

Knoll Alman Ilac ve Ecza Tic. Ltd. Sti., PK 937 Firuzaga Defterdar, BASF is Hani Yokusa No. 3, pg. 108   IT

TURKMENISTAN
Ashkhabad

Ram Representative Office-Turkmenistan, Hotel Ak Altin Plaza, Office B, Office Building, pg. 742   IT

TUVALU
Funafuti

Westpac Banking Corp. - Tuvalu, c/o National Bank of Tuvalu, pg. 1497   IT

UGANDA
Kampala

Alliance Air Ltd., pg. 1417   IT
Barclays Bank of Uganda Ltd., pg. 165   IT
CIBA-GEIGY Sales & Distribution Company Limited, pg. 979   IT
CIBA-GEIGY Trading and Marketing Services Co Ltd-Technical Advisory Office, pg. 980   IT
Gailey & Roberts (Uganda) Ltd., pg. 1437   IT
Gestetner Limited, P.O. Box 7693, pg. 1115   IT
Interfreight Forwarders Uganda Limited, pg. 1022   IT
Interfreight Investments Limited, pg. 1022   IT
Shell Uganda Ltd., Shell House, 7th St., Plot No. 7/11, Industrial Area, pg. 1137   IT
Stanbic Bank Uganda Limited, 45 Kampala Road, pg. 1294   IT
Standard Chartered Bank Uganda Ltd., 5 Speke Rd., pg. 1295   IT
The World Bank, 1 Lumumba Avenue & 4 Natasero Rd., pg. 1190   PV

UKRAINE
Cherkassy

Reemtsma Cherkassy Tyutyunova Fabrika, Oktyabrskaya Str. 170, pg. 1101   IT

Kiev

Akerlund & Rausing, Turgenevskaja Str. 38, pg. 33   IT
Robert Bosch Ltd., Ul. Mariny Raskowoj 11, pg. 205   IT
Leo Burnett Kyiv, Suite #24, pg. 185   PV
Representation of CIBA-GEIGY Services Ltd., Technical Advisory Office, pg. 984   IT
Rep. of CIBA Industrial Marketing Services Ltd., ul. Fjodorova 20/ap. 406, pg. 984   IT
Coeclerici Trading S.p.A., Gospitalnaja UL 12, pg. 304   IT
Commerzbank AG Representative Office-Kiev, Wulyzja Puschkinska 34, pg. 311   IT
ComputerWorld Kiev Comizdat Publishing Company, 15 Vossoyedeanenija Pr-f, pg. 569   PV
DMB&B LLC/Kiev, 8b Bolshaya, pg. 304   PV
Durkopp Adler Ukraine Ltd., ul. Terjochina 4, pg. 469   IT
Electricite de France, 13 Terechtchenkovskaia Rd., Ap. 2, pg. 437   IT
Honeywell, Reytarskaya 8, pg. 834   PB
ING Bank Kiev, Gogolevskaya Street 37/2, pg. 649   IT
S.C. Johnson Kiev Corp., pg. 593   PV
KONE Elevators, Ul. Akademika Koroleva, pg. 747   IT
Lotus Logistica S.r.l., Gospitalnaja UL 12, pg. 304   IT
Novo Nordisk A/S, Central Museum of Ukraine, 37, B. Khmelnitskogo Str., pg. 987   IT
RZB Kiev, 26, b-r L. Ukrainsky, 7th Fl./66, pg. 1084   IT
Ram Representative Office-Ukraine, 252053, 31 Artyoma Str. Apt. 8, pg. 742   IT
Reemtsma Kiew Tyutyunova Fabrika, Volodarskogo Str. 11, pg. 1101   IT
Reemtsma Ukraine, ul. Kreschatik 7/11, pg. 1101   IT
Representation of CIBA-GEIGY Services Ltd., vul. Artema Street 1-5, pg. 984   IT
Sogecred S.A., Bulvar Lesi Ukrainki 34, pg. 137   IT
Ukrainian Mobile Communications, pg. 721   IT
Ukron, Serpova st. 3, pg. 608   IT
Utel, pg. 721   IT
Vertretung der BASF in der Ukraine, u.l. P.Lumumby 4/6, pg. 110   IT
WestLB Kiev, ul. Krasnoarmejskaja 9/2, Entrance 7a, pg. 1493   IT
World Bank, 26, Shovkovychna St., Suites 2 & 3, pg. 1189   PV
Zeneca Kiev, Taras Shevchenko, 58A, pg. 1526   IT

Krivoy Rog

Svedala Ukraine, pg. 1325   IT

Mariupol

Lotus Logistica S.r.l., Prospekt Lunina, 2/A, pg. 304   IT

Rubezhnoye

Ingecol, pg. 983   IT

UNITED ARAB EMIRATES
Abu Dhabi

Abu Dhabi Company for Onshore Oil Operations, pg. 1140   IT
Abu Dhabi Gas Industries, pg. 1140   IT
Al Otaiba-Costain Company, P.O. Box 4272 Sector MN4, Plot 4F, pg. 337   IT
Arthur D. Little International, Inc., pg. 671   PV

PB - *U.S. Public Companies Volume*
PV - *U.S. Private Companies Volume*
IT - *International Public & Private Companies Volume*

Geographic Index-Non U.S.

UNITED ARAB EMIRATES
DIRECTORY OF CORPORATE AFFILIATIONS

Ballast Nedam Dredging, pg. 134 IT
Banque Paribas-United Arab Emirates, Airport St., pg. 320 IT
Bin Ham Trading Agencies, P.O. Box 46844, Bin Ham Building, 3rd Floor, pg. 550 IT
CRSS International, Inc., pg. 1415 IT
Computer Network Systems, pg. 739 IT
Crest Engineering Overseas, Inc., P.O. Box 7444, pg. 5 IT
DeLeuw, Cather International Ltd., P.O. Box 6736, pg. 842 PV
Dumez S.A. Emirates, Al Masaood Tower, pg. 823 IT
Emirates Technology Company (EMITAC), pg. 817 PB
Honeywell Middle East Ltd., Sheikh Faisal Building, Khalifa Street, pg. 835 PB
Jotun Abu Dhabi (L.L.C.), P.O. Box 3714, pg. 715 IT
The Kanoo Group Commercial Division Abu Dhabi, pg. 108 IT
Laing Abu Dhabi, P.O. Box 984, pg. 797 IT
MSA Middle East, P.O. Box 46338, pg. 1115 PB
Marcam U.A.E., pg. 1043 PB
Mitsui & Co., Ltd., Al-Harbroush Bldg., 1st Fl., No. 12 Corn, pg. 882 IT
Mobil Oil Abu Dhabi Inc., P.O. Box 7695, pg. 1119 PB
Otis International, Ltd., P.O. Box 6322, pg. 777 PB
Parker Hannifin Corporation, pg. 1263 PB
Swiss Bank Corporation, Gibca Building, 7th Floor, Sh. Khalifa Street, pg. 1330 IT
Tarmac (Abu Dhabi) Ltd., P.O. Box 6464, pg. 1355 IT
Technip-Geoproduction, Al Oteba Tower, Hamadan Street, pg. 1361 IT
Telefonaktiebolaget LM Ericsson Technical Office UAE, pg. 1371 IT
UBS Representative Office Ltd., ADNIC Building, 5/F, Shaikh Khalifa St., pg. 1441 IT
Varco BJ Drilling Systems, Hilal Mubarak Bldg., Al Salam St., pg. 1709 PB
Varco BJ Oil Tools, Hilal Mubarak Bldg., Al Salam St., pg. 1709 PB
Weatherford Bin Hamodah, Gasos Warehouse, Sector M-21, pg. 1750 PB

Deira

Middle East Finance Co. Ltd., Al Shaya Building, Al Ittihad Street, Dubai-Sharjah Road, pg. 583 IT

Dubai

ANZ Grindlays Bank plc United Arab Emirates, pg. 99 IT
AST Middle East Limited, Location RA 5/34B-R-7, pg. 1182 IT
Acer Computer (M.E.) Ltd., pg. 22 IT
Air Malta - Dubai, City Tower 2, Office No. 1904, pg. 38 IT
Air Products (Middle East) Inc., pg. 31 PB
Al-Futtaim Willis Faber (Private) Ltd., Al-Futtaim Tower, Level 3, No. 305, pg. 1509 IT
Al Futtaim-Wimpey (Pte.) Ltd., P.O. Box 1811, pg. 1355 IT
Al-Naboodah Laing (Private) Ltd., P.O. Box 4588, pg. 797 IT
Allainz Versicherungs-AG (Dubai Branch), pg. 60 IT
Allen-Bradley Company, Al Moosa Tower, Sheikh Zayed Road, pg. 1398 PB
ARCO Dubai, Incorporated, Level 33, Trade Center Tower, pg. 144 PB
BASF Kanoo Gulf FZE, Gulf Representative Office, Kanoo Bldg., 1st Fl., Alkhifaf Area, pg. 106 IT
BHP Steel Europe Middle East Ltd., Office 2003, Level 20, Dubai World Trade Center, pg. 227 IT
Bank Brussels Lambert, Dubai Representative Office, Ste.505, Juma Al Majid Bldg., Khalid Ibn Walid Road, Bur Dubai, pg. 148 IT
Bank of America NT&SA, Juma Al Majid Bldg., 6th Fl., Khalid Bin Walid St., pg. 182 PB
Banque Paribas-Dubai, Khalid Bin Al Walid St., pg. 320 IT
Brother International (Gulf) Corporation, Warehouse No. WD-1&2,R/A No. 8, Jebel Ali Free Zone, pg. 229 IT
Burgmann Middle East, pg. 234 IT
Chemiforward General Trading Co., No. 634 Al Ghurair Ctr., pg. 1255 IT
Christensen Gulf Services (Private) Limited, P.O. Box 1518, pg. 1174 IT
CIBA-GEIGY Regional Center, pg. 979 IT
CIBA-GEIGY Trading and Marketing Services Co Ltd-Pharmaceuticals Scientific Office (Gulf), pg. 980 IT
Citicorp Gulf Finance Ltd., pg. 378 PB
Citizen Watches Gulf Co., P.O. Box 16772, pg. 294 IT
Corro-Coat U.A.E. Ltd., pg. 715 IT
Costain Middle East, Holiday Inn Comercial Tower, Crown Plaza, Ste. 1606, pg. 337 IT
Crosland Filters Ltd., P.O. Box 290, pg. 786 IT
Daewoo Corp. - Dubai, First No. 1701, 17th Flr. Al Moosa Tower, pg. 358 IT
Danzas United Arab Emirates, Dubai Cargo Village, Room 2050 A, pg. 383 IT
Det Norske Veritas, pg. 398 IT
Dubai Petroleum Company, pg. 533 PB
ESAB Middle East, Al. Jahra Bldg., 6th Fl., P.O. Box 8964, pg. 282 IT
Emirates Can Company Ltd., pg. 465 PB
Emirates Technology Company (EMITAC), Block B Arenco Bldg., Zabei Rd., pg. 817 PB
Enso (Middle East), pg. 457 IT
FSI-Middle East, P.O. Box 389, pg. 1500 IT
Fugro-Middle East, 1509 Dubai International Trade Center, pg. 430 PV
Fuji Photo Film Co., Ltd., Dubai Office, No. 4G-17, L.O.B. 4, P.O. Box 17212, pg. 524 IT
Future Technology Worldwide L.L.C., Suite 220, Hyatt Regency Galleria, pg. 1194 IT
Gibbs Gulf Insurance Consultants Limited, Gamal Abdul Nasser Square, pg. 581 IT
Goldstar Middle East Co., Ltd., P.O. Box 16782 Jebel Ali, pg. 779 IT
Habib Bank Ltd., UPPL Building, Creek Side, pg. 585 IT
Intermarkets Public Relations (ME), New Juma Al-Majid Bldg., Hyundai Showroom, pg. 680 IT
Intermarkets U.A.E., New Juman Al Majid Bldg., Hyundai Show Room, pg. 680 IT
Intermarkets UAE, New Juma Al Majed Bldg., Dubai-Sharjah Road, pg. 1062 PV
Janssen-Cilag, World Trade Center, Level 25, pg. 929 PB
John Crane Middle East- Central Region, pg. 1339 IT
Jotun Polymer Inc., P.O. Box 16911, pg. 715 IT
Jotun U.A.E. Ltd., pg. 716 IT
Juma Al Majid, pg. 1368 IT
Kodak (Near East), Inc., pg. 554 PB
KONE Middle East GIBCA Ltd., B.M.T.C. Building, 1st Floor, Murraqabat Road, Port Said, pg. 747 IT
Kvaerner Eureka a.s. Dubai Branch Office, pg. 767 IT
Kvaerner Ships Equipment a.s Dubai Branch, World Trade Centre Bld., 28th Floor, pg. 768 IT
Laing Emirates, P.O. Box 4588, pg. 797 IT
Makita Gulf FZE, pg. 832 IT
Mathieu S.A., pg. 846 IT
Microsoft Corporation (Dubai Branch), pg. 1108 PB
Milchem International Limited, 74 Al Abbas Bldg., P.O. Box 6746, pg. 167 PB
Mitsui & Co., Ltd., Ste. No. 640, 6th Fl. Al-Ghurair Center, pg. 382 IT
Moulinex Middle East, AL NASR Building, oud Mitha Road, Flat 110-111/1st Fl., pg. 896 IT
NCT Middle East, P.O. Box 17071, pg. 914 IT
NYK-Dubai, Dubai Drydocks Industrial Estate, pg. 941 IT
Neste Oy Dubai, Sheikh Zayed Road City Twr. 2, Level 21, pg. 915 IT
Nokia Mobile Phones (Gulf), Jebel Ali DA4, RIA 8, pg. 952 IT
Nokia Telecommunications, P.O. 61031, pg. 953 IT
Novell Middle East, Dubai World Trade Center, 17th, Fl., P.O Box 9313, pg. 1204 PB
Oceaneering International AG, Jebel Ali, P.O. Box 346, pg. 1211 PB
Omsco Industries, Trade Centre, Ste. 503B, pg. 1231 IT
Panalpina Gulf LLC, pg. 1023 IT
SKF Intertrade Rep. Office, pg. 1158 IT
Shell Markets (Middle East) Ltd., Shell Bldg., Dubai Side, pg. 1141 IT
Smith International Gulf Services Limited, P.O. Box 24983, Oilfeld Supply Center, Shed Number 2, pg. 1478 PB
Sodexho International, pg. 1275 IT
Standard Chartered Bank, Al Mankhool Road,eet, pg. 1294 IT
Sumitomo Rubber Industries-Dubai, pg. 1317 IT
Tamra DMB&B, Old Chamber of Commerce Bldg., pg. 305 PV
Tamrock Middle East, Holiday Center, Office No. 1206, pg. 1353 IT
Terumo-Dubai, Arabift Tower, Off. No. 1308, pg. 1376 IT
3M Gulf Ltd., Hamarain Centre, Gate 4, 4th Fl., Deira, pg. 1606 PB
Toyota Motor Corporation, Dubai Liaison Office, Flat No. 702, Al-Futtaim Tower, P.O. Box, pg. 1413 IT
UBS Representative Office Ltd., ARBIFT Tower, Office 404, pg. 1441 IT
Utell International-United Arab Emirates, Airlines Centre, Flame Roundabout, pg. 1099 IT
Weatherford Oil Tool Middle East Ltd., 18th Floor, pg. 1750 PB
WestLB Dubai, City Tower II Building, Sheikh Zayed Road, pg. 1493 IT
The Yokohama Rubber Co., Ltd., pg. 1521 IT
Zeneca Pharma International, pg. 1527 IT
Zurich Life Insurance Company, pg. 1529 IT
Zurich Life Insurance Company Limited, pg. 1532 IT

Ras al Khaimah

Union Cement Co., pg. 1201 IT

Sharjah

Amoco Ras Al Khaimah Oil Co., Al Rostimani Bldg., King Faisel Rd., pg. 102 PB
Amoco Sharjah LPG Co., Al Rostamani Bldg., King Faisel Rd., pg. 102 PB
Amoco Sharjah Oil Co., Al Rostamani Commercial Bldg., King Faisel Road, pg. 102 PB
Banque of Sharjah, Building Al Bourj Ave., pg. 319 IT
Crawford Door AB, pg. 269 IT
Emirates Technology Company (EMITAC), pg. 817 PB
Honeywell Middle East Ltd., Dr Jaffar Bldg., King Faisal, Road 11, pg. 835 PB
Radio-Holland Group Middle East, P.O. Box 4592, pg. 1152 IT
Readymix Gulf Ltd., pg. 1092 IT
Standard Chartered Bank, pg. 1294 IT

UNITED KINGDOM

Aberdeen

ABB Vetco U.K. Ltd., Bridge of Don Industial Estate, Broadfol, pg. 5 IT
ARC South Wales, Canal Road, pg. 592 IT
Aberdeen Scaffolding Company Ltd., Alterns Indus. Estate, Harness Rd., pg. 1285 IT
Abertay Paper Sacks Ltd., Mugieemass Rd., Bucksburn, pg. 122 IT
Aker Contracting plc, Blackness Rd., Alten Industrial Estate, pg. 42 IT
Anixter Aberdeen, Kirkhill Ind Estate, Howe Moss Dr., pg. 116 PB
BHP Petroleum Ltd., St. Magnus House, Guild St., pg. 225 IT
BJ Process & Pipeline Services Ltd., Badentoy Ave., Badentoy Park, pg. 161 PB
N.G. Bailey & Co. Ltd.-Aberdeen Branch, The Parkway, Woodside Rd., pg. 132 IT
Bailey Telecom LTD - Aberdeen, The Parkway, Woodside Road, pg. 133 IT
Claymore Chemicals Ltd., Unit 1, Airways Industrial Estate, pg. 1086 IT
Core Laboratories (Scotland), Howe Moss Drive, pg. 1004 PB
Det Norske Veritas, Veritas House, Hareness Circle, pg. 397 IT
Dresser Drilling & Production Services, Howe Moss Crescent, Kirkhill Industrial Estate, pg. 529 PB
Ervin Abrasives Ltd., Green Bank Rd., pg. 382 PV
Ferranti Syseca, Johnstone House, Rose St., pg. 1384 IT
John Fyfe Ltd., Whitemyers Av., pg. 166 IT
Gardner Cryogenics, Westhill Industrial Estate, pg. 32 PB
Gearhart Geo Consultants Limited, Howemoss Dr., pg. 776 PB
Gearhart Geodata Services (Overseas) Limited, Howemoss Dr., pg. 776 PB
Gearhart (United Kingdom) Limited, Howemoss Drive, pg. 776 PB
Gearhart Wireline Services, Ltd., Howemoss Dr., pg. 776 PB
Gray Tool Co. (Europe), A-2, A-3 Wellhead Industrial Centre, pg. 5 IT
Gulf Offshore N.S. Ltd., 41 Regent Quay, pg. 769 PB
Kvaerner Earl and Wright, Inc., 5-9 Hadden St., pg. 771 IT
Kvaerner FSSL, Howe Moss Avenue, pg. 767 IT
Kvaerner H&G Offshore Ltd., Aberdeen, The Regent Centre, Regent Rd., pg. 771 IT
Kvaerner National Ltd., St. Magnus House, Guild Street, pg. 768 IT
Kvaerner Oil & Gas Services, Regent Centre, Regent Road, pg. 768 IT
Kvaerner Professional Services Ltd., 5-9 Hadden Street, pg. 768 IT
M/D Totco Instrumentation, Silverburn Place, Bridge of Don Industrial Estate, pg. 1709 PB
Macfish Limited, Watermill Road, pg. 491 IT
George Meller Ltd., Unit 4, Marcar Commercial Park, Denmore Rd., pg. 712 IT
Milchem Drilling Fluids Limited, Scouter Head Rd., pg. 167 PB
Nabors Drilling & Energy Services UK, Ltd., pg. 1149 PB
Noble Drilling (U.K.) Ltd., Farburn Industrial Estate, Dyce, pg. 1187 PB
Nodeco, Ltd., pg. 1750 PB
Nowsco Well Service Ltd.-Europe, Africa, Middle East, Badentoy Avenue, Badentoy Park Industrial Estate, pg. 990 IT
Oceaneering International Services, Ltd., Pitmedden Rd., Dyce, pg. 1211 PB
P&O Scottish Ferries Ltd., Jamieson's Quay, pg. 1034 IT
Riley Advertising (Aberdeen) Ltd., Unit 4, Deemouth Centre, South Esplanade, pg. 1117 IT
Safe Service Ltd., 21, Waverly Place, pg. 277 IT
Scotoil Services Limited, Sandilands Centre, Links Rd., pg. 663 IT
Sea Oil Homco Ltd., Kirkton Ave., pg. 1034 IT
Seaforth Maritime Limited, Seaforth Centre, 30 Waterloo Quay, pg. 776 PB
Shandwick Scotland Ltd., 12 Queens Rd., pg. 1226 IT
Smith International (North Sea) Ltd., Woodside Road, pg. 1478 PB
Smith Red Baron (Oil Tools Rental) Ltd., Blackness Avenue, pg. 1478 PB
Sovereign Oil & Gas PLC, 87 Waterloo Quay, pg. 915 IT
Sparrows Offshore Services Ltd., Denmore Rd., pg. 1285 IT
Stolt Comex Seaway Ltd., pg. 1301 IT
Sub Sea International, Greenwell Base, pg. 529 PB
Talisman Energy (U.K.) Limited, Belmont House, 1 Berry St., pg. 1352 IT
Texaco North Sea U.K. Co., Langlands House, Huntley St., pg. 1584 PB
Weatherford (U.K.) Limited, Howemoss Terrace, Kirkhill Industrial Estate, pg. 1750 PB
Weatherford (U.K.) Ltd., Kirkhill Industrial Estate, Walton Road, pg. 1750 PB
Willis Corroon Scotland Limited, 46 Queens Road, pg. 1503 IT
Wilson Supply International (U.K.) Ltd., 40 Abbotswell Rd., pg. 1181 PV

Abertillery

Merton Containers, Glandwr Industrial Estate, Aberbeeg, pg. 123 IT

Abiemore

Leisure Resorts Management, Delfaber Village, pg. 168 IT

PB - *U.S. Public Companies Volume*
PV - *U.S. Private Companies Volume*
IT - *International Public & Private Companies Volume*

1792
Geographic Index-Non U.S.

Abingdon

ARC Conbloc Limited, Appleford Rd., pg. 592 — IT
Bruce Hardwood Floors, Ltd., 185 Milton Place, pg. 1634 — PB
Bundy Group, Lambourn Court, pg. 1341 — IT
Collmark-Diagnostics, Blacklands Way, pg. 1524 — IT
John Crane Group, Lambourn Court, Abingdon Business Park, pg. 1338 — IT
Crowcon Detection Instruments Limited, Two Blacklands Way, pg. 589 — IT
Dinol Protectol Ltd., Nuffield Way Conduit Place, 100 Oak St., pg. 982 — IT
Dowty Aerospace, Lambourn Court, pg. 1337 — IT
Dowty Group, Lambourn Court, pg. 1340 — IT
E.B.I. Foods Ltd., 8 Suffolk Way, pg. 491 — PB
John Crane Polymer Division, Lambourn Court, pg. 1338 — IT
Krupp Industries Ltd., Kimber Rd., pg. 510 — IT
Lilly Industries, Inc., 152 Milton Park, pg. 995 — PB
Linde Hydraulics Ltd., pg. 810 — IT
Linde Refrigeration Ltd., 7, Nuffield Way, pg. 811 — IT
Messier-Dowty, Lambourn Court, pg. 1340 — IT
NAPS United Kingdom, P.O. Box 83, pg. 913 — IT
Oxford Instruments-Industrial Analysis Group, 19/20/22 Nuffield Way, pg. 1018 — IT
Oxford Instruments-Medical Systems, One Kimber Road, pg. 1018 — IT
Oxford Instruments-Research Instruments, Tubney Woods, pg. 1018 — IT
Perstorp Form Ltd., 161 Milton Park, pg. 1038 — IT
Pig Improvement Group Ltd., Fyfield Wick, pg. 376 — IT
R&D Systems Europe Ltd., 4-10 The Quadrant, pg. 1564 — PB
TI GROUP PLC, Lambourn Court, pg. 1337 — IT
Willis Corroon Hinton Limited, The Firs, Marcham Road, pg. 1502 — IT
Zeneca Diagnostics, Blacklands Way, pg. 1524 — IT

Accrington

The Baxenden Chemical Co., Ltd., pg. 1774 — PB
GEC Engineering (Accrington) Ltd., Blackburn Road, pg. 544 — IT
Hambledon Studios Ltd., Hambledon House, Marlborough Rd., pg. 485 — IT
Walter Holland & Son, Baxenden, pg. 968 — IT
Machine Fabricators, Victoria St., pg. 231 — IT

Addlestone

Chep in Europe, Unit #2, Weybridge Bus. Park, Addlestone Road, pg. 212 — IT
Chep UK Limited, pg. 212 — IT
EXAR Corp.-Europe, Orion House, 49 High St., pg. 598 — PB
GKN-Brambles Enterprises, Ltd., Unit #2, Weybridge Bus. Park, Addlestone Road, pg. 212 — IT
Pandrol International Limited, 63 Station Rd., pg. 280 — IT
Sequent Europe Ltd., Weybridge Business Park, pg. 1460 — PB

Adlington

AMEC Civil Engineering Ltd., Chapel Street, pg. 16 — IT

Ahringham

BWI Inex Vision Systems, Atlantic St., pg. 130 — IT

Albourne

Britannic Aviation Limited, Unit 1, Jammeson Estate, pg. 215 — IT

Alcester

Amcor Europe, 8 Arden Court, Arden Road, pg. 72 — IT
Dynacast International Limited, Tything Rd., Arden Forest, pg. 299 — IT
Perstorp Components, Tything Road East, Arden Forest Industrial Estate, pg. 1040 — IT
Rockwell Automotive (U.K.) Ltd., Park Lane, Great Alne, pg. 1400 — PB
Uddeholm Limited, Kinwarton Farm Rd., pg. 1472 — IT

Alderley Edge

Zeneca Pharmaceuticals, Alderley House, pg. 1524 — IT

Aldermaston

APD Cryogenics, Five Jupiter House, Calleva Indus. Park, pg. 894 — PB
Guest International (England) Ltd., 4 Vulcan House, Calleva Park, pg. 768 — PB
Wandel & Goltermann Sales Ltd., Portland House, Aldermaston Park, pg. 1486 — IT

Aldershot

AVX Ltd., Campbell Ho., 294 High St., pg. 776 — IT
BOC Distribution Services Ltd., Victoria House, Victoria Rd., pg. 121 — IT
BritCair, Ltd., Stafford House, Station Rd., pg. 1091 — PB
Linde Cryogenics Ltd., pg. 811 — IT
Lord Corp. (Europe) Ltd., The Brook Trading Estate, pg. 676 — PV

Wynn's-Precision (U.K.)Ltd., Unit F, Manaway Industrial Complex, pg. 1783 — PB

Alfreton

Birchwood Concrete Products Ltd., Birchwood Way, Cotes Park Industrial Estate, pg. 219 — IT
Countdown Clean Systems Limited, Keys Rd., Nix Hill Industrial, Estate, pg. 802 — IT
Derbyshire-Alfreton Branch, 35/37 High Street, pg. 394 — IT
Hepworth Refractories Ltd., 1 Swanwick Court, pg. 615 — IT
NFT Distribution, Azalea Close, Clover Nook Industrial Estate, pg. 968 — IT
Syntron Europe Limited, Birchwood Way, Cotes Park Industrial Estate, pg. 1563 — PB

Alperton

Viglen Limited, Alperton Lane, pg. 1468 — IT
VIGLEN TECHNOLOGY PLC, Viglen House, Alperton Lane, pg. 1468 — IT

Alton

Charwell Pharmaceuticals Limited, Charwell House, Wilsom Rd., pg. 1283 — PB
FLS Aerospace Support Ltd., pg. 475 — IT
Pronova Biopolymer Ltd., Westbrooke House, High St. 76, pg. 964 — IT
Pronova Polymer Ltd., pg. 961 — IT

Altrincham

Thomas Allen Ltd., Station House, Stamford New Rd., pg. 1032 — IT
BWI PLC, P.O. Box 95, pg. 130 — IT
BRAMMER PLC, 1 Tabley Court, Victoria St., pg. 212 — IT
Danisco Pack Ltd., Nelson House, Park Road, pg. 243 — IT
Ferrymasters Limited, Station House, Stamford New Rd., pg. 1033 — IT
GretagMacbeth (UK) Ltd., Macbeth House, Pacific Road, pg. 966 — PB
J.P. MacDougall & Co. Limited, Manchester Rd., pg. 663 — IT
P&O European Transport Services Ltd., Station House, Stamford New Rd., pg. 1033 — IT
P&O Roadtanks Limited, Station House, Stamford New Rd., pg. 1034 — IT
Smurfit Limited, Victoria House, 2 Victoria Street, pg. 1271 — IT
UPM-Kymmene UK plc-Northern Office, 8 Ambassador Place, Stockport Rd., pg. 1431 — IT
VG Data Systems Ltd., Tudor Rd., pg. 1595 — PB
VG Laboratory Systems Ltd., No.1 St. George's Court, Hanover Business Park, pg. 1595 — PB
VG Masslab Ltd., Tudor Rd., pg. 1110 — IT
Wisaforest (UK) Ltd., 8 Ambassador Place, Stockport Rd., pg. 1430 — IT

Amersham

Alcan Consumer Products, Raans Rd., pg. 51 — IT
BABCOCK INTERNATIONAL GROUP PLC, Badminton Court, Church Street, pg. 130 — IT
Boise Cascade Sales Ltd., 7C Hill Ave., pg. 243 — PB
ESS-FOOD UK Ltd., 12 Broadway, pg. 430 — IT
HALMA P.L.C., Misbourne Ct., Rectory Way, pg. 589 — IT
Ortho Clinical Diagnostic Systems Limited, Manderville House, 62 The Broadway, pg. 931 — PB
Thomas & Betts Manufacturing Ltd., White Lion Road, pg. 1598 — PB

Andover

Britax-Excelsior Limited, Church Hill Way W., pg. 216 — IT
ESAB Automation Ltd., Units 1-3 Crown Way, Walworth Industrial Estate, pg. 282 — IT
Fortnum & Mason (Export), South Way, pg. 500 — IT
Isovel International Ltd., Walworth Indusustrial Estate, Walworth Rd., pg. 585 — IT
Pitkin Guides, Healey House, Dene Road, pg. 1094 — IT
Preformed Line Products(Great Britain) Ltd., East Portway Industrial Estate, pg. 1321 — PB
TSB Trust Co. Ltd., Charlton Place, pg. 813 — IT
Trion Ltd., Reith Way, pg. 1639 — PB
R. Twining & Co., Ltd. (UK), South Way, pg. 92 — IT

Antrim

Hewlett-Packard Ireland Ltd., Carrickfergus Industrial Ctr., 75 Belfast Rd., pg. 820 — PB
Northern Ireland Limited, Monkstown Trading Estate, Doagh Road, pg. 970 — IT
Premier Power Ltd., Ballylumford Power Station, Islandmagee, Larne, pg. 119 — IT

Ardrossan

Northern Ireland Trailers, The Harbour, pg. 1033 — IT
Saztec Europe Ltd., North Crescent Road, pg. 1435 — PB

Armagh

DDL Electronics Ltd., pg. 473 — PB
DDL Europe Ltd., pg. 473 — PB

Arundel

Tarmac Topblock Limited, Ford Airfield, pg. 1355 — IT

Ascot

American Bank Note Company, DHI Centre, 13-14 Hermitage Parade, High St., pg. 68 — PB
GN Rathdown, Goodwood Works, 17 London Road, pg. 537 — IT
NSC European Operations, Kingsride Ct., pg. 1522 — PB
Network Systems Limited, Kingsride Court, pg. 1522 — PB
Owens-Corning Fiberglas (U.K.) Ltd., 8 Crossways, Silwood Road, Sunninghill, pg. 1237 — PB
Polysius Ltd., The Brackens, London Rd., pg. 512 — IT
Technitron Plc., Unit A, Silwood Park Buckhurst Rd., pg. 1000 — IT

Ashford

Bell & Howell Ltd., (UK) Mailhandling Div., 33-35 Woodthorpe Rd., pg. 201 — PB
Blackhawk Automotive Limited, Leacon Road, pg. 805 — PB
BRAKE BROS PLC, Enterprise House, Eureka Science & Business Park, pg. 210 — IT
Enerpac Ltd., Leacon Road, pg. 125 — PB
Houchin Aerospace Limited, Hilton Road, pg. 1344 — IT
Letraset Ashford, Kingsnorth Industrial Estate, pg. 461 — IT
Letraset Export, Kingsnorth Industrial Estate, pg. 461 — IT
PPF International Limited, pg. 1434 — IT
SICO Europe Limited, Henwood Industrial Estate, pg. 997 — PV
Steel Moulds Ltd., Westwell Leacon, pg. 1355 — IT
Stena Line Limited, Charter House, pg. 1300 — IT
Target Technology Ltd., Unit 3, Brunswick Industrial Centre, pg. 853 — IT

Ashtead

Rowenta U.K. Ltd., 9th Street, pg. 569 — IT

Ashton under Lyne

Barcrest Ltd., Margaret St., pg. 170 — IT
Hawke Cable Glands, Oxford St., W., pg. 851 — IT
Hunt-Seco Engineering Ltd., Cavendish St., pg. 549 — PV

Aston

Lincoln Electric (U.K. Ltd.), Mansfield Rd., pg. 997 — PB

Atherstone

TNT U.K. Limited, TNT Express House, Holly Lane, pg. 1343 — IT
Vendhalf Ltd., 8 Newborough Close, pg. 1184 — IT

Auchtermuchty

Russell pH Limited, Station Rd., pg. 1592 — PB

Audenshaw

Brother International Corporation (Europe) Ltd., Brother House, 1 Tame St., pg. 229 — IT
CMT Steels & Supplies, Unit 4, Shepley North Indust. Estate, pg. 265 — IT

Avonmouth

Avonmouth Terminal, Royal Edward Dock, pg. 692 — PB
Castle Cement Ltd. (Port Of Bristol), Royal Edward Dock, pg. 1201 — IT
ISC Chemicals Ltd., St. Andrews Rd., pg. 1113 — IT
Imperial Tobacco Ltd., Southern Trading Div., pg. 666 — IT
Kato Cranes (UK) Ltd., 202 Burcott Road, pg. 1420 — IT

Axminster

Amtech Division, pg. 672 — IT
Goulds Pumps U.K. Ltd., pg. 861 — PB

Aycliffe

Eaton Limited Axle Operations, Durham Way, pg. 559 — PB
NIFE Power Systems Ltd., Howden Way, Aycliffe Industrial Estate, pg. 53 — IT

Aylesbury

Aylesbury Automation Ltd., P.O. Box 2, Mandeville Rd., pg. 297 — IT
CLAYHITHE P.L.C., Mandeville Rd., pg. 297 — IT
Elmtube Ltd., pg. 1511 — IT
Ginn & Co. Limited, Prebendal House, Parson's Fee, pg. 1094 — IT
ICC Chemical (UK) Limited, 7, Prebendal Ct., Oxford Rd., pg. 554 — PV
ISS Cleaning Services Ltd., The Firs, Whitchurch, pg. 657 — IT
Intertec Limited, 7 Premendal Ct., Oxford Rd., pg. 554 — PV
Kerry Ingredients UK Ltd., Gatehouse Rd., pg. 732 — IT
Mando Marketing Limited, 27 Faraday Rd., pg. 1482 — IT
Mannesmann Demag Hamilton Ltd., pg. 837 — IT
Oral-B Laboratories Limited, European Area, Gatehouse Rd., pg. 745 — PB

Geographic Index-Non U.S.

Puritan Maid Ltd., Sloan House, 24-30 New Street, pg. 210   IT
Rexel Limited, Gatehouse Rd., pg. 675   PB
Rothmans (UK) Ltd., Oxford Rd., pg. 1130   IT

Aylesford

SCA Euroliner U.K., New Hythe House, New Hythe Ln., pg. 1326   IT
SCA Recycling, New Hythe House, New Hythe Ln., pg. 1327   IT
SCA Recycling Maybank, New Hythe House, New Hythe Ln., pg. 1327   IT

Bagshot

Sun Microsystems Europe, Inc., Bagshot Manor, Green Lane, pg. 1531   PB

Balderstone

British Aerospace Defence Limited (Military Aircraft), Samlesbury Aerodrome, pg. 217   IT

Baldock

Able Translations Limited, Meeting House Lane, pg. 221   PB

Ballinamore

Lilly Industries, Inc., Willowfield Road, pg. 995   PB

Ballyclare

Dunbrik (Ulster) Limited, 20 Ballypalady Rd., pg. 1079   IT
Hollybank Bleach & Dye Works Ltd., 19/21 Hollybank Rd., pg. 798   IT
The North Down Brick Company Limited, 20 Ballypalady Rd., pg. 1079   IT
The Portrush Columnar Basalt Company Limited, 20 Bally Palady Rd., pg. 1079   IT

Ballymena

The Braidwater Spinning Company Ltd., James Street, pg. 797   IT
Dale Farm Dairies Ltd., Pennybridge Industrial Estate, Larne Rd., pg. 968   IT

Banbridge

Balievey Ltd., 245 Castlewellan Road, pg. 797   IT

Banbury

Countrywide Porter/Novelli, 51 The Green, South Bar, pg. 1225   PB
FERGUSON INTERNATIONAL HOLDINGS, Balliol House, Banbury Business Park, pg. 479   IT
Alex Lawrie Factors Ltd., Beaumont House, Beaumont Rd., pg. 813   IT
Mannesmann Demag Material Handling Ltd., New Factory Industrial Estate, pg. 837   IT
Mannesmann Holdings U.K. Ltd., pg. 840   IT
Mattessons Walls Ltd., Malthouse Walk, pg. 1434   IT
Minalex, Southam Rd., pg. 52   IT
Perstorp Flooring (UK) Ltd., 39 The Green, pg. 1039   IT
S & A Lesme Callebaut, Synya House, Daventry Rd., pg. 252   IT
Water Engineering Ltd., Aynho Road, Adderbury, pg. 399   IT

Banff

Glenglassaugh Distillery, pg. 619   IT

Bangor

MRNI, pg. 554   IT

Barking

Ballast Wiltshier Plc - London Region, Wingham House, 16/30 Wakering Road, pg. 135   PB
Coral Racing Ltd., Glebe House, Vicarage Dr., pg. 170   IT
PTP Aerial Platforms Ltd., Maybell Indus. Estate, pg. 1285   IT
Stora Transport (UK) Ltd., Ripple Road, pg. 1303   IT
William Warne Limited, India Rubber Mills, Gascoigne Road, pg. 1160   IT

Barnet

Maclean Hunter Limited, Maclean Hunter House, Chalk Lane, pg. 1124   IT

Barnsley

McLean Homes Northern Limited, Wellscroft House, pg. 1355   IT
Schiess (UK) Ltd., Redbrook Business Park, Wilthorpe Rd., pg. 860   IT
Van Leeuwel Tubes Ltd., Downings House, Doncaster Rd., pg. 1450   IT
Van Leeuwen Tubes Ltd., Doncaster Road, pg. 1450   IT

Yorkshire Brick Company, Wombwell Lane, pg. 591   IT

Barnstaple

IBL (Ballscrews) Ltd., Westacott Rd., Whiddon Valley Indus. Estate, pg. 469   IT
Parker Hannifin (U.K.) Ltd. Instrumentation Products Div., Riverside Rd., pg. 1264   PB
Selkirk (HVAC) Europe, Bassett House, High Street, pg. 1795   PB
Xomox U.K. Limited, Riverside Rd., pg. 578   PB

Barrow-in-Furness

Sovereign Chemical Industries Limited, pg. 802   IT

Barton-under-Needwood

Espe Window Systems Ltd., Espe House, Barton Turns, pg. 1302   IT

Barton-upon-Humber

Colin Booth Ltd., Humber Road, pg. 1251   IT

Basildon

Coated Specialities Ltd., Chester Hall La, pg. 849   PB
GEC Sensors Ltd., Christopher Martin Rd., pg. 544   IT
Gilbarco Ltd., Crompton Close, pg. 545   IT
Konica Business Machines (UK) Ltd., 6 Miles Gray Rd., pg. 749   IT
Morse Controls Ltd., Christopher Martin Road, pg. 857   PB

Basingstoke

Alberto-Culver Company (U.K.) Limited, Houndsmill Industrial Estate, pg. 38   IT
Ampex Great Britain Limited, Ampex House, Beechwood, pg. 104   PB
Arjo Wiggins Appleton plc, P.O. Box 88, Gateway House, pg. 567   IT
Arjo Wiggins Europe Holdings, Ltd., P.O. Box 88, Gateway House, Basing View, pg. 567   IT
Arjo Wiggins Finland Holdings, P.O. Box 88, Gateway House, Basing View, pg. 567   IT
Arjo Wiggins Overseas Ltd., P.O. Box 88, Gateway House, Basing View, pg. 567   IT
Arjo Wiggins Research and Devel. Ltd., P.O. Box 88, Gateway House, Basing View, pg. 567   IT
Asea Hagglunds (U.K.) Ltd., Kingsland Industrial Pk., Bilton Road, pg. 8   IT
BOCM Silcock Ltd., BOCM Silcock Ho., Basings Vw., pg. 1434   IT
Barclays Mercantile Business Finance Limited, Churchill Plaza, Churchill Way, pg. 165   IT
Chattem (U.K.) Ltd., Guerry House, Ringway Ctr., Edison Rd., pg. 342   PB
Custom Accessories Europe Ltd., Custom House, pg. 298   PV
De La Rue Holographics Limited, Stroudley Road, Daneshill Industrial Estate, pg. 387   IT
De La Rue Identity Systems Limited, De La Rue House, Jays Close, pg. 387   IT
De La Rue Payment Systems Division, De La Rue House, Jays Close, Viables, pg. 387   IT
Thomas De La Rue and Company Limited, De La Rue House, Jays Close, pg. 386   IT
De La Rue Transaction Systems Division, De La Rue House, Jays Close, Viables, pg. 387   IT
Devlin Electronics Limited, Unit D1, Grafton Way, pg. 207   IT
ECI Telecom (UK) Limited, ISIS House, Reading Road, pg. 644   IT
Elanco Products Limited, Kingsclere Road, pg. 993   PB
Elliott Turbomachinery Ltd., 120 Thornycroft Indus. Estate, Worting Rd., pg. 373   PV
Eurodis Bytech Electronics Limited, 12A Cedarwood, Chineham Business Park, pg. 1247   IT
Eurodis Bytech OnBoard Limited, 12a Cedarwood, Chineham Business Park, pg. 1247   IT
Exploration Computing Limited, Houndsmill Road, pg. 776   PB
Gearhart Tesel Limited, Houndsmill Road, pg. 776   PB
B.F. Goodrich Component Services, Ltd., Cherrywood, Chineham Business Park, pg. 752   PB
Hyster Europe Ltd., Berk Ho., Basing View, pg. 1149   PB
ITW Electronic Component Packaging, West Ham Industrial Estate, pg. 868   PB
ITW Fastex, Viables Estate Jays Close, pg. 868   PB
ITW Nexus UK, Viables Estate, Jays Close, pg. 868   PB
Intercosmetic (Great Britain) Limited, Wella Rd., pg. 1490   IT
The Kendall Co. (UK) Ltd., Chineham Business Park, 2 Elmwood, Crockford Lane, pg. 1647   PB
Lansing Linde Ltd., Kingsclere Rd., pg. 810   IT
Eli Lilly and Company Limited, Kingsclere Road, pg. 993   PB
Lilly Industries Limited, Kingsclere Rd., pg. 994   PB
Linde Holding Ltd., pg. 811   IT
Luwa Filter and Shelter Ltd., pg. 617   IT
Macmillan Distribution Ltd., Houndmills, pg. 1479   IT
Macmillan Education Ltd., Houndmills, pg. 1479   IT
Measurements Group U.K. Ltd., pg. 1722   IT
Monsanto Export Limited, Monsanto House, Chineham Court, Chineham, pg. 1125   PB
Monsanto P.L.C., Monsanto House, Chineham Court, Chineham, pg. 1126   IT
Montal (Insurance) Limited, Monsanto House, Chineham Court, Chineham, pg. 1126   PB

Motorola Communications Services Limited, Viables Industrial Estate, pg. 1139   PB
Motorola Information Systems Limited, Viables Industrial Estate, pg. 1139   PB
Motorola Ltd., Jays Close, pg. 1140   PB
PDA International/United Kingdom, Rowan House, Woodlands Business Village, pg. 1031   IT
Perstorp Pharma Ltd. Wound Care Division, Studio 1, Intec 2, pg. 1037   IT
Portals Ltd., Overton Mill, Overton, pg. 386   IT
Quaife Papers, Ltd., Gateway House, Basing View, pg. 567   IT
Racal-Datacom Ltd, Landata House, pg. 1082   IT
Robinson-Nugent Ltd., Unit 9A, Intec Two, Wade Road, pg. 1395   PB
SMS Europe, Deane House, pg. 1463   PB
SMS United Kingdom, Ltd., Sarum Gate, Sarum Hill, pg. 1464   PB
Sanden International (Europe) Ltd., Humpshire International Business Park, pg. 1184   IT
Smiths Industries Aerospace & Defence Systems Limited-Basingstoke, Winchester Rd., pg. 1267   IT
Sony Broadcast & Communications Limited, Jays Close, pg. 1283   IT
Strategic Systems International Limited, Faraday Rd., pg. 1065   IT
Sun Life Assurance Company of Canada (U.K.) Limited, Basing View, pg. 1319   IT
Sun Life of Canada Group of Companies, Basing View, pg. 1319   IT
Sun Life of Canada Home Loans Company Limited, Basing View, pg. 1320   IT
Sun Life of Canada Nominees Limited, Basing View, pg. 1320   IT
Sun Life of Canada Unit Managers Limited, Basing View, pg. 1319   IT
The Sunlight Service Group Ltd., Roentgen Road, Daneshill East, pg. 385   IT
Taylor Made (Great Britain) Ltd., Annecy House, The Loddon Centre, Wale Road, pg. 1181   IT
Tesel International Services Limited, Houndsmill Rd., pg. 777   PB
Tesel Overseas Services Limited, Houndsmill Rd., pg. 777   PB
Tesel PLC, Houndsmill Rd., pg. 777   PB
Tesel Services Limited, Houndsmill Rd., pg. 777   PB
Tesel Wireline Services Limited, Houndsmill Rd., pg. 777   PB
Trane Ltd., Gastons Wood Reading Rd., pg. 92   PB
TransInstruments, Lennox Rd., pg. 857   PB
United Agricultural Merchants Ltd., Basingview, pg. 1434   IT
Velsicol Chemical Limited, Chineman Business Park, 8 Cedarwood, pg. 1135   PV
Vendhall Ltd., Unit 17, The Basingstoke Enterprise Centre, pg. 1184   IT
Viewlogic Systems, Ltd., Daneshill House, Chineham Court, pg. 1548   PB
Wiggins Teape Paper Ltd., P.O. Box 88, Gateway House, Basing View, pg. 567   IT
Wiggins Teape (Stationery) Ltd., P.O. Box 88, Gateway House, pg. 567   IT

Bath

BEAZER GROUP PLC, St. James House Sq., Lower Bristol Road, pg. 181   IT
The Andrew Brownsword Collection, Kelston Park, pg. 496   PV
The Classic Card Company, Ltd., James Street West, pg. 496   PV
Hanson Properties Limited, Beazer House, pg. 593   IT
Horstman Timers & Controls Limited, Newbridge Road, pg. 297   IT
Herman Miller, Ltd., Lower Bristol Rd., pg. 1112   PB
Portals (Bathford) Ltd., Bathford Mill, pg. 386   IT
Victoria House Publishing, Ltd., 4 North Parade, pg. 1368   PB
Work Base, Ltd., Lower Bristol Rd., pg. 1112   PB

Bathgate

Ewos Ltd., Westfield, pg. 349   IT
Taylor Instrument Ltd., 31 A North Bridge St., pg. 6   IT

Batley

Fox's Biscuits Ltd., P.O. Box 10, pg. 968   :T
Layezee Beds, Grange Road, pg. 1249   IT
Perstorp Analytical Lumac Ltd., Unit 301, Batley Enterprise Centre, pg. 1039   IT

Beaconsfield

Anglo Dutch Dredging Co. Ltd., The Old Rectory, Windsor End, pg. 134   IT
Perkin-Elmer Ltd., Post Office Lane, pg. 1279   PB

Beckenham

Aloette Cosmetics (UK) Ltd., pg. 57   PB

Bedford

Activ Training Ltd., Activ House, 45 Bromham Rd., pg. 859   PB
Beazer Homes (Bedford) Limited, Wootton House, pg. 182   IT

PB - *U.S. Public Companies Volume*
PV - *U.S. Private Companies Volume*
IT - *International Public & Private Companies Volume*

Camford Design Ltd., Research & Development Center, Ampthill Road, pg. 507   IT
Concorde Express, Unit 2, Westgate, Staines Road, pg. 707   IT
Danfoss Randall Limited, Ampthill Road, pg. 377   IT
Dusenbery Europe Ltd., Shuttleworth Rd., pg. 350   PV
Eaton Limited Commercial & Military Controls Operations, Elstow Rd., pg. 559   PB
Exel Logistics, The Merton Centre, 45 St.Peters St., pg. 901   IT
Georg Fischer Castings, P.O. Box 128, pg. 489   IT
Gordon Fraser Gallery, Eastcotts Road, pg. 496   PV
Irvin Aerospace Ltd., Redding's Wood, Ampthill, pg. 640   IT
Jacobs Suchard Ltd., Miller Rd., pg. 1289   PB
London Brick Company Ltd., pg. 593   IT
Nobel Systems Ltd., Murdock Rd., pg. 1290   IT
Oilgear Towler Ltd. (Bedford), Shuttleworth Rd., Goldington, pg. 1215   PB
Pre-Star Ltd., Ampthill Rd., pg. 507   IT
Rank Amusements Limited, Melbourne House, pg. 1087   IT
Texas Instruments Limited, Manton Lane, pg. 1586   PB
Tricom Supplies Ltd., pg. 838   IT
Wyseplant Ltd., Chawston, pg. 1035   IT

Bedlington

Welwyn Components Limited, Welwyn Electronics Park, pg. 1344   IT

Bedworth

LEX HARVEY LTD., King's House, King St., pg. 599   IT
Harvey Plant Limited, King's House, King Street, pg. 910   IT
Lex Harvey, King's House, King's Street, pg. 807   IT

Beeston

Barratt East Midlands, Broadgate House, Humber Rd., pg. 168   IT
Chambers Packaging, Stapleford Lane, pg. 123   IT
SHL Technology Solutions, 3 Padge Road, pg. 1154   IT

Belfast

Aggregates (Ulster) Limited, 22-30 Hopefield Ave., pg. 1079   IT
Albright & Wilson Northern Ireland, Ltd., Imperial Buildings, 72 High Street, pg. 49   IT
Bank of Ireland Corporate & International Banking, 7 Donegall Square Nth., pg. 153   IT
Belfast Terminal, Airport Rd., pg. 692   PB
Bewleys Oriental Cafes Limited, Unit 17 Donegall Arcade, pg. 254   IT
Bradstock Insurance Brokers Limited, Bulloch House, 2 Linehall St., pg. 210   IT
CEM Computers Limited, Victoria Business Park, West Bank Rd., pg. 1247   IT
CSD Hathaway Limited, pg. 799   PB
Calor Gas Northern Ireland Ltd., Airport Road West, pg. 1155   IT
Cardiac Services Company, 95A Finaghy Rd., S., pg. 816   PB
Gilbeys of Ireland, Gilbey House, 58 Boucher Road, pg. 409   IT
Guinness Northern Ireland Limited, P.O. Box 50, Apollo Rd., pg. 412   IT
HAC Catherwood & Sons (Belfast) Limited, 22-30 Hopefield Ave., pg. 1080   IT
Hathaway Advanced Power Limited, pg. 799   PB
Hughes Tool Company Limited, Montgomery Rd., Castlereagh, pg. 167   PB
Lambert Smith Hampton, Clarence House, 4/10 May St., pg. 797   IT
LAMONT HOLDINGS PLC., Lamont House, 429 Holywood Rd., pg. 797   IT
Lombard and Ulster Limited, 40 Linenhall St., pg. 910   IT
Lowden & Partners Limited, 328 Antrim Rd., pg. 1079   IT
Northern Bank Limited, P.O. Box 183, Donegall Square West, pg. 906   IT
RMC Catherwood (Surfacing) Limited, RMC House, Upper Dunmurry Ln., pg. 1079   IT
Ready Mixed Concrete (Ulster) Limited, RMC House, Upper Dunmurry Ln., pg. 1079   IT
William Reay (Belfast) Ltd., Delta House, Duncrue Crescent, pg. 390   IT
Sanderson NI Limited, Aldersgate House, University Road, pg. 1184   IT
Saville Tractors (Belfast) Ltd., pg. 817   IT
Savilles Auto Village Ltd., pg. 817   IT
Shandwick Northern Ireland Ltd., 425 Holywood Rd., pg. 1226   IT
Shorts Brothers PLC, Airport Road, pg. 200   IT
Stena Line Limited, Belfast Harbour, Commissioner's Harbour Office, pg. 1300   IT
Stena Line Limited, Passenger Terminal, Ballast Quay, pg. 1300   IT
Talza Ltd., 2 Marshalls Rd., pg. 296   IT
Thrige-Scott Ltd., 314 Ravenhill Road, pg. 1387   IT
Ulster Bank Commercial Services (NI) Limited, 11 Donegall Square South, pg. 911   IT
Ulster Bank Insurance Services Limited, Ulster Bank House, Shaftesbury Square, pg. 911   IT
Ulster Bank Limited, 47 Donegall Place, pg. 911   IT
Ulster Bank Trust Company, 35-39 Waring St., pg. 911   IT
Ulster Waste Limited, RMC House, Upper Dunmurry Ln., pg. 1079   IT
WF Corroon-Belfast, 78-86 Dublin Road, pg. 1501   IT

Willis Corroon Harris Marrian Limited, Willis Corroon House, 78-86 Dublin Road, pg. 1502   IT

Bellshill

Anixter Glasgow U.K., Unit 5, Motorlink Ringhead Estate, pg. 116   IT
WILLIAM GRANT & SONS DISTILLERS LTD., Phoenix Crescent Stroth Clyde Bus. Pk., pg. 557   IT

Belper

Curtagil Ltd., Derby Road, pg. 519   IT
Dalton & Co. (Synthetic Products) Ltd., Derby Road, pg. 519   IT
Fuchs (UK) p.l.c., Derby Road, pg. 518   IT
Hepworth Heating Ltd., Nottingham Rd., pg. 615   IT
Hepworth Home Products Limited, Nottingham Rd., pg. 615   IT
Phoenix Oil Company (UK) Limited, Derby Road, pg. 519   IT
Silkolene Lubricants Plc, Derby Road, pg. 519   IT
Silkolene Plc, Derby Road, pg. 518   IT

Bembridge

Pilatus Britten-Norman Ltd., Bembridge Airport, pg. 998   IT

Berkshire

Biogen Limited, Ocean House, The Ring, pg. 231   PB

Berwick-upon-Tweed

Ballast Wiltshier Plc - Scotland, Unit 3, North Road, pg. 135   IT
Jus-rol Ltd., Tweedside Trading Estate, pg. 411   IT

Betchworth

SmithKline Beecham Pharmaceuticals, Research Division, Brockham Park, pg. 1264   IT

Beverley

Bevaloid Ltd., P.O. Box 3, pg. 1113   IT
Yorkshire Marine Containers Limited, Belprin Rd., Swinemoor Lane, pg. 1214   IT

Bexhill-on-Sea

Chandlers Printers Limited, pg. 1511   IT

Bexley

Pharmax Ltd., 5 Bourne Rd., pg. 670   PB
WOOLWICH PLC., Watling St., pg. 1514   IT

Bicester

CCH Editions Limited, Telford Road, pg. 1514   IT
Lawter Intl., Ltd., Murdock Rd., pg. 981   IT
Micromedia Limited, Units 7-8, Telford Rd., Launton Indust. Estate, pg. 201   IT
Nellcor Puritan Bennett (UK) Limited, 10 Talisman Business Center, pg. 1040   PB

Bideford

Dartington Crystal, Alverdiscott Industrial Estate, Alverdiscott Rd., pg. 124   IT

Biggleswade

Metal & Pipeline Endurance, 7-8 Eldon Way, pg. 16   IT

Billericay

Totes U.K. Limited, Eastman House, Radford Crescent, pg. 111   PV
Willis Corroon Construction Risks Limited, 14 Woodbrook Crescent, pg. 1502   IT

Billingham

Tioxide Europe Limited, Haverton Hill Rd., pg. 663   IT

Billingshurst

Dynex Technologies (U.K.), Daux Rd., pg. 1591   PB
General Combustion Ltd., Brookers Rd., pg. 705   PB
Premier Industrial (U.K.) Ltd., Unit 4 Daux Rd., pg. 1068   IT

Bilston

Babcock Industrial & Electrical Products Ltd., Oxford St., pg. 472   IT
Babcock Transformers Ltd., Oxford St., pg. 472   IT
Barton Handling & Storage Systems Ltd., Mount Pleasant, pg. 264   IT
Beazer Homes (Birmingham), Beazer House, Hare St., pg. 182   IT
Beldray Limited, P.O. Box 20, pg. 968   PB
Cannon Industries Ltd., Gough Rd., pg. 543   IT

General Manufacturing Div., Oxford St., pg. 472   IT
STILL Materials Handling Ltd., pg. 811   IT

Bingham

Brian Pulfrey Ltd., Moorbridge, pg. 1267   PB

Bingley

BRADFORD & BINGLEY BUILDING SOCIETY, P.O. Box 88, pg. 210   IT
Damart, Bowling Green Mills, pg. 376   IT
Fairbank Brearley, Church St., pg. 268   IT

Birchills

Caparo Industries Plc., Caparo House, pg. 265   IT

Birkenhead

Dunlop Marine Safety Ltd., Corporation Rd., pg. 126   IT
Valvoline Oil Co. Ltd., Dock Rd., pg. 140   PB

Birmingham

Aero Engine Equipment Group, Warwick Rd., pg. 127   IT
AGIE UK Ltd., 21, Roman Way, pg. 488   IT
Alcan Specialty Aerospace, pg. 51   IT
Algemene Bank Nederland, 35 Waterloo Street, pg. 11   IT
Allied Domecq Leisure, Tamebridge House, pg. 63   IT
Anixter-Birmingham, Unit 120, Saltley Trading Estate, pg. 116   PB
Apricot Computers, 111 Hagley Rd., pg. 873   IT
Armstrong Screws & Fixings Ltd., 72-84 Great Barr St., pg. 265   IT
Autolease Fleets Limited, Burgess House, Coventry Rd., pg. 216   IT
Autolease Limited, Burgess House, Coventry Rd., pg. 216   IT
Avesta Sheffield Distribution Ltd., The Avenue, pg. 221   IT
Babcock Worsley Limited, 65 Livery St., pg. 472   IT
N.G. Bailey & Co. Ltd.-Birmingham Branch, Etna House, Grosvenor St., pg. 132   IT
Bailey Telecom LTD - Birmingham, Etna House, Grosvenor Street, pg. 133   IT
Bass International Brewers, Cape Hill Brewery, pg. 170   IT
Bass Taverns Ltd., Cape Hill, pg. 170   IT
Belliss & Morcom, Icknield Square, pg. 1065   IT
Bill Switchgear Ltd., Aston Ln., Perry Barr, pg. 390   IT
Birfield Plant of GKN Hardy Spicer, Station Works, Old Walsall Rd., pg. 534   IT
Birmingham, Wellesley House, 37 Waterloo Street, pg. 910   IT
Boxmag-Rapid Ltd., pg. 1511   IT
Bristol Street Motors Limited, Bristol Street House, 156/182 Bristol St., pg. 216   IT
British Bakeries (Midlands) Limited, 115 Golden Millock Rd., pg. 1396   IT
CAIB UK Limited, Imperial House, 350 Bournville Lane, pg. 212   IT
Cadbury International Limited, pg. 248   IT
Cadbury Limited, pg. 248   IT
Canning-Lippert Ltd., Argyle Works, Great Baw Street, pg. 526   IT
Castle Cement Limited, Park Square, 3160 Solihull Parkway, pg. 1201   IT
Charles Winn (Valves) Limited, 70 Warwick St., pg. 1651   PB
Cincinnati Milacron U.K. Limited, Kingsbury Rd., pg. 368   PB
CUNA Mutual Group-Great Britain, Crest House, 7 Highfield Road, pg. 296   PV
Dallas Semiconductor Corporation Ltd., Unit 26, W. Midlands Freeport, pg. 478   IT
Daventry International Rail Freight Terminal, 2308 Coventry Road, pg. 1226   IT
Delta Circuit Protection & Controls Ltd., MEM Works, Reddings Ln., pg. 390   IT
Delta Electrical Systems Ltd., Premier St., pg. 390   IT
Delta Repetition Components Ltd., Argyle St., pg. 391   IT
DOLLAND & AITCHISON LTD., 1323 Coventry Rd., pg. 414   IT
Dolland & Aitchison Services Ltd., 1323 Coventry Rd., pg. 414   IT
Dollands Photographic Holdings Ltd., 1323 Coventry Rd., pg. 414   IT
Ducost Engineering Ltd., Swan Office Centre, 1506-1508 Coventry Road, pg. 585   IT
Dunlop Adhesives, Chester Rd., pg. 125   IT
Dunlop Aircraft Tyres Div., pg. 125   IT
Dunlop International Projects, pg. 126   IT
Dunlop Tyres UK Ltd., Fort Dunlop, pg. 1317   IT
EIP Metals Limited, Heath St. S., pg. 426   IT
Export Sales & Distribution, MEM Works, Reddings Ln., pg. 390   IT
Farr Filtration, 272 Kings Road, pg. 614   PB
Financial Collection Agencies, GN House, First Floor, Holloway Head, pg. 471   IT
Forward Insurance Brokers Limited, Burgess House, Coventry Rd., pg. 216   IT
Foseco Plc, 285 Long Acre, Nechells, pg. 234   IT
H.B. Fuller Coatings Ltd., 95, Aston Church Rd., pg. 686   PB
GKN Automotive Ltd., P.O. Box 4128, Chester Road, pg. 534   IT
GKN Hardy Spicer Ltd., Chester Rd., pg. 534   IT
GLYNWED INTERNATIONAL PLC, Headland House, 54 New Coventry Road, pg. 554   IT

PB - U.S. Public Companies Volume
PV - U.S. Private Companies Volume
IT - International Public & Private Companies Volume

1795

Godwins Limited, Auchinleck House, Broad St., pg. 119   **PB**
Samuel Groves & Co., Ltd., Norton Street, pg. 1791   **PB**
Haden Drysys Environmental Ltd., Swan Office Centre, 1506-1508 Coventry Rd., pg. 585   **IT**
Haden Drysys International Ltd., Swan Office Centre, 1506-1508 Coventry Rd., pg. 585   **IT**
Haden Drysys Ltd., Swan Office Centre, 1506-1508 Coventry Rd., pg. 585   **IT**
Haden King Limited, Swan Office Centre, 1506-1508 Coventry Rd., pg. 585   **IT**
Hamblin Contact Lenses, 1323 Coventry Rd., pg. 414   **IT**
Hamblin Optical Services Ltd., 1323 Coventry Rd., pg. 414   **IT**
Harmo Industries, Ltd., Wharfdale Rd., pg. 1579   **PB**
Harrison Drape, Bradford Street Works, pg. 851   **IT**
John Heath & Co. Limited, 230 Bradford St., pg. 64   **PV**
Henderson Unit Trust Management Limited, 6th Fl., Charles House, 148-149 Great Charles St., pg. 609   **IT**
Arthur Holden & Sons Plc, pg. 663   **IT**
Hollandia Weathershields Limited, 1 Pennine Way, pg. 1463   **IT**
Hopkins & Bailey Ltd., 3 Windsor Industrial Estate, Rupert St., pg. 1226   **IT**
Houghton Vaughn plc, Legge St., pg. 541   **PV**
ISS Food Hygiene Ltd., Albert Street, pg. 657   **IT**
Ipsen Abar UK Limited, Unit 1A, Nechells Business Centre, pg. 1149   **IT**
Keter (UK) Ltd, Unit 4, pg. 732   **IT**
Kodak Limited-Midland Business Centre, Bank House, Cherry St., pg. 553   **PB**
Krups, 190 Camden Street, pg. 896   **IT**
Lambert Smith Hampton, 50 Newhall St., pg. 797   **IT**
LANDOR CARTONS, 45 Devon St., pg. 801   **IT**
LAUGHTON & SONS, LTD., Warstock Rd., pg. 804   **IT**
Leeds & Northrup Ltd., Wharfdale Rd., pg. 727   **PB**
LINPAC MOULDINGS LIMITED, 3180 Park Square, Birmingham Business Park, pg. 811   **IT**
MEM Ltd. 500V, MEM Works, Reddings Ln., pg. 390   **IT**
Edward Marsden Limited, Bordesley Green Rd., pg. 663   **IT**
McCarthy Bailey Limited, Etna House, Grosvenor St., pg. 133   **IT**
Mikron (Birmingham) Ltd., Chelmsley Wood Industrial Est., Unit 12, Waterloo Ave., pg. 867   **IT**
Motaproducts Automotive Limited, pg. 561   **PB**
Moulinex/Swan Ltd., Albion Street, pg. 896   **IT**
NYK Line-Birmingham, Containerbase, College Road, Perry Barr, pg. 942   **IT**
National Westminster Home Loans Limited, Priory House, 38 Colmore Circus, pg. 910   **IT**
Newey & Eyre Ltd., Donne Ho, Calthorpe Rd., pg. 125   **IT**
Polypenco Ltd., 64 Gravelly Industrial Park, Tyburn Road, Erdington, pg. 354   **IT**
Premisys Communications Limited, Birmingham Business Park, 2050 The Crescent, pg. 1323   **PB**
Purac Biochem (UK) Limited, 50-54 St. Paul's Square, Ste. 17, pg. 244   **IT**
RGB Stainless Ltd., pg. 1186   **IT**
RMC Surfacing Limited-Midlands Area, Railway Sidings, Aston Church Rd., pg. 1080   **IT**
Ready Mixed Concrete (West Midlands) Limited, RMC House, Queslett Rd., pg. 1080   **IT**
Riley Advertising (Birmingham) Ltd., Lopex Suite, Centre Court, 1301 Stratford Rd., pg. 1317   **IT**
Rockwell Light Vehicle Systems (U.K.) Limited - Access Control Systems, Fordhouse Lane, pg. 1401   **PB**
Rockwell Light Vehicle Systems (U.K.) Ltd. - Roof Systems, Fordhouse Lane, pg. 1401   **PB**
Rover Group Holdings Plc, International House, Bickenhill Lane, pg. 178   **PB**
Rover Group Limited, International House, pg. 178   **IT**
SPI plc, Ocean House, Wholesale Markets Precinct, pg. 491   **IT**
S.U. Automotive Limited, pg. 561   **PB**
Sanderson GA Limited, 1-2 Venture Way, pg. 1184   **IT**
Sandvik Coromant U.K., pg. 1186   **IT**
Sandvik Ltd., Manor Way, Halesowen, pg. 1186   **IT**
Sandvik Process Systems Ltd., Hereward Rise, pg. 1187   **IT**
Sandvik Saws and Tools U.K., pg. 1187   **IT**
Sandvik Steel U.K., pg. 1187   **IT**
Serck Heat Transfer, Warwick Rd., pg. 125   **IT**
Severn Trent Overseas Holdings Limited, 2297 Coventry Road, pg. 1226   **IT**
SEVERN TRENT PLC, 2297 Coventry Road, pg. 1225   **IT**
Severn Trent Property Limited, 2308 Coventry Road, pg. 1226   **IT**
Severn Trent Systems Limited, 2800 The Crescent, pg. 1226   **IT**
Severn Trent Technology Limited, 2308 Coventry Road, pg. 1226   **IT**
Severn Trent Water International Limited, 2308 Coventry Road, pg. 1226   **IT**
Severn Trent Water International (Overseas Holdings) Limited, 2308 Coventry Road, pg. 1226   **IT**
Severn Trent Water Ltd., 2297 Coventry Rd., pg. 1225   **IT**
Shell UK Oil (Birmingham), Fuel Farm, Birmingham Intl. Airport, pg. 1139   **IT**
Sheller-Clifford Ltd., Spring Rd., pg. 1691   **IT**
Smith & Nephew Consumer Products Ltd., Alum Rock Rd., pg. 1263   **IT**
South East Asia Companies, MEM Works, Reddings Ln., pg. 390   **IT**
State Bank of India, 67-73 Constitution Hill, pg. 1297   **IT**
Stoner Associates Europe Limited, 2800 The Crescent, pg. 1226   **IT**
Sturge, Lifford, Lifford Chemical Works, Lifford Lane, pg. 1113   **IT**
The Sumitomo Bank, Ltd.-Birmingham Representative Office, Bank House, Cherry St., pg. 1309   **IT**

Symix Systems Inc., Birmingham Bus. Ctr., 2460 Regents Ct., The Crescent, pg. 1547   **PB**
TI Reynolds Rings Limited, P.O. Box 763, Hay Hall, Redfern Rd., pg. 1338   **IT**
Takenaka (U.K.) Ltd., Birmingham, The Flag House, 16 Graham Street, pg. 1352   **IT**
Titex Tools Ltd., pg. 1187   **IT**
Toby Restaurants Ltd., Cape Hill, pg. 170   **IT**
TRANSTEC PLC, 2650 Kings Court, The Crescent, pg. 1418   **IT**
Tucker Fasteners Ltd., 177 Walsall Rd., pg. 234   **PB**
Universal Steel Tube Co. Limited, Bertha Road Greet, pg. 873   **PV**
VDO Instruments Ltd., pg. 839   **IT**
Valor Ltd., Wood Lane, pg. 925   **IT**
WF Corroon-Birmingham, Rutland House, Edmund Street, pg. 1501   **IT**
WAGON INDUSTRIAL HOLDINGS PLC, Birmingham Business Park, 3100 Solihull Parkway, pg. 1484   **IT**
Willis Corroon Credit Limited, Rutland House, Edmund Street, pg. 1502   **IT**
Willis Corroon Midlands Limited, Rutland House, Edmund Street, pg. 1502   **IT**
Wind River Systems UK Ltd., Aston Science Park, Aston Triangle, pg. 1771   **PB**

Birtley

Solvitol Limited, Shadon Way, Portobello Industrial Estate, pg. 858   **IT**

Bishops Stortford

Bewleys Coffeeman Limited, 1 The Priors, London Road, pg. 254   **IT**
Campbell Catering International Ltd., 1 The Priors, London Road, pg. 254   **IT**

Bishopston

Compaq Computer Mfg. Ltd., Erskine Ferry Road, pg. 418   **PB**

Blackburn

Mathew Brown plc, Lion Brewery, pg. 1211   **IT**
Channel Master (UK) Limited, Glenfield Park, Site 2, pg. 228   **PV**
East Lancashire Cablevision Limited, Glenfield Park, Site 2, Northrup Ave., pg. 1123   **IT**
Grau Limited, pg. 561   **PB**
H & H Refrigeration Ltd., Cunliffe Rd., Whitebirk Industrial Estate, pg. 1035   **IT**
Meggitt Petroleum Systems (UK), Harwood Street, pg. 853   **IT**
Porritts & Spencer Ltd., Oakfield House, 93 Preston New Road, pg. 1202   **IT**
Presspart Manufacturing Ltd., Whitebirk Estate, pg. 124   **IT**
Roe Lee Paper Chemicals Co. Ltd., Sett End Road, pg. 1086   **IT**
SCAPA GROUP PLC, Oakfield House, 93 Preston New Rd., pg. 1202   **IT**
Scapa Mouldings Ltd., Victoria Works, Parker St., pg. 1202   **IT**
Scapa Scandia Ltd., Cartmell Rd., pg. 1202   **IT**
Senior Heat Treatment-Blackburn, Whitebirk Industrial Estate, pg. 1221   **IT**
Silicone Engineering, Greenbank Business Park, pg. 853   **IT**

Blackpool

AD Plastics Ltd., Clifton Rd., pg. 499   **PB**
Lyons Biscuits, Devonshire Road, pg. 619   **IT**
Superform Metals, pg. 52   **IT**

Blackwood

Lansing Linde (Blackwood) Ltd., pg. 810   **IT**
Penny & Giles Studio Equipment Ltd., Newbridge Rd. Industrial Estate, pg. 207   **IT**

Blaenavon

Eurofoil Ltd., Kays & Kears Industrial Estate, pg. 868   **PB**
Metallised Films & Paper, Ltd., Gilchrist Thomas Indus. Estate, pg. 154   **PB**
Van Leer Metallized Products Ltd., pg. 1147   **IT**

Blaenrhondda

Stelco Hardy, pg. 222   **IT**

Bletchley

Felton Worldwide Ltd., Castle Tower Works, Bilton Rd., pg. 1696   **PB**
Jeumont-Schneider Industrial Systems (JSIS), P.O. Box 370, pg. 706   **IT**

Blyth

Welwyn Systems Limited, Kitty Brewster Estate, pg. 1344   **IT**

Bognor Regis

LEC Refrigeration Plc, pg. 1251   **IT**
Rosemount Ltd., Heath Place, pg. 577   **PB**
Solartron Metrology Ltd., Steyning Way, pg. 1130   **PB**
Weir Electronics Limited, Durban Rd., pg. 1241   **IT**

Bolton

APPH (Bolton) Ltd., Great Bank Road, pg. 112   **IT**
British Aerospace Defence Limited (Dynamics), Lostock Lane, pg. 217   **IT**
The Collapsible Tube Co. Limited, pg. 267   **IT**
Davidsons Waste Paper, Folds Rd., pg. 123   **IT**
Eurodis HB Electronics Limited, Lever St., pg. 1247   **IT**
Ingersoll-Rand Sales Company Limited UK, P.O. Box 2, Chorley, New Rd., Horwich, pg. 878   **PB**
Kontite, U.K., pg. 780   **PB**
Synres-Almoco UK Ltd., 68 St. George Rd., pg. 356   **IT**
Watson Steel & Co. (Constructional Engineers) Ltd., Lostock Lane, pg. 16   **IT**
Wire Machinery Div., Albion Works, Waterloo St., pg. 473   **IT**

Bookham

PHOTO-ME INTERNATIONAL PLC, Church Rd., pg. 1055   **IT**

Bootle

Scanland Agencies Ltd., 163 Derby Rd., pg. 967   **IT**

Borden

Molex Electronics Ltd., Molex House, Farnham Rd., pg. 1122   **PB**
Printed Motors Ltd., Bordon Trading Estate, pg. 448   **IT**

Borehamwood

Adecco UK plc, Adecco House, Elstree Way, pg. 24   **IT**
Bailey Telecom LTD - London, One Elstree Way, pg. 133   **IT**
Elstree Computing Ltd., 12 Elstree Way, pg. 796   **IT**
Harman Audio, Unit 2, Borehamwood Industrial Park, Rowley Ln., pg. 787   **PB**
Jacques Onona & Co. Limited, 1 Penta Court, Station Road, pg. 491   **IT**
Pizza Hut (UK) Ltd., One Imperial Pl., Elstree Way, pg. 1499   **IT**
Pizza Hut (UK) Ltd., One Imperial Pl., Elstree Way, pg. 1637   **PB**
O.C. Summers Ltd., Manor Way, pg. 796   **IT**
THORN LIGHTING GROUP PLC, Elftree Way, pg. 1385   **IT**
Wanson Co. Ltd., 7 Elstree Way, pg. 472   **IT**

Bourne

Allied Domecq Leisure, Sutherland House, 3 Dukes Meadow, pg. 63   **IT**
Ballast Phoenix Ltd., Victoria Stables, South Road, pg. 133   **IT**
Dunkin' Donuts U.K. Limited, Sutherland House, 3 Dukes Meadow, pg. 63   **IT**
Landis & Staefa Building Control (U.K.) Ltd., 2 Dukes Meadow, pg. 800   **IT**
Landis & Staefa Energy Management (U.K.) Ltd., 2 Dukes Meadow, pg. 801   **IT**
Lex Autosales, Lex House, Boston Drive, pg. 807   **IT**
Lex Bodycentres, Lex House, Boston Drive, pg. 807   **IT**
Lex Retail Group, Lex House, Boston Drive, pg. 807   **IT**
LEX SERVICE PLC, Lex House, Boston Drive, pg. 806   **PB**
Pacific Scientific Ltd., 8 Boston Drive, pg. 1250   **IT**
Rechem International Ltd, Astor House, Station Rd., pg. 1228   **IT**
SHANKS & MCEWAN GROUP PLC, Astor House, Station Road, pg. 1228   **IT**

Bournemouth

DeVilbiss Distributed Products Division, Ringwood Rd., pg. 867   **PB**
Dog Breeder's Insurance Company Ltd., 9, St. Stephens Court, St. Stephen's Road, pg. 90   **IT**
Holton Machinery Limited, Albany House, Elliott Road, pg. 1017   **IT**
Lloyds Bowmaker Finance Ltd, Holland House, Oxford Rd., pg. 813   **IT**
NM Funds Management (Europe) Ltd. United Kingdom, One Chaseside, pg. 908   **IT**
Uni-Rents Ltd., pg. 1512   **IT**

Brackley

Traub-Heckert UK Ltd., Warwick House, Link 40 Business Park, pg. 1419   **IT**

Brackmills

British Pepper & Spice Co. Ltd., Phosili Rd., pg. 236   **IT**
Erta (Arnold) UK Ltd., 29 Lyveden Rd., pg. 354   **IT**

Bracknell

Applied Automation U.K. Ltd., pg. 835   IT
BMW (GB) Ltd., Ellesfield Ave., pg. 178   IT
The Barden Corporation (U.K.) Ltd., East Hampstead Rd., pg. 468   IT
Birmingham Midshires Ltd., Eastern Gate, Bants Bridge, pg. 176   IT
CKS Partners/London, Eagle House, pg. 195   PV
Chiron Vision UK, The Enterprise Ctr., Easthampstead Rd., pg. 350   PB
Cognos Ltd., Westerly Point, Market St., pg. 306   IT
Dell Computer Corporation, Berkshire Court, Western Road, RG12 1RE, pg. 496   PB
Dell Computer Corporation Ltd., Milbanke House, Western Rd., pg. 496   PB
Electro Scientific Industries Ltd., Duke House, The Pavillions, Downmill Rd., pg. 569   PB
Esselte Meto Ltd., 43 Western Road, pg. 461   IT
Ethyl Petroleum Additives Ltd., London Rd., pg. 595   PB
Gandalf Digital Communications Ltd., Gandalf House, Duncastle Road, pg. 540   IT
Gandalf International Ltd., Gandalf House, Duncastle Road, pg. 540   IT
HFC Trust & Savings Ltd., Cory House, 8th Flr., The Ring, pg. 842   PB
Hewlett-Packard Ltd., Cain Rd., pg. 821   PB
Hewlett-Packard Ltd., Miller House, The Ring, pg. 821   PB
Honeywell Ltd., Arlington Business Park, pg. 835   PB
Household Finance Ltd., Cory House, 8th Flr., The Ring, pg. 842   PB
Household Intl. (U.K.) Ltd., Cory House, 8th Flr., The Ring, pg. 842   PB
ISS Contract Cleaning Services (South), Oakmeade Place, Terrace Road South, pg. 657   IT
Johnson & Johnson Professional Products Ltd., The Braccans, London Rd., pg. 931   PB
LSI Logic Europe plc, Grenville Pl., The Ring, pg. 971   PB
Mentor Graphics (UK) Ltd., Mentor House Western Ctr., pg. 1087   PB
Micron Europe Ltd., Centennial Ct., E. Hammpstead Rd., pg. 1105   PB
NMB (U.K.) Limited, Unit 17, Western Centre, Western Road, pg. 868   IT
Northern Telecom Inc., 1st Fl., Columbia Centre, Market St., pg. 970   IT
Novell United Kingdom, Novell House, London Rd., pg. 1204   PB
Powell Duffryn (Finance) Limited, Powell Duffryn House, pg. 1066   IT
POWELL DUFFRYN PLC, Powell Duffryn House, pg. 1065   IT
Quantum Peripheral Products, Ltd., 10/11 Bracknell Beeches, Old Bracknell Lane, pg. 1350   PB
RACAL ELECTRONICS PLC, Western Rd., pg. 1082   IT
Racal Radio Limited, Western Road, pg. 1082   IT
Rockwell Semiconductor Systems Limited, Berkshire Court, Western Road, pg. 1402   PB
SQA Europe, Ltd., Asmec Centre, Eagle House, The Ring, pg. 1361   PB
3M United Kingdom, PLC, 3M House, pg. 1607   PB
VideoServer, Limited, Avis House, Park Rd., pg. 1720   PB
VMark Software, Ltd., Bracknell Beeches, Unit 6, Old Bracknell Ln., pg. 129   PB
Windsor Healthcare Ltd., Ellesfield Ave., pg. 199   IT

Bradford

AE Goetze Automotive, St. Johns Works, Neville Rd., pg. 1334   IT
Alcan Enfield Alloys Ltd., Bowling Back Ln., pg. 51   IT
ALLIED COLLOIDS GROUP PLC., Cleckheaton Rd., pg. 62   IT
Allied Colloids Ltd., Low Moor, pg. 62   IT
Bailey Fire Protection, Cutler Heights Lane, pg. 133   IT
BRITISH MOHAIR HOLDINGS PLC Midland Mills Valley Road, pg. 219   IT
British Mohair Spinners Limited, Valley Rd., pg. 219   IT
Courtaulds Fibres Ltd., Westcroft Road, pg. 339   IT
Joseph Dawson Ltd, Cashmere Works, pg. 385   IT
FINE ART DEVELOPMENTS PLC, Dawson Ln., Dudley Hill, pg. 485   IT
Fine Art Graphics Ltd., pg. 485   IT
Flender Power Transmission Ltd., Thornbury Works, Leeds Rd., pg. 400   IT
Grattan PLC, pg. 1015   IT
Jet Tours U.K., 69/75, Boston Manor Road, pg. 560   IT
Kass Homes Limited, Totan Business Centre, Towngate, Wyke, pg. 219   IT
Low Moor Securities Ltd., Low Moor, pg. 62   IT
George Meller Ltd., Unit 2, Block C, City Way Industrial Estate, pg. 712   IT
NATIONAL & PROVINCIAL BUILDING SOCIETY, Provincial House, pg. 906   IT
Ranco Europe Plymouth UK, pg. 1243   IT
N. Schlumberger & Co. (U.K.) Ltd., Hillam Road Industrial Estate, Canal Road, pg. 1206   IT
Standard Wool (UK) Limited, Bowling Mills, Five Bowling Old Ln., pg. 1502   IT
Supervisory & Industrial Process Control Limited, Control House, Caledonia St., pg. 133   IT
Switchgear & Instrumentation Ltd., Bowling Park Works, Ripley Road, pg. 133   IT
YORKSHIRE BUILDING SOCIETY, Yorkshire House, Yorkshire Dr., pg. 1522   IT
Yorkshire Ltd., Howard House, 6 Bank Street, pg. 1522   IT

Braintree

RFI Shielding Limited, Warner Dr., pg. 1241   IT
Willcox & Gibbs, Ltd., 44 Springwood Drive, pg. 1177   PV

Branbury

EMTEC Magnetics U.K. Limited, 40 The Green, pg. 743   IT

Brentford

AST Europe Limited, AST House, 2 Goat Wharf, pg. 1182   IT
Agfa-Gevaert Limited, 27, Great West Rd., pg. 174   IT
Alfa-Laval Co. Ltd., Great West Rd., pg. 1380   IT
BITOR Europe, Data General Tower 3rd Flr., 8BS, pg. 1046   IT
Bull Information Systems Ltd., Great West Rd., pg. 318   IT
Bull Pension Trustees Ltd., Great West Rd., pg. 318   IT
Bull Worldwide Information Systems Ltd., Great West Rd., pg. 318   IT
Campbell Distillers Limited, 924 Great West Rd., pg. 567   IT
Data General Limited, Data General Tower, Great West Rd., pg. 486   PB
Delsey Luggage Ltd., 313 Boston Manor Road, pg. 192   IT
A.B. Dick-Itek, Westling House, 981 Great West Rd., pg. 791   PV
Heidelberg Graphic Equipment Ltd.-Heidelberg UK, 69/76 High Street, pg. 605   IT
Integris Ltd., Great West Rd., pg. 318   IT
Inter-Continental Hotels, IHC House, The Thameside Centre, pg. 1178   IT
Mannesmann Demag Ltd., pg. 837   IT
Merisel Europe, No. 1 West Cross Centre, West Cross Way, Great West Rd., pg. 1096   PB
Merisel U.K., Syon Gate Way, Great West Rd., pg. 1096   PB
New Holland Ltd., 950 Great West Rd., pg. 484   IT
Parsons Group International Limited, Parsons House Kew Bridge Rd., pg. 842   PV
AB Pharos Marine Ltd., 77 High St., pg. 1290   IT
Rank Video Services Ltd., P.O. Box 70, Phoenix Park, pg. 1087   IT
Samsung Europe Headquarters, Great West House, Great West Road, pg. 1183   IT
SmithKline Beecham Consumer Brands, One New Horizons Court, Harlequin Ave., pg. 1264   IT
SmithKline Beecham Pharmaceuticals, One New Horizons Court, Harlequin Ave., pg. 1264   IT
SmithKline Beecham Pharmaceuticals, International Division, SB House, Great West Rd., pg. 1264   IT
SMITHKLINE BEECHAM PLC, SB House, Great West Rd., pg. 1264   IT
Spectra-Physics Holdings Plc, 77 High St., pg. 1290   IT
Tarmac Construction Intl., Westlink House, pg. 1355   IT
Tie Rack Corporate Neckwear, Capital Interchange Way, pg. 1389   IT
TIE RACK PLC, Capital Interchange Way, pg. 1389   IT
Tie Rack Trading Limited, Capital Interchange Way, pg. 1389   IT
Utell International, Utell House, 2 Kew Bridge Way, pg. 1098   IT
World Brands Duty Free, 924 Great Roadn, pg. 567   IT
Zenith Data Systems Ltd., Great West Rd., pg. 318   IT

Brentwood

Barratt Eastern Counties, 200 North Service Road, pg. 168   IT
BETACOM PLC, Brentwood House, 169 Kings Road, pg. 193   IT
Briggs & Stratton U.K. Limited, Hubert, pg. 252   IT
Cereal Industries Group, Kindsgate, 1 King Edwards Rd., pg. 92   IT
Cleanaway Limited, The Drive, Warley, pg. 212   IT
Ford Automotive Leasing Limited, Eagle Way, pg. 665   PB
Ford Credit Funding plc, Eagle Way, pg. 665   PB
Ford Financial Trust Limited, Eagle Way, pg. 666   PB
Ford Fleet Financing Limited, Eagle Way, pg. 666   PB
Ford Lease Financing Limited, Eagle Way, pg. 666   PB
Ford Motor Company Limited, Central Office, Eagle Way, pg. 666   PB
Thermos Limited, Ongar Road, pg. 938   IT
Thyssen Haniel Logistics, Hubert Rd., pg. 1388   IT
XTRA (U.K. Leasing), Limited, Wilson's Corner, pg. 1787   PB

Bridgend

Biomet Ltd., Waterton Industrial Estate, pg. 232   PB
Bridgend Paper Mill, Llangynwynd, pg. 672   PB
Carters (J&A) Ltd., South Rd., pg. 911   PB
Fiskars UK Ltd., Bridgend Business Centre, pg. 493   IT
GORICON Metallurgical Services Ltd., Picton St., Kenfig Hill, South Wales, pg. 1459   IT
Harman Motive Ltd, Bennett St., pg. 787   PB
Ready Mixed Concrete (Wales) Limited, RMC House, Trews Field, Tondu Way, pg. 1080   IT
Rexel Engineering Ltd., Bettws. Rd., Llangeinor NR, pg. 675   PB
Spectrum Technologies Limited, Mid-Glamorgan Science Park, pg. 218   IT

Bridgnorth

Senior Phoenix RFS Limited, Stanmore Industrial Estate, pg. 1221   IT

Bridgtown Cannock

Parker Hannifin, Walkmill Lane, pg. 1260   PB

Bridgwater

AEP/Borden Global Packaging (U.K.) Ltd., Colley Lane Estate, pg. 5   PB
Beazer Homes (Bridgwater) Limited, The Grange, Middle Rd., pg. 182   IT
Bonded Fibre Fabric Ltd., Bath Rd., pg. 798   IT
Courtaulds Films Holdings Ltd., Bath Road, pg. 339   IT

Bridlington

Britax (P.M.G.) Limited, Bessingby Industrial Estate, pg. 216   IT
Kitchens of Sara Lee-United Kingdom, pg. 1434   PB

Brierley Hill

Trinova Limited Aeroquip Automotive Operations, pg. 25   PB

Brigens

CAPL, Parc Crescent, Waterton Ind. Estate, pg. 1152   IT

Brigg

Glanford Brigg Generating Station, Scawby Brook, pg. 660   IT

Brighouse

Halifax Rack & Screw Cutting Co., Ltd., Coronation Works, Armytage Rd., pg. 448   IT
Kent Introl Ltd., Armytage Road, pg. 7   IT
Wellman Fibers Ltd., Upper Bonegate, pg. 1753   PB

Brightlingsea

Ormandy & Stollery Electronic Components Limited, Osec House, Chapel Rd., pg. 892   IT

Brighton

Bowthorpe EMP Limited, Stevenson Road, pg. 207   IT
Grand Metropolitan Community Relations, 64/65 North Rd., pg. 408   IT
International Factors Limited, Sovereign House, Church St., pg. 813   IT
M B M Technology Limited, Victoria Rd., pg. 892   IT
Mark IV Instruments Ltd., The Hyde, pg. 482   PB
Navigator and General Insurance Co. Ltd., 113, Queen's Rd., pg. 110   IT
Notifier Ltd., 45 Franklin Rd., Portslade, pg. 1307   PB
Vital Signs, Inc., pg. 1723   PB
West Instruments, pg. 1045   PB

Bristol

Albright & Wilson UK Limited, Portishead Docks, pg. 49   IT
Allied Domecq Spirits & Wine, The Pavilions, Bridgewater Rd., Beminster Down, pg. 63   IT
AlliedSignal Truck Brake Systems, Douglas Road, pg. 54   PB
Anixter Bristol, Bristol House, Temple Street, pg. 116   PB
Avdon (GB) Ltd., 178, South Liberty Lane, pg. 1030   IT
N.G. Bailey & Co. Ltd.-Bristol Branch, Lodge Causeway, pg. 132   IT
Bailey Telecom LTD - Bristol, Causeway House, Lodge Causeway, pg. 133   IT
Barratt Bristol, Barratt House, Almondsbury Business Ctr., pg. 168   IT
Bay 6 (Building Materials) Limited, RMC House, Paulton, pg. 1080   IT
Bristol, 33-35 Queen Square, pg. 910   IT
BRISTOL & WEST BUILDING SOCIETY, P.O. Box 27, Broad Quay, pg. 216   IT
Bristol Brewery, Countership, pg. 1212   IT
British Aerospace Airbus Limited, Filton House, Filton, pg. 217   IT
Canon (SW) Business Systems Ltd., Canon House, Lakeside, pg. 263   IT
Cobelplast (U.K.) Ltd., pg. 1207   IT
Coleman U.K., Inc., Unit 2, Parish Wharf Estate, Harbour Rd., pg. 691   PV
Colston, Grosvenor House, 149 Whiteladies Road, pg. 1298   IT
D & B Software Ltd., P.O. Box 2732, Kings House, pg. 532   IT
DRG Cartons Ltd., Filwood Rd., Fishponds, pg. 927   PB
Dalgety Agriculture, Limited, 180 Aztec West, pg. 376   IT
Essilor Limited, Cooper Rd., pg. 462   IT
Charles E. Ford, Limited, Avonmouth Old Dock, pg. 1356   IT
Great Mills (South) Limited, Unit 1, Aldermoor Way, Longwell Green, pg. 1080   IT
Hamptons Residential, Broad Quay, pg. 216   IT

PB - *U.S. Public Companies Volume*
PV - *U.S. Private Companies Volume*
IT - *International Public & Private Companies Volume*

Harveys of Bristol Limited, 12 Denmark St., pg. 63   **IT**
Henderson Unit Trust Management Limited, 33 Wine Street, Third Fl., pg. 609   **IT**
Hewlett-Packard Ltd., Bldg. 2, Filton Rd., pg. 821   **PB**
Imperial Investments Ltd., Bull Wharf, Redcliffe St., pg. 593   **IT**
IMPERIAL TOBACCO GROUP, LTD., P.O. Box 244, pg. 666   **IT**
Imperial Tobacco Ltd., Cigar Div., pg. 666   **IT**
J.V. Laing-GTM Europe, Green Lane, pg. 823   **IT**
Kato Cranes, pg. 1325   **IT**
Knorr-Bremse Systems for Commercial Vehicles Ltd., Douglas Road, Kingswood, pg. 738   **IT**
Kodak Limited-Western Business Centre, Manulife House, Marlborough St., pg. 553   **PB**
LMG Finance Ltd., pg. 68   **IT**
Lawson Mardon Bristol Ltd., pg. 68   **IT**
Lawson Mardon Carton Ltd., pg. 68   **IT**
Lawson Mardon Group International Ltd., pg. 68   **IT**
Lawson Mardon Packaging Ltd., pg. 69   **IT**
Lawson Mardon Packaging UK Ltd., pg. 69   **IT**
Lawson Mardon Pharmaflex Ltd., pg. 69   **IT**
Lawson Mardon Pre-Press Ltd., pg. 69   **IT**
Lawson Mardon Star Ltd., pg. 69   **IT**
Lawson Mardon Sutton Ltd., pg. 69   **IT**
Lawson Products Ltd., 300 The Quadrant, Ash Ridge Rd., pg. 980   **IT**
Leaf United Kingdom Ltd., Carlyle Rd., pg. 638   **IT**
London Life, 100 Temple Street, pg. 100   **IT**
Lucas Ingredients, Moravian Rd., pg. 376   **IT**
Manville Great Britain Ltd. (Bristol), 1 Redcliffe Street, pg. 927   **PB**
Matthew Clark Brands, Whitchurch Lane, pg. 848   **IT**
MATTHEW CLARK TAUNTON, LTD., Church Lane, pg. 848   **IT**
Mead Packaging Ltd., 500 Woodward Ave., pg. 1077   **PB**
National Westminster Insurance Services Limited, 37 Broad St., pg. 910   **IT**
National Westminster Life Assurance Limited, Trinity Quay, Avon Street, pg. 910   **IT**
National Westminster Unit Trust Managers Limited, Trinity Quay, Avon Street, pg. 910   **IT**
OCE Graphics (U.K.) Limited, pg. 994   **IT**
Oxford Instruments-Plasma Technology, North End, pg. 1018   **IT**
RMC Concrete Floors Limited, London Rd., Wick, pg. 1080   **IT**
RMC Concrete Products Limited-Western, London Rd., Wick, pg. 1080   **IT**
RMC Surfacing Limited-South West Area, London Rd., pg. 1080   **IT**
Ready Mixed Concrete (Western) Limited, 82-87 Feeder Rd., pg. 1080   **IT**
Resins & Organics Division, Albright & Wilson Limited, Avonmouth Works, pg. 49   **IT**
Rexam Medical Packaging, Winterbourne Rd, pg. 1106   **IT**
Rexam Medical Packaging Bristol, 113 Dixon Road, pg. 1106   **IT**
Riley Advertising (Bristol) Ltd., Hanover House, Queen Charlotte Street, pg. 1117   **IT**
Rockwell Automation Limited, Northavon Business Centre, Dean Road, Unit 17, pg. 1399   **PB**
Rolls-Royce Military Aero Engines Ltd., P.O. Box 3, pg. 1127   **IT**
Sequent Computer Systems (United Kingdom), 31-33 Corn St., pg. 1460   **PB**
Severn Furnaces Limited, Brunnel Way, pg. 883   **PB**
Signfix Ltd., Bath Rd., Upper Langford, pg. 862   **IT**
SOMERFIELD PLC, Whitchurch Lane, pg. 1280   **IT**
Somerfield Stores Ltd., Whitchurch Lane, pg. 1280   **IT**
Sparrows Industrial Services, Ltd., Brookgate, pg. 1285   **IT**
Spillers Milling, Equinox South, Great Park Road, pg. 376   **IT**
Strachan & Henshaw Ltd., P.O. Box 103, pg. 1489   **IT**
Tenneco Malros Ltd., Rockingham Works, Avonmouth, pg. 1580   **PB**
Tenneco Organics Ltd., Rockingham Works, Avonmouth, pg. 1580   **PB**
Thule Ltd., 5C Business Centre, Unit 4 & 5, Concorde Dr., pg. 436   **IT**
Turbo-Union Ltd., pg. 367   **IT**
Unilever Export Ltd., Greyfriars, pg. 1434   **IT**
WF Corroon-Bristol, Howard House, Queens Avenue, pg. 1501   **IT**
Western Roadstone Limited, London Rd., Wick, pg. 1079   **IT**
Willis Corroon South Limited, Howard House, Queens Avenue, pg. 1503   **IT**
Wondertex Limited, The Sion, Crown Glass Pl., pg. 1080   **IT**

Brixworth

Bran & Luebbe (G.B.) Ltd., Scaldwell Rd., pg. 1380   **IT**
Ilmor Engineering, Ltd., Quarry Rd., pg. 724   **PB**

Broadstairs

Sericol International Ltd., Westwood Rd., pg. 235   **IT**

Brodmin

Natural Stone Products Limited, pg. 1355   **IT**

Bromborough

Candy Domestic Appliances Limited, New Chester Rd., pg. 260   **IT**
PPF Intl. Ltd., Food Industries Div., pg. 1434   **IT**
SAB WABCO Ltd., Thermal Road, pg. 271   **IT**

Unichema Chemicals Ltd., pg. 1434   **IT**

Bromley

BHP Steel Europe Middle East Ltd., King's House, 32-40 Widmore Road, pg. 227   **IT**
Ballast Wiltshier Plc - Construction Specialists Div., Prospect House, 19-21 Homesdale Road, pg. 135   **IT**
Korsnas Sales Ltd., Kings House, 32-40 Widmore Rd., pg. 759   **IT**

Bromsgrove

AAH Meditel Limited, Rigby Hall, pg. 591   **IT**
Kemira Safety Ltd., Unit 14B, Harris Business Park, Hanbury Road, Stoke Prior, pg. 729   **IT**

Brough

British Aerospace Defence Limited (Military Aircraft), pg. 217   **IT**

Brownhills

Quinton Hazell PLC, Brownhills, pg. 561   **PB**

Broxburn

Kerry Ingredients, Broxburn, East Mains Industrial Estate, pg. 732   **IT**

Brynmawr

Anacomp Magnetics Wales Ltd., Intermediate Rd., pg. 107   **PB**

Buckhaven

Trafalgar House Offshore Fabricators Limited (Methil Works), Wellesley Rd., pg. 773   **IT**

Buckingham

Antiference Ltd., pg. 1511   **IT**
CEM (Microwave Technologies) Ltd., Unit Two Middle Slace, Buckingham Industrial pk., pg. 277   **PB**
HBO & Company (UK) Limited, Lacemaker House, Chapel St., pg. 770   **PB**
Kawasaki Motors (UK) Ltd., 1 Dukes Meadow, Millboard Rd., pg. 726   **IT**
Respalex International Ltd., The Gate House, pg. 967   **IT**

Burgess Hill

CAE Electronics plc, Albert Dr., pg. 238   **IT**
EAO-Highland, Albert Drive, pg. 444   **IT**
Ericsson Data UK Ltd., Telecommunications Centre, Ericsson Way 67, pg. 1366   **IT**
Mindscape International, Priority House, Charles Avenue, pg. 1026   **IT**
Schering Holdings Ltd., pg. 1204   **IT**
VG Ionex Ltd., Charles Ave., pg. 1110   **IT**

Burnaston

Toyota Motor Manufacturing (UK) Ltd., pg. 1414   **IT**

Burnham-on-Crouch

Mini Instruments Limited, Eight Station Industrial Estate, pg. 392   **IT**

Burnley

Blanella Ltd., pg. 554   **IT**
Hepworth Industrial Plastics Ltd., Pollard Moor, Padiham, pg. 515   **IT**
Pipeline Induction Heat Limited, Pipeline Center, Farrington Rossendale Rd., pg. 1084   **PB**
Smurfit Paper & Box Mills (Burnley) Ltd., Caldervale, pg. 1271   **IT**
Tenneco-Walker (U.K.) Limited, Liverpool Rd., B.L. BB126HJ Rose Grove B, pg. 1580   **PB**
David Whitehead & Sons Ltd., Chaddesley House, Manchester Rd., pg. 818   **IT**

Burton

Quinton Hazell PLC, Burton Latimer, pg. 561   **PB**

Burton on Trent

Allied Domecq Retailing Limited, 107 Station St., pg. 53   **IT**
BTR Silvertown Ltd., Horninglow Rd., pg. 125   **IT**
Bass Brewers Ltd., 137 High St., pg. 170   **IT**
Bass Leisure, 3 The Maltings, Wetmore Rd., pg. 170   **IT**
Grolsch (UK) Ltd., Trent House, 137 High Street, pg. 559   **IT**
Pirelli U.K. Tyres Limited, Derby Rd., pg. 1059   **IT**
Qualitas Bathrooms Ltd., Hartshorne Rd., Woodville, pg. 197   **IT**
Van Leer (UK) Ltd., pg. 1147   **IT**

Bury

Ahlstrom Machinery Ltd., Bridge House, Heap Bridge, pg. 35   **IT**
Akerlund & Rausing Ltd., 82a Bolton St., pg. 33   **IT**
Albany International Ltd., Pilsworth Mill, pg. 37   **PB**
Bury Cooper Whitehead Ltd., Hudcar Mill, Hudcar Ln., pg. 1202   **IT**
Kemira Coatings, Heavy Duty Division, Radcliffe Road, pg. 729   **IT**
P&S Textiles Ltd., Fernhill Mill, Hornby St., pg. 1202   **IT**
Senior Hargreaves Limited, Lord St., pg. 1221   **IT**
Simon-Holder Ltd., Brandesholme House, Brandesholme Road, pg. 1251   **IT**
Uniform Ltd., Stubbins Vale Mill, pg. 1202   **IT**
Winterburn Ltd., Riverside Works, Woodhill Rd., pg. 1596   **PB**

Bury Saint Edmunds

Barenbrug U.K. Ltd., 33 Perkins Road, Rougham Industrial Estate, pg. 167   **IT**
CMI International, Shepherd's Grove Indus. Est., pg. 279   **PB**

Bushey

Graseby Ionics Ltd., Park Ave., pg. 1267   **IT**

Buxton

LeaRonal UK Ltd., Ashbourne Rd., pg. 982   **PB**
RMC Concrete Products Limited-Central, Dale Rd., Dale Holes, pg. 1080   **IT**
RMC Industrial Minerals Limited, Hindlow, pg. 1080   **IT**

Byfleet

Ferrosan Healthcare Ltd., Beaver House, York Close, pg. 989   **IT**
ING Farm Finance, Appex Court, Camphill Road, pg. 650   **IT**
Modo Merchants Ltd., Rosemount Ave., pg. 886   **IT**
Paines & Byrne, Limited, Yamanouchi House, Pyrford Road, pg. 1519   **IT**
Yamanouchi Pharma Ltd., Yamanouchi House, Pyrford Road, pg. 1519   **IT**
Yamanouchi U.K. Limted, Yamanouchi House, Pyrford Road, pg. 1519   **IT**

Caerphilly

Van Leer Metallized Products Ltd., pg. 1147   **IT**

Calne

H A Coombs Limited, Porte Marsh Rd., pg. 1160   **IT**
SKW Metals U.K. Ltd., Molypress Division, Portemarsh Industrial Estate, One Harris Rd., pg. 1465   **IT**

Camberley

Air Hanson Limited, Business Aviation Centre, Blackbushe Airport, pg. 592   **IT**
Astronautics U.K., 28 Tekels Ave., pg. 93   **PV**
BMC Software, Limited, Compass House, 207-215 London Road, pg. 163   **PB**
Beazer Homes (Yately) Limited, West House, Plough Road, pg. 182   **IT**
Bourns Electronics, Ltd., 90 Park St., pg. 161   **PV**
Charles Church, Charles Church House, Knolls Road, pg. 182   **IT**
The Continuum Company, Inc. (Europe), 423 London Rd., pg. 423   **PB**
Dionex (U.K.) Ltd., 4, Albany Ct., pg. 510   **PB**
EASAMS Ltd., Lyon Way, Frimley Rd., pg. 543   **IT**
Fluor Daniel Limited, Fluor Daniel Centre, Watchmoor Park, Riverside Way, pg. 660   **PB**
International Gas Apparatus Limited, Blackbrisle Business Park, Vigo Lane, pg. 1149   **PV**
S.C. Johnson, Frimley Green, pg. 593   **IT**
Kentucky Fried Chicken (Great Britain) Ltd., Wicat House, 403 London Rd., pg. 1637   **PB**
M4 Data Ltd., Lyon Way, Frimley Rd., pg. 1523   **PB**
Motorola Ltd., Frimley Road, pg. 1140   **PB**
Nokia Mobile Phones (UK) Ltd., Ashwood House, Pembroke Broadway, pg. 952   **IT**
Nokia Telecommunications Ltd., Unit 12 Admiralty Way, pg. 953   **IT**
Edmund Nuttall Ltd., St. James House, Knoll Rd., pg. 630   **IT**
Periphonics Voice Processing Systems Ltd., Albany Court, Albany Park, pg. 1279   **PB**
Preferred Direct, 403 London Rd., pg. 464   **IT**
L.A. Rumbold Limited, Doman Rd., pg. 216   **IT**
SHL Learning Technologies, Yorktown House, 8 Frimley Road, pg. 1154   **IT**
SHL Vision Solutions, 80 Park Street, pg. 1154   **IT**
Sandoz Pharmaceuticals (UK) Ltd., pg. 985   **IT**
Storno Limited, Frimley Rd., pg. 1140   **PB**
Sun Microsystems Ltd., Watchmoor Park, Unit 8, pg. 1532   **IT**
Systems Integration, U.K., Yorktown House, 8 Frimley Road, pg. 1154   **IT**
Toshiba Electronics (UK) Ltd., Riverside Way, pg. 1406   **IT**
Toshiba (U.K.) Ltd., Toshiba House, Frimley Rd., pg. 1407   **IT**

PB - U.S. Public Companies Volume
PV - U.S. Private Companies Volume
IT - International Public & Private Companies Volume

Cambridge

Acorn Computers Ltd., Acorn House, Vision Park-Histon, pg. 1002 — IT
Amgen Limited, 240 Cambridge Science Park, pg. 101 — PB
Amtech Limited, Mercers Row, pg. 106 — PB
Brite Voice Systems Europe, 4 The Cambridge Business Park, pg. 257
Cambridge Consultants Limited, Science Park, Milton Rd., pg. 671 — PV
Check Point Software Technologies (UK) Ltd., St. Johns Innovation Centre, Cowley Rd., pg. 342 — PB
Chefaro Props Ltd., Cambridge Science Park, pg. 44 — IT
CIBA Agriculture, Whittlesford, pg. 978 — IT
CIBA Polymers, pg. 292 — IT
Coherent (U.K.) Ltd., Cambridge Science Park, Milton Rd., pg. 396 — PB
Datascope Medical Co., Ltd., Lakeview Court, Spitfire Close, pg. 488 — PB
EECO, Switch, Trafalgar Way, Bar Hill, pg. 1631 — PB
Elsevier Trends Journals, 68 Hills Road, pg. 1100 — IT
Enzymatix Ltd., Cambridge Science Park, pg. 733 — PB
Genera Technologies Limited, St. John's Innovation Centre, St. John's Innovation Park, pg. 1226 — IT
Genus Europa Ltd., P.O. Box 841, pg. 733 — IT
Hydro Agri (UK) Ltd., Science Park, Milton Rd., pg. 962 — IT
Innovir (UK) LTD, 22 Science Park, pg. 1703 — IT
Intervet (U.K.) Ltd., Cambridge Science Park, Milton Rd., pg. 45 — IT
Logica UK Ltd., Betjeman House, 104 Hills Rd., pg. 814 — IT
Noise & Vibration Systems, 1 Cambridge Business Park, Cowley Road, pg. 1431 — IT
Nokia Telecommunications Ltd. Transmission Systems Product Development, Heffers Building, 6 Cambridge Business Park, Milton Road, pg. 953 — IT
Olivetti Research Ltd., Old Addenbrookes Site, 24a Trumpington St., pg. 1003 — IT
Omnifit Ltd., Two College Park, pg. 589 — IT
Organon Laboratories Ltd., Cambridge Science Park, Milton Rd., pg. 45 — IT
Pharmacia & Upjohn LKB Biochrom Ltd., Cambridge Science Park, Milton Road, pg. 1048 — IT
Pharmaco Intl. Ltd., Clarendon Road, pg. 1285 — PB
Q-ARC Limited, Saxon Way, Bar Hill, pg. 856 — PB
Roltech, Norman Park, Bar Hill, pg. 462 — IT
THE ROXBORO GROUP PLC, Byron House, pg. 1130 — IT
SAIC UK Limited, Poseidon House, Castle Park, pg. 976 — PV
TVT, P.O. Box 41, pg. 791 — PV
Topexpress, Ltd., Poseidon House, Castle Park, CB3 0RD, pg. 976 — PV
Toshiba Cambridge Research Centre Ltd., 260 Cambridge Science Park, pg. 1406 — IT

Cannock

Britool Ltd., Church Bridge Works, Walsall Rd., pg. 570 — IT
Pneumatic Div., Walkmill Lane, Bridgtown, pg. 1264 — PB
Thyssen Umformtechnik U.K. Ltd., pg. 1387 — IT
Ultra Electronics Magnetics, Fallow Park, Rugeley Rd., pg. 1431
Ultra Electronics Weapons Systems, Fallow Park, Rugeley Road, pg. 1431 — IT

Canterbury

Ballast Wiltshier Plc - South East Region, Hall Place, Church Hill, pg. 135 — IT
Chartham Papers, pg. 1107 — IT

Canvey

Vent-Axia Limited-Controls Division, Thames Estuary Estate, pg. 1267 — IT

Cardiff

A.F. & D. Mackay Ltd., Pinebrook 85 B, Mill Road, pg. 966 — IT
AXA Insurance, Burke Terr., 114-116 St. Mary St., pg. 19 — IT
Ascom Telecommunications Ltd., Cypress Drive, pg. 87 — IT
AB Automotive Electronics Limited, Forest Farm, Whitchurch, pg. 1344 — IT
Avana Bakeries Ltd., Pendyris St., pg. 1396 — IT
Bailey Telecom LTD - Cardiff, pg. 133 — IT
Ballast Wiltshier Plc - South West Region, 33 Lambourne Crescent, pg. 135 — IT
Barratt South Wales, Oak House, Penarth Rd., pg. 168 — IT
British Dredging Aggregates Limited, Avondale House, Avondale Rd., pg. 1081 — IT
Chartered Trust Plc., 24-26 Newport Rd., pg. 1296 — IT
Gloucester Railway Carriage & Wagon Company Ltd., Cambrian Works, Parkfield Place, pg. 473 — IT
Matsushita Electric (U.K.) Ltd., Wyncliffe Road, pg. 847 — IT
Memory Lane Cakes Ltd., Maes-y-Coed Rd., pg. 410 — IT
Powell Duffryn Standard Limited, Cambrian House, pg. 1065 — IT
Red Dragon Radio, Radio House, West Canal Wharf, pg. 452 — IT
Takenaka (U.K.) Ltd., Cardiff, 3rd Floor, Park House, Greyfriars Road, pg. 1352 — IT
Valeo Wiping Systems, pg. 240 — IT
WF Corroon-Cardiff, 3-7 Columbus Walk, Brigatine Place, pg. 1501 — IT

Willis Corroon Financial Planning Limited, 37 Columbus Walk, Brigantine Place, pg. 1502 — IT
Willis Corroon Wales Limited, 37 Columbus Walk, Brigantine Place, pg. 1503 — IT
Wotton Roadstone Limited, Wenvoe Quarry, pg. 1079 — IT

Carlisle

Breed UK Limited, Norfolk St., pg. 251 — PB
Carlisle Coated Stone, Stephenson Industrial Estate, Willowholme, pg. 1079 — IT
Circuit Foil U.K. Ltd., Service Center, pg. 80 — IT
Enesco Limited, Lorne Cresent, pg. 1508 — PB

Carshalton

Vinamul Ltd., Mill Lane, pg. 1434 — IT

Castleford

Cott Europe (Castleford), California Drive, pg. 338 — IT
Hickson & Welch Ltd., Wheldon Road, pg. 619 — IT
HICKSON INTERNATIONAL PLC, Wheldon Rd., pg. 618 — IT

Chalfont Saint Giles

Florasynth Limited, Wentworth House, 2/4 High St., pg. 173 — IT
NYCOMED AMERSHAM PLC, Amersham Place, pg. 992 — IT

Chandlers Ford

Barratt Southampton, Abacus House, 13a Oakmount Road, pg. 168 — IT
Russ Berrie (U.K.) Limited, Templars House, Lulworth Close, pg. 223 — PB
York Technology Ltd., York House, School Lane, pg. 1376 — IT

Chapel Town

ANGUS Chemie Gmbh, Unit 7, Rotunda Business Park Centre, pg. 75 — PV

Charlestown

Svedala Ltd. Plant, pg. 1325 — IT

Chatham

Black Horse Financial Services Ltd., Mountbatten House, Military Rd., pg. 813 — IT
Panduit Limited, 61-65 Revenge Rd., pg. 836 — PV

Cheadle

Airstream Products Limited, Airstream House, Brook St., pg. 1267 — IT
Brite Voice Systems Group, Ltd., Brite Court Park Rd., Gatley, headle, pg. 257 — PB
Cussons (U.K.) LTD., Cussons House, Birdhall Lane, pg. 1024 — IT
James Gant & Company Limited, pg. 485 — IT
Laporte Hygiene, Duke Ave., Stanley Green, pg. 802 — IT
TOSOH Europe B.V., Sinclair House, Station Rd., pg. 1408 — IT

Cheam

Metsa-Serla Tissue Ltd., St. George House, pg. 864 — IT

Chelmsford

Alarmcom Ltd., Baddow Park, West Hanningfield Road, pg. 1246 — IT
Britvic Soft Drinks Limited, Britvic House, Broomfield Rd., pg. 1499 — IT
Corporate Computers (MID) Plc, pg. 757 — IT
EEV Ltd., Waterhouse Lane, pg. 543 — IT
EWA Ltd., St. Mary's Green, pg. 1482 — IT
L.P. Foreman & Sons Ltd., Willow Works, Roxwell Rd., pg. 543 — IT
GEC-Marconi Communication Networks Ltd., Elettra House, Westway, pg. 544 — IT
GEC-Marconi Communications Ltd., Marconi House, New St., pg. 544 — IT
GEC-Marconi Research Centre, West Hanningfield Rd., Great Baddow, pg. 544 — IT
Geotek Europe, Wren House, Hedgerows Business Park, pg. 740 — PB
H.M.Z. U.K. Ltd., Connah Goldsworthy & Co. Accts., pg. 1134 — IT
Marconi Radar & Control Systems Ltd., Chobham Rd., Frimley, pg. 544 — IT
National Band Three Ltd., Wren House, Hedgerows Business Park, pg. 740 — IT
Quarterdeck Office Systems UK Limited, The Widford Hall, Widford Hall Ln., pg. 1351 — PB
Repsol Petroleum Ltd., East Saxon House, Duke Street, pg. 1105 — IT
VRG Information Systems (UK) Plc, pg. 757 — IT

Cheltenham

Alusuisse-Lonza UK Ltd., Imperial House, Lypiatt Rd., pg. 68 — IT
Bovis Home Ltd., Bovis House, Lansdown Rd., pg. 1032 — IT
Delta Schoeller, The Moors, Tewkesbury Rd., pg. 390 — IT
Dowty Aerospace Hydraulics, Cheltenham, Arle Court, pg. 1337 — IT
Eagle Star, Lagrange Bishops Ckeve, pg. 110 — IT
FormFlo Limited, Lansdown Industrial Estate, pg. 267 — IT
Mary Glasgow Publications Ltd., Ellenborough House, Wellington Street, pg. 1514 — IT
Hollingsworth & Vose Co. U.K. Ltd., Postlip Mills, pg. 535 — PV
Kraft Jacobs Suchard, St. Georges House, Bayshill Rd., pg. 1290 — PB
Lonza (UK) Ltd., Imperial House, Lypiatt Rd., pg. 67 — IT
Thomas Mercer Chronometer Ltd., 16a Lansdown Place, pg. 260 — PB
Portal Publications Ltd., Manchester Park, Tewkesbury Road, pg. 503 — PB
Royal Bank Leasing Ltd., RoyScot House, The Promenade, pg. 1132 — IT
RoyScot Trust plc, RoyScot House, The Promenade, pg. 1132 — IT
Smiths Industries Aerospace & Defence Systems Limited-Product Support, Bishops Cleeve, pg. 1267 — IT
Smiths Industries Aerospace & Defence Systems Limited-Civil Systems Div., Bishops Cleeve, pg. 1267 — IT
Terry's Group, St. Georges House, Bays Hill Rd., pg. 1290 — PB
Stanley Thornes (Publishers), Ellenborough House, Wellington Street, pg. 1514 — IT
Ultra Electrics, Kingsditch Lane, pg. 1431 — IT
Willis Corroon South Limited, Stirling House, College Road, pg. 1503 — IT

Chertsey

Bilfinger + Berger U.K. Ltd., The Old Bank House, 11 London Street, pg. 196 — IT
COMPASS GROUP PLC, Cowley House, Guildford Street, pg. 324 — IT
Leisure Sport Limited, Thorpe Park, Staines Road, pg. 1080 — IT
Oracle Corporation U.K. Ltd., Oracle Park, Bittams Lane, pg. 1213 — PB
Perfect Pizza Ltd., The Forum, Hanworth Lane, pg. 1213 — IT
Rainbow Technologies, Ltd., 4 The Forum, Hanworth Ln., pg. 1359 — PB
THORN Group, 37 Windsor St., pg. 1385 — IT
THORN PLC, 124 Bridge Rd., pg. 1385 — IT

Chesham

Adhesive Solutions Limited, Moor Road, pg. 234 — IT
Alcan Ekco, 90 Asheridge Rd., pg. 51 — IT
Industrial Adhesives Ltd., Moor Rd., pg. 234 — IT
No Frills (DIY) Limited, Townsend Rd., pg. 1080 — IT

Cheshunt

St. Albans Sand & Gravel Co. Limited, Delamare Rd., pg. 1079 — IT
Spinhill Properties Ltd., Tesco House, Delamare Rd., pg. 1376 — IT
Spinhill Properties PLC, Tesco House, Delamare Rd., pg. 1376 — IT
Tesco Capital Ltd., Tesco House, Delamare Rd., pg. 1376 — IT
Tesco Insurance Ltd., Tesco House, Delamare Rd., pg. 1376 — IT
TESCO PLC, Tesco House, Delamare Rd., pg. 1376 — IT
Tesco Property Holdings Ltd., Tesco House, Delamare Rd., pg. 1376 — IT
Tesco Stores Hong Kong Ltd., Tesco House, Delamare Rd., pg. 1376 — IT
Tesco Stores Ltd., Tesco House, pg. 1376 — IT

Chesire

Carefree Camping Limited, Canute Court, Toft Road, pg. 465 — IT

Chessington

ALLIANCE UNICHEM PLC, UniChem House, Cox Ln., pg. 57 — IT
Callaway Golf (U.K.) Limited, Units C63 & C64, Barwell Business Park, pg. 295 — PB
Mitsui & Co., Ltd., Oakcroft Road, pg. 881 — IT
OMRON Systems U.K. Ltd., Victory House, Cox Lane, pg. 1006 — IT

Chester

Barratt Chester, 2 Vicar's Ln., pg. 168 — IT
BICC Cables Limited, Heronsway, Chester Business Park, pg. 120 — IT
BolsWessanen UK Holding Ltd., pg. 752 — IT
British Aerospace Airbus Limited, pg. 217 — IT
Cheshire Wholefoods Plc, Sealand Rd., pg. 752 — IT
Continental Can Company Ltd., pg. 1207 — IT
Continental Can Company (Wrexham) Ltd., pg. 1207 — IT
Continental Can UK Holding Company Ltd., pg. 1207 — IT

PB - *U.S. Public Companies Volume*
PV - *U.S. Private Companies Volume*
IT - *International Public & Private Companies Volume*

IRD Mechanalysis (U.K.) Limited, Sealand Indus. Estate, Bumpers Ln., pg. 790   PB
Kemira Ince Ltd., Ince, pg. 728   IT
Komatsu UK, Ltd., Durham Road, pg. 744   IT
MBNA International Bank Limited (MBNA International), Stansfield House, Chester Business Park, pg. 1023   PB
NEBS Business Stationery, Chester West Employment Park, pg. 1171   PB
Nucletron UK Ltd., Nucletron House, Chowley Oak, Tattenhall, pg. 389   IT
Raytheon Corporate Jets, Broughton, pg. 1366   PB
Shell Chemicals U.K., Heronbridge House, Chester Business Pk., pg. 1139   IT
Shell Specialty Chemicals, Heronbridge House, pg. 1139   IT
White Cap U.K. Ltd., pg. 1207   IT
Wrexham Land Company Ltd., pg. 1207   IT

Chester le Street

Durham Chemicals Ltd., Birtley, pg. 598   IT
Hydro Aluminium Century Ltd., Durham Rd., pg. 962   IT
SLD Pumps Limited, Portobello Trading Estate, pg. 1160   IT

Chesterfield

AAH Medical, Broombank Bus. Park, Broombank Rd., pg. 591   IT
Birtley Engineering Ltd., Wheatbridge Road, pg. 1139   IT
British Electrical Repairs Ltd., Central Services, Wharf Ln., pg. 390   IT
Cromdane Steel & Engineering Limited, pg. 101   IT
David Eshelby Limited, Park Rd., Holmewood Industrial Estate, pg. 219   IT
Fusion Meters Limited, Smeckley Wood Close, Chesterfield Trading Estate, pg. 1226   IT
GKN Sheepbridge Stokes Ltd., Sheepbridge Works, pg. 535   IT
Krupp Hoesch Steel Ltd., Speedwell Industrial Estate, pg. 516   IT

Chichester

Anda Products Limited, Terminus Rd., pg. 1267   IT
Britax Wingard Limited, Kingsham Rd., pg. 216   IT
Old El Paso, East Walls, pg. 408   IT
D. Rowe & Co. Ltd., pg. 1512   IT
Shippams, East Walls, pg. 408   IT
Wiley Europe Limited, Baffins Lane, pg. 1768   PB

Chippenham

BRUNEL HOLDINGS PLC, Avon Reach, pg. 230   IT
Home Automation Group Ltd., Bumpers Way, pg. 390   IT
Peak Technologies-Europe, 3 Prince Rupert House, Cavalier Ct., Bumpers Farm, pg. 890   IT

Chipping Campden

Atlas Stone Products Limited, Westington Quarry, pg. 592   IT

Chipping Norton

Bio-Logic Systems Corporation Ltd., Dickenson House, Albion St., pg. 230   PB

Chipping Sodbury

ARC Limited, The Ridge, pg. 592   IT
Beazer Homes (Bristol) Ltd., Beazer House, The Ridge, pg. 182   IT
Greenways Landfill, The Ridge, pg. 592   IT

Chirnside

Dexter Nonwovens Division, Duns, pg. 505   PB

Chobham

Metco Ltd, pg. 1307   IT

Chorley

British Aerospace Defence Limited (Royal Ordnance), Euxton Lane, pg. 217   IT
Multipart Distribution, Pilling Lane, pg. 807   IT
Pontin's Limited, P.O. Box 100, pg. 1211   IT

Christchurch

FLS Aerospace (Lovaux) Ltd., Bournemouth Intl. Airport, pg. 475   IT
Metrosonics Ltd., 2 Airfield Way, pg. 207   IT
Penny & Giles Aerospace Ltd., 6 Airfield Rd., pg. 207   IT
Penny & Giles Position Sensors Ltd., 15 Airfield Rd., pg. 207   IT
Penny & Giles Computer Products, One Airfield Way, pg. 207   IT
Perstorp Unidur Ltd., Airfield Way, pg. 1039   IT

Chryston

DEVRO INTERNATIONAL PLC, Moodies Burn, pg. 408   IT

Church Stretton

Kruger Tissue (Industrial) Limited, Manchester House, pg. 762   IT

Cinderford

Runnymede Dispersion Ltd., Ruspidge Works, pg. 371   IT

Cirencester

BRANN LTD., Phoenix Way, pg. 212   IT

Clacton-on-Sea

Babcock Robey Limited, Telford Rd., Gerge Lane Indus. Estate, pg. 472   IT
Bowers International Ltd., pg. 1511   IT
Titman Tip Tools, Kennedy Way, Valley Rd., pg. 231   IT

Claygate

VDM (U.K.) Ltd., 111, Hare La., pg. 509   IT

Clayton

Anchor Chemical Group PLC, Clayton Ln., pg. 32   PB

Cleckheaton

BBA Friction LTD., Hunsworth Lane, pg. 112   IT
Birkett Cutmaster Limited, pg. 268   IT
Francis W. Birkett & Sons Limited, pg. 268   IT
Critchley, Sharp & Tetlow, Prospect Mills, Prospect Rd., pg. 268   IT
Dell Baler, P.O. Box 30, Hightown Rd., pg. 268   IT
Flexitalic Ltd, pg. 413   PV
Freudenberg Vileda Ltd., pg. 507   IT
Qualters & Smith, P.O. Box 30, Hightown Rd., pg. 268   IT
Rigby Metal Components Limited, Rawfolds, pg. 891   IT
United Packaging PLC, Dewsbury Road, pg. 1344   IT
Vileda LP, pg. 506   IT
Vileda Ltd., pg. 507   IT

Clevedon

Amper P.l.c., 108 Strode Rd., pg. 1157   IT

Cleveland

Darchem Engineering Ltd., Stillington, Stockton on Tees, pg. 1489   IT

Clifton

Ballast Wiltshire Plc - South West Region, Promenade House, The Promenade, pg. 135   IT

Clitheroe

Castle Cement Ltd. (Clitheroe), pg. 1201   IT

Clonmeh

Moy Insulation Ltd., Ardfinnan, Clonmeh, pg. 123   IT

Clwyd

Air Products PLC, Acrefair, pg. 32   PB

Clydebank

John Brown Engineering Limited, pg. 772   IT

Coaley

APV U.K. Plc, P.O. Box 4, pg. 1240   IT

Coatbridge

Castle Cement Ltd. (Strathclyde), Hollandhurst Rd., pg. 1201   IT
MSA (Britain) Limited, East Shawhead, pg. 1114   PB
NYK Line-Glasgow, Containerbase, Gartsherrie Road, pg. 942   IT
Shanks & McEwan (Northern) Ltd, A8 Edinburgh Rd., pg. 1228   IT

Cobham

Van Leer (U.K.) Limited, Sperry House, 78 Portsmouth Rd., pg. 1147   IT

Coinbrook

Steelcase Strafor (U.K.) Ltd., 14 Newlands Dr., SL3 0DX, pg. 1038   PV

Colchester

Astralux Dynamics Ltd., pg. 1511   IT
CIBA Bunting Ltd, Westwood Park, Little Horkesley, pg. 975   IT

Cortaulds Packaging Ltd., Mulberry House, Stephenson Rd. Severalls Business Park, pg. 339   IT
Droyhurst Limited, Severalls Lane Industrial Estate, pg. 341   IT
Dynapert Limited, Mason Road, pg. 234   PB
Lancaster plc, Charter Court, pg. 705   IT
Ready Mixed Concrete (Eastern Counties) Limited, RMC House, Whitehall Rd., pg. 1080   IT
SIMS Portex Limited, Whitehall Rd., pg. 1267   IT
Triumph Adler (U.K.) Ltd., Ipswich Rd., pg. 1004   IT
Woods of Colchester Ltd., Tufnell Way, pg. 545   IT

Coleorton

Resco UK, pg. 924   PV

Coleshill

Adtec (UK) Ltd, 19A The Courtyard, Gorsey Lane, pg. 278   IT
Glynwed Pipe Systems, De Montfort House, High Street, pg. 554   IT
Maxon Combustion Systems, Ltd., Chantry House High Street, pg. 717   PV

Colinton

Fort Lock UK, Ltd., 19 Fernielaw Ave., pg. 419   PV

Colnbrook

AMEC Construction Services Ltd., Lakeside Industrial Estate, pg. 16   IT
Anixter UK, Anixter House, Prescott Road, pg. 116   PB
BancTec Ltd., ScanData House, pg. 177   IT
G.G. Baxters, Fulcrum Building, Horton Road, pg. 619   IT
Sundstrand International Corp., Prescot Rd., pg. 1534   PB

Colne

SILENTNIGHT HOLDINGS PLC, Silentnight House, Salterforth, pg. 1249   IT

Colwich

ITT Flygt Ltd., Colwick Industrial Estate, pg. 860   PB

Colwyn Bay

Quinton Hazell PLC, Colwyn Bay, Conway Rd., pg. 561   PB

Congleton

Congleton Board, Buxton Rd., pg. 123   IT
Graham Precision Pumps Ltd., The Forge, pg. 757   PB
Graham Vacuum & Heat Transfer Ltd., The Forge, pg. 757   PB
Smurfit Cartons (Congleton) Ltd., Sutherland Works, pg. 1271   IT

Cookley

Steel Wheels, Ltd., Bridge Road, pg. 1619   PB

Corby

British Steel Seamless Tubes, OCTG Sales, pg. 221   IT
British Steel Tubes & Pipes, P.O. Box 101, pg. 221   IT
Celebration Arts Group Limited, Mercury House, Princewood Rd., pg. 78   PB
Certech International Ltd., Earlstress Indus. Estate, 92 C & D Brunel Road, pg. 308   IT
Curver Consumer Products Ltd., Curver Way, Willow Brood Indus. Estate, pg. 353   IT
Dulmison (U.K.) Limited, Macadam Rd., pg. 893   IT
FlowMole Limited, Earlstrees Ind. Estate, 33 Maylan Road, pg. 1701   PB
Pechiney Cebal Packaging Ltd., 77/78, Earlstross Road, pg. 1031   IT
Spirol Ind. Ltd., Princewood Rd., Carlstrees Ind. Estate, pg. 1026   PV

Corsham

Altus Engineering (Corsham) Ltd., Stokes Rd., pg. 390   IT
Bath & Portland Stone Limited, Head Office, Moor Park House, pg. 592   IT
Bowman Distribution-Europe, Leafield Trading Estate, pg. 190   PB
Wansdyke Securities Limited, pg. 1160   IT
Waterford Foods Investments Limited, Potley La., pg. 102   IT

Coseley

Hoogovens Steel Service Center Ltd., pg. 754   IT

Coulsdon

Jane's Information Group, 163 Brighton Rd., pg. 1601   PB

Coventry

AGA Gas Ltd., AGA House, Willenhall Lane, pg. 13   IT
Alcan Metal Centres, Springfield Rd., pg. 51   IT

PB - U.S. Public Companies Volume
PV - U.S. Private Companies Volume
IT - International Public & Private Companies Volume

1800

Alvis Aerospace & Transmissions Limited, The Triangle, pg. 69 IT
Alvis Industries Limited, The Triangle, pg. 69 IT
Alvis Logistics Limited, Unit 5, Quinn Close, Manor Park, pg. 69 IT
Alvis Vehicles Limited, The Triangle, pg. 70 IT
Ampco Metal Ltd., 17, Binns Cl, Torrington Av, pg. 67 PV
Armstrong Engineering Limited, Sir Henry Parkes Rd., pg. 265 IT
AutoCIM Plc, 757 IT
Buehler U.K. Ltd., pg. 575 PB
Camford Automotive Systems Ltd., Capmartin Rd., pg. 507 IT
Comdisco United Kingdom. Ltd., pg. 408 PB
Cornercroft Engineering Limited, Aceworks Parkside, pg. 265 IT
Courtaulds Engineering Ltd., pg. 339 IT
Courtaulds European Fibres, P.O. Box 143, pg. 339 IT
Courtaulds Fibres Ltd., P.O. Box 143, pg. 339 IT
Dunlop Aerospace Group, Holobrook Ln., pg. 125 IT
Dunlop Automotive UK, Holbrook Ln., pg. 125 IT
Dunlop Aviation Div., Holbrook Ln., pg. 125 IT
FSW Ltd., Unit 32, Lythalls Lane Industrial Estate, pg. 1466 PB
Georg Fischer (Great Britain) Ltd., Paradise Way, pg. 491 IT
Georg Fischer Sales Ltd., Paradise Way, pg. 490 IT
GPT Ltd., New Century Park, pg. 544 IT
Jaguar Cars Finance Limited, Browns Lane, pg. 910 IT
Jaguar Cars Limited, Brown's Lane, Allesley, pg. 666 PB
Judd (UK) Limited, Oban Rd., pg. 1219 PB
Key Plastics UK, Bayton Rd., pg. 618 PV
Norman Levy Associates Overseas, Station Tower, Station Sq., pg. 664 PV
Lex Commercials, Lex House, Torwood Close, pg. 807 IT
Lex Transfleet, Lex House, Torwood Close, pg. 807 IT
Matra Datavision Ltd., pg. 796 IT
Nadella U.K. Limited, Progress Close, Leofric Business Park, pg. 878 PB
NASTECH Europe Ltd., Torrington Ave., pg. 904 IT
Peugeot Motor Co. Plc, P.O. Box 227, Aldermoor House, pg. 1021 IT
Porta Systems Limited, Rowley Dr., pg. 1317 PB
Reinshagen U.K., Groveland Industrial Estate, Longford Rd., pg. 723 IT
Rolls-Royce Industrial & Marine Gas Turbines Ltd., Ansty, pg. 1127 IT
SPS Technologies Ltd., Burnaby Road, pg. 1420 PB
Sanderson CFL Limited, CFL House, Manor Road, pg. 1184 IT
Sandvik Hard Materials Ltd., pg. 1186 IT
Serck Controls Limited, Rowley Drive, pg. 297 IT
Severn Trent Laboratories Limited, STL Business Center, Torrington Avenue, pg. 1226 IT
Systematic Drill Head Co. Ltd., Willenhall Lane, pg. 585 IT
The Torrington Company Limited, Torrington Ave., pg. 878 PB
Transfleet Services Limited, The Oaks, Torwood Close, Westwood, pg. 911 IT
Volumatic Limited, Taurus House, pg. 590 IT

Cowes

Strainstall Engineering Services Limited, Denmark Road, pg. 1344 IT

Cowley

Unipart Group Limited, Unipart House, pg. 218 IT

Cradley Heath

CMT Engineering Ltd., P.O. Box 36, Congreaves Rd., pg. 265 IT
CMT Engineering Insulation, pg. 265 IT
Tube Fittings, pg. 265 IT

Craigavon

Hyster (NI) Ltd., Carn Industrial Estate, pg. 1150 PB
Irlandus Circuits Limited, Annesborough No. 3, pg. 473 PB

Craigellachie

Macallan Glenlivet, Macallan Distillery, pg. 619 IT

Cramlington

Cascade (U.K.) Ltd., Bassington Indus. Estate, pg. 311 PB
DeZurik International Ltd., Nelson Way, Nelson Industrial Estate, pg. 727 PB
Dunlop Industrial Hose Ltd., Bassington Industrial Estate, pg. 125 IT
Eaton Limited Forge Division, Nelson Way, pg. 559 PB
Forbo CP Ltd., pg. 497 IT
Forbo UK Ltd., pg. 498 IT
Hyclone Europe Ltd., Nelson Industrial Estates, pg. 1037 IT
Lonrho Textiles Ltd., Nelson Industrial Estate, Nelson Way, pg. 817 IT

Cranfield

Nissan European Technology Centre Ltd., Cranfield Technology Park, pg. 945 IT

Cranford

ALPHA AIRPORTS GROUP PLC, Europa House, 804 Bath Rd., pg. 65 IT

Cranleigh

Flouro-Precision Coatings, Unit 19, Hewitts Industrial Estate, pg. 1338 IT

Crathorne

VIRGIN HOTEL, Crathorn Hall, pg. 1468 IT

Crawley

AMI, Astral Towers, Betts Way, pg. 707 IT
APV Pasilac, pg. 1240 IT
Babcock Energy Limited, 11 The Boulevard, pg. 130 IT
Babcock King - Wilkinson Limited, 11 The Blvd., pg. 131 IT
Babcock Spraymixer Ltd., 11 The Boulevard, pg. 472 IT
Babcock Turnkey Operations Ltd., 11 The Boulevard, pg. 472 IT
Babcock Woodall-Duckham Ltd., 11 The Boulevard, pg. 472 IT
Barringer Instruments-U.K., Ltd., Unit 3, Lloyd'd Court, pg. 192 PB
BOWTHORPE PLC, Gatwick Rd., pg. 207 PB
Check Technology Limited, 3/4 Satellite Business Village, Fleming Way, pg. 342 PB
Decra Roof Systems (U.K.) Ltd., pg. 658 IT
DuraCell Batteries Limited, Mallory House, Hazelwick Ave., pg. 743 PB
Farah Manufacturing (U.K.) Limited, Unit 2a, Gatwick Gate Estate, Charlwood, pg. 613 PB
Foxboro Great Britain Limited, Unit C, Churchill Court, Manor Royal, pg. 1243 IT
Hewlett-Packard Limited, Churchill Ct., Gatwick Rd., pg. 821 PB
ITW Spit Fixings, Crompton Way, pg. 869 IT
Network Equipment Technologies, Ltd., Manor Court, Manor Royal, pg. 1169 PB
Novo Nordisk Pharmaceuticals Ltd., Novo Nordisk House, Broadfield Rd., pg. 988 IT
Pharmacia & Upjohn Limited, P.O. Box No. Eight, Fleming Way, pg. 1049 IT
Process Plant Contracting Div., Woodhall-Buckham House, 11 The Blvd., pg. 472 IT
Racal Radar Defence, Manor Royal, pg. 1082 IT
Radiometer Ltd., The Manor, Manor Royal, pg. 1084 IT
Radiometer (UK) Ltd., The Manor, Manor Royal, pg. 1084 IT
Redland Technologies Ltd., Sussex Manor Business Park, Gatwick Road, pg. 1091 IT
Sherwood Medical Industries Ltd., pg. 82 IT
Simrad Optronics Ltd., 3 Oakwood Industrial Park, pg. 770 IT
Southern Tree Surgeons, Ltd., Turners Hill Rd., pg. 119 PV
Telegan Gas Monitoring Limited, The Fleming Centre, Fleming Way, pg. 590 IT
Thermo Electron Ltd., Woolborough Ln., pg. 1596 PB
Toshiba Medical Systems Ltd., Manor Court, Manor Royal, pg. 1407 IT
VG Instruments plc, 29 Brighton Rd., pg. 1595 PB
VG Precision Ltd., Gatwick Rd., pg. 1595 PB
Van den Bergh Foods Ltd., Brooke House, Manor Royal, pg. 1434 IT
Varian-TEM Ltd., Gatwick Road, pg. 1710 PB
Vent-Axia Ltd., Fleming Way, pg. 1267 IT

Crayford

Aisin (UK) Limited, Unit 32, Rich Industrial, Estate, Crayford Road, pg. 39 IT
C. Cakebread, 149 Crayford Road, pg. 460 IT
Dussek Campbell Ltd., Thames Rd., pg. 234 IT

Crewe

Air Products PLC, Fourth Avenue, pg. 32 PB
JSB Electrical PLC, Holmes Chapel, pg. 453 IT
Rolls-Royce Motor Cars Limited, Pyms Lane, pg. 1467 IT
Rolls-Royce Motor Cars Limited, Mulliner Park Ward, Pyms Lane, pg. 1467 IT
Rolls-Royce Motor Cars Limited Sales & Marketing, Pyms Lane, pg. 1467 IT
Rolls-Royce Motor Cars Limited, Specialist Engines, Pyms Lane, pg. 1467 IT
Rolls-Royce Motor Cars Pacific Operations, Pyms Lane, pg. 1467 IT
Rolls-Royce Motor Cars UK Operations, Pyms Lane, pg. 1467 IT
Vickers Precision Components, Pyms Lane, pg. 1467 IT
Vickers Precision Machining, Pyms Lane, pg. 1468 IT

Crewkerne

VARTA Ltd., Unit 1, Cropmead Industrial Estate, pg. 1452 IT

Crieff

Glenturret Distillery Limited, The Hosh, pg. 619 IT

Crossgates

Vickers Defense Systems, Barnbow Works, Manston Ln., pg. 1467 IT

Croydon

ASSA Ltd., 75 Summer Rd., pg. 17 IT
Alpnet, Rothschild House, Whitgift Centre, pg. 58 PB
American Life Insurance Co., UK, American International Bldg., 2-8, Altyre Rd., pg. 85 PB
American Power Conversion, Keeley House, 22-36 Keeley Rd., pg. 89 PB
Ascom Hasler Ltd., Commerce Way, pg. 87 IT
Assi Pulp & Paper Sales (UK) Ltd., Prudential House, Wellesley Road, pg. 967 IT
BI Commercial Finance Limited, Alhambra House, 9 St. Michael's Rd., pg. 153 IT
Baltek Ltd., 64 High St., pg. 172 PB
Bank of Ireland Discounting, Alhambra House, 9 St. Michael's Road, pg. 153 IT
Bristol-Babcock Ltd., 218 Purley Way, pg. 474 IT
Canatom Heavy Water Limited, Grosvenor House, 125 High St., pg. 1587 PB
Canon Business Service (UK) Ltd., 59 Imperial Way, Croydon Airport Industrial Estate, pg. 262 IT
Centronic Limited, Centronic House, King Henry's Dr., pg. 892 IT
Chambourcy Food Co. Ltd., 154a Tredegar Road, pg. 920 IT
Continental Life Insurance plc, 64/70 High St., pg. 1011 PB
Direct Line Insurance plc, Direct Line House, 1 Edridge Rd., pg. 1132 IT
EMAP Maclaren, Maclaren House, 19 Scarbrook Rd., pg. 451 IT
Europ Assistance Holdings Ltd., 252, High Street, pg. 91 IT
Europ Assistance Insurance Ltd., 252, High Street, pg. 91 IT
Europ Assistance Ltd., 252, High Street, pg. 90 IT
Humphreys & Glasgow (Atlantic) Limited, Grosvenor House, 125 High St., pg. 1587 PB
Humphreys & Glasgow Europe Ltd., Grosvenor House, 125 High St., pg. 1587 PB
Humphreys & Glasgow International PLC, Grosvenor House, 125 High St., pg. 1587 PB
Humphreys & Glasgow (Overseas) Limited, Grosvenor House, 125 High St., pg. 1587 PB
Integrol, 145 London Road, pg. 1298 IT
Kvaerner H&G Offshore Ltd, Davis House, 69-77 Robert Street, pg. 771 IT
Landis & Staefa Communications (U.K.) Ltd., 40 Purley Way, pg. 800 IT
MJN, Staveley House, 11 Dingwall Road, pg. 1299 IT
Monomet Limited, 50 Beddington Ln., pg. 1079 IT
National Utility Service Ltd., Carolyn House, 8-12 Dingwall Rd., pg. 787 PV
Nestle U.K. Ltd., St. Georges House, pg. 922 IT
Philips Consumer Electronics, Philips Center, 420-430 London Road, pg. 1055 IT
Philips Lighting Ltd., City House, 420 London Rd., pg. 1055 IT
Process & Energy Consultants Ltd., Grosvenor House, 125 High St., pg. 1588 PB
Process Control Instrumentation Div., 218 Purley Way, pg. 473 IT
Pullen Pumps Division, 58, Beddington Lane, pg. 271 IT
Rohm & Haas (UK) Ltd., 2 Masons Ave., pg. 1404 IT
Royal Bank Invoice Finance Limited. Exchange Court, 3 Bedford Park, pg. 1132 IT
RoyScot Factors Limited, 3 Bedford Pk., pg. 1132 IT
RoyScot Finance Group plc, Exchange Ct., pg. 1132 IT
SNC-Lavalin Europe Ltd., Amp House, Dingwall Road, pg. 1163 IT
Sedgwick Noble Lowndes Group Limited, P.O. Box 144, Norfolk House, pg. 1218 PB
Shipley Europe Limited, pg. 1404 PB
Smiths Industries Aerospace & Defence Systems Limited-Newmark, Vulcan Way, pg. 1267 IT
STAVELEY INDUSTRIES PLC, Staveley House, 11 Dingwall Rd., pg. 1298 IT
Superdrug Stores PLC, 118 Beddington Lane, pg. 734 IT
Systech Solutions Ltd., 112 Gloucester Road, pg. 853 IT
Tolley Publishing Ltd., Tolley House, #2 Addiscombe Road, pg. 1095 IT
Trafalgar House Construction Ltd., Mitcham House, 681 Mitcham Rd., pg. 773 IT
Trafalgar House Technology Limtied (Mitcham House), 681 Mitcham Rd., pg. 774 IT
Univar Europe N.V., Suffolk House, George St., pg. 1147 IT

Crumlin

Flexonics Automotive, pg. 1220 IT
Redland Tile & Brick, 61 Largy Rd., pg. 1091 IT

Cumbernauld

Ashfield Medical Systems, Limited, 52 Grayshill Rd., pg. 689 PB
Beazer Homes (Glaston) Limited, Beazer House, 1 Napier Park, pg. 182 PB
Diesel ReCon UK, 2/10 Napier Place, pg. 469 PB
Robert Horne Paper (Scotland) Limited, pg. 757 IT
JLG Industries (United Kingdom) Limited, Westfield Industrial Estate, pg. 918 PB
MPC Cumbernauld, 2 Grayshill Rd., pg. 851 IT

PB - *U.S. Public Companies Volume*
PV - *U.S. Private Companies Volume*
IT - *International Public & Private Companies Volume*

Modern Structural Plastics Ltd., 1-9, Telford Rd., pg. 444   IT
Oki (UK) Ltd., 3 Castlecary Rd., Wardpark North, pg. 999   IT
Omsco Industries Limited, Dunswood Road, pg. 1231   IT

Cwmbran

Alfa-Laval Agri Ltd., Oakfield, pg. 1380   IT
Just Rubber plc., Somerset Industrial Estate, pg. 1202   IT
Lucas Light Vehicle Braking Systems, Grange Works, pg. 819   IT
Palmer Environmental Limited, Ty Coch House, Llantarnam Park Way, pg. 589   IT
Saunders Valve Co. Ltd., Grange Road, pg. 1379   IT

Dalkeith

Ferranti Syseca, Thornybank, pg. 1384   IT

Darbyshire

THORNTONS PLC, Thornton Park, Somercotes, pg. 1386   IT

Darlaston

Armstrong Fastenings Ltd., Station St., pg. 265   IT

Darlington

AMEC Construction Ltd., Industrial Engineering Div., Haughton Rd., pg. 16   IT
Anixter Darlington, 7 Houndgate, pg. 115   PB
Durham Tube, Brookside Works, Middleton St. George, pg. 1221   IT
Flymo Ltd., Aycliffe Industrial Estate, pg. 444   IT
Patons & Baldwins Limited, McMullen Rd., pg. 300   IT
SAB WABCO Ltd., Howden Way, Aycliffe Industrial Estate, pg. 271   IT
Taylor Woodrow Construction (Northern) Ltd., Lingfield Way, pg. 1358   IT
Whessoe Computing Systems Ltd., Brinkburn Rd., pg. 1498   IT
Whessoe Projects Ltd., Brinkburn Rd., pg. 1498   IT
Whessoe Systems & Controls Ltd., Brinkburn Rd., pg. 1498   IT

Dartford

Euroflex Screen Print Supplies Ltd., pg. 412   PV

Darwen

Chapman Industries plc, Grimshaw Bridge, Eccleshill, pg. 1420   IT

Datchet

Honeywell-Measurex International Systems Ltd., Measurex House, Slough Rd., pg. 833   PB

Daventry

Boge (UK) Ltd., pg. 835   IT
Cummins Engine Company, Ltd., Royal Oak Way South, pg. 469   PB
Ingersoll Milling Machines Overseas Ltd., 4 Scotia Close, pg. 562   PV
Skega Ltd., Whittle Close, Drayton Fields, pg. 1324   IT

Deeside

Computational Systems, Ltd., Unit 22, Rowleys Dr., Deeside Enterprise Centre, pg. 573   PB
Dexter Packaging Products Div., Parkway Deeside Indus. Pk., pg. 505   PB
Hydro Coatings Ltd., Tenth Ave., pg. 963   IT
Iceland Frozen Foods plc., Second Ave., pg. 658   IT
ICELAND GROUP PLC, Second Ave., pg. 658   IT
Remsdaq Limited, Second Ave., Deeside Indus. Park, pg. 300   PV
Van Leer (UK) Ltd., pg. 1147   IT

Denham

VB Automotive Batteries Ltd., P.O. Box 402, Broadwater Park, pg. 1452   IT

Derby

The British Van Heusen Company Limited, Viyella House, Nottingham Rd., pg. 299   IT
Brown & Sharpe Limited, Derby Road, Melbourne, pg. 260   PB
Carrington Viyella Garments Ltd., Viyella House, Nottingham Rd., pg. 299   IT
Elastogran UK Limited, Alfreton Industrial Estate, pg. 108   IT
Fletcher Smith Ltd., Norman House, Friar Gate, pg. 202   IT
Fluid Connectors Group, Parker Hannifin (U.K.) Ltd., Haydock Park Rd., pg. 1261   PB
Griffith Laboratories Limited, Cotes Park Estate, pg. 481   PV
Guilford Europe, Ltd., Cotes Park, pg. 769   PB

Herr Voss Ltd., Ten Nottingham Rd., Eastgate House, pg. 962   PV
LK Limited, East Midlands Airport, Castledonnington, pg. 1418   IT
Microfine Minerals Ltd. Mica Works, Raynesway, pg. 1459   IT
Nenplas Extrusions Homelux, Airfield Industrial Estate, pg. 851   IT
Rolls-Royce & Associates Limited, P.O. Box 31, pg. 472   IT
Rolls-Royce-Commercial Aero Engines Ltd., pg. 1127   IT
Ross & Catherall Ceramics Limited, Denby, pg. 1467   IT
SAPA Ltd., Saw Pit Lane, pg. 444   IT
SIG Holdings (UK) Ltd., Meteor Centre, Mansfield Road, pg. 1156   IT
SIG Packaging Technology (UK) Ltd., Meteor Centre, Mansfield Road, pg. 1156   IT
Salem Engineering Co., Ltd., Milford House, pg. 962   PV
Senior Control Engineering Limited, Alfreton Rd., pg. 1220   IT
Senior Davis Derby, Alfreton Rd., pg. 1220   IT
Shell of Castle Donington, East Midlands Intl. Airport, pg. 1139   IT
Svedala Ltd. Derby, pg. 1325   IT
WILLIAMS HOLDINGS PLC, Pentagon House, Sir Frank Whittle Rd., pg. 1079   IT
Zyma Healthcare, Units 4 & 10, Wimsey Way, pg. 986   IT

Desford

Caterpillar Logistics Services Limited, Peckelton Ln., pg. 317   PB
Caterpillar (U.K.) Limited, pg. 317   PB

Detling

A. Wood & Sons (Delting), Aerodrome Estate, pg. 491   IT

Devizes

Carters (J&A) Ltd., Prince Maurice Ct., Hambleton Ave., pg. 911   PB

Dewsbury

Carlton Cards, Ltd., pg. 78   PB
Emergi-Lite Safety Systems Ltd., Wesley Place, The Ring Rd., pg. 725   IT
Rust Craft Greeting Cards (U.K.) Limited, Mill Street East, pg. 78   PB

Didcot

Aztec Environmental Control Limited, 8 Hawksworth, pg. 1225   IT

Docking

Hillshog (United Kingdom) Ltd., pg. 982   IT

Dolgarrog

Aluminum Corporation, pg. 51   IT

Doncaster

Beazer Homes (Doncaster) Limited, Beazer House, Kirk Sandall Industrial Estate, pg. 182   IT
BRIDON PLC, Carr Hill, pg. 215   PB
Case United Kingdom Limited, pg. 1579   PB
Cementation Mining Limited, P.O. Box 22, Bentley House, pg. 772   IT
Crompton Lighting Ltd., Wheatley Hall Rd., Wheatley, pg. 124   IT
Emhart (U.K.) Ltd., Crompton Rd., Wheatley, pg. 234   PB
Intro Marketing Limited, The Old Freight Depot, Roberts Road, pg. 858   IT
Kvaerner Boving Limited, Kvaerner House, Ten Pound Walk, pg. 772   IT
PEM Intl. Ltd., Unit E. Sandall Lane, pg. 1270   PB
Pegler-Hattersley Plc, St. Catherines Ave., pg. 1395   IT
Rockware Glass Ltd.-Wheatley Factory, pg. 124   IT
VECTOR INDUSTRIES, LTD., 2B Sidings Court, pg. 1461   IT

Dorchester

Dorchester Transport Services (Lee Line Commercials), Poundbury West Industrial Estate, pg. 591   IT
Integrated Photomatrix Ltd., The Grove Trading Estate, pg. 448   IT

Dorking

Brambles (U.K.) Ltd., Abinger House, Church St., pg. 212   IT
Friends Provident, Pixham End, pg. 464   IT
Komori Currency Technology U.K. Limited, Sondes Place, Westcott Road, pg. 745   IT
The Ockley Brick Co. Ltd., Smokejacks Brickworks, Wallis Wood, pg. 197   IT
UNUM Limited, Milton Court, pg. 1700   PB

Dorset

Bridport Aviation Products, The Court, Bridport, pg. 215   IT

Bridport-Grundy Marine, The Court, Bridport, pg. 215   IT
Bridport-Grundy Netting Limited, The Court, Bridport, pg. 215   IT
Bridport-Gundry Ltd. (U.K.), The Court, West St., pg. 215   IT
BRIDPORT-GUNDRY P.L.C., The Court, West St., pg. 215   IT
Abbot Brown & Sons Ltd., pg. 1511   IT
Hamworthy Industramar Limited, Fleete Corner, pg. 1065   IT
Penny & Giles Drives Technology Ltd., 1 Airspeed Road, pg. 207   IT

Douglas

Bank of Bermuda (Isle of Man) Limited, 12/13 Hill St., pg. 151   IT
Bank of Ireland (IOM) Limited, Christian Rd., pg. 153   IT
Baring (Isle of Man), P.O. Box 174, St. James's Chambers, pg. 648   IT
Bermuda Trust (Isle of Man) Limited, 12/13 Hill Street, pg. 151   IT
The Derbyshire (Isle of Man) Ltd., Celtic House, Victoria St., pg. 395   IT
The Douglas Steam Saw Mill and Timber Company Limited, Lake Rd., pg. 1079   IT
Robert Fleming (Isle of Man) Limited, 5 Mount Pleasant, pg. 493   IT
Gray Tool Co. (Europe), Douglas Industrial Estate, pg. 5   IT
Island Aggregates Limited, Treger House, 23 Circular Rd., pg. 1079   IT
Isle of Man Bank Limited, 2 Athol St., pg. 910   IT
Lloyds Bank Finance (Isle of Man) Ltd., Victory House, Prospect Hill, pg. 813   IT
Manx Telecom Limited, Queen Victoria House, 41-43 Victoria St., pg. 223   IT
Midland Bank Trust Corporation (Isle of Man) Limited, Celtic House, Victoria Street, pg. 580   IT
NatWest International Trust Corporation (Europe) Limited, 11/13 Hill St., pg. 911   IT
NatWest International Trust Corporation (Isle of Man) Limited, 33 Athol St., pg. 911   IT
Pfizer Ringaskiddy Production Company, 50 Athol St., pg. 1283   PB
The Royal Bank of Scotland (I.O.M.) Limited, Victory House, pg. 1133   IT
Royal Insurance Service Co. (Isle of Man) Ltd., 19 Athol St., pg. 1130   IT
Royal Skandia Life Assurance Ltd., P.O. Box 159, Skandia House, pg. 1257   IT
Service Investments, Finch Rd. 12, pg. 534   IT
Standard Bank Investment Corporation (Isle of Man) Limited, P.O. Box 220, Exchange House, 54-58 Athol St., pg. 1294   IT
Ulster Bank (Isle of Man) Limited, 45 Victoria Street, pg. 911   IT
Warburg Asset Management Isle of Man Ltd., 12-13 Hill St., pg. 1331   IT
Willis Corroon Douglas Limited, Ten Finch Road, pg. 1502   IT
Willis Corroon Management Limited-Isle of Man, Ten Finch Road, pg. 1503   IT

Dover

C.G. Hibbert Ltd., Channel View Road, pg. 63   IT
Hoverspeed Ltd., International Hoverport, Western Docks, pg. 1214   IT
P&O European Ferries Ltd., Channel House, Channel View Rd., pg. 1033   IT

Driffield

Moorland Foods, Skerne Rd, pg. 619   IT
Premier Building Group, Catwick Lane, pg. 1   IT

Droitwich

Battenfeld Gloenco Extrusion Systems Ltd., Berry Hill Industrial Estate, Kidderminster Road, pg. 825   IT
Britax Vega Limited, Kingswood Rd., Hampton Lovett Industrial Estate, pg. 216   IT
Eclipse Combustion Ltd., Wassage Way, Hampton Lovett Indus. Estate, pg. 361   PV
Fuji Hunt Photographic Chemicals (U.K.) Ltd., Site 7, Kidderminster Rd., pg. 524   IT
Nu-Way Ltd., pg. 1512   IT
Olin UK Ltd., Site 7, Kidderminster Rd., pg. 1220   PB
Plastools Ltd., Unit 10, N. Bank, Berry Hill Industrial Estate, pg. 391   IT
Rexel Business Machines Ltd., P.O. Box 12, West Bank, pg. 675   PB
Wolseley Building Distribution - Europe, Vines Lane, pg. 1511   IT
WOLSELEY PLC, Vines Lane, pg. 1511   IT

Dronfield

Gunstones Bakery, Stubley Lane, pg. 968   IT
LAND INSTRUMENTS INTERNATIONAL LTD., pg. 798   IT

Dudley

Addison Saws Limited, Crackley Way, Pear Tree Industrial Park, pg. 448   IT
Air Movement Group Ltd., Peartree House, Peartree Lane, pg. 1267   IT

PB - *U.S. Public Companies Volume*
PV - *U.S. Private Companies Volume*
IT - *International Public & Private Companies Volume*

Clydesdale Engineering, Marriott Rd., pg. 265 — IT
Clydesdale Forge Co., Marriott Rd., pg. 265 — IT
Clydesdale Whitehouse & Co., Marriott Rd., pg. 265 — IT
Do It All, Falcon House, The Minories, pg. 203 — IT
Meggitt Composites, Netherton, pg. 853 — IT

Duffield

DERBYSHIRE BUILDING SOCIETY, Duffield Hall, pg. 394 — IT
The Derbyshire (Premises) LTD., Duffield Hall, pg. 395 — IT

Dukinfield

Nordsea Gas Technology Ltd., Broadway, Globe Lane Industrial Estate, pg. 1455 — PB

Dumbarton

Babcock Calorizing Ltd., Glasgow Rd., pg. 130 — IT
Diamond Power Specialty Ltd., Glasgow Rd., pg. 472 — IT
J&B Scotland, Strathleven, Gooseholm Rd., pg. 410 — IT
Methode Electronics Europe Limited, Block 14, Vale of Leven Industrial Estate, pg. 1101 — PB
Polaroid (U.K.) Ltd.-The Vale, Vale of Leven Industrial Estates, pg. 1314 — PB
Stewart & Son of Dundee Limited, 2 Glasgow Road, pg. 63 — IT
Wm. Teacher & Sons Limited, 2 Glasgow Road, pg. 63 — IT

Dumfries

Duralay Accessories, Dumfries Ind. Estate, pg. 113 — IT
The Gates Rubber Company Ltd., Edinburgh Rd., Heathhall, pg. 1397 — IT
Guthrie International, Irongray Road, pg. 113 — IT

Dundee

N.G. Bailey & Co. Ltd.-Dundee Branch, Unit 26, Prospect III Bus. Ctr., pg. 132 — IT
Delta Capillary Products, Alexander St., pg. 390 — IT
TRAK Microwave Co. Ltd., Dunsinane Avenue, pg. 1563 — PB
Andrew Valentine Holdings Limited, Arrol Rd. West, pg. 78 — IT
Van Leer Tay Ltd, pg. 1147 — IT
Willis Corroon Scotland Limited, 285 Queen Street, pg. 1503 — IT

Dunfermline

Bourns Electronics, Ltd., Hillend Industrial Estate, pg. 161 — PV
De La Rue Fortronic Limited, Ridgeway, Donibristle Industrial Estate, pg. 387 — IT
Heil Europe, Hillend Industrial Estate, pg. 521 — PB
OCLI Optical Coatings Ltd., Ridge Way, Hillend Industrial Pk., pg. 1227 — PB
Solectron Scotland Limited, Queensferry Rd., pg. 1483 — PB
Triumph Adler/Roytype (UK) Ltd., Donibristle Indus. Park, pg. 1004 — IT

Dungannon

Moygashel Ltd., Moygashel Mills, pg. 798 — IT
POWERSCREEN INTERNATIONAL PLC, Coalisland Road, pg. 1066 — IT

Dunstable

Baldwin (UK) Ltd., Unit 13 Apex Business Centre, Boscombe Road, pg. 170 — PB
Thomas De La Rue and Company Limited, French's Ave., pg. 386 — IT
Framatome Connectors U.K. Ltd., Connector House, Eyncourt Rd., pg. 503 — IT
General Motors Overseas Corp., High St. N., pg. 722 — PB
IBP Ltd., Unit 25, Verey Rd., pg. 391 — PB
M/A-COM Limited, pg. 8 — PB
Reed Travel Group, Church Street, pg. 1097 — IT
Reed Travel Publishing, Church Street, pg. 1097 — IT
Senior Heat Treatment Limited, Ashton Lodge, Ashton Rd., pg. 1221 — IT
Thomas & Betts Ltd., Foster Ave., pg. 1598 — IT
Yokohama HPT Ltd., Unit 7 Humphreys Rd., pg. 1521 — IT

Durham

AEI Cables, Birtley, Chester-le-Street, pg. 1344 — IT
Cleveland Structural Engineering Limited, P.O. Box 27, pg. 772 — IT
Dinol Protectol Ltd., Montalbo Road, pg. 982 — IT
Environmental Elements Limited, P.O. Box 17, pg. 587 — PB
Evenwood Engineering, Evenwood, pg. 231 — IT
Multi-Arc (U.K.) Ltd., No. 1 Industrial Estate, Medomsley Rd., pg. 1198 — IT
Ready Mixed Concrete (Northern) Limited, RMC House, Littlebum Industrial Estate, pg. 1080 — IT
Specialty Filaments Ltd., St. Helen's Aukland Industrial Estate, pg. 77 — PV

Dursley

Lister-Petter Ltd., Long St., pg. 125 — IT

Dyfed

Camford Pressings Ltd., Llethri Rd., pg. 507 — IT
Europe, Marshfield House, Fford-Y-Morfa, pg. 1540 — PB
Stena Line Limited, Fishguard Harbour, pg. 1300 — IT

Earley

Legacy Storage Systems Corp., Unit 15, Suttons Business Park, pg. 805 — IT

East Cowes

GKN Westland Aerospace Limited, Castle St., pg. 535 — IT

East Grinstead

Bowker-Saur Ltd., Maypole House, Maypole Road, pg. 1094 — IT
Disco Hi-Tec U K Ltd., 151 London Rd., pg. 413 — IT
Reed Business Information-East Grinstead, Windsor Court, pg. 1094 — IT
Rentokil Initial plc, Felcourt, pg. 1285 — IT
Rentokil Ltd., Felcourt, pg. 1285 — IT
Scott Limited, Scott House, pg. 960 — PB
VG Microscopes Ltd., Birches Industrial Estate, pg. 1595 — PB
VG Scientific Ltd., Birches Industrial Estate, pg. 1595 — PB
VG Semicon Ltd., Birches Indus. Estate, pg. 1595 — PB
Veritas DGC INC, Digicon Bldg., Portland Rd., pg. 1137 — PV

East Hanney

Mentor Medical Systems, U.K., Oxford Rd., pg. 1086 — PB

East Kilbride

Ademco Microtech Security Ltd., 2 Redwood Crescent, pg. 1307 — PB
Avex Electronics Ltd., 2 Young Pl., pg. 545 — PV
Courier International, Ltd., Three Colvilles Pl. Kelvin, pg. 453 — PB
DMC Telecom U.K. Ltd., pg. 508 — PB
Gray Tool Co. (Europe), P.O. Box 6, pg. 5 — IT
Hewlett-Packard Ltd., 1/3 Springburn Pl., pg. 821 — PB
Imperial Tobacco Ltd., Northern Trading Div., One Tennant Ave., pg. 666 — IT
Instrument Specialties Europe Ltd., 2 Kelvin Park S., Kelvin S. Business Park, pg. 565 — PV
JVC Manufacturing U.K. Ltd., 2 Glenburn Rd., pg. 847 — IT
Joy Manufacturing Company (UK) Ltd., East Kilbride Plant, Peel Park Place, pg. 789 — IT

East Molesey

Dahl Brothers Ltd., Scandia Works, Armfield Close Molesey Ave., pg. 359 — IT
Tennant Maintenance Systems, Limited, Central Ave., pg. 1577 — PB

Eastbourne

Berk Pharmaceuticals Ltd., St. Leonard's House, St. Leonard's Rd., pg. 1111 — IT
EIP GROUP PLC, 6 Alder Close, pg. 426 — IT
Intergen Beauty Products, 51/55 Brampton Rd., pg. 591 — IT
Private Patients Plan Limited, PPP House, 20 Upperton Road, pg. 1020 — IT
Rorer Health Care Ltd., Brampton Rd., pg. 1112 — IT
SSP Pumps Ltd., Birch Road, pg. 1380 — IT
Taylor & Goodman Ltd., Three Faraday Close, Hampden Park Trading Estate, pg. 1285 — IT
White Knight Products Limited, pg. 268 — IT

Eastleigh

Allders Nuance, 8498 Southampton Rd., pg. 1334 — IT
B & Q Plc, Portswood House, 1 Hampshire Corporate Park, pg. 733 — IT
Chloride Electronics Ltd., Barton Pk., pg. 287 — IT
Fortis (U.K.) Limited, Bishopsgate House, pg. 499 — IT
The Games, Parham Drive, Boyatt Wood, pg. 707 — IT
Pascon Ltd., Bournemouth Rd., pg. 124 — IT
Pirelli Construction Company Ltd., Leigh Road, pg. 1059 — IT
SMH (UK) Ltd., Omega House, Southampton Road 112, pg. 1161 — IT
William R. Selwood Ltd., School Lane, pg. 124 — IT
Warner-Lambert, Lambert Ct., Chestnut Ave., pg. 1739 — PB

Ebbw Vale

Aero Motive (U.K.) Ltd., Rassau Industrial Estate, pg. 1776 — PB

Eccles

Gardner Avon, Hardy St., pg. 1381 — IT
L. Gardner & Sons Ltd., Barton Hall, Hardy Street, pg. 1381 — IT
L. Gardner Group PLC, Barton Hall, Hardy Street, pg. 1381 — IT

Edenbridge

Kiloheat Ltd., Enterprise Way, pg. 1055 — PB
Lewis & Towers Limited, Fircroft Way, pg. 1344 — IT

Edgware

GKN Freight Services Ltd., Mattey House, 128/136 High Street, pg. 534 — IT
Sumitomo Electric Europe S.A. - Edgware, pg. 1314 — IT

Edinburgh

Adam & Company Group plc, 22 Charlotte Sq., pg. 1132 — IT
Adobe Systems Limited, Aldus House, West One Business Park, pg. 20 — IT
Adobe Systems UK Limited, 39 Palmerston Place, pg. 20 — PB
Aidsun Limited, 26 Orwell Terrace, pg. 1172 — IT
N.G. Bailey & Co. Ltd.-Edinburgh Branch, 5 South Gyle, Crescent Lane, pg. 132 — IT
Bailey Telecom LTD - Edinburgh, 5 South Gyle Crescent Lane, pg. 133 — IT
Brown Brothers & Company Ltd., Rosebank Works, Broughton Rd., pg. 1466 — IT
Cannongate Technology Limited, Abbey Brewery, Holyrood Rd., pg. 1211 — IT
Cumberland Life Assurance Co. Limited, pg. 665 — IT
Datastream International (Scotland) Ltd., Miller House, 18/20 George St., pg. 1326 — IT
DAWSON INTERNATIONAL PLC, Level 4, Saltire Court, pg. 385 — IT
Edinburgh, Kintore House, 74-77 Queen Street, pg. 910 — IT
Edinburgh Terminal, Imperial Dock, pg. 692 — PB
Financial Collection Agencies, Scott House, 2nd Floor, 8-10 South Andrew Street, pg. 471 — IT
Fountain Head Brewery, Scottish Cottage, pg. 1212 — IT
GEC Ferranti Defence Systems Ltd., Crewe Toll, Ferry Rd., pg. 544 — IT
GPC Market Access Scotland, 14 Charlotte Square, pg. 1225 — IT
The Gates Rubber Company Limited, NCR House, 5th Floor, 2, Roseburn Gardens, pg. 1397 — IT
Geographia Ltd., 12, Duncan St., pg. 927 — IT
Grange Glazing Limited, 26 Orwell Terrace, pg. 1173 — IT
Guardian Baillie Gifford, Ltd., 1 Rutland Ct., pg. 486 — PV
JOHN MENZIES PLC, 108 Princes Street, pg. 707 — IT
John Menzies Retail, Hanover Buildings, Rose Street, pg. 707 — IT
John Menzies (UK) Limited, Hanover Buildings, Rose Street, pg. 707 — IT
John Menzies Wholesale, Hanover Buildings, Rose Street, pg. 707 — IT
Lawson Mardon Thyne Ltd, Langmuir Works Sighthill, pg. 69 — IT
The Leith Agency, The Canon Mill, Canon St., pg. 1152 — PV
Liquid Gas Equipment Ltd., KeithHouse, 2 Redheughs Rigg, pg. 1489 — IT
M & S Toiletries Ltd., 100 Bankhead Crossway, North, pg. 591 — IT
Marine Harvest McConnell, Craigcrook Castle, pg. 202 — IT
Morgan Grenfell (Scotland) Limited, 35 St. Andrew Sq., pg. 405 — IT
Norske Skog (UK) Limited, 47A George St., pg. 967 — IT
Northumberland Group Ltd., Rutland Square House, 12 Rutland Square, pg. 162 — IT
The PR Centre Limited, 9-11 York Place, pg. 1226 — IT
Personal Performance Consultants UK Limited (PPC), 1/3 St. Colme Street, pg. 1502 — IT
Riley Advertising (Edinburgh) Ltd., 26 Great King St., pg. 1117 — IT
Royal Bank Development Capital Limited, 26 St. Andrew Square, pg. 1132 — IT
THE ROYAL BANK OF SCOTLAND PLC, 42 St. Andrew Square, pg. 1132 — IT
Royal Scottish Assurance plc, 31 St. Andrew Sq., pg. 1132 — IT
Scottish Equitable, Edinburgh Park, pg. 28 — IT
Scottish & Courage Beer Div., Abbey Brewery, Holyrood Rd., pg. 1212 — IT
Scottish & Courage Beer Production Limited, Abbey Brewery, Holyrood Rd., pg. 1212 — IT
Scottish & Courage Breweries (Sales) Limited, Abbey Brewery Rd., Holyrood Rd., pg. 1212 — IT
Scottish & Courage Breweries (Services) Limited, Abbey Brewery, Holyrood Road, pg. 1212 — IT
SCOTTISH & NEWCASTLE PLC, Abbey Brewery, Holyrood Rd., pg. 1212 — IT
Scottish Brewers Limited, Abbey Brewery, Holyrood Rd., pg. 1212 — IT
SCOTTISH WIDOWS' FUND & LIFE ASSURANCE SOCIETY, 15 Dalkeith Rd., pg. 1212 — IT
Sequent Computer Systems (Scotland), 1-3 St. Colme St., pg. 1460 — PB
Shandwick Scotland Ltd., 20 Stafford St., pg. 1226 — IT
STANDARD LIFE ASSURANCE, 3 George Street, pg. 1297 — IT
Sumitrust Ivory & Sime Limited, One Charlotte Square, pg. 1318 — IT
Swiss Bank Corporation, 66 Hanover Street, pg. 1330 — IT
TSB Bank Scotland Plc, Henry Duncan House, 120 George St., pg. 813 — IT
Templeton Investment Management, Ltd., Saltire Castle, 20 Castle Terrace, pg. 680 — PB
Toyo Trust Baillie Gifford Limited, 1 Rutland Court, pg. 1411 — IT

PB - U.S. Public Companies Volume
PV - U.S. Private Companies Volume
IT - International Public & Private Companies Volume

1803

Geographic Index-Non U.S.

United Distillers PLC, Distillers House, 33 Ellersly Road, pg. 412
V.A.G. Finance Ltd., pg. 817   IT
Vision Group plc, Aviation Hill, 31 Pinkhill, pg. 519   PB
Waverly Vintners Limited, Abbey Brewery, pg. 1212   IT
Willis Corroon Scotland Limited, 31 Drumsheugh Gardens, pg. 1503   IT
Xilinx Development Corporation, 52 Mortonhall Gate, Frogston Rd. E., EH16 6TJ, pg. 1786   PB

Egham

CMC (UK) Limited, Milton House, 1st Floor, 27 Station Road, pg. 414
Dataproducts International Ltd., Dataproducts House, 136-138 High St., pg. 621   PB
Dennison Transoceanic Corporation, Elvaco House, High St., pg. 154   PB
HADEN MACLELLAN HOLDINGS PLC, Haleworth House, pg. 585   IT
Johnson Wax Research and Development, c/o J. Wax Africa & Near East, Milton Park, pg. 593   PV
Procter & Gamble (Health & Beauty Care) Limited, Rusham Park, Whitehall Ln., pg. 1332   IT
RHM Grocery Ltd., Sharwood House, Church Rd., pg. 1396   IT
RMC GROUP P.L.C., RMC House, Coldharbour Lane, Thorpe, pg. 1078   IT
Scientific Software-Intercomp (U.K.) Limited, Monarch House, Crabtree Office Village, Eversley Way, pg. 1444   PB
J.A. Sharwood & Company Limited, Sharwood House, Church Rd., pg. 1396   IT
Vick International Ltd., Rusham Park, Whitehall Ln., pg. 1333   PB

Ellesmere Port

ASEA BICC Capacitors Ltd., pg. 7   IT
DSM Resins UK Ltd., 5 Civic Way, pg. 355   PB
Fabdec Ltd., Grange Road, pg. 301   PV
Freeman Distribution Ltd., 5 Civic Way, pg. 355   IT
Van Leer (UK) Ltd., pg. 1147   IT
Zeneca Ellesmere Port Works, Oilsites Road, pg. 1524   IT

Ellon

Barratt Construction, Golf Road, pg. 168   IT

Elstead

Phoenix Technologies Ltd., Oak House, Shackleford Road, pg. 1292   PB

Enfield

B.E. International Foods Ltd., Grafton House, Stackingswater Lane, pg. 380   IT
Cerplex Ltd., Bilton Way, pg. 332   PB
Delta Cables Holdings Ltd., Millmarsh Ln., Brimsdown, pg. 390   IT
Delta Crompton Cables Ltd., Millmarsh Ln., Brimsdown, pg. 390   IT
Delta Crompton Holdings Ltd., Millmarsh, Brimsdown, pg. 390   IT
Delta Encon Ltd., Millmarsh Ln., pg. 391   IT
Delta Enfield Cables (Holdings) Ltd., Brimsdown, pg. 390   IT
Delta Enfield Ltd., Millmarsh Ln., pg. 390   IT
Delta Enfield Metals Ltd., Millmarsh Ln., pg. 390   IT
Delta Precision Ltd., Millmarsh Ln., pg. 391   IT
Enfield Winding Wires Ltd. (Enamel & Textile), Lockfield Ave., Brimsdown, pg. 390   IT
Ferguson Limited, Crown Rd., pg. 1384   IT
G.E. Lighting Ltd., Lincoln Rd., pg. 713   PB
G.E.-Thorn Lamps Presscaps Division, Lincoln Road, pg. 713   IT
Henkel Chemicals Ltd., Henkel House, 292-308 Southbury Road, pg. 612   IT
E. & E. KAYE LIMITED, Queensway, pg. 727   IT
Lombard Bank, 339 Southbury Road, pg. 910   IT
Lombard Tricity Finance Limited, Tricity House, 284 Southbury Road, pg. 910   IT
WLT Travel UK Ltd, 400 Great Cambridge Rd., pg. 22   IT

Epping

Flexible Lamps Ltd., Rubbolite House, Centre Dr., pg. 1113   PV

Epsom

Alfax Paper of United Kingdom, Limited, pg. 872   PV
Fina Exploration Ltd., Fina House, 1, Ashley Avenue, pg. 1044   IT
Fina plc, Fina House, 1, Ashley Avenue, pg. 1043   IT
Lancaster Group Ltd., pg. 186   IT
Rheometric Scientific Ltd., Surrey Business Park, Weston Rd., Kin Lane, pg. 1387   PB
VAW (UK) Ltd., VAW House, 2 High St., pg. 1466   IT

Erdington

B.E.L. Products, Units 1 & 3, Erdington, Industrial Park, Chester Road, pg. 851   IT
D.C. Services (Electrical), Units 1 & 3, Erdington, Industrial Park, Chester Road, pg. 851   IT

Douglas Kane Hardware, Units 2 & 4, Erdington, Industrial Park, Chester Road, pg. 851   IT

Erith

John Shelbourne & Co. Ltd., Anchor Bay Wharf, Manor Rd., pg. 337   IT

Esher

BAe-Sema Limited, Biwater House, Portsmouth Road, pg. 217   IT
James Burn International Limited, Douglas Road, pg. 1507   PB
CPC (United Kingdom) Ltd., Claygate House, Littleworth Rd., pg. 225   PB

Evesham

Associated Spring SPEC, Ltd., Unit 16, Bond Indus. Estate, Wickhamford, pg. 190   PB
Bomford Turner Limited, Salford Priors, pg. 35   PB
Evesham Foods, Four Pools Industrial Estate, pg. 968   IT
Willmotts Limited, Swan Lane, pg. 88   IT

Ewell

ITW Compular, Nine Cheam Rd., pg. 868   IT

Exeter

ARC South Western, Regional Office, Grace Road, pg. 592   IT
Ertl U.K. Ltd., Units 2, 3 & 5, Alphinbrook Rd., pg. 1684   PB
Hardings Machine Tools, pg. 502   PV
Howmet Exeter Casting, Kestral Way, pg. 213   PV
Ready Mixed Concrete (South-West) Limited, Ashton Rd., Marsh Barton, pg. 1080   IT
SOUTH WEST WATER PLC, Penninsula House, Rydon Lane, pg. 1287   IT
Sparex International Ltd., pg. 1512   IT
The Vapormatic Co. Ltd., pg. 1512   IT
Westbrick Limited, Harrington Lane, pg. 1355   IT

Exhall

Thermal Processing Group Ltd., Thermal House, Colliery Lane, pg. 1338   IT
Thermal Processing Group Ltd. (Coventry), Thermal House, Colliery Lane, pg. 1338   IT

Exmouth

Dihurst Holdings Ltd., pg. 1511   IT

Eynsham

James Burn Binders, Stanton Harcourt Rd., pg. 1507   IT

Faldingworth

Oerlikon Logistics Ltd., pg. 998   IT

Falkirk

Barratt West Scotland, Mayfield House, 7 Maggie Woods Loan, pg. 168   IT
Campbell Lee Computer Services Ltd., McKinven House, Meeks Rd., pg. 1043   PB
Daniel Industries Ltd., Lochlands Indus. Estate, pg. 483   PB
Novellus Systems, Ltd., The Forum, Collander Business Park, pg. 1204   IT
RMC Catherwood (Scotland) Limited, 29 Wellside Pl., pg. 1079   IT

Fareham

Bettis UK Limited, Brunel Way, pg. 483   PB
Exxon Chemical Olefins Inc., pg. 602   PB
GEC Aerospace Ltd., Abbey Works, pg. 543   IT
Hyrolec Management Limited, 6 Pennent Park, Standardway, pg. 1016   PB
Labinal Aero & Defense Systems Ltd., Fort Wallington, pg. 786   IT
Lloyd Instruments Ltd., Whittle Ave., Segensworth W., pg. 100   PB
Meggitt Avionics, 7 Whittle Avenue, pg. 853   IT
Microturbo Ltd., Fort Wallington, pg. 787   IT
Searle Manufacturing Co., Newgate Lane, pg. 88   IT
Vicon Industries (U.K.) Ltd., Brunel Way, Segensworth East, pg. 1719   PB

Faringdon

Bertrand Faure Seating Ltd., White Horse Business Park, pg. 193   IT
Laporte Absorbents (Baulking) Limited, Baulking, pg. 802   IT

Farnborough

BTU Europe, 14 Armstrong Mall, pg. 164   PB
British Aerospace Defence Limited, Lancaster House, P.O. Box 87, pg. 217   IT

British Aerospace (Liverpool Airport) Limited, Warwick House, P.O. Box 87, pg. 217   IT
BRITISH AEROSPACE P.L.C., Warwick House, Farnborough Aerospace Centre, pg. 217   IT
European Business Development, pg. 423   PB
European Group, 279 Farnborough Rd., pg. 423   PB
Genicom Limited, Unit B13 Armstrong Mall, pg. 729   PB
LIC Care Ltd., Unit B11, Armstrong Mall, South Wood Summit Centre, pg. 551   IT
Lee Valley Developments, Warwick House, P.O. Box 87, pg. 218   IT
National Remote Sensing Centre Limited, Delta House, Southwood Crescent, pg. 545   IT
Solartron Ltd., Victoria Rd., pg. 1130   IT
Sulzer Infra (UK), Westmead, pg. 1306   IT
Sulzer (UK) Holdings Limited, Westmead, pg. 1307   IT
Sulzer (UK) Ltd., pg. 1307   IT
Thomson Directories, Thomson House, 296 Farnborough Rd., pg. 1689   PB
Weston Aerospace Ltd., Victoria Rd., pg. 1130   IT

Farnham

Earth Observation Sciences Limited, Broadmede Farnham Business Pk., Weydon Ln., pg. 1230   PB
Exxon Chemical Limited, pg. 602   PB
Lynwood Scientific Developments Limited, Lynwood House, pg. 1144   PB
MacDonald Dettwiler Limited, Broadmede Farnham Business Pk., Weydon Ln., pg. 1229   PB
Plascoat Systems Limited, Trading Estate, pg. 129   IT

Faversham

Saphir Produce Limited, Eurocentre, Whitstable Road, pg. 491   IT

Felixstowe

BFP Wholesale Ltd., Dock Road, pg. 1142   IT
British Fermentation Products Ltd., Dock Rd., pg. 1143   IT
The Felixstowe Dock & Railway Co., European House, The Dock, pg. 1033   IT
KymTrans UK, 306/7 Trelawny House, The Dock, pg. 1430   IT
Nedlloyd Lines U.K. Limited, pg. 1145   IT
P&O Harbours Ltd., c/o The Felixstowe Dock &, Railway Company, pg. 1034   IT
Powell Duffryn Storage Limited, pg. 1065   IT

Feltham

D.I.C. (UK) Ltd., Park House, 643-651 Staines Road, pg. 372   IT
Data General Limited, pg. 486   PB
Esselte UK Ltd., Spur Road, pg. 461   IT
Hall Aggregates (South East) Limited, RMC House, 55 High St., pg. 1079   IT
Konica UK Ltd., Plane Tree Crescent, pg. 749   IT
Lombard NatWest Commercial Services Limited, Smith House, Elmwood Ave., pg. 910   IT
MPL Pumps Ltd, Victoria Road, pg. 1380   IT
Marlin Lighting Limited, Hanworth Trading Estate, Hampton Rd. W., pg. 453   IT
E. Moss Limited, Fern Grove, pg. 58   IT
Nordisk Aviation Products Ltd., Browells Lane, pg. 964   IT
North American Van Lines Ltd., 15-16 Chestnut Way, pg. 1192   PB
RMC Engineering & Transport, RMC House, High Street, pg. 1080   IT
Ricoh UK Ltd., Ricoh House, 1 Plane Tree Crescent, pg. 1116   IT
Schindler, pg. 1205   IT
Sorbus (U.K.) Limited, 13 Mount Rd., pg. 204   PB
Stream International Limited, Four New Square, pg. 518   IT
Taywood Homes Ltd., Greenham Park House, Chertsey Road, pg. 1359   IT

Filey

Dale Power Systems plc, Electricity Buildings, pg. 1344   IT

Filton

Reflectone U.K. Ltd., pg. 218   IT
Sowerby Research Centre, pg. 218   IT
Watson Steel & Co. (Steelwork) Ltd., pg. 16   IT

Finchampstead

SHL Clarion Education, North Court, The Ridges, pg. 1154   IT

Fleet

Brooktree Ltd., 119 Fleet Rd., pg. 1398   PB
Cat Pumps (UK) Ltd., 27 Station Industrial Estate, pg. 336   PV
Hayes Microcomputer Products Ltd., Millenium House, Fleet Pk., Barley Way, pg. 801   PB
Octel Communications Ltd., Octel House, Ancells Rd., pg. 1018   PB

Fleetwood

Pandoro Ltd., Dock St., pg. 1034   IT

PB - *U.S. Public Companies Volume*
PV - *U.S. Private Companies Volume*
IT - *International Public & Private Companies Volume*

Shakespeare Monofilament U.K. Ltd., Beacon Rd., Poulton Industrial Estate, pg. 940   PB

Flintshire

Warwick International Ltd., Mostyn Holywell, pg. 1459   PB

Folkestone

Carter-Wallace Limited (United Kingdom), Wear Bay Rd., pg. 310   PB
DAWSON HOLDINGS PLC, Cannon House, Parkfarm Road, pg. 385   IT
Sims Medical Distribution Limited, Park Farm Rd., pg. 1267   IT

Foots Cray

Dayton Progress Intl., Powerscroft Rd., pg. 617   PB

Frome

ARC Pipes Limited, Divisional Office, Mells Road, pg. 592   IT
ARC Southern, Regional Office, Stoneleigh House, pg. 592   IT
Cuprinol Limited, Adderwell, pg. 1501   IT
J.W. Singer & Sons, Cork St., pg. 391   IT
United Kingdom Plant, pg. 443   PB

Gainsborough

Dexion Ltd., Corringham Road Industrial Estate, pg. 893   PB
Spraysafe Automatic Sprinklers Limited, Corringham Rd. Indus. Estate, pg. 327   PB
Wedco Technology U.K. Ltd., Sandars Rd., Heapham Road Industrial Estate, pg. 854   PB

Gateshead

Ballast Wiltshire Plc - North East Region, Endeavour House, Colmet Court, 7th Avenue, pg. 135   IT
R.R. Donnelley U.K.-Gateshead Division, 7th Avenue, Team Valley Trading Estate, pg. 519   PB
Drums Ltd., pg. 1146   IT
Eimco (Great Britain) Ltd., Earlsway, Team Valley, pg. 1353   IT
Huwood International, Kingsway, Team Valley Trading, Estate, pg. 473   IT
Kvaerner Computing & Consultancy Ltd., 13/14 Kingsway House, pg. 767   IT
Palintest Limited, Palintest House, pg. 589   IT
Sevcon Limited, Kingsway, pg. 1563   PB
Thomas De La Rue Ltd., Kingsway South, Team Valley Trading Estate, pg. 386   IT

Gatwick

Caledonian Airways Ltd, Caledonian House, pg. 219   IT
Nordisk Aviation Products Ltd., At London Gatwick, Bay 5000 B (Airside), pg. 964   IT

Gerrards Cross

Alcan Chemicals Europe, Chalfont Park, pg. 51   IT
Baco Leisure Products, Chalfont Park, pg. 51   IT
British Alcan Aluminium plc, Chalfont Park, pg. 51   IT
Lee Products Ltd., 3 High St., pg. 657   PV

Gillingham

Akzo Chemie UK Ltd., Pier Rd., pg. 47   IT
Aldrich Chemical Co., Ltd., The Old Brickyard, pg. 1472   PB
Bio-Kil Laboratories Limited, Old Brickyard Industrial Estate, pg. 802   IT
Hochiki Europe U.K. Ltd., Gillingham Business Park, 5 Ambley Green, pg. 623   IT

Girvan

Gentech International Ltd., pg. 1511   IT

Glasgow

Ademco MicroTech Limited, 2 Redwood Crescent, Peel Park Campus, pg. 1307   PB
Askit Laboratories Ltd., pg. 1120   IT
N.G. Bailey & Co. Ltd.-Glasgow Branch, Bairds Brae, pg. 132   IT
Ballast Wiltshire Plc - Scotland, 10 Lynedoch Place, pg. 135   IT
Bradstock Insurance Brokers Limited, Festival House, 177/179 W. George St., pg. 210   IT
British Bakeries (Scotland) Limited, 783 Duke St., pg. 1396   IT
CTS U.K., Ltd., Blantyre Indus. Estate High Blantyre, pg. 286   PB
Christie's Scotland Ltd., 164-166 Bath St., pg. 290   IT
Clydesdale Bank PLC, 30 St. Vincent Pl., pg. 906   IT
Coats Patons Plc, Pacific House, 70 Wellwaton St., pg. 299   IT
Edgcumbe Instruments Ltd., Main Street, pg. 207   IT
Ellis & McDougall Lifts Ltd., 86, Broad St., pg. 747   IT
Flexible Ducting Limited, Cloberfield, pg. 1267   IT
Fuji Electric (Scotland) Ltd., 3 Redwood Place, pg. 522   IT

GA Ltd., Woodside House, 14 Woodside Terr., pg. 630   IT
GEC Naval Systems Ltd., South St., pg. 544   IT
Glasgow Terminal, Rothesay Dock, pg. 693   PB
THE HIGHLAND DISTILLERIES COMPANY PLC, 106 W. Nile St., pg. 619   IT
Highland Malt Distilling Limited, 106 West Nile Street, pg. 619   IT
ITW Red Head, 118 Coltness Rd., pg. 869   PB
Inter-Globe Security Services Ltd., 266 Clyde St., pg. 593   IT
International Correspondence Schools Ltd., Eight Elliott Pl., Clydeway Centre, pg. 784   PB
International Correspondence Schools (Overseas) Limited, Eight Elliott Pl., Clydeway Centre, pg. 784   PB
Intertext Group, Ltd., Intertext House, Eight Elliott Pl., pg. 784   PB
Keystone Valve (U.K.) Ltd., 91 Meiklewood Rd., pg. 1650   PB
The Walter Kidde Co. Ltd., 455, Hillington Rd., pg. 593   PB
Kodak Limited, Scottish Business Centre, Pegasus House, pg. 553   PB
Kvaerner Govan Ltd., 1048 Govan Road, pg. 772   IT
Lambert Smith Hampton, 97/99 W. Regent St., pg. 797   IT
Logitech Ltd., Erskine Ferry Rd., pg. 1084   IT
The Media Shop (Scotland), 5 Royal Exchange Sq., pg. 853   IT
Minebea Electronics (UK) Ltd., Kelburn Business Park, pg. 868   IT
Morrison Bowmore Distillers, Ltd., Springburn Bond, Carlisle St., pg. 1322   IT
Murray Johnstone Limited, 7 W. Nile St., pg. 1674   PB
National Australia Group (UK) Limited, 6 Nelson Mandela Place, pg. 906   IT
NORIT (UK) Ltd., Clydesmill Pl., pg. 958   IT
George Outram & Company Ltd., 195 Albion St., pg. 817   IT
Quorum Graphic Design Consultants Ltd., Nine Lynedoch Crescent, pg. 1226   IT
R & J Garroway Limited, Netherfield Chemical Works, pg. 802   IT
The Rawlplug Company Limited, Thornliebank Indus. Estate, Skibo Dr., pg. 925   IT
Ready Mixed Concrete (Scotland) Limited, Hawbank Rd., College Milton, pg. 1080   IT
Riley Advertising (Scotland) Ltd., Baxter House, 9 Claremont Terrace, pg. 1117   IT
Robertson & Baxter Limited, 106 W. Nile St., pg. 619   IT
Royal Bank Insurance Consultants Ltd., 152 W. Regent St., pg. 1132   IT
RoyScot Financial Services, George House, 36 N. Hanover St., pg. 1132   IT
The School of Accountancy, Eight Elliott Pl., Clydeway Centre, pg. 784   PB
James Scott Mechanical & Electrical Services Ltd., 80-110 Finnieston St., pg. 16   IT
Scott Packing & Warehousing Limited (Scotland), Kilsyth Rd., pg. 1034   IT
Scott Stern Associates Limited, Eight Minerva Way, pg. 1482   IT
Scottish & Universal Newspapers Limited, Hellenic House, 87-97 Bath St., pg. 817   IT
SCOTTISH ENTERPRISE, 120 Bothwell St., pg. 1212   IT
Shandwick Scotland Ltd., Nine Lynedoch Crescent, pg. 1226   IT
Sodexho Services (UK) Ltd., Buchanan Tower, Buchanan Business Park, Cumbernauld Rd., pg. 1275   IT
Struers Ltd., Erskine Ferry Rd., pg. 1084   IT
TML Metrology Centre for Scotland, Unit 2, Block 57, Hillington Ind. Estate, pg. 260   PB
Taylor Woodrow Construction (Scotland) Ltd., Park House, 245 Blythswood Court, pg. 1358   IT
Vascutek Limited, pg. 1307   IT
WF Corroon-Glasgow, 160 West George Street, pg. 1501   IT
WEIR GROUP PLC, 149 Newlands Rd., Cathcart, pg. 1488   IT
Weir Pumps Ltd., 149 Newlands Road, pg. 1489   IT
Weir Westgarth Ltd., 149 Newlands Road, pg. 1489   IT
The Whyte & Mackay Group Plc., 310 St. Vincent St., pg. 675   IT
Willis Corroon Credit Limited, 160 West George Street, pg. 1502   IT
Willis Corroon Scotland Limited, 160 West George Street, pg. 1503   IT
Yamaichi-Murray Johnstone Ltd., Seven W. Nile St., pg. 1516   IT
Yarrow Shipbuilders Ltd., South St., pg. 545   IT

Glenrothes

B-Mat Ltd., Queensway Estate, pg. 184   IT
Bermo Scotland, Ltd, Westwood Park, Glover Road, pg. 136   PV
CRC, Nasmyth Rd., Southfield Ind. Est., pg. 242   IT
Canon Manufacturing U.K., Ltd., James Watt Ave., pg. 262   IT
Compugraphics International Limited, Eastfield Industrial Estate, pg. 802   IT
Eaton Hydraulics Limited, KY7 4NW, pg. 558   PB
Interconnection Products, Whitehill Indus. Estate, 72 Whitecraigs Rd., pg. 1005   PB
Sandusky Limited, Viewfield Industrial Estate, pg. 965   PV
Semtech Ltd., Whitehill Estates, pg. 1456   PB
Spanoptic Limited, Telford Rd., pg. 892   IT

Glossop

Firth-Rixson Superalloys Ltd., Shepley St., pg. 488   IT

Gloucester

BTR Permali RP Ltd., Bristol Rd., pg. 124   IT
Babcock Electrical Projects Ltd, Brunswick House, Brunswick Sq., pg. 471   IT
Babcock Minerals Engineering Ltd., Babcock House, Bristol Rd., pg. 472   IT
Babcock-Moxey Ltd., Babcock House, Bristol Rd., pg. 472   IT
Bensons, Bensons House, 104 Bath Road, pg. 460   IT
Bohlin Instruments Ltd., Unit 6, The Corinium Ctr., pg. 207   IT
Bristol Organics, Ltd., Sharpness Docks, pg. 1472   PB
COBE Laboratories Ltd., Athena 3, Olympus Business Park, pg. 667   IT
CHELTENHAM & GLOUCESTER PLC, Chief Office, Barnett Way, pg. 283   IT
Dowty Aerospace Propellers, Anson Business Park, Cheltenham Road E., pg. 1337   IT
Europa Insurance Company Ltd., Barton House, Eastgate Street, pg. 90   IT
Everbright Fasteners Ltd., Hempstead Lane, pg. 585   IT
Hamworthy Compressor Systems Limited, Chequers Bridge, pg. 1065   IT
Hitachi Zosen Europe Ltd., Pavilion 2A, Olympus Business Park, pg. 623   IT
Industrial Fasteners Ltd., Hempsted Ln., pg. 585   IT
MTS Systems Ltd. (UK), Tricorn House, Cainscross, Stroud, pg. 1029   PB
Messier-Dowty Customer Support Centre- Europe, Gloucester Office, Cheltenham Road, pg. 1340   IT
Messier-Dowty Ltd., Cheltenham Road, pg. 1340   IT
Moog Controls Ltd., Ashchurch Tewkesbury, pg. 1128   PB
Northern Star Insurance Company Limited, Barton House, Eastgate Street, pg. 90   IT
Permali Ltd., 125, Bristol Rd., pg. 126   IT
J. Rothschild Assurance Holdings, J. Rothschild House, Dollar St., pg. 1178   IT
Simon Access (U.K.) Ltd., Gloucester Trading Estate, Hucclecote, pg. 1251   IT
Western Staff Services (U.K.) Ltd., 46/50 Southgate St., pg. 1760   PB

Godalming

Akerlund & Rausing, Lammas Gate, 84A Meadrow, pg. 33   IT
British Aerospace Defence Limited (Military Aircraft), Dunsfold Aerodrome, pg. 217   IT
MTI U.K., Riverview House, Weyside Bank, pg. 1028   PB
Weyburn-Bartel Ltd., Elstead, pg. 1334   IT

Godmanchester

Nokia Mobile Phones UK Sales Ltd., Headland House, The Chord Business Park, pg. 952   IT

Goole

Timloc Building Products Ltd., Rawcliffe Road, pg. 467   IT

Gorgie

Scotch Premium Meat, Two New Market Rd., pg. 607   PB

Gosport

Cyanamid of Great Britain Ltd., Cyanamid House, Fareham Rd., pg. 81   PB
Morganite Special Carbons Limited, Quay Ln., pg. 891   IT
Polarcup United Kingdom Ltd., Rowner Rd., pg. 639   IT
Southern Graphite Services Limited, Quay Ln., pg. 891   IT

Grangemouth

Rohm & Haas (Scotland) Limited, pg. 1404   PB

Grantham

Commercial Hydraulics Kontak Ltd., Belton Park, Londonthorpe Rd., pg. 411   PB
Fenland Foods, Turnpike Close, Earlesfield Industrial Estate, pg. 968   IT
Grantham Road Services, Harlaxton Rd., pg. 591   IT
Oliver Rubber Europa Ltd., 28 Market Place, pg. 1505   PB
H.J. Tinsley & Co. Limited, Spittlegate Lavel, pg. 891   IT

Granton

United Wire Limited, Granton Park Ave., pg. 1202   IT

Gravesend

Britannia Refined Metals Ltd., Botany Rd., pg. 827   IT
W.T. Henley, Crete Hall Rd., pg. 1344   IT
Paper Sacks Limited, Northfleet, pg. 759   IT
Zest Equipment Ltd., Unit T., Springhead Enterprise, Park, Springhead Rd., pg. 231   IT

Grays

Ashby & Horner Joinery Ltd., 795 London Rc., pg. 1032   IT
Ashby & Horner Masonry Ltd., 795 London Rd., pg. 1032   IT

PB - *U.S. Public Companies Volume*
PV - *U.S. Private Companies Volume*
IT - *International Public & Private Companies Volume*

Castle Cement Ltd. (Grays), Thurrock Marine Terminal, Oliver Close, pg. 1201   IT
Grays Terminal, London Rd., pg. 693   PB
Lafarge Aluminates Co. Ltd., 730 London Rd., pg. 790   IT
Lafarge Aluminous Cement Co. Ltd., 730 London Rd., pg. 790   IT

Great Dunmow

Saab Automation Ltd, Unit 6 Zone B, Industrial Estate, pg. 686   IT

Great Harwood

Ashworth Young & Co., Ltd., Vulcan Works, Back Glebe St., pg. 1035   IT

Great Yarmouth

CAC U.K., Baker House, Viking Road, pg. 1593   PB
Weatherford U.K. Ltd., Harfrey Industrial Estate, Harfrey Rd., pg. 1750   PB

Greenford

Burroughs Wellcome Intl. Ltd., Glaxo Wellcome House, Berkeley Avenue, pg. 552   IT
Butler's Warehousing & Distribution Ltd., P.O. Box 14, Rockware Ave., pg. 1033   IT
Cooper, McDougall & Robertson Ltd., Glaxo Wellcome House, Berkeley Avenue, pg. 552   IT
E & D Taylor (Insurance Brokers) Limited, Greenford House, 309 Ruislip Road East, pg. 1358   IT
The Floating Technology Co, Greenford House, 309 Ruislip Road East, pg. 1358   IT
Guerlain Ltd., 22 Aintree Rd., pg. 780   IT
IBM United Kingdom Product Sales Limited, Rockware Ave., pg. 898   PB
THE TETLEY GROUP LIMITED, 325 Oldfield Lane N., pg. 1377   IT
Ultra Electronics Controls, 417 Bridport Road, pg. 1431   IT
ULTRA ELECTRONICS HOLDINGS PLC, 419 Bridport Road, pg. 1431   IT
Ultra Electronics Sonar & Communications Systems, The Metropolitan Centre, 419 Bridport Road, pg. 1431   IT

Greenock

Kvaerner Kincaid Ltd., 21 Main St., pg. 772   IT

Greenwich

Vickerys Holdings Ltd., 53 Norman Rd., pg. 1593   PB

Greetland

Bondina Ltd., pg. 507   IT
Broadtex Ltd., pg. 507   IT
Freudenberg Holdings Ltd., pg. 507   IT
Freudenberg Nonwovens Ltd., pg. 505   IT
Vilene Ltd., pg. 507   IT

Grimsby

Bluecrest Freebooker Ltd., Bluecrest House, Fishdock Rd., pg. 202   IT
CCL Industries Limited, South Humberside Industrial Estate, pg. 239   IT
CIBA Grimsby, Pyewipe, pg. 980   IT
Courtaulds Fibres Ltd., P.O. Box 24, pg. 339   IT
Frionor (England) Ltd., Marsden Rd., pg. 516   IT
Humberside Holdings Ltd, Spurn House, Immingham Dock, pg. 1065   IT
Immingham Storage Co. Ltd., Immingham Dock, pg. 1251   IT
Killingholme Wharfage Co. Ltd., North Killingholme Haven, pg. 1251   IT
Lindsey Oil Refinery, Killingholme, pg. 1043   IT
SCM Chemicals - Europe, pg. 593   IT
UB Frozen & Chilled Limited, Ross House, Wickham Rd., pg. 1442   IT

Groby

Redland Aggregates Ltd., Bradgate House, pg. 1090   IT
Redland Readymix Ltd., Bradgate House, pg. 1091   IT

Groole

Watts Bros. (A. Suthrell), Off Larsen Rd., M62 Trading Estate, pg. 591   IT

Guildford

ARCO British Limited, London Sq., Cross Lanes, pg. 144   PB
Autodesk Ltd., Cross Lanes, pg. 149   PB
BOC Process Plants Ltd., 30 Priestley Rd., pg. 121   IT
Ballast Wiltshier plc - South East Region, Parallel House, 32 London Road, pg. 135   IT
Barratt Southern Counties, Barratt House, Chestnut Ave., pg. 168   IT
Bullfrog Productions Ltd., 20 Nugent Road, pg. 569   PB
Canon Research Centre Europe Ltd., 20 Alan Turing Rd., Surrey Research Park, pg. 262   IT
Colgate-Palmolive Ltd., Guildford Business Park, Middleton Rd., pg. 398   PB
Cornhill Insurance PLC, 57, Ladymead, pg. 60   IT
Criterion Software Ltd., 20 Alan Turing Rd., Surrey Research Park, pg. 262   IT
European Cellars Ltd., Moorfield Rd., pg. 1499   IT
IKOS, U.K., The Surrey Research Park, 19 Frederick Sanger Rd., pg. 566   PB
iPTest (Holdings) Limited, 15 The Pines Broad St., pg. 972   PB
Kredietfinance Corporation Ltd., 14-15 Quarry St., pg. 761   IT
Lambert Smith Hampton, 242 High St., pg. 797   IT
Monmouth Pharmaceutical, Ltd., The Surrey Research Park, 3 & 4 Huxley Rd., pg. 1394   IT
Ocelot International U.K. Ltd., Pannell House, Park Street, pg. 996   IT
Ranger Oil (U.K.) Ltd., Ranger House, Walnut Tree Close, pg. 1086   PB
Retix United Kingdom, 60 Priestley Rd., pg. 1717   PB
Sanderson Brookstreet Limited, 5 Huxley Rd., pg. 1184   IT
Spar Space Systems, Ranger House, Walnut Tree Close, pg. 1288   IT
Telecom Solutions (Europe) Limited, 2 The Billings, pg. 1547   PB
Vokes Ltd., Henley Park, pg. 125   IT

Guiseley

Denison Colour Limited, Springhead Mills Springfield Road, pg. 78   PB

Gwent

Ekco International Housewares, Ltd., 66 Newport Road, pg. 566   PB
Peter's Savoury Products, Bedwas House, pg. 410   IT
Terram Limited, Mandiland Park, pg. 113   IT

Haddenham

McCormick (UK) Plc., Thame Road, pg. 1067   PB

Hadnall

Simon-Diasol, Unit 22, Hardwicke Industrial Estate, pg. 1251   IT

Halesowen

Analog Devices Ltd., 1st. Floor, Midland House, New Rd., pg. 108   PB
Barratt Central, Midland House, New Rd., pg. 168   IT
Barratt West Midlands, Midlands House, New Rd., pg. 168   IT
Rieter Automotive Great Britain Ltd., pg. 1117   IT
Whitlenge Drink Equipment Limited, Chancel Way, Halesowen Industrial Park, pg. 1445   PB

Halifax

Butler Newall Limited-Butler Machine Tool Div., Westholme Rd., pg. 448   IT
Dominion Machinery Co. Ltd., Denholmgate Rd., pg. 231   IT
FKI PLC, West House, pg. 471   IT
HALIFAX PLC, Trinity Road, pg. 589   IT
Holset Engineering Company, Ltd., 131 Parkinson Lane, pg. 469   PB
Horsfall & Bickham Limited, pg. 268   IT
Kluber Lubrication Great Britain Ltd., pg. 506   IT
SKW Chemicals UK Ltd., Focus House, Central St., pg. 1466   IT
Sagar-Richards Limited, Ellen Home, pg. 88   IT
Smith Wires Limited, pg. 268   IT

Halisham

Marlow Ropes Limited, South Rd., pg. 426   IT

Halsall

Breeder's Seeds Ltd., pg. 975   IT

Halstead

CIBA Corning Diagnostics Limited, Colchester Rd., pg. 978   IT
Electric Motor Developments (Halstead) Ltd., pg. 1511   IT

Hammersmith

Colourings, pg. 199   IT

Hammondsworth

Ballast Wiltshier Plc, Manor Court, High Street, pg. 134   IT
Bytex DataCom Ltd., Two Manor Ct., pg. 1522   PB

Hampton

Bausch & Lomb U.K. Ltd., 74 Oldfield Rd., pg. 195   PB
Bell (U.K.) Communications Limited, 3 Thames St., pg. 204   PB
Bell (U.K.) Services Limited, 3 Thames St., pg. 204   PB
Kvaerner Paladon Ltd., Station Road, pg. 768   IT
Sorbus Europe, Ltd., Three Thames St., pg. 204   PB

Handforth

Bush Beach Engineering Ltd., pg. 835   IT

Hanley

Faltec Doors Ltd, St. James Court, Statham Street, pg. 269   IT

Harefield

Chiron U.K. Ltd., Salamander Quay W., Park Ln., pg. 350   PB
Kao Corporation GmbH (London Office), Quay West, Salamander Quay, pg. 718   IT

Harlow

Addison-Wesley Longman Ltd., Edinburgh Gate, pg. 1027   IT
Analog Devices Ltd. - Eastern Sales Office, Oakwood House, South Rd., pg. 108   PB
Anixter Harlow, Athena Estate, Edinburgh Way, pg. 115   PB
BNR Europe Limited, London Rd., pg. 969   IT
Callitheke International Ltd., Templefields House, River Way, pg. 409   IT
Checkpoint Systems UK Limited, 13, Ash Industrial Estate, Flex Meadow, Pinnacles W., pg. 343   PB
A.C. Cossor Electronics, Limited, The Pinnacles-Elizabeth Way, pg. 1366   PB
Gan Life and Pensions PLC, Gan House, pg. 565   IT
IDV UK, Templefields House, River Way, pg. 409   IT
Longman Group (Overseas Holding) Limited, Longman House, Burnt Mill, pg. 1025   IT
Longman Group UK Ltd., Longman House, Burnt Mill, pg. 1025   IT
Longman Penguin Limited, Longman House, Burnt Mill, pg. 1025   IT
M/A-COM Greenpar Connectors, Cambridge Road, pg. 8   PB
Nortel Technology Limited, London Road, pg. 970   IT
Norton Healthcare Limited, Gemini House, Flex Meadow, pg. 915   IT
The Panther Car Co., Ltd., Horsecrost Rd., The Pinnacles, pg. 1292   IT
Perchem Ltd., West Rd., Templefields, pg. 47   IT
Pitney Bowes Ltd., The Pinnacles, pg. 1304   PB
Raytheon Marine Sales & Services Co., The Pinnacles, Elizabeth Way, pg. 1366   PB
Synthomer, Ltd., West Road, Templefields, pg. 370   IT

Harpenden

Cherry Electrical Products, Ltd., Coldharbour Lane, pg. 346   PB
Powell Duffryn International Fuels Ltd., 1st Fl., Mardall House, 9/11 Vaughan Rd., pg. 1065   IT
TAC (UK) Ltd., 42 Coldharbour Ln., pg. 670   IT
TAC (UK) Ltd., 42 Coldharbor Ln., pg. 670   IT

Harrogate

CRInc. - Wellman Ltd., 9 Windsor C., Clarence Dr., pg. 1753   PB
Handy & Harman (Europe) Ltd., pg. 780   PB
Kemira Kemi (UK) Ltd., Orm House, 2 Hookstone Park, pg. 728   IT
Schlatter Ltd., York Place, pg. 1206   IT

Harrow

Alcoa Europe Limited, Portman House, 104 College Road, pg. 62   PB
Ashby & Horner Ltd., Raeburn House, Northolt Rd., pg. 1032   IT
Baker/OTS International Ltd., 100 College Rd., pg. 168   'T
Bovis Construction Group, Hovis House, Northolt Rd., pg. 1032   IT
Bovis Construction Ltd., Bovis House, Northolt Rd., pg. 1032   IT
British Tissues Limited, Lowlands House, 43-51 Lowlands Rd., pg. 672   PB
Daewoo UK Ltd., Templar House, 82 Northolt Rd., pg. 358   IT
Dart Industries Ltd., 130 College Rd., pg. 1322   PB
B.F. Goodrich Aerospace, Unit B1, Neptune Rd., pg. 752   PB
Kodak Limited, Headstone Dr., pg. 553   PB
Ladbroke & Co. Ltd., Imperial House, Imperial Drive, pg. 787   IT
Ladbroke Racecourse Management Ltd., Imperial House, Imperial Drive, pg. 787   IT
Ladbroke Racing Ltd., Imperial House, Imperial Drive, pg. 787   IT
Michelin Tyre P.L.C., Davy House, Lyon Road, pg. 322   IT

PB - *U.S. Public Companies Volume*
PV - *U.S. Private Companies Volume*
IT - *International Public & Private Companies Volume*

1806

Geographic Index-Non U.S.

Millipore (U.K.) Ltd., Millipore House, 11-15 Peterborough Rd., pg. 1113 **PB**
The Music and Video Club Limited, Congress House, Lyon Road, pg. 733 **IT**
Pasco Engineering Limited, 118-122 College Rd., pg. 1355 **IT**
Rockwell Automation Limited, 132-134 College Road, pg. 1399 **PB**
SPAR (UK) LTD., 32-40 Headstone Dr., pg. 1288 **IT**

Hartlebury

Larch-Lap Limited, Hartlebury Trading Estate, pg. 925 **IT**

Hartlepool

Decoflex Limited, Hartepoole Industrial Estate, pg. 889 **IT**
Expamet Building Products, Stranton Works, pg. 467 **IT**
Expamet Fencing, P.O. Box 14, Stranton Works, pg. 467 **IT**
Expanded Metal Industrial, Stranton Works, pg. 467 **IT**
FMU Ltd., Hartlepool Trading Estate, pg. 113 **IT**
Industrial Building Components Ltd., Longhill Industrial Estate (North), pg. 467 **IT**
Owens Corning Polyfoam UK Limited, Hunter House, Industrial Estate, pg. 1237 **PB**
STADIUM LIMITED, Stephen House, Brenda Road, pg. 1293 **IT**

Hartley Wintney

Amdahl International Management Services Limited (European Headquarters), Dogmersfield Park, pg. 527 **IT**

Harwich

Stena Line Limited, Parkeston Quay, pg. 1300 **IT**

Haslemere

Vertex International Ltd., Clembro House, Weydown Road, pg. 1718 **PB**
Zeneca Seeds, Fernhurst, pg. 1524 **IT**

Haslingden

Duralay Ltd., Broadway, pg. 113 **IT**
Lipe Limited, pg. 561 **PB**
Medex Medical Inc., St. Crispin Way, pg. 689 **PB**
P&S Filtration Ltd., Broadway Mill, pg. 1202 **IT**

Hastings

Ibex Engineering Co. Ltd., Drury Lane, Ponswood, pg. 1380 **IT**
Madden & Layman Limited, 221-229 London Rd., St. Leonards-on-Sea, pg. 196 **PB**
VG Electronics Ltd., Theaklen Dr., pg. 1595 **PB**
VG Electrovac Ltd., Theaklen Dr., pg. 1595 **PB**
VG Engineering (Hastings) Ltd., Menzies Road, pg. 1595 **PB**
VG Special Systems Ltd., Sidney Little Rd., pg. 1595 **PB**
Vacuum Generators Ltd., Maunsell Rd., pg. 1595 **PB**

Hatfield

Black Horse Agencies Ltd., Black Horse House, Salisbury Square, pg. 813 **IT**
Davall Group Ltd., Travellers Ln., pg. 426 **IT**
Frere-Bourgeois UK Ltd., pg. 302 **IT**
Hewlett-Packard Ltd., Centec 2, Beaconsfield Rd., pg. 821 **PB**
Liebherr-Great Britain Ltd., Travellers Lane, pg. 808 **IT**
Mitsubishi Electric (UK) Ltd., Travellers Lane, pg. 873 **IT**
New Brunswick Scientific (UK) Ltd., Edison House, 163 Dixons Hill Rd., pg. 1170 **PB**
Raytheon Corporate Jets, Inc., 3 Bishop Square, pg. 1366 **PB**
Smurfit Corrugated (UK) Limited, Great Braitch Lane, pg. 1271 **IT**
Steelinter (UK) Ltd, pg. 302 **IT**
United Continental Steels Ltd U.C.S., pg. 302 **IT**
Videojet Ltd., Videojet House, 153 Dixons Hill Road, pg. 546 **IT**

Havant

Apollo Fire Detectors Limited, 36 Brookside Road, pg. 589 **IT**
DataCard Europe Ltd., New Lane, pg. 312 **PV**
Dawson-Keith Limited, Deekay House, Brockhampton Lane, pg. 1344 **IT**
De La Rue Cash Handling Product Group, Langstone Gate, Solent Rd., pg. 387 **IT**
De La Rue Systems Ltd., Langstone Gate, Solent, pg. 387 **IT**
Deep Sea Seals Ltd., 4 Marples Way, pg. 1339 **IT**
DELARUE SYSTEMS LIMITED PLC, Long Stone Gate, Solent Rd., pg. 388 **IT**
John Cranes Marine International, 4 Marples Way, pg. 1339 **IT**
KENWOOD APPLIANCES PLC, New Lane, pg. 730 **IT**
Lewmar Marine Holdings Ltd., Southmoor Lane, pg. 1461 **IT**
Norsk Hydro a.s. Petrochemicals Division, Station Road, North St., pg. 964 **IT**
Vickers Systems Division, P.O. Box 4, pg. 25 **PB**

Wessex Advanced Switching Products Ltd., Southmoor Lane, pg. 208 **IT**

Haverhill

Genzyme Fine Chemicals, 37 Hollands Rd., pg. 733 **PB**
I.F.F. (Great Britain) Ltd., pg. 899 **PB**
Methode Mikon Limited, Boundary Road, pg. 1101 **PB**
New Market Foods, Little Wratting, pg. 1170 **IT**
AB Stratos Limited, Hollands Road, pg. 1344 **IT**

Hawick

Barrie Knitwear, Burnfoot Industrial Estate, pg. 385 **IT**
Pringle of Scotland Ltd, Victoria Mill, pg. 385 **IT**

Haydock

Hoogovens Aluminium Building Systems Ltd., Haydock Lane, pg. 755 **IT**

Hayes

Anixter London Hayes, Unit 4 Chailley Estate, Pump Lane, pg. 115 **PB**
Antec International, Chaley Estate, Unit 4, Pump Lane, pg. 117 **IT**
Entertainment UK Ltd., 243 Blyth Road, pg. 733 **IT**
Gray Tool Co. (Europe), 72-74 Statton Road, pg. 5 **IT**
H.J. Heinz Company, Limited, Hayes Park, pg. 806 **PB**
Metier Management Systems, Metier House, 23 Clayton Rd., pg. 1010 **IT**
Myton Limited, Bridge House, Westmount Centre, pg. 1358 **IT**
Rock Falls Technology, Chaley Estate, Unit 4, Pump Lane, pg. 116 **PB**
STB-Europe, The Aeolian, 4 Mondial Way, pg. 1421 **PB**
SAFEWAY PLC, 6 Millington Rd., pg. 1169 **IT**
Safeway Stores plc, Argyll House, 6 Millington Road, pg. 1169 **IT**
Spar Aerospace (U.K.) Limited, Springfield Road, pg. 1288 **IT**

Haywards Heath

Lloyds Bank Insurance Services Ltd., 7 Perrymount Rd., pg. 813 **IT**
Lloyds Private Banking & Financial Services, Capital House, 1/5 Perrymount Rd., pg. 813 **IT**
Worcester Controls (UK) Ltd., Burrell Rd., pg. 125 **IT**

Heanor

Matthew Walker Ltd., Heanor Gate Rd., pg. 968 **IT**

Heckmondwike

Rieter Automotive Carpets Ltd., pg. 1117 **IT**

Helston

Seacore Limited, Lower Quay, Gweek, pg. 31 **IT**

Hemel Hempstead

Aladdin Industries, Ltd., Six Grovelands Business Ctr., pg. 31 **PV**
Amway (Europe) Ltd., Unit 3 Ground Fl., Mark House, pg. 69 **PV**
Avica, Boundary Way, pg. 853 **IT**
Bio-Rad Laboratories Ltd., Bio-Rad House, Mayland Ave., pg. 230 **PB**
Bio-Rad Lasersharp Ltd., Bio-Rad House, Mayland Ave., pg. 230 **PB**
BISS Limited, Maylands Avenue, pg. 1737 **PB**
Boral (UK) Ltd., Cleveland House, Cleveland Rd., pg. 203 **IT**
Butlin's Limited, One Park Lane, pg. 1086 **IT**
Crosfield Electronics Limited, Three Cherry Trees Lane, pg. 532 **PB**
Currys Group plc, Maylands Avenue, pg. 414 **IT**
Dacon Electronics Plc., One Enterprise Way, pg. 395 **PB**
Dexion Group plc, Maylands Ave., pg. 893 **PB**
Dexion Ltd.-Storage Div., Maylands Ave., pg. 893 **PB**
DIXONS GROUP PLC, Maylands Avenue, pg. 413 **IT**
Dixons Stores Group Ltd., Maylands Avenue, pg. 414 **IT**
Epson (U.K.) Ltd. (E.U.L.), Campus 100, Maylands Avenue, pg. 1219 **IT**
Fasson Adhesive Products, Ltd., Eastman Way, pg. 154 **PB**
Fasson U.K. Ltd., Eastman Way, pg. 154 **PB**
Finnigan MAT Ltd., Paradise, pg. 1596 **PB**
Fisher Frozen Foods Limited, Focus 31, Mark Road, pg. 491 **IT**
Hoogovens Aluminium U.K. Ltd., Swallowdale Lane, pg. 755 **IT**
Kodak Limited, Kodak House, Station Rd., pg. 553 **PB**
Kodak Limited, Swallowdale Ln., pg. 553 **PB**
Kodak Limited-Marketing Education Center, Gadebridge Lane, pg. 553 **PB**
John Laing International Ltd., Amber House, Wood Ln., pg. 796 **IT**
MDIS GROUP PLC, Boundary Way, pg. 826 **IT**
Mastercare Limited, Maylands Avenue, pg. 414 **IT**
Microscience Limited, Maylands Ave., pg. 230 **PB**
Parker Hannifin Corporation, Parker House, 55 Maylands Ave., pg. 1261 **PB**
Parkworld Holidays Ltd., One Park Lane, pg. 1086 **IT**

Pneumatic Scale Europe, pg. 118 **PV**
Presstech Controls Limited, Presstech House, Maxted Rd., pg. 789 **IT**
Schauman (UK) Ltd., Stags End House, Gaddesden, Row, pg. 1429 **IT**
Sensormatic Limited, Senator House, 23 Mark Rd., pg. 1458 **PB**
Simon & Schuster International (UK) Limited, Campus 400, pg. 778 **PV**
Spectra-Physics Ltd., Boundary Way, pg. 1290 **IT**
Utimaco Safeware plc, Hamilton House, 6th Fl., 111 Marlowes, pg. 1444 **IT**
WF Corroon-Hemel Hempstead, Unit 1, Clifton Court, pg. 1501 **IT**

Henfield

Shamrock (Great Britain) Ltd., pg. 196 **PB**

Henley-on-Thames

Hallmark Cards Ltd., Hallmark House Station Rd., pg. 496 **PV**
Stelrad Div., Newtown Rd., pg. 267 **IT**
Stelrad Group Limited, Newtown Rd., pg. 267 **IT**
Stelrad Overseas Limited, Newtown Rd., pg. 267 **IT**
Tonka Europe, Limited, 17 Market Place, pg. 798 **PB**

Hereford

H.P. BULMER HOLDINGS PLC, The Cider Mills, Plough Lane, pg. 232 **IT**
Dairy Supplies Hereford Ltd., The Cattle Market, pg. 1380 **IT**
Denco Ltd., Holmer Rd., pg. 16 **IT**
Inco Alloys Limited, Holmer Rd., pg. 672 **IT**
IncoTest, pg. 673 **IT**
Incotherm Limited, pg. 673 **IT**
Opella Ltd., Rotherwas Industrial Estate, Twyford Rd., pg. 391 **IT**
Sealed Air (FPD) Limited, Netherwood Road, Rotherwas Industrial Estate, pg. 1451 **PB**

Hertford

Avdel Textron, Mundells, Garden City, pg. 1590 **PB**
De La Rue Cash Handling Product Group, Unit 10, Caxton Hill Ind. Estate, pg. 387 **IT**
Hutchison Telecommunications (UK) Limited, The Chase, John Tate Road, pg. 218 **IT**
Smith Corona (U.K.) Ltd., pg. 1007 **PV**

Heston

European Area, Worldwide House, Unit 19, Airlinks Industrial Estate, pg. 281 **PB**

Hexham

The Northumberland Concrete Company Limited, Barrasford Quarry, Barrasford, pg. 1355 **IT**

Heywood

Ames Crosta Babcock Ltd., Gregge St., pg. 471 **IT**
Industrial Latex Compounds Ltd., Burns Mill, Manchester St., pg. 523 **PB**
Leesona, Unit 309., pg. 774 **IT**
Salford Electrical Instruments Ltd., Dawson St., pg. 545 **IT**
Water Engineering Division, pg. 472 **IT**

High Wycombe

AXA Equity & Law Life Assurance Society Plc, Amersham Rd., pg. 19 **IT**
Ademco, Cressex Industrial Estate, 12-13, Blenheim Rd., pg. 849 **PB**
Allergan Limited, The Crown Ctr., Coronation Rd., pg. 46 **PB**
Archer Technicoat Limited, Progress Rd., pg. 893 **IT**
Battenfeld UK Ltd., 6, The Valley Centre, pg. 826 **IT**
Biffa Waste Services Limited, Coronation Road, pg. 1225 **IT**
Biomedical Sensors (Holdings) Ltd., 5 Manor Courtyard, Hughenden Avenue, pg. 1283 **PB**
Costar UK Ltd., 10 The Valley Center, pg. 448 **PB**
D & B Software Ltd., Holmers Farm Way, pg. 532 **IT**
Datarange Communications plc, Kingsmead House, Abbey Barn Rd., pg. 956 **PV**
Dun & Bradstreet Ltd., Holmers Farm Way, pg. 536 **PB**
EG & G Sealol Inc., Coronation Rd., pg. 544 **PB**
Elkem Ltd. - Materials, Elkem House, 4A Corporation St., pg. 447 **IT**
Fallek Chemical Company (UK) Limited, 57-61 West Wycombe Rd., pg. 553 **PV**
Federal Express (U.K.) Ltd., 35/37 Amersham Hill, pg. 604 **PB**
HMT Rubber Glas Ltd., Elite Works, Wellington Road, pg. 914 **IT**
Hall & Co. Limited, Central Region, RMC House, Coronation Rd., pg. 1079 **IT**
Harrison & Sons Ltd., Harrison House, Coates Ln., pg. 817 **IT**
Hyundai Car (UK) Ltd, St. John's Place, pg. 807 **IT**
Instron Limited, Coronation Rd., pg. 883 **PB**
Instron Schenck Testing Limited, Coronation Road, pg. 883 **PB**

Janssen-Cilag Ltd., Wycombe Rd., pg. 929 **PB**
Krupp Widia U.K. Ltd., 5, The Valley Center, Gordon Rd.,
pg. 510 **IT**
Lorex Pharmaceuticals Ltd., P.O. Box 53, pg. 818 **IT**
Olicom UK Limited, Swan House, Peregrine Business Park,
pg. 1001 **IT**
Oxford Instruments-Microanalysis Group, Halifax Road,
pg. 1018 **IT**
PPP Beaumont PLC, Prospect House, Crendon Street,
pg. 1020 **IT**
RHM Technology Ltd., Lincoln Rd., pg. 1396 **IT**
Rank Hovis Limited, The Lord Rank Ctr., Lincoln Rd.,
pg. 1396 **IT**
SELIX F. SCHOELLER LTD., Wooburn Green,
pg. 1209 **IT**
G.D. Searle & Company Limited, Lane End Rd.,
pg. 1126 **PB**
Ultra Electronics Command & Control Systems, Knaves
Beech Business Center, Loudwater, pg. 1431 **IT**

Hillingdom

Milupa Ltd., pg. 991 **IT**

Hillsborough

Great Yorkshire Gold, Radio House, 900 Herries Rd.,
pg. 451 **IT**
Hallam FM, Radio House, 900 Herries Rd., pg. 451 **IT**
Kemira N.I. Limited, 5 Ballygowan Rd., pg. 728 **IT**

Hinckley

Burgess Architectural Products Limited, Brookfield Road,
pg. 1344 **IT**
CCM Limited, Rugby Rd., pg. 1261 **IT**
IRPC Hinton Limited, Stockwell House, pg. 1502 **IT**
Lift Truck Distribution, Unit 2a Maizefield, Hinckely Fields
Industrial Estate, pg. 807 **IT**
Personal Performance Consultants UK Limited (PPC),
Florence House, St. Mary's Road, pg. 1502 **IT**
SKETCHLEY PLC, Rugby Rd., pg. 1261 **IT**
Sketchley Retail Ltd., P.O. Box 7, pg. 1261 **IT**
SpeedFam Limited, Brindley Rd., pg. 1498 **PB**
Zodiac Holdings Ltd., pg. 69 **IT**
Zodiac Print Processes Ltd., pg. 69 **IT**

Hindhead

British Car Auction Group, Expedier House, Portsmouth
Rd., pg. 1649 **PB**

Hirwain

Sheer Pride Ltd., pg. 817 **IT**

Histon

Geraghty & Miller International, Inc., Suite A, Conqueror
House, Vision Park, pg. 607 **IT**

Hitchin

Aydin Europe Ltd., 1/3 Hunting Gate, pg. 158 **PB**
Aydin International U.K., 1/3 Hunting Gate, pg. 158 **PB**
BERG Electronics Connector Systems Ltd., The Maltings,
Bridge Street, pg. 213 **IT**
GESTRA (U.K.) Ltd., 9-11 Bancroft Court, pg. 550 **IT**
Kerry Ultrasonics Limited, Hunting Gate, Wilbury Way,
pg. 589 **IT**
SDRC U.K. Limited, Milford House, Priory End,
pg. 1525 **PB**

Hockley Heath

Bowater Windows, 4 Hockley Court, 2401 Stratford Road,
pg. 1106 **IT**

Hoddesdon

Alcan Metal Centres, Bingley Rd., pg. 51 **IT**
Analytical Development Company Limited, Pindar Rd.,
pg. 589 **IT**
Frigoscandia Food Process Systems Ltd., Scania House,
pg. 607 **PB**
Frigoscandia Ltd., Scania House, pg. 607 **PB**
Hathaway Instruments Limited, pg. 799 **PB**
ITT Jabsco, Belcon Industrial Estate, Bingley Road,
pg. 860 **PB**
Lockheed Martin Solartron Systems, Pindar Rd.,
pg. 1009 **PB**

Hollingworth Hyde

AlliedSignal Laminate Systems, 16C Etherow Industrial
Estate, Woolley Bridge Rd., pg. 53 **PB**

Holmes Chapel

AG Stanley Limited, Victoria Mills, Macclesfield Road,
pg. 202 **IT**

Holmwood

Zyma (United Kingdom) Limited, Mill Rd., pg. 986 **IT**

Holyhead

Anglesey Aluminium Limited, Penrhos Works, pg. 1063 **PB**
Anglesey Aluminium Limited, Penrhos Works, pg. 1119 **IT**
Stena Line Limited, Stena Line Limited House, Station
Approach, pg. 1300 **IT**

Hook

AAH Retail Pharmacy Limited, Vantage House, Meridian
Office Park, Osborn Way, pg. 591 **IT**
Integrated Network for Computer Administration Ltd.,
Vantage House, Meridian Office Park, pg. 591 **IT**
Trimble Navigation Europe Ltd., Trimble House, Meridian
Office Park, pg. 1638 **IT**

Horley

ABS Pumps Ltd., Station Road, pg. 270 **IT**
Delta Air Lines UK, Oakfield Court, Consort Way,
pg. 497 **PB**

Horsforth

Sandoz Chemicals (UK) Ltd., pg. 984 **IT**
Sandoz Products Ltd., Calverley Lane, pg. 985 **IT**

Horsham

Allied Domecq Spirits & Wine (UK) Ltd., Prewetts Mill,
pg. 63 **IT**
Applied Implant Technology, Foundry Ln., pg. 123 **PB**
CIBA Pharmaceuticals, Wimblehurst Road, pg. 981 **IT**
Ericsson Ltd., Viking House, Foundry Lane, pg. 1367 **IT**
EUROTHERM PLC, Leonardslee, pg. 465 **IT**
Novellus Systems, Ltd., Unit 1 eb, Bishops Weald House,
Albion Way, pg. 1204 **PB**
Phase Components Ltd., Unit 5, The Genesis Center,
Redkiln Way, pg. 93 **PB**
SOR Europe, Ltd., 2 Star Rd., pg. 957 **PV**
Swedish Ericsson Company Ltd., Viking House, Foundry
Lane, pg. 1370 **IT**
System Sensor, 3 Horsham Gates, North St.,
pg. 1307 **IT**
Thorn-Ericsson Telecommunications Limited, Viking House,
Foundry Lane, pg. 1370 **IT**

Horsmonden

W.H. Boddington & Co. Ltd., pg. 1511 **IT**

Horwich

Ingersoll-Rand Co., Ltd., Chorley New Rd., pg. 878 **PB**
Ingersoll-Rand Holdings Ltd., Chorely, New Rd.,
pg. 878 **PB**

Houghton le Spring

Evode Clearex Ltd., Houghton-le-Spring Industrial Estate,
pg. 802 **IT**
Intervet Laboratories Ltd., The Elms, The Thicket,
pg. 45 **IT**
Wadkin Durham, Fence Houses, pg. 231 **IT**

Hounslow

AAR Europa, Cardinal Point, pg. 1 **PB**
Aer Lingus, Aer Lingus House, 83 Staines Rd., pg. 28 **IT**
Air Canada, Cardinal Point, Radires Pk., London Heathrow
Airport, pg. 37 **IT**
Amdahl (UK) Ltd., Viking House, pg. 527 **IT**
Amerford Intl. (U.K.) Ltd., Unit 5, Silver Jubilee Way,
pg. 1388 **IT**
Boeing International Corp., Ground Fl., Cardinal Point-
Newall Rd., pg. 242 **PB**
Eaton Limited, Eaton House, Staines Road, pg. 558 **PB**
Ebara Pumps United Kingdom Limited, 2 Ariel Way,
Heathrow Causeway, pg. 432 **IT**
Ebara UK Ltd., 7 Ariel Way Heathrow Causeway,
pg. 432 **IT**
B.F. Goodrich Chemical (U.K.) Ltd., The Lawn-100,
Lampton Rd., pg. 752 **PB**
ISS Airport Services Ltd., Room 0140A, Ground Floor,
pg. 657 **IT**
ISS U.K. Ltd., 44-50 Bath Rd., pg. 657 **IT**
KONE Lifts Ltd., 168-170 Wellington Road South,
pg. 747 **IT**
Nippon Express (U.K.), Ltd., Unit 7, Parkway Trading
Estate, Cranford Lane, pg. 934 **IT**
Oki Europe Ltd., Central House, Balfour Rd., pg. 1000 **IT**
Safety-Kleen U.K., Ltd., Box 14 Worton Road, Isleworth,
pg. 1426 **PB**
Speedwing Logica Limited, Heathrow House, pg. 814 **IT**
E.R. Squibb & Sons Ltd., Squibb House, 141-149 Staines
Rd., pg. 256 **PB**
Squibb Europe Inc., Squibb House, pg. 256 **PB**
Squibb Surgicare Ltd., Squibb House, pg. 256 **PB**

Hove

Wayland (Publishers), 61 Western Road, pg. 1514 **IT**

Hucknall

K & M Hauliers, The Aerodrome, Watnall Road,
pg. 591 **IT**

Huddersfield

Chemviron Specialty Chemicals, 1-3 Upperhead Row,
pg. 1091 **PB**
Dawson Fur Fabrics Ltd., Wakefield Rd., pg. 385 **IT**
English Card Clothing Co. Limited, pg. 268 **IT**
Graham Builders Merchants Limited, 96 Leeds Rd.,
pg. 124 **IT**
HEYWOOD WILLIAMS GROUP PLC, Waverley Edgerton
Rd., pg. 618 **IT**
Holset Engineering Co. Ltd., Huddersfield Works,
Turnbridge, pg. 469 **PB**
Hopkinsons Ltd., pg. 1489 **IT**
Mikron U.K. Ltd., Tandem Industrial Estate, pg. 867 **IT**
Simpson International (UK) Ltd., Rubber Room Location,
Units 7-10, Ringway, pg. 1475 **PB**
Joseph Sykes Brothers Ltd., Acre St. Lindley, pg. 268 **IT**
Zeneca Huddersfield Works, pg. 1524 **IT**

Hull

Hanson White Ltd., South Orbital Trading Park, Hedon Rd.,
pg. 1035 **IT**
Milltech, pg. 1356 **IT**
NORTHERN FOODS PLC, Beverley House, St. Stephen's
Sq., pg. 967 **IT**
Reckitt & Colman Products, Dansom Ln., pg. 1090 **IT**
Resdispace Ltd., Valletta St., pg. 1285 **IT**
Seven Seas Limited, Hedon Rd., pg. 593 **IT**
Van Leer (UK) Ltd., pg. 1147 **IT**
Viking Radio, Commercial Rd., pg. 452 **IT**

Hulme

Simon-Carves Ltd., Sim-Chem House, pg. 1251 **IT**

Humberside

BEMROSE CORPORATION, North Bar House,
pg. 185 **IT**

Huntingdon

ABB Kent-Taylor Ltd., Howard Rd., Eaton Socon, pg. 7 **IT**
ABB Process Analytics Ltd., Howard Rd., Eaton Socon,
pg. 7 **IT**
Bailey Telecom LTD - Huntingdon, 7 Avro Court, Lancaster
Way, pg. 133 **IT**
Decision Data U.K. Ltd., Unit 1, Blackstone Rd.,
pg. 645 **IT**
Georg Fischer Plastics Ltd., Redwongs Way, pg. 490 **IT**
Gates Hydraulics Ltd., Station Road, pg. 1397 **IT**
Geotronics Ltd., Mensura House, Blackstone Rd.,
pg. 1290 **IT**
C E Johansson Ltd., Mensura House, Blackstone Rd.,
pg. 1290 **IT**
Kao Protoscan Plc, The Ermine Centre, Lancaster Way,
pg. 718 **IT**
Kent Industrial Measurements Limited, Howard Road, Eaton
Socon, pg. 2 **IT**
Munters Ltd., Blackstone Road, pg. 669 **IT**
Munters Moisture Control Services, Blackstone Road,
pg. 669 **IT**
Munters UK, Blackstone Rd., pg. 669 **IT**
Networks and Peripherals Ltd., Unit 1 Blackstone Road,
Stukeley Meadows, pg. 645 **IT**
Nokia Telecommunications Ltd., Lancaster House,
Lancaster Way, pg. 953 **IT**
Standard Products Limited, St. Johns Street, pg. 1505 **PB**

Hyde

Lion Steel Equipment Ltd., Johnson Brook Rd.,
pg. 488 **IT**

Hythe

L SIMS Portex Limited, Portex House, 1 High St.,
pg. 1267 **IT**

Ibstock

Garryson-Insley Ltd., Spring Rd., pg. 448 **IT**

Ilford

Britannia Music Co. Ltd., 60-70 Roden St., pg. 1052 **IT**
Gould Instrument Systems, Ltd., Seven Roebuck St.,
pg. 1592 **PB**
Kelvin Hughes Limited, New North Rd., pg. 1267 **IT**

Ilfracombe

Coutant Lambda Limited, Kingsley Ave., pg. 1241 **IT**
Pall Ilfracombe Ltd., Station Rd., pg. 1254 **PB**

Ilkeston

CHARNOS PLC, Corporation Rd., pg. 280 **IT**
Stanton Plc, pg. 1177 **IT**

PB - *U.S. Public Companies Volume*
PV - *U.S. Private Companies Volume*
IT - *International Public & Private Companies Volume*

1808

Ilkley

N.G. BAILEY & CO. LTD., Denton Hall, pg. 132 IT
Spooner Industries Ltd., Moorland Engineering Works, pg. 231 IT

Immingham Dock

G.D. Holmes Limited, Dock Offices, pg. 802 IT
Hydro Agri (UK) Ltd., pg. 962 IT
Hydro Chemicals Ltd., Immingham Dock, pg. 963 IT
Hydro Magnesium Ltd., Immingham Dock, pg. 963 IT
Stora Transport (UK) Ltd., Western Access Road, pg. 1303 IT

Innerleithen

The Ballantyne Cashmere Company Ltd, Caerlee Mills, pg. 385 IT

Inverness

McDermott Scotland, pg. 1068 PB
Moray Firth Maltings, Longman Rd., pg. 1211 IT

Ipswich

BOCM PAULS Limited, 47 Key St., pg. 598 IT
Cinram U.K. Ltd., 2 Central Avenue, Ransomes Europark, pg. 293 IT
Crane Limited U.K., Nacton Rd., pg. 458 IT
Delta (Manganese Bronze) Ltd., Handford Works, Hadleigh Rd., pg. 391 IT
Fisons Horticulture, Paper Mill Ln., pg. 1110 IT
Gas-Fired Products (U.K.) Ltd., 4-6 Chapel Lane, pg. 440 PV
P&O Roadways Ltd., Waveney House, Handford Rd., pg. 1034 IT
Pauls plc, 47 Key St., pg. 598 IT
RANSOMES PLC, Ransomes Way, Ransomes Europark, pg. 1087 IT
Sandoz Crop Protection Ltd., pg. 984 IT
Seawheel Ltd., Western House, Hadleigh Rd., pg. 1285 IT
United International Ferry Freight Ltd., Western House, 4th Fl., Hadleigh Rd., pg. 1285 IT
United Transport Containers Ltd., Western House, Hadleigh Rd., pg. 1285 IT
WF Corroon-Ipswich, Friars Street, pg. 1501 IT
Willis Faber (Underwriting Management) Limited, Friars Street, pg. 1504 IT

Irvine

Caledonian Paper Plc, Meadowhead Rd., pg. 1430 IT
Hyster Ltd., Industrial Estate Portland Rd., pg. 1150 PB
SCI UK Ltd., 1-5 Compton Way, pg. 1417 PB
Seagate Technology (U.K.), Limited, Riverside Business Park, 1 Brewster Place, pg. 1450 PB
Wilson Sporting Goods Co., Ltd., Ayr Rd., pg. 73 IT
Wilson Sporting Goods Co. Ltd., Ayr Road, pg. 73 IT

Islay

Bunnahabhain Distillery, pg. 619 IT

Isleworth

Aero Service (Great Britain) c/o Western Geophysical Co., P.O. Box 18, pg. 1004 PB
Avery Flight International Limited, Isleworth Business Centre, St. John's Road, pg. 215 IT
Comdisco United Kingdom Limited, One Centaurs Business Park, Grant Way, pg. 408 PB
Core Laboratories (UK), Wegesco House, P.O. Box 18, 455 London Rd., pg. 1004 PB
Gillette Europe, Gillette Corner, Great West Rd., pg. 744 PB
Gillette Industries, Ltd., Gillette Corner, Great West Road, pg. 745 PB
Gillette Products Division-Europe AMEE, Gillette Corner, Great West Rd., pg. 745 PB
Gillette UK Ltd., Gillette Corner, Great West Rd., pg. 745 PB
Greenham Construction Materials Limited, Wang Building, 661 London Road, pg. 1358 IT
Greenham Trading Limited, Greenham House, 671 London Road, pg. 1358 IT
Litton Avionics Systems, 288-290 Worton Rd., pg. 1005 PB
JOHN MOWLEM & COMPANY PLC, White Lion Court, Swan St., pg. 896 IT
Safteywear Limited, Isleworth Business Centre, St. John's Road, pg. 215 IT
Strand Lighting Limited, Grant Way, pg. 1087 IT
Svedala Ltd. Middlesex, pg. 1325 IT
Wang (UK) Limited, Wang House, 661 London Rd., pg. 1738 PB
Western Geophysical (Great Britain), Wesgeco House, 455 London Rd., pg. 1005 PB

Iver

Pinewood Studios Limited, Pinewood Rd., pg. 1086 IT

Ivybridge

Dutton-Forshaw (Land Machinery) Ltd., pg. 817 IT
Westmac Ltd., pg. 817 IT

Jarrow

Goldstar Electric U.K. Ltd., Simonside Industrial Estate, Shaftsbury Avenue, pg. 779 IT

Jedburgh

L.S. Starrett Co. Ltd., Oxnam Road, pg. 1511 PB

Jersey

PIONEER Poland U.K. L.P., pg. 312 IT

Keighley

Bolivar Stamping Ltd., Crown Works, pg. 390 IT
Grinding Machine-U.K., Cross Hills, pg. 1005 PB
Magnet Ltd., Royd Ings Ave., pg. 188 IT
S.O.S. Newall, Park Studios, pg. 1166 IT

Kempston

Hubbell, Ltd., Woburn R. Industrial Estate, pg. 845 PB
Robertson Tooling Ltd., Elstow Road, pg. 449 IT
Stone Vickers, Warrior Works, Viking Way, pg. 1467 IT
TML Metrology Centre for Bedford, 1-3 Singer Way, pg. 260 PB

Kettering

Sealed Air Limited, Telford Way, pg. 1451 PB
WEETABIX LIMITED, Weetabix Mills, pg. 1488 IT

Kew Bridge

Drake & Scull Engineering Ltd., 1 Thameside Centre, pg. 572 PB

Kidderminster

Amada United Kingdom Limited, Spennells Valley Rd., pg. 70 IT
Ashland Chemical Ltd., Oldington Vale Trading Estate, pg. 139 PB
Klark-Teknik Plc, Klark Industrial Park, Walter Nash Road, pg. 1045 PB
Kromschroder (U.K.) Ltd., Unit 159, Frederick Road, Faru Industrial Estate, pg. 1149 IT
National-Standard Co. Ltd., Stourport Rd., pg. 1161 PB
UK Petroleum Products Ltd., pg. 1065 IT

Kidlington

Elsevier Advanced Technology, The Boulevard, Langford Lane, pg. 1100 IT
Elsevier Science Limited, The Boulevard, Langford Lane, pg. 1100 IT

Kilburn

Thomas Robinson Group Plc, Kilburn Hall, pg. 231 IT

Killingholme

North Killingholme Cargo Terminal, Clough Lane, pg. 1251 IT

Kilmarnock

Blackwood Brothers Ltd, Bonnyton Works, Western Rd., pg. 385 IT

Kings Langley

Astra Pharmaceuticals Ltd., Home Park, pg. 94 IT
Wander Ltd., Ovaltine Works, Station Rd., pg. 973 IT

Kings Lynn

Campbell Grocery Products Ltd., Hardwick Rd., pg. 299 PB
Campbell's (U.K.) Limited, Hardwick Rd., pg. 299 PB
Cooper Roller Bearing Co., Ltd., Wisbech Rd., pg. 946 PB
Dow Chemical Co. Ltd., Cross Bank Rd., pg. 523 PB
Master Foods, Hansa Road, pg. 707 PV
Sun Electric U.K. Ltd., Oldmedow Rd., pg. 1481 PB
Warner-Jenkinson Europe, Oldmeadow Road, pg. 1696 PB

Kings Norton

Triplex Safety Glass Limited, Eckersall Road, pg. 1056 IT

Kingsthorpe

Lex Komatsu Forklift (UK), Logistic House, Horsley Road, pg. 807 IT

Kingston

Glynwed Metal Services Ltd., Amari House, 52 High St., pg. 554 IT
Nikon U.K. Ltd., 380 Richmond Rd., pg. 932 IT

Kingston upon Thames

BENTALLS PLC, Anstee House, Wood Street, pg. 187 IT
BRENNTAG (UK) Ltd., Brenntag House, 45 c, High St., Hampton Wick, pg. 1458 IT
Combined Ins. Co. of America, 15 Fairfield West, pg. 118 PB
Croner Publications, Ltd., London Rd., pg. 1514 IT
Elida Faberge, Three Jamess Road, pg. 1434 IT
GATX Finance (UK) Ltd., Thames Chambers, 2 Clarence St., pg. 691 PB
Gensym Ltd., Surrey House, 34 Eden St., pg. 731 PB
Kelly (UK) Services Ltd., Argyll House, 23 Brook St., pg. 949 PB
Krupp MaK (London) Ltd., Rennel House 40, Mill Place, pg. 509 IT
Lever Brothers Ltd., P.O. Box 69, Port Sunlight, pg. 1434 IT
Rockware Plastics Ltd., Lower Ham Rd., pg. 124 IT
Universal Leaf (UK) Ltd., Kingstons House, pg. 1695 PB
WF Corroon-Kingston, 12-42 Street, pg. 1502 IT
Willis Corroon Construction Risks Limited, Willis Corroon House, 12-42 Wood Street, pg. 1502 IT
Willis Corroon Credit Limited, Willis Corroon House, 12-42 Wood Street, pg. 1502 IT
Willis Corroon Limited, Willis Corroon House, Wood Street, pg. 1502 IT
Wolters Kluwer U.K., Croner House, 145 London Road, pg. 1514 IT

Kingston-upon-Hull

Akzo Coatings PLC, Sculcoates Ln., pg. 43 IT
Armstrong Fastenings Ltd., Clough Rd., pg. 265 IT
Donaldson Filter Components Ltd., Oslo Road, Sutton Fields Estate, pg. 517 PB
Humbrol Limited, pg. 159 PV
Ideal-Standard Ltd., P.O. Box 60, National Ave., pg. 92 IT
Kingston Cable Distributors, Unit 4C/4D, Amerstam Road, pg. 530 PB
Major Co. Ltd., Fountain Road, pg. 234 IT
Milchem Drilling Fluids Limited, Unit 102, Bankside Industrial Estate, pg. 167 PB
North Sea Ferries Ltd., King George V Dock, Hedon Rd., pg. 1035 IT
Smith & Nephew Medical Ltd., pg. 1263 IT

Kingswinford

Ballast Wiltshier plc - North West Region, LPC House, The Pensett Estate, pg. 135 IT
Crosland Plant, pg. 786 IT
Hydro Aluminium Rolled Products Ltd., Gibbons Industrial Park, Dudley Rd., pg. 963 IT
Intralox Ltd., Building 69, Third Ave., Pensnett Trading Estate, pg. 643 PV
Kennametal Hertel Limited, P.O. Box 29, pg. 951 PB
Remtox (Chemicals) Limited, No 22, First Avenue, pg. 802 IT

Kinross

Todd & Duncan Ltd., Lochleven Mills, pg. 385 IT

Kirk

Investment Engineering Ltd., Sidings Rd., Lowmoor Rd. Industrial Estate, pg. 391 IT

Kirkby

Charcon Tunnels, Southwell Lane, pg. 336 IT

Kirkcaldy

Butler Building Systems Ltd., Mitchelston Industrial Estate, pg. 271 PB
Forbo Nairn Ltd., pg. 497 IT
Robert Hutchison Limited, pg. 598 IT
G.L. Rexroth (Scotland) Ltd., pg. 838 IT

Knaresborough

Unitex Limited, Halfpenny Ln., pg. 1267 IT

Knoll Rise

Stevens & Brotherton Ltd., S & B House, 2, Vinson Close, pg. 1392 PB

Knottingley

Hickson Timber Products Ltd., Sowgate La., pg. 619 IT
Rockware Glass Ltd., Headlands Ln., pg. 124 IT
Rockware Glass Ltd.-Headlands Factory, Headlands Lane, pg. 124 IT
Rockware Glass Technical Centre, Headlands Ln., pg. 124 IT

PB - *U.S. Public Companies Volume*
PV - *U.S. Private Companies Volume*
IT - *International Public & Private Companies Volume*

Geographic Index-Non U.S.

Knutsford

Eurocamp Independent Limited, Toft Rd., pg. 465   IT
EUROCAMP PLC, Canute Ct., Toft Rd., pg. 464   IT
Eurocamp Travel Limited, Canute Ct., pg. 465   IT
Ilford Limited, pg. 905   PB
NNC Ltd., Booths Hall, Chelford Rd., pg. 545   IT
P.A. Ross (Food Brokers), Ltd., Ruskin Chambers, Drury Lane, pg. 753   IT
Sunsites Limited, Canute Ct., pg. 465   IT

Korby

Peavey Electronics Ltd, Great Folds Rd., pg. 846   PV

Lanark

Hoover Ltd.-Floor Care Manufacturing Facility, Somervell St., pg. 260   IT

Lancaster

Elsevier Electronic Publishing Services, Cameron House, White Cross, pg. 1100   IT
Forbo Contract Fabrics Ltd., Lune Mills, pg. 497   IT
Forbo Lancaster Ltd., Lune Mills, pg. 497   IT
Zeneca Resins Hillhouse International, Thornton, pg. 1524   IT

Lancing

Eschmann Equipment, Peter Rd., pg. 1267   IT
Link-Miles Limited, Churchill Industrial Estate, pg. 1385   IT
Scorpio Power Systems Limited, 2 Chartwell Road, Churchill Industrial Estate, pg. 1344   IT
SIMS Portex Limited, Peter Rd., pg. 1267   IT

Langley

Aluminum UK Limited, Waterside Drive, pg. 1172   IT
Amalgamated Glass Limited, Waterside Drive, pg. 1172   IT
Ferdee Limited, Waterside Drive, pg. 1172   IT
Gafsen Limited, Waterside Drive, pg. 1172   IT
Hayes Laminate Glass Co. Ltd., Waterside Drive, pg. 1173   IT
Image (Glassware) Limited, Waterside Drive, pg. 1173   IT
Kerosean Limited, Waterside Drive, pg. 1173   IT
London and Southern Glass Distributers Limited, Waterside Drive, pg. 1173   IT
London Architectural Glass Ltd., Waterside Drive, pg. 1173   IT
Marcus Summers Structural Glazing Ltd., Waterside Drive, pg. 1173   IT
P and B Stockglass, Waterside Drive, pg. 1173   IT
Panal Shopfront Systems Limited, Waterside Drive, pg. 1173   IT
Pentax U.K. Ltd., Pentax House, Heron Dr., pg. 85   IT
Rieter-Scragg Ltd., pg. 1117   IT
Scientific Atlantic Limited, Home Park Estate, pg. 1443   PB
Security Glass Group PLC, Waterside Drive, pg. 1173   IT
Solaglas, Waterside Dr., pg. 1173   IT
Thermax, Waterside Dr., pg. 1173   IT

Larbert

Exabyte Scotland Limited, 1 Central Blvd., pg. 597   PB

Larkfield

Kimberly-Clark Limited, pg. 959   PB

Larne

Curran Plant, Inner Mill, Circular Rd., P.O. Box 4, pg. 672   PB
Inver Mill, Inner Mill, Circular Rd., pg. 672   PB
Invercon Papermills Ltd., pg. 672   PB
Stena Sealink Line, Sea Terminal, pg. 1300   IT

Launceston

Abru Aluminium Limited, Pennygillam Industrial Estate, pg. 615   IT

Leabrooks

H.B. Fuller U.K., Ltd., Amber Business Centre, Greenhill Lane, pg. 687   PB

Leamington Spa

Scholastic Publications Ltd., Westfield Road, pg. 1441   PB

Leatherhead

ASHTEAD GROUP PLC, Ashtead House, Business Park 8, pg. 88   IT
Bergvik Sales Limited, Manor House, 1 The Crescent, pg. 904   PB
Denver Process Equipment, Ltd., Stocks House, 9 No. St., pg. 1326   PB
Encore Computer (UK) Ltd., Mole Business Park, Randalls Rd., pg. 580   PB
Integrated Device Technology Europe, Inc., Prime House, Barnett Wood Lane, pg. 884   PB

Kodak Limited-Southern Business Centre, Swan House, Swan Crescent Ct., pg. 553   PB
qad.united kingdom ltd., Egham Lodge, 24 Bridge St., pg. 1345   PB
Svedala Ltd., pg. 1325   IT
WWF Paper Sales U.K., Ltd., Claire House, Bridge St., pg. 1145   PV

Lechlade

Brake Cables Ltd, Mill Lane, pg. 472   IT

Lechworth

T.H. Dixon & Co. Ltd., Dixon House, Works Rd., pg. 231   IT

Ledbury

Clyde Petroleum plc, Coddington Court, pg. 577   IT

Leeds

APV Baker Limited, Coal Road, Seacroft, pg. 1240   IT
ASDA GROUP PLC, Asda House, Great Wilson St., pg. 17   IT
Anglo/CDT, Moorfield Industrial Estate, Moorfield Road, pg. 287   PB
Anixter Leeds, Suite 21, Concourse House, Dewsbury Road, pg. 115   PB
Aquaterra Environmental Consultants, Newton House, Newton Rd., pg. 697   IT
N.G. Bailey & Co. Ltd.-Leeds Branch, 7 Brown Lane West, pg. 132   IT
Bailey Telecom LTD, 7 Brown Lane West, pg. 133   IT
Ballast Wiltshier Plc - Northern Region, Richardshaw Drive, pg. 135   IT
Barratt Leeds, Premier House, 14 Royds Hall Road, pg. 168   IT
Battenfeld UK Ltd., Northern Area Office/Showroom, 12 West Vale, Brown Lane West, pg. 825   IT
CDT International, Moorfield Road, pg. 287   PB
Gray Tool Company, c/o Barry Ingham, 63 Whitehouse Ave., pg. 6   IT
Henkel Nopco Ltd., Nopco House, Kirstall Road, pg. 613   IT
Hoesch Woodhead Ltd., 177 Kirkstall Rd., pg. 508   IT
Ker Monolithics, Whitehall Estate, pg. 789   IT
Kodak Limited, Friends Provident House, 13-14 South Parade, pg. 553   PB
Komori U.K. Limited, Kirkstall Industrial Park, Kirkstall Road, pg. 745   IT
Lambert Smith Hampton, 18 Park Pl., pg. 797   IT
Leeds, Lion House, 41 York Place, pg. 910   IT
MLP UK Ltd., Unit 12 Riverside Place, Business Park, Bridgewater Rd., pg. 874   IT
Manville Great Britain Ltd. (Leeds), 60 Green Road Meanwood, pg. 927   PB
Monk Bridge Division, pg. 673   IT
Oilgear Towler Ltd., Oaklands Road, pg. 1215   PB
Pirelli Focom Ltd., Unit 10, Hunslet Trading Estate, pg. 1059   IT
Pland Stainless Ltd., pg. 817   IT
POULTER COMMUNICATIONS PLC, Rose Wharf, East St., pg. 1065   IT
Radio Aire, 51 Burley Rd., pg. 452   IT
Ready Mixed Concrete (Yorkshire) Limited, RMC House, Elland Rd., pg. 1080   IT
Riley Advertising (Leeds) Ltd., Ste. 26c, Joseph's Well, Hanover Way, LS3 1AB, pg. 1117   IT
Rocol Limited, Rocol House, pg. 892   IT
SLD Genlite Limited, Treefield Industrial Estate, pg. 1160   IT
SLD Skidhire Limited, Treefield Industrial Estate, pg. 1160   IT
Sanderson PSS Limited, South Point, South Accommodation Rd., pg. 1184   IT
Sandoz Holdings Great Britain Ltd., Calverley Lane, pg. 984   IT
Shandwick North Ltd., The Design Innovation Centre, The Calls, pg. 1226   IT
Sulzer (UK) Pumps Ltd., Manor Mill Lane, pg. 1306   IT
Time Retail Finance, Airedale House, 423 Kirkstall Road, pg. 734   IT
Toyota Industrial Equipment (UK) Ltd., Gelderd Rd., Gildersome, pg. 1414   IT
United Provincial Newspapers Ltd., Wellington St., pg. 1443   IT
WDS Limited, Pollard Lane, pg. 88   IT
Willis Corroon Credit Limited, Willis Corroon House, 30 Park Place, pg. 1502   IT
Willis Corroon North Limited, Willis Corroon House, 30 Park Place, pg. 1502   IT
Jonas Woodhead Limited, 177 Kirkstall Rd., pg. 268   IT
Yorkshire Bank, 20 Merrion Way, pg. 906   IT
YORKSHIRE CHEMICALS PLC, Kirkstall Rd., pg. 1522   IT
Yorkshire Post Newspapers Ltd., Wellington St., pg. 1443   IT

Leicester

ARC Central, Ashby Road East, pg. 592   IT
Akerlund & Rausing Ltd., 26 High St., pg. 33   IT
Arami UK Ltd., Enkalon House, Regent Road, pg. 45   IT
Astra Charnwood, Bakewell Rd., pg. 93   IT
Bardon (England) Ltd., pg. 166   IT
Bostik Ltd., Ulverscroft Rd., pg. 1409   IT
Camloc International, 15 New Star Rd., pg. 610   PB

Campbell Catering Limited, Castle Donnington, pg. 254   IT
Camtec Electronic Ltd., Camtec House, Vaughn Way, pg. 1365   IT
J.M. Clarke (Electrical Engineers) Limited, 64-66 Percy Rd., pg. 448   IT
Coats Limited, Desford Rd., pg. 299   IT
Coherent Optics (Europe) Ltd., Unit 28 Ashville Way, pg. 396   PB
Colex International, Ltd., Unit G1, Valley Way, pg. 796   PV
DCE Group, Humberstone Ln., pg. 125   IT
Enka UK Ltd., Regent Road, Enkalon House, pg. 46   IT
Ford & Slater Group Ltd., pg. 1434   IT
Gas Springs Division, 15 New Star Road, pg. 610   PB
Gencor ACP Ltd., Wharf Way, Glen Parva, pg. 705   PB
KME UK Limited, 9117 Tuxford Rd., pg. 720   IT
Kitsons Insulation Products (U.K.) Limited, Kitsons House, Century Way, pg. 1237   PB
Metalastik Vibration Control Systems, pg. 126   IT
Mettler-Toledo Ltd., 64 Boston Rd., pg. 4   PV
Northern Dairies, Smisby Rd., Ashby de la Zouch, pg. 968   IT
G. Perry & Sons Ltd., Hall Lane, pg. 1489   IT
Rank Taylor Hobson Limited, P.O. Box 36, 2 New Star Rd., pg. 1087   IT
Ruddles Brewery Ltd., Langham, Oakham, pg. 559   IT
Russell Castings Limited, Bonchurch St., pg. 449   IT
S & P Coil Products Limited, SPC House, Evington Valley Rd., pg. 590   IT
SEAC Limited, 46 Chesterfield Rd., pg. 590   IT
SPS Technologies Limited, 191 Barkby Rd., pg. 1420   PB
Sachs Automotive Components Ltd., pg. 835   IT
ServiceMaster Ltd., ServiceMaster House, Leicester Road, pg. 1462   IT
Speizman Industries Limited (Europe), Unit 2, 173 Barkby Rd., pg. 1498   PB
Standard Cressall Limited, Evington Valley Rd., pg. 590   IT
Tesa Reference Standards Div., Tesa Metrology Limited, Bradgate St., pg. 260   IT
United Marketing (Leicester) Ltd., Lyn House, pg. 234   PB
Viking Direct Holding Co., Units A & B, Bursom Industrial Park, pg. 1721   PB
Viking Direct Limited, Bursom Industrial Park, Towell Road, pg. 1721   PB
Wadkin Agencies, Green Lane Rd., pg. 231   IT
Wadkin Leicester, Green Lane Works, Green Lane Rd., pg. 231   IT
Wadkin Plc, Green Lane Works, Green Lane Rd., pg. 231   IT
Wadkin Tooling, 331 Humberstone Ln., pg. 231   IT
Walker's Crisps, Ltd., Feature Road, pg. 1278   PB
Willis Corroon Midlands Limited, Peat House, 1 Waterloo Way, pg. 1502   IT

Leigh-on-Sea

Mte-TURCK Ltd., 20 Stephenson Rd., pg. 449   IT

Leighton Buzzard

AGEMA Infrared Systems Ltd., Arden House, West St., pg. 1289   IT
Camden Motors Ltd., Fitzroy House, 69-79 Lake St., pg. 165   IT
E.C.E. Distribution Services, Spinney Pool, Billington Rd., pg. 591   IT
RMC Roadstone Limited-Midlands and South East, Arden House, West St., pg. 1079   IT

Letchworth

Avnet Access Ltd., Jubilee House, Jubilee Road, pg. 155   PB
Avnet Time Ltd., Jubilee House, Jubilee Road, pg. 155   PB
Camford Engineering PLC, Blackhorse Rd., pg. 507   IT
Hertfordshire BTR Ltd., Works Rd., pg. 126   IT
Geo. W. King Ltd., Blackhorse Rd., pg. 507   IT
Neosid Limited, Icknield Way West, pg. 1344   IT

Lewes

Boart Longyear Limited, Southernham House, Southernham, pg. 76   IT
Ferrosan Operations Ltd., Unit 24, Cliffe Industrial Estate, pg. 989   IT
W. Lunnon & Company Limited, pg. 757   IT

Leyland

BTR Farington Ltd., pg. 125   IT
Heating Replacement Parts and Controls Ltd., pg. 1511   IT
The Leyland & Birmingham Rubber Group, Golden Hill Ln., pg. 125   IT

Lichfield

GKN Bound Brook Ltd., P.O. Box 3, pg. 534   IT
GKN Powder Metallurgy Division, P.O. Box 3, pg. 534   IT
Gill's Cables Limited, pg. 268   IT

Lincoln

AAH Builders Supplies Limited, 76 South Park, pg. 591   IT
Babcock Robey Limited, Witham House, P.O. Box 23, pg. 472   IT
Bucyrus-Europe Ltd., Becor House, Green Lane, pg. 177   PV

NON-U.S. LOCATED COMPANIES
UNITED KINGDOM

Butterley Aggregates Limited, 17-21 West Parade, pg. 1079 IT
Georg Fischer (Lincoln) Ltd., Station Road, pg. 488 IT
Lincs. Surfacing Contractors Limited, Dowding Rd., Allenby Rd. Industrial Estate, pg. 1079 IT
MPC Wragby, Wragby, pg. 851 IT
New Farm Crops, Market Stainton, pg. 983 IT
Richardson Electronics (Europe) Ltd., Inspring House, Searby Rd., pg. 1388 PB
Roadstone Surface Dressing Limited, Dowding Rd., Allenby Rd. Industrial Estate, pg. 1081 IT
Rose Bearings Ltd., Doddington Road, pg. 869 IT

Linwood

Foam Plus Limited, S. James's House, Linwood Rd., pg. 341 IT

Lisburn

C.R. Bailey (Belfast) Ltd, pg. 1146 IT
De La Rue Smurfit (NI) Ltd., 13 Ballinderry Road, pg. 386 IT
Reynolds Systems (N.I.) Limited, Grand Street, Hilden, BT27 4TX, pg. 1387 PB

Littleborough

Courtaulds Aerospace, Summit, pg. 338 IT
Fisher Quality Foods Limited, Whitelees Road, pg. 491 IT
Tygaflor Ltd., Gate #5, Rock Nook Mill, Todmorden Rd., Summit, pg. 344 PB

Littlehampton

THE BODY SHOP INTERNATIONAL, Watersmead, pg. 199 IT
Eurotherm Drives Ltd., New Courtwick Lane, pg. 466 IT
Excellon U.K., Dominion Way, pg. 594 PB

Liverpool

A.F. & D. Mackay Ltd., 8C, Telegraph House, 29/35 Moor Lane Crosby, pg. 966 IT
Ayrton Saunders, Speke Hall Indus. Estate, 10 Spindus Rd., pg 591 IT
Bayex Ltd., Solicitors 7th Floor, 100 Old Hall Street, pg. 1177 IT
Canon (Mersey) Business Machines Ltd., New Zealand House, 18 Water Street, pg. 263 IT
Crown Sacks & Systems (Aintree) Ltd., Brookfield Dr., pg. 759 IT
Crown Sacks & Systems (Holdings) Ltd. U.K., Brookfield Dr., pg. 759 IT
Derbyshire-Liverpool Branch, 6 Dale Street, pg. 394 IT
EuroChem Division, Kirkby Bank Rd., Knowsley Industrial Park (North), pg. 166 PB
Imperial Tobacco Ltd., Liverpool Trading Div., pg. 666 IT
The Jacob's Bakery Ltd., Long Lane, pg. 381 IT
Kodak Limited-Chemical Division, Acornfield Rd., pg. 553 PB
Liverpool Airport Public Limited Company, South Terminal, Liverpool Airport, pg. 217 IT
Liverpool Coated Stone, Logwood Mill Industrial Pk., Stretton Way, pg. 1079 IT
NYK Line-Liverpool, Port of Liverpool Bldg., Pier Head, pg. 942 IT
Petrolite Limited, Knowsley Industrial Park, N., Kirkby Bank Rd., pg. 166 PB
Radio City, pg. 452 IT
Royal Life Holdings Limited, Box No. 30, pg. 1130 IT
Scientific Hospital Supplies Holdings Ltd., pg. 992 IT
Vernons Pools Limited, Fortune House, Park Lane, pg. 787 IT
John West Foods Ltd., pg. 1434 IT
Whitecable, Wilson Road, Huyton Industrial Estate, pg. 462 IT
Willis Corroon North Limited, 373 Lancaster House, Mercury Court, pg. 1502 IT

Liversedge

Owens-Corning Veil U.K. Limited, P.O. Box 30, pg. 1237 PB
Rigby-Maryland (Stainless) Ltd., Crystal Works, Union Rd., pg. 780 PB

Livingston

Abbey Chemicals, Ltd., Nettlehill Rd., pg. 271 PV
Analog Devices Ltd., 4th Floor, Pentland House, Almondvale South, pg. 108 PB
Banta Global Turnkey, 2 Fraser Road, pg. 188 PB
Beazer Homes (Edinburgh), Beazer House, Royston Road, pg. 182 IT
Byard Kenwest Engineering Limited, Muir Rd., pg. 336 IT
Canon (Scotland) Business Machines Ltd., 5 Fleming Road, pg. 263 IT
Jabil Circuit, Ltd., Simpson Pkwy., Kirkton Campus, pg. 920 PB
Laidlow Drew Ltd., 1 Lister Road, pg. 1455 PB
Mentor Graphics (UK) Ltd., 2nd Fl., Lomond House, pg. 1087 PB
NEC Semiconductors (UK) Limited, Deans West Industrial Estate, pg. 900 IT
NL Specialty Chemicals Ltd., Nettlehill Rd., pg. 271 PV
Network Systems Limited, 12 Grampian Court, pg. 1522 PB

Russell Corp. UK Limited, Deans S. W. Industrial Estate, One Dunlop Sq., pg. 1413 PB
Wyman-Gordon Limited, Houston Road, pg. 1782 PB

Llandudno

Simon Laboratories, Tyn-Y-Coed, pg. 1251 IT
Simon Petroleum Technology Ltd., Llandudno, pg. 1251 IT

Llanelli

Brockhouse Modernfold Limited, Bethesda Rd., pg. 426 IT
Delta Enfield Wires Ltd., Copperworks Rd., pg. 390 IT
Delta Welding Equipment Ltd., Copperworks Rd., pg. 390 IT

Llantrisant

Electronic Harnesses (U.K.) Ltd., Unit 5, Llantrisant Bus. Pk., pg. 1313 IT
FRAM Europe Ltd., pg. 53 PB

Lochgelly

Andrew Antennas, pg. 113 PB

Lolworth

Transico Inc., European Operations, Slate Hall, Unit 1, Close Hall Farm, pg. 1631 PB

London

AAF Consultants Ltd., Seven Queen St., pg. 1 IT
AAF INDUSTRIES PLC, Seven Queen St., pg. 1 IT
ABN-Amro Securities (U.K.) Ltd, 5-9, Well Court, pg. 12 IT
ACC Long Distance U.K. Ltd., 414 Chiswick High Road, pg. 3 PB
ADT Limited, 5 Hannover Square, pg. 1649 PB
AFI Hotels Limited, 166 High Holborn, pg. 556 IT
AGA Gloucester House, 5759 Gloucester Place, pg. 5 PV
AMEC Process & Energy, One Golden Lane, pg. 16 IT
AMP Asset Management Plc, 55 Moorgate, pg. 100 IT
AMS Management Systems UK Ltd, 51-55 Gersham St., pg. 87 PB
ANZ Grindlays Bank plc United Kingdom, Minerva House, Montague Close, pg. 99 IT
ANZ McCaughan Securities Limited United Kingdom, 7th Floor, 3 Finsbury Square, pg. 99 IT
ARC ADVERTISING, 195 Euston Rd., pg. 17 IT
AXA Marine & Aviation Insurance UK Ltd., 106 Fenchurch St., pg. 19 IT
AXA Re United Kingdom, Fourth Fl., Ste. 3, 3 Minster Ct., pg. 19 IT
ABBEY NATIONAL PLC, 215/221 Baker St., pg. 19 IT
Acclaim Entertainment, Ltd, Morean House, 112-120 Brompton Rd., pg. 15 PB
Accor UK, One Shortland, pg. 21 IT
Acer UK Limited, pg. 22 IT
Acxiom Corporation, 60-68 St. Thomas St., pg. 18 PB
Advertising Age International, Cowcross Court, pg. 285 PV
AEGON Financial Services Group (UK) Ltd., Lanark Square, Crossharbor, pg. 28 IT
AEGON Insurance Company (UK) Limited, 136, Fenchurch St., pg. 28 IT
Aetna Capital Management Investment Limited, 85 London Wall, pg. 27 PB
Air Malta - London, Air Malta House,314-316, Upper Richmond Road, pg. 38 IT
Air Malta - London, Malta House, Ticketing & FareOffice, pg. 38 IT
Airborne Leisure Ltd., Lakeside House, Squires Ln., pg. 1035 IT
Ajinomoto Europe Sales G.m.b.H., London Representative Office, 9/10 Grafton St., pg. 40 IT
Aker Engineering plc (AE), Bedford House, 69-79 Fulham High St., pg. 42 IT
Alexander & Alexander Services (UK) Plc, 8 Devonshire Sq., pg. 118 PB
Algemene Bank Nederland, 61, Threadneedle St., pg. 11 IT
Alginate Industries, 22 Harietta St., pg. 1091 PB
Alliance & Leicester Building Society, 49 Park Lane, pg. 57 IT
ALLIANCE LEICESTER BUILDING SOCIETY, 49 Park Lane, pg. 57 IT
ALLIED DOMECQ PLC, 24 Portland Place, pg. 62 IT
Alpha Airports Group Plc, 205 The Vale, pg. 65 IT
ALVIS PLC, 215 Vauxhall Bridge Road, pg. 69 IT
Amalgamated Metal Corporation Plc, Adelaide House, London Bridge, pg. 1071 IT
Amalgamated Metal Trading Ltd., Adelaide House, London Bridge, pg. 1071 IT
Amerada Hess (U.K.) Ltd., 33 Grozenor Pl., pg. 65 PB
American Express Bank Ltd., 60 Buckingham Palace Rd., pg. 74 PB
American Express Europe Limited, Portland House, pg. 74 PB
American Institute for Foreign Study, 37 Queen's Gate, pg. 57 PV
American International Underwriters (UK) Ltd., 120 Fenchurch St., pg. 85 PB
American Precision Industries (U.K.) Ltd., 100 New Bridge St., pg. 90 PB
Amoco Chemical (UK) Ltd., Amoco House, West Gate, Ealing, pg. 103 PB

Amoco Fabrics (U.K.) Ltd., Amoco House, West Gate, pg. 103 PB
Amoco Services, Inc., Amoco House, West Gate, pg. 103 PB
Amoco (U.K.) Exploration Company, Amoco House, West Gate, pg. 102 PB
Amoco (U.K.) Ltd., Amoco House, West Gate, Ealing, pg. 103 PB
Ampleflow Ltd., Chiswell St., pg. 1499 IT
Amsterdam-Rotterdam Bank N.V., 101 Moorgate, pg. 10 IT
Ana Trading & Takashimaya UK Ltd., 6-8 Old Bond St., pg. 1350 IT
Anglesey Aluminium Ltd. (ANGLESEY), P.O. Box 133, pg. 1062 PB
Anglo American Corporation of South Africa Limited (London), 40 Holburn Viaduct, pg. 77 IT
Anheuser-Busch Europe, Inc., 1 Newton St., pg. 115 PB
Anheuser-Busch European Trade Ltd., 1 Newton St., pg. 115 PB
Henry Ansbacher Holding PLC, Priory Hse., One Mitre Sq., pg. 487 IT
Apple Expo-The Macuser Show, Greater London House, Hampstead Rd., pg. 452 IT
Archer Group Holdings plc, Two Minister Court, pg. 337 PB
GW Archer & Co., 8 Henrietta Place, pg. 409 IT
Archer Managing Agents Limited, c/o Archer Group Holdings plc, Two Minister Court, pg. 337 PB
Area Headquarters-EUROPE & MIDDLE EAST, Berger House IF, 36-38 Berkeley Sq., pg. 393 IT
Armstrong Electra Ltd., Page St., Mill Hill, pg. 796 IT
The Arndale Property Trust Ltd., 220 Tottenham Court Rd., pg. 1034 IT
Arnold Projects Services Limited, Phoenix House, 18 King William Street, pg. 764 IT
Arrington-Hillgate International, Shropshire House, pg. 85 PV
Asahi Bank London Branch, 30 Cannon St., pg. 82 IT
Asahi Finance (U.K.) Ltd., Princes House, 95 Gresham Street, pg. 83 IT
Asahi Life Investment Europe Ltd., The Dresdner Bank House, 125 Wood St., pg. 85 IT
Asahi Property U.K. Ltd., The Dresdner Bank House, 125 Wood St., pg. 85 IT
ASCOT HOLDINGS PLC, Bury House, 31 Bury Street, pg. 87 IT
The Ascott Mayfair, 49 Hill Street, pg. 1212 IT
Ashby & Horner Furnishings Ltd., 32 Earl St., pg. 1032 IT
Ashdown Press Ltd., Unit 4, Rich Industrial Estate, Crimscott St., pg. 1226 IT
Ashikaga Bank-London Branch, 7th Floor, Bishopsgate Exchange, pg. 88 IT
Ashland Oil Intl. Ltd., 58 St. James's St., pg. 139 PB
ASSOCIATED BRITISH FOODS PLC, Weston Centre, Bowater House, 68 Knightsbridge, pg. 92 IT
Associated Newspaper Holdings Ltd., Northcliffe House, pg. 366 IT
The Associated Press, Ltd., 12 Norwich St., pg. 92 PV
Atalanta (U.K.) Ltd., Imperial House, pg. 94 PV
Attendor Raw Materials Ltd., 14, Queen Anne's Gate, pg. 710 IT
Audits & Surveys Worldwide, 6 Duke of York St., pg. 147 PB
Aurum Press Limited, 33 Museum St., pg. 1089 IT
Austin Reed Limited, 103-113 Regent St., pg. 796 PB
Australia & New Zealand Banking Group Limited United Kingdom, Minerva House, pg. 100 IT
Automotive Finance Limited, 8 Balderton St., pg. 665 PB
JOHN AYLING AND ASSOCIATES LIMITED, 27 Soho Square, pg. 103 IT
B of B (Europe) Limited, Two Broadgate, pg. 151 IT
BAA PLC, 130 Wilton Road, pg. 103 IT
BACSI (UK) Limited, Inveresk House, Aldwych, pg. 203 PB
B.A.T INDUSTRIES P.L.C., Windsor House, 50 Victoria St., pg. 110 IT
B.A.T International Finance Ltd., Windsor House, 50 Victoria St., pg. 111 IT
BB Securities Ltd., 10 Aldersgate Street, 6th Floor, pg. 142 IT
BBA GROUP PLC, 70 Fleet Street, pg. 112 IT
BBC MAGAZINES, 80 Wood Lane, pg. 114 IT
BCA, 87 Newman Street, pg. 192 IT
BDDP Holdings (UK) Ltd., 4-6 Soho Sq., pg. 117 IT
BDG/McColl, 24 St. John St., pg. 1482 IT
BFCE London, 4-6 Throgmorton Ave., pg. 161 IT
BHF-Bank, 61 Queen Street, pg. 119 IT
BHP Minerals, Brook House, 229 Shepherds Bush Road, pg. 224 IT
BHP Petroleum Ltd., Devonshire House, pg. 225 IT
BHS Plc, 129 Marylebone Rd., pg. 1304 IT
BICC Developments Ltd., Three Angel Square, pg. 120 IT
BICC PLC, Devonshire House, Mayfair Place, pg. 120 IT
The BIS Group Limited, 20 Upper Ground Rd., pg. 204 PB
BNA International Inc., Heron House, 6th Fl., 10 Dean Farrar St., pg. 182 PV
BNP Public Limited Co. (London), 8-13 King William St., pg. 164 IT
BNP UK Holdings Ltd., 8-13 King William St., pg. 164 IT
BP Chemicals Ltd., Britannic House, 1 Finsbury Circus, pg. 220 IT
BP Exploration Company Limited, Britannic House, 1 Finsbury Circus, pg. 220 IT
BP International Ltd., Britannic House, 1 Finsbury Circus, pg. 220 IT
BP Oil International Limited, Britannic House, 1 Finsbury Circus, pg. 220 IT
BPA International - London, 35 Piccadilly, pg. 107 PV
BSA International Inc., Royex House, Aldermanlary Sq., pg. 108 PV

Geographic Index-Non U.S.

PB - *U.S. Public Companies Volume*
PV - *U.S. Private Companies Volume*
IT - *International Public & Private Companies Volume*

BSN London, Santander House, 100 Ludgate Hill, pg. 144 **IT**
BST-BDDP, 4-6 Soho Square, pg. 117
BT Cablesystems Limited, 81 Newgate Street, pg. 222 **IT**
BT (CBP) Limited, BT Centre, 81 Newgate St., pg. 222 **IT**
BT Communications Management Limited, 81 Newgate Street, pg. 222 **IT**
BT Limited, 81 Newgate Street, pg. 222 **IT**
BT Property Ltd., BT Centre, 81 Newgate St., pg. 222 **IT**
BT Subsea Cables Limited, 81 Newgate Street, pg. 222 **IT**
BT (Worldwide) Ltd., BT Centre, 81 Newgate St., pg. 222 **IT**
BTR PLC, Silvertown House, pg. 124 **IT**
Babcock Hydro-Pneumatics Ltd., 10/18 Spurgeon St., pg. 471 **IT**
Babcock International Investments Ltd., Cleveland House, St. James Sq., pg. 472 **IT**
Babcock Plant Leasing Ltd., 165 Great Dover St., pg. 472 **IT**
Bain & Company (Securities) Ltd., 115 Houndsditch, pg. 406 **IT**
Bain Hogg Group plc, Lloyds Chambers, 1 Portsoken St., pg. 671 **IT**
Bain Hogg Insurance Brokers, Lloyds Chambers, 1, Portsoken St., pg. 671 **IT**
Balfour Beatty Limited, One Angel Square, pg. 120 **IT**
Balfour, Williamson & Co. Ltd., Roman House, Wood St., pg. 817 **IT**
Bally Group (UK) Limited, Bally House, 27-29 Beak St., pg. 997 **IT**
Bally Shoe Co. Ltd., Bally House, 27-29 Beak St., pg. 997 **IT**
Bally UK Sales Ltd., Bally House, 23-29 Beak St., pg. 997 **IT**
Banca March S.A., 30 Eastcheap, pg. 136 **IT**
Banca Nazionale del Lavoro, 33/35 Cornhill, pg. 137 **IT**
Banca Popolare di Milano, 51 Moorgate, pg. 137 **IT**
Banco di Napoli-London, One, Moorgate, pg. 140 **IT**
Banco di Sicilia, 99 Bishopsgate, pg. 140 **IT**
Banco do Brasil S.A.-London, P.O. Box 131, 34 King St., pg. 141 **IT**
Banco Hispano Americano Limited, 15, Austin Friars, pg. 140 **IT**
Banco Nacional de Mexico, Banamex House, 3 Creed Courts, pg. 574 **IT**
Banco Santander, Santander House, 100 Ludgate Hill, pg. 144 **IT**
Bancomer London Branch, 15 Austin Friars, pg. 145 **IT**
Bank Brussels Lambert, London Branch, 6 Broadgate, pg. 147 **IT**
Bank Hapoalim B.M., 8-12 Brook St., pg. 149 **IT**
Bank Hapoalim (London), 8-12 Brook St., pg. 149 **IT**
Bank Leumi (UK) P.L.C., 4-7, Woodstock St., pg. 150 **IT**
Bank of America NT&SA, 1 Alie St., pg. 182 **PB**
Bank of Boston Ltd., Bank of Boston House, 39 Victoria St., pg. 184 **PB**
Bank of Ireland Asset Management (UK) Limited, 36 Queen Street, pg. 153 **IT**
Bank of Ireland Investment Managers Limited, 36 Queen Street, pg. 153 **IT**
Bank of Montreal - England, 11 Walbrook St., pg. 155 **IT**
The Bank of New York, 46 Berkeley St., pg. 179 **PB**
The Bank of New York Capital Markets, Limited, 46 Berkeley St., pg. 179 **PB**
Bank of Tokyo-Mitsubishi (UK) Limited, Finsbury Circus House, 12-15 Finsbury Circus, pg. 158 **IT**
Bank of Yokohama London, 40, Basinghall Street, pg. 159 **IT**
Bankers Trust International Limited, 1 Appold St., Broadgate, pg. 186 **PB**
Bankers Trust Investment Management Ltd., 1 Appold St., Broadgate, pg. 186 **PB**
Bankers Trust New York Corporation, 1 Appold St., Broadgate, pg. 186 **PB**
Bankgesellschaft Berlin (UK) plc, 1 Crown Court, pg. 160 **IT**
Banque Francaise de L'Orient, 50 Curzon Street, pg. 314 **IT**
Banque Indosuez, 122 Leadenhall Street, pg. 314 **IT**
Banque Internationale a Luxembourg S.A., London Branch, Shackleton House, pg. 162 **IT**
Banque Paribas-U.K., 68 Lombard St., pg. 320 **IT**
Bantam Books Ltd., Century House, 61/63 Uxbridge Rd., Ealing, pg. 191 **IT**
Bantam Paperbacks UK, Century House, 61/63 Uxbridge Rd., Ealing, pg. 191 **IT**
Bantam Press UK, Century House, 61/63 Uxbridge Rd., Ealing, pg. 191 **IT**
Edward Barber & Co., Paxton Road, pg. 1651 **PB**
Jack Barclay Ltd., pg. 817 **IT**
BARCLAYS BANK PLC, 54 Lombard St., pg. 164 **IT**
Barclays Bank Trust Co. Ltd., 54 Lombard St., pg. 164 **IT**
Barclays Financial Services Co. Ltd., 54 Lombard St., pg. 164 **IT**
Barclays Insurance Brokers International Ltd., 54 Lombard St., pg. 164 **IT**
Barclays Insurance Services Co. Ltd., 54 Lombard St., pg. 165 **IT**
Barclays Life Assurance Co. Ltd., 54 Lombard St., pg. 165 **IT**
Barclays Property Holdings, 54 Lombard St., pg. 165 **IT**
Barclays Stockbrokers Ltd., 54 Lombard St., pg. 165 **IT**
Barclays Unicorn Ltd., Gredley House, 11 Broadway, pg. 165 **IT**
Barclays Unicorn Ltd., 54 Lombard St., pg. 165 **IT**
Baring Asset Management, 155 Bishopsgate, pg. 648 **IT**
Baring Brothers, 60 London Wall, pg. 648 **IT**
Baring, Houston & Saunders, 9 Devonshire Square, pg. 648 **IT**
Baring Venture Partners, 60 London Wall, pg. 648 **IT**

Barratt London, Warton House, 150 High St., pg. 168 **IT**
BARTLE BOGLE HEGARTY LIMITED, 660 Kingly Street, pg. 169 **IT**
Bass Holdings Ltd., 20 N. Audley St., pg. 170 **IT**
Bass Investments PLC, 20 N. Audley St., pg. 170 **IT**
BASS PLC, 20 N. Audley St., pg. 169 **IT**
Bayerische Hypotheken-und Wechsel-Bank A.G., 41 Moorgate, pg. 176 **IT**
Bayerische Landesbank - London Branch, Bavaria House, 13/14 Appold St., pg. 176 **IT**
Bayerische Vereinsbank AG-London Branch, 1, Royal Exchange Bldgs., pg. 181 **IT**
Bear, Stearns International Limited, One Canada Sq., pg. 198 **PB**
Bechtel Ltd., Bechtel House, 245 Hammersmith Rd., pg. 128 **PV**
Beeton Rumford Ltd., Exhibition Centre, Warwick Rd., pg. 1032 **IT**
Belgolaise, South Quay Plaza 2, 183 Marsh Wall, pg. 548 **IT**
Bennie Lifts Ltd., 142-170 Vauxhall St., pg. 747 **IT**
Benson & Hedges Limited, 13, Old Bond St., pg. 539 **IT**
BERG Electronics Corp., 3 Shortlands, Hammersmith International Centre, pg. 213 **PB**
Berglen Associates Limited, Masons House, pg. 1054 **PB**
Berglen Distributors Limited, Masons House, pg. 1055 **PB**
Berglen Group Limited, Eight Wimpole St., pg. 1055 **PB**
BERISFORD PLC, 1 Baker Street, pg. 188 **IT**
Berk Spencer Acids Ltd., Abbey Mill Works, Canning Rd., pg. 1113 **IT**
Berkeley Magazine Ltd., Berkeley Square House, pg. 1368 **PB**
Berlitz Schools of Languages Ltd., 9-13 Grosvenor St., pg. 222 **PB**
Bermuda International Investment Mangagement (Europe) Limited, 3rd Fl, Austin Friars House, 2-6 Austin Friars, pg. 151 **IT**
Bermuda International Securities (UK) Limited, 3rd Floor Austin Friars House, 2-6 Austin Friars, pg. 151 **IT**
Bermuda Trust (UK) Limited, 3rd Fl, Austin Friars House, 2-6 Austin Friars, pg. 151 **IT**
Bett-Technology in Educations, Greater London House, Hampstead Rd., pg. 452 **IT**
J. Bibby & Sons Plc, 16 Stratford Pl., pg. 167 **IT**
Biro BIC Ltd., Whitby Ave., pg. 1273 **IT**
BLACK & EDGINGTON LTD., 30 Marshgate Lane, pg. 197 **IT**
Blazer Plc, #8 St. John Hill, pg. 896 **IT**
BLUE CIRCLE INDUSTRIES PLC, 84 Eccleston Square, pg. 197 **IT**
The Boeing Company, 101-102 Jermyn St., pg. 242 **PB**
Boeing International Corporation, Tenterden House, 3 Tenterden St., pg. 242 **PB**
The Bombay Spirits Company, 151 Marylebone Rd., pg. 409 **IT**
Booker Agribusiness Ltd., 85 Buckingham Gate, pg. 202 **IT**
Booker Entertainment, 141 Sloane St., pg. 202 **IT**
Booker Overseas Trading, 21/24 Chiswell St., pg. 202 **IT**
BOOKER PLC, 85 Buckingham Gate, pg. 202 **IT**
Booker Tate, 37/41 Bedford Row, pg. 202 **IT**
Bookers Sugar Co., 21/24 Chiswell St., pg. 202 **IT**
Bounty Books, Michelin House, 81 Fulham Road, pg. 1093 **IT**
Bovis International Ltd., The Chambers, Chelsea Harbour, pg. 1032 **IT**
Bovis Urban Renewal Ltd., Liscartan House, 127 Sloane St., pg. 1032 **IT**
Box Hill Systems Europe Ltd., Suite 2, 97 Onslow Square, pg. 249 **PB**
Bradstock Blunt & Crawley (Aviation) Ltd, 90 Fenchurch St., pg. 210 **IT**
Bradstock Blunt & Crawley Ltd., 90 Fenchurch St., pg. 210 **IT**
Bradstock Blunt & Thompson, Lloyds Brokers, Bradstock, House, pg. 210 **IT**
Bradstock Blunt (Plastics) Ltd., 52/53 Russell Square, pg. 210 **IT**
Bradstock Financial Services Ltd., 52/53 Russell Square, pg. 210 **IT**
BRADSTOCK GROUP PLC, 18 London St., pg. 210 **IT**
Brandeis Brokers Ltd., 4 Fore St., pg. 1030 **IT**
Brandeis Ltd., 4 Fore St., pg. 1030 **IT**
Brasoil U.K. Ltd., 197, Knightsbridge 1st Fl., pg. 1042 **IT**
Brent Leisure Limited, Units 1 & 2, Brent Crescent Rd., pg. 905 **IT**
Bridgewater Paper Limited, 195 Knightsbridge, pg. 20 **IT**
Brierley & Partners, 45 Berkeley Street, pg. 168 **PV**
Brierley Investments Ltd., 3rd Floor, 10 Eastcheap, pg. 215 **IT**
British Airways Cargo, P.O. Box 99, World Cargo Centre S-126, pg. 219 **IT**
British Airways Holidays Ltd., Speedbird House, pg. 219 **IT**
BRITISH AIRWAYS PLC, Speedbird House, Hounslow, Heathrow Airport, pg. 218 **IT**
British American Offshore Limited, 79 Park St., pg. 1410 **PB**
British Arab Commercial Bank Ltd., 30 Gresham Street, pg. 579 **IT**
British European Associated Publishers Ltd., Glenthorne House, Hammersmith Grove, pg. 1445 **IT**
BRITISH FILM INSTITUTE, 21 Stephen St., pg. 219 **IT**
THE BRITISH LAND COMPANY PLC, 10 Cornwall Terrace, pg. 219 **IT**
The British Land Corporation Limited, 10 Cornwall Terrace, pg. 219 **IT**
THE BRITISH PETROLEUM COMPANY P.L.C., Britannic House, 1 Finsbury Circus, pg. 219 **IT**
BRITISH PRINTING COMPANY LTD., 7/10 Scando Street, pg. 220 **IT**

BRITISH RAILWAYS BOARD, Euston House, 24 Eversholt St., pg. 220 **IT**
British Steel General Steels Division, 9 Albert Embankment, pg. 220 **IT**
BRITISH STEEL PLC, 9 Albert Embankment, pg. 220 **IT**
BRITISH TELECOMMUNICATIONS PLC, BT Centre, 81 Newgate St., pg. 222 **IT**
Broadcasting Dataservices Ltd., Network House, Ariel Way, pg. 114 **IT**
Brother Finance (U.K.) plc, 4th Floor, N. Suite, Warworth House, pg. 229 **IT**
Brown & Root Energy Services, 150 The Broadway, pg. 775 **PB**
Brown & Root Limited, Brown & Root House, 150 Broadway, pg. 775 **PB**
Brown Brothers Harriman Limited, Veritas House, 125 Finsbury Pavement, pg. 173 **PV**
John Brown - Engineering & Construction Sector, 20 Eastbourne Terrace, pg. 772 **IT**
Bulkitalia (U.K.) Ltd., 144/146, New Bond St., pg. 304 **IT**
BUNZL PLC, 110 Park St., pg. 232 **IT**
Leo Burnett Limited, The Leo Burnett Building, 60 Sloane Ave., pg. 185 **PV**
THE BURTON GROUP PLC, 214 Oxford St., pg. 237 **IT**
Bush Boake Allen Ltd., Blackhorse Lane, pg. 1666 **PB**
Business Computing Show (JV with Montbuild Ltd.), Greater London House, Hampstead Rd., pg. 452 **IT**
Business Magazine, 234 King's Rd., pg. 1025 **IT**
BUTLER LUTOS SUTTON WILKINSON, William Blake House, 8 Marshall St., pg. 237 **IT**
Butler's (Grinders & Operators) Ltd., Shad Thames, pg. 1033 **IT**
BUTTERFIELD DAY DEVITO HOCKNEY LTD., 47 Marylebone Ln., pg. 237 **IT**
Butterworth & Co. Publishers Ltd., Halsbury House, 35 Chancery Lane, pg. 1095 **IT**
Butterworths British and Irish Legal, Halsbury House, 35 Chancery Lane, pg. 1095 **IT**
C. Cakebread, Unit 3, Elizabeth Industrial Estate, pg. 460 **IT**
C-E International, P.O. Box 196 12 Norwich St., pg. 5 **IT**
CACI N.V., Kensington Village, Avemore Road, pg. 272 **PB**
CBS Broadcast Services Ltd., Bowater House-2nd Fl., pg. 275 **PB**
CBS Pension Trustees U.K. Limited, Mitre House, 160 Aldersgate St., pg. 275 **PB**
CCF Foster-Braithwaite, 3 London Wall Bldgs., pg. 342 **IT**
CCF London, Peninsular House, 8th Fl., 36 Monument Street, pg. 342 **IT**
CCL Ltd., 220 Tottenham Court Rd., pg. 1034 **IT**
CCM Framlington Group Plc, 155 Bishopgate, pg. 342 **IT**
CDP, 33-34 Soho Sq., pg. 239 **IT**
CDP & Partners Ltd., Aquila House 33-34, Soho Square, pg. 393 **IT**
The CDP Media Co. Ltd., Aquila House 33-34, Soho Square, pg. 393 **IT**
C.I. Property & Investments Limited, 8 King St., pg. 290 **IT**
CIBC Contractors UK Limited, Cottons Centre, Cottons Lane, pg. 257 **IT**
CIBC Finance plc, Cottons Centre, Cottons Lane, pg. 257 **IT**
CIBC Investment Management Limited, Cottons Centre, Cottons Lane, pg. 257 **IT**
CIBC Limited, 55 Bishopsgate, pg. 257 **IT**
CIBC Mortgages plc, Cottons Centre, Cottons Lane, pg. 257 **IT**
CIBC Securities Europe Limited, Cottons Centre, Cottons Lane, pg. 257 **IT**
CIBC Unit Trust Managers plc, Cottons Centre, Cottons Lane, pg. 257 **IT**
CIBC (U.K.) Holdings Limited, Cottons Centre, Cottons Lane, pg. 257 **IT**
CLT UK Radio, 74, Newman Street, pg. 561 **IT**
CME KHBB, 82 Charing Cross Rd., pg. 241 **IT**
C.M.I. Defence Systems Ltd., pg. 302 **IT**
COMSIP Ltd., 90-100 Sydney St., pg. 53 **IT**
CTel Corporation (Europe), Africa House 5th Floor, pg. 643 **IT**
C.W.A. Holdings Ltd., pg. 1434 **IT**
Cable & Wireless Communications plc, 124 Theobolds Rd., pg. 247 **IT**
CABLE AND WIRELESS PLC, 124 Theobalds Rd., pg. 247 **IT**
CADBURY SCHWEPPES P.L.C., 25 Berkeley Square, pg. 247 **IT**
Canada Maritime Limited, 105 Victoria St., pg. 259 **IT**
Canberra Cruises Limited, 77 New Oxford St., pg. 1033 **IT**
CANNON RUBBER LTD., Ashley Rd., pg. 261 **IT**
CAPARO GROUP LTD., 103 Baker St., pg. 264 **IT**
Capital House Investment Management Limited, 24 Chiswell St., pg. 1132 **IT**
Cariplo London, 6 Lombard St., pg. 275 **IT**
CARLTON COMMUNICATIONS PLC, 25 Knightsbridge, pg. 272 **IT**
Carlton Film Distributors, 127-133 Wardour St., pg. 272 **IT**
Carnegie International Limited, Gate House 1, Farrington St., pg. 272 **IT**
Carot Insight, 8-10 Drydon St., pg. 1342 **IT**
W.I. Carr, 122 Leadenhall Street, pg. 314 **IT**
Casio Electronics Co., Ltd., Unit 6, 1000 North Circular Rd., pg. 274 **IT**
Castell Safety International Limited, Kingsbury Works, Kingsbury Rd., pg. 589 **IT**
Catamaran Cruisers Ltd./Bateaux London, Charing Cross Pier, Victoria Embankment, pg. 1274 **IT**
Central Japan Railway Company-London Office, Bow Bells House, Bread St., pg. 279 **IT**
Centre Reinsurance Representative Limited, The Zurich Building, 90 Fenchurch St., pg. 1530 **IT**

Century Employers Life Assurance Company Limited, Century House, 50 Bailey, pg. 685 IT
Century Life, Century House, 50 Bailey, pg. 685 IT
Century Life Insurance Limited, Century House, 50 Bailey, pg. 685 IT
Century Pensions Limited, Century House, 50 Bailey, pg. 685 IT
Charlwood Alliance Holdings Ltd., 220 Tottenham Court Rd., pg. 1034 IT
Charter Clinic Nightingale, 11-19 Lisson Grove, pg. 1036 PB
Charter Medical of England Ltd., 111 Kings Rd., pg. 1036 PB
CHARTER PLC, 7 Hobart Place, pg. 280 IT
Charterhouse Bank Ltd., 1 Paternoster Row, pg. 342 IT
Chartwell Advisers Limited, Fountain House, 130 Fenchurch St., pg. 337 PB
Chartwell Holdings Limited, c/o Archer Group Holdings plc, Two Minister Court, pg. 337 IT
Chartwell Land Plc., 66 Chiltern St., pg. 733 IT
Chase Futures & Options, Inc., John Adams St., pg. 341 PB
Chase Investment Bank Holdings Limited, Woolgate House, Coleman St., pg. 339 PB
Chase Investment Bank Limited, Woolgate House, Coleman St., pg. 339 PB
Chase Leasing Limited, Three Shortlands, pg. 339 PB
The Chase Manhattan Bank, N.A., 125 London Wall, pg. 339 PB
Chase Manhattan Capital Markets (U.K.) Ltd., Woolgate House, Coleman St., pg. 339 PB
Chase Manhattan Equities Limited, Woolgate House, Coleman St., pg. 339 PB
Chase Manhattan Futures (U.K.), Woolgate House, Coleman St., pg. 339 PB
Chase Manhattan Gilts Ltd., Woolgate House, Coleman St., pg. 339 PB
Chase Manhattan Milbank, Ltd., Woolgate House, Coleman St., pg. 339 PB
Chase Manhattan Trustees, Ltd,, Woolgate House, Coleman St., pg. 339 PB
Chase Netting (U.K.) Ltd., Chemical Bank House, 180 Strand, pg. 341 PB
Chase Trade Finance, Ltd., Woolgate House, Coleman St., pg. 339 PB
Chelsea Harbour Ltd., 4 Carlton Gardens, pg. 1034 IT
ChemBank Depository Nominees, Ltd., Chemical Bank House, 180 Strand, pg. 341 PB
Chembank Nominees Limited, Chemical Bank Bldg., 180 Strand, pg. 341 PB
Chemco Equipment Finance Limited, Chemical Bank House, 180 Strand, pg. 341 PB
Chemical Bank Pension Plan Trustee, Ltd., Chemical Bank House, 180 Strand, pg. 341 PB
Chemical Securities Limited, Chemical Bank, 180 Strand, pg. 341 PB
Chesebrough-Pond's Ltd., Victoria Rd., pg. 1436 IT
Chevron (U.K.) Ltd., Two Portman St., pg. 348 IT
Chiba Bank, Ltd.-London Branch, 1 King St., pg. 283 IT
Chiba International Ltd., 1 King St., pg. 283 IT
Chichibu Onoda Cement Corporation-United Kingdom, 3rd Floor, Bow Bells House, Bread Street, pg. 284 IT
Chieftain Exploration (U.K.) Ltd., Blackfriars House, 19 New Bridge House, pg. 284 IT
Chieftain International North Sea Limited, Royex House, Aldermanbury Square, pg. 284 IT
Chile Copper Ltd., York House, 23 Kingsway, pg. 303 IT
Chiyoda Life Europe Limited, Swed Bank House, 1st Fl., 42 New Broad Street, pg. 287 IT
CHLORIDE GROUP PLC, 15 Wilton Rd., pg. 287 IT
Chloride Group plc, pg. 287 IT
Cho Hung Bank, London Branch, 1 Minster Ct., pg. 288 IT
Christian Lacroix U.K., 45-49 Mortimer St., pg. 782 IT
Christiania Bank-London Branch, Lloyds Chambers, 6th Fl., One Portsoken Street, pg. 289 IT
Christie, Manson & Woods Limited, 8 King St., pg. 290 IT
CHRISTIES INTERNATIONAL PLC, 8 King St., pg. 289 IT
Christie's South Kensington Limited, 85 Old Brompton Rd., pg. 290 IT
Chubu Electric Power Co., Inc. (London Office), Nightingale House, 65 Curzon Street, pg. 290 IT
Chugai Pharma Europe Ltd., Flanders Rd., Turnham Green, pg. 291 IT
Chugai Pharma U.K. Ltd., Mulliner House, Flanders Rd., Turnham Green, pg. 291 IT
Chuo Trust International Limited, Triton Court, 14 Finsbury Square, pg. 291 IT
CIBA-GEIGY Scientific Publications, 100 Wigmore St., pg. 979 IT
Cigna G.B. Holdings, Ltd., 8-11 Lime Street, pg. 363 PB
Cigna International Investment Advisors, Ltd., ENDK House, 16 Finsbury Circus, pg. 357 PB
Cigna Reinsurance Company (U.K.) Limited, CIGNA House, 8 Lime St., pg. 363 PB
Cigna Services U.K. Limited, Cigna House, 8 Lime St., pg. 363 PB
Cinco, Salisbury House, 2nd Floor, Room 480, pg. 716 IT
The Cirio Co. Ltd., Section D, Plantation House, 31-35 Fenchurch St., 6th Fl., pg. 655 IT
CitiBank Savings, St. Martin's House, Hammersmith Grove, pg. 378 PB
Citicorp Insurance Group, St. Clare House, 30-33 Minories, pg. 378 PB
Citicorp International Bank Ltd., 335 Strand, pg. 378 PB
CitiCorp Investment Bank Ltd., Cottons Center Hays Lane, pg. 379 PB
CitiCorp Scrimgeour Vickers, Cottons Center Hays Lane, pg. 379 PB

CitiCorp Venture Capital Ltd., Cottons Center Hays Lane, pg. 379 PB
The City of London Real Property Company Limited, 5 Strand, pg. 798 IT
Clarins (UK) Ltd., 4 Queen St., pg. 295 IT
Classic Papers Ltd., Greenwich Industrial Estate, Woolrich Road, pg. 864 IT
Clinical Research Center, Europe, 2nd Floor, Albany House, 180 Albany Street, pg. 525 IT
Club Mediterranee U.K. Ltd., 106-108, Brompton Road, pg. 298 IT
Clyde Petroleum - London, Buchanan House, 3 St. James' Square, pg. 578 IT
Coastal States Petroleum (U.K.) Limited, 34 Grosvenor St., pg. 391 PB
Coca-Cola Great Britain & Ireland, #1 Queen Caroline St., pg. 392 PB
A. COHEN & CO. P.L.C., Clareville House, pg. 306 IT
Colbourne Insurance Co. Ltd., 60 Fenchurch St., pg. 391 PB
C.J. COLEMAN HOLDINGS LTD., Port Soken House, 155 Minories, pg. 306 IT
Coley Porter Bell, 11A W. Halkin St., pg. 1482 IT
Columbia Pictures International Television, 19/23 Wells St., pg. 1282 IT
Columbia Tri-Star Films (UK), 25 Golden Square, pg. 1281 IT
Comalco (UK) Limited, 20 Regent St., pg. 307 IT
Commerce International Trust Limited, Cottons Centre, Cottons Lane, pg. 257 IT
Commercial and Political Risk Consultants, Lloyds Chambers, 1, Portsoken St., pg. 671 IT
COMMERCIAL UNION PLC, St. Helen's 1 Undershaft, pg. 308 IT
Commerz Asset Management (UK) plc, pg. 311 IT
Commerzbank AG London Branch, Commerzbank House, 23 Austin Friars, pg. 311 IT
Commonwealth Bank of Australia, Senator House, 85 Queen Victoria St., pg. 313 IT
Community Psychiatric Centers of London (Unlimited), Priory Lane, Roehampton, pg. 1716 PB
Compass Group-UK Division, Queen's Wharf, Queen Caroline Street, pg. 324 IT
Comshare Ltd., 22 Chelsea Manor St., pg. 425 IT
Comtext International, Bishopsgate Court, 4 Norton Folgate, pg. 335 IT
Con-Carriers Ltd., 40A Victoria Way, pg. 373 IT
Concert Communications Company, BT Centre, 81 Newgate Street, pg. 223 IT
Conoco (UK) Ltd., Park House, 116 Park St., W1Y 4NN, pg. 531 PB
Conran Octopus Limited, 37 Shelton Street, pg. 1093 IT
Conso Group, London Showroom, 1/3 Chelsea Harbour Design Centre, pg. 434 IT
Continental Insurance Co. (U.K.) Limited, 77 Gracechurch St., pg. 1011 PB
E.J. Cook SCD Partnership, Spur House, Morden Rd., pg. 336 IT
COOKSON GROUP PLC, 130 Wood St., pg. 328 IT
Corgi Books Ltd., Century House, 61/63 Uxbridge Rd., Ealing, pg. 191 IT
Cornhill Insurance Plc, 32 Cornhill, pg. 60 IT
Corporate Computers Plc, pg. 757 IT
Cosmo Securities (Europe) Limited, Garden House, 18 Finsbury Circus, pg. 335 IT
Costain Engineering & Construction Limited, 111 Westminster Bridge Rd., pg. 336 IT
COSTAIN GROUP PLC, 111 Westminster Bridge Rd., pg. 336 IT
Cott Europe (London), 5 Princes Gate, pg. 338 IT
Country 103.5, 7, Hurlingham, pg. 561 IT
County & District Properties Limited, 46 Green St., pg. 337 IT
County NatWest Limited, 135 Bishpsgate, pg. 910 IT
Courtaulds Coatings Ltd., 50 George Street, pg. 338 IT
Courtaulds Nippon Paint Limited, pg. 937 IT
COURTAULDS PLC, 50 George St., pg. 338 IT
COURTAULDS TEXTILES PLC, 13/14 Margaret Street, pg. 339 IT
Coutts & Co., 7th Floor, Princess House, 27 Bush Lane, pg. 910 IT
Crawford & Company International, Inc., 12th Fl., One Minster St., pg. 458 PB
Credit Agricole (CNCA) London, 135 Fleet St., pg. 341 IT
Credit Lyonnais Capital Markets plc, Broadwalk House, 5 Appold St., pg. 344 IT
Credit Lyonnais United Kingdom, Broadwalk House, 5 Appold Street, pg. 344 IT
Credit Suisse Financial Products, pg. 345 IT
Credit Suisse Financial Products, One Cabot Square, pg. 1333 IT
Creditanstalt Export Finance Ltd., pg. 348 IT
Culverdale Investments Limited, pg. 703 IT
Cunard Line Ltd., 30-35 Pall Mall, pg. 773 IT
The Cunard Steam-Ship Company p.l.c., 30-35 Pall Mall, pg. 772 IT
DB U.K. Finance p.l.c., 6, Bishopgate, pg. 404 IT
DBC Europe, 37/39 Lime St., pg. 485 IT
DBS Securities UK Ltd., 7th Floor, Finsbury Circus House, pg. 351 IT
DCD (U.K.) Container Services Ltd., pg. 596 IT
DG Bank-London Branch, 10 Aldersgate St., pg. 352 IT
DKB Financial Products (UK) Limited, DKB House, 24 King William Street, pg. 361 IT
DKB International Public Limited Company, DKB House, 24 King William Street, pg. 361 IT
DKB Investment Management International Limited, DKB House, 24 King William Street, pg. 362 IT
DMB&B/London, 123 Buckingham Palace Rd., pg. 304 PV
DMG Exhibition Group Ltd., Northcliffe House, 2 Derry Street, pg. 366 IT

DRI Europe (U.K.) Ltd., Wimbledon Bridge House, Hartfield Road, pg. 1072 PB
DSM Energy (U.K.) Ltd., 150 Brompton Road, pg. 354 IT
Daewoo Securities (Europe) Ltd., 4th Fl., City Keys, 110 Middlesex St., pg. 359 IT
Dai-Ichi Kangyo Bank, Ltd.-London, DKB House, 24 King William Street, pg. 360 IT
Dai-ichi Life Insurance Agency Europe Limited, Level 4, 155 Bishopsgate, pg. 362 IT
Dai-ichi Life International (U.K.) Limited, Level 4, 155 Bishopsgate, pg. 362 IT
Dai-ichi Life Property (London) Limited, Level 4, 155 Bishopsgate, pg. 363 IT
Dai Nippon Printing Co. (UK) Ltd., 2nd Fl., 15 Berkeley Street, pg. 363 IT
Daido Life Europe Ltd., 82/86 Fenchurch St., pg. 364 IT
Daihatsu Diesel (Europe) Ltd., 6th Fl. Peninsular House, pg. 364 IT
DAILY MAIL & GENERAL TRUST PLC, Northcliffe House, 2 Derry St., pg. 366 IT
Daiwa Asset Managements (Europe) Ltd., 4F, Condor House, 14 St. Paul's Churchyard, pg. 374 IT
Daiwa Bank (Capital Management) Ltd., 6th Fl., 4 Broadgate, pg. 373 IT
Daiwa Bank-London, Fifth Fl., 4 Broadgate, pg. 373 IT
Daiwa Europe Bank plc, Condor House, 14 St. Paul's Churchyard, pg. 375 IT
Daiwa Europe (Gilts) Limited, 5 King William Street, pg. 375 IT
Daiwa Europe Limited, 5 King William St., pg. 375 IT
Daiwa Institute of Research Europe Ltd., 5F, 5 King William Street, pg. 375 IT
Daiwa International Capital Management (U.K.) Limied, Condor House, 14 St. Paul's Churchyard, pg. 375 IT
Dalgety Food Ingredients Ltd., 14 Clifford Street, pg. 376 IT
DALGETY PLC, 100 George St., pg. 376 IT
Dalgety Spillers Foods Ltd., 100 George Street, pg. 376 IT
DANKA BUSINESS SYSTEMS PLC, Masters House, pg. 379 IT
Datapoint (U.K.) Ltd., Datapoint House 400 N. Circular Rd., pg. 384 IT
Datastream International Ltd., Monmouth House, 58-64 City Road, pg. 1325 IT
THE DAVIS SERVICE GROUP PLC., 4 Grosvenor Place, pg. 385 IT
De Beers Central Selling Organization, 17 Charter House St., pg. 77 IT
DE LA RUE PLC, 6 Agar St., pg. 386 IT
Deborah Services, Riverside Rd., pg. 1285 IT
Decca International, 50 New Bond St., pg. 1053 IT
The Decca Record Co. Ltd., 50 New Bond St., pg. 1053 IT
Deeko Plc., 2-30 Garman Rd., Tottenham, pg. 672 PB
DELTA PLC, One Kingsway, pg. 389 IT
Deltair U.K. Investments Ltd., Beaufort House, 15 Botolph St., pg. 497 PB
Deminex UK Oil and Gas Limited, 68 Knightsbridge, pg. 1461 IT
Den norske Bank AS, London Branch, 20 St. Dunstans Hill, pg. 392 IT
Dentsu Europe Ltd.-London, Berger House, 1 Floor, 36-38 Berkeley Square, pg. 393 IT
Derwent Publications Ltd., Rochdale House, 128 Theobald's Rd., pg. 1601 PB
Desoutter Brothers (Holdings) plc, 319 Edgware Road, pg. 96 IT
Det Norske Veritas, Palace House, 3 Cathedral Str., pg. 397 IT
Deutsche Bank AG (London), 6, Bishopsgate, pg. 404 IT
Devimco Ltd., 1, Shortlands, pg. 21 IT
DEWE ROGERSON LIMITED, 3-1/2 London Wall Bldgs., London Wall, pg. 408 IT
DIAGEO PLC, 8 Henrietta Place, pg. 408 IT
THE DIALOG CORPORATION PLC, The Communications Bldg., 48 Leicester Square, pg. 412 IT
The Walt Disney Company Ltd., 31 Soho Square, pg. 514 PB
Dixie Benders Limited, River Park House, 225 High Rd., pg. 672 PB
Dixons Finance Plc, 29 Farm St., pg. 414 IT
Dolland & Aitchison - South East (London) Ltd., Draper House, 17 Elephant & Castle, pg. 414 IT
The Dominic Group Ltd., Brewery, Chiswell St., pg. 1499 IT
Dominion Insurance Ltd., 52-54, Leadenhall St., pg. 784 IT
DOMINO, Middlesex House, 34-42 Cleveland St., pg. 415 IT
R.R. Donnelley Pindar, Donnelley House, 25 Worship St., pg. 519 PB
DORLING KINDERSLEY HOLDINGS PLC, 9 Henrietta Street, pg. 416 IT
Dorling Kindersley Ltd., 9 Henrietta St., pg. 417 IT
The Dovercourt Motor Co. Ltd., pg. 817 IT
Dow Jones International Marketing Services (U.K.) Ltd., London Intl. Press Centre, pg. 525 PB
Dow Jones Markets Limited, Winchmore House, 12-15 Fetter Lane, pg. 525 PB
Dow Jones Markets Technical Services Limited, AP House, 12 Norwich St., pg. 525 PB
Draycott Partners, Ltd., 12-14 Masons Ave., pg. 738 PV
Dresdner Bank AG, 125 Wood St., pg. 419 IT
Alfred Dunhill Cognac S.A., 8 Henrietta Place, pg. 409 IT
Dunhill Scotch Whisky Sales Limited, 8 Henrietta Place, pg. 409 IT
Dunlop Holdings plc, Silvertown House, pg. 124 IT
E-Z-EM Ltd., 1230 High Rd., pg. 540 PB
EBC AMRO Bank Ltd., 10 Devonshire Square, pg. 10 IT
EIS GROUP PLC, 6 Sloane Sq., pg. 426 IT

EMAP Images, Priory Court, 30-32 Farrington Court, pg. 451
EMAP Metro, Mappin House, 4 Winsley St., pg. 451 IT
EMI GROUP PLC, 4 Tenterden St., pg. 426 IT
EMI Music, 30 Gloucester Pl., pg. 427 IT
EMI Music Publishing, 127 Charing Cross Rd., pg. 427 IT
EMI Records (UK), EMI House, 20 Manchester Sq., pg. 427 IT
EMI Records (UK), Studios Div., 3 Abbey Rd., pg. 427 IT
Eagle Star, 60 St. Mary Axe, pg. 110 IT
Eagle Star Insurance Co., 60 St. Mary Axe, pg. 110 IT
Earl's Court & Olympia Ltd., Exhibition Centre, Warwick Rd., pg. 1033 IT
Eastman Kodak Company-European Region, 245 Hammersmith Rd., pg. 551 PB
The Economist Group Limited., 25, St. James's St., pg. 1026 IT
Daniel J. Edelman Ltd., Haymarket House, 28-29 Haymarket, pg. 363 PV
Edison Mission Energy Limited, Lansdowne House, Berkeley Square, pg. 564 PB
The Education Show, Greater London House, Hampstead Rd., pg. 452 IT
EIB London Branch, 68 Pall Mall, pg. 465 IT
Eisai Europe Ltd., Trafalgar House, Hammersmith Intl. Office Center, pg. 435 IT
Elf Petroleum U.K., 197 Knightsbridge, pg. 446 IT
Elite Information Systems, Inc., 100 Fetter Ln., 4th Fl., pg. 258 PB
B. ELLIOTT PLC., Elliott House, Victoria Rd., pg. 448 IT
EMAP Architecture Ltd., 33-39 Bowling Green Lne., pg. 451 IT
EMAP Business Communications Division, Meed House, 21 John St., pg. 451 IT
EMAP Business Information/EMAP Heighway, Meed House, 21 John St., pg. 451 IT
EMAP Business International Ltd., Meed House, 21 John St., pg. 451 IT
EMAP Computing Ltd., Greater London House, Hampstead Rd., pg. 451 IT
EMAP Consumer Magazines, Mappin House, 4 Winsley Street, pg. 451 IT
EMAP Elan, Victory House, Leicester Pl., pg. 451 IT
EMAP Fashion Ltd., 67 Clerkenwell Rd., pg. 451 IT
EMAP Finance & Freight Ltd., 33-39 Bowling Green Lane, pg. 451 IT
EMAP Media, 33-39 Bowling Green Lane, pg. 451 IT
EMAP Media Ltd., 33-39 Bowling Green La., pg. 451 IT
EMAP Radio, Scriptor Court, 155 Farringdon Rd., pg. 451 IT
Emerson Electric U.K. Ltd., 39 Portman Square, pg. 576 PB
EMESS PLC, 20 St. James's St., pg. 453 IT
Endecotts Ltd., Lombard Rd., pg. 488 IT
Energizer Eveready U.K., Ever Ready House, 93 Burleigh Gardens, pg. 1360 PB
Engelhard Metals Ltd., Engelhard House, pg. 582 PB
Enserch Exploration (UK) Ltd., Enserch House, 8 St. James's Square, pg. 1587 PB
Enskilda Ventures Limited, Scandinavian House, 2-6 Cannon Street, pg. 1259 IT
Entores Ltd., City Wall House 79-83 Chiswell St., pg. 661 IT
Equifax Europe, 1-6 Clay St., pg. 588 PB
Equiscot Limited, 39 Portman Square, pg. 412 IT
Ericsson Network Engineering Ltd., World Trade Center, Europe House, pg. 1367 IT
Ernest Linsdell Limited, CIGNA House, 8 Lime St., pg. 363 PB
Erste Bank - London Branch, 68 Cornhill, pg. 459 IT
Esselte Europe, 4 Buckingham Gate, pg. 460 IT
Esso Exploration and Production UK Limited, Esso House, 96 Victoria Street, pg. 602 PB
Esso Petroleum Company, Limited, Esso House, 94-98 Victoria Street, pg. 602 PB
Esso UK plc, Esso House, Victoria St., pg. 602 PB
EURO RSCG Healthcare, 69 Monmouth St., pg. 603 IT
EURO RSCG Wnek Gosper, 11 Great Newport St., pg. 603 IT
Euromarketing, Cowcross Ct., pg. 285 PV
European Brazilian Bank Ltd., Bucklersbury House, 11 Walbrook, pg. 183 PB
European Magazines Limited, 2 Hatfields, pg. 651 IT
European Rubber Journal, Cowcross Ct., pg. 285 PV
Eurotunnel Finance Limited, One Canada Square, Canary Wharf, pg. 466 IT
THE EUROTUNNEL GROUP, One Canada Square, Canary Wharf, pg. 466 IT
Eurotunnel Services Limited, One Canada Square, Canary Wharf, pg. 466 IT
Everest Reinsurance, Ltd., 40 Lime Street, pg. 597 PB
EXPAMET INTERNATIONAL PLC., Clifton House, 83/89 Uxbridge Rd., pg. 467 IT
Expopesca, Meed House, 21 John St., pg. 452 IT
The Export-Import Bank of Korea, Unit 13H, Plantation House, 31-35 Fenchurch St., pg. 468 IT
Express Newspapers plc, Ludgate House, 245 Blackfriars Rd., pg. 1443 IT
Exquisite Form Brassiere (GB) Ltd., 30 Market Place, Oxford Circus, pg. 14 IT
Extel, Fitzroy House, 13-17 Epworth St., pg. 1025 IT
FCA!, 112 Dorset Street, pg. 470 IT
F.E.P. U.K. Limited, Hill House, 1 Little Newstreet, pg. 795 IT
FSSL Ltd., Monarch House, Victoria Rd., pg. 772 IT
FT Information, Fitzroy House, 13-17 Epworth Street, pg. 1025 IT
Fairways and Swinford (Travel) Ltd., Sea Containers House, 20 Upper Ground, pg. 1214 IT
Fairways & Swinford Travel Ltd., 37 Abbey Rd., St. Johns Wood, pg. 1213 IT

Falmer Press Ltd., 1 Gunpowder Square, pg. 1358 IT
Federal Products U.K. Ltd., Unit One, The Hertfordshire Business Centre, pg. 594 PB
Fergusson, Wild & Co. Ltd., Three St. Helen's Pl., pg. 1458 IT
Ferraris Piston Services Ltd., 12 Great Eastern Road E15, pg. 1395 IT
Fiat Auto (UK) Ltd., Berkeley Square House, pg. 483 IT
Fiduciary Trust International Limited, 30 Old Burlington Street, pg. 621 PB
Financial Collection Agencies (UK) Limited, 5th Floor, Solent House, pg. 471 IT
Financial Dynamics Ltd., 30 Furnival St., pg. 117 IT
Financial Security Assurance (U.K.) Limited, One Angel Court, pg. 623 PB
The Financial Times Ltd., 1 Southwark Bridge, pg. 1025 IT
Financial Training Company, DeBramley Rd., pg. 1514 IT
FINCO-London, 3 Cloth St., pg. 654 IT
Finmare-UK, Italian General Shipping, St. Clare House 28-35 Minories, pg. 655 IT
First Chicago Limited, 90 Long Acre, pg. 628 PB
First Marathon (U.K.) Limited, 7 Old Park Lane, pg. 487 IT
Fishing UK, Meed House, 21 John St., pg. 452 IT
Fleet PR Ltd., Three Grosvenor Gardens, pg. 1227 IT
Fleetfoot Ltd., 52 High Holburn, pg. 1035 IT
Fleishman-Hillard Europe, 25 Wellington St., pg. 411 PV
Fleishman-Hillard U.K. Limited, Covent Garden, 25 Wellington St., pg. 411 PV
Fleming Asset Management Limited, 25 Copthall Ave., pg. 493 IT
Fleming International Fixed Interest Management Limited, 25 Copthall Ave., pg. 493 IT
Fleming Investment Trust Management Limited, 25 Copthall Ave., pg. 493 IT
Fleming Investments Limited, 25 Copthall Ave., pg. 493 IT
Fleming Martin Limited, 25 Copthall Avenue, pg. 493 IT
Fleming Private Asset Management Limited, 20 Finsbury St., pg. 493 IT
Robert Fleming & Co. Limited, 25 Copthall Ave., pg. 493 IT
Robert Fleming Asset Management Limited, 25 Copthall Ave., pg. 493 IT
ROBERT FLEMING HOLDINGS LTD., 25 Copthall Ave., pg. 493 IT
Robert Fleming Insurance Brokers Limited, Staple Hall, Stone House Court, pg. 493 IT
Robert Fleming Management Services Limited, 25 Copthall Ave., pg. 493 IT
Robert Fleming Securities Limited, 25 Copthall Ave., pg. 493 IT
Robert Fleming (Stock Lending) Limited, 25 Copthall Ave., pg. 493 IT
FLEXTECH P.L.C., Tyman House, 16 Bonny St., pg. 495 IT
Florisloane Ltd., 15 Sloane Street, pg. 782 IT
Fluidised Combustion Contractors Ltd., 165 Great Dover St., pg. 472 IT
For Eyes plc, R/13m Aldgate Bars Sedgwick Centre, pg. 414 IT
Ford Personal Import Export Ltd., 8 Balderton St., pg. 666 PB
Forte Hotels (UK) Limited, 166 High Holborn, pg. 556 IT
FORTNUM & MASON PLC, 181 Piccadilly, pg. 500 IT
Forum Europe plc, Orion House, 5 Upper St. Martin's Ln., pg. 420 PV
Forward Trust Group Limited, 145 City Road, pg. 579 IT
Fosroc Expandite Ltd., Chase Rd., pg. 234 IT
Foster Wheeler Petroleum Development Corp., Ltd. (England), Greater London House, P.O. Box 160, pg. 677 PB
Foster's Finance European Region, Greenly House, 40 Duke's Place, pg. 500 IT
Fotolab Limited, 13 Cheval Pl., pg. 1389 IT
FoxVideo Limited, 20th Century House, 31-32 Soho Square, pg. 926 IT
Lynne Franks Ltd., 327-329 Harrow Rd., pg. 117 IT
Fred Perry Sportswear Ltd., Bridport Rd., pg. 620 IT
French Railways Ltd., pg. 1165 IT
Frontel Communications Services, Kampton Point, 68 Staines Rd. W., pg. 684 PB
Fruit of the Loom Limited, 17 Exeter St., pg. 686 PB
Fuji Capital Markets (U.K.) Limited, River Plate House, 7-11 Finsbury Circus, pg. 521 IT
Fuji Electric (U.K.) Ltd., 40 George St., pg. 522 IT
Fuji International Finance PLC, River Plate House, 7-11 Finsbury Circus, pg. 521 IT
Fuji Investment Management Company (Europe) Limited, River Plate House, 7-11, Finsbury Circus, pg. 521 IT
Fuji Leasing (UK) Limited, River Plate House, 7-11 Finsbury Circus, pg. 521 IT
Fuji Photo Film (U.K.), Ltd., 125 Finchley Road, pg. 525 IT
Fujisawa Ltd., 2nd Floor, Albany House, 180 Albany Street, pg. 524 IT
FULLER, SMITH & TURNER PLC, Griffin Brewery, Chiswick Lane South, pg. 529 IT
Furukawa Electric Co., Ltd. London, 3rd Floor, 56 Queen's Gate, pg. 531 IT
Furukawa Research & Engineering Europe Ltd., 2nd Floor, 56 Queen's Gate, pg. 531 IT
GDRU, Ltd., 6 Newcomen St., pg. 733 PB
G.E. Lighting Europe, 3 Shortlands, pg. 713 PB
GEC Estates Department, Kemble House, Kemble St., pg. 543 IT
GEC-General Signal Ltd., pg. 727 PB
GGK International's Executive Board, 76 Dean St., pg. 1335 IT
GGK London Ltd., 76 Dean St., pg. 1335 IT

GGT ADVERTISING LTD., 82 Dean St., pg. 532 IT
GGT DIRECT ADVERTISING, 82 Dean Street, pg. 532 IT
GPC Connect (London), Burwood House, 14 Caxton St., pg. 1225 PB
GPT Holdings Ltd., 1 Stanhage Gale, pg. 1248 IT
G.T. Global Fund Management Ltd., 14th Floor, Alban Gate, 125 London Wall, pg. 809 IT
Gable House Estates Ltd., Ten Cavandish Pl., pg. 787 IT
Gan Insurance Company Limited, Gan House, 12 Arthur Street, pg. 565 IT
Gan UK plc, Gan House, 12 Arthur St., pg. 565 IT
Ganton House Investments Limited, Chancel House, Neasden Ln., pg. 787 IT
GEERS GROSS ADVERTISING LIMITED, 110 St. Martins Lane, pg. 542 IT
Gefinor Finance S.A., Gefinor House, 18B Charles Street, pg. 542 IT
THE GENERAL ELECTRIC COMPANY, P.L.C., 1 Stanhope Gate, pg. 543 IT
General Electric International Operations, Shortlands, pg. 713 PB
General Mills Europe Limited, Bedford Row, pg. 718 PB
General Re Europe Limited, 16/18 London St., pg. 726 PB
Generale Bank - London, Bavaria House, 13-14, Appold St., pg. 547 IT
Georg Jensen Silver Ltd., 15 New Bond St., pg. 1134 IT
Gestetner Holdings PLC, 66 Chiltern St., pg. 1114 IT
Gestetner Investments Limited, 66 Chiltern St., pg. 1114 IT
Girobank, 49 Park Lane, pg. 57 IT
GLAXO WELLCOME PLC, Lansdowne House, Berkeley Square, pg. 552 IT
Goldman Sachs International Limited, Peterborough Ct., 133 Fleet St., pg. 462 PV
Goldway Ltd., Chemical Bank House, 180 Strand, pg. 341 PB
W.R. Grace Ltd., Northdale House, North Circular Rd., pg. 756 PB
Graham Miller Group Limited, 12th Fl., Minster Ct., pg. 458 PB
Graham & Trotman, pg. 1513 IT
Grain D'or, Units 16, Townsend Industrial Estate, pg. 968 IT
GRANADA GROUP PLC, Stornoway House, 13 Cleveland Row, pg. 556 IT
Grand Metropolitan Finance Plc, 8 Henrietta Place, pg. 408 IT
Grand Metropolitan Plc, 8 Henrietta Place, pg. 408 IT
Grand Metropolitan PLC-Group Internal Audit:London, 33 Welbeck Street, pg. 408 IT
THE GREAT UNIVERSAL STORES P.L.C., Leconfield House, Curzon Street, pg. 557 IT
Greenaway-Harrison Ltd. d/b/a Greenaways, Greenaway House, 14, Bonhill St., pg. 817 IT
Don Gresswell Ltd., Bridge House, Grange Park, pg. 1687 IT
Grey Europe/London, Wells Point, 79 Wells St., pg. 765 PB
Griffin Bacal International B.V., Griffin Bacal Ltd., 20-22 Stuckeley St., pg. 480 PV
Griffin Bacal Ltd., 20-22 Stuckeley St., pg. 480 PV
Grolier International Limited, 96 Lonard Street, pg. 795 IT
Grosvenor Theatrical Productions Ltd., 166 High Holborn, pg. 556 IT
Grundy Worldwide, Grundy House, One Barthouse Crescent, pg. 1025 IT
Gruner + Jahr of the UK, Portland House, pg. 190 IT
Guardian & Observer, 119 Farringdon Rd., pg. 577 IT
GUARDIAN ROYAL EXCHANGE PLC, Royal Exchange, pg. 577 IT
Guest Computer Services Ltd., 21, New Street, pg. 90 IT
Guinness Brewing Worldwide Ltd., Park Royal Brewery, pg. 412 IT
Guinness Enterprises Ltd., 39 Portman Square, pg. 412 IT
Guinness Mahon Holdings Plc, 32 St. Mary at Hill, pg. 159 IT
Guinness Plc, 8 Henrietta Place, pg. 412 IT
Guinness Publishing Ltd., 338 Euston Road, pg. 412 IT
Guinness Yokohama Leasing Limited, 32 St. Mary at Hill, pg. 159 IT
Gulf Conference, Meed House, 21 John St., pg. 452 IT
The Guthrie Corporation, PLC, Six Devonshire Sq., pg. 113 IT
H & C Timber & Building Supplies Ltd., One Great Tower Street, pg. 598 IT
H.D.H. Ltd., Windsor House, 1270 London Road, pg. 795 IT
H.D.S. UK Ltd., Windsor House, 1270 London Road, pg. 795 IT
HSB Engineering Insurance Limited, Aldgate House, 33 Aldgate High St., pg. 795 PB
HSBC Asset Management Europe Limited, 6 Bevis Marks, pg. 579 IT
HSBC Asset Management Limited, 6 Bevis Marks, pg. 579 IT
HSBC Forfaiting Ltd., 4th Floor, 10 Lower Thames Street, pg. 579 IT
HSBC Gibbs Ltd., Bishops Court, 27/33 Artillery Lane, pg. 579 IT
HSBC Greenwell, Thames Exchange, 10 Queen Street Place, pg. 580 IT
HSBC HOLDINGS PLC, 10 Lower Thames Street, pg. 579 IT
HSBC Insurance Holdings Limited, Bishops Court, 27-33 Artillery Lane, pg. 580 IT
HSBC International Trade Finance Ltd, 6 Arthur Street, pg. 580 IT
HSBC Investment Bank Limited, Thames Exchange, 10 Queen Street Place, pg. 580 IT

PB - U.S. Public Companies Volume
PV - U.S. Private Companies Volume
IT - International Public & Private Companies Volume

1814

Geographic Index-Non U.S.

HSBC Investment Services Limited, 6 Bevis Marks, pg. 580 **IT**
HSBC Markets Limited, Thames Exchange, 10 Queen Street Place, pg. 580 **IT**
HSBC Private Equity Europe Limited, 10 Lower Thames Street, pg. 580 **IT**
HSBC Unit Trust Management Limited, 6 Bevis Marks, pg. 580 **IT**
Habib Bank Ltd., 97 Cannon St., pg. 585 **IT**
Habitat Group, 196 Tottenham Court Rd., pg. 660 **IT**
Hakuhodo U.K. Ltd., 7-10 Chandos Street, pg. 588 **IT**
Halliburton Mfg. & Services Ltd., 17 Hanover Sq., pg. 777 **PB**
Hamlyn/Octopus, Michelin House, 81 Fulham Road, pg. 1093 **IT**
Hampshire Chemical Ltd., Northdale House, N. Circular Rd., pg. 498 **PV**
HAMPTON TRUST PLC, 20 Albert Embankment, pg. 591 **IT**
Hansa Re & Marine Insurance Co., (UK) Ltd., Plantation House, Ste. 5/G/A, 31-35 Fenchurch St., pg. 1425 **IT**
HANSON PLC, One Grosvenor Pl., pg. 592 **IT**
Hanson Properties Limited, One Grosvenor Place, pg. 593 **IT**
Hanwa Co., Ltd.-London Branch, 5th Fl., Finland House, 56, Haymarket, pg. 595 **IT**
Hapag-Lloyd (U.K.) Holdings Ltd., pg. 596 **IT**
Harmsworth Media Ltd., Northcliffe House, 2 Derry Street, pg. 366 **IT**
The Harp Lager Co. Ltd., Park Royal Brewery, pg. 412 **IT**
Harris & Dixon (Insurance Brokers) Ltd., 21, New Street, Bishopsgate, pg. 90 **IT**
Harris & Dixon Insurance Holdings Ltd., 21, New Street, Bishopsgate, pg. 90 **IT**
Harris & Dixon Reinsurance Brokers Ltd., 21, New Street, Bishopsgate, pg. 90 **IT**
Harvey Harris & Co. Ltd., 301 Mare St., pg. 414 **IT**
Harris Trust & Savings Bank, Bucklersbury House, 1st Fl., Three Queen Victoria St., pg. 154 **IT**
HARRISONS & CROSFIELD PLC, One Great Tower St., pg. 598 **IT**
Harry's Bar Ltd., 3 S. Audley St., pg. 1213 **IT**
THE HARTSTONE GROUP PLC, 4 Brent Cross Gardens, pg. 599 **IT**
Harvey & Thompson Ltd., 2 Merrow St., pg. 312 **PB**
Charles Haswell and Partners Limited, 99 Great Russell Street, pg. 1226 **IT**
Hatema Ltd., 70 Old St., pg. 540 **IT**
Hawker Instruments Ltd., 18 St. Jame's Sq., pg. 125 **IT**
Haworth U.K. Ltd., 10 New Oxford Center, pg. 512 **PV**
Haymarket Exhibitions Ltd., 55 North Wharf Rd., pg. 114 **IT**
Heckett Multiserv-Eastern Region, Commonwealth House, 2 Chalkhill Rd., pg. 793 **IT**
HENDERSON ADMINISTRATION GROUP PLC, 3 Finsbury Ave., pg. 609 **IT**
Henkel Chemicals Ltd., Merit House, The Hyde, pg. 612 **IT**
Henkel Ltd., Henkel House, 292-308 Southbury Road, pg. 613 **IT**
The Henley Centre, Nine Bridewell Pl., pg. 1482 **IT**
HEPWORTH PLC, Five Queen St., pg. 614 **IT**
The Herald & Weekly Times Ltd., 1 Maltravers St., pg. 925 **IT**
Heritable Group, Plc, 52 Berkeley Sq., pg. 447 **PB**
Hewlett-Packard Limited, Bridewell House, 9 Bridewell Pl., pg. 821 **PB**
Hildegund Ltd., pg. 312 **IT**
HILLSDOWN HOLDINGS PLC, Hillsdown House, 32 Hampstead High St., pg. 619 **IT**
Hine U.K., 13 Grosvenor Crescent, pg. 782 **IT**
Hitachi Zosen Europe Ltd., 6th Fl., 38 Finsbury Sq., pg. 623 **IT**
Hoare Govett Limited, Security Pacific House, 4 Broadgate, pg. 183 **PB**
The Hobart Manufacturing Co., Limited, Hobart House, pg. 1322 **IT**
The Hokkaido Takushoku Bank, Ltd. (London), 33 Lombard St., pg. 627 **IT**
The Hokuriku Bank, Ltd.-London, 2nd Flr., Atlas House, 1 King Street, pg. 627 **IT**
Holloway White Allom Ltd., 43 S. Audley St., Grosvenor Sq., pg. 796 **IT**
Holmen Paper Ltd., 5 Stanhope Gate, pg. 885 **IT**
Holmes Products Corp., Lakeside House, Squires Ln., pg. 1035 **IT**
John Holt Group Ltd., 138 Cheapside, pg. 817 **IT**
Homebase Ltd., Stamford St., pg. 534 **IT**
Honda Motor Europe Ltd., Livingston House, 12 Finsbury Square, pg. 635 **IT**
Honggroup Nominees Limited, 10 Lower Thames Street, pg. 580 **IT**
Hoogovens (UK) Ltd., pg. 754 **IT**
HORACE SMALL APPAREL PLC, Masters House, 107 Hammersmith Rd., pg. 635 **IT**
Hoskyns Group Plc, Hoskyns House, 130 Shaftesbury Ave., pg. 264 **IT**
HOWELL HENRY CHALDECOTT LURY & PARTNERS, Kent House, 14-17 Market Pl., Great Titchfield St., pg. 637 **IT**
Hufvudstaden (U.K.) Ltd., 15 Lower Regent St., pg. 478 **IT**
Hunter Plastics Ltd., Nathan Way, pg. 430 **IT**
The Hunterskil Howard Group plc., pg. 1511 **IT**
HUNTING PLC, 3 Cockspur St., pg. 640 **IT**
Hypertac Limited, Waterloo Rd., pg. 1267 **IT**
Hypo Trade Finance Ltd., 41 Moorgate, pg. 176 **IT**
IBJ International plc, Bracken House, One Friday Street, pg. 676 **IT**
IBM Information Services Limited, 389 Chiswick High Road, pg. 897 **PB**

IBM United Kingdom International Product Sales Limited, 40 Basinghall, pg. 897 **PB**
IC Insurance Limited, 1 Adam Street, pg. 1524 **IT**
ICAT (Integrating CadCam), Greater London House, Hampstead Rd., pg. 452 **IT**
ICI Finance PLC, Cash Management Group, ICI Group Headquarters, pg. 663 **IT**
ICL PLC, 1 High Street, pg. 528 **IT**
ICV Limited, Skandia House, 23 College Hill, pg. 1326 **IT**
IDC Multi User Expertise Center, 99 Grey's Inn Road, pg. 571 **PV**
IDC United Kingdom, 99 Grays Inn Rd., pg. 571 **PV**
IDG Communications Ltd., 99 Gray's Inn Rd., pg. 570 **PV**
IDV Africa & Latin America, 8 Henrietta Place, pg. 409 **IT**
IDV Asia Pacific, 8 Henrietta Place, pg. 409 **IT**
IHI Europe Ltd., Floor 9A, No. 1 Minster Court, Mincing Lane, pg. 689 **IT**
IMC/A.K. Fans Ltd., 32/34 Park Royal Rd., pg. 868 **IT**
INA Underwriting Agency Limited, Cigna House, 8 Lime Street, pg. 363 **PB**
ING Bank London, 60, London Wall, pg. 650 **IT**
ING Baring Securities, 60 London Wall, pg. 649 **IT**
ING Barings, 60 London Wall, pg. 650 **IT**
ING Lease (UK), 99, Gresham Street, pg. 650 **IT**
ING Lease (UK), 107, Cheapside, pg. 650 **IT**
ING (London) Futures & Options, 75, King William Street, pg. 650 **IT**
ING Real Estate, 72, New Bond street, pg. 650 **IT**
IPC MAGAZINES LIMITED, King's Reach Tower, Stamford Street, pg. 651 **IT**
ISS London Ltd., 10 The Circle, Queen Elizabeth St., pg. 657 **IT**
ISS Servisystem Ltd., 10 The Circle, pg. 657 **IT**
IVO Energy Limited, 18 Saville Row, pg. 661 **IT**
IVO Generation Services (UK) Ltd., 18 Savile Row, pg. 661 **IT**
Ikegami Electronics UK, Kestrel Ct., Pound Rd., pg. 660 **IT**
Ilco Unican (U.K.) Ltd., 7th Fl., Plantation House, Fenchurch St., Ste. 144, pg. 1432 **IT**
Illustrated London News, Sea Containers House, 20 Upper Ground, pg. 1214 **IT**
IMPERIAL CHEMICAL INDUSTRIES PLC, 9 Millbank, pg. 662 **IT**
Inchcape Family Investment, 2a, Eastcheap, pg. 671 **IT**
Inchcape Inspection & Testing Services, St. James House, 23 King St., pg. 671 **IT**
Inchcape Management Services Ltd., St. James House, 23 King St., pg. 671 **IT**
INCHCAPE PLC, St. James's House, 23 King Street, pg. 671 **IT**
Inchcape plc, Bain Clarkson House, 15 Minories, pg. 671 **IT**
Inchcape Shipping Services, St. James's House, 23 King St., pg. 671 **IT**
Inco Europe Limited, 1-3 Grosvenor Place, pg. 673 **IT**
INCSTAR Ltd., Ste. 1, Bulldog House, Reading Rd., pg. 483 **IT**
Independent Radio Features Limited, Communications House, Gough Square, pg. 525 **PB**
Indosuez Capital Emerging Markets, 122 Leadenhall Street, pg. 314 **IT**
Indosuez Capital Ltd., 122 Leadenhall Street, pg. 314 **IT**
Indosuez Capital Securities (UK) Ltd., 122 Leadenhall Street, pg. 314 **IT**
Indosuez Carr Futures Inc., 122 Leadenhall Street, pg. 314 **IT**
Indosuez Structured Finance International, 122 Leadenhall Street, pg. 314 **IT**
The Industrial Bank of Japan, Limited (London Branch), Bracken House, One Friday Street, pg. 675 **IT**
Inso Corporation, Ltd., Woodstock House, Gibbara Mews, pg. 882 **PB**
Insurance Company of North America (U.K.) Limited, CIGNA House, 8 Lime St., pg. 363 **PB**
Intalcable-UK, World Trade Center, Europe House, Ste. 172, pg. 656 **IT**
Inter-Continental Hotels Corporation, Hyde Park Corner, pg. 1178 **IT**
Interactive Video Systems Limited, 24 Ray St., pg. 1089 **IT**
Interbrand, 40 Long Acre, pg. 1225 **PB**
Intermarkets Europe Advertising Ltd., The Kiln House, 210 New Kings Rd., pg. 1214 **IT**
International Creative Management Ltd., 388/396 Oxford St., pg. 554 **PV**
International Distillers & Vintners-Europe, 8 Henrietta Place, pg. 409 **IT**
International Distillers & Vintners Ltd., 8 Henrietta Place, pg. 409 **IT**
International Flavours & Fragrances I.F.F. (Great Britain) Ltd., Commonwealth House, Hammersmith International Centre, pg. 899 **PB**
International Maritime Satellite Organisation (INMARSAT), 40 Melton St., pg. 222 **IT**
International Marketing & Promotions, London, 123 Buckingham Palace Rd., pg. 304 **PV**
International Press Distributors Ltd., Windsor House, 1270 London Road, pg. 795 **IT**
International Thomson Business Publishing, 216 Boundary Row, pg. 1601 **PB**
International Thomson Publishing Limited, 101 Ave. Rd., pg. 1600 **PB**
Invesco Europe Ltd., 11 Devonshire Sq., pg. 685 **IT**
INVESCO GROUP ASSET MANAGEMENT LTD., 11 Devonshire Sq., pg. 685 **IT**
Invesco Ltd., 11 Devonshire Sq., pg. 685 **IT**
Investcorp International Ltd., 65 Brook St. West, pg. 686 **IT**
Ishikawajima Europe B.V., Floor 9A, No. 1 Minster Court, Mincing Lane, pg. 689 **IT**

JGC Corporation (UK) Ltd., 35 Dover Street, pg. 697 **IT**
JIB Group plc, Jardine House, 6 Crutched Friars, pg. **IT**
JL Property Holdings Ltd., Page St., pg. 796 **IT**
JT International Europe Limited, East Wing, 3rd Floor, 3 Shortlands, pg. 703 **IT**
JT (UK) Ltd., 3 Shortlands, Hammersmith International Centre, pg. 703 **IT**
JVC (U.K.) Ltd., JVC House, JVC Business Park, 12 Priestley Way, pg. 847 **IT**
The Jaeger Company's Shops Ltd., Jaeger House, 57 Broadwick Street, pg. 300 **IT**
Jaeger Holdings Limited, Jaeger House, 57, Broadwick St., pg. 300 **IT**
Japan Airlines Company, Ltd., Hanover Court, 5 Hanover Square, pg. 701 **IT**
The Japan Development Bank-London Representative Office, Level 12, City Tower, 40 Basinghall St., pg. 702 **IT**
Japan Energy (U.K.) Ltd., 39 Dover St., pg. 702 **IT**
Jardine Credit Insurance Ltd., Jardine House, 6 Crutched Friars, pg. 705 **IT**
Jardine Insurance Brokers International Limited, Jardine House, 6 Crutched Friars, pg. 705 **IT**
Jardine Insurance Brokers Ltd., Jardine House, 6 Crutched Friars, pg. 705 **IT**
Jardine Insurance Services Limited, Jardine House, 6 Crutched Friars, pg. 705 **IT**
Jardine (Lloyd's Underwriting Agents) Ltd., Jardine House, 6 Crutched Friars, pg. 705 **IT**
J. Jarvis & Sons P.L.C., 57 Great Eastern St., pg. 705 **IT**
Jauch & Huebener, Reinsurance Brokers Ltd., Aldgate House, pg. 118 **PB**
Jefferies International Limited, 46 New Broad St., 3rd Fl., pg. 925 **PB**
Jewson Ltd., Aldwych House, 81 Aldwych, pg. 864 **IT**
Jewson Property Holdings Ltd., Aldwych House, 81 Aldwych, pg. 864 **IT**
John Hancock Advisers International, Ltd., 34 Dover St., pg. 590 **PV**
Axel Johnson Ltd., 14, Queen Anne's Gate, pg. 711 **IT**
Axel Johnson Ore & Metals Ltd., 14, Queen Annes Gate, pg. 712 **IT**
JOHNSON FRY HOLDINGS PLC, 20 Reagent St., pg. 713 **IT**
Johnson Fry Plc, 20 Lower Regent St., pg. 713 **IT**
JOHNSON MATTHEY PUBLIC LIMITED COMPANY, 2-4 Cockspur Street, pg. 713 **IT**
Ernest Jones (London) Limited, 15 Stratton St., pg. 1248 **IT**
Jotun-Henry Clark Ltd., 142 Minories, pg. 715 **IT**
Jupiter International Group PLC, pg. 312 **IT**
Justerini & Brooks Ltd., 8 Henrietta Place, pg. 409 **IT**
K Advertising, 83-89 Whitfield Street, pg. 1422 **PB**
K-Tel Entertainment (U.K.) Ltd., Windmill Court, 192 Windmill Lane, pg. 938 **PB**
Kansai Paint Europe Limited, Bastion House, 140 London Wall, pg. 723 **IT**
Kawasaki Heavy Industries (UK) Ltd., 3rd Fl., Bracton House, 34-36 High Holborn, pg. 726 **IT**
Kawasaki Steel Co., 8th Floor, London Intl. Press, Center, 76 Shoe Lane, pg. 726 **IT**
Kelco International Ltd., Westminster Tower 3, Albert Embankment, pg. 1091 **PB**
Kelly Services (U.K.) Ltd., Rodwell House, 100 Middlesex Street, pg. 949 **PB**
KELLY WEEDON SHUTE PARTNERSHIP, 37 Golden Square, pg. 727 **IT**
Kemira Coatings Ltd., Lea Bridge Estate, Argall Ave., pg. 729 **IT**
Kentships, Sugar Quay, Lower Thames St., pg. 1356 **IT**
Keppel (UK) Ltd., 17 Carlisle Street, pg. 731 **IT**
Kerr-McGee Oil (U.K.) PLC, 75 Davies Street, pg. 952 **PB**
Ki Pacific Asset Management, 9 Park Pl., pg. 1674 **PB**
Kim Eng Securities (London) Limited, 6th Floor, 20 St. Dunstan's Hill, pg. 733 **IT**
Kimball U.K., Inc., 21-27 Marylebone Lane, pg. 958 **PB**
KINGFISHER PLC, North West House, 119 Marylebone Rd., pg. 733 **IT**
Kiss FM, Kiss House, 80 Holloway Rd., pg. 452 **IT**
Kleinwort Benson Ltd., 20 Fenchurch Street, pg. 420 **IT**
Knight Wendling Ltd., 13-14, Cornwall Terrace, pg. 627 **PV**
Kobe Steel Europe, Ltd., Alton House, 174/177 High Holborn, pg. 741 **IT**
Korn/Ferry International, Regent Arcade House, 252 Regent St., pg. 633 **PV**
Kredietbank London Branch, Exchange House, 7th Fl., Primrose St., pg. 760 **IT**
Kredietfinance (U.K.) Ltd., 7th Fl., Exchange House, Primrose St., pg. 761 **IT**
Kruger Sales Limited, Convoys Wharf, Prince Street, pg. 762 **IT**
Kubota Corp.-London Office, 11/12 Hanover St., pg. 763 **IT**
Kubota Finance (UK) PLC, 11/12 Hanover St., pg. 763 **IT**
Kuwait Petroleum International (KPI), 80 New Bond St., pg. 766 **IT**
Kvaerner a.s London Office, Ryder Court, 14 Ryder Street, pg. 771 **IT**
Kvaerner Earl and Wright, Inc., Portland House, Stag Place, pg. 771 **IT**
Kvaerner Energy a.s. Business Area Hydropower, Ryder Court, 14 Ryder Street, pg. 767 **IT**
Kvaerner EnviroPower Ltd., Ryder Court, 14 Ryder Street, pg. 767 **IT**
Kvaerner FSSL Ltd., Monarch House, pg. 767 **IT**
Kvaerner Havtor (UK) Limited, 30 St. James's Street, pg. 771 **IT**
Kvaerner Holding UK Ltd., Ryder Court 14 Ryder Street, pg. 771 **IT**

PB - U.S. Public Companies Volume
PV - U.S. Private Companies Volume
IT - International Public & Private Companies Volume

Geographic Index-Non U.S.

1815

Kvaerner-John Brown Ltd., 20 Eastbourne Terrace, Paddington, pg. 773 IT
Kyoei Fire & Marine Insurance Co. (U.K.) Ltd., 1 College Hill, pg. 777 IT
The Kyoei Life Europe Co., Ltd., pg. 777 IT
The Kyoei Life Insurance Co., Ltd.-London Office, Condor House, 14 St. Paul's Churchyard, pg. 777 IT
The Kyoei Mutual Fire & Marine Insurance Company, London Respresentative Office, pg. 777 IT
Kyowa Hakko U.K. Ltd., CP House 97-107, Uxbridge Road, pg. 778 IT
LGC Communications Ltd., 33-39 Bowling Green Lane, pg. 451 IT
LGT Asset Management PLC, 14th Floor, Alban Gate, 125 London Wall, pg. 810 IT
LL&E (UK) Inc., 40 A Dover St., pg. 269 PB
LTCB and F&C Investment Management Co. Limited, 8th Floor,Exchange House, Primrose Street, pg. 816 IT
LTCB International Limited, 55 Bishopsgate, pg. 816 IT
Ladbroke Casino (Holdings) Limited, 10 Cavendish Place, pg. 787 IT
Ladbroke City & County Land Company Limited, Ten Cavendish Pl., pg. 787 IT
LADBROKE GROUP PLC, Chancel House, pg. 787 IT
Ladbroke Group Properties Ltd., Chancel House, Neasden Ln., pg. 787 IT
John Laing Construction Ltd., Page St., Mill Hill, pg. 796 IT
John Laing Developments, Ltd., Page St., Mill Hill, pg. 796 IT
JOHN LAING PLC, Page St., Mill Hill, pg. 796 IT
John Laing Services Ltd., Page St., pg. 796 IT
Laing Management Ltd., Page St., pg. 796 IT
Laing Technology Group Ltd., Page St., Mill Hill, pg. 796 IT
LAMBERT SMITH HAMPTON, 19/25 Argyll St., pg. 797 IT
Lambert Smith Hampton, 76 Cannon St., pg. 797 IT
The Lancet Limited, 42 Bedford Square, pg. 1100 IT
LAND SECURITIES PLC, 5 Strand, pg. 798 IT
Land Securities Properties Limited, 5 Strand, pg. 798 IT
Lane Safe Deposit Co. Ltd., Slerting House, 305-307 Chiswick House Rd., pg. 1033 IT
Lansdown Conquest, 4 Flitcroft St., pg. 1482 IT
LASMO North Sea PLC, 101 Bishopsgate, pg. 804 IT
LASMO PLC, 101 Bishopsgate, pg. 803 IT
Cyrus J. Lawrence (UK) Limited, 23 Great Winchester St., pg. 405 IT
Lazard Brothers & Co. Ltd., 21 Moorfields, pg. 1026 IT
Le Shuttle Holidays Limited, One Canada Square, Canary Wharf, pg. 466 IT
Leased Hotels Limited, 166 High Holborn, pg. 556 IT
Ledu Ltd., 12 Barmeston Road, pg. 821 IT
Legal & General Assurance Society Limited, Temple Ct., 11 Queen Victoria St., pg. 805 IT
Legal & General Finance Plc, Temple Ct., 11 Queen Victoria St., pg. 805 IT
Legal & General Financial Services Limited, Temple Ct., 11 Queen Victoria St., pg. 805 IT
LEGAL & GENERAL GROUP PLC, Temple Court, 11 Queen Victoria St., pg. 805 IT
Legal & General Investment Management (Holdings) Limited, Temple Ct., 11 Queen Victoria St., pg. 805 IT
Legal & General Mortgage Services Limited, Temple Ct., 11 Queen Victoria St., pg. 805 IT
Legion Ltd., Capitol House, 159 Hammersmith Road, pg. 795 IT
Legion UK Ltd., Capitol House, 159 Hammersmith Road., pg. 796 IT
Leonard Lifts Ltd., Leonard House, 84 Leven Rd., pg. 748 IT
Letraset UK, 195-203 Waterloo Road, pg. 462 IT
Liberty of London, Inc., 26 Great Marlborough St., pg. 807 IT
Liberty of London Prints Limited, 313 Merton Rd., pg. 807 IT
LIBERTY PLC, 210-220 Regent St., pg. 807 IT
Liberty Retail Limited, 25 Great Marlborough St., pg. 807 IT
Life Sciences International Plc, Crown House, 51 Aldwich, pg. 1594 PB
Lillywhites Ltd., 24-36 Regent Street, pg. 706 IT
Lipton Tea Company Ltd., Leon Ho., High St., pg. 1434 IT
Arthur D. Little Ltd., Berkeley Square House, Berkeley Square, pg. 671 PV
Liverpool Shoe Co. Ltd., Lakeside House, Squires Ln., pg. 1035 IT
Lloyds Associated Air Leasing Ltd., 71 Lombard St., pg. 813 IT
Lloyds Bank Commercial Properties Ltd., 71 Lombard St., pg. 813 IT
Lloyds Bank Export Finance Ltd., Hay's Lane House, One Hay's Ln., pg. 813 IT
Lloyds Bank Unit Trust Managers Ltd., 71 Lombard St., pg. 813 IT
Lloyds Bank UK Management Ltd.-Corp. Banking & Treasury, St. Georges House, 6-8 Eastcheap, pg. 813 IT
Lloyds Development Capital Ltd., 48 Chiswell St., pg. 813 IT
Lloyds Equipment Leasing Ltd., 57 Southwark St., pg. 813 IT
Lloyds Industrial Leasing Ltd., 57 Southwark St., pg. 813 IT
Lloyds International Banking, Hay's Lane House, One Hay's Ln., pg. 813 IT
Lloyds Leasing Ltd., 57 Southwark St., pg. 813 IT
Lloyds Merchant Bank Ltd., 48 Chiswell St., pg. 813 IT
LLOYDS TSB GROUP PLC, 71 Lombard St., pg. 812 IT
Lockheed Corporation (International) S.A., Eighth Fl., Berkeley Sq. House, Berkeley Sq., pg. 1009 PB
Loders & Nucoline Ltd., Cairn Mills, pg. 1434 IT
Loewe Hermanos (U.K.) ltd, 149 New Bond St., pg. 782 IT
LOGICA PLC, Stephenson House, 75 Hampstead Road, pg. 814 IT
Logica UK Ltd., 68 Newman St., pg. 814 IT
London & Scandinavian Metallurgical Co. Limited, 45 Wimbledon Hill Rd., pg. 735 PV
London Bureau Ltd., London Press Center, 76 Shoe Lane, pg. 1176 PB
London City & International Limited, 11 Holburn Viaduct, pg. 817 IT
London City & Westcliff Properties, 11 Holburn Viaduct, pg. 817 IT
LONDON INTERNATIONAL GROUP PLC, 35 New Bridge St., pg. 815 IT
London Representative Office (ESLON), 197 Knightsbridge, pg. 1042 IT
Long-Term Credit Bank of Japan, Ltd. - London Branch, 55 Bishopsgate, pg. 816 IT
Lonhro Exports Ltd., Roman House., Wood St., pg. 817 IT
Lonhro Finance Plc, Cheapside House, 138 Cheapside, pg. 817 IT
Lonrho (CIS) Ltd., pg. 817 IT
LONRHO PLC, Cheapside House, 138 Cheapside, pg. 817 IT
L'Oreal (UK) Limited, 30 Kensington Church St., pg. 819 IT
Louis Vuitton U.K. Ltd, 149 New Bond St., pg. 783 IT
The Lowe Group, Bowater House, 68-114 Knightsbridge, pg. 678 PV
Lowe Howard-Spink, Bowater House, 68-114 Knightsbridge, pg. 678 PV
LUCASVARITY PLC, 44-46 Park Street, pg. 819 IT
Ludgate Communications, 111 Charterhouse Street, EC1M 6AA, pg. 1157 PV
Ludgate Group Limited, 111 Charterhouse Street, pg. 1157 PV
Luncheon Vouchers Ltd., 50 Vauxhall Bridge Rd., pg. 21 IT
Luxo U.K. Ltd., 4, Barmeston Road, pg. 822 IT
MAN GHH (Great Britain) Ltd., 4-5 Grosvenor Place, pg. 824 IT
MEC UK Limited, Bow Bells House, Bread St., pg. 873 IT
MFI FURNITURE CENTER PLC, Southon House, 333 The Hyde, Edgeware Rd., pg. 827 IT
MIL (UK) Limited, Two Braodgate, pg. 151 IT
MPL Powerware Systems, Ltd., pg. 126 IT
MPSI Systems Ltd., 85-87, Jermyn St., pg. 1027 PB
MRI UK, 10 Jamestown Rd., pg. 727 PV
MTV Europe, Centro House, 20-23 Mandela Street, pg. 779 PV
MacDonald & Co. (Publishers) Ltd., Greater London House, Hampstead Road, pg. 1615 PB
Macmillan Children's Books Limited, 18/21 Cavaye Place, pg. 1479 IT
Macmillan London Ltd., 18-21 Cavaye Place, pg. 1479 IT
Macmillan Ltd., 25, Ecclestone Place, pg. 1479 IT
Magnet World Travel Ltd., 18-30 Clerkenwell Rd., pg. 544 IT
Mannesmann Engineers & Contractors Ltd., pg. 837 IT
Manulife International Investment Office, 125 London Wall, pg. 841 IT
Map Securities Ltd., Philpot Lane 2-3, pg. 335 IT
MAPFRE London Ltd., Philpot Lane 2-3, pg. 335 IT
MAPFRE Re Management Services U.K. Company Limited, Philpot Lane 2-3, pg. 335 IT
Marathon Oil U.K., Ltd., Marathon House, 174 Marylebone Rd., pg. 1662 PB
Mardev, 151-153 Wardour Street, pg. 1094 IT
Market Access Limited, 7 The Sanctuary, Parliament Square, pg. 1225 PB
Marketforce (UK) Limited, 247 Tottenham Court Road, pg. 651 IT
MARKS & SPENCER PLC, Michael House, 37-67 Baker St., pg. 842 IT
F.A. Marsden Ltd., 30/34 New Bridge St., pg. 739 PB
Marshall Pickering Holdings, Ltd., Middlesex House 34-42 Cleveland St., pg. 927 IT
Marshalls Finance Limited, Lloyds Chambers, 1 Portsoken St., pg. 222 IT
Martin Marietta International, Inc., Kingsbury House, 15-17 King St., pg. 1010 PB
Martin Marietta International, Inc., 3 Shortlands, Hammersmith, pg. 1010 PB
Marubeni U.K. Plc., 120 Moorgate, pg. 845 IT
Masco Corporation Limited, Banda House, pg. 1054 PB
Mase Westpac Limited, Five Lloyds Ave., pg. 1497 IT
Masterdrive Management Ltd., pg. 817 IT
McDonald's Hamburgers Limited, 11-59 High Road, East Finchley, pg. 1069 PB
MEDEVA PLC, 10 St. James's Street, pg. 852 IT
THE MEDIA CENTRE, 123 Buckingham Palace Road, pg. 852 IT
THE MEDIA SHOP LIMITED, 14-16 Regent Street, pg. 853 IT
MEDIAPOLIS, Commonwealth House, 1-19 New Oxford Street, pg. 853 IT
MediaVest, 123 Buckingham Palace Road, pg. 692 PV
Medical Imaging Systems Limited, Unit 12, Kingsbury Indust. Estate, Church Lane, pg. 589 IT
Medscreen Limited, 1A Harbor Quay, 100 Preston's Road, pg. 1286 PB
Mees & Hope Corporate Finance Ltd., Princes House, 95, Gresham Street, pg. 12 IT
Mees & Hope Investment Management Ltd., Princes House, 95 Gresham St., pg. 12 IT
Mees & Hope Securities Ltd., Princes House, 95, Gresham Street, pg. 12 IT
Meiji Seika Kaisha, Ltd., Salisbury House, Finsbury Circus, pg. 855 IT
The Meijiseimei International, London Ltd., Ste. B, Level 7, No. 6 Broadgate, pg. 854 IT
The Meijiseimei Property U.K. Ltd., Ste. B., Level 7, No. 6 Broadgate, pg. 855 IT
George Meller Ltd., Northfield Avenue Orion Park, Ealing, pg. 712 IT
Mellon Europe-London, Six Devonshire Sq., pg. 1086 PB
Melody Radio, 180 Brompton Road, pg. 593 IT
William M. Mercer Limited, Telford House, pg. 1049 PB
Mercury Asset Management Group plc, 33 King William St., pg. 1331 IT
Mercury Fund Managers Ltd., 33 King William St., pg. 1331 IT
Merial Ltd., 27 Knightsbridge, pg. 1092 PB
Merita Bank Ltd. London Branch, Kansallis House, 19 Thomas More St., pg. 859 IT
Merrell/Chisholm, Suite 203, Holywell Centre, 1 Phipp Street, pg. 543 PV
Merrill Burrups Worldwide, St. Ives House, Lavington St., pg. 1097 PB
Metallgesellschaft Ltd., 4th Floor, 3 Quays, Tower Hill, pg. 948 IT
Metro Group, 53 Great Suffolk Street, pg. 1482 IT
Metropole Hotels (Holdings) Ltd., pg. 817 IT
Metzeler Antivibration Systems, Ltd., Silverton House, Vincent Sq., pg. 130 IT
Meyer Forest Products Ltd, Aldwych House, 81 Aldwych, pg. 864 IT
Meyer International Finance & Property PLC, Aldwych House, 81 Aldwych, pg. 864 IT
Meyer International Group Pension Trust, Aldwych House, 81 Aldwych, pg. 864 IT
Meyer International Overseas Investments Ltd., Aldwych House, 81 Aldwych, pg. 864 IT
MEYER INTERNATIONAL PLC, Aldwych House, 81 Aldwych, pg. 864 IT
Micro Warehouse Limited, 46 Church Lane, pg. 1104 PB
Midland Bank PLC, 27-32 Poultry, pg. 580 IT
Milchem Drilling Fluids Ltd., 6 Babmaes St., pg. 167 PB
Milcom Communication & Electronics Ltd., pg. 1139 PB
Miller Freeman PLC, Miller Freeman House, pg. 1443 IT
Miller Patterson Aldred Mitchell, 31 Kingly Street, pg. 1152 PV
Miller/Shandwick Communications Ltd., 4 Bouviere Street, pg. 1226 IT
MIRROR GROUP PLC, One Canada Square, pg. 869 IT
Mitchell Beazley, Michelin House, 81 Fulham Road, pg. 1093 IT
Mitsubishi Chemical (U.K.) Plc., Jupiter House, Triton Court, 14 Finsbury Square, pg. 871 IT
Mitsubishi Heavy Industries Europe, Ltd. (MHIE), Bow Bells House, Bread St. (Cheapside), pg. 874 IT
The Mitsubishi Trust & Banking Corporation, 24 Lombard Street, pg. 876 IT
Mitsubishi Trust International Limited, 24 Lombard Street, pg. 877 IT
Mitsui & Co. Europe Ltd., Temple Court, 11 Queen Victoria St., pg. 880 IT
The Mitsui Trust and Banking Company - London, 5th Fl., 6 Broadgate, pg. 883 IT
Mitsui Trust International Ltd., 3rd Floor, 41 Tower Hill, pg. 883 IT
Mitsukoshi Ltd.-Europe Head Office, Dorland House, 14-20 Regent St., pg. 884 IT
Mitsukoshi (U.K.) Ltd., Dorland House, 14-20 Regent St., pg. 884 IT
Mobil Europe, Inc., Mobil Ct., Three Clements Inn, pg. 1119 PB
Mobil Europe, Ltd., Mobil Ct., Three Clements Inn, pg. 1119 PB
Mobil Holdings (Europe), Ltd., Mobil Ct., Three Clements Inn, pg. 1119 PB
Mobil North Sea Limited, Mobil Ct., 3 Clements Inn, pg. 1119 PB
Modem Media U.K., County Mark House, 50 Regent St., pg. 1641 PB
Moet & Chandon (London) Ltd, 13 Grosvenor Crescent, pg. 783 IT
Money Magazine Limited, Berkeley Square House, Berkeley Square, pg. 1368 PB
Samuel Montagu & Co. Limited, 10 Lower Thames Street, pg. 580 IT
Monteith Travel Services LTD, 27 Hammersmith Grove, pg. 1510 IT
Moody's Investors Service Ltd., 2 Minster Court, Mincing Lane, pg. 537 PB
Moore Business Forms U.K. Ltd., 81 Southwark St., pg. 889 IT
Moore Paragon U.K. Limited, Moore House, 75-79 Southwark St., pg. 889 IT
Morgan Grenfell & Co. Limited, 23 Great Winchester St., pg. 405 IT
Morgan Grenfell Asset Management Limited, 20 Finsbury Circus, pg. 405 IT
Morgan Grenfell Group PLC, 23 Great Winchester St., pg. 405 IT
Morgan Grenfell Laurie Ltd., Fitzroy House, 18-20 Grafton St., pg. 405 IT
Morgan Guaranty Trust Company, 60 Victoria Embankment, pg. 1130 PB
Morgan Guaranty Trust Company, 28 King St., pg. 1130 PB
J.P. Morgan Investment Management Inc., 28 King St., pg. 1131 PB
J.P. Morgan Securities Ltd., 60 Victoria Embankment, pg. 1131 PB

PB - *U.S. Public Companies Volume*
PV - *U.S. Private Companies Volume*
IT - *International Public & Private Companies Volume*

1816
Geographic Index-Non U.S.

J.P. Morgan Sterling Securities Ltd., 60 Victoria Embankment, pg. 1131 **PB**

Morgan Stanley International, 25 Cabot Square, pg. 1133 **PB**

MOSS BROS GROUP PLC, 8 St. Johns Hill, pg. 895 **IT**

MultiServ International Ltd., Piccadilly House, 33 Regent St., pg. 793 **PB**

Murco Petroleum Ltd., Winston House, Dollis Pk., pg. 1142 **PB**

Murphy Eastern Oil Co., Winston House, Dollis Park, pg. 1142 **PB**

Murphy Petroleum Ltd., Winston House, Dollis Park, pg. 1142 **PB**

NAC Reinsurance International Limited, New London House, 6 London Street, 7th Floor, pg. 1144 **IT**

NCE Group, Thomas Telford House, 1 Heron Quay, pg. 451 **IT**

NCNB National Bank, London Branch, 26 Austin Friars, pg. 1166 **PB**

NDC International Ltd., Inc., Crown House, 72 Hammersmith Rd., pg. 1156 **PB**

NEC Europe Ltd., NEC House, One Victoria Road, pg. 900 **IT**

NEC Industries (UK) Plc., Ste. 131, Victoria House, Southampton Row, pg. 900 **IT**

NEC (UK) Ltd., NEC House, 1 Victoria Rd., pg. 901 **IT**

NETG Limited, One Hogarth Business Park, pg. 784 **PB**

NFC PLC, 66 Chiltern St., pg. 901 **IT**

NIG Skandia PLC, Crown House, 145 City Road, pg. 1258 **IT**

NKK Europe Ltd.-London Office, 4th Fl., West Block, 11 Moorfields, pg. 903 **IT**

NLI Insurance Services (Europe) Limited, 20 Little Britain, pg. 936 **IT**

NLI International PLC, 20 Little Britain, pg. 935 **IT**

NLI Properties UK Limited, 20 Little Britain, pg. 936 **IT**

NYK Bulkship (Europe) Ltd., 45 Old Bond Street, pg. 941 **IT**

NYK International PLC, 1 King Edward Street, 7th Floor, pg. 941 **IT**

NYK Line (Europe) Ltd., 1 King Edward St., 7th Floor, pg. 942 **IT**

Nacional Financiera, 19th Floor, 1 Angel Court, pg. 904 **IT**

Namco Europe Ltd., 25/27 Mossop St., pg. 905 **IT**

National Australia Life, 91 Gresham Street, pg. 906 **IT**

National Bank of Greece S.A., 50, St. Mary Axe., pg. 907 **IT**

National Bank of Pakistan-London, 18 Finsbury Circus, pg. 908 **IT**

National Bank of Pakistan-London, 30 Sloane Street, pg. 908 **IT**

The National Magazine Company Ltd., 72 Broadwick St., pg. 518 **PV**

National Mobile Radio Limited, 110 Grafton Rd., pg. 1140 **IT**

National-Oilwell/Dreco Europe LTD, First Fl., Kingsland House, 122 Regent St., pg. 1158 **IT**

NATIONAL WESTMINSTER BANK PLC, 41 Lothbury, pg. 910 **IT**

National Westminster Bank Plc, 135 Bishopsgate, pg. 910 **IT**

NationsBank (United Kingdom) Branch, 103 Mount St., pg. 1166 **PB**

NatWest Capital Markets Limited, 135 Bishopsgate, pg. 910 **IT**

NatWest Corporate Investments Limited, 135 Bishopsgate, pg. 910 **IT**

NatWest Export Finance Limited, National Westminster Tower, 25 Old Broad St., pg. 910 **IT**

NatWest Financial Products plc, 135 Bishopsgate, pg. 910 **IT**

NatWest Futures Limited, 135 Bishopsgate, pg. 910 **IT**

NatWest Gilts Limited, 135 Bishopsgate, pg. 910 **IT**

NatWest Investment Management Limited, 135 Bishopsgate, pg. 910 **IT**

NatWest Markets Corporate Limited, 135 Bishopsgate, pg. 910 **IT**

NatWest Securities Limited, 135 Bishopsgate, pg. 910 **IT**

NatWest Specialist Finance Limited, 135 Bishopsgate, pg. 910 **IT**

NatWest Stockbrokers Limited, 55 Mansell St., pg. 910 **IT**

NatWest U.K., Drapers Gardens, pg. 910 **IT**

NatWest Ventures Limited, 135 Bishopsgate, pg. 910 **IT**

NatWest Wood MacKenzie & Co Limited, 135 Bishopsgate, pg. 911 **IT**

Nedlloyd Group Holdings UK Ltd., pg. 1145 **IT**

Neste Exploration Ltd., 30 Charles 11 St., pg. 915 **IT**

Neste Gas Ltd., 30 Charles 11 St., pg. 915 **IT**

Neste Petroleum Ltd., 30 Charles II Street, pg. 915 **IT**

Neste Production Limited Sovereign Oil & Gas PLC, The Chambers, Chelsea Harbor, pg. 915 **IT**

Neste (UK) Ltd., 30 Charles 11 St., pg. 915 **IT**

News International plc, 1 Virginia Street, pg. 927 **IT**

NewsEdge Corp., 12A Pinsbury Lane, pg. 1180 **PB**

NEWSQUEST MEDIA GROUP, 1 Kingsway, pg. 927 **IT**

NEXIS UK, 6 Bell Yard, pg. 1096 **IT**

Nichimen Europe plc, Latham House, 16 Minories, pg. 928 **IT**

Nicholson Leslie International Limited, 6 Braham St., pg. 119 **PB**

Nicholson Leslie Limited, 6 Braham St., pg. 119 **IT**

Nielsen UK, Unit 7, Frogmore Estate, pg. 462 **IT**

Nihon Keizai Shimbun Europe Ltd., Bush House North West Wing, pg. 929 **IT**

The Nikko Bank (UK) Plc, Nikko House, 17 Godliman Street, pg. 930 **IT**

Nikko Europe Plc, 55 Victoria Street, pg. 930 **IT**

Nikko International Capital Management (U.K.) Ltd., Nikko House, 17 Godliman St., pg. 930 **IT**

Nippon Credit Bank Ltd.-London, City Tower, 40 Basinghall Street, pg. 933 **IT**

Nippon Credit International Limited, Level 4, Finsbury Dials, 20 Finsbury St., pg. 933 **IT**

Nippon Express Tours (Europe) Ltd., Bond Street House, pg. 934 **IT**

Nippon Meat Packers U.K. Ltd., 1st Fl., Ste. 3, World Trade Centre, St. Katharine's Way, pg. 936 **IT**

Nippon Oil Exploration U.K. Limited, Dorland House, 18-20 Regent St., pg. 937 **IT**

Nippon Oil (U.K.) Public Limited Company, Pollen House, 10-12 Cork St., pg. 937 **IT**

Nippon Paint (Europe) Ltd., Level 8, City Tower, 40 Basinghall Street, pg. 937 **IT**

Nippon Steel Corporation-London Office, Bucklersbury House, 11th fl., 3 Queen Victoria St., pg. 940 **IT**

Nipson Printing Systems Ltd., 190 Strand, pg. 316 **IT**

Nishimatsu Construction Co., Ltd.-London Office, 9 Cavendish Pl., pg. 943 **IT**

Nissan International Finance (Europe) Limited, 5 Arlington Street, pg. 945 **IT**

Nissho Iwai Europe plc, Bastion House, 140 London Wall, pg. 948 **IT**

Nomura Asset Management (International) Limited, 8th Floor, Nomura House, 1 St. Martin's-le-Grand, pg. 955 **IT**

Nomura Bank International PLC, Nomura House, 1 St. Martin's-le-Grand, pg. 956 **IT**

Nomura Capital Management (U.K.) Limited, Nomura House, 1 St. Martin's-le-Grand, pg. 956 **IT**

Nomura Europe Plc, Nomura House, 1 St. Martin's-le-Grand, pg. 957 **IT**

Nomura International PLC, Nomura House, 1 St. Martin's-le-Grand, pg. 957 **IT**

Nomura Option International Plc, Nomura House, 1 St. Martin's-le-Grand, pg. 957 **IT**

Nomura Research Institute Europe Limited, Nomura House, 1 St. Martin's-le-Grand, pg. 956 **IT**

NORD/LB London, 71 Queen Victoria St., pg. 958 **IT**

NORD/LB Norddeutsche Securities, 71 Queen Victoria St., pg. 958 **IT**

Nordic Service Centre, 14 Waterloo Pl., pg. 1328 **IT**

Norinchukin International plc, 1st Floor, 4 Broadgate, pg. 958 **IT**

Normaco Ltd., 14, Queen Anne's Gate, pg. 712 **IT**

Norske Skog (UK) Ltd., 5, Stanhope Gate, pg. 967 **IT**

Nortel Properties Limited, 1B Portland Place, pg. 970 **IT**

Northern Telecom, 1B Portland Place, pg. 970 **IT**

The Northern Trust Co., 155 Bishopsgate, pg. 1197 **PB**

Norvista, 227 Regent Street, 3rd Floor, pg. 486 **IT**

Novotel UK Ltd., One Shortland, pg. 21 **IT**

Oak Dedicated Limited, c/o Archer Group Holding plc, Two Minister Court, pg. 337 **IT**

Obayashi Corporation-London, 2nd Floor, 25/28 Old Burlington Street, pg. 995 **IT**

Office Angels Limited, 3 Shortlands, pg. 1221 **PB**

Olivetti U.K. Ltd., Olivetti House, 86-88 Upper Richmond Rd., pg. 1003 **IT**

Olympus Optical Co. (U.K.) Ltd., 2-8 Honduras St., pg. 1005 **IT**

Olympus (U.K.) Ltd., pg. 1005 **IT**

OMRON Electronics Ltd., 1 Apsley Way, pg. 1006 **IT**

Orbis Insurance Agencies Limited, Cigna House, 8 Lime Street, pg. 363 **IT**

Orbital Park Limited, One Canada Square, pg. 466 **IT**

Ord Minnett Group Limited, First Fl., One College Hill, pg. 1497 **IT**

ORIX Corporate Finance Limited, 33 Lombard St., pg. 1009 **IT**

ORIX Europe Limited, 33 Lombard St., pg. 1009 **IT**

Osaka Gas Co.-London Office, Nash House, St. George St., pg. 1012 **IT**

Osprey, Michelin House, 81 Fulham Road, pg. 1093 **IT**

OSPREY PARK LTD., Osprey House, 10 Little Portland St., pg. 1012 **IT**

Otis Elevator PLC, 43/59 Clapham Rd., pg. 1691 **PB**

Outokumpu Copper Ltd., Outokumpu House, 10 Hammersmith Broadway, pg. 1017 **IT**

Outokumpu Rawmet (U.K.) Ltd., Outokumpu House, 10 Hammersmith Broadway, pg. 1017 **IT**

Outokumpu (U.K.) Ltd., Outokumpu House, 10 Hammersmith Broadway, pg. 1016 **IT**

P&O Bulk Carriers Ltd. (Bermuda), 58-72 Upper Ground, pg. 1033 **IT**

P&O Bulk Shipping Ltd., 58-72 Upper Ground, pg. 1033 **IT**

P&O Cruises Limited, 77 New Oxford St., pg. 1033 **IT**

P&O Properties International, 4 Carlton Gardens, pg. 1034 **IT**

P&O Property Developments Ltd., 4 Carlton Gardens, pg. 1034 **IT**

P&O Property Holdings Ltd., 79 Pall Mall, pg. 1034 **IT**

P&O Vending, Mulliner House, Flanders Rd., pg. 1034 **IT**

PB Leasing Ltd., Aviation House, 129 Kingsway, pg. 1304 **IT**

P.H.I. Engineering Ltd., 29-33, Tooley St., pg. 398 **IT**

PMC Eastern Europe LTD, 52 Minories, pg. 334 **IT**

PPIC UK Ltd., pg. 720 **IT**

PPM Ventures Ltd., 1 Waterhouse Sq., pg. 1073 **IT**

PTT Netherlands (UK) Ltd., pg. 720 **IT**

PTT Telecom Netherlands (UK) Inc., pg. 720 **IT**

PaineWebber International Inc., 1 Finsbury Av, pg. 1253 **IT**

Palace Theater London Limited, Cambrdige Circus, pg. 1089 **IT**

Pall Mall Support Services Limited, 125 Acre Ln., Brixton, pg. 385 **IT**

PanAgora Asset Management Limited, One Broadgate, pg. 936 **IT**

Panalpina World Transport Limited, pg. 1023 **IT**

Panmure Gordon & Co. Ltd., Nine Moorfields Highwalk, pg. 1166 **PB**

Panmure Gordon Bankers Ltd., 26 Austin Friars, pg. 1166 **PB**

Paragon Communications (UK) Ltd., Film House, 142 Wardour St., pg. 1226 **IT**

Paramount British Pictures Ltd., 45 Beadon Road, Hammersmith, pg. 777 **PV**

Paramount Television Ltd., 45 Beadon Rd., pg. 777 **PV**

Parcelforce, pg. 1064 **IT**

Parfums Christian Dior (Ireland) Ltd, c/o Parfums Christian Dior, (U.K.) Ltd, 13 Grosvenor Crescent, pg. 783 **IT**

Parfums Christian Dior (U.K.) Ltd., 13 Grosvenor Crescent, pg. 783 **IT**

Paribas Limited (ex. B.P.C.M.), 33 Wigmore St., pg. 321 **IT**

Parsons Brinckerhoff Ltd., 4 Roger Street, pg. 841 **PV**

Pauruinierre Gordon & Co. Ltd., New Broad Street House, 35, New Broad Street, pg. 1493 **IT**

Payne Stracey Ltd. (direct marketing), 80 Clerkenwell Rd., pg. 1152 **PV**

Pearson New Entertainment Europe, Kingsgate House, 536 King Road, pg. 1026 **IT**

PEARSON PLC., 3 Burlington Gardens, pg. 1025 **IT**

Pearson Professional Limited, Maple House, 149 Tottenham Court Road, pg. 1026 **IT**

Pegg Haindl Ltd., Thameside House, 100 Rainville Road, pg. 1026 **IT**

The Penguin Publishing Co. Ltd., 27 Wrights Lane, pg. 586 **IT**

THE PENINSULAR AND ORIENTAL STEAM NAVIGATION COMPANY, 79 Pall Mall, pg. 1032 **IT**

PENTLAND GROUP PLC, Pentlomds Ctr. Lakeside, Squires Ln., pg. 1035 **IT**

Pentland Shipping Services, Ltd., Pentland Centre, Lakeside Ho., pg. 1035 **IT**

Pepper, Hamilton & Scheetz, City Tower, 40 Basinghall St., pg. 851 **PV**

Permoglaze Paints, Ltd., pg. 47 **IT**

Perrier UK Ltd., 6 Lygon Place, pg. 919 **IT**

Personal Performance Consultants UK Limited (PPC), 85 Gracechurch Street, pg. 1502 **IT**

Petroleos de Venezuela UK, S.A., 7 Old Park Lane, 4th Fl., pg. 1046 **IT**

Petroleum and Facilities Engineering Ltd., pg. 1444 **PB**

Philadelphia National Limited, Merchant Bank, Philadelphia National House, pg. 447 **PB**

George Philip Limited, Michelin House, 81 Fulham Road, pg. 1093 **IT**

Philips Electronic & Associated Industries, Ltd., Arundel Great Ct., pg. 1055 **IT**

Phoenix Securities Limited, 99 Bishopgate, pg. 405 **IT**

Phonogram Ltd., 50 New Bond St., pg. 1053 **IT**

Pignone Engineering Ltd., 25, Green St., pg. 991 **IT**

Pillar Building Products ltd., Cleveland House, 19 St. James's Sq., pg. 267 **IT**

Pillar Electrical plc, Cleveland House, 19 St. James's Sq., pg. 267 **IT**

Pillar Engineering Ltd., Cleveland House, 19 St. James's Sq., pg. 267 **IT**

Piper, Jaffray & Hopwood Incorporated, London, 76 Cannon St., pg. 1303 **PB**

Pirelli UK plc, 40 Chancery Ln., pg. 1059 **IT**

Pitman Publishing Ltd., 128 Long Acre, pg. 1025 **IT**

Plenum Publishing Company, Ltd., New Loom House, 101 Black Church Lane, pg. 1311 **PB**

Plough (UK) Ltd., 17 Cavendish Sq., pg. 1439 **IT**

PolyGor Ltd., 13-14 St. George, pg. 1053 **IT**

PolyGram International Ltd., 8 St. James Sq., pg. 1053 **IT**

PolyGram Record Operations Ltd., 13-14 St. George, pg. 1053 **IT**

Pony Sports UK Ltd., Lakeside House, Squires Ln., pg. 1036 **IT**

Porti and Outdoor Advertising Ltd., 14, New Burlington Street, pg. 394 **IT**

Portland Holidays Ltd., 218 Great Portland St., pg. 1602 **PB**

THE POST OFFICE, 148 Old Street, pg. 1064 **IT**

Post Office Counters, pg. 1064 **IT**

Powerfin UK, Barrington House, Gresham Street 59-67, pg. 1415 **IT**

Price's Patent Candle Co. Ltd., 110 York Road, pg. 1139 **IT**

Priestley Footwear Ltd., Lakeside House, Squires Ln., pg. 1036 **IT**

Primark Investment Management Services, Limited, Monmouth House, 58-64 City Road, pg. 1326 **PB**

Prime Communications Ltd., Three Grosvenor Gardens, pg. 1226 **IT**

Priory Hospitals Group, Priory Lane, pg. 1716 **PB**

Private Electricity Company Ltd., Metro Power Office, City Cloisters, 188-196 Old St., pg. 1460 **IT**

Product Plus International, Unit 9, S. Bank Bus. Centre, Ponton Rd., pg. 1225 **PB**

Professional Publishing Ltd., Alhambra House, Charing Cross Rd., pg. 1601 **IT**

Prudential Assurance Co. Ltd., 250 Euston Road, pg. 1073 **IT**

PRUDENTIAL CORPORATION PLC, 142 Holborn Bars, pg. 1073 **IT**

Prudential Portfolio Managers Limited, 142 Holborn Bars, pg. 1073 **IT**

Qantas Airways Ltd., Quntas House, 395 King St., pg. 1075 **IT**

Quaestor Investment Management Ltd., River Plate House, 7-11 Finsbury Circus, pg. 1520 **IT**

Quantum International Ltd., 21 Soho Sq., pg. 1158 **PB**

Quilter & Co. Ltd., St. Helen's, pg. 343 **IT**

Quorium Capital Management Ltd., Bastion House, 140 London Wall, pg. 1493 **IT**

PB - *U.S. Public Companies Volume*
PV - *U.S. Private Companies Volume*
IT - *International Public & Private Companies Volume*

RNBNY Branch Office-London, 30 Monument St., pg. 1381 **PB**
The RTZ Corporation PLC, 6 St. James's Sq., pg. 1118 **IT**
RTZ Pillar Ltd., Cleveland House, 19 St. James's Sq., pg. 267 **IT**
RZB London, 36-38 Botolph Lane, pg. 1084 **IT**
Radio Connections, Scriptor Ct., 155 Farringdon Rd., pg. 452 **IT**
THE RANK GROUP PLC, 6 Connaught Place, pg. 1086 **IT**
Rank Holidays & Hotels Limited, 6 Connaught Place, pg. 1087 **IT**
Rank Investments Limited, 6 Connaught Pl., pg. 1087 **IT**
Rank Leisure Holdings plc, 6 Connaught Place, pg. 1087 **IT**
Rank Overseas Holding Limited, 6 Connaught Place, pg. 1087 **IT**
Rank RX Holdings Limited, 6 Connaught Pl., pg. 1087 **IT**
Ravenseft Industrial Estates Limited, 5 Strand, pg. 798 **IT**
Ravenseft Properties Limited, 5 Strand, pg. 798 **IT**
Ravenside Investments Limited, 5 Strand, pg. 798 **IT**
J.H. Rayner (Mincing Lane) Limited, Berisford Wing, 1 Prescot St., pg. 188 **IT**
Raysil Gowns Ltd., 17-18 Margaret St., pg. 300 **IT**
Raytheon Overseas Ltd., 31 Davies St., pg. 1366 **PB**
The Reader's Digest Association (Ireland) Limited, Berkeley Square House, Berkeley Square, pg. 1368 **PB**
The Reader's Digest Association Limited, Berkeley Square House, pg. 1368 **IT**
Reader's Digest (Family Insurance Services) Limited, Berkeley Square House, Berkeley Sq., pg. 1368 **IT**
Reader's Digest New Country Development Limited, Berkeley Square House, Berkeley Square, pg. 1368 **IT**
Reader's Union Limited, Berkeley House, Berkeley Square, pg. 1368 **IT**
Ready Mixed Concrete (London) Limited, RMC House, Townmead Rd., pg. 1080 **IT**
REALLY USEFUL HOLDINGS LIMITED, 19/22 Tower St., pg. 1089 **IT**
The Really Useful Theater Company Limited, 20 Greek St., pg. 1089 **IT**
RECKITT & COLMAN PLC, One Burlington Lane, pg. 1089 **IT**
Reckitt & Colman Products Ltd., One Burlington Ln., pg. 1090 **IT**
Red Carnation Gums Ltd., 5, Sir John Lyon House, High Timber St., pg. 1034 **IT**
Reed Books, Michelin House, 81 Fulham Road, pg. 1093 **IT**
Reed Elsevier Legal Division, Halsbury House, 35 Chancery Lane, pg. 1095 **IT**
REED ELSEVIER PLC, 25 Victoria Street, pg. 1093 **IT**
Reed International P.L.C., 25 Victoria Street, pg. 1093 **IT**
Reed MIDEM Organisation-UK, Metropolis House, 22 Percy Street, pg. 1096 **IT**
Reed Technology and Information Services (Europe), 39A Bowling Green Lane, pg. 1096 **IT**
Reliance National U.K. Limited, Plantation House, Fenchurch St., pg. 1374 **PB**
Repsol Exploracion U.K., Ltd., 5 Prince's Gate, pg. 1105 **IT**
Repsol Quimica, 5, Princes Gate, pg. 1105 **IT**
Repsol (U.K.) Ltd., 5, Princes Gate, pg. 1105 **IT**
Republic National Bank of New York (U.K.), 30 Monument Street, pg. 1381 **PB**
The Research Group, Holford Mews, Cruikshank St., pg. 704 **PV**
Research International, 6/7 Grosvenor Place, pg. 1482 **IT**
Retail Solutions, Greater London House, Hampstead Rd., pg. 452 **IT**
REUTERS HOLDINGS PLC, 85 Fleet Street, pg. 1105 **IT**
Reuters Limited, 85 Fleet Street, pg. 1105 **IT**
Reuters Television Limited, Cumberland Ave., pg. 1105 **IT**
Revlon International Corporation, 86 Brook St., pg. 690 **PV**
REXAM PLC, 114 Knightsbridge, pg. 1106 **IT**
R.J. Reynolds Tobacco (England) Limited, 57 Chiswell St., pg. 1355 **PB**
Rhone Poulenc Performance Resins & Coatings Division, 33 Ashley Place, pg. 1113 **IT**
Richard Shops Holdings Ltd., #1 Garrick Rd., pg. 1217 **IT**
Riggs A P Bank Limited, 21 Great Winchester St., pg. 1390 **PB**
RILEY ADVERTISING LIMITED, Riley House, 4 Red Lion Ct., Fleet St., pg. 1117 **IT**
Riley Advertising (London) Ltd., Riley House, 4 Red Lion Ct., Fleet St., pg. 1117 **IT**
RIO TINTO PLC, 6 St. James's Sq., pg. 1118 **IT**
The Ritz Hotel (London) Limited, Piccadilly, pg. 773 **IT**
Rockware Group Plc, Silvertown House, Vincent Sq., pg. 124 **IT**
Rogers & Cowan Brand Placement, 43 King St., Covent Garden, pg. 1226 **IT**
Rogge Global Plc, 5-6 St. Andrew's Hill, pg. 1674 **PB**
The Rolex Watch Co. Ltd., Heathend Rd., pg. 1126 **IT**
ROLLS-ROYCE PLC, 65 Buckingham Gate, pg. 1126 **IT**
Roose & Partners, 100 Gray's Inn Road, pg. 1377 **IT**
ROTHMANS UK HOLDINGS LIMITED, 15 Hill St., pg. 1129 **IT**
J. Rothschild Investment Management Limited, 27, St. James's Pl., pg. 1178 **IT**
J. Rothschild Wolfensohn & Co., 15, St. James's Pl., pg. 1178 **IT**
Rowan Drilling (U.K.) Limited, 79 Park St., pg. 1410 **PB**
Rowe & Pitman Ltd., One Finsbury Ave., pg. 1331 **IT**
Rowe & Pitman Money Broking Ltd., One Finsbury Ave., pg. 1331 **IT**
Rowe Price-Fleming International Inc., 25 Copthall Ave., pg. 493 **IT**

Royal & Sun Alliance Insurance Group, 1 Cornhill, pg. 1130 **IT**
ROYAL & SUN ALLIANCE INSURANCE GROUP PLC, 1 Bartholomew Lane, pg. 1130 **IT**
Royal Bank of Canada, 71-71a Queen Victoria St., pg. 1131 **IT**
Royal Copenhagen Ltd., 70 St. John St., pg. 1135 **IT**
Royal Copenhagen Porcelain & Georg Jensen Silver, 70 St. John St., pg. 1135 **IT**
Royal Insurance (UK) Ltd., 34 Lime St., pg. 1130 **IT**
Royal Mail, 76 Turnmill St., pg. 1064 **IT**
Ruhrgas UK Exploration and Production Limited, pg. 1149 **IT**
Rumenco, Sugar Quay, Lower Thames St., pg. 1356 **IT**
Rust Limited, Three Shortlands, Hammersmith Industrial Centre, pg. 1366 **PB**
S-E-Banken Luxembourg S.A., London, Scandanavian House, 2 Cannon Street, pg. 1259 **IT**
SBC CableComms, pg. 1416 **PB**
SBC Portfolio Management International Limited, 31 St. James's Square, pg. 1330 **IT**
SBC Warburg & Co. Ltd., 1 Finsbury Avenue, pg. 1331 **IT**
SBC Warburg Futures & Options Ltd., One Finsbury Ave., pg. 1331 **IT**
SBC Warburg Group Management Ltd., One Finsbury Ave., pg. 1331 **IT**
SBC Warburg Group plc, 1-2 Finsbury Ave., pg. 1330 **IT**
SBC Warburg Securities Ltd., One Finsbury Ave., pg. 1331 **IT**
SBCM Limited, 4th fl., Temple Ct., 11 Queen Victoria St., pg. 1310 **IT**
SCOR UK Group, 3, America Square, pg. 1153 **IT**
SEI Corporation, 6/7 Queen St., 3rd Fl., pg. 1417 **PB**
SHL Systemhouse Europe Ltd., 137 Stamford Street, pg. 1154 **IT**
S I Properties Limited, 765 Finchley Rd., pg. 1267 **IT**
SIA (UK) Ltd., Unit 2a, Elisabeter Indus. Estate, pg. 444 **IT**
SMC International U.K. 7392, 120 Wilton Rd., pg. 1717 **PB**
SMM Group, pg. 1316 **IT**
SR International Business Insurance Company Ltd., 71-77 Leadenhall Street, pg. 1333 **IT**
STC Investments Limited, Bridge House, Putney Bridge, pg. 528 **IT**
STC Properties Limited, Bridge House, Putney Bridge, pg. 528 **IT**
STC Technology Limited, Bridge House, Putney Bridge, pg. 529 **IT**
Saga Petroleum UK Limited, 123 Buckingham Palace Road, pg. 1169 **IT**
J. SAINSBURY PLC, Stamford House, Stamford St., pg. 1170 **IT**
ST. IVES PLC, St. Ives House, Lazington St., pg. 1177 **IT**
ST. JAMES'S PLACE CAPITAL PLC., 27 St. James's Place, pg. 1177 **IT**
St. Katharine by the Tower Limited, Ivory House, St. Katharine by the Tower, pg. 1358 **IT**
Sakura Finance International Limited, Ground and 1st Floors, 6 Broadgate, pg. 1180 **IT**
Sakura Global Capital Limited, Orient House, 42-45 New Broad Street, pg. 1179 **IT**
Sakura Trust Internaional Limited, Ground and 1st Floor, 6 Broadgate, pg. 1180 **IT**
Sampson Tyrrell Enterprise, Six Mercer St., pg. 1482 **IT**
H. Samuel Limited, 15 Stratton, pg. 1248 **IT**
San Francisco Insurance Company (U.K.) Limited, Three Quays Tower Hill, pg. 59 **IT**
Sangam Books Ltd., 57 London Fruit Exchange, pg. 1026 **IT**
Sanpaolo-London Branch, Wren House, 15 Carter Ln., pg. 692 **IT**
Santa Fe Braun (U.K.) Ltd., Parnell House, 19/28 Wilton Rd., pg. 765 **IT**
Santa Fe Minerals (U.K.), Inc., Parnell House, 19/28 Wilton Rd., pg. 766 **IT**
Sanwa Business Credit (UK) Limited, City Place House, 55 Basinghall Street, pg. 1190 **IT**
Sanwa Financial Products (UK) Co. Ltd., City Place House, 55 Basinghall Street, pg. 1190 **IT**
Sanwa Financial Services Limited, City Place House, 55 Basinghall Street, pg. 1190 **IT**
Sanwa International plc, City Place House, 55 Basinghall Street, pg. 1190 **IT**
SASIB Beverage UK Ltd., 28 Chase Rd., pg. 1195 **IT**
SavaCentre Limited, Stamford House, Stamford St., pg. 1170 **IT**
Save & Prosper Group Limited, One Finsbury Ave., pg. 493 **IT**
Scandinaviska Enskilda Banken London, Scandinavian House, 2-6 Cannon St., pg. 1259 **IT**
Schering-Plough Holdings Ltd., 182-204 St. John St., pg. 1439 **PB**
Schlumberger PLC, One Kingsway, pg. 1439 **PB**
Scholl (UK) Ltd., 182-204 St. John St., pg. 1439 **PB**
SCHRODERS PLC, 120 Cheapside, pg. 1210 **IT**
Scope Ketchum Communications Ltd., Towerhouse, 14 Southampton St., pg. 617 **PV**
ScotiaMocatta, Mocatta House, 4 Crosby Sq., pg. 156 **IT**
Sea Containers British Isles Ltd., Sea Containers House, 20 Upper Ground, pg. 1214 **IT**
Sea Containers Services Ltd., Sea Containers House, 20 Upper Ground, pg. 1214 **IT**
Seafood Europe, Meed House, 21 John St., pg. 452 **IT**
Seagram Europe and Africa, 5-7 Manderville Place, pg. 1217 **IT**
SEARS PLC, 40 Duke St., pg. 1217 **IT**
Security Insurance Co. (U.K.) Ltd., 40 Lime St., pg. 1232 **IT**
Security Pacific EuroFinance, Inc., The Adelphi, John Adam Street, pg. 183 **PB**

Security Pacific Hoare Govett (Holdings) Limited, Security Pacific House, Four Broadgate, pg. 183 **PB**
SEDGWICK GROUP PLC, Sackville House, 143-149 Fenchurch Street, pg. 1217 **IT**
Sedgwick Limited, Sedgwick House, The Sedgwick Centre, pg. 1218 **IT**
Sedgwick Oakwood Underwriting Agents Limited, Sackville House, 143-149 Fenchurch Street, pg. 1218 **IT**
Sensory Systems Ltd., 293/303 Edgware Rd., pg. 1074 **PV**
Sequent Computer Systems (United Kingdom), 10 Maltravers St., 10th Fl., pg. 1460 **PB**
Seven-Up Europe, 2 Basil St., pg. 1278 **IT**
Seymour Distribution Ltd., Windsor House, 1270 London Road, pg. 796 **IT**
Shandwick Communications Ltd., 114 Cromwell Rd., pg. 1226 **IT**
Shandwick Consultants Ltd., Aldermary House, 10-15 Queen St., pg. 1227 **IT**
Shandwick Interactive Ltd., 4 Bouverie Street, pg. 1227 **IT**
SHANDWICK INTERNATIONAL PLC, 61 Grosvenor St., pg. 1226 **IT**
Shandwick International Plc, 18 Dering Street, pg. 1226 **IT**
Shandwick Public Relations Ltd., 3 Grosvenor Gardens, pg. 1226 **IT**
Shandwick United Kingdom, 18 Dering St., pg. 1226 **IT**
Sharp Electronics (U.K.), 5 Vere St., pg. 1230 **IT**
Sharplan Lasers (Europe) Ltd., 141-155 Brent St., pg. 429 **IT**
Shell International Petroleum Co. Ltd., Shell Centre, 2 York Rd., pg. 1139 **IT**
Shell UK Ltd., pg. 1139 **IT**
Sheraton Hotels (England) Limited, The Kiln House, 210 New Kings Rd., pg. 1512 **PB**
Shimizu International Finance (UK) Ltd., 45 Old Bond St., pg. 1234 **IT**
Shimizu (UK) Ltd., 45 Old Bond St., pg. 1234 **IT**
Shiseido U.K. Co., Ltd., 8 Cork St., Mayfair, pg. 1236 **IT**
Shoko Chukin Bank, Bow Bells House, Bread St., pg. 1236 **IT**
Siemens Nixdorf Information Systems Ltd., Siemens House, pg. 1245 **IT**
SIGNET GROUP PLC, Zenith House, The Hyde, pg. 1248 **IT**
Sigurd EBS Ltd., pg. 312 **IT**
Sikkens Ltd., pg. 47 **IT**
Sime Darby Commodities Limited, Hibernia Chambers, London Bridge, pg. 1250 **IT**
SIMON ENGINEERING PLC, Simon House, 6 Eaton Gate, pg. 1251 **IT**
Simon Marketing, Ltd., 7 Moor St., pg. 1001 **PV**
SIMONS PALMER DENTON CLEMMOW & JOHNSON LTD., 19-20 Noel St., pg. 1252 **IT**
Simplex Piling Limited, 3rd Fl., Cherrydown Ave., pg. 219 **IT**
Sims Medical Distribution Limited, New Universal House, 303 Chase Rd., pg. 1267 **IT**
Singapore Tourist Promotion Board - London, 1st Floor, Carrington House, 126-130 Regent Street, pg. 1254 **IT**
The Singleton of Auchroisk, 8 Henrietta Place, pg. 409 **IT**
Sino-Health Ltd., 133 Houndsditch, pg. 1255 **IT**
Sinochem International Oil (London) Co. Ltd., Westminster Tower (11th Fl.), 3 Albert Embankment, pg. 1255 **IT**
Sinochem (U.K.) Ltd., 2nd Fl., Kingsburg House, 15/17 King St., pg. 1256 **IT**
Skadden, Arps, Slate, Meagher & Flom, One Canada Square, Canary Wharf, pg. 1004 **PV**
Skandia Insurance (UK Contact Office) Ltd., Skandia House, 23 College Hill, pg. 1256 **IT**
Skandia Investment Management Ltd., Skandia House, 23 College Hill, pg. 1258 **IT**
Skandia Marine Insurance Company (UK) Ltd., Marlon House, 71-74 Mark Lane, pg. 1257 **IT**
Skandia Property (UK) Ltd., Skandia House, 23 College Hill, pg. 1258 **IT**
Skandia (UK) Holding Ltd., Skandia House, 23 College Hill, pg. 1258 **IT**
Skandia UK Insurance plc, Skandia House, 23 College Hill, pg. 1258 **IT**
Skanska London, 5 Hyde Park Gate, pg. 1261 **IT**
SKYEPHARMA PLC, 105 Piccadilly, pg. 1262 **IT**
SLEEPEEZEE LIMITED, 61 Morden Rd., Merton, pg. 1263 **IT**
The Pierre Smirnoff Company, 151 Marylebone Rd., pg. 411 **IT**
SMITH & NEPHEW PLC, Victoria Embankment, 2 Temple Place, pg. 1263 **IT**
J. Smith & Sons (Clerkenwell) Ltd., St. John's Sq., pg. 391 **IT**
W.H. SMITH GROUP PLC, Audrey House, Ely Pl., pg. 1264 **IT**
Smiths Industries Aerospace & Defence Limited-Head Office, 765 Finchley Rd., pg. 1267 **IT**
Smiths Industries Industrial Group, 765 Finchley Rd., pg. 1267 **IT**
SMITHS INDUSTRIES PLC, 765 Finchley Rd., pg. 1266 **IT**
Smythe Dorward Lambert, 55 Drury Lane, pg. 1225 **PB**
Smythson of Bond Street, 40 New Bond Street, pg. 707 **IT**
Societe Generale Equities International, Exchange House, Primrose St., pg. 1274 **IT**
Softimage (U.K.) Ltd., pg. 1108 **PB**
Sony Music Entertainment (UK) Limited, 10 Great Marlborough St., pg. 1284 **IT**
Sony Music International, 1 Red Place, pg. 1284 **IT**
Sotheby's Asia, 34-35 New Bond St., pg. 1487 **PB**
Sotheby's Europe, 34-35 New Bond St., pg. 1487 **PB**
South African Airways, St. George's House, 61 Conduit Street, pg. 1417 **IT**

Speedbird Express, P.O. Box 99, World Cargo Centre S-126, pg. 219 **IT**

Speedwing Consulting, Speedwing House, Heathrow Airport, pg. 219 **IT**

SQUIRES ROBERTSON GILL, 9 Cavendish Pl., pg. 1291 **IT**

Stag Brewery, Lower Richmond Rd., pg. 115 **PB**

Standard Bank London Limited, Cannon Bridge House, 5th Floor, 2525 Dowgate Hill, pg. 1294 **IT**

The Standard Bank of South Africa Limited, 5th Floor, Cannon Bridge House, pg. 1294 **IT**

Standard Chartered Bank, 1 Aldermanbury Sq., pg. 1294 **IT**

Standard Chartered Bank, 37 Gracechurch Street, pg. 1294 **IT**

Standard Chartered Bank, 22 Billiter Street, pg. 1294 **IT**

STANDARD CHARTERED BANK PLC, 1 Aldermanbury Sq., pg. 1294 **IT**

Standard Chartered Equitor Limited, Clements House., 4/F Street, pg. 1296 **IT**

Standard Chartered Leasing Company Ltd., The Adelphi, John Adam St., pg. 1296 **IT**

Standard Commercial Tobacco Co. (U.K.) Ltd., 42 Grosvenor Gardens, pg. 1502 **PB**

Stansand Limited, Sir John Lyon House, 5 High Timber St., pg. 1377 **IT**

Stant Corporation, 28 Grosvenor St., pg. 1397 **IT**

State Bank of India, State Bank House, 1, Milk Street, pg. 1297 **IT**

State Bank of India, Nash House, St. George Street, pg. 1297 **IT**

State Bank of India, 630 Finchley Road, pg. 1297 **IT**

State Street Bank & Trust Co., London, 1 Canada Square, pg. 1513 **PB**

State Street Bank-London Branch, One Canada Square, pg. 1513 **PB**

State Street Global Advisors (U.K.) Limited, Almack House, 28 King St., pg. 1513 **PB**

Statoil (UK) Ltd., Swan Gardens, 10 Piccadilly, pg. 1298 **IT**

Kyle Stewart Ltd., Merit House, Edgware Rd., pg. 630 **IT**

STOLT-NIELSEN S.A., Aldwych House, 71-91 Aldwych, pg. 1301 **IT**

Stolt-Nielsen Limited, pg. 1301 **IT**

Stolt-Nielsen Shipping Limited, pg. 1301 **IT**

STOREHOUSE PLC, Marylebone House, 129-137 Marylebone Rd., pg. 1304 **IT**

Storno Cellular Services Ltd., 110 Grafton Rd., pg. 1140 **PB**

Straits Petroleum Limited, 53, St. George's Rd., Wimbledon, pg. 712 **IT**

Strategic Marketing Services London, Mulliner House, Flanders Road, pg. 1625 **PB**

Stratus Computer, Ltd., Central House Lampton Rd., pg. 1524 **PB**

Stratus Computer, Ltd., 3rd Fl., Beaufort House, 15 St. Botolph St., pg. 1524 **PB**

Subscription Services Ltd. (SSL), 148 Old Street, pg. 1064 **IT**

Sullivan Powell & Company Ltd., 34, Burlington Arcade, pg. 539 **IT**

The Sumitomo Bank, Ltd.-London Branch, Temple Court, 11 Queen Victoria St., pg. 1309 **IT**

Sumitomo Chemical (U.K.) plc, 22 City Rd., pg. 1312 **IT**

Sumitomo Electric Europe Limited, 30 Dorset Sq., pg. 1314 **IT**

Sumitomo Electric Finance U.K. Ltd., 30 Dorset Sq., pg. 1314 **IT**

Sumitomo Finance International plc, 4th Fl., Temple Ct., 11 Queen Victoria St., pg. 1310 **IT**

Sumitomo Life International (UK) Limited, 13F, 1 Angel Court, pg. 1315 **IT**

Sumitomo Life Realty (U.K.) Limited, 13F, 1 Angel Ct., pg. 1315 **IT**

Sumitomo Metal Industries Ltd. (European Office), 33 Cavendish Square, pg. 1316 **IT**

Sumitomo Sitix Europe Plc., 33 Cavendish Square, pg. 1317 **IT**

The Sumitomo Trust & Banking Co., Ltd., 155 Bishops Gate, pg. 1318 **IT**

Sumitomo Trust International Plc., 3rd Fl., 155 Bishopsgate, pg. 1318 **IT**

The Sun, pg. 927 **IT**

Sun International Production Company Limited, 80 Hammersmith Rd., pg. 1530 **PB**

SUN LIFE AND PROVINCIAL HOLDINGS PLC, 107 Cheapside, pg. 1318 **IT**

Suntory U.K. Ltd., 25, St. James's St., pg. 1322 **IT**

Sutcliffe Catering Group Ltd., Mulliner House, Flanders Rd., pg. 1035 **IT**

Svenska Handelsbanken London, Trinity Tower, 9 Thomas More Street, pg. 1327 **IT**

Swan Hellenic Ltd., 77 New Oxford St., pg. 1035 **IT**

Swedbank London, 42/45 New Broad St., pg. 1328 **IT**

Swiss Bank Corporation, Swiss Bank House, 1 High Timber St., pg. 1330 **IT**

Swiss Bank Corporation, 30A Charles II Street, pg. 1330 **IT**

Swiss Reinsurance Company UK Ltd., 71-77 Leadenhall Street, pg. 1333 **IT**

TBWA PAYNE STRACEY, 80 Clerkenwell Rd., pg. 1336 **IT**

TM Management Services Limited, 150 Leadenhall St., pg. 1392 **IT**

TMD CARAT ADVERTISING LIMITED, New London House, 172 Drury Ln., pg. 1342 **IT**

TMD Direct, New London House, 172 Drury Ln., pg. 1342 **IT**

TPS Public Relations Ltd., 3 Grosvenor Gardens, pg. 1226 **IT**

TSB Hill Samuel Bank Holding Co Plc, 100 Wood St., pg. 813 **IT**

Taisei Europe, Ltd., No. 3, Hanover Square, pg. 1347 **IT**

Taiyo Life International (U.K.), Ltd., Condor House, 14 St. Paul's Churchyard, pg. 1349 **IT**

The Taiyo Mutual Life Insurance Co., Condor House, 14 St. Paul's Churchyard, pg. 1349 **IT**

Takashimaya (UK) Ltd., Brook Street House, 47 Davies St., pg. 1350 **IT**

Takenaka (U.K.) Ltd., London, Tavistock House, South Tavistock Square, pg. 1352 **IT**

Takugin Finance International Ltd., 33 Lombard St., pg. 627 **IT**

Tarmac Construction Major Projects Limited, 27 Hammersmith Grove, pg. 1355 **IT**

Tate & Lyle Industries Limited, Sugar Quay, Lower Thames St., pg. 1356 **IT**

Tate & Lyle International, Sugar Quay, Lower Thames St., pg. 1356 **IT**

Tate & Lyle International Finance Limited, Sugar Quay, Lower Thames St., pg. 1356 **IT**

Tate & Lyle Investments Limited, Sugar Quay, Lower Thames St., pg. 1356 **IT**

TATE & LYLE PLC, Sugar Quay, Lower Thames St., pg. 1356 **IT**

Tate & Lyle Sugars, pg. 1356 **IT**

Tatung Co., 7 Salcombe Lodge, Lissenden Gardens, pg. 1357 **IT**

TAYLOR & FRANCIS GROUP LTD., 1 Gunpowder Sq., pg. 1357 **IT**

Taylor Woodrow Developments Ltd., 4 Dunraven Street, pg. 1358 **IT**

TAYLOR WOODROW PLC, 4 Dunraven St., pg. 1358 **IT**

Taylor Woodrow Property Company Ltd., International House, pg. 1359 **IT**

The Telegraph plc, 1 Canada Square, Canary Wharf, pg. 632 **IT**

Telsi Ltd., 19, Berkeley Street, pg. 1248 **IT**

Tennant KVK Ltd., 69 Grosvenor Street, pg. 371 **IT**

Tenneco Aviation Limited, Leconfield House, Curzon St., pg. 1580 **PB**

Tenneco Europe, Leconfield House, Curzon St., pg. 1580 **PB**

Tenneco International Finance Limited, Leconfield House, Curzon St., pg. 1580 **PB**

Tenneco United Kingdom Holdings Limited, Leconfield House, Curzon St., pg. 1580 **PB**

Tequila UK Ltd., Compass House, 22 Redan Pl., pg. 118 **IT**

Terra Nova Insurance Company Ltd., Terra Nova House, 41-43 Mincing Lane, pg. 27 **IT**

Texaco Britain Limited, 1 Westferry Circus, pg. 1584 **PB**

Texaco Limited, 1 Westferry Circus, pg. 1584 **PB**

Texaco Overseas Tankship Ltd., 1 Westferry Circus, pg. 1584 **PB**

The Sakura Bank - London Branch, Ground and 1st Fl., 6 Broadgate, pg. 1179 **IT**

Thomas Tilling Limited, Silverman House, Vincent Sq., pg. 124 **IT**

The Thomson Corporation PLC, The Quadrangle, P.O. Box 4YG, pg. 1601 **IT**

Thomson Finance Ltd., Four Stratford Pl., pg. 1601 **PB**

Thomson Holidays Ltd., Greater London House, Hampstead Rd., pg. 1602 **IT**

Thomson Information Services Ltd., The Quadrangle, 180 Wardour St., 1st Fl., pg. 1601 **PB**

Thomson Tour Operations Ltd., Greater London House, Hampstead Rd., pg. 1602 **PB**

Thornton & Co. Ltd., Swan House, 33 Queen Street, pg. 420 **IT**

Threadneedle Asset Management, 60 St. Mary Axe, pg. 110 **IT**

Threadneedle Investment Managers Limited, 60 St. Mary Axe, pg. 110 **IT**

Threadneedle Property Fund Managers Limited, 60 St. Mary Axe, pg. 110 **IT**

Three Quays Marine Services Ltd., 13-17 Long Lane, pg. 1035 **IT**

3I GROUP PLC, 91 Waterloo Rd., pg. 1386 **IT**

Tiffany & Co., 25 Old Bond Street, pg. 1609 **IT**

Tilbury Container Service Ltd., Beagle House, Braham St., pg. 1035 **IT**

Time-Life International Ltd., Time & Life Bldg., New Bond St., pg. 1615 **PB**

Times Newspapers Ltd., P.O. Box 495, pg. 927 **IT**

Tioxide Group Limited, Lincoln House, 137-143 Hammersmith Rd., pg. 663 **IT**

Tobacco Insurance Co. Ltd., 1 Threadneedle St., pg. 110 **IT**

Todd-AO Europe Holding Ltd., pg. 1619 **PB**

Todd-AO Filmatic Ltd., pg. 1619 **PB**

Todd-AO U.K., pg. 1619 **PB**

Together Ltd., pg. 1015 **IT**

TOHO Life International (UK) Ltd., 30-34 Moorgate, pg. 1390 **IT**

TOHO Life Properties (UK) Ltd., 30-34 Moorgate, pg. 1390 **IT**

Tokai Bank Europe plc, Mercury House, Tritan Court, 14 Finsbury Square, pg. 1391 **IT**

Tokai Capital Markets Limited, Mercury House, Triton Court, pg. 1391 **IT**

The Tokio Marine & Fire Insurance Company (U.K.) Limited, 150 Leadenhall St., pg. 1392 **IT**

The Tokio Marine Capital Research Limited, 150 Leadenhall St., pg. 1393 **IT**

Tokio Marine Europe Limited, 150 Leadenhall St., pg. 1393 **IT**

Tokio Marine Property Limited, 150 Leadenhall St., pg. 1393 **IT**

The Tokyo Electric Power Company-London, 31 St. James Square, pg. 1394 **IT**

Tokyo-Mitsubishi International plc, 6 Broadgate, pg. 158 **IT**

Tomen (U.K.) Plc., 13 Charles II St., pg. 1395 **IT**

TOMKINS PLC, E. Putney House, 84 Upper Richmond Road, pg. 1395 **IT**

Toppan Printing Co. (UK) Ltd., Gillingham House, 38-44 Gillingham St., pg. 1399 **IT**

Toray Europe Ltd., 7 Old Park Lane, pg. 1400 **IT**

Toray Industries, Inc.-Europe Office, 7 Old Park Lane, pg. 1400 **IT**

Toronto-Dominion Bank (United Kingdom) Ltd., Triton Court, 14-18 Finsbury Square, pg. 1401 **IT**

Toshiba International Finance (UK) plc, Audrey House, Ely Place, pg. 1406 **IT**

Total Oil Great Britain Ltd., 4 Lancer Square, pg. 1409 **IT**

Total Oil Marine p.l.c.-TOM, 16 Palace Street, pg. 1409 **IT**

Touche Remnant Holdings, Ltd., 3 Finsbury Ave., pg. 609 **IT**

Tourism Malaysia - London Office, 57, Trafalgar Square, pg. 833 **IT**

Toyo Trust International Limited, 36 Quenn St., pg. 1411 **IT**

Toyota Motor Corporation, London Representative Office, 9 Clifford St., pg. 1413 **IT**

Toyota Motor Finance (UK) PLC, 9, Clifford St., pg. 1414 **IT**

Trade Promotion Services Ltd., Exhibitions House, Warren Lane, pg. 451 **IT**

Trafalgar House Corporate Development Ltd., 1 Berkeley St., pg. 773 **IT**

Trafalgar House Engineering, 20 Eastbourne Terrace, pg. 773 **IT**

Trafalgar House Group Services Ltd., 1 Berkeley St., pg. 773 **IT**

Trafalgar House PLC, 1 Berkeley St., pg. 772 **IT**

Trafalgar House Property Ltd., 1 Berkeley St., pg. 773 **IT**

Transatlantic Holdings Inc., Fountain House, 130 Fenchurch Street, pg. 84 **PB**

Transatlantic Holdings, Inc.-London, Fountain House, 130 Fenchurch St., pg. 85 **PB**

Transnet Group, St. George's House, 61 Conduit St., pg. 1418 **IT**

TRANSPORT DEVELOPMENT GROUP PLC, Windsor House, 50 Victoria St., pg. 1418 **IT**

Transworld Publishers Ltd., 61-63 Uxbridge Rd., pg. 191 **IT**

Travel U.K., 66 Newman Street, pg. 647 **PV**

Tridex Systems Ltd., 42 Kingsway, pg. 193 **PV**

Triton Resources UK, pg. 1640 **PB**

Trusthouse Forte plc, 6 Sackville St., pg. 170 **IT**

Tunnel Refineries Limited, Sugar Quay, Lower Thames St., pg. 1356 **IT**

Turbomeca Ltd., 4/5 Grosvenor Pl., pg. 787 **IT**

Turegum Insurance Company, The Zurich Bldg., 90 Fenchurch St., pg. 1530 **IT**

Turner International U.K. Ltd., 247/249 Vauxhaul Bridge Rd., pg. 1646 **PB**

The Tussauds Group Limited, Maple House, 149 Tottenham Court Road, pg. 1026 **IT**

Twelve Islands Shipping Company, 8 Henrietta Place, pg. 409 **IT**

U.A.C. Holdings Ltd., U.A.C. House, Blackfriars Road, pg. 1434 **IT**

UAC International Ltd., U.A.C. House, Blackfriars Road, pg. 1434 **IT**

UBS Asset Management London Ltd., Triton Court 14, Finsbury Square, pg. 1440 **IT**

UBS Asset Management (UK) Ltd., Mercury House, Triton Ct., 14 Finsbury Square, pg. 1440 **IT**

UBS Limited, 100 Liverpool St., pg. 1440 **IT**

UBS Phillips & Drew International Investment Ltd., Triton Court, 14 Finsbury Square, pg. 1440 **IT**

UCM Timber PLC, City House, 190 City Road, pg. 967 **IT**

U.I.C. Insurance Co. Ltd., 63, Mark Lane, pg. 1043 **IT**

UN (Overseas) Ltd., Ludgate House, 245 Blackfriars Rd., pg. 1443 **IT**

UPM-Kymmene UK plc, Kymmene House, 4 Stratford Place, pg. 1430 **IT**

Ultramar Canada Inc.-London Office, Skandia House, 23 College Hill, pg. 1663 **PB**

UNIGATE PLC, Unigate House, pg. 1433 **IT**

Unilever (Commonwealth Holdings) Ltd., Unilever House, Blackfriars, pg. 1434 **IT**

UNILEVER PLC, Unilever House, pg. 1433 **IT**

Unilever U.K. Central Resources Limited, Unilever House, Blackfriars, pg. 1434 **IT**

Unilever U.K. Holdings Ltd., Unilever House, Blackfriars, pg. 1434 **IT**

Union Bank of Switzerland, 100 Liverpool Street, pg. 1441 **IT**

United Asset Management-London Office, Clutha House, 10 Storey's Gate, pg. 1674 **PB**

United Gas Co. Ltd., 21 Tothill St., pg. 1701 **PB**

United Molasses Company, Sugar Quay, Lower Thames St., pg. 1356 **IT**

UNITED NEWS & MEDIA PLC, Ludgate House, 245 Blackfriars Road, pg. 1443 **IT**

Universal Leaf Services Ltd., 2 Alric Ave., SW3, pg. 1695 **PB**

Universal Studios Artists (England) Ltd., 139 Piccadilly, pg. 1216 **IT**

Universal Studios Music Ltd., Universal Bldg., 138 Piccadilly, pg. 1217 **IT**

Universal (U.K.) Limited, Condor House, 14th St., Pauls Churchyard, pg. 1444 **IT**

UNUM European Holding Company Limited, Limited Hamilton House, One Temple Ave., Victoria Embankment, pg. 1700 **PB**

Urban Outfitters UK, Limite, 47 Beak St., pg. 1700 **PV**

Urethanes Technology, Cowcross Ct., pg. 285 **PV**

Geographic Index-Non U.S.

Usher-Walker Group Ltd., Usher-Walker House, 1 Datapoint Business Centre, pg. 371   IT
VNU Business Publications Ltd., pg. 1445   IT
Vector Marine Holdings, 55 Park Lane, Suite 14, pg. 1461   IT
Venice Simplon-Orient-Express Ltd., 20, Upper Ground, pg. 1213   IT
Verbatim-U.K., Prestige House, 23-26 High St., pg. 872   IT
Veuve Clicquot (UK) Ltd, Fifth Fl., 79 Knightsbridge, pg. 783   IT
Viacom Intl. Ltd., 40 Conduit St., pg. 779   PV
Vickers Medical, Vickers House, Millbank Tower, pg. 1467   IT
VICKERS PLC, Millbank Tower, pg. 1466   IT
Vickers Properties Limited, Anchor & Hope Lane, pg. 1467   IT
Victoria Joinery Ltd., Magdalen Rd., Earlsfield, pg. 796   IT
Videotron Holdings Plc, 76 Hammersmith Rd., pg. 247   IT
Virgin Music Group, Kensal House, 553/579 Harrow Road, pg. 427   IT
Voest-Alpine (U.K.) Ltd., 5th Fl., 36 Broadway, pg. 1472   IT
W & A Gilbey, 8 Henrietta Place, pg. 409   IT
WCRS, #5 Golden Square, pg. 603   IT
WF Corroon-Europe, 55 Gracechurch Street, pg. 1502   IT
WF Corroon-London, 55 Gracechurch Street, pg. 1502   IT
WF Corroon-United Kingdom & International, 55 Gracechurch Street, pg. 1501   IT
WHS, Southwark Bridge Office Village, pg. 1299   IT
WPP GROUP PLC, 27 Farm Street, pg. 1482   IT
Wackenhut U.K., Ltd., 875 Sidcup Rd., pg. 1732   PB
Waddington & Duval (Holdings) Ltd., Brewhouse St., pg. 129   IT
Wako International (Europe) Limited, 4th Floor, 155 Bishopgate, pg. 1485   IT
The Wall Street Journal Europe, London Intl. Press Centre, 76 Shoe Lane, pg. 525   PB
Walthamstow Plant, pg. 672   PB
Warner Music International (Europe) Ltd., 83 Baker St., pg. 1615   IT
WASSALL PLC, 39 Victoria St., pg. 1486   IT
Waste Management International plc, Hammersmith Intl. Center, 3 Shortlands, pg. 1745   PB
Wausau Insurance Company (U.K.), Ltd., 7th Floor, 7 Birchin Lane, pg. 789   PV
Waverly Europe Ltd., Kiln House, 210 New Kings Rd., pg. 1748   PB
Waverly House Limited, 12A Golden Square, pg. 796   IT
WEATHERALL GREEN & SMITH, 22, Chancery Ln., pg. 1488   IT
Weatherford Enterra Business Development Group, Ltd., pg. 1750   PV
The Weber Group, 2 Endell St., WC2H 9L, pg. 1157   PV
Welbeck Golin/Harris Communications Ltd., Covent Garden, 43 King St., pg. 1226   IT
E.J. Welton & Co. Limited, 85 Gracechurch Street, pg. 1502   IT
Wendy Cushing Trimmings, Unit G7, Chelsea Harbour Design Centre, pg. 434   PB
Wentworth Import & Export Ltd., 124/130 Wandsworth Road, pg. 491   IT
West Merchant Bank Ltd., 33-36 Gracechurch Street, pg. 1493   IT
Western Asset Global Management, 155 Bishopsgate, pg. 985   PB
WestLB London Branch, 51 Moorgate, pg. 1493   IT
WestLB UK Limited, 51 Moorgate, pg. 1494   IT
Westminster Cable Company Limited, 87-89 Baker Street, pg. 222   IT
Westminster Insurance Agencies Limited, 2 White Lion Court Cornhill, pg. 565   IT
Westpac Banking Corporation-European Div., 63 St. Mary Ave., pg. 1497   IT
WHITBREAD PLC, Chiswell Street, pg. 1498   IT
Whitehall Laboratories Ltd., 22/24 Torrington Place, pg. 82   PB
Williams de Broe Holdings Ltd., 6 Broadgate, pg. 148   IT
Willis Corroon Construction Risks Limited, 55 Gracechurch Street, pg. 1502   IT
Willis Corroon Continental Europe Limited, 55 Gracechurch Street, pg. 1502   IT
Willis Corroon Credit Limited, 55 Gracechurch Street, pg. 1502   IT
WILLIS CORROON GROUP PLC, Ten Trinity Sq., pg. 1501   IT
Willis Corroon Risk Consulting Limited, Ten Trinity Square, pg. 1503   IT
Willis Corroon Risk Management Limited, Ten Trinity Sq., pg. 1503   IT
Willis Faber & Dumas (Agencies) Limited, Lloyd's Building, One Lime Street, pg. 1503   IT
Willis Faber & Dumas Limited, Ten Trinity Sq., pg. 1503   IT
George Wimpey International Ltd., Hammersmith Grove, pg. 1510   IT
GEORGE WIMPEY PLC, Three Shortland, pg. 1510   IT
Wimpey Group Services Ltd., Hammersmith Grove, pg. 1510   IT
Wimpey Homes Holdings Ltd., Hammersmith Grove, pg. 1510   IT
Wimpey Property Holdings Ltd., Hammersmith Grove, pg. 1510   IT
Woolworths plc, Woolworth House, 242-246 Marylebore Rd., pg. 734   IT
Workgroup Computing Show, Greater London House, Hampstead Rd., pg. 452   IT
World Business New Zealand House, 15th Fl., pg. 1189   PV
World Expo Corporation, 99 Gray's Inn Rd., pg. 571   PV
World Trade Centre In London Ltd., Europe House, pg. 1359   IT
F.E. Wright Group, 109 Borough High St., pg. 818   IT

Wunderman Worldwide Limited, Greater London House, Hampstead Rd., pg. 1199   PV
YRI (Europe) Ltd., 74-78 Finsbury Pavement, pg. 1517   IT
Yamaichi Asset Management (Europe) Ltd., 74-78 Finsbury Pavement, pg. 1517   IT
Yamaichi Bank (UK) Plc, Guildhall House, 81-87 Gresham St., pg. 1517   IT
Yamaichi Capital Management (Europe) Ltd., 74-78 Finsbury Pavement, pg. 1516   IT
Yamaichi Gilts Ltd., Finsbury Court, 111-117 Finsbury Pavement, pg. 1517   IT
Yamaichi Information Systems Co., Ltd., Ste. 13, 01/02 Exchange Tower, 1 Harbour Exchange Sq., pg. 1516   IT
Yamaichi International (Europe) Ltd., Finsbury Court, 111-117 Finsbury Pavement, pg. 1516   IT
Yasuda Life International (London) Ltd., River Plate House, 7-11 Finsbury Circus, pg. 1520   IT
Yasuda Properties (U.K.) Ltd., River Plate House, 7-11 Finsbury Circus, pg. 1520   IT
Yellow Frog, 34-42 Cleveland St., pg. 416   IT
Yellow Pages Sales Limited, BT Centre, 81 Newgate St., pg. 222   IT
Yeomans & Partners Ltd., 152/154 Coles Green Rd., pg. 1035   IT
Young & Rubicam Holdings Ltd., Greater London House, Hampstead Rd., pg. 1199   PV
ZENECA GROUP PLC, 15 Stanhope Gate, pg. 1524   IT
Ziff-Davis U.K., Cottons Centre, Hay's Ln., pg. 1276   IT
ZOMBA RECORDING CORP., 165-167 High Road, pg. 1529   IT
Zurich International (UK) Limited, The Zurich Building, 90 Fenchurch St., pg. 1532   IT
Zurich Investment Management, 1 Fleet Place, pg. 1532   IT
Zurich Re (UK) Limited, The Zurich Building, 90 Fenchurch St., pg. 1532   IT

Loughborough

British Gypsum Ltd., East Leake, pg. 122   IT
Brush Electrical Machines Ltd., pg. 124   IT
Brush Transformers Ltd., P.O. Box 20, pg. 124   IT
Dunlop Precision Rubber Division, Ashbey Rd., pg. 125   IT
KSB Limited, pg. 721   IT
Ladybird Books Ltd., Beeches Rd., pg. 1025   IT
Mattel (UK) Ltd., Derby Road, pg. 1059   PB
Munradtech Generators Limited, Gelders Hall Road, Shepshed, pg. 1344   IT
Stahl GB Limited, Bakewell Rd., pg. 1524   IT

Loughton

OCE (U.K.) Limited, Langston Rd., pg. 995   IT
OCE (U.K.) Finance Limited, Langston Rd., pg. 995   IT
OCE (U.K.) Printing Systems Limited, Langston Rd., pg. 995   IT

Lowestoft

Kvaerner Humberoak Ltd., 2 Tower Road, pg. 767   IT
Richards (Shipbuilders) Ltd., Crown Works, Horn Hill, pg. 1356   IT
Sanyo Industries (U.K.) Limited, Oulton Works, School Road, pg. 1192   IT

Ludlow

ByPy Hydraulics and Transmissions Ltd., pg. 1511   IT
Bypy Hydraulics & Transmissions Ltd., 8 Lingen Rd. Industrial Estate, pg. 201   IT

Lurgan

Lurgan Fibre Ltd., pg. 1146   IT

Luton

AAH Distribution Services Ltd., Unit 7, Cosgrove Way, Dallow Rd., pg. 591   IT
ABB Kent Plc, Lea Rd., pg. 2   IT
Anritsu Europe Ltd., Thistle Rd., Windmill Trading Estate, pg. 77   IT
Barratt North London, Barratt House, 668 Hitchin Road, pg. 168   IT
Britannia Airways Ltd., Luton Airport, pg. 1601   PB
CEPSA U.K., Ltd., Norwich House, 37, Upper George St., pg. 323   IT
Cerner Solutions Center -SNI Health Solutions Div., Cresta House, Alma Street, pg. 331   PB
Columbus Dixon Ltd., pg. 444   IT
Continental Microwave (Holdings) Plc, 1 Crawley Green Rd., pg. 1289   IT
Continental Microwave Ltd., 1 Crawley Green Rd., pg. 1289   IT
Continental Microwave Technology Ltd., 171 Camford Way, pg. 1289   IT
A.T. Cross U.K. Ltd., Concorde House, Concorde St., pg. 461   PB
Electrolux (Commercial Equipment) Ltd., P.O. Box 18, pg. 444   IT
Electrolux Group, pg. 444   IT
Electrolux Ltd., pg. 444   IT
Husqvarna Ltd., P.O. Box 10, pg. 444   IT
IBC Vehicles Ltd., Kimpton Rd., pg. 693   IT
Kent Meters Ltd., Pondwicks Rd., pg. 2   IT
Kent Process Control Ltd., Bramington Business Park, pg. 2   IT
LAPORTE PLC, Laporte House, Kingsway, pg. 801   IT

Life Science Laboratories Ltd., North Luton Industrial Est., Sedgewick Road, pg. 1594   PB
Magec Aviation Ltd., Luton International Airport, pg. 544   IT
Pechiney Packaging Food & General Lines, Ltd., 100 Capability Green, pg. 1031   IT
SKF (U.K.) Ltd., Sundon Park Road, pg. 1159   IT
Scholl Consumer Products Ltd., 475 Capability Green, pg. 1209   IT
Senior Heat Treatment-Luton, Unit 7, Caleb Close, Dunstable Rd., pg. 1221   IT
Vauxhall Motors Limited, Griffin House, pg. 724   PB
Whitbread Beer Company, PorterTun House, 500 Capability Green, pg. 1498   IT
Whitbread Property, Oakley Rd., Leagrave, pg. 1498   IT
Whitbread Pub Partnerships, Whitbread House, Park St. W., pg. 1498   IT
Whitbread Restaurants & Leisure, Whitbread House, 14 Park St. W., pg. 1498   IT

Lutterworth

Freudenberg Engineering Ltd., pg. 505   IT
Freudenberg Limited, pg. 507   IT
Freudenberg LP, pg. 506   IT
Freudenberg Properties and Services Ltd., pg. 507   IT
IBSTOCK PLC, Lutterworth House, pg. 658   IT

Lytham Saint Anne's

Fairclough Homes Ltd., 6 Clifton Sq., pg. 16   IT
UMC Industries, Ltd., Dock Rd., pg. 457   PB

Macclesfield

CIBA Additives, Hulley Rd., pg. 978   IT
CIBA Dyes & Chemicals, Hulley Road, pg. 975   IT
CIBA-GEIGY (Insurance Services) Limited, Hulley Road, pg. 977   IT
CIBA-GEIGY Plc, Hulley Rd., pg. 978   IT
CIBA Pigments, Hulley Road, pg. 292   IT
CIBA Vision Lens Care Production Ltd., Hurdsfield Industrial Estate, pg. 981   IT
Georg Fischer Disa Engineering Ltd., London & Manchester House, Park Green, pg. 489   IT
Zeneca Pharmaceuticals, Macclesfield Works, Hurdsfield Industrial Estate, pg. 1524   IT

Maesteg

Standard Products Limited, pg. 1505   PB

Maidenhead

ACL Drayton, Cordwallis St., pg. 1241   IT
Abbott Laboratories Ltd., North Road, pg. 14   PB
Appliance Components Limited, Cordwallis St., pg. 1241   IT
Avery Label Systems Ltd., Gardner Rd., pg. 153   PB
Bestobell Service Co. Ltd., Marsh Gate Estate, pg. 853   IT
Costain Building & Civil Engineering Limited, Costain House, Nicholsons Walk, pg. 336   IT
Costain Civil Engineering Ltd., Costain House, Nicholsons Walk, pg. 336   IT
Costain Construction Limited, Costain House, Nicholsons Walk, pg. 336   IT
Costain Marine International Limited, Costain House, Nicholsons Walk, pg. 336   IT
Datapro Services, McGraw Hill House, Shoppenhangers Rd., pg. 1072   PB
Fujitsu Microelectronics Ltd., Hargrave House, Belmont Rd., pg. 528   IT
GATX Terminals Ltd., Nicholson House, High Street, pg. 693   PB
Grosvenor Casinos Ltd., Stafferton Way, pg. 1086   IT
KS Winston Ltd., KS House, Cordwallis Park, Cookham Rd., pg. 861   IT
Kenner Parker Europe, Hargrave House, Belmont Rd., pg. 797   IT
Lambert Smith Hampton, One Station Approach, pg. 804   IT
LAURA ASHLEY HOLDINGS PLC, 150 Bath Road, pg. 804   IT
Laura Ashley Ltd., 150 Bath Road, pg. 804   IT
McGraw-Hill Book Co. (U.K.) Ltd., Shoppenhangers Rd., pg. 1072   PB
McGraw-Hill International Publications Co. Ltd., Shoppenhangers Rd., pg. 1072   PB
Memco Limited, Memco House, Waldeck Rd., pg. 589   IT
Nortel Limited, Stafferton Way, pg. 970   IT
OASiS Group plc, Tectonic Place, Holyport Rd., pg. 1544   PB
Odeon Cinemas Ltd., Stafferton Way, pg. 1086   IT
Pacific Scientific, Ltd., Howarth Road, pg. 1250   PB
Park Lane Tobacco Company Ltd., Park House, Park St., pg. 1101   IT
Perstorp Analytical Ltd., Highfield House, Foundation Park, pg. 1039   IT
Perstorp Analytical NIRSystems-European Liason Office, Highfield House, Foundation Park, pg. 1039   IT
Rank Entertainment Limited, Stafferton Way, pg. 1087   IT
Rank Leisure Machine Services Ltd., Stafferton Way, pg. 1087   IT
Seagate Technology (U.K.) Sales Limited, 107 King Street, pg. 1450   PB
SEIKO UK Limited, Hattori House, Vanwall Rd., pg. 1218   IT
Symantec (UK) Ltd., St. Cloud's Gate, pg. 1546   IT
Syntellect Europe, 21 Marlowe Rd., pg. 1550   PB

PB - *U.S. Public Companies Volume*
PV - *U.S. Private Companies Volume*
IT - *International Public & Private Companies Volume*

1820

Geographic Index-Non U.S.

Top Rank Limited, Stafferton Way, pg. 1087 — IT
Toys "R" Us (UK) Ltd., Vanwall Park, pg. 1626 — PB
Unipen Ltd., Nicholson House, High Street, pg. 693 — PB
Unitank Storage Co. Ltd., Nicholson House, High Street, pg. 693 — PB
Weight Watchers Foods Central Europe B.V., Kidwells Pk. House, Kidwells Pk. Dr., pg. 807 — PB
John Wyeth & Brother Ltd., Huntercombe Lane, pg. 82 — PB

Maidstone

Ballast Wiltshier Plc - South East Region, Tovil Green, Tovil, pg. 135 — IT
Genzyme Biochemicals Ltd., Coleman House, King St., pg. 733 — PB
Mobil Data Services, Ltd., Pegasus Place, Lodge Rd., pg. 1119 — IT
Mount Isa Holdings (UK) Ltd., Watson House, Centre 3000, 20/20 Business Park, pg. 827 — IT
RAYOVAC Limited, Galleon House, King St., pg. 912 — PV
Rayovac/Vidor Limited, Galleon House, pg. 912 — PV
WHATMAN PLC, Whatman House, St. Leonards Road, pg. 1498 — IT
Willis Corroon South Limited, Medway House, London Road, pg. 1503 — IT
Zeneca Agrochemicals and Seeds, Yalding, pg. 1524 — IT

Maldon

Chief Industries UK Ltd., Bentall Industrial Estate, pg. 236 — PV
Chief Industries UK Ltd, Beckingham Business Park, Tolleshunt Major, pg. 236 — PV
Green Flour Mills Limited, pg. 598 — IT
Trace Elliot Limited, Galliford Rd., pg. 942 — PB

Malvern Link

Applied Curing Technology, Ltd., Unit 5, Link IndustrialEstate, pg. 1189 — PB

Manchester

ABS Submersible Division, Section 3, Richmond Rd., Trafford Park, pg. 270 — IT
AMEC Development Ltd., Sunlight House, pg. 16 — IT
ACCO Eastlight Limited, Ashton Rd., pg. 674 — PB
Acorga Mining Chemicals Business, PO Box 42, pg. 1524 — IT
Algemene Bank Nederland, Pall Mall Court, 61, King Street, pg. 11 — IT
Alliance Paper Group PLC, Mercury Way, Mercury Park, Barton Dock Road, pg. 863 — IT
American Appraisal (U.K.) Ltd., Suite 1E, Portland Bldgs., 127/129 Portland St., pg. 50 — PV
Arndale Communications Ltd., Arndale House, pg. 1034 — IT
BDH ADVERTISING LIMITED, Oakland House, Talbot Rd., Old Trafford, pg. 118 — IT
BSL Engineering Limited, Catford Rd., pg. 212 — IT
BSL Limited, Claverton Court, Claverton Rd., pg. 212 — IT
N.G. Bailey & Co. Ltd.-Manchester Branch, 321 Ordsall Lane, pg. 132 — IT
Bailey Telecom LTD - Manchester, 321 Ordsall Lane, pg. 133 — IT
Ballast Wiltshire Plc - North West Region, Laser House, Waterfront Quay, pg. 135 — IT
Bank Hapoalim (Manchester), Seven Charlotte St., pg. 149 — IT
Bank Leumi (UK) PLC, 4th Floor, Blackfriars House, Parsonage Gardens, pg. 150 — IT
Barratt Manchester, Worrall House, 683 Chester Rd., pg. 168 — IT
Brother Holding (Europe), Brother House, 1 Tame Street, pg. 229 — IT
Brother U.K., Ltd., Shepley St., Guide Bridge, pg. 230 — IT
Donald Brown (Brownall), Stretford Rd., pg. 390 — IT
CMB Sonoco Composites, Stokes St., pg. 1486 — PB
CV Home Furnishings Limited, Newton Mill, Lees St., pg. 299 — IT
CV Woven Fabrics Limited, P.O. Box 31, pg. 299 — IT
CARBO PLC, Lakeside, Trafford Park Rd., pg. 268 — IT
Chloride Industrial Batteries Ltd., pg. 125 — IT
CIBA Clayton, PO Box 2, pg. 975 — IT
The Clayton Aniline Company, Ashton New Rd., Clayton, pg. 981 — IT
COATS VIYELLA PLC, Lees St., pg. 299 — IT
Componenta International Ltd., 5 Ennis Close, pg. 1421 — IT
Costain Environmental Services Limited, Gateway House, Styal Road, pg. 336 — IT
Costain Oil, Gas & Process Limited Process Contracting Division, Costain House, Styal Road, pg. 336 — IT
Costain Urban Enterprises Limited, Costain House, Styal Road, pg. 337 — IT
DalKeith Knitwear Limited, P.O. Box 31, pg. 299 — IT
Deutsche Bank AG (Manchester), Ship Canal House, 98, King St., pg. 404 — IT
Eaton Limited Transmission Division, P.O. Box 11, Worsley Rd. North, pg. 559 — PB
Euroc Brick Ltd., Adamson House, Pomona Strand, Throstle Nest Ln., pg. 1199 — IT
FEB Ltd., pg. 982 — IT
Fermec Holdings, Ltd., Barton Dock Road, Stretford, pg. 312 — PB
Ferranti Air Systems Ltd., Concord Business Park, pg. 384 — IT
Financial Collection Agencies, Bracken House, 5th Floor, Charles Street, pg. 471 — IT
Flexibox Ltd., Nash Rd., pg. 426 — IT

GGT Direct Manchester, Oakland House, Talbot Rd., pg. 532 — IT
Godwins Limited, Blackfriars House Parsonage, pg. 119 — PB
Granges Automotive (UK) Ltd., Graeme House, Wilbraham Rd., pg. 444 — IT
GUARDIAN MEDIA GROUP PLC, 164 Deansgate, pg. 577 — IT
Albert Hartley Limited, P.O. Box 31, pg. 299 — IT
A Heald Limited, Three Elm Grove, Didsbury, pg. 102 — IT
Hellermann Insuloid, Leestone Rd., pg. 207 — IT
Henderson Unit Trust Management Limited, Royal London House, 2nd Fl., 196 Deansgate, pg. 609 — IT
Hewlett-Packard Ltd., Heathside Park Rd., pg. 821 — PB
International Water Limited, Oakland House, Talbot Road, pg. 1444 — IT
Kellogg Company of Great Britain Ltd., The Kellogg Building, Talbot Road, pg. 947 — PB
Knowsley SK Ltd., Trafford Park Rd., pg. 681 — PB
Kratos Group Plc/Kratos Analytical ltd., Barton Dock Rd., pg. 1232 — IT
Kredietbank Manchester Branch, National House, 6th Floor, 36, St. Ann Street, pg. 760 — IT
Lambert Smith Hampton, 79 Mosley St., pg. 797 — IT
LANCASHIRE DAIRIES LTD., 50 Derby St., pg. 798 — IT
Langwood (Prepared Vegetables) Limited, Three Elm Grove, Didsbury, pg. 102 — IT
Makro Self Service Wholesalers Ltd., Charles House, Albert St., pg. 1156 — IT
Manchem Ltd., Ashton New Rd., pg. 1113 — IT
Manchester, Clarence House, Clarence Street, pg. 910 — IT
Manox Ltd., Manox House, Coleshill St., pg. 1113 — IT
Mansfield Knitwear Limited, P.O. Box 31, Lees Street, pg. 300 — IT
Marcam U.K., Northern Region, Parkway One, Parkway Buss. Ctr., Princess Road, pg. 1043 — PB
Marquette Electronics (G.B.) Ltd., pg. 1047 — PB
Mitchell Shackleton & Co. Ltd., Green Lane Patricroft, pg. 783 — PV
Mono Pumps Ltd., pg. 529 — PB
Network Systems Limited, 13th Fl., Ste. B, 111 Piccadilly, pg. 1522 — PB
Newsquest Media (Manchester), Lancaster Buildings, 77 Deansgate, pg. 927 — IT
North West Radio, Piccadilly Plaza, 127-131 The Piazza, pg. 452 — IT
Numetrix Ltd., Denzell House, Denzell Gardens, Dunham Rd., pg. 990 — IT
Oldham Crompton Batteries Ltd., Edward St., Denton, pg. 125 — IT
Optiroc Ltd., Adamson House, Pomona Strand, pg. 1200 — IT
Osman Textiles, P.O. Box 7, pg. 300 — IT
P&O Shopping Centres Ltd., Arndale House, pg. 1034 — IT
Pasolds Limited, P.O. Box 31, pg. 300 — IT
Personal Performance Consultants UK Limited (PPC), Centurion House, 129 Deansgate, pg. 1502 — IT
Piccadilly Radio, Castle Quay, Castlefield, pg. 452 — IT
Portals Packaging Tapes, Bridge Street, Horwich, Nr. Bolton, pg. 386 — IT
Process Equipment, Oakland House, Talbot Road, pg. 1444 — IT
Process Instrumentation, Oakland House, Talbot Road, pg. 1444 — IT
RMC Surfacing Limited-North West Area, Smith Fold Ln., Little Hutton, pg. 1080 — IT
Rank Brimar Ltd., Greenside Way, pg. 1087 — IT
RENOLD PLC, Renold House, Styal Rd., pg. 1103 — IT
Percy L. Rigby & Sons Limited, 3 Elm Grove, Didsbury, pg. 102 — IT
Riley Advertising (Manchester) Ltd., Trafford House, Chester Rd., Stretford, pg. 1117 — IT
Rotunda Plc, Holland St., pg. 1202 — IT
Royal Bank Insurance Services Ltd., 49 Peter St., pg. 1132 — IT
Senior Service Tobacco Ltd., Virginia House, Gregory St., pg. 539 — IT
Sequent Computer Systems (United Kingdom), The World Trade Ctr., 8th Fl., Exchange Quay, Salford, pg. 1460 — PB
Serv-Tech Europe, Thornley House, Carrington Business Pk., pg. 1460 — PB
Shandwick North Ltd., Albion Wharf, Albion Street, pg. 1227 — IT
Sharp Electronics (U.K.) Ltd., Sharp House, Thorp Road, pg. 1230 — IT
Smurfit Fibreboard Converters Ltd., Worsley St., pg. 1271 — IT
Smurfit Packaging Products, Bolton Street, pg. 1271 — IT
Sulzer Papertec Manchester Ltd., pg. 1306 — IT
Svedala Ltd. Wythenshawe, pg. 1325 — IT
Svenska Handelsbanken Manchester, St. John's Court, 66 Quay Street, pg. 1327 — IT
Syseca Ltd, Southmoor House, Southmoor Road, pg. 1384 — IT
T & N PLC, Intl. Office Center, Styal Rd., pg. 1334 — IT
Tappan International Sales Ltd., Daisy Works, 345 Stockport Rd., pg. 444 — IT
TEXAS HOLDINGS LTD., Barton Hall, pg. 1381 — IT
Tootal Clothing Ltd., Lees St., pg. 300 — IT
Tootal Group plc, Lees St., pg. 300 — IT
Tootal Textiles Holdings Ltd., Lees St., pg. 300 — IT
Tootal Textiles Ltd., Lees St., pg. 300 — IT
Tootal Thread Ltd., Lees St., pg. 299 — IT
Trafford Coated Stone, Moseley Rd. N., pg. 1080 — IT
Trafford Park Bakery, Ashburton Rd. W., pg. 968 — IT
Tyco Valves Limited, 71 Princess St., pg. 1651 — PB
VG Analytical Ltd., Floats Rd., pg. 1110 — IT
VG Tritech Ltd., Crewe Rd., pg. 1111 — IT
Vantona Ltd., Lees St., pg. 299 — IT

WF Corroon-Manchester, Centurion House, 129 Deansgate, pg. 1502 — IT
Waterford Foods Limited, 3 Elm Grove, pg. 102 — IT
Weir Materials Ltd., Park Works, pg. 1489 — IT
Willis Corroon Credit Limited, Centurion House, 129 Deansgate, pg. 1502 — IT
Willis Corroon North Limited, Centurion House, 129 Deansgate, pg. 1503 — IT
Wormald Ansul U.K. Ltd., Park Works., Grimshaw Ln., pg. 1651 — PB
Wormald Holdings U.K. Limited, Park Works Grimshaw Ln., pg. 1651 — PB
Zeneca Biocides, PO Box 42, Hexagon House, pg. 1524 — IT
Zeneca Specialties, Headquarters, PO Box 42, pg. 1524 — IT

Mansfield

British Sterilizer Ltd., Unit 2, Bleakhill Way, Hermitage Lane Ind. Est., pg. 551 — IT
Tom Cobleigh plc, Phoenix House, Oak Tree Lane, pg. 1087 — IT
Scott Western Ltd., Ind. Est., Kings Mill Way, pg. 552 — IT
The Sterilizing Equipment Co. Ltd., Hermitage Lane Industrial Est., Kings Mill Way, pg. 552 — IT

Maple Cross

Trebor Bassett Ltd., Hertford Place, Denham Way, pg. 248 — IT

Margate

Charles River U.K., Ltd., Manston Rd., pg. 195 — PB

Market Drayton

APP Chemicals Limited, Unit 1, Maer Lane Industrial Estate, pg. 234 — IT
Palethorpes, P.O. Box 1, Maer Lane, pg. 968 — IT

Market Harborough

Eagle-Picher Fluid Systems Limited, Taith House, Rockingham Rd., pg. 355 — PV
HP Foods, 45, Northampton Rd., pg. 380 — IT
Synington Company, Springfield St., pg. 753 — IT
Tungstone Batteries Ltd., pg. 124 — IT

Marlborough

Finnfeeds International Ltd., Market House, Allesbury Ct., High Street Rd., pg. 349 — IT

Marlow

Alpha Industries, USA, Ltd., 19-21 Chapel St., pg. 57 — PB
The Anvil Consultancy, Alexander House, Mere Park, Dedmere Rd., pg. 1224 — PB
Avery Intl. Adhesive Prods., Ltd., 48 West St., pg. 153 — PB
Carnation Foods Ltd., Danesfield House, pg. 919 — IT
Chomerics Europe/U.K., Parkway, pg. 1262 — PB
Costain Homes Limited, 67/71 High St., pg. 336 — IT
GVG Limited, 1567 — PB
HMV Limited, Riley House, Riley Rd., pg. 427 — IT
LMC Associates Ltd., Insurance House, Station Road, pg. 864 — IT
Lex Vehicle Leasing, Globe House, Parkway, pg. 807 — IT
Lex Vehicle Leasing Limited, Globe House, Parkway, Globe Park, pg. 910 — IT
Liebert Ltd., Globe Park, pg. 577 — PB
Litton UK Ltd., 6 First Ave., pg. 1005 — PB
Lyell Holdings Limited, Park Way, pg. 1785 — PB
Maritz Europa Limited, pg. 704 — PV
Maritz Ltd. (Britain), Globe Park, pg. 704 — PV
Protim Solignum Ltd., Fieldhouse Ln., pg. 234 — IT
Protimeter plc, Meter House, pg. 207 — IT
Protocall Ventures, Park House, 5 Mere Park, pg. 740 — PB
Rank Xerox Limited, Parkway, pg. 1087 — PB
Rank Xerox Limited, Parkway, pg. 1785 — PB
Ranks Hovis McDougall Limited, Chapel House, Liston Rd., pg. 1395 — IT
SAS Software Ltd., Wittington House, pg. 967 — PV
Saab Great Britain Ltd., Saab House, Globe Park, pg. 687 — IT
Saab-Scania Finance Ltd, Saab House, pg. 688 — IT
Tektronix U.K. Limited, Fourth Ave, Globe Park, pg. 1568 — PB
Tyco Toys (UK) Ltd., Tyco House, Third Ave., Globe Park, pg. 1059 — PB
VELO Limited, Rehal House, 4 Station Road, pg. 420 — IT
Volvo Car UK Ltd., Globe Park, pg. 1477 — IT

Marple

Werner & Pfleiderer (U.K.) Ltd., 117 Stockport Road, pg. 511 — IT

Matlock

Firth-Rixson Forgings, Daley Dale, pg. 487 — IT
Tarmac Roadstone Ltd., John Hadfield House, Dale Rd., pg. 1355 — IT

Maybole

CAPS, Murray Gardens, pg. 1152 — IT

PB - *U.S. Public Companies Volume*
PV - *U.S. Private Companies Volume*
IT - *International Public & Private Companies Volume*

Meiksham

Cooper-Avon Tyres, Ltd., pg. 445   PB

Meir

USF Ltd., Whittle Road, pg. 61   PB

Melbourn

DONCASTERS PLC, 28-30 Derby Road, pg. 416   IT

Mendlesham

Lumipaper Ltd., The Airfelt Norwich Road, pg. 458   IT

Mersey

Advanced Design Electronics Limited, Dixon Road, Knowsley Industrial Park North, pg. 287   IT
Schauman Panels Ltd., Units 34/37, Vulcan Industrial Estate, pg. 1429   IT

Merstham

Canusa Systems Limited, Darby House, Bletchingley Road, pg. 1231   IT
Westinghouse Cubic Limited, 177 Nutfield Rd., pg. 466   PB

Merthyr Tydfil

Hoover Ltd.-White Goods Manufacturing Facility, Pentrebach, pg. 260   IT
Hoover Major Appliances, Pentrebach, pg. 260   IT
United Flexible, Abercanaid, pg. 1221   IT

Mexborough

Morphy Richards Appliances, pg. 554   IT
Morphy Richards Consumer Electronics, pg. 554   IT

Middlesbrough

N.G. Bailey & Co. Ltd.-Middlesbrough, Sotherby Road, pg. 132   IT
Chemoxy International plc, All Saints Refinery, Cargo Fleet Rd., pg. 88   IT
Downings Steel Ltd., Skippers Lane Industrial Est., Brunel Rd., pg. 1450   IT
Fine Organics Limited, Teesside Site, pg. 802   IT
King Wilkinson Ltd., Endeavour House, Cleveland Centre, pg. 131   IT
Marlow Foods Ltd., Station Road, pg. 1524   IT
Nordic Synthesis Limited, Seals Sands Rd., pg. 297   PB
Norsea Pipeline Ltd., Seal Sands, pg. 1044   IT
Northern Aggregates Limited, Tirrem House, 16 High St., pg. 1079   IT
Seal Sands Chemicals Ltd., Seal Sands Road, pg. 297   PB
Seal Sands Storage Ltd., pg. 1251   IT
TFM, Radio House, Yale Crescent, Thornaby, Stockton on Tees, pg. 452   IT
Tees Storage Company Limited, Seal Sands, pg. 693   PB
Teesside Holdings Limited, Queens Sq., pg. 1065   IT
Trafalgar House Offshore Fabricators Limited (Port Clarence), Port Clarence, pg. 773   IT
Trafalgar House Offshore Fabricators Limited (Linthorpe Dinsdale), pg. 773   IT
Van Leeuwen Tubes Ltd., Brunel Road, Skippers Lane Industrial Estate, pg. 1450   IT
Zeneca Bio Products, P.O. Box 2, Belasis Avenue, pg. 1524   IT

Middleton

British Aerospace Regional Aircraft Limited, pg. 218   IT
ISS Contract Cleaning Services (North), Arndale Chambers, Arndale Centre, pg. 657   IT
Industrial Latex Adhesives Ltd., Greenside Way, Chadderton Industrial Estate, pg. 523   PB

Middlewich

AMEC Engineering Ltd.-C.V. Buchan (Concrete) Ltd., Kings Lane, pg. 16   IT
Abu Garcia (UK) Ltd., Unit 5, Aston Way, Middlewich Motorway Estate, pg. 822   PV
British Salt, Cledford Lane, pg. 1298   IT
VG Gas Analysis Systems Ltd., Aston Way, pg. 1595   PB
VG Isotech Ltd., Aston Way, pg. 1110   IT
VG Quadrupoles Ltd., Aston Way, pg. 1111   IT

Mildenhall

Lamb Technicon UK, Leyton Ave., pg. 1004   PB

Milford Haven

Dowty Automotive Gaskets, Thornton Trading Estate, pg. 1338   IT

Milton Keynes

Amway (U.K.) Limited, Ambassador House, Queensway, pg. 70   PV
Balzers Ltd., Bradbourne Dr., pg. 997   IT

Beiserdorf UK Ltd., pg. 183   IT
Bergquist UK. Limited, Unit 27 Darin Ct., pg. 135   PV
Billion (UK) Ltd., pg. 836   IT
Componedex Ltd., Avant Business Centre, 23 Denbigh Road, pg. 1365   IT
Durco Process Equipment Ltd., 28 Heathfield, Stacy Bushes, pg. 659   PB
Hirose Electric UK Ltd., Crownhill Business Ctr., 16, Vincent Avenue, pg. 620   IT
Huls (U.K.) Ltd., Featherstone Rd., Wolverton Mill S., pg. 1456   IT
ISS Contract Clean Midlands Ltd., Unit 10, Drakes Mews, pg. 657   IT
Iggesund Board Sales Ltd. (Waltham Abbey), Sunningdale House, 47 Caldecotte Lake Drive, pg. 886   IT
Iggesund Converters Ltd., Northfield Drive, pg. 886   IT
Jotun Decorative Coatings Ltd., 16, Alston Drive, Bradwell Abbey, pg. 715   IT
K.J.P. Ltd., pg. 1512   IT
Kara Foods, Unit 15, Tanners Drive, pg. 968   IT
Laing Homes Ltd., Caldew House, Gwarnonde Dr., pg. 796   IT
Lista UK Ltd., pg. 812   IT
MVC Milton Keynes, Brunleys, Kiln Farm, pg. 851   IT
Makita International Europe Ltd., Michigan Drive, Tongwell, pg. 832   IT
Makita (U.K.) LTD., Michigan Dr., pg. 832   IT
Mercedes-Benz (United Kingdom) Ltd., Mercedes-Benz Centre, Delaware Dr., pg. 369   IT
Minolta (UK) Ltd., Precedent Drive, pg. 869   IT
Mobil Oil Company, Ltd., Mobil House, 500-600 Witan Gate, pg. 1119   PB
NEC Electronics (UK) Limited, Cygnus House, Sunrise Pkwy., pg. 901   IT
NEFF (UK) LIMITED, Grand Union House, Old Wolverton Road, pg. 912   IT
Pharmacia & Upjohn Ltd., Davy Ave., pg. 1050   IT
Pittler (U.K.) Ltd., pg. 1128   IT
Process Analytics, 72 Tanners Drive, Blakelands, pg. 6   IT
Radix Micro Devices, Plc, Three Clarendon Dr., pg. 907   PV
Rexroth Pneumatics Ltd., pg. 839   IT
Rockwell Automation Limited, Pitfield, Kiln Farm, pg. 1399   PB
Rockwell Automation Ltd. U.K. Drive Systems, Denbigh Rd., pg. 1400   PB
Rockwell Switching Systems Limited, Bouverie Square, 252 Upper Third Street, pg. 1402   PB
Rohm Electronics (U.K.) Limited, Whitehall Ave., pg. 1125   IT
SKF Engineering Products Limited, 2 Tanners Dr., pg. 1158   IT
Santa Fe Braun (U.K.) Ltd., 500 Elder Gate, pg. 765   IT
Scania (Great Britain) Ltd., Tongwell, pg. 687   IT
Stone & Webster Engineering Ltd., 500 Elder Gate, pg. 1520   PB
Super Homes Ltd., Cardew House, Garanorde Dr., pg. 796   IT
Telma Retarder Ltd., 31 Clarke Rd., pg. 786   IT
Time/System (UK) Ltd., Crownhill Business Center, 6 Vincent Avenue, pg. 73   IT
Tuck Tape Ltd., pg. 183   IT
V.A.G. (United Kingdom) Ltd., pg. 1475   IT
VMark Software, Ltd., Power House, Davy Ave., pg. 1475   PB
Volkswagen Financial Services (UK) Ltd., pg. 1475   IT
Volkswagen Group United Kingdom Ltd., pg. 1475   IT
WD-40 Company Ltd., PO Box 440, Brick Close Kiln Farm, pg. 1726   PB
Jervis B. Webb Company Ltd., Dawson Road, pg. 1157   PV

Mirfield

Mitchell Cotts Chemicals Limited, P.O. Box 6, Steanard Lane, pg. 88   IT

Mitcham

AAR Aviation Services U.K., 35 Willow Lane, pg. 1   PB
G.E. Lighting Limited, Miles House, 79 Miles Rd., pg. 713   PB
HSS Hire Service Group PLC, 25 Willow Ln., pg. 385   IT
Jotun Polymer (UK) Ltd., 54 Willow Lane, pg. 714   IT
PG Technology, Ltd., Mill Green Rd., pg. 424   PB
Plasro Plastics Limited, pg. 268   IT

Mold

Castle Cement Ltd. (Mold), Padeswood, pg. 1201   IT

Montrose

Plasboard Plastics Limited, Unit 8, Broomfield Industrial Estate, pg. 341   IT
Varco (U.K.) Ltd. Drilling Systems, Forties Rd., pg. 1709   PB
Varco (U.K.) Ltd. Oil Tools, Forties Rd., pg. 1709   PB

Moreton-in-Marsh

Manus (Great Britain) Ltd., London Rd., pg. 1380   IT

Morley

Filter Division, Parker Hannifin (U.K.) Ltd., Peel Street, pg. 1260   PB

Morriston

Morganite Electrical Carbon Limited, 52 Clase Rd., pg. 891   IT
Morganite Special Carbons Limited-Materials Division, One Upper Forest Way, pg. 891   IT

Mountain Ash

AB Connectors Limited, Abercynon, pg. 1344   IT
Sanken Power System, Abercynon, pg. 1189   IT
AB Test House Limited, Abercynon, pg. 1344   IT

Musselburgh

Bruntons Areo Product, Ivereste, pg. 268   IT

Nailsea

Readymixed Drypack Limited, The Sion, Crown Glass Pl., pg. 1080   IT

Neasden

Luxottica U.K. Ltd., Iron Bridge Close, Great Central Way, pg. 822   IT

Nelson

Decoport Ltd., Edward St., pg. 124   IT
IPC Corporation (UK) Ltd., Suite 608 Lomeshaye, pg. 651   IT
Smith & Nephew Medical Fabrics, Brierfield Mills, Brierfield, pg. 1263   IT
Suter Equipment Limited, Glenfield Mill, 61/71 Hallam Rd., pg. 88   IT

Netherfield

Kappler Europe, Ltd., Kappler Close, pg. 607   PV
Nottingham Coated Stone, Private Rd. No4, Colwick Industrial Estate, pg. 1079   IT

New Barnet

Amalgamated Shoe Co. Ltd., Kingmaker House, Station Rd., pg. 1035   IT

New Malden

AMEC Building Ltd., Apex Tower, High Street, pg. 16   IT
Decca, Burlington House, 118 Burlington Rd., pg. 1003   PB
INTERNATIONAL TOOL & SUPPLY, PLC, 61 Woodside Road, pg. 684   IT
OMRON Terminals (U.K.) Ltd., 58/62 Coombe Rd., pg. 1006   IT
Spillers Foods, Spillers House, 1 Blagdon Road, pg. 376   IT

New Milton

Parker Bath Company Ltd., Queensway, Stem Lane, pg. 1536   PB

New Parks

GEC Power Instrumentation & Control Ltd., Scudamore Road, pg. 53   IT

Newark-on-Trent

Iggesund Timber Sales Ltd., 25, Lombard St., pg. 886   IT
RHP Bearings Limited, Northern Rd., pg. 904   IT

Newbridge

Uniroyal Englebert Tyres Ltd., pg. 327   IT

Newbury

Advanced Logic Research, Inc. (U.K.) Limited, 16 Kingfisher Court, Hambridge Rd., pg. 704   PB
Analog Devices Marketing Ltd., Rothwell House, Pembroke Rd., pg. 108   PB
Atochem UK Ltd., Colthrop Way, pg. 446   IT
Bayer UK Ltd., Strawberry Hill, pg. 175   IT
C.D.I. Technologies, Ltd., Space House, 8-10 Westhills, pg. 1055   PB
Cabletron Systems, Inc.-Europe, Network House, Newbury Business Park, pg. 288   PB
Ciprico Intertnational Ltd., 7 Clearwater Place, Lower Way, pg. 370   PB
P C Cox (Newbury) Ltd., Turnpike Road, pg. 113   IT
De La Rue Systems (UK), Pool House, Horizon W., Hambridge Rd., pg. 387   IT
Eurotherm Gauging Systems Ltd., Abex Road, pg. 466   IT
Nationwide Refrigeration Supplies Limited, Bone Lane, pg. 88   IT
Newport Ltd., Newbury Business Park, 4320 First Ave., London Rd., pg. 1179   PB
Richmond House, Bath Road, pg. 1144   PB
Utah Scientific/Artel, 6 Votec Centre, Hambridge Lane, pg. 86   PV
VODAFONE GROUP PLC, The Courtyard, 2-4 London Rd., pg. 1469   IT

Newcastle under Lyme

Lucas SEI Wiring Systems, Ltd., pg. 1313 **IT**
Newcastle Plant, Lower St., pg. 672 **PB**
Norton Pampus Limited, Chesterton Works, Loomer Rd., pg. 1175 **IT**
T.H.E., Rosevale Business Park, pg. 707 **IT**

Newcastle upon Tyne

Bailey Maintenance Services, Newcastle Business Park, 23/24 Amethyst Road, pg. 133 **IT**
N.G. Bailey & Co. Ltd.-Newcastle Branch, 23/24 Amethyst Road, pg. 132 **IT**
Barratt Commercial, Wingrove House, Ponteland Rd., pg. 168 **IT**
BARRATT DEVELOPMENTS PLC, Wingrove House, Ponteland Road, pg. 167 **IT**
Barratt Homes, Wingrove House, Ponteland Road, pg. 168 **IT**
Barratt Newcastle, Barratt House, Airport Industrial Estate, pg. 168 **IT**
Barratt Northern, Barratt House, Airport Industrial Estate, pg. 168 **IT**
Eldon Laboratories Limited, 4 Pooley Close, pg. 58 **IT**
Fisher Seafoods (Grosforth) Ltd., Unit 1, St. Nicholas Hospital, Jubilee Road, Grosforth, pg. 491 **IT**
Great North Radio, pg. 451 **IT**
Huwood Electric Ltd., Shelley Rd., pg. 473 **IT**
Huwood Mining Supports Limited, Longrigg, Swalwell, pg. 473 **IT**
Leech Homes Limited, City House, 1-3 City Road, pg. 593 **IT**
Metro FM, pg. 452 **IT**
Michell Bearings, Scotswood Rd., pg. 1467 **IT**
The Newcastle Breweries, Ltd., The Tyne Brewery, pg. 1211 **IT**
Northern Rock Asset Management Limited, Bulman House, Regent Center, pg. 968 **IT**
Northern Rock Financial Services Limited, Northern Rock House, pg. 968 **IT**
Northern Rock Homes Limited, 3a Regent Rd., pg. 968 **IT**
NORTHERN ROCK PLC, Northern Rock House, Gosforth, pg. 968 **IT**
Northern Rock Unit Trust Limited, Bulman House, Regent Center, pg. 968 **IT**
PRC (UK) Ltd., Portland Road, pg. 339 **IT**
Procter & Gamble Ltd., Hedley House, Gosforth, pg. 1332 **PB**
RMC Roadstone Limited-Northern, 8/9 Blezard Business Pk., Brenkley Cross, Seaton Burn, pg. 1079 **IT**
Rolls-Royce Power Engineering plc, NEI House, Regent Centre, pg. 1127 **IT**
Vickers Defence Systems, Armstrong Works, Scotswood Road, pg. 1467 **IT**
Willis Corroon North Limited, Blackfriars Court, Dispensary Lane, pg. 1503 **IT**

Newhaven

Artex Ltd., Artex Ave., pg. 122 **IT**
Hennessy U.K. Ltd, Avis Way, pg. 782 **IT**
Parker Pen PLC, Parker House, Estate Rd., pg. 745 **PB**
Stena Line Limited, Port Administration Offices, Beach Road, pg. 1300 **IT**

Newmarket

BLP Components Ltd., Exning Rd., pg. 1130 **IT**
Bloodstock & General Insurance Services Limited, 162 High Street, pg. 1502 **IT**
Brimax Books Limited, Units 4/5, Studland Park Industrial Estate, pg. 1093 **IT**
Graseby Microsystems Ltd., Exning Rd., pg. 1267 **IT**
Pauls Malt Limited, pg. 598 **IT**

Newport

Access Equipment Ltd., Audley Ave., pg. 1128 **PV**
Aluminum Precision Extruders Ltd., Pant Glas Industrial Estate, Bedwas, pg. 961 **IT**
Atlantic Service Co. (U.K.) Ltd., P.O. Box 6, Crumlin Gwent, pg. 165 **PB**
Blue Coral Quaker State International, High Street, pg. 1348 **PB**
British Alcan Rolled Products Limited, Rogestone, pg. 51 **IT**
EAC Transport (UK) Limited, pg. 431 **IT**
AB Electronic Assemblies Limited, Tregwilym Industrial Estate, Rogerstone, pg. 1344 **IT**
Gwent Steel Ltd., Newport Industrial Estate, Lake Road, pg. 512 **IT**
Mitel Telecom Limited, Mitel Business Park, Portskewett, pg. 870 **IT**
Newbridge Networks Limited, Coldra Woods, Chepstow Road, pg. 924 **IT**
Penny & Giles Electronic Components Ltd., Unit 35/36, Nine Mile Point Industrial Estate, pg. 207 **IT**
Plasma-Technik Ltd., pg. 1308 **IT**
John Rusling Ltd., Old Hall, Station Rd., pg. 1128 **PV**
A. Schulman Inc. Limited, Croespenmaen Industrial Estate, Crumlin, pg. 1441 **PB**
A. Schulman Inc. Limited, Croespenmaen Industrial Estate, pg. 1441 **PB**
Senior Heat Treatment-Newport, Birds Industrial Estate, Pontymister, Risca, pg. 1221 **IT**
Serck Audco Valves, Audley Rd., pg. 125 **IT**

Newport Pagnell

Aston Martin Lagonda Design Limited, Tickford St., pg. 665 **PB**
Aston Martin Lagonda Group Limited, Tickford St., pg. 665 **PB**
Aston Martin Lagonda Limited, Tickford St., pg. 665 **PB**
Welcome Break Group Limited, # 2 Vantage Ct., pg. 686 **IT**

Newquay

Simoniz International Plc, Treloggan Industrial Estate, pg. 235 **IT**

Newry

Glen Electric, pg. 554 **IT**

Newton

SCHOLL PLC, 100 Capability Green, pg. 1209 **IT**

Newton Abbot

David & Charles plc, Brunel House, pg. 1368 **PB**
Nashua Photo Limited, Brunel Rd., pg. 1152 **PB**
WBB Devon Clays Ltd., Park House, Courtenay Park, pg. 1487 **IT**
WBB Technology Ltd., Park House, Courtenay Park, pg. 1487 **IT**
WATTS BLAKE BEARNE & CO. PLC, Park House, Courtenay Park, pg. 1487 **IT**

Newton Aycliffe

Great Mills (North) Limited, Bede House, St. Cuthberts Way, Aycliffe Industrial Estate, pg. 1080 **IT**
Hydro Polymers Ltd., School Aycliffe Lane, pg. 963 **IT**
Perstorp Ferguson Ltd. Industrial Flooring, Aycliffe Industrial Estate, pg. 1037 **IT**
Perstorp Ferguson Ltd.-Polyols Sales, Aycliffe Industrial Estate, pg. 1038 **IT**
Perstorp Ferguson Ltd.-Chemitec & Compounds, Aycliffe Industrial Estate, pg. 1037 **IT**
Perstorp Ltd., Aycliffe Industrial Estate, pg. 1040 **IT**
Perstorp Warerite Ltd., Aycliffe Industrial Estate, pg. 1039 **IT**
WHESSOE PLC, Heighton La., pg. 1498 **IT**

Newton-le-Willows

SASIB Bakery UK Ltd., pg. 1194 **IT**
Titan Wheel International Ltd., No. 6 Deacon Industrial Estate, pg. 1619 **PB**

Newtown

Dowty Bonded Seals, Unit 6, Dyyfryn Industrial Estate, pg. 1338 **IT**
Elkay Electrical, Mochdre Industrial Estate, pg. 1267 **IT**

Newtownabbey

Campbell Catering NI Limited, Valley Business Centre, Church Road, pg. 254 **IT**
Castlereagh Pharmaceuticals, 155/157 Glenville Rd., pg. 591 **IT**
Nashua Photo Delmont Ltd., 8 Mitchelin Rd., pg. 1152 **PB**

Newtownards

B.H. McCleery & Co. Ltd., Moss Road, pg. 797 **IT**
Northern Ireland Carpets Ltd., Comber Rd., pg. 797 **IT**

Norfolk

Air UK Engineering, Norwich Airport, pg. 39 **IT**
BESPAK PLC, Bergen Way, pg. 193 **IT**
Enterra Oil Field Services, Ltd., Harfreys, Harfreys Industrial Estate, pg. 1750 **PB**
RMC Concrete Products Limited-Eastern, Yaxham Rd., pg. 1080 **IT**
Readicrete Limited, 1 Thorpe Rd., pg. 1080 **IT**

North Braddesley

AEP/Borden Global Packaging (U.K.) Ltd., pg. 5 **PB**

North Shields

Elfab Limited, Alder Road, West Chirton Industrial Estate, pg. 589 **IT**
Formica Limited, Coast Rd., pg. 129 **IT**
Velva Liquids Ltd., Northumberland Dock, pg. 1251 **IT**

Northallerton

Four-F Nutrition, pg. 1356 **IT**
Micronized Food Products, Darlington Rd., pg. 1356 **IT**
E Wood Limited, Standard Way, pg. 858 **IT**

Northampton

Adhesive and Display Products Limited, pg. 757 **IT**

Avon Cosmetics Ltd., Nunn Mills Rd., pg. 156 **PB**
Barratt Northampton, Alexandra House, Queenswood Office Park, pg. 168 **IT**
British Timken Div., Main Rd., pg. 1617 **PB**
Burnett Polymer Engineering, Gladstone Close, pg. 851 **IT**
Carlson Marketing Group (U.K.) Limited, Belgrave House, 1 Grey Friars, 7th Fl., pg. 212 **PV**
Contract Papers (Holdings) Ltd, pg. 757 **IT**
Contract Papers Limited, pg. 757 **IT**
Cosworth Engineering Ltd., St. James Mill Road, pg. 1466 **IT**
Gelman Sciences, Ltd., Brackmills Bus. Park, Caswell Rd., pg. 1253 **PB**
Hartmann & Braun (UK) Ltd., pg. 835 **IT**
Robert Horne Group Plc, pg. 757 **IT**
Robert Horne Paper Company Limited, pg. 757 **IT**
Hospital Management & Supplies Limited, Brooke House, 4, The Lakes, pg. 58 **IT**
Krupp Materials Handling Ltd., pg. 511 **IT**
The Lummus Co. Ltd., G House, Lady's Lane, pg. 6 **IT**
Manitowoc Europe Ltd., St. James Mill Road, pg. 1041 **PB**
NRG Group Limited, Gestetner House, 4 Rushmills, pg. 1114 **IT**
Navstar Systems Ltd., Mansard Close, pg. 1547 **PB**
Price/Stern/Publishers, Ltd., John Clare House, pg. 1215 **IT**
Remington Consumer Products, Ltd., 3A Mercury Dr., pg. 921 **PV**
Rex-Rotary UK Limited, Gestetner House, 4 Rushmills, pg. 1114 **IT**
Rockware Glass Reclamation Centre, Four Harborough Rd., pg. 124 **IT**
Ross Systems (UK) Limited, 7 Rushmills, pg. 1406 **PB**
Rothenberger (UK) Ltd., Moulton Park, Industrial Estate, 14/18 Tenter Rd., pg. 1129 **IT**
Savory Paper Ltd, pg. 1212 **IT**
Scottish & New Castle Retail, Riverside House, Riverside Way, pg. 757 **IT**
Howard Smith Papers Ltd, pg. 757 **IT**
WILSON CONNOLLY, Thomas Wilson House, Tenter Road, pg. 1510 **IT**

Northfleet

Britannia Refined Metals Retirement Plan Ltd., Botany Rd., pg. 827 **IT**
M.I.M. Technology Marketing Limited, Botany Road, pg. 827 **IT**

Northolt

Kidde Fire Protection Ltd., Belvue Rd., pg. 1499 **IT**

Northwich

AMEC PLC, Sandi Way House, Hartford, pg. 16 **IT**
BPB Paper & Packaging Ltd., Davidson House, Gadbrook Park, pg. 122 **IT**
Cambridge Research Biochemicals Limited, Gadbrook Park, pg. 1524 **IT**
Eden Vale, Warrington Rd., pg. 968 **IT**
Zeneca Resins, Lostock Works, pg. 1524 **IT**

Northwood

ADT Phone & Modern Security, Zettler House, 201 Pinner Road, pg. 1649 **PB**
The Glacier Metal Co. Ltd., Argyle House, Joel Street, pg. 1334 **IT**

Norton

Morganite Thermal Ceramics Limited, Woodbury Ln., pg. 893 **IT**
Pratten Construction, Charlton Rd., pg. 219 **IT**

Norwich

Atlas Aggregates Limited, 5 Guardian Rd., pg. 1079 **IT**
Bally's Shoe Factories (Norwich) Ltd., Hall Rd., pg. 997 **IT**
BERNARD MATTHEWS PLC, Great Witchingham Hall, pg. 189 **IT**
Canon (Anglia) Office Automation Ltd., Canon House, White Lodge Business Park, pg. 262 **IT**
Elsevier Geo Abstracts, Regency House, 34 Duke Street, pg. 1100 **IT**
Grolier Limited, 29 Morgan Way, pg. 795 **IT**
Group Lotus Ltd., Potash Lane, pg. 1071 **IT**
Lotus Cars Ltd., Potash Lane, pg. 1071 **IT**
Lotus Engineering, Potash Lane, Hethel, pg. 1071 **IT**
Mills Manufacturing Technology, Bowthorpe Industrial Estate, Barnard Rd., pg. 585 **IT**
Nacanco Ltd., Salhouse Rd., pg. 1029 **IT**
NORWICH UNION LIFE INSURANCE, 25-27 Surrey St., pg. 970 **IT**
Riley Advertising (Norwich) Ltd., 2nd Fl., St. John's House, 25 St. John Maddermarket, pg. 1117 **IT**
Rockware Plastics Ltd., Paddock St., pg. 124 **IT**
Wavetek Limited, Hurricane Way, Norwich Airport, pg. 1155 **PV**

Nottingham

Ballast Wiltshier Plc - East Midland Area, Ascot House, Ascot Park Estate, pg. 135 **IT**
Blue Hawk Ltd., Pasture Lane, Ruddington, pg. 122 **IT**

PB - *U.S. Public Companies Volume*
PV - *U.S. Private Companies Volume*
IT - *International Public & Private Companies Volume*

THE BOOTS COMPANY PLC, Thane Rd. West, pg. 202 — IT
Boots Contract Manufacturing, One Thane Road, pg. 202 — IT
Boots Healthcare International, Central Park, Lenton Lane, pg. 202 — IT
Boots Opticians, St. Mary's Court, pg. 202 — IT
Boots Properties, One Thane Road, pg. 203 — IT
Boots The Chemists, One Thane Road, pg. 203 — IT
Bradstock Insurance Brokers Limited, Hine House, 25 Regent St., pg. 210 — IT
Britains Petite Ltd., Chelsea St., pg. 789 — PB
British Gas Energy Centres Ltd., P.O. Box 99, pg. 279 — IT
Byron Mediplastics Limited, Hucknall Industrial Estate, Daniels Way, pg. 789 — PB
Childrens World, Alan House, Clumber Street, pg. 1304 — IT
Chronos Richardson Limited, Arnside Rd., pg. 1299 — IT
Crosland Filters Ltd., Glaisdale Dr., pg. 785 — IT
Crosland Plant, pg. 786 — IT
Gala Leisure Ltd., New Castle House, Castle Blvd., pg. 170 — IT
Helly-Hansen (UK) Ltd., St. Mary's Hall, pg. 1011 — IT
Home Brewery plc, Mansfield Rd., pg. 1211 — IT
Imperial Tobacco International Ltd., Lenton Industrial Estate, Thane Road, pg. 666 — IT
Intermotor, Occupation Road, pg. 1503 — PB
Juki (Europe) G.m.b.H.-U.K. Office, Minerva House (Ground Floor), Spaniel Row, pg. 717 — IT
Kodak Limited, Mansfield Rd., pg. 553 — PB
Lambert Smith Hampton, 4 Regent Street, pg. 797 — IT
Lenton Foods, Lenton Lane, pg. 968 — IT
Luxfer, Colwick, pg. 51 — IT
The Pizza Factory, Finch Close, Lenton Lane, pg. 968 — IT
Poole Wood Equipment Ltd., Crown House, Traffic St., pg. 231 — IT
Pork Farms/Bowyers, Queens Dr., pg. 968 — IT
Raleigh Industries Ltd., Triumph Rd., pg. 394 — IT
Ready Mixed Concrete (East Midlands) Limited, RMC House, Long Ln., pg. 1080 — IT
Richard Simon and Sons Limited, Park Lane, pg. 789 — PB
Riley Advertising (Nottingham) Ltd., Riley House, Pelham Rd., Sherwood Rise, pg. 1117 — IT
Riverside Bakery, Crossgate Dr., pg. 968 — IT
Sandiacre Screw Ltd., Bradley St., pg. 585 — IT
Senior Conflow, Triumph Rd., pg. 1220 — IT
Senior Entex, Glaisdale Dr., pg. 1220 — IT
Smiths Flour Mills Ltd., P.O. Box 3, pg. 968 — IT
Speedo (Europe) Ltd., Ascot Works, Ascot Rd., pg. 1036 — IT
Stora Building Products, Scanda House, Acton Close, pg. 1303 — IT
Sturmey-Archer Limited, Triumph Rd., pg. 394 — IT
Tetra Europe Limited, Rock House, Stockhill Lane, pg. 1226 — IT
Toplis Painters Limited, Tower House, 96 Rolleston Dr., pg. 337 — IT
Toray Textiles Europe Ltd., Leonard Street, pg. 1400 — IT
TWIL Handling & Display Ltd., New Eastwood, pg. 184 — IT
Warner's (United Kingdom) Limited, Blenheim Industrial Park, Dabell Ave., pg. 1738 — PB
Watlow Limited, Thornfield Industrial Estate, Hooton St., pg. 1154 — PV
ZF Great Britain Ltd., Abbeyfield Rd., pg. 1522 — IT

Nuneaton

Cogsdill-Nuneaton, Ltd., Tenlons Rd., pg. 250 — PV
Quinton Hazell PLC, Nuneaton, Hazel Way, Bermuda Rd., pg. 561 — PB
Sandvik Rock Tools Ltd., pg. 1187 — IT
Thetford (Aqua) Products, Ltd., Centrovell Indus. Estate, Caldwell Rd., pg. 352 — PV

Oadby

Emhart International Ltd., Lyn House, 39 The Parade, pg. 233 — PB
Rimoldi (Great Britain) Ltd., 26 Mandervell Rd., pg. 1118 — IT
Union Special (UK) Ltd., 22, Manderwell Rd., Industrial Estate, pg. 717 — IT

Okehampton

G.R. Spinks & Co. Ltd., Exeter Road, pg. 1143 — IT

Old Woking

Medelec Limited, Manor Way, pg. 1467 — IT
Vickers Air-Shields, Unit 9, Manor Way, pg. 1467 — IT

Oldbury

Albright & Wilson Intertrade Ltd., P.O. Box 3, Albright & Wilson House, pg. 49 — IT
ALBRIGHT & WILSON PLC, 210-222 Hagley Rd. W, pg. 49 — IT
Bohler U.K. Ltd., Taylors Ln., pg. 1471 — IT
Bridgestone/Firestone U.K. Ltd., Bridgestone House, Birchley Trading Estate, pg. 214 — IT
M. Myers & Son plc, pg. 154 — PB
Phosphates Division, Albright & Wilson Limited, P.O. Box 80, Trinity St., pg. 49 — IT
Senior Engineering Products Business Area, Popes Lane, pg. 1220 — IT
Senior Flexonics Ltd., pg. 1221 — IT
Star Tubes (UK) Ltd, Unit 3, Park Lane Industrial Estate, pg. 1088 — IT

TP Manipulations, Popes Lane, pg. 1222 — IT
Tube Products, Popes Lane, pg. 1222 — IT
Western Aggregates Limited, Wolverhampton New Rd., pg. 1079 — IT

Oldham

Chemviron Carbon, 113 High St., pg. 293 — PB
Cobden Chadwick (UK) Ltd., Century Works, HAvelock St., pg. 488 — IT
Compoflex, Delph, pg. 1221 — IT
Dreamland Appliances Limited, Vine Mill, Middleton Rd., pg. 925 — IT
FERRANTI TECHNOLOGIES LTD., Waterhead, pg. 480 — IT
GEC Dynamics Limited-Missiles & Ordnance, Derker St., pg. 544 — IT
Geotek Communications, Inc., Old Bank House, 59 High St., pg. 740 — PB
K-Tron Great Britain, Ltd., 4 Southlink Business Park, pg. 938 — PB
Kidde Thorn Fire Protection Limited, Hollins Rd., pg. 1500 — IT
Luwa (UK) Ltd., pg. 618 — IT
MEM Ltd. 250 V, Whitesgate, Broadway, pg. 390 — IT
Moorside Division, pg. 673 — IT
Park Cakes Ltd., Ashton Rd., pg. 968 — IT

Oldsleworth

Helene Curtis UK, Inc., Bridge Wharf Rd., pg. 1434 — IT

Onchan

Coutts & Co (Isle of Man) Limited, Summerhill Road, Coutts House, pg. 910 — IT
Dowty Aerospace, Isle of Man, School Road, pg. 1337 — IT

Ormskirk

L.O. Jeffs Ltd., School Lane, Haskayne, pg. 542 — IT

Orpington

E.J. Brooks Europe Ltd., St. Mary Cray, 53 High St., pg. 172 — PV
Colorcon Ltd., Murray Road, pg. 139 — PV
Cyborg Systems (UK) Ltd., Central Ct., pg. 299 — PV
Enso Marketing Co. Ltd., Enso House, New Mill Rd., pg. 457 — IT
Enso Publication Papers Limited, Enso House, New Mill Rd., pg. 457 — IT
Forchem Limited, Enso House, New Mill Road, pg. 458 — IT
Graseby Andersen Ltd., River House, St. Mary Cray, pg. 1267 — IT
Graseby Specac Ltd., River House, pg. 1267 — IT
Southern Watch & Clock Supplies Ltd., pg. 817 — IT

Ossett

New Food Ingredients, Owl Lane, pg. 797 — PV
RHM Ingredient Supplies Limited, Owl Lane, pg. 1396 — IT
RHM Ingredients, Ltd., Owl Lane, pg. 797 — PV
VOAC Hydraulics Ltd., 66 Wakefield Rd., pg. 1264 — PB

Ottery Saint Mary

Ottermill Switchgear Ltd., Mill St., pg. 1198 — PB

Oxbridge

Lincoln National (UK) plc, The Keys, 101-105 Oxford Rd., pg. 998 — PB

Oxford

AP & T Ltd., Seacourt Tower, Floor 2, pg. 620 — PB
B.H. BLACKWELL LTD., Beaver House, Hythe Bridge Street, pg. 197 — IT
Blackwell Publishers Ltd., 108 Cowley Road, pg. 197 — IT
Blackwell Science, Osney Mead, pg. 197 — IT
Butterworth-Heinemann Limited, Linacre House, Jordon Hill, pg. 1094 — IT
Elsevier Editorial Services, Mayfield House, 256 Banbury Road, pg. 1100 — IT
Heinemann Educational Publishing, Halley Court, Jordan Hill, pg. 1094 — IT
Heinemann English Language Teaching, Halley Court, Jordan Hill, pg. 1479 — IT
Intermagnetics General (Europe) Limited, P.O. Box 181, pg. 894 — PB
International Rectifier Company (Great Britain) Ltd., Hurst Green, pg. 907 — PB
A.C. Nielsen Co., Ltd., Nielsen House, pg. 1183 — PB
The Oxford Collection Ltd., 1-3 Golden Cross, pg. 807 — IT
Oxford Instruments-Accelerator Technology Group, Osney Mead, pg. 1018 — IT
Oxford Instruments-NMR Instruments, Osney Mead, pg. 1018 — IT
OXFORD UNIVERSITY PRESS, Great Clarendon Street, pg. 1018 — IT
Reed Educational and Professional Publishing, Halley Court, Jordan Hill, pg. 1094 — IT
Sharp Laboratories of Europe, Ltd., Oxford Science Park, Edmund Halley Road, pg. 1230 — IT
Standex Holdings Limited, Stanton Harwat, pg. 1507 — PB
Yamanouchi Research Institute (U.K.), Littlemore Hospital, pg. 1519 — IT

Oxton

Ajax Magnethermic U.K. Ltd., Holland Rd., pg. 113 — IT

Padiham

Perseverance Mills Ltd., Albion Mills, pg. 1202 — IT

Paisley

CIBA Pigments, Hawkhead Rd., pg. 292 — IT
GIBCO/Bio-Cult Diagnostics, Ltd., 3 Washington Rd. Abottsvion Indus. Estat, pg. 505 — PB
Life Technologies (Europe) Ltd., Renfrew Rd., pg. 505 — PB

Penarth

HICKING PENTECOST PLC, Avon House, 19 Stanwell Road, pg. 618 — IT

Penn

Materials Research Ltd., St. John's Estate, Tyler's Green, pg. 1283 — IT

Penrith

Shap Concrete Products Limited, Shap, pg. 1080 — IT

Perth

Barratt East Scotland, Belhaven House, Marshall Place, pg. 168 — IT
GENERAL ACCIDENT FIRE AND LIFE ASSURANCE CORPORATION P.L.C., Pitheavlis, pg. 542 — IT
Matthew Gloag & Son Limited, West Kinfauns, pg. 619 — IT
Kanthal Ltd., pg. 724 — IT
United Distillers Blending & Bottling Ltd., Inveralmond, pg. 412 — IT
United Distillers UK Plc, Cherrybank, pg. 412 — IT
Woods of Perth, 3 Mill St., pg. 290 — IT

Perthshire

The Gleneagles Hotel, Auchterarder, pg. 412 — IT

Peterborough

APV Baker Plc, Westfield Road, pg. 1240 — IT
ACCO Europe Plc, Bretton Way, pg. 674 — PB
British Sugar plc, Oundle Rd., pg. 92 — IT
Chloride Electronics Ltd., Southgate Way, pg. 287 — IT
Choice Publications Ltd, Apex House, Oundle Rd., pg. 451 — IT
EMAP Nationals, Bushfield House, Orton Center, pg. 451 — IT
EMAP Response Ltd., Wentworth House, Wentworth St., pg. 451 — IT
Elliott Group Limited, Glebe Ct., Glebe Works, pg. 385 — IT
EMAP Apex, Apex House, Oundle Rd., pg. 451 — IT
EMAP PLC, One Lincoln Ct., Lincoln Rd., pg. 451 — IT
EMAP Properties, Lincoln Court, pg. 451 — IT
EMAP Pursuit Publishing, Bretton Court, pg. 451 — IT
Frontline, Park House, 117 Park Rd., pg. 114 — IT
Frontline- Distribution Division, Park House, Park Rd., pg. 451 — IT
Frontline Ltd., Park House, 117 Park Rd., pg. 114 — IT
Furon Ltd., Crusader House, High St., Maxey, pg. 689 — IT
Goss Graphic Systems Ltd., Bretton Way, pg. 466 — PV
Hotpoint Ltd., Celta Rd., pg. 544 — IT
Kalmar Kockum Ltd., 24, Stapleton Rd., Orton Southgate, pg. 1421 — IT
MB-Clarke Ltd., Padholme Road East, pg. 386 — IT
Metzeler (UK) Ltd., North Westwood Industrial Estate, pg. 1059 — IT
Park Air Electronics Ltd., Northfields, Market Deeping, pg. 1198 — PB
Pearl Group Plc, The Pearl Centre, Lynch Wood, pg. 100 — IT
Peter Brotherhood Ltd., Lincoln Rd., pg. 1596 — PB
Peterborough Quarries Limited, West End, Maxey, pg. 166 — IT
Princeton Gamma-Tech U.K. Ltd., 2, The Metro Center, pg. 1016 — IT
Redring Electric Ltd., Redring Works, Celta Road, pg. 545 — IT
Seymour International, Park House, 117 Park Rd., pg. 452 — IT
Varity Perkins, Frank Perkins Way, pg. 820 — IT

Peterhead

Guardian PTS Ltd, One Dales Industrial Estate, pg. 1231 — IT

Peterlee

NSK-AKS Precision Ball Europe Ltd., Davy Dr., North West Industrial Estate, pg. 903 — IT
NSK Bearings Europe Ltd., 3, Brindley Road, S.W. Industrial Estate, pg. 903 — IT
Roballo Engineering Co. Ltd., North West Industrial Estate, Mill Hill, pg. 509 — IT
Weiser (U.K.) Ltd., North West Indus. Estate, pg. 1055 — PB

PB - *U.S. Public Companies Volume*
PV - *U.S. Private Companies Volume*
IT - *International Public & Private Companies Volume*

1824

Geographic Index-Non U.S.

Pilsworth

Kemira Coatings, Heavy Duty Division, 5 Broadlands Crescent, pg. 729   **IT**

Pinner

Applied Technology (UK), 25 Gladsdale Dr., pg. 1004   **PB**
Initial Textile Service, Initial House, 150 Field End Rd., pg. 1285   **IT**

Plymouth

Acheson Colloids Company, Prince Rock, pg. 12   **PV**
Air Conditioner Division, Porsham Close, Belliver Indus. Estate, pg. 1406   **IT**
Ash Instruments Division, Dentsply Ltd., Penny Cross Close, pg. 499   **PB**
Bailey Telecom LTD - Plymouth, Trevol Business Park, Torpoint, pg. 133   **IT**
The Barden Corp., (U.K.) Ltd., Plymbridge Road Estover, pg. 468   **IT**
British Aerospace (Systems and Equipment) Ltd., Clittaford Rd., Southway, pg. 217   **IT**
Canusa Systems Limited - EMI, Bergstrand House, Parkwood Close, pg. 1231   **IT**
Canusa Systems Limited - EMI, Bell Close, Newnham Industrial Estate, pg. 1231   **IT**
Gleason Works Ltd., Plymouth Rd., pg. 746   **PB**
Hellerman Electric, Pennycross Close, pg. 207   **IT**
Kawasaki Precision Machinery (UK) Ltd., Ernesettle Lane, pg. 726   **IT**
Ranco Controls Ltd., Southway Dr., pg. 1243   **IT**
Remo Precision Tools Ltd., pg. 469   **IT**
Toshiba Consumer Products (U.K.) Limited, Northolt Ave., Ernesettle, pg. 1406   **IT**
Vi-Spring Limited, Ernesettle Lane, pg. 925   **IT**
Western Trust & Savings Holdings Ltd., The Moneycentre, pg. 841   **IT**
The Wrigley Company Ltd., Estover, pg. 1781   **PB**

Pontefract

Cott Europe (Pontefract), Knottingly Road, pg. 338   **IT**
Phildas Ltd., P.O. Box 10, pg. 585   **IT**

Pontyclun

Ondawel (G.B.) Ltd., pg. 1490   **IT**

Pontypool

Avesta Sheffield Ltd., P.O. Box 1, pg. 222   **IT**
Parke-Davis & Company, Ltd., Usk Road, pg. 1739   **PB**
Trico Ltd., NP4 OXZ, pg. 1397   **IT**

Pontypridd

Forest Fasteners, Treforest Industrial Estate, pg. 265   **IT**

Poole

Davy International, 551/553 Wallisdown Rd., pg. 773   **IT**
Hamworthy Allweiller Limited, Fleets Corner, pg. 1065   **IT**
Hamworthy Combustion Equipment Limited, pg. 1065   **IT**
Hamworthy Combustion Systems Limited, Fleets Corner, pg. 1065   **IT**
Hamworthy Engineering Limited, Fleets Corner, pg. 1065   **IT**
Hamworthy Heating Limited, Fleets Corner, pg. 1065   **IT**
Hamworthy Industramar Limited, pg. 1065   **IT**
Hamworthy Marine Limited, Fleet's Corner, pg. 1065   **IT**
Hamworthy Pumps and Compressors Limited, Fleets Corner, pg. 1065   **IT**
Heatric Ltd., 46 Holton Road, pg. 853   **IT**
Link House Advertising Periodicals Ltd., Link House, West St., pg. 1443   **IT**
Parker Electromechanical-Digiplan Division, 21 Balena Close, pg. 1263   **PB**
Poole Lighting Limited, Cabot Ln., pg. 453   **IT**
Powell Duffryn Tools Limited, Fleets Corner, pg. 1066   **IT**
Sieger Ltd., pg. 618   **IT**
Sieger TPA Ltd., pg. 618   **IT**
Sigma Chemical Co., Ltd., Fancy Rd., pg. 1472   **PB**
Sowester Limited, 6 Stinsford Road, pg. 968   **PB**
Telxon Limited, Old Orchard, High Street, pg. 1574   **PB**
United Advertising Publications plc, 25 West St., pg. 1443   **IT**
Van Leer Packaging Systems Ltd., pg. 1147   **IT**
Wayfarer Transit Systems Ltd., 10 Willis Way, pg. 853   **IT**

Port Talbot

Smurfit Giftwrap, Unit 5, Rutherglen Centre, Seaway Parade, pg. 1271   **IT**
Trafalgar House Technology Limited (Kenfig Industrial Estate), Margam, pg. 773   **IT**

Portadown

Kilmeaden Foods Limited, Unit 4, Carn Industrial Estate, pg. 102   **IT**
Polarcup United Kingdom Ltd., 180 Gilford Rd., pg. 638   **IT**

Portslade

Le Carbone (Great Britain) Ltd., South Street, pg. 1030   **IT**

Portsmouth

De La Rue Cash Handling Product Group, Walton Road, Farlington, pg. 387   **IT**
Ferranti Naval, Jackson Close, pg. 544   **IT**
GEC-Marconi Dynamics Ltd., Broad Oak Works, The Airport, pg. 544   **IT**
Hart, Fenton & Co. Ltd., 70 Broad Street, pg. 1214   **IT**
IBM United Kingdom Holdings Limited, Alencon Link, pg. 897   **PB**
IBM United Kingdom Limited, P.O. Box 41, North Harbour, pg. 898   **PB**
ITW Switches-Europe, Norway Rd., Hilsea Indus. Est., pg. 869   **PB**
J & N Wade Limited, Great Western House, 34 Isambard Brunel Rd., pg. 341   **IT**
Marconi Underwater Systems Ltd., Elettra Ave., pg. 544   **IT**
Matra Marconi Space NV, Anchorage Rd., pg. 545   **IT**
Pall Europe Ltd., Europe House, Havant Street, pg. 1254   **PB**
Pall Industrial Hydraulics Ltd., Europa House, Havant Street, pg. 1254   **PB**
Pall Process Filtration Ltd., Europa House, Havant Street, pg. 1254   **PB**
Wightlink Ltd., 70 Broad St., pg. 1214   **IT**
Zurich Insurance Company, Zurich House, Stanhope Rd., pg. 1531   **IT**
Zurich Life Assurance Company Limited, Hippodrome House, 11 Guildhall Walk, pg. 1532   **IT**

Potters Bar

Albany Life Assurance Company Limited, Canada Life Place, pg. 255   **IT**
CLGB Property Company Limited, Canada Life Place, High Street, pg. 255   **IT**
Canada Life Assurance Company of Great Britain Limited, Canada Life Place, pg. 255   **IT**
The Canada Life Assurance Company (U.K.) Limited, Canada Life Place, High Street, pg. 255   **IT**
Canada Life Financial Services Company Limited, Canada Life Place, High Street, pg. 255   **IT**
The Canada Life Group (U.K.) Limited, Canada Life Place, High Street, pg. 255   **IT**
Canada Life Holdings (U.K.) Limited, Canada Life Place, High Street, pg. 255   **IT**
Canada Life Management (U.K.) Limited, Canada Life Place, High Street, pg. 255   **IT**
Canada Life Trustee Services (U.K.) Limited, Canada Life Place, High Steet, pg. 255   **IT**
Canada Life (UK) Ltd., Canada Life Place, pg. 255   **IT**
Canada Life Unit Trust Managers Limited, Canada Life Place, High Street, pg. 255   **IT**
Nippert-Dawson Limited, Unit 21, Cranborne Industrial Estate, pg. 1017   **IT**
Soundcraft Electronics, Ltd, Cranborne House, Cranborne Industrial Estate, pg. 787   **PB**

Poyle

Steelcase Strafor (UK) Ltd., Unit 4, pg. 569   **IT**

Poynton

Lightnin Mixers Limited, London Road South, pg. 727   **PB**

Prescot

Giddings & Lewis Ltd, Randles Rd., pg. 1389   **IT**

Prestatyn

Kwik Save Group plc, Warren Dr., pg. 704   **IT**

Preston

Addison Tube Forming Limited, Unit 188, Walton Summit Industrial Estate, pg. 448   **IT**
Barratt Manchester, 333 Garstang Road, pg. 168   **IT**
British Aerospace Defence Limited (Military Aircraft), Warton Aerodrome, pg. 217   **IT**
British Aerospace Defence Limited (Systems & Services), Warton Aerodrome, Mill Lane, pg. 217   **IT**
DATEL TECHNOLOGIES LTD., Old Docks House, 90 Watery Lane, pg. 384   **IT**
GEC Reinforced Plastics Ltd., Mill Lane, pg. 544   **IT**
Goss Graphic Systems Ltd., Greenbank St., pg. 466   **PV**
Robert Hudson (Machinery Sale & Service) Ltd., pg. 817   **IT**
Nederman Ltd., P.O. Box 503, 91 Walton Summit, pg. 283   **IT**
New Tech Coatings, Units 9 & 10, Old Mill Estate, pg. 124   **IT**
Powerplan Systems Ltd, pg. 1512   **IT**
Preston Coated Stone, Red Scar Industrial Estate, Longridge Rd., pg. 1079   **IT**
Red Rose Radio, The Radio Station, pg. 452   **IT**
Studio Cards Ltd., Birley Bank, pg. 485   **IT**
Summit Gravure Ltd., Unit 171, Walton Summit Industrial Estate, pg. 498   **IT**
Willis Corroon North Limited, Stuart House, Caxton Road, pg. 1503   **IT**

Prestwick

British Aerospace Flying College Ltd., Prestwick Airport, pg. 217   **IT**

Prudhoe

Hammerite Products Limited, pg. 1501   **IT**

Pudsey

Senior Heat Treatment-Pudsey, Grangefield Industrial Estate, Richardshaw Rd., pg. 1221   **IT**
Smurfit Cartons (Leeds) Ltd., Manor Works, Robin Lane, pg. 1271   **IT**

Purfleet

Danzas (UK) Ltd., Stonehouse Lane, pg. 383   **IT**

Purley

EMC Computer Systems, EMC House, 814 Brighton Rd., pg. 545   **PB**
EMAP Direct, Beech House, 840 Brighton Road, pg. 451   **IT**
EMAP Enterprise Events, Whitecliff House, 852 Brighton Rd., pg. 451   **IT**
Valmet Paper Machinery (UK) Ltd., 120 High Street, pg. 1448   **IT**

Putney

ICL PLC, ICL House, 1 High St., pg. 528   **IT**

Quenington

H.J. Godwin Ltd., pg. 1511   **IT**

Radcliffe

Hall Brothers (Whitefield) Limited, Dumers Lane, pg. 1739   **PB**
Radcliffe Paper Tubes, Outwood Rd., pg. 123   **IT**

Rainham

ABM Investment Ltd., 89/95 Ferry Ln., pg. 1465   **IT**
Jonathan James Limited, New Road, pg. 1358   **IT**
SKW Metals U.K. Ltd., Murex Division, 89/95 Ferry Ln., pg. 1465   **IT**

Reading

A.F.N. Ltd., Falcon Works 400, London Rd., Isleworth, pg. 1063   **IT**
Acheson Industries (Europe) Ltd., Sun LifeHouse, pg. 12   **PV**
Activision UK, Blake House, Manor Farm Rd., pg. 17   **PB**
Agmet Ltd., 38 Bennet Road, pg. 369   **PV**
BG PLC, 100 Thames Valley Park Dr., pg. 118   **PB**
BG Plc Exploration & Production Ltd., 100 Thames Valley Park Drive, pg. 119   **IT**
Babcock Materials Handling Ltd., Babcock House, Rose Kiln Ln., pg. 131   **IT**
N.G. Bailey & Co. Ltd.-Reading Branch, 138-140 City Rd., pg. 132   **IT**
Ballast Wiltshier Plc-South West Div., 54 Suttons Business Park, pg. 135   **IT**
Bank of Ireland Home Morgages Limited, Plaza West, Bridge St., pg. 153   **IT**
Barbeque King, 16 Richfield Ave., pg. 1507   **PB**
Beauty International Ltd., pg. 185   **IT**
Berkshire Brewery, Imperial Way, pg. 1212   **IT**
Brush Wellman Ltd., 4 & 5 Ely Rd., pg. 266   **PB**
Celloglas Limited, Headley Rd. East, pg. 69   **IT**
Clarify Ltd.-United Kingdom, Wyvols Court, Swallowfield, pg. 382   **PB**
Clouston Foods Eurpoe, 924 Oxford Road, pg. 492   **IT**
Copygraphic Harris Ltd, pg. 757   **IT**
Danka Europe Ltd., Danka House, London Road, pg. 379   **IT**
Dataproducts Ltd., Unit 1, Heron Industrial Estate, Spencer, pg. 621   **IT**
Digital Equipment Co., Limited, Digital Park I, Imperial Way, pg. 507   **IT**
Dynapac Construction Equipment Ltd., 16 North Street, pg. 1420   **IT**
Dynapac (UK) Ltd., 14 Tessa Road, pg. 1420   **IT**
ECC Overseas Investments Limited, 1015 Arlington Business Park, pg. 455   **IT**
FW Management Operations Ltd., Station Rd., pg. 677   **PB**
Ferro Metal & Chemical Corporation Ltd., 179, Kings Rd., pg. 861   **PV**
Foster Wheeler Energy Limited, Foster Wheeler House, Station Rd., pg. 677   **PB**
Foster Wheeler Ltd. (England), Foster Wheeler House, Station Rd., pg. 677   **PB**
Chr. Hansen (UK) Ltd., 476 Basingstoke Rd., pg. 289   **IT**
Headley Reading Ltd., pg. 68   **IT**
I.D.M. Electronics Ltd., 30, Suttons Park Ave., Suttons Park Industrial Estate, pg. 946   **PB**
ITW Limited-Buildex Europe, 37 Suttons Business Park, pg. 868   **PB**
Intermec UK Ltd., Attenborough House, 15 Bennett Rd., pg. 1005   **PB**

PB - *U.S. Public Companies Volume*
PV - *U.S. Private Companies Volume*
IT - *International Public & Private Companies Volume*

Keithley Instruments Ltd., The Minster, 58 Portman Rd., pg. 947 **PB**
Kloeckner Pentapack Ltd., 268 Edgar Rd., pg. 737 **IT**
Kloeckner Pentaplast Ltd., Station Rd., Theale, pg. 737 **IT**
Lamborghini Great Britain, pg. 1063 **IT**
MB General Packaging Div., 7 Cheapside, pg. 266 **IT**
MB Overseas Limited, Queens House, Forbury Rd., pg. 267 **IT**
MSI Data Limited, United Kingdom, Data House 85-87 Basingstoke Rd., pg. 1546 **PB**
McDougalls Catering Foods Limited, McDougal House, Imperial Way, pg. 1396 **IT**
Metal Box plc Beverage Can Div., Queens House, Forbury Rd., pg. 267 **IT**
Micropolis Corp., Four Worton Dr., pg. 742 **PV**
NE Technology Ltd., Bath Road, pg. 1174 **IT**
Porsche Cars Great Britain Ltd., 26-30, Richfield Ave., pg. 1063 **IT**
Program Lighting Ltd., 27/28 Suttons Industrial Park, pg. 1152 **IT**
Rockwell-Collins (U.K.) Ltd., Suttons Business Pk., pg. 1400 **PB**
Sally Hair & Beauty, Unit 4, Area 10, pg. 38 **PB**
SAS, 27/28 Suttons Industrial Park, pg. 1152 **IT**
SAS HOLDINGS LIMITED, 27/28 Suttons Business Park, pg. 1152 **IT**
SAS International, 27/28 Suttons Industrial Park, pg. 1152 **IT**
Silicon Graphics Ltd., Arlington Business Park, 1530 Lakeside, pg. 1474 **PB**
Smith's Crisps, 121 King's Rd., pg. 1278 **IT**
Springborn Testing & Research (UK) Ltd., 10 Portman Rd., pg. 1027 **PV**
TMC, TMC House, 130 Queens Rd., pg. 1482 **IT**
Tate & Lyle Specialty Sweeteners, pg. 1356 **IT**
Tempatron Limited, 5 Darwin Close, pg. 1241 **IT**
Thames Side-Maywood Limited, 17 Stadium Way, pg. 590 **IT**
THORN Business Communications Ltd., Baird House, pg. 1385 **IT**
THORN Europe, Baird House, pg. 1385 **IT**
Union-Transport, Reading Cargo Centre, Hyperion Way, pg. 1120 **PV**
Unitech Plc, Apex Plaza, Forbury Rd., pg. 1241 **IT**
Universal Coatings Ltd., pg. 69 **IT**
VTEL Europe, Ltd., Apex Plaza, pg. 1703 **PB**
WF Corroon-Reading, Abbot's House, Abbey Street, pg. 1502 **PB**
Willis Corroon Credit Limited, Abbot's House, Abbey Street, pg. 1502 **IT**
Willis Corroon South Limited, 1 St. John's Gate, pg. 1503 **IT**
Woodward Governor (U.K.) Ltd., 350 Baskingstoke Rd., pg. 1777 **PB**
Wynn Oil (U.K.) Limited, Thames Court, 2 Richfield Ave., pg. 1783 **PB**

Redditch

AT&T ISTEL Global Messaging Services Ltd., pg. 11 **PB**
AT&T ISTEL Limited, P.O. Box 5, Grosvenor House, Prospect Hill, pg. 11 **PB**
Alcan Tubes, Studley Rd., pg. 51 **IT**
The Aro Corporation, East Moon Moat Industrial Estate, pg. 877 **PB**
Blakenhurst H.M. Prison, Hewell Lane, pg. 451 **PB**
Carpenter Technology (U.K.) Limited, Unit 48, Eagle Rd., pg. 308 **PB**
DSM United Kingdom Limited, Kingfisher House, Kingfisher Walk, pg. 353 **IT**
Dimensional Stone Limited, Park Farm Industrial Estate, Crossgate Rd., pg. 1081 **IT**
GKN PLC, P.O. Box 55, Ipsley House, pg. 534 **IT**
Graseby Best Ltd., pg. 1267 **IT**
Grau Limited, Arrowdale Rd., pg. 561 **PB**
Gunnebo Ltd., Woolaston Road, Park Farm North, pg. 578 **IT**
HDA Forgings Ltd., Windsor Rd., pg. 126 **IT**
Halfords, Ltd., Icknield Street Dr., Washford West, pg. 203 **IT**
Heath Spring Company LTD, Heath House, Hewell Rd., pg. 857 **PV**
Intech EDM Ltd., Unit 12, Padgets Lane, pg. 489 **IT**
International Radiator Services Ltd., Washford Indus. Estate, Claybrook Dr., pg. 126 **IT**
Linde Gas U.K. Ltd., pg. 811 **IT**
Quinton Hazell PLC, Redditch, Arrowdale Rd., Off Studley Rd., pg. 561 **PB**
Rahbek-Food Limited, Oxleasow Road, pg. 491 **IT**
Reddiwire Limited, 9 Dunlop Road, Hunt End, pg. 184 **IT**
Shakespeare Company United Kingdom, Broad Ground Rd., pg. 940 **PB**

Redhill

BGS Systems, Ltd., Bridge Gate, 55-57 High St., pg. 161 **PB**
DMG Business Media Ltd., Queensway House, 2 Queensway, pg. 366 **IT**
Forum (Holdings) Ltd., Forum House, 41-51 Brighton Road, pg. 41 **IT**
Lombard North Central PLC, Lombard House, 3 Princess Way, pg. 910 **IT**
Redhill, Betchworth House, 63-65 Station Road, pg. 910 **IT**
J.W. Spencer Engineering Ltd., Spencer Way, pg. 124 **IT**
TDK UK LTD., TDK House, 5-7 Queensway, pg. 1337 **IT**

Technology for Communications International, Ltd., Sterling House, 27 Hatchlands Rd., pg. 1555 **PB**
Toyota (Great Britain) Limited, The Quadrangle, 106-118 Station Rd., pg. 1414 **IT**
Xyrofin (UK) Ltd., 41-51 Brighton Rd., pg. 350 **IT**

Reigate

Beazer Homes (Reigate) Ltd., 33 London Rd., pg. 182 **IT**
Cigna Staff Pension Investments Limited, Crusader House, pg. 363 **PB**
Eurodis Electron Group, 17 Birkheads Rd., pg. 1247 **IT**
Eurodis Electron PLC, 17 Birkheads Rd., pg. 1247 **IT**
Lafarge Plasterboard Ltd., Wray Coppice, pg. 791 **IT**
Edward Mendell Co., Lonsdale House, 7-11 High St., pg. 1269 **PB**
Milk Products Holdings (Europe) Ltd., Bancroft Pl., 10 Bancroft Rd., pg. 923 **IT**
Redland Capital PLC, Redland House, pg. 1090 **IT**
Redland Finance PLC, Redland House, pg. 1090 **IT**
Redland Funding PLC, Redland House, pg. 1090 **IT**
Redland Global Funding PLC, Redland House, pg. 1090 **IT**
Redland International Funding PLC, Redland House, pg. 1090 **IT**
Redland International Limited, Redland House, pg. 1091 **IT**
Redland Overseas Funding PLC, Redland House, pg. 1091 **IT**
Redland Plasterboard Holdings, Wray Coppice, Oaks Road Wray Common, pg. 789 **IT**
REDLAND PLC, Redland House, pg. 1090 **IT**
Redland Preferred Stock PLC, Redland House, pg. 1091 **IT**
Redland Properties Ltd., Redland House, pg. 1091 **IT**
Redland Roof Tiles Ltd., Redland House, pg. 1091 **IT**
Redland Sterling Funding PLC, Redland House, pg. 1091 **IT**
Redland Universal Funding PLC, Redland House, pg. 1091 **IT**
Redland U.S. Funding PLC, Redland House, pg. 1091 **IT**

Renfrew

AMEC Construction Scotland Ltd., Meadowside St., pg. 16 **IT**
Babcock Construction Limited, Renfrew Works, Porterfield Rd., pg. 130 **IT**
Babcock Energy Limited, Renfrew Works, Porterfield Rd., pg. 131 **IT**
Babcock Energy Limited, Technology Centre, High Street, pg. 131 **IT**
Babcock Power Limited-Research Div., High St., pg. 472 **IT**
Babcock Power-Production Div., pg. 472 **IT**
Babcock Welding Products Limited, French St., pg. 472 **IT**
HOWDEN GROUP PLC, Old Govan Rd., pg. 636 **IT**
James Howden Group Limited, Old Govan Rd., pg. 636 **IT**
Robinson Nugent (Scotland) Limited, 4 Fountain Avenue, pg. 1395 **PB**
Smith & McLaurin Limited, Cartside Mllls, Kilbarchan, pg. 1107 **IT**
Van Leer (UK) Ltd., pg. 1147 **IT**

Retford

Babcock Jenkins Ltd., pg. 472 **IT**
Hall & Co. Limited, Midlands & North Region, RMC House, New St., pg. 1079 **IT**

Rhondda

Wolsey Electronics Limited, Dinas Isaf East, pg. 1344 **IT**

Rhymney

M.C. Sheet Metal Ltd., pg. 1117 **IT**

Richmond

ADC Metrica, Spencer House, pg. 4 **PB**
AES Electric, Burleigh House, 17-19 Worple Way, pg. 5 **PB**
AES Silk Road, Burleigh House, 17-19 Worple Way, pg. 5 **PB**
Burger King (UK) Limited, 20 Kew Road, pg. 411 **IT**
Chemie Linz UK Ltd., 12, The Green, pg. 356 **IT**
Compaq Computer Limited, Hotham House, 1 Heron Square, pg. 418 **IT**
Intermarkets International, Rosedale House, Rosedale Road, pg. 1062 **PV**
KTI Gas Processors Ltd., Burford House, pg. 837 **IT**
Kinetics Technology International Ltd., pg. 837 **IT**
Kintech (U.K.) Ltd., pg. 837 **IT**
MacMillan Bloedel Meyer Ltd., Lion House, pg. 829 **IT**
Mills & Boon Ltd., Eton House, 18-24 Paradise Rd., pg. 1402 **IT**
Northumberland Group Ltd., 18 Parkshot, pg. 162 **IT**
PROUDFOOT PLC, 5 Hill Street, pg. 1071 **IT**
Reed Exhibition Companies, Oriel House, pg. 1096 **IT**
Reed Exhibition Companies (UK) Ltd., Oriel House, 26, The Quadrant, pg. 1097 **IT**
Southcorp Wines Europe, 12 King St., pg. 1287 **IT**
Tarmac ServiceMaster, 37-39 Kew Foot Road, pg. 1462 **IT**
Tenneco United Kingdom, Inc., Castle Yard House, 1 Castle Yard, pg. 1580 **PB**

Western Data Systems Intl., Ltd., 22 The Quadent, pg. 1165 **PV**

Richmond upon Thames

Lubrizol Ltd., Palm Court, 4 Heron Square, pg. 1017 **PB**

Rickmansworth

Buxton Mineral Water Company Ltd., pg. 919 **IT**
Comet, Comet House, Three Rivers Court, pg. 733 **IT**
Costain Building Products Limited, Langwood House, High Street, pg. 336 **IT**
Mead Coated Board U.K. Limited, Hertford House, pg. 1076 **PB**
Nissan Motor (GB) Ltd., The Rivers Office Park, Denham Way, pg. 945 **IT**
Senior Construction Services Limited, 59/61 High St., pg. 1220 **IT**
SENIOR ENGINEERING GROUP, PLC., Senior House, 59/61 High St., pg. 1220 **IT**
Trafalgar House Technology Limited (Maple Cross House), Denham Way, Maple Cross, pg. 774 **IT**

Riddings

Laporte Electronics, Amber Business Centre, pg. 802 **IT**

Ringwood

Militair Aviation Limited, Militair House, Christchurch Road, pg. 215 **IT**

Ripley

Butterley Brick Ltd., Wellington St., pg. 592 **IT**
Butterley Engineering Ltd., Engineering Works, pg. 585 **IT**
Crowngap Construction Ltd., Lutidine House, pg. 1033 **IT**
Sermatech (U.K.) Limited, High Holborn Rd., Codnor, pg. 1570 **PB**

Ripon

Wolseley Centers Ltd., pg. 1511 **IT**

Risley

Bechtel Water Technology Ltd., Chadwick House, Warrington Road, pg. 128 **PV**
NWW Properties Limited, Chadwick House, Warrington Road, pg. 1444 **IT**

Rochdale

Alexander Drew & Sons Ltd., Stotts Mill, Bridge Fold Rd., pg. 798 **IT**
Farrel Ltd., Queensway Castleton, pg. 614 **PB**
TBA Industrial Products Ltd., pg. 1334 **IT**
Whipp & Bourne Ltd., Switchgear Works, pg. 473 **IT**

Rochester

APV Rosista Ltd., Commissioners Rd., Strood, pg. 1241 **IT**
Aquaseal Ltd., Kingsnorth House, pg. 1355 **PB**
CSA, Ltd., Knight Rd., pg. 424 **IT**
GEC Avionics Ltd., Airport Works, pg. 543 **IT**
Magnetic Technologies Europe, Ltd., pg. 1420 **PB**
RSI International, Ltd., Knight Rd., pg. 424 **PB**
STI International Limited, 34 Riverside, pg. 1095 **PB**

Romford

Alcatel Business Systems UK, P.O. Box 3, South Street, pg. 55 **IT**
AB Electronic Limited, Spring Gardens, pg. 1344 **IT**
P.C. Henderson Limited, Tangent Works, pg. 615 **IT**
Repsol Derivados Carless Refining & Mktg. Ltd., St. James's House, Eastern Rd., pg. 1104 **IT**
Stolt Tank Containers Limited, pg. 1301 **IT**

Romsey

Brookes & Gatehouse, Ltd., International Marine House, Abbey Park, pg. 1461 **IT**
McLean Homes Southern Limited, Rivermead House, pg. 1355 **IT**
Universal Calibration Laboratories Ltd., Universal House, Greatbridge Rd., pg. 390 **IT**

Ross-on-Wye

Energy Control Products, Unit C, The Beaver Centre, Ashburton Industrial Estate, pg. 1338 **IT**
John Crane Industrial Gaskets, Alton Road, pg. 1338 **IT**

Rossendale

AIRTOURS PLC, Wavell House, Holcombe Road, pg. 39 **IT**

Rotherham

Aven Tools Ltd., Aven Industrial Estate Maltby, pg. 234 **PB**
Beatson Clark plc, The Glass Works, Greasbrough Road, pg. 1344 **IT**

PB - *U.S. Public Companies Volume*
PV - *U.S. Private Companies Volume*
IT - *International Public & Private Companies Volume*

1826

Geographic Index-Non U.S.

Brooke Cutting Tools Ltd., Hellaby Industrial Estate, Denby Way, Hellaby, pg. 228   IT
Eldon Electric Ltd., Barbot Hall Industrial Estate, Mangham Rd., pg. 436   IT
Firth-Rixson Rings Ltd., P.O. Box 22, Sheffield Rd., pg. 488   IT
Form Fittings Ltd., pg. 1511   IT
I.G. Technologies Ltd., The Ickles, Sheffield Rd., pg. 1030   IT
Laporte Fluorides, Gin House Ln., pg. 802   IT
London & Scandinavian Metallurgical Co. Ltd., Fullerton Road, pg. 735   PV
Parker Hannifin plc, Barbados Way, Hellaby Industrial Estate, pg. 1263   PB
Rawmarsh Foods, Claypit Lane, pg. 968   IT
Salem Automation Limited, Sycamore Rd., pg. 962   PV

Rowley Regis

Willenhall Steel Stockholders Ltd., pg. 79   IT

Royal Leamington Spa

Dictaphone Co. U.K. Ltd., Regent Square House, The Parade, pg. 1045   PV
Glynwed Consumer & Construction Products Ltd., Clarence St., pg. 554   IT
Lunn Poly Ltd., York House, Clarendon Ave., pg. 1601   PB
MRB-Schumag (U.K.) Ltd., Berrington Rd., pg. 399   IT
RMC Mortars Limited, Holly House, 74 Upper Holly Walk, pg. 1080   IT
Technip UK Ltd., 53 Mill Street, pg. 1361   IT

Royston

Cresswell Lighting Limited, York Way Industrial Estate, pg. 453   IT
Endevco UK Ltd., Melbourn, pg. 853   IT
Johnson Matthey Noble Metals Business Unit, Orchard Road, pg. 713   IT
Johnson Matthey PLC, Orchard Rd., pg. 713   IT
Johnson Matthey P.L.C., Orchard Rd., pg. 713   PB
Sealed Air Cambridge, Saxon Way, Melbourn, pg. 1451   PB
TRU-LON Printed Circuits (Royston) Limited, Newark Close, York Way Industrial Estate, pg. 1290   IT

Ruddington

NSK-RHP Europe Limited, Ruddington Fields Business Pk., Mere Way, pg. 904   IT
NSK-RHP European Technology Co. Limited, Ruddington Fields Business Pk., Mere Way, pg. 904   IT
NSK-RHP UK Limited, Ruddington Fields Business Pk., Mere Way, pg. 904   IT

Rugby

Bourton Group, Bourton Hall, Bourton on Dunsmore, pg. 162   PV
Durkopp Adler (UK) Ltd., Unit 8, Glebe Farm Industrial Estate, pg. 469   IT
GEC Education Liaison, Dunchurch, pg. 544   IT
GEC Electrical Projects Ltd., Boughton Rd., pg. 53   IT
GEC Management College, Rugby Rd., pg. 544   IT
GECC Group, Boughton Rd., pg. 53   IT
GEConsult Ltd., Mill Rd., pg. 544   IT
Hospal Ltd., Unit G Forum Dr., pg. 668   IT
Lodge Ignition Limited, 5 Triton Park, pg. 1267   IT
Lumonics Limited, Cosford Lane, Swift Valley, pg. 1315   IT
Morgan Matroc Limited Rugby Division, St. Peter's Rd., pg. 893   IT
R.A. Brand & Co. Limited, Swift Valley Trading Estate, pg. 458   IT
Svedala Ltd. Warwickshire, pg. 1325   IT
WAGO Limited, Triton Park, Swift Valley Industrial Estate, pg. 209   IT

Rugeley

Armitage Shanks Limited, Armitage, pg. 197   IT
EDL Industries Ltd., Redbrook Lane, pg. 821   IT

Ruislip

Fanuc U.K. Limited, No. 1 Station Approach, pg. 478   IT
Oneida Silversmiths, U.K., Penbroke House, Penbroke Rd., pg. 1226   PB

Runcorn

AAH Pharmaceuticals Limited, West Lane, pg. 591   IT
AAH plc, Hampton Court, Tudor Road, Manor Park, pg. 591   IT
APPH Aviation Services Ltd., 1 Rokeby Court, pg. 112   IT
APPH Ltd., 8 Pembroke Court, pg. 112   IT
CCL Pharmaceuticals, Astmoor Industrial Estate, pg. 239   IT
CCL Pharmaceuticals, 6 Seymour Court, pg. 239   IT
Duni Ltd., pg. 421   IT
Herbert Ferryman, West Lane, pg. 591   IT
Gyproc Insulation Ltd., Norwich Rd., Whitehouse Industrial Estate, pg. 123   IT
Hillcross Pharmaceuticals, West Lane, pg. 591   IT
Hills Pharmaceuticals, West Lane, pg. 591   IT
Hosokawa Micron Ltd., Rivington Road, Whitehouse Industrial Estate, pg. 636   IT
Hussey Seating Systems (Europe) Ltd., Astmoor Industrial Estate, pg. 550   PV

ICI Chemicals & Polymers Ltd., pg. 663   IT
Life Sciences International (Europe) Limited, Chadwick Rd., pg. 1594   PB
PSC Bar Code Ltd., 13 Howard Ct., pg. 1246   PB
Packaging & Container Manufacturers Ltd., Edison Rd., Astmoor Industrial Estate, pg. 356   IT
Rexam Graphics, pg. 1107   IT
Runcorn Terminal, Percival Ln., pg. 693   PB
Scanglas Ltd., 25/26 Arkwright Road, Astmoor Industrial Estate, pg. 1237   IT
Vestric Ltd., West Lane, pg. 592   IT
Zeneca Resins, PO Box 8, pg. 1524   IT

Rutland

Lands' End Direct Merchants UK Limited, Pillings Rd., pg. 978   PB

Ryde

Trucast Ltd., Marlborough Road, pg. 1467   IT

Saffron Walden

Procter & Gamble (H & B Care) Ltd.-Mfg. Div., Shirehill Industrial Estate, pg. 1332   PB

Saint Albans

Autologic Information International Ltd., Alban Park, Hatfield Rd., pg. 1724   PB
Enraf-Nonius Ltd., Unit 11, Sandridge Park, Porters Wood, pg. 389   IT
HSBC Gibbs Benefit Consultants Limited, Antony Gibbs House, Ridgmont Road, pg. 579   IT
Marconi Instruments Ltd., Longacres and Fleetville, pg. 544   IT
Thomas Mercer Ltd., Eywood Rd., pg. 260   PB
Nationwide Trust Ltd., Nationwide House, pg. 912   IT
Pasta Foods Limited, Unit 1, Verulam Industrial Estate, London Road, pg. 1396   IT
Pharmacia & Upjohn Biotech, 23, Grosvenor Road, pg. 1047   IT
Polaroid (UK) Ltd., Ashley Road, pg. 1314   PB
Ready Mixed Concrete (Transite) Limited, The Willows, Barnet Rd., pg. 1080   IT

Saint Andrews

GB Papers Limited, Guardbridge, pg. 672   PB

Saint Austell

Teddington Controls Limited, Daniels Ln., pg. 1160   IT
The West Company Group Limited, Bucklers Lane, Holmbush, pg. 1756   PB
The West Company (UK) Ltd., Bucklers Lane, Holmbush, pg. 1756   PB

Saint Helens

Almetex, Parr Industrial Estate, pg. 51   IT
Delta Fluid Products Ltd., Delta Rd., Parr, pg. 391   IT
Owens-Corning Building Products UK Ltd., pg. 1237   PB
Pilkington Finance Limited, Prescot Rd., pg. 1056   IT
PILKINGTON PLC, Prescot Road, pg. 1056   IT
Pilkington Properties Limited, Prescot Road, pg. 1056   IT
Pilkington United Kingdom Limited, Prescot Rd., pg. 1056   IT

Saint Helier

AGIP (Africa) Ltd., pg. 428   IT
AGIP (North Africa & Middle East) Ltd., pg. 428   IT
AGIP (Overseas) Ltd., pg. 428   IT
ANZ Grindlays Bank (Jersey) Limited, West House, West's Centre, Peter Street, pg. 98   IT
ANZ Grindlays Trust Corporation (Jersey) Limited, Philip Malzard House, 15 Union Street, pg. 99   IT
Alusuisse-Lonza Capital Ltd, pg. 68   IT
BBME Trustee (Jersey) Limited, 1 Grenville Street, pg. 580   IT
BDL Banco di Lugano, 24 Union Street, pg. 1439   IT
BHF-BANK (Jersey) Ltd., 6 Wests Centre, pg. 119   IT
BL Jersey Ltd, 28/34 Hill Street, pg. 150   IT
BNP - Jersey Trust Corp. Limited, BNP House, Anley Street, pg. 163   IT
Bank of Ireland (Jersey) Limited, Templar House, Don Rd., pg. 153   IT
Bank of Montreal Trust Company (C.I.) Ltd., 18 Grenville St., pg. 155   IT
The Bank of Nova Scotia Channel Islands Limited, Kensington Chambers, 46-50 Kennsington Place, pg. 156   IT
The Bank of Nova Scotia Trust Company Channel Islands Limited, Kensington Chambers, 46-50 Kensington Place, pg. 157   IT
BankAmerica Trust Co. (Jersey) Ltd., Union House, Union St., pg. 183   IT
Bankers Trust New York Corporation, West House Peter Street, pg. 186   PB
Banque Bruxelles Lambert (Jersey) Ltd., Huguenot House, 28 La Motte Street, pg. 148   IT
Banque Bruxelles Lambert Trust Company Ltd., Huguenot House, 28 La Motte Street, pg. 148   IT
Barclays Bank Finance Co. (Jersey) Ltd., P.O. Box 191, 29/31 The Esplanade, pg. 165   IT

Bermuda Trust Executors (Jersey) Limited, Commercial House, Commercial Street, pg. 151   IT
Bermuda Trust (Jersey) Limited, Commercial House, Commercial Street, pg. 151   IT
Bermuda Trust (St. Helier) Limited, Commercial House, Commercial Street, pg. 151   IT
The British Bank of The Middle East, One Grenville Street, pg. 579   IT
Bull S.A. Financiere Ltd., Normandy House, Grenville St., pg. 316   IT
Cantrade Private Bank Ltd., Union Street 24, pg. 1439   IT
Capital House International Investment Management Limited, Capital House, Bath St., pg. 1132   IT
Chase Bank & Trust Co. (C.I.), Ltd., P.O. Box 185, Grenville St., pg. 339   PB
The Chase Manhattan Bank, N.A., P.O. Box 127, Grenville Street, pg. 340   PB
Citibank (Channel Islands) Ltd., pg. 378   PB
Confederation Bank (Jersey) Limited, 28/34 Hill St., pg. 326   IT
Coutts & Co (Jersey) Limited, 23/25 Broad Street, pg. 910   IT
Robert Fleming Management (Jersey) Limited, Queens House, Don Rd., pg. 493   IT
Flemings (Jersey) Limited, Queen's House, Don Road, pg. 493   IT
Forbo Invest Ltd., pg. 497   IT
HSBC International Trustee Limited, 1 Grenville Street, pg. 580   IT
HSBC Nominees (Jersey) Limited, 1 Grenville Street, pg. 580   IT
HSBC Private Banking (C.I.) Limited, 1 Grenville Street, pg. 580   IT
HSBC Trustee (Jersey) Limited, 1 Grenville Street, pg. 580   IT
Henderson Financial Management (Jersey) Limited, La Motte Chambers, pg. 609   IT
Hepworth Ceramic Overseas Ltd., Oak Walk, St. Peter, pg. 615   IT
Hyposwiss Schweizerische, 24 Union Street, pg. 1440   IT
ING Trust (Jersey), Kensington Chambers, 4650 Kensington Place, pg. 650   IT
Intrafin Services Ltd., pg. 181   IT
Kleinwort Benson (Jersey) Limited, P.O. Box 76, Wests Centre, pg. 420   IT
The Kyoei Life Investment Jersey Co., Ltd., pg. 777   IT
Lion International Management Limited, 1 Grenville Street, pg. 580   IT
Lloyds Bank (Jersey) Ltd., 9 Broad St., pg. 813   IT
Lloyds Bank Trust Company (Channel Islands) Limited, Waterloo House, Don St., pg. 813   IT
Midland Bank International Finance Corporation Limited, 28-34 Hill Street, pg. 580   IT
Midland Bank Trustee (Jersey) Limited, 1 Grenville Street, pg. 580   IT
MIL (Jersey) Limited, Commercial House, Commercial Street, pg. 151   IT
Montagu Management Services (Jersey) Limited, 1 Grenville Street, pg. 580   IT
Montagu Nominees (Jersey) Limited, 1 Grenville Street, pg. 580   IT
Morgan Grenfell (Jersey, C.I.) Limited, 12 Dumaresq St., pg. 406   IT
National Westminster Bank Finance (CI) Limited, 27 Broad St., pg. 911   IT
NatWest International Trust Corporation (Jersey) Limited, 23/25 Broad St., pg. 911   IT
Ocelot International Ltd., 2nd Floor, Sir Walter Raliegh House, pg. 996   IT
Repsol Oil International, No. 1 Le Couteur Ct., Mulcaster St., pg. 1105   IT
The Royal Bank of Scotland (Jersey) Ltd., 71 Bath St., pg. 1133   IT
The Royal Bank of Scotland Trust Company (Jersey) Limited, Capitol House, Bath St., pg. 1133   IT
SNAM International Ltd., La Motte Chambers, pg. 429   IT
Shell Fuel Supplies, Jersey Airport, pg. 1141   IT
Standard Bank (Jersey) Limited, One Waverley Place, pg. 1294   IT
Standard Chartered Bank (C.I.) Limited, Standard Chartered House, pg. 1294   IT
Swiss Bank Corporation, 40 Esplanade, pg. 1330   IT
Taiyo Investment (Jersey), Ltd., Rutland House, Pitt St., pg. 1349   IT
Tokai Airfinance Europe Limited, P.O. Box 301, Queen's House, pg. 1391   IT
UBS Jersey, 24 Union Street, St. Helier, pg. 1440   IT
Verein West Overseas Finance (Jersey) Ltd., pg. 181   IT
Warburg Asset Management Jersey Limited, Forum House, Grenville St., pg. 1331   IT
Westpac Banking Corporation (Jersey) Ltd., Charles House, Charles St., pg. 1497   IT
Yasuda Life Global Investment (Jersey) Limited, Kleinwort Benson House, West Centre, pg. 1520   IT

Saint Ives

Knurr (UK) Ltd., Burrel Road, pg. 739   IT

Saint Leonards

Computing Devices Co. Ltd., Castleham Road, pg. 331   PB

Saint Mary Cray

Coates Brothers PLC, Cray Avenue, pg. 1409   IT

PB - *U.S. Public Companies Volume*
PV - *U.S. Private Companies Volume*
IT - *International Public & Private Companies Volume*

Saint Neots

Dufaylite Developments Limited, Cromwell Road, pg. 1160   IT
EPL Plant & Access, Barford Rd., pg. 796   IT
Perstorp Components, Cromwell Rd., pg. 1040   IT
G.L. Rexroth Ltd., pg. 838   IT
Stabilus Ltd., pg. 835   IT

Saint Peter Port

ANZ Bank (Guernsey) Limited, pg. 98   IT
Allied Colloids Insurance Ltd., pg. 62   IT
Assicurazioni Generali (Insurance Managers) Ltd., Sarnia House, Le Truchot, pg. 90   IT
BGL Trustees Ltd., 26 Glategny Esplanade, pg. 162   IT
Bain Hogg Insurance Management Guernsey Ltd., Level 6, pg. 671   IT
Banco Santander (Guernsey) Ltd., St. Andrew's House, pg. 144   IT
Bank of Bermuda (Guernsey) Limited, Bermuda House, St. Julian's Ave., pg. 151   IT
Banque Belge (Guernsey) Ltd., Banque Belge House, pg. 547   IT
Banque Belge Trust Company Ltd., Lancaster Court, Forest Lane, pg. 547   IT
Banque Paribus Suisse (Guernsey) Ltd., La Plaiderie House, pg. 320   IT
Barclays Bank Finance Co. (Guernsey) Ltd., P.O. Box No. 269, Cambria House, New Street, pg. 165   IT
Baring Trustee (Guernsey) Ltd., P.O. Box 71, Arnold House, St. Julian's Avenue, pg. 648   IT
Bermuda Trust (Guernsey) Limited, Bermuda House, St. Julians Ave., pg. 151   IT
The CA Hungary Investment Partners Ltd., pg. 347   IT
CIBC Bank and Trust Company (Channel Islands) Limited, Ste. 4, Albert House, South Esplanade, pg. 257   IT
Cairngorm Insurance Ltd., pg. 235   IT
Canadian Imperial Bank of Commerce Trust Co. (Channel Islands) Ltd., Albert House, Suite 4, pg. 257   IT
Caparo Insurance Ltd., pg. 265   IT
Chemical Bank (Guernsey) Limited, P.O. Box 198, St. Julian's Court, pg. 341   PB
Cigna International Fund Managers (CI) Ltd., St. Julian's House, pg. 364   PB
Coutts & Co (Guernsey) Limited, Coutts House, Le Truchot, pg. 910   IT
Derwent Insurance Limited, Dixcart House, Sir William Place, pg. 1226   IT
Duferco Intl. Investment Holding Ltd., pg. 654   IT
Dynatech Data Communications Ltd., Rue du Commerce, Bouet, pg. 1591   PB
Dynex Technologies, Inc., Rue du Commerce, Bouet, pg. 1591   PB
Eastman Christensen (China) Limited, P.O. Box 187, Le Truchot, pg. 167   PB
The First National Bank of Boston (Guernsey) Limited, Valley House, Hirzel St., Ste. 9, pg. 185   PB
Gefina International Ltd., Sarnia House, Le Truchot, pg. 91   IT
Generali Worldwide Insurance Company Company, Sarnia House, Le Truchot, pg. 91   IT
Goethe Management Ltd., 26, Glategny-Esplanade, pg. 162   IT
Guernsey International Fund Managers Limited, P.O. Box 255, Barfield House, St. Julian's Avenue, pg. 648   IT
Guernsey International Investment Management Limited, Bermuda House, St. Julian's Avenue, pg. 151   IT
Hanson Bank Ltd., Hirzel House, Smith Street, pg. 592   IT
Henderson Administration (Guernsey) Limited, Barfield House, pg. 609   IT
Ilva Finance, 14 New St., pg. 654   IT
Imperial Fund Managers, Albert House, Ste. 4, So. Esplanade St., pg. 257   IT
Italimpianti Intl.-UK, 14 New Street, pg. 655   IT
J&H Marsh & McLennan Management Services (Guernsey) Ltd., Leriche House, P.O. Box 34, pg. 1049   PB
Kleinwort Benson (Guernsey) Limited, P.O. Box 44, The Grange, pg. 420   IT
LGT Asset Management Ltd., Suite 5 North, P.O. Box 366, pg. 810   IT
Management International (Guernsey) Limited, Bermuda House, St. Julians Ave., pg. 151   IT
Management International (Jersey) Ltd., Bermuda House, St. Julian's Avenue, pg. 151   IT
Midland Bank Trustee (Guernsey) Limited, 22 Smith Street, pg. 580   IT
Morgan Grenfell (Guernsey, C.I.) Limited, Morgan Grenfell House, Lefebvre St., pg. 406   IT
NRG International Ltd. (Bermuda), P.O. Box 268, pg. 1116   IT
NatWest International Trust Corporation (Guensey) Limited, Natl. Westminster House, Le Truchot, pg. 911   IT
NatWest Investment Management Channel, Commerce House, Les Banques, pg. 910   IT
Neste Insurance Ltd., 2 Grange Pl., pg. 915   IT
Northside Insurance Company Ltd., pg. 1015   IT
Rabobank Guernsey Ltd., St. Andrew House, 3rd Fl., Le Bordage, pg. 1082   IT
Renishaw Investments Limited, Orbis House, 20 New St., pg. 1103   IT
Royal Bank of Canada (Channel Islands) Limited, P.O. Box 48, pg. 1131   IT
The Royal Bank of Scotland (Guernsey) Limited, St. Andrews House, Le Bordage, pg. 1133   IT
The Royal Bank of Scotland Trust Company (Guernsey) Limited, St. Andrew's House, pg. 1133   IT
Royal Insurance Service Co. (Guernsey) Ltd., Dixcart House, P.O. Box 160, pg. 1130   IT

Willis Corroon Management Limited-Guernsey, P.O. Box 384, 4th Floor, The Albany, South Esplanade, pg. 1503   IT
Willis Corroon Secretarial Services Limited-Guernsey, P.O. Box 384, 4th Floor, The Albany, South Esplanade, pg. 1509   IT
Yorkshire Guernsey, Valley House, Hospital Lane, pg. 1522   IT

Saint Sampson

Gestetner Asia Pacific Limited, Garenne Park, pg. 1114   IT

Saint Saviour

The Jersey Tobacco Distributors Ltd., Rue de Pres Trading Estate, pg. 111   IT

Sale

Barber & Colman Ltd., Marsland Rd., pg. 1243   IT
Senior Colman Limited, 236 Marsland Rd., pg. 1220   IT
Snap-on Tools Limited, Palmer House, 150-154 Cross St., pg. 1481   PB

Salford

Addey Milner Limited, Two Ways House, Boston Court, pg. 1462   IT
Raab Karcher (U.K.) PLC, pg. 1458   IT
Raschig (U.K.) Ltd., 124 Dovepeys Rd., pg. 827   PV
Venesta International Packaging Limited, Langley Rd., Pendleton, pg. 267   IT
Venesta Packaging Group Ltd., Langley Rd., Pendleton, pg. 267   IT

Salisbury

Dunlop Hiflex Ltd., Churchfields Indus. Estate, P.O. Box 2, Telford Rd., pg. 125   IT

Saltcoats

A.T. Mays (U.K.), Nineyard Street, pg. 212   PV

Sandbach

Hepworth Minerals and Chemicals Limited, Brookside Hall, Congleton Rd., pg. 615   IT
PACCAR Financial Limited, Moss Lane, pg. 1247   PB

Sandwich

Howmedica International Limited, Ramsgate Rd., pg. 1283   PB
Pfizer Group Limited, Ramsgate Rd, pg. 1283   PB
Pfizer Limited, Ramsgate Rd., pg. 1283   PB

Sandy

BRITISH BUILDING & ENGINEERING APPLIANCES PLC, 63-65 London Rd., pg. 219   IT
Morgan Matroc Limited Park Royal Division, Cambridge Rd., pg. 893   IT

Sanquhar

Hydro Aluminium Century Ltd., Blackaddie Road, pg. 962   IT

Santry

Bewleys Franchising Limited, 4 St. Johns Court, pg. 254   IT

Saxilby

Kemira Agro U.K. Ltd., pg. 728   IT
Kemira Ltd., pg. 728   IT

Scarborough

Erskine Systems Limited, Lee De Forest House, Salter Road, pg. 1344   IT
Hawkins Structures, Dunslow Rd., pg. 256   IT
McCain Foods (GB) Limited, Havers Hill, pg. 850   IT

Scunthorpe

CCL Industries Limited, Foxhills Industrial Park, Atkinson Way, pg. 239   IT
Caparo Merchant Bar plc, pg. 265   IT
Citizen Systems & Peripherals Europe, Tanashi Dori, pg. 294   IT
Corro Clark Coatings Ltd., Flixborough Ind. Estate, pg. 715   IT
Firth-Rixson Castings Ltd., Dawes La., pg. 487   IT

Selby

Sturge Biochemicals, Denison Rd., pg. 1113   IT

Selford

PDA International/United Kingdom, Magnetic House, 51 Waterfront Quay, pg. 1031   PB

Selkirk

Laidlaw & Fairgrieve Ltd, Riverside Mills, pg. 385   IT

Seven Oaks

Wilson Supply International (U.K.) Ltd., Oak House, London Rd., pg. 1181   PV

Sevenoaks

Ascom Tele-Nova Ltd., Clockhouse Court, pg. 87   IT
BAS Components Limited, 2 Cramptons Road, pg. 1344   IT
Balfour Timber Ltd., 15 Pembroke Road, pg. 260   IT
EAC Timber (UK) Ltd., pg. 431   IT
The East Asiatic Company UK (Holdings) Limited, pg. 431   IT
East Asiatic Insurance Brokers (UK) Limited, pg. 431   IT
Erskine House Group Plc, Erskine House, Oak Hill Road, pg. 864   PB
Falstria Services Company Limited, pg. 431   IT
MARLEY PLC, Seven Oakhill Road, pg. 843   IT
Principal Investment Management Ltd., 16 South Park, pg. 1020   IT
Ready Mixed Concrete (South East) Limited, 116 London Rd., pg. 1080   IT
Swiss Life (UK), 101 London Road, pg. 1332   IT
Swiss Life (UK) Group, 101 London Road, pg. 1332   IT
Swiss Life Unit Trust Management, 101 London Road, pg. 1332   IT

Shaftesbury

Dorset Chilled Food Products Ltd., Longmead Industrial Estate, pg. 968   IT

Shalford

Mercia Diagnostics Limited, Mercia House, Broadford Pk., pg. 323   PB

Sheerness

MoDo Distribution Ltd., 104 Anchor Lane, pg. 887   IT

Sheffield

ANI Aurora Plc, Meadow Hall Rd., pg. 101   IT
Acme United Ltd.-Surmanco Division, 15-33 Cavendish St., pg. 17   PB
Avesta Sheffield Ltd., Stevenson Rd., pg. 221   IT
Avesta Sheffield Ltd., Cyclops Works, Carlisle St., pg. 221   IT
N.G. Bailey & Co. Ltd.-Sheffield Branch, Rutland Rd., pg. 132   IT
Batchelors Foods, Ltd., Wadsley Bridge, pg. 1434   IT
Bekaert Building Products Ltd., P.O. Box 119, pg. 184   IT
Billing Stainless, 3 Sanderson Street, pg. 222   IT
Binghams Cooked Meats Ltd., 148-154 Western Rd., pg. 968   IT
BROOKE INDUSTRIAL HOLDINGS PLC, Shepcote Lane, pg. 228   IT
Buck & Hickman Limited, Bank House, 100 Queen St., pg. 1032   IT
CARCLO ENGINEERING GROUP PLC, Carclo House, P.O. 224, Fife Street, pg. 268   IT
Crusteel Ltd., Rutland Way, pg. 293   PV
Davy International, Prince of Wales Rd., pg. 773   IT
The Davy Roll Co. Ltd., P.O. Box 123 Stevenson Rd., pg. 773   IT
Derbyshire-Sheffiels Branch, 15 Barkers Pool, pg. 394   IT
Dormer Tools Ltd., pg. 1186   IT
Dormer Tools (Sheffield) Ltd., pg. 1186   IT
Electrical Carbon Limited, Claywheels Ln., pg. 891   IT
Elkem Ltd., 301 Glossop Road, pg. 447   IT
FIRTH-RIXSON PLC, Smithfield House, pg. 487   IT
Hartons Group Plc., Shoreham House, Shoreham Street, pg. 1210   IT
Earle M. Jorgensen Company/United Kingdom, Units 7-9 Provincial Park, Nether Lane, pg. 600   PV
Lambert Smith Hampton, 6a Campo Ln., pg. 797   IT
Laporte Minerals, Cavendish Mill, pg. 802   IT
Lee Steel Strip Limited, pg. 268   IT
Lee Steel Wire Limited, pg. 268   IT
R.J. Mellor & Co. Ltd., 20 Julian Road, pg. 519   IT
Metinox Steel Ltd., pg. 1186   IT
Morgan Europe, Old Lane, Halfway, 519-5GZ, pg. 761   PV
Oughtibridge Mill, Spring Grove Mills, Oughtibridge, pg. 672   PB
Pennine Foods, Drakehouse Crescent, pg. 968   IT
Presto Engineers Cutting Tools Ltd., Albertworks, Heningstone Road, pg. 951   PB
R.F.A. Group Ltd., Bullhorse Works, Manchester Rd., pg. 231   IT
RFA Group Limited, Bullhouse Works, Manchester Rd., pg. 219   IT
Ross & Catherall Limited, Forge Lane, pg. 1467   IT
Sanderson CBT Limited, Sheffield Science Park, pg. 1184   IT
Sanderson Computer Services, Parkway House, Parkway Ave., pg. 1184   IT

PB - *U.S. Public Companies Volume*
PV - *U.S. Private Companies Volume*
IT - *International Public & Private Companies Volume*

1828

Geographic Index-Non U.S.

Sanderson Computers Limited, Parkway House, Parkway Ave., pg. 1184   IT
Sanderson Cotswold Limited, Parkway House, Parkway Ave., pg. 1184   IT
Sanderson Insight Limited, Parkway House, Parkway Ave., pg. 1184   IT
SANDERSON TECHNOLOGY LTD., Parkway House, Parkway Ave., pg. 1184   IT
Shefcut Tool & Engineering Ltd., Long Acre Close, Holbrook Industrial Estate, pg. 250   PV
Sheffield Coated Stone, Stephenson Rd., pg. 1079   IT
Thermal Processing Group Ltd. (Sheffield), 60 Cyclops Street, pg. 1338   IT
Tinsley Wire (Sheffield) Ltd., P.O. Box 119, Shepcote Lane, pg. 185   IT
Trebor Bassett Ltd., Livesey St., pg. 248   IT
S.H. Ward Inc., Sheaf Brewery, pg. 1454   IT
Ward Surfacing Limited, Albion Works, Savile St., pg. 1081   IT
Thos. S. Ward Contracting Limited, Albion Works, Savile St., pg. 1081   IT
Thos. W. Ward Roadstone Limited, Albion Works, Savile St., pg. 1079   IT
Willis Corroon North Limited, Willis House, Peel Street, pg. 1503   IT

Shepton Mallet

Svedala Ltd. Somerset, pg. 1325   IT

Sherborne

Baumann Springs & Pressings (UK) Ltd., E. Mill Ln., pg. 171   IT

Shirley

Lucas Electrical and Electronic Systems, Stratford Road, pg. 819   IT

Shrewsbury

Vickers Aerospace Components-Fabrications Facility, Whitchurch Road, pg. 1467   IT

Sidcup

Gambro Ltd., Lundia House, 124 Station Rd., pg. 668   IT

Sittingbourne

Bose U.K., Ltd., Trinity Trading Estate, pg. 161   PV
Shell Research Ltd., Sittingbourne Research Centre, pg. 1139   IT
Thermo Electric Intl. Ltd., Unit 17E, Eurolink Industrial Estate, pg. 1080   PV
U.K. Paper Plc, UK Paper House, Kemsley, pg. 495   IT
Whistable Times, 19/21 High St., pg. 452   IT

Skelmersdale

AlliedSignal Ltd. Turbochargers, Potter Place, West Pimbo, pg. 53   PB
Asco (UK), 2 Pit Hey Place, pg. 575   PB
Emerson Electric U.K. Ltd., Gerrard Pl., East Gillibrands, pg. 576   PB
Forbo Scanachrome Ltd., Three & Five Gorsey Pl., pg. 498   IT
New England Laminates (U.K.) Ltd., Pinfold Place West Pimbo, pg. 1258   PB
Procter & Gamble (H & B Care) Ltd.-Mfg. Div., Pimbo Rd., W. Pimbo, pg. 1332   PB
Raydex/CDT, Gadden Place, pg. 287   PB
Thermal Processing Group Ltd. (Skelmersdale), 18 Westgate, pg. 1338   IT
Turtle Wax Manufacturing Ltd., P.O. Box 102, Gillibrands Road, pg. 1110   PV

Skelton

Fisher Chilled Foods, Skelton Park, pg. 491   IT

Skipton

CAP Nationwide Motor Research, CAP House, Carleton Rd., pg. 451   IT

Sleaford

Staples Disposables Limited, East Road Industrial Estate, Woodbridge Rd., pg. 341   IT

Slough

Acacia Technologies UK/Europe, 183-187 Bath Road, pg. 420   PB
Accord Energy Ltd., Charter Court, 50 Windsor Road, pg. 279   IT
Air Transport Avionics Limited, 7/9 Willow Road, Poyle Trading Estate, pg. 1344   IT
Ascom Timeplex Ltd., Timeplex House, Station Road, pg. 87   IT
BPB INDUSTRIES PLC, Langley Park House, pg. 122   IT
Balacke-Durr Ltd., Monarch House, 1a Herschel Street, pg. 400   IT
Ballast Wiltshier plc - Airport Services Div., 5 Kingfisher Court, pg. 135   IT

Barlow International Investments Plc, Extram House, 1A Albert St., pg. 167   IT
Barlow Tractor International, 1A Albert St., pg. 167   IT
Bestobeli Aviation, 127/135 Farnham Road, pg. 853   IT
Black & Decker International, Westpoint, The Grove, pg. 234   PB
Bredero-Shaw, 21 Progress Business Centre, Whittle Parkway, pg. 529   PB
R.J. Brown & Associates (UK) Limited, Raglan House, 8-24 Stoke Rd., pg. 772   IT
Call Connections Limited, 260 Bath Road, pg. 222   IT
Calor Gas Ltd., Appleton Park, Riding Court Road, pg. 1155   IT
Camco Europe, Slough Trading Estate, 432 Perth Ave., pg. 276   PB
Caterpillar Financial Services (U.K.) Limited, Regal Court, 42-44 High St., pg. 315   PB
Cellnet Solutions Limited, 260 Bath Road, pg. 222   IT
CENTRICA PLC, Charter Court, 50 Windsor Road, pg. 279   IT
Concurrent Computer Corporation, 227 BAth Road, pg. 430   PB
Coopers Payen Ltd., pg. 1334   IT
Cow Proofings Limited, Eastbourne Rd., pg. 124   IT
John Crane UK Ltd., Crossbow House, 40 Liverpool Road, pg. 1338   IT
Dexter Electronic Materials, 80 Heron Rd., pg. 505   PB
Dexter, U.K. Ltd., Unit 9, Poyle 14, Newlands Drive, pg. 505   PB
Fidelio Software U.K. Ltd., 6-8 The Grove, pg. 1106   PB
Geosource International (Nederland) B.V., 3-5 The Grove, pg. 777   PB
Geosource U.K. Limited, 3-5 The Grove, pg. 777   PB
Goldstar United Kingdom, Goldstar House, 264 Bath Road, pg. 779   IT
Grace Construction Products, Ajax Ave., pg. 755   PB
Hanovia Limited, 145 Farnham Rd., pg. 589   IT
Herbalife (UK) Limited, Perth Ave., pg. 809   PB
ISS Mediclean Ltd., Norfolk House, Christmas Lane, pg. 657   IT
Icore International Limited, Leigh Rd., pg. 1267   IT
Industrial Components-Gravenhage B.V., 3-5 The Grove, pg. 777   PB
Interface Systems International, 959 Weston Rd., pg. 890   PB
Inverness UK LTD., 950-951 Yeovi Road, pg. 574   PV
John Crane EAA, Crossbow House, 40 Liverpool Road, pg. 1338   IT
Kidde-Graviner Ltd., Mathisen Way, Poyle Rd., pg. 1500   IT
Kintetsu Euro Transport Ltd., Unit 2, Poyle 14, Newlands Dr., pg. 735   IT
Kintetsu World Express (U.K.) Ltd., Unit 2, Poyle 14, Newlands Dr., pg. 735   IT
Kopex International Limited, 675 Ajax Avenue, pg. 1267   IT
Kvaerner Engineering (UK) Ltd., Raglan House, 8-24 Stoke Rd., pg. 772   IT
Kvaerner Professional Services Limited, Raglan House, 8-24 Stoke Road, pg. 768   IT
Lambert Smith Hampton, 44/46 Windsor Rd., pg. 797   IT
Lifetime Assurance Co. Limited, 34 High Street, pg. 153   IT
Mannesmann Kienzle Autocom Ltd., pg. 839   IT
Mars Confectionery, Dundee Rd., pg. 707   PV
Meggit Mobrey Ltd., 190/196 Bath Road, pg. 853   IT
Motorola Ltd., 110 Bath Rd., pg. 1140   PB
OKI Semiconductor (U.K.), Unit 5 Shaftesbury Court, 18 Chalvey Park, pg. 1000   IT
Oki Systems (UK) Ltd., 550 Dundee Rd., pg. 999   IT
Panasonic Industrial U.K. Ltd., 280-290 Bath Road, pg. 847   IT
Pechiney UK Ltd., Pechiney House-The Grove, pg. 1031   IT
PictureTel International Corporation-Europe/Middle East/Africa, 258 Bath Road, pg. 1295   IT
Plunt Acrow Ltd., Waterman House, Colnbrook By-Pass, pg. 88   IT
Racal Instruments Ltd., 480 Bath Rd., pg. 1082   IT
Rockwell International Limited, St. Martin's Place, 51 Bath Road, pg. 1401   PB
Sara Lee Household & Personal Care-U.K., 225 Bath Road, pg. 1435   PB
Satchwell Control Systems Ltd., Farnham Rd., pg. 1241   IT
Sciaky Electric Welding Machines Ltd., 212 Bedford Ave., pg. 1211   IT
Scott's Hotels Limited, Ditton Rd., pg. 1213   IT
Spectral Technology Group Ltd., 667 Ajax Ave., pg. 1189   PB
Summa Four Limited, 246 Bedford Ave., pg. 1527   PB
Tefal UK Ltd., Station Rd. 11-49, pg. 569   IT
Telecom Securicor Cellular Radio Limited, 260 Bath Road, pg. 222   IT
3Com, Ltd., 224 Berwick Ave., pg. 1604   PB
Union-Transport, Skyway 14 Calder Way, SL3 0BQ, pg. 1120   PV
Uniroyal Chemical Ltd., Kennet House, Four Langley Quay, pg. 460   PB
Xyvision Limited, 246 Bedford Ave., pg. 1787   PB

Smethwick

European Industrial Services, Heath St., pg. 231   IT
GEC Avery Ltd., Warley, pg. 543   IT
McLean Europe, 4 Bevan Way, pg. 1791   PB
SPS Technologies Limited, Cranford St., pg. 1420   PB

Snaith

Senior Foster Wheeler Construction Division, Pontefract Rd., pg. 1221   IT

Snodland

Townsend Hook Ltd., Snodland Paper Mill, pg. 1271   IT

Solihull

BARDON GROUP PLC, 6th Fl., Radcliffe House, Blenheim Ct., Lode Ln., pg. 166   IT
Birmid Holdings Ltd., pg. 1387   IT
Hewlett-Packard Limited, Avon House, 435 Stratford Rd., pg. 821   PB
Lamb Sceptre Ltd., 23 Monkspath Business Park, pg. 1004   PB
Lex Autocentres, Waterside, Richmond Road, pg. 807   IT
Lucas Aerospace, Brueton House, New Rd., pg. 819   IT
Lucas Aftermarket Operations, Stratford Rd., pg. 819   IT
LucasVarity plc, Stratford Rd., pg. 819   IT
Novo Nordisk Bioindustries UK Ltd., 4 the Courtyard, 707 Warwick, pg. 989   IT
Paperflow Services Limted, Ashbourne Way, pg. 1226   IT
Rover Finance Holding Limited, Avon House, 435 Stratford Road, pg. 911   IT
SSI Medical Systems, Inc., The Courtyard, Warwick Rd., pg. 828   PB
Sasol Chemicals Europe Limited, 1 Hockley Court, 2401 Stratford Rd., pg. 1196   IT

Somerset

Arthur Hart Webbing, Viney Bridge Mills, Crewkerne, pg. 215   IT
Kruger Tissue (Consumer) Limited, Isleport Business Park, pg. 762   IT

South Queensferry

Hewlett-Packard Ltd., pg. 821   PB
Taunton Cider Scotland, Holst House, Edinburgh Rd., pg. 849   IT

Southall

AlliedSignal Aerospace Service Corporation, Unit 3A, Harlequin Centre, Southall Lane, pg. 52   PB
Anixter Heston, Unit 7, Christopher Road, pg. 116   PB
Harper Freight International, 2 Rubastic Road, pg. 373   PB
Krupp Machinery Ltd., Unit 10Great W. Indstrl Park, Windmill Lane, pg. 510   IT
MacGregor Golf UK, Ltd., The Harequin Center, Southall Lane, pg. 73   IT
Quaker Oats Limited, 13 Bridge Rd., pg. 1348   PB
State Bank of India, Kings House, The Green, pg. 1297   IT
Taylor Insurance Brokers Limited, Taylor House, 345 Ruislip Road, pg. 1358   IT
Taylor Woodrow Civil Engineering Ltd., Taywood House, 345 Ruislip Road, pg. 1358   IT
Taylor Woodrow Construction Holdings Limited, Taywood House, 345 Ruislip Road, pg. 1358   IT
Taylor Woodrow Construction Limited, Taywood House, 345 Ruislip Road, pg. 1358   IT
Taylor Woodrow Construction (Southern) Ltd., Taywood House, 345 Ruislip Road, pg. 1358   IT
Taylor Woodrow International Ltd., 345 Ruislip Road, pg. 1358   IT
Taylor Woodrow Management & Engineering Limited, Taywood House, 345 Ruslip Road, pg. 1358   IT
Taylor Woodrow Management Ltd., Taywood House, 345 Ruislip Road, pg. 1359   IT
Taylor Woodrow Services Ltd., Taywood House, 345 Ruislip Road, pg. 1359   IT
Taymech Limited, Taywood House, 345 Ruislip Road, pg. 1359   IT
Taywood Engineering Ltd., Taywood House, 345 Ruislip Road, pg. 1359   IT
Teledyne United Kingdom, The Harlequin Centre, Southall Lane, pg. 44   PB

Southam

Dywidag-Systems (U.K.) Ltd., Westfield Rd., pg. 425   IT

Southampton

AC Rochester Corporation, West Bay Rd., New Dock, pg. 721   PB
AC Rochester Overseas Corporation, West Bay Road New Dock, pg. 722   PB
ARC Marine Limited, Regional Office, Burnely Wharf, pg. 592   IT
Aberdare Cables Limited, Western Esplanade, pg. 1059   IT
N.G. Bailey & Co. Ltd.-Southampton Branch, Commodore House, 16/18 Millbrook Road East, pg. 132   IT
Borden (U.K.) Ltd., Chemical Works, Rownhams Road, pg. 159   PV
CIBA Vision Ophthalmics, Park West, Flanders Rd., Hedge End, pg. 981   IT
CIBA Vision (UK) Ltd., Park West, Royal London Park, Flanders Road, Hedge End, pg. 981   IT
Dawmec Limited, Unit 6, Waterloo Industrial Es, tate, pg. 88   IT
Dimplex UK, pg. 554   IT

Geographic Index-Non U.S.

Duphar Laboratories Ltd., Gaters Hill GB West end, pg. 1278 **IT**
Glover Webb Ltd., Hamble Lane, pg. 535 **IT**
Gould Electronics Ltd., Foil Div., Bursledon Rd., Thornhill, pg. 1592 **PB**
Midland Bank Trust Company Limited, 13/F, Norwich House, Nelson Gate, Commercial Road, pg. 580 **IT**
Midland Life Limited, Norwich House, Nelson Gate, Commercial Road, pg. 580 **IT**
Midland Unit Trust Management Limited, Norwich House, Nelson Gate, Commercial Road, pg. 580 **IT**
Minipack Systems Limited, pg. 1067 **PB**
Morgan Matroc Limited Transducer Products Division, Bursleson Rd., pg. 893 **IT**
NYK Line-Southampton, Berth 204/206, pg. 942 **IT**
P&O Lines Ltd., Dukes Keep, Marsh Lane, pg. 1034 **IT**
Pirelli Enfield Supertension Cables Ltd., Western Esplanade, pg. 1059 **IT**
Pirelli PLC, Western Esplanade, pg. 1059 **IT**
Professional Life Assurance Co. Ltd., P.O. Box 26, Skandia House, pg. 1257 **IT**
Ready Mixed Concrete (South-Coast) Limited, 110/120 Bitterne Rd., pg. 1080 **IT**
SadCo Ltd., pg. 589 **PV**
Skandia Life Assurance Co. Ltd., P.O. Box 37, Skandia House, pg. 1258 **IT**
Skandia Life PEP Managers Ltd., Skandia House, Portland Terrace, pg. 1258 **IT**
Skandia Trust, Skandia House, Portland Terrace, pg. 1258 **IT**
Solvay Veterinary Ltd., Solvay House, Flanders Road, Hedge End, pg. 1280 **IT**
South Coast Shipping Company Limited, Canute Chambers, Canute Rd., pg. 1079 **IT**
Statim Finance Limited, Galen House, pg. 591 **IT**
Stena Line Limited, Test Road, Eastern Docks, pg. 1300 **IT**
Totton Pumps Ltd., pg. 1512 **IT**

Southend-on-Sea

Bradstock Group Services, Princess Caroline House, 1 High St., pg. 210 **IT**
Keymed (Medical & Industrial Equipment) Ltd., KeyMed House, Stock Rd., pg. 1005 **IT**
Morganite Electronic Instruments Limited, Priory Crescent, pg. 891 **IT**

Southport

Baumann, Hinde & Co., Ltd., pg. 817 **IT**

Southwater

Arun Technology Ltd., Unit 16, Southwater Industrial Estate, pg. 1130 **IT**
Eberline Instrument Company Ltd., Unit ZZ, Southwater Ind. Est., Station Road, pg. 1596 **IT**
Thermo Electron Ltd., Unit ZZ, Southwater Ind. Est., Station Rd., pg. 1596 **PB**

Spalding

GEEST PLC, West Marsh Road, pg. 542 **IT**
Hillsdown Ltd., Bridge Rd., Long Sutton, pg. 619 **IT**
Metalair-Filliat Limited, pg. 1065 **IT**
Metalair Limited, Sutton Bridge, pg. 1065 **IT**
Sutton Bridge Wharfage Co. Ltd., West Bank, pg. 1251 **IT**

Speke

Dista Products Ltd., Fleming Rd., pg. 993 **PB**

Spennymoor

Tomado Ltd., Green Lane Industrial Estate, pg. 184 **IT**

Speyside

Glenrothes Distillery, pg. 619 **IT**
Tamdhu Distillery, pg. 619 **IT**

St. Albans

Cirrus Logic (UK) Ltd., One Stroud Wood Bus. Ctr., pg. 375 **PB**

Stafford

Evode Group Ltd., Common Rd., pg. 802 **IT**
Evode Ltd., Common Rd., pg. 802 **IT**
GEC Computer Services Ltd., The Hollies, Newport Rd., pg. 544 **IT**
Stanhope Pension Trust Ltd., P.O. Box 20, Lichfield Rd., pg. 545 **IT**
Taylor Woodrow Construction (Midlands) Ltd., St. Albans Road, Stafford, pg. 1358 **IT**

Staines

Ardath Tobacco Co. Ltd., Millbank, pg. 111 **IT**
British-American Tobacco Co. Ltd., Millbank, pg. 111 **IT**
British Gas Services Ltd., Lakeside House, 30 The Causeway, pg. 279 **IT**
British Gas Trading Ltd., 17 London Road, pg. 279 **IT**
Del Monte Foods International Limited, Del Monte House, London Rd., pg. 388 **IT**
Inchcape Motors International, 40 Church St., pg. 671 **IT**

Industrial Acoustics Company, Ltd., Central Trading Estate, pg. 875 **PB**
Lotus Development Ltd., Lotus Park, The Causeway, pg. 896 **PB**
Measureaim, Ash House, Fairfield Ave., pg. 1283 **PB**
Pfizer Hospital Products Group Pension Trustees Ltd., Ash House, Fairfield Ave., pg. 1283 **PB**
Pfizer Hospital Products, Ltd., Ash House, Fairfield Ave., pg. 1283 **PB**
Scottish Courage Limited, Ashby House, 1 Bridge St., pg. 1212 **IT**
Sony (U.K.) Ltd., Sony House, South St., pg. 1284 **IT**

Stallingborough

IVO CM Services Ltd., Hobson Way, pg. 661 **IT**
Stora Transport (UK) Ltd., Redwood Park Estate, Kiln Lane, pg. 1303 **IT**

Stamford

Castle Cement Ltd. (Stamford), Ketton, pg. 1201 **IT**
Costain Dow Mac, Barholm La., pg. 336 **IT**
Newage International Ltd., Barnack Road, pg. 469 **PB**
S.O.S. NEWALL LIMITED, Foundry Road, pg. 1166 **IT**

Stanford-le-Hope

Durox Building Products Limited, Linford, pg. 1080 **IT**

Stanley

Nippon Silica Glass Europe Ltd., 2 Greencroft Industrial Park, Annfield Plain, pg. 1408 **IT**
Standard Chartered Bank, pg. 1294 **IT**

Stanmore

AMP of Great Britain Limited, Merrion Ave., Terminal House, pg. 9 **PB**
GEC-Marconi Ltd., The Grove, Warren Lane, pg. 544 **IT**
Klaxon Signals Limited, 502 Honeypot Lane, pg. 590 **IT**
Marconi Defence Systems Ltd., The Grove, Warren Lane, pg. 544 **IT**
Marconi Electronic Systems Ltd., The Grove, Warren Lane, pg. 544 **IT**
Matra Marconi Space UK Holdings, pg. 796 **IT**

Stannington

Arnold Wragg (Bolts & Nuts) Ltd., 691 Stannington Rd., pg. 586 **IT**

Stansted

AIR UK LTD., Stansted House, Stansted Airport, pg. 38 **IT**
Air UK Engineering Ltd., Airways House, Stansted Airport, pg. 39 **IT**
Air UK (Leisure) Ltd., Airways House, Stansted Airport, pg. 39 **IT**
FLS Aerospace Engineering Ltd., Long Border Rd., pg. 475 **IT**
FLS Aerospace Ltd., Long Border Road, pg. 476 **IT**
Heavylift Cargo Airlines Limited, Building 16A, London-Stansted Airport, pg. 773 **IT**
Shell UK Oil (Standsted), Stansted Airport, pg. 1139 **IT**

Stevenage

British Aerospace Defence Limited (Dynamics), Six Hills Way, pg. 217 **IT**
Confederation Financial Services (UK) Limited, Bank House, Primmett Rd., pg. 1319 **IT**
Confederation Life Insurance Company (U.K.), Limited, Lytton Way, pg. 1319 **IT**
Confederation Mortgage Services Limited, Bank House, Primmet Rd., pg. 1319 **IT**
Confederation Pension Investment Management Limited, Lytton Way, pg. 1319 **IT**
Du Pont (U.K.) Ltd., Wedgewood Way, pg. 533 **PB**
Hanson Amalgamated Industries, Southgate House, pg. 592 **IT**
Hanson Building Division, Southgate House, pg. 593 **IT**
Iroquois Capital Limited, Bank House, Primmett Rd., pg. 326 **IT**
T.J. Kenton & Company, CES Training Centre, Caxton Vay, pg. 552 **PB**
Kinetica Limited, Wedgewood Way, pg. 533 **PB**
Lindustries Ltd., Southgate House, pg. 593 **IT**
Lucas Milhaupt - Europe, pg. 780 **PB**
The Manufacturers Life Insurance Company (UK) Limited, ManuLife House, St. George's Way, pg. 841 **IT**
ManuLife Management Ltd., ManuLife House, St. George's Way, pg. 841 **IT**
Matra Marconi Space UK Ltd., pg. 545 **IT**
Newport Electronics Ltd., Cavendish Road, pg. 816 **PV**
SLD HOLDINGS LTD., Southgate House, pg. 1160 **IT**
Sun Banking Corporation, Bank House, Primmett Rd., pg. 1319 **IT**
Taylor Instrument, Gunnels Wood Road, pg. 6 **IT**

Stevenston

Nobel's Explosives Company Limited, Nobel House, pg. 663 **IT**

Stirling

Scottish Aggregates Limited, 6 Union St., Bridge of Allan, pg. 1079 **IT**
Scottish Amicable PLC, pg. 1073 **IT**
Zeneca Grangemouth Works, Earle Road, pg. 1524 **IT**

Stockport

ABM Chemicals Ltd., Unity Works, Polacre Ln., pg. 1113 **IT**
Adidas (UK) Ltd., The Adidas Center, Pepper Rd., Hazel Grove, pg. 25 **IT**
Beazer Homes (Stockport) Limited, Stockport Road, pg. 182 **IT**
Bowden Bros & Co., Ltd., Newby Road Industrial Estate, Hazel Grove, pg. 1149 **IT**
British Trimmings Ltd., pg. 434 **PB**
Buss Waeschle Ltd., Andrew House, 26, Mellor Road, pg. 490 **IT**
C & K Colours (UK) Ltd., Battersea Road, Henton Mersey, pg. 460 **PB**
Capseals, Limited, Oakwood Rd., pg. 1486 **PB**
Cussons Group Ltd., Cussons House, Bird Hall Lane, pg. 1024 **IT**
Cussons International Ltd., Cussons House, Bird Hall Lane, pg. 1024 **IT**
Encore Computer (UK) Ltd., Regents House, Heaton Lane, pg. 580 **IT**
Ferodo Ltd., Chapel-en-le-Frith, pg. 1334 **IT**
GenRad (ADS), Manchester, Orion Business Park, Bird Hall, Cane, Monmouth House, Monmouth Road, pg. 731 **PB**
James & Bloom Limited, Compstall Mill, Andrew St., pg. 1160 **IT**
Kemira Coatings Ltd., Station Rd., pg. 729 **IT**
Kemira Polymers, Station Rd., pg. 729 **IT**
Matra Marconi Space, First Ave., Poynton Industrial Estate, pg. 545 **IT**
Mirrlees Blackstone (Stockport) Ltd., Hazel Grove, pg. 125 **IT**
National Tyre Service Ltd., 80-82 Wellington Rd., pg. 328 **IT**
Neste Chemicals UK Ltd., Cambridge House, 37 Bramhill Lane South, pg. 914 **IT**
Nordson U.K., Ltd., Ashurst Dr., Cheadle Heath, pg. 1189 **PB**
Nutricia Dietary Products Ltd., pg. 992 **IT**
PATERSON ZOCHONIS PLC, Cussons House, pg. 1024 **IT**
Rockwell Automation Limited, Applicon House, Exchange Street, pg. 1399 **PB**
Roehlen England, Unit 6, Cromwell Rd. Trading Estate, pg. 1507 **PB**
Sonoco U.K. Ltd., Inc., pg. 1487 **PB**
Standex International Limited, Unit 6, Cromwell Rd. Trading Estate, pg. 1507 **PB**
T.P.T. Ltd., pg. 1487 **PB**
Williams Fairey Engineering Ltd., Crossley Road, pg. 1500 **IT**
Woodbank (UK) Ltd., Woodbank House, Hollingworth Rd., pg. 488 **IT**

Stocksbridge

Avesta Sheffield Precision Strip Ltd., pg. 222 **IT**
Hepworth Building Products International, Hazlehead, pg. 615 **IT**
Hepworth Building Products Limited, Hazlehead, pg. 615 **IT**

Stockton on Tees

Ballast Wiltshier Plc - North East Region, P.O. Box 112, The Moat, pg. 135 **IT**
British Chrome & Chemicals Ltd., Urlay Nook, pg. 598 **IT**
Davy International, Ashmore House, pg. 773 **IT**
Elta Plastics Limited, Elta House, Yarm Road, pg. 929 **IT**
Envirodyne Limited, Salters Lane, pg. 586 **PB**
Grayston, White & Sparrow Ltd., Harewood Works, Middlesbury Rd., pg. 1285 **IT**
McLean Homes North East Ltd., Bowesfield Lane, pg. 1355 **IT**
Tabuchi Electric U.K. Ltd., Tabuchi House, Teeside Industrial Estate, pg. 1346 **IT**

Stoke on Trent

APV Chemical Machinery Limited, Cooper St., Hanley, pg. 1240 **IT**
Autopress Composites Limited, New Street, Biddulph Moor, pg. 354 **IT**
Century Oils Ltd., New Century St., pg. 518 **IT**
Century Oils Ltd., pg. 518 **IT**
Cookson Matthey Ceramics PLC, Uttosceter Road, pg. 713 **IT**
Cookson Matthey Print, William Clowes St., Burslem, pg. 713 **IT**
Crawford Door Ltd., Whittle Road, pg. 269 **IT**
Creda Ltd., Creda Works, Blythe Bridge, pg. 543 **IT**
GEC Industrial Controls Ltd., pg. 53 **IT**
Great Mills (Central) Limited, Berryhill Trading Estate, Victoria Rd., pg. 1080 **IT**
Hills Precision Components Ltd., Humber Road, pg. 1021 **IT**
IL Wastepaper (UK) Ltd, Campbell Rd., pg. 378 **IT**
Kanthal Ltd., pg. 724 **IT**

The Langer Biomechanics Group (UK) Ltd., Brookhouse Way, The Green Cheadle, pg. 978　**PB**
Norton Advanced Ceramics Limited, King St., pg. 1174　**IT**
Norton Chemical Process Products (Europe) Limited, King St., pg. 1175　**IT**
Norton PLC, King Street Fenton, pg. 1175　**IT**
Norton UK Pensions Limited, Kings Road, Fenton, pg. 1175　**IT**
ROYAL DOULTON PLC., Minton House, London Rd., pg. 1135　**IT**
Royal Doulton (UK) Limited, Milton House, London Road, pg. 1135　**IT**
Senior Moducel Limited, King St., Fenton, pg. 1221　**IT**
Springett Coated Stone, Tunstall Wharf, Valley Rd., Ravensdale, pg. 1080　**IT**
Waterford Wedgwood UK Plc, Barlaston, pg. 1487　**IT**

Stoke Poges

THE ALBERT FISHER GROUP PLC, C Sefton Park, pg. 491　**IT**

Stone

ABB Metering Systems, Stonefield Works, Oulton Rd., pg. 2　**IT**

Stonehouse

Amicon Ltd., Upper Mill, pg. 1113　**PB**
Danfoss Flowmetering Limited, Magflo House, Ebley Road, pg. 377　**IT**
ABB Kent Taylor Ltd., Oldends Lane, pg. 2　**IT**

Stourbridge

Astec Europe Limited, High Street, Woolaston, pg. 93　**IT**
British Steel Service Centres Ltd., 96 Stourbridge Road, Lye, pg. 221　**IT**
The Bronx Engineering Company Limited, pg. 862　**IT**
CiMatrix Ltd., St. James Court, Bridgnorth Rd., pg. 1395　**PB**
Hughes & Spencer Steel Ltd., Mill Race Lane, pg. 79　**IT**
METALTECH INTERNATIONAL PLC, Dudley Rd., pg. 862　**IT**
Newsquest Media (Central), St. John's House, St. John's Road, pg. 927　**IT**
Oxford Hoist Company Ltd., High Street, pg. 1536　**PB**
Sunrise Medical, Inc., High Street, pg. 1536　**PB**

Stourport

BWP Controls, Baldwin Road, pg. 472　**IT**
European Cables Controls Div., Baldwin Road, pg. 472　**IT**
Magco Ltd., Baldwin Road, pg. 473　**IT**
Morgan Materials Technology Limited, Bewdley Rd., pg. 894　**IT**
Morgan Matroc Limited, Bewdley Road, pg. 893　**IT**
Parsons Chain Company Ltd., pg. 473　**IT**

Strabane

Adria PLC, Beechmount Ave., pg. 280　**IT**

Stranraer

Stena Line Limited, Sea Terminal, pg. 1300　**IT**

Stratford-on-Avon

Charmilles Technologies Ltd., Arden Street, pg. 489　**IT**
Nenplas Mouldings, Masons Rd., pg. 851　**IT**
PPP Lifetime plc, PPP Lifetime House, Elm Court, pg. 1020　**IT**
Pedershaab Ltd., Timothy's Bridge Rd., pg. 475　**IT**
Saville Tractors Ltd., pg. 817　**IT**
Video Display Corporation Limited, Unit 2, Avenue Farm Industrial Estate, pg. 1720　**PB**
Watveare Ltd., pg. 817　**IT**
Welcombe Hotel, pg. 1213　**IT**

Streatham

Smith Meters Ltd., 170 Rowan Rd., pg. 593　**IT**

Street

CLARKS INTERNATIONAL, 40 High St., pg. 296　**IT**

Stretford

D. Anderson & Son Ltd., Barton Dock Road, pg. 659　**IT**

Stroud

Cumberland Engineering-Europe, John Brown Plastics Mach. Ltd., Bath Rd., pg. 774　**IT**
Egan Europe (John Brown Plastics Machinery Ltd.), Bath Rd., pg. 774　**IT**
Hobourn Automotive Limited, pg. 561　**PB**
Hobourn-Eaton Steering Ltd., Priory Rd., pg. 559　**PB**
Quaker Chemical Limited, Bath Rd., Woodchester, pg. 1347　**PB**

Sudbury

Edward Baker Limited, pg. 598　**IT**

CIBA Corning Diagnostics Limited, Northern Rd., pg. 978　**IT**

Sudley

Beazer Homes (Redditch) Limited, Beazer House, Birmingham Rd., pg. 182　**IT**

Suffolk

Ling Electronics Ltd., 44A Suffolk Enterprise Ctr., Russell Rd., pg. 1077　**PB**

Sunbury

Braun (U.K.) Ltd., Dolphin Estate, Windmill Road, pg. 744　**IT**
Howden Airdynamics Group Limited, 111 Windmill Rd., pg. 636　**IT**
Siemens plc, Siemens House, Windmill Rd., pg. 1247　**IT**
THORN SECURITY GROUP, LTD., Security House, The Summitt, pg. 1386　**IT**

Sunbury-on-Thames

Scan-Optics, Ltd., Dolphin Estate, Windmill Rd., Unit Two, pg. 1436　**PB**

Sunderland

Acxiom Corporation - Publicity Centre, Hendon Rd., pg. 18　**PB**
Corning Consumer Limited, pg. 448　**PB**
Corning Limited, Wear Glass Works, pg. 449　**PB**
Grove Europe, Crown Works, pg. 592　**PB**
Haskel Energy Systems Ltd., North Hylton Rd., pg. 798　**PB**
Homeworthy Furniture Ltd., North Hylton Rd. Trading Estate, pg. 1249　**IT**
Maintenance Building & Signage, pg. 1454　**IT**
Nike (U.K.) Limited, 1 Victory Way, pg. 1184　**PB**
Nissan Motor Manufacturing (UK) Ltd., Washington Road, pg. 945　**IT**
Steels Engineering Ltd., Leechmere Works, pg. 400　**IT**
VAUX GROUP PLC, pg. 1453　**IT**
Vaux Inns Ltd., pg. 1454　**IT**
Vishay Components (U.K.) Ltd., Pallion Industrial Estate, P.O. Box 37, pg. 1722　**PB**

Sunning Hill

R. Hirschmann Electronics UK Ltd., Kingswick House, pg. 1108　**IT**

Sunningdale

Anglo-Austrian Magnesite, Ltd., Dale House, London Rd., pg. 903　**PV**

Surbiton

Hedsorboard Ltd., Tolworth Tower, Ewell Rd., pg. 864　**IT**
Linatex Limited, Wilkinson House, Galway Road, pg. 598　**IT**
Standard Commercial (U.K.), Standard House, Weyside Pk., pg. 1502　**PB**
TT GROUP PLC, Clive House, 12-18 Queens Rd., pg. 1344　**IT**
Unicliffe Limited, Tolworth Tower, Ewell Rd., pg. 1283　**PB**
VoltDelta Europe Limited, Park House, Wick Rd., pg. 1724　**PB**
Wilson Sporting Goods Company Limited, One Tanners Yard, pg. 73　**IT**

Sutton

Cahners Publishing-United Kingdom, Quadrant House, The Quadrant, pg. 1096　**IT**
Engelhard Metals Ltd., Chancery House, St. Nicholas Way, pg. 582　**PB**
ICIS LOR-Europe, Quadrant House, The Quadrant, pg. 1094　**IT**
Reed Business Information, Quadrant House, The Quadrant, pg. 1094　**IT**
Reed Travel Publishing-UK, Quadrant House, The Quadrant, pg. 1097　**IT**
Utell International-United Kingdom, Quadrant House, The Quadrant, pg. 1098　**IT**

Sutton in Ashfield

Pretty Polly Limited, Unwin Road, pg. 1434　**PB**

Sutton Coldfield

The Aluminum Powder Company, Forge Lane, pg. 735　**PV**
Capital Controls Ltd., Park Lane, pg. 1225　**IT**
Clevedon Rivets & Tools Ltd., 11 Reddicap Trading Estate, pg. 297　**IT**
Fedders International, Unit 4, Priory Business Park, London Road, pg. 615　**PB**
GKN Driveline Ltd., Unit 5, Kingsbury Business Pk., Kingsbury Rd., Minworth, pg. 534　**IT**
Haslimann Taylor, Knights House, 2 Parade, pg. 1226　**IT**

ISS Darenas Ltd., Daren House, Kingsbury Road, pg. 657　**IT**
Rockwell Automation Limited, Bank House, Westhaven Road, pg. 1399　**PB**

Swadlincote

Dowty Woodville Polymer, Hearthcote Road, pg. 1338　**IT**
Robert Morton Aerospace Limited, Unit 1, Boardman Industrial Estate, pg. 1160　**IT**

Swallowfield

Chips and Technologies, Inc., Wyvols Court, Old Basingstoke Road, pg. 349　**PB**

Swanley

Adams Rite (Europe) Ltd., Unit 6, Moreton Industrial Estate, pg. 17　**PV**
Fitch Food Services Ltd., 5 Pedham Place Estate, Wested Lane, pg. 202　**IT**
IRCON, Ltd., Unit 6 Park Rd., pg. 1209　**IT**
Simon Petroleum Technology Ltd., Horizon House, Azalea Dr., pg. 1251　**IT**

Swansea

Alcan Wire, Port Tennant, pg. 51　**IT**
Alcoa Extruded Products (UK) Ltd., P.O. Box 68, Waunarlwydd Works, pg. 62　**IT**
Alcoa Manufacturing (G.B.) Ltd., P.O. Box 68, Waunarlwydd Works, pg. 62　**PB**
Escalade International Ltd., Unit 1 Beaufort Road, Swansea Enterprise Park, pg. 591　**PB**
ITW Paslode, Queensway, Fforestfach, pg. 869　**PB**
Signode, Queensway, pg. 869　**PB**
Siliconix Ltd., Morriston, pg. 367　**IT**
Viskase United Kingdom Limited, Kingsway, pg. 586　**PB**

Swanton

Wm. Briggs & Co. Limited, Lee St., pg. 299　**IT**

Swindon

Allied Dunbar Assurance plc, Allied Dunbar Ctr., pg. 110　**IT**
Anchor Foods Limited, P.O. Box 82, pg. 923　**IT**
Apex Service Stations Limited, Burmah Castrol House, Pipers Way, pg. 234　**IT**
BCA, Guild House, Farnsby Street, pg. 192　**IT**
BancTec UK Limited, 15-18 Cherry Orchard West, pg. 177　**PB**
Benckiser Ltd., pg. 185　**IT**
Biomet Ltd., Murdock Road, pg. 232　**PB**
Burmah Castrol Chemicals Division, pg. 234　**IT**
Burmah Castrol Chemicals Ltd., Burmah Castrol House, Pipers Way, pg. 234　**IT**
Burmah Castrol Lubricants Division, pg. 234　**IT**
BURMAH CASTROL PLC, Burmah Castrol House, Pipers Way, pg. 234　**IT**
Burmah Castrol Trading, Ltd., Burmah Castrol House, Pipers Way, pg. 234　**IT**
Burmah Oil Investments Holdings Ltd., Burmah Castrol House, Pipers Way, pg. 234　**IT**
Castrol Ltd., Burmah Castrol House, Pipers Way, pg. 234　**IT**
Castrol Overseas Ltd., Burmah Castrol House, Pipers Way, pg. 234　**IT**
Castrol (U.K.) Limited, Burmah Castrol Home, Pipers Way, pg. 234　**IT**
Clarion Shoji (U.K.) Ltd., Unit 1, Marshall Rd., pg. 296　**IT**
DEA UK, pg. 654　**IT**
Dana Distribution U.K., Great Eastern House, Stratton St. Margaret, pg. 480　**PB**
Drugasar Ltd., Deans Road, pg. 1210　**IT**
Early Learning Centre, South Marston Industrial Estate, pg. 707　**IT**
Emerson Electric Indus. Controls Ltd., Elgin Drive, pg. 576　**PB**
Ericsson Components, Pagoda House, Westmead Drive, Westlea, pg. 1366　**IT**
GEC Plessey Semiconductors, Cheney Manor, pg. 544　**IT**
Hexcel, U.K., Unit 27, Techno-Trading Estate, pg. 824　**PB**
ITW Magnaflux Limited, South Dorcan Industrial Estate, pg. 868　**PB**
Intel Corporation U.K. LTD., Pipers Way, pg. 887　**PB**
Intergraph (UK) Limited, Delta Business Park, Great Western Way, pg. 892　**PB**
Linton and Hirst Limited, Parsonage Road, Stratton St. Margaret, pg. 1344　**IT**
Magnet Developments Limited, Magnet House, Blackworth Industrial Park, Highworth, pg. 1344　**IT**
Meggitt Electronic Components Ltd., Westmead Industrial Estate, pg. 853　**IT**
NP Automotive Coatings (Europe) Ltd., Britannia Park, Radway Road, pg. 937　**IT**
NATIONWIDE BUILDING SOCIETY, Nationwide House, Pipers Way, pg. 912　**IT**
Nationwide Life, Kingsbridge Point, pg. 912　**IT**
Nokia General Communications Ltd., Bridgemead Close, pg. 954　**IT**
Ohmeda Ltd., Faraday Rd., pg. 121　**IT**
PHH Vehicle Management Services, United Kingdom, PHH Centre, Windmill Hill, White Hill Way, pg. 322　**PB**
Piher International Ltd., Westmead Industrial Estate, pg. 853　**IT**
Pilkington's Tiles Ltd., pg. 124　**IT**

PB - *U.S. Public Companies Volume*
PV - *U.S. Private Companies Volume*
IT - *International Public & Private Companies Volume*

Geographic Index-Non U.S.

1831

Press Construction Ltd., Utilities Div., pg. 16   IT
Reader's Digest European Systems Group, Limited, Pegasus House, pg. 1368   PB
Redpoint Thermalloy Limited, Cheney Manor, pg. 207   IT
Sauer-Sundstrand Ltd., Cheney Manor, pg. 1198   IT
Scherer DDS Ltd., Euro Way, Blagrove, pg. 1438   PB
R.P. Scherer Limited, Frankland Road, pg. 1438   PB
Shorrock Security Ltd., Unit # 1, Orbit Ctr., pg. 1285   IT
Spectrol Reliance LTD., Garrard Way, pg. 352   PV
Square D Company United Kingdom Limited, Cheney Manor, Trading Estate, pg. 1209   IT
Three-Five Systems Limited, Cherry Orachard North, pg. 1604   PB
Torin Limited, Greenbridge, pg. 1267   IT
Tylan (UK) Ltd., Unit 19, Westmead Industrial Estate, pg. 1113   PB
Vivitar (Europe) Ltd. Hanimex-Vivitar, pg. 1061   IT
T.D. Williamson (U.K.) Ltd., Faraday Rd., Dorcan Way, pg. 1180   PV
Zimmer Limited, Elgin Industrial Estate, Dunbeath Rd., pg. 257   PB

Syston

Evode Specialty Adhesives Ltd., Wanlip Rd., pg. 802   IT
Laporte Alphagary LTD., Wanilp Rd., pg. 802   IT

Tadcaster

John Smith's Tadcaster Brewery, pg. 1212   IT
Stora Newton Kyme Ltd., Newton Kyme, pg. 1302   IT

Tadley

Kollmorgen Hightech Ltd., Servo House, pg. 966   PB

Tamworth

Berendsen Fluid Power Ltd., Sandy Way, Amington Industrial Estate, pg. 1284   IT
NEWMOND PLC, Litchfield Rd. Industrial Estates, pg. 924   IT
Smurfit Paper Mills (Tamworth) Ltd., Lichfield Road, pg. 1271   IT
Spline Gauges Ltd., Piccadilly, pg. 482   PB
Swish Products Ltd., Lichfield Road Industrial Estate, pg. 925   IT
Weber Marking Systems Ltd., Cavendish 7, 8 & 9, Litchfield Rd. Industrial Estate, pg. 1157   PV

Tarvin

PolyMedica Industries UK, Ltd., Tarvin Sands Complex, pg. 1315   PB

Taunton

Bowthorpe Thermometrics, Crown Industrial Estate, Priorswood Road, pg. 207   IT
K-Swiss Europe Ltd., 40 High St., pg. 937   PB
Pearsalls Sutures, Tancred Street, pg. 215   IT
Power Development, Crown Industrial Estate, Priorswood Rd., pg. 207   IT
Taunton Cider Company P.L.C., Norton Fitzwarren, pg. 849   IT

Teddington

Livingston U.K. Limited, 2-6 Queens Rd., pg. 212   IT
Livingston UK Ltd., 2-6 Queens Rd., pg. 212   IT
Pearson Television Ltd., Teddington Studios, Teddington Lock, pg. 1026   IT
Sodra Cell (UK) Ltd., 16-20 The Causeway, pg. 1276   IT
Thames Television Ltd., Broom Rd., pg. 1026   IT
Woodmark Ltd., 109 Fairfax Rd., pg. 967   IT

Telford

ABB Power Ltd., Darby House, pg. 2   IT
Augat Ltd., Hortonwood 1, pg. 1598   PB
Bailey ICS plc, pg. 449   IT
Bischof & Klein (U.K.) Ltd., Rd. 2, Hortonwood Industrial E, state, pg. 122   IT
Bundy U.K. Ltd., Halesfield 9, pg. 1341   IT
CBS (Automotive & Industrial) Ltd., Unit F Halefield 14, pg. 113   IT
GKN Defence Ltd., P.O. Box 106, pg. 534   IT
GKN Sankey Engineering Products, P.O. Box 83, pg. 535   IT
GKN Sankey Industrial Products, P.O. Box 86, pg. 535   IT
GKN Sankey Ltd., P.O. Box 20, pg. 534   IT
GKN Squeezeform, P.O. Box 106, Hadley Castle Works, pg. 534   IT
GKN Wheels, P.O. Box 85, pg. 535   IT
Gibson Greetings International Limited, Gibson House, Unit A, Hortonwood 30, pg. 742   PB
Horton Automatics, Ltd., #12 Hortonwood 32, pg. 823   PV
MacDermid G.B., Stafford Park 18, pg. 1030   IT
Makita Manufacturing Europe LTD., Hortonwood Industrial Estate, Road 7, pg. 832   IT
The Miller Group Limited (Telford), Unit G9, Hortonwood 32, pg. 869   PB
NEC Technologies (UK) Ltd., Castle Farm Campus, Priorslee, pg. 900   IT
Nature's Sunshine Products, Inc., Unit 5 Hortonwood 32, pg. 1167   PB
New York Life (U.K.) Limited, Windsor House, Telford Centre, pg. 795   PV

OMRON Telford Ltd., Unit A, Hortonwood 2, pg. 1006   IT
Rockwell Automation Limited, Hortonwood 30, pg. 1399   PB
Sealed Air (FPD) Limited, Stafford Park 9, pg. 1451   PB
Suhner Electronics Ltd., Telford Rd., pg. 637   IT
Tatung UK Ltd., Stafford Park 10, pg. 1357   IT
Telford Foods Ltd., Haldane, Halesfield 10, pg. 753   IT
Tesa Metrology Limited, PO Box 418, Halesfield 8, pg. 260   PB
VG Engineering (Telford) Ltd., Road 7 Strafford Park, pg. 1595   PB
VARI-FORM, Halesfield 9, pg. 1341   IT
Vickers Systems Div., Lang Pneumatic Products, Halesfield 6, pg. 25   IT
Ymos (UK) Ltd., pg. 302   IT

Tenbury

Margetts Foods Limited, Clee Hill Rd., pg. 732   IT

Tenterden

Miller's Publications, The Cellars, High Street, pg. 1093   IT

Testwood

Van Leeuwen Tubes Ltd., Unit 'A' The Phoenix Centre, Eddystone Rd., pg. 1450   IT

Tetbury

Defontaine U.K. Ltd, Malmesbury Business Park, pg. 509   IT

Tewkesbury

Blount U.K. Limited, Six Station Dr., Bredon, pg. 239   PB
Andrew Brownsword Gifts, Ltd., Shannon Way, pg. 496   PV
CHAPTER ONE GROUP LIMITED, Green Ln., pg. 280   IT
De La Rue Card Technology Limited, Alexandra Way, Ashchurch Business Ctr., pg. 387   IT
Engineered Seals, Ashchurch, pg. 1338   IT
Fisax, Unit E4, Northway Trading Estate, pg. 103   PV
John Crane Polymer Engineering, Ashchurch, pg. 1338   IT
Micro Circuit Engineering Limited, Alexandra Way, pg. 1267   IT
Reifenhauser Ltd., Sun St., pg. 1101   IT
TNT Logistics UK, Unit B, Fitzhamon Museum Building, pg. 1343   IT

Thakeham

Chesswood Produce Ltd., Chesswood Nurseries, pg. 1396   IT

Thame

Angus Fire Armour Limited, Thame Park Road, pg. 1500   IT
Atlet Ltd., Jefferson Way, pg. 97   IT
Booker Tate Ltd., pg. 1357   IT
CPM International, Aylesbury Rd., pg. 1225   PB
CRC, 19 Thame Park Business Ctr., Wenner Rd., pg. 241   IT
The Grand Pub Company Limited, Mill House, pg. 956   IT
Inntrepreneur Pub Company Limited, Mill House, Aylesbury Road, pg. 956   IT
Kubota (U.K.) Limited, Dormer Rd., pg. 763   IT
Leyland DAF Ltd., Eastern Bypass, pg. 1247   PB
Memec PLC, pg. 1458   IT
Nordson U.K., Ltd., Wenman Rd.,Thame Park Industrial Estate, pg. 1189   PB

Thames Ditton

Policy Management Systems Europe, Ltd., 2 A.C. Court, pg. 1315   PB

Thamesmead

Plant Construction Plc, Hailey Rd., pg. 585   IT

Thatcham

Nitto U.K. Limited, Unit 2, Berkshire Business Centre, pg. 951   IT
WF Corroon-Global Support Unit, Thatcham House, Turner's Drive, pg. 1502   IT
WF Corroon-Thatcham, The Old Coach House, Turner's Drive, pg. 1502   IT
Zitel International Corp., 16 Thatcham Business Village, pg. 1794   PB

Theale

Arlington Securities plc, Arlington House, Arlington Business Park, pg. 217   IT
ECC International Ltd., 1015 Arlington Business Park, pg. 455   IT
ECCI Europe, 1015 Arlington Business Pk., pg. 455   IT
ENGLISH CHINA CLAYS PLC, 1015 Arlington Business Park, pg. 455   IT
Fiskars Electronics Ltd., Commerce Park, pg. 492   IT

Thetford

Alpha Therapeutic U.K. Ltd., Howlett Way, Fison Way Industrial Estate, pg. 558   IT
Breckland Farms, Mundford Farm, Cranwich Rd., pg. 1170   IT
Howard Long International Ltd., Brandon Road, pg. 491   IT
Perry Equipment Ltd., Rymer Point, pg. 855   PV

Thornhill

Gould Electronics Ltd., Circuit Protection, Bursledon Rd., pg. 1592   PB

Thrapston

SS Coils Limited, 18 Cottingham Way, pg. 88   IT

Tilbury

Alternative Transport Services Ltd., pg. 1144   IT
Fibo ExClay Ltd., Focal House 18-19 Berth, pg. 1200   IT
P.J. Parmiter & Sons Ltd., pg. 1512   IT
Powell Duffryn Shipping Ltd., Powell Duffryn House, 21 Berth, Tilbury Docks, pg. 1065   IT

Tipton

Alcan Metal Centres, Birmingham New Rd., pg. 51   IT
Babcock Construction Limited, Birmingham New Road, pg. 130   IT
Conex-Sanbra Ltd., Whitehall Rd., pg. 390   IT
ELSTER (UK) Ltd., pg. 1149   IT
Ervin Amasteel Uk. LP, George Henry Rd., pg. 382   PV
Jeavons Engineering, Ltd., Lower Church Lane, pg. 1149   IT
Midland Tool and Design Limited, Barnfield Road, pg. 1344   IT
Senior Heat Treatment-Tipton, Coneygre Industrial Estate, Burnt Tree, pg. 1221   IT

Todmorden

DSM Compounds UK Ltd., Perseverance Works, Halifax Road, pg. 355   IT
Warmen International Limited, Halifax Road, pg. 967   IT

Tonbridge

Standex Electronics (U.K.) Ltd., 40 Morley Rd., pg. 1507   PB
Wallace & Tiernan, Priory Works, pg. 1444   IT

Torpoint

Select Gauges, pg. 260   PB

Torrington

Dartington Crystal, pg. 124   IT

Totnes

Dundridge College Limited, Dundridge House, pg. 544   IT
Sewells International Ltd., Cart Business Centre, Darington, pg. 451   IT

Towcester

GEC-Marconi Materials Technology Ltd., Caswell, pg. 544   IT

Trawden

Wadkin Colne, Lodge Home, pg. 231   IT

Trenent

Weber Marking Systems Ltd., MacMerry Industrial Estates, pg. 1157   PV

Tring

Grass Roots Group plc, Pennyroyal Court, Station Rd., pg. 1482   IT

Tromode

KWB Controls Ltd., pg. 391   IT

Trowbridge

Cow & Gate Nutricia Ltd., pg. 991   IT
Galenco Ltd., pg. 991   IT
Nutricia Holdings Ltd., pg. 992   IT

Tunbridge Wells

British Reserve, Adriatic House, 6 Vale Ave., pg. 61   IT
De Lage Landen Factors Ltd., Belvedere House, Vale Ave., pg. 1082   IT
Lamberts Healthcare Ltd., 1 Lamberts Road, pg. 989   IT
PPP HC, Phillips House, Crescent Rd., pg. 1020   IT

PB - *U.S. Public Companies Volume*
PV - *U.S. Private Companies Volume*
IT - *International Public & Private Companies Volume*

1832

Plant & Tools Ltd., pg. 1512 — IT
Private Patients Plan Limited, Phillips House, Crescent Road, pg. 1020 — IT
Private Patients Plan Limited, Priplan House, Crescent Road, pg. 1020 — IT
SPA-Aluminium Ltd., Unit 1, Chapman Way, pg. 964 — IT

Tuxford

Dosco Overseas Engineering Limited, pg. 604 — IT
Hollybank Engineering Company Limited, pg. 604 — IT

Twickenham

Dexter Specialty Materials, Ltd., Booth House, 15 Church St., pg. 505 — PB
Hydro Aluminium U.K. Ltd., Bridge House, 69 London Rd., pg. 963 — IT
MacMillan Bloedel Pulp & Paper Sales Ltd., Regal House, London Rd., pg. 829 — IT
Magnesium Elektron, Regal House, London Rd., pg. 51 — IT
Norsk Hydro (U.K.) Ltd., Bridge House, 69 London Road, pg. 964 — IT
Swift Adhesives Ltd., St. George's House, Church Street, pg. 370 — IT

Twyford

Borland UK, 8 Pavilions, pg. 246 — PB
Mentholatum Co., Ltd., Longfield Rd., pg. 1126 — IT
Mentholatum (Overseas) Ltd., Longfield Rd., pg. 1126 — IT
Tilbury Douglas Plc, Tilbury House, Ruscombe Park, pg. 634 — IT
Tin Plate Containers, Ltd., Longfield Rd., pg. 1126 — IT

Uckfield

Gunnebo Mayor Ltd., Bellbrook Business Park, pg. 578 — IT
Millbank Electronics Group Ltd., Bellbrook Industrial Estate, pg. 64 — PV
RAM Golf UK, Bell Lane, pg. 908 — PV
Sussex Clinical Research Consultants Ltd., pg. 986 — IT
VG Microtech Ltd., Bellbrook Business Park, pg. 1595 — PB
Woodpax Limited, Sheffield Park, pg. 458 — IT

Uddingston

JLG Industries (Europe), Kilmartin Place, pg. 918 — PB

Ulverston

Ashley & Rock Ltd., pg. 1511 — IT

Uttoxeter

Elkes Biscuits, Dove Valley Bakeries, Cheadle Rd., pg. 968 — IT

Uxbridge

Acuson Ltd., pg. 18 — PB
Allen & Hanburys Limited, Stockley Park West, pg. 552 — PB
Apple Computer (UK) Ltd., 6 Roundwood Ave., pg. 121 — PB
Armstrong Europe Services, Armstrong House, 3 Chequers Square, pg. 132 — PB
Armstrong World Industries Ltd., Armstrong House, 3 Chequers Sq., pg. 132 — PB
Blockbuster Entertainment Corporation Limited (U.K.), 45 Riverside Way, pg. 776 — PV
Robert Bosch Ltd., Broadwater Park, N. Orbital Rd., pg. 205 — IT
Bristol-Myers Company Limited, Swakeley House, Milton Rd., pg. 255 — PB
Burger King, Europe/Middle East/Africa, Cambridge House, Highbridge Industrial Estate, Oxford Rd., pg. 411 — IT
CNT International, One Roundwood Ave., pg. 421 — PB
Cape Plc., Iverlang, pg. 280 — IT
Coca-Cola & Schweppes Beverages Ltd., Charter Place, Vine St., pg. 393 — PB
Duncan Flockhart & Co. Limited, Stockley Park West, pg. 552 — IT
Fiserv Europe Limited, 5 Roundwood Ave., pg. 647 — PB
Fujitsu Europe Ltd., 2, Longwalk Road, pg. 528 — IT
Gamma Holding (UK) Ltd., pg. 540 — IT
Glaxo Laboratories Limited, Stockley Park West, pg. 552 — IT
Glaxo Pharmaceuticals UK Ltd., Stockley Park West, pg. 592 — IT
Glaxochem Ltd., Stockley Park West, pg. 552 — IT
Grand Metropolitan Corporate Property, 106 Oxford Road, pg. 408 — IT
Grand Metropolitan Estates Ltd., 106 Oxford Road, pg. 408 — IT
GrandMet Foods UK, Harman House, 1 George Street, pg. 408 — IT
Hasbro Bradley UK Limited, Two Roundwood Ave., pg. 797 — PB
Hasbro Europe UK Limited, Two Round Wood Ave., pg. 797 — PB
Hewlett-Packard Ltd., Harman House, No. 1 George St., pg. 821 — PB
Konami (UK) Ltd., Konami House, 54A Cowley Mill Road, pg. 746 — IT
Lincoln Assurance Limited, The Quays, 101-105 Oxford Rd., pg. 998 — PB
Merloni Domestic Appliances Ltd, Merloni House, 3 Cowley Business Park, pg. 860 — IT
Milupa Ltd., Milupa House, Hillingdon, pg. 991 — IT

Nyborg Engineering Ltd., Longbridge Way, Cowley Mill Rd., pg. 444 — IT
PAREXEL International Limited, River Ct., 50 Oxford St., pg. 1258 — PB
Pillsbury U.K. Ltd., Oxford House, 97 Oxford Rd., pg. 411 — IT
Rank Film Laboratories Limited, North Orbital Rd., pg. 1087 — IT
SCA Packaging Ltd., Packet Boat House, Packet Boat House, Packet Boat Ln., pg. 1326 — IT
Arthur Sanderson and Sons Ltd., 100 Acres Oxford Road, pg. 540 — IT
Tandem Computers Ltd., Tandem House, 7 Roundwood Ave.,Stockley Park, pg. 418 — PB
Toshiba International (Europe) Ltd., 1 Roundwood Ave., Stockley Park, pg. 1406 — IT
Unisys Limited, Baker Court, Baker Road, pg. 1671 — PB
Wisaforest (UK) Ltd., 6 Belmont Chambers, 28, Bakers Road, pg. 1429 — IT

Wadebridge

Bach-Simpson (UK) Ltd., Trenant Estate, pg. 944 — PB

Wakefield

AMEC Mining Ltd., Fairmine House, Wakefield 41, pg. 16 — IT
Bombardier Prorail Ltd., Horbury, pg. 200 — IT
Brotherton Chemicals Ltd., Calder Vale Rd., pg. 356 — PB
Deborah Services, Ten South Par, pg. 1285 — IT
Nacanco Ltd., pg. 1029 — IT
Northern Dairies Ltd., Raines House, Denby Dale Rd., pg. 968 — IT
RMC Panel Products Limited, Waldorf Way, Denby Dale Rd., pg. 1080 — IT
Senior Foster Wheeler Industrial Boiler Division, Calder Vale Rd., pg. 1221 — IT
Senior Green Economiser Division, Calder Vale Rd., pg. 1221 — IT
Senior Luke Materials Handling Division, Calder Vale Rd., pg. 1221 — IT

Wallasey

Volclay Limited, Birkenhead Rd., Seacombe, pg. 64 — PB

Wallingford

Vetrotex Ltd., Unit A 3 Beadle, Trading Estate, pg. 1177 — IT

Wallington

Barratt South London, Grosvenor House, 110 Manor Road, pg. 168 — IT
Barratt Southern, 2nd Floor, Grosvenor House, pg. 168 — IT
Elscint Cryomagnetics Ltd., Parkhouse Estate, Tower Road, pg. 450 — IT
Master Builders Materials Ltd., pg. 1465 — IT
Sidwell & Company Ltd., Rosemount Towers, pg. 1160 — IT

Wallsend

George Angus & Co. Ltd., pg. 507 — IT
Apax Autoparts International Ltd., pg. 507 — IT
Freudenberg Angus LP, pg. 505 — IT
Freudenberg Household Products LP, pg. 505 — IT
Freudenberg Technical Products Ltd., pg. 507 — IT
Gaco Ltd., pg. 507 — IT
Kockums Computer Systems (UK) Ltd., Armstrong Technology Center, Davy Bank, pg. 278 — IT
Press Offshore Ltd., Howdon Yard, pg. 16 — IT
TSL Group PLC, pg. 1176 — IT

Walsall

Barton Aluminum Foundries, pg. 264 — IT
Barton Conduits, Birchills, pg. 264 — IT
Barton Engineering Ltd., Birchills, pg. 264 — IT
Binks-Bullows, Ltd., Pelsall Road, pg. 229 — PB
Bowthorpe-Hellermann Distributors, Brickyard Rd., pg. 207 — IT
Caparo Industries Plc, pg. 264 — IT
Clydesdale Jones Co., Alumwell Industrial Estate, pg. 265 — IT
Crabtree Electrical Industries Limited, Lincoln Works, pg. 592 — IT
Delta EMS Ltd., Goscote Ln., pg. 391 — IT
Georg Fischer Disa Ltd., Portland Street, pg. 489 — IT
GEC Card Technology Ltd., Sartec House, West Bromwich Rd., pg. 544 — IT
GKN Driveshafts Ltd., pg. 534 — IT
ITW Proffitt & Co. Ltd., Bentley Ln., pg. 869 — PB
InterTAN U.K. Ltd., Tandy Center, Lea More Lane, pg. 910 — PB
MCKECHNIE PLC, Leighswood Rd., Aldridge, pg. 851 — IT
PM Services Ltd., Sertec House, West Bromwich Rd., pg. 545 — IT
Paxton, Green Ln., pg. 851 — IT
Senior Heat Treatment-Aldridge, Shenstone Dr., Northgate, pg. 1221 — IT
Stamco (U.K.) Ltd., Bath House, Bath Street, pg. 1124 — PB
Sterling Tubes Ltd., pg. 1187 — IT

Waltham Cross

ESAB Group (UK) Ltd., Hertford Rd., pg. 282 — IT

Hales Waste Control Limited, Delamare Rd., pg. 1081 — IT
Powerflex, Hertford Rd., pg. 1221 — IT
Senior TIFT Limited, Hertford Rd., pg. 1221 — IT

Walton-on-Thames

Air Products PLC, Hersham Place Molesey Rd., pg. 32 — PB
Akzo Chemie U.K. Ltd., 1-5, Queens Road, Hersham, pg. 47 — IT
Allegro MicroSystems Europe Limited, Balfour House, Churchfield Rd., pg. 1188 — IT
Analog Devices Ltd., Walton House, Station Ave., pg. 108 — PB
Barry Controls Ltd., Molesey Road Hersham, pg. 125 — IT
Birds Eye Walls Ltd., Station Ave., pg. 1434 — IT
Hunter Douglas Ltd., Wellington House, New Zealand Ave., pg. 640 — IT
The MacNeal-Schwendler Co. Ltd., Case House, 85/89 High St., pg. 1032 — PB
Thomas Nelson & Sons Ltd., Nelson House, Mayfield Rd., pg. 1601 — IT
Parfums Givenchy Ltd, Old Esher Rd., pg. 783 — IT
Sanken Electric Europe Limited, Balfour House, Churchfield Road, pg. 1188 — IT
Square D Company Europe, Balfour House, Churchfield Rd., pg. 1209 — IT

Wantage

Crown Cork & Seal Company, Inc.-Corporate Technologies, Downsview Road, pg. 464 — PB
MB Group plc Engineering Div., Denchworth Rd., pg. 267 — IT
Metal Box plc., Research & Development Div., Denchworth Rd., pg. 267 — IT

Wardley

CMT Dynamics, pg. 265 — IT
Caparo Steel Stockholders Ltd., Overend Rd., pg. 265 — IT

Ware

Isuzu Truck (UK), Thundridge Business Park, pg. 807 — IT
Rank Cintel Ltd., Watton Road, pg. 1087 — IT
Vaughn-Harmon Ltd., The Matlings, Hoe Lane, pg. 788 — PB

Wareham

Brooklyns Limited, Sanford Ln., pg. 1355 — IT

Warley

GKN Computer Services Ltd., Cranford House, Cranford Street, pg. 534 — IT
Talco, Woodlane Cradley Heath, pg. 614 — PV

Warminster

LYONS SEAFOODS LIMITED, Barrow House, Bishopstrow, pg. 824 — IT

Warrington

AAH Consumer Products Ltd., Hamilton House, Birchwood Lane, pg. 591 — IT
AMD (U.K.) Ltd., The Genesis Centre, Garrett Field, Science Park South, pg. 21 — PB
Alcan Recycling, P.O. Box 108, Latchford, pg. 51 — IT
Alcan Specialty Extrusions, Latchford Works, pg. 51 — IT
Angelica International Ltd., Ashton Rd., Golborne, pg. 113 — PB
Anixter Warrington, Unit 15 Chesford United Trading Estate, pg. 116 — PB
Aqualon (UK) Limited, D Genesin Centre, Garriette, Birchwood, pg. 810 — PB
BNFL, Risley, pg. 120 — IT
Bently Nevada (UK) Ltd., 2 Kelvin Close, pg. 134 — PV
British Aerospace (Consultancy Services) Limited, 620-622 Birchwood Blvd., pg. 217 — IT
Joseph Crosfield & Sons Ltd., pg. 1434 — IT
Europtics Limited, Helsby, pg. 530 — IT
Frialator International, Unit 4, Heaton Ct., pg. 1065 — PB
THE GREENALLS GROUP PLC, Wilderspool House, pg. 558 — IT
Impell Corporation U.K. Ltd., Genesis Centre Garrett Field, pg. 6 — IT
Interox Solvay, Baronet Works, P.O. Box 7, pg. 1278 — IT
Krauss-Maffei (Air Defence) Ltd., pg. 836 — IT
Krauss-Maffei Holdings Ltd., pg. 836 — IT
Krauss-Maffei (U.K.) Ltd., Krauss-Maffei House, Birchwood Blvd., pg. 836 — IT
Morton International Limited, Chesford Grange, Woolston, pg. 1135 — PB
North West Water Limited, Dawson House, pg. 1444 — IT
Pacific Nuclear Transport Limited (PNTL), Risley, pg. 305 — IT
Pacific Nuclear Transport Ltd., Riseley, pg. 949 — IT
Peters Stubs Ltd., Causeway Avenue, pg. 88 — IT
Rylands Whitecross Ltd., P.O. Box 29, Battersby Lane, pg. 185 — IT
Smurfit Corrugated Cases (Warrington) Ltd., Orford Lane, pg. 1271 — IT
UNITED UTILITIES PLC, Birchwood Pt. Bus. Park, pg. 1444 — IT
Vulnax International Ltd., 50 Melford Court, Hardwick Court, pg. 47 — IT

PB - *U.S. Public Companies Volume*
PV - *U.S. Private Companies Volume*
IT - *International Public & Private Companies Volume*

Warrwaton

The Menswear Company, Harvard Ct., pg. 300   IT

Warwick

Behr Industrial Equipment Ltd., pg. 422   IT
Benford Limited, The Cape, pg. 1066   IT
BRITAX INTERNATIONAL PLC, Seton House, Warwick Technology Pk., pg. 216   IT
Calor Group plc, Athena Drive, pg. 1155   IT
Ceatron Technology Ltd., The Manor, Hasseley Business Centre, pg. 148   PB
Commercial Hydraulics Keelavite, Ltd., Tachbrook Park Drive, pg. 411   PB
Durr Control Systems Ltd., pg. 422   IT
Durr Ltd., Broxell Close, pg. 422   IT
Hydro Aluminium Prolifer UK Ltd., Warwick, Titan Business Ctr., pg. 963   IT
Hydro Aluminium Systems U.K., Unit 3, Titan Business Centre, Tachbrook Park, pg. 963   IT
Marcam U.K., Headquarters, Seton House, Warwick Technology Park, pg. 1043   PB
Millward Brown International, Olympus Ave., Tachbrook Park, pg. 1482   PB
Nicolet Limited, Budbrooke Rd., pg. 1594   PB
Potterton Myson, Brooks House, Coventry Rd., pg. 197   IT
Scholastic Book Fairs, Ltd., Westfield Road, pg. 1440   PB
Sensormatic CamEra Ltd., Rossmore House, Haseley Manor, pg. 1457   PB
Volvo Bus Limited, Hawkes Dr., pg. 1477   IT
Volvo Trucks (Great Britain) Ltd., Wedgnock Ln., pg. 1478   IT
Wicona UK Ltd., Titan Business Ctr., Tachbrook Park, pg. 965   IT

Washington

Bundy U.K. Ltd., One Spire Road, pg. 1341   IT
John Gibson (Plastics) Ltd., pg. 355   IT
Littelfuse Ltd., 3 Rutherford Road, pg. 1001   PB
RAYOVAC UK Limited, Stephenson Estate, pg. 912   PV
Swallow Hotels Limited, Swallow House, Parsons Road, pg. 1454   IT
Thermon U.K. (Ltd.), 18 Tower Rd., pg. 1081   PV

Waterbeach

Cambridge Vacuum Engineering Ltd., Denny Industrial Centre, pg. 1337   IT
Thermal Processing Group Ltd. (Cambridge), Denny Industrial Estate, pg. 1338   IT

Waterford

Asahi Chemical Industry - London, 22 The Courtyards, Hatters Lane, pg. 84   IT

Waterlooville

Anaren Microwave, Ltd., 12 Somerset House, Suite 16 & 17, pg. 111   PB
James Crean Holdings (UK) Ltd., Birch House, Parklands Business Park, pg. 341   IT

Watford

Abloy Security Ltd., 2-3 Hatters La., pg. 17   IT
Alcon Laboratories (UK) Ltd., pg. 918   IT
Alkor Plastics Ltd., Odhams Trading Estate, St. Alban's Road, pg. 1278   IT
Alvis-Unipower Limited, Watford Business Park, 34 Greenhill Crescent, pg. 69   IT
Beko U.K. Ltd., 40 Caxton Way, pg. 742   IT
Bell Cablemedia plc, Colne House, pg. 116   IT
Boeing Computer Services - Europe, 5 Millfield House, pg. 242   PB
Construction Research Communications, pg. 451   IT
Cylinder Div., Parker Hannifin plc, 6 Greycaine Rd., pg. 1263   PB
Dennison plc, Colonial Way, pg. 153   PB
Elscint (GB) Limited, Colonial Business Park, pg. 450   IT
Graseby Dynamics Ltd., Park Avenue, pg. 1267   IT
Graseby Medical Ltd., Colonial Way, pg. 1267   IT
Graseby Security Ltd., Park Avenue, Bushey, pg. 1267   IT
Hilton International Hotels (U.K.) Ltd., Millbuck House, pg. 787   IT
Iveco-Ford Truck Ltd., Iveco House, Station Road, pg. 484   IT
McKechnie Consumer Export, Spur House, Otterspool Way, pg. 851   IT
Mothercare World UK Ltd., Cherry Tree Rd., pg. 1304   IT
Novilon Ltd., pg. 498   IT
PAXAR Europe Ltd., Croxley Business Park, 4 Awberry Court, pg. 1267   PB
George Philip Limited, 1 Marlin House, Marlin's Meadow, pg. 1094   IT
Price/Costco, Inc.-United Kingdom Region, pg. 452   PB
Rhone-Poulenc Chemicals Ltd., Oak House, Reeds Crescent, pg. 1112   IT
Sanyo U.K. Limited, Sanyo House, Otterspool Way, pg. 1193   IT
Schweppes Europe Limited, 28 Clarendon Road, pg. 248   IT
Senior Heat Treatment-Watford, Otterspool Way, pg. 1221   IT
Sharp Electronics (U.K.), Sherbourne House, The Croxley Center, pg. 1230   IT

Sharp International Finance (U.K.) PLC., Sherbourne House, The Croxley Center, pg. 1230   IT
Spur Shelving, Spur House, Otterspool Way, pg. 851   IT
Sun Chemical Ltd., Sandown Road, pg. 371   IT
Swedish Royal Refrigeration Ltd., 17-19 Greycaine Rd., pg. 444   IT
Teac UK Ltd., 5 Marlin House, Marlins Meadow, pg. 1360   IT
Thomson Regional Newspapers Ltd., Hannay House, 39 Clarendon Rd., pg. 1601   PB
Trio-Kenwood Europe Ltd., Kenwood House, Dwight Rd., pg. 731   IT
Trio-Kenwood U.K. Limited, Kenwood House, Dwight Rd., pg. 731   IT
USB Pharma Ltd., Stes. 10 & 12 The Courtyards, Croxley Business Park, pg. 1681   PB
Veeco Instruments Ltd., Unit 8, Colne Way Court, Colne Way, pg. 1711   PB
Volvo Penta U.K. Ltd., Otterspool Way, pg. 1478   IT

Watton-at-Stone

JARVIS PLC, Frogmore Park, pg. 705   IT

Wednesbury

Glynwed Engineering Ltd., Victoria Steel Works, Bull Lane, pg. 554   IT
Glynwed Metals Processing Ltd., Victoria Steel Works, Bull Ln., pg. 554   IT
Glynwed Steel Tubes Ltd., Victoria Steel Works, Bull Lane, pg. 554   IT
Midland Coated Stone, Holyhead Industrial Estate, Western Way, Off Bull Ln., pg. 1079   IT
Nettlefolds Ltd., Wooden Rd. West, pg. 231   IT
Prodorite Ltd., Lea Brook, pg. 99   PB

Wellingborough

Booker Wholesale Foods, Equity House, Irthlingborough Rd., pg. 202   IT
Cosworth Engineering, Wellingborough Plant, Booth Dr., pg. 1467   IT
Gestetner Manufacturing Limited, 170 Sinclair Drive, pg. 1114   IT
Graseby GK Interest Ltd., Vaux Rd., Finedon Rd., Industrial Estate, pg. 1267   IT
ITW Devcon, Brunel Close, Park Farm Estate, pg. 868   PB
ITW Irathane Intl. Ltd., Brunel Close, Park Farm Industrial Estate, pg. 868   PB
Inter-Tel Equipment UK, Ltd., Nine Enterprise Ct., Newton Close Park Farm, pg. 888   IT
Sigmaform (U.K.) Ltd., Park Farm Industrial Estates, Sywell Rd., pg. 1363   PB

Welshpool

Floform Ltd., Henfaes Lane, pg. 88   IT
Rockwell Automation Limited Electro-Craft, Unit 13-14, Severn Farm Industrial Estate, pg. 1400   PB

Welwyn Garden City

Air Call Communications Ltd., 1 Boulevard, pg. 1470   IT
DSM EPP UK Ltd., 83 Bridge Road East, pg. 354   IT
Danish Bacon Company plc, Denmark House, pg. 429   IT
Graseby Allen Ltd., 6 Little Mundells, pg. 1267   IT
Integrated Systems, Inc., Ltd., 1st Fl. Gatehouse, Fretherne Rd., pg. 886   PB
JEOL (U.K.) Ltd., JEOL House, Silver Court, pg. 697   IT
Loctite (UK) Ltd., Watchmead, pg. 611   IT
Nicholas Laboratories Ltd., pg. 1121   IT
Norton Abrasives Limited, Bridge Rd. East, pg. 1174   IT
Norton Company UK Limited, Bridge Road East, pg. 1175   IT
Polycell Products Limited, 30 Broadwater Rd., pg. 1501   IT
Roche Products Ltd., 40 Broadwater Rd., pg. 1121   IT
Roche Registration Limited, pg. 1122   IT
Stafford-Miller Limited, Broadwater Rd., pg. 237   PB
Thresher, Sefton House, 42 Church Rd., pg. 1498   IT

Wembley

Hasselblad (UK) Ltd., York House, Empire Way, pg. 1468   IT
Herta (U.K.) Ltd., pg. 920   IT
Hirst Research Centre, East Lane, pg. 544   IT
JVC Professional Products (U.K.) Ltd., Alperton House, Bridgewater Rd., pg. 847   IT
M.W. Kellogg Limited, Kellogg Ho, pg. 528   PB
Osram Ltd., East Lane, pg. 1244   IT
Senior Foster Wheeler Power Division, Olympic Office Centre, 8 Fulton Rd., pg. 1221   IT
Senior Thermal Engineering Limited, Olympic Office Centre, 8 Fulton Rd., pg. 1221   IT

West Bromwich

ARENA LIGHTING LTD., Cornwalace Street, pg. 80   IT
Brockhouse C & F Machining Limited, Victoria Works, Howard St., pg. 426   IT
Brockhouse Forgings Limited, Hill Top, pg. 426   IT
Cladding & Decking (UK) Ltd., Shawstreet, pg. 754   IT
Delta Engineering Holding Ltd., Greets Green Rd., pg. 390   IT
Delta Extruded Metals Co. Ltd., Greets Green Rd., pg. 391   IT

HOW GROUP LIMITED, Intersection House, 110 Birmingham Rd., pg. 636   IT
IBP, Greets Green Rd., pg. 391   IT
Kemira Coatings Ltd., Kelvin Way, pg. 729   IT
Phoenix Steel Tube, Great Bridge St., pg. 1221   IT
Precision Drawn Tube, Phoenix St., pg. 1222   IT
Senior Bigwood Limited, Phoenix St., pg. 1220   IT
Senior Heat Treatment-West Bromwich, Unit 4, Kelvin Way Industrial Estate, pg. 1221   IT
Senior Tube Limited, Phoenix St., pg. 1221   IT
Truline Treetex Limited, 23 Kelvin Way, Trading Estate, pg. 1152   IT
Unifix Ltd., Hilltop Industrial Estate, Shaw St., pg. 231   IT
Walsall Conduits Ltd., Dial Lane, pg. 80   IT
Warwick Finspa Limited, Golds Green, pg. 426   IT

West Calder

Central Blocks Limited, Westwood Works, pg. 1079   IT

West Drayton

ACL Drayton, Chantry Close, pg. 1241   IT
Acco-Rexel Group Services PLC, The Lodge, Harmondsworth Lane, pg. 674   PB
Continental Europe, Church Road, pg. 1442   IT
Continental Tyre & Rubber Group Ltd., pg. 328   IT
DMR Group Limited, Heathrow Boulevard IV, pg. 528   IT
Drayton Control (Engineering) Limited, Chantry Close, pg. 1241   IT
The Flight Data Company Ltd., The Lodge, Harmondsworth Lane, pg. 207   IT
GTE Internetworking UK Limited, One Heathrow Blvd., pg. 696   PB
RAM Mobile Data Limited, Heathrow Blvd., 280 Bath Rd., pg. 208   PB
Totalizator Systems (UK) Limited, 241 Horton Rd., pg. 900   PB
United Biscuits Asia Pacific, Church Road, pg. 1442   IT
UNITED BISCUITS (HOLDINGS) PLC, Church Rd., pg. 1442   IT
United Biscuits (UK) Limited, Church Road, pg. 1442   IT

West Malling

Rhone-Poulenc Rorer Ltd., 50 Kings Hill Ave., pg. 1110   IT

West Thurrock

Henderson Hardware Ltd., Lyndale Estate, London Road, pg. 615   IT
Simpson International (UK) Ltd., 131 Parkinson Ln., pg. 1475   PB

Westerham

Aqualisa Products Limited, The Flyer's Way, pg. 925   IT
MoDo Paper Ltd., General Wolfe House, 83 High Street, pg. 887   IT
MoDoCell Ltd., General Wolfe House, 83 High St., pg. 887   IT

Westhoughton

Ames Europe Ltd., pg. 540   IT

Weston

Perrier Group of Canada Ltd., 650 Bar Mac Dr., pg. 919   IT

Weston-super-Mare

GKN Westland Industrial Products Ltd., Winterstoke Rd., pg. 535   IT
Mitchell Cotts Remanufacturing Limited, Winterstoke Rd., pg. 88   IT

Wetherby

ARC Northern, Regional Office, Clifford House, pg. 592   IT
MERISTEM PLC, 4 Deighton Close, pg. 858   IT
PREMIER FARNELL PLC, Farnell House, Sandbeck Way, pg. 1068   IT
Rolled Alloys Ltd., Thorp Arch, Trading Estate, pg. 941   PV

Weybridge

Amari Plastics Plc, Holmes Ho., 24-30, Baker St., pg. 554   IT
American Software (UK) Ltd., Europe/Middle East/Africa, St. Georges Business Center, Locke King Road, pg. 91   PB
Automotive Export Supplies Limited, Hangar T184, Sopwith Drive, Brooklands Business Park, pg. 70   IT
Cambridge-Lee (Europe) Ltd., 1 Camphill Industrial Estate, pg. 202   PV
CARADON PLC, Caradon House, 24 Queens Road, pg. 266   IT
CERAMLO Ltd., Ham Moor Lane, Addlestone, pg. 499   PB
Digital Link U.K. Limited, pg. 508   PB
J.R. Freeman & Son Limited, Members Hill, Brooklands Rd., pg. 539   IT

PB - *U.S. Public Companies Volume*
PV - *U.S. Private Companies Volume*
IT - *International Public & Private Companies Volume*

1834

Gallaher International Limited, Members Hill, Brooklands Rd., pg. 539 — IT

Gallaher Investments Limited, Members Hill, Brooklands Rd., pg. 539 — IT

GALLAHER LIMITED, Members Hill, Brooklands Rd., pg. 539 — IT

Gallaher Overseas Limited, Members Hill, Brooklands Rd., pg. 539 — IT

Gallaher Tobacco Ltd., Members Hill, Brooklands Rd., pg. 539 — IT

Interleaf UK, Ltd., Ideal House, 210 Shepherds Bush Rd., pg. 893 — PB

Lloyds Abbey Life PLC, 205 Brooklands Rd., pg. 813 — IT

NBS Limited-Card Services Division, 105 Oyster Ln., pg. 898 — IT

NBS Limited-Personalization Systems Division, 7 Canada Road, pg. 898 — IT

Toshiba Information Systems (U.K.) Ltd., Toshiba Court, Weybridge Business Park, pg. 1406 — IT

Xilinx Ltd., Benchmark House, 203 Brooklands Rd., pg. 1786 — PB

Weymouth

BHC Aerovox Ltd., 20-21 Cumberland Dr., Granby Industrial Estate, pg. 26 — PB

Ultra Electronics Ocean Systems, Waverley House, Hampshire Road, pg. 1431 — IT

Whetstone

Chemical Construction Products, Ste. 4, Best House, Grange Business Park, Enderby Rd., pg. 867 — PB

ITW Engineered Polymers, Ste. 4, Best House, Grange Business Park, pg. 868 — PB

Oakley Young/4th Dimension, Whiteacres, Whetstone Business Park, pg. 1482 — IT

Soabar Marking Systems Ltd., Unit 7, Ashville Way, pg. 154 — PB

White Waltham

Analogic Ltd., 17 Grove Park, Waltham Road, pg. 109 — PB

SKY Limited, 17 Grove Park, Waltham Road, pg. 109 — PB

Whitehaven

Detergents Division, Albright & Wilson Limited, P.O. Box 15, Marchon Works, pg. 49 — IT

Whitley Bay

MacGREGOR (GBR) Ltd., 86/90 Front Street, pg. 670 — IT

Whitstable

Huyck Ltd., Thanet Way, pg. 124 — IT

Whyteleafe

Givaudan-Roure Ltd., Godstone Rd., pg. 1120 — IT

Widnes

Albright & Wilson UK Limited, P.O. Box 1, pg. 49 — IT

Alumina Company Limited, Ditton Rd., pg. 51 — IT

Anglo Blackwells Ltd., Ditton Rd., pg. 1465 — IT

BetzDearborn Ltd., Foundry Lane, pg. 227 — PB

Laporte Absorbents Europe, pg. 802 — IT

Laporte Fluorides, pg. 802 — IT

Laporte Wood Preservation, pg. 802 — IT

North West Aggregates Limited, North West House, Spring St., pg. 1079 — IT

Quickmix Concrete Company Limited, RMC House, St. Mary's Rd., pg. 1080 — IT

Ready Mixed Concrete (North West) Limited, RMC House, St. Mary's Rd., pg. 1080 — IT

Wigan

Dobson Park Industries Plc, Dobson Park House, Manchester Rd., Ince, pg. 789 — PB

Gridweld, Woodhouse Lane, pg. 185 — IT

Rockware Glass Ltd.-Wigan Factory, Webster St., pg. 124 — PB

Shearings Limited, Miry Ln., pg. 1087 — IT

Volex Accessories Limited, Leigh Rd., pg. 593 — IT

Wigston

Linread North Bridge, Viking Road, pg. 852 — IT

Willenhall

McLean Homes North London Ltd., Crestwood House, Birches Rise, pg. 1355 — IT

Monmer Foundry Limited, St. Annes Rd., pg. 390 — IT

PSM International, Longacres, pg. 852 — IT

Howard E. Perry & Co. Ltd., Strawberry Lane, pg. 79 — IT

Willenhall Manufacturing, Neachells Lane, pg. 265 — IT

Willerby

Selles Medical Limited, Great Gutter La., pg. 58 — IT

Wilmslow

Ciba Pharmaceuticals, Stamford Lodge, Altrincham Rd., pg. 981 — IT

General Surety & Guarantee Ltd., Hawthorne Hall, Hall Road, pg. 1531 — IT

GRAYSTONE PLC, Emerson Court, pg. 557 — IT

Zeneca Pharma, King's Court, Water Lane, pg. 1524 — IT

Wimborne Minster

COBHAM PLC, Brook Road, pg. 301 — IT

Meggitt Holdings plc., Six Poole Rd., pg. 124 — IT

MEGGITT PLC, Farrs House, pg. 853 — IT

Rollalong Limited, Woolsbridge Industrial Estate, Old Barn Farm Road, pg. 593 — IT

Winchester

Ballast Wiltshier Plc - South West Region, Winnall Close, pg. 135 — IT

Denplan Limited, Denplan Court, Victoria Road, pg. 1020 — IT

Dickinson Control Systems, Ltd., Winnal Trading Estate, Unit E., Moorside Rd., pg. 231 — IT

W.H. Dickinson Engineering Ltd., Winnal Indus. Estate, Moorside Rd., pg. 231 — IT

FLS Aerospace Ltd., Worthy Park House, Abbots Worthy, pg. 475 — IT

Hall Aggregates (South Coast) Limited, 46 Jewry St., pg. 1079 — IT

IBM United Kingdom Laboratories Limited, Hursley Pk., Hursley, pg. 897 — PB

Windlesham

THE BOC GROUP PLC, Chertsey Road, pg. 121 — IT

Lilly Research Centre Limited, Erl Wood Manor, pg. 994 — PB

Windsor

Airstream Finance Limited, Sceptre Gate, pg. 420 — IT

Black Horse Relocation Services Limited, 59-60 Thames St., pg. 813 — IT

British & Soviet International Carbon Limited, Morgan House, Madiera Walk, pg. 894 — IT

British Bakeries Limited, RHM Ctr., 2730 King Edward Ct., pg. 1396 — IT

Commercial Systems Limited, 3-7 William Street, pg. 1184 — IT

Excalibur Technologies International, Ltd., The Courtyard, New Lodge, pg. 598 — PB

Graseby Goring Kerr Ltd., Vale Rd., pg. 1267 — IT

HFC Bank Plc, North St., Winkfield, pg. 842 — PB

ITW Limited, St. Marks House, St. Marks Road, pg. 868 — PB

Keeler Limited, Clewer Hill Road, pg. 589 — IT

Leverton Group Ltd., pg. 1434 — IT

Lotus Development (U.K.) Limited, Consort House, Victoria St., pg. 896 — PB

Manor Bakeries Limited, King Edward House, 27/30 Kind Edward Ct., pg. 1396 — IT

MORGAN CRUCIBLE CO. PLC, Morgan House, Madiera Walk, pg. 890 — IT

Morgan Trans Limited, Morgan House, Madiera Walk, pg. 894 — IT

Morganite International Limited, Morgan House, Madiera Walk, pg. 894 — IT

PHARMACIA & UPJOHN, INC., 67 Anma Rd., pg. 1047 — IT

RHM Foods Limited, Chapel House, 69 Alma Rd., pg. 1396 — IT

Saab Aircraft International Ltd., Leworth House, pg. 687 — IT

SIEBE PLC, Saxon House, pg. 1240 — IT

Skil (Great Britain) Ltd., Fairacres Indus. Estate, Deadworth Rd., pg. 577 — PB

Smurfit Investments U.K. Limited, Mercer House, Thames Side, pg. 1271 — IT

Sorin Biomedica Ltd., 42 Thames St., pg. 483 — IT

Sun Healthcare Group International Ltd., Exceler Healthcare, Exceler House, SL4 6AF, pg. 1531 — PB

Vorwerk (U.K.) Ltd., pg. 1481 — IT

Woodward-Clyde International, Woodside House, Woodside Rd., Winkfield, pg. 1658 — PB

Winsford

Colin Stewart Minchem Limited, Weaver Valley Road, pg. 858 — IT

FIAT OM, pg. 811 — IT

VG Elemental Ltd., Road Three, pg. 1110 — IT

VG Microtrace Ltd., Road Three, pg. 1111 — IT

Winslow

Kronos (UK) Ltd., pg. 271 — PV

Wirral

Cabot International Services Corp., Lodge Lane, Port Sunlight, pg. 289 — PB

Costain Oil, Gas & Process Limited Pipeline & Offshore Division, Port Causeway, Bromborough, pg. 336 — IT

Lubrizol Limited, Dock Road South, pg. 1016 — PB

E.R. Squibb & Sons Ltd., Reeds Lane, Moreton, pg. 256 — PB

Thermal Ceramics Limited, Tebay Rd., pg. 893 — PB

Westminster Contractors Ltd., Dockyard Road, Off Oil Sites Road, pg. 135 — IT

Wisbech

Oil-Dri (U.K.) Ltd., Bannister Row, pg. 1215 — PB

Wishaw

Svedala Ltd. Plant, pg. 1325 — IT

Witham

Hugh Baird & Sons Limited, Witham Plant, Station Maltings, pg. 428 — PB

Beazer Homes (Colchester) Limited, The Grange, 10 Collingwood Rd., pg. 182 — IT

Beazer Homes (Colchester) Limited, New Collingwood House, Collingwood Road, pg. 182 — IT

Crompton Instruments Ltd., Freebournes Rd., pg. 125 — IT

Fisons Consumer Health Plc, pg. 1110 — IT

INSPECTORATE PLC, Two Perry Rd., pg. 679 — IT

Smith Flow Control Limited, Six Waterside Business Park, Eastways Industrial Estate, pg. 590 — IT

Smurfit Cartons (Witham) Ltd., Freebournes Road, pg. 1271 — IT

Witney

Buckhorn Ltd., Witney Trading Estate, Sta. Lane, pg. 1143 — PB

OXFORD INSTRUMENTS PLC, Old Station Way, pg. 1018 — IT

Oxford Magnet Technology Limited, Wharf Road, pg. 1018 — IT

Sifan Systems Limited, Windrush Industrial Estate, Northwood Rd., pg. 1267 — IT

Smiths Industries Hydraulics Company Limited, Windrush Industrial Park, Windrush Park Rd., pg. 1267 — IT

Steelweld U.K., Lea View House, Two Rivers Estate, pg. 71 — IT

Witton

IMI PLC, P.O. Box 216, pg. 646 — IT

Xpelair Ltd., Deykin Ave., pg. 545 — IT

Woking

ACI Europe Ltd., White Rose Court, Oriental Road, pg. 129 — IT

B.A.T (UK & Export) Ltd., Export House, pg. 111 — IT

Bell Atlantic Financial (U.K.) Limited, Dukes Court, Dukes St., pg. 204 — PB

Canon Audio Ltd., Unit 6, Genesis, Business Park, Albert Dr., pg. 262 — IT

Costain International Limited, Costain House, West St., pg. 336 — IT

Costain Mining Limited, Chobham House, Christchurch Way, pg. 336 — IT

Crown Financial Management Limited, Dukes Court, Duke St., pg. 468 — IT

Galleon Ltd., Fulham House, Goldworth Rd., pg. 114 — IT

Hall & Co. Limited, Southern Region, Vale Farm Rd., pg. 1079 — IT

Hoesch Limited, Cavendish House 36-40, Goldworth Rd., pg. 515 — IT

Hogan Systems Europe, Hogan Business Centre, Church St. W., pg. 422 — PB

Ideal Homes Holdings Plc, Goldsworth House, The Goldsworth Park Centre, pg. 773 — IT

LTX (Europe) Limited, Woking Business Park, Albert Drive, pg. 972 — PB

Leasing Solutions International, Ltd., Continental House, West End, pg. 983 — PB

Mannesmann Supplies & Services Limited, pg. 838 — IT

Mannex (London) Ltd., pg. 838 — IT

Phillips Petroleum Co. Europe-Africa, Phillips Quadrant, 35 Guildford Rd., pg. 1291 — PB

Storage Technology Limited, StorageTek House, Woking Business Park, pg. 1523 — PB

TCI/US West, Unit One, Genesis Business Park, pg. 1555 — PB

The Victoria Wine Company Limited, Brook House, Chertsey Rd., pg. 63 — IT

JAMES WALKER & CO. LIMITED, Lion House, Oriental Road, pg. 1485 — IT

Wokingham

Addison-Wesley Publishers Ltd., Finchampstead Rd., pg. 1027 — IT

Bailey Telecom LTD - Wokingham, Unit 16, The Metro Centre, Toutley Road, pg. 133 — IT

Bang & Olufsen United Kingdom Ltd., Unit 630, Winnersh Triangle, Wharfdale Rd., pg. 146 — IT

BioWhittaker UK Ltd., BioWhittaker House, 1 Ashville Way, pg. 297 — PB

Cerberus Ltd., Trinity Court, pg. 1246 — IT

Citizen Watch (U.K.) Ltd., Quoin House, Fishponds Road, pg. 294 — IT

Comtest Limited, Unit 4, Weller Drive, Hogwood Industrial Estate, pg. 1596 — PB

Data Translation Ltd., The Mulberry Business Ctr., pg. 1079 — PB

Data Translation Networking Limited, pg. 1079 — PB

PB - U.S. Public Companies Volume
PV - U.S. Private Companies Volume
IT - International Public & Private Companies Volume

1835

Geographic Index-Non U.S.

EG & G Fiber Optics, Sorbus House, Mulberry Business Park, pg. 544 — PB
First Brands (Europe) Ltd., 5 Metro Centre, Toutley Rd., pg. 627 — PB
Fisher-Price House, Oaklands Park, Fishponds Rd., pg. 1058 — PB
General DataComm Limited, Molly Millars Lane, pg. 708 — PB
Harris Systems Ltd., Eskdale Rd., Winnersh, pg. 791 — PB
Hewlett-Packard Ltd., Eskdale Rd., pg. 821 — PB
Hewlett-Packard Ltd., Customer Information Centre, King St. Ln., pg. 821 — PB
Hewlett-Packard Ltd., Nine Mile Ride, pg. 821 — PB
Inamed Ltd., Unit 4 Forest Court, pg. 874 — PB
Intercare Products Ltd., 7, The Business Centre, Molly Miller Lane, pg. 983 — IT
KLA Instruments Ltd., 4 The Business Center, Molly Millars Lane, pg. 939 — PB
Lee Spring Co., Ltd., pg. 1118 — PV
Mannesmann Tally Ltd., pg. 840 — IT
Memorex Telex (U.K.) Ltd., Eskdale Road, pg. 858 — IT
Mizuno (UK) Ltd., Mizuno House, 612 Reading Rd., pg. 885 — IT
J.R. Phillips & Co., Ltd., Mulberry House, pg. 1499 — IT
Symbol Technologies Limited, Fishponds Road, pg. 1546 — PB
Vorwerk Carpets Limited, pg. 1481 — IT

Wolverhampton

Anglo-Swiss Aluminium Company Ltd., pg. 68 — IT
British Steel Seamless Tubes-Wednesfield Works, Waddens Brook Ln., Wednesfield, pg. 220 — IT
CCL Pharmaceuticals, Pond Lane, pg. 239 — IT
Clydesdale Walton Co., Tettenhall, pg. 265 — IT
Dowty Aerospace, Wolverhampton, Wobaston Rd., pg. 1337 — IT
FAG (UK) Limited, Heath Mill Rd., pg. 469 — IT
Ferro (Great Britain) Limited, Ounsdale Road, pg. 619 — PB
Fortress Interlocks Limited, 148-150 Birmingham New Rd., pg. 589 — IT
GKN Technology Ltd., Birmingham New Rd., pg. 535 — IT
James Gibbons Format Limited, Colliery Road, pg. 1344 — IT
Graco UK Limited, 34 Wednesfield Rd., pg. 757 — PB
Marston Ring Div., pg. 425 — PV
Ovako Steel Ltd., Neachells Lane, pg. 1157 — IT
Plasmar Ltd., Neachells Lane, pg. 1202 — IT
Royal Ordnance Specialty Metals Ltd., P.O. Box 27, pg. 217 — IT
Schenectady Europe, Ltd., Four Ashes, pg. 970 — PV
Sinclair Collis Limited, Lower Walsall St., pg. 593 — IT
Spicer Europe, Stafford Rd., pg. 480 — IT
Tarmac Construction Limited, Construction House, Birch St., pg. 1355 — IT
Tarmac Homes Midlands Ltd., 4th Flr., Norwich Union House, Waterloo Rd., pg. 1355 — IT
TARMAC PLC, Hilton Hall, Hilton La., Essington, pg. 1355 — IT
Tarmac Quarry Products Ltd., P.O. Box 8, Millfields Rd., pg. 1355 — IT
Tarmac Topmix Limited, Millfields Rd., pg. 1355 — IT
Thatcher Alloys Ltd., Unit 49, Wombourne Enterprise Park, pg. 1017 — IT
Yale Europe Materials Handling Corporation Ltd., Waddens Brook Lane, pg. 1150 — PB
Yale Security Products, Ltd., Wood St., pg. 1499 — IT

Woodbridge

Girdlestone Pumps Limited, pg. 967 — IT

Woodford

British Aerospace Regional Aircraft, Avro Intl. Aerospace Div., Woodford Aerodrome, Chester Rd., pg. 218 — IT

Woodgate Valley

Hall & Kay Fire, Sterling Park, Chapgate Lane, pg. 1298 — IT

Woodley

ADC Telecommunications U.K. Limited, 126/128 Crockhamwell Road, pg. 4 — PB

Wootton Bassett

Plantronics A.G., c/o Plantronics Limited, Interface Business Park, pg. 1308 —
Plantronics Ltd., Interface Business Park, Bincknoll Lane, pg. 1308 — PB

Worcester

Babcock FATA Ltd., Gregory's Bank, pg. 472 — IT
British Alcan Building Products Ltd., Blackpole Trading Estate, pg. 51 — IT
Cosworth Castings Ltd., Hylton Rd., pg. 1467 — IT
Cosworth Castings Ltd., Warndon, Buckholt Dr., pg. 1467 — IT
Froude Consine, Blackpole Industrial Estate, Blackpole Road, pg. 472 — IT
Longwall International Limited, Brumyard Rd., pg. 789 — PB
Metal Box plc., Food Packaging, Woodside, Perrywood Walk, pg. 267 — IT
MISYS PLC, Burleigh House, Chapel Oak, pg. 870 — IT

OCG Microelectronic Materials Limited, Site 7, Kidderminster Rd., pg. 1220 — PB

Workington

British Steel Engineering, pg. 220 — IT
Cumbrian Storage Ltd., Prince of Wales Dock, pg. 1251 — IT
Ectona Fibres Limited, P.O. Box 20, pg. 552 — PB
Fischer & Porter Ltd., Salterbeck Trading Estate, pg. 449 — IT
Iggesund Paperboard (Workington) Ltd., pg. 886 — IT
Pentagon Chemicals limited, Northside, pg. 88 — IT

Worksop

Cinch Connectors Ltd., Shireoaks Rd., pg. 786 — IT
Labauto Ltd., Shireoaks Rd., pg. 785 — IT
Redland Distribution Limited, Shireoaks, pg. 1090 — IT
Rockware Glass Ltd.-Worksop Factory, Sandy Ln., pg. 124 — IT

Worthing

Eurotherm Controls Ltd., Faraday Close, pg. 466 — IT
Eurotherm Process Automation Ltd., Broadwater Trading Estate, Southdownview Way, pg. 466 — IT
Eurotherm Recorders Ltd., Dominion Way, pg. 466 — IT
Griffin Credit Services, 21 Farncombe Road, pg. 579 — IT
Lemo U.K., 12 North Street, pg. 806 — IT
London & Edinburgh Insurance Group Limited, The Warren, Warren Rd., pg. 795 — PB
The Marylebone Optical Co. Ltd., 35 Brougham Rd., pg. 414 — IT

Wotton-under-Edge

RENISHAW PLC, New Mills, pg. 1103 — IT
Renishaw plc, Old Town, pg. 1103 — IT
Wotton Travel Limited, 4 High St., pg. 1103 — IT

Wrexham

Brother Industries (U.K.) Ltd.-Ruabon Factory, Vauxhall Industrial Estate, pg. 229 — IT
Caparo Wire Company Ltd., P.O. Box 87, pg. 265 — IT
GKK Plastics Ltd., Vauxhall Industrial Estate, Ruabon, pg. 230 — IT
ICW Limited, Llay Industrial Estate, Miners Road, pg. 1563 — IT
Morgan Matroc Limited Unilator Division, Vauxhall Industrial Estate, pg. 893 — IT
Owens-Corning Fiberglas (G.B.) Ltd., Bryn Lane, pg. 1237 — PB
Portec (U.K.) Ltd., Vauxhall Industrial Estate, pg. 1318 — PB
ROR Rockwell Limited, Rackery Lane, Llay, pg. 1399 — IT
Rexam Custom, Wrexham Industrial Estate, pg. 1107 — IT
Sharp Manufacturing Company of U.K., Sharp House, pg. 1230 — IT
Sharp Precision Manufacturing (U.K.) Ltd., Forward House, Davy Way, pg. 1230 — IT

Wymondham

Lemken Tri-AG Limited, Howard, pg. 1387 — IT
Vishay Components U.K. Ltd., pg. 1722 — PB
Wymondham Oil Storage Company Limited, Stansfield Rd., pg. 693 — PB

Yarmouth

Wilson Supply International (U.K.) Ltd., Great Yarmouth Marine Base, pg. 1181 — PV

Yeovil

Alfa-Laval Cheddar Systems Ltd., 10, Oxford Rd., pg. 1380 — IT
GKN Westland Helicopters Limited, pg. 535 — IT
GKN Westland Technologies Limited, pg. 535 — IT
Moore Products Co. (U.K.) Ltd., Copse Rd., Lufton Indus. Estate, pg. 1129 — PB
Normalair-Garrett Ltd., Westland Rd., pg. 54 — PB
Westland System Assessment Limited, 91 Preston Road, pg. 535 — IT

York

Armstrong Patents Co., Ltd., Manor Lane, Shipton Road, pg. 265 — IT
Barratt York, Richmond House, Millfield Ln., pg. 168 — IT
R.R. Donnelley, Limited-York, Boroughbridge Rd., pg. 519 — PB
Eden Vale Food Ingredients, Station Lane, pg. 968 — IT
Hagglunds Drives Ltd, Foxbridge Way, pg. 670 — IT
MPC Stamford Bridge, Stamford Bridge, pg. 851 — IT
MVC Pickering, Westgate Carr Rd., pg. 851 — IT
Nanoquest Defence Products Limited, Green Park Business Centre, pg. 268 — IT
Nestle Lyons Maid, pg. 918 — IT
Nestle-Rowntree Ltd., pg. 921 — IT
Smith & Nephew Research Ltd., York Science Park, pg. 1263 — IT
Superbreak Mini Holidays Group Ltd., 5th Floor, Ryedale Building, pg. 465 — IT

URUGUAY

Montevideo

AGA S.A., P.O. Box 1915, pg. 13 — IT
Abiatar S.A., Av. Dr. Francisco Soca 1444, pg. 208 — PB
Agroindustrias La Sierra S.A., pg. 448 — PB
Alcan Aluminio del Uruguay S.A., Casilla de Correo 789, pg. 50 — IT
Amway Uruguay, San Jose 954, pg. 70 — PV
Apoint S.A., Avda. Gral. Flores 2422, pg. 333 — IT
BASF Uruguaya S.A., Camino Ariel 4620, pg. 107 — IT
BNL de Uruguay, 25 de Mayo 575, pg. 136 — IT
BNP (Uruguay) SA, Edificio Presidente, Rincon 477, Piso 9, pg. 164 — IT
Banco de Montevideo, Rincon esq. Misiones 1399, pg. 403 — IT
Banco do Brasil S.A.-Uruguay, Calle 25 de Mayo, pg. 141 — IT
Banco Exterior, S.A., Rincon 493, pg. 81 — IT
Banco Santander Uruguay S.A., Cerrito 449, pg. 143 — IT
Banco Surinvest S.A., Rincon 530, pg. 1082 — IT
Bank of Boston, Zabala 1463, pg. 184 — PB
Banque Europeenne pour l'Amerique Latine (BEAL) S.A., Rincon 477 p. 7, pg. 1493 — IT
Banque Paribas-Uruguay, Rbla 25 de Agosto 318, pg. 320 — IT
Becton Dickinson Uruguay, Urolban SA Montevideo, AV 18 De Julio 984P4, pg. 200 — PB
Briole S.A., Sante Fe 1191, pg. 1462 — IT
Bull del Uruguay S.A., Av. Dr. Luis A de Herrerra 2802, pg. 315 — IT
Bull del Uruguay S.A., Av. Dir. Luis A. de Herrera, pg. 318 — IT
Cia Ericsson Uruguay S.A., Plaza Cagancha 1335, Piso 11 - Esc. 1102, pg. 1368 — IT
CIBA-GEIGY Services SA-Orctc Sucursal Montevideo, Casilla de Correo 12230, pg. 980 — IT
CIBA-GEIGY Uruguaya S.A., Casilla de Correo 605, pg. 980 — IT
Colgate-Palmolive, Inc., Camino Colman 5360, pg. 398 — PB
Compania Dowson, 25 de Mayo 455 4to Piso, pg. 179 — PB
Compania Ericsson S.A., Mercedes 1787, pg. 1365 — IT
Conatel, S.A., Ejido 1690, pg. 817 — PB
Coutts & Co (Uruguay) s.a., Calle Gabriel Otero 6462, pg. 911 — IT
Daewoo Corp. - Montevideo, Juncal 1305, Apt. 1102, pg. 358 — IT
Embotelladora del Uruguay, S.A., Martin Fierro 2579, pg. 1277 — PB
Ericsson Suc. Uruguay, 21 Septiembre 2980, pg. 1367 — IT
EURO RSCG Norton, Avda. Echevarriarza 3380, pg. 603 — IT
Hapoalim (Latin America) S.A., Florida 1251 Esquina, Soriano, pg. 150 — IT
IMSA S.A., Ave. Libertador 1670, 2nd Fl., pg. 447 — PB
Johnson & Johnson de Uruguay, S.A., Casilla de Correo 273, Camino Carasca 5436, pg. 930 — PB
Kodak Uruguay, Ltd., Yi 1532, pg. 555 — PB
Laboratorios Americanos S.A., General Aguilar 1331, pg. 81 — PB
Leumi Le-Israel (Latin America), 25 de Mayo 549, pg. 150 — IT
MADD Agency, Jose Ellauri 724, pg. 1200 — PV
MAPFRE Soft America, S.A., 18 de julio, 841, pg. 335 — IT
Microcosmos, S.A., Cuareim 2052, pg. 570 — PV
NRG Latin America S.A., Cerrito 534, Piso 1, pg. 1116 — IT
NRG South America S.A., Cerrito 534, Piso 1, pg. 1116 — IT
Nestle Del Uruguay S.A., Carlos Crocker 2883, pg. 921 — IT
Nucleo Publicidad, Jose Enrique Rodo 1668, pg. 186 — PV
Owens-Corning Fiberglas S.A., Costa Rica Street, No 1685, Suite 2, pg. 1237 — PB
Pablo Ferrando S.A.C.e.I., Avenida Italia 2877, pg. 822 — PB
RNBNY Representative Office-Montevideo, 25 de Mayo 467/102, pg. 1381 — PB
RAI Corporation Uruguay, Galeria Diri, Ave. 18 de Julio, pg. 655 — IT
Republic National Bank of New York (Uruguay) S.A., 25 de Mayo 471, pg. 1381 — PB
Roche International Ltd., pg. 1121 — IT
SBC Ltda., Edificio Regidor, Rincon 602-P 6, pg. 1330 — IT
SGS (Uruguay) Limitada, Edificio Premier, 468 Calle Rincon, 1 Piso, pg. 1154 — IT
SKF Uruguay S.A., Cerro Largo 1066, pg. 1159 — IT
Sandoz Quimica y Farmaceutica S.A., pg. 985 — IT
Sapac Corp., Ltd., pg. 1122 — IT
Shell Uruguay Ltd, San Fructuoso 927, pg. 1142 — IT
Suarez & Clavera/DMB&B, Saito 1210 C.P. 11,200, pg. 305 — PV
SUDAMTEX DE URUGUAY, S.A., Edificio Artigas, Rincon 487, pg. 1304 — IT
Supermar Uruguay Limitada, Santa Fe 1123, pg. 1154 — IT
Texaco Uruguay Sociedad Anonima, 18 De Julio 985 Piso 4, pg. 1584 — PB
3M Uruguay, Casilla de Correo 239, pg. 1607 — PB
Topps Latin America S.A., Plaza Independencia 811 P.B., pg. 1622 — PB
Turbomeca Sud Americana, Rincon 487 Edificio Artigas, pg. 787 — IT
Van Leer Uruguay, pg. 1147 — IT
Viceversa/Young & Rubicam, Rio Branco 1494, pg. 1200 — PV
Volt-Autologic Directories S.A., Cebollati 1470, Piso No. 2, pg. 1724 — PB
Zeneca Uruguay, Bulevar Artigas 2029, pg. 1527 — IT

PB - *U.S. Public Companies Volume*
PV - *U.S. Private Companies Volume*
IT - *International Public & Private Companies Volume*

Geographic Index-Non U.S.

Punta del Este

Hapoalim (Latin America) S.A., Calle 28 y Golero, pg. 150   IT
Leumi Le-Israel (Latin America), Ave. Gorlero, Calle 28, Edeflcio Torre de las Americas Local 006, pg. 150   IT
RNBNY Representative Office-Uruguay, Avenida Gorlero y Calle 28, pg. 1381   PB
Republic National Bank of New York (Uruguay) S.A., Avenida Gorlero y Calle 28, pg. 1381   PB
SBC Ltda., Calle 27 y Gorlero, pg. 1330   IT

UZBEKISTAN

Kasan

CIBA-GEIGY Limited-Representative Office, ul. Krasnoselskaja 51a, pg. 978   IT

Tashkent

CCF Uzbekistan, 21 rue Akhunbabaev, Bureau 105, pg. 342   IT
CIBA-GEIGY Limited-Representative Office, GSP-4, 700000, ul. Amir Timura 62, pg. 977   IT
CIBA-GEIGY Limited-Representative Office, Unus Abad District, 700000, pg. 977   IT
CIBA-GEIGY Limited-Representative Office, Tschilansar 2, 26, kw. 17, pg. 977   IT
CIBA-GEIGY Limited-Representative Office, Furkat ul. 1, pg. 977   IT
CIBA-GEIGY Services AG, Ciba-Geigy Limited, GSP-4, 700000, ul. Amira Timura 62, pg. 979   IT
Novo Nordisk A/S, 62/35 Navruz Street, pg. 987   IT
Ram Representative Office-Uzbekistan, Maveraunahr (Former Proleterskaya), pg. 742   IT
The Sakura Bank - Tashkent Representative Office, 3rd Floor, Internatinal Banking & Finance Ctr., pg. 1180   IT
Tashkochauto, 47 Oibek Str., pg. 742   IT
Vertretung der BASF in der Republik Uzbekistan, Beethoven Strasse 3, pg. 109   IT
The World Bank, 43, Academician Suleimanova St., pg. 1190   PV

VANUATU

Port Vila

ANZ Bank (Vanuatu) Limited, ANZ House, Kumul Highway, pg. 98   IT
BHP Steel Building Products Vanuatu, Behind Bon Marche, Number 2, pg. 227   IT
Banque d'Hawaii (Vanuatu) Limited, pg. 1248   PB
Westpac Banking Corp. - Vanuatu, Kumul Hwy., pg. 1497   IT

VENEZUELA

Altimira

Construcciones Pitt-Des Moines Venezuela, C.A., Avenida San Juan Bosco, Entre 5ta., Transversal, pg. 1304   PB

Anaco

Helmerich & Payne de Venezuela C.A., Apartado 16, pg. 808   PB
Otis Engineering International, C.A., Apartado 53, pg. 777   PB
Santa Fe Drilling Co. of Venezuela, C.A., Apartado 34, Carretera Negra Kilometro 9, pg. 765   PB

Anzoategui

Petrolite Suramericana, S.A., Zona Industrial Los Montones, 3ra. Etapa, pg. 166   PB

Barinas

Drillers Inc., DI de Venezuela, Urbanizacion Franciso-Miranda, Final Calle Apure #15-61, pg. 765   PB

Barquisimeto

Caramelos Royal C.A., pg. 919   IT
Hewlett-Packard de Venezuela, C.A., Carrera 19 con Calle 33, Torre La Previsora, pg. 819   PB
John Crane Venezuela, Zona Industrial 2, Carrera 5, pg. 1340   IT

Cagua

Cealco C.A., Ave. Grand Mariscal de Ayacucho, pg. 606   PB
Productos Stahl Polyvinyl CA, Zona Industrial, Valle Abajo, pg. 1525   IT

Caracas

ADC Telecomunicaciones Venezuela, S.A., Edificio Meme Grande-Piso 4, Av. Francisco De Miranda, pg. 4   PB
AFIA Venezuela, C.A., Edificio Centro Seguras La Paz, Piso 7, pg. 363   PB
AGA Gas C.A., pg. 13   IT

AGA Venezolana C.A., Apartado 62351, pg. 14   IT
AJL Park, Torre Multinvest, Piso 4, Plaza La Castellana, Chacao, pg. 389   PV
ARS/DMB&B, Edificio ARS, Diego Cisneros, 1071, pg. 303   PV
ATA S.A., Edificio Teatro Altamira, PH2 Oeste Altamira Sur, pg. 53   IT
Abbott Laboratories C.A., 2da Av. Edificio Plumrose, pg. 13   PB
Acer de Venezuela, pg. 22   IT
Administradora Plumrose C.A., pg. 431   IT
Adriatica de Seguros C.A., Avenida Andres Bello, Ed. Adriatica, pg. 61   IT
Aguador S.A., pg. 721   IT
Alfa-Laval Venezolana S.A., P.O. Box 47723, pg. 1380   IT
Alimentos Heinz C.A., Edif. Torre Uno, Penthouse, Calle Orinoco, Las Mercedes, pg. 806   PB
Alimentos Kellogg S.A., Apartado 168 Maracay, Edo Aragua, pg. 947   PB
Aliven S.A., Edificio Centro Altamira, Av. San Juan Bosco, Pisos 12 y 13, pg. 447   PB
Alpine Technologies de Venezuela, C.A., Apartado Postal 70796, pg. 360   PV
Anseven, Centro Cristobal, pg. 654   IT
Ascensores Schindler de Venezuela S.A., pg. 1205   IT
Asea Brown Boveri S.A., pg. 8   IT
The Associated Press de Venezuela, S.A., Apartado A de Correo, pg. 92   PV
Atkinson International Venezuela, Avenida Luis Roche, Quinta Santa Elena, pg. 1045   IT
Autodesk Venezuela, Centro Cristopal, Piso 7, Av Principal de Bello Monte, pg. 150   IT
Avon Cosmetics de Venezuela, C.A., Apartado 60404, pg. 156   PB
BASF Venezolana, S.A., Multicentro Macaracuay, Piso 10, Av. Principal de Macaracuay, pg. 107   IT
BK Investments, Edificio Polar, Mezzanina 2, Plaza Venezuela, pg. 179   IT
Banco do Brasil S.A.-Venezuela, Av. Francisco de Miranda-Ed. Centro Lipo, pg. 142   IT
Banco Mundial, Torre Oeste, Piso 15, Edificio Parque Cristal, Oficina 15-05, pg. 1189   PV
BANCO PROVINCIAL S.A. BANCO UNIVERSAL, Centro Financiero Provincial, pg. 142   IT
Banco Santander, Avda. Urdaneta, Esq. Animas y Pl. Espana, pg. 144   IT
Bank Hapoalim (Caracas), Edificio Parque Cristal, Torre Oeste, Piso 5, Oficina 4, pg. 149   IT
Bank of America NT&SA, Edificio Torre Cavendes, Piso 2, Avenida Francisco de Miranda, pg. 182   PB
The Bank of New York, Edificio Polar, Mezzanina 2, Plaza Venezuela, pg. 179   PB
Bankers Trust New York Corporation, Apartado 61028, Torre Fundo Comun, Penthouse B, pg. 186   PB
Banque Paribas-Venezuela, Edificio Cavendes, Avenid Francisco de Miranda, pg. 321   IT
Bariven, S.A., Av. Francisco de Miranda, Cruce con Calle San Ignacio de Loyola, pg. 1045   IT
Bayer Quimicas Unidas S.A., Av. Fco. De Miranda, pg. 175   IT
Bayerische Vereinsbank AG, Calle Beethoven, Colinas de Bello Monte, pg. 180   IT
BEAL - Caracas, Edifico Delta P.H.-A, Av. Francisco de Miranda, pg. 1493   IT
Bienes y Servicios Biserca, Centro de Arte La Estancia, Avda. Santa Ana, pg. 1045   IT
Bitumenes Orinoco, S.A. (BITOR), Edificio Bitumenes Orinoco, Calle Cali, pg. 1045   IT
Black & Decker Holdings de Venezuela, C.A., Apartado No. 61860, pg. 234   PB
Borg & Beck de Venezuela SA, pg. 835   IT
Borsig de Venezuela C.A., Edificio Torre Phelps, Piso 15, pg. 399   IT
Braun Transworld Corp., Edificio Torreon, Piso 6, pg. 765   PB
Bristol-Myers de Venezuela, S.A., pg. 255   PB
Leo Burnett Venezuela, C.A., Centro Plaza, Torre B, Niveles 7,8,9,10, pg. 186   IT
C.A. Vencemos Pertigalete, Edifico Las Fundaciones, Piso 16, pg. 791   PB
CGA-HBS, Multicentro Empresarial del, Este, Avenida Libertador Torre Miranda, pg. 53   IT
CIED Centro Internacional de Educacion y Desarrollo, El Hatillo, con calle El Angel de la Tahona, pg. 1045   IT
Canyon Venezuela CA, Edif. El Cigarral-Piso 9-A, Ave. Principal Colinas de Bello Monte, pg. 302   PB
Cementos Caribe C.A., Tamanaco, Torre A, Piso 2, pg. 629   PB
Cemex, S.A. de C.V. - Caracas, Edificio las Fundaciones, Av. Andres Bello, pg. 278   IT
Centro de Idiomas Berlitz de Venezuela, Av. Fca De Miranda, Piso 1, Torre Oeste, pg. 222   PB
Chesebrough-Pond's C.A., Calle Bernadette Los Ruices Edf Pons, pg. 1436   IT
Chicle Adams S.A., P.O. Box 647, pg. 1739   PB
Chocolates Nestle S.A., pg. 920   IT
Cigna de Venezuela Intermediarios de Reaseguras, S.A., Torre Banco de Lara-Piso 11-OFF.11D, pg. 364   IT
Circle Freight Venezuela S.A., Edificio Centro Parima, Piso 8, OFC 804, pg. 373   PB
Club Med S.R.L., Avenida DCO Miranda Esc., pg. 298   IT
Colgate-Palmolive Co. Anonima, Avenida Diego Cisneros, Antes Ave. Principal Los Ruices, pg. 398   PB
Commerzbank AG-Caracas Representative Office, Centro Cremerca, piso 2, pg. 311   IT
Compania Anonima de Seguros "Avila", Edificio Seguros Avila, Apartado 1 007, 1010, pg. 364   PB
Compania Anonima Ericsson, Av. Francisco de Miranda, Torre Banco de la Construccion, Piso 8, pg. 1365   IT
Compania Anonima Tocars, Edificio Cars, Avenida Los Ilustres, pg. 1413   IT

Compania Giva S.A., pg. 744   PB
Componentes Delfa, C.A., Quinta Mariana, Avenida Orinoco, pg. 724   PB
Computerworld Venezuela, Edificio Mary Stella Post Box, Av. Carabobo c/c. Boyaca, pg. 569   PV
Comtrade International C.A., Torre Oxal, Piso 1, Oficina A, Avda. Venezuela, El Rosal, pg. 303   IT
Constructora Venezolano de Vehiculos, C.A., pg. 723   PB
CORPORACION GRUPO QUIMICO, S.A.C.A., Av. Francisco De Miranda, Edificio Parque Cristal, Torre Oeste, pg. 331   IT
Corporation MS 90 de Venezuela S.A., pg. 1108   PB
Corpoven, S.A., Avenida Libertador, Sector la Campina, pg. 1045   IT
Covigal SA, pg. 981   IT
Cyanamid de Venezuela CA, Centro Cyanamid, Calle 1-2 Manzana C3, pg. 80   PB
DG Venezuela C.A., 134-A Av. Libertador-Chacao, pg. 485   IT
Daewoo International - Caracas, pg. 358   IT
Dai-Ichi Kangyo Bank, Ltd.-Caracas, Centro Financiero Latino, Piso 25, Avenida Urdaneta, pg. 361   IT
Daisy de Venezuela C.A., pg. 686   IT
C.A. Danzas Venezolana, Avenida Casanova, Edificio Cediaz, pg. 383   IT
Dateline, C.A., Sabana Grande, Avenida Francisco Solano, pg. 817   PB
Deltaven S.A., Av. Francisco de Miranda, Centro Lido, pg. 1045   IT
Det Norske Veritas, C.C.C. Tamanaco, Oficina C-709, pg. 397   IT
Digital Equipment de Venezuela, Torre ING Bank, Centro Letonia, pg. 508   IT
Digital Microwave de Venezuela, C.A., pg. 508   PB
Distribuidora de Productos Sandoz S.A., pg. 982   IT
Dit Harris S.A., Edificio Torre Cari, 2da Avenida de la Urbanizacion, pg. 1361   IT
Dow Jones Markets de Venezuela, C.A., Boulevard Plaza, Penthouse #3, Esquina Jesuitas, pg. 525   PB
Dow Chemical CA, 1 Ra. Transv. Edf., pg. 524   PB
Du Pont de Venezuela C.A., Apartado 61.582, Edificio Los Faraes, pg. 532   IT
Dunkin' Donuts Venezuela, pg. 63   IT
C.A. Electrolux, Apartado 1.561, pg. 444   IT
Eniac C.A., Plaza Venezuela, Edif. Polar, PISO 5, pg. 1043   PB
Envases Internacional S.A., Apartado 5849, Carmelitas 101, pg. 906   IT
Equipos Percom, C.A., Sabana Grande, Sector Las Delicias,Avenida Los Mangos, pg. 817   PB
Especialidades Alimenticias S.A., pg. 920   PB
Etoxyl, C.A., Calle La Gruta, Edificio Corimon, pg. 1219   IT
EURO RSCG-Venezuela, Av. Diego Cisneros, Centro Colgate, pg. 603   IT
Fabrica Nacional de Cementos, Centro Letonia, Torre ING Bank, Piso 6 Ave. Principal la Castellana, pg. 791   PB
First RepublicBank Dallas, N.A. Representative Office, Torre America Pisco 7, No. 704, Avenida Venezueala Urb, Bello Monte, pg. 1165   PB
Fondo Educativo Interamericano FEI C.A., pg. 1027   IT
Foster Wheeler Caribe Corporation, C.A., Torre Forum, Piso 4, Ave. Principal de las Mercedes, pg. 677   PB
Foto Interamericana de Venezuela S.A., Apartado Postal 80658 Ave. La Guairit, pg. 552   PB
GO International de Venezuela, S.A., Centro Integral Santa Rosa, PH Officiana 506, Av. Principal, pg. 776   PB
General Motors de Venezuela C.A., Apartado 666, pg. 722   PB
General Motors Venezolana C.A., Centro Ciudad Comercial Tamanaco, pg. 723   PB
Gerber de Venezuela, Calle Hans Neuman, EDF Coriman, pg. 973   IT
Gestetner SA, Calle 9, Edificio Gestetner, pg. 1115   IT
Gillette de Venezuela S.A., Av. Libertador, etre calles, Elice y La Joya, Torre Miranda II, pg. 744   PB
Henkel Venezolana S.A., Piso 8-Oficina 85, Ave. Ppal. de Altamira, pg. 614   IT
Hewlett-Packard de Venezuela, C.A., Los Ruices Norte, 3A Transversal, pg. 819   PB
Hilos Magic H.M. de Venezuela CA, Torre Credival 12th Fl., Segunda Avenida Campo Allegre, pg. 840   IT
Honeywell C.A., Avenida Principal los Cortijos, de Lourdes, pg. 834   PV
IDC Venezuela, pg. 571   IT
ING Bank Caracas, Centro Letonia, Torre ING Bank, Piso 16, Av. Eugenio Mendoza, pg. 649   IT
Inaven, C.A., Edificio Torre La Primera, Av. Generalismo Francisco de Miranda, pg. 363   PB
Industrias Quimicas Carabobo, C.A., pg. 982   IT
Industrias Wyeth S.A., Apartado Postal 70048, pg. 81   PB
Insumos Ferroviarios C.A., Torre B, Piso 10, Oficina 1006, pg. 425   IT
Intergraph Servicios de Venezuela, C.A., C.C.C. Tamanaco, Torre C. Piso 11, pg. 891   PB
International Flavors & Fragrances de Venezuela C.A., Edificio Galipan, Entrada B, Piso 1, Oficianas B Y C, pg. 899   IT
Interven, S.A., Edif. Petroleos de Venezuela, Torre Sur, pg. 1045   IT
Inversiones Gengibral-Rep. Office of PWT in Venezuela, Torre Hener, Oficina 2A, Calle Gusicaipuro-El Rosal, pg. 1030   IT
Inversiones Isica, C.A., Apartado Aereo 609, pg. 1271   IT
Inversiones La Libertad, C.A., Edf. Centro La Paz - Piso 7, Av. FCO. de Miranda, pg. 364   PB
Inversiones Moore CA (Venezuela), pg. 890   IT
Inversiones Ortrac C.A., pg. 1022   IT
Italimpianti Intl.-Venezuela, Edif. Atlantico de Los Palos, Ave. Andres Bello Piso 6, pg. 655   IT
Itsemap Venezuela C.A., Av. Libertador, pg. 333   IT

PB - *U.S. Public Companies Volume*
PV - *U.S. Private Companies Volume*
IT - *International Public & Private Companies Volume*

J.M.C./Young & Rubicam, Torre Banaven (Cubo Negro), Torre C, Piso 5, Oficina 51, pg. 1200 **PB**
Johnson & Johnson de Venezuela, S.A., Apartado del Este 60349, pg. 930 **PB**
S.C. Johnson & Son de Venezuela, C.A., Apartado 70.041, pg. 593 **PV**
KSB Venezolana C.A., pg. 721 **IT**
Kelko Quaker Chemical, S.A., Avda. Francisco de Miranda, Edificio Parque Cristal, Piso 7, pg. 1346 **PB**
Kendall de Venezuela, C.A., Edificio Stugis, Piso 3, Avenida Chicago, pg. 1648 **PB**
Kodak Venezuela, S.A., Ave. La Guairita La Trinidad, pg. 555 **PB**
KONE Ascensores C.A., 4ta. Transversal de Horizonte, pg. 747 **IT**
Korn/Ferry International, Edif. Mene Grande II, Piso 2, Oficina No. 26, pg. 633 **PV**
La Federacion Compania de Seguros, C.A., Centro Plaza, Tower D, Avds. Francisco de Miranda/Los Palos, pg. 355 **IT**
Laboratorios Pharmacia & Upjohn, C.A., Apartado 60.752, pg. 1049 **IT**
Laboratorios Substantia, C.A., Apartado Postal No. 5828, pg. 1739 **PB**
Lagoven, S.A., Edif. Lagoven, Av. Leonardo Da Vinci, pg. 1045 **IT**
Lever S.A., Av. Libertador, pg. 1438 **IT**
Arthur D. Little de Venezuela, C.A., Edifico Banco de Lara-PH1, Avenida Principal de La Castellana, pg. 670 **PV**
Loctite de Venezuela, C.A., Centro Comercial Los Samanes, Piso No.1, Ofc. 102, pg. 611 **IT**
Loffland Brothers de Venezuela, C.A., pg. 1149 **PB**
Lucent Technologies Venezuela S.A., Av. Francisco de Miranda, Edificio Parque Cristal, pg. 1019 **PB**
Lummus Co. Venezuela C.A., Centro Plaza, Torre A, Av. Francisco de, pg. 6 **IT**
MBT de Venezuela, C.A., pg. 1465 **IT**
Makro Comercializadora S.A., Prolongacion Avenida Romulo, Gallegos, Carretera Petare-Guarenas, pg. 1155 **IT**
Mannesmann Venezolana S.A., pg. 838 **IT**
MANTEX, S.A.C.A., Viscosa Venezolana S.A., 2DA, Ave. de Campo Alegre, pg. 840 **IT**
Maraven, S.A., Edificio La Estancia, Av. La Estancia, pg. 1045 **IT**
Marqint Marcas Internacionales SA, Ave. Principal Boleita Norte, pg. 410 **IT**
Mathieu Venezuela, Piso 4, Oficina 45-A, Avenida Vera Cruz, pg. 846 **IT**
McCormick de Venezuela, C.A., Apartado 75, 093, pg. 1067 **PB**
Mead Johnson de Venezuela, S.A., Edificio Torre Sucre Piso 11, pg. 256 **PB**
Medicas Yoma, Calle Comercio Edificio Teca, pg. 822 **PB**
Memorex Telex de Venezuela, C.A., Av. Francisco de Miranda, Centro Seguros La Paz, Piso 3, pg. 857 **IT**
Mitsui de Venezuela C.A., Edificio Cavendes, Piso 10, Avenida Fran, pg. 882 **IT**
Molinos Caracas Maracaibo S.A., Edificio Ctr., Plz. Torre A, Piso 10, Ur, pg. 411 **IT**
Molinos Nacionales, C.A. (Venezuela), Apartado #70.384, pg. 901 **PB**
Molovenca, Calle Bolivar, Edif. NO 94, 3 piso, pg. 1031 **IT**
Monsanto (Venezuela) C.A., Avenida Francisco de Miranda, Edificio Parque Cristol, pg. 1126 **PB**
Morgan Grenfell (Venezuela), Torre Alfa, P.H., Avenida Principal de Sanfa Sofia, pg. 406 **IT**
J.P. Morgan Venezuela, S.A., Centro Profesional Eurobldg., Piso 6, Oficina 6-B, pg. 1131 **IT**
Motorola de los Andes y el Caribe, Calle Guacaipuro, Edificio Forum, Piso 6, pg. 1139 **PB**
Motorola Electronica de Venezuela S.A., pg. 1139 **PB**
Multipak De Venezuela C.A., P.O. Box 5826y, pg. 869 **PB**
Nalco de Venezuela, C.A., Av. Ppal. Eugenio Mendoza, pg. 1150 **PB**
Nature's Sunshine Products de Venezuela, pg. 1166 **PB**
Nestle Venezuela S.A., pg. 922 **IT**
Nissho Iwai de Venezuela C.A., C. C. El Parque, Torre Seguros Caracas, Piso 10, pg. 948 **IT**
Nordson International de Venezuela, C.A., Edif. La. Piramide, Piso 4, Of. 406, pg. 1189 **PB**
Norsk Hydro Venezuela C.A., Centro Banaven, Torre D, Piso 2, Oficina D-24, pg. 964 **IT**
Novell Venezuela, C.A., Av. La Estancia, Torre Las Mercedes, Piso 6, pg. 1204 **PB**
Novo Nordisk Bioindustrial SA, Torre Diamen, Piso 7, Officina 75, pg. 989 **IT**
Olin Quimica, S.A., Galipan Bldg., Piso 2, Avenida Francisco Mirada, Entrance C, pg. 1220 **PB**
Olivetti de Venezuela C.A., Ed. Olivetti, Calles Los Laboratorios, Los Ruices, pg. 1003 **IT**
Optimizacion ADD, Avenida Venezuela, pg. 1200 **PV**
Organon Venezolana SA, Centro Comercial Diana, Primer Piso, Calle Suapure, pg. 45 **IT**
Oster de Venezuela S.A., Edificie Principal No. 2, Pis 2 3 ra Tra, pg. 1533 **PB**
PDV Marina, S.A., Av. Libertador con Calle Los Mangos, pg. 1045 **IT**
Pajias Milani, S.A., pg. 411 **IT**
Palmaven, S.A., Edif. Palmaven, Av. Tamanaco, pg. 1045 **IT**
Panalpina C.A., pg. 1022 **IT**
Panalpina Transportes Mundiales C.A., pg. 1023 **IT**
Papeles Venezolanos, S.A., Urb. El Rosal, Avienda Las Mercedes con calles, pg. 762 **IT**
Parker Hannifin de Venezuela, S.A., Edificio Draza PB., Esq Calle Miraima con, pg. 1263 **PB**
Pequiven, S.A., Apartado 2066, Av. Francisco de Miranda, pg. 1045 **IT**

PETROLEOS DE VENEZUELA S.A., Edif. Petroleos de Venezuela, Torre Este, Av. Libertador, pg. 1045 **IT**
Pfizer S.A., Multicentro Empresarial del, Este, Torre Libertador, Nucleo A, pg. 1282 **PB**
Plumrose Latinoamericana C.A., pg. 431 **IT**
Prestaciones Venezolanas, Avenida Este 6, Colon a Doctor Diaz, pg. 1275 **IT**
Procter & Gamble de Venezuela C.A., Ave. La Estancia, pg. 1332 **PB**
Productora de Alcoholes Hidratados, C.A. (PRALCA), Calle Hans Newman, Edif. Corimon, 1 ER Piso, pg. 1220 **PB**
Productos CIBA-GEIGY SA, Apartado Postal 68.097, pg. 983 **PB**
Productos Quaker, C.A., Centro Plz.Torre C, pg. 1348 **PB**
Productos Roche S.A., pg. 1121 **IT**
Proyeparsons, C.A., Torre La Noria, Paseo Enrique, Las Mercedes, Apto. 60632, pg. 842 **PV**
RNBNY Representative Office-Caracas, Avenida Casanova, pg. 1381 **IT**
Radio-Holland de Venezuela S.A., Avda. Ppal Colinas de Bello Monte, pg. 1152 **IT**
Raychem de Venezuela, CA, Edificio Segre II, Segundo Piso, Calle 6, pg. 1362 **PB**
Representacion del Deutsche Bank AG (Caracas), Plaza Venezuela, Torre Phelps, Piso 21, Of. d, pg. 405 **IT**
Repsol Exploracion, Centro Ciudad Comercial Tamanaco, pg. 1105 **IT**
Rexroth SA, pg. 839 **IT**
Rhone-Poulenc de Venezuela, Av. Principal de Chuao, Edificio Los Roques, Pisos 6 y 7, pg. 1113 **IT**
Alfonso Rivas Co., C.A., Edificio Aquila, Avenida Veracruz concalle cali, pg. 447 **PB**
Robert Bosch SA, Avenida Republica Dominica, pg. 206 **IT**
Rockwell Automation de Venezuela, C.A., Avenida Gonzalez Rincones, pg. 1399 **IT**
SKF Venezolana S.A., Calle 8, Edifico EI, pg. 1159 **IT**
SNC-Lavalin, Ave. Francisco de Miranda, Torre Centro Lido, pg. 1162 **IT**
Sandoz Venezuela S.A., pg. 985 **IT**
Sandvik Venezuela C.A., Apartado de Correo No. 80026, pg. 1188 **IT**
Seguros Saint Paul de Venezuela, C.A., Edificio Centro Seguos La Paz, Piso 7, Aven. Francisco de Miranda, pg. 363 **IT**
Servicios Empresariales Seremca CA, pg. 21 **IT**
Shell Quimica de Venezuela, C.A., Edificio Centro Banaven, Av. La Estancia, Torre C, Piso 7, pg. 1142 **IT**
Shell Venezuela SA, Avenida la Estancia, Edificio Centro Banaven, Torre C, pg. 1142 **IT**
Siemens S.A., Avenida Don Diego Cisueios, pg. 1248 **IT**
Sistemas Ericsson C.A., Av. Francisco de Miranda, Ctro. Emp. Parque del Este, Piso 7, pg. 1370 **IT**
Sistemas Oracle de Venezuela, Av. Francisco de Miranda, Centro Plaza Torre A, pg. 1228 **IT**
Skil Venezolana S.R.L., Edificio Principal 1, Prinipal de Los Ruices, pg. 578 **PB**
Smith International de Venezuela, C.A., Av. Libertador, Edif. Xerox, Piso 12 A, pg. 1478 **IT**
SmithKline & French, C.A., Calle La Guairita, Edificio Los Frailes, pg. 1265 **IT**
Sociedad Venezolana de Electrificacion C.A. (SVECA), Apartado 6649, Carmelitas, pg. 3 **IT**
Sonoco de Venezuela C.A., Apartado de Correos 325, pg. 1487 **PB**
Standard Chartered Bank (Venezuela), pg. 1296 **IT**
Stanhome Panamericana, C.A., Apartado 60595, Chacao-Edo Miranda, pg. 1508 **PB**
Suiza de Reseguros Venezuela C.A., Edificio Torre la Noria, Piso 8-Norte, Paseo Enrique Eraso, pg. 1333 **IT**
Sulzer de Venezuela S.A., pg. 1306 **IT**
The Sumitomo Bank, Ltd.-Caracas Representative Office, Av. Francisco de Miranda, pg. 1309 **IT**
Superenvases Envalic C.A., Avenida Romulo Gallegos, pg. 1387 **PB**
Swiss Bank Corporation, Edificio Torre Europa, Piso 2, Avenida Francisco de Miranda, pg. 1330 **IT**
Syseca, Centro Commercial Los Cedros, Piso 4 Oficina 43, pg. 1384 **IT**
Systemhouse de Sur America, C.A., Centro Integral Santa Rosa, PH.6, Urb. Santa Rosa de Lima, pg. 1154 **IT**
TN Media, Av. Principal de las Mercedes, pg. 1641 **PB**
Technologia Medica del Caribe, C.A., Santa Monica, Calle Lisandro Alvardo, pg. 823 **PB**
Tecnofluor Inc., c/o Tecnoconsult, Avenida Sur 11, No. 33, pg. 661 **IT**
Tempus SRL, Ave. Fco Miranda Centro, Plaza C Piso 16, pg. 1348 **PB**
Thomson-CSF de Venezuela C.A., Centro Gerencial Mohedano Piso, 11, oficina 21, Av. Chaguaramos con, pg. 1384 **IT**
3M Manufacturera Venezuela S.A., Apartado 2083., Puente Brion A Luis Razetti, pg. 1607 **IT**
Tokio Marine de Venezuela, C.A., Edificio Parque Cristal, Torre Oeste Piso 12, Oficina 12-03, pg. 1393 **IT**
Toshiba de Venezuela, C.A., Torre Britanica de Seguros, Officina D, Piso 4, Ave. Jose Felix Sosa, pg. 1406 **IT**
Toyota Motor Corporation, Caracas Representative Offices, c/o Compania Anomina Tocars, Edificio Cars, Avenida Los, pg. 1413 **IT**
UBS Representative Office, Edificio Bancaracas, Piso 8, Plaza de la Castellana, pg. 1441 **IT**
Union Carbide Comercial C.A., Edificio Union Carbide Venezuela, pg. 1667 **IT**
United Distillers Curiel de Margarita, S.A., Centro Coinasa Piso 6, Av. San Felipe entre 2a Transversal, pg. 412 **IT**
Utell International-Venezuela, Av Libertador, Centro Comercial, Libertador, pg. 1099 **IT**
Valores Santander, S.A., Av. Tamanaco; Urb. El Rosal, pg. 144 **IT**

Van Raalte de Venezuela C.A., pg. 686 **PB**
Veneasistencia C.A., Avda. del Libertador, pg. 334 **IT**
Venepastas C.A., pg. 922 **IT**
Venezolana Empacadora C.A., pg. 431 **IT**
Vida Herbal Suplementos Alimenticios, C.A. (Venezuela), Edificio Playdeca, Final Calle Bolivar, pg. 809 **PB**
Voest-Alpine International de Venezuela C.A., Avenida la Estancia, pg. 1472 **IT**
Wackenhut de Venezuela, S.A., Calle La Industria, Edif. Mijal, pg. 1731 **IT**
Wander de Venezuela S.A., pg. 986 **IT**
Wang Latin America S.A., AV. Eugenio Mendoza Con 1 ra., Transvrsal, Edf. Banco de Lara, pg. 1738 **IT**
The West Company Venezuela C.A., Av. Romulo Gallegos, Cruce Con, 1 Av. Santa, Eduvigis Edif Pascal, pg. 1756 **PB**
West Merchant Bank Limited, Torre Clement, Of. 5A, of. SA Av. Venezuela, pg. 1493 **IT**
Westinghouse Electro-Metalurgica, C.A., Apartado 1889, Edificio Banco Exterior, 6 Piso, pg. 275 **PB**
Whitehall Venezuela, Edificio Oficentro - Piso 10, Avda. Principal, pg. 81 **PB**
Willis Faber & Dumas, Edifico Impres, Piso 8, Oficina 809, pg. 1510 **IT**
Xerox de Venezuela, C.A., Final Av. Libertador, pg. 1785 **PB**
Zurich International de Venezuela C.A. de Corretaje de Reaseguros, Torre Taeca, Piso 6, Av. Guaicaipuro, Urb. El Rosal, pg. 1532 **IT**

Chacaito

Informatica, Negocios y Tecnologia, S.A., Ave. El Bosque, pg. 976 **PV**
La Venezolana de Vida Compania Anonima de Seguros, Edificio Easo, Avenida Francisco de Miranda, pg. 363 **PB**

Chacao

Laboratorios Pfizer de Venezuela S.A., Multicentro Empresarial, del Este, Torre Libertador, pg. 1282 **PB**
Eli Lilly y Compania de Venezuela, S.A., Multicentro Empresarial Del Este, pg. 994 **PB**
Pfizer Bioquimicos S.A., Multicentro Empresarial del, Este, Torre Libertador, Nucleo A, pg. 1282 **PB**

Chuao

Young & Rubicam C.A., Centro Banaven Torre C, Piso 5, Oficina 51, pg. 1200 **PV**

Ciudad Guayana

C.V.G. Aluminio del Caroni, S.A., Apartado 115, Puerto Ordaz, Edo. Bolivar, pg. 1386 **PB**
Supervisora de Instalaciones Tecnicas SRL, pg. 837 **IT**

Ciudad Ojeda

Otis Engineering International, Carreterra K, Bariao Libertad, pg. 777 **PB**

Cumana

Toyota de Venezuela C.A., Urbanizacion Industrial El Penon, pg. 1413 **IT**

Guacara

Ejeven S.A., Urb. Industrial Pruinca, pg. 559 **PB**

Guarenas

Hilana C.A., 1RA, Averiida Calle B, Centro Industrial Del Este, pg. 947 **IT**
SmithKline Beecham (Venezuela) S.A., 2nd Avenida; Centro Industrial del Este, pg. 1266 **IT**

La Victoria

Productos CIBA-GEIGY SA, pg. 983 **IT**

Las Mercedes

Bombas Goulds de Venezuela C.A., Calle, California, Qta., pg. 861 **FS**

Los Morochas

ENSCO Drilling (Venezuela), S.A., pg. 585 **PB**

Los Taques

Intevep, S.A., Edif. Sede Central, Urb. Santa Rosa, pg. 1045 **IT**

Maracaibo

C-E International (Technological Branch), Av. 5 De Julio Con Av. 13A, Apartado 233, pg. 5 **IT**
C.M.S. Compania Anonima, Calle 146, No. 64-120, pg. 1174 **IT**
Carbozulia, S.A., Calle 77 con Av. 11, Edificio Lagoven Maracaibo 4001, pg. 1045 **IT**
Compania Hallbourton De Cementacion, Avenado 17 n108, pg. 776 **PB**

PB - *U.S. Public Companies Volume*
PV - *U.S. Private Companies Volume*
IT - *International Public & Private Companies Volume*

1838